INTERNATIONAL

WHO'S WHO IN MUSIC

AND MUSICIANS' DIRECTORY

INTERNATIONAL WHO'S WHO IN MUSIC

EDITORIAL DIRECTOR:
ERNEST KAY, D.Litt.

EDITOR:
Adrian Gaster, B.A. (London), Mus.B., M.A. (Cantab), A.R.C.M.

CONSULTANT EDITOR:
Peter Townend

EDITORIAL MANAGER:
Patricia McClatchie

PRODUCTION MANAGER:
Nicholas Law

EXECUTIVE SALES MANAGER:
Roger W. G. Curtis, M.A. (Cantab)

RESEARCHER:
Sheila Ellwood

All communications to: I.W.W.M., International Biographical Centre,
Cambridge CB2 3QP, England

INTERNATIONAL WHO'S WHO IN MUSIC AND MUSICIANS' DIRECTORY

NINTH EDITION

Edited by
ADRIAN GASTER

Distributed by
GALE RESEARCH COMPANY
Book Tower
Detroit, Michigan 48226

INTERNATIONAL WHO'S WHO IN MUSIC
Cambridge, England

Distributed exclusively in
the United States and Canada by
Grand River Books,
Detroit, Michigan, USA

First Published
1935
Second Edition
1937
Third Edition
1950
Fourth Edition
1962
Fifth Edition
1969
Sixth Edition
1972
Seventh Edition
1975
Eighth Edition
1977

Ninth Edition
1980

ISBN 0 900332 51 4

Printed and bound in the UK
by The Garden City Press Limited
Letchworth, Hertfordshire SG6 1JS

CONTENTS

FOREWORD BY THE EDITOR

In this, the Ninth Edition of the *International Who's Who in Music and Musicians' Directory*, the lives and main achievements of more than 10,000 musicians are recorded - composers, performers, teachers, critics, scholars, administrators and others connected with musical life. There are more than 2,000 new entries in the biographical section and the Appendices, which retain the format of the previous edition, have been updated and corrected to the best of my ability.

Every biographee was sent a typescript of his or her entry for correction and approval and such corrections have been incorporated in the final copy. Sometimes the typescripts have not been returned, either because biographees thought it unnecessary where the typescript was correct, but sometimes because we have been ignorant of changes of address. If every biographee or organisation would put the International Biographical Centre on its mailing list, so that changes of address could be recorded here, it would be of the greatest help.

Some (not many) have complained that career or creative output have not been comprehensive. A cursory glance at the book will show that space is severely limited, so that a biographee who attaches a long curriculum vitae or a complete list of compositions to a questionnaire runs the risk of having either or both curtailed unless some indication is given of the relative importance of each piece of information. In the absence of such information, I have had to use my own judgment and have, in general, concentrated on later events or compositions.

Since the eighth edition there have, inevitably, been many losses to record. Perhaps the most important has been the death at the age of 92 of the French composer, conductor, scholar and teacher, Nadia Boulanger. I have been struck by the number of eminent musicians throughout the world who studied with Mlle. Boulanger. Her influence has extended over half a century and will, through her pupils, extend many years into the future.

Other grievous losses have been sustained by the deaths of such fine musicians as Pierre Bernac, Leopold Stokowski, Andre Kostelanetz, Arthur Fiedler & Richard Rodgers.

It only remains for me to thank all those who have helped to produce the Ninth Edition. I am grateful to the Editorial Director, Dr. Ernest Kay, for entrusting me with this absorbing, if demanding task, and to all my colleagues for their constant and prompt response to my requests for information and assistance. I must particularly thank Patricia McClatchie, the Editorial Manager, for her unremitting cooperation, tolerance and patience.

A word of thanks, too, to all those, too numerous to name individually, who have offered information and advice. If I have not always been able to act on the advice, that does not mean that I am not grateful for it.

Last, but by no means least, I must express my gratitude to my secretary, Heather Shaw, whose help has been invaluable.

None of the above are responsible for any errors that may have crept in: for these, the Editor must accept sole responsibility.

ADRIAN GASTER

International Biographical Centre,
Cambridge CB2 3QP,
England.
May 1980.

NUMBERING OF THE REFERENCE BOOKS MENTIONED IN INTERNATIONAL WHO'S WHO IN MUSIC

The numbers at the end of the majority of entries denote other reference books in which the subject is listed. The following is a 'key' to this information

1. Who's Who (UK)
2. Who's Who in America
3. Who's Who in Music (UK)
4. International Who's Who in Music (America)
5. Who' Who of America Women
6. Who's Who in the East (USA)
7. Who's Who in the South and Southwest (USA)
8. Who's Who in the Midwest (USA)
9. Who's Who in the West (USA)
10. International Who's Who in Poetry (UK)
11. Directory of American Scholars
12. Who's Who in American Education
13. Who's Who in the Theatre (UK)
14. Grove's Dictionary of Music and Musicians (UK)
15. Who's Who in Australia
16. International Who's Who (UK)
17. Who's Who in New Zealand
18. Who's Who of Southern Africa
19. Who's Who in Europe (Belgium)
20. Who's Who in American Theatre
21. International Blue Book (UK)
22. Personalities Caribbean
23. International Who's Who in Community Service (UK)
24. Dictionary of Scandinavian Biography (UK)
25. Dictionary of African Biography (UK)
26. Dictionary of Caribbean Biography (UK)
27. World Who's Who of Women (UK)
28. Men of Achievement (UK)
29. Dictionary of International Biography (UK)
30. Who's Who in the World (USA)

TABLE OF ABBREVIATIONS

AA	Associate of Arts
AAGO	Associate, American Guild of Organists
AAUP	American Association of University Professors
AAUW	American Association of University Women
AB	Bachelor of Arts
ABC	American Broadcasting Corporation
ABSM	Associate, Birmingham and Midland Institute School of Music
Acad.	Academy; Academic
ACCO	Associate, Canadian College of Organists
Accomp.	Accompanist, Accompaniment
ACT	Australian Capital Territory
ADCM	Archbishop of Canterbury's Diploma in Church Music
Admin.	Administration
Admnstr.	Administrator
Advsr.	Advisor
Advsry.	Advisory
AFM	American Federation of Musicians
Agcy.	Agency
AGO	American Guild of Organists
AGSM	Associate, Guildhall School of Music and Drama
AK	Alaska
ALA	American Library Association
Ala.	Alabama
ALAM	Associate, London Academy of Music
Alta.	Alberta
ALCM	Associate, London College of Music
AM	Master of Arts
Am.	America, American
AMus.TCL	Associate, in Music, Trinity College of Music, London
App.	Appearance, Appeared
Appt.	Appointment
Apr.	April
Apt.	Apartment
APTA	American Piano Teachers Association
ARAM	Associate, Royal Academy of Music
ARCM	Associate, Royal College of Music
ARCO	Associate, Royal College of Organists
ARMCM	Associate, Royal Manchester College of Music

ARNCM	Associate, Royal Northern College of Music
Ariz.	Arizona
Ark.	Arkansas
Arr.	Arranger, Arrangement
ASCAP	American Society of Composers, Authors and Publishers
Assn.	Association
Assoc.	Associate; Associated
Asst.	Assistant
ASTA	American String Teachers Association
ASUC	American Society of University Composers.
ATCL	Associate, Trinity College of Music, London
Aug.	August
Aust.	Australia, Australian
Auth.	Authority
Aux.	Auxiliary
Ave.	Avenue
b.	Born
BA	Bachelor of Arts
Balt.	Baltimore
BBA	Bachelor of Business Administration
BBC	British Broadcasting Corporation
BC	British Columbia
BCL	Bachelor of Civil Law
BD	Bachelor of Divinity
Bd.	Board
BE	Bachelor of Education
Beds.	Bedfordshire
Berks.	Berkshire
BFA	Bachelor of Fine Arts
Biog.	Biography; Biographical
BJ	Bachelor of Journalism
Bldg.	Building
BLS	Bachelor of Library Science
Blvd.	Boulevard
BMus	Bachelor of Music
BMusEd	Bachelor of Music Education
Br.	Branch
Brit.	Britain; British
BS	Bachelor of Science
BSc	Bachelor of Science
BSM	Bachelor of Sacred Music
BST	Bachelor of Sacred Theology
BTh	Bachelor of Theology
Bucks.	Buckinghamshire
c.	children; circa
Calif.	California
Cambs.	Cambridgeshire
Can.	Canada; Canadian

Cantab.	Cantabrigian (Cambridge University degrees)	DD	Doctor of Divinity
CAPAC	Composers, Authors & Publishers of Canada.	DDR	Deutsche Demokratik Republik
Capt.	Captain	Dec.	December
Cath.	Catholic	dec.	Deceased
CB	Companion of the Bath	Del.	Delaware
CBC	Canadian Broadcasting Corporation	Deleg.	Delegate
		Dept.	Department
CBE	Commander, Order of the British Empire	Dev.	Development
		DFC	Distinguished Flying Cross
CBS	Columbia Broadcasting System	DFM	Distinguished Flying Medal
		Dict.	Dictionary
CCNY	City College of New York	Dip.	Diploma
CeBeDeM	Centre Belge de Documentation Musicale	Dipl.	Diplomate
		Dir.	Director
Cert.	Certificate; Certified	Dist.	District
CGGB	Composers Guild of Great Britain	Disting.	Distinguished
		Div.	Division
Ch.	Church	div.	Divorced
Chapt.	Chapter	DLit	Doctor of Letters
Chgo.	Chicago	DLitt	Doctor of Literature
Chmbr.	Chamber	DMus	Doctor of Music
Chmbr. of Comm.	Chamber of Commerce	Doct.	Doctorate; Doctoral
		DPh	Doctor of Philosophy
Chmn.	Chairman	Dpty.	Deputy
Cinn.	Cincinnati	Dr.	Doctor; Drive
Cmdr.	Commander	DRSAM	Diploma, Royal Scottish Academy of Music
Co.	County; Company		
C of E	Church of England	DSc	Doctor of Science
Col.	Colonel	DSC	Distinguished Service Cross
Coll.	College		
Colo.	Colorado	DSM	Distinguished Service Medal
Comp.	Composition; Composer		
Cond.	Conductor	DSO	Distinguished Service Order
Conf.	Conference		
Congl.	Congregational	DST	Doctor of Sacred Theology
Conn.	Connecticut	DTh	Doctor of Theology
Cons.	Consultant; Consulting		
Conserv.	Conservatory		
Contbn.	Contribution		
Contbr.	Contributer	E	East
Conven.	Convention	Econ(s).	Economic(s)
Coop.	Cooperative; Cooperation	Ed.	Editor; Edition; Editorial
Coord.	Coordinator; Coordinating	EdB	Bachelor of Education
Corp.	Corporation	EdD	Doctor of Education
Corres.	Correspondent; Corresponding	EdM	Master of Education
		Educ.	Education
Coun.	Council	Educl.	Educational
Cres.	Crescent	EEC	European Economic Community
Ct.	Court		
Ctr.	Centre	Elec.	Electric; Electrical
Ctrl.	Central	Ency.	Encyclopaedia
CUNY	City University of New York	Engl.	English
		Engr.	Engineer
C'wlth.	Commonwealth	Engrng.	Engineering
Czech.	Czechoslovakia	Episc.	Episcopal; Episcopalian
		EPTA	European Piano Teachers Association
d.	Daughter	esp.	Especially
DAR	Daughters of the American Revolution	ESTA	European String Teachers Association
DBE	Dame Commander, Order of the British Empire	Estab.	Established
		Etc.	Et cetera
DC	District of Columbia	Exec.	Executive
DCL	Doctor of Civil Law	Exhib.	Exhibit; Exhibition
DCM	Distinguished Conduct Medal	Exhibnr.	Exhibitioner
		Ext.	Extension

Fac.	Faculty	GCSM	Graduate, Guildhall School of Music and Drama
FAO	Food and Agriculture Organization		
FBSM	Fellow, Birmingham and Midland Institute School of Music	Glam.	Glamorganshire
		GLCM	Graduate, London College of Music
FCCO	Fellow, Canadian College of Organists	Glos.	Gloucestershire
		GM	George Medal
Feb.	February	Gov.	Governor
Fed.	Federal	Govng.	Governing
Fedn.	Federation	Govt.	Government
Fest.	Festival	Grad.	Graduate
FGSM	Fellow, Guildhall of Music and Drama	Grp.	Group
		GRSM	Graduate, Royal Schools of Music
Fla.	Florida		
FLCM	Fellow, London College of Music	GSM	Guildhall School of Music and Drama
Fndg.	Founding	Gt.	Great
Fndn.	Foundation	GTCL	Graduate Diploma, Trinity College of Music, London
Fndr.	Founder		
FRAM	Fellow, Royal Academy of Music		
		Gtr.	Greater
FRCCO	Fellow, Royal Canadian College of Organists		
		Hants.	Hampshire
FRCM	Fellow, Royal College of Music	Herts.	Hertfordshire
		Hd.	Head
FRCO	Fellow, Royal College of Organists	HHD	Doctor of Humanities
		HI	Hawaii
FRMCM	Fellow, Royal Manchester College of Music	Hist.	History
		Histl.	Historical
FRNCM	Fellow, Royal Northern College of Music	Histn.	Historian
		Hlth.	Health
FRSA	Fellow, Royal Society of Arts	Hon.	Honorary; Honour
		Hosp.	Hospital
Ft.	Fort	HQ	Headquarters
FTCL	Fellow, Trinity College of Music, London	Hunts.	Huntingdonshire
		Hwy.	Highway
Ga.	Georgia	IA	Iowa
Gall.	Gallery	ID	Idaho
GB	Great Britain	ILEA	Inner London Education Authority
GBE	Knight (or Dame), Grand Cross Order of British Empire	Ill.	Illinois
		Inc.	Incorporated
GBSM	Graduate, Birmingham School of Music	Ind.	Indiana
		Incl.	Include; Including
GC	George Cross	Inclng.	Including
GCB	Knight, Grand Cross of the Bath	Ind.	Industry
		Indl.	Industrial
GCIE	Knight, Grand Commander, Indian Empire	Indpls.	Indianapolis
		Info.	Information
GCMG	Knight, Grand Cross Order of St. Michael and St. George	INR	Institut National de Radiodiffusion (Belgium)
		Insp.	Inspector; Inspection
		Instn.	Institution
GCVO	Knight, Grand Cross, Royal Victorian Order	Int.	International
		ISCM	International Society for Contemporary Music
Gdns.	Gardens		
GDR	German Democratic Republic	ISM	Incorporated Society of Musicians
Gen.	General	ITA	Independent Television Authority
Geog.	Geography		
Geo. Wash. Univ.	George Washington University		
GFR	German Federal Republic	Jan.	January

JB	Jurum Baccalaureus	Mag.	Magazine
JD	Doctor of Jurisprudence	Maj.	Major
JP	Justice of the Peace	Man.	Manitoba
Jr.	Junior	Mar.	March
Jrnl.	Journal	Mass.	Massachusetts
Jt.	Joint	MAT	Master of Arts in Teaching
		Math.	Mathematical
Kan.	Kansas	Maths.	Mathematics
KBE	Knight Commander, Order of the British Empire	MBA	Master of Business Administration
KCB	Knight Commander, of the Bath	MBE	Member, Order of the British Empire
KCIE	Knight Commander, Indian Empire	Mbr.	Member
		Mbrship.	Membership
KCMG	Knight Commander, Order of St. Michael and St. George	Md.	Maryland
		ME	Maine
		MEd	Master of Education
KCSI	Knight of the Star of India	MENC	Music Educators National Conference
KCVO	Knight, Royal Victorian Order	Meth.	Methodist
		Met.Opera	Metropolitan Opera
Kt.	Knight	MFA	Master of Fine Arts
Ky.	Kentucky	Mgmt.	Management
		Mgr.	Manager
LA	Los Angeles	Mich.	Michigan
La.	Louisiana	Middx.	Middlesex
Lancs.	Lancashire	Min.	Minister, Ministry
Lang.	Language	Minn.	Minnesota
LBSM	Licentiate, Birmingham and Midland Institute School of Music	Misc.	Miscellaneous
		Miss.	Mississippi
		MIT	Massachusetts Institute of Technology
LCM	London College of Music		
Ldr.	Leader	ML	Master of Laws
Lectr.	Lecturer	MLA	Modern Language Association
Leics.	Leicestershire		
Lincs.	Lincolnshire	MLitt	Master of Literature; Master of Letters
LHD	Doctor of Humane Letters		
Lib.	Library	MLS	Master of Library Science
Libn.	Librarian	MM	Military Medal
Lic.	License; Licentiate	MMus	Master of Music
Lit.	Literature	Mo	Missouri
Lit Hum	Literae Humaniores (Classics)	Mod	Modern
		Mon.	Monmouthshiree
LittB	Bachelor of Letters	Mont.	Montana
LittD	Doctor of Letters	MP	Member of Parliament
LLB	Bachelor of Laws	Mpls.	Minneapolis
LLCM	Licentiate, London College of Music	MRE	Master of Religious Education
LLD	Doctor of Laws	MRSM	Member, Royal Society of Musicians
LLM	Master of Laws		
LMusTCL	Licentiate in Music, Trinity College of Music, London	MS	Manuscript
		MSM	Master of Sacred Music
		MSS	Manuscripts
LPO	London Philharmonic Orchestra	MST	Master of Sacred Theology
		Mt.	Mount
LRAM	Licentiate, Royal Academy of Music	MTA	Music Teachers Association
LRSM	Licentiate, Royal Schools of Music	Mtn.	Mountain
		MTNA	Music Teachers National Association
LSO	London Symphony Orchestra	MTNC	Music Teachers National Conference
Lt.	Lieutenant		
Luth.	Lutheran	Mus.	Museum
		MusB	Bachelor of Music
m.	Married	MusD	Doctor of Music
MA	Master of Arts	MusM	Master of Music

N	North	Phil.	Philharmonic
NAACP	National Association for the Advancement of Coloured People	Phila.	Philadelphia
		Philos.	Philosophy
		Phys.	Physical; Physics
NACWPI	National Association of College Wind and Percussion Instructors	Physn.	Physician
		Pitts.	Pittsburgh
		Pk.	Park
Nat.	National	Pkway.	Parkway
NB	New Brunswick	Pl.	Place
NBC	National Broadcasting Corporation	Postgrad.	Postgraduate
		PQ	Quebec
NC	North Carolina	PR	Public Relations
ND	North Dakota	PRS	Performing Right Society Ltd.
NEA	National Education Association		
		Pres.	President
Neb.	Nebraska	Presby.	Presbyterian
Nev.	Nevada	Prin.	Principal
Nfld.	Newfoundland	Prod.	Producer; Production
NGPT	National Guild of Piano Teachers	Prof.	Professor
		Profl.	Professional
NH	New Hampshire	Profn.	Profession
NJ	New Jersey	Prog.	Program
NM	New Mexico	PTA	Parent-Teacher Association
Northants	Northamptonshire	Pt.-time	Part-time
Notts.	Nottinghamshire	Publr.	Publisher
Nov.	November	Publs.	Publications
NS	Nova Scotia	Pvte.	Private
NSO	National Symphony Orchestra		
NSW	New South Wales	QC	Queen's Counsel
NT	Northern Territory	Qld.	Queensland
Num.	Numerous		
NY	New York		
NYC	New York City	RADA	Royal Academy of Dramatic Arts
NZ	New Zealand		
		RAF	Royal Air Force
		RAM	Royal Academy of Music
OBE	Officer, Order of British Empire	RC	Roman Catholic
		RCA	Radio Corporation of America
Oct.	October		
Off.	Officer	RCM	Royal College of Music
OH	Ohio	RCN	Royal Canadian Navy
Okla.	Oklahoma	RCO	Royal College of Organists
OM	Order of Merit	Rdr.	Reader
Ont.	Ontario	Recip.	Recipient
Orch.	Orchestra	Ref.	Reference
Orchl.	Orchestral	Relig.	Religion
Ore.	Oregon	Rels.	Relations
ORTF	Office de Radiodiffusion et Television Française	Rep.	Representative
		Repub.	Republic
OSA	Order of St. Augustine	Res.	Resident; Residence
OSB	Order of St. Benedict	Ret'd.	Retired
OSD	Order of St. Domonic	Rev.	Reverend
OSF	Order of St. Francis	RI	Rhode Island
Oxon.	Oxfordshire	RMCM	Royal Manchester College of Music
		RN	Royal Navy
Pa.	Pennsylvania	RNCM	Royal Northern College of Music
Parl.	Parliament		
Parly.	Parliamentary	RPO	Royal Philharmonic Orchestra
PC	Privy Councillor		
PEI	Prince Edward Island	RSAMD	Royal Scottish Academy of Music and Drama
Pembs.	Pembrokeshire		
Perf.	Performance; Performer	RSCM	Royal School of Church Music
PhB	Bachelor of Philosophy		
PhD	Doctor of Philosophy	Rsch.	Research

Rte.	Route		TTD	Teachers Training Diploma
Rt.Hon.	Right Honourable		TV	Television
Rt.Rev.	Right Reverend		TVA	Tennessee Valley Authority
S	South			
s.	Son			
SA	Société Anonyme		UAR	United Arab Republic
SA	South Australia		UCLA	University of California at Los Angeles
SABC	South African Broadcasting Corporation		UK	United Kingdom
SACEM	Société des Auteurs, Compositeurs et Editeurs de Musique		UN	United Nations
			Undergrad.	Undergraduate
			UNESCO	United Nations Educational, Scientific, and Cultural Organization
Salop.	Shropshire			
Sask.	Saskatchewan			
SB	Bachelor of Science		UNICEF	United Nations International Children's Emergency Fund
SC	South Carolina			
ScB	Bachelor of Science			
ScD	Doctor of Science		Univ.	Universty
Schl.	School		USA	United States of Ameica
Sci.	Science		USAF	United States Air Force
SD	South Dakota		USN	United States Navy
Sec.	Secretary		USNR	United States Naval Reserve
Sect.	Section			
Sem.	Seminary		USSR	Union of Soviet Socialist Republics
Sept.	September			
Serv.	Service		UT	Utah
Sev.	Several			
Sgt.	Sergeant			
SI	Order, Star of India		VA	Veterans Administration
SJ	Society of Jesus		Va.	Virginia
SM	Master of Science		Var.	Various
SNO	Scottish National Orchestra		Vic.	Victoria
			Vis.	Visiting; Visitor
Soc.	Society		Vol.	Volunteer; Voluntary
SPAM	Society of Polish Artists and Musicians		VP	Vice President
SPNM	Society for the Promotion of New Music		VPO	Vienna Philharmonic Orchestra
			VSO	Vienna Symphony Orchestra
Sr.	Senior			
St.	Street		Vt.	Vermont
Staffs.	Staffordshire			
STB	Bachelor of Sacred Theology			
STD	Doctor of Sacred Theology		W	West
STM	Master of Sacred Theology		w.	With
Str. Quartet	String Quartet		WA	Western Australia
SUNY	State University of New York		Warwicks.	Warwickshire
			Wash.	Washington
Supvsr.	Supervisor		Wash. DC	Washington, D.C.
Symph.	Symphony		Wilts.	Wiltshire
			Wis.	Wisconsin
			Wk.	Week
Tas.	Tasmania		Wm. & Mary Coll.	William & Mary College
Tchr.	Teacher			
TCL	Trinity College of Music, London		WNO	Welsh National Opera
			Worcs.	Worcestershire
TD	Teachers Training Diploma		WVa.	West Virginia
Tech.	Technical		Wyo.	Wyoming
Techn.	Technician			
Tenn.	Tennessee			
Tex.	Texas		YMCA	Young Men's Christian Association
ThD	Doctor of Theology			
ThM	Master of Theology		Yorks.	Yorkshire
Transl.	Translation; Translator		Yr.	Year
Treas.	Treasurer		YWCA	Young Women's Christian Association
Trng.	Training			

INTERNATIONAL WHO'S WHO IN MUSIC AND MUSICIANS' DIRECTORY

AALTONEN, Erik Verner (Erkki), b. 17 Aug. 1910. Hämeenlinna, Finland. Composer; Conductor; Violinist; Teacher. Educ: Sibelius Acad., 1929-47; Orchl. cond. examination, 1947. M. Ilta Annikki Tyyne Virtanen, 2s., 1 d. Debut: as cond., 1948. Career: Guest cond. in Finland & other countries, 1948-69; Prin., Music Inst., Kemi, 1966-73; Violinist, Helsinki Symph. Orch., 1936-66. Comps: 5 symphs.; 2 piano concertos; Violin concerto; 2 Ballet suites for orch.; Folk music for orch. & ensembles; 1 ballet; music for films, radio, etc. Mbrships: Composers' Copyright Bureau, Helsinki; Finnish Composer Union. Hons: Silver medal of City of Helsinki; Gold medal as cond. of Coll. orch. Hobbies: Painting. Address: Ohjaajantie 3 A 3, 00400 Helsinki 40, Finland.

AANEN, Greet, b. 8 Apr. 1947. Hoornaar, Netherlands. College Music Teacher; Accompanist (Piano & Harpischord); Soprano Soloist. Educ: Studied Piano, Schl. Music & Singing. Conserv. of Music; still studying Harpsichord & Cond. Career: Cond. of an operatic choir w. num. perfs; choral radio apps. Hobbies: Reading; Exploration of Nature; Cooking. Address: Wyfsprongweg 118, Lunteren, Netherlands.

AAQUIST JOHANSEN, Svend, b. 7 Dec. 1948. Lyngby, nr. Copenhagen, Denmark. Composer; Conductor; Pianist. Educ: Univ. of Copenhagen; Royal Danish Conserv., Copenhagen. Debut: 1969. Career: Occasional TV apps. & regular transmission on radio of perfs. of own works or of perfs. as cond. or musician. Comps. incl: Salut Salut, 1970; Smmermusik (chmbr. orch.), 1971; Solla Famlre Dosl, 1972; Ketjak, 1973: Wiegenlied (Bertolt Brecht), 1974; Unite (wind ensemble or orch. without strings) 1974; Symph. for Orch., 1976; The Lilacs Shall Bloom in May, They Shall! for cello solo, 1978; Two Movements (flute & piano), 1977. Mbrships. incl: VP, Danish Comps. Soc.; Nat. Music Coun. of Denmark; Nordic Comps. Coun. Ed., Dansk Musiktidsskrift, ISCM periodical, 1971-72. Recip., 3 yr. Comps. Stipendium, Danish Art Fund, 1974-76. Mgmt: Soc. for the Publication of Danish Music, Valkendorfsgade 3, DK-1151 Copenhagen, Denmark. Address: Haraldsgade 58, DK 2100 Copenhagen, Denmark.

AAS, Ernst, b. 16 Dec. 1910. Honningsvaag, Norway. Pianist; Chief of Division, Ministry of Fisheries. Educ: Can. Oecon 1937; Autodidact. 2 c. Career: Played swing music in bands in Oslo, 1930's; Piano entertainer, Oslo restaurants; Concerts. Norwegian radio & TV; Chief of Div., Ministry of Fisheries. Comps: Guri Malla; Signal March (recorded). Mbrships: Norwegian Musicians Union. Hons: Winner Comp. Competitions or Guri Malla & Signal March. Hobbies: Still Music; Painting. Address: Vaekeroveien 205, Oslo 7, Norway.

AAS, Gunnar, b. 10 Feb. 1947. Oslo, Norway. Percu. Educ: Veitvedt Musikkonservatorium w. Jan Hanseth; Timpani studies w. Bengt Arsenius; Pvte. studies w. Walter Shubert & Bobben Hagerup. m. Hanne Revold, 1 s. Career: Norwegian Opera Orch. (3 yrs. as extra, 2 yrs. full time); Var. radio & TV apps. w. Norwegian Broadcasting Orch.; currently at The Norwegian Theatre. Recordings w. The Norewgor Broadcasting Orch. & Oslo Phil. Orch. Mbrships: Norwegian Musicians Union. Hobbies: Music; Family; Making own percussion instruments. Address: Kirkesvingen 10, Olso 9, Norway.

ABBADO, Claudio, b. 1933. Italy. Conductor. Educ: Conserv. Giuseppe Verdi, Milan; Musica; Acad., Vienna, Austria. Career: Cond., La Scala Orch., Milan, 1968-76; Musical Dir., ibid., 1972-76; Guest Cond., Prin. Orchs. in Europe & Am.; Cond., Vienna Festival, 1961-; Salzburg Festival, 1965-; Edinburgh Festival, 1966-; Prague Spring, 1966-; Lucerne Festival, 1966-; Holland Festival; Venice Festival; Prin cond., LSO, 1979-. Hons: Sergel Koussewitzky Prize, Berkshire Music Festival, USA, 1958; Dimitri Mitropoulos Prize, 1963; Diapason Prize, 1966, 1967; Grand Prix du Disque, 1967; Deutsche Schallplatten Prize, 1968. Address: Vla Nirone 2/A, 20123, Milan, Italy.

ABBEY, Elizabeth, b. 27 July 1946. Cleveland, Ohio, USA. Bassoonist; Teacher. Educ: B Mus, 1969, M Mus, 1972, Univ. of Md.; PhD studies, Univ. of Md. & Mich. State Univ.; studied bassoon & contrabasson w. noted tchrs. m. Michael D Sherline. Career: Ed. & Educl. Dir., Fereol Publs., 1968-73; Free-lance Columbia Union Coll., Takoma Pk., Md., 1972-73; Prin. Bassoon, Grand Rapids Symph. Orch., 1973-74, Jackson Symph. Orch., 1974 76; Contrabassoon, Lansing Symph. Orch., 1973-76; on Ed. Staff, Checklist of the Wind Instrument Collection of the Smithsonian Institution, publd. 1974-75. Mbrships. incl: Int. Double Reed Sco.; Am. Musicol. Soc.; Music Lib. Assn. Recip. acad. hons. Hobbies incl: Tennis & Cycling. Address: 1106F Univ. Village, E. Lansing, MI 48823, USA.

ABBOTT, Anthony William, b. 26 Dec. 1941. Cheltenha, UK. Assistant Registrar, Royal College of Music. Educ: Emanuel Schl., London; TCL; RAM; GRSM; LRAM; ARCM; ARCO; ARAM. Career: Asst. Dir. of Music, Emanuel Schl., London, 1966-70; Musical Dir., Haywards Heath Operatic Soc., 1966 67; Organist & Choirmaster, St. John's Ch., Merton, London, 1960-63; Balcombe Parish Ch., Sussex, 1965-66, Keymer Parish Ch., Sussex, 1966-; Cond., The Hurstpierpoint Singers, 1977-. Mbrships: ISM; RAM Club; RCM Union Surrey Co. Cricket Club. Hobbies: Cricket; Reading; Motoring; Choir-Training. Address: ''Water Musik'', Blunts Wood Rd., Haywards Heath, Sussex, UK. 3.

ABBOTT, Kenneth John Dearie, b. 28 July 1919. Leigh-on-Sea, Essex, UK. Professor of Music; Director of Music. m. Ruby Mary Marchant, 3 s., 1 d. Educ: RCM; DMus (London); FRCO; ARCM. Career: Organist, Luton Parish Ch.; Berkhamsted Schl.; Hd. of Music, Ambassodor Coll.; Prof. of Music, RAF; Dir. of Music, City Temple Ch., London; Examiner, Assoc. Bd., Royal Schls. of Music. Mbrships: ISM; RCO; RAF Club. Hobbies: Sailing; Golf; Swimming. Address: The Old Rectory, Aston Clinton, Bucks., UK.

ABEL, David W., b. 24 Feb. 1914. NY, USA. Music Educator; Conductor; violinist. Educ: BA, Brooklyn Coll., 1935; MA, Schl. of Educ., NY Univ., 1947; L'Ecole Monteux, 1950; studied w. Koussevitsky. m. Edity Bellman, 1 s. Career: Cond., NY Adirondack Symph.; Asst. Cond., Honolulu Symph., NYC Tchrs. Symph.; Dir. & Organizer of Orchs. & Bands, NYC Bd. of Educ. Secondary Schl.; Organizer dir., Bronxwood Inst. for Adult Educ., 1976. Contbr. to: Music Educators Jrnl.; High Points; The Instrumentalist. Mbrships: Phi Delta Kappa; Am. Fed. of Musicians, Local 802. Hobby: Films. Address: 118 Riverside Drive, NY, NY 10024, USA.

ABEL, Jenny. Husum, N. Sea, Germany. Concert Violinist. Educ: High Schl. for Music, Freiburg/Breisgau, Cologne; Berne

Conserv. of Music w. Max Rostal; private study w. Henryk Szerying; Dip. w. hons., Berne. Debut: Bach and Mozart Concertos, aged 8. Career: Soloist in most European countries, USA & S America; Appts. w. many well-known orchs., at fests., on TV and radio; solo & duo recitals. Recordings incl: 1st recording of Siegfried Wagner's Violin Concerto; Complete Brahms & Bartok violin sonatas. Hons: Deutscher Schallplattenpreis, 1977. Address: Lautenbacherstr. 17, D 7562 Gernsbach, German Fed. Repub.

ABEL-STRUTH, Sigrid, b. 24 July 1924. Breitscheid, Germany. Professor of music education.- Educ: doctorate degree. Caree: lectr., Coll. of Educ., Bielbfeld/Westphalia, 1971-3; Inst. for music educ., J. W. Goethe univ., Frankfurt, from 1973. Publs: Musikalische Grundausbildung, 1967; Materialien zur Entwicklung der Musikpädagogik als Wissenschaft, 1970; Musikalischer Beginn in Kindergarten and Vorschule, 3 vols., 1970-77; Ziele des Musiks-Lernen, 1978; Musikpädagogik in Forschung and Lehre, ed. 1972. Contbr. to: Musik kund Bildung; MUSICA. Mbrships: Int. soc. of music educ.; union of German schl. music tchrs.; circle for music educ. rsch.; work grp. on music educ. & trng. for German music coun. Address: D-6236 Eschborn, Dörnweg 36, German Fed. Repub.

ABENDROTH, Walter, b. 29 May 1896. Hanover, Germany. Composer; Critic. m. Hilda Schlegl, 1945, 2 s., 2 d. Career: Mil. Serv., 1916-18; Critic & Ed., Allgemeine Musikzeitung, Cologne, 1929-30; Critic & Chief Ed., Berlin Allgemeine Musikzeitung, 1930-34; Music Advsr., Berliner Lokalanzeiger, 1934-44; Dir., Die Zeit mag., Hamburg, 1946-55; Cultural Corresp., Symph.; Concerto for Orch.; Viola, Violin, Piano & Cello Concertos; Divertimento for Chmbr. Orch.; Fantasy Concerto for Small Orch. & Harpsichord Obbligato; 5 String Quartes; Var. Chmbr. Music pieces, especially for Viola; Songs. Publs: Biographies of H. Pfitzner & A. Bruckner; Deutsche Musik der Zeitwende; Die Symphonien Anton Bruckners; Vom Werden & Vergehen der Musik; Vier Meister der Muisk; Selbstmord der Musik; Bildbiographie Anton Bruckner; Kleine Geschichte der Musik; Ich warne Neugierge (Autobiog); Arthur Schopenhauer; Rudolf Steiner & die heutige Welt. Address: Haus Rechenau, 8161 Hammer (Fischbachau); Oberbayern, W. Germany.

ABERCROMB, Jillian Dawn, b. 19 Dec. 1935. Poole, Dorset, UK. Violinist; Teacher. Educ: RCM (senior univ. scholarship), 1954-58; ARCM (pfte.); ARCM (violin); GRSM. m. Eric Abercromb, 1 b. Career violin & piano tchr., St. Helen's Schl., Northwood, 1958-59; peripatetic tchr., Oxfordshire, 1959-; vis. tchr., St. Helen's Schl., Abingdon, 1964-66; lectr., Bulmershe Coll. of Higher Educ., 1974-78; tchr., King Jame's Coll., Henley, 1977-; co-prin., Reading Concert Orch., 1967-77; freelance player for num. orchs. incl. Oxford Pro Musica, Orchestra da Camera, Engl. Bach Fest. Orch. Purcell Orch. Oxford Symph. Orch. & Slough Phil. Orch.; ldr., num. operatic & choral socs., music clubs in outer London area. Mbrships: RCM Union; ISM; Musicians' Union. Hobbies: Yoga; Walking; Conservation; Vegetarianism. Address: 10 Hamilton Ave., Henley-on-Thames, Oxon. RG9 1SM, UK.

ABERCROMBIE, Alexander, b. 7 Sept. 1949. London, UK. Composer; Pianist. Educ: M Mus, RCM. m. Barbara Dix. Debut: Park Lane Grp. Concerts, London, 1972. Career: has given num. premieres of works by Ravel, Skalkottas Xenakis, Finnissy & other comps. Mbr., ISM. Hons: 2nd Prize, Gaudeamus Int. Perfs. Competition, 1972; 1st Prize, Stroud Fest. Comps. Competition, 1968. Hobbies: Mathematics; Natural Sciences. Address: Dormy House, 2C Kent Rd., Birkdale, Southport, UK.

ABERG, Kerstin, b. 11 May 1940. Stockholm, Sweden. Pianist. Educ: Music Tchr. Dip., Royal Acad. of Music, Stockholm, 1961; Piano Tchr. Dip., ibid., 1965; studied w. Prof. Gunnar Hallhagen, Alexander Liberman, Gerald Moore, Dorothy Irving, Erik Werba. m. Torkel Aberg, 1 s. Debut: Stockholm, 1968. Career: Free-lance Pianist, Soloist, Vocal & Instrumental Accomp.; Duo Perfs. w. Dorothy Irving, Soprano, & w. Elemar Lavotha, cello; var. TV Apps., num. Radio Solo & Chmbr. Music Perfs., Sweden. Recip. Medal of the Royal Acad. of Music, Stockholm, 1968. Mgmt: Tonkontakt Lyttkens & Aberg, Uppsala, Sweden. Address: 7 Envagen, 752 52 Uppsala, Sweden.

ABERT, Anna Amalie, b. 19 Sept. 1906. Halle (Saale), DDR. Prof. musicol. Educ: Univ. Berlin, DPh 1934; State pvte. cert. for violin, Kiel, 1935. Career: 1935 Asst. Musicol. Inst. Kiel Univ.; 1943 Lectr. Kiel Univ.; 1962 Prof. Kiel; since 1971 ret'd. Mbrships: Int. Musicol. Soc.; Int. Soc. for Music Rsch.; Inst. for Mazart Rsch. Salzburg. Publs. incl: What is taken for granted in Heinrich Schütz's sacred hymns, 1935; Claudio Monteverdi and the Musical Drama, 1954; Christoph Willibald

Gluck, 1960; Mozart's Operas, 1970; Richard Strauss, his Operas, 1972. Contbr. to: Ency: Music past and present; Ency. de la Pléiade; New Oxford History of Music; Acta Musicologica; Music Rsch. Address: Wrangelstr. 21, D2300 Kiel, German Fed. Repub.

ABRAHAM, Gerald Ernest Heal, b. 1904. Educ: MA, FTCL. m. Isobel Patsie Robinson, 1 d. Career: Asst. Editor, Radio Times 1935-39; Dep Editor, The Listener 1935-42; Chmn., Mus. Section, The Critics Circle 1944-46; Alsop Prof. of Music, Liverpool Univ., 1947-64; BBC 1962-67. Ed., Monthly/Mus Record., Second; Secy. Ed. Bd. New Oxford History of Music Publs: This Modern Stuff; Nietzsche; Studies in Russian music; Tolstoy; Masters of Russian Music (w. Calvocoressi); Dostoevsky; 100 Years of Music; On Russian Music; Chopin's Musical Style; Beethoven's 2nd Period Quarters; 8 Soviet Composers; Tchaikovsky, Rimsky-Korsakov; Design in Music. Hobbies: Walking; Languages. Address: Old School House, Ebernoe (Perworth) Sussex. UK.

ABRAHAMS, Frank, b. 8 Nov. 1947. Phila., Pa., USA. Choral Conductor; Music Educator. Educ: B Mus Ed, Temple Univ. Phila., Pa., 1969; MM, New England Conserv., Boston, Mass., 1972. m. Ellen Meyers Abrahams, 1 s., 1 d. Career: Dir. of Choral Activities, Malden HS, Mass., 1969-75; Dir., Malden Community Chorus, Mass., 1971-73; Music Educ. Fac., New England Conserv., Boston, Mass., 1972-; Supvsr. of Music Educ., Town of Stoneham Pub. Schl., Mass., 1975-; var. recordings as mbr. of Temple Univ. Choirs & New England Conserv. Chorus. Mbrships. incl: Music Educators Nat. Conf.; Mass. Music Educators Assn. Contbr. to Mass. Music News. Address: 20 Dana Rd., W Peabody, MA 01960, USA.

ABRAHAMSON, Bergljot, b. 27 March, 1909. Grimstad, Norway. Teacher. Educ: Peabody Conserv. of Music, Balt., Md. (violin, chorus, Aural trng., music appreciation); Univ. of Ariz., Tucson; ASU at Tempe, Ariz., State Univ. of Fla., Gainesville, Fla.; State Tchrs. Coll., Albany, NY; Grand Canyon Coll., Phoenix, Ariz.; John Hopkins Univ., Balt., Md.; Univ. of Miami, etc. Career: Tchr., NY, Md., Fla. & Ariz. (piano, harp, accordion, harmonica, etc.). Comps: Souvenirs of Spitzbergen. Recordings: Whispering Hope. Publs: Scandinavia Revisited, 1958; $90 Circle Tour, 1979. Contbr. to newspapers. Mbrships: Life, NEA, NY State, Ariz., Fla., Md. State Tchrs. Assn.; Dept. of ELM Schl. Prins. NY & Ariz.; Ariz. Schl. Admin.; Ariz. Retired Tchrs. Assn. Hobbies: Stamp collecting; Hiking; Fancy work. Address: PO Box 1642, Clewiston, FL 33440, USA. 2, 8, 9, 23, 27.

ABRAM, Blanche Schwartz, b. 28 June 1925. NYC, USA. Pianist; Teacher of Music. Educ: BA, Bklyn. coll.; NY Univ.; studied piano, comp. & analysis w. noted tchrs. m. Irving Abram, 2s., 2d. Debut: NYC. Career: many concerts & broadcasts, USA & Caribbean; Pianist, co-dir., Am. Chmbr. Ensemble; pianists, Drucker Trio; Fac. Mbr., NY Unic. (formerly), Hoftstra Univ. (currently), & 92nd St. YMHA (currently, also Chmn. of Piano Fac. for many yrs.); Advsr. to Supt. of Schls. on cultural remedial affairs, Roosevelt Schl. Dist. Publs: Educating Young Musicians - A Guide for Students, Teachers, and Pianists, 1960. Contbr. to Clavier Music Mag. Mbrships. incl: MENC; Coll. Music Soc. Hons. incl: Outstanding Musical Contribution, 92nd St. YMHA, 1966. Hobbies incl: Folk Dancing. Mgmt: Celia Goodstein Mgmt. Address: 2320 Surrey Ln., Baldwin, NY 11510, USA. 4.

ABRAMOWITSCH, Bernhard, b. 5 Jan. 1906. Hamburg, Germany. Concert Pianist; Music Educator. Educ: studied w. Paul Strecker and Heinrich Sthamer, Hamburg. m. Eva Koretz, 1 s., 1 d. Debut: Hamburg, 1926. Career: num. concerts in Germany & USA; Soloist w. var. orchs.; radio & TV broadcasts; Tchr., Univ. of Calif. (Berkeley), Mills coll. (Oakland) & Holy Name Coll., Oakland; Pvte. tchng. Calif. Recordings: Roger Sessions' 2nd Sonate & 'From My Diary'; Ernst Krenek's 4th Sonata; Schubert; B flat major Sonata. Address: 966 Keeler Ave., Berkeley, CA 94708, USA 3.

ABRAMOWITZ, Jonathan, b. 15 Mar. 1947. Greenbelt, Md., USA. Violoncellist. Educ: BM, MS, DMA, Juilliard Schl., NYC. Debut: Carnegie Recital Hall, May 1967, Career: Num. Solo orch. & chmbr. Music perfs. & Recitals in US, Europe & TV; Master classes and Residencies at maj. univs. in USA. Hons : 1st Prize, Nat. Soc. of Arts & Letters String Competition, 1964; Medallist, Geneva Int. Perfs. Competition, 1966. Mgmt: Larney Goodkind, 30 E 60th St., New York, NY, USA. Address: 685 W. End Ave., NY, NY 10025, USA.

ABRAMS, David, b. 6 Aug. 1949. Brooklyn, NY, UA. Assistant Professor. Educ: BA, 1971, MM, 1976, DMA, 1979, Eastman Schl. of Music. Career: Mbr., Rochester Phil. Orch. 1970-74; Mbr., Wisconsin Art Quintet, 1974-76; Instructor of

Clarinet & Theory, Univ. of Wis., Stevens Point, 1974-76; Asst. Prof. of Clarinet & Theory, State Univ. of NY/Onondaga Community Coll., 1976-. Recordings: sev., incl. Anthology of Am. Music. Mbrships: Int. Clarinet Soc.; Nat. Assn. of Coll. Wind & Percussion Instructors; Phi Mu Alpha Sinfonia; Co-fndr., Central NY Clarinet Congress. Hobby: Chess. Address: 1313 Butternut St., Syracuse, NY 13208, USA.

ABRAMSON, Jean Margaret, b. 12 Nov. 1926. Laurium, Mich., USA. Pianist; College Professor; Lecture-Recitalist. Educ: incls: B Mus, Chgo. Musical Coll., 1948; M Mus, 1951, D Mus, 1965, Univ. of Rochester, NY; studies w. var. noted tchrs. in USA, also master classes under Paul Badura-Skoda & Viola Thern, Vienna, Austria, 1972-73. Career: Instructor, piano, Suomi Coll., Hancock, Mich., 1948-50, music, Mary Hardin-Baylor Coll., Belton, Tex., 1952-54; Prof., Wartburg Coll., Waverly, 1954-; Lecture-Recitals on var. topics. Contbr. to Iowa Music Tchr. Bullentin. Mbrships: MTNA-IMTA; Coll. Msuic Tchr. Bulletin. Mbrships: MTNA-IMTA; Coll. Music Soc.; Delta Kappa Gamma; AAUP. Hobby: Embroidery. Address: 319 11th St. NW, Apt. 4, Waverly, IA 50677, USA 27.

ABRAMSON, Robert M, b. 23 Aug. 1928. Phila., Pa., USA. Composer; Conductor; Pianist; Harpsichordist; Teacher. Educ: BM, 1965; MM, 1966, Manhattan Schl. of Music, NYC. Career incls: Assoc. Prof., Harford Conserv. of Music, Conn., 1964-; Chmn., Theory Dept., Manhattan Schl. of Music, 1970-; Dir., The Music Workshop, NYC, 1960-; Lecture demonstrations & seminars on eurhythmic techniques in music educ., 195-69; Cond. of sev. film scores, recordings, concerts, musicals; Sev. piano perfs. in concerto & recitals & on radio & TV. Comps. incl: Dance Variation (piano & orch); The Countess Kathleen; Three Old Songs Resung. Recordings incl: Carols for All Seasons. Mbr., sev. musical assns. Author of sev. texts, arrs. & reviews. Recip., num. hons. Address: 250 W 94th St., NY, NY 10025, USA.

ABRAVANEL, Claude, b. 16 July 16 July 1924. Montreux, Switz. Director of a Music Library; Lecturer, Rubin Academy of Music, Jerusalem. Educ: piano, Pierre Souvairan, Conserv. of Berne, & Dinu Lipatti, Conserv. of Geneva; piano, Yvonne Lefebure, comp., Arthur Honegger, Tchr. Dips., piano, counterpoint, fugue, Ecole Normale de Musique, Paris. m. Sara Treves, 3 children. Comps: Four Psalms for voice & orch. Author: Claude Debussy: A Bibliography, 1974. Contbr. to jrnls. Mbrships: Israel Comps. League; Acum. Comps. & Authors Assn. in Israel Musicol. Soc. Address: Ramban St. 55, Jerusalem, Israel.

ABREU, Eduardo, b. 19 Sept. 1949. Rio de Janeiro, Brazil. Concert Guitarist. Educ: Studied Guitar w. Adolfina Raitzin Tavora (pupil of Segovia); studied Harmony, Comp. etc. w. var. masters. Debut: Rio de Janeiro, 1963. Career: Apps. in most major cities of Europe & N & S Am., inlcng. Buenos Aires, 1965, Paris & London, 1968, NYC, 1970, & also in Aust. Recordings for Decca & CBS. Mgmt: Basil Douglas Ltd., 8 St. Georges Terrace, London NW1, UK.

ABREU, Maria (Carlota). b. 18 June 1916. Porto Alegre, Brazil. Pianist; Musicologist; Music Critic; Journalist. Educ: Piano dip., Instituto de Belas Artes da Universidade de Porte Alegre, 1937. m. José Maria Santiago Wagner (1939-78), 1 s., 2 d. Debut: Porto Alegre, 1943. Career: concerts in sev. cities in Argentian & Brazil incl. Buenos Aires & Rio de Janeiro; perfs. on radio, Buenos Aires & Rio de Janeiro; Prof. of piano, Academia de Musica Lorenzo Fernândez (Rio de Janeiro) & Escola de Artes da Universidade do Rio Grande do Sul (Porto Alegre); Ed., Musical Dir., Rede Globo (Rio de Janeiro) of prog., Concertos da Juventude. contbr. of num. reviews, criticisms, articles to var. jrnls., mags. & newspapers. Hons: Hispanidad Prize (Instituto de Cultura Hispanica), Madrid, 1967. Hobby: Collecting Paintings & Posters. Address: Praia do Flamengo 300, apt. 503, BR-22210 Rio de Janeiro, RJ, Brazil.

ABREU, Sergio, b. 5 June 1948. Rio de Janeiro, Brazil. Concert Guitarist. Educ: Studied Guitar w. Adolfina Raitzin Tavora (pupil of Segovia); studied Harmony, Comp. etc. w. var. masters. Debut: Rio de Janeiro, 1963. Career: Yearly tours of Europe, N & S Am., 1967-; 4 Aust. tours. Contbr. to: Guitar review, NY, Num. recordings. Hons: First Prize, Paris Int. Guitar Competition, 1967. Hobbies incl: Guitar constructions; A coustical research on musical instruments. Mgmt: Basil Douglas Ltd., 8 St. George's Terrace, London NW1, UK (Europe); M L Byers Inc., One Fifth Ave, NY, NY 10003, USA (N Am.). Address: Av. Copacabana 1246, Apt. 1205, 22070 Rio de Janeiro, Brazil.

ACCIAI, Giovanni, b. 4 Feb. 1946. Albisola Superiore, Savona, Italy. Teacher; Musicologist. Educ: BA, Schl. of Paleografia et Filologia Musicale at Pavia Univ. m. Ferrari Carla,

1 d. Debut: Dirig. of Corale Univ. di Torino in concerts in Poland. Career: Tchr. Musical Hist. at Conservatorio G. Nicolini of Piacenza; Chorus Master of Corale Univ. de Torino. Comps: Soundtrack for First Triennial Exhibition of Bow Instruments, Cremona, 1976. Contrbr. to La Cartellina, choral reviews. Mbrships: Italian Soc. Musicology; Int. Assn. of Gregorian Chant (Cremona). Address: Via Maria Luigia d'Austria, 39-29100 Piacenza, Italy. 1.

ACHUCARRO, Joaquin, b. 1932. Bilbao, Spain. Pianist. Educ: Indachu Coll., Bilbao, Madrid Conserv., Chigiana Conserv., Siena; Saarbruken Conserv. m. Emma Jiménez, 1 s., 1 d. Career: app. at Masaveu, Spain, 1950, Viotti Int., Italy, 1953; Liverpool Int. Piano Concerto Competition, 1959, Cheltenham Fest., 1966 & 69; toured Africa, 1967; app. in USA w. LA Phil., 1969; toured S Am., 1958, 60, 62, 64, 67, & 69; world tour, 1970, inclng. UK, India, Philippines, USA, Mexico, Columbia, Spain, & Scandinavia. Mbr: Bilboan Soc. Hobbies: Swimming; Mycol., Bicycling. Address: Apartado 1332, Bibao, Spain. 3.

ACKERMANN, Pavel, b. 6 Mar. 1935. Prague, Czech. Clarinettist; Teacher of Music. Educ: Grad. Prague Conserv., 1958; Grad., Acad. of Musical Art, 1962, m. Jana Veverkova, 1 s., 1 d. Debut: w. Prague Chmbr. Orch. Prague, 1962, 1st clarinettist w. Prague Chamber Orch., 1959-. Career: solo concerts & recitals in Prague, Split (Yugoslavia), Berlin, Dresden & Leipzig; TV recordings, Prague & Berlin; num. recordings for Czech. Radio, Prague, 1959-; recording for Radio Dresden, 1963. Recordings: Mozart's Serenade in B flat, 1961. Mbrships: Concert Artists Sect., (Union of Czech Composers); Czech. Sci. Soc. HOns: Bronze Medal, Int. Competition, Warsaw, 1955; 1st Class Dip., Prague Spring Fest, 1959; Gold Medal & 1st Prize, Nat. Concours, Bratislava, Czech., 1961; Dip., Helsinki, 1962; B Smetana Hon. Medal, Czech. Music Yr., 1974. Hobby: Aquarium. Mgmt: Pragokocert, Mel tézcké ném 1, Prague 1, Czech. Address: W. Piecka 89, 130 00 Prague 3, Czech. 4.

ACTON, Charles, b. 25 Apr. 1914. Music Critic; Journalist; Broadcaster; Lecturer. m. Carol Acton. Career: w. Thos Cook & Son (London & Haifa); Farming; Charcoal mfr.; Rep. for Ency. Britannica; Sales mgr., Tripod Harvesting; Music Critic, The Irish Times, 1955-; Gov. Royal Irish Acad. Music, 1955 (Coulson Gov. from 1958). Contbr. to The Irish Times and various periodicals in Ireland, UK. USA. Publs: Irish Music and Musicians. Mbrships: Critics Circle, London; RIAM; Feis Ceoil; NUJ; DOP (past hon. sec.); RDS; Nat. Lib. Soc.; Conetemporary Irish Art Soc.; Cambridge Univ. ADC (Life member). Addres: Carrickmines Station, Dublin 18, Eire. 3, 28.

ADAM, Jennifer Adele, b. 5 Oct. 1943. Port Augusta, S Aust. Woodwind Teacher. Educ: Hornsby Girls High Schl.; Balmain Tchrs. Coll., Sydney; NSW Conservatorium of Music; Pvte. pupil of Pamela Weston, London for clarinet. Career: Primary tchr., NSW Dept. Educ., Music Advsr., ibid., Pt.-time univ. lectr. in music educ., Macquarie Univ., 1967; Woodwind tchr., Harrow Educ. auth., London. Mbrships: Incorp. Soc. Musicians; Aust. Soc. Music Educ.; Int. Clarinet Soc.; Nat. Flute Assn. Inc., USA; Clarinet & Saxophone Soc. of GB; Clarinet Soc. of NSW; Sydney Flute Soc.; Assn. of Conservatorium (NSW) Ex-Students & Friends. Hobbies: Music; Travel; Photography; Country walking. Address: 15A Bracknell Gdns., London, NW3 7EE, UK.

ADAM, Jenö, b. 12 Dec. 1896. Szigetsentmiklos, Hungary. Composer; Conductor; Educator. Educ: Univ. of Budapest; Acad. of Msuic, Budapest; studied under Felix Weingartner, Basel, Switz. m. Olga Römet, 1 d. Debut: Budapest, 1927. Comps. incl: 2 operas; chmbr., music; orchl. & choral works; works for chmbr. orch., mixed choir & solo voices. Recordings: Qualiton LPX 11291 & LP 10028. Publs. incl: song-books for schls.; From the Scale to the Symphony, 1943; On Music, 1953-55. Mbrships: Int. Soc. for Music Educ.; Int. Folk Music Coun., Hungarian Sect. Hons: Meritorious Artist of the Hungarian Repub., 1955; Kossuth Prize, 1957. Address: Moszkva-ter 14, 1122 Budapest, Hungary.

ADAMS, Brenda Jane, b. 10 April 1954. Toronto, Ont., Can. Bassoonist; Manager. Educ: BMus (Perf.), Univ. of Toronto; as recip. of artist grant from the Can. Coun., studied w. William Waterhouse, UK. m. Stephen Baker Eprile, 1 c. Debut: Shakespearian Fest., Stratford, Ont., 1974. Career: Apps. w. Calgary Phil., Thunderbay Symph., CJRT Orch., Can. Opera Co., Huronia Symph.; Radio perfs.; Mgr., Toronto Chmbr. Winds, Can. Mbrships: Am. Fedn. of Musicians; Int. Double Reed Soc. Hons: Opera scholarships, Univ. of Toronot, 1973, '74; Music Talent Scholarship, ibid., 1975. Hobbies: Handspinning and its assoc. crafts; Tennis. Address: 62 Oriole Gardens, Apt. 10, Toronto, Ont. M4V 1V7, Can.

ADAMS, David Stephen, b. 10 Dec. 1909. Edinburgh, Scotland, UK. Retired Music Publisher. Educ: James Clark Schl., Edinburgh; FRCO; LRAM. m. Doris Raftree, 2 d. Career: Dir., Boosey & Hawkes Ltd.; Dir., Boosey & Hawkes Music Publishers Ltd.; Former Pres., Boosey & Hawkes, Inc., NY, USA. Mbrships: Exec. & Gen., Coun. Mbr., PRS; Coun. Mbr., Mech. Rights Soc. Ltd.; Hon. Mbr., Music Publishers Assn., UK; Pres., Music Publishers Assn. of Am., 1959; Hon. Mbr., Phi Mu Alpha Sinfonia, Columbia Univ., NY, 1958; Fellow, Royal Philatelic Soc. Hobbies: Music; Philately; Photography. Address: 4 Wildcroft Manor, Wildcroft Rd., Putney, London SW 15, UK.

ADAMS, John, b. 23 Jan. 1953. Meridian, Miss., USA. Composer; Percussionist. Educ: w. Fred Coulter, Wesleyan Coll. & Mercer Univ., Macon, Ga., 1969-70; w. James Tenney & Leonard Stein at Calif. Inst. of the Arts, Valencia, 1970-73; BFA, ibid., 1973: grad. studies w. Charles Knox at Ga. State Univ., Atlanta, 1973-74. m. Margrit von Braun. Comps. incl: Northern Summer, for Organ & 2 percussion, 1975; Songbirdsongs, Bk.1, for piccolo & percussion, 1974-75; Wind Garden, for flute & percusstion, 1975-77; Celestial Silence, for 2 SATB choruses, harp & percussion, 1977; Three on Hira, for flute & Koto (or harp) & percussion, 1977-78. num. awards & hons. incl. Grant from Nat. Endowment for Arts, 1974; Composer in Residence, Ossabaw Island Project, 1975, & at Hambidge Ctr., 1976-77; Winner, Nat. Fed. of Music Clubs Young Comps. Contest, 1978. Hobbies: Backpacking; Photography. Address: 218 Driveway, Fairbands, AK 99701, USA.

ADAMS, John M, b. 15 Feb. 1936. Cirencester, UK. Violist. Educ: RCM, 1959-61; ARCM. m. Elizabeth Harding, 2s., 1 d. Debut: soloist in Berlioz's Harold in Italy, 1974. Career: mbr. Halle Orch., 1961; sub-prin. viola, ibid., 1967; prin. viola, ibid., 1970. Recordings: A Little Music for a Few Friends by Italian comps. (w. Halle Wind Quintet). Hobbies: Reading; Astronomy. Address: 93 Fog Ln., Didsbury, Manchester M20 OSL, UK.

ADAMS, Kenneth Gaither, b. 5 Jan. 1946. Balt., Md., USA. Clarinettist. Educ: B Mus. Ed., Howard Univ., Wash. DC, (Clarinet w. Lawrence Bocaner), 1968; Mus. M., Manhattan Schl. of Mus., NYC (Clarinet w. Leon Russianoff, Saxophone & Flute w. Harvey Estrin, Flute w. Hal Archer), 1970. Career: Instr. of Clarinet, Howard Univ., 1967-68; Instr. of Clarinet, Manhattan Schl. of Music, 1969-70; Instr. of Woodwinds, Roosevelt Public Schl. System, 1970-71; Cons., Talent Unlimited, 1973: Instr. of Woodwinds & Theory, York Coll., 1972-74. Profl. Experience: Aspen Fest. Orchestra, 1966; Wash. Chamber Player, 1967; Nat. Orchestral Assn., 1969; Soc. of Black Composers Showcase, 1971: Symph. of the New World Quintet, 1970-71; Apple Hill Chamber Players, 1972; Sympy. of the New World, 1970-74; Urban Phil. Soc. 1973; Fest. Orch. of Jamaica, 1973: New Metro. Woodwind Quintet, 1971-74. Recordings: Hank Johnson, Septa Records; Ornette Coleman, WBAI Radio Stn.; Sound Track for Alvin Ailey Special Mbr., profl. orgs. Hobbies: Woodworking; Plants; Pocket Billiards; Sports Cars. Address: 315 E. 162nd St., No. 1, Bronx, NY 10451, USA.

ADAMS, Leslie, b. 1932. Cleveland, Ohio, USA. Composer; Choral Conductor; Music Educator. Educ: BM, Oberlin Coll.; MA, Calif. State Univ., Long Beach; PhD, Ohio State Univ. Debut: Concert of works presented by Ira Aldridge Soc., Steinway Hall, 1962, Judson Hall, 1963, NYC. Career: Fac. Mbr., Kan. Unv. Composition: Largo for Horn & Piano; Hosanna (Choral); Madrigal (Choral). Var. unpublished works for piano, horn, chorus, A Kiss in Xanadu (ballet). Publs: Problems of Composing Choral Music for High School Use, 1973. Contbr. to profl. jnrls. Mbrships: Afro-Am. Music Opportunities Assn.; Am. Choral Dirs. Assn.; Am. Music Ctr., Ind.; Pi Kappa Lambda; Phi Delta Kappa; Phi Mu Alpha Sinfonia. Hons: Winner, 1974 Choral Composition Competition, The Christian Arts, Inc.; Piano Concerto chosen for perf., 1974 Black Composers Symposium, Houston, Tex.; Piano concerto premiered for bi-centennial concert of Am. music, 1976. mgmt: Elaine Schuman-LeMoyne, 140-39 34th Ave., Flushing, NY 11354, USA. Address: 9409 Kempton Ave., Cleveland, OH, USA 8.

ADAMS, Park 'Pepper', b. 8 Oct. 1930. Highland Park, Mich., Usa. Composer; Arranger; Baritone Saxophonist. Educ: Wayne State Univ. m. Claudette Nadra Adams, 1 step-son. Career: featured artist on radio, Sweden, Denmark, France, Belgium, Netherlands & Norway; num. profl. apps. w. own group & w. orchs. inclng. Stan Kenton, Thelonious Monk, Benny Goodman, Thad Jones-Mel Lewis (1966-77); solo apps. w. Phila. Orch., Rochester Symph., NY, Toronto Symph. & Am. Symph.; Pres., Excorent Music, ASCAP. Comps: 29 works recorded & publd. Recordings: num., inclng. 15 LPs under own name. Mbrships: Bd. of Govs., Nat. Acad. of Recording Arts & Scis., NY Chapt.,

1978-80. Recip., num. hons., inclng: All-Stars'-All-Star Award, Playboy Mag., 1975, & Downbeat Int. Jazz Critics Poll, 1979. Hobbies: Literature; Art; Sport; Cinema; Photography. Address: c/o Radio Registry, 850 7th Ave., NYC, NY 10019, USA. 2.

ADAMS, Peter, D, b. 16 Feb. 1942. Newburgh, NY, USA. Musician (French Horn). Educ: BM, Berklee Coll. of Music, Boston, Mass.; Univ. of Mass. Debut: W. Birmingham Symph. Orch. Career incls: French Horn w. num. orchs. inclng: Birmingham Symph. Orch. Montreal Symph. Orch., Can.; Va. Symph. Orch.; Asbury Pk. Municpal Band; Relief Band, Harrah's Club, Reno, Nev. & Lake Tahoe, Calif.; TV apps. w. Birmingham Symph. Orch.; Film for Overseas Educ. Series w. Va. Symph. Orch. Recordings w. USMA Band, West Point, NY. Mbr. Int. Horn Soc. Address: 46 Wilkin St., Newburgh, NY 12550, USA.

ADAMS, Stanley, b. 1910. Brierley Hills, Staffs., UK. Music Adviser; Pianist; Conductor; Composer. Educ: studied pvtely. w. Edith Chambers; Royal Manchester Coll. of Music; LRAM; Assoc. Birmingham Schl. of Music m. Adelaide Clarke, 1 s., 1 d. Career: Dir. of Music, W. Riding of Yorks, 1954-62; Music ADvsr., City of Birmingham Educ. Committee, 1962-; Orchestral & Choral Cond.; Solo Pianist w. BBC & City of Birmingham Symph. Orchs. Compositions: The Infant King (carol sequence for Christmas); Festival Fancies (string pieces for children); 60 hymns for juniors. Hobbies: Gardening; Motoring. Address: 133 Oxford Rd., Moseley, Birmingham, UK. 3.

ADMSKY, Vladimir, b. 15 Feb. 1908. Kelske, Vinice, Mělník, Bohemia. Conductor; Composer. Educ: Pub. Music Schl. Libechov; study with Profs. Pavel Dedecek & Zdenek Hula. m. Anna Bausova, 3 children. Career: Bandmaster & Music Tchr., Kostelec on Labe; Ed. of popular & brass music for Czech Radio, Prague, 1945-65; Cond., small radio brass band 'Svitorka'; Instr., amateur brass bands; Ed. of folklore & brass music for publng. house Panton. Compositions: over 20 works incl. songs & traditional dances, polkas, waltzes, etc., many of these recorded on Panton label. Publ: We Play for Dance & Listening, 1961. Contbr. to: Lidova tvorivost mag.; Brass Orch. bulletin. Mbrships: Union of Authors; Union of Exec. Music Artists. Recip: Dips. for work w. Czech Radio, & for conducting & instrng. in music. Hobbies: Water sports; Yachting. Address: 120 00 Prague 2, Jugoslavska 29/620, Czechoslovakia.

ADAMSON, Janis-John, b. 10 Oct. 1924. Timosov, Russia. Cellist. Educ: Latvian State Conserv., Riga; w. Prof. Atis Teichmanis, Germany. m. Betty Adamson, 1d. Debut: at age 6. Career: Latvian Nat. Opera, Riga; Latvian Ballet Co. Orch., Stuttgart; Indpls. Symph. Orch.; Starlight Musicals, Ind., etc. Mbrships: Am. Fed. of Musicians. Hobby: Talent Scouting for Min. Vikings, profl. football team. Address: 820 N Graham Ave., Indpls., IN 46219, USA.

ADDIE, Fiona. Pianist. Educ: GRSM; LRAM; studied w. Vivian Langrish, Louis Kentner, & Marcel Gazell (Belgium). m. Dr. H. M. E. Cardwell, 1 d. Career: broadcasted for 20 yrs.; Mbr., Klaviol Piano Trio w. Peter Beaven & (late) Irene Richards, 1957-64; toured S. Africa, Rhodesian & Uganda w. Irene Richards, 1963; Played Beethoven's Triple Concerto w. Cape Town Symph. Orch.; toured Uganda for Brit. Coun.; played piano concertos, Cape Town, S Africa. & Bulawayo, Rhodesia, 1965; has given recitals in Wigmore Hall & many colls. & schls. thru'out Brit. Isles, also plays for Chmbr. Music Socs.; has Sonata Ensemble w. Peter Beavan; on Music Staff, St. Paul's Girl's Schl., 1966-. Mbr: ISM. Hobbies: Animals; Gardening. Address: Hill End Farm, Luppitt, Honiton, Devon, UK. 3.

ADDINSELL, Richard, b. 13 Jan. 1904. London, UK. Composer. Educ: RCM; Herford Coll., Oxford. Compositions. incl: film music for Dangerous Moonlight, (Warsaw Concerto), Goodbye Mr. Chips, The Greengage Summer, Roman Spring Of Mrs. Stone, 30 others; Stage works incl: Happy Hypocrite, Come Of Age (NY), num. others, in collaboration w. Clemence Dane; Num. Stage revues & many songs w. Joyce Grenfell. Recip. Polish Silver Cross Of Merit. Address: 1 Carlyle Mansions, Cheyne Walk, London SW3, UK. 1, 13.

ADDISON, John, b. 16 Mar. 1920. W. Chobham, Surrey, UK. Composer. Educ: ARCM. m. Pamela Druitt, 1 s., 1 d. Career: Cond. of own music, Royal Albert Hall (prom), Royal Fest. Hall, etc. Comps: Orchl. & Chmbr. works incl: Carte Blanche (ballet suite); Trumpet Concerto; Serenade for Wind Quintet & Harp, Inventions for Oboe & Piano; Conversation Piece for 2 Soprano Voices, Harpsichord & Harp; Divertmento for 2 trumpet, horn & trombone; Concerto for trumpet & strings. Film Music; Over 60 scores inclng. Tom Jones, Sleuth; Theatre Music: Beckett, Ionescu, etc. Mbrships: CGGB; Comps. & Lyricists Guild of Am.; Screen Comps. of Am.; Songwriters Guild, UK. Hons:

Sullivan Prize for Comp. Acad. Award for Tom Jones; Anthony Asquith Award for A Bridge Too Far, 1978. Hobbies: Skiing; Tennis; Mountain Walking. Mgmt: Liz Keys, London Mgmt, UK; Marc Newman, Hollywood, USA. Address: 18060 Boris Dr., Encino, CA 91316, USA.

ADELSON, Bonnie Lynn, b. 4 Mar. 1944. Oakland, Calif., USA. Solo Tympanist; Percussionist. Educ: BA, San Francisco State Coll.; Juilliard Schl. of Music. Career: Solo Tympanist, Carmel Bach Fest., Calif., Puerto Rico Symph. Orch., Harkness Ballet Orch., NY., Broadway Show, Man Of La Mancha; Zagreb Radio-TV Symph. Orch., Zagreb Phil., Jugoslavia, 1968-73; Radio-TV Luxembourg Symph. Orch., 1973-. Recordings: Concerto for 4 Tympani & Orch., Boris Papandopulo; Concert, for Jazz Ensemble, String Quartet & 4 Tympani, Ozren Depolo; num. w. Radio-TV Luxembourg Symph. Orch., Vox Records. Mbr. Am. Fedn. of Musicians, Local 6, San Francisco, Local 802, NYC. Recip. Scholarship to San Francisco State Coll., 1961-65. Hobbies: Homemaking; Piano; Reading. Addres: c/o Radio-Tele Luxembourg Symph. Orch., Luxembourg.

ADKINS, Anthony, b. 14 Jan. 1949. Northampton, UK. Concert Pianist. Educ: RCM (w. Eric Harrison & Bernard Roberts), 1967-72; ARCM (piano perf.); State Conserv. of Music, Cracow, Poland (w. Jan Hoffman), 1974-75. m. Kazimiera Brynkus. Debut: Wigmore Hall, London, 1973. Career: concerts at Wigmore Hall, Purcell Room, Fairfield Halls; extensive tours of UK; perfs. in Germany, Austria & Netherlands; tchr., var. colls., 1968-. mbr., ISM. recip., Chopin Fellowship form Polish Govt. Hobbies: Arts; Travel; Walking. Address: 151 Lichfield Ct., Sheen Rd., Richmond, Surrey TW9 1AY, UK.

ADLER, Barbara Walz, b. 28 Feb. 1943. Signaw, Mich., USA. Organist; Educator. Educ: BM, 1945, MMus, 1966, Univ. of Mish.; MSc, Kan. State Ichrs. Coll., 1967; DMa, Univ. of Kan., 1971. m. Richard C. Adler, 1 s., 1 d. Career: Asst. Prof. of Music, Univ. of HI, Honolulu, 1969-73; Organist, Ch. of the Holy Apostles, Hilo, HI, 1973-77. Mbrships: HI Concert Soc. (Pres.); HI Assoc. of Music Socs. (Sec.); AGO; Pi Kappa Lambda; Mu Phi Epsilon. Hobbies: Sailing; Hiking; Skin Diving; Gardening; Childbirth Education. Address: 1179 Kahoa Rd., Hilo, HI 96720, USA.

ADLER, Kurt Herbert, b. 2 Apr. 1905. Conductor; Opera Impressario. Educ: Acad. of Music, Vienna, Austria; Conserv. & Music-Histl. Inst., Univ. of Vienna. Career: Cond., Max Reinhardt Theatre, Vienna, 1925-28; Cond., Germany, Italy & Czechoslovakia, 1928-37; Asst. Cond. to Toscanini & Instr., Mozarteum, Salzburg Festivals, 1936-37; Cond. Chgo. Opera Co., USA, 1938-42; Cond., NY Opera Co., 1945; San Fran. Opera Co., 1943-; Artistic & Musical dir., ibid., 1953-56; Gen. Dir., 1956-; Prod. Spring Opera, San Fran.; Gen. Dir., Western Opera Theater; Hd., Merola Opera Prog.; Artistic Advsr., San Fran. Conserv. of Music, 1949-51; Guest Cond., var. orchs. in USA & Italy, 1938-58. Mbrships: Trustee, Nat. Opera Inst., 1969-70. Hons: Mus. D., Coll. of the Pacific, 1956; var. decorations from Austria, Germany & Italy. Address: San Fran. Opera Assn., War Mem. Opera House, San Fran., CA, USA.

ADLER, Peter Herman, b. 2 Dec. 1898. Czechoslovakia. Conductor. Educ: Univ. of Prague; Prague Conservatory. Debut: New York Philharmonic, Carnegie Hall, 1940 (US). Career: Music & Artistic dir./Cond., NBC-TV Opera Theater, WNET Opera Theater, Balt. Symph., Metropolitan Opera, Julliard Am. Opera Ctr., Leningard Symph., Prague Symph. Recordings: On RCA Victor label. Contbr. to: New York Times, Sunday Arts & Leisure; Opera News; Saturday Review. Hons: US TV Acad. Awards Nominations, 1971. Mgmt: Columbia Artists Mgmt. Inc. Address: 260 West End Ave., NY NY 10023, USA. 2.

ADLER, Samuel H., b. 4 Mar. 1928. Mannheim, Germany. Composer; Conductor; Professor. Educ: B Mus, Boston Univ., USA; MA, Harvard Univ.; studied Comp. w. var. masters. m. Carol Ellen Stalker, 2 d. Career: Prof. & 1st Cond., 7th Army Symph. Orch., 1952; Prof. of Comp., N. Tex. State Univ., 1956-66; Cond., Dallas Lyric Theatre & Dallas Chorale; Guest Cond., num. symph. orchs. & operas, worldwide; now Prof. of Comp. incl: 5 Symphs.; 4 Operas; 6 Str. Quartets; var. Sonatas; 3 Cantatas. Recordings for major Cos. Publs. incl: Anthology for the Teaching of Choral Conducting. Contbr. to num. profl. jrnls. Mbr., Profl. assns. Hons. incl: D Mus, Southern Meth. Unv.; 4 Pulitzer Prize nominations; num. commissions. Address: 54 Railroad Mills Rd., Pittsford, NY 14534, USA. 6.

ADMON, Jedidiah, b. 5 Nov. 1894. Jerusalem, Palestine. Composer for Ohel Theatre. Educ: grad., Teurs. Seminary, Jerusalem; Ecole Normale de Music, Paris; 4 yrs. pvte. study w. Nadia Boulanger. m. Esther, 4 c. Debut: Paris, 1930. Career:

Music for films; Lectures; TV & radio apps.; var. musicals for Nat. Theatre Habima. Var. recordings. Contbr. to: Alliance Revue; Jewish Music Forum. Mbrships: Pres., Israel Comps. Soc., 1940-47; Fndr. & Pres. of Comps. & Authors financial org. ACUM, & pres., Israel Comps. Soc., 1950-56. Hons: Nat. Govt. Prize, 1974 (Israel). Address: Maharal Str. No. 6, Tel Aviv, Israel.

ADNI, Daniel, b. 6 Dec. 1951. Haifa, Israel. Concert Pianist. Educ: Paris Conservatoire. Debut: Wigmore Hall, London, 1970. Career: Concerts w. LPO, New Philharmonia, RPO, Halle Orch., Liverpool Phil., Bournemouth Symph., Scottish Nat.; some BBC Orch.; Frequent BBC Radio Broadcasts, BBC 2 TV recital, Gala Perf., 1973. Recordings exclusively for EMI -Chopn, Debussy, Mendelssohn (Complete Songs Without Words), Ravel. Greig. Recip., First Prize for Piano, Solfege, Sight Reading of Paris Conserv., 1969. Hobbies: Cinema; Theatre; Sports; Bridge. Address: Harold Holt Ltd., 122 Wigmore St., London W1H 0NQ, UK. 3, 28.

ADOLPH, Heinz, b. 1915. Berlin. Composer; Conductro; Plays Piano, Organ, Oboe & Violin. Educ: Orch. Schl.; State Acad. for Music, Berlin. m. Elaga Richter, 1 s., 1 d. Career: army & war serv. w. music corps, 1936-46; 1st Cond., Theatre in Lippstadt, 1946; 1st Cond., Theater am Nollendorfplats, Berlin, 1947; Cond., Ice Ballet, Holiday on Ice, Maxi & Ernst Baier, 1950-57; Freelance Composer & Arr. for films, stage & recordings, 1957-; w. Recording-Prods., Teldec, Hamburg, 1961-. Compositions incl: music for ballets; 1 piano concerto; cantata; The Cornet; Little Symphonie 1961; chmbr. music; songs; music for films; many arrs. for operettas & musicals for records. Recip. of Grand Prix of Bilbao for music of short film Sunday Morning, 1966. Hobbies: Walking; Swimming; Ping-Pong; Motoring. Address: Bantschow 32, 2 Hamburg 64, German Fed. Repub. 3.

ADOMINÁN, Lan, b. 29 Apr. 1905. near Mogiliov-Podolsk, Ukraïne. Composer; Conductor; Violinist. Educ: Musikvereinschule, Czernowitz, Bucovina; Peabody Conserv. of Music, Balt., USA; Curtis Inst. of Music, Phila. m. Maria Teresa Toral. Career: Cond. & instrumentalist; Radio & film work; comps. performed by St. Louis Orch., NBC Orch., Nat. Orch. (ORTF) & other major orchs. Comps. incl: Le Matin des Magiciens (large orch. & choir of 12 flutes); 8 symphs. var. orchl. works; opera, La Mascherata; Lieder; chmbr. music Mbr., Mexican Soc. of Comps. & Authors (part of CISAC). Hons: Premio Silvestre Revueltas, Nat. Univ. of Mexico, 1975; 1st Prize, Latin Am., Goethe Inst., Munich, German Fed. Repub., (for instrumental septet), 1975. Hobby: Work. Address: Georgia 152, Mexico 18, DF, Mexico.

ADORJAN, András György, b. 26 Sept. 1944. Budapest, Hungary. Flautist. Educ: studied w. J-P Rampal, Int. Summer Acad., Nice, 1964-68; w. Aurele Nicolet, State Music Acad., Freiburg, 1968-70; Dip. in Dentistry, Copenhagen, 1968. m. Marianne Henkel, 3 children. Career: Soloist w. Royal Opera. Stockholm, Gürzenich-Orch., Cologne, SWF Radio Symph. Orch., Baden-Baden & Bavarian Broadcast Symph. Orch., Munich. Recordings incl: Erato; Nippon Columbia; RCA Victor Publs: var. eds. for Musica Rara, London & Ed. Billaudot, Paris. Hons: incl: Prize, Int. Flute Competition, Montreux, 1968; Premier Grand Prix, Concours Int. de Flûte, Paris, 1971. Mgmt: Wilhelm Hansen Koncertdirektion, Copenhagen. Address: c/o Sinfonieorch. des Bayerischen Rundfunks, D-8 München 2, Postfach, German Fed. Repub.

AESCHBACHER, Niklaus, b. 30 Apr. 1917. Trogen/AR, Switz. Musical Director. Educ: Grad. summa cum laude, Zürich Conserv. m. Elisabeth Rüetschi. Debut: Tonhalle, Zürich, 1938. Career: Musical Dir., Stadttheater, Bern, 1949-54, 68; Prin. Dir., NHK-Symph. Orch., Tokyo, Japan, 1954-56; Gen. Music Dir., Kiel, 1959-63, Detmold, 1964-72; Prof., Leiter der Opernschule an der NWD-Musicakadamie, Detmold, 1972-. Comp. radio opera, Die roten Schüle. Recordings: Peter Mieg's Konzert für 2 Klaviere; H Sütermeister's Max & Moritz & Die schwarze Spinne. Publs: sev. musical eds. Mbrships: Schweiz. Tonkünstler; SUISA; Schweiz. Bühnenkünstler. Recip. Kulturpreistraeger der Lippischen Landeszeitung, 1973. Address: Friedr. Ebertstr. 5, D-493 Detmold (Schanze), German Fed. Repub.

AFFEL, John Kweku, b. 21 Sept. 1936. Himan, Ghana. Teacher. Educ: 4 yr. Tchr. Trng. Educ.; Music Educ. Dip. m. Christiana Cobbinah, 5 d. Debut: w. choral comp. Wo So Ye Bi. Career incl: featured on radio & TV progs. w. choirs inclng. Konenda Adehye Singers & Sekondi Vocal Band. Comps. incl: Beposo Kurow Hyeren; Arise & Shine; Do na di; Kontonkurowi; Aka bi (More beyond); Akyedze; Dabi asem ntsi; over 50 hymn tunes. Has recorded for Ghana Broadcasting Corp. & TV. Mbrships: Ghana Music Tchrs. Assn.; Arts Coun. of Ghana;

Nat. Instr., Ghana United Vocal Bands. Hobbies: Tailoring; Gardening. Address: HIMAN, PO Box 108, Prestea, Ghana. 23, 28.

AFROUZ, Novin, b. 1 Sept. 1942. Tehran, Iran. Concert Pianist. Educ: Piano dip., Conserv. of Milan, Italy; Piano virtuosity degree, Conserv. of Geneva, Switz. Debut: Sala G Verdi, Milan, Italy. Career: Concers (recitals & w. orch.), Europe, Asia & Africa; Sev. Int. Music Fests. Comps: Turkoman Dances. Sev. recordings. Mbrships: Int. Women's Club; Zonta. Hobbies: Painting; Writing poetry. Address: Mosasagh Ave., Pahlevan Ave. 60, Tehran, Iran.

AFZELIUS, Björn Svante, b. 27 Jan. 1947. Jönköping, Sweden. Composer; Author; Singer; Guitarist. Educ: Univ. of Lund. 1 d. Debut: Malmoe, Nov. 1970. Career: Toured Scandinavia w. Hoola Bandoola Band, 1970-76; w. Björn Afzelius Band, 1976-79; Appts., UK, German Dem. Repub., Cuba; Num. radio & TV apps. Comps: Over 45 songs; music for 2 musicals 3 movies & 1 play. Recordings: 4 albums w. Hoola Bandoola Band; 5 albums w. Björn Afzelius Band, etc. Publs: Songbooks. Contbr. to: Swedish music mags. Hons: Govt. Scholarships; Record of the Year Award, Aftonbladet, 1976. Hobbies: Lits.; Travelling; Sports. Address: Kastellgatan 12, 41122 Gothenburg, Sweden.

AGBENU, Victor Nicholas, b. 1 Dec. 1945. Bayive/Atiavi, Volta Reg., Ghana. Music Tutor in Cello, Piano & African Drums. Educ: Dip. Music Educ., Specialist Coll., Winneba, Ghana, 1973. m. Victoria Agbenu, 1 s. Debut Ghana Broadcasting Studio, 1975. Career: Radio apps. Comps: Mina Miawodeka Le Ghana (Let Unity Prevail in Ghana); Miawoezo (You Are Welcome); Xexeame Lolo; Ghana Lom (Ghana Loves Me); Morzola; Sports Anthem. Mbrships: Ghana Music Tutors Assn., Winneba; Ghana Assn. of Musicians, Arts Coun., Accra. Hons: Winner, Nat. Patriotic Songs Competition, NRC, 1975; Winner, Sports Anthem Competition, Sports Coun. of Ghana for Supreme Coun. of Sports for Africa, 1976. Hobbies incl: Comp. Address: Mt. Mary Coll., PO Box 19 Somanya, Ghana.

AGER, Laurence Mitchell, b. 18 Nov. 1904. Palegate, Sussex, UK. Composer; Writer. Educ: AIB; ACCS; ARCO. m. Doris Park, 1 s. Career: Organist & Choirmaster at chds. & Dir. of choral grps., 1918-55; Music Master, Temple Grove Schl., 1939-45; Music Critic, Hastings Observer & other papers, 1959-. Comps: many partsongs, songs, piano & organ pieces & arrs. Contbr. to var. jrnls. inclng: Comp.; Musical Times; Musical Opinion; Strad; Lady. Mbrships: Comps. Guild of GB; PRS; Dolmetsch Fndn. Address: 8 Oaklea Close, Old Roar Rd., St. Leonards-on-Sea, E Sussex TN37 7HB, UK. 3, 4.

AGERSNAP, Harald, b. 2 Mar. 1899. Vinding, Vejle, Denmark. Pianist; Cellist; Chorusmaster. Educ: Royal Acad. of Music, Copenhagen, 1914-18. m. Rudie Agersnap, 1s. Career: Cellist in var. orchs.; Repetiteur at Royal Danish Ballet; Chorus master, Royal Theatre, Copenhagen, 1934-68. Comps: Songs; Str. Quarter. Mbr., Soc. of Danish Comps. Hon: Kt. of Danarbrog. Address: 40 Ordruphojvej, 2920 Charlottenlund, Denmark.

AGOSTI, Guido, b. 11 Aug. 1901. Forli, Italy. Pianist. Educ: Conserv. & Univ. of Bologna; Dip. of pianofote. m. Lydia Grauen. Career: concerts, Italy, NY, Mexico, S Am., Egypt, Lebanon, Switz., Turkey, Belgium, Germany, Hungary, Romania, Portugal; apps. w. many noted perfs.; Piano & Chmbr. music Prof., Venice & Rome State Conservs., Nat. Acad. of Sant Cecilia, Rome; Piano Master Classes in many places inclng: Franz Liszt Hoschschule, Weimar, Germany, Juilliard Schl., NYC, USA. Comps: works for piano & for voice & piano. Publs: Osservazioni intorno alla tecnica pianistica; transcriptions & eds. of var. musica; works. Recip. num. hons. inclng: Hon. Mbr. RAM, London; VP, Nat. Acad. of Santa Cecilia, Rome; VP, Rubinstein Competition, Israel. Hobby: Collecting books on city of Paris. Address: Via Filippo Civinini 61, 00197 Roma, Italy.

AGUIAR, Ernani Henrique Chaves, b. 30 Aug. 1950. Estado do Rio, Petropolis, Brazil. Cathedral Choir Director; Assistant Director of Young Symphony Orchestra. Debut: w. Petropolis Cathedral Choir, 1968. Career: Dir., Petropolis Cathedral Choir; Asst. Dir., Young Symph. Orch., Rio de Janeiro; num. concerts, dir. & violinist, Brazil & Italy. Comps. incl: works for piano, string quartets, duets, soloists & choirs. Mbrships: incl: Order Brazilian Musicist. Hons: Prize Mesbla, Congress Young Musicists, Rio de Janeiro, 1970; 'Capellae Choralis Magistrum, Honoris Causa', S Maria a Peretola, Florence, Italy, 1975. Mgmt: Abrarte-Assoc. Brasileira de Arte, Rua Dr. Sa Earp 280, Petropolis, RJ, Brazil. Address: Rua 16 de Marco 167 Apto. 401, 25.600 Petropolis, Estado do Rio, Brazil.

AGUIRRE, Diana V, b. 5 June 1941. San Diego, Calif., USA. Specialist in Renaissance Instruments & Vocal Compositions of

same period. Educ: B Mus, Univ. Southern Calif. Career incls: Apps: MENC, Shrine Auditorium Concert, 1958; Old Globe Madrigal Singers & Silvergate Consort, Nat. Shakespeare Fest., Globe Theatre, San Diego, Calif., 1961-76. San Diego Symphonic Chorale, San Diego Civic Theatre. Comps: Nymph's Reply to the Passionate Shepherd (voice); The Bait (voice). Num. recordings. Contbr. to Pan Pipes Mag. of Sigma Alpha Iowa. Recip. Award for Outstanding Madrigal Singer of Yr., San Diego City Coll., 1960. Hobbies: Aviculture; Costume Design. Address: 1424 Essex St., San Diego, Calif., USA.

AGUSTSSON, Herbert H, b. 1926. Graz, Austria. Composer; Horn Player. Educ: studied w. Franz Mixa & A. Michl, Graz (Grad., 1944). Career: 1st Horn, Graz Phil. Orch., 1944-51, & Icelandic Symph. Orch., 1952-; Tchr. & Choral Cond., Iceland, 1952-. Compositions incl: Seven Inventions, op. 11, for clarinet & bassoon; Quartetto breve, op. 15, for viola, oboe, horn & bassoon; Five Songs, op. 13, for soprano, horn & piano; Kammermusik for 9 wind instruments; Three Spiritual Songs for bass & orch.; Concerto breve, op. 19, for orch.; Movimenti ritmici, op. 16, for orch.; Shades of Colour, op. 17, for orch.; Tempi mutabile, op. 18, for orch.; Suite for Orchestra, op. 19; Psalms in the Atomic Age for soprano & chmbr. ensemble; Prayer for male choir. Address: c/o Islenzk Tonverkamidstöd, Laufasveg 40, Reykjavik, Iceland.

AGYEI, Yawa Grace, b. 25 April 1938. Anfoega Bume, VR, Ghana. Singing Teacher. Educ: Music Tchrs. Cert., Music Schl. STC Winneba; Dip. course, ibid, 1964-66; LRSM (London), 1967. Debut: As soloist, STC Assembly Hall, 1965. Career: Tchr., LA Mid Schl., Anfoega Bume Vr Ghana, 1960; Tchr., LA Mid Schl., Vakpo Vr Ghana, 1961; Music Tchr., EP Tr. Coll. Amedzofe Vr Ghana, 1963-64; Music Tchr., Anfoega Tr. Coll., Anfoega, 1966-72; Voice Tutor, Cond., Chapel Choir, Nat. Acad. of Music, Winneba, 1973-78; Var. apps. as Cond. & Adjudicator, Ghana. Mbrships: Ghana Nat. Assn. of Tchrs.; Music Tchrs. Assn. (Ghana); Int. Soc. for Music Educs. Hobbies: Sewing; Gardening; Fold Dancing; Folk Drumming; Folk Song Collecting. Address: Westminster Choir Coll., Princeton, NJ 08540, USA.

AHARONI, Avraham, b. 4 Mar. 1924. Vilna, Poland. French Horn Player. Educ: Mizrachi Tchrs. Sem.; Rubin Acad. of Music Jerusalem, Israel. m. Sarah Aharoni, 3 children. Career: Ldr., Horn Sect., Jerusalem Symph. Orch. of Israel Broadcasting Authority; num. solo & chmbr. music perfs. on Radio; toured Europe w. Israel Phil., 1971; has played under major Conds. inclng. Klemperer, Bernstein, Kertes & Krips. Compositions (recorded): Arrs., mainly for Wind, broadcast by Israel Radio. Recordings: Num. Solo & Chmbr. music tapes for Israel Radio. Hobby: Interest in & Reading of Scientific & Technical Publications. Address: 8 Shamay St., Jerusalem 94631, Israel.

AHERN, David Anthony, b. 2 Nov. 1947. Sydney, Australia. Composer; Conductor; Lecturer. Educ: NSW Conserv. of Music; Rheinische Musikschule, 1968. Debut: Cond. own comp. at Sydney Cell Block Theatre, 1966. Career: Formed Teletopa Live Electronic Music Grp., 1970; Performed in Aust., Manilla, London, NY & Japan; Regular Broadcaster on New Music over ABC Radio. Comp. of orchl., chmbr., solo wind & electronic music; Lectr., Expmtl. Music, Sydney Coll. of the Ars. Recordings incl: After Mallamé. Contbr. to profl. jrnls.; Music Critic, Daily & Sunday Telegraphs, Sydney. Mbrships. incl: Artistic Dir., AZ Music; ISCM (Sydney); Fellowship of Aust. Comps. Hobbies: Cooking; Travel. Address: 46 Rosser St., Balmain, Sydney, Australia.

AHLÉN, Carl-Gunnar, b. 3 Sept. 1938. Stockholm Sweden. Music Critic. Educ: Fil. kand. Divorced, 2 d. Career: Radio & TV broadcaster, Swedish Radio, 1963-; Music Critic, Svenska Dagbladet, 1965; Sr. Music Critic, ibid., 1967-; Publr., quarterly music jrnl. Musik och Ljudteknik, 1973-74; Record prod., mainly histl. re-issues for CBS & EMI; recordings for Deutsche Gramophone at Drottninsholm Ct. Theatre; Special Courses in Art of Performance, Univs. of Uppsala, Lund & Stockholm. Mbrships: Pres., Ljudtekniska sallskapet, 1967-74; VP, ibid., 1974-75; Sec. Swedish Sect., ISCM, 1970-75. Address: Hornsgatan 148/3, S-117 28 Stockholm, Sweden.

AHLGRIMM, Isolde, b. 31 July 1914. Vienna, Austria. Harpischordist; Professor of Harpischord, Musikhochschule, Vienna. Educ: Staatsakademie fur Musik (now called Musikhochschule), Vienna, div. Career: Concerts in most Euwopean countries; Teheran & USA; Num. TV & radio apps. Recordings: Complete Works for Harpischord of J S Bach (Philips); Recordings for Amadeo, Belvedere, Deutsche Schallplatten, Tudor & Musical Heritage Soc. Publs. incl: Reprint of Grundrichtiger ... Unctericht der Musickalischen Kunst ... by Daniel Speer, Ulm 1687 & 1697, 1974 by Ed. Peters, Leipzig. Contbt. to profl. jrnls. Mbr. Wiener Bachgesellschaft.

Recip. of Das goldene Ehrenzeichen fur Verdienste um die Republik Osterreich, 1975. Hobby: Nature Lover. Address: Strudelhofg. 17,A-1090 Vienna, Austria.

AHLSKOG, Gunnar Mathias, b. 6 June 1914. Nedervetil, Finland. Organist; Choirmaster; Music Master. Educ: ch. musician and music tchrs. exams. m. Elsa Nygaard, 3 d. Career incls: num. concerts as Choir Dir & Organist, Scandinavian countries & USSR; Organist, Cantor, Swedish Parish of Vasa; Music Reporter, Vasabladet. Mbrships: Chmn., Ch. Musicians Soc. of Finland; Nordiska kyrkomusikraadet; Synod, 1963-77; Hymn Book Committee, 1975-. Hobbies: Fishing; Sports. Address: Almavägen 25-27, 65610 Smedsby, Finland.

AHLSTROM, David, b. Feb. 1927. Lancaster, NY, USA. Composer; Writer; Teacher. Educ: BM, MM, Cinn. Conserv. of Music; Dips. Piano, Piano Tuning; PhD Comp., Eastman Schl. of Music, Univ. of Rochester. m. Doris Rohl Ahlstrom, 1 s. Career incls: Vis. Lectr. var. univs. in USA; Assoc. Prof. of Comp. & Theory, Eastern Ill. Univ., Charleston, 1967-76. Comps. incl: Scherzo for Cup Muted Trumpet, Winds & Percussion; Var. operas. Num. recordings. Publs. incl: Creative Sound as the Ground of Music, 1974. Contbr. to profl. jrnls. Mbrships: Nat. Opers Assn.; Nat. Soc. of Lit. & the Arts; Music Educators Nat. Conf. Recip. Danforth Fndn. Grant, 1965. Hobby: Walking. Address: 62 Oakwoood St. No. 4, San Francisco, CA 94110, USA. 4.

AHLSTEDT, Linda Foxx, b. 1 Oct. 1947. Ithaca, NY, USA. Music Teacher (Orff Specialist). Educ: BM, State Univ. Coll. of NY at Fredonia; Med. Univ. of Md.; studied piano w. Claudette Sorel; Orff Cert. Practicum 1, Alfred Univ. special course cert. Orff Inst., 1976-77. m. Douglas Ahlstedt. Career: Dept. of Defense Schls. Music Speicalist, Okinawa, 1969-70; Macedon Flem. Schl., NY, 1970-72, Music Specialist, Daly City Schls., Calif., 1972-73, Edgemont Schl. Dist., Scarsdale, NY, 1973-76. Mbrships: Am. Orff-Schulwerk Assn.; Sigma Alpha Iota; Kappa Delta Pi. Hobbies incl: Skiing; Golf; Making Folk Instruments; Opera. Address: c/o Deutsche Oper am Rhein, 4000 Dusseldorf, German Fed. Repub.

AHN, Yong Ku, b. 18 Feb. 1928. Wonsan, Korea. Violinist. Educ: Coll. of Music, Seoul Nat. Univ.; Musikhochschule, Munich; Akademie für Music, Vienna. m. Chung Hyun Kim, 3c. Debut: Seoul. Career: Prof., Seoul Nat. Univ.; Fndr., Ahn Strng. Sintonetta; Music Dir., Columbia Chmbr. Orch.; tchr. of violin, viola & chamber music on fac. of Peabody Inst. of John Hopkins Univ.; tchr. of Kyung Wha Chung, Young Uck Kim & other notable artists. Address: 5017 Durham Ct., Columbia, MD 21044, USA.

AHNSJÖ, Claes H, b. 1 Aug. 1942. Stockholm, Sweden. Opera singer (lyric tenor). Educ: Music Acad. (opera schl.) 1969. m. Helena Jungwirth, 2c. Debut: as Tamino in Magic Flute, Stockholm, 1969. Career: Royal Theatre, Stockholm, 1969-73; Bavarian State Opera, Munich. 1973-; apps. on TV; roles include Fenton in Merry Wives of Windsor & Tom in Rake's Progress. Recodings: works by Haydn, Mozart, Schubert, Bruckner, Donizetti & Nicolai. Hon. Kammersänger, 1977. Hobbies: Cooking; Mountain wandering. Address: Hofmarkstr. 21G, 8033 Planegg/Munich, German Fed. Repub.

AHRENDT, Karl F., b. 7 Mar. 1904. Toledo, Ohio, USA. Composer; Violinist; Professor; Administrator. Educ: B Mus, Cinn. Conserv. of Music, 1936; M Mus, 1937, PhD, 1946, Eastman Schl. of Music; pvte. music study in Berlin & Paris, 3 yrs. Career: Assoc. Prof. Music, Fla. State Univ., 1937-44; Dir., Schl. of Music & Prof. of Music, Augustana Coll., Rock Island, Ill., 1946-50 & Ohio Univ., Athens, 1950-67; Prof. of Music, ibid., 1967-74; Disting. Prof. Emeritus, 1974-. Comps. incl: Johnny Appleseed (orch.), 1951; Pastorale (strings), 1976; (also recorded) Montage (orch.), Publs: Affirmation for wind ensemble, 1976; Montage for orch., 1977. Mbr., musical assns. Hons. incl: 1st Prizes, Roth & Ohio Music Tchrs. Assn. Comp. Competitions, 1972. Hobbies: Travel; Gardening. Address: 5 Old Peach Ridge Rd. Athens, OH 45701, USA.

AHRENS, Joseph Johannes Clemens, b. 17 Apr. 1904. Sommersell, Westf., Germany. Composer. Educ: State Acad. for Ch. & Schl. Music, Berlin; State exams, Organist & Choir Dir., & Tchng. post at colls. m. Gisela Schroeder, 2 d. Career: Emeritus Prof., Hochschule for Music & Arts, Berlin; Comps. incl: 30 organ pieces; 7 choral partitas; concert for organ & wind instruments; Trilogia Sacra (Domus Dei, Regnum Dei, Civitas Dei, also Verwadlungen 1-3); 7 Masses; 27 Latin & German Motels & choir pieces. Mbr., Acad. of Art, Berlin. Hons. incl: Ehrengast der Deutschen Akadamie Villa Massimo, Rome, & Silberne Pontifikats-Medaille, Rome, both 1968. Hobby: Gardening. Address: Hüningerstr. 26, D-1000 Berlin 33, German Fed. Repub.

AHSEFJAH, Bijan, b. 9 June 1940. Tehran, Iran. Opera & Stage Director. Educ: Conserv. of Music as singer & Dir. m. Wendy Ahsefjah, 4c. Career: Singer & Stage Dir. in num. opera houses; Prod. & Dir., num. classical & modern works incl. Gianni Schicchi, Lucia di Lammermor, Tosca, La Bohéme, Falstaff, Carmen & Salome. Hons: Dr. Fuchs-Corbett Fndn. Scholarship; Cinn. Conserv. of Music Scholarship. Mgmt: AIM; Basil Horsfield. Address: Tehran Opera, Ave. Arfa, Tehran, Iran.

AITAY, Victor, Budapest, Hungary. Violinist. Educ: Royal Acad. of Music; studied violin w. Bela Bartok, Zoltan Kodaly, chmbr. music w. Leo Weiner & Ernst Von Dohanny; Artist Dip., Franz Liszt Royal Acad. of Music, Budapest, 1939. m. Eva Vera Kellner, 1 d. Career: Organizer, Ldr., Aitay Str. Quartet which toured Europe; Recitalist & Soloist w. symph. orchs., Met. Opera Assn., NYC, 1948-54; Concertmaster, Chgo., Symph. Orch., 1954-; Co-Concertmaster, ibid. 1962-; Concertmaster, Ravinia (Ill.) Music Fest., 1960-; Prof., 1st Int. String Congress; Prof., Violin, DePaul Univ. Chgo., 1962-; Ldr., Chgo. Symph. Str. Quartet; Cond., Music Dir., Lake Forest (Ill.) Symph. Orch.; has given num. performs. at Casals Fest. on invitation of Pablo Casals. Address: 212 Oak Knoll Terr., Highland Park., IL 60035, USA. 2.

AITKEN, Hugh, b. 7 Sept. 1924. New York, NY, USA. Composer; Teacher. Educ: BS, Juilliard Schl. of Music, 1949; MS, ibid., 1950. m. Laura Tapia, 1s., 1 d. Career: Fac., Juilliard Schl. of Music, NYC, USA, 1960-70; Currently Prof. of Music, William Paterson Coll., Wayne, NJ. Comps. incl: Works for string orch., band, bassoon, violin, contrabass & piano; Four Pieces, Four Hands (piano); Suite in Six (band); Suite (clarinet). Contbr. to Notes, jrnl. of Music Lib. Assn. Mbrships: ASCAP; Am. Music Ctr., Hegel Soc. of Am. Recip. num. hons. Hobbies: Reading; Chess; Hiking; Cuisine. Address: William Paterson Coll., Wayne, NJ 07470, USA.

AITKEN, Robert M, b. 28 Aug. 1939. Kentville, NS, Can. Flautist; Composer; Conductor. Educ: BMus (comp.), Univ. of Toront, 1961; MMus (comp.), ibid., 1964; studied flute w. Nicholas Fiore, Marcel Moyse, Julius Baker, Jean-Pierre Rampal & others. m. Marion Ross, 2d. Debut: Prin, flute, Vancouver Symph., aged 19. Career incl: num. solo apps. w. orchs. in Can., USA & Europe; num. solo & chmbr. music recitals on CBC radio & TV, USA, Japan & throughout Europe; mbr. CBC Symph. Orch., 1960-64; co-prin. flute, Toronto Symph., 1965-70; Fndr., Mus. Dir., Music Today Shaw Fest., Ont., 1970-72; Fndr., Artistic Dir., New Music Concerts, Toront, 1971-; num. tchng. posts. Comps. incl. orchl., instrumental & electronic works. num. recordings incl. Bach sonatas, complete flute works of Kazuo Fukushima & Doppler. Hons. incl: prizewinner, Councours. Int. de Flûte de Paris, 1971; Prix de la Recherche Artistique, France, 1972. Mgmt: Ingpen & Williams, London; Concertmaster, Toronto. Address: 14 Maxwell Ave., Toronto, Ont. MSP 2B5, Cen.

ÄKERLIND, Curt Ossian Nils, b. 15 Oct. 1012. Stockholm, Sweden. Piano Soloist & Accompanist; Orchestra & Choir Conductor. Educ: studied w. Profs. Olof Wibergh, H Gillgren, G Nordqvist & Vladimir Oulianski, Music Acad. m. Gunn Akerlin, 4 children. Debut: Stockholm, 1939. Career: Swedish Radio, 1936-55; currently Tchr., Music Schl., Kalmar, Sweden. Comps. incl: Concerto Antique for flute, strings, harp; Romance (solo violin & orch.); Nocturne (solo harp & orch.); many marchest; piano works; etc. Recordings incl: Warzawa Conserto by Addinsell (piano soloist); also backing many singers w. Curt Akerlinde ensemble or orch. Hons. incl: 1st Prize for comps., for Castingmarsch, Kalmar, 1973. Hobby: Cycle racing.

AKERS, Howard E. b. 17 July 1913. Ladonia, Mo., USA. Composer; Arranger; Teacher; Tromobonist. Educ: Curtis Inst. of Music; Murray State Coll.; Ill. Wesleyan Univ.; Chgo. Music Coll.; Millikin Univ.; Berkshire Music Ctr.; BMus; BMusEd.; MMus.; Perf. Dip. m. Va. Lois Wahlgren, 1 s. Career: Music Clinician in 33 states; Music Supvsr.; Petersburg, Ill., Schls.; on Fac., Springfield, Ill., Coll. of Music & Allied Arts, Wash. State Univ., Ctrl. Wash. Coll., Eastern Wash State Coll.; Tech., Northport (NY), LA, & Seattle pub. schls.; Prof., Union Coll., Millikin Univ., Chgo. Musical Coll. & Seattle Pacific Coll.; Ed. of Carl Fischer, Inc., NY; has own pvte. brass studio. Comps: over 110 works inclng. The Showman; In Prospect Park; March for a Festival; Bandland fiesta; Music Campers Marsh. Recordings; Band Marches on Decca; num. schl. coll. & educl. recordings. Contbr. to jrnls. in field. Mbrships. incl. ASCAP; Phi Kappa Phi; Phi Mu Alpha; Kappa Kappa Psi; Sigma Chi; MENC; Coll. Band Dirs. Nat. Assn. Hobbies: Camping; Fishing; Hiking. Address: 202 Federal Ave. E, Seattle, WA 98102, USA. 2, 8, 9.

AKON, Alfred, b. 15 Aug. 1905. Hartford, Conn., USA. Violist; Conductor; Arranger. Educ: Studied violin w. Jacques

Gordon, conducting w. Pierre Monteux. comp. w. Vittorio Giannini & Frederick Jacobi. m. Mary Holloway. Career: Has played w. San Francisco Symph. Orch., NBC Symph., Gordon String Quartet; Solo Viola concerts; Cond., Akon Strings, & Guest Cond. Compositions; Orchl. Suite Pucelliana, 1954; num. other orchl. & string arrangements. Hobbies: Travel; Reading. Address: Logan Ct., Box 213, Rte. 1, King, N Carolina, 27021, USA.

AKPABOT, Samuel Ekpe, b. Oct. 1932. Etinan, South Eastern State of Nigeria. Musical Educator; Composer. Educ: MA, Univ. Chgo., PhD, Mich. Stae Univ.; FTCL; ARCM. m. Beatrice d'Almaida, 3 children. Career incls: Sr. Music Prod., Nigerian Broadcasting Corp., 1959-62; Artists in res., African Studies Ctr., Mich. State Univ., 1973-75; Dir., Chapel Music, Univ. of Ife, Nigeria, 1970-73; Assoc. Prof., of Music, Univ. of Ife, Nigeria, 1970-73; Assoc. Prof. of Music, Coll. of Educ., Uyo, Nigeria, 1975-; Guest Lectr. & Cond. num. Univs. Comps. incl: Verba Christi-Sacred Cantata for soloists, chorus & orch., 1975. Recordings: Sam Akpabot in a Lighter Mood. Publs. incl: Ibibio Music in Nigeria Culture, 1975. Contbr. to profl. jrnls. Hons. incl: 1st Prize, music for 3 min. commercial jingle, Cannes Film Festival, 1956. Hobbies: Sportswritings; Cricket; Football. Address: Coll. of Educ., PO Box 1017, Uyo, South Eastern Nigeria.

AKULA, Appal Raj, b. 20 Aug. 1930. Andhra Pradesh, Visakhapatnam, India. Music Director; Composer; Conductor. Educ: Studied Carnatic Music & acquired working knowledge of Western music w. notations. m. Mrs. Satyavathi, 3s., 1d. Career: Music Dir., Devuditchina Bhartha (Telegu movie), 1968; Instrumentalist, sev. film orchs., Madras; Composed music & conducted for many film recordings of var. langs.; Appts. on stage, film, TV & radio, Madras; Composed music for songs; Currently, working as Music Dir. for 3 films. Mbrships: Life., Cine Musicians Union, Madras; Past Sec., ibid. Hobbies incl: Painting; Photography.

ALAIN, Marie-Claire, b. 10 Aug. 1926. St. Germaine-en-Laye, France. Organist. Educ: Institut Notre Dame a St. Germaine-en-Laye; Conservatoire Nat. Superieur de Musique; Music Tchrs. Dip. m. Jacques Gommier, 2 c. Debut: Dpty. Organist at Ch. of St. Germaine-en-Laye, 1937. Career: Appts. in over 1,500 concerts in Europe, USA, S Africa, etc. since 1955; Prof. of Haarlem Summer Schl., Netherlands, 1956-72, Conserv. of Music, Rueil-Malmaison. Recordings: Complete organ works of J S Bach & Buxtehude; 16 organ concertos of Handel, etc. Hons. incl: Edison Prize, 1968; 14 Grand Prix du Disque; Chevalier de la legion d'honneur, 1974; Officier des Arts et Lettres, 1978. Address: 37 Chemin de la Butte, 78620 L'Etang-la-Ville, France.

ALBANES, Antonio, b. 24 May 1938. Malaga, Spain. Guitarist; Professor, Guildhall School of Music. Educ: studied harmony, counterpoint & fugue, comp., Madrid, Spain; AGSM (guitar), UK. m. Maria-Jesus Molina, 1s., 1d. Debut: Velez Malaga, Spain. Career: Radio Nacional de España, Madrid; Spanish TV; BBC, Newcastle-upon-Tyne; concerts, Madrid, Barcelona, Alicante, Malaga, Valladolid, Segovia, Toledo, etc., London, Canterbury, Birmingham, etc. Hons: 1st Prize, harmony competitions, Cheltenham, Chelmsford, St. Albans, etc. Hobbies incl: Listening to music; Theatre; Travel; Swimming. Address: 90/92 Redcliffe Gdns., Chelsea, London SW10, UK.

ALBANESE, Licia, b. 22 July 1913. Bari, Italy. Operatic Soprano. Educ: studies w. Giuseppina R Baldassare Tedeschi; Mus D, St. Peters Univ., Jersey City. m. Joseph Gimma. Debuts: as Madame Butterfly, Milan, 1934, Royal Theatre, Parma, 1935; Metrop. Opera, NYC, 1940. Career incls: operatic apps., Italy & USA; app. at Royal Opera House, Covent Gdn., Fest. of King George VI. Recordings incl: La Boheme w. Beniamino Gigli. Mbrships: incl: Trustee, Bagby Music Lovers Fund; Advsry. Coun., 3rd St. Music Schl. Settlement. Hons. incl: DHL, Manhattan Coll.; LLD, Seton Hall Univ.; Lady, Grand Corss, Order of the Holy Sepulchre. Address: 800 Park Ave., NY, NY 10021, USA, 2.

ALBAROSA, Nino, b. 27 Aug. 1933. Messina, Italy. Musicologist. Educ: LittD; Dip. in Pianoforte; Specialisation in Musical Paleography. Appt: Instr., Hist. of Music, Fac. of Pedagogy, Univ. of Studies, Parma. Mbrships: Int. & Italian Musicol. Socs.; Int. Assn. of Study of Gregorian Chant. Contbr. to: Orpheus; Riuista Italiana di Musicologia; Gregorian Studies; Die Musik in Geschichte und Gegenwart. Address: via Casalmaggiore 58, 26100 Cremona, Italy.

ALBEE, David Lyman, b. 19 Jan. 1940. Detroit, Mich., USA. Concert Pianist; Artist-Teacher of Piano; Professor of Piano Literature Chamber Music Coach. Educ: BMusEd, Univ. of

Evansville; MMus, Univ. of Ill.; DMA Univ. of Tex., Austin, m. Fay Egbert, 1 s., 1 d. Debut: Detroit. Career: Extensive solo & chmbr. music concerts in USA, incl. solo appearance w. Detroit Symph. Orch.; Radio & TV appearances; Artist-Tchr. of Piano, Drake Univ.; Nat. Music Camp; Black Hills Fine Arts Ctr.; Baylor Univ.; Pianist, Fine Arts Trio, 1964-72; Piano master classes & workshops throughout USA, Assoc. Prof. of piano, Baylor Univ.; Pianist, Baylor Trio. Recordings: Piano trios by Walter Piston & Charles Ives w. Fine Arts Trio, 1971. Contbr. to: Am. Music Tchr.; The Piano Quarterly. Mbrshisp: Pi Kappa Lambda; Phi Mu Alpha Sinfonia; NMTR Recip. Bendetson Netzborg Piano Award, 1964 & Fac. Rsch. Grant, Drake Univ., 1969. Fac. Rsch. Grant, Baylor Univ., 1976. Fac. Rsch. Grant, Baylor Univ., 1976; Hobbies: Fishing. Jogging. Address: Schl. of Music, Baylor Univ., Waco, TX 76703, USA 8.

ALBERSHEIM, Gerhard, b. 17 Nov. 1902. Cologne, Germany. Pianist; Musicologist; Teacher. Educ: Osterreichische Staatsprüfung fur Musiklehrer, Vienna, 1930; PhD in Musicol., Univ. of Vienna, 1938; pvte. instrn. in Cologne & Vienna. m. Erna Eder. Career: Pvte. Tchr., piano, coaching, theory, 1929-; Fac. of LA Conserv. of Music & Art, 1947-53; Asst., then Assoc., then Full Prof. of Music, UCLA, 1953-56, then Calif. State Univ., LA, 1956-70; Prof. Emeritus; Concert accomp. of Elisabeth Schumann, Ezio Pinza, Jussi Björling, Richard Lewis, Dietrich Fischer Dieskau, etc. Recordings: Schönberg op. 15, Die Hängenden Gärten w. Belva Kibler. Publs: Zur Psychologie der Toneigenschaften, (Strassbourg, 1939, Baden-Baden, 1975); Zur Musikpsychologie, vol. 33, Taschenbücher zur Musikwissenschaft, Wilhelmshaven, 1974, '79. Ed., Music Sect., The College & Adult Reading List, NY, 1962. Contbr. to profl. jrnls. Mbr., sev. profl. orgs. Address: Brachmattstrasse 22, CH-4144 Arlesheim, Switz. 4, 9.

ALBERT, Karel, b. 16 Apr. 1901. Antwerp, Belgium. Composer; Music Teacher. Educ: Dip. Tchr., Tchrs. Coll., Antwerp; Royal Flemish Conserv.; Dip. of Music Tchr., State Secondary Schl., 1st & 2nd Degrees. m. Irma Payot, 1 d. Career: Musical Collaborator, Flemish People's Theatre, 1924-32; Tchr. of Music, State Secondary Schl., 1928-34; Sec., Musical Dept., Belgian Radio, Brussels, 1933-38; Vice-Dir., Flemish Dept., Belgian Radio, 1938-61. Compositions incl: Works for Orch., Violin & Chamber Orch.; Piano; Vocal Settings; Sev. Ballets; Chambermusic; an Opera Buffa. Recordings: Evening; Mister Jim; Flowering Lotos (Piano); Sev. Choral to Beethoven; Singing as Reading; Follow the Guide (1978). Contbr. to num. mags. & profl. jrnls. Mbrships: SA BA M; CeBeDeM; Union of Belgian Comps.; Red Cross of Belgium. Hons: Kt., Ordre de la Couronne; Off. Ordre de Leopold II; Stella della Solidarieta; Silver Medal, Red Cross. Hobbies: Chess; Theatre; Television. Address: Rotterdamstreet 41/2000 Antwerp, Belgium. 3, 14, 19, 28.

ALBERT, Stephen, b. 6 Feb. 1941. NYC, NY, USA. Composer. Educ: Eastman School of Music, Rochester, NY; BMus, Phila. Musical Acad.; Studies w. Darius Milhaud; Elic Siegmeister; Bernard Rogers; Joseph Castaldo; George Rochberg. m. Marilyn Silagy Albert, 1 d., 1 s. Career: Works perfd. by Chgo. Symph. Orch., Phila. Orch., RAI Orch., Rome, Bershire Music Ctr., Orch., Tanglewood. Comps: Illuminations (2 pianos, 2 harps, brass & percussion); Supernatural Songs (soprano & chmbr. orch.); Bacchae (chorus & orch.); Wolf Time (soprano & players); Orchestrabook (orch); Cathedral Music (2 amplified flutes, 2 amplified celli, brass, percussion, elec. guitar, harp, 2 pianos, elec. organ); Voices Within (orch); Chamber Music. Publs: Illuminations, 1968; Bacchae, 1969; Voices Within, 1975. Mbrships: ASCAP; Am. Music Ctr. Hons: 1st Prize BMI Hemisphere Competition, 1960; Bearnes Prize, Columbia Univ., 1961; Prix de Rome, 1965-66, 1966-67; Guggenheim Grant, 1968-69; Ford Fndn., Grant, 1967-68; Martha Baird Rockefeller Grants, 1966, 1969, 1974; Fromm Fndn., Berkshire Music Fest. Commission, 1975; MacDowell Fellowship. Hobbies: Postal History of USA & Canada; Squash; Gardening. Address: Sherry Rd., Harvard, MA 01060, USA.

ALBRECHT, George Alexander, b. 15 Feb. 1935. Bremen, Germany. Music Director. Educ: Pvte. studies w. Hermann Grevesmuhl, Paul van Kempen, Prof. Kurt Eichhorn, Prof. Maria Landes-Hindemith. Career: Repetitor, Theatre in Bremen, 1958; Kapellmeister, Theatre in Bremen (2), 1959 & '60; Kapellmeister, Nds. Staatstheater, Hannover, 1961; Gen. Music Dir., Landeshaupstadt, Hannover, 1965. Mbr., Rotary Club of Hanover. Recip. Prix d'execellence, Accademia Chigiana, Siena, 1964. Address: Berkowitzweg 2, 3 Hannover, German Fed. Repub.

ALBRECHT, Gerd, b. 19 July 1935. Essen, Germany. Conductor. Educ: Univ. & Acad. at Hamburg. m. Ursula Albrecht-Schöffler, 2d. Career: Opera perfs. & concerts in Berlin, Munich, Vienna, Hamburg, Cologne, Brussels,

Rotterdam, Rome, Oslo & Zürich; Prin. cond., Zürich Tonhalle Orch., (1975-80); concert tours of USA, 1977, & S Am. 1978. Mgmt: Konzert-Direktion Hans Adler, Berlin. Address: Wundtstr. 52, 1 Berlin 19, German Fed. Repub.

ALBRIGHT, Janet Elaine (Murray), b. 26 March 1933. Ardmore, Pa., USA. Pianist; Violist; Composer; Harpischordist. Educ: MusB, (piano) Beaver Coll., Pa.; MA, Music Theory, Colo. Coll., Colo.; Conserv. of Geneva; Harpsichord w. Isabel Nef (Switz.); New Schl. of Music, Phila., Pa.; Viola w. Max Aronoff. m. William E Albright III, 1 s., 1 d. Career: Artistic Dir., Hello Symph. (Educl. concerts for children by Farifax Symph.); Dir., Puppetell Prodns., John F Kennedy Center for the Perf. Arts, Wolf Trap Farm Pk.; Artist, Tchr. trainer & Cons., Arlington Co. Humanities Project; Prin. Viola, Alexandria Symph. Orch., 1977-; Fac., N Virginia Community Coll. (piano & harpsichord). Comps: Textures I for string orch.; 'Twas the Night Before ... A Christmas Fantasy, for puppets & orch.; Hello Symph. Mbrships: ASCAP; DC Fedn. of Musicians; Mu Phi Epsilon. Hons: Recip., grants; 1st Prize, Friday Morning Club Comp. Contest for Textures I. Hobbies: Skiing; Swimming Instructor. Address: 3505 Queen Anne Drive, Fairfax, VA 22030, USA.

ALBRIGHT, Philip H, b. 7 July 1927. Winfield, Kan., USA. Professor of Double Bass; Orchestral Musician (Double Bass). Educ: B Mus, Eastman Schl. of Music, Univ. Rochester, 1949; Perfs. Cert. ibid., 1949; MA, Wash. Univ., 1959; DMus. Arts, Eastman Schl. of Music, Univ. Rochester, 1969. m. Annette Nahmensen, 2 s., 1 d. Career: Performed w. num. orchs. inclng. Rochester Phil., St. Louis Symph.; Prof. of Double Bass, Schl. of Music, Ball State Univ., Ind., 1959-. Orchl. recordings w. Rochester Phil. & St. Louis Symph. Orch. Publs: Original Solo Concertos for the Double Bass, 1969. Contbr. to num. profl. mags. Mbrships. incl: Am. Fedn. of Musicians; Phi Mu Alpha Sinfonia. Address: 24 Berwyn Rd., Muncie, IN, 47304, USA.

ALBU-BAIRD, Margaret Cecilia, b. 13 Mar. 1907. Johannesburg, S Africa. Solo Pianist & Teacher. Educ: studied w. Sydney Rosenbloom, Johannesburg, 1921-24, at RCM, 1925, & 2 yrs. w. Leff Pouishnoff, 1929; LTCL; LRAM; ARCM. m. John Logie Baird (dec.), 1 s., 1 d. Debut: Grotrian Hall, London, 1929. Career: num. engagements w. major orchs. in UK; apps on TV; recitals & concerts in S Africa, Netherlands etc.; talks & lectures; tour of 29 towns in S Africa, 1962; lectr. in piano, Performing Arts Schl., Technikon, Natal. Contbr. of num. articles to newspapers. mbr., S African Soc. of Music Tchrs. (committee, Natal branch). Hobby: Gardens. Address: 2 Derrence Ct., 137 Brand Rd., Burban, Natal 4001, S Africa.

ALBUQUERQUE, Armando, b. 20 June 1901. Porto Alegre, Brazil. Head Professor of Composition. Educ: Studied Violin w. Oscar Simm; Harmony w. Joao Schwartz; Grad., Conservatório de Música do Instituto de Belas Artes, Porto Alegre. m. Dalva Albuquerque, 3 children. Career: Profl. Musician, Sao Paulo, Rio & Porto Alegre; Musical Advsr., Univ. Radio Broadcasting, Porto Alegre; Tchr., Fed. Univ. of Rio Grande Sul, 1966-; Prof. of Comp., Instituto de Artes, Fed. Univ. of Rio Grande Sul. Comps. incl: Instrumental & Vocal Music; Chmbr. Music' Pieces for Symphony & String Orch. Publs: A Obra Musical de Natho Henn, revision & analysis, Ed. Movimento, 1974. Mbr. num. profl. orgs. Address: Rua Lopo Goncalves 607, 90 000 Porto Alegre, Brazil. 3.

ALCH, Mario, b. 20 Mar. 1920. Highland, Ill., USA. Singer & Voice Teacher. Educ: Wash. Univ., St. Louis, Mo.; BS in Music, Juilliard Schl., NYC; MA in Music, Columbia Univ., NYC. m. Monika Alch, 1 s., 1 d. Debut: Broadway show, Ballet Ballads, NYC, 1948. Career: 20 yrs. ldng. operatic Tenor, Bern, Aachen, Cologne, Dusseldorf, Kassel, Braunschweig, Hannover, Hamburg, Frankfurt, Munich, Stuttgart, Zürich, Graz, Linz, Salzburg, Klagenfurt, Innsbruck & Vienna; TV & Radio Apps. in Graz, Vienna, Salzburg, Austria, Hamburg, Hannover & Munich; Currenlty Prof. of Music, Ohio State Univ., Columbus, Ohio. Mbrships: AGMA; AAUP NATS; MNTA; Hobbies: Sports. Address: 878 Lenore Ave., Comlubus, OH 43224, USA.

ALDENBJORK, Herbert Ernfrid, b. 14 Dec. 1939. Helsingborg, Sweden. Director of Music (Violin, clarinet, piano). Educ: Royal Coll. of Music, Stockholm, 1960-66; Dir. of Music (Military), 1966; Dip., Radio Conserv., 1969; Prof. of Music, 1970. m. Monica von Knorring, 2 d. Career: Headmaster & Cond., Laxa Music Schl., Ronneby Music Schl. & Sala Music Schl.; Soloist & cond. at var. concerts in Sweden. Composition: Om Sommaren Skona (Swedish folk melody for 2-part choir & small orch.); arr. 1974. Recip: Vastmanlands Landstrings Stipendium, 1974. Hobbies: Langs., Lit.; Sports. Address: Johannesbergsgat, 17, 733 00 Sala, Sweden.

ALDERSON, Geoffrey, b. 5 Jan. 1927. Bradford, Yorkshire, UK. Musical Director; Composer; Arranger; Instrumentalist. m.

Patricia Agnes, 3 s., 1 d. Career: BBC Northern Dance Orch. 1954-63; BBC Staff Arranger & Composer, 1963-67; Cond. 'Midnight Strings' sect. of BBC Radio Orch.; Geoff Alderson Orch.; Geoff Alderson Big Band Num. light music compositions inclng. background lib. pieces. Address: 'Rookfield', 2 Howard Rd., Swanage, Dorset BH 19 2QJ, UK.

ALDRIDGE, Carol Tinker, b. 25 Apr. 1924. Rochester, NY, USA. Trumpet Player; Teacher of Instrumental Music; Director of Bands & Orchestras. Educ: BMus, 1945, MMus, 1950; Eastman Schl. of Music, Univ. of Rochester. m. John C Aldridge, 1 s. Career: Trumpeter, Louisville Phil., All-Univ. Symph. & Rochester Community Players Orch.; Trumpet Soloist, Honeoye Falls Bands; Dir. of Bands & Tchr. of Instrument, Louisville (Ky.), Royalton-Hartland Ctrl. Schl. & Greece Ctrl. Schl. Dist.; w. Schl. Band of Am. on 3 European concert tours. Contbr. to NY State Schl. Music News. Life Mbr: Sigma Alpha Iota; MENC; NEA. Mbr., Greece Ctrl. Tchrs. Assn. Hobbies incl: Photography; Travel. Address: 1585 Calkins Rd., Pittsford, NY 14534, USA. 27.

ALDRIDGE, J Tinker, b. 20 Sept. 1952. Rochester, NY, USA. Arts Adminstrator; Music Educator (Horn & Guitar). Educ: BMus, Eastman Schl. of Music; MMus, ibid. Career: Asst. Dir., Barley Schl. of Music. Mbr. Music Educators Nat. Conf. Address: 1585 Calkins Rd., Pittsford, NY 14534, USA.

ALDRIDGE, Maisie. Christchurch, Hants., UK. Teacher of Piano; Music Editor; Writer on Music. Educ: RCM, London; ARCM; Piano w. Arthur Alexander, London; Jeanne Manchon, Paris France. Publs. incl: The Kingly Classics Grades I-V (w. Honor Phillips); The Kingly Book of Nursery Rhymes, 1956 (w. Olive Rees); The Augener Carol Book, 1960 (w. Olive Rees); The Bass Clef Book, 1960; The Kingly Classics, Repetoire Pieces, 1967; The Young Pianists' Handel, Book 1, 1969; Easy Russian Piano Music, Books 1 & 11, 1974. Contbr. of reviews & articles to Music in Educ. Mbr. ISM. Hobbies: Reading; Gardening; Walking. Address: 43 Upper Addison Gdns., London W14 8AJ, UK. 3, 4.

ALDULESCU, Radu, b. 17 Sept. 1922. Piteasca, Rumania. Cellist; Concert Soloist; Virtuoso. Educ: Dip. Bach, Theoretic Lyceum; Absolv. & dip., RAM, Bucharest, 1942. m. Corenco Galina, 1 child. Debut: Radio Symph. Orch., Bucharest, 1942. Career: Performed in num. countries inclng: England, France, Holland, Denmark, Spain, Italy, Switzerland, USSR, Turkey, Israel, Iran, S. Africa. Ctrl. & S. Am.; Tchr., European Conserv. of Music, Paris; Vis. Tchr., Italy, Spain, E & W Germany, England. Compositions incl: 3 Cadenzas, Boccherine B flat cello concerto. Num. recordings inclng: 3 Bach Sonatas. Mbrships: Accademia Philarmonica, Bologne; Accademia Tiberina, Rome; Legion d'Oro, Rome. Recip. num. int. prizes. Hobby: Motocar notation. Address: Maconlaan 26 (Campagne), Maastricht, 5001, Netherlands.

ALEKSANDAR, Petrović, b. 23 Feb. 1927. Belgrade, Yugoslavia. Painist; Composer; Bandleader. Educ: Secondary Music Schl. w. Danica Kauzlarić, 1d. Debut: in Radio Orchestra, Belgrade, 1952. Career: Bandleader of many dance orchs. Comps. many for fests. in Yugoslavia inclng. Zagreb, Split, Rijeka, Belgrade & for children's fests. at Zagreb & Rijeka. Recordings w. many orchs. in Yugoslavia. Publs: Yugoslav Composers & Music Writers; K. Kovacević, Musical Creations in Croatia, 1945-65. Mbrships: Union of Yugoslav Comps; Croation Musicians' Organization. Hons: Jury Prize, Split, 1958; Rijeka Prize, 1974; 1st prize, MIK, 1974, '78. Hobbies: Fishing; Autosport. Address: Zrtava Fasizma 4/V, 51000 Rijeka, Yugoslavia.

ALEMANN, Eduardo Armando, b. 12 Jan. 1922. Buenos Aires, Argentina. Composer; Editor; Music Critic. Educ: 10 yrs. piano w. John Montes; 5 yrs. clarinet w. F Martorella; 2 yrs. clarinet w. R Spatola; harmony w. E Leuchter; comp. w. W Graetzer & H Veerhoff; organ w. H Zeoli; chmbr. music w. L Spiller; early music at Stanford Univ., USA, etc. m. Leonor Forsthuber, 3 c. Career: Clarinettist of a woodwind quintet for almost 20 yrs., for which he wrote much music; Comp., 1940-. Comps. incl: Serenade for woodwinds; Encuentro; 12 short pieces for 2 recorders; Tropidanza; Arlequin trists; Spectra; Divertimento; Micropoems; Sonatina; 2 pieces for solo recorder. Many recordings. Music Critic & Ed., Argentinisches Tageblatt. Hons. incl: 1st prize at the ARS, NY, 1972; 1st prize, Arg. Nat. Arts Fund Comp. Contest, 1973, '75; 2nd prize, Barry, 1977. Address: Parana 523, 1640 Martinez, Argentina. 2.

ALESSANDRO, Victor Nicholas, b. 27 Nov. 1915. Conductor. Educ: Eastman Schl. of Music, Univ. of Rochester, NY, USA; Mozarteum, Salzburg, Austria; Acad. of St. Cecilia, Rome, Italy. Career: Musical Dir., Okla. Symph., 1938-51; San

Antonio Symph. Orch. & San Antonio Grand Opera Festival, 1951-. Hons: Alice M. Ditson Award, Columbia, 1956; Nat. Music Coun. Award. 1964. Address: San Antonio Symph. Soc., 600 Hemisfair Plaza Way, Suite 102, San Antonio, TX 78205, USA.

ALEXANDER, Ashley Hollis, b. 1935. Luceine, Okla., USA. Trombonist; Conductor; Educator. Educ: BMusEd, Okla. State Univ., 1957; MMus, N Tex. Univ., Denton, 1971. m. Metcha Franke Alexander, 3 s., 1 d. Career incls: Asst. Prof. of Music Univ. of Northern Ia., 1972-; Dir. of Bands, Perry, Okla., 1962-64; Dir. of Instrumental Music, Edison, Tulsa, 1964-69; currently Cond., Univ. of Northern Ia. Symphonic & Jazz Bands; Prin. Trombone, 2nd & 3rd. Trombone & Prin. Trumpet, Tulsa Phil. Orch.; Bass Trombone, N Tex. Orch.; Staff musician, Delta Recording Studio, Ft. Worth, Tex.; Dir., Symph. & Jazz Bands, Mt. San Antonio Coll., Walnut, CA; Recordings incl: The Vanguards Georgia Camp Meeting arrangemens, cond. & perf.). 1966; Dixieland & All That Jazz, 1970; Thursday Night Dues, 1973; Contbr. to profl. jrnls. Mbrships. incl: MENC; Nat. Assn. Jazz Educators; Coll. Band Dirs. A Nat. Assn.; Ia. Bandmasters Assn.; Kappa Kappa Psi; Phi Mu Alpha. Recip., var. hons. Hobbies incl: Pvte. pilot; Boats. Address: 20725 Loyalton, Walnut, CA 91789, USA.

ALEXANDER, Haim, b. 9 Aug. 1915. Berlin, Germany. Composer; Pianist; Harpischordist. Educ: Sternsches Conserv., Berlin; Grad.; Palestine Conserv. & Acad. of Music, 1945; higher studies, Freiburger Career: Tchr. of Piano & Theory, Rubin Acad. of Music, Jerusalem, 1945-; Assoc. Prof., Composition & Theory, & Hd. of Dept. of Theoretical Subjects, ibid, 1972-; Assoc. Prof., Theoretical Subjects, Dept. of Musicol., Univ. of Tel-Aviv, 1972-; full Prof., ibid., 1976-; Compositions incl: works for piano, mixed choir, chmbr. ensemble & full orch., sev. pieces being based on oriental folklore. Mbrships: Directory of Bd., Rubin Acad.; Soc. of Authors, Composers & Music Eds. of Israel (ACUM Ltd.); CISAC; League of Composers of Israel; Bnai-Brith Lodge, Jerusalem. Hons. incl: 1st Zimra Prize for choral work, 1952; Pres. Prize for choral work, 1955; 1st Prize, Israel Music Inst. for Soundfigures for Piano, 1966; 1st Prize, Artur Rubinstein Int. Piano Master Competition for Patterns for piano, 1973. Hobbies: Gymnastics; Swimming; Bridge. Address: 55 Tschernichowsky St., 92582, Jerusalem, Israel.

ALEXANDER, John, b. 21 Oct. Meridian, Miss., USA. Opera Singer (tenor). Educ: BM, Cinny. Conserv. of Music Duke Univ. m. Sue Travis, 1d. Debut: Metropolitan Opera, NY, in Cosi fan Tutte, 1961. Career: Leading tenor in num. opera houses inclng. Metropolitan Opera, NY, NY City Opera, San Francisco, Phila., Cinn., Covent Garden, London, Vienna State Opera; 5 operas w. NBC TV. Recordings incl. Norma & Anna Bolena. Mbrships. incl. Bd. of Governors, AGMA; Manhasset Yacht Club. Hon: Dr. Performing Arts, 1968. Mgmt: Columbia Artists, NY. Address: 46 Pickwick Rd., Manhasset, NY 11030, USA. 2.

ALEXANDER, Josef, b. 15 May 1910. Boston, Mass., USA. Composer; Professor of Music; Pianist. Educ: AB, MA, Harvard Univ.; Dip., Grad. Artist's Degree, New England Conserv. of Music. m. Hannah Margolis, 4 s. Debut: Jordan Hall, Boston, Mass. Career: as concert pianist apps. throughout Eastern USA & w. symph. orchs. inclng. People's Symph., Boston; as composer works perf. by most major orchs. in USA and some in Europe, inclng. Finnish Radio Orch. Comps: Epitaphs for Orchestra; 4 symphs.; Salute to the Whole World, for narrator & orch.; 3 Symphonic Odes for Men's Chorus & Orch.; 3 Overtures; num. comps. for solo piano, voice & piano, chamber & choral music; (recorded) Songs for Eve; 3 pieces for 8 instruments; Burlesque Fugue for Trumpet & Piano & 3 Diversions for Tmpani & piano; Incantation for piano. Contbr. of review of music books for Glanville Press. Mbr. of profl. Assns. Hons. incl: ASCAP Panel Awards annually, 1960-79; 2 Harvey Gaul comp. prizes; sev. Fellowships & Grants. Hobbies: Travel; Collecting Antiques & works of art. Address: 229 W 78th St., New York, NY 10024, USA.

ALEXANDER, William P., b. 8 Nov. 1972. Lompoc, Calif., USA. Professor of Music; Composer in Residence. Educ: BA, Univ. of Calif. at Santa Barbara; MA, EdD, George Peabody Coll. Career: Prof. of Music & Comp. in Res., Edinboro State Coll., Pa. Comps: (orch.): Symphonic Suite; The Morning Trumpet; (band): Adagio & Scherzo; Prologue & Repartee; (opera): The Monkey's Paw Mbrships: Am. Musicol. Soc.; Coll. Music Soc.; sonatas, quartets, etc. Erie Phil. Bd. of Dirs.; Comp. mbr., Am. Music Center. Publs: Music Heard Today, 1966, 69; Toward a Musical Classroom (ed.), 1969. Hobbies: Gardening; Tropical fish; Collecting art. Address: 116 Terrace Dr., Edinboro, PA 16412, USA. 12.

ALEXANDRA, Liana, b. 27 May 1947. Bucharest, Romania. Composer. Educ: Acad. of Music, Bucharest; Int. courses of music & comp., Weimar (1973) & Darmstadt (1974, '78). Career incls: Univ. Asst., Dept. of Comp., Acad. of Music. Comps: Chmbr. music; symph. & concertante music; vocal-symph. music; film music. Sev. recordings. Contbr. to: Romanian mags. & reviews. Mbrships: Romanian Comps. Union; GEMA, West Berlin; Int. Soc. Frau und Music. Hons: Prize of Romanian Comps. Union, 1971, '75; 1st Prize, Carl Maria von Weber, Dresden, 1979; Prize of Comps. Union of Romania, 1979; Laureate, Int. Gaudeamus Competition, Bilthoven, Netherlands, 1979. Hobbies: Mountain climbing. Address: str. Luceafarului nr. 2 ap. 1, sector 6, Bucharest 76128, Romania.

ALEXANDROV, Anatoly, b. 25 May 1888. Moscow, Russia. Composer; Pianist. Educ: Fac. of Philos., Moscow Univ.; Grad. as composer, Moscow Conserv., 1916. m. Nina Gueyman, dec., 2 d. (1 dec.). Career: Prof. of composition, 1926-; as Pianist, perf. own works in many Russian towns, 1915-. Compositions: 102 opera in var. genres, inclng. 4 operas (Two Worlds, Bela, Wild Bara, & Left-hander) symphs., piano music, vocal music, film & theatre scores. Recordings incl: Quartet No. 4 (perf. by Borodin Quartet); Dithyramb for double-bass & piano (perf. by composer & Rodion Azarkhin). Publs: Memoirs of N Medtner, & S Tanejeff. Contbr. to musical mags. Mbr: Union of Soviet Composers. Hons. incl: Order of Red Banner, 1943; Hon. Art Worker of RSFSR., 1946; Order of Lenin, 1953; People's Artist of RSFSR., 1967; People's Artist of USSR, 1971: Dr. of Arts, 1971. Hobbies: Readings; Boating; Walking; Touring; Gardening. Address: 10 Gottwald St., Apt. 54, 125047, Moscow, USSR.

ALI, Ahmed Mohamed, b. 11 Feb. 1915. Alexandria, Egypt. Composer; Violinist. Educ: Music Tchrs. dip., 1938. M. Badee'Ah Sadek, 5c. Debut: children's songs, Alexandria radio, 1936. Career: Chmn. of Music Lib., Nat. Coun. for Culture, Arts & Letters, Kuwait. Comps: about 100 songs recorded in all Arab radio & TV stations; num. arrs. Recordings: Kuwaiti Folklore Music (tapes). Publs: Series of Essays on Singing in Kuwait, Alam Al Pann mag. Mbrships: SACEM, Paris; Int. Musicol. Soc.; Syndicate of Profl. Musicians, Cairo. Hons: 2 decorations from the Bey of Tunisia, 1951, '55. Hobbies: Reading; Drawing. Address: c/o Nat. Coun. for Culture, Arts & Letters, Kuwait.

ALI, Naushad, b. 25 Dec. 1919. Lucknow, India. Composer. Educ: Matriculation. m. Aliya Khatoon, 9c. Career: has composed music for 57 films; many apps. for charitable causes. Recordings: Songs & background scores for films; orchl. pieces. Mbrships: Pres., Cine Music Dirs. Assn.; Bombay; Mbr., Governing Body of Indian Performing Right Soc.; Maharashtra State Angling Assn., Bombay. Hons: 17 num. awards for film music, 2 Diamond Jubilees, 9 Golden Jubilees & 24 Silver Jubilees. Hobbies: Hunting; Angling; Kite Flying. Address: Ashiana, Carter Rd., Bandra, Bombay 400050, India.

ALIAPOULIOS, Paul A., b. 16 Dec. 1935. Manchester, NH, USA. Associate Dean; Professor of Music Educations. Educ: BA, Univ. of NH, 1957; MMus, 1961, DMA, 1970, Boston Univ. m. Mary Janet Aliapoulios, 3 s. Career: Choral Cond., Ch. Choirs, Community Choruses, Univ. Chorus, All State Choruses; Adjudicator, Maine, NH, Mass., Conn., Va., NC, SC, Ohio, Ind., Wis., Ill.; Baritone soloist, recital, oratorio, opera, Ch.; Assoc. Dean & Prof. of Music Educ., Schl. of Music, Northwestern Univ. Recordings: (as Cond.) Mozart Requiem. Contbr. to: Am. Music Tchr., (Choral Ed.); NC Music Educ.; Fanfare. Mbrships: Phi Mu Alpha (Gov. Province 37); Pi Kappa Lambda; Music Tchrs. Nat. Conference; Coll. Music Soc. Hons: Outstanding Educs. in Am., 1971. Hobbies: Bridge; Tennis; Sailing; Reading. Address: 1314 Hinman Ave., Evanston, IL 60201, USA.

ALISTER, Kathleen Cameron. Cape Town, S Africa. Harpist. Educ: studied w. Francis Foster, W G Ross. m. James Fulton. Career: Recitals, Israel, S Africa; Radio Perfs., Europe, Israel, Can., USA; Prin. Harp, S African Broadcasting Corp. Nat. Symph., 1952-64; Fndr., Kathleen Alister Trio, 1962; became Nederburg Harp Trio, 1973. Concerts in Holland, UK, Radio Perfs., BBC; Instructor of Harp, Univ. of Witwatesrand, & S African Dept. of Educ.; Judge, Int. Harp Contests, Israel, USA. Recordings: Interludes; Trios for Flute, Viola & Harp. Mbrships: Musical Advsr., Fndr., Hon. Life Mbr., Harp Soc. of S Africa; Hon. Assoc. Mbr., Clarsach Soc., Scotland. Hobbies: Dress Designing; Sewing; Crafts. Address: 87 Dundalk Ave., Parkview, Johannesburg 2001, S Africa.

ALLAIRE, Gaston Georges, b. 18 June 1916. Berlin, NH, USA. Pianist; Organist; Musicologist; Professor of Music History. Educ: BM Univ. of Montreal, 1946; MA, Univ. of

Conn., 1956; Ph.D., Boston Univ., 1960. m. Fleurette Turcotte, 2 children. Career: Invited Lectr., Univ. of Toronto, 1971; Piano, organ recitals, local network, Radio Can.; Organ recitals, nat. network, ibid. Compositions: Commissioned music for TV film The Man of the Beach, 1953; Noel! Noel! Noel! (anthem). Publs: The Theory of Hexachords, Solmization & the Modal System, 1972; Ed., Magnificats by Claudin de Sermisy, 1970, Holy Week Music by Claudin de Sermisy, 1972. Contbr. to profl. jrnls. Mbrships: Past Pres., Past Didr., Can. Folk Music Soc.; Int., French, Am. Musicol. Socs. Hons: Sight Reading Trophy, 1939; Rsch. Grant, Can. Coun. of the Arts, 1961; Fulbright Post-doct. Rsch. Grant. 1962; Rsch. Grant, Can. Coun. of the Arts, 1973-74. Hobbies: Reading; Travel; Stamp collecting. Address: 80 Edgett Ave., Moncton, NB E1G 7B2, Canada.

ALLAN, Anthony, b. 9 Oct. 1933. Shanghai, China. Classical Guitarist; Lutenist. Educ: GSM; Akademie für Musik und darstellende Kunst (Vienna); ARCM; AGSM. m. Margaret Edity Allan, 1 s., 2 d. Debut: Brisbane, Aust., 1962. Career: Broadcasts for Aust. Broadcast Commission (radio & TV), lute and guitar solo recitals; Recitals for Musica Viva (Aust.); Fndr., Dir., Renaissance Consort. Recordings: Four Centuries of Lute and Guitar; Early Music from Renaissance Europe. Hobbies: Making viols, lutes, rebecs. Address: 42 Brigalow Ave., Kensington Gdns., Adelaide, SA 5068, Aust.

ALLAN, Jean Mary, b. 27 Sept. 1899. Channelkirk, Oxton, Berwickshire, Scotland, UK. Music Librarian. Educ: Pvte. studies; MA, Univ. of Edinburgh, 1924; Fellow, Library Assn., 1932. Contbr. to: Ency. Int.; Die Musik in Geschichte und Gegenwart; Grove's Dictionary of Music and Musicians; The Library Review. Mbrships: Hon. Treas., 9 yrs., Hon. Mbr., Scottish Library Assn.; Edinburgh Bibliographical Assn. Hobbies: Reading; Music; Gardening; Animal study & welfare; Writing. Address: The Old Manse, 45 Lanark Rd., Slateford, Edinburgh EH14 1TL, UK.

ALLEN, Betty, b. 17 Mar. 1930. Campbell, Ohio, USA. Opera & Concert Singer. Educ: Wilberforce Univ., Ohio, 2 yrs.; Dip., Hartford Conserv. of Music, 1952. m. R Edward Lee III, 1s., 1d. Debut: concert, Town Hall, NY, 1958; opera, Teatro Colon, Buenos Aires, 1964. Career: num. concert & opera apps., Far E, Europe, Scandinavia, N & S Am. Recordings incl: St. Matthew Passion (Bach); Songs & Songs with String Quartet (Weigl); Alexander Nevsky (Prokofiev); Treemonisha (Scott Joplin). Mbrships: Sigma Alpha Iota; Cosmopolitan Club. NY. Hons. incl: LHD, Wittenberg Univ., 1971. Hobbies: Cooking; Collecting prints & spoons. Mgmt: Columbia Artists Mgmt. Inc. (David Kleger Personal Rep.), 165 W 57 St., NY, NY 10019, 5, 6.

ALLEN, Frank Edward, b. 29 Nov. 1936. Birmingham, UK. Clarinetist. Educ: Bordesley Green Tech. Schl., Rugby Coll. of Arts; ABSM; LMus. TCL; pvte. study w. Jack Bryner. m. Christine Garforth, 2 s. Career: 2nd Clarinet, BBC Welsch Orch.; Bass Clarinet, Birmingham Symph. Orch.; Prin. Clarinet, ibid. 1 yr.; currently Bass Clarinet, ibid; perfs. as extra player w. most Engl. Orchs. Recordings: Numbers as Bass most Engl. Orchs. Recordings; Numbers as Bass Clarinet w. City of Birmingham Symph. Orch. Mbrships: Fndr., Mercian Wind Quintet. Mercian Ensemble. Hobbies: Photography. Address: 799 Chester Rd., Erdington, Birmingham 24, UK.

ALLEN, Harold, b. 30 Mar. 1917. Grenfell, Aust. Composer. Educ: BEc, Sydney Univ., NSW; pvte. study w. Peter Racine Fricker & Elizabeth Lutyens. m. Una Allen (Stebbins), 3 s. 1 d. Compositions incl: Morning (soprano & ensemble); Only its Own (soprano & ensemble); Spelt from Sibyl's Leaves (soprano chorus & ensemble); The White River (mezzo soprano, ensemble of guitars & percussion); Sound of Rain (guitars); The Wintry Places (soprano), guitar & clarinet); Fire Opal (solo clarinet); var. chamber comps.; Sonata for Clarinet & Piano; Trio for clarinet viola & piano. Mbrships: Composers' Guild of Gt. Brit.; Aust. Performing Rights Assn. Address: Foxcombe, Charlwood Drive, Oxshott, Surrey, KT22 OHB, UK 3.

ALLEN, Ivy M, b. 8 June, 1932. Memphis, Tenn., USA. Music Educator; Conductor; Flautist; Cellist. Educ: BS in Music Educ., Memphis State Univ., 1954; Secondary Cert. in Perf., De Shazo Coll. of Music, 1954; Grad. study, Ind. Univ. Schl. of Music MME, St. Louis Inst. of Music, m. Jocleta Dalton, 1 s. 2d. Career: Music Educator, 25 yrs; Now Orch. Dir., McCluer HS, Florissant, Mo. & Asst. Prof., Applied Instrumental Music, Band & Orch., Dir., Florissant, Valley Community Coll. Musical Career: Sr. Flute Recital, Memphis State Univ., 1954; Cellist, St. Louis Phil. Orch., 1960-63, Univ. City Symph. Orch., 1965-68, St. Louis Gateway Fest. Orch., 1968-; Tenor, St. Louis Chmbr. Chorus & St. Louis Symph., 1963-65; Christ Ch. Cathedral Men & Boys Choir, 1963-65; Flute Soloist, 1973,

Cond., 1970-, Florissant Valley Community Coll. Symph. Contbr. to profl. jrnls. Mbrships: NEA; Am. Fedn. of Musicians. Hobby: Study of history. Address: 540 N & S Blvd., St. Louis, MO 63130, USA.

ALLEN, Jane, b. 15 June 1928. Dallas, Tex., USA. Concert Pianist; Educator. Educ: Pvte. study w. Paul van Katwijk, 1941-47; Southern Meth. Univ. Schl. of Music, 1944-46. m. Melvin Ritter, Concert Violinist. Career: Pvte. Tchr., St. Louis, Mo., 1952-; Ritter-Allen Duo (violin & piano), 1959-; Official Pianist, St. Louis Symph., 1961-64; Hd., Piano Dept., Sewanee Summer Music Ctr., Tenn., 1963, 1964, 1968; Artist in Res., Piano Fac., Stephens Coll., 1966-75; St. Louis Conserv. of Music, 1975-; Am. Acad. of the Arts in Europe, 1975-; Univ. Missouri, St. Louis, 1976; Soloist, St. Louis Symph. & Balt. Symph.; Annual Concert Tours, USA & Canada; Recitals, NY Town Hall, 1959, 1960, 1961, 1963 (twice) 1966, 1968, 1977; European Tours, 1962, 1969, 1973. Mbrships: Sigma Alpha Iota (Hon.); Nat. Music Tchrs. Assn. Hons: Artists Presentation Soc. Award, St. Louis, 1958; Mason & Hamlin Tchr. Award. 1970. Hobbies: Cooking; Needlework. Mgmt: Albert Kay Assocs., 58 W 58th St., NY,NY 10019, USA. Address: 7471 Kingsbury Blvd., St. Louis, MO 63130, USA. 3, 27, 139.

ALLEN, Larry Dale, b. 7 Apr. 1947. Dayton, Ohio, USA. Music Educator; Oboist; English Hornist; Director of Instrumental Music. Educ: BME, Baldwin-Wallace Conserv. of Music, 1969; MM, Hartt Coll. of Music, 1971; Studied w. Robert Bloom, Galen Kral & Bart Lucaccelli. m. Judith Ann Kreeger. Career: Music Educator, W Hartford Public Schls.; Prin. Oboist, New Britian Conn. Symph. Orch.; Engl. Hornist, Hartford Symph. Orch.; Dir. of Instrumental Music, Trinity Coll. Publs: Beginning Electronic Music in the Classroom, 1974: Cons., Sounds, The Raw Material of Music, 1976. Contbr. to profl. jrnls. Mbrships: NEA CMEA; MENC. Recip. Northmont Educl. Assn. Scholarship, 1965. Hobbies: Rock Climbing; Amateur Radio; Tennis. Address: 118 Pondview Dr., Southington, CT 06489, USA.

ALLEN, Susan Ellen Hamman, b. 5 Apr. 1921. Dallas, Tex., USA. Pianist; Educator. Educ: Bachelor Public Schl. Music, Southern Meth. Univ., 1942; Master Liberal Arts, ibid., 1973; studied w. Paul Van Katwijk. Div., 1 d. Mbrships: Pro Musica (Treas., Dallas); Mu Phi Epsilon (Nat. Convention Chmn.); Pres., Tex. Music Tchrs. & Dallas Music Tchrs. Assns.; Pres., Van Katwijk Club. Hobbies: Oil Painting; Needlepoint. Address: 3137 Caruth Blvd., Dallas, TX 75225, USA. 3, 7, 27.

ALLEN, Thomas, b. 10 Sept. 1944. Seaham Harbour, UK. Opera & Concert Singer. Educ: ARCM Hons. m. Margaret, 1 s. Debut: Welsh Nat. Opera, 1969. Career: apps. on TV, w. Welsh Nat. Opera, at Covent Gdn. & at Glyndebourne, Aldeburgh, Leeds, Edinburgh & European Festival & Proms; roles incl: Figaro (both Mozart's & Rossini's); Count Almaviva; Papageno; Billy Budd; Guglielmo; Belcore; Marcello & Schaunard; Silvio; Valentin; Demetrius; Ned Keene. Recordings: Orff, Carmina Burana; Bizet, Carmen; Purcell, Dido & Aeneas, Come Ye Sons of Art; Berlioz, L'Enfance du Christ, Beatrice et Benedict, Faust, Alexander's Feast, Peter Grimes. Mbrs., Stage Golf Soc. Hons: Queen's Prize, 1967; Gn. 1967; Gulbenkian Fndn. Fellowship, 1968. Hobbies. incl: Ornithol.; Golf; Sailing; Walking. Mgmt: John Coast. Address: Ranworth Cottage, Sheath Lane, Oxshott, Surrey, UK.

ALLERS, Franz, b. 6 Aug. 1905. Carlsbad, Czechoslovakia. Conductor. Educ: Univ. of Berlin; Prague Conserv., Berlin Hochschule fuer Musik; Degree in Conducting. m. Janne Furch Allers, 1d. Career: Asst. cond., Bayreuth & Paris, Wagner Fest.; Gen. Music Dir., Aussing, Czech.; in US Ballet Russe; many Broadway & TV prodns; Cond., Metropolitan Opera, NY, 1963-; Conducted most major symph. orchs. in Am. & Europe inclng. NY Phil., Phila. Orch., Cleveland Orch., Chgo. Symph., Royal Phil., London, Munich Phil., Residentie Orkest, Hague; Gen. Music Dir., State Opera Comique (Staatstheater am Gaertnerplatz), Munich, 1973-77; USA Concert tours w. Tonkuenstler Orch., Vienna, 1978 & 1980. Recordings: RCA Victor; Columbia Records; Capitol Records; CBS London; Eurodisk & Electrola, Germany, etc. Contbr. to var. profl. jrnls. Mbrships: The Bohemians; NY Musicians Club; IPA. Hons: Antoinette Perry Award, NY., 1957 & 62. Mgmt: Columbia Artists Mgmt., 165 W 57 St., NY, Ny 10019; Alex Saron, PO Box 29, Blaricum, Holland. Address: 139 W 94th St., NY, NY 10025, USA. 3, 6.

ALLING, Ruth Stevenson, b. 26 Nov. 1892. Bryant, Ill., USA. Music Educator. Educ: Pvte. Music Study w. Hd. of Music Dept., Steinman Coll., Dixon, Ill.; Advanced Piano Trng. w. Harold Stewart Briggs, Scranton, Pa. Career: Tchr., Piano, 50 yrs.; Fndr., Lo-Kno-Pla Music Inst., Corpus Christi, Tex.; Lectr.

piano; Conducted workshops in many cities inclng. Chgo., 1939 & Mt. Royal Coll., Calgary, Can., 1974. Comps: Scores of tchng. pieces incl. in publd. tchng. materials of the Lo-Kno-Pla Approach. Publs: Through the Door of Music Land, 1928; How to Make Money Teaching Piano to Beginners, 1971, 2nd ed. 1974; Author of num. publs. comprising the Lo-Kno-Pla Approach to Piano; Author of 12 tchrs. manuals of instruction. Contbr. to: Iowa Music Tchr. Mbrships: Sec.-Treas. & VP, Iowa State Music Tchrs. Assn. Hobbies: Travel. Address: c/o Lo-Kno-Pla Music Inst., PO Box 6767, Corpus Christi, TX 78411, USA. 5.

ALLISTER, Jean Maria, b. 26 Feb. 1932. Ballymoney, Antrim, N. Ireland, UK. Singer. Educ: LRAM; Hon. RAM; FRAM. m. Dr. René Atkinson, 1 s. Debut: Royal Albert Hall, London. Career: Oratorio singer, UK; Tours of Germany, France, Belgium, Netherlands, Austria, Spain, Sweden & USA; Perfs. w. Covent Garden, Glyndebourne & Sadlers Wells Theatre Cos.; 1st perf. of John Gardener, The Visitors, at Aldeburgh Fest.; Stage prod. of Delius, Koanga; has sung under num. noted conds. Recordings; Delius, Koanga (w. LSO); Stravinsky, Mass; Gilbert & Sullivan, Readers Digest Series; Mikado (Wells). Mbrships: Equity; ISM; Brit. Fedn. Music Fests. Hobbies: Theatre; Winemaking; Gardening; Cine Filming. Address: Elm Farm, Crouch Lane, Goffs Oak, Waltham Cross, Herts. EN7 6TH, UK.

ALLITT, John Stewart, b. 13 May 1934. Coulogne, France. Art Historian; Author. Educ: Univs. of Leeds & London, UK; BA; Dip. Theol.; Dip. Ed. m. Eleanor Judith Cobb, 3 d. Career incls: Sr. Lectr. in Art Hist., Ctrl. Schl. of Art & Design, London, 1965-; Has revived works of Mayr, inclng. L'Amor coniugale (w. A. Gazzaniga), 1973, & La Passione, 1974, O Te Deum, 1976, & of Donizetti, inclng. Les Martyrs, 1975; Ave. Maria; L'angelo & la chiesa, & Miserere (1843), 1976; mbr. St. Annes' Centre for the study of the Arts, 1978. Publs: incl: Donizetti & the Tradition of Romantic Love, 1975; L'importanza di Simone Mayr nella formazione culturale musicale di Donizetti, 1976. Contbr. to Donizetti publs. Mbrships. incl: other Donizetti assns. Hons: Italian State Scholarships, 1971, 75. Hobbies. incl: Sailing; Walking; Family. Address: St. Annés Centre, Holmhurst St. Mary, Baldslow, St. Leonards-on-sea, East Sussex, TN37 7PU, UK.

ALLSEBROOK, Ruth. Leamington Spa, UK. Singer. Educ: RCM, London; ARCM; LRAM. m. James Murray Brown, 1 s., 1 d. Debut: London. Career: Opera, oratorio & recital work in UK; Tours in Europe, USA, Aust. etc.; TV apps. in Hong Kong. Recordings for Radio Hong Kong, NZ BC & Radio NZ. Mbr. ISM. Hobby: Breeding Dachshunds. Mgmt: Choveaux Mgnt. Address: "Kinlochbervie," 58 Bolton Ave., Richmond, N. Yorks., UK. 3, 27.

ALLSOP, Alfred Henry, b. 1899. Ashbourne, UK. Organist; Pianist. Educ: Grammar Schl., Ashbourne; Ptve. studies; Royal Coll. Music, London & Southwark, Manchester & Ripon Cathedrals. Career: Organist; Choirmaster; Radio broadcast, Speed the Plough, Masham. Compositions: Songs. Mbrships: ISM; Royal Coll. Music Union; Royal Coll. Organists. Recip. 1st. Prize, Hymn Tune, Rutland Triennial Exhib. Arts. Hobby: Golf. Address: 28 Bondgate Ct., Ripon, N Yorks., HG4 1QZ, UK, 3.

ALM, Folke, b. 19 Oct. 1917. Karlskrona, Sweden. Organist; Conductor; Master of Cathedral Music. Educ: pvte. studies w. Alf Linder (organ) & Algot Haquinius (piano); High Schl. of Music, Stockholm, 1939-43. m. Märit, 1 s., 1 d. Career: Organist at Varbert, 1945-63; Master of Music at the Cathedral of Lund, 1964-; Fndr., Oratory choir & orch. of Lund Cathedral; perfs. of works by Bach, Handel, Mendelssohn, Dvorak, Haydn, Mozart, Brahms, Bruckner & Stravinsky; 1st cond., Established Swedish Ch. Soc. of Choirs. Recordings: Folke Alm plays Bach at Lund Cathedral Organ, 1974; Kormosaik, the Prin. choir of Lund Cathedral sings. Mbrships: Royal Acad. of Music, 1976. Hons: Harriet Cohen Bach medal, 1962; NY TIDS culture prize, 1961; Lund Univ. Silver Medal. Hobbies: Travel; Italian lang. Address: Karl XI gatan 11 B, 22220 Lund, Sweden.

ALMASY, László, b. 6 Jan. 133. Budapest, Hungary. Solo Pianist; Professor. Educ: Dip. of Comp., 1959, Dip. for Solo Pianist & Prof., 1960, Acad. of Music Liszt Ferenc, Budapest. m. Lily Poór, 1 s., 2 d. Debut: on Hungarian Radio, 1959. Career: Solo Pianist, Nat. Philharmonia; Prof., Acad. of Music Liszt Ferenc; Pianist, Hungarian Radio; apps. on Hungarian & for. TV progs.; many concert tours, Austria, Algeria, Bulgaria, Czech., Finland, France, Italy, Yugoslavia, Poland, Morocco, GDR, GFR, USSR, Tunisia. Recordings incl: Saint-Saens, Carnival of the Animals; Zsolt Durko, Fire Music. Mbrships: Assn. of Hungarian Artists of Music. Mbrships: Assn. of Hungarian Artists of Music; Fndn. Mbr., Liszt Ferenc Soc. Fndn. Mbr., Hungarian Kodály Soc., 1978. Hons. incl: awards for interpretation of new Hungarian works, Copyright Off. of

Comps., 1962 & 67. Address: 1122 Budapest XII, Varosmajor u. 40, Hungary.

ALMEIDA, Laurindo, b. 2 Sept. 1917. Brazil. Guitarist; Composer. Educ: Nat. Schl. of Music, Rio de Janeiro. m. Maria M Ferreira (dec.). Career incls: Soloist, Stan Kenton Orch., 1947-50; Guitarist, motion picture prods., 1949-; Owner/Operator, Brazilliance Music Publng. Co., 1952-. Comps. incl: musical soundtracks for TV. Film scores incl: Maracaibo, 1956; Goodbye My Lady, 1957. Recordings: Decca; Capital; World Pacific. Mbrships: Am. Songwriters Assn.; Comps. Guild of Am.; ASCAP; Bd. of Govs. for Classical Music, Nat. Acad. of Recordings Arts & Scis. Address: 4104 Witzel Dr., Sherman Oaks, CA 91403, USA. 2.

ALMEIDA PRADO, Jose António Rezende de, b. 8 Feb. 1943. Santos, Brazil. Composer; University Teacher. Educ: Dips., piano, harmony, comp., arts, Conserv. Musical Santos; w. Camargo Guanieri & Dinora de Carvalho, Brazil; Olivier Messiaen & Nadia Boulandger, Paris. Debut: Mozart's Rondo Concerto w. Mus. Art São Paulo Orch., 1954. Career: Concerts, TV Cultura Sao Paulo; TV Globo Rio; Teatro Municipal Sao Paulo & Rio; Eglise St. Andre, Chartes; Purcell Room, London; Ctr. Int. Percussion, Geneva; Lectr., Univ. of Campinas (Unicamp), Brazil. Comp. incl: Cartas Celestes (pinao); Auora (piano & orch.). Recordings incl: Turibio Santos-Musique bre'silienne pour guitare. Mbr. profl. orgs. Hons. icnl: 1st prize, Independence 150th Anniversary, 1972. Hobbies incl: Collecting butterflies. Address: Rua Boaventura do Amaral 912/202, Campinas, Brazil.

ALMGREN, Tore Oscar, b. 7 May 1935. Stockholm, Sweden. Pianist; Conductor; Teacher; Producer. Educ: Royal Acad. of Music, Stockholm, 1957; studied piano w. Prof. Guido Agosti, Rome, 1957-58. m. Ingrid Bergenholtz, 2 d. Debut: Stockholm, 1960. Career: concerts in Sweden, UK & Germany; radio perfs.; Prof., Inst. for Nat. Concerts (Rikskonserter). Comp., film music for Secret Stockholm, 1963. Publs: Spela Piano; Elva Pianostycken, 1965. Mbr., Rotary Club. Recip. Italian State Scholarship, 1960. Hobbies: Flying; Fishing. Address: Stradstigen 11, 641 00 Katrineholm, Sweden.

ALOTIN, Yardena, b. 19 Oct. 1930. Tel-Aviv, Israel. Composer; Piano Tchrs. Dip., Israel Acad. of Music, Tel-Aviv; Tel-Aviv Music Tchrs. Sem. m. Yochanan Rywerant. Career: Comp.-in-Res., Bar-Ilan Unv., 1975-76. Comps.: works for chmbr. ensembles, piano & a cappella choir, inclng: Sonata & Sonatina for violin & piano; 6 Duets for 2 violins; Sonata for solo cello; Fugue for string trio; String quartet; Passacaglia for piano; Suite for piano; 3 preludes for piano; 6 pieces for children (piano); Yefei Nof (a capella choir); Hinei Ma Tov (a capella choir) Cantata for a cappella choir; The Painful Exile for vioce & orch. Mbr., Israel Comps. League. Recip., Nissimov Prize, 1952. Address: 13 Kikar Malchei Yisrael, Tel-Aviv, Israel.

ALTMAN, Elizabeth, b. 6 July 1948. Leeds, UK. Pianist. Educ: Mus B, Univ. of Manchester; Assoc. Royal Manchester Coll. of Music; RAM; LRAM. m. John Altman, 2 d. Debut: Purcell Rm, London, 1975. Career: apps. as recitalist & soloist throughout UK; TV & radio broadcasts, 1958-. Mbrships: ISM; Leeds Univ. Sr. Common Rm.; Brit. Lizst Soc. Hons. incl: 2nd Prize, BBC Piano Competition. Hobbies: Indoor Plants; Antiques; Teachinig; Washing Nappies & Household Chores. Addess: 8 Oakland Pk., Leeds 8, UK.

ALTMANN, Günter, b. 14 June 1925. Berlin, Germany. Musicology; High school teacher. Educ: Tchng. cert., 1943; Berlin Conserv., 1946-47; High Schl. for Music, Berlin-Charlottenburg, 1947-51 (Schl. music, piano, comp.). m. Waldtraut Janetzki, 2 s. Career: Lect. in Piano, Theory, Hist. of Music, Inst. for Advancement of Music, Berlin, 1951-; Tchr., High Schl. Choral works; Songs; Canons, Cantatas. Publs: Musikalische Formenlehre, 1959; biog. pieces. Contbr. to var. profl. jrnls.; record sleeve notes. Mbrships: Union of Comps. & Musicologist of the German Dem. Repub. Hons: Pestalozzi Medal, 1960 & '70; Th. Neubauer Medal; Medal of Hon., of the Union of Comps.; Service Medal of Germna Dem. Repub., 1977. Address: DDR 1125 Berlin, Berliner Str. 140, German Dem. Repub.

ATLWEGG, Raffaele, b. 17 Nov. 1938. Tettenhall, UK. (Swiss nat.) Cellist. Educ: 1st MB, St. Thomas' Hosp., London Univ.; Conserv. St. Cecilia, Rome; Concert Dip.; Said Conserv.; study w. John Shinebourne, London; Paul Grümmer, Switzerland; & Pablo Casals (Zermatt summer course). m. Barbara von Schulthess, 2 children. Career: Int. soloist & chmbr. musician, 1958-60; Ldr. of cellos, Zürich Tonhalle Orch. & Mbr., Tonhalle String Quartet; Tchr. of Concert Class, Zurich Acad. of Music, 1960-1975; Tchr. of Concert Class, Basel Acad. of Music, 1971-1975; Fndr. & Tchr. of Cello,

Chmbr. Music & Orch. Classes, Schl. of Music, Canberra, Australia, 1968-70. Conducts Master classes for cello, Laudinella, St. Moritz, Switz.; 1963-; State Expert for Music, Switz., 1975-. Recordings: Bach, C Major Suite (Dynamic); Martinu - Duo for Violin & Cello; Bruckner & Martinu Quintets. (PECLA & KM). Mbrships: Schweizer Musiker-Verband; Schweizerischer Tonkünstlerverein; Schweizerischer Musikpädagogischer-Verband; Kiwanis. Recip: 1st Prizes, Nat. Piano Comp., Wolverhampton, 1947. Hobbies: Skiing; Reading; Cycling; Swimming; Rowing. Mgmt: Ariette Drost, Holland; Paul Kreye, Germany; Kon zertdirektion, Klaus Menzel, Zürich, Switzerland; Musica Viva, Australia. Address: Schlossbergstrasse 27, 8702 Zollikon (Zürich), Switzerland.

ALVA, Luigi, b. 10 Apr. 1927. Lima, Peru. Opera Singer. Educ: music study w. Roas Mercedes de Morales, Peru; Singing Schl., Scala Theatre, Milan, Italy. m. Anna Maria Zanetti, 2 s. Debut: Municipal Theatre, Lima, 1950. Career: performances in all major Opera Houses in Europe, Am., Japan, Australia, etc.; appearances at important musical festivals & in opera, films & TV. Recordings incl: operatic works by Mozart, Rossini & Verdi on EMI, Decca, Deutsche Grammophon & Philips labels. Hons: Off., Order of Merit, Peru, 1962; Cmndr., Orden del Sol, ibid., 1963; Viotti d'Oro, Vercelli, 1975; Palcoscenico d'Oro, Mantova, 1976. Hobbies: Photography; Filming. Address: Via Moscova 46/3, 20121 Milan, Italy.

ALVAREZ, Luis Manuel, b. 31 Mar. 1939. Yabucoa, Puerto Rico. Ethnomusicologist; Composer; Guitar Teacher; Music Professor. Educ: BA, Unv. Puerto Rico; BMus, Conserv. of Puerto Rico; MA, Ind. Univ. USA; PhD, ibid. div. 2 s., 1d. Career: Comps. performed in maj. concert ctrs. & instns. of Puerto Rico & on WIPR TV. Compositions incl: Seis Piezas Breves (clarinet & flute); Cancion Tonta (art song); Media Luna (art song). Num. recordings. Mbrships: Music Soc. of Puerto Rico Soc. of Contemporary Music. Hons: Commission to compose orch. work for Puerto Rico Symphonic Orch. given by Festival Casals Inc., 1974. Hobbies: Electronics; Chess; Fishing; Swimming; Dancing. Address: calle Capetillo 307, Rio Piedras 00923, Puerto Rico.

ALVIN, Juliette, b. Limoges, France. Solo 'Cellist; Music Therapist. Educ: Nat. Conserv. of Music, Paris; Sorbonne. m. Prof. W. A. Robson, 2s., 1d. Career: w. Music Dept., Univ. of NC, USA, 1951; Dir., Course in Music Therapy, GSM; Chmn.-Fndr., Brit. Soc. for Music Therapy, London, 1958; has lectured on music in educ., music therapy, & special educ., var. univs. in UK, USA, Japan, & S. Am.; Rsch. Binfield Park Hosp., 1970. Publs: 'Cello Tutor for Beginners; Musical Theory & Instrumental Technique; Music for the Handicaped Child; Music Therapy. Contbr. to: Musical Times; Music Educ.; Time Educl. Supplement; special educ. & profl. med. papers. Mbrships: London Violincello Club; Hospitality Club (Univ. of London). Hons: 1st Excellence Prize & Gold Medal, Nat. Conserv. of Music, Paris; Hon. Fellow Guildhall Schl. of music & drama. Hobbies: Tennis; Walking; Theatre. Address: 48 Lanchester Rd., London N6, UK. 3.

ALWYN, Kenneth, b. 28 July 1928. London, UK. Conductor, Composer. Educ: RAM; ARAM; GRSM. m. Mary Law, 2 d. Career incls: Assoc. Cond., Sadlers Wells Theatre Ballet, 1952-56, Royal Ballet, Covent Gdn., 1956-59; Cond., Let's Make an Opera, BBC TV; presented & conducted Omnibus, BBC TV, Tchaikovsky; Cond., revival of Hiawatha trilogy, 1975; concerts & recordings w. major orchs., Britian, Europe, N Am. & Japan, Prin. Cond., BBC N Ireland Orch. & regular broadcaster & introducer for BBC. Recordings: Decca. Mbr., ISM. Hobby: Flying. Address: Horelands, Broadford Bridge, N Bilingshurst, Sussex, UK. 14.

ALWYN, William, b. 1905. Composer; Professor of Composition. Educ: FRAM, 2 s. Career: Prof. of Composition, RAM, 1926-54; Chmn., Composers' Guild of GB, 1949, 50, & 59. Compositions incl: 15 sin fonietta for strings; symphs., 2 operas, Juan of the Lberine and Mis Julie; 3 concerti grossi; Concerto for Harp; Overture; Derby Day; var. works for orch., chmbr. ensemble, piano etc.; many film scores inlng. Odd Man Out, The Way Ahead, The True Glory & The Magic Box. Mbrships. incl: Savile Club; Island Sailing Club. Hons: CBE, 1978. Address: Lark Rise, Blythburgh, Halesworth, Suffolk, UK. 1, 4.

AMADUCCI, Bruno, b. 5 Jan. 1935. Lugano-Veganello, Switzerland. Conductor. Educ: Ecole Normale de Paris; Conserv. G. Verdi, Milan. m. Donatella Gusberti-Noseda, 1 d. Career: has appeared At Met. Opera, NYC, Théâtre Nat. de l'Opera, Paris, Staatsoper, Vienna & Deutsche Oper, Berlin, & on TV & radio broadcasts in many countries. Recordings: Cimarosa's Maestro di Cappella; Vivaldi's Le Stagioni; Mozart's Jupiter Symph.; Tchaikovsky's Piano Concerto; a series of Overtures by Rossini & Mozart; works of Vivaldi & Lully. Publs: L'Amfiparnaso de Orazio Vecchi, 1951; Walter Jesinghaus, 1970; Music of the five composers of the Puccini Dynasty; La musica nella Svizzera Italiana e la presenza della Radiorchestra, 1973. Contbr. to sev. Swiss newspapers. Mbrships: Pres. of Committee for recording of neglected works, Int. Assn. Music Libs.; Pres., Ricerche musicali nella Svizzera Italiana; Lions Club Lugano. Hons: Grand Prix du Disque (Opera), for Maestro di Capella recording, Paris, 1955; Concorso nazionale Italiano per direttori e concertatori d'opera, Trieste, 1960. Maschera d'argento prize, 1976. Hobbies: Clocks; French Wines Collect. Mgmt: Casella postale 1042, CH 6901 Lugano, Switzerland. Address: Via Praccio 33 a., CH 6900 Lugano-Massagno, Switz.

AMATI, Orlanda (Elinor Barbara d'Amato). New Jersey, USA. Pianist. Ec: BS, The Juilliard Schl., NY, 1954; MA, Columbia Univ., 1961. Educ: pvte. study w. Alberta Masiello, Carl Friedberg, Lonny Epstein & David Saperton (piano); w. Robert Mann (ensemble); w. David Barnett (Comp.). Debut: Jt. recital w. brother, Steinway Hall, NY, age 11. Career: Concert perfs., Newark, NJ, 1957; W. Orange, NJ, 1958; Judge, Nat. Fed. of Music Clubs, NJ Fest., 1957-67; Lectr., Fac., Manhattan Schl. of Music, 1962-63; Fac. & Judge, NGPT & Am. Coll. of Musicians, Austin, Tex., 1962-. Comp: The Paper Piazzetta (suite for piano). Publs: Transcriptions of Italian Renaissance Music, 1959; Girándula, wheel of light (1st collect. of poetry), 1972; contbr. of poetry to var. coll. publs. Mbrships: Kappa Delta Pi; Pi Lambda Theta; Recording Sec., MTA of Northern NJ, 1957-59; Sec., Gdn. State Guild, 1960. Hobbies: Chess; Fencing; Painting. Address: 394 Highland Ave., Orange, NJ 07050, USA 27.

am BACH, Rudolf, b. 6 June 1919. Trogen, Switz. Pianist; & Professor. Educ: Studied, 3 yrs. Music Conserv., Zürich; Pvte. student, Prof. Emil Frey, Zürich; Tchrs. Dip., (piano), 1938, Soloist's Dip., summa cum laude, 1939; Studies w. Prof. Frederic Lamond, (student of Franz Liszt), London, 1940. m., 2 children. Career: Tchr., Piano, Collegium, Winterthur, Switz., 1939; Piano Recitals, Zürich, 1941-43, '45, 1948-73; Concert lours & Recitals, GB, 1951, '56, '68, France, Germany, Austria, Spain, Canda, (1967); Radio Recitals incl., Radio London, 1958, (Swiss Comps.), Radio Zürich; Works perfd. incl. 3 Siécles de Pianoforte, 40 Concertos, & var. works by F. Busoni, R. Strauss, Scriabin, Ravel, Prokofieff, etc. New Recordings incl: Anthologie Schwezer Musik, Hug Sonate op 39, Monapartita op 48a; Concerto da Camera, the Inspiration of Great Composers, Felix Mendelssohn, Songs without words & works by Franz Liszt. Mbrships: Assn., Swiss Musicians, 1940-; Union Suisse des Artistes & Musiciens, (USDAM), 1943-; Musica Helvitia, Basle. Hons: 1st prizes, Hegar, (Zürich Conserv.), Schumann, Geneva, 1938; 1st prize, Int. Competition, Geneva, 1940. Hobby: Playing Chmbr. music in Trio. Mgmt: Konzertgesellschaft Zürich, Steinwiesstr, 2, 8032 Zurich. Address: Goldanerstr, 24, 8006 Zürich, Switz.

AMBROSIUS, Hermann, b. 25 July 1897. Hamburg, Germany. Composer; Pianist; Director; Music Teacher. Educ: Studied Theory & Piano w. Hans Grisch, Leipzig, 1918; Music Ed., w. Schering, Abert & Kroyer (w. exams), Univ. of Leipzig, 1919; Instrument teaching w. Pianist, Alfred Szendrei, Leipzig; Master Class w. Hans Pfitzner, Acad. of Arts, Berlin, 1921-23. m. Else Roth, 1924, Eva von Modrszewski, 1973, 1 s. Debut: (Comp.), Symph. for Big Orch., Eleuisches Fest. for Orch., Young Comps. Concert, Leipzig, 1924. Career: Sound Dir., Radio Leipzig until Leipzig, 1944; Tchr., comp. & Theory, Music Schl., Leipzig; Music Ed., Elect Apprentices, Ballbearing factory, Leipzig W. Comps. incl: Sinfonia Gloria Dei, 1974; 5 Klavierkonzerte, Violinkonzert; Konzert fur Flöte, Fagott & Gitarre; Sinfonie g-moll, 1963 (num. other symphs.); Der Deutsch Schwarzwald, Suiet fur gr. Bläsorch., 1955; Choir Music, Faust, Sinf. Dichtung nach Goethe, 1923; Festgesang im Frühling, 1954; Was ihr dem Geringsten, 1951; Sangerspruch, 1954; Num. songs piano works & works for other instruments incl. organ. Num. Recordings. Contbr. to num. profl. jrnls. Hons. Mbr., Zupborch., BDR. Hobbies: Construction; Mathematics; "Electrics". Address: 7707 Enge Herm. Hessestrasse, 19 German Fed. Repub.

AMBROS-WIENCEK, Beata, b. 30 Oct. 1937. Dabrowa, Tarn, Poland. Conductor. Educ: Music High Schl., 1950-55; Cracow Conserv., Dept. of theory, comp. & condng. (Dip.BA) 1955-60., n. Kazimierz Wiencek, 1s. Debut: Dip. concert, Cracow. Career: Cond. of opera & operetta, Cracow, 1962-65; Cond., musical theatre, Lodz, 1965-78; Cond. of music theatre, Szczecin, 1978-; app. at 17th Int., Competition for Young Conds., Besancon, France, 1967. Mbrships: Assn. of Polish Musical Artists (SPAM). Hons: Music Course, Vacanze Musicali, Venice, 1964. Hobbies: Climbing; Tourism. Address: ul. Reymonta 5, 71-276 Szczecin, Poland.

AMELING, Elly, b. 8 Feb. 1938. Rotterdam, Netherlands. Concert Singer; Soprano. Educ: Conserv. of Music, 'Sgravenhage, Netherlands; w. Pierre Bernac, Paris, m. A W Belder. Debut: Europe, 1964; USA, 1968. Career: Song recitals, concerts w. orchs. & opera on all 5 continents. Recordings incl. works by Beethoven, Bach, Handel, Haydn, Mozart Mendelssohn Bruckner, Mahler, Schubert, Schumann, Brahms, Wolf, Vivaldi, Fauré, Poulenc, Martin. Hons: Stereo Review, 1969, '73, '77; Kt., Order of Oranje Nassau; Preis der Deutschen Schallplattenkritik; Grand Prix du Disque. Hobbies: Dogs; Travel. Mgmt: De Koos, 416 King's Rd., London SW10 OLJ, UK. Address: c/o Mgmt.

AMELLER, André Charles Gabriel, b. 2 Jan. 1912. Arnaville, France. Conservatory Director; Conductor; Composer. Educ: Nat. Higher Conserv. of Music, Paris. m. Melle Jacqueline Guyon, 2 s., 2 d. Debut: Nat. Opera Theatre, Paris, 1938. Career incls: Dir., Nat. Music Conserv., Dijon, 1953-; Cond., Concert Soc., ibid.; Pres., Musical Confedn. of France. Comps. incl: Cyrnos (opera); Fingal's Spear (lyric drama); Séléné's Dance (ballet). Mbrships. incl: Gen. Deleg. for France & VP, Int. Soc. for Music Educ.; Committee, European Assn. of Dirs. of Acads., Conservs. & Higher Schls. of Music. Hons. incl: Kt., Legion of Hon.; Cmdr., Nat. Order of Merit. Hobby: Philately. Address: 82 rue du 22 Septembre, 92400 Courbevoie-Becon, France.

AMEMIYA, Yasukazu, b. 18 July 1939. Tokyo, Japan. Timpanist; Percussionist. Educ: BFA, Tokyo Nat. Univ. of Fine Arts & Music, m. Gyokuran Amemiya. Career incls: Apps. w. Yomiuri Nippon Symph. Orch., 1962-; Apps. over Nippon TV, 1971; Solo Percussion Perf. over NHK (Summer Prayer) for solo percussion. Recording of Natsu Nabutsu. Mbrships: ASCAP; Percussive Arts Soc. Hons. incl: 2nd Hons. in Woodwind & Brass Instrument Contest sponsored by Asahi Newspapers, 1954; 1 yr. Scholarship for study & rsch. abroad awarded by Japanese Min. of Cultural Affairs, 1974. Hobby: Collecting Percussion Instruments. Address: 5-17-14 Ohkura Setagaya-ku, Tokyo 157, Japan.

AMEND, Erwin, b. 12 Aug. 1919. Weilburg, Germany. Violinist; Composer. Educ: State Music Acad., Frankfurt/Main; studied w. Prof. Josef Peischer, Mrs. Alma Moodie, Mrs. Guyla Bustabo, Prof. Fritz Malats, Prof. Karl Holler, Kurt Hessenberg, Gerhard Frommel. m. Klare Ulrich, 1 c. Debut: Frankfurt/M, 1937; Cologne, 1938; Breslau/Silesia, 1938. Career: Concermaster, City Stage, Mainz; Radio, TV Comp. Comps: Variationen über ein Thema von Rameau, orch.; Musik f. Streicher; Konzert, trumpet & orch.; Str. Quartet; Diverimento, 9 brass & percussion; Passionmusik, soloist, choir & orch.; opera Der Soldat Postnikow; Sonatine, violin & piano; Sonatine, trumpet & piano. Mbrships: German Comps. Grp.; GEMA. Hobbies: Readings; Arts. Address: 1 Bastion Martin, Mainz, German Fed. Repub.

AMFITHEATROF, Daniele, b. 29 Oct. 1901. Composer & Conductor. Educ: Royal Conserv. of Music, Santa Cecilia, Rome, Italy, 1915; Conserv. of Music, Petrograd, USSR, 1917. Appts: Asst. Conductor, Augusteo Symph. Orch., Rome, Italy, 1924-29; Conductor, & Exec., Symph. & Orch.; EIAR, Italian Broadcasting Co., Genoa, Milan, Triesta & Turin; Guest Conductor, Rome, Naples, Budapest, Vienna, Paris, Brussels, (Pasdeloup & Lamoureux Orchs.), 1929-37; Assoc. Conductor, Mpls. Symph. Orch., USA, Guest Conductor, Boston Symph. Orch., Mass., LA Philharmonic Orch., 1937-38; Composer & Conductor, originial film music, Hollywood, MGM; 20th Century-Fox; Paramount; Republic; Columbia; Warner Bros.; Disney; Selznick Int.; over 70 films, 1939-59. Mbr. profl. assns. in field. Num. creative works incl: Symphonic works; Choral works; Operas; Chmbr. Music. Recip. of Order of Cmdr. of Italian Star of Solidarity. Address: 11807 Dorothy St., Los Angeles, CA 90049, USA.

AMIRAN-POUGATCHOV, Emanuel, b. 1909. Russia. Composer. Educ: Studied w. Yoel Engel & Prof. David Shor, Russia, Prof. S Rosowsky, Israel, Sir Granville Bantock & Alec Rowly, UK. Career: Co-Fndr. w. Prof. Leo Kestenberg, Music Tchrs. Sem., Tel-Aviv; Off. i/c musical activities, Israel Defence Forces, 1948; Dir. Supvsr., of Music Educ., Min. of Educ. & Culture until ret'd., 1975; Fndr. & Chmn., VP, 1972, Les Jeunesses Musicales in Israel. Comps. incl: Hashomer (The Guard, orchl.); Evel (orchl.); A Symphonic Movement; Achrei Moti (After My Death, cantata); Nahanu Ami (cantata for mixed choir & orch.); piano pieces; theatre music; num. songs. Address: 39 Harav Friedman St., Tel-Aviv 62 303, Israel.

AMMANN, Benno, b. 1904. Lucerne, Switz. Composer. Educ: Conserf. of Leipzig; studies w. Honegger, Roussel & Milhaud for comp., also w. Boulez, Messiaen & Stockhausen. Carerr: Electronic Studio R7, Rome; Electronic Studio IPEM,

Ghent; Inst. for Sonologie, State Univ. of Utrecht, 1973-76; Electronic Music Ctr., Columbia Univ., Princeton; apps. as cond. w. sev. leading European orchs. Comps: Chamber choral music, Cantatas (Flight from the Depth), ballets & electronic music. Address: Faubourg St. Alban 43, 4052 Basle, Switz.

AMOYAL, Pierre, b. 29 June 1949. Paris, France. Violinist. Educ: 1st Prizes, Violin & Chmbr., Music, Conserv. Nat. Superieur de Musique, Paris; Heifetz Master Class Hon. Dip., Univ. of Southern Calif., USA. Debut: w. Georg Solti & Orch. de Paris, 1972. Career: has played w. leading orchs. in most European cities, inclng. UK, also in USSR, Can., USA, Hong Kong, Japan, tours of S Am., S Africa, Asia & Middle E; Prof. Paris Nat. Conserv. 1977-. Recordings: Lalo, Symphonie Espagnole; Mendelssohn, Violin Concerto; 3 Tartini Concerti; 2 Prokofiev Concerti for Violin; Saint-Saens, Concerto, Rondo Capricciosi & Havanaise; 2 Prokofiev Sonatias; Bruch Violin Concertos; Faure Sonatas; Tartini Sonatas. Hons: Prix Ginette Neveu, 1963; Pric Paganini, 1964; Prix Georges Enesco, 1970; Grand Prix du disque, 1973 0 77. Hobbies: Photography; Lit.; Sports. Mgmt: Bur. de Concerts De Valmalete, 11 Ave. Delcassé, Paris 75008, France. Address: 21 rue des Hortensias, Mennecy 91450, France.

AMRAM, Aharon, b. 1937. Zanaa, Yemen. Singer. Educ: Eli Kourtz Conser., Tel Aviv, 2 yrs.; Personal resources in Yemenite Folklore. m. Sara, 5 c. Debut: Beit Handar, in Rosh Haayin, Israel. Career: Num. public perfs.; Org., trained & Cond. Youth Choirs; European tour w. Pa'amonim Group (The Bells), 1963; TV apps., Belgium & The Netherlands. Comps: Num. Yemenite Songs incl: Asalaiot. Recordings: 25 LP's. Mbrships: ACUM Ltd.; Société d'Auteurs, Compositeurs et Editeurs de Musique, Israel; Confederation Internale des Societes d'Auteurs et Compositeurs. Hobby: Music. Address: Stamper 92, Petah-Tikva, Israel.

AMRAM, David Werner, b. 17 Nov. 1930. Phila., Pa., USA. Composer; Conductor; French Horn Player. Educ. incl: Oberlin Coll. Conserv. of Music; BA, Geo. Wash. Univ.; Manhattan Schl. of Music, 1955-58; studied w. var. noted tchrs. Career incl: Ldr. w. George Barrow, Amram-Barrow Jazz Quartet since early 1950's; Musical Dir., NY Shakespeare Fest., 1956-58; Cond.-in-Res., NY Phil. Orch., 1966-67; Guest Cond. w. many orchs. Comps: incidental music for about 30 Shakespearean prods.; 6 film scores; sev. Broadway & off-Broadway plays; 2 operas; num. chamber & orch. pieces. Author; Vibrations: The Adventures & Musical Times of David Amram (autobiog.), 1968. Address: 461 Ave. of the Ams., NY, NY 10011, USA.

AMUNDRUD, Lawrence, b. 18 Sept. 1954. Watrous, Canada. Concert Pianist. Educ: B Mus, Univ. of Regina, 1976; MMus, ibid, 1978; Studied piano w. Thomas Manshardt. Debut: Performed Franck's Symphonic Variations w. Saskatoon Symph. Orch., 1972. Career: Mbr. French Horn Sect., Regina Symph. Orch., 1970-; Prin. Horn, ibid., 1970-71 Season; Toured Southern Sask. as chmbr. music player on piano & french horn, 1973. Mbr. Am. Fedn. of Musicians, Local 446, Hobbies: Reading; Listening to gramophone recordings of gt. singers (Patti, Chaliapin, Melba, etc.). Address 14 Dunning Cres., Regina, Sask., Canada S43 3W1.

AMUNDSEN, Signe, b. 9 June, 1899. Oslo, Norway. Singer. Educ: studied w. Mimi Hviid, Oslo, Waldemar Bernardi, Paris & Antonino Votto, Milan. m. Anders Finsland. Debut: as Norina in Don Pasquale (Lecco), Oslo, 1920. Career incls: apps. at ldng. Italian, French, Scandinavian & Netherlands opera houses; sang Agnese in Beatric di Tenda (w. Arangi-Lombardi) at the Bellini Centenary, Catania, 1935; represented Norway, Music Fest., Copenhagen, 1938; sang at 1st reception at Waldorf-Astoria for UN Delegs., 1946. Recordings: Grieg songs. Contbr. to: newspapers; radio progs.; lectures. Address: Bygdoy allé 20, Oslo, Norway.

AMZALLAG, (Eilam) Avraham, b. 28 Sept. 1941. Casablanca, Morocco. Composer; Flautist. Educ: Music Tchrs.' Seminar, Tel Aviv; Israel Music Acad., Univ. of Tel Aviv; Musicol. Fac., ibid.; BA Music. m. Nava Eilam, 1 s. Debut: Israel Broadcasting Serv., 1969. Career: Achoti Kala (My Sister, My Bride), musical play for Inbal Dance Theatre; Kad (The Jar), for Inbal Dance Theatre. Comps: Taksim (flute solo), 1970; Maavakim Ba-Yam (Struggels in the Sea, symphonic orch.); Music for Flute & Percussion; Meditations (oboe solo); 200 for 5 (4 wind instruments), 1976; Midbarit (flute solo), 1973. Mbr., Israel Comps. League. Address: 264 Bnei Efraim, Neot Afeka, Tel Aviv, Israel.

ANAGNOSON, James, b. 4 Feb. 1947. Boston, Mass., USA. Concert Pianist; Piano Teacher. Educ: BMus, Eastman Schl. of Music, 1968; MSc, Juilliard Schl., 1970. m. Judith Anne Crocker. Career: num. perfs. as part of Anagnoson-Kinton Duo in Can., USA & Europe; perfs. on TV; radio recordings for BBC, CBC, Hilversum radio; Can. premiere of Stravinsky's 2 piano version of Dumbarton Oaks Concerto; num. works comp. for the Duo; fac. mbr., examiner, Royal Conserv. of Music, Toronto. Hons: scholarships at Eastman Schl., 1964-68, Chautauqua Music Schl., 1971, '73, & Aspen Music Schl., 1969, '70. Address: 7 Huntley St., Apt. 202, Toronto, Ont., M4Y 2PS, Can.

ANDERSEN, Diane-Bricault, b. 5 July 1934. Copenhagen, Denmark. Concert Pianist; Prof. Royal Conserv. of Music, Mons, Belgium. Educ: Musical Educ. in France, Denmark and Royal Conserv. of Music, Brussels. m. André Gertler. Debut: Danish Radio, 1942. Career: Concerts and recitals, apps. on TV and radio in Europe, USSR, Australia w. ldng. orchs. and conds. Recordings: Complete piano works of G. Pierné & L. Cherubini; complete Songs without Words by Mendelssohn; (w. André Gertler) Complete comps. for violin and piano by Bartok, etc. Hons: 1st Prize, Piano and Chambr. Music, Brussels Conserv.; Harriet Cohen Bach Medal, 1962; Grand Prix du Disque, Acad. Charles Cros, Paris, 1967. Hobbies: Archaeology; Swimming; Practising piano. Address: Ave. d'Overhem 28. 1180 Brussels, Belgium. 27.

ANDERSÉN, Harald Fridolf, b. 4 Apr. 1919. Helsinki, Finland. Choir Conductor; Organist; Lecturer. Educ: BA. m. Rode Birgita Maria Wirén, 2 s., 1 d. Career: Cond., Finnish Radio Chamber Choir, Klemetti Institute Chamber Choir & Cantemus, chamber choir of Sibelius Acad.; Tours w. Klemetti Chamber Choir & Cantemus in most European countries & USA; Reformer of Finnish choral tradition; Lectr., Hd. of Ch. Music Dept., Sibelius Acad. prof., 1978. Minor litugical comps. Recordings: num. w. above choirs. Publs: (compiler) Mass Music used in the liturgy of the Swedish-speaking Lutheran Church in Finland, 1968; Hymanal (w. T Kkuusisto), 1976. Mbr., Bd. of Music of Finnish State. Hons: Pro Finlandia medal; Harriet Cohen Int. Music award, 1967; Dr., Theology, 1975; Music award of the Finnish State, 1976; 1st cultural prize ever awarded by Soc. for the Advancement of Public Educ. Address: Västra Braheg. 4a B 15, 00510 Helsingfors 51, Finland.

ANDERSEN, Karsten, b. 16 Feb. 1920. Oslo, Norway. Conductor; Concert Violinist. Educ: studied in Norway & Italy. m., 2 children. Career: Orch. Cond. & Musical Dir., Stavanger, 1945-64, & Harmonien Soc., Bergen, 1964-; Chief Cond., Iceland Symph. Orch., 1973-; Guest Cond., orchs. in most European countries & Am. Recordings: sev. w. Bergen Symph. Orch., for Philips. Address: Svartediksvei 7A, 5000 Bergen, Norway.

ANDERSEN, (Marjorie) Elnore Crampton, b. 23 Feb. 1933. Detroit, Mich., USA. Violinist; Teacher. Educ: B Mus, Univ. Mich.; Violin studies w. Emily Mutter Adams & Karl Chase, Detroit; Gilbert Ross, Ann Arbor; studied w. Sally G Thomas, NYC; Meadowmount Schl. of Music. m. Carl Marius Andersen, 1 s., 2 d. Career: Violin Soloist & 1st Violinist, Williamsburg Gov's Palace Ensemble, Va.; Frequent soloist in Tidewater, Va., area; Violinist, Williamsburg String Trio & Peninsula Symph.; Formerly mbr. of Indpls. Symph. & Norfolk, Va., Symph.; Tchr. & and ensemblist var. grps., 1959-61; Co-fndr. w. Rebecca Siegel of Williamsburg Youth Symph. Mbrships: Pi Kappa Lambda; Sigma Alpha Iota. Address: 116 Caran Rd., Williamsburg, VA., USA.

ANDERSEN, Martin, b. Mar. 1889. Violin Educator. Educ: violinist pupil of Nanny Raffenberg. Royal Chambermusician Peder Moller, Emil Telmany, Prof. Vojtcek Frait (Prague), Max Rostal, 1955; conductor pupil of Nicolai Malko; studies in theory w. composer Christian Danning, etc. Appts: Violin Educator, 1918-; State-guaranteed Violin Educator, 1940; w. Malm Concerthall Symph., 1925-27; Fndr., 1929-63; Fndr. & Dir. The Fuenen Chamber Orch., 1931; Fndr. of Odense Town Orch., Denmark & on Danish Radio w. The Funen Chamber Orch., inclng. 1st performance of num. new Danish compositions. Var. concert tours. Mbr., The Danish Soc. of Musicpedagogues. Publs: (books) Hjemmemusikken og dens betydning pa Fyn, 1956; Erindringer fra mit lives eventyr; Mit Liv i Musikken, 1970; conbtr. to Leksikon for opdragere. Num. paintings at pub. art exhibs. Hons. incl: Ridder of Dannebrog. at the command of King Frederik IX, 1954. Address: Sohusvaenet 13, 5270 Odense N, Denmark.

ANDERSON, Beth, b. 3 Jan. 1950. Lexington, Ky., USA. Composer; Pianist; Accompanist; Improvisor. Educ: Perf. maj. Univ. Ky., 1968; BA Mus, Univ. Calif., Davis, 1971; MFA, Mills Coll., 1973; MA, ibid., 1974. Career incls: Piano & Voice Tchr., Oakland, Calif., 1971-75; Performing mbr., Hysteresis, women's Conserv. New Music Ensemble & 1974 Cabrillo Festival, Calif. Comps. incl: Queen Christina (opera), 1973; Tower of Power (organ), 1973. Num. recordings. Publs: Ed.

Publr., EAR Mag. 1973-. Conbtr. to profl. mags. Mbrships: League of Women Corps.; Coll. Music Soc. Recip. num. grants & awards. Hobby: Astrolo. Address: 326 Second Ave. NY, NY 10003, USA.

ANDERSON, Edwin D, Jr., b. 14 July 1933. Hingham, Mass., USa. Bass Trombonist. Educ: B Mus, Eastman Schl. of Music, Univ. of Rochester. m. Virginia Morrison, 1 s., 1 d. Career: Bass Trombonist, Buffalo Phil., NY, 1959-64. Cleveland Orch., 1964-. Recordings: w. Cleveland Orch. Mb., Int. Trombonists Assn. Address: 3337 Clarendon Rd., Cleveland Heights, OH 44118, USA.

ANDERSON, Garland Lee, b. 10 June 1933. Union City, Ohio, USA. Pianist; Composer. Educ: Ind. Univ., Bloomington; AB, Earlham Coll.; Univ. of Miami, Fla.; Univ. of Edinburgh, UK div., 1 d. Debut: Edinburgh, UK, 1954, Career: has perf. at many colls. & univs.; Music Dir., WGLM Radio, 1963-66; has made radio & TV broadcasts; has received commissions for works from Phi Mu Alpha Sinfonia, Richmond Symph. Orch. & Dr. Cecil Leeson. Comps. incl: Three Preludes for piano; saxophone & piano (recorded); Sonata for tenor saxophone & piano; sonata for baritone saxophone & piano, 1976; Prelude for piano. Mbrships: Am. Soc. of Comps., Authors & Publrs. Hons: Nat. Endowment for the Arts, Grant to compose opera, 1976-77. Address: 316 N Mulberry St., Muncie, IN 47305, USA.

ANDERSON, Gillian Bunshaft, b. 28 Nov. 1943. Brookline, Mass., USA. Musicologist; Conductor. Educ: BA, Bryn Mawr Coll., 1965; MM Univ. of Ill. at Urbana, 1969. m. Gordon Wood Anderson. Career: Lib. of Congress, Music Div., 1978-; Nat. Public Radio, 1976-77; Kennedy Ctr., White House; Nat. Archives; Nat. Portrait Gallery; Am. Philosophical Soc. etc.; Cond., Colonial Singers & Players. Recordings: Political & Patriotic Music of the Am. Revolution; Frances Hopkinson, America Independent; Daniel Bayley, A New Royal Harmony. Publs: Freedom's Voice in Poetry & Song, 1977; The Music of the American Revolution; Frances Hopkinson, America Independent or The Temple of Minerva, 1977. Contbr. to num. Profl. jrnls. Mbrships: Am. Musicol. Soc.; Music Library Assn.; Sonneck Soc.; Trustee, Bryn Mawr Coll. Hon: Pi Kappa Lambda, 1967. Hobbies: Bryn Mawr Coll., Mountain Climbing; Bread Baking; Sex; Gossip. Address: 1320 N Carolina Ave. N E, Washington, DC 20002, USA.

ANDERSON, Gordon Athol, b. 1 May 1929. Melbourne, Aust. Musicologist. Educ: BA, BMus, MMus, DMus, Univ. of Adelaide. m. Laurel Alice Heath, 2 d. 1 s. Career: Sr. Master in Langs. & Music, Pulteney Grammar Schl., Adelaide, SA, 1957-69; Post Doct. Fellowship, Flinders Univ. of SA, 1970-72; Lectr. in Music, Univ. of New England, 1973-74; Snr. Lectr. in Music, ibid., 1975-76; Assoc. Prof. in Music, ibid., 1977-. Num. publs. incl: The Motels of the thirteenth century manuscript La Clayette; Newly identified Clausula-motels in Las Huelgas manuscript; Nove geniture: three variant settings of a Notre-Dame conducts, Symbolism in texts of thirteenth century music. Contbr. to num. profl. publs. Mbrships: Fellow, Aust. Acad. of the Humanities; Musicol. Soc. of Aust. (Pres., 1977); Int. Musicol. Soc.; Am. Musicol. Soc.; The Mediaeval Acad. of Am.; Aust. Soc. for Music Educ. Hobbies: Reading; Concergoing; Jazz music. Address: Dept. of Music, Univ. of New England, Armidale, NSW 2351, Aust. 4.

ANDERSON, Harry L(ancelot), b. 14 Mar. 1910. Guadalajara, Mexico. (Brit. national). Musicologist; Pianist; Piano Teacher. Educ: San Diego Tchrs. Coll.; USA; pvte. study of Piano, Theory & Comp., Calif. & London, UK. m. Mary Lee Caldwell, Career: Recitals & broadcasts, San Diego, NYC, S Africa & NM, also in Ceylon during RAF serv., WWII; Lecture course on dev. on keyboard music, San Diego, Rsch. into hist. of piano playing & esp. of piano recording as histl. documentary; large collection of source material. Recordings: Pieces by Medtner; works of Morris Ruger (pvte.) Contbr. to: Saturday Review; Musical Courier; Phonograph Monthly; Music Lovers Guide; Recorded Sound, UK. Hobbies: Reading; Handicrafts. Address: 4080 32nd St., San Diego, CA 92104, USA.

ANDERSON, James Granville, b. 6 Sept. 1946. Manchester, UK. Tubist; Professor. Educ: ARCM; Royal Manchester Coll. Debut: Concert Hall Broadcasting House. Career: joined Bournemouth Symph. Orch. when aged 20, 3 yrs.; free-lance, 3 yrs.; currently Prin. Tuba, BBC Symph. Orch.; Prof., GSM. Contbr. to: Sounding Brass. Hobbies: Photographer; Squash; Reading. Address: 58 Seabright Rd., Barnet, Herts., UK.

ANDERSON, Jay, b. 9 Sept. 1920. New Haven, Conn., USA. Guitarist; Singer. Educ: Longy Schl. of Music (solfege, harmony, counterpoint, comp.). m. Robert B Anderson, 3d. Career: local radio & TV apps., 1950-67; Resource tchr.; taught live & on TV; tchr., 2 Japanese schls., 1967. Comps:

91st Psalm (SSA); Echo Below; Softly, Softly Fell the Snow; Reflections; Bird in the Willow Tree; Song in the Mist; Spring. Mbr., exec. Bd., League of Women Comps. Hobby: Writing Book containing many unpubl. children's pieces. Address: 389 Kailua Rd., Apt. 201, Kailua, HI 96734, USA.

ANDERSON, Karen, b. 25 May 1945. Cardston, Alta., Can. Violinist. Educ: BS, Mannes Coll., NYC, 1970. Career: Rehearsal Pianist, Performing Arts Ctr., St. Paul, Minn., 1971-72; Sect. Violist, 1971-72, Prin. Violist (May & June), 1972 & 73, Civic Orch. of Mpls., Minn.; temporary Sect. Violist, Westchester Symph., NY; jobbing 7 chmbr. music experience (violin & viola) Mpls. & NYC, (viola) Edmonton & Milwaukee; Sect. Violist, 1972-73, Asst. Prin. Violist, 1973-74 & 74-75, Edmonton Symph. Orch., Atla.; Sect. Violist, Milwaukee Symph., Wis., 1975-. Hobby: Chamber Music. Address: 1007 N Cass, Milwaukee, WI 53202, USA.

ANDERSON, Kenneth, b. 6 Dec. 1903. London, UK. Violinst; Teacher. Educ: Mus B, Edinburgh Univ.; ARCM; FTCL. m. (1) Kathleen Prenter (dec.) 3 d; (2) Margot Bouch. Career incls: Asst. Music Master, Sedbergh Schl., 1940-64; Cond., Westmorland Orch., 1945-56; var. schl. music appts., Middx. & Surrey, 1964-73; Ldr., Guildford Symph. Orch., 1968-74; Violin Tchr., Guildford Co. Schl. of Music, 1968-. Comps: violin pieces & exercise; schl. orch. music & songs; transcriptions. Mbrships: ISM; European Str. Tchrs. Assn. Hobby: Reading. Address: Bankside, Sunnydell Ln., Farnham, Surrey, UK. 3.

ANDERSON, Margaret Ann Bissell (Peggy), b. 2 June, 1927. Larchmont, NY., USA. Piano accompanist. Educ: Pvte. piano & organ study w. var. tutors. m. Paul D. Anderson, 1 s. 1 d. Career: Piano accompanist for vioce, choir & instrumentalists, 1940-; Own weekly piano prog., Radio KCRS, Midland, Tex., 1942-44; Mbr., Radio House Chorus, Univ. of Tex., Austin, 1945-47. Mbrships: Musicians Club, Midland; Var. Ch. Choirs, Providence, RI., Austin & Midland, Tex.; Midland-Odessa Symph. Chorale, 1962-; Midland Symph. Chorus, Also piano rehearsal accompanist, 1953-55. mbr., AAUW. Hobbies: Theatre musicals; Chorus work; Archaeol.; Anthropol.; Camping. Address: 1410 Community Lane, Midland, TX 79701, USA.

ANDERSON, Michael Stothart, b. 26 Aug. 1934. Dumfries, Scotland, UK. Music Librarian. Educ: Dumfries Acd.; Edinburgh Univ.; MA, 1952; LRAM, 1961; Assoc. of the Lib. Assn., 1964. Career: Asst. Libn., Edinburgh Univ., 1959-62; Libn., Reid Music Lib., Edinburgh Univ., 1962-. Mbrships: Lib. Assn.; Int. Assn. of Music Libs. Hobbies: Scots Hist.; Travel. Address: 9 Polwarth Gdns., Edinburgh, EH11 1JS, UK.

ANDERSON, Nicholas Maurice William, b. 29 Mar. 1941. Exeter, UK. Music Producer, BBC. Educ: Oxford Univ.; Durham Univ. Career: Lectr. in Music, Bede Coll., Durham, 1966-68; Lectr., WEA (Northern Div.) 1966-68; Decca Record Co., 1969-71; Music Prod., BBC, 1971-. Contbr. to Musical Times, Grove's Dictionary of Music & Musicians; Recorder & Music Mag.; The Guardian; Northern Echo; Early Music Mag.; The Gramophone Mag. Mbr. Royal Musical Assn. Addres: 3 Cranbourne Ct., Albert Bridge Rd., London SW11, UK.

ANDERSON, Nicola Charlotte, b. 15 Nov. 1940. Manchester, UK. Cellist. Educ: Tchr's ARCM. m. Andrew Milne, 2 d. Debut: ISM Young Artists Recitals, Wigmore Hall, Mar. 1963. Career: Recital Work; Mbr. sev. Chamber Orchs. inclng. Prin. cellist, Midland Chambr. Orch., & Manchester Camerata; Birmingham Bach Soc. Orch. Subprin. of English Sinfonia; Hobbies: Family; Gardening. Address: Brook Furlong S Rd., Oundle, Peterborough PE8 4BP, 3, 27.

ANDERSON, Robert David, b. 20 Aug. 1927. Shillong. Assam, India. Conductor' Writer' Editor. Educ: MA, Gonville & Caius Coll., Cambridge, UK, 1954. Career: Asst. Ed., Record News, 1954-56; Asst. Master & Dir. of Music, Gordonstoun Schl., 1956-62; Cond., Moray Choral Union; Asst. Cond., Spoleto Fest., 1962; Cond., St. Bartholomew's Hosp. Choral Schl., 1965-; Assoc. Ed., The Musical Times, 1967-; Critic., The Times, 1967-72; Contbr., to BBC Music Mag. & Concert Calendar, 1969-72; TV Prog. on Paganini for BBC2, 1971. Recordings: Mozart Accred. Music. Mbrships: Hon. Sec., Egypt Exploration Soc., 1971; Royal Musical Assn. Publs: Catalogue of Egyptian Antiquities in the British Museum, III, Musical Instruments, 1976. Hobby: Modulating from music to Egyptol. Address: 54 Hornton St., London W8 4NT, UK.

ANDERSON, Ronald K, b. 19 Aug. 1934. Kansas City, Mo., USA. Trumpet Soloist; Teacher. Educ: BME, Ctrl. Mo. State Coll., 1955; BS, Juilliard Schl. of Music, 1957; MS, ibid., 1958; MA, Columbia Univ., 1963; EdD, ibid., 1970. m. Felicitas Capalo, 1 s., 1 d. Debut: Trumpet Recital, Town Hall,

NYC, 1966. Career incls: Trumpet recital, Tully Hall, & Carnegie Recital Hall, NYC; Solo apps. in USA & Europe; Former mbr., NY Pro Musica Antique & Am. Brass Quintet; Fac: SUNY, Stony Brook; SUNY, Purchase; Vt. Comps. Conf. Num. recordings. Publs. incl: Ed., Solo Piece for Trumpet by Stefan Wolpe, 1968. Contbr. to Music Jrnl. Mbr. Bd. Dirs., Int. Soc. for Contemporary Music. Num. awards. Hobby: Small farm w. trout stream. Address: 251 W 92 St., Apt. 11-B, New York, NY 10025, USA.

ANDERSON, Ronald Kinloch, b. 16 Oct. 1911. Edinburgh, Scotland, Pianist; Teacher; Writer; Lecturer; Harpischordist; Artistic Director of Gramophone Recording. Educ: Mus B, Edinburgh Univ., 1932; ARCM. Debut: London, 1938. Career: Apps. & broadcasts as solo pianist in UK & Continent, 1938-45; Pianist of Robert Masters Quartet, 1946-58; Prof. of Pianoforte, TCL, 1946-63; Harpischordist w. Menuhin Festival Orch., 1957-63; Writer & Broadcaster on Music, 1973-. Compositions incl: Songs & arrangements. Recordings as harpsichordist w. Menuhin Festival Orch. etc. Contbr. to profl. mags. Mbrships. incl: ISM. Hons. incl: Audio Award, 1974. Hobbies: Music; Gardening Address: 19 Parkhill Rd. London NW3, UK.

ANDERSON, Ross, b. 2 Jan. 1929. Borchington, UK. Conductor; Accompansit; Musical Administrator. Educ: RCM; Royal Schl. of Ch. Music. m. Jean Anderson, 1 s., 1 d. Career: Guest Cond., BBC Concert Orch., BBC Reg. Orchs., Choral & Operatic socs. throughout Brit. Isles; Apps. at Three Choirs, Edinburgh, & Canterbury Fests; Gilbert & Sullivan For All. Comps: Incidental music for "Good Friday" (Masefield), & "Song of Adam" (Lamb); Ch. music; Songs; "Bachelor's Eve" (W End Revue). Mbrships: Exec. Comm., & Chmn., Music Advsry. Panel, SE Arts Assn. Address: Tabard House, Godwyn Gdns., Folkestone, CT20 2JZ, UK.

ANDERSON, Stig, b. 25 Jan. 1931. Mariestad, Sweden. Music Publisher; Record Producer; Lyric Writer; Manager. Educ: Tchrs. HS, Stockholm. m. Gudrun Anderson, 3 children. Comps. (w. Bjorn Ulvaeus & Benny Andersson): Waterloo; Honey Honey; I do I do I do I do; SOS; Mamma Mia; Fernando. Mbrships: Bd., Swedish Publrs. Assn.; Swedish IFPI Org. Hons: Billboad's Trendsetter Award, 1974; Winner, Eurovision Song Contest, Brighton, UK, 1974. Address: c/o Polar Records AB, Baldergatan 1, Fack, 10041 Stockholm, Sweden.

ANDERSON, Warren DeWitt, b. 19 Mar. 1920. Brooklyn, NY USA. Professor. Educ: BA, Haverford Coll., 1942; MA, PhD, Harvard Univ., 1947, '54; BA (Oxon.), 1947. m. Anne Bacon Worden, 2 s., 1 d. Career: Prof. of Comparative Lit., Univ. of Mass. at Amherst. Publs: Ethos & Education in Greek Music, 1966; Word-Accent & Melody in Ancient Greek Musical Texts, 1973. Contbr. to: Musical Times; Music Review; Research Chronicle of the Royal Music Assn.; 74 articles in Grove's Dict., 6th ed. Mbr. Am. Musicol. Soc. Hobby: Translation. Address: 27 High Point Dr., Amherst, MA 01002, USA. 2.

ANDERSON, William Miller, b. 26 Nov. 1940. Pulaski, Va., USA. Educator. Educ: BMus, MMus, Eastman Schl. of Music; PhD, Univ. of Mich. m. Lee Ann Stephens Anderson. Career: Associate Professor of Music Educ. & Ethnomusicol. & Coord. of Grad. Studies, Schl. of Music, Kent State Univ. Recordings w. Eastman Wind Ensemble; Hovhaness Symph. No. 4; Giannini Symph. No. 3; Marching Along; Screamers. Publs. incl: Teaching Asian Musics in Elementary & Secondary Schools; An Introduction to the Musics of India & Indonesia, 1975; Music and Related Arts for the Classroom, 1978. Contbr. to jrnls. Mbrships. incl: Comm. of Rsch. in Music Educ., Ohio Music Educ. Assn., 1971-; Life Mbr., MENC & Phi Mu Alpha Sinfonia; Soc. for Asian Music; Am. Orff-Schulwerk Assn. soc. for Ethnomusicology. Recip. acad. hons. Hobby: Photography. Address: Schl. of Music, Kent State Univ., Kent, OH 44240, USA.

ANDRÉ, Maurice, b. 21 May 1933. Ales, Gard, France. Trumpeter. Educ: Nat. Conserv. of Music, Paris. m. Lilianne Arnoult, 4 children. Debut: 1954. Career: Soloist w. prin. orchs. in France & abroad; Tours of Germany, Scandinavis, N & S Am., etc. specialising in 17th Century & contemporary music; Prof., Nat. Conserv. of Music, Paris, 1967-. Recordings: num. classical & modern music, Hons. incl: Chevalier, Legion of Hon.; 1st Prize, Trumpet & Hons. Prize, Cornet, Paris Conserv.; 1st Prize, Geneva Int. Competition, 1955; 1st Prize, Munish Int. Competition, 1963; Schallplattenpreis, Berlin, 1970. Hobbies: Pen-drawing; Gardening; Swimming. Address: 77137 Prestes-en-Brie, France.

ANDREAE, Hans, b. 24 May 1908. Zurich, Switz. Musician; Professor of Music. Educ: Concert Dip., Cologne Schl. of Music; Counterpoint Dip., ibid. m. Rosmarie Metzenthin, 4 children.

Debut: W. Adolf Busch, Germany, 1932. Career: Prof. of Music, Zurich Conserv.; Performed var. festivals inclng: Salzburg, Lucerne, Stresa, Edinburgh, Vienna, Engadin, etc.; Chmbr. music concerts most European countries & USA; Radio & TV apps. in Switz., England, Austria & Germany. Num. recordings w. harpischord, piano & organ. Contbr. to newspapers & jrnls. Mbrships: Schweizarischer Tonkunstlerverein; Musikpadagogischer Tonkunstlerverein; Musikpadagogischer Verband der Schweiz. Hobbies: Mountaineering; Swimming. Address: Justrain 50, 8706 Meilen, Switz.

ANDREAE, Marc Edouard, b. 8 Nov. 1939. Zürich, Switzerland. Conductor; Composer; Publisher. Educ: Dip. in cond., piano, Conservatory, Zürich; Studied comp. w. Nadia Boulanger; w. Franco Ferrara, S Cecilia, Rome; Dips., Siena, master courses. Career: Chief Cond., Swiss & Italian Radio & TV orchs.; Cond., major European orchs., inclng. Berlin, Munich, Hamburg, Cologne, Frankfurt, Paris, Rome, Milan, Genoa, Zürich, Basle, Geneva, Belgrade, Lubljana. Compositions. R Schumann/Andreae, Symphony in G Minor; CM v. Weber/Andreae, F Schubert/Joachim, Symphony in C Major (Op. 140); Rossini; Ouverture, Matilde di Shabran. Recordings of works by var. comps. inclng. Schubert, Schumann, Mussorgsky, Witt. Mbrships: Commission, Soc. of Swiss Musicians; Swiss Musi Pedagogues. Hons: Winner, competition for conds., Zürich; Prize, Italian Music Critic for Recordings, 1974; 22nd Prize for studies, Italian govt. Hobbies: Greek; archaeol.; Sport. Mgmt: Spectrum Concert Bur., Nürnberg, & Konzertgesellschaft, Zürich, Switzerland. Address: Casa Felix, 6901 Vernate, Switzerland.

ANDREASSEN, Eyvind, b. 26 Oct. 1945. Fredrikstad, Norway. Musician (horn). Educ: Pvte. studies w. Froydis Ree Wekre & Prof. Vitaly Boyanovsky, Conserv. of Leningrad; Military Musician Exam., Halden, Norway. m. Bente Fleksem, 1 d. Career: Soloist, Oslo Phil., Bergen Symph.; Chmbr. music, radio & TV; 4 yrs., Military Band of Halden; 3rd horn, Norwegian Broadcasting Orch., Oslo, 1971-. Recordings: Wind Quintet; Chmbr. Music. Mbrships: Int. Horn Soc. Hobbies: Sports; Norwegian beer. Address: Ostgardvn. 2A, N-1600 Fredrikstad, Norway.

ANDREASSEN, Mogens Steen, b. 3 Oct. 1916. Copenhagen, Denmark. Oboe Player. Educ: Conservatoire Nat., Paris, France. m. Elisabeth Mygdal-Meyer, 2 s. Debut: Copenhagne, 1936. Career: Leading Oboe, Danish Radio Symph. Orch., 1937-46, Royal Danish Orch., 1946-; Assoc. w. Royal 1937-46; Perfs. of chmbr. music, TV, radio throughout Europe; Solo perfs., radio & w. var. orchs. Var. recordings of chmbr. music & symphs. Hons: Scandinavian Prize, 1936; Silver Medal, Geneva, Switz. 1947; RD (Order of Knighthood). Hobbies: Music; Books; Travel; Country house. Address: Ordrupvej 86, 2920 Charlttenlund, Denmark.

ANDREIS, Josip, b. 19 Mar. 1909. Split, Yugoslavia. Professor of French, Italian & Music History. Educ: Dip., Fac. of Leters, Zagreb, 1931; Dip., Acad. of Music, ibid., 1947. m. Vesna Pasini, 2 s. Career incls: Asst. Prof., Zagreb Acad. of Music, 1947-52; Assoc. Prof., ibid., 1952-60; Full Prof., 1960-72; Ret'd., 1972. Publs. incl: Introduction to the Aesthetics of Music, 1944; History of Music, 3 eds.; History of Croatian Music, 1962, new ed. 1974. Contbr. to var. profl. jrnls. Mbrships. incl: Corres. Mbr., Yugoslav Acad. of Arts & Scis., 1954; 75; Regular Acad. Mbr., 1975; Pres., Assn. of Croatian Comps., 1952-53, 1955-56. Recip. var. hons. Address: Ul. Socijalističke revolcije 42/III, 41000 Zagreb. Yugoslavia.

ANDRESS, Will K, b. 28 Aug. 1938. El Dorado, Ark., USA. Choral Director; Singer (tenor). Educ: B Mus Centenary Coll., La., 1961; M Ch Mus, Southern Bapt. Theol. Sem., 1963; M Mus, E Car. Univ., 1969; D Mus, Fla. State Univ., 1971. m. Julia Hamiter Andress, 1 s., 1 d. Career incls: Oratorio soloist num. Eastern & Southern States of USA; Choral Clinitian in 8 states; Cond., 5 int. choral tours inclng. concert for Pope Paul VI, 1972; Music Dir., 1st United Meth. Ch., Shreveport, La.; Dir., Centenary Coll. Choir. Contbr. 16 articles to Opus II; 48 articles to Ch. Musician. Mbr. num. profl. orgs. inclng: Phi Delta Kappa; Nat. Opera Assn.; Am. Choral Dirs. Assn. Recip. Gold Key, Fla. State Univ., 1971. Hobbies: Tennis; Golf. Address: 316 Maggie Ln., Shreveport, LA 71106, USA.

ANDREW, Donald James Clifford. Barnstaple, UK. Oboist. Educ: RAM, London, ARCM. Debut: BBC, Bristol, 1945. Career incls: 1st UK Broadcast Perf. of Haydb Oboe Concerto, Bristol, 1947; Liverpool Phil. Orch., 1948-49; Prin. Oboe, BBC Revue Orch., 1950-54, Leighton Lucas Chamber Orch., 1955-57, Ballet Rambert, 1958-59; Mbr. of Wind Band, Stratford-upon-Avon, 1959-60; Prin. Oboe, Salders Wells Opera Co.,

1960-63; Has played for all leading London orchs. & and othes; Has given many broadcast recitals, schls. broadcasts, etc.; Recital, Purcell Room - Festival Hall, 1972. Mbrships: Musicians Union; London Musical Club. Hons: IBC Diploma, 1976. Mgmt: James Fox, London Musical Club. Address: London Musical Club, 21 Holland Park, London, WII, UK. 3, 4, 28.

ANDREWES, John Hampden, b. 31 Jan. 1915. Canterbury, UK. Music Publisher. Educ: Gonville & Caius Coll., Cambridge Univ., 1933-35; RCM, 1938-40, 46-47. m. Olivia Sarel, 1 s., 1 d. Career: Mbr., Ballet Rambert, 1936-40; Free-lance Cond., esp. ballect, 1947-53; Music Ed., Boosey & Hawkes Music Publrs., 1953-74; Music Promotion w. special resp. for promotion of new music, 1958-74; Fndr., Musical Dir., Finchley Children's Music Grp., 1959-; Publishing Mgr., 1977. Recordings incl: Malcolm Williamson, Julius Caesar Jones (opera); Gordon Crosse, Meet My Folks; R R Bennett, The Aviary/The Insect World. Mgmt: Adza Vincent Ltd., 11a Ivor Pl., London NW1, UK. Address: Enfield House, Windmill Hill, Londn NW3, UK. 3.

ANDREWES, Richard Michael, b. 7 April 1943. Kidderminster, UK. Librarian. Career: Int. Inventory of Musical Sources (RISM), 1967-70; Librarian, RAM 1971-73; Librarian, Pendlebury Lib. of Mulsic, Cambridge, 1974-. Contbr. to Musical Times. Mbrships: Int. Assn. of Music Libraries; Viola da Gamba Soc. Address: 6 Selwyn Rd., Cambridge, UK.

ANDREWS, Donald John, b. 29 May 1929. Singleton, NSW, Aust. Guitarist; Composer; Arrangor. Educ: guitar studies in Spain. m. Monica Scott. Career incls: Guitarist w. Aust. Broadcasting Commn., 16 yrs.; perf. w. Sydney Symph. Orch.; Ldr., own chmbr. music grps. broadcasting via transcription serv. to 13 European countries; Examiner, Aust. Music Exams. Bd. Comps: num. film scored; guitar works. Recordings: incl. num. commercial. Publs. incl: Don Andrews Guitar Series (about 30 vols.); curricular & instructional materials; guitary transcripts. Mbrships: Musical Assn.; APRA. Hobby: Gardening. Address: 7 Castlefield St., Bondi, NSW, Aust. 2026.

ANDREWS, Pamela L, b. 15 Aug. 1943. Aurora, III., USA. Double Bassist; University Professor. Educ: BS, Univ. of III., Champaign Urbana; MM Univ. of Miami, Fla. Career: Double Bassist, N Fla. Chmbr. Orch., Jacksonville Symph., & Savannah Symph., currently; Fac. Artist, Brevard Music Ctr., NC; Prof. of Double Bass, Fla. State Univ.; Dir. of String Instruction & Chairperson, String Dept., ibid. Mbrships. incl: Sec., Pi Kappa Lambda, 1973-; Fla. Pres., Am. String Tchrs. Assn., 1975-; Phi Kappa Phi. Contbr. to profl. jrnls. Recip., Stiven Award, Am. Fedn. of Musicians, 1966. Address: 1805 Salmon Dr., Tallahassee, FL 32303, USA.

ANDRIĆ, Stojan. b. 18 Aug. 1912. Zajecar, Yugoslavia. Composer. Educ: Musical Acad., Belgrade. m. Milena, 2 children. Career: Prof. of Music; Cond. of Chorus & Symph. Orch., Radio Nis, & of Nat. Theatre, Nis; radio perfs. of works. Comps: 2 Fugues for orch.; 20 Romances (6 recorded); 9 Rukovets (Switas) for chorus; Switas for orch., set of children's choruses; set of revolutionary songs & Song of rebuilding for mixed Pro Musica & some daily papers. Mbrships: Savez Kompozitora Yugoslavije; Udruženje Muzićkih Umetnika. Recip., October Prize, Town of Nis, 1959. Hobby: Fishing. Address: V Kongres 22/1, 18000 Nis, Yugoslavia.

ANDRIENKO, Kalena Czaczka, b. 1 Nov. 1920. Vienna, Australia. Pianist; Piano Teacher. Educ: Pvte. piano studies w. Alida Hecker, Maria Dombrowski, Berlin; Staatliche Musiklehrer prufung, Staatliche Hochschule fur Musik, Berlin; Lysenko Music Inst., Lviv, W Ukraine w. Roman Sawytsky & Wasyl Barwinsky; w. Viola. Thern Musikschule der Stadt Wien; Staatiche Hochschule fur Musik, Munich w. Joseph Pembaur, Career: Co-Fndr., Ukrainian Music Inst. of Am. Inc., 1952: Fac. Mbr., ibid., 1952-; Publishing Dir., ibid., 1976. Mbrships: NGPT; Assoc. Music Tchrs. League of NY Inc.; Assoc. Mbr., NY Singer Tchrs. Assn.; Ukrainian Lit. & Art Club. NY. Address: 118 Ave. D, Apt. 10B, New York, NY 10009, USA.

ANDRIESSEN, Louis, b. 6 June 1939. Utrecht, Netherlands. Composer. Educ: Royal Conserv., The Hague Ldr., brass orch. De Volharding currently Tchr. of instrumentation & orchestration, Royal Conserv., The Hague Compositions incl: Lttrospezione II for orch.; Ittrospezione III (Concept I & II); Nocturnen for soprano & orch.; Registers for piano; Series for 2 pianos; Sonata for flute & piano; sweet for recorders; Anachronie I for large orch.; Contra Tempus for orch.; de Staat, for voices & 27 instruments; works for theatre and film; sev. comps. recorded. Contbr. to De Gids. Mbr., Soc. Dutch Comps. (treas. & committee mbr.). Hons: 1st prize International

Rostrum of Comps. for de Staat; Gaudeamvs Prize, 1959. Address: Keizersgracht 740, Amsterdam, The Netherlands.

ANDRUS, Donald George, b. 13 Sept. 1935. Seattle, Wash., USA. Composer; Associate Professor Music & Coordinator of the Electronic Music Studio, Calif. State Univ., Long Beach. Educ: BA, Western Wash. State Coll., 1957; MA, Univ. of Wash., 1960; D Mus A, Univ. of Ill., 1968; studied composition, acoustics, analysis, piano & organ w. var. tchrs.; worked in electronic music studios at Univs. of Ill., Utrecht (Netherlands, Rijksuniversiteit), Calif. (San Diego), & Wis. Digital Music, Stanford Univ., Nórsk studio for Elektronisk Musikk. m. Gretel Yvonne Shanley, 1 s. Career: formerly on facs. of Univ. of Ill. & Univ. of Wis.; electronic composition for tape, Psssh, played in Severance Hall, Cleveland, Ohio, 1967, at 1st Fest. of Music of the Ams., Rio de Janeiro, Brazil, 1969, & ISCM Concert, Oslo, Norway, 1969; The Aardvark Shuffle for contrabass & 4-channel tape, commissioned by Bertram Turetzky & premiered by him in Long Beach, Calif., 1974. Compositions publd.; Imbrications for Four Performers; Gradual & Alleluia of the Acoustics of Tamtam Sounds, 1968. Mbrships: LA Chapt., Int. Soc. for Contemp. Music Am. Soc. Univ. Comps; Electronic Music Asscn. of LA. Electronic Music Assn. of LA. Recip. of sev. grants. Address: 21516 Encina Rd., Topanga, CA 90290, USA. 8, 4, 9.

ANGAS, Richard, b. 18 Apr. 1942. Cobham, Surrey, UK. Bass.-baritone. Educ: RAM; Acad. of Music & Dramatic Art, Vienna. m. Rosanne Creffield, 1 s. Debut: w. Scottish Opera. Career: has sung as guest w. all major Brit. opera cos., inclng. Royal Opera House prods. of Wozzeck & world premiere of Henze's The River; Concert Singer w. ldng. int. orchs.; frequent broadcaster; currently under contact w. theatre in Koblenz and Rhein; sings as guest in other German theatres. Recordings: EMI; DGG; CBS. Mbrships: ISM; Equity. Hons. incl: Richard Tauber Memorial Scholarships; Kathleen Ferrier Award, 1962. Hobbies: Squash; Tennis; Walking; Cooking. Address: 121 Coningham Rd., London W12, UK.

ANGELL, Warren Mathewson, b. 13 May 1907. Brooklyn, NY, USA. Dean of Music; Pianist; Organist; Singer; Conductor; Composer. Educ: BM Syracuse Univ., 1929; MM, ibid., 1933; Ed D, Columbia Univ., 1944. Career: Radio & TV apps. w. Fred Waring Pennsylvanians, Robert Shaw Chorale, 1942-44; Dean of Music, Okla. Baptist Univ., 1936-73. Comps. incl: (recorded) This Is The Day The Lord Hath Made; Christmas Means Thinking of Jesus; Hallelujah! I Love Him; Glorius Is Thy Church O Lord. Pubis: Vocal Approach, 1950; The Beginning Vocalist, 1959; Choir Clinic Manual, 1952; Look Up, You Singers 1978. Contbr. to: Southwestern Musician; Ch. Musician. Mbr. num. profl. orgs. Hons: Warren M Angell Coll. of Fine Arts named in hons.; Warren M Angell Day in Okla. & Mo., 1973; Hon. DMus, Soutwest Baptist Coll., 1973; Hon. DMus, Okla. Bapt. Univ., 1975. Hobbies: Fishing; Golf; Swimming. Address: 1920 N Bell, Shawnee, OK 74801, USA. 2, 7.

ANGERDAL, Lars Göran, b. 28 Aug. 1937. Örebro, Sweden. Organist; Choirmaster. Educ: Studied Univs. of Uppsala & Stockholm, Sweden; Studied Ch. Music & Music Educ., Royal Acad. of Music, Stockholm, 1957-62; Studied at Musikhochschule Berlin, Germany, 1962-63. m. Sonja Birgitta Malmström, 2 d. 1 s. Career: Organ Concerts, Scandinavia, Germany, Switz., France, England, USA; Choir Concerts, Scandinavia, Germany Australia, Italy; TV & Radio apps., Sweden & USA; Lectr., Sweden & USA; Asst. Organist & Choirmaster, Uppsala Cathedral, Sweden, 1967-. Recordings: Organ Music, Uppsala Cathedral. Mbr., profl. orgs. Pubis: Edited organ & choir music of other comps. Contbr. to: Svensk Kyrkomusik; Sohlmans Musiklexikon; The Am. Organist. Address: Fiskgjusevägen 16, S-752 56 Uppsala, Sweden.

ANGERER, Paul, b. 16 May 1927. Vienna, Austria. Conductor; Composer. Musical Educ: Acad. for Music, Vienna; Vienna; Vienna Conserv. m. Anita Rosser, 2 s., 2 d. Career incls: Solo Violist, Vienna Symph. Orch., 1953-57; Cond., Vienna Chamb. Orch., 1956-63; Comp. & Cond. Wieher Burgtheater, 1960-70; 1st Con., Bonn Theatre, 1964; Musical Dir., Ulm Theatre, 1966-68; Opera Dir., Salzburger Landestheater, 1967-72; Ldr., SW German Chmbr. Orch., 1971-; Artistic Dir., Hellbrunner Spiele, 1970-71; Permanent Guest, Orch. sinfonica di Bolzano e Trento, 1960-; Prof., 1978. Comps. incl: Quintett für Flöte, Oboe, Klarinette, Horn & Fagott, 1956; Toccaten für Cembalo, Gloriatio für kontrabass & dammerorch., 1957; "Inklination der Ariadne des Monteverdi", für Orch., (also Ballet), 1967. Trio I "Brushestcke", for flute, oboe & cello, 1971; Harfenstück I, 1971; "Recordatio" for 14 string instruments, 1972; Harfenstück II, 1972; Klavierstck I & II, 1973; "Floskein", trio for violin, violin cello & piano, 1973; Harfenstück III, 1974; Stage music for var. theatre; Film & TV music. Recordings incl:

Mozart piano concertos (cond.); Beethoven piano concertos (cond.); Bach Brandenburg Concertos (var. instruments). Ed., Diletto musicale. Contbr. to Maske & Kothurn. Hons. incl: Theordor Korner Prize, 1958; 1st Prize, Salzburg opera competition, 1959. Hobby: Collecting musical instruments & antiques. Address: Esteplatz 3, 1030 Vienna, Austria. 28.

ANGERMAN, Evelyn Carlson, b. 30 Mar. 1927. Dekalb, Ill., USA. Professor of Music; Clarinetist. Educ: BME, Northwestern Univ.; Advanced study, W Mich. Univ., N Ill. Univ. m. Robert F. Angerman, 1 s., 1 d. Career: Prin. Clarinetist, Battle Creek Symph., Kalamazoo Concert Band; Bass Clarinetist, Kalamazoo Symph. & Grand Rapids Symph.; Clarinetist, Kalamazoo Symph. Woodwind Quintet; Prof., Music, Kalamazoo, Coll. Recording: Bartok Concerto for Orchestra, w. Kalamazoo Symph. Pubis: Prog. Annotator, Kalamazoo Symph., 1950-60. Mbrships: Sec., Kalamazoo Concert band Bd.; Mbr., Kalamazoo Fedn. of Musicians Bd.; Past Pres., Sigma Alpha Iota Alumnae; Pi Kappa Lambda. Hobbies: Golf; Bridge. Address: 1405 Baker Dr., Kalamazoo, MI 49001, USA. 5.

ANGERMANN, Gerda, b. 10 Aug. Hamburg, Germany. Cellist. Educ: pvte. study of piano, violin, viola, organ & cello; studied w. Heinrich Schüchner, HS, Hamburg; master classes w. Enrico Mainardi. m. Karl Henke. Debut: Hanover, 1963. Career: concerts in Hanover, Bamberg, Munich, Stuttgart, Hamburg, Montreal, Manila, Dortmund & montreux Fest., 1974, '76; num. broadcasts in Germany & Switzerland; Cellist, Ensemble Divertimento Hamburg Hamburg & Hamburg String Trio. Recordings incl: Sonata op.6, S.Barber; Sonata in D minor, J. Woelfl; Capriccio, L.Foss; Sonata in G minor, M. Reger; Concerto in A minor, Op. 33, R Volkamnn; Concerto, Op.58, A. Casella. Hobbies: Sailing; Tailoring; Plants. Mgmt: Karl Kenke, zum Forellenbach 11, 2 Hamburg 74, German Fed. Repub.

ANGERMÜLLER, Rudolph Kurt, b. 2 Sept. 1940. Bielefeld, Germany. Music Editor; Music Librarian. Educ: MA; PhD, 1970; Grad., Försterling Conserv. of Music, Bielefeld. m. Hannelore Johannböke, 1 d. Career: Asst., Musicol. Inst., Univ. of Salzburg; Chief Ed., New Mozart Ed., & Libn., Int. Mozarteum Fndn., 1972-. Pubis: Untersuchungen zur Geschichte des Carmen-Stofes, 1967; Antonio Salieri, Sein Leben & seine weltlichen Werke unter besonderer Berücksichtigung seiner grossen Opern, 3 vols., 1971, 1972, 1974. Contbr. to: Bulletin of the Int. Mozarteum Fndn.; Mozart-Jahruch; Haydn-Johrbuch; Die Musikforschung; Osterreichische Musikzeitschrift; Wiener Figaro; Musical Times; Deutsche Jahrbuch für Musikwissenschaft; num. other profl. jrnls. & books. Mbrships: Int. Musicol. Soc.; Soc. for Music Rsch.; Austrian Musicol. Soc. Hobby: Collecting Old Books & Copperplate Engravings. Address: 92a Moostr., 5020 Salzburg, Austria.

ANNMO, Erland J, b. 5 Oct. 1920. Fengchen, China. Headmaster of The School of Music and Art in Jonkoping, Sweden. Educ: Pvte. studies in violin, singing, ch. music; Grad. Music Tchr., RAM, Stockholm, 1949; Grad. Cond., ibid., 1951. M. Sonja Rosentrom, 3 s. Career: Headmaster of Municipal Music Schls. in Sundbybert, Stockholm & Jonkoping; Cond., symph. orchs. & choirs; Prod. of Broadcasting Music Prog. for Schls.; Lectr. in courses & confs. Contbr. to profl. jrnls. etc. as music columnist. Mbrships: Pres., Riksforbundet Sveriges Musikpedagoger, 1953-; VP, Pres., & Sec., Nordisk Musikpedagogisk Union, 1960-64; Mbr. num. cultura socs. Reicp. Swedish Royal Medal. Address: Kallarpsgatan 23, 552 59 Jonkoping, Sweden.

ANNOVAZZI, Napoleone, b. 14 Aug. 1907. Florence, Italy. Orchestra Conductor; Pianist; Organist; Composer. Educ: M. Fascarini Coll., Venice; Studied piano, organ & comp., Conservatorio B. Marcello, Venice & Conservatorio G. Rossini, Pesaro. Debut: as pianist, aged 10 yrs.; as cond., aged 17 yrs. Career: Vienna State Opera; Munich State Opera; Royal Theatre La Monnaye, Brussels; Opera House, Rome; San Carlo Naples; Teatro Regio, Parmo, San Carlo, Lisbon; Gran Teatr del Liceo, Barcelona; Bella Arte, Mexico; Opera Bucharest; Opera Zagreb; Opera Sofia; Vienna, Madrid, Lisbon, Paris, Munich, Rome, Turin, Milan, Warsaw orchs., etc.; Fndr. & Cond., Chmbr. Orch. of Barcelona, 1946-48. Compositions: La lampada, one-act opera; Num. songs, choral & symph. works; Realizations of ancient Italian music Recordings: Madame Butterfly; La Traviata; Haydn Symph. no. 4. Pubis: Songs for voice & piano; 12 Symphonies of Manfredini, 1964; Overture of l'Eroe cinese by Galuppi. Recip. of hons. Hobbies: Painting; Stamp collecting. Address: Via Colleferro 16/10, 00189 Rome, Italy, 3, 28.

ANSCHÜTZ, Sonia Sylvia Carolina. Antwerp, Belgium. Concert Pianist; Professor of Piano. Educ: Royal Conserv. of Music,; Brussels, div. Debut: 1948. Career incls: Perfs., num. European countries; Prof. of Piano, Royal Conserv. of Music,

Mons, Int. Piano Class, Cuenca, Spain. Recordings incl: Recital of Russian Music; Liszt; Hungarian Rhapsodies Nos 1 & 2; Richard de Guide; Concerto for Piano & Orch., Hons. incl: Num. Prizes, Royal Concerts of Music, Brussels, 1946-52; Cmdr., Royal Assn. of Profl. Artistes, Belgium. Address: rue des Francs 82, 1040 Brussels, Belgium.

ANSTEY, Albert John, b. 3 Oct. 1928. Kingston-on-Thames, Surrey, UK. Church Organist & Choirmaster; Theatre Organist. Educ: TCL; studied w. Dr. Alan W. Bunney. m. Audrey Jane Anstey, 1d. Career: Ch. Organist, Kingston, Brentford, Tonbridge; currently Organist, Vale Royal Ch., Tunbridge Wells & Dir., Vale Royal Singers; var. recitals on organ, inclng. Wells Cathedral, 1973; own progs. of light organ music, BBC Radio Medway. Hobby: Photography. Address: 69 Higham Lane, Tonbridge, Kent, UK.

ANTAL, Istvan, b. 27 Jan. 1909. Budapest, Hungary. Pianist. Educ: Dip for Piano, Staatlich Akademische Hochschule für Musik, Vienna, Austria; Student of Prof. Leonid Kreuzer, ibid. m. Katalin Perjési. Debut: Cluj, Romania, 1925. Career: Concerts in Budapest, Vienna, Rome, Athens, Cologne, Berlin, Stockholm, Bucharest, Warsaw, Moscow, Leningrad, Dubrovnik, Zagreb; TV Apps in Budapest, Berlin; Radio Pers. incl: Budapest, Vienna, Leipzig, Stockholm, Weimar, Bratislava, Bucharest. Recordings: Works of Beethoven inclng. Hammerklavier, Sonata Op. 111, Variation Diabelli, Imperial Concerto; 2 records of Bartok; Works of Liszt, Brahms & Schumann. Mbrships: Liszt Soc., Budapest; Chopin Soc., Warsaw. Hons: Polonia Restituta, 1949; Liszt Prize 1, 1954; Merited Artist, Hungarian Peoples Repub., 1956; Gold Medal, Order of Merit of the Repub., 1957; Prize for Interpretation of Contemporary Music, Fedn. Hungarian Musicians, 1959; Medal of Merit of the Repub., 1969. Hobbies: Sports; Model Railways. Address: Budapest 13, Szent István Körüt 22, Hungary.

ANTAL, Livia, b. 10 July 1929. Budapest, Hungary. Lyric Soprano. Educ: Music Acad. of Budapest/Univ. of Music; Dip., operatic singer, 1951. m. Péter Földes. Debut: w. Hungarian Phil., 1954. Career: soloist of Hungarian Phil. & Inst. of Concerts of Hungarian State; apps. in Hungary & at Florence, Parma, Rome, Spoleto, Naples, Brussels, Paris, Basle, Vienna, Leipzig, Halle, Erfurt, Prague, Brno; Warsaw, Poznan, Sofia etc.; perfs. on radio in Hungary, France, Belgium, Switzerland, Austria etc. num. fest. apps. sev. recordings. Mbrships: Assn. of Hungarian Musicians; Kodaly Soc., Hungary; Academie du Chant Francais. recip. Artijus prize, Hungary, 1975. Mgmt: Interconcert, Budapest. Address: Október 6 u. 19, 1051 Budapest, Hungary.

ANTESBERGER, Günther, b. 25 April 1943. Klagenfurt, Austria. Music Producer. Educ: Tchrs. Trng. Coll.; Music Acads. & Univs. of Graz & Vienna; Mag. Phil. (Music & Englis Philology); PhD. m. Gertraud Antesberger, 2 d. 1 s. Career: Prod. of music progs., radio & TV, 1967; Music Prod., Austrian Radio; Tchr., Klagenfurt Conserv. of Music Comps. (recorded) Scenae pro Oriente for Chmbr. Orch.; Mexican Suite for recorded quintet; Lyric Scenes for piano & clarinet; Choirs; Brass wind music. Recordings: Folk music; Choirs; popular masses; num . folk song arrs. Publs: Klagenfurter Musikleben in der ersten Hälfte des 19 Jahrhunderts. Contbr. to: Vida musical en Venezuela. Mbrships: Österreichischer Komponistenbund; var. local institutions. Hons: Forderungspreis für Musik des Landes Kürnten. Hobbies: Travel; Langs.; Music-ethnology. Address: A-9020 Klagenfurt, Weidenweg 27, Austria.

ANTHONY, James Raymond, b. 18 Feb. 1922. Providence, RI, USA. Professor; Musicologist. Educ: BS, Columbia Univ., 1946; MA, ibid., 1948: Dip., Univ. of Paris, France, 1951; PhD, Univ. of S Calif., 1964. m. Louise Macnair, 1 s., 2 d. Publs: French Baroque Music, 1973; Church Music in France, 1661-1750 (w. Norbert Dufourcq), Chapt. VII of The New Oxford History of Music, 1975. Montéclair cantatas. BK. III, 1978. Contbr. to var. music jrnls. inclng: Musical Quarterly; Jrnl. of Am. Musicol. Soc.; Royal Music Assn. Recherches. Mbrships: Coun., Am. Musicol. Soc., 1976-78; French Musicol. Soc.; Coll. Music Soc.; MTNA; AAUP. Hobbies: Hiking; Travel. Address: 800 N Wilson Ave., Tucson, AZ 85719, USA.

ANTHONY, Marian, b. 27 Jan. 1922. Hyderabad, India. Musician; Violinist. Educ: Studied violin, theory, conducting w. Dr. J H Lushwitz, Dir. of Music, Hyderabad State Symph. Orch. m. Mary Esther, 1 s. 4 d. Debut: Schl. Concert, Hyderabad, at aged of 10. Career: 1st Violinist, Hyderbad State Symph. Orch.; 1st Violinist, Bombay Phil. Orch. & Madrigal Singers; Concert Master, Delhi Symph. Orch.; Performed for Indian films; Soloist on All India Radio; Tchr. of Violin. Fndr. Mbr.,

Delhi Symph. Soc. Hobby: Badminton. Mgmt: Delhi Symph. Soc. Address: B/8 Ashoka Hotel, N Delhi, India.

ANTONOWYCZ, Myroslau, b. 1 Mar. 1917. Dolina, Ukraine. Musicologist. Choir Conductor. Educ: PhD, 1951; Conserv. (Lembert, Russian Lvov, Ukranian Lviv); Musicol., (Lemberg, Utrecht, Harvard Univ.) m. Karla E Jungblut, 2 d. 1 s. Career: Radio & opera singer, 1939-43; Orch. & Choir Cond., DP Camp, 1946-48; Prof., Liturgical music, Ukranian Priest Seminary, Culemborg, 1948-50; Choir Cond., ibid., 1948-50; Cond., Utrecht Byzantin Choir, 1951-; Perfs. in Amsterdam, Brussels, London, Paris, Rome, Montreal, New York, Toronto, Washington; Musicol. Rsch., Utrecht Univ., Netherlands. Recordings: Dureco, Amsterdam, Te Deum; Omega; Metronome; Vega. Publs: Die Motette Benedicta es von Joquin des Prez und die Missen super Benedicta, Utrecht 1951; Works by Josquin des Prez; The Chants form Ukrarian Herimologia, Bilthoven 1974; Ukranian "Partesny" Concertos, Winnipeg, 1974. Contbr. to: MGG (Musik in Geschichte und Gegenwart); Algemene Muziek-Encyclopedia, Antwerp 1957-63; Kirchenmusikalisches Jahrbuch; Tijdschrift (Magazine) voor Nederlands Muziekgeschiedenis. Mbrships: Int. Musicol. Soc.; Vereniging voor Nederlandse Muziekgeschiedenis. Address: Castellumlaan 28, de Meern, Netherlands.

ANTUNES, Jorge, b. 23 Apr. 1942. Rio de Janeiro, Brazil. Professor of Composition; Composer; Conductor; Violinist. Educ: B Phys., M Comp., Violin, Univ. of Brazil; M Comp., Inst. Torcuato Di Tella de Buenos Aires; Electronic & Electroacoustic msuic courses; Doct., Sorbonne, Paris, 1977. m. Mariuga Lisboa Antunes, 2s. Career: Prof. of Comp., Univ. of Brasilia; Dir., Electronic Music Lab., & Expmtl. Music Grp., ibid.; TV & radio apps: num. recordings. Comps. incl: Cromonfonética, 1969; Tartina MCMLXX, 1970; Nascer Aqui, 1970-71, Macroformóbiles 1, 1972-73; Castastrophe Ultra-Violette, 1974. Recordings: Jorge Antunes, Musica Electronica. Mbrships: Movemento Candango de Mlusica Contemporanea Hons. incl: 1st Prize, Premio Angelicum di Milano, 1971: 1st Prize, Concurso Nacional de Composicao, Rio de Janeiro, 1972 & '76; 2nd Prize, Concurse de Composicao de Paraiba, 1977. Hobby: Painting. Address: Univ. de Brasilia, Depta de Música, 70.000 Brasilia, DF, Brazil.

ANZAGHI, Davide, b. 29 Nov., 1936. Milan, Italy. Composer; Music Educator. Educ: Dip., Pianoforte Choral & Orchl. Direction & Composition, Conserv. of Milan. Debut: Municipal Theatre, Treviso, 1970. Compositions incl: Segni & Ritografia (piano); Limine & In-Chiostro (string trio); Riturgia, Limbale, Ausa, Egophonie (orch.); Alena & Remota (ensemble); Aulografia (flute); Aur'ore (Chorus & orch.). Hons. incl: Awards for piano composition, Treviso, 1970 & Olivier Messaien Prize, 1974. Address: via B. Panizza 11, 20144 Milan, Italy.

APEL, Willi, b. 10 Oct. 1893. Konitz, Germany. (American Nat.) Emeritus Professor of Musicology. Educ: Univs. of Bonn, Munich, Berlin; Studied piano w. Leonid Kreutzer, Edwin Fischer. m. Ursula Siemering. Career: Lectr., Music, 1926-30; Went to USA, 1936, Tchr., Longy Schl. of Music, 1936-43, Harvard Univ. & Radcliffe Coll., 1938-42, Boston Ctr. for Adult Educ., 1937-50; Prof. of Music, Indiana Univ., 1950-63, Emeritus Prof., ibid., 1964-. Publs: The Notation of Polyphonic Music 800-1600, 1942; Harvard Dict. of Music, 1944; Historical Anthology of Music, (w. A T Davidson), 2 vols., 1946, 50; Masters of the Keyboard, 1947; French Secular Music of the Late 14th Century, 1950; Gregorian Chant, 1950; Harvard Brief Dict. of Music, 1960; Gesiche der Orgel- und Klavier-musik bis 1700, 1967. Hons. incl: Fellow, Medieval Acad. of Am.; Gold Medal, Monteverdi Fest., Venice, 1968. Address: Franz-Joseph-Strass 71, 8000 Munich 40, German Fed. Repub. 2, 16.

APFEL, Ernest, b. 6 May 1925. Heidelberg, Germany. Musicologist. Ec: Univ. of Heidelberg. m. Waltraud Eimer. Publs: Der Diskant in der Musiktheorie des 12.-15. Jahrhunderts, 1953; DPh Univ. Heidelberg, 1953; Studien zur Satztechnik der mittelalterlichen englischen Musik, 1959; Privatdozent Univ. des. saarlandes Saarbrücken, 1962; 1963 Dozent; Beitrage zu einer Geschichte der Satztechnik von der fruhen Motette bis Bach, 1964, Teil II mit Grundlinien der Entwicklung bis zur Neuzeit, 1965; apl. Prof., 1969; Antage und Struktur der Motetten im Codex Montpellier, 1970; Zur Vor - & Fruhgeschichte der Sumphonie, Begriff, Wesen & Entwicklung - vom Ensemble - zum Orchestersatz, 1972; prof. auf Lebenszeit, 1972; Grundlagen einer Geschichte der Satztechnik, Teil II: Polyphonie und Minodie, Voraussetzungen und Folgen des Wandels um 1600, 1974. bis zum 16. Jahrhunbert, 1974; Studien zur Theorie und Geschichte der mlusikalischen Rythmik und Metrik, w. C. Dahlhaus, 1974. Contbr. to: Archiv fur Musikwissenschaft; Die Musikforschung;

Acta Musicologica. Mbrships: Soc. for Music Rsch.; Int. Musicol. Soc. Address: Fasaneweg, Postfach 20, D 6601 Scheidt, German Fed. Repub. 19.

APGAR, Lawrence (Clarke), b. 15 Feb. 1907. Westfield, NJ, USA. Organist; Pianist; Carillonneur. Educ: AB, Yale Univ.; AM (Music) Harvard Univ.; MusB, Curtis Inst. of Music; AAGO (Ch M). m. Margaret Elinor Parsons, 3 s. Career: Organist & Choir Dir., St. Stephen's Ch., Providence; Organist & Carillonneur, Duke Univ.; Hd., Dept. of Music, Western Coll., Oxford, Ohio; Assoc. Prof. of Music, Earlham Coll.; Cond., Univ. Glee Club, Providence; Carillonneur, Rainbow Bridge, Niagara Falls, Ont., Can. Contbr. to: Union Seminary Quarterly. Mbrshisp: Dean, State Dir., Regional Dir., AGO. Hons: Prize for entrance exams. in piano playing, Yale Univ., 1924. Hobbies: Modern Architecture; Tropical Plants; Philately. Address: Friends House, 17340 Quaker Lane, Sandy Spring, Maryland, USA.

APIVOR, Denis, b. 14 Apr. 1916. Collinstown, W Meath, Eire. Composer. Educ: studied comp. w. Alan Rawsthorne & Patrick Hadley, 1937-39. m. Rima Austin, 2 children. Career: Composer, words commnd. by Royal Ballet, Sadlers Wells, BBC etc. Comps. incl: Opera, Yerma, 1959; Symph. No. 2, 1963; Tarot, 1968; Southern Flora, 1973; Concerti, Clarinet, 1945; Chamber, Landscape (Eliot), 1953; Crystals, 1964; Exotics Theatre, 1972; Fern Hill (Dylan Thomas), 1973; Ballet, Mirror for Witches; Blood Wedding; Corporal Jan, 1968; Other, Seis Canciones (Iorca), 1945; Variations for solo Guitar, 1958; Bouvard & Pécuchet, opera in 4 acts, 1971-74; Violin Concerto No. 2, 1975; Gello Concerto No. 2, 1976. etc. Contbr. to T S Eliot (Ed., Braybrooke); The Musicians Role in Ballet; Dancing Times; Jrnl. of CGGB; Jrnl. of Recorded Sound. Mbrships: CGGB; Perf. Rights Soc. Hobbies: Walking. Gardening. Address: 44 South Hill Pk., London NW3, UK. 3.

APOLIN, Stanislav, b. 20 Feb. 1931. Sec u Blovic, Czechoslovakia. Violinicellist; Professor. Educ: Conservatorium Brno, 1945-49; Acad. of Art, 1949-53; Postgrad. study w. Prof. Vasa Cerny, 1953-56; Study w. L. Rostropowich, Moscow, USSR. m. Milena Pokludova, 1 s. Career: Concert perfs. in UK, Ireland, Sweden, Denmark, Norway, German Fed. Repub., German Democratic Repub., USSR, Bulgaria, Poland, Rumania, Yugoslavia, Egypt, Austria, Switzerland, Iceland, Turkey; Mbr., Smetana Piano Trio; Prof., Acad. of Art, Prague; Prof., Conservatoire, Lucerne, Switzerland. Recordings: Britten, Sonata in C Op. 65; 2 Concertos by. D. Milhaud; Tchaikoswky, Variations Rococo Op. 33. Mbr., Union of Czech Composers & Interpreters. Mgmt: Pragokoncert, Czechoslovak Arts & Entertainment Agcy., Maltezske nam. 1, Prague 1. Address: Hrubeho A22/1202, 182 00 Prague 8, Czechoslavkia.

APOSTLE, Nicholas, b. 24 May 1930. Kenton, Ohio, USA. Performing Musician; Teacher. Educ: BA, Ohio State Univ.; MA, Columbia Tchrs. Coll.; Nat. Orchl. Assn.; Tanglewood Music Camp, Lenox, Mass. m. Anne Kasparian Apostle, 3 s. Career: 1st Oboist, Boston Pops Tour Orch. & Radio City Music Hall Orch. Num. Broadway shows & freelance (TV etc.); Currently w. Long Island Woodwind Quintet, Num. freelance recordings. Mbrships: Pres., Ohio State Chap., Phi Mu Alpha; Kappa Kappa Psi; Recording Arts. Recip., Tanglewood Scholarship. Hobbies: Hiking; Bicyling; Gardening. Address: 84 Muttontown Rd., Syosset, NY 11791, USA.

APPEL, Toby, b. 22 Nov. 1952. Elmer, NJ, USA. Violist. Educ: Curtis Inst. of Music, Phila., Pa. Debut: Carnegie Recital Hall, 1971. Career: Solo recitals, Phila., NY, Wash. etc., at age 15; Participant, Marlboro Festival, 1970; Asst. Prin. Violist, St. Louis Symph. Orch., at age 17; Recital, Alice Tully Hall, 1974; joined Lenox Quartet at age 18; Asst. PRof. & artist in red., SUNY, Binghamton, currently; mbr., Chmbr. Music NW, Portland, Ore.; Var. radio & TV appearances; 1/2-hour prog. of msuic written by Ezra Laderman for TV Recordings; Opus 20, Haydn Quartets 1-6; Leon Kirchner Quartet Concerto. Hobbies: Collecting antique cars; Chinese cooking; Woodworking; 5-string banjo. Address: R.D. 2 Rockwell Rd., Vestal, NY 13850, USA.

APPER, Elie, b. 22 July 1933. Ukkel, Belgium. Saxophonist; Professor Saxophone. Educ: Brussels Conserv. m. Eliane Tondeur, 1 s. Debut: Belgian Army Band & Belgian Saxophone Quartet, 1954. Career: Num. appearance w. Belgian Army Band & Belgian Saxophone Quartet in France; Luxemburg, Switzerland, Germany, Holland, UK, Canada, USA, S Africa & Scandinavia; Prof. of Saxophone, Brussels Conserv.; Vis. Lectr., Saxophone, N Tex. State Unv.; USA; Soloist, Belgian Musique Royale des Guides. Recordings: Var. works w. Belgian Saxophone Quartet & Musique des Guides. Hobbies: Photography. Fishing. Address: Molenstraat 26, 1660 Lot, Belgium.

APPERSON, Ronald R, b. 18 Feb. 1936. Portland, Ore., USA. Tuba Player. Educ: BA, Wash. State Univ., Pullman; M Mus.,

Northwestern Univ. Evanston, Ill.; 1 yr. postgrad. study (tuba), ibid. m. Sylvia Mueller, 1 s., 1 d. Career: Tubist, Corpus Christi Symph., Tex., 2 yrs.; Cond., Tex. A & I Coll. Brass Ensemble; TV apps., Tex., Tubist, Hartford, Conn., Symph. Orch., Brass Quintet, Brass Quartet, Bras Trio (fndr.), 1965-; apps. on local TV & at Carnegie Hall & Lincoln Ctr., NYC; Solo recitals, Conn. & Mass.; Brass Clinician & High Schl. Music Adjudicator, ibid.; subject of radio prog., Hartford, 1971. Recordings: Var. tapes of solo recitals. Mbrships: Phi Mu Alpha Sinfonia (Advsr., Hartt Coll. of Music, 7 yrs.); Tubaist, Universal Brotherhood Assn. Hons: Scholarships, Northwestern Univ. & Wash. State Univ.; Winner, Met. Opera Touring Co. audition, 1964; invited to play in Eastern Inst. Orch., Am. Symph. Orch. League, 1965-66, 1974. Hobbies: Making Mutes for Brass Instruments, especially Tuba, Trombone & French Horn; Gardening & Vegetable Growing; Landscaping. Address: 58 Hungary Rd., Granby, CT 06035, USA.

APPLEBAUM, Stan, b. 1 Mar. 1929. Newark, NJ, USA. Composer; Arranger; Conductor; Pianist; Educator; Author. Educ: Studied of comps., piano & conducting w. var. tchrs. Comps. incl: Marrakech Bazaar, for symphonic band; 5 Preludes for Trumpet; Str. Quartet; Cantata; 8 works for Chorus; Piano Concerto; 3 musical comedies; 4 musical playlets for children. Recordings: Over 500 arrangements of pop songs as singles and albums for all labels, many which attained No. 1 worldwide. Publs. incl: Transcriptions of Gymnopedies I, II, III by E. Satie; Voices From Kaluga; Hometown Hoedown; Cimmaron; 2's- n-3's. Mbrships: Chairman Tech. & Info. Committee, SAMPAC; On Board of Govs., NARAS, 802 AFM, SAG, AFTRA, ASMA. Hons. incl: Clio, for Pan Am Makes the Going Great, 1969; Mag. Award, for music for Eastern Airlines, 1970. Hobbies: Swimming; Reading; Farming; Construction. Address: 330 W 58th St., NY, NY 10019, USA.

APPLEBY, David P, b. 16 Oct. 1925. Belo Horizonte, Brazil. Professor; Pianist. Educ: BA, Univ. of NC, 1946; MA, 1949, BM, Southern Meth. Univ.; MSM, Southwestern Bapt. Theol. Sem.; PhD, Ind. Univ., 1956. m. Martha Dobson Appleby, 1 d. Career incls: solo concerts & recitals, Brazil, Japan & USA; Soloist w. Houston Symph. Orch., Amarillo Symph. Orch. & Ft. Worth Symph. Orch., all in Tex.; Fac., Nat. Music Camp, 1963-69; Coord., Piano & Theory, Morehead State Ulniv., 1969-71; 1974-; Prof. Music, E. Ill. Univ.; Fulbright Scholar & Lectr., Brazil, 1975 & 77. Publs: History of Church Music, 1965. Contbr. to: Contemp. Latin Am.; musical jrnls. Mbrships: Ill. State Music Tchrs. Assn.; Music Tchrs. Nat. Assn.; Am. Coll. of Musicians. Recip. var. rsch. awards in Brazil. Hobbies: Chess; Swimming. Address: 1020 Williamsburg Dr., Charleston, IL 61920, USA.

APPLETON, Clyde R, b. 21 Nov. 1928. Climax Springs, Mo., USA. Music Educator. Educ: BA, Pk. Coll., 1954; M Mus Ed, Univ. of Ariz., 1957; PhD, NY Univ., 1971. Career: Pub. schl. music Tchr., Mo., Iowa & Ariz., 11 yrs.; Formerly on facs. of Shaw Univ., W Carolina Univ., NY Univ., Kittrell Coll. & Purdue Univ.; Assoc. Prof. of Creative Arts, Univ. of NC at Charlotte, 1978-; Comps: Blues for Emmett Till (music for song), 1956; Carpenter in Alabama (music for song), 1958. Mbrships. incl: Music Educators Nat. Conf.; Nat. Assn. of Jazz Educators; Soc. for Ethnomusicol. Contbr. to profl. jrnls. Hons. incl: Kappa Delta Pi Outstanding Tchr. Awards in Elementary Educ., Purdue Univ., 1975, '76, '77, '78; Dept. of Creative Arts Excellence in Tchng. Award at Purdue Univ., 1974. Address: 2010-3 Canterwood Dr., Charlotte, NC 28213, USA. 4, 28, 29.

APPLETON, Jon Howard, b. 5 Jan. 1939. Los Angeles, Calif., USA. Composer. Educ: BA, Reed Coll., 1961; MA, Univ. of Ore., 1965; Columbia-Princeton Electronic Music Ctr., 1966. m. Elizabeth Winebert, 1 s., 1 d. Career incls: Dir., Stiftelsen Elektronmusikstudion, Stockholm, 1976-. Comps: This Is America; The Sydsing Camklang; Georganna's Farewell. Recording: The World Music Theatre of Jon Appleton. Ed: The Development & Practice of Electronic Music, 1975. Contbr. to: Nutida Musik; Perspectives of New Music. Mbrships: ASCAP; Coll. Music Soc. Hons: Guggenheim & Fulbright Fellowships; ASCAP awards. Hobby: Pacific ethnomusical. Address: EMS, Kungsgatan 8, 111 43 Stockholm, Sweden. 6.

APPLEYARD, John David, b. 18 Feb. 1933. Alexandria, Egypt. Trumpeter. Educ: RCM, ARCM, B Mus, London Univ. Career incls: Prin. Trumpet, London Fest. Ballet Co., 1958-60; Sub.-Prin. Trumpet, Royal Oper House, Covent Gdn., 1962-66; Co-Prin. Trumpet, Sadlers Wells Opera, 1966-75, Engl. Nat. Opera, 1975-; Lectr. in Music, Middx. Polytechnic, 1974; Trumpet Tutor, ILEA Ctr. for Young Musicians, 1975. Mbrships: Org. annual Christmas Carol Brass Band & Voice Ensemble in aid of Cancer Rsch., 1956-. Hobbies: Photography; Squash; Tennis. Address: 6 South Hill Pk., London NW3 2SB, UK.

APPLIN, Nancy Ann, b. 28 Apr. 1950. Dansville, NY, USA. Music Education Specialist (Vocal, Instrumental & String). Educ: Music Educ. Degree, Mansfield State Coll.; John Paul Christianson Choral Inst. Dip., Chautauqua Inst.; Dip., Voice & German Leider, Mozarteum, Salzburg, Austria; 3 Dips. Grad. Work, Saratoga-Potsdam Choral Inst. Career: Mbr. All-Co. (Livingston Co.) Chorus & NY State Sectional All-State Ormandy & w. Phila. Orch.; Tchr. since 1972-; Cond., sev. chorus grps. Mbrships: Sigma Alpha Iota; Music Educators Nat. Cond.; NEA; Am. Fedn. of Tchrs.; Oswego Classroom Tchrs. Assn. Hobbies: Skiing; Cooking; Travel. Address: 45 E 7th, Oswego, NY 13126, USA.

ARAI, Yoshiko, b. 27 Apr. 1949. Fukuoka, Japan. Violinist. Educ: Conserv. Nat. Superieur de Musique, Paris, France. m. Seppo Kimanen, 1 s., 1 d. Career: Perfs. of chmbr. music, recitals & apps. as soloist, Finland, France, Japan, Sweden & Norway; mbr., Trio Tateno; Mbr. Helsinki Chmbr. Soloists; Mbr., Finnish Sect., ISMC. Recip., 1st Prize, Conserv. Nat. Superieur de Musique, Paris, 1969. Hobby: Cooking. Mgmt: Festium Oy, Partiotie 34, 00370 Helsinki 37, Finland. Address: Topeliuksenkatu 3 b 44, 00260 Helsinki 26, Finland.

ARANT, Everett Pierce, Jr. b. 3 Dec. 1938. Orangeburg, SC, USA. Professor of Voice & Chorus. Educ: AB, Wofford Coll.; Converse Coll. Schl. of Music; M Mus., Yale Univ. Schl. of Music; Ed D, Music Educ., Univ. of Ga.; Voice study w. John Richard McRae, Benjamin DeLoache, m. Sylvia Raymel Harley, 2 d. Career: Tenor Soloist, All-Am. Chorus European Tour, 1960: Opera, Operetta, Musicals & Concerts, Eastern USA; Cond., Ga. Univ. Men's Glee Club & Univ. Chorus; Asst. Prof., Voice & Choral Music, Ga. Univ. Mbrships: Mbr., Nat. Bd. of Dirs., Intercollegiate Musical Coun.; State Chapt. Pres., Lt. Gov., Nat. Assn. of Tchrs. of Singing; MENC; Phi Mu Alpha; Pi Kappa Lambda. Hons: Blue Key; Scabbard & Blade, 1960. Hobbies: Carpentry; Bicycling; Bridge. Address: 500 Brookwood Dr., Athens, GA 30601, USA.

ARAPOV, Boris Alexandrovich, b. 12 Sept. 1905. St. Petersburg, Russia. Composer. Educ: Leningrad Conserv. under Prof. V. V. Shcherbacher. m. Todorova Tatjana Pavlovna, 2d. Career: Tchr., Leningrad Conserv., 1934; Prof., ibid., 1940; Hd., Instrumental Dept., ibid., 1951-74; Hd. of Comp. Dept., ibid., 1974. Comps. incl: Hodja Nasreddin (Uzbek opera); The Frigate Victory, 1958; Rain (chamber opera), 1965; Concerto for orch., 1969; Portrait of Dorian Gray (ballet), 1971; 4 Symphonies; Violin Concerto (recorded), 1967; Piano sonata (recorded); Mbrships: Exec., Leningrad Section, Soviet Comps. Union Contbr. to var. profl. publs. Hons. Honoured wkr. of Arts of Uzbek SSR, 1944; of RSFSR, 1957; Order of Red Banner of Labour, 1953; People's Artist of RSFSR, 1976. Hobbies: Travel; Painting; Oriental art and poetry. Address: Prospekt J. Gagarina 35 kw 65, Leningrad 196142, USSR.

ARBIZU, Ray Lawrence, b. 10 Aug. 1929. Phoenix, Ariz., USA. Opera Tenor; Educator. Educ: BA, MA, Ariz. State Univ.; Univ. of Southern Calif.; Akademie für Music, Vienna, Austria. m. Annie Marion Albrechty Arbizu, 4 s., 4 d. Career: Perfs. in Bonn & Essen Perm. Houses, 1962-67; Recitals & opera perfs., USA & Germany; Tours in many US & European cities inclng. Bonn, Hanover, Vienna, Salzburg, Düsseldorf, Köln, Los Angeles, Chgo., NYC, St. Louis, Boston, Soloist, Utah Symph., 1975, '77; Lead Tenor, Am. Nat. Opera Co., 1967-68; Guest perfs., num. US cities; Coll. Prof., N Ariz. Univ., 1968-70; BYU Provo, Utah, 1970-79. Mbrships: Nat. Assn. of Tchrs. of Singing; Nat. Opera Assn.; MENC. Hons: Fulbright Schlr., 1960. Hobbies: Boxing; Football. Mgmt: BYU Artists Bur., BYU, Provo, UT, USA. Address: 661 W 700 N, Orem, UT 84057, USA. 9.

ARCHER, Malcolm David, b. 29 Apr. 1952. Lytham, Lancs., UK. Assistant Organist; Music Master. Educ; RCM, 1970-72; Organ Scholar, Jesus Coll., Cambridge, 1972-75; ARCM, 1971; FRCO, 1973; BA (Cantab.) 1975; MA, ibid., 1979; Cert. Ed., ibid., 1976. Career: Cond.; Cambridge Univ. Musical Soc. Second Orch., 1975; Asst. Dir. of Music, Magdalen Coll. Schl., Oxford, 1976-78; Asst. Organist, St. Clement Danes Ch. & Hampstead Parish Ch., London; Cond.; Isis Singers of Oxford, 1976-78; Asst. Organist, Norwich Cathedral & Music Master, Norwich Schl., 1978-; Organ recitalist & continuo player. Comps: Dormi Jesu. Recordings: The Organs of Jesus Coll., Cambridge; John Ireland and his contemporaries. Mbrshisp: FRCO. Hons: R J Pitcher Scholarship (RCO); Organ Scholarship, Jesus Coll., Cambridge. Hobbies: Football; Cooking; Real ale; Travel. Address: 58A The Close, Norwich, NR1 3EH, UK. 4.

ARCHER, Norman, b. 18 Feb. 1923. Whaley Bridge, UK. Cellist. Educ: Studied w. Kathleen Moorhouse, Royal Manchester Coll. of Music; Pvte. Study w. Peter Muscant; ARMCM (Vlc. T). Career: Served w. RAF, 1942-46; Cellist,

Scottich Symph. Orch., 1949-50; Yorks. Symph. Orch., 1950-55; Peripetetic Cellist, Berks. Educ. Auth., 1955-75; Peripatetic Cellist, SW Surry Educ. Authority, 1978. Mbr. ISM. Hobbies: Travel; Study of German Lang.; Collecting Rare Classical Recordings. Address: 234 Courthouse Rd., Maidenhead, Berks., SL6 6HE, UK. 4.

ARCHER, Richard Donald, b. 3 July 1947. Leicester, UK. Teacher. Educ: BA, Univ. of Durham; Grad. Cert. Ed., Christ's Coll. of Educ., Univ. of Liverpool; FRCO; FTCL Organ; LRAM Piano Accomp.; ARCM Organ Perf.; FRCO (CHM). Career: Organist, local chs.; Recitals; Violist, Leicester Symph. Orch.; Leicester Phil. Choir; Cond. Hinkley Choral Union. Mbrships: ISM; Pres., Leicester & Distric Organists' Assn., 1975-. Hons. incl: 1st Prize, Richmond Fest. Organ Competition, London, 1972. Hobbies: Walking; Reading. Address: 553 Welford Rd., Knighton, Leicester, LE2 6FN, UK.

ARCHER, Violet Balestreri, b. 24 Apr. 1913. Montreal, PQ, Canada. Educator; Composer; Pianist. Educ: Lic. in piano, McGill Univ., 1934; B Mus, ibid., 1936; RCCO, 1939; B Mus, Yale Unv., 1948; M Mus, ibid., 1949. Career incl: Concert, Radio & TV appearance throughout USA & Canada. Compositions: Over 140 works for piano, organ, orchestra, choir, chmbr. music, etc. Num. works recorded by Int. Serv. of Canadian Broadcasting Copr. Mbrships: Prof. Emeritus., Div. of Theory & Comp., Univ. of Alta.; Canadian & Am. Music Ctrs.; Canadian Assn. of Univ. Tchrs.; Canadian Musicians Assn.; Canadian Folk Music Assn.; Int. Folk Music Coun.; Pi Kappa Lambda; Hon., Sigma Alpha Iota; Canadian Music Tchr. Contbr. to: Showcase; Piano Quarterly; Canadian Music Tchr.; Liberte 59. Hons. incl: D Mus, McGill Univ., 1971; Recip. Queen's Jubilee Silver Medal, 1977. Hobbies: Readings; Hiking; Films & Drama. Address: 10805 85th Ave., Edmonton, Alta., Canada T63 2L2. 5, 9, 23.

ARCHIBALD, James Montgomery, b. 3 Apr. 1920. London, UK. Film Producer, Writer & Director. Educ: MA, Merton Coll., Oxford, Hon. FTCL. m. Shelia Elizabeth Maud Archibald, 2 s. Career: films incl. entertainment features, sociol. documentaries, etc.; films made w. particular ref. to music & dance; Opus; Sweet Thames; Music!; Enigma Variations; Rehearsal; Festival. Recordings: Facade, Sir Wm. Walton ldng. the London Sinfonietta w. Peggy Ashcroft & Paul Scofield; Music in Scotland. Mbrships. incl: Chmn., Nat. Music Coun. of GB, Worshipful Co. of Musicians; Fellow, Royal Anthropol. Inst.; FRSA; Brit. Acad. of Film & TV Arts. Hons: MBF; Georges Auric Medal, 1971. Hobbies: Music, Sailing. Address: 35 Morpeth Mansions, Morpeth Terrace, London SW10 1EU, UK. 4.

ARCHIBALD, Margaret Helen, b. 3 Feb. 1949. London, UK. Clarinettist; Soprano; Teacher. Educ: GSM, 1967-70; RAM, 1971-72; GGSM; LRAM; ARCM. Debut: Wigmore Hall, Londno, 1974. Career: Freelance; Stanford Concerto, Queen Elizabeth Hall, 1975; Leeds Nat. Musicians' Platform, 1977; mbr. of Brompton Oratory choir. Mbrships: Musicians' Union; Brit. Actors' Equity; ISM. Hons: Dove Prize, GSM, 1970; Recital Dip., & Hawkes Prize, RAM. Hobbies: Walking; Reading; Dinner parties. Address: 66A Parkhill Rd., London NW3 2YT, UK.

ARCHIBEQUE, Charlene, b. 15 July 1935. Mt. Sterling, Ohio, USA. Professor; Choral Director. Educ: Oberlin Conserv., BME, Univ. of Mich., MA, San Diego State Univ.; DMA, Univ. of Colo. 1 d. Career: Prof., Music Dept., & Dir., Choral Activities, San Jose Stae Univ.; Choral Dir., San Jose Symph.; Clinician; Adjudictor; Guest Cond. Staff, Aspen Music Fest., 1978. Comps: Folk song arrs.; Eds., Distler's Mörchechorliederbuch. Recordings w. Univ. choral grps., US Hon. Choir. Contbr. to profl. jrnls. Mbrships. incl: Past Pres., N Calif. Choral Dirs. Assn.; Am. Choral Dirs. Assn.; MENC; Nat. Assn. of Tchrs. of Singing; Calif. Music Educators Assn.; Phi Beta Phi; Pi Kappa Lambda; Mu Phi Epsilon; Tau Beta Sigma. Hons: Dir., US Hon. Choir European tours, 1973, '74; 1st Place Winner, as Cond., Calif. Bay Area Coll. Chorale, Hague Int. Choral Fest. Hobbies: Reading; Cooking; Travel. Address: 1201 Weymouth Dr., Cupertino. CA 95014, USA.

ARCUSA, Ramon, b. 10 Dec. 1936. Barcelona, Spain. Composer; Producer; Arranger, former Singer. Educ: 4 yrs. piano study, later self taught. m. Shura Hall. Career: Singer in the 1960's w. Manuel de la Calva in Duo Dinamico. Comps. about 500 recorded by 25 singers or groups. Mbrships: Sociedad Autores España. Hons. incl: winner, Eurovision Song Fest., 1968. Address: Clara del Rey 39, Madrid 2, Spain.

ARDEN-GRIFFITH, Paul, b. 18 Jan. 1952. Stockport, UK. Opera, Oratorio & Concert Singer (tenor). Educ: Royal Manchester Coll. of Music; Royal Northern Coll. of Music;

GRSM (Tchrs.), piano & singing; ARMCM (Tchrs.), piano & singing, & performers, singing. Debut: Trained Dancer Puck in Britten's Midsummer Night's Dream, Sadlers Wells Theatre, 1973. Career incl: Pantomime, York, 1971-72; w. Engl. Nat. Opera, London Coliseum, 1975; World Premiere of Henze's 'We Come to the River', Covent Gdn., 1976; Brit. Premiere of Britten's 'Paul Bunyan', Aldeburgh Festiva, 1976; freelance prin. artist in UK & abroad. Mbr: Inc. Soc. of Musicians. Recip: Gwilym Gwalchmai Jones Schlrship. for Singing, RMCM, 1974. Hobbies: Travel, Yoga; Painting. Address: 19 Hillbrook Rd., Offerton, Stockport, Cheshire, SK 1 4JW, UK.

ARDLEY, Neil Richard, b. 26 May 1937. Wallington, Surrey, England, UK. Composer. Educ: BSc, Bristol Univ., 1959; m. Bridget Mary Gantley, 1 d. Career: Dir., New Jazz Orch., 1964-70; Own Orch., 1969-; Num. Concerts, Festivals & Radio Apps.; Arts Coun. Tours of England, 1975. Comps. incl: The Greek Variations, 1969; A Symphony of Amaranths, 1971; Kaleidoscope of Rainbows, 1974-75; The Harmonies of the Spheres, 1977-78. Recordings incl: New Jazz Orch., 1965; 68; Willpower, 1974. Publs: Ed., Jazz: A Little Guide, 1968. Mbrship: Musician's Union. Hobbies: Eating; Drinking. Address: 13a Priory Ave., Bedford Pk., London W4 1TX, UK.

AREL, Bülent, b. 23 Apr. 1919. Istanbul, Turkey. Professor & Director of Music Studios, State University of New York, Stony Brook. Educ: Dip. in Comp., Piano & Cond., State Conserv. of Ankara; studied sound engrng. w. Jose Bernard & Willfried Garrett. div., 3 c. Career: Pioneered combination of conventional instruments w. live electronic music, 1957. Pioneer wk., music for string quartet & tape, 1957. Dir., Electronic Music Studios, SUNY; Staff Mbr., Columbia-Princeton Electronic Music Ctr.; Fac. Mbr., Yale Univ., Columbia Univ., & SUNY at Stony Brook. Compositions: (Publd.) num. works for conventional instruments & electronic media; (Recorded) Mimiana II; Frieze, For violin & piano; Fragment; Stereo Electronic Music Nos. 1 & 2; Music for a Sacred Service: Prelude & Postlude. Contbr. to Opus. mbr. Ed. Committee, Am. Comp. Alliance. Hons: Rockefeller Rsch. Grant, 1959; Num. commissions for electronic music. Nat. Endowment for the Arts award, 1974-75; State Univ. Research Grant, 1975. Hobbies: Mobile Making; Airplane Modelling. Mgmt: BMI. Address: Music Dept., SUNY, Stony Brook, NY 11790, USA.

ARENDS, Henri Joseph, b. 8 May 1921. Maastricht, Netherlands. Conductor; Professor of Music. Educ: Cond. courses, Mozarteum, Salzburg (w. Carlo Zecchi); Accademia Chigiana, Siena (Paul Van Kempen); Conserv., Maastricht. m. Augusta Johanna De Wit, 5 c. Career: Asst., 2nd Cond., Amsterdam Concertgebouw Orkest & Choirmaster, Toonkunst Choir, 1953-57; 1st Cond., Musical Dir., N Holland Phil.; Fndr., Heart's Desires Fest.; Guest Cond., Netherlands & abroad; Cond., Radio Orchs. of Hilversum, Helsinki, Paris, Nice, Geneva; Cond., FOK Orch., Prague; Cond., Phils. of Brno, Ostrawa, Krakow, Lodz, Katowice, Gdansk, etc.; Apps. w. orchs. in S Africa & USA; Res. Guest Cond., Cape Town Symph. Orch., 1975-. Recordings incl: Kosmos-Symph. of Johan Franco; Brahms - Hungarian Dances; Grieg - Norwegian Dances.

ARENS, Rolf-Dieter, b. 16 Feb. 1945. Zinnwald, Germany. Pianist; Univ. Lectr. Educ: Dip. piano & chmbr. music, Leipzig, 1968; Dip., Budapest, 1966. m. Sabine Pleissker, 1 d., 1 d. Debut: at age 9. Career: concerts in Europe, S America, Asia; radio & TV apps. Mbrships: Comp. & Musicians Union of German Dem. Repub. Hons: 2nd prize, Weltfestspiele 1968; Sonderpreis, Paris, 1971. Hobbies: reading; sport. Mgmt: Künstleragentur der DDR, Berlin. Address: DDR-7113 Markkleeberg/Leipzig, Thälmannstr. 71, German Dem. Repub.

ARGOV, Alexander, b. 5 Nov. 1914. Bialystok, USSR. Composer. Educ: Pvte. study of Piano, Comp. & Orchestration. m. Esther, 2 children. Debut: 1948. Career: Comp. for State, Films, TV, Radio, etc. Comps: 6 Musicals, incnlg. King Solomon & the Cobbler; 7 Films inclng. Pas Question le Samedi; choreographic music; music for theatre (12 plays); over 600 songs (most of works also recorded). Mbrships: ACUM; Israeli Comps. League. Hobby: Photography. Address: 35 Sirkin St., Tel-Aviv, Israel.

ARHINE, Moses C'Kwamenah, b. 10 Aug. 1934. Obuasi, Cape Coast, Ghana. Teacher of Music Theory, Voice & Piano. Educ: Tchrs. Cert., Govt. Trng. Coll. Peki; LTCL. m. Hannah Araba Amaning, 3 children (1 dec.). Debut: Cond., Bawku Presby. Ch. Choir, 1969. Career: Currently i/c of Music Educ., Gbewaah Trng. Coll., Pusiga. Comps: Te Winam; O Wum Ya Yesy Piad La; Boma Le Loly; Hugh Greer; Kalabile Te Yampana. Mbrships. incl: Upper Reg. Sec., Ghana Music Tchrs. Assn.; Ghana Nat. Music Assn.; Choirmaster, Meth. Ch. Choir,

Bekwai-Ashanti; Hobbies: Gardening; Reading; Table Tennis. Address: Ghana Education Service, PO Box 110, Bekwai-Ashanti, Ghana. 28.

ARIE, Raffaele, b. 22 Aug. 1922. Sofia, Bulgaria. Opera & Concert Singer. Educ: studied med. for 3 yrs.; Maestro of Music Acad. m. Elisabeth Geiger. Debut: Teatro alla Scalla. Career: apps. in all major operatic & concert houses. Recorded for HMV & Decca labels. Hons: 1st Prize, Concours Int. d'execution Musicale, Geneva, 1946; Italian Gold Stage (Oscar for Opera), 1970. Hobbies: Documentary films; Philately. Address: largo Murani, 2-Milan, Italy.

ARIEN, Jan Arthur Gaston, b. Antwerp, Belgium. Impressario; Concert Manager. Educ: Royal Flemish Conservatorium, Antwerp. m. M. Verdonck, 1 d. Career: Fndr., Office International de Concerts & Spectacles, 1928; Fndr.-Pres., Antwerp Phil. Orch.; Fndr.-Dir., Antwerp Phil. Soc.; Organizer, Int. Theatre Festival of Antwerp, 1958-; Organizer of num. European tours inclng. Vienna Symph. Orch., Vienna Phil. Orch., Wiener Sängerknaben, orig. Am. prod. of Porgy & Bess; Belgian rep. of num. artists inclng. F. Chaliapine, Alfred Cortot, Benjamino Gigle, Anna Pavlova, Tito Schipa, Richard Tauber, before 1940, Vladimir Ashkenazy, Victoria de los Angeles, Francois Glorieuz, Herbert von Karajan, Yehudi Menuhin, Arthur Rubinstein, Isaac Stern, Elisabeth Schwarzkopf, after 1945. Francois Huybrechts; Edith Vokkaert; Ria Bollen. Pres., Assn. Européene des Directeurs de Bureaux de Concerts & Spectacles. Recip., O O Crown, K O Leopold II & K O Leopold. Hobby: Numismatics. Address: Office International, Huidevettersstr. 38-40, B2000 Antwerp, Belgium.

ARJAVA, Ritva Leena, b. 29 July 1932. Helsinki, Finland. Concert Pianist. Educ: studied w. mother in Helsinki, w. Marguerite Long, Paris, 1950-51, w. Bruno Seidlhofer Vienna, 1952-56, & w. Jan Hoffman, Cracow, 1964. m. Pastor Aarno Sainio, 1 s. Debut: St. Michael, Finland, 1945. Career: Recitalist & Soloist, Helsinki & other Finnish cities, Stockholm, Copenhagen, Vienna, Warsaw, Bialogh, Paris, & E. Berlin; has made radio broadcasts in num. cities & TV made recordings in Finland, Warsaw & Copenhagen; Tchr. Conservatorium, Helsinki, 1976-; Mbrships: Sec., Finnish Soloist Assn., 1969-71; Concert Centrum; Zonta Int. Hons: Int. Dinu Lipatti Mem. Purse Medal & Prize, London, 1955. Hobbies: Painting; Swimming in a hole in the ice. Mgmt: Maire Pulkkinen Musik Fazer, Helsinki 10, Finland. Address: Alppikatu la, Helsinki 53, Finland.

ARLEN, Walter, b. 31 July 1925. Vienna, Austria. Composer; Music Critic; Professor of Music History. Educ: BSc Mus, Geo Peabody Coll. of Tchrs., Nashville, Tenn.; MA Mus, UCLA. Career: Music News Ed., Los Angeles Times, USA, 1961-70; Prof. of Music Num. Univs. inclng: UCLA; Calif. State Univ., Los Angeles; Fndr. of Music Dept., Chmn. & Prof., Loyola Marymont Univ., 1968-75; Regular Music & Reviewer, Los Angeles Times. Mbrships: 1st VP, Nat. Assn. of Comps., USA; Admnstr. & Artistic Dir., Am. Acad. of Arts in Europe; Charter Mbr. & 1st VP, Nat. Assn. of Am. Comps. & Conds. Hobbies: Hiking; Skiing. Address: 515 S. Barrington Ave., Los Angeles, CA 90049, USA.

ARLT, Wulf, b. 5 Mar. 1938 Breslau, Poland. Musicologist. Professor of Music History. Educ: Musical., Univs. Koln & Basel; Dr. phil. 1966; Habil, 1970. m. Hannalore Hardt, 5 children. Career: Dir., Schola Cantorum Basiliensis, 1970; Prof. of Music Hist., Univ. of Basel. Publs. incl: Ein Festoffizium des Mittelalters aus Beauvais in seiner liturgischen und musikalischen Bedeutung, 1970; Ed., Palaographie der Musik, 1974. Contbr. to profl. mags. Mbrships: Schweizerische Musikforschende Gesellschaft Deutsche für Gesellschaft Musikforschung; Am. Musicol. Soc. Address: Rebgasse 17, CH-4132 Mutten, Switz.

ARMA, Paul, b. 22 Oct. 1905. Budapest, Hungary. Composer; Musicologist; Pianist. Educ: Studied w. Bela Bartok, Acad. of Music Franz Liszt, Budapest, m. Edmee Louin, 1 s., 1 d. Debut: Pianist w. Trio of Budapest. Career: Var. Appts. incl: Orch. & Choir Cond. in Berlin & Leipzig, 1930-32; Musical Rsch., Univ. of Paris, 1949-; Prod. ORTF. Num. Comps. incl: Concerto pour Quatuor a Cordes, 1946-47; Divertimento No. 3 pour Flute ou Violin Solo, 1952; Quatre Transperences pour Bande Magnetique, 1967; Trois Mobiles pour Clarinette, 1971; Huit resonances, (dedicated to Alexander Solzhenitsyn), 1971. Num. Recordings incl: Divertimento, de concert No. 1; Quand La Mesure est Pleine; Sept Transparences. Var. Publs. incl: Chantons Les Vielles Chandons d'Euorpe, 1946; Mouvement dans le Mouvement, 1970; The Faber Book of French Folk Songs, 1972. Mbrships: SACEM; SDRM; Soc. des Gens de Lettres de France. Recip. num. Hons. Hobby: Sculpture. Address: 3 Impasse des Saubergeaux, Ⱶ 92160 Antony, France.

ARMENIAN, Raffi, b. 4 June 1942. Cairo, Egypt. Conductor; Pianist; Composer. Educ: BSc, Univ. of London; Dip., Acad. of Music, Vienna, for piano perf., conducting & comp. Career: Can. Opera Co. (6 prods.), Music Dir., Stratford (Ont.) Festival, 1973-76; Fndr. & cond., Stratford Ensemble, 1974-; Music Dir., Kitchener-Waterloo Symph. Orch., 1971; num. Can. Broadcasting Co. radio & TV apps.; Resident Cond., Can. Opera Co., 1976-78; has conducted Berg's Violin Concerto in Menuhin's Man & his Music series. Concerts in Belgium & Austria. sev. recordings. Hons: Can. Silver Jubilee Medal, 1977. Address: 306-300 Regina St., N Waterloo, Ont., Can. N2J 3B8.

ARMHOLD, Adelheid, b. 4 Mar. 1900. Kiel in Holstein, Germany. Concert & Oratorio Singer. Educ: Conserv., Hamburg (piano) & w. Edmund Schmid; singing w. tchrs. of the Italian (Alexander Scarueo), French (Alexander de Rival) & German (Maria Ivogün) schls. m. 1) Pranas Domsaitis (dec.), 2) Kazys Zvironas. Career: Perfs. all over Europe under ldng. conds. inclng. Furtwängler, Klemperer, Ansermet, Scherchen, Wood, Boult, Schuricht & Mengelberg. Comps: The Great Invocation. Recordings: songs by Schumann, Brahms; Agathe in extracts from Der Freischütz. Publs: Singing, based on Irregragable Laws, 1963. Contbr. to Musical America. Mbrships: Sr. lectr., Univ. of Cape Town, S Africa, 1949-65. Address: 632 Omaha St., Kahala, Honolulu, HI 96816, USA.

ARMON, William Henry, b. 5 Apr. 1923. Tooting, London, UK. Violinist. Educ: ARAM. m. Peggy Stretton Downes, 1 s., 1 d. Career: Leader, BBS Concert Orch., 1954-62; BBC Solo Broadcasts; Freelance Ldr. Recordings. Concerto in A Major, Michael Haydn Little Orch.; Concerto in E Major, Bach & Concertante E flat Major, Mozart, Little Orch. of London, Leslie Jones. Hons: Catterall, Waley & Edward Cooper Prizes, RAM. Hobbies: Swimming; Golf; Fishing. Address: High Leigh, Traps Lane, New Malden, Surry, UK.

ARMOUR, Eugene, b. 4 Nov. 1929. Brooklyn, NY, USA. Professor of Music. Educ: Juilliard Schl. of Music, NYC; BS, MA, PhD, Schl. of Educ., NY Univ. Career: Assoc. Prof. of Humanities (Music), Professor of Music, NYC Community Coll., CUNY. Publs: Ed., Musical Styles Through the Ages, 1967; An Introduction to Musical Concepts, 1970, '76. Mbrships. incl: Perf. Arts Coun., CUNY; Music Coun., ibid.; MENC; Am. Musicol. Soc.; Am. Music Ctr. Hobbies incl: Bridge; Tennis; Swimming; Chess. Address: Dept. of Humanities & Perf. Arts, NYC Community Coll., 300 Jay St., Brooklyn, NY 11201, USA.

ARMSBY, Maurice, b. 29 Dec. 1932. Barton Mills, UK. Music Adviser. Educ: Ely Cathedral Choir Schl.; Cambridge Univ.; MA; ARCO. m. Doreen Christy. Career: Nat. Service, Royal Signals Band; Tchr. var. pvte. & State Schls., incl. RAF Schls. in Aden & Ghana; Lectr., Bishop Otter Coll., Chichester; Lay Clerk Chichester Cathedral; currently Music Advsr., Lancs. Educ. Committee, Area 1. Mbr., Music Advsrs. Nat. Assn. Hobbies: Travel (motor carvan); Tennis; Golf; Skiing; Concert-going; Owl Collecting. Address: 35 Douglas Ave., Stalmine, Blackpool FY6 0NB, UK.

ARMSTRONG, David, b. 12 May 1927. Shoeburyness, Essex, UK. Composer; Conductor; Pianist. Career: Prod., ABC TV, 1956; Scottish TV, 1957-58, Granada TV, 1959-61, Radio Telefis Eireann, 1961-. Comps. incl: incidental music to TV plays; scores for revue, documentary film Irish Harvest, 1965; Suite for light orch.; English Landscapes; piano solos, Black Valley Nocture & Horizons; Dialogue for piano & orch.; opera, Deirdre; Symph. in D Minor; var. songs for children's TV; song cycle, Scala a Disillusione; music for documentary film, Ane Iyle Callit Rachlaine; String quartet; Tone poem, Bealachoisin. Contbr. to: Comp.; World of Music. Mbrships: Comps. Guild of GB; Irish Actors Equity Assn.; Assn. of Irish Comps. Address: 85 Clonkeen Rd., Blackrock, Co. Dublin, Eire.

ARMSTRONG, Karan. b. Havre, Mont., USA. Soprano, Opera, Symphony. Concert. Educ: BA, Concordia Coll., Moorhead, Minn., 1964. m. Dana Tefkin. Debut: Musetta, San Francisco Spring Opera, 1966. Career incls: Sang w. maj. cos. in Strasbourg, France, Balt., Cinn., Ft. Worth, Hartford, Houston, Lake George, Memphis, Milwaukee Florentine, NY Met. & City Opera, Omaha, Portland, San Antonio, San Diego, San Francisco Spring, Santa Fe, USA; TV, Boston Pops Salute to Cole Porter. Mbrships: Mu Phi Epsilon; Met. Opera Nat. Coun. Hons: 1st Pl., San Francisco Opera Auditions, 1965; 1st Pl., Met. Opera Auditions, 1966. Hobby: Needlepoint. Mgmt: Columbia Artists Mgmt., 165 W 57th St., NY, NY 10019, USA.

ARMSTRONG, Peter McKenzie, b. 12 Mar. 1940. Suffern, NY, USA. Pianist; Lecturer. Educ: Harvard Coll., Cambridge,

Mass.; Dip., Longy Schl. Music, Cambridge, 1964; B Mus, Emerson Coll., Boston, 1968; M Mus Arts, Yale Schl. Music, New Haven, 1972. m. Ellen M. O'Connor. Career incls: App., Town Hall, NYC, 1952; Soloist w. Phila. Symph. Orch., Worcester Fest., Mass., 1955; num. Broadcasts, radio Boston; Recitals, Gardner Mus. & Jordan Hall, Boston, Wadsworth Atheneum, Hartford, & var. colls.; Lectr., Music, Trinity Coll., Harvard. Recordings: w. soprano Olga Averino Mbr. profl. orgs. Hons. incl: Winner, NY Music Educ. League Piano Competition, 1952. Hobby: Math. diversions. Address: Wallingford Rd., Durham, CT 06422, USA.

ARMSTRONG, Richard, b. 7 Jan. 1943. Leicester, UK. Conductor; Musical Director. Educ: Corpus Christi Coll., Cambridge. Career: Music Staff, Royal Opera House, Covent Gdn., London, UK 1966-68; Welsh Nat. Opera, 1968; Musical Dir., Welsh Nat. Opera, 1973. Hons: Janacek Medal. Hobbies: Walking; Food; Wind. Mgmt: Ingpen & Williams, London. Address: 1 Beachcliff, Penarth, Glamorgan, UK.

ARMSTRONG, (Sir) Thomas Henry Wait, b. 15 June 1898. UK. Organist; Music Educator. Educ: MA, D Mus., Keble Coll., Oxford Univ.; FRCM. Career: Organist, Thorney Abbey, 1914; Sub-Organist, Peterborough Cathedral, 1915; Mil. Serv., WWI, 1917-19; Sub-Organist, Manchester Cathedral, 1922; Organist, St. Peter's Eaton Sq., London, 1923; Organist, Exeter Cathedral, 1928; Cramb Lectr. in Music, Univ. of Glasgow, 1949; Student of Chirst Ch., Oxford, 1939-55; Student Emeritus, ibid., 1955-; Choragus of the Univ. & Lectr. in Music, 1937-54; Cond., Oxford Bach Choir & Oxford Orchl. Soc.; Organist, Christ Ch., Oxford, 1953-55; Prin., RAM, 1955-68. Hons: Kt.; FRCO; FRAM. Address: The Old Rectory, Newton Blossomville, Turney, Beds., UK.

ARMSTRONG,-SEXTON, Sheila Ann, b. 13 Aug. 1942. Ashington, UK. Singer. Educ: RAM; FRAM, 1972; Hon. RAM; Hon. MA, Newcastle. div. Debut: in Cosi fan tutte, Sadler's Wells, London, 1965. Career incls: Star of BBC prod. of die Fledermaus; Perfd. w. most major orchs. in Am. & Europe; num. TV, radio concert & recital apps. Recordings: w. most major cos. & conds.; Rachmoninov, The Bells (w. Previn); Vaughan Williams, Sea Symph. (w. Sir A Boult). Recip., Hon. RAM, 1969; Kathleen Ferrier & Mozart Prizes, 1965; prizes for Bells & Sea Symph. Hobbies: Interior decoration; Antique keys; Dressmaking. Mgmt: Harrison & Parrott Ltd. Address: Sandcroft, Esher Green, Surrey, UK.

ARNADOTTIR, Katrin, b. 30 May 1942. Reykjavik, Iceland. Violinist; Violin Teacher. Educ: Tchrs. Coll., Kirksville, Mo., USA, 1962-63; BA, Univ. of Iceland, 1967; Dip., Reykjavik Music Conserv., 1969; Int. Summer Acad., Nice, France, 1973 & '74, Int. String Workshop, Exeter, UK, 1975 & Cambridge, 1976; Kató Havas Workshop, 1976. div., 1 s. Career: Violinist, Icelandic Symph. Orch., 1961-; & Stavanger Symph. Orch., 1974-75 season; Tchr., Children's Music Schl., Reykjavik, 1967-. Mbrships: Sec., Orch. Committee, Soc. of Musicians in Icelandic Symph. Orch., 1973-74; var. committees, Icelandic Musicians Union; Treas., 1972-73, VP, 1973-75, Icelandic Tour Guides Assn.; ESTA. Hobbies incl: Travelling; Arts. Address: Horgshlid 10, Reykjavik, Iceland.

ARNATT, Ronald, b. 16 Jan. 1930. London, UK. Condutor; Composer; Organist; Harpsichordist; Teacher. Educ: FTCL., 1951; FAGO., 1952; B Mus., Durham Univ., UK, 1954. m. Carolyn Freeman Woodward, 2 d. Career: Came to USA, 1947; Organist & Choirmaster, var. Chs., Wsh. DC., 1947-54; Fac. Mbr., Am. Univ., ibid., 1951-54; Fndr. & Cond., Wash. Cantata Chorus; Dir. of Music & Organist, Christ Ch. Cathedral, St. Louis, Mo., 1954-; Dir. of Music, Mary Inst., ibid., 1964-68; Fndr., St. Louis Chamber Chorus (now Ronald Aratt Chorale), 1956; Fndr., St. Louis Chamber Orch., 1959; Assoc. Prof. Music. & Dir. Choral Activities, Univ. of Mo., St. Louis, 1968-; Has given recitals as Concert organist thru'out USA & toured UK in 1967. Cond. & music dir., Bach Soc. of St. Louis, 1974-. Compositions incl: Easter Triumph; Communion for the People; Short Mass for the People; Plainsong Preludes; num. anthems, canticles, Carols, organ & other Ch. Music. Recording: The King of Instruments. Contbr. to profl. jrnls. Mbrships incl: ASCAP; Am. Fedn. Musicians; Standing Commission on Ch. Music, Episc. Ch.; MENC. Hons. incl: Canforth Fndn. Grant, 1967; D Mus., Westminster Choir Coll., Princeton, NJ, 1970. Address: 412 S Gore Ave., St. Louis, MO 63119, USA. 8.

ARNELL, Richard Anthony Sayer, b. 15 Sept. 1917. London, UK. Composer; Lecturer; Conductor; Writer. Educ: Royal Coll. of Music. m. Charlotte Jennings. Debut: 1st pub. performance of The New Age Overture, Carnegie Hall, NYC, 1940. Career incl: Prof. of Composition, Trinity Coll. of Music, London, 1948-; Vis. Prof., Bowdoin Coll. & Houston Univ., USA, 1967-70; Gov., London Int. Film Schl. Recordings incl: Ballet;

Punch & the Child Serenade Great Detective; Roundelay; Organ Works, 1975. Contbr. to: Composer; Emerson Quarterly Review, etc. Mbrships: Past Chmn., Coun., CGGB; Brit. Acad. of Film & TV Arts; Inc. Soc. of Musicians; VP, Young Musicians Symph. Orch. Soc. Address: c/o Westminster Bank, 115 Old Brompton Rd., London, SW7.

ARNELL, Robert G, b. 4 July 1900. Brooklyn, NY, USA. Clarinetist; Professor. of Theory, Harmony & Composition. Educ: Curtis Inst.; Paris Conserv., France. m. Lucille J Arnell, 1 s. Career: Prof. of Music, Pitts. High Schl., 1932-42; Toured USA as solo clarinetist w. Sigmund Romberg, comp. & cond.; Clarinetist w. NBC Symph., directed by Arturo Toscaninini; Appeared w. Pitts. Symph.; Solo Clarinetist, Radio City Music Hall, NYC. Comps: Dedicated a Moon Song to 1st Astronaut to land on the Moon. Mbr. Am. Fedn. of Musicians, Local 60 Pitts., Pa. & NYC. Hobby: Teaching Children to appreciate music. Address: 2604 Brownsville Rd., Pittsburgh, PA 15227, USA.

ARNER, Gotthard, b. 21 Apr. 1913. Arby, Sweden. Organist; Professor of Music. Educ: RAM, Stockholm; Studied w. Fritz Heitmann, Berlin. m. Barbro Manthen. Debut: 1942. Career: Organist, Vaxjoe Cathedral, 1936; Organist, Stockholm Cathedral (Storkyrkan), 1953; Prof. of Organ, RAM, Stockholm, 1957-; Mbr. of Jury of Int. Competition of Organ Improvision, Haarlem, Holland, 1967 & Krakow, Poland, 1973; Concerts in all Scandinavian Countries, Germany, Holland, Switzerland, Italy, Spain, France, E Germany, Poland & USA. Publs: Organ & Choir Arrangements, Proprius, Stockholm. Mbr. RAM, Stockholm. Address: Skomakargatan 30, S-111 29 Stockholm, Sweden.

ARNETOVA, Renata, b. 22 Sept. 1936. Prague, Czechoslovakia. Pianist. Educ: Conserv. of Music, Prague; Acad. of Music, ibid.; Conserv. of Music Moscow. Debut: Premiere of 3rd Concerto for piano of Kabalevsky, Prague, 1954. Career: Concert apps. in Czech. & abroad, 1954-; Radio broadcasts, Czech. Radio, 1964-. Recordings: Slavicky -Sonata 'Reflection above the life'; Beethoven - Sonatas 1 & 31. Hons: 1st Prize, Czech Youth Music Comp., 1960; Lond-Thibaud comp., Paris, 1965. Hobbies: Philos.; Nature. Mgmt: Pragokoncert. Address: byt 53, Pocernicka 513/56, 108 00 Praha 10, Malesice, Czechoslovakia.

ARNO, T. Michael, b. 31 Oct. 1936. Beckenham, UK. Concert Recorder Player. Educ: LGSM. m. Mary Thomson Clark, 2 d. Career: Many apps. throughout UK as soloist & as a mbr. of num. chmbr. ensembles; Apps., Germany, Austria & Italy; num. broadcasts. Recordings: Music by Blow (w. Alfred & Mark Deller), 1966; Music by Purcell (w. Accademia Monteverdiana), 1967; Music by 17th Century German Composers (w. Collegium Saggitari), 1968; 17th & 18th Century Englis Music, 1973. Contbr. to: Recorder & Music Mag. Hons: Silver Medal, GSM, 1972. Hobbies: Cycling; Winemaking. Address: 29 Kingswood Rd., Shortlands, Bromley, Kent, UK.

ARNOLD, David John, b. 13 Nov. 1951. London, UK. Percussionist; Senior Professor of Percussion. Educ: GRSM; ARCM; LRAM. Career: Percussionsist, RPO; Sr. Prof. of Percussion, GSM. Mbr., RCM Union. Recip., Schlrship., RCM, 1969. Addrss: 70 Grossways, Gidea Park, Ramford, Essex RM2 6AS, UK.

ARNOLD, Dênis Midgley, b. 15 Dec. 1926. Sheffield, UK. University Professor. of Music. Educ: BA; B Mus; MA; ARCM; (piano perf.). m. Elsie Millicent Dawrent, 2 s. Career: Lectr. in Music, Queen's Univ. of Belfast, 1951-60; Rdr. in Music, ibid., 1960-64; Sr. Lectr. in Music, Hull Univ., 1964-66; Vis. Prof., Univ. of Calif. at Berkeley, USA, 1966; Docenta, Hist. of Music, Acad. Chigiana, Siena, Italy, 1967-68; Prof. of Music, Nottingham Univ., UK, 1969-75; Prof. of Music, Oxford Univ., 1975-; Frequent Radio talks on music for BBC. Publs. incl: G. Gabrieli, Opera Omnia, vols. I-VI, 1957-74; Monteverdi, 1963; Marenzio, 1965; A. Gabrieli, Drei Motetten, 1965; Marenzio, 10 Madrigals, 1966; Co-Ed., Monteverdi Companion, 1968; A. Gabriel, 10 Madrigals, 1970; Giovánni Gabrieli and Veneham Music fo the High Renaissance 1979; Co.-Ed., Beethoven Companion, 1971; Giovanni Gabrieli, 1974 Joint Ed., Music & Letters, 1976-. Contbr. to num. profl. jrnls. inclng. Musical Quarterly, Monthly Musical Record. Mbrships: RMA; Int. Musicol. Soc.; Gesellschaft für Musikforschung; Soc. Italiana di Musicol. Recip., Hon. RAM., 1971. Hons. Fellow, Brit. Acad., 1976; Foreign Mbr. Italian Nat. Academia dei Luncei, 1976; Premio Gableo Galilei for Italian Studies, 1977. Hobby: Eating & Drinking. Address: c/o Faculty of Music, University of Oxford, Oxford, UK.

ARNOLD, John Phillip, h 21 Oct. 1944. Hampstead, London, UK. Conductor. Educ: LRAM Cello Tchr., 1966. m. Gillian Rose.

Debut: Royal Ballet, 1968. Career: Freelance Cond. w. Royal Ballet, BBC Orchs. (Welsh Scottish, N Ireland, Studio Strings), CBSO, & orchs. in France, Italy, Poland, Netherlands & Switz. Comps: Cello Concerto, 1966: Scherzo for strings, 1964; Short Suite for Strings, 1962 & '66. Mbr., ISM. Hons: 1st Prize, Lugano Int. Conds. Competition, Switz., 1978; 2nd Prize, Besancon Int. Conds., Competition, France, 1973. Hobbies: Tennis; Riding; Squash; Badminton; Gardening. Address: 10 Hocroft Ave., London NW2 3EH, UK.

ARNOLD, Malcolm, b. 21 Oct. 1921. Northampton, UK. Composer. Educ: RCM. m. 2 s., 1 d. Career: Prin. Trumpet, LPO, 1942-44, 1946-48; Mil. Ser., WWII, 1944-46; Composer & Cond., 1948-. Compositions incl: Beckus the Danipratt (overture), 1943; 1st Symph., 1949; 2nd Symph., 1953; 3rd Symph., 1957; 4th Symph., 1960; 5th Symph., 1961; 6th Symph., 1967; Ten Concertos; Homage to the Queen, Coronation Ballet performed at Covent Gdn., 1953; Film music for Bridge on the River Kwai, 1958; Inn of the Sixth Happiness, 1959. Hons: Cobbett Prize, 1941; Mendelssohn Oscar for music of Bridge on the River Kwai; Ivor Novello Award for music in Inn of the Sixth Happiness. Address: Meadowcroft, The Hill, Monkstown, Co. Dublin, Eire.

ARNOLD, Robert Eugene, b. 8 Nov. 1927. Mobile, Ala., USA. Organist;.Pianist; Harpsichordist; Educator. Educ: BA, B Mus, Univ. Ala.; MA, Columbia Univ. Career incls: Organist, Trinity Ch., NYC; Metropolitan Museum of Art Concerts; Trinity Radio Choir,, CBS & WQXR; Apps. at Carnegie Hall, Town Hall & Lincoln Ctr. w. NBC Symph.; The Dessoff Choirs; The Cantata Singers; Festival Orch. of NY; Symph. of the Air; NY Phil.; Robert Shaw Chorale; Dir., Patchoque Schl. of Music & Dance; VP, Schlicker Organ Co. Num. recordings. Mbrships. incl: Dean. NY Chapt., Am. Guild of Organists. Contbr. to The Diapason; Am. Organist; NY Times. Hobbies: Yachting; Skiing. Address: 890 West End Ave., New York, NY 10025, USA.

ARNSTED, Jørgen Voigt, b. 28 June 1936. Orbaek, Denmark. Tubaist; Professor of Tuba. Educ: Pvte. studies; w. Paul Bernard & Fernand Lelong, Paris, 1970; Degree as Prof. in Tuba, Fionia Conserv., 1968-70. m Inga Arnsted, 3 c. Debut: 1965. Career: Soloist, Copenhagen, Odense, Danish Radio, Arhus, Paris, Int. Brass Congress Montreux, Danish TV, Stocholm, Katowice; Organizer, First Danish Tuba/Euphonium Workshop, 1977: Solos written for him by Vagn Holmboe, Sven Erik Werner, Henrik Colding Jorgensen; Tubaist, Odense Orch.; Prof. of Tuba, Danish & Swedish Conservs., 1966-. Contbr. to: Dansk Musik Tidsskrift; Tuba Tidende. Mbrships: Tubist Univ. Brotherhood Assn.; Danish Tuba Club; Fndr., ibid. Hons: 1st Prize, Solo Contest for brass players, First Int. Brass Symposium Montreux, 1974. Hobbies: Orientation. Address: Dragebakken 539, DK 5250 Odense SV, Denmark.

AROM, Simha, b. 16 Aug. 1930. Düsseldorf, Germany. Ethnomusicoloist. Educ: Jerusalem Acad. of Music, 1949-51; Conserv. Nat. Sup. de Musique, Paris, 1951-54; 1st prize for French Horn, ibid., 1954; Doct., Ethnol., Sorbonne, Paris, 1973. Career: Fndr., Dir., Boganda Nat. Mus., Bangui, Ctrl. African Repub., 1963-67; Hd. of Rsch., Nat. Ctr. for Scientific Rsch., Paris. Recordings: The Music of the Ba-Benzele Pygmies, Music of the Central African Republic; UNESCO Collection; Musiques Banda. Collection Musée de l'Homme, Vogue, (Grand Prix du Disque, Acad. Charles Cros); Aka Pygmy Music, UNESCO, Philips, etc. Publs: Les mimbo, génies du piégeage et le monde Surnaturel des Nqbaka-ma'bo, 1974; Conte et Chantefables Ngbakama'bo, 1970; 2 films, L'arc musical ngbaka & Les enfants de la danse, 1970. Contbr. to: Revue de Musicol, 1969, 73, The World of Music (UNESCO), etc: Bibliothéque de la SELAF; Ethnomusicology. Mbrships: French Musicol. Soc.; Int. Musicol. Soc.; Int. Folk Music Soc.; Int. Committee of Mus. & Musical Instrument Collections, (CIMCIM); Int. Coun. of Mus. (ICOM). Address: 6 Rue Malar, 75007, Paris, France.

ARONOFF, Frances Webber, b. 30 Sept. 1915. Columbia, SC, USA. Professor of Music Education. Educ: BA, Ohio State Univ.; MA, Tchrs. Coll., Columbia Univ.; EdD, ibid.; Dip. & Postgrad. Dip., Juilliard Schl. of Music; Certified Tchr., Eurythmics, Solfege, Improvisation, Dalcroze Schl. of Music, NY Div. Career: Workshops & lecture-demonstrations in Univs., Schl. systems, nat. & int. profl. orgs. (Puerto Rico, Buenos Aires, Argentina, Venezuela, Moscow, USSR, Jerusalem & Haifa, Israel); Prof. of Music & Music Educ. NY Univ. Recordings: Num. demonostration videotapes, Tchr. Performance Ctr., NY Univ. Publs: Music & Young Children, Holt, Rinehart & Winston, 1969; Spanish Edn., Recordi Americana, Buenos Aires, 1974. Contbr. to: Music Educators Jrnl.; The Music Ldr.; Le Rythme; Tarbut. Mbrships incl: Phi Beta Kappa; Union Internationale des Professeurs de la Rythmique Jaques-Dalcroze; Music Educators Nat. Conf.; Int.

Soc. for Music Educ.; College Music Soc. Hons: Scholarships, Inst. Musical Art, Juilliard Schl. of Mus., 1933-36; Cook-Burrows Fellowship, Tchrs. Coll., 1964-65. Hobbies: Sewing; Baking; Travelling. Address: 4 Washington Sq. Village, NY, NY 10012, USA.

ARONOFF, Josef, b. 13 June 1932. Budapest, Hungary. Violinist; Conductor; Lecturer. Educ: Franz Liszt Acad. of Music, Budapest, GSM, London; AGSM; LRAM. m. Astrid Gray, 2 s., 1 d. Career: Radio & TV apps. in Hungary, Austria, UK, Portugal, France & Aust.; Prof., Royal Manchester Coll. of Music, 1965-70; Hd. of Strgs., Queensland Conserv. of Music, 1970-75; Musical Dir., Conserv. Chamber Orch., 1970-75; Musical Dir., Artemon Ensemble & Orch., 1971-; Concertmaster & Dir. of Instrumental Studies, Darling Downs Inst. of Advanced Educ., 1975-77; Cond., Allegri Players, 1975-77; Sr. Lectr., Adelaide Coll. of Arts & Educ., 1977-79; Prof., GSM, 1979-; Musical Dir., South Western Symph. Orch., 1977-79.; Mbrships: ISM; ISCM; ASME; AUSTA. Hons: Sheriff Prize, 1959; Alfred Gibson Prize, 1960; Louis Pecskay Prize, 1960. Hobbies: Sailing; Swimming. Mgmt: M G Associates. Address: c/o GSM, Barbican, London EC2Y 8DT, UK. 28, 29, 30.

ARONOVSKY, Sulamita, b. 5 May 1929. Kaunas, Lithuania. Pianist. Educ: Dip. of Distinction, Vilnius State Conserv.; MA, Moscow State Conserv. m. A Aronovsky, 1s. Career: Perfs. solo & w. orchs.; broadcasts, USSR, Eaff, Vilnius & Moscow Conservs.; currently Sr. Lectr. of Prin. Study Piano, Royal Northern Coll. of Music, Manchester, UK. Mbrships: EPTA; ISM. Address: 16 Beech Court, Willow Bank, Fallowfield, Manchester 14, UK.

ARPIN, John Francis Oscar, b. 3 Dec. 1936. Port McNicoll, Ont., Can. Pianist; Arranger; Composer; Publisher. Educ: B Mus; Assoc., Royal Conservatory of Music, Toronto. m. (1) Anne, 1 s., 1 d., (2) Paulette, 2 d. Career: Musical Dir., 2 TV shows, CTV Network; Num. radio appearances; Num. solo concerts. Compositions incl: Jenny's Tune; Toronto Blues; Cumberland Stroll; Jogging Along; To Love Again; Pass my Way Again; Centennial Rag; My Love & I; Was it Worth Singing About?; Sweet Sunshine. Recordings incl: 7 LP's. Contbr. to: The Ragtimer. Mbrships: Dir., Ragtime Soc. Incorp. Mgmt: John Aprin Enterprises Incorp. Address: 2726 Vic. Pk. Ave., Willowdale, Ont., Can., M2JH 4A7.

ARRAND, Dick (Richmond) Henry, b. 3 July 1929. Gainsborough, Lincs., UK. Lecturer in Archgaeology; Brass Band Conductor, Adjudicator, Writer, Historian & Lecturer. Educ: Nottingham Univ. Inst. of Educ., BEd, Bishop Grosseteste Coll. m. Elizabeth Patricia Corrigan (div.), 3 s. Career incls: Band of HM Welsh Guards, 1947-48; Profl. Tromobonist, 1948-50; Cond., 1951-; 1947-76; currently Cond., Coventry Fest. Bands & Profl. Coach to var. other bands. Contbr. to: Brit. Bandsman; Brass Band News; The Dick Arrand Column in Brit. Mouthpiece. Mbrships: Sec. & The Ed. of Jrnl., Band Hist. Soc.; Fndr. Mbr., Adjudicators Assn.; Nat. Brass Band Club. Hons. incl: num. prizes as Cond. at band contests. Hobbies incl: Archaeological Excavation; Politics; Paleography. Address: 32 Bristol Rd., Birmingham B5 7XX, UK.

ARRAU, Claudio, b. 6 Feb. 1903. Chile. Pianist. Educ: Chilean Govt. Grant to study w. Martin Krause (pupil of Liszt), Berlin, Germany, 1919-20. Debut: Concert, Santiago, 1908. Career incl: USA Concert debut, 1923; num. concert tours in var. countries incl: USA, 1941- (annually); USSR, 1968; Australia 1947, 58, 61, 64, 70, 72, 74; S. Africa 1949, 52, 56; S & N Am. Europe & Israel, 1951, 53, 58, 61, 64, 70, 72; India, Sri Lanka & Singapore 1955-56; World Tour, 1958, 68, 75; Recordings: 5 Beethoven Concertos; 2 Brahms; the 32 Beethoven Piano; the works for piano & Orch. by Chopin; solos by Liszt, Chopin, Schumann, Brahms, Schubert, Mozart. Hons: Liszt & Ibach prizes; Int. Congress of Pianists Award, Switzerland 1927, Hans von Bulow Medal, 1978. Address: c/o Harold Holt Ltd., 124 Wigmore St., London, W. 1.

ARRIEU, Claude, b. 30 Nov. 1903. Paris, France. Composer. Educ: Nat. Higher Conserv. of Music, Paris, Num. comps. incl: (operas) The Princess of Babylon, 1953-55; Cymbeline, 1958-63; Balthazar of Living Death, 1966; (ballet) Commedia Umana, 1960; (symphonic) Mascarades, for orch., 1929; Concerto in E, for violin & orch., 1938; Suite for Strings, 1959; Classic Variations, for strings, 1970; (music for plays) Loire, 1934; The Merchant of Venice, 1961; (chmbr. music) The Little Duck, 1928; Sonata, for violin & piano, 1948; Trio, for piano, violin, violincello, 1957; Capriccio, for clarinet & piano, 1970; (piano) 4 Studies-Caprices, 1954; (vocal) The Sand of the Hour-Glass, 1958. Hons. incl: Kt., Legion of Hon. Hobby: Painting. Address: 32 bis Rue Pérignon, Paris 15e, France.

ARROYO, Martina. Operatic Soprano. m. Emilio Poggioni, Career incls: apps. at ldng. opera houses inclng. Covent Gdn., Vienna State Opera, Metrop. Opera, Teatro Colon, San Fran.; Soloist w. great orchs. inclng. Vienna, Berlin & NY Phi. Orchs. & Concertgebouw; apps. at Vienna, Berlin, Ravinia, Saratoga, Helsinki, Tanglewood Fests. Recordings: DGG; EMI; Columbia. Recip., Oustanding Alumna Award, Hunter Coll., NYC. Mgmt: Maurice Feldman, 745 5th Ave., NY, NY 10022, USA. 2.

ARTEEL, Freddy, b. 8 Feb. 1938. Roeselare, Belgium. Clarinettist. Teacher. Educ: Higher Dip., Royal Conserv., Brussels (clarinet); cond. w. D Sternefeld, Antwerp. m. Van Es Jozina, 2 d. Career: Prof. of clarinet, Royal Conserv. of Ghent, 1st clarinet & soloist, Antwerp Phil. Orch.; Mbr. Woodwind Trio D'ard, 1957-63, Clarinet Quartet of Belgium, 1959-61; Woodwind Quintet of Antwerp, 1961-77; Chambr. music ensemble, Contracts, 1975-; solo & chambr. music apps. for TV & radio in Europe & N. Am. sev. recordings. Hons: Laureate, competitions at Darmstadt & Geneva. Hobbies: Sailing; Tennis. Address: Parklaan 20a, 2232 Schilde-Antwerp, Belgium.

ARTHUR, Edna Margaret Aubrey, b. 25 May 1928. Edinburgh, UK. Violinist. Educ: Waddell Schl. of Music, Edinburgh; RCM; ARCM. m. Bryce Gould, 1 s., 1 d. Career incls: solo broadcast w. BBC Scottish Symph. Orch.; Prin. Violinist, Scottish Baroque Ensemble & Scottish Chmbr. Orch.; solo TV broadcasts, Edinburgh Fest., 1975; New Music Group of Scotland & Mr. Topham's Diary; Tchr., RSAM; Glasgow; Tchr. & Cond., Waddell Schl. of Music; String coach, Edinburgh Yooth Orch. Recordings: Scots Fiddle-High Style (Scottish Records SRCM 117 stereo). Mbrships: Committee, BBC Scottish Music Advsry. Bd.; Edinburgh (Comp.) Musical Fest.; ISM; European String Tchrs. Assm. Hons. incl: W H Reed Prize, 1948; Queen's Silver Jubilee Medal, 1977. Hobbies incl: Knitting; Reading. Mgmt: Pro Arte Musica, 6 Lonsdale Terrace, Edinburgh. Address: 19 Craighleith View, Edinburgh EH4 3JZ, UK.

ARTUS, March Stuttle, b. 29 Mar. 1931. Kan. City, Mo., USA. School Choir Director. Educ: B Mus, Univ. of Tex. A & I Univ., Kingsville. m. Paul H. Artus, 1s., 1 d. Career: Tchr., Jr. High Schl. & at High Schl. Level, 1952-60; Dir. of Music, Pkwy. Presby. Ch., Corpus Christi, Tex., 1961-72; Choir Dir., Cunningham Jr. High Schl., Corpus Christi, Tex., 1972; Cond. of Workshops for Tchrs., Corpus Christi Schl. System, 1973, 74, 75; Choir Dir., Drama Tchr. & Guitar Instructor; Haas Jr. High Schl., Corpus Christi, Texas, 1977-. Mbrships: MENC; Am. Choral Diro. Assn.; Tex. Choral Dirs. Assn.; Tex Music Educators Assn.; Delta Kappa Gamma. Recip. Superior rating for Choir, Corpus Christi Choir Fest, 1974-78. Hobby: Travel. Address: 6622 Sahara, Corpus Christi, TX 78412, USA.

ARTZT, Alice, b. 16 Mar. 1943. Philadelphia, Pa., USA. Concert Guitarist. Educ: BA, Columbia Univ.; Musicology & Comp., Grad. Dept. ibid., studied w. Julian Bream, Ida Presti, Alexandre Lagoya; comp. w. Darius Milhaud. Debut: Wigmore Hall, London, 1969. Career: num. Concert Tours covering most of W. Europe, N. Ctrl. & S Am., Far E, Africa & Aust.; num. radio & TV broadcasts; perfs. w. var. orchs. inclng. Vienna Symph. Orch. Recordings: Gemini 1018, 1019, London; Klavier 555, USA; Meridian E77006, London and other recs. on Meridian label. Publs: The Art of Practicing, Musical New Services, London. Guitar Transcriptions, Columbia Music USA. Contbr. to: Guitar Review; Jrnl. of the Am. Lute Soc. Mbrships: Guitar Fndn. of Am.; NY Classic Guitar Soc.; Am. Lute Soc. Hobbies: Travel, Reading, Listening to Records. Mgmt: Helen Jennings Ltd., 60 Paddington St., London W1M 3RR, UK. Address: Apt. 26, 180 Claremont Ave., NY, NY 10027, USA.

ARUHN, Britt-Marie. Opera & Concert Soprano. Educ: Stockholm Opera Schl. Career: prin. coloratura & lyrical soprano, Royal Opera, Stockholm; apps. at opera houses in Dresden, London, Munich, Bordeaux, Vienna, Copenhagen etc.; roles incl. Sophie (Rosekavalier), Gilda (Rigoletto), Zerbinetta (Ariadne auf Naxos), Musetta (Boheme), Rosina (Barber), Violetta (La Traviata) & Olympia (Tales of Hoffman); regular oratorio & recital perfs. Mgmt: Artistsekretariat Ulf Törnqvist, Norrtullsgatan 26, 4tr., 11345 Stockholm, Sweden. Address: c/o mgmt.

ARZRUNI, Sahan, b. 8 June 1943. Istanbul, Turkey (Armenian nationality). Pianist; Composer; Ethnomusicologist. Educ: Istanbul Conser., 1949-61; BMus, MS, Juilliard Schl. of Music, 1964-68. Career: num. piano recitals, N & S Am., Europe, Middle East and USSR; TV apps. London, Germany; weekly radio prog., NY; perfs. w. Victor Borge. Comps: Piano works; Christmas motet (recorded). Recordings incl: Haydn's sonatas for piano w. violin; Bartok's For Children; An Anthology of Armenian piano music. Publs: Music Textbook for Elementary Schools, 1963. Contbr. to: Music Journal; Ararat.

Mbr., Bd. of Dir., Soc. for Asian Music. Hobbies: Cookery; Photography. Mgmt: Edgewood Organization, Inc., NYC. Address: 215 E 80th St., LD, NY, NY 10021, USA.

ASCHAFFENBURG, Walter Eugene, b. 20 May 1927. Essen, Germany. Composer; Professor. Educ: BA, Oberlin Coll. Ohio, USA, 1951; MA, Eastman Schl. Music, Univ. of Rochester, NY, ibid., 1952; Dip. in Theory & Comp., Hartford Schl. Music, Conn., 1945. m. Nancy Dandridge Cooper, 2 d. Career: Prof. of Comp. & Music Theory, Oberlin Coll. Conserv. Music, Ohio. Compositions: Bartleby (opera), 1968; The 23rd. Psalme (for tenor, oboe, mixed chorus & organ), 1968; 3 Dances (for orch.), 1972. Mbrships: ASCAP; Am. Music Ctr.; Am. Soc. Univ. Comps.; AAUP (former chapt. pres.); Am. Civil Liberties Union. Hons: Award, Fromm Music Fndn., 1953; Fellow, Guggenheim Mem. Fndn., 1955-56, 73-74; Award & Citation, Nat. Inst. Arts & Letters, 1966. Address: 49 Shipherd Circle Oberlin, OH 44074, USA. 2, 8.

ASCHER, Ruth Jeanette, b. 20 Nov. 1913. Nordrach, Baden, Germany. Pianist; Lecturer in Music. Educ: Univs. of Heidelberg & Reading; Trinity Coll., Dublin; MusB; ARCM (Performer's); LGSM (w. gold medal); piano tchr.'s dip., Germany. Debuts: soloist in Cambridge, Oxford, Reading, Wigmore Hall, London, 1968, '70. Career: part-time tutor in music, Oxford Univ. Dept. of External Studies; tchr., Reading Univ. Music Dept.; senior music mistress, Queen Anne's Schl., Caversham (retired). mbr., ISM. Hons: Accomp. prize, 1935, Gold Medal, 1937, GSM. Hobbies: Reading; Travel; Sightseeing. Address: 9 St. Anne's Rd., Caversham, Reading, Berks. RG4 7OA, UK.

ASHBEE, Andrew, b. 22 Aug. 1938. Snodland, Kent, UK. Tchr.; Musicologist. Educ: RAM, 1957-61; GRSM, 1960; B Mus, Univ. of London, 1961; PhD, Fac. of Music, ibid., 1966; ARCM (Flute performing), 1959. m Brenda Ann Hawkins, 1963, 1d., 1s. Career incls: Hd. of Music Dept., Rochester Grammar Schl. for Girls, 1968-; Organist-Choirmaster, Christ Ch., Lower Birling, 1957-; Cond., Weald Singers, Maidstone, 1968-; Pt.-time Music Tutor, Open Univ., 1971-; Tchr. of Flute, Theory & Music Hist., Kent Jr. Music Schl., 1961-70. Mbrships: Royal Musical Assn.; Viola da Gamba Soc.; ISM. Publs. incl: Consort Music of Four Parts (Musica Britannica xxvi, 1969); John Jenkins: Consort Music in 6 parts (w. Nicholson), 1976; Jenkins: Consort Music in 4 parts, 1978. Contbr. to profl. publs. Hobbies incl: Philately. Address: 214 Malling Rd., Snodland, Kent, UK.

ASHFIELD, Robert James, b. 28 July 1911. Chipstead, Surrey, UK. Cathedral Organist. Educ: Royal Coll. of Music; D Mus, London Univ.; FRCO. m. Mary Elizabeth Lee, 2 d. Compositions: Choral Suite: Cantiones Roffenses; Ch. & Organ Music. Address: Rochester, Kent, UK. 3. 2 Grange Way.

ASHKENASI, Shmuel, b. 11 Jan. 1941. Tel-Aviv, Israel. Violinist; Professor of Music. Educ: Tel-Aviv Music Acad.; Curtis Inst. of Music. m. Lucile Ashkenasi. Debut: w. Berlin Phi. under Karl Böhm, Berlin Fest., 1963. Career: concerts in USA, Europe, Israel, S Am., USSR, Japan, Prague; 1st Violinist, Vermeer String Quartet; Prof., Northern Ill. Univ. Recordings: Paganini Concertos 1 & 2 w. Vienna Symph., DGG. Hons. incl: Winner, Merryweather-Post Contest, Wash. DC, 1958; 2nd Prize, Tchaikovsky Int. Competition, 1962. Address: c/o Music Dept., Northern Ill., Univ. Dekalb, IL 60614, USA.

ASHKENAZY, Vladimir, b. 6 July 1937. Gorky, USSR. Pianist. Educ: Moscow Ctrl. Music Schl.; Moscow Conserv. m. Thorunn Sofia Johannsdottir, 2 s., 2 d. Career: concert apps. throughout the world, solo recitals & w. major orchs. Has made num. recordings for Decca Records. Hons: 2nd Prize, Chopin Int. Competition, 1955; 1st Prize, Brussels, 1956, & Tchaikovsky, 1962. Int. Competitions. Mgmt: Harrison/Parrott Ltd., 22 Hillgate St., London W7 8SR, UK. Address: Brekkugerdi 8, Reykjavik, Iceland.

ASHLEY, Douglas Daniels. Kan. City, Mo., USA. Assoc. Professor. Educ: BM, MM, PhD, Northwestern Univ.; Conserv. of Vienna (piano dip.). Debut: Erzhergog Karl Palace, Vienna, 1967. Career: Assoc. Prof., Fine Arts, College of Charleston, S Carolina. Publs: ed., num. contemporary piano works. Mgmt: Marjorie Dutton, London, UK. Address: Dept. of Fine Arts, Coll. of Charleston, Charleston, S Carolina, USA. 29.

ASHTON, John Howard, b. 11 July 1938. Pitts., Pa., USA. Trumpeter; Composer; Conductor. Educ: BFA, Carnegie Mellon Univ., 1960; MFA, ibid., 1961; Cath. Univ. Am., 1962-65; WVa Univ., 1972-75. m. Bonnie Faye Gallaher, 3s., 1 d. Career incld: Asst. 1st trumpet, New Orleans Phil.; Asst. Prof., Univ. Neb. & Fairmont State Coll., Fndr., music dir., Fairmont Coll. Community Symph. Orch. Comps. incl: Theme & 5 Variations (piano solo); Trumpet Sonata; The Request for Sick Leave (text

Scot Morris) (song cycle baritone & piano). Mbr. profl. orgs. Recip: 1st Prize WVa Univ. comp. contest unpubld. clarinet quintet, 1961; NACWPI prize, Trumpet Sonata, 1963. Aid to Artist grant, WV Arts Coun., Music for Com. Orch., 1977. Hobbies incl: Sailing. Address: 1109 Alexander Pl., Fairmont, WV 26554, USA. 7.

ASKENASE, Stefan, b. 10 July 1896. Poland (now Belgium citizen). Concert Pianist. Educ: Coll. in Lemberg; Acad. of Music, Vienna, Austria. Career: Mil. Serv., Austrian Army, 1915-18; Tchr., Cairo Conserv., Egypt, 1922-25; Res. in Brussels, Belgium, 1925-; Prof., Royal Conserv. of Music, ibid., 1957-61; Concert perfs. in tours of Europe & num. other countries. Recordings of var. works made on Deutsche Grammophon Gesellschaft label. Address: c/o Wilfrid van Wyck Ltd., 80 Wigmore St., London W1, UK.

ASKER, Björn. Stockholm. Operatic & Concert Baritone. Educ: Royal Acad. of Music, Stockholm; study w. Tito Gobbi. Career: Prin. baritone, Royal Opera, Stockholm; concert & operatic apps. in Copenhagen, Helsinki, Kiel, Florence, Parma, Moscow, Mexico City & Jerusalem; roles incl. Don Giovanni, Count di Luna (Il Trovatore), Figaro & Almavava (Marriage of Figaro), Amonasro (Aide), Escamillo (Carmen), Telramund (Lohengrin), Alberich (Ring), Klingsor (Parsifal) & Bluebeard (Duke Bluebeard's Castle); num. concert & oratorio perfs. Mgmt: Artistsekretariat Ulf Törnqvist, Norrtullsgatan 26, tr. 4, 11345 Stockholm, Sweden. Address: c/o mgmt.

ASKONAS, Lies, b. 13 Aug. 1913. Vienna, Austria. Artist's Manager. Educ: studied Hist. of Art, Univ. of Vienna. m. Neville Shepherd. Hons: German Order of Merit; Pro Artibus (Sweden). Hobby: Gardening. Address: Hanging Lands, Ashtead. Surrey, UK.

ASLANIAN, Vahe, b. 13 Mar. 1918. Dorchester. Mass., USA. Professor of Music; Music Editor; Choral Conductor. Educ: Mus B, Boston Univ., 1940; MA, Claremont Grad. Schl., 1950; DMA, Stanford Univ., 1965. m. Charlotte Deane Ellingsworth, 2 d., 2 s. Career: Tchr., Hartnell Coll., Salinas, Calif., 1950-; Choral Conductor & Adjudicator; Lectr. Recordings: Mission Music at San Juan Bautsta w. Hartnell-Community Chorus. Publs: Ed., Chamber Mass (Vivaldi), Mass in F (L. Leo), NigaraSum (Victoria), etc. Mbrships: incl: Pres., Music Assn. of Calif. Community Colls., 1974-76, Moneterey Peninsula Chmbr. Music Soc., 1974-75; Coll. Music Soc. Publs. incl: Te Deum Laudamus, Leonardo Leo (ed.), 1976. Contbr. to profl. jrnls. Hons. incl: Martha Rockfeller Grant-in Aid, 1958-59; Fulbright Grant for Study in Italy. Address: 181 San Benancio Rd., Salinas, CA 93901, USA.

ASRIEL, Andre, b. 22 Feb. 1922. Vienna, Austria. Composer; Pianist. Educ: LRAM; LRCM; Staatsexamen, W Berlin; Musikhochschule; piano studies w. Grete Minterhofer, Vienna, Franz Osborn, London; comp. studies w. R.Stöhr, Vienna, Hans Eisler, Berlin. m. Katya Benner, 1 s. 1 d. Career: Tchr. of Theory, Hochschule für Musik, Hans Eisler, E Berlin, 1951-67; Prof. of Theory & Comp., ibid., 1967-. Comps: num. political choral songs; chansons; lieder; chambr. music (especially w. guitar); music for approx. 30 film stage & broadcasting prods. sev. recordings. Publs: Jazz - Analysen und Aspekte, 2nd ed., 1977. Contbr. to Musik und Gesellschaft, Berlin. Mbr. Verband der Komponisten der DDR (on presidium of Berlin district). Hons: Nat. Prize of GDR, 1951; Vaterlandischer Verdienstorden, 1975. Hobbies: Jazz; Science Fiction. Address: Frankfurter Tor 1, 1034 Berlin, German Dem. Repub.

ASSALY, Edmund Philip, b. 4 Jan. 1920. Rosetown, Sask., Can. Composer; Pianist; Conductor. Educ: Assoc., Toronto Conserv. of Music; LRSM. m. Gretta Assaly. Debut: Sakatoon, Sask., Can. Career: Comp., Arr., Pianist, CBC; Regular Recitalist. CBC Radio; featured in CBC Special Prog.; 1st Recitalist, Tour Series, Can. MTA; Musical Dir., Cond., McGill Univ. Stage Shows, 1957-67; Comp., Recorded Film Tchr., Univ. of Wis., USA. Compositions: (recorded) Sonata for Violin; Mount Royal Fantasy; Ballet des Sports; Ballet des Souris; var. TV music. Recip. Can. Broadcasting Award for Comp., 1963. Hobbies: Films; Theatre; Golf. Address: 1229 N Prospect, Milwaukee, WI 53202, USA.

ASSELBERGS, Alphons Julianus Maria, b. 28 May 1914. Bergen op Zoom, Netherlands. Extraordinary Professor of Musicology. Educ: Ordained as RC Priest, 1938; Inst. Pontificio di Musica Sacra, Rome, Italy; Studied piano w. Alfredo Carello, Stefan Askenase; D Mus; Rijksuniv. Utrecht, 1966. career: Sev. Concerts & radio recitals; Extraordinary Prof. of Musicol., Cath. Univ. Nijmegen, 1967-79; prog. emeritus, ibid., 1979-. Mbrships: Vereniging voor Nederlandse Muziekgeschiedenis; Gessellschaft fur Musikofoschung. Publs: Dr. Jan Pieter Heije of De Kunst en het Leven, 1966; Estetische Vragen Bij Actieve

Deelname, 1967. Address: Oude Kleefsebaan 417, Berg en Dal, Netherlands.

ASTBURY, Ida Pauline, b. 20 Aug. 1922. Harborne, UK. Music Teacher. Educ: SRN, Gen. Hosp., Birmingham; Whitelands Coll., Putney; TCM, LTCL (CMT). Career: QAIMNS/R, 1944-48; Music Tchr., Fulham, 1950-57; Hd. of Music Dept., Thornbury Grammar Schl. (now Marlwood), 1957-75; Cond., Thornbury Music Club Choir, 1963-74; Hd. of House, Marlwood Schl., 1974-; Choirmistress, St. Mary's Ch., Olveston, 1963-76; Cond., Tyndale Choral Soc., 1978-. Mbrships: Co.-Fndr., Thornbury Music Club, 1963; Chmn. Thornbury Music Club, 1974-78; ISM. Hobby: Gardening. Address: 9 Fort Lane, Dursley, Glos. GL11 4LG, UK.

ASTILL, Gary, b. 16 July 1955. Nottingham, UK. Peripatetic Instrumental Teacher of Upper Strings. Educ: LCM, 1973-76; GLCM; LLCM (Violin Tchrs.); Post Grad. Cert. in Educ., Trent Polytechnic, Clifton, Nottingham. Career: Peripatetic Instrumental Tchr. of Upper Strings for Derbyshire Educ. Committee; Mbr., Derby Cathedral Orch. Hobbies: Motoring; Gardening; Collecting fine violin bows. Address: 63 Mansfield Rd., Heanor, Derbyshire DE7 7AQ, UK.

ASTON, Peter George, b. 5 Oct. 1938. Birmingham, UK. Univeristy Teacher; Composer; Conductor. Educ: Tettenhall Coll.; Birmingham Schl. of Music; Univ. of York; D. Phil.; GBSM.; FTCL.; ARCM. m. Elaine Veronica Neale, 1 s. Career: Lectr. in Music, Univ. of York, 1964-72; Snr. Lectr., ibid., 1972-74; Prof. of Music, Univ. of D Anglia, 1974-; Dir., The Tudor Consort, 1959-65; Cond., The English Baroque Ensemble, 1967-70; Aldeburgh Festival Singers, 1974-. Compositions: 2 Song Cycles; Chamber Music; Opera; Ch. & Choral Works; Eds. of Baroque Works. Recordings: Meller's Life Cycle; num. Choral Works. Publs: The Music of York Minster, 1972; co-author, Sound and Silence, 1970, German ed., 1972, Contbr. to var. profl. jrnls. Mbrships: Royal Musical Assn., Comps. Guild of GB. Hobbies: Assn. Football; Cricket; Chess. Address: Univ. of E Anglia, Music Centre, School of Fine Arts and Music, Norwich, UK. 3.

ASTOR, Franklin O. b. 23 May 1915. New Kensington, Pa., USA. Professional Brass Performer; Educator. Educ: BS, Ind Iniv., Pa.; M Mus. Ed., Temple Univ.; Post Grad. Work, Columbia Univ.; Studied Trumpet w. James Morrow, Pitts. Symph. & Horn w. Larry Stitt, Ind. Univ. m. Thelma Gould, 1s., 1 d. Career: Profl. Brass Perf., 30 yrs.; over 1000 radio progs.; CBS; Tchr., 35 yrs.; Prof., Music Educ., Glassboro State Coll., 1958-80; Organized & Conducted Tours to European Music Fests.; Conducted Tours to Europe, Africa & Asia; Apps. as Guest Cond. & Clinician, NJ, Del. & Pa.; App., Sev. TV Shows, CBS, Pa. Recordings: Recorded w. Oscar Dumont & Johnny Austin, Angel & Capital Records. Contbr. to MENC Jrnl.; Instrumentalist Mag.; Brass Quarterly. Mbrships: Coll. Band Dirs. Nat. Assn.; MENC; Am. Fedn. of Musicians; Am. Fedn. of Tchr.; NEA; NJ Assn. of Tchr. Educ.; AAUP. Hobbies: Travel. Address: 306 Hamilton Rd., Glassboro, NJ08028 USA.

ASTRAND, (Karl) Hans (Vilhelm), b. 5 Feb. 1925. Bredaryd, Sweden. Music Historian. Educ: Filosofie licentiatexamen (Romance langs.), Lund Univ. 1958; studied organ w. Gunnar Ek, double bass w. Sune Pettersson. m. Birgitta Helga Margareta Örle. Debut: choir cond., Malmö, 1953. Career: Sec., Royal Swedish Acad. of Music, 1973-. Publs: Chief ed., Schlman'd Dict. of Music, 5 vols., 1975-79. Contbr. to: Nutida Musik; ARTES; music critic of Kvällsposten, Malmö, 1950-, etc. Mbrships: Royal Swedish Acad. of Music, 1970 ; Corres. mbr., Real Academia de Bellas Artes de San Fernando, Spain, 1976-. recip., Palmes académiques, France, 1979. Address: c/o Musikaliska akademien, Blasieholmstorg 8, 11148 Stockholm, Sweden. 30.

ASTUTTI, Nestor Eugerio, b. 11 Sept. 1932. La Plata, Buenos Aires, Argentina. Professor of Percussion. Educ: Chem. Techn.; Conserv. of Music, La Plata City; Superior Inst. of Art, Buenos Aires. m. Noemi Ciarlantini, 3 s., 2 d. Debut: Teatro Argentino, La Plata. Career: Teatro Colon Orch.; Phil. Orch., Buenos Aires; TV apps.; Broadcasting Municipal-Buenos Aires (LS1); Rivadavia Radio (LS5); pvte. assns.; Youth & Nat. Orchs.; Ritmus Percussion Ensemble; Nat. Conserv. of Music; Conserv. of Music Juan Jose Castro; Lectures, Argentina Cath. Univ., 1971-75, Educ. Room of Teatro Colon, 1976. Recordings: Music of Argentinian Composers; film music. Mbr. profl. orgs. Hobbies incl: Recording world folk music. Address: Viamonte 938-2'A, Buenos Aires, Argentina.

ATHANASIADES, Georges, b. 27 July 1929. Saint-Maurice, Switz. Priest (Canon Regular of St. Maurice); Theologian; Professor; Organist; Concert Performer. Educ: Univs. of Heidelberg & Freiburg (Germany); Conserv. of Lausanne

(Switz.) Debut: 1953. Career: Prof.; Adjudicator; Organ Recitals. Comps: Toccata (organ) recorded Fono Gesellschaft Bach), Teldec. Publs: Initiation á la musique par le disque IV-V (Lausanne, Suisse, 1956); Das Klingende Buch der Musik des Musiciens Suisses; Société Suiss de Pédagogie Musicale; Consociatio Internationalis Musicae Sacre, Rome. Mgmt: Franz Günther Büscher, Heidelberg: Antonio Cristofari, Rome. Address: Abbaye, 1890 Saint-Maurice, Switz.

ATHERTON, David, b. 3 Jan. 1944. Blackpool, UK. Conductor. Educ: MA, Cantab.; LRAM; LTCL; LGSM. m. Ann Gianetta Drake, 2d. Debut: Royal Opera House, Convent Garden, 1968. Career: Res. Cond., Royal Opera House, 1968-; Musical Dir. & Fndr., London Sinfonietta, 1968-73; Guest Cond., orchs., UK, Persia, Lebanon, France, Spain, Italy, Portugal, Belgium, Germany, Holland, Iceland, Canada, Russia; Japan, Korea & Hong Kong, USA, Sweden, Aust., NZ, Yugoslavia, Israel. Recordings: num. recordings w. LSO, Engl. Chamber Orch., L ondon Sinfonietta Philarmonia Orch. Recordings incl: Complete Works for Chamber Ensemble by Arnold Schoenberg. Publs: Ed., Pandora Suite & Don Quixote Suite, Gerhard; Arranger: Pandora (for Royal Ballet); Gerhard. Ed., The Complete Instrumental & Chamber Music of Arnold Schoenberg & Roberto Gerhard, 1973. Contbr. to Revised Musical Companion. Mbr., ISM. Hons: Edison Award, Grand Prix du Dusque; Special award. Comps. Guild, Cond. of The Year, 1971. Hobbies: Squash; Reading; Travel. Mgmt: Harold Holt Ltd. Address: c/o Harold Holt Ltd., 122 Wigmore St., London W1H 0DJ, UK.

ATHERTON, Joan, b. 6 Apr. 1948. Blackpool, UK. Violinist. Educ: GRSM; ARCM. m. David Edwards. Career: Prin. Mbr., London Sinfonietta, 1970-; Soloist, Chmbr. Music (Nash Ensemble) & Chmbr. Orchs. Recordings. incl: Complete Chmbr. Works of Schoenberg w. London Sinfonietta. Mbr. ISM. Recip. Tagore Gold Medal, 1970. Hobbies: Swimming; Tennis; Walking; Reading. Address: 18 Asmuns Pl., London NW11 7XG, UK.

ATHERTON, Robert, b. 9 Dec. 1910. Blackpool, UK. Composer; Lecturer; Teacher; Adjucator. Educ: Durham Univ. & pvtely; RMus; LRAM: ATCL. m. Lavinia Burton, 1s., 1d. Career incl: organist & choirmaster, Parish Ch., St. Annes-on-Sea, 1937-; Cond., Blackpool Symph. Orch., 1943-; Tchr., Liverpool Matthay Schl., 1955-71; Musical Dir., St. Annes Operatic Soc., 1971-; WEA lectr., 1941-; Cond. & fndr., Robert Atherton Choir, 1951; cond., Burnley Municipal Choir, 1956-; adjudicating tours of Can., 1975, '77. Comps: Sine Nomine (overture for orch.); Intermezzo for small orch.; Strg. Quartets; Anthems; organ music. Mbr. Rotary. Hobby: Literature. Address: 35 Mere Rd., Blackpool FY3 9AU, UK.

ATKINS, John Gordon, b. 23 Apr. 1933. Brierley Hill, UK. County Music Adviser. Educ: Cert. of Educ., Bristol Univ.; LTCL (CMT); LRAM; ABSM; FLCM. m. Shirley Ann Atkins, 1s., 1 d. Career: Music Master & Hd. of Dept., var. schls.; Music Advsr., Co. Borough of Warley; Music Advsr., W Sussex. Comps:In His Hands, a spiritual sequence. Recordings: Part songs & carol a arrs.; Christmas Carls by Ann Chcrale; Arun chorale, (Chrysal's). Contbre. to Education; Times Educ. Supplement; Sussex Life. Mbrships: Schl. Music Sect. Exec., ISM; Nat. Assn. of Educl. Advsrs. & Insps. Hon: Birmingham Schl. of Music Prize for Highest Marks in Paperwork, 1966. Hobbies: Singing; Conducting (Choir & Orch.); Gardening; Wearing Out Beach. Address: "Sea Point," Limmard Way, Summerley, Felpham, Bognor Regis, Sussex, UK. 3.

ATKINS, Terence Edward, b. 29 July 1946. S Woodford, London, UK. Church Musician; Music Teacher (Organ, Piano, Double Bass). Educ: RCM & Univ. London, 1965-69; Univ. of Birmingham, 1969-70; Organ Scholar, St. George's Chapel, Windsor Castle, 1967-69; B Mus; GRSM; ARCO; ARCM; Post-grad. Cert. in Educ. Career: Organist & Choirmaster: St. Peter's Ch., Maney, Sutton Coldfield, W Midlands, 1970-75; Chipping Barnet Parish Ch., Herts., 1976-; Dir. of Music, Nicholas Hawksmoor Schl., Boreham Wood, Herts; cond. Barnet Cantata Choir; Pvte. & Schl. Music Tchr., Birmingham & London. Mbrships: Hymn Soc. of GB & Ireland; Am. Hymn Soc. Hobbies: Hymnology; Antigrarian, Lit. Deltiology; Address: 108A Wood St., Barnet, Herts. EN5 4BY, UK.

ATKINSON, Charles M, b. 15 Aug. 1941. Crockett, Tex., USA. Musicologist; Clarinettist. Educ: BFA, Univ. of New Mexico, 1963; MM, Univ. of Mich., 1965; PhD, Univ. of N Carolina, 1975; Juilliard Schl., of Music, 1967-69. m. Margaret Livingston Atkinson, 1 s., 1 d. Career: Asst. Prof., Univ. of Calif., 1973-78; Assoc. Prof., Ohio State Univ., 1978-; perf., 5 Compositions from Irvine (recorded). Publs: Die einstimmigen Melodien der Sanctus und Agnus Dei mit ihren

Tropen. Contbr: Jrnl. of Am. Musicol. Soc.; Notes; Handwörterbuch der musikalischen Terminologie; Speculum; Jrnl. of Music Theory; AMS Newsletter. Mbrships: Coun., Am. Musicol. Soc.; Int. Musicol. Soc.; Mediaeval Acad. of Am.; Music Lib. Assn. Hons: Elliot Prize, Mediaeval Acad. of Am., 1979; Alfred Einstein award of Am. Musicol. Soc., 1978. Hobbies: Spending time with wife & chilren. Address: 372 Fallis Rd., Columbus, Ohio, USA.

ATKINSON, Clarence Frederic, b. 11 Aug. 1934. Te Kopuru, New Zealand, Viola Player. Educ: Studied w. Winifred Stiles, NZ; Nannie Jamieson, UK; Max Rostal & Radovan Lorkovic, Switzerland; GSM, London. Career: Performed w. NZ Symph. Orch.; Bournemouth Symph. Orch.; Rheinisches Kammerorch, Cologne; Bern Symph. Orch.; Bern Chmbr. Orch.; Chmbr. Ensemble of Bern Radio; LPO; Currently w. LSO. Num. Orchl. recordings mostly w. LSO Contbr. to Nat. Geographic; NZ Railway Observer; Rails, NZ. Hobbies: Chmbr. Music; Railways; Civil Aviation; Gardening. Address: 19 Queensbridge Pk. Islworth, Middx. TW7 7LY, UK.

ATKINSON, Neville Thomas. Newcastle on Tyne, Northumberland, UK. Director of Music. Educ: MA, B Mus, Leeds Univ.; ATCL. Career: Var. teaching, lecturing & conducting appts., Yorks., 1957-68; Dir. of Music, Perse Schl. for Girls, Cambridge, 1968-; Asst. Dir., Jr. Music Schl., LCM, 1975-; Examiner, ibid., 1967-. Contbr. to: Music in Educ.; Music Review; Musical Opinion; Music Tchr.; etc. Recip. Hons. F.L.C.M. (1978); Prize, Madrigal Soc., 1956. Hobbies: Detective fiction; Mod. Brit. painting. Address: 41 Panton St., Cambridge, CB2 1HL, UK.

ATKINSON, Robert James, b. 16 Sept. 1922. Detroit, Mich., USA. French Hornist; French Horn Designer; Expert in Brass Instruments. Designed or built the first Am. Dual Bore Doubld Deskant Horn; NBC Orch. of the Nation Series; Horn Instructor, Univ. of Wichita, 1941-44; 1st, 3rd & 4th Horn, Indpls. Symph., 1944-47; Prin. Horn, Wichita Symph., 1948-49; Hornist, Utah Symph. under Abravanel, 1961-65; Prin. Horn, Atlanta Chmbr. Orch., 1966-67; currently Mgr., Atkinson & Son Music Co. Recordings: orchl. works, RCA Victor & Vanguard. Publs: Solid Rocket Engine Mandrels of Plastic, 1963. Conbtr. to: Int. Horn Soc. Mbrships: Int. Horn Soc.; Sr., Soc. of Mfg. Engrs., USA.; Am. Soc. of Metals. Hobbies: Golf; Fishing; Camping; Hiking; Swimming. Address: Atkinson & Son Music Co., 4350 Lankershim Blvd., N Hollywood, CA 91602, USA.

ATLAS, Dalia. Haifa, Israel. Conductor. Educ: Israel Acad. of Music, Tel-Aviv; Dips., Rubin Acad., Jerusalem, Benedetto Marcello Conserv., Venice, Basle Conserv.; studied conducting Pierre Boulez. m. Josef Atlasowitz, 2s., 1 d. Career incl: Permanent cond., Israel Pro Musica Soloist & Technion Symph. and Chorus; Guest cond., Israel Phil. Orch. & leading orchs. in UK, USA, Aust., Canada, Finland, etc.; Guest Prof., Israel & other Am. Univs.; recordings for Israel Radio, BBC, ABC, etc. Mbrships: Int. Musicol. Soc.; Artists Soc. in Israel. Hons. incl: Silver Medal and Special Citation, Dmitri Mitropoulas Competition, 1964; Finalists' Medal, Guido Cantelli Conds. Competition, 1963; 4th Prize, 3rd Conds. Comp., Royal Liverpool Phil. Soc. UK, 1964; Leopold Stokowsky Prize, & Villa Lobos Vermeil Medal, Comp. Conds.; Rio de Janerio, 1978; 1st recip. Eugene Ormandy Award, Phila. 1979; Leonard Bernstein award, Tanglewood, USA, 1966 & 75. Hobbies incl: Swimming; Graphology; Poetry; Philosophy. Mgmt: Ibbs & Tillet, UK; Albert Kay, USA; Lodding; Scandinavia; Fazer, Finland; ABC, Aust. Address: POB 7191, Haifa, Israel. 5.

ATOR, James Donald, b. 15 Oct. 1938. Kansas City, Mo., USA. Saxophonist; Composer. Educ: BME, Drake Univ., 1960; MM, Wichita State Univ., Kan., 1964; D Mus A, N Tex. State Univ., Denton, 1971. m. Mary Louise Ator, 2d. Career: Profl. Musician, 1957-; Mbr., US Mil. Acad. Band, Westpoint, NY, 1960-62; Asst. Prof., Wichita State Univ., Kan., 1960-62; Asst. Prof., Wichita State Univ., Kan., 1966-69, Millikin Univ., Decatur, Ill., 1971-73, Ind.-Purdue Univ., Ft. Wayne, Ind., 1973-; Chmn., Dept. of Theory & Comp., ibid. Comps: Woodwind Quartet, 1969; Enuffispluntee, 1971; 4 Haiku for Mezzosoprano & Piano, 1972; Life Cycle, 1973; Haikansona, 1974. Mbrships: ASCAP; Am. Fedn. of Musicians; Midwest Music Theory Soc.; Am. Soc. of Univ. Comps.; Coll. Music Soc. Hons. incl: Winner, Young Artist Contest, Des Moines Symph., 1959 also num. fellowships. Hobbies: Model Building; Fishing. Address: 1925 Coronet Dr., Ft. Wayne, IN 46805, USA.

ATSUMI, Takayori Paul, b. 8 Jan. 1934. Tokyo, Japan. Educator; Cellist. Educ: BFA, Kunitachi Music Coll., Tokyo; M Mus, New Engl. Conserv. of Music, Boston, Mass., USA. m. Sally Bigelow, 1s., 1 d. Debut: Soloist w. Kunitachi Phil. Orch.,

May 1956. Career incls: Recitalist, both solo & w. orchs.; has played w. sev. well-known orchs., USA & Japan; Prin. 'Cellist, many orchs. inclng. Phoenix Symph. Orch., 1964- & Flagstaff Summer Fest. Orc., 1965-; Fndr., Pres., Ariz. Cello Soc., 1970-; has played w. sev. chmbr. grps. inclng. New Art Quartet, 1965-; Phoenic 'Cello Quartet, Phoenix Symph. & Phoenix Str. Quartet, has taught at sev. univs. & music schls., also at workshops; Fac. Assoc.-Assoc. Prof., Ariz. State Univ., Tempe, 1964-. Recorded for Ariz. 'Cello Soc., Ltd., 1970. Contbr. to profl. publs. Mbrships. incl: MENC; NEA; ASTA; Vloloncello Soc. of NY; NASM; Coll. Music Soc.; Phi Mu Alpha Sinfonia; VP Higher Educ. Sect., Ariz. Music Educs. Assn., 1973-. Hobbies: Chess; Sports; Books. Address: 1872 E. Concordia Circle, Temple, AZ 85282, USA.

ATTFIELD, Helen Margaret, b. 18 Feb. 1946. Lutterworth, Leics., UK. Singer (Contralto). Educ: LRAM; Recital Dip. m. William Knight. Debut: Wigmore Hall, 1970. Career: Apps. w. Engl. Opera Grp. inclng. world premiere of Death in Venice; WNO; Engl. Nat. Opera; Festivals incl: Eng. Bach. Festival; Bath; Cheltenham; Aldeburgh; Fishguard; Petersfield. Oratorio & recitals at all maj. London halls & throughout the country. Recordings. Engl. Nat. Opera: The Rheingold (Flosshilde); The Valkyrie (Schwertleite). Hons. incls: 2nd Prize, 17th Int. Vocal Concours at 's Hertogenbosch, Holland, 1970. Hobbies: Theatre; Tennis; Handicrafts. Mgmt: Ingpen & Williams. Address: 22 Whitehall Pk., Rd., Chiswick, London W4, UK.

ATTWELL, H. M., b. 27 Jan. 1943. Clevedon, Somerset, UK. Violin Teacher; Direcotor of Music. Educ: BA, Exeter; LRAM (Violin Tchng.). m. Patricia Anne Vernon, 2 s., 1 d. Career: Royal Marine Band, 1960-70 (Ldr., Plymouth Group Orch., 1966-70); Violin Tchr., Dir. of Music, Elizabeth Coll. Mbrships: ISM; Chmn., Guernsey Tchrs. Music Group; Ldr., Choral & Orchl. Soc.; Ldr., Demos String Quartet. Hons: Cassell Prize (Royal Marine's Band), 1960. Hobbies: Squash; Vehicle upkeep. Address: Shalom, 3 Marettes Villas, St. Martins, Guernsey, UK.

ATZMON, Moshe, b. 30 July 1931. Budapest, Hungary. Conductor. Educ: Tel-Aviv Conserv., Israel; grad., Tel-Aviv Acad. Music, ibid. Career: Cond., BBC Orch., LPO, RPO, LSO, Royal Liverpool Phil.; Chief Cond., Sydney Symph. Orch., Australia, 1969-72; Cond., Vienna Phil. Orch., Salzburg Festival, 1967; Cond., Berlin, Vienna, Madrid, Helsinki, Israel, Stockholm, Oslo, etc.; Chief Cond., NDR Orch., Hamburg. W. Germany, 1972-76; Artistic Dir., Basle Symph. Orch., 1972-; chief Cond., Music Advisor, Metropolitan Symph. Orch. of Tokyo. Hons: Cond. Prize, GSM, 1963; 1st Prize, Liverpool Int. Conds. Competition, 1964. Address: c/o SA Gorlinsky Ltd., 35 Dover St., London W1Z 4NJ, UK.

AUBERT, Eric Louis, b. 3 May 1921. Bellingen, NSW, Aust. Lecturer in Pianoforte, Acoustics & Accomplishment. Educ: DSCM, NSW State Conservatorium of Music, Sydney, 1948. m. Jane Eleanor Mary Albert, 1 s., 1 d. Career: Perfs. for Aust. Broadcasting Commission, inclng. Pianists of Aust. & 3 apps. in concertos w. Sydney Symph. Orch., 1941-; Accomp., Sydney Symph. Orch., 1950-56; Lectr. in Pianoforte, Acoustics & Accompaniment, Newcastle Br., NSW State Conservatorium of Music; Dpty. Prin., ibid, currently. Recordings: 3 short piano works by Aust. comps. Mbrships: Aust. Soc. for Music Educ. Hobbies incl: Elec. constrn.; Tennis; Swimming. Mgmt: Dpty. Prin., Newcastle Br., State Conservatorium of Music, NSW, Aust. Address: 65 Kenrick St., Merewether, NSW 2291, Aust.

AUBERT, Roger Stephan, b. 14 Dec. 1913. Geneva, Switz. Performer & Teacher of Piano & Harpsichord; Director of Music Broadcasting. Educ: Geneva Business Schl.; Dip., Geneva Conser.; Paris Nat. Conserv., 1936 (Tchrs., Lazare-Levy, Cortot-Sauer). m. Rosemary P Stack, 2s. Career: Concert apps. in W. Europe & USA, 1939-49; Dir. of Music, Swiss Broadcasting Corp, 1973-; Vice Chmn., Geneva Opera, 1965-. Recordings: Forte-Piano music from late Bach to early Beethoven (radio recordings). Contbr. to: Micromegas (Le Locle, Switz.); Sev. studies on Time & Music. Mbrships: Swiss Musicians Assn.; Wagner Soc. (Geneva Chapt.); Liszt Soc. (Geneva Chapt.) Hobbies: Photography; Sailing; Architecture. Address: Radio-House, 66 Bd. Carl-Vogt, 1211 Geneva -8, Switz.

AUBEUX, Louis, b. 28 Oct. 1917. Beaulieu sur Layon, Maine et Loire, France. Cathedral Organist & Canon. Educ: Litt B; Grad., Cesar Franck Schl., Paris. Career: Organist, Angers Cathedral; Canon, ibid.; Dir., Chorale Plantaganet for 25 yrs.; Admnstrs., Musique Sacrée L'Organiste. Comps. (publs.): Motets A Cappella; Organ Pieces. Author, The Organ & Its Construction. Contrb. to: Sacred Music, Paris; Caecilia, Strasbourg; Stella Maris, St. Malo. Address: 10 Rue du Parvis St. Maurice, 49000 Angers, France.

AUBREY, Elizabeth, b. 19 Mar. 1951. Dallas, Tex., USA. Teacher of Music History; Performer (voice, recorder, psaltery, Krummhorn) of early music. Educ: BA, Grinnall Coll., Iowa, 1973; MMus, Univ. Md., 1975; PhD Cand., Musicol., ibid. Career: Music hist. fac., Anne Arundel (Md.) Community Coll.; Prin. Singer, A Newe Jewell, renaissance consort. Mbrships: Am. Musicol. Soc.; Mediaeval Acad. of Am.; Coll. Music Soc.; Register of Early Music. Hons: Mill Contest Award for Cond., 1973; Doct. Fellow, Univ. of Md. Hobbies: Backpacking; Ch. works; Canoeing; Working w. children. Address: 9515 Riley Rd., Silver Spring, MD 20910, USA.

AUERSPERG, Johannes, b. 29 Jan. 1934. Salzburg, Austria. Contrabassist; Conductor. Educ: Dip., Musikhochschule Mozarteium, Salzburg. m. Urder Auersperg, 3 s., 1 d. Career: Soloist on TV; Cond. of var. orchs. & youth orchs.; Prof., Musikhochschule, Graz; Recordings on disc & radio. Hobbies: Ping-pong; Skiing; Swimming. Address: 1180 Vienna, Pözhleinsdorferstr. 77, Austria.

AUFDEMBERGE, Clarence T, b. 25 June 1939. Lincoln, Kan., USA. Assistant Professor. of Humanities. Educ: BS Educ., Concordia Tchrs. Coll., Ill.; PhD Musicol., Univ. Kan. m. Reva A Pflughoft, 2 s., 1 d. Career incls: Tchr. & Min. of Music, Immanuel Luth. Ch. Wis. Rapid, 1962-65; Vis. Lectr. in Music Hist., Ind. Univ.; Asst. Prof. of Humanities, Northern Ariz. Univ., Flagstaff. Comps. incl: Ed. Melchoir Franck, Christe du bist der helle Tag; Publs: Vollständiges Werk-Verzeichnis der Kompositionen von Melchoir Franck, 1975. Contbr. to profl. jrnls. Mbrships. incl: Am. Musicol. Soc. Recip. NDEA Fellowship, Univ. Kan., 1968-70. Hobby: Collector of Evangelical Hymnbooks. Address: Box 6031, Northern Ariz. Univ., Flagstaff, AZ 86001, USA.

AUGÉR, Arleen J., b. 13 Sept. 1939. LA, Calif. USA. Soprano. Educ: Calif. State Univ., Long Beach, Calif., 1957-63, BA, 1963; Voice training w. Ralph Errole. m. Dr. Wolfgang Augér. Career incls: Music tchr., Calif., Colo. & Ill., 1963-67; Mbr., Vienna State Opera, 1967-74; num. apps., USA & Europe; Radio & TV apps.; App., Bolshoi Theatre, Moscow, 1971; La Scala, Milan, 1974, Met., NY, 1978; Lieder recitals; Num. fest. apps.; Japanese tour, 1974; 1979; USA tour, 1977, Israel tour, 1979, Master classes, etc. Num. recordings. Hons: Max Reinhardt Medal, Salzburg Fest., Austria; Recip., Orphée d'Or, as Konstanze, Die Entführung aus dem Serail; 5 times, Wiener Flötenuhr; Annual Award 1972 for best Mahler recording; Deutscher Schallplattenpreis; Grand Prix du Disque; Premio della Critica Discografica Italiana. Hobby: Music. Address: D 6000 Frankfurt/Main 1, Oeder Weg 77, German Fed. Repub. 2.

AUGUSTEIJN, Henri Paul, b. 5 July 1921. Axel, Holland. Flute Teacher. Educ: Conserv., Amsterdam Muzieklyceum, Govt. Dip., Flute Tchr. 10 c. Career: Pvte. & Music Schl. Flute Tchr.; var. Perfs.; Mgr., Stichting Kunst in de kamer. Mbr. Royal Dutch Musicians Assn. Address: 424 Herengracht, PO Box 5054, 1007 AA Amsterdam, Netherlands.

AULIN, (Thor) Leif, b. 31 Jan. 1935. Boden, Sweden. Violist. Educ: Grad. w. Dips. in Violin & Viola, Royal Coll. of Music, Stockholm, 1965; Repertory studies in Viola & Str. Quartet w. Lillian Fuchs, Manhattan Schl. of Music, 1965-66. m. Margareta Petersroon, 1 s., 1 d. Debut: Violin recital, Stockholm, 1963; US debut as viola soloist in Berlioz, Harold in Italy, 1966. Career: Former mbr., Stockholm Phi. w. Antal Dorati; Solo Violist, Gothenburg Opera, 1972-; Chmbr. music concerts, Sweden & Denmark. Mbrships: Philatelic Music Circle; W. Peterson-Berger Fndn. Hons: Fellowship, Sweden-Am. Fndn., 1965. Hobbies: Squash; Philately. Mgmt: Gösta Schwarck, Dalgas Blvd. 48, 2000 Copenhagen, Denmark. Address: Sangspelsgatan 3 VII, 422 41 Hisings Backa, Sweden.

AURIC, Georges, b. 15 Feb. 1899. France. Composer. Educ: Paris Conserv.; Schola Cantorum, Paris, Career: Mbr. of "Les Six" Movement in France; Music Critic, Marianne publ., 1936; Paris-Soir newspaper; Dir., Reunion des theatres lyriques nat., 1962-68. Compositions incl: film music for Rene Clair's A Nous la Liberte, 1932; Jean Cocteau's L'Aigle a Deux Tetes, 1948; Ballet music - Le Peintre & Son Modele, 1949; Phedre, 1950; Chemin de Lumiere, 1952; Coup de Feu, 1952; Opera - Le Masque; Sonata for piano & unaccompanied 4-pt. chorus, 1950; num. songs & pieces for piano. Mbrships: Pres., Int. Confedn. of Socs. of Authors & Composers, 1968-70; Acad. des Beaux-Arts. Hons. incl: Cmndr., Legion d'Honneur. Address: 90 rue du Faubourg St. Honoré, Paris 8, France.

AUSTIN, Arthur William, b. 2 Jan. 1912. NYC, USA. Violinist. Educ: BS, MA, JD, BM, MM, D Mus, NY Conserv. of Music, NY Univ. m. Ann Amron Austin, 1 d. Debut: Carnegie Hall. Career: Played w. Serge Koussevitsky, Tanglewood, Mass., Leopold Stokowsky, Robin Hood Dell, Pa., & Frederica Stock Sr., Grant Pk., Ill. Comps: NY Suite; Quartette G Maj.; Quartette C Minor; Concerto in C Maj. Recordings: Bach Suite; Bach Double Concerto; St. Sarn Concerto; Bruch G Minor Concerto. Mbrships. incl: Bohemians; Good Fellowship; Nat. Bd., Chatauqua; VP, NCTB, Contbr. to Music Age. Hons. incl: Griffith Schlrship., Newark, NJ. Hobbies incl: Tennis. Address: 151 E 80 St., NY, NY 10021, USA.

AUSTIN, Dorothea, b. 22 July 1922. Vienna, Austria. Professor of Music. Educ: Vienna Conserv. of Music; ARCM (Perf.), London; LRAM (Tchr.), London; MA, Queens Coll. m. Dr. Harry Austin (dec.), 3 d. Career: Perf.; Comp.; Asst. Prof. of Music, Queensborough Community Coll.; Apps. on TV. Comps. Choral work & woodwind quintets performed at Queens Coll.; Comp. for viola d'amore, piano & tape performed at NY Univ., & Colden Auditorium, Queens Coll. Mbrships: Coll. Music Soc.; Am. Musicol. Soc.; Performing Arts Assn. Partial transl., Anthol. of Renaissance Music. Hons. incl: Tobias Matthay Schlrship., Prof. H Fryer, London. Hobby: Painting. Address: 247 Cornwell Ave., Valley Stream, NY 11580, USA.

AUSTIN, Louis F, b. 22 Aug. 1930. Menomonie, Wis., USA. Teacher; Performer (flute, recorder, baroque flute, krummhorn); Director of Midwest Workshops. Educ: Beloit Coll.; Cert. by Am Recorder Soc. as Tchr.; Am. Conserv. of Music. Chgo. m. Donal E Austin, 1 s., 3 d. Career: TV as pantomimist, WTMJ-TV Milwaukee, Wis.; Singer, Dancer, Announcer w. Music w. Hormel Girls, CBS & ABC radio; Instrumentalist w. Chgo. Baroque Ensemble & var. other grps. Music Review Ed., Am. Recorder Mag. Mbrships: Bd. Dirs., Am. Recorder Soc.; Cons. to Bd. of Offs., Chgo. Chapt., Am. Recorder Soc. Hobbies: Ballet; Swimming; Plumbing. Address: 112 S Clinton Ave., Oak Pk., IL 60302, USA. 5.

AUSTIN, Richard Russell, b. 25 Aug. 1943. Sydney, Aust. Composer. Educ: RCM. m. Virginia Anne Stevens, 3d. Career: incls. arrs. for recordings, theatre & comps. for variety of instrumental combinations perfd. on BBC radio & in var. concert halls & theatres. Comps: Mandy the Actor's Cat, a musical entertainment (recorded). Contbr. to Composer. Mbrships: Compo. Guild; Committee, Aust. Musical Assn.; Periscope Hon. Comps. Prize, RCM, 1967. Hobbies: Reading; Drama; Inter-cultural studies. Address: 119 Amyand Pk., Rd., Twickenham, Middx., UK.

AUSTIN, William W. b. 18 Jan. 1920. Lawton, Okla., USA. Professor of Musicology. Educ: AB, Harvard Univ., 1939; AM, ibid., 1940; PhD, ibid., 1951. m. Elizabeth Jane Hallstrom, 2 d. Career: Goldwin Smith Prof. of Musicol., Cornell Univ., USA. Publs. inlc: Music in the 20th Century, 1966; Susanna, Jeanie and The Old Folks At Home. Songs of Stephen C Foster From His Time to Ours, 1975. Contbr. to var. profl. jrnls. & mags. inclng: Musical Quarterly. Mbrships. incl: Int. Musicol. Soc.; Am. Musicol. Soc.; Int. Webern Soc. Hons: Dent Prize, IMS, 1967; Kinkeldey Prize, AMS, 1967. Hobbies: Keyboard Perf., especially in Chmbr. Music; Comp. of Songs & Choruses. Address: Music, Cornell, Ithaca NY 14853, USA. 2.

AVELING, Valda, b. 16 May 1920. Sydney, Australia. Concert Artist (Piano, Harpsichord & Clavichord). Educ: Pers. & Tchrs. Dips., NSW State Conservatorium of Music, 1936. Debut: Town Hall, Sydney, w. Sir Malcolm Sargent, 1938. Career: Appearances w. all leading Orchs. & at all Music Festivals in UK; Frequent concert & record collaboration w. Richard Bonynge & Joan Sutherland; Num. Recitals as Duo w. Evelyn Barbirolli (oboe); Num. Tours, Europe, Canada & Far East inclng. tour of Germany as jt. soloist w. Yehudi Menuhin; Perf. Rome Harpsichord Festival, Italy, 1971, 1972; 4 visits to Aust. for Aust. Broadcasting Commission (latest 1976). returned via USA giving recital at Univ. of Indiana. 1976. Recordings incl: Scarlatti Sonatas for Harpsichord; Scarlatti Sonatas for EMI, issued 1976. Chio Mi Scordi di Te, Mozart; Harpsichord Pieces, Thomas Morley; The Collection of Historic Instruments at the Victoria & Albert Museum, London; Music for Four Harpsichords; Harpsichord Continuo; num. other recordings. Contbr. to Music & Musicians. Mbr. Inc. Soc. Musicians. Hons: FTCL. Hobbies: Cooking; Gardening; Reading. Mgmt: Ibbs & Tillett. Address: 15 Priory Rd., London NW6 4NN, UK. 3.

AVERI, Peter Warwick, b. 14 Sept. 1934. Kilbirnie, Wellington, NZ. Concert Manager; Organ Recitalist; Conductor. Educ: LTCL. m. Dr. Kathleen Averi, 2d. Debut: Wellington Ch. Organist, aged 11. Career: Ldng. NZ organ recitalist & broadcaster; Organist & Choirmaster, sev. chs., 30 yrs. inclng. St. Andrews 1st Presby. Ch., Wellington; sometime Cond., Wellington Harmonic Soc. Wellington Gilbert & Sullivan Soc.; Official Accomp., Orpheus Choir & Wellington Competition Soc.; Concert Mgr., NZ Symph. Orch. Comp: NZ Liturgy Choral

Setting. Recordings: 3 vols. Golden Hymns; 2 Organ recitals & as accompanist to sev. solo artists. Pres., Wellington Orphans Club, 1966. Hobbies: Motoring; Cooking. Address: P O Box 3482, Wellington, NZ.

AVERY, James Allison, b. 23 Sept. 1937. Hutchinson, Kan., USA. Pianist. Educ: B Mus, Univ. Kan., 1959; M Mus, Ind. Univ., 1962. Staatkiche Hochschule für Musik 1963-66, Freiburg. m. Beverly Bakkum Avery, 2 children. Career: Performed at concerts in maj. European cities & USA; Performed w. Ctr. for New Music, Univ. Iowa, on campus & on tour; Currently Assoc. Prof. of Music, Univ. Iowa. Recordings: Num. solo recordings in Germany & USA. Mbr. Pi Kappa Lambda. Contbr. to: contemporary keyboard. mag. Hon. incl: Prizewinner in Int. Competition for Interpreters of Contemporary Music, 1965; Num. Scholarships & Grants. Hobbies: Langs. (German, Italian, Norwegian & French). Address: Schl. of Music, Univ. of Iowa, Iowa City, IA 52242, USA.

AVIDOM, Menahem, b. 6 Jan. 1908. Stanislau, Austria. Composer. Educ: BA, Am. Univ. of Beirut; music study, Paris. m. Suzanne, 2 d. Compositions incl: 9 symphs.; 5 operas; num. instrumental & vocal works. Publs: music critic, Jerusalem Post, 1958-73. Mbrships: Chmn., Israel Composers League, 1955-72; Admin. Coun., Int. Confedn. of Socs. of Authors & Composers, Paris. Hons: Life-Fellow, Int. Inst. Arts & Letters, 1958; Israel State Prize, 1961; Tel-Aviv Municipality Prize, 1947; 1958; Israel Phil. Orch. Prize, 1952; Acum Prize, 1963. Hobbies: Painting; Chess. Address: 30 Samadar St., Ramat-Gan, Israel.

AVIS, Marjorie, b. 13 July 1912. Bristol, UK. Singer (Soprano). Educ: ARCM, perfs. dip., RCM, London. Career: BBC Singers; Singing Together, BBC Schls. Broadcasting: Solo broadcasts; Concert perfs. of Oratorio; Lieder, Engl. Songs, etc.; Prof. of Singing, Guildhall Schl. of Music & Drama, London. Recordings: Village Romeo & Juliet by Delius (cond. Sir Thomas Beecham); Pirates of Penzance by Gilbert & Sullivan. Mbrships: ISM; British Actors' Equity Assn.; Life mbr., BBC Club. Address: Holmwood East, 41 South Road, Westan-Super-Mase, Avon, UK. 3.

AVISS, Peter Ronald Frampton, b. 20 Nov. 1950. Croydon, Surrey, UK. Composer. Educ: LGSM. div., 2d. Comps: Missa Brevis & 3 Cavalier Songs, both broadcast on BBC Radio 3. Mbrships: Comps. Guild of GB; ISM. Address: 3 Shaftesbury Rd., Canterbury, Kent CT2 7LE, UK.

AVITHAL, Theodor, b. 13 Jan. 1933. Bacau, Romania. Conductor; Professor. Educ: Orchl. Cond. Dip., State Conserv. of Music, Bucharest. m. Ursula Reyher, 1 d., 1 s. Debut: Jassy, Romania, 1955. Career: Permanent Cond., Moldava State Phil., Jassy, 1955-59; Regular Cond., St. Louis, Mo., USA. Phil., 1963-70; Res. Guest Cond., Acting Music Dir., Wichita, Kan., Symph., 1970-71; Cond., Music Dir., Univ. - N Ark. Symph., Fayetteville, 1971-74; Cond., Univ. of Wis. Symph., Milwaukee, 1974-; Guest Perfs., Belgium, Holland, Germany, Israel, Romania, Switz., USA. Mbrships: Am. Fedn. of Musicians; AAUP; Am. Symph. Orch. League. Mgmt: Premier Int. Presentations. Address: 4425 N Maryland Ave., Milwaukee, WI 53211, USA. 2, 8, 28.

AVNI, Tzvi Jacob, b. 2 Sept. 1927. Sarrbrucken, Germany (Israeli citizen, 1935-). Composer; Music Educator. Educ: Dip., Tel-Aviv Music Acad. in Music Theory & Comp., 1958; Columbia Univ., NY, USA, 1962-64; Tanglewood, summer 1963. m. Pnina (dec. 1973). Compositions incl: Sonata for Piano, 1961; Wind quintet, 1959; String Quartet No. 1 -Summer Strings, 1962; 3 Psalm Canticles for Mixed Choir, 1965; Meditations on a Drama for Chmbr. Orch., 1966; Prayer for String Orch., 1962; Chaconne for Harp, 1965; Holiday Metaphors for Symph., Orch., 1970; Vocalise (Electronic music), 1964. Recordings of var. compositions on CBS, RCA & Vox-Turnabour labels. Publs: An Orchestra is Born, 1969; Bronsivalaw Huberman, 1972; Contemp. music in Israel, in Dictionary of 20th Cent. Music; Ed., Guitite, 1966-. Mbrships: Nat. Committee for Culture & Art; Tel-Aviv Committee for Lit. & Art; Music Advsr., Bat Dor Ballet Co. Hons: 1st Acum Prize, 1966; Liberson Prize, 1969; Engel Prize, 1973 (all for compositions). Hobby: Wood Carving. Address: 7 Zangwill Str., Tel-Aviv 62599, Israel.

AVORGBEDOR, Dan Kodzo, b. 18 Aug. 1952. Seva, Ghana. Accompanist (Piano); Musician (Violoa, African Drums, Percussion Instruments). Educ: Gen. Dip. in Music, Univ. Ghana; MA, NE Missouri State Univ.; PhD Cand., Ethnomusicology, Ind. Univ., Bloomington. Career: Mbr. of Ghanaian contingent at Int. Fest. of Youth Orchs. & Perf. Arts, London, Scotland, 1975; Lecture-Demonstration tours in Ill.;

TV interviews of African Music, Ill.; Contbr. to: Sankofa; Weekly Spectator; Kirksville Daily; Transition. Mbrships: Am. Musicol. Soc.; Royal Anthropological Instr.; Am. Piano Tchrs. Guild; Int. Folk Music Coun.; Phi Mu Alpha. Hons: 2nd Prize, Sports Anthem Comp., Ghana, 1976. Hobbies: Billiards; Fishing; Photography. Address: Evermann Apts., No. 680, Bloomington, IN 47401, USA.

AVOTRI, Kenneth Kafui Kwaku, b. 25 July 1951. Hohoe, Ghana. Composer; Violinist; Organist. Educ: Gen. Dip. in Music, Univ. of Ghana, Legon, 1975. Career incls: Organist, Kpandu Secondary Schl., 1968-73; Organist, 1968-, Choirmaster, 1972-, Hohoe EP Ch.; Guest Choirmaster, Madina EP Ch., 1974-; Organist, Trinity Coll. Presbys., Legon; Teaching Asst., Music Dept., Inst. African Studies, Univ. of Ghana. Comps. incl: Nutifafa (choral); Yehowafe Lolo Lolo (choral), 1973; Hadzidzi vivie Nuto (choral), 1973; Midoto (choral), 1974; Dzifo Gbowo na vu (chorus & orch.), 1974, also recorded; Mawu fe Gbogbo (full orch.), 1976. Hobbies: Goalkeeping; High Jumping. Address: Commonwealth Hall, Univ. of Ghana, Legon, Accra, Ghana.

AVRIL, Edwin Frank, b. 6 May 1920. Brooklyn, NY, USA. Professor of Music. Educ: BA, San Fran. State Univ.; MA & EdD, Tchrs. Coll. Columbia Univ. m. Dorothy Vernon, 1s., 1d. Career: 1st Bassoon, num. orchs. in USA inclng: Sacramento Phil. Orcho., Calif., Marquette Municipal Band, Mich.; Riverside Symph., NYC; Northern Mich. Symph.; Cond., Coco-Cola Recreation Band, Redding. Calif. Comps. inlc: Cantata 1040, Sleepers Wake, setting of income tax form, 1978; Studies in Contemporary Style, 1972. Recordings incl: Toccara Moderne (accordion), 1967. Contbr. to newspapers & profl. mags. Mbrships. incl: Chmn., World Educ. Coun.; Masons; Phi Mu Alpha Sinfonia; Phi Delta Kappa. Recip. num. awards. Hobbies: Collecting musical instruments & toy trains; Travel. Address: 409 Swarthmore Rd., Glassboro, NJ 08028, USa.

AVSHALOMOV, Jacob. Tsingtao, China. Composer; Conductor; Educator; Educ: Mus B, MA Reed Coll., Portland, Ore. m. Doris Felde, 2 s. Career: w. Music Dept., Columbia Univ., 1947-54; Asst. Prof., 1954; Cond., Portland Jr. Symph. Orch., 1954-; has premiered works by many comtemp. composers. Mbrships: League of Composers; Am. Composers Alliance; Int. Soc. Contemp. Music. Hons. incl: NY Critics Circle Award for premiere of Tom of Bedlam (by Robert Shaw), 1953; Naumberg Recording Award for Sinfonietta (by Scherman, premiered by him at Town Hall, NY, 1946), 1956; Alice M. Ditson Cond.'s Award, 1966; DFA, Univ. of Portland, 1966; appointed by Pres. Johnson to Nat. Coun. for Humanities, 1968. Address: 2741 SW Fairview Blvd., Portland 1, OR, USA. 3.

AXARLIS, Stella b. 5 Mar. 1944, Alexandria, Egypt. Greek-Australian Opera Singer. Educ: Univ. Melbourne, Aust. Debut: Aida in Germany. Career: Soloist, Aust. Broadcasting Co.; Lieder Recitals; Operatic perfs. in Hagen, Germany, 1968-70; W Deutsche Oper am Rheim until 1979; Guest perfs. in maj. German opera houses inclng: Berlin, Hamburg, Munich, Cologne; Perfs. in Vienna, Paris, London, Brussels, Rome, Amsterdam, Rotterdam, Luxembourg, Sydney & Melbourne. Hons. incl: 1st Prize, Met. Opera Auditions, Sydney, 1965; Winner var. other competitions w. 1st prizes & medals. Hobbies: Swimming; Fast Cars; Reading. Mgmt: Columbia Artists, NYC, USA; Dr Raab, Vienna; R Schulz, Munich; Music Int., London. Address: Bruhnstr. 5, 4 Düsseldorf, W Germany.

AXWORTHY, Thomas V, b. 1 Dec. 1948. Whittier, Calif., USA. Musician: Oboe, English Horn, Clarinet, Saxophones, Flute, Early Instruments. Educ: BA, Musicol, MA Cand., Calif. State Univ., Fullerton; Tchrs. Cert., Am. Recorder Soc. m. Lisa Lowery Axworthy. Career: Studio Recording Artist; Orch. Perf. & Soloist; Clinician & Lectr. on Early Music & Early Instruments; Teacher. Fndr., Dir., Whittier Wind Ensemble & Brass Choir, S Calif. Early Music Consort; Mbr., 1920's Vaudeville Saxophone Quintet, 'Sax-in-a-Bag'; Orange Co. Sax. Quartet; Canto Antiguo. Publs: Arrs. for saxophone ensembles; Woodwind quintet arrs. of Peter & the Wolf, The Entertainer. Mbrships: Int., Am. Musicol. Socs.; Am. Recorder Soc.; Dolmetsch Fndn.; Galpin Soc.; Int. Double Reed Soc. Address: 16123, Orsa Dr., La Mirada, CA 90638, USA.

AYERS, Henri, b. 21 Jan. 1951. Lachute, Que., Canada. Tubaist, of Quebec Symph. Orch.; Geodetic Surveyor. Educ: Diplôme des Etudes Collegiales; BA, BASc Geodesiques. m. Marie Damphousse, 1 s. Career: Radio Canada, TV & Radio. Mbr., Am. Fedn. of Musicians. Hons: Premier Prix en Tuba, Conservatoire de Musique de Quebec. Hobbies: Hockey; Football; Baseball; Tennis. Address: 1850 Bvd. Benoit XV, Quebec 3, Que. G1L 2Z7, Can.

AYLING, Marjorie b. 18 June 1938, Blyth, Northumberland, UK. Lecturer in Music Education. Educ: BA Music, St. Mary's Coll., Durham Univ.; ARCM (Piano Perfs.), 1961; ARCM (Viola Tchrs.), 1962. m. Peter Ayling, 2 s. Career: Music Tchr., Tiffin Girls Schl., Kingston; Lectr., Stockwell Coll. of Educ., Bromley, Kent; Prin. Lectr. & Hd. of Music Dept., Philippa Fawcett Coll. of Educ., London; Freelance Lectr. in Music Educ.; Chief Examiner for A Level Music, Univ. of London. Mbrships: ISM; Orff Schulwerk Soc.; Soc. for Rsch. in Psychol. of Music & Music Educ. Contbr. to Recorder Music Mag. Hobbies: Old Engl. Sheepdog; Conversion & Cultivation of old Devon Cottage w. 2 acres; Cooking for gatherings of 5-50; 17 ft. Old Salmon Fishing Boat; Swimming; Books. Address: 99 Lee Rd., Blackheath, London SE3 9DZ, UK.

AYSCUE, Brian b. 25 Apr. 1948, Camden, NJ, USA. Saxophonist; Clarinettist; Composer; Musicologist; Critic. Educ: clarinet studies w. Anthony Ciccarelli; saxophone studies w. Ciccarelli & Sigurd Rascher; comp. w. Joel Thome; BA, Glassboro State Coll., 1970. 1 s. Career: Clarinettist & bass clarinettist w. Lucien Cailliet, 1966-67; perfs. w. Rascher Saxophone Ensemble, 1968, '69; Clarinettist w. var. local orchs.; saxophone soloist. Comps. incl: 3 Pieces for alto saxophone solo; Permutations I, for flute, oboe, clarinet, trumpet, tenor saxophone; The Plane of Peace, for tenor saxophone & piano; First Butterfly, for solo flute. Contbr. to: The Saxophone Symposium (record reviewer); Woodwind World Brass & Percussion. Mbrships: ASCAP; Am. Musicol. Soc.; N Am. Saxophone Alliance; MENC; Int. Clarinet Soc.; Hons: Pep Boys Educl. Foundation Scholarship, 1967; John Phillip Sousa Band Award, 1966. Hobbies: Study of Art, Philosphy & Classical Lit.; Swimming; Jogging. Address: 1217 Sylvan Dr., Haddon Heights, NJ 08035, USA.

AZCURRA, Pedro Roberto, b. 22 Jan. 1940. Ambeños, Buenos Aires, Argentina. Professor of Guitar. Educ: Schl. of Music, Buenos Aires, 1958; Studies w. Maestro Adel Carlevaro, 1970; Univ. of Comahue, 1969. m. Angélica Diaz, 3 children. Career: Recitals on TV & Radio Neuquen, Argentina; Recital, La Cultural Cipoleña, 1974; Recital, Univ. of Neuquen, 1975; Dir., Guitar Section, Schl. of Music. Comps: Miviesa raza (song in matopéyico rhythm): Yo no me iré de picon (song); El canto del Limay (trémolo); Baigorrita (samba); Araucano... tema (song). Contbr. to: Diario Sur Argentino. Mbrships: Ateneo-Cultural of Neuquen; Pres., Comahue Guitar Assn. Hons: 1st Prize, Fest. of Unpublished Songs, Zapala, Neuquen; Medals from the Provincial Govt. for his work in Buenos Aires. Hobbies: Travel; Talking about music. Address: San Martin 900, Neuquen-Capital, Argentina.

B

BAASCH, Robert Jefferson, 12 Apr. 1916, Springfield, Mass., USA. Flautist, Musician; Music Educator. Educ: BS, Univ. of Miami, Fla.; & Colo. Univ., NY; MA, Profl. Dip., EdD, Columbia Univ. m. Lucile Graf. Career; Profl. Flautist, 1943-; former Fac. Mbr., Columbia Univ.; Hd., Dept. of Woodwinds, LI Inst. of Music, NY; Dir. of Music, (Ret'd), Malverne Pub. Schls., LI, NY. Contbr. to: Woodwind World (columnist); Woodwind Instrumentalist; Music Jrnl. Mbrships: Phi Mu Alpha Sinfonia; Am. Fedn. of Musicians. Hons: NY Phil. Scholarship (flute), 1935; Univ. of Miami Music Scholarship, 1938-41. Hobbies: Art Illustrator; Cartoonist; Painting. Address: 1 Woodward Dr., Oyster Bay Cover, NY 11771, USA. 4, 29.

BABAJANYAN, Arno Arutyunovich, b. 22 Jan., 1921, Erevan, USSR. Composer. Educ: Erevan & Moscow Conservs. Career: Asst. Prof., Erevan Conserv., 1956. Compositions incl: Variations for Piano, 1937; Prelude, 1939; Sonata for Piano, 1943; Dance Vagarshapat, 1944; Polyphonic sonata for piano, 1946; Heroic Ballade for Piano & Orch., 1942; Sonata for Violon & Pinao, 1959; My Heart is in the Mountains (operetta), 1962; variety, jazz, film & theatre music. Hons: State Prize, 1951; Honoured worker of ARts of Amenian SSR, 1956; People's Artist, ibid., 1962. Address: Armenian Composers Union, 25 Ulitsa Demerchana, Erevan, USSR.

BABAYEV, Sabir, b. 30 Dec. 1920, Tashkent, Uzbekistan, USSR. Composer. Educ: Tashkent Conserv. Career: Exec., Uzbek Composers Union; Sec., Soviet Composers Union. Compositions: Two Suites for Symph. Orch., 1946-47; Two poems & Festival Overture for folk instrument orch., 1950-52; Concerto for chang (Uzbek folk instrument) & Orch. of folk instruments, 1952; Contata, Cotton Farmers of Uzbekistan, 1955; Segokh (Symphonic poem on folk themes), 1956; Love of Motherland (musical drama), 1957; During the Festival (symphonic poem), 1958; Khamza (opera), 1961; Uzbek Poetic Songs, 1966. Hon: Merited Worker of Arts of the Uzbek SSR. Address: Uzbek Composers Union, Tashkent, USSR.

BABB, Jeffery William, b. 5 Jan. 1926, Tottenham, London, UK. Conductor; Secretary of National Association of Youth Orchestras. Educ: pols., philos. & econs., Oxford Univ.; profl. coaching from Ernest Read & Sir Adrian Boult; LRAM; LTCL. m. Dorothy Joan Pryce, 7 children. Debut: 1962. Career: Schl. Music Tchr., 1951-, currently Dir. of Music, Wintringham Schl., Grimsby; Cond. of Youth Orchs.; Ochl. courses, Engl. & Int.; Mbr., conducting staff, Int. Arbeiskreis für Music. Comps: var. orchestrations & arrs. for schl. & youth orchs.; var. unpubld. comps. Contbr. to jrnls. Mbrships: ISM; Royal Musical Assn.; Schls. Music Assn. Address: 30 Park Dr., Grimsby, S Humberside, UK.

BABBITT, Milton Byron, b. 10 May 1916, Phila., Pa., USA. Composer; Educator; Music Theorist. Educ: SEssions, 1936-38; MFA, Princeton Univ., 1942; DM, Middlebury Coll., NY Univ., 1968, Swarthmore Coll., 1969, New England Conservatory 1972. m. Sylvia Miller, 1 d. Carrer: Currently WS Conant Prof. Musc, Princeton Univ. & Mbr. Composition FAc., Juilliard Schl. Compositions incl: Three Compositions for Piano; Compositions incl: Three Compositions for Piano; Compositions for Four Instruments; Composition for Twelve Instruments; Composition for Viola & Paino; Du; String Quartet No. 2; Woodwin Quartet; Two Sonnets. Contbr. to var. profl. jrnls. Mbrships incl: Phi Beta Kappa; Coll. Music Soc.; Acoustical Soc. of Am.; Audio Engrng. Soc.; Dir., Electronic Music Ctr., Columbia & Princeton Univs.; Ed. Bd., Perspectives of New Music. Hons: Joseph Bearns Prize, 1942; NY Critics Circle Citations, 1949, 1964; Award, Nat. Inst. Arts & Letters, 1959; Guggenheim Fellowship, 1960-61; Gold Medal, Brandeis Univ., 1970. Hobbies incl: Analytical Philos.; Math. Studies; Watching Football. Address: Woolworth Centre, Princeton Univ., Princeton, NJ 08540, USA, 2.

BABIKIAN, Virginia, b. 20 Sept. 1930, Everett, Mass., USA. Concert & Opera Soprano. Educ: Boston Univ.; B Mus 1951, M Mus 1952, Westminster Choir Coll., Princeton, NJ; Opera studies w. B oris Goldovsky & others, 1954-57; studies in Perugia & Rome, Italy, & Barcelona, Spain. m. George Reynolds Stein, 3 d. Debut: Spoleto, Italy, 1957. Career incl: Min. of Music, River Oaks Bapt. Ch., Houston, Tex., 1952-56; Concert Artist, 1958-; Solo concert perfs. w. num. major orch. inclng. NY Phil., Vienna Symph., Nat. Orch. of Columbia, S Am.; leading roles w. Houston Grand Opera, Wash. Opera, Rome Opera Co. & other cos.; apps. at Fests. & Community & Civic

Concerts; recitals thru'out USA; num. concert tours, Europe, Caibbean, S Am. & Orient; Artist-in-Res. & Assoc. Prof., Houston Bapt. Univ., Tex., 1965-; Vocal Coach & Asst. Cond., Houston Symph. Chorale, 1971-. Recordings incl: Milhaud, Les Choephores; Haydn, 7 Last Words of Christ; Orff, Carmina Burana. Mbrships incl: Am. Guild of Musical Artists; Sigma Alpha Iota. Recip. num. profl. awards & hon. Hobbies: Bridge; Sports; Stamps. Mgmt: Alkahest Attractions, Inc., 1175 Peachtree St., NE, Atlanta, GA 30309. Address: 8603 Ariel, Houston, TX 77074, USA.

BABINSKI, Ludwig, b. 29 June 1909, Vienna, Austria. Bandmaster; Composer; Arranger; Violinist; Pianist, etc. Educ: theoretical studies, violin, piano, sax., clarinet, Wiener Volkskonservatorium; Dipl-Kaufmann, Hochschule für Welthandel, Vianna, 1930. m. Friederike Babinski, 1 d. Debut: w. own 'Saloon' orch., 1923. Career: Musician in well-known Viennese Orchs.; in Ankara, Turkey, playing for Pres. Ataturk, 1935-38; Own band, 1939-; Bandmaster, 1. saxophonist, duet-arr., comp., Radio Vienna, 1943-45; Bandmaster of Vienna Radio Orch., 1950-57; Freelance collaborator, Radio Vienna, 1957-70; Babinski-Schrammein, Radio Vienna, 1970-. Compositions: Singing Strings; Vienna in Spring; Augarten Porzellan; Vetraumtes Wien; Rupf-u.Zupf-Polka; Traum-Melodie, etc. Recordings on: Philips, Columbia; Polydor; Amadeo; Elite Special, etc. Mbrships: Vp, Osterreichischer Komponistenbund; VP, Fachgruppe Kapellmeister/Gewerk-schaft für Kunst u. freie Berufe. Hons: Prof. decree by Austrian Pres., 1972. Hobbies: Photography. Address: Siemensstrasse 161, 1210 Vienna, Austria.

BABY, Lucile, b. 23 Mar. 1930, Quebec, Canada. Musician (Harpist). Educ: BA, BMus., Laval Univ., Que.; Dips. from the Conserv. of Music, Province of Que. m. Francois Baby, 4 c. Career: 1st Harpist, Que. Symph. Orch. & Kingston Symph. Orch., Ont.; CBC Radio & TV apps. Hobbies: Camping; Chess. Address: 2090 Brulart, Sillery, PQ G1T 1G3, Canada.

BACELAR, José Gabriel, b. 24 Apr. 1924, Cervaes, Portugal. Tchr.; Concert Guitarist. Educ: Coll. of Musical Educ. & Gregorian Inst., Paris, France; Dip., Inst. of Musicol., Univ. of Paris. Career incl: Radio Johannesburg, Lourenco Marques, Lisbon; Illustrated interviews, ORTF; Concerts in Portugal, Mozambique, S Africa & France; Tchr. of classical guitar, Acad. of Chmnbr. Music, Paris. Contbr. to Harmony Review, Paris. Mbrships: French & Int. Musicol. Socs. Participator, Int. Congress on 18th Century Portuguese Art, Braga, 1973. Hobbies incl: Lyric poetry; Stormy seas; High, snowy mtns.; Bird songs. Address: 31 Rue Esquirol, 75013 Paris, France.

BACH, Maria, b. 11 Mar. 1896, Vienna, Austria. Composer. Educ: Music Acad. of Vienna. Career: Appts. in concerts in Italy, Japan, Buenos Aires; Performed on radio in Vienna & Helsinki. Comps., incl: 3 Orchesterlieder, 1963; Marcia Funebra, 1968; Impressioni Italiane, 1969. Num. recordings inclng: piano pieces, string quartet, etc. Mbrships: AKM, Wien; Austro Mechana; Osterreichischer Komponistenbund; Wiener Frauenklub; Lyceumklub; Beta Sigma Phi. Recip. num. awards inclng: Premio Int. para Compositores Buenos Aires, 1962. Hobbies: Painting; Poetry; Singing. Address: 1010 Wien, Karntnerstr. 12, Austria.

BACHERINI BARTOLI, Maria Adelaide, b. 23 Feb. 1935, Civitavecchia, Italy. Librarian. Educ: Scoula di Paleografia musicale di Cremona; musical studies w. Prof. Piera Corsi. Career: Hd., Musical Dept., Biblioteca Nazional Centrale di Firenze. Contbr. of bibliographical articles to profl. jrnls. & reviews. Address: Via di Novoli 81, 50127 Florence, Italy.

BACHLEDA, Andrzej, b. 9 Sept. 1923, Zakopane, Poland. Singer. Educ: Dip., Conserv. of Musik, Katowice, 1952. m. Maria Gasienica-Wawrytko. 2 s., 1 d. Debut: Philharmony, Krakow. Career: Apps. w. leading orchs., Austria, Italy, Germany, Belgium, Switz.; & USSR; Soloist, Warsaw & Cracow Phils., 1950-; Soloist, Cracow Choir & Chmbr. Orch., & vocal recitals, NYC, Phila., & Wash., USA, 1966; Jacquino, Fidelio, Minn. Orch., 1968; Solo, Karol Szymanowski's 'Harnasie,' Minn. Orch., 1971; Vocal recitals, USA, 1975. Recordings: Chopin Songs. Hobbies: Tennis; Skiing. Mgmt: Pagart, Warsaw. Address: 15 Grudnia, 8-D, Zakopane, Poland.

BACHMANN, George Theodore Jr., b. 31 Mar. 1930, Annapolis, Md., USA. Librarian. Educ: BA, Hist., Univ. Md.; MA, Hist., ibid; MSLS, Cath. Univ. of Am., Wash. DC; Studied w. var. tchrs. Recorder, Viola da Gamba & Harpsichord. m. Marjorie Adale Bachmann, 2 s., 2 d. Debut: Balt., Md., 1962. Career: Public recitals w. early music grps. in Balt., Md. & Wash. DC; Mbr., Balt. Ars Antiqua; Hd. Libn., Western Md. Coll., Westminster, Md. Contbr. of review articles & bibliographies to Jrnl. of Am. Viola da Gamba Soc.; Ed.,

Newsletter of Viola da Gamba Soc., 1973-74. Mbrships: Viola da Gamba Soc., 1973-74. Mbrships: Viola de Gamba Soc. of Am.; Am. Recorder Soc. Address: 71 Pennsylvania Ave., Westminster, MD 21157, USA.

BACHMANN, Reinhard Werner, b. 13 Oct. 1923, Frohburg, Germany. Musicologist; Lecturer. Educ: Martin-Luther Univ., Halle-Wittenberg, 1948-52; Music Rsch. Inst., Uiv. of Halle, 1952-55; PhD, 1959. m. Elenor Landgraf. Career: Lectr., VEB Friedrich Hofmeister Musikverlag, Leipzig, 1956-; Sr. Lectr., VEB Deutscher Vёrlag für Music, Peipzig, 1968-. Publs. incl: Die Anfänge des Streichinstrumentenspiels, 1964, 66; The Origins of Bowling & the Development of Bowed Instruments, 1969; Probleme musikikonographischer Forschung und der Edition von Bildquellen, 1977; Herausgeber der von Heinrich Besseler und Max Schneider begrundeten, 1961. Contbr. to: Grove's Dict. 6th ed.; profl. jrnls. Mbrships: Int. Gesellschaft fur Musikwissenschaft; Folk Music Coun., Verband der Komponisten und Musikwissenschaftler der DDR. Address: Leninstr. 49, 72 Borna, German Dem. Repub.

BACIU, Ion, b. 1931. Conductor; Educator. Educ: Ciprian Porumbescu Conserv., Bucharest. Debut: as Cond., Bucharest Univ. Choir. Career: Cond., Ploiesti Phil. Orch., Moldova Phil. Orch., Jassy, 1962-, & orchs in many European countries, USA, Can., etc.; has app. w. noted soloists inclng. Ciccolini, & Tortellier; tours incl USA & Canada., 1967, & German Fed. Repub., 19781; Agregate in Orchestration, Jassy Conserv.; Rector, George Enesco Conserv, Jassy. Hons. incl: State Schlrship. for post-grad. studies at Musical Acad., Vienna. ADdress: Str. Cuza Voda nr. 29, Jassy, Romania.

BACK, Sven Erik, b. 1919, Sweden. Composer; Violinist; Conductor; Head of Swedish Radio Music School, Edsberg Castle. Career: Mbr. of Monday Group during 1940s. Compositions incl: String Quintet (Exercises); Sinfonia da Camera; Transjädarna (The Crane Feathers-a chmbr. opera); A game around a game; Fageln (The Birds-an opera); Favola for clarinet & percussion; Ikaros (ballet); Movements (ballet); Intrade for Orchestra; O Altitudo I for organ; O Altitudo II for orch. & organ; In Principio (electronic music, commissioned by Swedish Radio); much choral music; quartets. Recordings incl: Fageln.

BACKES, Lotte, b. 2 May 1901, Cologne/Rhine, Germany. Pianist; Organist; Composer. Educ: Conservs., Strasbourg & Dusseldorf; studies w. Prof. E Eckert, Geneva; concerts w. Siegfried Wagner. 1934-37; studies in comp., Acad. of ARts, Berlin. Debut: Piano recital, Dusseldorf, 1922. Career: num. radio broadcasts, choir concerts, recitals for piano & organ, featuring own comps. in Germany, USA, Cand., UK, Poland, Romania, USSR, Egypt, Cyprus, Malta etc. num. comps. Recordings: 3LPs of organ music. Contbr. to Ars Organi. Hons: Ch. music medal, St. Cacilia soc., 1947. Address: Kurfürstenstr. 17, Berlin 30, German Fed. Repub.

BACON, Denise, b. Newton, Mass., USA. Pianist; Music Educator. Educ: Soloist Dip., Longy Schl. of Music; Studied w. Mieczyslaw Horszowski; BM, MM, New England Conserv. of Music. Debut: Boston Pops Orch., 1942. Career: Limited concert career; Fndr. Dana Schl. of Music, 1957 & Kodaly Musical Trng. Inst., 1969; Dir., Kodaly Musical Trng. Inst., 1969-77; Fndr.-Dir. Kodaly Center of American, 1977-. Publs: Let's Sing Together, 1971; 46 2-Pt. Am. Exercises, 1973; 50 Easy 2-Pt. Am. Exercised, 1977; 185 Union Pentatonic Sight-Reading Exercises, 1978. Contbr. to num. profl. jrnls. Mbrships incl: Int. Kodaly Soc.; Int. Folk Music Coun.; Music Educators Nat. Conf. Hons: Recip. Braithmayer Fellowship Award 1967. Hobbies: Chmbr. Music; Reading; Travel; Gardening. Address: 15 Denton Rd., Wellesley, MA 02181, USA.

BACON, Madi, b. 15 Feb. 1906, Chgo., Ill., USA. Teacher; Professor; Conductor. Educ: PhB, 1927, MA, 1941, Univ. of Chgo.; Northwestern Univ.; San Fran. Conserv. of Music, 1928-30. Debut: Cond., Elizabethan Madrigal Singers, Chgo., 1932. Career; Elizabethan Madrigal Singers, Middle W, 1931-43; N Shore Choral Soc., 1936-46; Roosevelt Univ. Chorus, 1941-46; Univ. of Calif. Ext. Chorus, 1946-56; Fndr.-Cond., San Fran. Boys Chorus; Staff, San Fran. Opera, 1948-72; Prof. & Dean, Schl. of Music, Roosevelt Univ., 1941-46; Lectr. & Dir., Music Ext., Univ. of Calif., 1946-53; num. apps. on radio & TV, Chgo. & San Fran.; var. recordings. Mbrs.; sev. musical assns. Contbr. to Musica Am. Recip., var. hons. Hobbies incl: Mtns. Address: 1120 Keith Ave., Berkeley, CA 94708, USA, 3, 9, 12.

BACON, Ralph, b. 19 June 1934, Doncaster, UK. Conductor; Instrumental Teacher. Educ: GSM; ARCM. m. Barbara Mary Plowright, 1 s., 2 d. Career: Royal Engr. Band, Chatham, 1952-56; Violin Tchr., Doncaster Educ. Committee, 1957-64;

Dir. of Music, Doncaster Grammar Schl., 1965-657; String Tchr., Somerset, 1968-73; currently Sr. Instrumental Tchr., Derby & Cond., Derby Concert & Phil. Orchs. Publs: Ed., 'Christmas Fantasia', Appleby & Fowler, 1963. Statham St., Derby, UK.

BACON HARTY, Carol, b. 17 Jan. 1937, Harrogate, Yorks., UK. Flute Teacher & Freelance Performer. Educ: ARCM, RAM, London, 1957, 1 d., 1 s. Debut: Fest. Ballet Orch., London, 1957. Career: Concert recitals, broadcasts & TV apps., Jamaica, 1958-68; Aust. Ballet Co., 1965; Regularly played for Jamaican Nat. Dance Co., inclg. visit to Expo 67, Montreal, Can.; Recitals & tchng., Vancouver, Can., 1969-70; Specialist Flute Tchr., Canterbury areas, UK, Freelance perf., Recitals, Kent Music Schl., Orchl. playing, UK, 1970-. Recordings: Queenie's Daughter, 1963; Carols & Spirituals, 1975. Committe Mbr., E Kent Div., ISM. Address: 87 Rough Common Rd., Canterbury, Kent, UK.

BACON-SHONE, Frederic, b. 30 Nov. 1924, London, UK. Pianist; Organist; Harpsichord Player; Oboist; French Horn Player; Teacher. Educ: BA, London Univ., 1949; MA, Columbia Univ., 1953; PhD, Univ. of S Calif., 1976; LGSM (perf.), 1946. m. Robin Sue, 3 s., 1 d. Career: Keyboard Concerts, recitals, in London, W USA & Can.; Dir., Blomstedt & Willcocks Workshops, Loma Linda Univ., Calif. 1975-. var. tchng. posts incl: Vis. Prof., Columbia Univ., 1959, Instructor, Covina-Valley Unified Schl. Dist., Covina, Calif., 1960-; grad. student, Univ. of S Calif., Los Angeles, Calif., 1963-76. Comps: Psalm 121; Easter. Recording: Vivaldi, Chmbr. Mass. Publ: Form in tghe Chamber Music of Frederick Delius, 1976. Mbrships: Am. Musicol. Soc.; Am. Guild of Organists; MENC; Calif. Tchrs. Assn. recip. 4 silver medals for piano perf., GSM. Hobbies: Astronomy; Backpacking; Photography. Address: 6940 Abel Stearns Ave., Riverside, CA 92509, USA.

BÁCS, Ludovic, b. 19 Jan. 1930, Petrila, Rumania. Conductor. Educ: Konservatorium Gluj-Napoca; Conservatorium P J Ceaikowski, Moscow. m. Ercse Gyöngyver, 2 c. Debut: Moscow. Career: Radio, TV & stage apps., Romania, Moscow, Berlin (GFR), Spain, DDR, Hungary, Yugoslavia, Poland, Netherlands, Switz., Bulgaria. Comps: Codex Caioni (Old Music); Suite of Romanian Old Dances. Recordings: Vieru, Iona (opera); Wagner, Verdi Arias from Operas; Bentolu, Iphigenia; Bach, Die Kunst der Fuge, etc. Contbr., sev. reviews. Hons: Ordinul Meritul Cultural; Medalia Muncii; Medalia, 23 Aug. Hobbies: Films; Running. Address: Dinicu Golescu No. 31 sc III ap. 87, Sector 7, Bucharest, Romania.

BADINGS, Henk, b. 17 Jan. 1907, Bandoeng, Indonesia. Composer. Educ: Dr. Eng., Tech. Univ., Delft, Netherlands, 1931. m. Jeanette Margaretha Tukke, 1 c. Debut: Amsterdam, 1930. Career: Prof. of Comp. & Co-Dir., Musieklyceum, Amsterdam, 1935-41; Dir., State Conserv., The Hague, 1941-45; Freelance Comp., 1945-60; Dir., Electronic Music Studio, Univ. of Utrecht, 1960-64; Lectr., Acoustics & Info. Theory, ibid, 1960-74; Prof. of Comp., Musikhochschule, Stuttgart, 1962-72. Compositions: 14 Symphs.; 25 Concerti, 25 orchl. works of var. forms: 72 Chamber works; 6 Sonatas, 4 Sonatinas, 15 volumes of little pieces, for piano; 2 Concerti, 10 Solors, for organ; 10 works for organ & var. instruments; 144 choral songs; 4 Oratorios; 8 Cantatas; 25 volumes of songs; 6 Operas; 8 Ballets; var. Film Scores & Theatre Music; 30 Electronic works; 24 31-Tone works. Publs: De hedendaagsche Nederlandsche musiek; Het Palaeogeen in den Indischen Archipel; Tonaliteitsproblemen in de nieuwe musiek; Elektronische muziek. Contbr. to num. profl. jrnls. Mbr. Royal Flemish Acad. of Arts. Recip. num. hons. Hobbies: Geology; Plastic Arts, Address: Huize 'Hugten,' Hugten 5, Maarheeze, Netherlands, 16, 19.

BADINGS, Vera Maria, b. 5 Mar. 1938, Santport, The Netherlands. Solo Harpist; Head Professor of Harp, Amsterdam Conservatory. Educ: Dip. w. distinction for sound (Orch.), & Dip. w. distinction for gen. musical & instrumental qualitites (Soloist), Amsterdam Conserv. Career: Orch. Harpist, NOS radio symphs., 1 regional symph., currently w. Concertgebouw Orch.; regular Soloist w. or without orchs. or ensembles, live, radio or TV performs.; appeared live on Eurovision; invited annually to participate in Hollad Fest. Recordings: sev. w. Concertgebouw Orch. Mbr. of var. orgs. Recip. Prize of Excellence, Amsterdam Conserv., 1962. Mgmt, AFC Drost. Pr. Hendriklaan 13, Amsterdam, The Netherlands. Address: Lijnbaansgracht 325, Amsterdam, The Netherlands.

BADINSKI, Nikolai, b. 19 Dec. 1937, Sofia, Bulgaria. Composer; Teacher; Violinist. Educ: Dip., Music Acad., Sofia; Dip. (comp), Master Class, Acad. of Arts, Berlin, German Dem. Repub.; master classes, Dip., Music ACad., Siena; Int. Courses for New Music, Darmstadt. Career; perfs. in USA, Berlin, Stockholm, Sofia, Lisbon, Leipzig, Dresden, Italy & Switz.; num. radio perfs.; guest prof., Univs. of Stockholm & Copenhagen; lectures in many European countries; tchr., violinist, concertmaster, adviser on musical educ. at Univs. (conservs.) in German Dem. Repub. & Bulgaria. Comps. incl: Ballets; Die Ruinen unter Sofia; sev. concertos for instruments & orch.; Wind Quintet; Concerto con Clavicembalo Avec douze, for 12 strgs.; Organ album, Diverstities; 3 strg. quartets; other orchl., chmbr. & electronic music. Mbrships: ISCM; GEMA; German Composers Union; GEMA. Hons. incl: 1st prize Int. competition for comps. G B Viotte, 1977, & Intl. Competition for Comps., karlheinz Stockhausen, Italy, 1978. Address: Carmerstr. 15, 1 Berlin 12, German Fed. Repub.

BADURA-SKODA, Eva, b. 15 Jan. 1929, Munich, Germany. Musicologist. Educ: Univ. of Heidelberg, Vienna, Innsbruck; PhD, 1953; 3 yrs. study, Hochschule für Musik, Wien. m. Paul Badura-Skoda, 4 c. Career: Freelancing Lectr. & Writer, until 1962; Summer Schl. Lectr., Mozarteum, Salzburg; Prof., Univ. of Wis., 1964-74; Guest Prof., Boston Univ., 1976, Queen's Univ., Kingston, Can., Spring 1979. Publs: Mozart - Interpretation, 1957; Interpreting Mozart on the Keyboard, 1961; Mozart's c moll Konzert, 1971. Contbr. to Musicol. jrnls.; Grove's Dict., 6th Ed., etc. Mbrships: Int. Musicol. Soc.; Haydn Inst., Cologne; AIBM, etc. Hons: 3 Univ. grants. Address: Zuckerkandlgasse 14, 1190 Vienna, Austria.

BADURA-SKODA, Paul, b. 6 Oct. 1927, Austria. Pianist. Educ: Study of Conducting & Piano, State Conserv., Vienna; Master class of Edwin Fischer, Lucerne. m. Eva. Career: Concert pianist, 1948-, incl. tours throughout the World & solo appearances w. num. leading orchs.; Held annual master classes, formerly in Edinburgh & Salzburg, recently at Vienna Festival; Artist in Residence, Univ. of Wis., USA & master classes, Madison, Wis., 1966-. Compositions: A Mass in D; Cadenzas to paino & Violin Concertos by Mozart & Haydn. Publ: co-author w. wife, interpreting Mozart on the Keyboard; Edits. of works of Schubert, Mozart & Chopin. Recip: 1st Prize, Austrian Music Compeition, 1947. Address: 5802 Julia St., Madison, WI 53705, USA.

BAEKKELUND, Kjell, b. 6 May 1930, Oslo, Norway. Pianist. Educ: studies w. Nic Dirdal & Ivar Johnsen, Oslo, Gottfried Boon, Stockholm, Bruno Seidlhofer, Vienna, Hans Richter-Haaser, Detmold, olana Kobos, London, & Wilhelm Kempff, Postano. 1 s. Debut: 1938. Career: Concerts in USSR, S Am., Spain, Singapore, Iran, Poland, Germany, Yogoslavia, India, Portugal, France, Thailand, Hungary, Egypt, Netherlands, Turkey, Italy, China, Korea, UK etc. Recordings incl. concertos by Rachmaninoff (No 2), Liszt (No 1(, Tchaikovsky (No. 1), Schumann; works by Grieg, chamber music etc. Publs: ARt of Chaos, 1968; From Bach to Beatles, 1974; Meeting with Music, 1975; Norwegian Composers, 1977. Contbr. to newspapers & jrnls. Mbrships: Chmn, sev. committees on art & artists for Norway's leading political party: Norwegian Cultural Coun. Hons: Prize, Scandinavian Musicians competition, 1953; Finest pianist of yr., London, 1953; Paderewski medal, London, 1958; Medal, Danish Discofil Assn., 1959. Hobbies: Literature; Country Cottage. Address: Oberst Rodes vei 44 F, Oslo 11, Norway.

BAEKVANG, Peter, b. 6 Aug. 1941, Roskilde, Denmark. Musician; Trumpeter. Educ: Dip. Soloist, Royal Danish Acad. of Music, 1967; ARCM, 1969. Debut: Copenhagen, 1969. Career: Special Recitals of Baroque Music & Performing of Mod. Comps. for Trumpte; Performed w. Royal Danish Orch.; Perf., Aarhus Symph. Orch., Denmark, 1971-. Recip. of Prize to Study w. Prof. Richard Walton, FRCM at RCM, London, 1967. Hobbies: photography; Baroque Trumpets; Hist.; Amateur Bands; Teaching. Mgmt: Aarhus Symph. orch., Denmark. Address: P B Lundsvej 39, 8660 Skanderborg, Denmark.

BAER, Madeleine, b. 11 Nov. 1928, Brugg, Switz. Lyric Soprano. Educ. incl: Zürich Acad. of Music; Grad., Acad. of Music, Geneva; Acad. of Music, Vienna. m. Jordan Nalbantow. Debut: Kammeroper, Vienna; Opera House, Basle. Career incl: at Opera House, Zürich, 1960-69; perfs. at Staatsoper Hamburg, Staatsoper Berlin, Opera Houses Basle & Berne, Grand Théâtre Geneva; vocal recitals in Zürich, Vienna, Basle, Frankfurt, etc.; broadcasting recordings from Zürich, Basle, Berne, Geneva, Vienna, Stockholm, Cologne; almost exclusively Concert & Oratoria Singer, Switz., Germany & France, 1969-. Mbrships: Swiss Musicians Soc.; Soc. of Friends of Music, Braunwald; Lyceum Club. Zürich. Hons. incl: 1st Prize, Soc. of Friends of Music, Vienna, 1954, INt. Competition, Verviers, Belgium, 1959. Hobbies: Folklore Painting; Home Crafts. Mgmt: Conert-Agcy. Klaus Menzel, Zürich; Concert-Agcy. F G Büscher, Heidelberg. Address: Im Brächli 31, CH-8053 Zürich, Switzerland.

BAER, Walter Karl, b. 7 April 1928, Zürich, Switz. Composer; Music Educator. Educ: Piano Tchrs. Dip., Conserv. & Music Acad. of Zürich; musicol. studies, Zürich Univ.; studies comp., solo singing, choir direction, chmbr. music & piano w. var. tchrs. m. Anna-Margrit Wehrli, 2 s, 2 d. Career: Hd., Schl. Music Dept., Conserv. & Music Acad. of Zürich; perfs. of var. comps. for Swiss Radio; Concert perfs. of orchl., ch. & other comps. Comps: Num. works, 1957-, inclng. From Unreality to Unreality, 1972; Expansionen, 1973; Meeting, 1974; 5 Sätze für Klarinette, Violine & Violincello, 1974; Somnium Daedali, 1976; Message, 1977; Sonatina Nostalica, 1977; Psalmus Nonus, 1978. Recordings: Tapes for Swiss Broadcasting Corp. Publs: Christmas Songs & Pieces for Children; Verzauberungen, 1975. Mbr., Swiss profl. Assn. of Comps. & Interpreters. Hons: Prizes in 2 Swiss Comp. Contests, 1974; 1st prize of 10 Swiss towns, 1975. Address: Schlösslistr. 12, 8044 Zürich, Switz.

BAERTSOEN, Jean-Claude, b. 26 Aug. 1923, Brussels, Belgium. Composer. Educ: Harmony, Counterpoint, Fugue, Conserv. of Brussels. m. Charlier Germaine, 2 children. Career incls: Music Critic, La Peuple, 1946-62; Dir., Acad. of Music, Nivellas; Prof. of Harmony. Royal Conserv., Brussels. Comps. incl: Music for films: Andre Modeste Gretry; Suite Belge; Sculpture Aujourd'hui, Le roi du rail, etc.; Comps. for voice & piano, guitar, piano; Opera radiophonic, La Jeune Veuve. Num. recordings inclng: Concerts for Les Jeunesses Musicales de Belgique. Publs: Collaborator to Music in Belgium; Num. reviews. Mbr. num. profl. orgs. Hons. incl: Special Prize for Music, Film Festival of Antwerp, 1958 & 68. Hobby: Photography. Address: Rue Josse Impens, 11, 1030 Brussels, Belgium, 19.

BAERVOETS, Raymond Oscar, b. 6 Nov. 1930, Brussels, Belgium. Composer. Educ: Royal Conserv. of Music, Brussels; Dip., Acad. of St. Cecilia, Rome, 1962. Comps. incl: Improvvisazioni Concertainti (cello etc.); 5 Pieces for String; Notturno (chmbr. orch.); Les Dents de la Terre (The Earth's Teeth) (soloists & 2 orchs.); Psalm 129 (baritone & strings); Musica - 1972 (chmbr. orch.); Concerto for viola & orch.; La Chasse Fantastique (ballet); Metamorphoses (orch.); Magnificat (soprano & orch.); Invenzioni (piano); Immagini; Espaces; Memoria (orch.). Recordings incl: Concerto for violin & orch.; concerto for Guitar & Orch.; Concerto for Alto & Orch. Mbrship: Dir., Cultural Ctr. Concerts, Brussels. Hons. incl: Prix Koopal, Belgian Govt., 1962; City of Trieste Prize, 1965, Prix C Huysmans, 1978. Address: 51 via Cilicia, 00179 Rome, Italy, & 255 Ave. Moliere, 1060 Brussels, Belgium. 19.

BAEZ, Joan, b. 1941, Staten Island, NY, USA. Folk Singer. Educ: Schl. of Fine & Applied Arts, Boston Univ. m. David Harris (div.), 1 s. Career: began as singer in coffee houses; Ballad Room, Club 47, 1958-68; Gate of Horn, Chgo., 1958; Newport, RI. Folk Fest., 1959-60; Town Hall & Carnegie Hall, NY, 1962, 67, 68; concerts at black colls., southern USA, 1963-; tours, Europe, 1970, 71, 72, USA, 1970, 71, 72, 73. Dem. Repub. of Viet Nam, 1972; num. TV apps., num. recordings, 1960-72; A & M Record Co., 1972-. Publs: Daybreak, 1968; Coming Out (w. Harris), 1971. Fndr., \ ', Inst. for Study of Non-Violence, 1965, 16.

BAGIN, Pavol, b. 11 May 1933, Kosica, Czech. Artistic Principal & Conductor of the Opera of the Slovak National Theatre, Bratislava. Educ: Grad., Pedagogical Univ.; Univ. of Muses' Arts, Bratislava, 1955-59. Grad., Orch & Operatic Conducting, Dr. L. Rajter's Schl., 1959. m. Viera Baginova, 2 children. Debut: w. Slovak Phil. Orch., Bratislava. Career: Chief Cond., Mil. Artistic Ensemble, Bratislava, 1957-69; Dir., Admin. of Arts, Min. of Arts & Culture, 1969-71; Chief Dramatist & Chief Artistic Cond., Opera, Slovak Nat. Theatre, Bratislava, 1971-; Cond., sev. Czech. orchs.; has appeared in USSR, German Dem. Repub., Poland, Hungary, Bulgaria & Yugoslavia; has given 1st perfs. of many Slovak comps. Comps. Scherzo for piano; 4 Slovak Dances for orch.; Quartet for strings Juvenile Suite for piano; Arr. of sev. Slovak folk-songs (recorded by Orch. of Czech Broadcasting Corp.). Many recordings. Contbr. to sev. mags. Mbrships: Czech. Committee of Composers' Assn.; Bd. of Dir. & Chmn., Slovak Composers' Assn.; Chmn., Committee of Slovak Music-Fund; Chief, Creative Comm. of Concert Artists, Slovak Composers' Assn. Recip. Vit. Nejedly Prize for artistic activity, 1966. Hobbies: Lit.; Sports. Address: Pod Rovnicami 3, 800 00 Bratislava, Czech.

BAHNER, Gert, b. 26 March 1930, Neuweise/Erzgebirge, Germany, conductor; pianist. Educ: cond. exam, Leipzig acad., 1954. Debut: Berlin, 1957. Career: Komische Oper, Berlin, 1954-58; chief cond. Postdam, 1958-62; chief cond./gen. music dir., Karl-Marx Stadt, 1962-65; chief cond., Komische Oper, Berlin, 1965-74; chief cond., Leipzig opera, 1974-. Mbrships: Comp. Union of German Dem. Repub.; Theatre Union of German Dem. Repub. Hons: Kulturpreis der DDR, 1971. Hobbies: Sport; motor cars. Address: DDR-102 Berlin, Mollstr. 14. German Dem. Repub.

BAILES, Anthony James, b. 18 June 1947, Bristol, UK. Lutenist, Guitarist. Educ: Bulmershe Coll. of Further Educ., Reading, Berks.; Studied guitar w. Michael Watson, Bristol; Lute w. Diana Poulton, London, Gusta Goldschmidt, Amsterdam and Eugen Dombois at Schola Cantorum Basiliensis, Basel. m. Anne van Royen. Debut: Purcell Room, 1971. Career: Solo concerts and recording tours throughout Europe and Scandinavia; worked extensively as accomp. to many singers; gave 1st perf. of Richard Rodney Bennett's Times Whiter Series at Aldeburgh Fest., 1975. Num. Recordings. Contr. to Swedish Mag. Sgls Tidskriften. Mbrships: Lute Soc.; Svenska Gitarr och Luta Sallskapet. Hons: Art Council Grants, 1971, 72. Hobbies: Reading. Address: Hochstrasse 78, CH-4053 Basel, Switz. 2, 4.

BAILEY, Elizabeth Blitch, b. 16 June 1939, Valdosta, Ga., USA. Librarian; Pianist; Organist; Soprano Singer. Educ: BA, 1961, M Libnship., 1970, Emory Univ.; postgrad. in musicol., Univ. of NC, 1961-63. m. William B Bailey, (div.), 1 d. Career: Subject: Specialist/Instr., bibliog. for fine arts & non-Engl. philol., Lib., Univ. of Ala., Huntsville, 1970-; Organist, Univ. United Meth. Ch., 1971-. Contbr. to profl. jrnls. Mbrships. incl: Am. Musicol. Soc.; Music Lib. Assn.; Coll. Art Assn.; Bd. of Dirs., Treas., 1975-76, Huntsville Chmbr. Music Guild. Hobbies: Yarn arts; Swimming & diving. Address: 4311 Boxwood Ct., Huntsville, AL 35805, USA. 27.

BAILEY, Exine Margaret Anderson, b. 4 Jan. 1922, Cottonwood, Minn., USA. Professor of Voice; Professional Singer. Educ: BS, Univ. of Minn., 1944; MA, 1945, Profl. Dip., 1951, Columbia Univ. m. Arthur Albert Bailey. Debut: Times Hall, sponsored by Nat. Assn. of Comps. & Conds. Career incls: perf. as Soloist w. Arturo Toscanini, Frank Black & NBC Symph., NBC Radio, NYC, also w. Lyn Murry, CBS, NYC; Soloist for major chs. & temples, NYC & area; master classes; apps. w. orchs. & in recital; adjudication throughout USA; Soloist w. Helmuth Rilling, Bach's St. Matthew Passion. Recordings: RCA Victor (under Toscanini). Publs: articles in profl. jrnls. Mbrships. incl: Nat. Voice Chmn., Music Tchrs. Nat. Assn.; Pres., Ore. Music Tchrs. Assn.; Nat. Comm. on Vocal Pedagogy, Nat. Adjudicator, Nat. Assn. of Tchrs. of Singing. Recip., profl. hons. Hobbies: Art; Music; Reading. Address: 17 Westbrook Way, Eugene, OR 97405, USA, 5, 8, 9, 27.

BAILEY, Leon, b. 11 Apr. 1931, Portsmouth, UK. Music Lecturer. Educ: Queen's Coll., Taunton; GRSM, London; LRAM; ARCM; LTCL; LMus TCL; FTCL. m. Kathleen Dorothy Andrews, 3 d. Careers: Peripatetic Tchr.; Staffs. Co. Coun., 1953-58; Hd. of Music, Cannock Grammar Schl., 1958-65; Lectr. & Sr. Lectr., Music, W. Midlands Coll. of Educ., 1971-74; Subject Hd. (Music), Div. of Creative and Performing Arts, Newcastle-upon-Tyne Polytechnic, 1974-. Comps: A Shanty Sequence (Curwen). Hons: Maud & Mary Gooch Organ Scholarship, RAM, 1948-51. Hobbies: Concerts; Operas; Theatre; Reading; Gardening; Comp. & Arranging; Collecting. Address: 11 Gt. N. Rd., Brunton Pk., Gosforth, Newcastle-upon-Tyne NE3 2EB, UK. 3.

BAILEY, Norman Stanley, b. 23 Mar. 1933, Birmingham, UK. Opera & Concert Singer (Varitone). Educ: BMus, Rhodes Univ., S Africa; Performer's & Tchrs. Lic., Singing, ibid.; Dip. in Opera, Lieder & Oratoria, Vienna State Acad., Austria. m. Doreen Simpson, 2 s., 1 d. Career incl: Prin. Baritone, Linz; Deutsche Oper Am Rhein; Sadlers Wells Opera, 1967-71; regular performances at major opera houses inclng: La Scala, Milan; Royal Opera House Covent Gdn.; Bayreuth Festival; Vienna State Opera; Aust. Opera; Metropol. Opera, NYC; Paris Opera; Edinburgh Festival, etc.; num. appearances on BBC-TV, Sev. Recordings notably in Wagnerian opera. Mbrships: Baha'i World Community. Recip: CBE, 1977, Sankley Memorial Aize, 1977; Prize Winner, Int. Song Competition, Vienna, 1960. Hobbies incl: Chess; Squash. Mgmt: S A Gorlinsky Ltd., London. Address: Quarry Hangers, White Hill, Bletchingley, Surrey RH1 49Z, UK. 1, 21.

BAILEY, Robert, b. 21 June 1937, Flint, Mich., USA. Musicologist; Associate Professor of Music. Educ: BA, Dartmouth Coll., 1959; Studied piano w. Friedrich Wührer, Staatliche Hochschule für Musik, Munich, German Red. Repub. 1959-60; Studied piano w. Edward Steuermann, Juilliard Schl., NY, & musicol., Princeton Univ., 1960-62; MFA, Princeton Univ., 1962; PhD, ibid., 1969. Career: FAc., Dept. of Music, Princeton Univ., 1962-63; Fac., Dept. of Music, yale Univ., 1964-; Assoc. Prof., ibid., currently; Vis. mbr., Music Dept., Univ. of Calif., Berkeley, 1970-71. Currently working on new critical ed. of Wagner's Tristan & Isolde for Neue Wagner-

Gesamtausgabe. Contbr. to Notes, Music Lib. Assn.; Musical Times; Grove's Dict. Mbrships: Phi Beta Kappa; Coun. mbr., Am. Musicological Soc., 1972-; Int. Musicological Soc. Hons: Travel Grant, Am. Philosophical Soc., 1970; Younger Humanist Fellowship. Nat. Endowment for Humanities, 1972-73. Hobbies: 19th century Engl. & German art; Americana of fed. period. Address: Dept. of Music, Staeckel Hall, Yale Univ., New haven, CT 06511, USA.

BAILEY, Teresa, b. 1 Apr. 1955, Dayton, Ohio, USA. Recorder Player; Seminary Student. Educ: Univ. of Dayton; BA, Valparaiso Univ., 1975. Career: Played w. small grps. for benefits & ch. servs.; Solo apps. w. Valparaiso Univ. Schola Cantorum, the Dayton Art Inst. & var. chs. Mbrships: Reg. Coord., Lutheran Soc., for Worship, Music & the Arts; Am. Recorder Soc.; Dayton Bach Soc. Contbr. to Recorder Review. Hobbies: Reading; photography; Choral singing. Address: 311 Fountain Ave., Dayton, OH 45405, USA.

BAILLIE, Isobel, b. 9 Mar. 1895, Hawick, Scotland, UK. Singer. Educ: Dover St. HS for Girls, Manchester; Pvte. Music study in Manchester & Milan, Italy. m. Henry Wrigley, 1 d. Career: Solo soprano, num. appearances in concerts, TV & Radio. Recording artist for EMI. Hons: BE; ME; Hon. DLit; RAM; RCM; RMCM; Silver Plaque, Worshipful Co. of Musicians, London. Mbrships: Past Warden, ISM. Address: 524 Stretford Rd., Manchester 16, Lancs., UK.

BAIN, Wilfred Conwell, b. 20 Jan. 1908, Shawville, PQ, Can. Pianist; Musician; Conductor; Educator. Educ: AB, Houghton Coll., 1929; Westminster Choir Coll., 1931, BMus; AM, NY Univ., 1936; EdD (music), 1938; Hon. DMus, Temple Univ.; Dmus, Am. Conserv.; D Fine Arts, Westminster Choir Coll.; LLD, Ind. State Univ. m. Mary Freeman. Career incl: Dean, Ind. Univ. Schl. of Music, 1947-73; Artistic Dir., Ind. Univ. Opera Theatre, 1973-77; Gen. Mgr., ibid., 1947-73; Cond., Choral Concert Groups; Choral Cond., Dallas Houston, Texas Symph. Urchs., Ind. Symph.; Sec. & Auditions Chmn., Int. Fests. Bd. Mbrshps: Phi Delta Kappa; Phi Sigma Kappa; Pi Kappa Lambda; Phi Mu Alpha, Hon. Kappa Kappa Psi; Pres., Soc., MTNA. Hons. incl: Gold Medal, Nat. Soc. of Arts & Letters, 1972; Ysaye Medal. Hobby: Painting. Address: 3570 S Ocean Blvd., Palm Beach, FL 33480, USA. 2, 8, 12.

BAINES, Francis Athelstan, b. 11 Apr. 1917, Oxford, UK. Composer; Leader, Consort of Viols; Double-vass Player; Professor. Educ: RCM. m. June Hardy, 2 s., 1 d. Career: Composer; Ldr., Jaye Consort of Viols; Double-bass Player; Prof., RCM; Perf., hurdy-gurdy, ancient bagpipes, pipe & tabor. Comps: 2 sumphs.; Violin Concertino; Many chmbr. works. Recordings: Jaye Consort on Arion, Pye, Argo, Vox, HMV Harmonia Mundi. Contbr. to Early Music Mag. Hon. RCM, 1973. Address: 25 Cleveland Rd., London SW 13, UK.

BAIRD, Nora, b. 13 Mar. 1900, Belfast, UK. Music Teacher; Organist; Accompanist; Adjudicator. Educ: LRAM; LTCL; (piano tchr.); LTCL (organ perf.). Career: Chief piano tchr., St. Margaret's C of E Schl., 1928-73; Mbr. Tchng. Staff, Queensland Conserv., 1957-75; Organist, Valley Presby. Ch., 1942-; Attended summer schls., Seascale, Matlock & St Albans, UK, also Master Class, Vienna, 1962; Attended the Observer Conds. Course, Bromley, Kent, also Vienna & Edinburgh Fests. 1962. Mbrships: Royal Schls. Music Club, Hon. Sec.; Aust. Broadcasting Committee, Exec.; Hons: 2 Bursaries estab. in her name: Lf. Mbr. Music Tchrs. Assn., 1928-; Presentation from Royal Schls. Music Club; MBE, 1980. Hobbies: Travel; Correspondence; Stamp-collecting. Address: 352 Newmarket Rd., Newmarket, Queensland 4051, Aust.

BAIRD, Tadeusz, b. 26 July 1928, Grodzisk, Mazuria, Poland. Composer. Educ: Music studies in Warsaw. m. Alina Sawicka-Baird. Compositions incl: 2 Symphs., 1950, 1952; Piano Concerto, 1949. Concerto for orch., 1953; Divertimento (4 wind instruments), 1957; String Quartet, 1958; Espressioni Varianti (violin & orch.), 1959; Erotiques (soprano & orch.), 1961; Epiphany Mjsic (orch.), 1963; Four dialogues for oboe & chmbr. orch., 1964; Tomorrow (one-act opera), 1966; Sinfonia brevis, 1968; 3rd Symph., 1969; Psychodram (orch.), 1972; Elegeia for orch., 1973; Concerto for Oboe & orch., 1973; Concerto Lugulre for viol. & orch., 1975; Double concerto for cello, harp & orch., 1976; String Quartet, 1978; num. chmbr. music pieces, instrumental works; choral & solo songs; incidental music for stage & films. Hons. incl: Stae Prize (for 1st Symph.), 1951; Olympics Prize (for 2nd piano sonatina), 1952; City of Cologne Music Prize, 1963; State Prizes, 1964, '70; Union of Polish Comosers Prize, 1965; 3 First Prizes, Int. Tribune of Composers, UNESCO, Paris; City of Warsaw Music Prize, 1970; Mbrship. Academy of GDR, 1978;

num. decorations. Hobbies: Cars; Theatre. Address: Lipska 11 m 4, 03-904, Warsaw, Poland.

BAISLEY, Robert William, b. 5 Apr. 1923, New Haven, Conn., USA. Professor of Music; Concert Painist. Educ: BMus, Yale Univ.; MA, Columbia Univ. m. Jean I Shanley, 3 d. Career: Prof. of Music, Pa. State Univ.; Concerts w. major orchs., chmbr. grps. & solo recitals throughout NE, Ctrl. & S areas of USA. Lecture-recitalist, var. univs. Recordings: 5 major films for educl. TV. Author of 2 monographs for MENC. Mbrships: Coll. Music Soc.; MENC; Am. Musicological Soc. Hobbies: Gardening; Photography. Address: 454 Park Lane, State Coll., PA, USA, 6.

BAJALOVIĆ, Mirjana, b. 12 Nov. 1943, Belgrade, Yugoslavia. Violinist. Educ: Dip. cum laude, Belgrade Acad. of Music; Dip. (studied w. Galamian & Makanowitzky), Juilliard Schl. of Music, USA. m. Vojislav Kovacević, 1 s. Debut: Belgrade, 1964. Career: Recital & TV hour, Belgrade, 1964; Soloist w. orch. under Fielder, 1966; Freelance, NY, 1968-71, playing w. Princeton Chmbr. Orch., Pro Arte Symph., Am. Symph., etc.; Mbr., NJ Symph., 1971-75; currently w. Symph. Orch. of City of Duisburg (German Opera on the Rine); Recitals, NY & Boston; Apps. w. chmbr. grps., US & Europe. Mbrships: Am. Fend. of Musicians; Deutsche Orchestervereinigung. Recip. var. hons. Mgmt: Critics choice Artist Mgmt., 1697 Broadway, NY 10019, USA. Address: Gutenbergstr. 6, D-4100 Duisburg, German Red. Repub.

BAKER, (Dame) Janet Abbott, b. 21 Aug. 1933, Hatfield, Yorks., UK. Singer. Educ: Hon. DMus, Birmingham, 1968, Leicester, 1973, London, 1974, Oxford, 1975, Hull, 1976. m. James Keith Shelley. Career: apps. in concert halls, opera & fests. throughout the world. Has made num. recordings. Fellow, St. Anne's Coll., Oxford. Hons: Kathleen Ferrier Award, 1956; Queens Prize, RCM, 1959; Shakespeare Prize, Hamburg, 1972; CBE, 1970; DBE, 1976. Hobbies: Reading; Gardening. Address: 124 Wigmore St., London W1H OAX, UK.

BAKER, Julius, b. 23 Sept. 1915, Cleveland, OH, USA. Flautist. Educ: Eastman Schl. of Music; Dip., Curtis Inst. of Music, 1937. m. Ruth Thorp. Career: Mbr., Cleveland Orch., 1937-41; 1st Flautist, Pitts. Symph., 1941-43, CBS Symph., 1943-51, Chgo. Symph., 1951-53; Mbr., Bach Aria Grp., 1947-65; Fac. Mbr., Juilliard Schl. of Music, 1954-; Solo Flute, NY Phil. Orch., 1965-; num. recordings. Address: Crosby Rd., RFD 1, Brewster, NY 10509, USA, 2.

BAKER, Kathryn June, b. 8 July 1946, St. Thomas, Ont., Can. University Music Teacher (Organ, Theory & Piano). Educ: MusBac, Univ. of Western Ont., London; MA, Eastman Schl. of Music, USA; AMus, Organ Perf., Western Conserv. of Music, London, Ont., Can., ARCT, Piano Perf., Toronto Conserv. of Music. Career: Tchr., Preparatory Theory, Eastman Schl. of Music, Rochester, NY, USA; Tchr., Theory, Organ, Piano, FAc. of Music, Univ. of Western Ont., London, Can., 1970-. Organist & Choir Dir., Redeemer Lutheran Ch., London, Ont., 1970-76; Music Dir., Wellington St. Unit Ch., London, Ont., 1977-78. Mbrships: Am. Guild of Organists; Soc. for Music Theory.; Coll. Music Soc.; Num. hons. Hobbies: Sewing; Swimming. Addres: 432 N Martin Ave., Tucson, AZ 85719, USA, 4, 27.

BAKER, Larry, b. 7 Sept. 1948, Fort Smith, Ark., USA. Composer; Conductor. Educ: MM, Comp., Cleveland Inst. of Music, 1973; BME, BM, Comp., Ikla. Univ., 1971; Studied comp. w. Spencer Norton & Donald Erb. Career: Griffin State Memorial Hosp., 1969-71, Music Therapy Aide; Hd. of Music Div. of Cuyahoga Community Coll. Saturday ARts Prog., 1971-72; Perf., Portfolio V, Cleveland Inst. of Music, 1972; Ohio Fest. of Contemporary Performing ARts Series, 1972; Grad. Asst. in Theory, Cleveland Inst. of Music, 1972-73; Dir., Contemporary Music Ensemble, Mbr. of Theory-Comp. Fac., ibid., 1973-; Cleveland Comps' Guild Concerts, 1972-74; Num. perfs. of own comps. Comps: Form 1, 1971; The Journey, 1971; Sontata, 1971: Background Music for Richard III, 1971; From the Worlds of the Imperium -1, 1972; Trimophony, 1972; Groupe, 1973; Night Ancestor I, 1972; Before Assemblage I, 1973; Before Assemblage III, 1973; Echo image, 1975; Hommage à Dali, 1975; Columns, 1976, mbr. num. profl. socs. Hons: Ranney Scholarship, 1072-73; Vermoan Comps. Conf. Scholarship, 1972-73; Cleveland Phila. Commission, 'Echo Image', presented 1975; Ind. Chmbr. Orch. Commission, 'Columns', 1976. Nat. Endowment for the Arts Fellowship-Grant, 1976. Address: 2496 Derbyshire Rd., Apt. II, Cleveland, OH 44106, USA.

BAKER, Norman Louis, b. 8 Dec. 1941, Milwaukee, Wis., USA. Clarinettist. Educ: BMus, Juilliard Schl. of Music, 1964; MMus, Cleveland Inst. of Music, 1968. Career: Programme

Coordinator for 3 yrs. Atlanta Symp.; chmaber music grant, Nat. Endowment for the Arts, Washington, DC, 1970-72; Prin. clarinet, Atlanta Symph.; fac., Georgia State Univ. Recordings: w. Atlanta Symph. Mbrships: Nutritional Acad., Des Plaines, Ill. Hobbies: Alexander Technique; Nutritional Counselling. Address: 4307 Rickenbacker Way NE, Atlanta, GA 30342, USA.

BAKER, Richard Douglas James, b. 15 June 1925, Willesden, London, UK. Radio & Television Broadcaster; Author. Educ: MA, Peterhouse, Cambridge; studied piano, 1932-39. m. Margaret Celia Baker, 2 s. Debut: As Actor, 1948, as BBC Announcer, 1950. Career: Actgor 1948-49; Tchr., 1949-50; BBC TV Newsreader, 1954-; Panellist on BBC's 'Face the Music', 1965-; Presenter of TV Concerts, 1960-; Presenter, 'These You Have Loved'; Radio 4, 1972-77; Presenter, BAker's Dozen, Radio 4, 1978k-; num. concert appearances as Narrator. Recordings as Narrator of Peter & the Wolf; Young Persons Guide to the Orchestra, CFP 185. Publs: The Magic of Music, 1975; Guide to Good Music, 1979. Mbrships: Savage; Barrick; London Phil. Orch. Coun., Coun. of Friends & Covent Garden. Hons: OBE, 1976. Hobbies: Gardening; Sailing. Mgmt: Bagenal Harvey, 15 Charterhouse St., London EC1. Address: 12 Watford Rd., Radlett, Herts., UK.

BAKER, Robert, b. 23 Aug. 1920, London, UK. Clarinettist. Educ: Charterhouse; RCM, 1938-39, 1946; ARCM. m. Ruth Gipps, 1 s. Career: Prin. clarinet, City of Birmingham Symp. Orch., 1946-57; freelance player in London w. all leading orchs., 1957-; mbr., London Mozart Players, 1957-76, Menuhin Fest. Orch. & London Chanticleer Orch. Mbrships: Musicians' Union; ISM. recip., Manns Prize, RCM, 1946. Address: Allfarthings, Hermitage Rd., Kenley, Surrey CR2 5EB, UK.

BAKER, Samuel, b. 28 May 1907, Prenton, Birkenhead, UK. Organist. Educ: Lichfield Theological Coll.; ARCO; LTCL; Comp. w. George Oldroyd. m. Evelyn Perry Brown, 2 s. Career: 2nd Asst. Organist, Chester Cathedral; Asst. Organist & Acting Organist, Derby Cathedral; Asst. Cond., Derby Choral Union; Dir. of Music, Adams' Grammar Schl., Newport Salop; Extra Mural Lectr., Birmingham Univ.; Organist, St. Mary's Colegiate Ch. & St. Chad's Ch., Shrewsbury. Mbr. Savage Club. Hobbies: Sport; Art; Reading. Address: Heathfield, St. Dogmaels, Cardigan, Dyfed, UK.

BAKHSHI, Anand Prakash, b. 21 July 1930, Rawalpindi, W Pakistan. Lyricist; Singer. m. Kamla, 4 c. Career: Writer of approx. 2,000 film songs. Mbrships: All India Film Writers Assn. Hons: 4 Gold, 2 Silver discs fro Gramophone Co. of India. Hobbies: Reading books, mags. & Urdu lit. Address: 201 Costebelle, 687 Perry Cross Rd., Bandra, Bombay, India.

BAKKE, Ruth, b. 2 Aug. 1947, Bergen, Norway. Composer; Organist; Teacher. Educ: Univ. of Bergen; Music Degree, Univ. Oslo; Organist Examen, Bergen Conserv. of Music; BA Mus, Texas Lutheran Coll., USA, MA Mus, Wash State Univ. Career: Organ recitals in USA; Apps. on Radio & TV in Norway; Tchr., Bergen Conserv. of Music; Organist & Choir Dir., Bergen; Fndr., 5 children's & youth choirs. Comps. incl: Sonata (organ); Chromocumuli (large symph. orch.); The Girl in the Elfs Dance (soprano, flute, violin); Des Kaisers Neue Kleider (chmbr. ensemble). Recordings: Tapes available from Soc. of Norwegian Comps. & Norwegian Chapt., ISCM. Mbrships: Soc. of Norwegian Comps.; Ny Musikk, NOrwegian Chapt., ISCM; Norwegian Guild of Organists. Hons: incl: 1st Prize, Comp., Ch. & Arts Fest., Tex. Luth. Coll., 1970. Hobbies: Track Sports. Address: Fagerasvei 13, 5032 Minde, Norway, 4, 29, 30.

BAKKEGARD, Benjamin David, b. 19 Jan. 1951, Austin, Tex., USA. Orchestral Musician; horn player. Educ: BA, Mus. Calif. State Univ., Fresno; Calif. Standard Sec. Teaching Credential (Music), 1974. m. Karen Moats Bakkegard. Career: Co-Prin. First Horn, Baltimore Symph. Orch.; Perfs. w. Chgo. Symph. Orch.; Lyric Opera of Chgo.; Chgo. Opera Studio; Fresno Phil. Recordings w. Chgo. Symph. Orch. and Baltimore Symph. Orch.; var. studio recordings. Mbrships: Pres. and VP, Gamma Pi Chapt., Phi Mu Alpha Sinfonia. Hons: Brass Honors Award, CSUF; Los Angeles Horn Club Competition Award, 1971; Colo. Phil. Orch., 1972; Music Acad. of the West, 1973; Am. Wind Symph. Orch., 1974. Hobbies: Backpacking; Water Skiing; House Renovation. Address: 2243 Eutaw Place, Baltimore, MD 21217, USA.

BAKKER, Anne Johanna, b. 19 May 1938, Amsterdam, Netherlands. Cellist. Educ: BFA & MFA, Calif. Inst. of the Arts, Lost Angeles; MMus, Va. C'wlth. Univ., Richmond. Career: Cellist, Winipeg Symph. Orch., Royal Winnipeg Ballet Orch. & CBC Winnipeg Radio Orch., Man., 5 yrs.; Prin. Cellist, Edmonton Symph. & Alta. Chmbr. Players, 3 yrs.; currently

Fac. Mbr., Va. C'wlth Univ., String Tchr., Va. Union Univ. & Mbr., Richmond Symph. Orch. Mbr., Am. Fedn. of Musicians. Hobbies: Swimming; Camping; Cooking. Address: PO Box 5005, Richmond, VA 23220, USA.

BAKKER, Marco, b. 8 Feb. 1938, Beverwijk, Netherlands. Singer. Educ: Amsterdam Conserv. m. Patrician Anne Madden, 1 s. Debut: in Montevardi's Orfeo, Holland Fest. Career: Soloist, Dutch Opera, Amsterdam, Wexford Fest., Ireland, Glyndebourne Fest., UK, Scottish Opera, UK; num. radio & TV perfs.; has had own opera/cinima/classical prog. on TV, past 2 yrs. Recordings: num. LP records, opera, operetta, oratorio & musical comedy. Hons: Bass & Baritone Winner's Hergotenbosch Int. Singing Contest, 1966; 2nd Prize, Munich, 1968; 1st Prize, Rio de Janeiro, 1969. Hobby: Sports. Mgmt: Pieter G Alferink, Apollolaan 81, Amsterdam. Address: Jan van Scorelpark 5, Schoorl, Netherlands.

BAKST, Ryszard, b. 1926, Warsaw, Poland. Pianist; Professor. Educ: MA, PI Tchaikovsky's Moscow State Conserv. div., 1 s. Career: on fac., State HS of Music, Wroclaw, Poland, 1947-50, State Advanced Schl. of Music, Wroclaw, 1950-53, Stae Acad. of Music, Warsaw, 1953-68, & Royal Manchester Coll. of Music, UK, 1969-; has made concert tours in France, Czechoslovakia, Norway, Denmark, Bulgaria, Rumania, Finland, China, USSR, Can.; USA, Japan, Indonesia, India, Yugoslavia, Hungary, Cuba, Israel, GB, etc., 1947-70; num. tchng. posts incl. RMCM/RNCM, 1969-. Recordings: works by Beethoven, Schumann, Chopin, Szymanowski, Paderewski, Zarembski, etc.). Mbrships: Assn. of Polish Musicians; Frederic Chopin Soc. Recip. of prize in 4th Int. Chopin Competition, Order of Polinia Restituta. Address: 104 Park Rd., Prestwich, Manchester, UK.

BALADA, Leonardo, b. 22 Sept. 1933, Barcelona, Spain. Composer; Professor. Educ: Proesorado, Conserv. Liceo, Barcelona, 1954; Dip., comp., Juilliard Schl., NY, USA, 1960. div. 1 s. Career: Commissions from leading orgs.; works performed by leading orchs. & soloists; Prof. of Comp., Carneyle Mellon Univ., Pitto., Pa. Comps. reserded: Guernica (orchl.); Maria Sabina (oratorio); Cumbres (for band); Geometria; Cuatris; Mosaico; Violin Sonata; Analogias for guitar; Apuntes for four guitars. Comps. publd. incl: Homage to Casals; Homage to Sarasate, for orch.; Sinfonia en Negro-Homage to M Luther King; Ponce de Leon (narrator & orch.) Contbr. to La Vanguardia Espanola. Mbrships: ASCAP; Am. Music Ctr. Hons: 1st Prize, City of Zaragoza Int. Comp. competition; City of Barcelona Comp. Prize. Mgmt: G Schirmer Inc. & Belwin Mills, Publrs., NY USA. Address: Music Dept., Carnegie Mellon Univ., Pittsburgh, PA 15213, USA. 2.

BALAKIAN, Lucy Boyan, b. 10 Sept. 1907, Constantinople. Turkey. Pianist; Teacher. Educ: Geneva Conserv. Music, Switzerland; Juilliard Schl. Music, NY, USA; Seminars at Mozarteum, Salzburg. m. Krikor G. Balakian (dec.). Career: Tchr., piano. Mbrships: Fac. mbr. & adjudicator, Nat. Guild Piano Tchrs.; Pres., Associated Music Tchrs. League NY 1971-73; Past VP. Piano Tchrs. Congress NY & Profl. Music Tchrs. Guild.; Am. Coll. Musicians; Fla. State & Nat. Music Tchrs. Assn.; Int. Soc. Music. Educ.; Juilliard Alumni Assn.; Fla. Symph. Guild.; Civic Music; Friday Musicale; Hon., Profl. Music Tchrs. Guild, NJ. Hon: ASsociated Music Tchrs. League NY estab. Lucy Boyan Balakian annual schlrship. award. Hobbies: Reading; Walking; Bridge; Painting. Address: 2727 N Atlantic Ave., Apt. 412, Daytona Beach, FL 32018, USA. 4, 5.

BALANCHIVADZE, Andrei Melitonovich, b. 1 July 1906, St. Petersburg, Rissia. Composer. Educ: Tiflis & Leningrad Conservs. Compositions incl: Ballet music for Heart of the Mountains, 1938; music for 20 films incl: Georgy Saakadze, David Guramishvili, Lost Paradise, They Descended from the Mountains, Mameluk; Opera - Mzia, 1949; 3rd Concerto for piano & string orch., 1953; Concerto for bassoon & orch., 1954; Ruby Stars (ballet), 1951; Orchl. works, incl: Lake Ritza, The Sea, Rhapsody, Ballade; 2nd Symph. (orch. & piano), 1959; Stranitsy Zhizni (Pages of Life - ballet), 1961; 4th Concerto for pinao & orch.; 1962; Evening, miniature for string quartet, 1964; Fantasia for piano, 1964; Muvri (ballet), 1965. Hons: State prizes for compositions, 1944, 1946; People's Artist of Georgian SSR. Address: Georgian Composers Union, 22 Prospekt Rustaveli, Tbilisi, USSR.

BALASANYAN, Sergei Artemyevich, b. 26 Aug. 1902, Ashkabad, Turkmen, Russia. Composer. Educ: Moscow Conserv. Career: Sec., RFRSR Composers Union; Exec., USSR Composers Union; Asst. Prof., 1961-65; Prof., 1965-. Compositions incl: The Vose Uprising (opera), 1939; Kova the Blacksmith (opera), 1941; Leili & Medjnun (ballet), 1947; Two Sonatinas for piano, 1948; Tadjik Suite (Symph. Orch.). 1949; Bakhtior & Nisso (opera), 1954; Seven Armenian Songs

(Symphonic Suite), 1955; Afghan Suite, 1956; 9 Songs by Komitas for Voice & Symph. Orch., 1957; 3 Songs by Sayatnova for Voice & Symph. Orch., 1957; Islands of Indonesia (6 Symphonic pictures for orch.), 1959, 1961: Rhapsody on a Theme of Rabindranath Tagore; 4 Songs of Africa; 2 Songs of Latin America; Shakuntala (ballet); 1961. ons: Honoured worker of Arts of Tadjik SSR, 1939; People's Artist, ibid., 1957; State Prize, 1949; Honoured Worker of Arts of RSFSR, 1964; var. Soviet medals & decorations. Address: Moscow Sect., RSFSR Composers Union, 4-6 Tretya Miusskaya ulitsa, Moscow, USSR.

BALASSA, George, b. 30 Jan. 1913, Budapest, Hungary. Clarinettist. Educ: Univ. Degree in Philos. & Art; Artist Dip., Liszt Ferenc Acad. of Music, Budapest, 1936. m. Elisabeth Balassa. Debut: 1936. Caree; Mbr., var. Symph. Orchs. inclng. Wintertur, Switzerland, 1937-38; Solo Clarinettist, Hungarian State Symph. Orch., 1945-68; Permanent Soloist, Hungarian Radio; Assoc. Fndr. & Mbr., Budapest Wind Quintet, 1948-54; Prof., Liszt Ferenc Acad. of Music, Budapest, 1949-. First Hungarian Perf. Béla Bartok's Contrasts, 1946. Recording: I. Sárközy, Sinfonia Concertante per Clarinetto Solo. Publs incl: Methodology of Clarinet Playing, 1973; Tutor for Clarinet (w. K Berkes), 2 vols.; Concertos for Clarinet by C Stamitz, A Dimler, J B Vanhal; Sonata for Clarinet by F Danzi; 3 Quartets for Wind Instruments by Gambaro; Wind Quintet by M Haydn; Quartet for Clarinet & Strings, Vanhal; Concertos by I. Pleyel, F Tausc; 4 Sonatas by F A Hoffmeister; Trios for woodwind by F Devienne. Contbr. to: Hungarian Music. Mbrships: Exec. Committee; Trade Union of Hungarian Music Tchrs; Union of Hungarian Artists of Music. Hons: Liszt Ferenc Prize, 1953. Hobby: Stamp Collecting. Address: 4 1023 Budapest, Harcsa u. 1, Hungary.

BALASSA, Sándor, b. 20 Jan. 1935, Budapest, Hungary. Composer; Music Director Hungarian Radio. Educ: STudied Choral Leadership, Béla Bartók Conserv., Budapest; Comp. Dip., Liszt Acad, ibid. m. Irene Balogh, 1 s, 1 d. Debut: 1955. Career: Radio Broadcasts incl: Legen (21 Stations), 1971; Requiem for Lajos Kassák (30 Stations), 1972 73; xenia (BBC), 1974; Works perfd abroad: Chant of Glarus (full orch.), comps. on commission from The Koussevitzky Music Fndn. Comps. incl: The Man Outside (opera in 5 movements); Antinomia (Trio for Soprano, Clarinet, Cello), recorded; Xenia (nonet) recorded; Trio for Violin, Viola & Harp; Legend (recorded); Motet - for Mixed Choir; Requiem for Lajos Kassák (recorded); Iris (orch.), recorded; Cantata Y (recorded); Lupercalia (orch.) recorded; Tabulae (Chmbr. orch.), recorded. Mbrshps: Assn. of Hungarian Musicians; Artisjus. Hons: (for Requiem) Critics' Prize, Hungary, 1972; Disting. Comp. of Yr., UNESCOs Int. Rostrum of Comps., Paris; Erkel Prize, 1972; Critics' Prizes, for Tabulae & Quintetto per percussion, 1974, 76-78; Merited Artist of the Hungarian People's Repub. Hobbies: Nature; Mountains. Address: 26 Rákóczi str., Budakeszi 2092, Hungary.

BALAZS, Arpad, b. 1 Oct. 1937, Szentes, Hungary. Composer. Educ: Conserv., Szeged; Grad. Comp., Budapest Acad. of Music, 1964. m. Agnes Malovecz, 1 s. Compositions incl: 21 songs for choir, 1958-74; Burlesca (flute & piano), 1970; Songs from Borsod (suite for female choir), 1971; Songs on Budapest (canata), 1972; Fourteen Easy Pieces for Piano, 1972; Overcoming Winter (canata), 1974. Recordings incl: Memento; Song on Budapest; Song from Borsod; Song on the Song; Greeting at Daybreak; O Maria. Mbrships: Pres., Foreign Affairs Comm., Ctrl. Coun. of Hungarian Choirs; Warsaw Int. Chopin Soc.; Assn. of Hungarian Musicians. Hons. incl: Gold Medal of Order of Labour, 1975. Address: H-1022 Budapest, 11 Tovis u 4, Hungary.

BALDASSARRE, Joseph Anthony, b. 10 Oct. 1950, Cleveland, Ohio, USA. Guitarist; Guitar Teacher; Musicologist. Educ: Cleveland Inst. of Music; MBE, Baldwin-Wallace Coll.; MA, Kent State Univ., Ohio; Pvte. studies w. Miguel Rubio, Spain. m. Karen Lynn Schulze, 2 d. Career: Tchr., Baldwin-Wallace Coll., Berea, Ohio; Tchr. of Guitar, Music Hist., Boise State Univ., Idaho; Feature Perf., KYW TV & Radio Road Show, 1961-65; Mbr., Boise Phil. Orch., String Bas Sect., & Guitar Soloist, 1976; Lecture/recitals on Early Music, Lute, & Hist. of the Spanish Guitar. Studio recordings as soloist, overdub artist & backup musician. Mbrships: Lute Soc. of Am. Hons. incl: Full Scholarship, Cleveland Inst. of Music. Hobbies: Early Music, etc. Address: 9704 Telfair Dr., Boise, ID 83704, USA.

BALDWIN, John, b. 12 Apr. 1940, Arkansas City, Kan., USA. Percussionist. Educ: BME, Univ. of Wichita, 1963; MME, Wichita State Univ., 1965; PhD, Mich. State Univ., 1970. m. Alison Anne Comstock, 2 c. Career: mbr. num. orchs. inclng. Wichita Symph., Aspen Fest., Boise Phil., Boise Civic Opera, Boise City Band, Boise Symphonette; var. solo & chamber music perfs.; currently Assoc. Prof. of Percussion, Boise State

Univ. Comps: Odo, for women's chorus; Allegro, for keyboard percussion ensemble; over 60 arrs. for keyboard percussion ensemble. Publs: co-ed., Scoring for Percussion, 1969. Contbr. to profl. jrnls; percussion ed., School Musician. Mbrships: MENC; Percussive Arts Soc. (State chmn., Wis. & Idaho Chapts.); Nat. Assn. of Coll. Wind & Percussion instructors; Idaho Music Educ. Assn.; MTNA; etc. Hons. incl: Outstanding Young Man of Am., 1976; Cert. of Excellence, MENC. Hobbies: Outdoor activities; Fishing; Hiking. Address: Music Dept., Boise State Univ., 1910 Univ. Dr., Boise, ID 83725, USA. 29.

BALDWYN, Rodney Clifford, b. 18 May, 1927, London, UK. Organist; Harpsichordist. Educ: Birmingham Schl. of Music; LRAM; ARCM. m. Freda Smith, 1 d. Debut: Organ Music Soc., London. Career: Recitals, major cathedrals and concert halls, Royal Fest. Hall and Queen Elizabeth Hall, London; recitals in Europe and Scandinavia; broadcasts, Danish Radio, ORTF Paris, KRO Hilversum, Bavarian Radio; Bach cycle, Milan; 3 Choirs Fest.; Bruges Organ Week; Dir. of Music Music, St. Mary's Convent Schl., Worcs; Dir., Melodes Jevenales Girls' Choir. Recording: Pye. Publs: CPE Bach organ sonatas. Contr. to: Music in Educ.; Organists' Review; Elgar Newsletter. Mbrships. incl: RCO; Chmn., Worcs. Organists Assn. Hons: Gold Medal, Pedrazzi Soc., Modena, Italy. Hobbies: Archaeology; Puppetry; Art. Address: 76 Bridge Str., Pershore, Worcs., UK.

BALEA, Ilie, b. 25 June 1923, Brasov, Romania. Musicologist; Music Critic; Producer; Teacher. Educ: Municipal Conser. of Music, Brasov, 1940-42; Theatre Inst., Cluj, 1949-50. Debut: Asst. prod., Eugene Onegin, 1951. Career: Musical sec., 1948-51; Gen. stage dir., Cluj Opera, 1951-; Lectr., Conserv. at Cluj, 1951-75; prin. stage dir., Opera Theatre, Ankara, Turkey, 1974-75; Fndr. & ldr., Opera Studio, Gong 49, at Conserv., Cluj; operas prod. incl. over 50 works by Wagner, Bizet, Tchaikovsky, Prokoviev, Britten, Glodeanu etc. Publs: The Dialogue of Arts, 1969; (transl.) The Magic Flute. Contbr. to num. profl. jrnls. & magazines. Mbrships: Union of Musicologists & Comps. of Romania; SACEM, Paris. Hons: State Prize, 1954; Work Order, 1954; Order for Cultural Merit, 1969. Hobbies: Books; Cycling. Address: str. Rakoczı 11 ap. 1/A, 3400 Cluj-Napoca, Romania.

BALES, Dorothy Johnson, b. Ketchikan, Alaska, USA. Violinist; Professor; Writer. Educ: MMus, Boston Univ.; BMus, New England Conserv.; BA, Univ. Ore. m. Prof. Robert F. Bales. Debut: Jordan Hall, Boston, 1948. Carnegie Recital Hall, NY, 1961; Salle Chopin Pleyel, Paris, 1952; Brahmssaal, Vienna, 1972. Career incls: Soloist with Boston Pops; Orch. de l'Althenée, Geneva; Soloist, Mass. bi-centennial concert, Kennedy Center, Washington, DC, 1975; soloist, Nat. Gallery of Art, Washington, DC, 1978; Concert tours, Arts Prog. of Assn. of Am. Colls., 1964-68; radio and TV apps.; Asst. Prof. of Music, Emmanuel Coll., Boston, 1969-74; Lectr. in Music, ibid, 1974-; Visiting Prof., Univ. of Mass., Amherst, 1978. Publs: Rounds on Records, 1960. Contbr. to: Music Educators Jrnl.; Am. String Tchr. Mbr. Num. profl. orgs. Recip. num. hons. Hobbies: Chmbr. Music; Sports; Reading. Address: 61 Scotch Pine Rd., Weston, MA 023193, USA. 5, 27.

BALISSAT, Jean, b. 15 May 1936, Lausanne, Switzerland. Composer; Conductor. Educ: Lausanne & Geneva Conserv. m. Annette Moret, 1 s., 1 d. Career: Music Critic, Lausanne Gazetta, 1957-60; Cond., Comp., Prof. of Comp. & Orchestration, Fribourg Conserv., 1972-. Comps. incl: Symphonie, 1959; Sinfonietta, for string orch., 1960; Variations concert for 3 percussions & orch., 1969; Concertino, for percussion & orch., 1972; Les Gursks, symphonic poem for harmony or brass band, 1973; Fête des Vignerons, 1977 for 2 chorus orch., 2 harmonies & 2 brass bands, 1974-76. Mbrships: incl. Assn. of Swiss Musicians. Hobby: Model railways. Address: 1099 Corcelles-le-Jorat, Switzerland. 19.

BALKE, Jon Georg, b. 7 June, 1955, Ottestad, Norway. Pianist; Composer. Educ: Pvte. studies w. var. tchrs. Debut: Club 7, Oslo, 1973. Career: Sev. Scandinavian TV & radio shows; num. European Jass Fests.; Jass-Jamboree, Warsaw, 1974; The Jass Yatra, Bombay, 1978; Cascais Jazz Fest., 1975. Num. comps. Recordings: Clouds in my Head, w. Arild Anderson Quartet, 1974; Hifly, w. Karin Krob & Archie Shepp, 1977; Num. Norwegian recordings. Hobbies: Sealife; Woodcrafts. Address: Hans N Hanges 91-23, Oslo 4, Norway.

BALKWILL, Bryan Havell, b. 2 July 1922, London, UK. Conductor. Educ: FRAM. m. Susan Elizabeth Roberts, 1 s., 1 d. Career: Assoc. Cond., Glyndebourne, 1953-59; Res. Cond., Royal Opera House, Convent Garden, 1959-65; Musical Dir., Sadler's Wells, 1966-69; TV Operas; BBC Radio Concerts; Concerts & Opera all over the British Isles & in France, Germany, Belgium, Sweden, Portugal, Russia, Bulgaria, South

Africa, Canda, etc; Prof. of Music, Ind. univ., 1977-. Recordings: Operatic Recital w. Sir Geraint Evans; Sadler's Wells Highlights from Madam Butterfly. Freelance, 1970-Mgmt: Artist Int. Mgmt., 3 & 4 Albert Terr., London NW1 7SU, UK. Address: 8 The Green, Wimbledon Common, London, SW19 5A2, UK.

BALL, Charles H, b. 18 Dec. 1931, Madisonville, Ky., USA. Professor. Educ: BA, BS, Western Ky. Univ.; MMus, Mich. State Univ.; PhD, George Peabody Coll. m. Lois Ann Johnson, 2 s., 1 d. Career: Prof. & Hd., Dept. of Art & Music Educ., Univ. of Tenn., Knoxville. Publs; Musical Structure & Style, 1975. Contbr. to Music Educator's Jrnl. Mbr., MENC (Chmn., Nat. Comm. on Grad. Study in Music Educ.). Hobbies: Photography; Sailing. Address: 210 Sutton Ln., Knoxville, TN 37919, USA. 2, 7.

BALL, Christopher, b. 7 July 1936, Leeds, UK. Conductor. Educ: RAM; GSM; RMCM; ARMCM; ARAM. Career: Asst. Cond., Vancourver Symph. Orch.; Cond., Royal Ballet; Guest Cond., BBC Northern Symph. Orch., BBC Scottish Orch., City of Birmingham Symph. Orch., Ulster Orch.; Cond. Convent Garden; Prof. of Clarinet, RAM, 1961; Dir., Early Music Consort, Warwick Univ. TV Appearances as Solo Clarinettist, Comoposer, Arrange & Accomp.; Woodwind Ensemble Coach, Morley Coll.; Dir., Praetorius Consort. Compositions: Ed., The Praetorius Consort series of early music; var. comps. & arrangements for clarinet & piano. Recordings: The Praetorius Consort; Seamus Crumhorn (pop music played on early instruments) London Baraque Trio; Westminter Harpsichord Trio. Contbr. to: Early Music; Recorder & Music Mag.; The Province (Vancouver). Hons: Hiles Gold Medal; John Solomon Prize; Ricordi Prize; ARAM. Hobby: Photography. Mgmt: Ibbs & Tillett, 124 Wigmore St., London W1. Address: Top Flat, 122 Wigmore St., London W1, UK. 3, 28.

BALL, Clifford Evans, b. 27 June 1899, Birmingham, UK. Teacher & Performer, Carillon, Pianoforte, Organ. Educ: B Mus., Birmingham Univ., 1921; Dip. w. Hons., Nat. Schl. of Carillon Art, Malines, Belgium, 1924. m. Ivy Muriel Reddall, 1 s. Debut: St. Rombout's Cathedral, Malines, 1922. Career: Carollonneur, Bournville Village Trust, & gen. musical work Messrs. Cadbury, Bournville, 1924-65; Regular Carollon & Organ Recitals ibid., 1924-; Num. TV & Radio perfs. w. Carillon; Recitals in Belgium, France, Holland, Scotland & Ireland; Tchr. of Pianoforte, Birmingham Schl. of Music, 1945-64; Tour of 10 States in USA, 1961; Recitals in NZ & Aust.; Cons. for large Carillon presented by Gt. Brit. to Aust. people, Canberra, 1970. Comps: Num. works for Carillon reproduced & played in USA. Recordings: Var. discs made of perfs. by BBC. Mbrships: Past-mbr., Soc. des Amis du Carillon, Belgium. Hons: Prizes, Int. Carillon Compeitions Amsterday, Holland, 1934, Utrecht, Belgium, 1953. Hilversum, Holland, 1959. Hobbies: Golf; Gardening; Walking; Water-Colour Painting. Address: 20 Middle Park Rd., Weoley Hill, Birmingham B29 4NE, UK. 1.

BALLANTINE, Christopher John, b. 30 Aug. 1942, Johannesburg, S Africa. Professor of Music; Head of Department of Music. Educ: BMus Hons. (Wits.); MLitt (Cantab.); DMus (Cape Town). Career: Journalist, The Star, Johannesburg, 1960-61; Music Critic, ibid, 1966; Freelance writer on music, England, 1970-71; Tchr. of Music & English, St. John's Coll., Johannesburg, 1971; Sr. Lectr. in Music, Univ. of Natal, Durban, 1972-73; L G Joel Prof. of Music & Hd., Dept. of Music, ibid, 1974-; Examiner; Vis. Schlr., Columbia Univ., Vis. Schlr. Grad. Centre, City Univ., New York, 1978; Cons. & Supervisory Hd. to the Dept. of Music, Univ. of Zululand, 1979-. Publs: Music and Society - The Forgotten Relationship, 1975; Towards a Theory of the Modern Symphony - an Approach through Symphonic History, 1980. Contbr. to: African Music; New Society; Music Review; Musical Quarterly; Symposium; S African Music Ency. Mbrships: Committee of Hds. of S African Music Depts., 1974-; Natal Perf. Arts Count. (Oper Committee), 1974-; Durban City Con. Ad Hoc Music Committee, 1977-; Coll. Music Soc. (USA), 1978-; Durban Music Fndn., 1979-. Recip., awards, scholarships & bursaries. Hobby: Film-groing. Address: Dept. of Music, Univ. of Natal, Durban 4001, S Africa.

BALLARD, Jeremy Howard Reeves, b. 10 Oct. 1938, Hemel Hempstead, Herts, UK. Violinist. Educ: Pupil of Sascha Lasserson. m. Kay, 3 s., 2 d. Debut: Sept. 1978, London. Career: Fndr. of Arioso Quartet; Spent sev. years in the Royal Marines & played as soloist for the Queen at num. functions; Prin. 2nd violin w. City of Birmingham Symph. Orch; Violin tutor, Birmingham Schl. of Music. Hons: Casel Prize, 1957. Hobbies: Watercolour painting; Chess; Family. Address: 26 St. Agnes Rd., Mosely, Birmingham B13 9PW, UK.

BALLARDIE, Quintin, b. Hoylake, Cheshire, UK. Violist. Educ: RAM. m. 3 children. Career: Prin. Viola. LPO, 1963-71; Prin.

Viola & Artistic Dir.; Eng. Chamber Orch.; Recitals of Chamber Music. Mbr. Musicians Union. Hon: FRAM. Hobby: Sailing. Address: 9 North Side, London, SW4., UK. 3.

BALLENGER, Kenneth Leigh, b. 28 July 1921, Des Moines, Iowa, USA. Professor of Voice; Musical Director. Educ: BA, Hardin Simmons Univ., Abilene, Tex.; BMus, ibid.; MMus. Eastman Schl. of Music, Rochester, NY. m. Inez Ward, 1 s., 1 d. Career incl: USO tour of Germany & Holland, 1964; 5 stage & TV appearances, Mexico City, 1968; NYC Town Hall & Arthur Godfrey Show, then tour of W Europe, 1971; Tour of Germany, Switzerland & Austria, 1974: Community Concert in Vernon, Tex. & US Chmbr. of Comm., Wash. DC, 1975 (all as Dir. of Uarkettes grp.). Recordings: 4 Albums of Uarkette selections. Contbr. to: Am. Music Tchr.; Nat. Opera Assn. Jrnl. Mbr.; MTNA. Hons: 2 Commendations from Ark. Gen. Assembly. Hobbies: Foreign Stamps; Photography; Gardening. Address: 506 Hawthorn, Fayetteville, AR 72701, USA. 7, 125, 139.

BALLIF, Claude André François, b. 22 May 1924, Paris, France. Professor of Analysis. Educ: Conservs. Bordeaux 1942, Paris 1948, Berlin, 1955. m. Elisabeth Geze, 4 c. Debut: Paris 1953, Berlin 1956, Darmstadt 1957. Career: Lectr., French Inst. of Berlin 1955, Hamburg 1957; Prof. of Analysis, »Ecole Normale de Musique, Paris 1963, Conserv. Reims, 1964, Paris, 1971. Comps: Chmbr. music, violin & symph. works. Recordings: 5 records. Publs: Introduction à la Métatohelité, 1956; Berlioz, 1969; Voyage de mon Oreille, 1979. Contbr. to: Revue Musicale, Paris. Mbr., Société des Auteurs et Compositeurs de Musique. Hons: 1st Prize, Comp., Concours Int. Geneva 1955; Honegger Prize, Paris, 1974. Address: 5 rue d'Argont, Paris 75002, France, 19.

BALMER, Hans, b. 6 Jan. 1903, Birrwil, Argovie. Musician (piano & organ). Educ: Dip., 1926; studies w. Robert Casadesus & Nadia Boulanger, Paris. m. Alice von Tscharner, 2 c. Comps: 4 Songs of Love, for baritone & piano; Dreams of a Young Lady, for voice & saxophone quartet. Publs: Sequences, 5th ed., revised & enlarged, 1976; Spiel und Denktechnik für Klavier. Address: unterm Schellenberg 143, 4125 Riehen, Switz.

BALOGH, Endre, b. 28 June 1954, LA, Calif., USA. Concert Violinist. Educ: UCLA; Pvte. studies, Joseph Borisoff Piastro, Manuel Compinsky, (Yehudi Menuhin Schl., London, 1964); Mehli Mehta. Debut: LA, age 15, NY, age 16; London (Wigmore Hall), age 18. Career: Soloist, var. Am. Symphs. incl: LA Phil., Denver Symph., Wash. Nat. Symph. & Seattle Symph.; European tour, 1973; Num. recitals, USA & Europe; apps. w. Berlin Phil, Rotterdam Phil., Frankfurt Symph., Tonhalle Orch. (Zürich), Basel Symph. Contbr. to: LA Times. Hons: Num. scholarships; First Prize & Grand Prize, Denvery Symph. Solo Competition, age 13; Top violin prize, Merriweather Post Contest, age 13. Hobbies: Prof. Hypnotist; Stained glass window making; Oriental carpet collecting. Mgmt: Columbia Artists Mgmt. Inc., NY. Address: 318 N Detroit St., LA, CA 90036, USA.

BALOGH, Olga Mitana, b. 19 Oct. 1917, Budapest, Hungary. Violinist. Educ: Southwestern Coll. of Music; Muzart Conserv. of Music; pvte. studies w. Vlado Kolitsch & Joseph Piastro. m. Feenc Balogh, 1 s. Career: Soloist, tchr., chamber musician; violinist on radio - staff of NBC & CBS; Hollywood Motion Picture Studio recordings; TV, Opera & Symph. Orchs.; mbr., Los Angeles Phil. & Hollywood Bowl Symph. Orchs., 1943-77; concert tours to Asia, Europe, Can. & throughout USA. num. recordsing w. major symph. orchs. & as violinist in film recording orchs. Mbrships: Vp, Hollywood Wilshire Community Concert Assn.; Calif. Strg. Tchrs. Assn. Hobbies: Gourmet Cooking; Prestidigitation (magic); Travelling; Chess; Reading. Address: 316 N Detroit St., Los Angeles, CA 90036, USA.

BALOGHOVÁ, Dagmar, b. 13 Dec. 1929, Ilava, Czech. Pianist; Professor. Educ: Grad., Musical Fac., 1952. 1 s. Debut: Prague, 1952. Career: Concerts in most European Countires, in Turkey & USA, inclng. TV & radio apps.; Prof., Acad. of Fine Arts, Prague. Recordings: Piano concertos by Prokoviev (No. 2), Martinu (No. 1), Shostakovich (No. 1), Bartok (No. 1); works by Liszt, Beethoven etc. Publs: Revision of piano work by Bedrich Smetana. Contbr. to: Hudebni rozhledy; Gramorevue. Hons: Czech Musical Fund prize, 1967; Prize of the Capital, Prague, 1975; Nat. Prize of Czech Nat. Coun., 1976; Meritorious Artist, 1979. Mbrships: Presidium, Assn. of Czech Comps.; VP, Assn. of Czech. Concert Artists; Prague Spring Soc. Hobby: Gardening. Mgmt: Pragoconcert. Address: Nerudova 32, 11800 Prague 1, Czech.

BALSAM, Artur, b. 8 Feb. 1906, Warsaw, Poland. Concert Pianist; Teacher. Educ: Conserv., Lodz, Poland; State Acad. of Music, Berlin. m. Ruth Miller. Debut: Lodz, age 12. Career: Num. concerts, recitals; Soloist w. maj. orchs., inclng. London

Philharmonia, LSO, LPO, Warsaw, BBC Orch., RPO, NBC Orch. & radio orchs. of Warsaw, Berlin, Hilversum, Milan, Vancouver, Munich, etc; Num. chmbr. music concerts w. Menuhin, Milstein, Francescatti, Oistrach, Rostropovitch, others, w. Budapest, Vegh, Koeckert, Kroll string quartets; Tchr., Manhattan Schl. of Music, NY, Eastman Schl. of Music, & Boston Univ. Compositions: Num. cadenzas for Mozart piano concertos, B. Minor Concerto of Paganini. Recordings: Complete piano works of Mozart, Haydn; Complete violin sonatas, cello sonatas, of Beethoven; Complete Hummel sonatas; 12 Mozart concertos; Num. misc. solo & chmbr. works. Publs: Eds. of 4 Mozart concertos, 2 Mozart concertos. Mbship: The Bohemians Club, NYC. Hons: 1st Prize, Piano Competitions, Berlin, 1930, 31. Hobbies: Stamp collecting; Driving. Address: 258 Riverside Dr., NY, NY 10025, USA.

BALSIS, Edwardas Kosto, b. 20 Dec. 1919, Nikolaev, Ukraine. Composer. Educ: Kaunas Conserv. Career: Chmn., Lithuanian Composers Union: Sec. & Exec. Mbr., USSR Composers Union; Asst. Prof., 1960-. Compositions incl: Piano Sonata, 1949; Vilnius (poem for symph. orch.), 1950; Heroic poem (symph. orch.), 1952; String Quartet in G Minor, 1953; 1st Concerto for Violin & Orch., 1954; Dance Suite of Lithuanian Folk Dances for Symph. Orch., 1957; 2nd Concerto for Violin & Orch., 1958; Egle, Queen of the Snakes (ballet), 1960; Cantata for Choir & Symph. Orch., 1961; Film music: The Bridge, Blue Roads, 1957; Adonas Wants to Become a Man, 1959; Living Heores, 1960; The Cannonade, 1961; Old Sailor's Slongs, Going on a Long Sea Voyage, 1964. Hons: Honoured Worker of the Arts of Lithuanian SSR, 1959; People's Artist, ibid., 1965; Order of Banner of Labour, Badge of Hon. Address: Lithuanian Composers Union, 6 Ulitsa Reshitoyu, Vilnius, Lithuanian SSR, USSR.

BALTSA, Agnes, b. Lefkas, Greece. Opera Singer. Educ: Dip. in voice & theatre, Athens Music Acad. m. Gunter Missenhardt. Debut: Cherubino in Marriage of Figaro, Frankfurt, Germany. Career: Mbr., Vienna State Opera & German Opera, Berlin; guest appearances in Houston, Barcelona, Trieste, Amsterdam, Covent Gdn. London; Easter & Summer Festival, Salzburg; La Scala, Milan; Hamburg State Opera, etc. Recordings incl: Missa Solemnis; Ascanio in Alba; Mozart Requiem, etc. Hons: Prize Winner. George Enescu Competition, Roumania, 1964; Maria Callas Stipendium, 1964. Mgmt: Music & Arts SA, Zürich. Address: Tobelhofstr. 2, CH-8044 Zürich, Switzerland.

BAMBER, Dennis, b. 7 Dec. 1947, South Bend, Ind., USA. Performer & Teacher (saxophone). Educ: BMus, MMus, Ind. Univ. m. Virginia Baran. Debut: Wash. DC, 1972. Career: Radio perf. w. Wolftrap Orch., Wash. DC, 1972; Soloist, Midwest Chmbr. Orch., 1976; Owner, The Woodwind (profl. music store). Recordings: Debussy Rapsodie; Charles Koechlin, Études for Saxophone & Piano; Desenclos, Prelude, Cadence & Finale; Pierre Max Dubois, Dix Figures et Danse; Bernhard Heiden, Solo for Alto Saxophone & Piano. Contbr. to: The Schl. Musician; The Saxophone Service. Mbrships: Int. Saxophone Congress. Hons: Bronze Medal, Int. Saxophone Competition, Geneva, Switz., 1972. Hobbies: Racquetball; Swimming. Address: 40733 US 31 North, South Bend, IN 46637, USA.

BAMBERGER, Carl, b. 21 Feb. 1902, Vienna, Austria. Orchestra Conductor. Educ: Univ. of Vienna; Theory, piano, w. Heinrich Schenker, Vienna. m. Lotte Hammerschiag-Bamberger. Career: Opera Cond., German Operhouses, 1924-31; Guest Cond., Russia, France, Estonia, Finland, Egypt, Austria, Czech., USA, S Am., etc.; Musical Dir., Spring Festival, Columbia, SC, USA, 1942-50; Eremitage Chamber Concerts, Montreal, Canada, 1950-52; Fndr., Music Dir., Mannes Coll. Orch., 1938-; Opera Guest Cond., Acad. Vocal Arts, Phila.; Guest Cond., Chgo. Lyric Opera. NYC Opera, Boston Philharmonia, Stuttgart Radio, Germany; Guest cond., Louisiana State Univ. Var. recordings. Author, The Conductor's Art, 1965. Contbr. to: Ency. Am.; Photographic Jrnl., PSA. Hons: Hon DMus, Mannes Coll. of Music, NYC. Hobby: Photography. Address: 171 W 79 St. NY, NY 10024, USA.

BAMBERGER, David, b. 14 Oct. 1940, Albany, NY, USA. Director; Producer. Educ: Yale Univ. Schl. of Drama; Université de Paris; BA, Swarthmore Coll. m. Carola Beral, 1 s. Career: Stage Dir. (Prodr.) for the following: NYC Opera: The Barber of Seville, The Magic Flute, Der Rosenkavalier. Nat. Opera, Santiago, Chile: Rigoletto, Lucia di Lammermoor. Cinn. Summer Opera: Madame Butterfly, Don Pasquale. Pittsburgh Opera: Don Pasquale. Hartford Opera Co: The Flying Dutchman. Oberlin Music Theater, Ohio: Prodr.-Dir. (British terminol: Gen. Mgr.-Prodr.): Don Giovanni, Four Saints in Three Acts, Madame Butterfly, Cosi Fan Tutte, The Gondoliers, Die Fledermaus, Menotti's Tamu-Tamu (first prodn. after its world premiere); Gen. Mgr. & Artistic Dir., Cleveland Opera Co.; directed La Traviata, La Boheme, Daughter of the Regiment, etc., Nonopera prodns. incl. first maj. NY prodn. of Sophocles' Oedipus at Colonus & Am. Nat. Tour for the Nat. Shakespear Co. of Much Ado about Nothing. Contbr. to: Opera News. Recip., H H Powers Travel Award, 1979. Address: 1289 Andrews Ave., Cleveland, OH 44107, USA.

BAMBERGER, Lotte, b. 13 July 1904, Vienna, Austria. Violist. Educ: Grad., Vienna Acad. of Music. m. Carl Bamberger. Debut: w. Kolbe Str. Quartet, Vienna. Career: quartet tours throughout Europe; solo apps., Vienna; ASst. 1st Viola. Israel Symph. Orch.; orch. & chmbr. music apps. in USA; w. Busch Quartet for 1 yr.; currently Tchr., viola & chmbr. music, Mannes Coll. of Music, & free-lance Orchl. Musician. Has recorded w. Marlboro & Bklyn. Phil. Orchs. Hobbies: Sports; Gymnastics. Address: 171 W 79th St., NY, NY 10024, USA.

BAMFORD, Stephanie Catherine, b. 29 Aug. 1946, Maidenhead, UK. Pianist. Educ: BA(Music), Univ. of Liverpool; ARCM (piano perf.), aged 11, youngest ever to obtain this diploma; RAM (recital medal). m. Dr. Charles Vyvyan Howard, 1 d. Debut: Colston Hall, Bristol, 1957. Career: Conert apps. UK and abroad; Radio and TV apps.; Accomp. for Max Rostal's Int. Master Classes in Cologne and Aldeburgh and Sir Peter Pears' Courses for Singers in Aldeburgh, 1973-; Official accomp. for BBC TV's Young Musician of the Year Competition. Mbrships: ISM. Hons: Foundation Scholarship RCM, 1961; Prizewinner, Nat. piano playing competition, 1963; Liszt competition, 1968; French Govt. Scholarship, 1965; Undergraduate scholarship, Univ. of Liverpool, 1970, 1971; Awards, Countess of Munster, Leverhulme and Martin Funds. Hobbies: Ornithol; Collecting cacti; Langs. Address: 38 Beresford Rd., Oxton, Birkenhead L43 1XJ, UK. 4, 27.

BAMPTON, Rose E, b. Cleveland, Ohio, USA. Concert & Opera Singer. Educ: BMus, Curtis Inst. of Music, Phila.; LHD, Drake Univ., DesMoines, Iowa. m. Wilfred Pelletier. Debut: Met. Opera, NYC, 1932. Career: Met. Opera, NYC, 1932-50; Convent Garden, London, UK, 1937; Teatro Colon, Buenos Aires, Argentina, 1945-50; Chgo. Opera; San Fran. Opera; Voice Fac., Manhattan Schl. of Music, 1962; Julliard Schl., 1974-. Recordings: Gurrelieder (Stokowski); Fidelio (Toscanini); Operatic Arias (Wilfrid Pelletier). Hons: LHD Holart & Wm. Smith Colls., Geneva, NY, 1978. Hobbies: Tennis; Riding; Swimming; Collecting Antique Earrings. Address: 322 E 57th St., NY, NY 10022, USA.

BANAN, Gholam-Hossein, b. 1911, Tehran, Iran. Music Teacher; Traditional Folk-Singer. Educ: Course w. traditional folk-singers eg. Seyt & Rassai. m. P Araz, 2 children. Career: Art Cons. in radio: Tchr. in music schl. Comps: approx. 400 comps. recorded w. grps. of profs. of traditional bolk-singing in Iran eg. Khaleghi, Colonel Naziri. Publs: Tchng. records of traditional Iranian music. Contbr. to Radio Folk Magazine. Mbr., National Music Company. Hobbies: Sports; esp. boxing. Address: 64-Av 156, Tehran Pars, Western Tehran, Iran.

BANCROFT, B. Richard, b. 17 Mar. 1936, White Plains, NY, USA. Professor of Music. Educ: BS, SUNY, Fredonia; MS, Univ. Wis.; EdD, NY Univ. m. Hoyce Ann Aldrich, 1 s., 1 d. Career: Prof. Music, Westminster Coll., New Wilmington, Pa; Prof. Music, Lakeland Coll., Sheboygan, Wis. Comps: Sketches; Piano; Soliloquy, Solo Trumpet; Brass Row, Brass Quintet; Epitaphs, for Wind Ensemble; Tangents, for Brass; Canticle, for Peace, for Choir & Winds. Recordings: Black Maskers Suite (arr. Sessions); Autumn from The Seasons (arr. Glazounov). Publs: Contbrng. Ed., Dictionary of Eminent American Educators. Contrbr. to jrnls. Mbrships: CBDNA; MENC; Pres., Pa. Coll. Bandmasters Assn.; Kappa Delta Pi; Phi Mu Alpha Sinfonia; Coll. Music Soc. Recip: 1st prizes, Wis. Comp. Contests. Hobbies: Tennis; Photography; Billiards. Address: 1736 2nd Street, Sheboygan, WI 53081, USA. 6.

BANDA, Edo, b. 6 Apr. 1917, Budapest, Hungary. Violoncellist; Professor at the Academy of Music. Educ: Acad. of Music, Budapest. m. Ida Gádor, 1 s., 2 d. Career: toured throughout Europe giving stage & broadcast performs. as Soloist & as Mbr. of Tatrai Quartet. Mbrships: Assn. of Hungarian Musicians; 'Feszer' Club of Artists. Recip. Kossuth Prize, 1958. Mgmt: Országos Filharmonia, Budapest V. Vörösmarty-tér 1, Hungary. Address: RD No 3 Randall Dr., New Castle PA 16105, USA.

BANGS, Carl Oliver III, b. 20 Feb. 1945, Pasadena, Calif., USA. Conductor; Carillonneur; French Horn Player. Educ: BA, Univ. of Kan., 1966; Royal Carillon Schl., Mechelen, Belgium, 1965; Univ. of Chgo. Divinity Schl., 1967; M Div, Pacific Schl. of Relig., 1969; MA, Univ. of Calif., Santa Barbara, 1974. Career: ASst. Carillonneur, Univ. of Chgo., 1967; Free-lance French Horn Player; Cond., Berkeley Chmbr. Orch. Comps: Leopold's Passacaglia for Carillon; Mimemata. Mbrships: Am.

Fend. of Musicians Local 6; Guild of Carillonneurs in N Am.; Am. Symph. Orch. Conds. Guild. Address: 843 Cornell Ave., Albany, CA 94706, USA.

BANK, Jacques, b. 19 Apr. 1943, Borne, Netherlands. Composer. Educ: Amsterdam Conserv. m. C de Jong, 2 children. Comps. incl: Blind Boy Fuller (recorder, piano and optional voice); Emcee, text by Thomas Nicolaas (choir); Memoirs of a Cyclist (2 recorders); Song of Sitting Bull (recorder and organ); Put Me on My Bike (recorder, baritone and choir); Blue Monk (clavichord); Blue Mosque (bass recorder); Monk's Blues (piano, choir and wind); Little Blue Monkey (organ); Fan It (orch.); Wave (recorder and percussion); Last Post (bass clarinet and piano); Stint (bass clarinet); Thomas, text by Dylan Thomas; Frieze (percussion); Variations on a Theme of Purcell (organ 4 hands); Mesmerised, text by G.M. Hopkins (voice, 3 trumpets, piano, percussion); Alexandre's Concerto (piano and orch.). Mbr. Soc. of Dutch Comps. Recip. Prize for Comp., Amsterdam Conserv., 1974. Address: Kelbergen 69, Amsterdam, Netherlands. 4.

BANKS, Eric, b. 2 Apr. 1932, S Shields, Co. Durham, UK. Conductor; Director of Music. Educ: FLCM; LRAM; LGSM; ARCM. m. Jean Banks, 2 s., 1 d. Dareer: Euphonium Player RAF Ctrl. BAnd, 1949-58; currently Dir. of Music, RAF (current rank of Squadron-ldr.) & Guest Cond. at choral & bass band fests., Adjudicator. Comps: nm. works for brass & mil. band; ch. choral music. Recordings: Invicta Records; EMI; Electrola. Mbrships: MPRS; MCPS. Hons: Silver Medal, Worshipful Co. of Musicians, London, 1967; MBE. Hobbies: Caravanning; Ten Pin Bowling; Squash; Gardening. Address: Hq Music Servs., RAF, Uxbridge, Middx., UB10 0R2, UK.

BANT, George Edward, b. 3 June 1934, Montreal, PQ., Canada. Composer; Arranger; Conductor; Pianist; Organist. Educ: BSc., Sir George Williams Univ., Montreal Can.; BMus, Univ. of Toronto, Can. m. Birte Mortensen, 5 d. Career: Cond., var. TV Apprs., USA; Regular TV Apps., Can. TV Network, CBC TV, NBC TV, USA. Compositions; SEven Come Eleven Theme For Birte; Roses in December; Symph. No. 1 piano & orch.; ballet Blue SA.; film score Petals in The Sun; Sandra; Blues To End All Blues. Recording Eddie Bant At The Seven Eleven (Naturally). Mbr. Royal Can. Coll. of Organists. Hobbies: Philately Chemistry; Sailing. Address: 4121 Bon Homme Rd. Woodland Hills, CA 91364, USA.

BANTER, Harald, b. 16 Mar. 1930, Berlin, Germany. Composer; Conductor; Music Editor; Univ. Teacher. Educ: Studied comp. at Music Schl. m. Ingeborg Hölken, 2 children. Debut: WDR Cologne, 1952, w. own orch. Career: Dir. of Entertainment Music Section, WDR, and Deputy Dir. of Music Dept. Comps: More than 1,000 for Radio, TV, Films and Theatre. Recordings: w. Philips and Electrola. Mbrships: Bd. of Dirs., GEMA and German Comps. League. Hobbies: Music; Nature; Chess. Address: Wieselweg 10, D5000 Cologne 91, German Fed. Repub. 4, 30.

BANTICK, John Howard, b. 22 Dec. 1939, Edgware, Middx., UK. Singer (tenor) & singing teacher; Conductor. Educ: RAM; GRSM; LRAM; ARCM; LTCL. m. Carole Anne Ash. Debut: Wingmore Hall, London, 1972. Career: Hd. of Music, Hatfield Schl., 1962-72; solo oratorio apps.; ad hoc work w. BBC Singers; Chorus Master, Welwyn Garden City Music Soc., 1972-; Dir., Sing through Messiah; Adjudicator; pvte. tchr. of singing, piano, theory & musicianship. Publs: A Handbook on Singing, 1980. Mbrships: Equity; ISM. Hons: Ricordi Opera Prize, RAM, 1971; Van Someren Godfrey Eng. Song Recital Prize, RAM, 1969. Hobbies: Softly (retriever dog); Gardening; DIY. Address: 3 Dancote, Pk. Ln., Knebworth, Herts. SG3 6BP, UK.

BARACH, Daniel Paul, b. 8 Feb. 1931, Weirton, W. Va., USA. Biolist; Professor of Viola. Educ: BM Mich. State Univ., 1953; MM, Univ. of Ill., 1957; Postgrad. study, Eastman Schl. of Music, Univ. of Rochester.; Pvte. study w. William Primrose, Lillians Fuchs, Francis Tursi, others. m. Marilyn Höppe, 2 d. Debut: Radio apps., Music from Interlochen Series. Career: Violist, Aspen Fest. Orch., 1953, 54; Houston Symph., 1954-55; Mpls. Symph., 1957-64; Marlboro Music Fest.; Violist, Musica Viva Ensemble, NEd Fox Chmbr., Players, Pac. Violist, Interlochen Nat. Music Camp; Solo, cmbr. concerts. Minn., var. NY univs.; Prof., Viola, SUNY, Oswego, Sheldon String Trio in Residence, SUNY, Oswego. Recordings w. Musica Viva. Mbrships: Past Mbr., MENC, NY State Music Assn., Am. Str. Tchrs. Assn.; Phi Kappa Phi; Viola Research Sec. of Am.; Viola d'Amore Soc. Hons: Outstanding Student at Mich. State Univ., 1953, Ny State Grant for improvement of undergraduate educ., 1978. Hobby: photography; Travel. Address: 160 W. 4th St. Oswego, NY, NY 13126, USA.

BARATI, George, b. 3 Apr. 1913, Gyor, Hungary. Composer; Conductor. Educ: Grad. Tchrs. & State Artist Dips., Franz Liszt Conserv. of Music, Budapest. m. Ruth Carroll, 1 s (from previous marriage), 2 d. Career incls: Fndr-Cond., Princeton Ensemble & Princeton Choral Union, NJ; Cond., Alexandria, La. Military Sympn., Barati Chmbr. Orch. of San Francisco; Music Dir., Honolulu Syphm., 1950-68. Comps. incl: (orch.) Symph.; Polarization; (chmbr. music) Octeta; Str. Quartets No. 1 & 2. Recordings for var. cos. Contbr. to: Maths & Music; Music Jrnl. Mbrships. incl: MacDowell Colony; Am. Comps. Alliance. Hons. incl: D Mus, Univ. of Hawaii, 1954; Naumberg Award, 1959; Guggenheim Fellowship in comp., 1965. Hobbies incl: Swimming; Ping pong. Address: Villa Montalvo, PO Box 158, Saratoga, CA 95070, USA. 2, 3, 9.

BARBAG-DREXLER, Irena, b. 9 Jan. 1920, Przemysl, Poland. Concert pianist; Piano teacher; Musicologist. Educ: Tchrs. Dip.; Dip., piano perf.; DPhil (musicol.), Univ. of Vienna, 1966. m. Dr. Severin Barbag (dec.). Debut: Aged 7 at Przemysl, Poland. Career: Recitals & perfs. w. orchs. & radio recordings in Austria, Italy, German Red. Repub., Switz., France, Sweden & UK; played in 2 short films, Liszt's Liebestraum & Beethoven's Spring Sonata; lectr. & pianist at Int. Schubert Symposium, Vienna, 1974, & Int. Liszt Symposium, Eisenstadt, 1975; num. radio lectures; Prof. at Acad. of Music & Performing Arts, Vienna. Contbr. to num. profl. publications inclng. Chopin Yearbook, 1970, Beethoven Almanac, 1970, Liszt Studies, 1975 & to educl. jrnls. Mbrships: Ex. Bd., Int. Chopin Soc.; Ex. Committee, IMC; European Liszt Ctr. Hobbies: Performance & Musicology. Address: Rasumofskygasse 16/11, 1030 Vienna, Austria.

BARBER, Samuel, b. 9 Mar. 1910, Pennsylvania, Pa., USA. Composer; Organist. Educ: pvtely. & at Curtis Inst. Career: began appearing as Organist at age 12. Compositions incl. Symphonies Nos. 1 & 2; Adagio for Strings; Essays Nos. 1 & 2 for orch.; Concerto for cello & orch.; Medea (ballet); Sonata in E flat minor for piano; The School for Scandal; Dover Beach; Vanessa (opera); Concerto for violin & orch.; Capricorn Concerto; Knoxville; Summer of 1915; Souvenir; Prayers of Kierkegaard; Die Natale; Piano. Concerto; Andromache's Farewell; Anthony & Cleopatra (opera). Hons. incl: Pulitzer Fellowship; Am. Prize of Rome; Pulitzer Prize for Vanessa, 1958; DMus., Harvard Univ.; Pulitzer Prize, 1963. Mgmt: G Schirmer Inc., 609 Fifth Ave., NYC, NY, USA.

BARBERIS, Mansi, b. 25 March 1899, Iassy, Romania. Composer; Teacher of Singing; Pianist; Violinist. Educ: Music Acad. of Iassy, 1918-22; music studies, Berlin, 1922-23, Paris, 1926-27, Vienna, 1937. m. Georg Placinteanu, 1 s, 1 d. Career incls: Founding Mbr., George Enescu Orch.; Mbr., Moldova Symph. Orch.; Mbr., Femina Str. Quartet of Iassy. Comps. incl: operas, The Princess From Far Away, Sun Set, & Kera Dudura; TV serial, The Mushatins Itinéraire dacique; La charette aux paillasses (opera); 19 vocal symphonic poems, 15 symphonic works; 25 Instrumental chmbr. works; 5 choral pieces; 80 songs for voice & piano. Mbr., Comps. Union. Hons. incl: Sev. comp. prizes; Prize for Cultural Merit, 1969. Address: str. Taras Sevcenko nr. 37 A, Sector 2, Cod 70269 Bucharest, Romania.

BARBIER, Guy, b. 10 June 1924, Namur, Belgiu. Conductor; (Composer). Educ: Studied violin, chamber music, solfège, harmony, hist. of music, Royal Music Conserv., Brussels, 1942; Dip. d'Excellence, Cond., Vienna Music & Arts Acad., 1955, (studied w. Hans Swarowsky). M. Nicole Floris, 2 children. Debut: 1957. Career: Cond., most maj. symph. & Opera Orchs., inclng., Gewandhaus Orch., Leipzig, Israel Phil. Orch., Tokyo Phil., Berlin Symp. Orch., Gayern Opera Orch., München, Montreal Symph. Orch., Belgian Nat. Orch., Colonne & Lamoureux Orchs., Paris, LPO, New Symph. Orch. & philomusica, London, etc.; Permanent Cond., Nat. Belgian Opera, 1968, Lyon Opera, 1967; Num. Int. Concert Tours, inclng., Ballet of 30th century w. Maurice Bejart, (Perf., Sacre du Printemps, Stravinsky), & S. Am., Mexico, Paris, London, Berlin, Rome, Barcelona, Palermo, Munich, Athens, Tel Aviv, Jerusalem, Osaka, Tokyo, etc.; Cond., var. Fests., inclng., Int. Opera Fest., Wexford, 1971; Fndr. & dir., Orch. Mozart de Bruxelles; Currently, Tchr. of conds., Royal Conserv. of Music, Liège, Belgium. Recording: Favourite Overtures of the LPO, (Classics for Pleasure); Concerto d'Aranjuez, w. Philomusica of London. (Music for Pleasure). Hobby: Gardening. Address: 58A Ave. Léopold, 1330 Rixensart, Belgium.

BARBIER, René August Ernest, b. 12 July 1890, Namur, Belgium. Musical Director; Organist; Conductor. Educ: Prix de l'Acad. Belgique; Medal for Organ studies; 2st prize, Royal Conserv., Liège. m. Henriette Baudhuin, 3 s. Career: Tchr., harmony, Royal Conserv., Liège, 1916-; Cond., Nat. Orch., Symph. Orch. (RTB), & var. Chorales. Compositions: Num.

works inclng., Melodies, Sonate violon piano; 2 petites suites pour 2 guitares; 3 mouvements symph., orch. à cordes; Pièce concertante, saxo et piano; Poème, violoncello piano; Messe à 3 voix (2 voix); num. ballets, operettas, concertos, oratorios, cantatas etc. Recordings: Num. on RTB and. w. Decca & Alpha labels. Mbrships: Vp, SABAM; Acad. Royal des sciences des lettres et des beaux Arts de Belgique; Soc. Order of Leopold. Hons: Chevalier et Officier des Odres nat. de la Couronne et Grand Officer Ordre de Leopold. Off., Acad. de France; Civic Cross (1st class). Hobby: Painting. Address: Résidence Pacific, 14 Rue Willems App 24 c 03, 1040 Brussels, Belgium.

BARBIERI, Fedora, b. 4 June 1919, Trieste, Italy. Operatic Mezzo-soprano. Educ: studies w. Luigi Toffolo, Maestro Bugamelli. m. Luigi Barlozzetti, 2 s. Debuts: Ch. of San Giusto, Trieste: Teatro Comunale, Florence, 1940. Career: Royal Theatre, Rome, 1941-42; La Scala, 1942; Teatro Verdi, Florence, 1945; Uk tour w. La Scala Co., 1950; Mbr., Metrop. Opera Co., NYC, 1950-. Address: c/o Metrop. Opera Co., Lincoln Ctr. Plaza, NY, NY 100232, USA. 2.

BARBINI, Ernesto, b. 15 July 1911, Venice, Italy. Conductor; Pianist; Organist; Operatic Coach; Composer. Educ: Conserv. of Music, Venice; Conserv. of Music, Padua; Masters degree in piano & organ; Dr., comps. & cond. Career: organ & piano concerts in Italy; cond., symph. concerts in Venice & opera in sev. Italian cities; operatic coach & cond., Chgo., 1938; staff mbr. & cond., Metropolitan Opera Co., NY, 1945; staff mbr., opera dept., Univ. of Toronto & cond., Can. Opera Co., 1053; perf. at Rome Opera House, La Scala, Naples, Brussels, Paris, etc.; now Musical Dir., Royal Conserv. Opera Schl., Toronto, & ldng. cond., Musical advsr., Can. Opera Co.; num. apps. on radio & TV. Hons: Gold medal, Conserv. of Padua; Kt. Off., Order of Merit (Italy); Kt. Commander, ibid. Address: 467 Briar Hill Ave., Toronto, Ont. M5N 1M8, Can.

BARBIROLLI, (Lady) Evelyn, b. 24 Jan. 1911, Wallingford, Rerks., UK. Oboe Player. Educ: RCM, London; Hon. RAM; Hon. FTCL; HOn. MA (Leeds); Hon. RNCM. m. Sir John Barbirolli (dec.). Career: Solo oboe w. Covent Garden Touring Co., 1931-32, SNO, 1933-37, Glyndebourne Fest. Orch., 1934-38, & LSO, 1935-39; 1st perf., re-discovered Mozart Oboe Concerto, Salzburg, Austria, 1948; Prof., RAM. Comps: var. arrs. & ed. Recordings incl: Concertos Corelli-Barbirolli & Marcello; Recital for Oboe & Harpsichord w. Valda Aveling. Publs: Orchestral Studies and Bach Studies, 1952; Oboe Technique, 1957; The Oboist's Companion, 3 vols., 1977. Contbr. to: Jrnl. of Int. Double Reed Soc., etc. Mbrships: ISM (Pres., 1980). Hobbies: Collecting 18th century glass, Photography. Mgmt: Ibbs & Tillett, 450-452 Edgware Rd., London, W2, UK. Address: 28 Ivor Pl., London NW1 6DA, UK. 3, 27.

BARBLAN-OPIENSKA, Lydia, b. 12 Apr. 1890, Morges, Switz. Singer. Educ: Freiburg in Breisgau. m. Henryk Opienski, Debut: w. Albert Schweizer, 1910. Career: Singer & Voice Tchr.; Co-fndr., Motet and Madrigal. Comps: Songs. Publs: var. articles on Paderewski & on singing. Mbrships: Assn. des Musiciens Suisses; mbr. d'Honneur, Swiss Soc. of Musical tchrs. Hons: Polish Gold Cross of Merit; Officer of Acad., France; Bourgeoise d'Honneur de la Ville de Morges. Address: 100 Grand-Rue, 1110 Morges, Switz.

BARBOSA-LIMA, Carlos, b. 17 Dec. 1944, Säo Paulo, Brazil. Guitarist. Educ: Benedito Moreira, Isaias Savio, Brazil; Andres Segovia, Spain; Abel Carlevaro, Montevideo, Uruguay. Debut: Säo Paulo, 1957. Career: Extensive tours of N Am.; Tours in S Am., England, France & Sweden; Master Classes, Hartford, Conn., USA, 1973-74; Artist-in-res. & Prof., Carnegie-Mellon Inst. Recordings incl: Scarletti Guitar Recital, 1971. Hons Mbr., Wash. Guitar Soc., DC. Author of num. transcriptions Contbr. to Guitar Review. Hons. incl: Premio Señora Andrews Segovia, Premio Santiago Vásquez, & Premio del Inst. Cultura Hispánica de Madrid, int. Guitar Contest, Orense, Spain, 1968. Hobbies incl: Soccer. Mgmt: Shaw Concerts Inc. Address: 1995 Bdwy., NY, NY 10023, USA.

BARBOTEU, Georges-Yves, b. 1 Apr. 1924, Algiers, Algeria. Professor; Solo French Horn Player. Educ: Nat. Higher Conserv. of Music, Paris; Algiers Conserv. m. Gilda Escolin, 1 s., 1 d. Career incls: French Horn Solo, Paris Orch., 1970-76; Prof., Nat. Higher Conserv. of Music, ibid., 1970-. Comps. incl: (for horn) Classic Studies; 4 Duets; 4 Quartets; Limits, experimental piece for horn & orch.; (for other instruments), Astral, for brass quintet & metronome; Divertissement, for tuba & brass quartet. Recordings incl: Hindemith: Concerto for horn & orch.; Mouret: Double Concerto; Fanfares from 6 Centuries; Carl Maria Von Weber: Concertino in E. Mbr. Int. Horn Soc. Recip. var. hons. Hobbies: Comp.; Cooking. Mgmt: Annie Devalmalete. Address: 18 Rue Guersant, Paris 75017, France.

BARBU, Filaret, b. 16 Apr. 1903, Lugoj, Romania. Composer; Conductor; Professor. Educ: Grad., New Conserv., Vienna, Austria. m. Lucia Jurma, 1 s., 1 d. Career: Cond., Ion Vidu choir at Lugoj, 1926-39; Prof., Special Music Schl., Bucharest, 1946-63. Comps: Operettas; Choral Music; Symph. Poems; Ballet music; Orchl. music; Oratorio; film music. Recordings: arias & chorus from own comp., operetta, Ana Lugojana. Publs: Traian Grozavescu, monograph, 1935; Portative of Banat, 1942. Contbr. to: Muzica; Armonia; Luceafarul; Rasunetul etc. Mbrships: Union of Romanian Comps. Hons: 3rd prize, Ion Vidu comps. competition; State prize of Romanian Socialist Republic, 1952; Order of Cultural Merit, 1969. Address: Str. Pescarilor 8, 1900 Timisoara, Romania.

BARD, Ysabelle, b. 13 Sept. 1889, Villars sours Yens, above Morges, Switzeland. Singer; Elocutionist. Educ: Geneva Conserv.; Coll. of Educ., Paris, Brussels. Debut: 1919. Career: Soloist, Paris Symph. Orch., Ribaupierre Orch.; Tchr., Chatelard Schl., Les Avants, St. George's Schl., Carens, etc. Mbrships: Assn. of Swiss Musicians; Swiss Soc. of Music Tchrs. Recip. Prize, Geneva Conserv., 1914. Hobbies: Travel; Nature. Address: 5b ave. Belmont, 1820 Montreux, Switzerland.

BARDOSSI, Elizabeth Jane, b. 24 Mar. 1956, Niskayuna, NY, USA. Violist. Educ: Univ. of Ore. Career: tour as Mbr., LI Youth Orch., 2 yrs., w. broadcasts in Denmark, Norway, NZ & Aust.; Violist, Eugene Symph., Ore.; Prin. Violist, All-Country Fest., 1970, LI String Fest., 1970, 72. Hobbies: Sewing; Belly Dancing; Acting; Reading; Fashion & Stage Design. Address: 27 Tappen Dr., Huntington Stn., NY 11746, USA.

BARDWELL, William (Bradley), b. 26 Aug. 1915, Kingston-on-Thames, UK. Composer. Educ: ARCM; studied Theory & Comp. w. R O Morris, RCM, 1934-37; studied Piano w. Solomon, 1934-37; studied Comp. w. Nadia Boulanger, Paris, France, 1937-39. m. Begoña López-Berasategui. Career: Comp. in London & Spain (1969-); Music for BBC Radio & TV plays; Cond. of own works. Compositions incl: Symph. No. 1 (BBC 1971); Symph. No. 2; Nocturne for Violin & String Orch.; Harpsichord Concerto (BBC 1973); Hymn to St. John the Baptist; Sonata for Tuba & Piano (BBC 1972); Judecca; Chamber Oratorio; Three Chinese Cantatas (BBC 1955); Dardi d'Amore (for a cappella choir) (BBC 1969); Serranillas: Song Cycle (BBC 1967, 1969); Antiphony, Double Wind Quintet (BBC 1973); String Quartet No. 1 (BBC 1963); String Quartet No. 2 (BBC 1978); Canzona I (for guitar); Fantasia for Flute, Viola & Harp. Mbrships: Composers' Guild of GB. Hobbies: Barrelling & Bottling the Best Local Wines. Address: Lista de Correos, Aspe (Alicante), Spain. 3.

BARELA, Margaret Mary, b. 19 Oct. 1946, Albuquerque, NM, USA. Pianist; Chamber Player; Accompanist; Former Violinist & Organist. Educ: BM, Univ. of NM, 1968; MMus, 1970, & DM, 1976, Ind. Univ. Career: Num. solo & accompanying recitals, Albuquerque, Bloomington, Sioux City, Lubbock, 8 yrs; 6 solo apps. w. var. Albuquerque orchs.; Soloist, Sioux City Symph, 1975; Vis. Asst. Prof. of Piano & Piano Lit., Tex. Tech. Univ., Lubbock; Former Organist, Immaculate Conception Cath. Ch., Albuquerque, 7 yrs.; Former Violinist w. orchl. experience in Albuquerque, 9 yrs. Mbrships: Pi Kappa Lambda; Mortar Bd. Hons. incl: Outstanding Freshman, Pi Kappa Lambda, Univ. of NM. Hobbies: Sewing; Cooking. Address: 3102 4th St. Apt. 117 , Lubbock, TX, USA.

BARENBOIM, Daniel, b. 15 Nov. 1942, Buenos Aires, Argentina (now Israeli citizen). Concert Pianist; Condcutor. Educ: piano & music study w. Prof. Enrique Barenboim (father), Nadia Boulanger, Edwin Fischer & Igor Marketvitch. m. Jackqueline du Pre, 1967. Debut: Buenos Aires, age 7; Career incl: Perf. of Bach Concerto, Salzburg Mozarteum, age 9; regular concert perfs., Europe, 1954-; annual tours of USA, 1957-; other tours of Japan, Australis & S. Am.; cond. or soloist w. New Philharmonica Orch., LSO, NY Phil.; Phila. Orch., Israel Phil., Vienna Phil., Berlin Phil., etc.; Frequent tours w Engl. Chmbr. Orch.; Appeared in Series of Master Classes on BBC-TV, London; Presented Festival of Summer Music, S. Bank, London, 1968-69; Leading role in Brighton Festival, 1967-; regular perfs. at Edinburgh Festival. Recordings incl: complete Mozart piano concertos & late symphs., w. Engl. Chmbr. Orch. complete Beethoven Sonatas & Concertos, w. New Philharmonia Orch., under Klemperer. Address: c/o Hardol Holt Ltd., 122 Wigmore St., London WI, UK.

BARFORD, Philip Trevelyan, b. 23 Nov. 1925, Leeds, UK. Senior Lecturer in Music. Educ: BMus, 1949; MA (PHilos.), 1950, Univ. of Leeds. m. Gwynneth Elizabeth Morgan, 2 s. Career incl: Sr. Lectrt. in Music, Inst. of Extension Studies, Univ. of Liverpool. Publs: The Keyboard Music of C P E Bach, 1965; Mahler - Symphonies and Songs, 1970; Brucknew -Symphonies, 1978. Contbr. to: Music and Letters; Music

Review; Musica; Monthly Musical Record, etc. Mbr., Royal Musical Assn. Hobbies: Mountain Walking. Address: Gwynfyd, Fron Deg, Pantymwyn, Mold, Clwyd, UK.

BARKER, Noelle, b. 28 Dec. 1928, Aberdeen, Scotland, UK. Soprano. Educ: MA, Aberdeen Univ., 1948; Dartington Hall; Amsterdam Conservatory; Munich Acad.; studied w. Hans Hotter. m. Christopher Peake, 3 children. Debut: Royal Fest. Hall, London. Career: oratorio, lieder & contemp. music w. Indng. choral socs. & ensembles; apps. at 3 Choirs & other fests.; sang w. Engl. Opera Grp., London Sinfonietta, Dreamtiger ensemble; broadcasts on BBC & European stns.; Hd., Singer Dept., GSM, London, 1977-. Recordings: complete solo vocal works of Messiaen, Argo; jazz songs, Jupiter Records. Publd: Co-Ed., Pathodia Sacra e Profana, Constantijn Huygens. Mbrships: ISM; Committee, Pk. Kane Grp. Hons: FGSM, 1974. Hobbies: Chamber Music; Skiing; Tennis; Breadmaking; Dressmaking; Swimming. Address: 2 Cannon Pl., London NW3 IEJ, UK. 3.

BARKER, Philip Stanley, b. 21 May 1913, Earl Shilton, Leics., UK. Banjoist. Educ: Pvte. study w. Dr. Ben Burrows; LMusTCL. m. Gladys Margaret Cox. Career: Mbr.; Troise & Banjoliers, 1948-49; Variety Artiste, 1946-50, Concert Artiste, 1950-; Solo broadcasts, BBC, BFN Hamburg, Radio Can.; 1931-; Music Dir., Church Stretton Arts fest. Compositions incl: Jackpot, Tickled Pink, Etude in F., Idyll, Andante in C (banjo solos); Allergro in D (guitar solo); Caprice No. 1, Gavotte (mandolin solos). Contbr. to Fretwire mag. Mbrships: Adjudicator, Brit. Fedn. of Banjoists, Mandolinists & Guitarists; Civil Serv. Club. Hobbies: Sketching; Chess; Crosswords; Country mansions; Sports. Address: Ardencroft, Sandford Ave., Church Stretton, Salop, UK. 3.

BARKIN, Elaine Radoff, b. 15 Dec. 1932, NYC, USA. Composer; Educator. Educ: BA, Queens Coll., 1954; MFA, 1956, PhD, 1970, Brandeis Univ.; Cert., Comp. & Piano, Berlin Hochschule for Musik, 1957. m. George Jean Barkin, 3 s. Career: Tchr., Univ. of Mich., 1970-74; Princeton Univ., 1974, UCLA, 1974- (currently Prof., comp./theory(; Co-Ed., Perspectives of New Music, 1963-. Comps: String Quartet; Six Piano Pieces; Plus ca change (str. & percussion); PRIM Cycles (flute, clarinet, violin, cello); Sound Play (violin); Mixed Modes (clarinet, violin, viola, cello, piano); Inward & Outward Bound (14 players); Two Dickinson Choruses; Ebb Tide (2 vibrophones); String Trio; For Suite's Sake, for harpsichord. Recordings: String Quartet (CRI). Contbr. to jrnls. Mbrships: Am. Soc. Univ. Comps., Am. Comps. Alliance; Int. Soc. Contemp. Music. Recip. var. hons. Address: 12533 Killion St., N Hollywood, CA 91607, USA, 5.

BAR-LEV, Assaf, b. 5 June 1936, Faifa, Israel. Music Educator; Bassoonist; Pianist. Educ: Emerson Coll.; Studied Piano w. Verdina Shlonsky; Bassoon w. Mordechai Rechtmann; Israel Initiation Musicale, Methode E Willems. m. Marquerite Bar-lev, 3 children. Career: Perfs. w. Israeli Phil. Orch., 1957-62; Lausanne Chmbr. Orch., 1962. Recordings incl: Haydn Operas conducted by A Dorati; Bach B Minor Mass. Mbrships: Unon Suisse des Artistes Musiciens; Brit. Musicians Union. Recip. Medal in Int. Competition, Geneva, 1961. Hobbies: Gardening; Swimming; Outings & Music-making w. family; Philosophy; Education. Address: Chalet Clairval, 8 Ave. Guillemin, CH-1009, Pully, Lausanne, Switzerland.

BARLOW, Jeremy, b. 25 July 1939, London, UK. Flautist; Recorder Player; Harpsichordist; Composer; Editor; Musical Director. Educ: RCM, 1957-58; Trinity Coll., Cambridge, 1958-61; RAM, 1961-63. m. Jane Hollowood, 3 s., 1 d. Career: Flautist, Nat. Symph. Orch. of Iceland, 1963-64; Royal Shakespeare Co., 1965-; Nat. Theatre Co., 1969-73; Dir. of Music, Sheffield Crucible Theatre, 1971-74; Music Prod., Gramophone Dept., BBC Radio, 1966-71; Mbr., Martin Best Consort, 1972-; Dir., Barlow Baroque Playes, 1975-; Dir., The Broadside Band, 1979-. Recordings w. Martin Best Consort & Martin Best. Publs: Ed., Holcombe, 3 Airs for Flute; Roseingrave, Flute Sonata No. 2 in D; Weldeman, Sonatas for Flute; Hebden, Flute Sonata No. 1 in D, etc. Cntbr. to profl. jrnls. Mbrships: PRS; Mechanical Copyright Protection Soc.; Royal Musical Assn; Savile Club. Hons: Augustus Manns prize for conducting, RAM, 1961. Hobby: Psychology. Address: Meadow Lodge, Binsted, ARundel, Sussex, UK.

BARLOW, Stephen William, b. 30 June 1954, Seven Kings, Essex, UK. Conductor; Keyboard Player; Percussionist; Counter-tenor. Educ: BA, Trinity Coll., Cambridge, 1975; FRCO. Career: Prin. Timpanist, Nat. Youth Orch., 1971-73; Cond., Cambridge Univ. Bach Soc., Cambridge Univ. Chmbr. Orch. & Cambridge Univ. Chmbr. Choir, 1974-75; Cond., Southern Sinfonia, 1975-; Dir., New London Chmbr. Grp., 1976-; Asst. Organist to Martindale Sidwell, Hampstead Parish

Ch. & St. Clement Danes, 1975-76. Address: 31 Chichester Dr., Chelmsford, Essex CM1 5RY, UK.

BARNDORFF, Bjarne, b. 7 Oct. 1941, Kobenhavn, Denmark. Organist; Kantor. m. Birgit, 1 s., 1 d. Career: Radio Programmer (Accordion). Mbrships: Dansk Organist Og Kantorsamfund (DOKS); Dansk Musikpaedagogisk Forening; Dansk Musikerforbund. Hons: Danish Champion (Accordion), 1963. Mgmt: Mariendal Kirke, Kolh. Address: Stenmaglevej 141, 2700 Bronshoi-Kobenhavn, Denmark.

BARNES, John, b. 17 Oct. 1904, Leslie, Fife, Scotland, UK. Musician (Double Bass, Guitar, Tenor Banjo, Trombone). Educ: var. instrumental & sight reading tchrs.; also studied arrs. div. Career: trombonist, Army Service Corps.; tchr. of strings, Mark Winn Schl. of Music. num. recordings w. var. groups. mbr. Toronto Musicians Assn. Hobbies: Photography; Hunting; Fishing. Address: Box 44, Keene, Ont., Can.

BARNES, Richard, b. 26 Mar. 1947, Croydon, UK. Director of Music; Publisher; Conductor; Baritone; Keyboard Player. Educ: chorister, Westminster Abbey, 1956-61; choral scholar, King's Coll., Cambridge; BA, 1968; MA, 1973; ARCO, 1965; ARCO (CHM), 1972. m. Diana Hosken. Career: Dir. of Music, Dorchester Abbey, 1979-; Dir., Renaissance Singers, 1977-; Dir. of Cathedral Music (publishing firm); cond., Hill Singers, Wimbledon, 1971-77, Epsom Chbr. Choir, 1976-80; Organist, Holy Trinity; Brompton, 1973-79; Dir. of Music, N E Surrey Coll. of Technology, 1973-79. Recordings: w. King's Coll. Choir, Cambridge, & Guildford Cathedral Choir. Publs: num. eds. of ch. music. Contbr. to record sleeves. mbr., ISM. Hons: John Brook Prize, 1972; John Steward of Rannoch Scholar in sacred music, 1968. Hobbies: Travel; Coins; Cricket. Address: 8 Manor Farm Rd., Dorchester-on-Thames, Oxon. OX9 8HZ, UK.

BAROLSKY, Michael, b. 19 July 1947, Wilna, Lithuania, USSR. Composer; Pianist; Teacher of Harmony Analysis & Electronic Music. Educ: Music Acad. of Wilna, Pvte. studies in Moscow; Courses of Contemporary Music, Darmstadt & Switz. m. Shulamit Berliner. Debut. Moscow, 1966. Career: Tchr., Ed. of Music Progs. on radio; Performer in live electronic concerts. Comps: incl: Recitative & Melody (piano, flute & violoncello), 1966; Exodus (orch.), 1969; Photogenesis I (Brass quintet & percussion), 1973; Notturno (piano & tape), 1974; Chries & Whispers (orch. & tape), 1975; Blue Eye, Brown Eye (opera), 1975. Mbr., League of Israeli Comps. Hobby: Painting. Address: 8 Modigliani Str., Tel-Aviv, Israel.

BARON, Carol Kitzes, b. 29 June 1934, NY, USA. Pianist; Musicologist. Educ: BA, Queen's Coll., 1957; Yale Univ. Grad Schl., 1957-58; Master's Degree, Queen's Coll., 1977; MPhil. Grad. Ctr., CUNY, 1979. m. Samuel Baron, 1 d., 2 s. Career: apps. as accomp. & in chamber music w. leading performers throughout USA & Can.; WXQR. sev. recordings. Publs: Ed., Pieces for Young Pianists, by Alec Wilder, Vol. 1, 1969, Vol. 2, 1970; Ed.; Symphonie, La Tempete et la Calme by Louis Massoneau, 1979. Contbr. to: Current Musicology; Centerpoint. Hons: Phi Beta Kappa, 1956; fellowships & scholarship. Mbrships: Am. Musicol. Soc.; Int. Musicol. Soc.; Sonneck Soc. Hobbies: Reading; Sailing; Travelling. Address: 321 Melbourne Rd., Great Neck, NY, NY 11021, USA.

BARON, John Herschel, b. 7 May 1936, Milwaukee, Wis., USA. Musicologist; Teacher; Violinist; Conductor; Critic. Educ: Ba, Harvard Coll., 1958; MA, ibid., 1959; Tanglewood, Berkshire Music Ctr., 1958-59; studied violin w. Bernice S. Baron, Ruth Posselt, Charlotte Chambers & Alexander Schneider; PhD., Brandeis Univ., 1967. m. Doris Ann Solomon, 1 d. Career: Instructor, Boston Univ., 1964-65; Asst. Prof., UCLA, 1967-68, Univ. of Calif., Davis, 1968-69 & Tulane Univ., 1969-; Fndr. & Cond., Tulane Chmbr. Orch., 1970-75. Comps. have been perf. at pub. concerts. Publ: Ballet des Fées de la Foret de St. Germain (monograph). Mbrships: Regional Off., Am. Musicol. Soc.; Int. Musicol. Soc.; Am. Music Lib. Assn.; Am. Soc. for Ethnomusicol.; Coll. Music Soc.; Spanish Musicol. Soc.; Sonneck Soc. Contr. to: JAMS, ACTA, Muskal Quarterly, etc. Alex. von Humholdt Fndn., fellowships, 1965-66, 1976; Nat. Endowment for the Huamnities, 1972, Am. Coun. of Learned Socs., Fellowships, 1975-76. Hobby: Philately. Address: Music Dept., Newcomb Coll., Tulane Univ., New Orleans, LA 70118, USA.

BARON, Samuel, b. 27 Apr. 1925, Brooklyn, NY, USA. Flautist; Conductor; Teacher. Educ: Brooklyn Coll.; BS, Juilliard Schl. of Music, 1948. m. Carol Kitzes, 1 s., 1 d. Career: Apps. w. NYC Symph.; NYC Opera; Minneapolis Symph.; NY Chmbr. Soloists; Contemporary Chmbr. Ensemble; Bacharia Grp.; 1946-; Concerts, recordings & int. tours w. NY Woodwind Quintet, 1949-69; Prof. of Music, SUNY, Stony Brook; Tchr. of

Flute, Juillard Schl. of Music. Comps: Transcription of Art of Fugue byBach for Chmbr. Music Perf. (recorded). Num. recordings. Publs. incl: Bach Sonatas in A maj. & minor. Mbrships: Coll. Music Soc.; VP, Nat. Flute Assn. Hons. incl: Order of Monisaraphon, Cambodia, 1962. Hobby: Chess. Mgmt: Sheldon Soffer. Address: 321 Melbourne Rd., Gt Neck, NY 11021, USA. 2.

BARR, Raymond Arthur, b. 1 Jan. 1932, Pittsburgh, Pa., USA. Musicologist. Educ: BS, Pa. State Univ., 1953; MS, Univ. Wis., 1961; PhD, ibid., 1968; Carnegie Inst. of Technology; Freie Universitat, W Berlin, Germany. Career: Music Fac., NYS Univ., Geneseo, NY, 1968-71; Music Fac., Univ. Miami, Coral Gables, Fla., 1971-; Publs: Num. articles in 6th Ed. Groves Dictionary of Music & Musicians. Mbrships: Exec. Bd., Sec., Treas., Southern Chapt., Am. Musicological Soc.; Coll. Musc Soc.; Fac. Advsr., Phi Mu Alpha; Music Educators Nat. Conf. Pres. Southern Chapter Am. Musicol. Soc. Hons: Dankstipendium, German Academic Exchange, Berlin, 1962-64; Rsch. Grant, SUNY, 1970. Hobbies: Swimming; Skiing; Tennis; Chess. Address: 5840 SW 57 Ave., Miami, FL 33143, USA.

BARR, Robin Noel, b. 24 Dec. 1940, Glasgow, UK. Lecturer; Concert Agent; Violinist. Educ: Univ. of Glasgow, 1959-65; MA; BMus; Royal Scottish Acad. of Music; ATCL. Career: Lectr., RSAMD, 1965-; Extramural Lectr., Univ. of Glasgow; Concert Agent; Dir., Pro Arte Concert Mgmt. Contbr. to: ISM Jrnl.; local newpapers. Mbrships: ISM; Chmn., Kilmardinny Music Circle; Pres., Glasgow Music Soc. Hobbies: Mountain goat spotting. Address: Auchenreoch, Main St., Gartocharn, G83 8RT, UK. 3.

BARRATT, Carol Ann, b. 16 Feb. 1945, Derbyshire, UK. Composer; Teacher; Pianist. Educ: RCM; ARCM (piano tchng.); GRSM. m. Karl Jenkins. Career: writing songs w. husband; TV jingles; comps. perf. in concert hall & on radio. Comps: Song cycle & chmbr. works. Recordings: var. songs. Publs: 1977-79 Chester's Piano Books, Nos. 1-5; Chesters Concert Pieces, Books 1 & 2; A Feast of Easy Carols. Contbr. to: Composer; Music Tchr. Mbrships: ISM; Iptec. recip., Martin Musical Scholarship for Comp., 1967. Hobbies: Words; Walking; Animals; Cooking. Address: Flat 3, Melina Ct., Gipsy Lane, Putney, London SW15, UK.

BARRATT, Clifford, b. Salisbury, UK. Conductor; Organist; Adjudicator; Composer. Educ: LRAM; Univ. of London; Cambrdige Inst. of Educ.; studied w. Sir Walter Alcock, J A Sowerbuts & Leff Pouishnoff; BA; GRSM; LCL; ARCM; FRSA. Career incl: Sub-Prof., RAM, 1951; Piano Accomp., Children's Hour, 1952-54; Music Off. Dpty., BBC, RPO, Philharmonia, 1952-58; 6th Form Master, S Hackney Schl., 1963-64; Lectr., Hackney Coll. of Further Educ., 1964-66; Music Advisor & Artistic Dir., Gateshead MBC, 1966-; Cond., Newcastle-upon-Tyne Operatic Soc. Comps. incl: light operas (Something for Nothing, A Christmas Carol, etc.); Marche Francaise for orch.; Arrs. for brass band of Dvorak's Symphs. contbr. to articles in var. jrnls. MbrshipsL Liszt Soc.; Royal Soc. of Arts. Hons. incl: Bronze medal, Vienna Mozart Fest., 1964. Hobbies: Mozart; Liszt; Clocks; Opera; Squash. Address: Hillcrest, West Park Rd., Gateshead NE8 45P, Tyne and Wear, UK. 2, 23, 28, 29, 30.

BARRAUD, Henry, b. 23 Apr. 1900, Bordeaux, France. Composer. m. Denise Parly, 3 children. Career: Former Musical Dir. & Dir., Nat. Prog., French Radio, 1944-65. Compositions incl: Three Symphs.; Four Operas; Three Concertos for Piano, Flute & Trumpet; Two Rhapsodies for Orch.; Oratorio, Le Mystère des Saints Innocents; Cantatas; Te Deum (Orch. & Choir), Pange Lingua (Orch. & Choir), La Divine Comédie (Dante), Le Testament, Villon; Orch. Pieces: Divertimento, Offande à une Ombre, Trois Etudes, Une Saison en Enfer,, Ouverture pour un Opera interdit; Poème (Orch.); Concert for Strings; Chamber Music: String Quartet, Saxophone Quartet, String Trio, Sonatina for Piano & Violin; var. Lieder & Piano pieces. Publs: La France & la Musique Occidentale; Berlioz; Pour Comprehdre les Musiques d'Aujourd'hui; Les Cing Grands Operas. Hons: Off., Légion d'Honneur; Cmdr., Ordre des Arts & Lettres; Grand Prix Nat. de la Musique, 1959; Great Prize for Symph. Music (SACEM). Address: 20 Rue Jean Daudin, 75015 Paris, France.

BARRELL, Bernard, b. 15 Aug. 1919, Sudbury, Suffolk, UK. Composer; Lecturer; Teacher. Educ: FTCL; LMusTCL. m. Joyce Howard Barrell. Comps: Recorder Trio (Op. 16); Cambridge Suite (Op. 22, Recorder & Piano); 5 Dances (Op. 40, Guitar & Recorder); Music for 2 (Op. 43); Missa Brevis (Op. 31, for Flute & Guitar); Prelude & Fugue (Op. 36, for Organ); Soliloquies for Cello (Op. 39); Divertimento for Solo Oboe (Op. 53); Missa Brevis for SATB a cappella (Op. 41); Epitaph for Zoltan Kodaly (Op. 49); Music for Brass Trio (Op. 55). Mbrships. incl: E

Anglian Rep., Comps.' Guild of GB. Contbr. to Comp. Address: 37 Graham Rd., Ipswich, Suffolk IP 1 2QE, UK. 4.

BARRELL, Joyce Howard, b. 26 Nov. 1917, Salisbury, Wilts, UK. Composer: Guitar teacher; Accomp. Educ: Pupil of Dr. Ben Burrows, Miss Grace Burrows, Leicester Univ. and Mr. Harold Craxton. m. Bernard Barrell. Career: Var. tchng. appts. - esp. guitar. Compositions incl: Child of Our Time, carol, Op. 43; Dialogue for Flute and Viola da Gamba, Op. 20; Prelude for Harp, Op. 23; The Three Inns, 2 Guitars, Op. 48; Tranzmusik for Piano, Op. 33; Trio tor Recorders, Op. 10; 8 Studies for Guitar, Op. 31; Strata for 3 Guitars, Op. 40; The Fires for Piano, Op. 51; Trio for Clarinet, Viola and Piano, Op. 44; String Trio, Op. 36. Mbr. CGGB. Address: 246 Tuddenham Rd., Ipswich, Suffolk IP4 3BH, UK.

BARRERA, Carlos Gomez, b. 19 May 1918, Chetumal, Mexico. Composer. Educ: Nat. Schl. of Agric., Chapingo. Compositions incl: Himno a Chapingo, 1954; March de las Reservas de Quintana Roo, 1943; Un sueñno fue; Inutil es fingir; Solo con mi dolor; milagro de amor; Por que has tardado?; Falsos juramentos; Que me casique, Dios; Mentira; Tu eres mi destino; Por un punado de oro; Fantasia for piano & orch. (film score for La edad de inocencia, 1963); Leyenda de Chetumal; Isla mujeres; Cozumel; var. film scores. Mbrships. incl: Adminstr.-Gen., Soc. of Authors & Composers of Mexico, 1954-63; Dir.-Gen., Soc. of Authors & Composers of Music, S de A, 1963-; Sec.-Gen., Exec. Comm., Composers Sec., Union of Cinematographic Prodn. Workers of Mexico, 1958-; Sec.-Gen.; Ctrl. Comm., ibid., 1968-70; Pres., Ctrl. Am. 1960-; Fellow, Mexican Soc. of Geog. & Stats., 1973. Recip. of ONIX Trophy, Ibero-Am. Univ.

BARRETT-AYRES, Reginald, b. 7 May 1920, Aberdeen, UK. Head of University Music Department; Instrumentalist (Piano; Organ; Trumpet; Violin). Educ: B Mus, Edinburgh Univ.; Moray House Coll. Educ. m. Dorothy Ewing (dec.); m. Esther Mary Craig, 1 s., 2 d. Career: Music Master, Ackworth Schl., 1942-45; Glasgow Acad., 1945-51; Lectr., Music, ABerdeen Univ., 1951-56; Sr. Lectr. & Dept. Hd., ibid., 1956-70; Rdr. in Music & Dept. Hd., 1970-; TV & Radi apps. 1945-. Comps. incl: The Proposal (opera); Hugh Miller (opera); Series 3 Communion Service; Violin Concerto, 1977; The Secret Sin of Septimus Brope (opera). Recordings incl: Love Poems of Ancient Egypt. Publs: Critical Ed. of the Quartets of Joseph Haydn (First 14), Score and parts, 1977; Joseph Haydn & the String Quartet, 1974. Contbr. to var. jrnls. Hobbies incl: Stage prod.; Travel. Address: 15 Sunnyside Terr., Aberdeen, Scotland, UK.

BARROW, Rebecca Anne, b. 12 Feb. 1942, Mattoon, Ill., USA. Teacher & Performer (Piano). Educ: B Mus, Millikin Univ. Ill.; MSc. Juilliard Schl. of Music; Pvte. studies w. Elizabeth Travis, Krwin Freundlich, Jacob Lajeiner, Mo Agosti; Studied in Rome. career: Sr. Fac. Mbr., NC Schl.of Arts; Solo perf. w. Austin Tex., Symph.; Chgo. Businessmen's Orch.; Series of Concerts in Mexico in collaboration w. El Organismo de Promocion Internacional de Cultura; Num. duorecitals. Recordings: The Twentieth Century Double Bass w. Lynn peters. Mbrships: Pi Kappa Lambda; Phi Kappa Phi. Hons. incl: Brewster-Allison Award, 1962; Fullbright grant to Italy, 1968-69. Hobbies: Reading; Plants. Address: 104 Cascade Ave., Winston Sale, NC 27107, USA. 27.

BARRY, Barbara Rosamond, b. 2 June 1949, London, UK. Professor; Pianist. Educ: BMus, Univ. of London; MMus, ibid.; Perfs. course at TCL; ATCL; LTCL. Debut: St. John's, Smith Sq., London. Career: Profl. freelance for London Schl. of Contemporary Dance & Laban Dance Ctr. until 1975; Fndr. of modern dance choreographic & dance group for shcl. children in Lond's East End; formerly lectr. in music & communications studies, Waltham Forest Coll., London; now Prof. of Music History, GSM, & tutor in musical analysis, Univ. of London, Goldsmith's Coll. Contbr. to: Composer; Music & Musicians; Times Educl. Supplement; Symposium. Mbrships: Soc. for Music Theory, USA; Coll. Music Soc., USA; Nat. Assn. of Tchrs. in Further & Higher Educ. Hons: Priness Helena Victoria Silver Medal, TCl, 1967. Hobbies: Theatre; Films; Opera; Ballet; Aleatoric Cooking. Address: Flat 2, Dover house, Cormont Rd., London, SE5 9RG, UK.

BARRY, Gerald Anthony, b. 28 April 1952, Ennis, Co. Clare, Island. Composer. Educ: MusB, 1973, MA, 1975, Dip. Music Tchng., Univ. Coll., Dublin; Royal Conserv., The Hague; State Acad. of Music, Cologne; Vienna Acad. of Music, etc. Career: Comps. broadcast throughout Europe & elsewhere under auspices of UNESCO Int. Rostrum of Comps. Comps. incl: Things That Gain By Being Painted; Decolletage; Mr. Volans His Rest; Monocule; Belacquered; Kpippenspiel; A Piano Concerto; All The Dead Voices, for soprano, alto, orch., etc. Mbrships:

Fndr. Mbr., Assn. of Irish Comps.; PRS: Mechanical Coypright Soc. Hons. incl: Grants awarded by Dutch, Irish & German Govts. Hobby: Belacquering. Address: Clarehill, Clarecastle, Co. Clare, Repub. of Ireland. 4.

BARRY, Kathleen Marie, b. 25 May 1934, Manchester, UK. School Teacher. Educ: Tchrs. Cert., Maria Assumpta Trng. Coll., London; 3rd yr. Tchrs. Supplementary Course, TCM; ATCL (piano perf.), 1955; A Mus TCL, 1957; ARCM (singing tchr.), 1958; LTCL (piano perf.), 1960; FTCL (piano), 1962. m. Kevin Milton Barry, 2 s., 1 d. Career incl: Dpty. Headmistress, Ss. Peter & Paul Second. Schl., Lincoln; UK, 1959-63; Hd. of Music Dept., Winckley Sq. Girls' Grammar Schl., Preston, UK, 1963-68, Iona Coll. Girls' Schl., Havelock N, NZ, 1968-71; 1 solo piano recital & sev. duet recitals w. Marie Stothart, NZ Radio (Napier). Ed. Musical Educ. of the Under Twelves, 1959-60. Mbr., ISM. Hobbies: Chmbr. music; Walking. Address: 803 Hastings St. N, Hastings, NZ. 3.

BARSHAI, Rudolph Borisovich, b. 1 Oct. 1924, Labinskaya, Krasnodar Territory, USSR. Conductor. Educ: Moscow Conserv. Career: performer in Chmbr. Ensembles w. leading musicians inc. Shostakovich, Richter, Oistrakh & Rostropovich; Fndr., Moscow Chmbr. Orch., 1955-; num. for. tours. Compositions: Orchns. & Arrs. for Chmbr. Orch. of works by contemporary composers & other works.

BARSHAM, Dinah, b. 2 Oct. 1937, London, UK. University Lecturer. Educ: RAM, London; BMus; PhD; LRAM. m. Gerald Hendrie, 2 s. Career: Lectr. in Music, Homerton Coll., Cambridge, 1962-63, Manchester Univ., 1965-67, The Open Univ., 1970-. Recordings: As Cond., for Open Univ. Publs: Joint Ed., new Gilbert & Sullivan Soc. Contbr. to: Die Musik in Gegenwart und Geschichte; Grove's. Mbrships: Musician's Union; AUT. Hons: State Scholarship, 1956; RAM Hist. of Music Prize, 1957; RAM Club Prize, 1960. Hobby: Family. Address: 19 Madingley Rd., Cambridge, CB3 OEG, UK.

BARSTOW, Josephine, b. Sheffield, UK. Opera Singer. Educ: BA Hons., Birmingham Univ.; London Opera Ctr. m. Ande Anderson. Debut: Opera for All. Career: Apps., all opera houses, UK, Met., NY, Dallas, Sante Fe, Miami, Baltimore, France, Geneva, East Berlin, Turin. Recording: The Knot Garden. Hobby: Gardening; Outdoor interests: Walking. Mgmt: John Coast, London. Address: c/o John Coast, 1 Park Close, Knightsbridge, London SW1X 7PQ, UK.

BART, Lionel, b. 1 Aug. 1930, UK. Composer & Lyricist. Compositions incl: Lyrics for Lock Up Your Daughters, 1959; Music & lyrics for Fings Ain't Wot They Used T'be, 1959; Music, lyrics & book for Oliver!, 1960 (film version 1968); music, lyrics & dir., Blitz!, 1962, Music & lyrics, Maggie May, 1964; num. film scores incl: Serious Charge; In the Nick; Heart of a Man; Let's Get Married; Light Up the Sky; The Tommy Steele Story; The Duke Wore Jeans; Tommy the Toreador; Sparrers Can't Sing; From Russia With Love; Man in the Middle; composer of num. popular songs. Hons: Ivor Novello Awards as song writer, 1957 (3); 1959 (4); 1960 (2); Variety Club Silver Heart as Show Bus. Personality of the Yr., Boradway, USA, 1960; Antoinette Perry Award (Tony) for Oliver!, 1962; Gold Disc for soundtrack of Oliver!, 1969. Address: Neo-Cortic Prods., Page House, 91 Shaftesbury Ave., London W1, UK.

BARTA, Mihaly, b. 6 Feb. 1954, Budapest, Hungary. Violinist. Educ: Dip., Ferenc Liszt Acad., Budapest. Career: Conerts in London, Paris, Frankfurt, Cologne, Tokyo; Recordings for major German Radio Stations; Ldr., Kodaly String Quartet. sev. recordings in Hungary, Germany & Japan. Mbr., Hungarian Kodaly Soc. Hons: Franz Liszt prize for Kodaly Quartet, 1970; as soloist, 2nd prize, Joseph Szigeti Int. Competition, Budapest, 1973; Gold Medal of Belgian Ysaye Soc., 1973; Special Prize of the jury at Tchaikovsky Competition, 1974. Mgmt: Interkoncert, Budapest. Address: Rajk L.U. 49/B, 1133 Budapest, Hungary.

BARTAK, Zdenék, Jr. b. 31 Aug. 1954, Prague, Czech. Composer; Arrange; Pianist; Tubist; Singer. Educ: Grad., State Conserv. of Music, Prague. m. Jana Bartáková. Comps. incl: Je Ráno; Bily Stul; Ucitelka Zpevu; Jak Bude Dnes; Létej; Damarád; Aprisl Girl, musical theatre, 1977; Jedeuzcté prinházzui, musical theatre, 1979. Num. recordings. Mbrships: ASsn. for Comps'. Protective Rights (OSA), Czech.; Org. for Protection of Prof. Artists (OAA); Suaz če shych shladatelü a honcertüch unilcü - Ahtiv inladych (SCSKY). Hons. incl: 1st Prize, Song for the Star Competition, 1975, 77; 1st prize for voice & song Jan zit, Intertalent 1976. Hobbies: Reading musical reviews; Sports. Address: Nebovidská 4/461, 11800 Prague 1 - Malá Strana, Czech. 3.

BARTELINK, Bernard G M, b. 24 Nov. 1929, Enschede, Netherlands. Organist; Composer. Educ: Dutch Inst. for Ch.

Music, Ultrecht, examination 1950; Amsterdam. Conserv., examination 1952; studied Organ w. Albert de Klerk, Anthon van der Horst, Gaston Litzize. m. Catharina J T Stolwyk, 2 s. Career: Num. recitals inclng. Westminster Cathedral, UK, 1970, Nat. Cathedral, Washing. DC 1971, Royal Fest. Hall, London, UK, 1973; Mbr. of Jury, Int. Organ Improvisation Contest, Haarlem, 1969; Tchr. of improvisation, Int. Ch. Music Week, Kristiansand, Norway, 1974; Tchr., Organ & Improvisation, Dutch Inst. for Ch. Music Ultrecht; Organist, Roman Cath. Cathedral of St. Ba Vo. Haarlem; Organist, Concertgebouw Orch., Amsterdam, Compositions incl: Voluntary for a Festal day (organ); Zaligsprekingen (Beatitudes, Latin text) (low voice & organ); Toccata per Organo. Recording: Famous Organ Works of Bach. Contbr. to Gregoriusblad. Hons: Prix d'excellence for Organ, Amsterdam Conserv., 1954; Winer Int. Organ Improvisation Contest, Haarlem, 1961. Hobbies: Walking; Reading; Listening to Good Music. Address: Marsstraat 99, Haarlem, Netherlands.

BARTH, Guido, b. 15 Dec. 1937, Stuttgart, German Fed. Repub. Violist; Musicologist. Educ: studied w. Prof. Emil Kessinger, exam. as perf. artist, 1967. Acad. of Music, Stuttgart; Dr phil. cand. (musicol., Egyptol. & art hist.). Tubingen Univ. m. Margot Horné, 3 s., 1 d. Career: participant in series Concerts of Young Artists, Germany; apps. as chmbr. music player, Germany & Western Europe; perfs. as Soloist; Soloist w. Stuttgart State Opera; w. Pandula Str. Quartet has made num. concert tours in Europe, radio broadcasts & recordings, & given 21 world premieres of expmntl. & microinterval music. Has made chmbr. music recordings w. var. ensembles. Hobby: Lit. Address: 7000 Stuttgart 1, Alexanderstr. 21 A, German Fed. Repub.

BARTHA, Dénes (Richard), b. 2 Oct. 1908, Budapest, Hungary. Musicologist; Professor. Educ: PhD., Univ. of Berlin, Germany, 1930. m. Susan Bartha, 1 s., 2 d. Career: Music Lign., Nat. Lib., Budapest, 1930-; Lectr., F. Liszt Acad. Music, ibid., 1934; Assoc. Prof., ibid. 1945; Prof., 1948-; Vis. Prof., Smith Coll., USA, 1964, Harvard, ibid., 1964, 66, Cornell, 1965-66, Pitts., 1967. A. W. Mellon prof. of music 1969-. Publs. incl: Benedictus Ducis, 1930; Die unger Doppelschalmei von Jánoshida 1934; Das Musiklenhrbuch einer ung Klosterschule, 1934; A xviii század magyar dallamai, 1935; Beethoven, 1939; A Zenetörténet Antológiája, 1948, '74; Haydn als Opernkapellmeister, 1960. Contbr. to var. profl. jrnls. Mbrships. incl: int. Soc. Musicol. (cound., 1961-); Am. Musicol. Soc. (coun., 1970-). Recip., Edward Dent Medal, IMS, 1963. Hobbies: Collector, phono records; Mountaineering. Address: 5600-D Fifth Ave. Pittsburgh, PA 15232, USA. 2.

BARTLE, Graham Alfred Reginald, b. 6 Nov. 1928, Ballarat, Vic., Aust. Lecturer. Educ: BA, Dip. Ed., Melbourne Univ., 1953, Bmus, ibid, 1964; MMus, 1971; FICL, 1949. m. Ruth Marian Walker, 1 s., 3 d. Career: Tchr., Yallourn HS, Vic., 1954-57, Univ. HS, Melbourne, 1958-62; Lectr. in Music, Secondary Tchrs. Coll., Melbourne, 1962-65; Sr. Lectr. in Music, Univ. of Melbourne, 1966-; Deputy Dean, FAc. of Music, ibid, 1978-; Chmn., Music Standing Committee of the Vic. Inst. of Secondary Educ. Publs: Music in Australian Schools, 1968; Chapt. in The Teacher's Role in Curriculum Design, 1974. Contbr. to: Aust. Jrnl. of Music Educ.; Careers, Victoria. Mbrships. incl: Chmn., Vic. Chapt., Aust. Soc. of Music Educ., 1972-73; Fndn. mbr., ibid, 1967; Int. Soc. for Music Educ.; Kodaly Educ. Inst. of Aust.; Int. Kodaly Soc.; MENC; ISM; Examiner, Aust. Music Examinations Bd.; Can. Music Educators Assn.; Aust. Inst. of Music Thcrs. Hons: Ormond Exhib., Univ. of Melbourne, 1958; Comp. Prize, ibid, 1960. Hobbies: Gardening; Home Decorating. Address: 10 Chaucer Cres., Canterbury, Vic., 3126, Aust.

BARTLETT, Ian James, b. 20 Sept. 1934, London, UK. Lecturer. Educ: BA, 1956, MA, 1960, Brasenone Coll., Oxford; Post-grad. Cert. in Educ., Inst. of Educ., Unv. of London, 1958; RAM, 1956-57; ARCM (piano tchr.), 1957; LRAM (piano perf.), 1961; MMus., King's Coll., Univ. of London, 1974. m. Anne Verne Lucas, Career: Dir. of Music, Bilborough Grammar Schl., Nottingham, 1958-62; Banbury Schl., Oxon., 1965-70; Lectr. in Music, Bretton Hall Coll. of Educ., Yorks., 1961-65; Dir., N Oxon. Jr. Music Schl., 1966-70; Prin. Lectr. in Music, Goldsmiths' Coll., Univ. of London, 1970-. Publs: Arr. for Piers Press and Chester's. Contr. to num. profl. jrnls. and mags. Mbrships: Royal Musical Assn.; Soc. for Rsch. in Psychol. of Music and Music Educ.; NATFHE. Hobbies: Athletics; Theatre. Address: 31 Brooklands Ave., Sidcup, Kent, UK.

BARTLETT, Loran Wayne, b. 7 Feb. 1932, Dallas, Ore., USA. Professor of Music; Performer in bassoon, clarinet, saxophone, recorder. Educ: BA (Music Educ.), BA (Music), Eastern Wash State Coll., Cheney, 1954; M Mus Ed., Oberlin Coll. Conservatory of Music, Oberlin, Ohio, 1955; PhD, Univ. of Iowa, Iowa City, 1961. m. Lois Ann Fox Bartlett, 2 s., 2 d. Career: 3nd clarinet, alto saxophone, bas clarinet, Spokane Phil. Orch., 1951-54; 1st bassoon, Little Rock, Ark., Symph. Orch., 1955-65; 1st bassoon, Greeley Phil. Orch., Colo., 1965-; Bassoon, Ginsburg ARts Woodwind Quintet, 1965-; Assoc. Prf., Ark. Polytechnic Coll., Russelville, 1955-65; Prof. of Music, Chmn., Woodwind Dept., Univ. of Northern Colo., Greeley, 1965-; Clinician, judge or perf., var. states. Mbrships: MENC; State Chmn., Div. Chmn., NACQPI; Music Tchrs. Nat. Assn.; Blue Key; Kappa Delta Pi; Phi Mu Alpha Sinfonia; Kappa Kappa Psi. Hobbies: Woodworking; Camping; Hiking; Christian activities. Address: Schl. of Music, Univ. of Northern Colo., Greeley, CO 80631, USA.

BARTON, June, b. Bendigo, Vic., Aust. Coloratura Soprano. Educ: studied in Aust.; RCM (w. Clive Carey & Henry Cummings); studied w. Maria Carpi, Geneva. m. Ian Sloane, 3 s. Career: concerts throughout Aust., Europe, Asia & UK; apps. w. Sadler's Wells Opera Co. & opera cos. in Europe & Asia. sev. recordings. mbr., ISM. Hons: num. prizes incl. winner, 1960 SunAria, Melbourne, & 1961 Shell Aria, Canberra. Hobbies: Cooking; Bridge. Mgmt: Friedrich Paarsch, Düsseldorf, German Red. Repub. Adress: c/o Sloane, F C O, King Charles St., London, SW1 UK. 27.

BARTON, Todd, b. 2 July 1949, Oakland, Calif., USA. Director of Music. Educ: BMus, Conserv. of Music at Univ. of the Pacific, Stockton, Calif., 1971; MA, Univ. of Oregon, 1978. m. Terrell Barton. Career: Dir. of Music, Oregon Shakespeare Fest. Comps: Diastems for alto recorder; Improv 11 XII 74, music for the play, Margaret, Queen of England, 1977; arr. or comp. music for most of Shakespeare's plays. Recording: An Elizabethan Pleasure Garden. Contbr to: Pro Musica. Mbrships: Am. Musicol. Soc.; Soc. for the STudy of Alchemy and Early Chemistry. Hons: Close Fellowship, 1976, 77. Hobbies: Translating Latin; Rennaissance Philosophy. Address: PO Box 763, Ashland, OR 97520, USA,

BARTON-ARMSTRONG, John, b. 8 Apr. 1923, Stockton-on-Tees, UK. Composer. Educ: BMus, Univ. of Durham; studied comp. w. Norman Demuth & Edmund Rubbra. Career: Design & Sales Engineer, 1951-64; comp. studies & practice, 1964-; Consultant in Electronics, aviation & public relations. Comps. Opera, Hamlet, 1st symph.; Forest Impressions, orchl. suite (recorded); num. comps. in different media. Contbr. to: Composer. Mbrships: CGGB. Hobbies: Rowing; Rugby; Squash; Swimming; Walking. Address: Ingledene, 41 Cambridge Rd., Ashford Common, Middx. TW15 1UF, UK.

BARTOS, Jan Zdenek, b. 4 June 1908, Dvur Kralove nad Labem, CSSR. Professor of Composition. Educ: Comp. Prague Conserv., 1935-39; Dip. ibid., 1935 m. Zdenka Jezkova-Bartosova, 1 s., 1 d. Debut: Radio Brno, 1935. Career: Violinist: Sak's Phil. Orch.; Prague Symph. Orch.; Concert Master; Messagerie Maritime, Marseilles; Theatre Orch., Prague; Porfc. in Germany, Holland, Austria, USA & S Am. Comps. incl: Over 180 works inclng. 5 symphs., 2 operas & 11 string quartets. Num. recordings. Publs. incl: On the Development of Musical Forms and Genres, 1964; Music Colls SoS, 1969. Contbr. to profl mags. Hons. incl: State Decoration For Outstanding Work, 1955, Artist of Mesto, Vaclavaske namesti 3/III, Schody, 110 00 Praha, CSSR.

BARTSCHI, Werner, b. 1 Jan. 1950, Zürich, Switz. Pianist; Composer. Educ: Volksschule und Gymnasium, Zürich; Matura Typ A, 1968. Career: Concerts in Switz., Germany, Austria, Holland, UK, France and Italy; TV Apps. in Switz.; Broadcasts from Switz., Holland and Germany; Fndr. (w. Peter Schweiger), Snom and Zasch, theatre grp; Concerts and broadcasts as cond. in Switz. and Germany. Recordings for DGG and EMI. Publs: The Inevitable Music of John Cage (w. others), 1969. Mbrships: Bd., Artist's House, Boswil; Pro Musica, Zürich Sect. of IGNM; Schweizerischer Ronkünst-lerverein; Leos Jánacek Gesellschaft, Zürich. Address: Hadlaubstr. 120, CH 8006 Zürich, Switz. 30.

BARTZ, Huub, b. 6 Aug. 1936, St. Jansteen, Netherlands. Professor. Educ: studies in organ, choir direction, Gregorian Chant & theory. m. J. Bongaarts, 3c. Career: Prof. at Sweelinck Conserv., Amsterdam; Tchr. of organ, choir direction, Gregorian Chant, solfége, counterpoint, harmony & analysis; choir dir. for TV and radio. Mbrships: Vereniging van Nederlandse Muziekgeschiedenis; Societé Int. de Musicol.; Gesellschaft fur Musikforschung. Hons: many prizes in nat. & int. choir competitions with the Oosterhouts Kamerkoor. Recordings: works of the modern Dutch comp., Daan Manneke. Address: Wyde Omloop 63, Oosterhout, Netherlands.

BARTZ, Jerzy, b. 28 May 1936, Warsaw, Poland. Acoustic Engineer; Drummer; Percussionist. Educ: Master's degree,

Polytechnic Coll. Debut: 1957. Career: radio, TV, stag & film apps. w. num. ldng. Polish jazz grps. (Namyslowski, Kurylewicz, Nahorny, Novi Singers, Wróblewski); as acoustician, Sci. Worker, Acad. of Music. Recordings: w. Namyslowski, 1958; sev. records w. Doduś Matuszkiewicz Swingtet, 1960-63; Novi Bossa Nova w. Novi Singers, 1968; num. pop. & rock recordings. Publs: New Drum Rhythms, 1971; School for Drums, 1976. Contbr. to: Archiwum akustyki; Przekroj. Mbr., Polish Jazz Soc. Hobby: Travel. Address: Kaniowska 2, 01-529, Warsaw, Poland.

BARWICK, Steven, b. 2 Mar. 1921, Lincoln, Neb., USA. Pianist; Music Educator. Educ: BA & BMus., Coe Coll.; MMus., Eastmen Schl. of Music, Rochester, NY; MA & PhD., Harvard Univ. Debut: London, 1961. Career: Concert Tours in Europe & USA; Prof., Piano & Music Lit., Southern Ill. Univ., Carbondale, Ill. Publs: Motets from Mexican Archives, 1956-58; The Franco Codex of the Cathedral of Music, 1965; Contbr. to Musical Quarterly; Essays on Music. Mbrships: Am. Musicol. Soc.; Music Tchrs. Nat. Assn.; Pi Kappa Lambda; Phi Mu Alpha Sinfonia. Hons: John Knowles Piano Travelling Fellowship. Harvard, 1945-47; DFA, Coe Coll., 1969. Hobbies: Antique Collecting; Cooking; Foreign Travel. Address: 709 W Elm, Carbondale, IL 62901, USA.

BARYLLI, Walter, b. 16 June 1932, Vienna, Austria. Violinist. Educ: HS for Music & Dramatic Art, Vienna; Violin study w. F von Reuter, Munich. Debut: Munich, 1936. Career: Concert tours throughout Europe & overseas; Mbr., Vienna State Opera Orch. & Vienna Phil., 1938-; currently ldr. of both orchs.; Ldr., Barylli Quartet, 1945-; Prof. of Violin, Vienna Conserv., 1969-. Var. recordings issued. Hons: Kreisler Prize (twice won). Address: Rennweg 4/14 Vienna, A-1030 Austria.

BARZENICK, Walter, b. 23 Nov. 1922, Maywood, Ill., USA. Clarinettist. Educ: BMus., Northwestern Univ., Evanston, Ill., 1949; MMus, ibid., 1950; studied clarinet w. Wesley Shepard, Tony Sirmarco, Dominco De Caprio, Sidney Forest & Simion Bellison. m. Margaret E Barzenick, 2 c. Career: Over 50 recitals covering major lit. for clarinet; perfs. w. num. symph. orch. in Ill. & La.; Prin. clarinet, Baton Rouge Symph., 1950-; Clinician, recitalist, consultat & adjudicator in S & SW USA; Prof. of music, Southeastern La. Univ., Hammond. Publs: The Clarinet, 1969; Interesting Events in the History of the Clarinet, 1972; Symphonic works played by Baton Rouge Symph., 1950-79. contbr. to The Instrumentalist. Mbrships: La. Music Educators Assn.; La. Bandmasters Assn..; Am. Fed. of Musicians; Nat. Assn. of Coll. Wind & Percussion Tchrs.; Int. Clarinet Soc.; past Pres., Optimist Club of Hammond. Hons: Phi Mus Alpha Sinfonia, 1946; Pi Kappa Lambda, 1950; Purple Heart & 4 battle stars, 1944. Hobbies: Tennis; Reading; Advsr. to univ. groups. Address: 100 Elm Dr., Hammond, LA 70401,USA. 7, 11.

BARZIN, Leon Eugene, b. 27 Nov. 1900, Brussels, Belgium. Conductor. Educ: studied w. father, Pierre Henrotte, Eugene Meergerlin, Eugene Ysaye; comp. studies w. Lilienthal. m. Eleanor Close, 2 s., 1 d. Career: Solo Violist, NY Phil., 1920-29; Asst. Cond., Am. Orchl. Soc., 1928-29; Music Dir., Nat. Orchl. Assn., 1930-57, 69-76, Hartford Symph., 1940-45, NYC Ballet, 1948-58, WQXR, 1940-45; Guest Cond. w. orchs. in USA & Europe; Dir. & Prod., Fun With Music, WABC TV, 1939-40; formed Phil. Soc. of Paris; created Les Musicoliers -prog. for Children, France, 1968, & Baalbeck Fest., Lebanon. Var. recordings inclng. Mozart's Haffner Symph. Contbr. to: Musical Am.; New Yorker. Mbrships: incl: Bohemians. Hons: incl: Legion of Hons., France; Lebanese Gold Medal. Hobbies: Tennis; Golf; Fishing. Address: 53 Rue de Monceau, Paris VIII, France. 2.

BASELT, Franz Bernhard Bernd, b. 13 Sept. 1934, Halle (Saal), DDR. Musicologist. Educ: Music Acad. Halle 1953/1955; Martin Luther Univ. Halle-Wittenberg 1955/1958; PhB, DPh, DSc. m. Elfriede Baselt, 1 s., 1 d. Career: Lectr. Martin Luther Univ. Halle-Wittenberg, Dept. Musicol. Mbrships: Assn. for Comp. and Musicologists DDR; Mbr. bd. Int. Handel Soc., Halle, DDR. Publs: incl: G. Ph. Telemann, The Modern Demon Lover, kassel, 1969; Thematical, Systematical Catalogue of Handel's Works, vol. 1, Leipzig, 1976; J A Hiller, Biographies of Famous Contemporary Musicologists and Musicians, Leipzig, 1784, re-ed. Leipzig, 1975. Address: Marx-Engels Plaz 1, 402 Halle (Saal), DDR.

BASKERVILLE, David, b. 15 Aug. 1918, Freehold, NJ, USA. Conductor; Composer; Writer; Professor of Music. Educ: BA,Univ. of Wash., 1940; MA, 1955, PhD, 1965, UCLA. m. Roberta M Baskerville, 2 children. Career: Staff Comp.-Cond., NBC Hollywood; Comp.-Arr.-Orchestrator, Paramount Pictures, 20th Century Fox; TV Prod.; BBC London; 3 for. tours producing,writing & directing musical revues; currently Prof. of

Music, Univ. of Colo., Denver. Comps: 26 works for band/orch.; 12 comps./arrangements recorded (Columbia, UK; Venice, USA). Contbr. to: Instrumentalist; Music Jrnl.; Music Educators Jrnl.; Downbeat. Mbrships: Cons., Bd., Nat. Assn. of Jazz Educators; ASCAP; MENC. Recip., Music Award, Lord Mayór of London, UK, 1961. Hobbies: Theatre; Golf; History. Address: 8011 W 72nd Pl., Arvada, CO 80005, USA.

BASS, Warner Seeley, b. 6 Oct. 1915, Brandenburg, German. Professor of Music & Music Education; Conductor. Educ: MA (equivalent), Univ. of Berlin; MM, State Acad. of Music, Berlin; MA, NY Univ., USA; MusB, NY Coll. of Music. m. Marion Corda Bass. Career: Cond. & Comp. of stage music, State Opera, Kassel, Germany; Cond., Kulturbund Theatre, Berlin; worldwide apps. as Guest Cond. w. major orchs.; Assoc. Cond., Am. Symph. orch., (Leopold Stokowski), 1962-64; Vis. Prof., Southampton Coll., Long Island Univ., 1965; Music Dir. & Prof., NY Coll. of Music; Assoc. Prof., NY Univ., 1968-69; Assoc. Prof., CUNY, 1969-75; Prof., ibid., 1975-. Compositions: Overture & Fugue, 'Song of Hope'; Adagio for Str. Orch., Trumpet & Percussion, 'Taps'; Suite for Str. Orch., Serenata Concertante (violin & string orch.); The 96th Psalm (chorus & organ). Recordings: Var. arrs. for RCA Victor Co. Mbrships: ASCAP; Coll. Music Soc.; Am. Symph. Orch. League. Recip., Outstanding Educators of Am. Award, 1971, 1972; Community Leaders & Noteworthy Americans Award, 1975. Hobbies: Literature; Languages; Philosophy. Address: 260 W 72nd St., NY, NY 10023, USA. 6.

BASSETT, Henrietta Elizabeth (Beth), b. 25 Mar. 1932, Dallas, Tex., USA. Music Teacher. Educ: BA, Baylor Univ., Waco, Tex., 1952; piano & organ studies, ibid., & w. pvte. tutors in Waco & Dallas; cert. tchrs., music tchrs. Nat. Assn. & Am. Coll. of musicians. Debut: recitals in Dallas, Waco & Mesquite. Career: radio app., piano solos, 1944; pianist; Mesquite High Schl. chorus, 1945-49; ch. pianist, 1945-; ch. organist, 1952-; Dir., musicals, plays, etc. Publs. incl: The Water Wheel; Ten Little Indians - Two Pianos 10 Players; Stepping High; Sleepy; Fireworks; Christmas Contata - The First Christmas; 3 Theory Workbooks. Contbr. to: Clavier; Piano Wuarterly; The Organist; Am. Home Organist; Piano Guild Notes. Mbrships: Fac., NGPT (Austin); Nat. ASsn. of Organ Tchrs. Indiana; Mesquite Area MTA; chmn., Mesquite area Ctr. for Nat. Piano & Organ Playing Auditions; Dir., Adminstr., Beth Bassett Music Camp Acad., 1948. Hons: Nat. Piano-Playing Audition winner, 1946-48; 1st place cash award for The First Christmas, 1st place cash award for Name That Tune, 1976, Am. Coll. of Musicians, 1967; superior ratings for comp. entries, Am. Coll. of Musicians, 1965-76. Hobbies: Bell Collecting; Music. Address: Rte. 2, Box 180, Sunnyvale, TX 75182, USA.

BASSETT, Leslie Raymond, b. 22 Jan. 1923, Hanford, Calif., USA. Composer; University Professor. Educ: BA, Fresno State Univ., 1947; MMus, Univ. of Michigan, 1949; École Normale de Musique, Paris, 1950-51; A.MusD, Univ. of Michigan, 1956. m. Anita Denniston, 1 s. (1 dec.) 1 d. Career incl: Chmn., Dept. of Comp., Univ. of Michigan, 1970; Albert A Stanley Dist. Univ., Prof. of Music, 1977. Compositions incl: Variations for Orch. (recorded); Echoes from an Invisible World for orch.; Sextet for piano and strings (recorded); Concerto for 2 Pianos and orch.; Sounds, Shapes and Symbols for band; Wind Music for wind sextet; Music for saxophone and piano (recorded). Publs: Manual of 16th Century Counterpoint, 1967. Mbrships incl: Am. Composers Alliance; MTNA; Pi Kappa Lambda; Phi Mu Alpha. Hons. incl: Pulitzer Prize, 1966; Guggenheim Award, 1973; Prix de Rome, 1961-63; Disting. Alumnus Award, Fresno State Univ., 1978; Sn. Fellow, Michigan Soc. of Fellows, 1978. Address: 1618 Harbal Dr., Ann Arbor, MI 48105, USA. 2.

BASSETT, Ralph Edward, b. 25 Dec. 1944, Long Beach, Calif., USA. Operatic Bass-baritone. Educ: studied w. Allan Lindquest, Merola Opera Program; coached by Ernest St. John Metz. m. Margaret Bassett, 4 c. Debut: NYC Opera, 1978. Career: Community Concerts; Western Opera Theatre; Kansas City Lyric; San Diego; Reno, Nevada; Augusta, Georgia; Miami Beach, Florida; NYC Opera. Mbr., AGMA. Hons: Martha Baird Rockefeller Grant, 1976, 78; Euterpe Opera Singer of the Yr., 1979; Loren L Zachary Auditions, trip to Europe, 1978. Hobbies: Karate; Cooking; Sailing. Mgmt: Kazuko Hillyer Int., Inc. Address: 70-12 Loubet, Froest Hills, NY 11375, USA.

BASSO, Alberto, b. 21 Aug. 1931, Turin, Italy. Musicologist. Music Educator. Educ: Grad. in Law. Appts. incl: Prof., Hist. of Music, Conserv. of Turin, 1961-74; Lib. Dir., ibid., 1974-. Mbrships: Int. & Am. Musicol. Socs.; Pres., Italian Musicol Soc., 1973-; VP, ibid., 1968-73; Admnstrve. Coun. Royal Theatre of Turin, 1969-. Publs: The Giuseppe Verdi Conservatory of Turin: History & Documents, 1971; History of the Royal Theatre of Turin, 1789-1936, 1976; The Age of Bach & Handel, 1976. Ed., La Musica, 6 vols. (histl. ency. & dictionary), 1966-71; Ed., Hist. of the Opera, 6 vols., 1977. Address: Via Umberto I, 15 bis, 10020 pecetto Torinese, Italy.

BASTER-SORS, Janina, b. 20 Oct. 1932, Krakow, Poland. Pianist. Educ: Dip. Artist of Music, Acad. of Music, Cracow; Docent, ibid. m. Ferenc Sors, 1 s. Debut: Piano duet w. Docent Janusz Dolny at Festival of Highest Artistic Schls., Poznan, 1955. Career: Concerts on radio, TV & w. Phil. in Poland, Austria, Rumania, Czech., Italy, USSR & var. other countries. Apps. at num. festivals inclng: Festival of Mod. Music, Wroclaw. Recordings for Polish radio & E Polish & E German TV. Mbr. Soc. of Polish Artists & Musicians. Hons. incl: Golden Cross of Merit, 1975. Hobbies: Collecting exlibrises; theatre. Mgmt: Polish Artistic Agcy., Pagart, Warsaw. Address: Krakow, ul Garncarska 14 m 3, Poland.

BASTIAN, Dudley Stuart, b. 15 July 1939, Perth, Western Aust., Aust. Organist & Choirmaster; Teacher of Music. Educ: MusB. Dip. Ed., Univ. of Western Aust.; FRCO(CHM); LTCL; LMus. m. Beverley Joy Hatch, 3 s., 1 d. Career: Tchr. of Organ, Piano, Violin, Theory & Comp.; Dir. of Music, Penrhos Coll., Como; Area rep., Inc. Guild of Ch. Musicians; Music Dir., Annual Choir Schls. for Jr. Choristers; Cond., Bible Soc. Hymnfest, 1977-78; Recitalist, Organ, Piano & Harpsichord; Special Commissioner, & Chmn., Western Aust., Br., RSCM; Dir., RSCM Cont., Guildford, 1973. Recording: RSCM Golden Jubilee. Pub: Guild of Young Artists 25th Anniversary, 1967. Contbr. to profl. jrnls. Mbrships incl: Fndr., Organ Soc. of Western Aust., & Paringa Choral Soc.; Western Aust. Music Tchrs. Assn. Hons. incl: John Brook Prize, London, 1970. Hobbies: Swimming; Gardening; Interio Decorating. Address: 3 Baker Ave., Perth, Western Aust. 6000, Australia.

BATCHELOR, Phyllis, b. 1 Feb. 1920, Healesville, Vic., Aust. Pianist; Composer; Teacher. Educ: AMus, A., Melbourne Univ.; LRSM (London, UK). m. Ivan Pietruschka, 1 s., 1 d. Career: Recitalist; Soloist w. Melbourne Symp. Orch.; num. broadcasts as Solo Recitalist & Accomp. for Aust. Broadcasting Commission. Compositions (recorded): Variations on an Original Theme (piano); Sonatina for Piano; Sonata (flute & piano); Suite in Three Movements (flute & piano); Lyrics from the Chinese (voice, flute & piano); 14 Songs for Soprano Voice & Piano; num. piano pieces & songs. Mbr., Fellowship of Aust. Comps. Hobby: Painting in Oils. Address: 46 Mount St., Heidelberg, Vic., Aust. 3084.

BATE, Jennifer Lucy, b. 11 Nov. 1944, London, UK. International Concert Organist. Educ: BA Mus, Bristol Univ.; FRCO; LRAM (org. perf.), ARCM (org. perf.). Career: Worldwide concert tours with TV and radio apps.; Apps. at Int. Fest. in France, Italy, Belgium, Czechoslavakia, Scandinavia, Far East, Australia, USA, S America, W Indies etc.; Regular broadcasts for BBC, incl. at Royal Fest. Hall and Promenade Concerts. Num. Recordings inclng: Hindemith, Reger, Liszt, Elgar and Schumann. Contbr. to: Grove's Dictionary; Musical Times; Organists Review. Mbrships: ISM; Philatelic Music Circle. Hons: J. F. Read Prize (RCO); Young Musician, 1972. Hobbies: REading; Cooking; Philately. Address: 35 Collingwood Ave., Muswell Hill, London N10 3EH, UK.

BATE, John Richard, b. 22 Apr. 1936, Bromley, Kent, UK. Conductor. Educ: MA in Econs., Caius Coll., Cambridge Univ.; TCM; BMus., 1961, GTCL, 1960; FRCO, 1962. Debut: Queen Elizabeth Hall, 1975. Career: Dir. of Music; var. schls.; Organist; Fndr. & Cond., Barnet Orch., Hendon, 1968; John Bate Choir of Richmond & Putney, 1964; Cantanti Camerati of Richmond, 1968. Richmond Opera, 1972; Dpty. Chorus Master, New Philharmonia Chorus, 1974; Cond., TCM Vocal Ensemble, Lonson Soloists Ensemble & Chmbr. Orch., 1975; Cond., John Bate Orch., 1977; Snr. Lectr., Kingston Polytechnic, 1978. Recording: W G Whittaker Centenary Recording, 1975. Mbrships: ISM. Hons: Ricordi Conducting Prize, 1961; Hon. Fellow, TCL, 1978. Hobby: Languages. Mgmt: Nicholas Choveaux. Address: 5 Grena Rd., Richmond, Surrey, UK. 3.

BATE, Philip Argall Turner, b. 26 March 1909, Glasgow, Scotland, UK. Musicologist; WRiter. Educ: BSc (Pure Science), Univ. of Aberdeen; pvte. music studies. m. Yvonne Mary Leigh-Pollit. Career: Num. radio & TV programmes; Dir., BBC TV; Musicologist; Writer. Publs: Instruments of the Orchestra Series - The Oboe, 1956, 62, 75; The Flute, 1969, 75; Trumpet & Trombone, 1966, 72, 78; (revised, F. G. Rendall). The Clarinet, 1971. Contbr. to profl. publs. Mbrships: Fndr. Chmn., The Galpin Soc., 1948-53, 2nd Term, 1973-77; currently Pres., ibid. Hons: Hon. MA (Oxon); FSA. Hobbies: Collecting Fossils; Railways. Address: 11 Halton Rd., London N1 2EN, UK.

BATES, Thomas Eugene, b. 4 Aug. 1939, Florence, Ala., USA. Chmn., Div. of Music Education & Therapy; Percussionist. Educ: Bmus, MMus & EdD, NE La. Univ. m. Carol Anita Williamson, 1 d. Mbrships: Am. Musicol. Soc.; Percussive Arts Soc.; Phi Delta Kappa; Phi Mu Alpha; Alpha Phi Omega (Chmn., Fac. Advistory Committee); Coll. Music Soc.; Omicron Delta Kappa; MENC. Hobbies: Electronics; Woodworking; Competitive target shooting. Address: 705 Woodland Ave., Winchester, VA 22601, USA. 7.

BATTIER, Marc, b. 21 Dec. 1947, Brive-la-Gaillarde, France. Composer. Educ: music studies w. G G Englert (Paris), M Kagel & G Ligeti (Darmstadt); MMus, M (computer science), PhD. Career: in charge of electroacoustic music studios, Univ. & Paris VIII. Comps: (tapes) Lisses, 1971; Vistas, 1972; Aire Tù, 1972; Cosa Materiale, 1977; Re Cosa Materiale, 1977; Objets Empruntés, 1977; Geometrie d'hiver, 1978; (live synthesizers & computers); Cosa Mentale, 1975; Washington Square Waves, 1975; New York Licks, 1977; FD&C Blue No. 2, 1979; (tape & instruments) Tension de l'Air, FD&C Blue No. 1, flute & tape, 1977; FD&C No. 1, 1979; Les Papiers d'Ivry, piano & tape, 1979. Publs: co-author, Un repertoire d'informatique, une Bibliographie Indexe, 1978. Contbr. to: jrnls. & conferences. Mbrships: Groupe Art et Information de Vincennes, Univ. de Paris VIII; Audio Engineering Soc.; Coll. Music Soc.; Société Francaise de Musicologie. Address: 6 rue Berthelot, 94200 Ivry-sur-Seine, France.

BATTIPAGLIA, Diana Mittler, b. 19 Oct. 1941, NYC, NY, USA. Chairman of Music; Pianist. Educ: BS & MS, Juilliard Schl. of Music; DMA, Eastman Schl. of Music. m. Victor A Battipaglia. Career: Pinao Soloist, NY Phil., New Haven Symph., NYC Sumph., Dr.'s Orch.; Solo & chmbr. recitals, Lincoln Ctr. Lib., NY Histl. Soc., Mass., Rochester, Buffalo, Carnegie Recital Hall & over WNYC & WFUV Radio, NYC; Chmn. of Music, Choral Dir., Flushing HS, NY. Recordings: Best of Offenbach. Mbrships: Woodwind Committee of Music, Bur. of Bd. of Educ., MENC; Delta Kappa Gamma. Publs: Franz Mittler - Composer, Pedagogue, & Practical Musician, 1974. Contbr. to profl. jrnls. Recip., sev. hons. Hobbies: Travel; Reading; Gardening. Address: 108-57 66 Ave., Forest Hills, NY 11375, USA. 27, 29.

BATTIPAGLIA, Victor, b. 8 Nov. 1940, NYC, USA. Clarinettist. Educ: BS, Juilliard Schl. of Music, 1963; MA, Columbia Univ., 1964; DMA, Eastman Schl of Music, Univ. of Rochester, 1975. M. Diana Mittler. Debut: Carnegia Recital Hall, 1979. Career: Clarinettist in Orchs. and Chamber Music Grps; Orchl. perfs. at Carnegie Hall, Lincoln Center, Alice Tully Hall; Broadcasts over WNYC-FM-NYC, etc.; prin. clarinettist, Con Brio Chmbr. Ensemble & Wind Quintet; w. ARs Viva. Publs: The Double-Lip Embouchure in Clarinet Playing, 1975. Mbrships: Am. Fend. of Musicians; Int. Clarinet Soc. Hons: Scholarship Awards, Juilliard Schl. of Music, 1960-63; Fellowship, Berkshire Music Centre, Tanglewood, 1960-61; Fellowship, Eastman Schl. of Music, 1973-74. Hobbies: Jogging; Walking; Reading; Collecting; photographic records. Address: 108-57 66th Ave., Forest Hills, NY 11375, USA. 4.

BAUD-BOVY, Samuel, b. 27 Nov. 1906, Geneva, Switz. Conductor; Musicologist. Educ: DLit, Univ. of Geneva; Conserv. of Music & Inst. Jacques-Dalcroze, Geneva; Cond. w. F Weingartner & H Scherchen. m. Lyvia Angst, 1 s, 1 d. Career: Dir., Societé de Chant Sacré, Geneva; Dir., Conserv. of Music, Geneva, 1957-70; Prof. of Cond., ibid., 1942-74; Collaborator, Orch. de la Suisse Romande, Radiosuisse Romande, Soc. romande de spectacles; Rep., Grand Theatre, tours & concerts in Europe. Publs: Chansons populaires grecques du Dodécanèse, 2 vols., 1935-38; La chanson grecque Dodécanèese, 1936; Études sur la Chanson Cleftique, 1958; Chansons populaires de Crète occidentale, 1972. Contbr. to var. profl. Jrnls. Mbr., profl. orgs. Hons. incl: Prix de musique de la Ville De Genève 1975; Hons. Doc., Univ. of Thessalonique, 1977. Address: 14 Bld. des Tranchées, 1206 Geneva, Switz. 19.

BAUDO, Serge. Conductor; Composer. Educ: Conserv. of Paris. m. Madeline Reties. 2 c. Career: Musical Dir., Radio Nice, France; has cond. num. operas, orchs. & fests. inclng: Berlin Opera, Paris Opera & Opéra-Comique, La Scala, Vienna State Opera, Berlin Philharmonic, Prague Philharmonic, BBC London Orch., Aix-en-Provence Fest.; Co-Fndr. (w. Charles Munch), Orch. de Paris; Cond., ibid, until 1970; currently Musical Dir., Orch. de Lyon, Lyons. Compositions incl: film scores, notably Le Monde sans soleil; symphonic & stage works. Recordings incl: works of Saint-Saens Debussy, Honneger Ravel. Address: c/o Orchestre de Lyon, Hotel de Ville, 69000 Lyons, France.

BAUER, Guilherme, b. 1 July 1940. Rio de Janiero, Brazil. Composer; Violinist. Educ: Padre Antonio Vieira Coll., Rio de

Janeiro; Violin, Nat. Music Schl. of Universidade Federal, Rio de Janeiro. Career: Violinist, Nat. Orch., Rio de Janeiro, Brazil; Artistic Dir., ARS Contemporanea Ensemble. Compositions: Espelho Paovisorio; Animus; Fragmentos. Mbrships: Brazilian Soc. of Contemporary Music; Musicians Order of Brazil; Musicians Syndicate. Address: Rua Gustavo Sampaio 460/1102, Leme ZC 07 Rio de Janeiro RJ, Brazil.

BAUER, Kurt, b. 19 Apr. 1928, Kempten, Germany. Professor; Pianist. Educ: STudy w. H Brehme, W. von Horbowski, Walter Gieseking. m. Heidi Bauer-Bund, 3 children. Debut: 1952. Career: Pianist, Solo & Piano Due Bauer-Bung; 1,000 concerts; 150 radio apps.; Prof., Musikhochschule Hannover. 3 recordings. Mbrships: Deutscher Tonkünstlerverband. Hons: Bayer Staatspreis, 1966; Przes, int. competitions, Munich, 1952, Geneva, 1953, Vercelli & Bolzano, 1954; Duo piano competitons, Munich, 1955, Vercelli, 1953. Hobbies: Skiing; Touring. Mgmt: Konzertdirektion Drissen, Mainz. Address: Di3252 Bad Muender 13, Deisterstr. 26, Germa Red. Repub.

BAUER, Robert Paul, b. 24 Jan. 1950, Port Colborne, Ont., Can. Composer; Classical Guitarist; RAdio Music Producer. Educ: BMus, Univ. of Toronto. m. Karen Way. Career: Radio Music Prod., CBC; Fndr. mbr., New music group, Array; num. concert & radio perfs.; commissions from CBC & others. Publd. comps: White Line on a Green Fenc (guitar); Mao (guitar & mandolin); Nondescript (guitar & tape); Two Laments (guitar); Willy Rag & Sakasodik (saxophone Quartet); sev. unpubld. comps. Recordings: Willy Rag & Sakasodic (w. Pual Brodie Saxophone Quartet); Guitar Extensions (w. William Kuinka). Mbrships: Can. Music Ctr.; Can. League of Comps.; Performing Rights Organization of Can. recip., Can. League of Comps. award, 1972. Hobbies: Recording Electronics; Swimming; Reading. Address: 15 Queensdale Ave., Toronto, Ont., Can. M4J 1Y1.

BAULT, Diane Lynn, b. 14 June 1937, Kearney, Neb., USA. Classic Guitarist; Violinist. Educ: BA, Univ. Fla.; Concordia Conserv. Music, Fargo, ND; Master Classes under Manuel Lopez Ramos, 1970-76. m. Edward I. Bault, 2 s. Debut: Violinist, Frago, ND, 1953; Gainesville, Fla., 1961. Career: Classical Guitar Concerts, Mobile, Prichard, Point Clear & Fairhope, all Ala.; Classic Guitar Instr., Univ. S. Ala., Mobile. Mbrships: Clara Schumann Club; Int. Soc. Classical Guitar; Sigma Alpha Iota. Hobbies: Art; Sculpture; Painting water colours. Address: 133 Oaklane Dr., Theordore, AL 36582, USA.

BAUMANN, Herbert, b. 1925, Berlin, Germany. Composer; Conductor. Educ: Berlin Classical HS; studied w. Blacher & Celibidache, Int. Music Inst. m. Marianne Brose, 2 s. Career: Cond. Tchaikovsky Symph. Orch., 1947; Composer & Cond., German Theatre, Berlin, 1947-53, Schiller Theatre, Berlin, 1953-70, & Bavarian Drama Co., Munich, 1971-; Mgmt. of Galerie-Konzerte, Munich. Compositions incl: Berliner Kantate; Psalmen-Triptchon; Variations on an English Folk Song; Rotor; Italian Suite; String Quartet in C; Concerto for guitar & strings; Divertimento for wind instruments; 2 chmbr. concertos; Musica per sei, Brass Quintet, 7 Songs on Peace; Fantasie for guitar (recorded). Mbr. of Tonkünstlerband München. Hobbies: Films; Photog. Address: Lindenstrasse 16, D 8011 Vaterstetten bei München, German Red. Repub. 3.

BAUMANN, Max Georg, b. 20 Nov. 1917, Kronach, Germany. Composer. Educ: Passed examination in Orchl. Cond.; studied Comp. w. Prof. B. Blacher & Prof. K. F. Noetel. m. Hildegard Schwarz. Career: Choir Dir. & Cond., Stralsund Stadttheater, 1947; Prof. of Music, 1960-. Compositions: Passion; Libertas Cruciata; Pelleas & Melisande (ballet); Lucas Cranach (Oratorio); var. Chapel Masses & comps. for Organ. Recip., Art Prize, City of Berlin, 1953. Hobby: Chess. Address: 2d Waltharistr., 1 Berlin 39, German Fed. Repub.

BAÜMGARTEN, Chris, b. 16 Dec. 1910, Berlin, Germany. Composer; Song Producer; Lecturer. Musical Educ: Hochschule for Musikerziehung & Kirchenmusik, Berlin Charlottenburg; Akademische Hochschule für Musik, Berlin; State exams. for organists & choristers. Career: Lectr. & Music Prod., Theatre schls. in Weimar, Leipzig, Berlin, Hannover, Stockholm, Götelovs and Amsterdam. Courses for interpretation for singing actors at schls. & theatres in Germany & abroad; Dir., studio for singing actors, Berlin, & attached to Berlin theatres; Musical Prod. for radio, TV & films; On jury for competitions. Compositions: Num. stage & film musicals; About 300 songs to texts of modern lyricists; Hallo, Du, 1971; Songs in Poesie & Purzelbaum, 1972. Recordings: Die lasterhaften Lieder des Francois Villon, 1963; Du bist min..., old German love songs sung by actors, 1965; Chat Noir am Alex, literary songs interpreted by actors, 1967. Contbr. to jrnls. Mbrships:

Verband der Theaterschaffenden, German Democratic Repub.; Deutscher Komponistenverband. Hobbies incl: Chmbr. music; Jazz; Painting. Address: Karl Marx Allee 20/, 102 Berlin, German Democratic Republic.

BAUMGARTNER, Rudolf, b. 14 Sept. 1917, Zürich, Switzerland. Musician; Conservatory of Music Director; Festival Artistic Director. Educ: Univ. of Zürich; Conservs., Zürich, Lucerne, Vienna, Paris; Dips. for Virtuosity & Teaching. m. Katharina Sallenbach, 1 d. Debut: Zürich. Career: Dir., Lucerne Conserv. of Music; Artistic Dir., Int. Fest. of Music, Lucerne; Fndr. & Dir., Chamber Orch., Fest. Strings, Lucerne. Recordings: Polydor; Philips; Decca; Ariola-Eurodisc. Publs: Eds. of baroque music. Address: Klusstrasse 8, 8032 Zürich, Switzerland.

BAVEL, Zamir, b. 8 Feb. 1929, Tel-Aviv, Israel. Professor of Mathematics & Computer Science; Composer; Violinist. Educ: Tchrs. Dip., Levinsky Tchrs. Coll., Tel-Aviv, 1947; Dip. in Comp. & Violin, Shulamit Conserv., ibid.; BS in EDuc., BAs in Music & Maths., Southern Ill. Univ., USA, 1954; MA in Maths., ibid., 1955; PhD, Univ. of Ill., Urbana, 1965; m. Patricia F. Bavel, 2 s., 1 d. Comps: (recorded) Israeli Rhapsody; Erev Bakfar; other instrumental & vocal works. Publs: Num. instrumental works & songs, books & articles in other fields. Hobbies: Track & Field; Bridge; Chess. Mgmt: ACUM, Tel-Aviv, Israel. Address: 2559 Missouri, Lawrence, KS 66044, USA. 8.

BAXTER, William Hubbard, Jr., b. 14 Nov. 1921, Birmingham, Ala., USA. Music Educator (voice, musicol. & music theory). Educ: BA, Birmingham Southern Coll., 1942; BMus, Birmingham Conserv. of Music, 1947; SMM, Union Theol. Sem., 1949; PhD, Univ. of Rochester, 1957. m. Virginia Spranger, 1 s. Career: Asst. Prof. of Music, w. Kentucky State Coll., 1949-51; Asst. Prof., Assoc. Prof., Prof. of Music, Birmingham S Coll., 1953-. Publs: Agostini Steffani: A study of His Life & Work, 1957; Basic Studies in Music, 1968. Contbr. to: Intellect; Choice. Hobby: Photography. Address: 1244 Greensboro Rd., Birmingham, AL 35208, USA.

BAZELON, Irwin A., b. 4 June 1922, Evanston, Ill., USA. Composer; Conductor; Author. Educ: BA, De Paul Univ., 1944; MA, ibid, 1945; Mills Coll., Calif., 1945-47. m. Cecile Gray Bazelon. Career incls: Cond., Detroit Symph. Orch.; Music for film Survival, 1967 NBC-TV prods.; Am. Shakespeare Fest. Theatre, Stratford, Conn. Comps. incl: Short Symph.; Symph. No. 5; Brass Quintet; A Quiet Piece (orch.); Churchill Downs Concerto; Propulsions; Double Crossings. Num. recordings. Publs: Knowing the Score, 1975. Mbrships: ASCAP. Hons. incl: 1st Prize, Blossom Music, Clevland Symph. Fanfare Competition, 1970. Hobby: Horseracing. Address: 142 E 71st St., NY, NY 10021, USA.

BAZLIK, Igor, b. 5 Dec. 1941, Banská Bystrica, Czechoslovakia. Composer. Educ: Dip., Acad. of Musical Art, Bratislava. m. Milota Bázliková, 1 s. Compositions: 5 works for flute & piano; a musical comedy: 'Gooser's'; Adventure by Harvest; Musica stovaca for symph. orch.; Symphonietta for full orch.; About 150 pop songs recorded by radio, TV & Supraphon & Opus record cos.; many arrs. of folk songs for symph. or chmbr. orch.; about 200 works for theatre, puppet shows, radio & TV broadcasts inclng. TV series, & films. Musical: Full Pockets of Money. Mbr: Union of Slovak Composers. Hons: Prize, Slovak Musical Fund, 1972; many prizes in pop song competitions on TV & radio; 2nd place, Fest. of pop songs 'Lyre of Bratislava', 1973. Hobbies: Amateur Sport; Touring. Address: 80900 Bratislava. Stromova 31, Czechoslovakia.

BEALE, Everett Minot, b. 7 July 1939, Rockland, Mass., USA. Symphonic Musician (Percussionist). Educ: BM, New England Conserv. of Music, 1962. m. Carol Hallworth, 2 d. Career: Assoc. Mbr., Boston Symph. & Boston Pops Orch.; Prin. Percussion, Boston Ballet & Boston Opera Orchs.; Hd., Percussion Dept., Univ. Lowell, Mass., 1968-; Num. TV concerts Recordings w. Boston Symph. & Boston Pops Orch. Publs: The Playing and Teaching of Percussion Instruments, 1975. Contbr. to profl. jrnls. Mbr. Phi Mu Alpha Sinfonia. Hons. incl: Mbr. of World Symph. Orch., 1971. Hobbies: Antique Clock Collecting & Repair; Tropical Fish; Horseback Riding. Mgmt: Mgmt. in the Arts, 551 Tremont St., Boston, Mass., USA. Address: 39 Alcott St., Acton, Mass., USA.

BEAMENT, James William Longman, b. 17 Nov. 1921, Crewkerne, UK. Professor; Acoustician; Syndic of Cambridge University Press. Educ: BA, MA & SCD, Cantab.; PhD, London. m. Juliet Barker, 2 s. Career: Rsch. Sci.-Univ. Rdr.-Univ. Prof., all Cambridge Univ., Mbr. of Fac., Bd. of Music, Cambrdige Univ.; many radio talks on hearing & music. Ed: Biological Receptor Mechanisms, 1962. Contbr. to: many sci. jrnls.;

Grove's Dictionary, 6th ed.; Everyman Ency. Mbrships: Soc. of Expmtl. Biol.; Fellow, Inst. of Biol.; Comps.' Guild of GB; Soc. for Psychol. of Music. Hons: Sci. Medal, Zool. Soc., 1962; FRS, 1964. Hobby: Playing double bass. Address: Queens' Coll., Cambridge, UK. 1.

BEAN, Hugh Cecil, b. 1929, Beckenham, UK. Violinist. Educ: FRCM; studied w. Albert Sammons & André Gertier. m. Mary Harrow. Career: Prof., RCM, 1954; Ldr., Philharmonia & New Philharmonia Orchs., 1957-68; Assoc. Ldr., BBC Symph. Orch., 1967; currently w. Music Grp. of London; Mbr. of Sonata Team w. David Parkhouse. Recordings incl: Elgar's Violin Concerto & Violin Sonata; Vaughan Williams' Lark ascending; Vivaldi's Concerti op. 8/1-4; var. recordings w. David Parkhouse & Music Grp. of London. Hons: CBE; Cobbett Gold Medal; Double Premier Prize, Brussels Conserv. Hobbies: Model Aircraft; Model Railways. Address: 30 Stone Park Ave., Beckenham, Kent, UK. 3.

BEAN, Shirley Ann, b. 30 Oct. 1938, Kansas City, Mo., USA. Assistant Professor of Music Theory, History & Literature. Educ: AA, Kan. City Jr. Coll., 1958; BME, 1960, MMus, 1963, Univ. of Kan. City; DMA, Univ. of Mo.-Kan. City, 1973. Career: Music Instr., Shawnee Mission HS Dist., 1963-65; Dir. of Music, var. churches, Kan. City area, 1963-69; Asst. Prof., Univ. of Mo.-Kan. City, 1969-. Contbr. to profl. jrnls. Mbrships: Am. Musicol. Soc.; Univ. of Mo.-Kan. City Alumni Assn.; Kan. City Alumnae Chapt., Sigma Alpha Iota; Sec.-Treas., Alpha Psi Chapt., Pi Kappa Lambda. Hons: Sword of Hon., Sigma Alpha Iota, 1971; Standard Oil Fndn. Award for Excellence in Undergrad. Tchng., 1973. Hobbies: Bold-Note Project for partially sighted; Gardening. Address: 24 E. 70th St., Kansas City, MO 64113, USA. 138.

BEAN, Thomas Ernest, b. 11 Feb. 1900, Colne, UK. Orchestral Manager, now ret'd. m. Eleanor Child, 1 d. Career: Gen. Mgr., Halle Concert Soc., 1943-51, Royal Festival Hall, 1951-65; Sec., London Orch. Concert Bd., 1965-70. Publs: Future of the Hallé Orch., 1945. Contbr. to: Nat. Press. Mbrships: Hon. Fellow, Inc. Soc. of Musicians. Hons: CBE; Austrian Order of Merit (Officer Class). Hobbies: Reading; Gardening. Address: 5 Pixholme Ct., Dorking, Surrey, UK. 1.

BEAN, William, b. 5 Feb. 1927, Darlington, Co. Durham, UK. Organist; Pianist; Singer. Educ: STudied w. Drs. Kitson & Conway. Career incls: Sub-Organist, Ely Cathedral & Music Staff, King's Schl., Ely, 1947-50; Dir. of Music, Eagle House, Preparatory Dept. of Wellington Coll., 1950-65; Organist & Master of Choir, Royal Memorial Chapel Royal Military Acad., Sandhurst, 1965-70; Dir. of Music, Handcross Pk. Schl., 1970-. Comps. for own choirs. Recordings of Organ Solos, organ & Military Bands., w. own choirs. Contbr. to num. pubis. inclng: Musical Times; ISM Mag. Mbrships. incl: ISM, RSCM; MMA. Hobbies: Music; Reading; Travel. Address: Handcross Pk. Schl., Handcross. Nr. Haywards Heath, Sussex, RH17 6HF, UK.

BEAR, Peter Ronald, b. 19 Nov. 1940, Ipswich, UK. Educationalist; Violinist; Violist. Educ: Tchrs. Cert., Bretton Hall Coll. of Educ. m. Joan Kathleen Trudgett, 1 s., 2 d. Appts: Sr. Peripatetic Tchr., Doncaster CBC, 1968-; Hd., Doncaster Schls. Music Ctr., 1970-; Fndr., Dir., Boyce Chmbr. Orch., 1969-; Adjudicator, Dir., orchl. courses. Mbrships: Rural Music Schls. Assn. Hobbies: Drawing; Painting; Architecture; Climbing; History of Lutherie. Address: 159 Zetland Rd., Doncaster, S Yorks, UK.

BEARD, Kenneth Bernard, b. 9 June 1927, Oldham, UK. Cathedral Organist. Educ: MusB, Manchester Univ.; MA Cambrdige Univ.; Royal Manchester Coll. of Music; FRCO (CHM); ARMCM. Career: Organist, St. Michael's Coll., Tenbury, 1952-59, & Southwell Minster, 1959-. Hons: Organ Schlr., Emmanuel Coll., Cambridge. Address: 4 Vicars St., Southwell Notts., UK.

BEARER, Elaine Louise, b. 1 Apr. 1947, Morristown, NJ, USA. Composer; Conductor; Musicologist (Horn, Violin, Viola, Piano). Educ: BM Manhattan Schl. of Music, 1970; MA, NY Univ., 1973; PhD, ibid.; Cert. d'Assistance, Fontainebleau Am. Conserv. Career incl: Instr., San Francisco State Univ., 1973-75; Asst. Prof., Lone Mountain Coll., San Francisco 1973-74; Perfs. in San Francisco incl: Jewish Commun. Ctr., var. Chs., Grapestake Gall. Comps. incl: 5 Pieces for Organ, 1974; Three Songs of Innocence, 1974. Mbrships: Fontainebleau Alumni Assn.; Am. Musicol. Soc. Hons: Scholarship, Manhattan Schl. of Music; Univ. Fellow, NY Univ. Hobbies: Horseback Riding; Skiing; Tennis. Address: 1850 Gough 501, San Francisco, CA 94109, USA.

BEASLEY, Rule, b. 12 Aug. 1931, Texarkana, Ark., USA. Music Educator; Musician (bassoon); Composer. Educ: BA,

Southern Meth. Univ., Dallas, TEx., 1952; MusM, Univ. of Ill., Urbana, 1958; Juilliard Schl. of Music. m. Lida Oliver, 2 s. Career: Prof. of Music, Centenary Coll. of La., Shreveport, 1958-66; Prin. Bassoon, Ft. Worth Symph. & Opera Orch., 1968-73; Prin. Bassoon, Shreveport Symph., 1958-66; Assoc. Prof. of Music, N Tex. State Univ., Denton, 1966-73; Instructor of Music, Santa Monica Coll., Calif., 1973-78. Comps. incl: Elegy for orch.; Lyric Overture for orch.; Concerto for Euphonium; Concerto for Tuba; Quintet for Brass. Contbr. to: The Instrumentalist. Mbrships: Phi Beta Kappa; Am. Soc. of Univ. Comps. Hobbies: Golf; Cycling. Address: 1127 Pacific St., Santa Monica, CA 90405, USA. 4.

BEAT, Janet Eveline, b. 17 Dec. 1937, Streetly, UK. Composer; Teacher. Educ: BMus, MA, Birmingham Univ. Career: Tchr., Royal Scottish Acad. of Music & Drama. Comps. incl: Inventions for Woodwind (flute, oboe & clarinet), 1966; Seascape with Clouds, for solo carlinet, 1978; Piangam, for piano & tape, 1979; Noctuary, for clarinet & piano, 1979. Publs: Monteverdi & the opera orchestra of his time, The Monteverdi Companion, 1968; Edits. of Carissimi's Jephte, 1974, Carissimi's Nisi Dominus, 1974 & Handel's Let God ARise, 1978. Contbr. to profl. publs. Mbrships: CGGB; Royal Musical Assn. Recip., G D Cunningham Award, 1962. Hobbies: Reading; Cats; Military models. Address: 5 Letham Dr., Glasgow G43 2SL, UK. 3.

BEATH, Betty, b. 19 Nov. 1932, Bundaberg, Qld., Aust. Composer; Teacher; Accompanist; Examiner. Educ: Dip. Mus., QCM; TMusA; AMusA; LTCL; AMusA (singing); Registered Tchr. m. David Cox, 1 s., 1 d. Career: Music Specialist, St. Margaret's Girls' Schl.; Accomp., Qld. Conserv. of Music; Examiner, AMEB. Comps. incl: Seawatcher (song); Abigail & the Rainmaker, Abigail & the Bushranger (musicals for children); In This Garden (song cycle); Marco Polo (music drama for children); sev. commissions. Publs: Articles on Schl. Opera; In Lands of Spice & Magic (Indonesia). Mbrships: Musicol. Soc. of Aust.; Aust.-Indonesia Assn.; Greek Community of St. George. num. hons. & awards. Hobbies: Indonesian Culture; Greek & Chinese Culture; Nature; Walking; Gardening; Animals; Languages. Address: 8 St. James St., Highgate Hill, Qld., 4101, Aust.

BEAUDRY, Jacques, b. 10 Oct. 1929. Sorel, PQ, Can. Symphony & Opera Conductor. Educ: Royal Conserv. of Music, Brussels, Belgium; studied w. René Defossez, Paul Van Kempen, Willem Van Otterloo; BA, Univ. of Montreal. m. Pauline Bonneville. Career: Prof., Orch. Conducting, Univ. of Montreal; Toured Europe as Cond., Montreal Symph. Cond.; Opera-Comique, & Paris Opera House, NY Metropolitan Opera, 1967-; Radio Perfs. in Can., Belgium, Holland, Italy; Czechoslovakia, Norway, Luxembourg, France; Concerts, ibid., & USSR, Guatemala, Poland, Switzerland, Greece, Monaco, USA; TV apps., Can., France. Hobbies: Skiing; Swimming; French Wines & Cuisine. Mgmt: David Haber Artists Mgmt. Inc., 1235 Bay St., Toronto, Ont., M5R 3K4 Canada. Address: 246 Willowdale Ave., Montreal, PQ, H3T 1G7 Canada.

BEAUMONT, Adrian, b. 1 June 1937, Huddersfield, UK. University Lecturer & Composer. Educ: Univ. Coll., Cardiff; BA (First class hons. in Music); MMus, 1961; D Mus., 1973; ARCM. (oboe perf.); comp. pupil of Nadia Boulanger. m. Janet Price. Career: Lectr. in Music, Univ. of Bristol, 1961-78; Snr. Lectr., ibid, 1978-; Fndr./Cond., Bristol Bach Choir, 1967-78. Publd. Compositions: Songs for Little Children(Set One); Sonata for Brass Quintet; Anthem 5, The Spacious Firmament and Awake, Put on Thy Strength; Partsongs; Songs of all Seasons; Welsh Folk-Song Arragements; preliminary Exercises for the Oboe. Mbrships: Assn. of Univ. Tchrs.; ISM; CGGB; Musicians' Union. Hobbies: Fell-Walking; Conducting; Gardening. Address: 73 Kings' Dr., Bishopston, Bristol BS7 8JQ. UK.

BEAUREGARD, Cherry Niel, b. 6 Oct. 1933, Filmore, Utah, USA. Tubist. Educ: Staatliche Hochschule für Musik, Munich, German Red. Repub., 1956-68; BA, Brigham Young Univ., 1959; MMus, 1964, DMusA, 1970, Eastman Schl. of Music, Univ. of Rochester. m. (1) 1 d., 1 s., (2) Sharon Niemeyer, 1 d. Career: Bavarian State Opera Orch., Munich, 1960-62, Rochester Phil. Orch., NY, 1962- w. Eastman Brass Quintet, 1964-, making yearly tours of USA & Can., also radio & TV broadcasts, Mexico, Peru, Chile & Ecuador, 1967, tour of Israel, 1972, apps. as Tuba Solist in Rochester; Asst. Prof., Tuba, Eastman Schl. of Music, 1972-. Recordings: German & Engl. Music of the Late Renaissance for Brass; Canto VII for Tuba Solo (Samuel Adler). Mbr. profl. orgs. ADdress: 135 Pershing Dr., Rochester, NY 14609, USA.

BEAVEN, Peter Richard, b. 17 Jan. 1954, Plymouth, Devon, UK. Conductor; Organist; Teacher. Educ: GTCL; LTCL; var. tchrs. incl. Dr. Harry Gabb, James Gaddarn, Charles Proctor & Bernard Keeffe. m. Janice Ballard. Career: Artistic Dir., Sunbury

Fest. Chorus & orch.; cond., Feltham Choral Soc. & Middx. Fed. of Townswomens Guild Choir; Dir. of Music, Sunbury Parish Ch.; staff, GSM; pvte. tchr. mbr. ISM. Hobbies: Motoring; Sailing; Gastronomia. Address: Rose Cottage, Green St., Sunbury-on-Thames, Middx. TW16 6RE, UK.

BECK, Conrad, b. 16 June 1901, Lohn, Schaffhausen, Switz. Composer. Educ: Conserv. Dip. Piano & Counterpoint; Studied in Paris w. Jacques Ibert, Albert Roussel; Arthur Honegger & Nadio Boulanger. m. Friedel Ehrsam. Career: Hd. of Music, Basle Radio Stn., 1938-66. Comps. incl: Aeneas Silvius Symph.; Chmbr. Cantata (sonets of Louisa Labé); Herbstfeuer; Sonnenfinsternis, Death Over Basel. Mbrships: Assn. of Swiss Comps. (VP); Int. Assn. for Contemporary Music; Swiss Alpine Club. Hons: Assn. of Swiss Musicians, Comps. Prize, 1954; City of Basle Arts Prize, 1964: Commander of the order of merit, Monaco, 1973. Hobby: Mountaineering. Address: St. Johann Vorstadt 82, Basel, Switz.

BECK, Gordon James, b. 16 Sept. 1938, London, UK. Jazz Pianist; Composer; Arranger. Educ: 5 yr. Aircraft Engrng. Apprenticeship; Design Draughtsmanship. Career: 1962-69 app. w. var. well known Jazz grps. inclng. Tubby Hayes Quintet; Debut of own trio at Ronnie Scott Club accompanying var. Am. instrumentalists & singers; TV apps. & studio work; 1969-75, 3 1/2 yrs. w. Phil Woods, USA, inclng. USA tour; Festival, TV, radio, club apps. thro'out world; solo concert debut, 1978. Comps. incl: Here Comes the Mallett Man; They're Coming. Num. recordings incl. The French Connection, 1978. Mbrships: PRS; MCPS; Songwriters Guild; European Jazz Fedn. Hobbies: Mechanics; Astronomy; Wildlife. Address: 14 Second Drive, Litt Downham, Near Ely, Cambs., UK.

BECK, Harold, b. Wanganui, NZ. 'Cellist; Conductor. Educ: Canterbury Univ. Schl. of Art, NZ; Sidney Conserv. of Music, Aust. m. Rhoda, 1 d. Career: Cond., Nat. Broadcasting SErv. Orch., Christchurch, NZ, 1931-37; Prin. 'Cellist, Sydney Sumph. Orch., 1938-39, & Melbourne Symph., 1940-48; Cond., Conserv. Symph. Orch. & Mbr. of Univ. Str. Quartet, 1940; Acting Cond., Aust. Broadcasting Commission Orch., 1940-47; Broadcast Lectr., Aust. Music Exam. Bd., 1942-47; Lectr. & Mbr. of Army Educ. Serv. Str. Quartet, 1942-45; Prin. 'Cellist, Halle Orch., 1949-55; External Examiner, Royal Manchester Coll. of Music, UK, 1950-51; Prin. 'Cellist, LSO, 1955-58; Soloist w. major orchs. in UK, Aust. & NZ. Address: 60 Carlton Hill, St. John's Wood, London NW8, UK. 3.

BECKER, Heinz, b. 26 June 1922, Berlin, Germany. Musicologist; University Professor. Educ: Cert. in clarinet (cond., comp., piano), Hochschule for Musik, Berline-Charlottenburg; Humboldt Univ., Berlin, 1947-51; Dr. phil., Berlin, 1951, inaugurated, Univ. of Hamburg, 1961; pvte. study w. Hermann Grabner. m. Dr. Gudrun Weidmann, 1 child. Career: Full Prof., Ruhr Univ., Bochum, 1966. Publs. incl: Klarinettenkonzerte des 18 Jahrhunderts, 1957; Der Fall Heine - Meyerbeer, 1958; Glacomo Meyerbeer, Briefwechsel & Tagebücher, I-III, 1959, 70, 75; Gaschichte der Instrumentation, 1964; zur Entwicklungsgeschichte der antiken u. mittelalterlichen, 1976; Beiträge zur Geschichte der Oper, 1969; Die Couleur Locale in der Opera des 19, Jahrhunderts, 1976; num. articles. Mbr., profi. assns. & advsry. bodies. Hons: Beirat Stiftung PreuBischer Kulturbesitz, 1975; Beirat Deutsche Bibliothek Frankfurt, 1975. Address; D 4630 Bochum-Querenburg, Askulapweg 26, German Fed. Repub.

BECKER-GLAUCH, Irmgard, b. 16 Nov. 1914, Bochum, Germany. Musicologist. Educ: studied at Univs. of Tübingen, Breslau, & Heidelberg; Dr. phil., 1941. 1 d. Career: w. Staatliches Inst für Deutsche Musikforschung, Berlin, 1942-43; Asst. Seminar for Comp. Musicol., Hamburg Univ., 1943; Lectr., State Coll. for Music, Weimar, 1944-45, & Peoples Coll., Hamburg, 1946-55; Dir., Music Lib. & Studio for New Music, Brit. Ctr. Die Brücke, Hamburg, 1948-53; Archive Mgr., Joseph Haydn Inst., Cologne, 1955-; radio lectures for var. stns. in Germany. Publs: Die Bedeutung der Musik für die Dresdener Hoffestebis in die Zeit Auguste des Starken, 1951; eds. of sev. works by J Haydn. Contbr. to var. publs. Mbrships: Soc. for Music Rsch., Kassel; Austrain Soc. for Musicol., Vienna. Address: Wilhelm-Waldeyer Str. 2, D-5000 Cologne 41, German Red. Repub.

BECKETT, James Brian, b. 21 Mar. 1950, Dublin, Ireland. Composer; Pianist; Pianoforte Teacher. Educ: Royal Irish Acad. of Music; BMus, Trinity Coll., Dublin; ARIAM. Debut: Dublin Festival of 20th Century Music, 1972. Career: Tchr. of Piano, Royal Irish Acad. of Music. Comps. incl: 2 Sonatas (piano solo); 2 Sonatas (cello & piano); Chmbr. Music (Tanatos, 4 cellos, 2 clarinets, mundane egg string quartet, flute, clarinet); Song Cycle (Caddy). Mbrships: Sec., Assn. of Young Irish Comps.,

1972-74; Coun. Mbr., Music Assn. of Ireland, 1973. Hons: Chmbr. Music Prize, Comps. Feis Ceol., 1970; Vandeleur Acad. Scholarship, 1973. Hobbies: Chess; Sailing. Address: 25 Flower Grove, Dun Laoghaire, Co. Dublin, Eire.

BECKETT, Sibthorpe Leopold, b. 16 Dec. 1920, Kingston, Jamaica, W Indies. Choral & Orchestral Conductor. Educ: Kingston Coll.; Cambridge Schl. Cert. m. Edna Lucille Thomas, 2 d., 1 s. Career: Fndr., Res. Cond., Dir. of Music Jamaica Phil., 1940; Fndr., Cond., Y Choral Grp., 1943; Co-Fndr., Sec., Treas., Jamaica Guild of Organists, Choirmasters & -Assocs., 1944; Cond. num. Concerts; Music Critic, Daily Express, Daily Gleaner. Mbrships: Int. platform Assn.; PR Dir., Kingston YMCA; Y's Men's Club; Past Pres., ibid.; Past Dist. Gov., ibid. Hons: Silver Musgrave Medal, inst. of Jamaica, 1963; Order of Distinction, Govt. of Jamaica, 1973. Hobbies: Swimming; Reading, Law. Address: YMCA HQ, 21 Hope Rd., Kingston 10 Jamaica. 22.

BECKIE, Donal Wayne, b. 24 March 1938, Greenville, Ill., USA. College Teacher; Associate Professor of Music; Recitalist; Clinician; Conductor. Educ: BMus, Conserv., Univ. of the Pacific, Stockton, Calif.; MMus, DMus, Ind. Univ., Bloomington, Ind. m. Carolyn June Watson, 1 s., 1 d. Debut: Clarinet Soloist, Berkeley Young Peoples Symph. Orch., 1956. Career: Tchr., Tennyson High Schl., 1960-65; Dir. of Bands, Woodwind Tchr., Gettysburg Coll., Gettysburg, Pa.; Woodwind, music hist. & music educ., Dir. of Bands, Acting Chmn., Fine Arts Dept., Susquehanna Univ., 1968-; Recitalist; Adjudicator; Cond.; Woodwind Specialist, tchr., ensembles coach & music historian, Pa. Governor's Schl. for the Arts, 1973-; Woodwind Specialist, Pa. Alpiners German Band. Num. recordings. Contbr. to: NACWPI. Mbrships: Phi Delta Kappa; phi Mu Alpha Sinfonia; Phi Beta Mu; Int. Clarinet Soc.; NACWPI, MENC, Hons. incl: Outstanding Prof. Award, Gettysburg Coll., 1968. Hobbies: Cross county skiing; Bowling; Woodworking; Reed making. Address: RD 2 Orchard Hills, Selinsgrove, PA 17870, USA.

BECKMAN, Fokke Ph., b. 5 May 1931, Zandvoort, Netherlands. Violinist. Educ: Dip., state examinations. m. P. H. Buis, 2 c. Career: 4 yrs. w. Haarlem Symph. Orch.; 22 yrs. w. Utrecht Symph. Orch.; 8 yrs. w. Radio Phil., Hilversum; TV apps. w. string orchs. num. recordings w. string orch. Mbrships: Soc. of Radio & TV Musicians. Hobbies: Tennis; Sailing. Address: L.v.d. Tongelaan 16, 1251 N W Laren, Netherlands.

BECKWITH, John, b. 9 Mar. 1927, Victoria, BC, Can. Composer; Writer; Pianist; Professor. Educ: MusB, MusM, Univ. of Toronto; pvte. study w. Alberto Guerrero (piano) & Nadia Boulanger (comp.). div., 1 d., 2 s. Career: Prof. (Dean, 1970-77), fac. of music, Univ. of Toronto. Comps. incl: Night Blooming Cereus (chmbr. opera), 1953-58; The Shivaree (opera), 1965-66, 78; Concerto Fantasy (piano & orch.), 1959; Flower Variations & Wheels (orch.), 1962; Circle w. Tangents (instrumental ensemble), 1967; Quartet, 1977; Taking a Stand (instrumental ensemble), 1972; Keyboard Practice (4 players, 10 keyboards), 1979; Johah (soloists, choir, orch.), 1963; Sharon Fragments (choir), 1966; The Sun Dance (choirs, speakers, organ, percussion), 1968; piano, vocal & college music. sev. recordings of own works. Publs: (co-ed) The Modern Composer & His World, 1961, & Contemporary Canadian Composers, 1975. Contbr. to newspapers & profl. jrnls. Mbrships: Bd., Can. Music Ctr., Can. Opera Co., New Music Concerts, etc. num. hons. & award. Address: c/o F c. of Music, Univ. of Toronto, Toronto, Ont. M5S 1A1, Can. 14.

BEDBROOK, Gerald Stares, b. 23 May 1907, London, UK. Musicologist; Pianist. Educ: Dulwich & Kings Coll., London. Career: Lectr., Medieval Music & Early Keyboard, Trinity Coll.; Lectr., Oriental Music, Schl. of Oriental Langs., Inst. of Contemporary Arts Soc.; TV apps. Comps: (Ed.) Four Toccatas - Claudio Merulo, 1954; Marco Antonio di Bologna - Recerchari, Motetti, Canzoni, 1954; Giovanni Gabrieli - Werke für Tastinstrumente, 1957. Publs: Keyboard Music from the Middle Ages, 1949, 1973; Liszt in London. Contbr. to num. profl. publs. Mbrships: Liszt Soc. (Hon. Mbr.); Patron, The Paderewski Museum, Morges, Switz.; Town Mbr., Royal British Club. Address: Royal British Club, Rua da Estrela 8, 1200 Lisbon, Portugal.

BEDFORD, David, b. 4 Aug. 1937, London, UK. Composer; Arranger; Teacher (Piano, Saxophone & Trombone). Educ: RAM. m. Susan Pilgrim, 2 d. Num. Compositions. Recordings: 2 Poems of Kenneth Patchen for Choir; music for Albion Moonlight, Soprano arr. 7 instruments; The Tentacles of the Dark Nebula, Tenor, arr. 8 strings; 18 Bricks, 2 elec. Guitars; You asked for it, solo Guitar; Trona, arr. 12 instruments; Nurses

Song, 10 Guitars. Hons: ARAM, 1970. Hobbies: Table Tennis; Astronomy. Mgmt: Universal Ed. Address: 39 Shakespeare Rd., Mill Hill, London, NW7 4BA, UK. 3.

BEDFORD, Steuart John Rudolf, b. 31 July 1939, London, UK. Conductor; Pianist. Educ: RAM; BA, Oxford Univ.; FRCO; FRAM. m. Norma Burrowes. Debut: as orchl. cond., Oxford, 1964; as opera cond., Sadlers Wells, 1967. Career: on staff, RAM, 1965-; Glyndebourne Fest., 1965-67; Engl. Opera Grp., now Engl. Music Theatre, Aldeburgh & London, 1967-73; Artistic Dir. & Res. Cond., EMT & Aldeburgh Fest., 1975-; Freelance Cond., w. Metropolitan Opera, NY, Santa Fe Opera, Teatro Colon, Buenos Aires, Brussels, Lyons, etc.; Cond., Welsh Nat. Opera, Royal Opera House Covent Garden; BBC; Netherlands Radio; Belgian Radio, etc. Sev. recordings. Recip. Medal, Worshipful Co. of Musicians. Hobbies: Golf; Skiing. Mgmt: Harrison/Parrott Ltd., 22 Hillgate St., London 38, UK. Address: c/o Mgmt. 4, 30.

BEECHAM, (Sir) Adrian, b. 3 Sept. 1904, Lucerne, Switz. Composer. Educ: Mus Bac, Durham Univ., 1926; TCM. m. Barbara Joyce, 2 s., 1 d. Comps: 4 songs; Little Ballet Suite; Ruth (sacred contata); 4 part songs. Mbrships: Savage Clug; ISM. Hobby: Country life. Address: Compton Scorpion Manor, Shipston on Stour, Warwickshire, UK.

BEECHEY, Gwilym Edward, b. 12 Jan. 1938, London, UK. Lecturer; Organist; Harpischordist; Musical Scholar. Educ: MA., Mus B, Ph.D (Cantab.); FRCO; FTCL; FLCM; LRAM; ARCM. Compositions: Intermezzo for Organ, 1970; Chorale Prelude 'In dulci jubilo', 1973; Ave Maria, gracia Dej plena, 2073. Editions incl: Thomas Arne, 8 Keyboard Sonatas, 1969; Haydn Symps. 34, 46, 50, 51, 54, 56, 59, 69, 1968-73; C F Abel, Sonata in E minor, Op. 6 no. 3, 1972; Sonata in G major, Op. 6 no. 6, 1972; Symph. in E flat, Op. 14, no. 2, 1972; F Barsanti, 2 Sonatas for treble recorder & continuo, 1973; Henry Lawes, Hymns to the Holy Trinity, 1973; Six romantic pieces for clarinet & piano, 1976. T I inley, Jr. Anthem; Lot Good Arise; Recent Researches in the Music of the Classical Era, 1977; T. Morley, Motet Ndo Mortem Peccatoris, 1977; Musica Britanica XXX, 1976. Contbr. to var. profl. jrnls. Hobbies: Lit.; Theatre; Topography; Cricket. Address: 15 Hamlyn Ave., Hull HU4 6BT, UK. 3. 28.

BEEKS, Graydon Fisher, Jr., b. 15 Oct. 1948, Long Beach, Calif., USA. Musicologist; Conductor. Educ: BA, Pomona Coll., Claremont, Calif., 1969; MA, 1971, PhD Cand., Univ. of Calif., Berkeley. m. Serena Elizabeth Evans. Career incls: Teaching Asst., Univ. of Calif., Berkeley, 1970-72; Fndr. Cond., Berkeley Vocal Ensemble, 1970-73; Assoc., Univ. of Calif., 1977-78; Dir. of Music, St. Clement's Episcopal Ch., Berkeley, 1976-78; Instructor in Music & Dir. of Choral Activities, Vassar Coll., 1978-. Publs. Sub-Ed., new ed. Grove's Dictionary of Music & Musicians, 1974-76; Handel's Chandos Anthems: The 'Extra' Movements, 1978. Mbrships: Am. Musicol. Soc.; Coll. Music Soc.; Am. Guild of Organists Hobby: Sports. Address: Box 448, Vassar Coll., Poughkeepsie, NY, NY 12601, USA.

BEER, Anton de, b. 27 Oct. 1924, Haarlem, The Netherlands. Conductor; Composer; Pianist; Organist; Harpsichordist; Archiphonist. Educ: Dip., Acad. of Music, Amsterdam. m. Elisabeth Pelganta, 5 children. Debut: Organist, 31 tone organ, Teylers Mus., Haarlem, 1952. Career incls: Accomp. to singers & instrumentalists; Cond., maj. choral socs., youth & profl. orchs.; Apps. as solo pianist in Neatherlands, Germany & Austria; Choral & orchl. organist in Europe, USA, Can., Aust. & TV apps. Comps. incl: Sonatina & Var. comps. for 31 tone organ. Contbr. to profl. mags. Mbrships. incl: Pres., Huygens-Fokker Fndn. Hobbies: Chess; Swimming; Mod. Lit.; Vis. Mus. & Theatres. Mgmt: Nederlands Impresariaat, Amsterdam. Address: Kleine Houstraat 116, The Netherlands.

BEERMAN, Burton, b. 12 June 1943, Atlanta, Ga., USA. Assistant Professor of Music. Educ: B Mus., Fla. Stae Univ., 1966; M Mus., Univ. of Mich., 1968; DMA., ibid. 1971 m. Stella Celeste, 1 s. Career incl: Aswt. Prof. of Music Comps. & Hist., Bowling Green State Univ.; Dir., Univ. Electronic Music Studio. Comp: Mixtures (voices, instruments & tape), 1973; Frame (6 flutes), 1973; Sensations (clarinet & tape, Advance Recordings label). Mbrships: Am. Comp. Alliance; Broadcast Music, Inc.; Am. Soc. of Univ. Comps.; Ohio Theory-Comp. Tchrs. Hons: 1st Prize, comp. for flute, Pitts. Flute Club, 1971; Composition Impressions of Birth chosen for perf. at Gaudeamus Int. Fest. Bilthoven, Holland, 1969. Hobby: Photography. Address: Coll. of Musical Arts, Bowling Green State Univ., Bowling Green, OH 43403, USA.

BEESON, Jack Hamilton, b. 15 July 1921, Muncie, Ind., USA. Composer; Educator. Educ: BMus, 1942, MMus, 1943, Eastman Schl. of Music, Rochester Univ.; Grad. study, ibid &

Columbia Univ.; Study, piano, cello, clarinet & percussion. m. Nora Bette Sigerist, 1 s (dec.), 1 d. Debut: As actor in own opera, My Heart's in the Highlands, NET, 1970. Comps. (over 50 publd.) incl: Hello Out There; The Sweet Bye & Bye; Lizzie Borden; My Heart's in Highlands; Captain Jinks of the Horse Marines; Dr. Heidegger's Fountain of Youth (operas); Symphony No. 1 in A; 3 Choral Rounds; Two Settings from The Bay Psalm Book (all recorded). Contbr. to jrnls. & Grove's Dict., 6th Ed. Mbrships: SEc., Alice M Ditson Fund; VP, Int. Contemp. Music Exchange; Chmn., Music Publ. Comm., Columbia Univ. Press; Co-acting Pres., 1975-76 CRI, Inc.; Vice Chmn., Comps. Forum; Am. Acad./Inst. of Arts & Letters. Hons: Rome Prize, 1948-50; Fulbright Fellowship, 1949; Guggenheim Fellowship, 1958-59; Marc Blitzstein Award, Nat. Inst. of Arts & Letters, 1968; Gold Medal, Nat. Arts Club, 1976. Hobbies: Swimming; Sailing. Address: 40£ Riverside Dr., NYC, NY 10025, USA. 2, 14.

BEESTON, Michael Harding, b. 11 May 1948, Blackpool, UK. Violist; Teacher. Educ: studied w. Frederick Riddle at RMCM; GRSM. m. Janet Bond, 1 d. Career: mbr. BBC Scottish Symph. Orch.; prin. viola, Scottish Chmbr. Orch.; violist, Edinburgh Quartet, w. whom perf. in UK, Germany Holland, Scandinavia & S Am.; apps. on radio & concert platform as soloist; perfs. at Edinburgh fest. & Vienna Conserv; pt.-time tchr., RSAMD. Recording: Shostakovich Piano Quintet w. Edinburgh Quartet & Roger Woodward. Hons: Webster Memorial Prize, 1970. Hobby: Dev. & Appreciation for Good Things of Life. Address: 119 Craigleith Rd., Edinburgh EH4 2EH, UK.

BEGG, Heather, b. Nelson, NZ. Operatic Mazzo Soprano. Educ: Attended St. Mary's Music Coll., Aukland, 1950-53, Sydney Conservatorium of Music, Aust., 1954-56 & Nat. Schl. of Opera, London, UK, 1957-59; Studies Voice w. Florence Norberg, London. m. W J King. Debut: Auckland, NZ, 1954. Career: Prin. ezzo Soprano, Nat. Opera of Aust. 1954-56, Carl Rosa Opera Co., London, UK, 1960, Sadler's Wells Opera. London, 1961-64, NZ Opera Co., 1964-66; Guest Artist, Royal opera, Covent Gdn., London, UK, Sadler's Wells & Scottish Opera, 1967-71; Res. Mezzo Soprano, Royal Opera, 1972-76; Res. Mezzo Soprano Aust. Opera, 1976-; Guest artist, opera houses in France, Can., Am., Salzburg Fest.; Concert artist & recitalist on stage, radio & TV, UK, NZ, & Aust.; Unitel Film, Le Nozze di Figaro. Recordings incl: Les Troyens; Mefistofele; I Puritani; The Little Sweep. Hons: Sydney Sun Aria Winner, 1955; Recip., NZ Govt. Music Bursary, 1956; Countess of Munster Scholarship, 1959; OBE, 1978. Hobbies: Tapestry; Photography; Painting, Gardening. Address: c/o Aust. Opera, PO Box R223, Royal Exchange, NSW 2000, Aust. 23, 27, 29, 30.

BEGLARIAN, Grant, b. 1 Dec. 1927, Tiflis, Georgia, USSR. Composer; Editor; Administrator. Educ: B Mus., Univ. of Mich., 1950; M Mus., ibid., 1952; DMA, 1958, Boston Univ., 1947; studied w. Aaron Copland, Berkshire Music Ctr., 1959. m. Joyce Heeney, 1 s., 1 d. Career: Field Rep., Ford Fndn., 1961-65; Pres., Musi-Book Assocs., 1960-65; Dir., Contemporary Music Proj., Ford Fndn., 1965-69; Dean Schl. of Perf. Arts, Univ. of So. Calif., 1969-. Compositions: Sinfonia for Strings, 1974; Diversions for Viola, Cello & Orch., 1972; Fables, Foibles & Fancies, 1971; And All the Hills Echoed, 1970; A Hymn for Our Times, 1969; Divertiments for Orch., 1967; Woodwind Quintet, 1966. Ed. of all publs. of the Contemporary Music Proj., 1965-69. Mbrships incl: ASCAP; Coll. Music Soc.; Am. Music Ctr., etc. Hons: The Ysaye medal, 1971; The Gershwin Meml. Award, 1959; Ford Fndn. Composers Award, 1959. Hobbies: Reading. Address: Univ. of So. Calif., LA, CA 90007, USA.

BEHR, Jan, b. 1 Apr. 1911, Krnov, Czechoslovakia. Conductor (Piano, Violin, Bassoon). Educ: LLD, German Univ. of Prague; Acad. of Music, Prague; Masterclass Piano w. Franz Langer; Conducting w. George Szell. m. Elizabeth Eichnar, 1 d. Debut: La Traviata at German Opera House, Prague, 1936. Career: Res. Cond., Met. Opera, NY, 1951-; Apps. at Aspen, Colo., Music Festival; Cinn. Opera; Orchestre National de Belgique, Brussels. Num. recordings on Columbia & Urania. Address: 514 West End Ave., New York, NY 10024, USA.

BEHREND, Louise, b. 3 Oct. 1916, Wash. DC, USA. Violinist; Teacher. Educ: Inst. Musical Art, Mozarteum, Salzburg, Austria; Dip., Juilliard Grad. Schl., NY, USA. Debut: Town Hall, NYC, 1950. Career: Num. perfs. as soloist & recitalist; Var. tours inclng. US & Far East; Mbr., Fac., The Juilliard Schl., 1943-; Mbr., Music Fac., NY Univ., 1967-; Bd. of Dirs., Harlem Schl. of the Arts, NYC, 1969-; Fndr. & Dir., Schl. for Strings, NYC, 1970. Contbr., 1 Chapt., The Suzuki Concept, 1973. Contbr. to Allegro, 1971-72. Mbrships: VP, Suzuki Assn. of the Ams.; Am. String Tchrs. Assn. HOns: 3 Fellowships, Juilliard Grad. Schl., 1939-41; Medal of Hon., Soc. Eugene Ysaye, 1971. Address: 155 W 68th St., NY, NY 10023, USA.

BEHREND, Siegfried, b. 19 Nov. 1933, Berlin, Germany. Professor of Music; Guitarist; Conductor; Composer. Educ: Klindworth Scharwenka Conserv., Berlin, Germany. m. Claudia Brodzinska. Debut: Leipzig, 1953. Career: Has appeared in almost all the Concert Halls around the World, inclng., Berlin Phil., NY Phil., Vienna Concert House, Mozarteum, Grosses Festspielhaus, Salzburg etc: to about 200 Films; Has made about 4000 Radio Recordings throughout the World. Fndr., Dir., Int. Music Fest., Altmuhtal, Germany. Comps: approx. 100 publd, & many of these recorded for Radio, TV or Records; Approx. 1000 arrs., num. of which have been recorded for Radio, TV of Records. Recordings: DGG (now exclusively); EMI; Nippon Crown; Nippon Columbia; Da Camera; Thorofon; Suparaphon; Acanta; Bellaphon, w. 80 LPs altogether. Contbr. to: Guitar Review, NY; Gitarre Information, Munich, etc. Mbrships: incl: Hon. Life mbr., Am. Guitar Fndn., Japan Guitar Assn., NZ Guitar Assn. Hobby: Fishing. Mgmt: Informations und Veranstaltungsdienst Siegfried Behrend, 1 Berlin 33. Address: Johannisbergerstr. 4, 1000 Berlin 33, German Fed. Repub.

BEHRENS, Jack, b. 25 March 1935, Lancaster, Pa., USA. Composer; Pianist; Administrator. Educ: BSc (Comp.), 1958, MSc (Comp.), 1959, Juilliard Schl. of Music, NYC; PhD, Comp., Harvard Univ., Cambridge. m. Sonja Peterson. Career: Lectures & Lecture-Recitals, USA, Can. & UK; Perfs. as Pianist & Cond., USA & Can., incl. Radio & TV apps.; Comps. perfd., USA & Can.; Artistic Dir., A New Music/Dance Ensemble for Young Audiences of Kern County - Perf. Laboratory, 1973-75. Comps: In A Manger (SATB); The Older Order Amish (film score); Happy Birthday, John Cage. Recordings: The Feast of Life (piano); Opus One (No. 13). Contbr. to: Notes; Studies in Music from the Univ. of W Ont.; The Piano Quarterly. Mbrships: ASCAP; Am. Musicol. Soc.; Nat. Assn. of Comps., USA; Can. League of Comps. Address: Fac. of Music, Univ. of Western Ont., London, Ont., Can. N6A 3K7.

BEHRENS, Richard Hermann, b. 7 July 1925, Rustenburg, TVL, S Africa. Professor of Music; Head of Music Department; Director; Organist; Musicologist. Educ: BA, Univ. of Stellenbosch; BMus, ibid; ODMS; LTCL m. Irma Katharine Schutte, 5 c. Career: Lectr. & Sr. Lectr., 1948-64, Hd. of Music Dept. & Dir. of Conservatoire, 1961-, prof. of Music, 1965, Univ. of Stellenbosch. Mbrships: Chmn., Committee of Heads of Univ. Music Dept.; Music Committee, Univ. of S Africa; S African Soc. of Music Tchrs.; S Africa Acad. for Arts & Science. Hon: Merit Award, Cape Tercentenary Gndn., 1979. Address: 13 Kronendal Ave., Stellenbosch 7600, S Africa.

BEILBY, John Frederick, b. 3 March 1945, York, UK. Senior Lecturer in Music; Examiner; Adjudicator. Educ: Univ. of London; MTC (London); currently Univ. of Leeds, MPhil. in preparation; LCM; GLCM: FLCM; LRAM; LTCL. Career: Snr. Lectr. in Music, Mabel Fletcher Coll., Liverpool; Examiner; Adjudicator. Contbr. to: LCM Mag. Mbrships: Fellow, Royal Soc. of Arts; ISM; LCM Soc.; RSCM. Hons: Bromley-Drry Gold Medal Memorial Prize, 1967. Hobbies: Theatre; Travel; Reading. Address: 92 Kingfisher Way, Upton, Wirral, Merseyside L49 4PS, UK.

BEIMAN, Melvyn, b. 2 Jan. 1932, Brooklyn, NY, USA. Musician, English Horn, Oboe. Educ: BS, NY. Univ.; MA Hunter Coll., NY. m. Frances Marian Beiman, 2 d. Career: Former Asst. Prof. of Music, Rutgers, The State Univ., Newark, NY; Mbr. Jeffrey Woodwind Quintet; Prin. Oboe, The Chmbr. Symph. of NJ; Oboe Soloist, The Orch. Da Camera, Berlin, NJ; English Horn & Oboe Soloist, The NJ Symph. Recordings: English Horn Soloist, The Wind Music of Alan Hovhannes, Mbrships: Am. Fed. of Musicians; AAUP. Hobbies: Fishing; Motoring. Address: 124 Mohawk Dr., Cranford, NJ07016, USA.

BEIRER, Hans, b. 23 June 1911, Vienna, Neustadt, Austria. Heldentenor. Educ: Univ. Vienna, Phil., Medicin.; State Music Acad. Vienna, song, drama. Debut: Linz. m. Terry Rofrana. Career: Tours throughout Austria, German, France, Italy, UK, Lebanon, Spain, Portugal, USA, Japan, South Am., Radio, TV apps., Otello 1961, Tannhäuser - Beirut. Recordings: var. operas. Mbrships: German Theatre Company; Hons. mbr. grand Opera paris; Hon. mbr. German Opera Berlin. publs. incl: Fairy Tales, 1976. Hons: Federal German Merit Cross, 1st class; Great Federal German Merit Cross, w. a gold band, May market for watercolours, Mannheim. Hobbies: Poetry; Painting. Address: Mahlerstr. 13,A 1010 Vienna Austria.

BEITAMOUNI, Mohammad Mujab, son of Khalil, b. 23 Dec. 1937, Damascus, Syria. Music Teacher (piano, flute, recorder, choir, elementary/preparatory music). Educ: Syrain Cert. of Secondary Educ.; Examination Cert. of Music Instr. m. Britta Kristina Mossesson. Debut: Gothenburg. Career; Syrian TV & Radio. Comps: Num. Arabic songs & sketches; Instrumental

pieces, some w. Swedish text. Mbrships: Riksforbundet Svariges Musikpedagoger/Nat. Confederatin of Sweden Music Pedagogues. Recip. 5 yrs. scholarship granted by Syrian Educ. Min., 1963. Hobbies: Music; Poetry; Swimming. Address: Golvläggaregatan 4A, S-412 62 Gothenburg, Sweden.

BEJINARIU, Mircea, b. 26 Oct. 1950, Cluj-Napoca, Romania. Assistant Lecturer. Educ: Schl. of Music, Bluj-Napoca (Piano); Conserv. of Music G. Dima, Cluj-Napoca; MA, Musicol., ibid; Drd. Musicol., ibid. Publs: Co-Author, Musical Folklore in the Huedin Area, 1978. Contbr. to num. Musicol., Song to Romania Nat., Fest., 1979; Prize Musicol., Union of Composers & Musicol.; Romania, 1979. Hobbies: Films; Books. Address: Str. Ploiesti 34, R-3400 Cluj-Napoca, Romania.

BELAMARIĆ, Miro, b. 9 Feb. 1935, Sibenik, Yugoslavia. Conductor; Composer. Educ: Studied Cond., Musical Acad., Zagreb, 1962; studied comp., ibid., 1975. m. Angelika Rüttjerodt. Debut: w. Zagreb Phil., Croatian Nat. Theatre, Zagreb. Career: Vienna State Opera; Craz Opera; Prague Nat. Theatre; Brno Opera; Salzburg Summer Fest.; Athens Fest.; Teatro Reggio - Torino; Teatro La Fenice, Venezia; Teatro Verdi, Triests; Opera Mainz; Fest. Bordeaux, etc. Comps: The Love of Don Perlimdlin, opera; Variation for Piano & Orch.; Vocal & Chmbr. music (recorded). Hons: Zagreb City Prizes for Music, 1975; Critics Prize, 1969, 1976. Address: Opera HNK, Zagreb 41.000, Yugoslavia.

BELANGER, Marc, b. 30 July 1940, Que., Canada. Violinist; Violist; Arranger; Composer; Teacher; Conductor. Educ: Baccalaureat de Rhetorique; Conseratoire de Quebec, Canada. m. Hélène Arcand, 1 s., 2 d. Début: Que. Symph. Orch. career: Mbr. of the Que. Symph. Orch., 16 yrs., from 1957 (viola solo for the last two seasons); Arranger-Cond. for Radio broadcasts during 1964-68; Tchr., Conserv. of Que., 1971-, at Montreal's Univ., 1973-; Mbr. of the CBC Chamber Orch. of Que. & Mbr. of the CBC Orch. of Montreal, 8 yrs.; Many public appearances w. folk singer Gilles Vignealt. Guest cond., Montreal CBC Orch., Jan. 76. Compositions: Modulation Perpetuelle, recorded for the CBC, Moncton. Recordings incl: Instrumental Record for Strings & Rythm (Le Groupe Marc Belanger); Espoir, Reverie Sentimentale; Mélodie pour vi-tar; Fendu en Quartes; Gigue et variations; Gigue Olympique. Mbrships: Que. Musicians Assn.; Musicians Guild of Montreal. Hobbies: Home decorating & finishing; Composing. Address: 31 des Trembles, Domaine des Haut-Bois, Ste-Julie, Chambly, Quebec, Canada Ja 260.

BELCHER, John Theodore, b. 3 Dec. 1937, Orpington, UK. Organist & Choirmaster. Educ: RCM, 1956-58; BA, 1961, MA, 1965, Cert. in Educ.; 1962, Cambridge Univ.; FRCO, 1962; CHM, 1964; ARCM (organ perf.), 1958. Career: Organist & Choirmaster, Knockholt Parish Ch., 1956-61, Holy Trinity Ch., Folkestone, 1963-67; Asst. Organist, Chester Cathedral, & Dir. of Music, Chester Cathedral Choir Schl.., 1967-71; Organist & Master of the Choiristers, St. Peter's Ch., Bournemouth, & Vis. Music Master, Winchester Coll., 1971-. Publs: The Organ, 1966 (A History of the Organs of Holy Trinity Ch., Folkestone), 1966; The Organs of Chester Cathedral, 1970; The Organs of St. Peter's Ch., Bournemouth, 1976. Mbr., RCO; ISM. Hobbies: Church arch.; Swimming. Address: St. Peter's Ch., Bournemouth, UK.

BELCOURT, Emile, b. Canada. Opera Singer. Educ: Acad. of Music, Vienna. Career: Early opera appearances in Germany & France; Leading role in Ravel's L'Heure Espagnole, Covent Gdn., 1963; Mbr., Engl. Nat. Opera, 1963-, inclng. leading roles in Orpheus in the Underworld; Die Fledermaus; Bluebeard; La vie Parisienne; Patients; The Violins of St. Jacques; Lucky Peter's Journey; Salome; The Coronation of Poppea; The Makropolos Case, etc.; lead in stage musicals - Man of La Mancha & Kiss Me Kate; Can. Opera debut in Heloise & Abelard, 1973; recent performances incl. title role in Philidor's Blase le Sazitier, Inst. Francais. Recordings incl: role of Loge in The Rhinegold, w. Engl. Nat. Opera (EMI). Address: c/o Engl. Nat. Opera, London Coliseum, St. Martin's Ln., London WC2N 4ES, UK.

BELINFANTE-DEKKER, Martha Suzanna Betje, b. 12 Aug. 1900, Amsterdam, Holland. Singing, speech & voice pedaagogue; Composer. Educ: Singing study w. Ina Santhagens Waller, Joh. Dresen-Dhont, Berthe Sereon & Rose Schonberg, Ida Mollinger, Acad. of Dramatic Art. Piano & theory study w. Paul F. Sanders & husband. m. Dan. Belinfante, 1923. Career: Dir., Muziekschool Watergraafsmeer, Amsterdam, 1945-; developed & patented method of breathing, etc., following loss of own voice due to Asthma & Bronchitis. Pretjes; num. folk-songs; Zo geneest U zelf Uw astma en bronchitis; var. adult games incl: De wethouders v. Waterwelde; de zangers; de dansers; O mens; Vader Tijd. Recip. Prize for best children's poems, 1933. Address: Pythagorasstraat 27, Amsterdam-O. Holland.

BELINSKÝ, Isai (Ysaye), b. 17 Jan. 1900, Irkutsk, Russia. Oboist. m. Pola Belinsky (dec.) Educ: Moscow Conserv.; studied w. Prof. L Bleuzet, paris. Career incls: played w. ldng. symph. orchs. through Europe & Am.; w. NBC Symp. Orch. under Arturo Toscanini, NYC Symph. under Leopold Stokowski; Tchr., Mexican Nat. Conserv. of Music, Mexico City; Film, The Oboe Player; Engl. Horn Player. Publs. incl: Solo Oboe & English Horn With Piano Accompaniment; The Professional Oboist, 1960; Visual Fingering Chart for the Oboe, 1972; The Complete Oboist, 1976. Contbr. of column, The Oboist Looks at his Problems, to Int. Musicians Mag. Mbrships: NYC Musicians Union Local 802; Local 10, Chgo.; Nat. Soc. of Lit. & the Arts, Wash. DC. Address: 81-11 Pettit Ave., Elmhurst, NY 11373, USA.

BELIY, Victor Arkadyevich, b. 14 Jan. 1904, Berdichev, Ukraine. Composer. Educ: Moscow. Conserv. Compositions incl: Instrumental works - Lyric Sonatina, 1929; Sonata for Piano, 1941; Sonata for Piano No. 4, 1946; 16 Preludes on Folk Themes of the USSR, 1947; Two Pieces for Piano on Byelorussian Themes, 1950; Sonata for Violin & Piano, 1953; works for voice & piano - 26 Works, 1926; War Cycle (words by E Toller), 1929; Ten Chuvash Songs, 1933; Leavetaking, 1935; Song of the Partisan Girl, 1935; The Little Airman, 1935; Winter Road, 1936; Sea Song, 1939; Ballade of Captain Gastello, 1941; Lenin's Birthday, 1949; choral works -Hunger march, 1930; Suite on Chuvash Themes, 1936; Two Fragments from poem V I Lenin, 1938; Three Roads, 1939; Slav. Suite, 1942; Two Choral Works on Russian Folk Themes, 1945; num. songs. Mbrship: Bd., USSR Composers Union. Ons: State Prize, 1952; Honoured Artist of Byelorussia, 1955; Honoured Worker of the Arts of RSFSR, 1956; Order of Red Banner of Labour, 1947; Badge of Hon., 1964. Address: Composers Union of USSR, 8-10 Ulitsa Nezhdanovoi, Moscow, USSR.

BELKIN, Alan Ivor, b. 5 July, 1951, Montreal, Canada. Composer. Pianist; Organist; Teacher. Educ: BA, Sir Geo. Wms. Univ; MA, McGill Univ; Study under Bernard Lagace (organ), David Diamond (composition). Debut: Sarah Fischer Concert, 1969. Hons: Scholarships from Quebec Govt. and Juilliard Schl. Address: 5052 Bessborough, Montreal, Quebec HAV 253, Canada.

BELL, Arnold Craig, b. 23 Jan. 1911, Lancaster, UK. Retired Schoolmaster; Author. Educ: Tchrs. Dip. m. Edith France Walker, 1 d. Comps: arrs. of Negro Spirituals; 4 pieces from Handel & Scarlatti for oboe & piano; First lessons in Handel. Publs. Handel, A Chronological Thematic Catalogue, 1972; Handel before England, 1975; The Songs of Schubert, 1964; The Lieder of Brahms (in prep.). Contbr. to: Music Review, Penguin Music Magazine. mbr. prog. soc. of Harrogate Music Club. Hobbies: Cricket; Walking; Countryside. Address: Folly Hall, Thornthwaite, Harrogate, Yorks. HG3 2QT, UK.

BELL, David M., b. 11 Aug. 1954, Waukesha, Wis., USA. Conductor; Teacher; Composer & Arranger; Church Musician. Educ: BA, N Ill. Univ., 1975; Public Schl. Tchrs. Cert. in Music, ibid, 1975; MMus (Choral Cond.), Univ. of Cinn. Coll. Conserv. of Music. m. Lois Jean Bell. Career: Music Dir., Dayton Liederkranz Turner Soc. Choruses, 1979-80; Public Schl. Music, Dayton, Ohio, 1979-80; Formed Cinn. Singer's Ensemble, Cinn., 1978; Perf. w. Chgo. Symph. Chorus & Cinn. May Fest. Recording: w. Chgo. Syjph. Orch., Missa Solemnis (Beethoven). Mbrshis: Am. Choral Dirs. Assn.; Am. Musicol. Soc. Hons: Outstanding Masters Student in Choral Cond., Univ. of Cinn., 1979; Pi Kappa Lambda, 1979; Grad. Assistantship, Univ. of Cinn., 1978-79; Full Univ. Grad. Scholarship, ibid., 1977-78. Hobbies: Cross-country skiing; Backpacking; Touring. Address: 1596D Beaver Ridge Dr., Kettering, OH 45429, USA.

BELL, Derek Fleetwood, b. 16 Nov. 1923, Belfast, UK. Composer; Teacher; Performer on Piano, Harps, Oboe, Oboe d'amore, Cor anglais, Cimbalom, Dulcimer, Santur, Tuned Percussion Instruments & Tanpura. Educ: Sr. Cert. Exam., N Ireland Min. of Educ.; ARCM, 1955-54; LRAM, 1957; BMus, Dublin, 1959; studied w. many noted tchrs. Debut: Belfast, 1947. Career incls: prin. Cor anglais, City of Belfast Orch.; Prin. Harp. BBC N Ireland Orch.; Répétiteur, N Ireland Opera & Ulster Opera; Guest Soloist w. var. orchs.; TV apps. in UK, Germany, France, Finland, USA, Can. Comps. incl: Symph. No. 1 in E flat; Three pieces for oboe & piano; songs; piano sonatas; incidental music; etc. Recordings incl: O'Carolan's Harp Music; Carolan's Receipt Vol II (solo harp album); var. recordings w. Chieftains. Contbr. to var. publs. Mbr. profl. org. Hobbies incl: Yoga. Mgmt: Kinetic Music, London. Address: 144 Malon Ave., Belfast 9, UK. 28.

BELL, Donald Munro, b. 19 June 1934, Burnaby, BC, Can. Concert & Opera Singer. Educ: RCM; pvt. studies w. Prof. Carl

Ebert, Opera Studio Berlin (2 yrs.), Prof. Hermann Weissenborn (voice trng.), Berlin, 5 yrs., Prof. Edith Boroschek-Duesseldorf (voice), 7 yrs. 1 s. Debut: Concert, Wigmore Hall, London, 1958; Opera, Bayreuth, 1958. Career: Düsseldorf Opera, 1964-67; Glyndebourne, 1973-75; Apps., most European Music fests.; Tours, 17 countries. Sev. recordings. Recip., Arnold Bax Medal, 1955. Mgmt: AIM, 3 & 4 Albert Tce., London NWI 7SU, UK; Hart/Murdock, 195 College St., Toronto, Ont., Can.

BELL, S Aaron, b. 24 Apr. 1924, Muskogee, OK, USA. Arranger; Composer; Bassist; Pianist; Tubist. Educ: BA, Xavier Univ., New Orleans, La.; MA, NY Univ.; MED, EdD Cand.; Columbia Univ. m. DeLores Orton Bell, 1 s., 2 d. Career incls: Staff Mbr., NBC, 2 yrs.; Broadway shows, inclng. Golden Boy, Apple Tree, Compulsion, Golden Rainbow; Res. Comp., LaMama Theatre; Mbr., Buffalo, Cleveland & NY Symphs.; film soundtracks: Anatomy of Murder, Cool World, Paris Blues, Billy the Kid; Guest Lectr., var. colls.; sev. TV apps. Comps. incl: incidental music to plays by Ed Bullins; African Springtime; Congo; Let the Rain Fall; Oh-So; Watergate Sonata; Bicentennial Symph. Recordings: Flying Dutchman; Herold; RCA; MGM; Columbia. Mbrships. incl: ASCAP; Nat. Soc. of Lit. & the Arts; Phi Delta Kappa. Hons. incl: Int. Jazz Critic Poll Award for Best Bassist, 1959; ASCAP Comp. Awards, 1969-75; Best jazz Tuba Player, Down Beat Poll, 1960-61; Int. Fest. of Plays Award, Milan & Venice, 1972. Address: 444 S Columbia Ave., Mt. Vernon, NY 10053, USA.

BELL, Sebastian, b. 19 Oct. 1941, Oxford, UK. Flautist. Educ: RAM, 1957-60. m. Elizabeth Harrison, 2 c. Career: Sadlers WElls Opera Co. Orch., 1960-63; Prin. flute, BBC Welsh Orch., 1963-67; currently Prin. flute, London Sinfonietta; Prof., RCM. Hons: solo instrumentalists prize, Harriet Cohen Int. Music Awards, 1964, 65; Hon. RCM. Address: 93 Popes Grove, Twickenham, Middx., UK.

BELLHOUSE, Alan Robert, b. 28 June 1914, Sydney, NSW, Australia. Musician; Author; Conductor. Educ: BA, Univ. of Sydney; State Conservatorium of Music, Sydney; MusD, IUA, Aust. m Dulcie Sybil Holland, 1 s., 1 d. Career: Cond., var. choirs; Cond., N. Shore Symph., Sydney, 1946-77; Fndr., Cond., N Shore Youth Orch. (ret'd. 1977); Dir. of Music, Newington Coll., Sydney (ret'd. 1972). Comps: To Music; In Judah, Long Ago (part songs). Publs. incl: Musical Form for Beginners, 1966; Opera for Beginners, 1968; Harmony for Beginners, 1969; Senior School Harmony & Melody (w. Dulcie Holland), 1970; Musical Biographies for Beginners 1974; Ballet Music for Beginners, 1974; The Operatic & Concert Overture for Beginners, 1975; Asian Music for Beinners, 1977. Mbrships: Chmn., Music Comm., NSW Chapt., Aust. Coll. of Educ.; 1st Life Mbr., N Side Arts Fest.; Chmn., Music Comm. 1st N Sydney Community Fest., 1975; Aust. Soc. of Authors. Hons: Mbrship, The Order of Aust., 1976. Hobbies: photography; Cricket. Address: 67 Kameruka Rd., Northbridge, NSW 2063, Australia. 15, 21, 25.

BELLUGI, Piero, b. 14 May 1924, Florence, Italy. Conductor. Educ: Florence Conserv. of Music; Accademia Chigiana, Siena; Akademie des Mozarteum, Salzburg, Austria; Berkshire Music Ctr., Tanglewood, USA. div., 4 c. Debut: Teatro Scala, Milan, 1960. Career: Permanent Cond., Radio Symph. Orch. Turin. 1969-. Recordings: Philips; Columbia; RAI. Mbrships: Hon. Mbr. Accademia Nazionale Cherubini. Mgmt: Musart, 31 Via Manzoni, Milan, Italy. Address: 50027 Strade in Chianti, Florence, Italy.

BELMAS, Xenia, b. 6 Feb. 1896, Chernegott, Ukraine, Russia. Opera Singer. Educ: Imperial Acad. - Conserv., Kiev. m. Dr. Alexandre Kitchine Debut: Odessa - Paris Grand Opera. Career: Belgium (Symph. Concert); Kiev (Opera House); Berlin (Beethoven Salle); Rhine tour; Australia (Williamson Melba Co.); Poland; S Africa. Sev. recordings. Mbr.; S Africa Soc. of Music Tchrs. Hons: 1st Prize, Imperial Acad., Kiev. Address: 474 Bartle Rd., Umbilo, Durban, S Africa.

BELOTTI, Gastone, b. 2 Aug. 1920, Venice, Italy. Musicologist. Educ: Litt.D; studied musicol. w. Fausto Torrefranca, & piano w. Gino Tagliapietra. m. Maria Teresa Flores d'Arcais, 2 children. Publs: FF Chopin, l'uomo, 3 vol. 1974. Contbr. to musical publs. in USA, Austria, Poland & Italy. Mbrships: Sec.-Gen., Italian-Polish Friendship Soc.; Corres., Towarzystwo imienia Fryderyka Chopina, Warsaw; Academician, Adam Mickiewicz Acad., Bologna. Recip. of Order of Kthood. to merit of Polish Culture, 1972. Hobbies: Gardening; Photography. Address: via Antonio Medin 3, 135100 Padua, Italy.

BELT, Philip R., b. 2 Jan. 1927, Hagerstown, Ind.; USA. Fortepiano Maker. Educ: Apprentice to Frank Hubbard, 1965-67. m. Maribel Meisel, 5 children. Career: Builder, 18

fortepiano replicas & sev. harpsichords; Restoration work for Yale Univ., Boston Mus. of Fine Arts, Toledo Art Mus., pvte. individuals; Dev. Belt-Stein fortepiano kit, 1971; Lectr. on early piano restoration & reconstruction. Publs: Belt-Stein Fortepiano Kit Manual, 1972. Contbr. to Grove's Dictionary. Hobby: Building model airplanes. Address: 26 Stanton St., Paweatuck, CT06379, USA.

BENAGLIA, John Angelo, b. 26 Apr. 1938, NYC, NY, USA. Teacher of Recorder, Guitar, Harpischord, Handbells, Orff Dulcimer, & Folk Singing. Educ: Johns Hopkins Univ., Balt., Md., 1956-58; BMus, Cath. Univ., Wash. DC, 1965; Career: Pvte. Music Tchr., 1959-; Schl. Music Tchr., Potomac Schl., 1966-; Music Dir., Capitol Hill Consort, 1961-; Workshops in grp. recorder technique/consort playing, 1966, 74, 76. Comps: Five Vignettes (recorder quartet), 1969. Mbrships. incl: Cert. Tchr., Am. Musicol. Soc.; Orff Schulwerk Assn. Contbr. to Am. Recorder Soc. Mag., 1975. Hobbies incl: Camping. Address: 1837 19th St. NW, Wash. DC 20009, USA.

BENCE, John Michael, b. 11 Oct. 1942, London, UK. Organ Teacher; Teacher. Educ: ALCM; BSc, Leicester Univ. m. Helen Mary Rushton, 3 children. Career: Dir. of Music. Longslade Coll., Organist, Choirmaster, St. Mary de Castro, Leicester; Dir., Longslade Singers; Harpsichord Maker specialising in Italian reproductions. Contbr. to: Times Educl. Supplement; Musical Opinion. Mbrships: RCO; RSCM. Hobbies: Organ Building; Church Activities; Youth Work. Address: 126 Shanklin Dr., Leicester LE2 3QB, UK.

BENDER, Anna Catherina, b. 6 Dec. 1919, Piet Retief, S Africa. Pianist; Keyboard Player. Educ: BA, Univ. of Pretoria; Educ. Dip., Normal Coll., Pretoria; LTCL & FTCL (piano perf.) m. Dr. A S Brink, 2 d. Debut: City Hall, Pretoria, 1927. Career: Regular broadcasts for S AFrican Broadcasting Corp. since age 15; accomp., & orchl. pianist, Nat. Symph. Orch. & Radio Johannesberg, 1950-69; Lectr. in Art Song & Repetiteur, Opera Schl., The Technikon, Pretoria, 1975-; Ed., Opus, 1969-73; hon. profl. advsr., Cultural Hist. Museum, Petoria, 1979. Recordings: as accom. to Gaspar Cassado, Jean-Pierre Rampal & singers from leading European opera houses. Publs: Vir die Musiekleier, 1949. Mbrships: S African Soc. of Music Tchrs.; Harp Soc. of S Africa; committee of Nederburg Prize for Opera, Transvaal. Hobby: Collecting Africana. Address: PO Box 85083, Emmarentia 2029, Johannesburg, S Africa.

BENEDICT, Audrey Cecile, b. 15 Aug. 1901, Hepburn, Ohio, USA. Musician (Piano, Organ, Voice); Music Teacher. Educ: Studied music, Thiel Coll., Pa., 3 yrs.; studied voice w. Prof. T M Philips of Dennison Univ., 6 yrs., Arturo Bimboni, Dir., Juilliard Schl. NYC, Dr. Jackson of Ariz. State Univ., Dr. Kratz of Miami Univ., Oxford, Ohio. m. Paul A. Benedict (dec). Career: Ch. Soloist; Soloist, Frigidaire RAdio progs. & Dir. Harmonaires (radio advertising) 4 yrs.; Soloist, Youngstown Symph. & Dayton Phil. Orchs., Ohio; Fndr. & Dir., Fontana Schl. of Fine Arts, Calif. Dir., TV Sows, Rocket to Stardom, Hollywood, Calif.; Affiliated Tchr. Piano, Sherwood Music Schl., Chgo., Ill. Mbrshps: Am. Coll. Musicians; Nat. Guild Piano Tchrs. (Past Chmn.); Former Tri-Co. Chmn. of Music, BPW, Calif.; Pres.'s Conf. on Educ., 1954; Gov.'s Conf. on Educ. in Calif.; Dir., Nat. Delphian Soc. Hons. incl: Winner, Soprano Class & 2nd place, Grand Championships, Nat. Welsh Eisteddfod, 1938; Named disting. Citizen, Ohio, 1974. Hobbies: Painting; Composition. Address: 1216 E Market St., Warren, OH 44483, USA.

BENEŠ, Jiři, b. 24 Sep. 1928, Komarno, Czech. Viola Player; Musicologist. Educ: PhD, Univ. of Brno, 1952; grad., Conserv. of Brno, 1953; Dip., Janácek Acad. of Musical Arts, 1958. m. Zdenka Bubenícková, 1 s. (by previous marriage), 1 d. Debut: as viola player, Brno, 1952. Career: State Phil. Orch., Brno, 1951-69; Moravian Quartet, 1965-; apps. on TV & radio with Moravian Quartet in Czech., German Fed. Repub., Sweden, Italy; tours of most European countries; Tchr., Conserv., 1969-; Recordings; num. chamber music records. Contbr. to profl. jrnls., radio. prog. notes, sleeve notes etc. Mbrships: Union of Czech. comps. & concert artists; Czech. Musical (Janácek) Soc. Hons: Italian Quartet prize, 1965; Janácek medal, 1978. Hobbies: Running; Sledging. Mgmt: Pragokoncert, Prague. Address: Filipova 19, 63500 Brno, Czech.

BENFIELD, Warren A., b. 12 Feb. 1913, Allentown, Pa., USA. String Bassist; Teacher; Professor. Educ: Curtis Inst. of Music, Phila., Pa. m. Corinne Ponsford, 1 s., 1 d. Career: Mpls. Symph. Orch., 1934-37; St. Louis Symph. Orch., 1937-42, Prin. Bassist, 1938-42; Phila. Orch., 1942-49, Co-Prin. Bassist, 1948-49; Mbr., Chgo. Symph. Orch., 1949, Prin. Bassist, 1949-52; ARtist-Tchr., AF of M Congress of Strings, 1959-72; Prof., String Bass, Northwestern Univ., Evanston,

Ill.; Tchr. of String Bass, DePaul Univ., Chgo., Ill. Publs: The Art of Double Bass Playing (w. James S Dean); Excerpts Twentieth Century Music. Mbrships: The Cliff Dwellers; Am. String Tchrs. Ass.; Pi Kappa Lambda; Curtis Inst. Allumni Assn. Hobbies: Golf; Travel; Bridge. Address: 357 W Grove St., Lombard, IL 60148, USA. 2.

BENGTSSON, Erling Blondal, B. 8 Mar. 1932, Copenhagen, Denmark. Cellist; Professor. Educ: Dip., Curtis Inst. of Music, 1950; studied w. Gregor Piatigorsky. m. Merete Bengtsson, 2 s. Debut: w. Tivoli Orch., Copenhagen 1942. Career: apps. as soloist all over Europe, Can., USA, USSR, Africa; tchr., Curtis Inst. of Music, 1950-53; Prof. at Royal Danish Conserv. of Music, Copenhagen, 1953-; Prof. at High Schl. for Music, Cologne, 1978-. Recordings: Haydn, D maj. concerto; Nystroem, Symphoni Concertante; many solo & chamber music works; concertos & solo works by Scandinavian comps. Contbr. to: My Musical Self-Portrait, 1966. mbr. Royal Swedish Acad. of Music, Stockholm. Hons: Harriet Cohen Musical Prizes, 1954; Morisson Gold Medal for cellists, London, 1955. Hobbies: Collecting modern Scandinavian paintings & sculpture. Mgmt: Wilhelm Hansen, Denmark, & Norman McCann, UK. Address: Gyrstingevej 13, 2700 Copenhagen, Brh. Denmark.

BENGTSSON, Ingmar (Lars Olaf), b. 2 March 1920, Stockholm, Sweden. Musicologist. Educ: Solo class piano, Royal High Schl. of Music, Stockholm, 1937-40; BA, Uppsala & Stockholm Univ., 1941; Licentiate, 1945, PhD, 1955 (Uppsala). m. Britta Ridderstad, 1 c. Debut: Stockholm, 1942. Career: Pianist, harpsichordist, accomp., 1940-60; Tchr., Uppsala Univ., 1947-; Prof., 1964; Hd., Swedish Musicological Soc., 1961-; Hd., Berwald Committee, 1963-. Num. publs. Contbr. to: Svenska Dagbladet, Stockholm (Music Critic, 1943-59); Svensk tidskrift för musikforskning. Mbrships: Kingl. Musikaliska Akademien, 1960-; Kingl. Vitterhets Historie och Antikvitets Akademien, 1970-; Det danske videnskabernes samfund, 1978; Gustav Adolfs akademien, 1978-; Int. Musicol. Soc., Dir., 1963-77, etc. Hons. incl: Gold Medal, Swedish Royal Acad. of Music. Hobbies: Sailing; Skating; Gardening; Mushrooms; Music. Address: Djurgaardsvaegen 158, S-115 21 Stockholm, Sweden.

BEN-HAIM, Paul, b. 5 July 1897, Munich, Bavaria. Composer. Educ: Music Acad. & Univ. Munich, 1925-16 & '18-20. m. Helena Acham, 1 s. Debut: Cond. own orchl. comp. in public concert, 1921. Career: Asst. of Bruno Walter & Hans Knappertsbusch, (Munich Staatsopera), 1920-24; Cond. in Augsburg, -1932; Emigrated to Israel, 1933. Compsitions incl: 2 symphs. & 8 other symph. works; The Sweet Psalmist of Isreal (rec. by Columbia w. NY Phil., Leonard Bernstein cond.); Chamber music; Sonata for violin (rec. by Y Menuhin); Concerts for Violin, Cello, piano & choral music; Many songs & solo pieces. Concerto for strings; Pastoralerariée for clarinets, harp & strings; To the Chief Musician (Variations for Louisville Orch.); etc. Recordings: 1st Symph.; From Israel, suite for orch., etc. Mbrships: Hon. Pres., League of Comps. in Israel; Hon. Chmn., AKUM Ltd. Hons. incl: Israel State Prize, 1957; Cross of Merit, 1st class of the German Fed. Repub., 1968. Hobbies: Reading. Address: 11 Aharonowitz St., Tel-Aviv, Israel. 14, 16.

BENIC, Vladimir, b. 3 Oct. 1922, Zagreb, Croatia, Yugoslavia. Conductor. Educ: Acad. of Music, Zagreb; Studied w. Clemens Kraus in Salzburg, w. George Snell in Cleveland. m. Vera Kalan, 1 s. Career: Cond. for Operas & Symph. Concerts in num. Countires; Musical Dir., Rijeka Opera & Symph. Orch. Hons: Rijeka City Prize, 1962; The Repb. Croatia Award, 1967; Opera Bienalle Ljubljana, 1978. Address: Ulica zrtava fas. 2/1, 51000 Rijeka, Yugoslavia. 3.

BENJAMIN, Thomas Edward, b. 17 Feb. 1940, Bennington, Vt., USA. Composer; University Professor. Educ: BA, Bard Coll., MA Harvard Univ.; MFA, Brandeis Univ.; PhD, Eastman Schl. of Music. m. Elizabeth Clein, 1 s., 1 d. Career incl: Prof. of Theory & Composition, Schl. of Music, Univ. of Houston. Published Compositions incl: 4 Pieces for 3 Flutes; After-Dinner Pieces; Adoramus Te; Four by Two; Laudate Dominum; The Fruit of Love; Two Choral-Preludes; Two Motets; Rag; Music for Brass Quintet; Te Deum; The Righteous Nation. Publs: The Structure of Tonal Music (co-author), 1971; Techniques & Materials of Tonal Music (co-author), 1975. Model Counterpoint in the late Sixteenth-Century Style, 1976. Contbr. to Opera Cues; Forum. Mbr. of var. profl. assns. Hons. incl: Performance Award, Delius Contest, 1975; ASCAP Standard Music Award, 1975. Hobbies: Running; Cooking; Tennis. Address: 2629 Cason St., Houston, TX 77005, USA. 7

BENKER, Heinz, b. 13 Mar. 1921, Landshut, Bavaria. Secondary School Professor & Composer; Training College Director. Musical Educ: Kirchenmusikschule, Regensburg; Staatliche Hochschule für Musik, Munich. m. Gertrud Benker (Schmittinger), 2 d. Career: Secondary Schl. Prof. & Comp.; Dir., musical trng. coll.; Free-lance Collaborator, TV III, Bayerischer Rundfunk. Comp. of orchl. works, music for youth, choral works, chmbr. music, organ works, songs, opera. Publs: Von Note zu Note, 1967; Vom Ton zum Klang, 1969; Leichte Klaviermusik aus fünf Jahrhunderten, 1969. Contbr. to Neue Musikzeitung. Mbrships: Deutscher Komponistenverband; VDMK; 1st Chmn., Verband Bayerischer Schulmusikerzieher; GEMA. Recip., Culture Prize, E Bavaria, 1964. Hobbies: Travel; Good Wine. Address: Hippelstr. 57 b. 8000 Munich 82, German Fed. Repub.

BENKO, Daniel, b. 29 July 1947, Budapest, Hungary. Lutenist; Guitarist; Lute Teacher. Educ: Liszt Ferenc Acad. of Music, Budapest. Debut: Munich. Career: 25 TV progs., Hungarian TV, 70 radio progs., Hungarian Radio, & 210 live concerts as soloist & w. Bakfark Consort, 1973-76; Num. TV, radio, & concert apps. abroad. Recordings: Complete lut works of Balefarle (5 LPs); Vivaldi Lute Concertos & & Trios; Early Hungarian Songs; Verse Chronicals; College Music in Hungary (w. Balefarle Consort); also participator in other recordings. Contbr. to profl. jrnls. Hobbies: Collecting instruments; Folk dancing; Modern dancing; Good food. Mgmt: Interkoncert, Budapest, Hungary. Address: 1025 Budapest, Verhalom u.20, Hungary.

BENKO, Gregor, b. 4 Aug. 1944, Cleveland, Ohio, USA. Administrator & President, International Piano Archives. Educ: Pvte. study. Career: Radio & TV apps., regarding piano playing, pianists of the past & histl. perf. style; Curator of Archives, Int. Piano Archives, Univ. of Md., Lectr. on evolution of perf. styles; Tchr., perf. practice, based on histl. recordings, 1977-78. Recordings. Over 40 modern LP re issues of historic piano perfs. Contbr. to: 78 RPM; Antique Records; Grove's; High Fidelity, Stereo Review, etc. Mbrships: Dir., Am. Liszt Soc.; Music Lib. Assn.; Music Tchrs. Nat. Assn.; Assn. for Recorded Sound Collections. Hobby: Hand Bookbinding. Address: Babb House, Ivor, VA 23866, USA.

BENNER, James, b. 19 July 1925, Ithaca, NY, USA. Pianist; Vocal Coach; Accompanist. Educ: BA, Cornell Univ., 1947; MA, Columbia Univ., 1948; studied Piano w. John Kirkpatrick, Gaston Dethier & Egon Petri. m. Frances Yeend. Career: Coach & Accompanist for many leading singers on int. Concert Tours; Freelance Vocal Coach, NYC, 1948-67; Pianist for Obernkirchen Children's Choir (Schammbürger Märchensänger) from Bückeburg, Germany, 1954-; Ten tours of N Am., extensive tours of S Am., Middle East, Fart East & S Africa in this capacity; Mbr., Music Fac., W Va. Univ., Morgantown, 1967-. Compositions: (recorded) Arrs. of Folk Songs for Obernkirchen Children's Choir. Recordings: Frances Yeend Sings; Holiday in Japan (Obernkirchen Children's Choir). Address: 421 Richwood Ave., Morgantown, WV 26505, USA.

BENNER, Lora, b. 23 Sept. 1907, Milwaukee, Wis., USA. Pianist. Educ: Carre Musical Coll.; Univ. of Wis.; St. Louis Inst. of Music; Chgo. Musical Coll.; Juilliard Schl. of Music. m. Philip Edward Benner. Career: Public apps. from age 5; Recitals; Radio progs.; Calif. & Wis. Comps: Music for Piano Students; Three Suites for Piano. Publs: Blue and Gold Books, 1960; Handbook for Piano Teaching, 1975; Theory for Piano Students (5 books) 1959; Teachers Reference, 1974; Make Your Own Scales & Arpeggios, 1959. Contbr. to: Clavier; Am. Music Tchr.; Piano Guild Notes; APTA Mags. Mbrships: ASCAP; NGPT; APTA (Fndr. & Pres.). Address: 1739 Randolph Rd., Schenectady, NY 12308, USA. 23, 27.

BENNETT, Keith Michael, b. 1 Mar. 1942, London, UK. Dir. of Music; Conductor; Accompanist; Continuo player; Organist. Educ: Brasenose Coll., Oxford, 1961-64; MA, DPhil (Oxon); TCL, 1964-65; ARCO. m. Pamela Harding, 1s. Career: Dir. of Music, St. Dunstan's Coll., Catford; Sr. Lectr. in Music, Bath Coll. of Higher Educ., 1979-. Contbr. to Music & Letters. Mbrships: ISM; Royal Musical Assn.; RCO. Hons: Organ Scholar, Brasenose Coll. Hobbies: Arts; Gardening; Wine. Address: 39 Blythe Hill, London SE6 4UL, UK.

BENNETT, Lawrence Edward, b. 27 Sept. 1940, Rock Is., Ill., USA. Tenor Singer; Choral Conductor; Musicologist. Educ: BA, Carleton Coll., Northfield, Min., 1962; MA, NY Univ.; PhD cand. m. Nancy J. Debut: Carnegie Recital Hall, 1968; Career incls: Mbr., Western Wind Vocal Sextet performing vocal chmbr. music of Renaissance, Baroque, early Am. & Contemp. comps. throughout USA; Inst. of Music, Choral Cond., Uppsala Coll., E Orange, NJ. Recordings: Claudio Monteverdi Madrigals (soloist); Early American Vocal Music (w. sextet). Publs:

Western Wind American Tune-Book. Contbr. to musical publs. Mbrships: Am. Musicol. Soc.; Sonneck Soc. Hobbies: Artist; Tennis; Volleyball. Address: 310 W 107 St., NY, NY 10025, USA.

BENNETT, Richard Rodney, b. 29 Mar. 1936, Broadstairs, Kent, UK. Composer; Pianist. Educ: RAM, w. Lennox Berkeley & Howard Ferguson; ARAM; FRAM; French Govt. Schlrships. for study w. Pierre Boulez, Paris. Career incl: Prof. of Compositions, 1963-65. Compositions incl: Two operas commnd. by Sadlers Wells -The Mines of Sulphur, 1965; A Penny for a Song, 1967; The Approaches of Sleep, 1959; Suite Francaise, 1961; London Pastoral, 1962; Jazz Calendar, 1964; Symph. no. 1, 1965; Epithalamion, 1966; Symph. No. 2 (commnd. by Leonard Bernstein & 1st perf. by NY Phil. Orch., 1968); Piano Concerto, 1968; Jazz Pastoral, 1969; Guitar Concerto, 1971; Music for num. films incl: Indiscreet; Only Two Can Play; Far From the Madding Crowd; Billion Dollar Brain; Billy Liar; Nicholas & Alexandra. Recip: Arnold Bax Soc. Prize for Commonwealth Composers, 1964. Ralph Vaughan Williams Award as composer of the yr., 1965. Hobbies: Cinema; Modern jazz. ADdress: c/o London Mgmt., Regent House, 235-241 Regent St., London W.1, UK.

BENNETT, Robert Russell, b. 15 June 1894, Kansas City, Mo., USA. Composer; Arranger; Conductor. Educ: instrumental studies w. parents; studied comp. w. Carl Busch & Nadia Boulanger. m. Louise Merrill, 1 d. Career: orchestrations for num. stage shows, films, TV, records. Comps: Sights & Sounds; Abraham Lincoln (symph.); Sonata for Organ; Hexapoda (violin & piano); A Song Sonata (violin & piano). Recordings: Victory at Sea; Symphonic picture of Gershwin's Porgy & Bess. Author: Instrumentally Speaking 1974. Mbrships: ASCAP; Pres., Bohemians & NAACC; Liederkranz Club. Hons. incl: LHD. Franklin & Marshall Coll., 1965. Hobby: Tennis. Address: 65 W 54th St., NY, NY 10019, USA. 2.

BENNETT, W I B, b. 7 Feb. 1936, London, UK. Flautist. Educ: studied w. Geoffrey Gilbert, GSM; French Govt. Schlrships. to study w. Claratgé & J P Rampal, Paris. m. Rhuna Martin, 2 d. Career: apps. w. BBC Northern Orch., Sadlers Wells Orch., LSO, Engl. Chmbr. Orch., Acad. of St. Martin-in-the-Fields, Vesuvius, Prometheus & Melos Ensembles; num. broadcasts & solo apps. throughout world; Master Classes in Canterbury, London, USA, Manila, Can., etc. Recordings incl: Mozart Flute Quartets; Vivaldi Flute & Piccolo Concertos; Boulez Flute Sonatine & other mod. works; many works by Bach. Recip. FGSM. Hobbies: Winemaking; Cockroach baiting. Address: 13 St. Peter's Sq., London W6, UK.

BENNETT, Wilhelmine, b. 14 June 1933, Carmi, Ill., USA. Composer. Educ: BM, Jordan Conserv.; MM, DMus, Northwestern Univ.; Post-doctoral studies, Columbia Univ. & Freiburg Hochschule für Musik. div. Career: Radio & TV progs., (Chigao, Berkeley, Bloomington) in connection w. career. Comps: Hyperbolex; 5 Quick Visions of the Apocalypse. Mbrships: Int. League of Women Comps. (Bd. of dirs.). Hons: Faricy Award, 1962; Fullbright Scholarship, 1965-66; Nat. Coun. of Arts Award, 1966. Hobbies: Backpacking; Cross Country Skiing; Writing plays. Address: Box 512, West Branch, IA 52358, USA.

BENNION, Krista Louise, b. 24 Jan. 1961, Redwood City, Calif., USA. Violinist. Educ: Studied w. Anthony Doheny, Yehudi Menuhin, Isadore Tinkleman, Stuart Canin, David Cerone & Ivan Galamian; Chmbr. musc w. Heiichiro Ohyama; San Fran. Conserv. of Music. Debut: w. San Fran. Symph. at age 15. Career: Soloist, San Fran. Symph. Orch., 1976; Seattle Symph. at Centrum Music Fest., 1977; Palo Alto Chmbr. Orch., 1970, 74, 78; Fremont-Newark Phil., 1978. Sev. recordings. Hons: Palo Alto Chmbr. Orch. Soloist Competition, 1974; San Fran. Symph./Pepsi Cola Young Musicians Award, 1976; Fremont-Newark Phil. Young Artists Competition. Hobbies: Backpacking; Winemaking; Conversation. Address: 1310 Bay Laurel Dr., Menlo Pk., CA 94025, USA.

BENOIT, Jean-Christophe, b. 18 Mar. 1925, Paris, France. Singer. Educ: Nat. Conserv. of paris. m. Monique Linval. Career: Appearances in leading opera houses of France & abroad, & at Festivals of Aix-en-Provence, Salzburg, Bordeaux & Holland. Mbr.; Speleo Club de Paris. Recip: Cmndr., Order of Civil Merit. Hobbies: Entomol.; Biospelegraphy. Address: 12 rue de Milan, Paris 9, France.

BENOLIEL, Bernard John, b. 25 Sept. 1943, Detroit, Mich., USA. Composer. Educ: Piano, trumpet, Detroit Inst. of Musical Art; Comp., Univ. Mich.; Studied w. Stefan Wolpe. Career: Sec. Ralph Vaughan Williams Trust; Musical Advsr. to British Music Info Centre. Comps. incl: Eternity Junctions-Five Poems of Emily Dickinson (chorus), 1968; The Black Tower (soprano &

chmbr. ensemble), 1968; Two Movements for Piano, 1969; String Quartet, 1969-76; The After-War (chorus & organ), 1970; With St. Paul in Albion (amplified cello & organ), 1974; The Intolight)chorus & organ) 1976; Symphony in One Movement, 1972-73; Piano Quintet (w. baritone voice), 1975-79. Contbr. to: Temp. Mbr. CGGB, Hons: Bennington Comps. Conf. Schlrship., 1969; Tanglewood Fellowship, 1970; Arts Coun. Bursary for creative work, 1978. Hobbies incl: Metaphysics, Analytical Psychology, English & Am. Lit. Address: 68 Elm Park Gdns., Chelsea, London SW10, UK.

BEN-OR, Nelly, Warsaw, Poland, Pianist; Teacher of the Alexander Technique. Educ: Tchr.'s & Perf.'s Dips., Rubin Acad. of Music, Jerusalem, Israel; Tchr.'s Dip., Alexander Fndn., London. m. Roger Clynes, 1 d. Debut: Katowice, Poland, when aged 13. Career: recitals, concerto perfs., chmbr. music, broadcasts, Israel, Europe, USA, Aust.; Prof., GSM; Vis. Tchr., univs. & music acad., USA & Europe. Mbr., ISM. Recip. 1st Prize. Mozart Competition, Israel. Address: 23 Rofant Rd., Northwood, Middx., UK.

BENSELIN, Margaret Mary, b. Leigh-on-Sea, Essex, UK. Concert Pianist; Conductor Professor of Piano. Educ: RAM; LRAM; ARCM; studies w. Cyril Smith. Career incls: recitals, Wigmore Hall, London, 1967, 1970; BBC London; num. other recitals & concerto perfs.; 9 recitals for Henry Wood Proms Circle; London premieres of Rubbras Eight Preludes & Labux Concertino; Musical Dir. & Cond., New Malden & Dist. Choral Soc., & Thameide Singers, 1966-69; Lectr. in Piano Technique, Richmond Adult Coll., 1970-. Mbrships. incl: ISM; Coun., Soc. of Women Musicians; Inter-Varsity Club Brit. Fend. of Music Fests. Hons. incl: Gold Medals, Hastings Recital Competition, London Music Competition, 1976; 25 other first prizes in profl. piano competitions. Hobbies incl: Landscape Gardening; Woodwork; Reading. Address: Crotchet Rest, 41 Malden Green Ave., Worcester Pk., Surrey, UK. 27.

BENSON, Clifford George, b. 17 Nov. 1946, Grays, Essex, UK. Pianist - Solo & Chamber Music & Accompaniment. Educ: ARCM Perfs. m. Dilys Morgan Davies, 1 d. Debut: (solo) Royal Fest. Hall, 1969; (chmbr.) Purcell Room, 1969. Career: many BBC Radio broadcasts & Swiss, German & Dutch recordings; Apps. on BBC-TV, Swiss & Bavarian TV; Bath, Edinburgh, Durham, Cheltenham, Aix-en-Provence, Flanders & Aldeburgh Fests.; Tours of most of Europe, Middle E, Persia; Mbr., Nash Ensemble, 1972-; Soloist, Constance Lambert's Piano Concerto. Prom, 1975. Recordings (w. Nash Ensemble) incl: A Victorian Musical Evening; 3 Sonatines for Violin & Piano; Fauré Sonatas for Cello & Piano. Hons. incl: Munich Int. Duo Competition, 1970. Hobbies incl: Tennis. Address: 80 Quarry Hill Rd., Tonbridge, Kent TN9 2PE, UK.

BENSON, Joan, b. St. Paul, Minn., USA. Concert artist on clavichord & 18th century piano; Lecturer in Music. Educ: Master's degree, Univ. of Ill.; Protégée of Edwin Fischer, Switz.; Study in clavichord music w. Fritz Neumeyer (Germany), Valda Aveling (UK) & Santiago Kastner (Portugal); Advanced study in Vienna, Paris, Italy & Germany. Career: Concerts, lects. & apps. in fests. & on TV & radio throughout USA, Europe & Middle East; Repertoire incls. music from 15th century to contemporary; Special emphasis & perf. on antique instruments; Lectr. in Music, Stanford Univ; Fac., Univ. of Ore. Recordings: Joan Benson - Clavichord; Music of C P E Bach, played on clavichord & early piano. Mbrships: Am. Musicol. Soc.; Neue Bach Gesellschaft. Recip., Kate Neal Kinley Award for perf. Mgmt: Joan Benson, 2795 Central Blvd., Eugene, OR 97403, USA. Address: Schl. of Music, Univ. of Ore., Eugene, OR 97403, USA.

BENSON, Warren F., b. 26 Jan. 1924, Detroit, Mich., USA. Composer; Teacher. Educ: BMus., Univ. of Mich., 1949; MMus., ibid, 1950. m. Patricia L. Vander Valde, 1 s., 3 d. Career incls: Dir. of Band & Orch., Mars Hill Coll., NC, 1952-53; Prof. of Music & Comp.-in-Res., Ithaca Coll., NY, 1953-67; Prof. of Comp., Univ. of Rochester, EAstman Schl. Music, ibid, 1967-. Comps. incl: Love is (double antiphonal choir); Helix (tuba & wind ensemble); Recuerdo (obos & engl. horn & wind ensemble); The Solitary Dancer (wind ensemble); Shadow Wood (soprano & wind ensemble); Capriccio for Violin, Viola, Cello & piano; Concert for Horn & Orch.; Five Lyrics for mezzo soprano & flute; Largo Toh; Embers; The Dream Net. Var. Recordings. Author, Creative Projects in Musicianship, 1967. Contbr. to var. profl. jrnls. Mbrships: ASCAP; MENC; Macdowell Colony Assocs.; Am. Music Ctr.; Hon. Mbr., Phi Mu Alpha Sinfonia. Recip., Alpha Sinfonia Recip, Lillian Fairchild Award for Comp., 1971. Hobbies: Poetry; Camping. Address: Eastman Schl. Music, Univ. of Rochester, 26 Gibbs St., Rochester, NY 14604, USA. 6.

BENT, Ian D., h. 1 Jan. 1938, Birmingham, UK. University Lecturer in Music. Educ: St. John's Coll., Cambridge, BA,

BMus, MA; PhD (Cantab.). m. (1) Margaret Bassington, 1 s., (2) Caroline Coverdale. Career: Lectr. in Music & Sub-Dean, Fac. of Music, King's Coll., Univ. of London; Prof. of Music, Dept. of Music, Univ. of Nottingham. Publs. incl: Two Medieval Alleluias (ed.), 1970; The Medieval Lyric; Poetic Individuality in Middle Ages. Contbr. many articles on medieval music to profl. jrnls. Mbrships: Royal Musical Assn.; Am. & Int. Musicol. Soc. Address: Music Dept., Univ. of Nottinham, Nottingham, Notts., UK. 3.

BENTLEY, Arnold, b. 11 Jan. 1913, Padiham, Lancs., UK. Reader in Education (Music), Rading University. Educ: BA Hons., 1935, Dip. Ed., 1936, PhD, 1963, Reading Univ.; arcm, 1940; LRAM, 1946. Career: Tchr. until 1948; Lectr., Music. Weymouth & Trent Pk. Trng. Colls., 1948-49; Lectr., Music Educ., Reading Univ., 1949; Sr. Lectr., ibid, 1964; Rdr., ibid, 1973; Vis. Prof., num. univs. Compositions: Songs to Sing & Play, 1964; 16th Century Trios & Quartets for Wind Instruments, 1964. Pubs: Musical Ability in Children & its Measurements, 1966; Measures of Musical Abilities, 1966; Aural Foundations of Music Reading, 1966; Monotones: A Comparison with Normal Singers, 1968. Music in Education - A Point of View, 1975. Contbr. to num. profl. jrnls. Mbrships: 1st Chmn., Rsch. Commission, Int. Soc. for Music Educ., 1968-72; Chmn. & Fndr., Soc. for Rsch. in the Psychol. of Music & Music Educ.; ISM. Hobbies: Walking; Swimming. Address: 17 Highmoor Rd., Caversham, Reading RG4 7BL, Berks., UK. 3.

BENTLEY, Keith, b. 27 June 1946, Middlesbrough, UK. Pianist; Conductor; Lecturer; Adjudicator. Educ: Royal Manchester Coll. Music, 1962-69; ARMCM Dip.; GRSM (Special Merit in Perf.); ARMCM (Teachers). m. Julie Andrews, 2 c. Debut: Cond., Flotow's 'Martha', Manchester Opera Co., 1964. Career: 1st BBC Broadcast, piano, 1962; Chorus Master, Yorks. Opera, 1967-72; Music Dir., Manchester Opera Co., 1964-67; Centurion Opera Grp., 1967-69; Cleveland Opera, 1972-78; Head of Music, Cleveland Tech. Coll., 1970-; Dir., Redcar Jr. Coll. of Music, 1976-. Hons: Ricordi Book Prize, Piano, 1967. Address: 69 Borough Rd., Redcar, Cleveland, Yorks, TS10 SEQ, UK. 4.

BENTLEY, Lionel Reginald, b. 17 Feb. 1908, London, UK. Violinist. Educ: RCM; Hond. RAM; studied w. Carl Flesch et alia. m. Christina Howell. Debut: Wigmore Hall. Career: Ldr., Amici Quartet; Mbr., London Harpsichord Ensemble, London Horn Trio; Ldr., Boyd Neel & London Chmbr. orchs. Solo & chmbr. broacasts & concerts; String ensemble coaching; Adjudicating; Prof. of Violin, RAM. Recordings: Amici Quartet. Mbrships: ISM; Little Shp Club. Hobby: Interior decorating. Address: 30 Cranhurst Rd., London NW2 4LN, UK. 4.

BENTOIU, Pascal, b. 22 Apr. 1927, Bucharest, Rumania. Composer. Educ: Law studies, Bucharest, 2 yrs.; prvte. musical studies w. Mihail Jora. m. Annie-Maria Deculescu, 1 d. Debut: first comp. perf. 1954. Career: num. perfs. at the Rumanian Radio & TV, 1955-; also BBC (l'Amour Médecin & Hamlet), RAI (Iphigenia's Immolation, Hamlet), ORTF (l'Amour Médecin, Sonata for violin & piano), etc.; Hamlet (Opera Municpal de Marseille, 1974); l'Amour Médecin (Bucharest Opera, 1965, Cluj Opera, 1967). Comps. incl: Concertos for piano, Op. 5, Op. 12; Sonata for violin & piano; L'Amour Médecin, opera in one act. Two Str. Quartets; Hamlet, oera in two acts. 2nd Syph. Opus 20 (1st perf. Bucharest, 1975); staging of Hamlet, Bucharest Opera, 1975; Songs for voice & piano op 21 & op 24, 1978; Eminesciana III - Concerto for orch., 1977; Third symphony op. 22. Var. recordings & tapes. Publs: Musical Icon & Its Meaning, 1971; Apertures Toward the World of Music, 1973. The Musical Thought, Bucharest Musical Eds., 1975. Mbr., Rumanian Comps. Union. Recip. sev. awards & hons. inclng. Georges Enesco Prize, Rumania Acad. for 'Hamlet', 1974 & Comps. Union Prize for Symphonic Music, 1976 & 78. Address: Aleea Parva 5, app. 60 of. post. 74, Bucharest, Rumania.

BENTON, F. R. 'Dick', b. 3 Oct. 1928, Chgo., Ill., USA. Jazz Pianist; Musical Director; Educator. Educ: BME, Morningside Coll., Sioux City, Iowa; MA, Sam Houston State Coll., Huntsville, Tex.; Doct. Study, Univ. of SD, Vermillion, 1970. Currently PhD Cand., UNL, Ed.Adm., ACI. m. Pat. 2 s. Career: Musical Dir., KVTV Channel 9, Sioux City, Iowa, 1954-57; Piano w. Warren Covington & Tommy Dorsey Orch.; Solo backing for num. artists; Dir., Schl. Stage Bands, 1973; Superintendent of Schls., Stuart, Neb., 1973-. Cojpositions: Shadows of Clouds; Zombie Boogie; March Zapitch. Recording: Rhapsody in Blue. Publs: Tone Producing Terminaology for Stringed Instruments, 1954. Mbrships: Phi Mu Alpha; Kappa Kappa Psi; Alpha Tau Delta. Hobbies: Law; Nutrition; Parachute Jumping. Address: 2600 S. Lyon, Sioux City, IA, USA.

BENTON, Patricia, b. 20 Mar. 1907, Tarrytown, NY, USA. Pianist. Educ: Dip. in Music, Miss Mason's Schl., & Westchester Conserv. of Music. m. Nikolai Mednilcoff, 1 d. Career: TV & radio apps., Scottsdale & Phoenix, Ariz. Comps: Love Me From Now On; White Wisteria Face; Barky the Dog; Tiptoe the Cat; Manhattan Mosaic; Miracle of Roses; Merry-Go-Sounds at the Zoo. Ariz. State Pres., Mbrhsips: ASCAP; Am. Guild of Musicians & Authors; Phi Sigma Alpha. Publs: Musical Therapy for Orthopaedic Cases, 1943. Hons: Complete collect. of poetry & musical career established at Boston Univ., 1965; Songwriters Hall of Fame. Hobby: All the arts. Address: 7849 E Glen Rosa, Scottsdale, AZ 85251, USA. 27, 9, 2.

BENTON, Rita, b. 28 June 1920, New York, NY, USA. Musicologist; Music Librarian. Educ: BA, Hunter Coll.; Dip. in Piano, Juilliard Schl. of Music; MA in Musicology, Univ. of Iowa; PhD in Musicology, ibid, 1961. M. Arthur Benton, 3 c. Career: Tchr. of Theory & ear-trng., High Schl. of Music & ARt, NYC, 1939-40; Music Libn., Univ. of Iowa Libs., 1957-; ASsoc. Prof. of Music, Univ. of Iowa, Summer 1966 & Autumn 1969; Prof. of Music, 1975-; Cons. & Project Reviewer, Nat. Endowment for the Humanities, 1975-. Publs: Fontest artis musicae, (Ed.-in-Chief), 1976; Directory of Music Research Libraries; 1967-72; French Song from Berlioz to Duparc, by Frits Noske, transld. & revised by Rita Benton; Ignace Pleyel: A Thematic Catalogue of his Compositions, 1977. Contbr. var. profl. jrnls. Mbrships: Am. Musicol. Soc., Sec., 1972-78; Pres., Commission of Rsch. Libs., Int. Assoc. of Music Libs., 1964-75; Pres. Music Lib. Assoc., 1962-63. Hons: Fulbright award, Univ. of Paris, 1968; NEH project award, 1977. Hobbies: Ceramics; Travel. Address: Schl. of Music, Univ. of Iowa, Iowa City, IA 52242, USA.

BEN-TOVIM, Atarah, b. Abergavenny, Wales, UK. Concert Presenter; Writer & Broadcaster; Flautist. Educ: RAM; Paris (French Govt. Scholarship); ARCM; LRAM; ARAM. m. Dougles Boyd, 1 d. Career: Prin. flute, Royal Liverpool Phil. Orch., 1964-76; num. radio & TV apps.; originator of Atarah's Band Children's Concerts. sev. recordings. Publs: Atarah's Book, 1976; Children & Music, 1979; Atarah's Bandkits, 1978-. Conbr. to: Guardian; Times Educ. Supplement; Music & Musicians etc. sev. hons. & awards; MBE, 1980 (Serv. Childrens Music). Mgmt: Childrens Concert Centre, Regent St., Haslingden, Rossendale, Lancs., UK. Address: c/o mgmt.

BENTZON, Johan, b. 1 Feb. 1909, Svendborg, Denmark. Flutist. Educ: Dip. of Flute & Organ, Danish Royal Acad. of Music, 1930. m. Astrid Giessing, 4 d. Career: Flutist, Soloist, Chmbr. Music & Orch., Mbr., Radio Symph. Orch., Radio Denmark, 1944-72; Chmn., ibid, 1950-53; Broadcasts in Denmark, Norway, Sweden, Holland, Finland & Switzerland. Recordings: Records of contemporary & classical Chmbr. Music. Publs: Var. essays on musical & philosophical subjects. Mbrships: ISCM (Bd. Mbr., Danish Sect. 1932-55, Pres. 1953-54); IMC Exec. Committee 1954-55; Pres. 1953-54); IMC Exec. Committee 1954-58, 1960-66; Danish Music & Youth (Chmn. 1964-68); Danish Coun. for Music Educ. (Chmn. 1972-74); Danish State Music Coun. 1972-. Hobbies: Philosophy; Philately; Gardening. Address: Emdrup Banke 159, 2100 Copenhagen, Denmark.

BEN-YOHANAN, Asher, b. 22 May 1929, Kavalla, Greece. Composer; Music Educator. Educ: incl: studied oboe & piano; comp. studies w. Paul Ben-Haim, Israel, Aaron Copland, USA, Luigi Nono, Italy; Gustave Reese, NY Univ. & others; MMus, Univ. of Mich., USA. m. Shoshana Swibel, 1 s., 1 d. Career: comps. perf. in Israel, Europe & USA & many radio recordings; Hd., Music Dept., Thelma Yellin Music & Arts HS, Tel-Aviv; Lectr., Dept. of Musicol., Bar-Ilan Univ. Compositions incl: Two Movements for Orch., 1959; String Quartet, 1962-64; Soliloquy for Violin, 1977; Music for Orch., 1967 (commission, Israel Comps. Fund); Chamber Music for Six, (commission, Israel Fest., 1968); Quartetto Concertato (Piano, clarinet, trombone & cello); Mosaic (soprano & 10 players); Concerto for String Orch.; Songs of the Scorching Summer (baritone & piano). Author, Music in Israel, A Shor Survey, 1975. Mbrships incl: Bds., Israel Soc. of Comps., Authors & Music Publrs., Millo Artists' Club; Mbr. of the Board, League of Composers, Israel; Pi Kappa Lambda. Hons. incl: Morse Fellowship in Comp., Univ. of Cinn., USA, 1971; Acum Prize (twice). Address: 4 Bloch St., Tel-Aviv, Israel. 28.

BENZI, Roberto, b. 12 Dec. 1937, Marseilles, France. Conductor. Educ: Baccalaureat, Sorbonne, Paris; pvte. studies w. André Cluytens & Fernand Lamy. m. Jane Rhodes. Debut: Bayonne, France, 1948. Career: Guest Cond., worlwide; Music Dir., Orch. of Bordeaux-Aquitaine, 1973-; 2 French films, Prélude à la Gloire, 1949 (1st Prize, Cannes Festival 1950) & L'Appel du Destin, 1952. Compositions: Orchestrations of Brahms op. 23; Schumann variations & Brahms op. 24; Handel

variations (both orginally for piano), 1970 & '73. Recordings: about 20 recordings w. LSO, Orch. Lamoureux, Paris Opera, The Hague Phil., Bucharest Phil. Mbr., Acad. de Neuilly sur Seine. Chevalier de l'Ordre Nat. du Mérite; Chevalier de la Legion d'honneur. France. Hobbies: Cycling; Zool. Address: 15 rue Général Gordonnier, 92200 Neuilly sur Seine, France. 3, 19.

BEN ZWIE, Yitzchak, b. 1 June 1922, Buktzaz, Poland, (Israeli citizen). Composer; Singer; Educ: Grad. in Educ.; studied w. comp. P. Chaifa; Music Tchrs. Sem., Oranim Kiryat Tivon Kibbutz Profl. Assn., 2 yrs.. m. (3) Johana Gillman, 2 s., 4 d. Career: State & pvte. Tchr. of Music, 14 yrs.; radio apps. & progs. of music. Comps. incl: (some publ.'d & recorded) Hed Ha' Tabor (symph. suite); Suite for Ensemble, Choir & Soloists; Wind Quartets; ballet, Hed Hazibor in Ein Dor; songs. Publs. incl: 16 Choral Songs of New Israel, 1962; Jerusalem in Poland, 1966. Mbr., Israeli Comps. League. Recip., var. grants & travel awards. Hobbies incl: Inventing; Science; Ballet; Nature; Hiking. Mgmt: (self) YBZ Recording & Publishing Co. Haifa. Address: PO Box 4684 Haifa, Israel.

BERANEK, Vratislav, b. 30 Jan. 1926, Kladno, Czechoslovakia. Music Teacher; Radio Editor. Educ: Educ. Fac., Charles Univ., Prague, 1945-49. m. Věra Bubeniçcková. Career: Music Tchr., elem. music schl., 1950-61; Ed., Dept. of Music for Children & Youth, Radio Prague, 1961-. Publs: Music Reading Book for Youth, 1960 & 65; Little Encyclopedia of Music for Children (w. Jan Brychta, illustrator), 1968; Ten Questions-Biographies of Ten Composers, 1969. Contbr. to: Aesthetic Education Mag. Mbrships: participates in int. confs. of int. Soc. for Music Educ.; Czech. Music Soc. Address: Na Kuthenca 7, 160 00 Prague 6-Dejvice, Czechoslovakia.

BERBERIAN, Ara, b. 14 May, Detroit, Mich., USA. Opera & Concert Singer (Bass). Educ: AB (Econs.), LLB, Univ. of Mich. m, Virginia Kalfaian, 2 s, 1 d. Debut: Turnau Opera, Woodstock, NY, 1958. Career: apps. w. most regional US Opera Cos.; Concert w. over 50 N Am. Symph. Orchs.; Took part in 4 World Premieres on CBS-TV Network; NYC Opera, 1962-; San Fran. Opera, 1966-; Metropolitan Opera Debut, 1979. Recordings: B Minor Mass; 3 albums of songs by Alan Houhaness, w. comp. at piano. Hobbies: Tennis; Woodworking; Gardening. Mgmt: Harold Shaw. Address: 28415 Streamwood Ln., Southfield, MI 48034, USA. 2.

BERBERIAN, Cathy, b. Attleboro, Mass., USA. Singer; Actress; Composer; Teacher; Translator. Educ: NY Univ.; Columbia Univ.; La Meri Dancing Schl., Conserv. G Verdi, Milan, Italy; studied Voice w. Giorgina del Vigo, Milan, Acting w. Herbert Graf. Peter Brook. m. Luciano Berio (div.), 1 d. Debut: Naples, Italy, 1957. Career: Apps at La Scala, Milan, Convent Garden & Royal Fest. Hall, London, UK, Hamburg Opera, Germany, Concertgebouw, Holland, Stockholm Opera, Sweden & at major Music Fecto. thru'out world, TV Specials incl. apps. in Hamburg, Oslo, Vienna, Munich, Paris & USA; Tchr. of Master Classes in Can., Germany & Italy. Comp: Stripsody, 1966; Morsicat(h(y, 1971; Awake & Readjoyce, 1971. Recordings incl: REcital 1 for Cathy; Stravinsky Songs; Magnificathy; Monteverdi, Orfeo; Beatles Arias; Berio Selections; Visage; Circles. Mbr., Artistic Commission Soc. Italiana Musica Contemporanea. Hons. incl: Wiesbaden Festival Prize, 1970, 1973; Grammy Nomination, 1971, 1973 & 1974. Hobbies: Collecting Art Noveau & Edwardiana; Cooking. Mgmt: Allied Artists, London, UK. Address: Via Moscata 7, Milan, Italy 20154, 2, 3, 5, 19, 27.

BERBERIAN, Hratch, b. 13 Jan. 1927, AThens, Greece. Violinist; String Pedagogue; Musicologist; Lecturer. Educ: Dip.-César Franck, Ecole Superieure de Musique, Paris; MMus, Boston Conserv. of Music; Doct. Cand., Univ. of Iowa. m. Arpinee Sanoukian, 3 d. Career: Recitals & Chmbr. Music perfs. in Middle East, France & USA; Toured w. Boston Pops Orch., Pablo Casals Fest. Orch. & Goldowski Opera Orch., 1961-66; RAdio apps., 'Commentary on the Classics', Prof. of Music, South Dakota State Univ., 1967-. Mbrships: Am. String Tchrs. Assn. Hons: First Prize, 'Nicola Dale' Middle East Violin Competition, 1945. Hobbies: Astronomy; Ping-Pong; Travelling. Address: 702 Medary AVe., Brookings, SD 57006, USA.

BERDAHL, Arthur Clarence, b. 26 Sept. 1906, Canton, SD, USA. Professor of Music Emeritus; Assistant Principal Bass. Educ: AB, Augustana Coll., 1927; MA, 1931, PhD, 1936. Univ. of Iowa; Berkshire Music Ctr., Hollywood Bowl w. Klemperer; Study w. Philip Greeley Clapp, Edwin Evans, (Univ. of Iowa), Koussevitsky, Copland. Hindemith, Chapple (Berkshire Music Ctr.), Alfred Hertz (San Fran.). m. Mildred Stomme, 2 s. (1 dec.). Career: Tchr., HS, 1927-30; Coll. & Univ. Tchr., Music, Conducting, 1930-71; Prof. of Music

Emeritus, Calif. State Univ., Fresno; Asst. Prin. Bass, Fresno Phil. Orch.; Cond., Fresno State Coll. Symph., 1932-54; Univ. of Iowa Symph., summers, 1936, '54; Fresno Community Chorus, 1956, '60; Guest Cond., var. city, schl. orchs.; Fndr., Music Dir., Ctrl. Calif. Symph. Assn., 1936-37. Unpublished compositions for voice, chorus, orch., solo piano pieces, 1 string quartet. Tech. Cons., illustrated Home Library Encyclopedia (1955), New Wonder World Encyclopedia (1959-62). Mbrships. incl: MENC; Nat. Soc. for Arts & Letters; aaup; Phi Mu Alpha; Luth. Soc. for Music, Worship & Arts; Standard Schl. Broadcast Advsry. Bd., 25 yrs. Hons: Alumni Achievement Award, Augustana Coll., 1972. Hobbies: Reading; Theatre & acting; Vacations in High Sierras; Swimming. Address: 440 E Harvard Ave., Fresno, CA 93704, USA. 3, 9, 11, 12.

BEREAU, Jean-Sébastien, b. 25 Dec. 1934, Soissons, Aisne, France. Conservatory of Music Direcor; Conductor. Educ: Louvre Schl.; Nat. Higher Conserv. of Music, Paris. m. 3 children. Career: Dir., Metz Conserv., 1963; Dir., Rouen Conserv & Rouen Chmbr. Orch., 1967; Dir., Strasbourg Conserv. of Music, 1973-. Comps. incl: Concert Music, for oboe & orch.; Sextet (wind instruments); Triptych. for bassoon & orch. Var. recordings w. Rouen chmbr. orch. Mbrships. incl: vp, Autonomous Syndicate of Conserv. Dirs., Chmbr. Music Soc., Strasbourg. Kt., Order of Arts & Letters, 1970. Hobbies incl: Natural hist. Address: 70 Ave. des Vosges, 67000 Strasbourg, France.

BERENBOICK, Lester Willard, b. 14 May 1921, Weehawken, NJ, USA. Professor of Church Music; Organist; Choral Director. Educ: BS, MS, Juilliard Schl. of Music; Dip. & Postgrad. Dip., Guilmant Organ Schl. Career: Organist & Choir Dir., Trinity Luth. Ch., Grantwood, NJ, Trinity Episc. Ch., Cliffside Park, NJ, W End Presby. Ch., NYC, Presby. Ch., Madison, NJ; Prof., Ch. Music. Organist & Choral Dir., Drew Univ. Comps: Engl. version of Marius Monnikendam's Via Sacra; Organ, vocal works. Recordings w. Drew Theol. Schl. Choir & as soloist. Contbr. to Music Ministry jrnl. Mbrships: Soc. of Arts, Scis. & Letters, Paris; AGO; AAUP; Hymn Soc. of Am.; Choristers guild; Fellowship of United Meth. Musicians; Am. Choral Dirs. Assn.; Presby. Fellowship of Musicians. Hons: Silver Medal, Soc. of Arts, Scis. & Letters, Paris, 1974. Hobbies: Travel; Gardening; Bridge; Bicycling. Address: 220 Park Ave., Convent Stn., NJ 07961, USA.

BERENDES, (Sister) M Benedicta, IHM, b. 28 Nov. 1927, NYC, USA. Musicologist; Pianist; Organist. Educ: BM, Marywood Coll., Scranton, Pa., 1955; MM, Univ. of Notre Dame, 1962; MA Cand.; PhD, Univ. of Pitts., 1973; Choirmaster Cert. - AGO, 1962. Career: currently Dir., Cert. Progs. for Liturgical Music co-sponsored by Diocese of Scranton & Marywood Coll. Mbrships: Am. Musicol. Soc.; AAUP; Nat. Pastoral Musicians Assn. Recip. 1st Prize, NCMEA Musicol. Contest, 1962. Address: Marywood Coll., Box 864, Scranton, PA, 18509, USA. 4, 27.

BERENS, Fritz, b. 26 Apr. 1907, Vienna, Austria, Symphony Orchestra Conductor; Composer; Pianist; Accompanist. Educ: Dip., Conserv. of Music, Vienna. m. Lois Treadwell Berens, 1 d. Career: Operatic & Ballet Cond., Germany & Austria, 1929-; Symph. Cond., USA, 1939-; Assoc. Prof. of Music, Tex. Christian Univ., Ft. Worth, 1966-73; Ret'd., 1973; Pvte. Tchr. of piano, conducting, comp. Comps: Symphonic; Chmbr. music; Ballets; Songs. Address: 3809 Winifred Dr., Ft. Worth, TX 76133, USA.

BEREZNICKA-PNIAK, Urszula, b. 12 July 1941, Rdwne, Poland. Percussionist. Educ: Dip., Music Acad., Lidz; MA. m., 1 s. Career: soloist on film, TV, radio & w. orch.; currently Mbr., Lodz Phil. Orch. Hobbies: Travel; Theatre. Address: Marusakowny 6/16, 940-41 Lodz, Poland.

BERG, Bengt Johan Daniel, b. 26 Nov. 1935, Vadstana, Sweden. Organist. Educ: RCM, Stockholm; Studied organ w. Alf Linder; Higher Organists Dip., 1955; Higher Choirmasters Dip., 1959; Music Tchrs. Dip., 1959; Studied w. Flor Peeters, Belgium; Dip., Antwerp, 1967; Dip. (Soloists), Stockholm, 1971. Debut: Organ Scholar, Swedish Broadcasting Corp., Stockholm, 1962. Career: O Broby, Emmisiöv, 1959-61; Hedvig's Norrköping, 1962-64; Matteus, Stockholm, 1964-; Recitals in Sweden, Finland, E & W Germany, Belgium & UK. Recordings incl. organ works by Messiaen, Vivaldi, Bach, etc. Mbr. Exec. Committee, Stockholm Diocesan Ch. Musicians Soc. Recip. 3rd Prize & Audience Award, 1967 Int. Organ Competition, Bruges. Address: Västmannagatan 92v, S-11343 Stockholm, Sweden.

BERG, Christopher Babcock, b. 17 June 1952, New Haven, Conn., USA. Performer of Classical Guitar & Lute. Educ: BM,

MM, Classical Guitar, Peabody Conserv. of Music, Baltimore, Md., USA; studies w. Aaron Shearer, 1971-77; studies w. Dr. Carolyn Raney & Gregg Smith. m. Janice Zamos Berg. Career: Soloist, TV prog., taped & broadcast by WBAL TV, Baltimore, 1974; Soloist w. Md. Ballet Co., 1975-76; Soloist & 1st Guitar w. Peabody Guitar Ensemble; Num. recitals in Baltimore, Phila., Conn. & NY, inclng. concerts for classical guitar socs.; concerto apps. w. Skitch Henderson & Stamford Symph.; Perf. as lutenist w. var. early music ensembles; Asst. Prof. of Music, Univ. of SC. Mbrshps: Guitar Fndn. of Am.; Am. Str. Tchrs. Assn.; Coll. Music Soc. Hons. incl: 1st guitarist to receive MM from Peabody Conserv.; 1st prize, Music Tchr. Nat. Assn. Comp., 1977. Hobbies: Calligraphy; Etymology; Backpacking. Mgmt: Gary McGee Assocs., 156 West 72nd St., NY. Address: 133 Chaunticleer Rd., Columbia, SC, 29204, USA.

BERG, Gunnar, b. 11 Jan. 1909, St. Gallen, Switzerland. Composer. Educ: Royal Danish Conserv. m. Béatrice Duffour, 1 d. Debut: Copenhagen, 1945; 1st work performed in Royal Danish Conserv., 1936. Career. incls: Am. Seminar, Salzburg, 1950; Paris, 1948-57; Concert w. own works, cercle Paul Valéry, Paris, 1953; Apps. w. wife, most European countries; Ballet in Holland Fest., 1956. Comps. incl: (publs.) Gaffky's I-X, for piano (also recorded); for clarinet & violin (also recorded); Frise for piano & chmbr. orch. Recordings incl: Ten Japanese Woodcuts; Filandre. Mbr. Dansk Komponisforening. Address: Lindved gl. Skole, 8783 Hornsyld, Denmark.

BERG, Olav, b. 25 Sept. 1949, Hedrum, Norway. Composer. Educ: Studies in Comp. w. Antonio Bibalo; 1 yr. study w. Lennox Berkeley, London. Career: Sev. radio perfs. of chmbr. & orchl. works. Comps. incl: Pezzo per Orchestra, 1974; STring Quartet, 1975; Movimento Sinfonico, 1977; Four Pieces for Orch., 1978. Mbr., Soc. of Norwegian Comps. Hons: 1st Prize, Comp., Assn. for the Int. Competition of Amateur Symph. Orchs., Liège, Belgium, 1976. Address: Langgt, 36, 3190 Horten, Norway.

BERG, Reidun, b. 7 June, 1936, Bergen, Norway. Producer/Reporter; Pianist. Educ: Grad., Nordwestdeutsche Musikakademie, Detmold, W Germany; Piano-dip. exam., Oslo Conserv. of Music; Pvte. studies w. Hans Richter-Haaser, Carlo Zecchi & Robert Riefling. m. Prof. Kare Berg. Debut: Oslo, 1957. Career: Radio & TV apps., Norway, USA & Italy; Recitals, Norway, USA & Germany; Soloist w. Symph. Orchs. of Oslo & Bergen; Prod./Reporter, Music Dept., Norwegian Broadcasting, 1968-. publs: Norwegian translation of The Wonderful World of Music (B Britten & I Holst), 1970. Contbr. to: Programbladet. Mbrshps: Chmn., Norwegian State Music Coun., 1977-; Norwegian Soc. of Artists; Norwegian Soc. of Soloists. Hons: German State Fellowship, 1961-63; Italian State Fellowship, 1961. Address: Tollef Gravs vei 95a, 1342 Jar, Norway.

BERGAAS, Mark, b. 7 Feb. 1951, Mpls., Minn., USA. Musicologist; Organist. Educ: BA, St. Olaf Coll.; MA, M Phil & PhD, Yale Univ. m. Mary Carol Bergaas. 1 d. Career: Freelance Organist, Mpls., Minn. & New Haven, Conn.; Co-Arr. (w. wife), musical Amity Parish; Asst. Prof. Music History, Univ. of Alabama, Tuscaloosa. Publs: Compositional Style in the Keyboard Works of Hugo Distler (1908-1942), 1979. Mbr., Am. Musicol. Soc.; Soc. for Music Theory. Address: 1745 River Rd., No 31-B, Tuscaloosa, Alabama 35401, USA.

BERGAMO, Petar, b. 27 Feb. 1930, Split, Yugoslavia. Composer. Educ: Studied Comp. under Prof. Stanojlo Rajicic, Belgrade Coll. of Music; Dip. & MA, ibid. Career: Lectr., Comp. & Orch., Belgrade Coll. of Music. Comps. incl: Unknown (Suite for Mixed Chorus); I Symphony, 1956-57; Variazioni sul tema interroto (Piano), 1957; Navigare necesse est (Overture-Fantasy), 1959-60; Concerto abbreviato (solo clarinet), 1966; Ritrovari per tre (piano, violin & cello), 1971; all comps. broadcast on Yugoslav jrnls. & newspapers. Mbr., Union Yogoslav Comps. Hons. incl: 7 July Prize (highest nat. prize) for concert music, 1963. Hobbies: Photography & Sailing. Address: 1040 Vienna, Fleischmanngasse 3/12, Austria.

BERGANZA, Teresa, b. 16 Mar. 1935, Spain. Singer (mezzo-soprano). Educ: Study w. Lola Rodriques Aragon, m. Felix Lavilla. Debut: Madrid, 1955. Career incl: Leading opera roles in var. countries incl: The Marriage of Figaro, Glyndebourne, 1958; The Barber of Seville, Convent Garden, 1960; La Scala, Milan; Rome Opera: Metropol. Opera, NY; Chgo. OPera HOuse; San Fran. Opera, etc.; Festival appearances at Edinburgh, Holland; Concert tours of W. Europe, N & S Am., Israel. Repertoire incl. wide operatic range together with lieder & Spanish folk songs num. recordings. Hons: Premio Lucrezia Arana; Premio extraordinario del Conserv. de Madrid; Grand Cross of Isabel the Catholic. Address: Joaquin Maria Lopez, 29, Madrid 15, Spain.

BERGE, Sigurd, b. 1 July, 1929, Vinstra, Norway. Composer. Debut: Helsinki, 1959. Comps: Approx. 50 comps., inc: Chroma (orch.); Yang-Guan, woodwind quintet for the Young; Flute-Solo, Oboe-Solo, Horncall; Illuxit (choir), all recorded; Between Mirrors, (violin & strg. orch.); Raga (oboe & orch.); Electronic pieces; Juvenes; Spring dance, recorded. Publs: Soundforming, 1973; Soundforming with the Tape Recorder, 1974; Piano School, 1978. Hons: Oslo City musical prize; Baerum musical prize; 3 nat. prizes. Address: Kierschowsgate 3, Oslo 4, Norway.

BERGER, Arild, b. 22 Aug. 1941, Oslo, Norway. Pianist; Jass Pianist. Educ: Pvte. studies, 11 yrs. m. Anne Kari Berger, 1 s, 1 d. Debut: Oslo's Jazz Clubs, 1956-57. Career: Sev. radio & TV perfs. (NRK); apps. w. Norwegian groups as Jazz Pianist. Comps: Dixieland; Swing; Mainstream; Bop. Recordings: 5, in Norway. Mbrshps: Norwegian Jazz Soc.; Norwegian Music Union. Hobbies: Art; Joining the family. Address: Skysetv. 5D, 1481 Li, Norway.

BERGER, Georg Wilhelm, b. 4 Dec. 1929, Rupea-Brasov, Rumania. Composer Musicologist. Educ: Conserv. of Music, Bucharest. m. Lucia Berger, 1 s. Debut: 1954. Career: sev. musicol. broadcasts on Rumanian TV. Compositions: 11 Symphs., 1960, 63, 64, 65, 68 (recorded), 69 (recorded), 70, 71, 74, 76 & 76; Symphonic Poem, 1959; Concerto for STr. Orch., Variations for Chmbr. Orch.; Oratorio 'Stefan Fortuna'; Lyric Cantata 'Dintre sute de catarge'; Fest. Music for Flute & Orch.; Concerto for violin & Orch. (recorded); Concerto for 2 Violins & Orch.; Concerto for Cello & Orch. (recorded); Concerto for Violin & 2 Quartets; 12 Str. Quartets (the 6th recorded); Sonata for Violin Solo (recorded); Sonata for Viola & Cello; Sonata for Flute, Viola & Cella; Sonata for Violin & Piano. Publs: Muzica sinfonica (baroca-classica), 1967; Muzica simfonica (romantica, 1830-1890), 1972; Quartet de coarde de la Haydn la Debussy, 1970; Ghid pentru muzica instrumentala de camera, 1965; Muzica simfonica (romantica-moderna, 1890-1930), 1974; Muzica Simfonica Moderna Contemporana, 1950--75. Contbr. to: Muzica; var. newspapers. Mbr: Sec., Union of Rumanian Composers; Hons: Prince Rainier III Prize, Monaco, 1964; 1st Prize Int. Concours for str. quartet compositions, 1965; 1st Prize Queen Elizabeth of Belgium Int. Musical Concours, 1966; George Enesco Prize for Compositions, Rumanian Composers. Address: Boul. 1 Mai No. 148, App. 3, Bucharest, Rumania.

BERGER, Melvin H., b. 23 Aug. 1927, NYC, USA. Violist; Writer. Educ: B Mus., Eastman Schl. of Music, Univ. of Rochester, 1951; MA, Columbia Univ., 1952; additional study in the Associateship Prog. of London Univ.; Private study w. Raphael Bronstein & Nathan Gordon. m. Gilda Schulman, 2 d. Debut: Carnegie Recital Hall, NYC, 1962. Career: TV & Radio appearances on all major US networks; Recital & concerto appearances throughout the USA, plus several concerts in England. Compositions: Basic Viola Technique, MCA, 1966; 3 Fourteenth Century Dances for Viola & Tambour, MCA, 1964; Doulce Memoire for Viola & Piano, MCA, 1968; Viola Solos, MCA, 1967. Recordings: Vaughan Villiams 'Suite for Viola & Orchestra' & Robert Starer 'Concert for Viola, Strings & Percussion', w. Engl. Chamber Orch. under John Snashall, by Pye. Publs: (books) Science & Music, 1961 in USA & 1964 in UK; Music in Perspective, 1962; Masters of Modern Music, 1970; The Violin Book, 1972; Jobs in the Fine Arts & Humanities, 1974; The Story of Folk Music, 1976. Contbr. to: Book of Knowledge, ency.; Am. String Tchr.; The Instrumentalist; Jrnl. of the Music Educators Nat. Conf., World Book Ency. Hobbies: Travel; Reading; Collecting antique microscopes. Address: 18 Glamford Rd., Great Neck, NY 11023, USA.

BERGER, Roman, b. 9 Aug. 1930, Cieszyn, Poland. Composer; Pianist. Educ: Dip., Piano, Acad. of Musical Arts, Bratislava, Czech., 1956; Dip., Comp., ibid, 1965. m. Ruth Strbova. Debut: Comp., Bratislava, 1962; Piano, ibid, 1956. Career: Prof. of Piano, Conserv., Bratislava, 1956-65; Fellow, Sound Laboratory, Czech. TV, 1965-66; Sec., Union of Slovak Comps., 1966-69; Bratislava, 1969-73. Comps: Suite, strings, piano, percussion; Konvergenzioni I, violin, II, viola III, violoncello; Memento after the Death of MF; Transformations, symph.; Elegia in memoriam Jan Rucka, Eptaf to Kopernic, electronic works; 20 short film scores; var. stage music. Mbr. Union of Slovak Comps., 1966-72. Recip. var. Hons. for Comp. Address: 83.000 Bazovskeho 11/8, Bratislava, Czech.

BERGER, Theodor, b. 1905, Traismauer-Danube. Composer; Conductor. Educ: Music Acad., Vienna. m. Karin Bornhofen. Compositions: Homerian Symphony; Symphonia parabolica; Jahreszeiten-Sinfonie; Concerto Manuale; Violin Concerto; Aquafonien; Frauenstimmen im Orchester; Music for Faust II; 2 ballets; La Parola; Malinconia; Chronique Symphonique; Rondo Ostinato; Imperssionen; sev. quartets; Gold medal of Hon. of City of Vienna. Address: Prinz Eugenstrasse 38, Vienna IV, Austria.

BERGH, Oivind, b. 3 Dec. 1909, Hamar, Norway. Conductor; Violinist. Educ: Matriculation degree. m. Rigmor Hansen. Debut: Oslo, 1935. Career: Violinist & Conductor, Music HS of Dresden; Mbr., Oslo String Quartet, 1938-44; Conductor, & Artistic Ldr., Norwegian Broadcasting Orch., 1946-; over 5,000 radio concerts performed; Guest Cond., num. countries in W. Europe, Iceland & USA. Recordings: num. records w. Norwegian Braodcasting Orch., 7 LPs, 'Light Music of Norway'. Publ: Modern Dance Music, 1945; contbr. of num. music articles to Scandinavian newspapers & mags. Hons: Kt., Dannebrog Order, Denmark, 1960; Off., Ordre de Leopold II, Belgium, 1965; Cavaliere Officiale dell'Ordine Al Merito della Repub. Italiano, 1965; Verdienstkreutz 1 Klasse, 1970; Kt. FALK order, Iceland, 1970, Knight of St. Olav's Order, Norway. Hobbies: Travel; Photography & movie making. Address: Elvefaret 34, Roa, Oslo 7, Norway. 19.

BERGH, Sverre, b. 2 Nov. 1915, Hamar, Norway. Composer. Educ: studied comp. w. Fartein Valen, organ w. Arild Sandvold & piano w. E Westher. m. Eva Bergh, 2 children. Career: Musician, Oslo, 1936-46; Pianist & Arr., Norwegian State Broadcasting, 1946-62; Musical Dir., Folketeatret, Oslo, 1952-57, Den Nationale Scene, Bergen, 1957-76; Mng. Dir., Gergen Int. Fest., 1976-. Comps. incl: chmbr., orchl. & piano music; incidental music to plays & films; choral music. Comps. recorded: String Quartet No. 1; Village Sketches for orch.; sev. piano pieces & orchl. works. Address: Storhavgen 16,5000 Bergen, Norway.

BERGLUND, Paavo Allan Engelbert, b. 14 Apr. 1929, Helsinki, Finland. Conductor. Educ: Sibelius Acad., Helsinki; Vienna & Salzburg. m. Kirsti Kivekäs, 1 s., 2 d. Career: Violinist, Finnish Radio Symph. Orch., 1949-56; cond., ibid., 1956-62; prin. cond., ibid., 1962-p71; prin. cond., Bournemouth Symph. Orch., 1972-79; prin cond., Helsinki Phil. Orch., 1975-79. Recordings: num. incl. all Sibelius symphs. (inc Kullervo Symph.); Shostakovich Symphs. Nos. 5, 6, 7, 10, 11; Smetana, Ma Vlast. Publ: A Comparative Study of the Printed Score & the Manuscript of the Seventh Symphony of Sibelius, 1970. Hons: Finnish State Award for Music, 1972; hon. OBE, 1977. Address: Munkkiniemenranta 41, 00330 Helsinki 33, Finland.

BERGMAN, Erik, b. 24 Nov. 1911, Nykarleby, Finland. Composer; Professor. Educ: studied musicol., Helsinki Univ.; Dip. in comp., Sibelius Acad., 1938; studied comp. W. Heinz Tiessen, Berlin, & Wladimir Vogel, Switz.; further studies in many European countries & studies of folk music in the Balkans, Turkey, Egypt & Far E. m. Solveig von Schoultz. Career: Cond., Akademiska Sangföreningen (male chorus, Helsinki Univ.), 1950-69, & Sällskapet Muntra Musikanter, 1951-78; Music Critic, Hufvudstadsbladet, Helsinki, 1947-; prof. of Comp., Sibelius Acad., 1963-76. Comps. incl: orchestral works, chmbr. works, works for choir & orch. or instrumental ensemble, & works for solo instruments. Comps. recorded: Aubade for orch; Concertino da camera, chmbr. work; Aspects, Sonatine, Intervalles for piano, Exsultate for organ, Energien for harpsichord; Lapponia, Missa, Faglarna, Svanbild, Vier Galgenlieder, Nox, Bon appetit for choir. Mbrships: For. Mbr., Swedish Acad. of Music; Bds., Finnish Sect., ISCM, 1952-67; Mbr., State Expert Comm. on Music, 953-71. Recip. of Int. Sibelius Prize of Wihuri Fndn., 1965; Phil. Dhc, 1978. Hobbies: Photography; Travel. Address: BErg. 22, C, Helsinki 10, Finland.

BERGMAN, Janet Louise Marx, b. 15 June 1920, St. Louis, Mo., USA. Flautist; Flute Prof., Fac. of Am. Conserv. of Music. Educ: studied w. Laurent Torno & John F Kiburtz & in Schlrships Symph. under Edward Murphy. m. Albert Soloman German, 1 s., 2 d. Career incls: has played w. many bands & orchs., inclng. St. Louis, Okla. City & New Orleans Symphs. & Women's Symph., Chgo.; toured Mich. & Wis. w. Women's Sinfonetta; 1st Flute & Solist, St. Louis Little Symph. (at age 19), Okla. City Symph., City Symph. Chgo., Chmbr. Orch. Chgo., has played for theatre prodns., inclng., Schubert Theatre. Was 1st woman in history of opera to march in army band in 'La Boheme' (played piccolo); Mbr., Aeolian Woodwind Ensemble 1965-76; since 1963, 1st Flute, City Symph. of Chgo.; Flute Inster., FAc. of Chgo. Conserv. Coll., 1968-; Adjudicator or Judge for sev. contests. inclng., Flute Concours Montreal. St. Louis Radiokmox, Am. FEd. Music Clubs. Publs: Do's & Don'ts of Flute Playing, 1967. Mbrshps: Am. Fedn. of Musicians; Organized Women Musicians; Educl. Off., N Side Chapt., Chgo., Nat. Hlth. Fndn., 1975-76. Recip of 1st Place Prize, Solo Competition, Nat. Contest, Little Rock, ARk; 1st Place Solo Competition State Contest, Columbia Mo., 1939.

Hobbies incl: Interior Decorating, Antique & Art Collecting, Bicycle Riding. Address: 1817-G W Hood, Chicago, IL 60660, USA.

BERGONZI, Carlo, b. 13 July 1924, Busseto, Parma, Italy. Opera Singer. Educ: Parma Conserv. Debut: as baritone, Figaro, Barber of Seville, Lecce, 1948; as tenor, title role, Andrea Chenir, Teatro Petruzzelli, Bari, 1952. Career: apps. in var. Italian opera houses inclng. La Scala Milan; US debut at Lyric Opera, Chgo., in Il Tabarro & Cavalleria Rusticana; played Radames in Aida & Manrico in Il Trovatore, Met. Opera, NYC, 1955-56; apps. in all major European opera houses, also in USA & S Am. 16.

BERGQUIST, Peter, b. 5 Aug. 1930, Sacramento, CA, USA. University Professor (musicology, theory, bassoon). Educ: Eastman Schl. of Music, Rochester, NY, 1948-51l BS, Mannes Coll. of Music, NYC, NY, 1955-58; MA, PhD, Columbia Univ., NYC, NY, 1958-64. m. Dorothy Bergquist, 2 d. Career: Faculty, Schl. of Music, Univ. of Oregon, 1964-; profl. perfs. as bassoonist in NY, Rochester & Oregon. Recordings: New Music for Woodwind Quintet w. Univ. of Oregon Woodwind Quintet, 1972. Publs: Transl. of Pietro Aaron, Toscanello in Musica, 1970. Contbr. to var. profl. jrnls. Mbrships: Am. Musicol. Soc., Nat. count., chapt. sec. & chmn.; Coll. Music Soc.; Music Lib. Assoc.; Int. Musicol. Soc.; Soc. for Music Theory. Hons: Ersted Award for Disting. Tchng., Univ. of Oregon, 1972. Hobbies: Travel; Gardening; Wine collecting. Address: 3195 Portland Str., Eugene, OR 97405, USA.

BERGSAGEL, John Dagfinn, b. 19 Apr. 1928, Outlook Sask., Can. Musicologist. Educ: BA, Univ. of Man., 1949; BMus, St. Olaf Coll., Minn., USA, 1950; Grad. study, Cornell Univ., Oxford Univ., UK, ram; LRAM, 1954; PhD, Cornell, 1957; MA (Oxon.), 1964. m. Charlotte Sorensen, 4 c. Career: Tchr., Concordia Coll., Minn., 1954-55; Ohio Univ., 1955-59; Tutor in hist. of music, Oxford Univ., 1962-67; Lectr., New Coll., ibid., 1966-67; Sr. lectr. in musicol., Manchester Univ., 1967-70; Inst. of Musicol., Univ. of Copenhagen, Denmark, 1970-; Exec. Ed., Early Engl. Ch. Music, 1961-76; Ed. Bd., ibid., 1976-. Publs: The Early Tudor Masses, 1963; Engelske Anthems fra det 16 Aarhundrede, 1974. Contbr. to num. musical publs. Mbrships: Am., Danish & Int. Musicol. Socs.; Royal Musical Assn.; Plainsong & Medieval Music Soc. Hons: Friends of Music Prize in Comp., Cornell Univ., 1953; Can. Coun. Sr. Arts Fellowship, 1959; Gulbenkian Fndn. Grant, 1960; Royal Danish Acad. of Scis. & Letters, 1978. Address: Batzkes Bakke 9, 3400 Hillerod, Denmark. 14.

BERGSTRØM-NIELSEN, Carl, b. 28 July 1952, Denmark, Copenhagen. Composer; Performer (French horn). Educ: Inst. of Musicol., Copenhagen. Career: perfs. & organizational work, Group for Alternative Music, 1971-77; Rep., Young Nordic Music Fest., 1975, 78; Pers. w. Group for Intuitive Music, Denmark & Belgium, 1976-; Perfs., ISCM Danish Sect. Comps: 11. September; Fanfares for Everyday Life, 4 Horns; Sonata for Horn Quartet Postcard Music; Fire-Music. Contbr. to: bladet; Dansk Musiktidsskrift. Hons: 5000 dkr. from State Arts Fndn., 1977. Address: Hostrups Have 24, DK-1954 Copenhagen, Denmark.

BERIO, Luciano, b. 24 Oct. 1925, Oneglia, Italy. Composer; Conductor. Educ: Dip., Conserv. Giuseppe Verdi, Milan. m. Talia, 4 c. Career: has composed & conducted for most major orchs. & ensembles of USA & Europe; has composed for num. ldng. contemp. performers, inclng. Holliger, Gazzeloni, Trampler, Globokar, Dempster, Berberian; Prof. of Comp., Mills Coll., Harvard Univ. & Juilliard Schl. Comps. incl: Sequenzas I-VIII; Gesti; Laborintus II; Omaggio a Joyce; Allez Hop; Sinfonia; Recital I (for Cathy); Agnus; Concerto for 2 Pianos; Variazioni per Orch.; Melodrama; Points on the curve to Find. num. recordings. Contbr. to num. jrnls. Mbr., Accademia Philharmonia Romano. Recip., num. hons., inclng: Grand Prix du DCisque, 1972; Montreux, 1970. Mgmt: Allied Artists, 36 Beauchamp Pl., London SW3. Address: Il Columbaio, Radicondoli, Siena, Italy.

BERK, Betty Jean Thomas, b. 30 Aug. 1915, Ludlow Falls, Ohio, USA. University Music Teacher; Pianist; Organist. Educ: BMus., Uiv. of Dayton, Ohio, 1944; MMus., Eastman Schl. of Music, 1950; PhD., ibid., 1963. m. Samuel F. Berk, 1 step-d. Career: prof., Theory, Music Hist., Piano, Univ. of Dayton, Ohio; perfs. on WHIO radio, Twenty Fingers & Two Grands, & as Piano Soloist, WING radio; Adjudicator, NGPT & Ohio Music Educators Assn. Comp: Dearest Jesus. Publs: Analysis of Two Scriabin Sonatas, 1950; Harmonic Materials & Treatment of Dissonance in the Pianoforte Music of Frederic Chopin, 1963. Mbrships: AGO (Dean, Dayton Chapt. 1957-58); Ohio Fedn. of Music Clubs (Student Advsr. 1972-74); Sigma Alpha Iota (Moderator, Student Chapt. 1965-73); Am. Musicol. Soc.;

Dayton Music Club; MENC; Ohio Music Educators; NGPT. · Recip., Sword of Honor, Nat. Guild of Piano Tchrs.; Hall of Fame. Sigma Alpha Iota. Hobbies: Hiking; Swimming; Reading. Address: 4434 Berquist Drive, Dayton, OH 45426, USA. 5, 8, 23, 27.

BERK, Ernest, b. 12 Oct. 1909, Cologne, Germany. Composer; Performer, Violin & Ethnic Percussion. Educ: Mod. Ballet Dip., Rheinische Musikshcule, Cologne; FGSM. m. (1) Lotte Berk, 1 d.; (2) Ailsa Berk, 1 s. Career incl: has composed music for 18 documentary films & feature film The Last of the Longhaired Boys; Fndr., Lyra Ventura orch. of improvised music; Music in our Time, Camden Fest., 1974-75; Own electronic music studio (tchng. & composing), 1955-; Prof., GSM, 1959-; num. fests., concerts, TV shows. Comps., over 200 major works inclng. ballet music. Recordings: Initiation; Gemini. Contbr. to Sound. Mbr., PRS. Hobbies: Sailing; Motorcycling. Address: 143 The Grampians, London W6, UK.

BERKELEY, (Sir) Lennox Randal, b. 12 May 1903, Oxford, UK. Composer. Educ: BA Oxford; pupil of Nadio Boulanger, Paris. m. Elizabeth Bernstein, 3 s. Compositions: Orchestral; Chamber Music; Opera; Piano; Choral Music, etc. Recordings: Piano Music, Voice & Piano, Voice & String, Lyrita; Violin Concerto, EMI; Third Symphony (LPO), Lyrita; Guitar Sonatina & Theme & Variations, RCA; Four Poems of Ronsard (Peter Pears), Decca, 1974; 1st Symph. & Concerto for 2 Pianos & Orch. Lyrira; Divertimento Serenade & Partita, Lyrita; Ronsard Sonnets, Decca. Mbrships: Inc. Soc. of Musicians; performing Right Soc., Hons: Collard Fellowship in Music, 1946; Cobbet Medal for Chamber Music, 1950; CBE, 1958; Composer of the Yr. Award, Composers' Guild, 1972; Recip. Knighthood, 1974. Hobby: Reading. Address: 8 Warwick Ave., London 2S, UK 1.

BERKELEY, Michael Fitzhardinge, b. 29 May, 1948, London, UK. Composer. Educ: Westminster Cathedral, Chorister under George Malcolm; RAM; studies w. Richard Rodney Bennett; comp., piano & singing studies. Career: BBC Radio 3 announcer, 1974-; has presented concerts on BBC 2 TV. Comps. incl: Mass for Men's Voices & Organ, 1974; Meditations for Str. Orch., 1975, (recorded); Concerto for oboe & Strg. Orch., 1976; Strg. Trio, 1976; FAntasia Concertante, 1977; The Wild Winds, soprano & small orch., 1978; Primavera, overture for full orch., 1979. Contbr. to: Observer; The Listener; Vogue. Hons: Guiness prize for Comp., 1977; Assoc. comp. to Scottish Chmbr. Orch., 1979. Hobbies: Walking; Squash; Reading. Address: 26 Lady Margaret Rd., London, NW5, UK.

BERKENSTOCK, James Turner, b. 9 Oct. 1942, Joliet, Ill., USA. Musician; Teacher. Educ: BS, George Peabody Coll. for Tchrs., Tenn.; MM, Northwestern Univ., 1966; PhD, ibid, 1975. m. Jean Wideroe Berkenstock, 1 s. Career: Prin. Bassoonist, Lyric Opera of Chicago, 1968-; Mbr. of Contemporary Chmbr. Players, Univ. of Chicago, 1967-; Asst. Prof. of Music, Northern Ill. Univ., 1978-; Fndg. VP, The Orch. of Ill., 1978. Recordings: num. recordings with Contemporary Chmbr. Players; Symphs. No. 6 & 8, Mahler. w. Chicago Symph. Orch. Publs: Joseph Haydn in Literature: A Bibliography in Haydn Studies, 1974. Mbrships: Am. Musicol. Soc.; Chmn., Lyric Opera Orch. Mbrs'. Committee. Hobbies: Gardening. Address: 3626 Thayer St., Evanston, IL 60201, USA.

BERLEANT, Arnold, b. 4 Mar. 1932, Buffalo, NY, USA. Professor of Philosophy(Aesthetics), CW Post Centre, Lond Island University. Educ: BMus., Eastman Schl. of Music, Univ. of Rochester, 1953; MA, ibid, 1955; PhD, State Univ. of Ny Buffalo, 1962. m. Riva Berleant-Schiller, 1 s., 2 d. Publs: The Aesthetic Field, A Phenomenology of Aesthetic Experience, 1970. Contbr. to: Jrnl. of Aesthetics & Art Criticism; Philos. & Phenomenol. Rsch.; Jrnl. of V alue inquiry. Mbrships: Trustee, Am. Soc. for Aesthetics, 1972-74; Exec. Comm., Am. Soc. for Value Inquiry, 1973-75; Sec. Treas., Am. Soc. for Aesthetics. Recip. of Geo. Eastman Hon. Schlrship. Hobbies: Chmbr. Music; Sailing. Address: 25 Highfield Rd., Glen Cove, NY 11542, USA. 6, 12.

BERLIN, Edward Alan, b. 26 June 1936, New York, NY, USA. Musicologist; Teacher; WRiter; Editor. Educ: BA in Econs., Queens College, NY, 1959; MA in Music Hist., Hunter Coll., NY, 1965; PhD in Musicology, City Univ. of Ny, 1976. m. Andrée de Plata, 3 d. Career: Prof. & Lectr. of music at Herbert H. Lehman Coll., Hunter Coll., Brooklyn Coll., Richmond Coll. & York Coll.; Ed. for Schirmer Books & Holt, Rinehart & Winston; Freelance writer, rschr. & ed. Publs: Ragtime: A Musical & Cultural History, 1979; Ed. 6th ed. of Baker's Biographical Dictionary of Musicians, 1978. Contbr. to: Notes; The Balck Perspective in Music; Jrnl. of Jazz Studies; Current Musicology; Jrnl. of Rsch. in Music Educ. Mbrships: Am. Musicol. Soc.;

Sonneck Soc.; Coll. Music Soc.; Music Lib. Assn.; Maple Leaf Club. Hons: George N. Shuster Award, 1965. Address: 26 Horton St., Malverne, NY 11565, USA.

BERLIN, Irving, b. 11 May 1888, Russia (USA Res., 1893). Composer; Song Writer. Educ: NYC. m. Ellin Mackay, 1926, 3 d. Career incl: Pres., Irving Berlin Music Corpn. Compositions incl: Stage musicals - Annie Get Your Gun; Miss Liberty; Mr. President; Call Me Madam; Film musicals - This is the Army; Easter Parade; Popular songs incl: Alexander's Ragtime Band; Oh, How I Hate to Get Up in the Morning; Always; Reaching for the Moon; White Christmas; God Bless America; Blue Skies; What'll I Do; All Alone; Remem ber; Everybody's Doing It; There's No Business Like Show Business; How Deep is the Ocean. Hons: DMus.; Medal of Merit for This is the Army; Special gold medal for God Bless America. Address: Irving Berlin Music Corpn., 1290 Ave. of the Americas, NY, NY, USA.

BERLIN, Richard Merrill, b. 10 Mar. 1947, Balt., Md., USA. Trumpeter; Instructor in Trumpet, Music Theory & Music History. Educ: BS, Univ. of Md., Coll. Pk., 1968; MMus, Cath. Univ. of Am., Wash. DC. m. Glenda Diane Fried Berlin. Career: Prin. Trumpet, Prince George Symph. Orch. 1970-72; 2nd Trumptet, Greensboro Symph. Orch., 1972-76; Prin. Trumpet, Salisbury Symph. Orch., 1973-76; Co-Prin. Trumpet, Piedmont Brass Quintet, 1974-75; Brass Art Quintet, 1972-76; Trumpet Instructor, Univ. of NC at Greensboro, 1972-76, Wake Forest Univ., 1973-76; Asst. Prin. Trumpet, Jerusalem Symph. Orch., 1976-; Solo Trumpet w. Israel Bach Soc., Trumpet w. Jerusalem Big Band, 1976-; Solo trumpet w. Jerusalem Brass Quartet, 1977-. Solo recitals; Solo apps. w. orchs. & bands; Master classes. Mbrships. incl: Int. Trumpet Guild; Phi Mu Alpha Sinfonia. Hobbies: Bicycling. Address: c/o Jerusalem Symph. orch., Israel Broadcasting Authority, Jerusalem, Israel.

BERLJAWSKY, Joseph, b. 6 May 1911, Przemysl, Poland. Music Educator; Teacher of Violin & Viola; Coach of Chamber Music. Conductor; Musicologist. Educ. incl: Grad., Vienna Acad. of Music; DMus, Univ. of Montreal, Can. m. Paula Mansfield, 3 s. Debut: Vienna. Career: Soloist & chmbr. musician, Radio Vienna; 2nd Solo Violinist, Vienna Musica Viva; Asst. Concertmaster, Wiener Konzertorchester; Fndr.-Cond., Montreal Orchl. Soc. (now Montreal Musica Viva), 1954-. Mbrships: Cons. Mbr., Acad. de Musique, Quebec; Am. Musicol. Soc.; Life, Musicians' Guild of Montreal. Contbr. to mags. Hobby: Painting in watercolours. Address: 448A Riverdale Ave., Ottawa, Ont., K1S 1S2, Canada.

BERMAN, Bart, b. 29 Dec. 1938, Rotterdam, Holland. Pianist; Teacher of Piano. Educ: Muziek Lyceum, Amsterdam; Solist's Examination, 1961; Prize of Excellence, 1964. m. Hélène Julia Cohen, 3 children. Debut: Arnhem, 1960. Career: Num. recitals & concerts w. orch.; Apps. on Dutch radio; Concert tours of UK. France, Italy, W Germany, Sweden, Switzerland, Eire & Israel. Comps: 28 Cadenzas to Piano Concertos by Haydn, Mozart & Beethoven Recording: Modern Dutch Piano Comps., 1978. Mbrshps: KNTV; Vereniging van Docenten. Recip. of 1st Prize, Gaudeamus Int. Competition for Perfs. of Contemporary Music, 1970. Mgmt: Nederlands Impressariaat, Amsterdam. Address: Reeweg 122, Hendrik Ido Ambacht, The Netherlands.

BERN, Julian, b. 5 Dec. 1911, Skuodas, Lithuania. Pianist; Composer; Professor of Music. Educ: State Conserv. of Music, Memel; Ecole Normale de Musique, Paris, study w. Nadia Boulanger, Alfred Cortot; Hons. Dip., State Conserv.; Riga. m. Marianne A. Katzenstein, 1 s., 1 d. Career: Concert perfs., Israel, Middle East, Europe, USA & Ethiopia; Recital, Wigmore Hall, London, 1953; Num. tours of Europe, USA, & radio, TV perfs. in USA, 1961-; Artist-in-Res., Cornell Coll., Iowa. Compositions incl. song cycles, piano works, suites for flute & piano, violin & piano, & arrs. Mbrships: MTNA; IMTA. Hons: Govt. Grant for study in Paris, 1928; Iowa Arts Coun. Grant, 1972-73. Hobbies: Yoga; Swimming; Books. Address: Cornell Coll., Mt. Vernon, IA, USA. 12.

BERNARD, Michelle, b. 29 Jan. 1928, Alger, Algeria. Musicologist; Organist. Educ: Dr. Oceanography; Organ study., Nice Conserv.; Musicology w. L F Tagliavini; Organ Acads., St. Dié (France) & Pistoia (Italy). m. Francis Bernard, 2 c. Career incls: Fndr., Dir., Centre d'Etudes Organistiques M Bernard. Publs: Eléments pour une politique de la musique à Nice, 1979; La facture d'orgue italienne dans le Sud de la France et son répertoire musical (Orgues Méridionales), 1980. Contbr. to: Diapason; Jeunesse & Orgue. Mbrships: French & Italian Musicol. Soc.; Gesellschaft d. Orgelfreunde. Address: 35 avenue Ratti, F-06000 Nice, France.

BERNARDI, Mario, b. 20 Aug. 1930, Kirkland Lake, Ont. Canada. Conductor; Pianist. Educ: Dips. in Piano, Organ,

Comp., Conservatorio B Marcello, Venice, Italy. m. Mona Kelly, 1 d. Career: Music Dir: Sadler's Wells Opera, 1966-69; Nat. Arts Ctr., Ottawa, 1969-; Guest Cond. for operas, concerts; NYC Opera; San Francisco Opera; Chgo. Symph. etc.; Dir. of Music: Ottawa Univ.; Laurentian Univ. Recordings: Hansel & Gretal (Humperdinck); 3 recordings; Several other recordings. Mbr. Savage Club, London. Recip. of Companion of the Order of Can., 1972. Address: c/o Nat. ARts Ctr., Ottawa, Ont., Canada. 2.

BERNARDO, José Raul, b. 3 Oct. 1938, Habana, Cuba. Composer; Conductor; Pianist. Educ: PhD, Columbia Univ., NY; MM, Miami Univ.; BMus, Conservatorio Nacional, Habana, Cuba; BArch, MArch, Columbia Univ. Comps: The Child, lyric tragedy, 1st perf. Lake George Opera Fest., 1974; Sonata for Amplified Piano; Canciones Negras; Bruges La Mort, music for film, 1975; Lethargia for Amplified Piano & Toy Organ. Num. recordings. Publs: Cap-A-Pie, a musical, 1975. Contbr. to New Outlook for the Blind; Architectural Record; Forum; News. Mbr. of var. profl. orgs. inclng: Am. Inst. of Architects. Recip. num. fellowships. Hobbies: Painting; Body Bldg. Mgmt: Michael Tannen's Office, 36 E 61 St. New Yrok, NY, 10021. Address: 240 W 98 St., New York, NY 10025, USA. 6.

BERNATHOVA, Eva, b. Budapest, Hungary. Concert Pianist. Educ: Prof. Dip., 1949, Performing Artist Dip., 1950, Franz Liszt Acad. of Music, Budapest. m. Joseph Bernath. Career incls: Has toured in Europe, USA, Far E, India, Japan, Aust., NZ; Soloist w. many world famous orchs.; Perfs. of chmbr. music w. Janacek & Prague STr. Quartets; Prof., TCL, UK, 1970-. Recordings incl: Solo works; Concerti w. orch.; Chmbr. music. Hons: Grand Prix Nat. du Disque Francais, Paris, 1964; Grand Prix du Disque, Acad. Charles Cros, Paris, 1970; Hon. FTCL, 1973. Hobbies: Reading; Langs.; Table tennis. Address: 8 Purley Ave., London, NW2 1SJ, UK. 3, 27.

BERNHEIMER, Martin, b. 28 Sept. 1936, Munich, Germany. Music Critic & Editor; University Teacher. Educ: BA, Brown Univ.; grad. study, Munich Conserv.; MA, NY Univ. m. Lucinda Pearson, 1 s., 3 d. Career: frequent TV & radio broadcasts, NY & Los Angeles; Met. Opera Quiz broadcast; Met. Opera auditions, KCET; Music Critic & Ed., Los Angeles Times; Tchr., NY Univ., UCLA & Univ. of Southern Calif., Calif. Inst. for the ARts. Contbr. to: 50 periodicals in Am. & Europe; liner notes for RCA Victor, Columbia, London Records. Hons: outstanding serv. to art of opera in Los Angeles, Sigma Alpha Iota, 1971; ASCAP Deams Taylor Award, 1974; Juror, Nat. Book Awards in Arts & Letters, 1974. Address: Los Angeles Times, Times Mirror Sq., Los Angeles, CA 90053, USA. 2, 9.

BERNIER, Francoys J M, b. 12 July 1927, Quebec, PQ, Canada. Conductor. Educ: A(BA, Laval Univ.; Music Schl., ibid.; Music Conserv. of Quebec. Career: Music Tchr., Coll. Classique, Gravelbourg, 1950; Dir. of Progs., CFRG, ibid.; Musical Prod., Radio Can., Montreal, 1953-60; Prod., 'L'Heure du Concert', TV Prog., ibid.; Musical Dir., Montreal Festival, 1956-59; Gen. Dir., Quebec Symph. Orch. & Dir. of STudies, Conserv. of Music, Quebec, 1959-69; Prof. & Fndr., Dept. of Music, Univ. of Ottawa, 1969-; Chmn., ibid., 1969-76; Cond., major orchs. in Can. & France, inclng. Orch. Colonne; Phil. of ORTF; Bordeaux Phil. Orch., etc. Mbrships. incl: Past Pres. & Dir., Can. Music Coun.; Int. Soc. of Music Educ. Hobbies: Reading, Sports. Address: RR 1, Les Eboulements, Co. Charlevoix, Quebec, PQ, Can.

BERNIER, René, b. Mar. 1905, St.-Gilles-lez-Bruxelles, Belgium. Composer. Mbr., Royal Acad. of Belgium, 1963; Musicol. student, Princess Marie-Jose National Foundation, 1937-38. m. Juliette B ernier Craps. Debut: w. Les Synthetistes. Career: Hon. Examiner of musical educ. (EM & EN), 1945-68; Hon. Prof., Royal Conservs. of Liege & Mons, 1939-70; Jury of the Concours du Conservatoir National Superieur de Paris & Concours Int. d'Execution Musicale, Geneva, etc. Comps. incl: Symphs. (ballets), choral, vocal & instrumental works; Chmbr. Music. Var. recordings. Contbrbr. to var. profl. jrnls. Mbrships. incl: Royal Acad. of Belgium; Mbr., Commission de la Biographie Nationale. Hons: Prix Fuerison (musical comp.), 1935; Prix Koopal (musical comp.), 1969; Prix Quinquennal de la SABAM (musical comp.), 1965; Grand Off. of the Order of Leopold & the Order of the Grown; Off. of Nat. Order of Merit of France; Chev. Légion d'Honneur (France). Hobbies: Lit.; Vis. Museums & Exhibitions. Address: avenue Emile Duray, 62, 1050 Brussels, Belgium. 19.

BERNSDORFF-ENGELBRECHT, Christiane Helene, b. 6 Jan. 1923, Erwinen/Ostpreussen, Kreis Bartenstein, Germany. Musicologist; Music Critic; Lecturer. Educ: Land Music Schl., Strassburg/Elsass; PhD, 1956. m. Hans Bernsdorff, 1 s. Career: Musical Asst. 1956-58; Jrnl. Ed., Schott, Mainz, 1958-59, Merseburger, Berlin, 1959-69; Music Critic,

Tagesspiegel, Berlin, 1960-62, Deutsche Zeitung, Bonn, 1963-65, Rhein Merkur, Cologne, 1963-65; Features Ed., Recklinghauser Zeitung, 1963-65; Music Critic, Westfalenblatt, 1966-; Lectr., Music History, Westphalian Land Ch. Music Schl., Herford, 1971-. Author, Die Kasseler Hofkapelle im 17. Jahrhundert und ihre anonymen Musikhandschriften auf der Kasseler Landesbibliothek, 1958; Einführung in die evangelische Kirchen-musik, 1979. Contbr. to: Theater in Kassel, 1959; Reclams Klaviermusikführer, Vol. 1; Kongressbericht Hamburg 1956, 1958; Num. ency.'s, dictionaries, profl. jrnls. Mbrships: Int. Musicol. Soc.; Soc. for Musicol.; Int. Heinrich-Schutz Soc.; Soc. of Friends of the Organ. Hobby: Breeding Shetland Ponies. Address: 6 Im Königsfeld, 4973 Vlotho-Exter; Westf., German Red. Repub.

BERNSTEIN, Jacob, b. 4 Sept. 1905, Kaunas, Lithuania. Musician (cello). Educ: Conservs. of Moscow & Leipzig; cello study w. Julius Klengel. Career: Solo cellist under Arturo Toscanini; Concert tours of USA, Far E, S Am. & Europe. Compositions; Candenzas for major cello concerti; var. transcriptions for cello. Mbrships: VP, Cello Soc., NY. Hons: Citation for outstanding contbn. during Far E Tour, 1959. Address: Hotel Bretton Hall, W 86th St., NY, NY 10024, USA.

BERNSTEIN, Leonard, b. 25 Aug. 1918, Lawrence, Mass., USA. Conductor; Pianist; Composer. Educ: AB, Harvard Univ., 1939; Grad., Curtis Inst. Music, 1941. m. Felicia Montealegre Cohn (d. 1978), 1 s., 2 d. Career incls: Fac., Berkshire Music Ctr., 1948-55; Hd., Conducting Dept., ibid, 1951-55; Prof., Music, Brandeis Univ., 1951-56; Co-Cond., NY Phil., 1957-57; Music Dir., ibid, 1958-59; Laureate Cond. for Life, 1969; Num. Tours w. Orchs., sev. Continents. Compositions incl: Symph. No. 1, Jeremiah; Symph. No. 2, Age of Anxiety; Symph. No. 3, Kaddish, 1963; Chichester Psalms for mixed Chorus, Boys' Choir, 1965; Musical Score for Broadway Prod., On The Town, Wonderful Town, Candide, West Stide Story, 1957; film, On the Waterfront, 1954; Serenade for Violin & Str. Orch. w. Percussion, 1954; 5 Anniversaries for Piano, 1954; Mass, A theatre piece for singers, players & dancers (fox opening of John F. Kennedy Ctr. for Perf. Arts), 1971; Dybbuk, (ballet), 1974; Songfest, 1977. Publs: The Joy of Music, 1959; Leonard Bernstein's Young People's Concerts for Reading & Listening, 1962, rev. edit., 1970; The Infinite Variety of Music, 1966; The Unanswered Question, 1976. Recip., var. hons. Address: 1414 Av. of Americas, NY, NY 10019, USA. 2.

BERNSTEIN, Seymour, b. 24 Apr. 1927, Newark, NJ, USA. Pianist; Composer; Educator. Educ: Mannes Coll. of Music; Juilliard Schl. of Music; Fontainebleau Conservatoire, France. Debut: NYC, USA, 1954. Career: Concerts in UK, Europe, Asia, Can., S Am., USA; Perfs. in Carnegie Hall, Town Hall, Tully Hall, Avery Fischer Hall; Perfs. w. Chgo. Symp., NJ Symph., Tokyo Phil.; Apps. on Num. TV & radio stations throughout world. Compositions: (publd.) Birds, Book 1, 1972; Birds, Book 2, 1973; Concerto For Our Time, 1973; Toccata Française, 1969; New Pictures at an Exhibition, 1974; Insects, 1976. Mbrships: ASCAP; Assoc. Music Tchrs. League; Bohemian Club; Nat. Fedn. of Music Tchrs.; NGPT. Hons: Griffith Artists Award, 1945; Prix Jacques Durand, Fontainebleau Conservs., 1953; State Dept. Grants, 1955, 60, 61, 67; Rockefeller Grants, 1958 & 59; Nat. Fedn. of Music Clubs Award. Hobbies: Photography. Mgmt: Melvin Kaplan Inc., 85 Riverside Drive, NYC, 10024. Address: 10 W 76th St., NY, NY 10023, USA.

BEROFF, Michel, b. 1950, Epinal, Vosges, France. Concert Pianist. Educ: Nancy & Paris Conservs. Debut, Paris, 1966. Career: has app. on TV, & at fests. in Portugal & Iran, 1967, also at Royan & Oxford Bach Fests, 1968; has lectured & given recitals & concerts in var. European & S Am. countries; has app. w. London Symph. Orch. Colonne, & toured w. Paris Orch., NY Phil. & BBC Symph.; toured Japan & S Africa. Recordings incl: Prokofiev's Visions fugitives; Messiaen's Quatuor & Vingt Regards; Debussy's Preludes, Estampes, Pour le piano. Hons: 1st Prize, 1962, & Excellence Prize, 1963, both Nancy Conserv.; 1st Prize, Paris Conserv., 1966; 1st Prize, Olivier Messiaen Competition, Royan. Address: 114 rue des Dames, Paris 17, France. 3.

BERRY, Corre, b. 27 Mar. 1929, Bastrop, Tex., USA. Voice Teacher; Musicologist. Educ: BA, 1950, MA, 1952, BMus, 1953, Baylor Univ.; MMus, New England Conserv. of Music, 1958; PhD, N Texas State Univ., 1974. Career: 20 yrs. tchng. experience, Sam Houston State Univ., Southwestern Univ. (Tex), Baylor Univ., Northeastern Univ. Contbr. to: The Music Review; NATS Nat. Assn. of Tchrs. of Singing) Bulletin. Mbrships: Am. Musicol. Soc. (Chmn, SW Chapter, 1977-79); NATS; Pi Kappa Lambda; Alpha Chi; Pi Delta Phi; Mu Phi Epsilon. Address: 1425 Ave.O, Huntsville, TX 77340, USA. 7.

BERRY, Lemuel Jr., b. 11 Oct. 1946, Oneonta, NY, USA. Chairman, Division of Humanities; Chairman, Department of Music. Educ: BA, Music Educ., Livingstone Coll., NC; MA, Music Educ., Univ. Iowa; PhD, ibid. m. Christine Elizabeth Elliott, 1 s. Career: Chmn., Div. of Humanities, Fayetteville State Univ., 1973-75; Chmn., Dept. of Music, ibid., 1973-; TV apps. incl: Jim Burn's Show, Wilmington, NC; Educ. TV, Fayetteville State Univ. Recordings incl: Galpin Soc.; Int. Soc. for Music Educ. Contbr. to mags. reviews, etc. inclng. Schl. Musician. Hobby: Collecting old recordings & music. Address: 313 Stuart Ave., Fayetteville, NC 28301, USA.

BERRY, Wallace Thomas, b. 20 Aug. 1927, Glasgow, UK. Music Teacher; Music Adviser. Educ: Royal Scottish Acad. of Music; Dip. in Musis Educ. RSAM, 1947; Hordanhill Tchrs. Trng. Coll.; LRAM, 1950. m. Jean Kelsey, 1 s., 2 d. Career incls: Music Tchr., Glasgow Corp., 1950-56; Asst. Music Org., Roxburgh Co. Coun., 1956-60; Music Org., Clackmannan Co. Coun., 1960-65; Music Advsr., Ayr Co. Coun., 1965-75, Strathclyde Reg. Coun. (Ayr Div.), 1975-. Comps: incidental music to Saroyan's Opera! Opera! Publs: A First Minor Reader, 1963. Contbr. to: Music in Education. Mbrships. incl: 1st Sec., Assn. of Music Advsrs. in Scotland; Adjudicator, Brit. Fedn. of Music Fest.; Music Advsrs. Nat. Assn. Hobbies: Golf; Gardening. Address: 38 Sunningdale Ave., AyrKA7 4RQ, UK. 4, 28.

BERRYMAN, Alice Davis, Pianist; Educator; Composer. Educ: Studied w. Wager Swayne, Paris, Drance, Emile Scharvtz, Paris Conservatoire & w. Rudolph Ganz, Switzerland; New Coll., Oxford, UK, 1969. m. Cecil Wells Berryman, dec., 3 s. Debut: Princess Theatre, NYC, USA. Career: Ran piano conservatoire w. husband, Omaha, Neb., 50 hrs.; Pvte. Tchng., 1960-; Judge, num. musical auditions, for NGPT in USA; Oncerts in NY, Omaha, New England & Paris; Piano recitals w. husband & ensemble concerts w. sons. Compositions: Alice in Wonderland Suite (Melody Music Co.); Spanish Dance; Birds in the Linden Tree; The Dragon w. the One Green Eye; Slumber Song for Little Dragons; Swinging on the High Trapeze Lavell. Contbr. to: Musical Observer. Mbrships: Omaha, Neb. & Nat. MTAs; (Pres., Omaha 1977-78); Fac. Mbr., NGPT, Nat. Mbrship. Committee; Advsry. Mbr., Marquis Biog. Soc. Hons: Musical Schlrship., Paris, 1912; Hall of Fame Piano Guild, 1968; Cert of Profl. Advancement, 1959. Hobbies: Travel; Photography. Address: 5018 Izard, Omaha, NB 68132, USA. 2, 5, 8.

BERTA, Joseph Michel, b. 5 May 1940, Glendale, Calif., USA. Professor of Music; Solo Clarinetist. Educ: BA in Music, Univ. of Calif., Santa Barbara, 1962; MA in Musicol. & Perf., ibid, 1965; studied clarinet w. Mitchell Laurie & Clayton Wilson; studies in clarinet lit. & perf. w. Rudolf Jettel, Vienna, Austria; Calif. Jr. Coll. Tchng. Credential, 1966. m. Pamela Jane Nichols, 1 d. Career: Clarinetist, First Clarinetist & Soloist w. sev. orchs.; First Clarinetist, w. Music from Bear Valley Fest., Calif., summers, 1970, 71, 73; Berta-Lafford Clarinet-piano duo - num. perfs. yrly., Fla. tours in 1972 & 73 & Calif. tour in 1974; Toured Europe as First Clarinetist of the Am. Community Symph. Orch., summer 1968; Instr., pvte. woodwind lessons, 1968-; Tchng. Asst., Univ. of Calif., Santa Barbara, 1964-65; Prof., Prairie View A & M Coll., Tex.; Prof., Alan Hancock Coll., Santa Maria, Calif., Cond.; San Luis Obispo Co. Hon. Band., Calif.; Prof., Hobart & Wm. Smith Colls., Geneva, NY. Mbrships incl: Nat. Assn. of Coll. Wind & Percussion Instructors; Geneva Rotary Club; MENC. Recip. var. hons. Hobbies: Sports; History. Address: 55 Ver Planck St., Geneva, NY 14456, USA.

BERTA, Miroslav, b. 5 Nov. 1926, Zagreb, Yugoslavia. Musician (Clarinet, Saxophone, Accordion, Electric Organ); Composer. Educ: Music Acad., Zagreb; recognised Stage Artist. m. Branka Berta, 1 s., 1 d. Debut: Radio-TV, Zagreb. Career: Comps. performed on radio & TV, Zagreb, & in theatres. Comps. incl: (solo accordion & orch./soloist) Cavrljanje; Pozdrav parizu; (ballets) Mornarske Vragolije; Klik-Klak; Baletni divertisman; (puppet musical) Brod se zelenom bradom; 1 albums for solo accordion; works for fests; (recorded) Planinske polke i valceri. Recordings of own works. Mbrships: Croatian Comps. Soc.; Soc. of Operatic & Symph. Musicians. Hobby: Fishing. Address: Kranjceviceva 38, 41000 Zagreb, Yugoslavia.

BERTALOT, John, b. 15 Sept. 1931, Maidstone, UK. Lecturer; Organist; Choir Master. Educ: RCM, Major Organ Scholar; Lincoln College, Oxford, organ scholar; Corpus Christi Coll., organ scholar; MA, FRCO (CHM)., FRCCO, ARCM, Hon. RSCM. Career: Organist, St. Matthew's Ch., Northampton, cond., Northampton Symph. Orch. & Northampton Bach Choir, 1958-64; Sen. Lectr., RNCM, Organist & Master of Choristers, Blackburn Cathedral, 1964-; Fndr. cond. Blackburn Bach Choir (renamed John Bertalot Singers); Special Commissioner,

RSCM; Adjudicator, Nat. Fed. of Music Socs., Examiner, RSM. Recordings: The Organ of Blackburn Cathedral; O Glorious Serpent; The John Bertalot Singers in Concert. Hobbies: Photography; Work. Address: 28 Mellor Lane, Mellor, Blackburn, Lancs, UK. 16.

BERTHELOT, John, b. 8 Oct. 1942, New Orleans, La., USA. Composer; Arranger. EDuc: BM Ed., Loyola Univ., New Orleans, 1965; MMus, La. State Univ., Baton Rouge, 1967; MEd., Univ. of New Orleans, 1977; summer study at Eastman Schl. of Music & MIT. m. Rose Marie Costanza. Career: Record Prod. for Clifton Chenier, New Orleans, New Orleans Parade & The All-Star Marching Band. Comps: Essay for Orch.; Cityscape; Spring Song Cycle for soprano & woodwinds; Chamber Jazz Suite; The Roach (recorded); The Streetcar (recorded); Dap (recorded); Music for the Children of New Orleans, Vol. 1 (recorded); Louisiana Boys (recorded); Sonatina for french horn. Contbr. to Wavelength. Mbrships: Am. Music Ctr.; ASCAP; Nat. Acad. of Recording Arts & Scis. Hons: 1st place, Sam Houston State Univ. Jazz Comp. contest, 1967. Hobby: Reading. Address: PO Box 13977, New Orleans, LA 70185, USA.

BERTHOLD, Charlotte, b. 17 Jan. 1939, Loban, Germany. Mezzo Soprano, Opera & Concert (piano). Educ: Acad. of Music, Leipzig, German. Studied w. Willy Domgraf-Fassbaender, Munich. Debut: Gera, Germany. Dareer: Hannover, Lobeck, Wuppertal, State Opera House, Munich; Opera House, Zurich; Perfs. in London, Stockholm, Strasbourg, Bordeaux, Venezia, Japan & Chgo., USA, num. TV & radio apps. Recordings: Humperdinck's Jansel & Gretel (Eurodisc). Hobby: Horses. Mgmt: Schulz, Munich; Bueker, Hannover. Address: In de Wasseri 12, CH-8047 Zürich, Switzerland.

BERTINI, Gary, b. 1 May 1927, Birzewo, Bessarabia. Composer-Conductor; Music Director; Music Adviser. Educ: Verdi Conserv., Milan, Italy, 1946-47; Tel-Aviv Coll. of Music Educ., 1950; Nat. Conserv. of Music, & Inst. of Musicol., Univ. of Paris, Paris, France, 1954; studied w. Arthur Honneger, Normal Schl. for Music, 1951-54. m. Rosette, 2 d. Debut: w. Israel Phil., 1955. Career: 1st app. in USA, w. NY Phil. & Isaac Stern as soloist, for Am. Culture Fndn., 1959; app. at Bath Fest., 1965, London Proms, 1967. Hamburg Opera, 1971 & w. Berlin Phil., 1973; did Ashmedai by Yosef Tai w. Scottish Opera, 1971; Fndr. (1965) & Music Dir., Israel Chmbr. Orch.; Fndr. (1955) & Music Advsr., Rinat Chmbr. Choir; Music Advsr., Batsheva Dance Co. Compositions: Horn Concerto; Violin Sonata; stage music for Wozzeck, King Lear, 12th Night & Blood Wedding; ballet & film music. Recordings: Webern's Cantata No. 1 (w. ECO, Heather Harper & John Aldiss Choir) & Five Pieces op. 10; Shostakovitch's Concerto for violin & orch.; Debussy's l'Après-midi d'un Faune & Printemps. Recip. of Kt. of Order of Merit, Italy, 1967. Mgmt: Columbia Artists, NY; Harold Holt Ltd., UK; Concerto Winderstein, Munich; Alex Saron. The Netherlands. Address: Israel Chmbr. Orch., Ibn Gvirol 103, Tel-Aviv, Israel. 3, 4.

BERTOLINO, Ercole Mario, b. 10 Sept. 1934, Palermo, Italy. Bass-Baritone; Basso Buffo. Educ: Conserv. V Bellini, Palermo; Conserv. G Verdi, Milan; studies w. Mario Basiola, Milan, & Guiseppe Danise, NY. m. Constance Demitriu Bertolino, 2 d., 1 s. Debut: as Marcello (Boheme), Milan, 1955. Career: Mbr., Metropolitan Opera, NY; apps. in N Am., S Am., Europe & F East. num. recordings. Mbrships: AGMA; AFTRA; AGVA; SIAE. Hons: 1st prize, Int. Voice Contest, Assn. Lirica Concertistica, Italy. Hobbies: Cooking; Playing w. my children. Address: 100-26 67th Rd., Forest Hills, NY 11375, USA.

BERTOUILLE, Gerard Victor, b. 26 May 1898. Composer; Music Critic. Educ: LLD; PhB; pupil of Souris, Absil, de Bourgignon & Marsick. m. Suzanne Purnal, 1 s., 1 d. Debut: 1932. Career: Var. radio & TV appearances. Num. comps. inclng: Sonate pour piano; 4 préludes et fugues; 4eme sonate pour violon et piano. Recordings: Fantaisie pour Orchestre; Quintette pour instruments à vents. Publs: L'Expression Musicale, Ed. G. Houyoux; L'Art entre ses Disciplines et ses Libertés, Ed. Laconti SA. Contbr. to: Phare (Sunday); Le Matin (Antwerp); Clef pour la Musique (Brussels). Mbrships: Société des Compositeurs belges; Gaulois Circle. Hons: Chevalier de l'Ordre de Leopold; Chevalier de l'Ordre de la Couronne. Address: 19 rue d'Dcosse, 1060 Brussels, Belgium.

BERTRAM, Hans Georg, b. 27 Aug. 1936, Giessen, Germany. Composer; Organist; Pianist; Conductor. Educ: Stipendit der Studiensiftung; Dr. phil., Univs. of Tübingen & Würzburg, 1963; Staatliche Hochschule für Musik, Stuttgart, State exam. in ch. music, 1960. m. Hanna Bertram (Mueller), 3 s., 1 d. Career: Organist, 1950-; Organ concerts in Germany, 1957-; Organ concerts in Italy & other European countries, 1961-; Cnd., own & other works, var. German towns; Guest

Lectr., holiday courses, Univ. of Urbino, Italy, 1961-64; Choirmaster & Organist, Evangelische Petruskirche, Giessen, 1963-78; Area Rep., ch. music coun., Frankfurt, 1965-78; Kirchenmusikdirektor, Evangel. Stadtkirche Esslingen and Dozent, Kirchenmusikschule, Esslingen, 1978-; Performances of works in var. counties; Broadcasts of works from most W German radio stns. Composer of choral works, organ works, chmbr. music, orchl. works, oratorios, Violin Concerto. Author of Material-Struktur-Form; Studien zur musikalischen Ordnung bei J N David, 1965. Contbr. to: Festschrift for J N David, 1970; Neue Zeitschrift für Musik; Musik & Kirche; Osterreichische Musikzeitschrift. Hons. incl: Prize, Int. composer-organist competition, Zwolle, Netherlands, 1972. Hobbies: Chmbr. music; Walking; Swimming. Address: Mülbergstr, 39, 7300 Esslinger, Germand Fed. Repub.

BERTRAND, Nanon, b. 11 Sep. 1937, Soissons, France. Harpsichordist; Fortepianist; Lyric Accompaniest. Educ: Nat. Music Conserv., Bourges; Nat. Music Conserv., Paris; harpsichord acad., St. Maximin; fortepinao congress, Wellesley; harpsichord symposium, Mnpls. div. 2, 2 d. Debut: as lyric accomp., 1957. Career: num. recitals on harpsichord & fortepiano in USA & France; tour of France, Germany & USA as commp. to Alain Germain Ballet Co. Contbr. to Diapason. Mbrships: Société Françcaise de Musicologie; Société des Amis du Musée du Conservatoire. Hons: Prix Special de la ville de Bourges, 1952; 2nd prize for piano, Conserv. of Paris, 1956. Hobbies: Sailing (has crossed Atlantic); Photography. Address: 16 ave. de Bouvines, 75011 Paris, France.

BESSELINK, Maria, b. 25 Feb. 1937, Dieren, Netherlands. Educ: Dips., Solo Singing, Brabant conserv. Tiburg and Maastrichts Conserv.; studied w. Luigi Ricci, Janine Micheau. Debut: City Théatre, Aachen. Career: Opera Perfs. and concerts in Netherlands, Germany, Belgium, Drance, Italy. Professor Solo Singing, Conserv. of Music & Stage Acad., Maastricht. Recip. Grand Prix Lyrique, Lille, France, 1968. Address: 32 Bemelerweg, Cadier en Keer, Netherlands.

BEST, (Alan) Barrie, b. 8 Nov., Winnipeg, Man., Can. Executive Director, Society for the Preservation & Encouragement of Barber Shop Quartet Singing in America, Inc. m. Mary Anne Scheneck, 1 s., 2 d. Career: Tenor in amateur quartets & Chorus Dir. of amateur grps. Recordings: as Tenor of 'West Coasters' Medalist Quartet is on SPEBSQSA Int. Contest Recordings of 1957 & 58, Decca Records. Contbr. to: The Harmonizer (monthly publ. of SPEBSQSA). Mbrships. Nat. Bd. of Regents, Inst. Div., US Chmbr. of Comm.; Exec. Committee, Inst. of Logopedics, Wichita; Am. Soc. of Assn. Execs.; Kenosha Rotary Club. Hobby: Golf. Address: 514 69th ST., Kenosha, WI53140, USA. 8.

BEST, Hubert, b. 24 Mar. 1952, Durban, S Africa. Cathedral Organist. Educ: BA, Rhodes Univ., S Africa; RAM; BMus (London); ARCO. Dareer: Organist & Master of the Choristers, Birmingham Cathedral. Mbr., ISM. Address: 32 Salisbury Rd., Birmingham 613 8JT, UK.

BEST, Roger, b. 28 Sept. 1938, Liverpool, UK. Musician (viola); Professor at Royal College of Music, London. EDuc: ARMCM. m. Bronwen Naish, 5 children. Debut: Manchester, 1955. Career: w. Hallé Orch., 1958-60; Prin viola, Northern Sinfonia Orch., 1961-73; World Premieres of Viola Concertos written by Malcolm Arnold, 1972 & Richard Rodney Bennett, 1973; Mbr., Alberni String Quartet. Mbrships: ISM; Musicians Unions. Hons: Open Scholarship, RMCM, 1955; Hiles Gold medal, 1958; Barbert Trust Scholarship to Birmingham Univ., 1960; Hon. RCM. Hobbies: Painting; Golf. Mgmt: Dido Senger. Address: 9 Granard Rd., Wandsworth Common, London SW12, UK. 4.

BESTER, Elizabeth Joan, b. 22 June 1929, Theunissen, S Africa. Music Teacher (piano, recorder, theory). Educ: BA, STD, Stellenbosch Univ.; ATCL; LTCL. m. Adriaan Bester, 4 c. Mbrships: S African Soc. of Music Tchrs.; S African Tchrs. Assn. Hobbies: Photography; Flower Arrangements; Gardening; Farming. Address: Semper Idem, PO Box 108; Theunissen 9410, S Africa.

BESTOR, Charles, b. 21 Dec. 1924, NYC, USA. Composer; Educator; Writer. Educ: Yale Univ., 1943-44; BA, Swarthmore Coll., 1948; BS, Juilliard Schl. of Music, 1951; MMus, Univ. of Ill., 1952; D MusA, Univ. of Colo., 1974. m. Ann Bestor, 3 s., 3 d. Comps. incl: Piano Sonata (recorded); Little Suite for Beginning Strings; Concerto Grosso for percussion & orch.; Improvisation I for tape recorder alone; Improvisation II for instruments & electronic tape; My Love & I for a capella chorus; Poem for choir, soprano soloist & electronic synthesizer; Music for the Mountain for orch.; Concertino for Trumpet & Band;

Variations for violin & piano duo w. electronic synthesizer (recorded). Contbr. to jrnls. & encys. Mbrships. incl: Grad. Commission, Nat. Assn. Schls. of Music; Nat. Coun., Coll. Music Soc. Address: 2887 Northwood R., Salt Lake City, UT 84117, USA. 2.

BETENBAUGH, Gordon Murray, b. 30 June 1941, Clinton, SC, USA. Minister of Music & Fine Arts; Organist; Choirmaster. Educ: Bm, Westminster Choir Coll., Princeton, NJ; MM, Peabody Conserv., Balt., Md. m. Helen Louise Reckenzaun, 2 d. Career: ch. & coll. positions, Pa., Md., Ak. & Neb.; toured over 30,000 miles w. Choirs, 1965-; served as Cond. or on fac. for fests. & workshops; currently Min. of Music & Fine Arts, Westminster Presby. Ch., Lincoln, Neb. & Instr. of Organ, Union Coll. Contbr. to: Music; AGO; Jrnl. of Ch. Music; Clavier; Choristers Guild Letters; The Harpsichord; Overtones. Mbrships. incl: AGO; Nat. Sec., Am. Guild of Engl. Handbell ringers; Choristers Guild; Int. Harpsichord Soc., RSCM. Hobbies: Reading; Travel; Water Sports. Address: 2620 Surrey Ct., Lincoln, NB 68512, USA.

BETJEMAN, Paul, b. 26 Nov. 1937, London, UK. Composer; Teacher. Educ: BA, Oxford; Berklee Schl. of Music, Bostgon; Harvart (MAT); Pvte. study (comp.) w. Stefan Wolpe; Electronic & Computer Music w. Vladimir Ussachevsky, Mario Davidoosky, Charles Dodge, 1967-72. Career: Pueblo, electronic music & concrete sound for play, produced Arena Stage, Wash. DC, 1971; Forbidden, electronic score for ballet, commissioned by Harkness Ballet Co., 1974. Comps: String Quartet, 1969; Rattler, 1970; 3 Songs on Scriptural Texts, 1973; Hawthorn, 1972; Hawthorn 2, 1974; Hawthorn 3, 1975; Slow Burn, 1976. Mbr. Am. Music Ctr. Recip. Nat. Endowment for Arts Fellowship Grant, 1975. Address: Riverdale Schl. of Music, Bronx, NY 10471, USA.

BETTENS, Etienne, b. 8 July 1931, Lausanne, Switzerland. Bass Singer; Teacher. Educ: Dips. for Music Teaching & Singing, Fribourg & Geneva Music Conservs. m. Anne-marie Buffat, 1 s., 1 d. Debut: 1956. Career incls: Concerts, recitals, recordings, radio, theatre, Switzerland & abroad; Roles incl. oratorio, opera & songs. Recordings incl: Madrigals (Monteverdi); Cantata No. 6 (H Sutermeister); Cantata No. 4 (J S Bach); Mass in C Minor (Beethoven); Sunday Vespers (Mozart). Co-ed., On the Discovery of Music, 1967. Hons: Galland Prize, 1961; Swiss Young Musicians' Prize, 1962. Virtuoso Prize, 1962. Hobbies: Teaching; Cooking; Sport. Address: Chemin de Champ-Rond 37, 1010 Lausanne, Switzerland.

BETTERIDGE, Leslie, b. Lichfield, Staffs., UK. Composer; Adjudicator; Conductor; Organist & Choirmaster. Educ: FRCO. m. Doris Mabel Parsons. Dareer: Organist & Choirmaster, St. Barnabas, Oxford, St. John's Upper Norwood, London, St. Michael & All Angels, Croydon; Cathedral of the Most Holy Trinity, Bermuda; Cond.; Bermuda Phil. Soc., 7 yrs. Comps. publd: Missa Sancti Barnabae, for unaccompanied voices; Variations for organ on 'Veni Emmanuel'; Three Compline Anthems - Visit, We Beseech Thee, O Lord; Look Down O Lord; Be Present, O Merciful Lord; Two Fanfare Anthems of Praise - O Praise the Lord (Psalm 117) & O Praise God in His Holiness (Psalm 150). Author of sev. publd. short stories & contbr. to var. mags. & jrnls. Mbrships: PPGO (Oxon.); Naval & Mil. Club, London. Hobbies: Chess; Swimming; Motoring. 3, 28.

BETTINELLI, Bruno, b. 4 June 1913, Milan, Italy. Composer. Educ: Dips. in Composition, Piano, Choral Music & Song & Vocal Polyphony. m. Maria Luisa Nasturzio, 1 s., 1 d. Career: perfs., La Scala (Milan), Fenice (Venice), Civic Theatre (Bologna), etc.; also Italian & for. radio broadcasts, Italian TV, Carnegie Hall (NYC), etc. Compositions incl: 6 symphs.; 3 orchl. concertos; 3 piano concertos; 2 cantatas for choir & orch.; Episodi for orch.; Varianti for orch.; choral & vocal works w. orchl. & chmbr. accomp.; 2 str. quartets; var. chmbr. works. Compositions recorded Salmo IV; 2 Invenzioni for Str.; Symph. for Strs.; Fantasia for Piano. Contbr. to: var. musical jrnls. & reviews. Mbrships: Acad. of St. Cecilia, Rome; Cherubini Acad., Florence; Accademia 'Degli Agiati', Roverto. Hons. incl: Winner of 12 competitions, 1938-64; Prize, Acad. of St. Cecilia, 1940; Angelicum Prize, 1943; Bolzano Prize, 1959; Trieste Prize, 1964. Hobbies: Mountaineering. Address: Via Compagnoni 7, Milan, Italy.

BEUTE, Sjoerd, b. 31 Aug. 1942, Valburg, Netherlands Tenor Singer; Teacher of Singing & Voice Production. Educ: Univ. Educ. Dip.; BA (Musicol. & German). m. Idelette van den Heever, 2 d. Debut: Bloemfontein, S Africa, 1964. Career: Prog. Supvsr., S African Broadcasting Corp.; pt.-time apps. in concerts, opera, oratorio, & as radio recitalist, 1964-71; Freelance singer, 1971-; Solo recitals, Lieder concerts, opera perfs., boradcasts, etc.; Roles incl. tenor part in Verdi,

Requiem, & Belmonte, Mozart, Il Seraglio; Concert & opera tours, apps. as recitalist in Europe. Recordings incl: Stephen O'Reilly, Cantata Unitates; concert progs. Hons: Var. medals & bursaries. Hobbies: Outdoor Life; Photography; Gardening; Travel. Address: 7 Kingfisher St., Rhodesfield, Kempton Park, 1620, S Africa.

BEVAN, Clifford James, b. 25 Jan. 1934, Manchester, UK. Musician; Author; Administrator; Composer. Educ: LRAM; ARCM; LMusLCM. m. Jeannette Lunt, 3 s., 1 d. Career: Freelance trombonist & arr., 1960-61; Pianist. Chief Arr. & Musical Dir., The Temperance Seven, 1961-74; Tuba, Royal Liverpool Phil. Orch., 1964-71; Orch. Mgr., 1966-68; Gen. Mgr. Manchester Mozart Orch., 1968-71; Freelance tubist, author & comp., 1972-75; Music Off., Southern Arts Assn., 1975-75; Dir. Bournemouth Fest. of Dance; Organiser, Youth & Music Solent; Freelance Comps: Several comps. for films, small ensembles, children, choirs & bands. Publs: The Tube Family, 1977. Contbr. to profl. jrnls. Mbrships: Comps. Guild of GB; Performing Right Soc. Hons. incl: Edward Hecht Prize, 1958. Hobbies: Photography; Travel. Address: 10 Clifton Terrace, Winchester, Hants SO22 5BJ, UK. 3.

BEVAN, Maurice Guy Smalman, b. 10 Mar. 1921, London, UK. Singer. Educ: Attended Shrewsbury Schl. & Magdalen Coll., Oxford; FTCL; ARCM. m. Anne Alderson, 1 d. Career: Vicar Choral, St. Paul's Cathedral, 1948-; Fndr. Mbr., The Deller Consort; Oratorio & Recitals, BBC; Soloist, GB, Europe, USA, Israel & Brazil. Compositions: Editions of Engl. Vocal Music of the 17th and 18th Centuries. Recordings: Purcell's Fairy Queen; Handel's Acis & Galatea; Many recordings for RCA, Vanguard, Abbey & Harmonia Mundi. Contbr.to: Jrnl. of the Am. Musicol. Soc.; Die Musik in Geschichte und Gegenwart; Grove's Dictionary of Music & Musicians, Number 6. Hobby: Cooking. Mgmt: Ibbs & Tillett. Address: 45 Court Way, Twickenham, Middx. TW2 SA, UK.

BEVERSDORF, Samuel Thomas, b. 8 Aug. 1924, Yoakum, Tex., USA. Composer; Conductor; Orchestral Performer; Teacher. Educ: BMus, Univ. Tex., 1945; M Mus., Eastman Schl. of Music, 1946; D Mus, ibid., 1959. Norman Beeson Beversdorf, 2 s., 2 d. Debut: Cond., Austin (Tex.) Symph., 1944; Comp., Houston Symph. Orch., 1946. Career incls: Apps. w. orchs, inclng: Pittsburgh Symph.; Met. Opera.; Recitals, solo apps. at music convens. & univs. in USA & Can. Compositions incl: Sonata for Violincello & Piano, 1969. Num. recordings. Contbr. to profl. jrnls. & mags. Recip. num. awards. Hobbies: Family Activities; Fishing; Boating; Tennis; Travel; House & artifact design. Address: R12 Box 227, Cedar Crest, Bloomington, IN 47401, USA.

BEVINS, Karl A., b. 30 May 1915, Wellman, Iowa, USA. Clarinettist; Saxophonist; Teacher. Educ: BS Electrical Engineering, Ga. Tech.; Clarinet & Woodwinds w. num. pvte. tchrs.; Piano studies, Atlanta Conserv.; Harmony, Arr. & Cond., Univ. of Iowa Summer Schl. Career incls: Prin. Clarinet, Atlanta Phil. Orch., 1935, 36, Atlanta Pops Orch., 1945-, Atlanta Symph. Orch., 1945-66; 1st Clarinet, Municipal Theatre of The Stars, 1954-; Solo Clarinet, Band of Atlanta; Asst. in Instrumental Music Dept., Cond., Public Schls., Wash., Iowa, 1933-34; Pvte. studio, 1933-; Instructor of Clarinet, Music Dept., Ga. State Univ., 1964-; Student Cond., Ga. Tech. Band, 1936-39; Asst. Dir., Hq. Band Ga. State Guard, 1941-46. Contbr. to: Podium; Int. Musician. Mbrships: Pres., Iota Chapt., Kappa Kappa Psi; Exec. Bd., Atlanta Fedn. of Musicians, 1954-, etc. Hons: 1st Place, Clarinet Solo, Iowa High Schl. Music Fest., 1933; 2nd Place, Clarinet Solo, Nat. High Schl. Music Fest., 1933. Hobbies: Hiking; Swimming. Address: 110 Laurel Forst Circle NE, Atlanta, GA 30342, USA.

BEYNON, Ivor James, b. 28 Mar. 1919, Swansea, UK. Musician; Adjudicator; Teacher (clarinet, saxophone, piano, accordion). Educ: TCL, 1947-49; LRAM; ARCM; LTCL; LLCM; (TD): ABCA (TD); LBCA., m. Margaret Mary. Career: Profl. Free Lance Musician; Adjudicator, Brit. Fedn. of Music Fests; Has played Accordion w. major chamber music ensembles and symph. orchs in UK; has recorded w. var. orchs. and dance bands. Comps: Air and Toccatina; Rhapsody for Two; Danses Exotiques; Toby (all for accordion). Publs: Harmony for Accordionists, 1949; The Complete Piano Accordion Tutor, 1979. Contbr. to: Grove's Dictionary; var. profl. jrnls. and mags. Mbr: ISM. Hobbies: Gardening; Studying Philos. Address: 16 Dickerage Rd., Coombe Hill, Kingston, Surrey KT1 3SS, UK.

BEZUCHA, Jerzy, b. 13 Sept. 1949, Cracow, Poland. Drummer. Educ: Middle Schl. of Music; Profl. card as Solo Drummer, Polish Assn. of Art, 1971. m. Wieslawa Bezucha. Debut: Hard Bop Trio, Wroclaw Jazz Fest., 1970. Career: TV & radio perfs. w. Z Seifert Quintet, Jazz Band Ball, Old Metropolitan Band, Dzamble, Klaus Lenz Band (German Dem.

Repub.), K Sadowski Organ Grp., Polish Radio Jazz Studio Big Band, Z Namyslowski Quintet, Nove Singers, W Nahorny Quartet, Janusz Muniak Quartet; Film & theatre music. Appts. at sev. jazz fests; Recordings w. 2 grps. Mbr., Polish Jazz Assn. Recip., 2 music prizes. Hobbies incl: Record lib. Address: 31-161 Cracow, Szlak 18/5, Poland.

BIALES, Albert, b. 27 Sept. 1929, Cleveland, Ohio, USA. Professor; Musicologist; Performer (trumpet). Educ: BSc, MA, Ohio State Univ.; PhD, Univ. of Calif., Los Angeles; studies at Univs. of Cologne & Munich, 1960-61. m. Barbara, 4 d. Career: Free-lance trumpeter, Los Angeles, Lake Tahoe, 1956-62; Prof., Coll. of St. Catherine, St. Paul, Minn, 1962-. Publs: Ed., Giovanni Priuli, Sacrorum Concentuum pas prima (1618); Concentus Mu, Vol. II, Veröffentlichungen der musikgeschichtlichen Abteilung des Deutschen historischen Instituts in Rom, 1973. Cont. to var. profl. jrnls. Mbrships: Am. Musicol. Soc.; Coll. Music Soc. Hons: Fulbright Grant for Study in Germany, 1961-62. Address: 1763 Beechwood, St. Paul, MN 55166, USA.

BIANCHI, Lino, b. 14 May 1920, Vedano Olona, Varese, Italy. Musicologist, Composer. Educ: Dip. in Comp., G Rossini Conserv., Pesaro, 1945. M. Gabriella Limentani. Career incls: Artistic Dir., Centro Oratorio Musicale, Rome, 1949-63, Edizione De Santis, Rome, 1960-, GP da Palestrina Fndn., 1973-; num. broadcasts on Palestrina, Carissimi & other comps., Italian radio & TV, 1952-. Comps: Il Principe Felice, 1-act opera; Uruel, 3-act dramatic commentary. Recordings: (as cond.) Works by Carissimi, Stradella, A. Scarlatti & D. Scarlatti. Publs. incl: Ed., Complete works of G. Carissimi, & of G P da Palestrina; Ed., Complete oratorios of A. Scarlatti, 1964-, & A. Stradella, 1969-; Carissimi, Stradella, Scarlatti & l'orat. music 1969; A Scarlatti (w. R Pagano), 1972. Contbr. to musical encys. & jrnls. Address: Circonvallazione Clodia 82, 00195 Rome, Italy.

BIANCO, Anthony, b. 3 Sept. 1917, New Haven, Conn., USA. Bass Violist; Teacher. Educ: studied bass viol, theory, solfeggio & harmony w. noted tchrs. m. Angela Irene Boccella, 7 children. Career incls: New Haven, Bridgeport & Hartford Symphs., 1936-4¢; Nat. Orchl. Assn. under Leon Barzin, also playing w. New Opera Co., NY, & for NBC radio progs., 1941-44; Prin. Bass for Fritz Reiner, Wm. Steinberg, 26 seasons, also Chautauqua Symph. Orch., 1944-56; recitals & solo apps. w. orchs.; joined fac., Chatham Coll. Summer Day Camp., 1956; Bass instr., Sr. Lectr., Carnegie-Mellon Univ.; Mbr., Pitts. Symph. Orch. In orchl. recordings under Reiner, Steinberg & Previn. Mbr., Am. Fedn. of Musicians. Hobbies: Walking; Swimming; Reading. Address: 3833 Ridgeway Dr., Allison Park, PA15101, USA.

BIANCONI, Lorenzo Gennaro, b. 14 Jan. 1946. Minusio/Muralto, Switz. Musicologist. Educ: PhD, Univ. of Heidelberg, 1974; studied music theory w. Luciano Sgrizzi, Lugano, Switz. Career: Collaborator, Repertoire Int. des Sources Musicales, Italy, 1969-70; Mbr., German Inst., Venice, 1974-76; Guest Asst., German Inst., Rome, 1976; Guest Prof. Princeton Univ., USA, 1977; Prof. of History of Opera, Bologna Univ., 1977-; Prof. of History of Music, Moderata Univ., 1977-78; Co-Ed., Rivista Italiana di Musicologia, 1973-. Publs: P M Marsolo, Madrigali a 4 voci (1614), 1973; B Marcello, Sanates pour clavecin (ed. w. Sgrizzi), 1971; Il Verso, Madrigale & 3 e a 5 voci (1605-19), 1978. Contbr. to musical reviews. Mbrships: Am., It. & Int. Musicol. Soc.; Gesellschaft für Musikforschung. Address: 151 via S Gottardo, CH-6648 Minusio, Switzerland.

BIBA, Otto, b. 9 Aug. 1946, Vienna, Austria. Archivist; Lecturer. Educ: Univ. of Vienna. m. Monika Saiche, 1 c. Career: Archivist, soc. of Friends of Music, Vienna; lectr., inst. for organ rsch. & documentation coll. of music & arts, Vienna. Publs: Der Piarstenorden in Osterreich, 1975; approx. 60 eds. of music from the baroque, classic & romantic period. Contbr. to: Jahrbuch für Osterreichs Kulturgeschichte; Die Musikforschung; Ars Organi; The Diapason; Singende Kirche; Osterreichische Musikzeitchrift etc. Mbrships: int. soc. of organ enthusiasts; int. Joseph-Haydn trust; int. Bruckner soc.; int. Chopin soc.; Austrian organ forum; Franz Schmidt circle, Vienna. Address: 1080 Wien, Josefstädterstr. 29, Austria.

BIBALO, Antonio, b. 18 Jan. 1922, Trieste, Italy. Composer; Pianist. Educ: Dip., piano; comp., Trieste, 1938-50; TCL, 1953-56. m. Crete Lys. Debut: Pianist, Italy 1937, London, 1954. Career: Works perd. on TV & stage, Germany, Italy, UK, Sweden, Denmark etc. Comps: 3 piano concertos; var. symph. music & chmbr. music; Operas; The Smile at the Foot of the Ladder (H Miller short story), 1969; Miss Giuliz (from Strindberg), 1975; Ballet; Pinocchio; TV ballets; Apollo, 1971; Flames, 1973; Symph. No. 2, 1978; Fairy-tale Opera, Askeladden. Mbr., Norwegian Composers Assn. Hons. incl:

Norwegian Music Culture Prize, 1975. Hobbies: Astron.; Microbiology. Mgmt: Wilhelm Hansen, Copenhagen. Address: 9on28, 3260 Ostre Halsen, Norway.

BIBBY, Gillian, b. 31 Aug. 1945, Lower Hutt, NZ. Composer; Keyboard Performer. Educ: BA, 1968, B Mus, 1969, MA (Musicol.), 1970. Univ. of Otago; studies w. var. masters inclng. comp. w. K Stockhausen, Berlin, 2 yrs., Cologne 3 yrs., German Fed. Repub. m. Roger Wilson. Career: Radio perfs. of comps., NZ & German Fed. Repub.; TV apps. & progs. on new music, NZ; Piano recitals & Lieder recitals w. husband Roger Wilson on radio, & throughout NZ, in Aust. & in Germany, 1973-75; Co-Fndr. Ensemble (comp.-perf. grp.), C ologne, 1973, apps. in Germany, 1973-76; Mozart Fellow, Univ. of Orago, NZ, 1976. Numb. Comps. incl: Aie! A Conversation Piece (tape). Mbr., profl. orgs. Contbr. to Contact. Hons. incl. num. prizes for comp., NZ & Germany. Hobbies incl: Whittling; Fiddling; Painting. Address: c/o Univ. of Otago Music Dept., PO Box 56, Dunedin, NZ.

BIBERIAN, Gilbert Emanuel, b. 19 Feb. 1944, Istanbul, Turkey. Composer; Guitarist. Educ: LMus, TCL. m. Marianne Joeger. Debut: Wigmore Hall, London, 1969. Career: Cond., Omega Players; Fndr., Omega Guitar Quartet; Num. solo concerts & apps. w. Orchs. & Broadcasts in UK. Portugal, USA, & Canada. Comps: incl: Prelude & Fugue for Guitar; Suite for Guitar Quarter; Epigrammes for Voice & Guitar; Angelus for 32 musicians. Recordings w. Omega Guitar Quartet. Contbr. to: Guitar mag. Recip: The John Halford Composition Award. Hobbies: Painting; Lit.; Table Tennis. Mgmt. Helen Jennings Concert Mgmt. Address: 7 Alberon Gdns., London NW11, UK.

BICK, Donald A., b. 18 July 1948, Wilkes-Barre, Pa., USA. percussionist; Conductor; Assistant Professor of Music. Educ: BMus, Eastman Schl. of Music, Rochester, NY, 1970; MMus, Univ. of Md., Coll. Park, Md., 1974. m. Rebecca Tiger. Career: Rochester Phil. Orch., 1969-60; US Marine Band, 1970-71; Richmond Symph. Orch., 1975-; Contemporary Music Forum, 1973-; Asst. Prof. of Music, Va. Commonwealth Univ. Contbr. to: Percussive Notes Mag. Mbrships: Percussive Arts Soc., (VP & Ed., Va. Chapt.); Nat. Assoc. of Coll. Wind & Percussion Instructors. Address: 3967 Fauquier Ave., Richmond, VA 23227, USA.

BICKERSTAFF, Robert Graham, b. 26 July 1932, Sydney, Aust. Opera & Concert Singer; Teacher. Educ: NSW Conserv. of Music, Syndey; Univ. of Melbourne Conserv., Vic. m. Renée Goossens, 1 stepson. Debut: Marseille Opera, France. Career: Prin. baritone, Sadler's Wells & Engl. Nat. Opera, 1964-70; apps. at Covent Garden, Paris, Marseille, Nice, Bordeaux, Toulouse, Liege & w. Welsh Nat. Opera; perfs. w. Pittsburgh Opera; roles incl: Amonasro, Escamillo, Macbeth, Simon Boccanegra, Scarpia, Count Almaviva (Mozart), Wotan, Eugen Onegin, etc.; oratorio & recital perfs.; apps. on radio & TV. Mbr., ISM. Hons: hon. ARAM. Hobbies; Reading; Sailing; Outdoor Activities. Mgmt: Jeniter Eddy, Kew, Vic., Aust. Address: 87 Blues Point Rd., McMahon's Point, Sydney, NSW 2060, Aust.

BICKNELL, Nixon S, b. 10 Aug. 1932, Muskogee, Okla., USA. Organist; Pianist; Choral Conductor; Teacher of Music Theory & History; Music Critic. Educ: MusB. Westminster Choir Coll., Princeton, NJ; MSacMus, Union Theol. Sem., NYC. m. Saundra L Reber, 2 s., 1 d. Career: Organ recitals throughout north-eastern USA; Cond., oratorios & other choral works, Metrop. NY, NJ area; Profl. Accomps. & chmbr. music perf.; Music Tchr., grades 7-12, extensive work w. student choruses; Vocal Coach; Organ Tchr.; Music Dir., Montclair Chorale & Oratorio Soc. of NJ. Recorded Keyboard works of Orlando Gibbons. Contbr. to: Montclair Times (Music Cricit); MUSIC AGO/RCCO Mag. Mbrships: AGO; Am. Assn. of Choral Conds. Hobby: Reading hist. Address: 161 Lloyd Rd., Montclair, NJ 07042, USA.

BIDART, Lycia de Biase, b. 28 Nov. 1910, Espirito Santo, Vitoria, Brasil. Pianist; Composer. Educ: Music w. Maestro Viovanni Giannetti; Piano w. Magdalena Tagliaferro. m. Joao Baptista Bidart, 2 d. Debut: Comp., 1930; Cond., 1931. Career: W. Angelus Symphonic Poemetto, Italy, 1948; Radio Roquete Pinto, 1953, w Canaan, Poema Sinfonico & Pieces for Piano & Songs. Compositions incl: Canaan conducted by Wm. Pickerill, Capetown, S Africa, 1945; Missa Pro Sposi for Organ, Strings & Flute, 1960 (recorded); Dedicando for Flute, Clarinet & Horn, 1975 (recorded). Mbrships: SBAT; Circulo de Arte Vera Janacopoulos. Hobby: Gardening. Address: Rua Santa Heloisa N 11 - Z C 20, Rio de Janeiro, RJ, Brazil.

BIDDLECOME, Robert Edward, b. 9 May 1930, Somerville, NJ, USA. Musician (Trombone, Bass Trombone, Euphonium). Educ: Trombone Dip., 1952, BMus, 1967, Master of Sci.,

1971, Juilliard Schl. of Music. m. Jacqueline Lee Blow (div.), 5 s., 1 d. Career: US Army Band, 1952-61; Goldman Band, NY City Ballet Orch., (Bass Trombone), 1964-; Bass Trombone, Am. brass Quintet, 1962-; Bass Trombone, Am. Symph.´Orch., 1970-; Res. Artist & Fac., Aspen Music Fest., 1970-; Asst. Dean, Aspen Music Schl., 1971-. Num. recirdings as mbr. of Am. Brass Quintet, etc. Mbrships: Players Gov. Coun., Am. Symph. Orch. (Treas. 1975, 76, Pres., 1977, 78-); Bd. of Dirs., Chmbr. Music Am., 1978-. Hobbies: Flying; Photography; Fishing; Cooking. Mgmt: (Am. Brass Quintet) Melvin Kaplan, Inc., 50 Riverside Dr., NY, NY 10023, USA. Address: 210 W 70th St., Apt. 804, NY, NY 10023, USA.

BIDLO, Karel, b. 13 Jan. 1904, Hluboka, Czechoslovakia. Bassoonist; Professor. Educ: Prague Conserv. of Music. m. Anna Pokoma, 1 s. Career: Bassoon Soloist; Solo Bassoon, Czech Phil. Orch., 37 yrs.; Mbr., Prague Wind Quintet, 27 yrs.; Prof. & Mbr., Chmbr. Ensemble of Profs., Prague Conserv. of Music, Num. recordings incl. music by Bach, Vivaldi, Martinu, Mozart, Weber, Pauer, Telemann, Zelenka. mbrships: Guild of Czech Composers & Concert Artists. Hons: Merited Artist of Czechoslovakia; Holder, Order of Work. Hobbies: Restoring antique clocks; Fishing. Address: Biskupcova 25, 130 00 Prague 3 - Zizkov, Czechoslovakia.

BIELAWA, Herbert Walter, b. 3 Feb. 1930, Chgo., Ill., USA. Composer; Pianist; Professor of Music. Educ: Bmus, BS, Univ. of Ill., 1954; M Mus, ibid., 1958. m. Sandra Solderlund, 1 s., 1 d. Career: Asst. Prof. of Music, 1966-70. Assoc. Prof., 1970-. San Fran. State Univ. Publd. comps: num. organ, choral, band works. Comps. recorded: Spectrum for Band & Tape, Capitol Records, 1970, Cornell Univ., 1971; Concert Fanfare for band, Educl. Record Ref. Libr., 1971; Fife & Dr.m, Crusade Enterprises, 1973. Contbr. to musical jrnsl. Mb.ships. incl: ASCAP; Pi Kappa Lambda; Am. Soc. of Univ. Comps. Address: 81 Denslowe Dr., San Fran., CA 94132, USA. 9.

BIELAWSKI, Ludwik Augustyn, b. 27 July 1929, Chojnice, Poland. Ethnomusiocologist. Educ: Poznan Univ.; Ph.D, Inst. of Art. Polish Acad. of Scis., Warsaw, 1965; Asst. Prof., ibid, 1974. m. Krystyna Kowalewska, 1 s. Career: Assoc. w. Action of Gathering Musical Folklore, 1951; Rsch. Worker, 1955; Hd., Study of Documentation of Polish Folklore, Inst. of Art, Polish Acad. of Scis., Warsaw; Ed. Musicol. books. Publs: Rytmika polskich piesni ludowych, 1970; Ed., Adolf Chybinski, Karol Szymanowski a Podhale, 1959; Ed., Adolf Chybinski, O polskiej muzyce ludowej. Wybor prac entograficznych, 1961; Ed., Jadwiga i Marian Sobiescy, Polska muzyka ludowa i jej problem. Wybor pract, 1973. Ed., Polish Folk Songs & Music, 1974-75; Ed; Ze studiów nad metodami etnomuzykologii, 1975; Zonal Theory of Time & its Significance for Musical Anthropology, 1976; Ed., Studia etnemuzykologicane, 1978. Contbr. to num. Profl. Jrnls. Mbrships: Union of Polish Comps., Musicol. Sect.; Study Grp. of Folk Music, Systematization, Int. Folk Music Coun.; Soc. for Ethnomusicol., USA; Polish Anthropol. Soc. Address: 24 m 6 ul. Dluga, 00-238 Warsaw, Poland.

BIENIECKA, Wanda, b. 18 Nov. 1925, Bialystok, Poland. Opera Singer; Soprano. Educ: MA, State Higher Musical Schl., Warsaw; Dips. of merit, Italy; Stuided w. Ada Sari. m. (dec.). Career: Nat. Filharmony, Poland & abroad; Musical concerts & int. fests. in Polish theatres & abroad; Radio & TV recordings, Poland & abroad; Disc recordings. Mbrships: Polish Assn. of Musicians; Trade Union of Workers of Culture & Art. Hons: Italian Schlrship., 1961-64; Paderewski Fndn. Schlrship., NY. Hobby: Sport. Address: 00-102 Warsaw, Marszalkowska St. 111 A ap. 225, Poland.

BIERLEY, Paul Edmund, b. 3 Feb.´1926, Portsmouth, OH, USA. Tubist; Author. Educ: studied w. William J Bell; BAero Eng, Ohio State Univ. m. Pauline Jeanette Allison, 1 s., 1 d. Career: Tubist, Columbus Symph. Orch., 1964-, World Symph. Orch., 1971, Detroit Concert Band, 1973; Tubist, 1960-, Asst. Cond., 1961-76, Rockwell Int. Concert Band. Has recorded w. var. ensembles. Publs: John Philip Sousa; A Descriptive Catalog of His Works, 1973; John Philip Sousa: American Phenomenon, 1973. Contbr. to: music jrnls.; record jacket notes; radio & TV. Mbrships. incl: Assoc., Advsr. to Rsch. Ctr. Committee, Am. Bandmasters Assn.; Assoc., Am. Schl. Band Dirs. Assn. Sonneck Soc; Bd. of Advisors, Detroit Concert Band. Recip. Edwin Franko Boldman Mem. Citation, 1974. Address: 3888 Morse Rd., Columbus, OH 43219, USA.

BIGG, John, b. 13 Sept. 1930, West Wickham, Kent, UK. Pianist. Educ: RCM; ARCM; LRAM; Ecole Marguerite Long, Parisp; pvtly. w. Ilona Kabos & Harold Crzxton. Career: Pianist in Res. & Prof. of Piano, Coll. Conserv. of Music, Univ. of Cinn., USA, 1968-71 (Vis. Pianist & Prof. of Piano, 1967-68); Piano Tutor, RSCM, 1966-68; Currently Piano Organist, Inner London Educ. Authority Music Ctr.; Piano Supervisor, ILEA Ctr. for Young Musicians; Tutor, City Lit. Inst.; Prof., RAM; Examiner, Assoc. Bd. of RSM. Mbrships: ISM. Hons: French Govt. Scholarship for piano, 1953-54. Hobbies: Reading Cinema; Theatre. Address: 102 Pickhurst Rise, West Wickham, Kent BR4 OAW, UK. 3.

BIGGS, Ann Elizabeth, b. Aug. 1920, Parkersburg, W Va., USA. Associate Professor of Music. Educ: BA, Maryville Coll., Tenn.; BMus, MMus, Coll.-Conserv. of Music, Univ. of Cinn., OH; Ecoles d´Art Americaine, Fontainebleau, France; Northwestern Univ.; pvte. study w. Maggie Teyte. Career: w. Union Univ., Jackson, Tenn. Mbrships: Sigma Alpha Iota; Alpha Delta Kappa; AAUW; Nat. Assn. of Tchrs. of Singing. Hons: Sword of Hon., Sigma Alpha Iota, 1967; Woman of Yr., Jackson Bus. & Profl. Women's Club, 1973. Hobbies: Reading; Needlepoint. Address: 301 Morningside Dr., Jackson, TN 38301, USA. 27.

BIGGS, Charlene Marie, b. 23 Jan. 1953, Toronto, Ont., Can. Pianist; Chamber Musician; Vocal Coach. Educ: Assoc., Royal Consev. of Music, Toronto; 2 yrs. study for BMus (perf.), Univ. of Toronto. Debut: aged 11 yrs., Royal Conserv. of Music. Career: w. Toronto Symph. Orch., aged 14; Radio recitals, Can.; Recital, Purcell Room, South Bank, London; Recital, Glasgow Univ.; w. Bowkun, Bowkun & Biggs; Vocal Coach, Cond., Toronto Opera Repertory; Has worked w. Can. Opera Co.; Official Pianist, Can. Nat. Music Fest.; Played piano & celeste for TV prodn. of The Medium. Mbrships: Richard III Soc.; Ont. Science Fiction Club. Hobbies incl: Politics. Address: 620 Jarvis St., Apt. 208, Toronto, Ont. M4Y 2R8, Can.

BIGGS, Edward George Power, b. 29 Mar. 1906, UK. Organist. Educ: RAM. Career: Organist & Soloist, Sir Henry Wood's Fest. Orch., Queen's Hall; Free-lance Concert Organist, USA. Recordings: many recital recordings on historic organis; has recorded for RCA Victor & Columbia. Hons: Fellow, Am. Acad. of Arts & Scis.; DMus., Acadia Univ., NS, Can., & New Engl. Conserv., Boston, Mass.; DFA, Co. Co., Iowa; FRAM; FRCO. 16.

BIGOT, Pierre, b. 27 May, 1932, Rouen, France. Band director. Educ: Studies in organ, comp. & conducting. m. Marie Madeline Pigeon, 3 c. Career: Asst. Dir., Nat. Police Music, 1964-68; Dir., ibid, 1968-; Mbr. of sev. examination bds. Comps: Instrumental works; works for band or fanfare, (4 recorded). Hons: Musical Confed. of France, 1070 & 74; Nat. Order of Merit; Combat Cross; Polic Medal of Hon. Address: Musique de la Police Nationale, Place du Gén. Leclerc, 92420 Vaucresson, France.

BIKEL, Theodore, b. 2 May 1924, Vienna, Austria. Guitarist; Folk Singer. Educ: Univ. London, UK. m. Rita Wainberg, 2 s. Career: Performed in A Streetcar Named Desire, The Love of Four Colonels, Tonight in Samarkand, The Rope Dancers, The Lark, The Sound of Music, The Rothchilds, Jacques Brel, Zorba, The Defiant Ones, The African Queen, The Little Kidnappers: Apps. on TV & in USA. Recordings incl: An Actor's Holiday; Folk Songs of Israel; Silent No More; Theordore Bikel for the Young. Publs: Folksongs & Footnotes, 1960. Contbr. to var. jrnls. Mbrships: Press., Actors' Equity Assn.; Co-Chmn., Am. Jewish Congress Govng. Coun. Mgmt: William Morris Agcy. Inc., 1350 Ave. of the Americans, NYC. Address: c/o William Morris Agcy. Inc., 1350 Ave. of the Americas, New York, NY 10019, USA.

BIKLE, Charles Henry, b. 19 June 1941, Harrisburg, Pa., USA. Musicologist; Cellist; Meterologist. Educ: BA, Gettysburg Coll. Pa., 1963; BS, Univ. of Utah, Salt Lake City, 1964; BMus., 1969, MA, 1974, Ph.D Cand., 1975, Univ. of Mich., Ann Arbor. Career: Profl. Meterol., USAF; Co-Fndr. & Co-Mgr., Concentus Musicus, Univ. of Mich., 1968-72; Pvte. Tchr. of cello, music hist., music theory, 1969-; Tchr. of music theory & cello, Plymouth State Coll., NH, 1972-73. Mbr., Am. Musicol. Soc. Publs: incl: Odes for St. Cecilia's Day (1691-1695) (John Blow). Hons. incl: Rackham Prize, Award for Adv. Acad. Schlrship., Univ. of Mich., 1971-72. Hobbies incl: Automotive mechanics. Address: 216 Mason St., Ann ARbor, MI 48103, USA.

BILEK, Ales, b. Metylovice, Czechoslovakia. Pianist. Educ: Conserv. of Brno; Dip., Acad. of Music, Prague; Postgrad. study, chmbr. music, ibid. m. Bedriska Matulova. 1 d. Debut: Brno, 1953. Career: Concert tours, Europe, Canada, Venezuela; Tchr., Shawnigan Summer Schl. of the Arts, Can.; Tchr., Univ. of the Andes, Merida, Venezuela. Mbr., Forester Trio. Recordings as Pianist, & as Mbr., Forester Trio, of music by Liszt, Martinu, Hanus, Franck, Schumann; Radio recordings. Mbrships: Mozart Soc.; Forester Soc. Hons: 3rd Prize, Smetana Int. Piano Competition, Spring Fest., Prague, 1957. Mgmt:

Progokoncert, Prague. Hobbies: Chess; Cooking; Skiing. Address: Africka Str. 28, 160 00 Prague 6, Czechoslovakia.

BILGER, David Victor, b. 16 Apr. 1945, Reading, Pa., USA. Performer; Saxophone Instructor; Clarinet Teacher. Educ: BMus., Ithaca Coll., Ny; Univ. of Hartford, Conn.; Lebanon Valley Coll., Annville, PA; Union College. m. Dorinne Potter Bilger, 1 s. Debut: Bath, Ny, 1968. Career: Perfs. w. Bilger Duo in colls. & HSs, music & art fests., chs. & women's clubs, artist recital series; Guest soloist w. orchs. & wind ensembles; Saxophone Instructor & Dir. of Saxophone Ensemble, Lebanon Valley Coll.; Saxophone & Clarinet Tchr., Bilger Music Studio, Shillington, Pa.; Saxophone Clinician; Perfs., 5th World Saxophone Congress, London 1976; Carnegie Recital Hall, NY, w. Rascher Saxophone Quartet, 1978. Recordings incl: Siguard Rascher Saxophone Ensemble, 1975; The Bilger Duo, Vol. 1, 1976, & the Bilger Duo plays Recital Favorites, Vol. 2, 1978. Mbr., var. musical assns. Contbr. to profl. jrnls. Recip., sev. hons. Hobbies incl: Water skiing. Address: 124 High Blvd. E, Shillington, PA 19607, USA.

BILK, Bernard Stanley (profl. name: Acker Bilk), b. 28 Jan. 1929, Pensford, Somerset, UK. Musician; Band Leader; Publishing Company Director; Jazz Agency Proprietor. m. Jean Hawkins, 1 s., 1 d. Debut: Meth. Chap., 1933. Career: formed own band in Pensford, c. 1953; Clarinet Player, Ken Colyer's Band, London, 1954; returned disillusioned, to Pensford to form own band, the first Paramount Jazz Band, with which returned to London in May 1957; has made num. TV & radio apps. Composed num. works, most famous being Stranger on the Shore, which was top of the charts for 53 weeks. Has made num. recordings, EMI & (currently) Pye Records. Num. tours inclng: Aust.; Singapore; Germany; Holland & France. Mbrships: PRS; Hon. Mbr., Luton Football Club. Recip. of Ivor Novello Award, 1961.4 gold discs; 1 silver disc; MTA Record Award, 1976; Ivor Novello Award, etc. Hobbies: Fishing; DArts. Mgmt: (Miss Pamela Sutton) Acker's Int. Jazz Agcy., 5 Carlisle St., London W1V 5RG, UK.

BILLAUDOT, Gerard, b. 18 Sept. 1911, paris, France. Publisher. m. Nicole Balas, 6 c. Career: Music Publisher. Address: 14 rue de L'Echiquier, Paris 10, France.

BILLETER, (Otto) Bernhard, b. 26 July 1936, Zurich, Switz. Pianist; Organist; Musicologist; Organ Teacher. Educ: Music HS, Surich, 1955-57 & 61-64; Acad. for Music, Vienna, 1958-61; Piano, Lehrdiplom, Zurich, 1967, & Reifprüfung, Vienna, 1960; Organ, Konzertdiplom, Zurich, 1964; Dr.phil., Univ. of Zurich, 1970. m. Verena Blumganz, 3 children. Career: Organist, ch. in Qurich-Unterstrass; Tchr. of Piano, Lucerne Conserv.; Mbr., Zurcher Klavierquintett. Recordings: Hindemith, Keyboard Works I, 1 & 2, Konaert auf der Bussard-Orgel von Zurzach; Orgellandschaften der Schweiz 1; Dvorak & Boccherini Piano Quintets; Tartini, 4 Violin Sonata (w. Andrej Lütschg). Publs. incl: Frank Martin. Ein Aussenseiter der neuen Music, 1970; Die Harmonik bei Frank Martin, Untersuchungen zur Analyse neurer Musik. Contbr. to many publs. in field. Mgmt: Concerts Int., Gianna Guggenbuehl, Meilen, Switz. Address: An der Specki 33, CH-8053 Zurich, Switz.

BILLINGTON, Harry George Read, b. 7 Mar. 1930, Sydney, Aust. Inspector of Schools. Educ: BA, Sydney Univ.; Dip. T Mus, NSW State Conserv. & Sydney Tchrs. Coll. m. Elaine Audrey, 2 s., 2 d. Career: Schl. Music Tchr.; Inspector of Schls. (music); Rsch. in music curriculum dev. Publs: Creative Music Making, 1975; Sounds & Western Music, 1976; Your World of Sound, 1978. Contbr. to profl. jrnls. & papers read at Nat. & State Confs. on music in educ. Mbrships: Int. Soc. of Music Educ.; Aust. Soc. of Music Educ.; Assn. of Music Educators & Lectrs.; Aust. Coll. of Educ.; Bd. of Governors, NSW State Conserv. of Music. Hobbies: Record & Book Collecting; Travel. Address: 6 O'Brien's Rd., Hurstville, 2220 NSW, Aust.

BIMBERG, Siegfried, Wolfgang, b. 5 May 1927, Halle, DDR. Musicologist; Psychologist; Comp.; Cond. Educ: Univ. 1951, State exam; 1953 Doctorate; 1956 DSc.; 1957 Lectr.; 1964 Prof. m. Dr. Ortrud Bimberg, 1 s. Debut: Halle, 1952. Career: Sci. work Halle Univ. 1952; Berlin Univ. 1956; since 1961 Halle Univ.; Ldr. Chmbr. Choir Univ. Halle; Concert tours through Europe; Radio, TV prod. w. works; folklore, renaissance, contemporary. Comp. incl: Opera, The Little Singing Horse, 1961; Cantatas; Songs; Ballads; Choir works; Recordings of own comps. in Nova & Eterna lavels. Mbrships: var. profl. orgs. Publs. incl: Research in Tonal Hearing as a Basis for Musical Receptiveness, 1963; Just Before Musical Creation, 1976; Ed.; Der Komponist und sein Adressat, 1976. Hons. incl: Bela Bartok Prize, 1970; Handel Prize, 1971; Cond. Prize Bulgarian Music Soc., 1975. Address: Ernestusstr. 35, Halle, 402, German Dem. Repub.

BING, (Sir) Rudolf, b. 9 Jan. 1902, Vienna, Austria. Opera Manager. Educ: Vienna. m. Nina Schelemskaya. Career: w. var. operatic & concert houses & agencies, Germany, 1921-33; Gen. Mgr., Glyndebourne Fest., UK, 1934-49; Artistic Dir., Edinburgh Int. Fest., 1947-49; »Gen. Mgr., Metrop. Opera Assn., NYC, USA, 1950-72. Dir., Columbia Artists Mgmt. Inc., NY. Publ: 5000 Nights at the Opera, 1972. Hons. incl: OBE; Kt. Legion of Hon.; Grand Off., Order of Merit, Italy; Order of Merit, Germany; Grand Silver Medal of Hon., Austria; kbe, 1971. CBE. Address: 165 W 57th St., NY, NY 10019, USA.

BINNS, Margaret, b. Huddersfield, Yorks, UK. Violinist. Educ: ARCM, 1933; LRAM, 1934, London. m. Alfred Crowther, 1 s., 1 d. Career: Played w. lemare String Orch., A W Kaye Symph. Orch., Douglas Hall Orch., N Phil. Orch.; Dpty., BBC N Orch.; Ldr., Huddersfield Phil. Orch., 1947-, & String Ensemble, Huddersfield Schls., 1948-49; Violinist, Rogeri Pianoforte Trio, 1960-. Mbrships: Former Pres., Wednesday Club; Past Mbr., Mrs. Sunderland Musical Festival Committees. Hons: W Riding Music Scholarship 1932. Hobbies: Reading; Travelling; Sailing. Address: The White House, Northgate, Honley, Nr. Huddersfield, Yorks., UK. 3. 27.

BINGE, Ronald, b. 15 July 1910, Derby, UK. Composer. m. Vera Simmons, 2 children. Career: Guest Cond. for own works, BBC, Norwegian, Danish & Czech. radio stns. Comps. incl: Saturday Symphony; Concerto for Saxophone; Elizabethan Serenade; The Watermill; Festival Te Deum; Thames Rhapsody; Cornet Carillon (brass band); Old London (mil. band). Mbrships: Dir., PRS; VP, Songwriters Guild; Comps., Guild; Royal Phil. Soc. Recip. Novello award, 1957. Hobby: Painting. Address: N Barham House, E Hoathly nr. Lewes, Sussex BN8 6QL, UK. 3.

BINKLEY, Thomas Eden, b. 26 Dec. 1931, Cleveland, OH, USA. Performer of Early Music. Educ: Univs. of Colo., Ill. & Munich; BMus, 1955. m. (1) 1 dp; (2) Raglind Herrel Binkley, 1 d. Career: organizer, Munich, 1960, current Dir., Studio der frühen Musik (Early Music Quartet) performing on lute, other early plucked instruments & winds. Has made approx. 30 recordings of medieval & renaissance music, most w. Teldec or EMI-Electrola. Publs: Music, Sound & Sensation (transl.), 1968. Contbr. to var. publs. Mbrships: Am. Musicol. Soc.; Brit. Goat Soc. Hobbies: Gardening; Small animals. Mgmt: Colbert Artists Mgmt., 111 W 57th St., NY, USA. Address: Rudolfstr. 20, Basle, Switzerland.

BINKOWSKI, Bernhard, b. 2 Mar. 1912, Neisse, Germany. Music Professor. Educ: State exam. in Music & English; Advanced studies, High Schl. Prof. Unser Liederbuch, 11 vols., 1955-70; Musik um uns, 5 vols. plus 11 records, 1970-78. Contbr. to: Musik & Bildung; ISME Yearbooks; RILM. Mbrships: German Nat. Assoc. of Music Tchrs.; ISME; Chmn., Music in Schl. & Music Tchr. Trng. Hobbies: Foreign Langs.; Mountaineering. Address: 706 Schorndorf, Hungerbühlstr. 25, German Fed. Repub.

BINNINGTON, Stephen, b. 2 June 1953, Beverley, UK. Teacher; Freelance Organist & Accompanist. Educ: post-grad. cert. in Educ.; St. John's Coll., York. RCM; GRSM; ARCM; ARCO; LRAM. Career: Concert tours of German Fed. Repub. & Ont., Can., while a student; organ recitals in UK; Dir. of Music, Port Regis Schl., Dorset, 1976; tour of German Fed. Repub. as accomp. w. Dorchester Choral Soc., 1977; cond., Silton Singers, 1979. Contbr. to: Western Gazette. Mbrships: ISM; RCO; RCM Union. Hobbies: Reading; Sports; Hist. of Engl. & French Cultures. Address: Port Regis, Motcombe Pk., Shaftesbury, Dorset SP7 9QA, UK.

BINNS, Malcolm, b. 29 Jan. 1936, Nottingham, UK. Pianist. Educ: ARCM. Debut: London, 1957. Career: Regular Perf., LOP & Royal Philharmonic Soc. seasons, Festival Hall, London; Perf., Henry Wood Promenade Concerts (9 seasons), BBC Radio & TV; Recital & Concerto appearances throughout Europe. Perf., var. Recordings. Mbrships: ISM. Hons: Medal, Worshipful Co. Musicians, 1956; Chappell Gold Medal, 1956; Arnold Bax C'with. Medal, 1959. Mgmt: Ibbs & Tillett. Address: 233 Court Rd., Orpington, Kent, UK.

BIRCHER, John Charles, b. 14 Oct. 1947. Phila., Pa., USA. Percussionist; Educator. Educ: BME, E Carolina Univ.; MME, Univ. of SC; DMA Cand., Northwestern Univ. m. Julia McCoy Bircher, 2 s. Career: Prin. Percussionist, Columbia Phil. Orch.; Percussion Asst. Prof., Univ. of SC, Columbia. Contbr. to: Instrumentalist; NACWPI Jrnl.; PAS Jrnl. Mbrships: Pres., State Chapt., Percussive Arts Soc.; Pi Kappa Lambda. Hobbies: Hogging; Motivational Studies. Address: 3919 Parkman Dr., Columbia, SC 29206, USA.

BIRD, Carol Henrietta, b. 12 Nov. 1918, Sterling, NY, USA. Music Educator (Trombone, Trumpet, Alto Horn, Baritone Horn,

Piano, Music Theory, Music History, Music Appreciation; Choir Dir.) Educ: BSM, Eastern Baptist Coll., Pa. 1945; MMus., Manhattan Schl. of Music, NYC 1953; Juilliard & Eastman Schls. of Music; Ithaca Coll.; Studied in Europe. Studied Humanities, Univ. of Edinburgh, UK; Mozarteum, Salzburg, Austria. Career incls: Music Tchr., Nyack Coll., 1945-53; Perf. as Trumpeter, Carnegi Hall, NYC, 1940-44. Soprano, Rochester Oratorio Soc., 1955-57; Choir Dir., 1st Baptist Ch., Newark, NY, 1954-; Currently Supvsr. of Vocal Music, Public Schls., NYS; Elementary Supvsr. of Vocal Music, Lyons Ctrl. Schl., 1957-; Dir., Wayne County Elementary Music Fest., Lyons Central Schl., 1971-. Mbr. num. civic & profl. orgs. inclng: Music Educators Nat. Assn,; NY State Music Tchrs. Assn.; Rochester Civic Music Assn.; NY; Assoc. Mbr., Smithsonian Nat. Instn. Recip, several scholarships. Hobbies: Travel on Educl. Tours in USA & Europe; Ballet; Theatre; Symph. Orch. Concerts; Opera; Photography. Address: 416 Colton Ave., Newark, NY 14513, USA. 4, 27.

BIRD, Hubert C., b. 12 Oct., 1939, Joplin, Mo, USA. Composer; Singer; Professor. Educ: BMus (voice, comp.), Pittsburg State Univ., 1962; BMus Ed, (choral), ibid, 1963; MS in Music (comp.), ibid, 1966; Dr. Musical Arts (comp.), Univ. of Colo., 1977. m. Rosemary Small, 1 d. Career: College prof. Comps: The Cricket Sang, 1965; Blessed is the Nationa Whose God is the Lord, 1976. Recordings: Songs of Faith, w. Bruce Porter, accomp., 1978. Mbrships: Am. Soc. of Univ. Comps; Am. Soc. of Comps. Authors & Publrs.; NH Music Tchrs. Assoc.; Music Tchrs. Nat. Assn.; NH Music Ed. Assn.; etc. Hons: 1st Prize, Nat. competition for the comp. of ch. anthems, 1973; Nat. prizewinner in anthem comp. competitin for US Bicentenniel, 1975; nat. recognition in competition for cmbr. works, 1978. Hobbies: Photography. Address: 68 Blossom St., Keene, NH 03431, USA. 6, 23.

BIRDWELL, Edward Ridley, b. 20 Apr. 1936, Houston, TEx., USA. Musician (French Horn); Arts Administrator; Dpty. Dir., Carnegie Hall, NYC; Former Assistant Dean with Aspen Music School & Festival. Educ: Bmus, Houston Conserv. of Music, Tex.; M Mus, Univ. Houston. m. Nancy Jamison, 2 s. Career: Concerts w. Am. Brass Quintet in USA, Europe & Asia, 12 yrs.; Apps. at maj. univs. & concert halls; In cover story profile, NY Times Wkly. Mag., Jan. 1974; In 3 PBS films on Am. Brass Quintet; App. w. Am. Brass Quintet in TV film for USA Information Agcy. to be released in Europe; Num. radio apps. w. Am. Brass Quintet on WQXR NY. Mbrships. incl: Treas. & Bd. Dirs., Am. Symph. Orch. NYC. Hobbies: Sailing; Fishing; Tennis. Mgmt: Melvin Kaplan Inc., 85 Riverside Dr., New York, NY 10024. Address: 173 Riverside Dr., New York, NY 10024, USA.

BIRENBAUM, Jack Abraham, b. 28 Oct. 1913, LA, Calif., USA. Violinist. Educ: Univ. of the West, LA, Calif., 2 yrs.; studied w. J Clarence Cook, Henri J Van Praag, Jascha Gegna, Calmon Lubowski, Peter Meremblum, LA Div., 2 d. CAreer: Played w. Motion Picture STudio & had own grp. playing for dances & weddings, 1934-36; played w. var. bands & grps., 1938-39; Played w. Paul Nabors dance grp. at Mapes Hotel, Reno, Nev., 1947-50; Played w. num. orchs. in & around LA area, sev. community orchs., 1950-60; Sev. concerts w. the Bakersfield Symph., summer concerts w. Burbank Symph., concerts at Redlands Bowl under Farbman, LA Orch. under Roy White, COTA under Don Ray, Valley Symph. under Elmer Bernstein, 1960-65; Phoenix Symph. Orch. under Guy Taylor, 1966-67; Kans. City Phil. under Hans Schweiger, 1967-68; Phoenix Symph. Orch. under var. conds. inclng. Roger Wagner & Arthur Fiedler, 1969-73; Engaged w. sev. orchs. in LA area, 1973-, & COTA Symph. Orch. Mbr., Musicans Union, local 47. Hobbies: Hiking; Tennis; Ballroom dancing. Address: 4752 Haskell Ave., Encinco, CA 91436, USA.

BIRET, Idil, b. 21 Nov. 1941, Ankara, Turkey. Pianist. Conserv. Nat. Superior, Paris, 1st prizes in Piano Supérieur, Piano Accomp., & Chamber Music classes. m. Sefik Büyükyüksel. Debut: Paris, 1952 (w. Wilhelm Kempff). Career: Concert apps. in Europe, USA, Canada, Africa, Aust. & Asia; Invited by Emil Gilels to tour USSR; perfs. w. leading orchs. under direction of prominent conds.; apps. at Fests. of Montreal, Persepolis, Royan, La Rochelle, Athens, Gstaad, Eastbourne & Istanbul; mbr. of the Jury of the Int. Piano Competition for Contemporary Music, 1969 & 71; mbr. of the Hury of the Queen Elizabeth Piano Competition, Belgium, 1978. Recordings: Works by Beethoven, Brahms, Bartok, Schumann, Boulez, Boucourechliev, Chopin, Rachmaninoff, Ravel, Stravinsky, etc. Hons: Lily Boulanger Memorial Fund, Boston, 1954 & 64; Harriet Cohen - Dinu Lipatti Golden Medal, London, 1959; Polish Artistic Merit, 1974; Chevalier de l'Ordre Nat. du Mérite, France, 1976; State Artist of Turkey, 1973. Mgmt: Ibbs & Tillett, UK; Camille Kiesgen, France. Hobbies: Simming; Travelling; Reading (lit. & hist.); Painting on glass;

Flea Markets. Address: 255 Moda cad., Kadiköy, Istanbul, Turkey; 1 Ormonde Terr., London NW8, UK.

BIRMINGHAM, Hugh Myers, Jr., b. 5 Feb. 1929, Olive Branch, Miss., USA. Musicologist; Pianist. Educ: Bmus, 1951, MA, 1955, N Tex. State Univ., PhD, Ind. Univ., 1973. div., 1 s. Career: Taught at Clinch Valley Coll., Memphis State Univ., Ind. Univ., Univ. of Southern Miss., Univ. of St. Thomas at Houston, Tex. Mbr., Am. Musicol. Soc. Hobby: Vegetable Gardening. Address: 151 E. Goodman, Olive Branch, MS 38654, USA.

BIRNIE, Tessa Daphne, b. 19 July 1934, Ashburton, NZ. Concert Pianist. Educ: LRSM. Debut: Paris. Career: Concert tours of USSR, UK, Europe etc.; soloist w. ldng. orchs & on radio networks; num. premieres incl. 1st world perf. of the 450 piano works of Schubert, 1978, & unpubld. music from 14th century onwards; initiated Aust. Soc. of Keyboard Music & jrnl., Key Vive. Publs: num. articles on musicol. Contbr. to Key Vive. Mbrships: Fndr., Pres., Aust. Soc. for Keyboard Music; Patron, Tauranga Young Musicians, NZ. Hons: Beethoven Medallion, awarded by German Fed. Repub. Govt., 1974. Hobbies: Reading; Swimming; Photography; Arts; Languages. Mgmt: Horn Mgmt., Sydney, Aust. Address: 9 Glenroy Ave., Middlecove, Sydney, Aust. 2, 14, 15, 27, 30.

BIRNSTINGL, Roger, b. 12 Jan. 1932, London, England. Bassoonist. Educ: Bedales, RCM, London; ARCM. m. Judith Pearce. Career: w. London Symph. Orch.; Music Group of London; London Wind Soloists. Mbrships: ISM. Hons: FGSM; Tagore Gold Medal. Address: 60 Fitzjohn's Ave., London, NW3, UK.

BIRTWISTLE, Harrison, b. 1934, Accrington, Lancs., UK. Composer. Educ: Royal Manchester Coll. of Music; RAM. Career: Dir. of Music, Cranbourne Chase Schl., 1962-65; Vis. Fellow, Princeton Univ., USA, 1966; co-fndr., The Pierrot Players. Compositions incl: The Mark of the Goat (cantata), 1965; The Vissions of Francesco Petrarca (sonnets for bariton & orch.), 1966; Punch & Judy (opera), 1966; Orch. works - Chorales for Orch., 1963; 3 Movements with Fanfares, 1964; Nomos, 1968; The Triumph of Time, 1970; Choral works - Narration: Description of the Passing of a Year, 1964; Carmen Paschale, 1965; num. works for instrumental ensemble, incl: Refrains & Choruses, 1957; The World is Discovered, 1960; Ring a Dumb Carillon, 1965; Verses for Ensembles, 1969. Works performed at leading European Festivals. Address: 22 Trafalgar Rd., Twickenham, Middx., UK.

BISCARDI, Chester, b. 19 Oct. 1948, Kenosha, Wis., USA. Composer. Educ: BA, MA, Univ. Wis., Madison; Università di Bologna; Conservatorio di Musica 'G B Martini'; MMus, comp., Schl. of Music, Univ. Wis., 1974; MMA comp., Schl. of Music, Yale Univ., 1976. Career incls: Teaching Asst., Schl. of Music, Univ. Wis., 1973-74; Teaching Fellow, Schl. of Music, Yale Univ., 1975-76. Comps. incl: They had ceased to talk (violin, viola, horn in f & piano), Trusting Lightness (soprano & piano), 1975; Tenzone (2 flutes & piano), 1975; Music for the Duchess of Malfi (chmbr. ensemble & voices), 1975. Mbr. Phi Kappa Phi. Hons. incl: Charles E Ives Scholarship, Nat. Inst. of Arts & Letters, 1975-76; Rome Prize, Am. Acad. in Rome, 1976-7-. Address: 194 Mansfield St., New Haven, CT 06511, USA. 2.

BISHOP, John Edward, b. 23 Feb. 1935, Bristol, UK. Head of Birmingham School of Music; Recital Organist. Educ: MA, MusB, St. John's Coll., Cambridge Univ., DMus, Univ. of Edinburgh; Dip. Musical Educ., Univ. of Reading; FRCO. (CHM); ADCM. Career: Organist & Asst. Dir. of Music, Worksop Coll., Notts. Dir. of Music, ibid.; Head of Organ Div., Birmingham Schl. of Music; Hd., ibid.; Senior Lectr. & Tutor for Admissions, ibid.; Hon. Dir. of Music, Cotham paris Ch., Bristol; Dir. of Music, Henleaze UR Ch., Bristol; Examiner & Lctr., num. Radio apps. as Solo Organist. Mbrships: ISM; Music Masters' Assn.; Sheffield Organists' & Choirmasters' Assn. (Pres.) Birmingham Organists' Assn. (Pres.) Hons: Exhibition in Music, St. John's Coll., Cambridge Univ., 1953; John Stewart of Rannoch Scholarship in Sacred music, Cambridge Univ., 1954. Hobbies: Walking; Ecclesiology; Savouring Towns & Cities; Railways. Address: Birmingham School of Music, paradise Circus, Birmingham B3 3HG, UK.

BISHOP, Martha, b. 31 July 1937, North Wilkesboro, NC, USA. Cellist; Viola di Gambist. Educ: MA, Musicol. & BA Instrumental Music, Univ. NC. m. Walter H Bishop, 2 s., 1 d. Career: Cellist; Atlanta Symph.; Chattanooga Symph.; Viola da Gamba Soloist; Atlanta Symph. Emory Univ. Orch.; Workshops in Viola da Gamba w. NC, Fla., Ga.; Concerts in NY, NC, Ga., Gla., Tenn.; Fac: Emory Univ.; Ga State Univ.; Ga. State Coll. Contbr. to profl. jrnls. inclng: Viol. Mbrships: Pi Kappa Lambda; Regioanl Chmn. & Bd. Dirs., Viola da Gamba Soc. of Am. Hobbies:

Builder, Ed. & Perf. on Renaissance & Medieval instruments. Address: 1859 Westminster Way, NE, Atlanta, GA 30307, USA.

BISHOP, Ronald Taylor, b. 21 Dc. 1934, Rochester, NY, USA. Tubist. Educ: BMus, Perfs. Cert in Tuba, Eastman Schl. of Music; MscMusEd, Univ. of Ill. Champaign-Urbana. m. Marie Elizabeth Milburn, 1 s. Debut:' as soloist, San Fran. Symph. Orch., 1965. Career: Tubist, Eastman Symphonic Wind Ensemble, Am. Wind Symph., Buffalo Phil. Orch., US Army Field Band, San Fran. Symph., San Fran. Opera Orch., Eastman Brass Quintet, Camara Brass Quintet, Cleveland Brass Quintet; currently Prin. Tuba, Cleveland Orch. Has made var. recordings inclng: Highlights from the Ring (Wagner); Romeo & Juliet (Prokofiev); Porgy & Bess (Gershwin); Carmina Burana (Orff). Mbr., Tubist Universal Brotherhood Assn. Hobbies incl: Carpentry; Water sports. Address: 5595 Liberty Rd., Chargin Falls, OH 44022, USA.

BISHOP-KOVACEVICH, Stephen, b. 17 Oct. 1940. Concert Pianist. Educ: studied w. Myra Hess & Lev Shorr. Debuts: San Fran., 1951; London, 1961. Career: concert tours of UK, USA & Europe; apps. w. num. major orchs., inclng. London, Israel, New York, & Los Angeles Phil. Orch., LSO, Amsterdam Concertgebouw & BBC Symph. Orchs.; Soloist, complete Mozart Piano Concertos, 1969-71; apps. at Berlin, Edinburgh, Salzburg Fests; Dedication and world premiere of Richard Rodney Bennett's Piano Concerto, 1969, and John Taverner's Piano Concerto, 1979. Recordings: 20 receords for Philips. Hons: Edison Award for recording of Bartok's 2nd Piano Concerto. Hobbies: Cinemas; Chess; Tennis. Mgmt: Harrison/Parrott Ltd., 22 Hillgate St., London W8 7SR, UK. 1.

BISTER, Eero Olavi, b. 15 Nov. 1919, Valkjarvi, Finland. Violinist; Conductor; Concertmaster. Educ: Dip., Violin Perf., Sibelius Acad., 1949; Cond. Exam. ibid., 1967. m. Aune Sanelma Syvajarvi, 2 s., 2 d. Career: Concertmaster, Tampere Orch., 1946-70; Cond., Kouvola Orch. Mbrships: Union of Musicians, Finland; Lions Club, Kouvola. Hobby: Tennis. Address: Impivaarantie 16, Kouvola 20, Finland.

BITETTI, Ernesto, b. 20 July 1943, Rosario, Argentina. Classical Guitarist. Educ: MMus., Univ. Nacional de Litoral, ARgentina, 1964; STudied Guitar, Conducting, Chorus, Piano, Flute & Comp. m. Graciela Sanchez. Debut: Rosario, 1956. Career: Soloist, w. Num. Leading Orchs. inclng. Engl. Chmbr. Orch., Spanish Radio-TV Orch., Israel Chmbr. Ensemble, Syndey Sumph., Osaka Phil., Colon Phil. of Liverpool, Peruvian Symph., Nat. Phil. of Manial, Radio Hamburg & St. Louis Symph.; Toured Euorpe, UK, Ctrl. & S Am., USA, Can., Asia, Australia & NZ. Recordings incl: Contemporary Music for Guitar; Casteinuovo-Tedesco: Guitar Concerto in D; Rodrigo: Aranjuez Concerto; Weiss; Suite in A; Bach: Suite in D; Four Centuries of Spanish Guitar Music; Four Centuries of Italian Guitar; Torroba Sonatina; Works by Alleniz & Paganini. Music. Hons. incl: 1st Prize, Hebrew Soc. of Buenos Aires, 1961; Gentleman of the Order of the Screw, Benito Quinquela Martin, 1969; Conqueror of Bronze, Argentine Govt., 1971; ACE Award for best perf. in NY, 1975-76. Hobbies: Painting; Sports. Mgmt: Herlert Barrett Mgmt., 1860 Brodway, NY, USA; Dekoos, London, UK; Falmalete, Paris, France. Address: General Gallegos 3, 8th Floor C, Madrid 16, Spain.

BITSCH, Marcel, b. 29 Dec. 1921, Paris, France. Composer. Educ: Lic. in Letters; Nat. Higher Conserv. of Music, Paris. Career: Tchr., La Fontaine High Schl., Paris, 1952-71, César Franck Schl., 1955-58; Prof. of Counterpoint & Fugue, Nat. Higher Conserv. of Music, Paris, 1956-. Comps. (publs) incl: Concerto for piano & 13 wind instruments; 2nd Concerto, for piano & orch.; Concertino, for piano & chmbr. orch. Recording: The Art of the Fugue of J. S. Bach (w. Claude Pascal). Publs. incl: Manual of Tonal Harmony, 1957; Treatise on Counterpoint (w. Noël Gallon), 1964; The Art of J S Bach's Fugue, 1967. Mbr. French Musiol. Soc. Hons. incl: 1st Grad Prix, Rome, 1945.

BITTER, Marietta, b. 14 Oct. 1904, Weehawken, NJ, USA. Harpist. Educ: Bryn Mawr Coll., 1 yr.; Inst. of Musical Art (now Juilliard Schl.), 1 yr. m. Water Abel, 2 s. CAreer: Concerts; Solo Recitals; Mbr., Am. Symph. Orch. under Stokowski; much work in theatres; NYC; Extensive teaching. Contbr. to: Harp News; Am. Harp Jrnl. Mbr., Am. Harp Soc. (Pres. Metropolitan NY Chapt.). Hobbies: Cooking; Grandchildren. Address: 167 E 71st St., NY, NY 10021, USA.

BITTMAN, Emil, b. 16 July 1927, Bucharest, Rumania. Physician; Amateur Violinist. Educ: MA, Med. Fac., Bucharest, 1951; PhD., Doctor in Med. Scis., 1956; Musical Schl., Bucharest, 1945. m. Silvia Cahana, 1 d. Debut: Perf. in The Musical Schl., 1942. Career: Amateur Musician w. num. stage,

TV & radio apps. w. the Chamber Orch. of Physicians from Bucharest. Mbrships: Union of Med. Socs. from Rumania; Int. Soc. of Gastroenterol.; Amateur Chamber Music Players, Vienna, Va., USA. Hobbies: Chamber Music. Address: Daniceni Sts. 18, Bucharest, Romania. 29.

BIXLER, Martha Harrison, b. 9 Aug. 1927, Springfield, Mass., USA. Musician (Recorder, Harpsichord, Krummhorn, Rackett, Sackbut, Piano); Teacher, Recorder & Harpsichord. Educ: MA, Brooklyn Coll., BA, Smikth Coll., MusB, Yale Univ.; Preparing MA, Booklyn Coll., CUNY; 15 yrs. Piano study; 6 yrs. Harpsichord study; also studied Clarinet, Voice, Recorder, Sackbut; Tchrs. Cert., Am. Recorder Soc. m. Richard C Sacksteder, 2 d. Career: Concert apps. NYC & thru'out USA w. NY Pro Musica, Manhattan Consort, Trio Flauto Dolce & The Renaissance Winds; TV apps. w. NY Pro Musica Renaissance Band, Today Show, NBC. Recordings: Has recorded on several labels. Publs. incl: Ho Boys, Ho, arranged for Soprano & Alto Recorders, 1962; Non Nobis Domine, William Byrd; Four Resolutions, arranged for Three Recorders (w. P Skrobela), 1970; 9 medieval Songs, 1977. Contbr. to The Am. Recorder. Mbr., Am. Recorder Soc. (Past VP & Mbr. Bd. of Dirs.). Hobbies: Engl. Folk Dancing. Address: 670 West End Ave., Apt. 9-B, NYC, NY 10025, USA.

BIZONY, Celia, b. Berlin, Germany. Singer; Teacher; Harpsichordist. Educ: Tchrs. & Lectrs. Dip., Lyceum, Berlin; Stern Conserv. of Music, ibid.; Univ. of Geneva, Switzerland; Neues Wiener Conserv., Austria; Columbia Univ., USA. m. Bela Bizony (decd.) 1 s. Debut: Song Recital w. Conrad van Bos. Career: RAdio & TV Appearances, USA & Canada; Co-Fndr., Dir. & Performer, Music Antica e Nuova Ensemble, UK; Radio Broadcasts, ibid., Tchr., Neues Wiener Conserv., Austria, McGill Univ., Canada, Queen's Univ., Ont., ibid.; Prof. of Voice, Mt. Allison Univ., Frayn, 1955; Prof., GSM, London, UK & Lectr., Morley Coll., ibid., 1956-60. Compositions: Part Songs for Chamber Choir; var. works for voice, strings & harpsichord. Var. recordings. Publication: The Family of Bach, A Brief History, 1975. Mbr., Inc. Soc. Musicians. Hons: Gustay Hollander Medal, Stern Conserv.; FGSM, 1967. Hobbies: Reading; Drawing; Country walks; Research in early music. Address: Flat 2, Grove Ct., 243 Willesden Lane, London NW2 5RX, UK.

BJARNASON, Grimur, b. 12 Jan. 1955, Reykjavik, Iceland. Drummer; Percussionist. Educ: Grad., Coll., 1972. m. Erla Walterdottir, 3 c. Career: Háskölabiö Concert Hall, 1972; Austurbájarkiö Concert Hall, 1974; Num. tours, Iceland; Toured USA, 1973; Var. TV apps. Recordings: The Three Swans. Contbr. to: Melody Maker; New Musical Express. Mbrships: RIH, The Icelandic Musicians Union. Hobbies: Skiing; Rod fishing. Address: Stelkshölar 6, Reykjavik 109, Iceland.

BJELINSKI, Bruno, b. 1 Nov. 1909, Trieste, Italy. Composer; Professor of Music. Educ: Grad. comp., Zagreb Acad. of Music. m. Lierka Pleslić-Bjelinski, 2 s. Career: Mbr. People's Liberation Theatre on Island of Vis; Tchr., Music Schl. in Split; Prof., Zagreb Acad. of Music, 1945. Comps. incl: (Orchl.) Five Inventions for Chmbr. Orch., 1966; Fifth Symph. (Symph. for Thalia), 1969; (Chmbr. Ensembles) Sonata for clarinet & paino, 1966; Scherzi di notte for wind quartet, 1969; (Piano) Piano Concertino (recorded); (Concertos) Concerto for horn, strings & percussion, 1967; (Operas & ballets) Peter Pann, ballet, 1966; The Bells, chmbr. opera, 1973; Orpheus of the 20th Century, opera, 1979; (Vocal comps.) Candomblé, 1972 (recorded); (For children) Concert for a Small Boy, 1973; (Brass) Promenade Concert, 1974. Mbr., League of Yugoslavian Comps. Address: Suacićev Trg 12, 41000 Zagreb, Yugoslavia.

BJERRE, Jens, b. 13 Oct. 1903, Arhus, Denmark. Organist; Pianist; Composer. Educ: The Royal Danish Conserv. of Music; 2 yrs. in Paris w. Lazare Levy & Louis Aubert. m. Helga Oehlenschlaeger, 2 c. Career: Organist, Garnisons Ch.; var. Organ concerts. Compositions: Music for plays on Danish Radio; Ballet for the Royal Theatre, 'La Dame Aus Camelias' & music for Shakespeare's As You Like It'; Ballet for TV, The White Supper (Rostand); Works for orch., chamber music, songs, works for choir. Recordings: Songs Serenade for flute, oboe, viola. Mbrships: KODA; Danish Composers Soc.; Danish Organists Soc. Hons. incl: Koda Prize. Hobbies: Travelling. Address: Frimestervej 75, 2400 Copenhagen NV, Denmark.

BJONER, Ingrid, b. Kraakstad, Norway. Opera & Concert Singer. Educ: Conserv. of Music, Oslo, Norway; Hochschule für Musik, Frankfurt/M, Germany; Grad. Pharmacist, Univ. Oslo, 1951. m. Thomas R Pierpoint. Debut: Donna Anna in Don Giovanni, Oslo, 1957. Career: Mbr. Wuppertal Opera, 1957-59; Deutsche Oper am Rhein, Düsseldorf, 1959-61; Dramatic Soprano, Bayerische Staatsoper, München, 1961-; Guest apps. at Festival Bayreuth, Salzburg, Vienna, Hollywood

Bowl, USA, Met. Opera NY, La Scala, Milan; Currently w. Baerische Staatsoper, & w. Wiener Staatsoper, Staatsoper Hamburg, Opera Berlin West, Cologne Opera, La Scala, Milan; Concert apps. worldwide. Num. recordings. Hons. incl: Order of St Olav, Norway; Bavarian Order of Merit. Address: Gregers Grams vei 33, Oslo 3, Norway. 2, 5.

BJOREID, Bjorg Leerstang, b. 2 May 1925, Porsgrunn, Norway. Singer (soprano). Educ: Matriculation Examination; Tchr's. Cert. Examination; Pvte. studies. m. Gunnar Bjoreid, 2 d. Debut: Univ. Aula, Oslo. Career: Recitals, oratorios, TV & radio apps.; App. at Bergen Int. Festival & Rikskonsertene (State concerts); concerts and TV apps. in USA, 1978. Recordings: Soloist w. Bel Canto chorus & Sverre Valen chorus. Mbr. Norwegian Soc. of Musicians. Hons: Porsgrunn City Culture Prize, 1978. Hobbies: Lit.; Travel; Skiing; Swimming. Address: Prestealleen 73, 3920 Eidanger, Norway.

BJÖRKLUND, Björn, b. 21 Apr. 1926, Lilleström, Norway. Organist. Educ: MA. m. Gerd Björklund, 3 children. Mbrships: Pres., Norwegian Organist Union, 1962-73; Pres., Scandinavian Organist Union, 1965-70; Presidency, World Organist Union, 1968-73. Ed., Norwegian Church Music (monthly mag.), 1962-73. Address: H Ruuds v 3 Raelingen, 2000 Lilleström, Norway.

BJÖRLIN, (Mats) Ulf Stefan, b. 21 May 1933, Stockholm, Sweden. Conductor; Composer; Pianist. Educ: Conserv. de Paris; studied under Nadia Boulanger & Igor Markevitch. m. Mercedes Lampert, 2 s. Career: Mjusical Dir., Royal Dramatic Theatre, Stockholm, 1963-68; Free-lance Cond. throughout Europe, 1968-. Comps: 2 operas; sev. ballets; num. pieces of incidental music for theatre, film & TV. Recordings: EMI. Mbr., Swedish Comps. Union. Address: Flaravägen 11, 8132 Lidingo (Stockholm), Sweden.

BJORLING, Rolf Warner David, b. 25 Dec. 1928, Jonkoping, Sweden. Opera Singer. Educ: RAM, 1953-55. 3 c. Debut: Pinkerton in Butterfly, Gothenburg, Sweden, 1961. Career: Apps. in Deutsche Oper Berlin, San Francisco, NY, Hamburg, München, Frankfurt, Brussels, Amsterdam, Paris, Stockholm, Oslo & Helsingfors. Recordings on EMI, RCA & Karusell (Deutsche Gram.). Recip. Royal Order of Vasa from King of Sweden, 1974. Hobbies: Golf; Fishing; Spectator Sports. Mgmt: Joanne Rile, 119th N 18th St., Philadelphia, Pa., USA & Ulf Tornquist, Nortullsgatan 26, Stockholm, Sweden. Address: Langangsvagen 44, 18275 Stocksund, Sweden.

BJORNSSON, Arni, b. 23 Dec. 1905, Lon, Kelduhverfi, Iceland. Composer; Pianist; Flautist. Educ: Dip., comps. & paino, Reykjavik Music Conserv., 1935; Performer's Dip., Royal Manchester Coll. of Music, UK, 1946. m. Helga Thorsteindottir, 2 d. Career: Flautist, Icelandic Symph. Orch., 1952-; Prof. of piano & theory, Reykjavik Conserv. of Music, 1952-; Recitals, Orchl. concerts, broadcasts on Radio & TV. Compositions: Musica Islandica: Piano Sonata No. 1; 2 Romances for Violin & Piano; Variations on 4 Icelandic Folk Songs for Flute & Piano; Festival Cantata for male chorus, tenor solo & piano; num. songs, marches, etc. Recording issued of sev. comps. Contbr. of music articles to var. newspapers & Musical mag. Mbrships: Hon. Mbr. Tonskaldefelag Islands (Soc. of Icelandic Composers); STEF (Assn. of Composers & Copyright owners); FIH (Icelandic Musicians Union); ARMCM. Recip. Prizes for Compositions, 1966, 1972. Address Horgshlid 10, Reykjavik, Iceland.

BLACHER, Deanna, b. 20 Sep. 1940, Cape Town, S Africa. Castanet Virtuoso. Educ: studied w. Elsa Brunelleschi, London, La Quica & Juanjo Linares, Madrid. m. Neville Cohn, 2 s. Career: Duo recitals w. pianists Michael Isador, Lamar Crowson, Allan Sternfield, etc.; soloist w. orchs. incl. Israel Phil.; dedicatee of num. works; gave world premiere of Valetin Ruiz's Fantasia for Castanets & Orch., Cape Town, 1976; many other orchl. concerts; num. radio & TV perfs.; fac. mbr., Rubin Acad. of Music, Jerusalem. Fndr. mbr., Spanish Dance Soc. Hobbies: Travel; Reading. Mgmt: Nicholas Choveaux, UK. Address: POB 39231, Tel Aviv, Israel.

BLACK, Donald Fisher, b. 3 Feb. 1941, Detroit, Mich., USA. Professor of Music; Organ Recitalist. Educ: BS, Wayne State Univ., 1962; MEd., ibid., 1968; Choirmaster Cert. Am. Guild of Organists. Debut: Concert Organist, 1957; Concert Pianist, Detroit, 1958. Career: Recitals in Detroit, Mich.; Cleveland, Ohio; Univ. of Western Ont., Can.; Clarion State Coll., Pa. Mbr. Music Educators Nat. Conf. Hobbies: Reading; Collecting Histl. Pictures of Keyboard Instruments. Address: Clarion State Coll., Dept. of Music, Clarion, PA 16214, USA.

BLACK, Edwin Clair, b. 5 Aug. 1938, Kittaning, Pa., USA. French Horn Player. Educ: BA, Montclair State Coll.; MA, Tchrs.

Coll., Columbia Univ.; Dip., US Navy Schl. of Music; 2 summer scholarships, Tanglewood Music Fest. m. Kathryn Black, 1 s. Career: TV specials featuring NJ Symph. sev. recordings. Contbr. to Tempo Magazine, NY. Mbrships: Int. Horn Soc.; MENC. Hons: Cond. & Mus. Dir., Lakeland Symph. Soc., 1975-; solo recital, Lincoln Centre, 1975. Hobbies: Swimming; Tennis. Address: 61 Nestro Rd., W Orange, NJ 07052, USA. 6.

BLACK, Gordon McCully, b. 29 Nov. 1913, St. John, NB, Can. Teacher; Recitalist. Educ: BA, Mus Bac., Mt. Allison Univ., Sackville, NB; LST, Bishop's Univ., Lennoxville, PQ; BST, ibid; ARCO; Assoc., RCCO; studied w. Pauline Biederman, Harold Hamer, Charles Peaker, Weldon Kilburn, Jean Hamilton, Dr. George Thalben-Ball, Angus Morrison. Career: Chief Supvsr. of Music Teaching, City Schl. System, St. John, NB; Teaching Staff, Conserv. of Music, Mt. Allison Univ., Sackville, NB; Dir., Albert Coll. Conserv. of Music, Belleville, Ont.; Organist, Old St. Basil's Ch., Toronto, Ont., St. Peter's Cathedral, Peterborough, Ont.; Univ. Organist, Bishop's Univ., Lennoxville, Que. Contbr. to Educl. Review. Mbrships: Ont. MTA; NB. MTA. Hons: Alumni Award, Highest Gen. Standing, Arts Course, Mt. Allison Univ.; Highest Grade (in Can.). Local Ctr. Examinations, Piano, McGill Univ., Montreal, PQ; Lansing Lewis Memorial Prize, Bishop's Univ. Hobbies: Swimming; Gardening. Address: Brentwood One, 310 Woodward Ave., St. John, NB E2K 2L1, Can.

BLACK, Neil, b. 28 May, 1932, Birmingham, UK. Oboist. Educ: Exeter Coll., Oxford Univ. m. Jill Heningsley, 3 children. Career: Soloist & chmbr. music player w. var. ensembles inclng. Engl. Chmbr. Orch., Acad. of St. Martin's in the Fields, London Mozart Players. Recordings: Oboe concertos by Mozart, Bach, Vaughan-Williams & Vivaldi. Mgmt: John Wright. Address: 102 Dulwich Village, London, UK. 3, 14.

BLACK, Ralph, b. 11 July 1919, Knoxville, Tenn., USA. Arts Administrator. Educ: BS, Houghton Coll., 1941. m. Eva Landsberger, 3 s., 1 d. Career: Gen. Mgr., Chattanooga Symph., Tenn., 1950-51, Buffalo Phil. Orch., NY, 1951-55, Nat. Symph., Wash. DC, 1955-60, Balt. Symph., Md., 1960-63, Nat. Ballet, Wash. DC, 1963-73; Exec. Dir., Am. Symph. Orch. League, Vienna, Va., 1973-; Gen. Dir., Shenandoah Valley Music Fest., Woodstock, Va., 1974-78; Dir., Am. Arts Alliance, Wash. DC & Nat. Music Coun., NYC. Contbr. to: Black Notes; Symph. News; publ. of Am. Symph. Orch. League. Mbrships: Congressional Country Club, Bethesda, Md.; Fndng. Chmn., Assn. of Am. Dance Cos.; Asst. Sec./Treas., Am. Symph. Orch. League. Hons: Silver Baton Award, Bell System, Am. Telephone & Telegraph Co. Hobby: Sailing. Address: 7005 Winslow St., Bethesda, MD 20034, USA. 2.

BLACK, Stanley, b. 14 June 1913, London, UK. Conductor. Composer; Pianist; Arranger. Educ: Matthay Schl. of Music. m. Edna Kaye, 2 children. Career: Cond., BBC Dance Orch., 1944-52; Musical Dir., Assoc. Brit. Pictures Corp., Elstree Studios, 1958-63; BBC TV apps. Guest Cond., NZ, Aust., 1967; Prin. Cond., BBC Northern Ireland Orch., 1968-69; Assoc. Cond., Osaka Phil. Orch., 1971; Prin. Cond., NZ Proms, 1972, 74. Comps. incl. over 100 film scores num. recordings. Contbr. to: Melody Maker; Today's Cinema; etc. Hons: Life Fellow, Int. Inst. Arts & Letters, Zurich, 1962; Jr. Novello Award, 1963; var. Gold Records. Hobbies: Theatre; Riding. Address: 118/120 Wardour St., London W1, UK.

BLACKBURN, Andrew Stewart, b. 22 July 1954, London, UK. Organist; Harpsichord Player. EDuc: Bmus, Melbourne Univ.; studied w. Roy Shepherd, June Nixon & in Paris w. Jean Langlais. m. Jean Penny. Career: Asst. organist, St. Paul's Cathedral, Melbourne; organist & Dir. of Chapel music, Melbourne Ch. of Eng. Girls Grammar Schl.; Dir. of Choir, Trinity Grammar; regular recitals, St. Paul's Cathedral & elsewhere; mbr. & co-fndr., Terpodian Trio. Mbrships: RCO; Aust. Musicolog. Soc.; Organ Histl. Trust of Aust.; Victorian Organists Soc. Hons: Ormond Exhibition, 1972; Davis Memorial Prize, 1973. Hobbies: Reading; Walking. Mgmt: Artpreneur, Melbourne. Address: 50 Palmerston Cres., S Melbourne, Vic. 3205, Aust.

BLACKETT, Joy E., b. 29 Sept. 1944, Devonshire, Bermuda. Concert & Opera Mezzo-soprano. Educ: B Mus, Juilliard Schl. of Music; MS, ibid. Divorced, 1 s. Debut: Town Hall Recital, 1971. Career: Apps. incl: Milwaukee Symph., Seattle Symph., Musica Aeterna Orch., Am. Symph., Indpls. Symph.; Apps. w. San Francisco Opera, Opera South, Santa Fe Opera, Wolf Trap Fest., Aspen Music Fest., Ibermusica, Madrid, Spain; Num. solo recitals on Uni. Artists series throughout USA; Cons., Advsry. Panel, Opera Sect., Nat. Endowment for Arts, Wash. DC; Lectr. in Music, Douglass Coll., Rutgers Univ., 1973-76; Perf. &

Lectr., Nat. Assn. of Tchrs. of Singing, Univ. Wis., 1975. Nums. recordings. Hons. incl: Nat. Opera Inst. Grant, 1972. Hobbies: Reading; Camping; Fishing. Mgmt: Kazuko Hillyer Int. Inc. Address: 90 Riverside Dr., PHC, NY, NY, 10023, USA.

BLACKING, John Anthony Randoll, b. 22 Oct. 1928, Guildford, Surrey, UK. Ethnomusicologist; Socail Anthropologist. Educ: BA, 1953, MA, 1957, King's Coll., Cambridge; PhD & DLitt., Univ. of Witwatersrand, Johannesburg. m. (1) Brenda Eleonora Gebers (div., 1975) 4 d. (2 dec.), 1 s.; (2) Zureena Rukshana Desai, 2 d. Carer: Musicol., Int. Lib. of African Music, 1954-57; Lectr., 1959-65, Prof., 1966-69, Univ. of Witwatersrand; Prof., Western Mich. Univ., Kalamazoo, 1970-72; Prof. & Hd., Dept. of Social Anthropol., Queen's Univ. of Belfast, 1970-; Fndr. & Cond. of Univ. of Witwatersrand Choir, 1960-65. Recordings: Music from Petauke, Zambia, Ethnic Folkways Records (2 LPs). Publs. incl: Venda Children's Songs, 1967; How Musical is Man?, 1973; Ed., World Anthropology, the Performing Arts, 1979. Contbr. to num profl. jrnls. Mbrships. incl. Fellow, Royal Anthropol. Inst., Current Anthropol.; Assn. of Social Anthropols. of UK & C'wlth. Hobbies: Music; Philately. Address: 18 Dleaver Pk., Belfast, N Ireland BT9 5HX, UK.

BLACKMAN, Paul Anthony, b. 7 July, 1953, W Ryde, Sydney Aust. Orchestral Musician (Bassoon & Contrabassoon). Educ: STudied w. John Cran, Sydney, attaining Assoc. Music Aust.; studied w. Albert Hennige, Detmold, Germany. m. Helen Isabel Farhall. Career: Bassoonist & Contrabassoonist, N Z Symph. Orch., 1973-78; Prin. Bassoon, Tas. Symph. Orch., 1978. Comps: String Quartet; Bassoon Concertino; Trio for Violin, Cello & Piano. Hobbies: Tennis; Music Comp.; Golf; Photography. Address: 1 Liverpool Cres., West Hobart, Tas. 7000, Aust. 30.

BLACKMORE, George Henry James, b. 24 Jan. 1921, Chatham, UK. Organist (Electronic, Theatre & Concert Organs). Educ. incls: studies w. many pvte. tchrs.; ARCO, 1941; FRCO, 1952. m. Joyce Annie Patricia Hampton, 1 s. Debut: Majestic Theatre, Rochester, 1939. Career: Organist at var. chs. & theatres, 1937-59; frequent radio broadcasts from cinemas & BBC Theatre Organ, 1941-; many film, TV & recording sessions w. orchs.; Exploitation & Recorded Music Rep., Bosworth & Co. Ltd., 1960-68; Music Advsr. & Chief Demonstrator, Hammond Organ (UK) Ltd., 1968-74; Promotions, Marketing & Sales Mgr., CG Conn Organs (UK) Ltd., 1977-. Comps: novelties for piano & orch.; marches; intermezzi; mood music. Has made LP's for sev. cos. Publs. (albums for organ): Tune Time for Electronic Organ, 1964; Traditional Airs of the British Isles, 1964; Hits of Yesteryear, 1965; Goilden Standards, 1965. Mbr. Profl. org. Recip. var. hons. Address: 4 Englefield, Round Green, Luton, Beds. LU2 7TD, UL. 3.

BLACKSHAW, Christian, b. 18 Jan. 1949, Cheadle Hulme, Cheshire, UK. Pianist. Educ: Royal Manchester Coll. of Music, 1965-70; RAM, UK, 1972-74. Debut: London, 1969; Leningrad, 1971; Rome & Madrid, 1975. Career: Recital, Concerto, Radio & TV apps. Hons: Queen's 1st Prize, London, 1968; Perfs. Dip. w. distinction & Dayas Gold Medal, Royal Manchester Coll. of Music, 1969; Recital Dip. & Macfarren Gold Medal, RAM, 1973; 1st Prize, Alfredo Casella Int. Piano Competition, Naples w. Clara Haskil Mozart Prize, & Pres. of Italy's Gold Medal, 1974. Hobby: Music. Mgmt: Ibbs & Tillett Ltd., 125 Wigmore St., London W1H OAX, UK. Address: c/o Mgmt.

BLACKWELL, Anna Gee, b. 24 Dec. 1928, Springfield, Ohio, USA. Pianist; Organist; Vocalist; Composer; Teacher. Educ: Wilberforce Univ., Ohio, 1947-48; Wittenberg Univ., Springfield, Ohio, 1963-64; Wright State Univ., Dayton, Ohio, 1970-72; Cert., Nat. Piano Fndn; Sinclair Coll., Dayton, Ohio, 1977-78. m. Harold Benson-Jerry Blackwell Sr., 2 s., 3 d. Debut: Detroit, 1943. Career: RAdio Station WIZE, 1940-44; Accomp., Wright State Chmbr. Singers, 1970-71; Dir., Pianist, Organist, St. John Baptist Ch., Springfield, for 20 yrs.; Organist, Ctrl. Chapel, AME Ch., 6 yrs.; TV Channel 2, Dayton, 1976-77; Tchr., Kiefer Jr. High Schl., Springfield, Ohio, 1973-. Comps: incl: Because You're You; Boogie Woogie Breakdown; Ebony Waters; Because You have Said We're Through; They'll Come Back Someday; There's A New World Coming; Psalm 150. Publs: Twenty-Two Days of Music in Europe. Recording: Dir., St. John Baptist Ch. Choir, St. John Sings. Mbrships: NGPT (Chmn. Springfield Chapt.); Ohio Fedn. of Music Clubs; Am. Coll. of Musicians; MENC; Xenia Music Club. Recip. num. hons. Hobbies: Sewing; Rug-making; Walking. Address: 244 Northwood Dr., Yellow Spring, OH45387, USA. 5.

BLACKWELL, Glenda Rue Moseley, b. 26 Nov. 1940, Butler, Ala., USA. Teacher (Piano, Organ, Music Theory, Composition). Music Studios Owner & Director. Educ: BMus, Auburn Univ.,

1963; postgrad., Univ. of Chattanooga, Yamaha Music Schl., Nat. Symposium, music for the very young, Chgo.; Tchr. Accreditation, Ala. Music Tchrs. Assn., NGPT, Yamaha Learning Explorations. 2 s. Career: Tchr., elem. & jr. HS, Birmingham, Ala., & Chattanooga; Organist, 1st Bapt. Ch., Prattville; Adjudicator, piano fests., Ala. Music Tchrs. Assn., NGPT. Comps: Passacaglia for Piano; Overture 'Cocytus to Lethe' (orchl.); Madrigal (concert choir); backbround music, Auburn Players prods.; organ works. Mbrships. incl: Chmn., Autauqua Co. Div., NGPT; prog. committee, Perf., Montgomery Music Study Club; Charter Mbr., Treas., Piano Tchrs. Forum, Montgomery; Charter Mbr., Chmn., Music Committee, Bd. of Dirs., Coun. on Arts & Humanities, Prattville. Hobbies: Crewel; Crocheting; Fishing; Sports. Address: 542 Julia Ct., Prattville, AL 36067, USA.

BLACKWELL, William Neal, b. 28 Nov. 1942, Memphis, Tenn., USA. Professor of Music (Horn); Art Consultant; Conductor; Music Librarian. Educ: Bmus, & MMus., La. State Univ.; Cand. PhD, Univ. Iowa. m. (1) Pamela Signor (div.) (2) Dorothy White. Career: Admnstr., Lending Libr., Soc. for Commissioning New Music; Dir., The New Music Ensemble; Tchr., Miami-Dade Jr. Coll. & Univ. Iowa; Vis. Prof. of Music, La. State Univ.; Currently pvte. tchr. Publs: Compiler & Ed., Catalogue of Lib. of Soc. for Commissioning New Music, 1976. Contbr. to profl. mags. Mbrships. incl: Phi Kappa Phi; Phi Mu Alpha; Pi Kappa Lambda; MLA. Recip. num. awards. Hobbies: Reading & Collecting Detective Fection; Engl. Hist. Address: 6108 Goodwood Ave., Baton Rouge, LA 70806, USA.

BLADEN, Anthony William, b. 18 Jan. 1924, Worcester, UK. Violinist; Voilist; Pianist; Free-lance Journalist. Educ: Birmingham Schl. of Music; ARCM; AMSM (Violin-perf.). m. Eileen Ruth McDermott. Career: Former Prin. Viola, BBC W of England Players & BBC Scottish Radio Orch.; Former Asst. Master, King's Coll., Taunton; Solo Viola & chmbr. music broadcasts, BBC W Reg., 1962-65; Considerable free-lance tchng. Mbrships: Past Committee Mbr., ISM; Music Masters' Assn.; Past Vice-Chmn., Bristol Br., & Mbr., SW Dist. Coun., Musicians' Union. Contbr. to Somerset Co. Gazette & other newspapers. Recip., schlrships., Birmingham Schl. of Music, 1939-45. Hobbies incl: Reading. Address: 31 Abbey Close, Curry Rivel, Langport, Somerset TA10 OEL, UK.

BLADES, James, b. Peterborough, UK. Orchestral Timpanist; Tutor; Lecturer; Author. Educ: Prof. of Percussion, RAM, London; MMus., Surrey Univ. m. Joan Goossens, 1 child. Recordings: L P Blades on Percussion; Discourses ABK 13, 1974. Publs: Orchestral Percussion Technique, 1961-73; Percussion Instruments and their History, 1970-75. Contbr. to Saturday Book, 1969. Recip. IBE, 1972. Hobby: Mechanics. Address: 191 Sandy Lane, Cheam, Surrey SM2 7EU, UK.

BLAHA, Ivo, b. 14 Mar. 1936, Litomysl, Czech. Composer. Educ: Dip., Acad. of Arts, Prague, 1958, 1970. m. Lidmila Vrhelova, 2 d. Career: Tchr., Acad. of Arts, Prague. Comps: 2nd String Quartet; What Beauty in the World (cantata cycle for children's choir); Spring Play (suite for wind quintet); Concerto for Percussion Instruments & Orch.; 3 Toccata Studies for Piano; Concerto for Violin & Orch.; 2 Inventions for Flute Solo. Mbr., Union of Czech. Comps. Address: Jablonecká 418, Prague 9, Czech.

BLAIN, Albert Valdes, b. Apr. 1921, Havana, Cuba. Classic Guitarist; Concert Artist; Teacher. Educ: Engrng., Univ. Ala. & Columbia Univ., NY, USA, 3 yrs.; Guitar w. Julio Martinez Oyanguren & Andres Segovia; Juilliard Schl. Music; Tchrs. Dip., Greenwich Hs. Music Schl., NY. m. Lilia Hurtado Echemendia, 1 s. Debut: Carnegie Recital Hall, 1941. Career: Concert apps. throughout USA & Canada; TV & Radio apps., 1940-64; Fac. mbr., NY Univ., Mannes Coll. Music, Bronx Community Coll., Bklyn. Coll. & Kingsborough Community Coll. Recordings: w. brother Roland, Rollette Records. Author: 700 Years of Music for Classic Guitar, 1967. Contbr. to profl. jrnls. Fellow. Soc. Classic Guitar, NY. Phila. & Cinn. Address: 25 W 13th St., NY, NY 10011, USA.

BLAIR, Bert Alvin, b. 19 Mar. 1927, Mason, Ohio, USA. Music Educator; Conductor; (Piano; Viola). Educ: BS, Coll. Conserv. of Music, Univ. Chmn., 1950; MMus, Miami Univ., 1958; Mbr. Inst. for Advanced Study in Music Lit., Univ. Iowa, 1966. m. Dorothy Denman Blair, 1 s, 5 d. Carer: Active in string & orchl. music educ. for 27 yrs.; Cond., Lima Symph. Orch. Coordinator of Strgs. & orch., Lima City Schls. Contbr. to Triad. Mbrships: Pres., Dist 12, Ohio Music Educ. Assn.; Treas., Ohio String Tchrs. Assn.; Pres., Eta Chapt., Phi Mu Alpha Sinfonia; Nat. Schl. Orch. Assn.; MENC. Hons. incl: Conds. Award, Lima Symph., 1964. Hobbies: Painting; Wood-working; Carpentry; Cooking; Photography; Canoeing; Golf. Address: 416 S Charles St., Lima, OH 45805. USA.

BLAIR, Betty Woodruff, b. 5 Jan. 1920, Little Falls, NY, USA. Music Educator; Falutist; Teacher. Educ: BS, MA, Ithaca Coll., NY.; studied Flute at grad. level, Juilliard Schl. of Music, Eastman Schl. of Music, & Syracuse Univ., NY. m. Thomas P Blair, 2 d. Career: Fndr. & Dir., Ctrl. NY Little Symph.; Guest Cond., Area All State & Co. Orchs. & NY State Music Camp Orch; Music Dept. Chmn., Cazenovia, NY; Asst. Prof. Music, SUNY at Potsdam, NY; Mbr., Utica, NY, Symph. & Opera Orch. Contbr. to NY State Schl. Music Assn. Manual; NY State Music News, 1946-56. Mbrships: NY State Schl. Music Assn. (1 Term, Exec. Coun.); MENC; Music Club of Utica; Local No. 51. Musicians Union. Hobbies: Skiing; Singing; Hiking; Swimming; Sailing. Address: 17 Chateau Dr., Whitesboro, NY 13492, USA.

BLAIR, Roger Phillip Ian, b. 2 Nov. 1948, Newcastle-upon-Tyne, UK. Director of Music; Timpanist; Teacher. Educ: RCM; LRAM; ARCM; GRSM; postgard. cert., Bretton Hall Coll. of Educ.; BA Open Univ. m. Wendy Ann Wallis, 1 s. Career: Dir. of Music, Bishop Reindorp Schl., Guildford; prin. timpanist, Guildford Phil. Orch.; percussion tchr., Charterhouse & Cranleigh Schls. Mbrships: Musicians' Union; ISM; Nat. Assn. of Schlmasters. recip., City Livery Award, 1971. Address: Sunstar, 19 Sandfield Terr., Guildford, Surrey, UK.

BLAKE, Christopher Hugh, b. 5 Jan. 1949, Christchurch, NZ. Music Arts Administrator. Educ: Bachelor of Engnrng., Univ. of Canterbury; BMus, ibid; BMus, Univ. of Southampton, UK. Career: Former Mgr., Canterbury Orch., Christchurch, NZ; currently Planning Mgr., Nat. Opera of NZ. Comps. recorded: Tasman Octet, 1975; Viola on Skye, for solo viola, 1976; Ribbonwood is Home, for solo piano, 1978; Regions, for Wind Quintet, 1978; Towards Peace, for solo clarinet, 1978. Contbr. to: CANZ Newsletter. Mbrships: Assoc., Australasian perf. Rights Assn.; Comps. Assn. of NZ; Service Mbr., Am. Symph. Orch. League. Hobbies: Reading; Writing; Cats; Gardening. Address: CPO Box 4101, Auckland, NZ.

BLAKE, David Leonard, b. 2 Sept. 1936, London, UK. University Professor; Composer; Pianist; Conductor. Educ: BA, MA, Gonville & Caius Coll., Cambridge Univ.; Deutsche Akademie der Künste, Berlin, GDR. m. Rita Blake, 2 s., 1 d. Comps., publd. by Novello, Schott & Oxford Univ. Press. Hobbies: Squash; Indian Cooking. Mgmt: Novello. Address: 33 Heslington Lane, York, UK. 3.

BLAKE, Frances Ann Georgina, b. 15 Mar. 1926, Coonoor, S India. Peripatetic String Teacher; Accompanist. Educ: ARCM, Tchng., Pianoforte & Violin, 1946. Career: Tchr. of Piano, Violin, Theory Musical Appreciation, schls. in Berks. inclng. Berks. Music Schl., 1951-70; Strings Tchr., Surrey, 1970-71; Tchr., Herts Co. Coun., 1971-; Mbr., Herts Tchrs. Orch.; Peripatetic Strings Tchr., Violin & Viola, Dacorum Div. of Herts; perfect of Studies & Tchr. of Piano, Violin & Viola, London Oratory Jr. Choir; Ldr.; Welwyn Garden City Music Soc. Orch., 1977-. Mbr., Dacorum Oboe Quartet, giving concerts in schls.; Accomp., Chipperfield Choral Soc. Comp. of arrs. & original works for jr. string orchs. Mbrships. incl: ISM. Hobbies incl: Tennis. Address: 10 Connaught Close, High St. Green, Hemel Hempstead, Herts, UK.

BLAKE, Rex Etherton, b. 13 Apr. 1926, Darwen, UK. Music Adviser. Educ: BA, Univ. of Durham; Dip. Educ., Univ. of Durham Inst. of Educ. m. Averil Taylor, 2 s. Career: Music Master, The Grammar Schl., W Bromwich, 1951-53; prin. Music Master, Berwickshire High Schl., 1953-66; Fndr., 1st Co. orch. in Scotland, Berwickshire, & 1st in N Ireland, Armagh; Co. Music Advsr., Co. Armagh, 1966-73; Music Advsr., Southern Educ. & Lib. Bd., 1973-; Fndr., S Ulster Youth Orch., 1975; Adjudicator, var. music fests., 1967-; Orchl. Cond., 1959-. Comps. incl: Pageantry (march) for full orch., 1963; Celtic Cavatina for strings & harp. for BBC TV N Ireland, 1971. Mbr. Nat. Assn. of Insps. & Educl. Advsrs. Hobby: Photography. Address: 46 Castle Gdns., Castle Demesne, Richill, Co. Armagh, UK. 3.

BLAKEMAN, Virginia Louise, b. 1 Aug. 1949, Sandusky, Ohio, USA. Violist. Educ: BMus, New England Conserv., 1971; MMus, Yale Univ. Schl. of Music, 1974; Scholarship participant, Tanglewood, Blossom & Meadowbank Music Fests. Career: Prin. Violist, NY String Seminar, Carnegie Hall, 1970, 71; Participant, Marlboro Music Fest., 1973-74; Boston freelance musician; Mbr., Musica Viva (new music ensemble), Boston Pops; Prin. Violist, Rochester Phil., 1974-; Soloist w. Colo. & Rochester Phils. Hons. Benjamin H. Delson Award, Tanglewood, 1970. Hobbies: Reading; Swimming; Hiking. Address: 18 Rundel Pk., Rochester, NY 14607, USA.

BLAM, Rafailo, b. 11 Oct. 1910, Belgrade, Yugoslavia. Violinist; Professor of Violin. Educ: Dip., violin & violin tchng.,

Acad. of Music. m. Ivanka, 1 s., 1 d. Career: num. concerts in Yugoslavia & other countires as mbr. of Radio Belgrade Orch.; soloist in Yugoslavia, UK, Turkey, etc.; TV apps.; Cond., Nikola Tesla chorus, Belgrade; Musical Ed., Prosveta, Belgrade. num. comps. for choir & vocal soloists. mbr. Yugoslav Comps. Soc. Address: Braće Jugovića 8/II, 11000 Belgrade, Yugoslavia.

BLANC, Ernest Marius Victor, b. 1 Nov. 1923, Sanary, Var. France. Opera Singer (baritone). m. Eliane Guirard, 1 s. Debut: Marseilles Opera, 1950. Career incl: Mbr., Paris Opera, 1954-58; Prin. roles in opera houses in France & abroad, inclng. Bayreuth, 1959; La Scala, Milan, 1959-60; Carnegie Hall, NYC, etc.; Repertoire incl: Tannhauser; Loghengrin; Parsifal; Don Giovanni; Aida; Rigoletto; Il Trovatore, etc. Hobby: Mechanics. Address: Blvd. des Baguiers, Notre-Dame-des-Routes, 83200 Toulon, France.

BLANC, Johnny, b. 1939. Operatic Tenor. Deubt: 1965. Career: Prin. tenor, Royal Opera House, Stockholm; apps. in Denmark, Norway, Finland, Germany, UK, USA, Portugal, etc.; roles incl. Cavaradossi (Tosca), Florestan (Fidelio), Siegmund (Walküre), Don Carlos, Don José (Carmen) & Eisenstein (Die Fledermaus). Mgmt: Artistsekretariat Ulf Törnqvist, Norrtullsgatan 26, tr. 4, 11345 Stockholm, Sweden. Address: c/o mgmt.

BLANDFORD, Jeremy Richard, b. 23 Apr. 1943, Bishop's Stortford, UK, Organ Recitalist; Organ, Harpsichord & Pianoforte Accompanist. Educ: MA (Cantab); GRSM; FRCO; LRAM (organ perf.); ARCM (pianoforte teaching). m. Susan Marsland, 2 s. Career incls: Organist & Master of Music, St. Mary's Parish Ch., Southampton, 1968-; Dir., St. Mary's Singers, 1974-; Organ Tchr., Southampton LEA, 1971-; Vis. Tutor, La Saints Union Coll. of Higher Educ., Southampton, 1972-; Organist, Southampton Choral Soc., 1973-; Music Staff, King Edward Vi Schl., Southampton, 1975-; Recital tours of USA, France & Smitz; Public perfs. of Messiaen's maj. organ suites. Recordings: Carols from Cambridge, Clare Coll. Singers & Orch. w. organ. Recip. RAM Richards Organ Prize, 1963. Hobbies: Motoring; Theatre; Hist.; Current Affairs. Address: 3 Plover Cl., Chilworth Pk., Lordswood, Southampton, UK. 3.

BLANK, Allan, b. 27 Dec. 1925, NYC, USA. Composer; University Teacher. Educ: BA, NYU, 1948; MA, Univ. of Minn., 1950; Tchrs. Coll., Columbia Univ., 1955-56, '66-67; Univ. of la., 1966-67; Juilliard Schl. Music, 1945-47; Princeton Seminar in Adv. Musical Studies, summer 1960. m. Margot Blank. Career incl: Assoc. Prof., Virginia Commonwealth Univ., Richmond, Va. Compositions incl: Tell Me Where Is Fancy Bred; 2 Simple Canons for 2 Flutes; Escapades: Songs for Rote & Piano Duet; Give Ear to my Words, O Lord; Aria Da Capo; Music for Orch.; Meditation for Orch.; Concert Piece for Band; 13 Ways of Looking at a Blackbird; 2 Parables by Franz Kafka; Poem; Moments in Time: 3 Pieces for Oboe & Piano; Music for Violin; 1961; The Frogs; 2 Bagatelles for 2 Bassoons; 4 Bagatelles for Oboe & Clarinet; A Song of Ascents: For Solo Viola; Variations for Clarinet & Viola; 4 Piec es for 2 Trumpets & 3 Trombones. Mbrships: Bd. Govs., Am. Comps. Alliance, 1968-70; Am. Soc. Univ. Comps.; Am. Music Ctr. Recip: Am. Artists Series Commn . 1975 for chmbr. work to be performed 1976. Address: 3210 Marlboro Drive, Richmond, Va., USA.

BLANK, Jorg D, b. 9 Dec. 1952, Rinteln, German Fed. Repub. Violinist. Educ: studied w. Tibor Varga, Saschko Gawriloff, Renato de Barbieri; Dip. for violin, Conserv. M. Paganini, Genoa. m. Hannelore Blank. Debut: soloist in Beethoven's violin concerto, Dortmund. Career: Soloist in Germny, Italy, Switz. & Austria; apps. on TV & radio; currently ldr., Pfälzischen Phil. Orch., Ludwigshafen. mbr. European Strg. Tchrs. Assn. Hons: 1st German violinist to play on Paganini's violin (Die Kanone), 1973. Hobbies: Meditation; Dogs. Address: von Denisstr. 17, 6703 Limburgerhof, German Fed. Repub.

BLANKENBURG, Walter, b. 31 July 1903, Emleben bei Gotha, Thuringen, Germany. Emeritus School & Church Music Director. Educ: PhD, Musicol.; Exams in Theol. & Philol. m. Annemarie Weber, 4 c. Career: Retired Dir., Protestant Ch. Music Schl., Schlüchtern; Land Ch. Music Dir. Publs: Geschichte der melodien des evgl. Kirchengesangbuchs, 1957; Leiturgia; Handbuch des evgl. Gottesdienstes IV, 1961; Einführung in Bachs h-moll-Messe, 1950, 1974. Contbr. to: Die evangelische Kirchenmusik, 1968; Musik & Kirche; Wege der Forschung, CLXX, 1970; Musik in Geschichte & Gegenwart; musical encys. Mbrhips. incl: Int. Bach Soc. (Bd. of Dirs.); Int. Musicol. Soc. HOns: Dr. h.c., Theol. Fac., Marburg Univ. Hobbies: Numismatics; Collecting Old Songbooks & Choirbooks. Address: 35D Bahnhofstr., 649 Schlüchtern, German Fed. Repub. 14.

BLANKERS, Laurens A(rthur), b. 20 Jan. 1933, O'Brien Co., la., USA. Organist; Cellist; Gambist; Music Educator; Music

Librarian. Educ: BA, Univ. of Northern Ia., 1955; MMusEd, Univ. of Colo., 1969; MLS, George Peabody Coll., 1974. Career: Music Educator, primary & secondary schls., Ia., Neb. & Wyo., working esp. w. schl. orchs.; Ch. Organist, num. yrs.; Cellist, num. community orchs.; Cond., Sheridan, Wyo., Summer Community Orch., 1970-72; Music publishing, Nashville, Tenn. Contbr. to: Music for Band, Orch. & String Orch., Music Educators Nat. Conf. listing 1971; NSOA Bulletin. Mbrships: Nat. Schl. Orch. Assn. (Nat. Bd., 1970-72; New score review committee; orch. score chmn. to Music Educators Nat. Conf., 1973; Bicentennial Repertoire Commission); Am. Guild Organists (Fndr., Past Dean, N Platte Chapt.) Phi Mu Sinfonia, BX Chapter. Hobbies: Reading; Singing; Cooking; Collecting Books; Recordings. Address: Box 294, George Peabody Coll., Nashville, TN 37203, USA.

BLANKS, Fred Roy, b. 31 May 1925, Schwäbisch Gmünd, Germany (now Aust. citizen). Industrial Chemist; Music Critic. Educ: BSc., Univ. of Sydney. m. Christine Margaret Hellman, 1 s., 1 d. Career: Aust. Corres., Musical Times (UK), 1955-; Music Critic, Sydney Morning Herald, 1963-; Music critic, Aust. Jewish Times & other publs; lectr. to var. music & other organizations. Mbrships: Musicol. Soc. of Aust.; Royal Soc. of NSW. Address: 19 Innes Rd., Greenwich, NSW 2065, Aust.

BLATTER, Alfred Wayne, b. 24 Dec. 1937, Litchfield, Ill., USA. Composer; Arranger; Theorist; Horn Player; Editor; Administrator. Educ: Bm, Univ. of Ill., 1961; MM, ibid., 1965; DMA, ibid., 1974; studied horn, condng., comp., & theory pvtely. m. Marilyn Dvorak Blatter, 1 d., 1 s. Career: US Army Band, 1962-65; fac., Marshall Univ., 1966-69; fac., Univ. of Ill., 1969-79; Hd., Dept. of Music, Drexel Univ., Phila., 1979-; US Panellist, Int. Conf. on New Musical Notation, Ghent, 1974; Sr. Ed., Media Press. Comps: Suite for 10 brass; 5 sketches for trombone, 2 piano; Fanfare for 12 trumpets; 2 solos for Euphonium; Dream within a Dream for tenor, piano & paino interior; Study in Time & Space for Stg. Quartet; Cameos for Tuba. Mbrships: Soc. for Music Theory; Am. Soc. of Univ. Comps.; Mid-West Theory Soc.; Central Mid-West Theory Soc. (steering committee). Hobbies: Model Railroading; Electornics; Carpentry. Address: 153 Latches Ln., Media, PA 19063, USA.

BLATTMANN, Hans, b. 18 Oct. 1922, Dübendorf, Zürich, Switz. Violoncellist; Viola da Gambist; Soloist; Music Master. Educ: Dips. as Violincello Master, 1944, Violincello Soloist, 1945, Consedrv., Zürich. m. Thea Blattmann-Strobel, 1 d., 1 s. Career: Recitals as violincello, viola da gamba & recorder soloist in Switz., F & W Germany, Italy, Poland, Netherlands & Bulgaria. Comps. incl: (organ): Toccata; Kleines Vorspiel und Fuge; (piano): Kleine Suite, Sonate; (2 pianos): Kleine Stücks; (guitar): Kleine Sonate; (violincello solo): Kleine Sonatine; other works for string trios & recorders. Mbrships. incl: Schweizerischer Tonkünstlerverein. Hobby: Mbr., Ancient Mystical Order Rosae Crucis; Verband Deutscher Musikerzighet & Konzertierender Kunstler. Address: Thomas-Borchwede Weg 10, D 4770 Soest (Westfalen), German Fed. Repub.

BLAZER, Walter, b. 8 Jan. 1918, Brooklyn, NY, USA. Singer; Voice Teacher. Educ: Juilliard Schl. of Music, NYC; Am. Theatre Wing, NYC. m. Maria Vernole, 1 s., 1 d. Debut: Opera, Rome; Oratorio, Carnegie Hall. Career: Wagner, Rome RAI, Milan RAI Opera Co.'s; Soloist w. Phila. Orch.; Recitalist w. maj. Concert Orgs., Europe & USA; num. Leading Roles, Opera & Oratorio; Voice Tchr.; Chmn., Int. Seminar on vocal technique & methodology at Estate Fiesolana fest., Florence, Italy, 1979. Recording: Tenor Soloist, Messiah. w. Masterwork Chorus. Contbr. to NATS Mag. Mbrships: Nat. Assn. of Tchrs. of Singing; Fac., Manhattan Schl. of Music, NY. Named Winner, Young Artists Recitals, Brooklyn, 1946. Hobbies: Hiking; Camping; Cycling. Address: Box 803, 34 Norman Rd., Upper Montclair, NJ 07043, USA.

BLAZHKOV, Igor Ivanovich, b. 23 Sept. 1936, Kiev, USSR. Conductor; Musicologist. Educ: Grad. Dip., Kiev Conserv., 1959. m. (1) Galina Mokreyeva, dec.; (2) Irene Lozovik, 1 s. Debut: Kiev, 1958. Career: Cond., Ukraine State Symph., Kiev, 1958-62, Leningrad Phil., 1963-68, ballet The Twelve, Leningrad, 1964, opera The Captain, Kiev, 1970; Artistic Dir., Cond., Kiev Chmbr. Orch., 1969-76; Guest cond., Ukraine Concert Agency, 1978-; Perfs. in 2 Films; num. TV, Radio Perfs. Recordings: Schoenberg, Serenade, op. 24; Ives, Tone Roads No. 3; Hindemith, Kammermusik No. 1; Stravinsky, Song of The Nightingale; Britten, Variations On a Theme Of Frank Bridge; Shostakovich, 5 Fragments, op. 42, 2 Pieces, op. 11, 2nd & 3rd Symphs.; Cimarosa, Maestro di Capella; Haydn, Sinfonia Concertante in B Flat; Telemann, Schulmeister; A. Scarlatti, Sinfonia 4 & 5; Dittersdorf, Sinfonia Concertante; Grabovsky, Symphonic Frescoes; Jubarenko, 1st Symph.; var. orthers. Contbr. to: I F Stravinsky, The Articles & Letters, 1973; Ruch Muzyczny. Mbr. var. profl. orgs. Hons: Honoured

Artist, Ukrainian Soviet Socialist Republic, 1973; Ukrainian Cond. Prize, 1959. Hobby: Books; Photography. Address: Apt. 16, 79 Jchkalov St., Kiev 54, USSR 252054.

BLECH, Harry, b. 2 Mar. 1910, London, UK. Musician; Conductor. Educ: Ctrl. London Fndn.; FTCL; FRMCM; RAM. m. Marion Manley, 1 s., 3 d. Career: Early concerts as solo violinist; Mbr. BBC Symph. Orch., 1930-36; Fndr. & Ldr., Blech String Quartet, 1933-50; Fndr. & Cond., London Wind Players, 1942-; Fndr. & Cond., London Mozart Players, 1949-; Musical Dir. & Fndr., Haydn-Mozart Soc. Recordings incl: Symph. No. 35 in C, Mozart; Divertimento in D, Mozart; Symph. No. 35 in D, Mozart; Symph. No. 90 in C, Haydn; Symph. in C, Mozart; Piano Concerto in A (w. soloist Michael Roll). Mozart. Recip. OBE, 1964. Hobbies: Lit., Chess. Address: 'The Owls' 70 Leopold Rd., Wimbledon, London SW19, UK. 1.

BLENDINGER, Herbert, b. 3 Jan. 1936, Ansbach, Germany. Solo Violist; Composer. Educ: State High Schl. for Music, Munich. m. Sigrid Blendinger, 2 c. Debut: Nurenberg. Career: Num. perfs. & solo apps. as Violist in Europe & for Radio & TV. Comps: Konzert für Viola Und Streichorchester; Sonate für Viola und Cembalo; Concertino für Violine und Streichorchester; Concerto tonale für Violoncello und grosses Orchester; Konzert für Streichquartett und grosses Orchester; Var. Str. Quartets. Ch. Music - Introduktion und Chaconne für Viola und Orgel. Recordings: Bayern Radio, Munich, WDR, Cologne, SW Radio & Saar Radio. Mbr., Bayern Grp. of Sound Artists, (VDMK). Hons: Saltire Cup, Edinburgh, 1960; Var. Prizes incl. Nurenburg, 1962, Schumann prize, Dusseldorf, 1967, Bayern 1967, Förderungspreis für Musik, 1975; Mgmt: Orlando Verlag, Richard Gartenmaier, Munich. Address: Oberholz 6, 813 Starnberg, German Fed. Repub.

BLEUMERS, Bart, b. 11 Sept. 1943, The Hague, Holland. Violinist. Educ: Amsterdam Conserv. m. Carien v. d. Schoor, 1 s., 1 d. Career: Third Concertmaster, Residentie Orch. in The Hague, 1975-; 1st Concertmaster (Ldr.) & Soloist, Overijssels Phil. Orch. in Enschede; Num. recitals of works from Barok to contemporary music in concert halls & on radio; Tchr. Conserv. of Arnhem. Hobby: Playing Piano. Address: Jan Prins str. 28, Hengelo (O), The Netherlands.

BLEZZARD, Judith Helen, b. 29 July 1944, Bradford, W. Yorks., UK. University Lecturer in Music. Educ: BA, BMus, PhD, Leeds Univ.; LRAM (Pfte. tchng.). Career: Cond., Liverpool Univ. Singers; Lectr. in Music, Liverpool Univ., 1972-. Contbr. to: Musical Times; Early Music; Music & Musicians. Mbrships: Royal Musical Assn.; ISM. Hobby: Silence. Address: Dept. of Music, The University, P O Box 147, Liverpool L69 3BX, UK.

BLIESENER, Ada Elizabeth Michelmann, b. 9 Oct. 1909, Quincy, Ill., USA. Cellist; Educator. Educ. incls: BMus (cello), 1931, Bmus (comp.), 1933, Am. Conserv. of Music, Chgo.; MMus(cello), 1963, MMus (comp.), 1966, Univ. of Ill., Urbana. Career incls: Pvte Tchr., cello & piano, 1927-, tchr. piano, Birmingham, Ala., 1973-74; now retired and writing. Asst. Prof., cello & theory, Bethany Coll., Lindsborg, Kan., 1966-70; Cellist w. var. ensembles, orchs., music socs., etc., 1929-, Birmingham Symph. Orch., 1972-74; Comps. publd: Prelude for Piano. Mbrships. incl: Am. Soc. of Univ. Comps.; Nat. Assn. of Comps., USA. Recip. var. hons. Address: 119 Ike Rd., Rte. 1, Brownsboro, AL 35741, USA. 5, 27.

BLITZSTEIN, Marc, b. 2 Mar. 1905, Philadelphia, Pa., USA. Composer. Educ: Univ. of Pa.; Curtis Inst. Compositions incl: The Cradel Will Rock (opera); No for an Answer (opera); The Airborne (symph.); Regina (musical play). Hons. incl: Guggenheim Fellowship, 1940; grant from Am. Acad. of Arts & Letters.

BLIZINSKI, Marek Bohdan, b. 22 Mar. 1947, Warsaw, Poland. Guitarist; Composer; Arranger. m. Thereese Koryl, 1 s. Debut: Warsaw, 1971. Career: Perfs. w. Zbigniest Namystouski, Michat Urbaniak, Novi Singers, Tomasz Stanko; Radio Perfs., Poland Radio, TV, Film Composer. Compositions: The Glass Mountain: A Strange Story; High Jump; Spring Song; Travelling in Colourful Summer. Recordings: num., Jazz, pop. Poland. Mbrships: Assn. of Authors & Comps. of Light Music; Soc. of Authors; Jazz Soc. Hons: Musicians Test, Warsaw, 1966; as mbr., Cond., grp. Four, 1st Place, Glivice Fest., 1967; Best Instrumentalist, ibid; 3rd Prize, Jazz On The Order Fest., Wroclaw, 1971. Address: 00-344 Warszawa ul. Dobra 26 m 13, Poland.

BLOCH, Alexander, b. 11 July 1881, Selma, Ala., USA. Violinist; Conductor; Composer. Educ: Columbia Univ., 1897-98; studied violin w. Eduard Herrmann, NYC, Ottakar Sevčik, Vienna & Leopold Auer, Petrograd (now Leningrad). m. Blanche Bloch, 1 s., 1 d. Debut: NYC, 1913. Career:

Concertmaster & Soloist w. Symph. Orch. in Tiflis in the Caucasus; Concertized extensively w. Mrs. Bloch, pianist, in Easter & Southern US, specializing in sonata recitals; Tchng. Asst. to Prof. Auer during his residence in USA; Cond. of Educl. Alliance Symph. Orch., NYC & Chatham Choral Soc., NY; Hd. of Violin Dept., Wash. DC Coll. of Music & Rollins Coll. Conserv., Winter Pk., Fla.; Cond., Symph. Orch. of Ctrl. Fla., Winter Pk., 1936-43; Guest Cond., NBC Symph. & Nat. Symph. Orch.; Cond., Fla. West Coast Symph. Orch., Sarasota, 1950-62. Unpublished works which have been performed: 'Roeliff's Dream' (children's operetta), libretto by Mrs. Bloch; 'The Lone Tree' (Christmass operetta), libretto by Arthur Davison Ficke; Transcriptions: Bach Adagio in C Minor (violin & strings); Vitali Chaconne (full orch.); Art songs to poems by Shelley, Edna St. Vincent Millay & Arthur Davison Ficke. Publs: var. tech. works for violin. Contbr. to Musical Am. & other profl. mags. Mbrships: The Bohemians, NYC; The Beethoven Soc., NYC, etc. Hobbies: Music & Reading. Address: Springhill Farm, Hillsdale, NY 12529, USA.

BLOCH, Augustyn, b. 13 Aug. 1929, Grudziadz, Poland. Composer; Organist. Educ: MA in Organ & Comp., State Coll. Music, Warsaw. m. Halina Lukomska. Debut as Organist, 1955. Career: Recordings of own comps. for Polskie Radio & WDR Köln. Compositions incl: Piano Variations, 1953; Organ Sonata, 1954; Espressioni per soprano ed orchestra, 1959; Meditations for soprano, organ & percussion, 1961; Voci (1 act ballet), 1962; A Cable for children's choir, 2 pianos & percussion, 1963; The Awaiting (1 act ballet), 1963; Dialoghi per violino ed orchestra, 1964; Ayelet Jephthah's Daughter (mystery opera in 1 act), 1967; Gilgamesz ballet music in concert version, 1969; Enfiando, 1970; Salmo gioioso, 1970; The Sleeping Beauty, Opera in 1 Act for children, 1973; Jubilate for Organ, 1974. Contbr. to Polish Music Quarterly. Mbrships: Treas., Union Polish Comps., 1967-69; VP, Union Polish Authors & Comps. 'Zaiks', 1965-71. Hons. incl: UNESCO Prize for 'Dialoghi', 1969; Polish Min. of Culture Prize for 'Enfiando', 1971; Prince Rainier II Of Monaco Prizes for Meditations, 1962, The Awaiting, 1964. Hobbies: Rowing; Gardening. Address: 00-788 Warsaw, Wybieg 14, Poland. 3.

BLOCK, Phyllis Ray, b. 26 Apr. 1925, Krugersdorp, S Africa. Violinist; Teacher (piano & violin). Educ: BMus, Univ. of the Witwatersrand; tchrs. dip. (piano, 1944, violin, 1943), TCL. m. Leon Bloc, 1 s., 1 d. Career: Ldr., Jewish Guild Orch., Johannesburg; apps. as soloist & accomp. at local functions; freelance journalist. Mbrships: Convocation (Univ. of the Witwatersrand); S African Soc. of Music Tchrs. Hons: 3 gold & 1 silver medals for violin playing, Nat. Eisteddfod of S Africa & Afrikaans W Rand Fest. of Arts, 1944. Hobbies: Writing; Knitting; Embroidery; Gardening; Reading; Cooking. Address: 3 Neethling St., Monument Extension 1, Krugersdorp 1740, S Africa.

BLOCKER, Robert Lewis, b. 4 Sept. 1946, Charleston, SC, USA. Educator; Concert Pianist. Educ: BA, Furman Univ.; MMus, DMA, N Tex. State Univ. m. Delaney Muikey, 1 s. 1 d. Debut: Charleston Symph. Orch., Dock St. Theatre, 1963. Career: num. radio, TV & concert engagements; Chmn., Fine Arts Div., Brevard Coll., NC. Contr. to: Piano Guild Notes, Southwestern Musician. Mbrships: incl: Bd. of Dir., Texas Assn. of Schls. of Music; Chmn. College, Div., Section XXI, Texas Music Educators' Assn., Pi Kappa Lambda; Phi Mu Alpha Sinfonia; TKE; Fellow, United Meth. Musicians; Alpha Phi Gamma. Hons. incl: San Antonio Tuesday Musical Club Competition, 1969. Hobbies: Raquetball; Touchfootball. Address: Music Dept. Chmn., Stephen F Austin State Univ., Nacodoches, TX 75961, USA.

BLOEMENDAL, Coenraad Robert, b. 30 April 1946, Amsterdam, Holland. Cellist. Educ: Dip., US, Amsterdam; Dip., Amsterdam Conserv. of Music, 1969; Post grad. studies w. Janos Starker & William Primrose, Ind. Univ. m. Barbara Schogt. Debut: REcital in Amsterdam, aged 16. Career: Recitals, concerts and chmbr. music perfs. in Can., USA, S Am. & Europe; radio & TV apps. incl. CBC Can., Radio France, Radio Holland, W Deutsche Rundfunk, Piadro Mexico. Sev. recordings. Hobbies: Painting; Photography; Hiking; Swimming. Address: 71 Hocken Ave., Toronto, Ont., Can.

BLOMBERG, Erik, b. 6 May 1922, Järnskog, Sweden. Composer; Music Teacher. Educ: Musical Acad., Stockholm. m. Kerstin Blomberg (dec.) 2 d. Debut: Swedish Radio, 1964. Career: w. Swedish Radio. Comps: 4 Symphs.; 1 Opera; 3 Piano Sonatas; Works for Soloists, Choir & Orch., String Orch., Wind Orch. Mbrships: Soc. of Swedish Comps. (FST); STIM. Recip. num. Scholarships. Hobby: Life of nature. Address: Granitvägen 184, 75243 Uppsala, Sweden.

BLOOD, Denis Jeffrey, b. 7 Jan. 1917, Dublin, Ireland. Composer; Pianist; Organist. Educ: Hertford Coll., Oxford;

Univ. of Southern Calif., USA; ARCM; B Mus. Career: Solo Organist & Pianist, Radio City Music, Hall Corp., 1950-62. Comps. incl: Bravade (overture); Improvisations; Missa Brevis; Cappricio for piano & orch. Mbr., London Orchl. Assn. Recip. Wm. E Bigg Prize for Solo Piano, 1937. Address: c/o London Orchl. Assn., 13/14 Archer St., London W1, UK. 3.

BLOOD, Esta, b. 25 Mar. 1933, New York City, USA. Composer; Teacher of Piano. Educ: Manhattan Schl. of Music, NYC. m. Robert Blood, 1 s. Comps. incl: String Quartet: Variations on an Armenian Theme; Trio; Bulgarian Trio (flute, violin & piano); Violin & Piano: Nocturne; Improvisations on (9) Shaker Tunes; Fall Starsong; A Psalm of David; Jack and the Beanstalk (2 winds, 2 strings & narrator); The House the Jack Built; Happy Birthday to US. Publs: Piano Solo; Balkan Suite (G K Schirmer), 1970; Piano Solo for 2nd yr. students; Five-legged Spider (Pro Art Publn.); 3 variations for 2 pianos, 8 hands, 1978. Contbr. to profl. mags. Mbr. Am. Soc. of Comps., Authors & Publrs. Hobby: Balkan & Middle-Eastern Folkdancing. Address: 1218 Regent St., Schenectady, NY 12309, USA.

BLOOM, Julius, b. 23 Sept. 1912, Brooklyn, NY, USA. Performimg Arts Administrator. Educ: BA, Rutgers Univ., 1933; post-grad. studies in philos., NY Univ., 1934-36; pvte. musical educ. m. Emily Leah Spicer, 2 s. Administrator of performing arts ctrs., Brooklyn Inst. of Arts & Scis., Brooklyn Acad. of Music, 1936—57; Carnegie Hall Corp., NY, 1960-. Publs: The Year in American Music, 1946-47, 1947. Mbrships: Pres., Brooklyn Music Schl., 1956-62; 1st VP (1943-46), acting pres. (1946-47), Am. Platform Guild; Exec. Sec., Nat. Assn. of Concert Managers, 1953-57; Pres., Assn. of Coll. & Univ. Concert Managers, 1962-64; Phi Beta Kappa, 1932-. Hons: LHD (hc), Buena Vista Coll., Stormlake, Ia, 1975; Ordre des Arts et Lettres, France, 1978. Address: 1207 Dorchester Rd., Brooklyn, NY 11218, USA.

BLUM, (Robert) Stephen, b. 4 Mar. 1942, Cleveland, USA. Music Historian; Pianist. Educ: MusB, Oberlin Coll., 1964; PhD, Univ. of Ill., Urbana-Champaign, 1972. Career: Assoc. Prof., York Univ., 1977-; Asst. Prof., Univ. of Ill., Urbana, 1973-77; Asst. Prof., Western Ill. Univ., 1969-73. Contbr. to: Grove's Dict., 6th ed.; Musical Quarterly; Ethnomusicology; Colelge Music Symposium; Asian Music; Yearbook of the Int. Folk Music Coun.; Eight Urban Musical Cultures, 1978; Report of the 12th Congress of the IMS. Mbrships: Soc. for Ethnomusicol. (Coun., 1971-73, 1979-81); Int. Folk Music Counc.; Int. Musicol. Soc.; Am. Musicol. Soc; Soc. for Asian Music; Can. Assn. of Univ. Schls. of Music. Address: York Univ., 4700 Keele St., Downsview, Ont., Can. M3J 1P3.

BLUME, Helmut, b. 12 Apr. 1914, Berlin, Germany. Professor; Pianist; Broadcaster. Educ: grad., Staatliche Akademische Hochschule für Musik, Berlin, 1938. m. Ljerka Putić. Debut: Berlin, 1926. Career: Dean, fac. of music, McGill Univ., 1963-76; now Prof. Emeritus, ibid.; broadcaster (radio & TV) for CBC, 1944-63. Recording: Form in Song, 1960. Contbr. to: CBC's Music To See (TV), Story of Music, Opera Stars & Stories, Int. Concert, etc. (radio), 1950-6 J. Mbrships: Can. Music Coun.; Can. Assn. of Univ. Schls. of Music. Hons: 1st Award, 22nd Am. Exhibition of Educ. Radio/TV progs., Ohio State Univ., 1958; FRCA, 1976; Can. Centennial Medal, 1976; Prof. Emeritus, McGill Univ., 1979. Address: 20 Windsor Ave., Westmount, Que. H3Y 2L6, Can. 2.

BLUNDELL, William Thomas, b. 24 Apr. 1900, Halewood, Lancs., UK. Orchestral Musician (Flute; Piccolo; Alto Flute); Musicologist; Arranger. Now Retired. Educ: Pvt. & Military Musical Educ. m. Isobel Roberts Temple, 1 s. Career: Prin. Flute, Folkestone Municipal Orch.; Mbr., SNO; Mbr., BBC Symph. Orch.; First Broadcast as Flute Soloist. Manchester, 1933; Catalogue Ed., BBC Music Lib., 1953-65. Publs: Ed., BBC Ctrl. Music Lib. Catalogues, 7 Volumes, 1965-67. Hobbies: Chess; Philately. Address: 16 Coleherne Mews, London SW10 9EA, UK. 3.

BLY, Randi Jean, b. 7 Apr. 1952, Bklyn., NY, USA. Professional Flutist & Piccoloist. Educ: Bmus, Shenandoah Conserv. of Music, Winchester, Va.; Madison Coll., Harrisonburg, Va. m. Carl Anthony Bly. Career incls: Soloist, Shenandoah Conserv. Orch. & Wind Ensemble, 1970-74; The Richmond Symph., Va., 1972-; The Richmond Ballet Orch. 1974-; Richmond Sinfonia, 1974-; Richmond Woodwind Quintet, 1975-; Richmond Civic Opera, 1975-; Instructor of Flute, Univ. of Richmond 1974-. Mbrships: Am. Symph. Orch. League; Am. Fedn. of Musicians; Sigma Alpha Iota. Hons. incl: Woodwind Level Winner, Collegiate Artist Competition, Southern Div., Music Tchrs. Nat. Assn., 1976. Hobbies incl: Horseback riding. Address: 143B Pemberton Rd., Richmond, VA 23233, USA.

BLYTH, Alan, b. 27 July 1929, London, UK. Music Critic & Editor. Educ: MA, Oxford Univ. m. Ursula Zumloh. Career: Contbr. as Critic, The Times, 1963-; Assoc. Ed., Opera, 1967-; Music Ed., Ency. Britannica, 1971-76. Publs: The Enjoyment of Opera, 1969; Colin Davis, A Short Biography, 1969; Janet Baker, A Short Biography, 1972. Contbr. to: The Gramophone; Musical Times; Musical America; BBC; The Listener. Mbrships: Cricics' Circle. Hobbies: Gardening; Wine; Collecting 78 rpm Vocal Records. Address: 11 Boundary Rd., London NW8 0HE, UK. 3.

BLYTON, Carey, b. 14 Mar. 1932, Beckenham, Kent, UK. Composer/Arranger; Music Editor; Lecturer. Educ: Univ. Coll., London Univ.; TCM 1953-57, AMusTC, LTCL (TTD), FTCL (Comp.); Bmus (London) Royal Danish Acad. of Music, Copenhagen, 1957-58. m. Mary Josephine Blyton, (Mills), 2 s. Career: Music Ed., Mills Music Ltd., 1958-63; Freelance Comp./Arranger., 1963-; Mbr. Professional Staff, TCM, 1963-73; Music Ed., Faber Music Ltd., 1964-74 (Ed., work of Benjamin Britten, 1964-70); Prof. of Comp. for Films, TV & Radio, GSM 1972-. Compositions: (publd.) Num. Orchl. & Instrumental Works inclng. Cinque Port, The Hobbit, On Holiday; music for Solo Guitar; num. Vocal works inclng. Carols, Madrigals, Children's Songs; (Recorded) Num. works, mainly for Wind or Chamber Ensemble; incid. music for TV plays & documentary films. Publs: Faber Book of Nursery Songs (w. D Mitchell); Bananas in Pyjamas. Contbr. to num. profl. jrnls. Mbrships incl: Performing Right Soc.; Mechanical-Copyright Protection Soc.; CGGB; BAFTA. Hons: Sir G. Bantock Prize for Comp., TCM, 1954, Sir W. Churchill Endowment Fund Scholarship, 1957. Hobbies: Reading; Fishing; Keeping Tropical Fish. Mgmt: Frazer-Skemp Mgmt., Ltd. Address: Hawthornden, 55 Goldsel Rd., Swanley, Kent BR8 8HA. 3, 23.

BOAL, Dean, b. 20 Oct. 1931, Longmont, Colo., USA. Pianist; Music Administrator. Educ: BMus; BME; M Mus; Doct. Musical Arts. m. Ellen TeSelle, 2 s. Career: Pres., Community Assn. Schls. for the Arts, St. Louis; St. Louis Conserv.; Formerly Chmn., Music Dept., State Univ. Coll., Fredonia, NY; Prof., Piano; Dean & Pianist, Peabody Conserv. Music, Balt.; Bradley Univ.; Hastings Coll.; Concertized, solo recitals, chmbr. music & orchs.; Duo recitals w. cellist wife; Dir., pilot study on electropiano lab., featured in Time Mag., 1 Nov. 1968. Publs: Concepts & Skills for the Pianio Book I, 1969, Book II, 1970. Contbr. to profl. jrnls. Mbrships. incl: Pi Kappa Lambda; Patron, Mu Phi Epsilon. Hobbies incl: Swimming; Chess. Address: 7445 Oxford Dr., St. Louis, MO 63105, USA.

BOATENG, Stephen Geoffrey, b. 1 Oct. 1926, Adukrom Akuapim, Gold Coast. Music Educator. Educ: BMus, Leningrad Stae Conserv., USSR; LTCL, Trinity Coll. of Music, UK. Career incl: Tchr. of Harmony, Counterpoint, Orchestration & Choral Condng.; Sev. appearances as Cond., Ghana TV. Compositions: 10 Choral Works broadcast on Ghana Radio). publ; Rudiments of Music, Grade 1, 1972. Mbrship: Local Sec., Int. Music Coun. Hobby: Gardening. Address: Arts Coun. of Ghana, PO Box 2738, Accra, Ghana.

BOBBE, Jerry Alan, b. 9 Mar. 1949, Chicago, Ill., USA. Musician (Violoncello). Educ: Roosevelt Univ., Chgo., Ill.; Chgo. Musical. Coll., ibid. Debut: Orchestra Hall, Chgo. Ill., 1970. Career: Solo performance w. Chgo. Civic Orch. at Orchestra Hall, Chgo., also Prin. Cello, 1968-70; TV appearances WGN-TV, Chgo., Ill.; Assoc. Prin. Cello, Milwaukee Symph. Orch., Milwaukee Wis., 1971-72; Prin. Cello, Fla. Gulf Coast Symph. Orch., Fla., 1972-. Mbrships: Am. Fed. of Musicians, Chgo., Ill. & Tampa, Fla. Hons: Three scholarships, Chgo. Musical Coll., Roosevelt Univ., Chgo., Ill.; Scholarship, Chgo. Symph. Orch.; Winner, Chgo. Symph. String Comp. Hobbies: Golf; Coin Collecting. Address: 1525 W. 187th St., Homewood, IL 60430, USA.

BOCKMANN, Alfred, b. 10 Jan. 1905, Essen, W Germany. Pianist; Comp. Prof. Educ: Conserv.; Music Acad. Cologne. Debut: Essen, 1924. Career: 1938/1952 Tchr. Essen; since 1952 Prof. comp. Franz Liszt Acad. Weimar; var. Radio recordings of piano comps., ballet suites and orch. music. Comp. incl: Choir works; piano music; music for folkloric instruments; Sinfonietta for large orch.; Ballet music; 2 Operas. Hons: Prof., 1962. Address: Helmholzstr. 29, 53, Weimar/Thür., DDR.

BODART, Eugen, b. 8 Oct. 1905, Kassel, W. Germany. Composer; conductor. Educ: Acad. of Music, Leipzig; studied w. Emil Nicolaus von Reznicek, Paul Graener. m. Elisabeth Jacob, 1 c. Career: Cond., Radio Kassel, 1926-29; Landestheater Altenburg, Thüringen, 1932-33; 2nd Cond., Nat. Theater, Weimar, 1933-35; 1st Cond., Opera, Köln, 1935-39; Generalintendant, Generalmusikdirektor Altenburg/Thüringen, 1939-43; Generalmusikdirektor, Ldr.,

Acad. Concerts, Mannheim, 1942-45; Fndr., Kurpfalzisches Kammerorchester; Generalmusikdirektor, Pfalzoper Kaiserslautern, 1956-. Compositions incl: operas Hirtenlegende, Der abtrunnige Zar, Spanische Nacht, Der leichtsinnige Her Bandolin, Sarabande, Kleiner Irrtum; works for orch.; solo, piano Concerti; arr. over 80 works of the Mannheimer Schule; Arr. D.v. Dittersdort, Concerto for Oboe, D'amore & orch. Recordings: Spanische Nacht (Electrola). Mbr. Rauberhohle, Mannheim. Hobbies: Bibliophile; Antique Procelain. Address: 8082 Grafrath/Amper, Kirchweg 28, German Fed. Repub. 19.

BODEN, Daphne, b. 28 Jan. 1942, Woking, UK. Harpist. Educ: ARCM Perf.'s Dip.; premier Prix de Harpe, Royal Conserv. of Music, Brussels, Belgium. m. Gordon Turner (dec.) Debut: London, 1969. Career: num. recitals & lecture-recitals, UK & Europe; radio & TV broadcasts; apps. w. major Brit. orchs.; Vis. Tchr., RCM Jr. Dept. Recordings: Harp Recital, VIP Records. Contbr. to: Making Music. Mbr., ISM. Hons. incl: Jack Morrison Harp Prize, 1966. Hobby; Horseback riding. Mgmt: Ibbs & Tillett, 124 Wigmore St., London W1, UK. Address: 82 Addison Rd., London W14 8ED, UK.

BODENSTEIN, Nancy Marie, b. 21 Mar. 1940, Milwaukee, Wis., USA. Teacher & Performer. Educ: B Mus, Lawrence Coll., 1962; MMus, New Engl. Conserv. of Music, 1964; DMusA, Boston Univ., 1975. Appts: Boston Women's Symph., 1965; Class Piano Instr., Newton (Mass.) Elem. Schls., 1964-69; Tchng. Fellowship, Boston Univ., 1969-71; Asst. Prof., Salem State Coll., 1971-; perfs., workshops & lectures in histl. & Polish dance, orch. & chmbr. musician, piano, harpsichord & all clarinets; Choreographer for stage prods. Contbr. to var. educl. projs., handbooks, etc. Mbrships incl: Asst. Dir., Cambridge Ct. Dancers; Bd. of Dirs., 1974-77, New Engl. Conserv. of Music Alumni Assn ; Krakowiak Polish Dancers; N Shore Phil. Orch. Recip. acad. hons. Address: Salem State Coll., Salem, MA 01970, USA.

BODER, Gerd Wilhelm Karl, b. 13 Juen, 1933, Saarbrücken, Germany. Composer; Pianist; Conductor. Educ: High Schl. for Music, Saarbrücken; studied Comp., Nat. Conserv., Paris, France. Career: Msuic Tchrs., Tchrs. Sem., Lebach, 1959-61; Freelance Comp., 1961-75; Music Tchr., Homburg/Saar, 1975-. Comp. incl: Woodwind Trio, op.- 1 9 Istanti for str. quartet; 2nd Horn Quartet; Brühler Concerto; Concerto for 2 Pianos & Orch.; Concertino for Trumpet, Piano, Percussion & Strings; Contornos virtuosos for Flute & Str. Orch. op. 51. Recordings for German radio stations, also radios Hilversum, Paris, Lausanne & Brussels. Mbr., profl. assns. Hons. Villa Massino Rome, 1961; Comp. Prizes, Stuttgart, 1963, 68; Comp. Prize, Monaco, 1969; Marler Comp. Prize, 1971. Kunstpreis de Saarlandes, 1976. Address: z. Zt. Saarbrüken, Gersweilerstrasse 9, German Fed. Repub.

BODLEY, Seoirse, b. 4 Apr. 1933, Dublin, Ireland. Composer; Statutory Lecturer in Music; Conductor. Educ: Royal Irish Acad. of Music; Univ. Coll., Dublin; Staatliche Hochschule für Musik, Stuttgart; DMus.; LTCL. m. Olive Murphy, 3 c. Career: Statutory Lectr. in Music, Univ. Coll., Dublin. Comps: Orchl., Vocal, Chmbr. Music. Recordings incl: Symphony for Chamber Orchestra; Music for Strings; String Quartet; Prelude, Toccata & Epilogue; Three Satires; Mass of Life. Contbr. to profl. jrnls; Critical introductions to reprints of The Irish & Highland Harps & Grattan Flood (R B Armstrongg); A History of Irish Music (Irish Univ. Press. Mbrships. incl: Chmn., Dublin Fest. of 20th Century Music; Assn. of Irish Comps.; Chmn., Folk Music Soc. of Ireland. Hons: Macaulary Fellowship in Musical Comp., 1962. Address: 17 Villiers Rd., Dublin 6. Ireland.

BODO, Arpad, b. 8 Mar. 1942, Szeged, Hungary. Pianist; Piano Teacher. Educ: Dips., Franz Liszt Acad. of Music, Budapest, 1966. m. Eva Layber. Debut: Franz Liszt Acad. of Music, 1966. Career: Many radio apps. on Hungarian Broadcasting Corp. as soloist & accomp.; Recitals, German Dem. Repub., Czechoslovakia & Poland; Participant, Int. Leeds Pianoforte Competition, 1969. Mbrships: Liszt Soc. of London; Sec., Pecs-Szekszart Sect., Hungarian Liszt Soc. Hobbies: Nature; Lit.; Tennis; Philos. Address: 7601 Pecs, PF 144, Hungary. 28, 30.

BODY, John (Jack) Stanley, b. 10 Oct. 1944, Te Aroha, NZ. Composer. Educ: MMus (Auckland). Comps: Turtle Time for voice & 4 instruments; 4 Stabiles, for piano; 23 Pages, for orch.; Kryptophones, electronic (recorded); Music Dari Jalan, electronic (recorded); Marvel Not Joseph, for choir (recorded). Mbrships: Australasian Performing Right Assn.; Comps. Assn. of NZ. Hons: Prix de Bourges, for electro-acoustic music, 1976. Hobbies: Field recording, esp. traditional music. Address: 92 Stanley Ave., Te Aroha, NZ.

BOEHM, Jan Szczepan, b. 21 Dec. 1929, Pedagogical Academy Teacher. Educ: Grad., State HS of Music, Warsaw, 1955. m. Hildegarda Nowak, 2 d. Career: Tchr., Coll. of Music, Olsztyn, 155-. Pedagogical Acad., Olsztyn, 1974-; Music Reviewer, Olsztyn newspapers, 1955-68. Publs. incl: Feliks Nowowiejski, 1968. Bibliografia organow fromborskich, 1969; Bibliografia utworow muzycznych o tematyce Kopernikowskiej Skomponowanych do 1974, 1975. Podstawowe formy ksztaltowania myslenia muzycznego, 1975. Mbrships: Musicol. Sect., Polish Comps. Assn.; Polish Histl. Assn. Recip., Gold Order of Merit, 1975. Hobbies: Picture Postcads & stamps on Musical Themes; Cycling. Address: al. Wojska Polskiego 74b/3, 10-290 Olsztyn, Poland.

BOEHM, Karl-Walter, b. 6 June 1938, Nürnberg, Germany. Helden tenor. Educ: w. Prof. Mangold, Berlin. Debut: Radames, Aida, Aachen 1969. Career: Apps., Argentina, Austria, Belgium, Brazil, France, Italy, Netherlands, Hungary, UK, Germany, USA. Recordings: Rienzi; Herod, Salome. Hobby: Yoga. Address: Haüs am Branich II, D6905 Schriesheim, German Fed. Repub.

BOEHM, Mary Louise, b. 25 July 1928, Sumner, Iowa, USA. Concert Pianist. Educ: BMus, Northwestern Univ., Evanston, Ill.; MMus, Univ. of Neb.; Special Student, New Schl. of Soc. Rsch., NYC; Pvte. study w. Robert Casadesus, Paris, France & w. Walter Gieseking, Conserv. of Saarbrücken, Germany. m. Kees Kooper. Debut: European-Paris; Am.-Chgo. & NYC. Career: Num. concerts in major cities in Am., Europe & S. Am.; Series of Radio Concert on Educl. Network; Coast-to-Coast TV broadcasts w. CBS & wkly. TV show, NYC; Fndr., Concert Artists Repertoire Grp. & Master Players of NY Recordings incl: David Diamond/R Palmer Quintets for Piano, Winds & Strings; Moscheles Concerto C Major/Kalkbrenner Fantasy Concerto for piano & violin, Johann Pixis, Concerto in E minor, Kalkbrenner; Amy Beach; Concert in C sharp minor; D.G. Mason, Aelude & Fugue for pinao & orch. Contbr. to Pan pipes as record reviewer. Mbrships: Sigma Alpha Iota; Pi Kappa Lambda; Nat. Music Coun. Hons. incl: Northwestern Univ. awards; Fulbright Travel Grant; Special Merit Award for Recording, 1973. Hobbies: Art; Geology. Mgmt.. Suite 609, Carnegie Hall, NY, NY, USA. Address: 210 Riverside Dr., NY, NY 10025, USA.

BOEHMER, Konrad, b. 24 May 1941, Berlin, Germany. Composer. Educ: PhD Musicol., Univ. of Cologne, 1966; studied Comp. w. Gottfried M Koenig until 1961. Debut: Paris, 1963. Career: At Electronic Music Studio, Radio Cologne, 1961-64; Sci. & Artistic Collaborator, Studio of Electronic Music, Univ. of Utrecht, 1966-68; Tchr. Music Theory, Music Sociol. & Comp., Royal Acad. of Music, The Hague; Cond., var. concerts of own works throughout Europe. Comps. incl: Variation (orch.), 1969, perfd., BBC; Potential (piano), 1963; Information (percussion & pianos), 1964-66; Aspekt (electronic), 1964-66 (also recorded): Jugend (16 voices, 12 instruments), 1966-67; Weg (music theatre), 1968; Vietnam Songs (voice & small orch.), 1972-73 (also recorded); Canciones del Camino (recorded). Lied wit de verte for soprano and orch; Adem (breath) for flute; Sestina for oboe. Publs: Zur Theorie der Offenen Form, 1967; Zwischen Reihe & Pop., 1970; Gehoord & Ongehoord, 1974. Contbr. to books, num. jrnls., Radio & TV progs. Mbrships: Bd., Dutch Author Rights Union BUMA; Pres., Dutch Union of Comps. Hons: Prize, Dutch Radio AVRO, 1966; Prize, 5th Biennale, Paris, 1967. Hobbies: Composing; Study of Social History of Music. Address: Singel 402, 101b AK, Amsterdam, Netherlands.

BOEHNLEIN, Frank, b. 2 Feb. 1945, Bedford, Ohio, USA. Pianist; Composer; Music Educator. Educ: B Mus, Rollins Coll.; MusD, Arts, Cleveland Inst. of Music & Case-Western Reserve Univ. m. Sherry Ingles Boehnlein. Career: Tchr., St. Mary of the Plains Coll., Dodge City, Kan.; Asst. Prof., Theory & Comp., Tex. Women's Univ., Denton, Tex. Compositions: Aftermath for 3 choirs, dancers & ensembles; Canto for Str. Quartet; Piano Sonata; Missa L'Homme Arme for a Capella 12 part choir. Mbrships: ASCAP; Cleveland Comps. Guild; Tex. Comps. League; Am. Soc. of Unv. Comps. Hons: Aid from Presser Fndn., 1963-67, Comps. Conf., 1970 & 73. Ford Fndn., 1971 & nat. Endowment for the Arts, 1973. Hobbies: ESP; Philos.; Dance. Address: P. O. Box 962, Denton, TX 76201, USA.

BOELEE, Bram, b. 5 Jan. 1927, Rotterdam, Netherlands. Pianist. Educ: Toonkunst Music Schl., Rotterdam; studied cond. & paino w. Eduard & Marinus Flipse; Proficiency Cert. & Nat. Dip., Amsterdam Conserv., w. Willem Andriessen, 1946-48; studied w. Lazare Lévy & Marguerite Long, Paris, France & Alfred Cortot, Lausanne, Switzerland. m. M-E L Meijers. Debut: w. Rotterdam Phil. Orch., Radio Hilversum, 1950. Career: Num. concert perf. w. all Dutch Orchs. & under major Dutch & foreign Conds.; Concerts in Holland, UK, Germany, Italy, Sweden & Denmark, 1968-69; app. in 1st pub. concert,

Doelen Concert Hall, Rotterdam; num. perfs. for Radio & TV. Netherlands & other European countries. Recordings: Chopin, 1964, 1965; Saint-Saens (2 pianos & orch.). records w. Choirs; record of Piano-Duet. Contbr. var. jrnls. Mbr., Netherlands Music Coun. Hons: Scholarship, French Govt.; Dr. Julius Röntgen Prize, Amsterdam, 1950; Prize Winner, Int. Music Contest, Geneva, 1951, 1954. Hobby: Listening to.& Making Music. Address: Weidebloemestraat 22, Berkenwoude z.h., Netherlands.

BOER, Nico, b. 6 Dec. 1938, Haarlem, Netherlands. Opera & Concert Tenor. Educ: studied w. Coby Riemersma & Ruth Horna, Amsterdam Conserv.; studied w. Johannes den Hertog, opera studio for young soloists, Netherlands Opera Co., 3 yrs. m. Rini Frijn, 2 s. Debut: as Ferrando, Cosi Fan Tutte, Amsterdam. Career: opera apps. w. Netherlands Opera, 1970-, w. Royal Flemish Opera, Antwerp, 1975, also many concert, oratorio, operetta, & TV apps. Roles incl: Mozart, Tamino (Magic Flute), Basilio & Curizio (Marriage of Figaro), Belmonte & Pedrillo (Abduction from the Seraglio), Don Ottavio (Don Giovanni); Beethoven, Jacquino (Fidelio); Bizet, Don José (Carmen); Henze, Lord Barrat (Der Junge Lord); Weber, Max (Der Freischütz). Mbr., Royal Netherlands Musical Artists Soc. (KNTV). Mgmt: Artists Rep. Will. J. T Visser, 1e Hugo de Grootstraat, 20 Amsterdam, Netherlands. Address: Schoenerstraat 51, Zaandam, Netherlands.

BOERINGER, James, b. 4 Mar. 1930, Pittsburgh, Pa., USA. Organist; Composer; Writer. Educ: Dr. of Sacred Music, Union Theological Seminary Schl. of Sacred Music, NY; MA, Columbia Univ.; BA, Coll. of Wooster, Ohio. m. Grace Nocera, 3 d., 1 s. Career incl: Asst. Prof., Okla. Baptist Univ., Shawnee, 1962-64; Assoc. Prof., Susquehanna Univ., Selinsgrove, Pa., 1964-77; Prof., ibid., 1977-; Chmn., Music Dept., ibid., 1978-; Publs. incl: num. eds. of works by baroque & classical comps.; eds. of early Am. music esp. humn tunes; complete works of John Stanley, Vol. 1. Contbr. to num. profl. periodicals & jrnls. Hons. incl: Philips Distinguished Visitor, Haverford Coll., Pa. Mbrships: former nat. off., Am. Guild of Organists, Organ Historical Soc.; Fndr., Int. Soc. for Organ History & Preservation. Address: RD1, Box 380, Selingsgrove, PA 17870, USA.

BOETTICHER, Wolfgang, b. 9 Aug. 1914, Bad Ems, Germany. Musicologist; Pianist; Organist. Educ: PhD, Univ. of Berlin, 1939; PhD habil, ibid., 1943; Prof., 1955. Career: Prof. of History of Music & Dir., Inst. of Musicol., Univ. of Göttingen. num. scientific publs. in German, Englsh, French, Slovene, Polish & Italian (see bibliography in Festschrift Wolfgang Boetticher, 1974). Mbrships: Dolmetsch Soc.; Gesellschaft für Musikforchung, etc. Hons: (w. Hans Pfitzner) Schumann Prize, Zwickau, 1942. Address: Dahlmannstr. 10, 34 Göttingen, German Fed. Repub.

BOEYKENS, Walter, b. 6 Jan. 1938, Gornem, Antwerp, Belgium. Professor; Clarinettist. Educ: Conserv. of Music, Brussels. m. Gerda Van Gils, 2 d., 1 s. Debut: 1956. Career incl: Prof., Conservatorium, Antwerp; Prof., Academie d'Eté, Nice, France; solo clarinettist, Brussels Radio; gave first perf. of Domaines, by Boulez, Brussels, 1969. Recordings: works by Mozart, Weber, Boulez, Stravinsky, Messiaen, Girtelinek etc. Mbrships: 51 Club Int. Hobby: conducting symphonic bands. Address: Luipegem 19, 2680 Bornem, Belgium.

BOGAJEWICZ, Ireneusz, b. 2 Mar. 1921, Pniewy, Poland Violinist; Composer. Educ: MA, Music Acd., Poznan, Poland. m. Hlelena Bogajewicz, 2 c. Career: Mbr., Symph. Orch., Poznań; Mbr., Nat. Philharmonie, Warsaw; Concert Master, Orch. Nat. Opera, ibid; Soloist, Polish Radio & TV; Soloist in Estrada Kameralna by Warsaw Nat. Philharmonie; Fndr., Dir., & Soloist, Warsaw Strings Orch.; Mbr., Montreal Symph. Orch., 1965-; Mbr., McGill Chmbr. Orch., Montreal; TV & Radio Soloist, Can. Recordings: His own comps., (Pop) in Polskie Nagrania, Poland. Mbrships: Am. Fedn. of Musicians; Zaix, (Comps. Club, Poland). Recip., 3rd Prize, Polish Music Schls. Bach Competition, Poznań, 1950. Address: 1770 Tillemont St., Brossard, PQ, Canada.

BOGDANY-POPIEL, Wanda, b. 25 May 1928, Tranowskie Góry, Poland. Librarian; Musicologist. Educ: Licenciée es Sciences (musicol). m. Jerzy Popiel. Career: Hd., Music Dept., Nat. Lib. of Warsaw. Publs: in the series, La Bibliographie des Périodiques Polonais Musicaux (Bibliografia Polskich Czasopism Muzycznych), vol. 3, Ruch Muzyczny 1857-62, 1957; vol. 4. Gazeta Muzyczna i Teatralna 1865-66, Przeglad Muzyczny 1877, 1955; vol. 12, Muzyka Polska 1934-39, 1967; vol. 15, Muzyka 1950-55, 1977. Mbr., Musicol. Sect. Address: ul. Podleśna 48 m. 23, 01673 Warsaw, Poland. ▪

BOGGIO, Shelby Richard, b. 22 Feb. 1945, NYC, USA. College Professor; Flautist. Educ: BS, Mannes Coll. Music; MMus, Syracuse Univ.; MusAD, Boston Univ. m. Kathleen Dietin Boggio, 1 s. Career: Prin. Flautist, Jamaica Symph. Orch., Amsterdam Symph., Utica Symph., Rome Civ. Band, Utica Civ. Band, Gilbert & Sullivan Opera Co. NY & Balalaika Symph. NY. Mbrships: MENC; Bach Soc.; Nat. Flute Assn.; Nat. Assn. Coll. Wind & Percussion Instructors; Coll. Music Soc.; NY State Schl. Music Assn. Hobbies: Skiing; Bicycling; Tennis; Gourmet Cooking; Trap Shooting. Address: 121 Adena Rd., W. Newton, MA 02165, USA.

BOGGS, Jon William, b. 27 Sept. 1940, S Bend, Ind., USA. Trumpet Player; Professor. Educ: BME, Ind. Univ.; MMus, Univ. Mich.; PhD, ibid. m. Carla T, 1 s., 1 d. Career: 1-hr. jazz progs., WMFS-WMFT TV, Milwaukee, Wis., Mar. 1971 & Mar. 1972; Weekly jazz prog., WUWM Radio, Milwaukee, winter 1971. Recordings: UWM Jazz Ensemble Live Ed., Encyclopedia of Band Instruction. Publ: Music Instruction in Detroit from 1874-1929, 1970. Contbr. to: S. Carolina Musician; Instrumentalist; Vermont Music Educator; Wis. Schl. Musician; NAJE Educator; Assoc. Prof. of Music, Converse Coll., Spartanburg, SC. Mbrships: MENC; Nat. Assn. Jazz Educators; Pi Kappa Lambda. Hobbies: Jazz; Fishing. Address: Converse Coll., Spartanburg, SC 29301, USA.

BOGGS, Martha Daniel, b. 4 July 1928, Abilene, Tx., USA. Clarinettist; Educator. Educ: Bmus, 1948; MMus, 1961; Advanced grad. study in musical., 1970-74. m. A D Boggs, 2 s., 1 d. Career: Asst. Prof. in Woodwind & Music Lit., Hardin-Simmons Univ., 1961-; prin. Clarinet, Abilene Phil. Mbrships: Sigma Alpha Iota; Int. Clarinet Soc.; Am. Musicol. Soc. Hobby: Genealogy. Address: 2654 Garfield Ave., Abilene, TX., USA. 5, 7, 29.

BOGIANCKINO, Massimo, b. 10 Nov. 1922, Rome, Italy. Concert Pianist; Musicologist; Opera Director. Educ: MA, Conserv. & Acad. of St. Cecilia, Rome; Studied w. A Caslla, Rome & A Crtot, Normal Schl. of Music, Paris. m. Judith Matthias. Career incls: Prof. of Hist. & Aesthetics of Music, Conserv. of St. Cecilia, Rome, 1957-67; Ed., Encyclopaedia dello Spettacolo, 1957-62; Artistic Dir., Roman Phil. Acad., 1960-63; Artistic Dir., Teatro dell'Opera, Rome, 1963-67; Prof., Hist. of Music, Univ. Perugia, Italy 1968-; Dir., Festival of Two Worlds, Spoleto, 1968-71; Dir. of Concert Progs., Acad. of St. Cecilia, Rome, 1971; Artistic Dir., Teatro alla Scala, Milan, 1972-75; Gen. Mgr., Teatro Communale Maggio Musicale Fiorentino, Florence, 1975-. Contbr. of essays to profl. jrnls. etc. Address: Via Solferino 15, Florence, Italy.

BOGIN, Abba, b. 24 Nov. 1935, NYC, USA. Pianist; Conductor. Educ: piano studies w. Isabella Vengerova, orch. w. Samuel Barber & Gian-Carlo Menotti, chmbr. music w. Wm. Primrose & Gregor Piatigorsky; Dip., Curtis Inst. of Music, Phila., Pa.; cond. studies w. Pierre Monteux, L'Ecole Monteux, Hancock, Maine. m. Masako Yanagita, 2 c. from previous marriage. Debut: Town Hall, NYC, 1947. Concerts in USA, Canada, Mex., Europe, Far East as Pianist; Soloist w. major symph. orchs. inclng. NY Phil.; Phila., Chgo., San Fran., Houston, Nat. Buffalo Symph. Orchs., etc.; Soloist, Bell Telephone Hour (USA) & Coca-Cola Hour (Mex.); appearances as Cond. w. Am. Symph. Orch., Boston Symph. Orch. Pops. Wiesbaden (Germany), Lake George Opera, NY City Ctr. Light Opera, CBS Symph., etc.; Cond. & Musical Dir. of 24 Broadway Musical Theatre prodns. inclng. 'Most Happy Fella', 'How to Succeed in Business Without Really Trying,', etc. Recordings incl: Complete Sonatas for Cello & Piano, Beethoven & Brahms (w. Janos Starker, Cellist); Cond., Cast albums of Broadway musicals 'Greenwillow' & 'Mrs. Patterson'. Mbr., var. profl. orgs. & Cons. to NY State Coun. on the Arts Hons incl: Naumburg Award, 1947; YM-YWHA, NYC Award, 1948. Mgmt: Raymond Weiss Artists Mgmt., NYC, NY. Address: 838 West End Ave., NY, NY 10025, USA.

BOGUSLAWSKI, Edward, b. 22 Sept. 1940, Chorzów, Poland. Composer; Teacher. Educ: State Coll. of Music, Katowice; State Acad. of Music, Katowice; BA, 1964; Dip. in comp., 1966. m. Barbara Sliwakowska, 2 c. Debut: Warsaw, 1964. Career: Tchr. of comp. & music theory, State Acad. of Music, Katowice. Comps: Apokalipsis; Signals; Intonazione II; Canti; oboe concerto; Musica per Ensemble MW-2; Pictures, for solo flute; Metamorphoses; Per Pianoforte; The Devel's Sonata (opera). Mbrships: Assn. of Polish Comps.; Int. Lib. of Contemporary Music, Fontainebleau, France. Hons: 1st prize, competition, 1966; 2nd prize, Malawski competition, 1970; 1st prize, Polish competition for comps., 1975; 2nd prize, Min. of Culture & Arts, 1975; Katowice District prize, 1979. Hobby: Painting. Address: Gajowa 12/9, 41500 Chorzów, Poland.

BOHAN, Edmund, b. Christchurch, NZ. Tenor Singer. Educ: MA, Univ. of Canterbury, NZ, 1960. m. Gillian Margaret Neason, 1 setps., 1 d. Career: Concerts, opera & broadcasting, NZ & Aust., 1958-63; Uk, 1964-, also in Ireland, on continent; Britten's War Requiem, Rio de Janiero; in Anvil film of Barber of Seville sang Count Almaviva, 1974. Recordings: St. Matthew Passion Excerpts; A Gilbert & Sullivan Spectacular. Publs: The Writ of Green Wax, 1970; The Buckler, 1972 (children's histl. novels). Contbr. to jrnls. & encys. Mbrships: ISM; Equity. Hobbies: Reading; Writing; Gardening. Address: 124 Faraday Rd., Wimbledon, London SW19 8PB, UK.

BOHANA, Roy, b. 3 June 1938, Caernarfon, UK. Music Director; Conductor. Educ: BMus, BA (celtic studies), Univ. of Wales. m. Mina Bancheva, 1 d. Career: Music Dir., Welsh Arts Coun., 1961-; Cond., Welsh Nat. Choir, Investiture of HRH The Prince of Wales, 1969; Fndr.-Cond., Cardiff Polyphonic Choir, 1964-75; touring USA & Can., 1961, 67, 69, 73, Japan, 1970; Guest Cond., var. orchs. & choirs inclng. Romanian Madrigal Choir, Bucharest, 1968, 73, Fest. of Male Voices, London, 1969, 70, 72, 74; concerts, broadcasts, TV apps., w. var. UK orchs.; Adjudicator, var. events inclng. Llangollen Int. Fest., 1964-, Royal Nat. Eisteddfod of Wales, 1965-. Has recorded for EMI & Cambrian Recordings. Ed: Composers of Wales series. Contbr. to Artists in Wales, 1974. Mbrships. incl: Music Panel, Brit. Coun., 1974-; Coun., ISM, 1972-. Recip. MBE, 1974. Hobbies: Philately; Photography; Gastronomy. Address: 5 Minehead Ave., Sully, Penarth, S. Glamorgan, UK.

BOHLIN, Folke, b. 21 Sept. 1931, Uppsala, Sweden. Senior Lecturer in Musicology & Head of the Musicological Department, Lund University; 1971-; Conductor, Lunds studentsangförening (Lund University Male Chorus) 1972-. Educ: M. Theol., 1960; PhD., Uppsala Univ., 1970. m. Eva Svanholm, 4 children. Publs: Liturgisk sang i Svenska Kyrkan, 1697-1897, 1970; Olaus Ericis sangbok (ed.), 1967; Johan Lindells Masson kortelingen Abo 1784 (ed.), 1968; Melodier till julepistoln i svensk tradition, 1970. Contbr. to: Svensk tidskrift för musikforskning; Jahrbuch für Hymnologie und Liturgik; Ed., Arsboken Svenskt gudstjänstliv (annual). Address: Kvarnkroken 4, S-222 47 Lund, Sweden.

BÖHM, Karl, b. 28 Aug. 1894, Austria. Conductor. Educ: Karl Franzens Univ., Graz; studied w. Eusebius Mandyczewski, Vienna. Career: Cond., Graz City Theatre, 1917-21. Munich State Opera, 1921-27, Vienna Phil. Orch., 1933-, & w. many other noted orchs. inclng. Berlin & NY Phil. Orchs.; Gen. Music Dir., Darmstadt, 1927-31, Hamburg, 1931-33; Dir., Dresden State Opera, 1932-42, Vienna State Opera, 1943-45, 54-56; Guest Cond. at many opera houses, Europe & USA; Cond. at many noted fests. Many recordings. Hons. Mbr: Mozarteum, Salzburg; Music Acad., Graz, Music Soc. of Steiermark, Soc. for Music Theatre, Vienna; Concerthouse Soc., Vienna; Cultural Circle, Vienna; German Opera, Berlin; Vienna Phil. Orch. Recip. num. awards, & hons. inclng: Hon. Senator, Karl-Franzens Univ.; Great Badge of Hon. in Silver; Great Disting. Serv. Cross in Gold w. Star; etc. 16.

BÖHME, Baldur, b. 7 Feb. 1932, Weimar, Germany. Composer; Violin Teacher. Educ: pvte. study of piano, violin & comp.; studied violin & comp., Thuer. Landeskonservatorium; Dip., Franz Liszt Coll., Weimar. m. Bergliot Böhme, 2 s., 3 d. Debut: Weimar, 1947. Career: 2nd Concert Master, Gewandhaus, Leipzig, 1952; 1st Violin, State Opera, Berlin, 1953-68; Comp., also concerts w. piano trio, 1958-66; Violin Tchr., Franz Liszt Music Coll., Weimar 1966-. Num. comps. inclng: Small Fantasie for violin & piano; symphs.; Im Morgenlich (3 songs, text by Fritz Goehme); piano works for children; Fantasy piece for sole violin; 6 songs after poems from Goethe; Divertimentos for Chmbr. orch.; etc. Mbr., Union for German Comps. & Musicols. Address: Erfurterstr. 56, 53 Weimar, German Dem. Repub.

BÖHME, Erdmann Werner, b. 8 Dec. 1906, Salzwedel (Altmark), Germany. Press Correspondent. Educ: studied musicol., Univ. of Freigburg in Br. & Greifswal; Dr. phil., 1931; studied piano, trumpet, organ. m. Hildegrad Schroeder. Career: Cond., Lüneburg Symph. Orch. Comps: song settings & piano accomps. Publs: many musical eds. & articles on musicol. topics. Contbr. to: Deutsche Musikforschung; Der Convent; etc. Mbrships: Soc. for Music Rsch., Kassel-Wilhelmshohe; Humboldt Soc. for Musicol., Art & Educ. Hobby: Sport; Water painting; Piano; Elec. Organ. Address: Ahornweg 6, D-5307 Wachtberg-Niederbachem über Bonn-Bad Godesberg 1, German Fed. Repub.

BÖHMELT, Harald, b. 23 Oct. 1900, Halle, Germany. Composer; Conductor. Educ: Univ. of Halle. m. Ursula, 2 c. Career: Cond. & Dir., Symph. Orch. for Opera, until 1932; Film Comp., 1932-. Comps: More than 75 for Films; 2 works for Theatre; comp., music for musical, Ein Mann Kommt in die Stadt; Der Zanberer, A Musical Comedy, Vienna 1940. Hobbies: Books; Antiques. Address: Lamontstr. 13, 8 Munich 80, German Fed. Repub.

BOHN, Elsebeth, b. 16 Oct. 1931, Copenhagen, Denmark. Violinist. Educ: Dip., Royal Acad. of Music, Copenhagen; studied w. Prof. Max Rostal, Will. Pleeth, m. Gregers Gamborg, (Pianist). Debut: Copenhagen, 1953. Career: Former Mbr., Tivoli Symph.; Radio Pers. w. husband; Chmbr. Music, Recitals, throughout Denmark, Soloist, var. orch.'s 1st Violin, Danish State Radio Orch. Recordings: w. husband; Niels Viggo Bentzon, Capricietta & Square Root of Three, d'Ambrosio, Canonetta; Poul London, Epsidoe; Albeniz, Tango. Recip. Travelling Aid, Danish State Radio. Address: 4 Lipkesgade, 2100 Copenhagen. Denmark.

BOILES, Charles Lafayette, b. 15 June 1932, Ada, Okla., USA. Ethnomusicologist. Educ: BS, Juillard Schl. of Music; PhD, Tulane Univ. m. Maria Cristina Vázquez Boilès, 2 d. Career: Ethnomusicologist, Instituto de Antropologia, Universidad Veracruzana, Jalapa, Veracruz, Mexico; Assoc. Prof. of Folklore & Ethnomusicol., Ind. Univ., Bloomington, USA. Author, Man. Magic, & Musical Occasions, 1975. Contbr. to: La Palabra y el Hombre; Yearbook for Inter-Am. Musical Rsch.; Jrnl. of Soc. for Ethnomusicol.; Musique en jeu; Versus. Mbrships: Book Review Ed., Soc. for Ethnomusicol., 1970-72; Coun., 1974-77. Hons. incl: Jaap Kunst Prize, Soc. for Ethnomusicol., 1966. Hobby: Int. cuisine. Address: Box 36, Ada, OK 74820, USA.

BOJANOWSKI, Jerzy, b. 29 Aug. 1936, Chorzow, Poland. Manager; Jazz Writer; Concert Organizer. Educ: MS (aircraft engrng.). Warsaw Inst. of Techno.; pvte. study of piano & guitar. m. Ewa, 1 s. Career: Fndr. Stodola traditional jazz club; Author, jazz progs. on Polish Radio & biog. notes in jazz concert progs.; Chief Organizer, Warsaw Old Jazz Meeting. Contbr. to: Jazz Forum. Mbrships: Gen. Bd., Polish Jazz Soc.; Warsaw Stodola Club. Hobby: Gliding. Address: Barcelonska 7 m 19, 02-762, Warsaw, Poland.

BOK, Josef, b. 15 Nov. 1890, Nechanice, Czechoslovakia. Flautist; Pianist; Composer. Educ: Instrument Conserv., Prague; Conserv. for Comps., Prague; Orch. Conds. Schl., Prague. 1 s. Career: Many Recitals as Flute Soloist & Pianist, USSR & Czechoslovakia; Mbr., Opera House Orch., Moscow, USSR; Soloist, Sergel Kusevickij Orch., Moscow, 1913-19; Mbr., Opera House Orch., Brno & Prof., State Conserv. of Brno. Czechoslovakia, 1919-39; Prof., State Conserv. of Music, Prague, 1939-; Prof., Musical Arts Acad., Prague, 1946-62. Compositions: 14 Virtuoso Cadences for Flute; Lyric Songs; Camer Music-String Trio; Str.-Quartet; Little Beer; Concerto for Trombone; Fade Leaves; Ostrava Miners. Publs: Big School for Flute Playing; Little School for Flute Playing; The Flute Origin & History. Mbrships: Protection Union of Comps.; Union of Comps. & Concert Artists. Hons: Deserving Artist, 1963. Address: Dobrovského 924, 250 82 Uvaly u Prahy, Czechoslovakia.

BOKCHENKO, Luba, b. 4 July, 1941, Leningrad, USSR. Harpist. Educ: High Schl. of Music, Moscow; Conserv., Odessa, USSR. Career: Soloist/Harpist, Orch. of Royal Opera, Copenhagen. Address: Saxogade 1 - 1, 1662 Copenhagen V, Denmark.

BOKELUND, Per, b. 18 June 1936, Frederiksberg, Copenhagen, Denmark. Violinist. Educ: Dip., Royal Conserv. of Music, Copenhagen. Debut: Copenhagen, 1958. Career: Mbr. Royal Danish Orch.; Solo Concerts in Sweden, UK, Germany, Belgium, France, Italy; Radio Perfs. in Denmark, Sweden, Belgium, France. Hobbies: Literature; ARt. Mgmt: Wilheim Hansen, Copenhagen. Address: 10 Skraningen, 2700 Copenhagen, Denmark.

BOLCOM, William Elden, b. 26 May 1938, Seattle, Wash., USA. Composer; Pianist. Educ: BA, Univ. Wash., Seattle, 1958; MS, Mills Coll., Calif., 1961; DMus Arts, Stanford Univ., 1964; Paris Conserv., 1965. m. Joan Morris. Career: Concert perfs. throughout USA & Europe w. Joan Morris, many recordings. Film score, Hester Street; Perfs. as comp. incl: Morning & Evening Poems: Open House (song cycle w. orch.), St. Paul 1975. Compositions incl: 12 Etudes for piano 1966; Frescoes for 2 keyboard performers, 1971; Piano quartet, Chmbr. Music Soc., NY, 1977; Piano Concerto, NY, Carnegi Hall, 1978. Recordings as pianist incl: Piano works of George Gershwin; Bolcom Plays His Own Rags; Black Host; num. recordings as comp. Publs. incl: Music Exclusively. Contbr. to profl. mags. Hons. incl: Henry Russel Award, Univ. of Mich., 1977. Mgmt: Harold Shaw Concerts Inc. Address: 3080 Whitmore Lake Rd., Ann Arbor, MI 48103, USA. 2, 6.

BOLDORINI, Raquel, b. 26 Mar. 1943, Montevideo, Uruguay. Pianist. Educ: Grad., Nat. Conserv. of Music, Uruguay, 1966; studied w. Maria Tipo, Leon Fleisher & Marguerite Long. m. Carlos Herbert Moreno, 1 s. Career: Recitals at Kennedy Ctr.,

Wash., DC; NY; Buenos Aires. Recording of Latin Am. Comps. Hons: Viotti Int. Contest, Italy, 1965; Recife S Am. Competition, Brazil, 1970; Lalenicz Int. Contest, Argentine, 1969; Latin Am. Competition, Chile, 1974; Aspen Musical Fest., 1975. Hobby: Photography. Mgmt: Carlos Moreno. Address: Libertad 2667 A 3, Montevideo, Uruguay.

BOLDREY, Richard Lee, b. 6 Dec. 1940, Richmond, Ind., USA. Vocal Coach; Concert Pianist; Accompanist; Conductor; Teacher. Educ: Bmus, Roosevelt Univ., Chgo., 1963; piano studies w. Rudolph Ganz & Robert Goldsand, 1 d., 1 s. Debut: Beethoven Concerto No. 1 w. Richmond (Ind.) Symph., 1958. Career: Perfs. of concertos w. sev. orchs. inclng. Bach Concertos w. Chgo. Symph. Orch., 1977; Pianist, organist, tympanist w. Robert Shaw Chorale, 1964; Accomp. many top artists inclng. Mattiwilda Dobbs & Robert Merrill; fac., N Part Coll., Chgo., 1974-; now asst. cond., Opera Midwest. Hobbies: Chess; Genealogy. Address: 6166 N Sheridan, Apt. 24-D, Chgo., IL 60660, USA.

BOLEN, Jane Moore, b. 17 Mar. 1928, Sialkot, W Pakistan (then India). Exec. Dir.; Private piano & theory teacher; Choir Director. Educ: AB, Erskine Coll.; Due West, SC: MMus, Converse Coll., Spartanburg, SC; PhD, Fla. State Univ., Tallahassee; Summer schl., Westminster Choir Coll., Princeton, NJ; Arts Mgmt. Inst. Harvard Univ. Career: Exec. Dir., Greenwood Coun. of the Arts; Choir Dir., A.R. Presbyterian Ch. Comps: Master's thesis, Ballet Suite for Chambr. Orch. Publ: Dissertation, The Five Cembalo Concertos of John Christian Bach, 1974. Mbrships: Delta Kappa Gamma; Pi Kappa Lambda; Am. Musicol. Soc.; MTNA. Address: 210 W Cambridge Ave., Greenwood, SC 29646, USA.

BOLET, Jorge, b. 1914, Havana, Cuba. Concert Pianist. Educ: MusB., Curtis Inst. of Music, Phila., Pa., USA. Career: instr., Curtis Inst., 1938-42; Asst. Mil. Attaché, Cuban Embassy, Wash. DC, 1943-45; Mus. Dir., GHQ, Tokyo (US Army), 1946; Mus. Dir., Japanese Première Gilbert & Sullivan's 'The Mikado', Tokyo, 1946; Prof. of Music, Indiana Univ. Schl. of Music, 1968; performed piano soundtrack of film 'Song Without End' (story of Franz Liszt), 1960. Hons: Naumburg Prize, 1937; Josef Hofmann Award, 1938; Caballero, Order of Carlos Manuel De Cespedes. Address: Apartado 5, Fuenterrabia, Spain.

BOLLERT, Werner, b. 9 Nov. 1910, Berlin, Germany. Musicologist. Educ: Univ. of Heidelberg & Berlin; Dr. Phil., 1935. m. Irene Fellmann. Career: asst. Musikwissenschaftliches Inst., Free Univ. Berlin, 1948-54; Acad. Asst., Staatliches Inst. für Musikforschung, Berlin, 1954-74; Ret'd., 1974. Publs. incl: Sing Akademie zu Berlin (Festschrift), 1966; Musikleben, in: Berlin & die Provinz Brandenburg im 19 & 20 Jahrhundert, 1968; Carl Maria von Webers Briefe an Gottfried Weber, in: Jahrbuch des Staatlichen Inst. für Musikforschung, 1972, 73. Contbr. to Musik in Geschichte & Gegenwart; Neue deutsche Biographie; Enciclopedia dello Spattacolo; Musica; Fono Forum; Die Musikforschung. Mbr. num. profl. orgs. Address: Hermannstr. 8, 1000 Berlin 37, German Fed. Repub.

BOLOGNINI, Remo E, b. 21 Oct. 1898, Buenos Aires, Argentina. Violinist. Educ: Conserv. Santa Cecilia, Buenos Aires; last pupil of Eugene Ysaye, Brussels. m. Natalia Arostegui. Career incls: 40 concerts in Argentina; sonata recital w. Arturo Rubinstein, Buenos Aires; recitals in Columbia, Uruguay, Paris, Rome, Berlin, Cologne, Brussels, London, Alsace-Lorraine, Cuba & Netherlands; 4 times Soloist under Arturo Toscanini, Carnegie Hall, Soloist w. Sir Thos. Beecham, ibid.; Concert Master, NBC Orch. under Toscanini, 23 yrs.; Asst. Cond., Balt. Symph. Orch., Md., 4 yrs. Recordings: w. NBC. Recip., Award, Ysaye Fndn. Hobby: Wrestling. Address: 295 Ctrl. Pk. W, NY, NY 10024, USA.

BOLT, Klaas (Roelofj), b. 6 Mar. 1927, Appingedam, Netherlands. Organist. Educ: State Examinations for Music, Organ. Career: Ch. Organist, St. Bavo Ch., Haarlem, 1953; Lectr. of Organ, Sweelinck Conserv., Amsterdam. Recordings incl: var. examples of Historic Dutch Organis:-Krewerd (1531); Noordbroek, Schnitger Freytag-orgen; Arp Schnitger organs in Uithuizen, Nieuw Sscheemda & Godlinze; Christian Muller organs at Amsterdam, Beverwijk & Alkmaat; Haarlem; St. Bavo; Lohman organ, Farmsum; Arp Schnitger organ, Der Aakerk, Groningen; Organ Bonifacius kerk Medemblik; Organ Oude kerk, Amsterdam. Mbrships: Advsr., Dutch Reformed Ch. Organ Committee (for bldg. new organs & restoring historic organs); promoter & organizer of tours of historic organs. Hons: Winner, Haarlem Organ improvisation Contest, 1956-57. Address: c/o Grote of St. Bavorkerk, Oude Groenmarkt. Haarlem, The Netherlands.

BOLT, Michael Sidney, b. 2 Sept. 1946, Swansea, UK. Teacher of Violin & Piano. Educ: BA; cert. in Educ.; LTCL. m. Sandra Elvira Mason. Career: mainly concerned w. children & music; writing, arranging & prod. of children's musicals (operettas & light shows). mbr., ISM. Hobbies: Amateur Recording; Hi-Fi; Records; Theatre. Address: 19 St. Davids Dr., Leigh-on-Sea, Essex SS9 3RQ, UK.

BOLTE, Barbara Anne, b. 5 Nov. 1952, Ottawa, Can. Musician (Oboe, Cor Anglais). Educ: BMus, Univ. of Toronto, 1974; Dip., Musikhochschule, Freiburg, after studies w. Heinz Holliger, 1976. Career: Recitals, Freiburg, Paris, London, Toronto, Ottawa; recording for CBC; Mbr., Ensemble Intercontemporain w. Pierre Boulez, 1976-77. Hobbies: Studying Shakespeare; Folk & Traditional Music; Swimming. Address: 4 Bie St., Ottawa, Ont. K2G 0K7, Can.

BOLZ, Harriett, b. Cleveland, Ohio, USA. Composer; Pianist; Lecturer. Educ: BA, Case Western Reserve Univ.; MA, Ohio State Univ. m. Harold August Bolz, 3 s. Career: Comps. performed throughout major cities of USA. Recordings incl: Four Christmas Songs; Two Madrigals for Christmas; That I May Sing; Sweet Jesus; Carol of the Flowers. Contbr. to PEN Woman Mag. Mbr. num. profl. orgs. inclng: ASCAP; Phi Beta. Recip. num. nat. awards in comp. Hobbies: Travel; Knitting; Sewing. Address: 3097 Herrick Rd., Columbus, OH 43221, USA. 5, 8, 27.

BOLZONELLO ZOJA, Elsa, b. 12 Mar. 1937. Agugliaro (Vicenza), Italy. Organist. Educ: studied piano, organ & composition at C. Pollini Conserv., Padua; studied w. Luigi Ferdinando Tagliavini, Bologna; at Int. Summer Acad. for Organists, Haarlem for 5 yrs. Career: Pers., (organ), at home & abroad; participant in many Int. Fests.; Interested in old music; works for safekeeping & restoration of artistic organ; Fndr. & Dir., Cycles (Spring & Autumn), Organ Concerts, Ch. of Caselle d'Altivole (Treviso), 1968 ; Prof., Organ & Organ Composition, A. Boito Conserv., Palma, 1969-. Recordings: Italian works of 18th century on histl. organ ('Gaetano Callido', 1791), Borca of Cadore for Ricordi. Contbr. to L'Organo (review). Mbrships: Hon. Inspector for Preservation of Old Organs, Sewing. Address: Via Morello, 7-31033, Castelfranco Veneto (Treviso), Italy.

BOMAN, Arild, b. 15 Aug. 1940, Drammen, Norway. Music/media; Sociologist; Composer; Keyboard musician. Educ: Mag. art, Sociology, Oslo Univ.; studies w. Ruud, Lorentzen, also in TV/Music prod. etc; 1 s. Career: Cond. of own orchs., radio, TV & film apps., 1960-. Comp., Project leader of cultural studies, Inst. for Social Rsch., Oslo. Comps: Film, Theatre, TV & multi-media works; Diade I (orch.); Diade II (orch.) Mr. Gorgon; music for film, Red-Blue Paradise; Videographic Music Piece No. 2; Ecumens; Interludium, etc. Publs. incl: Television and Interaction; Action TV. An Experiment with Videographics and Music Communication, 1974; Models of International Cultural Interactin. Contbr. to Encys. & profl. publs. Mbrships. incl: Norwegian Sect., Int. Soc. for Contemporary Music; Norwegian Union of Musicians. Hobbies: Walking; Cross-wounty skiing. Address: 3074 Skoger, Norway.

BOMM, Urbanus Johannes, b. 28 June 1901, Lobberich (Nettetal), Germany. Benedictine Monk; Abbot; Musicologist; Choirmaster. Educ: Unis. of Bonn & Göttingen; PhD; studied piano w. Arthur Laugs & Joseph Streiffeler, singer w. Jörg Hendrik, musicol. w. Friedrich Ludwig. Career: Ldr. of monastic choir, 1931-64; Abbot, Maria Laach Monastery, 1964-77. Publs: Dissertation, Der Wandel der Modalitätsbestimmung etc., 1929; sev. articles & reviews: Contbr. to: Archiv für Liturgiewissenschaft; Musica Sacra, Cologne; Liturgie und Mönchtum. Mbrships: Int. Musicol. Soc.; Gesellschaft für Musikforschung; Consociatio Internationalis Musicae Sacrae. Address: Abtei 5471 Maria Laach Abbey über Andernach, German Fed. Repub.

BON, William Frederik, b. 15 June 1940, Amersfoort, Netherlands. Conductor; Composer. Educ: Dip. Conducting & Comp., Conserv. Amsterdam, The Hague; Dip. Conducting: Siena Accademia Chigiana; Salzburg Mozarteum. m. Annet Bon-Sorgdrager, 1 s. Career incls: Main Cond., Chmbr. Orch., Amsterdam Sinfonietta, 1973; Cond. of num. Dutch Symph. Orchs.; Guest Cond. throughout Holland & abroad. Comps. incl: Var. chmbr. music works; Symphonies 1 & 2, 1969, 70; l'Ete, texte Verlain for altmezzo & orch., 1976. Num. recordings. Mbr. of num. profl orgs. Hons. incl: Visser Neerlandia Award, 1967. Hobby: Filming. Mgmt: Rob Green, Dutch Impressariaat, van Breestraat 77, Amsterdam. Address: Weesperzijde 23, Amsterdam, Netherlands.

BONAZZI, Elaine, b. Endicott, NY, USA. Mezzo-Soprano; Opera & Concert Singer; Teacher of Voice. Educ: BM, Eastman Schl. of Music; Pers. Cert., ibid.; Opera, Hunter Coll., NYC. m. Jerome Carrington, 1 s. Debut: Santa Fe Opera, 1958. Career: Performed w. Maj. operas in USA inclng: NYC Opera; Wash. Opera Soc.; Santa Fe; World & USA premieres of 17 operas; Soloist w. Num. orchs. inclng. NY Phil.; Phila. Orch; Spoleto Fest., 1974; Netherlands Opera, 1978: Berlin Bach Fest., 1976. App. on TV over CBS, NBC & ABC. Num. recordings. Contbr. to Kennedy Ctr. Performing Arts Mag. Mbr. Mu Phi Epision. Hons. incl: Sullivan Fndn. Grant, 1963. Hobbies: Cooking; Reading; Sailing. Mgmt: Thea Dispeker, 59 E 54 St., NYC. Address: 650 West End Ave., New York, NY, USA.

BOND, Victoria, b. 5 June, 1950, Los Angeles, Calif., USA. Conductor; Composer. Educ: BA, Univ. Southern Calif.; MM, Juilliard Schl. of Music; DMus, ibid., 1977. m. Stephan H Peskin. Career: Music Dir. & Cond., New Amsterdam Symph. Orch. & Pitts. Youth Orch.; Exxon/Arts Endowment Cond., Pitts. Symph. Compositions: Equinox (full orch.); Tarot (chorus & percussion orch.); From an Antique Laud; Peter Quince at Clavier. Recordings: Sonata for cello. Contbr. to: Int. Musician; Parade Magazine. Mbrships: ASCAP; Mu Phi Epsilon; Am. Symph. Orch. League. Hons: ASCAP Award, 1978, 79; Victor Herbert Award, 1975. Address: Gaetway Towers, Apt. 4-0, Pitts., PA 15222, USA. 5.

BONDEVILLE, Emmanuel, b. 29 Oct. 1898, Rouen, France. Composer; Musical Director. m. Jacqueline Petitalot, 1955, 2 s. Career: Dir. of Artistic Broadcasts, Radiodiffusion Française, 1935-45; Dir., Monte Carlo Opera, 1945-49; Dir., Nat. Comic Opera Theatre, 1949-52; Dir., Nat. Opera Theatre, 1952-70. Compositions: Le Bal des Pendus, 1930; L'Ecole des Maris, 1935; Illuminations, Sonate pour Piano; La Cloche Felée; Trois Pochades; La Rhapsodie Foraine; Le Parson de Saint-Anne; Illustrations pour Faust, 1942; Madame Bovary, 1951; Gaultier-Garguille, 1953; Symphonie Lyrique, 1957; Symphonie Choréographique, 1965. Mbrships: Acad. of Fine Arts; Permanent Sec., ibid, 1964-; Hon. Pres., Nat. Comm. of Music, 1964-. Recip: Grand Prix of Music, Soc. of Authors, 1966. Address: Palais Mazarin, 25 Quai de Conti, Paris 6e, France.

BONDI, Anna Maria, b. 11 Apr. 1931, Rome, Italy. Singer (Soprano). Educ: Dip. Instituto Magistrale Superiore; Dip, Liceo Musicale Morlacchi di Perugia; Studied w. Gabriella Bezanzoni, Tito Schipa, Lotte Schone. Debut: Concert, Perugia, 1968; Opera, Rome, 1963. Career: First Soprano, Rome Comic Opera, 1963-66; Opera in Firenze, Rome, Sassari, Perugia, Pescara, Tripoli & in France; Concerts in Italy, France, Germany, UK & Africa; Festivals in France; Radio pers. over ORTF-RAI. Recordings in Germany & France incl: Scarlatti (opera arias); Cantatas (Mannheim Schl.) Charpentier (motets). Address: 40 Ave. Isaac Pereire, 77220 Gretz Tournan, France.

BONDI, Eugene B, b. 18 May 1953, Berkeley, Calif., USA. Cellist. Educ: B Mus, Ind. Univ.; MMus, Univ. of S Calif.; Studied w. Colin Hampton, Janos Starker, Gregor Piatigorsky. Career: Solo perfs. w. Santa Barbara, Houston & San Francisco Symphs.; Solo recitals, NY, Los Angeles, Honolulu; Currently Asst. Prin. Cellist, Honolulu Symphy. Recording: David Baker; Sonata for piano & string quintet. Hobby: Cooking. Address: 3534 Sunvalley Rd., Houston, TX 77025, USA.

BONELL, Carlos Antonio, b. 23 July 1949, London, UK. Guitarist. Educ: RCM. m. Pinuccia Rossetti, 2 s. Debut: Wigmore Hall, London. Career: num. fests. as Soloist; Guest Soloist w. Halle Orch., Royal Phil. Orch., London Symph. Orch., etc.; frequent broadcaster. Comps: Spanish Folk Songs & Dances. Recordings: for CBS & Enigma Classics. Mbr., Musicians Union. Hobbies: Reading; Walking. Mgmt: Harold Holt. Address: 60 Burghley Rd., London NW5, UK

BONELLI, Alessandro, b. 8 Oct. 1947, Venice, Italy. Oboist; Professor of Chamber Music. Educ: Dip. oboe, Conservatorio Benedetto Marcello, Venice. m. Patricia Dunkerley. Career: 1st Oboe & Soloist w. orch. inclng: Gulbenkian Chmbr. Orch., Lisbon; San Pietro A Majella, Naples; Michelangelo, Florence; Orch. Sinfonica of Teatro La Fenice, Venice; 5 tours w. above orchs. in USA (300 concerts) & prin. cities & festivals of Europe; Radio & TV apps. in Italy, Switzerland, Germany, France, Portugal, Ireland, Belgium; Currently 1st Oboe & Soloist w. Chambr. Orch. I Soloisti Veneti, 1970-; Prof. of Chmbr. Music, Padova Conserv. Num. recordings. Publs. incl: The Young Oboist. Hobby: Politics. Address: S Marco 2960, Venice, Italy.

BONELLI, Ettore, b. 21 Oct. 1900, Venice, Italy. Violinist; Professor; Editor; Composer. Educ: Dip. Violin. Conservatorio Benedetto Marcello, Venice. m. Maria Antonietta Grimaldo, 2 children. Career: Violin Soloist several quartets in Italy; Prof. of Violin, Viola & Chmbr. Music; Conservatorio of Cagliari, Sardinia, 1922-24; Padova Conservatorio, 1924-52; Violin

Prof. Venice Conservatorio, 1953-70. Comps. incl: 12 pezzi per Oboe & Pianoforte, op 44. Researched, revised & edited over 95 works of Italian 18th century comps. Mbrships. incl: Accademia di Musica Antica di Venezia; Accademia Filarmonica di Bologna. Hons. incl: Gold Medal of Min. of Educ. for Cultural & Musical Activities, 1969. Address: Castello 5477, Venice, Italy.

BONIS, Ferenc, b. 17 May 1932, Miskolc, Hungary. Musicologist. Educ: Ferenc Liszt Acad. of Music, Budapest. m. Terézia Csajbók. Career: Music Prod., Hungarian Radio, 1950-70; Ldr., Music Dept., Youth Radio, 1970-; Scientific Collaborator, Musicological Inst. of Hungarian Acad. of Scis., 1961-73; Musicological Committee, ibid, 1973-; Prof., Musicological Fac., Ferenc Liszt Acad., 1972-; Ed., Magyar Zenetudomány (Hungarian Musical.), 1959-; Ed., Magyar Zenetörténeti Tanulmányok (Studies of Hist. of Hungarian Music), 1968-. Publs. incl: Erkel Ferenc, 1953, 2nd edit., 1954; A Vietórisz kódex szvit-táncai, 1957; Zoltán Kodálys Werke: Schriften, 1962; Bartók & Wagner, 1969; Beethoven & die ungarische Musik, 1970-; Béla Bartók, His Life in Pictures & Documents, 1972; Elemente der ungarischen National romantik in Bartóks und Kodalys Kunst; Vermächtnis und Umwertmy, 1979. Contbr. to var. musical mags. & publs. Mbrships: Int. Musicological Soc.; Curatorium, Int. Jugend-Kulturzentrum, Bayreuth; Pres., Hungarian Kodály Soc. Recip. Ferenc Erkel Prize, 1973. Address: Belgrád rakpart 27.1.5. H-1056 Budapest, Hungary.

BONNEAU, Paul, b. 14 Sept. 1918, Moret S./Loing, Seine et Marne, France. Composer; Conductor. Educ: Nat. Conserv. of Music, Paris, 1932-45. 2 d. Daniele Risso. Career: Dir., Music, Army, 1945; Cond., Symph. Music, RTF & ORTF (1300 concerts), 1944-; Musical Dir., Operettas & Comedies, Châtelet Theatre, Paris, & var. theatres in provinces, 1948-; Dir., var. Musical perfs., Europe & S. Am. Compositions: Num. for Orch.; Var. Operettas, Songs, Pieces & Arrangements; More than 50 Film Scores. Var. Recordings. Num. publs. Mbrships: SACEM; SDRM; SACD. Hons: Var. from nat. Conserv., Paris inclng. 1st prize, Harmony, 1937; 1st Prize for Fugue, 1942; 1st prize for Comp., 1945. Address: 4 Rue Lyautey, 75016, Paris, France.

BONSOR, (James) Brian, b. 21 Aug. 1926, Hawick, Roxburgh, UK. Music Educator & Adviser. Educ: Moray House Coll. of Educ., Edinburgh; LRAM; LMus, TCL. m. Mary Hargreaves, 1 s., 1 d. Career: Asst. Tchr., Hawick HS, 1948-61; Asst. Co. Music Organiser Roxburgh, 1961-66; Prin. Tchr. of Music, Hawick HS, 1966-70; Music Advsr., Roxburgh & Selkirk, 1970-75; Regional Adviser in Music, Border Region 1975 ; Musical Dir., Soc. of Recorder Players, 1967-; Tutor & Dir., Recorder in Educ. Summer Schl., 1959-. Comps. incl: The Shades of Night (comic opera), 1952; Beguine, 1959; Hoe-Down, 1960; Three into Five, 1971; var. pieces & arrs. for recorder. Recordings made of var. works. Contbr. to: Recorder & Music mag.; Mbrships: ISM; Music Advsrs. Nat. Assn.; Assn. of Music Organisers in Scotland; Soc. of Recorder Players; Dolmetsch Fndn. Address: Grove House, 37 Weensland Rd., Hawick, Roxburgh, TD9 9NW, UK.

BONYNGE, Richard, b. 1930, Sydney, Aust. Conductor. Educ: studied piano. m. Joan Sutherland. Debut: as cond., Santa Cecilia Orch., Rome, Italy, 1962; as opera cond.; Faust., Vancourver, 1963. Career incls: Artistic Dir., Prin. Cond., Sutherland/Williamson Int. Grand Opera Co., Aust., 1965; Artistic Dir., Vancouver Opera Assn., 1974-; Musical Dir., Aust. Opera, 1975-. Many recordings inclng: La Sonnambula; Faust; The Messiah; Tales of Hoffman; etc.; num. orch. works; ballet. 16.

BOODY, Charles G, b. 11 Aug. 1939, Dawson, Minn., USA. Musicologist. Educ: BA, Macalester Coll., St. Paul, Minn., 1961; MA, Major in Musicol., Univ. of Minn., 1968; Studies towards PhD, ibid, 1971. m. Nancy Lee Hayden, 2 d. Career: HS Instructor, 1961-64; Teaching Assoc. & Rsch. Fellow, Univ. of Minn., 1964-70; Instructor in Music Hist. & Instrumental Music, Austin Coll., Sherman, Tex., 1970-. Compositions: Freedom Trail (Folk Song arrangement); What Tidings Bringest Thou, Messenger? (ed. of 15th century Engl. Carol). Contbr. to: Current Musicology; Choral Journal (Book Review Ed. 1968-73); Jrnl. of Research into Music Education; Jrnl. of Band Research; Student Musicologists at Minn. Mbrships: Am. Musicological Soc.; Coun. for Rsch. in Music Educ.; Nat. Assn. Coll. Wind & Percussion Instructors; Am. Choral Dirs. Assn.; Music Educators Nat. Conf.; Coll. Band Dirs. Nat. Assn.; Electronotes Music Club; Pi Kappa Lambda, 1973. Hobbies: Performance of Medieval & Renaissance Music; Recorder Playing. Address: 1028 S. Walnut, Sherman, TX, USA.

BOOGAARTS, Jan, b. 10 May 1934, Helmond, Netherlands. University Lecturer; Choir Director; Organist; Organ Specialist. Educ: Conserv., Tiburg; Royal Conserv., The Hague; Inst. of Musicol., Utrecht. m. Dorine Sniedt, 2 s., 1 d. Career: Radio recordings for BBC, England; AVRO, NOS, KRO, NCRV, The Netherlands; Sud-Deutscher Rundfunk; ORTF France; Polish Radio; DDR radio for choir & organ; TV Holland Festival; visiting professorships throughout Europe. Recordings incl: Plainsong; Ordo Missae Instauratus Concilii Vaticani II; Motets of BVM of Renaissance Period; Matins for Holy Saturday. Contbr. to profl. jrnls. Mbrships. incl: Nat. Rep., CIMS; Bd., Vereniging voor Latijnse Liturgie; Advsr. to Monumentencommissie van de Provincie Gelderland. Address: Die Magerhorst, Duiven, Gelderland, Netherlands.

BOOKSPAN, Martin, b. 30 July 1926, Boston, Mass., USA. Critic; Commentator; Lecturer; Author. Educ: BSc, Harvard Coll.; violin, Boston Music Schl.; harmony, hist., orchestration, etc., Harvard. m. Janet S Sobel, 2 d, 1 s. Career: Music Dir., Program Dir., WBMS Boston; Music Dir., Program Dir., Program Cons., WQXR NY; Commentator for all Live From Lincoln Center & Great Performances musical telecasts. Publs: 101 Masterpieces of Music and Their Composers, 1968, 73; Zubin -The Zubin Mehta Story (Co-author), 1978. Contbr. to: High Fidelity; Musical Am.; House Beautiful; The New York Times (Tape Critic & Columnist, 1963-65); Stereo Review (Contributing Ed., 1958-76); The New York Times Guide to Recorded Music. Mbrships: The bohemians; Bd. of Dirs., Am. Music Center & Nat. Music Coun. Hons: Letter of Distinction from Am. Music Center, 1977. Hobbies: Spectator Sports; Reading; Videotaping old movies. Address: c/o ASCAP, 1 Lincoln Plaza, NY, NY 10023, USA. 6.

BOON, Klaas Willem, b. 18 Apr. 1915, Den Helder, Holland. Professor & Soloist of Viola. Educ: Pvte. study of violin w. Willem Boon, Dick Mesman & Oscar Back. m. Ina Overkamp, 1 child. Career: Soloist w. num. orchs. incl. Concertgebouw Orch. in concertos by Walton, Serly, Hindemith, Henkemans, Bartok, etc.; Duo w. wife (pianist); Fndr., Netherlands Pianoquartet. Recordings: Chamber Music on Philips label. Hobbies: Playing Chamber Music; Crossword Puzzles; Walking in the open air. Mgmt: Impresario International Concert Admin., Sandtmannlaan 2b, Naarden. Address: Botticellistraat 9, Amsterdam, Netherlands.

BOONE, Clara Lyle (pseudonym for comp., Lyle de Bohun), b. 6 Sep. 1927, Stanton, Ky., USA. Music Publisher; Composer; Teacher. Educ: BA, Ctr. Coll. of Ky.; Mat. Radcliffe Coll. & Harvard Grad. Schl. of Educ.; piano & voice studies w. var. tchrs.; comp. studies w. Walter Piston, Cecil Burleigh & Darius Milhaud. Career: Music publisher, Arsis Press for Women Comps.; Tchng. at all levels in 5 States & in DC. Comps: Annunciation of Spring, suite for piano or orch.; Motive & Chorale, for orch.; The Americas Trio for flute, clarinet & bassoon; Songs of Estrangement, for str. quartet & soprano (recorded); num. songs & choral comps. Contbr. to Jrnl. of Integrated Educ.; Bulletin of the Harvard Grad. Schl. of Educ. Mbrships: Music Publishers Ass. of US; Radcliffe & Harvard Clubs of Wash.; corres. sec., S E Civic Assn. Hons: Music Prize, Ctr. Coll. of Ky., 1949; 3 Paul Revere Awards, Music Publishers Assn. of US, 1976. Hobbies: Cycling; Hiking; Middle East Studies. Address: 1719 Bay Street, S E, Wash., DC 20003, USA.

BOONIN, Joseph Michael, b. 18 Nov. 1935, Philadelphia, Pa., USA. Music Publisher. Educ: AB, Univ. Pa., 1957; MS, Drexel Univ., 1959. m. Nanch Z Boonin, 1 s., 1 d. Career: Grad. Instructor in Music, Univ. Pa., USA, 1958-59; Music Cataloguer, NY Public Lib., 1960-62; Sales Mgr. & Lib. Cons., Alexander Broude Inc., NY, 1962-69; Pres., Joseph Boonin Inc., Publrs. & Distributors of Music & Books, 1969-. Publs: An Index to the Solo Songs of Robert Franz, 1970. Contbr. to num. profl. jrnls. Mbrships. incl: Dir., Music Publrs. Assn., 1973-; Music Lib. Assn. Address: c/o Joseph Boonin Inc., PO Box 2124, S. Hackensack, NJ 07606, USA.

BOOS, Elizabeth L, b. 26 Mar. 1934. Musicologist. Educ: BA, Am. Univ., Wash. DC; SMM, Schl. of Sacred Music, Union Theol. Sem., NYC; PhD Cand., Ind. Univ. Career: Organist, Luth. Ch. of the Reformation, Wash. DC; has taught at Univs. of Cincinnati & Western Ont.; Western III. & Am. Univs.; & Pikeville Coll. Ed., Fevin, Sancta Trinitas, 1968. Contbr. of profl. papers & articles. Mbrships: Am. & Int. Musicol. Soc.; Coll. Music Soc. Hons: Fulbright Schlr., 1966-67. Hobbies: Study; Tennis. Address: 222 Senator Pl., Cincinnati, OH 45220, USA.

BOOTH, Bernard Joe, b. 12 July 1928, El Paso, Tex., USA. Music Administrator & Consultant; Clarinettist & Saxophonist. Educ: BS, Hardin-Simons Univ., 1950; MA, Univ. of Tex., El

Paso, 1958. m. Reta, 3 children. Career: Elem. Band Dir., El Paso Pub. Schls., 1950, 1952-55; US Army Bands, 1950-52; Band Dir., Burges HS, El Paso, 1955-64; El Paso Symph. Orch., 11 yrs.; var. Dance Bands, 30 yrs. Mbrships: Tex. State Tchrs. Assn.; Past Regional Chmn., Tex. Music Educators Assn.; Past Regional Band Chmn., ibid; Nominating Comm., Tex. Bandmasters Assn., 1971, 77; Nat. Band Assn.; El Paso Educ. Assn.; El Paso Elem. Prins. & Supvsrs. Assn.; Accreditation Comm., Southern Assn. of Colls. & Secondary Schls., 1973, Nat. Assoc. of Jazz Educators. Address: 8512 Turrentine, El Paso, TX 79925, USA.

BOOTH, Dian Atherden, b. 24 Feb. 1939, Sydney, Aust. Violinist. Educ: NSW Conserv. of Music High Schl.; BA in Psychol., Melbourne Univ.; Dip., Sydney Conserv. of Music. Debut: Melbourne, 1967; London, 1972. Career: Solo recitals & radio & TV apps., Aust.; Ldr., Aust. Youth Orch., Chmbr. Orch. & Symph. Orch.; Ldr., Orch. of Royal Ballet, UK, 1970-73; Ldr., Adelphi Str. Quartet. Contbr. to The Musician. Involved in the issue of women in the musical profession. Hobby: Travel. Mgmt: Ruth Ticher Concert Mgmt. Address: 16 Hornsey Rise, London N19, UK.

BOOTH, Philip, B. 6 May 1942, Wash. DC, USA. Opera Singer - Bass. Educ: AB, Wash. & Lee Univ., Lexington, Va.; Special Student, Eastman Schl. of Music, Rochester, NY, 1965-66. m. Sandra Bush Booth, 1 d. Debut: John F Kennedy Center for the Perf. Arts, Grand Opening, 1971 - Handel, Ariodante. Career: San Fran. Opera, 1971-74; Metropolitan Opera, 1975-. Recordings: Ezra Pound, Le Testament De Villon; Virgil Thompson, The Mother of Us All. Hons: The John Graham Award, Wash. & Lee Univ., for contribution to the Fine ARts, 1964; Gramma Fisher Award, Metropolitan Finals, 1970; Nat. Opera Institute Award, 1972-73. Hobbies: Cooking; Reading; Walking. Mgmt: Herbert Barrett Mgmt. Address: 170 W End Ave., Apt. 24-N, NY, NY 10023, USA.

BOOTH, Philip Alexander, b. 10 June 1953, Southport, UK. Pianist; Composer; Pipe & Tabor Player. Educ: MA, St. John's Coll., Cambridge; pupil of Grace Wilkinson; LRAM. Debut: Wigmore Hall. London, 1976. Career: Many apps. as soloist & w. Grace Wilkinson & Lyn McLarin; Cotswold Wind Ensemble, often playing own music. Comps: Fugal Fantasy for ogran (recorded), 1974; piano music; vocal music; chamber music, esp. featuring wind instruments. Mbrships: ISM; Convenor, Hereford Group, Campaign for Homosexual Equality. Hobbies: Humorist; Writer; Musician for Breinton Morris Dancers. Address: Green Crize Farm, Hoarwithy Rd., Hereford HR2 8AB, UK.

BOPP, Joseph Georges, b. 5 Sep. 1908, Mulhouse, France. Flautist. Educ: Conservoi, Strasbourg & Basle; studies w. René Le Roy, Paris. m. Marguerite Bannwarth, 4 s. Career: Solo flute w. Basle Symph. Orch.; Cond.; Mozartgemeinde, Basle; Prof. & Dir., Acad. de Musique, Basle. sev. recordings. Pubis: Eds. of works by Handel, Mozart, Vinci, Telemann, Bach, Berbiguier & Schers. mbr. Ambassador Club, Basle. Hons: 1st price, Strasbourg Conserv. Hobby: Collecting Flutes. Address: Melchtalstr. 15, 4102 Binningen, Switz.

BOR, Edward Boris, b. Bexhill-on-Sea, Sussex, UK. Violinist. Educ: RAM (Scholarship); ARCM; ARAM; Pvte. studies w. Max Rostal. m. Edith O'Hanrahan, 3 children. Career: Mbr. maj. orchs. in London & provinces inclng: Bath Fest. Orch. directed by Yehudi Menuhin; Ldr. of Chmbr. Music Ensemble & Tchr. at Univ. Coll. of Wales, 1948-67; Lectr. in Music in charge of String work, Cambs. Coll. of Arts & Technol., 1967-; Ldr., Cambridge Players, 1967-, & other ensembles. Num. recordings w. NSO & Bath Fest. Orch. Mbrships: European String Tchrs. Assn.; ISM Hobbies: Reading; Walking. Address: 10 Glisson Rd., Cambridge CB1 2HD, UK.

BOR, Hilda, b. 7 May 1910, London, UK. Musician; Pianist. Educ: pvte. & at RAM. Debut: London & provinces, 1924. Career: comes from family of musicians; public apps. as pianist at an early age; 1st Promenade concert, 1924; 1st broadcast at age 17; elected ARAM at age 18; prof., Tobias Matthay Piano School, age 20; fndr., organiser of City lunch time concerts at Royal Exchange, London, during WW II; num. recitals, chambr. music & concert apps.; perfs. on radio. sev. pre-war recordings. Mbrships: FRAM; ISM; vice-chmn., City Music Soc. num. prizes at RAM. Hobbies: Reading; Dogs. Address: 197 Hills Road, Cambridge, CB2 2RN, UK.

BOR, Margot, b. 10 Nov. 1917, Bexhill, Sussex, UK. Pianist; Teacher; Writer. Educ: LRAM; ARAM. Career: Accomp.; Ensemble Player; Broadcasts; Recitals, Tour, USA; Tchr., Dartington Hall Coll. Arts, 1946-50, Homerton Coll., Cambridge, 1970-. Publs: Still The Lark, a life of Elizabeth Linley (co-author), 1962; Revision of Concise Encyclopaedia of

Music, 1973. Contbr. to Groves Dictionary Music. Mbr., ISM. Hons: Elizabeth Stokes Schlrship., RAM, 1933; Emma Levy Schlrship., ibid, 1937; Sterndale Bennett Prize, 1936. Hobbies: Reading; Walking; Rsch. in 18th century musical & theatrical life. Address: 197 Hills Rd., Cambridge CB2 2RN, UK.

BØRCH, Poul, b. 11 Nov. 1921, Nykobing F. Denmark. Organist. Educ: Royal Danish Conserv. of Music, 1938-43. m. Dorrit Elizabeth Huusom, 3 s. Debut: 1945. Career: Recitals & concerts in Denmark, Sweden, German Fed. Repub., Belgium, Poland & USA; broadcasts on Norwegian & Danish radio. Recording: Niels la Cour, Archetypon. Address: Paludan Müllersvej 1, 5230 Odense M, Denmark.

BORDA, Germán, b. 27 Jan. 1935, Pogotá, Colombia. Composer. Educ: Comp. Dirp., Acad. Music, Vienna, Austria, 1968. m. Pilar Caballero, 1 s. Career: Tchr., Andes Univ., Bogotá; Nat. Univ., Bogotá; Music Critic, 'el Tiempo', Bogotá; Radio Progs., HJCK; TV Progs.; Apps. maj. theatres, Bogotá, & Miami, USA. Comps. incl: 20 Preludes for piano; 10 micropiano pieces; 2 string quartets; 5 quartets for wind instruments; Harmonies for wind quartet; 'Pequeño Requiem' for wind ensemble; 'A la Recherche de temps perdu' 5 works for choir & orch. Contbr. to var. jrnls. Mbr., Assn. Compositores Colombianos Música Culta. Hobbies: Lit.; Walking. Address: Calle 118 no. 54-77. Bogotá, Colombia, S Am,

BORG, Kim, b. 7 Aug. 1919, Helsinki, Finland. Professor; Singer; Composer. Educ: MSc (chem.); studied singing & music, Finland, Sweden, Denmark, Austria, Italy, USA. m. Ebon B, 2 c. Debut: Helsinki, 1945. Career: Profl. Singer, 1949-, appearing in major opera houses & concert halls in 26 countires of Europe, N & S. Am., Asia, Aust., Africa. Comps: str. quartet; str. trio; 4 serious songs for medium voice & str. orch.; Variazioni for soprano & orch.; Ophelia Sings (soprano, flute & viola); Ein alter Clown (tenor, basson & harpsichord); Laulelmia Saimaata (bass & orch.) Recordings for major cos. Publs: Soumalainen Laulajanaapinen, 1972. Contbr. to musical publs. Mbrships: Pres., Det Danske Sangselsab; Teosto; Solistforeningen 1921. Recip. decorations, Finland, Ausitra & Denmark. Hobby: Interscandinavian Coop. Address: Osterbrog. 158, DK 2100, Copenhagen, Denmark. 2, 19.

BORKH, Inge, b. 26 May 1921, Mannheim, German Fed. Repub. Opera singer. Educ: Vienna, Milan. m. Alexander Welitsch. Debut: Switz. Career: Perf. in var. Opera houses, Vienna, München, Stuttgart, Berlin, Beyruth, Milan, Chgo., San Fran., New York. Recording: Turandot; Antigonae; Gurre Songs. Hons: Great Record Prize, 1961. Address: CH 9405 Wienacht, St. Gallen, Switz.

BORKOWSKI, Marian, b. 17 Aug. 1934, Pabianice, Poland. Composer; Musicologist; Pianist; Teacher. Educ: MM, Warsaw Univ.; Paris Univ.; Sorbonne; Coll. de France; Comp., Dip., Acad. of Music, Warsaw; Paris Conserv.; Dip., Acad. of Music, Siena. m. Maria Borkowska, 2 s. Debut: Polish Radio, Warsaw, 1961. Career: Lectr., Acad. of Music, Warsaw, 1968-75; Asst. Prof. & Vice-Chmn., Dept. of Comp., Orch. Conducting & Theory, ibid., 1975-78; Assoc. Prof. & Pro-Rector, Acad. of Music, Warsaw, 1978-. Comps. incl: Toccata for Piano; Visions for Cello; Limits for orch.; Dram for orch., Variant for chmbr. ensemble. Mbrships: Vice-Chmn., Warsaw Br., Union of Polish Comps.; Chmn., Music Bd., Assn. of Polish Mariner Painters; ZAIKS. Hons. incl: 3rd Prize, Comp. Contest K Szymanowski, Warsaw, 1974; Prize of Minister of Culture & Arts, 1976. Hobbies: History; Theatre; Travel; Sport; Philosophy. Address: 00-362 Warsaw, ul, Galczynskiego 5 m. 17, Poland.

BÖRNER, Klaus, b. 22 June 1929, Senftenberg, Germany. Piniast; Harpsichordit; Conductor; University Professor. Educ: Acad. of Music, Weimar, 1946-50; Staatliche Privatmusiklehrerprufung, 1949; Conserv. of Music, Lausanne, Switzerland, 1950-52; 1st Prize, Virtuoso Exam., 1952; courses w. Alfred Cortot; Edwin Fischer; Wilhelm Kempff. m. Helga Kibat, 1 s., 1 d. Debut: Weimar, 1950. Career: Concerts, TV & radio pers. as soloist, chmbr. musician & w., orchs., Europe, Am., Africa, Asia, 1951-; Dir. & tchr., int. music camps; Prof. of Piano. J. Guttenberg Univ., Mainz. Comps: Trio (horn, violin, piano). Recording: Accomp., series 'Jugend Musiziert'. Contbr. to profl. jrnls. Mbr., profl. assns. Hon. incl: 1st prices, Int. Piano Contets, Barcelona, 1956, Mailand-Monza, 1967. Hobby: Photography. Address: Nibelungenstr. 38 D-4040 Neuss, German Fed. Repub.

BORNYI, Lajos, b. 27 July 1931, Debrecen, Hungary. Music Educator; Clarinetist; Composer; Conductor. Educ: Franz Liszt Acad. of Music, Budapest, Hungary; Artist Dip., Fac. of Music, Univ. of Toronto, Can., 1960; MMus Schl. of Music, Yale Univ., USA, 1965. m. Veronica Bótai, 2 c. Debut: Mesey Hall,

Toronto. Career: Soloist, var. CBC orchs., Halifax Symph. Orch., Hamilton Phil., Fac. of Music Trio Univ. of Toronto; Cond., Sault Ste. Marie Symph. Orch. Comps: Mini Concerto for Musica Fracta (orchl.); Time, Orchyd, My Fish (unaccomp. flute); Dreams (soprano & orch.); Northern Lights (orchl.); 1984, Sounds, Visions (unaccomp. clarinet). Mbrships: OSSTF; CAPAC; ORMTA; AFM. Hobbies incl: Ches. Mgmt: Ont. Arts Count. Address: 153 Kohler St., Sault Stre. Marie, Ont. P6A 3V2, Canada.

BOROUCHOFF, Israel, b. 1 Dec. 1929, Kiustendil, Bulgaria. Flautist. Educ: Juilliard Schl. of Music, 1 s., 1 d. Career: Solo Flutist, St. Louis Symph., USA, 1958-66. Chmbr. Symph. of Phila., 1966-68; Performed w. Israel Phil., 1954-55, Casals Fest. Orch., Puerto Rico & Caracas, Venezuela, 1959; num. solo recitals & chmbr. music perfs.; Mbr., Woodwing Arts Quintet, 1968-74; Mbr., Richards Quintet, Mich. State Univ., & Prof. of Flute & Assoc. Prof. of Music, ibid., currently. Recordings incl: Prokofiev Sonata & Reinecke Sonata. Mbrships. incl; Pres., Nat. Flute Assn., USA. Contbr. to Woodwind World. Hons. incl: Grant, Israel-Am. Cultural Fndn., 1955. Hobby: Photography. Mgmt: Albert Kay Assocs., NYC. Address: Dept. of Music, Mich. State Univ., E. Lansing, MI 48824, USA.

BORRIS, Siegfried, b. 4 Nov. 1906, Berlin, Germany. Composer; Musicologist. Educ: D Phil., Univ. of Berlin; HS of Music, Berlin, pupil of Paul Hindemith. m. Sabine Jahnke, 4 c. Career: Lectr., HS for Music, Berlin, 1929-45; Prof., ibid, 1945-. Compositions incl: 5 Symphs.; 8 solo concertos; 10 cantatas; 3 ballets, 2 radio operas; 2 masses; num. chmbr. music pieces, songs, choral works, etc. Publs. incl: Elementary Music instructions, 1951, 2nd edit., 1973; Moder Jazz, 1962; Key for the Music of Today, 1967; Music LIfe in Japan, 1967; The Great Orchestras, 1969; Operas of the 20th Century Vol. I, 1963, Vol. II, 1973; Introduction into Modern Music, 1974; Pop-Music, 1977. Mbrships: Pres., German Music Coun. Recip: Bundesverdienstkreuz 1st Class, 1972. Hobby: Chess. Address: 1 Berlin 33, Scholerneralles 32, German Fed. Repub. 19.

BORROFF, Edith, b. 2 Aug. 1925, NYC, USA. Musicologist; Pianist; Harpsichordit; Composer. Educ: MusB, Am. Conserv. of Music, Chgo., 1946; MusM, ibid., 1948; PhD, Univ. Mich., 1958. Debut: Piano Recital, NYC, 1939. Career incls: Prof. of Music, num. univs. inclng: Univ. Wis., Mich. Univ., Univ. of NC; Prof., SUNY, Binghamton, 1973-. Compositions incl: Oboe Variations, 1966; Horn Sonata, 1970. Publs: Author of 6 books inclng: Music in Perspective (w. M Irvin), 1976; 31 Articles; 21 Papers. Mbrships: Coll. Music Soc.; Am. Musicol. Soc.; Soc. for Ethnomusicol.; Renaissance Soc.; Mu Phi Epsilon. Recip. num. rsch. awards. Hobbies: Making Jig-saw Puzzles; Heraldry. Address: 900 Lehigh Ave., Binghamton, NY 13903, USA.

BORST, David Thomas, b. 10 Mar. 1933, NYC, USA. Professor of Bassoon & Music Education; Principal Bassoonist. Educ: BS, SUNY, Fredonia; Univ. of Buffalo; DMA. Eastman Schl. of Music. m. Ingrid Martha, 1 s., 3 d. Career: Prof. of Bassoon & Music Educ., Ind. Univ. of Pa.; Prin. Bassoonist, Johnstown Symph. Orch., Pa.; Bassoonist, Buffalo Phil., Erie Phil., Amherst Symph.; Mbr., Ind. Univ. of Pa. Woodwind Quintet & Reed Trio, Eastman Chmbr. Orch.; TV Special, The Johnstown Symph. Presents the Borst Family, 1976. Author, The Scale & Chord Finder, 1967. Mbrships. incl: MENC; Int. Double Reed Soc. Hobbies: Camping; Sailing. Address: 500 Locust St., Ind., PA 15701, USA.

BÖRTZ, Daniel, b. 8 Aug. 1943, Hässelholm, Sweden. Composer. Educ: Royal Acad. of Music, Stockholm; also in USA, W. Germany, Holland, France, Italy. Comps. incl: Il Canto dei Canti de Salomone, soprano & 7 instrs., 1965; Voices, 3 sopranos, symph. orch. & tape, 1966-68; Josef K., words by Franz Kafka, recitation, & vocal soloists, choir, organ, symph. orch., 1969; Str. Quartet No. 2, 1971; Nightwinds for vocal quartet, 1972; Sinfonia 1, 1973; Wind of Dawn, male choir, 1976; Dialogo 3, 2 pianos, 1978; Prelude for brass, 1978. Recordings: Monologhi 2, bassoon, 1966; Nightclouds, string orch., 1975; Monologhi 5, soprano, 1976; etc. Contbr. to: Sohlmans Lexikon; Bonniers Lexikon; Altmann Tonkünstler Lexikon; Nutida Musik; Konsertnytt; Tonfallet. Mbrships: Soc. of Swedish Comps.; ISCM. Recip. num. hons. Address: Bergvägen 24, S-196 30 Kungsängen, Sweden.

BORUP, Lars, b. 3 June 1944, Copenhagen, Denmark. Clarinettist; Teacher. Educ: Dip., Royal Acad. of Music, Copenhagen 1968; soloist class, ibid., 1968-70. m. Aina Bentzon, 2 c. Debut: Copenhagen 1970. Career: Gothenburg Opera Orch., 1967; Royal Lifeguards Band, 1967-79; Aarhus Symph. Orch., 1969-; 1st solo clarinet, ibid., 1972-; TV &

radio apps. in Denmark; apps. as soloist w. orch.; num. chmaber music apps.; mbr., East Jutland Woodwind Quintet & Aarhus Woodwind Trio. Recording: Otto Mortensen, Woodwind Quintet. Hons: Wilhelm Hansen prize, 1970. Hobbies: Ornithology; Photography; Salmon & Trout Fishing. Address: Egebjergvej 155, 8220 Brabrand, Denmark.

BORWICK, Susan Harden, b. 12 Feb. 1946, Dallas, Tex., USA. Musicologist; Music Theorist. Educ: BMus, (music theory & comp.), Baylor Univ., Waco, Tex.; BME (vocal music), ibid.; PhD (musicol.) Univ. of N. Carolina, Chapel Hill. m. Douglas B Borwick, 1 s. Career: grad. study w. W S Newman, Howard Smither, James W Pruett, Calvin Bower & Andrew Hughes; Asst. Prof., Music Hist., & Theory, Baylor Univ., 1972-76; Coordinator, Div. of Music Hist., 1976; Asst. Prof. of Music Theory, Eastman Schl. of Music, Univ. of Rochester, NY, 1977-; current research on German opera between WWI & WWII. Contbr. to: MLA Notes; Vinquist/Zaslaw, Performance Practice Bibliography; The Baylor Line. Mbrships: Am. Musicol. Soc. (sec.-treas.), SW Chapt., 1974-76; Soc. for Music Theory; Coll. Music Soc. (life mbr.); Music Lib. Assn. Hons: NDEA Title IV 3 yr. fellowship, 1968-71; Outstanding Woman Musician, 1968; Pi Kappa Lambda. Hobbies: Conducting; Travel. Address: 349 Cromwell Dr., Rochester, NY 14610, USA.

BOS, Chris, b. 7 Oct. 1920, Utrecht, Netherlands. Musician; Organ, Carillon, Harpsichord. Educ: Organ Dip., Conserv., 1947; Dip. Gen. Music Educ., Gehrels Inst., 1947; Dip, NKV (Guild of Carillon Players), 1954. m. A L A de Vries, 2 d. Debut: Organ, 1940; Carillon, 1947; Harpsichord, 1954. Career incls: Prof. of Schl. Music, Conserv. of Utrecht, 1947; Municipal Carillon Player, Utrecht, 1954-. Compositions incl: Passacaglia (carillon). Recordings incl: Muzikale Improvisatie, 1954. Contbr: Man & Melody; Bell & Clapper. Mbr. num. profl. orgs. Hons: Num. awards. Hobbies: Painting; Drawing; Photography; Chess; Playing Irish Harp & Bagpipes. Address: Buys Ballotstraat 28, Utrecht, Netherlands.

BOSANQUET, (Rosamund) Caroline, b. 2 Mar. 1940, Bangor, N. Wales, UK. Senior Music Lecturer; Cellist. Educ: LRAM cello piano; BMus, Dunelm. Career: Lectr. in Music, Cello Specialist, Cambs. Coll. of Arts & Technol.; Cello Tchr., Homerton Coll. Cambridge; has given regular chmbr. music & solo cello concerts in Cambridge, London & elsewhere. Contbr. to: ISM Music in Ed. Comm., 1976; European & Am. String Tchng. Assns: Int. Soc. for Music Educ; CNAA. Hobbies: Gardening; Reading. Address: 171 Gwydir St., Cambridge, UK.

BOSE, Maria Teresa Lapere, b. 27 Oct. 1932, Edinburgh, UK. Piano & Singing Teacher. Educ: LRAM (piano); Study of Bel Canto, Studio of John & Aida Dickens, Studio of Lucille Bensted, & Freiburg Musik Schule. m. Nitai Chandra Bose, 2 s. Career: Perfs. of Spanish & S. Am. songs w. Spanish guitarist, London clubs, halls, town halls & hotels; Currently, tchng. Mbrhis: ISM; Metropolitan Entertainers Assn., London. Address: 8 Buckstone Dell, Edinburgh 10, UK.

BOSHKE, Nathalie, b. 22 Jan. 1893. Concert Violinist. Educ: Juilliard Schl.; studies w. Sevcik, Leopold Auer & Eugene Ysaÿe. m. Edward F. Brown (dec.), 1 s., 1 d. Debut: St. Petersburg, Russia, 1912. Career: Soloist, Russion Symph., NYC, Los Angeles Phil.; tours, Asia 1924 & 52, Europe, 1956; Fndr., Southampton Music Fest., 1953; 16 annual sonata recitals, Donnell Lib., NYC, to present; concert apps., USA. Can., S Am., Russia, Java, China, Japan, Norway, Sweden, Denmark. Recordings: RCA Victor; Nipponophone. Recip., Medaille Eugene Ysaÿe, 1972. Address: 1158 Fifth Ave., NY, NY 10029, USA. 6.

BOTEZ, Dumitru D, b. 10 Mar. 1904, Roman, Romania. Conductor; Professor; Composer. Educ: Grad., Law Fac., Univ. of Tasi; Grad. (majors, violin & conducting, also studied piano & viola), Tasi Acad. of Music. m. Elena, 1 d. Debut: Cond., Romanian Broadcasting Chorus, 1945. Career: Msuic Tchr., var. instrs., 1930-48; Violinist, Broadcasting Orch., 1933-45; Cond., Broadcasting Chorus, 1945-51, Bucharest Phil. Chorus, 1953-69; Dir., radio musical progs., 1947-50; Conducting Prof., 1949-, Rector, 1959-63, Bucharest Acad. of Music; cond., over 1500 choral concerts inclng. premiere perfs. of over 500 works. Comps. incl: 180 choral works. Recordings: Romanian Choral Literature; many radio & TV tapes. Publs. incl: 4 anthols. on choral msuic; Choral Triptic, 1976; Choral Conducting Treatise, in press. Contbr. to num. publs. Active Mr., musical orgs. Recip. many awards & decorations. Address: 39 Schitu Magureanu, Bucharest VII, 7000 Romania.

BOTTA, Rudolf, b. 30 Aug. 1918, Moragy, Hungary. Senior Lecturer in Violin, Chamber Music & the Art of Teaching. Educ: Tchrs. Dip. (perf.), Conserv., Belgrade; var. courses inclng.,

Cond. Course, Pécs, Hungary, Solfége Course, Hungary. m. Leontine Botta, 3 children. Career: 'Pro ARte' Str. Quartet, 1938-39; Hd., Bonyhad Jr. Music Schl., 1953-56; Violin Tchr.,Hungary State Music Schl., Szeksard, 1955-56; Violin Tchr., later, Sr. Lectr., RMCM, 1957-73; Sr. Lectr., Violin, Chamber Music, Art of Teaching., Royal Northern Coll. of Music, 1973-; Cond., var. Orchs., 1953-68; Int. Adjud., 1955-; Radio & TV broadcasts incl., BBC Radio, Christmas Eve, 1956, Granada TV, 1957, Hungarian Radio, 3 times, 1956. Recording of Bonyhad Music Schl. Orch., Radio Budapest, 1956 (as Cond.). Publs: Modern Basic Violin Method, 1971; Systematic Vibrato Studies, 1972; Various Technical Studies for Violin, 1971-73. Contbr. to: Gazette Littéraire Paris; Catholic Sunday, Cleveland, USA; etc. Hons: Kt. of the Hungarian 'Szent Laszlo' order, 1963. Mbrships: Pres., Hungarian Cultural Soc., Manchester; Pres., Anglo-Hungarian Bartok Soc., ibid. Hobbies: Fencing; Swimming; Gardening. Address: 35 Goodward Rd., New Mills, Stockport, SK 12 4AT, UK.

BOTTAZZI, Ana Maria Trenchi de, b. 29 May 1938, Buenos Aires, Argentina. Pianist. Educ: BA, MMus, PhD, Univs. in Buenos Aires & USA; Conserv. Nat. de Paris, France, 1952-56. m. Brungo Giulio Bottazzi, 1 s., 1 d. Debut: Buenos Aires, 1942. Career: Concerts in almost every country & in 4 continents, - 1963; num. radio & TV apps.; Resumed playing after severe car accident NYC, 1974. Comps. of sev. works for piano & chmbr. music. Mbrships: Pres., Germaine Pinault Int. Musical Soc. Ltd. Hons. incl: 1st Prize for best for. student, Paris Prize, St. Louis Competition, 1965. Hobbies incl: Swimming. Address: 109 Forest Rd., Centereach, NY 11720, USA.

BÖTTCHER, Eberhard Fritz, b. 1 Nov. 1934, Berlin, Germany. Composer; Oboist. Educ: Stadt Konservatorium, Berlin, 1952-56; Comp. Studies w. Prof. Friedrich Metzler. m. Ingrid Böttcher, 2 d. Career: Oboe Player, sev. symph. orch., German Dem. Repub. 1956-58, Sweden 1958-68, Norway 1968-. Comp. incl: Sonatina for violin & paino; Trio for oboe, viola & paino; Concertante Suite for accordion; Two Movements for Wind Quintet; Fantasia Sinfonica for Orch.; Concerto for horn & strings; Lyric Suite for piano; Introduction & Allegro for String Quartet; Latin Madrigals, for choir; Solo Sonata for cello; 3 songs for tenor & guitar. Sev. radio recordings. Mbrships: VDMK, German Dem. Repub.; STIM; NY Musikks Comp. Group; Soc. of Norwegian Comps. Hons: Carl Maria von Weber Prize, Dresden, 1957. Mgmt: Norwegian Music Information Centre, Oslo 1, Norway. Address: Ilevollen 3 E, N-7000 Trondheim, Norway.

BOTTENBERG, Wolfgang Heinz Otto, b. 9 May 1930, Frankfurt/Main, Germany. Professor of Music; Composer. Educ: Theol. HS, Vallendar, 1952-58; B Mus., Profl. Cert. in Music, Univ. of Alta., Canada; M Mus., Univ. of Cinn., USA, 1962; DMA, 1970. m. Joanna Heinrich, 2 s. Career: HS Tchr., Calgary & Alberni, BC, 1963-65; Lectr. & Asst. Prof. of Music, Acadia Univ., 1965-73; Asst. Prof. of Music, Sir George Williams Univ., Montreal, 1973-. Comps: Partita, Good Christian Men Rejoice; Trio for Recorders; Three English Carols (piano duet); Moods of the MOdes; var. pieces for organ, choral works, etc. Contbr. to: The Canadian Composer; CAUsm Jrnl. Mbrships: Pi Kappa Lambda; Canadian League of Comps.; Assoc. Comp., Canadian Music Ctr. Hobbies: Water colour painting; Instrument building. Address: 44 Charles Ave., Pointe Claire, PQ, Canada H9R 4K5.

BOTTGER, Max Lee, b. 10 Oct. 1930, Grand Island, Neb., USA. Public School Director of Orchestras, Bands, & Stage Bands; Minister of Church Music; Pipe Organist; Choir Director. Educ: BA, Hastings Coll., Neb.; MA, Northern Colo., Greeley. m. Betty Joy Balius, 2 s., 1 d. Career: Dir. of Instrumental Music in pub. schls., 1956-; Ch. Pipe Organist, since age 15; Organist & Choirmaster, Hastings, Lyons, & Lincoln, Neb.; Band Clinician; Judge of Bands; Cooperating Tchr., Tchr. Trng. Progs. Peru State Coll., Univ. of Neb., Neb. Wesleyan Univ. & Union Coll. Mbrships. incl: MENC; Neb. Music Educators Assn. Contbr. to Neb. Music Educator. Hobbies incl: Hunting. Address: 1660 Woodsview, Lincoln, NB 68502, USA.

BOTTJE, Will Gay, b. 30 June 1925, Grand Rapids, Mich., USA. Composer; Professor of Music; Flutist; Conductor. Educ: BS, MS, Juilliard Schl. of Music; D Musical Arts, Eastman Schl. of Music; studied at Amsterdam Conserv. & Ultrecht State Univ., Netherlands, & Stiftleson Electronic Music Studio, Stockholm, Sweden. m. Joyce Thompson, 3 children. Career: Prof. of Music (Theory & Comp.), & Dir. Electronic Music Studio, S III. Univ., Carbondale. Comp. (publd.): Over 85 works inclng. Facets (piano & large wind ensemble), 1973, Designs (2 flutes, violincello & piano), 1974, (tapes): 14 pieces of electronic music, 1963-, (recorded(What is a Man; The Ballad

Singer Chiaroscuros, 1974; In a Word (1975); From Winds & The Farthest Spaces, 1976; Concerto for tuba & orch., 1977; Rooms, 1978. Contbr. to: Instrumentalist; School Musician. Mbrships: Am. Comps. Alliance (BMI); Am. Soc. Univ. Comp.; AAUP. Hons. incl: Thor Johnson Brass Composition Contest, 1955; Creative Rsch. Awards, S III. Univ., 1960, 1964, 1967-68, 1971; NACWPI Composition Contest, 1974. Address: 914 Taylor Dr., Carbondale, IL 62901, USA.

BOTVAY, Karoly, b. 29 Dec. 1932, Sopron, Hungary. Cellist. Educ: Dip. (perf. & tchr.), Franz Liszt Acad., Budapest. m. Agnes Gadanyi, 2 s. Debut: (as soloist) Cambridge; Wigmore Hall, London. Career: Cellist, Bartók Str. Quartet, 1960-77; worldwide tours. & apps. at num. fests. w. Bartók Quartet; solo career, 1977-; tchr., Int. cello master classes, Aldeburgh, 1978, 79; tchr., Int. Bartók Seminar, Hungary, 1979; num. apps. at recitals & concerts incl. Royal Fest. Hall. Recordings: 48 w. Bartók Quartet. Hons: Bach prize, 1950; Bart&k prize, 1951; Liége prize, 1964; Liszt award, 1964; Nat. Kossuth award, 1970. Hobbies: Photography; Swimming; Gardening. Mgmt: Interkoncert, Budapest. Address: Mártonhegyi ut. 41, 1124 Budapest, Hungary.

BOUCHARD, Antoine, b. 22 Mar. 1932, St. Philippe-de-Neri, PQ, Canada. Organist; Professor of Organ. Educ: BA, LTh., Laval Univ., Quebec; Study in Can. w. Abbé Destroismaisons, Claude Lavoie; in Paris w. Simone Plé-Caussade, Gaston Litaize, Antoine Reboulot. Career: Concerts, fests. in Quebec City, Montreal, Paris, Concerts, Can. & USA; Radio perfs., CBC & ORTF; Series of concerts on 20 European Historical ograns, Radio Can.; Cons., Organ Prof. & Dir. Schl. of Music, Laval Univ., Quebec. Recordings: Music by Dandrieu & Buxtehude; Radio recordings: Noëls Françcais du 18e Siécle; Bach et Pachelbel; Anthologie I. Contbr. to Can., European jrnls. Address: 908 Parc Belvedére, Place Normandie GOS 3LO, PQ, Canada. 4.

BOUCHET, Gabriel, b. 7 July 1937, Paris, France. Percussionist. Educ: Basle, Paris, Strasbourg; dip. for piano & percussion. m. Giséle Lalvyaux, 2 c. Debut: as percussionist w. Berne Symph. Orch. Career: 1st percussionist w. Berne Symph. Orch. Career: 1st percussionist, ORTF Orch., Strasbourg, 1966-73; 1st percussionist, Strasbourg Phil. Orch.; mbr., Percussions of Strasbourg. Recordings: 8 w. Percussions de Strasbourg. Hobbies: Swimming; Tennis. Address: 47 rue de Chambord, 67000 Strasbourg Robertrau, France.

BOULAY, Laurence, b. 19 Jan. 1925, Boulogne sur Seine, France. Professor; Harpsichord player. Educ: Dr. (musicol.) Univ. of Paris; Conserv. Nat. Supérieur de Musique de Paris. Career: num. concerts in France; tours of Europe, USA, Can. & Japan; Prof., Conserv. Nat. Supérieur de Musique de Paris. Recordings: more than 40 records. Publs: ed., num. scores of French 18th century chmbr. music. Contbr. to Recherches. Hons: Five 1st prizes from Conserv. Nat. Supérieur de Paris; sev. Grands Prix du Disque. Address: 127 Av. J B Clément, 92100 Boulogne, France.

BOULDING, Keith Ronald Rex, b. 4 July 1925, Dartford, Kent, UK. Military Director of Music. Educ: LRAM; ARCM; FVCM; BBCM., psm. m. Phyllis Eileen Boulding, FVCM, 2 d. Career: Musician, RAMC Band, Trumpet w. Brit. Expeditionary Force Band; Bandmaster, The Devonshire Regiment, 1950-58; Bandmaster Devonshire & Dorset Regiment, 1958-; Staff Bandmaster, Brigade of Guards, 1962-63; Dir. of Music, Royal Tank Regiment, 1963-69; Royal Signals, 1969-. Compositions: Regimental March of The Devonshire & Dorset Regiment; March, Saffron; March, Fifty Years Young; Concert March, The Rotarians; Fanfare, Golden Jubilee; Fanfare, Eboracum. Recordings: Begone Dull Care, EMI; On Tour w. The Band of The Royal Corps. of Signals, Eros; Spirit of England, Indigo; Let's Go Skating. Mbr., Kneller Hall Club. Recip., Sommerville; Prize, Royal Mil. Schl. of Music, 1947. Hobby: Golf. Address: St. Brelades, 18 Bayfran Way, Blandford Forum, Dorset, UK.

BOULEZ, Pierre, b. 26 Mar. 1925, Montbrison, France. Composer; Conductor. Educ: Conservatoire de Paris. Career: Music Dir., NY Phil., 1971-77; Chief Cond., BBC Symph. Orch., 1971-75; Dir., Institut de Recherche et Coordination Acoustique Musique, Paris, 1976. Recordings w. CBS. Publs: Penser la Musique Anjourd'hui; Reléve D'Apprenti. Contbr. to var. mags. & jrnls. Mgmt: Ingpen & Williams Ltd. Address: 757 Baden-Baden, Postfach 22, German Fed. Repub.

BOULT, (Sir) Adrian Cedric, b. 8 Apr. 1889, Chester, UK. Conductor; Musical Director. Educ: Christ Church, Oxford, (MA, D Mus); Leipzig Conserv. (non Hochschule). m. Anne Mary Grace Bowles, 3 step-c. Debut: West Kirby, Lancs., 1914. Career: Staff, RCM, 1920; Cond., Patron's Fund,

1919-29; Musical Dir., Birmingham City Symph. Orch., 1924-30; Dir. of Music, BBC, 1930-42, & 1959-60; Cond., BBC Symph. Orch., 1930-50; Cond., LPO, 1950-57, Pres. 1966-; Has been Cond., throughout the World, and conducted all permanent Orchs. in UK; Dir. of num. Schls. for Conductors; Cond., Bach Choir, 1928-33, Prom. Concerts, 1942-50, & num. other Fests., Services, Concerts, Coronations, etc. Recordings: Pye, Westminster, Lyrita, EMI. Publs: The Point of the Stick, a Hnadbook on the Technique of Conducting, 1920, rev. Ed., 1968; (joint), Bach's Matthew Passion, 1949; Thoughts on Conducting, 1963; My Own Trumpet (autobiography), 1973. Contbr. to: Music & Letters; Musical Times, etc. Pres., ISM; Nat. Youth Orch., 1947-57; Schls. Music Assn., 1947-; Royal Scottish Acad. of Music, 1959-; Life Mbr., Athenaeum Club. Hons. incl: CH, 1969; Kt., 1937, FRCM; Hon. Mus. D., Edinburgh, Cambridge; Hon., GSM, TCL, RAM (mbr.); Gold Medal, Royal Phil. Soc., 1944; Harvard Medal w. Dr. Vaughan Williams, 1956. Mgmt: Ibbs & Tillett, London. Address: Fox Yard Cottage, West Str., Farnham, Surrey, GU9 7EX.

BOULTON, John, b. 3 Aug. 1909, Manchester, UK. Critic; Reviewer; Lecturer. Educ: MSc, Univ. of Manchester. Career: Ed. Cons. to Music Review; Former Univ. Ext. Lectr. in Music Appreciation, Univs. of Manchester & Cambridge; Co-fndr. Hallé Mag. Contbr. to: Music Review; Hallé Mag. Committee Mbr., Hallé Concerts Soc. Address: Rings, Shalford, Braintree, Essex, CM7 5HX, UK.

BOUQUET, Marie Thérèsa, b. 26 Jan. 1939, Dieppe, France. Musicologist. Educ: Dr. of European Studies, Univ. of Paris (Sorbonne); Dip., Practical Schl. of Adv. Studies; Dip., Paris Music Schl.; Nat. Conserv. of Music, Paris. m. Boyer Gustavo. Appts. incl: Jurist, Nat. Conserv. of Music, Paris, at confs. & concerts in France, Switzerland & Italy. Compositions: 6 pieces for piano; transcriptions of var. 17th & 18th century works. Mbrships: French & Italian Musicol. Socs. Publs. incl: Music & Musicians of Turin from 1648 to 1775, 1969; Music & Musicians of Annecy, 1969. Recordings incl: var. concerto & Sonati for strings & orch. on Durium, Cetra & Erato labels. Mbrships. incl: Sociétes Francaise et Italienne de Musicologie; Académie Florimontana. Address: Cascina Pivia, Fraz. Montariolo, 10090 Sciolze, Italy.

BOURDE, André Jean, b. 11 Oct. 1921, Marseille, France. University Professor & Administrator. Educ: Agrégé d'histoire, Dr. és Lettres, Paris; PhD, Cambridge; studied piano w. Madeleine de Valmaléte & organ w. Marcel Prévot & André Marchal. Career: Prof. & Dir. of Musical Rsch. Sect., Univ. d'Aix-Marseille I; currently giving harpsichord recitals & courses in muscol., Univ. of Provence. Contbr. to: Revue de Musicologie; Revue CMR XVII. Mbr., French Soc. of Music. Address: Institut d'Art, 21 rue Gaston de Saporta, 1300 Aix en Provence, France.

BOURGEOIS, Derek David, b. 16 Oct. 1941, Kingston-on-Thames, UK. Composer; Univ. Lecturer in Music. Educ: Magdalene Coll., Cambridge, 1959-63; RCM, 1963-65; MA; DMus, 1971. m. Jean Berry. Compositions: 4 Symphs.; Concertos for clarinet, bass tube, double bass, 3 trombones; Tone Poem The Globe; Symphonic variations; dance variations; Rumpelstiltskin (opera); 2 Brass Band Concertos; Concerto for Brass Quintet & Brass Band; 2 Brass Quintets; Concerto Grosso for Brass Decet; 2 Violin Sonatas; Clarinet; Sonata; String Quartet; Sonata for two pianos; Organ Symphony; Choral works incl.: Jabberwocky; Agincourt; Pied Piper of Hamelin; Triumphal March. Mbrships: Exec. Committee, Composers Guild; Chmn., SW Branch of same. Hons: BBC Monarchy 1000 Competition, 1973; Sontori Prize for Strings Competition, 1976. Hobbies: Fine Wines; Golf; Gardening. Address: The Vines, Hewelsfield, Lydney, Glos GL15 6XE, UK.

BOURLIGUEUX, Guy, Charles Corentin Jean, b. 15 Nov. 1935, Metz, France. Organist; Musicologist. Educ: studied, num. Univs., France & Spain; Lic. és Lettres.; Dip., higher studies of Spanish lang. & llt.; Agrégé de L'Université; Musicol. Rsch., w. Profs. J Chailley & Dufourcq. Lit. rsch. w. Prof. Aubrun; ancien mbr. sci. section, casa de Valázquez. Madrid. Career: Tchr., Lycée Henri-IV, Paris, Sévigné Coll., Paris, Fac., Lettres et Scis. Sorbonne, Paris, Univs. of Nantest & Angers, TV advert. ctr., W. Univs., France, Conserv. & Inst. of European Studies, Nantes; Contbr. ot num. articles to: Annuario Musical; Archivos Leoneses; Grove's Dictionary, etc. Mbrships. incl: San Fernando Royal Acad. of Fine Arts, Madrid. Corr. mbr., Sup. Commission for hist. monuments. Organ section; French Musicol. Soc.; Int. Consortium of Sacred Music; former mbr. Admin. Coun., Friends of the Organ, Soc. francaise de musicologie; var. Archeol. Socs. Hons: Chevalier des Palmes Académiques, Chevalier des Arts etc Lettres. Address: Villa Euterpe, 3 Place d'Auteuil, 44700 Orvault, France. 6.

BOURNE, Bramwell Bernard, b. 28 July 1945, Edgware, Middx., UK. Organist; Teacher of Organ, Piano, Brass & Theory. Educ: ARCM (Organ Tchng.); LRAM (Organ perf.). Career: Ch. Organist-Choirmaster; Organ Tchr. & Recitalist; Tchr. of Piano, Brass & Theory. Comp. of anthems & introits. Mbrships: RCO. Hobby: Collecting & reparing clocks. Address: 43 Victoria Cres., Parkstone Poole, Dorset BH12 2JQ, UK.

BOURNE, Iris, b. Nottingham, UK. Soprano Singer. Educ: RAM. m. David Bourne. Career: concerts, oratorios, opera, recitals, UK, France, Spain, Can. Recip. Hon. ARAM. Hobbies: Cooking; Viticulture. Address: 152 Worrin Rd., Shenfield, Essex, UK.

BOURTON, Robert John, b. 20 Apr. 1942, Shifnal, Salop, UK. Bassoonist. Educ: St. Dunstan's Coll., London; ARCM. m. Honorah Josephine Taylor, 1 s. Career: Hallé Orch., UK, 1962-63; Prin. City of Birmingham Symph. Orch., 1963-66; Co-Prin., Royal Opera House, Covent Gdn., 1966-70; Co-Prin., LSO, 1970-. Recip. Coun. Wind Prize, RCM, 1962. Hobbies: Collecting Antiques; Collecting Musical Stamps; Kite-flying. Address: 32 Vallance Rd., Alexandra Pk., London N22, UK.

BOVET, Guy, b. 22 May 1942, Neuchatel, Switz. Organist; Composer. Educ: 1st Prize of Virtuosity, Conserv. of Geneva, 1962, 1 d. Career: Concert artist, Europe & Am., 1962-. Comps: Organ pieces; Concerto for Organ & Orch. Recordings: Historical Organs of Switz. Contbr. to: The Organ Yearbook; L'Orgue; Musik & Gottesdienst; Ed., La Tribune de l'Orgue. Recip., 10 int. prizes, 1962-74. Address: La Maison du Prieur, 1349 Romainmotier, Switzerland.

BOWDEN, Mary Lucas Williams (Jeanne Francis Harper), b. 26 Jan. 1928, Montgomery, Ala., USA. Music & Music Theory Teacher (piano, chord organ, dulcimer). Educ: BS, Univ. of Ala.; piano & theory studies w. Joanne Raulin, comp. w. Robert W Dumm. m. Warren Franklin Bowden, 1 d. Comps. incl: Somebody Bigger than You & I; Younger than Springtime; Medieval Hymn of Praise; Portrait of My Love; The Petals; In the Fields in Springtime; Do You Hear What I Hear; The Stable in Bethlehem (Gregorian chant); Nobody Knows the Trouble I've Seen. Publs: The Complete Dictionary of Authentic & Plagal Scales, 1976. Contbr. to: Clavier; Robert Dumm Review. Mbrships: Pres., Mt. Vernon Music Club, 1975-77. Recip., Nobel Peace Prize, 1976. Hobbies: Cooking; Entertaining. Address: 1609 Baltimore Rd., Alexandria, VA 22308, USA. 5.

BOWDEN, Pamela, b. Rochdale, Lancs., UK. Contralto. Educ: Assoc., Royal Manchester Coll. of Music; later Fellow, ibid. m. D J P Edwards, 1 s., 1 d. Career: concert & opera apps. throughout UK & Europe; tours of W Indies, Middle E, Scandinavia; seasons w. Glyndebourne Opera, Covent Gdn. Opera, Engl. Opera Grp.; num. int. fest. & broadcasts on radio & TV. Recordings: HMV; Pye; Decca. Mbrships: Coun. & Exec. Committee, ISM. Recip., 1st Prize, Concours Int. d'Execution Muscale, Geneva, 1954. Hobbies: Reading; Gardening; Watching Motor Racing. Mgmt: Choveaux Mgmt., Mancroft Towers, Lowestoft, UK. Address: 11 Wickliffe Ave., London N3, UK.

BOWEN, Kenneth John, b. 3 Aug. 1932, Llanelli, Wales, UK. Tennor Singer; Professor at Royal Academy of Music; Adjudicator. Educ: MA, MusB (Cantab); BA (Wales); Hon. RAM; ARCM. m. Angela Evenden, 2 s. Career: Apps. throughout UK incl: Promenade Concerts, 3 Choir Fests. & other maj. Fests. Apps. abroad incl: Berlin, Brussels, Geneva, Madrid, Oslo, Paris, Rome, Stockholm, Israel, USA & Can.; Royal Opera, Covent Garden, London; w. Sadlers Wells Opera at Coliseum; Welsh Nat. Opera; Glyndebourne Touring Opera; Engl. Opera Grp.; Phoenix Opera; Handel Opera Soc.; Kent Opera. Num. recordings. Hons. incl: Queen's Prize, 1961; 1st Prize, Munich Int. Competition, 1962. Hobbies: Golf; Collecting Books, Pictures & Gramophone Records. Address: 44 King Henry's Rd., London NW3 3RP, UK.

BOWEN, William Meirion, b. 6 Apr. 1940, Swansea, W. Wales, UK. Lecturer; Writer; Musical Director. Educ: B Mus, Birmingham Univ., 1962; Cambridge Univ., 1962-63; ARCM Piano Tchng., 1961; ARCO, 1962. Career: Lectr., Liberal Studies, Croydon Coll. of Art, 1963-65; Prod., BBC Radio, 1965-67; Dir. of Music, Kingston Polytechnic, 1968-78; Musical Advsr., London Schl. of Contemporary Dance, 1977-; Freelance jrnlsm.; The Times Educl. Supplement, 1963-, The Guardian, 1967-, Music & Musicians, etc.; Formed percussion/music theatre grp., The Elec. Candle, 1969, w. perfs. at Wigmore Hall, 1970, Queen Elizabeth Hall, 1972, BBC Radio, 1973, & var. fests. Mbr., musical assns. Contbr. to 2 books & var. periodicals. Hons. incl: Barber Postgrad. Schlrship., 1962. Hobbies incl: Cricket. Address: FLat 4, 60 Lavender Gdns., London SW11, UK.

BOWERS, Jane Meredith, b. 17 Sept. 1936, Mpls., Minn., USA. Musicologist; Baroque Flautist. Educ: BA, Wellesley Coll., 1958; MA, 1962, PhD, 1971, Univ. of Calif. Berkeley; studied flute w. James Pappoutsakis, Boston & Frans Vester, The Hague, Baroque flute w. Frans Grüggen, The Hague. Career: Asst. Prin. Flute, Oakland Symph. Orch., 1962-65; Instructor, flute & music lit., Univ. of NC, Chapel Hill, 1968-72; Asst. Prof., musicol. & music hist., Eastman Schl. of Music, Rochester, NY, 1972-73, 74-75; concert tour, Bowers/Wolf Duo, summer 1975; Vis. Prof.; Portland State Univ., Ore., summer 1976 & 1977-78; Vis. Prof., Cornell Univ., 1979. Ed., Michel de la Barre, Pièces pour la flûte traversiére (1702). Contbr. to var. publs. Mbrships. incl: Review Ed., Ed. Bd., Am. Musical Instrument Soc., 1976-. Recip. acad. hons. Address: 429 W 48th St., NY, NY 10036, USA.

BOWERS-BROADBENT, Christopher Joseph, b. 13 Jan. 1945, Hemel Hempstead, UK. Organist; Composer. Educ: Chorister, King's Coll., Cambridge, 1954-58; RAM; ARAM; m. Deirdre Cape, 1 d., 1 s. Career: Organ Recitalist; Comp.; Organist, St. Pancras Ch., London. Compsotions incl: The Pied Piper of Hamelin (children's opera); Worthy is the Labm (oratorio); The Hollow Men (cantata); Te Deum; collected Church Pieces, 1972. Mbrships: RCO. Hobby: Painting. Mgmt: Clarion Concert Agency Ltd., London N19. Address: 94 Colney Hatch Lane, London N10, UK.

BOWIE, Edgar William Lorimer Ormond, b. 19 Mar. 1926, Church Stretton, Salop., UK. Teacher; Flautist; Conductor. Educ: Engl. Music Pedagogue, 1960; Dansk Musikpedagog, 1966. m. Anne-Lise Andersen, 1 d. Career: Engl. Flautist Res. in Copenhagen; Tchr., Flute, Kobenhavns Musikhojskole, 1963-66, Danmarks Musikskole, 1970; Music Fac., N Zahles Seminarium, & John F. Kennedy, & Dag Hammarskjold Schls. Mbr. Dansk Seminariernes Musiklaererforening; ISME. Hobbies: Sport; Painting; Photography. Address: Nansensgade 78 B 2 tv, Copenhagen, Denmark.

BOWKUN, Heléna, b. 12 Dec. 1951, Toronto, Can. Painist. Educ: Royal Conserv. of Music, Toronto; BMus (perf.), Univ. of Toronto; Academie Maurice Ravel, St. Jean de Luz, France. m. Brad Warnaar. Debut: Full solo recital incl. own comps., Royal Conserv. of Music, aged 9 yrs. Career incls: Perfs. w. Toulouse Symph., Toronto Symph. Orch., other French & Can. orchs.; Recitals & Chmbr. Music Concerts, Can., Europe & USA; TV & radio apps., USA & France; sev. perfs. w. violinist Steven Staryk; Tchr., piano, chmbr. music & music theory, George Brown Cull., var. colls. & summer schls., Ont.; currently on staff of the Royal Conserv.; scholarships for Univ. tuition. Hobbies: Animals; All arts (especially embroidery); Swimming; Skating; Movies; Theatre; Ballet. Address: 16 Maxwell Ave., Toronto, Ont. M5P 2B5, Can.

BOWKUN, Julia, b. 1 June 1954, Toronto, Ont., Can. Cellist. Educ: 1 yr., Univ. of Toronto; Pvte. study. Career: Asst. Prin. Cellist, Chmbr. Players of Toronto, 1977-78; w. Toronto Symph. Orch.; Mbr., Ensembles Canada & Bowkun; Tchr., 6 yrs. Hons: Scholarship for Congress of Strings, Am. Fedn. of Musicians, 1971. Hobbies: Sewing; Interior Decoratin. Address: 620 Jarvis St., Apt. 308, Toronto, Ont., Can.

BOWKUN, Sandra, b. 1 June 1954, Toronto, Ont., Can. Flautist. Educ: Royal Conserv. of Music, Toronto; studied w. Jean-Pierre Rampal, Maxence Larrieu (France), William Bennett (London, UK), Robert Aitken, Nicholas Fiore (Can.); Arts & Sci. degrees. master classes in USA w. Julius Baker & others. Career: Prin. flute, E York Symph., 1974-79; mbr., Trio Toronto (now Bowkun); freelance soloist, chmbr. musician & tchr; double-bass player from age 10. Hobbies: Photography; Yoga. Address: 14 Pendrith St., Toronto, Ont. M6G 1R7, Can.

BOWLES, Anthony Philip, b. 18 Sept. 1931, London, UK. Musical Director; Conductor; Composer; Pianist. Educ: RAM, 1948-53; LRAM; ARCM. Career: Musical Dir., many shows inclng. London prod. Jesus Christ Superstar, 1972-. also of Stuttgart Ballet Co., 1973-74; on staff, GSM; Comps. incl: Winter's Tale (film-score), 1968; Leo the Last (film-score), 1969; Red (film-score), 1976; Mandrake (show music), 1969; Musical Dir., original recording & London theatre prod. of Evita. Music for many TV plays inclng. No, No; War & Peace. Recip. FGSM, 1974. Hobbies: Sailing; Food & wine. Mgmt: Fraser & Dunlop. Address: 15 Lonsdale Sq., London N1 EN, UK.

BOWLES, David Graham Alexander, b. 4 July, 1945, Southampton, UK. Bass Tuba Player. Educ: ARCM, 1967; Royal Military Schl. of Music, 1962-63. Career: 9 yrs. army band service; 32 radio broadcasts; 12 TV apps. Recordings: 3 s. brass & military bands. Mbrships: ISM; Tubists Union Brotherhood Assn. Hobbies: Driving; Politics; Accordion Playing. Address: Portland Ct., 40 Kent Rd., Southsea, Hants., UK.

BOWLES, Edmund Addison, b. 24 Mar. 1925, Cambridge, Mass., USA. Musicologist; Specialist in Medieval Musical Instruments & Performance Practices; Tympanist. Educ: Ba, Swarthmore Coll.; MA, Yale Univ.; Dip., Berks. Music Ctr., Tanglewood, Mass. m. Marianne von Recklinghausen, 1 s., 1 d. Career incls: Asst. Mgr. Dept. Arts & Scis., Mgr. of Profl. Activities, Univ. Rels., Sr. Prog. Dir. for Humanities, Ligs. & Mus., IBM Corp., 1959-. Publs. incl: Musikleben und Aufführungspraxis des 15. Jahrhunderts, 1976. Contbr. to reviews & papers to profl. jrnls. Mbr. num. profl. orgs. Hons. incl: Grant-in-Art, Nat. Endowment for the Humanities, 1971-72. Hobby; Orchl. Playing. Address: 5 Sage Court, White Plains, NY 10605, USA. 11.

BOWLES, Paul, b. 30 Dec. 1910, New York City, USA. Composer; Author. Educ: Univ. of VA; Study in Berlin & Paris. m. Jane Bowles (dec.). Career incl: Music Critic, NY Herald Tribune, 1942-45. Compositions incl: music for films & theatre incl: Doctor Faustus; The Glass Menagerie; Twelfth Night; Cyrano de Bergerac; Watch on the Rhine, etc.; Ballet scores for Yankee Clipper; Pastorela; Colloque Sentimentale; Operas -Denmark Vesey; The Wind Remains; Terma; var. sonatas, concertos & other pieces. Recordings incl: Sonata for flute & piano; music for a farce; Sonata for 2 pianos; Concerto for 2 pianos, wind & percussion; Night without sleep. Publs. incl: novels - The Sheltering Sky; Let It Come Down; The Spider's House; Up Above the World; Love with a few Hairs, transl. from Arabic; non-fiction - Their Heads are Green; Yallah!; Without Stopping; var. collects. of short stories, poetry. Hons: Guggenheim Fellowship; Rockefeller Grant. Address: 2117 Tanger Socco, Tangier, Morocco.

BOWLING, F Lee, b. 2 Nov. 1909, Guymon, Okla., USA. Physician; Musician (clarinet, piano, violin, saxophone); Educator. Educ: PhC, BS, MD, Univ. of Colo.; MS, Univ. of Denver; MPH, Harvard Univ.; studied music pvtely; Conducting w. Dr. J De Forrest Cline at Univ. of N Colo. m. Ruth Clarke Cottrell, 3 s. Career: Mgr., Univ. of Colo. Band & Symph. Orch.; Organizer, 1st Rocky Mountain Intercollegiate Band; Fndr. & Organizational Dir. of life of Nat. Intercollegiate Bands; sponsored by Kappa Kappa Psi & Tau Beta Sigma; Int. Plenipotentiary Rep. for Development of Int. Collegiate Bands. Contbr. to: The Baton; The Podium. num. Mbrships. Hons: Disting. Service to Music Award; Award of Merit; Life mbr., Kappa Kappa Psi; Life Mbr., Am. Fedn. of Musicians. Address: 1001 E Oxford Ln., Englewood, CO 80110, USA. 1, 9, 23, 29.

BOWMAN, David Samuel, b. 20 Sept. 1940, Llandudno, Wales, UK. Director of Music. Educ: Mus B, Manchester Univ.; Assoc., Royal Manchester Coll. of Music; Dip. Ed.; Magdalene Coll., Cambridge; FRCO. m. Jill Dorothy Clowes. Career: Music Master, Up Holland Grammar Schl., Wigan, 1964; Dir. of Music, Preston Grammar Schl., 1966; Dir. of Music & Organist, Ampleforth Coll. & Abbey, York, 1970-. Mbrships: AMA; RCO. Hons: Hargreaves Prize, Manchester Univ., 1960; Choral Exhib., Magdalene Coll., Cambridge, 1964. Hobbies: Skiing; Gardening; Fell-walking; Bad Television; Reading. Address: Woodland House, Gilling E, York, UK.

BOWMAN, James Thomas, b. 6 Nov. 1941, Oxford, UK. Counter-Tenor. Educ: MA, New Coll., Oxford Univ.; Dip. in Educ. Debut: opening of Queen Elizabeth Hall, London, 1967. Career: Engl. Opera Grp., 1967; Sadlers Wells Opera, 1970;; Royal Opera Covent Gdn; Aust. Opera, 1978, Paris Opera, 1979. Educl. TV apps. Mbrships: Am. Fedn. of Musicians; Am. Harp Soc.; NEA; Ohio Educ. Assn.; Columbus Educ. Assn.; Ctrl. Ohio Tchrs. Assn. Hobbies: Reading; Sewing; Cycling; Camping; Folk Music. Mgmt: Columbia Artists Mgmt., NY. Address: 194 Wetherby Gdns., London, SW5, UK.

BOWMAN, Robert, b. 10 Jan. 1925, Leeds, Yorks., UK. Tenor singer; Radio & Record Producer; Writer; Conductor; Teacher of Singing; Lecturer; Adjudicator. Educ: AGSM. m. Micky Bowman, 2 s. Debut: Royal Opera House, Covent Gardent, 1958. Career: Prin. tenor at Royal Opera House, Covent Garden, 1958-68; Guest artist, ibid., 1968-. Comps: Dick Turpin, a musical (w. Nigel Brooks). Recordings: Highlights from Falstaff, Billy Budd; sev. films; num. TV apps. Mbrships: Savage Clug; BBC Club; Yorks. Dialect Soc. Hons: Schl. tenor prize; Mirsky Memorial Prize for Lieder; Alfred & Catherine Howard Prize. Hobbies: Reading; Langs.; Physical Exercise. Address: 27 Mayfield Rd., Sutton, Surrey SM2 5DU, UK.

BOYCE, Merel David, b. 11 Nov. 1922, Hazen, Ark., USA. Band Director. Educ: BME, LA State Univ.; Univ. Ore.; Cinn. Conserv. Music; Reed Coll.; Ark. Tech.; Clarinet w. Emil Schmachtenberg, Cinn., & Rocco Zottarelle, St. Louis, Mo. m. Jeanne L. Foster, 4 c. Career: Bandmaster & commanding off., 106th Army Band, Ark. Nat. Guard (rank of Chief Warrant Off., CW3). Contbr. to: Schl. Musician; Instrumentalist. Mbrships:

ASBDA; MENC; Phi Mu Alpha Sinfonia. Hobbies: Fishing; Swimming; Boating; Collecting recordings; Cooking; Collecting special recipes. Address: 7101 Amherst, Little Rock, AR 72205, USA.

BOYCHUK, Albert, b. 10 Oct. 1915, Brandon, Man. Canada. Bandmaster. Educ: Theory & Harmony. Brandon Coll.; Corresp. Courses in theory, harmony, arr., orchn., & 12-tone comp. m. Mary Elizabeth, 2 d. Career: Brandon Concert Orch., 1934; Asst. Bandmaster, HMCS Naden Band, Esquimault, BC & overseas, 1940-46; Bandmaster, Vancourver Fire Dept. Band, 1946-; Musician (woodwinds & guitar), Musicians Fedn. Band Local 145, Vancouver, 1946-; Dir., Collingwood Boys & Girls Band, 1960. Recordings: Band arr. of Warsaw Concerto; HCMS Naden Band broadcasts, recorded by BBC for AEF Progs., 1944-45. Mbrships: Life Am. Fend. of Musicians; Active Army, Navy & Air Force Veterans in Canada. Hons. incl: 1st Prize clarinet, Brandon Music Fest., 1936; 1st Prize, Nat. Exhib. Sr. Bands, 10 times from 1955-73; 1st Prize Vancouver Sea Fest., 1969-73; 1st Prize N Vancouver Parades, 1965-74. Hobbies: Restoring old bldgs.; Electronics. Address: 2146 W 33rd Ave., Vancouver BC, vM 1B9, Canada.

BOYD, Anne Elizabeth, b. 10 Apr. 1946, Sydney, Australia. Composer; Flautist; Lecturer in Music. Educ: BA, Univ. of Sydney, DPhil, Univ. of York; NSW Conserv. of Music. Debut: Adelaide Fest. of Arts, 1966. Career: fest. perfs. incl. Adelaide Fest. of ARts, 1966, 68 & 76 Opening Season Fest. of Sydney Opera House, 1973, Edinburgh & Windsor Fests., 1974; Lectr. in Music, Univ. of Sussex. Comps. incl: String Quartets 1 (recorded) & 2; As Far as Crawls the Toad for 5 young percussionists; The Voice of the Phoenix for solo piano, guitar, harp, harpsichord, full orch. & optional synthesizer; As it leaves the Bell, piano, 2 harps & 4 percussion (recorded); Angklung for piano (recorded); As I Crossed a Bridge of Dreams for unaccomp. SATB, Chorus. Contbr. to: Music Now; Musical Times; Miscellanea Musicol.; Aust. Jrnl. of Music Educ. Mbrships: APRA; Fellowship of Aust. Comps.; Aust. Comps. Guild. Hons. incl: Frank Albert Prize for Music, Univ. of Sydney, 1967. Hobbies: Walking; Swimming; Drinking. Publr: FAber Music Ltd. Address: Swanborough Manor, Swanborough near Lewes, Sussex, BN7 3PF, UK.

BOYD, Franklyn, b. 27 Nov. 1925, Luton, Beds., UK. Singer; music Publisher. m. Daphne Richardson, 1 s., 1 d. Career: Dance band singer; Soloist w. own radio progs., BBC; Published music of Burt Bacharach. Sev. solo recordings. Mbrships: PRS; ASCAP; BMI. Hobby: Cruising the Canadian lakes in Chris Craft. Address: Suit 2214-85, Thorncliffe Park Dr., Toronto, Ont., M4H 1L6, Can.

BOYD, Heather Lilian Elaine, b. 17 May 1932, Comber, Nr. Belfast, N Ireland. Music Teacher. Educ: N Foreland Lodge Schl.; Lic. Royal Acad. Music; Dip. Educ., Music Teaching, Stranmillis Trng. Coll. m. Trevor Dempster Boyd, 5 c. Mbrships: Incorp. Soc. Musicians; Lit. Drawingroom Circle; Holywood Music Festival, Co. Down; Belfast Naturalists' Field Club; Royal N of Ireland Yacht Club; Jt. Hon. Sec., UPNI. Hobbies: Sailing; Gardening; Nature Rambles; Reading; Drama; Music; Stone Polishing. Address: Ringreagh, 8 Craigdarragh Road, Helen's Bay, Co. Down, N Ireland.

BOYD, Jack, b. 9 Feb. 1932, Indpls., Ind., USA. Choral Director; Composer; Editor. Educ: BS, Abilene Christian Coll., 1955; MusM, N Tex. State Univ., 1959; PhD, Univ. of Iowa, 1971. m. Joann Orr, 1 s., 2 d. Career: Composer & Cond., animated film set 'Tales From The Great Book'; Composer & Cond., outdoor drama 'Stars in My Crown', Kenlake Amphitheatre, Kt., Composer & Cond., network relig. radio prog. 'Herald Of Truth', Composer, over 100 works & arrangements of folk & popular music; Ed. of The Choral Jrnl. Publs: Rehearsal Guide For The Choral Director, 1970; Teaching Choral Sight Reading 1975; The Lord's Singing (in preparation). Contbr. to: Choral Jrnl; Music Jrnl; Iowa Music Educator; Southwestern Musician; Hi-way. Mbrships: Am. Choral Dirs. Assn; Tex. Choral Dirs. Assn. Hobbies: Hunting; Freelance writing; Travel. Address: 541 Coll. Drive, Abilene, TX 79601, USA.

BOYD, Malcolm, b. Newcastle-upon-Tyne, UK. Lecturer in Music. Educ: BMus.; MA; ARCO. m. Beryl Gowen, 2 c. Career: Nat. Service; Tchr.; Lectr.; Univ. Coll., Cardiff. Publs: Harmonizing 'Bach' Chorales, 1967; Bach's Instrumental Counterpoint, 1967; Palestrina's Style, 1973; The Music of William Mathias, 1978; composers of Wales 4, Contbr. to: Musical Times; Music & Letters; The Music Review; Tempo; La Musica; Sohlman's Musiklexikon; Grove's Dictionary of Music & Musicians. Mbrships: Royal Musical Assn.; RCO. Hobby: Gardening. Address: 211 Fidlas Rd., Llanishen, Cardiff CF4 5NA, UK.

BOYD, Rodney C, b. 27 Sept. 1943, Baton Rouge, La., USA. Bassoonist; Music Educator. Educ: BMusEd, La. State Univ.; MS, Ill. State Univ.; DMA cand., Boston Univ. m. Sylvia Louise Kendrick. Career: Formerly bassoonist w. var. orchs. inclng. Bloomington-Noraml Symph. Orch., S. Ark. Symph. Orch., Greenville Symph. Orch. & Twin Cities Symph. Orch.; Currently solo bassoonist, Topeka Civ. Symph. Orch.; Mbr. & mgr., Washburn Arts Woodwind Quintet, 1973-; Asst. Prof., music, Washburn Univ., Topeka Kan.; Num. solo & ensemble apps., pub. educl. TV & elsewhere. Contbr. to: Nat. Assn. Coll. Wind & Percussion Instructors Jrnl. Mbr. profl. orgs. Recip. fellowships. Hobbies incl: Photography. Address: 2715 SW 19th St., Topeka, KS 66604, USA.

BOYDELL, Brian, b. 17 Mar. 1917, Dublin, Ireland. Professor of Music; Composer. Educ: BA (Cantab.), 1938; BA, Univ. of Dublin, 1939; MusB, LRIAM, ibid., 1941; ibid, 1942; MusD, 1959; RCM; royal Irish Acad. of Music. m. Mary Jones, 3 s. Career: Adjudicator, num. music festivals incl. the Canadian 'Chain', Over 500 boradcasts made on musical subjs.; Cond., Dublin Orchestral Players, 1942-68; Dir., The Dowland Consort, 1958-69; Guest Cond., RTE & Other Symph. Orchs.; Prof. of Music, Univ. of Dublin. Compositions incl: Violin Concerto; 3 String Quartets; Orchestral & Symphonic Music; Chamber Music; Vocal & Choral Music; Music for Films; Symphonic Inscapes. Publs: 400 years of Music in Ireland. Contbr. to: Grove's Dictionary; Sohlmann's Musiklexikon; Ency. Americana, etc. Mbrships: Irish Arts Coun.; Fndr.-Coun., Music Assn. of Ireland, 1948-. Hons: Fellow, Trinity Coll., Dublin, 1972. Hon. DMus, Nat. Univ. of Ireland, 1974. Hobbies: Fishing; Gardening. Address: Trinity Coll., Dublin 2, Eire.

BOYDEN, David Dodge, b. 10 Dec. 1910, Westport, Conn., USA. Musicologist; Professor of Music. Educ: AB, Harvard Univ., 1932; MA, ibid, 1938; Hartt Sch. of Music, 1936-37. m. Ruth Grant Quimby, 2 s. Publs: History & Literature of Music, 1948; Ed., Geminiani, The Art of Playing on the Violin (1751), Fasc. Ed., 1952; A Manual of Counterpoint, 2nd. ed., 1953; Introduction to Music, 1956 2nd ed., 1970; The History of Violin Playing, 1965; Catalogue of the Hill Collection...Oxford, 1969. Contbr. to num. jrnls., encys., dictionaries. Mbrships: Am. Musicological Soc., (VP. 1954-56, 1960-62); Galpin Soc.; Royal Musical Soc. Hons: Guggenheim Grants, 1954-55, 1967, 1970-71; DMus, Hartt Schl. of Music, Hartford, Conn., 1957; Fulbright Rsch. Scholar, Oxford Univ., UK, 1963. Hobbies: Tennis; String Quartets; Bicycling. Address: 1208 Shattuck Ave., Berkeley, CA 94709, USA. 2.

BOYLE, Diana, b. 22 May 1954, London, UK. Solo & Chamber Music Concert Pianist. Educ: RCM (fndn. scholar); grad. studies w. Enrique Barenboim (Tel Aviv) & Artur Balsam (NY). Debut: S Bank, London, 1979. Career: recitals throughout UK, Ireland, Spain & USA; radio recordings for BBC, RTE (Dublin) & CBC (Montreal). mbr., ISM. recip., Fulbright Scholarship, 1976. Hobbies: Reading; Current Affairs; Watching Sport. Address: 16 Deodar Rd., Putney, London, SW15, UK.

BOYLE, Hugh, b. 28 Apr. 1916, Electrical Engineer. Career: Lectr. in Maths., E. Ham. Coll. of Technol., 1965-; London Rep. & Contbng. Ed., The Harpsichord. Mbr., Royal Musical Assn. Publs: Intervals, Scales & Temperaments, 1963. Contbr. to Hi-Fi News Annual 1963. Hobby: Study of musical instruments & intonation. Address: 405 Green Lane, New Eltham, London SE9, UK.

BOYLE, Rory David Alasdair, b. 9 Mar. 1951, Ayr, Scotland, UK. Composer; Teacher. Educ: chorister, St. George's Chapel, Windsor; Eton Coll.; RSAMD (comp., piano, clarinet, organ); DRASMD (comp.). m. Victoria Lloyd, 1 s. Comps. incl: Toccata for Organ (recorded); 2 symphs.; clarinet concerto; opera; chmbr. music; Augustine (children's opera). Mbrships: Performing Right Soc.; ISM; Musicians Union. Hons: BBC Scotland Comps. Prize, 1971; Royal Phil. Soc. prizes, 1973, 75. Hobbies: Stamp Collecting; Football. Address: The Willows, Walhampton School, Lymington, Hants. SO4 8RE, UK.

BOYSEN, Bjørn Fougner, b. 3 Dec. 1943, Oslo, Norway. Organist. Educ: Organ Tchrs. Dip., Oslo, 1966; Univ. of Oslo. m. Ingrid Haugsand, 2 s. Debut: Oslo, 1966. Career: recitals throughout Scandinavia; 5 tours of UK; 2 recitals, BBC; num. recitals on Norwegian radio & TV, most recently on a prog. about Norwegian comp. Ludvig Mathias Lindeman; Tchr. of Organ, Music Acad., Oslo. Recordings: Contemp. Music from Norway, Jubilate Deo, Organ Music by Arild Sandvold. Contbr. to: Organ Yearbook; Festskrift for Arild Sandvold's 80th yr.; Norsk Kirkemusikk; Rondo. Recip., Prize, Norwegian Sect.;

Nordic Music Competition, 1973. Hobby: Sailing. Address: Huk Aveny 18, Oslo 2, Noway.

BOZEMAN, George L, Jr., b. 10 Nov. 1936, Pampa, Tex., USA. Organbuilder; Organist-Choirmaster. Educ: N. Tex. Univ.; St. Louis Inst. of Music, Mo., Schl. of Music, N. Tex. Univ.; Acad. of Music, Vienna, Austria. Career: Var. Ch. positions, Tex. & Mass.; apprenticed to organbuilder Otto Hofmann, Austin, Tex., 1959-61; later worked w. Joseph E. Blanton, Albany, Tex., Robert L. Sipe, Dallas, Tex., & Fritz Noack, Georgetown, Mass.; Fndr., own film, 1971. Contbr. to: The Tracker (Organ Histl. Soc.); Diapason; The Organ, London; Music (AGO-RCCO). Mbrships: AGO; formerly Exec. Coun., Boston chapt. Organ Histl. Soc.; Int. Soc. Organbuilders; Boston Organ Club. Recip., Fulbright Grant, Austria, 1967-68. Hobby: Cooking. Address: RFD 1, Deerfield, NJ 03037, USA.

BOZIC, Darijan, b. 29 Apr. 1933, Slavonski Brod, Yugoslavia. Composer; Conductor. Educ: MMus. m. Marija Erceg, 2 s., 1 d. Career: Violist, Slovene Opera & Slovene Philharmonia, 1953-68; Cond., Slovene Opera, 1968-70; Artistic Dir., Slovene Philharmonia, 1970-74; w. RTV, Ljubjana, 1974-. Comps. incl: Concerto for trombone & orch.; Concerto for trumpet & orch.; Audiostructgurae for piano & orch.; Audiospectrum, for orch.; Cries for narrator, brass quintet & tape; Protest Song for voice, piano, double bass & 3 tape recorders. Deaf Windows, TV ballet; Ares-Eros, musical comedy. Recordings: Helidon, Ljubljana; Desto, NYC. Recip., Yugoslav RTV Prizes for incidental (1964 & 70), tape (1970), and chamber (1968) music. Hobbies: Skiing; Dogs. Address: Strossmayerjeva 8, Ljubljana, Yugoslavia.

BOZICEVICH, Ronald, b. 8 Feb. 1948, Wheeling, W. Va., USA. Double Bass Player. Educ: Oberlin Conserv.; Juilliard Schl. of Music. m. Sylvia (Hallock) Boziecevich. Career: w. Cinn. Symph., Soloist, Botlesini Duo Concertante, 1973. Address: 7327 Jethve Ln., Cincinnati, OH 45243, USA.

BRACALI, Giampaolo, b. 24 May 1941, Rome, Italy. Composer; Pianist; Conductor. Educ: Dip. Piano, Conservatorio di Santa Cecilia, Rome, 1960; Dip. Comp., ibid., 1963. m. Barbara Bersh, 1 s. Debut: Accademia di Santa Cecilia, 1965. Career: Comps. performed by Nat. Acad. Orch. of Santa Cecilia, Rome, Italy; Symph. Orchs. of Radiotelevisione Italiana, Rome, Turin & Milan; Orch. Pomeriggi Musicali, Mialn; Currently Cond., Manhattan Schl. of Music, NYC, USA; Comp. Fac., ibid. Compositions incl: Quintetto for strings & guitar, 1974; Pezzo for orch., 1977. Mbr. Am. Comps. & Conds Assn Hons incl 1st Prize, F M Naplitano Int. Comp. Competition, 1964. Hobby: Sailing. Address: 601 Kappock St., Riverdale, NY 10463. USA.

BRACEFIELD, Hilary Maxwell, b. 30 June, 1938, Dunedin, NZ. Lecturer; Critic. Educ: MA (Engl. & Music), Dip. Mus., Univ. of Otago; Dip. Tchgn., Christchurch Tchrs. Coll.; LTCL. Career incl: Tchr., Bayfield High Schl., Dunedin; lectr., Worcester Coll. of Higher Educ.; senior lectr., Ulster Polytechnic; joint ed., Contact mag., Today's Music, 1971-. Contbr. to: Music & Musicians. Mbrships: Royal Musical Assn.; ISM (local ctr. treas., 1978-). Hobbies: Film; Theatre; Reading. Address: Music Dept., Ulster Polytechnic, Newtownabbey, Co. Antrim BT37 0QB, N Ireland.

BRACY, Katherine Branfield, b. 13 Mar. 1938, Alliance, Ohio, USA. Harpist; Teacher. Educ: BMus, Oberlin Conserv. of Music, 1959; MMus, Baylor Univ., 1965; Hard study, Summer Harp Colony of Am., Camden, Me. m. Carl Cluster Bracy. Career: Instr. in Music & Hd. of Harp Dept., Univ. of Tex., Austin, 1960 65; Prin. Harpist, Austin Symph.; 1960-65; 2nd Harpist, Houston Symph., 1964-65; Akron & Youngstown Symphs., Ohio, 1965-67; Prin Harpist, Columbus Symph., 1969-; Prin. Harpist, Lakeside Summer Symph., 1964-; Elem. Schl. Tchr., 1965-; Mansfield & Licking Co. Symphs.; Num. Recital & Educl. TV apps. Mbrships: Am. Fedn. of Musicians; Am. Harp Soc.; NEA; Ohio Educ. Assn.; Columbus Educ. Assn.; Ctrl. Ohio Tchrs. Assn. Hobbies: Reading; Sewing; Cycling; Camping; Folk Music. Address: 6612 Merry Ln., Columbus, OH 43229, USA.

BRADBURY, Colin, b. 4 Mar. 1933, Blackpool, UK. Clarinettist. Educ: RCM, 1951-56; ARCM Dip. (Clarinet Perf.). Debut: soloist w. Nat. Youth Orch., Edinburgh Fest., 1951. Career: Prin. Clarinet, BBC Symph. Orch., 1960-; Prof. of Clarinet, RCM, 1963-; regular concerto apps. w. BBC Symph. Orch. Recip. Tagore Gold Medal, best student of yr., RCM, 1956. Hobbies: Electronics; Brewing. Address: 56 Castlebar Rd., Ealing, London 35 22D, UK.

BRADBURY, John, b. 19 May 1944, Manchester, UK. Musician (Violin). Educ: Royal Manchester Coll. of Music;

FRMCM. m. Eira West. Career: Currently Ldr., City of Birmingham Symph. Orch.; Free-lance activities incl: VLN/PNO Duo w. Eira West; Alpha Trio; Ruggieri String Quartet; Concertos & Orchl. Viennese Concert Direction. Mgmt: Elisabeth Ashe Mgmt. Address: 63 Meadow Hill Rd., Kings Norton, Birmingham B38 8DA, UK.

BRADLEY, Ian Leonard, b. 11 Aug. 1925, Aukland, NZ. Professor; Conductor; Organist. Educ: BEd, 1962, EdD, 1969, Univ. of BC; MEd, Western Wash. State Col., 1966. m. Patricia Anne Bradley. Career incls: num. CBC radio & TV broadcasts as Cond. of local schl., community & ch. choirs; Ed., BC Music Educators Jrnl. Publs: Canadian Music for Schools, 1974; A Selected Bibliography of Musical Canadiana, 1974; Twentieth Century Canadian Composers, 1975; Twentieth Century Canadian Composers, Vol. II, 1976; A Bibliography of Canadian Native Arts, 1977. Contbr. to num. profl. jrnls., USA & Can. Mbrships. incl: Exec., BC Music Educators Assn.; Con. Music Ed. Assn.; MENC. Hobbies: Music; Canadian Indian Arts & Crafts. Address: 2574 Vista Bay Rd., Victoria BC, Can. J8P 3E8. 4, 12.

BRADSHAW, David, b. 31 Oct. 1937, Wash., DC, USA. Concert Pianist; Piano Teacher; Lecturer. Educ: BS, Juilliard Schl., NYC. Debut: Alice Tully Hall, NYC, 1970. Career: Solo recitalist, Carnegie Hall, NYC, Constn. Hall, Wash. DC, Town Hall, NYC, The White House, Wash. DC, San Fran. Music Ctr., Cornell Univ., The Juilliard Schl., ETC; Solorist w. orchs. inclng. Nat. Symph., Wash., DC; Radio perfs. inclng. WQXR, WNCN, WBAI, NYC; TV apps. inclng. NBC, ABC, WSLN; var. recordings. Mbrships. incl: Co-Fndr., Pres., 1970-74, Vp, 1976, Alton Jones Assocs. Ltd.; Nat. Guild of Paino Tchrs. Author of prog. notes. Hons. incl: Nat. Soc. of Arts & Letters Award. Hobbies incl: Collecting records. Address: 170 W. 73rd St., NYC, NY 10023, USA.

BRADSHAW, Merrill Kay, b. 18 June 1929, Lyman, Wyo., USA. Composer; Educator. Educ: AB, Brigham Young Univ., 1954; MA, ibid, 1955; MMus, Univ. of Ill., 1956; DMusA, ibid, 1962. m. Janet Spilsbury, 7 c. Career: Instructor, Assoc. Prof., Prof. Music, Brigham Univ., 1957-; Fellow in Music & Asst. in Music, Univ. of Ill., 1956, 1961; Instructor for Music Theory, Airforce Band, Chanute Air Force Base, Ill., 1962. Comps. (publ.) incl.: Echoes, choir; 6 Songs for Sing With Me; 8 Paino Pieces for Music for Worship; 6 Paino Pieces for Miniature Preludes; 20 Piano Pieces for Mosaics; 2 Hymns; (recorded) 10 Piano Pieces for Mosaics/Peace memorial, 1974; The Title of Liberty (musical) 1975; Mormon Hymn Fantasies, 1978; The Resotration; Lovers & Liars; Modules for Musicianship; Four Mountain Sketches; Symph. No. 5, 1979. Contbr. to: Clavier Mag.; Utah Music Educator; Brigham Young Univ. Studies. Mbrships: Music Tchrs. Nat. Assn.; MENC; Int. Webern Soc. ASCAP; Phi Kappa Phi; Local Chapt. Pres., ibid, 1968. Hons: Recip. var. Scholarships & Fellowships; Karl G Maeser Creative Arts Award, 1967-68. Hobbies: Hiking; Fishing; Gardening; Shakespeare. Address: 248 4 3140 N., Provo, UT 84601, USA. 9.

BRADSHAW, Murray C., b. 25 Sept. 1930, Hindsdale, Ill., USA. Musicologist. Educ: Mmus; AAGO; ChM; PhD. m. Doris Hogg, 2 s., 1 d. Publs: The Origin of the Toccata (Am. Inst. of Musicol.), 1972, The Falsobordone: A Study in Renaissance & Baroque Music, 1976. Contbr. to: The Musical Qtly.; The Music Review; The Diapason; Music. Mbrships: Am. Musicol. Soc.; Int. Musicol. Soc.; Ctr. for Medieval & Renaissance Studies; AGO. Hobbies: Jogging; Swimming; Reading; Chess. Address: c/o San Francisco Opera House, San Francisco, CA, USA.

BRADSHAW, Richard James, b. 26 Apr. 1944, Rugby, Warwicks., UK. Conductor. Educ: BA, London. Career: Chorus Dir., Glyndebourne Fest. Opera; Dir. Music, Higham, 1966-; Dir., New London Ensemble & Chorus, 1972-; Saltarello Choir, 1972-75; Regular apps. in all maj. London concert halls, through UK & Europe, & at maj. fests.; Rep. of GB, Gala concert, 1974 Arbeitsgemeinschaft Europaischer Chorverbunde, Oslo; Num. & regular broadcasts for BBC. Recordings: Bruckner; Verdi; Brahms. Hobbies: Wine; Ecclesiastical architecture; Contemporary painting & sculpture. Mgmt: Undine Concannon, 8 the Limes, Linden Gdns., London W2, UK. Address: 13 Woodleigh Ct., Stuart Cres., London N22, UK. 1.

BRADY, Kathleen Teresa, b. 13 Feb. 1934, Traralgon, Vic., Aust. Educ: Dip., music, Univ. of Melbourne; perfs. degree in harpsichord, Quebec City, Can. Debut: Quebec City. Career: Appts. in var. colls. & univs.; perfs. as harpsichord & pianist in sev. countries; inaugural piano recital for Robert Blackwood Hall, 1972; radio perfs. in Can., Aust., & London; TV apps. in Can.; specialises in 19th century keyboard interpretations. sev.

recordings as soloist esp. of 19th century keyboard works. Publs: established Musica Australiana Press; facsimile MS of C E Horsley's Str. Quartet. Contbr. of talks on radio about 19th century Aust. musical life. Mbrships: ISM; Musicol. Soc. of Aust. Hons: Harmony prize, 1952; 1st prize, Dandenong Comps. competition, 1956; bursary, Imperial Order of Daughters of the Empire, 1965. Hobbies: Reading; Antiquarian books; Gardening; Cooking; Antiques; collecting keyboard & Aust. msuic. Address: 6/17 High St., Mont Albert, Vic. 3217, Aust.

BRAEM, Thuring Lukas, b. 10 Apr. 1944, Basel, Switzerland. Conductor; Composer. Educ: MA, Univ. Calif., 1973. m. Penny Boyes Braem, 1 d. Debut: Cond., Radio Orch. Basel, 1970. Career incls Fndr.-Cond., Students' Chmbr. Orch., Basel, Switzerland, 1965-70; Mbr., Santa Fe Opera, 1971; Conserv. Orch., Basel, 1973-; Concerts & radio apps. as cond., comp., lect. & accomp. in Switzerland & USA; Dean of dept., Musik Akademie Basel. Compositions incl: Textures, 1973. Recordings incl: Children's Songs, 1975. Contbr. to Basler Volksblatt. Mbr. Schweizer Tonkunstlerverin. Recip. num. prizes in USA & Switzerland. Hobbies: Plays; Films; Lit.; Skiing. Address: Musik-Akademie der Stadt Basel, Leonhardsstrasse 6, CH-4051 Basel, Switzerland.

BRAGA, Henriqueta Rosa Fernandes, b. 12 Mar. 1909, Rio de Janeiro, Brazil. Musicologist; Lecturer; Pianist; Conductor; Professor of Music History. Educ: Dip. Piano Tchr., Nat. Inst. of Music, Univ. of Rio de Janeiro; Dip. Maestro, Nat. Schl. of Music, Univ. of Brazil; DMus & Titular Prof., Schl. of Music, Fed. Univ. of Rio de Janeiro; Titular Prof., Villa Lobos Inst., Guanabara Schl. of Music. Career incls: Prof. of Music Hist., var. univs. inclng: Fed. Univ. of Rio de Janeiro, 1936-; Music Hist. Progs., Radio Roquette Pinto, Rio; Organist & Choir Cond., Fluminese Evangelical Ch. Comps. incl: Sonhemos (voice & piano). Publs: incl: Canticos do Natal, 1947. Contbr. to profl. jrnls. Mbr. num. profl. orgs. Hons. incl: Alexandre Levy Medal, 1964. Address: Rua Desembargador Isidro, 126 Bloco A Apt. 701, Tijuca, 10.000 Rio de Janeiro, Brazil. 4.

BRAGA, Robert, b. 30 Nov. 1915, London, England. Teacher (violin & viola); Musician (viola). Educ: LRAM. m. Rosemary Beckett, 2 s. Career: Free lance player w. London Phil. Orch., 1947-67; mbr. of Peter Mountain String Quartet, 1956-66; Tchr. of violin & viola to Univ. of Liverpool. Mbrships: ISM. Hobbies: Reading; Ornithology. Address: 20 Southwood Rd., Liverpool L17 7BQ, UK.

BRAHN, Lux, b. 4 Jan. 1946, Lachen, Schwyz, Cwitz. Clarinettist. Educ: Clarinet Dip., Zürich (studied w. Rolf Kubli); Salzburg Mozarteum, Paris & Hannover. m. Arthur Genswein, 1 s, 1 d. Career: num. concerts as soloist & chmbr. musician, France, Belgium, Italy, Germany, Austria, Switz.; num. radio & TV broadcasts, Vienna, Cologne, Brussels, Zurich, Genoa, Paris; Mbr. Zürcher Solisten 't' Ensemble européen de la musique contemporaine (Paris); Recordings: Clarinet Quintets by Mozart, Welex and Brahms; Trios by Beethoven and Brahms. Mbr., var. ensembles. Recordings: Rimpahon, Zurich; Music Pick; Da Camera. Mbr., Swiss Musicians Union. Hons. incl: Prize, Expo 64, Lausanne; 3 times, Prize, Kiefer-Hablutzel Fndn.; Migros Fndn. Hobbies: Literature; Film. Address: Dufourstr, 32, CH-8702 Zollikon, nr. Zürich, Switzerland. 4.

BRAILSFORD, Clive Robert, b. 26 Oct. 1945, Fareham, Hants., UK. Music Teacher; Organist; Pianist. Educ: GSM; London Univ.; Exeter Univ. Inst.; BMus (London); GGSM; ARCO; ATCL; Cert. Educ. m. Eileen Elizabeth Peacey, 2 s. Career: Organist, Wisley Ch., Surrey, 1957; Pianist, Pack Club, Southsea; Pianist, Oriana passenger liner; Piano Tchr., Catford Inst., 1971; Deputy Hd. of Music, Sir Walter St. John's Schl., Battersea, 1978. Hons: Schl. Organ Prize, GSM, 1965. Hobbies: Chess; Reading; Tuning keyboard instruments. Address: 2 Vicarage Gardens, Mitcham, Surrey CR4 3BL, UK.

BRAIN, Gary Clifford Dennis, b. 12 Aug. 1943, Palmerston N, NZ. Principal Timpani; Percussionist; Director. Educ: Staatliche Hochaschule für Musik, Berlin; NZ Symph. Trainee Scheme. m. June Anne Brain, 1 d, 1 s. Debut: NZ Nat. Youth Orch. Career: Prin. Timpanist, Percussionist, NZ Symph. Orch.; Dir. NZ Percussion Ensemble; Dir., Music Players '70 (TV apps.); Dir., TV & films soundtracks & radio prodns., Tutor, Vic. Univ., Wellington. Comps: Quartet, violin & percussion; Sonata, Vere et Violin, for solo violin; Three Movements for String Orch. Recordings: Music Players '70; Sonata two pianos & percussion; Bartok; Composition Five Percussion Electronic Sounds, John Rimmer; Dances from Electra, Edwin Carr. Publs: History of Percussion, 1977. Contbr. to: Newspapers. Mbr. Soc. for Music Educ. Hons: Scholarships. Hobbies: Fishing; Art; Family; Philosophy. Mgmt: Music Fedn. of NZ. Address: 30 Anne St., Highland Pk., Wellington 1, NZ.

BRAINARD, Paul Henry, b. 18 Apr. 1928, Musicologist. Educ: BA, MA, Univ. of Rochester; PhD, Univ. of Göttingen. m. Ingrid Kahrstedt, 1 s. Publs: Le sonate per violino di Giuseppe Tartini, 1975; Neue Bach-Ausgabe, Sweries II, Vol. 7; Easter Oratorio, 1977, Vol. 8; Ascension Oratorio, 1978, Series I, Vol. 16; Cantatas 21, 76, 2, 135, forthcoming. Contbr. to: Jrnl. Am. Musicol. Soc.; Die Musikforschung; Notes. Mbrships: Int. & Am. Musicol. Socs.; Germn. Soc. for Music Rsch.; New Bach Soc. Hobbies: Photography; Carpentry. Address: Brandeis Univ. Dept. of Music, Waltham, MA 02154, USA. 2.

BRAININ, Norbert, b. 12 Mar. 1923, Vienna, Austria. Violinist; Leader of Amadeus String Quartet. Educ: studied w. Max Rostal & Carl Flesch; GSM. m. Kathe Kottow, 1 d. Career: Fndr., Ldr., Amadeus String Quartet, 1947-. Recordings: principally DGG. Hons. incl: Carl Flesch Prize for solo violin, GSM, 1948; CBE, 1960; Doct., Univ. of York, 1968. Address: 9 The Ridgeway, London NW7, UK. 1.

BRAITHWAITE, Nicholas Paul Dallon, b. 26 Aug. 1939, London, UK. Conductor. Educ: RAM; Bayreuth Festival Masterclasses; Acad. of Music, Vienna. Debut: BBC Scottish Symph. Orch., 1966. Career: Assoc. Cond., Bournemouth Symph. Orch., 1967-70; Assoc. Prin. Cond., Sadlers Wells Opera, 1971-74; Music Dir., Glyndebourne Touring Opera, 1977-; Guest Cond. w. Norwegian State Radio Orch., 1976-; BBC Symph. Orch.; BBC Scottish, Norther & Welsh Orchs.; City of Birmingham Symph.; Welsh Nat. Opera; Scottish Nat. Orch.; Ulster Orch.; Halle Orch.; Philomusica; Radio Symph. Orch. of Helsinki; Oslo Phil.; RPO; Hambrug Staatsoper; Coven Garden. Recording: Cooke Symph. No. 3, w. London Phil. Orch. (Lyrita Records). Mbrships: ISM; Musicians Union. Recip. FRAM, 1970. Hobby: Scale model aircraft. Mgmt: Stafford Law Associates. Address: 42 Muswell Ave. London N10 2EL, UK.

BRAKSTAD, Anna, b. 23 Sept. 1944, Bergen, Norway. Horn Player (French Horn). Educ: Royal Danish Acad. of Music, Copenhagen; Leningrad Conserv. Career: 4th Horn, Odense Town Orch., Denmark; 2nd Horn, Sjoellands Symph. Orch., Copenhagen. Mbrships: Int. Horn Club. Address: Gardfestevej 20, 2300 Copenhagen, Denmark.

BRAM, Marjorie, b. 28 June 1919, Phila., Pa., USA. Performer; Conductor; Author; Educator. Educ: BS, Temple Univ., MA, Columbia Univ.; Cert. in condng., Mozarteum, Salzburg, Austria. Career: performer on viols da gamba, viola d'amore, rebec, Medieval fiedel, violin (baroque & contemporary) & viola. Publs: Sound Dimensions for New Players (instrumental prog., 19 student books, 1 tchs. manual), 1971. Contbr. to num. profl. publ. incl: Music Educators Jrnl., The instrumentalist, Jrnl. of the Viola da Gamba Soc. of Am., Strad mag. (UK). Mbrships: Viola da Gamba Soc. of Am. (pres., 1970-72, Bd. of Dirs., 1972-78, Bd. of Advsrs., 1978-); Viola d'Amore Soc. of Am.; Am. Musicol. Soc. American String Tchrs. Assn. etc. Hons: life mbr., NJ Music Educators Assn.; 1st prizes in comp., Temple Univ., 1939, '40. Hobbies: Gardening; Photography; Swimming; People. Address: 3611 22nd Ave. W, Bradenton, FL 33505, USA. 5, 6, 7, 27, 29.

BRAMMER, Sheila Elizabeth, b. 19 Sept. 1952, Hyde, Cheshire, UK. Teacher. Educ: GRNCM (piano, singing, oboe); postgrad. cert. of Educ., Homerton Coll., Cambridge. m. Paul Morrison. Career: Hd. of Music in a comprehensive schl.; pvte. tchr. of piano, oboe, recorder, harmony & counterpoint. Mbr., ISM. Hobbies: Music; Dancing; Concert-going; Creative Crafts; Squash Racquets. Address: 9 Radnormere Dr., Cheadle Hulme, Stockport SK8 5JX, UK.

BRAMSEN, Ludvig Ernst, b. 12 Dec. 1910, Vedbaek, Denmark. Double Bass Player. Educ: studied engrng., B & W, Copenhagen, 5 yrs.; Royal Danish Conserv. of Music, 1933-38. m. Margrethe Balslev (née Nissen), 2 s, 1 d. Career: Mbr., Young Musicians Orch., 1938-48; w. Emil Telmányi, Endre Wolf & Collegium Musicum chmbr. orchs., 1st Asst., Royal Theatre (opera), Copenhagen, also Soc. Wkr. (Childrens Welfare), Copenhagen Municiaplity, 1943-48; Mbr., Danish State Radio Symph. Orch., 1948-73. Ed. (in collaboration), Danish literature of fiction & poetry, 1900-1950, vols. 1-3, 1959-63. Now working for Gyldendal. Hobby: Personal-hist. work. Address: Overgade neden Vandet 33/1. Copenhagen, 1414, Denmark.

BRANCO, José Mário, b. 25 May 1942, Oporto, Portugal. Compser; Singer; Author; Actor. Educ: pvte. w. Michel Puig (Paris), Escola Parnaso (Oporto). div. 2 s. Debut: 1967, 1st record publd. Career: num. apps. in France, Switz., Belgium, Italy, Netherlands, Germany, UK & Portugal; solo concerts. Comps: Music for 3 films; 70 titles publd. and recorded, 1967-69. Recordings inc. 7 LPs. Mbrships: Sociede Portuguesa de Autores; SACEM; Fndr. of groups Organon,

69/1 Gac. num. awards for records, 1978. Hobby: Crossword Puzzles. Address: Rua Pedro Nunes 27-10/F, Lisbon, Portugal.

BRAND, Geoffrey Edward, b. 9 May 1926, Gloucester, UK. Conductor, Arranger, Adjudicator. Educ: ARAM; LRAM; ARCM. m. Violet Brand, 1 s., 1 d. Career: Trumpet player, Royal Phil. Orch., Royal Opera House Orch., etc., 1949-55; Music Prod., BBC Radio & TV, 1955-67; Prod., Int. Light Music Festival, 9 yrs.; Orchestral Cond., BBC, etc.; Profl. Cond., Black Dyke Mills & other Brass Bands; Music Advsr., Nat. Youth Brass Band of Gt. Britain, 1967-; Fndr. & cond. of City of London Brass; Ed., the British Bandsman & Music Ed., R Smith & Co., 1967-; Lectr., Extra-Mural Dept., Univ. of London; Examiner, TCL; World-wide Adjudicator. Num. Recordings w. bands, choirs & orchs. for major recording cos. Contbr. to: The British Bandsman; Times Educl. Supplement; Music Coll. Mag. Mbrships: Mbrs. Fund Committee, Performing Rights Soc.; Middlesex Cricket Club; ISM. Hons: Vivian Dunn Orchestral Prize, RAM, 1949; John Solomon Wind Prize, RAM, 1949. Hobbies: Cricket; Theatre; Boating; Reading; Travel. Address: 7 Moor Lane, Rickmansworth, Herts, UK.

BRAND, Max (Maximilian), b. 26 April 1896, Lemberg, Austria. Composer & Librettist (Opera & Ballet); Musician (Piano, Organ, Electronic Synthesizer). Educ: Rosenberg inst., St. Gallen, Switz.; Pupil of Franz Schreker, Vienna Conserv., Austria; State Acad. of Music, Berlin. Debut: Winterhur Fest., 1922. Career: Fndr., Mimoplastic Ballet Theatre, Vienna, Austria; Co-Dir., Opera Prods., Raimund Theatre, ibid; Prod., avant-gards films, ibid; for many yrs. Dir., Music & Theatre Wing, Caravan of East & West Inc., NYC. Comps. incl: Night Music; Tragoedietta, ballet; Five Ballads for Voice & Six Instruments (recorded); Maschinist Hopkins (recorded); The Gate, scenic Oratorio (recorded); The Wonderful One-Hoss-Shay (recorded); Night on the Bayous of Louisiana; The Astronauts, electronic; ballet, instrumental & electronic music. Contbr. to var. jrnls. & newspapers. Mbrships: Audio Engrng. Soc. Inc.; GEMA. Hons: 2nd Prize for Film Music, Venice Film Fest., 1933. Address: Studio of Electronic Studies, Chimanigasse 10, A-2103 Langenzersdorf, Austria.

BRAND, Myra Jean, b. 4 Sept. 1936, Dallas, Ore., USA. I chr. of music, Ore. Coll. of Educ. (Asst. Prof.); Singer. Educ:- BMus, Williamette Univ., Salem, Ore., 1968; MMus., Univ. of Ore., 1971; Candidate for DMus Arts, ibid., 1979. m. Malcolm L. Brand, 1 s., 1 d. Career incls: Prof. of Music, Ore. Coll. of Educ., 1968-; Solo apps., w. Salem Symph., 1974, 75, 77, 78. w. Eugene Symph., 1976; w. Boise Phil., 1977; w. Portland Junior Symph., 1976; Morning Musicale Series, Salem, 1970; var. operatic & oratorio roles on W. Coast & recitals of solo & chmbr. music. Mbrship incls: NATS (Gov. of Ore., 1977-79); Cascade Chap. Pres., 1973-75; Mu Phi Epsilon; Pi Kappa Lambda; ACDA, AAUP. Hons. incl: 1st Recip. Mu Phi Epsilon Scholarship, 1956; Winner, Close Award Competition, Univ. of Ore., Eugene, 1975. Hobbies: Family activities; Travel. Address: 720 McGilchrist SE, Salem, OR 97302, USA.

BRANDMAN, Israel, b. 1 Dec. 1901, Kamenetz, Podolsk, USSR. Conductor; Violinist; Composer. Educ: Dips. in comp., violin & conducting; Schl. of Music, Vienna. m. Berta, 2 c. Debut: 1910, Russia. Career: Cond. since 1918; apps. as violinist & cond. in Vienna, Czechoslovakia & Israel. Comps: Sonata for violin & piano; Variations on a Theme by Engel for piano & orch.; Variations for a String Quartet. Mbrships: Israeli Organisation of Comps. Address: Acad. Floom, 134 Tel Aviv, Israel.

BRANDON, Heather, b. 21 Nov. 1931, London, UK. Music Lecturer; Choral Director; Pianist. Educ: GTCL; FTCL; LRAM; LTCL (perf.). m. Edward William, 1 s. Career: Nat. broadcast artist, SABC on piano & w. Oriana Choir; TV apps; Dir., Oriana Choir & Durban Symphonic Choir. Contbr. to: Arts Review (SABC); Mercury; Daily News. Mbrships: Exec., Burban City Coun. Music Mgmt. Committee; hon. sec., Durban Music Soc.; S African Soc. of Music Tchrs. recip., TCL Silver Medal, 1947. Hobbies: Squash; Sailing; Riding; Conservation. Address: 21 Sherborne Pl., Durban N, Natal, S Africa.

BRANDSE, Wilhelmus Cornelis, b. 17 Aug. 1933, Utrecht, Holland. Compser; Professor. Educ: Muzieklyceum, Amsterdam; Conservatorium, Utrecht; Highest Dip. for Theory, 1950. m. Annie Bakker, 4 c. Career: Prof. Sled. Conservatorium, Zwolle, 1959-; Prof. of Comp., Utrecht Conservatorium, 1265-69. Comps. incl: Sonatine for flute & piano, 1975; Five Willem Brandt Songs, 1975; Freemason Music for Accordion, 1975; Pocket Music for piano, 1975; Gezelschapspel (pieces for 2, 3 & 4 pianos), 1976. Mbrships. incl: Neo. Toonkunsenaarsregister & var. Dutch Music Assns.; Mbr., Staatsexamens for Music. Address: Apeldoornseweg 16, Hattem, Holland.

BRANDT, Hans Henrik, b. 16 May 1944, Aarhus, Denmark. Flautist; Recorder Player. Educ: pvte. studies w. Erik Thompson, Copenhagen, & Severino Gazzelloni, Rome. m. Lise Mücke Brandt. Career: TV & radio apps. for the last 15 yrs.; mbr., Vestjysk Kammerensemble, 1967-. Comps: Christ rose from the dead (recorded). Recordings: own improvisations; works by Nielsen, Lutoslawski & Britten. Hobby: Ornithol. Address: Sonderengen 50, 6700 Esbjerg, Denmark.

BRANDT, Jerome, b. 6 Nov. 1937, Philadelphia, Pa., USA. Tenor-Counter Tenor. Educ: BA, Univ. of Pa., 1969. m. Rachel S. Brandt, 1 s., 1 d. Career: Mbr., The Suffolk Owls, 5-part vocal ensemble, perfs. at Univ. Museum, Univ. of Pa. Fest. Baroque Music, Saratoga Springs, NY. Mbr. Univ. of Pa. Collegium Musicum, Men's Chorale of All-Phila. Boys Choir, & Prin. Tenor & asst. to choimaster, Ch. of St. Martin-in-the-Fields, Chestnut Hill, Pa. Mbrships: Int. Heinrich Schütz Soc. Hons: 3rd Prize, Repertoire Contest, Nonesuch Records. Hobby: Playing chamber music (viola). Address: 2589 Murray Ave., Hungtingdon Valley, PA 19006, USA.

BRANDT, Michel, b. 11 Jan. 1934, Rennes, France. Conductor. Educ: Dip., Paris Conserv.; Dip., Ecole Normale de Musique de Paris. m. Rosemarie Wright, 2 s. Debut: Aarhus, Denmark. Carer: Cond., Staedtebund Theater, Biel-Solothurn, 1961-64, Cologne Opera House, 1964-71; Sr. Lecturer, Royal Northern Coll. of Music, Manchester, Uk, 1973-; Guest Cond., Royal Ballet; Concerts in Denmark, Holland, France, Germany, Italy, Ireland, Israel, Switzerland, USA. Comps: Film & State Music for French Radio & TV. Comédie de l'Ouest & var. film cos. Recordings: on RCA, Decca & EMI. Recip. Prize Int. Competition for Conds., Bescancon, 1960. Hobbies: Art; Do It Yourself. Address: 84 Filsham Rd., Hastings, UK.

BRANGJOLICA, Ivo, b. 19 Nov. 1928, Dubrovnik, Yugoslavia. Professor of music & piano. Educ: Dip. Mus., Music Schl., Zagreb, Dip. Mus, Acad. of Music, Zagreb. Career: Apps. at fests. at Dubrovnik, Belgrade, Zagreb, Titograd, Mostar, St. Stefan-Budva; TV apps. in Zagreb, Belgrade, Titograd & Sarajevo; Radio broadcasts in Zagreb, Dubrovnik, Sarajevo & Titograd. Mbrships: Soc. of Music Tchrs. of Croatia; Soc. of Creative Artists of Croatia. Hobbies: Swimming; Gardening. Mgmt: Koncertna poslovnica, Dubrovnik Festiv. od Sigurate 1, Dubrovnik, Yugoslavia. Address: Sredenj kono 10, 50 000 Dubrovnik, Yugoslavia.

BRANSCOMBE, Peter John, b. 7 Dec. 1929, Sittingbourne, Kent, UK. University teacher; Musicologist. Educ: Dulwich Coll.: MA, Worcester Coll., Oxford; PhD, Bedford Coll., London. m. Marina Elizabeth Riley, 2 s., 1 d. Career: Apps. on BBC radio & TV & Scottish TV; Lectr. in German, Univ. of St. Andrews, 1959-69; Sen. Lectr., ibid, 1970-. Publs: Part-author & co-ed., Schubert Studies: Problems of Style & Chronology; Translr. of Mozart & his World in Contemporary Pictures, 1961; co-translr. of Mozart, A Documentary Biography, 1965. Contbr. to var. profl. jrnls. Mbrships: Royal Musical Assn.; Modern Humanities Rsch. Assn.; English Goethe Soc. Hons: Gov., RSAM, 1967-73; Music Committee, Scottish Arts Coun., 1974-; Scottish Arts Coun. 1976-. Hobbies: Riding; Natural Hist. Address: 55 George St., Cellardyke, Anstruther, Fife, KY10 3AS, UK.

BRANSFORD, Mallory Watkins, b. 9 Mar. 1912, Smoot, W Va., USA. Organist; Choirmaster; Professor. Educ: BM, Oberlin Coll., 1934; MM, Butler Univ., 1936; BMusEd, ibid, 1944; grad. study in Ind. Univ., 1947-49; Doct. Fellow, Walden Univ., 1974-75; PhD, ibid, 1975; 2 Certs., Christiansen Choral Schl.; var. seminars & workshops; studied organ w. Marcel Dupré. m. Helen Elizabeth Zahn, 1 s., 1 d. Career: Min. of Music, Ct. St. United Meth. Ch., Rockford, Ill., 1936-42; Music Specialist, Indpls. Pub. Schls., 1943-; Chmn., Organ Dept., Jordan Coll. of Music, Butler Univ., 1944-; Min. of Music, Ctrl. Ave. Meth. Ch., 1949-51; Zion Evangelical United Ch. of Christ, 1951-; Organist, Supreme Coun. of Scottish Rite Cathedral, 1960-. Comps. & Arr., Sacred Choral Music. Recording: Choral & Organ Favourites, 1978. Publs: Manual of Organ Instruction (to be publd. 1975); articles on Ch. Choir systems. Mbrships: AGO (Dean, 2 yrs.); Nat. Assn. Choral Dirs.; MENC; Phi Mu Alpha Sinfonia; Mason. Recip., Hon. Masonic 33rd Debree, Phila., 1971; Disting Service Award, MENC. Hobbies: Gardening, Photography. Address: 4705 Melbourne Rd., Indianapolis, IN 46208, USA. 8.

BRANSON, David, b. 13 July 1909, King's Lynn, Norfolk, UK. Pianist; Composer. Educ: LRAM; RCM. Debut: Steinway Hall at age 11. Career: Performed on radio in UK & Eire; TV film of Sussex Ensemble, 1966; Concerts in prin. UK cities; Mbr., Lydian & Cecilia Hansen Trios; Radio work incls: recitals, concertos & ensembles; Perf. & lectr. in USA, 1966. Compositions incl: Two Spanish Imperssions (orch.) Mediterranean (piano & strings); The Mortal Pastime (tenor, harp & strings); many songs. Publ: John Field and Chopin, 1972. Contbr. to Music, Music in Schls., etc. Mbrships: Brit. Fedn. of Music Festivals; PRS. Art exhibs., Royal Acad. & Royal Watercolour Soc. Hobbies: Swimming; Films (artistic). Address: Rock House, Exmouth Pl., Hastings, Sussex TN34 3JA, UK. 14.

BRASCHOWANOWA, Lada, b. 11 Feb. 1929, Sofia, Bulgaria. Musicologist. Educ: Classical High Schl., Basel, Switz.; State Acad. of Music, Sofia, Bulgaria. m. Stefan Stantchev, 1 s. Debut: Sofia, 1946. Career: Piano tchr.; musicologist & music publr., 1949-; mbr. of Assn. of Bulgarian Comps. & Musicologists, 1951-; mbr. of Assn. of Music Tchrs., 1953-; mbr. of the Jury of the Int. Music Competition in Munich, 1975. Publs: Mozart, 1958; Berlioz, 1958; Handel, 1959; The Song -A beloved comrade of youth, 1963; Great Composers' Childhood & Adolescence, 1971; Carl Orff, 1974; co-author, Text book on Music, 1976; Readings in Literature on Music with Analyses, (co-author), 1964, etc. Contbr. to num. profl. jrnls. Mbrships: Int. Assn. for Music; Assn. for Musical Rsch.; Assn. of the Bulgarian Comps. & Musicologists. Hobbies: Travelling. Address: 1504 Sofia, Boulevard Russki 17, Bulgaria.

BRASIL, Arthur, b. 14 Mar. 1949, Petrópolis, Brazil. Pianist. Educ: studied w. Myriam Dauesberg; Inst. of Music, Salvador, Bahia; Tex. Christian Univ. Inst. of Music. Debut: Rio de Janeiro, 1968; NY, 1972. Career: num. concerts & recitals in Brazil, Canada, USA, France, Spain, Italy, etc. Mbrships: Ordem dos Músicos do Brasil; Abrarte Cultura Artistica de Petropolis. Hobbies: Dumb-bell exercises; Skiing; Travelling; Books & Records. Address: Abrarte Cultura Artistica de Petrópolis, Rua Dr. Sá Earp 280, Petrópolis, CEP 25.600, Brazil.

BRASSENS, Georges, b. 22 Oct. 1921, France. Musician; Compser. Educ: Coll. de Sète; Lycée de Montpellier. Career incl: Writer & singer of songs in cabaret & music halls, 1952-; Wrote music & songs & acted in film Porte des Lilas, 1956. Compositions incl. num. songs - La Mauvaise Réputation; Le Gorille; Le Fossoyeur; Hecatombe, etc. Publs: La Tour des Mirales (novel); La Mauvaise Réputation (collect of songs). Hons: Grand Prix du Disque, 1964; Poetry Prize, Acad. Françcaise, 1967. Address: 138 Blvd. du Montparnasse, Paris 14e., France.

BRATT, C Griffith. b. 21 Nov. 1914, Balt., Md., USA. Organist; Choirmaster; Professor of Music; Composer. Educ: Univ. of Balt.; Johns Hopkins Univ.; Univ. of Utah; Peabody Conserv. of Music; Artist's Dip. in organ; MMus.; DMus; AAGO. m. Mary E Wallis, 4 c. Career: Num. concerts in USA as Organist & Choral Dir.; weekly organ recitals on radio, 1953-58; Organist-Choirmaster, St. Michael's Cathedral; Prof. of Music & Comp.-in-Rex., Boise State Univ. Comps: 3 operas, 'Rachel', 'Montezuma', & 'Season for Sorrow', 2 Symphs., The Lyric & The Bimodal; 2 Cantatas; Pieces of 8 (24 piano works); 70 organ works inclng. Four Voluntaries (for organ), Six Seasonal Preludes, & Voluntaries for the Church Year (3 Vols.); sev. choral works. Publs: Evolution of Harmony, 1965. Contbr. to sev. mags. Mbr. Dean of local chapt. & State Chmn. for 20 yrs., AGO. Hons. incl: Allied Arts Award for 'Rachel'; Disting. Alumni Award, Peabody Conserv.; Nat. Fedn. of Music Award; Award for Serv. to Music, Gov. of Idaho. Hobbies: Fishing; Travel. Address: 1020 N 17th St., Boise, ID 83702, USA.

BRAUER, Dieter, b. 16 Sept. 1935, Lübben, Germany. Concert pianist. Educ: Hans Eisler Coll. of Music, Berlin 1953-58; Masters Degree, 1963. m. Eva Dryoff, 1 d. Career: asst. & hd. asst. lectr. Hans Eisler Coll. of Music, 1963-75; lectr. at same Inst. from 1975; Concerts in E Europe, USSR, Scandinavia, China, Korea; num. radio apps. Recordings: 'Musik für Kinder', - works by Kochan, Spies, Schwaen, Finke, Wagner-Régeny; works by Kabalewski, Meyer, Gerster, Thilman, on 'Schola'. Contbr. to var. profl. jrnls. Mbrships: comps. & musicians union of German Dem. Repub.; Chopin Soc., Berlin; Johannes R Becher Club. Berlin; Arts Trade Union of German Dem. Repub. Hons. incl: J R Becher Medal, 1972 & 76. Address: 1058 Berlin, Gleimstr. 10, German Dem. Repub.

BRAUN, Edgar J., Conductor; Music Director. Educ: Cond. w. Pierre Monteux; Musicianship & Comp. w. Ernest Bloch; Masters & Doct. Degrees, Univ. of Calif. Career: Cond., San Fran. Chmbr. Orch., 1966-; Music Dir., ibid; Cond., USA; Guest Cond., Netherlands, Salzburg, Mexico, Argentina, Vienna, Paris, Lisbon, Poland. Address: c/o San Francisco Chamber Orch., San Francisco, Calif., USA.

BRAUN, Peter Micheal, b. 2 Dec. 1936. Composer; Pianist; Conductor; Lecturer. Educ: Music Colls., Cologne & Detmold. Career: W. German Radio, Cologne, 1959; Darmstadt Summer Course, 1960; World Fest. of ICSM, Basle, 1970; Warsaw

Autumn Fest., 1970; Donau Musiktage, 1971; Wittener Tage für Neue Kammermusik, 1974. Comps. incl: 4 Pieces for Chamber Ensemble; Reprise for piano; Spuren for optional voices/instruments; Monophonie for guitar; Thesis-Medium for piano.; Summer Pieces for violin & piano; Transfer to full orch.; Variete for full orch.; Planctus for piano; Problems & Solutions for string orch. Contbr. to German-lang. music jrnls. Mbrships: GEMA; German Comps. Union; German Sect., ISCM. Hons. incl: Johann-Stamitz-Prize, 1975; Villa Massimo, Rome, 1976. Address: Am Kuttenbusch 24, 5040 Brühl, German Fed. Repub.

BRAUNINGER, Eva J (Miller), b. 8 July 1931, Fredonia, Kan., USA. Teacher of Strings; Principal String Bass. Educ: BMus, Wichita State Univ., Kan.; MMus, Eastman Schl. of Music, Rochester, NY; Additional study, Ind. Univ., Bloomington, Ind. m. James E Brauninger, 2 s., 1 d. Career: Former mbr., Hormel All-Girl Orh., CBS TV; Mbr., Wichita Symph.; Prin. String Bass, Des Moines Symph. Orch., 1963-; Tchr. of strings. Mbrships: Mu Phi Epsilon; Guest Lectr., Am. String Tchrs. Assn. Hobbies: Sewing; Camping; Swimming; Cycling. Address: 3108 Giles St., W Des Moines, IA, USA.

BRAUNINGER, James Edward, b. 2 Mar. 1927, Kansas City, Mo., USA. Violinist; String Teacher; Conductor. Educ: BM, Eastman Schl. of Music, Rochester Univ.; MM, Univ. of Tulsa; Doct. study, Ind. Univ. m. Eva Miller, 2 s., 1 d. Career: String Tchr., Des Moines,(Iowa) Schls.; Former Cond., 13 yrs., Des Moines Youth Symph. Mbrships: Past State Pres. & Past Ed., Newsletter, Am. String Tchrs. Assn.; MENC. Hobby: Hi-fi. Address: 3108 Giles St., W Des Moines, IA 50265, USA. 12.

BRAUS, Dorothea, b. Heidelberg, Germany. Concert Painist. Educ: Pvte. lessons w. Prof. Conrad Ansorge, Berlin. m. H Steinberg. Debut: Berlin, Germany. Career: Apps. w. orchs. inclng: Vienna Phil.; Berlin Phil.; Leipzig Gewandhaus; Prague Phil.; Tours of Europe; Apps. on Engl. & European radio stns.; Jt. recitals w. Leon Goossens; Apps. w. LPO & London Mozart Players. Num. recordings on Decca Mbr. ISM. Hobbies: Mtn. Climbing; Dressmaking. Address: 65 Lancaster Ave., Hadley Wood, Barnet, Herts., UK. 27.

BRAUSS, Helmut F, b. 19 Oct. 1930, Milan, Italy. Concert Pianist. Educ: Handel Conserv., Munich, Germany; Hochschule für Musik, Heidelberg; pvte. studies w. Prof. Elly Ney & Prof. Edwin Fischer. m. Friedegard Zahn, 1 s., 1 d. Debut: Munich, 1952. Career: Num. Recitals, Broadcasts & Orchl. Concerts, Germany, Ital, Switzerland, Austria, France, Belgium, Netherlands, Scandinavia, Ireland, UK & USA; apps. in Can. w. Sask. Fest. Orch., Edmonton Symph., Vancouver & Winnipeg CBS Orchs., & in most major ctrs.; Iniator & Organist, 1 yr. Beethoven Fest., Sask., 1970; specialist in music of Beethoven, Brahms & Schumann; currently Prof. Music, Univ. of Alta. Recordings: Works by Mozart, Beethoven, Schubart, Schumann, Brahms on PBS and Poulenc on CBS (Can.). Publ: Article Musik aus Sweiter Hand publd. in num. German-lang. newspapers & mags. Hobbies: Woorwork; Swimming; Chess. Address: Dept. of Music, Unv. of Alberta, Edmonton/Alta. Can. T6G 2E6.

BRAVNIČAR, Matija, b. 24 Feb. 1897, Tolmin, Yugoslavia. Composer. Educ: Dip., Acad. of Music, Ljubljana. m. Gizela Pavsic, 1 s. Career: Prof., Acad. of Music, Ljubljana (ret'd); Past Pres., Yugoslav Comps. Soc. Comps. incl: 3 symphs.; Hlapec Jernej in njegova pravica, opera, 1948; Suonata in modo antico, 1953; Elegia notturna, 1955; Berceuse interrompue, 1955; Tango for violin & piano, 1957; Hymnus Slavicus, 1965. Comps. recorded: Symphs. 2 & 3; Fantasia rapsodica for violin & orch. Contbr. to: var. jrnls. & newspapers. Mbrships: Slovene Acad. of Scis. & Arts; Slovene Comps. Soc. Hons: Preseran Prize, 1963; Yugoslav Comps. Soc. Prize, 1954 & 70; State Prize, 1959. Hobbies: Numismatics; Collecting Art; Gardening. Address: Titova 4, 61000 Ljubljana, Yugoslavia.

BRAY, Roger, b. 29 Mar. 1944, Sheffield, UK. University teacher. Educ: King's Coll. Choir Schl., Cambridge; King Edward's Schl. Birmingham; MA, DPhil, Magdalen Coll., Oxford. m. Juliet Borwn, 1 s., 1 d. Career: Lectr. & Asst. Prof. in Music, Univ. of Victoria, BC, Canada, 1968-70; Lectr. in Music, Univ. of Manchester, 1970-79; Prof. of Music, Univ. of Lancaster, 1979-. Publs: Tudor Music, 1979; Gen. Ed., Harvester Series of Musical Manuscript Microfilms. Contbr. to var. profl. jrnls. Hons: J. I. Halstead Scholarship in Music, Oxford, Univ., 1965-68. Address: Dept. of Music, University of Lancaster, Bailrigg, Lancaster, LA1 47W, UK.

BREAKWELL, George W, b. 8 May 1931. Fairchance, Pa., USA. Director of Music Education; Choral Conductor; Organist. Educ: B Schl. Music, Coll. of Wooster, Ohio, 1953; MA, Columbia Univ., NYC; New England Conserv. of Music, Boston,

Mass. Career: Music Educator, 25 yrs.; Choral Cond. w. ensembles appearing in NYC; Organist, chs. in Pa., Ohio, Mass, NH & NY; Guest Cond. for fests. in NH, Pa., Mass. & NY; Apps. w. Nat. Choral Coun., Aver Fisher Hall, NYC; Adjudicator for Competition Fests.; Dir. of Music Educ., Lynbrook Schls., NY; Musical Dir., Lynbrook Chorale. Mbrships. incl: Life, Am. Choral Dirs. Assn.; AGO; MENC. Hobby: Travel. Address: 118-53 Metropolitan Ave., Kew Gdns., NY 11415, USA.

BREAM, Julian, b. 15 July 1933. UK, Musician (Guitar & Lute). Educ: RCM. Debut: Cheltenham, 1947; London debut, 1950. Career incl: tours of Europe, Am., Japan & Australia; Perfs. at Festivals incl. Aldeburgh, Edinburgh, Three Choirs, King's Lynn, Holland, Ansbach, Berlin & Stratford (Canada); Rschr. in Elizabeth lute music, leading revival of works for lute; Promoter of contemporary Engl. works for guitar; Fndr., Int. Summer Schl., Wilts., 1965. num. recordings. Address: c/o Basil Douglas Ltd., 8 St. George's Terr., London NW1 8XJ, UK.

BREDICEANU, Mihai, b. 14 June 1920. Brasov, Romania. Conductor; Composer. Educ: BA (Law), Bucharest Univ.; Dr. (maths), ibid.; Grad., Bucharest Conserv. in piano, comp. and condng. m. Dina Cocea. Debut: Bucharest State Opera, 1946. Career: Gen. Mgr. & music dir., Bucharest Phil. Orch., 1958-; Vis. Prof., Coll. of Visual & Perfng. Arts, Syracuse, NY, 1971-; Permanent Cond., Bucharest Phil. Orch., 1958-; Cond., opera perfs. all over Europe; Cond. Bucharest Phil. Orch. European Tour; guest cond., num. orchs. in Europe, USA, S Am. etc.; cond. at num. Int. Fests; developed & formulated the structural polytempi theory; invented the Polymetronome. Comps: Stage, music, ballet music, symph. & chambr. music. num. recordings. Contbr. to profl. jrnls. Mbrships: Romanian Comps. Union; SACEM. Hon s: num. awards incl. George Enescu Comp. Prize, 1945, Artist Emeritus of SR of Romania & Grand Prix du Disque, 1974. Hobbies: Dogs; Walking. Mgmt: ARIA, Bucharest; Maurice Werner, Paris. Address: 9 Dumbrava Rosie, 70254 Bucharest, Romania. 2.

BREE, Peter, b. 23 Sept. 1949. Driebergen-Rijsenburg, Netherlands. Oboist. Educ: Univ. of Groningen (Engl. lang. & lit.); pvte. studies w. Han de Vries; Sweelinck Conserv., Amsterdam, 1972-79; solo examination, ibid., 1979. Debut: 1964. Career: prin. oboe, Dutch Radio, 1977-79; freelance, mainly solo & chambr. music, 1979-; recitals in Netherlands, Belgium, UK & France; dedicatee of sev. works written for him. Recordings: for Dutch Radio w. Jonathan Katz, John Alley & Lodewijk Collette. Mbrships: Koninklijke Nederlandse Toonkunstenaars Vereniging; ISM. Hobbies: Horse Riding; Deep Sea Diving; Photography; Literature; Travel. Address: Marnixstraat 378 Bel, 1016 XX, Amsterdam, Netherlands.

BREGMAN, Robert J, b. 4 Sept. 1943. NYC, USA. Music Publisher & Distributors. Educ: BA, Miami Univ. of Ohio; JD, NY Univ. Law Schl. div., 1 d. Career: Pres., Alexander Broude Inc., music publr. & distributor. Mbrships: Phi Beta Kappa; Am. Bar Assn.; NY State Bar Assn.; The Bohemians; Zeta Beta Tau Fraternity. Hobby: Aviation. Address: 225 W 57th St., NY 10019, USA.

BRENDEL, Alfred, b. 5 Jan. 1931. Wiesenberg, Czechoslovakia. Pianist; Writer. Educ: State Dip. (Piano), Vienna, Austria, 1947; Piano studies w. Sofija Dezelic, Zagreb, Ludovika von Kaan, Graz, Paul Baumgartner, Edward Steuermann, Edwin Fischer, m. 1) Iris Heymann-Gonzala (div.), 1 d.; 2) Irene Semler, 1 s., 1 d. Career: Concert tours in Europe, USA, Latin Am., Aust., Japan, Israel; Apps. at most major Fests., and w. most major orchs. in Europe and USA. Recordings incl: Repertory from Bach to Schoenberg, incl. Beethoven's complete piano solo works and concertos, Schubert's piano works 1822-28, works by Mozart and Liszt. Publs: Musical Thoughts and Afterthoughts, 1976-77. Contbr. to num. profl. periodicals. Num. Hons. incl: Grand Prix du Disque; Hon. DMus. Univ. of London, 1978. Hobbies: Literature, Theatre, Film, Romanesque and late Baroque Architecture, Masks, Unintentional Humour. Address: c/o Ingpen & William, 14 Kensington Court, London, W8, UK. 1, 2, 3, 4.

BRENNER, Rosamond Drooker, b. 23 Mar. 1931. Cambridge, Mass., USA. Organist; Choir Director; Educator; Composer. Educ: AB., Radcliffe Coll., Cambridge; MA., Grad. Schl., ibid; PhD in Music Hist., Brandeis Univ., 1968; Profl. Cert. in Organ, Geneva Conserv. of Music, Switzerland, 1959; Vienna Acad. of Music, Austria; Fontainebleau Schl. of Music, France; Longy Schl. of Music, Cambridge, Mass. m. Alfred E. Brenner, 1 s., 2 d. Career: Organ recitalist, TV & radio broadcasts, Boston & Chgo.; Lecture-recitals, ibid & Memphis, Tenn.; Fac., Am. Conserv. of Music, Chgo., 1971-; Fac., Columbia Coll., Chgo.; Fac. Boston Conserv. of Music; Organist-Choir Dip., Phillips Cong. Ch., Watertown, Mass. Compositions incl: Love & Unity;

Be Calm, Be Strong, Be Grateful; Rejoice; Darkness Hath Fallen; The Desire; The Day in Over. Contbr. to var. Music Publs. Mbrships. incl: Assoc., AGO; III. MTA; Am. Musicological Soc. Hobbies: Swimming; Walking; Reading. Address: 726 N Pk., Blvd., Glen Ellyn, IL 60137, USA. 27.

BRESGEN, Cesar, b. 16 Oct. 1913. Florence, Italy. Comp. Educ: München Music Acad. dip., comp., organ. m. Eleonore Jorham, 2 s. Career: Mozarteum Salzburg; Prof. since 1939. Comp. incl: Orch. pieces; Chmbr. music; Organ music; Operas; Oratoria; Ballets; Choral pieces. Recordings: Death Dance; Organ pieces; Chmbr. music; Death mass; Requiem. Mbrships: Austrian Comp. League (OKB); Lion's Int.; Int. Music Assembly; Int. Org. Mozarteum. Publs. incl: Improvisation, 1961; In The Beginning There Was Rhythm, 1976. Hons: Great Austrian State Prize, 1976; Music Prize München, 1941. Hobbies: Mycology; Folklore; Mountain climbing; Skiing. Address: Rupertiweg 192,5084 Grossgmain, Austria.

BRESNICK, Martin, b. 13 Nov. 1946. NYC, USA. Composer; Assistant Professor of Music. Educ: AB, Univ. of Hartford, 1967; MA, 1968, DMA, 1972, Stanford Univ.; Acad. of Music, Vienna, 1970. m. Anna Barbara Broell, 1 d. Career: works performed by Kiel Phil. Orch., & San Fran. Symph. Orch., 1972, Rome Orch. RAI, 1975, Münster Symph., 1976; Asst. Prof. of Music, Yale Univ. Comps: Trio for 2 Trumpets & Percussion, 1970; Ocean of Storms, 1971; 3 Intermezzi (violincello solo), 1971; B's. Garlands (8 violonceli recorded), 1973. Contbr. to Mosaic. Mbrships: ASCAP; Am. Soc. of Aesthetics & Art Criticism; Coll. Music Soc. Recip., musical & acad. awards. Address: Dept. of Music, Yale Univ., New Haven, CT 06520, USA.

BRETSCHGER, Frederick, b. 27 Oct. 1953. Buffalo, NY, USA. Double Bass Player. Educ: Cleveland Inst. of Music; Julllard Schl. of Music. Career: Prin. Double Bass, Indpls. Symph. Orch.; orchl. & chmbr. bass player. Recordings: w. Buffalo (NY) Phil. mbr., Indpls. Symph. Soc. Hobbies: Backgammon; Card Playing; Hiking; Swimming; Racquet Sports. Address: 4927 N Ctrl. Ave., Indpls., IN 46205, USA.

BRETT, Charles Michael, b. 27 Oct. 1941. Maidenhead, UK. Solo Counter Tenor; Teacher. Educ: Winchester College; King's Coll., Cambridge (choral Scholar); MA, Cantab. m. Brigid Barstow, 1 s., 1 d. Career: Asst. Music Master, Eton College, 1963-68; Dir. of Music, Malvern Coll., 1968-76; Cond. Malvern Musical Soc., 1969-76; Dir. of Music, Westminster Schl., 1976-; concert apps. in Britain and many European countries, at prin. music fests. & on BBC, etc. var. recordings. Mbrships: ISM; Nobleman & Gentlemen's Catch Club. Hobbies: Reading; Antiques. Mgmt: Clarion Concert Agency. Address: 5A Dean's Yard, London, SW1, UK.

BRETT, Philip, b. 17 Oct. 1937. Edwinstowe, UK. University Teacher; Conductor. Educ: MA, PhD & Mus B, Cambridge Univ., UK. Career: Fellow, King's Coll., Cambridge & Asst., Lectr., Music Fac., 1963-66; Asst. Prof. of Music, Univ. Calif., Berkeley, USA, 1966-71; Assoc. Prof., ibid., 1971-78; Prof., ibid., 1978-. Publs. incl: William Byrd, Consort Songs for Voice & Viols, 1970; Mass for Five Voices, 1973; Gen. Ed., The Byrd Edition. Contbr. to num. prof. mags. jrnls. & bulletins. Mbrships: Coun. Mbr., Am. Musicol. Soc., 1973-76; Royal Musical Assn.; Plainsong & Mediaval Music Assn. Hons: Archibald T Davison Medal for Musicol. (The Harriet Cohen Int. Musical Awards), 1969. Hobbies: Running; Yoga. Address: 980 Middlefield Rd., Berkeley, CA 94708, USA.

BRETTINGHAM SMITH, Jolyon, b. 9 Sept. 1949. Southampton, UK. Composer; Lecturer in Analysis & Music Theory. Educ: Magdelene Coll., Cambridge; Univ. Heidelberg; Comp. w. Isang Yun, Hochschule für Musik und darstellende Kunst Berlin. Career: Mbr., Gruppe Neue Musik Berlin. Career: Mbr., Gruppe Neue Musik Berlin & live electronic improvisation ensemble No-Set, 1971-; Radio perfs., 1972-; Lectr. in Analysis & Music Theory, Freie Univ., Berlin, 1973-. Comps. incl: Death of Cuchlain, opera, 1972-73; Earth Magic, for orch., 1974; Dancing Days, 1975. Monograph, 1975; Densities, 1976; Mandrake Roote, 1976; Num. graphic scores for improvisation ensembles, No-Set, Hons. incl: 1st prize for opera, Nuremberg, 1973: Scholarship of Italian Govt. to work w. Donationi in Bologna, 1975. Hobbies: Flying; Photography; Travel; Very Long Walks; Film; Theatre; Bldg. Scale Models; Ancient Hist. & Mythologies. Address: Brandenburgische Str. 81, D 1000 Berlin 31, Germany.

BREUER, Janos, b. 8 June 1932. Budapest, Hungary. Musicologist; Critic. Educ: Choir Conducting & Musicol., F Liszt Acad. of Music, Budapest. m. Zsuzsanna Falus-Breuer. Career: Concert Critic, 1958-; Musicol. Collaborator, Assn. of Hungarian Musicians & Hungarian Music Coun., 1958-; Critic,

Hungarian Daily Newspaper Nepszabadsag, 1961-; Ed., Hungarian Musicol. Review, Magyar Zene, 1961-. Num. recordings. Publs. incl: 30 ér magyar zenekulturája, 1975; Kodaly-dokumentumok I Nemetorszag, 1976; In Memoriam Dmitrij Shostakovich, 1976: Kodaly: Psalms Hungaricus, 1977; Zenei irások a Nyugatban, 1978; A Budapest Filharmóniai Társaság, 1978; Bartók és Kodály, 1978. Contbr. to profl. jrnls., etc. Mbr. Assn. of Hungarian Musicians. Address: Rajk Laszlo-utca 33, 1136 Budapest, Hungary.

BREWER, Linda Judd, b. 13 Nov. 1945. Arkansas City, Kansas, USA. Assistant Professor; Cellist. Educ: DMA, Univ. of Texas, cello studies w. George Neikrug & Phyllis Young, 1978; MM, ibid, cello studies w. Adolphe Frezan, chmbr. music studies w. Andor Toth & Leonard Shure, bass studied w. Stuart Sankey, 1969; BM, Univ. of Kansas, cello studies w. Raymond Stuhl; chmbr. music studies w. Raymond Cerf & Karel Blaas. Career: Asst. prof, UKniv. of Wis., 1974-; Soloist w. Aspen Phil. Orch., 1972; mbr. of Aspen Fest. Orch., 1971 & '72; Prin. cellist, Kansas Univ. Orch., 1964-65 & 1965-66; solist w. Oklahoma City Symph. & Kansas Univ. Orch., Hons. incl: 1st place, Aspen Cello Composition, 1972; Regional winner, NMTA Collegiate Artists Auditions, 1970; Holtzschue String Award, 1st Prize. Address: Dept. of Music, Univ. of Wisconsin, La Crosse, WI 54601, USA.

BREWER, Virginia, b. 9 Dec. 1943. Oboist. Educ: BA, Coll. of Notre Dame, Belmont, Calif., 1965; MS, Juilliard Schl., NYC, 1967. m. Edward Brewer, 1 s., 1 d. Debut: Carnegie Recital Hall, NYC, 1974. Career: Solo apps. w. Mozart Fest. Orch., NYC, 1974, Nat. Orch. Assn., NYC, 1968, San Fran. Symph., San Mateo, Calif., 1961: Mbr., Musica Sacra, Bach Collegium of NY, L'Ensemble du Sacré Coeur; freelance work. Recordings: Desto; Columbia; Music Minus One; Vox. Mbr., Local 802, Am. Fedn. of Musicians. Hobby: Embroidery. Address: 250 W 104th St., NY, NY 10025, USA.

BREZNIKAR, Joseph John, b. 17 June 1950. Cleveland, Ohio, USA. Guitarist; Teacher of Guitar. Educ: BA, Cleveland State Univ.; MMus, Univ. of Akron; Studied classical guitar w. Sophocles Papas, Carlos Barbosa-Lima & Abel Carlevaro. m. Christine Meszaros. Debut: Edwin J Thomas Hall, Akron, Ohio, 1975. Career: Perfs. on stage, radio & TV in USA & Brazil; Tchr. of Guitar, Firestone Conserv., Univ. of Akron. Publs: Virginal Music for Guitar, 1978. Mbrships: NY Soc. of Classic Guitar; Wash. Guitar Soc.; Am. String Tchrs. Assn.; Guitar Fndn. of Am. Hobby: Composing music for classical guitar. Address: 572 Malvern Rd., Akron, OH 44303, USA.

BRICCELTTI, Thomas Gaetano, b. 14 Jan. 1936. Mt. Kisco, NY, USA. Conductor; Composer. Educ: Piano w. Dr. Jan Dansereau; Cond. w. Dr. Richard Lert; Comp., Samuel Barber & Alan Houhaness, 1 s., 1 d. Career: Music Dr., Cond., St. Petersburg, Fla., Symph. Orch.; Assoc. Cond. num. orchs. inclng: Indpls. Symph. Orch.; Ind. Chmbr. Orch.; Cleveland Inst. Univ. Circle Orch.; Omaha Symph. Orch. Compositions incl: 40 instrumental & vocal works. Num. recordings. Mbrships: ASCAP; Am. Symph. Orch. League; NAACC. Hons: Prix de Rome, 1958-59; Ford Fndn. Comp. Fellowship, 1959-60, 1960-61. Hobbies: Classic, Antique & Vintage Cars (Italian)l; Horticulture. Mgmt: Columbia Artists Mgmt. Inc. Address: 4912 S Harrison St., Ft. Wayne, IN 46807, USA. 2, 8.

BRICKMAN, Joel Ira, b. 6 Feb. 1946. NYC, USA. Composer; Educator. Educ: Montclair State Coll.; Juilliard Schl. of Music; BMus, 1968, MMus, 1970, Manhattan Schl.of Music. Career: Tchr., pub. schls., Bergen Co., NJ; Fac., Mbr., Manhattan Schl. of Music, 1971-; & Marymount Coll., Tarrytown, NY, 1972-; Guest, radio prog., Comps. Forum; Guest Cond. of own works; perfs. of comps. in USA, Europe & S. Am. Comps. incl: Of Wonder (SATB, a cappella choir); Suite for Woodwind Quintet; Prelude & Caprice for Solo Accordion. Dialogue for Oboe & wind Ensemble; Concert Overture; Prelude & Dityramb; Thousands of Days. Mbrships: ASCAP; Nat. Assn. Am. Comps. & Conds.; Am. Music Ctr.; AAUP, Coll. Music Soc. Hons: Winner, Manhattan Schl. of Music Comp. Contest, 1970; Comp. Prelude & Caprice chosen as World Accordion Competition Solo, 1973. Hobbies incl: Photography; Mapreading; Tennis. Address: 90 Edison Court, Monsey, NY 10952, USA.

BRICKMAN, Miriam, b. 6 Dec. 1933. Gt. Barrington, Mass., USA. Concert Pianist. Educ: BA, Queens Coll.; MS, Juilliard Schl. of Music. Debut: Town Hall, NYC, USA, 1968. Career: Soloist, Carnegie Recital Hall; Apps. in Libs., Mus., Colls. in USA; Performed on ships to Aust., NZ, & S. Pacific; TV apps. in USA & Tokyo, Japan; Piano soloist w. Huntington, Long Island, Symph.; Violinst, Puerto Rico Symph.; Originated piano dramas combining live lit. dramatizations of poetry & dramas in 5 langs. 2nd VP, Alton Jones Assocs. Endorsed by US Dept. of State for SE Asian tour, 1977; Tully Hall recital, 1979; Tours US &

South Am. Hobbies: Swimming; Ice Skating; Skiing; Ping Pong; Bridge; Backgammon; Scrabble; Collecting Shells & feathers. Mgmt: Eastman Boomer, 433 E 51 St., NY, NY 10022, USA. Address: 210 Lakeview Pl., Riverdale, NY 10471, USA.

BRIDCUT, John Creighton, b. 13 June 1952. Redhill, US. Journalist; Impresario. Educ: BA, Keble Coll., Oxford. Career: Asst. Lit. Ed., The Spectator, 1970-71; Music Critic, ibid., 1974-76; Fndr.-Dir., Fest. of Engl. Song, 1973-; Music Critic, What's on in London, 1975-; Music Reporter, BBC World Service. Hobbies: Singing. Address: 37 Rodney Court, Maida Vale, London W9, UK.

BRIDGE, Geoffrey Stuart, b. 26 Aug. 1936. Accrington, UK. Oboist. Educ: St. Andrews Univ.; RCM; Aberdeen Coll. of Educ.; studied oboe w. Leon Goossens & Sidney Sutcliffe, cond. w. Sir Adrian Boult; LRAM. m. Hilary Spencer Young. Debut: Manchester, 1962. Career: solo artist for Arts Coun. in Scotland; freelance oboist w. num. orchs.; solo & chmbr. music broadcasts for BBC; cond., many amateur & student groups, some profl. groups; now Hd., Woodwind teaching for Hampshire Co. Coun. Contbr. to BBC on woodwind subjects; talks on avant-garde music & wind music of 18th century. mbr., ISM. Hobbies: Cooking; Photography; Walking; Cars; Medical Matters. Address: 25 Eveley Cl., Whitehill, Bordon, Hants., UK.

BRIDGE, Jean Ann, b. 26 Mar. 1936. Norwich, UK. Teacher of Violin & Viola. Educ: Bretton Hall, Yorks; RCM; ARCM; Rural Music Schl., Kent. m. David G Bridge. Career: Tchr., St. Bees Schl., 1962-69, Cumbria Co. Coun., 1962-; Ldr., W Cumberland Orch., 1962-72, Martinu Trio (flute, violin, piano), 1970-74; Mbr., Lakeland Sinfonia, 1972-75; Pvte. Tchng. Mbrships: Local Committee, ISM; European String Tchrs. Assn. Hobbies: Walking; Collage; Sketching; Antiques; Writing Children's Stories. Address: 28 Abbey Vale, St. Bees, Cumbria, UK.

BRIDGES, Thomas Whitney, b. 17 Nov. 1930. Macedon, NY, USA. Music Librarian; Musicologist; Performer on Flute & Recorder. Educ: AB, Hamilton Coll., Clinton, NY; MA, Univ. of Calif. at Berkeley; MSLS, Drexel Univ. m. Patricia Gaspari. Career: Tchr. of Music Hist., Theory & Appreciation, Univ. of Ill., Univ. of Wash., Univ. of Pa.; Music Libn., State Univ. Coll. Fredonia, NY, 1973-. Mbrships: Music Lib. Assn.; Am. Musicol. Soc.; SUNY Librns.' Assn.; Audubon Soc.; conservation orgs.; Contbr. to Grove's Dict. of Music & Musicians, 6th ed. Hobbies: Birdwatching; Gardening. Address: 79 Ctrl. Ave., Fredonia, NY 14063, USA.

BRIGGS, Howard, b. 29 Aug. 1942. Preston, UK. Conductor; Singer; Teacher; Adjudicator. Educ: Cathedral King's Schl., Worcester (ACP); Vic. Univ., Manchester Coll. of Educ. (Cert. Ed.); Huddersfield Schl. of Music; LTCL; ALCM. m. Susan Longden, 1 d. Debut: Birmingham Town Hall. Career: Circuit Concert Artist, 1964-; Hd. of Choral Music, Chethams Schl. of Music, 1973-77; Dir. of Music, Hereford Cathedral Schl., 1978-. Recordings: var. as singer & cond. Contbr. to: The Hereford Times; Evening News, etc. mbr. ISM. Hobby: The Countryside. Address: 4 Castle St., Hereford HR1 2NL, UK.

BRIGGS, John Stewart, b. 9 May 1948. Bingley, Yorks., UK. Pianist. Educ: RMCM (w. Colin Horsley); ARMCM; pvte. study w. Sulamita Aronovsky. Career: recitals & concertos in UK & W Europe; TV & radio perfs.; 1st UK profl. pianist to give master classes for amateur pianists. Recordings: Romantic Piano Music, 20th century Piano Music. Contbr. to: var. local radio classical magazine progs. Hons: semifinalist, Royal Overseas League competition, 1972; Polish State Scholarship, 1971: Martin Fund Scholarship, 1972. Hobbies: Oriental Art; Interior Design/Decor. Address: 9 Priestthorpe Rd., Bingley, W Yorks., UK.

BRIGHT, Alma Louie. Redditch, Worcestershire, UK. Soprano; Pianist; Conductor. Educ: Birmingham Schl. of Music & Coll. of Educ.; Lic. Royal Acad. Music; Cert. Educ.; Pvte. studies. m. Walter Evelyn Clarke, 5s. Debut: Birmingham Town Hall. Career: Dir., Redditch Choral Soc., 1963-; Artistic Dir., Midlands Opera, 1963-; Musical Dir., Redditch Bach Club, 1943-46; Broadcasts: Songs at the Piano; Accompanist; Soprano Soloist; Mbr., BBC Midland Singers. Mbr., Incorp. Soc. of Musicians. Hobbies: Gardening; Geology. Address: The Ave., 1 Alcaster Rd., Studley, Warwicks., B80 7AN, UK.

BRIGIDO, Odemar, b. 31 Jan. 1941. Rio de Janeiro, Brazil. Composer; Teacher. Educ: Nat. Music Schl., Brazil Univ.; Music Schl., Rio Fed. Univ.; Dips. in comp., conducting, orchestration, Brazilian musical folklore, music hist., fugue; Master of choral counterpoint. m. Guilhermina Brigido. Debut: as comp., 1963. Career incls: Tchr., orchestration, comps. & Brazilian musical folklore; Roquete Pinto Radio Conf. on Maués brasilian indian music. Comps. incl: Te Deum (oratorio); Fantasia do Nordeste (piano & clarinet); Brasilian Suite for orch. Orchestrator, Dorme Coraçao (A Rebello) & Banho de Cheiro (O Souza) for recording Alice Ribeiro na Cançao do Brasil, vol. II., Mbr., Ordem dos Musicos do Brasil. Reicp. 1st as orchestrator, Music Fest., Nova Friburgo City, 1972. Hobby: Parapiscol. Address: Rua Mariz e Barros 513, ap. 504, Niterói-24000, RJ, Brazil.

BRILIOTH, Helge. Operatic Tenor. Debut: as Don Jose. Career: apps. in Sweden, Paris, London, Bayreuth, Vienna, Rome, Moscow, NY Metropolitan, etc.; roles include Siegmund, Siegfried, Tristan, Parsifal, Lohengrin, Walter, Florestan etc. Mgmt: Artistsekretariat Ulf Törnqvist, Norrtullsgatan 26 tr. 4, 11345 Stockholm, Sweden. Address: c/o mgmt.

BRILL, Joan Rothman, b. 3 May 1930. Greenport, NY, USA. Concert Pianist. Educ: BA, Southampton Coll., Lond Island Univ.; MMus., SUNY, Stony Brook; Juilliard Schl. of Music. m. Robert J. Brill, dec., m. Oliver W. Petty, 2 d. Debut: Carnegie Recital Hall, 1958. Career: Adjunct Lectr., Southampton Coll., Lond Island Univ.; num. perfs., NYC & Long Island; Piano Soloist; Clearwater Symph., Fla., 1974; Perf. in Brill-Gaffney Trio. Mbrships: Local 802, Am. Fedn. of Musicians; John Drew Theatre, E. Hampton; Prog. Chmn., Music Committee, ibid, 1950-70; S. Fork Concert Assn., Exec. Bd., ibid., 1950-. Recip. num. Hons. Hobbies: Sailing; Ice Skating; Fishing; Mgmt: Virginia Page (Allied Promotions), 55 Horton Dr., Huntington Station , NY 11746, USA. Address: 69 N Main St., E Hampton, NY 11937, USA.

BRINCK, Eva. Odense, Denmark. Opera Singer (Lyric Soprano); Singing Teacher. Educ: Studied Singing, Lied, Oratorio & Opera w. var. tchrs., Acad. of Music, Vienna, Austria. m. 1) Georg Incze, 1 s, 2) Sven Hilleman. Career: Small part singer, vienna State Opera, 1 yr.; Singer, Philips Opera Studio, Salzburg; Municipal Theatre, Bonn, German Fed. Repub.; Leading Lyric Soprano, Opera House, Hanover, 7 yrs.; Guest perfs., Volksoper, Vienna, Hamburg State Opera, Cologne Opera House, La Fenice, Venice, Festspiele Salzburg, Bregenz & Aix-en-Provence; now Singing Tchr., Royal Conserv. of Music, Copenhagen, Denmark. Recordings: Works by Mozart, Haydn, Dittersdorf & Alban Berg. Address: Fuglebakkevej 23, DK-2000, Copenhagen, Denmark.

BRINDEL, Bernard, b. 23 Apr. 1912. Chgo., Ill., USA. Composer. Educ: BMus, MMus, Chgo. Musical Coll.; studied w. Max Wald, Isaac Levine, Paul Held. m. June Rachuy, 1 s., 1 d. Career: Dir. of Music, Temple Sholom, Chgo.; Tchr. of music theory & comp., Morton Coll., Cicero, Ill., 1954-. Chgo. Musical Coll., 1964-54, Nat. Music Camp., Interlochen, Mich., 1955-67. Comps. str. quartets; choral works; solo songs; concertos for cello & orch.; sonatas for violin, piano; orchl. works; cantatas; saxophone solos. Recordings: Children's Songs. Mbrships: Int. Soc. for Contemp. Music; Music Educators Assn. Recip. Am. Fedn. of Music Award, 1973. Address. 2740 Lincoln Ln., Wilmette, IL 00091, USA. 0.

BRINDLE, Reginald Smith, b. 1917. nr. Preston, Lancs., UK. Composer. Educ: Univ. Coll., N Wales; studied composition St. Cecilia Acad., Rome; studied pvtely, w. Pizzeti & Dallapiccola. m. Giulia Borsi, 1 s., 3 d. Career: Collaborator, Italian Radio & 3rd Prog., 1957-; Prof. of Music, Univ. of Surrey, Guildford, 1970, & currently, Univ. of Bangor, N. Wales; Writer on contemp. music. Compositions incl: Cosmos; Homage to H G Wells; Creation Epic; Apocalypse for full orch.; Via Crucis, An Epitaph for Alban Berg for strings; Concerto for 5 instruments & percussion; Grafico de la Patenera for soprano, chorus & small orch.; February Run (electronic music). Publs: European Music in the 20th Century; Serial Composition; Contemporary Percussion. Contbr. to: Encyclopedia Britannica; Enciclopedia Dello Spettacolo; jrnls. Hobbies: Painting; Travel. Address: c/o Univ. of Bangor, Bangor, N. Wales, UK.

BRINDLEY, Gerry H, b. 26 Aug. 1935. Oldburg, Worcs., UK. Teacher; Performer. Educ: Organ scholar, Selwyn Coll., Cambridge, 1956-59; BA, MA (Cantab.); ARCM; FRCO. m. Maria Watkin, 4d. Career: Music tchr., ch. organist & choir master, Ventnor, Isle of Wight, 1959-60; Musical Dir., Half Moon Bay Ltd., Montego Bay, Jamaica, 1962-70; num. radio & TV perfs. on Jamaica Broadcasting Corp.; Music tchr., Cornwall Coll., Montego Bay, 1968-70; Vocal tchr., Brockton High Schl., Toronto, 1971-77; Hd. of Music, Lakeview Senior Schl., Toronto, 1978-. Mbrships: Toronto Musicians Assn.; Toronto Music Tchrs. Assn. Hobbies: Golf; Contract Bridge; Reading; Arranging. Address: 75 Snowhill Cres., Agincourt, Ont. M1S 3T4, Can.

BRINER, Andres, b. 31 May 1923. Musicologist; Music Critic. Educ: studied Musicolo., Hist. of Music Theory, German Lit.,

Univ. of Zürich, Switz. m. Diana E. Craig, 4s. Career: Asst. Prof. for Music Hist., Music Dept., Univ. of Pa., Phila., USA, 1955-64; First Music Critic, Neue Zurcher Zeitung, Switz., 1964-. Publs: Paul Hindemith, 1971. Contbr. to var. periodicals inclng. Schweizer Musikzietung. Mbrships: Int. Musicol. Soc.; Schweizer Musikforchende Gesellschaft. Mgmt: Neue Zrcher Zeitung. Address: Hadlaustr. 45, CH 8006, Zürich, Switzerland.

BRINGS, Allen, b. 24 Feb. 19334. New York City, USa. Composer; Pianist. Educ: BA, Queens Coll.; MA Columbia Univ.; Mus AD, Boston Univ.; graduate study at Princeton Univ.; studies in piano w. Sylvia Lopez; Berkshire Music Center, Tanglewood. m. Genevieve Chinn, 1 c. Career: Apps. in USA & Europe w. Genevieve Chinn in progs. of music for piano, 4 hands. Comps. incl: chmbr. concertos for piano & orch., violin & percussion, flute & strings; sonatas for piano, viola & piano, solo violin; Capriccio & Notturno for orch.; Variations on Quiet Theme for band. Recordings: Contemporary Am. Music for Piano, 4 hands, w. Genevieve Chinn. Contbr. to: Contemporary Music Newsletter. Mbrships: incl: Am. Soc. of Univ. Comps.; Am. Musicol. Soc.; Coll. Music Soc.; Nat. Assn. of Comps. USA; Am. Soc. for Comps., Authors & Publrs. Hons: Student Comps. Radio Award from Broadcast Music, Inc., 1957; ASCAP Awards annually from 1975. Hobbies: Tennis, Mgmt: Int. Concert Admin. Address: 199 Mountain Rd., Wilton, CT 06897, USA.

BRINKMANN, Reinhold, b. 21 Aug. 1934. Wildeshausen, Germany. Professor of Musicology, Educ: State exam. in schl. music, Hochschule für Musik, Hamburg, 1958; Univs. of Hamburg & Freiburg im Breisgau, 1956-66; DrPhill., Univ. of Freiburg im Breisgau, 1967; Habilitation, Berlin, 1970. Career: Prof., Free Univ., Berlin, 1970; Full Prof., Univ. of Marburg/Lahn, 1972-. Publs: Arnold Schönberg, Drei Klavier-Stücke, op. 11 - Untersuchungen zur freien Atonalität bei Schönberg, 1969: Ed., Arnold Schönberg, Sämtliche Werke, Bd. 4A: Werke für Klavier zu zwei Händen (w. E Steuermann), 1968; Ed., Arnold Schönberg, Sämtliche Werke, Bd. 4B: Skizzen & Fragmente, 1975. Contbr. to: Archiv für Musikwissenschaft; Darmstädter Beiträge zur Neuen Musik; Publs. of Inst. für Neue Musik & Musikerziehung, Darmstadt; Die Musikforschung; Neue Zeitschrift für Musik; Jahrbudi Staatl. Just. für Musik forshung, Berlin, v.a. Address: Hirtenweg 20, D 3551 Reddehausen, German Fed. Repub.

BRISTOW, Daniel LeRoy, b. 21 Aug. 1924. Fort Worth, Tex., USa. Conductor; Composer; Music Educator. Educ: Grad., Juilliard Schl. of Music, NY; BS & grad. study, Columbia Univ., NY Univ. & Univ. of Houston, m. Dorothy Marie. 1 s., 1 d. Career: Violinist w. NBC Symph., Houston Symph., Vancouver Symph.; Cond., Oak Ridge Civil Chorale, Sentinel youth Symphonic Choir (Spokane World's Fair Expo 74); Cond. of premiere performances. Compositions: Christmas Overture (Symph. Choir); 125th Psalm (Symph. Choir); Harlequinade Ballet (Pain-Orch.); Intermezzo for 2 violins; Renaissance (paino); Sing Ye a Song of Harvest (Choral; O'er the Fields we Go, (Choral). Publs: Full score arrs. & orchn. of musical version of Dicken's Great Expectations, 1974. Mbrships: MENC; Canadian Music Educators Assn.; Am. Fedn. of Musicians. Recip. var. Schlrships. for master classes. Hobbies: Electronic; Amateur radio. Address: 4456 Canterbury Cres., N. Vancouver, BC, Canada V7R 3N6.

BRITAIN, Radie, b. 17 Mar. 1908. Silverton, Tex., USA. Composer; Pianist; Organist. Educ: BMus, Am. Conserv.; D Mus, Fine Arts Conserv., Amarillo, Tex.; adv. study, Chog. Univ. m. Theodore Morton, 1 d. Debut: Munich, Germany. Publd. comps. incl: orchl. works; choral works; piano pieces; violin pieces. Recorded comps: Prelude to a Drama for Orch.; Lament (medium orch.). Nt. Music Ed., Penwomen Mag. Mbrships: ASCAP; Nat. Soc. Am. Pen Women; Hon. SAI; Etude Club; State Fedn. of Music Clubs of Tex.; Tex. Tchrs. Assn. Hons.; Nat. Band Assn. Hons: Juilliard Publn. Award for orchl. comp. Heroic Poem; over 50 int. & nat. comps. awards. Hobby: Writing. Address: 1945 N. Curson Ave., Hollywood, CA 90046, USA. 2, 3, 5, 6.

BRITTEN, David Ralph, b. 20 June 1953. Auckland, NZ. Composer; Conductor. Educ: BMus (Auckland). Comps. incl: Overlap, for chmbr. orch.; Fanfare 2, for brass & Renaissance instruments; Kare, for full orch.; Variations on a Theme of Lilburn, for Chmbr. Orhc.; The Way You Want It, for string quartet & vibraphone; Tinkers' Curse, for solo trumpet, sev. works in the electronic media. Publs: As Asst. Ed., Price Milburn Music Ltd. Mbr., Comps. Assn. of NZ. Hons: Bishop Memorial Prize in Comp., 1971, '73. Hobbies: Tennis; Chess; Tramping; Oil Painting. Address: 52 Savoy Rd., Glen Eden, Auckland 7, NZ.

BRITTON, Allen Perdue, b. 25 May 1914. Elgin, Ill., USA. Musicologist; Music Educator. Educ: BSc, MA, Univ. of Ill.; PhD, Univ. of Michigan, 1949. m. Veronica Fern Wallace. Career: Music Tchr., Public Schls., Griffith, Indiana, 1939-41; mbr. of Music Fac., Eastern Ill. Univ., 1938-50; Asst. Prof., Univ. of Michigan, 1949-53; Assoc. Prof., ibid., 1953-59; Prof., ibid, 1959-; Asst. Dean, ibid, 1960-62; Assoc. Dean, ibid, 1962-69; Acting Dean, 1969-71; Dean, ibid, 1971-; Chmn., Dept. of Music Educ., ibid, 1959-69. Publs: Ed., Journal of Research in Music Education, 1953-72. Contbr. to var. profl. jrnls. Mbrships: Music Educators Nat. Conf., Pres., 1960-62; Am. Musicol. Soc., mbr. of Coun. 1964-65; Soc. for Ethnomusicology; Int. Folk Music Coun.; Sonneck Soc. Address: 1475 Warrington Drive, Ann Arbor, MI 48103, USA. 2.

BRITTON, David James, b. 20 Jan. 1942. Westfield, Mass., USA. Concert Organsit; Associate Professor of Organ; Recording Artist. Educ: BMus, Oberlin Conserv. of Music, 1963; MMus, Eastman Schl. of Music, 1964; Dr. Musical Arts, ibid., 1973. Debut: St. Michael's Cathedral, Springfield, Mass., 1959. Career: Soloist, Eastman-Rochester Phil., 1964; Recitals for noted chs., coll.s & univs. in USA & for num. convens. of the Am. Guild of Organists; Organist, Immanuel Presby. Ch., Los Angeles, 1973-75. Recordings: Masterworks for organ by Jean-Jacques Grunenwald & Jean Langlais; Toccatos & Fugues of the N. German Baroque; Sonatas I & II for Organ. Publs: Abbe Georg Joseph Vogler His Life and His Theories on Orgna Design. Mbr. num. profl. orgs. Hons. incl: Perfs. Cert. in Organ, Eastman Schl. of Music, 1966. Hobbies: Antiquities; Camping. Mgmt: Artist Recitals, 3427 Fernwood Ave., Los Angeles, CA 90093, USA. Address: 503 Conneticut St., San Francisco, CA 94107, USA.

BRITTON, Donald, b. 2 Nov. 1919. London, UK. Coordinator of Instrumental Music. Educ: MA, MusB, DipEd., Emmanuel Coll., Cambridge; ARCM; ARCO; ALAM (Hons.) m. Pearl Creed, 2 d. Career: Asst. Music Master, Winchester Coll., & Examiner for Cambridge Univ. Local Exams. Syndicate; Dir. of Music, Melbourne Grammar Schl., Aust., & Examiner, Aust. Music Exam. Bd., & Aust. Coll. of Organists; Coord. of Instrumental Music in Schls., Qld., Aust. Comps: 2 Pieces for pianoforte, 1938; Anthem for Choir & Organ, 1958; Mass for Choir & Organ, 1975. Mbrships. incl: Aust. Soc. for Music Educ. Hons. incl: Hon. Sr. Schlr., Emmanuel Coll., Cambridge, 1948-. Hobbies incl: Piano & organ recitals. Address: 26 Lindsay St., Ashgrove, Qld. 4060, Australia. 3.

BRITTON, Noel Eric John, b. 20 Dec. 1915. Lecturer; Violinist; Violist. Educ: RMCM; GSM; AGSM; (violin); AGSM (viola-silver medal); ARCM. m. Margaret Britton, 1 s., 1 d. Career: Lindisfarne Coll., 1939: RAF, 1940-46; Yorkshire Symph., 1948-53; peripatetic music tchr., Isle of Wight, 1953-71; lectr., Colchester Inst., 1971-. mbr., ISM, European Str. Tchrs. Assn. Hons: Orchestral Wakefield Prize; Alfred Gibson Memorial prize; The Sherriffs Violin Prize. Hobbies: Photography; Reading. Address: Nimrod, The Green, Gt. Bentley, Colchester, Essex CO7 8PA, UK.

BRIXEL, Eugen Johann Carl, b. 27 Mar. 1939. M Schoenberg, Morvia, Czech. Clarinet Player & Teacher; Composer. Educ: State Acad. Music, Vienna, Austria, 1955-62; PhD, Univ. Vienna, 1967. m. Eva Leeb, 2 d. Career: Lectr., Hochschule für Musik & darstellende Kunst, Graz. Comps: Politik im Walzertakt (1st perf. Bad Ischel 1968); Orch. works; Festival-Overture, Salzkammergut-Suite, Concertino bravuroso; Songs; Chmbr. Music; Perspektiven (3 clarinets). Publs. incl: Clarinet Bibliography, 1976; Alta Musica 1 (ed. w. W Suppan), 1975; Austrian Military Music, 1976. Contbr. to profl. jrnls. Gen. Sec., Soc. Rsch. & Promotion Brass & Wind Music. Hobbies incl: Theatre; Walking. Address: A-8010 Graz, Carnerigasse 11/5, Austria.

BROCK, Peggi. London, UK. Musician (Piano, Violin, Accordin). Educ: Liberal Arts Course, Ursuline Coll., Wimbledon, London, 4 yrs.; Arts & Langs., Frau Doctor Schudel-Benz Pvte. Schl., Zürich, Switz.; Dips. w. Distinction for Typewriting & German corres., Pitman's Secretarial Schl., London; w. Dr. Kasics-Durigo, Zurich Conservatorium, 2 yrs.; w. Prof. Jose Berr, a pupil of Busoni, 3 yrs.; specialized study of the Swiss Nat. Accordion & the Chromatic Accordion; Govt. Grant for study of Piano & Violin, Trinity Coll. of Music, London, 3 yrs. (earned both Licentiate & Fellowship Dips.); w. John Nowell, Fac. of Oxford & of Salzburg, specializing in adv. pianoforte techniques & the study of the methods of famous concert techniques & the study of the methods of famous concert virtuosos, 4 yrs. Career: Perfs. at London musical events w. an original sextet devised, arranged & conducted by the late Hungarian Composer Mathias-Seiber; Coached &

accompanied profl. Lieder singers; Num. piano & other recitals w. a London orch.; Considerable broadcasting & prodn., experience; On perm. tchng. staff, Trinity Coll., 1957-77; Much contract tchng. w. professionals. War serv. w. ENSA. Recordings: Accordion Act, Peggi & Veda Brock, London Home & Forces 'Break for Music', BBC, 1940. Hons: Highest Mauss, Wimbledon Fest. Painoforte, 1928. Hobbies: Painting; Drawing; Violin; Walking; Skiing; Swimming. Address: 120 Sutherland Ave., London W9, UK. 3, 27.

BROCK, Petr, b. 2 Oct. 1932. Brno, Bohemia. Professor of Msuci; Flautist. Educ: Konservatory of Music; Univ. of Musical Arts. m. Zdenka Brockova, 2 children. Debut: W. Prague Chmbr. Orch. Career: Appeared on TV Music Shows, 50 Sonatas for Radio Prague. Recordings: W A Mozart, flute quartets; A Rejcha-Fr. Krommer, flute quartets; Records of contempory music. Mbr. SCSKU (Union of Czechoslovak Comps.) Recip 1st. Prize Wien for recording of Mozart. Hobby: Music. Mgmt: Pragokoncert Praha. Address: 100 00 Praha 10, ul. 28. pluku 34, CSSR.

BROCKHAUS, H(einz) Alfred, b. 12 Aug. 1930. Krefeld, Germany. Musicologist. Educ: studied musicol., Coll. of Music, Weimar & Berlin, also Humboldt Univ., Berlin; Dip. in Musicol., 1956; Dr. Phil., 1962; Dr. Phil. (2nd degree), 1966. m. Ingrid Brockhaus (nee John). Career: w. Humbolt Univ., 1956-. Publs. incl: Hans Eisler, 1961: Dimitri Schostakovisch, 1962; Sergy Prokofjew, 1963; Michael Glinka (ed.), 1962. Contbr. to var. publs. in field. Mbrships. incl: Int. Soc. for Musicol.; active in exec. of affiliated socs. in GDR. Address: Nalepastr. 187, 116 Berlin, German Dem. Repub.

BROCKLEBANK, Arthur, b. 20 Jan. 1930. Greenock, Renfrewshire, UK. Prinicipal Music Adviser. Educ: RSAMD; LRAM; LTCL. m. Henrietta Aitken, 1 d. Debut: Stevenson Hall, Glasgow, 1952. Career: Tchr. of Music, Hermitage Acad., 1954-67; Advsr. in Music, Ross & Cromarty, 1967-75; Prin. Music Advsr., Highland Region, 1975-. Contr. to: Aberdeen Evening Express; Times Educl. Supplement. Mbrships: Educl. Inst. of Scotland; Bd. of Dirs., N E Scotland Music Schl., Ltd. Hons: Piano Scholarship, 1952. Hobbies: Caravanning; Photography. Address: Highways, Pitglassie, Dingwall, Ross-shire, UK. 3.

BROCKLEHURST, John Brian. University Sr. Lecturer. Educ: BA, Nottingham Univ.; MA, Sheffield Univ.; DMus, ibid.; LRAM; ARCM. Career: Univ. Reader in Music Educ., & Sr. Tutor PGCE Course, Univ. of Birmingham, UK. Publs: Music in Schools, 1962; Pentatonic Song Books, 1968, 1976; Response to Music, 1971. Contbr. to: Music & Letters; Educl. Review; Music Tchr. Address: Fac. of Educ., Birmingham Univ., PO Box 363, Birmingham, B15 2TT UK. 3.

BROCKLESS, Brian, b. 21 Jan. 1926. London, UK. Conductor; Composer; Organist; Teacher. Educ: RCM; BMus; ARCM; ARCO; pvte. study w. Matyas Seiber; Accademia Musicale, Siena. m. Jennifer Wright, 1s. (by former marriage). Career: Concerts w. Engl. Chmbr. Orch., RPO, Northern Sinfonia; Italian tours w. London Schubert Orch.; concerts in Romania, Stockholm, Palermo, Brussels & Venezuela; choral & orchl. perfs. for BBC & for Belgian & Swedish radio; Dir. of Music, St. Bartholomew-the-Great Priory, Smithfield, 1961-71, 1971-; Lectr., Univ. of Surrey; Prof., RAM; fest. adjudicator. Comps: Prelude, Toccata & Chaconne; Introduction, Passacaglia & Coda; Fantasia, Adagio & Fugue (all for organ); English Elegy for strng. orch.; Ch. music, songs & chmbr. music. Recordings: Quires & Places where They Sing; Mozart sacred music (w. Jill Gomez). Contbr. to: Choir; Composer; RAM Mag. Mbrships: ISM; RAM Club; Dir., Dolmtesch Fndn. Hons: ARAM; Conducting prize, Siena, 1963. Hobbies: Reading; Ornithology; Cricket. Address: 2 Grove Heath N, Ripley, Surrey GU23 6EN, UK.

BROCKMAN, Thomas, b. 12 Jan. 1922. Greenville, SC, USA. Concert Pianist; Teacher; Professor of Piano. Educ: Curtis Inst. of Music; Grad., Juilliard Schl. of Music, 1948; Study w. Olga Samaroff, Edwin Fischer. Robert Casadesus & Nadia Boulanger. Debut: Carnegie Hall, NYC, 1950; London 1952. Career: 7 European tours; Apps., BBC radio, Danish W. German, French, Swiss & Dutch radio; Num. US concerts inclng. perfs. w. maj. orchs. Mbrships: Past Pres., Xi Chapt., Rollins Coll., Pi Kappa Lambda. Hobbies: Reading history & biography; Collecting records. Address: 271 Virginia Dr., Winter Park, FL 32789, USA. 7, 28.

BROCKPÄHLER, Renate, b. 9 Mar. 1927. Hettstedt, German Dem. Repub. Westfalian Folksong Archivist. Educ: Westfalian Schl. of Music, 1948-51; DPh, 1959. Mbrships: Gesellschaft für Musikforschung; Deutsche Gesellschaft für Volkskunde; Kommission für Lied-, Musik- & Tanzforschung, ibid. Publs:

Handbuch zur Geschichte der Barockoper in Deutschland, 1964. Contbr. of sev. articles on folkmusic to periodicals. Address: D 4400 Münster, Saarbrücker Str. 123, German Fed. Republic. 4.

BROCKWAY, Oliver M W, b. 7 Jan. 1946. Horn Player; Arranger; Composer. Educ: RAM, 1964-68. Career: Free-lance, playing w. LSO, RPO, & other London & provincial orchs.; Vis. Horn Tchr., Bedales Schl., ILEA schls. Comps. incl: Chorale & Variations (4 horns); Purcell Variants (4 horns); Rondo for Brass (band). Arrs. incl: Bach's Fugue IV a 5 for Brass Quintet; Mendelssohn's Capriccio Brilliant for brass band w. solo piano; Handel Sonata for Euphonium for brass band; Eccles Sonata in G Minor for brass band w. solo horn or euphonium; Handel Sonata for Solo Trumpet for brass band. Contbr. to: Sounding Brass; Horn Call. Address: 3 Wynnstay Gdns., London W8 6UP, UK.

BRODACKI, Krystian Wladyslaw Szymon, b. 23 July 1937. Warsaw, Poland. Journalist; Pianist. Educ: Warsaw Univ.; Fac. of Mech: Engrng., Cracow Polytechnic Schl. m. Maria Klara Jarocinska, 1 s. Debut: as musician, 1971. Career: Jrnlst., Polityka, 1967-69; Artistic Mgr., HAGAW Assn. Grp., 1971-73; TV & radio apps. in Poland, German Dem. & Fed. Republs., Austria & Czech. Recordings: w. HAGAW Assn., Poland & German Dem. Repub. Contbr. to: Jazz-Forum; PT-Innowacje; Non-Stop Radar; Razem: Mbrships: Gen. Coun., Vice-Chmn. of Critics Div., Polish Jazz Soc.; Polish Jrnlsts. Assn. Recip., 1st Prize, Int. Jazz Critix Competition, Jazz Forum, 1967. Hobbies: Italian Civilisation; Swimming; Tennis. Address: Al. Lotnikow 19 m. 55, 02-668 Warsaw, Poland.

BRODAL, Jon Eilif, b. 23 Oslo, Norway. Violinist; Teacher. Educ: Studies w. Leif Halvorsen in Oslo, 1929-33, w. Carl Flesch & Harmann Kaplan (violin), Berlin, Paul Juon & Wilhelm Forch (theory), Romuald Wikarski (piano), Maurice, Hewitt, Paris, Frederick Grinke, London. m. Emly de Lange, 2 c. Debut: Oslo, 1929. Career: Tchr., Bergen Music Acad., 1943-52; apptd. to the Musikkselskabet Harmonien Orch, 1945: 1st ldr., ibid, 1947-; ldr., Norwegian Opera, 1963-65; Ldr., Filharmonisk Selskap Orch., Oslo, 1965-; num. apps. in Norway & on Norwegian & Danish radio; mbr. of Brodel-Hindar-kvartetten, 1945-50; mbr. of Harmoniens Strykekvartett. Contbr. to: Musikknytt. Mbrships: Norwegian Musicians Union. Hons: Kings Reward Medal, 1976; Mark of Hon. of Filharmonisk Selskap Assn. Hobbies: Photography; Woodcarving; Reading. Address: Kongen 14, 1412 Sofiemyr, Norway.

BRODER, Teodor, b. 15 Oct. 1933. Lodz, Poland. Pianist; Composer. Educ: Grad., Piano & Comp., The New Jerusalem Conservatoire & Acad. of Music, Jerusaelm, Israel, Grad., Piano, Conserv. di St. Cecilia, Rome, Italy & Comp. from Accademia Nazionale di St. Cecilia, Rome, Italy. Career: Stage & radio apps. in Israel & some concerts in Rome, Italy, 1958-60; Works performed in Israel by Kol Israel Orch., Israel Chmbr. Ensemble & Haifa Chmbr. Ensemble. Compositions (publd.): Six Rubaiyyat of Omar Khayyam for voice, flute & clarinet; 3 studies for strings. Contbr. to: Tatzlil. Mbrships: Soc. of Authors, Comps. & Eds. of Music in Israel; Israel Assn. of Musicians & Musci Tchrs. Hons: Hon. Mention, Artur Malawski Mem. Competition, Poland, 1962; Premio d'Atri, Acad. di St. Cecilie, 1960. Address: 34402 Haifa, 25A Rachel St., Israel.

BRODERICK, Golda Avril, b. 24 Apr. 1919. Wales, UK. Music Teacher. Educ: Trained w. Gwen Lea-Dennis; Assoc., London Coll. of Music. m. Albert John Broderick, 2 s., 1 d. Career: Tchr. of piano, guitar, piano-accordian, violin, theory. Mbrships: Assoc., Imperial Soc. of Tchrs. of Dancing; Incorp. Soc. of Musicians; Music Tchrs. Assn. Hobbies: Dancing; Singing. Address: 2 Whittlesea Path, Harrow Weald, Harrow, Middx., HA3 6LP, UK.

BRODIN, Lena Birgitta Elise, b. 20 June 1941. Gothenburg, Sweden. Instrumental Music Teacher (piano, violin, viola, recorder); Composer; Teacher of Relaxation. Educ: Dip. (piano tchr.), 1966; Gen. music tchr. dip., 1966; Rhythmics tchr. dip., 1969. m. Gunnar Jonsson, 1 d. Career: Tchr., Communal Music Schl., Stockholm, 1969-; tchr., Adult Schl., Stockholm, 1969-; mbr. of a state investigation for grp. tchng., 1977; courses given in Sweden, Denmark & Finland on grp. tchng. Comps: small works for students of violin, cello & piano, ensembles; recorder music. Publs: Fela Med Färg 1 & 2 (violin book for grp. tchng.), 1973; Fritt Fram 1 & 2 (paino book for grp. tchng.), 1975; Spelsugen (Beginners book for recorder), 1976; Teacher's Guide to Group Teaching, 1976. Mbrships: Violin Tchrs. Assn.; Piano Tchrs. Assn.; Chamber Music Assn. Hobbies: Playing Chmbr. Music; Skiing; Skating; Swimming. Address: Baggensgaten 15 II, 111 31 Stockholm, Sweden.

BRODY, Elaine, b. 21 Apr. 1923. NYC, USA. Musicologist; Pianist. Educ: AB, Wash. S. Coll., NYU, 1944; AM, Columbia Univ., 1960; PhD, NYU NY 1964. m. David Silverberg, 1 d. Career: Musicol.; Pianist; Presented Music in the Romantic Era on TV; var. lectures in USA; Mbr., Education committee Met. Opera Guild. Publs. incl: Music in Opera, 1970; The German Lied & Its Poetry (co-author), 1971, Music Lovers Guide to Europe (6 books) co-author, 1974; The Music Guide to Gt. Britian: The Music Guide to Austria & Germany; Music in the Romantic Era; The French Revival (French Music from 1870-1925). Contbr. to: Musik in Geschichte & Gegenwart; Grove's Dictionary: Notes; Music Review; Symposia; Studies in Romanticism, etc. Mbr. Phi Beta Kappa (sec., NYU chapt., 10 yrs.); Am. Musicological Soc., Int. Musicological Soc., etc. Hobbies: Work; Travel related to work. Address: 35 E 84th St., NY, NY 10028, USA. 11.

BROEKSTRA, Hendrik Jan, b. Jan. 1924. Zaandijk, Netherlands. Manager. Educ: Conserv. (Piano & Schl. Music); Solo-studies w. Prof. Hauser in Vienna. m. Leonora Johanna Gompertz, 4 c. Debut: As pianist, w. Frysian Orch., 1949. Career: Pianist w. sev. orchs., in recitals & as accomp.; num. radio perfs.; Tchr. of schoolmusic; Hd. of Music Dept. RONO; Gen. Mgr., Het Brabants Orkest, 8 yrs.; Mgr., Div. Perf. Artists, Nederlandse Omroep Stichting, Hilversum. Num. publs incl: Alma Musica 12th Ed.; Wolters-Noordhoff; Groningen & Musiek in de Brugklas. Address: Ruthardlaan 35, 1406 RR Bussum, Netherlands.

BROFSKY, Howard, b. 2 May 1927. NYC, USA. Musicologist; Professor of Music. Educ: PhD, NY Univ. m. Miriam Brofsky, 1 s., 1 d. Career: NY Univ.; Univ. of Chgo.; Univ. of BC; Prof. of Music, Queens Coll., Listening: Developing Musical Perception, 3rd ed., 1975, w. accompanying set of 7 LP records, Contbt. to: Musical Quarterly; Jrnl. of Am. Musicological So.; Rivista Italiana di Musicologia. Mbrships: Int. Musicological Soc; Am. Musicological Soc.; Soc. for 18th Century Studies; Coll. Music Soc. Address: 186 Riverside Dr., NY, NY 11024, USA. 2.

BROIDO, Arnold Peace, b. 8 Apr. 1920. NYC, USA. Music Publisher. Educ: BS, Ithaca Coll., 1941; MA, Columbia Univ., 1954. m. Lucille Tarshes 3 s. Career: Ed. & Prod. Mgr., Boosey & Hawkes Inc., 1945-55; VP & Gen. Mgr., Century Music & Mercury Music Corp., 1955-57; Dir. Publs. & Sales, Frank Music Corp., 1962-68; VP, Boston Music Co., 1967-69; Pres., Theodore Presser Co., Bryn Mawr, Pa., 1969-; Chmn., Elkan-Vogel Inc., 1970-. Publs: Co-author, Music Dictionary, 1956; Invitation to the Piano, 1959, Assoc. Ed., Univ. Soc. Ency. of Piano Music; articles in the field. Mbrships. incl: ASCAP (Dir. 1972-); Am. Music Ctr. (Bd. of Dirs. 1968-72, 1978); Music Publrs. Assn. (Sec. & Bd. of Dirs., 1965-70, First VP 1970-72, Pres. 1972); Int. Publrs. Assn. (VP Music Sect. 1972-); Music Ind. Coun. (Pres. 1900-08, VP, 1909-70), BJ. of Educ., Union Free Schl. Dist. 21, Rockville Ctr., NY (VP & Dist. Clerk 1967-69); Treas. & Dir., ASCAP Fndn., 1972. Address: 908 Wootton Rd., Bryn Mawr, PA 19010, USA. 2.

BROJER, Robert, b. 17 Apr. 1919. Reichwaldau, Czechoslovakia. Guitar Teacher. Educ: Studied Guitar & Violin at Acad. of Music, Vienna; State Dip. for Tchrs. of Music. m. Michaela Mahler, 1 s., 1 d. Career: Guitar Tchr., Konservatorium der Stadt, Wien. Comps. incl: For 2 Guitars; Kinderstucke; Miniaturen; Kleine Musik; Fantasie a-moll; For 1 ¢ Guitar: 5 Bagatellen; 3 Orginalstudien f.G; Thema mit Variationen; Sonatine; Comps. published under R Brojer & pseudonym A Morena. Publs. incl: Der Weg zur Gitarre, Barenreiter-Verlag, Kassel, 1973. Mbr. IAM, Kassel, W Germany. Hons: Awarded title of Prof. 1968. Hobbies: Making Music; Transcribing Tabulatures etc. in view of publishing. Address: Medekstrasse 31, 1-3400 Klosterneuburg, Austria.

BRONSON, Bertrand Harris, b. 22 June 1902. Lawrenceville, NJ, USA. Musicologist; Folklorist; violinist. Educ: AB, LHD, Univ. of Mich.; MA, Harvard Univ.; BA, MA, Univ. of Oxford; PhD, Yale Univ.; D és L, Univ. Laval; LHD, Univ. of Chgo.; LLD, Univ. of Calif. m. Mildred Sumner Kinsley. Publs: The Ballad as Song, 1968; The Traditional Tunes of the Child Ballads, vols. 1-4, 1959-72; The Singing Tradition of Child's Popular Ballads, 1976; Chapt. on Music & Literature in Relations of Literary Study, 1967. Contbr. of essays & reviews to music & folklore jrnls. Hons: Rice Univ. Medal of Hons., 1962; GuggenheimFellow, 1943, '44 & '48; Am. Coun. Learned Socs. Award, 1959; Wilbur Cross medal, Yale Univ., 1970. Mbrships: Corr. Fellow, Brit. Acad.; Am. Acad. of Arts & Scis.; Int. Folk Music Coun.; Fellow, Am. Folklore Soc; Modern Langs. Assn., Am. Exec. Coun. Emeritus. Hobbies: Lute, Recorder & Violin playing. Address: 927 Oxford St., Berkeley, CA 94707, USA. 2.

BROOK, Barry Shelley, b. 1 Nov. 1918. NYC, USA. Musicologist; Professor. Educ: BSS, CCNY, 1939; MA, Columbia Univ., 1942; Dr. de l'Université, Univ. of Paris, 1959. m. (1) 1 s., 1 d.; (2) Claire Kessler. Career incls: Prof. of Music, Queens Coll., & Exec. Off. of PhD Prog. in Music, Grad. Schl. CUNY, 1967-; Ed.-in-chirf, RILM Abstracts of Music Lit., 1967-; Ed. for Music, 18th Century: A Current Bibliography, Philol. Quarterly, 1971. Publs. incl: La symphonie française dans la seconde moitié du XVIIe siécle, 3 vols., 1962; Thematic Catalogues in Music; an annotated bibliography, 1972. Ed. many scholarly eds. of musical works. Contbr. to num. profl. publs. Mbr. num. profl. orgs. Recip. num. hons. inclng: PhD, Univ. of Adelaide, Aust., 1974. Hobby: Tennis. Address: 50 Ctrl. Park W, NY, NY 10023, USA. 2, 11, 14.

BROSTER, Eileen, b. 23 June 1935. London, UK. Concert Pianist; Teacher. Educ: RCM (w. Frank Merrick & Cyril Smith); ARCM. m. Reginald Chaplain, 1 s. Debut: Wigmore Hall, London. Career: Soloist w. ldng. orchs.; recitals throughout UK; num. radio & TV perfs. for BBC. mbr., ISM. Hobbies: Yoga; Reading; Concerts. Address: 199 Beehive Ln., Redbridge, Ilford, Essex, UK. 27.

BROTHERS, Lester D., b. 10 July 1945. Hanford, Calif., USA. Musicologist. Educ: BA Mus, Calif. State Univ., Fresno, 1967; MA Mus, PhD Mus, Univ. of Calif., Los Angeles, 1970 & '73. m. Janet Elizabeth Nelson Brothers, 1 s., 1 d. Career: Lectr. in Music, Calif. State Univ., 1973-74; Asst. Prof. of Music, N. Texas State Univ., 1974-. Contbr. to var. profl. jrnls. Mbrships: Int. Musicol. Soc.; S. Ctrl. Renaissance Conf., Exec. Committee, Ed. Bd.; Pi Kapp Lambda; Phi Kappa Phi; Phi Mu Alpha Sinfonia. Hons: UCLA Alumni Assn. Dist. Graduate Award, 1973: Ingolf Dahl Award, Pacific Coast Chapts. of the Am. Musicol. Soc., 1973. Hobbies: Clarinet; Piano; Reading. Address: 2608 Sherwood Land, Denton, TX 76201, USA. 28, 29.

BROTHWOOD, Constance Edna, b. 9 Mar. 1925. Durban, S Africa. Concert Pianist. Educ: RAM; ATCL, 1944; LTCL, 1945; FTCL, 1948. m. John N Ley. Debut: as soloist w. Durban Symph. Orch., 1935. Career incls: num. solo recitals and apps. w. all major S African orchs. under var. conds. inclng. Dr. Anton Hartman, Gideon Fagan, Frits Schuurman, Antal Dorati, Brydon Thompson & Sir Malcolm Sargeant; recordings for Brussels Radio & in Jerusalem for Kol Israel; Official Accomp., S Africa Broadcasting Corp., 1949-70. Recordings: S African Broadcasting Corp. transcriptions. Mbrships: S African Soc. of Music Tchrs.; Wild Life Soc. of Natal; Natal Cornish Assn. Recip., 3 Gold Medals, Natal Soc. for the Advancement of Music, 1943-44. Hobbies: Dog-breeding; Riding; Nature Study. Address: 401 Kensington, N Ridge Rd., Durban 4001, S Africa.

BROTT, Alexander, b. 14 Mar. 1915. Montreal, Can. Composer; Conductor; Professor. Educ: Lic. Mus., McGill Univ., 1932; degree, Que. Acad. of Music, 1933; grad., Juilliard Schl. of Music, NY, 1937; postgrad., ibid., 1938; DMus, Chgo. Univ., 1960; LLD, Queen's Univ., 1973. m. Lotte Goetzel, 2 s. Career: Prof. of Music, McGill Univ.; Cond., McGill Chmbr. Orch. & Kingston Symph. Orch. Comps. incl: symphonic works, concerti, solo, vocal & chmbr. music. Recordings: Works by Haydn, Mozart, Schubert, Beethoven. sev. recordings of own comps. Mbrships: McGill Univ. Fac. Club; Musicians' Guild; Société de musique contemporaine; CAPAC; FRSA. num. hons. Address: 5459 Earnscliffe Ave., Montreal, Que. H3X 2P8, Can.

BROTT, Boris, b. 14 Mar. 1944. Montreal, Canada. Music Director & Conductor. Educ: Conservatoire de Musique, Montreal, Canada; McGill Univ., Montreal; studied cond. w. Pierre Monteux, Igor Markevitch, Leonard Bernstein & Alexander Brott. Debut: As violinist, Montreal Symph., 1949; as cond., Nat. Symph. Orch., Mex., 1958. Career: Fndr., Phil. Youth Orch. of Montreal, 1959: Asst. Cond., Toronto Symph., 1963-65; Prin. Cond., Northern Sinfonia, UK, 1964-68; Asst. Cond., NY Phil., 1968-69; Music Dir., & Cond., Lakehead Symph., 1968-72 & Regina Symph., 1971-73; currently Music Dir., & Cond., BBC Welsh Symph. Orch., 1972; CBC. Num. award winning radio & TV series for CBC. Num. series & specials for CBC & CTV in Canada & ITV & BBC in UK. Var. recordings. Recip. sev. hons. & awards. Address: Hamilton Pl., 50 Main St., W Hamilton, Ont., Canada. 2, 14.

BROTT, Denis, b. 9 Dec. 1950. Montreal, PQ, Can. Concert Cellist; Professor of Cello. Educ: incls: Grad., Conserv. of PQ, Montreal; Artist Dip., Ind. Univ., USA; Piatigorsky's Master Calss, Schl. of Performing Arts, Univ. of Southern Calif.; studies w. many noted cellists, also conducting w. Igor Markevitch w. Julie Ann Stephanie Shoshana Fraser Debut: Carnegie Recital Hall, NYC, 1968. Career incls: radio & TV broadcasts, Can., UK, Europe; currently Prof., NC Schl. of Arts.

Sev. recordings for CBC. Mbr. Violoncello Soc. Inc. Recip. num. awards & study grants inclng: Top Prize, 22nd Int. Cello Competition, Munich. Hobby: Photography. Address: Interlochen Arts Acad., Interlochen, MI 39643, USA.

BROUGH, George. b. Boston, Lincolnshire, UK. Pianist; Organist; Harpsichordist. Educ: MA, Oxford Univ., UK; ARCM, FRCO, DMus, Oxford Univ. m. Judith Penelope Petit, 1s. 1d. Career: Asst. Conductor & Coach, Canadian Opera Co.; Opera Coach, Fac. of Music, Univ. of Toronto, Ont.; Soloist & Accompanist, Canadian Broadcasting Corp., 1950-; Harpsichordist, Toronto Chmbr. Players; Accompanist, Toronto Mendelssohn Choir; Examiner, Royal Conserv. of Music, Toronto; Accompanist & Opera Coach, Banff Schl. of Fine Arts, Banff, Alberta, 1965-. Recordings: Accompanist to David Zafer (Violin) & Paul Brodie (Saxophone); Festival Singers of Canada; Toronto Mendelssohn Choir; 3 recordings w. winners of Canadian Broadcasting Corp. Talent Festival. Mbr., Royal Canadian Coll. of Organists. Address: 4 N Sherbourne St., Toronto, Ont. M4W 2T1, Canada.

BROWN, Alan Martin, b. Dec. 1941. London, UK. University Lecturer. Educ: MusB, MA, PhD, Gonville & Caius Coll., Cambridge; LRAM; FRCO, m. Judith Penelope Petit, 1s. 1d. Career: Fellow, Fitzwilliam Coll., Cambridge, 1965-73; Lectr. in Music, Sheffield Univ., 1973-. Comps: Three Christmas Carols. Publs: Tisdale's Virginal Book (transcribed & ed.), 1966; William Byrd; Keyboard Music (transcribed & ed.), vols. 27, 28, Musica Britannica. Mbr., Royal Musical Assn. Recip. Wm. Barclay Squire Prize, 1964. Hobbies: Walking; Gardening; Go (the game). Address: 71 Watson Rd., Sheffield, S10 2SD, UK.

BROWN, Beatrice, b. 17 May 1917. Leeds, UK. Conductor; Violist. Educ: BA, Hunter Coll., NYC, 1937; MA, NY Univ., 1940; Dip., Music Schl. Settlement, NYC, 1940. m. Morris Rothenberg. Debut: NY Phil. Orch., Carnegie Hall, NYC, 1955. Career incls: Violist, RCA Victor Symph., 1944-56; NY City Opera Co., 1948-62; Brooklyn Philharmonia, 1950-62; Westchester Symph. Orch., 1955-62; Am. Symph. Orch. under Stokowski, 1963-64; Music Dir. & Cond., Scranton Philharmonia Orch., Pa., 1963-72; Ridgefield Orch., Conn., 1969-; Mbr.; Dept. of Music, Bronx HS of Sci., NYC, 1970-; Adj. Asst. Prof., Lehman Coll., NYC, 1972-74. Mbrships: Hon., Phi Beta Kappa & Kappa Mu Epsilon; Hunter Coll. Hall of Fame, 1972. Hobby: Sports. Mgmt: Albert Kay, 58 W 58th St., NYC. Address: 39 Glenbrook Rd., Stamford, CT 06902, USA.

BROWN, Beryl Edith, b. 8 Sept. 1905. Farnham, Surrey, UK. Piano Teacher. Educ: Studies of Pianoforte teaching, aural trng., harmony & counterpoint; Assoc., Royal Coll. Music, London, 1927. Career: Schl. & pvte. tchr. of pianoforte up to dip. standard. Mbr., Incorp. Soc. of Musicians. Address: 23 Wick Lane, Christchurch, Dorset, BH23 1HT, UK.

BROWN, Christine, b. 22 Nov. 1930. Leeds, UK. Senoir Lecturer in Music; Pianist; Virginals Player. Educ: LLB, Univ. of Leeds, 1959; Dip. in Philos. of Educ., Univ. of London Inst. of Educ., 1973; ARCM, 1951; GRSM, 1952; FTCL, 1971. Career: Sr. Lectr. in Music, Bretton Hall Coll.; Yorks. Area Organiser EPTA Piano Tchrs. Assn. Publs. (piano): First Album; Second Album; Third Album; Fourth Album; Play at Sight, Parts I to VI. Contbr. to: Making Music; Music in Educ.; Jrnl. of ISM. Hons: Fndn. Schlrship., RCM, 1948; Winner, Yorks. Symph. Orch. Concert Soloists' Competition, 1954. Hobbies: Reading: Old keyboard instruments. Address: 10A Chandos Gdns., Leeds LS8 1LW, UK.

BROWN, Christopher Roland, b. 17 June 1943. Tunbridge Wells, UK. Composer. Educ: MA, King's Coll., Cambridge Univ.; RAM, London; Hochschule für Music, Berlin, Germany. m. Anne Smillie, 1 s., 1 d. Career: Compositions played thru'out Brit., in USA, Europe & Aust.; Perfs. at Three Choirs, Bath & Nottingam Festivals; num. Radio Broadcasts. Compositions: Three Medieval Lyrics; David; Hymn to the Holy Innocents; Hodie Salvator Apparuit; Elegy; Three Shakespeare Songs; Four Madrigals; The Snows of Winter; Missa Brevis; Ch. Music; Carols; Nocturne for Organ. Mbrships: CGGB (Exec. Committee). Hons: Westminster Abbey 900th Anniversary Jubilate Award, 1966; Theodore Holland Award, RAM, 1967. Guinness Prize for comp., 1974; Collard Fellowship, Musicians Co., 1974. Hobbies: Photography; Opera; Do-it-Yourself; Playing Games. Address: Sedge Roof, 10 High St., Bluntisham, Cambs., UK. 3. 139.

BROWN, Colin Stewart, b. 13 Dec. 1944. Dounby, Orkney Isles, UK. Accompanist; Piano Soloist; Music Teacher. Educ: Royal Scottish Acad. Music, Glasgow; Conservatorio di S. Cecilia, Rome; Royal Acad. Music, London; Lic., ibid.; Dip. Music Educ.; LTCL. m. Margaret Elaine Kerss, 1 s., 1 d. Career:

Appears w. Ian Wallace in An Evening with Ian Wallace Show; Solo perfs. at music clubs. Mbrships: Soloists' Br., Incorp. Soc. of Musicians; Musicians' Union; SSTA. Recip. Italian Govt. schlrship. to study piano w. Vincenzo Vitale & Rodolfo Caporali at Conservatorio di S. Cecilia. Hobbies: For. Cooking; Travel; Playing viola; Singing. Address: Villa d'Este, 35 Ochiltree, Dunblane, Perthshire, UK.

BROWN, David Clifford, b. 8 July 1929. Gravesend, UK. University Reader. Educ: BA, BMus, MA, Sheffield Univ.; PhD, Southampton Univ.; LTCL (piano perf.). m. Elizabeth Valentine, 2 d. Career: Music Libn., London Univ., 1959-62; Lectr.-Rdr., Music, Southampton Univ., 1962-. Publs: Thomas Weelkes: A Biographical & Critical Study, 1969; Mikhail Glinka: A Biographical & Critical Study, 1974; John Wilbye, 1974. Jr. Ed: Thomas Weelkes: Collected Anthems, 1966; Tchaikovsky: A Biographical & Critical Study, Vol. I, The Early Years (1840-1874), 1978. Contbr. to profl. jrnls. Mbrships: Royal Musical Assn.; Address: 56 Pentire Ave., Southampton SO1 2RS, UK. 28.

BROWN, Earle, b. 1926. Lunenburg, USA. Composer; Lecturer. Educ: studied engrng., Northeastern Univ., Boston, Mass.; Schillinger Schl. of Music, Boston, studied composition pvtely. Career: Composer; Project for Music for Magnetic Tape, NY, 1952-55; Composer in Res., Kunstler Prog., W. Berlin, 1970-71, & Peabody Conserv. of Music, Balt., 1968-70 & 71-72; specializes in graphic music, new notations, open form & new scoring for improvisation. Compositions incl: Three Pieces for Piano; Perspectives; Folio & Four Systems; Music for 'Cello & Piano; Available Forms I & II; Nine Rarebits; Corroborree; Modules I & II; Synergy II; Syntagm III. Publs: Notation & Performance of New Music, 1964; Form in New Music, 1965. Mbrships: Broadcast Music Inc.; Am. Music Ctr. Hons. DMus.; Peabody Conserv.; Guggenheim Fellowship, 1965-66. Hobbies: Skiing; Tennis; Driving Good Automobiles. Address: c/o Universal Edition, 2-3 Fareham St., London W1, UK. 3.

BROWN, Gavin William, b. 18 Apr. 1925. Battersea, London, UK Organist; Teacher; Dir., Jr. Exhibitioners Course & Co-ordinator of Aural Trng. Royal Academy of Music. Educ: Organ Schlr., Christ Ch., Oxford; MA; B Mus; FRCO. m. Florence Jones, 3 d. Career: Organist, Brighton Parish Ch., 1949-74; Vis. Music Tchr., Lancing Coll., 1958-76; Prof., RAM, 1960-; Examiner, Assoc. Bd. of Royal Schls. of Music, 1964-; Special Commnr., Royal Schl. of Ch. Music, 1968-; Accomp., Brighton & Hove Harmonic Soc., 1975-; Broadcast organ recitals, 1960-65. Mbrships: ISM; RCO; Brighton & Dist. Organists Assn.; Royal Soc. of Musicians. Recip. Hon. RAM. Hobby: Railways. Address: 118 Holmes Ave., Hove, Sussex BN3 7LE, UK, 3, 28.

BROWN, Gerald. b. Douglas, Ariz., USA. Director of National Symphony & National Youth Symphony, Costa Rica. Educ: Ariz. State Univ.; studies toward MA in French Horn, Juilliard Schl. of Music, NYC. Career: spent 3 yrs. in Bolivia as Peace Corp Volunteer, reorganizing orch.; moved to Costa Rica to re-organize orch. at request of Vice-Min. of Culture, Guido Saenz, & has developed Nat. Youth Symph. to train future musicians. Address: c/o Nat. Symph. Orch., Apdo 5015, San Jose, Costa Rica.

BROWN, Harold, b. 31 Oct. 1909. NYC, USA. Choral Conductor; Composer; Violist; Violinst; Eductor (Specialist in Renaissance Music). Educ: BA, MA, Columbia Univ.; studied Violin w. L J Bostelmann, Prof. H. Dittler; Nat. Orchl. Assn.; studied Conducting w. Leonard Berstein, Seymour Lipkin, Leon Barzin, studied Comp. w. Nadia Boulanger, Aaron Copland, Bernard Wagenaar, Rubin Goldmark; Pius X Schl. of Liturgical Music. m. Nancy Clemens, 2 d. Career: Fndr. & Musical Dir., Renaissance Chorus of NY, 1954-; Violist, Balt. Symph. Orch., NYC Ctr. Orch., Mansfield State Coll., Pa., 1957-61. Comps: (publd.): Choral Setting No. 1; Prelude for Piano; Music for Educl. Film, 'Your Child is a Genius!' Recordings: w. Renaissance Chorus: Isaac, Motets from Choralis Constantinus No. 3; Des Pres, Missa Una Musca de Bruscaya; Ockeghem, Missa Mi-mi; Martini, Magnificat; Finck, Missa de Beata Virgine. Publs: var. choral comps.of Ockeghem & Finck. Contbr. to: Partisan Review; The Nation: Film Music Notes. Charter Mbr., Am. Comps.' Alliance. Hons: Mosenthal Fellow in Music Comp., Columbia Univ., 1930. Address: 2225 Milford Pl., Spolane, WA 99201, USA.

BROWN, Howard Fuller, b. 24 July 1920. Arkona, Ont., Canada. University Teacher. Educ: BA, Univ. of Toronto; MusBac., ibid.; MA, Univ. of Mich.; Studied piano w. Lubka Kolessa, Fac. of Music, Univ. of Toronto. Career: Fac. mbr., Dept. of Music, Mt. Allison Univ., Sackville, NB, 1950-67. Co-Prof. (w. Derek C. Oppen) of The Gustafson Piano Library, a set

of tapes of an important pvte. collect. of piano records belonging to Ralph Gustafon, 1971-. Recip., Schlrship. from Royal Soc. of Canada for study in UK, 1957-58. Address: Dept. of Music, Bishop's Univ., Lennoxville, PQ J1M 1Z7, Canada.

BROWN, Howard Mayer, b. 13 Apr. 1930. LA, Calif., USA. Professor of Music. Educ: AB, Harvard Univ., 1951; AM, ibid., 1954; PhD, ibid., 1959. Career: instructor in Music, Wellesley Coll., Mass., 1958-60; Asst. Prof., Assoc. Prof., Prof., Univ. of Chgo., 1960-72; King Edward Prof. of Music, Univ. of Chgo., 1974-; Alexander D. White Prof.-At-Large. Cornell Univ., NY, 1972-76. Ferdinand Schevil Disting. Service Prof. of Music, Univ. Chgo., 1976-. Publs. incl: Instrumental Music Printed Before 1600, 1965; w. Joan Lascelle, Musical Iconography, 1972; 16th Century Instrumentation, 1973; Rebellishing 16th Century Music, 1977; Music in the Renaissance, 1977. Contbr. to: Jrnl. of the Am. Musicol. Soc.; Acta Musicologica; La Musica Encyclopedia; Musical Quarterly; Die Musikforschung; Musical Times; Music Lib. Assn. Notes; Renaissance News; Early Music. Mbr., Off., num. profl. orgs. Recip. num. hons. Address: 1415 E. 54th St., Chgo., IL 60615, USA.

BROWN, James Gopsill, b. 12 Apr. 1929. Leeds, UK. Oboist. Educ: Hon.RCM. m. Marion Taylor, 3s. Career: Oboist w. Royal Opera House Orch., Covent Garden, 1951-53; Netherlands Opera, 1954; London Mozart Players; Bath Festival Orch.; English Chamber Orch.; London Wind Solists. num. recordings. Publs: 370 Exercises for the Oboe, 1966; Solos for the Oboe, 1977; Ed., Sonata by Widerkehr, 1970. Address: 2 Parkgate Crescent, Hadley Wood, Barnet, Herts., UK.

BROWN, James Gopsill, b. 12 April 1929. Oboe Player. Educ: Hon. RCM. m. Sandy Brown. Career: Mbr., Engl. Chmbr. Orch. Publs: 370 Finger Exercise for the Oboe; Two Books of Solos for the Oboe; Oboe Duets; Oboe Trios; Ed., Rossini & Chopin Variations. Address: 6 7A Lordship Rd., London N16, UK

BROWN, James Murray, b. 8 Mar. 1913. Galashiels, Scotlands. University Lecturer; Pianist. Educ: Univ. Edinburgh; BMus, Dunelm; DMus, ibid.; FTCL; LRAM. m. Ruth Allsebrook, 1 s., 1 d. Career: Sr. Lectr. in Music, Durham Univ.; Examiner for Trinity Coll. of Music; Pianist, Recitals & Lecture Recitals w. Ruth Allsebrook, Soprano. Publs: Handbook of Musical Knowledge for Trinity Coll. of Music; Workbook for the Examinations of Trinity Coll. of Music; Mbrships: ISM; Fedn. of Music Festivals. Hobbies: Painting; Gardening (specially growing Alpines). Address: Kinlochbervie, 58 Bolton Ave., Richmond, N Yorks., UK.

BROWN, James William, b. 8 Aug. 1928. Streatham, London, UK. Musician (Horn, Wagner Tuba, Alphorn); Professor. Educ: RSAMD. m. Arline Mary Wendy Robinson, 2 d. 1 s. Debut: w. Scottish Orch., 1945. Career: Scottish Orch., Prin. horn, RPO, 1959-70; Prin. horn, LPO, 1955-58; perfs. w. Royal Opera House Orch. & Philharmonia Orch.; Prof., RAM, 1964-; chmn. RPO, 1963-66; Recordings incl. 4 Mozart Horn Concertos. Mbrships: Musicians' Union; ISM; Savage Club. Hons: OBE, 1967; hon. RAM. Hobbies: Gardening; Model Boats; Golf. Mgmt: Conchord Mgmt. Ltd. Address: The Cottage, Gibson's Hill, London SW16, UK.

BROWN, Jasmin Alexandra Thalia Jane, b. 4 Mar. 1952. Wellington, Somerset, UK. Music Teacher. Educ: Tchng. Cert., Newton Pk. Coll., Bristol Univ., 1970-73; CAAT, Newcastle, 1979; A Mus TCL, 1978; Cand. for L Mus TCL. Career: Tchr., 1974-; Asst., Newcastle Festival Off., 1979; Music Dept., Oxford Univ. Press, 1979-; Running student dance co., Dance Variations; Front of House Staff, Royal Opera House. Mbr., Incorp. Soc. of Musicians; Soc. of Friends. Hobbies: Choreography; Swimming; Work for Soc. of Friends (Quakers). Address: 64 Priory Gdns., Highgate, London, N6, UK.

BROWN, Keith, b. 21 Oct. 1933. Colorado Springs, Colo., USA. Trombonist; Conductor; Educator. Educ: BM, Univ. of Southern Calif., 1957; MM, Manhattan Schl. of Music, 1964. m. Leslee Scullin Brown, 1 s., 2 d. Career: NY Brass Quintet, 1958-59; Assoc. 1st Trombone, Phila., Orch., 1959-62; 1st Trombone, Met. Opera, 1962-65; Aspen Festival, 1957-69; Casals Fest. Orch., Puerto Rico, 1958-; Marlboro Festival, 1970-; Chmn., Brass Dept. Music Acad. of the West, num. Solo & Chmbr. Music perfs. w. Leonard Berstein, Karl Richter, Chmbr. Music Soc. of Lincoln Center, 1969-, etc.; Prof. of Music, & Cond., Temple Univ., Phila., Pa., 1965-71, Ind. Univ., 1971-. Recordings: num. orchl.; Solo incl. NY Brass Quintet in Concert, Golden Crest, Stravinsky Conducts, Columbia, Yehudi Wyner Serenade For 7 Instruments, Composer's Recordings. Publs: 10 volumes orchl. studies for trombone & tuba; num. eds. of solo, brass ensemble works, study materials. Mbrships: MENC; Phi Mu Alpha Sinfonia; Pi Kappa Lambda. Recip. var.

hons. Hobbies: Tennis; Handball; Sailing. Address: Schl. of Music, Ind. Univ., Bloomington, IN 47401, USA.

BROWN, Leon Ford, b. 18 Jan. 1918. Taylorsville, NC, USA. Musician; Composer; University Professor. Educ: BFA, Okla. State Univ., Stillwater, Okla.; MA, Educ: BFA, Okla.; MA, Cath. Univ. of Am., Wash. DC. m. Juanita Smead, 2 s., 1 d. Career: Tchr. in pub. schls.; Tchr., US Navy Schl. of Music; Prof. of Music (Trombone), N. Texas State UKniv. Comps: 05 misc. comps. & arrs. for chorus, brass, brass ensemble, bands. Publs: Handbook of Selected Literature for the Study of Trombone at the University-College Level, 1972. Contbr. to var. profl. jrnls. Mbrships: BdDirs., Int. Trombone Assn.; NACWPI; Tex. Music Educators Assn.; Tex. Assn. of Coll. Tchrs.; Phi Mu Alpha; Kappa Kappa Psi; Pi Kappa Lambda. Hons: Hon. Prof., N. Texas State Univ., 1976. Hobbies: Antique collecting; Fishing; Golf; Gardening. Address: 2907 Nottingham, Denton, TX 76201, USA. 7, 29.

BROWN, Malcolm Hamrick, b. 9 Nov. 1929. Carrollton, Ga., USA. Musicologist. Educ: BMus, Converse Coll., 1951; MMus, Univ. Mich., 1956; PhD, Fla. State Univ., 1967; Moscow Conserv. of Music, USSR, 1962; Monterey Inst. of Int. Studies, 1978. m. Shirley Ann Wood, 2 d. Career: Chmbr. & Prof. of Musicology, Ind. Univ. Schl. of Music, Bloomington, Ind., USA. Publs: Ed., Papers of the Yugoslav-Am. Seminar on Music, 1970; Articles & reviews in profl. jrnls. Mbrships: Am. Musicol. Soc.; Int. Musicol. Soc.; Am. Assn. for Advancement of Slavic Studies. Recip. num. grants & fellowships. Hobbies: Jogging; Tennis. Address: 6701 E. Bender Rd., Bloomington, IN 47401, USA.

BROWN, Melaine Vadas, b. 26 Feb. 1956. Cinn., Ohio, USA. Music Therapist (Harp). Educ: BMus, Music Theraphy, Univ. of Ga.; studied w. Linda Wellbaum, Cinn. Coll. Conserv. of Music Prepatory Dept.; Harp studies w. Marlene Ledet, Univ. of Ga. m. Thomas Brand Brown. Career: Perfs. w. Athens Avante Garde Soc. & at 1978 Nat. Convention of Nat. Assn. of Music Therapy. Mbrships: Sigma Alpha Iota; Nat. Assn. of Music Therapy. Hobbies: Drawing; Theatre; Swimming. Address: K-205 University Village, Athens, GA 30602, USA. 4.

BROWN, Myrne Weeks, b. 4 July 1937. Flautist. Educ: BM, Univ. of UT, 1958; MM, N Tex. State Univ. 1973. M. Newel Kay Brown, 2 s., 3 d. Career: Ark. Symph., 1968-70; Prin. Flute, Wichita Falls Symph., Tex., 1974-; Pt.-time Tchr., N Tex. State Univ. & Midwestern Univ. of Wichita Falls, 1974-. Recording: Dialogue & Dance by N K Brown, 1968. Mbrships. incl: Nat. Flute Assn.; Mu Phi Epsilon; Phi Beta Kappa; Phi Kappa Phi; N Tex. Flute Club; Pi Kappa Lambda. Hobbies: Research; Handwork. Address: 805 Laguna, Denton, TX, USA.

BROWN, Oren Lathrop, b. 13 Apr. 1909. Somerville, Mass., USA. Teacher of Singing & Voice Therapy. Educ: BMus (voice), MA (comp.), Boston Univ. m. Julia Lukas, 2d., 1 s. Career: Tchng. posts at Principia Coll., S Illinois Univ., Missouri Univ., Wash. Univ. & Mannes Coll. of Music & Union Theological Seminary, NY; Prof. of voice & Hd., Music Dept., Shurtleff Coll., Alton, Ill, 1947-54; Lctr. in Voice Therapy Wash. Univ. Schl. of Medicine, St. Louis, 1952-68; Consultant in Otolaryngology, St. Louis City Hospital; Music Advsr. National Staff of USO during the war; Lctr. & Clinician at num. coll. clinics; 6 yrs. chmn. of Committee on Vocal Educ. of Nat. Assn. of Tchrs. of Singing (NATS); Dir., Oren Brown Voice Seminar at Zuoz, Switz., 1977, '78, & Amherst, Mass., 1972-76; pvte. tchr., NY. Contbr. to NATS Bulletin. Mbrships: NATS; NY Singing Tchrs. Assn.; Int. Assn. for Experimental Rsch. in Singing; Bohemians. Hobbies: Ornithology; hiking; swimming. Address: 2109 Broadway, NY, NY 10023, USA.

BROWN, Patricia Anne, b. 7 Jan. 1945. Brisbane, Aust. University Music Lecturer. Educ: BA (music), Univ. of Qld., 1967; MA (music), ibid., 1969; dip., librarianship, Univ. of NSW, 1970. m. Roger Covell. Career: 1st music libn., Nat. Lib. of Aust., Canberra, 1970-72; Lectr. in music, Univ. of NSW, Sydney, 1973-; apps. in over 20 operatic roles since 1970 w. Univ. of NSW Opera, incl. Miss Jessell (Turn of the Screw), Medoro (Handel's Orlando), in Monteverdi's The Return of Ulysses & in Barry Conyngham's Edward John Eyre; soprano soloist in sev. contemporary concert works. Recording: soprano soloist in opera, Edward John Eyre. Contbr. to profl. publ. inclng. Aust. Jrnl. of Music Educ.; Sydney Morning Herald; Studies in Music; Musicology. Mbrships: Musicol. Soc. of Aust.; Aust. Soc. for Music Educ.; Int. Assn. of Music Libs.;p Aust. & NZ. Hon: winner of Robert Dalley-Scarlett Scholarship, 1969-70. Hobbies: Singing; Bushwalking. Address: Music Dept., Univ. of NSW, PO Box 1, Kensington, NSW 2033, Aust.

BROWN, Raymond, b. 20 June 1920. Hope Mills, NC, USA. Singer; Conductor; Teacher. Educ: Univ. NC; Juilliard Schl. of Music; Degrees: Peabody Conserv. & Johns Hopkins Univ. m. Nina Trew. Career: Perfs. in operas, oratories, recitals in Eastern USA; Tours as Choir Dir., Europe, Israel, USA; Prof. of Music & Dir. of Choral Music, Pa. State Univ. Mbrships: Alpha Phi Omega; Nat. Assn. of Tchrs. of Singing; Coll. Music Soc.; Am. Choral Dirs. Assn. Hons: Hon. Citizen, Delphi; Recip. of Alpha Phi Omega Disting. Serv. Award, 1975. Address: 214 Eisenhower Chapel, PA. State Univ., Univ. Pk., PA 16802, USA. 6.

BROWN, Rayner, b. 23 Feb. 1912. Des Moines, Iowa, USA. Organist; Composer. Educ: BMus., MMus., Univ. of S. Calif. m. Barbara Patrick, 1 s., 1 d. Career: Organist, Wilshire Presby. Ch., LA; Prof., Music, Biola Coll., Calif.; Emeritus Prof., ibid., 1977. Num. comps. incl: Trio for Flute, Clarinet & Viola; Symbols for 2 Clarinets; concerto for Organ & Band; Prelude & Fugue for Brass Choir; Variation for Piano, 4 Han, 1975; Concertino for Harp & Brass Quintet. Recordings of own comps. incl: Concerto for 2 Pianos, Brass & Percussion; Symph. for Clarinet Choir; Brass Quintet No. 2; Sonata for Flute & Organ; 5 Pieces, Organ, Harp, Brass Choir. Mbrships: Past Dean, LA Chapt., AGO; ASCAP. Hons: Annual Award, for Composition, ASCAP, 1965-. Address: 2423 Panorama Terrace, Los Angeles, CA 90039, USA.

BROWN, Richard S, b. 10 Sept. 1947. Phila., Pa., USA. Percussionist; Educator. Educ: BMusEd, Temple Univ.; MMus, Cath. Univ., Wash. DC. m. Carol Ann Schack, 1 s. Career: Mbr.; US Army Band, Wash. DC, 1969-72; played w. Chmbr. Symph. of Phila.; Prin. Percussionist, Grand Teton Music Fest. Orch., Jackson Hole, Wyo., summer; Percussionist, Houston Symph. Orch., Houston Grand Opera & Houston Ballet; Asst. Prof. of Percussion, Shepherd Schl. of Music, Rice Univ., Houston, Tex.; Fac., Univ. of St. Thomas. Recordings: w. Houston Symph., US Army Band & Chmbr. Symph. of Phila. Mbr., Percussive Arts Soc. Address: 4231 Tennyson, Houston, TX 77005, USA.

BROWN, Stephen Butler, b. 24 June 1945. Newton, Mass., USA. Educator; Pianist. Educ: Artist's Dip., Piano, Conservatorio di San Pietro & Maiella, Naples, Italy, 1966; BA, Tufts Univ., 1967; MMA, Yale Univ. Schl. of Music, 1970. m. Eleanor Howells Brown, 1s. Career: Solo & Ensemble Perf. in USA & Europe; Soloist, Boston Pops, 1967; Performed in num. festivals, progs. etc. inclng: Sarasota Music Festival, Fla.; Tanglewood, Lenox, Mass.; Am. Inst. of Musical Studies, Graz, Austria. Duo-pianist w. Eleanor Howells Brown. Mbrships: Coll. Music Soc.; Recip. num. Fellowships & Awards. Hobbies: Reading; Genealogy. Mgmt: Keene Artists Mgmt. Address: 120 Orchard Lane, Columbus, OH 43214, USA.

BROWN, Susan Barbara Comstra, b. 25 Oct. 1949. Rochester, NY, USA. Trumpet Player; Teacher (Trumpet, Music Education; Brass Methods). Educ: BMus, Eastman Schl. of Music, 1971. m. Guy Ralph Brown, 1s, 1 d. Career: Trumpet Player; Rochester Phil. Orch.; Rochester Chmbr. Orch.; Opera Under the Stars Orch. Recordings: Eastman Wind Ensemble, Sousa March Record (Mercury); Rochester Phil. Orch., Music of David Amram (RCA). Mbr. Pi Kappa Lambda. Hobbies: Interior Decorating & Remodeling. Address: 1116 E. Whitney Rd., Fairport, NY 14450, USA.

BROWN, Timothy Charles, b. 9 Dec. 1946. Newcastle-upon-Tyne, UK. School Director of Music; Counter-Tenor Singer; Conductor. Educ: Choral Scholar, MA, King's Coll., Cambridge; Cert. Ed., Westminster Coll., Oxford; Lay Clerk, New Coll. Oxford, 1968-69. Career: Hd. of Music, Hinchingbrooke Schl., Huntingdon & Mbr. of The Scholars, 1968-72; Dir. of Music, Oundle Schl., 1973-; Cond., Cambridge Phil. Soc., 1975-. Has recordedw. King's Coll. Choir & The Scholars. Hobbies: Walking; Painting; Rowing. Address: Gardener's Cottage, Bramston House, Oundle, Peterborough, UK.

BROWNE, Murray, b. 5 Sept. 1907. London, UK. Author; Composer; Pianist. Educ: Regent St. Polytech., London. widower, 1 d. Career: Musical Dir., Ralph Reader; Entertainer on piano, Windmill Theatre; has done TV work, 1947-, & radio work, 1948-; Author for Holton & Longacre, Newnes & Odhams Press; currently Feature Writer on music, art & lit., Kent Life (S. Eastern Mags. Ltd.); has composed material for other perfs. Compositions publd. incl. ballads & dance music, also has ballet in MS. Publs: Pianoforet Tutor for Beginners. Mbrships: PRS; Mechanical Copyright Soc.; Brit. Song Writers Guild; Savage Club; London Sketch Club; Pres., Canterbury Soc. of Art & Canterbury Guild of Guide-Lectrs.; Late Chmn., Canterbury Writers Club & Whitstable Art Soc. Hobbies: Painting; Lit. Address: 1 Westgate Grove, Canterbury, Kent, UK.

BROWNE, Sandra, b. 27 July 1947. Point Fortin, Trinidad, W. Indies. Singer Educ: BA, Vassar Coll., Poughicelpsie, Trinidad; 2

yrs. at Royal Conserv., Brussels; 2 yrs. at Royal Manchester Coll. of Music. m. Piers Hart. Debut: May, 1972. Career: Num. concerts, recitals & opera perfs. in UK & abroad; radio & TV broadcasts. Recordings: American Collection; Spanish Collection; w. Michael Isador as accomp. Hons: Kathleen Ferrier Memorial Scholarship, 1971; RMCM Gold Medal for Voice, 1972. Hobbies: Lighting bonfires; Letter writing; Squash; Knitting; Travel; Lying on Tropical beaches; Good company. Address: c/o Ingpen & Williams 14 Kensington Ct., London W8 5DN, UK.

BROWNING, Alan David Jeffrey, b. 24 Jan. 1955. Bristol, UK. Lecturer in Music; Extramural Tutor. Educ: Clifton Coll., Bristol; Trinity Coll., Cambridge (Open Exhibition), MA; Westminster Coll., Oxford; Univ. of Birmingham. Career: Rsch. Student, Univ. of Birmingham; Extramural Tutor, Univ. of Birmingham; Lectr., Univ. of Leicester; Dir., Fayrfax Singers, New Bristol Chmbr. Group. Mbr., Royal Musical Assn. Address: 6 Harley Place, Clifton, Bristol BS8 3JT, UK.

BROWNING, Francesca Alsing, b. 24 Dec. 1905. San Francisco, Calif., USA. Piansit; Violinist; Music Eduator; Supervisor. Educ: BA, Univ. of Calif.; Dip., Sherwood Music Schl., Chgo.; cert. in pedagogy, Effa Ellis Perfield Schl., NY; piano studies at Mills Coll., Oakland, Calif., Temple Univ. & Mozarteum, Salzburg. m. Edgar S Browning (dec.) Debut: San Francisco, 1918. Career incl: violin soloist, KPO radio, Dorian Trio, KROW radio; 1st violinist, Univ. of Cailf. Symph. Orch.; mbr., San Francisco Phil. Orch.; has played in San Francisco Symph.; Adjudicator; piano classes in num. elementary schools.; lectr.; pvte. music studio, San Francisco & Berkeley, Calif.; fac., Univ. of Calif. Extension div., fac., Music & Arts Inst., San Francisco. num. mbrships. incl: Pres., San Francisco branch, Music Tchrs. Assn. of Calif., 1945-46; Pres., Dist II, Calif. Assn. of Profl Music Tchrs. 1971-72; NGPT; MTNA. Hons: Alpha Mu Sinfonia, 1941; Am. Coll. of Musicians, NGPT, Nat. Honor Roll, 1974, '75, '76. Hobbies: Photography; Travel; Flowers; Gardening; Drama. Address: 1967 28th Ave., San Francisco, CA 94116, USA.

BROWNING, John, b. 23 May 1933. Denver, Colo., USA. Concert Pianist. Educ: Juilliard Schl. of Music, NYC. Debut: Denver, 1943. Career: Concert pianist w. NY Phil. & leading orchs. in USA, Europe, Mexico, USSR, etc.; recital tours throughout the world; Am. Govt. rep., World's Fair, Brussels, 1958; Gave World premiere of Samuel Barber's 1st Piano Concerto w. Boston Symph. Orch. (opening week of Lincoln Ctr., NYC). Recordings incl. num. classical & contemporary piano works, on Capitol, Columbia, Desto & RCA labels. Hons. incl: Steinway, Centennial Award, Nat. Fedn. of Music Clubs, 1954; Queen Elizabeth Int. Councours Award, Brussels, 1955. Hobbies: Films; Swimming. Mgmt: Herbert Barrett Mgmt., 1860 Broadway, NYC. Address: c/o Ingpen & Williams, 14 Kensington Ct., London, W8 5DN, UK.

BROWNRIDGE, Angela Mary, b. 24 Oct. 1944. Concert Pianist. Educ: BMus. Edinburgh Univ.; LRAM; ARCM. m. Arthur Johnson, 1 s. Debut: Wigmore Hall, London. Career: toured as Soloist w. Leicestershire Symph. Orch., Germany & Norway, aged 14; apps. w. orch. throughout UK; Solo Recital Broadcasts, BBC Radio 2 & 3, Recorded: Mandy the Actors Cat, w. Sandor Elés. Mbrships: ISM; Musicians Union. Hons. incl: Tovey Mem. Prize for perf., 1965. Hobbies: Riding; Swimming. Mgmt: Ruth Ticher Concert Mgmt. Address: 118 Audley Rd., Hendon, London NW4 3HG, UK.

BROZEN, Michael, b. 5 Aug. 1934. NYC, USA. Composer. Educ: Bard Coll.; Berkshire Music Ctr., Tanglewood; BS, MS, Juilliard Schl. Compositions: Canto, orch., Theodore Presser Co.; Dark Night, Gentle Night, soprano, tenor & orch., Theodore Presser Co.; Five Alleluias, chorus, Theodore Presser Co.; In Memorian, soprano & string orch., Theodore Presser Co. Recordings: In Memorian, Composers Recordings Inc. Contbr. to: reviews & articles, Musical Am. & High Fidelity mag. Mbrships: ASCAP; Am. Music Ctr.; Am. Fed. Musicians. Hon: Howard Hanson Commission, 1968; Annual ASCAP Award, 1968-72; Grant & Letters, 1969; Ingram Merril Fndn. Frant, 1969 & '&; Guggenheim Fellowship, 1971; Special Cit. of the Koussevitzky Int. Recording Award, 1971. Res. Grant, Wurlitzer Fndn., New Mexico, 1975. Address: 86 Horatio St., NY, NY 10014, USA.

BRUBECK, David Warren, b. Dec. 1920. Concord, Calif., USA. Musician. Educ: Pacific & Mills. Colls. m. Iola Whitlock, 5 s., 1 d. Career: formed trio, 1950; formed Dave Brubeck Quartet, 1951. Comps: about 250 songs; Points of Jazz (ballet); Elementals (orchl.); The Light in the Wilderness (oratorio); The Gates of Justice (cantata); Truth Is Fallen (cantata). Num. recordings. Hons. incl: PhD, Univ., of Pacific Fairfield Univ.; num. trade mag. awards. Hobbies: Nature study; Hiking; Gardening; Camping. 16.

BRUCE, F Neely, b. 21 Jan. 1944. Memphis, Tenn., USA. Assoc. Prof. of Music; Conductor; Pianist; Composer; Scholar of Early Am. Music. Educ: BMus, Univ. of Ala.; MMus, Univ. of Ill., DMusArts, ibid. m. Phyllis Ruth Bruce 1 s. 2 d. Career: Prof., Schl. of Music, Univ. of Ill., Urbana-Champaign, 1968-74; Prof. Choral Music, Wesleyan Univ., 1974-. Num. perfs. as pianist & harpsichordist; Mbr., Contemporary Chmbr. Players, Univ. of Ill.; Perfs. as accompanist; Fndr. & Dir., Am. Music Grp., Univ. of Ill., choral org. devoted to perf. of Am. music; Dir., Prod., many theatrical prodns. Var. compositions, recordings & publs. Contemporary reviews in profl. jnrls. Mbrships: Am. Musicol. Soc.; Am. Soc. of Comps. Authors & Publrs. Recip. num. grants & fellowships. Hobbies: Jogging; Swimming; Tennis. Address: RR 12, Box 304, Bender Rd., Bloomington, IN 47401, USA.

BRUCE, Margaret, b. 28 June 1943. Vancouver, Can. Pianist. Educ: ARCM (perf. & tchr.); studied w. Liza Fuchsova & Peter Gellhorn. m. Hon. H L T Lumley-Savile, 3 (triplet)s. Debut: Wigmore Hall, London, 1968. Career: perfs. in Can., Czech., UK; piano duettist & piano duo w. Peter Gellhorn; works by Sir Lennox Berkeley, Herbert Howells, Peter Gellhorn & Jean Couthard specially written for her. Recordings: Solo recital; duets; 2 piano recital. Hons: James Caird Scholarship for study in Vienna, 1966; prizewinner, RCM, 1962. Hobbies: Tai Chi Chuan; Reading. Mgmt: Gordon Dunkerley, 102 Newgate St., London EC1B 1JB. Address: 38 Carlyle Square, London SW3 6HA, UK.

BRUCE-PAYNE, David Malcolm, b. 8 Aug. 1945. Banbury, Oxon., UK. Organist. Educ: RCM; ARCM; BMus, London Univ.; FRCO (chm.). m. Susan Mary Baker, 1 d. 2 s. Career: 2nd Asst. Organist, Westminster Abbey Choir Schl., 1968-74; Organ Tutor & Course Instructor, RSCM; Organ Recital & Choral Conducting Tour of USA & Canada, 1972, 73, 75 & 77. Organist, Master of the Choristers, Birmingham Cathedral 1974-77; Dir. of Music, King Edwards Schl., Birmingham, 1974-76. Concert tour, W Indies, 1977. Contbr. to Musical Opinion. Hons. incl: W T Best Memorial Scholarship, Worshipful Co of Musicians; Sawyer Prize, RCO. Hobbies: Golf; Fishing. Mbrships: Life Mbr. RCM. Mgmt: Arts Image Ltd., Hartford, Conn., USA; Terry Slasberg Agency, London W12 8LW, UK. Address: 47 Rotten Rd., Edgbaston, Birmingham, B16 0SG, UK.

BRUDERHANS, Zdenek, b. 29 July 1934. Prague, Czechoslovakia. Lecturer in Music. Educ: Dip., Prague Conserv.; M Mus, Prague Acad. of Music. m. Eva Holubarova, 1 s., 1 d. Debut: Prague, 1957. Career: Concert flautist; fests. inc. Prague, Brno, Cannes, Avignon, Adelaide; Tours, recitals & radio recordings in 12 European countries & Austrilia. Recordings: Flute recital (Bach, Haydn, Hindemith, Messiaen); Martinu Flute Sonatas; Valentini: Flute Concerto; Flute Anthology. Contbr. to: Miscelania Musicologica. Mbrships: Australian Musicol. Soc., Czechoslovaklan Club of South Australia. Hons: Grand Prix, Int. Competition of Wind Instruments, Prague, 1959. Address: 2 McLaughlan Ave., Brighton 5048, South Australia. 29.

BRUEGGEN, Frans, b. 30 Oct. 1934. Amsterdam, Netherlands. Performer on Recorder & Transverse Flute; Conductor; Musicologist. Career incls: was Prof. of Recorder, Transverse Flute & Old Music, Royal Conserv., The Hague; Erasmus Prof., Harvard Univ., 1972-73; Regent's Prof., Univ. of Calif., Berkeley, 1974. Recordings: Telefunken; Phillips. Publs: var. eds. w. Schott (London), Zen-On (Tokyo) & Broekmans & Van Poppel (Amsterdam). Mgmt: Horowitz Mgmt., 24 Montagu Sq., London W1H 1RE,

BRÜGGEMANN, Kurt, b. 30 Mar. 1908. Berlin, Germany. Composer; Conductor. Educ: Studied Philos. Musicol., Hist. of Art, Univ. of Berlin; Studied Comp. w. Paul Graener, Prussian Acad. of Arts m. Waltraute Macke. Career: Lectr., State Acad. Music Educ. & Sacred Music, Berlin; Prof. of Music, Wilson Univ., NC, USA; Comp., Cond., Concerts Theatre, Radio, TV & Films, Comps: Num. works listed in Die Musik in Geschichte und Gegenwart, Vol. 15 - publd., Basle, Paris, London, NY. Recordings: Num., in Fidula-Verlad, Boppard, Rhein, Recip., 1st State Prize for Composition. Address: D-8221 Erlstätt bie Traunstein, Oberbayern, German Fed. Repub. 14.

BRUGGEMANN, W., b. 25 Feb. 1936. Hamburg, Germany. Composer. m., 4c. Career: Comp. for popular folksingers, German-speaking area. Over 1600 comps. incl: One day in my life (piano concerto); Romance (Brass Orch.); Down Town (Symphonic pop suite); Austrian folk mass. Recordings incl: Der frohe Wanderer; Frühling, Sommer Herbst und Winter; Heimweh nach meinen Bergen, bei euch is schön, Bergkameraden. Publs: Schoolbook for accordion. Hons: 2nd Prize, European Broadcasting Union, Geneva, for Capriccio Brillante, 1970. Address: 4020 Puchenau, Linz, Austria.

BRÜGGER, Roger Werner, b. 15 Apr. 1942. Wettingen, Switzerland. Pianist. Educ: Dip, Trng. Coll. for Tchrs.; Akademisches Hauptseminar of Hochschule für Musik und darstellende Kunst., Vienna; Pvte. studies in Zürich & Vienna. Debut: Zurich. Career: Performed in concerts in W Germany, France, Holland, Hungary, Italy, Austria, Rumania, Spain, Switz., Czech., USSR; Radio & TV in Switz., W Germany, France & Austria; Prof., Konservatorium Winterhur. Hons: Dip., Int. Competitions, Geneva & Vercelli. Hobbies: Lit.; Theatre; Films. Address: Sonnrainweg 14, CH 5430 Wettingen AG, Switz.

BRUGK, Hans Melchoir, b. 24 Nov. 1909. Munich, Germany. Composer. Educ: studies comp. & directing. Acad. of Musical Arts, Munich, 1935-38. m. Marianne Popp, 1 d. Career: Prof., var. grammar schls.; Lectr., Richard Strauss Conserv., Munich, 1963-75. Comps: songs; choral works; 3 masses; Deutsches Te Deum (oratorio); music for brass bnad; chmbr. music; chmbr. music for winds; orchl. works; organ music. Recordings: Die Hoschzeit zu Kana (cantata for soloist & mixed choir a capella). Mbrships: Union of Germany Comps: Mbr., GEMA; Verband Müncher Tonknstler in VDMK. Hons: Friedland Prize, 1963; Rosenheim Culture Prize, 1963. Hobbies: Wandering; Mtn.-climbing. Address: Blumenstr. 5, 8204 Brannenburg, German Fed. Repub. 14, 19, 28.

BRUHN, (Hans) Christian, b. 17 Oct 1934. Wentorf, Lauenburg, Germany. Composer; Arranger; Producer. Educ: stuied in Hamburg w. Prof. E. G. Klussmann. 2 s. Career: Musician in sev. bands. Comps incl: Midi-Midinette, 1960; Zwei kleine Italiener, 1962; Mitsou, 1963; Liebeskummer lohnt sich nicht, 1964; Marmorstein und Eisen bricht, 1965; Lord Leicester, aus Manchester, 1966; Monsieur Dupont, 1967; Wärst du doch in Düsseldorf geblieben, 1968; Hinter den Kulissen von Paris, 1969; Wunder gibt es immer wieder, 1970; Akropolis Adieu, 1971; Der Pariser Tango, 1971; Der Stern von Mykonos, 1973; Ein indiojunge aus Peru, 1974; Es war einmal ein Jäger, 1975 Der Zarund das Mädchen, 1976; Mille Columbes, 1977; Heidi, 1978. Altogether about 1000 songs recorded. song cycles; James Tierleben, Heinrich Heine, Wilhelm Busch; Suite-Cantate Der Rhein; Das Lied von der Elbe. Contbr. to Musiktelegram, München; James Kruss Almanach, Hamburg, 1976. Mbrships: Deutscher Komponisten Verband; Verband Deutscher Musik Bearbeiter; Isartal-Verein München. Recip. var. awards inclng. 3 rd Winner G. Prix Eurovision, 1970. Address: Irmgardstr. 11, D8 Munich 71, German Fed. Repub. 1. 3.

BRUM, Oscar da Silveira, b. 27 Jan. 1926. Lage do Muriae, Rio de Janeiro State, Brazil. Trombonist; Band Director. Educ: Studied comp. & cond., Conservatorio Brasileira de Musica; Studied trombone, Escola Nacional de Musica de Univeridade Federal, Rio de Janeiro. m. Cledia da Cunha Brum, 3 s., 1 d. Debut: Orquestra Sinfonica da Casa do Estudante do Brasil (amateur); Orquestra Sonfonica Brasileira; Band Dir., Musician Capt. of Mil. Police, Guanabara State. Compositions: Introduction, Divertissement & Fuge for Symphonic Orch. (monothematic & modern); 1 Lied; 1 Antique Suite for Piano; 1 Overture-Concertante for Symphonic Band. Mbrships: Int. Trombone Assn.; Order dos Musicos do Brasil. Hobbies: Watching football & news serv. int. or nat., TV or radio; Waling. Address: Rua Encanamento 215, Nova Iguacu, RJ, Brazil.

BRUNELLE, Philip Charles, b. 1 July 1943. Faribault, Minn., USA. Music Director & Principal Conductor, Minnesota Opera Company. Educ: BA, Univ. of Minn.; studied piano w. Theodore Bergman & Paul Freed, conducting w. George Schick & organ w. Arthur B. Jennings. m. Carolyn Jane Olsen, 2 s., 1 d. Career: Orch. Pianist, Minn. Orch. (formerly Mpls. Symph. Orch.), 1965-71; Music Dir., Plymouth Congl. Ch. & Plymouth Music Series, 1969-; Music Dir. & Prin. Cond., Minn. Opera Co., 1970-; Music Coord., Minn. State Arts Coun., 1972-. Compositions (publd.): arranged El Capitan by Sousa & The Mother of Us All by Virgil Thomson for chmbr. orch.; Cantique de Paques by Honegger for chorus & organ & Psalm 24 by Paul Pierne for chorus, brass & organ. Recorded Postcard From Morocco. Mbrships: Opera Am. (in name of Minn. Opera); Bd. Mpls. Chapt., AGO. Recip. of Martha Baird Rockefeller conducting schlrships., 1969 and British Fndn. Summer Fellowship, 1975. Hobbies: French Cooking; Tennis. Address: 4211 Glencrest Rd., Minneapolis, MN 55416, USA.

BRUNERYE, Mare, b. 24 Mar. 1935. Paris, France. Professor. Educ: Licenciέ és Lettres (hist.), Université de Paris; Licenciέ en Droit, ibid.; grad., musical educ. & choral song; dip. & higher degree, Schola Cantorum de Paris. Career: Prof., hist. of music & organology, Conserv. Nat. de Réegion de Metz; Prof. of Letters, Coll. Classique de Jongquiére, Que., Can.; Prof., musical educ. & choral song. Mbrships: Société française de musicologie; Société des Agrégés de l'Université; Soc. des Amis de l'oeuvre et de la pensée de G Migot. Hons: Première

BRUNO, Joanne (Joanna). Orange, NJ, USA. Opera & Concert Singer (Lyric Soprano). Educ: MS, Juilliard Schl. of Music; pvte. study of Voice w. var. tchrs., USA & Italy. Debut: Spoleto, Italy. Career: Apps. in leading roles at Paris Opera, Netherlands Opera, Spoleta Fest., Italy, Triesta, Scottish Opera, Chgo. Lyric Opera, NYC Opera, Hawaii Opera, Houston Grand Opera, Sant Fe Opera & Zagreb, Yugoslavia. Hons: Minna K. Ruud Award, 1968; Nat. Arts Club Award, NY, 1968; Liederkranz Fndn. Scholarship Concert, 1968; Eastern Regional Finalist, Met. Opera Auditions, 1969; Martha B. Rockefeller Fndn. Grant, 1970. Hobbies: Reading; Tennis; Swimming. Mgmt: Columbia Artists Mgmt Inc. (CAM), 165 W 57th St., NY, NY 10019, USA. 2.

BRUNSMA, Donna Louise, b. 3 June 1932. Beech, Grove, Ind., USA. Opera Rehearsal Assistant & Coach; Concert Accompanist; Organ Recitalist; Organist Choirmaster (Piano, Organ, Harpsichord). Educ: BMus, Eastman Schl. of Music; Juilliard Schl. of Music; Schl. of Sacred Music, Union Theol. Sam., NYC; Academie Internationale d'Ete, Nice. Debut: Recital Accomp. w. Jerome Hines, 1956. Career incls: Apps. as Accomp.-Coach & Organist-Choirmaster in NYC at Sarah Lawrence Coll.; Met. Opera Nat. Co., etc.; Radio & TV apps. in NYC; Radio Jerusalem; Radio Svizzera; RAI-TV, Italy. Currently, Musical Asst., Maggio Musicale Fiorentino & at Accademia Chigiana (Siena). Mbrships. incl: Mu Phi Epsilon. Recip. Study Grant in Italian Opera, Inst. of Int. Educ., 1967. Hobbies: Rsch. on Italian & Portuguese Histl. Organs; Tuscan Gastronomy. Address: Lungarno Guicciardini 5, Florence, Italy.

BRUSCANTINI, Sesto, b. 10 Dec. 1919. Civitanova Marche, Italy. Opera Singer. Educ: Dr. of Law, Marcerata Univ.; studied wingint w. Maestro Luigi Ricci, Rome. Debut: Geronimo, Il Matrimonio Segreto, La Scala, Milan, 1948/49. Career: began as a Bass, specializing in buffo roles; gradually changed to Baritone; alternating between buffo & serious baritone roles, 1960-; has sung in all major opera houses, Europe, UK, N & S Am.; roles incl. Pere Germont, Rigoletto, Falstaff, Iago, Posa & Renato (all Verdi) & Figaro (Rossini). Num. recordings inclng: Rossini, La Cenerentola (2 recordings); Mozart, Marriage of Figaro & Cosi fan Tutte; Verdi, La Traviata; Bizet, The Pearl Fishers. Hons. incl: Lyons Club award, 1970. Hobbies: Photography; Amateur film making. Address: Via dei Sansovino, 6, Rome, Italy. 14.

BRUUN, Mogens Erik Soelberg, b. 8 Oct. 1923. Copenhagen, Denmark. Viola; Violin. Educ: Danish Royal Acad. of Music. m. Kirsten Dolmer, 1 s. Debut: Copenhagen, 1955. Career: Mbr., Danish Royal Orch.; Viola, Copenhagen Str. Quartet, concerts all over Europe, USA, Can. Recordings: Quartets by Haydn, Mozart, Mendelssohn, Tchaikowsky, Carl Nielsen, Holmbe, Gade, Hornemann etc. Hons. incl: Jacob Gades Award, as mbr. of Copenhagen Str. Quartet. Address: Vester Sogade 68, 1601 Copenhagen V, Denmark.

BRUZDOWICZ-TITTEL, Joanna, b. 17 May 1943. Warsaw, Poland. Composer; Pianist; Cellist. Educ: MA, Higher Conserv. of Music, Warsaw; Study w. Olivier Messiaeh, Nadia Boulanger & Pierre Schaeffer. m. Horst-Jürgen Tittel. Career: Comp. since age 12; Comps. performed throughout Europe, Latin Am., USA, Can., Japan, Morocco, S. Afica, Turkey; 2 operas Belgian TV; Lectr. on contemporary, esp. electronic, music. Comps: La Colonie Penitentiare (opera), 1968; Lews Troyennes (opera), 1972; 7 symphs.; 20 chmbr. works; 11 pieces of electronic music; music for film & theatre prods. Mbr., var. music assns. Contbr. to profl. jrnls. Recip., 2nd Prize, Comps. Union of Poland Competition, 1967. Hobbies incl: Film; Travelling; Linguistics. Address: B-1982 Duisburg, Roelandsheide 22, Belgium.

BRYAN, John Howard, b. 24 Feb. 1952. Ilford, Essex, UK. Musician (viol, psaltery, renaissance wind instruments, portative organ & medieval percussion). Educ: BA, BPhil. Univ. of York, UK. m. Margaret McCaul. Career: w. Landini Consort, 1973. Career: mbr. of Landini Consort; apps. at fests. in York, Harrogate, Cheltenham, Aldebugh, Ludwingsburg, Zadr (Yugoslavia); radio braodcasts on BBC, WDR, NDR. Recordings: Nowell, Nowell - medieval & renaissance Christmas music; Songs & Dances of 14th Century Italy; The Play of Daniel. Contbr. to: Music in Education. Mbrships: York Early Music Fest., Dir. Hobbies: Travelling; Eating. Address: 86 Micklegate, York YO1 1JZ.

BRYAN-TURNER, Edward Lorimer, b. 20 Nov. 1925. Staten Island, NY, USA. Violinist; Music Teacher; Music Draftsman.

Educ: Pre-med. course, Tulane Univ.; Violin study w. Prof. Nicholai Zadri, Loyola Univ.; Violin & vocal study w. var. pvte. tutors. m. Catherine Elizabeth Thorn. Career: Amateur mbr., Symph. Orchs. & Chamber Ensembles, Wash. Area; Savannah Symph. Orch.; Tchr., piano & violin Savannah Home for Girls; Tchr., Solfege, Chatham Br., Ga. State Prison; Specialist music drafter, developing new clefs for transciptions for viola & piano, 1964-; Inventor of Automatic Music Stand, exhib. at Savannah Arts Festival, 1965. Publs: Transcriptions for unaccompanied viola of a wide range of classical music incl. Beethoven, Mozart, Schubert, Liszt, Tchaikowski; J S Bach & Handel, Prelude for unaccompaniedn viola. Mbrships: Amateur Chamber Music Players, Inc.; Viola Rsch. Soc. Dir., Am. Equity Assn. Hobbies: Removing rubbish from streets; Medical Writing. Address: 304 Bonaventure Rd., Thunderbolt, GA 31404, USA.

BRYANT, Carolyn, b. 26 July 1944. Musicologist. Educ: BA, Dickinson Coll., 1966; MA, NY Univ., 1973. Career incls: Freelance Ed./Proof rdr., Columbia Records, 1971-72; command. to prepare exhib. & catalogue on band music, Travelling Exhib. Serv., Smithsonian Instn., 1974-75; Ed., wind instrument articles, Grove's Dict., 6th ed. Publs: incl: And the Band Played On, A Survey of Bands in America, 1776-1976, 1975. Contbr. to: Musical Quarterly, Grove's Dict., 6th ed. Mbrships: Am. Musicol. & Recorder Socs. Address: 4405 Colfax St. Kensington, MD 20795, USA.

BRYANT, Celia Mae, b. 11 Aug. 1913. Porum, Okla., USA. Professor of Music. Educ: BMus, Univ. of Okla.; MusM, ibid.; Postgrad. study w. Frank Mannheimer. m. (div.) 3 d. Career: Perf. & Lectr., in 48 States.; USA; Prof. of Piano, Univ. of Okla., Norman, 1948-; Vis. Prof. of Piano, Univ. of Mich. Div. Interlochen Ctr. for Arts. Mich., summers, 1972-73. Contr. to: Clavier Mag., 1961-. Mbrships. incl: Pres., Music Tchrs. Nat. Assn., 2 terms, 1969-73; Nat. VP, ibid, 1965-69; Bd. of Dirs., Nat. Music Coun., 1971-73; Pres , 2 terms, Okla. Music Tchrs Assn., 1961-65; Chmn., MacDowell Allied Arts Club, 1965-. Hons: Nat. Citation, Phi Mu Alpha Sinfonia, 1972; Outstanding Musician in Okla. Award, Gov. of Okla., 1973; Selected 1 of 9 outstanding Music Educs. in nation, Mu Phi Epsilon, 1962. Hobbies: Reading Historical Novels; Sports. Address: 614 Okmulgee, Norman, OK 73069, USA. 2, 5, 7, 27, 29.

BRYANT, Raymond, b. 5 Mar. 1908. Lutterworth, Leics., England, UK. Player & Professor of the Horn; Coach; Conductor; Adjudicator. Educ: MA, Oxon; RCM. m. Florence Sargent, 1 s. Career: Mbr. of Scottish, Glyndebourne, LSO, BBC Symph. & Concert Orchs.; Prof. of Horn, GSM; Vis. Prof., RAM; Horn Tchr., Middx. Polytech., Trent Pk.; Brass & Chmbr. Music Coach & Cond. for Youth Orchs. & Summer Schls. Mbr. ISM. Contbr. of Sect. on Wagner Tubas to Groves Dictionary of Music & Musicians. Hobbies: Chess; Tennis. Address: 12 Warner Rd., London N8, UK.

BRYANT, Ruth Audrey, b. 13 Apr. 1918. Hanworth, Middlesex, UK. Principal Lecturer & Music Director. Educ: Tchrs. Trng. Course Cert., RAM. Career: Pupil Tchr., St. Michaels', Bognor Regis, 1937-38; Accomp., Margaret Morris Schl. of Dancing, Edinburgh, 1939, Tolmers Pk., Stanford Ct., Worcs., 1941-43; Northcliffe & Music Mistress, St. Michael's, Burton Pk., Petworth, 1947-51; Dir. of Music, Edgehill, Windsor, NS, Can., 1951-53; Lectr. in Music, Coll. of Sarum St. Michael, Salisbury, UK, 1954-63; Dir. of Music & Prin. Lectr., bid., 1964-78; 2 piano recitals w. Anne Ramey, Radio NS. Mbrships. incl: ISM; The Pipers Guild. Hobbies incl: Motoring. Address: 6 Wylye Ct., Pk. Lane, Salisbury, Wilts. SP1 3N5, UK. 4.

BRYCE, Owen, b. 8 Aug. 1920. Woolwich, UK. Musician; Trumpet; Band Leader; Lecturer; Journalist; Broadcaster. m. 1 s., 3 d. Career: Fndr. Mbr., George Webb's Dixielanders; Ldr., own band, 1956-; Company Dir., radio & TV. Num. recordings w. George Webb & w. Original Dixielanders, Publs: Let's Play Jazz, 1962; Lets Play Jazz, BK 2. 1978. Contbr. to all maj. musical, educl. jrnls. Hons: Dip., for judging int. song fests., 1962-64. Polish Govt. Hobbies: Boating. Address: 31x' c/o Windy Nob, Staleys Rd., Borough Green, Sevenoaks, Kent, UK.

BRYDEN, John Carrick McClure, b. 16 June 1947. Edinburgh, Scotland, UK. Pianist. Educ: Emmanuel Coll., Cambridge; BAMus; MAMus; Piano Studies w. Peter Katin; Guido Agosti, etc. Chigiana Acad. of Music, Siena; Master Classes w. Claudio Arran, Bonn; ARCM; ARCO. m. Margaret Greenlaw, 1 d. Debut: Purcell Room, London, 1971. Career: Solo Pianist, Chmbr. Musician, Accomp., num. recitals in UK & Salle Cortot, Paris & Chiziana Acad., BBC Broadcasts; Tchr. of Piano, Dartington Coll. of Arts, Devon, 1976-; ISM Outstanding Young Musicians Series, Wigmore Hall. Mbr. ISM. Recip. of Martin Musical Scholarship, 1969. Hobbies: Langs.; Walking; Reading. Mgmt: Pro Arte. Address: 45 Hunter's Moon, Dartington, Totnes, Devon, TQ9 6JT, UK.

BRYDEN, John Rennie, b. 22 Aug. 1913. Detroit, Michigan. Professor. Educ: BA, Transylvani Coll., 1937; MA, Harvard Univ., 1942; PhD, Univ. of Michigan, 1951. m. Helen Elaine Hume, 1 s., 1 d. Career: Asst. Prof., Univ. of Illinios, 1951-53; Asst. Prof. of Music, Wayne State Univ., 1953-58; Dir., Humanities Prog., ibid, 1956-58; Chmn., Dept. of Humanities, 1958-64; Acad. Dean, Transylvania Coll., 1964-71; VP for Acad. Affairs, ibid, 1965-71; Prof. of Humanities, ibid, 1964; provost, 1971-75; full-time tchr., 1975-78; ret'd. 1978. Publs: Index of Gregorian Chant, w. D. G. Hughes, 1969; String Duos, 1959. Contbr. to: Am. Music Tchr.; The Am. Organist. Mbrships: Am. Musicol. Soc., etc. Address: 760 Malabu Drive, Lexington, KY 40502, USA.

BRYDON, Roderick b. 1939. Edinburgh, UK. Conductor. Educ: St. Mary's Cath. Choir Schl.; Daniel Stewart's Coll., Edinburgh; BMus, Edinburgh Univ.; Chigiana Acad., Siena; Acad. for Music & Representative Arts, Vienna; ARCM. m. Pamela Batchelor, 1 s., 1 d. Career: Assoc. Cond. Scottish Nat. Orch.; Cons., Sadler's Wells Opera & Scottish Opera; Music Dir., Scottish Opera for All; Guest Cond. w. many orchs. inclng. Royal Opera, Copenhagen, Netherlands Opera, Nuremberg Phil. & Radio Eireann. Mbr. ISM. Recip. of sev. schlrships. Hobbies: Reading; Studying Other Arts. Address: London Road, Harston, Cambridgeshire, UK. 3.

BRYDSON, John Callis, b. 8 Aug. 1900. Kegworth, UK. Lecturer & Teacher of Music; Composer. Educ: BMus, Durham Univ.; LTCM. m. Lilian Ellen Bagguley, 1 s. Comps: var. educl. piano albums; unison & part song & anthems; Organ Sonatina; var. arrs for organ. Publs: Composition of Melody; Exercises in Harmony; Five Lesson Course in Two Part Writing; Study & Composition of the Two Part Writing; Study & Composition of the Two Part Invention; Teaching & Training of Aural Culture; Phrasing (w. exercise). Contbr. to: Musical Times; Music Tchr.; Choir Jrnl. Mbrships: Comp. Mbr., PRS; ISM; Royal Soc. of Tchrs. Address: 252 Leicester Rd., Loughborough, UK. 3.

BRYMER, Jack, b. 27 Jan. 1915. South Shields, UK. Musician (Clarinettist). Educ: DipEd, London Univ. m. Joan Richardson, 1 s. Career: Prof., RAM, 1950-59; Prof., Kneller Hall, 1967-71; Prin. Clarinet, Royal Phil., 1957-63, BBC Symph. Orch., 1963-71 & London Symph., 1971-; Fndr. Mbr., Wigmore Ensemble; Dir., London Wind Soloists; Mbr., Tuckwell Wind Quintet; Mbr., Robles Ensemble. Recordings: Mozart Concert (3 versions); Weber Conartino; Krommer Concerto; Debussy Rhapsody; Wagner Adagio; Brahms 5th Beethoven (Per. & Wind); Complete Wind Music of Mozart, Beethoven, Haydn, J C Bach, etc. Complete WInd Music to BBC scripts for talks. Hons. Hon. RAM, 1956; OBE, 1960; MA, Newcastle, 1973. Hobbies: Golf; Gardening; Swimming. Address: Underwood, Ballards Farm Rd., So. Croydon, Surrey CR2 JA, UK.

BRYN-JONES, Delme. Brynamman, Wales, UK. Baritone; Operatic Singer. Educ: GSM; Vienna Acad. m. Carloyn Dryn Jones, 1 d. Debut: Opera for All, Arts Coun. of GB. Career incls: debut at Glyndebourne, Covent Gdn.; Welsh Nat. Opera, 1963: Am. debut, San Francisco, 1967; regular apps. in major baritone roles, Covent Gdn., 1963-; guest apps. in Vienna, Germany, Am., Edinburgh, etc.; broadcasts incl. Brit. premiere of Henze's The Bassarids & HTV's 1-hr. documentary on life & career made in 1973. Recordings: Cambrian Recordings; Decca. Contbr. to: Artists in Wales, 1976. Mbr., Gorsedd of Bards, Royal Nat. Eisteddfod, Wales. Hobbies: Welsh Cobs; Rugby. Mgmt: Colbert Artists Mgmt., 111 W. 57th St., NYC, NY 10019; Greenan Artists Mgmt., 19b Belsize Pk., London NW3. Address: 57 Elm Ave., Eastcote, Ruislip, Middx. HA4 8PE, UK.

BUBAK, Bohdan, b. 10 Apr. 1946. Praha, Czechoslovakia. Compser. Educ: Dip. Comp., Acad. of Music, Prague, 1969. Debut: W. String Quartet, Prague, 1969. Career: Insp. of Culture; Tchr.; TV w. Folk Grp., Kramari; Soloist on TV. Comps: Suite for Orch. & String Quartet; Chmbr. Music; Folk Songs. Recordings of Folk Songs. Mbrships: Pragoconcert; Jazz Club, Praha. Hobby: Lyrics for Songs. Address: P O Box 19, 11121 Praha, Czechoslovakia.

BUBAK, Josef, b. 14 Feb. 1902. Mnichovo Hradiste, Czech. Composer; Trumpeter. Educ: Grad., Conserv. of Prague, 1932. m. Vladimira Risplerova, 1 s., 1 d. Career: Mbr., Czech. Broadcasting Serv., Prague. Comps: chmbr. music in quarter-tone, sixth-tone & 12-tone systems; wind quintet; songs; string-quartet in half-tone system. Mbr., Czech. Soc. of Comps. Publs: Czech. Patent for Quarter-tone Piston Trumpet. Address: Slezska 61, 130 000 Prague 3, Czechoslovakia.

BUCCI, Jane, b. 28 Dec. 1929. El Dorado Springs, Mo., USA. Soprano Singer. Educ: AB, Vassar Coll.; pvte. study, NYC. m. Earl M Bucci, 1 s., 2 d. Debut: Town Hall, NYC, 1967. Career: concerts apps., upstate NY & New Engl.; Soloist, recitals, chambr. music, choral & orchl. works; has appeared w. Albany, Schenectady & Utica symphs.; pub. broadcasting serv. radio & TV apps; Fndr. & Artistic Dir., Am. Comps. Forum, Schenectady (concert series w. living Am. comps. attending perfs. of their works). Has recorded tapes for broadcast concerts. Hobbies: Hiking; Bicycling; Reading. Address: 914 St., Davids Lane, Schenectady, NY 12309, USA.

BUCH, Hans Joachim, b. 11 Oct. 1935. Dusseldorf, Germany. Director of Higher Education. Educ: DrPhil, Musicology, Univ. Bonn, 1961. Publs: Die Tänze, Lieder & Konzertstüeke des Werner Fabricius, 1961; Bestandsaufnahme der Werke Clemens Thiemes in Die Musikforschung, 1963. Mbrships: Assn. for Musical Research, Kassel. Address: Nordstrasse, 92, D 4020, Mettmann, German Fed. Repub.

BUCHANAN, Dorothy Quita, b. 28 Sept. 1945. Christchurch, NZ. Composer; Violinist; Pianist. Educ: MusB(Hons), B(Hons), Canterbury Univ., Christchurch, 1975. m. (1) Scott, 1 d; (2) James Rginald Bradley. Career: TV app., Seven Artists in review, 1974; Regular apps. w. Christchurch Symph. Orch. & Canterbury Orch.; 1st person appointed NZ Comp.-in-Schs., NZ Govt., var. TV interviews, radio presentations, lectures. Comps. recorded: Three Jacques Prevert Settings; Four Duos for Violin & Cello; Song from Exxlesiastes; Mass & Motet in English. Music for educl. use (operas, chmbr. music, orchl. works, songs) forthcoming. Mbrships. incl: Comps. Assn. of NZ; Australasian Performing Rights Assn. Hons. incl: John Cowie Reid Mem. 2nd Prize, 1974; Queen Elizabeth II Arts Coun. Grant, 1974. Address: 9 Otara St., Fendalton, Christchurch, NZ.

BUCHER, Josef, b. 14 Aug. 1929. Willisau, Switz. Organist. Educ: Concert Dip., Conserv. Zürich; Kapellmeister Dip., Wiener Musikakademie. m. Jacqueline Bucher, 2s., 1d. Career: Organ concerts in most European countries & Can.; Cond. of var. choruses; var. recordings; Prof. & Hd. of Dept., Folkwang HS of Music, Essen, Germany; Organist & Chorus Master, Liebfrauenkirche, Zürich. Mbr., Schwiezer Tonkünstlerverein. Hobbies: Skiing; Swimming; Photography. Address: Vogelsangstr. 5, CH 8006, Zürich, Switz.

BUCHOME, Ferose (Home), b. 13 June 1922. Karachi, Pakistan. Concert Pianist. Educ: BA, Univ. of Bombay; LRSM; studied piano w. Cyril Smith, London, Alfred Cortot, Lausanne & Paris, Mme. Bascourret de Gueraldi, Paris. Debut: Bombay, 1945. Career: Recitals, Naples, Rome, Florence, 1950, Paris, 1951; Fndng. Mbr., Hon. Sec., Dir., of Music Fndn. of Pakistan; Fndr.-Dir., Karachi Acad. of Music. Comps. incl: Fantasia on Oriental Themes. Recip. var. hons. Hobbies: Reading; Writing; Theatre-going. Address: 5 Buch Terr., Preedy St., Karachi-3, Pakistan.

BUCHT, Gunnar, b. 5 Aug. 1927. Danderyd, Sweden. Composer. Educ: DrPhil, 1953. m. Bergljot Krohn Bucht. Career: Asst. Prof. Musicol., Univ. of Stockholm, 1965-70; Cultural Attache, Swedish Embassy, Bonn, 1970-73; Prof., Composition, Royal Coll., of Music, Stockholm, 1975-. Compositions: 7 Symphs; The Pretenders (opera), 1966; Eine lutherische Messe (for soloists, choir, children's choir & orch.), 1973; Winter Organ (for orch.), 1974; Journées oubliées (orch.) 1975; Au delá (orch.), 1977: chamber & electronic music. Contbr. to World of Music. Mbrships: Pres., Swedish Comps. Union, 1963-69; VP, Bd, Int. Soc. Contemporary Music, 1969-72; RAM, Stockholm. Recip., Hon. Award, City of Stockholm 1970. Address: Burge Hablingbo 620 11 Havdhem, (Gotland), Sweden. 19.

BUCHTEL, Forrest Lawrence, b. 9 1899. St. Edward, Neb., USA. Composer; Teacher. Educ: AB, Simpson Coll.; MS in Educ., N Western Univ.; BMus, Vander Cook Coll. of Music; MMus, ibid. m. Jessie Helene Macdonald, 1 s., 3 d. Career: Music Tchr., Grand Rapids, Mich., 1921-25; Emporia State, Kan., 1925-30; Lane Tch., Chgo., 1930-34; Amundsen HS, Chgo., 1934-54; Vander Cook Coll. ofMusic, 1931-. Compositions incl: Num. overtures, marches, etc. for bands; solo works for woodwind, brass & strings; arrangements of Band & instrumental works by leading Am. composers, etc. Mbrships: Am. Bandmasters Assn.; Sinfonia - Phi Mu Alpha; Phi Beta Mu; Kappa Kappa Psi; Delta Upsilon. Hons: Disting. Alumnus Award, Simpson Coll., 1966: Vander Cook Coll. 1971. Hobby: Bowling. Address: 1116 Cleveland St., Evanston, IL 60202, USA.

BUCIL, Milan Bohumil, b. 4 Apr. 1936. Prague, Czech. Trombonist; Pianist; Composer; Conductor; Educator. Educ: BA, Prague; Grad., Prague Conserv. of Music; BMus, BEd, Toronto. Career: TV & film; Comedy, Prague, 1965: A Man

Next to You, Berlin, 1966; num. stage & radio apps., Europe & N Am.; assoc. w. Classical Stage Prods., Toronto, & Int. & Multicultural Theatre, Fests. in Ont. Comps: scenic music; stage music; chmbr. music; songs; Jazz suite; num. arrs. Contbr. to var. newspapers. Mbrships. incl: Am. Musicol. Soc.; Comps., Authors & Publrs. Assn. of Can. Ltd.; Toronto Musicians Assn. Hobbies: Fine Arts; Literature; Outdoor Living; Travel. Address: 344 Military Trail, W Hill, Ont., Canada M1E 4E6.

BUCK, David L, b. 7 Apr. 1937. Jamestown, NY, USA. Instrumental Music Teacher; Band Director. Educ: BS, State Univ. Coll., Fredonia, NY; State Univ. Coll., Oneonta, NY; Paterson Coll., Wayne, NJ; MS, 1978; State Univ. Coll., Oneonta, NY. m. Mary Selleck, 2 d., 1 s. Debut: Jamestown Municipal Band. Career: incls: Trumpeter, Buffalo Phil. Orch., NY, 1959; 1st Trumpet, Fredonia Coll. Symphonic Band, 1955-59, Fredonia Coll. Symph. Orch., 1958-59; Trumpet, US Mil. Acad. Band, W Point, NY 1959-62; Instrumental & Choral Music Dir., Milford Ctrl. Schl., NY, 1962-64; Instrumental Music Tchr. & Band Dir., N Rockland Ctrl. Schl. Dist. Stony Point, NY, 1964-Trumpeter & Section Ldr., 119th Army Reserve Band, NY Army Nat. Guard, Peekskill, NY. Mbrships. incl: MENC; NY State Schl. Music Assn. Hobbies incl: Photography. Address: 1 Utopiano Ave., Suffern, NY 10901, USA.

BUCK, Ole, b. 1 Feb. 1945. Fredriksberg, Copenhagen, Denmark. Composer. Educ: Jydske Musik Konservatorium, 1965-69. m. Anne Behrndt, 1 s., 1 d. Debut: Tivoli, Copenhagen, 1965. Comps: Kalligrafi; Fioriture; Signes; Masques; Felix Is Icomen In. Mbr., Danish Composers Soc. Address: Skydebanegade 12 111 tv, 1709 Copenhagen, Denmark.

BUCK, Wayne Richard, b. 11 June 1948. Violinicellist; Professor of Music History; Musicologist. Educ: BM, MM, PhD Cand., Northwestern Univ. m. Carole D Bemler, Career: num. recitals, Chgo. & Fargo, ND; Prin. Cellist, Fargo-Moorhead Symph., Orch.; Prof., Concordia Coll., Moorhead, Minn., 1975-. Mbrships: Am. Musicol. Soc.; Phi Kappa Lambda. Hobbies: Cabinetmaking; musicol instrumental repair; Ecological endeavors. Addess: 1546 11th St. N, Fargo, ND 58102, USA.

BUCKLEY, Emerson, b. 14 Apr. 1916. NYC, USA. Music Director; Conductor; Artistic Director. Educ: AB, Columbia Coll., Columbia Univ., 1936; LHD, Univ. of Denver, Colo., 1959. m. Mary Henderson Buckley, 2 s. Career: Music Dir./Cond. of: Ft. Lauderdale Symph. Orch., 1963-; Gtr. Miami Opera Assch., 1950; Balt. Opera, 1972-75; Seattle Opera Assns., 1964-74; Naumburg Concerts, 1963-73; Cinn. Summer Opera, 1971; NY City Opera Co., 1955-67; Ctrl. City Opera Fes., 1956-69, etc.; Has cond. concerts & opera in every maj. city in N Am.; Cond. world premier of 'The Ballad of Baby Doe', 1956; Apptd. first Musical Dir. of the Empire State Music Fest. cond. Toscanini's Symph. of the Air, 1955; Music Admnstr., Chgo. Opera, 1956; Musical Dir. for 9 yrs. of radio, TV stn WOR, & the Mutual Broadcasting System in NY; Fac. Mbr. &/or Lectr., Columbia Univ., Univ. of Chgo., Univ. of Denver, Univ. of Miami; Music Dir. of the Opera Theatre of the Manhattan Schl. of Music, 1958-70; Cond., San Francisco Opera, 1975; Cond., Houston, 1976. Recordings incl: (operas) The Ballad of Baby Doe, & The Crucible. Hons. incl: Alice M Ditson Conds Award, Columbia Univ.; Chevalier de l'ordre des Arts et des Lettres, French Govt., 1970; Am. Patriot Award, State of Fla., 1971. Mgmt: Herbert Barrett Mgmt: NYC. Address: Greater Miami Opera Association, 1200 Coral Way, Miami, FL 33145, USA. 2, 7.

BUCKLEY, Geoffrey, b. 3 Apr. 1930. St. Annes-on-Sea, UK. Concert Pianist. Educ: Royal Manchester Coll. of Music. m. Patricia Artingstoll, 2 s. Career: Hd. of Piano Dept., Welsh Coll. of Music & Drama; Cardiff; Free-lance Soloist & Chmbr. Music Player. Has recorded on Open Univ. Mbr., ISM. Recip. Dayas Gold Medal, 1949. Hobbies: Cooking; Chess. Address: Beech Ct., Lakeside, Cardiff, UK.

BUCKLEY, Mary Henderson, b. 17 Dec. 1912. Longueuil, PQ, Canada. Violinist; Professor of Voice. Educ: LMus, McGill Univ., Montreal, PQ, Canada; Pvte. study w. C Waldeman Alves, Paul Althouse, Renato Bellini & Antoinetta Stable. m. Emerson Buckley, 2 s. Debut: Metropolitan Opera, 1946. Career: Many radio perfs., NBC & WOR TV; Concerts, USA & Canada; Perfs. w. Boston, Toronto, NY Philharmonic Orchs. & Little Orch. Soc.; Prof. of Voice, Univ. of Miami, Fla. Recordings: Allegro; Mbrships: AGMA; MENC; VP, Miami Chapt., NATS. Hobbies: Swimming; Cooking; Needlepoint. Address: 19640 NE 20 Ave., N Miami Beach, FL 33162, USA.

BUDASHKIN, Nikolia Pavlovich, b. 6 Aug 1910. Russia. Composer. Educ: Moscow Conserv. Compositions incl: 1st Symph., 1937; Sonatina for Piano, 1937; Holiday Overture, 1937; Russian Rhapsody, At the Fair; Russian Fantasia; Second Rhapsody; Thought. Hons: Hon. Art Worker of RSFSR; Order of Red Star, 1943; State Prizes for Composition, 1947, 1949. Address: Union of Composers, 8-10 Nezhdanova St, Moscow, USSR.

BUDDEN, Julian Medforth, b. 9 Apr. 1924. Hoylake, Cheshire, UK. Musicologist; Music Organizer. Educ: BMus, London; MA, Queen's Coll. Oxford; RCM; TCM. Career: Music Lib. Clerk, 1951, Asst. Music Info., 1955, Music Prof., 1956, Chief Prod., Opera, 1971, External Servs. Music Organiser, 1976, BBC. Publs: The Operas of Verdi, Vol. 1 (from Oberto to Rigoletto), 1973, vol. II, 1978. Contbr. to: musical & lit. jrnls. Address: 94 Station Rd., London N3 2SG, UK.

BUDDEN, Roy Thomas, b. 1913. Bridport. Conductor. Educ: LGSM. Career: Fndr. & Cond., Capriol Orch. of London, 1949-, & Hendon Str. Orch., 1943-; Dir. of Music, Working Men's Coll., London, 1949-; Cond., Lloyds Choir, 1950-54; Morley Coll. Students' Orch., 1945-49, Divertimento Wind Players, 1952-54. WelwynMusic Soc., 1952-, Berla Players Opera Soc., 1954-61, Marylebone Opera Soc., 1955-. Colchester Operatic Str. Players, 1965-, & Ipswich Operatic Soc., 1967-; Dir. of Music, Univ. Coll., London, 1960-64; Chmn. & Cond. Youth Music Ctr., 1967-; has app. on BBC TV & Radio & at Aldeburgh Fest.; frequent Guest Cond.; has conducted many premiers of works; has written articles, record sleeve notes & analytical notes on musical topics. Mbr: ISM (Perf.). Address: 33 Holly Park Gdns., London N3 3NG, UK. 3.

BUEHRER, Urs, b. 13 Dec. 1942. Neuhausen am Rheinfall, Switz. Composer; Organist; Pianist; Professor of Music. Educ: Dip. Piano, Dip. Harmony & Counterpoint, Zürich Conserv.; Dip, Organ, Acad. of Music, Basel. m. Delphine Buehrer Champion, 2 c. Career: Piano & organ concerts & radio apps., many w. own comps.; Prof. of Harmony, Solfége & Piano. Comps. incl: 14 Orgelschoräle; Quartet for flute & strings (recorded); Suite for harpsichord (recorded). Mbrships: Assn. of Swiss Musicians; Swiss Assn. of Music Profs. Hons: Int. prize for organ comps. Gambarogno-Lago Maggiore, 1964; Prize. Stroud Fest., 1976 (piano comp.). Hobbies: Travel; Wandering. Address: Nonnenmattstr. 16, CH-4107 Ettingen, (bei Basel), Switz.

BUFF, Iva Moore, b. 28 Aug. 1932. Musicologist; Performer on Keyboards. Educ: BMus, PhD, Eastman Schl. of Music, BA, Univ. of Rochester; MA, Smith Coll. m. Frank P Buff. Debut: Tarrytown, NY, 1949. Career: Tchr., Brearley Schl., NYC; Postdoctl. Fellow & Rsch. Assoc. in Musicol., Eastman Schl. of Music; Piano Tchr.; Performer on piano, harpsichord & clavichord: var. chmbr. recitals. Publs; The Chamber Duets & Trios of Carrissmi, 1973. Contbr. to music broadcasts. Mbrships. incl: Am. Musicol. Soc.; Coll. Music Soc.; AAUW. Hobbies: Photography; Travel. Address: 90 Roby Dr., Rochester, NY 14618, USA.

BUGHICI, Dumitru, b. 14 Nov. 1921. Iasi, Rumania. Professor; Composer. Educ: George Enescu Conserv., Iasi, 1935-38; H A Rimski Korsakov Conserv., Leningrad, USSR, 1950-55. m. Rodica Bughici, 1 s., 1 d. Debut: Suite for violin & piano, 1953. Career: Comps. & Prof. of Musical Forms, Ciprian Porumbescu Conserv., Bucharest, 1955-; Participant in radio & TV broadcasts on music. Compositions incl: Concert for trumpet & orch. (jazz rhythm), 1975; Concertino for piano & orch., 1975; Symph. 1970; 1975-76; Concerto for violin & orch. no. 2, 1977; Quartet no. 1977; Jazz divertisment for quartet, 1978. Num. recordings inclng: The Monument (symphonic poem). Publs. incl: Dictionary of Musical Forms & Genera, 2 nd. ed., 1978. Contbr. to profl. mags. Mbr. Comps. Union of Rumania. Hons. incl: The Prize of Rumania Acad., 1967. Hobby: Football. Address: Str Jules Michelet Nò. 15, Bucharest 7000, Romania.

BUJARSKI, Zbigniew, b. 21 Aug. 1933. Muszyna, Poland. Composer. Educ: Dips. in comp. & teaching, Higher Schl. of Music. m. Agnieszka Kamińska, 2 d. Debut: Synchrony 1, 1958. Career: Stage music; 6 pieces of film music; Music for TV Theatre. Comps. incl: Strefy; (recordings) Krzewy Plonace; Kinoth; Kom Pozycja Kameralna (chmbr. music); Contraria; Studium; El Hombre. Mbrships: Union of Polish Comps.; Zaiks, Union of Authors & Comps. of Stage Music. Hons: 3rd Prize, Competition for Young Comps. Warsaw, 1961; 2nd Prize, G Fitelberg Competition, 1963; 4th Prize, Int. Tribune of Comps., Paris, 1967. Hobbies: Art; Hist.; Ethnography; Skiing. Address: 31-456 Kraków, Ul. Ugorek 8 m 49, Poland.

BUKETOFF, Igor, b. 1915. Hartford, Conn., USA. Symphony Conductor. Educ: BA, & MS, Juilliard Schl. of Music, NYC. m. Maragret Elizabeth Smith, 1 d. Career: on Fac., Juilliard Schl. of Music, 1935-45, Chaugauqua Schl. of Music, summers 1941-47, & Columbia Univ., 1943-47; Cond., Broadway Co. on tours, Am & Europe, 1947-48, Fort Wayne Phil. Orch., 1948-66, & Young People's Concerts, NY Phil., 1948-53; Guest Cond. w. var. orch. Europe, S. Am. & USA; Music Dir., Iceland State Symph., 1964-65; w. Contemp. Composers Project, Inst. of Int. Educ., 1967-70; Fndr. & Chmn., World Music Bank, 1957-; Artistic Dir., St. Paul Opera Assn., 1968-. Recordings: w. Olso Phil. & Iceland State Symph. for RCA. Mbr.: (VP) Bax Soc. Hons: MusD; Alice M Ditson Award for Am. Conds.; Alice M Ditson Grant, 1957; Alice M Ditson Annual Award, 1967. Address: 500 East 85 St., NYC, NY 10028, USA. 3.

BUKOJEMSKA, Ewa Maria, b. 18 Sept. 1949. Krakow, Poland. Musician; Pianist. Educ: Dip. Secondary Schl. of Music, Cracow, 1968; MMus, High Schl. of Music, Cracow; Ajunct of Piano, ibid., 1974. Debut: Public Concert, 1955, at age of 6 yrs. Career incls: Film for TV; Num. progs. for TV & radio in Poland; About 400 recitals & concerts w. orch. in Poland, Czechoslovakia, USSR & France, 1975-76. Num. recordings. Contbr. to: Polish Ed. of Music. Mbrships: Soc. of Polish Music Artists; Soc. of Polish Masters. Hons. incl: Lili Boulanger Prize, Paris, 1975. Hobbies: Lit.; Cinema; Theatre; Fine Arts; Spanish & French Langs.; Visiting Monuments. Mgmt: Plish Agcy. of Artists, Pagart, Warszawa, P1 Zwyciestwa 9, Poland. Address: ul. Jozefa 44/4, 31056, Krakow, Poland.

BULATOFF, Paul, b. 26 Dec. 1948. Hong Kong. Violinist; Composer; Paganini Specialist. Educ: Conserv., Utrecht. m. Susan Baxter. Owner of Paganini Documentation - all publ. works by Paganini, facsimiles of autograph music manuscripts, manuscript copies, letters, etc., gramophone & tape recordings, etc. Ed. of works by Paganini, adds accompaniments to incomplete works. Publs. by Zimmermann, Curci, Zaniban. Mbrships: Istituto di Studi Paganniniani. Hobbies: Beetles. Address: Hora Siccamasingel 286, 9721 HX Groningen, The Netherlands.

BULL, Storm, b. 13 Oct. 1913. Chgo., Ill., USA. Professor. Educ: Sorbonne, Paris; Univ. of Budapest, Hungary; Am. Conserv. Music, Chgo.; Chgo. Musical Coll.; Ecole Normale de Musique, Paris; Liszt Acad. Music, Budapest. m. Ellen Elizabeth Cross, 2 s., 1 d. Debut: Soloist w. Oslo Phil., Norway, 1929. Career: 1st western hemisphere perf. of Bartok 2nd Piano Concerto, Chgo. Symph. Orch., 1939; Grieg centennial soloist, NY Phil., 1943; Concert Pianist, 1935-42; USNR, 1942-45; Asst Prof. of Piano, Baylor Univ., Waco, Tex., 1945-47; Prof. of Music, Hd., Div. of Piano, Coll. of Music, Univ. of Colo., Boulder, 1947-. Publs: Contemporary Composers, Vol. I, 1964, Voll. II, 1974; Musikkens Verden, 1951, '63. Contbr. to var. profl. jrnls. Mbrships. incl: Music Tchrs. Nat. Assn.; Music Educators Nat. Conf.: Pres. Colo. Music Tchrs. Assn. 1950-52; Hon. Mbr., Am. Coll. Musicians, Boulder Area Music Tchrs. Assn. Hons. incl: Silver Beaver, Boy Scouts of Am., 1968; Dioting. Achievement Award, Scandinavian Am. Fndn., Denver Salina Star Rte., Sunshine Canyon, Boulder, CO 80302, USA. 2, 4, 7, 9, 11.

BULLARD, Alan, b. 4 Aug. 1947. London, UK. Composer; Lecturer. Educ: RCM; Nottingham Univ.; ARCM (piano tchng.); BMus, London; MA, Nottingham. Career: Lectr., London Coll. of Music, 1970-75, Winchester Schl. of Art, 1973-75, Schl. of Music, Colchester Inst., 1975-. Comps. publd. by Novello, OUP, Banks, Schott; Unpublished works available from composer. Mbrships. incl: Comps. Guild of GB; PRS; Nat. Assn. of Tchrs. in Further & Higher Educ.; ISM; Nat. Coun. for Civil Liberties. Recip. 2nd Prize, Wangford Fest. Comps. Competition, 1974; 1st prize, ibid, 1978. Hobbies: The countryside. Address: Swiss Cottage, 4 Ponders Rd., Fordham nr. Colchester, Essex CO6 3LX, UK.

BULLOCK, (Sir) Ernest, b. 15 Sept. 1890. Wigan, Lancs., UK. Organist; Music Educator. Educ: Music study w. Sir Edward Bairstow. m. Margery Newborn, 1919, 2 s., 1 d. Career: Asst. Organist, Leeds Parish Ch.; Organist, Micklefield Ch. & Adel Ch.; Sub-Organist, Manchester Cathedral, 1912; Mil. Serv., WWI, 1915-19; Organist, St. Michael's Coll., Tenbury, 1919; Organist, Exeter Cathedral, 1919-27; Organist & Master of the Choristers, Westminster Abbey, 1928-41; i/c of music & Cond., Coronation of King George VI, 1937; Gardiner Prof. of Music, Univ. of Glasgow & Prin. Royal Scottish Acad. of Music & Drama, 1941-52; Dir., RCM, 1953-60. Compositions incl: Vocal & choral works; Part songs; Organ & Ch. Music. Mbrships: Past Pres.; Inc. Soc. of Musicians; Past Pres., RCO. Address: Welby Cottage, Long Crendon, Aylesbury, Bucks., UK.

BULLOCK, William Joseph, b. 25 Dec. 1943. Crawfordsville, Ind., USA. Educator; Choral Director. Educ: BMusEd, Fla. State

Univ., 1966; MA, ibid, 1968; PhD, ibid, 1971. m. Jane Lee Wilson, 1 s., 1d. Career: Prof. of Music & Coordinator of Vocal & Choral Music, Tarrant Co. Jr. Coll., Forth Worth, Tex., Northeast Campus; Choral Dir. Contbr. to: Jrnl. of Rsch. in Music Educ., 1973; Southwestern Musician/Tex. Music Educator, 1971; Assoc. Prof. of Music & Dir. Choral Activities, Univ. S Miss.; Dir., Six Flags Over Texas & Six Flags over Mid-Am. Choral Fests. Mbrships. incl: Am. Choral Dirs. Asscn: Am. Choral Fndn.; Phi Mu Alpha Sinfonia; Pi Kappa Lambda; Music Educators Nat. Conf. (Rsch. Mbrships.); Phi Kappa Phi; Phi Delta Kappa; Kappa Delta Pi; Tex. Jr. Coll. Tchrs. Asscn.; Phi Eta Sigma (Jrnl. of Aesthetic Educ.). Hons: Arion Award; Prospective Tchr. Fellowship, US Higher Educ. Act of 1965; FAc. Senator, Fac. Senate Chmn., Fac. VP, Tarrant Co. Jr. Coll.; 2nd VP, Tex. Jr. Coll. Tchrs. Assn. Hobbies: Tennis; Record Collecting. Address: 3011 Magnolia Pl., Hattiesburg, MS 39 401, USA. 7, 28.

BULLOUGH, John Frank, b. 15 Oct. 1928. Wash. DC, USA. Music Historian; Conductor; Organist. Educ: AB, Geo. Wash. Univ., Wash. DC, 1954; Choirmaster Choir, AGO, 1956; M. Sacrid Music, Schl. of Sacred Music, Union Theol. Sem., NYC, 1958. m. Dorothy Baines, 1 s., 2 d. Career: Asst. Prof. Music & Speech, Hartford Sem. Fndn., Conn., 1958-64; Dir. of Music, 1st Ch. of Christ (Ctr. Ch.) Hartford, Conn., 1960-64; Asst. Prof.-Prof. Music, Fairleigh Dickinson Univ., Teaneck, NJ, 1964-; Organist & Choirmaster, St. Paul's Episc. Ch., Englewood, NJ, 1973-; Exec. VP, Bd. Trustees, Bergen Phil Orch., 1973-; num. apps., Radio & TV, as Cond. & Speaker on musical subjects. Contbr. to: New York Times; Muslim World; The Hymn; Bergen Phil. Orch. Prog. Booklet. Mbrships: Coll. Music Soc.; Hymn Soc. of Am.; AAUP; AGO (Dean, Hartford, Conn. Chapt., 1963-64). Hobby: Sailing. Address: 488 Fairidge Terrace, Teaneck, NJ 0766, USA.

BUMBRY, Grace, b. 4 Jan. 1937. St. Louis, Mo., USA. Opera Singer. Educ: Boston, Chgo. & Northwestern Univs. Debut: Amneris, Aide, Paris Opera, 1960. Career: Basle Opera, 1960-63; Carmen, Paris Opera & Japanese tour; Royal Opera, Brussels; Die Schwarze Venus, Tanhäuster, Bayreuth Fest., 1962; Vienna State Opera, 1963; Covent Gdn., 1963, 68 & 69; Salzburg Fest., 1964; Met. Opera, 1965: La Scala, 1966. Has recorded. Hons: Richard Wagner Medal, 1963; DH, Univ. of St. Louis. Hobbies: Interior decoration, Clothing design. 16.

BUMBULIS-MELLINS, Valija, b. 15 Sept. 1937. Riga, Latvia. Singer; Assistant Professor. Educ: BMus, Chgo. Conserv. Coll., Ill., USA, 1962; MMus, ibid., 1964; Royal Conserv. Music, Toronto, Can., 1956-58. m. Bumbulis, 1 d. Debut: Carnegie Recital Hall, 1967. Career: Recitals, Carnegie Recital Hall, 1971, 74 & 78. Soloist w. Chgo. Symph. Orch., Battle Creek Symph., EMU Civ. Symph. Orch., Capital Univ. Orch., & Kalamazoo Symph. Orch.; Recitalist Toronto, Detroit, Cleveland, Chgo. etc.; Broadcast, Radio Free Europe. Recording: Arnold Sturm's songs (Coronet), 1976. Mbr. profl. orgs. Hons. incl: Gleemen Award, 1962. Hobbies incl: Tennis; Swimming; Art. Address: 6700 Cabot Dr. L-14, Nashville, TN 37209, USA.

BUNA, Roy Peter, b. 29 June 1951. Toronto, Ont., Can. Music Teacher; Night Club Performer. Educ: studied w. Eli Kassner. m. Carol Ann Bowman. Career: perfs. all over Can.; apps. on TV Benefit Telethons. Recordings: TV & radio commercials; sidesman on var. records. Hobbies: Films; Plants; Karate. Address: 23 Yarrow Rd., Toronto, Ont. M6M 4E2, Can.

BUNCH, Meribeth A., b. 20 Apr. 1938. Aulander, NC, USA. Professor of Voice; Consultant in Voice. Educ: BMus, Salem Coll., Winston-Salem, NC, 1960; MSM, Union Theological Sem., NYC, 1962; PhD, USC, 1974. Pvte. vocal study w. Joan Jacobowsky, William Vennard, Esther Andreas; Pvte. vocal coaching w. Shibley Boyes, Gwendolyn Koldofsy, James Low, Martin Katz. Career: Recitals in NC, NY, Pa., LA; Instr. in Music, Wilson Coll., Chambersburg, Pa., 1963-66; Instr. in Anatomy, Dental Schl., Univ. of Southern Calif., LA, 1967-72; Instr. in Voice, Music Schl., ibid, 1969-74; Instr. in Anatomy for interns & Residents, Huntington Mem. Hosp., Pasadena, Calif., 1970-74; Asst. Prof. of Music, Univ. of Del., Newark, 1974-; Var. lects. inclng. Guest, Sanford Professorship, Yale Univ., 1974. Book reviews ed., Nat. Assn. of Tchrs. of Singing; AAAS; AAUP; Ed. Bd. NATS Bulletin. Hobby: Tournament tennis. Address: Dept. of Music, Univ. of Del., Newark, DE 19711, USA.

BUNGER, Richard Joseph, b. 1 June 1942. Allentown, Pa., USA. Pianist; Theorist; Composer. Educ: BMus, Oberlin Coll. Conserv., 1964; MMus, Univ. of Ill., 1966. m. Melinda Jean Lowrey Bunger, 1 s. Career: Leading specialist in 20th century music; Perf., recorder & lectr. on this repertoire throughout USA, in UK & on Continent. Comps: Chmbr. music; Songs;

Choral works; Piano works. Recordings: The Perilous Night & Other New Sounds in American Music Reflections; Akwan (concerto by Olly Wilson, recorded w. Balt. Symph.); Early Keyboard Music by John Cage. Publs: The Well-Prepared Piano, 1976. Vols. 1-10, Japanese Ed., 1978. Contbr. to: profl. publs. Mbrships: Nat. Coun., Am. Soc. of Univ. Composers; Bd. of Dirs., Nat. Assn. of Am. Comps. & Cond. Int. Soc. for Contemporary Music; Pi Kappa Lambda; Am. Fedn. of Musicians. Hons: Grant, MB Rockefeller Fund for Music, Inc.; Fellowship, Bennington Composers' Conf. Mgmt: Anni Peters Agcy. Address: 5286 Townsend Ave., LA, CA 90041, USA.

BUNKE, Jerome Samuel, b. 8 Sept. 1945. Albany, NY, USA. Clarinetist; Professor; Record Producer. Educ: BMus, MS, Juilliard Schl.; PhD, NY Univ. m. Jane Bassewitz. Debut: NY Town Hall. Career: TV & Radio Appearances, NY, Kan. City & Tokyo; Concert Clarinetist, Carnegie Recital Hall, Japan Phil Symph. Orch.; NHK Yomiuri Nippon Symph. Orch., Tokyo, Kyoto, London Woodwind Workshop, Chautauqua Festival, Wash., Toronot, Harvard Univ. Recordings incl: Robert Keys Clark; Concerto for Clarinet; Brahms; Clarinet Sonata No. 1, Clarinet Sonata No. 2; Schumann; Fantasiestucke & Romances; Weber; Grand Duo Concertant; Bernstein; Sonata; Wanhal; Sonata; Vaughan Williams; Studies in English Folksong; Mozart; Concerto; Wilson; Sonatine; Wagner; Adagio; Tuthill; Pieces; Delmas; Promenade; Weber; Music for Clarinet & Piano. Contbr. to Maine Music Educators Jrnl.; Conn. Music Educators Assn. Mag.; etc. Hons: Concert Artists Guild Award, 1968. NY Univ. Fndrs. Day Award, 1972. Hobbies: Photography; Reading; Sailing; Sports. Mgmt: Thea Dispeaker Mgmt., 59 E 54th St., NY, NY 10022. Address: 382 Central Park W, NY, NY 10025, USA. 2.

BUNNEY, Herrick. Barnes, Surrey, UK. Master of Music, St. Giles' Cathedral; Conductor; Organist. Educ: BMus; FRCO; ARCM. m. Mary Cutting, 1 s., 1 d. Carerr: Organist & Master of Music, St. Giles' Cathedral, Edinburgh; Cond., Edinburgh Univ. Singers; Organist, Univ. of Edinburgh; Recordings: St. Giles Cathedral (Gt. Cathedral Organs); Music in St. Giles. Contbr. to Inc. Soc. Musicians Jrnl. Mbrships: Coun., RCO; Chmn., Edinburgh Youth Orch.; Prog. Panel, Edinburgh Festival Soc.; Inc. Soc. Musicians. Mbr., Victorian Order, 1964. Address: 3 Upper Coltbridge Terr., Edinburgh EH12 6AD, UK.

BURAL, Nemai Chand, b. 28 Nov. 1930. Calcutta, W Bengal, India. Singer; Educator. Educ: Sangeet-Gunakar (MMus equivalent); Sangeet-Varidhi (MusD equivalent); BA. m. Sandhyarani Bural, 1 s. 3 d. Debut: All India Music Conf., 1953. Career incls: Singer in radio, 1952-, stage, film, TV, etc., 1965-; Prof. & Hd., Dept. of Indian Classical Music, Visva-Bharati Univ., Santiniketan. Comps: publd. in leading musical jrnls., 1961-. Num. recordings. Publs: incl: Sangeet Nayak, 1970; The Language of Music, 1974. Contbr. to acad. & pub. jrnls. Mbrships: incl: Solo for Ethnomusicol., Can., 1972; Assoc. Fndr. Mbr., Indian Musicol. Soc. Hons: incl: Fellow in Dhrupad, 1970; Gov.'s Medal, 1953-54. Hobbies: Special studies on experimental Indian music. Address: Visva-Bharati Univ., Santiniketan, 731235, India.

BURCH, Robert William, b. 28 Jan. 1929. Lyttelton, NZ. Horn Player, Educ: MusB, Vic. Univ. of Wellington, 1951; studied comp. b. Benjamin Frankel & horn w. Raymond Bryant, GSM, London, UK, 1951-54. m. Leah Chloe Burch, 1 s., 1 d. Career: 2nd Horn, NZ Symph. Orch. Comps: chmbr. music esp for wind instruments; vocal & choral pieces. Recordings: Capriccio for saxophone quartet; Serenade for Wind Quintet. Mbrships: Committee, Comps. Assn. of NZ; Chmn., Alex Lindsay Mem. Award Trust. Hobby: Yachting. Address: 20 Rimu Rd., Kelburn, Wellington, 5 NZ.

BURDA, Antonin, b. 5 June 1902. Uherské Hradiste, Czech. Author. Educ: Studied musicol. & phonetics, Charles Univ., Prague, 1937-46; Studied violin, cello, piano, solo singing (tenor). m. Jaromíra Dedecková, 1 d. Career: Stenographer, Národní listy; Sub-Ed., econs., ibid, Národní politika & Svobodné noviny; Asst.; Tatra Waggon Works, Prague, 6 yrs.; Sub-Ed., maths. & physics, Publishing House of Czech. Acad. of Scis. (now named Academia), until 1968. Comp: Missa Brevis in honorem St. Venceslai; Double Passion (1st after Matthaeus & 2nd after John); About 20 songs; Harmonization of Czech. folk & choral songs. Publs. incl: The Czech. Contribution to the Modern Theory of Music, T B Janovka & his Clavis, 1964: Aurelius Augusinus: De musica libri sex, 1967: A M S Boethius: De institutione musica, 1974 (trans. w. commentaries); The theory of Music during the Barock time in the Czech. countries (1974); Plutarchos Peri musikés, 1976; Philodémos Peri musikés, 1977: Bellermanniani Anonymi, 1978; Aristotelis Problemata, sect. XIX, 1978 (transl. w. commentaries). Contbr. to: Die Musikforschung; Hudebni veda. Recip. of hons. Address: Kotenvni 2, 150 00 Prague 5, Smívhov, Czech.

BURDA, Pavel, b. 7 Apr. 1942. Bohemian Budweis, Czechoslovakia. University Professor; Timpanist; Percussionist; Conductor. Educ: Dip. Prague Conserv. of Music; MMus, SUNY, USA; Postgrad., State Acad. of Music, Hamburg, W Germany. Career incls: Num. TV shows; Timpanist, Symph. Orch. of Vit Nejedly; Toured w. orchs. in Eastern & Western Europe & N Africa; Solo Timpanist, Brazilian Symph. Orch.; Prin. Timpanist-Percussionist, Orch. de Camera, NY; Solo Timpanist, Fest. Casals Orch., San Juan, PR, 1976. Fac. Mbr. Dept. of Music, Univ. Wis., USA; Dir., Cond., The Music with Percussion Ensemble. Comps. incl: Incidental Music for Vysinuta Hrdlicka, Theatre on the Balustrade, Prague, 1963-65. Num. recordings as soloist on Orion label. Mbrships: Am. Fedn. of Musicians; Coll. Music Soc.; Percussive Arts. Soc. Recip. Fellowship to Tanglewood, 1970. Hobby: Travel. Address: 3003 N Farwell Ave., Milwaukee, WI 53211, USA.

BURDEN, John Harold, b. 13 Apr. 1921. London, UK. Professor of Horn, TCL & GSM. Educ: Blundell's Schl.; Trent Coll.; RAM (Ross Scholar). m. Anita Jane Deane, 2s; 2 d., 1 s. by previos marriage. Debut: w. LSO. Career: Prin. horn, LSO, Engl. Chmbr. Orch., Sinfonia of London, Menuhin Fest. Orch.; fndr. mbr., Virtuoso Ensemble of London & London Horn Trio; solo perfs. abroad & on TV & radio; formerly prin. horn, Geoff Love, Ron Goodwin, Jack Parnell, etc. orchs. Recordings: num. & varied w. above orchs. Publ: Horn Playing, a New Approach, 1970. Mbrships: Royal Soc. of Musicians; ISM; Royal Phil. Soc. Hons: Coronation Medal, 1952; hon. FTCL. Hobbies: Gardening; DIY. Address: Shimber Beris, 103 Shirkoak Pk., Woodchurch, nr. Ashord, Kent, UK.

BURGAN, Arthur, b. 29 June 1923. Rotherham, UK. Instrumental Tutor; Double Bass Player; Violist; Violinist. Educ: Northern Schl. of Music, ARCM (viola tchng.). m. Kathleen, 1 s., 1 d. Career: Senior Instrumental Tutor, Hull; freelance double bass player, 1948-; lectr. in maintenance & repair of stringed instruments. Publs: Basic String Repairs, 1974, '79 Contbr. to: News & Views, jrnl. of European Str. Tchrs. Assn. Mbrships: NAS; Musicians Union; European Str. Tchrs. Assn. Hons: FNSM, 1966; FRSA, 1974. Hobbies: Camping; Walking; Reading; Repairing Stringed Instruments. Address: 23 Hull Rd., Cottingham, E Yorks. Hu16 4PN, UK.

BURGER, Bernard, b. 22 Feb. 1932. Amsterdam, Netherlands. Conductor; Pianist; Oboist. Educ: Amsterdam Conserv.; Acad. Music, Mozarteum, Salzburg, Austria; Curso Panam. Direccion d Orquesta, Mexico. m. 1) Sigrid Reichert (dec.); 2) Ineke Franssen, 1 s. Debut: Amsterdam. Career: Guest Cond., Hamburger Symph., Germany; Stadtisches Sinfonierorchester, Innsbruck, Austria; Orc. de Chmbr. de Toulouse, France; Orquesta de Bellas Artes & Orquesta Nacional de México; Overijssels Phil Orch.; & Het Gelders Orch., TV & Radio apps., Mexico, Holland, Gemany, etc. Recordings: Dellini Messa di Gloria, Dvorak's Te Deum, Beethoven's Choral Fantasy (Mirasound). Contbr. to jrnls. Mbr., Koninklijke Nederlandse Toonkunstenaars Vereniging. Hobbies: Lit.; Yoga. Mgmt: Nederlands Impresariaat, Amsterdam. Address: Henry Dunantlaan 9, 7548 AA Boekelo Enschede, Netherlands.

BURGER, Hester Aletta Sophia, b. 30 Sept. 1913. Worcester S Africa. Teacher; Composer. Educ: MMus, Univ. of Pretoria; ATCL; LTCL. m. J F Burger, 1 d. Career: piano tchr. in high schls. for 34 yrs.; wrote text & play for Repub. Fest. for Eastern Cape Province, 1965, & language fest., 1975; retired 1977. comps: Passion Oratorio, 1968; Christmas Oratorio, 1972: Christmas Oratorio, 1974. Hobbies: Flowers; Books; Grandsons; Bowls. Address: Old Age Home, Lettie Theron, 7200 Hermanus, S Africa.

BURGESS, Grayston, b. 7 Apr. 1932. Cheriton, Kent, UK. Conductor; Countertenor. Educ: MA, King's Coll. Cambridge. m. Katherine Mary Bryan, 3 d. Debut: London, 1955. Career: Oberon in Britten's Midsummer Nights Dream, Covent Gdn.; 'Downland' TV prog.; Handel Opera Soc. perfs.; BBC Henry Wood Proms; num. radio broadcasts. Recordings: as Singer/Cond., Purcell Consort of Voices, 20 recordings (Argo & Turnabout). Mbrships: ISM; Choir Benevolent Fund. Hobbies: Sport; Gardening; Riding; Walking; The Countryside. Address: Pencombe Hall, Pencombe nr. Bromyard, Herefordshire, UK. 3.

BURGHARDT, Hans-Georg, b. 7 Feb. 1909. Breslau/Schlesien, Germany. Composer; Pianist; Music Teacher. Educ: studied musicol., piano theory & comp. w. noted tchrs.; State Pvte. Music Tchr.'s Exams., piano, 1932, comp. & theory, 1933. m. Margarete Burghardt (dec.). Debut: 1930. Carer: Free-lance Comp., Pianist, Song Accomp. & Music Tchr., 1930-; Music Tchr., colls. of Bresau, Jenna & Halle-Saale Univs., 1941-; concerts, radio broadcasts for Radio DDR; now ret'd. Comps. incl: 2 piano concertos; Concerto for 2 pianos & orch.; Sonata for 2 pianos; Sonata for violin & piano. Mbr., Union of German Comps. & Musicols. in GDR. Hons. incl: Pestalozzi Medals, Bronze, 1962, & Silver, 1971. Hobbies incl: Playing harmonium. Address: Liebenaulerstr. 19, 402 Halle-Saale, German Dem. Repub.

BURGHAUSER, Jarmil Michael, b. 21 Oct. 1921. Plsek, S Bohemia, Czech. Composer; Musicologist. Educ: Prague Conserv. of Music, 1940-44; Master Class of Cond., ibid, 1944-46; Charles Univ., Prague, 1945-48. Career: Choirmaster & Cond., Nat. Theatre, Prague, 1946-53; Freelance Comp. & Musicologis, 1953-; Comp., Film, stage & TV music, 1945-; Audiovisual presentations w. SCARS grp., 1969-. Comps. incl: Operas, The Miser, Karolinka and the Liar; Ballets, The Servant of Two Masters & Tristram and Izalda; Cantatas, The Mystic Trumpeter & The Pensive Country; Orchl. works, Seven Reliefs, The Ways, Colours in Time; Chmbr. music. Publs. incl: Antonín Dvorak, Thematic Catalogue, 1960; Antonín Dvorak, 1967; Introductions to editions of works of A Dvorak, L Janacek & J B Kittl; Editl. Bd. mbr., complete critical editions of A Dvorak, Z Fibich & L Janacek. Chmbn., Comps. Sect., Guild of Czech. Comps., 1969. Mbrships: VP, Dvorak Soc. of GB. Recip. sev. prizes. Address: Klindá 25, 162 00 Prague 6, Czech. 3.

BURGON, Geoffrey, b. 15 July 1941. Hambledon, UK. Composer. Educ: GSM; studied pvtely. w. Lennox Berkeley. m. Jan Garwood, div., 2 children. Compositions: works for theatre, ballet, orch., chorus, chmbr. ensemble, children, film, TV & radio. Hons: Prince Pierre of Monaco Award. 1967; Wainwright Schlrship., 1963. Mgmt: Harrison & Parrott. UK Address: 22 Hillgate St., London W8, UK 4.

BURIAN, Karel Vladimir, b. 23 May 1923. Prague, Czechoslovakia. Professor. Educ: Study of comp. w. Rudolf Karel; Music sci. & hist. w. J Hutter & J Plavec. m. Jarmila Kopejtkova (dec.), 1 d. Publs: Num. biogs., novels on W A Mozart, B Smetana, A Dvorak; books on music inclng: Verdi, 1948; G Rossini, 1963: A Toscanini, 1967; L Stokowski, 1976; A Short History of English Music, 1948; The Story of World Opera, 1961: Basic Works of Verismo-Opera, 1968; The World Opera Theaters, 1973; Stars of Ballet, 1971. Film strips: Czech. Music of Baroque, Classicism & Revivalist Period, 1973; Music & Motion, 1974, Contbr. to jrnls., mags. Hons. incl: Annual Prize of Supraphon, 1971, '76, '77. Hobby: Hist. & theory of painting & architecture. Address: Zapotockeho 264, 251 01 Ricany u Prahy, Czech.

BURKE, Martin Teasdale, b. 15 Feb. 1908. Ealing, London, UK. Teacher; Pianist; Organist; Conductor. Educ: Tobias Matthay Pianoforte Schl.; RAM, London; ARAM; LRAM; ARCO; Study w. Amy Grimson. Career: Organist, St. Benedict's Ch., Ealing, 1935-37; Organist & Choirmaster, St. Saviour's Ch., Lewisham, 1937-40; Cond., Alan Turner Opera Co., 1900, Sub Prof. of Piano, RAM, London, 1930-40; Cond., Leigh Choral Soc., 1938-39; RAF, 1940-46; Cond., Buckingham Music Soc., 1948-58; Mbr., Music Staff, Stowe Schl., 1946-68. Mbrships: ISM; Ret'd. Mbr., Music Masters Assn. RAF Club. Recip., Chappell Gold Medal, 1939. Hobbies: Gardening; Reading; Travel. Address: Cielo e Mar, Porthilly View, Padstow, Cornwall, UK. 3.

BURKE, Paul, b. 30 Oct. 1941. Wombwell, Barnsley, Yorks., UK. Concert Pianist; Teacher. Educ: RAM, London; Mbr. Nat. Youth Orch. GB; Studied w. Frank Herrick, Llona Kabos, Fanny Waterman & Louis Kentner. m. Monika Caser, 1 s., 1 d. Debut: Vaduz, Liechtenstein, FL. Career: Var recitals for BBC Radio, Sheffield; Concerts in UK, Austria & Liechtenstein; Professional Staff; Stadtische Musikschule, Feldkirch & Stella Matutina Kolleg, Feldkrich. Mbrships: ISM; Gesellschaft der Musikfreunde, Feldkirch, Vorarlbert, Austria. Recip. of W Riding Music Scholarship to RAM, London. Hobbies: Attending Concerts; Philately. Address: Kirchgasse 14, A-6804 Altenstadt, Feldkirch, Vorarlberg, Austria.

BURKHART, Herman Peter, b. 3 June 1921. Brooklyn, NY, USA. Double Bass Virtuoso. Educ: BA, Univ. of Tulsa; Schlrship. student of Anselm Fortier; Study of orch., Leon Barzin. m. Jenny Guncelle, 1 s., Career: Prin. Bass., Kan. City Phil. St. Louis Symph., Pitts. Symph., Adolph Busch Chmbr. Players, Bolshoi Ballet; Num. solo perfs. w. orch. & recitals; Mbr., Music Fac., Memphis State Unv. Recordings: 12 Handel Concerti Grossi, w. Adolph Busch Chmbr. Players; Var. works w. St. Louis Symph.; String bass solos. contbr. to profl. jrnls. Hobbies: Fishing; Hunting. Address: 530 S Prescott, Memphis, TN, USA.

BURKO, Louis, b. 28 Aug. 1932. Vladimerzecz, Poland. Conductor, Arranger; Organist; Pianist. Educ: LRSM Berkshire Music Ctr., Tanglewood, Mass., USA; studied w. Michel Hirvy.

div., 1 s., 1 d. Career: Cond., Arr., Pianist; over 300 Radio Apps. w. The Lou Burko Orch.; Music Dir., Shaare Zion congregation; TV Apps., Cond., Pianist. Mbrshi&ps: Musicians Guild of Montreal; Hond. Mbr., Zoltan Kodaly Acad. & Inst.; Hon. Patron, L'Assomption Coll. of Music. Hons: Silver Medal, Piano, Toronot Conserv. of Music, 1946; Scholarship. ibid. Hobbies: Swimming; Cross-Country Skiing. Address: 5500 Borden Ave., Apt. 909, Montreal, PQ, Can.

BURLEIGH, Cecil, b. 17 Apr. 1885. Wyo., NYC, USA. Composer; Emeritus Professor; Violinist. Educ: Klindworth - Scharwenka Conserv., Berlin, Germany; Chgo. Musical Coll. m. Jessie Jennings Burleigh. Debut: Aeolian Hall, NYC. Career: Composer; Violinist; Emeritus Prof., Univ. of Wis., Madison. Compositions: 92 violin pieces; 35 songs; 40 piano pieces; 3 violin concertos; 2 violin sonatas; Evangeline for small orch. Recordings: Moto Perpetuo; Giant Hills. Mbr., ASCAP. Recip., Doct., Am. Conserv. M. Music, Chgo., Ill. Contbr. to Etude. Hobbies: Painting; Reading Classics. Address: PO Box 2116, Madison, WI 53701, USA. 2, 4.

BURLES, Charles, b. 21 June 1936. Marseilles, France. Singer. Educ: Studies w. Leon Cazauran & Pierre Mercadel. m. Berthe Davin, 3 s. Debut: Toulon, 1958. Career: 'All Tenor Roles of opera & operetta, Marseilles; Apps. all over France, Belgium, Italy, Spain; Paris debut, Comic Opera, 1969: TV apps., ORTF. Recordings incl: La Belle Héléne; Lakmé; William Tell; The Barber of Seville. Hons: Golden Orpheus, 1971; Cmdr., Order of Merit, 1974. Hobby: Painting. Mgmt: Mlle. Pongy, 27 rue Ste. Victorine, 13003 Marseille, France. Address' 5-7 rue Felix Ebové, 13002 Marseille, France.

BURN, Frederick Henry. Haverick, Cumbria, UK. Music Teacher; Organist; Choirmaster. Educ: LTCL (CMT); MRST; studied w. W Broome & Dr. F H Wood. m. Dorothy Bosanko, 1 s., Career: Music Master, Wilson Shcl., Workington (1960), Richmond Schl., Whitehaven (1963), Millom Comprehensive Schl. (1968); Examiner in Music, N Regional Examination Bd., 1973-78; on panel of examiners, Joint Matriculation Bd., 1973-78; organist, Haverigg Meth. Ch.; organist & choirmaster, Millom Parish Ch., Bootle Parish Ch. num. unpubl. comps. used in chs. & schls. in the county. Hobbies: Tennis; Photograp;hy. Address: 7 Atkinson St., Haverigg, Millom, Cumbria LA18 4HA, UK.

BURNAU, Suanna Jeannette Flake, b. 22 Jan. 1938. Conway, Ark., USA. Mezzo-Soprano; Educator. Educ: BSE, 1960, MEd, 1970, Univ. of Ark.; Univ. of Mo. at Kan City Conserv. div., 1 d. Career: concerts, radio, TV, plays, ch. & temple soloist; 21 operatic roles; 13 musical comedies; Oratorio soloist & soloist w. orch.; Kan. City Lyric Opera Co.; Ark. State Opera Co.; Kan. City Starlight Theatre. Ark. Symph., Kan City Civic Orch: Tchr. var. schls. Mbrships incl: Nat. Assn. of Tchrs. of Singing; MENC; VP, Ark. Tan Chapter, Alpha Delta Kappa Int.; NEA. Recip., Chatham Opera Schlrship., SW Dist., Am. Fedn. of Music Clubs, 1962. Hobbies incl: Travel; Reading; Mineralogy. Address: 7007 Gingerbread Lane, Little Rock, AR 72204, USA. 5, 7, 27.

BURNESS, John Frederick, b. 11 May 1933. London, UK. Bassoon Player. Educ: Hon. RCM. m. Patricia Brady, 1s. Career: RAF Ctrl. Band; Sadlers Wells, 3 yrs.; Royal Opera House, Covent Garden, 3 yrs.; Bournemouth Symph. Orch., 3 yrs.; Bassoon & Double Bassoon player, BBC Symph. Orch., 1965-. Comps: 4 Easy Pieces for Bassoon; Variations for Solo Bassoon. Publ: Bars Rest, 1975. Mbrships: VP, Chesham Arts Fest.; Chmn., Music Panel, Nat. Assn. of Boys Clubs, 1957-77. Hons: Doris Hudson Orchl. prize, 1949; Alice Bonwick Bequest, RCO, 1948. Hobbies: Ch. & organ music; Railways; Pubs. Address: 19 Treachers Close, Chesham, Bucks., HP5 2HD, UK.

BURNHAM, Andrew, b. 19 Mar. 1948. Workshop, UK. Conductor; Freelance teacher. Educ: BA, New Coll., Oxford, 1969; MA, ibid., 1978; ARCO (CHM). Career: Chorus master, Engl. Sinfonia, 1973; Chorus master, Nottingham Harmonic Soc., 1973; Fndr., Musical Dir., The Trent Orch., 1979. Mbr., Incorp. Soc. of Musicians (Solo Perfs. Sect.). Recip. sponsorship by E. Midlands Arts Assn., 1977. Hobbies: Reading; Writing; Liturgy. Mgmt: Cantata Music Promotions Ltd. Address: 289 Derby Rd., Nottingham, UK.

BURNSWORTH, Charles Carl, b. 27 June 1931. Niagara Falls, NY, USA. College Professor; Chora; Conductor. Educ: BS, Music Educ., SUNY, Fredonia; MS, Music Educ., Univ. of Ill.; DMA, Boston Univ., Boston Univ., Dip., US Naval Schl. of Music; profl. cond. study w. Robert Shaw & Richard Burgin. m. Carole Scranton, 2 s., 1 d. Career: num. Radio & TV appearances (local-domestic), cond. Univ. Choir; TV prog., Zürich, Switz., 1968; Dir., NY chmbr. choir, concerts in Switz.,

1978. (w. Ostschweizer Kammerorchester) Cond. of Univ. Choir on 5 LP recordings; LP recording of Schubert - Mass c major, & Mozart, Missa Brevis (K 220), w. NY chmbr. Choir & Ostschweizer kammerorchester, 1978. Elected to Common Coun., City of Oneonta, NY. Publs: Choral Music for Women's Voices, 1968. Contbr. to music jrnls. & local newspaper music reviews. Mbrships: MENC; Pi Kappa Lambda; Exec. Coun., NY State Schl. Music Assn.; Sec., NY State Choral Dirs. Guild. Recip. var. hons. Hobby: Golf. Address: 14 Suncrest Terr., Oneonta, NY 13820, USa. 23, 29.

BURROWES, Norma Elizabeth, b. 1944. Bangor, Co. Down, N. Ireland, UK. Singer. Educ: Sullivan Upper Schl., Holywood, N Ireland; Queen's Univ., Belfast; Royal Acad. of Music. m. Steuart Bedford. Special subject: Opera; Lieder; Oratorio, Mbr., ISM. Hons: Tankard Lieder Prize; Worshipful Co. of Musicians Award; Van Someren-Godfrey Prize, RAM; Gulbenkian Schlrships., 1970. Address: Auguste Cottage, Hammers Lane, London NW7, UK.

BURROWS, David, b. 5 Feb. 1930. Honolulu, Hawaii, USA. Historian of Music Educ: BMus., Eastman Schl. of Music, Univ. of Rochester, 1951; AM, Harvard Univ., 1952; PhD, Brandeis Univ., 1961. m. 2 s., 1 d. Career: Tchr., Yale, 1960-67; NY Univ., 1967-. Publs: Ed. - The Practical Harmonist at the Harpsichord, by Francesco Gasparini; The Italian Cantata, 1: Antonio Cesti; Antonio Cesti; Four Chamber Duets; The Wellesley Edition Cantata Index Series; 1: Antonio Cesti. Contbr. to encys., jrnls. Mbrships: Am., Int. Musicol. Socs.; Soc. for Enthnomusicol. Hons: Fulbright Awards for study in Italy, 1958-60, 1973. Address: Dept. of Music, Grad. Schl. of Arts & Sci., NY Univ., Washington Sq., New York, NY 10003, USA.

BURROWS, Donald Ivan, b. 28 May 1930. Luton, Beds., UK. Teacher; Lecturer. Educ: MA, Univ. of Birmingham; RCM; ARCM; FRCO. m. Helene van Aertselaer. Career: Dir. of Music, Padgate Coll. of Educ., Lancs.; Dir. of Music Christ Ch. Coll. of Educ., Canterbury, Kent; Staff tutor & Sr. Lectr. in Music, Open Univ., Milton Keynes, Bucks. mbr., ISM. Address: 1 Portman Rd., King's Heath, Birmingham B13 0SM, UK.

BURROWS, Donald (Donwald) James, b. 28 Dec. 1945. London, UK. Teacher; Conductor; Musicologist; Continuo Player; Harpsichordist. Educ: MA, Trinity Hall, Cambridge Univ. m. Marilyn Jones, 2 s. Career incls: Dir. of Music, John Mason Schl., Abingdon, Oxon; Cond., Abingdon & Dist. Musical Soc.; Organist, St. Nicholas' Ch., Abingdon; Lectr., Abingdon Coll. of Further Educ.; Tchr., Abingdon Music Schl.; cond. wantage choral soc.; schlmaster Student, Merton Coll., Oxford, Hilary Term, 1979; Harpsichordist, Abingdon Consort w. perfs. in Cambridge & Oxford. Publs: Ed., Handel, Anthem on the Peace, First Ed., 1978/9. Contbr. to Musical Times; Music & Letters. Mbrships: Royal Musical Assn.; RCO. Hobbies: Archaeol.; Steam Locomotives. Address: 24 Rookery Close, Shippon, Abingdon, Oxon OX13 6LZ, UK.

BURROWS, James Stuart, b. 7 Feb. 1933. Cilfynydd, Wales, UK. Opera Singer (tenor). Educ: Trinity Coll., Garmarthen; Tchrs. Cert., Univ. of Wales. m. Enid Lewis, 1 s., 1 d. Debut: Welsh Nat. Opera, Cardiff, 1963. Career: Operatic apps., Royal Opera Covent Garden, Paris Opera, Vienna State Opera, Hamburg Opera, Geneva Opera, San Fran. Opera, Huston Opera, Santa Fe Opera, Metropolitan Opera NY, Boston Opera, Salzburg Fest.; BBC TV films of Faust, La Boheme, Rigoletto; Concerts & recitals w. sev. Am. Symphs. & Vienna Phil. Orch. Num. recordings. Hons: Blue Riband Nat. Eisteddfod of Wales, 1959. Mgmt: AIM Ltd., London. Address: 35 st. Fagans Dr., St. Fagans, Cardiff CFS 6EF, UK.

BURROWS, John, b. 3 Aug. 1941. Newcastle under Lyrre, UK. Musical Director; Conductor; Pianist; Composer; Arranger. Educ: BMus., Manchester Univ., ARCO; GRSM; ARMCM. m. Rita Sandford, 1 s., 1 d. Career: Mbr., Music Staff, Sadlers Wells Opera Co., 1965-70; Assisted in preparation of & prompted 'Ring cycle, London Coliseum, 1970-73; Musical Lambeth (1976); Once More with Music (1976-77), A Chorus Line (1977-78); Love All, 1978; Wizard of Oz, 1978-79; UK tour of Gilbert & Sullivan, 1979; Arranger/Composer, BBC TV (inclng. Beethoven biog. series, Take Three Girls, Put Out More Flags, Casanova, Black & Blue. Recordings: Cowardy Custard; Sullivan Songs; Liza of Lambeth; Cole; Treasure Island. Mbr., PRS. Mgmt: Orch. Advisory Mgmt., 10 Parkland's Way, Worcester Pk., Surrey, UK. Address: 158 Balls Pond Rd., London N1 4AA, UK.

BURRY, Lloyd Noah French, b. 6 Aug. 1929. St. John's, Nfld., Can. Organist; Pianist. Educ: TCL, Nfld.; Grad., Royal Conserv. of Music, Toronot; Yamaha Int. Cert. of Achievement. m. Helga Burry, 2 s. Career: Kiwanis Fest., Toronto, 1950;

Organ Recital & Concert, Jones Hall, Houston, Texas, 1968; Ch. Organist, Recitalist, Can. incl. Bandshell Recital, Can. Nat. Exhibition, Toronto, 1969; Yamaha Can. & Yamaha Int. Concert tour, Can., 1976; Concert artist on organ for Hammond Int., incl. tours of USA & Can.; Jazz Pianist & Organist; TV & radio apps., Can. & USA. Comps: Helga. Recordings: Lloyd Burry at the Organ; Lloyd Burry Night Train; Lloyd Burry at Town & Country. Mbrships: Am. Fedn. of Musicians; Comps., Author & Publrs. Assn. of Can. Hons: Winner, 8th Int. Yamaha Electrone Fest., Toronto, 1971. Hobbies: Tennis; Hockey; Ceramics; Ice Skating; Soccer. Address: Apt. A-3844, 36 Terrace South, St. Petersburg, FL 33711, USA.

BURT, Amanda M, b. 31 July 1916. Duluth, Minn., USA. Musicologist; Harpist; Organist. Educ: AA, BA, MA, PhD. m. Howard J Burt, 1 d. Career: Staff Organist, Cypress Gdns., Fla.; Assoc. Prof. of Music. Publs: Notes and Stuff, 1971; Iceland's Twentieth Century Composers and a Listing of Thier Works, 1975, 1977: 29 articles on Iceland & comps. in Grove's Dictionary of Music and Musicians. Contbr. to Musart; Baton. Mbrships: Fac. Advsr., Phi Beta; Phi Kappa Lambda; Mortar Board; Phi Kappa Phi; Wash. Harp Soc.; Nat. Harp. Soc.; Nat. Coll. Music Soc.; Pres. Va. Chapt. Coll. Music Soc. Hons: 5 special grants to rsch. Icelandic music from George Mason Univ. Fndn. Hobbies: Beachcombing; Swimming; Biking. Address: Assoc. Dean of Fine Arts, Manatee Jr. Coll., Bradent FL 33506, USA. 4, 27.

BURT, Francis, b. 28 Apr. 1926. London, UK. Composer; Professor. Educ: RAM, 1948-51; Hochschule für Musik, Berlin, 1951-54. m. Lina Burt. Career: Prof. of Comp., Hochschule für Musik und darstellende Kunst, Vienna, 1973-. Comps. incl: Iambics for orch. Op. 5; Volpone (opera), Op.9; Espressione orchestrale, Op.10; Der Golem (ballet), Op.11; Fantasmagoria per Orch., Op.12; Barnstable (opera), Op.13; Unter der blanken Hacke des Monds, for baritone & orch. Hons: Mendelssohn scholarship, 1954; ARAM, 1957; Körner prize, 1973. Hobbies: Reading; Walking; Eating; Drinking; Good Friends. Address: Mayerhofgassse 12/20, 1040 Vienna, Austria.

BURTENSHAW, Leonard John, b. 9 July 1941. Sydney NSW, Aust. Snr. Lectr.; Hd. of Music Educ., NSW State Conserv. of Music; Guest Orch. Cond.; Organist. Educ: PhD, Colo.; MMus, Sydney; BMus, Adelaide Univ.; RAM; Mozarteum, Salzburg; Conducting w. Adrian Boult, Eugene Goossens & Carl Melles. Career incls: Cond. w. major symph. orchs. in Aust; Organ Recitals for Aust. Broadcasting Commission Hd. of Music Educ. Dept., State Conservatorium of Music, Sydney; Organist & Choirmaster, St. Stephen's Ch., Sydney. Num. recordings. Contbr. to profl. jrnls. Mbr., NSW Chapt. ASME; AGO; MENC. Hons. incl: num. scholarships & Conds. prize, RAM. Hobby: Sailing. Address: Univeristy Club, 972 Broadway, Boulder, CO 80302, USA. 28.

BURTON, Barbara h 25 Jan 1950 Chgo. Ill. USA. Percussionist. Educ: Juilliard Schl., NYC. m. Marvin Tuten. Career: apps. w. num. orchl., vocal, operatic & ballet grps., inclng: NY Phil.; NJ Symph.; Brooklyn Phil.; Harlem Phil.; City Ctr. Ballet Orch.; Queens Opera Assn.; Chgo. Symph. Chorus; Dance Theatre of Harlem; Chgo. Ballet Co., Alvin Ailey Dance Theatre. Comps. background music for cartoons, TV advt. Recordins: w. Wayne Shorter, Blue Note Records; Weather Report, Columbia Records; free-lance recordings, var. labels. Mbrships: incl: Nigerian Fest. Comm.; Percussive Arts Soc.; Am. Fedn. of Musicians. Recip., num. acd. awards. Hobby: Floriculture. Address: Apt. 6D, 615 Ft. Washington Ave., NY, NY 19940, USA.

BURTON, Nigel Mark, b. 9 Apr. 1947. Southampton, UK. University Lecturer; Singer; Pianist; Organist. Educ: MusB, 1969, MA, 1972, Gonville & Caius Coll., Cambridge; MusB, 1976; MA, 1977, Trinity Coll., Dublin. studied w. Bernard Roberts (piano), Gwendoline Hanson (singing), Arnold Richardson (organ), FRCO, 1970. Career: Jr. Lectr. in Music, Trinity Coll., Dublin, 1974; Dir. of Ch. Music, ibid., 1975; Lectr., ibid, 1977; Lectr. in Music, Univ. of Reading (specialising in 19th century Brit. music), 1979-. Contbr. to Music & Musicians. Hobbies: Amateur Theatricals; Food; Wine. Address: St. Patrick's Hall, Reading, Berks., RG2 7HB, UK.

BURTON, Thomas Eldin, b. 26 Oct. 1913. Fitzgerald, Ga., USA. Composer; Pianist. Educ: BA, Post-Grad. Degrees, Atlanta Conserv. Of Music, Ga., 1938; Dip., Juilliard Grad. Schl., 1946. Debut: Carnegie Recital Hall, NYC, 1949. Career: about 200 Radio Piano Concerts, Atlanta, about 50 Stage Apps., playing own works, NYC. Compositions incl: (publ.) Sonata For Viola & Piano; Sarabande In G Major; A Wish; The Lord's Prayer; (publd. and recorded) Sonatinas, For Flute & Piano, Violin & Piano; Fiddlestick; Quintet For Piano & Str.

Quartet; Concerto for piano w. orch.; Concerto for flute w. Orch. Recordings: 53 Piano Solos, var. comps., Classic Eds. Recordings; Golden Crest Records. Contbr. to: Atlanta Historical Soc. Bulletin; The Northside Press, Atlanta. Mbrships: Comps., Grp. of NYC; Past Pres., ibid., 2 terms; The Bohemians. Georgia State Dept., of Archives & Hist. Hons: Best Song, Best Piano Piece, Ga. Fedn. Of Music Clubs, 1938; Fellowships In Comp., Juilliard Grad. Schl., NYC, 1943-46, won NY Flute Club Compeition, 1948. Address: 5050 Bay Shore Rd., Sarasota, FL 33580, USA.

BUSBY, Gerald, b. 16 Dec. 1935. Abilene, Tex., USA. Composer; Pianist; Teacher; Actor. Educ: BA, Yale Univ.; Studied piano, comp. & music theory, Yale Music Schl. Debut: Town Hall, NYC, 1966. Career: Piano recitals & soloist w. orch.; Instr., Dept. of Music, Princeton Univ., 1973-77; Commission from Paul Taylor, Choreographer, for dance score Runes, 1975 (Premiered: Paris, 1975); Comps. incl: Noumena for Solo Flute; An Am. Magnificat for Organ, Trumpet & SATB w. Soloists; Fantasy for Violin & Piano; Tantalus (vibraphone); Alhambra (rondo for guitar); Ancient of Days (Organ, SATB); Touch (piano); A Wedding Waltz (piano). Hons. incl: Grant from Nat. Endowment for the Arts for comp. of Rumes, 1976. Hobby: Cooking. Mgmt: STE Agency, NYC. Address: Chelsea Hotel, 222 W23, NY, NY 10011, USA.

BUSBY, Joan. Middlesbrough, UK. Mezzo-Soprano/Contralto Singer; Teacher of Singing. Educ: BSc, MSc, Edinburgh Univ.; pvte. music study, Edinburgh & Glasgow; ARCM; FTCL. m. John Busby, 3 children. Career: Recitalist for music socs. & Soloist w. choral socs., throughout Scotland; regular broadcasts, BBC Scotland; leading roles for local opera cos.; w. Scottish Opera chorus, 1 yr.; Mbr., John Currie Singers, 4 yrs, inclng. tour of Israel; currently Mbr., Trio Felice (voice, piano, viola), & Hill Square Consort; premiered leading role in James Douglas 'The Seven Deadly Sins, Stirling Fest. & Edinburgh Fest., 1974. Mbrships: ISM, Scottish Opera Club. Hobbies incl: Scottish country dancing. Address: Easter Haining; Ormiston, E Lothian, EH35 5NJ, UK.

BUSCH, Gudrun, b. 7 Sept. 1930. Wuppertal, Germany. Lecturer in Musicology; Assistant High School Director. Educ: Grammar Schl. Tchrs. Degree; Musikhochschule, Cologne; Univs. of Cologne & Bonn, PhD in Musicol. Career: Lectr. in Musicol., Robert Schumann Inst., Dusseldorf, Rhineland State Music Acad.; Asst. Dir., Balderichstrasse City Gymnasium, Moenchengladbach; Vis. Asst. Prof., Schl. of Music, Univ. of Iowa, USA, Summer Schl. 1968 & 1969-70. Publ: CPhE Bach & seine Lieder, Kölner Beitrage zur Musikzeitung. Mbrships: Gesellschaft fur Musikforschung; Int. Musicol. Soc.; Am. Musicol. Soc.; Lessing Soc. Hobbies: Art; Travel; More Music. Address: Roermonder Str. 58, D-4050 Moenchengladbach, German Fed. Repub.

BUSCH, Hans Peter. b. 4 Apr. 1914. Aachen, Germany. Stage Director (Producer); Educ; Max Reinhardt Seminar, Vienna, Austria; Geneva Univ., Switzerland. m. Carolyn Lockwood, 2 s. Debut: Parsifal prod., Teatro Colon, Buenos Aires, 1934. Career: Asst. Stage Dir. (Prod.), Florence, Buenos Aires, Rio de Janeiro, Verona & Glyndebourne; Dir., prods. in var. countries inclng: Italy, Argenitine, Switzerland, Belgium, Sweden, Denmark, Netherlands, USA, Canada, Cuba, German Fed. Repub.; Dir., TV opera profs., NBC, NY, & in Hamburg, German Fed. Repub.; Stage Dir. (Prod.), Metropol. Opera, 1956-60, Covent Garden, 1959, San Carlo Opera, Naples, 1969; Prof. of Music & Stage Dir., Ind. Univ. Bloomington, Ind.; Guest Prof., Hamburg, Hanover, Juilliard Schl., NY, etc.; Prod., Sante Fe Opera, NM, & on tour w. co. & I. Stravinsky, Berlin Festival & Belgrade, 1961. Publs: Rsch. on Verdi letters & authentic documents, forthcoming; Num. articles in var. langs. Address: Schl. of Music, Ind. Univ., Bloomington, IN 47401, USA.

BUSCH, Otto, b. 14 Oct. 1901. Dortmund, German Fed. Repub. Professor of Music. Educ: Acads. of Music in Dortmund & Leipzig; Cert. Matriculation, Leipzig. m. Maria Hennes, 1 s. Comps. incl: 89 works for organ, string quartet, string quintet, piano solo & two pianos, violin & piano, piano trio, piano quintet, orchl. concerts, songs for solo vioces & piano or orch., 3 concertos for string orch., incl. Num. recordings from radio & public concerts worldwide. Publs. incl: Praludium und Fuge in a, 1930. Mbr. Deutscher Komponistenverband, Berlin, 1929-74. Hobbies: Study of Mod. Pianting; Hist.; Biol.; Mod. Philos. & Lit. Address: Hindenburgstrasse 17, Bad Liebenzell, German Fed. Repub.

BUSH, Adrian John, b. 3 June 1944. Southampton, UK. Harpsichoard Player. Educ: LTCL; GTCL. m. Celia Katharine Moore. Debut: Purcell Room, London, 1969. Career: Arno-Bush Duo (recorded & harpsichord), 1964-; num. apps. at Purcell

Room; BBC Radio 3 broadcast, 1975. Has made 2 recordings w. Michael Arno for Saga label. Recip. Raymond Russell Prize for Harpsichord, 1964. Mgmt: Choveaux. Address: 4 Waterloo Cottage, Church St., Leatherhead, UK.

BUSH, Alan, b. 22 Dec. 1900. London, UK. Professional Musician; Composer; Conductor; Pianist. Educ: RAM, London, 1918-22; Univ. of Berlin, 1929-31; DMus, Lond., 1969; DMus, Honoris Causa Dunelm, 1971; FRAM, 1938; studied comp. w. John Ireland; piano w. Benno Moiseivich, Mabel Lander, Artur Schnabel & Harold Rubens, m. Nancy Head, 3 d. (1 dec.). Debut: Concert of own comps., piano recital, Wigmore Hall, London, 1927; as Cond. Promenade Concert, Queen's Hall, 1930. Career: Played solo pianoforte part in Piano Concerto Op. 18, BBC Male Choir & Symph. Orch., cond. by Sir Adrian Boult, 1938; World Premiere Operas Wat Tyler, Leipzig Opera House, 1953, Men of Blackmoor, German Nat. Theatre, Weimar, 1956, The Sugar Reapers, Leipzig Opera House, 1966 (libretto Barrie Stavie); Deutsche Staatsoper, Berlin, 1970. Compositions: Operas; Children's Operas; Orchestral Works; Chamber Music; Pianoforte Solos; Songs; Choral Works. Recordings: Dialetic for String Quartet, Aeolian String Quartet, Decca; Voices of th Prophets, Cantata for Tenor & Piano, Peter Pears & Alan Bush, ARGO RG 439; Variations, Nocturne & Finlae for Piano & Orch. (soloist David Wilde), Pye GCC 4073. Publs: Strict Counterpoint in Palestina Style, 1948. Mbrships: Chmn., Composers Guild of GB, 1948-49; Chmn., Workers' Music Assn., 1936-41; Pres., ibid, 1941-. Hons: Carnegie Award for String Quartet in A Minor, 1924; Arts Coun. Prize in Fest. of Britain Opera Comp., for the Opera Wat Tyler, 1951; Handel Prize, City Coun. of Halle, German Dem. Repub. for Byroм Symph., 1962. Address: 25 Christchurch Cres., Radlett, Herts., UK. 3, 14.

BUSH, Geoffrey, b. 23 March 1920. London, UK. Composer; Pianist; University Lecturer. Educ: MA, DMus, Oxford Univ. m. Julie Kathleen McKenna, 2 s. Career: Lectr. in Music. Oxford Univ. Extra Mural Dept., 1947-52; Staff Tutor in Music, London Univ. Extra Mural Dept., 1952-64; Sr. Staff Tutor, ibid, 1964-; Vis. Prof. in Music, Kings Coll., London, 1969-. Music Advsr., John Ireland Trust, 1969-. Compositions: 2 Symphonies; 3 Operas (The Equation; If The Cap Fits; Lord Arthur Saville's Crime); Songs; Piano Music; Concertante Works for Piano, Oboe, Cello, Trumpet; Overtures for Orch.; Christmas Cantata; Choral Music; Wind Quintet; Chamber Music. Recordings: Music fo orch.; overture (Yorick); Magdalen Magnificant; Two Songs. Publs: Musical Creation & The Listener, 1954, '66; Ed., Piano & Chamber Music of Sterndale Bennett, 1972, Invitation to the Partsong, vol. 1, 1973, Vol. 2, 1975, Vol 3, 1978. Contbr. to: Musical Times; The Composer. Mbrships: Composer Guild of GB (chmn., 1957; coun., 1960); Royal Musical Assn. Recip., Royal Phil. Prize for overture Yorick, 1959. Hobbies: Tennis; Walking; Watching Cricket; Bridge; Detective Stories; Theatre. Address: 43 Corringham Rd., London NW11, UK. 3, 14.

BUSH, Michael, b. 8 Oct. 1932. Aughton, UK. Conductor; Music Advisor. Educ: ARMCM, piano tcrs., dip., 1952; Royal Manchester Coll. of Music, 1949-54; ARCM, piano perfs. dip., ibid, 1953; LRAM, piano accompanists dip., 1957; RAM, 1954-57; ARAM, 1964. Career incls: Prof., Jr. Exhibitioners' Dept., RAM, 1964-68; Cond., Neri Orch., 1957-63; Mbr. of Advisory Staff, Liverpool Educ. Comm., 1968-; Cond., Sedere Singers, 1973-78; Cond., Liverpool Schls. Symph. Orch. 1974-. Publs: 2 Spanish Carols arranged for SSA. Mbrships: ISM; Music Advsrs. Nat. Assn.; Nat. Assn. of Insps. of Schls. & Educl. Advsrs. Hons: Read & Ricordi Cond. Prizes, 1956. Address: 40 Bertram Dr., Meols, Wirral, Merseyside, L47 0LH, UK. 3.

BUSH, Milton Louis, b. 22 July 1925. New Orleans, La., USA. Band Director; Trombonist; Composer/Arranger. Educ: BA, Southeastern La. Coll., 1947; BMus, ibid, 1947; MMusEd, La. State Univ., 1948; postgrad. Juilliard Schl. of Music, 1948. m. Rita Alice Rogers, 1 d, 2 s. Career: Itinerent Tchr., Instrumental music elementary public schls, New Orleans, La., 1948-49; Dir., band, Behrman High Schl., New Orleans, 1949-66; Band Dir., Kennedy High Schl., New Orleans, 1966-68; Prof., Univ. of New Orleans, 1968-; Mbr., New Orleans Summer Pops Orch., 1949-; Co-Cond., ibid, 1960-; Mbr., New Orleans Opera Orch., 1948-68. Comps: Ballard for Trombone; Mill Mountain Roanoke; Num. Band Arrs. Recordings: Trombones Beaucoup - Swing Low Album. Mbrships: Pres., New Orleans Summer Pops Orch. Inc., 1957-77; Dir., Community Concerts Assn.; Mbr., Louisiana Bandmasters' Assn.; MENC; La. Music Educs. Assn. (Pres., 1972-74); Coll. Band Dirs. Assn. (La. State Chmn., 1976-78); Phi Mu Sinfonia; Phi Beta Mu. Hons. incl: Band Dir. of The Year, 1974. Address: 1932 Wildair Dr., New Orleans, LA 70122, USA.

BUSHOUSE, M. David, b. 12 Jan. 1941. Kalamazoo, Mich., USA. Professor of Music. Educ: BMus, Univ. of Mich., 1965; MMus, ibid, 1966; studies w. Louis Stout, Harry Berv (Horn). m. Sandra L Bushouse, 2 s. Career: Instructor of Music, Morehead State Univ., Kentucky, 1966-69; Prof. of Music (horn), Univ. of Kansas, 1969-; Horn player w. Kansas Brass Quintet, Kansas Woodwind Quintet. Comps: Arr. of Haydn, Concerto No. 2. Mbrships: Int. Horn Soc.; NA CWPI; MENC. Hobbies: Jogging; Camping; Hiking. Address: Schl. of Fine Arts, Univ. of Kansas, Lawrence, KS 66045, USA.

BUSSI, Francesco, b. 14 Sept. 1926. Piacenza, Italy. Musicologist; Pianist; Lecturer; Translator. Educ: BA, Cath. Univ. of Milan, 1948; Dip. in Piano. Conserv. of Piacenza, 1949; Dip., Histl. Musicol., Univ. of Parma, 1953: Dip., Choral Music, Conserv. of Parma, 1954; studied w. G C Paribeni (comp.), G Tagliapietra & E Calace (piano). m. Maria Villa, 2 d. Career: Instructor in Music Hist., A Boito State Conserv. of Music, Parma, 1955-59; Music Critic, Libertá daily, Piacenza, 1962-; currentlyFull Instructor, Hist. of Music & Libn., G Nicolini State Conserv. of Music, Piacenza. Publs. incl: L'Antifonario-Graduale di S. Anotonio in Piacenza, 1956; Umanitá e arte di Gerolamo Parabosco, 1962; Il Cantore spagnolo Pietro Valenzola e i suoi madrigali Italiani, 1966; Piacenza - La Musica, 1966; La Produzione sacre di Cavalli e i suoi rapporti con quella di Monteverdi, 1967; Catalogo del Fondo musicale del Duomo di Piacenza, 1967; Amilcare Zanella, emulo di Busoni e paladino di Rossini, 1971; Due importanti Fondi musicali piacentini, 1971; L'Opera veneziana dalla morte di Monteverdi alla fine del '600, 1974. Ed., Compositions for 2 + 6 voices, G. Parabosco, 1962; Ed., Missa pro defunctis, F Cavalli, 1974; Transl., New Oxford History of Music, vols, II & IV, (into Italian), 1963 & 69. Contbr. to: num. profl. jrnls.; var. musicol. anthols.; Grove's Dictionary; Die Musik in Geschichte und Gegenwart, Ricordi Encyclopedia of Music; etc. Mbrships: Italian Musicol. Encyclopedia of Music; etc. Mbrships: Italian Musicol. Soc.; Int. Music Lib. Assn Address: Strada Guastafredda 45, 29100 Piacenza, Italy, 14.

BUSTANTI, Linda Maria, b. 27 June 1951. Rondonia, Porto Velho, Brazil. Concert Pianist. Educ: Ballet Dip., Rio de Janeiro; studied Theory & Harmony w. Esther Scliar, & Piano w. Arnaldo Estrella, Rio de Janeiro; post-grad. work. Tchaikowsky Conserv., Moscow, USSR. m. Marcos Louzada. Debut: Brazil, aged 11. Career: Num. perfs. in UK, 1972-, inclng. recitals, BBC recordings, & concerto apps. w. New Phil., Bournemouth Symph., Royal Liverpool Phil., & other major orchs.; 1st London appearance. Royal Festival Hall, 1976; concerts in S. Am. & Europe; tour of USSR, 1976. Hons. incl: 1st Prizes, Nat. Piano Compeition, Brazil, 1966, 68; Semi-finalist, Leeds Int. Piano Competition, UK, 1972. Hobbies incl: Antiques; Record Collecting. Mgmt: Tower Music, 125 Tottenham Ct. Rd., London W1P 9HN, UK.

BUSWELL, James Oliver, b. 4 Dec. 1946. Ft. Wayne, Ind., USA. Violinist; Conductor; Professor of Music. Educ: BA, Harvard Univ.; Juilliard Schl. of Music. m. Sara Kaye, 1 s, 1 d. Debut: NY, 1967. Career: Recitals, solo apps. w. Orch. & Chmbr. music perfs. throughout USA, Can., UK, Italy; Prof. of Music, Ind. Univ., Bloomington, Ind., USA. Sev. recordings. Mgmt: Columbia Artists Mgmt., NY. Address: 3930 E 10th St., Bloomington, IN 47401, USA.

BUTINA, Roman, b. 5 Aug. 1937. Zagreb, Yugoslavia. Organist; Keyboardist; Composer. Educ: Dip., Intermediate Music Schl. m. Ljerka Miladinova, 1 s., 1 d. Debut: 1956. Career incls: Mbr., Dalmatia vocal grp., 12 yrs., touring Yugoslavia & Eastern & Western Europe; Ldr. & Organist, The Blue Stars grp., 1970-72; Perf. on Hammond Organ & Elec. Piano, Laguna Hotel & occasionally Zagreb-Intercontinental Hotel, 1973-. Comps. recorded & publd: num. popular tunes & songs. Recordings incl: Magic Sound of Hammond Organs No. 1; Evergreens No. 2; Hammond Top Hit Melody No. 3; With Soul and Heart No. 6; Harmonica Pops No. 1. Publs. incl: Ed., With Song Through Zagorje, 1960; Ed., Greetings Tyrol, 1969; Ed., Ancient Croation Songs, 1972; Ed., World Folk Songs, 1975. Contbr. to: Yugoslavian musical jrnls. Mbrships: Yugoslav & Croation Comps. Assns.; Union of Artist of Croatia, Zagreb. Hons. incl: 2nd Prize, Zagreb Fest., 1971. Hobby: Philately. Address: Turopolijska 36. 41000 Zagreb, Yugoslavia.

BUTLER, Douglas Lamar, b. 17 May 1944. Toccoa, Stephens, GA, USA. Organist; Harpsichordist; Accompanist; Conductor/Choirmaster; Mixed media Productions. Educ: BMus, Stetson Univ., DeLand, Fla., 1966; MEd, Univ. of Fla., Gainesville, 1968; DMus A, Univ. of Ore., Eugene, 1973. Career: Concert Organ tours throughout USA, 1973-; Soloist, lectr., Nat. Convention of AGO, 1978; Performer, lectr., Cornell Unv., 1979; Broadcasts of solo organ, Nat. Public

Radio, 1976-. Recorded music of Fantini, Frescobaldi & Telemann w. trumpeter Fred Sautter. Mbrships. incl: AGO; Am. Musicol. Soc. Hobbies: Art; Cooking. Mgmt: Artist Recitals Inc., Los Angeles, Calif. Address: 629 SE Franklin, 26, Portland, OR 97202, USA.

BUTLER, Mark H, b. Feb. 1949. Brighton, UK (Canadian Citizen). 2nd Violin, Chilingirian Str. Quartet. Educ: ARCM. London; Studio w. Leonard Hirsch. Debut: Wigmore Hall, London, UK, 1972. Career: As mbr. of Chilingirian Str. Quartet, broadcasts throughout Europe (EBU, BBC, BBC TV, var. European stations), USA (NPR), NZ & Australia (ABC). Worldwide tours. num. recordings. Mbr. var. profl. orgs. Hobbies: Meteorolgy. Mgmt: Basil Douglas Ltd., London. Address: 5310 Rocky Point Rd., Victoria, BC, Can.

BUTT, David, b. 7 Jan. 1936. Salisbury, UK. Flautist. Educ: RAM; FRAM, 1975. m. Valeria Butt, 2 s., 1 d. Career: currently Prin. Flute, BBC Symph. Orch. Prof., RCM London; Principal Flute, London Bach. Orch. Contbr. to: Music in Educ. Mbr., ISM. Address: 8 St. Martins Ave., Epsom: Surrey, UK.

BUTT, James Baseden, b. 6 Apr. 1929. Northwood, Middx., UK. Composer. Educ: London Univ., 1944-47; Dartington Hall Schl. of Music, 1949-52. m. K A Kelly, 2 s. Debut: Northwood, 1935. Has written incidental music for prodns. of 12th Night, Brer Rabbit, The Rock, etc. & his works have been performed by var. artists. Compositions (publd) incl: (songs) Four Canadian Cowboy Songs, for baritone & piano; The Fairies Song, for soprano & alto; Christmas Carol, soprano & piano; Sunset,I soprano & piano, or harp; I Got Me Flowers, soprano & piano, or harp; When I am Dead, soprano & piano; (sacred songs) Psalm I, Psalm 150, Courage, for voice & organ, or piano; River of Life, An Evening Hymn; (pianoforte music) Little Boy Dances-African Suite, Indian Suite, American Suite, & English Suite; (instmntl. music) Winsome's Folly, Suite No. 1 for oboe, clarinet, horn & bassoon, & Suite No. 2 for Flute, oboe, clarinet, horn, bassoon; Suite for Horn & Orch.; var. choral music & recorded music. Whimsy for brass bands; Concerto for 4 brass bands. Contbr. to all English Musical Mags. & daily papers. Mbrships: CGGB; PRS. Hons: Dartington Open Scholarship, 1951. Hobbies: Motoring; Swimming; Marionettes. Address: Gramercy House, 12 Northfield Rd., One House, Stowmarket, Suffolk, UK. 3.

BUTTERLEY, Nigel Henry, b. 13 May 1935. Sydney, Aust. Composer; Pianist; Lectr. in Contemporary Music, Newcastle Conserv. Compositions publd: First Str. Quartet, 1965; Meditations of Thomas Traherne (orch.), 1968; Second Str. Quartet, 1974; Violin Concerto, 1970; Watershore, 1977. Noctures for 4 Doublebasses, 1978. Compositions publd. & recorded: Laudes, 1963; In the Head the Fire, 1966; Explorations for Piano & Orch., 1970; Letter from Hardy's Bay, 1971; First Day Covers (w. Barry Humphries), 1973. Hons: Italia Prize for radiophonic comp. for In the Head the Fire, 1966. Address: 57 Temple Street, Stanmore, NSW 2048, Aust.

BUTTERWORTH, Arthur Eckersley, b. 4 Aug. 1923. New Moston, Manchester, UK. Composer; Conductor; Teacher. Educ: Royal Manchester Coll. of Scottish Nat. Orch., 1951. Career: Freelance Cond., 1965-; Num. broadcasts as cond. of BBC Orch.; Tchr. of Comp. & Orchestration; Currently Perm. Cond., Huddersfield Phil. Soc.; Musical Dir., Nat. Youth Brass Band of GB. Comps. incl: Music for Brass Bands & Orch.; Song Cycles; Chmbr. Works; Educl. Music, 3 Symphs.; violin, organ concertos. Some recordings of Brass Band & Choral Music. Publs: Scoring for Brass Band, 1978. Contbr. to profl. jrnls. Mbrships: ISM; Comps. Guild of GB. Hobbies: Country-living; Animals (Mbr. RSPCA); Steam Trains. Address: 'Pohjola', 11 Dales Ave., Embsay, Skipton, Yorks BD23 6PE, UK. 1, 28.

BUTTERWORTH, David Neil, b. 1934. London, UK. Conductor; Composer; Lecturer; Writer. Educ: Nottingham Univ.; London Univ.; GSM; studied horn w. Ian Berrs & Francis Bradley; BA; MA. m. Anna Barnes, 3 d. Career: Fndr. & Cond., Erato Orch., 1959-; Lectr., Kingston Coll. of Further Educ., 1964-68; Second. Schls. Choir, 1970-; Dir., of Music, Edinburgh Coll. of Commerce, 1968-; Hd., Music Dept., Napier Coll., Edinburgh, 1968-; cond., Glasgow Orchl., Soc., 1975-. Comps. incl: Rumplestiltzkin (musical fairy tale); 3 Orchestral Pieces; Horn Concerto; Summer Music for Strings; Kettlebury Hill for oboe & orch.; Ghost Cantata; The Bluebird Line; num. instrumental pieces & songs; incidental music for plays. Publs: 400 Aural Training Exercises; The Symphonic Works of Aaron Copland; A Musical Quiz Book; A Musical Anthology; Short History of American Music; Haydn; Dvorak. Recip. of Conducting Prize, GSM. Hobbies incl: Collecting Records &

Books; Hellenic Studies; Bonfires; Jigsaw Puzzles. Address: 24 Napier Rd., Edinburgh EH 19 5AY, UK. 3.

BUTTRESS, Edward Crossley, b. 18 Feb. 1910. Cullen, Scotland, UK. Research Chemist (Retired); Musician (French Horn); Teacher; Adjudicator; Festival Organiser; Educ: Manchester Coll. of Technol.; FVCM. 2 s. Career: Cond., Northern Military Band, 1937-39; Musical Dir., Clayton Aniline Works Band, 1945-56; Musical Dir., Eccles Borough Band, 1956-65; Tutor in Brass, Manchester Educ., 1956-; Musical Dir. & Mgr., NW Area Youth Band, 1963-; Organiser, Nat. & Regional Brass Band Festivals, 1968-; Profl. Coach, many other Bands inclng. Argyll & Sutherland Highlanders (Bonnybridge) Band, Crewkerne Youth, Radcliffe Borough; Adjudicator (Instrumental), GB & Europe; Cond., num. Bands in TV & Radio perfs. Publs: Managing Dir. & Ed., British Mouthpiece (Weekly Brass Band jrnl.). Contbr. to brass band jrnls. Mbrships: Nat. Coun. Brass Bands Assns. (Gen. Sec.); British Fedn. Brass Bands (VP); NW Area Brass Bands Assn. (VP & Chmn.). Recip., Silver Medal, Worshipful Co. of Musicians, London. Address: 60 Whalley House, Wood Road, Manchester M16 9RL, UK. 1.

BUTTREY, John, b. 16 Aug. 1931. Sydney, Aust. Singer. Educ: MusB, Univ. Cambridge, 1962; MA, ibid., 1965; PhD, ibid., 1967; NSW Conservatorium of Music; Pvte. tuition w. Roy Henderson. Career: Concert singer & mbr. of Daller Consort; Singing apps. all over Europe; Toured w. Deller Consort in USA, S Am. & Israel; Broadcast talks on Engl. theatre music for BBC; Devised recordings of music & poetry for Purcell Consort of Voices. Recordings incl: Purcell, The Fairy Queen; Num. recording of madrigals & ch. music. Contbr. to num. profl. mags. inclng: Music & Letters. Mbrships: Elgar Soc.; ISM; Royal Musical Assn. Hobby: Musicol. Address: 34 Disraeli Gdns., Bective Rd., London SW15, UK.

BYERS, Harold, b. 16 Aug. 1944. Portland, Ore., USA. Violinist; Baroque Violinist. Educ: BMus, Oberlin Coll. Conserv.; Juilliard Schl.; Studies w. David Cerone, Paul Makanowitzky, Ivan Galamian. m. Dorothy Furber Byers. Career: Cazenovia, Atlanta & Columbus String Quartets; Chmbr. Symph. of Phila.; Atlanta & Cinn. Symphs.; Baroque Chmbr. Players; Bellermine Piano Trio. Hobbies: Photography; Bicycling; Hi Fidelity. Address: 854 rue de la Paix B6, Cinn., OH 45220, USA.

BYNUM, Raymond Tapley, b. 14 Aug. 1906. Springdale, Ark., USA. High School & College Band Director & Teacher; Flautist. Educ: BA, Hardin Simmons Univ.; BMus, ibid.; DMus (hon.), Okla City Univ. m. Mary Catherine Adamson. 2 s., 2 d. Career: tchr., band dir., Abilene High Schl., 1926-46; Prof. of music & Dir. of bands. McMurry Coll., 1946-72; approx. 50 concert tours incl. Europe (1955), Mexico (1964, '71); adjudicator & clinician; now guest cond. & cons. in Abilene area. Contbr. of num. articles on teaching methods to Texas Music Educator & other jrnls. Mbrships: Texas Music Educators Assn. (past pres.); Texas Bandmasters Assn. (past pres.); Am. Bandmasters Assn. Hons: Texas Bandmaster of the Year, 1968; Phi Beta Mu Hall of Fame, 1978; num. other hons. Hobbies: Rose Culture; Chess. Address: 1501 North 14th, Abilene, TX 79601, USA. 7.

BYRNE, Andrew William Arthur, b. 12 Mar. 1925. London, UK. University Teacher. Educ: Royal Acad. of Music; DMus (Lond.); FRAM. m. Celia Swann, 3 d. Career: Prof., RAM, 1954-66; Lectr. in Music, Reading Univ., 1965-; Sr. Lectr. ibid, 1974-. Compositions (Publd.): Suite for clarinet & piano; 2 pieces for clarinet & piano; 3 Bagatelles for flute & piano; 4 pieces for oboe & piano; Suite for 3 equal-pitch instruments. Publs: Contributions to Assoc. Board Graded Wind Music Series. Mbrships: ISM until 1974; Composers Guild; Brit. Fedn. of Music Fests. Hons. incl: Charles Lucas Prize; Wm. Wallace Exhib. Address: Manor Cottage, Burghfield, Reading, Berks. RG3 3TG, UK. 4.

BYRNE, Peter, b. 21 Nov. 1932. Grimsby, Lincs., UK. Director of Music; Organist & Choirmaster (Piano, Viola, organ). Educ: BMus, Univ. of London, Goldsmiths' Coll.; ARCM. m. Anne Josephine Lavery, 1 s., 2 d. Career: Mbr. Nat. Youth Orch. (viola) 1949-51; Music Tchr., Cardinal Wiseman Schl., Ealing, 1959-64; Organist & Choirmaster, Ch. of Holy Ghost & St. Stephen, Shepherds Bush, London, 1960-63; Organist & Choirmaster, St. Benedict's Abbey, Ealing, 1963-68; Dir. of Music, Salvatorian Coll., Harrow, 1965-; Musical Dir., Cecilian Players, Ealing, 1969-74; Mbr., RMA. Hobbies: Langs.; Travel; Hist.; Archaeol. Address: 27 Lancaster Gdns., Ealing, London W13 9JY, UK. 3. 28, 4.

C

CAAMANO, Roberto, b. 7 July 1923, Buenos Aires, Argentina. Composer; Pianist. Educ: Nat. Conserv. of Buenos Aires, 1939-46; Prof. Superior de Piano; Prof. de Comp. m. María Teresa Stafforini, 4 children. Career: Pianist, 1944-; Concerts throughout Argentina, USA, Spain, Italy, Switzerland. Germany, sev. Latin Am. counties. Comps. incl: Mafnificat; 1st Piano Concerto; Music for Strings; Quintet; Cantata de la Paz; Tripartita; Harp Concerto. Recordings incl: Magnificat; Suite for String Orch. Author, The History of the Teatro Colón, 3 vols., 1969. Mbr. var. profl. orgs. Recip. many hons. Hobbies: Gardening; Linguistics. Mgmt: Barry Editorial SRL, Talcahuano 860, Buenos Aires, Argentina. Address: Jusan B Alberdi 1275, Buenos Aires 1406, Argentina.

CABALLÉ, Montserrat, b. 12 Apr. 1933, Barcelona, Spain. Opera & Concert Singer. Educ: Conserv. del Liceo, Barcelona; studied w. Eugenia Kemeny. m. Bernabé Marti, 1 s., 1 d. Debut: Carnegie Hall, as Lucrezia Borgia, 1965. Career: Apps. at Covent Garden, Glyndebourne, Metropolitan (NY), La Scala, Mexico City & ldng. opera houses throughout the world; roles incl. Maria Stuarda, Luisa Miller, Violetta (La Traviata), Norma, Marguerite (Faust) & Desdemona (Otello); apps. on radio & TV. num. recordings. Hons: Cross of Lazo de Dama, Order of Isabel the Catholic, Spain. Mgmt: Columbia Artists Mgmt., Inc., 165 W 57th St., NY, NY 10019, USA.

CABLE, Howard Reid, b. 15 Dec. 1920, Toronto, Can. Conductor; Composer; Arranger; Musical Director; Producer. Educ: Assoc., Royal Conserv. of Music, Toronto, 1939; Degree in conducting & bandmastership. m. (1) Dawn Darroch (div.), 2 s., 2 d., (2) Marie Pendleton Gauley (Div., 1 step d., (3) Peggy Feltmate, 1973. Career incls: Composer of incidental music, CBC Radio & TV, 1941-; Dir. of Musical Progs. 1942- Cond., Howard Cable Concert Band, 1952-. Compositions incl: (publs.) Newfoundland Rhapsody, concert band, 1956; Stratford Suite, concert band, 1964; These Things Shall Be, chorus & orch., 1968; Sea to Sea, score, 1968. Recordings incl: Sea to Sea, 1968. Mbr. var. profl. orgs. Hobbies: Hiking; Boating; Reading. Address: 18 Prideaux St., PO Box 810, Niagara-on-the-Lake, Ont., Can. 2.

CÁCERES, Oscar, b. 4 Apr. 1928, Montevideo, Uruguay. Guitarist. Debut: 1941. Career: 1st European Tour, 1957; Musical Researcher; Concerts given in France, England, Spain, Germany, Belgium, Norway, Turkey, 1967; Soloist, var. rests.; Tchr., Master Class, Int. Music Fest. of Annecy, 1969-; Tchr., Int. Music Univ., Paris, 1969-. Recordings: Great Studies for Guitar, 2 vols.; Leo Brouwer by Oscar Cáceres; Music for 2 Guitars (w. Turibio Santos); Latinoamerican Recital. Author, Oscar Cáceres Collection. Mgmt: Raymond de Saint-Ours, Paris; Basil Douglas, London. Address: 138 Bis Rue léon Maurice Nordmann, 75013 Paris, France.

CADDY, Ian Graham, b. 1 Mar. 1947, Southampton, UK. Baritone. Educ: RAM, 1965-70; LRAM; ARCM. Debut: London, 1974. Career: Opera for All; Lent Opera; New Opera Co.; Phoenix Opera; Glyndebourne; Engl. Nat. Opera; opera, oratorio, recitals throughout GB, also Austria, Wexford & Versailles Fest; Eng. Nat. Opera; Denmark, Eire, France, Germany; Netherlands, Yugoslavia; ITV; RTV, Yugoslavia; BBC TV & radio; Danish Radio; Radio Oslo; Radio Eireann; Yugoslav Radio. Recordings incl: L'Amor Coniugale Mayr; Jigs-Reele & Songs of the Bottle, Holbrooke; Vivaldi's Dixit Dominus. Hons. incl: Ricordi Prize, 1967; Vaughan Williams Trust Award, 1969; Countess of Munster Musical Trust Award, 1970; RAM Pres. Prize, 1970. Hobbies: Paino; Photogr£aphy. Mgmt: Ibbs & Tillett, London. Address: 8 Cosway Mansions, London NW1, UK.

CADENHEAD, Elizabeth Margaret Gay, b. 8 Nov. 1936, Aberdeen, Scotland. UK. Teacher. Educ: Dip. Musical Educ., Royal Scottish Acad. of Music; Further tchr. trng., Aberdeen Coll. Educ. Career: Prin. tcht. of music, Milne's HS, Fochabers; Ch. Organist & Choir mistress, St. James' Ch., Lossiemouth; Former conductor, Keith Phil. Choir. Contbr. to: News bulletin for inclusion in Church Music Quarterly for Scottish Affiliated Chs. Mbrships: Incorp. Soc. of Musicians (HLR Inverness Br.); Scottish Committee, RSCM; Music convenor, Moray Arts Club; Moray Music Festival Committee. Hobbies: Field Club Activities; Gardening; Recorder playing; Madrigal Ensemble Singing. Address: 8 Woodside Rd., Fochabers, Moray, IV32 7HD, UK.

CADUFF, Sylvia, b. 7 Jan. 1938, Chur, Switz. Orchestra Conductor; Professor of Conducting & Orchestral Studies; Bern Conservatory. Educ: Piano Dip., Lucerne Conserv.; studies w. Herbert von Karajan, Berlin Conserv.; studies conducting in Lucerne, Salzburg & Hilversum s. Karajan, Kubelik, Matacic & Otterloo. Debut: w. Tonhalle-Orchester, Zürich. Career: Guest Cons., Switz., Germany, Scandinavia, UK, Yugoslavia & USA w. var. orchs. inclng. Munich Phil., RSO Berlin, RPO (London), NY Phil. Orch. Mbrships: Swiss Musicians Assn.; Swiss Conds. Union. Hons. incl: 1st Prize, Mitropoulos Competition, NY, USA. Mgmt:' Konzertgesellschaft GmbH, Zürich, Switz. Address: Belleriverstrasse 31, 6006 Lucerne, Switz.

CAFFAGNI, Mirko, b. 16 Aug. 1934, Modena, Italy. Technical Manager of Tile Manufacturing Plant. Educ: Degree, Electrotech. Engrng., 1961; Autodidact in lute playing; Studied Musicology, Univ. Bologna. m. Paola Soffritti, 2 children. Career: Lute or Solo Player in about 100 concerts in var. Italian Consorts of Early Music. Publs: Ed. of Capricci armonici sopra la Chitarriglia Spagnuola di Gio Battista Granata. Modena, Berben, 1962; Lute & Chitarrone, tablature of Alessandro Piccinini (libre primo 1623). Contbr. to profl. jrnls. Mbrships: Societa Italiana di Musicologia; Societa Italiana del Flauto Dolce; Antiquae Musicae Italicae Studiosi, Bologna. Hobbies: Agriculture; Oenology. Address: Sassuolo (Moderna); Viale della pace 96, Italy.

CAGE, John, b. 5 Sept. 1912, Los Angeles, Calif., USA. Composer; Author; Artist. Educ: Pomona Coll.; Study of composition, harmony & counterpoint w. Buhlig, Weiss, Schoenbert & Cowell. m. Xenia Andreyevna Kashevaroff, 1935 (div. 1945). Career: Tchr. of Composition, New Schl. for Soc. Rsch., NYC, 1955-60; Musical Dir., Merce Cunningham & Dance Co., ibid, 1944-68; Fellow, Ctr. for Adv. Studies, Wesleyan Univ., 1960-61; Vis. Rsch. Prof., Schl. of Music, Univ. of Ill., 1967-69; Artist in Residence, Univ. of Calif., Davis, 1969. Compositions incl: The Seasons (ballet), 1949; Atlas Eclipticalis (Commnd. for Montreal Festival), 1961. Publs. incl: The Life & Works of Virgil Thomson (co-author), 1958; Silence, 1961; A Year from Monday, 1967; Notations, Not Wanting to Say Anything About Marcel. Hons. incl: Guggenheim Fellow, 1949. Address: 107 Bank St., NY, NY 10014, USA.

CAHILL, Teresa Mary, b. 30 July 1944, Maidenhead, UK. Singer (Lyric Soprano). Educ: AGSM (Piano); LRAM (Singing); London Opera Ctr. m. John A Kiernander. Debut: Glyndebourne, 1970; Covent Gdn., 1970. Career: Opera: Glyndebourne, Eng. Nat., Covent Gdn.; Dabut at La Scala, Milan, 1976; Concerts incl: Edinburgh Festival; Proms.; RFH; w. all London Orchs.; Boston Symph. Orch.; Halle, RLPO, Danish Radio Orch.; Stockholm Phil.; BBC Orchs. Num. recordings. Mbrships: ISM; Equity. Hons: Silver Medal, Worshipful Co. of Musicians, 1966; John Christie Award, Glyndebourne, 1970. Hobbies: Photography; Arts; Cooking; Collecting Antique Furniture. Mgmt: Ingpen Williams, Ltd. Address: 65 Leyland Rd., London SE 12, UK.

CAIMI, Florentino J, b. 11 Aug. 1943, Ridgway, Pa., USA. Band Director; College Instructor. Educ: BSMusEd, Mansfield State Coll., Pa., 1964; MA, 1969, DEd cand., Pa. State Univ. m. Carol C Caimi, 1 s., 1 d. Career: Performing profl. musician & cond., 1960-; Vocal & Instrumental Music Tchr., Jersey Shore Schl. Dist., 1964-66; Supvsr. of Music, Instrumental Music Tchr., Muncy, Pa. Schl. Dist., 1967-73; on staff, Clarion Coll. summer band camp, 1973-74; Cond. of Band & Instr., Lock Haven State Coll., 1973-. Co-Author, Literature & Materials Guide to Instrumental Music, 1974. Contbr. to: The Instrumentalist. Mbrships: incl: Coll. Band Dirs. Nat. Assn.; Nat. Band Assn. Recip. acad. hons. Address: 300 Frederick St., Flemington, PA 17745, USA.

CAIN, David, b. 18 Oct. 1941, Stoke-on-Trent, UK. Composer. Educ: BSc, London Univ. m. Marianne Cain, 1 d. Career: Comp./Prod., BBC Radiophonic Workshop, 1965-74; Comp.-in-Res., Cumbria Educ. Committee, 1974-76. Comps. incl: Incidental music for BBC radio drama inclng. The Hobbit, War of the Worlds, Much Ado About Nothing, & Prometheus Bound; Forbidden Fruit, for tenor & guitar; Cantata for Guitar; Moses, opera for schl. orch. & brass band w. soloists & chorus. Recordings incl: Music for Four Radio Plays; The Magnificent Eleven. Mbrships: Comps. Guild; Performing Rights Soc. Hobbies incl: Cond.; Cockermouth Mechs. Brass Band. Address: Prospect House, Kirkgate, Cockermouth, Cumbria, UK.

CAIN, James Nelson, b. 6 Jan. 1930, Arcadia, Ohio, USA. Orchestra Manager. Educ: BA, Ohio State Univ.; Pvte. studies, piano, violin & cello. m. Marthellen Jones, 2 s., 2 d. Career: Fndr.-Mbr., Prestige Concerts, Columbus, Ohio, 1948-62; Exec. Dir., Aspen (Colo.) Music Fest. & Schl., 1962-68; Asst Mgr., St. Louis Symph. Orch., 1968-71; Mgr., ibid., 1971-. Contbr. to Columbus Citizen. Address: 718 N Grand Blvd., St. Louis, MO 63103, USA. 6.

CAIRD, George, b. 30 Aug. 1950, Montreal, Can. Oboist. Educ: Peterhouse, Cambridge, 1973-76; BA (Cantab.); RAM, 1969-72; LRAM; ARCM; Nordwestduetsche Musikakademie, Detmold, 1972-73. m. Sarah Verney, 2 s. Career: Oboist w. London Baroque Soloists, Albion Ensemble, Vega Wind Quintet, Claydon Ensemble, Pelican Trio. mbr., ISM. Hobbies: Silence; Caldling. Mgmt: Basil Douglas Ltd., London. Address: 2 Berkeley Pl., London SW19 4NN, UK.

ČAKSTE, Aija, b. 6 Jan. 1924, Riga, Latvia. Pianist. Educ: Coll. of Riga; Studied w. G Boon, Stockholm; Conservatoire, Riga. Debut: Stockholm, 1951. Career: Concerts in Latvia, Scandinavia & W Gemany. Address: Nackrosvaj 28, 17131 Solna, Sweden.

CALAME, Blaise, b. 1922, Geneva, Switzerland. Violinist. Educ: Polytech. Schl., Zürich; Royal Conserv. of Brussels; studied w. Carl Flesch, Leon Nauwinck, Georges Enescu, & Zino Frandescatti. m. Genevieve Griaule, 1 s., 1 d. Career: has given concerts in all musical ctrs. of Europe; made world tour in 1962-63; tours USA yearly; has app. at fests. in Venice, Dubrovnik, Aix-en-Provence, Carthage, Stradivari, Stresa, etc.; toured Japan & S Am., 3 times each, also China; plays Stradivarius of 1722 (The Mendelssohn); involved in acoustical rsch.; inventor of Calacoustic. Hons: 1st Prize for Violin; 1st Prize for Chmbr. Music; Harriet Cohen Musical Award; Ysaÿe Gold Medal. Hobby: Owning Rolls Royce. Address: 8, rue Gay-Lussac, Paris éme, France. 3.

CALDER, David Lewis, b. 2 Sept. 1945, Dunedin, NZ. Composer; Songwriter; Instrumentalist. Educ: MA (French Lit.) Auckland Univ.; mainly self-taught musically. m. Fran Campbell, 1 s. Debut: in Princess Ida, aged 9. Career: Country musician & entertainer in all NZ media, 1967-70; folk musician, UK, 1971. Comps: all exist as taped perfs.; music for NZ films; Partita in C minor for Whales & Humans. Mbrships: Comps. Assn. of NZ; Charter mbr., Aerial Railway Music Cooperative Inc. Hons: winner, Australasian Performing Rights Assn. Rock Comps. Award, 1977. Address: Moehau Community, Port Charles RD, Coromandel, NZ.

CALDWELL, Bruce, b. 23 Aug. 1941, Tacoma, Wash., USA. Music Educator; Professional Trombonist, Pianist. Educ: BMusEd, Standard Gen. Tchng. Cert., Univ. of Wash. m. Jo Perella, 3 children. Career: Prin. Trombonist, Seattle World's Fair Band, 1962; Ldr. & Pianist, Bruce Caldwell Dance Orch., 1958-70; Dir. of Bands, Madrona Jr. HS, Edmonds, Wash., 1964-70; Asst. Dir., Univ. of Wash. Marching Band, 1965-; Dir. of Bands, Woodway Sr. HS, Edmonds, 1967-. Records, Wash. Marching Band, Woodway HS Bands. Contbr. to Lyre. Mbrships: MENC; Chmn., Wash. All-State Band, Wash. Music Educators Assn.; NEA; Am. Fedn. of Musicians; Advsr. Husky Marching Band Alumni Assn., Univ. of Wash. Hons: Woodway HS Band apps. incl. Truth or Consequences TV show, Nixon Inaugural Parade, Walt Disney World, Spokane World Fair. Hobby: Swimming. Address: 739 14th Way SW, Edmonds, WA 98020, USA.

CALDWELL, John Anthony, b. 6 July 1938, Bebington, Cheshire, UK. University Lecturer (Organ, Harpsichord). Educ: BA, 1960, BMus, 1961, DPhil, 1965, Keble Coll., Oxford; Liverpool Matthay Schl. of Music; FRCO, 1957. m. Janet Susan Kellar, 1 s., 1 d. Career: Asst. Lectr., Bristol Univ., 1963-66; Univ. Lectr., Oxford Univ., 1966-; Fellow, Keble Coll., Oxford, 1967-. Recordings: Machaut, Mass (organ part). Publs: Ed., Early Tudor Organ Music, vol. 1, 1966; English Keyboard Music Before the Nineteenth Century; Medieval Music. Contbr. to: Music & Letters; Musical Times; Organ Yearbook; Early Music; Grove's Dict., 6th Ed. Mbrships: Coun., Plainsong & Medieval Music Soc. Address: 23 Squitchey Lane, Oxford, UK.

CALLAGHAN, Jean, b. 4 Mar. 1942, Sydney, Aust. Mezzo Soprano Singer; Researcher. Educ: BA, Univ. of WA; LMusA; FTCL. Career: Soloist in opera, oratorio, concert & radio in Perth, WA; pvte. singing tchr.; rsch. on writings on vocal technique & on influence of language of nat. musical style. Contbr. to Aust. Jrnl. for Music Educ. Mbrships: Inaugural Pres., Mastersingers Guild, WA; Aust. Musicol. Soc.; Aust. Soc. for Music Educ. Address: 20 Crescent Ln., London SW4, UK.

CALLAHAN, James Patrick, b. 15 Jan. 1942, Fargo, ND, USA. Teacher (piano, organ, music theory); Performer (piano, organ); Composer. Educ: BA, St. John's Univ., Minn., 1964; Vianna Acad. of Music; Salzburg Mozarteum; MFA (piano), PhD (comp.), Univ. Minn. Career: 3 organ recitals at St. Thomas Ch., 5th Ave., NYC; The Organ Music of James Callahan performed by comp., radio prog. Minn. Pub. Radio Network; Yrly. apps. on Pvte. coll. Concert Series, 1968-75 (pinao & organ), KTCA-TV. Comps. incl: Parish Worship (choir, congregation & organ), 1966; Variations for Organ, 1974. Recording: Handel: St. John Passion, Gregorian Inst. of Am. No. EL-32 (organist). Contbr. to

Piano Quarterly. Mbr. of Minn. Comps. Forum. Address: Music Dept., Coll. of St. Thomas, St. Paul, MN 55101, USA.

CALLAWAY, Frank Adams, b. 16 May 1919, Timaru, NZ. Professor of Music; Head, Department of Music; Conductor; Administrator; Examiner. Educ: Dunedin Tchrs. Coll.; Univ. of Otago; Royal Acad. of Music, London; TCL; MusB, Univ. of NZ; FRAM; FTCL; ARCM. Career incls: Hd., Music Dept., King Edward Tech. Coll., Dunedin, 1942-53; Rdr. in Music, Univ. of WA, Aust., 1953-59; Fndn. Prof. of Music & Hd., Dept. of Music, bid., 1959-; Mbr., Orchs. of NZ Broadcasting Corp.; Guest Cond., Nat. Symph. Orch. of NZ, WA Symph. Orch., SA Symph. Orch., Manila Symph. Orch.; Permanent Cond., WA Univ. Choral Soc., 1953-, WA Orch., 1953-64. Ed. & Fndr., Studies in Music, & The Aust. Jrnl. of Music Educ.; Gen. Ed., Challenges in Music Educ., Jt. Ed., Australian Composition in the Twentieth Century; Gen. Ed., Music Series, Monographs, etc. Mbrships. incl: Int. Soc. for Music Educ., Bd. of Dirs., 1958-, Pres., 1968-72; Treas., 1972-. Hons. incl: Hon. DMus, Univ. of WA; Fellow, Aust. Coll. of Educ.; Fndn. Chmn., WA Arts Coun.; OBE, 1970; CMG, 1975. Address: 31 Langham St., Nedlands, WA 6009, Aust.

CALONNE, Jacques, b. 10 Aug. 1930, Mons, Belgium. Composer; Painter; Poet. Educ: 1944-45 Mons Conserv.; 1945-46 Brussels Royal Conserv.; 1946-49 Music Acad. Etterbeek; 1954 Darmstadt, Int. Holiday Course w. Pierre Boulex and Karl Heinz Stockhausen; 1947-49 Brussels Royal Art Acad. Comps. incl: Mutations, for 2 and 5 pianos, 1972-75, Paris, 1976; Incomplete, for violoncello, and 12 other soloists, 1973; 3 Works for film. Mbrrships: Art group COBRA, 1949-51. Contbr. to: var. profl. jrnls. Hons: Comp. Prize Darmstadt, 1962; Invitation to live one year in Berlin, DAAD (Berlin Artist Program), 1972-73. Hobbies: Songs by Salon, from his Boarding school repertory. Address: Rue Lebeau, 59, B-1000 Brussels, Belgium.

CALVERT, Morley Frederick, b. 11 June 1928, Brantford, Ont. Can. Teacher. Educ: BMus (music educ.), McGill Univ.; AMus (trumpet perf.), ibid.; LRSM (piano tchr.). m. Olga Stathatos, 1 s., 2 d. Career: 22 yrs. tchng. instrumental music in Montreal, Can., high schls.; 7 yrs. at Barrie Ctrl. Collegiate, Barrie, Ont.; Hd., instrumental music dept., Barrie Ctr. Collegiate. Comps: 14 works for brass band; Introduction, Elegy & Caprice; Romantic Variations; A Song for Out Time (Band & chorus); Suite from the Monteregian Hills, for brass quintet (recorded); An Occasional Suite, for brass quintet; 3 Dance Impressions, for brass quintet. Mbrships: Am. Bandmasters Assn.; CAPAC. Hon: subject of TV prog. on The Music of Morley Calvert, 1975. Hobbies: Painting; Golf; Skiing. Address: 11 Campfire Ct., Barrie, Ont. L4M 5Gz9, Can.

CAMAJANI, Giovanni, b. 5 May 1915, New York City, USA. Conductor; Pianist accompanist; Coach. Educ: BС (Music), NY Univ., 1937; MA, ibid., 1941; PhD, 1916; FTOL, 1945. m. Margaret Alma Chase, 1 s., 1 d. Career: Am. Asst., Verona Opera Festival, Italy; Guest Cond., Tuskegee Choir, Ala.; Assoc. Prof., Hd. of Vocal Dept., San Fran. State Univ.'s Opera Repertory Theatre; Assoc. Cond., Pacific Opera Co., San Fran.; Cond., Bach Cir., LA; Fndr.-Dir., Schola Cantorum & Brass Ensemble of San Fran.; collaborator w. Pierre Monteux, presentations of San Fran. Symph.; Cond. of num. Am. premiers w. Mbrs. of San Fran. Symph. Recordings: Music of Ernest Bascon. Contbrng. Ed., Ency. Americana, 1945-50. Contbr. to: Ramparts; Music Mag.; Grove's Dictionary; Liturgical Arts Quarterly; Quondom Mbr., Soc. Geografica Italian; AAAS; Medieval Acad. of Am.; Phi Delta Kappa. Recip. var. grants & schlrships. Hobbies: Theatre; Trave; Art; Books. Address: 124 Presidio Ave., San Fran., CA 94115, USA. 12.

CAMBISSA, Giorgio, b. 17 May 1921, Bodio, Switz. Composer; Conductor; Director; Artistic Director. Educ: Doctor of Arts; Master of Comp. m. Sonia Marmolja, 1 c. Career: Collaborated in G Verdi Theatre, Trieste; Cond.; Tchr., Genoa, Parma, Milan; Dir. of Conserv. C Monteverdi, Bolzano, Italy; Artistic Dir., F Busoni Int. Piano Competition. Comps: (Theatre) Favola Bella Bella Addormen; (Ballet) Tata; (Ochl.) Cinque Pezzi; Four Concertos; Concerto for Trio & Orch.; Rapsodia Greca; Concerto Breve for Cello & Orch.; Piccola Cantata; Chmbr. music. Publs: Armonia Complementare, 1957; Elementi di Analisi Formale, 1957. Hons: 1st Prize, Comp., Reine Elisabeth, 1961, etc. Address: Piazza Domenicani 25 I, 39100 Bolzano, Italy.

CAMDEN, Anthony J, b. 26 Apr. 1938, London, UK. Oboist. Educ: RCM; ARCM; FGSM. m. Diane Camden, 1 s., 1 d. Career: Fndr. Mbr., London Virtuosi, 1972-; Prin. Oboe, Northern Sinfonia orch., City of Birmingham Symph. Orch., & LSO, 1974-; Chmn., Bd. of Dirs., LSO, 1975-. Recordings: Grace Williams Oboe Concerto (w. LSO under Sir Charles Groves); Honneger Concerto for cor anglais & flute; Haydn Divertisseme for solo oboe & strings; Mozart Oboe Quartet; Eleman Trio (w. James Galway). Publs: Spare time for Music-Woodwind Section. Recip. Sullivan Prize, RCM, 1960. Hobby: Cricket. Address: Birchwood, Barnet Ln., London N20, UK.

CAMERON, Alexander, b. 25 Mar. 1922, Dundee, Scotland, Cellist. Educ: LRAM; FRAM. m. Elizabeth Lawson, 1 s., 2 d. Career: Prin. Cellist, Royal Opera House Orch., Covent Gdn.; Prin. Cellist, LPO, 1963-. Recip., prizes, RAM. Hobby: Golf. Address: 43 Tybenham Rd., Merton Pk., London SW19, UK. 3.

CAMERON, Alexandra Esther, b. 8 Feb. 1910, Qld., Aust. Pianist; Music Educator; Administrator. Educ: BMus, Univ. of Melbourne; BEd., MEd., Univ. of Melbourne. Career: music tchr. in secondary schls; Lectr. in methods of class teaching of music, Univ. of Melbourne; Inspector of Music for secondary schls., Educ. Dept., Melbourne, 1963-73; org. sec., Melbourne Youth Music Coun.; hon. mgr., Melbourne Youth Orch.; hon. org. sec., Aust. Youth Music Fest. Publs: Music Appreciation for Australian Schools, 1958; Singing Together, 1965. Contbr. to profl. jrnls. Mbrships. incl: Aust. Soc. for Music Educ. (fndn. life mbr.); Vic. Music Tchrs. Assn. (life mbr.); Aust. Strng. Assn.; Aust. Coll. of Educ.; Aust. Fed. of Univ. Women; Lyceum Club, Melbourne. Hons: MBE, 1979; sev. scholarships. Hobbies incl: Reading; Writing; Travel; Work among Young People Through Music. Address: 1/21 Yerrin St., Balwyn, Vic. 3103, Aust.

CAMERON, Archie André, b. 22 Dec. 1957, Greensboro, NC, USA. Violist. Educ: Dip. in Viola, NC Schl. of Arts, 1976; studied violin w. Julie Kohl & viola w. Victor Stern, Eastern Music Fest., & viola w. Sally Peck & Paul Doktor, NC Schl. of Arts. Debut: Basilica Santa Francesca Romano, Rome, Italy, 1977. Career: Former Mbr., Greensboro NC Symph.; Mo. Symph. Soc. Chmbr. Orch., 1978; Perf. in major centres of Am. & Italy; Mbr. of orch. of L'Opera di Teatro Regio, Torino, Italy, 1978-. Hons: Winner, 1977 Rome Fest. Orch. Concerto Competition. Mbrships: Bd. of Dirs., Eastern Music Fest.; Am. Symph. Orch. League. Recip. scholarships. Hobbies: Running; Swimming; Dancing. Address: 1002 Julian St., Greensboro, NC 27406, USA. 28.

CAMERON, John, b. Coolamon, NSW, Aust. Baritone Singer; Tchr. Educ: Syney Conservatorium of Music; AMusA Dip. m. Patricia Cameron. Debut: Germont, La Traviata, Covent Gdn., 1949. Career: Prin. Singer, Covent Gdn., Glydebourne, Sadlers Wells & German opera houses; radio & TV broadcasts in oratorio & opera; Recitalist; Int. Concert Singer; Sn. Lectr., Royal Northern Coll. of Music, Manchester. Num. recordings inclng: Mendelssohn, Elijah; Vaughan Williams, Sea Symphony; Handel, Solomon; Berlioz, L'Enfance du Christ; Purcell, King Arthur; Walton, Belshazzar's Feast; Elgar, Dream of Gerontius; Mozart Mass No. 14, in C Major; Gay, Beggar's Opera; major Gilbert & Sullivan operas; etc. Mbrships: Fndr. Mbr. & Pres., Aust. Musical Assn. Hobbies: Motoring; Chess. Address: Lindum Lodge, 13 Stamford Rd., Bowdon, Altrincham, Cheshire, UK. 3, 28.

CAMILLERI, Charles Mario, b. 7 Sept. 1931, Hamrun, Malta. Composer; Conductor. Educ: BMus, Univ. of Toronto, Can. m. Doris Vella, 1 s., 1 d. Comps. publd. & recorded: Missa Mundi; Piano Trio; Mantra; Taqsim; Hemda Etudes; Times of Day; Maqam; Cosmic Visions; Ritual Meditations. Recordings: Vista; Argo. Contbr. to: Musical Opinion; Organists' Review; etc. Mbr., Comps. Guild of GB. Recip., num. hons. Hobbies: Fishing; Walking; Swimming. Mgmt.: Ruth Ticher, London. Address: Villa L'ghana, St. May's St., San Pawl, Tat-Targa, Malta.

CAMMAROTA, Lionello, b. 6 Sept. 1941, Naples, Italy. Musicologist. Educ: laureate of letters, Univ. of Rome; studied comp. w. father & Renator Parodi & conducting w. Franco Ferrara & Igor Markevitch. m. Marisa de Paoli, 1 c. Career: Lect. in Hist. of Music, Nat. Acad. of Dramatic Art, S D'Amico, Rome, 1966-73, subsequently at Conserv., S. Cecilia, Rome. Publs: L'Espressionismo e Schönberg, 1965; Il Terminorum Musicae Diffinitorium di J. Tinctoris, 1968; Giandomenico del Giovane da Nola, 1973; L'Orchestrazione dell'Orfeo di Monteverdi, 1976. Address: via Mario Fascetti 67, 00136 Rome, Italy.

CAMMAROTA, Robert Michael, b. 25 June 1949, NY, NY, USA. Musicologist; Performer on Modern & Baroque Oboe & Shawm; Educ: BA, Hunter Coll., CUNY, 1971; MA, 1973, PhD Cand., NY Univ.; Grad. Schl. of Arts & Scis.; pvte. studies, oboe (w. Bert Lucarelli) piano, classical guitar. Career: Mbr., Borromini (baroque) Ensemble, 1974-75; Free-lance Oboist, NYC; Adj. Instructor, Fine Arts Dept., Fordham Univ., Bronx, NY, 1973-77; Fac., New Schl. for Social Rsch., NYC, 1975. Contbr. to: The Acad. Am. Ency. Mbr., Am. Musicol. Soc. Hons: Deutscher Akademischer Austauschdienst, 1978-80. Hobbies: Tennis; Photography; Travel. Address: 215 W 92nd St., NY, NY 10025, USA.

CAMP, Max W, b. 4 July 1935, Arab, Ala., USA. University Professor. Educ: BMus, Univ. of Ala.; MMus, Geo. Peabody Coll.; DMusEd, Univ. of Okla.; Alos studied piano, Univ. of Ind. & pedagogy, Eastman Schl. of Music. Career: Lects. & workshops on piano pedagogy presented at colls., univs. & to piano tchr. grps. at state, divisional & nat. level throughout th eS., & in major cities inclng. NY, Carnegie Recital Hall, LA, St. Louis & Phila.; Adjudicator for piano auditions & contests; Prof., piano & piano pedagogy, Univ. of SC, Columbia. Contbr. to: Clavier Mag.; The Am. Music Tchr. Mbrships: Pres., Southern Div., Music Tchrs. Nat. Assn.; Pres., SC Music Tchrs. Assn.; Pi Kappa Lambda; Am. Coll. of Musicians Bd. of Judges. Hobby: Tennis. Address: Dept. of Music, Univ. of SC, Columbia, SC 29208, USA.

CAMPANELLA, Michele, b. 5 June 1947, Napoli, Italy. Pianist. Educ: Piano Dip. m. Beatrice Tita, 2 c. Career: Perfs., Europe, USA, Aust., S Am., Japan, w. Schippers, Abbado, Mackerras, Stein, Prêtrê, etc. Recordings incl: Liszt Concertos; Totentanz; Hungarian Phantasy; 19 Hungarian Rhapsodies; Wagner Transcriptions; Parafrasi; Original pieces; Saint Saens 4th Concerto; Tchaikowsky 1st Concerto. Hons: Winner, Casella Competition, 1966; 2 Awards, Liszt Acad., Budapest, for Liszt recordings. Address: Via Vittorio Emanuele 1, Brescia, Italy.

CAMPBELL, David, b. 15 April 1953, Hemel Hempstead, UK. Clarinettist. Educ: RCM, 1971-75; GRSM; ARCM; LRAM. Debut: Wigmore Hall, London, 1975. Career: Mbr., Nat. Youth Orch. of GB; Mbr., The Fires of London, London Sinfonietta, Nash Ensemble & London Mozart Players; Duo w. pianist, Andrew Ball, Concerts in London & provinces; Apps., Major fests.; BBC radio; 2 tours of S Am. Mbrships: ISM; Musicians Union. Hons: Frederick Thurston Prize, RCM, 1975; Mozart Memorial Prize, 1975; GLAA Young Musician, 1977. Hobbies: Squash; Motoring; Cooking. Mgmt. Astra Blair, Music & Musicians Artists Mgmt. Address: 4 St. Olaf's Rd., London SW6, UK.

CAMPBELL, Frank Carter, b. 26 Sept. 1916, Winston-Salem, NC. USA. Chief of Music Division, NY Public Library. Educ: BMus, Salem Coll., Winston-Salem, NC; MMus, Eastman Schl. of Music, Rochester, NY. Career: Catalogue, Sibley Lib., Eastman Schl. of Music, Rochester, NY, 1943; Libn., Lib. of Congress (Music Div.), Wash., DC, 1943-59; Prof. of Music Hist., Am. Univ., 1950-53; Music Critic, Wash. Evening Star, 1953-59; Asst. Chief, NY Public Lib. (Music Div.), NY, 1959-66; Chief, ibid., 1966-. Publs: Notes, Jrnl. of the Music Lib. Assn. (Assoc. Ed., 1950-67, Ed., 1971-74). Mbrships. incl: Music Lib. Assn. (Sec., 1948-50, Pres., 1967-69); Am. Musicol. Soc.; Int. Assn. of Music Libs. Address: 1 Nevada Plaza, Apt. 16A, NY, NY 10023, USA.

CAMPBELL, John Coleman, b. 1 July 1935, Hereford, Tex., USA. Assoc. Professor; Organist. Educ: BA, Hardin-Simmons Univ., 1957; MMus, Univ. of Okla., 1964; Perfs. Cert, 1969, D Mus Arts, 1975, Eastman Schl. of Music; studied w. Mildred Andrews Boggess, Arthur Poister, Russell Saunders, Michael Schneider, Hugo Ruf. m. Lillie Spurgin, 2 s. Career: Solo organ recitals, NYC; Buffalo, Schenactady & Rochester, NY; Louisville, Berea & Harlan, Ky.; Kent & Cinn., Ohio; Cologne, German Fed. Repub.; Baton Rouge, La.; Okla. City & Norman, Okla.; Abilene, Amarillo, Fort Worth & Houston, Tex. Mbrships: AGO; Pi Kappa Lambda; Phi Mu Alpha. Hons: Leo Potishman Award, 1952; Study Grant, German Govt., 1969-70. Hobby: Audio Electronics. Address: 1609 Wishbone, Abilene, TX 79603, USA.

CAMPBELL, Kenneth, b. 17 Aug. 1922, Crayford, UK. Teacher of Singing; Opera Director; Impressario. Educ: Upton Coll.; GSM. m. Jean Isabel Campbell, 1 d. Career: Trained num. successful singers; fndr., Piccola Opera, 1960, 25 operas prod. & directed in original lang. Mbrships: ISM; Concerto Artistes Assn. Hobbies: Walking; Gardening; Siamese Cats. Addess: The Ferns, 88 Station Rd., Crayford, Dartford DA1 3QG, UK.

CAMPBELL, Lewisson, b. 28 July 1924, Paeroa, NZ. Lecturer; Pianist; Trumpet player. Educ: TCL (piano); studies interrupted by war & uncompleted for MusB, Auckland Univ. Career: Reular broadcaster in NZ, 1953-63; freelance in Sydney, 1963-69; Prin. Trumpeter, Elizabethan Trust Sydney Orch., 1970-77; Lectr., Brass Dept., NSW State Conserv. of Music, 1974-; Comps: Light music recorded & broadcast by NZ radio; Chambr. music for brass. Recording: 1 jazz album w. Gene Wright (str. bass). Publs: Brass books of Etudes & suites & fanfares awaiting publication. Mbr., Burmese Cat Soc. of Australasia. Hobbies: Reading Joseph Conrad; Brown Burmese Cats; Photography; Chess; Walking. Address: 65 Glover St., Mosman, NSW, Aust.

CAMPBELL, Margaret Jane, b. 15 June 1957, Shoreham by Sea, UK. Flautist. Educ: RCM, 1975-77; ARCM. Career: Prin.

Flute, City of Birmingham Symph. Orch., 1977-; Concerto apps. w. City of Birmingham Symph. Orch.; Mbr., Koenig Ensemble, (broadcasts on BBC, German & Italian radio). Mbrships: ISM. Hons: Oxford Fest. Concerto Competition, 1976; Douglas Whittaker Prize for Flute, 1976 & '77 (RCM); Eve Kisch Prize for Flute, 1977 (RCM). Hobbies: Reading; Keeping fit; Playing cello. Address: The Roses, Waddesdon, Aylesbury, Bucks., UK.

CAMPBELL, Margaret (Jean), b. London, UK. Author on Musical Subjects. Educ: Art Schl., London. m. Richard Barrington Beare, 3 children. Career: Talks & interviews, BBC Radio & Southern TV. Mbrships: Soc. of Authors; Fndr., Oxford Fndn. for Histl. Musical Instruments; Committee, The Galpin Soc.; Committee & Gov., The Dolmetsch Fndn. Publs: Dolmetsch: the Man & his Work, 1975; Great Violinists (in preparation); Ed., The Brit. Jrnl. of Music Therapy. Contbr. to: Grove's Dict., 6th ed.; Time; Daily Telegraph; The Strad; Music in Educ.; Recorder & Music Mag.; The Consort. Recip., Winston Churchill Mem. Travelling Fellowship, 1971. Hobbies incl: Singing. Address: White House, 160 Piccotts End, Hemel Hempstead, Herts., UK. 27.

CAMPBELL, Richard Gene, b. 21 Feb. 1932, Inglewood, Calif., USA. Ethnomusicologist; Curator of Musical Instruments. Educ: BFA, Univ. of Utah, 1955; PhD, Freie Universität Berlin, 1968. m. Olivia Erfurth, 2 s. Debut: as pianist, 1941. Career: Radio & concerts, LA, Calif. & Portland, Ore., 1938-55; Orch. & choral cond., 195-60. Publs: Zur Typologie der Schalenlanghalslaute, 1968; Musical Instruments from Five Continents, 1976; Friedmann, Aron - Der Synagogale Gesang. Leipzig, 1978. Mbrships: Phi Mu Alpha; Soc. for Ethnomusicology; Ont. Folk Music Coun.; Soc. for Asian Music; Gesellschaft für Musikforschung. Hobbies: Model railroading; Tennis; Skiing. Address: Fasanenstrasse 37, 1000 Berlin 15, German Fed. Repub.

CAMPBELL, Robert Gordon, b. 24 May 1922, Magnolia, Ark., USA. Music Educator; Administrator. Educ: BA, Hendrix Coll., 1943; BMus, Univ. of Texas, 1948; MMus, ibid., 1950; PhD, Indiana Univ., 1966. m. Nancy Patterson, 3 d., 1 s. Career: Instructor of Music, Univ. of Texas, 1950-52; Prof. of Music & Chmn., Div. of Fine Arts, S Ark. Univ., 1952-. Contbr. of program notes for S Ark. Symph. Concerts, 1974-. Mbrships. incl: Music Tchrs. Nat. Assn. (Exec. Bd., 1968-72); Ark. State Music Tchrs. Assn. (Pres., 1967-68); Am. Musicol. Soc.; Coll. Music Soc.; Music Lib. Assn.; MENC; Ark. Music Educrs. Assn.; Pi Kappa Lambda. Hobbies: Travel; Birdwatching; Walking. Address: Box 1398, Southern Ark. Univ., Magnolia, AR 71753, USA. 7, 12, 28, 29.

CAMPBELL, William Alexander, b. 2 Feb. 1913, Dayton, Pa., USA. University Music Administrator. Educ: BM, Eastman Schl. of Music, Rochester Univ., 1935; MA, NY Univ. 1941; Grad. Study, Eastman Schl. of Music & Syracuse Univ.; Dips., Niles Bryant Schl. of Piano Tuning & Technics, Army Music Schl. m. Alice Louise Williams, 2 d. Career: Supvsr. of Music, Oneida, NY 1000 41, Organist & Choir Dir., 1st Presby. Ch., Oneida, 1936-41; Music Tchr., East HS, Auburn, NY, 1941; AUS, 1942-46; Bandleader, var. army bands; Dir., Instrumental Music & Theory, St. Lawrence Univ., 1946-47; Dir. of Bands, Cornell Univ., 1947-66; Chmn., Music Dept., Ore. State Univ., Corvallis, 1966-78; Prof. Emeritus, ibid., 1978-. Mbrships: Coll. Music Soc.; MENC; AAUP; Ore. Music Educators; Ore. Music Admnstrs. Hobbies: Fishing; Camping. Address: 1017 Alder Creek Dr., Corvallis, OR 97330, USA. 2, 9, 28.

CAMPOLI, Alfredo, b. 20 Oct. 1906, Rome, Italy. Violinist. Educ: studied w. father, Romeo Campoli, Concert Master, Accademia Santa Cecilia, Rome. m. Joy Burbridge. Debut: aged 11. Career: played in series of Int. Celebrity Sub. Concerts, aged 15; has toured throughout the world; broadcasts, Savoy Hill, since the 1930's. Recordings: for Decca, HMV & Pye for past 40 yrs. Mbrships: Hon. Mbr. RAM, 1978. Hons. incl: Gold Medal, London Musical Fest., aged 15. Hobbies: Competitive Bridge; Photography; Recording. Address: 50 Eversley Pk., Rd., Winchmore Hill, London N21, UK.

CAMPOS, Anisia, b. Rio de Janeiro, Brazil. Pianist; Teacher. Educ: Studies in Paris, France, & Austria. Career: Perfs. in Europe, S Am., & Can.; Piano Master Classes & lectures, Ecole Superieure de Musique Vincent d'Indy, Montreal, PW, Cand.; Int. Summer Courses, Orford Arts Ctr., (Jeunesses Musicales du Can.); Mbr. of Fac., Conserv. of Musique, Quebec; Tchr., Univ. of Ottawa. Hobbies: Photography; Gardening. Address: 2660 Flaubert, Laval, PQ, H7E 2L4, Canada.

CAMUS, Raoul F, b. 5 Dec. 1930, Buffalo, NY, USA. Musicologist; Conductor. Educ: BA, Queens Coll., CUNY, 1952; MA, Columbia Univ., 1956; PhD, NY Univ.,

1969. m. Amy Edith Platt, 1 s., 2 d. Publs: Military Music of the American Revolution, 1976; Military Band in the United States Army prior to 1834, 1969. Contbr. to: Jrnl. of Band Rsch. Mbrships: Treas., Sonneck Soc.; Am. Musicol. Soc.; Coll. Band Dirs. Nat. Assn.; Company of Military Historians; Int. Military Music Soc. Hons: Queens Coun. on the Arts Award, 1975. Hobby: Model trains. Address: 14-34 155th St., Whitestone, NY 11357, USA. 6.

CANARINA, John Baptiste, b. 19 May 1934, New York, NY, USA. Conductor (Piano, Double Bass). Educ: BSc, 1957; MSc, 1958; Juilliard Schl. of Music, NY. Career: Asst. Cond., NY Phil., USA, 1961-62; Cond. & Music Dir., Jacksonville, Fla., Symph. Orch., 1962-69; Dir., Orchl. Activities, Drake Univ., Des Moines, Iowa, 1973-; Guest cond. num. orchs. inclng: RPO; Bratislava Radio Symph. Orch.; Belgian Radio Orch.; BBC Welsh & Scottish Symph. Contbr. to Tempo, 1972. Mbrships: Am. Symph. Orch. League; Sir Thomas Beecham Soc.; Arturo Toscanini Soc.; Berlioz Soc. Recip. Ford Fndn. Grant, 1964. Hobbies: Theatre; Films; Baseball. Address: 36 Verdi Ave., Tuckahoe, NY 10707, USA. 4.

CANETTY-CLARKE, Janet Constance, b. 1 Dec. 1935, Eccleston, Lancs., UK. Pianist/Accompanist; Lecturer; Choral Conductor. Educ: RAM; BMus, London Univ.; GRSM; LRAM; ARCM. m. Peter Canetty-Clarke, 1 s., 1 d. Career: Lectr., Extra-Mural Depts. of London, Surrey & Sussex Univs.; Pt.-time Lectr., W Sussex County Coun.; Cond., Ditchling Choral Soc.; apps., BBC; Concert apps., The Royal Albert Hall (1969), Fairfield Halls Croydon (1971, '76), Purcell Room London (1975), Wigmore Hall London (1977), St. Martin-in-the-Fields, London (1977), The Maltings, Snape (1976, '79). Recordings: The Brilliant and The Dark (Malcolm Williams); Dances for 2 pianos (Howard Blake). Mbrships: Solo Perfs. Sect., ISM; Tutors' Panel, Nat. Fedn. of Women's Insts. Hobbies: Theatre; Ballet. Address: Deanlands Place, Horsted Lane, Sharpthorne, W Sussex, RH19 4HX, UK.

CANNON, Dwight W, b. 7 July 1932, Pomona, Calif., USA. Conductor; Trumpeter; Composer; Professor. Educ: BMus, De Paul Univ.; MA, San Jose State Univ.; PhD (in progress), Univ. of Calif., San Diego. m. Nancy, 2 s., 1 d. Career: Chgo. TV & Recording Artist; On tour w. Freddy Martin Orch., Ralph Marterie Orch.; Cond., San Jose State Univ. Opera Orch., Jazz Ensembles, Concert Band; Principal Trumpet, Santa Clara Phil., San Jose Symph., La Jolla Civic Phil., Chgo. area orchs.; Cond., Man of La Mancha, Music Man, Carousel, Guys & Dolls, Anything Goes, Carnival, Most Hally Fella, Carlysle Floyd's Sussanah, Westside Story. Compositions incl: Chronometers for Percussion; A Play For Concert Band; Music for 1-13 Trumpets & 4-Channel Tape; Ex Pluribus Unum; Rich is Nice; Goodbye Yesterday; CIN for jazz ensembles. Mbr., Phi Mu Alpha Sinfonia. Hobbies: Scuba diving. Poetry. Address: Music Dept., San Jose State Univ., San Jose, CA 95192, USA.

CANNON, Jack Philip, b. 21 Dec. 1929, Paris, France. Composer; Conductor; Professor of Composition. Educ: RCM, FRCM. m. Jacqueline Playfair Laidlaw, 1 d. Career: Comp.; Cond.; Lectr.; Tchr.; Cond., BBC Foreign Radios, Lectr. in Comp., Sydney Univ.; Prof., RCM. Comps. incl: Missa Chorea; Lord of Light; Dr. Jekyll & Mr. Hyde, Morvoren, The Man; Son of Man; Te Deum; The Temple from Venus (operas); Son of God; Fleeting Fancies; Songs to delight; Symphonic Study, Spring; Concertino for Piano & Strings; Oraison Funèbre de l'Ame Humaine; Lord of Light; String Quartet; Clarinet Quintet; Piano Trio; Three Rivers; Sonata per Ballo; Sonatine Champêtre; L'Enfant s'Amuse; Galop Parisien; Cinq Chansons de Femme (all broadcast/perfd.) Contbr. to: Musical Times; Musical Opinion, etc. Mbr., Royal Musical Assn.; Savile Club. Hons: (String Quartet), Grand Prix, Critics Prize, Paris, 1965; FRCM, 1972; Commissioned by Queen Elizabeth II to write Te Deum, 1975. Address: 25 Ansdell St., Kensington Square, London W8 5BN, UK. 14.

CANTAGREL, Gilles, b. 20 Nov. 1937, Paris, France. Musicologist; Music Critic. Educ: BSc; LittB; Story of Art, Univ. of Paris; Gen. & applied physics, Conserv. of Arts et Métiers, paris; École Normale de Musique, Paris; Conserv. National Supérieur, Paris. m. Marie Dominique Bertola, 2 s. Career: Chmn. of new eds., Diapason Eds.; Ed., musical Collection Diapason; TV & Radio apps., Belgium & France. Publs: Livre d'Or de l'Orgue Français, 1976; Guide Pratique du discophile, 1978; Guide du disque classique, 1978. Contbr. to: Le Monde; L'Express; les Nouvelles litteraires; L'Audiophile; Nouvelle Revue du Son. Mbr., Société Française de Musicologie. Address: 22 bis, rue Pétrarque, 75016 Paris, France.

CANTER, Robin, b. 20 June 1952, London, UK. Oboist. Educ: Dartington Coll. of Arts; RAM; LRAM; Freiburg Hochschule für Musik, Perfs. Dip. m. Elizabeth Routier. Debut: Wigmore Hall, 1976. Career: Apps., Purcell Room, Queen Elizabeth Hall; British Coun. tours of Africa, Spain, Germany, Middle East,

Yugoslavia, Greece & Cyprus; num. radio & TV broadcasts. Mbr., ISM. Hons: Silver Medal, Geneva Int. Oboe Competition; Prizewinner, Gaudeamus Int. Modern Music Competition. Hobbies: Painting; Sailing. Mgmt: Ruth Ticher Concert Mgmt. Address: 46 Springfield Rd., Guilford, Surrey GU1 4DP, UK.

CANTOR, Joseph, b. 12 Feb. 1913, Amsterdam, Netherlands. Solo Cellist. Educ: Conservatorium. m. Valentina Marie Buchowski, 1 s., 1 d. Debut: Gebouw van K en W, The Hague. Career: Solo concerts w. all radio orchs. of Holland; films & TV; Solo Cellist, Radio Phil. & Promenade Orch.; Cellist w. Pro Arte Trio (Cor de Groot, piano, Nap de Klijn, violin). Has made many recordings w. Paul Godwin, Gregor Serban, Benediet Silverman, Stanley Black, Residentie Orch. Mbrships: Anouh; KNTV. Hobbies: Playing Jewish & Tzigane music; Reading; Tennis; Walking; Trave. Address: Frans Halslaan 15, Hilversum, Netherlands.

CANTOR, Montague, b. 10 Dec. 1909, London, UK. Composer; Musicologist; Instructor in Music. Educ: BMus, Manhattan Schl. of Music; MA, PhD, NY Univ.; studied comp. w. Arnold Schoenberg, Paul Hindemith, Roger Sessions. m. Miriam Kornbleet, 1 s., 2 d. Career: Instructor, Brooklyn Coll., 1952-64, Lehman Coll., 1968-69, Queens Coll. 1969-74; Tchr., pvte. music schls.; former M BR., Schola Cantorium of NY, Vinaver Chorus, cast of US première of Peter Grimes, 1946; apps. in opera, light opera & num. plays & musicals. Comps: Suite for Clarinet Unaccompanied. Publs: Ed., A History of Music, 1965. Mbr., Am. Musico. Soc. Hobbies: Acting; Singing; Walking; Travel. Address: 568 Bedford Rd., Pleasantville, NY 10570, USA.

CANTRELL, Derrick Edward, b. 2 June 1926, Sheffield, UK. Cathedral Organist. Educ: MA, BMus, Oxford Univ.; FRCO m. Nancy Georgina Bland, 4 c. Career: Organist, Manchester Cathedral, 1962-77; Lectr., Royal Northern Coll. of Music. Recording: Manchester Cathedral Organ. Recip., Sawyer & Limpus Prizes, RCO. Address: 159 Old Hall Lane, Manchester M14 6HJ. UK.

CAPOBIANCO, Tito, b. 28 Aug. 1931, La Plata, Argentina. Opera Stage Director. Educ: Masters Degree, Law & Music, Buenos Aires. m. Elena Denda, 2 s. Career: Univ. Prof., Chile; Stage & Technical Dir., Teatro Colon, 4 yrs.; Gen. Dir., Chile Opera Co., 4 yrs.; Artistic Dir., La Plata, 3 yrs., Cinn. Opera, 5 yrs.; Res. Stage Dir., NYC Opera; Prof. of Acting & Interpretation, Acad. of Vocal Arts Phila.; Dir. & Fndr., Am. Opera Ctr., Juilliard Schl.; Prof. of Opera Dept. & Dir., Phila. Musical Acad., Las Palmas Fest.; Gen. Dir., San Diego Opera Co., 1975-; Prod. of many operas. Mgmt: Clifford Stevens, 1650 Broadway, NY, NY 10019, USA. Address: c/o San Diego Opera, Box 988, San Diego, CA 92112, USA. 2.

CAPPS, Ferald Buell Jr., b. 2 Sept. 1943, Phoenix, Ariz., USA. Oboist; English Horn Player. Educ: BA, Ariz. State Univ., Tempe; MM, Temple Univ., Phila., Pa. m. Margarete Capps, 1 s., 1 d. Career: Solo Engl. Horn, Aspen Fest. Orch., Aspen, Colo.; Prin. Oboe, Santa Fe Opera Co., NM, Phila. Lyric Opera Co., Pa.; Soclo Engl. Horn, Chmbr. Symph. of Phila., Minn. Orch., Mpls. Comps. incl: Duex, duet dor oboe & clarinet; 3 sketches, oboe, bassoon, clarinet & piano; Sonata in 2 Movements, clarinet & piano. Recordings incl: Complete Orchestral Works of Ravel. Mbrships: Phi Mu Alpha; Kappa Kappa Psi; Blue Key. Hons: Charter Mbr., Oboe, Schl. Band of Am., 1961. Hobbies incl: Outdoor activities. Address: 301 Janalyn Circle, Golden Valley, MN 55416, USA.

CAPPS, William, b. 21 Mar. 1941, St. Louis, Mo., USA. French Horn Player & Professor. Educ: B Mus, Perf. Dip., Curtis Inst. of Music; Perf. Dip., Hochschule für Musik, Berlin, Germany; MMus, DMA, Cath. Univ., Wash., DC. m. Marilyn R Capps, 2 s. Career: Prin. Horn, Phila. Little Symph., Berlin Chmbr. Orch., Tokyo Phil. Orch.; Assoc. Prin. Horn, RIAS Orch. of Berlin; Assoc. Prof. of French Horn, Fla. State Univ. Schl. of Music. Mbr., Int. Horn Soc. Hobby: Tennis. Address: 2011 Seminole Dr., Tallahassee, FL 32301, USA.

CAPUANA, Franco, b. 29 Sept. 1896, Fano, Italy. Conductor. Educ: Naples Conserv. of Music. m. Emy Callo. Career incl: Cond. of leading orchs. & at opera house inclng: La Scala, Milan; Rome; Florence; Naples; Covent Gdn., London; Buenos Aires; Vienna; Berlin; Tokyo; etc. Mbr: Acad. of St. Cecilia, Rome. Hons: Chevalier, Legion of Hon., France; Grand Order of Merit, Repub. of Italy. Hobbies: Antiques; Period furniture; Books. Address: Via di Villa Albani 26A, Rome, Italy.

CAPURSO, Alexander, b. 22 May 1910, Bari, Italy, University Professor of Music. Educ: Phila. Musical Acad., USA; Pa. State Univ.; Temple Univ.; Univ. of Ky.; BMus, MA, PhD; Pvte. instruction in violin since age 6. m. Martha Honerkamp, 1

s., 1 d. Career: Hd., Music Dept., Univ. of Ky.; Dir., Schl. of Music, Syracuse Univ.; Assoc. Chmn., Creative Arts Div., San Fran. State Univ.; Pres., Stanislaus State Coll., Calif.; Hd., Music Dept., Calif. Polytech. State Univ.; Cond., var. univ. orchs.; Cond., Music Dir., Syracuse Symph. Orch., Santa Maria Symph. Orch., Calif.; Guest Cond., num. US orchs. Publs. incl: Music & Your Emotions (co-author), 1952; Curricular Planning for the Gifted Child (co-author), 1960; Contbr. to profl. jrnls. & mags. Mbrships. incl: Am. Psychol. Assn.; NY, Calif. Psychol. Assns.; Am. Musicol. Soc.; Nat. Soc. of Music & Arts; MTA; MENC. Hons: DMus., Phila. Music Acad., 1957; LLD, Okla. City Univ., 1967; Disting. Prof., Univ. of Ky.; Hall of Fame, Univ. of Ky. Alumni; Knighted by Italian Govt., 1970. Hobbies: Collecting Italian violins, oriental art; Study of Renaissance. Address: 260 Westmount Ave., San Luis Obispo, CA 93401, USA. 2.

CARABO-CONE, Madeleine, b. 2 June 1915. Violinist; Author; Educator; Creator, Original Pre-Instrumental Teaching Method 'The Carabo-Cone Method', A Sensory-motor Approach to Music Learning. Educ: Juilliard Grad. Schl.; Am. Conserv., Chgo. m. Harold Simon Cone, 1 s., 1 d. Debut: Town Hall, NY, 1939. Career incls: Vis. Prof., num. colls.; Solo Concerts, US & Wigmore Hall, London, 1970; 1st woman 1st violin sect., Cleveland Orch.; Toured Europe, Lectr.-Demonstration, Carabo-Cone Method; Lectr. Tour, Canada, 1973. Publs. incl: Concepts for Strings, 1966. Contbr. to jrnls. Hons. incl: Music Therapy Award, Mu Phi Epsilon, 1974. Hobby: Langs. Mgmt: (Distbrs. Carabo-Cone Method Series), Belwin-Mills, Melville, NY 11146, USA. Address: Q Sherbrooke Rd., Scarsdale, NY 10583, USA.

CARAPETYAN, Armen, b. 11 Oct. 1908, Isfahan, Iran. Musicologist; Editor; Publisher. Educ: BA, Asbury; MA, PhD, Harvard Univ.; Sorbonne, Paris. m. Harriette Esther Norris, 1 s., 1 d. Career: series of broadcasts as Violinist, perf. of early sonatas, Boston, 1933-44; Gen. Ed., Corpus Mensurabilis Musicae, Musicol. Studies & Documents; Ed., Musica Disciplina; Publr. of above as well as Corpus Scriptorium de Musicae, Musicol. Studies & Documents, Early Keyboard Music & Miscellanea. Address: CP 515 San Silvestro, Rome, Italy. 2, 28.

CARAPEZZA, Paolo Emilio, b. 11 Oct. 1937, Rome, Italy. Musicologist; University Professor. Educ: Dr. Classical Lit.; Est. Univ. Lectr. in Hist. of Music; Univ. degree, 1961. m. Marisa Maraventano (d. 1974), 2 children. Career: Dir., Inst. of Musicology, Palermo Univ., 1970-; Gen. Ed., Collage, 1963-70; Gen. Ed., MRS, corpus of Sicilian Renaissance Music, 1970-; Gen. Ed., Puncta, series of studies in musicology, 1974-. Publs. incl: Studi e documenti sul Wozzeck di Alban Berg, 1965; Le Costituzioni della Musica, 1974; Figaro e Don Giovanni; due folli giornate, 1974. Mbrships: Accademia di Scienze, Lettere e arti di Palermo; Societe Italiana di Musicologia. Address: Via Lombardia 4, 1-90144 Palermo, Italy.

CARATELLI, Sebastian, b. 24 Aug. 1913, Rome, Italy. Flautist; Instructor of Flute & Theory. m. Ann Sacchi Caratelli. Career: Flautist, NBC Symph. Orch. & Cleveland Orch.; Soloist Flautist, Pitts. Symph. Orch. & Detroit Symph. Orch.; Asst. Cond., Am. Arts Orch., NY; Sev. radio solo apps. & recitals; 4 Carnegie Hall recitals, NYC; European tours. Recordings: B minor suite (Bach); Masterpieces for the Flute; Contemporary Sonatas; Early American Music. Publs: Reminiscences of a Musician. Recip., schlrships., NY Phil.-Symph. Schlrship. Soc., & Nat. Orchl. Assn. of NY. Hobbies: Writing; Lit. Address: 135 Old Courthouse Rd., New Hyde Pk., NY 11040, USA.

CARD, June, b. 10 Apr. 1942, Dunkirk, NY, USA. Opera Singer, Lyric Coloratura. Educ: BS; Grad. Work, Mannes Coll. of Music, NYC. m. Manfred Lutgenhorst. Debut: Singer, Broadway Musicals, 1959; Opera, NYC Opera, 1963. Career: Pef. in 3 Broadway Shows; Singer in USA, Ireland, Brussels, Geneva, Antwerp, Vienna State Opera, Munich Opera, Hamburg, Berlin, Dusseldorf, Koln, Frankfurt, Persia, etc. Recip. title of Bayerische Kammersangerin bestowed by State of Bavaria for servs. in opera. Mgmt: Agentur Schulz, 8 Munchen 23, Martiusstr. 3, Germany. Address: 8 Munchen 81, Arabellastr. 5/1411, German Fed. Repub.

CARDER, Richard Holland, b. 14 Sept. 1942, Gravesend, UK. Music Teacher (Clarinet & Blockflute); Composer. Educ: GSM, 1961-64; Birmingham Schl. of Music, 1967-69; ABSM; LTCL; BMus, Trinity Coll., Dublin; Cert. Educ., Newton Pk. Coll., Bath, 1973. Debut: Minehead Fest. Orch., 1972. Career: Tchr., Birmingham, Bristol & Bath: Covenor, Player, Awuarum Sulis Venti; Winds on the Waters; The Spheres of Sul. Comps: Songs & Carols; Old Nick the Nuke, 1978; Tryptych for 2 Clarinets. Publs: The Music of Decadence (1979). Contbr. to Egologist. Mbrships incl: ISM; Trustee, Nat. Musical Mus. Hons: Comp. Prize, Mid-Somerset Fest., 1974. Hobbies: Gardening;

Ecology; Swimming. Address: Tre Loregyonen, 76 Lower Oldfield Pk., Bath, Avon, UK.

CARDEW, Cornelius, b. 7 May 1936, Winchcombe, UK. Composer; Pianist. Educ: Chorister, Canterbury; FRAM; Acad. of St. Cecilia, Rome. Career: Asst. to Karlheinz Stockhausen, 1958-60; Creative Assoc., Ctr. for Creative & Perf. Arts, Buffalo, NY, USA, 1966-67; Prof. of Comp., RAM, 1967-. Comps. incl: February Pieces for Piano; Treatise; Schooltime Compositions; The Great Learning; Thälmann Variations for piano. Contbr. to profl. publs. Address: 7 Agar Grove, London NW1, UK. 3.

CARDINAAL, Carlos, b. 31 July 1948, 's-Hertogenbosch, Holland. Cello Soloist. Educ: Dip., Chamber Music., Conservatorium Malagna; Solo Dip., Cello, Conservatorium Madrid. Debut: Malagna, 1963. Career: Concerts in Spain, France, Germany, Holland; Radio recordings for RNE, Madrid, ORTF, Paris, NOS Holland; Cello Soloist, Gewestelyck Orch. Mbr., Royal Dutch Artists Soc. Hons: 1st Prize, Chamber Music, 1966; Prix d'Excellence, Conservatorium Madrid, 1968; Matrimonio Luque Prize, Spain, 1968. Address: 368 H. Tollensstr., Delft, The Netherlands.

CARDNELL, Valerie Flora, b. Bexley, Kent, UK. Soprano. Educ: TCL; FTCL; LTCL; LRAM. Career: Prof. & Examiner, TCL; Prof. Singing, Coll. Educ., Bognor Regis, 1965-; Prof. Singing, Avery Hill, 1970-; Solo Singer, BBC, 1955-; Radio & TV Apps. throughout Western Europe; Special subjects, Oratorio, Recitals, Music Therapy for Children. Mbrships: ISM; Brit. Soc. Music Therapy. Hons: Elizabeth Schuman Lieder Prize, 1954; Ricordi Opera Prize, 1955; Silver Medal, Worshipful Co. Musicians, 1956; Prize Winner, Int. Singing Competition, 'sHertogenbosch, Holland, 1957. Hobbies: Victoriana; Floral arrangement. Address: 20 Woodside Close, Tolworth Rise, Surbiton, Surrey KTT5 9JU, UK. 3.

CAREWE, John Maurice Foxall, b. 24 Jan. 1933, Derby, UK. Conductor. Educ: GSM; Conserv. Nat., Paris, France. m. Rosemary Philipps, 2 d. Career: Fndr., New Music Ensemble, & Music Today, 1956; Prin. Cond., BBC Welsh Orch., 1966-71; Musical Dir., Prin. Cond., Brighton Phil. Soc. 1974-. Recordings: Histoire du Soldat (Stravinsky); Creation du Monde (Milhaud); Façade (Walton); Leopardi Fragments (Davies); Music for Albion Moonlight (Bedford). Recip., Bablock Prize, 1959; Hon. ARAM. Hobby: Photography. Address: Brighton Philharmonic Soc., 50 Grand Parade, Brighton, Sussex BN2 2QA, UK.

CAREY, Gerald Vernon, b. 19 Dec. 1936, New Orleans, La., USA. Professor of Music; Flautist. Educ: BMus, Eastman Schl. of Music, 1959; MMus, ibid., 1961; DMA Cand., Univ. Ill. m. Tanya Lesinsky, 2 children. Career: Prin. Flute, Milwaukee Symph. Orch., USA, 1961-64; Buffalo Phil., 1959-61; Rochester Phil., 1958-61; Prin. Flute, Eastman Phil. & Eastman Symphonic Wind Ensemble, 1958-61; Prof. of Music, Western Ill. Univ. Sev. recordings as flutist: 21 albums w. Camerata Woodwind Wuintet. Mbrships: Phi Mu Alpha Sinfonia; Nat. Flute Assn.; Am. Musical Instrument Soc.; Galpin Soc. Recip. num. awards. Address: 507 Meadow Dr., Macomb, IL 61455, USA.

CARFAGNO, Simon Albert, b. 8 Jan. 1906, Scottdale, Pa., USA. Composer; Concert Violinist; Symphony Conductor. Educ: BA, Univ. of Calif., LA; PhD, ibid; Studied w. Arnold Schonberg, Nadia Boulanger & Eleazar de Carvalho; Berkshire Music Ctr., Tanglewood, Mass. Debut: Violin Soloist, Hollywood Bowl Orch. Career: Toured as soloist, Western USA; Performances w. Carfagno String Quartet in concerts & on radio for 14 yrs.; Conductor, Chico Symph. Orch. for 5 yrs.; Prof. of Music, Chico State Univ.; Concertmaster, LA Symph. Orch.; 1st violinist, LA Philharmonic Orch. Compositions: String Trio in E; Gettysburg, 1863, cantata for symph. orch., mixed chorus & 4 solo voices; Salmagundi Suite for violin & piano; Sonata for flute & piano; Toccata for piano; Favola, prelude No. 3, for piano; Nonet, chmbr. music work for viola, woodwinds & 4 pitched drums; Fuga-Canone, for cello; Quartetto II, for 2 violins, viola & cello; God of our Nation, hymn. Mbrships: Chmn., Artist Comm.; Paradise Community Concerts; Am. Fedn. of Musicians. Recip., Pro Musica Prize, 1942. Hobbies: Oil painting; Sculpure; Photography; Gardening; Fencing. Address: 5037 Russell Drive, Paradise, CA 95969, USA. 9, 12.

CARFI, Anahi, b. 5 Dec. 1946, Buenos Aires, Argentina. Violinist. Educ: Dip. & Medal of Hon., Manuel de Falla Conserv., Buenos Aires. m. Riccardo Chailly. Career: Appts: Teatro Colon Buenos Aires; El Maggiori Centry Sinfonici Sudamericani; Regiodi Torino; San Remo; Cagliari; 1st Violin, Di Spalla, La Scala, Milan, Italy. Recordings: Brahms Trio; Hindemith Sonata. Address: Viale Bianca Maria 17, Milano, Italy.

CARIDIS, Miltiades, b. 9 May 1923, Danzig, Poland. (Greek Citizen). Conductor. Educ: Dip. in Conducting, Music Acad., Vienna, Austria, 1947. m. Sonja (Dengel) Caridis, 1 d. Career: Permanent Cond. in Graz. Cologne, Vienna; Permanent Cond., Danish Radio-Symph.-Orch., Copenhagen; Cond.-inChif, Philharmonia Hungarica; Artistic & Music Dir., Phil. Soc., Oslo, 1969-75; Cond. in Chief, Duisburg Symph. Orch., W Germany, 1975-. Recordings: Amadeo; Ariola; Philips; Teldec; Somerset. Addrss: Himmelhofgasse 10, Ober St. Veit, A-1130, Vienna, Austria.

CARLEVARO, Abel, b. 16 Dec. 1918, Montevideo, Uruguay. Composer; Classical Guitarist. Educ: Univ. of Montevideo; studied Harmony, Comp., Orchestration; studied Guitar w. Andrés Segovia, 9 yrs. div. Career: Creator of new advanced instrumental guitar technique; Dir. Int. Guitar Seminars; Tech. Dir., Int. Guitar Seminar, Porto Alegre. Brazil, 1972-74; frequent Jury Mbr., int. competitions; Master Course, Arles, Arles, France, 1975. Comps. incl: Perludios Americanos; Cronomias I(Sonata); Estudios (Homenaje a Villa-Lobos); Concierto del Plata (guitar & orch.). Mbr., ASCAP. Recip., 3 Prizes for the Best Records. Mbmt: Barry, Talcahuano 860, Buenos Aires, Argentina. Address: Casilla de Correo 1695, Montevideo, Uruguay.

CARLSON, Lenus Jesse, b. 11 Feb. 1945, Jamestown, ND, USA. Opera Singer; Baritone. Educ: BA, Moorehead State Coll., Minn., 1967; Profl. Study Prog., Juilliard Schl., NY, 1970-74. m. Linda Jones. Debut: w. Minn. Symph., 1966. Career: Met. Opera Debut, 1974; European Debut, Netherlands Opera, Amsterdam, 1974; UK Debut, Scottish Opera, Edinburgh Fest., 1975; Dallas Opera, 1972-73; Wash. Opera, 1973-74; Boston Opera, 1973; Covent Garden Opera, 1976. Hobbies: Tennis; Chess; Wood Carving; Reading. Mgmt: AIMS, London, UK; Colombia Artists, NY, USA. Address: 782 W End Ave., NY, NY 10025, USA. 2.

CARLSON, Lilian, b. 22 July 1936, Stockholm, Sweden. Pianist. Educ: RAM, Stockholm; Piano Pedagog, 1961; Staatliche Akademie für Musik and Darstellende Kunst, Vienna, Austria. m. Olle Nyquist, 1 d. Debut: Stockholm, 1961; Wigmore Hall, London, UK, 1967. Career: As Soloist, Chmbr. Musician & Accomp. toured Scandinavia, GB, Austria, Germany & Liberia; Radio & TV apps.; Performed w. Manoug Pakistan, Karine Georgian, Vivian Joseph, Halina Lukomska & Elisabeth Soderstrom. Recordings incl: A Tribute to Gottfrid Boon (piano solo); The Ten Yes. (piano & clarinet). Mbrships. incl: Swedish Pianopedagogue Assn. Stockholm, 1961. Hobbies: Lit.; Art; Piano Playing; Gardening. Address: Varvsgatan 12, 2 tr., 11729, Stockholm, Sweden. 27.

CARLSON, Paul Bollinger, b. 11 Feb. 1932, Chgo., Ill., USA. Professor of Music; Violinist. Educ: BMus, Chgo. Conserv., 1954; MMus, Northwestern Univ. 1958; DMusA, Univ. of Mo. Kan. City, 1964. m. Laura R Carlson, 1 s., 1 d. Debut: Kimble Hall, Chgo., 1953. Appts: Violin Soloist, Chgo. Soncerv. & Northwestern Chmbr. Orchs.; Concertmaster, Springfield Mo. Symph. Orch.; Prof., Kan. State Coll., Pitts. & 1st Violin, Res. Str. Quartet. Contbr. to profl. jrnls. Mbrships: Music Tchrs. Nat. Assn.; Exec. Bd., Kan. Music Tchrs.; ASTA. Hons: Young Artist Contest Soc. of Am. Musicians, 1952; Reg. Winner, Nat. Fedn. of Music Clubs, 1953. Address: 526 S Georgia, Pittsburgh, KS 66762, USA. 8.

CARLSTEDT, Jan A, b. 15 June 1926, Orsa, Sweden. Composer. Educ: RCM, Stockholm, 1948-52; RCM, London, 1952-53. m. Marie Janice, 3 children. Comps: 5 String Quartets; Solo works for violin & cello; 3 Wind Quintets; Duos for 2 violins; Quartet for oboe & strongs; Quintet for flute, oboe & strings; 2 Symphs.; Concerto for cello & orch.; Choral works. Comps. recorded: String Quartets 1 - 4; String trio; Sinfonietta for 5 wind instruments; Sonata for solo violin; Sonata per Archi; Symph. No. 2; Choral works. Contbr. to: Nutida Musik; Muik-Revy, etc. Mbrships: Royal Swedish Acad. of Music; Samtida Musik; Soc. of Swedish Comps. Hon: The Alfvén Prize, 1875. Hobby: Nature. Address: Bodalsvägen 22, S18¢136 Lidingö, Sweden.

CARLTON, Anita, b. 3 Apr. 1933, Yoakum, Tex., USA. Pianist; Teacher. Educ: BMus, Univ. of Tex., 1952; MMus, Univ. of Mich., 1954; Dip., Conserv. Americaine, 1961; study w. Robert, Jean & Gaby Casadesus, annette Dieudonne, Clifford Curzon & Nadia Boulanger. Career: Instr., Univ. of Tex., Arlington, 1955-61; Asst. Prof., ibid., 1962-66; Asst. to Jean Casadesus, SUNY, Binghamtown, 1966-69; Artist-in-Residence, Univ. of Sci. & Arts of Okla., 1979-; Recitals & perfs. w. var. orchs. in USA, Mexico & Europe. Publ: Functional Piano 9, 1964. Mbrships: Pi Kappa Lambda; Mu Phi Epsilon; Coll. Music Soc.; Nat. Harriett Hale Woolley Award, 1961; Fribourg Award, 1961; Schlrships. to Conserv. Americaine, 1962-63, 1967. Hobbies: Poetry; Needlework. Address: 909 S 17th St., Chickasha, OK 73018, USA.

CARLYLE, Joan Hildred, b. 6 Apr. 1931, UK. Operatic Soprano. m. Robert Duray Aiyar, 1 d. Career: Prin. Lyric Soprano, Covent Gdn., 1955-; many apps. at fests. & abroad inclng. Salzburg, Met. Opera, Teatro Colon (Buenos Aires). Roles incl: Oscar, Ballo in Maschera; Sophie, Marschallin, Der Rosenkavalier; Nedda, Pagliacci; Mimi, La Bohème; Titania, Midsummer Night's Dream; Pamina, Magic Flute; Countess, Marriage of Figaro; Zdenka, also title role, Arabella; Suor Angelica; Desdemona, Othello; Jenifer, Midsummer Marriage; Donna Anna; Reiza, Oberon; Adrianna Lecouvreur; Russalka; Elizabetta, Don Carlos; etc. sev. recordings. Hobbies: Gardening; Travel; Preservation of the countryside; Interior design; Cooking. 16.

CARMACK, Murray, b. 11 Feb. 1920, Nanton, Can. Pianist; Composer; Music Educator. Educ: ARCT, 1938; LRSM, 1938; FTCL (solo piano perf.), 1953; AM, Harvard Univ., USA, 1968; BMus, Dunelm, 1970. m. (1) Edith Holroyd Paull (dec.), (2) Mary Dudman (div.), 2 d. Career incls: Solo piano recitals, CBC, 1947-53; Dir., Carmack Recorder Ensemble, 1962-65; Prof., GSM, 1967; Acad. Chmn., Music Prog., Douglas Coll., BC, Can., 1970-74; Music Supvsr., Burns Lake Schl. Dist., BC, 1974-; Dir., BC Harvard Alumni. Comps. of 2 string quartets & miscellaneous music for piano, voices, recorders. Publs: We Like to Sing (w. Kurth & McManus), 1954; Sing me a Song (w. Kurth & McManus), 1956; Contbr. to Musical Times; Times, etc. Recip., var. hons. Hobbies incl: Reading. Address: Ita Wegman Institut, CH 4144, Arlesheim, Switz. 4.

CARMAN, Ofelia, b. 11 Aug. 1909, Buenos Aires, Argentina. Pianist; Piano Teacher. Educ: Conservatorio Nacional de Musica, Buenos Aires; Dip., Profesora Superior de Piano y Armonía, 19290; Piano w. Vincenzo Scaramuzza; Harmony & Counterpoint, Erwin Leuchter & Athos Palma. Deubt: w. Alfredo Casella, piano duet, 1930. Career: 1st Piano recital, 1933; Perfs. & recitals, Buenos Aires & other cities in Argentina, 1933-; Soloist, Phila. Symph. Orch., Univ. of Pa., 1942; Perfs. & recitals, N & S Am., Paris; Tchr., Escuela de Orquesta y Coro Infantiles, Conservatorio Nacional de Musica, Buenos Aires; Masterclass; Pvte. tchr., Germany; currently, Tchr., Musikschule der Stadt Troisdorf & Pädagogische Hochschule Rheinland; Music seminar, Abteilung Bonn; Num. radio & TV apps. Recordings: Sonata in F major K 494 & 533, Mozart; Variations in C major, K 264 Lison dormait, Mozart. Contbr. to: La Nación, Buenos Aires. Mbr., Verband deutscher Musikerzieher und konzertierenden Künstler VDMK, Bonn. Hons: Quien es quien enla Argentina, Editorial Kraft, Buenos Aires. Address: Rathausstr. 2, 5300 Bonn 3, German Fed. Repub.

CARMEL, Dov, b. 26 Oct. 1933, Budapest, Hungary. Teacher; Composer. Educ: Music Inst., Oranim Schl. of Educ.; Pvte. studies, violin, comp., orch., arr., cond. m. Meira Sherf, 4 c. Debut: Comps. Workshop, Tel Aviv, 1970; Studio Neue Musik, Berlin, 1974. Career: Music Tchr., Harei-Efraim High Schl., 1957-71; Meggido Music Inst., 1960-71; Musical Dir., Gevatron Singers, 1966-74; Mbr., staff of Music Inst., Oranim Schl. of Educ., 1972-. Comps. incl: Chants of Spring; The Evening Wind; Arise, Ye North; Evenings Eyelids; Meadows; Terzettino; Fractures; Adagio for Brass; Meditation for a Lonely Flute; Brasschoir; Penkahaedron; Caleidoscope. Recordings of own comps. by Israel Broadcasting Authority. Mbrships: Israel Comps. League; ACUM; Nat. Union of Musicians; Nat. Union of Tchrs. Hons: ACUM Prize, 1969; Kibbutzim Cultural Bd. Prize, 1972. Address: Dalya 18920, Israel.

CARMEN, Marina, b. 17 July 1942, Santander, Spain. Classical Guitar Concert Artist; Teacher; Composer. Educ: Grad., Madrid Conserv. m. Philliph T Gioconda. Career: Performed on Radio TV Espanola; Radio Stns. WAXR, WNYC; Concerts in maj. Spanish cities; France, Italy, Morocco, Japan & USA. Compositions incl: Trio for guitar, cello & flute; Num. comps. for Guitar; Songs for voice & guitar; The Old Men and the Sea (opera). Recordings incl: XIX Century Music for the Guitar. Contbr. to Ritmo. Mbrships: ASTA; SACE; Profl. Staff Congress, CUNY. Hobbies: Swimming; Reading. Address: 333 Pearl St., Apt. 17K, New York, NY 10038, USA.

CARMIGCHELT, Henk W, b. 15 Sept. 1933, Zutphen, Holland. Conductor. Educ: Piano Dip., Conserv. of The Hague; Conducting Dip., Conserv. of Utrecht. m. Jos Kraasenberg, 2 s. Career: Cond., Het Gelders Orch.; Overyssels Phil. Orch.; var. choirs in oratorio, etc.; Music Cons., Culturele Raad voor Gelderland; Adjudicator; Broadcaster, NOS. Contbr. to var. jrnls. Mbrships: Koninklyke Nederlandse Toonkunstenaars Bereniging. Hobbies: Tennis; Fishing; History. Address: Leeuweriklaan 15, Zutphen, Holland.

CARNER, Mosco, b. Nov. 1904, Vienna, Austria. Conductor; Musical Author; Critic (piano, cello & clarinet). Educ: PhD, Vienna Univ.; Neues Wiener Konservatorium. m. Debut: Danzig Stats

Theater. Career: Conducted all maj. London Orchs. & BBC Symph. Orch.; Broadcaster of talks on music. Publs: Dvorak, 1940; A Study of 20th Century Harmony, 1942; Of Men and Music, 1944; The Waltz, 1948; Puccini: A Critical Biography, 1958; '74, Letters of Giacomo Puccini, 1974; Alban Berg: The Man and the Music, 1975. Contbr. to num. mags., reviews, etc. Recip. Silver Medal, Italian Govt., 1964. Hobbies: Reading; Swimming; Motoring. Address: 14 Elsworthy Rd., London NW3 3DJ, UK. 1.

CAROLL, Ann (TREGENNA, Zilla; LAKE, Anna), b. 1 Feb. 1911, Clapham, London, UK. Singer. Educ: LRAM. Career: Solo singer, Christmas Concerts, Garrison Theatre, Ctrl. Burma, WW 1, 5-10 yrs. old; Adult debut. Soloist, Carol Concert, Queen's Hall, London; Prin. Roles, Carl Rosa Opera Co. & BBC Operatic Sect. inclng. 1st perf. in Engl., Dvorak's 'Russalka'; Gala Symph. & Operatic Concert, Winter Gdn. Theatre, London; Concerts throughout UK. Mbrships: ISM; Fndr. Mbr., Women of the Yr. Annual Luncheon. Hobby: Philosophy. Address: c/o Nat. Westminster Bank, 21 Hanover Sq., London W1, UK. 3.

CARPENTER, Gary, b. 13 Jan. 1951, Clapton, London, UK. Conductor; Composer; Pianist. Educ: LRAM (com.); ARCM (Piano); Pvte. study comp., piano & conducting. Career: Arr. & Assoc. Music Dir. for film The Wicker Man (Brit. Lion), 1972; Film music for Das Feverrote Spielmobil, Bayerische Rundfunk, 1973-74; Music for plays incl: Good & Faithful Servant; Nighlight; Pianist & Cond., Vereinitgen Stadtischen Buhnen Krefeld, Monchengladbach, 1974-76; Pianist & Cond., Nederlands Dans Theater, Holland, 1976-. Mbrships: Musicians Union; Comps. Guild of GB. Recip. var. comp. awards. Hobbies: Cinema; Lit.; Scuba Diving; Table Tennis; Hist. & Geog. of Tex.; Astronomy; Chess. Address: c/o Nederlands Dans Theater, Koningstraat 118, Den Haag, Holland.

CARPENTER, Hoyle D, b. 8 Aug. 1909, Stockton, Calif., USA. Musicologist; Organist. Educ: MusR, Univ. of the Pacific; MusM, Eastman Schl. of Music; PhD, Univ. of Chgo. m. Rose Mick. Publs: Teaching Elementary Music without a Supervisor, 1959; Poster Sets Music in American History, 1970; Opera, 1970; 18th Century Composers, 1970; Famous Musical Amateurs, 1970; What Makes a Good Musicians, 1973; Contbr. to var. musical publs. incl: Acta Musicologica; Anuario Musical; Civil War History. Mbrships: Pres., NJ MTA, 1961-63; Sec., Eastern Div., Music Tchrs. Nat. Assn., 1962-64; MENC; Am. & Int. Musicological Socs.; Renaissance Soc. of Am.; AGO; Pi Kappa Lambda; AAUP. Recip. Rsch. Grants, Glassboro State Coll., 1968, 1971. Address: 512 S Woodbury Rd., Pitman, NJ 08071, USA.

CARPENTER, Nan Cooke, b. 29 July 1912, Louisa County, Va., USA. University Professor. Educ: BMus, Hollins Coll., 1934; MA, Univ. of N Carolina, 1941; MA, Yale Univ., 1945; PhD, ibid., 1948. Career: Prof. of English, Univ. of Mont., Univ. of Ga., 1948-78; Hd., Dept. of Comparative Lit., Univ. of Ga., 1974-78; Prof., music hist., Syracuse Univ., 1965-66. Publs: Rabelais and Music, 1954; Music in the Medieval and Renaissance Universities, 1958, ' '77; John Skelton, 1968. Contbr. to profl. publs. Mbrship: Modern Lang. Assn.; Renaissance Soc. of Am.; Am. Musicol. Soc.; Comparative Lit. Assn.; Phi Beta Kappa; Amici Mori; Univ. Womens Club (London). Hons: Ford Fellowship, Cambridge, 1954-55. Address: Park Hall, Univ. of Ga., Athens, GA 30602, USA. 5, 7, 11.

CARPENTER, Thomas H, b. 27 Sept. 1927, Kingfisher, Okla., USA. Prof. of Music & Chmn. of Dept. of Music, SUNY, Coll. at Fredonia. Educ: BA, Univ. Mo., 1952; MA, ibid., 1954; D Mus Arts, Boston Univ., 1965. m. Emily Gay Capenter, 2 s., 2 d. Career: Instr. of Music, Univ. of Maine at Machias, 1954-58; Asst. Prof. & Chmn. of Fine Arts, Mass. State Coll., Worcester, 1958-65; Assoc. & Prof. of Music & Chmn., Dept. Music Educ., E Car. Univ., USA, 1965-73; Prof. of Music, SUNY, Coll. of Fredonia, 1973-; Chmn., Dept. of Music, ibid., 1973-. Publs: Utilizations of Instructional Television in Music Education, 1969; Televised Music Instruction, 1973. Contbr. to profl. jrnls. Mbrships. incl: Phi Mu Alpha-Sinfonia; Pi Kappa Lambda; Kappa Delta Pi; Music Educ. Nat. Conf. Hobby: Photography. Address: 12 Sunset Dr., Fredonia, NY 14063, USA.

CARR, Colin Michael, b. 25 Oct. 1957, Liverpool, UK. Cellist. Educ: Yehudi Menuhin Schl., 1966-74; studied cello w. Christopher Bunting, Maurice Gendron & William Pleeth; ARCM hons. (perf.). m. Louise de Coetlogon Williams. Debuts: London, 1975; Amsterdam, 1976; Berlin, 1978; NY, 1979. Career: apps. in all London major concert halls; Aldeburgh, Brighton, Windsor, Edinburgh, Gstaad, Como, S Bank Fests.; also at Berlin Phil. Hall, Sev. concerts, Amsterdam Concertgebouw; apps. on British Dutch & German radio & TV; tours of USA. Mbr.

INTERNATIONAL WHO'S WHO IN MUSIC

117

ISM. Hons. incl: 1st Prize, Royal Overseas League Music Competition, 1974; 3 times Martin Scholarship Fund winner, 1973-78; Gulbenkian Music Fellowship, 1977; Young Concert Artists Competition winner (USA), 1978. Hobbies: Liverpool F.C. Supporter; Natural Foods. Mgmts: De Koos (Europe); Young Concert Artists Inc. (USA). Address: c/o De Koos Concert Mgmt., 416 King's Rd., London SW10 OLJ, UK.

CARR, Ian, b. 21 Apr. 1933, Dumfries, Scotland, UK. Trumpeter; Flugelhorn Player; Composer/Arranger; Writer. Educ: BA. m. Sandra Louise Carr, 1 d. Career incls: Co-Ldr., Don Rendel-Ian Carr Quintet; 1963-69; Fndr. Mbr., New Jazz Orch., 1964-68; Ldr., Nucleus, 1969-; num. radio, TV & fest. apps. throughout Europe & Scandinavia. Comps. incl: Solar Plexus, 1970; Labyrinth, 1973; Will's Birthday Suite, 1974. Recordings incl: Snakeships Etcetera, 1974; Alleycat, 1975. Mbrships. incl: Music Panel, Gtr. London Arts Assn.; Brit. Sect., Int. Soc. for Contemporary Mus. Publs: Music Outside, 1973. Contbr. to periodicals. Hons: 1st Prize, Int. Jazz Fest. Montreux, Switz., 1970. Hobbies incl: Walking. Mgmt: David Apps, 189 Regent St., Suite 309, Triumph House, London W1. Address: 34 England's Lane, London NW3, UK.

CARR, Jennifer Elizabeth, b. 21 Oct. 1935, Great Witley, Worcs., UK. Flautist. Educ: Guildhall Schl. of Music; AGSM; Hochschule für Musik, Berlin; Abschlussprüfung. m. Clifford Caesar. Debut: British Ctr., Berlin, 1963. Career: RIAS, Berlin; BBC TV, London. Mbrships: Inc. Soc. of Musicians; Musicians Union. Hobbies: Sculpture; Dress Design. Address: 8 Trehern Rd., Mortlake, London SW14, UK. 3.

CARR-BOYD, Ann Kirsten, b. 13 July 1938, Sydney, Australia. Composer. Educ: BMus, Univ. Sydney, 1960; MA, ibid., 1963; RCM. m. Peter Murray Carr-Boyd, 3 d. Career: pvte. Piano Tchr. Tutor in Music, Dept. Music, Sydney Univ., 1967-73; Currently full-time Comp. Comps. incl: Look at the Stars (14 piano pieces) 1970, Gold (orch.), Couperin (chmbr. ensemble); Catch 75 for chmbr. ensemble w. voice. Contbr. to: Aust. Dictionary of Biog; Grove 6. Mbrships: APRA; FAC; Comps. Guild of Aust. Hons. incl: Albert H Maggs Comp. Award, Aust., 1975. Mgmt: J Albert & Son, 139 King St., Sydney 2000, Aust. Address: 1 McMahons Rd., Northwood, NSW, 2066, Aust.

CARRERAS, José Maria, b. 5 Dec. 1946, Barcelona, Spain. Opera Singer. 1 s., 1 d. Educ: Gennaro, Lucrezia Borgia, Barcelona, 1970. Career: Don Carlo (Film Version, Dir. Herbert von Karajan), 1980; Sev. radio & TV apps., Italy, France, Spain, Austria, USA. Recordings: Early Verdi Operas; Don Carlos; Aida; Werther; Ballo in Maschera; Turandot; Boheme; Lucia di Lammermoor; Pagliacci; Cavalleria Rusticana; Simon Boccanegra. Hons: Verdi Singing Competition, 1971; Sev. recording awards; Recip. awards by sev. Opera Cos., Italy, France, Austria & Spain. Hobby: Sport (tennis). Address: Infanta Carlota 23, Atico 1°, Barcelona, Spain.

CARRINGTON, Jean, b. 23 May 1918, London, UK. Cellist. Educ: The Study, Wimbledon, UK; studied w. Effie Richardson, Antonia Butler, Emmanual Feuermann. ARCM. m. (1) Robert Carrington, 2 s. m. (2) Lt. Col. F de Weld Simon. Career: Cello Tchr., Ardingly Coll., Roedean Schl., 1948-63; Charterhouse, 1967-, Hurstpierpoint Coll., 1971-; Pvte. Cello Tchr.; Organiser, Orchl. & Choral Summer Schl., Termonfechin, Co. Louth, Ireland, 1968-. Mbr., ISM. Hobbies: Grandchildren; Gardening; Walking; Reading Detective Stories. Address: Ladymead, Hurstpierpoint, W Sussex, UK.

CARRINGTON, Philip Rodney, b. 26 Sept. 1948, Melbourne, Aust. Teacher of & Performer on Violin & Viola; Conductor. Educ: Melbourne Univ.; studied violin w. Hermia Barton, John Glickman, Jan Sedivka. Debut: Assembly Hall, Melbourne, 1971. Career incls: premiered Leslie Howard's opera Hredidar the Fool (cond. & repetiteur, Melbourne Univ. orch. & choral soc.) & Violin Sonata, Antony Kitchen's String Quartet & Perfluvio for viola, flute & percussion, & Richard Excel's Gnomon II for solo violin; string master, Aquinas Coll., 1978-. Recordings: Bach Partita 3; Bach Sonata for unaccompanied violin no. 1. Contbr. to: New Music. Mbrships: Cond. of str. orch. & tutor of chmbr. music, Dorian le Gallienne Music Soc.; Res. Cond., Melbourne Univ. Symph. Orch. Hons. incl: Winner, Dandenong Eisteddfod Concerto Competition, 1971. Address: 16 Clapham St., Balwyn, Vic., 3103, Australia.

CARRINGTON, Simon Robert, b. 23 Oct. 1942, Salisbury, UK. Musical Director; Singer, Contrabassist; Arranger. Educ: MA, King's Coll., Cambridge; Tchng. Cert., New Coll., Oxford. m. Hilary Stott, 1 s., 1 d. Career: Musical Dir., The King's Singers, app. in all major UK fests. on BBC & ITV, many radio broadcasts, toured Aust. (1972, '75, '76, '79), USA (1973, '74, '75, '77, '78), Europe & Japan. Comps: sev. arrs. for

The King's Singers. Recordings: w. The King's Singers: French Collection: Madrigal Collection; Contemporary Collection; Concert Collection; etc. Mbrships: ISM; Royal Soc. of Musicians; Folio Soc. Hobbies: Vintage Cars; Gardening; Walking; Inland waterways; Eating. Mgmt: Noel Gay Org. Address: 7 Woodcote Pk. Rd., Epsom, Surrey, UK. 3, 4.

CARRITT, R Graham, b. 25 Sept. 1892, Dulwich, London. UK Professor of Music; Lecture-recitalist; (Piano). Educ: New Coll., Oxford Univ.; piano pupil of Katharine Goodson & George Woodhouse; ARCM. m. C N Begg. 3 c. Career: Prof., RCM, London; British Council Tours; Associated Bd. Tours; Pupils at Westminster Schl.; Recitals, Grotian Hall, Schls., Colls.; Lectr. in Adult Educ., London Univ. Ext.; Music w. talks,.BBC, Var. publs. on Norway, Denmark, Baltic Countries, Czechoslovakia. Contbr. to The Musical Record; Edited RCM mag. Mbr., Inc., Soc. Musicians. Hons: Chevalier of 3 Stars of Latvia for musical liaisons. Hobbies: Translating Italian stories; Croquet; Playing Scrabble. Address: 19 Culford Mansions, London SW3, UK.

CARROLL, Charles Michael, b. 5 Mar. 1921, Otterbein, Ind., USA. Professor of Music. Educ: BMus, Ind. Univ., 1949; MMus, 1951, PhD, 1960, Fla. State Univ. m. Mary Rosenbush, 2 s., 2 d. Career: Prof. of Music & Musicologist, Ind. Univ., Fla. State Univ., Pensacola Jr. Coll., St. Petersburg Jr. Coll.; Music Critic, Tallahassee Democrat, 1950-53, St. Petersburg Independent, 1976-. Publs: The Great Chess Automation, 1975. Contbr. to profl. publs. Mbrships. incl: Exec. Bd., 1974-77, VP, 1977-79, Pres., 1979-80, Am. Soc. for 18th Century Studies, SE Region; Nat. Coun., 1977-80, Assoc. Ed., 1975-, Coll. Music Soc.; Am. Musicol. Soc. Hobbies: Gardening; Chess. Address: 1701 80th St. N, St. Petersburg, FL 33710, USA. 7.

CARTER, Elliott Cook, Jr., b. 11 Dec. 1908, USA. Educator; Composer. Educ: AB, AM, Harvard Univ.; Ecole Normale de Musique, Paris. m. Helen Frost-Jones, 1939, 1 s. Career: Musical Dir., Ballet Caravan, 1937-39; Critic, Modern Music, 1937-42; Tutor, St. John's Coll., Annapolis, 1939-541; Tchr. of Composition, Peabody Conserv., 1946-48, Columbia Univ., 1948-50; Queen's Coll., NY, 1955-56; Prof. of Music, Yale Univ., 1960; Andrew White Prof.-at-large, Cornell Univ., 1967-. Compositions incl: Symph., Double Concerto; Variations for orch.; Piano Concerto; Woodwind Quintet; Sonatas for piano & cello, flute, oboe, cello & harpsichord; 2 String Quartets; Ballets-Pocahontas; the Minotaur; Concerto for Orch., 1970; choral & incidental music. Hons. incl: Pulitzer Prize; Sibelius Medal, 1960; Hon. degrees from var. Univs.; Gold Medal, Nat. Inst. of Arts & Letters, 1971. Address: Mead St., Waccabuc, NY 10597, USA.

CARTFORD, Gerhard Malling, b. 21 Mar. 1923, Ft. Dauphin, Madagascar. Musicologist. Educ: BMus, St. Olaf Coll., Northfield, Minn.; MSM, Schl. of Sacred Music, Union Theol. Sem., NYC, 1950; PhD, Univ. of Minn., 1961. m. Pauline Edna Ferguson, 2 s., 1 d. Career: Ch. Musician (Organist & Choir Dir.), 1951-61; Prof. of Music & Chmn. of Dept., Tex. Lutheran Coll., Seguin, Tex., 1961-74; Asst. Prof. of Liturgy, Ch. Music & the Arts, Luther Theol. Sem., St. Paul, Minn. 1974-. Comp. of Liturgical music, choral anthems & hymns. Mbrships. incl: Lutheran Soc. for Worship, Music & the Arts. Contbr. to profl. jrnls. Hons. incl: Fulbright Schlr., Norway, 1950-51. Hobbies incl: Carpentry. Address: 2279 C'wlth. Ave., St. Paul, MN 55108, USA.

CARTLEDGE, Lucy Amelia, b. 4 Mar. 1956, London, UK. Flautist (perfromer & teacher). Educ: RCM (w. John Francis); ARCM (perfs. & tchrs.). m. Nicholas Hooper. Career: works w. husband as flute & guitar duo; tours of UK & France, playing for music clubs, fests., univs., etc.; selected by Julian Bream for Yehudi Menuhin's organization Live Music Now; as flautist also does freelance work w. var. orchs. & chmbr. ensembles. mbr., ISM. Hobbies: Yoga; Craft Work; Swimming. Mgmt: Live Music Now. Address: 47 Vicarage Rd., Oxford OX1 4RE, UK.

CARTWRIGHT, Patricia, b. Manchester, UK. Viola Player; Pianist; Teacher; Composer. Educ: GSM; Univ. of London; BMus; LRAM; ARCM; AGSM. Career: viola player, Guarnerius Str. Quintet, Hampstead Piano Quarter; Philharmonia Orch., BBC Concert Orch. & English Sinfonia; many tours & broadcasts, incl. TV in USA. Comps: Passacaglia for Str. Quintet; Intermezzo for Piano Quartet; Prelude, Air & Fugue, for Wind Quintet; choral pieces. Mbrships: ISM; Dir., Henley Summer Music Schl. Hons: Goldsmiths' Piano Scholarship, GSM; Sir Frederick Bridge Scholarship, Univ. of London. Hobbies: Travel; Driving; Theatre; Cinema; Tennis; Swimming; Handicrafts. Mgmt: Concert Agency (for Guarnerius Str. Quintet). Address: 18 Asmuns Hill, London NW11 6ET, UK.

CARUCCI, James, b. 20 Mar. 1942, Newark, NJ, USA. Musician; Flautist (Orchestral & Chamber Music). Educ: BA, Flute &

Music Educ., Montclair State Coll., NJ; MM, Flute, Applied Music, Manhattan Schl. of Music, NYC. div. 2 s. Career: Solo perfs. at NY Flute Club & NY Histl. Soc.; Solo Flautist, Pitts. Wind Symph. & Denver Symph. Orch., Currently freelance musician & tchr. in NY & NJ. Mbrships: Local 802, Am. Fedn. of Musicians, NYC; Sinfonia. Recip. Robert Lombardi Memorial Scholarship, 1962. Hobbies: Sports; Astronomy; Theatre. Address: 217 Newark Ave., Lyndhurst, NJ, USA.

CARUS, Louis, b. 22 Oct. 1927, Kasauli, India. Violinist. Educ: Brussels Conserv.; Peabody Conserv., Balt., USA; LRAM. m. Nancy Reade Noell, 2 s., 1 d. Debut: Glasgow, 1952. Career: SNO, 5 yrs.; Solo, Chamber Music & Tchng. career, Scotland; Hd., String Dept., RSAM; Mbr., Scottish Trio, Scottish Piano Quartet, Clarina Ensemble, New Music Grp. of Scotland; Ldr., Northern Sinfonia Orch.; Sub-Ldr., Monteverdi Orch.; Prin., Birmingham Schl. of Music. Recordings: Shostakovich & Beethoven Piano Trios. Contbr. to: daily papers; Strad Mag.; Inc. Soc. Musicians Jrnl. Mbrships: Warden, Inc. Soc. Musicians, 1973-74. Hons: FRSAMD; hon. RAM. Hobbies: Gardening; Sketching; Picture Collection; Travel. Mgmt: Helen Jennings Concert Agcy., London. Address: 24 Barlows Rd., Edbaston, Birmingham B15 2PL, UK. 3.

CARVALHO, Dinora, b. 1 June 1908, Uberaba, Minas Gerais, Brazil. Composer. Educ: Conserv. of Music, Sao Paulo m. Jose Bittencourt Muricy. Career: Piano recitals in France, Italy, S Am.; Fndr., woman's wind orch., Sao Paulo. Comps. incl: Symphonic pieces; 4 piano & orch. works; Chmbr. music; 80 piano pieces; works for cello, harp, violin, flute, clarinet, oboe; De Profoundis, mass; choral works. 4 ballets; theatre music; 60 songs; guitar pieces. Recordings incl: Piano Sonata No. 1. Mbrships. incl: Brazilian Acad. of Music. Contbr. to newspapers. Recip., var. hons. Address: Rua Itacolomi 380 Apt. 62, Higieuopolis, Sao Paulo, Brazil.

CARVALHO, Reginaldo, b. 27 Aug. 1932, Guarabira, Paraiba, Brazil. Composer; Professor; Violin Player; Organist. Educ: Grad. music, Rio de Janeiro, 1952; Contemporary Music Studies, 1952-56; Psychol.; Pedagogy, Paris; Electroacoustic Music, Ctr. Bourdan, ORTF, France. m. Liliane Penne Vilar de Carvalho, 3 s. Debut: Brazil, 1951. Career: Artistic dir. of var. choirs in Brazil & Europe; Prof., Coll. Pedro II, Rio de Janeiro; Musical Dir., Radio Eldorado, Radio Brasilia; Rep. for Brazil at World Congress for Choir Singing, Paris & Roime. Comps. incl: Sonoridades, 1969. Tape recordings of all electroacoustical works. Publs. incl: Children's Theatre. Contbr. to profl. jrnls. Mbr. num. profl. orgs. Hons: 1st Prize, Best Music for Stage Plays, 1956-72. Hobbies: Sound Picture Collages; Folkloric Rsch.; Reading. Address: Rua Goias, 999 Sul Teresina, CEP 64000, Piaui, Brazil.

CARY, Bob, b. 28 Feb. 1940, Providence, RI, USA. Composer; Arranger; Band Leader; Musician (Trumpet, Trombone). Educ: Berklee Schl. of Music, 1957-60. Debut: Homestead Showbar, Providence, 1956. Career: Played w. num. bands incl. Tommy Dorsey, Buddy Morrow, Jimmy Dorsey; Mgr., Bob Carey Orch. Sev. recordings incl: Live at Soho's. Contbr. to: Big Band Mag. Mbr., Bix Biederbecke Memorial Soc. Address: Apt. 203, 71 Parkwoods Village Dr., Don Mills, Ont. M3A 2YI, Can.

CARY, Tristram Ogilvie, b. 14 May 1925. Lxford, UK. Composer; University Lecturer; Conductor; Electronics Engineer. Educ: MA, Oxon; AMus, TCL; LMus, ibid.; Hn. RCM. m. Doris Enid Jukes, 2 s., 1 d. Debut: Piano Comp. performed 1949. Career: Commissions for BBC & films, 1955-73; Num. feature fiims, theatre scores & TV serials; Fndr., Electronic Music Studio, RCM, 1967; Vis. Comp., Univ. Adelaide, 1974; Sr. Lectr. in Comp., ibid. Compositions incl: Narcissus; Trios. Num. recordings. Contbr. to profl. mags. inclng: The Composer. Mbrships. incl: Coun. Mbr., CGGB. Hobbies: Food; Wine; Swimming; Sailing; Conversation. Address: c/o Dept. of Music, Univ. of Adelaide, S Australia 5001.

CASADESUS, Gaby, b. 9 Aug. 1901, Marseilles, France. Concert Pianist; Teacher. Educ: Paris Conserv. m. Robert Casadesus, 2 s., 1 d. Debut: Monte Carlo. Career: Soloist w. ldng. orchs. of the world; num. perfs. of 2 piano music w. husband. Bd. of Jurors for Piano Conserv. and all Brussels comps.; conducts master classes, Fontainebleau Am. Schl.; Royal Acad. (France); Curtis Inst. (USA). Recordings: num. Mozart concertos; Bach concertos; works by Faure, Debussy, Ravel, Satie, Schmitt, R Casadesus, Bartok. Hons: Chevalier of Legion d'Honor, France. Mgmt: Y Dandelot, Paris; CAMI, NYC. Address: 54 rue Vaneua, Paris, France.

CASADESUS, Marius Robert Max, b. 24 Oct. 1892, Paris, France. Violinist; Composer. Educ: Conserv. Music, paris (violin). 1 d. (dec.). Career: Soloist in symph. Concerts. Europe, USA; recitals for 13 yrs. as Violin/Piano duo. w. his nephew, Robert Casadesus, Num. compositions incl: symphs. & Chamber Music. Num. recordings. Hons: Commandeur, l'Ordre de la Légion d'Honneur, Medaille d'Or du Mérite Civique; Off., order of Arts & Lettore, 1974; Grande Medaille de Vermeil de la Ville de Paris, 1917. Address: No. 8 Place des Quatre Frères Casadesus, 75018 Paris, France.

CASCARINO, Romeo, b. 28 Sept. 1922, Phila., Pa., USA. Composer; Pianist; Conductor; Teacher. Educ: BMus, Phila. Conserv. of Music, 1943. m. Dolores Ferraro. Career: Cond. & Musical Dir., Co-Opera Co., 1950-57; Arranger, Somerset Records 101 Strings, 1956-63; Hd., Theory & Comp. Depts., Combs Coll. of Music, Phila. Major comps. incl: Blades of Grass (Eng. horn & strings); Fanfare & March (band); Acadian Land (Orch.); Little Blue Pigeon (song); Prospice (ballet); William Penn (opera); Soniferous Nuance (piano). Comps. recorded: Sonata for Bassoon & Piano; Pymalion; 8 songs. Mbrships: ASCAP; Sinfonia Fraternity. Hons. incl: Orpheus Award, Phi Mu Alpha Sinfonia Fraternity, 1975; Guggenheim Fellowships, 1948, '49; Hon. Doct., Combs Coll. of Music, 1960. Hobby: Cooking. Address: 17 Zummo Way, Norristown, PA 19401, USA.

CASH, Louise, b. 23 Sept. 1939, Worcester, Mass., USA. Singer (Mezzo-Soprano); College Music Teacher. Educ: AB, Emmanuel Coll., 1959; MMus, Boston Univ. Schl. Fine & Applied Arts, 1962. m. Philip Cash, 3 s., 1 d. Debut: Concert, Wigmore Hall, London, UK, 1971. Career: Prin. singer w. Assoc. Artists Opera Co., New England Regional Opera, Cambridge Opera, Artist Int.; Soloist w. choral socs.; recitalist; Asst. Prof., Music, Emmanuel Coll.; Chmn., Dept. Music, ibid., 1975-. Mbr. profl. orgs. Recip: Cabot Trust Grant, 1970. Hobbies incl: Reading; Theatre; Belly Dancing. Address: 13 Debra Lane, Framingham, MA 01701, USA.

CASHMORE, Donald, b. 12 July 1926, London, UK. Conductor; Organist; Composer. Educ: BMus, BSc, Univ. of London; FRCO; LRAM; ARCM. m. Margaret Elizabeth Hamilton. Career: Dir. of Music, Emanuel Schl., London, 1956-61; Prin. Lectr. in Music, Ealing Coll. of Higher Educ., 1961-; Cond., Kingsway Choral Soc., 1952-63, City of London Choir, 1963-, & Brompton Choral Soc., 1974-. Comps: (cantatas) This Child Behold; Jerusalem; num. anthems, carosl & part songs. Contbr. to: Musical Times. Recip., Sawyer Prize, ARCO, 1949. Address: 22 Vallis Way, Ealing, London W13, UK.

CASO, Fernando H, b. 28 July 1943. Professor of Music History & Theory. Educ: BA, Univ. of Puerto Rico; MM, Ind. Univ. Mbrships: Am. Musicol. Soc.; Treas., VP, Puerto Rico Musical Soc. Hobbies: Collecting Puerto Rican Paintings; Tennis; Reading; Ballet. Address: Calle Barranquitas No. 52, Apt. 3-A, Condado Santurce, PR 00907 Puerto Rico.

CASSELLS, Ian McIntosh, b. 14 Apr. 1945, Dunfermline, Scotland, UK. Schoolmaster; University Research Worker (Organ, Harpsichord, Recorder, Crumhorn, Cornamusa, Doltzaina, Kortholt, Rackett, Shawm, Bombard, Cornett, Viola da Gamba). Educ: George Watson Coll., Edinburgh; Pembroke Coll.; Cambridge; BA; MA; FLS; FCPS. Career: Fndr. & Dir., several Early Music Consorts. Mbr. Conchological Soc. Hobbies: Conchology; Langa.; Hist.; Brasses; Palaeography & Calligraphy; Windmills & Sundials, Hilwalking. Address: Pembroke Coll., Cambridge CB2 1RF, UK.

CASSILY, Richard, b. 14 Dec. 1927, Wash., DC, USA. Opera Singer (tenor). Educ: Peabody Conserv. of Music, Baltimore, Md., 1946-52. m. Helen Koliopoulos, 3 d., 4 s. Career: apps. at Mosk major opera houses incl. NYC, Berlin, Hamburg, Covent Garden, Vienna, La Scala, Paris, Metropolitan, NY. TV films of Peter Grimes, Elektra, Otello, Fidelio, Meistersinger & Wozzeck. num. recordings. Hons: Kammersinger, Hamburg, 1973. Mgmt: Lies Askonas, London; Columbus Artists Mgmt. Inc., NY. Address: c/o Metropolitan Opera House, Lincoln Center, New York City, NY 10024, USA.

CASSUTO, Alvaro Leon, b. 17 Nov. 1938, Porto, Portugal. Conductor; composer. Educ: PhD, Univ. Lisbon, 1964. Kappelmeister Dip., Vienna Conserv., 1965. Debut: Comp., Sintra Festival w. Sinfonia Brava No. 1, 1959; Cond., Oporto Symph., 1961. Career: Cond. in England, USA, Denmark, Greece, Brazil, Israel, Switzerland & Czechoslovakia. Comps. incl: Song of Loneliness, 1972 (Ed. G Shirmer); To Love and Peace, 1973 (Ed. G Schirmer). Contbr. to daily newspapers & publs. in Portugal. Hons. incl: Portuguese Press Award, 1970. Mgmt: Sheldon Soffer Inc., 130 W 56th St., New York, NY 10019, USA. Address: Av. de Sintra 826, Cascais, Portugal.

CASTEL, Nico, b. 1 Aug. 1931, Lisbon, Portugal. Singer (tenor) specializing in character roles. Educ: BA, Temple Univ., Phil., Pa.; Caracas Univ.; Pvte. tchrs., USA, Milan, Mainz, Germany. m. Nancy, 1 d. Debut: Fenton in Falstaff (Verdi), Santa Fe Opera, 1958. Career: Has sung w. major opera cos. of USA;

NY Opera, 12 seasons; Mbr., Metropolitan Opera; Recitals; Tours, Europe, S Am., USA; Diction Coach, Metropolitan Opera; Trilingual Diction Tchr. for singers, NYU Queens Coll., Am. Inst. of Musical Studies, Graz, Austria & Mannes Schl. of Music; Fndr. & mbr., Metropolitan Opera Madrigal Singers. Mbrships: Am. Guild of Musical Artists; Am. Fedn. of TV & Radio Artists; Screen Actor's Guild. Hons: 1st Winner, The Joy in Singing Competition, 1958. Hobbies: Languages; Photography; Cooking. Mgmt: Ludwig Lustig & Florian, 111 57th St., NY, NY 10019, USA. Address: 170 West End Ave., NY, NY 10023, USA.

CASTLEMAN, Charles Martin, b. 22 May 1941, Quincy, Mass., USA. Violinist. Educ: BMus., Curtis Inst. of Music; AB, Harvard Univ.; MA, Univ. of Pa.; Phd. Cand., Bryn Mawr Coll. m. Heidi Waldron Castleman. Debut: Town Hall, NYC, 1951. Career; has toured in USA., Mexico, Can., UK, France, Germany, Netherlands, Switz., Austria, Sweden, & USSR; apps. as Soloist, Boston, NYC, Chgo., Phila., Moscow State, Belgian Nat. orchs., Dir., PMA Saratoga Str. Quartet Prog. Violinist w. Raphael Trio, 1974. Recordings: Reger String Trios; Martin Trios. Contbr. to: Anvario Musicale; Music Jrnl. Mbrships: Bd. Mbr., Curtis Inst. Alumni Assn.; Bohemians; BEI. Hons: Silver Medal, Queen Elisabeth of Belgium Contest, 1963; Laureate, Tchaikovsky Contest, 1966. Hobbies: Bridge; French Lit.; Cycling. Mgmt: Colbert Artists Mgmt. (solo), Wm. Judd Mgmt. (trio); USA; ICA, Amsterdam, Europe. Address: 1630 Waverly St., Philadelphia, PA 19146, USA. 14.

CASTRILLON, Maria Teresa, b. 2 Nov. 1935, Mexico City, Mexico. Concert Pianist; Piano Teacher. Educ: MMus; Concert pianist & tchng. dip., Conserv. of Mexico; Dip., Vienna Acad.; Courses, Spain & Italy. m. Ing. Alfonso Malo, 3 d. Debut: Ravel Concerto, w. Mexico Symph. Orch. Career: Apps., Mexico, Vienna & Paris; TV app., Mexico; Radio apps., Madrid, Paris, Brussels & Vienna. Contbr. to sev. profl. jrnls. Mbr., Interamerican Music Critics Assn., Wash. Hons: Gold Cross, Austrian Govt. Hobby: Children. Mgmt: Associación Manuel M Ponce, Mexico D.F. Bucareli 12. Address: Espíritu Santo 75, Coyoacán, México 21, D.F. Mexico.

CASWELL, Kenneth, b. 16 Mar. 1917, Normanton, Yorks., UK. Teacher. Educ: Leeds Coll. Music; LLCM; LTCL; Studied w. Arthur Hinchcliffe. m. Olive Slack. Career: Mbr., Studio Choir, BBC (N), 1947, Radio Luxembourg, 1951; Full time Singing & Music Specialist, WRCC; Evening Inst. Choral Tchr., ibid., 20 yrs.; Musical Dir., Normanton Operatic Soc. & Featherstone Musical & Dramatic Soc.; Organist & Choirmaster, Pontefract, Pontefract Ctrl. Meth. Ch., Oxford St. Meth. Ch., Wakefield Belle Isle Congl. Ch., Leeds; Fndr., Cond., W. Riding Singers Broadcasting Choir. Mbrships: Inc. Soc. Musicians; Music Tchrs. Soc. of GB.; Life Fellow, Int. Inst. Arts & Letters. Hons: Silver Bowl & Silver 1st Prize, Sunderland Music Competition, Huddersfield, 1947. Hobbies: Gardening; Driving. Address: 1 Lawn's Close Bungalows, Altofts, Normanton, WF6 2NR, Yorks., UK. 3.

CATHCART, David Paul, b. 7 June 1949, Bradford, UK. Orch. Conductor. Educ: GGSM. Career: Fndr. & Prin. Cond., Lambeth Orch.; Prin. Cond. & Artistic Dir., Metropolitan Symph. Orch.; Guest Cond., num. orchs. in GB & Europe; Broadcasts, BBC radio. Recordings incl: Schubert's Symph. 3, 8, 9; Weber Clarinet Concerto 2, Beethoven Symph. 9. Publs: Ed. of Schubert Symph. 8 'Unfinished', 1979. Address: 56 Bennerley Rd., London, SW11 6DS, UK.

CATLOW, John Rolf Aldred, b. 10 Nov. 1940, Simonstone, Lancs., UK. Cellist & voice (baritone). Educ: Royal Manchester Coll. of Music; ARMCM (tchrs. & performers dips.). m. 1 s., 1 d. Career incl: Cellist, London Symph. Orch.; Co-prin. Cellist, Hallé Orch.; Prin. Cellist, Engl. Nat. Opera (current). Recordings incl. Engl. Nat. Opera (current). Recordings incl. Engl. Nat. Opera (Wagner, Ring). Hons: Pinson Prize (Bach playing) & Hiles Gold Medal (rochl. playing), Royal Manchester Coll. of Music, 1962. Hobbies: Lieder & Oratorio singing. Home Brewing & Wine Making. Address: 24 Surrey Rd., Harrow, Middx., HA14NA, UK.

CATTIN, Giulio, b. 22 May 1929, Vicenza, Italy. Professor of Classic Letters & Liturgical History. Educ: Laureate in Classic Letters, Cath. Univ. of Milan; Grad. study in Hist. of Music & Fndns. of Renaissance & Mediaeval Polyphony; Dip., organ. Career: Prof., Hist. of Music, Univ. of Padua. Publs: Johannis De Quadris Opera, 1972; Il Primo Savonarola-Pise e prediche dal codice Borromeo, 1973; Italian Laude from MS Cape Town 3.6.12, 1977; Il Medioevo I, 1979. Contbr. to Acta Musicologica; Quadrivium; Benedictina, etc. Mbrships: Soc. Int. de Musicol.; Soc. Italiana di Musicol.; Am. Musicological Soc. Address: Borgo S. Lucia 43, Vicenza, Italy.

CAUDLE, Theresa, b. 22 Mar. 1957, Surrey, UK. Performer on Cornetto & Baroque Violin. Educ: GSM. Career: Ldr., London Cornett & Sackbut Ensemble; BBC recordings w. same & w. others inclng: Musica Reservata, London Pro Musica, Hamburger

Bläserkreis für alte Musik & The Consorte of Musicke. Recordings: w. London Cornett & Sackbut Ensemble & Pro Cantione Antiqua. Address: Whitehill Lodge, Bletchingley, Surrey, UK.

CAVALCANTI, Nastor de Hollanda, b. 26 Nov. 1949, Rio de Janeiro, Brazil. Teacher of Comp. & Classic Guitar; Composer. Educ: Schl. of Music, Fed. Univ. of Rio de Janeiro; Private Study - music theory, comp. & classic guitar. Comps. incl: Guitar: Estudos Inegavelmente Cromáticos, 1978; Piano: Os Cabocolinhos, 1978; Choral: Noturno & Cantos de Trabalho, 1975; Strings: Quarteto Agonico No. 1 & No. 2, 1975; Chmbr. Orch: A Lenda do Tabuleiro da Xadrez, 1974; Septet: Contradiçao, 1975; Orch: Contradiçao 2, 1977. Mbr. num. profl. orgs. Recip. var. hons. & prizes. Hobbies: Listening to Records; Reading; Composing; Watching Films & TV; Talking to a few people. Address: Rua Prof. Álvaro Rodrigues 284, Apt. 102, Botafogo 60, 20 000 Rio de Janeiro, Brazil.

CAVARRA, Robert N, b. 23 Feb. 1934, Denver, Colo., USA. Organist; Professor; Organ Consultant; Harpsichordist; Theatre Organist. Educ: BA, St. Thomas Sem., Denver, 1956; Grad. Study, Pontifical N Am., Coll., Rome, Italy, 1957-58; BM, Univ. of Colo., Boulder, 1961; MM, ibid., 1963. m. Barbara Sedlmayr Cavarra, 3 s., 1 d. Career: Assoc. Prof., Colo. State Univ., Ft. Collins: Organ Recitalist. Composer, Suite For Organ. Recordings: Organist, Prod., Christmas at Colo. State Univ., Volumes I & II; Organist, Kodaly, Missa Brevis, Classic Chorale of Denver. Contbr. to: The CSU Alumnus Mag.; The Art of The Organ. Mbrships: AGO, 1947-; Dean, Ft. Collins Chapt., ibid., 1967-69. Named to Iota Kappa Lambda, 1963. Hobbies: Camping; Model Railroading. Address: 1717 Hillside Dr., Ft. Collins, CO, USA. 60.

CAVDARSKI, Vančo, b. 3 Mar. 1930, Vladimirovo, Yugoslavia. Orchestral Conductor. Educ: Tchrs. Coll., Skopje; Violin & Piano, Zagreb Music Schl.; Dip. Orchl. Cond., Belgrade Music Acad., 1957; studied w. Hans Schmidt-Isserstedt, Staatliche Hochschule für Musik, Hamburg, Germany. m. Elisabeth Katharine Lythgoe, 2 s. Career: Viola Player, Belgrade Phil. Orch., 1953-57; Cond., Macedonian Phil. Orch. & Nat. Opera & Ballet Co., Skopje; Musical Dir., Macedonian Phil., 1965-70; Assoc. Cond., Aust. Opera Sydney, 1970-72; Musical Dir./Cond., Christchurch Symph. Orch., NZ, & Chief Cond., Tasmanian Symph. Orch., Aust., 1973-; apps. w. Royal Liverpool Phil. & BBC Northern Orch., UK, Leningrade Phil., USSR, George Enescu Phil. orch., Bucharest, Rumania, Sydney Symph. Orch., Aust., & var. NZ orchs. TV apps. in Yugoslavia & Australia; num. concerts thru' out Europe. Recordings: Num. recordings for Aust. Broadcasting Commission. NX Broadcasting Commission & Yugoslav Radio. Hons: 2nd Prize, Liverpool Int. Conds. Competition, UK, 1962; October Prize for Music, Macedonia, 1962, Aust. Nat. Critics Award, 1975. Mgmt: Ingpen & Williams, Ltd., London. Address: 4 Braeside Crescent, Sandy Bay, Hobart, Tasmania, Aust. 15.

CAVE, Michael, b. 17 May 1944, Springfield, Mo., USA. Pianist; Fortepianist; Composer. Educ: studied w. noted tchrs.; BMus, Cali. Inst. of the Arts; MMus, Univ. of Southern Calif. m. Judyth Walker, 1 d. Debut: Rolla, Mo. Career incls: on fac., UCLA; concerto apps. & solo recitals inclng. cycle of Mozart Piano Concertos w. Mozart Fest. Chmbr. Orch. (also broadcast), 1973-74. Comps. incl: Ecclesiastes, (two sopranos, str. qt., oboe, horn, piano) 7 movements. Lines to the Sea (soprano, Engl. horn & piano); Elegy for soprano, oboe & piano; Woodwind Quintet; Pandora's Box (children's opera). Recordings: Mozart on the Fortepiano: Michael Cave Compositions. Mbrships: Bd., Nat. Assn. of Comps. of USA; Calif. Music Tchrs. Assn. Recip. var. hons. Address: 1525 Walnut Ave., Venice, CA 90291, USA.

CAVIN, Mile, b. 15 Feb. 1936, Evansville, Ind., USA. Professional Clarinetist (also Saxophone & Flute). Educ: BMus, Ind. Univ., 1959; pvte. study w. Anthony Gigliotti, 5 yrs.; Reed-making w. Kalmen Opperman; coaching w. var. Separated, separated, 2 d. Debut: Carnegie Recital Hall, NYC, 1968. Career: 1st Clarinet w. Met. Opera Nat. Co., Le Grand Ballet Classique de France, Radio City Music Hall, NYC, Am. Ballet Theatre & Harkness Ballet, also w. USN Band, Wash., DC; Soloist w. Chmbr. Shmbr. Symph. & USN Band; Solo recitals var. venues, NYC; Mbr., Manhattan, & Lyric Woodwind Quintets; featured soloist & orchl. player, Broadway shows. Mbr., Phi Mu Alpha Sinfonia. Hobbies: Bicycle Riding; Photography. Address: 354 S Evergreen Drive, Ventura, CA 93003, USA.

CAWOOD, Elizabeth Marion, b. 14 Sept. 1941, Harlan, Ky., USA. Opera Singer (Lyric Soprano); Voice Teacher. Educ: BMus, Ind. Univ., Bloomington; MMus, Univ. of Ky., Lexington; Acad. of Music, Munich Germany, 2 yrs.; Tulane Univ., Fla. Debut: Cologne Opera House, 1969. Career: has app. in Munich & Stuttgart, Germany, & in Tenn., Ky., Va., Ind., Fla., Ark. & NY, USA; Pvte. Tchr. of Voice & Lang. Pronunciation & profl. singer,

Tenn., Ky. & Ark.; Instructor in Voice & Artist in Res., David Lipscomb Coll., Nashville. Mbrships: Nat. Assn. Tchrs. of Singing; Delta Kappa Gamma. Hons. incl: 1st in Dist., Met. Opera Auditions. W Va., 1963, '64. Hobbies incl: Reading; Hiking; Tennis. Address: David Lipscomb Coll. Music Dept., Nashville, TN 37203, USA. 4.

CAZEAUX, Isabelle Anne-Marie, b. 24 Feb. 1926, NY, USA. Professor of Musicology. Educ: BA, Hunter Coll., NY; MA, Smith Coll., Mass.; MS in Lib. Sci., Columbia Univ.; PhD, in Musicol., ibid.; grad. study, Sorbonne, Paris; École normale de Musique, ibid, etc. Career incls: Hd., Music & Phonorecord Cataloguing Sect., NY Pub. Lib., 1957-63; Fac., Bryn Mawr Coll., 1963-; currently Alice Cater Dickerman Prof. & Chmn., Music Dept., ibid.; Pt.-time Fac. of Musicol. & Music Hist., Manhattan Schl., 1969-; Vis. Prof. of Music, Douglass Coll., Rutgers Univ., New Brunswick, NJ, 1978. Publs: Collaborator, Anthologie de la Chanson Parisienne au 16e Siècle, 1953; Ed., Chansons by Claudin de Sermisy, 1967; French Music in the 15th & 16th Centuries, 1975. Contbr. to var. musical publs. Mbrships. incl: Former Mbr. of Coun. & of Committee on the Status of Women in Musicol., Am. Musicol. Soc.; Former Mbr., Committees on Cataloguing & Bibliography, Music Lib. Assn.; Int. & French Musicol. Socs. Hons. incl: var. Fellowships, Scholarships & Educl. Grants. Address: 415 E 72nd St., NY, NY 10021, USA.

CECCATO, Aldo, b. 18 Feb. 1934, Milan, Italy. Conductor; Music Director. Educ: Verdi Conservatory, Milan; Musikhochschule, Berlin; Accademia Chigiana, Siena. m. Eliana de Sabata, 2 s., Debut: Milan. Career: Music Dir. & Cond., Detroit Symph. Orch., USA; Guest, major symph. orchs. & opera houses in world. Recordings: Traviata; Maria Stuarda; Grace Bumbry Italia Album; John Ogdon, Mendelssohn Piano Concertos. Hobbies: Russian lit.; Stamps; Tennis. Address: 770 Pemberton Rd., Grosse Pointe Park, MI 48230, USA.

CECCHINI, Penelope C, b. 8 Oct. 1943, Kokomo, Ind., USA. Piano Professor. Educ: BM, Butler Univ., Ind., 1965; Aspen Inst. of Music, Colo., 1965; MM, Mich. State Univ. 1966; ABD of PhD, ibid., 1970. Career: Soloist, Indpls. Symph. Orch.; Ft. Wayne Phil. Orch., Ind.; Mich. State Univ. Orch.; Univ. of Wisconsin; Eau Claire Symph. Orch.; TV apps. w. Indpls. Symph. Orch.; Guest Pianist, Congress of Strings Fac., Schubert Quintet, E Lansing, Mich.; Artists Series Concerts, Univ. Western Ont., Can.; Pioneered 1st piano workshops for high schl. pianists in Wis. State; Public solo recitals, accomp. instrumentalists, vocalists & apps. in Chmbr. grps. Mbrships: Sigma Alpha Iota; Phi Kappa Phi; Assn. of Univ. of Wis. Facs; Pi Kappa Lambda. Recip. num. hons. & prizes. Hobbies: Travel; Handwork; Antiques. Address: 218 McKinley Ave., Eau Clair, WI 54701, USA.

CECCONI-BATES, Augusta, b. 9 Aug. 1933, Syracuse, NY, USA. Composer; Public School Music Teacher. Educ: BA, 1956, MA 1960, Syracuse Univ.; Studied comp. w. Robert Palmer. m. Robert N Bates Sr., 3 stepchildren. Debut: Syracuse Univ., 1956. Career: Pub. Schl. Music Tchr., 1968-; Prof. of Music, Maria Regina Coll., Syracuse, NY, 1964. Comps. incl: Cantata for Mixed Chorus; Soprano & Tenor Solos w. Orch. Accomp.; sev. songs for soprano, bass & chmbr. grp., & for baritone & piano; works for piano solo inclng. 2 suites; 2 sonatas for violin & piano; 2 works for woodwind ensemble; 2 sorks for woodwind quartet; Cinque Stanze da Poliziano for soprano & tenor w. piano accomp.; Sonata for French Horn & piano. Mbr., musical socs. Recip., var. hons. Address: Toad Harbor, Shaw Rd., Bos 49D, W Monroe, NY 13167, USA.

CELIS, Fritz, b. 11 Apr. 1929, Antwerp, Belgium. Conductor; Professor of transportation. Educ: studied piano, harp, counterpoint, fugue, & orchl. conducting in Antwerp, Brussels, Cologne & Salzburg. m. Liane Jespers, 2 d. Debut: Royal Opera, Brussels, 1954. Career: Cond., Royal Opera of Brussels; Guest Cond., France, Spain, Germany, Netherlands, Czech.; Music Dir. & 1st Cond., Royal Flemish Opera, Antwerp, 1959-; Prof., Royal Flemish Conserv. of Music. Comps. incl: Elegy for orch.; Music for strings; 3 Symph. Movements; Variazioni (for Chmbr. orch.); Sonate (for violin & piano); Sonate (for cello & piano); Notturno e dansa (for 4 flutes); Episodes for viola & harpsichord. Address: Smolders Blockstraat 36, B-2520 Edegem, Belgium.

CERNAUSKAS, Kathryn Birute, b. 15 Sept. 1948, Hanover, Germany. Flautist. Educ: Wayne State Univ.; BMus, Univ. of Toronto; St. Cecilia's Conserv. of Music, Rome, Italy; studied w. J.-p. Rampal, M. Moyse & Gazzelloni. Career: var. apps. on CBC radio; num. solo recitals & chmbr. music concerts. Hons: Can. Coun. Grant 1971 & 72; Chalmers Award, 1971 & 72. Address: 2651 Lloyd Ave., N Vancouver, BC V7R 3X3, Can.

CERNY, William Joseph, b. Dec. 1928, NYC, USA. Concert Pianist; Accompanist; University Professor. Educ: BA, Yale Univ.,

1951; BMus, Yale Schl. of Music, 1952; MMus, ibid., 1954. m. Mary Ann Cunningham, 4 d. Debut: Steinway Hall, NYC, 19544. Career: Profl. Pianist & Accomp. for ldng. concert artists, 1954-59; Fac. Mbr., Eastman Schl. of Music, 1959-72; Chmn. & Prof. of Music, Music Dept., Univ. of Notre Dame, 1972-. Recordings: Music Saxophone Sacophone & Piano (2 vols.). Scott Joplin Rags, 1975. Contbr. to: Notes. Mbrships: Pi Kappa Lambda; Phi Beta Kappa. Phi Mu Alpha; Am. Musicol. Soc.; Coll. Music Soc. Recip. of highest awards of Music Educ. League of NY, 1951. Hobbies: Boating; Carpentry. Address: 2918 Caroline St., S Bend, IN 46614, USA.

CERVETTI, Sergio, b. 9 Nov. 1940, Uruguay. Composer. Educ: BA, Peabody Conserv., Balt., Md., USA; MA. Career: Comp. & pianist. Comps: 6 Sequences for dance; Five Episodes, Cello, Violin Piano; String Quartet. Recordings: Guitar Music, Aria suspendida. Contbr. to: Melos. Mbrships: BMI; Am. Philatelic Soc. Hons: Comp. in Res., DAAD, W Belin, 1969-70; 2nd Prize, Comp., Maracaibo Music Fest., 1977. Hobbies: Stamp Collecting; Oenologist. Address: 96 Park Place, Brooklyn, NY 11217, USA.

CERVIN, Helle, b. 2 Mar. 1943, Rakvere, Esthonia, Sweden. Music Educator; Soprano Singer. Educ: Exam. as music tchr., Acad. of Music; studied vocal interpretation w. Ingalill Linden, Lucie Frateur, Erik Werba, Mozarteum, Salzburg; Masterclass of singing, Acad. of Gothenburg. Henrik Herik Cervin, 1 s., 1 d. Debut: 1961. Career: Recitals in Sweden, Belgium, German Fed. Repub., Italy; broadcasts for Swedish & German Germany stns.; Music Dir., Tchr., Music Schl. of Falkenberg. Recordings w. Broadcasting Choir of Gothenburg. Recip. Esthonian Culturprize, 1969. Address: Hansagård, S-31100 Falkenberg, Sweden.

CERVIN, Henrik, b. 3 Apr. 1934, Arstad, Sweden. Music Director; Organist; Conductor. Educ: Organist, Canton & Music Tchr. Exams., Royal Acad. of Stockholm; Organ Dip., Alf Linder; studied w. Flor Peeters, 1967. m. Helle Aro, 1 s., 1 d. Debut: 1965. Career: many recitals, Sweden, Engl., Belgium, German Fed. Repub., Italy, also on Swedish & Northern German broadcasting stns.; Music Dir., Organist, Falkenberg, 1965-; Cond., Motetchoir, Falkenberg; Prof., Summer Acads. & Music Fests., Falkenberg, 1966-; one of initiators tchrs. at Weeks of Organ, Stenbrohult. Has recorded for Swedish Broadcasting. Ed., Organum 61 & 62. Hons. incl: Prize of Arts, Falkenberg, 1975. Address: Hansagard, S-31100 Falkenberg, Sweden.

CEULEMANS, Yvon Constant Jean (Ivo), b. 18 Mar. 1905, Antwerp, Belgium. Composer; Hon. Dir. of the Municipal Academy for Music, Hoboken, Antwerp. Educ: Royal Conserv. (Flemish), Antwerp, studied violin w. Peter Saenen, comp. w. Frans D'haeyer & Karel Candael; Tchr., music solfege & violin (all levels), 1925, MusAc, Hoboken. m. Magdalena J Seynhaeve. Comps. incl: Sonatine for clar. (viola) & piano; Lullaby for violin & piano; 3 Bagatelle for Harp solo; Suite for 2 trumpets, horn & trombone; 4 melodies; Capriccio for violin (viola) & piano; Corale e Variazioni for cello (CB) & piano; Suite française, Paul Bazelaire (or chl. score); 10 Melodies for children; Study VIII for Drum Couletier (pianoscore); Recordings: Quartetto per Clarinetti, Choral songs; Quartetti per archi, Concerto per violino & orch.; Suite per trumpet, Fr. horn & fagotto. Divertimento (orch); 'Mystic portrait', Cycle for soprano, quintetto ad archi. Publs: Notenleerlessen, (Method of music reading), Ed. De Sikkel, Vol. 1, 1966, Vol. II, 1969, Vol. III, 1971. Contbr. to sev. profl. jrnls. Hons: Karel Boury prize for children's songs. Royal Acad. of Ghent, 1954; 2nd prize, SABAM for 1st Quartetto per archi, 1956. Hobbies: Art; Nature. Address: Avenue Coghen 176, B-1180, Brussels, Belgium.

CEZAR, Corneliu, b. 22 Dec. 1937, Bucharest, Romania. Composer; Piano Teacher. Educ: Schl. of Music No. 1, Bucharest; Bucharest Conserv. m. Adina Cezar, 1 d. Career: Musical Sec., Romanian Opera of Bucharest, 1963-66; Piano Tchr., Schl. of Music No. 2, Bucharest, 1966-. Comps. incl: Cronica; Galileo Galilee (opera); Taaroa; Lieder for baritone & piano; La porte; Notre pain; Woyczeck; Golem; Les couleurs de l'immortalité; Hersale Dubrovner; Pericle; La couronne du soleil; Rota; Endlessday; Children's pieces for piano, etc. Contbr. to: Scînteria; Contemporanul; Muzica, etc. Address: Str. Anton Pann,on. 48A, Cod 74236, Bucharest 4, Romania.

CHACKSFIELD, Frank, b. 9 May Battle, Batle, Sussex, UK. Musical Director; Composer. Educ: Study of piano since age 7; Exams., Piano & Theory, local Trinity Coll. of Music; Organ study w. J R Sheehan-Dare. m. Jeanne Lehmann. Career: Cond., concerts, London & Europe; Radio, TV, concert apps., UK, Europe & Japan, Radio, TV apps., USA; Weekly BBC radio series. The Frank Chacksfield Hour, w. strings of BBC Radio Orch. Compositions Sea Mist; Cuban Boy; Blue Train; Catalan Sunshine; Candid Snap. Recordings: Approx. 80 LPs, & singles. Mbrships: Performing Rights Soc.; Mechanical-Copyright Protection Soc.; NARAS.

Hons. Cash Box Award, for Most Promising New Orch., 1953; Gold discs, for million sales of Limelight & Ebb Tide; NME Awards for same. Mgmt: Edward Sommerfield, London. Address: Allegro, Elm Walk, Farnborough Park, Kent, UK.

CHADWICK, Eric, b. 23 Nov. 1928, Manchester, UK. Conductor; Chorus Master; Solo Organist; Organ Teacher. Educ: RMCM, 1945-50; ARCO, 1946; FRCO, 1948; ARMCM (Perf. & Tchr.), 1948. Debut: as Solo Organist, Town Hall Manchester, 1949; as Cond., City Hall, Sheffield, w. Hallé Orch. & Sheffield Phil. Chorus, 1957. Career: Organist, St. Luke's Parish Ch., Weaste, 1948- & Hallé Concerts Soc., 1950-63; BBC recitalist, 1952-; Organ Prof., RMCM, 1954-72; Organist & Musical Advsr., Univ. of Manchester Inst. of Sci. & Technol., 1955-; Chorus Master, The Sheffield Phil. Chorus, 1955-, Huddersfield Choral Soc., 1962-69. Hallé Concerts Soc., 1956-66, Montgomery Co. Chorus, 1956-65; Sr. Lectr., Royal Northern Coll. of Music, 1973-; Guest Cond., RPO, Hallé Orch., Royal Liverpool Phil. Orch., City of B'ham Symph. Orch. Engl. Nat. Orch.; Northern Sinfonia Orch., Sheffield Phil. Orch.; appearances in Vienna, Brussels, Berlin, Munich, Lisbon, Zurich, Boston; TV appearances, BBC & ITV. Recordings for EMI & Pye (Nixa). Hons: Heywood Silver Medal, RMCM, 1950; Hon. Fellow, ibid., 1962. Var. hobbies. Address: 44 Broadway, Fairfield, Froylsden, Lancs., M35 6FE, UK. 3, 21.

CHAHIN, Myra, b. 4 July 1946, London, UK. Violoncellist. Educ: RAM; LRAM; (tchr. cello & piano); ARCM; studied w. Maurice Gendron, Civic Acad. of Saarbrücken; Staatliche Hochschule für Musik. m. Christopher Williams. Career: Tchr. of Cello, Yehudi Menuhin Sch.; Freelance Cellist w. major orchs.; num. recital apps. inclng. Purcell Room & Wigmore Hall, London; app. on BBC Tortelier masterclass series; recital on Malta TV. Contbr. to Somerset Music Maker. Mbrships: Musicians Union; ISM. Hons: German Govt. Exchange Scholarship, 1967-68. Hobbies: Reading; Country walking; Learning Russian. Address: 9 Portway, Wells, Somerset, BA5 2BA, UK.

CHAI, Nakyong Tjong, b. 16 Sept. 1933, Seoul, Korea. Pianist; Teacher; Head of Keyboard Department. Educ: BMus, Coll. of Music, Seoul Nat. Univ.; MMus, Univ. of S Calif., USA; grad. piano study, HS for Music, Munich, Germany. m. David S Chai, 1 d. Career: Num. recitals in Germany, Korea & USA; Soloist s. orchs. inclng. Seoul Nat. Symph. Orch.; TV & radio perfs. & lectr., KBS (Korea); Soloist w. La Mirada Symph. Orch., Calif., num. TV perfs.; Fac. mbr., Rio Hondo Coll., Calif.; Hd. of Keyboard Dept. Saddleback Coll., Calif. Contbr. to Korea Times LA Branch; Hollywood Bowl Review. Mbrships: Music Educs. Assn. of Calif.; Calif. Piano Assn.; Dir., Korean Musicians Assn. of Calif. Hons: Pres. Award, Seoul, 1956. Hobbies: Reading; Travel. Address: 1861 Arbolita Dr., La Habra, CA 90631, USA.

CHAIKOVSKY, Boris Alexandrovich, b. 10 Sept. 1925, Moscow, USSR. Composer. Educ: Moscow Conserv. Comps. incl: Sonatina for Piano, 1944; Suite for cello, 1946; 1st Symph., 1947; The Star (Opera), 1949; Fantasia on Russian Folk Themes, 1950; Slav Rhapsody, 1951; Sonata for Piano, 1952; Symphonietta for string orch., 1953; Trio, violin, cello & piano, 1953; Cappricio on English Themes, 1954; 1st Quartet, Quarter, 1954; Trio for Strings, 1955; Ceoncertino for Clarinet & Orch., 1957; Sonata for cello & piano, 1957; Overture for 40th Anniversary of October, Revolution, 1957; Sonata for violin & piano, 1959; 2nd Qurtet, Aruqrter, 1961; 2nd Symph., 1962; Piano Quintet, 1962. Mbrship: Exec., Moscow Sect., Composers Union of RSFSR. Recip. State Prize, 1969. Address: Composers Union of RSFSR, 8-10 Nezhdanovoy, Nexhdanovoy, Moscow, USSR.

CHAILLEY, Jacques, b. 24 Mar. 1910, Paris, France. Composer; Musicologist. Educ: Dr. ès Lettres; comp. studies w. Nadia Boulanger, Claude Delvincourt; Conserv. of Paris; cond. w. W Mengleberg & Pierre Monteux; musicol. w. A Pirro & A Smijers. m. Helene Pompei, 1 s., 2 d. Career incl: subdir., Conserv. de paris, 1937; prof., ibid., 1947; Dir., Inst. of Musicol., Univ. of Paris, 1952; Gen. Inspector for music, Min. of Educ., 1973. Comps. incl: Str. Quartet, 1939; Symph., 1945; opera, Thyl de Flandre, 1953; ballet, La Dame à la Licorne, 1957; songs, choral & ch. music. sev. recordings of own works. Publs: 25 books. Mbrships: Pres., Nat. Music Committee, UNESCO, 1963-66; pres. or VP, num. profl. socs. num. hons. inclng. Off. de la Létion d'Honneur. Address: 5 rue Rèmy-Dumoncel, 75014, Paris, France. 19, 28.

CHAILLY, Luciano, b. 19 June 1920, Ferrara, Italy. Composer; Musical Director. Educ: Dip. in Violin, Ferrara, 1941; BA, Univ. of Bologna, 1943; in Composition, Milan Conserv., 1945. m. Anna Maria Motta, 1 s., 2 d. Career: Dir. of Musical progs., Italian TV, 1950-67; Artistic Dir., La

Scala Theatre, Milan, 1968-71; Dir., Regio Theatre, Turin, 1972; Dir., Angleicum, Milan, 1972-74; Dir., Arena, Verona, 1974-76; Gen. Dir., La Scala, Milan, 1976-; Prof. of Comp., Conserv. of Milan, 1968-. Compositions incl: 12 lyric operas inclng: Una domanda di matrimonio, Il Mantello, Procedura penale, L'Idiota; var. symphonic works, choral music, chmbr. music, etc.; 3 ballets. Publs: I Personaggi, Il matrimonio segreto di cimaroso; Cronache di vita musicale; Taccuino segreto di un musicista. Hons. incl: The Garda Rose Award, 1973, Legion of Hon., 1974; San Francesco d'Oro, 1977. Hobbies: Tennis; Skiing; Stamp collecting. Address: Bianca a Maria 17, Milan, Italy.

CHAILLY, Riccardo, b. 20 Feb. 1953, Milan, Italy. Orchestral Conductor. Debut: Rome, 1969; w. LSO, Edinburgh Fest., 1979; w. Berlin Phil., Berlin, 1980. Career: Asst. to Claudio Abbado, Teatro la Scala, Milan, 1972-73. Recordings: Werther; William Tell; Mendelssohn Symphs. No. 2 & 3. Mgmt: Harrison/Parrott Ltd., 22 Hillgate St., London W8, UK. Address: c/o Mgmt.

CHALLUPPER, Joseph, b. 18 Feb. 1911, Horovice, CSSR. Solo Pianist; Composer. Educ: PhD, Univ., Charles IV, Prague; studied music Paris, Vienna, Geneva; Piano studies w. Conrad Ansorge (student of Liszt). w. K Hoffmaister, Prague. m. Rosalie Challupperova. Debut: Prague, 1929, Paris, 1933. Career: Piano recitals; Concerts in Paris, Vienna, Prague, Switzerland, w. Central Europe, & on Radio. Num. Compositions incl: Images de France, 1933-34; 4 Arabesques, 1934-36; Matterhorn, 1936; Jésus Jesus de Prague, 1939; Chansons, 1939-41; Intermezzo de Marionettes, 1948; Suite de Ballet, Ragtimes Regimes de Paris, 1963; To Louis Armstrong, 1965; A La Belle Reine, 1973; In Thermas Caroli IV, 1974; Thermalia, (Carlsbad Concert), 1974. Publs. incl: Essais sur Jazz. Kazz. 1955; Evolution séries series rhythmiques et las Musique de Danse, Allgemeine Allgeneine Musiklehre, 1969 Le Cours de Piano sur la Baoo de la Théorie l'Information, Il'Information, 1972; Les Pianistes-Compositeurs de l'École de Franz Liszt, L'Oeuvre Pédagogique Pedagogique de Carl Czerny et notre époque, 1974. Mbrships: Assn. des compositeurs d'oeuvres musicales, (OSA); Chopin Soc., Marienbad. Address: Jindr., Jindr., Hradec 67 67/1. CSSR.

CHAMBERS, Colin, b. 16 June 1933, Harrow, UK. Flautist. Educ: w. Gareth Morris, RAM; ARAM. m. Patricia, 3 s. Career: Sadler's Wells Opera Orch., 1955-59; City of Birmingham Symph. Orch. (Piccolo), 1959-60; LPO, 1960-76; Prin. Flute, Royal Liverpool Phil. Orch., 1976-; Tutor, Royal Northern Coll. of Music. Publs: Essential Repertoire for Flute. Address: 20 Glendydke Rd., Liverpool, L18 6JR, UK.

CHAMBLEE, James Monroe, b. 10 Jan. 1935, Raleigh, NC, USA. Professor of Music & Chairman, Department of Fine Arts. Educ: BA, Univ. of NC at Chapel Hill; MA, Columbia Univ., NY; PhD, Univ. of NC at Chapel Hill. m. Carla Anzelette Smith, 2 d., 2 s. Career: Prof. of Music, Gardner-Webb Coll., Boiling Springs, NC; Dir. of Summer Schl. Chorus, Univ. of NC at Chapel Hill; Dir. of Raleigh (NC) Oratorio Soc.; Choir Dir., Murfreesboro (NC) Baptist Ch.; Prof. of Music & Chmn., Dept. of Fine Arts, Chowan Coll., Murfreesboro, NC. Contbr. to: Am. Music Tchr.; Current Musicol. Mbrships: Am. Musicol. Soc.; Coll. Music Soc.; Music Lib. Assn.; Assn. of Choral Conds.; MTNA; NC Music Tchrs. Assn. (Chmn., voice sect.). Sev. acad. hons. Address: 112 Springlake Dr., Murfreesboro, NC, USA.

CHAN, Mary Elizabeth, b. 18 Dec. 1940, Wellington, NZ. University Lecturer. Educ: BA, Vic. Univ., Wellington, 1962; MA, ibid., 1963; PhD, Univ. of Cambridge, 1968. m. Henry Douglas Min-hsi Chan, 1 s. Career: Jr. Lectr. in English, Vic. Univ., 1963-64; Lectr., Massey Univ., NZ, 1967-71; Sr. Lectr., ibid., 1972-76; Lectr. in English, Univ. of NSW, 1976-78; Sr. Lectr., ibid., 1978-. Contbr. of scholarly articles to Music & Letters; Lute Soc. Jrnls.; Royal Musical Assn. Research Chronicle; Studies in the Renaissance, etc. Mbrships: Royal Musical Assn.; Musicol. Soc. of Aust.; Australasian Univs. Langs. & Lit. Assn. recip., postgrad. Travelling Scholarship, NZ Univ. Grants Committee, 1964. Hobbies: Piano; Theatre; Bush Walking; Chinese Art. Address: 71 Elliott St., Balmain, NSW 2041, Aust.

CHAN, Timothy Tai-Wah, b. 31 Aug. 1945, Hong Kong, China. Orchestra Conductor; Violinist; Teacher. Educ: BMus, San Francisco Conserv. of Music; MA, Calif. State Univ., San Francisco. m. Evelyn Man-Ching, 1 d. Debut: Hong Kong City Concert Hall, 1965. Career: Violinist, Oakland (Calif.) Symph. Orch.; Music Dir. & Cond., Chinese Am. Youth Orch., San Francisco; Pvte. tchr. Mbrships: Musicians Union, Local No. 6, San Francisco; Am. Fedn. of Musicians of USA & Can. Recip. Gold Medal (1st Prize), Music Festival Competition of Hong Kong, 1960. Hobbies: Philately; Table Tennis; Soccer; Hiking; Music;

Record Collecting; Chmbr. music. Address: 2366 45th Ave., San Francisco, CA 94116, USA.

CHANCE, Nancy Laird, b. 19 Mar. 1931, Cinn., Ohio, USA. Composer; Teacher of Piano. Educ: Bryn Mawr Coll.; Columbia Univ.; Post Coll.; var. pvte. tchrs. 3 s. Comps. incl: Motet for Double Chorus Divided, 1972; Bathsabe's Song, 1972; Darksong, 1972; Three Rilke Songs, 1973; Edensong, 1973; Daysongs, 1974; Ritual Sounds, 1974; Duos II; Declamation & Song; Ceremonial; Duos I. Mbrships. incl: ASCAP; League of Women Comps.; Am. Music Ctr. Inc. Hons: ASCAP Special Award, 1978-79. Hobby: Photography. Mgmt: Judith Finell. Address: 538 E 89th St., Apt. 3 E, NY, NY 10028, USA. 3.

CHANDLER, Mary, b. 16 May 1912, London, UK. Composer; Oboist. Educ: MA (Oxon.); LRAM; ARCM Career: Prin. Oboe, City of Birmingham Symph. Orch., 1944-58; Area Dir., Kent Music Schl., 1960-71; Examiner & Adjudicator. Compositions: Cantatas; Nativity Ode; Tobit's Hymn of Rejoicing; Concerto for Oboe d'Amore & Strings; Suite for Oboe & Piano from Purcell's Orpheus Britannicus; Part-songs; var. chmbr. & orchestral works broadcast from MSS on BBC. Contbr. to: Making Music; Music Tchr.; Composer; Times Educl. Supplement, etc. Mbrships: CGGB; Chmn., Assn. of Wind Tchrs., 1965-70. Recip: W W Cobbett Prize for Women Composers, 1967. Hobbies: Gardening; Walking. Address: Parson's Cottage, Bisley, Stroud, Glos. GL6 7BB. UK.

CHANEY, Harold, b. Mesa, Ariz., USA. Harpsichord Player; Organist. Educ: BMus, Mmus, DMusA, Univ. of Southern Calif.; Columbia Univ., NYC; Staatliche Hochschule für Musik, Hamburg, Germany. Debut: Town Hall, NY, 1967. Career: apps., Nat. Convention, AGO, Los Angeles, w. NY Phil. Orch., on CBS-TV; harpsichord recitals for educl.; TV; Solo Harpsichord Tour, Far E; Music Dir., St. Ignatius' Ch., NY; Adj. Prof. of Music, Staten Island Coll., NY. Recordings: Organ & Harpsichord Recital; Roussakis-Sonata for Harpsichord. Ed: Halsey Stevens, Partita for Harpsichord. Mbr., Pi Kappa Lambda. Hons: Fulbright Grant, 1960; Organ Scholarship, Univ. of Redlands. Address: 838 W End Ave., NY, NY 10025, USA.

CHANG, Yung-Kai James, b. 2 Feb. 1947. Shanghai, China. French Horn Player; Manager. Educ: BS, NE Missouri State Univ., Kirksville. m. Wang, Shaw-Wen, 1 d. Career: Horn player, Taiwan Provincial Symph. Orch.; Taipei Municipal Symph. Orch.; Pro Art Symph. Orch.; Gen. Mgr., Le Vent Music Co. Ltd., Taipei. Mbrships: Int. Horn Soc. Address: 37 Foo-Teh S. Rd., San-Chung City, Taipei, Taiwan.

CHANNON, Michael David Huddleston, b. 3 May 1939, Anniston, Ala., USA. Musicologist; Harpsichordist; Dir., Calisto Concerts Soc. Educ: Univ. of NM; TCL; Mozarteum, Salzburg. Career: USN Security Service, 1962-68; BBC Music Div., 1969-. Publs: Ed., Two Latin Anthems of Samuel Wesley, 1969; An Evening Service By Richard Portmann, 1970; The Complete Ch. Music of John Goldwyn (in prep.). Mbrships: Harpsidh ordist, Finchley Chamber Orch.; Brit. Museum Soc.; Pianist, Hendon Christian Sci. Ch.; Nat. Trust; Musical Advsr., Wessex Sinfonia. Recip. Nat. Defense Medal, USN, 1968. Hobbies: Reading; Bookbinding. Address: 26 Marlborough Rd., London, N19, UK. 28.

CHAPIN, Schuyler Garrison, b. 13 Feb. 1923. New York City, USA. Impressario: Music & Educ. Administrator. Educ: Longy Schl. of Music, Cambridge, Mass., 1940-41; DLit., Emerson Coll., 1976. m. Elizabeth Steinway, 4 s. Career: NBC Int., 1941-43, 1946-50; Gen. Mgr., Tex. & Jinx. 1950-52; Concert agt., 1952-59; Dir., Columbia Records, 1961-63; VP, Lincoln Ctr. for Performing Arts, NYC, 1963-68; Exec. Prod., Amberson Prods., 1969-72; Asst. Mgr., Metropol. Opera, 1972; Acting Gen. Mgr., ibid., 1972-73; Gen. Mgr., 1973-75; Dean, FAc. of the Arts, Colombia Univ., 1976-. Publs: Musical Chairs, A Life in the Arts, 1977. Mbrships: Century Assn.; Coffe House Club. Hons: Art Medal, 1944; Conspicuous Serv. Cross, 1951; LHD, NY Univ., 1974; LHD, Hobart & Wm. Wmith Colls., 1974. Hobbies: Bridge; Tennis; Reading; Swimming. Address: 901 Lexington Ave., NY, NY 10021, USA.

CHAPMAN, Clive, b. 18 Apr. 1930, London, UK. Lecturer. Educ: Hd. Chorister, Westminster Abby; Fitzwilliam Coll. Cambridge; MusB, MA (Cantab); Cert. Ed.; hon. FLCM. m. Margaret Celia Westrup, 1 s., 1 d. Career: sev. schooltchng. posts; lectr., Hockerill Coll., 1963-65; Sr. Lectr., Winchester Schl. of Art, 1965-70; Prin. Lectr. in Music, Hd. of Dept., Digby Stuart Coll., Roehampton, 1970-; Examiner, LCM, 1963-; Cond., Bishop's Stortford Operatic Soc., 1964-65; Cond., Andover Operatic Soc., 1967-69; special subject, 18th Century Eng. pantomime & its music. Contbr. to Soc. for Theatre Rsch.

Mbrships: Royal Musical Assn.; Purcell Club. Hobbies: Cooking; Talking; Walking. Address: Hatters, Old Woking Rd., W Byfleet, Surrey, UK.

CHAPMAN, Ernest Walter, b. 14 Apr. 1014, London, UK. Music Publisher; Critic; Concert Organizer. Educ: RCM; studied w. Herbert Howells, Frank Merrick, Frederick Thuston, Alan Bush. Career: Ed. Staffs, Boosey & Hawkes Ltd., 1932-47, Joseph Williams Ltd., 1932-47, Joseph Williams Ltd., 1947-51, Augener Ltd., 1958-63; Fndr. & 1st Ed., Tempo, 1939-47; Concert & Record Critic, Musical Events, 1958-73; Fndr., var. exec. posts, Contemporary Concerts Coordination; var. exec. posts. Macnaghten Concerts, 1957-; Governing Council, ibid., 1964; devised var. new types of concert prog. in England, 1960-64; investigated posthumous MSS of John Ireland, w. Norah Kirby, 1964. Author, John Ireland: A Catalogue of Published Works & Recordings, 1968. Contbr. to: Chambers' Ency.; Pelican Concerto Symposium; var. mags. & profl. jrnls. Address: 63, Bateman House, Kennington Park Gardens, London, SE17 3PF, UK.

CHAPMAN. John Peter Ford, b. 6 July 1928, Birmingha, UK. Tenor Singer. Educ: studied voice prod. w. Janet & Ivy Fitton. m. Sheila Martin, 1 s., 1 d. Career: concert apps., inclng. oratorio; radio & TV perfs.; mbr., Age of Gold, 1977-. Mbrships: ISM; Musicans' Union. Hobbies: Traditional Music & Customs; Early Civilisations; Drawing; Reading; Good Food & Wine. Mgmt: Age of Gold, 30 Grove Rd., Stratford-on-Avon, Warwicks. Address: 16 Gaveston Cl., Warwick, CV34 5HR, UK.

CHAPMAN, Neil, b. 8 June 1933, Underberg, S Africa. Conductor. Educ: Natal Tchrs. Dip.; LRAM. m. Emma Megaw, 1 d. Career: Lectr. in Music, Natal Tchrs. Trng. Coll., Pietermaritzburg, 1962-64; Musical Dir., Pietermaritzburg Phil. Soc., 1965-66; Asst. Cond. & Chorus Master, Performing Arts Coun., Transvaal, 1967-75; Music Staff (Cond., Choir Master, etc.), S African Broadcasting Corp., 1975-. Hobbies: Gardening; Tennis. Address: 47 Twelfth St. W., Menlo Pk., Pretoria 0081, S Africa.

CHAPMAN, Paul Rutledge, b. 3 Feb. 1948, Welwyn Garden City, Herts., UK. Musician (flute & piccolo). Educ: BA (Music), Sheffield Univ., 1969; Royal Coll. of Music, 1970-71; ARCM, 1969. Career incl: Flautist & Prin. Piccolo, Engl. Nat. Opera. Recordings: var. works w. London Mozart Players London Festival Ballet, Engl. Nat. Opera & London Concert Orch. Hobbies: Owning & maintaining Citroën Cars; Camping; Walking; Tennis. Address: 2 High Grove, Welwyn Gdn., City, Herts., UK.

CHAPPELL, Herbert, b. 18 Mar. 1934, Bristol, UK. Composer. Educ: MA, BMus (Oxford); studied w. Bernard Rose & Eon Wellesz. Career: Scripted & Produced Music Documentaries for BBC TV w. André Previn; Comp. scores for num. TV films. Compositions: Dead in Tune, for narrator & orch.; Max the Sheepstealer, opera for children; The Daniel Jazz; All That Jazz series; Magnificant & Nunc Dimittis; Overture 'Panache'; Irish Overture; Psalms for Today; George & the Dragonfly. Recordings: The Pallisers (theme), BBC; Panache Overture; Dead in Tune/George & The Dragonfly. Mgmt: London Mgmt., 235 Regent St., London W1, UK.

CHAPPELL, Ruth Ellison, b. 12 Dec. 1942, Leatherhead, UK. Flautist; Pianist; Violinist; Guitar Player; Teacher. Educ: GSM; studied flute w. Geoffrey Gilbert & James Galway; AGSM. Career: 1st flute, Surrey Phil. Orch.; mbr., Erato Chmbr. Orch.; solo apps. in Bach's B minor Suite & in concertos by Mozat & Pergolesi. Recordings for Dutch TV. Mbrships: ISM; Musicians' Union. recip. scholarship for 4th yr. at GSM, 1964. Hobbies: Langs.; Art; Ornitthol. Address: 17 Poplar Rd., Leatherhead, Surrey KT22 8SF, UK.

CHAPPLE, Stanley, b. 29 Oct. 1900, London, UK. Conductor; Pianist. Educ: Perf.'s Dip.; Gold Medal, London Acad. Music. m. Barbara Joyce Hilliard. Career: Guest Cond., major orchs., Europe & USA, 1950-54; Dir., Symph. & Opera, Univ. of Wash., 1948-71. Mbrships: Inc. Soc. Musicians, UK; Music Educators Nat. Conf., USA. Hon. DMus., Colby Coll., Me., 1950. Address: 18311 47th Pl. NE, Seattle, WA 98155, USA. 1, 14.

CHARALAMBOUS, Andreas, b. 10 Apr. 1940, Evrykhou, Nicosia, Cyprus. Lecturer in Music. Educ: Dip., Tchrs. Trng. Coll., Nicosia; Dips., Harmony, Counterpoint, Fugue, Orchestration, Musicology & Conducting, State Conserv., Salonica. m. 2 children. Career: Creator & Cond. of Pro Musica Choir & String Orch., Famagusta, Cyprus; Num. TV & radio apps., concerts, etc. Comps. incl: Cyprus Sketches (orch.); July 9th, Symphonic Poem (soloist, choir & orch.); The Song of Marriage (choir & orch.); Songs for solo Voices & orch.; The Storm (ballet music). Publs. incl: Try to

Teach Music, 1974. Mbr. num. profl. orgs. Recip. several awards. Hobbies: Birds; Travel. Address: Arsakios Akademy, Patrai,.Greece.

CHARD, Geoffrey William, b. 9 Aug. 1930, Sydney, NSW, Australia. Opera Singer (baritone). Educ: NSW Conserv. of Music. m. Margaret Elizabeth, 1 s. Debut: Don Giovanni, w. NSW Nat. Opera, 1952. Career incl: Prin. Baritone w. Welsh Nat. Opera, Australian Opera, Glyndebourne Festival Touring Opera, Aldeburgh Festival Opera, Sadlers Wells - Engl. Nat. Opera & Edinburgh Festival. Hobbies: Tennis; Squash; Golf. Mgmt: Music & Musicians Artists Mgmt, Maulden, Bedford. Address: 21 Regal Way, Kenton, Harrow, Middx., HA3 0RZ, UK.

CHARDON, Yves, b. 27 Dec. 1902, Paris, France. Cellist; Conductor. Educ: Conservatoire Nat. de Musique, Paris. m. (1) Henriette de Constant, 2 s., 1 d., (2) Iris Schoening, 1 d. Debut: Concerts Colonne, Paris. Career: Tours in France, Italy, Greece, USA as soloist; Mbr., Boston Symph. w. Serge Koussevitzky, USA; Chardon Strong Quartet, Boston, 10 yrs.; Currently, Mbr., String Trio of NY; 1st Cellist & Assoc. Cond., Mpls., Symph.; Guest Cond. in Paris, Havana, Phila., Chgo., etc.; Cond., Fla. Symphony, USA. Comps. incl: Sonata for Trumpet & Cello; Concertante for Prin. Viola, Oboe, Engl. Horn, Basson & Timpani. Recip., Palmes Académiques, French Govt. Mgmt: New Era Int. Concerts Ltd., London, UK. Address: 72 Sea Lane, Old Saybrook Manor, CT, USA.

CHARLES, S(arai) Robin, b. 2 Oct. 1951, New Westminster, BC, Can. Composer. Educ: incl: study w. Dr. Samuel Dolin, Clifford Poole, Glen Gardiner & others, Royal Conserv. of Music, Toronto. Career: copyist, Can. Broadcasting Corp., Can. Music Ctr. & pvte. comps.; profl. comp., 1979-. Comps: The Little Match Girl (chmbr. radio opera); Band Piece No. 1 - A Fanfare; But I'm Only Twelve Years Old (strg. orch. w. solo violin); Responsorial Psalm (voice w. instrumental ensemble); other vocal works. mbrships: PRO of Can.; Toronto Musicians Assn.; AFM. Hons. incl. comp. scholarships to Royal Conserv. of Music, Toronto, 1977-79. Hobbies: Languages (French, German, Greek, Hebrew, Aramaic). Address: 4 Rostrevor Rd., Toronto, Ont. M6C 3E6, Can.

CHARLOFF, Aaron, b. 9 Nov. 1941, Chatham, Ont., Can. Conductor; Composer; Pianist. Educ: BSc, Univ. of Man., Can., 1963; Music Dip., ibid., 1962. Career: Permanent cond., Tel Aviv Phil. Choir, Rubin Acad. of Music - Hebrew Univ. Symph. Orch. & Kibbutsim Youth Symph. Orch.; guest cond., Israeli Phil. Oroh., Kol Israel Radio Orch., Haifa Symph. Orch. Comps: Choral Pieces; Etude, for piano; Dialogues, for 2 bassoons; Fragments, for piano; Oboe's Lament. Mbrships: ACUM (Israel); Israel Comps. League. Hons: prize for comp., Fire & the Mountains, in Int. Competition on subject on the Holocaust, Israel, 1978. Address: c/o Rubin Acad. of Music, Jerusalem, Israel.

CHARLTON, David, b. 20 June 1946, London, UK. Music Historian; Lecturer. Educ: BA, Nottingham Univ.; PhD, Univ. of Cambridge; RAM. Career: Lectr. in Music, Univ. of East Anglia. Publs: A National Catalogue of Music Microfilms, 1972; Ed., Symphony in G minor (Méhul), 1979. Contbr. to num. profl. publs. Mbrships: Royal Musical Assn.; British Soc. for 18th Century Studies. Hobby: Sunbathing. Address: Music Centre, Univ. of E Anglea, Norwick, UK.

CHARNASSÉ, Hélène Renée., b. 1 Feb. 1926, Le Mans, Sarthe, France. Researcher. Educ: Nat. Higher Conserv. of Music, Paris; Lic. in Letters, Fac. of Letters, Sorbonne, Paris, 1963; Doct., ibid., 1966; Dip., Practical Schl. of Advanced Study, 1961. div., 1 child. Career: Rsch. Attachée, Nat. Ctr. for Sci. Rsch., Paris, 1962; Rsch. Chargé ibid., 1968; Hd. of Rsch., 1972; Collaborator w. Mme. de Chambure, Paris Conserv. Mus., 1962-73; Fndr. w. H Ducasse, ERATTO Team, 1973. Author, num. articles on old instruments, 16th & 17th century music. Address: CNRS, 27 rue Paul Bert, 94200 Ivry, France. 27.

CHARRY, Michael, b. 28 Aug. 1933, NY, NY, USA. Orchestra Conductor. Educ: Oberlin Coll. Conserv. of Music; Juilliard Schl. of Music; Study w. Jean Morel; BS, 1955, MS, Orchestral Cond., 1956, Hochschule für Musik, Hamburg, study w. Hans Schmidt-Isserstedt, 1956-57; Pierre Monteux Schl., Me., USA, summers, 1952-55. m. Jane Thoms, 1 s., 1 d. Career: Cond. & Pianist, Jose Limon Mod. Dance Co. Tours, Europe, 1957, S & Ctrl. Am., 1960, Far East, 1963; Asst. Cond., Santa Fe Opera. 1960; Asst. Cond. & Prin. Oboist, RI Phil., 1960-61; Apprentice Cond., Cleveland Orch. under George Szell, 1961-65; Asst. Cond., ibid., 1965-72; Musical Dir., Canton (Ohio) Symph., 1961-74; Prin. Guest Coind., Kan. City Phil., 1972-74; Guest Cond., num. orchs., USA, Finland, Netherlands; Guest Music Dir., Ala. Fest., 1975; Music Dir., Cond., Nashville Symph., 1976-, Peninsula Music

Fest., Wis., 1978-. Contbr. to Fine Arts Mag. Hons: sev. scholarships; Apprentice Cond., Cleveland Orch., 1961-65. Hobbies: Art collecting; Sailing; Chess. Address: Nashville Symph., 1805 W End Ave., Nashville, TN 37203, USA.

CHARTERIS, Richard, b. 24 June 1948, Chatham Islands, NZ. Musicologist. Educ: BA, Victoria Univ., Wellington, 1970; MA, Univ. of Canterbury, 1972; PhD, Univs. of Canterbury & London, 1976; ATCL, 1972. Career: Rothmans Post-Doctl. Fellow, Univ. of Sydney, 197678; Post-Doctl. Fellow, Univ. of Qld, 1979. Publs: John Caprario, A Thematic Catalogue of his Music, 1977. Contbr. to: Music & Letters; Royal Musical Assn. Rsch. Chronicle; Chelys; The Galpin Soc. Jrnl. Mbrships: Royal Musical Assn.; Viola de Gamba Soc. of GB; Lute Soc. Hons: Louise Dyer Award, 1975; Mary Duncan Scholarship, 1975. Address: Music Dept., Univ. of Sydney, NSW, Aust. 2006.

CHARTERS, Murray R, b. 11 Sept. 1943, Toronto, Can. Musicologist; Performer on Viols & Cello. Educ: MusB, Univ. of Toronto, 1966; MA, Univ. of Western Ont., 1972; AMus, Western Ont. Conserv. of Music, 1971. m. Judith Akiko Fukushima, 1 s., 1 d. Career: CBC TV, 1975, 1977; CBC Radio, 1977-79; Mbr., Hart House Consort of Viols., 1974-76; Mgr., ibid., 1975-76; Instr., York Univ., Toronto, 1975-76; Prin. cello, Newfoundland Symph. Orch., 1976-; Asst. Prof., Memorial Univl. of Newfoundland, 1976-. Mbrships: Royal Musical Assn.; Am. Musicol. Soc.; Viola da Gamba Soc.; Viola da Gamba Soc. of Am.; Am. Soc. for 18th Century Studies; Bd. of Dirs., Newfoundland Symph. Orch., 1978-79. Contbr. to The Musical Times, & Grove's Dict. of Music & Musicians, 6th Ed. Recip., Ont. Grad. Fellowship, 1969-71. Hobby: Photography. Address: 24 Gambier St.,°St. John's, Nfld. A1B 3G4, Can.

CHASE, Joseph Russell, b. 9 Mar. 1922, Eastham, Mass., USA. Accompanist; Piano Teacher; Music Therapist; Counselor. Educ: BSc., Calvin Coolidge Coll., Boston, Mass.; MEd, ibid.; Registered Music Therapist, Schl. for Musical Guidance. Career: Studio, Concert Accomp., Cape Cod Conserv. of Music; Piano Tchr,. 40 yrs.; Pvte. Music Therapist, 20 yrs.; Tchr., Piano & Theory, Cape Cod Conserv. of Music, 1963-70; Music Therapist, ibid., 2 yrs.; Tchr., Kingsley Schl., Boston, Parents' Schl. for Atypical Children, Chatham, Mass.; Co-Fndr., Cape Cod Conserv. of Music, Barnstable, Mass. Mbrships: Nat. Assn. for Music Therapy, Inc.; Nat. Assn. of Tchrs. of Singing, Inc.; Diplomate, Am. Assn. of Clinical Counsellors, Inc.; Nat. Alliance for Family Life, Inc.; NGPT; Leschetzky Assn.; ISME; MMTA; MTNA. Hons: Fndrs. Medal, NGPT, 1970; George B Baker Scholarship in Music, 1940. Hobbies: Painting; Writing; Hiking. Address: Salt Pond Rd., PO Box 228, Eastham, MA 02642, USA.

CHASE, Stephanie Ann, b. 1 Oct. 1957, Evanston, Ill., USA. Concert violinst. Educ: studied w. Fannie Chase, 1959-66; w. Sally Thomas, 1966-76; w. Arthur Grumiaux, 1976-; Juilliard Pre-Coll., 2 yrs.; Chmbr. music w. Josef Gingold. m. Robert Rothschild. Debut: Alice Tully Hall, Lincoln Center, NY, 1978. Career: has perf. w. Chgo., Denver, Pitts., Am., Nat., Dallas, Houston, Buffalo, Puerto Rican & SNO, etc.; has app. on many US TV shows inclng. David Frost Show; num. radio perfs.; was subject of Screen Gems documentary film, 1971. Hons. incl: Ima Hogg Young Artists Competition, 1978; 1st Prize, G B Dealey Award, 1978, Buffalo Symph. Young Artists Competition, 1978, Financial Federal Young Artists Competition, 1978. Hobbies: Collecting Frogs; Chmbr. music; Table tennis; Pinball. Mgmt: Columbia Artist' Mgmt. Inc., 165 W 57th St., NY, NY 10019, USA. Address: c/o Mgmt. 3.

CHASINS, Abram, b. 17 Aug. 1903, NYC, NY, USA. Composer-Pianist; Author; Teacher; Radio Executive. Educ: Columbia Univ.; Juilliard Schl.; Curtis Inst. of Music. m. Constance Keene. Debut: Phila., 1928. Career: 1st Am. contemporary composer to be perfd. by Toscanini, 1931; Apps. in recital & as soloist w. leading orchs. of Am. & Europe, & recorded extensively, 1926-46; Musical Dir., WQXR, 1941-65; currently, Artistic Dir., KUSC, Univ. of Southern Calif.; 1972-77. Composer of over 100 published works, mainly for solo piano & 2 pianos. Recordings incl: All Chopin Album; All Bach Album. Mbr., var. music assns. Publs. incl: Leopold Stokowski, A Portrait, 1979. Contbr. to var. publs. Recip., var. hons. Hobbies incl: Chess. Address: 200 E 78 St., NY, NY 10021, USA. 2.

CHATTERJEE, Pabitra Narayan, b. 8 Aug. 1918, Calcutta, Bengal, India. Former Sitarist; Music Director; Film Producer. Educ: Studied w. S D Das, Prin., Arjya Sangit Samaj Music Coll., 1927-39. m. Smt. Labayanaprava Chatterjee, 3 s., 2 d. Career: Joined All India Radio as vocalist & sitarist, 1936; Musician & Music Dir. for films, 1939; Trainer & Sitarist, HMV, 1940; Major apps. in films as music dir., 1945-; Prod. of 2 feature films 'Charankavi Mukunda Das', 1968 & 'Megh-Kalo', 1970. Comps. of solo sitar music & music for films & solo discs.

Mbrships. incl: Pres., Calcutta Cine Musicians Assn. Recip., var. hons. Hobbies incl: Reading. Address: 20/1 Banerjee Para Rd., Calcutta 700041, India.

CHATZIDAKIS, Manos, b. 1925, Greece. Composer. Compositions incl: Ballet music; Incidental music for theatre & films; Piano & orchl. works; popular songs; Theatre music incl. Lysistrata, The Birds & Plautos (Aristophanes); Films incl: Stella, 1956; Never on Sunday, 1960; Topkapi, 1964. Recip. num. nat. & int. awards, incl. Oscar, 1961.

CHAUN, Frantisek, b. 26 Jan. 1921, Kaplice, Czechoslovakia. Composer. Educ: Pvte. study, Klement Lavicky. m. Eva Farrenzenova, 1 s., 1 d. Debut: Prague, 1955. Career: Composer of radio, TV film music. Compositions recorded incl: Hommage á Dubuffet; 5 Pictures for Orchestra; Ghiribizzo, for piano & orch.; Kafka Trilogy, for large orch. Other compositions incl: Bruno II, for string quintet; Divertimento for 9 Wind instruments. Mbrships: Union of Czech Composers. Hons: 3 Czech. Radio Prizes, 1963, '69, '70; Medal of Capt. Jaros, 1966. Hobbies: Painting. Address: Polska 48, Prague 2, Czechoslovakia.

CHAVEZ, Carlos, b. 13 June 1899, Mexico City, Mexico. Composer; Conductor; Educator. Educ: studied w. Pedro Luis Orgazon, Juan Fuentes & Manuel Ponce. Debut: 1st perf. of concert of own works, Mexico City, 1921. Career: Fndr.-Cond., New Music Conserts, Mexico City, 1923-25. Mexico Symph. Orch., 1928-48; Dir., Nat. Conserv. of Music, 1928-29 & 34; Hd., Dept. of Fine Arts, 1933-34; Fndr.-Dir., Nat. Inst. of Fine Arts, 1947-52, Hd. Music Dept., ibid, 1973-; Fndr., Nat. Symph. Orch.; Guest Cond., symph. orchs. in N & S. Am., 1935-; Chas. Eliot Norton Prof., Harvard Univ., 1958-59. Compositions incl: Sextet w. piano; El Fuego Nuevo; Sonata II; Imagen Mexicana; HP (horsepower) premiered by Stokowski, Phila., Pa., 1932 (ballet); Sinfonria India, 1936; Concert for 4 horns, 1938; Piano Concerto, 1940; Violin Concerto, 1948; 3rd Symph., 1954; Panfilo & Lauretta (opera), 1957; 7th Symph. Publs: Towards a New Music, 1937. Hons. incl: Off. Legion of Hon., France; Cmdr., Order of the Crown of Belgium; Cross of the Star of Italian Solidarity; Order of Pole Star, Sweden; CAro de Boesi Prize, Caracas, Venezuela, 1954. Address: av. Pirincos, Lomas de Chapultepec, Mexico City DF, Mexico.

CHAZANOFF, Daniel, b. 1 Mar. 1923, Music Educator; Cellist; Conductor; Music Researcher. Educ: BSc, OH State Univ., 1949; MA, 1951, EdD, 1964, Columbia Univ. Career incls: Asst. Prin. Cello, Birmingham Symph., 1951-52; cello perfs. on radio & TV, Columbus, OH, NYC, Birmingham, Ala. & Rochester, NY; Music Cons., Videotape Series, NY State Educ. Dept., 1968 & 70; currently Music Supvsr., Rochester, NY, Pub. Schls. Publs: Ed., Music 'Round the School Year, 1966. Contbr. to: Strad; Music Jrnl.; Am. String Tchr.; Orch. News; Consumer Guide; Schl. Music News; Jrnl. of Synagogue Music. Mbrships. incl: MENC; Am. String Tchrs. Assn.; Am. Fedn. of Musicians. Hobbies: Walking; Reading. Address: 114 Penarrow Rd., Rochester, NY 14618, USA.

CHEADLE, William George, b. 11 Dec. 1938, Detroit, Mich., USA. Concert Pianist; Professor of Piano. Educ: Detroit Inst. of Musical Art; Artist Dip., Juilliard Schl. of Music, 1961; MS, ibid., 1964; grad. studies w. Adele Marcus & Sascha Gorodnitzk; ibid, m. Louise Cheadle, 1 s., 1 d. Debut: Town Hall, NYC, 1965. Career: Num. perfs. in NYC, Eastern seaboard & Midwest of USA as recitalist, guest soloist w. var. orchs., & part of duo-piano team w. wife Louise Cheadle; num. apps. on educl. & commercial TV & Radio; Master classes & lecture recitals in colls. & schls.; former Hd., Keyboard Dept., Amherst Summer Music Ctr.; Fac. Mbr., Westminster Choir Coll., Princeton, 1965-; currently Assoc. Prof. of Piano, & Theory Coord., Preparatory Div., ibid.; Alice Tull Hall, Lincoln Center Lib. of Perfng. Arts. Comps. incl: 8 Picture Postcards for Piano duet, 1978; Hommage a S.R., 1978. Mbr., Music Club of Princeton (Pres. 1970-73). Hons: Detroit News Music Fest. Award, 1953; Juilliard Scholarships, 1956-64; Kresge Fndn. Grants, 1956-60; Nat. Chopin Scholarship Prize, Kosciuszko Fndn., 1959; Concert Artists Guild Award, 1964. Hobbies: Photography; Records. Mgmt: Leeds Concert Bureau. Hobbies: Philately; Postcards. Address: 338 Hamilton Ave., Princeton, NJ 08540, USA. 28.

CHECKER, Maurice John, b. 10 Oct. 1933. Oboist; Performer on Oboe d'Amore & Cor Anglais. Educ: RCM; Paris. m. Susan Tunnell, 1 s., 1 d. Career: Oboist, London Phil. Orch., 1956-60; Prin. Oboe, BBC Welsh Orch., 1960-62; Cor Anglais, London Phil. orch., 1966-74; currently Mbr., Scottish Chmbr. Orch.; Fndr. mbr., Scottish Virtuosi. Hobbies: Sailing; Gardening; Bee-keeping. Address: 6 Gt. Stuart St., Edinburgh EH36AW, UK.

CHEMIN-PETIT, Hans (Helmut Gunter), b. 24 July 1902, Potsdam, Germany. Conductor; Composer; Professor. Educ: Studied Cello w. Hugo Becker, Hochschule für Musik Berlin: Comp. w. Paul Juon, ibid. m. Lena von Hippel, 2 d. Debut: Cellist, 1920. Career: Tchr., Acad. of Music, 1929; 1st Concert w. Berlin Phil. Orch., 1934; Cons., Magdeburg Cathedral Choir, 1939-43; Rebling Oratorio Choir, 1943-59, Berlin Phil. Choir, 1944-; Substitute Dir., Berlin Acad. of Music, 1965; Dir., Music Dept., Berlin Acad. of Art, 1968. Compositions incl: (stage König Nicolo, 1959; Konzert für Orgel, Streicher und Pauken, 1963; (orch.) Intrada e Passacaglia, 1963; Konzert für Violine & Orch., 1971; num. works for chamber orchs. & choirs. Mbrships. incl: German Composer League. Hons. incl: Art Prize, Berlin, 1964; Bundesverdienstkreuz, 1968. Hobbies: Antique Art; Drawing; Painting. Mgmt: Konzertdirektion Adler, Auguste-Viktoria Strasse 64, 1 Berlin 33, German Fed. Repub. Address: Ahrenshooper Zeile 66, 1 Berlin 38, German Fed. Repub.

CHEMPIN, Beryl Margaret, b. Birmingham, UK. Teacher; Accompanist; Lecturer; Adjudicator. Educ: Birmingham Schl. of Music, later w. Harold Craxton; FTCL; LRAM; ARCM: LTCL; ABSM. m. Bernard While, 2 d. Career: Tchr. of piano, Birmingham Schl. of Music & Birmingham Junior Schl. of Music; pvte. tchr.; solo perf. & accomp. at public concerts; lectr. & adjudicator; mbr. of lecturing panel, Int. Piano Tchrs. Consultants. Contbr. to: Musical Times; Music Teacher; newspapers. Mbrships: ISM; European Piano Tchrs. Assn.; Int. Piano Tchrs. Consultants., etc. Hon: Midland Woman of the Year, 1977. Hobbies: Reading; Langs.; Art; Cooking. Address: 54 Moorcroft Rd., Moseley, Birmingham B13 8LU, UK. 23, 27, 29, 30.

CHEN, Fu-yen, b. 12 Dec. 1940, Hsinchu, Taiwan, China. Ethnomusicologist. Educ: BA Music, Taiwan Normal Univ., 1967; MA Music, Wesleyan Univ., 1971; PhD Ethnomusicol., ibid., 1976. m. Theresa Yuping Teng, 1 child. Publs: Source Readings in Asian Music: East Asia. Contbr. to Asian Music. Mbrships: Soc. for Ethnomusicol.; Am. Musicol. Soc.; Int. Folk Music Coun.; Soc. for Asian Music. Hons: Dissertation Fellow, Woodrow Wilson Nat. Fellowship Fndn. Hobby: Reading. Address: 53-18 111 St., Corona, NY 11368, USA.

CHENETTE, Louis Fred, b. 2 April 1931, Powersville, Iowa, USA. Dean. Educ: BA, Wheaton Coll., Ill.; MMus, Northwestern Univ.; PhD, Ohio State Univ. m. Emily Louise Scanlan, 3 s., 2 d. Career: Dir. of Music, Antioch, Ill. High Schl., 1953-58; Instructor of Music, Bemidji, Minn. State Coll., 1958-59; Music business, Lyon & Healy, Chgo., 1959; Findlay, Ohio Coll., 1960-72; Chmn., Dept. of Music, ibid., 1963-65; Chmn., Div. of Fine Arts, ibid., 1965-67; Asst. Dean & Dir. of Instnl. Rsch., ibid., 1967-69; Asst. to Pres., ibid., 1969-72; Acting Pres., ibid., 1971-72; Dean, Jordan Coll. of Music, Butler Univ., 1972-. Contbr. to num. profl. publs. Mbr., num. profl. orgs. Hobbies: Fishing; Canoeing; Amateur Radio. Address: 4518 Dickson Rd., Indpls., IN 46226, USA.

CHENOWETH, Wilbur Rossiter, b. 1899, Tecumseh, Neb., USA. Composer; Concert Pianist & Organist; Musicologist. Educ: BMus., Univ. of Neb. Schl. of Music; studied piano w. Sigismond Stojowski & Alexander Lambert, NY, & organ & composition w. Pietro Yon. m. Louise Grainger, 2 s. (1 dec.), 2 d. Career: Prof. of Piano Organ & Composition, Univ. of Neb. & Organist & Choirmaster, 1st Plymouth Congregational Ch., Lincoln, Neb., 1928-38; Hd. of Piano Dept., Occidental Coll., LA, Calif., 1938-45; Organist & Choirmaster, Neighborhood Ch., Pasadena, Calif., 1938-62; Hd. of own schl. of piano & organ, 1948-64; made many apps. as Recitalist & lectr. Compositions incl: Variations on Lobe den Herren (for both orch. & piano); Fiesta (piano & orch. or 2 pianos); Vocalise (for voice & orch.); num. piano pieces, songs, choral works, etc. Mbr: Beach Club of Santa Monica. Hobby: Hiking. Address: 106 Winnett Pl., Santa Monica, CA USA. 3.

CHENYLLE-PROCTOR, Stuart John, b. 11 Nov. 1934, Ipswich, Suffolk, UK. Violinist; Teacher. Educ: Violin study, var. tutors; Cond. w. Ernest Read, Richard Austin & Leo Quayle; Harmony & Comp. w. Eric Thiman; studied horn. m. Anne Bell Chenylle-Proctor, 1 s., 2 d. Career: General playing for Symph. Orchs., Theatre Orchs., Ballet, Opera, Chmbr. Music Ensembles; Cond. Choral Socs., Chmbr. Orchs., Renaissance/Baroque Ensembles; Tchr., Violin, Viola & French Horn; Adjudicator, var. music Fests. Recordings: (as Cond.) St. Johns Passion; Mahler's Kindertotenlieder; Dido & Aeneas; brahms Requiem; 3 collections of var. orchl. works; var. 20th Century works (all tapes). Contbr. to: var. provincial papers as critic. Mbrships: ISM; Musicians' Union. Hobby: Hist. Address: Pennvanmarc, 3 Helena Ave., Victoria Park, Whitby Bay, Northumberland, UK.

CHERKASSKY, Shura, b. 7 Oct1911, Odessa, Russia. Concert Pianist. Educ: Curtis Inst. of Music, Phila., Pa. div.

Career: Has played in every continent w. all the prin. Conds. & Orchs. of the World; Frequent soloist, Salzburg Fest. Recordings: Num. w. var. Record Cos. Hobby: Travel. Address: c/o Ibbs & Tillett, 124 Wigmore St., London W1, UK. 3.

CHERRINGTON, Meta Miles Robson, b. 2 Dec. 1921, Harrogate, Yorks., UK. Piano & Singing Teacher. Educ: RAM; Studied Piano w. Ruth Gipps, A J Pritchard & Benjamin Kaplan; Singing w. Mark Raphael; EPTA. m. Clive Cherrington, 1 s. Mbr. ISM; LRAM. Hons: Prize for Distinction Grade VI, Margate Dist., Assoc. Bd., 1937; Silver Medal (piano) Grade VII, 2nd Distinction, 1938; 1st Prize, Bach. Competition, S London Schl. of Music, 1959. Hobbies: Social Work; Ch. Work; Music Tchng; Traning Choirboys. Address: 9 Helena Close, Hadley Wood, Barnet, Herts. EN4 OJA, UK.

CHERRY, Kalman, b. 9 Apr. 1937, Philadelphia, Pa., USA. Timpanist; Percussionist. Educ: studied percussion since 7 yrs. of age; Dip., Curtis Inst. of Music, 1958. m. Janet E Reusser. Career: Timpanist, Dallas Symph. Orch., 1958-; Perf., Marlboro Music Fest., Vt., w. Pablo Casals, & at Bethlehem Bach Fest., Pa.; Fac. Mbr., Southern Meth. Univ., & N Tex. State Univ.; Pvte. Instr. & Clinician. Has recorded. Mbr: Percussive Arts Soc. Address: 9535 Chiswell Rd., Dallas, TX 75238, USA.

CHERRY, Philip, b. 31 July 1923, Phila., Pa., USA. Chellist. Educ: MA, Tchrs. Coll., Columbia Univ.; BS, Juilliard Schl. of Music; studied cello w. Benar Heifetz, Felix Salmond. m. Ruth Alice Cerry, 1 s., 1 d. Career: Solo Cello, Buffalo Phil., Nat. Symph., St. Louis Symph.; Prof., Colo. Coll.; w. NY Str. Quartet, Fest. Casals Orchs., Symph. of Air; currently (1961) w. Met. Opera Orch. Recordings: Gotham Baroque Ensemble. Hobby: Painting. Address: 70 W 95th St., Apt. 196, NY, NY 10025, USA.

CHESHIRE, John Brian, b. 26 July 1937, Chester, UK. Composer; Teacher. Educ: LTCL; GTCL; Comp. Studies w. Humphrey Searle. m. Rosemary Julia Smith, 1 d. Comps. incl: (orchl.): 3 Pieces; Anagrams; March Wall; Adagio for Strings; (chmbr.): Serenade for High Voice & 9 Instruments; Poems for 6 Instruments; Concerto for 12 Instruments; Sonata for Solo Violin; (piano); 6 Sonatas; Fragments; Miniatures; Aphorisms; Saudades; Sonata for 2 Pianos; 3 Elegies; Incidental music to Viet Revue; Tale of the Cheshire Cat for Narrator, Piano & Optional Children's Choir; num. songs, short instrumental pieces, etc. Mbrships: Comps'. Guild of GB; Soc. for the Promotion of New Music. Contbr. of occasional talks to Radio 3. Hobbies inc: Cinema; Science Fiction; Home-brewing; Music of Stravinsky & Alkan. Address: 2 Bron Llan, Llanfairtalhaiarn, Abergele, N Wales, UK.

CHESLOCK, Louis, b. 25 Sept. 1898, London, UK. Composer; Violinist; Professor of Music. Educ: Tchrs. Certs., in Violin, 1917, in Theory, 1919, Artist Dip., 1921, Peabody Conserv. of Music. m. Elise Brown Hanline, 1 s. Career incls: world-wide perfs. of major works; Prof., Peabody Inst., 1916-. Comps. incl: The Jewel Merchants (opera, libretto J R Cabell); Symph. in D Major; Violin Concerto, D Major; French Horn Concerto, F Major; Sonata for Piano, free tonality; Sonata for Violoncello, G Major; String Quartt, C Major; sev. song cycles; Sonata for Violin & Piano; The Congo (Vachel Lindsay), chorus & orch.; Psalm 150, chorus, orch., organ. Publs: Violin Vibrato, 1931; H L Mencken on Music, 1961. Contbr. to num. US periodicals. Mbrships: ASCAP; AAUP. Hons. incl: Hon. Citizen, Balt., Md.; DMusA, Peabody Inst., 1964. Address: Peabody Inst., Mt. Vernon Pl., Baltimore, MD, USA. 2, 11.

CHESNAIS, Pierre Louis, b. 22 July 1924. Courbevoie, France. Administrator. Educ: Dip., Advanced Studies in Econ. & Fin. Scis.; Dip., Pol. Sci., ML. m. Marcelle Boutier, 4 c. Career: Dir., French Union of Perfs., 1948-68; Gen. Sec., Int. Fedn. of Actors, 1951-58; currently Gen. Sec., French Nat. Fedn. of Music; Gen. Del., French group IFPI (SNEPA). Publs: L'Acteur, 1957. Contbr. to Jurisclassim 'Spectacles'. Mbrships: Int. Assn. of Arts & Lit.; Chmn., Assn. Professionelle du Spectacle et da L' Audiovisuel. Hons: Kt., Nat. Order of Merit, 1971. Address: 3 rue du Professeur Guyon, 78430 Louveciennes, France.

CHESTERMAN, Henry David, b. 17 Apr. 1920, Bath, UK. Administrator; Concert Promoter. Educ: Dip., Mgmt. Studies. m. Jean Kenward, 2 s., 1 d. Career: Sales, Advertising, PR, Dunlop, 20 yrs.; Personal Asst. to Sir Robert Mayer, Youth & Music, 4 yrs.; Mgr., Ernest Read Music Assn., 1970-75; Tenor, LP Choir; Music & Drama Adminstr., Nat. Fed. of Women's Insts.; Music Critic, Bucks Examiner. Contbr. to: Musical Times; Music in Educ.; etc. Mbrships: Coun. & Exec., Nat. Fedn. of Music Socs.; Chmn., Music Sub-Committee, City of Westminster Arts Coun. Hobbies: Tennis; Walking; Theatre. Address: 191 Old Marylebone Road, London, NW1 5QN, UK.

CHEYETTE, Irving, b. 1 Aug. 1904, NYC, NY, USA. University Professor. Educ: BS, 1929, MA, 1930, EdD, 1936, Columbia Univ.; Inst. of Musical Art, 1925-27 & 1935-36. m. Ruth Netter Cheyette (dec.), 2 s. Career: Prof., Music Educ., Syracuse Univ., 1948-55; Fulbright Prof., Tokyo Univ., Fine Arts, Japan, 1954-55; Dir., Music Educ., SUNY, Buffalo, 1955-72; Adj. Prof., Fordham Univ., 1973-. Comps. incl: 4 & 20 Folk Tunes; Bridging the Gap Band Book; Four Tone Folios (3 vols.). Mbr., var. music assns. Publs. incl: Teaching Music Creatively in the Elementary School, 1969. Contbr. to profl. jrnls. Recip., var. hons. Hobbies incl: Writing Poetry. Address: 150 W End Ave., NY, NY 10023, USA. 3, 6.

CHIBA, Kaoru, b. 6 Mar. 1928, Ooita, Japan. French Horn Player. Educ: Tokyo Univ. of Arts; studied w. Dennis Brain. m. Reiko Honscho. Career: currently Prin. Hornist, NHK Symph. Recordings incl: Complete Mozart Horn Concertos. Mbr., Tokyo Horn Club. Hobby: Motoring. Address: 1-11-3 Nakaochiai, Shinjuku-ku, Tokyo, Japan.

CHIDELL, Anthony Derek, b. 20 Aug. 1942, Bulawayo, S Rhodesia. Horn Player. Educ: RAM. m. Angela Chidell, 1 d., 4 s. Career: Horn, Royal Shakespeare Co., 1961; London Mozart Players, 1962; LPO, 1963-71; LSO, 1971-; Prof. of Horn, GSM, 1972-. Recordings: Bach Brandenburg Concerto No. 1 in F, Thea Musgrave - Night Music; both w. Barry Tuckwell. Co-prod. of horn mouthpieces w. Paxman Horns. Hobbies incl: Motorcycling. Address: 66 Redston Rd., London N8 7HE, UK.

CHILDS, Barney, b. 13 Feb. 1926, Spokane, Wash., USA. Composer. Educ: BA, Univ. of Nev., 1949; BA, Oxford Univ., UK, 1951; MA, ibid., 1955; PhD, Stanford Univ., USA, 1959; studied Comp. w. Leonard Ratner, Carlos Chevez, Aaron Copland, Elliott Carter. div., 2 d. Career: Instructor-Asst. Prof., Engl., Univ. of Ariz., 1956-65; Dean, Deep Springs Coll., 1965-69; Comp.-in-Res., Wis. Coll.-Conserv., 1969-71; Fac. Fellow in Music & Lit., Johnston Coll., Univ. of Redlands, Calif., 1971-73; Prof. of Comp. & Music Lit., ibid., 1973-. Compositions: (publd.) About 40 works inclng. num. commissions; (recorded) Music recorded on var. labels inclng. CRI, Ars Nova, Advance. Publ: Co-Ed., Contemporary Composers on Contemparary Music (w. Elliott Schwartz), 1967. Contbr. to num. profl. jrnls. Mbrships: Am. Soc. Univ. Comps. (Nat. Coun., 1967-70, 1974-, Exec. Committee 1970-73); Am. Comps. Alliance; Am. Music Ctr.; Am. Music Soc., UK (Advsry. Bd.); Pi Kappa Lambda. Hons: Rhodes Scholarship, 1949; Fellow, MacDowell Colony, 1963, 1968, 1970, 1974, 1978. Address: School of Music, Univ. of Redlands, Redlands, CA 92373, USA. 9, 14.

CHILDS, Gordon Bliss, b. 22 Oct. 1927, Springville, Utah, USA. Professor of Music; Head of College Music Department. Educ: BA, Brigham Young Univ., 1950; MA, ibid., 1953; EdD, ibid., 1975; Univ. of Mont., 1976. m. Elaine Finlayson, 2 s. Career incls: Public Schl. Tchr., USA, 1950-60; Asst. Prof. of Music, Univ. Mont., 1956-60; Prof. of Music, Adams State Coll., Colo., 1960-; Soloist & cond. num. orchs. in USA inclng. San Luis Valley Symph. Contbr. to profl. mags. Mbrships: Am. Musicol. Soc.; Am. String Tchrs. Assn.; Music Educators Nat. Conf.; Colo. Music Educators Assn.; Phi Delta Kappa. Recip. Disting. Serv. Award, Missoula Jr. Chmbr. of comm., 1969. Hobbies: Fishing; Reading. Address: 5290 Sierra Vista Rd., Alamosa, CO 81101, USA.

CHILINGIRIAN, Levon, b. 28 May 1948, Nicosia, Cyprus. Violinist. Educ: ARCM; pvte. study w. Manoug Parikian. Career: Perfs. throughout N Am., Europe, Aust. & NZ; TV & radio apps., Europe; Num. fest. apps.; Recitals w. Chilingirian String Quartet, & w. Clifford Benson (piano). Recordings incl: Schubert String Quartets; Korngold String Quartets; Arriaga String Quartets; Schubert - 3 sonatinas for violin & piano. Mbr., ISM. Hons: 1st Prize, BBC Beethoven Competition, 1969; 1st Prize, Munich Int. Competition, 1971 (both w. Clifford Benson); Prize, Young Concert Artists, NY, 1976. Hobbies: Backgammon; Not travelling. Address: 50 Cromwell Rd., Beckenham, Kent, UK.

CHIMES, John William, b. 3 Nov. 1953, London, UK. Timpanist. Educ: RCM, London. m. Margaret Whiteley. Career: Prin. Timpanist, BBC Symph. Orch. Hobbies: Football; Driving; Cooking. Address: Hunters Rest, Weedon Hill, Hyde Heath, Bucks. HP6 5RN, UK.

CHINI, Tarcisio, b. 27 Aug. 1936, Zambana, Trento, Italy. Librarian. Educ: Grad. in Mod. Lit.; Dip. in Musicol.; Dip. in Organ. m. Carla Pisetta, 2 d. Publ: Le Opere Strumentali di Giovanni Cavaccio (in preparation). Contbr. to: Studi Trentini di Scienze Storiche; Bolletino Ceciliano. Mbrships: Italian Musicol. Soc.; Int. Assn. of Music Libs. Hobbies: Alpinism; Tennis. Address: Via Licata 6, Verona, Italy.

CHISSELL, Joan Olive, b. Cromer, Norfolk, UK. Music Critic. Educ: ARCM; GRSM. Career: Lectr. in Music for Extra-Mural Depts., London & Oxford Univs., UK, 1943-48; Piano Tchr., Jr. Dept., RCM, 1943-53; Asst. Music Critic, The Times, 1948-. Publs: Schumann, 1948; Chopin, 1965; Schumann's Piano Music, 1972; Brahms, 1977; Contbr. to: Benjamin Britten (A Symposium); Chmamber Music (Pelican); The Concerto (Pelican); var. profl. mags. & Radio Times. Mbrships: Royal Musical Assn.; RCM Union. Hobby: Boating on River Thames. Address: 7D Abbey Rd., London NW8, UK. 3, 14.

CHMARA-ZACZKIEWICZ, Ewa Barbara, b. 11 Dec. 1933, Poznan, Poland. Musicologist. Educ: Dip. Magister, Inst. of Musicol. at the Warsaw Univ., 1959; Research Grants-Hungary 1969 & Austria, 1975-76. m. Leon Zaczkiewicz. Career: Lectr. of Theory of Music at Sec. Music Schl. in Warsaw, 1955-66; Prelector of Wardaw Music Soc., 1961-71; Prelector of Nat. Philharmony, Warsaw, 1958-; Co-worker of number of publsrs. & institutions in the field of sci. works, jrnlsm., pedagogy, etc. Publs: incl: Do genezy nokturnu instrumentalnego przed Chopinen, in FF Chopin, Warsaw, 1960; Das Problem der Agogik der Nocturni von Field u. Chopin, in The Book of the 1st in Musicol. Congress, Warsaw, 1963; Twórczość wokalna M Kartowicza, in: Z zycia i twórcości Mieczyslawa Karlowicza, ed. W Dziebowska, Kraków 1970. Contbr. to many profl. publs. Mbrships: Mr. of Committee, Assn. of Polish Musicians; Union of Polich Comps.; The Warsaw Music Soc.; Int. Soc. for Music Educ. Hons. incl: Award of Meritorious Person actively engaged in cultural works, 1969; Medal of Merit from the Wardaw Soc. of Music, 1971. Hobbies: Theatre, etc. Address: Ziota 75/55, 00-819 Warsaw, Poland.

CHODOS, Gabriel, b. 7 Feb. 1939, White Plains, NY, USA. Pianist. Educ: BA, 1959, MA, 1964, UCLA; Dip. in Piano, Acad. of Music & Dramatic Art, Vienna, 1966; Piano studies w. Aube Tzerko. m. Yoriko Takahashi, 1 s. Debut: Carnegie Recital Hall, NYC, 1970. Career: apps. throughout USA; num. tours of Europe, Japan & Israel; apps. w. Chgo. Symph. Orch., Radio Phil. Orch. of Holland & Jerusalem Symph. Ordn. Recordings; Orion Records (USA); Victor Records (Japan). Hons. incl: Winner, Michaels Competition, 1967, Concert Artists Guild Auditions, 1970; Fulbright Scholarship, 1965-66; Martha Baird Rockefeller Grants, 1970, 74. Address: 245 Waban Ave., Waban, MA 02168, USA.

CHODURA, Frantisek, b. 22 Apr. 1906, Pribor, Czechoslovakia. Violinist; Conductor; Associate Professor; Master of Pedagogical & Musical Science. Educ: State Exams., Violin, Singing, Piano & Organ, Tchrs. Trng. Coll. m. Vera Lebedova, 3 s. Career: Mbr., S Bohemian Str. Quartet; Cond., S Bohemian Vocal Chmbr. Assn.; Assoc. Prof., Tchrs. Trng. Coll.; Cond., Tchrs. Symph. Orch.; Ret'd. 1972. Compositions: 20 Folk Songs for schools; 4 cantatas; Memories (str. quartet). All above broadcast by Czech radio, some by radio of GDR, Japan, GFR, Poland & Holland. Publs: Problems of Intonation applied to Receptive Musical Education at Schools, 1967; Problems of Educational Concerts in the Field of Chamber Music--String Quartet, 1969. Contbr. to Estetika vychova, Prague; Mbrships: Czech. Soc. for Musical Educ., Prague; VP, S Bohemian Grp. of Vocal Assns. Hons. incl: Medal of Vojtech Jirovec, 1963; Medal, 700th Anniversary of City Ceske Budejovice, 1965; Hon. of Tchrs. Trng. Coll. Dean, 1971; Mem. Medal, Tchrs. Trng. Coll., Ceske Budejovice, 1973. Hobby: Study of Slav nation's songs. Address: Cechova 51, Ceske Budejovice, Czechoslovakia.

CHORZEMPA, Daniel Walter, b. 7 Dec. 1948, Mpls., Minn., USA. Pianist; Organist; Musicologist; Conductor; Composer; Harpsichordist. Educ: BA, PhD, Univ. of Minn.; further musical trng., Cologne, German Fed. Repub. Career: Organ Instructor, Univ. of Minn., 1962-65; Piano & Organ Recitalist, Germany, Denmark, Italy, UK, etc., 1968-. Recordings incl: Organ music by Liszt, Bach, Haydn, Mozart & Handel; Beethoven Sonata Recital (piano). Publ: Ed., Reubke Organ Sonata, 1976. Mbrships: Phi Kappa Lambda; Phi Beta Kappa. Recip., J S Bach Prize, Leipzig, 1968. Hobbies: Mathematics; Architecture; Poetry; Renaissance History & Literature. Address: 5 Cologne 1, Hohestr. 114, German Fed. Repub.

CHOUINARD, Joseph Jerod, b. 7 May 1926, Middletown, Conn., USA. Music Librarian; Singer (bass). Educ: BA, MA (Music), Univ. of Conn.; MLS; Geneseo (NY). Debut: Chattanooga (Tenn.) Opera, 1955. Career: Tri-Cities Opera, Binghampton, NY, 1956-66; Apps., Aspen, Interlochen, Tanglewood Music Fests.; App., Summer Schi. for Singers, Oxford, UK, 1961; Fla. Int. Fest.; Allegheny Summer Music Fest., Pa., 1979; Ch. Soloist, NYC, Buffalo, NY. Contbr. to: Am. Reference Books Annual. Mbrships: Nat. Assn. of Tchrs. of Singing; Am. Musicol. Soc.; Music Lib. Assn.; Fontainebleau Alumni Assoc. Hobby: Compsoing music. Address: 71 Central Ave., Fredonia, NY 14063, USA.

CHOVEAUX, Nicholas, b. Bromley, Kent, UK. Concert & Artist Manager. Educ: FRCO; Matthay Schl; studies w. Arnold Grier. m. (1) Evelyn Mattinson (dec.), (2) Andrée Maillard-Back, 2 d. Career: Organist & Tchr. to 1948; Music Master, Dover Coll.; Organist & Choirmaster, Chelsea Old Ch., St. John's Ch., Wimbledon, & St. Bartholomew the Gt., Smithfield; Jt. Organiser, Karg-Elert Fest., St. Lawrence Jewry; Ensa Music Advsr.; Contemporary Music Promotion, Boosey & Hawkes, & A Lengnick & Co.; Concert & Artist Mgmt.; 1948-. Comps. incl: 3 pieces for Organ; 3 pieces for Violin & Piano; Prelude-Improvisation for Organ; Communion Service. Hobbies: Reading; Listening; Travelling. Address: Mancroft Towers, Oulton Broad, Lowestoft, Suffolk NR32 3PS, UK. 3.

CHOWDHURY, Salil, b. 19 Nov. 1923, Calcutta, W Bengal, India. Composer; Lyricist; Scenarist; Playwright; Film Director. Educ: Grad., Univ. of Calcutta. m. Sabita Chowdhury, 2 S., 5 d. Career: Musical Dir., cinema, 1950-, composing music for over 60 films in virtually all Indian langs.; num. apps. on stage, TV & radio. Comps: Over 500 songs recorded for films. Publs: sev. vols. of lyrics; plays; poems. Mbrships: Fndr., Cond., Bombay Youth Choir; Indian Peoples Theatre Assn.; Gen. Sec., Cine Music Dirs. Assn., Bombay. Hons. incl: Best Film Story, Asiatic Film Soc., London, 1953; Film Fare Award for Best Music Dir., 1957. Hobbies: Folk Music & Instruments; Sports. Address: Hingiri 2, Peddar Rd., Bombay 26, India.

CHRIPPES, Peter Gordon Charles, b. 21 Apr. 1945, Redditch, Worcs., UK. Percussion/Timpanist. m. Diane M Huckins. Career: currently Mbr., LPO. Num. recordings w. LPO, other orchs. & chmbr. orchs./groups. Hobbies: Model Railways. Address: 81 Harlands Rd., Haywards Heath, Sussex RH16 1LZ, UK.

CHRIST, William B, b. 22 Nov. 1919, Marion, Ill., USa. Music Administrator; Professor of Theory. Educ: BMus, Ill. Wesleyan Univ., Bloomington, 1941; MMus, Ind. Univ., Bloomington, 1949; PhD, ibid., 1953. m. Nelda McMurtrey Christ, 1 d., 1 s. Career incl: Dir., of Music, Asst. Prof. of Music Educ., Dir. of Chroal Music, Coll. of Music of Cinn., 1953-55; Asst. Prof. of Theory, Schl. of Music, Ind. Univ., 1955-59; Asst. Dean & Full Prof., ibid., 1963; Assoc. Dean, ibid., 1968-; now Dir. of Grad. Studies, ibid.; Ind. State Arts Commission, 1969-77 (chmn., 1971-72); District Dir., S Ind. District Metropolitan Opera Auditions, 1967-. Publs. incl: The Comprehensive Study of Music, consisting of 4 vols., plus Anthologies of Music from Plainchant to Stockhausen, 1976-79, Piano Reductions for Harmonic Study, 1979 & Basic Principles of Music Theory, 1979; The Materials & Structure of Music, 1967. Mbrships: Phi Kappa Lambda; Phi Kappa Phi; Phi Mu Alpha; Phi Delta Kappa; Am. Assn. of Univ. Profs.; Ind. Music Tchrs. Assn.; MENC; Music Tchrs. Nat. Assn.; Soc. of Music Theory. Recip. Orchl. Comp. Prize, 1952. Address: 4901 E Ridgewood Dr., Bloomington, IN 47401, USA.

CHRISTENSEN, Anker, b. 12 Nov. 1899, Copenhagen, Denmark. Violinist. Educ: studied violin & chamber music w. Thorvald Nielsen, solo violin w. Fini Henriques, Emil Telmanyi, Adolf Bak & Adolf Busch; studies at Music Schl. Eksamen, 1921, 1945. m. Jota Hagemeister, 2 s. Debut: 21 Oct. 1926. Career: 1st violin, Danish Radio Symph. Orch.; Soloist, Swedish, Norwegian & Swiss radio, & num. perfs. w. piano and orch., Danish radio. Var. comps. & recordings. Contbr. to Politiken's Leksikon. Mbr., (past committee) Danish Soloists Grp. Hons: Num. works dedicated by comps., inclng. Niels Viggo Bentzon, Rued Langaard, Thorvald Larsen, Jens Bjere; Ridderkorset, 1969. Hobby: Piano. Address: Borups Allé 201, Copenhagen NV, Denmark.

CHRISTENSEN, Dieter, b. 17 Apr. 1932, Berlin, Germany. University Professor of Ethnomusicology. Educ: Study of cello, Berlin State Conserv.; PhD, Musicol., Free Univ., Berlin, 1957. m. Nerthus Karger, 1 s., 1 d. Debut: RIAS radio, Berlin, 1949. Career: Prof., Columbia Univ., NYC. Recordings: Lappish folk songs, Kurdish folk music. Publs. incl: Die Musik der Kate und Sialum, 1957; Die Musik der Ellice-Inseln (w. G Koch), 1964; Co-ed., Hornbostel Opera Omnia, 1974. Contbr. to German & Int. profl. jrnls. Publs: Der Ring des Tlalocan, 1977. Mbrships: Exec. Bd. Mbr., Prog. Chmn., Edinburgh Conf., 1969, Regensberg Conf., 1975, Int. Folk Music Coun.; Chmn., Mbr., var. comms. & Book Review Ed., Jrnl. Soc. for Ethnomusicol. Hobbies: Agriculture; Electronics. Address: 464 Riverside Dr., New York, NY 10027, USA. 19.

CHRISTENSEN, Helge Ploug, b. 23 May 1918, Copenhagen, Denmark. Double Bass Player. Educ: Highest Degree of the Royal Danish Music Conserv. m. Ellen Margrethe Ploug Christensen, 1 s., 1 d. Debut: 1940. Career: many solo, ensemble and orchl. perfs. in concert halls & on Danish Radio; 1st bass player, Danish Broadcasting Symph. Orch.; lectr., Danish

Music Conserv. Recordings: w. Danish Broadcasting Symph. Orch., Danish Chambr. Orch. & Chambr. Orch. of Copenhagen Cathedral. Mbrships: Academic Ctrl. Organisation; Tchrs. Club, Royal Danish Music Conserv.; Danish solo players' club; Danish Music Pedagogues' Club. Hons: Danish Broadcasting Legacy Award; Kt., 1973. Address: Wibrandtsvej 90, 2300 Copenhagen, Denmark.

CHRISTIAN, Judith Anne, b. 8 Apr. 1955, Douglas, Isle of Man, UK. Pianist; Violinist; Teacher. Educ: Chetham's Hospital Schl. of Music; RNCM, 1973-77; GRNCM; studied w. Rysard Bakst. m. Julian Sutton, 1 s. Career: perfs. for num. music clubs throughout N W England; app. in Norway playing Beethoven's 1st piano concerto, 1980. mbr., ISM. Address: 6 Lezayre Pk., Ramsey, Isle of Man, UK.

CHRISTIAN, Susan Hendrick, b. 24 Feb. 1954, Denver, Colo., USA. Tchr., organ & piano. Educ: Baylor Univ., Waco, Tex. BS in Educ.; Master of Religious Educ., New Orleans Baptist Theological Seminar, 1979. m. John M. Christian. Debut: Vocal, Age 7; Piano, Age 11; Organ, Age 16. Career: Singer, Pianist, Weekly TV Prog., Va.; Miss Roanoke Valley Beauty Pageant, 1972; Piano Accomp., Special Music for Roanoke Valley Christmas Pageant, 1972; Soloist, Piano, Organ Accomp., Radio Prog. Little Country Ch., Mid-West & Eastern USA & Can., 1972, 1973. Contbr. to Am. Harp Soc. Jrnl. Mbrships: Sec., Baylor Univ. Schl. of Music Chapt. Am. Harp Soc.; Tex. State Music Educators Assn.; MENC. Recip. num. hons. Hobbies: Collecting Bells; Entertaining Children; Reading; Cheerleading; Travelling. Address: 246 Knoll Rd., Roanoke, VA 24019. 4, 7, 27, 29.

CHRISTIANSEN, Asger Lund, b. 23 May 1927, Copenhagen, Denmark. Professor of Cello; Composer. Educ: degree, Royal Danish Conserv. of Music, Copenhagen, 1943-47; studied w. Gaspard Cassado, Acad. Chigiana, Siena, Italy, 1947-48 m Jytte, 1 s., 1 d. Debut: Børno, Switz., 1947. Career: num. concerts throughout world as Soloist & Chmbr. Music Perf.; Mbr., Copenhagen Str. Quartet, 1st Cello, Phil. Orch., Copenhagen, 1949-59, & Royal Orch. (opera), Copenhagen, 1959-66; Prof., Aarhus, 1966-. Comps: Concertos for trombone & bassoon; Trio for flute, viola, cello; Quintet for clarinette & str. quartet. Recorded over 50 LPs. Publs: Musiklexicon for bedrevidende, 1976. Contbr. to num. publs. Dir: DMA (anthol. of Danish music on records); Soloist Assn., Tivoliphon (recording co.). Recip. Rider of Dannebrog. Mgmt: Daub Concerts, Copenhagen; Adler, Berlin. Address: Frederiksberg alle 25, Copenhagen 1820 V, Denmark.

CHRISTIANSEN, James, b. 26 Nov. 1931, Goomeri, Qld., Australia. Singer; Teacher; Conductor. Educ: Matriculation, Muirden Coll., Adelaide; Dip. Assoc., Univ. of Adelaide; FTCL. m. Marilyn Richardson, 6 children. Debut: ABC Concert Adelaide, 5 Aust. Career incls: Recitalist. Aust. Broadcasting Commission, 20 yrs.; BBC, 5 yrs.; Num. concert apps. in Aust., GB & USA. Cond: ABC Adelaide Singers; Adelaide Symph. Orch. Opera: Glyndebourne Festival; Wexford Festival; St. Paul Opera Assn., USA; State Opera, S Aust.; Tchr., Pvte. & Institutional, 20 yrs.; Adjudicator in GB, USA & Aust. Num. recordings. Recip. Qld. Univ. Music. Scholarship, 1953. Hobbies: Tennis; Gardening; Reading. Address: 28 Yeltana Ave., Wattle Pk., SA 5066, Aust.

CHRISTIANSEN-FERNALD, Beverly J, b. 22 Sept. 1936, Denver, Colo., USA. Singer; Teacher; Coach; Director. Educ: BMus, Univ. of Denver; Hochschule für Musik, Munich. m. Ralph J Fernald, 1 d. Career: Over 40 leading opera roles performed w. num. opera cos. inclng. NYC Opera; Conn. Opera Assn.; Chattanooga Opera Assn.; Denver Lyric Opera; Kan. City Lyric Theatre; num. concerts & oratorios; TV & radio apps.; Mbr., Milton Berle's Royal Quartet; Mbr., Vocal Fac., Metropolitan State Coll., Denver. Mbrships. incl: Mu Phi Epsilon; Altrusa Int. Hons. incl: Ford Fndn. Grant; Rockefeller Grant, 1962. Hobbies incl: Swimming. Address: 3812 Wright Ct., Wheat Ridge, CO 80033, USA.

CHRISTIE, Amalie, b. 21 Dec. 1913, Vang Hedemark, Norway. Pianist; Music pedagog. Educ: Kunstler Dip., Staatliche Akademische Hochschule für Musik, Berlin. m. Dan Lindholm, 3 c. Debut: Oslo, 1937. Career: Concerts, Norway, Sweden, Hungary, Germany & Switz.; Radio & TV pers., Norway. Publs: Mennesket og musikken, 1949; Beethoven, 1970. Mbrships: Norsk Tonekunstnersamfund; League of Norwegian pedagogs. Hons: 3 yrs. State Artist stipendium, 1968-; State Guaranteed income for artists, 1976-. Hobby: Mountain wandering. Address: Ruglandveien 87, 1342 Jar, Norway.

CHRISTIE, Catherine, b. Kirkcaldy, Scotland, UK. Soprano. Educ: Pvte. tuition in Scotland & London. m. I M Hughes, 2 s., 1 d. Career: Oratorio, recital, misc. stage, TV work & opera; perf. of Three Moons by John McLeod, 1969; 1st Scottish

perfs. of Henze's Being Beauteous, 1970 & Schoenberg's Herzgewachse, 1971; Singer in Green Grow the Rashes, dramatized arr. of Burn's peoms on stage, 1973, TV, 1974; Soloist, La Fête Etrange w. Scottish Ballet, 1975; Played Mam & Mary Ellis in Ivor by John Cairney, 1975. Mbrships: Equity; ISM. Hobbies: Reading; Walking. Address: 108 High St., Old Aberdeen, Aberdeen, UK.

CHRISTIE, George, b. 31 Dec. 1934, Glynebourne, Lewes, Sussex, UK. Opera Administrator. Educ: Eton; Trinity Coll., Cambridge. m. Mary Nicholson, 4 children. Occasional contbr. to mags. Address: Glyndebourne, Lewes, Sussex, UK. 1.

CHRISTOPHERSON, Larry Lee, b. 9 Feb. 1937, Burley, Idaho, USA. University Professor; Ethnomusicologist; Bassoonist. Educ: BMus, Univ. Mont., 1964; MMus, Northwestern Univ., 1968; DPh, ibid., 1973. m. Virginia Jean Johnson, 1 d. Career: Lectr., Univ. Ghana, Legon, Ghana, 1971-73. Asst. Prof. & Music Coord., York Coll. of CUNY, USA, 1973-; Assoc. Prof. & Coord. of Music Educ., Conserv. of Music, Capital Univ., 1977-. Contbr. to record reviews for Black Perspectives in Music, 1974; Video Tape as a Tool in Music Education and Musicological Research, rsch. Bulletin of Inst. of African Studies, Ghana. Mbrships. incl: Music Eduator's Nat. Conf.; Ohio Music Educator's Assn. Recip. Award, Outstanding Young Tchr. of Yr., 1966-67. Hobbies: Gardening; Reading. Address: 885 Francis Ave., Colombus, OH 43209, USA.

CHUANG, Marisa Yuen, b. 19 Mar. 1943, Kwalin, China. Piano Performer & Teacher; Cellist. Educ: Royal Schls. of Music, London, 1962; MA, Columbia Univ., 1966; DPh Candidate, Univ. of Mich.; Honor roll, NGPT, USA, 1970; Music Therapy Internship, Essex County Overbrook Hosp., NJ. m. Ven L Chuang, 1 d. Debut: as pianist, Chinese Univ. of Hong Kong, 1961. Career incls: apps., Hong Kong TV, 1960, Radio Hong Kong, 1958-60, Berea Coll., USA, 1965. Mbrships: NGPT; Psi Chi. Hons. incl: Distinction Award, RSM, 1961; Tchr. w. Merits, NGPT, 1970. Hobbies: Public Speaking; Skiing; Swimming. Mgmt: Arts House, 6842 Cathedral, Birmingham, MI 48010, USA.

CHUCHRO, Josef, b. 3 July 1931, Prague, Czech. Cellist. Educ: Conser. of Music & Acad. of Musical Arts, Prague. m. Zdenka Chuchrova-Brunova, 1 s. Debut: Prague, 1950. Career: concert activity as Soloist & Chmbr. Musician on all 5 continents; Prof., Conserv. of Music & Acad. of Musical Arts, Prague; Soloist, Czech. Phil. Orch.; Mbr., Suk Trio. Var. recordings. Mbr., Union of Czech. Comps. & Concert Artists, Prague. Hons. incl: 1st Prizes, Hanus Wihan Int. Competition, Prague, 1955, Pablo Casals Int. Competition, Mexico, 1959; Artist of Merit, 1976. Hobbies: Bridge; Chess; Teaching. Mgmt: Pragokoncert, Prague. Address: 3 Zizkov, Kriva 2620, 130 000 Prague, Czechoslovakia.

CHULAKI, Mikhail Ivanovich, b. 19 Nov. 1908, Simferopol, Crimea, Russia. Composer. Educ: Leningrad Conserv. Career: Tchr., Leningrad Conser., 1933; Moscow Conserv., 1948-; Sec., Union of Soviet Composers, 1948-57; Vice-Chmn., Committee for Arts Affairs, USSR Coun. of Mins., 1951-53; Dpty. Chief, Dept. for Arts Affairs of the USSR, Min. of Culture, 1953-55; Dir., Bolshoi Theatre, 1955-59, 1963-70; Sec. Union of Composers of RSFSR, 1959-63; Mbr., Supreme Soviet of RSFSR, 1963-71. Compositions incl: 3 Symphs.; Ballets - The Story of the Priest & His Servant Balda, 1939; The Imaginary Bridegroom, 1946; Youth, 1947; Cantata on the Banks of the Volhov River, 1943; A Symph. Cycle of Songs & Dances of Old France, 1959; Lenin is With US, 1960; Romances on Whitman's Verses, 1962. Hons: State Prizes, 1947, '48, '50; Badge of Hon.; Peoples Artist of RSFSR. Address: Boshoi Theatre, 1 Ploshchad Sverdlova, Moscow, USSR.

CHUN-WILSON, Seoung Lee, b. 18 Apr. 1931, Seoul, Korea. Mezzo-Soprano; College Voice Teacher. Educ: BMus., Univ. of Louisville Schl. of Music; MMus, Southern Meth. Univ. Schl. of Music; summer sessions at Music Acad. of the W, 1953, & Aspen Music Schl., 1955, 56, 57, & 58. m. Brian Wilson, 2 s., 2 d. Debut: Solo Voice Recital, Nat. Theatre, Seoul, Korea, 1960; in USA, Solo Recital, San Fran. Performing Arts Ctr., 1974. Career: Soloist, Seoul Nat. Symph. Orch., KBS Orch. Charleston Symph. Orch., Green Bay Symph., Sebastian Chmbr. Orch., & others; app. in leading rolws w. Ky. Opera Assn., W Bay Opera, & Peninsula Artist & Opera Co.; app. at Moravian Music Fest., 1974. Mbrships: Nat. Assn. Tchrs. of Singing; SAI. Mgmt: Int. Artists Mgmt., San Francisco. Hobbies: Knitting; Tennis; Cross-Country Skiing. Address: 937 St. Mary's St., De Pere, WI 54115, USA.

CHUNG, Kyung-Wha, b. 26 Mar. 1948, Seoul, Korea. Concert Violinist. Educ: pvte. tchrs. in Korea; Juilliard Schl. of Music, NYC; pvte. study w. Ivan Galamian. Debut: Seoul,

1957; European debut w. LSO, Royal Fest. Hall, 1970. Career: Perf. w. Korean Broadcasting Symph. Orch., 1958; Appts. w. major US Orchs., also major orchs. of N & S Am., Japan, Europe. Recordings: (w. orch.) Bruch 1/Scottish Fantasy; Tchaikovsky/Sibelius, Walton/Stravinsky (winner, Edison Award); Prokoviev 1 & 2; Elgar; Bartok 2; Saint-Saens 3; Vieuxtemps 5; Concertos & recital records. Contbr. to: High Fidelity. Hons: Jt. Winner, Edgar M Leventritt Int. Comp., 1968; named Star of the Yr. in Music by Münchner Abendzeitung, 1973. Hobbies incl: Ice Skating; Reading sci. fiction. Mgmt: Harrison/Parrott Ltd., 22 Hillgate St., London W8 7SR, UK. Address: c/o Mgmt.

CHUNG, Myung-Wha, b. 19 Mar. 1944, Seoul, Korea. Concert Cellist. Educ: BA, Juilliard Schl. of Music; Univ. of Southern Calif. Master Class w. Gregor Piatigorsky. m. Samuel Koo, 1 d., 1 s. Debut: w. Seoul Phil., Korea, 1957. Career: Soloist w. orchs. in N Am., E Asia, & Europe inclng. RPO, Halle Orch.; Orch. Swiss Romande, San Fran. Orch., Mexican Nat. Symph.; jt. apps. w. sister Kyung-Wha (violin) & brother Myung-Whun (piano); mbr. of trio w. above; TV apps., UK, USA, Korea. Recording: Tchaikovsky Rococo Variations. Contbr. to mags. & newspapers in Korea. Mbr., Cello Soc., USA. Hons: 1st Prizes, San Fran. Symph. Award, 1968, & Geneva Int. Musical Competition, 1971. Mgmt: Harrison/Parrott, 22 Hillgate St., London W8 7SR, UK. Address: c/o Mgmt. 30.

CHUNG, Myung-Whun, b. 22 Jan. 1953, Seoul, Korea. Pianist; Conductor. Educ: Mannes Schl. of Music & Juilliard Schl., NYC, USA; Dip. in piano & condng., 1974. Debut: w. Seoul Phil., 1960. Career incl: Concert performances w. London Symph. Orch., Berlin Radio Orch., Hague, Phil., New Philharmonia Orch., BBC Symph. Orch. & London Mozart Players; US Concert Tour, 1975-76; Debut as Cond., Korean Nat. Symph., 1971; Dir., NYC Youth Symph., 1976/; Dir., Juilliard Pre-Coll. Orch., 1976-77. Recordings incl: Haydn & Chopin Sonatas Hons. incl: 1st Prize, NY Times Radio Competition, 1970; 2nd Prize, Tchaikowsky Competition, Moscow, 1974. Hobbies: Sports; Cooking. Mgmt: (UK & world) Harrison/Parrott Ltd., London, (USA) Columbia Artist Mgmt. Address: 27 W 89th St., Apt. C, NY, NY 10024, USA.

CHURCHILL, John, b. 29 May 1920, London, UK. University Professor; Conductor. Educ: BMus, London Univ.; FRCO (CHM), GRSM, ARCM, LRAM. m. Jean Trevelyan, 2 s., 1 d. Career: Organist, St. Martin-in-the-Fields, London; Prof., RCM, London; Prof., Music, Carleton Univ., Ottawa. Can. Compositions: (arr.) Vaughan Williams: Psalm 23: Three Songs from Eastern Canada. Recordings: Academy of St. Martin-in-the-Fields, (Oiseau Lyre etc.). Publs: Congregational Singing, 1962; Pasquali: Figured Bass Made Easy, (Ed.), 1974. Contbr. to: Musical Times; RCM Mag. Mbrships: Can. Assn. of Univ. Tchrs.; Inc. Soc. of Musicians. Hons: Harding Prize, 1940; Hon. ARCM, 1966. Address: Carleton Univ., Ottawa, Ont., Can. 3.

CHURGIN, Bathia Dina, b. 9 Oct. 1928, NYC, NY, USA. Musicologist. Educ: BA, Hunter Coll., NYC, 1950; MA, Radcliffe Coll., 1952; PhD, Harvard Univ., 1963. Career: Vassar Coll., 1952-57, 1959-71; Instructor to Full Prof., Bar-Ilan Univ., Israel; Prof. and Fndng. Hd. of Dept., ibid., 1970-. Publs: The Symphonies of G B Sammartini, Vol. 1, The Early Symphonies, 1968; (w. Newell Jenkins) Thematic Catalogue of the Works of Giovanni Battista Sammartini, Orchestral & Vocal Music, 1976. Contbr. to profl. pbuls. Mbrships: Israel Musicol. Soc. (VP, 1972-74); Am. Musicol. Soc.; Int. Musicol. Soc. Hons: Rsch. Fellow, Am. Coun. of Learned Socs., 1964. Address: Dept. of Musicol., Bar-Ilan Univ., Ramat Gan, Israel. 5.

CHWALEK, Jan, b. 7 Jan. 1930, Wola Baranowska, Tarnobrzeg, Poland. Priest. Educ: studied Phil., Theol. & Musicol.; Dr. Theol. Publs: Budowa Organow. Wprowadzenie Do Inwentaryzacji I Dokumentacji Zabytowych Organow W Polsce (Organ Building. An Introduction into the Problems of Registering & Documenting Historial Organs in Poland), 1971, 2nd ed., 1973. Mbr: Zwiazek Kompozytorow Polskich. Address: ul. Nowotki 7, 20-039, Lublin, Poland.

CHYLINSKA, Teresa, b. 20 June 1931, Wojciechowice, Poland. Musicologist. Educ: DMusicol., Jagiellonian Univ., 1953. dlv., 1 s. Career: Gen. Ed., Complete Ed. of Karol Szymanowski's Works, Polish version, 26 vols., Engl.-German version, 17 vols. Publs: Incl: Szymanowski's Letters, Szymanowski's Writings, Ed., 1958; Karel Szymanowski Album, Polish & Eng. Versions, 1973; The Story of a Friendship, The Correspondence of Karol Szymanowski & Pawel & Zofia Kochanski (ed.), 1971; Concert Guide (w. S Haraschin & B Schäffer), 1973; Between composer and publisher. Correspondence of Karol Szymanowski 2nd Universal Edition, Ed., 1978. Mbrships: Musicol. Sect., Polish Composers' Union;

Polish Soc. of Book Eds. Address: ul. Syrokomli 16 m. 10, 30-102 Cracow, Poland. 30.

CIANI, Dino, b. 1941, Fiume, Italy. Pianist. Educ: studied w. Marta del Vecchio, Geneva & Alfred Cortot; St. Cecilia Conserv., Rome. Career: has made concert tours in Germany, Switz., Hungary & Italy. Hons: 1st Prize, Ciovanni Concertist Competition, 1960; 2nd Prize, Liszt-Bartok Competition, Budapest, 1961. Address: c/o Lies Askionas, 19a Air St., Regent St., London WI, UK. 3.

CICCOLINI, Aldo, b. 15 Aug. 1925, Naples, Italy. Pianist. Educ: special 4 yrs. schlrship. to study piano & comp., Naples Conserv., 1934. Career incls: Prof. of piano. Naples Conserv., 1947; debut at Carnegie Hall, 1950; recitals & concerns in Europe, N & S Am., Near E. USSR; radio & TV broadcasts; apps. at major fests.; appointed Prof., Conservatoire National Supérieur de Musique, Paris, 1971. Recordings incl: Grieg recital; complete Saint-Saëns Piano Concertos; complete piano works of Eric Satie (in progress). Hons. incl: 1st Prize, Marguerite Long/Jacques Thibaud competition, 1949. Mgmt: Ibbs & Tillett, 124 Wigmore St., London W1H ODJ, UK.

CIGLIČ, Zvonimir, b. 20 Feb. 1921, Ljubljana, Yugoslavia. Composer; Conductor; Professor of Composition. Educ: Acad. of Music, Ljubljana; Mozarteum, Salzburg, Austria; Asst., Orch. Lamoureux, Paris, France. m. Ana Korez-Ciglic. Debut: (as Comp.) 1939; (as Cond.), 1947. Career: Cond., Ljubljana, Sarajevo, Subotica & Maribor, Yugoslavia & num. other European countries; TV, radio & film music. Comps. incl: Dancer's Schore (recorded); Suite in ancient style for Piano; Bacchanal; (also recorded) Adagio Amoroso; Concertino for harp & string orch.; Sinfonia Appassionata; Vision; Two songs; Phoenix Sylvestris for orch. Publs: Ed., Selected Works of Slovene Composers. Contbr. to var. jrnls. Mbr., profl. assns. Prize for Comp., Presidium of People's Assembly of Slovenia, 1948. Address: Ljubljana, ul. Talcev5/1, Yugoslavia.

CIKKER, Jan, b. 29 July 1911, Banska Bystrica, Czechoslovakia. Composer; Music Educator. Educ: Banska Bystrica Conserv.; Master Schl. of Composition, Prague; Study of conducting w. Felix Weingartner, Vienna. Career: Prof. of Theory of Music, Bratislava Conserv., 1939-51; Dramaturgist, Opera House, 1945-48; Prof. of Composition, Schl. of Musical Arts, 1951-. Compositions incl: Sonatina for Piano, 1933; Symphonic Prologue, 1934; 2 String Quartets; Capriccio, 1936; Cantus Filiorum (cantata), 1940; About Life (Trilogy of symphonic poems); Concertino for piano & orch., 1942; Bucolic Poem (ballet music), 1944; Operas - Juro Janosik, 1954; Beg Bajazid, 1957; Resurrection, 1962; Mr. Scrooge, 1963; A Play About Love & Death, 1967. Hons. incl: Czech Peace Prize, 1951; Herder Prize, Vienna Univ., 1966; Madach Prize, Hungary, 1966. Address: Fialkove udolie c. 1042, Bratislava, Czechoslovakia.

CIMASZEWSKI, Tadeusz, b. 6 June 19036, Wilno, Poland. Tenor. Educ: MA, Coll. of Music, Wroclaw. m. Krystyna Czaplarska. Debut: Opera of Gdansk, 1961. Career: Major opera stages of Wroclaw, Gdansk, Krakow, Bytom. TV Wroclaw, Radio Warsaw & Gdansk; Concerts at Sofia, Bulgaria, Berlin & throughout Poland. Mbrships: Polish Musicians' Assn. (Chmn., Revision Commission, Wroclaw Sect.); Bd., Lower Silesian Br., ibid., Chmn., Artistic Coun., ibid.; Chmn., PMA, Wroclaw Opera. Recip. Yrly. Schlrship., Walter Felsenstein Opera Staging, Berlin. Hobbies: Tourism; Sports. Address: 50-419 Wroclaw, ul. Traugutta 111/113, Poland.

CIMBRELIUS, Bengt Ivar, b. 30 May 1922 Simrishamn, Sweden. Church Organist. Educ: Organist's & Precentor's Exam., Gothenburg, 1940. Elem. Schl. Tchrs. Cert., Lund, 1945; Organist, Precentor, Music Dir., Royal Acad. of Music, Stockholm, 1951; BA, Lund Univ., 1955; Grad. in Musical Sci., ibid., 1967; Organ study w. Helmut Walcha; Composition, John Fernstroem; Viola, Ferenc Piler. m. Ingar Hallquist, 3 children. Career: Elem. Schl. Tchr., Simrishamn, 1945-48; Elem. Schl. Tchr., Organist & Precentor, Oxie, 1948-59; Music Tchr., Trng. Coll., Gaevle, 1953; Lectr., Music Hist., Acad. of Music, Malmoe, 1954-55; Permanent Organist, town bldg. for Sveriges Pastoratsförbund, Diocese of Lund, 1962-; Organ Recital, Radio Denmark, 1973. Compositions: Toccata in G (organ), 1952; Recordings: The Organs of St. Peter, Malmoe. Contbr. to Swedish jrnls. Hons: Musica Sacra Badge for Conds., Riksföbundet Svensk Kyrkomusik, 1969. Hobby: Seamanship. Address: Langkroksvägen 32, 28100 Haessleholm, Sweden.

CIOBANU, Gheorghe, b. 4 Feb. 1909, Padureni, Ilfov, Romania. Professor. Educ: Bucharest Conserv. of Music, 1931-38, 1943-45; DMusicol. m. Filofteia Dimitriu, 1 d. Career incls: Prof. of Music, 1939-52; Researcher in

Archives of Folklore of Soc. of the Romanian Comps., 1936-49; Prin. Researcher, Folklore Inst., 1949-54; Sect. Hd., ibid., 1954-68, Bucharest; Lectr., Folkore, Jassy Conserv., 1965-68; Reader, ibid., 1968-72. Publs. incl: The Laoutars of Clejani, 1969; Studies in Byzantine Music & in Ethnomusicology, 1974; Sources of Romanian Music, Vols. 1-3, 1976-78. Contbr. to var. profl. jrnls. Mbr., Union of Comps. & Musicologists. Hons: Ciprian Porumbescu Prize, Romanian Acad., 1957; Order of Cultural Merit, 3rd Class, 1969; Prizes of Union of Comps. & Musicologists, 1956, '75, '78. Hobby: Sci. Rsch. Address: Barajul Dunarii no. 3, B1 M 35 sc. 6 ap. 241, Sector 4, Bucharest, Romania.

CIOFFARI, Richard J, b. 27 Dec. 1943, Detroit, Mich., USA. Conductor; Pianist; Double Bassist; Composer. Educ: BMus, MMus, Univ. of Mich. m. Estelle L Dobbins. Career incls: Assoc. Prof., Bowling Green State Univ., Ohio; Former Prin. Bassn, NC Symph. & Univ. of Mich. Philharmonia; Former Cond., Bowling Green State Univ. Chmbr. Orch. & Opera Theater; Studio Tchr., recitalist, coordinator of string instruction, ibid. Comps. incl: Rhapsody for Tuba & Orchestra, 1975; Fantasy for Flute, Strings, & Harp, 1975; Divertimento for Brass Quintet, 1978. Mbrships: Int. Soc. of Bassists; Pi Kappa Lambda; Phi Kappa Phi. Hons. incl: co-winner, Nat. Schl. Orch. Assn. Roth Comp. Contest, 1972. Hobby: Amateur radio. Address: 15431 Sand Ridge Rd., Bowling Green, OH 43402, USA.

CIOMPI, Giorgio, b. 27 Jan. 1918, Florence, Italy. Concert Violinist. Educ: Grad., Paris Conserv., France; Performing Artist Dip., ibid; Advanced Studies w. George Enesco & Diran Alexanian. m. Adriana Prat, 2 s. Debut: Milan, 1935; NYC, 1948. Career: Many Concert Tours w. Maj. Orchs. in Europe & USA as Recitalist & Soloist; Mbr., Albeneri Trio, 16 yrs.; First Violinist, Ciompi Quartet, Duke Univ., Durham, NC, USA; Participant, Casals Fest., Aspen Fest.; Former Hd., Strings Dept., Cleveland Inst. of Music; Former Mbr., Toscanini NBC Orch.; Artist in Res., Duke Univ., Durham, NC. Recordings incl: Chmbr. Music Lit. & Piano Trios. Mbrships: NY Bohemians; Musicians Union; ASTA. Hons: Premier Prix, Conservatoire Paris, 1934; Fedn. of Music Clubs Award, 1968; Recognition of Honor, Puerto Rico Govt., 1970. Address: 3614 Westover Rd., Durham, NC 27707, USA.

CIORTEA, Tudor, b. 28 Nov. 1903, Brasov, Romania. Composer; Professor. Educ: Dip., Acad., Econ. Scis., Cluj. Romania; Dip., Fac., Law, Univ. of Brussels; Studied comp. w. Paul Dukas & Nadia Boulanger, Music Schl., Paris; Dip., comp., Music Conserv., Bucharest. m. Vera. Debut: 1927. Career: Under Dir., Press Dept., Foreign Min., 1944-40; Prof., Musical form & comp., Conserv. of Music, Bucharest, 1948-. Compositions: 3 Suites et 4 Sonates pour piano; Sonates pour diverses instruments; 4 String Quartets; Passacaglia et Toccata pour grand orch.; Variations pour piano et orch.; Concerto pour clarinette et orch.; Octuor pour cordes, piano et instruments à vent; var. others. inclng. num. songs. Recordings; Concerto pour orch. à cordes; Octuor; Quatre chansons de Maramures; Quatuor à cordes No. 2; Lieder. Publs: Les Quatuors de Beethoven, 1968. Contbr. to: Muzica, Bucharest, & var. other jrnls. Mbrships: Romanian Comps. Union; Cttee., Romanian Music (CIM). Hons: 1st mention, Georges Enesco comp. contest, 1946; State Prize, 1955; George Enesco Prize, Romanian Acad., 1964; var. other prizes. Hobbies: Mountaineering; Swimming. Address: Boul. Gheorghiu-Dej No. 67, Bucharest VI, Romania.

CIRCELLI, Michele (Padre Egidio), b. 5 Feb. 1920, San Bartolomeo in Galdo, Benevento, Italy. Professor of Organ Music; Organist & Choirmaster. Educ: Dip., Pontificio Istituto di'Musica Sacra, Rome; Dip., Santa Cecilia State Conserv. of Music, 1952. Debut: Organ concert, Rome, 1952. Career: Prof. of Organ, Polyphony & Gregorian Chant, var. Roman insts.; Participator, var. live transmissions, Italan Radio & TV; Designer of 60 organs; Dir., restoration of var. 18th century organs; 80 organ concerts, Italy, Germany, Yugoslavia & Israel. Compositions (publs) incl: Missa Mater Gratiarum, for 3 mixed voices, 1960. Contbr. to: Miscellanea, Regensburg; Bollettino Ceciliano, Rome. Mbr. var. profl. orgs. Hobby: Electronics. Address: Via S. Maria Mediatrice, 25, 00165 Rome, Italy.

CIRONE, Anthony J, b. 8 Nov. 1941, Jersey City, NJ, USA. Percussionist; Professor. Educ: BS, MS, Juilliard Schl. Music. m. Josephine J Cirone, 1 s., 1 d. Career: Percussionist, San Fran. Symph., Assoc. Prof. of Music, Calif. State Univ., San Jose. Compositions incl: Double Concerto for Two Percussion & Orch.; 5 items for Soprano & percusssion; A Sacred Mass for Chorus & Percussion; Portraits in Rhythm; 50 Studies for Snare Drum; Portraits in Melody; 50 Studies for Marimba; The Orchestral Snare Drummer; Portraits for Timpani; Sonata 3 for Clarinet & Percussion; Sonata 4 for Violin, Piano & percussion; The Orchestral Mallet Player; The Orchestral Timpanist. Recordings:

76 Pieces of Explosive Percussion by Sonic Arts Symph. Percussion Consortium. Author, Orchestral Techniques of the Standard Percussion Instruments. Contbr. to: The Instrumentalist; Percussive Arts Soc.; Brass & Percussion World. Mbrships: ASCAP; Bd. Dirs., Percussive Arts Soc., 1970-72. Hobby: Organic Gardening. Address: PO Box 612, Menio Park, CA 94025, USA.

CISAŘ, Miroslav, b. 2 Dec. 1929, Prague, Czechoslovakia. Musician; Conductor; Brass Band & Folklore Ensemble. Educ: People's Conserv.; Pedag. Univ. m. Vera Plackova, 2 s. Debut: 1945. Career: Film, radio recordings of folk & popular music. Compositions incl. ballet music, gymnastic music & works for brass band. Over 250 recordings of folk, popular & brass band music. Contbr. to books & Melodie mag. Mbrship: OSA. Hons: 1st Prize, 1971, 2nd Prize, 1972, Radio Contest; 15 prizes, folklore dancing & gymnastic music contests, 1955-74. Hobbies: Gardening & bee-keeping. Address: Nad ostrovem 4, Prague 4 - Podolí, 14700, Czechoslovakia.

CITRON, Pierre, b. 19 Apr. 1919, Paris, France. Professor of French Literature. Educ: Agrégation des lettres, Dr.-és-lettres, Paris Univ. m. Suzanne Grunbach, 4 children. Career: Prof. of French Lit., Univ. of Paris, Sorbonne nouvelle. Publs: Couperin, 1956; Bartok, 1963; Ed., Berlioz, Memoires, 1969; Ed., Berlioz Correspondance Générale, Vol. 1, 1972; Vol. 2, 1975; Vol. 3, 1978. Mbrship: French Soc. of Musicol. Address: 17 rue J-J Rousseau, 95330 Domont, France.

CIUCIURA, Leoncjusz, b. 22 July 1930, Grodzisk Mazowiecki, Poland. Composer. Educ: Dip., State Coll. of Music, Warsaw. m. Sylwia Grelich. Debut: Concert, State Coll. of Music, Warsaw. Comps. incl: Fonodiagra, for 7 perfs. & 10 instruments, 1968; Intarsio series, 1 - woodwinds, for solo flute, oboe, clarinet & bassoon w. instrumental grps., 1969-71; 2 -bass, for solo trumpet, horn & trombone w. instrumental grps., 1971-73; 3 - Strings, for solo violin, viola, cello & harp, w. instrumental grps., 1973-75; 4 - keyboard, for pianoforte, organ solo w. instrumental grps., 1976-78; Rencontre, optional instrumental ensemble, 1979-81. Mbrships: Union of Polish Comps.; ZAIKS. Hons. incl: Concertino da Camera 1st Prize, Int. Comps. Competition, Prague, 1962; Ornamenti, Polish Broadcast & TV Prize, 1963. Address: Grodzisk-Mazowiecki, Zwirki & Wigury 5, Poland.

CIVIL, Alan, b. 13 June 1929, UK. Musician (horn); Composer. Educ: Music study w. Aubrey Brain, London & Willy von Stemm, Hamburg. Career: Prin. Horn, RPO, 1952-55; Co-Prin. Horn. w. Dennis Brain, Philharmonia Orch., 1955-57; Prin. horn, ibid., 1957-; Prof. of horn, RCM; Solo horn, BBC Symph. Orch., 1966-; Guest Prin. Horn w. Berlin Phil. Orch.; Mbr. of sev. Chmbr. Music Ensembles, incl. London Wind Quitet, London Wind Soloists, Wigmore Ensemble. Prometheus Ensemble, Alan Civil Horn Trio, Music Grp. of London; Soloist in Horn Concertos in N & S Am. & Europe. Recording artist. Compositions incl: Symph. (brass & percussion), 1950; Wind Octet, 1951; Wind Quintet, 1951; Horn Trio in E Flat, 1952; Divertimento for Trombone Quartet; Suite for Two Horns; Songs; Music for Brass Ensemble; Horn studies, etc. Address: Downe Hall, Downe, Kent, UK.

CLAMPIN, Ailsa Rose, b. 29 Aug. 1952, Wellington, Somerset, UK. Pianist. Educ: RAM, 1971-75 (w. Max Pirani); profl. cert., RAM; further study w. Guy Jonson; Univ. of E Anglia, 1978-81. Career: concert tours in Norway incl. apps. for British Coun. in Oslo. Mbrships: ISM; Norwich Gramophone Soc. Hons: piano profs. prize, Albanesi medal, Claude Beddington Prize, Alexander Roller Prize, all RAM; Norwegian Govt. Scholarship to study Norwegian music, Oslo Univ., 1977-78; award from Ralph Vaughan Williams Trust. Hobbies: Norwegian Lang. & Culture; Walking; Cycling. Address: Treasure Hill House, Penwood, Burghclere, Newbury, Berks. RG15 9EH, UK.

CLAPHAM, John b. 31 July 1908, Letchworth, UK. Musicologist. Educ: BMus, Univ. of London, 1934; DMus., ibid., 1946; RAM. m. Mary Wright, 4 c. Career: Lectr., Univ. Coll. of Wales, Aberystwyth, 1946-62; Sr. Lectr., Univ. of Edinburgh, 1962-69; Rdr., ibid., 1969-75. Publs: Antonin Dvorak: Musician & Craftsman, 1966; Smetana (Masta Musicians Series), 1972. Contbr. to: Musical Qtly.; Music & Letters; Musikforschung; Proceedings of the Royal Musical Assn.; Debbinveda; Musica; The Music Review; The Musical Times; The Listener, Grove's Dictionary of Music & Musicians, etc. Mbrships: Int. Musicol Soc.; Royal Musical Assn.; Soc. of Authors; Assn. of Univ. Tchrs. Hons: FRAM, 1959; Fndr. Mbr. of the Antonin Dvorak Soc. of Prague, 1959; Silvr Medal & Dip. of the Czechoslovak Soc. for Int. Rels., 1966. Hobby: Photography. Address: 26 Fernbank Rd., Redland, Bristol BS6 6PU, UK. 3.

CLAPP, Lois Steele, b. 28 Sept. 1940, Newburgh, NY, USA. Choir Dir., First Bapt. Ch., Gloucester, Mass.; Staff Organist, St. Joachim's, Rockport, Mass. Educ: New England Conserv. of Music, Boston, Mass., 2 yrs.; Camerata Schl., Mus. of Fine Arts, Boston; Harvard Univ., Cambridge, Mass. m. Dr. Ronald B Clapp, 1 s., 2 d. Career: Specialist in baroque music; Organist & Choir Dir., St. Mary's Episcopal Ch., Rockport, Mass.; Accomp., Rockport Community Chorus; Perfs. & workshops, Univ. of Maine & Machias; Perfs., Conn. & Mass.; Pvte. tchr. of organ & harpsichord; Comps: St. Mary's mass. Recordings w. New England Conserv. Chorus & Boston Symph. Orch. Mbrships: Boston Chapt., Am. Guild of Orgnists; Am. Musicol. Soc. Hobbies incl: Gardening; Needlework. Address: 90 Main St., PO Box 270, Rockport, MA 01966, USA.

CLAPP, Stephen H, b. 27 Nov. 1939, Tall Mann, NY, USA. Assoc. Prof., Univ. of Texas at Austin; Adjunct Assoc. Prof., Oberlin Conserv. Educ: BMus, Oberlin Coll., 1961; Artist Dip., Juilliard Schl. of Music, 1963; MMus, ibid., 1965. m. Linda Daman, 3 children. Career: Mbr., Beaux-Arts String Quartet (tours in Europe & N Am.); Concert Master, Aspen Fest. Chmbr. Symph., Austin Symph. & Nashville Symph.; Former solo recitals & chmbr. music tours in Europe, N & S Am. Publs: The American String Tchr., 1978-80. Mbrships: Am. String Tchrs. Assn.; Am. Fedn. of Musicians; Music Tchrs. Nat. Assn.; Pi Kappa Lambda; Phi Mu Alpha. Hosn: Josef Gingold Award, Cleveland Soc. for Strings, 1959; Juilliard Schl. Apprenticeship in violin & chmbr. music, 1964-66; 1st Chmbr. Music Award, Water W. Naumburg Fndn., 1965. Hobbies: Hiking; Restoration of old homes w. character. Address: 1407 W 9th St., Austin, TX 78703, USA. 7.

CLARE, Beatrix, b. Lambeg, N Ireland. Cellist & Viola da Gamba. Educ: Blackheath Conserv. of Music, Guildhall Schl. of Music & Drama. Royal Acad. of Music, London; Accademia Musicale Chigiana, Siena, Italy. Debut: 1st Broadcast, age 13. Career: Solo concerts & ensemble work, UK & num. European countries; 1st TV app., as soloist 1974; Music journalist & coach. Hobbies: Schlrships to schls. above; Num. awards both as cellist & pianist. Hobbies: Needlework; Painting; Dancing. Address: 6 Market St., Lewes, Sussex, UK. 3, 27.

CLARE, Derek John, b. 1923, Peterborough, UK. Music Master; Composer; Organist. Educ: RCM; GRSM; ARCM; ARCO; LTCL. m. Doreen Estelle Allin. Career: Pupil Asst. Organist, Peterborough Cathedral, 1948-50; Dir. of Music, Peterborough Youth Coun., 1950-53; Asst. Dir., Music, Haileybury Coll., Hertford, 1951-59; Examiner, Royal Schls. of Music, 1958; Dir., Music, Stonyhurst Coll., Iancs., 1960-63, The Schl., Wellingborough, 1963-68; Dir. of Music, Choir Schl., lay Clerk, Music Master, Eton Coll., 1968-77; Choirmaster, organist, S Flpins Schl., Darley Dale., Radio & TV apps. Extensive tours as Ictr., recitalist. Compositions: Concertino Accompagnato; Spring, Chroal Suite; Variations on a Nursery tune; O Lord Support Us; Var. Carols & Folksongs arrs. Hons: FRSA. Hobbies: 18 Century Music; Touring; Architecture; Antiques. Address: Bluntisham House, Bluntisham, Cambs., UK.

CLARE, Maurice, b. 30 Dec. 1914, Dundee, UK. Violinist. Educ: Morgan Acad.; pvte. studies w. Sevčik, Flesch, Hess, Enesco. m. Marta Zalan. Debut: Wigmore Hall, London, 1930. Career: Fndr., Dir., NZ Broadcasting Serv. Orch., 1940-42; Touring soloist, 1952-62; Ldr., Boyd Neel Orch., 1947-52; Ldr., Vic. Symph. Orch., 1962-64; Prin. Lectr., Violin, Northern Schl. of Music, Manchester (Royal Northern Coll. of Music), 1965-; Dir., Camerata String Orch., London, UK, 1967-70; Fac. Mbr., Nat. Youth Orch. Assn. of Can.; Master Tutor, Chetham's Schl. of Music, Manchester, 1973-. Recordings incl: Telemann Fantasias. Hobbies: Art; Cooking. Address: 15 Northchurch Rd., London N1, UK. 3.

CLARE, Renée, b. 27 June 1920, London, UK. Orchestral & Solo Violinist; Teacher of Violin & Viola. Educ: ARCM; studied w. Arthur Bent & Albert Sammons; orchl. trng. w. Sir Malcolm Sargent. m. Edward Robert Spratt, 1 s. Debut: 1943. Career incls: Soloist w. ENSA, freelancing between tours, WWII; w. Boyd Neel Str. Orch.; 1st Violin, Sadler's Wells Opera Co., Solo Recitalist, 1945-54; currently Prof., RAM, tchng. at sev. schls. & colls., Ldrd., Southgate Tech. Coll. Orch. & Kensington Concordia, Coach, Enfield Young Symph. Orch., Soloist at recitals & concerts. Mbrships: ISM; Musicians' Union. Recip. Prize Bow for best violinist, RCM, 1942. Hobbies: Travelling; Reading; Caravanning. Address: 37 River Bank, London N21 2AB, UK.

CLARK, Frances Oman, b. 28 mar. 1908, Goshen, Ind., USA. Music Educator; Pianist. Educ: AB, Kalamazoo Coll., 1928; Postgrad., Am. Acad. of Fontainebleau, 1930-31; Juilliard Schl. of Music, summers, 1934-37 & '40. Career: Pvte. Piano Tchr., Sturgis, Albion & Kalamazoo, Mich., 1932-45; Piano Pedagogy, Kalamazoo Coll., 1945-55; Chmn., Piano &

Piano Pedagogy Depts., Westminster Choir Coll., Princeton, NJ, 1955-60; Fndr. & Dir., New Schl. for Music Study, Princeton, NJ, 1960-; Lectr., Clinician & Master Tchr. for music workshops, convens. & study cour000 of music educators. Publs: Author & Compiler, Frances Clark Lib. for Piano Students, 1953-. cContbr. to: Clavier Mag.; 1966-. Mbrships: Music Tchrs. Nat. Assn.; NGPT; Nat. Soc. of Arts & Letters; Pres., NJ MTA, 1960; Sigma Alpha Iota. Hons: MusD, Kalamazoo Coll., Mich., 1962. Hobbies: Sailing; Gardening; Photography. Address: PO Box 407, Princeton, NJ 08540, USA. 5.

CLARK, Harold Ronald, b. 17 Apr. 1924, Walkeringham, UK. Musician. Educ: RAM; GRSM; LRAM; studied w. York Bowen. m. Joan Hall, 1 s. Career: Sr. Music Master, St. Paul's Schl.; Examiner, TCM; Music Critic, Peterborough Standard; Accomp., Peterborough Music Fest., 1956-73; Asst. Cond., Peterborough Phil. Soc., 1960-67; Organizer, Annual Summer Recital Series, Peterborough Cathedral, 1964-; Piano Tchr., Peterborough Tech. Coll. Comps.; Sketches for Young Pianists. Contbr. to: RAM Mag.; Philatelic Music Circle Bulletin. Mbrships: RSM; ISM; RCO; RAM Club; TCM Guild; FIAL. Recip., Review Week Prize, RAM, 1949. Hobby: Musical Philately. Address: 42 Glebe Rd., Peterborough PE2 8BG, UK.

CLARK, J Bunker, b. 19 Oct. 1931, Detroit, Mich., USA. Musicologist. Educ: BMus, Univ. of Mich., 1954; MMus, ibid., 1957; PhD, 1964. m. Marilyn Jane Slawson. Career: Instr. of Theory & Organ, Stephens Coll., Columbia, Mo., 1957-59; Lectr. in Music, Univ. of Calif., Santa Barbara, 1964-65; Prof., Music Hist., Univ. of Kan., 1965-. Publs: Transposition in 17th Century English Organ Accompaniments & the Tranposing Organ, 1974; Anthology of Early Am. Keyboard Music, 1787-1830, Vols. 1 & 2. Contbr. to: The Am. Organist; The Choral Jrnl.; Music & Letters; Musica Disciplina; Notes: Jrnl. of the Am. Musicol. Soc.; The Musician's Guide; Grove's Dictionary (new ed.) Mbrships: Chmn., Mid-W. Chapt., Am. Musicol. Soc., 1974-76; Pres., Univ. of Kan. Chapt., 1971-72, & Kan. Conf., 1973-74, AAUP; Royal Musical Assn.; Int. Musicol. Soc.; Music Lib. Assn.; Phi Kappa Lambda. Hons: Fulbright Schlrship. to UK, 1962-63; Grant, Nat. Endowment for Humanities, 1972-73. Address: Music Hist. Dept., Univ. of Kan., Lawrence, KS 66045, USA.

CLARK, James John III, b. 22 Feb. 1941, Syracuse, NY, USA. Tenor Singer. Educ: BA(music), Montclair State Coll., NJ; pvte. piano & violin studies; vocal studies w. Armen Boyagian, Uta Graf & Mary Ledgerwood. m. Evelyn Reilly, 2 s., 1 d. Debut: Carnegie Hall, NY, 1971. Career: ldng. tenor, Opera Theatre Dept., Manhattan Schl. of Music; Metropolitan Opera Studio; perfs. w. Milwaukee Symph. & Florentine Opera Co.; NY City Opera debut, 1978. mbr., Am. Guild of Musical Artists. Hobbies: Jogging; Weight Lifting; Chamber Music. Address: 118 Indiana St., Maplewood, NJ 07040, USA.

CLARK, Jane, b. 17 April 1928, London, UK. Harpsichordist. Educ: GSM; LGSM. m. Stephen Dodgson. Career: Concerts, broadcasts & lectures in Europe & USA. Contbr. to: Early Music; Records & Recording. Mgmt: Ibbs & Tillet. Address: 4 Scarth Rd., London SW13 OND, UK.

CLARK, June, b. 3 June 1933, St. Albans, Herts., UK. Concert Pianist; Composer; Teacher. Educ: LRAM dip.; RAM, studies w. Cyril Smith. m. David Pepin, 2 s. Debut: as duo-pianist w. Joan Ryall, Bayreuth, Germany, 1958-59. Career incls: in duo w. Joan Ryall has made many broadcasts for BBC, apps. at St. Pancras Arts Fest., 1962, Cheltenham Fest., 1963, Wigmore Hall, 1963, 64, Holland, 1967. Comps. incl: Let Us Light a Candle (carol); educl. piano works & schl. songs. Mbr., ISM. Hons: 1st Prize as duo, Int. Competition for Interpreters of Contemp. Music, Utrecht; Prize for Best Perf. of Contemp. Dutch Work. Hobbies: Photography; Dressmaking; Ch. arch.; Gardening. Address: 3 Fryth Mead, St. Albans, Herts. AL3 4TM, UK. 3, 27.

CLARK, Patricia, b. 14 Sept. 1929, Glasgow, Scotland, UK. Singer. duc: RSAM; Dip., SNAM; RAM; ARCM. m. D R Matten, 2 d. Career: created role of Nausicaa in Lennox Berkley's opera, The Castaway; sang s. Scottish Opera, Engl. Opera Grp., Handel Opera Soc.; num. operatic & recital broadcasts. num. recordings. Hobby: Playing the Piano Rather Badly. Address: 65 Crescent West, Hadley Wood, Herts., UK.

CLARK, Sondra Rae Scholder, b. 20 Jan. 1941, Breckenridge, Minn., USA. Musicologist; Critic; Teacher; Pianist; Annotator. Educ: BM, Juilliard Schl., NYC; MA, Calif. State Univ., San Jose; PhD, Stanford Univ., Calif. m. Gordon L Clark. Career: Nationally recognised specialist on music of Charles Ives; Tchng. Grad., Musicol. & Thesis Writing, Calif. State Univ., San Jose; Critic, Oakland Tribune, San Fran. Peninsula Newspapers Inc.; Annotator, San Jose Symph.; Pianist, The Am. Sampler

Ensemble. Mbrships: Am. Musicol. Soc.; Music Critics Assn. Contbr. to newspapers & profl. jrnls. Hons: Ella Moore Shiel Fellow, Stanford Univ., 1967-68. Hobbies: Calif. Mission Indian basketry. Address: 208 Diablo Ave., Mtn. View, CA 94043, USA.

CLARK, William Charles Sydney, b. 12 May 1946, Thurmaston, Leics., UK. Violist; Teacher. Educ: Royal Acad. of Music; LRAM, 1967. m. Deirdre, 1 s. Career incl: Violist, Engl. Nat. Opera Co. & freelance; music tchr. Hon: York Bowen Viola Prize, 1967-68. Hobby: Walking. Address: 10 Ash Grove, Allington, Maidstone, Kent, UK.

CLARKE, Andrew Henry Alan, b. 9 Oct. 1954, London, UK. Teacher of Pianoforte & Violin. Educ: Postgrad. Cert. Educ., Coll. of Ripon & York St. John; GRSM, Royal Coll. of Music; Assoc., ibid. Career: Dir., Thor Oak Schls. Orch.; Mbr., Essex Chmbr. Orch. Mbrships: Incorp. Soc. of Musicians; EAEB CSE Rep. for Thurrock. Hobbies: Literature; Creative writing. Address: 27 Tennyson Ave., Grays, Essex, RM17 5RG, UK.

CLARKE, Frederick Robert Charles, b. 7 Aug. 1931, Vancouver, BC, Canada. Professor of Music; Church Organist; Harpsichordist. Educ: ARCT (piano), 1948; ARCT (organ) w. Gold Medal, 1951; ACCO, 1951; BMus, Univ. of Toronto, 1951; FCCO, 1952; DMus, Univ. of Toronto, 1954. m. Martha Claire Mundy, 1 d. Career: Profl. Ch. Organist, 1950-; Sometime Examiner for Royal Conserv. of Toronto & The RCCO; Cond., St. Catharines Civic Symph., 1957-58; Cond., Kingston Choral Soc. & Symph., 1958-; On staff of Music Dept., Queen's Univ., Kingston, 1964-; currently Prof. of Music, ibid. Compositions publd.: 11 Anthems for choir & organ; a number of short pieces for organ & piano. One of the Music Eds. of the 1971 Hymn Book for the Anglican & United Churches of Canada. Contbr. to music jrnls. Mbrships: RCCO (sometime Chmn. of Examinations); Canadian Assn. of Univ. Schls. of Music; Ont. Registered Music Tchrs. Assn. Hons: Commissioned to write Festival Te Deum for choir & orch. for Kingston Tercentenary; CBC Choral Composition Prize, 1968. Hobbies: Sailing, etc. Address: 260 Indian Rd., Kingston, Ont. K7M 1T7, Canada.

CLARKE, Harold Richard, b. 28 June 1914, Cambridge, UK. Flautist; Director of Wind Music, Trinity Coll. of Music. Educ: Wind Scholar, TCM; Open Wind Scholarship, RCM; LTCL; LRAM; Hon. FTCL, 1963. m. Margaret Scott Cree, 1 s., 1 d. Career: Prin. Flute, Sadlers Wells, Royal Opera House, BBC Midland Orch., Jacques Orch.; etc.; Prof. of Flute & Dir. of Wind Music; TCM; Woodwind Organizer, ILEA; Musical Dir., Court Ensemble & Musica da Camera. Orchl. recordings w. Royal Opera House Covent Gdn., LSO, LPO, RPO. Publs: Orchestral Extracts for Flute, 1974. Contbr. to 'Making Music'. Mbr., RSM; ISM. Hobbies: Cooking. Address: 78 Trinity Rd., London, SW17 7RJ, UK. 3.

CLARKE, Stephen Lionel, b. 4 Dec. 1951, Cheltenham, UK. Pianist; Piano Teacher. Educ. pvte. piano study w. Frank Britton & Guy Jonson, London; LRAM, 1971. m. Christine Wilson. Career: Pvte. Tchr.; Piano Tchr., Alice Ottley Schl., Worcester; Piano Tchr., Downs Schl., Colwall. Mbr., ISM. Hobbies: Gardening; Travel; Walking. Address: Payford Bridge, Redmarley, Gloucestershire, UK.

CLARKE, Terry, b. 20 Aug. 1944, Vancouver, BC, Can. Drummer; Percussionist. Educ: 5 yrs. study w. Jim Blackley. m. Susan Piltch. Career: apps. on all major TV networks in USA & Can.; now freelance in Toronto, Ont., recording, radio, TV & film work. Recordings incl: John Handy Live; John Handy Album; Spirituals to Swing; Big Band Jazz; Moe Koffman plays Bach; num. recordings for CBC. Contbr. to Tempo (Can.). Hobbies: Photography; Cooking. Address: 222 Glen Manor Dr. W, Toronto, Ont. M4E 2X6, Can.

CLARO-VALDES, Samuel, b. 31 July 1934, Santiago, Chile. Musicologist. Educ: Lic. in musical scis. & arts, Univ. of Chile, 1960; MA, Dept. of Music, Columbia Univ., NY, USA, 1964. m. Patricia Swinburn, 2 s., 3 d. Publs. incl: Antología de la Música Colonial en América del Sur; Catálogo del Archivo Musical de la Catedral de Santiago de Chile. Contbr. to many profl. pbuls. Mbrships: Chilean Acad. of Hist.; Corres., Royal Acad. of Hist. of Spain; Int. Musicol. Soc. Address: Martin de Zamora 4245, Santiago 10, Chile.

CLAUSEN, Bruce Edward, b. 22 Sept. 1948, Palo Alto, Calif., USA. Composer; Horn Player. Educ: BA, Ambassador Coll., Univ. of S Calif. Comps. incl: Sonata for Four Horns; Rhapsody for Piano; Two Preludes & Fugues for Piano; The Ballad of Reading Gaol (concert overture); Epitaph (concert overture); Epigenisis (concert overture); Sonata for Three Horns; Concerto for Horn; Var. TV & radio incidental scores. Mbrships: Am. Soc. of

Comps., Authors & Publrs.; Acad. of TV Arts & Scis.; Am. Film Inst.; IMA Sinfonia, Pres. Epsilon Chapt., USC, 1968. Hons: Information Film Prods. of Am. Bronze Award, 1973. Address: 676 Rio Grande St., Pasadena, Calif., USA. 29.

CLAUSETTI, Eugenie, b. 7 Jan. 1905, Italy. Music Publisher. Educ: JD. Career: Mng. Dir., G Ricordi & Co., Milan, 1944-. Mbrships: Pres., Soc. of Italian Music Publrs.; Pres., SEDRIM (Italian Soc. for Collect. of Performing Rights of Authors & Composers); VP, Publrs., Music Sect.; Pres., Arti Grafiche Ricordi. Address: G Ricordi & Co., s.p.a., Via Berchet 2, Milan, Italy.

CLAVIE, Léopold-Charles, b. 11 Dec. 1904, Marseille, France. Physician; Psychologist. Educ: Bach. degree, Janson de Sailly, Paris; Doctorate, Faculté de Médeceine de Paris; Paris-Neuilly Conservatory (piano prize), 1919-21. m. Gisèle Dérieux, 3 c. Debut: Casablanca, Morocco. Career: Tchr. of Hist. of Music, Casablanca Conserv.; Num. pub. & radio confs.; Musical critic in num. papers. Publs: Du Classicisme au Jazz (First study about Am. Jazz), 1933, 2nd edn., 1946; Num. articles in var. reviews. Mbr., French Soc. of Musicol. Hons: Academic Palms Officer. Hobby: Music recording. Address: 11 rue de Pondichery, Paris 75015, France.

CLAXTON, Andrew Edgar Kyle, b. 22 Jan. 1950, London, UK. Teacher (Piano & Brass); Pianist; Tuba Player; Composer; Arranger. Educ: Nat. Youth Orch. of GB, 1966-67; RAM, 1968-72; Bretton Hall Coll. of Educ., 1972-73; GRSM; LRAM; Cert. Ed. m. Marguerite Donald, 1 s. Career: peripatetic brass tchr., Oxon Co. Coun., 1974-; pvte. piano & brass tchr.; prin. pianist & tuba player, Oxford Pro Musica, 1974-, Ed. & proprietor of The Mounted Horse Music Press, publishing instrumental music for schl. children. Recording: Tubby the Tuba, 1974. Mbrships: ISM; Soc. for Rsch. in Psychol. of Music & Music Educ. Hobby: Spontaneity. Address: 1 Andrew Rd., Wallingford, Oxon. OX10 8AE, UK.

CLAYTON, Herbert Kenneth, b. 29 Jan. 1920, Rushden, Northants., UK. Pianist; Composer; Conductor; Educationalist. Educ: TD, Daneshill Training Coll.; Dip. Ed., Univ. of London, Inst. of Educ.; ARCM; LRAM; studied w. Greville Cooke, Gilbert Thomas, Dr. Norman Spranklin. m. Joan Paget. Career: tchng. posts, Nottingham schls., 1949-54; Musical Dir., Cranley Girls' Operatic Soc., 1950-54; Headmaster, Worcs. Co. Coun., 1954-57, Essex Co. Coun., 1957-65, London Borough of Havering, 1965-75; lectr., tchrs. inservice training. Comps: Bows & Belles (operetta); Sonatine, for piano; Tangita, for 2 pianos; Shepherd's Tune & Evening, for piano & recorders. Mbrships: life mbr., Nat. Assn. of Head Tchrs.; life mbr., Assn. for Therapeutic Educ.; life mbr., Nat. Union of Tchrs.; sec., Nottingham Music Fest. Soc. Hons: 3 Exhibitions, TCL, 1931-34; life Fellow, Royal Soc. of Arts. Hobbies: Swimming; Walking. Address: 62 Mimosa Ave., Merley, Wimborne, Dorset BH21 1TT, UK. 23, 28, 29.

CLEALL, Charles, b. 1 June 1927, Heston, UK. Her Majesty's Inspector of Schools, Scottish Education Department, 1972-. Educ: BMus (London), 1952; MA (Wales), 1967; ADCM; FRCO (CHM); GTCL; LRAM (organ perf.); HonTSC; Jordanhill Coll. of Educ., Glasgow. m. Mary Turner, 2 d. Career incl: Organist & Choirmaster, St. Luke's Ch., Chelsea, 1945-46; Command Music Advsr., RN, Plymouth, 1946-48; Choral Scholar, Westminster Abbey, & Prof., TCL, 1949-52; Cond., Glasgow Choral Union, 1952-54; BBC Music Asst., Midland Region, 1954-55; music master, Glyn Co. Schl., Ewell, 1955-66; Cond., Aldeburgh Fest. Choir, 1957-60; Organist & Choirmaster, Holy Trinity, Guildford, 1961-65; Lectr., Froebel Inst., 1967-68; Music Advsr., London Borough of Harrow, 1968-72; Warden, Educ. Sec., ISM, 1971-72. Publs. incl: Voice Production in Choral Technique, 1955 (revised 1970); The Selection & Training of Mixed Choirs in Churches, 1960; Music & Holiness, 1964; John Merbecke's Music for the Congregation at Holy Communion, 1963; Plainsong for Pleasure, 1969. Mbrships: ISM; Soc. of Recorder Players; MCMS; RSCM; RCO, etc. Hons: Limpus Fellowship Prize, RCO, 1953; Int. Competition Prize, of St. John the Divine, NYC, 1954. Address: 29 Colthill Circle, Milltimber AB1 0EH, UK. 1.

CLEEVE, Stewart Montagu, b. Southsea, UK. Musician, Violin & Viola d'Amore; Teacher of Strings & Piano; Professor. Educ: Royal Military Acad.; Woolwich Military Coll. of Sci.; Heatherly Art Schl.; LGSM; LRAM. m. Isabell Ruth. Debut: Wigmore Hall, London, 1958. Career: Solo Violin w. RA Orch., 1935; Opening Violin Recital, AIR, 1934; Toured India & Ceylon; Haslemere Festival; Perf. for HM The Queen Mother, St. James' Palace, 1964; designer & recitalist on Cleeve Viola d'Amore; Prof. & Examiner, TCL. Compositions: Whitgift Suite, for small orch.; 4 sonatas for Viola d'Amore; num. works in MS. Contbr. to: Musical Times; The Strad; The Consort; The Gunner.

Mbrships: ISM; ESTA; Dolmetsch Fndn.; Fndr., Viola d'Amore Soc.; Trinity Coll. Guild; Victorian Soc.; Kensington Soc.; SPAB. Hons: Hon. FTCL; Chevalier of the Crown of Roumania, 1920; 2 1st Prizes, Portsmouth Music Festival, 1926. Hobbies: Collecting & Restoring Old Pianos; Modelling; Watercolour Sketching & Portraiture; Travel; Gardening. Mgmt: Ibbs & Tillett, London, UK. Address: Cliffe House, 1 Parkside Ave., Wimbledon Common, London SW19, UK. 3.

CLELLAND, Lamond, b. 19 July 1921, Gateshead, Durham, UK. Flautist; Music Teacher. Educ: DipEd, Bristol Univ.; LTCL. m. Georgina Mary Bagnall, 1 s. Career: Recitals & broadcasts w. The Vincian Trio & sonata recitals; Concerto perfs. incl. broadcasts; Flutist, var. orchs. in London, Bournemouth Symph. Orch., 11 yrs.; Cond.-trainer, Youth Orchs. & Bands; Flute master-class tchr.; Tchr. of woodwind & brass. Comps: 18th Century works, revival by realisations, editions, orchestrations & arrangements; Schl. units - arrangements for Orch., woodwind, wind band, etc. Recording: For Your Delight (Butt), w. Vincian Trio. Publ: Still the Lark (w. Margot Bor). Contbr. to: Making Music. Mbrships: ISM. Hobbies: Chess; Bridge; Harpsichord Making. Address: Tocwood, 35 Seend Cleeve, Melksham, Wilts., UK. 3.

CLEMENS, Earl L, b. 11 June 1925, Dover, Ohio, USA. Oboist; Professor of Oboe. Educ: BPSM, Mt. Union Coll., 1949; MMus, Northwestern Univ., 1959; Postgrad. study, Ind. Univ. m. Idaleen Root, 2 s., 1 d. Career: Oboist, civic bands & orchs., clinics, Midwest States, 1939-; 1st Oboe, All Am. Band Masters Band, 1956-61; Tchr., pub. schl. music, Mich. & Ohio, 1946-59; Prof., Oboe, N III. Univ., 1959-; Oboe consultant, Custom Music Co., 1976-. Num. recordings, var. grps.; Quintet recordings w. N III. Univ. Quintet. Publs: Doctoring the Double Reeds, 1960, rev. ed., 1972; Oboe Teaching, 1977; num. arrangements of oboe pieces. Mbrships: Past Pres., Int. Double Reed Soc.; Bd. of Govs., Int. Music Camp; III. Music Educators Assn.; NEA. Hobby: Photography. Address: 220 W Royal Dr., DeKalb, IL 60115, USA.

CLEMENT, Andries, b. 29 May 1943, Eindhoven, Netherlands. Musicologist; Conductor. Educ: Master Perf., conducting, Conserv.; doctl. cand. in musicol. m. Gusta Westers, 2 children. Debut: 1960. Career: many concerts, Netherlands, Sweden, Hungary, Belgium Germany; Tchr., hist. of music & conducting, Conservs. of Zwolle & Amsterdam; currently Dir., Brabant Conserv. Mbrships: Bd., 's-Hertogenbosch Muziekstad; Nederlandse Vereniging voor Muziekgeschiedenis. Hobbies: Sports, esp. Lawn Tennis. Address: Kloosterlaan 20, Moergestel, Netherlands.

CLEMENT-CART, Marianne, b. 26 Feb. 1929, Le Locle, Switzerland. Flauist. Educ: Acad. of Music of Lausanne; Dip. Teaching; Dip. Virtuosity; Studied w. Marcel Moyse, Paris, France. m. Pierre-Paul Clement, 2 d. Debut: Flautist, Chmbr. Music Orch., Lausanne, 1949. Career: Regular Soloist, Chmbr. Music Orch., Lausanne, 1950; Piano recitals w. Denyse Rich (flautist); Guitar recitals w. Raoul Sanchez (flautist) (flautist). Num. concerts for Swiss radio at Sottens & Beromunster; TV concerts as Lisbon. Recordings of Bach & Handel w. Raoul Sanchez, guitarist; Soloist for M Corboz. Mbrships: Assn. of Musicians of Switzerland; Assn. of Music for Youth. Address: 16 Ave. du Leman, CH-1005 Lausanne, Switzerland.

CLENDENIN, William Ritchie, Sr., b. 23 July 1917, Sparta, III., USA. Musicologist; Organist. Educ: BMus, Univ. of III., 1940; SMM, Union Theol. Sem., NYC, 1942; PhD, Univ. of Iowa, 1952. m. Virginia June Van Zandt, 1 s. Career: Organ recitalist & Ch. musician, var. parts of USA; Asst. Prof. of Music, Queens Coll., Charlotte, NC & Iowa State Univ., Ames; Asst. Prof.-Prof. (1968) of Music, Coord. Grad. Studies in Music, Univ. of Colo., Boulder. Publs. incl: Music: History & Theory, 1965; Visual Aids in Western Music, 3rd ed., 1967; History of Music, 1974. Contbr. to profl. jrnls.; Cons.-Reviewer, Reprint Bulletin-Book Reviews, 1975. Mbr., profl. assns. Recip., Fellowship & Grants, Univ. of Colo. Hobby: Swimming. Address: 4703 Harrison Ave., Boulder, CO 80303, USA. 4, 9, 28.

CLEOBURY, Nicholas Randall, b. 23 June 1950, Bromley, UK. Conductor. Educ: BA, Worcester Coll., Oxford; FRCO. Career: Asst. Organist, Christ Ch., Oxford, 1973-76; Chorus Master & Cond., Glynebourne Opera; Asst. Dir., BBC Singers. Guest Cond., many orchs. incl: BBC Symph., Netherlands Chmbr., Engl. Chmbr. & Engl. Nat. Opera. Recordings: Num. continuo & Tippett choral music. Hons: Limpus Prize, FRCO, 1969. Hobbies: Theatre; Reading; Cricket. Mgmt: Ingpen & Williams. Address: 203 Latchmere Rd., London SW11 2LA, UK.

CLEOBURY, Stephen John, b. 31 Dec. 1948. Organist; Conductor. Educ: MA, MusB, St. John's Coll., Cambridge; FRCO.

m. Penelope Jane Holloway, 2 d. Debut: Royal Fest. Hall Organ, 1975. Career: Organist, St. Matthew's, Northampton & Cond., Northampton Bach Choir, 1971-74; Sub-Organist, Westminster Abbey, 1974-78; Master of Music, Westminster Cathedral, 1979-; Harpsichordist, Pianist. num. recordings. Mbrships: RCO; ISM. Hons. incl: Limpus Prize, ARCO, 1966; Limpus & Dr. F J Read Prizes, FRCO, 1968. Hobbies: Chess; Cricket; Reading Railway Timetables. Address: 15 Westbrook Rd., Blackheath, London SE3 ONS, UK.

CLIBURN, Van (Harvey Lavan, Jr.), b. 12 July 1934, USA. Pianist. Educ: Juilliard Schl. of Music, NYC. Debut: w. Houston Symph. Orch., 1952. Career incl: Soloist w. NY Phil. Orch., 1954, 1958; Concert tours of USA, 1955-, USSR, 1958; appearances in Brussels, Amsterdam, London, Paris, etc. Hons. incl: HHD, Baylor Univ.; num. prizes. Address: c/o Hurok Attractions Inc., 730 5th Ave., NY, NY 10019, USA.

CLICKNER, Susan Fisher, b. 15 Apr. 1934, Buffalo, NY, USA. Teacher; Performer. Educ: BMus, Ind. Univ., Bloomington; Dip., Curtis Inst. of Music, Phila., Pa. div.; B.A. div.; 3 d. Career: Apps. w. Boston Symph., Phila., Pa. div., 3 d. Career: Apps. w. Boston Symph., Phila. Orch., Ind. Symph., Buffalo Phil. Orch., Erie Symph., Trenton, Symph., Phila. Lyric Opera Co.; num. radio apps., Boston, Mass., Buffalo, NY, Phila., Pa., Indpls., Ind.; Concert tour, Switz. & France, 1974; num. apps. in E & Mid W Coast in oratoric & recital; Asst. Prof., Clark Univ., Worcester, Mass.; Voice Fac., New England Conser. of Music, Boston, Mass. Mbrships. incl: Bd. of Dirs., New England Reg., Nat. Assn. of Tchrs. of Singing. Recip., sev. hons. Hobbies incl: Antiques. Address: 64 Eastwood Rd., Shrewsbury, MA 01545, USA.

CLIFFORD, Daphne Monica, b. 17 Aug. 1926, Gt. Bealings, Woodbridge, Suffolk, UK. Music Teacher (Piano, Singing, Recorder); Accompanist. Educ: RCM; ARCM (Piano Tchr.); LRAM (Singing Performer); LTCL (Piano Performer). Career: Music Tchr. & Accompanist, East Anglia, 1948-54, 56-62; Tchr., Rhodesian Coll. of Music, 1954-55; Tchr., St. Joseph's Convent, Port of Spain, Trinidad, 1963-. Contbr. to: Trinidad Express: Caribbean Contact; Catholic News. Mbrships: Inc. Soc. Musicians. Prog. organizer, Trinidad Recital Club; Vice Chmn., Trinidad Music Tchrs. Assn. Hobbies: Horse Racing; Gardening; Cooking; Reading. Address: 2 Mary Ave., Diego Martin, Trinidad, W1. 3.

CLIFT, Dennis Richard, b. 31 Aug. 1919, London, UK. Trumperter; Conductor; Violinist. Educ: RCM; TCM; Kneller Hall. m. Betty Rouse, 2 s., 1 d. Career: Violinist, Bournemouth Symph. Orch., 1938-40; Trumpeter, Philharmonia Orch., 1949-54; Prin. Trumpet, LSO, 1955-61; Cond., Havering Youth Orch., & Havering Symph. Orch., 1961-77; Camberley Symph. Orch. & Hornchurch Youth Orch., 1961-77; Prof., Royal Military Schl. of Music, Kneller Hall, 1977-. Recordings: Chmbr. music; Bach Suites & Brandenburg Concertos. Mbr., ISM. Hobbies: Writing; Conducting. Address: 37 Buckingham Gdns., E Molesey, Surrey, UK.

CLINCH, Peter Gladstone, b. 26 June 1930, Geraldton, WA, Aust. College Lecturer; Clarinettist; Saxophone Player. Educ: LMus, MMus, Univ. of WA; preparing PhD thesis at Monash Univ. m. Joy Richmond, 2 c. Career: 30 yrs. perfs. at concerts, on radio & TV throughout Aust., UK, Europe & USA; soloist w. chmbr. ensembles; formed duo w. pianist Trevor Barnard; Sr. Lectr. in Music at Melbourne State Coll. Comp: Introspection for saxophone & tape (recorded). Recordings: num., incl. saxophone concertos of James Penberthy & William Lovelock. Publs: Clarinet Tutor, 1976; (ed.) Clarinet Concerto by Franz Tausch, 1978. Contbr. to: Studies in Music; Aust. Jrnl. of Music Educ.; The Clarinet. Mbrships: Pres., Clarinet & Saxophone Soc. of Vic.; Assoc. mbr., APRA. Hons: 2 Aust. Govt. Grants to study in Europe, UK, Can. & USA, 1972. Hobbies: Weight lifting; Football. Address: 57 Woodhouse Rd., Doncaster E, Vic. 3109, Aust.

CLINTON, Francis Gordon, b. 19 June 1912, Broadway, UK. Baritone. Educ: RCM, (ARCM). m. Phyllis Jarvis, 1 d., 2 s. Career: 35 yrs. singing inclng. major fests., tours of USA, Canada, Far East & N Africa. Many broadcasts inclng. Prom. Concerts; Soloist in Beecham 70th Birthday Concert; 50 apps. in Albert Hall, London; 20 apps. in Royal Fest. Hall, London inclng. inaugural concerts; Adjudicator, nat. & int. fests.; Examiner, Assoc. Bd., Royal Schls. of Music, 1959-; Prin., Birmingham Schl. of Music, 1960-73; Prof. of Singing, RCM; Bd. of Profs., ibid.; Chorus Master, City of Birmingham Symph. Orch. Chorus Recordings: L'Oiseau Lyre EMI. MBrships: Royal Phil. Soc.; ISM:; VP, Music & Choral Socs. Hons: FRCM: FRSM; Hon. RAM. Hobbies: Sport; Wild Life. Address: 42 Pembroke Croft, Birmingham 28, UK. 1, 3, 14, 21.

CLOAD, Julia, b. London, UK. Musician (pianist). Educ: studied w. Hilda Bor, RCM w. Cyril Smith, Liszt Acad. w. Lajos Hernadi.

Debut: Wigmore Hall, London, 1969. Career: concerto apps. w. BBC orchs., LPO, RPO & Hallé orchs.; recital & concerto apps. in London, Frankfurt, Darmstadt & Kaln. Recording: works by Bach & Mozart. Hons: Arts Coun. & British Coun. scholarships, 1970. Hobbies: Theatre; Reading. Mgmt: Ibbs & Tillett, London. Address: 40 Highfield Ave., London NW9 OPY, UK.

CLOTTU, Dagmar, b. 8 Feb. 1952, Bienne, Switz. Pianist. Educ: Tchrs. Dip., Bienne; Superior Musical Execution Dip., Neuchatel; Concert Dip. w. Paderevsky Prize, Geneva. Career: recitals & orchl. concerts in major cities of Switz. inclng. app. on Swiss French TV & recordings for Swiss German & Swiss French radios; London debut, 1976; Recording of Chopin & Liszt works. Life Mbr., LPO, Engl. Chmbr. Orch. & Edinburgh Fest. Clubs. Mbr., LSO Club. Hons: Prix Ville de Lausanne, when aged 12; Pembauer-Preis, 1975; Bronze Medal, Geneva, 1977. Hobbies: Learning orchl. scores; Attending fests. & rehearsals. Mbmt: John Higham, New Era Ltd. Address: Chemin des landes 22, 2503 Bienne, Switz.

CLOUD, Lee V, b. 24 May 1950, Winston-Salem, NC, USA. Bass-Baritone Singer; Composer. Educ: BA, Morehouse Coll. (comp. w. T J Anderson); MMus, (theory & comp.), Bowling Gn. State Univ.; PhD, Univ. of Iowa (studied comp. w. William Hibbard, Donald Jenni & Richard Hervig). Comps: Salutation, for piano & orch.; Songs of Death, for baritone & str. trio; Thesis, for str. orch.; Two for T, for solo flute; Music for Five; Gestures (piano); Music for voices, instruments, Choir & orch. Mbrships: Am. Soc. of Univ. Comps.; Am. Musicol. Soc.; MENC; Pi Mu Alpha. Hobbies: Tennis; Swimming. Address: 1215 Elm St., Grinnell, IA 50112, USA.

CLOW, Jo Ellen Thompson, b. 28 Aug. 1948, Tulsa, Okla., USA. Vocal Instructor. Educ: BMusEd., Bethany Nazarene Coll. m. Richard Charles Clow, 1 s. Career: Vocal Instructor, Public Schls. Junior High. Contbr. to: Notated Indian Chant (2) for Okla. Indian Curriculum Book. Mbrships: Okla. Music Tchrs. Assn.; Am. Choral Dirs. Assn.; Delta Kappa Gamma; Music Chmn., Okla. Educ. Assn.; Claremore Clasroom Tchrs.; Nat. Educ. Assn.; Rogers Country Educ. Assn.; Music Educs. Hons: incl: Scholarship, Delta Kappa Gamma, 1978. Hobbies: Sewing; Crafts; Gourmet cooking; Reading; Flowers & plants. Address: 3214 S Marion, Tulsa, OK 74135, USA.

CLYNE, Malcolm Edward, b. 6 Sept. 1943, Tunja, Colombia. Composer. Educ: BA, Bethel Coll., McKenzie, Tenn., USA, 1966; ThM, Dallas Theol. Sem., Tex., 1970; MM, N Tex. State Univ., Denton, 1975; Currently, doct. student in comp.. ibid. m. Janice Elizabeth Williams, 1 s. Comps. incl: Ricercare and Canonette for Brass Trio; 1st String Quartet; Sinfonietta for 12 Wind Instruments; Variations for Unaccompanied Clarinet; Woodwind Quintet; Sonata for solo violin; Sol. Deo Gloria, for mixed chorus (a capella); Phantasy for Guitar. Mbrships: Am. Musicol. Soc.; Am. Soc. of Ch. Hist.; Charter Mbr., Xi Sigma Chapt., Phi Mu Alpha Sinfonia Fraternity of Am.; etc. Address: 3330 Rosedale, Dallas, TX 75205, USA.

CNATTINGIUS, Claes Magnus, b. 5 Mar. 1933, Linköping, Sweden. Musicologist; Hd., Record Lib., Swedish Broadcasting Corp. Educ: BA, Univ. of Uppsala, 1956; Licentiate of Philos. in Musicol., Uppsala, 1962; studies in comp. (w. Vaughan Williams) & cond., London, 1951-52, '55; comp. (w. Marius Constant) & cond. (w. Igor Markewitch), Paris, 1959. m. Katarina Landahl, 2 s. Career: Royal Lib., Stockholm, 1962-68; Hd., Nat. Phonotheque, 1965-68; Swedish Broadcasting Corp., 1968-; Music critic, Dagens Nyheter (Stockholm), 1961-74. Publs: Notes sur les oeuvres de jeunesse de Claude Debussy, 1962; Contemporary Swedish Music (German & French versions 1962-63) revised ed., 1973. Mbrships: Int. Assn. of Music Libs. (sec., record lib. commission, 1965-78); Int. Assn. of Sound Archives (Bd., 1968-75); Pres., IAML/IASA Jt. Committee on Music & Sound Archives, 1978-. Hobbies: Travel; Gardening. Address: Skogsvägen 26, Täby, Stockholm, Sweden.

COATES, Dale Young, b. 17 Sept. 1942, Terrell, Tex., USA. Band Director. Educ: BM, E Tex. Baptist Coll., Marshall, Tex.; MME, N Tex. State Univ., Denton, Tex. m. Sandi Jean Sanders, 2 s. Career: Band & Choir, John Adams Jr. High Schl., Grand Prairier; Asst. Band Dir., Ennis High Schl., Tex.; Band Dir., Wills Point High Schl., Tex.; Band Dir., W Mesquite High Schl., Mesquite, Tex.; Jr. & Sr. High Orch. Dir., First Baptist Ch., Dallas. Recording w. several schl. bands. Mbrships: Tex. State Tchrs. Assn.; Tex. Music Educators Assn; Tex. Bandmasters Assn.; Phi Delta Omega. Hobbies: Antiques; Wood Refining; Making lamps for Band Instruments. Address: 2712 Sybil Circle, Mesquite, TX 75149, USA. 4.

COATES, Edith, b. 31 May 1908, Lincoln, UK. Operatic Mezzo-Soprano. Educ: TCM, London. Debut: Old Vic Theatre,

London. Career: Sadlers Wells/Engl. Nat. Opera; Royal Opera, Covent Gdn.; English Opera Group; Welsh Nat. Opera Co.; etc.; BBC Radio & TV. Recordings: EMI; HMV. Mbrships: ISM; Lansdowne Club; British Actors Equity. Hons: Hon. Fellow TCM; Hon. FTCL; OBE, 1977. Hobby: Reading. Address: Montrose, Cross Lane, Findon, Sussex BN14 0UQ, UK. 1, 3, 14.

COATES, Gloria Kannenberg, b. 10 Oct., Wausau, Wis., USA. Composer. Educ: BA, Theatre, Art, BMus, Comp., Voice, Columbia Univ., 1963; MMus, Comp., Musicol., La. State Univ., 1965; Mozarteum, Salzburg. 1 d. Career: Singer, Actress, Dir. & Comp., 1957-72; Arranger Prod., German-Am. Concert Series, Munich, 1971-79; Tchr., Music, Univ. of Wis. Comps. incl: Orchl. Chmbr. Music, Choral, Songs, Theatre & Electronic Planets, Three Movements for Chmbr. Orch.; Voices of Women in Wartime (cycle for soprano & chmbr. ensemble); Five Abstractions from Poems of Emily Dickinson for Woodwind Quartet; Music on Open Strings, Warsaw Autumn Fest., 1978; String Quartet No. 4; Music for Theatre inclng. Hamlet, Thieves' Carnival & St. Joan. Num. radio recordings, Int. fests. & concerts. Mbr., num. profl. orgs. Address: Savoy Haus 108, Tengstr. 20, 8 Munich 40, German Fed. Repub. 4, 27.

COATES, Leon, b. 15 June 1937, Wolverhampton, UK. Lecturer in Music. Educ: MA, St. John's Coll., Cambridge Univ.; LRAM (Piano Tchng.); ARCO. m. Heather Johnston. Career: Mbr., Nat. Youth Orch., 1954-56; Asst. Dir. Music, Leys Schl., Cambridge, 1962-63; Lectr. in Music, Edinburgh Univ., 1965-; Cond., Edinburgh Chmbr. Orch., 1965-75; Cond., Edinburgh Symph. Orch., 1973-; Broadcasts as Pianist & Harpsichordist; Harpsichord continuo player for Scottish Baroque Ensemble, 1971-. Comps: A Legend's Carol (cantata); Str. Quartet; 2 song cycles; piano & organ music; Viola Concerto. Recordings (BBC Archives) Harpsichord duets w. Peter Williams. Contbr. to: New Edinburgh Review. Mbr., CGGB. Recip., Ord Travel Scholarship, 1962. Hobby: Hill-walking. Address: 31 Scotland St., Edinburgh EH3 6PY, UK.

COATES, Tamara, b. 2 July 1928, London, UK. Oboist. Educ: Qualified as Physiotherapist, Kings Coll. Hosp. Study of oboe & piano, GSM; LRAM. m. (1) Dr. G W Miller, (2) G E Dewdney, 1 s., 3 d. Debut: Wigmore Hall, London, 1949. Career: Mbr., Melbourne Symph., Australia, & num. concerts, solo recitals & broadcasts, 10 yrs.; Freelance Oboe, all London chmbr. orchs. & BBC. Hobbies: Squash; Tennis; Painting. Address: 83 Corringham Rd., London NW11, UK.

COBB, A(lfred) Willard, b. 19 Dec. 1929, Baltimore, Md., USA. Concert Singer (tenor). Educ: BA, Tusculum Coll., Tenn., 1951; BMus, Oberlin Coll. Conserv., 1955; MMus, ibid., 1957; FTCL, 1962; LRAM, 1962; LTCL, 1963. m. Mary Evans. Career: Concert Singer in England & Europe; num. radio apps., incl. 2 BBC recitals; Mbr., Early Music Quartet, 1964-70; Tchr. of voice & early music, St. Louis Conserv. & St. Louis Univ. Num. recordings inclng: Songs of John Dowland; Carmina Burana. Contbr. to KWMU radio mag. Mbrships: Pi Kappa Lambda; NATS. Recip. num. awards. Hobby: Restoring Early Keyboard Instruments. Address: 5112 Westminster Pl., St. Louis, MO 63108, USA.

COBB, David Alan, b. 20 Feb. 1930, Quincy, Mass., USA. Double Bass Player; Teacher. Educ: pvte. studies. m. Janet S Cobb, 3 s., 1 d. Debut: as Double Bass Soloist w. Berkshire Symph. Orch., 1971. Career: Prin. Bassist, Albany, Vt. & Berkshire Symph. Orchs.; Tchr. of Double Bass, SUNY at Albany, Coll. of St. Rose at Albany & Niskayuna HS, Schenectady; Soloist, NE USA; sev. broadcasts. Comps: sev. double bass comps.; concerto for double bass. Hobbies incl: Sailing. Address: Waterbury Rd., Box 390, Nassau, NY 12123, USA.

COBB, Margaret Evelyn, b. 2 Sept. 1918, Hendon, London, UK. Organist; Pianist. Educ: BMus, London; FRCO; ARCM; LRAM; FTCL; LTCL; TCL; RAM. Debut: As pianist, Queen's Hall. Career: Organist, St. Stephen's, Paddington, London, UK, 1947-54; Organist, St. Philip's, Kensington, 1954-60; Organist, St. Lawrence Jewry, London, 1957-74; Soloist & recitalist, Rhodesia, S Africa, NZ & UK; Soloist, BBC Promenade Concert; Num. broadcast organ recitals. Hons: FRCO w. Turpin, Harding & Read Prizes; Haigh Prize, RCM; ARCCO w. Sawyer Prize. Hobby: Gardening. Address: 65 The Greenway, Ickenham, Middx. UB10 8LX, UK.

COBBE, Hugh Michael Thomas, b. 20 Nov. 1942, Farnham, Surrey, UK. Librarian. Educ: Studied Classical at Trinity Coll., Dublin, 1961-65; BA, ibid., 1965; MA, 1968; Corpus Christi Coll., Oxford, 1965-66. Career: Asst. Keeper especially concerned w. music manuscripts in the Dept. of Manuscripts, Brit. Lib. (formerly Brit. Mus.), 196778; Publs: Officer, British Library Reference Div., 1978-; Sec., Royal Musical Assn., 1977-. Publs: Edn., Samuel Wesley, Trio in F for Two Flutes & Piano Forte,

OUP, 1973. Contbr. to: Musical Times; Brit. Mus. Qtly.; Hermathena. Mbrships: Royal Musical Assn.; Fellow, Royal Geographical Soc.; Kildare St. Club, Dublin. Hobbies: Playing chamber music pvtly.; Travelling; Gardening; Railways. Address: 69 St. Paul's Rd., London N12LT, UK.

COBLEY, Martin Howard, b. 6 Mar. 1944, Cosby, Leics., UK. Piano Teacher. Educ: Grad.; Royal Acad. of Music, London, 1962-65; Lic., ibid.; GRSM; LRAM. m. June Mary Cobley, 1 d. Career: Music master, Dyson Perrins Ch. Second. Schl., Malvern Link, 1965-67; Roundhill HS, Thurmaston, Leics., 1967-70; Mkt. Bosworth HS, 1970-73; Hd. Music Dept., Henry Mellish Grammar Schl., Bulwell, Nottingham, 1973-78. Mbr., Incorp. Soc. of Musicians. Hobbies: Model making, esp. railways; Transp.; Painting. Address: 59 Enfield St., Beeston, Nottingham, UK.

COBOS, Henry Diaz, b. 12 Apr. 1931, El Paso, Tex., USA. Musicologist; Pianist; Education Administrator. Educ: Univ. of Tex., El Paso, 1948-50, 1952-53, 1955-58; BMus., Eastman Schl. of Music, Univ. of Rochester, NY, 1952; MMus, ibid., 1955; UCLA, 1958-61. Debut: Juarez, Chihuahua, Mexico, 1945; LA, Calif., 1960. Career: Perf., Mexican radio stn., at age of 11; Perf. w. El Paso Symph., age 18; Tchr., UCLA, 1972; Mbr., fac., Dominguez Hills State Univ., Calif., 1972-, E LA Coll., 1969-; Cons., Nat. Endowment for Humanities, Mexican Historic Music Proj., 1973-75; Dir., Financial Aids., E LA Coll., 1971-. Author of Musica colonial venezolana, 1972. Contbr. to: Heterofonia Revista bimestral musical; Notes of the Music Lib. Assn.; Die Musik in Geschichte & Gegenwart. Mbrships: Am. Musicological Soc.; Music Lib. Assn. Hobby: Collecting early Mexican paintings & archaeological pieces. Address: 824 N Oxford Ave., LA, CA 90029, USA.

COCHRAN, Jean Kathleen, b. 7 Oct. 1928, London, UK. Freelance Lecture & Writer; Tutor in Humanities & Renaissance Music. Educ: Bedford Coll. for Women, London Univ., 1947-50; Tchng. Dip., Inst. of Educ. & Trinity Coll. of Music, 1951; LRAM, 1968; Royal Acad. of Mus., 1959-60; ARCM, 1960. Career incls: Dir. of Music, ILEA schls., 1951-73; Profl. Accomp. to singers, 1950's; Guest Lectr., Piano Music, Hendon Coll. of Technol., 1961-63; Mbr., BBC Choir, 1961-69; Tutor in Humanities & Renaissance Music, Open Univ. incls: FRSA; ISM; Assoc. Mbr. PEN. Publs. incl: Guide to Listening for Young People, 1970. Contbr. to profl. jrnls. Recip., 3rd Prize, Open Competition Piano Midlands, 1946. Hobbies incl: Restoring antique furniture. Address: 65 Sunny Gdns. Rd., London NW14, UK.

COCK, Richard Alan Charles, b. 27 July 1949, Port Elizabeth, S Africa. Director of Music; Assistant Organist. Educ: BA (Music), Univ. of Cape Town; LRSM (Piano & Organ; FRCO (CHM). Career: Tchr. & Lay Vicar of Chichester Cathedral, UK; Dir. of Music, Prebendal Schl., Chichester; Asst. Organist, Chichester Cathedral. Mbrships: RCO. Hons: William Charles Kent Prize RSCM. Hobbies: Walking; Reading. Address: Prebendal School, Chichester, Sussex, PO19 IRT, UK. 4.

COELHO, Peter, b. 29 June 1906, Pomburpa, Goa, India. Violinist; Saxophonist; Clarinetist; Band LEader; Music Teacher; Arranger. m. Eufemia Lourenco-Coelho, 2 c. Debut: Elphinstone Theatre, Lahore, 1926. Career: Theatre Orch. Ldr., Violinist, Stage Shows, Operas, Ballets, Silent Films, India, 1926-; Radio, Film, Recording Pers., India & Burma, 1934-60; Perfs. w. own band & num. others, India & Burma; Music Tchr., Calcutta Boys' Schl., 1966-; Mbr. Calcutta Symph. Recordings: num., w. own band, & Violin Accomp., Soloist, w. var. Singers. Mbr. Calcutta Schl. of Music. Address: Bishop Cotton Boys School, St. Marks Rd., Bangalore, T60001, India.

COELHO MACIEL, Emanuel, b. 16 Oct. 1935, Belo Horizonte, Brazil. Music Teacher; Violinist; Violist. Educ: Schl. Music Mil. Police, Minas Gerais; BMus, Conserv. Minas Gerais & Univ. Arts Minas Gerais, 1957; Tchr. Music, Nat. Conserv. Music, Rio de Janeiro, 1960. Debut: 1st violinist, Symph. Orch. Minas Gerais, 1954. Career incls: Music Fac., Univ. Amazon, 1970-71; V-Dir., Schl. Music, Brasilia, Maestro, Jr. & Sr. Orchs., ibid., & 1st violinist, Orch. Ars-Brasiliense, 1972-75; Music Fac., Fed. Univ. Piaui, 1976-. Comps. incl: Prelude & Canon for Strings, 1965; Sun & Fair, 1971; Two Spacial Songs for soprano, piano & cello, 1974. Publ: Coleçao Saci-Pérere, 1962. Mbr. profl. orgs. Hobby: Popular Brazilian music. Address: Faculdade de Música da Univ. Fed. do Piaui, Terezina-Pl. Brazil.

COEN, Massimo, b. 11 Mar. 1933, Rome, Italy. Violinist; Teacher. Educ: Law degree, Rome Univ.; Violin Dip., St. Cecilia Conserv., Rome; pvte. study of chmbr. music & violin. m. Mirella Thau, 2 s., 1 d. Career incls: Fndr., Chmbr. Music Grps., I Solisti di Roma, 1961, & Quartetto Nuova Musica, 1963, giving

concerts & radio perfs. throughout Europe; Tour of USA & Can. as soloist w. Soc. Cameristica Italiana, 1969; Fndr., Music Schl., Rome; Music Tchr., Nat. Acad. of Dance; Discoverer, Ed., & Perf. of num. ancient Italian musical MSS. Recordings of Baroque & Contemporary music. Contbr. to Mondo Operaio. Mbr., profl. assns. & couns. Hons: Mbr., Int. Jury, Gaudeamus Fndn. Competition, Rotterdam, 1976. Mgmt: Studio Consul, Via Gallia 34, 00183 Rome. Address: Via Ipponio 8, 00183 Rome, Italy.

COENEN, Paul Franz, b. 8 Dec. 1908, Saarlouis, Saarland, Germany. Composer; Conductor (Piano, Organ, Violoncello, Viola, Violin, Clarinet). Educ: Univs. & Musical Acads. at Munich, Bonn, Berlin, Leipzig; Pvte. studies. 3 d. Debut: Perf. Radio Berlin, 1934. Career: Own concertos w. violoncellist Martin Grenlich in Berlin, Wittenberg (Elbe), Saarlouis, Leipzig; Perfs. on radio w. own comps. Comps. incl: Sonatas for Piano, op 12 & 53; Fantasia for Violin & Piano, op. 30; Sonata for Violoncello & Piano, op. 4; Sonata for Organ, op. 2. 2 operas: The Karamasows; The Priest of Evil. Contbr. to profl. jrnls. Mbrships: incl GEMA, German Comps. Grp.; Assn. of Music Educators; Soc. of Theatre Mbrs. Hobbies: 10 Langs.; Travel; Geog.; Hist. Address: 3 Hannover 21, Osteroder Weg 3, German Fed. Repub.

COFALIK, Antoni, b. 3 March 1940, Myslowice, Poland. Violinist. Educ: Dip. of Art, Prof. of Music, Coll. High Schl. of Music. Debut: Solo Violinist w. Krakow Phil. Orch., 1964. Career: Mbr., Cracow Trio, 1963-; Concerts, most countries of Europe., Am., Africa, Asia; Ldr., Artistic Dir., String Chmbr. Orch., All Antico; Radio & TV apps. Recordings w. Cracow Trio. Hons: Artistic Prize of Krakow, 1975; Gold Medal of Rome, 10th Anniversary of Cracow Trio, 1973; 1st prize, Karajan Competition for Young Musicians, 1975. Hobby: Success in violin tchng. Address: ul. Zakatek 13/8, 30-076 Crakow, Poland.

COFFIN, (Roscoe) Berton, b. 11 Apr. 1910, Fairmount, Ind., USA. Professor of Voice. Educ: BA, Earlham Coll., Richmond, Ind., 1932; BMus, Chgo. Musical Coll., Ill., 1935; MMus, Eastman Schl. of Music, Univ. of Rochester, NY, 1938; MA, Columbia Univ., NYC, 1946; EdD, Columbia Univ., NYC, 1950. m. Mildred Wantland, 1 d. Career: Gen. & widespread opera, orchl. appearances; Profl. NCB & RCA singing & recording w. Robert Shaw Chlorale in NY; VAr. other engagements in NY, Tex., Colo., etc.; Major career in the tchng. of singing; Currently Hd., Div. of Voice, Coll. of Music, Univ. of Colo., Boulder. Publs: The Singer's Repertoire, 5 vols., 1956-60; Program Notes of the Singer's Repertoire (co-auth.), 1964; Word-by-Word Translations of Songs & Arias, Pt. I (co-auth.), Pt. II (colleagues, w. Foreword), 1966 & '73; Phonetic Readings of Songs & Arias (co auth.), 1964; The Sounds of Singing; Vocal Techniques, 1976; Coffin's Favorable Vowel-Color Charts & Manuals for Male & Female Voices, 1976. Mbr. of sev. profl. orgs. Address: 4495 Osage Dr., Boulder, CO 80303, USA. 3.

COGGINS, Alan, b. 1932, Dagenham, Essex, UK. Pianist; Composer. Educ: RAM; LRAM; ARCM. m. Bettie Owen, 2 s. Career: Specialist, music & electronic sound scores for theatre, esp. contemporary dance. Recording: Sound Images, 1976. Mbrships: ISM; ICA. Hobbies: Skiing; Photography; Printing. Address: Parsloes, Recreation Ground, Stansted Mountfichet, Essex, UK.

COGGINS, Willis Robert, b. 20 Aug. 1926, Winston-Salem, NC, USA. Professor of Saxophone & Clarinet; Composer, Arranger & Editor of Pedigogical Works for Saxophone. Educ: BS, Davidson Coll., NC; MS, Univ. of Ill., Champaign-Urbana. m. Jessie Mae Tolson, 3 d. Career incls: Instr., Brevard Music Ctr., 1946-58; & Dir. of Bands, Conway Pub. Schls., SC, 1949-53; Prof., Univ. of Ill., Urbana, 1953-; currently Mbr., Champaign-Urbana Symph.; Soloist w. var. symphs., bands & ensembles. Author of 51 pedagogical works inclng: The Alto Saxophone Student (3 levels); Etudes for Saxophone (3 levels). Mbrships: Pi Kappa Lambda; Phi Mu Alpha. Address: Schl. of Music, Univ. of Ill., Urbana, IL 61801, USA.

COGHILL, Harry MacLeod, b. 14 Apr. 1944, Edinburgh, Scotland, UK. Opera Singer (Bass). Educ: Studied Singing, Royal Manchester Coll. of Music, 1967-71, w. Frederick Cox; ARMCM (Teaching & Perf.); student of John Hargreaves. m. Anna Sweeny. Debut: w. Engl. Nat. Opera, 1972. Career: Concert Tour, N Am., 1965; Mbr., Glyndebourne FEst. Chorus; Prin. Bass, Engl. Nat. Opera, 1971-; over 400 perfs., UK & abroad. Roles incl: Senceca, Monteverdi, L'Incoronazione di Poppea; Zeta, Lehar, The Merry Widow; Oroveso, Bellini, Norma; Kecal, Smetana, Bartered Bride; Blind Ballad Singer, Britten, Gloriana. Hons: Imperial League of Opera Prize & Ricordi Prize, Royal Manchester Coll. of Music, 1971. Hobby: Gold. Mgmt: H H H Ltd. (Concert Agcy.), 5 Draycott Pl., London SW3 2SF. Address: Derryheen, Hook Heath Rd., Woking, Wurrey, UK.

COGNAZZO, Roberto, b. 23 Dec. 1943, Montiglio, Asti, Italy. Musician; Musical Promoter. Educ: Grad. in Law; Dip. in Pianoforte. Deubt: Turin, 1968. Career incl: Concert pianist (solo & in chmbr. ensembles); Concert Organist; Tchr., Conserv. of Turin; Prog. Organizer for Chmbr. Music, Regio Theatre, Turin. Recordings: 1 bis del concertista, w. G Ferrari, cello (Cetra label); Manzoni's Musica notturna-Castiglioni: Movimento continuato, in La Musica Moderna (Fabbri Bros. label). Mbrships: Italian Musicol. Soc.; Ctr. of Piedmont Studies. Contbr. to Studi Piemontesi, etc. Recip: 1st Prize, 3rd Int. Festival del Duo, 1972. Address: Piazza Vittorio Vento 18, 10123 Turin, Italy.

COHEN, Albert, b. 16 Nov. 1929, NYC, USA. Professor of Music. Educ: BS, Juilliard Schl. of Music (violin), 1951; AM, PhD, NY Univ. (Musicol.), 1953, '59; Univ. of Paris, France, 1956-57. m. Betty Joan Berg Cohen, 1 s., 1 d. Career: Prof. of Music (Theory-Musicol.), Univ. of Mich., 1960-70; Prof. of Music & Chmn., SUNY, Buffalo, 1970-73; Prof. of Music & Chmn., Stanford Univ., 1973-. Publs: Transl. & Ed., G G Nivers, Treatise on the Composition of Music, 1962; Ed., E Moulinie Three Fantasies, 1963; Transl. & Ed., E Loulie, Elements or Principals of Music, 1965; Co-auth., Anthol. of Music for Analysis, 1965; Ed., J Millet, La Belle Methode, 1973. Contbr. to profl. jrnls. Mbrships: incl: Exec. Bd. Mbr., Coun. Mbr., Chmn. of Local Arrangements Comm. & Prof. Comm. at nat. meetings, Am. Musicol. Soc.; Int. Musicol. Soc.; Société Française de Musicologie, 1963. Recip. var. grants, fellowships. Address: Dept. of Music, Stanford Univ., Stanford, CA 94305, USA. 2, 11.

COHEN, Eta, b. Sunderland, UK. Violin Teacher; Lecturer on violin Pedagogy. Educ: Pvte. violin studies w. Alfred Wall, Carl Flesch, Max Rostal & Endre Wolf. m. Ephraim Smith, 2 d. Publs: Eta Cohen Violin Methods - Books I, II & III; Rounds for Violin. Contbr. to: Music in Educ.; ISM Jrnl. Mbrships: ISM; Comm. mbr., UK Coun. for Music Educ.; ESTA. Hobbies: Gardening; Walking. Address: 757 Scott Hall Rd., Leeds LS17 5PG, UK. 3, 27, 30.

COHEN, Norm, b. 13 Dec. 1936, NYC, USA. Chemist; Folklorist. Educ: BA, Reed Coll., 1958; MA, 1960, PhD, 1963, Univ. of Calif., Berkeley. m. Anne Elizabeth Billings Cohen, 1 s., 1 d. Career: Ed., JEMF Quarterly, John Edwards Mem. Fndn., UCLA, 1966-; Record Review Ed., Western Folklore, 1970-75; Exec. Sec., John Edwards Mem. Fndn. archive for commercially recorded & publd. Am. folk & folk-derived musics, 1968-. Publs: Uncle Dave Macon: A Bio-Discography (w. Ralph Rinzler); Long Steel Rail (Univ. of Ill. Press., 1979). Contbr. to: num. LP liner notes; var. folkloric & musical jrnls. Mbrships: Am., Calif., Tenn., Ky., NY, Pa., W Va. & Miss. Folklore Socs.; Soc. for Ethnomusicol. Address: 626 Haverford Ave., Pacific Palisades, CA 90272, USA.

COHEN, Raymond, b. 27 July 1919, Manchester, UK. Violinist. Educ: ARMCM; FRMCM. m. Anthya Rael, 1 s., 1 d. Career: Soloist in recitals and concerts w. major orchs. all over the world; Ldr., RPO, 1959-65; Mbr., Cohen Trio. num. recordings. Hons: Carl Flesch Award, 1946; Hon. RCM. Hobbies: Reading; Theatre; Antique collecting. Address: 6 Alvanley Gdns., London NW6 1 JD, UK. 14.

COHEN, Robert, b. 15 June 1959, London, UK. Cellist. Educ: Purcell Schl.; GSM. Debut: Aged 8. Career: Concert tours, USA, Germany, Israel, Rumania & Netherlands. Apps., Tanglewood, Aldeburgh & Harrogate Fests.; Apps. as soloist w. RPO, London Mozart Players; Concerts w. Yehudi Menuhin; BBC Radio & TV perfs.; Mbr., Cohen Trio. Recordings: Elgar Cello Concerto w. LPO. Mbrships: ISM. Hons: Suggia Prize Winner, aged 8; Winner, Young Concert Artists Int. Auditions, NY, 1978; Recip., Gregor Piatigorski Prize, Tanglewood Fest., 1978. Hobbies: Photography; Driving Cars; Squash. Mgmt: Young Concert Artists Inc., NY, USA. Address: 6 Alvanley Gdns., London, NW6 1JD, UK.

COHN, James (Myron), b. 12 Feb. 1928, Newark, NJ, USA. Composer; Musicologist; Inventor. Educ: incls: theory & comps. w. var. tchrs. inclng. Roy Harris; adv. comp. w. Bernard Wagenaar, 7 yrs.; BSc., 1949, MSc, 1950, Juilliard Schl. of Music; postgrad. course in Electronic Music, Hunter Coll., NYC, 1973. Career: Musicol., ASCAP, 1954-; Inventor of patented control devices for electronic musical instruments. Comps. publd. incl: Symphonies Nos. 3, 4 & 5; The Little Circus; Variations on The Wayfaring Stranger; Variations on John Henry; Kind of an Ode to Duty; One From One Leaves Two; Statues in the Park. Recordings: Recorded Music for Film, Radio & TV. Mbrships. incl: Am. Fedn. of Musicians; Am. Guild of Authrors & Comps.; Audio Engineering Soc. Recip. sev. awards. Address: c/o ASCAP, 1 Lincoln Plaza, NY, NY 10023, USA. 6, 28.

COKER, Paul Thomas, b. 7 Nov. 1959, London, UK. Pianist. Educ: Yehudi Menuhin Schl., 1969-77; RCM, 1977; ARCM (Perf.), 1977. Debut: age 6; London recital debut, Wigmore Hall, 1979. Career: Num. fest. apps.; Apps. abroad in Wash., Fontainebleau, Gstaad; TV apps., BBC, AVRO TV. Hons: Jt. Winner, Piano Sect., BBC Young Musician of the Yr. Competition, 1978; Winner, Nat. Fedn. of Music Socs. Concert Award, 1978. Hobby: Astronomy. Address: 51 Sittingbourne Ave., Bush Hill Pk., Enfield, Middx. EN1 2DB, UK.

COLBENTSON, Oliver, b. 14 Nov. 1927, Chgo., Ill., USA. Violin Soloist; Pedagogue. Educ: PhB, Univ. of Chgo.; BM, Manhattan Schl. of Music. m. Rose Wholers, 1 d. Debut: Town Hall, NYC, 1953. Career: Assoc. Concertmaster, Met. Opera, NYC, 1954-58; Annual Concert Tours in Europe w. apps. & broadcasts in most European capitals, 1955-58; Emigration to Europe, 1958, concert master & soloist; Pedagogue, Nuremberg Conserv., Germany, 1962-; Concert apps. in almost every country in the world, 1962-. Num. recordings. Contbr. of 7 articles on musical & technical ideas of Alexanian to Symphony, NYC. Mbr., Lions Int. Hon: Winner, Chgo. Musical Coll. Competition & app. w. orch. in Orch. Hall Chgo., 1944. Address: Virichow Str. 3, 85 Nürnberg, German Fed. Repub. 3, 29, 30.

COLD, Ulrik, b. 15 May 1939, Copenhagen, Denmark. Singer. Educ: Cand. jur., Univ. Copenhagen. m. Helle Hogh. Career: Oratorio, Lieder, Opera on radio & TV; Don Quichotte, Komische Oper, Berlin; Sarastro in Ingmar Bergman's film version of The Magic Flute; Marke, Fiesco, Padre Guardiano, Gurnemanz, Ochs, Falstaff, etc. Recordings: The Magic Flute; Rinaldo; Admeto; Hippolyte et Aricle; Danish Songs. Hons. incl: Aksel Schiotz Prize, 1978. Address: Bredgade 63, DK 1260, Copenhagen K, Denmark.

COLDING-JØRGENSEN, Birgit, b. 9 Feb. 1939, Kobenhavn, Denmark. Opera Singer (contralto); Professor of Music. Educ: Solfege Pedagogue, Det Kongelige Danske Musikkonservatorium, 1965; MA, Kobenhavns Univ., 1966. m. Henrik Colding-Jorgensen, 1 child. Debut: In Verdi's Rigoletto w. Den Jyske Opera, 1970. Career: Apps. on Denmark Radio incl: Barbare (H Colding-Jorgensen); Threni (Strawinskij); Gilgamesh (P Norgard); Messiah (Handel); Alto Rhapsody (Brahms); App. in Hallelujah (M Kagel), Det Kongelige Teater. Mbrships: Solisforeningen, 1921; Danish Section ISCM; Dansk Magisterforening. Hobbies: Music; Riding. Mgmt: Koncertdirektion Inge Daub, Marathonvej 18, DK 2300 Kobenhavn S, Denmark. Address: Hjulbaekvej 5, Tolstrup, DK 4174 Jystrup Midtsjaelland, Denmark.

COLDING-JØRGENSEN, Henrik, b. 21 Mar. 1944, Risskov, Denmark. Composer; Organist; Teacher. Educ: Grad. as Ch. Organist, 1966, & as Tchr. of Organ, 1967, Royal Danish Conserv. of Music. m. Birgit Colding-Jorgensen, 1 child. Career: Organ Tchr., Folkemusikskole, Copenhagen; Tchr. Music Theory, Fynske Music Conserv.; Tchr. of organ Royal Danish Conserv. of Music; Organist, Kildebronde Ch.; works performed on radio & TV. Comps. incl: (instrumental ensemble), 1968; Albert (solists, choirs & orch.), 1970, Intrada, 1971; Ave Maria, 1974; To Love the Music, 1975; A Little Te Deum, 1976. Mbr. var. profl. assns. Hons. incl: Num. Bursaries, Prizes & Commissions. Hobbies: Music; Philosophy; Psychology. Address: Hjulbaekvej 5, Tolstrup, DK 4174 Jystrup Msj., Denmark. 14.

COLE, Elmer Francis Wyatt, b. 4 July 1938, Walmer, UK. Flautist. Educ: ARCM (Perf.'s Dip.); pvte. study w. Albert Honey & Geoffrey Gilbert. m. Frances Nicholls, 1 s., 1 d. Career: Nat. Serv. w. Royal Artillery Band, Woolwich; studied under John Francis at RCM. Prin. Flautist, Engl. Nat. Opera at the London Coliseum, London Concert Orch. & Bristol Sinfonia; Soloist, concerts & music clubs; Chmbr. music w. Merle Ensemble (Agnes Kory). Recordings: Genin, The Carnival of Venice (complete variations); Faure, Sicilienne (w. John Parry, piano accomp.). Hobbies: Sailing; Reading; Inventing; Drawing & Painting. Address: 98 Dora Rd., Wimbledon, London SW19 7HJ, UK.

COLE, Elmertha Butler, b. 5 Oct. 1905, Wynne, Ark., USA. Teacher. Educ: BS in Educ., Lemoyne-Owen; AB in Educ., MI Coll., Holly Springs, Miss.; Bailey Schl. of Art-Sci. in Music; Organ w. Thomas Webber. m. Jefferson Cole, 1 d. Career: Ch. Min. of Music, Salem Gilfield Bapt. Ch., Tenn., 1923-58; Tchr., piano & organ, Memphis, Tenn. Mbrships: Nat. Guild of Piano Tchrs.; Life, YWCA. Contbr. to Pfund's Happy Note. Hons: Hall of Fame & Hon. Roll, Nat. Piano Tchrs. Guild. Hobby: Ch. music; Sunday School tchr. Address: 1033 S Orleans St., Memphis, TN 38126, USA. 5.

COLE, Howard, b. 20 Aug. 1913, Wayne Co., W Va., USA. Trombonist. Educ: grad., Curtis Inst. Music, Phila., Pa.,

1940. m. Rebecca Steger, 1 d. Career: Pitts., Pa., Symph. Orch. - Fritz Reiner, 1939-48; Phila. Orch. - Eugene Ormandy, 1948-69; Leopold Stokowski's All Am. Youth Orch., summer 1940, '41; NBC Symph. Orch., NYC, 1943; Chautauqua Symph. Orch., NY, 1945; Phila., Pa., La Scala Opera Co.; Phila. Civic Opera Co.; Westinghouse Musical Americana (Radio), 1940; Pitts. Civic Opera Co., summer 1946; Bass Trombone, Norfolk, Va., Symph. orch., 1929-33; Richmond, Va., Symph., 1933-36. Mbr., Am. Fedn. Musicians, local chapts., NYC & Phila., Pa. Hobbies: Photography (movies & stills); Short Wave Radio; Tape Recording; Reading. Address: Rte. 1, Box 9-B, Dunnellon, FL 32630, USA.

COLE, Vincent L, b. 19 June 1946, LA, Calif., USA. Composer; Conductor; Teacher. Educ: BA, UCLA, 1969; MA, Calif. State Univ., Northridge, 1975; PhD, UCLA, 1979. m. Joan Cole. Career incls: Tchr., Moorpark Coll. Comps: Woodwind Trio, 1971; String Quartet, 1971; Concrete Study for two-channel tape, 1973; Lamentation for oboe & tape, 1973; Mediatation for piano & tape, 1974; Cantata for soprano & orch., 1975; Distillations for solo cello, 1977; Chronikos for chmbr. ensemble, 1977; Wind Quintet, 1978; Songs of the Sea for chorus & orch., 1979. Mbrships: Nat. Assn. of Comps., USA; Am. Musicol. Soc. Hons: Atwater-Kent Comp. Award, 1977. Address: 16823 McKeever St., Granada Hills, CA 91344, USA.

COLE, Ward K, b. 17 Jan. 1922, Helena, Mont., USA. Professor of Music; Trumpeter; Conductor. Educ: BA (music), Univ. of Wash., Seattle, 1948; MA, profl. dip., Ed.D, Columbia Univ., 1952, '53, '54; post grad. study, Juilliard Schl. of Music. m. Carolyn J Clark. Career incl: trumpeter, Seattle Symph., 1946-49; Ted Weems Orch., 1949-51; Fred Waring Pennsylvanians, 1954-56; Toronto Symph., etc. sev. tchng. posts inclng. Hd., Dept. of Music, Fac. of Fine Arts, Univ. of Calgary, Alta., 1968-73; Prof. of Music, Univ. of Calgary, 1973-. Comps: Blues Muse; Bobcat Rock. Recordings: Messiaen's Turangalila Symph. w. Toronto Symph.; w. Fred Waring. Publs: arrs. & comps. for Stage Band, 1963-64. Contbr. to Can. Music Educators Jrnl. mbr. sev. profl. socs. Hons: Grad. Fellowship, Columbia Univ. Tchrs. Coll., 1952; Deutscher Akademischer Austauschdienst study award, 1974. Hobbies: Jazz perf.; Old Engl. Sheepdogs; Golf. Address: 2316 Sovereign Cres. SW, Calgary, Alota. T3C 2M2, Can. 2, 9.

COLE, William Charles, b. 9 Oct. 1909. Master of the Music at the Queen's Chapel of the Savoy since 1954. Educ: RAM; DMus; FRAM; FRCM; FRCO. m. (1) Elizabeth Brown Caw, 3 d.; (2) Winifred Grace Mitchell, 1 s. Career incl: Hon. Music Dir., Toynbee Hall, 1947-58; Prof. of harmony, comp., & lectr. in hist. of music, RAM, 1945-62; lectr., Royal Acad. of Dancing, 1948-62. Publs: Rudiments of Music, 1951; The Form of Music, 1969. Contbr. to musical jrnls. mbr. num. musical socs. & organisations. recip., MVO, 1966. Hobby: Stained Class. Address: Packways, Hindhead, Surrey, UK.

COLEBROOKE, Janet Mildred, b. 1 Oct. 1942, Brighton, UK. Reference & Accessions Assistant; Singer; Musical Director. Educ: RCM, 1960-65; ARCM tchng. dips., singing, cello, piano, 1961-62; GRSM, 1964. m. Michael Sodring. Career: Soloist, many oratorio perfs. & Lieder recitals; Dir., Opera Integra Addison Choir, The Addisonians; Ref. & Accessions Asst., BBC Music Lib. Mbr., ISM. Hons: Dir's. Special Prize, RCM, 1963; Marjorie Whyte Mem. Prize & Tagore Gold Medal, ibid., 1974. Hobbies: Cookery; Dressmaking; Stage costume designing; Gardening; Walking. Address: 19 Coombe Rd., Chiswick, London W4 2HR, UK. 3.

COLEMAN, Brian Robert, b. 24 June 1944, Sale, England. Singer; Director; Educationalist. Educ: Leys Cambridge, Coll. of St. Mark and St. John; Univ. of London, Inst. of Educ.; Univ. of East Anglia. m. Christine Coleman, 2 d. Career: var. singing, directing work for BBC, ORTF, RTB, EMI, Pye a.o.; Asst. dir. St. Michael's Coll. Tenbury, 1967-2; Dir. Authur Mellows Village Coll., Peterborough, 1972-76; Univ. of East Anglia, 1976; Musical Dir. Musica Deo Sacra, since 1967; Associate cond. Locinan Chmbr. Orch., since 1968. Recordings: var. Mbrships: Inc. Soc. of Musicians. Hobbies: Shooting; Vintage cars. Address: 3 The Nook, Helpston, Peterborough, Cambridge, UK.

COLERIDGE-TAYLOR, Avril Gwendolen, b. 8 mar. 1903, S Norwood, UK. Composer; Conductor; Accompanist (Piano); Authoress. Educ: GSM; TCL; var. tchrs. m. (1) Harold Christian Dashwood; (2) Bruce Somes-Charlton (div.), 1 s. Debut: (as Comp.) London, 1916; (as cond.) Eastbourne 1932. Career incls: Cond., Coleridge-Taylor Symph. Orch., 1943-50; Musical Dir., Fairbairn Hiawatha Prods., 1946-50; Guest Cond. of BBC Symph. Orch., BBC Concert Orch., 1936-60 &

prin. London Orchs. & Choral Socs., & provincial orchl. & choral socs.; Organizer & Cond.-Accomp., Fest. of Music, Amberley, Sussex, 1964, 65, 66; Fndr. & Cond., Malcolm Sargent Symph. Orch., 1971; num. talks, BBC. Publ: The Heritage of Samuel Colderidge-Taylor, 1976. Contbr. to profl. jrnls. Mbr., PRS. Hobbies incl: Walking; Reading; Psychology. Mgmt: Raymond Gubbay Mgmt. Address: c/o Nat. Westminster Bank, 1 Cavendish Sq., London W1, UK. 3.

COLES, James, b. 4 Oct. 1943, Gloucester, UK. Violinist. Educ: RAM; LRAM. Career: co-ldr., Bournemouth Symph. Orch.; Mbr., Montpellier Piano Trio; former mbr., Menuhin Fest. Orch. & Philharmonia Orch.; tchr., Birmingham Schl. of Music. Mbrships: ESTA; ISM. recip., Carnegie Prize, RAM. Hobby: Building. Address: Cornmill, Compton Abdale, nr. Cheltenham, Glos., UK.

ČOLIĆ, Dragutin, b. 8 Feb. 1907, Pozega, Yugoslavia. Professor. Educ: Dept. of Theoretical Subjects, Belgrade Music Schl.; State Conserv., Prague. Career: Tchr., Theoretical subjects, Stankovič Music Schl., 1937; Asst. Prof., Belgrade Music Acad., 1940; Assoc. prof., ibid., 1952. Comps. incl: (Chmbr. music) 3 String Quartets; Tema con Variazioni for piano; Suites for quarter-tone piano Nos. 1 & 2; Three Cycles of Solo Songs for voice & piano; (orchl.) Concertino for quarter-tone piano & string orch.; Symphonic poem, Nikoletina Bursac; Cycle of Songs, Circle of Tenderness, for bass & symph. orch.; Symph. for string orch. & percussion; Film Music; Theatre Music. Publs: Development of the theory of harmonic thinking, 1976. Contbr. to newspapers. Mbr., Assn. of Comps. of Sebia. Address: Lole Ribara 27, 11000 Belgrade, Yugoslavia.

COLIN, Georges Emile, b. 15 June 1921, Brussels, Belgium. Composer; Teacher. Educ: Royal Conserv. Music, Brussels. m. Albertine De Clerck (Jeanne Colin). 2 s., 2 d. Career: Tchr., Music Educ., Schaerbeek, Brussels; Tchr., Solfeggio & Harmony, Acad. Music, Anderlecht. Compositions incl: Cinq croquis d'élèves, pour Piano; Sonate pour Flûte et Piano; Concerto pour trompette et Orchestre; Cinq poèmes français de Rainer Maria, Rilke, pour voix et piano; Cantate pur le vif des Temps; La porte de pierre; Ryoan-Ji; Corps de Feu, pour Soprano, baryton, choeurs et orchestre. Publs: Neuf Chants Populaires, 1954; Chants et Danses Populaires, 1956; Doulce France; La flûte à alto: Méthode complète en 3 Vol. Hons: 1st prize, Concours de Composition Musicale de la Province de Brabant, 1964; 1st prize, Royal Conserv. of Music, Brussels. Address: Ave. Paul Deschanel, 120, B-1030-Brussels, Belgium. 3, 19.

COLIN, Jeanne, b. 9 Jan. 1924, Brussels, Belgium. Composer; Teacher. Educ: Royal Conserv. Music, Brussels. m. Georges Colin, 2 s., 2 d. Career: Tchr., Music Acad., Anderlecht. Compositions: Impovisation pour flûte solo; Caprice pour violonet orchestre; Tryptique pour Anches; Quatuor à cordes; Concerto pour flûte et orchestre; Concerto pour violon et orchestre. Address: Ave. Paul Deschanel, 120, B-1030-Brussels, Belgium.

COLLARD, Jean-Philippe, b. 27 Jan. 1948, Mareuil sur Aÿ, France. Pianist. Educ: Conserv. Nat., Paris. m. Christine Gelas, 2 c. Career: Concert apps., recitals, all over Europe, Am., Japan, USSR; num. radio & TV perfs. num. recordings incl. works by Fauré, Debussy, Franck, Milhaud, Rachmaninov, Schumann, Brahms, etc. Hons: Grand Prix du Concours Nat. des Artistes Solistes; Prix Albert Roussel; Prix Gabriel Fauré; Prix du Concours Int. Marguerite Long - Jacques Thibaud; Grand Prix du Concours Int. Cziffra. Hobbies: Tennis; Jogging. Mgmt: Bureau de Concerts de Valmaléte, Paris. Address: 160 Blvd. Malesherbes, 75017 Paris, France.

COLLEN, Jean McIntyre, b. 31 Aug. 1943, Glasgow, Scotland, UK. Music Teacher (Singing & Piano). Educ: BA, Hist. of Music, Univ. of S Africa; Studied singing w. Anne Ziegler & Webster Booth; Piano w. Sylvia Sullivan, Johannesburg; LTCL (Singing); LTCL (Piano). m. Errol Collen, 1 s., 1 d. Career: Mbr., Perf. Arts Coun. of Transvaal Opera; Taught at Kingsmead Coll., Johannesburg, 1965, 1968-70; Tchr., Wheathampstead Second. Modern Schl., 1966-68; Tchr., Selborne Coll., E London, 1973; currently pvte. tchr. & Cond., Choir of Trinity Congregational Ch., Yeoville, Johannesburg; Radio & TV apps. Mbrships: TCL Music Guild; S African Soc. of Music Tchrs. Hobbies: Ice Skating; Drama; Lit. Address: 25 Oxford Rd., Kensington, Johannesburg 2094, S Africa.

COLLETTE, Joannes M J F B, b. 20 mar. 1918, Blaricum, Netherlands. Musician, Flute, Recorder, Viola D Gamba, Fiddle, Organ, Piano, Harpsichord. Educ: Govt. Examinations, Flute, Music Theory; Organ Dip. m. de Vries, Folkertje, 5 c. Debut: The Hague, 1940. Career: Prof., Conservs. of Ultrecht, 1954, Tilburg, Arnheim, Maastricht, 1959; Radio, TV Apps., Holland, Germany, Austria, 1945-67; Concerts in Holland, Belgium, UK, Germany, Austria. Recordings: Muziekkring Obrecht; Syntagma Musicum. Publs: 12 Melodions Exercises for Descant Recorder;

Leidraad tot het spel op de Alblokfluit; 8 Melodische Studies Op De Altblokfluit; Melodische Studies Op De Altblokfluit. Hobbies: Building Copes of old Clavichords, Virginals, Harpsichords; Restoring Old Keyboards. Address: 6 Proost Abrahamstraat, Meerssen 5052, Netherlands.

COLLIER, Charles R, b. 10 Sept. 1935, Wash., DC, USA. Maker of Early Wind Instruments. Educ: Swarthmore Coll., Pa.; Univ. of Chgo.; Chgo. Art Inst.; Art Students League, NYC. m. Corlu Collier, 1 s., 1 d. Career: Painter; Graphics (Etcher); Maker of musical wind instruments, 1972-. Instrumments in prod. (w. var. tech. assts.): Mute Cornetto G; Mute Cornetto A; Mute Cornettino D; Renaissance Flutes, Bass G, Alto-tenor D, Descant in G or A; Renaissance Shawms, Alto in G, Treble in D, Tenor in C. Address: PO Box 9442, Berkeley, CA 94709, USA. 4.

COLLIER, Corlu, b. 6 Dec. 1927, Shanghai, China. Musician (early music); Teacher. Educ: BA, Univ. of Wash., Seattle, 1948; Grad. study, Grad. Lib. Schl., Univ. of Chgo., Ill.; pvte. study of voice, recorder, keyboard, guitar, etc. m. Charles R Collier, 1 s., 1 d. Career: Co-Fndr. of San Francisco Recorder Guild, 1950; Mbr. of Baroque Players (perf. group of the SF Recorder Guild), 1950-53; Duo with Freerk Mulders, Dutch classical guitarist, 1953-58; Berkeley Consort, 1967-69; Amici Musicae, 1972-. Mbrships: San Fran. Bay Area Chapt., Am. Recorder Soc., Rep. at Large, 1969-70; Co-Fndr. of Northern Calif. Chapt., Am. Orff-Schulwerk Assn., Rep. at Large, 1973-75. Address: 1615 Grant St., Berkeley, CA 94703, USA. 5.

COLLIER, Derek, b. 1929, London, UK. Concert Violinist; Professor of Violin. Educ: RAM; FRAM. m. Lila Git-Sen Wong, 1 s., 1 d. Career: Former Ldr., Bournemouth Symph. Orch.; Guest Ldr., RPO, NPO, LSP, Bournemouth Sinfonietta, Vic. Symph. Orch. (Can.); Soloist, Promenade Concerts, BBC & w. maj. Brit. orchs.; Concert tours of Con.; Engl. premieres of concertos by Boris Blacher, Dag Wiren & Rodrigo. Prof. of Violin, RAM. Comps: Num. works for violin & piano. Recital recordings for HMV, Pye & Decca. Hobby: Sport. Mgmt: Helen Jennings. Address: 9 Parkgate Cresc., Hadley Wood, Barnet, Herts., UK.

COLLINGS, Marcia Vivien Helen, b. 7 June 1940, Sydney, Aust. Music Teacher (Singing & Instrumental). Educ: Trained Primary Tchrs. Cert. (Vic.); Tas. Tchrs. Certs.; Music Tchrs. Cert. (Vic.). m. Rev. Ian Ernest Collings, 2 d., 1 s. Career: Var. TV & Radio apps.; Mbr., Melbourne Jr. Symph. Orch. (Playing flute & piccolo and as Libn.), 7 yrs.; Mbr., Launceston Orch., 1971-76; Mezzo Soprano leads, sev. stage musicals, Cond., Ch. Choirs, Pt. Melbourne, Moe, Launceston & Ararat; Cond., Moe Women's Choir & Moe Mixed Choir; Cond., var. schl. choirs; Cond., St. Stephen's Youth Choir, ISME Conference, Montreaux, 1976; Music & Art Tchr., Marian Coll., Ararat. Mbrships: Past Pres., Tas. Pvte. MTA; Past Pres., Tas. Schl. MTA; Mbr.; Programme Committee, Ararat Music Club; Musical Dir., Ararat Jr. Civic Choir & Ararat Musical Comedy Soc.; Committee Mbr., Ararat Competitions. Hons: Prizes, var. Eisteddfod perfs. & competitions w. children's singing groups & instrumental ensembles, woodwind solos & musical comedy solos. Hobbies: Craftwork, Needlework. Address: 277 Barkly St., Ararat, Vic. 3377, Aust.

COLLINS, Anne, b. 29 Aug. 1943, Meadowfield, Co. Durham, UK. Operatic & Concert Contralto. Educ: ARCM; LRAM. Debut: as Governess, The Queen of Spades, Sadler's Wells Opera, London Coliseum. Career: Mbr., Engl. Nat. Opera Co., 5 yrs.; sang at Covent Gdn., Engl. Opera Grp. at Aldeburgh in Albert Herring; lieder recitals for BBC radio; concerts w. major orchs. & choral socs. throughout UK; concerts in Belgium, France, Paris, Rome, Lisbon. Recordings: sang Erda in Rhinegold & Siegfried w. Engl. Nat. Opera under Goodall, EMI; Janácek's Glagolitic Mass, Decca; Monteverdi madrigals, Philips. Mbrships: Equity; ISM. Mgmt: Ibbs & Tillet. Address: Flat 10, 25 Queensgate Gdns., London SW7, UK.

COLLINS, Charles Frederick, b. 5 Jan. 1916, Newbury, UK. Professor of Music. Educ: RCM. m. Kathleen Anne Falconer, 1 s., 1 d. Career: Organist & Choirmaster, Dunedin Cathedral, NZ & var. parish chs., Organ Recitalist; Choral Cond.; Hd., Music Depts., var. London schls.; Examiner, 1956-, Prof. 1961-, London Coll. of Music. Contbr. to: Musical Times. Mbrships: ISM; Royal Coll. of Organists; London Assn. of Organists. Hobbies: Tennis; Travel; Reading. Address: 85 Grange Crescent, Chigwell, Essex, UK. 3.

COLLINS, Frances, b. London, UK. Piano Accompanist & Coach. Educ: Tobias Matthay Pianoforte Schl., ARCM, Accomp. m. George Cole. Career: Opera répétiteur, Zürich, Vienna, Stuttgart, Glyndebourne; Staff Coach, GSM, London; Mbr., Sheraton Piano Quartet. Mbr., ISM. Hobbies: Music; Walking; Travel. Address: 65 Gloucester Pl., London W1H 3PF, UK.

COLLINS, Richard Lee, b. 13 Oct. 1922, Louisville, Ky., USA. College Professor; Operatic Stage Director; Operatic Baritone. Educ: BA, Univ. of Louisville, Ky., 1944; MusB, Cinn. Conserv. of Music, Ohio, 1948; MA, Columbia Univ., 1953; MusD, Ind. Univ., 1974. m. (1) Marjorie Faith Collins., 1 s., d. (2) Diane Collins. Doubt: w. Punch Opera Grp., NYC, 1952. Career: over 40 maj. baritone roles w. opera cos. throughout the USA; Artistic Admnstr., State Opera Assn. of Fla., 1966-70; Dir. of Opera, Fla. State Univ., Tallahassee, 1965-70; Dir. of Opera & Prof. of Music, Millikin Univ., Decatur, Ill., 1970-76; Dir. of Opera, Memphis State Univ., 1976-78; Exec. Dir., Lowndes/Valdosta Arts Commission, 1978-. Publs: A Study of the Musical & Dramatic Treatment of Five Baritone Roles in Operas by Verdi, 1974. Mbrships: Pres., 1966-68, & served as VP & on Bd. Dirs., Nat. Opera Assn.; Nat. Assn. of Tchrs. of Singing. Recip., Evans Award, Cinn. Conserv. of Music, 1948. Hobbies: Numismatics & Tennis. Address: 407 Baytree Rd., PO Box 1966, Valdosta, GA 31601, USA.

COLLINS, Verne Edman, b. 9 Apr. 1935, Bowling Green, Ohio, USA. College Dean; Trombonist. Educ: BS in Educ., Bowling Green State Univ., 1957; MMus, Northwestern Univ., 1958; Eastman Schl. of Music, 1959; PhD (Ed D Music), Univ. of Mich., 1966. m. Charlotte A Collins., 1 s., 1 d. Career incls: Bass Trombonist, Toledo Symph. Orch., 1955-57, 1963-65; 1st Trombone & Soloist, Milwaukee Symph., 1957-58; apps. in Europe as Trombone Soloist, 1966, 60, & as Orchl. Cond., 1967, 68; Dir. of Bands, Shenandoah Conserv. of Music, Winchester, Va., 1958-63; Dean, ibid., 1965; Dean, Shenandoah Coll. & Conserv. of Music, 1972-. Comps. incl: Fantasy for Brass & Percussion (recorded). Publs: Books on educ. & music educ. Mbr., profl. assns. Address: 182 Hawthorne Drive, Winchester, VA 22601, USA.

COLLINS, Walter Stowe, b. 12 Jan. 1926, W Hartford, Conn., USA. Professor of Music. Educ: BA, Yale Univ., 1948; BMus, ibid., 1951; MA Univ. of Mich., 1953; PhD, ibid., 1960. m. Jane Katherine Reynolds, 1 s., 2 d. Career: US Army Air Corps, 1944-45; Master, Dir. of Choral Music, Hotchkiss Schl., 1948-51; Instructor in Music, Dir. of Choral Music, Auburn Univ., 1951-55; Teaching Fellow, Acting Dir., Men's Glee Club, Univ. of Mich., 1955-57; Asst. Prof. of Music, Dir. of Choral Music, Co-Fndr., Workshop in Choral Art, Univ. of Minn., 1958-60; Fndg. Chmn., Dept. of Music, Oakland Univ., 1960-66; Assoc. Prof., 1960-65, Prof. of Music, 1965-71, Dir. of Choral Music, 1960-65, Originator, Meadow Brook Schl. of Music, 1964-68, ibid.; Vis. Apps., Univ. of Mich., 1961, Univ. of the W Indies, Kingston, Jamaica, 1964, Prof. of Music, Assoc. Dean for Grad. Studies inc Music, Univ. of Colo., 1971-; Columnist, The Choral Jrnl., 1971-. Co-Ed., Thomas Weelkes, Collected Anthems, Musica Britannica, Vol. XXIII, 1966; Co-author, Choral Conducting - A Symposium, 1973. Contbr. to num. profl. jrnls. Mbr. & Off., num. profl. Orgs. Recip. var. Scholarships. Hobbies: Fly Fishing; Travel. Address: Coll. of Music, Univ. of Colo., Boulder, CO 80309, USA.

COLLINSON, Francis, b. 20 Jan. 1898, Edinburgh, Scotland, UK. Composer; Author; Senior Research Fellow. Educ: MusB, Edinburgh Univ., 1923; Studies under Sir Donald Tovey & Dr. T H Collinson. m. Elizabeth Grant, 1 d. Career: Musical Dir., London Theatres to C B Cochran & other mgmts; hon. Sr. Rsch. Fellow in Folk Music, Edinburgh Univ. Comps. incl: Rumpelstiltskin; Gaelic Suite for Strings; Engl., Scots & Gaelic Folk Songs arrs. Publs. incl: The Traditional & National Music of Scotland, 1966; The Bagpipe: The History of a Musical Instrument, 1975; Hebridean Folksongs, 1969 (Vols. 1 & 2; Vol. 3 in prep.). Contbr. to: Grove's Dictionary of Music & Musicians. Mbrships: Composers' Guild; Soc. of Authors. Recip. Italia Prize Award, 1950. Hobbies: Shooting; Fishing; Arboriculture. Address: The Ley; Innerleithen, Peeblesshire, UK. 3.

COLLINSON, Julian Carson, b. 27 Sept. 1944, Huyton, Lancs., UK. Musician (Clarinet; Piano); Teacher; Conductor. Educ: manchester Coll. Educ.; Liverpool Matthay Schl. Music; ARCM; LTCL. m. Elizabeth Anne Lawton. Career: Formerly, Cond., Liverpool Mount St. Orch.; Currently, Hd., Music, Comprehensive Schl.; Clarinet specialist, Liverpool Educ. Comm.; Cond., Liverpool Schls. Concert Band; Examiner, music colls.; Profl. orch. engagements. Mbrships: Musicians Union; ISM; Nat. Assn. Schlmasters. Hobbies: Studying Educ.; Psort; League Cricketer. Address: 141 Roby Rd., Huyton, Liverpool L14 3NU, UK.

COLLIS, Peter Evan, b. 14 Oct. 1947, Manchester, UK. Conductor; Lecturer. Educ: Cert., Bretton Hall Coll. of Educ.; BEd, Leeds Univ.; Adv. Dip. in Educ., MA, London Univ.; LTCL. Career: Fndr., Bretton Baroque Ensemble, Beech Consort; Mbr.; Univ. of Salford Contemp. Music Ensemble; currently Dir, Cockpit

Voices, Thames-side Singers, Mary Ward Chmbr. Choir; Mbr., Cockpit Ensemble; Musical Dir., Cockpit Youth Theatre; Managing Ed., Sing for Pleasure. Publs. Comps: Sound Map 1 (recorded); var. arrs. Contbr. to: Set to Music; Rondo. Mbrships: Vice Chmn., Sing for Pleasure; Nat. Exec., Schls. Music Assn. Hons: FRSA. Hobbies: Sport; Travel. Address: 1& Barham Close, Wembley, Middx., UK. 4.

COLLOT, Serge, b. 27 Dec. 1923, Paris, France. Professor; Viola Player. Educ: Conserv. Nat. Supérieur de paris; Comp. w. Arthur Honegger. m. Norbert Micheline, 2 c. Career: Prof. of Viola, Conserv. Nat. Supérieur de Paris; Mbr., Quatuor Parrenin, 1944-57; mbr., Quator Radio, 1957-60; mbr., Trio à Cordes Français, 1960-; Soloist at Pierre Boulez's Domaine Musical, 1953-70. Recordings: Quartets, Trios, Contemporary music. Hons: 1st prize for viola, Conserv., Paris, 1944; 1st Prize, chmbr. music, ibid., 1948. Mgmt: Mariedi Anders, San Francisco, USA. Address: Tour Gambetta, 2/313 Square H Regnault, 92400 Courbevoie, France.

COLQUHOUN, Neil, b. 29 Nov. 1929, Palmerston North, New Zealand. Music Educator; Teacher; Composer; Folksinger; Classical Guitarist; Musical Director. Educ: Music & Art, Christchurch Tchrs. Trng. Coll.; Canterbury Univ. Coll.; Auckland Univ. m. Barbie Colquhoun, 2 s., 1 d. Debut: Comp., Christchurch Trng. Coll. Choral Soc., 1950; Folksinger, Auckland Festival, 1957. Career incls: Hd. of Music Dept., Edgewater Coll., Pakuranga, Auckland; Music Direction & Comp: NZBC radio documentaries & folkmusic prog. series. Comps. incl: Lullabies; Men at Work. Num. recordings. Publs. incl: Soundscape Songbook, 1976. Contbr. to profl. mags. Mbrships. incl: Fndn. Pres., NZ Folklore Soc., Auckland. Hobbies: Painting; Collecting Native Plants & Pottery; Playing Jazz Piano; NZ Scenery & Hist. Address: 45 Chelmsford Ave., Auckland 5, New Zealand.

COLSON, Andrée, b. 5 Sept. 1924, Paris, France. Violinist. Educ: Nat. Higher Conserv. of Music, Paris; Chigiana Acad., Siena, Italy. m. Charles Meyer, 1 s., 1 d. Career: Fndr. & 1st Violin, Andrée Colson Instrumental Ensemble; Chmbr. music concerts, France & abroad; Num. int. tours; TV & radio apps. Recordings: Vernou Disques, France. Mbrships: Vernour Record Soc. Georges Colson Recording Ctr.; Vernou Int. Musical Days (fest. founded, 1975). Hon: Kt., Arts & Letters. Hobbies: Hunting; Riding; Printing. Address: Domaine de Vernou, BP 22, 37103 Langeais, France. 27.

COLSON, William Wilder, b. 17 July 1945, Kansas City, Mo., USA. Musician (Cello, Piano). Educ: BMus, Oberlin Coll. Conserv. of Music, Ohio, 1967; MMus, 1968, D Musical Arts, 1975, Univ. of Ill., Urbana. Comps incl: 8 Pieces for Flute, 1964; 6 Variations & a Fugue, 1966; My Last Duchess, 1966; 3 Blake Songs, 1967; Sinfonia Concertante, 1968; Sonata for Violin, 1968; The Wreath (song cycle), 1969; Serenade for Winds, 1970; Sonata for Violoncello & Piano, 1970; Concerto for Violoncello & Orch., 1974. Mbrships. incl: Pi Kappa Lambda; Ft. Worth Symph. Orch. Hons: 1st Prize & Devora Nadworny Award, Nat. Young Comps. Comp. Contest, Nat. Fedn. Music Clubs, 1966; Concerto Competition, Univ. of Ill., 1968. Address: 554 S Summit 418, Ft. Worth, TX 76104, USA.

COLUMBRO, Mary Electa, b. 16 Mar. 1934, Aurora, Ohio, USA. Pianist; Organist; Musicologist. Educ: BA, Notre Dame Coll., 1956; MA, Cath. Univ. of Am., 1966; PhD, Case Western Reserve Univ., 1974; studed piano w. Jean Meagher Miller, John B Paul, Andrius Kuprevicius. Publs: Ostinato Technique in the Franco-Flemish Motel, 1480-ca. 1562, 1975. Contbr. to: Musart; Marytoday; Studies in Medieval Culture; Music & Man; A Jrnl. of Interdisciplinary Studies. Mbrships: Nat. Cath. Music Educators Assn.; Nat. Chmn., Music Educ. Div., ibid.; Am. Musicol. Soc.; Am. Recorder Soc. hons: Kulas Fndn. Grant, 1970; Ranney Fndn. Scholarship, 1973-74; Newberry Lib. Rsch. Fellowship, 1973. Hobbies: Reading; Hiking; Collecting Medieval Manuscripts. Address: 4545 Coll. Rd., Cleveland, OH 44121, USA. 5, 27.

COLVILLE, Robin, b. 17 Sept. 1945, Glasgow, Scotland. Pianist. Educ: RSAM; w. Miles Coverdale & Lawrence Glover; Salzburg Mozaeteum w. Hans Lewygraf & Erika Frieser; Accademia Musicale Chigiana, Siena; DRSAM; LRAM; ARCM; Dip.; Salzburg Mozarteum. Career: concertos (esp. Mozart); Soloist & Accomp.; Piano duets & chmbr. music in Austria, Germany & UK inclng. BBC-TV, Austrian & Bavarian Radio; Piano Tchr., Horizons & Culture, Salzburg, 1975; Guest Prof., Orff Inst., Salzburg, 1976. Mbrships: ISM. Hons. incl: Austrian Govt. Schlrship. to Salzburg Mozarteum, 1972; Scottish Arts Coun. Bursary, 1974; ISM Young Artists Concert, 1976; Trust Award, 1973. Hobbies: Skiing; Travel; Walking; Cooking. Address: 54 Hornton St., London W8, UK.

COLWELL, Richard, b. 27 May 1930, Sioux Falls, SD, USA. Teacher. Educ: BFA, MM, Univ. of SD; EdD, Univ. of Ill. m. Ruth

Crockett, 1 s., 2 d. Career: Tchr., pub. schls., SD & Mont., E Mont. Coll., Univ. of Ill. Publs: The Teaching of Instrumental Music, 1969; Music Achievement Tests 1, 2, 3, 4, 1967-70; The Evaluation of Music Teaching & Learning, 1970; Concepts for a Musical Foundation, 1974; Silver Burdett Competency Tests 1-6, 1979. Contbr. to profl. jrnls. Mbrships: AERA; NCME; MENC; ISME; IMEA; PDK. Address: 406 W Michingan, Urbana, IL 61801, USA.

COMAN, Nicolae, b. 23 Feb. 1936, Bucharest, Romania. Composer; Professor of Harmony. Educ: Acad. of Music Ciprian Porumbescu, Bucharest; Dip. for musical comp., 1959. m. Lavinia Coman Tomulescu. Career: Scientific Rschr., Ethnographical Inst. of Romanian Acad., 1960-63; Prof. of Harmony, Acad. of Music Ciprian Proumbescu, 1963-; Over 50 musical progs.; TV & radio. Comps: (most recorded) Lyric Cantata, The Source of the Peace; One Piano concert w. orch.; 20 pieces for piano; 2 piano sonatas; 44 lieder for voice & piano (piano/flute, piano/clarinet, string quartet); 12 songs, etc. Contbr. to: România Literara; Revista Muzica; Contemporanul. Mbr., Romanian Comps. Union. Hons: Prize of the Romanian Comps. Union, 1969; Medal, 30 yrs. from liberation of Romania, 1974. Hobbies: Poetry; Chess. Address: Str. Delea Veche nr. 45, Sector 3, 73119 Bucharest, Romania.

COMBS, Sheila G, b. 11 Sept. 1950, Ft. Smith, Ark., USA. Organist; Cellist; Director of Choirs. Educ: BMusEd, John Brown Univ., 1968-72; MMus, E Texas State Univ., 1972-74. Career: Cellist, Ft. Smith Symph.; Dir. of Ch. Music & Organist; Dir. of Choirs. Mbrships: Fellowship of United Methodist Musicians; Am. Guild of English Handbell Ringers; Am. Guild of Organists; Mu Phi Epsilon; Am. Fedn. of Music Clubs. Hons: Presidential Scholarship, John Brown Univ., 1968-72; Assistantship in Music, E Texas State Univ., 1972-74. Hobbies: Swimming; Golf. Address: 2005 South 'Y' St., Ft. Smith, AR 72901, USA.

COMES, Liviu, b. 13 Dec. 1918, Serel-Transilvanny, Romania. Composer; Professor. Educ: Dips., Music Acad. Cluj, Romania. m. Valeria Comes, 2 d. Debut: 1950. Career: Prof., Ciprian Porumbescu Music Acad., Bucarest. Comps: Sonatas for piano, violin & piano, clarinet & piano; Wind Quintet; orchl. owks; Lieder; Choral works. Comps. recorded: Sonata for violin & piano; Ballad for mixed chorus. Publs: Palestrina's Melody, 1971, Italian transl., 1975. Recip. Romanian Acad. Prize, 1974. Address: Str. Olimpului 3, Sect. 5, Bucharest, Romania.

COMFORT, Abraham, b. 29 April 1931, Küstendil, Bulgaria. Violinist. Educ: Acad. of Tel-Aviv, Israel; studied w. Lorand Fenyves, O Partos & Michael Taube. m. Zipora Zwick, 1 s., 2 d. Debut: Küstendil, Bulgaria. Career: Ldr., Haifa Symph. Orch., 1954-56; Ldr. & Soloist, Israeli Chambr. Orch., touring Europe, USA, Latin Am. & appng. on TV & radio, 1956-62; currently ldr., Winterthur Symph. Orch. & Winterthur Str. Quartet. Recordings incl: Bernstein, Serenade for violin & strgs; Walton, Violin Concerto; Bartok, Violin Concerto No. 2. Hons: 1st prize, Israel-USA Fndn. Competition, Tel-Aviv, 1956. Hobbies: Painting; Chess; Ping-Pong; Jogging. Address: Fuchshalde 6, 8408 Winterthur, Switz.

COMINGS, George Francis, b. 12 May 1931, Oxford, NY, USA. Choral Director; Tenor Soloist; Clinician; Adjudicator; Guest Choral Conductor. Educ: BS, Music Educ., MS, Music Educ., SUNY, Potsdam, NY; Studied w. Julius Herford, Robert Shaw, Lara Hoggard, Brock McElheran, Nadia Boulanger, Aaron Copland, Stanley Chappel, Paul Christiansen in workshops & Summer Sems. m. Dorothy Jane Cummings, 2 s. Composed sev. Choral Arrs. Contbr. to: Schl. Music News (NYSSMA monthly); Choral Jrnl. (ACDA monthly). Mbrships: Life Mbr., MENC, Schl. Music Assn., NY, Am. Choral Dirs. Assn.; State Pres., NY State Chapt., ACDA, 1970-72; Rotary Int. Hons: Mbr., Dirs. Chorus, Kansas City, 1972; Mbr., Dirs. Chorus, Atlantic City (MENC), 1968; Guest Cond., County & State Choruses, 1969-; Paul Harris Fellow. Home Building (Built own home); Collecting 16th Century instruments. Address: 8841 Angel Rd., Greenfield Centre, NY 12833, USA.

COMISEL, Emilia, b. 28 Feb. 1913, Ploiesti, România. Professor; Ethnomusicologist. Educ: Music Acad. of Bucharest. div., 1 d. Career: Ethnomusicologist, 1936-; Prof., Music Acad. of Bucharest; Radio & TV Conferences; Scientific Rschr., Folklore Archives Dir. by Constantin Brailoiu, 1936-49, Folklore Institute, 1949-63, South-East European Institute, 1964-76. Recordings: approx. 5000 pieces (vocal & instrumental). Publs. incl: The Rumanian popular Ballada, in Studia memoriae Belae Bartók Sacra, 1956, '57, '59; La ballade populaire roumaine, 1959; La musique de la ballade roumaine, 1964; Le folklore calendaire et les catégories d'âge, 1973; Anthologies sonores - La coutume de d'hiver, 1974. Contbr. to profl. publs. Mbrships: Comps. Union of Romania; Int. Folk Music Coun.; Int. Musicol. Soc., Basel; Organisation Coun. of

Balkan Fest. of Ohrid, Yugoslavia; Société française d'anthropologie musicale, etc. Hons: Ordinul Muncii (activity decoration), 1965; Meritul cultural, 1969. Address: Aleia Baraj Bicaz 6, Bl. M 26, ap. 53, 774661 Bucharest, România.

COMISSIONA, Sergiu, b. 16 June 1928, Bucharest, Romania. Conductor. Educ: Conserv. of Romania, Bucharest. m. Robinne Comissiona. Career: Dir., Romanian State Ensemble, 1948-55; Prin. Cond., Romanian State Opera, 1955-58; Cond., Haifa Symph. Orch. & Israeli Chamber Orch., 1958-66; Artistic Ldr., Goteborg Symph. Orch., 1966-72; Musical Dir., Balt. Symph. Orch., USA, 1969-; Guest Cond., major orchs., USA & Europe; Music Advsr. Am. Symph. Orch., 1978-; Music Dir. Chautaugua Symph. Summer Fest., 1976-. Recordings: recordings w. Haifa Symph. Orch., Stockholm Phil., Suisse Romande, LSO, Balt. Symph. Orch. Hons. incl: Besançon Int. Competition, 1955; Romanian Order of Merit, 1956; humanistic sci. degree, Loyola Coll. Balt., USA; Hon. MusD, Peabody Conserv. of Music, 1972; D Fine Arts, W Maryland Coll., 1977. Hobbies: Mime; Cinema. Address: 39 Stanbury Ct., 99 Haverstock Hill, London NW3, UK.

CONANT, Isabel Pope, b. 19 Oct. 1901, Evanston, Ill., USA. Musicologist. Educ: AB, MA; PhD. m. Kenneth J Conant. Publs: Ed. of Literary Texts in Harmonica Musices Odhecaton, 1942; El Villancico Polifónico in Cancionero de Upsala, 1944; Music in Our Time: Trends Since the Romantic Era, 1946 (transl.); A Neapolitan Repertory of Sacred and secular Music, ca. 1480; The Manuscript Montecassino 871 (w. Masakata Kanazawa). Contbr. to profl. jrnls. Mbrships: Am. Musicol. Soc.; Int. Musicol. Soc.; Renaissance Soc. of Am.; Mediaeval Acads. of Am. Hobby: Travel. Address: 274 Grove St., Wellesley, MA 02181, USA.

CONANT, Robert (Scott), b. 6 Jan. 1928, Passaic, NJ, USA. Harpsichordist; Conductor; University Professor. Educ: BA, Yale Univ., 1949; MusM, Schl. of Music, ibid., 1956. m. Nancy Lydia Jackson, 1 d., 1 s. Debut: Town Hall, NYC, 1953. Career: Annual tours of US & Europe; Apps. w. NY Chmbr. Music Circle, Krainis Trio, Deller Trio, Fiori Musicali, etc.; Assoc. prof., 1967-71, Prof., 1971-, Chgo. Musical Coll. of Roosevelt Univ.; Dir., Fest. of Baroque Music, Greenfield Center, NY. Recordings incl: Elliott Carter Sonata. Mbr. music socs. Publs: Twentieth-Century Harpsichord Music: a Classical Catalog (w. Frances Bedford), 1974. Contbr. to profl. jrnls. Recip., Roosevelt Univ. Fellowship, 1971. Hobby: Photography. Address: 154 Maple Ave., Wilmette, IL 60091, USA. 8.

CONATI, Marcello, b. 26 Apr. 1938, Milan, Italy. Opera Conductor. Educ: Dip. in piano, comp. and cond. m. Licia Vallon. Career: Sn. Asst. Orchl. Dir., Zürich Opera House, 1961-71; Instructor in Stage Art, Conserv. of Piacenza, 1971-75, Conserv. Parma, 1975-; Permanent staff, isnt. of Verdi Studies, 1971-. Publs: Canti Popolari della Val d/Enza de della Val Cedra. Contbr. to: L'Opera; Musica Università; Discoteca; Gazzetta di Parma; L'Arena; La Musica a Verona, 1976; Il melodrama italiano dell' Ottocento, 1977; Rivista Italiana di Musicologia, etc. Mbrships: Grand Opera, Symphonic & Folklore Sects.; Gran Premio del Disco jury, 1969-; Fndr. Mbr. Italian Soc. of Ethnomusicol., 1974-. Hobbies: Archaeology; Folk Costume & Customs. Address: borgo Riccio de Parma 50, 43100 Parma, Italy.

CONDON, Denis Francis, b. 25 Sept. 1933, Hamilton, NSW, Aust. Lecturer. Educ: Dip. T Mus, NSW Conserv. of Music, 1954. Career: Music master, Fort St. Boys High Schl., 1959-70; Commonwealth Exchange tchr. in UK, 1962; lectr. in music, Kuring-gai Coll. of Advanced Educ., 1971-72; lectr. in music, Sydney Tchrs. Coll., 1973-; num. broadcasts; lecture-recitals at Adelaide Fest. of Arts, 1976, & Sydney Int. Piano competition, 1977; collector & possessor of large number of electric reproducing pianos, piano rolls & musical automata. Mbrships: ASME; Automatic Instrument Collectors Assn. (US); Player Piano Group (UK). Address: 47 Station St., Newtown, NSW 2042, Aust.

CONE, Edward T(oner), b. 4 May 1917, Greensboro, NC, USA. Composer; Pianist; Professor; Writer. Educ: AB, Princeton Univ., 1939; MFA, ibid., 1942. Career: Asst. Prof., Princeton Univ., 1947-52; Assoc. Prof., ibid., 1952-60; Prof., 1960-. Compositions: Excursions (for unaccompanied chorus), 1955; Silent Noon (for soprano), 1964; num. unpubld. works. Publs: Musical Form & Musical Performance, 1968; Ed., Berlioz, Fantastic Symph., 1971; Co-Ed., Perspectives on Schoenberg & Stravinsky, 1968, Perspectives on American Composers, 1971, Perspectives on Contemporary Music Theory, 1972; The Composer's Voice, 1974; Co-Ed., Perspectives of New Music, 1966-68; Advsry. Ed., ibid., 1968-72; Co-Ed., Perspectives on Notaion & Performance, 1975. Contbr. to: Perspectives of New Music; Musical

Quarterly; Am. Scholar. Recip., Guggenheim. Fellowship in Musical Comp., 1947-48; ASCAP-Deems Taylor Award, 1975. Hobbies: Bird-Watching; Travel. Address: 18 College Rd., W, Princeton, NJ, USA. 2.

CONNAH, Geoffrey Hall, b. 9 Aug. 1924, St. Helens, Lancs., UK. Pianist; Piano Teacher. Educ: Liverpool Univ.; Liverpool Matthay Schl. of Music; RAM, 1948-53; LRAM (performer's). Career: Accompanist to solo instrumentalists & in chmbr. ensembles; var. appearances at Wigmore Hall, London; BBC broadcasts w. solo instrumentalists. Mbrships: Solo & accompanist Sects.; ISM. Recip. Sub-Prof.'s Medal, RAM, 1952. Hobby: Collector. Address: 35A The Ave., Beckenham, Kent, BR3 2EE, UK.

CONNER, William James, b. 21 June 1951, Exeter, NH, USA. Journalist; Musicologist; Harpsichordist; Arts Administrator. Educ: Phillips Exeter Acad., 1969; BA, Grinnell Coll., 1973; Grad. work in musicol., Univ. of London, King's Coll., UK. Admnin. Asst. to Dir., Boston Univ. Schl. of Music. Publs: Ed. & Contb., Grove's Dictionary of Music & Musicians, 6th Ed.; Music & the World of Islam, Musical Times, 1976. Contbr. to num. profl. mags; Book review in Musical Times. Mbr. num. musicol. socs. Hobbies: Cooling; Architecture; Travel. Address: Boston Univ. Schl. of Music, 855 Comm. Ave., Boston, MA 02129, USA.

CONNOLLY, Justin Riveagh, b. 11 Aug. 1933, London, UK. Composer. Educ: ARCM; Yale Univ., Harkness Int. Fellowship, 1963-65. Career: Staff, RCM. London, 1967-. Compositions: (publd.) The Marriage of Heaven & Hell, fragments from William Blake, for solo voices, choir & orch.; Antiphonies (36 players); Cinquepaces (brass quintet); Obligati I, II, III; Poems of Wallace Stevens, I, II, III, (1966-70) for solo voice & chamber grp.; num. other works incl. electronic music & works for var. chamber grps. (recorded) Cinquepacae, brass quintet; Verses For 8 Voices; Triad III; Poems of Wallace Stevens I. Recip. Alfred Clements Memorial Prize, 1967. Address: c/o RCM, Prince Consort Rd., London SW7, UK. 3.

CONNOLLY, Martha Nixon Taugher, b. 7 Feb. 1939, Mt. Vernon, Ohio, USA. Mezzo-Soprano; Teacher & Performer of Voice & Piano. Educ: BMus, Univ. Mich.; MMus, Caht. Univ. Am. m. Joseph H Connolly (separated), 1 s. Debut: Piano, Philharmonia Hall, Buffalo, NY; Voice, Textile Mus., Wash., DC, 1971. Career: Lectr., voice, class voice, piano, Cath. Univ. Am., 1970-73; Lectr., voice, piano, theory, Mt. Vernon Coll., Wash., DC, 1973-; Vis. Tchr. of Voice, Univ. of Va., 1978-; Pers. in Opera, Oratorio & recitals, Wash.; Perfs. of modern music. Mbr. & Off., profl. orgs. Recip., Tchng. Asstship., Cath. Univ. Am., 1970-73. Address: 1512 Scandia Circle, Reston, VA 22090, USA. 27, 30.

CONNORS, Ann-Marie, b. 20 July 1951, Birmingha, UK. Soprano Singer. Educ: Scholarship to RCM, 1970-74; ARCM. Career: Concerts in UK incl. Royal Fest. Hall, Queen Elizabeth Hall, Purcell Room, Royal Albert Hall & Wigmore Hall, London, Brighton, Harrogate, Leeds & w. Hallé Orch., London Mozart Players & Royal Choral Soc.; Apps. abroad incl. Salzburg, Austria, Germany, France, Belgium, Denmakr, Sweden, Finland & Iceland. Recordings: in Schubert's Mass in G & as Crobylle in Thaïs. Hons: Mozart Memorial Prize (1st), 1973; Tagore Gold Medal, 1974; 1st Prize, Int. Mozart Competition, Salzburg, 1975. Hobbies: Reading; Walking; Swimming. Mgmt: Ingpen & Williams, London. Address: 53 Schubert Rd., Putney, London SW15 2QT, UK.

CONOMOS, Dimitri Emmanuel, b. 26 Sept. 1947, Sydney, Aust. Professor of Music History. Educ: BA, MA (Sydney); DPhil. (Oxon). m. Danae Comino. Career: Rsch. Fellow, Inst. of Patristic Studies, Thessaloniki, Greece; Vis. Fellow, Harvard Univ., Dumbarton Oaks Center for Byzantine Studies; Prof., Univ. of BC, Vancouver, Can. Publs: Byzantine Trisagia and Cheroubika of the 14th & 15th Centuries, 1974; Ed., Studies in Eastern Chant, 1979-. Contbr. to: Jrnl. of Am. Musicol. Soc.; Proceedings of Int. Musicol. Soc.; Grove's Dict., 6th Ed.; Proceeding of Int. Byzantine Studies Congresses; Studies in Music; Studies in Eastern Chant; Cantate Domino. Mbrships: Am. Musicol. Soc.; Byzantine Studies Assn. Address: 1111 Burnaby St., Vancouver, BC, Can.

CONSTABLE, John Robert, b. 5 Oct. 1934, Sunbury-on-Thames, Middx., UK. Piano Accompanist & Harpsichordist. Educ: studied w. Harold Craxton, RAM; LRAM; ARAM. m. Katharine Ingham, 2 d. Career: Repetiteur, Royal Opera House, Covent Gdn., 1960-; Prin. Keyboard Player, London Sinfonietta, since its formation. Many recordings w. London Sinfonietta, playing harpsichord continuo for operas & as accomp. on recital records. Mbrships: ISM; Musicians Union. Hobbies: Travel; Watching cricket. Address: 13 Denbigh Terr., London W11, UK. 3.

CONSTANT, Marius, b. 7 Feb. 1925, Bucharest, Roumania. Composer; Conductor. Educ: Bucharest Conser. of Music; Nat. Conserv. of Music, Paris, France. m. Sonia Millan, 1 s. Career: Musical Dir., French Radio, 1953, 1963-67; Musical Dir., Roland Petit ballet, 1956-63; & Paris Opera Ballet; Cond., Ars Nova Ensemble. Compositions: ballets - Haut-Voltage, 1956; Contrepointe, 1958; Cyrano de Bergerac, 1959; Concertino pour 3, 1961; Eloge de la Folie, 1966; Le Paradis Perdu; Music for Marcel Marceau's Candide, 1971; var. symphonic works inclng. Turner, 1961. Num. works recorded. Hons: 1st Prize for Composition, Paris. Conserv.; Chevalier, Legion of Hon.; Prix Italia, 1952; Grand Prix du Disque, 1956; Nat. Grand Prix of Music, 1968. Address: 18 rue des Fosses-St.-Jaceues, 75005, Paris, France.

CONSTANTIN, Rudolf, b. 16 Feb. 1935, Paris, France. Opera Singer (Baritone). Educ: Accademia di Canto und Conserv., Zürich. Debut: Aachen, Germany. Career: oper houses, Frankfurt, Berlin, Munich, Cologne, Stuttgart, Vienna, London, Paris; TV, Un Ballo in Maschera (ZDF); Num. radio apps.; Over 50 roles inclng. Scarpia, Rigoletto, Jago, Macbeth, Mandryka, Barak, Holländer. Mbrships: Hon., Rencontre Wagneriennes, Bordeaux; Amici di Verdi, Busseto, Italy. Hons: Award, Frankfurter Patronatsverein. Mgmt: Heli Teske, Waidmannstr. 276 Frankfurt, German Fed. Repub. Address: c/o Mgmt.

CONSTANTINESCU, Dan, b. 10 June 1931, Bucharest, Romania. Composer. Educ: Comp.'s Dip., Bucharest Conserv. of Music. Debut: Jassy Phil., 1957. Lectr. in Harmony & Comp., Bucharest Conserv. Comps. incl: Divertissement for string orch.; Ballad for orch.; Chmbr. Symph.; Symph. Consertante; Concerto for piano & string orch.; Concerto for 2 pianos & small orch.; 4 Sonatas; Trio for violin, clarinet, piano & percussion; 3 Quartets. Recordings: Piano part in var. works. Mbr. Romanian Comps. Union. Recp. Georges Enesco Prize, Romanian Acad., 1968. Hobbies: Ancient hist.; Archaeol. Address: Strada Corneliu Botez 3, Bucharest 9, Romania.

CONSTANTINESCU, Mihai, b. 22 Aug. 1926, Chisiniau, USSR. Violinist; Professor. Educ: Dip., Conserv. of Music, Bucharest. m. Emilia Constantinescu, 1 c. Career: Soloist, George Enescu Phil., Bucharest; Radio & TV apps.; Tours, USSR, Czech., Korea, China, German Dem. Repub., Vietnam, Poland, Bulgaria, France, Belgium, Hungary, Yugoslavia, German Fed. Repub., Italy, Cuba, Luxembourg, Spain, S Am.; Prof., High Schl. of Music Ciprian Porumbescu, Bucharest. Recordings: Works by Mozart, Beethoven, Pergolesi, Sabin Dragoi, Liviu Comes, Wilhelm Berger. Publs: 3 vols. of Poetry. Contbr. to: Musica; Romania Literara; Familia; Toris; Atheneum, etc. Mbr. of Literary Circle, George Calinescu (affiliate circle of Roumanian Acad.) Hons: 2nd Prize, Int. Concours of Weimar, 1942; Emerit-Artist. Hobbies: Poetry; Literature; Theatre; Plastic Arts; Astronomy; Dogs. Address: Sos. Giurgiului 96-102 BL.H1, Bucharest, Romania.

CONSTANTINIDES, Dinos (Constantine Demetrios), b. 10 May 1929, Ioannina, Greece. Composer; Violinist; Educator. Educ: dip., violin, Greek Conserv., 1949-50; dip., theory, ibid., 1956-57; dip., violin, Juillard Schl. of Music, 1958-60; MMus (Violin), Mich. State Univ., 1965-68; PhD, ibid. var. summer courses. m. Judith Hursh, 1 s., 1 d. Prof. of violin & comp., Louisiana State Univ., 1966-; Chmn., Louisiana State Univ. Fest. of Contemporary Music; co-fndr. & dir. of New Times; ldr., Baton Rouge Symph. Comps. incl: Diakos Suite, 1961; Symph. No. 1, 1967; Sonata for violin & piano, 1970; Antigone (music drama), 1973; Dedications for orchs., 1974; Fugue for Two Violins (1 act opera), 1975; Antitheses, 1977; 8 Miniatures for Tuba Quartet, 1978; Str. Quartet No. 2, 1979. Contbr. to: Louisiana Jrnl.; Monographs on Higher Educ. mbr. num. profl. orgs. num. hons. incl: 4 ASCAP awards for comp., 1976-80; fellowships, grants, commissions. Hobbies: old Films; Stamps; Wine. Address: 947 Daventry Dr., Baton Rouge, LA 70808, USA. 1, 2, 7.

CONTRERAS, Frank Rodriguez, b. 19 Dec. 1942, Santa Rita, NM, USA. Assistant Professor of Music; Organist. Educ: BMus, Millikin Univ., 1965; MMus, E Carolina Univ., 1966; Artist Dip., Am. Coll. Musicians (NGPT), 1966; DMA, W Va. Univ., 1977. Career: Perfs. throughout USA; UK tour as organist for Ch. of the Nativity, 1978; Soloist, Conven. Nat. Fedn. Music Clubs, 1969; Soloist, Conven., W Va. Music Tchrs. Assn., 1974; Concerto perfs. w. Pitts. Symph. Orch.; Asst. Prof. of Music (Piano & Theory), Univ. of Ala., Huntsville; Organist, Ch. of the Nativity, Huntsville, Adjudicator, Clinician & Accomp. Mbr., profl. orgs. Hons. incl: 1st, Comps. Competition, E Carolina Univ., 1966; Anne M Gannett Award, Nat. Fedn. Music Club, 1970. Hobbies incl: Swimming. Address: Music Dept., Univ. of Ala., Huntsville, AL 35807, USA.

CONYERS, David, b. 24 Aug. 1945, Bradford, UK. Tenor Singer. Educ: pvte. study of singing & piano, w. Prof. Joseph Hislop

m. Valerie Patricia, 1 d. Career: mbr., Scottish Opera chorus, 1973-75; freelance concert & oratorio singer, 1975-. Mbrships: Equity; ISM. Hobbies: Walking; Gardening. Address: 71 Pullan Ave., Eccleshill, Bradford, W Yorks. BD2 3RP, UK.

CONYNGHAM, Barry Ernest, b. 27 Aug. 1944, Sydney, Aust. Composer; Lecturer. Educ: BA (Sydney); MA; Univ. Medal; Comp. studies Europe, USA & w. Toru Takemitsu, Japan. m. Deborah, 1 s. Career: Comps. perfd. in Europe & Aust.; Lectr. in Comp., Music Dept. of Univ. of Melbourne, 1976-. Comps. incl: Dialogue for String Trio; Farben (choral), recorded; Crisis - Thoughts in a City, for two string orchs. & percussion (recorded); Three, for 2 groups of percussion & string quartet (recorded); Horizon; Water ... Footsteps ... Time (recorded); Ice Carving, for amplified violin & 4 string orchs. (recorded); Edward John Eyre, music theatre work (recorded); Sky; Without Gesture; Sky; Ned Mark II, Opera to text by Alan Seymour; The Apology of Bony Anderson, music theatre work to text of Murray Copland. Recordings: Snowflake; Through Clouds; To Be Alone. Hons. incl: Churchill Fellowship, 1970; Harkness Fellowship, 1972; Aust. Music Bd. Fellowship, 1975. Hobbies: Tennis; Drinking. Address: Fac. of Music, Univ. of Melbourne, Parkville, Vic. 3052, Aust.

CONZELMANN, Curt, b. 29 Oct. 1919, Basel, Switz. Violinist; Director of Music Acad. Educ: Music. Schl., Basel, TD 1942; Conserv. Basel, dip. soloist, 1944; Conserv. Luzern. m. Christa Roedel, 2 s. Career: Cond. Concert Hall Zürich; Cond. Festival Orch., Luzern; Mbr. Concert Hall Quartet, Zürich; Dir., Music. Acad. Olten. Recordings: Str. Quartets of great Opera Masters, Bonitzetti, Humperdinck, Gounod. Mbrships: Swiss Soc. for Musicians; Swiss Music Assn.; Collegium Musicum Zürich. Contbr. to: Program Concert Hall, Zürich. Hobbies: Riding; Sailing; Skiing. Address: Billrothstr. 14, CH 8008 Zürich, Switz.

COOK, Brian (Robert) Rayner, b. 17 May 1945, London, UK. Singer (Baritone). Educ: BA, Univ. of Bristol, 1966; ARCM, 1968. m. Angela Mary Romney, 1 s. Career: profl. since 1967; Baritone soloist, Henry Wood Centenary Concert, Royal Albert Hall, 1969; recital debut, Wigmore Hall, London, 1970; studio recital debut, BBC radio, 1970; profl. solo debut BBC TV, 1970; Foreign radio debut, 1972; Foreign TV debut, 1974; Henry Wood Proms debut, 1973; London operatic debut, Sadlers Wells, 1974. Recordings incl: Fauré Requiem; Dellius Fennimore & Gerdia (Baritone lead); Elgar's Caractacus; Walton's Gloria; Schütz's Seven Last Words from the Cross; Songs of Edward Elgar. Mbr., ISM. Recip., Kathleen Ferier Mem. Scholarship, 1969. Hobbies incl: DIY; 78 rpm Recordings; Laurel & Hardy Films; Playing Piano & Organ. Mgmt: Ibbs & Tillett, 450-52 Edware Rd., London W21EG. Address: 53 Friars Ave., London, N20 OXG, UK.

COOK, Deborah, b. 6 July 1938, Phila., Pa., USA. Opera Singer (Coloratura Soprano). Educ: pvte. study of piano & violin; studied voice w. Irene Williams, Phila. m. Dr. Robert L Kashoff (dec.), 1 s. Debut: Phila., Pa. Career: num. apps. w. leading cos. & w. leading orchs., Germany, Italy, Belgium, UK, USA, etc.; Rachel in world première of We Come to the River, Covent Gdn., 1976; currently w. Bayerische Staatsoper, Munich. Mbrships: AGMA; Brit. Actors' Equity Assn. Recip. WGN, Chgo.; Mona Van Mem. Award. Hobbies: Cooking; Sewing. Address: c/o Bayerische Staatsoper, Munich, German Fed. Repub.

COOK, Jean, b. Phoenix, Ariz., USA. Lyric Soprano. Educ: Music Acad. of the West; Univ. of S Calif.; UCLA; Pvte. studies w. William Eddy, Rudolf Spira. Debut: Pamina (Zauberflöte) Opernhaus Zürich, 1960. Carer: Has sung w. major Opera Cos. in Belgium, France, German Fed. Repub., Netherlands, Italy, Spain, Switz., USA; Num. roles; Recitalist; apps. w. Symph. Orch.; Voice Tchr. Sev. recordings. Hons: Award for Outstanding Achievement in Perf. Arts, Univ. of Calif., 1975; MB Rockefeller Fund, 2 grants. Mgmt: Mrs. Thea Dispeker, NY. Address: 780 Riverside Dr., 5A, NY, NY 10032, USA.

COOK, Josephine Mary, b. 24 Aug. 1952, Bury St. Edmunds, Suffolk, UK. Lyric Soprano. Educ: RCM; LRAM; ARCM; Hochschule für Musik, Vienna; Hochschule für Musik, Munich. Career: currently appearing at Städtischen Bühnen, Freiburg im Breisgau, German Fed. Repub. mbr., ISM. Hons: Austrian Govt. Scholarship, 1976-77; Bavarian State Govt. Scholarship, 1978-79; Churchill Fellow, 1979. Hobbies: Travel; People. Mgmt: Friedrich Paasch, Düsseldorf, German Fed. Repub. Address: Ailanthus, Gt. Barton, Bury St. Edmuns, Suffolk, UK.

COOK, Keith Linwood, b. 9 Sept. 1951, Warrenton, NC, USA. Violinist. Educ: BS (Mus.Ed.), Eastman Schl. of Music, 1973. Career: Mbr., Golden Strings of Minneapolis; soloist w. US Navy Band, 1968; radio perf. at Univ. of Minn. fac. recital, 1974. Contbr. to Jrnl. of Suzuki Assn. of the Americas; mbr. Phi

Mu Alpha Sinfonia. Hon: winner, Omega Psi Phi Talent Hunt, Wash., DC, 1967, '68. Address: 2929 Panthersville Road, Apt. P-13, Decatur, GA 30034, USA.

COOK, Melville, b. 18 June 1912, Gloucester, UK. Organist; Pianist; Conductor; Examiner & Adjudicator. Educ: FRCO; DMus, Durham Univ., 1940. m. Marin Weir Moncrieff. Career incls: Organist & Choirmaster, All Saints, Cheltenham, 1935-37, Leeds Parish Ch., 1937-56, Hereford Cathedral, 1956-66, All Saints, Winnipeg, Can., 1966-67, Metropolitan United Ch., Toronto, 1967-; Cond., Halifax Choral Soc. UK, 1948-56, 3 Choirs Fest., 1957-66, Winnipeg Phil. Choir, 1966-67, Metropolitan Fest. Choir, Can., 1968-; Mbr., Music Fac., McMaster Univ., Hamilton, 1973-77. Comps: Choral works. Recordings of organ music. Mbrships: RCO; ISM; Royal Can. Coll. Organists. Recip. Harding Prize, RCO, 1931. Hobby: Walking. Mgmt: Ibbs & Tillett, UK. Address: 6 Glen Gannon Drive, Toronto, Ont., M4B 2W4, Canada.

COOK, Peter Francis, b. 1 Sept. 1923. Associate Professor of Music. Educ: BMus, MMus, Oberlin Coll., OH; DMusA, Peabody Inst.m. Marjorie K Cook (div.), 4 s., 2 d. Debut: as Pianist, Carnegie Recital Hall, NYC. Career: Assoc. Prof., Austin Peay State Univ., Clarksville, Tenn. Comps: Folana; Southward Flows its River; Vespers in Silvara; Indian Summer; The Paddle Wheel; To a Southern Pine; Kanawha River; There's a Cricket in the House; Mice in Three Blind Keys; Plaint a Sundown. Mbrships: Hon., Phi Alpha Sinfonia. Address: Box 4426 APSU, Clarksville, TN 37040, USA.

COOK, Wayne Evans, b. 16 Dec. 1939, Pearsall, TX, USA. Professor. Educ: BMus, N Tex. State Univ., Denton, 1962; MSMusEd, Univ. of Ill., Urbana, 1964. m. Marlene Bruce Cook, 3 d. Career: Assoc. Prof. of Trumpet, Univ. of Wis., Milwaukee, 1966-; 1st Trumpet, Milwaukee Civic Band, Milwaukee Civic Symph. Orch., Fac. Chamber Orch., Univ. of Wis., Waukesha Symph. 1st Trumpet, Milwaukee Am. Legion Band and W Allis Concert Band; Fndr. & 1st Trumpet, Clarion Brass Quintet. Champaign-Urban Civic Symph. Orch., Dallas Symph. Orch., Ft. Worth Symph. Orch., Terre Haute Symph. Orch., Fac. Brass Quintet, Ind. State Univ., Milwaukee Brass Quintet, Milwaukee Symph. Orch. Trumpet Sect., Fac. Brass Trio, Univ. of Wis., Milwaukee Contemporary Chamber Ensemble, Wis. Brass Quartet. Mbrships. incl: Int. Trumpet Guild; Phi Mu Alpha Sinfonia. Contr. to: Encyclopedia of Band Instruction (forthcoming). Hobbies: Golf; Fishing; Tennis. Address: 5647 W Glenbrook Rd., Milwaukee, WI 53223, USA.

COOKE, Anthony John, b. 29 Jan. 1931, Birmingham, UK. Organist; Director of Music; Harpsichordist; Adjudicator. Educ: Organ scholar, Keble Coll., Oxford; MusB; MA; LRAM; FRCO (CHM); ADCM. Career: sev. posts as organist & choirmaster incl. Organist & Master of the Music, Edgbaston Parish Ch., 1958-64; Dir. of Music, King Edward's Grammar Schl., Aston, Birmingham, 1955-64; Organist & Dir. of Music, Leeds Grammar Schl.; var. cond. posts incl. Herefordshire Co. Primary Schls. Music Fest., 1962; Assoc. Cond., Bradford Old Choral Soc., 1967-69; Examiner in Music, Oxford Local Examinations, 1956-; Music rep., RSCM, Diocese of Ripon. Mbrships: ISM; Coun., Exec., Incorporated Assn. of Organists; RSCM Music dvsry. Bd., 1969-72; IAO exec., 1969-. Hobbies: Railways; Driving; Continental Travel. Address: 8 Wrenbury Ave., Cookridge, Leeds LS16 7EQ, UK.

COOKE, Arnold Atkinson, b. 4 Nov. 1906, Gomersal, Yorks., UK. Composer. Educ: BA, MA, MusB, MusD, Cambridge Univ.; Hochschule fur Musick, Berlin, Germany. Compositions: var. chamber & orchl. works, concertos, symphs., songs, choral pieces, Opera & Ballet. Mbrships: Composers Guild; Inc. Soc. Musicians; Soc. for Promotion of New Music. Hobbies: Reading; Walking; Gardening. Address: Phyllis Cottage, Five Oak Green, Whetsted Rd., Tonbridge, Kent, UK. 3.

COOKE, John William, b. 14 Sept. 1930, Barnstaple, UK. Adviser on Church Music. Educ: RCM; GRSM (Lond.); ARCM; ARCO. m. Mona Elizabeth Bennett, 2 s. Career: Music Master, Sandroyd Schl., 1952-54, Cottesmore Schl., 1954-63; Organist & Choirmaster, St. Mary's P/Ch., Southgate, Crawley, 1959-63, St. Paul's, Winchmore Hill, 1964-66, Cheshunt P/Ch., 1966-74; Cond., Crawley & Dist. Choir, 158-63, Christ Ch. (Enfield) Choral Soc., 1963-67; Mbr. of staff, Jr. Dept., RCM, 1961-73; Dir. of Music, Chestnut Schl., 1965-74; Northern Commissioner, Royal Schl. of Ch. Music, & Examiner, Assoc. Bd., Royal Schls. of Music, 1975-. Mbr., ISM. Address: 8 Broadoak Rd., Bramhall, Stockport, Cheshire SK7 3BW, UK. 3.

COOKE, Maxwell Joseph Lorimer, b. 14 Feb. 1924, Melbourne, Australia. Pianist; Harpsichordist; Music Educationalist; University Lecturer; Dean of Faculty. Educ: Dip.

Mus, MMus, Univ. Melbourne; Degre de Perfectionnement, Ecole Normalei de Paris. m. Brenda Brookman Barber, 1 s., 1 d. Career: Concerto perfs. w. Melbourne Symph. Orch. in Celebrity Concert Series; Regular radio apps. on ABC as piano & harpsicord soloist & accomp.; TV apps. w. local & overseas artists. Num. recordings. Publs. incl: Tone Touch & Technique, 1964; Musically Gifted Children, Training and Recognition, 1977. Contbr. to profl. jrnls. Mbrships. incl: Past Pres. Aust. Soc. for Music Educ.; Past Pres., Victorian Music Tchrs. Assn.; Chmn., Inst. of Music Tchrs. Num. hons. inclng: Wright Prize for Solo Perf., 1946. Hobbies: Tennis; Golf; Foreign Langs. Address: 35 Talbot Cres., Kooyong, Australia.

COOKE, Nelson, b. 21 Dec. 1924, Mayfield, NSW, Australia. Violoncellist; Conductor; Teacher; Coach. Educ: AMUSA; LMUSA; Studied w. Jascha Gopinko, Australia, Ivor James, London, Pablo Casals, France. m. Margaret Louise, 2 s. Debut: Forum Club, Sydney, 1940, Wigmore Hall, London, UK, 1952. Career: Prin. Cellist, ABC Sydney Symph. Orch., 1947; Concerto soloist, recitalist, radio apps., lects., Australia; Prin. Cellist, LSO, UK, 1962; Prin. Cellist, RPO, 1968; BBC Soloist Royal Fest. Hall, London, Wigmore Hall, London; Tours of USA, Australia, NZ, Israel, etc.; Assoc. Prof., Univ. of S Fla., USA, 1970; Cellist, Quartet, ibid.; Prin. Cellist, FGCS. Orch.; Concerto soloist, TV & radio apps., USA; Chmn., Music Dept., Univ. of S Fla., 1972; Hd., Instrument Dept., Canberra Schl. of Music, Aust., 1974; Cond., Canberra Youth orch.; Soloist, radio & TV apps., Sydney Opera House. Var. recordings. Recip., Harriet Cohen Int. Award, 1961. Hobbies incl: Aviation; Tennis. Address: Canberra Schl. of Music, Manuka, Canberra, ACT, Aust.

COOLIDGE, Richard Ard, b. 1 Nov. 1929, Williamsport, Pa., USA. Composer; Author; Pianist; University Professor. Educ: Peabody Conserv. of Music; John Hopkins Univ.; BMus, Cinn. Conserv. of Music; MMus, ibid., 1953; DMus, Fla. State Univ., 1963. m. Penny Coolidge, 1 s., 1 d. Career: Piano recitals and lectures (esp. early in career); Prof. of Music, Stephen F Austin State Univ., Tex. Publs. Comps: Arioso for trombone & piano; Visions of Things Past, for clarinet & piano; Weeping Dancer, for piano and treble clef instrument; Music for a Rhapsody by Shelley, for flute & piano; Curves of Gold, for trombone & piano; Triptych, for trombones; 3 songs of Night, for French horn & piano; Illuminations, for trombone & piano. Comps. recorded: Arioso, Weeping Dancer, Shelley Rhapsody. Publ: Owls, Pussycats, Cabbages & Kings; Musical Growth through Modern Songs & Piano Pieces, 1972. Contbr. to: Music Review (UK) and other prfl. jrnls. Mbr. var. profl. assns. Hons: Award winner of Delius Comp. Contest, 1976, 77, 78. Address: 2212 Dogwood, Nacogdoches, TX 75961, USA. 7, 23, 28, 29.

COOMBS, John Martin, b. 27 Jan. 1929, London, UK. Tenor; Composer; Translator; Writer. Educ: LCM & privately. m. Sheila Dempster, 1 s. (dec.), 1 d. Career: Mbr., BBC Singers, 1962-74; Tenor solo roles, var. opera cos. & ensembles. Compositions: Volpone (opera in 3 acts after Ben Johnson); The Major's Daughter (operetta); The Deluded Bridegroom (new libretto & musical adaption of Mozart's opera); var. other compositions, piano & vocal arrs. Publs: Translations of maj. German biogs. of Richard Strauss, 1964, Beethoven, 1970, Bach, 1975; Num. booklets record sleeve notes. Contbr. to: Opera; Die Zeit. Hobby: Boating. Address: 72 Clarendon Gardens, Wembley, Middx., UK. 3.

COOPER, David Edwin, b. 30 Jan. 1944. Music Librarian; Musicologist; Discographer. Educ: BMus, Univ. of Mich., 1966; MFA, OH Univ., 1968; MA, 1972, PhD Cand., Univ. of Kan.; MLS, Kent State Univ., 1973. Career: Univ. of Kan. Music Lib., 1970-72; Kent State Univ. Music Lib., 1972-73; SUNY at Buffalo Music Lib., 1973-75; C F Peters Corp., NYC, 1976-. Publs: International Bibliography of Discographies, 1975. Contbr. to profl. publs. Mbrships: Am. Musicol. Soc.; Music Lib. Assn.; Assn. of Recorded Sound Collects. Hobby: Collecting Records. Address: 100 LaSalle St., Apt. 2F, NY, NY 10027, USA.

COOPER, Imogen, b. 28 Aug. 1949, London, UK. Musician (pianist). Educ: Paris Cnserv.; study w. Alfred Brendel, London & Vienna. Career: Recitals throughout UK, incl. Bath, Harrogate & Cheltenham Fests.; Apps. w. major British Orchs.; Promenade Concerts; Concerts in Germany, Austria, Portugal & France; Frequent broadcaster, & TV apps. 1973-. Recordings: Schubert Four Hand Piano Music; Mozart Double Piano Concerto. Recip: Mozart Mem. Prize, 1969. Hobbies: Philos.; Hist.; Romanesque Architecture. Mgmt: Ingpen & Williams Ltd., 14 Kensington Ct., London W8. Address: c/o Mgmt.

COOPER, John Harris, b. 16 Jan. 1933, Leicester, UK. Lecturer in Music; Church Organist. Educ: BMus, 1960; MMus, 1968; ARCM; ARCO; FRCO (CHM). m. Richardis Ute Cooper,

1 d., 2 s. Career: RAF, 1951-53; Ch. Organist, 1949-, Holy Trinity, Leamington Spa, 1959-69, St. Mary-le-Tower, Ipswich, 1971-; Schl. Tchr., 1956-69, Leamington Coll. for Boys, 1959-69; Sr. Lectr., Music Dept., North-East Essex Tech. Coll., Colchester, 1969-; Cond., Leamington Spa Bach Choir, 1959-69; Ipswich Choral Soc., 1969-. Mbrships: RCO; Leicester Organists Assn.; past Pres., ibid.; Coventry Organists Assn.; Past Pres., Archdeaconry Rep., RSCM, Ipswich; Pres., Suffolk Organists Assn. Hons: Limpus Prize, RCO, 1954; Harding Prize, RCO, 1955. Hobbies: Sport, esp. Tennis, Cricket. Soccer. Address: 66, Corder Road, Ipswich, Suffolk.

COOPER, Joseph, b. 7 Oct. 1912, Westbury on Trym, UK. Concert Pianist; Lecturer. Educ: Organ Schol., Keble Coll., Oxford Univ.; MA (Oxon.); ARCM (solo piano); Study of piano w. Egon Petri. m. (1) Jean Greig, 1947, (dec. 1973), (2) Carol Borg, 1975. Debut: Wigmore Hall, 1947 (postponed from 1939 due to WW II). Career: Recitals throughout UK & Perfs. w. leading orchs.; Presenter of 'Concert Biographies'; Tours of Europe, Africa, India, Can.; Regular Contbr. to BBC progs. & Chmn., Face the Music, BBC TV. Compositor: Arrangement of Vaughan Williams Piano Concerto for 2 pianos. Recordings: Standard piano repertoire, & Hidden Melodies (own compositions of well-known tunes in styles of classical composers). Mbrships: Liveryman, Worshipful Co. of Musicians Garrick Club. Mbr., Music Panel, Arts Coun., & Chmn., Piano Subcomm., 1966-71. Hons: Ambrose Fleming Award, Royal TV Soc., 1961. Hobbies: Sailing; Walking. Address: Trocks Mill Cottage, Mill Hill, Barnes Common, London SW13, UK. 1, 3, 28.

COOPER, Lawrence, b. 14 Aug. 1946, LA, Calif., USA. Opera Singer. Educ: BA, Calif. State Univ., Northridge. Career: San Fran. Opera (Valentin, Marcello, Donner); Western Opera Theater; San Fran. Spring Opera; Can. Opera Co.; Denver Symph.; San Fran. Symph.; Honolulu Symph.; Columbus Symph., etc. Mbrships: AGMA; Can. Actors Equity. Hons: San Fran. Opera Auditions, 1971; Nat. Opera Inst., 1972. Hobby: Antique Cars. Mgmt: Columbia Artists (Nelly Walter). Address: Driftwood, Cooper's Falls, Washage, Ont. LOK 2BO, Can.

COOPER, Lewis Hugh, b. 31 Dec. 1920, Pontiac, Mich., USA. Professor of Music; Bassoonist. Educ: BM, Univ. of Mich. Schl. of Music. m. Nadillae V Savage, 1 d., 1 s. Career: Mbr. of Fac., Univ. of Mich., 1945-; currently, Prof. of Music (Bassoon), Schl. of Music, ibid.; Former Mbr., Detroit Symph., 17 yrs.; Charter Mbr., Univ. of Mich. Fac. Woodwind Quintet. Int. Expert in voicing, repair & design of bassoons; Acoustical Cons. in design & manufacture of bassoons. Mbrships. incl: AAUP; Am. Fedn. of Musicians; Int. Double Reed Soc. Publs: Essentials of bassoon Technique, 1968. Contbr. to profl. jrnls. Address: The Univ. of Mich. Schl. of Music, Ann Arbor, MI 48104, USA.

COOPER, Lindsay, b. 3 Mar. 1951, London, UK. Bassoonist; Composer; Oboist; Flautist; Pianist. Educ: Dartington Coll. of Arts; RAM; LRAM. Career; Freelance orchl. & session work; Mbr., Comus, 1971-72, Ritual Theatre, 1973; Musical Dir., Tokyo Kid Brothers' Musical The City, Royal Ct. Theatre, london; currently Mbr., grp. Henry Cow, recent apps. incl. Nancy Jazz Fest & Sigma Fest., Bordeaux, num. broadcasts inclng. BBC & ORTF. Collective comps. recorded w. Henry Cow; Linguaphonie; Upon Entering the Hotel Adloh; Archades; Deluge; Beginning: the long march; Morning Star. Recordings: Unrest V2011; In Praise of Learning V2027. Mbr., ISM. Hobbies: Politics; Feminism; Theatre; Reading; Collecting Old Postcards of Ferris Wheels. Address: c/o Virgin Records, 2-4 Vernon Yard, 119 Portobello Rd., London W11, UK.

COOPER, Martin Du Pré, b. 17 Jan. 1910. Winchester, UK. Writer on Music. Educ: BA, Oxford Univ. m. Mary Stewart, 1 s., 3 d. Career: Ed., Musical Times, 1953-56; Mbr., Editl. Bd., New Oxford Hist. of Music; Ed., Vol. X, ibid. Publs: Gluck, 1935; Bizet, 1938; Opéra Comique, 1949; Frecnh Music 1870-25, 1950; Russian Opera, 1951; Les Musiciens anglais d'aujourd'hui, 1952; Ideas & Music, 1966; Beethoven-the last decade, 1970. Music Critic, London Mercury, 1934-39, Daily Herald, 1945-50, The Spectator, 1946-54, Daily Tekgraph, 1950-76; Pres. Critics Circle, 1959-60; Hon. FTCL & RAM; CBE, 1972. Address: 34 Halford Rd., Richmond, Surrey, UK.

COOPER, Peter Douglas, b. 16 May 1918, Christchurch, NZ. Pianist. Educ: Canterbury Univ. Coll.; RAM; studied w. Ignaz Friedman & Edwin Fischer. Debut: Christchurch, NZ, 1939. Career: toured Russia, Europe, Am., Africa, India, Far E., Middle E., Australasia. Compositions: Tango-Caprice; Waltz in Memory of Ignaz Friedman (recorded); Spring Waters (recorded). Recordings: total of 12 for Pye & EMI. Publs: Style in Piano Playing, 1975. Mbrships: Pres., Medtner Soc. Hons: Recip. of Eric Brough Mem. Prize, RAM, 1947; Hon. FTCL. Mgmt: David

Jones, 76a Alderman's Hill, Palmers Green, London N13. UK. Address: c/o Bank of NZ, 1 Queen Victoria St., London EC4P 4HE, UK. 3.

COOPER, (Walter Thomas) Gaze, b. 11 June 1895, Long Eaton, UK. Composer; Teacher of Pianoforte & Composition. Educ: RAM; Nottingham Univ. Coll. m. Frances Lucky Kirkland, 1 d. Debut w. Bournemouth Symph. Orch. Career incls: many piano recitals of own work; perf., own 1st Piano Concerto, BBC; perf. w. State Orch., Poland. Fndr. & Cond., Nottingham Symph. Orch. for 35 yrs. Comps. incl: 9 symphs; 5 piano concertos; concertos for oboe, viola, horn; opera; Missa Brevis. Mbr., Performing Right Soc. Hobby: Chinese Art. Address: Dolphin Cottage, Town St., Hawksworth, Notts., UK.

COOVER, James B, b. 3 June 1925, Jacksonville, Ill., USA. Professor of Music. Educ: AB, Northern Colo. Univ., 1949; MA, ibid., 1950; MALS, Univ. of Denver, 1953. m. Jeanne A Walker, 1 s., 2 d. Career: Bibliographer & Asst. Dir., Bibliographical Ctr. for Rsch., Denver, Colo., 1950-54; Hd., George Sherman Dickinson Music Lib., Vassar Coll., Poughkeepsie, NY, 1954-67; Prof. of Music & Birge-Cary Chair, 1974-76; Dir., Music Lib., SUNY, Buffalo, 1967-; Cons. for Middle States Assn.of Colls. & Secondary Schls., 1961, '62, '66, '69, '74, '75, '78. NY State Coun. on Arts, 1965-68, Oberlin & Swarthmore Colls., Union Theological Sem. & Univ. of Louisville, 1957, '59, '62, '68. Publs: Music Lexicogrpahy, 1952, 3rd revised ed. 1971; Medieval & Renaissance Music, 1964, Supplement, 1973; The 'Rainbeau' Catalog, 1962. Contbr. to num. jrnls. inclng: Fontes Artis Musicae; Grove's Dictionary; Notes for Music Lib. Assn.; Jrnl. of Music Theory. Present Mbrships: Pres., Music Lib. Assn., 1959-60; Int. Assn. of Music Libs.; AAUP. Recip. of hons. Hobby: Photography. Address: 111 Marjann Terr., Buffalo, NY 14223, USA. 14.

COPE, David Howell, b. 17 May 1941, San Fran., Calif., USA. Composer; Writer; Performer on Piano, Cello & Contrabass. Educ: BMus, Ariz. State Univ.; MMus, Univ. of Southern Calif. m. Mary Jane Stluka, 4 s. Career: Perfs. at all major int. fests. of New Music, at Carnegie Hall (twice), Lincoln Ctr., Kennedy Ctr., Comps. Theatre; Guest Comp., over 20 univs. in USA; many radio & TV apps.; music on syndicated radio progs. Comps. incl: Streams for orch.; Re-Birth for concert band; Margins (chmbr. ensemble); Arena (cello' tape); Vortex for chmbr. ensemble; Contrasts for orch.; Requiem for Bosque Redondo for brass choir; Variations for piano & wind ensemble. Pubs: New Directions in Music, 2nd ed., 1976; New Music Notation, 1976; New Music Composition, 1976. Contbr. to jrnls. Mbrships: ASCAP. Recip. var. hons. Hobby: Editing. Address: 508 Edgehill Dr., Oxford, OH 45050, USA. 2, 18, 16.

COPELAND, Kenneth Thomas, b. 29 Sept. 1908, Highgate, London, UK. Violinist; Violist; Clarinettist. Educ: studied w. Prof. Spinks & John Mertens; Dip., Niles Bryant Schl. of Piano Tuning, Wash., DC, 1951. m. Edna Esther Pohl, 1 d. Carer incls: Musician, London, UK, etc., 1925-31; over 2000 concerts throughout Can., 1931-40; Mbr., RCA Band, 1952-62; 1st Violin Sect., Halifax (NS) Symphonette, Halifax Symph. Orch., Halifax Concert Orch., CBC Strongs, etc., 1952-65; Mbr., 1965-66, Mbr., Viola Sect, winter seasons, 1973-, Victoria Symph. Orch.; Prin. Viola, Atlantic Symph. Orch., Halifax, NS, 1966-73, Charlottetown Summer Fest. of the Arts, PEI, 1966-; num. TV broadcasts; Mbr., World Symph. Orch. Hobbies: Carpentry; Walking; Motoring; Nature. Address: 345 Arnold Ave., Victoria, BC, Canada V8S 3L6.

COPLAND, Aaron, b. 14 Nov. 1900, Brooklyn, NY, USA. Music Educator; Composer. Educ: Study of piano & composition w. pvte. tutors in US; Study w. Vines & Nadia Boulanger, Paris. Career: Organised Copland-Sessions Concerts, 1928-31; Dir., Am. Festival of Contemporary Music, Yaddo; Music Lectr., New Schl. of Soc. Rsch., NY, 1927-37; Toured S Am., 1941, 1947; Asst. Dir., Berkshire Music Ctr., Tanglewood, 1945; Charles Eliot Norton Prof., 1951-52. Compositions incl: 1st Symph., 1925; Concerto for Piano & Orch., 1926; Billy the Kid, 1938; Violin Sonata, 1943; Appalachian Spring (ballet), 1944; Rodeo (ballet); 1942; Symphonic Ode, 1955; Music for a Great City, 1963; Inscape for Orch., 1967. Publs: What to Listen for in Music, 1939; Our New Music, 1941; Music & Imagination, 1952; Copland on Music, 1960; The New Music 1900-1960, 1968. Hons. incl: Pulitzer Prize for Appalachian Spring, 1945. Address: c/o Boosey & Hawkes, 30 W 57th St., NY, NY 10019, USA.

COPPENS, Claude A, b. 23 Dec. 1936, Schaarbeek, Belgium. Pianist; Composer. Educ: JD, Brussels Univ., 1960; Royal Conser. Brussels, 1950. m. Hilda Ide, 1 s. Career incls: Concert tours, W & E Europe, N & S Am., N, Ctrl. & S Africa, Turkey, Iran; Soloist, recitals & concerts; Jury mbr., var. nat. & int.

competitions; Prof. of Piano, Royal Music Conserv., Ghent; Prof. of New Music in Practice, Brussels. Comps. incl: Piano music; Chmbr. music; Vocal music; Var. commissions for Belgian Broadcasting & Int. Fest. of Flanders. Var. recordings as pianist & comp. Contbr. to var. profl. jrnls. Mbrships: Charter Mbr., Round Table, Brussels; Fndr. Mbr., SPECTRA. Recip., var. hons. as pianist & comp. Hobbies incl; Lit.; Art exhibs. Address: Tuinwyklaan 49, 9000 Gent, Belgium.

COPPOLA, Carmine, b. 11 June 1912, NYC, USA. Flautist; Composer; Conductor. Educ: BMus, Columbia Tchrs. Coll.; Dip., Juilliard Schl.; BS, MMus, Manhattan Schl. of Music. m. Italia Pennino, 2 s., 1 d. Debut: NYC, (flute), 1929. Career: 1st Flutist, Radio City Music Hall, Detroit Symph. & NBC Toscanini Symph., NYC; Compositions incl: Danse Pagane; Orchestral Suite; Escorial (opera). Film music: Godfather Parts I & II; The People. Recordings incl: (cond. & comp.) Godfather Part II; Godfather's Wedding Album; Accordeon Concerto; Woodwind Quintet; Symph. Poem, Phantom Cavalry. Publ: A Manual of Flute Instruction, 1975. Contbr. to press. Mbr., profl. assns., USA & Italy. Hons. incl: Oscar for Godfather II score, Acad. of Motion Pictures, 1975. Hobbies: Travelling; Italian Cookery. Address: 19813 Gilmore St., Woodland Hills, CA 91364, USA.

COQUET, Odile, b. 3 Oct. 1932, Lyon, France. Composer; Pianist. Educ: Sorbonne; Grad., Conservs. of Lyon & Paris; studied w. Oliver Messiaen. Career: Placed, Concours of Musical Composition, Rome, 1960; works broadcast by Radio Luxembourg, 1960, Namur-Brussels, 1965, Radio Lyon, 1965, 66, 68 & 74. Compositions publd. incl: Gentil Coquelicot for piano; 25 Choeurs de Varèse; Trio d'anches; Little Suite for Piano; Fantasie for violin & piano; Romantic Waltz for stmp. orch.; Little Suite for orch. (recorded); Fantasie-Impromptu for solo violin & orch. (recorded); Petite suite for accordian, 1976. Mbr: Assn. of Women Grads. of Univ., Reid Hall, Am. Educl. Ctr., 1958-; SACEM, Paris, 1964-. Recip. of Bursary, St. Jacques-de-Compostelle Inst. of Spanish Music, 1960. Address: 9 rue Paul-Huvelin, 69110 Ste Foy/Lyon, France.

CORBITT, Gretchen Johnson, b. 20 Dec. 1920, Delway, NC, USA. Public School Teacher; Private Piano Teacher. Educ: Mars Hill Coll., NC; BA, Meredith Coll., Raleigh, NC; Univ. Ext. Conserv., Chgo., Ill.; Appalachian State Univ., Boone, NC. m. Rev. John C. Corbitt, 4 c. Career: Public Schl. Music Tchr.; Pvte. Piano Tchr.; Dir., Foothills Children's Theatre; Dir., N Cove Boychoir; Dir., W Marion Boys Choir. Contbr. to: Staff Notes, Int. Piano Lib.; Inc.; Children's Theatre Review & other jrnls. Mbrships: NGPT; Nat. MTA; NC MTA; Nat. Music Educators Conf.; NC Music Educators Cond.; Nat. Fedn. of Jr. Music Clubs; Nat. Fedn. of Boychoir; VP, McDowell Chapt., NC Symph.; Am. Theatre Assn. Hobbies: Reading; Cooking; Camping. Address: PO Box 303, Ridgecrest, NC 28770, USA.

CORBOZ, Michel Jules, b. 14 Feb. 1934, Marsens, Switzerland. Cond. Educ: Tchr. Trng. Coll., Freiburg; Conserv. Freiburg; Inst. Ribeaupierre, Lausanne. Debut: Lausanne, 1961. Career: Cond. Lausanne since 1953; Cond. concerts organized by himself. Comp. incl: Harmonization of popular songs; Motets; Cantata to Notre-Dame. Recordings incl: Monteverdi; Bach; Mozart; Charpentier. Hons. incl: Grand Priz de Disque, Acad. Charles V, 1967; Jacques Ranché Prize, 1968; Prize Acad. of the French record, 1969; Big Prize for record lovers; German record Prize. Hobbies: Soccer; Cars. Address: Mollie Margot 1099, Switzerland.

CORCORAN, Francis, b. 1 May 1944, Tipperary, Ireland. Composer. Educ: BA, Maynooth Coll.; BD, Pont. Universita del Laterano, Rome; BMus (NUI); BMus (Dublin Univ.); Hochschule für Musik, Berlin; pvte. studies w. Boris Blacher. m. Maria-Dorothea Steinkühler, 4 c. Career incls: Inspector of Music, Irish Dept. of Educ.; Lectr., Broadcaster on new music & aesthetics. Comps. incl: Symph. No. 1; Three Pieces for Orch.; Chmbr. Symph.; 2 String Quartets; Two Meditations for Speaker & Orch.; Ballet, Mac na Mara; Mythologies, for solo percussion; Sonata for Strings; Chmbr. Sonata. Recordings: Collection One. Contbr. of articles on music educ. Mbrships: Fndn. Sec., Assoc. of Irish Comps., Music Assn. of Ireland; PRS; MCPS; Assn. for the Promotion of Music in Educ. Hons: Sev. prizes, commissions, incl. DAAD Comp. Fellow, in Berlin, 1980. Hobbies: Squash; Mountain-walking; Languages; Philosophy. Address: c/o DAAD, 1 Berlin 12, Steinplatz 2, German`Fed. Repub.

CORDEIRO, Joseph, b. 1 Sept. 1926, Cumberland, RI, USA. Conductor; Violinist. Educ: BM; MA; AMusD; Soloist Dip. div. 1 d. Debut: Nat. Pell Fndn., RI Career: 6th Army Band; 6th Army Str. Quartet; Tokyo Symph.; New England Conserv. Orch.; Boston Opera Orch.; Teaching Specialist, Strings, Ga., Ariz.; Atlanta Opera Orch.; Assoc. Cond., Univ. of Ariz. Symph.; Tucson Symph.; Tucson Symphonette; ond., Tucson Little Symph., Univ.

of Wis., La Crosse Symph.; Ariz. Chmbr. Orch.; Atlanta Symph. Contbr. to: Wis. Schl. Musician; Ariz. News. Mbrships: Life, NEA; Life, MENC; Ariz. Music Educators; Wis. Music Educators; Am. String Tchrs. Assn.; Wis. Music Educators State Student Chmn.; Pres., Wis. String Tchrs. Assn. Hobbies: Tennis; Judo; Swimming. Address: Fine Arts Ctr., La Crosse, WI 54601, USA.

CORDERO, Ernesto, b. 9 Aug. 1946, NYC, USA. Composer; Classical Guitarist; University Professor. Educ: Grad. as Prof. of Guitar, Royal Conserv. of Music, Madrid, Spain; studied Comp., Chigiana Acad., Siena, Italy. m. Gloriela Munoz Arjona, 2 d. Career: Guitar Concerts, Puerto Rico, USA, Spain, Italy, Greece; Concert apps., Puerto Rican TV & Vatican radio; Prof., Univ. of Puerto Rico. Compositions: Preludes III & IV, 1970; Mapeyé, 1975, Publs: Danzas Puertorriquenas (w. L Egurbida), 1970. Mbrships: Ateneo Puertorriqueno; Italian Soc. Authors & Publrs., Rome; ASCAP. Hons. incl: 1st Prize, Int. Contest for Guitar Solos, Classical Guitar Soc. of Mich., 1972. Address: Cafeto St. num. 709, Highland Park, Rió Piedras, Puerto Rico.

CORDERO, Roque, b. 16 Aug. 1917, Panama. Composer; Conductor; Teacher. Educ: BA, Hamline Univ., Minn., USA; Study of composition w. Ernst Krenek; Conducting w. Dimitri Mitropoulos, Stanley Chapple, Leon Barzin. m. Elizabeth Lee Johnson, 3 s. Debut: Nat. Symph. of Panama. Career: Cond., Nat. Orch.of Panama, 1964-66; Guest Cond., Colombia, Chile, Brazil, Argentina & USA; Fac. Mbr., Music Dept., Ill. State Univ. Compositions incl: Quintet; String Quartet 1, 2 & 3, Musica Veine; 2nd Symph.; Adagio Tragico. Recordings of own compositions: Quintet; Violin Concerto; 9 Miniatures for orch. Publs: Curso de Solfeo, 1963. Contbr. to profl. jrnls. & Grove's Dictionary. Mbrships: Inter-Am. Music Coun. - Sec.-Gen., 1956-60; Panamanian Rep., Int. Music Coun., 2nd Symph., 2nd Inter-Am. Fest., Caracas; 1st Prize, for Rapsodia Campesina, Panama, 1953; Guggenheim Fellowship; 1949; Chamber Music Prize, Inter-Am. Contest for 3rd Strg Quartet, 1977. Hobby: Chess. Address: Music Dept., Ill. State Univ., Normal, IL 61761, USA. 14.

CORE, Howard A, b. 13 Oct. 1941, Wash., DC, USA. Importer & Dealer in Musical Instruments; Orchestral & Choral Conductor. Educ: BMus, Capital Univ., Columbus, Ohio. m. Myrna Lee Hyde, 2 children. Debut: Columbus, Ohio. Career: Pittsburgh Orch.; Westmoreland Symph. Orch.; Sales Mgr., Buffet Crampton Cie., USA; Gen. Mgr., Andrew Schroetter & Co. Inc. Comps: Sev. choral works; 3 works for instrumental grps. Contbr. to jrnls. Mbrships: Pres., Sinfonia Chapt., 1963; Off., sev. grps. Recip: Minor conducting prizes. Hobbies: Reading; Numismatics; Collecting Records; Astron. Address: 22 Mill Dam Rd., Smithtown, NY 11787, USA.

CORELLI, Franco, b. Ancona, Italy. Operatic & Concert Tenor. Educ: Pesaro Conserv; Maggio Musicale, Florence. Career incls: many apps. in European theatres inclng. La Scala, Minal, Teatro San Carlo, Naples, Covent Gdn.; London; debut as Met. Opera, NYC, Manrioc, Il Trovatore, 1961; regular apps. on Am. TV; recital tour w. Renata Telbaldi; major roles in many operas inclng: Carmen (Don Jose); Andrea Chénier; La Bohème; Turandot; Tosca; Ernani; Aida; Don Carlos; Forza del Destino; Cavalleria Rusticana; I Pagliacci; etc. Recip. 1st Prize, Spoleto Nat. Competition. 16.

CORENA, Fernando, b. 22 Dec. 1916, Geneva, Switz. Operatic Bass. Educ: Univ. of Fribourg. Debut: La Scala, Milan, 1947. Career incls: Ldng. Bass, Metrop. Opera, NYC, 1954-; apps. at Lyric Opera Chgo., 1956, Teatro Colon, 1958, Statsoper Berlin, 1957, Covent Gdn., San Fran. Opera, 1960, Vienna Statsoper, 1963, Grand Theatre Geneva, 1963 & 64, Rome Opera, 1965. Address: 15 Tatum Dr., Middletown, NJ 07748, USA. 2.

CORFIELD, Greta, b. 13 Aug. 1912, Oakengates, Shrops., UK. Mezzo-Soprano Singer; Painter. Educ: studied piano w. Hedley Hetherington, Wellington; studied singing w. Irene Jarman, Wellington, Frank Mullings, & Dame Eva Turner. m. Kenneth W Wiggins, 1 d. Career: began singing, 1944; has given many recitals throughout Midlands & N of Engl. & on BBC; Oratorio singer; joined Wolverhampton Opera Club, 1953, roles incl. Carmen, Aida, Nedda (I Pagliacci); Singing Tchr., 1961-; trained & presented Greta Corfield Singers. Hons: Gold Medal, Cheltenham Fest.; Herbert Wise Cup for operatic singing, Birmingham, 1950. Address: 'Albertina', 122 Haybridge Rd., Hadley, Telford, Salop TF14JJ, UK.

CORINA, John Hubert, b. 21 Apr. 1928, Cleveland, OH, USA. Educator; Composer; Oboist. Educ: BS, 1951, MA, 1956, Western Reserve Univ.; DMus, Fla. State Univ., 1965. m. Carol Lange, 2 s., 1 d. Career: Oboist, Ga. Woodwind Quintet, Univ. of Ga. Baroque Ensemble, Augusta Symph. Orch.,

1965-; currently Prof. of Music (comp., theory, oboe), Univ. of Ga. & Organist-Choirmaster, Emmanuel Episcopal Ch., Athens. Comps. incl: Dance Fugure (tenor & ensemble), 1973; Partita for Alto Saxophone & Piano, 1974; Sonet for Solo Oboe & Strings, 1974; Partita for Oboe & Percussion, 1975; Partita for Woodwind Quintet, 1976; Song Cycle, Songs of Day, for treble chorus & piano, 1977; Cantata, The Way of the Cross, for speaker, soloists, chorus handbells & organ. Contbr. to Jrnl. of the Int. Double Reed Soc. Mbrships. incl: MENC; ASCAP. Hobies incl: Golf. Address: 396 Hancock Ln., Rte. 3, Athens, GA 30605, USA.

CORKHILL, David, b. 29 Sept. 1946, Bebington, UK. Orchestral Percussionist/Timpanist. Educ: ARAM. Career: Timpanist, Engl. Chmbr. Orch., 1969-; Prin. Percussion, RPO, 1982-74; Currently Prin. Percussion, NPO; Percussionist, Early Music Consort of London; Philip Jones Brass Ensemble; Vesuvius Ensemble. Recordings: Chmbr. version of Chichester Psalms (Bernstein) w. Ledger & King's Coll. Choir, Cambridge. Acad. hons. Hobbies: Good food; Cooking & eating; Collecting Wine. Address: Milton, Lee Common, Gt. Missenden, Bucks., UK.

CORNER, Philip Lionel, b. 10 Apr. 1933, New York, USA. Musician; Composer; Performer; Teacher; Writr. Educ: BA, CCNY, 1955; MA, Columbia Univ., 1959; Paris Conserv. m. Julie Winter. Career incls: Comp. and/or Perf: Avant Garde Fest., 1963-75; OM Theatre, Boston, 1966-69; WBAI Radio, 1968-; Expmtl. Intermedia Fndn., 1970-; Comps. Forum, 1972-; Livingston Coll. Concerts, 1972-. Comps. incl: Crash Actions (sounding); 12-Tone Continuum (ear). Publs. incl: The Journal of The Idential Lunch, 1970. Contbr. to profl. mags. Mbrships. incl: Bd. Dirs., Comps. Forum. Recip. num. hons. Hobbies: Reading Poetry; Looking at Art; Meditating; Listening. Address: 145 W 96 St., New York, NY 10025, USA.

CORNIL, Dominique, b. 15 Jan. 1953, Lobbes, Belgium. Concert Pianist. Educ: Piano Conservatoire Royal de Mons, Belgium; Chmbr. music, Conservatoire Nat. Superieur de Paris. Career: Num. recitals & concerts for Belgian Radio & TV; Perf. w. var. orchs. inclng: RTB Symph. Orch.; Orch. Nat. de Belgique; Orch. de Liege; Orch. Phil d'Arvers; Symph. Orch. ORTF, Strasbourg; LPO; Chmbr. Orch. E YSAYE of Cologne; Zagreb Soloists; Ensemble P Kuentz. Recordings incl: Recitals of works of Haydn, Mozart, Scarlatti, Matiic, Franck & Rachmaninov. Hons. incl: Laureat of Concours Int. Reine Elisabeth, Belgium, 1975. Hobbies: Horseback Riding; Travel. Address: 16 Lagrattiere, 6558 Lobbes, Belgium.

CORP, Charles Leworthy, b. Horsham, UK. Concert & Operatic Tenor; Teacher of Singing. Educ: AGSM (Perfs.' & Tchrs.' Dip.). m. Penelope Birtles, 2 d. Career: Oratorios & recitals throughout Brit. Isles; Sadlers Wells Opera, 1971 & 1972; Handel Opera Soc.; Chelsea Opera Grp.; Sang in 1st perfs. of Lichfield Canticle (Rutter), 1972. House on Secker St. (Cole), 1974; Wall (Ulia Usher), 1978; Fest. apps. inclng. Engl. Bach. Cheltenham, Windsor, Leith Hill (Dorking), Petersfield & Newtown. Mbrships: ISM; Old Blues. Hons. incl: Flanders Gold Medal, GSM, 1969; Tenor Prize, 'S-Hertogenbosch Int. Competition, 1970. Hobbies incl: Gardening, English Singers 78 rpm records. Address: 53 Gracelfield Gdns., London SW16, UK.

CORREA Louis Patricio, b. 25 Aug. 1925, Calcutta, W Bengal, India. Musician (Cellist). Educ: w. father & Alex Schemansky, Calcutta; w. Thomas Kanitz, Max Mueller Bhavan, Delhi, 1968; Bhaven Seminar, Poona, 1971. m. Filomena Emilia, 3 s. Career: Mbr., Calcutta Symph. Orch.; Ldr., Cello Sect., Bombay Chmbr. Orch.; Soloist w. Delhi Symph. Orch.; extensive film work. Hobby: Collecting Coins. Address: 60 Bhaveshwar Bhuvan, Opp. Portuguese Ch.-Dadar, Bombay 400028, India.

CORREA DE AZEVEDO, Luiz Heitor, b. 13 Dec. 1905, Rio de Janeiro, Brazil. Musicologist; Music Teacher. Educ: Dip., Piano, Theory & Harmony, Inst. Nacional de Música, Universidade do Brasil, 1939. m. Violeta Pizarro Jacobina, 1 d. Career: Libn., Inst. Nacional de Música, Rio de Janeiro, 1932-39; Prof., Conserv. Brasileiro de Música, ibid., 1937-47 & Escola Nacional de Música, Universidade do Brasil, 1939-47 & 1966-67; Cons., Pan Am. Union, Wash., DC, USA & 1941-42; Prog. Specialist, UNESCO, Paris, France, 1948-65; Vis. Prof., Tulane Univ., New Orleans, La., USA, 1967-68, & Ind. Univ., Bloomington, 1969. Publs. incl: Dois Pequenos Estudos de Folclore Musical, 1938; Escala, Ritmo e Melodia na Música dos Indios Brasileiros, 1938; Brief History of Music in Brazil, 1948; Musica & Musicos do Brasil, 1950; Bibliografia Muscal Brasileira, 1952; La Musique no Brasil, 1956. Contbr. to num. books, dictionaries & profl. jrnls. Mbrships. incl: Int. Music Coun. (Exec. Bd., 1966-73, individual mbr. 1974-77); Acad. Brasileira de Musica; Acad. Nacional de Musica, Brasil; Int. Musicol. Soc.; Int. Folk Music Coun. (Exec.

BD. 1969-76. Hons: Int. Music Coun. Prize, 1977. Hobbies: Photography; Travelling. Address: 12 Rue de Galilé, 75116 Paris, France. 4, 14.

CORSARO, Frank Andrew, b. 22 Dec. 1924, New York City, USA. Stage Director. Educ: Yale Schl. of Drama; Actors' Studo. m. Mary Cross Lueders, 1 s. Debut: in Susannah, NYC Opera, 1958. Career incl: Dir. & Prod. of Opera for major cos. inclng. Cinn., Houston, Lake George, NYC Opera, St. paul, San Fran. Spring, Seattle & Wash., DC, USA; Spoleto Festival Italy; Film & Stage actor, inclng. role in Rachel Rachel, 1967. Publ: Soldiers Tale (adaptation of Ramuz; L'Histoire du Soldate), 1973; Maverik, 1978. Mbrships: Ed., Nat. Opera Inst., Kennedy Ctr., Wash., DC. Hobbies: Piano; Painting. Mgmt: Columbia Artists Mgmt., NY. Address: 33 Riverside Dr., NY, NY 10023, USA.

CORT, Lois-Alexandra Lund, b. 5 Dec., NYC, USA. Educator; Singer; Composer; Lecturer. Educ: BA in Psychol., & Educ., Russell Sage Coll.; HEW Intern in Gerontol., Univ. of Mich.; Opera Workshop, SUNY at Albany Conserv. of Music. m. Howard Lee Cort. Career incls: Exec. Dir., Gladys Rudd Eno Lund Mem. Benefit for Needy Aged Emergency Fund; Dir. & Operatic Contralto, Lois-Alexandra Concert Co.; Educator, Elem. Educ. & Mentally Retarded; Recording Artist & Ballad Comp., Lundcort Records. Recordings. incl: My Love Comes Softly (LP). Mbrships. incl: Am. Assn. for Ret'd. Persons; Columbia-Greene Humane Soc.; Pres., Ghent Women for Liberation; Publicity Chmn., Town of Ghent Bicentennial Commn.; AAUW; Shelter Mgr., Nat. Civil Defense. Hobbies incl: Siamese Cats; Horseback Riding; Singing; Swimming; Voluntary Work. Address: Pine Crest, Ghent, NY 12075, USA.

CORTI, Ottavio Giuseppe, b. 2 Oct. 1911, Zürich, Switzerland. Violist. Educ: studied w. Stefi Geyer. m. Leontine Browar, 2 s., 1 d. Debut: Stefi Geyer Quartet, 1940. Career: 1st Viola, Tonhalle Orch., 1944-; Solo Viola, Collegium Musicum, 1941, Zürich; Mbr., Kammermusiker Zurich, 1960-; Pvte. Tchr.; Tchr. Violin & Viola, Conserv. of Zürich, 1972-; var. solo perfs. in Europe, Am., Aust. Recordings: Quintets by Haydn, Goetz, Beethoven, Bruckner, Martinu, w. Kammermusiker Zürich. Mbrships: Swiss Musicians Union; Swiss Music Pedagogic Union. Hobbies: Travel; Movie Photography. Mgmt: Konzert Gesellschaft, Zürich. Address: 19 Bahnhofstr., 8702 Zollikon, Switz.

CORTI-COLLEONI, Mario Enrico, b. Florence, Italy. Composer; Conductor; Music Critic. Educ: Dip. in Composition, G Verdi Conserv. of Music. Career: Music Consultant, Voce Del Padrone, 1937-38; Music Critic, La Cultura, Grazio, Tempo, Espersso & Pagine Nuove; Radio Consultant, 1945; Tech. Dir., Ufficio Diffusione Internazionale Musicasti (EDIM), 1952-56; Fndng. Dir., Musicisti Organo Uff. elel Sindicato Nazionale Musicisti, 1953-56; Artistic Dir., Nat. Inst. for Ballet. Compositions incl: La Morte Di Salome (Oscar Wilde); Revue (ballet); Ritmi Made in Italy (ballet); La Fanciulla Dell'amore (1-act opera); La Commedia Del'Arte; La Lezione Di Canto for coloratura soprano & Tempi for flute & piano; Dawn Rhapsody for piano & small orch.; sev. piano pieces. Address: Via Margutta 51, Rome, Italy. 3.

CORTINA, Raquel, b. 23 Jan. 1946, Havana, Cuba. Singer; University Professor & Voice Department Head. Educ: BA, La. State Univ., 1968; MMus, Fla. State Univ., 1970; DMus, ibid., 1972. Debut: w. New Orleans Phil. Symph. Orch., 1971. Career incls: Opera, solo & chmbr. recitals; Concerts La., Miss. & Fla.; Radio & TV apps.; Soprano soloist, 'King David' (Honegger) & 'Les Noces' (Stravinsky) w. New Orleans Phil. Symph. Orch.; Assoc. Prof. & Voice Dept. Hd., Univ. New Orleans. Mbrships. incl: Bd., State La., Nat. Assn. Tchrs. Singing, 1975-77. Hons. incl: Mme. Outstanding Young Women of Am., 1973. Hobbies incl: Mtn. Hiking. Address: 7019 Crowder Blvd., Apt. 82, New Orleans, LA 70127, USA.

CORTINAS, Pedro, b. 11 Oct. 1943, Chihuahua, Mexico. Violinist; Conductor. Educ: Violin studies w. Abraham Chavez; Ivan Galamian & Max Rostal; Juilliard Schl. of Music, NY; Studied cond. w. Jean Morelle. m. Elisabeth Schaerli, 2 s. Career: apps. w. string quartet; Concertmaster, num. orchs. in USA, Can., Latin Am., Belgium & Germany. Hobbies: Tennis; Equestrian riding. Address: Fichtenweg 3, D-5912 Hilchenbach, German Fed. Repub.

CORUJO, Francisco, b. 25 Nov. 1909, Buenos Aires, Argentina. Violinist. Educ: Dentistry, Nat. Schl. of Odontology, Univ. of Brazil; Studied violin in Buenos Aires w. Rosa Taberné, Francisco Sitoula, Victor Vezzelli, Rio de Janeiro, Brazil w. Romeu Ghipsman; Graded by Conserv. of Music. Fed. Univ. Fluminense, Rio de Janeiro. m. Renet Damiao Corujo, 2 d., 3 s. Career: Violin, Phil. Orch., Rio de Janeiro; Leader Nat. Radio Symph. Orch., 1956-61; 1st Violin Quartet, Min. of Educ. & Culture

Radio, 1960-63; Leader Municipal Theatre Orch., Rio de Janeiro, 1961-69; Leader Brazilian Symph. Orch., 1967-. Mbr., Profl. Musicians Union, Rio de Janeiro. Hons: Musician of the Year, 1974 (Brazilian Musicians, Rio de Janeiro); Good Service Dip., 1974 (Guanabara State Govt.). Hobbies: Chess; Watching Football. Address: Rua Evarista da Veiga 47-901, ZC 06, Rio de Janeiro, Brazil.

CORY, Eleanor Thayer, b. 8 Sept. 1943, Englewood, NJ, USA. Composer. Educ: BA, Sarah Lawrence Coll., 1965; MAT, Harvard Grad. Schl. of Educ., MAT, 1966; MM, New England Conserv., 1970; DMA, Columbia Univ., 1975. m. Joel William Gressel. Career: tchng. positions, Columbia & Hofstra Univs., Brooklyn Coll., CUNY; currently Fac. Mbr. Baruch Coll., ibid.; Tchr., Yale Univ., 1978-. Comps. incl: Epithalamium for solo flute, 1973; Counterbrass, for brass, piano & percussion, 1978; Aria Viva for tenor & 5 instruments, 1977; Waking, for Soprano & 10 instruments. Contbr. to musical jrnls.; Ed. Committee, Theory & Practice; Assoc. Ed., Contemp. Music Newsletter. Mbrships. incl: Corres. Sec., League of Cmps. Int. Soc. for Contemp. Music; Am. Comps. Alliance; 2nd VP, ibid; Am. Music Ctr. Hons. Nat. Endowment for the Arts, 1976; NY State Coun. (CAPS Grant), 1976; MacDowell Colony Fellowship, 1977. Hobbies: Modern Dance, Tennis, Poetry. Address: 945 West End Ave., Apt. 8B, NY, NY 10025, USA.

COSCIA, Silvio (pen name Sylvius C), b. 27 Nov. 1899, Milan, Italy. French Hornist; Composer; Vocal Teacher. Educ: Higher Dips., French Horn & Comp., Giuseppe Verdi Conserv., Milan. m. Virginia Malnati. Career: Mbr., NY Met. Opera Assn. Orch., USA, 1929-634; Voice Fac., New Engl. Conserv., Boston, Mass., ibid., 1967-. Compositions (some under name C Silvius): Vocal Arias; Trumpet Duets; Septet; Quintets; Quartets; Trio; Duets; French Horn Method With 5 Concert Pieces. Author, Operative Italian Diction & Articulation Applied to Singing, 1969. Contbr. to La Follia, NY. Mbrships: ASCAP; Hon. Mbr., AFM. Hons: Silver Medal, Min. Foreign Affairs, Italy, 1964; Kt., Italian Repub., 1965. Address: 12 Riverside St., Apt. Watertown, MA 02172, USA.

COSMA, Octavian Lazar, b. 15 Feb. 1933, Tresnea Salaj, Romania. Musicologist; Professor. Educ: Rimsky Korsakov Conserv., Leningrad, USSR. m. Elena Cosma, 1 s., 1 d. Career: Counselor, Min. of Culture & Educ., 1959-63; Asst. & Lectr. Prof., Conserv. of Bucharest, 1959-. Publs: The Romanian Opera 2 vols., 1962; Enesco's Oedipus, 1967; The Chronicle of Romanian Music, vol. I, 1973, vol. II, 1974, vol. III, 1975; Vol. IV, 1976. Contbr. to var. profl. jrnls. Mbrships. incl: Romanian Union of Comps ; Am. Musicological Soc. Hons. Cipiran Porumbescu Prize, Romanian Acad., 1963; Prize, Romanian Union of Comps., 1968. Hobbies: Sport; Football; Tourism. Address: Cotroceni 5-7, Bucharest, Romania.

COSMA, Viorel, b. 30 Mar. 1923, Timisoara, Romania. Musicologist. Educ: Municipal Conserv., Timisoara; Ciprian Porumbescu Conserv., Bucharest. m. Coralia Cosma. Debut: as Cond., 1944; as Musicol., 1946. Publs. incl: Ciprian Porumbescu, 1957; Romanian Musicians Lexicon, 1970; Two Thousand Years of Music in Romania, 1976; Rumanian Performers Lexicon, 1976. Contbr. to int. musicol. jrnls. Mbrships: Int. Musicol. Soc.; Georg Friedrich Händel Soc.; French Musicol. Soc.; Chopin Soc., Warsaw. Hons. incl: Prize, Romanian Union of Comps., 1970; Prize, Acad. of Romania, 1971. Hobby: Motoring. Address: Str. Luterana nr. 3, Bucharest, Romania.

COSSA, Dominic, b. 13 May 1935, Jessup, Pa., USA. Opera Singer. Educ: BS & MA (Psychol.). m. Janet Edgerton, 2 c. Debut: NYC Opera, 1961. Career incl: Leading baritone w. Metropol. Opera, NYC Opera & San Fran. Opera. Recordings: Elixir of Love (Decca); Les Huguenots (Bd. of Govs.); Julius Caesar. Mbrships: AGMA, Bohemian Club, NYC. Hons. incl: Liederkranz Award & sev. 1st prizes. Hobbies: Collecting Antiques; Wine Making. Mgmt: Colbert Artists Mgmt. Address: 429 Hegi Dr., New Milford, NJ 07646, USA.

COSSETTO, Emil, b. 12 Oct. 1918, Trieste, Italy. Composer; Conductor. Educ: Dip. Cond., Music Conserv., Zagreb. m. Dunja Cossetto, 3 children. Career: Concerts w. choir & orchs. in Yugoslavia & abroad; Radio & TV apps. num. countries inclng: Italy, France, Switzerland, Austria, USSR; Cond.; Promenade choirs Joza Vlahović & Mos a Pijade, Zagreb. Comps. incl: Concert for Clarinet; Aria & Minuetto; Adagio Tarantella; Dances (violin & piano); The Rider (cantata). Contbr. to Zvuk (Music Revue); Oko, Zagreb; Num. jrnls. & newspapers. Mbrships: Pres., Soc. of Croatian Comps., 1968-70; Soc. of Croatian Musical Artists. Hons. incl: Gold Medal of Merit, 1975; Prizes for composing & conucting. Hobby: Music. Address: TRG Republike 3, 41000 Zagreb, Yugoslavia.

COSSOTTO, Fiorenza, b. 22 Apr. 1938, Crescentino, Italy. Operatic Mezzo-soprano. Educ: Dip., G Verdi Conserv. of Music, Turin, 1956. m. Ivo Vinco, 1 s. Career: Permanent Singer, La Scala, Milan, 1957-; apps. in oper houses of Venice, Florence, Naples, Rome, Milan, Barcelona, Paris, London & Vienna, as well as in USSR & at Edinburgh Fest. Address: Via Ezio Biondi 1, Milan, Italy. 2.

COSTA, Mary Pokora, b. 21 Apr. 1908, NYC, USA. Pianist; Teacher; Adjudicator. Educ: Grad., AM Virgil Piano Schl.; Schlrship., David Marnes, NYC; 12 yrs. study w. Heinrich Gebhard, Boston, Mass.; 3 yrs. study w. Bruno Eiser of Berlin Conserv.; studied w. Guy Maier, Alfred Mirovitch & Johanna Harris; Accredited Tchr., State of NY. m. Joseph L Costa, 1 s., 1 d. Career: weekly radio progs., WNYC, 1927-28; concerts throughout New England, 1930-43; currently Adjudicator for NGPT, Music Tchrs. Nat. Assn., MTAC, Schapiro Mem. Schlrship. (Alaska), & var. local coll. & schl. competitions; Mng. Co-Chmn., Orange Co. Youth Philharmonic Audtions & Young Musician's Contest of Orange Co. Contbr. to: Guild Notes; Woonsocket (RI) Call. Music Criticsm; prog. notes for var. concerts. Mbrships: Fac. Mbr., Hall of Fame, NGPT; Bd. of Dirs., Educ. Chmn. & Contest Chmn., Music Tchrs. Assn. of Calif.; Music Tchrs. Nat.Assn.; Prog. Chmn., Westchester (NY) Music Tchrs. Coun.; Am. Coll. of Musicians; NY Music Tchrs. Congress; Piano Audition Chmn., Musical Arts Club of Orange Co.; Pres., Beethoven Club of RI; Leschetizky Assn.; Maier Assn.; Abby Whiteside Assn. Hobbies: Art Collecting; Gardening. Address: 11812 Colony Dr., Santa Ana, CA 92705, USA. 3, 5.

COSTANTINO, Romola, b. 14 Sept. 1930, Sydney, Aust. Pianist. Educ: LRAM; DSCM (Sydney); BA, MMus, Sydney. m. George Enyi. Debut: Melbourne, 1950. Career: Aust.-wide tours as assoc. artist for Itzhak Perlman, Kyung-Wha-Chung, Gyorgy Pauk, Janos Starker, Herman Baumann, Felicity Palmer, Carl Pini, Ladislav Jasek, Rafaele Altwegg, Guy Fallot, etc.; Apps., all major Aust. musical centres as soloist w. ABC Orchs., in chmbr. music, recitals, TV & radio programs; apps. Adelaide Fest. of the Arts. Recordings: French Piano Music; Brahms viola/piano sonatas w. Robert Pikler. Contbr. to: Sydney Morning Herald (Music Critic, 1962-). Hons: Queen's Jubilee Medal, 1977; OBE for services to the Arts, 1978; Churchill Fellowship, 1970. Address: 5 Reginald St., Cremorne, NSW, Aust.

COSTERE, Edmond, b. 2 May 1905, Bourg en Bresse, France. Musicologist-piano. Educ: LLD; Dip., Soc. des Auteurs & Composeurs de Musique; Dr. of Musicol., Univ. of Paris. m. Anna Malzac, 4 c. Compositions: Pieces pour piano; Sonate alto & piano; Quatuor a cordes. Publs: Lois & Styles de Harmonies Musicales, 1954; Mort ou Transfigurations de l'Harmonie, 1962 (Tokyo 1978). Contbr. to: Polyphonic; Revue Musicale; Revue de Musicol.; Revue d'Esthetique; Ency. de la Musique de Fasquelle; Jrnl. Musical de Lausanne; Opera Int., etc. Mbrship: French Soc. of Musicol. Recip: Off., Legion d'Honneur, 1955. Hobby: Painting. Address: 24 rue de Falicon, Nice 06000, France.

COSTIN, William Lorne, b. 17 Aug. 1952, Amherst, NS, Can. Orchestral Musician - French Horn. Educ: BMus, Mt. Allison Univ., Sackville, New Brunswick, Can., 1974; Künstlerische Abschlussprüfung im Hauptfact Horn, Folkwang Hochschule Essen, German Fed. Repub., 1978 (w. Hermann Baumann). Career: Tibor Varga Chmbr. Orch., Sion, Switz.; Detusch Oper am Rhein (Duisburg Sinfoniker), Duisburg, German Fed. Repub. mbr. AFM. Hobbies: Winemaking; Photography. Address: PO Box 609, Amherst, NS B4H 4B8, Can.

ČOTEK, Pavel, b: 12 Mar. 1922, Frysava, Czech. Composer; Educator. Educ: Grad., State Conserv., Prague; Dip., Janacek Acad.of Arts & Music, Brno. m. Zdenka Tkana. Career: active, 1946-; Assoc. Prof., Philos. Fac., Palacky Univ., Olomou. Comps. incl: Sonatina for piano, 1960; Sonata for violin & piano, 1960; Sonata for violin & piano, 1962; Sonata for violin & piano, 1962; Portrait of a Bird, 1963; Concertino grosso, 1964; Symphonic Etudes, 1965; Concerto for 2 percussionists & orch., 1967; Responseria for organ & percussionists & orch., 1967; Responseria for organ & orch., 1969. Contbr. to: Hudebni rozhldedy. Mbrships: Union of Czech Comps. & Concert Artists; Committee, Czech Music Fund. Recip., num. Czech. comp. awards, 1946-. Hobbies: Dogs; Sports. Address: 18 Riegrova, 77200 Olomouc, Czechoslovakia.

COTRUBAS, Ileana, b. Galati, Romania. Concert & Opera Singer; Lyric Soprano. Educ: Scoala speciala de Musica, Bucharest; Ciprian Porumbescu Conserv., ibid; Musikakademie, Vienna, Austria. m. Manfred Ramin. Debut: as Yniold, Bucharest Opera, 1964. Career: Frankfurt Opera, Germany, 1968-71; Staatsoper, Vienna, Austria, 1970-; Covent Gdn., UK, 1971-; Saatsoper, Munich, Germany, 1973-; Lyric Opera, Chgo., USA, 1973-75; Opera Paris, 1974-75; La Scala, Mllan, Italy, 1975-; Metropolitan Opera, NY, 1977-; San Fran., 1978-;

Var. fests. Num. recordings. Hons: 1st Prize, Int. Singing
Competition, Hertogenbusch, Netherlands, 1965; 1st Prize,
Munich Radio Competition, 1966. Address: c/o Royal Opera
House Covent Garden, London WC2E 7QA, UK.

COTTON, Eric Beaumont, b. 17 Jan. 1916, Irlam,
Manchester, UK. Orchestral Bassoonist. Educ: Royal Manchester
Coll. of Music. m. Edna A D Devonshire. Career: Amateur
Violinist in early youth; Profl. Bassoonist, Halle Liverpool Phil.,
BBC Northern Orchs.; Prin. Bassoonist, Buxton, Carl Rosa Opera,
Bournemouth; Prin. Bassoonist, SNO, 1950. Mbr., Glasgow
Soc. of Musicians Recip., Iles Gold Medal, Royal Manchester Coll.
of Music, 1939. Hobbies: Golf; Simple card tricks. Address:
38 Westbourne Gdns., Glasgow, G129PF, UK.

COULING, Vivien, b. 14 Feb. 1931, Edinburgh, UK.
Cellist; Teacher of Alexander Technique. Educ: RCM; ARCM;
studied w. Pablo Casals, Prades, France; Constructive Tchng.
Centre, London. m. Gordon Mackie (dec.), 2 s. Career: Cello
soloist & chmbr. music perfs.; Tchr.of Alexander Technique, esp.
for musicians, UK, Paris, USA & Switz.; Staff mbr., Schl. of
Alexander Studies, London, 1977-. Mbrships: ISM; ESTA; Soc.
of Tchrs. of the Alexander Technique. Address: 18b Earl's Court
Square, London SW5 9DN, UK. 27.

COULSON, Richard, b. 20 June 1948, Gateshead, Co.,
Durham, UK. Concert Organist; Continuo Player. Educ: Newcastle
Schl. of Music; RCM, London; FRCO; GRSM; ARCM; LRAM. m.
Susan Fraser Wood, 1 s., 1 d. Debut: Westminster Cathedral,
London. Career: apps. in fests. such as the Bath Fest., Bath Bach
Fest., Edinburgh Fest., Bach in London Fest. & Int. Organ Fest., St.
Albans; recitals in cathedrals, chs. & concert halls; frequent radio
broadcasts. Recordings; var. Recip., num. prizes for organ &
continuo & Gtr. London Arts Assn. Young Musician award,
1973. Hobby: Photography. Mgmt: Terry Slasberg Assocs.
Address: 131 Gilders Rd., Chessington, Surrey, UK.

COULTHARD, Jean, b. 10 Feb. 1908, Vancouver, BC,
Canada. Composer; Teacher; Pianist. Educ: Univ. of BC; RCM;
LRSM; Juilliard Schl., NY; study w. Milhaud, Schoenberg,
Copland & Bartok. m. Donald Marvin Adams, 1 d. Debut:
Concert of original works, Vancouver, 1932. Career incl. num.
broadcasts on CBC. Comps. incl: Cradle Song, 1927; Threnody,
1935; Canadian Fantasy (orch.), 1939; Ballade: A Winter's
Tale, (large string orch.), 1942; Song of the Sea (orch.),
1942; String Quartet No. 1, 1948; Symph. No. 1,
-1950; Concerto for violin & orch., 1959; This Land, Choral
Symph., 1967; String Quartet No. 2, 1969; Music to St.
Cecilia (organ, strings & tape), 1969; Songs for the Distaff Muse
(soprano, alto, cello), 1972; Canada Mosaic, 1973;
Kalamalka (Lake of Many Colours), 1974; 4 Prophetic Songs,
1975; 3 duets for contralto & violin, 1977; 3 Shakespeare
Sonnets, 1977. Var. works recorded by artists incl. John Ogdon.
Contbr. to Canadian Music Tchrs. Jrnl. Mbrships: Canadian
League of Composers; Canadian Music Ctr.; Vancouver Women's
Musical Club. Recip: Alfred Clement Mem. Prize, 1951. Am.
W Coast Learned Socs. Award, 1949; Canadian Royal Soc.
Fellowship, 1955; Canada Coun. Fellowship, 1965.
Hobbies: Travel; Walking. Mgmt: BMI, Canada. Address: 2747
SW Marine Dr., Vancouver, BC, Canada.

COUSIN, Jack, b. 17 Oct. 1952, Boston, Mass., USA.
Bassist. Educ: Dip., New England Conserv. Debut: Concerto app.
w. Gtr. Boston Youth Symph., 1970. Career: Won audition for
Leopold Stokowsky's Int. Youth Orch., 1969; Soloist, Holyoke
Cymph., 1970, Red Fox Music Camp Orch., 1971; num.
recitals, Boston & LA; currently Bass player, LA Phil. Orch.
Contbr. to: LA Bass Club Newsletter. Mbr., Int. Soc. of Bassists.
Recip., musical awards & scholarships. Hobbies incl: Karate; Scuba
diving; Photography; Skiing; Science Fiction. Address: 4310
Raintree Circle, Culver City, CA 90230, USA.

COUSINS, John Edward, b. 2 Aug. 1943, Wellington, NZ.
Composer; University Teacher. Educ: MusB, Canterbury Univ. m.
Leonie Joan Cousins, 2 s. Comps. incl: I Sing of Olaf (secular
cantata; recorded), 1969; 3 Songs for voice & piano (publd.),
1970; Christmas Music (commnd. by NZ Radio; recorded on
Kiwi SLD 44.46); num. instrumental works recorded by NZ
Radio; electronic comps. on master tapes held by Univ. of
Canterbury Electronic Music Studio. Contbr. to: NZ Listener; Price
Milburn Gazette. Hobbies: Long Distance Running. Address: 4
Hackthorne Rd., Christchurch, NZ.

COVELL, Roger David, b. 1 Feb. 1931, Sydney, Aust.
University Teacher; Music Critic; Conductor. Educ: BA; PhD. m.
Patricia Anne Brown, 1 d., 3 s. Career: Hd., Music Dept., Univ.
of NSW, 1966-; Chief music critic, The Sydney Morning Herald,
1960-; Musical Dir., Univ. of NSW Opera, Grainger Consort.
Comps: Theatre music; choral pieces. Recordings: (as Cond.),
Barry Conyngham's Edward John Eyre. Publs: Australia's Music-

Themes of a new society, 1967; Music in Australia - Needs and
possiblities, 2 vols., 1970; Music in Australian libraries (co-
author), 1970; The Currency Lass (Ed. & Arr.), 1976. Contbr.
to: Studies in Music; Aust. Jrnl. of Music Educ.; Quadrant; Theatre
Aust., etc. Mbrships: Aust. Coun., Nat. Pres., Aust. Soc. for Music
Educ.; Musicol. Soc. of Aust. Hobbies: Music; Bush-walking.
Address: 9 Kubya St., Blackheath, NSW 2785, Aust.

COVERDALE, Miles, b. 6 July 1914, Hull, Yorks., UK.
Pianist; Teacher. Educ: pvte. study w. Harold Craxton; studies w.
Tobias Matthay, Tobias Matthay Pianoforte Schl. m. Joan
Rosemary Pye, 1 s. Debut: Wigmore Hall, London, 1949.
Career: Recitals & Concertos; Regular broadcasting since 1948,
all regions & London; Staff Mbr., Bangor Univ., 19390-40,
1946-47; Asst. Tchr. to Harold Craxton, 1948-58; Staff
Mbr., RSAMD, 1958-79; Master classes & Chmbr. music
coaching; Lecture recitals, UK & abroad. Mbr., ISM. Hons: Jessie
Mattay Memorial Scholarship, 1937. Hobbies: Sailing. Address:
East Brendon, Polruan by Fowey, Cornwall, UK. 3.

COVERT, John, b. 21 June 1937, Southampton, USA.
Professor of Music, (French Horn). Educ: BMus., Mus M., Eastman
Schl. of Music, USA. m. Mary Ann Covert, 1 s. Career: French
Hornist, Rochester Phil. Orch., 1961-64; Memphis Symph.
Orch., 1965-66, NE Pennsylvania Symph. Orch., 1972-; Fac.
Mbr., Memphis State Univ., Ithaca Coll., Eastman Schl. of Music.
(Summer 1973); Prof. of Music, (French Horn), Ithaca Coll.
Recordings: Recital Music for French Horn, Mark Records; Ithaca
Brass Quintet, Mark & Crest Records. Mbrships: MENC; Coll.
Music Soc.; Pi Kappa Lambda; Kappa Gamma Psi. Recip., Perf's
Cert., French Horn, Eastman Schl. of Music, 1960. Address:
215 N Cayuga St., Ithaca, NYC, USA.

COVERT, Mary Ann Hunter, b. 24 Sept. 1936, Memphis,
Tenn., USA. Pianist; Harpsichord Player; Associate Professor of
Music. Educ: Dip., Memphis Conserv. of Music, 1954; BM,
Okla. Bapt. Univ., 1957; Dip., NGPT, 1958; MA, Memphis
State Univ., 1965. m. John Covert, 3 s., 1 d. Debut: Carnegie
Recital Hall, NYC, 1971; Rome, Italy, 1974. Career incls:
Recitalist in chmbr. ensembles; apps. w. orchs. Comps. publs: Jr.
HS Choral works; recorded: Recital Music for Trumpet, Piano &
Organ; Recital Music for French Horn; Chamber Music (Ithaca
Brass Quintet). Recordings: Kent Kennan Concertino for piano &
wind ensemble; Rhapsody in Blue w. Ithaca Coll. Wind Ensemble;
Complete solo piano work of Karel Husa. Contr. to: Clavier. Mbr.
profl. orgs. Recip. var. hons. & awards. Hobbies: Reading;
Camping. Address: 215 N Cayuga St., Apt. 108, Ithaca, NY
14850, USA. 4

COWAN, Joan Yarbrough, b. 10 Sept. 1940, Boston, Mass.,
USA. Professor of Music; Concert duopianist. Educ: B Mus.,
Oberlin Conservatory of Music, Ohio; Studied at Mozarteum.
Salzburg, Austria, 1 yr.; LRAM & 3 yrs. study, Royal Acad. of
Music, London, UK. m. Robert Holmes Cowan. Debut: as mbr. of
duo-piano team Yarbrough & Cowan, Town Hall, NY, 1967.
Career: Over 200 concerts in 30 states, Europe & Mexico;
Appearances w. New Orleans Phil., Okla. City Symph. Orch.,
Atlanta Symph. Orch., Charlotte Symph. Orch., Augusta Symph.
Orch. & others; Broadcasts on Voice of Am., Armed Forces Radio &
Mutual Broadcasting System; Appearances on Educl. TV.
Recordings: Dynamisms for 2 pianos, by Wayne Barlow; Modern
Music for 2 pianos; Sonata for 2 pianos, Op. 13, by Vincent
Persichetti; Variations for pianos, Op. 54a, by Wallingford
Riegger; Fantasy for 2 pianos, Op. 9, by Nicolai Berezoskwy.
Contbr. to Music Jrnl. Mbrships: Pi Kappa Lambda; Music Tchrs.
Nat. Assn. Recip., All Am. Press Assocs. Award, Best Duopianists,
1966. Hobbies incl: Bicycling; Reading. Address: PO Box 465,
Montevallo, AL 35115, USA.

COWAN, Robert Holmes, b. 12 Jan. 1931, Enid, Okla.,
USA. Professor of Music; Pianist. Educ: BS, MS, Juilliard Schl. of
Music, NYC; DMA, Eastman Schl. of Music, Rochester; LRAM. m.
Joan Yarborough. Debut: Piano-duo w. wife, Town Hall, NYC,
1967. Career: Over 200 concert apparances in USA, Europe &
Mexico; appeared w. New Orleans Phil., Okla. City
Symph.,Atlanta Symph., Charlotte Symph., Augusta Symph.,
etc.; Broadcasts w. Voice of Am., Armed Forces Radio & Mutural
Broadcasting System; appearanced on Educl. TV. Recordings:
Dynamisms for 2 Pianos by Wane Barlow (MirroSonic); Modern
Music for 2 Pianos; Vincent Persichetti - Sonata for 2 Pianos, Op.
13, Wallingford Riegger-Variations for 2 Pianos, 54a; Nicolai
Berezowsky-Fantasy for 2 Pianos, Op. 9 (CRI label). Contbr. to
Music Jrnl. Mbrships: Pi Kappa Lambda; Nat. MTA. Recip: All-
Am. Press Assocs. Award, Best Duo-Pianists 1966. Hobbies:
Cycling; Reading. Mgmt: Ala. Concert Assoc. Ltd., PO Box 465,
Montevallo, AL 35115, USA. Address: PO Box 465,
Montevallo, AL 35115, USA.

COWAN, Sigmund Sumner, b. 4 Mar. 1948, New York City,
USA. Opera Singer (baritone). Educ: Univ. of Miami, 1963-64;

Univ. of Fla., Gainesville, 1965-68; Juilliard Schl., NYC, 1969-70; Manhattan Shcl. of Music, NYC, 1972-73. Debut: Teatro del Giglio, Lucca, Italy, 1974. Career incl: opera perfs., NYC Opera, Lake George Opera Fest.; Worlf Trap Farm Park of the Perf. Arts; Rochester Opera; Miamia Opera Guild; San Antonio Grand Opera; TV apps., NBC; Var. Orchl. concerts, inclng. Balt. Symph., Spoleto Fest. Orch., Nat. Symph., Rochester Phil., Fest. Chmbr. Orch. Mbrships: Am. Guild of Musical Artists; Phi Mu Alpha Sinfonia. Hons. incl: Int. Opera & Belcanto, Belgium, 1978. Mgmt: Sardos Artists Mgmt., 180 West End Ave., NYC, NY 10023, USA; Lies Askonas, 19A Air St., London W1R 6LQ, UK. Address: 215 W 7th St., NYC, NY 10023, USA.

COWDEN, Robert Hapgood, b. 18 Nov. 1934, Warren, Pa., USA. University Professor; Arts Administrator. Educ: AB, Princeton Univ., 1956; BMus., Eastman Schl. of Music, Rochester, NY, 1959; MMus., ibid., 1960; DMA, 1966; Perfs. Cert. in Voice & Opera, 1961; Dip., Musikhochschule Frankfurt/M, 1963. m. Jacqueline V Mailloux, 4 c. Debut: Chautauqua Opera Assn., 1957. Career: w. Chautauqua Opera Assn., 1957-61, '68; Stadt-theater Hildesheim, W Germany, 1963-65; Mt. Op. Nat. Co., 1965-66; TV series 'Masterpieces of Musical Theater' over ABC Detroit, 1971; Cultural host & commentator, WDET-FM (Detroit), 1973-74; Univ. Prof., Voice, Opera, Wayne State Univ., Detroit. Publs: trans., Albert Lortzing's Der Wildschhuetz, 1966; trans. Giuseppe Verdi's Un Ballo in Maschera Edwin F Kalmus, 1969; The Chautauqua Opera Assn., 1929-58; An Interpretative History, 1974; Checklist of Singers' Biographies, 1969. Contbr. to profl. publs. Mbr. of sev. profl. orgs. Recip. var. hons. Hobbies: Gardening; Bibliophile, etc. Address: School of Humanities & the Arts, San Jose State Univ., San Jose, CA 95129, USA.

COWDEROY, Peter Sutherland, b. 9 Oct. 1918, London, UK. Pianist; Composer; Accompanist; Professor of Piano & Theory. Educ: RAM, 1937-45; Aamo studies m. Max Pirani, Frenz Reizenstein & Adelina de Lara; Comp. studies w. M Pirani & B J Dale. Debut: Cowdray Hall, London, 1949. Career: Sub-Prof., RAM, 1942-45; Prof. of Piano, Welbley Pk. Schl. of Music, 1950-59; Pvte. Tchr., Colindale, 1960-68, currently in Bushey, Herts.; Solo Recitals, London & provinces; Accomp. for singers, instrumentalists; Chmbr. Music Perfs. Mbrships: RAM Club; VP, Stanmore Choral Soc., Middx.; Patron, Watford Music Fest., Herts. Recip. num. awards at RAM inclng: Thalberg Schlrships. for piano, 1939; Eyers Prize (aural trng.), 1940; Potter Exhib., Walter MacFarren Gold Medal, Westlake Mem. Prize for piano & Oliveria Prescott Prize (disting. comp.), all 1941. Hobbies incl: Philately; Singing solo tenor. Address: Adnam Cottage, 17 Finch Ln., Bushey, Watford, Herts. WD23AH, UK. 3, 28.

COWIE, Leroy, b. 1 Sept. 1940, Aberdeen, UK. Freelance Musician (Double bass). Educ: RAM; ARCM; Cert. Ed. m., 2 c. Career: Sub-Prin. Double Bass, BBC Scottish Symph. Orch., 1962-64; Co-Prin. Double Bass, Oslo Phil. Orch., 1964-65; Prin. Bass, Birmingham Symph. Orch., 1966-71; Freelance Double Bass, 1972-. Contbr. to: Contact (Modern Music mag., Birmingham). Mbr., Int. Inst. for String Bass. Hons: George VI Coronation Scholarship, 1958; West Midlands Arts Assn. Comp., 1971. Hobbies: Reading; Chess; Philosophy. Address: 9 Teddington Pk. Rd., Teddington TW11 8NB, UK.

COX, Alison Mary, b. 15 Feb. 1956, London, UK. Composer. Educ: Royal Northern Coll. of Music, Manchester; GRNCM. m. Anthony Gilbert. Comps: Trio for Strings; 2 Songs for counter-tenor, alto flute & viola; String Quintet; 3 Piano Pieces; 5 Pieces for Chmbr. Orch.; The Time Killing (opera); Incidental Music for th Caucasian Chalk Circle; 2 songs of Death, for baritone; Chien-Tang, music for a Chinese puppet play; Trilithon, for orch.; Music for film, The Outing (Denny Lawrence). Hons: Cecil Fifield Prize for Comp., 1974; Leo Grinden Prize for Comp., 1978; Award from Vaughan Williams Trust to study film music in Aust. Hobbies: Wildlife Study; Art; Writing; Reading; Travelling. Address: 52 Hague Bar, New Mills, NR. Stockport, SK12 3AT, UK.

COX, Clifford Laird, b. 30 Jan. 1935, New Kensington, USA. Professor of Music; Violist; Conductor; Adjudicator. Educ: BS, Ind. Univ. of Pa.; MEd, ibid.; Carnegie Mellon Inst.; Univ. of Buffalo; studied w. Nicolai Lopatnikoff. m. Joanne Hill Cox, 2 d. Career: Soloist w. Symphs. & Bands; TV App. as Cond.; opera The Cynic; Fndr., Dir., Edinboro Summer Orch. Camp; Host, Radio Progs. Crossroads of Classics, 1956-68; Bach to Bartok, 1972-; Prof. of Music, Edinboro State Coll.; Mbr. Erie Phil.; Dir., Presque Isle Str. Quartet; Cond., Edinboro Coll. Orch., Northwest Pa. Symph., num. Fest. Grps.; Adjudicator; Prin. Cond., Pa. Youth Orch., 1976 European Tour. Compositions: overture Psi; oper The Cynic. Author, Toward Classroom Music, 1969. Contbr. to MENC Jrnl. Mbrships: Phi Delta Kappa; Phi

Mu Alpha; Alpha Psi Omega; NEA; Apscuf/Pahe. Hons: Corrine Menk Wahr Award for Excellence in the Fine Arts, 1955; Corrine Menk Wahr Award for Initiative, 1956. Hobbies: Reading; Aeronautics; Electronics. Address: 222 Fairway Dr., Edinboro, PA 16412, USA.

COX, David (Vassall), b. 4 Feb. 1916, Broadstairs, Kent, UK. Composer; Pianist; Writer; Broadcasting Organiser. Educ: RCM; MA, BMus, Oxford Univ. m. Barbara Ellen Lee Butcher, 2 d., 1 s. Career: Music Orgnsr., External Servs. BBC, 1956-76. Comps. incl: (Opera) The Children in the Forest; (Choral) The Summer's Nightingale; Of Beasts; Songs of Earth & Air; This Child of Life; A Greek Cantata; (Song Cycle) 3 Songs from John Donne. Publs. incl: The Symphony, 1967; Debussy's Orchestral Music, 1974. Contbr. to profl. publs. Mbrships: PRS; MCPS. Hobbies: Lit.; Films; Photography; Swimming. Address: Linn Hey, Dunton Green, Sevenoaks, Kent, UK.

COX, John, b. 12 Mar. 1935, Bristol, UK. Opera & Play Producer. Educ: BA, Univ. of Oxford. Debut: L'Enfant et les Sortilèges, Sadlers Wells Opera Co. Career: Freelance Prod. of Plays, London, English provinces, Spoleto Fest.; Freelance Prod. of Opera, worldwide inclng. London, NY, Vienna, Sydney, Frankfurt; Dir., Music Theatre Ensemble, 1967-70, Edinburgh, Brighton, City of London Fests.; Formerly Dir., BBC TV; Dir. of Prod., Glyndebourne Fest. Opera, 1971-. Recordings: Direction for stereophonic sound, Coronation of Poppaea, Pritchard, & Otello, Barbirolli; Directed Ashcroft, Schofield in Facade, Walton. FRSA. Recip. Scholarship, Countess of Munster's Musical Trust, 1959-60. Hobbies: Fine arts; Gdns. Mgmt: AIM Ltd. Address. 7 W Grove, Greenwich, London SE10, UK.

COX, Renee S, b. 24 May 1952, Independence, Miss., USA. Assistant Professor; Double Bass Player. Educ: BMus, Oberlin Coll., 1974; MMus, Univ. of Mich. at Ann Arbor, 1976; studied double bass w. Jacques Posell, Lawrence Hurst & David Danesi. Career: perf. w. New Hungarian Quartet, Oberlin, 1974; sev. solo recitals; Asst. Prof. of Music Hist., Univ. of Tenn. at Chattanooga, 1976-; Dir. of Graduate Studies in Music, ibid., 1978-; prin. bass, Chattanooga Symph.; mbr., Tenn. Chmbr. Players. Contbr. of paper on Use of Mode in the Death Songs of Franz Schubert to S Chapt. of Am. Musicol. Soc., 1979. Mbrships: Pi Kappa Lambda; Am. Musicol. Soc.; Coll. Music Soc.; hon. mbr., Blue Key Honor Fraternity. Hons: Fac. Develop. grant, UTC, 1979-80; Univ. Fellowship, OSU, 1979-80. Hobbies: Academic Minor Philosophy; Women's Movement. Address: 101 Curl Dr., Apt. 1239, Columbus, OH 43201, USA.

COZAD, Joseph, b. 30 Nov. 1935, Topeka, Kan., USA. Guitar Instructor; Guitarist. Educ: BMusEd, Violin, Washburn Univ., Topeka, Kan.; Grad. Studies, Univ. of Mo., Kansas City, Conserv. of Music; Segovia Master Class, UL, Berkeley, Calif.; studied w. Walter Fritschy, Alirio Diaz, Oscar Ghiglia, Celin Romero, Pepe Romero, etc. m. Cynthia Bonner, 2 s., 1 d. Career: Tchr. of Guitar, Cons. of Music, Univ. of Mo. at Kansas City, 15 yrs.; Vis. Lectr., UMSL, Webster Coll., Washburn Univ.; Tchr., Penn Valley Community Coll., Park Coll. & Univ. of Kansas; Guest soloist w. Kansas City Phil. Mbrships: Alpha Psi Chapt., Phi Mu Alpha Sinfonia; Fndr. mbr., Am. String Tchrs. Assn. Address: 11517 Roe, Leawood, KS 66211, USA.

COZENS, John, b. 27 April 1906, Tottenham, UK. Choral Conductor. Educ: Toronto Conserv. of Music; Pvte. tchrs. m. Winifred Pitman, 1 d., 1 s. Career: Concert & radio singer (tenor), 1924-45; Cond., The Tallis Choir, 30 yrs.; Cond., Toronto Phil. Choir, Toronto Orpheus Choir; Currently Cond., Ont. Civil Service Choir. Comps: Var. choral comps. & arrs. Contbr. to var. Can. & USA musical jrnls. Mbrships: Hon. Sec., Can. Music Coun. (Sec. Treas., 30 yrs.); Past Pres., Toronto Branch, Ont. Registered Music Tchrs. Assn.; Ch. Music Soc. England; Plainsong & Mediaeval Music Soc. England; Arts & Letters Club of Toronto. Hons: Can. Music Coun. Medal, 1976; Canada's Centennial Medal, 1967; Queen's Silver Jubilee Medal, 1977. Hobby: Heraldic Art. Address: 188 Elmwood Ave., Willowdale, Ont. M2N 3M6, Can.

CRABB, Michael, b. 12 Apr. 1938, Rochford, Essex, UK. Teacher; Conductor; Organist. Educ: Tchrs. Cert. Educ., Coll. St. Mark & St. John; LRAM; LTCL; ACP. m. (1) 1 s.; (2) Anne Shipley. Career: Dir., Music Southend HS Boys; Cond., Southend Boys' Choir; Choirmaster & Organist; Holy Trinity Ch., Southch.; Dir. of Music, Southern High for Boys; 3 series broadcasts, BBC radio Music Workshop w. Southend Boys' Choir & conducted them in all maj. concert halls, cathedrals inclng. continental tours; Edinburgh Fest., 1976; Organ accomp., Royal Albert Hall, Purcell Room, var. London Chs.; St. Severin, Paris, Leiden Cathedral, Holland & Basilica Ottobeuren, Bavaria and var. Brit. Cathedrals. Recordings incl: w. Southend Boys' Choir, Carmina Burana, 1976. 2 Records of pop cantatas. Hobby: Sport (Tcnr.

schl. cricket team). Address: 40 Wimborne Rd., Southend-on-Sea, Essex, UK.

CRABTREE, Phillip D, b. 25 Feb. 1937, Des Moines, Iowa, USA. Musicologist; Conductor; Researcher-Editor; Publisher. Educ: AB, Cornell Coll.; MA, Univ. of Iowa; PhD, Univ. of Cinn. Career: Tchr.-Cond., publ. schls., 1959-65; Asst. Prof. of Choral Music & Musicol., Univ. of Hawaii, 1968-72; Assoc. Prof. of Musicol., Univ. of Cinn., 1972-; Ed., Roger Dean Publng. Co.; has ed. early music for chorus, brass & Collegium Musicum ensembles, inclng. works by Gioseffo Guami, Adriano Banchieri, Andrea Gabrieli, Claudio Merulo, Jacob Handl & John Taverner; is a specialist on music of the Guami family. Contbr. to Grove's 6 & jrnls. Mbrships: Am. Musicol. Soc.; Am. Choral Dir's Assn.; Neue Bach-Gessellschaft; Int. Heinrich Schütz Soc.; Music Educator's Nat. Assn.; Pi Kappa Lambda. Hobbies: Camping; Bicycling. Address: Coll.-Conserv. of Music, Univ. of Cinn., Cinn., OH 45221, USA.

CRAGER, Ted J, b. 27 Dec. 1925, Lockney, Tex., USA. Professor. Educ: BS, Tex. Technol. Coll., 1949; MEd, ibid., 1950; MA, Tchrs. Coll., Columbia Univ., 1954; EdD, ibid., 1955. m. Patricia Ray Bonham, 2 s., 2 d. Career: Profl. Trumpet Player, Symph. Orchs., TV, Radio, Theatres & Night Clubs, 1950-71; currently Radio, Theatres & Night Clubs, 1950-71; currently Prof. & Assoc. Dean, Schl. of Music, Univ. of Miami, Coral Gables, Fla. Comps: Tone Poem for Band, Tex. Tech. Band, 1950; Fanfare & Flourishes, W Tex. State Band, 1963; Jazz Suite, W Tex. State Jazz Band, 1962; Day Portrait, Univ. of Miami Brass Choir, 1966. Contbr. to: The Schl. Musician Mag.; The Fla. Music Dir. Mag.; The Selmer Bandwagon. Mbrships: Music Educators Nat. Conf.; NeA; Nat. Assn. Jazz Educators; Fla. Music Educators Assn.; Am. Fedn. Musicians; Audio Engrng. Soc.; Tex. Bandmasters Assn. (past VP); Tex. Assn. Music Schls. (past mbr., Bd. Dirs.); Tex. Music Educators Assn. (past mbr., Bd. Dirs.). Hobbies: Electronics; Audio Engrng.; Boating; Fishing. Address: 7305 SW 141 Terr., Miami, FL 33158, USA,. 7, 12.

CRAIG, Charles, b. 3 Dec. 1922, London, UK. Dramatic Tenor. Educ: Studied w. Sir Thomas Beecham. m. Dorothy Wilson, 1 s., 1 d. Debut: In Madam Butterfly, Covent Garden, 1959. Career: w. Carl Rosa Opera Co., 1952; Sadlers Wells Opera Co., 1955-59; Int. career, singing at all world's major Opera Houses, 1959-; Specialist in Italian opera; over 300 perfs. of Verdi's Othello. Sev. recordings. Mgmt: c/o S A Gorlinsky Ltd. Address: Whitfield Cottage, Whitfield, Brackley, Northants., UK. 3, 21.

CRAIG, Dale Allan, b. 19 Dec. 1939, Illiopolis, Ill., USA. University Teacher; Composer; Asian Music Researcher; Pianist. Educ: BMus, Millikin Univ., Decatur, Ill.; MA, Cornell Univ., Ithaca, NY; DMusA, Stanford Univ., Calif. m. Fannie Cheng Craig, 1 s. Career incls: Lectr. in Music, Chung Chi Coll., Chinese Univ. of Hong Kong; Chmn. of Music Dept., ibid., 1972-74; Dir., Hong Kong Archives of Chinese Music, 1971-; Leverhulme Fellow, Univ. of WA, Aust., 1976; Lectr. & Dir., Asian Music Prog., Queensland Conserv. of Music, Brisbane, Aust. Comps. incl: Byan Hwa (orch., speakers, dancers); Plum Blossoms (synthesizer, vibraphone, flute, violin, viola, basson, double bass); Cascades on Noh (flute & piano); Existence (cello & piano). Sev. recordings. Contbr. to profl. publs. Mbr. profl. orgs. recip. acad. hons. Mgmt: Dr. Franz Holford, J. Albert & Son, 39 King St., Sydney, Aust. Address: 15 Ebrill St., Jamboree Heights, Qld. 4074, Aust.

CRAIG, David MacLeod, B. 23 Dec. 1941, Woodstock, NB, Can. Broadcast Journalist; Conductor; Musician (brass). Educ: DMus, Metropolitan Collegiate Inst., London, UK. separated, 2 s. Debut: Sydney, NS, Can., 1962. Career: CFRB Radio, Toronto, Can. Comps: Overturesque, 1976; Bon Homme (Overture); The Valiant Ones (March); Poetic Symphony for Band. Contbr. to: profl. publs. Mbrships: Can. Band Dirs. Assn.; Toronto Musicians Assn. Hobbies: Composing; Electronics. Address: 75 Berkinshaw Cres. Don Mills, Ont. M3B 2T1, Can.

CRAIG, Leonard C D, b. 18 Apr. 1917, Toronto, Can. Retired Tuba & Bass Viol Player. Educ: Toronto Conserv. of Music. m. Elsie, 2 s. Career: perfs. w. Royal Can. Army Service Corps Band (overseas), Can. Guards Band, Oshawa Civic Band & var. military bands in Toronto. Address: 1538 Lakemount St., Oshawa, Ont. L1J 3Y2, Can.

CRAIG, Patricia, b. 21 July 1943, Kew Gardens, Queens, NY, USA. Opera Singer. Educ: BS, Music Educ., Ithaca Coll. Schl. of Music. Debut: Metropolitan Opera, 1978. Career: Metropolitan Opera; NYC Opera; Cinn. Summer Opera; Miami Opera; Balt. Opera; La Fenice, Venice, Italy; Theater Under the Stars, Atlanta, Ga.; CBS TV, The Questions of Abraham; NBC, Days of Our Lives. Hons: Metropolitan Opera Nat. Coun.

Auditions Finalist, 1968. Hobbies: Dogs; Plants; Entertaining; Theatre going. Mgmt: Robert Lombardo. Address: 121 W 72 St., NY, NY 10023, USA.

CRAIG, William James, b. 21 Aug. 1933, Kenora, Ont., Can. Pianist; Conductor. Educ: ARCM, Toronto; RAM. m. Constance Fisher. Debut: La Boheme, Sadlers Wells Opera Co. Career: Operatic perfs. w. Sadlers Wells Opera Co., Can. Opera Co., Vancouver Opera Assn.; Currently, Musical Dir., Opera Dept., Fac. of Music, Univ. of Toronto. Address: Plaza 100, 100 Wellesley St. E, Apt. 1012, Toronto M4Y 1H5, Can.

CRAMPTON, Freda Henrietta Carline, b. 23 Jan. 1906, Edinburgh, UK. Conductor; Violinist; Violist. Educ: RMCM. Career: Cond., Ross Orchl. Soc. from 1935, Newent Orchl. Soc. from 1940, Coleford Orchl. Soc., 1940-69, Hereford Orchl. Soc., 1954-69; Viola & Soloist w. Concords & Glos. String Quartets; Lectr. in musical hist., esp. 18th century. Hobbies: Collecting books; Stream railways. Address: The Mount, Symonds Yat, Ross on Wye, Herefordshire HR9 6DY, UK. 3, 27.

CRANE, Joelle Wallach, b. NYC, NY, USA. Composer; Singer (mezzo soprano). Educ: BA, Sarah Lawrence Coll., 1967; MA, Columbia Univ., 1969; Juilliard Schl. of Music; Piano, Comp., Vocal & Educ. study, num. tchrs. m. John Thomas Crane. Comps. incl: The Force That Through the Green Fuse, for soprano & oboe, 1965; Three Whitman Visions, 1976; Contemplations, for solo brass clarinet, 1978; Moment, for oboe solo; Concerto for Four Winds & Orch.; Cords; Five-fold Amen; Two Introits; 30 Ecumenical Responses. Contbr. to profl. publs. Mbrships: Am. Women Comps., Inc.; League of Women Comps.; Am. Music Center; Bibliothèque Internationale de Musique Contemporaine. Address: 782 West End Ave., NYC, NY 10025, USA.

CRANE, Robert, b. 24 Dec. 1919, Winchester, Mass., USA. Composer; Educator. Educ: BMus, Oberlin Coll.; Dip., Longy Schl. of Music; MMus, PhD, Univ. of Rochester. m. Jessie Starr, 3 d., 2 s. Career: on fac. of music, Univ. of Wis., Madison, Wis., 1950-. Comps. incl: (for orch.) A Dance Interlude; A Dance Rondo; Exsequiarum ordo, in memorian Berlioz; (for band) 5 Baroque Chorale Preludes; Passacaglia & Fugue; (for chorus) A Cradle Song; Missa de Angelis; (cantatas) Peter Quince at the Clavier; The Litany; (instrumental) 5 Christmas Chorale Preludes, for organ; Partita, Sonatina, for piano; Pastorale, for oboe & piano; Str. Quartet; Woodwind Quartet; Brass Octet; num. other works in same categories. mbr. profl. socs. Hons: Lili Boulanger Memorial Fund Award, 1942; Alumni Award, Phi Mu Alpha Sinfonia, 1952. Address: 1615 Adams St., Madison, WI 53711, USA. 2.

CRANMER, Margaret Valerie, b. 10 Mar. 1945, Salisbury, UK. Music Librarian. Educ: BA (music & hist.), Dunelm; postgrad. dip., librarianship, Univ. of Sheffield; gen. musical educ., esp. piano & flute playing. m. Frank Arthur Cranmer, 2 d. Career: Rowe Music Libn., King's Coll., Cambridge. Contbr. to: Grove's Dict., 6th ed.; Antique Finder. Mbrships: hon. sec., Galpin Soc.; Fellowship of Makers & Restorers of Historical Instruments; life mbr., Soc. of Indexers; life mbr., Dolmetsch Fndn.; Cambridge Lib. Group. Hobbies: Rsch. on the Eng. piano; Ballet; Gardening. Address: 116 Tenison Rd., Cambridge, CB1 2DW, UK.

CRANMER, Philip, b. 1 Apr. 1918, Birmingham, UK. Professor of Music. Educ: BA, BMus, MA, Oxford Univ.; FRCO. m. Ruth Loasby, 1 s., 3 d. Career: Staff Accomp., BBC Midland Region, 1948; Lectr., Birmingham Univ., 1950; Prof. of Music, The Queen's Univ., Belfast, 1954, Manchester Univ., 1970-74; Sec., Associated Bd., Royal Schls. of Music, London, 1974-. Comps: part-songs; organ comps. Author, The Technique of Accompaniment, 1970; Gen. Ed., Eulenburg Miniature Score, ed., 1976; Sight-reading for Young Pianists, 1978. Mbrships: Pres., Inc. Soc. Musicians, 1971; Coun., RCO, 1973. Recip., Hon. RAM, 1968; MA, Manchester, 1974; FRNCM; FRCM, 1976. Hobbies: Crossword puzzles & Handwriting. Address: 14 Bedford Sq., London WC1, UK. 1.

CRASNARU, George-Emil, b. 30 Aug. 1941, Bucharest, Romania. Vocalist (Bass). Educ: Grad., Conserv. of Bucharest, Ciprian Porumbescu. m. Irina Crasnaru, 1 s., 1 d. Debut: Osmin, Die Entführung aus dem Serail (Mozart), Romanian Opera of Bucharest, 1972. Career: Apps. throughout Europe, Can. & S Am., incl: Österreichische Gesellschaft für Musik (Vienna), Music Centers of Toronto & Montreal (Can.), Philharmonic of Prague, Deutsche Staatsoper (Berlin), Stockholm Phil.; Soloist, Romanian Opera of Bucharest; Num. radio & TV apps. Num. recordings. Mbrships: Romanian Assn. of Music & Theatre. Hons: Honorific Dip., Janacek Fest., Czech., 1977; Honorific Dip., Robert Schumann Fest., German Dem. Repub., 1969; Prize of Music Critic, Bucharest, 1976. Hobbies: Lit.; Record Library; Sport. Address: Soseaua Cotroceni 6, Sector 6, Bucharest, Romania.

CRAWFORD, Anne Margaret, b. 17 May 1939, Edinburgh, UK. Piano Accompanist. Educ: BMus, Edinburgh Univ.; Moray House; LRAM (tchr.); LRAM (accompanist); ARCM. m. Renton Thomson, 2 c. Career: Chmbr. Music accompanist & soloist in concertos, many music clubs in Scotland; Accompanist on sev. radio broadcasts inclng. violin & flute recitals; BBC panel of accompanists. Mbr., Incorporated Soc. of Musicians. Hons: Piano solo gold medal, Bach & Beethoven prizes & Horace Fellowes Chmbr. Music Trophy in 3 consecutive yrs., Edinburgh Competitive Festiva; McFarlane Schlrship., Glasgow Acad.; Tovey Mem. Prize, Edinburgh Univ.; ANdrew Fraser Schlrship., ibid. Hobbies: Walking; Reading. Mgmt: Pro Arte Musica - Scottish Concert Agcy. Address: 108 Speirs Rd., Bearsden, Glasgow, UK.

CRAWFORD, David Eugene, b. 16 July 1939, Fort Scott, Kan., USA. Professor of Musicology. Educ: BA, Univ. Kan.; MA, ibid.; PhD, Univ. Ill. m. Marilyn Shaw, 2 children. Career: Prof., Univ. Mich., USA, 1967-. Publs: Vespers Polyphony at Modena's Cathedral in the First Half of the Sixteenth Century, 1967; Sixteenth-Century Choirbooks in the Archivio Capitolars at Casale Monferrato, 1975. Contbr. to num. profl. jrnls. Mbrships: Am. Musicol. Soc.; Int. Musicol. Soc.; Music Lib. Assn. Hons: incl num. Fellowships. Hobbies: Golf; Skiing; Swimming. Address: 1204 Iroquois, Ann Arbor, MI 48104, USA. 11.

CRAWFORD, Dawn Constance, b. 19 Dec. 1919, Ellington Field, Tex., USA. Teacher; Composer. Educ: BA, Rice Univ., 1939; MA, Columbia Univ., 1954; BMus, Houston Conserv. Music, 1940; Grad. Study, Eastman Schl. Music. Career: Asst. Dir., Houston Conserv. Music, 1942-49; Fac., Dominican Coll. Music Dept., Houston, 1964-; Chmn., ibid., 1972-. Comps: The Pearl, chamber opera, 1971; Incidental music, Angna Enters' 'Love Possessed Juana', Houston Little Theatre, 1946. Publs: Manuals for Composers, 1946; Scale Fingerings for Keyboard Instruments, 1966; Sight-Singing Practice Manual, 1966. Contbr. to Notable American Women, 1607-1950, 1971. Mbrships: Am. Musicol. Soc.; Leschetizky Assn.; Houston Music Tchrs. Assn. (charter mbr.; Pres., 1944); Houston Chapt., Am. Guild Organists (charter mbr.; Treas.); Pi Lambda Theta; Pi Delta Phi. Hobbies: Woodworking; Gardening. Address: 13722 Hooper Rd., Houston, TX 77047, USA.

CRAXTON, Janet, b. 17 May 1929, London, UK. Oboist; Performer; Teacher. Educ: FRAM; Paris Conservatoire. m. Alan Richardson. Career: Prin. Oboe: Halle Orch., 1949-52; Mozart Players, 1952-54; BBC Symph., 1954-63; London Sinfonietta, 1969-. Num. recordings inclng: Handel Oboe Concertos; Vaughan Williams Blake Songs; Fantasy Quartet & 6 Metamorphoses after Orid (Britten); Wind Quintet (Schoenberg), etc. Publs: Mozart Oboe Quartet arr. for oboe & piano; First & Second Books of Oboe Solos (w. Alan Richardson); No. 4 of 4 pieces by Grieg arr. oboe & piano. Contbr. to Composers. Mbrships: ISM; Royal Soc. of Musicians. Recip. Cobbett Medal for Servs. to Chmbr. Music, 1975; Composers Guild Award, Instrumentalist of the Yr., 1978. Hobbies: Cooking; Gardening; Golf. Address: 14 Kidderpore Ave., London, NW3, UK.

CRAY, (Rev.) Kevin E, b. 20 June 1922, Erie, Pa., USA. Roman Catholic Priest; Pianist; Composer; Music Therapist. Educ: Cath. Univ. of Am., Wash. DC; St. John Univ., Collegeville, Minn.; SUNY, Fedonia; Chatauqua Instn., NY; BA (philos.); BMus; MMus; Nat. Cert. Tchr. of piano & comp. Career: on fac., Am. Coll. of Musicians, Austin, Tex.; former Music Critic, Erie Morning News. Comps: Mass of the Psalms (equal voices, organ); Mass 'Savior of the World' (equal voices, organ); Mass of St. Peter (unison choir, organ); Motets for a capella choir; Teaching pieces for young pianists. Mbrships: Music Tchrs. Nat. Assn.; Pres., NW Dist., Pa. Music Tchrs. Assn.; Erie Music Tchrs. Assn. Hobbies incl: Writing prose; Hiking. Address: 419 Stafford Ave., Erie, PA 16508, USA.

CRAYFORD, Helen Elizabeth, b. 3 Aug. 1953, Broadstairs, Kent, UK. Trumpeter; Pianist. Educ: LGSM (piano perf.), 1967; ARCM (piano tchr.), 1976; MA (music), Cantab., 1974; postgrad. course, RCM, 1974-76; study w. Nadia Boulanger, Paris, 1976-77. Debut: (trumpet) aged 4, soloist w. N E Kent Orch., Margate. Career: mbr. Gallina Brass, 1st all-female brass quintet, 1975-; apps. at Purcell Room as part of Park Lane Group 20th century music series & as GLAA Young Musicians, 1978; apps. w. Konig Ensemble (trumpeter & pianist), Ballet Rambert & Orch. of St. John's Smith Square; duos w. Robin Grice (viola) & Barbara Bolte (oboe). Mbr. ISM. Hons: French Govt. Scholarship, 1976; (w. Gallina Brass) winner, Royal Overseas League Ensemble Prize, 1976. Hobbies: Cinema; Theatre; Cooking; Swimming; Table Tennis; Badminton; Travel. Address: 75 Solent Rd., W Hampstead, London NW6, UK.

CREAMER, Alice DuBois, b. 16 Apr. 1915, Roadstown, NJ, USA. Musician (performer with piano, pipe organ, cello, recorder,

krummhorn, kortholt & viola da gambia); Sculptress; Researcher into old musical instruments. Educ: Pvte. studies & self-taught. m. Malcolm K Creamer, 1 d., 1 s. Career: Fmr. Tchr., piano; Organiser & Perf., Baroque Chamb. Ensemble, Cumb. Co. Hist. Mus., Dec., 1972, '73, (filmed for TV documentary, 1973); Played var. recitals w. recorder & krummhorn; Collector of old musical instruments which are restored for playing in local concerts; num. sculptures. Mbrships: Am. Recorder Soc.; Am. Viola da Gamba Soc.; Int. Soc. of Harpsichord Builders; Galpin Soc. of England; Curator, Hist. Instruments, Cumb. Co. Hist. Soc., Bridgeton Antiquarian League. Hobbies: Pottery; Spinning; Weaving; Painting; Re-building musical instruments. Address: RFD Apt. 5, Finley Rd., Bridgeton, NJ, USA.

CREE BROWN, Christopher John, b. 25 July 1953, Christchurch, NZ. Composer; Multi-Media Co-Ordinator. Educ: BMus, 1976; BA, 1977; BMus w. hons., 1977; Pvte. violin studies. Career incls: Theme music for film, Three Love Stories, & other film music. Comps: Piece for Piano & String Quartet, 1974; An Exercise for Oscillators, 1976; Piece for Piano, 1977; Piece for Solo Flute, 1977; Three Short Piano Pieces, 1977; Epitaph on a Tyrant for Soprano Solo & Chorus, 1977; Piece for String Orch. & Vibraphone, 1977; Piece for Piano, Prepared Tape & Live Electronics, 1977; Study I for Magnetic Tape, 1977; Study II for Magnetic Tape, 1977; Study III for Magnetic Tape, 1977. Mbrships: Comps. Assn. of NZ. Hons: Schl. Music Prize, 1971; Hymn Comp. Prize. 1974; Mozart Fellowship, Univ. of Otago, 1980. Hobbies: Drama; Reading; Art; People and Pubs. Address: 77 Puriri St., Riccarton, Christchurch 4, NZ.

CREED, Elizabeth Mary, b. 27 July 1933, London, UK. Music Librarian. Educ: ARCM (piano tchng. & perf.); Dip. of Educ., Reading Univ. Career: tchng. posts in schls. inclng: Norwich HS for Girls, Greycotes Schl., Oxford; Cambs. HS for Girls; joined Music Lib. Staff, London Univ.; currently Asst. Music Libn., ibid., on leave Feb.-Mar. 1976 to work in music lib. at Univ. of Witwatersrand, S Africa. Mbr., ISM. Hobbies: Tennis; Swimming; Ballet; Opera; Bridge; Theatre; Travel. Address: 31 Ormsby Lodge, The Avenue, London W4 1HS, UK.

CREED, Marcus Alan, b. 19 Apr. 1951, Eastbourne, UK. Repetiteur; Pianist; Singer; Conductor; Teacher. Educ: GSM; LGSM, MA, King's Coll., Cambridge; cert. Ed., Christ Ch., Oxford. Career: Repetiteur, Deutsche Oper, Berlin; Asst. Cond., Berlin Radio Chmbr. Choir; tchr., Berlin Hochschule für Musik. Recordings: Stravinsky, Cantiucm Sacrum (baritone solo); Play of Daniel (w. Clerkes of Oxenford). Mbr., ISM. Hobbies: Cricket; Books; Wine. Address: Goethestr. 57, 1 Berlin 12, German Fed. Repub.

CREES, Eric James, b. 30 Mar. 1952, London, UK. Assistant Principal Trombone; Professor of Trombone. Educ: BMus, Univ. of Surrey; LRAM; ARCM. m. Veronica Ann Black, 1 s. Career: Asst. Prin. Trombone, LSO; Prof. of Trombone, GSM. Recordings: Num., w. LSO, other orchs. & chmbr. groups. Contbr. to: Sounding Brass. Address: 2 Allenby Rd., London SE23, UK.

CREES, Kathleen Elsie, b. 22 Oct. 1944, Tollesbury, Maldon, Essex, UK. Early Keyboard Performer; Teacher; Composer. Educ: TCL; GTCL; FTCL; LTCL; ATCL (Piano); FTCL (Harpsichord); Cologne, Germany. Debut: Purcell Room. Career: Freelance Musician; Tchr., TCL; Lectr., Pianoforte, St. Paul's Schl., London, London Evening Institutes; Toured as Solo Pianist w. London's former Western Theatre Ballet Co.; Pianist, London Fest. Ballet; Film on mod. reprodns. of early keyboards instruments; Film series, EMI, etc.; Perf. on all TV networks & radio; Recitals on Clavichords, harpsichord & piano throughout UK; Tours of Aust., 1974, '78, '79, Can., 1979; Beethoven Trio, 1970-. 7 Recordings on clavichord & harpsichord. Publs: Jonathan & the Magic Clavichord (includes music); The Good Tempered Clavichord, 1974. Mbr., Musicians Union. Recip. many prizes & awards. Address: 9 Cressida Rd., Highgate, London N19 3JN, UK. 27.

CRENSHAW, Randel L, b. 24 Mar. 1955, San Diego, Calif., USA. Performer, Composer, Arranger of Early Music. Educ: BMus (perf.) cand., Willamette Univ., Salem, Ore. m. Linda Groves Crenshaw. Career: Perf. on Baroque & modern trumpet, cornett, recorder, Renaissance Windcap reeds, sackbut, shawm, pipe & tabor, guitar; playing works from Mediaeval through to Baroque periods; musician with Oregon Shakespearean Festival, Ashland, Ore., 1978; arranger with group Airborne, 1977-78. comps. incl: Fanfare for brass sextet; Portrait (chmbr. orch.); Father, Forgive Them (tenor solo & choir); Third Cage on the Left (guitar & flute); Beautivul Song; Praises; Psalm 92. Recordings: Music in May, 25th Anniversary Festival; San Francisco Honor Band, 2nd Annual Spring Concert; Valentines Concert, 1976. Mbrships: incl: Fndr. & Dir., Willamette Early Music Soc.; Am. Recorder Soc.; Portland Brass Soc. Hons. incl: 1st Cornet, Music in May fest., 1973; 1st Trumpet, 1976 All-Northwest College

Band Director's Honor Band. Hobbies: River rafting, basketball, songwriting. Address: 1861 SE 21st, No. 163, Albany, OR, 97231, USA.

CRESPIN, Régine, b. Marseilles, France. Opera Singer. Debut: Singing Kundry, in Parsifal, Fest. of Bayreuth. Career: She has sung in most maj. Opera Theatres of the World, inclng., The Vienna Opera Hse., Covent Garden, London, The Rome Opera, San Francisco Opera, Metropolitan Opera, La Scala, Milan, etc.; She has sung var. maj. roles, inclng., Phaedra in Pizetti, La Scala, Milan; The Marshall's Wife, in the Rosenkavalier, Glyndebourne Fest. & Metropolitan Opera, USA, & Vienna Opera; Brunnehilde, in the Walkyrie, at the 1st Easter Fest. of Salzburg, Mar. 1967, (Dir. by Herbert von Karajan); Carmen, Metropolitan Opera, NY. Has given recitals & concerts, Paris, NY. Recordings incl: recital Wagner, recital Schumann, Wolf, Debussy, Fauré, Les Nuits d'Eté de Berlioz, Les Troyens, (Dir., George Prêtre), etc. Hons: One of the 1st singers to record Die Walküre twice in one yr. Address: c/o 141 Blvd. St. Michel, Paris 5, France.

CRESSWELL, Lyell Richard, b. 13 Oct. 1944, Wellington, NZ. Composer. Educ: BMus, Vic. Univ. of Wellington, NZ; MMus, Univ. of Toronto; PhD, Univ. of Aberdeen. m. Catherine Mawson. Comps: Violin Concerto; Salm; Music for Skinheads; Macpherson's Rant; The Slaughter of the Innocents; Drones IV; Wa; In Memory of ... Mbrships: CGGB; Australasian Perf. Rights Assn.; Comps. Assn. of NZ. Hons: Commonwealth Scholarship, 1969-70; Dutch Govt. Bursary, 1974-75; Ian Whyte Award, 1978. Address: 52 Conway Rd., Cardiff CF1 9NU, UK.

CRESTON, Paul, b. 10 Oct. 1906, NYC, USA. Composer; Pianist; Organist; Conductor; Educator. m. Louise Gotto, 2 s. Career: Pianist, 1926-; Theatre Organist, 1926-30; Ch. Organist, St. Malachy's Ch., NY, 1934-67; Comp., 1932-; Comp. of Radio, TV & Film Music, 1942-66; Prof., NY Coll. of Music, 1964-68; Prof., Central Wash. State Coll., 1968-75. Compositions: piano, choral & chamber music, 5 symphs., 14 concertos, num. radio background scores, 20 TV scores & 2 film scores. Recorded Compositions incl: Str. Quartet; Partita; 2 Choric Dances; Dance Overture; Sonata for Saxophone & Piano; Symph. No. 2; Invocation & Dance. Author, Principles of Rhythm, 1961. Contbr. to var. profl. jrnls. Mbrships: Bd. Dirs., ASCAP, 1960-68; Pres., Nat. Assn. Am. Comps. & Conds., 1956-60; Exec. committee, Nat. Music Coun., 1950-68; Bd. Govs., Bohemians, 1950-68; Hon. Mbr., Kappa Kappa Psi; Pi Kappa Lambda; Phi Mu Alpha Sinfonia; Life Fellow, Int. Inst. Arts & Letters. Hons. incl: 1st Prize, Paris Int. Referendum for Symph. No. 1, 1952; Music Award, Am. Acad. Arts & Letters. Hobbies: Linguistics; Bowling. Address: PO Box 794, Ellensburg, WA 98926, USA. 2, 3, 4, 9, 28.

CREWS, George Norman, b. 12 Feb. 1946, Ft. Smith, Ark., USA (now Can. citizen). Harpist; Composer; Arranger; Teacher; Music critic. Educ: Univ. of Ill., 1964-67; Univ. of W Ont., 1967-72; Music Educ. prog., ibid. Career: perfs. as harpist w. num. orchs. in Can., musical theatres in Can. & Chgo.; apps. in TV backup orchs.; num. perfs. as Dining Room Entertainer, 1974-. Comps. incl: The Pleiades for chmbr. orch.; 4 short pieces for harp; Sun, for 2 horns & 2 flutes; Earthtune, for voice & harp; Chicago Sweet, for solo harp; sev. arrs. for harp. Contbr. to London Free Press; The Albertan; The Daily Gleaner. Mbrships: AFM; Am. Harp Soc. Hobbies: Cycling; Art work; Writing; Astrol. Address: No. A-7 - 80 Galbraith Drive SW, Calgary, Alta., Can.

CRIGHTON, Robert Garry, b. 7 Dec. 1942, Toronto, Can. Freelance Early Music Performer & Teacher (voice - Counter-tenor, Sackbut, Renaissance Winds, Plectrum Lutes). Educ: BA, Modern Langs. & Lit., Univ. of Toronto, 1964; Tchng. Certs., Ont. Coll. of Educ., 1965; pvte. music studies. 1 s., 1 d. Career: Secondary Schl. Tchr., 9 yrs. (Music Dept. Head, 7 yrs.); Pt.-time music instructor, Scarborough Coll. (Univ. of Toronto) & York Univ. (Toronto); Radio & TV apps.; Mbr., The Toronto Consort & The Musicians of Swanne Alley, w. frequent perfs., USA & Can.; Dir. & Singer, The Scarborough Singers; Alto Lay Clerk, St. James Cathedral, Toronto; Mbr., The City Waits (Toronto); Tchr. of medieval & renaissance ensembles, Fac. of Music, Univ. of Toronto & Royal Conserv. of Music, Toronto. Recordings w. The Toronto Consort. Contbr. to: Continuo. Mbr., Lute Soc. of Am. Hobbies: Playing Bulgarian dance-music and jazz. Address: 191 Scarborough Rd., Toronto, Ont., Can. M4E 3M7.

CRISTANCHO, Mauricio, b. 22 Oct. 1946, Bogotá, Colombia. Violinist; Violin Teacher; Composer. Educ: Bachelor of Humanities; Chemistry studies; Conserv. Nacional de Música, Colombia; Accademia Int. di Musica da Camera, Rome, Italy; Fundación Bariloche, Argentina; Music studies, Mexico City; Studies w. Profs. Ernesto Diaz, Alberto Lysy, Henryk Szeryng. m. Ruth M de Cristancho, 1 s. Career: Past Mbr., Camerata Bariloche; Past Mbr., Cuarteto Colombiano; Former soloist w. Colombian Symph. Orch., Colombiana de Arcos, Orquesta del

Conservatorio, Orquesta de Camada de la Ciudad de Mexico, etc.; Present Asst. Concertmaster, Colombia Symph. Orch.; Concertmaster, Orquesta Colombiana; Prof., Conserv. Nal. de Música, Bogotá; Dir. & Prof., Centro de Orientación. Musical Comps: (recorded) Sureño; Donald III; Marco; Ella; Relámpago (Colombian Music). Recordings: 4 LPs w. Orquesta Colombiana. Mbrships: Nat. Univ. of Colombia; Centro de Orientación Musical 'Francisco Cristancho'. Address: Carrera 20 No. 51-74, Bogotá 2, Colombia.

CRISWICK, Mary, b. 26 June 1945, Southend on Sea, UK. Mezzo-soprano; Guitar Teacher; Music Calligrapher. Educ: BA, Britol Univ., 1967; GSM. m. Alan Singer, 1 d. Career: apps. at folk clubs, restaurants; Guitar Tchr., City Univ., London, St. Paul's Girls Schl., 1970-74; currently Lead Singer, Florilegium Musicum de Paris, 1976 and L'ensemble Euterpe; French TV app., 1976 & 77. Recordings: w. Florilegium Musicum de Paris, CBS. Publs: num. arrs. & albums for guitar (Stainer & Bell, Breitkopf, Chester, Chappell & Max Eschig; Weinberger). Contbr. to: Musical Times; BMG; Guitar; Soundboard; Music Yearbook. Mbrships: ISM; PRS; Soc. for Rsch. in Psychol. of Music & Music Educ.; Lute Soc.; Galpin Soc.; Guitar Fndn. of Am. Hobbies: Cookery; Historical Dance; Lute; Piano. Address: 10 Rue Charles Pathe, 94300 Vincennes, France.

CROCHET, Sharon Brandstetter, b. 15 Mar. 1945, San Antonio, Tex., USA. Flautist; Composer; Commercial Business Broker. Educ: BA (Engl.), 1967; Real Estate License 1979; MMus, 1975. m. J James Crochet. Career: High Schl. tchr. & choir director to 1978. Comps. recorded: score arr. for screenplay, Mother, 1979; Christmas Ayre, 1971; Children's Songs, 1964; March for Miki, 1980; num. arr. of choral comps. w. orch. Mbr., Am. Musicol. Soc. recip., music scholarship, Univ. of Houston, 1963. Address: 2754 Raintree, Sugarland, TX 77478, USA.

CROLL, Gerhard, b. 25 May 1927, Dusseldorf, Germany. Professor of Musicology. Educ: PhD, Goettingen Univ., 1954; Habilitation, Univ. Münster/West., 1961. m. Renate Lessmann, 5 c. Career incl: Prof. of Musicol. & Dir., Inst. of Musicol., Salzburg Univ., 1966-. Publs. incl: Festmusiken der Renaissance, 1969; W A Mozart, Wege der Forschung vol. 233, 1977; Ed., W A Mozart, Der Schauspieldirektor, etc. Contbr. to: Die Musikforschung; Österreich Musikzeitschrift; Mozart-Jahrbuch; Musica Disciplina. Mbrships: Int. Musicol. Soc.; Gesellschaft für Musikforschung; Österreich Gesellschaft für Musikwissenschaft; Zentralinstitut für Mozartforschung. Hons: Mozartmedaille Wien 1968. Hobbies: Mountains; Family. Address: Wilhelm Kress Str. 19, A5020 Salzburg, Austria.

CROMBEEN, Marc-Anton Ernst, b. 18 Nov. ₁928, Laarne, Ghent, Belgium. Organist; Cembalo; Orchestral Director. Educ: Conserv. Ghent & Vienna (organ & cembalo); Orchestral Direction, Salzburg & Vienna; Octuor de Cuivres de Paris. m. Jane Depasse (div.), 1 s. Comps: A Modern Mass (recorded); Fugue for large Orch., 1962; Classical songs; Ballets; 2 Oratorios, La Chathedral Boraine, The Refugees. Mbrships: VP, Acad. Int. de Lutèce (Paris) Belgian Sect. Hons: Prize from Ghent, for Fugue for large orch.; Hon. mentions, Triest, Rome, Assisi. Hobbies: Horse riding (jumping & dressage). Address: Burggravenlaan 186, 9000 Ghent, Belgium.

CROMIE, Beatrice Florence Dickson, b. 11 Mar. 1946, Borsad, India. Administrator. Educ: St. Hilda's Schl., Ootacamund, S India. Career: Joined Ulster Orch. staff, 1970; Publicity & Planning Asst., 1972-73; Gen. Mgr., 1973-78; Admnstr. of Symphonia of Auckland, 1978-. Hobbies: Needlework, REading. Address: 9A, Cape Horn Rd., Auckland H, NZ.

CRONE, Tan, b. 2 Mar. 1930, Hertogenbosch, Holland. Pianist; Accompanist. Educ: Amsterdam Conserv.; 2 yrs. study w. Nadia Boulanger, Paris; New England Conserv. of Music, Boston, USA (MMus, Artist Dip.). Career: Concert Perfs., (solo & chmbr. music), Europe, S Am., USA; Repertoire Coach, Royal Conserv. of Music, The Hague; Official Accomp., Int. Music Contest, Munich. Mgmt: Nederlands Impresariaat, The Netherlands. Address: Nieuwe Looiersdwarsstraat 3, 1017 TZ Amsterdam, The Netherlands.

CRONQUIST, Robert Lee, b. 10 June 1929, Chgo., Ill., USA. Performer (French horn); Conductor; Stage Director; Scenic Designer. Educ: BA, MA, Western Reserve Univ.; Ariz. Univ.; Profl. trng. w. Louis Lane, Dr. F Karl Grossman, Dr. E Evans, Cleveland, Ohio; 14 yrs. m. Carol E Andrews, 1 child. Career: Perf., Phoenix, Ariz. Symph., Youngstown Symph.; Canton Symph., Akron Symph., Cleveland Orch.; Cond., Mansfield Symph., Musical Dir., ibid., 22 yrs.; Cond., Tuscarawas Orch., 6 yrs.; Cond.; Lakeside Symph. & Festival, 5 yrs.; Cond., Ohio State Festival; Asst. Prof., Kenyon Coll., 1956-57, W Liberty

State Coll., 1958-59, Ohio State Univ., Mansfield, 1973-. Mbrships: Am. Symph. Orch. League; Am. Musical Fedn. (Mansfield & Cleveland). Address: 28 Bartley Ave., Mansfield, OH, USA. 8.

CROPPER, Peter John, b. 19 Nov. 1945, Southport, UK. Violinist. Educ: Recital Dip., RAM, London; ARAM. m. Nina Martin, 1 s. Career: Ldr., Lindsay String Quartet. Recordings: Tippett String Quartets 1, 2 & 3; Mozart String Quartets C maj., Bb maj.; Beethoven String Quartets Op. 74 & 95. Mbr., ISM. Hobbies: Wine & Food; Old glass; Old watches. Mgmt: Ingpen & Williams. Address: 10 Stumperlowe Ave., Sheffield S10 3QN, UK.

CROSBIE, William Perry, b. 19 Aug. 1947, Exeter, NH, USA. Organist; Harpsichord Player. Educ: AB, Whittier Coll., 1969; DMusA cand., W Va. Univ.; studied piano & organ w. var. tchrs. m. Kate Russell Haddad. Career: Asst. Organist, 1956-61, Organist-Choirmaster, 1961-65, Organist Emeritus, 1975-, St. Margaret's Episcopal Ch., S Gate, Calif.; Asst. Organist-Chormaster, St. Paul's Cathedral, Los ANgeles, 1965-70; Organist-Choirmaster, St. Matthew's Episcopal Ch., Wheeling, 1970-; Chapel Organist, Interfaith Chapel, W Liberty State Coll., 1970-; Recitalist & Harpsichord & Organ Soloist; instr., W Liberty State Coll., 1970-. Mbrships: incl: Chmn., Music Committee of Centennial Commission, Music Cons., Episcopal Diocese of W Va.; RSCM; AGO; Am. Choral Dirs. Assn. Recip. var. hons. Address: The Mansion, Howard Place, Wheeling, WV 26003, USA.

CROSDALE, John, b. 4 Oct. 1929, Manchester, UK. Trumpet Player & Teacher; Conductor. Educ: Northern Schl. of Music; LRAM (trumpet & piano); Berkshire Music Ctr., Tanglewood, USA; Hilversum Radio cond. course, Netherlands. m. Susan Elizabeth Haggas, 2 d. Career: Trumpeter, Scottish Nat. Orch., Hallé Orch., BBC; tchr.; cond., sev. N W Music Socs. incl. New Sheffield Symph. Orch., Beethoven Soc., Gorton Phil. Orch., Mus. Dir., Didsbury & Wilmslow Amateur Operatic Socs.; brass coach for Trafford Educ. Authority & Hd. of Music, Stretford Girls' Grammar Schl.; lectr. to Halle Clubs. mbr., ISM. recip., cond. scholarship to Tanglewood, USA. Hobby: Golf. Address: 45 South Dr., Chorltonville, Manchester M21 2DZ, UK.

CROSHAW, Christine Mary, b. 7 Oct. 1942, Nuneaton, UK. Pianist; Professor. Educ: RAM, 1960-66; studied w. Vivian Langrish; LRAM. Career: Soloist, Ensemble Player & Accomp.; sev. recitals in chmbr. grps. & as accomp., Wigmore Hall & Purcell Room; Official Pianist, cello master classes, Int. Musicians Sem., Prussia Cove, Cornwall, 1973 , & Antonio Janigro's cello master classes, Int. Music Fests., Cascais, Portugal, 1973 & 74; Prof., TCM. Mbr., ISM. Recip. var. awards. Hobbies: Jazz; Antiques; Flying. Address: 21 College Cross, London N1, UK.

CROSLEY, Lawrence E, b. 19 May 1932, Oaklandon, Ind., USA. Composer. Educ: BMus, Eastman Schl. of Music, Univ. of Rochester, NY, 1957; MMus, ibid., 1960. m. Michal Ann, 6 c. Career incl: Hd. of Music & Post-Production Sound, Nat. Film Bd. of Can., 1978 . Comps: 165 film scores incl. Storm O'Brian; Poison Pen; David & Goliath; Counterfeiter; The Gentle Executioner; Canadian Diamonds; Seal Hunting at La Tabatiere; On the Sea; Expo '67; Profile, Canada; The Age of Exploration (series); The Tenth Decade (TV series); Cry of the Wild; Accident; Year of the Child; The Bioshpere, etc. Mbrships: Can. League of Comps; CAPAC; AFM; Phi Mu Alpha. Hons: over 33 awards to films w. music by L Crosley incl. The Man Who Skied Down Everest, Acad. Award (Oscar) for Best Documentary Feature, Hollywood, 1976. Hobbies: Farming. Address: RR 1, Low, Que. JOX 2CO, Can.

CROSS, Joan, b. Sept. 1900. Operatic Soprano. Career incls: Prin. Soprano, Old Vic & Sadler's Wells, London, 1924-44; Dir. of Opera, Sadler's Wells, 1941-44; later Prin. (resigned), Nat. Schl. of Opera, Morley Coll., London. Address: Brook Cottage, Yoxford, Saximundham, Suffolk, UK. 1.

CROSS, Norma, b. 10 Mar. 1917, Lawler, Iowa, USA. University Teacher. Educ: BMus, 1941, MFA, 1942. Univ. of IA. Career: Tchr. of Piano, Piano Pedagogy & Piano Accompaniment, Assoc. Prof., Univ. of IA; Soloist w. Univ. of IA Symph. Orch. Publs: Comprehensive Listing of Piano Literature & Teaching Materials, 3rd ed., 1968, 2nd supplement, 1974; rsch. for 3rd supplement, 1978. Mbrships. incl: Music Tchrs. Nat. Assn.; IA Music Tchrs. Assn.; Civic Music; Phi Beta Kappa; Phi Kappa Lambda. Address: 1015 Kirkwood Ave., Iowa City, IA 52240, USA. 4, 5, 8, 11, 12.

CROSS, Ronald, b. 18 Feb. 1929, Ft. Worth, Tex., USA. Professor of Music; Organist; Performer on Harpsichord, Recorder & Viola da Gamba. Educ: BA, Centenary Coll. of La.; MA & PhD, NY Univ.; further studies, Guilmant Organ Schl., NY, Conserv. of

Venice, Univ. of Florence, Chigiana Acad. (Siena), & Univ. of Vianna. Career: Prof. of Music (music hist. & theory. Cond., Collegium Musicum), Wagner Coll., Staten Island; Specialist, Renaissance music; Perf., early music; Organist-Choirmaster, var. chs., currently St. Paul's-St. Luke's Luth. Comps: Pastorale for Organ. Publs: Matthaeus Pipelare - Opera omnia, 3 vols., 1966-67. Contbr. to var. jrnls. in field, also Grove's Dictionary of Music & Musicians. Mbrships: Coll. Music Soc.; AAGO; Am. & Int. Musicol. Socs.; Viola da Gamba Soc. of Am.; Am. Recorder Soc.; Soc. for Ethnomusicol.; Am. Histl. Instrument Soc.; Am. Assn. of Engl. Handbell Ringers. Recip. of sev. awards. Hobby: Gardening. Address: 221 Ward Ave., Staten Island, NY 10304, USA. 6.

CROSS, William Samuel, b. 7 Mar. 1952, Almonte, Ont., Can. Musician (trombone). Educ: BMus, Univ. of W Ont., London, Ont., 1971-75; MM, Yale Univ., New Haven, Conn., 1975-77; Acad. of the West, Santa Barbara, Calif., 1975; Yale Summer Schl., Norfolk, Conn., 1976; Philip Jones Brass Ensemble SS, Horncastle, UK, 1977. Career: Past mbr., London (Ont.) Symph. Orch., Springfield (Mass.) Symph. Orch., Orch. of the Royal Winnipeg Ballet; apps. w. Hamilton Phil. Orch., Bolshoi Ballet (central Can. tour); currently trombonist, Orch. of the Nat. Ballet of Can. Mbr., Am. Fedn. of Musicians (Toronto & Ottawa). Hobby: Numismatics. Address: 18 Temple Ave., Toronto, Ont., Can. M6K 1C8.

CROSSE, Gordon, b. 1 Dec. 1937, Bury, Lancs., England, UK. Composer. Educ: MA Mus, St. Edmund Hall, Oxford. m. Elizabeth Bunch, 2 children. Career: Operas incl: Purgatory, The Grace of Todd, The Story of Vasco, Potter Thompson; 2 Concertos for violin & orch.; Ceremony for Cello & orch.; Ariadne (recorded) for oboe & ensemble; Memories of Morning-Night for mazzo-soprano & orch.; Changes (recorded), 2 Symphs.; The New World (recorded) for voice & piano; Works for Childrn's voice & insturments. Contbr. to var. profl. jrnls. Address: Brants Cottage, Wenhaston, Halesworth, Suffolk, UK. 1, 3, 16.

CROSSLAND, Anthony, b. 4 Aug. 1931, Nottingham, UK. Organist; Master of Choristers. Educ: MA, BMus, Christ Ch., Oxford; FRCO; ARCM. m. Barbara Helen Pullar-Strecker, 1 s., 2 d. Career: Asst. Organist, Christ Ch. Cathedral, Oxford, 1957-61, Wells Cathedral, 1967-71; Organist & Master of Choristers, ibid., 1971-. Recordings: as organ accomp. Music for Matins & Evensong from Wells Cathedral; as choir dir., Wells Cathedral Choir, 1975 & Anthems and Motets from Wells Cathedral. Hobbies: Readng; Photography. Address: 15 Vicar's Close, Wells, Somerset BA5 2UJ, UK. 1.

CROSSLEY, Paul Christopher Richard, b. 17 May 1944, Dewsbury, UK. Concert Pianist. Educ: BA, Oxford Univ., 1966; MA, ibid., 1970. Debut: Festival of Tours, 1968. Career: Concert pianist, Festivals of Tours, Bath, Cheltenham, Edinburgh, Harrogate; Recitals, UK, Europe, USA; Concertos w. major Brit. orchs. & in Europe. Recordings: num. incl. Messiaen piano works and works by Tippett, Franck, Faure, Stravinsky, Tchaikovsky, Weber and Janacek; (w. Arthur Grumiaux) Schubert Sonatinas & Faure Sonatas. Contbr. to: The Listener. Hons: Gulbenkian Fndn. Fellowship, 1971-74; 2nd Prize, Concours Olivier Messiaen, 1968. Hobbies: Parlour Games; Cinema; Reading. Mgmt: De Koos & Co., Ltd., 416 King's Rd., London SW10, UK. Address: 19 Westbourne Park Rd., London W2, UK. 1, 3, 14.

CROSSLEY-HOLLAND, Peter Charles, b. 28 Jan. 1916, London, UK. Composer; Professor; Ethnomusicologist. Educ: BA, St. John's Coll., Oxford, 1936; MA, ibid., 1941; BMus, 1943; Royal Coll. of Music, London; Schl. of Oriental & African Studies, Univ. of London. Debut: League of Arts Concerts, London, 1938. Career: Comp. own comps, BBC, radio & fests., UK; Appearances as medieval harpist, TV & radio; Num. broadcasts & lectures on music of Celts, Tibet & Orient; Asst. Dir., Inst. of Comparative Music Studies, Berlin, 1964-66; Vis. Lectr., Univ. of Ill., 1966; Vis. Prof. of Music, Univ. of Hawaii, 1968-79;p Lectr. thru' Prof. of Music, Univ. of Calif., LA, 1969-. Publd. Comps. incl: Cantata: The Sacred Dance; 2 songs for soprano & piano; 24 Rounds of Nature; Cantata: The Visions of Saint Godric; Des Puys d'Amors, songs for string orch. & harp.; Breton Tunes. Field recordings mainly on Tibetan music. Publs: Secular Medieval Music in Wales, 1942; Ed. & Co-author, Music in Wales, 1948; Music: A Report on Musical Life in England, 1949; The Pelican History of Music, Volume 1, Part 1, 1960. Contbr. to num. profl. jrnls. Address: 15554 Olden St., Sylmar, CA 91342, USA.

CROSTEN, William Loran, b. 7 Sept. 1909, Des Moines, Iowa, USA. Musicologist; Pianist; Educator. Educ: MusB, Drake Univ., 1930; AM, Univ. of Iowa, 1936; PhD, Columbia Univ., 1946; studied comp. w. Roger Sessions, m. Mary Perry Crosten, 1 s., 1 d. Publs: French Grand Opera, 1948, reprinted 1972. Contbr. to: Jrnl. of Am. Musicol. Soc.; Musical Quarterly; McGraw-Hill World Ency. Mbrships: Coll. Music Soc.;

Am. Musicol. Soc.; Musical Quarterly; McGraw-Hill World Ency. Mbrships: Coll. Music Soc.; Am. Musicol. Soc. Hons. incl: Guggenheim Fellowship, 1954-55; Drake Univ. Disting. Alumnus Award, 1964; Steinway Award for serv. to music, 1964. Hobbies: Travel; Photography; Environmental Studies. Address: Moose River Rd., Boonville, NY 13309, USA. 2, 4.

CROUCH, Margaret Cecelia Long, b. 12 Dec. 1937, Williamsport, Pa., USA. Harpsichordist; Musicologist. Educ: BMus (hist. & lit., harpsichord), 1971; MA (harpsichord), 1973; PhD (musicol.), 1978. m. David Glenn Crouch, 1 s. Career: Tchng. posts at Univ. of Calif., Santa Barbara, 1971-73, 1974-77, 1978-79, Schl. of Music, Univ. of Man., Winnipeg, 1977-78, & Calif. Lutheran Coll., 1979-80; Specialist in early keyboard music; num. recitals. Contbr. to profl. jrnls. & mags. Mbrships: Int. & Am. Musicol. Socs.; Coll. Music Soc.; Pi Kappa Lambda; Am. Guild of Organists; Sigma Alpha Iota. Recip., Univ. of Calif. Fellowship, 1973-74. Hobby: Reading in Philos. & Art Hist. Address: 7586 Hempstead Ave., Goleta, CA 93107, USA. 27.

CROW, Todd, b. 25 July 1945, Santa Barbara, Calif., USA. Pianist. Educ. incls: BA, Univ. of Calif., 1967; MS, Juilliard Schl. of Music, 1968; Music Acad. of W. m. Kinda Golsby, 1 s., 1 d. Debut: Wigmore Hall, London, 1975. Career: num. concerts in USA & Europe; recitals in London, Amsterdam, Edinburgh, Brussels; Am. Liszt Fests., 1971, 72; perf. at Alice Tully Hall, NY; num. apps. w. Comps. Str. Quartet & Concord Str. Quartet. Publs: Bartok Studies, 1976. Contbr. to: NOTES. Mbrships. incl: Am. Musicol. Soc.; Am. Liszt Soc. Recip. num. hons. Mgmt: New Era Int. Concerts Ltd., London. Address: Dept. of Music, Vassar Coll., Poughkeepsie, NY 12601, USA.

CROWE, Eyre Alexander, b. 28 Dec. 1947, Edinburgh, UK. Coach. Educ: BA, 1970, MA, 1976, Sidney Sussex Coll., Univ. of Cambridge; studied piano, 1953-66; violin, 1957-62, viola, 1962-66, & organ, 1962-66; LRAM (piano tchrs.), 1966. m. Felicity Helen Lambert. Career: Solo-Coach, Niedersächsisches Staatstheater, Hanover, German Fed. Repub., 1973-. Mbr., RCO. Recip., Finnish Min. of Educ. scholarship for rsch. into Sibleius's earlier comps., 1972. Hobbies: Walking; Reading; Squash. Address: Schäferweg 20, D-3012 Langenhagen 7, German Fed. Repub.

CROWE, Peter Russell, b. 25 Feb. 1942, Rangitikei, NZ. Ethnomusicologist. Educ: BMus, Vic. Univ.; div., 2 s. Career: specialist in Pacific ethnomusicol., esp. of Melanesia; Jt. Coord. of Oral Traditions prog., New Hebrides, for Cultural Ctr. at Port Vila. Comps: Bail Ha'i (5 new Hebrides songs for str. orch.); Magpies, Tuis Wetas, Whitebiat. Recording: Traditional music of the South Pacific. Publs: Report on Aoba, 1974; work in the North 1974-77, 1977. Contbr. articles on New Hebrides music & ritual to jrnls. Mbrships: Sec., Soc. for Oceanic Music; Comps. Assn. of NZ; Musicol. Soc. of Aust. Hons: Moli, 1976-77 (New Hebirdean hons.); Anzac Fellow, 1974. Address: 81 Ranfurly Rd., Auckland 3, NZ.

CROWN, Helen Barbara, b. 4 Apr. 1951, Cambridge, UK. Flautist (solo & orchestral). Educ: TCL w. Harold Clarke; FTCL; LTCL; pvte. study w. James Galway. m. Jonathan Bowden. Debut: Wigmore Hall, London, 1978. Career: recitals throughout UK; app. at Aldeburgh Fest.; perfs. in Calif. & Aust. Hobbies: Swimming; Cinema; Reading. Address: 49 Kingston St., Cambridge CB1 2NU, UK.

CROXFORD, Eileen, b. 21 Mar. 1924, Leighton Buzzard, Bucks., UK. Cellist. Educ: RCM; studied w. Effie Richardson, Ivor James, Pablo Casals. m. David Parkhouse, 2 s. Debut: Wigmore Hall; Royal Albert Hall. Career: Recitalist; Concerto Perf.; Fndr. Mbr., Music Grp. of London; Trours in Europe, N Africa, USA, Can., Far East; Prof., RCM; num. Broadcasts, BBC Sound, BBC TV. Recordings: Beethoven, Ghost Trio, Archduke Trio, Irish Songs; Schubert, Trout Quintet; Mendelssohn, Trio in D Minor, Bush Trio; Ravel Trio; Cello & Piano Sonatas by Dohnayi, Barber; Rachmaninoff, Kodaly, Debussy; Vaughan Williams, 2 Quartets, On Wenlock Edge, Studies on Folk Songs; Warlock, Curlew; Lennox Berkeley, Sextet; Elgar Quartet. Mbr. ISM. Hons: Alexander Prize, 1945; Queens Prize, 1948; Boise Fndn. Award, 1949. Hobbies: Cooking; Home; Family. Address: 63 Madrid Rd., London SW13, UK.

CRUFT, Adrian (Francis), b. 10 Feb. 1921, Mitcham, Surrey, UK. Composer. Educ: RCM, 1938-40, 46-47. m. Jocelyn Mather. Career: Double Bass Player, London orchs., 1947-69; co-Fndr. & Asst. Cond., London Classical Orch., 1951; Music Advsr., Scottish Children's Theatre, 1951-65; Cond., Purcell Club, 1955-57; Prof., theory, RCM, 1962-, orchestration, GSM, 1972-75; Examiner, Assoc. Bd., 1965-. Comps. incl: 4 cantatas; 3 overtures; 4 suites; works for orch., concert & brass band; works for solo

instruments & strings; Vaudeville/Opera; The Eatanswill Election, for unbroken male voices & piano; 2 masses; 2 Te Deum Laudamus; ch. & organ Music; chmbr. & recital music, esp. for wind & brass; educl. music. Num. recordings. Contbr. to musical publs. Mbrships: Royal Soc. of Musicians (Sec., 1966-70); Comps. Guild of GB (Chmn., 1966, Hon. Treas., 1968, Coun., 1969); Royal Soc. of Musicians; ISM; Royal Phil. Soc. Recip. var. hons. inclng: ARCM, 1964. Address: 1 The Retreat, S Worple Way, London SW14 8SS, UK.

CRUICKSHANK, Alistair Urquhart, b. 16 Nov. 1909, Lonmay, Scotland, UK. Teacher of Pianoforte. Educ: Lonmay Pub. Schl.; Fraserburgh Acad.; Pvte. studies of piano, organ & theory w. Mrs. Sim; Pvte. studies of Piano, organ, harmony & teaching w. James Hinchliffe; FIAL ATCL; Accredited tchr., ISM. m. Jessie Moir Imlach, 2 s. Mbr., Incorp. Soc. of Musicians (Pvte. tchrs. & music in educ. sects.). Hobbies: Walking; Reading; Swimming; Wine Making; Verse writing. Address: 7 Rose-in-the Bush Varavan Pk., Mawgan, Helston, Cornwall, UK.

CRUM, Dorothy Edith, b. 24 May 1944, Providence, RI, USA. Lyric Soprano; Assistant Professor of Voice. Educ: MM, Bowling Green State Univ., Ohio, 1969; Worth Abbey, London; DMA, Univ. of Colo., Boulder, 1977. Debut: Soloist, Balt. Comic Opera & Balt. Bach. Soc., 1969; Cond., Choral grp. w. the Boston Pops Orch., 1973. Career: Soloist, Wichita Choral Soc., USA, 1975. Roles incl: Musetta in La Boheme; Penelope in Golden Apple; Frasquita in Carmen. Publs: Creative Recitaling, 1978. Mbrships: Regional Gov., Nat. Assn. of Tchrs. of Singing; Am. Choral Cons.; Nat. Soc. of Lit. & the Arts; Cousteau Soc.; IAERS; Faculty Advisor, Sigma Alpha Iota at WSU. Recip. Rose Scholarship, Mich. State Univ., 1968; Grad. Teaching Assistantship, Univ. of Colo., 1976-77. Hobbies: Collecting antique ruby red & cobalt blue glassware; Skiing; Backpacking. Address: Wichita State Univ. Schl. of Music, Wichita, KS 67208, USA.

CRUMB, George, b. 24 Oct. 1929, Charleston, W Va., USA. Composer; University Professor of Composition. Educ: BM, Mason Coll. of Music, 1950; MMus, Univ. of Ill., 1952; DMA, Univ. of Mich., 1959; Hochschule für Musik, Berlin, 1955-56. m., 2 s., 1 d. Career: Prof., Composition, Univ. of Pa. Compositions (all recorded) incl: 5 Pieces for Piano; Night Music 1; 4 Nocturnes for Violin & Piano; Echoes of Time & the River: 4 Processionals for Orchestra; Night of the 4 Moons; Black Angels for Electric String Quartet; Makrokosmos Vol. 1. Mbrships: Broadcast Music, Inc. Hons: Pulitzer Pize in Music, for Echoes of Time & the River, 1968; Koussevitsky Int. Recording Award, 1971; Int. Rostrum of Composers (UNESCO) Award, 1971. Hobby: Reading. Address: 240 Kirk Lane, Media, PA, USA. 2.

CRUTCHFIELD, Edmund Allday, b. 23 July 1943, Northampton, UK. Clarinettist; Conductor. Educ: Dip., Huddersfield Schl. of Music; ARCM. Career: tchng., recitals, conducting; estab. Caterham Music Fest.; Dir., Surrey Sinfonia & Mozart Wind Ensemble. Contbr. to: Croydon Advt. Mbrships: ISM; Musicians Union. Hobbies: Photography; Cycling; Railways; Walking. Address: The Rostrum, 9 Nelson Rd., Caterham, Surrey, UK.

CRUZ, Ivo, b. 19 May 1901, Corumba, Bresil, Portugal. Orchestra Conductor; Composer. Educ: Law Grad., Univ. of Lisbon; Studied Comp. & Orch. w. Richard Mors, Munich, W Germany; Studied Musicl., Univ. of Munich. m. Maria Adelaide Soares Cardoso, 3 s., 1 d. Career: Fndr. & Chief Cond., Lisbon Phil. Orch. & Sociedade Coral de Duarte Lobo; Dir., Nat. Conservatoire; Pres., Nat. Musicians Union & Pro-Arte, Procurator, Corporative Chmbr.; Conducted Concerts in Portugal, Spain, France, Germany, Austria, Switzerland, Roumania, Belgium, Holland & Brazil. Comps. incl: Amadis Symph.; Queluz Symph.; Pastorale (ballet); Lusitanian Motifs; 1st Portuguese Concert; 2nd Portuguese Concert; The Poet's Loves; Triptych; Homages; Kaleidoscope; Sonata for Violin & Piano; Lunatic Ballads; Sentimental Songs. Recordings w. Da Vinci Records, NY & Educo, Calif. Publs: Ink Drops - A Project of Reform of the national Conservatoire. Mbrships: Alderman, Lisbon Municipality; Committee Mbr., Teatro de Sao Carlos; Higher Culture Inst. Hons: Cmdr., Order of St. James; Grand Off., Public Instruction; Kt. Order of Alfonson el Sabio. Hobby: Antiques. Address: Rua do Salitre 166, 2° Esq., Lisbon 2, Portugal. 16.

CRUZ, Richard H, b. 11 Feb. 1929, Rice, Tex., USA. Professor of Music; Trumpeter. Educ: BA, MA, Special Second. Life Dip. in Music. m. Bertha P Cruz, 4 children. Career: Prin. Trumpet w. Downey Light Opera, Laguna Arts Fest. Orch.; Soloist, Rio Hondo Symph. of Whittier; Prof., Fullerton Coll., Calif.; Guest Cond., Wildwood Music camp Symphonic Band, Guam Hon. Bands, var. Calif. grps. Mbrships: Pres., Music Assn.; Calif. Community Colls.; MENC; Assn. of Calif. Symph. Orchs.;

Southern Calif. Band & Orch. Assn. Hobby: Photography. Address: 910 N Oakdale, Fullerton, CA 92631, USA.

CRUZ-ROMO, Gilda, b. 12 Feb., Guadalajara, Mexico, Opera singer (soprano). Educ: Nat. Conserv. of Music of Mexico, Mexico City. m. Robert B Romo. Debut: Ortlinde (Walküre) Bellas Artes Opera Int., Mexico, 1962. Career: Metropolitan Opera debut as Madam Butterfly, 1970; Leading Soprano, ibid,m 1970-; Int. Opera, Mexico City, 1962-67; toured Aust., NZ, S Am.; Dallas Civic Opera, 1966-68, '69, '79; NYC Opera, 1969-72; La Scala rep. as Aida, USSR, 1974; Lyric Opera Chgo., 1975, '80; Leading roles, many cos. in USA & abroad, incl. Covent Gdn., La Scala, Vienna State Opera, Rome Opera, Paris Opera, Florence, Torino, Verona, Teatro Colon, Buenos Aires, Barcelona, Santiago; Concert apps., Can., Mexico, USA, Japan, Israel, USSR; TV apps. Recordings: Aida, Orange Fest. 1976. Mbr., Sigma Alpha Iota. Hons: 1st Prize, Metropolitan Opera Nat. Coun. Award, 1970; Recip., Critics Award Union Mexicana de Cronistas de Treatro y Musica; Best Singer, 1976-77 season Cronistas de Santiago de Chile. Mgmt: Harold Shaw, USA; John Coast, Europe. Address: 397 Warwick Ave., Teaneck, NJ 07666, USA. 2.

CSABA, Janos, b. 25 Mar. 1938, Kisujszallas, Hungary. Violist. Educ: BMus., Univ. of Tex., 1961; MMus., Eastman Schl. of Music, 1969; Dip. of Merit, Accademia Musicale Chigiana, Siena, Italy. m. Jerry Lorene Csaba, 2 d. Debut: Austin Tex., USA. Career: Viola, Austin, Tex., Montreal, PQ, Can., Ottawa, Ont., Symphs; Tchr., Western State Coll., Colo., USA, 1 yrs.; num. chmbr. Music Apps., Recitals. Recording: Music for Guitar & Strings. Hons: Scholarship, Tuesday Musical Club, San Antonio, Tex., 1960; Can. Coun. Grant, 1971. Hobbies: Sports; Photography; Woodworking; Gardening. Address: 2846 Grandeur Ave., Ottawa, Ont. K2B6YG, Can.

CSABA, Jerry L, b. 22 Mar. 1940, Houston, Tex., USA. Violinist. Educ: BM, Univ. of Tex. m. János Csaba, 2 d. Career: Mbr. Austin Tex., Symph., 1957-60, Montreal, PQ, Can., Symph., 1962-68, McGill Chmbr. Orch., 1965-68. Nat. Arts Ctr. Orch., 1969-74, Rochester Phil., 1968-79; Soloist w. Rochester Phil., McGill Chmbr. Orch., NAC Orch., Thirteen Strings; currently mbr., nat. Arts Centre Orch., Ottawa Baroque Ensenble, The Thirteen Strings. Recording: Music for Guitar & Strings. Hobby: Cooking. Address: 2846 Grandeur Ave., Ottawa, Ont. K2B 6Y9, Can.

CSÍKY, Boldizsár, b. 3 Oct. 1937, Tîrgu-Mures (Transylvania), România. Composer. Educ: Conserv. of Music George Dima, Cluj. 1 s. Debut: 1961. Career: Prof. of counterpoint & harmony in Music Schl.; Music Sec. of the State Phil. of Tîrgu-Mures. Comps: Two pieces for large orch.; Praeludium, Fugue & Postludium for Symph. Orch. (recorded); Four esquisses for string orch.; Old Translyvanian dances and songs; Chant des héros (Heldenlieder); Suite antique for strings & lute, etc. Recordings: Old Translyvanian dances and songs; Chant des héros (sur les mélodies du Sebastian Tinódy); The Mountain, Symph. Poem). Publs: Zenetudomanyi Irások (Hungarian) incl. Musicology Studies, 1977. Mbr., Union of Comps. of Romania. Hons: Prize of the Union of Comps., 1975; Medalia Meritul Cultural, 1969. Hobby: Mountain fishing. Address: Filarmonica de stat Tîrgu-Mures, str. G Enescu nr. 2, 4300 Tîrgu-Mures, Romania.

ČUBR, Antonin, b. 21 Aug. 1904, Litomysl, Czechoslovakia. Pianist; Organist; Musicologist; Critic. Educ: LLd, Charles Univ., Prague; Dip. of profl. pianist, Music Acad., Prague. m. Marie Pixová-Cubrová, Career: Practical performing as soloist, accompanist of singers & instrumentalists, 2 yrs.; Impressario, vocal concerts & recitals of Mrs. Marie Pixová-Cubrová 1946-49. Mbrships: Chmn., Ed. Bd. Critical Edition of Antonin Dvoiak's Works: Pres., Antonin Dvorak's Soc.; Sec., Soc. for Chmbr. Music, Prague. Address: Na Mlejnku 20, CS 147 00 Prague 4, Branik cp. - 993, Czechoslovakia.

CUCKSTON, Alan George, b. Horsforth, Yorks., UK. Harpsichordist; Performer on Fortepiano. Educ: MA & MusB, King's Coll., Cambridge. m. Vivien Broadbent, 3 d. Career: BBC Music Prog.; touring Europe, Can. & USA; Harpsichordist, The London Virtuosi, Acad. of St. Martin's in the Fields, New London Soloists Ensemble, Pro Cantione Antiqua, Northern Chmbr. Orch. & Yorks. Sinfonia. Recordings: Harmonia Mundi; Teldec RCA; EMI; DGG. Mbrships: Royal Musical Assn.; ISM. Address: Swinsty Hall, Feston, Harrogate HG3 1ST, UK. 16, 28.

CUENOT, Yves, b. 20 Mar. 1951, Besancon, France. Music Teacher of Piano & Organ; Concert Performer on Organ & Harpsichord. Educ: Laureate, Acads. of Music, Besancon & Dijon. Career: Organist, Cathedral & Protestant Ch. of Dijon; Dir. & Cond., L'Orch. Phil. de Dijon; Soloist in concerts organised by Cultural Assns. of Guadeloupe & Porto Rico; Vis. Tchr., Acad. of Music, Guadeloupe. Recordings: Recital Trompette et Orgue.

Mbrships: Responsable of the Assn. Heure Musicale du Dimanche. Address: 3 Rue Charles-de-Vergennes, 21000 Dijon, France. 30.

CUGLEY, Ian Robert, b. 22 June 1945, Richmond, Victoria, Australia. Composer; Lecturer; Percussionist. Educ: BMus, Univ. of Sydney. m. Jennifer Cugley, 4 c. Career: Lectr., NSW Conserv., 1967; Univ. of Tas. & Tasmanian Conserv. of Music, 1968-. Comps. incl: Mass in Honour of St. Catherine, 1971; Sonata Movement for Violin & Piano, 1972; Acquarelles for Piano, 1972; Sea Changes (opera for boys' voices) words by Gwen Harwood, 1974; var. misc. works for children. Num. recordings. Publs: Exploring Musical Language, 1974. Contbr. to profl. jrnls. Mbr. of profl. orgs. Hons: Alfred Hill award for Chmbr. Symph., 1971. Hobbies: Watercolour Painting; Graphics. Address: 39 Proctors Rd., Dynnyrno, Tasmania, Australia.

CULBERTSON, Melvin W, b. 9 Apr. 1946, Wheeling, W Va., USA. Tubaist. Educ: Univ. Calif., Long Beach; New England Conserv., Mass.; Juilliard Schl. of Music. m. Susan Brown, 1 s. Debut: Carnegie Recital Hall, NY, 1968; Career incls: Solo recitals: GB, Holland & USA; Solo perfs: Los Angeles; Boston; Phila.; Munich, Germany; Montreux, Switzerland; Master Instr. for Tuba & Chmbr. Music (brass), Montreux's Inst. for Advanced Music Studies; Brass Instr: Koninglijk Conserv., The Hague; Rotterdamse Muziek Schl.; Tubaist, Phil. Orch. of Ams., Mexico City, 1976; Tubaist (solo), The Hague Phil., Holland. Hons: 1st Place, Sigma Iota Competition, 1964, 65. Hobbies: Wrestling; Cooking. Address: Bottelroos 2, Berkel-Rodenrijs, Holland.

CULBREATH, Edward Blake, b. 7 Apr. 1941, NYC, USA. Cellist; Professor of Cello. Educ: HS of Performing Arts, NYC; BSc, Mannes Coll. of Music, NYC; MMus, Yale Schl. of Music. m. Julia Hoerner, 1 s., 1 d. Career: CBC Radio & TV broadcasts; Prin. Cellist, Syracuse Symph. Orch.; Vaghy String Quartet; Artist-in-Res., City of Kingston, Ont.; Prof. of Cello, McGill Univ., Montreal, PQ. Comps: Incidental music to CBC Radio adaptation of Romeo & Juliet. Recordings: Radio Can. Int. (RCI). Address: 4915 Blvd. de Maisonneuve Oues, Montreal 215, PQ, Canada.

CULLEN, John Gavin, b. 30 Apr. 1936, Dundee, Scotland, UK. Director of Music; Organist; Conductor; Harpsichordist. Educ: Christ's Coll., Cambridge; MA; FRCO; ARCM (rogan perf.). m. Mary Elaine Randolph, 2 s., 1 d. Career: Organist & Master of the Choristers, Aberdeen Cathedral, 1961-63; tchr., Aberdeen Grammar Schl., 1961-63; Dir. of Music, Abingdon Schl., 1964-67; Dir. of Music, Tonbridge Schl., 1967-; cond. & harpsichordist, Tonbridge Phil. Soc. Comps: A Scottish Suite, for chorus & orch.; ch. music; carol arr., etc. Recordings: Missa Brevis & Carols, Choral Evensong (Aberdeen Cathedral); And Did Those Feet (Tonbridge Schl. Choir & Organ). Contbr. to musical & ecclesiastical jrnls. Mbrships: ISM (Educ. sect.), Warden, 1979-80; Music Masters' Assn., Pres., 1977-78; H.M.C Music Curriculum Committee, Chmn., 1979-. Hobbies: Climbing; Gardening; Golf. Address: Hazlehead, 29 Dry Hill Rd., Tonbridge, Kent, UK.

CULSHAW, John Royds, b. 28 May 1924, Southport, UK. Author; Television & Recording Producer. Educ: Self-taught. Career: Classical Recording Prod., Decca, 1946-54; Capitol, 1954-56; Mgr., Classical Dept., Decca, 1956-67; Hd., Music Prog., BBC TV, 1967-75. Mbr., Arts Coun. of GB, Chmn., Music Panel ibid. Publs: Sergei Rachmaninov, 1949; A Century of Music, 1951; Ring Resounding, 1967; Reflections of Wagner's Ring, 1976. Contbr. to profl. jrnls. Mbrships: Soc. of Authors. Hons: Vienna Phil. Nicolai Medal, 1959; Schalk Medal, 1967; OBE, 1966. Hobby: Private flying. Address: 16 Arlington Ave., London, N1 7AX, UK. 1.

CUMMINGS, Diana, b. 27Apr. 1941, Amersham, UK. Violinist. Educ: Recital Dip., RAM; ARAM. m. Luciano Jorios, 2 s., 1 d. Debut: Wigmore Hall. Career: has toured throughout GB as soloist and chmbr. musician; num. TV & radio broadcasts; Ldr., Cummings String Trio & Engl. Piano Quartet. Mbrships: Musicians Union; ISM. Hons: incl: Prizewinner, Int. Peganini Competition, Geona, 1963. Int. Competition 'A Curci', Naples, 1967. Address: 2 Fairhazel Mansions, Fairhazel Gardens, London NW6, UK.

CUMMINGS, Diane M, b. 24 Mar. 1952, Williams, Ariz., USA. Violinist; Teacher. Educ: summer schl., Northern Ariz. Univ.; BMus, Ariz. State Univ., 1975; studied w. Kathleen Gregg, Clarence Shaw & Eugene P Lombardi; master classes w. Eudice Sahpiro, Sydney Harth, Bronstien. Debut: Soloist w. Flagstaf Symph., 1970. Career: w. Ariz. All-State Orch., 4 yrs.; w. full orch., 7 yrs. & chmbr. orch., 5 yrs., Flagstaff Summer Fest.; Sr. Violin Recital, Ariz. State Univ., 1975; in 1st violin sect. Phoenix Symph., 1975-76. Recorded recital of music by Handel,

Ibert, Bloch, Kerr & Franck, 1975. Mbrships: NEA; MENC; Sigma Alpha Iota, Gamma Mu Chapt. Hons. incl: Gold Medal, State Solo & Ensemble Fest., 1969. Hobbies incl: Ballet; Handicrafts. Address: 1920 N Talkington Dr., Flagstaff, AZ 86001, USA.

CUMMINGS, Henry, b. 22 Dec. 1906, Dublin, Eire. Baritone. Singer. Educ: RAM, London; FRAM; ARAM. m. Norah Newby, 3 c. by former marriage. Career: Oratorio, recitals, concerts, radio recitals, etc.; Appeared at maj. perfs. - Promenade Concerts, Three Choirs Fest. & major Choral Socs., etc. Var. recordings. Mbrships: RAM Club (Sec.); Assn. of Engl. Singers & Speakers. Recip., var. singing prizes. Address: 52 Carlton Hill, St. Johns Wood, London NW8 OES, UK.

CUMMINGS, Keith, b. Perth, W Australia. Violist. Educ: Royal Manchester Coll. of Music; FTCL; ARMCM. m. Ellen Madge Cummings, 2 s., 1 d. Career: Apps. w. London String Quartet; Prof., TCL. Hobby: Photography. Address: 18 Ellerdale Rd., London NW3 6BB, UK.

CUMMINGS, Winford Claude Jr., b. 1 Apr. 1919, Ft. Worth, Tex., USA. Musicologist; Violinist; Violist; Conductor. Educ: BMus, Univ. Tex., 1941; MA, Harvard Univ., 1949. m. Elizabeth Story, 1 s., 1 d. Career: Asst. & Assoc. Prof. of Music, Miami Univ., Ohio, USA, 1953-; Lectr., Ind. Univ., 1963; Prod. Ed., Music Progs. for WNYC, WIW, WCKY, Voice of Am.; Cond., New Music Ensemble in NYC, Wash., DC, Chgo. Recordings incl: Taped series for radio, Introduction to Music; David Cope's Music on Indian Themes. JAMS abstracts of papers read at regional meetings on 16th century theory. Mbrships: incl. Int. Musicol. Soc.; Am. Musicol. Soc. Hons. incl: Walter W Naumberg Fellow in Music, 1948-50. Address: 3 Patrick Dr., Oxford, OH 45056, USA.

CUNEO, Linda Boring, b. 15 Jan. 1945, Pitts., Pa., USA. Pianist; Musicologist. Educ: MusB, Oberlin Conserv.; MA, NY Univ.; MS, Juilliard Schl.; PhD Cand., NY Univ. studed w. S Hummel; D Danenberg; S Gorodnitzki; G Casadesus. m. Donald L Cuneo. Debut: Albany, NY, 1972. Career incls: apps. in NY inclng. perfs. at Alice Tully Hall & Town Hall; Guest apps. on CBS shows; concert tours w. Allnations Co., Israel, Rumania, Caribbean Islands; coll. circuit tour w. pianist Stanley Hummel, NY state, 1974-75; Taught music hist., Juilliard Schl., 1973-75. Recordings: Cuneo & Hummel: Music for Two Pianos. Mbrships: Am. Musicol. Soc.; Pi Kappa Lambda. Hobbies: Tennis; Photography; Golf; Films. Address: 7 rue d'Olivet, Paris 75007, France.

CUNNINGHAM, Juliet Elizabeth, b. 9 Dec. 1928, Gloucester, UK. Orchestral Double Bass Player. Educ: RCM, 1946-50; ARCM (double bass perf.). m. Bill Jones, 2 s., 2 d. Career: w. BBC Symph. Orch., 1950-; free-lance playing in London. Has recorded w. BBC Symph. Orch. Hobbies: Walking; Gardening; Cooking; Handicrafts. Mgmt: BBC. Address: 68 Swakeleys Dr., Ickenham, Middx., UK.

CUPERS, Jean-Louis (Georges Marie), b. 19 June 1946, Etterbeek, Brussels, Belgium. Philologist; Musicologist; Pianist. Educ: Lic. Philos. Lettres, Univ. Cath. Louvain, 1968; B Philos, ibid., 1971; DLitt, ibid., 1978; Lic. Musicol., 1972. Career: Perfng. on 18th & 19th century pianofortes (Musée Instrumental de Bruxelles): Recordings: Mendelssohn's Piano Concerto No. 1 in G Minor, 1967. Contbr. to: Revue des archéologues et historiens d'art de Louvain, 1971; Int. Review Aesthetics & Soc. Music, 1974; Mélanges de Musicol., Louvain, 1974. Mbrships: Int. Musicol. Assn.; Comm., Assn. Germanistes, Univ. Cath. Louvain; Assn. Profs. Langs. Vivantes (Soc. Francois Closset). Hons: Govt. Medal for the Piano, Acad. de Musique de Woluwé-St-Pierre, Brussels, 1966. Hobbies: Walking; Dancing; Playing the Piano. Address: 10 ave. Van Crombrugghe, 1150 Brussels, Belgium. 23, 28, 29.

CUPPER, Ralph John, b. 9 Aug. 1954, Norwich, Norfolk, UK. Concert Organist; Composer; Teacher. Educ: RAM, London, 1972-76; GRSM; LRAM (organ tchng.); ARCM (organ perf.); ARCO; Studes w. Lady Susi Jeans; Nicolas Kynaston & Bernard Bartelink. Career: Num. organ recitals in UK, incl. Southwark Cathedral, St. Michael's Ch. Cornhill, London, etc.; 2 concert tours of Germany, 1977-78. Contbr. to: Musical Times; RAM Club Mag. Mbrships: ISM; RAM Club; RCO, London. Hons: Frederick Keene Organ Perf. Prize, 1974 (RAM). Hobbies: Lang.; Engrng. (manufacturing dental equipment). Address: 73 Winchester Tower, Vauxhall St., Norwich, Norfolk NR2 2SF, UK.

CURESS, Richard, b. 3 Dec. 1893, Endersbach, Germany. Doctor of Music and Composition. Educ: PhD, DMus, Abitur, Univ. m. Dely Lederer, 2 c. Career incls: Dir., Acad. for Music, Münster & Kassel. Comps: 145 opera, Symph., Oratorios,

Concertos & Songs. Publs: Der Musikunterricht in der Schule, 1928; Entwukliengder Klavier variation von Gaboldi, J S Bach, 1927. Hons. incl: Lisztmedalia, Spohr Goetheplakette. Hobbies: Playing piano. Mgmt: GEMA, 1 Berlin 30, German Fed. Repub. Address: Auerstrasse 2F, 3500 Kassel, German Fed. Repub.

CURPHEY, Margaret, b. 27 Feb. 1938, Douglas, Isle of Man, UK. Opera Singer. Educ: Birmingham Schl. of Music. m. Philip Summerscales, 1 d. Debut: in Arts Coun's. Opera for All. Career: Prin. Soprano, Engl. Nat. Opera; Festival appearances at Glyndebourne, Valencia & in Bulgaria; Concerts w. Calgary Symph. Orch. & Halle Orch.; Broadcasts on BBC Radio. Recordings: Excerpts from Gotterdamerung; Die Walkyrie. Hon: Bronze Medal for Young Opera Singer, Sofia, Bulgaria, 1970. Hobbies: Sewing; Gardening; Cooking. Address: 9 Thames St., Walton-on-Thames, Surrey, UK.

CURRIE, John, b. 1934, Prestwick, UK. Chorus Master; Conductor. Educ: Ayr Acad.; Royal Scottish Acad. of Music; Univ. of Glasgow; MA; DipMusEd., RSAM; LTCL. m. Barbara Kirkwood, 1 s., 2 d. Career: Lectr., Dept. of Music, Glasgow Univ., 1964-71; Glasgow Music Critic, The Scotsman, 1962-; Chorus Master, Scottish Nat. Orch. Chorus, 1965-; Artistic Dir., John Currie Singers, 1968-; Dir. of Music, Leicester Univ., 1971-74; Chorus Dir. & Musical Assoc., Scottish Opera, 1974-; Chorus Master, Edinburgh Fest. Chorus, 1977-. Comps. incl: Song Cycle for baritone & orch.; Loon Woman; Symph. arrs. Scottish songs. Mbrships: CGGB; Musicians Union. Address: 4 Princess Gdns., Glasgow G12, UK. 3.

CURRO, John Ronald, b. 6 Dec. 1932, Cairns, Qld., Aust. Lecturer in Viola, Violin & Chamber Music. Educ: Violin w. Oscar Rosen, London, 1955; Klagenfurt Conserv., Austria, 1956-57, Santa Cecilia Conserv., Rome, Italy, 1957-58; Violin & Viola, Qld. Conserv., 1962-65; Viola w. Robert Pikler, Sydney, 1965-68; Cond. w. Ezra Rachlin, Brisbane, 1968-72, London, 1976. m. Carmel Cusack, 2 d. Career incls: lectr. in Violin, Viola & Chmbr. Music, Qld. Conserv. of Music, 1974-; Dir. of Music, Qld. Youth Orch., 1966- (3 Int. tours); Cond., Youth Orchs., Aust.; Musical Dir., Cond., sev. Aust. profl. opera Cos.; Radio recitalist; Violist, Lazaroff String Quartet, 1964-72; Duo (viola) w. Ladislav Jasek, 1968-69; Ldr., Mayne String Quartet (Univ. of Qld.), 1974-77; Prin. Viola, Univ. of Qld. Sinfonietta, 1973-. Recordings: Concerto for Viola (James Pemberthy). Mbr.; num. profl. orgs. Hons: Queen Elizabeth II Silver Jubilee Medal, 1977. Mgmt: Mr. F Chiesa, Novara, Italy. Address: 19 Moray St., New Farm, Brisbane, Qld., Aust.

CURRY, Carol Anne Isabelle, b. 27 June 1943, Orangeville, Ont., Can. Operatic Singer. Educ: Artist & Lic. Dips., Univ. of Toronto; Fac. of Music Opera Dip., Royal Conserv., Toronto. m. James Christopher Lightbourn. Debuts: Scottish Opera, Perth, 1969; Wigmore Hall, London, 1971; Alice Tully Hall, Lincoln Ctr., NYC, 1973; Can. Opera Co., Toronto, 1973. Career: Can. Broadcasting, USA. Mbrships: Actors Equity Assn. Hons: CBC Talent Fest., 1967; Gt. Lakes Reg., Metrop. Opera Auditions, 1969; Arts Bursary, Can. Coun., 1971 & 72. Hobbies: Reading; Writing; Cooking. Mgmt: Kathryn J Brown, Personal Mgmt., Toronto. Address: 611-188 Margaret Ave., Kitchener, Ont., Canada N2H 4J3.

CURRY, Diane, b. 26 Feb. 1942, Clifton Forge, Va., USA. Opera Singer (mezzo soprano). Educ: BMus, MMus, Westminster Choir Coll., Princeton, NJ, USA. Debut: NYC Opera, 1972. Career: Mbr., NYC Opera; apps. w. major opera cos., USA & Europe; Num. fest. apps.; Perfs. w. num. choral orgs. & orchs. in USA & Italy, concerts & oratorios. Recordings: Ariel Symph. Hobbies: Reading; Walking; Museums; Plants. Mgmt: Kazuko Hillyer Int. Address: 203 W 81 St., NYC, NY 10024, USA.

CURRY, Donna Jayne, b. 26 Jan. 1939, Los Angeles, Calif., USA. Concert Artist; Educator; Singer-Lutenist. Educ: BA, Whittier Coll., Calif.; Grad. studies, The Schola Cantorum Basiliensis; Pvte. studies. Debut: Wigmore Hall, London, 1971; Carnegie Recital Hall, NYC, 1971. Career incls: Lute, voice & guitar concerts in USA, UK, Germany, Switzerland & Hungary; Broadcasts & TV apps. in USA & abroad; Instr. of Lute: UCLA, 1978-; Mt. St. Mary's Coll.; Stanford Summer Schl.; Univ. of S Calif., 1976-; Lute Soc. Summer Schl., Cheltenham, UK. Var. recordings incl: Since First I Saw Your Face. Publs: An Anthology of Lute Songs, 1976. Contbr. to profl. jrnls. Mbr. num. profl. orgs. Recip. Honoraria, Renaissance Ctr. of Calif., 1970, 71, 72. Hobbies: Gardening; Cabinetry. Address: PO Box 194, Topanga, CA 90290, USA. 4, 5, 29.

CURSON, Theodore (Ted), b. 3 June 1935, Philadelphia, Pa., USA. Jazz Musician (trumpet, piccolo trumpet, flugelhorn); Performer; Composer; Publisher; President, Nosc Publishing Company, Jersey City. Educ: Granoff Music Conserv.,

1952-53. m. Marjorie N Curson, 1 s., 1 d. Career: Mbr., Charles Mingus' Jazz Workshop, 1959-60; Trumpeter w. Max Roach, Philly Joe Jones, Cecil Taylor, Eric Dolphy, etc., 1960-63; Bandleader, 1963-; appearances on radio, TV, clubs, fests. (inclng. Antibes, Lugano, Prague, Lucerne, Stockholm), 1961-; var. appearances at US fests., Univ. concerts Guest Instr., Univ. of Vt. Fest. of contemporary Music, 1968; Instr., Music, Warsaw Univ.; Guest Soloist, Danish Radio, etc.; Mbr., Schauspielhaus Theatre, Zürich, 1972-73. Sev. compositions & recordings. Publs: The New Thing: Nine Originals, 1966. Contbr. to Jazz Forum, Poland. Mbr., Am. Fedn. Musicians. Recip. sev. hons. & awards inclng: Winner, Trumpet Sect., Down Beat Int. Critics Poll, 1966; named New Jazz Artist, Jazz Podium, 1966. Address: 130 Arlington Ave., Jersey City, NJ 07305, USA. 2.

CURTIN, Phyllis, b. Clarksburg, W Va., USA. Singer. Educ: BA, Wellesley Coll., Mass.; MusD, W Va. Univ. m. Eugene Cook, 1 d. Debut: recital, Town Hall, NYC, 1950; opera, NYC Opera, 1953. Career: recitals around the world; ldng. roles, NYC Opera, Metrop. Opera, Teatro Colon, Vienna Staatsoper, La Scala, Glyndebourne et al.; Soloist w. ldng. symph. orchs. & in major fests.; Prof. of Voice, Yale Schl. of Music, New Haven, Conn.; Artist-in-Res., Tanglewood, Berkshire Music Ctr., Lenox, Mass. Recordings incl: Shostakovitch Symph. 14, w. Phila. Orch. under Ormandy; Wozzeck excerpts w. Boston Symph. under Leinsdorf. Recip., hon. docts., Marshall Univ. & Salem Coll., 1964. Mgmt: Columbia Artists, 165 W 57th St., NYC, NY 10019. Address: 129 Davis St., Hamden, CT 06517, USA. 2.

CURTIS, Alan, b. 17 Nov. 1934, Masone, Mich., USA. Harpsichordist; Conductor; Musicologist. Educ: BMus, Mich. State Univ., 1955; MMus, Univ. Ill., 1956. 2 children. Career: Cond. & Harpsichordist: Holland Festivals, 1974-75; Opening season Brussels Royal Opera, 1974; Broadcasts & Recitals all maj. European countries, USA & Can. Recordings incl: Cond., L'Incoronazione di Poppea (Monteverdi); num. works as Harpsichordist. Publs: Sweelinck's Keyboard Music, 1963; Dutch Keyboard Music. Contbr. to Tijdschrift VNM; Revue de Musicologie. Mbrships: Am. Musicol. Soc.; Vereniging voor Nederlands Muziekgeschiedenis. Hobbies: Gardening; Art Hist. Address: Dept. of Music, Univ. of Calif., Berkeley, USA.

CURTIS, James Gilbert, b. 27 Aug. 1904, Birkenhead, Merseyside, UK. Organist; Organist; Choirmaster; Recitalist; Teacher of Singing. m. Gladys Pearl Cooke. Career: Organist & Choirmaster, Eillaston-in-Wirral, 1925-50; St. Saviour's, Oxton, Birkenhead, 1951-76, Organist & Choirmaster, Holy Cross Ch., Woodchurch, 1976 (now retired); a Diocesan Rep., RSCM; Diocesan Organ Advsr.; Tchr. of Singing w. emphasis on remedial voice prod. Comps: Chorale Prelude on Wiltshire; Jesus by the Wonded Feet (anthem). Mbrships: incl: RCO; Coun., Past. Nat. Exec., Inc. Assn. of Organists, 1945-77; Hon. Sec. & Treas., IAO Benevolent Fund; Past Pres., Liverpool & Chester Organists Assns. Publs: Think Afresh About the Voice (w. A D Hewlett), 1970. Contbr. to profl. publs. Hobby: Motoring. Address: Lodore, 2 Coronation Rd., Hoylake, Wirral, Merseyside, L47 1HR, UK. 4.

CURTIS-SMITH, Curtis O B, b. 9 Sept. 1941, Walla Walla, Wash., USA. Composer; Pianist; Associate Professor of Music. Educ: BMus, Northwestern Univ., 1964; MMus, ibid., 1965. Comps. incl: A Song of Degrees, 1972 (2 pianos & percussion); Five Sonorous Inventions, 1973 (violin & piano); Rhapsodies, 1973 (piano); (Belles) Belle du Jour, 1974-75 (orch.); Suite in Four Movements, 1975 (harpsichord); Variations for Piano, 1975. Recordings: Five Sonorous Inventions, Gerald Fischbach, violin, C Curtis-Smith, piano; Rhapsodies, David Burge, piano. Contbr. to Woodwind World; Brass & Percussion. Hons. incl: Martha Baird Rockefeller Grant, 1974. Hobbies: Mountain Climbing; Hiking; Swimming. Address: 3409 W Mich., Apt. 6, Kalamazoo, MI 49007, USA.

CURZON, (Sir) Clifford Michael, b. 18 May 1907, London, UK. Concert Pianist. Educ: FRAM; studied w. Katharine Goodson, Artur Schnabel (Berlin), Wanda Landowska & Nadia Boulanger (both Paris). m. Lucille Wallace, 2 s. Debut: Queen's Hall Prom. Concerts under Sir Henry J Wood, when aged 17. Career: has made world-wide tours, playing w. leading orchs. & at major fests. Has recorded. Hons: CBE, 1958; DMus, Leeds Univ., 1970; D Litt., Sussex Univ., 1973. Hobbies: Gardening; Picture Collecting. Mgmt: Ibbs & Tillett, London; Harry Beall Mgmt., NY, USA. Address: The White House, Millfield Place, Highgate, London N6, UK.

CUSHMAN, Stephen, b. 16 Aug. 1938, Boston, Mass., USA. Musicologist; Organist; Assistant Professor. Educ: AB, Harvard Coll., 1960; MMus, New England Conserv., 1962; PhD, Boston Univ. Grad. Schl., 1973. m. Wasthi Brannstrom, 2 s.

Career: Asst. Prof. Music Hist., Wheaton Coll., Ill.; Chmn., Dept. Music Hist., ibid., 1976-; Organ recitalist, New England area, 1956-70. Mbrships: Am. Musicol. Soc.; Nat. & Mid W Chapts., ibid.; Nat. Wildlife Fedn. Hon: Musicol. Prize, Boston Univ. Grad. Schl., 1968. Hobbies: Ice skating; Organic Gardening. Address: 905 E Wakeman Ave., Wheaton, IL 60187, USA.

CUSTER, Arthur, b. 21 Apr. 1923, Manchester, Conn., USA. Composer; Educator; Arts Administrator. Educ: Assoc. in Sci., Univ. of Hartford; BA, Univ. of Conn.; MMus., Univ. of Redlands; PhD, Univ. of Iowa. m. Dolores Borgaard, 1 s., 3 d. Career incl: Dean, Phila. Musical Acad.; Dir., Arts in Educ. Proj., RI State Coun. on the Arts. Compositions incl: Orchestral - Passacaglia for Small Orch., 1957; Concert Piece for Orch., 1959; Symph. No. 1 (Sinfonia de Madrid), 1961; Found Objects II (Rhapsodality Brass!), 1969; Doubles for Violin & Small Orch., 1972; num. pieces of Chamber Music, works for voice & piano or chamber ensemble, etc. Recordings: The Music of Arthur Custer, Vols. 1 & 2; Sextet for Woodwinds & Piano (Serenus Recorded Edits.); Permutations for Violin, Clarinet & Cello/Two Movements for Woodwind Quintet (Composers Recordings Inc.); Film & TV Music. Contbr. to num. music jrnls. Mbrships: incl: VP, Eastern Div., Nat. MTA; MENC; Am. Composers Alliance; BMI. Recip: Publ. Award, Soc. for Publ. of Am. Music, 1963. Addresds: 4365 Post Rd., E Greenwich, RI 02818, USA. 6, 8.

CUSTER, Laurenz, b. 21 Apr. 1930, Frauenfeld, Switz. Pianist; Organist. Educ: Dips. in Piano & Organ, Winterthur Conserv., 1952; Univ. studies w. Paul Hindemith; Studies w. Marguerite Long, Nadia Boulanger, Dupré, Dona. Career: Recitals & apps. w. orchs. in Switz., Germany, France, Italy, S Am., S Africa. Recordings: Schaeuble; Mono partita (w. Rudolf am Bach); Dvorak, chamber music (w. Ensemble Fauté) Der virtuose Kontrabass (w. Yoan Goilav). Mbrships: Schweizerischer Musikpaëdagogischer Verband; Schweizerischer Tonkuënstlerverein. Hons. incl: 1st Prize, Rudolf Ganz Competition, 1956. Hobbies: Painting; Wandering. Address: Wielsteinstr. 56, CH 8500 Frauenfeld, Switz.

CUSTODIO, Bernardino F, b. 20 May 1914, Sta. Cruz, Manila, Philippines. Pianist; Conductor; Composer; Teacher. Educ: TD, Univ. of the Philippines; BMus., UNiv. of Santo Tomas; MA, ibid. Debut: Inauguration of the Philippine Repub., 1946. Career: Assoc. Cond., Manila Symph.; Prof., former Dir., Coll. of Music, UST; 1st Filipino Cond., Manila Symph., 1946; num. Perfs., Philippines. Contbr. to var. profl. jrnls. Mbrships: Int. Soc. for Music Educ. Nat. Music Coun. of the Philippines; Filipino Comps. League; Filipino Soc. for Comps. & Publrs.; Piano Tchrs. Guild. Hons: 1st Prize, Composition Contest, 1932; Ldr. Grant, US Educl. & Cultural Exchange Prog.; Award of Merit, Nat. Songfest.; Nat. Competition for Young Artists. Hobbies: Photography; Swimming; Sketching. Address: 5810 Jacobo St., Makati, Rizal, Philippines.

CUTHBERTSON, Eric, b. Erdington, Warwicks., UK. Musician; Violist. Educ: Birmingham Schl. of Music. w. Albert Sammons, London; Viola w. Lionel Tertis. m. Deirdre Cuthbertson, 1 s. Career: Hastings Municipal Orch., UK; Free lance, violin & viola, London; Mbr., Henry Hall's BBC Dance Orch., 4 yrs.; BBC Concert Orch., 1945-; Viola Mbr., LSO, 1950-; Broadcaster in Israel, USA & UK. BBC. Mbr. Stage Golfing Soc. Hobbies: Golf; Record Collecting. Address: 68 Reading House, Bayswater, London W2 6HE, UK.

CUTLER, Ivor, b. Glasgow, UK. Composer; Singer; Musician; Poet; Illustrator; Writer; Humorist; Teacher. 2 s. Debut: on BBC TV Tonight career: An Evening of British Rubbish, Comedy Theatre; Monday Night at Home, radio; Magical Mystery Tour, TV; Up Snday, TV; Dave Allen in search of the English Eccentric, TV; John Peel, radio, The End of the Peer Show, TV. Comps: 150 songs; music for Ken Russell's TV prod., Diary of a Nobody. Recordings: Dandruff; Velvet Donkey; Jammy Smears. Publs: Cockadoodledon't, 1966; Many Flies Have Feathers, 1974; A Flat Man, 1976; Meal One, 1973; Balookyklniypop, 1975. Contbr. to var. jrnls. Mbrships. incl: Equity; PRS. Address: c/o BBC Broadcasting House, London W1, UK.

CVETKO, Dragotin, b. 19 Sept. 1911, Vucjavas, Yugoslavia. Musicologist. Educ: Dip. & PhD, Philos. Fac.; Dip. Comp., Conserv. Ljubljana, Prague. m. Nives Polak, 3 c. Career: Full Prof. of Musicol., Univ. of Ljubljana. Comp. of music for piano, for organ, chamber music & songs. Publs: The History of Slovene Music, vol. I-III, 1958-60; Academia Philharmonicorum Labacensis, 1962; Jacobus Gaullus-Leben w. Werk, 1972; Ed., Gallus, Harmoniae morales, 1966 & Moralia, 1968, Musikgeschichte den Südslawen, 1975. Contbr. to var. reports, jrnls., reviews, etc. Mbrships: Inst. Musicol. Soc.; Am. Musicol. Soc.; Gesellschaft fur Musikforschung; Int. Assn. of Music Libs.; Slovene & Servian

Acad. of Sci. & Arts. Recip., Herdeer Prize, Vienna, 1972. Address: Gregorciceva 15, 61000 Ljubljana, Yugoslavia.

CVRCEK, Vaclav, b. 14 Mar. 1928, Nechod, Czechoslovakia. Bassoonist; Pianist. Educ: Dip.; Czech Conservatory, Prague. m. Zdenka Psutkova, 1 s. Debut: Hall of Artist's House, Prague. Career: Films w. Czech Phil. Orch.; Harmony of Czech Phil., Rejchas Wind Quintet; TV & radio appearances. Recordings: Beethoven; Mozart; Rejcha; Milhaud; Baird; Eben; Jezek; Malipiero; Vivaldi. Mbrships: Syndicate of Czech Composers, Prague; Mozart Community, Prague; Bertramka. Recip., Mozart Prize, Salzburg, 1973. Address: Chodske 9, Prague 2, Czechoslovakia.

CYERMAN, Claude, b. 22 Oct. 1947, Metz, France. Pianist; Assistant Professor. Educ: BEPC Dip.; Metz Conserv., 1962; Conserv. Nat. Superieur de Musique, Paris, France; Grad. studies, Ind. Univ., Bloomington, USA. m. Ruth, 1 d. Career: Num. recitals, France, USA, Canada, Switzerland; Concerts w. maj. orchs., France inclng. ORTF Radio & TV Symp; Num. TV & Radio apps., France & Luxembourg; Asst. Prof., Piano, DePauw Univ., Ind., USA. Hons. incl: Num. prizes & medals, Metz Conserv. & Conserv. Nat. Superieur Musique, Paris; Grand Prix, Concours Nat. des Jeunesses Musicales de France, 1963; 2nd Grand Prize, Int. Competition Marguerite Lond-Jacques Thibaud, Paris, 1971. Hobbies incl: Reading; Ping-Pong. Address: Schl. Music, DePauw Univ., Greencastle, IN, USA.

CYMERMAN, Lilian, b. 1 Mar. 1949, Szczecin, Poland. Music Instructor (Piano). Educ: Piano Instructors Dip., State Coll. Music., Stockholm. Mbr., Swedish Assn. Piano Instructors. Hobby: Playing other instruments inclng. harpsichord, violoncello, percussion instruments. Address: Solhemsvägen 17 1, 13700 Västerhaninge, Sweden.

CZAJKOWSKA, Teresa, b. 19 June 1920, Radom, Poland. Pianist. Educ: Dip., Tchr. Trng. Dept., State Higher Schl. of Music, Cracow, Instrumental Music Dept., State Higher Schl. of Music, Wroclaw; MA. m. Czajkowski Kazimierz. Debut: Symph. Orch. of Radom, 1959. Career: Piano Music Tchr. & Accomp., Josef Elsner Second. Schl. of Music, Warsaw; Piano Music Lectr., Higher Pedagogical Schl., Dept. of Musical Educ., Kielce; Solo piano concerts & accomps., Poland & abroad; Mbr. of Senate Committee for Didactics. Mbrships. incl: Polish Musicians Soc.; Musical Educ. Soc. of Poland. Contbr. to profl. jrnls. Hons. incl: Gold Cross of Merit, 1974; Golden Emblem of Polish Tchrs. Assn. Hobbies

incl: Collecting antique objects of art. Address: ul. Zywnego 12 m.8, 02-701 Warsaw-Mokotow, Poland.

CZAPIEWSKI, Bogdan Windenty, b. 8 Mar. 1949, Gdynia, Poland. Pianist. Educ: MA, Acad. of Music. m. Iwona Gorska, 1 s. Career: many recitals & concerts throughout Poland; Archival recordings for Polish Radio. Mbr., Polish Musicians Soc. Hons: Schlrship., Fryderyk Chopin Soc., 1971, Goansk Soc. of Art, 1973; 1st Distinction, Int. Piano Competition F Busoni, Bolzano, Italy, 1975; 6th Prize, Int. Piano Competition Vianna da Motta, Lisbon, Portugal, 1975. Hobbies: Philos., Psychol.; Belles-Lettres; Tourism. Address: Warszawska 35/9, 81-309 Gdynia, Poland.

CZAPINSKI, Kazimierz, b. 18 Feb. 1933, Zarnów, Poland. Organist. Educ: Organist Schl., Przemysl Higher State Schl. of Music, Warsaw. Career: Organist of Garwolin. Comps: Ch. songs; adaptations of Ch. songs for choir; Monography of State Amateur Music Centre, Lukas. Mbrships: Assn. of Polish Musicians. Hobbies: German Lang.; Travelling abroad. Address: 08-400 Garwolin, ul. Staszica 11, Poland.

CZIFFRA, Gyorgy, b. Budapest, Hungary. Concert Pianist. Educ: Franz Liszt Conserv. of Music, Budapest. m. Soleyka Cziffra, 1 s. Career: Recitals & Concerts in UK, USA, Can., France, Israel, Benelux, Italy, Switz., Japan & S Am.; apps. on radio & TV; fndr., biennale Concours Int. (for young pianists), Versailles, 1968; fndr. (w. son), Fest. of La Chaise-Dieu; Fndr., Auditorium Franz Liszt & Acad. of Music Franz Liszt, Senlis, France, 1973; pres., Frdn. Cziffra, 1975-. num. recordings. Hons: Chevalier de la Légion d'Honneur, 1973; Commander, Ordre des Arts et des Lettres, 1975. Address: 4 rue St. Pierre, 60300 Senlis, France.

CZYZ, Henryk, b. 16 June 1923, Grudziadz, Poland. Conductor; Composer. Educ: Law, Kopernik Univ., Torun, Poland, 1 yr.; Philos., ibid, 2 yrs.; Two Dips., Conducting; Composition, High Music Schl., Poznan, Poland. m. Halina Buczacka. Career: currently Chief Cond. of Düsseldorfer Symphoniker, Germany & Philharmonia, Lodz, Poland. Compositions: Study of Orchestra, Ed. PWM-Poland; Bialowlosa - Musical, Ed. PWM Poland; Doglovers Dilemma - Comic Opera, Ed. PWM Poland. Publs: Ucieczka Spod Klucza (Escape from Key). Mbrships: ZKP (Assn. of Polish Composers); SPAM (Assn. of Polish Musicians); ZAIKS. Hons: Grand Prix de Disques, 1968 & Edison Prize, 1969 (Penderecki's 'Lucacs Passion' & 'Dies Irae'). Hobby: Car. Address: Moliera 2-21 Warsaw 00076, Poland.

D

DACHINGER, Mark, b. 16 Mar. 1909, NYC, USA. Musician (Violin, Viola, Clarinet, Flute). Educ: studied violin pvtly. for 9 yrs.; studied viola, pvtly. & at Manhattan Schl. of Music, NYC., 4 yrs.; ensemble & orchl. trng., ibid. 6 yrs.; studied clarinet & flute for sev. yrs.; Cert. to teach strings & woodwinds, Be. of Educ., NYC. M Ray Goldblatt, 1 s. Career: Concert work w. Ossip Grabrilovitch, Antonia Bricco, Olin Downes & var. commercial perfs., Tchr. in Music Prog., Bd. of Educ., NYC, 4 yrs.; Pvte. tchng. var. commercial ensemble recordings. Mbr. Associated Musician of Gtr. NY. Hobbies: Sailing. Address: 120, 22 Asch Loop, Bronx, NY 10475, USA.

DACHWITZ, Curt, b. 23 Sept. 1931, Soest, Westphalen, Germany. Choral & Ensemble Director; Composer; Pianist; Orchestral Leader. Educ: Fachschule für Musik, Magdeburg; Koinservatorium Dresden. m. Irmgard Schöpke. Career: Ldr., Volkskunstenensemble, 1957; Ldr., Solistenensemble des FDGB, 1964; Choral & Ensemble ldr. & piano orchestral ldr., Tanz-u. Unterhaltungsorchester Magdenburg, 1973-. Comps. incl: Cantata, Der Sturmvogel, 1958: Die Legende v. Eulenspiegle u. dem goldenen Pflugeisen, 1960; Ballett, Afrika-Poem, 1961; Operetta, Georg stand abseitsz, 1962; music for revues, film, choir, cabaret etc. Mbrships: Ctrl. committee, Berlin, Verband der Komponisten und Musikwissenschaftler der DDR. Hons: Preis fur künsterlerisches Volksschaffen, 1961; Kunstpreis des Rates d. Bezirkes Magdenburg, 1968. Address: Heyrothsbergerstr. 8, 3104 Biederitz, German Dem. Repub.

DÄHLER, Jörg Ewald, b. 16 March 1933, Bern, Switz. Harpsichordist; Pianist; Hammerklavier player; Teacher; Conductor. Educ: Tchrs. Trng. Coll., Bern; Piano Dip., Conserv. of Bern; Harpsichord studies w. Prof. F Neumeyer. Career: Hd., Harpsichord & Thorough Bass Class, Bern Conserv., 1962-; Tchr., Acad. of Music, Basel, 1962-67; Cond., Bern Chmbr. Choir, 1974-. Sev. recordings. Mbrships: Rotary Club Bern; Schweizerischer Tonkünstlerverband. Hons: 1st Prize, harpsichord, Int. Music Contest, Munich, 1964, Hobby: Drawing. Mgmt: Eve Landis, CH-8706 Meilen, Switz. Address: Trechselstr. 6, CH-3005, Bernr, Switzerland.   •

DAHL ERIKSEN, Richard, b. 1 March 1918, Detroit, Mich., USA. Violinist; Violist. Educ: Dip., Royal Danish Acad. of Musich, 1938; Pvte. studies w. R Benedetti, Paris. m. (1) Ulla Eriksen, 1 d; (2) Prof. Grethe Krogh. Career: Mbr., DUTS Orch., 1963-; Asst., Danish Radio Symph. Orch., 1940; Mbr., Tivoli Symph. Orch., 1942; Mbr., Danish Radio Symph. Orch., 1948-; Fndr., Musica Vitalis Quartet. Recordings: Chmbr. music, incl. works by Nielsen & Holmboe. Publs: Carl Nielsen -6th Symphony (Ed.); Ed., Kundage Riisager - Variatins for clarinet, viola and basson. Contbr. to: Dansk Musiktidsskrift. Address: Primulavej 13, 2720 Vanlöse, Denmark.

DAHLIN, Inger Berg, b. 27 June 1935, Montevideo, Minn., USA. Violinist; Baroque Violinist: Hardanger Fiddler; Teacher. Educ: BA, 1957, grad. study, Univ. of Minn. m. Donald Arthur Dahlin, 2 s. Carrer: Concert Mistress, St. Paul Civic Symph., Minn.; Mbr., Musica Primavera (chmbr. ensemble), Norwegian Music Trio, Good Trio: has made concert tours & radio & TV broadcasts; Fac. Mbr., Shenandoah Conserv. of Music, Winchester, VA., 1959-61, Rymer Schl. of Music, Roseville, Minn. Mbrships: Mpls. & St. Paul Musicians Unions; Schubert Club; Thurs. Musical; Sigma Alplha Iota. Recip. acad. hons. Mgmt: Program Prods., Mpls. Address: 6747 79th Ave. N. Minneapolis, MN 55445, USA.

DAHNERT, Hans Karl Ulrich, b. 25 Nov. 1903, Dresden, DDR. Musicologist; Organ expert. Educ: Univ. Leipzig, 1932. M. Gudrun Dahnert, Dec. 1976. Mbrships: Assn. of Comp. and Musicologists DDR. Publs: The Organs of Gottfried Silbermann in the DDR, Leipzig, 1953; The Organ and Instrument Builder Zacharias Hildebrandt, Leipzig, 1961. Contbr. to: Rimann Music Ency., 12th ed.; Music and Society; Jrnl. for Instrument building; the Ch. Musician. Hobbies: Harpsichord playing; Interest in Art History. Address: Kaizer Str. 42 14, 8027 Dresden, German Dem. Repub.

DAKERS, Lionel, b. 24 Feb. 1924, Rochester, UK. Musician; Director of the Royal School of Church Music. Educ: Rochester Cathedral Choir Schl.; Pupil of Sir Edward Bairstow, RAM, 1047-51; BMus, (Dunelm) FRCO; FRAM; ADCM; FRSCM. M. Mary E Williams, 4 d. Career: Asst. Organist, St. George's Chapel, Windsor Castle, 1950-54; Asst. Music Master. Eton Coll., 1952-54; Organist, Ripon Cathedral, 1954-57;

Organist, Exeter Cathedral, 1957-72; Dir., RSCM, 1973-. Var. Comps. of ch. music. Recordings: Organ Music & w. Choir of Exeter Cathedral, HMV, Pilgrim, etc. Publs: Church Music at the Crossroads, 1970; A Handbook of Parish Music, 1976; Making Church Music Work, 1978. Contbr. to Musical Times; Organists' Review. Mbrships: RCO; Fellow, St. Michael's Coll., Tenbury; Savage Club. Hobbies: Book Collecting; Gardening; Continental Food: Travel. Address: Addington Palace, Croydon CR9 5AD, UK. 1,3.

D'ALBERT, Francois Joseph, b. 17 Sept. 1918, Györ, Hungary. Professor of Music; Concert Violinist; Composer; Conductor. Educ: State Artist & Prof. Dips., Royal Liszt Acad., Budapest; PhD, Peter Pazmany Univ., Budapest; studied Comp., Cond., Violin & Viola. Debut: Aged 6, Györ. Career: 5000 Concerts: Film, TV, radio & concert apps. in over 50 countries. Comps. publd. in Hungary, Switgerland, France, UK & USA. Recordings. Over 10 LP albums in USA. Contbr. to var. mags. all over world. Mbr. & Hoéns. incl: Winner, Geneva Int. Competition: Prox Heugel: Hubay Grand Prix; Gold Medal, Arpad Acad. Medal of Hon., DAR. Hobby: Swimming. Mgmt: Papsodia Concert Mgmt., Chgo., USA. Address: 2540 N. Spaulding Ave., Chgo., IL 60647, USA.

D'ALBERT, Julius, b. 26 Feb. 1892, Salgotarjan, Hungary. Musician: Composer; Conductor; Music Educator. Educ. Study of violin & composition. m. Maria Theresa de Varga, 2 s., 1 d. Career incl: Musician (violin & trumpet); Profl. Mil. Cond.; Prof. of Music; Fac. Mbr. Conserv. Coll., USA. Compositions: some 200 works, for violin, trumpet, string quartet, orch. & vocal pieces. Recording: Hubay's Lieder. Contbr. to var. European periodicals. Mbrships. incl: ASCAP; Hon., Chgo. Artists' Assn.; Hon., Phi Beta; Hon. Pres., Kodaly Acad. Hons. incl: Gold Medals for compositions. Hobbies: Golf; Swimming. Address: 2540 N Spaulding Ave., Chgo., IL 60647, USA.

DALBY, John Briggs, b. 8 Apr. 1910, Shipley, Yorks., UK. Organist. Retired. Administrator in Musical Education. Educ: Mus.B, London Univ.; FRCO; Choir Trng. Dip., RCO. m. Louisa Dixon, 1 s. Career: Organist & Choirmaster, sev. Chs., Yorks.; Organist, St. Machar's Cathedral, Aberdeen, 1938-55; Music Master, sev. schls., ibid; Supt. of music, City of Aberdeen, 1946-70; Asst. Musical Dir., Nat. Youth Orch. of GB, 1948-. Author, The School & Amateur Orchestra, 1966. Mbrships: Inc. Soc. Musicians; Hon. Life Mbr., Edinburgh Soc. Organists, Bradford Organists Assn. Hons: Fellow, Educl, Inst. of Scotland; Harding Prize, RCO, 1935; OBE, 1968; DMus, Univ. of Aberdeen, 1973. Hobbies: Photography; Hill Climbing. Address: Shieldaig, Hazelwood, Silverdale, Nr. Carnforth, Lancs. LA5 0TQ, UK 3.

DALBY, Martin, b. 25 Apr. 1942, Aberdeen, Scotland, UK. Head of Music BBC Scotland; Composer. Educ: BMus, Durham Univ.; ARCM. m. Flora Orr. Career: Viola, Orch. Del'Accademia Di Napoli, Italy, 1963-65; Music Prod., BBC Radio London, UK, 1965-71; Cramb Rsch. Fellow in Comp., Univ. of Glasgow, 1971-72; Hd. of music, BBC Scotland, 1972-. Compositions incl: 1 Symph.; 1 Str. Quintet; 2 Concertl; Var. Orch. works; 7 works for voice/var. instruments; 3 works for orch. & voices; 3 choral works; var. ch. music; 9 comps. for var. chmbr. ensembles; suite for organ; 3 comps. for var solo instruments, num. radio recordings. Contbr. to Listener. Mbrships incl: CGGB; Coll. Club. Univ. of Glasgow; PRS. Hons. incl: Prizes in Comp., RCM, 1962-63. Hobbies: Railways; Literature; Hill Walking; Mgmt: Novello & Co. Ltd., Music Publrs., 1-3 Upper James St., London W1R 4BP. UK Address: 5 Doune Quadrant, Glasgow G2O 6DL, UK. 3.

DALE, Gordon Alan, b. 13 July 1935, Wrexham, Wales, UK. Composer; Conductor; Teacher of Violin. Educ: DipEd, Worcester Coll. of Educ.; Birmingham Schl. of Music; FLCM. Career: Lectr. in Music, Stevenage Coll., 1965-69; Dorset Co. Music Advsr., 1969-73; Saxophone/Clarinet, City of Birmingham Symph. Orch.; Violin, Baroque Soloists of London; Cond., London Handel Orch., & Jacques Orch.; BBC TV Gala Perf. w. LPO. Comps. incl: Rugue for Brass Quartet; Recital Hors d'Oeuvre; Descants for Christmas; Five Folk Songs; A Dozen Duets; Violin Duets & Simple Sonata; Miniature Piano Concerto; Songs of Scotland; Songs for Children. Mbr., Comps. Guild of GB. Contbr. to Living Music. Hons: Royal Gdn. Party, 1973. Hobby: Fishing. Mgmt: Helen Jennings Concert Agcy. Address: 17 White Horse Sq., Hereford, HR4 0HD, UK. 3.

DALE, Mervyn, b. Worthing, Sussex, UK. Composer; Pianist. Educ: TCL & pvtly.; FLCM; LRAM; ARCM; LTCL; ALCM. Career: Made over 20,000 apps. on the West End Stage as Mbr. of London's Windmill Theatre Co.; Has appeared in many touring & summer shows & in films, on TV & Radio Comps. Has written over 200 songs, of which 50 are publd. inclng: 'Eight Nonsense Songs', '16 Silly Songs for Kids', 'The Centipede' &

Other Rhymes, 'Four English Lyrics'; Many songs for Unison, two, three & four part choir; Orchl. pieces, inclng. an Overture for full orch.; Piano music; Three musicals inclng. the books & music; An Operetta & a String Quartet. Harp Pieces: Concert pieces Nos. 1 & 2 for Solo Harp; Guitar Solos: Rhapsodie & Variations on a Theme; Reflections (suite of 6 pieces for solo piano); Two String Quartets; Concert Overture: Avrilyse. Sev. recordings available inclng. 'Let the Children Sing the Songs of Mervyn Dale'. Hons: Freedom of City of London, 1977. Hobbies: Horse-riding; Swimming; Walking; Travelling. Mgmt: New Era Int. Concerts Ltd. Address: c/o Edwin Ashdown Ltd., Music Publrs., 175-281 Cricklewood Broadway, London NW2 6QR, UK. 3. H.

DALE, Phyllis, b. 20 Jan. 1914, Wolverhampton, UK. Teacher of Pianoforte. Educ: Pvte. lessons for grade exams.; Assoc., Royal Coll. Music; LLCM; ALCM. Career: Gen. & Music specialist, Brierley Hill Grammar Schl., 1946-59; Vis. Tchr., Wolverhampton & Staffs. Tech. Coll., 1942-57; Music specialist, Holy Trinity Schl. Bilston; Wednesbury Pennfields Special Schl., Kings Hill, 1970-78; Choir trainer for annual carol concert at Civic Hall, Wolverhampton until 1972. Compositions: Piano concerto in C; Arrangements of songs & carols; music for dancing & keep fit. Mbrships: Incorp. Soc. of Musicians; Assoc. Mbr., D'Oyly Carte; Life mbr., Battersea Dogs' Home. Hons: Passed Grade VI w. credit, 1929. Hobbies: Theatre; Grand Opera; Gilbert & Sullivan; Needlework; Old time dancing. Address: 21 Pk. Ave., W Pk., Wolverhampton, W Midlands, UK. 3.

DALE, William Henry, b. 16 Nov. 1911, Yale, Okla., USA. Musicologist; Music Theorist; Educator. Educ: BS, Kan. State Coll.; MMus., Northwestern Univ.; PhD., Univ. of Southern Calif.; Univ. of Vienna. m. Alta Cowen Dale. Career: Tchr., Public Schls., 1932-43, Jr. Coll., 1939-43; Teaching Asst., Northwestern Univ., Univ. of Southern Calif.; Prof., Whittier Coll., 1949-77; Chmn., Music Dept., ibid., 1969. Emeritus Prof., 1977; Author, The MusicoPsychological Dramas of Vladimir I. Rebikov, 1961. Contbr. to Encyclopedia of Theatre, 1960. Mbrships: Int. Musicol. Soc.; Am. Musicol. Soc. Coll. Music Soc. MENC; Phi Mu Alpha Sinfonia. Hobbies: Travel; Comparative Arts; Intellectual History, Tennis. Address: 13703 E. Philadelphia, Whitter, CA 90601, USA. 4,9,12.

DALGAARD, Leif, b. 18 May 1945, Store Heddinge, Denmark. Master of the Clarinet & Guitar. Educ: Highest Degree, Royal Danish Acad. Music, 1967; State-Tested Music Tchr., 1969; Chmbr. Music Courses, Sweden, 1963, '64, '69; Further studies, Cologne, /éê, & France, 1970. Debut: 1970. Career: Concerts, Denmark & other countries; Radio perf.; Orgnst., musical guides for travellers visiting Vienna, Berlin, Paris, Leningrad & Moscow, 1966-; Fndr. of music & publng. house 'Edition Leif Dalgaard'. Contbr., cultural/critic, var. newspapers & mags., 1972-. Mbrships: Danish League Music Tchrs.; Danish Soc. Authors. Recip: Czech. Govt. Schlrship., 1969. Hobbies: Art; Writing. Address: Holmeg ardsplarken 25, 2908 Kokkedal, Denmark.

DALLIN, Leon, b. 26 Mar. 1918, Silver City, Utah, USA. Professor; Author; Composer; Violinist. Educ: BMus., Eastman Schl. of Music, Univ. of Rochester, NY; MMus., ibid.; PhD, Univ. of Southern Calif. m. Lynn Dallin. Career: 1st Violin, Brigham Young Univ. Str. Quartet; Guest Cond., Utah Symph., Long Beach Symph. Comps: Songs of Praise, soloists, chorus, orch.; Sierra Overture, band; var. solo & ensemble works. Publs: Techniques of 20th-Century Composition, 1957, 1964, 1974; Listeners Guide To Musical Understanding, 1959, 1968, 1972, 1977. Foundations in Music Theory, 1962, 1967; Basic Music Skills, 1971; Introduction to Music Reading, 1966; Music Skills for Classroom Teachers, w. Robert W Winslow, 1958, 1964, 1970, 1975 , 1979. Heritage Songster, w. Lynn Dallin, 1966; Folk Songster, w. Lynn Dallin, 1967; Christmas Caroler for Youth Pianists, w. Lynn Dallin, 1967. Mbrships: ASCAP; Int. Soc. for Contemporary Music; Music Educators Nat. Assn.; Coll. Music Soc.; Am. Musicol. Soc. Address: Music Dept., Calif. Univ., Long Beach, CA 90804, USA. 9.

DALOZE, Paule, b. 19 Apr. 1932, Brussels, Belgium. Singer. Educ: Dips., solfeggio, instruments, singing & lyric art, Royal Conserv., Brussels. m. Jean de middeleer. Career: Song Recitals in Belgium, Switz., Denmark, Germany & France; Prof. of singing at Acad. of music, Brussels & Royal Conserv., Brussels.; mbr., l'Ensemble Vocal de Bruxelles. Hons: Laureate of Mozarteum, Salzburg. Address: Vieux Marché aux Grains II, 1000 Brussels, Belgium.

DALRING, Arne, b. 4 Mar. 1918, Copenhagen, Denmark. Musician (Piano). Educ: Educationist: Alexander Stoffregen. Debut: Copenhagen, 19037. Career: Piano Soloist, num. films

inclng: Otte Akkorder & Mod Mig Pa Cassiopaia; Num. TV apps. inclng. Accomp. w. orch. to Vera Lynn, 1974; Soloist, Radio Paris, Swedish Radio, Radio Noray, Danmarks Radio. Recordings. Hobbies: Video Cassette Recordings: 8 mm Color Photography. Address: Ved Andebakken 4, 1.th., 2000 Copenhagen R., Denmark.

DALRYMPLE, Glenn Vogt, b. 18 Dec. 1934, Little Rock, Ark., USA. Physician, radiology & nuclear medicine; Musician, trombone & horn. Educ. incls: N Tex. State Univ., Denton, Tex., 1952-54; BS, Univ. of Ark., 1956; MD, ibid, 1958; Trombone studies w. Leon Brown. m. Mary Jo (June) Dalrymple, 1 d, 1 s. Career incls: Mbr., Little Rock Phil. Orch. (later Ark. Orch. Soc.), 1956-; Perfs. w. orchs. in Denver, Colo. & San Antonio, Tex., 1960-65; Mbr., Ark. Symph. Chmbr. Orch. Publs: (Medicine), 60 papers & 4 books. Contbr. to: The Horn Call; Num. Clinical & Scientific Medical Jrnls. Mbrships. incl: Int. Horn Soc.; Am. Fedn. of Musicians. Hobbies: Fishing; Target Shooting; Weight Lifting; Distance running. Address: 18 Athena Court, Little Rock, AR 72207, USA. 7,29.

DALSGAARD, Mogens, b. 12 Aug. 1942, Dronninglund, Denmark. Concert Pianist. Educ: N Jutland Conserv.; Royal Danish Conserv., Copenhagen; Studied w. Alicia de Larroca, Barcelona & Prof. Jarzy Lafeld, Warsaw. Career: Toured as Soloist in most European Countries & USA in 1970,71, 73, 74 & 75. Mbr. of Danish Soloist Soc. Hons: Hon. Prize, Assn. of Danish Music Critics, 1964; Gladsaxe Music Prize, 1966; One of top prizes in comp. for pianists from Nordic Countries, 1973. Hobby: Photography. Mgmt: Wilhelm Hansen, Gothersgade 9-11, Copenhagen. Address: Frederikssundsvej 112, 2700 Bronsoj, Copenhagen, Denmark.

DAMAIS, Emile, b. 4 Mar. 1906, Paris, France. Composer; Conductor; Musicologist. Educ: State Cert. for Music Teaching. m. Genevieve Goonlin, 3 children. Career: Cond.; Prof., Coll. of Music Educ.; Musical Dir., French Rural Music Ctr. Comps: 8 symphs.; 4 oratorios inclng. The Way of The Cross; Num. chmbr. music works; Dance of Dawn. Publs: The Piano Concerto; Handel; Important Stages in Musical Thought. Hons: Blumenthal Prize, 1946; Chambery Prize, 1962. Address: 5 rue Claude Mutrat, 92130 Issy-les-Moulineaux, France.

DAMARATI, Luciano, b. 6 Feb. 1942, Lucca, Italy. Organist; Conductor; Educator. Educ: Dips., organ, piano, comp. & orchl. cond.; organ w. Fernando Germani, choral cond. w. Nino Antonellini, musicol., at Chigiana Acad. of Music, Siena, orchl. cond. w. Franco Ferrara, further organ study w. Rene Saorgin. Career: Many concerts as organists & orchl. cond.; Tchr., Luigi Cherubini Conserv., Florence; broadcasts as comp. & choir cond. on Italian radio. Comps: Impressioni for viola & piano; Fugue, Prelude, Variations for organ; Meditazione & Contrasti for piano, etc. Contbr. to musical publs. Mbr., Italian Soc. of Musicol. Address: Piazza S Francesco n. 14,55100 Lucca, Italy. 28, 29.

D'AMATO, Michael, b. 30 June 1926, Zurrieq, Malta. Priest. Educ: LRSM (BranchA), 1961; AMusLCM, 1958. Dir. of Choir & Musical Services; Organ, Piano maintenance, repairs & tuning; Admnstr. of all local parish musical services. Comps: Mass for the Faithful; Band March for local fiesta & TV prog. Recordings: Folkloristic Choral Music. Contbr. to Organ Club Jrnl. Mbrships: Int. Soc. of Organ Builders; Organ Club (UK). Hobby: Reading. Address: 144 Main St., Zurrieq, Malta.

D'AMBROSE, Joseph, b. 31 Oct. 1938, Bklyn., NY, USA. Flutist; Concert Music Administrator. Educ: BS, Juilliard Schl. of Music NYC, 1961. Career: Flautist, Doyle Cart Opera, US Tour, 1961-62; Solo Flautist, Birmingham Symph., Ala., 1962-64; Fac. Mbr., Henry St. Settlement Schl. of Music, NYC, 1965-67; Flautist, Hurok Mgmt., The Royal Ballet & The Ukranian Ballet, 1967-68; Concert Music Admstr., Broadcast Music Inc., NYC, 1969-. Mbr., Assoc. Musicians of Gtr. NY. Editing of promotional brochures for BMI. Hobbies incl: Going to orchl. concerts, ballet, theatre & off-off Broadway Exmptl. Theatre. Address: 149 W 72nd St. Apt. 3C, NY, NY 10023, USA.

DAMGAARD, Harry, b. 4 Sept. 1934, Copenhagen, Denmark. Conductor. Educ: Dips., Royal Danish Music Conserv., 1954. m. Karin Elisabeth Damgaard, 2 d. Debut: Sjalland Symph. Orch., Copenhagen, 1971. Career: Cond., all big orchs. Scandinavia inclng. Swedish-Danish-Finnish Broadcasting Symph. Orch.; Stockholm Phil. Orch.; Swedish TV; Helsinki Stats Orch.; Goteborgs Symph. Orch.; Swedish Opera; 1st Cond., Finnish Nat. Opera, 1975-; Ballet Cond., ibid., 1973-. Hobby: Golf. Address: Hogbyvagen 88, 17546 Jarfalla, Stockholm, Sweden.

DAMGAARD, John, b. 30 Dec. 1941, AArhus, Denmark., Pianist; Lecturer. Educ: w. Georg Vasarhelyi, Ilona Kabos & Wilhelm Kempff. 1 child. Debut: 1965. Career: given concerts: Scandinavia, Germany, Holland, Belgium, France, Austria, Italy, Canada, USA, Mexico, Russia & E. Germany; Lectr., Royal Danish Acad. Music. Recordings: Chmbr. Music (Phillips); Danish Piano Music (Emi). Hon: Gladsaxe Prize, 1974. Mgmt: Gosta Schwarck. Address: Fyrrebakken 15,3460 Birkerod, Denmark.

D'AMICO, Fedele, b. 27 Dec. 1912, Rome, Italy. Music Critic; Historian. Educ: Grad., jurisprudence; pvte. studies w. Alfredo Casella (piano & comp.) m. Suso Cecchi, 1 s., 2 d. Career: Music Critic, num. jrnls., 1931-; Sec., Italian inst. of Hist.of Music, 19398-43: Ed., La Rassegna Musicale, 1941-44; Dir., Music Sect., Enciclopedia dello Spettacolo, 1944-57; Lectr., Hist. of Music, Univ. of Rome, 1963-; Co-Dir., Nuova Rivista Musicale Italiana, 1967-; Co-Dir., Italian Soc. of Musical., 1968-70. Publs: Cioacchino Rossini, 19398; Modest P Musorgsky, 1942; Goffredo Petreassi, 1942; I casi della musica, 1962. Contbr. to var. jrnls. & encys. Mbrships: Rome Phil. Acad.; Luigi Cherubini Acad., Florence. Address: Via Paisiello 27, Rome, Italy.

D'AMICO, Peter David, b. 9 Oct. 1949, Toronto, Ont., Can. Musician (Electric Guitar, Electric Bass, Piano Synthesizer); Writer; Arranger. Educ: Brebeuf & Seneca Colls., Toronto; pvte. studies in jazz & theory; drama coach, etc. Career: num. ratio & TV apps. solo, & w. groups, Tribe, o The Pair Extrordinaire. 93 songs publ. &/or recordes; sev. solo recordings & w. above groups. Hobbies: Golf; Table Tennis; Coin Collecting. Mgmt: Rhonda Taylor, Mgr., Boxer Prods., Ltd. Address: PO Drawer 887, Truro, NS B2N 5G6, Canada.

DAMM, Peter, b. 27 July 1937, Meiningen/Thür., Germany. Horn Player. Educ: Dip., Acad. of Music Weimar, 1957. m.Hildegard Noll, 3 d. Debut: as soloist, Berlin, 1956. Career: Solo Horn, Gera, 1957-57, Gewandhausorchester, Leipzig, 1959-59, Staatskapelle, Dresden, 1969-; has made apps. as solo horn in Hungary, Poland, Austria, Chile, at fests., etc. Recordings incl: Shumann, Konzertstük für 4 Horns; Brahms, Trio Es, op. 40 Concertos by Teleman & Leopold Mozard; R Strauss, Konzerte; Mozart, Konzerte; S Kurz, Konzert. Ed. var musical works for Breitkopf & Härtel, Peters, etc. Mbr., Int. Horn Soc. Recip. num. awards inclng: Critics Prize, V Biennale of Music, Berlin, 1975. Mgmt: Kéustler-Agentur der DDr, 108 Berlin, Krausenstr. 9-10. Address: Wachbergstr. 35, Box 197-41, DDR-8054 Dresden German Dem. Repub.

DAMMANN, Rolf, b. 6 May 1929, Cell a.d. Aller, Germany. Professor of Musicology. Educ: Studied musicol., Greiburg-Br. 1948, Kiel 1948-50, Freiburg-Br. 1950-52: Dr. Phil. m. Martha Krieger, 1 c. Career: Asserplanmässiger Prof., Freiburg, 1966; Prof., ibid, 1978. Publs: Der Musikergriff im deutschen Barok, 1967. Contbr. to: Archiv für Mjsikwissenschaft; Der Dom von Florenz. Mbrships: Int. Musicol. Soc.; Gesellschaft für Musikforschung; Hochschulverband. Address: 7818 Oberrotweil am Kaiserstuhl, German Fed. Repub. 19.

DANBY, Nicholas Charles, b. 19 July 1935, London, UK. Organist; Professor. Educ: studied w. Guy Weitz, RCM; LRAM; ARCM. m. Margaret Caton, 2 children. Career: Organist, Farm St. Ch., Mayfair; Prof., RCM & GSM; Organist, City Univ.; Asst. Curator of Organ, Royal Fest. Hall, num recordings. Mbr., ISM. Recip. hon. FGSM. Hobby: Travel. Mgmt: Ibbs & Tillett. Address 2 Durrington Park Rd., London SW20, UK.

DANCE, Dennis Linwood Vennor, b. 3 Mar. 1906, London, UK. Professor (ret'd); Examiner; Adjudicator. Educ: Privately then RAM, FRAM, FGSM, ARCM. Career: Mbr., BBC Staff partly responsible for putting first Music Mag. on Air; Chmn., N. London Music Fest.; Adjud., maj. fests. thru'out UK; Music Master, St. Leonard's Mayfield Schl., Sussex, 1963-; Prof. & Examiner, GSM, (ret'd). Mbrships: GSM; D Profs. Hobbies: Collecting family heirlooms; Riding; Swimming; Theatre; Opera. Address: 3 Byfields Croft, Bexhill-on-Sea, Sussex, UK 3.

DANCHENKO, Victor, b. 13 Nov. 1937, Moscow, USSR. Concert Violinist; Teacher. Educ: Ctrl. Music Schl., Moscow; Moscow State Conserv., dip., soloist & tchr.; postgrad., ibid. m. Nina Danchenko, 1d. Debut: in Kabalevsky concerto, Moscow, 1954.,Career: num. recitals, solo perfs. w. orch., TV & radio apps. in all major cities of USSR; recitals & solo perfs. in Bulgaria, Romania, Yugoslavia, Italy & Can. Recordings: 3 solo LPs; sev. chmbr music. Mbr., Union of Am., Musicians. Hons: num. 1st prizes in nat. & int. competitions incl: Gold Medal & hon. dip. of Eugene Ysaye Fndn., Brussels, 1967. Hobbies: Collecting Books & Records; Watching Soccer & Hockey. Mgmt. Int., Artists Mgmt., NY. Address: 25 Cedarcroft Blvd., 204, Wilowdale, Ont. M25 2Z3, Canada.

DANCO, Suzanne, b. 22 Jan. 1911, Brussels, Belgium. Operatic Soprano. Educ: Brussels Conserv. Career: apps. in European cities inclng. London, Paris. Am. debut, 1950. Recordings. Address: c/o London Records Inc., 521 W 25th St., NY, NY 10001, USA. 2.

DANCZOWSKA, Kaja, b. 25 Mar. 1949, Craców, Poland. Violinist; Teacher. Educ: studies w. Prof. Eugenia Uminska, Craców, 1957, Henryk Szeryng & Pawal Klecki, 1958, David Oistrach, moscow, 1970-72. Debut: 1960. Career: Concerts in all socialist countries, German Fed. Repub., UK, Italy, Switz., Finland, Sweden, N Am., Japan, Australia, etc.; apps. at fests. in W. Berlin, Bordeaux, Helsinki, & Bratislava; num. TV & radio broadcasts; Tchr., State Acad. of Music, Craców. num recordings inclng. Mozart concertos & Mozart/Beethoven sonatas. Hons. Prizes at Wieniaw Ski Memorial Contest, Poznan, 1967, Alberto Curzi Contest, Naples, 1969, Young Laureates Int. Contest, Bulgaria, 1969, UNO Gold Medal, Geneva, 1970, ARD Competition, Munich, 1975 0 Queen Elisabeth Int. Competition, Brussels, 1976. Mgmt: Pagart Warsaw. Address: ulica Csysta 15, 21131 Craców, Poland.

DANE, Jean R, b. 8 Apr., 1948, Hattiesburg, Miss., USA. Violist. Educ: BMus, New England Conserv. Music, 1973. Career: Past fac. mbr., Blair Acad. & Peabody Coll., Nashville, Tenn.; Violist, Blair String Quartet; Prin. Viola, Nashville Symph., 1972-74; Currently, Violist, Composers String Quartet, 1974- appng. in US, Canada, UK, Ireland, Norway, Denmark, Romania, Israel & India; Radio apps., BBC UK, Denmark, Israel & India; TV, India & Romania; Assoc. Music Columbia Univ., NYC. Contbr. to (Corres.) Boston Globe, 1970-72. Mbr., CSQ Soc. Chmbr. Music Inc. Hobbies incl: Drawing; Short Stories. Mgmt: Melvin Kaplan Inc. 85 RSD, NYC, NY 10024. Address: 21 W86 St. Apt. 410, NY, NY 10024, USA.

DANEELS, Francois, b. 4 Nov. 1921, Tubize, Belgium. Saxophonist; Professor of Music. Educ: 1st prize, solfége, sight-reading & transposition, saxophone (w. dist.), Royal Conserv. of Music, Brussels; studied harmony & counterpoint, Paris. m. Jeanne Kempen, 1 c. Career: Soloist w. Radio-TV (Belgium), in Germany, Sweden, Denmark, France, Switzerland, USA, Canada, UK; Prof., Royal Conserv. of Music, Brussels. Compositions: (publd.) Suite pour saxophone solo; Le Saxophoniste en Herbe. Recordings. Recip., Ruga Trophy, SABAM. Address: Bd. G. Geryck, 53, 1360, Tubize, Belgium.

DANEK, Victor Bartholomew, b. 26 Oct. 1914, Chgo., Ill., USA. Professor of Music; Music Director. Educ: BMus, MMus, Am, Conserv. of Music, Chgo.; DMus Ed, Ind. Univ. Bloomington. m. Marian D. Laut, 1 s. Career incls: Prof. of Music, Ind. Ctrl. Univ., Indpls., 1954-64: Fndr. & Cond., Indpls. Civic Symph., 1955-645: Prof., Ind. State Univ., Terre Haute, 1964-; Violinist, 1964-71, Dir. of Music, 1971, Terre Haute Symph. Orch. Mbrships: Music Tchrs. Nat. Assn.; MENC; Exec. Bd., Ind. Chapt., ASTA, 1976-; Phi Mu Alpha Sinfonia; Am. Fedn. of Musicians. Hobbies: Travel; Gardening. Address: 1903 Berne Ave., Terre Haute, IN 47804, USA. 3,8.

D'ANGELO, Paul James, b. 16 Apr. 1941, Quincy, Mass., USA. Conductor; Music Educator. Educ: BA, Univ. of Miami, Fla., 1963: MMus, New England. Conserv. of Music, Boston, Mass. 1966; Dip., Am. Conserv., Fontainebleau, France, 1963; studied cond. w. Frederik Prausnitz, harmony w. Nadia Boulanger, piano w. Jean Casdesus. Career: tchr., public schools for 10 yrs.; music dir., var. community & ch. orgs.; perfs. in music theatres & choral socs.; cond., Falmouth Interfaith Choir & accomp., Falmouth Chmbr. Orch., Falmouth, Mass.; former military band dir. for USA Coast Guard. Mbrships: Dir., New Engl. Conserv. Alumni Bd.; charter mbr. & alumnus, Gtr. Boston Youth Symph. Orch.; Am. Symph. Orch. League; Am. Musicol. Soc.; Phi Mu Alpha Sinfonia. Hons: full scholoarship in choral cond., Tanglewood, 1967; full scholarship for proficiency on clarinet while undergrad. Hobby: Reading. Address: 35 Federal Furnace Rd., Plymouth, MA 02360, USA.

DANIEL, Harian, b. 23 Feb. 1932, Fox, Ark., USA. Discographer-Historian. Educ: BGS, MA, Roosevelt Univ. Publs: Biblio-discography for G Ohrlin, Hell Bound Train, 1973; Brochure notes for recording by Puritan, Folk Legacy, Univ. of Ill. Campus Folksong Club. Contbr. to: JEMF Quarterly; Am. Folk Music Occasional; Jrnl. of Southern Folk Lore; Pa. Folklore Soc. Bulletin. Mbrships: Am. Folklore Soc.; Org. of Am. Histns.; Am. Histl. Soc.; Nat. Histl. Soc. Hons: Elected to Bd. of Advisors, John Edwards Memorial Fndn., Folklore & Mythol. Ctr., Univ. of Calif., Los Angeles. Hobbies: Popular Antiquities: Southern & Western Americana. Address: Box A3250, Chgo, IL 60690.

DANIEL, Oliver, b. 24 Nov. 1911, De Pere, Wis., USA. Musicologist; Pianist; Author; Critic; Business Executive. Educ: St. Norbett Coll., Wis., Studied piano in Amsterdam, Berlin Boston. Debut: Pianist, Boston, Mass., 1935. Career: Toured USA as Pianist, 1935-41; Prod. of Music Documentary & Dramatic Progs., CBS, 1947-54; VP, Concert Music Admin., Broadcast Music Inc., 1954-. Publs. incl: Ed., Deep North Spirituals, 1973. Contbr. to num. mags. & newspapers inclng. Sat. Review & Music Jrnl. Mbrships. incl: Int. Music Coun., US Nat. Commn. for UNESCO; Phi Mu Alpha. Hons: Laurel Leaf Award, Am. Comps. Alliance, 1956; Hon. DMus, New England Conserv. of Music, 1973. Address: PO Box 658, Scarsdale, New York, NY 10583, USA. 2.

DANIEL, Ralph Thomas, b. 10 Apr. 1921, Kerens, Tex., USA. Professor of Musicology; Director of Graduate Studies in Music. Educ: BMus., MMus., BA, N. Tex. State Univ., Denton, Tex., MA, PhD, Harvard Univ., Cambridge, Mass. m. Genevieve Barr Daniel. Career: Prof. of Musicol., Ind. Univ., Bloomington; Dir. of Grad. Studies in Music, ibid. Publs: The Harvard Brief Dictionary of Music, (w. Willi Apel), 1960; The Anthem in New England before 1800, 1966: The Sources of English Church Music, 1949-1660 (w. Peter le Huray), 1972; Ed. Paul Nettl; Selected Essays 1975. Contbr. to num. jrnls. inclng. Western Music (article), Ency. Britannica. Mbrships: Int. Musicological Soc.; Coun. mbr., Am. Musicological Soc.: Coll. Music Soc.: MENC; Music Tchrs. Nat. Assn.; etc. Guggenheim Fellowship, 1961-62. Hobbies: Swimming; Hiking. Address 1700 Longwood W., Bloomington, IN 47401 USA.

DANIEL, Sean, b. 27 Aug. 1939, Scranton, Pa., USA. Professional Baritone; General Director, Albuquerque Opera Theatre; Associate Professor, Univ. of New Mexico. Educ: BMus, Syracuse Univ., MMus Ed, Ind. Univ.; Dip., Goethe Inst., Murnau, German Fed. Repub. 1 s. Career: 8 perfs., Carnegie Hall; Mbr., Pro Musica Antiqua; Bethlehem Bach Fest., PBS TV; Greek Theatre; Tanglewood; Summer Stock; Hunter Coll. Recordings: B Minor Mass; Bishop of Brindisi. Publs: Ed., Univ. of NM, Music Dept. 'Bulletin'. Mbrships: AGMA; AEA; Pi Kappa Lambda. Hobbies: Tennis; Painting. Address: 1104 Wade Cr. NE, Albuqueque, NM 87112, USA.

DANIELL, Timothy Jenner, b. 4 Nov. 1948, Gloucester, UK. Schoolmaster; Pianist; Trombonist; Conductor; Singer (Bass). Educ: BMus, King's Coll., London; MTC, London Univ.; AKC, ibid; Chorister, Gloucester Cathedral. Career: Asst. Cond., Cheltenham Young Peoples' Orch., 1966-67: Accomp., E Herts. Choral Soc., 1975 -; Cond., King's Coll., London Choral Soc., 1969-70; Dir. of Music, St. Mary's HS, Chestnut, 1967-; Cond., The Limbourne Orch., 1973-75; Music Master, Chestnut Schl., Herts., 1971-76: Tchr, Lea Valley Music Ctr., 1976-; Coach, Lea Valley Youth Orch., 1978-; Vis. Lectr., City Univ.; Trombonist, Chelthenham YP Orch. Mbrships: ISM; Asst. Masters; Assn.; Ldr., Educl. Travel Ltd. Hobbies: Foreign Travel & Langs.; Cuisine; Maintaining Standards. Address: 41 Churchgate, Chestnut, Herts., UK.

DANIEL-LESUR, J Y, b. 19 Nov. 1908, Paris, France. Composer. Educ: Nat. Conserv. of Music, Paris. m. Simone Lauer, 1 s, 1 d. Debut: Paris, Career: Fndr., Groupe Jeune France, 1936; Mbr., ORTF, 1939; Dir., 'Schola Cantorum', 1957; Musical Cons., TV, 1961; Admnstr., Nat. Lyrical Theatre, 1970; Insp. Gen., Music, Ministry of Cultural Affairs, 1973. Compositions incl: Andres del Sarto (opera); Le Cantique des Cantiques: Symphony des Danses; Serenade; Le Bal du Destin (ballet) Symphony. Recordings: Erato, Philips, ORTF, etc. Publs: Pour ou Contre la Musique Moderne, w. Bernard Gavoty, 1957; Prix Samuel Rousseau, L'Acad. des Beaux Arts, 1973; Officier de la légion d'honneur; Cmdr., Ordre Nat. du Mérite; Off., Ordre, Arts & Lettres; President de L'Académie Charles Cros, 1978. Address: 82 Boulevard Flandrin, 75016 Paris, France.

DANIELOU, Alain, b. 4 Oct. 1907. Neuilly sur Seine, France. Musicologist; Institute Director. Educ: studied music & art in France & music, Sanskrit & philos. at trad. schls., Bernares, India. Career: Prof. & Vice Prin., Coll. of Music, Benares Hindu Univ., 1949-54; Dir., Adyar Lib. & Sanskrit Rsch. Ctr., Madras, 1954-56; Prof., French Inst of Indol., Pondicherry, 1956-59; Mbr., Ecole Française d'Extreme Orient, Paris, ¢959-; Dir., Inst. Inst. of, for Comparative Music Studies, Berlin & Venice, 1962-; Ed. of UNESCO Anthosl. of the Orient, 'Musical Sources' & 'Musical Atlas' (recordings). Publs: Introduction to the Study of Musicals Scales, 1942; Northern Indian Music, 1949; Ragas of Northern Indian Music 1968; Traité de Musicologie Comparee, 1958; Musical Traditions - India, 1966; Semantique Musicale, 1967; Music & Musicians in the Countries of the Orient, 1971; Musique du Cambodge et du laos, 1957; Tableau Comparatif des Intervalles Musicaux, 1958; Musique des Paranas, 1959: Gitalamkara, 1969: & num. works on Indian Hist., Religion &

Philos. Hobby: Painting. Address: Int. Inst. for Comparative Music Studies, Winklerstreasse 20, 1 Berlin 33, German Fed. Repub.

DANIELS, Melvin L, b. 11 Jan. 1931, Cleburne, Tex., USA. Music Educator. Educ: Air Force Base Schl. of Music Dip., 1952; BS, Abilene Christian Coll., 1955; MEd, ibid, 1956; EdD, N Tex. State Univ., 1964. m. Carolyn McClintock, 1 s., 1 d. Career: Hd., Music Dept., Abilene Christian Coll., Texas; Tchr. of the theory, comp. & orchestration. Composer of 47 publd. comps. & arrangements of strings, orch., chorus, brass choir & band. Mbrships: ASCAP; Am. Soc. Univ. Comps.; Phi Mu Alpha Sinfonia; Tex. Music Educators Assn. Recip., 1st Prize, Nat. Schl. Orch. Competition, 1968, 70, 78. Hobbies: Golf; Bicycling. Address: 401 NE 23rd., St., Abilene, TX 79601, USA.

DANKS, Harry, b. 18 May 1912, Dudley, Worcs., UK. Musician (viola & viola d'amore). m. Leonora Irene Shrimpton, 1 s., 1 d. Career: BBC Symph. Orch., 1937; Prin. viola, ibid., 1946-78: Dir., London Consort of Viols. Recordings: Vivaldi, 2 cercertos for viola d'amore. Publs: The Viola d'Amore, 1975 (2nd Ed., 1979). Contbr. to: Music & Letters; The Strad; Violins & Violinists; The String Teacher (USA); Melos. Hobby: Bookbinding. Address: 12 Beverly Gdns., Wembley Park, Middx. HA9 9QZ, UK.

DANKWORTH, Avril Margaret, b. 1 Apr. 1922, Southend-on-Sea, Essex, UK. Music Lecturer. Educ: Hockerill Trng. Coll. for Tchrs.; RCM, London; TCM, London; BMus. (London); GTCL; FTCL; ARCM; LRAM. m. Les Carew. Career: Music Tchr., Reading Grammer Schl., Berks., 1944-47; Music Lectr., Stockwll Coll., Bromley, Kent, 1952-63; Freelance Music Lectr., 1963-. Compositions: Play Songs & Play Tunes. Recordings: Play Songs & Play Tunes, Jupiter, 1968. Publs: Jazz: An Introduction to its Musical Basis, 1968; Make Music Fun, 1973; Voices & Instruments, 1973. Contbr. to: ISM; Music Tchrs. Assn., Schls. Music Assn. Hobbies: Walking; Cycling; Watersports, etc. Address: 56 Station Road., Long Marston, Tring, Herts, UK. 3, 27.

DANKWORTH, John Philip William, b. 20 Sept. 1927, UK. Composer, Musician. Educ: RAM, 1944-46; ARAM 1969; FRAM, 1973. m. Cleo Laine, 1 s., 1 d. Career: Closely involved w. post war development of British jazz, 1947-60; formed large jazz orch., 1953. Comps: works for combined jazz & symph. musicians incl: Improvisations (w. Matyas Seiber), 1959, Escapade, 1967; num. film scores incl. Saturday Night & Sunday Morning, Darling, The Servant, Morgan Accident; other works incl. Palabras, 1970. Hons: CBE, 1974; Variety Club Joint Show Business Award (w. Cleo Laine), 1977. Hobbies: Driving; Household Maintenance. Mgmt: Laurie Mansfield, Int. Artists Representation, 235 Regent St., London W1. Address: The Old Rectory, Wavedon, Milton Keynes MK17 8LT, UK.

DANN, Elias, b. 12 Mar. 1916, Kingston, NY, USA. Musicologist; Violinist; Conductor. Educ: PhD, Columbia Univ., NY; Violin dips., Manhattan Schl. of Music, NY, & Juilliard Grad. Schl., NY. Career: Cond. & Musical Dir., Nat. Co., ''Oklahoma;'' Dir. of Bands, Columbia Univ.; Prof. of Music Hist. of Musicol., Florida State Univ. Contbr. to: Grove's Dict., 6th ed.; Musical Quarterly; Music Lib. Assn. Notes; Jrnl. of Rsch. in Music Educ. Mbrships: Am. Musicol. Soc.; Coll. Music Soc. Hons: Phi Beta Kappa. Address 457 White Dr., A-1, Tallahassee, FL 32304., USA.

DANNATT, George, b. Aug. 1915, London, UK. Chartered Surveyor (retd. 1969); Music Critic; Painter. Educ: studied piano & comp. w. Harry Farjeon, Norman Franklin & Scott Goddard. m. Ann Doncaster. Career: After army service, resumed work as music critic w. News Chronicle, 1945-56, & Penguin Music Mag., 1946-49; has tended to specialize in music of John Ireland & of Arthur Bliss. Contbr. to: Cheltenham Fest. prog., 1976, on Bliss; biography & survey of the music in Complete Catalogue of the Music of Arthur Bliss, Novello, 1980; Contributor Ralph Hill's Pelican 'The Concerto' (1952)-Chopin Article; prog. notes; record sleeve notes; musical jrnls. Mbrships: Garrick Club; Critics' Circle; Royal Musical Assn. Hobbies: Walking & cycling in the country; Exploring inter-relatioinship of music & abstract painting. Address: East Hatch, Tisbury, Salisbury, Wiltshire, UK.

DANNATT, Norman Frederick, b. 27 Dec. 1919, Westcliff-on-Sea, UK. Music Adviser; Musician (Piano, Organ Percussion, Clarinet, Saxophone). Educ: Tchrs. Cert.; Assoc. of the Coll. of Preceptors; Dip. in the Visual Arts, London Univ.; FTCL; LTCL (Class Music Tchng.). m. Marjorie Laura Dannatt, 3 c. Career: Organist, Pall Mall Union Ch., Leigh-on-Sea, Christchurch Jerusalem, ENSA; Comp. to Peter Myers in London's West End theatrical prodns.; Tchr.; Music Adviser to the London Borough of Havering. Mbrships: Exec. Committee, Music Advisers' Nat. Assn. Hobbies: Calligraphy; Internationalism. Address: 13 Wych Elm Rd., Hornchurch, Essex RM11 3AA, UK.

DANSIE, Eric Blaise Kuuyanibe, b. 10 June 1940, Koyka, Lawra-Nandom, Ghana, W Africa. Music Teacher (Flute). Educ: Tchrs. Cert. A; Schl. of Music, Univ. Ghana, Legon, 1969: Cert. of Music, 1972: LRSM (Teaching). m. Esther Mary Dansie, 2 d. Career: Music Tutor, Ghana Secondary Schl., Tamale, 1972-75: Organiser, Arts Coun. Regional Br., Bolga, 1975-76; Perfs. on Flute in Concert Hall, TV & Radio w. maj. works inclng: Mozart Concertos (flute); Tchr., Dagaare Ch. Songs, Legon Music Soc.; Musical tour of Ghana inclng. Lincoln Ctr., NYC, Wash. Cathedral & num. maj. music ctrs. & univs., 1969. Mbrships. incl: Regional Commissioner, Scouts Assn., 1974-75: Arts Coun. of Ghana. Hobbies: Football; Swimming; Hiking. Address: Arts Coun. of Ghana, PO Box 116. Bolga, Ghana, W Africa.

DA-OZ, Ram, b. 17 Oct. 1929, Berlin, Germany. Composer. Educ: Grad. Musical Acad., Tel-Aviv, 1953. m. Shari Gross. Career: comps. perf. in Israel & abroad, 1955-. Comps: Changing Phantoms for chmbr. orch.; Rhapsody for piano & strgs.; Romances for violin & orch.; Piano trio; String trio; works for solo piano & piano duet; Improvisations on a song, for 10 instruments; Suite in Old Style; Simple Suite for recorders; songs, etc. Mbrships: Israel Comps. legue. Hons: ACUM prize, 1967; 2nd prize, IMI for piano, 1966; prizes from Haifa Municipality, 1964, 1978. Hobbies: Reading; Walking; Playing the piano. Address: Shaulst. 41, Nave Shaanan, Haifa, Israel.

DARA, Enzo, b. 13 Oct. 1938, Mantua, Italy. Lyric singer (Buffo Bass). Educ: studied at Mantua w. Bruno Sutti; Dip., Conserv. m. Ivana Cavallini. Debut: Reggio Emilia in L'Elisir d'Amore. Career: Apps. in opera houses in Italy (inclng. Milan, Rome, Venice & Turin), Algiers, N & S Am., Germany, Austria, Czech., UK; Roles incl. Almaviva (Marriage of Figaro), Gianni Schicchi, Batolo (Barber of Seville) & Dulcamaro (L'Elisir d'Amore) etc.; apps. on TV and films off Barber of Seville, L'Italiana in Algeri, La Cenerentola; radio apps. sev. recordings. Contbr. to Tempo di Musica. Hobby: Journalism. Mgmt: Stafford Law, London, Lombardo, NY. Address: via Achille Sacchi 15, 46100 Mantua, Italy.

DARASSE, Xavier, b. 1934, Toulouse, France. Organist; Composer. Educ: Paris Conserv.; studied composition w. Olivier Messiaen. Career: Prof. of Organ & Composition, Univ. of Toulouse; Cultural Advsr. & Prod. of Musical Progs., ORTF; Int. Perf. on organ. Compositions incl: Liszt's Evocation; Pablo's Modules; sev. recital records. Hons. incl: sev. 1st Prizes & Gold Medals while student; Prize for virtuosity & improvisation of Amis de l'orgue de Paris; Grand Prix de Rome. Address: c/o Louisville Phil. Soc., 333 W Broadway, Louisville, KY 40202, USA.

DARBELLAY, Etienne, b. 14 Oct. 1946, Lausanne, Switzerland. Pianist. Pianist; Professor; Pianist. Educ: Lic. es Letters, 1970, PhD, Musicol., w. L F Tagliavini, 1971, Fribourg Univ.; Prix de Virtuosite, Geneva Conserv., 1968; Study w. L Bronarski, Fribourg Conserv., D Bidal, Lausanne Conserv., & w. A Perret, Geneva Conserv.; Pvte. study w. Ervin Laszlo, Fribourg, & Margareth Chaloff, Boston USA. m. Chantal Evequoz, (Painter) 1 d., 1 s. Career: Solo recitals, concerts, Switzerland; Ed. staff, new ed., Historischbiographisches Musiker Lexicon der Schweiz, of E Refardt, 1971-73: Vis. Prof., Marlboro Coll., Vt., USA, 1972-74. Vis., Prof., Paris Conserv. Prof., Geneva Conserv., 1975-; Chargé de Cours, Univ. of Geneva; Assoc. Prof., Univ. Laval, Quebec, Canada. Composition: Piano Toccata (recorded Radio Geneva 1968). Publs: Critical ed., CPE Bach's T Sonatas, 1976; Critical ed., 2 Books of Toccate by Frescobaldi, 1977. Contbr. to Grove's Dictionary. Mbrships: IMS; Swiss, Italian Musicol. Soc. Hobbies: Philosophy; Sound recordings; Rock climbing. Address: Écolede Musique, Univ. Laval, Quebec, Canada G1K 7P4. 30.

D'ARCY-ORGA, Hüsnü Ates, profl. name ATES ORGA, b. 6 Nov. 1944, Kingston-on-Thames, Surrey, UK. Pianist; Lecturer; Writer; Record Producer. Educ: BMus (Dunelm); FTCL; LMus TCL; ATCL. m. Josephine Prior. Career: Freelance Critic, 1965-70; BBC Music Div., 1971-75; Lectr., Music Dept., Univ. of Surrey, 1975; Artistic Dir., Inst. of Armenian Music, 1976-. Comps: Ed., Choplin Piano Music; Ed., Beethoven, Sonata in C, WoO 51 Publs: The Proms, 1974; Chopin - His Life & Times, 1976; Records & Recording Classical Guides, 1977-78: Beethoven, His Life and Times, 1978. Contbr. to: num. profl. publs; Programme Annotator, LSO; Sleeve notes. Mbrships: Royal Musical Assn. Hobbies incl: Cats; Dogs, Astronomy; Occasional Gardening/DIY. Address: Spike Island, Wadhurst, E Sussex, UK. 30.

DARLING, Sandra, b. St. Petersburg, Fla., USA. Operatic Soprano. Educ: Fla. State Univ.; Juilliard Schl. of Music; BMus, Southern Meth. Univ.; New England Conserv., etc. m. James Wilson, 1 s., 1 d. Debut: in World Premiere of Natalia Petrovna, w. NYC Opera. Career incl: Leading roles w. NYC Opera, Nat. Am. Opera, Can. Opera, Ctrl. City Opera Co. Colo., Lake George Opera Festival, etc.; Soloist in Symph. Concerts at Carnegie Hall & Avery Fisher Hall, & w. Pitts., Detroit & Toledo Symph. Orch.; Leading Soprano, Am. Premiere of The Mountebanks; TV opera appearances on Stn. WBZ, Boston & Stn. WFAA, Dallas. Recordings: Soloist, Merry Christmas New York from the Radio City Music Hall. Hons. incl: Rockefeller Study Grant, 1964 & Travel Grant, 1966; Liederkrantz-Borden Award. Hobby: Animals. Address: 1245 Longfellow Ave., Teaneck, NJ 07666, USA.

DARLOW, Denys, b. 13 May 1921, London, UK. Organist; Harpsichord Player; Composer; Conductor. Educ: FROC. m. Sophy, 2 s., 1d. Career: London, Royal Fest. Hall; Queen Elizabeth Hall; Westminster Abbey; BBC Third Prog.; BBC TV; Cond. & Fndr., Tilford Bach Fest. Choir & Orch., 1952; Prof., RCM; Dir. of Music, St. Georges Ch., Hanover Sq., London: Apps. in Switz., Germany, France, Netherlands, Belgium, Ireland, Sweden, Am. & Singapore. Comps. incl: var. Anthems; Ed., Passion of Christ (Handel). Recordings: Portugese Baroque Music. Publs: Musical Instruments for Children, 1962. Mbrships: ISM, Solo Perfs. Committee. Hons: Hon. RCM; Hon. FLCM. Mgmt: Helen Jennings, London. Address: 15 Somerset Rd., Brentford, Middx., UK.

d'ARMAND, John, b. 15 Nov. 1935, Knoxville, Tenn., USA. Singer; Teacher; Broadcaster; Arts Administrator. Educ: BSc, Univ. of Tenn., 1958; BMus, Baldwin-Wallace Coll., 1963; MMus, Univ. of Ill., 1965; DMus A cand., Univ. of Cinn. m. Gretchen Schauf, 2 d. Career: Soloist w. leading orchs. & in premier perfs. of works by many contemp. comps.; Mbr., Robert Shaw Chorale; Exec. Dir. & Fndr., Paul Ulanowsky Mem. Fndn. for Chmbr. Musicians; Assoc. Prof. of Music, Univ. Of Mass.; Music Dir., WFCR. Recordings incl: Peter Maxwell Davies Eight Songs for a Mad king; Vaclav Nelhybel's Four Readings from Christopher Marlowe's Dr. Faustus; Dave Brubeck's Light in the Wilderness. Contbr. to jrnls. Mbrships. incl: AFTRA; AGMA; Am. Fedn. of Musicians; Coll. Music Soc. Address: Box 362, Old Stage Rd., S Deerfield, MA 01373, USA.

DARRELL, R(obert) D(onaldson), b. 13 Dec. 1903, Newton Ctr., Mass., USA. Writer. Educ: Harvard Coll. New Engl. Conserv. of Music, 1923-26. Publs: The Gramophone Shop Encyclopedia of Recorded Music, 1963; The Highroad to Musical Enjoyment, 1943; Schirmer's Guide to Books on Music & Musicians, 1951; Good Listening, 1953, '55; Tapes in Review, 1963. Contbng. Ed., High Fidelity mag., 1955-; past Ed., The Phonograph Monthly Review, Music Lovers' Guide, Gramophone Shop Supplement, Steinway Review of Permanent Music; Contbr. to: Disques; The Gramophone, NY Sunday Times; NY Herald-Tribune Book Review; Down Beat; Audiocraft. Mbrships: Audio Engrng. Soc.; Acoustical Soc. of Am.; Radio Club of Am. (Fellow); Assn. for recorded sound collections. Hons: New Engl. Conserv. Endicott Prize for 5 songs, 1925; John Simon Guggenheim Fellowship, 1939., Address: Balmoral, The Vly, Stone Ridge, NY 12484, USA. 2,3.

DARRENKAMP, John David, b. 9 July 1935, Lancaster, Pa., USA. Baritone Singer. Educ: Acad. of Vocal Arts, Phila., Pa. m. Joycelyn M. Darrenkamp, 2 d. Debut: as Sharpless, Mme. Butterfly, NYC Opera, 1969. Career: apps. in major opera houses, Barcelona, Mexico City, NY, Phila., Balt., San Diego, Los Angeles, Hartford, Wash., etc. Hobbies: All types of sports. Mgmt: Columbia Artists Mgmt. Inc. Address: 3224 Elmae Dr., Lancaster, PA 17601

DARTER, Thomas Eugene, Jr., b. 13 Feb. 1949, Livermore, Calif., USA. Composer; Keyboard Player; Educator; Conductor; Editor. Educ: BA, Cornell Univ., 1969; MFA, 1972, DMA, ibid., 1979. Debut: Chicago, 1973. Career: Ed., Contemporary Keyboard Magazine, 1975-; Dir., Roosevelt Univ. Contemporary Music Ensemble, 1972-75; Keyboard Player (esp. piano & synthesizer) & specialist in 20th century ensemble work, improvisation & jazz. Comps: Sonatina for solo trumpet, 1974; Dual for electric guitar & electric bass, 1976. Contbr. to: Choice; Music Jnl., Guitar Player; Contemporary Keyboard. Mbrships: Phi Beta Kappa; Phi Kappa Phi. Hons. 1st Prize, Nat Fedn. of Music Clubs Young Comps. Contest, 1969, 71; 2nd prize, ibid., 1974; Otto Stahl award for outstanding work in comop. prog., Cornell Univ. Music Dept. Hobbies: Drama; Films; Mythology; Microcomputers; Backpacking; Music. Address: 1671 Honfleur Dr., Sunnyvale, CA 94087, USA.

DARVAS, Gábor, b. 18 Jan. 1911. Szatmárnémeti, Hungary. Composer; Writer on Music. Educ: Acad. of Music, Budapest. m. Eva Sauer, 3 s. Career: Asst. Cond., Chile, 1939-48; Musicol., Hungary, 1948-. Comps. incl: Improvisations symphoniques pour Piano & Orchestre, 1963; Medalia, 1965; Sectio Aurea (for symphonic orch), 1965; A Torony (The Tower), 1967; Rotation for 5, 1968; Antiphon (tape music), 1970; Children's Music (for Soprano & toy instruments), 1970; Solitary Confinement 1 for percussion & tape), 1970; Passion Music (for mixed choir & tape), 1977; Bánat (Grief) for baritone, symph. orch. & tape, 1978. num. arrs. for orch. Publs: A zenekari muzsika mühelytikai (Workshop secrets of orchestral music), 1959; Evezredek hangszerei (Instruments of millennia), 1961; Zenei ABC (ABC of Music), 1963; Bevezetö a zene világába (Introduction to the World of Music), 1965-68; Pocket Dictionary of Music, 1974: From Totem Music to Violin Concerto (History of Music before 1700), 1977. Mbrships: Hungarian Comps. Assn; Hungarian Liszt Soc. Recip., Erkel Prize, 1955. Address: Budapest 1121, Hollós ut 3 Hungary. 4

DARWIN, Glenn, b. 15 Dec. 1912, Topeka, Kan., USA. Baritone. Educ: Eastman Schl. Music, Rochester, NY; Juilliard Schl. Music, NY. m. Martha Linnea, 1 s., 1 d. Debut: Carnegie Hall, 1937: Metro. Opera, Walter Damrosch's 'Man without a Country', 1938; NY Town Hall, 1940. Career incls: Boy Soprano, Kan City., Mo; Baritone, Broadway Stage roles; Starring TV roles, 1949-51; Num. Radio perfs; Concert Soloist w. num. orchs. inclng. NY Phil. Symph., Cleveland Symph; Soloist, USAF Band, WWII & Korea; Concertized, US, Canada, UK & Europe. Recordings incl: Pilgrim's Song & Colored Toys; num. as original 'Singing Sgt.', USAF Band. Hons: USAAF Commendation Medal, outstanding serv. as vocalist w. USAAF Band, 1943-46. Hobbies incl: Piano. Address: 13429 Rancherias, Apple Valley, CA 92307, USA.

DASHER, Richard Taliaferro, b. 10 Feb. 1923, Wash. DC, USA. Professor of Music & Music Education. Educ: BMus, 1955, MMus, 1960, Univ. of Miami, Fla. EdD, Univ. of Mich., 1968. m. Betty Joan Ketor, 3 s., 1 d. Career: Bandsman, US Army, 1955-57; Tchr., elem. schl. music, Dade City, Fla., 1957-59, Jr. HS Music, St. Lucie Co., Fla., 1959-60, HS Music, Ft. Lauderdale, Fla., 10960-65; Tchng. Fello Univ. of Mich., 1965-68; Tchr., Edinboro State Coll., Pa., 1968-. Publs: Toward a Musical Classroom (co-author), 1969; Black American Music, 1974; Music of the World 7 supplementary materials, 1975; Musical Theory, 1977. Contbr. to jrnls. Mbrships. incl: MENC; Pa. Music Educators Assn; Coll. Music Soc. Recip. acad. hons. Hobbies: Skiing; Reading Hist.; Playing Koto. Address: RD 1, Florek Rd., Edinboro, PA 16412, USA. 12

DASHOW, James, b. 7 Nov. 1944, Chgo., Ill., USA. Composer. Educ: BA, Princeton Univ., 1966; MFA, Brandeis Univ., 1969; Dip., Corso di Perfezionamento, Accademia Nazionale di Santa Cecilia, 1971. Career incls: Organizer & Dir., The Forum Players (contemp. music ensemble), Rome, tours incl: 10 Mediterranean cities, 1972, Scotland & Ireland, 1973: invited to teach computer synthesis of electronic music, Int. Summer Seminar, Istitutoi Mesicale F Canneti, 1974-76; establd. Studio di Musica Electronica Sciadoni, Rome, 1974; close assoc., Centro di Calcolo dell'Università di Padova. Comps. incl: Some Dream Songs (soprano, violin, piano); Whispers Out of Time (electronic); Effetti Collaterali (solo clarinet w. electronic accomp.); Mappings, (electronic). Mbrships: ASCAP Assoc., Audio Engrng. Soc. Recip. many hons., Address: Via della Luce 66,00153 Rome, Italy.

DATYNER, Harry, b. 4 Feb. 1923, La Chaux de Fonds, Switzerland. Pianist. Educ: Nat. Conserv., Paris, France. m. Bluette Blum, 1 s. Career: Concerts, Europe, N & S Africa, N & S Am; Prof. of Virtuosity, Geneva Conserv; Swiss Rep. as Jury Mbr., int. competitions, Montreal, Wash., Montevideo, Palma de Mallorca, Berlin Recordings: Shumann; Choplin Mbr. Neuchâtel Inst. Hons: 1st Prize, Musical Perf., Geneva, 1944; Prize, Neuchâtel Inst., 1972. Hobbies: Bridge; Chess. Address: 1245 Collouge Bellerive, Switzerland.,

DAUB, Inge, b. Braunschweig, Germany. Concert Manager. Educ: Univs., Germany & France, 2 yrs; Music tchr. exam., piano & recorder, Music Conserv., Compenhagen, Denmark. m. O C Olesen. Mbrships: Assn. Européenne des Directeurs de Bureaux de Concerts et Spectacles. Hobbies: Music; Lit. Address: Marathonvej 18, DK 2300 Copenhagen S, Denmark.

DAUTH, Ursula Alexandra, b. 9 June 1949, Überlingen, German Fed. Repub. Musicologist; Music Critic. Educ: Richard Strauss Conserv., Munich. 1968-70; Univ. Munich, 1969-70; Univ. Heidelberg, 1970-77; PhD, ibid, 1977. Career: Freelance Music Critic, 1975-; Music Critic, Die Rheinpfalz, Ludwigshafen/Rhein. Contbr. to var. newspapers. Mbrships:

Società Italiana di Musicologia. Hobbies: Movies; Antique Furniture. Address: Moizartstrasse 6, D-7770 Überlingen/See, German Fed., Repub.

DAVAN WETTON, Hilary John, b. 23 Dec. 1943, Strafford-upon-Avon, UK. Conductor. Educ: ARCM; MA, Brasenose Coll., Oxford Univ. m. Elizabeth Jane Tayler, 3 d. Career: Dir. of Music, St. Albans Schl., 1965-67, Carnleigh Schl., 1967-74, Stantonbury Educ. Campus & Theatre, 1974-79, St. Paul's Girls Schl., 1978; Cond., St., Albans Choral Soc., 1965-67, Working Symph. Orch., 1971-74, Guildford Choral Soc., 1968-; Sherwood Sinfonia, 1974-, Milton Keynes Chmbr. Orch., 1974-, Bucks. Youth Choir, 1974-, Milton Keynes Chorale, 1974-. Contbr. to: Musical Times; Oxford Mail; Music & Musicians. Mbr., Athenaeum. Recip. Ricordi Conducting Prize, 1967. Hobbies: Skiing; Golf. Address: 4 Church St., Little Horwood, Winslow, Bucks. MK13, UK.

DAVERNE, Gary Michiel, b. 26 Jan. 1939, Auckland, New Zealand. Conductor: Composer; Arranger; Record Producer; College Head of Commerce Department; (Clarinet, Piano, Percussion). Educ: Auckland Univ; Auckland Tchrs. Coll; LRSM; LTCL; FTCL. Debut: Mozart Clarinet Concerto w. Auckland Secondary Schls. Festival Orch., 1957. Career: Hd. of Commerce, Glendowie Coll., Auckland; Musical Dir. Arr. for NZ Day Pageant, 1974; Musical Dir., State Shows; TV; Res. Cond., Music Players of Auckland Symph. Orch. Cond North Shore Youth Orch.; 1978 Composer in schools. Comps. incl: 4 operas orchl. music; Chmbr. Music; Electronic Ballet Music; Popular Songs. Num. recordings. Mbrships. incl: Auckland Musicians Club; Pres., Comp. Assn. of NZ, 1978. Hobbies: Bridge; Chess; Hockey, Rugby. Address: 45 Wanganui Ave., Herne Bay, Auckland, New Zealand.

DAVEY, Malcolm, Solo Organist & Accompanist. Educ: Trinity Coll., London (Dr. Wm. Lovelock & Charles Sealey); pvtly. w. Dr. George Tootell, G T Pattman & Guy Eldridge; FRCO; LTCL; L (Mus) TCL; FTCL; Fellow, Int. Inst. of Arts & Letters, Switz., 1963. Career: Theatre Organist, 1936-39, 1950-54; Dir. of Music, Middle East Broadcasting Serv., 1945-47; Organ Recitalist in London & Provinces; Many concerts abroad & concerts for Palestine Broadcasting Serv., Egyptian State Braodcasting & S African Broadcasting Corp., also BBC; Dir. of Music, Tettenhall Coll., Staffs., 1950-74; organist, Darlaston Town Hall, Walsall,Staffs., 1962-74; organist, Central Ch., Queen Square, Brighton, 1976-; Vis. Master, Lancing Coll., Coll., Sussex, 1977-. Comps: Pieces for organ, piano, songs & anthems. Contbr. to: The Organ; Musical Opinion. Mbr., ISM; Cinema Organ Soc. Address: Glendale, Sea Lane, Angmering-on-Sea, West Sussex, BN16 1NE, UK. 3, 20, 30.

DAVID, Gyula, b. 6 May 1913, Budapest, Hungary. Composer; Professor. Educ: Liszt Ferenc Acad. Music, Budapest. m. Elisabeth Wolff, 2 c. Career: Prof., Liszt Ferenc Acad. Music, Budapest; Viola Player; Cond. & permanent Comp., Nat. Theatre, Hungary; Cond. & Artistic Dir., Ctrl. Art Ensemble, Hungarian Army; Ldr., Art Ensemble, Min. of Interior Affairs; Prof. of chamber music, Bela Bartok Conserv., 1964-66. Compositions: Sonatas for Piano, Flute & Piano, Violin & Piano; Concerto for Violin & Piano; Sonatina for Viola & Piano; Prelude for Flute & Piano; 4 Quintets for Wind Instruments; Quartet for Archi; Concerto for Viola. Hons: Erkel Prize, 1952, '55; Kossuth Prize, 1957; Munkaérdem Prize (Gold), 1973. Address: 1126 Budapest, Beethoven u. 7/a, Hungary.

DAVID, Johann Nepomuk, b. 30 Nov. 1895, Eferding, Austria. Composer; Professor. m. Berta Eybl, 2 s. Comps. incl; many works for orch. inclng. 8 symphs., concertos for flute, violin, violin & cello, etc; Chmbr. Music inclng. 3 sonatas for solo violin, sonata for flute & viola, sonata for 3 cellos, etc; organ works inclng. Partita über B-A-C-H, Zwei Fantasian und Fugen Choral werk; Vocal works inclng. 3 masses. Mbr: Acad. of Art, Berlin; Bavarian Acad. of Fine Arts. Hon. Mbr: Acad. of Music, Vienna; Vienna Concert House & Singing Acad. Soc.; Mozart Soc., Vienna. Recip. num. prizes & hons. inclng: Doct., Evanglica Theol. Fac., Univ. of Mainz. Address: 7 Stuttgart, Stafflenbergstr. 26, German Fed. Repub.

DAVID, José (Léon Georges), b. 6 Jan. 1913, Les Sables d'Olonne, Vendée, France. Composer; Teacher. Educ: Laur., sr., student, Conserv., Paris; Dip., Music Tchr. Exam., Paris. m. Janine Le Brun, 1 s. Debut: Perf. w. mixed Choir 'Au Large', Radio Francaise, 1937. Career: Num. perfs. of works thru'out Europe, inclng., Belgian & Spanish Radio, Morocco, Italy, UK (Wigmore Hall, 1951), USA, (NY, Carnegie Hall), etc; Prof., Nat. Conserv. Sup. de Musique, Paris. Compositions: Sonate piano et violon, 1955: Laudate Dominum, for 3 male voices & organ, 1960; impressions de Vendée, 1952; Etude et Danse, 1970; Deux Poémes, for voice & piano, 1973. Recordings:

Chansons du Pays d'Ouest, Les Compagnons. Publs: Traité d'Harmonie tonale, atonale et totale, (w. Nicolas Obouhow), 1947; Maurice Ravel, 2968. Contbr. to: Musique et Instruments; Revue du Bas-Poitou; L'Aurore; Le Jrnl. de la France; Le Deux-Sévrien de Paris; Foreword & Intro. ofr Internatioinal Encyclopedia of violin & keyboard. Mbrships; Bd., Nat. Conserv. Sup. de Musique, Paris; SACEM; SACD; Co-Fndr., Eurythmie grp., 1947. Hons: Var. Laurs. inclng., Inst. de France, 1941, SACEM, (Joubert prize), 1945, Nantes, (Pineau Chaillou Prize), 1958; Off., des Palmes Acad., 1972. Hobbies: Boats; Cycling. Address: 157 Blvd. Saint Germain, Paris 75006, France.

DAVID, Thomas Christian, b. 22 Dec. 1925, Wels, Austria. Composer; Conductor. Educ: Thomasschule, Leipzig Hochschule Mozarteum, Salzburg. m. Mansoureh Ghassri, 2 s., 4 d. Career: Head of Dept. of the Hochschule für Musik in Vienna; Cond. of num. orchs., incl. Riasorchester Berlin, the Munich Philharmonic, Niederösterreichische Tonkünstle-rorchester, Orchester des Österreichischen Rundfunks, etc. Comps. incl: Bagatellen & Sonate (piano); Fantasie, Dux Michael; 3 Intermezzi; 3 Canzonen; Concert for Oboe & Orch.; Concert for 9 Solo Instruments; & songs, based on Chinese stories, for voice & piano; Concert for Oboe & Orch.; choral works. Hons: Austrian State Prize, 1935: Prize of Vienna, 1973. Address: 1020 Vienna Fugbachgasse 16/3, Austria.

DAVIDSON, James Robert, b. 25 Apr. 1942, Pitts., Pa., USA. Professor of Music (Organ). Educ: BMus, Wheaton Coll.; BCM, MCM, DMA, Schl. of Ch. Music, Southern Bapt. Theol. Sem., Louisville, Ky. m. Rosemary Lynn Piersma, 1 s., 1 d. Career: Chmn., Music Dept., Tift Coll., Forsyth, Ga.; Min. through Music, Northminster Presby. Ch., Macon, Ga.; Musical Dir. for Summer Musical, Macon Little Theater. Publs: Dictionary of Protestant Church Music, 1975. Contbr. to Ga. Music News. Mbrships: Ga. State Chmn., AGO Coll. Div. Chmn., Ga., MENC; VP, Macon, Ga. Music Tchrs. Assn.; Hymn Soc. of Am.; Choristers Guild. Recip., Garrett Fellowship, Southern Bapt. Sem. Hobbies incl: Painting; Building. Address: 1158 Darlington Dr., Macon, GA, USA.

DAVIDSON, Joy Elaine, b. 18 Aug. 1940, Ft. Collins, Colo., USA. Mezzo Soprano: Operatic & Grad. work, Fla. State Univ. m. Robert S. Davidson. 2 s., 1 d. Debut: W. Met. Opera Nat. Co., 1965-66. Career incls: Apps. in USA w. NYC Opera; San Francisco Opera; Met. Opera, etc.; Apps. in Can. w. Edmonton Opera; Vancouver Opera; Apps. in Europe incl: Los Angeles Phil.; Boston Symph. etc., Mbr. SAI. Recip. 1st Prize, Int. Competition for Young Opera Singers, Sofia, Bulgaria, 1967. Hobbies: Swimming; Tennis; Cycling; Handcrafts; Indoor Sports. Mgmt: Columbia Artists Mgmt. Inc., NYC; Artists Int. Mgmt., London, UK., Address: 5751 S W 74th Ave., Miami, FL 33143, USA. 5, 7.

DAVIDSON, Louis, b. 16 Mar. 1912, New York City, NY, USA. Trumpet Player. Educ: Prof., Trumpet, Ind. Univ. Schl. of Music, 1963. m. Melba Alone Davidson, 2 children. Career: At age 14 played trumpet in Movies Theatres in NYC, USA; Age 15 Ships Musician on USS Leviathan; Age 16 2nd Trumpet, Cinn. Symph. Orch.; Age 23 Solo Trumpet, Cleveland Symph. for 23 yrs.; Perfs. Radio City, NBC Symph., Ballet Russe, etc. Comps: Transcriptions for trumpet incl: Romance in G, Beethoven. Num. recordings w. Cleveland Symph. Orch. Publs: Trumpet Techniques; Trumpet Profiles. Contbr. NY Brass Conf. Jrnl.; Holton Mag.; Symph. Mag. Mbrships: Am. Fedn. Musicians; Pi Kappa Lambda, Hobbies: Watching Football & Baseball; Golf. Address: 608 Kerry Dr., Bloomington, IN 47401, USA.

DAVIDSON, Norma Lewis, b. 12 Oct. 1929, Provo, Utah, USA. Violinist. Educ: BS, MS, in Psychol.; MMus in Violin, Southern Meth. Univ., Dallas, Tex.; Juilliard Schl. & Mannes Coll. of Music, NYC. m. W James Davidson, 2 s. Debut: Carnegie Hall, Town Hall, NYC. Career: Recording Artist for films; concert tours, USA, Mexico, Can., Columbia Artists, Community Concerts; weekly show, NBC TV; special tours & Lincoln Ctr. concerts celebrating Int. Women's Yr.; Artist-in-Res., Tex. Woman's Univ., Mannes Coll. of Music. Comps: works for violin & piano; violin duets. Recordings. Contbr. to: Southern Meth. Univ. Music News. Mbrships: Am. String Tchrs. Assn.; String Chmn., Music Tchrs. Nat. Assn.; Am. Psychol. Assn. Hons. incl: Comps. Cert., Denton, Tex., 1976. Hobbies: Swimming; Yoga; Reading. Mgmt: Don Vann, 811 W Oak, Denton, TX 76201, USA. Address: 1810 Williamsburg, Denton, TX 76201, USA. 5.

DAVIES, (Albert) Meredith, b. 30 July 1922. Conductor. Educ: RCM; Keble Coll., Oxford; Acad. of St. Cecilia, Rome. m. Betty Hazel Davies, 3 s., 1 d. Career incl: Organist & Master of the Choristers, Cathedral Ch. of St. Alban, 1947-49: Musical

Dir., St. Albans's Schl., 1948-49; Organist & Choirmaster, Hereford Cathedral, & Cond., City of Birmingham Symph. Orch., 1957-59; Cond., City of Birmingham Choir, 1957-64; Musical Dir., Engl. Opera Grp., 1963-65, Vancouver Symph. Orch., 1964-71; Chief Cond., BBC Trng. Orch., 1969-72; Cond., Royal Opera House at Covent Gdn., Sadler's Wells, BBC. Address: 8 Averill St., London W68/B, UK. 1.

DAVIES, Andrew Richard, b. 5 Mar. 1949, London, UK. Pianist; Adjudicator; Trombonist. Educ: Film Rsch.; Recording; Musical Ed.; Adjudicator for BBC Competition Young Musician of the Year, 1978. currently piano duo w. David Branson, TV & radio apps. Recordings: 18th & 19th Century piano music. Mbr., RAM Club; Green Room Club. Hobbies: Instrument renovation; Horticulture; Country matters. Address: Bredon, Coast Hill, Westcott, Dorking, Surrey, RH4 3LH, UK.

DAVIES, (Doris) Eiluned, b. London, UK. Concert Pianist; Teacher. Educ: RCM w. Kathleen Long, Gordon Jacob & C H Kitson; pvte. study w. Frida Kindler. Debut: Aeolian Hall, early 1930's. Career: num. recitals in UK, Germany & Spain; apps. at Boosey & Hawkes Concerts, Macnaghten concerts, Wigmore Hall, Nat. Gallery; perfs. w. BBC Symph. Orch., Liverpool Phil., BBC Welsh Orch., etc.; specialises in modern British music.; sev. comps. Recordings: 3 Bagatelles & Fugue in F sharp minor by Daniel Jones. Contbr. to Welsh Music. Mbrships: ISM; Brit. Music Soc.; Soc. for the Promotion of Welsh Music. Hon: Open Piano Scholarship to RCM, 1928. Hobbies: Foreign Langs.; Reading. Address: 40 The Limes Ave., New Southgate, London N11 1RH, UK.

DAVIES, Ffrangcon, b. 14 May 1925, Cardiff, Wales, UK. Concert Pianist. Educ: RAM w. Harold Craxton; studies w. Franz Osborn & Louis Kentner. m. Diana Redlich, 3 c. Debut: BBC Welsh Orch., 1936. Career: num. recitals in UK, Europe & Aust.; concerto perfs. w. BBC & other ldng. orchs. in UK & Aust.; num. broadcasts on radio & TV; chmbr. music apps.; apps. at fests., incl: Int. Adelaide Fest., 1978, & Beethoven Fest., Aust.; Master classes; Adjudicator; former Prof. of Piano, State Conserv. of Music, Sydney; now lectr. in piano for SA Dept. of Further Educ., Adelaide; tour of USSR, 1972. Hons: 2 scholarships & 5 prizes at RAM; Arts Coun. of GB Award, 1960. Hobbies: Martial Arts. Mgmt: New Era Int. Concert. Ltd., London. Address: c/o Adelaide C F E, Schl. of Music, Adelaide, SA, Aust.

DAVIES, Hazel Anne, b. 8 Apr. 1937, Cydweli, S Wales, UK. Organist. Educ: RAM; GRSM; LRAM; ARCM. m. David Gedge, 1 s., 1 d. Career: Broadcast Organ Recitals from Selby Abbey & Brecon Cathedral, BBC; Organ Accomp., Servs. from Selby Abbey & Brecon Cathedral etc.; Accomp., cathedral choir & singers on tours of Germany, Canada & USA; BBC Radio & TV. Recordings: Organ Recital from Bangor & Brecon Cathedrals; Christmas in Wales from Brecon Cathedral; Praise the Lord. (accompanying 19th century anthems); Sing Noel (Christmas carols). Hons: Thomas Threfall & John Williams (postgrad.), scholarships; Lady Wallis Budge Prize, RAM. Hobbies: Cooking; Interior Decoration; Motoring. Address: Garth Cottage, Pendre, Brecon, LD3 9EF, UK. 3.

DAVIES, Joan, b. London, UK. Pianist; Fortepiano Player. Educ: RAM; Hon ARAM; FRAM. w. Ivor Wallsworth. Debut: Wigmore Hall, when aged 16. Career: apps. throughout Brit. Isles, France, Italy, Hungary, Can., Czech.; many radio & TV broadcasts. Recordings for Abbey & Strobe. Contbr. to The Consort. Mbrships: Chmn., Royal Overseas League Prize; VP, Soc. of Women Musicians; The Prom Circle; Pres., Holmbury St. Mary Music Club; Brit. Mus. Soc., etc. Hobbies: Cooking; Gardening; Embroidery; Antiques; 16th century illuminated manuscripts; Medicine; Bird-watching. Mgmt: Ibbs & Tillett. Address: Leyland Cottage, Pevensey Bay, Sussex, UK. 3, 14.

DAVIES, John Huw, b. 26 Feb. 1935, Gilfach Goch, Wales. Singer; Broadcaster; Lecturer. Educ: TCM; GTCL; LTCL (singing); LTCL (TTD); ARCO. m. Rita Elisabeth Phillips, 1 s., 1 d. Career: over 400 broadcast & TV apps. inclng educl. prog., recitals; Soloist, major throughout Brit. Isles; num. concerts & broadcasts w. var. consorts; Prof., TCM; Lectr. on singing at many courses, etc.; Adjudicator, var. fests.; Sr. Music Advsr., Gwynedd County Coun. Contbr. to: Music Tchr.; Music & Musicians. Mbr., ISM. Hobbies: Golf; Reading. Mgmt: Helen Jennings. Address: Craig-y-don, St. David's Rd., Caernarfon, Gwynedd, UK.

DAVIES, John Leighton, b. 12 Feb. 1918, Cahir, Ireland., Professor of Clarinet. Educ: RAM; FRAM. m. Jean Kathleen Hills, 1 s., 1 d. Career: Prof., RAM, 1950-; Tutor, ibid, 1969; Soloist; Tchr., etc. Publs: Technical books for woodwind & brass. Mbrships: Royal Soc. of Musicians; Royal Phil. Soc.;

ISM. Hobbies: Food; Junk. Address: 11 Bruton Way, Ealing, London W13 0BY, UK.

DAVIES, Lyndon, b. 13 July 1944, Cardiff, UK. Pianist; Organist; Teacher. Educ: Pupil of Elsie Hankins, Bournemouth Schl. of Music; RAM, 1962-66: Pupil of Franz Reizenstein (piano) & Dr. Douglas Hopkins (organ); GRSM; LRAM (piano). Debut: Soloist, Beethovens First Piano Concerto w. Bournemouth Symph. Orch., conductor Charles Groves, 1957. Career: Broadcasts, BBC Children's Hour, 1958; Res. Music Tchr., Bedales Schl., Petersfield, 1966-70; Watford Schl. of Music, 1969-71; Musical Dir. & Organist, sev. variety shows & pantomimes, Bunny Baron Agcy.; Organist, 'Seeing and Believing', BBC TV; Organist, 'Geraldo in Concert', Royal Festival Hall, 1971; Organist, Geraldo's last major concert, Eastbourne, Sussex, 1974; Pt.-time tutor, Southern Music Trng. Ctr., Bromley, Kent 1973-75 ; part-time Lectr., Filton Tech. Coll., Bristol, 1975-77; part-time Lectr., St., Peters Coll., Birmingham, 1976-77; Broadcasts, BBC Radio 4 'The Organists Entertains'; Radio Oxford. Mbrships: Incorporates Soc. of Musicians; Royal Coll. of Organists. Hobbies: Photography; Country Walking; Electronics; Conservation; Elec. & Theatre Organs. Address: 7, Gorse Hill Rd., Poole, Dorset BH15 3QH, UK.

DAVIES, Maldwyn Thomas, b. 24 Oct. 1950, Merthyr Tydfil, Wales, UK. Lyric Tenor. Educ: BMus, Univ. Coll., Cardiff; Welsh Coll. of Music & Drama, Cardiff; LRAM; ARCM; LWCMD. m. Christine Margaret Powell. Debut: Purcell Room, London, 1979. Career: extensive tours performing opera & oratorio; num. apps. on radio & TV. Recordings: Handel, L'Allegro, Il Penseroso ed Il Moderato. Mbrships: ISM; Equity. Hons: Maisie Lewis Young Artist Fund Winner; ISM Young Artist finalist. Hobbies: Horses & Ponies; Squash; Reading. Mgmts: Ibbs & Tillet; Music Int.; Clarion. Address: 22A Clarence Rd., Windsor, Berks., UK.

DAVIES, Noel Anthony, b. 1 Jan. 1945, London, UK. Conductor. Educ: Hereford Cathedral Schl.; RCM; ARCM (Organ perf.), 1963: ARCM (Piano accomp.), 1966., Debut. Kentish Opera, Kent, 1967. Career: Apps. w. Welsh Philharmonia Orch., BBC Northern Symph. Orch., BBC Symph. Orch. & LSO & London Welsh Fest. Orch.; contracted to Engl. Nat. Opera, 1967-; Contracted to London Welsh Fest. Chorus, 1974-. Recording: Engl. Nat. Opera Gala Recording. Hons: G R Sinclair Choral Scholarship Hereford, 1955-63; Michael Mudie Cond. Award, RCM, 1966. Hobbies: Football; Wildlife; Cuisine. Mgmt: Trafalger Perry Ltd., 4, Goodwin's Court, London, W.C.2. Address: 20 Cricketfield Rd., London E5, UK.

DAVIES, Peter Maxwell, b. 8 Sept. 1934, Manchester, UK. Composer. Educ: Royal Manchester Coll. of Music; BMus, Manchester Univ.; studies w. Goffredo Petrassi, 1957. Career: Dir. of Music Cirencester Grammar Schl., 1959-62; Lecture tours, Europe, Aust., NZ, 1965; Comp. in Res., Univ. of Adelaide, 1966; Dir., Pierrot Players, 1967-70, Fires of London, 1970-; Fndr., Dir., St. Magnus Fest., Orkneys, 1977-. Comps. incl: Magnum Mysteriuym (chorus, instruments, organ); Str. Quartet; Veni Sancte Spiritus (chorus & orch.); Shepherd's Calendar (young singers & instrumentalists); Eight Songs for a Mad King; Taverner (opera); The Blind Fiddler (mezzosoprano & chmbr. ensemble); Salome (ballet), 1978; Symph. for Orch.; 1975: Kirkwall Shopping Songs for primary schl. children, 1979; num. piano pieces, instrumental works, choral works; realisations of 15th & 16th century comps.; music for the films, The Devils & The Boyfriend. Hons: Olivetti Prize, 1959; Koussevitksy Award, 1964; Koussevitsky Recording Award, 1966. Mgmt: Mrs. Judy Arnold, Flat 3,50 Hogarth Rd., London SW5, UK. Address: c/o Mgmt. 1b.

DAVIES, Peter Neville, b. 25 May 1928, Gorseinon, Wales. Music Inspector. Educ: BMus, Univ. Coll., Cardiff; GSM m. Heather Hathaway, 1 d. Career: Co. Music Advsr., Montgomeryshire, 1956-64 (formed Montgomery. Co. Youth Orch. & Choir; BBC Broadcasts w. Orch. & Choir; Appearance in TV Film 'Wales, This Land of Song'; For. Tour w. Orch. & Choir, Baden-Wurttemberg, 1964; City Music Advsr., Southampton, 1964-74; Music Insp., City of Birmingham, 1974- (formed City of Southampton Youth Orch. & Choir); Sev. BBC Radio Broadcasts; For. Tours w. Orch. inclng. Netherlands, 1972, Berlin, 1973, Hamburg, 1974. Recordings: 4 recordings w. City of Southampton Youth Orch. & Choir. Contbr. to Western Mail. Mbrships: Past Coun. Mbr., Nat. Youth Orch. of GB; Music Panel, Southern Arts Assn. Hons: Walford Davies Memorial Award, 1949; 1st Prize, Nat. Competition for Orchl. Conds., 1954. Address: Heathville, 22 Summerfield Rd., Holy Cross, Clent, Worcs., UK. 3, 28.

DAVIES, Philippa Claire, b. 20 Mar. 1953, London, UK. Flautist. Educ: BMus, ARCM; Studies w. William Bennett.

Debut: Purcell Room, London, 1977. Career: freelance flautist; solo apps. & w. num. orchs. inclng. Scottish Nat. Orch., London Symph. Orch., Royal Liverpool Orch., Philharmonia Orch., London Mozart Players, BBC N Ireland Orch. etc.; apps. w. Fires of London, Park Lane Music Players, Capricorn, Ars Nova & others; apps. at fests. at Flanders, Cheltenham, Edinburgh, Brighton, Bergen, Orkney & Montepulciano; radio broadcasts in UK & Belgium. Recordings w. orch. of St. John's, Smith Sq. Hons: num. scholarships & awards; Tagore Gold Medal; Eve Kisch flute prize; Finalist in Leeds Nat. Musicians' Platford, 1977; 3rd prize, Mozart Memorial Competition, 1978. Hobbies: Sports; Walking; Skiing; Climbing; Good food & wine. Mgmt: Terry Slasberg, London. Address: 99 Gt. Titchfield St., London W1, UK.

DAVIES, Ryland, b. 9 Feb. 1943, Cwm Ebbw Vale, Monmouthshire, UK. Opera & Concert Singer. Educ: Royal Manchester Coll. of Music, w. Frederik Cox, 1960-64. m. Anne Howells. Debut: Almaviva in the Barber of Seville, Welsh Nat. Opera, 1964. Career incl: Soloist w. Glyndebourne Fest. Chorus, 1964-66; Welsh Nat. Opera; Sadlers Wells Opera Engl. Nat. Opera N; Royal Opera House, Covent Gdn.; Salzburg Fest.; opera at San Fran. & Chgo., USA; Concerts at Tanglewood, San Fran., Hollywood Bowl, in Europe, Israel, S Am., etc. frequent guest apps. at Paris & elsewhere. Recordings incl: Belmonte in Il Seraglio; Hylas in The Trojans; Ferrando in Cosi Fan Tutte. Hons. incl: Fellow, Royal Manchester Coll. of Music; Imperial League of Opera Prize; Ricordi Prize, 1964; Boise & Mendelssohn Fndn. Scholarship, 1964. Hobbies: Antiques; Art; Cinema. Mgmt: Artists Int. Address: Milestone, Broom Close, Esher, Surrey, UK. 1,2,4,30.

DAVIS, Alan Roger, b. 16 May 1945, Birmingham, UK. Recorder Player; Teacher. Educ: BA (Oxon); MA (Birmingham); ARCM; LTCL. m. Eira Myfanwy Picton, 2d., 1s. Debut: Wigmore Hall, London, 1974. Career: Prof. of Recorder, Birmingham Schl. of Music, 1969-; Hd., Music Dept., King's Norton Girls' Schl., 1971-; Dir., Halcyon Consort, 1969-77; Jury mbr., 27th competition of German Broadcasting Co., 1978; Lectr., Swansea Bach Week, 1978-79. Recordings for BBC. Contbr. to: Birmingham Post; Recorder & Music. Mbrships: ISM; Soc. of Recorder Players. Hobby: Jazz. Address: 180 Shenley Fields Rd., Birmingham B29 5BP, UK.

DAVIS, Albert Oliver, b. 9 Apr. 1920, Cleveland; Ohio, USA. Composer; Pianist; French Hornist. Educ: BA, Ariz. State Univ., Tempe, 1943W: MA, ibid, 1951; Cleveland Inst. Music, Ohio; Western Reserve Univ., ibid; Cleveland Music Settlement. m. Olive Marie Wheeler Davis, 2 d. Career: Accompanist (piano), Thomas L. Thomas, 1963-73; French Hornist, Phoenix Symph., 1941-43; Comp.; Arranger, N am. Air Defense Command Band, Colo. Springs, 1961-64, Sun Devil Band, Ariz. State Univ., Tempe, 1948-67, Ohio State Marching Band, Columbus, 1968-72, Paul Burton Orch., Cleveland, Ohio, 1947-73; Chmn. Music Dept., Phoenix Coll., Ariz.; Musical Arranger, 1960-76. Compositions incl: Desert Star; Hollywood Serenade; Welsh Folk Suite; 2 Little Colts; Desert Pastrorale; Drummers Madness; Winter Scene; Rapsody Modernata; El Camino Real, Songs of Nyassaland, Fantasieona Danish Theme; scores of 8 musical comedies for HS Contbr. to Ariz. State Musical Newsletter, 1954-62. Mbrships. incl. ASCAP; St. Past Pres., Ariz. State Band & Orch. Dirs. Assn. Recip., hons. Hobbies: Travel; Model Trains; Golf. Address: 1329 E Catalina Dr., Phoenix, AZ 85014, USA.

DAVIS, Allan Gerald, b. 29 Aug. 1922, Watertown, NY, USA. Composer; Professor of Music, Lehman Coll. of the City Univ. of NY. Educ: BMus, MMus, Syracuse Univ., NY; Grad Studies at the Eastman Schl. of Music Rochester Univ., NY. Educ: BMus, MMus, Syracuse Univ., NY; Grad studies at the Eastman Schl. of Music, Rochester Univ., NY. Comps: The Sailing of the Nancy Belle, opera in one act, The Ordeal of Osbert, opera in one act, Razorback Reel for piano; Razorback Reel, version for band; Italian Festival Suite for brass choir & percussion; Festival Concerto for clarinet & orch., Hometown Suite for band; A Song for Daniel, for mixed chorus, brass choir, percussion & piano; A Psalm of Praise, for mixed chorus, brass choir & perc., The Departure, Opera in 3 Acts. Recording: Razorback Reel. Contbr. to profl jrnls. Mbr., ASCAP. Recip. var commissions. Hobbies: Record collecting; Swimming; Collecting memorabilia of 1939 World's Fair. Address: 210 Riverside Dr., NY, NY 10025, USA.

DAVIS, Andrew Frank, b. 2 Feb. 1944, Ashridge, UK. Conductor. Educ: MusB, MA, Kings Coll., Cambridge Univ.; Conservatorio di S Cecilia, Rome. m. Felicity Vincent. Career: Asst. Cond., BBC Scottish Symph. Orch., 1970-72; Assoc. Cond., New Philharmonia Orch., 1973-; Musical Dir., Toronto Symph. Orch., 1975-. Recordings w. LPO, RPO, NPO. Hobbies: Kite flying; Stained glass. Mgmt: Harold Holt Ltd., in N Am.,

Shaw Concerts Inc. Address: 1 Leighton Rd., London NW5, UK. 3.

DAVIS, Angela R, b. 26 Sept. 1947, St. John's Mich., USA. Violinist. Educ: BMus (violin), Univ. of Mich., Schl. of Music, 1969. m. Henk Sekreve. Career: w. Montreal Symph. Orch., 1969-71; Het Residence Orkest, The Hague, Holland, 1971-75; Concertgebouw Orch., Amsterdam, 1975-; Violin Tchr., Koninklijke Conservatorium for Music, The Hague, 1972-74. Hobbies: Sewing; Reading; Traveling. Address: 44 Haarlem, Holland, Marstraat.

DAVIS, Arthur David, b. 5 Dec. 1934, Harrisburg, Pa., USA. Conductor; Composer; Arranger; Publisher; Educator; Soloist Musician (Double Bass, Tuba, Piano). Educ: AA Manhattan Community Coll., BA, Hunter Coll., CUNY; MA, City Coll., CUNY; MA, NY Univ.; Manhattan Schl. of Music; Juilliard Schl. of Music. m. Gladys Davis, 3 c. Debut: Harrisburg, Pa., 1951. Career incls: Mbr. NBC, Westinghouse & CBS Staff Orchs; Soloist & Prin. Double Bass w. var. orchs.; Num. Movies, TV & Radio Commercials; Worldwide tours; Broadway Shows; Ldr., The Trio, 1968-; Fac., Univ. of Bridgeport, Conn. Comps. incl: Dialogue for Freedom; Reflections for 2 Double Basses & Cello. Num. recordings. Publs: The Arthur Davis System for Double Bass, 1976. Contbr. to: NY Times; Music Black, White & Blue; Coda. Mbrships. incl: Bd. Mbr.; Scarborough Schl. Advisory Arts Coun. Recip. num. awards. Hobbies incl: Karate; Fishing; Astronomy; Photography; Gardening; Gourmet. Address: KMV Enterprises Inc., PO Box 431, Crugers, NY 10521, USA. 2,6.

DAVIS, Charles Wheeler, b. 26 July 1915, Buffalo Ctr., Iopwa, USA. Bass Baritone; Voice Teacher; Director of Choral Activities; Director of Opera Workshop; Professor Music. Educ: BA, MA, Univ. of Iowa. m. Beverly Jean Davis, 3 s., 1 d. Career: Soloist in Der Fledermaus, Bartered Bride, Cosi fan Tutte, etc.; Recitalist; Choral Dir., pub. schls. in Iowa; Choral & Voice Tchr., Univ. of Iowa, Wash. State Univ., Univ. of NM, & Univ. of Alaska; Adjudicator & Clinician; Prof. of Music. & Hd., Dept. of Music, Univ. of Alaska, Fairbanks. Mbr. of Profl. Assns. Contbr. to profl. jrnls. Hobbies incl: Fishing. Address: Dept. of Music, Univ. of Alaska, Fairbanks, AK 99701, USA.

DAVIS, Sir Colin Rex, b. 25 Sept. 1927, Weybridge, Surrey, OK. Conductor. Educ: RCM. m. (/) April Cantelo, 1949 (div. 1964), 1 s., 1 d.; (2) Ashraf Naini, 1964, 2 s. Career: Cond., assoc. w. Kalmar Orch. & Chelsea Opera Grp.; Asst. Cond., BBC Scottish Orch., 1957-59; Cond., Sadler's Wells Opera House, 1960; Musical Dir., ibid, 1961-65; Chief Cond., BBC Symph. Orch., 1967-71; Musical Dir., Covent Garden, 1971; Guest Cond., Metropol. Opera, NY, 1966: Guest cond. & recordings made w. leading UK Orchs. Recip. CBE, 1965. Hobbies: Reading; Cooking; Gardening. Address: c/o Pears-Phipps Mgmt., 8 Halliford St., London N13HE, UK.

DAVIS, (Donald) Evan, b. 13 Mar. 1923, LA, Calif., USA. Professor of Music. Educ: Dip., LA Conserv. of Music, 1940; MMus., Northwestern Univ., 1948; DEd., Univ. of Ore., 1953; Cert., Vienna State Acad. of Music, 1961. m. (Clara) Janice Monks, 5 children. Career: Supvsr. of Music, Ashland (Ore) City Schls., 1948-51; Music Tchr., LA City Schls., 1947-48; Asst. in Keyboard Theory, Univ. of Ore., 1952; Asst. Prof. of Music, Ariz. State Coll., 1953-55, Ore State Coll., 1955-58; Assoc. Prof. of Music, Univ. of BC., 1958-65; Prof. of Music, Brigham Young Univ., 1965-. Compositions: 3 Children's Songs; The Family at Christmas; Rise We From Death Triumphant (sacred cabtata); Holy Lord, Our Grateful Prayer Now Hear; 4 Songs of Hugo Wolf (arr. for women's chorus); When Music Sounds. Publs: Music Handbook, 1958; Bringing Music to Children, 1965; An Analytical Study of Selected Contemporary American Choral Compositions & the Implications for Teaching Methods of Reading Music, 1969; Ed., Sing With Me, 1971. Contbr. to num. profl. jrnls. Mbrships: Ed., The Instructor, 1968-72; Past Pres., BC Music Educators Assn.; Fndng. Mbr. & Regional VP, Canadian Music Educators; VP, Utah Music Educators Assn.; Life, Menc. Recip. of num. rsch. grants & fellowships. Hobbies: Farming; Camping; Flying. Address: C-584 Harris Fine Arts Ctr., Brigham Young Univ., Provo, UT 84601, USA. 9, 28.

DAVIS, Evelyn Helen Johnson, b. 26 May 1915. Carrington ND, USA. College Professor of Music Education. Educ: BA, Concordia Coll., Moorhead, Minn.; MMus., Syracuse Univ., NY; PhD, Univ. of Md., Coll. Park, Md.; Voice Cert., Concordia Coll. Conserv.; Piano Cert., Fargo, ND; pvte. studies at Am. Conserv., Chgo. w. Susannah Coleman, Gilderoy Scott & Miriam Taylor. m. Joseph M. Davis, 3 s. Career: Music Tchr. in Pub. Schls. & pvte. colls. for 18 yrs. at Oral Roberts Univ., Augustana Coll., Wayland Jr., Coll; Vocal Soloist in maj. churches & orgs. in Md., Va. & Wash. DC; Lecture recitals on Norwegian Vocal Music. Publs: The Significance of Arthur

Farwell as an Am. Music Educator, 1972., Contbr. to music jrnls. Mbr. MENC. Hons: Dr. Burgess Award, 1935; Dr. Hagen Award, 1936; Rev. Gould Wickey Award, 1937; Hayes-Swarthout Award, 1943 ; Mu Phi Episilon Doctoral Grant, 1971. Hobbies: Swimming; Reading; Travel. Address: 7106 E 53rd Pl. S. Tulsa, OK 74145, USA.

DAVIS, Evelyn Marguerite Bailey, b. Springfield, Mo., USA. Church Organist & Pianist; Harpist; Vocal Soloist; Director of Youth Orchestra; Music Arranger; Teacher of Piano, Organ, Voice & Croma Harp. Educ: Piano studies, Springfield, Mo.; Organ & piano study w. Charles Cordeal, Webster Grove, Mo. m. James Harvey Davis. Debut: Organ & Voice recital, Hall for Performing Arts, Webster Groves. Career incl: Ch. Organist & Pianist; Dir., Ch. Youth Orch., Maplewood, Mo.; Harpist & Vocal Soloist; Dir. Youth orch., arr., Tchng. Bible, Bible Baptist Ch., St. Charles, Mo.; Accomp. at revival meetings, weddings, funerals, crusades; radio broadcasts, Springfield; Piano & Organ Tchr. Comps. incl: I am the Alpha & Omega (cantata); I Will Sing Hallelujah; Prelude to Prayer. Recordings: I am the Alpha & Omega; Sev. wedding concerts. Mbrships: Am. Guild of Organists; Nat. Guild of Piano Tchrs.; Int. Platform Assn.; Life Mbr., Int. Biographical Assn. Hobbies: Collecting music boxes; Interior Decorating w. Antiques; Flower arranging; Oil painting. Address: No. 4 Rancho Dr., Edgewood Acres, St. Charles, MO 63301, USA. 5,8,9,27,29.

DAVIS, Howard, b. 9 Apr. 1940, Wolverhampton, UK. Violinist. Educ: RAM; ARAM; LRAM. m. Virginia Black, 2 s. Career: Mbr., Alberni String Quartet, 1961-; Res. Quartet, Harlow, 1963-; Vis. artists-in-res., Univ. WA; Num. overseas tours. Recordings: Complete Schumann chmbr. music; Complete Rawthorne Quartets; Mendelssohn; Schubert; Haydn, etc. Mbr., ISM. Hobbies: Harpsichord bldg.; Painting; Photography. Address: Charlotte Cottage, 123 Sheering Rd., Old Harlow, Essex CM17 OJP.

DAVIS, Ivan, Concert Pianist. Educ: N. Tex. Univ.; N. Tex. Univ.; Dip. St. Cecilia Acad., Rome, Italy. m. Betty Lou, 1 d. Career: has played w. major orchs. & given recitals, USA, UK & Europe, has also given recitals in Can. & S Am.; Interested in hist. & perf. of opera; Artist-in-Res. & Prof. of Piano, 1966-71, & Univ. of Ind., 1971-. Recordings incl: Liszt's Piano Concerto 1 & 2; Rachmaninov's Piano Concert 2; Tchaikovshy's Piano Concerto 1; Chopin's Fantasie Impromptu, Etude 3, Barcarolle, Ballade 1 Waltzes 6 & 7, Nocturn 8, & Scherzo 3 Hons: 1st Prize, Casella Competition, Naples, 1958; Handel Award NYC, 1962; 1st Prize, Int. Liszt Competition, 1960-61; Busoni Competition, Boizana, 1959. Hobbies incl: Cooking; Theatre; Motion Pictures. Address: 416 Viscaya Ave., Coral Gables, FL 33134, USA. 3.

DAVIS, Keith C, b. 24 Jan. 1951, London, UK. Opera & Concert Singer; Counter-tenor. Educ: RCM. m. Jennifer Anne Young. Debut: Berlin, 1977; France (opera), 1978. Career: Solo counter-tenor, Westminster Catherdral 1970; soloist in Handelian opera and oratorio; apps. in Bach Passions & Cantatas; apps. in Amsterdam, Paris, Salzburg as well as Fairfield & Queen Elizabeth Halls, UK. Recordings: Sev. as soloist & w. Early Music Consort of Prof. Musica Antiqua. Hons: Chilver Wilson Prize for Singing, RCM. Hobbies: Taekwando; Fast Driving; Ancient Civilisation. Mgmt: Ibbs & Tillet, London. Address: 3 Copse Hill, Wimbledon, London SW20, UK.

DAVIS, Leonard, b. 26 Mar. 1915. Eastbourne, Sussex, UK. Conductor; Viola Player; Chamber Music Coach; Adjudicator. Educ: GSM. m. Luise, 1 s. Career: Viola player, both freelance & on contract w. BBC, Royal Phil. Orch., LPO, LSO, Sandlers Wells Opera Orch., etc.; Cond. of Orpington Symph. Orch., London Co-op Soc. Orch., Goldsmiths Youth Orch., Goldsmiths Trng. Orch. (Goldsmiths Coll.), etc.; Chamber Music Coach for Inner London Educ. Authority & London Borough of Bromley (Adult Educ.). Mbrships: Trustee, Musicians Union; ISM; Adjudicator, Brit. Fedn. of Music Fests.; London Continuative Tchrs. Assn. Hobbies: Cycling; Playing Chamber Music. Addresss: 82 Brightfield Rd., London SE12 82QF, UK.

DAVIS, Marilyn Johnson, b. 22 Feb. 1936, Carroll, Ohio, USA. Teacher of Piano, Theory & Composition; Pianist. Educ: Emory Univ.; Gulf Coast Jr. Coll.; Grad. work, Eastman Schl. of Music, New Schl. for Music Study, Princeton, NJ. m. Al J. Davis, 1 s., 1 d. Debut: Radio, 1952. Career: Tchr.; Sherwood Music Schl.; 15 yrs. experience as Hd. of Studio & Tchr.; num. workshops; recital w. Greg Kamback, 1965. Recording: Hit Music of the 40s and 50s. Publ: Method book to be published, 1977. Contbr. to S Johnson, Ed., Lovers of Chopin; local press. Mbrships incl: Nat. MTA; Ala. MTA; NGPT. Hobbies incl: Genealogy; Brailling for Musically Blind; Managing a Judaica Shop; Swimming; Composing; Painting. Mgmt: Davis Music Studio. Address: Davis Music Studio, Apt. N101, 2100 W Beach Dr., Panama City, FL 32401, USA.

DAVIS, Mark Llewellyn, b. 6 June 1906, Easton, Pa., USA. Organist (Church & Concert); Teacher (Piano, Organ, Voice Theory). Educ: Westminster Choir Coll., Princeton, NJ; studied w. var. masters inclng. Earle D Laros (Piano), Firmin Swinnen (Organ & Theory), Rome Fenton (Voice). Widower, 1 s., 1 d. Career: Organist & Oboist, Easton, Pa., Symph. Orch.; Organist-Choirmaster, Trinity Episc. Ch., Easton, 129-44; Hd., Music Dept. Moravian Coll. for Women, Bethlehem, Pa. Ctrl. Moravian Ch., Bethlehem, Pa., 1944-55; Cristo Rey Cath. Ch., Santa Fe, NM, 1944-55, Visiting Lectr. on Liturgy & Hymnology, Moravian Theological Seminary, Bethlehem, Pa., 1965-55. Cristo Rey Cath. Ch., Santa Fe, NM, 1959-60, Episc. Ch. of Holy Faith, ibid, 1960-66, St. Francis Cathedral, ibid, 1967-72; Former Lectr., Moravian Theol. Sem., Bethlehem, Pa.; Residence Studio, Voice & Organ, Carnegie Hall, NYC, 1955-59; Musical Dir., Santa Fe Civic Chorus, NM, 1959-; Substitute Hd., Music Dept., Inst. Am. Indian Art, ibid. 1966; Instr. in Organ Coll. of Santa Fe, 1971-; Var. Organ Recitals. Contbr. to the Moravian. Mbrships: Hymn Soc. of Am.; AGO; AAUP; Local 802, Am. Fedn. Musicians. Recip., 1st Prize, Organ playing, Sesquicentennial Exposition, Phila., Pa., 1926. Hobbies: Walking; Talking with People; Psychology. Address: 213 Country Club Gdns., Santa Fe, NM, USA.

DAVIS, Michael D, b. 29 May 1937, Hull, UK. Violinist. Educ: GSM; Staatiliche Hochschule für Musik, Cologne; ARCM; LRAM. m. Eileen Muldowney, 1 s. Debut: NY, 1959; London, 1962. Career: recitals & concerts, BBC Radio & TV; Soloist on European tours; Concertmaster, Scottish Nat. Orch., 1974-75; Artist Prof., Ohio State Univ., Columbus, USA, 1976-. Has recorded for BBC, Radio Hamburg, Hilversum, etc. Mbrships: NY Musicians Club; Pi Kappa Lambda. Hons: 1st Prize, Int. Carl Flesch Competition, 1957; Gold Medal, GSM, 1958. Hobbies: Hi-Fi, Sports Cars; Photography. Mgmt: Basil Douglas, London; David Schiffmann, London. Address: 125 W Dodridge Apt. 207, Columbus, OH, USA. 3.

DAVIS, Miles, b. 1926, Alton, Ill., USA. Jazz Trumpeter; Composer. m. Irene, 1 s., 1 d. Recordings incl: Jack Johnson; Miles Smiles; Miles Davis at Carnegie Hall; Bitches Brew; Sketches of Spain; Miles Ahead; Nefertiti. Mgmt: Harold E. Lovette, 120 E 56th St., NY 22, NY, USA. 3.

DAVIS, Sharon, b. 30 Sept. 1937, North Hollywood Calif., USA. Pianist; Editor; Composer. Educ: BMus, Univ. of Southern Calif.; MSci, Juilliard Schl. of Music. m. William Schmidt, 1 d. Debut: Duo recital w. cellist brother Douglas Davis, Carnegie Recital Hall, NY, 1961. Career: Extensive solo & ensemble apps. in S Calif. area; premiered & commissioned over 100 new works; toured US & Can. w. brother, 10 yrs. Comps. incl: Though Men Call Us Free (recorded); Three Poems of Wm. Blake (recorded); 11 transcriptions. Recordings: 7 recordings as soloist & chmbr. player. Mbrships: ASCAP; Pi Kappa Lambda. Hons: Scholarships to USC & Juilliard; Fulbright Grant for piano study in Paris, France, 1962-63. Hobbies: Photography; Back-packing. Address: 2859 Holt Ave., LA, CA 90034, USA.

DAVISON, Arthur Clifford Percival, b. Montreal, Can. Conductor. Educ: Conserv. of Music, McGill Univ.; Conserv. de Musique, Montreal; LRSM; ARCM; FRAM. m. 1) Barbara Hildred, 1 s., 2d; 2) Elizabeth Blanche. Career: Cond. of choral & orchl. socs., and solo violinist. w. leading orchs. in Can.; since 1948 has app. w. major symph. orchs. in UK & other countries; Dir., LPO; Mus. Dir. & Cond., Little Symph. of London, Virtuosi of Engl.; Nat. Youth Orch of Wales, Croydon Symph. Orch., etc; Music Advsr., Welsh Jt. Educ. Committee on Nat. Youth Orch. of Wales; Guest cond., Royal Danish Ballet, NYC Ballet; has cond. symph. concerts & given talks for CBC, BBC, Scandinavian & var. other European TVs; Dir., choral concerts & fests.; Adjudicator; Dir., conducting course, Goldsmith's Coll., London. Comps. incl: var. choral works; film scores. sev. recordings; Contbr. to jrnls. Hons: CBE, 1974; MMus, Univ. of Wales, 1974; Guild for Promotion of Welsh Music Award, 1977. Hobbies: Theatre-going; Reading; Fishing. Address: Glencairn, Shepherd's Hill, Merstham, Surrey RH1, 3AD, UK, 3.

DAVISON, Nigel St. John, b. 1 Dec. 1929, Merrut, India. University Lecturer; Organist. Educ: BA, 1953, MusB, 1954, MA, 1957, Peterhouse, Cambridge (organ); DMus, Edinburgh Univ., 1962; RCM, 1947-48; FRCO, 19054. m. Kristine Grahame Meikle, 3 s., 1 d. Career: Asst. Music Master, Oundle Schl., 1954-57; Asst. Dir. of Music, 1957-62 & Dir. of Music, 1963-67, Wellington Coll.; Lectr. in Music, 1967-71. Snr. Lectr., 1971-, Bristol Univ.; Musical Dir., Bristol Opera Co., 1967-77; Organist, The Lord Mayor's Chapel, Bristol, 1976-79. Publs. incl: Pierre de la Rue; Tye, etc. Contbr. to: Musical Quarterly; Music & Letters; Musical Times; The Music Review; The Oragan. Mbrships: ISM; RCO. Hobbies: Hillwalking; Sailing. Address: 4 Carnarvon Rd., Bristol BS6 7DP, UK.

DAVYE, John Joseph, b. 19 Oct, 1929, Milkton, Mass., USA. Conductor; Composer. Educ: BMus., Univ. of Miami, Fla., 1952; MMus, Ithaca Coll.,NY, 1965. m. Betty Bostick Davye, 1 s., 1 d. Career: Choral Cond. & Comp. of Choral of Chmbr. Music; Tchr., Public Schl. Music, Secondary Level, 1955-65; Dir. of Choral Activities, Assoc. Prof. of Music, & Tchr. of Music Theory, Conducting & Comp., Old Dominion Univ., Norfolk, Va., 1966-; Apps. w. his Choral Grps. on Coast-to-Coast Radio Network apps., Local, State Regional & Nat. Confs. & Convens. Choral Comps: (publd.) Psalm 93; Tenebrae Factae Sunt; The Spirit of the Lord God is Upon Me; Thy Glory Dawns, Jerusalem, Awake; A Child is Born to Us; Missa Brevis. Mbrships: Am. Choral Dirs. Assn.; Am. Soc. of Univ. Comps.; MENC; AAUP; Hon. Life Mbr. Iota Tau Chapt., Phi Mu Alpha Sinfonia Fraternity. Hons: Comps. Selected for Third & Fourth Annual Symposiums of Contemporary Am. Music, Univ. of Kansas, 1961 & '62 & for Second Annual Symposium of Contemporary Choral Music, Univ. of S Fla., 1970. Address: Old Dominion Univ., Norfolk, VA 23508, USA.

DAWES, Frank, b. 15 Feb. 1910, London, UK. Piano Teacher; Lecturer; Writer; Free Lance Journalist. Educ: ARCM (piano perf.). m. Elfrida Cheetham, 1 s. (dec.). Comps: educl. piano music. Arr. pieces for recorder. Ed: Clementi, Symphonies & piano works; Elizabethan Keyboard music; J C Bach, Sinfonia Concertante in F; S Wesley, 4th Symphony; original recorder works; Maurice Greene, The Song of Deborah & Barak; etc. Publs: Pattern Pieces, an introduction to form, 1956; Debussy Piano Music, 1969. Contbr. to Musical Times. Mbrships: Royal Musical Assn.; ISM; Royal Soc. of Tchrs. Hons: Chappell Gold Medal, piano; Boosey Gold Medal, singing. Hobbies: Photography; Country walking. Address: 19 Gaysham Ave., Ilford, Essex, 1G2 6TH, UK. 3, 28.

DAWNEY, Michael William, b. 10 Aug. 1942, Ilford, UK. Musicologist; Editor; Composer; Lecturer. Educ: BA, Univ. of Durham, 1963; BLitt, Lincoln Coll., Oxford, 1967; MPhil. Inst. of Dialect & Folk Life Studies. Univ. of Leeds, 1975. m. Louise Bateman. Career: Comps. incl: A Christmas Greeting; A Carolan Suite; Festival March; Echoes for Brass, London is a Fine Town; Now Welcome Summer; Finale for organ; 5 Irish Dances. Publs: incl: Doon the Wagon Way, 1973. The Iron Man, 1974; The Ploughboy's Glory, 1977. Contbr. to musical jrnls. Mbrships incl: Comps. Guild of GB, Royal Musical Assn. Recip., Irish Folk Song Soc. Gold Medal, 1975; HM Queen Elizabeth II Silver Jubilee Prize, 1977. Hobbies: Swimming, Cinema. Address: 118 Colin Gdns., Colidale, London NW9 6ER, UK 4,23,28.

DAWSON, David, b. 21 June 1939, Ashton-under-Lyne, Lancs., UK. Lecturer; Operatic Director. Educ: Cert. Ed., Mancester Univ.; GRSM, ARMCM, RMCM; LLCM (TD). m. Christine Ann Radford, 2 s. Career: Tchng. posts in Montgomeryshire & Hull, 1967-74; Lectr. in music, Bingley Coll., 1974-78; Sr. Lectr., Ilkley Coll., 1978-; Dir., Bradford Opera Group; Chief Examiner, O level music for London Univ.; cond.; accomp.; recorder player. Publ: Musical Ed., Songs for Living, 1972. Mbrships: ISM; Nat. Assn. of Tchrs. in Further & Higher Ed. Hobby: Mountaineering. Address: 12 Heaton Close, Eldwick, Bingley, W Yorks., BD16 3DW, UK.

DAWSON, Joan Copeland, b. 13 Dec. 1917, Sydney, Aust. Lecturer in Pinaforte. Educ: AMEB & Wm. Vicars' Scholarships to Sydney Conservatorium; AMusA; LRSM; LMusA; AMEB Travelling Scholarship, RCM, London; ARCM; Tchrs. Trng. Cert. m. Gladstone Bell (dec.). 1 s. Career: concert apps., Sydney & Newcastle; radio recitals, Aust. Broadcasting Commission; Lectr., aural trng., Sydney Conserv.; currently Lectr., NSW Conservatorium, Newcastle; Examiner, Aust. Musical Exam. Bd., 1949-, also Mbr. of Advsry. Bd., AMEB. Mbrships: Musical Assn. of NSW; NSW Pub. Sev. Profl. Offs. Assn.; Aust. Soc. Music Educ. Hobby: Philately. Address: 24 Bar Ceach Ave., Newcastle, NSW 2300, Aust.

DAWSON-LYELL, Julian, b. 18 Nov. 1947, Peebles, Scotland, UK. Pianist. Educ: RCM, 1965-68; GRSM; ARCM; Queen's Coll., Oxford Univ. 1968-71: BA (Oxon). Debut: Purcell Room, London, 1974. Career: Solo pianist, ensemble player & accomp.; London solo recitals, 1974, '75, '78, '79; tours of Germany, Italy, Southern Africa & Scandinavia; radio broadcasts for BBC & Italy; TV apps. in Italy, S Africa, & Iceland; apps. at fests. in Sorrento & Reykjavik. Comps: 4 songs (1955-57). Recordings w. flautist Manuela Wiesler of Boulez, Sonatine, Jolivet, Chat de Linos, & Francaix, Divertimento. Contbr. to The Strad. Mbr. Musicians Union. Hons: Semifinalist, Geneva pianoi competition, 1973; Winner (w, Capricorn ensemble), jury's special prize in Gaudeamus Competition for Interpreters of Contemporary Music, Rotterdam, 1975. Hobbies: Reading; Bridge; Langs. Address: 1 Lyndhurst Rd., London NW3, UK.

DAY, Ann Trent, b. 15 May 1948, Balt., Md., USA. Musicologist; Ethnomusicologist; Organologist. Educ: BMus, Converse Coll., 1970; AM, Univ. of Mich., 1974; Columbia Univ. Mbrships: Soc. for Ethnomusicol; Am. Musicol. Soc. Address: 338 E 83rd St., NY, NY 10028, USA.

DAYTON, Michael Owen, b. 22 Oct. 1948, Oakland, Calif., USA. Composer; Educator. Educ: AB, Calif. State Univ., Hayward, 1970; MMus, San Fran. Conserv. of Music, 1972; Juilliard Schl. of Music 1973-74; PhD, Union Grad. Schl., Yellow Springs, Ohio, 1975. m. Susan Dayton. Debut: Town Hall, NYC, 1973. Career: Comps. performed at concerts NYC, Aspen Music Fest., etc. Comps. incl: Epithlamium for 11 Woodwinds & Tape, 1969; Essay for Orch., 1972, Threnody for the Victims of Vietnam, 1973; Phantasmorgia (ballet suite), 1975; Fundaments, 1976. Contbr. to profl. jrnls. Mbr., profl. assns. Hons. incl: 1st Prize, Denver Ballet Co., 1974; 1st Prize, Fresno Orch. Contest, 1973. Hobbies: Ornithology; Hiking; Indian Lore. Address: 2048 Sierra Rd. Apt. 3, Concord, CA 94518, USA.

DEAHL, Robert W, b. 9 Oct. 1928, Pitts., Pa., USA. Professor of Music; Trombonist. Educ: BMus, MMus, Oberlin Coll. Conserv.; further studies, 'Mozarteum' Acad., Salzburg. Div. Career: Instr., Overlin Coll., 1957-58 0 Tex. Tech. Coll., 1958-59; Dir. Salzburg Div., Oberlin Conserv., 1959-64: Asst. Prof.-Prof., Asst. Chmn., Dept. of Music, Tex. Tech. Univ., 1964-; Ch. Choir Dir., 1964-70; 1st Trombone, Pitts. Youth Symph., Orch., 1946- 47, 583rd AF Band, 1953-56, USAF Band, TDY, 1953 & 54, Lubbock Symph. Orch., 1971-, Midland-Odessa Symph. Orch., 1972-74, & Roswell Symph. Orch., 1973-. Contbr. to musical jrnls. Mbrships: Tex. Music Educators Assn.; Int. Trombone Assn.; Am Musicol. Soc.; Coll. Music Soc.; Tex. Assn. of Coll. Tchrs.; Phi Mu Alpha; Kappa Kappa Psi; Pi Kappa Lambda. Hobbies: Travel; Photography. Address: 3610 46th, Lubbock, TX 79413, USA. 23.

DEÁK, Tamás, b. 27 Apr. 1928, Magyarország, Hungary. Professor of Trumpet; Composer; Conductor; Bandleader. Educ: Studies Law. m. Gabrielle Ernöházi, 1 s. Debut: (as Comp.) Hungarian Radio Pop Song Contest, 1959. Career: 1st Trumpet & Arr., Hungarian Radio Big Band, 1959-; Comp. for Film & TV cartoons, 1964-; Ldr., Deák Big Band; Prof., Bela Bartok Conserv. Comps: Amout 300 published & recorded works, 1960-; TV musicals; ballet music. Mbrships: Organization of Hungarian Musicians; Fndn. Hungarian Artist. Hons: 2nd Prize, Hungarian Radio Jazz Contest, 1959; 3rd Prize, 1956, 2nd Prize 1968, Hungarian Pop Song Contest. Hobbies: Skiing; Sailing; Gardening. Mgmt: Organization of Hungarian Musicians (as comp.) Artis Jus. Address: 1021 Budapest, Széher ut. 60, Hungary.

DEAKIN, Richard, b. 28 Mar. 1946, Drybrook, Glos., UK. Violinist. Educ: BA, Emmanuel Coll., Cambridge Univ.; RAM; FRCO; LRAM. m. Emma Ferrand. Debut: Wigmore Hall, 1972. Career: Recitals, Kirchman Soc., Purcell Romm.; Ldr., Chmbr. Orch. of St. John's, Smith Sq.; Tutor in violin, Royal Northern Coll. of Music, Manchester. Mbr., ISM. Hobbies: Gardening; Mountain Walking. Mgmt: H H H Concert Agcy. Address: The Homestead, Hartley Wintney, Nr. Basingstoke, Hants., UK.

DE ALMEIDA, Antonio, b. 1928, Paris, France. Conductor. Educ: BMus, Yale Univ., USA; Studied w. A Ginastera, Buenos Aires, Serge Koussevitsky, Paul Hindemith. m. Lynn Erdman, 2 s., 1 d. Career: Portuguest Radio, 1957-60; Musical Dir., Stuttgart Phil., 1962-64: Musical Dir., Paris Opera, 1964-; Guest Cond., Berlin Phil., Phila. Orch., LSO, RPO, BBC, Nat. Swiss Orch. (Romande): Leningrad Phil. Publs: Offrande Musicale Orchestral Series (Ed.); Complete Symphonies of Boccherini (Ed.); Thematic Catalogue Works by Offenbach. Hons: Chevalier des Arts et Lettres: Grand Prix du Disque. Address: 25 Rue des Grands Augustins, Paris 6 France. 14, 19.

DEAN, George Dixie, b. 25 Sept. 1916, London, UK. Accordionist; Composer; Teacher. m. Myra Wilcox Dean, 2 s., 1 d. Debut: aged 14. Career: num. perfs. on radio & for film background music; perfs. in Can., UK, France, Belgium, Netherlands, Germany during WW II in Canada's Meet the Navy show; missionary & perf. in Latin Am.; formerly Hd. Instructor, Pietro Deiro Accordion Schl., NY; tchr. of sev. of best Can. perfs. & tchrs.; Prin. Ontario Conserv. of Music. Comps: num. solos; complete accordion course, Hanon for Accordion. Recordings: The 3 Keyboards of Dixie Dean Accordion Melodies. Publs: Hanon for Accordion, complete course in 14 books. Contbr. to var. jrnls. Mbrships: Charter mbr., Can Accordion Tchrs. Assn.; Can. Dir., World Radio Missionary Fellowship. Hobbies: Golf. Address: 77 Moss Brook Cres., Scarborough, Ont. M1W 2W8, Canada.

DEAN, John Theodore, b. 25 June 1934, Perth, Aust. Violist. Educ: Dip. Mus., Melbourne Univ. Conserv.; MusB, Univ. of WA; pvte. studies w. Cecil Aronowitz, London. m.

Margot Hamilton Robertson, 2 d., 1 s. Career: Prin. violist, WA Symph. Orch., 1970-; Concerts, broadcast recitals for Aust. Broadcasting Commission; Interstate tours for Musica Viva Sc. as mbr. of Oriel String Quartette; Examiner, AMEB, 1976-. Mbrships: Aust. Soc. for Music Educ; Aust. Strg. Tchrs. Assn.; WA Music Tchrs. Assn. Hobbies: Skin Diving; Boating. Address: 71 Williams Rd., Nedland, Perth, WA 6009, Australia.

DEAN, Stafford Roderick, b. 20 June 1937, Kingswood, Surrey, UK., Operatic & Concert Bass. Educ: Opera Scholar, RCM. m. Carolyn Lambourne, 4 s. Debut: Zuniga, Carmen, Sadler's Wells Opera, 1964. Career: Prin. Bass, Sadler's Wells, 1964-70; Guest Artist, Convent Gdn., 1969-, Munich State Opera, Glyndebourne, Scottish Opera, Welsh Nat. Opera, Engl. Opera Grp.; has also appeared w. cos. in Hamburg, Prague, Berlin, Strasbourg, Bordeaux, Toulouse & Holland Fest.; concert apps. w. leading Brit. orchs., Stockholm, Brussels & Tanglewood (USA). Recordings. Hobbies: Tennis; Squash. Mgmt: Harrison Parrott Ltd, 22 Hillgate St., London W 8 7SR, UK.3.

DEAN, Talmage Whitman, b. 29 Jan. 1915, Russellville, Tenn., USA. Musician; Teacher; Composer; Administrator. Educ: BA, BM, Hardin-Simmons Univ., Abilene, Tex., 1940; MMus, Eastman Schl. of Music, Rochester, NY, 1941; PhD, USC, 1960. m. Frances Sibley, 3 d., 1 s. Career: Fac. Mbr., Hardin-Simmons Univ., 1941-43, 1946/56, 1946-56, Univ. of Tex., 1943-44: Lt., USNR, 1944-46; Dean. Schl. of Music, 1952-56; Chmn., Grad. Studies in Music, Southwestern Bapt. Sem., 1956-67; presently Dean Schl. of Music, Hardin-Simmons Univ.; Comp., Arr., Bapt. Radio & TV, 1957-63, Tex. Girls Choir, 1966- 67. Compositions: Bapt. Hour Choral Series: cantatas The Raising of Lazarus, organ & chorus, Proclaim The Word, brass & chorus, Pax Vobis, orch. & chorus; oratorio Behold The Glory of The Lamb orch. & chorus; over 50 short cantatas, anthems, & instrumental works. Author, Source Readings In The History Of Church Music, 1965. Contbr. to: Southwestern Musician; Southwestern Jrnl. of Theol.; Jrnl. of So. Bapt. Ch. Music. Mbr., Off., num. profl. & ch. orgs. Recip. num. hons. Hobbies: Hunting, Fishing. Address: Rt. 3, Box 313, Abilene, TX 79605, USA. 2,7.

DEAN, Winton Basil, b. 18 Mar. 1916, Birkenhead, UK. Author; Musicologist. Educ: MA, King's Coll., Cambridge, UK. m. Hon. Thaila Mary Shaw, 1 s., 1 d. Career: Ernest Bloch Prof. of Music, Univ. of Calif., Berkeley, 1965-66: Num. Broadcasts; Regent's Lectr., Univ. of Calif., Berkeley, 1977. Publs: incl: Bizet, 1948; Carmen, 1949; Introduction to the Music of Bizet, 1950 (3rd Ed. 1975); Franck, 1950: Handel's Dramatic Oratorios & Masques, 1959: Shakespeare & Opera, 1964; Georges Bizet, His Life & Work, 1965; Handel & the Opera Seria, 1969; Beethoven & Opera, 1971; The Rise of Romantic Opera, 1976; G. F. Handel: Three Ornamented Arias, 1976; Giulio Cesare in Egitto, 1977. Contbr. to var. profl jrnls. Mbrships: Music Panel, Arts Coun., 1957-60: Committee, Handel Opera Soc., 1955 - 60: VP, Coun., Royal Musical Assn., 1970-; Int. Musicological Soc. Recip., Hon. RAM, 1971; FBA, 1975. Hobbies: Shooting; Naval History. Address: Hambledon Hurst, Godalming, Surrey, UK. 1, 3, 2, 19.

DEANE, Basil, b. 27 May 1928, Bangor, N Ireland, Director of Music, Arts Council of Great Britain. Educ: BA, BMus, Queen's Univ., Belfast; MA, Manchester Univ.; MMus, Melbourne Univ.; PhD, Glasgow Univ.; hon. FRNCM. m. Norma Greig, 2s. Career: Prof. of Music, Manchester Univ. -1980; Dir. of Music, Arts Coun. of GB, 1980-. Publs: Roussel, 1962; Gherubini, 1964; Hoddinott, 1978. Contbr. to var. profl. jrnls. Hobbies: Chmbr. Music; History. Address: c/o The Arts Council, 105 Piccadilly, London, W1, UK. 1.

DEARNLEY, Christopher Hugh, b. 11 Feb. 1930, Wolverhampton, UK. Organist. Educ: MA, Worcester Coll., Oxford; BMus; FRCO. m. Bridget née Wateridge, 3 s., 1 d. Career: Asst. Organist, Salisbury Cathedral, 1954-57; Organist & Master of the Choristers, ibid., 1957-68; Organist, St. Paul's Cathedral, 1968-. Compositions: var. ch. music; arrangements & ods. of early ch. music. Recordings: EMI Great Cathedral Organ Series nos. 112 & 17; Organ Music From Salisbury Cathedral; num. choir discs. Publs: The Treasury of English Church Music, vol. 3; English Church Music, 1650-1750. Contbr. to var. ch. music jrnls. Mbrships: Pres. Int. Assn. of Organists, 1968-71; Chmn., Friends of Cathedral Music, 1971-; var. other ch. music socs. Hobbies: Sketching; Gardening. Address: 8B Amen Court, London EC4, UK.

DEARNLEY, Dorothy Alice, b. 30 Nov. 1914, Preston, Lancs., UK. Pianist; Organist; Folk Singer. Educ: Royal Manchester Col. of Music; ARCM; ALCM; Royal Schl. Ch. Music; London Acad. Music & Dramatic Art. 2 s. Career: Broadcasts, 1952-; Folk Singer, Liverpool Phil. Hall; Accomp.

to violinist & singers; BBC Documentary on own musical life, 1966; Small parts in plays on Granada, TV, 1970-; Concert tours (piano & organ) in Germany & Holland, 1972, 73 Comps: 7 Cheshire Folk Songs. Recordings: 15 Cheshire Folk Songs. Mbrships: ISM; Equity; Chester Br., Music Tchrs. Assn. Organists & Choirmasters Assn. RSCM. Hobbies: Gardening; Reading. Address: 11 North Dr., Heswall, Wirral L60 OBB, UK.

DEASEY, Michael Keith, b. 25 Jan. 1947, Sydney, Aust. Organist, Choirmaster & Conductor. Educ: Dip. Mus. Ed. NSW Conserv. of Music, 1964-67: RSCM, UK, 1969-71: FTCL; LRAM; ARCM; ARCO. Career: Asst. Organist, St. Andrews Cathedral, Sydney, 1967-69: Organist & Choirmaster, Selsdon Parish Ch., Surrey, UK, 1969-72: Organist & Master of Choristers St. Peter's Ch., Brockville, Ont., Can., 1973-; Dir., Brockville Choral Soc.; organ recitals, Aust., UK, Iceland, Can. & USA. Hons: 1st Prize, Ernest Truman Memorial Organ Contest, Sydney, 1967; W C Kent Prize for Organ Playing, RSCM, 1971. Hobbies: Swimming; Tennis; Skiing. Address: St. Peter's Church, 46 Park St., Brockville, Ont., Canada.

DEATHRIDGE, John William, b. 21 Oct. 1944, Birmingham, UK. Organist; Conductor; Musicologist. Educ: BA, MA, DPhil, London Coll., Oxford; FRCO. Career: concert activity & rsch., Munich, German Fed. Repub., 1972-; Dir. of Music, Pfarramt St. Wolfgant & Co-Ed., Richard-Wagner-Gesamtausgabe, Bavarian Acad. of Fine Arts. Publs: Wagner's Rienzi: a reappraisal based on a study of the sketches & drafts, 1977; Richard-Wagner-Werkverzeichnis (co-ed.), 1977. Contbr. to: Proceedings of Royal Musical Assn.; Music & Letters. Mbrships: Royal Musicalk Assn.; Gesellschaft für Musikforschung. Hobby: Cinema. Address: 8 Munich 22, Mannhardstr., 7, German Fed. Repub.

De·BARROS, Eudóxia, b. 18 Sept. 1937, Sao Paulo, Brazil. Concert Pianist; Teacher. Educ: Dip., Inst. Musical de Sao Paulo; Dip., Fest. at Salzburg, 1957; studies in Paris, USA, Brazil & Germany. Debut: aged 7, Sao Paulo. Career: apps. & tours in Brazil, USA & Mexico; Piano tchr., N Carolina Schl. of Arts, Winston, Salem, 1965-67; app. w. Orquestra Sinfonica Braileira, 1953. 17 recordings. Publs: Pianistic Technique. Contbr. to num. jrnls. Hons: 1st prize for soloist w. N Carolina Symph. Orch., 1966., Hobbies: Theatre; Concerts; Films. Address: Avenida Rebougas 1164, Ap. 16, 05402 Sao Paulo S P, Brazil.

DEBRAS, Louis G M, b. 30 Mar. 1938, Sint Niklaas, Belgium. Recording & Re-Recording mixer; Composer. Educ: Royal Flemish Conserv., Antwerp; Univ. of Ghent; Cologne Conserv., Germany; studied w. Karlheinz Stockhausen, Louis De Meester, Ton De Leeuw, Earl Brown, Daniel Sternfeld. m. 2 children. Career incls: Asst. of Rich Teitelbaum, Electronic music studio of York Univ., Toronto, Can. Compositions: Sequenza 1, flute, 2, oboe; Rotations, woodwind quarter; Studie 2, electronic work; Piece For Piano; 5 Little Pieces, piano; Sequenza 3, flute; Cantus Subtillis, oboe, Entelechie, orch.; Introspectrion 2, 3, orch.; electronic works Sound Structures, Apocatstase; Situations, piano; electronic work Cahier. Mbr: Belgian Comps. Assn. Hobby: Drawing. Address: 41 Bremstraat, 2700 St. Niklaas, Belgium.

de BREMAEKER, Angèle M, b. 3 Jan. 1893, St. Ulriks-Kapelle, Belgium. Poetess. m. Alfons van Frachen (dec.), 1s. Career: Author of num. poems set to music by prominent Belgian comps. incl. her son Victor van Frachen, who has written comps. on her poems for art songs, youth and folksongs, choral works a capella an accompaniment of piano & orch. Publs: Num. poems in editions of Music, daily & weekly papers & magazines. Mbrships: SABAM. Hons: Badge of Honour, Award of Honour, from Sabam; Ridder in de ordre van Koning Leopold II; Ridder in de Kroonordre. Hobbies: Reading; Studying; Painting; Cultivating Flowers. Address: Retreat St. Vincentius, Dorp 65, 9460 Aaigem, Belgium.

de BROMHEAD, Jerome Andrew, b. 2 Dec. 1945, Waterford, Eire. Composer. Educ: MA, Trinity Coll., Dublin. m. Dolores, 1s. Comps: Abstract Variations, for orch.; Danzostinato, for orch.; Blath in Aitinn, for choir; Iomramh, for choir; 2 str. quartets & var. other chmbr. works. Mbrships: Committee. Assn. of Irish Comps.; Music Assn. of Ireland; Royal Dublin Soc. Contbr. to Counterpoint. Hons: Feis Ceoil Comps. prize, 1975, '76: Seán O'Riada Memorial prize, 1976,'77; Dublin Symph. Orch. prize, 1978. Hobbies: Reading; Visiting Art Galleries; Theatre; Sailing. Address: Martello Cottage, Strand Rd., Killiney, Co. Dublin, Erie.

DECADT, Jean, b. 21 June 1914, Ypres, Belgium. Professor of Compositions; Director of Music Academy. Educ: Dips., Harmony, Counterpoint & Fugue, Royal Conserv., Ghent; Pvte. studies. m. Adeline Cromheecke, 2 d. Debut: Blankenberge.

Career: Prof. of Comp., Royal Conservatoir, Ghent; Dir., Acad. of Music, Harelbeke; Apps. in Ypres, Kortrijk, Antwerp & Ghent. Comps. incl: Trip for Woodwinds: Ballad on a Tree (soprano solo, flute, oboe & strings); Concerto No. 1 for alto saxophone & orch.; Canto Expressivo Molto Giuocanda for 4 saxophones. Num. recordings. Contbr. of articles to nat. & local press & profl. jrnls. Hons. incl: Koopal Prize of Belgian Govt., 1962; Kt., Order of Leopold, 1966; Kt., Order of Crown, 1967. Hpbbies: Paintings; Travel; Culture; Arts; Hist. Address: Pevernagestraat 89, B-8730 Harelbeke, W Vlaanderen, Belgium.

DE CESARE, Ruth, b. 2 July 1923, NYC, USA. University Professor, Composer. Educ: AB, Hunter Coll., NYC, 1943: MS, Queens Coll., ibid, 1960; PhD, Schl. of Educ., NY Univ., 1972; Mannes Schl of Music, 1936-41. M. Sam J. De Cesare (div.) 1 s. 1 d. Career: Tchr., Pub. Schls., NY, 1943, 1963-65; Tchr., NYC Bd. of Educ., 1966-69; Broadcaster, WPDQ, Jacksonville, Fla., 1944-45: Prod., educl. records, Bowmar, Calif., 1959-62: Tchr., Mills Coll. of Educ., NYC, 1960-62. Tchr., State Univ. of NY, Buffalo, 1962; Tchr., Adelphi Univ., NY, 1964-65; Prof., Ind. Univ. of Pa., 1979-. Publd. & Recorded Compositions: Latin Am. Game Songs; French Game Songs; Songs for the French Class; Songs for Italian, German, Spanish & Russian Classes; They Came Singing; Publd. Am. Tunes & Tales; Chula la Manana; Candu; El Rio; Dinah Oh; Lullay; My Horses Aint hungry; Piano Games. Contbr. to: Listen Mag.; Music Jrnl.; Music Educators Jrnl.; Am. Music Tchr.; NC, Pa. & Md. Music Educator; Piano Tchr. Chmn., Comm. for Music in Special Educ. Pa. Music Educators Assn. Phi Beta Kappa; Phi Delta Kappa. Recip., Cravath Fellowship, Juilliard Schl. of Music. NYC., 1942. Address: 545 Grandview Ave., Indiana, PA 15701, USA. 6,27.

DECHARIO, Tony Houston, b. 25 Sept. 1940, Girard, Kan., USA. Orchestra General Manager. Educ: BMus, Eastman Schl. of Music, Univ. of Rochester, 1962; MMus, ibid., 1963, Perfs.'s Cert. in Trombone, 1962. m. Mary Gill Roby, 1 s., 3 d. Career: 2nd Trombone, Kan. City Phil., 1963-64; 1st Trombone, Dallas Symph., 1964-65; 2nd Trombone, Rochester Phil., 1965-75; Gen. Mgr., ibid. Address: 199 Oak Ln., Rochester, NY 14610, USA.

DEČI, Josip, b. 1 July 1904, Stari Sivac, Yugoslavia. Composer. Educ: Grad., Fac. of Law, Univ. of Zagreb, 1931; studied under Vincent D'Indy. m. Anka Balen, 3 children. Debut: Paris, 1927. Comps. incl: Easter Egg (children's operetta), 1932; An Infant Prodigy (operetta), 1935; The Wedding of Mickey Mouse (children's operetta), 1937; Above the Clouds (musical comedy), 1960; A Story about a Golden Fish (puppet-play), 1974. Contbr. to Yugoslav & Dutch musical encys. Mbrships: Yugoslav & Croatian Comps. Assns. Hobby: Travel. Address: Solovljeva 5, 41000 Kagreb, Yugoslavia.

DECKER, Franz-Paul, b. 22 June 1923, Cologne, Germany. Conductor. Educ: State Inst. for Musical Educ.; Univ. of Cologne. m. Christa Terka, 2 d. Career: Cond., Cologne Opera, 1945; Municipal Dir. of Music, Krefeld, 1946; Prin. Cond., State Opera House, Wiesbaden, 1950; Permanent Dir., Wiesbaden Municipal Symph. Orch., 1953; Gen. Musick Dir., Bochum Orch., 1956-65; Chief Cond. & Artistic Dir., Rotterdam Phil., 1962-68: Music Dir. & Permanent Cond., Montreal Symph. Orch., 1967-; Prof. of Music in Res., Sir Geo. Wms. Univ., Montreal; Guest Cond. in all major music & orchl. works. Has recorded for D G G & EMI., Mbr: Rotary Club. Hons: Edgar Roquette Pinto Medal, Brazilian Govt., 1963; Herscheppend schep ik Medal, Netherlands, 1968; Bundesverdienstkreuz (Order of Merit), 1st Class. German Fed. Repub., 1971; D h.c., Concordia Univ., Montreal. Address: c/o Montreal Symph., Orch., Place des Arts, Montreal, PQ H2X 1Y9, Canada.

DECKER, Harold Augustus, b. 13 May 1914, Belleville, Kan., USA. Professor of Music. Educ: AB, MusM, & DMus, Morningside Coll. & Oberlin Conserv. of Music. m. Helene Crenshaw, 1 s., 1 d. Career: Hd. of Voice & Choral Depts., Wichita State Univ., Kan., 1944-57; Chmn., Choral Div., Univ. of Ill. Schl. of Music, 1957-; Vis. Prof., Univ. of Mich., Univ. of Southern Calif., Peabody Coll., & Oberlin Conserv. of Music; Dir. of state hon. choirs & choral workshops throughout USA. Mbrships: incl: Exec. Bd., Past Pres., Am Choral Dirs. Assn.; MENC. Publs: Choral Conducting - A Symposium, 1971. Contbr. to profl. jrnls. Hons. incl: Disting. Sev. Award, Am. Choral Dirs. Assn., 1975. Hobbies incl: Travel. Address: 1204 S Vine St., Urbana, IL 61801, USA. 2,8.

DECSÉNYI, Janos, b. 24 Mar. 1927, Budapest, Hungary. Composer. Educ: Comp. Dip., Acad. of Music Budapest. m. Eva Porász, 1 d. Career: Contbr. to the Music Dept. of the Hungarian Radio, 1951- & currently Acting. Mgr. of the

Symphonic & Dramatic Sec.; Ldr., Studio for Electronic Music of the Hungarian Radio, 1976-. Compositions: Stage Work: An Absurd Story, ballet, 1962 MS. Orchestral works: Five Csontváry Paintings, 1967; Melodia Hominis - for Chamber Orch., 1969; Thoughts - Tryptic Thoughts - by Day by Night, for Symph. Orch., 1971; The Plays of Thought, Cantata for Soprano Solo & Chamber Orch., 1972; Commentaries to Marc Aurel - for String Orch., 1973; Variations for Piano & Full Orch., 1976; Concerto boemo, 1976; Concerto grosso-per orch. camera, 1978, Choral Works: Three Children's Choruses, 1961; Three Elegies on Poems by Quasimodo, 1962 MS; New Year's Window, on Poems by Gyula Illyés, 1968 MS. Chamber Music: Metamorfosi per Soprano e Pianoforte, 1964 MS; Shakespeare's Monologues, for Bass Baritone Solo & Piano, 1968 MS Mbr., Assn. of Hungarian Musicians. Hons: Prize Winner, Vercelli competitions of Comps., 1956. Var. hobbies. Address: VII Wesselényi u. 65, 1077 Budapest, Hungary.

DEDEN, Otto, b. 19 Nov. 1925, Amsterdam, Netherlands, Composer; Conductor; Organist & Choirmaster. Educ: High Schl. of Ch. Music, Utrecht; studied comp. w. Henk Badings. m., S A M van Dijk, 4 children. Career: Apps. in Ch. servs. on Radio & TV; Choral concerts w. var. male, female & mixed choirs. Comps: 25 Mases; 50 Motets; Te Deum; Hymns, etc; Ballads; Oratorios; arrs. of Folk songs: (commissioins) Mysteria; Kain. Recordng: Raamconcerto, 1972. Hons: Ballade v.d Bezemsteel (Male voices) Maastricht, 2958. Hobby: Painting. Address: Polluxhof 16, Dordrecht, The Netherlands.

DEERING, Richard Jon, b. 15 July 1947, London, UK. Concert Pianist; Accompanist; Lecture-Recitalist; Adjudicator. Educ: GSM; TCL; FTCL; GTCL; LRAM; ARCM. m. Denise Heath, 1 s., 1 d. Debut: Wigmore Hall, London, 1973. Career: Performer & Adjudicator, UK, Asia, Australsia, Ctrl. & S Am., Caribbean, Iceland, Netherlands; Num. premieres of works by mostly British Comps. Recordings: English Piano Music; Elizabeth Lutyens 70th Birthday Recital; Beatles Concerto; Favourite Encores. Mbrships: ISM; Fedn. Brit. Music Fests.; RPS. Hobbies: Cricket; Walking; Public Debates. Mgmt: Ruth Ticher, 91 Woodville Rd., Ham, Richmond, Surrey, UK. Address: 41 Warwick Rd., Wanstead, London E11 2DZ, UK.

DEFFAYET, Daniel, b. 23 May 1922, Paris, France. Professor of Saxophone. Educ: Conservatoire National Superieur de Musique (violin & saxophone). m. Daniele Le Gac, 1 s, 1 d. Career: Int. soloist; Fndn. Mbr., Quatuor de Saxophones D Deffayet; Prof. of Saxophone, Conservatoire National Superieur de Musique, Paris. Num recordings. Mbrships: Pres., L'Association des Saxophonistes Francais. Address: 13 Bis Avenue Clodoald, Saint Cloud, 92210, France.

DE FILIPPI, Amedeo, b. 20 Feb. 1900. Ariano, Italy. Composer; Pianist; Conductor. Educ: Juilliard Grad. Schl. of Music.m. Della Posner, 1 s., 1 d. Career: Composer; Arranger & Orchestrator, Pathe Films, Judson Radio Prog. Co., Victor Phonograph Co., var. theatres & publrs., Staff mbr., CBS Inc., 1930-; Work w. Josef Pasternack, Eugene Ormandy, howard Barlow, Andre Kostelanetz, Sophie Braslau, Feodor Chiliapine, Lawrence Tibett, Llly Pons, Marjorle Lawrence, Helen Jepsen, Jascha Heifetz, Albert Spaulding; Orchestrator, ballets for Ballet Russe & Ballet Theatre; Works perf. by leading smph. orchs. Compositions incl: Orch. works, Wuite, Concerto for Orch., Symph., Twelfth Night Overture, Medieval Court Dances, Five Arabian Songs; Ballets, Les Sylphides, Carnaval, Jardins aux Lilas; Works for string orch., Diversioins, Serenade, Music for Recreation & Provencal Airs; Choral music; chmbr. music; Stage & film music. Num. recordings. Mbrships: Bohemians; ASCAP; Am. Music Ctr.; Nat. Assn. Am. Composers & Conds. Sonata for Viola & Piano performed on Contemporary Am. Music Festival, Princeton, 1936., Address: 4101 Wilkinson Ave., N. Hollywood, CA 91604, USA. 3,6,14.

deFRANCESCO, Amada Santos-Ocampo, b. 23 June 1927, Manila, Philippines. Pianist-Composer; Conductor. Educ: Music Tchr. Cert., St. Paul's Coll., Manila; BMus., Centro Escolar Univ., Manila; MMus, DePauw Univ., Greencastle, Ind., USA; post-grad. work, Ind. Univ. Schl. of Music, Bloomington. m. Rio deFrancesco. Debut: St. Paul's Coll. & Metrop. Theatre, Manila, Philippines. Career incls: TV & radio apps. in Manila; app. at Philamlife Auditorium, Manila, DePauw Univ. Recital Hall, Ind. Univ. Schl. of Music Recital Hall, etc.; gives Lecture-Recitals & Compositions Recitals; works have been played by well-known perfs. in the Philippines & USA; works have been taped for uses in free exercise gymnasts. Compositions incl: orchestral works, chmbr. music, vocal music, piano pieces & music for modern dance. Mbrships: League of Filipino Composers; AAUP; Pa. State Assn. for Hlth., Phys. Educ. & Recreation; Music Guild of State Coll.; Athletic Advsry. Bd. & Fac. Club, Pa. State Univ., FILSCAP; Cath. Soc. of Philippines; Pi Kappa Lambda. Recip. of 1st Prize, Piano Competition, 1936. Hobbies: Collecting

Clippings; Coins; Stamps; Cooking; Swimming; Playing Badminton & Table Tennis. Address: 1131-H, W Aaron Dr., State Coll., PA 16801, USA.

DE FRANK, Vincent, b. 18 June 1915, LI, NY, USA Conductor (Cellist). Educ: violin study w. Geo. Frenz, 1920-33: violoncello study w. Percy Such, 1933-37, Georges Miquelle, 1937-40; Juilliard Schl. of Music (cond. w. Albert Stoessel), 1934-35: Tchng. Fellowship (Cello), Ind. Univ., 1950-52. m. Jean Marie Martin, 2 s. Career: Fndr. & Cond., Memphis Symph., 1952-; Guest Cond., Memphis Opera Theatre, Memphis Ballet Soc.; Orchs in Nashville Tenn., Quincy, Ill., Jacson, Miss.; All-State Orch., Sewanee Summer Music Ctr., etc. Mbrships: Local 802 & 71, Am. Fedn. Musicians; Memphis Music, Inc; Am. Symph. Orch. League, etc. Hons: ASCAP Award, 1967; Memphis Symph. Award, 1973; Hon. Doct. of Music Degree, Southwestern Univ., Memphis, 1974. Hobbies: Fishing; Hunting. Address: 4748 Shady Grove Road, Memphis, TN 38117, USA. 2,7.

DE FREITAS, Frederico, b. 15 Nov. 1902, Lisbon, Portugal. Composer; Conductor. Educ: Piano & Comp. degree; studied w. Florent Schmitt, W. Mengelberg & Vittorio Gui. m. Consuelo Fernandez De Freitas, 1 d. Debut: in Lisbon. Career: Cond., Nat. Broadcasting Co., 1935-76. Comps. incl: Symphs., Symph. Poem, Mass, Operas, Choral & Vocal Music, Chmbr. Music & Piano Works; Transcriptions of Bach, Chaconne & piano part of M. de Flla's 7 canciones populares, both for orch.; Musical Consultant, Enciclopedia Verbo; Music Critic for newspaper, Novidades. num recordings. Mbrships: Pres., Sociedade Portuguesa de Autores; Hon. Mbr., Juventude Musical Portuguesa. Hons: 1st prize in Comp., Nat. Conserv., Lisbon; Domingos Bontempo, Nat. Broadcasting Co.; Carlos Seixas of SNJ; Comendador da Orden de Santiago da Espada; Red Cross. Address: Ave. E.U. America 122 4 E, 1700 Lisbon, Portugal.

DE FROMENT, Louis Georges Francois, b. 5 Dec. 1921, Toulouse, France. Conductor. Educ: Paris Conserv.; Toulouse Conserv. m. Jacueline Charles, 1 d. Career: Cond., ORTF Orch., Paris, 1949; Musical Dir., Casinos, Cannes & Deauville, until 1956; Artistic Advsr., Musical Dir., Vichy Casino, until 1969; Cond., Comic Opera Orch., Paris; Permanent Cond., Radio-Télé-Luxembourg Orch., 1958-. Recordings: 160 records, Decca, Vox, EMI, CBS. Hons. incl: Off. w. Crown, Civil & Military Order of Adolphe de Nassau, Luxembourg; Off., Order of the Crown, Belgium; Kt., Order of Merit, France. Hobby: Mathbox Collection. Mgmt: De Valmaléte, Paris. Address: 138 2ne A Unden, Résidence Debussy, Luxembourt, Grand Duche Luxembourg.

DE GABARAIN, Marina, b. 1928, San Sebastian, Spain. Deceased. Mezzo soprano-contralto. Educ: Milan & Paris. m. Gian-Carlo Villa, 1 d. Career; perfs. at num. opera houses incl. Barcelona & Covent Garden; Sung the Premier of Rossini's Cenerentola at Edinburgh & Glyndebourne fests.; roles include Bizet's Carmen, Verdi's Amneris in Aida, Strawinsky's Baba the Turk in the Rake's Progress, Acuzena in Il Trovatore, Preciosilla in La Forza del Destino, L'Italiana in Algiers, Premier of Castro's 'Blood Wedding' & Musorsky's Kovanchina at the Teatro Colon in Buenos Aires, Princes Iboly in Verdi's Don Carlos, Cenerentola's Premier at Monaco, Mascagri's Santurza in Cavalleria Rusticana; Roaina in Rossini's Il Barbiere de Seville, Falla's El Amor Brujo (Love the Magician) with Antonio & under L. Stowkowsky, Barbirolli, Ansermet, L. Maazel, Ataulfo Argenta; Repertory in concerts: German Lieder, French, Italian & Spanish Songs performed at the main Theatres such as Glyndebourne several times, Edinburgh Festival 3 times, Berlin Opera House; Opened the Season at the Theatre Finice in Venize w. Cenerentola de Rossini; Theatro Colon in Buenos Aires, Opera Houses in Barcelona (Theatro del Liceo), Rome, Naples, & sung & worked dedicately to establish opera in S Africa singing w. enormous success Carmen, Il Trovatore, concerts, etc. Mgmt: Ibbs & Tillett Ltd., 122-24 Wigmore St., London W1, UK. Address: c/o Mgmt.

DEGEN, Helmut, b. 14 Jan. 1911, Aglasterhausen, Germany. Composer: Professor of Composition of Theory. Educ: Music High Schl., Cologne, 1930-32: High Schl. for Music, 1932-33: Univ. of Bon, 1933-36. M. Maria Höfer, 2c. Career: as comp. in Germany & other countries. Comps: works for large orch., choir, chmbr. music inclng. str. quartet, piano trio & wind quintet; instrumental music for organ, cello, viola, violin, flute, etc. Contbr. to profl. jrnls. mbr. Deutscher Komponistenverband, Berlin. Hobby: study of the world's mountains. Address: Postfach 14, 7218 Trossingen, German Fed. Repub.

DE GOEDE, Nicolaas A J, b. 1 Apr. 1915, Amsterdam, Netherlands. Roman Catholic Priest. Educ: MA, Pontifical Inst. for Ch. Music, Rome, 1948; Doct., 1952. Career: Mbr.,

Congregation of the Priests of the Sacred Heart; Ldr. of Ch. Music & Prof. of Liturgy, Theol. House, Nijmengen; Tchr., Conservs., Tilburg, Rotterdam & Arnhem, also at Netherlands Inst. of Roman Cath. Ch. Music, Utrecht. Comps: var. pieces of ch. music. Recording: Proprius 7730, Stockholm. Publs: The Utretch Prosarium, 1965. Contbr. to: Ency. Catholica; Ency. van het Christendom; Gregoriusblad; etc. Mbrships. incl: Exec., Netherlands St. Gregory Soc., Hertogenbosch; ITR; KDOV. Address: Kerkstreaat 65, Nijmegen 3, The Netherlands.

deGRAAF, Gerard Albert Cornelis, b. 4 Feb. 1928, Amsterdam, Netherlands. Builder of Organs & Harpsichords. Educ: Orgelbaumeister. m. Aurora Manuela Nuez, 1 s., 1 d. Career: began own firm, Amsterdam, 1958, moving to Spain in 1970; has build approx. 50 new organs & 20 harpsichords, Netherlands, Belgium, German, Spain & USA; restorer of old Spanish organs. Publs: Literature on the Organ, 1957. Contbr. to: ISO - Information (ed.); Organ Year Book. Mbr., Int. Soc. of Organ Builders (ISO). Address: Mayor 49, La Almunia, Spain.

DEGRADA, Francesco, b. 23 May 1940, Miloan, Italy. Teacher of History of Music. Educ: Doct., Modern Letters, Univ. of Milan, 1964; Dip., Piano, G Verdi Conserv., Milan, 1961; Dip., Comp., ibid, 1965. m. Anna Pavan, 1 child. Career: Tchr., hist. of music, G Verdi Conserv., Milan, Fac. of letters, State Univ., Milan. Compositions: Editions of works by Antonio Vivaldi, Nicolò Porpora, F Durante, D Scarlatti, G B Pergolesi, J A Hasse, D Sarro, N Jommelli, etc. Recordings: w. Arcophon & Harmonia Mundi (France), A Scarlatti, Le Dodici sinfonie di concerto gross, (Text rev. & harpsichord); A Stradella, Cantage e Arie, (Text rev. & Harpsichord); G B Pergolesi, Tutte le opere strumentali, (Text rev. & harpsichord); G Carissimi, Dives Malus, (harpsichord & organ). Publs: Num. studies about Renaissance, Broque & Comtemp. Music, (in, Die Musik in Geschichte & Gegenwart, Vol. XV, 1973). Contbr. to: Rivista Italiana di Musicol.; Chigiana; Analecta Musicol.; Nuova Rivista Musicale Italiana; Distoteca, etc. Mbrships: Int. Musicol Soc.; Italian Musicol. Soc. Assn. Int. Bibliothèques Musicales; Soc. Int., Antonio Vivaldi. Hobby: Reading Classics. Address: Via De Amicis 33, 20123 Milan, Italy.

DE GRAY, Julian, b. 15 July 1905, Harrisburg, Pa., USA. Pianist; Harpsichordist; Teacher; Lecturer. Educ: AB, Columbia Univ., NY; studied w. Jean Hure, Lazare Levy, Tobias Matthay. m. Margaret Patterson. Debut: London, Wigmore Hall, 1929; NYC, Town Hall, 1930. Career: Concerts, Holland, Germany, Austria, 1931, USA, 1939-47: Inaugurated Cuban Branch, ISCM w. 2 Concerts of contemp. music, 1931; Prof. of Piano, Univ. of Miami, Fla., 1928-31, Bennington Coll., 1932-70, ret'd War, State Dept. Service, 1942-45; Guest Prof., Univ. of Minn., 1950-51; Pvte. Coach, NYC, 1932-. Mbr. Am Matthay Assn. Recip. Chappell Gold Medal, Matthay Pinoforte Schl., London, UK, 1928., Hobbies: Tennis; Skiing. Address: Town Hill Rd., Warren, CT 06754, USA.

DE GROOT, Cor, b. 7 July 1914, Amsterdam, Netherlands. Composer; Conductor; Pianist. Educ: Conservatorium Amsterdam. m. C De Haan, 1 s. Career: has made concert tours throughout the world. Comps. incl: works for orch., concertos, chmbr. music, songs, film & TV music. Has made about 40 LPs. Contbr. to var. publs. Mbrships. incl: Int. Conds. Course, Dutch Radio Broadcast; Int. S Rachmaninoff Soc.; Int. R Caradesus Soc. Recip. 1st Prize, piano competition, Vienna, 1936. Hobbies: Composing; Playing; Reading. Address: Laren (N H), Netherlands.

DE GROOTE, Andre, b. 28 Mar. 1940, Brussels, Belgium. Pianist. Educ: St. John's Coll., Johannesburg, S Africa; Conservatoire Royal, Brussels; Chapelle Muscale Reine Elisabeth. Debut: Johannesburg, S Africa, 1955; London, UK, 1973. Career: Concerts, TV & Radio apps. in S Africa, W Germany, Belgium, UK, USSR, Holland, Italy, France, Spain, Portugal, Brazil, Czechoslavakia, Yugoslavia & Iran. Recordings: Schumann, Sonata Op. 11 & Fanrasiestucke Op 111. Hons. incl: Prize, Tchaikowsky Competition, Moscow, 1966; Prize Queen Elisabeth Competition, Brussels, 1968; Prize, Int. Competition, Munich, 1970. Mgmt: Liesl Stary, Flat 2, 2 Mandeville Pl., London W1M 5LA, UK. Address: 100 Rue du Culot, B-6322 Mellery, Belgium.

DE HEER, Hans, b. 3 Apr. 1927, Klundert, Netherlands. Mathematician; Computer Scientist; Composer; Pianist. Educ: PhD, Maths.; Piano (Staatsexamen Dip.) Comp. m. Anne Jurriaanse, 2 children. Career: Sonatine for flute & guitar performed in Carnegie Hall & Lincoln Ctr., NY, USA; Concerto for guitar & string orch. broadcast from tape recordings by Durch & Belgian Radio; Etudes, solo guitar; 3 Sonatas, solo guitar; 3 Sonatinas, flute & guitar; Trio, flute, guitar & viola; 7 Preludes, solo guitar. Hons: Nat. Concours of Comp.of Netherlands for Chmbr. Music, 1967. Address: Badhuisweg 6-B, The Hague, The Netherlands.

DE HEN, Ferdinand Joseph, b. 16 Feb. 1933, Deurne, Belgium. Music Educator. Educ: Lic. Pol. & Diplomatic Scis.; Lic. Col. & Admnstrv. Scis.; Lic. in African linguistics; PhD. m. Rita E. L Goegebeur 1d. Career: num. educl. broadcasts (radio & TV) in low.land countries; Sci. Collaborator, Instrumental Mus., Brussels, 8 yrs.; Prof., Musicol., Univ. of Ghent, Hist. of Music, Chapelle Musicale Reine Elisabeth. Publs. incl: Beitrag zur Kenntnis der Musikinstrumente aus Belgisch Kongo & Ruanda-Urundi, 1960; Les Instruments de Musique dans l'Art & l'Histoire (w. R Bragard), 1967-71. Contbr. to: Gaplin Soc. Jrnl.; Gamma; Vlaams Muziektijdscjroft; Revue de Musicol. Belge; Current Anthropol.; MAN. Mbrships: German Soc. for Music Rsch.; Belgian Musicol. Soc.; Fellow, Royal Anthropol. Inst. Hobbies: Dogs; Horses. Address: Ronsen Heirweg 32, B-9700 Oudenaarde, Belgium.

DEHLAVI, Hosein, b. 29 Sept. 1927, Teheran, Iran. Composer. Educ: Dip., Accounting High Schl.; BS in Music (Comp.). m. Sousan Aslani, 3 children. Career: Dpty. Mgr., Educl. Dept., Fine Arts Min.; 135 Concerts in var. venues; Music for 3 documentary films; 11& TV progs., etc; Dir., Iran Nat. Conserv., 1962-71. Comps. incl: 3 published pieces; 40 works recorded on tape; (to be recorded) Bijan & Manije (ballet suite); Sabokböl (for Iranian orch.). Publs: Method of Tombak (Iranian instrument); Songs for Children. Contbr. to Iranian Nat. Music Mag. Mbr., Musicol. Inst., Iran (connected w. Fine Arte Min.). Hons: 4 Medals from the Shahinshah. Hobby: Mountain Climbing. Address: Ave. Eisenhower, Behdoudi Str., Line Nakhost 146, Teheran 14, Iran.

DEHNERT, Edmund John, b. 15 Feb. 1931, Chgo., Ill, USA. Musicologist; Composer; Pianist. Educ: BA, St. Mary of the Lake Univ., Ill., 1952; BMus, 1955, MMus, 1956, De Paul Univ., Chgo.; PhD, Univ. o Chgo., 1963. M. Donna Marie Wroblewski Dehnert, 3s., 1d. Career: incls: Pianist-Lectr., Pub. Broadcasting System, Chgo., 1967-; Rsch. & Scriptwriter, WTTW & WXXW TV stns., Chgo., 1969; radio broadcasts; Fellow, Nat. Humanities Inst., Univ. of Chgo., 1976-77. Comps: For the Dead Children of Auschwitz, 1975; Polonaise: Krakow, 1974, for piano, 1975; Pentatonic Sketches for Orch., 1975-76. Publs: Polish Music: The Spirit that Never Dies (co-author), 1975. Contbr. to musicol. jrnls. Mbrships: Am. Soc. of Univ. Comps.; Am. Musicol. Soc. Hons. incl: State of Ill. Res. Comps. Competition for Orchl. Work, 1975. Hobbies: Chess; Bridge. Address: 1121 Harvard Terrace, Evanston, IL, 60202, USA. 4,8,11,12,23,28.

DEIHL, Ned Charles, b. 23 July 1931, Hamilton, Ohio, USA. Professor; Director of Bands. Educ: BMus. Ed., Ind. Univ., Bloomington, 1954; MMus, Univ. of Mich., Ann Arbor, 1957; DEd, Pa. State Univ., 1963. m. Janette Martin Deihl, 2s., 1d. Career: Prof. & Dir. of Bands, Pa. State Univ.; guest cond. & adjudicator; adjudicator & cons. to Am. Schl. Bands in Mexico, Spain & Italy. Recordings: 2 of Penn State Blue Band. Publs: num. articles in profl. jrnls.; reports of funded rsch. projects; panelist at profl. meetings. Contbr. to: Jrnl. of Rsch. in Music Educ.; Music Jrnl.; Instrumentalist; Music Educators Jrnl.; Coun. for Rsch. in Music Educ. Mbrships: Am Bandmaster Assn., 1972; Pres., E Div., Coll. Band Dirs. Nat. Assn.; 1970; Pi Kappa Lambda; hon. life mbr., Phi Mu Alpha Sinfonia. recip. Mansfield (Ohio) Mastersingers Music Scholarship, 1951. Address: 217 Chambers Bldg., Pa. State Univ., Univ. Park, PA 16802, USA.

de JONG, Marinus, b. 14 Aug. 1891, Oosterhout N. Br., Netherlands, Composer, Piano Virtuoso. Educ: Dips. of Piano Counterpoint & Figue, Royal Flemish Conserv., Antwerp. m. Jeanne Corthals. Career: sev. Concert Tours of USA after WWI; concerts in Antwerp, Brussels, Berlin; Prof. of Piano, Counterpoint & Fugue, Lemmensinstituut, 1926; same at Royal Flemish Conserv., 1932. Compositions: var works for all instruments; major works incl. Operas, Oratorios, Symphs. & Chamber Music, Publs: Classic Harmonie in 6 parts, 1950 Mbrships: SABAM. Hons: recip. sev. musical prizes; Chevalier, Off., Royal Crown; idem., Order of King Leopold; Off. & Commander, Order of St. Gregoire le Grand. Hobby: Literature. Address: Weymouthlaan 14,2080 Kapellen, Belgium.

DE JONG, Willem Coenraad, b. 4 July 1908, Leiden, Netherlands. Minister of Religion (Ret'd); Cellist. Educ: Divinity & Musicol., State Univ., Utrecht (w. Prof. A A Smijers), 1929-34. Career: Cond., Utrecht Univ. Student Orch., 1930-34 & 1953; Min., Protestant Ch., Dutch E Indies (now Indonesia), 1935-50: Cond. Handel's Oratorio, The Triumph of Time & Truth, 1st perf. in Holland; Ed., Nieuwe Rotterdamsche Courant, Rotterdam, 1952-70: now devoted to musicol., specializing in the Baroque period &, since 1960, Handel in particular. Contbr. to: Mens en Melodie; Ouverture & other periodicals; Oosthoek's Algemene Ency. Address: 21 Van Beverningkstraat, The Hague-2013, Netherlands.

DEKANY, Bela, b. 22 Apr. 1928, Budapest, Hungary. Violinist. Educ: Franz Liszt Acad. Music, Budapest; Acad. Music, Vienna. m. Dorothy Browning, 1 s., 1 d. Debut: Budapest, 1947. Career: Recitals, Broadcasts as Soloist w. Orchs., Hungary, Austria, Switz., Aust. & UK; Formed Dekany String Quartet, Netherlands, 1960; Ldr., BBC Symph. Orch., London, UK, 1969-. Recordings: Var. w. Dekany String Quartet; Haydn String Quartets. Hobbies: Reading; Table Tennis; Walking. Address: 68 Woodside Ave., London N6, UK.

DEKKER, Gerard H Chr., b. 26 Dec. 1931, Utrecht, Netherland. Organist; Harpsichordist. Educ: Laureate, Organ, Choir Direction, Dutch Inst. of Cath. Ch. Music, Utrecht, 1956; Piano Dip., Brabants Conserv., Tiburg, 1959; Dip Theory, ibid, 1962; Solo Harpsichord Dip., Amsterdam Conserv., 1968. m. Cornelia J Dix, 2 c. Debut: Organ, KRO Radio Hilversum, 1955: Harpsichord, ibid, 1966. Career: Num. Radio, TV Concert, Fest. Perfs., Holland, Belgium, UK, Germany; Harpsichordist, Amsterdam Sinfonietta; & Ensemble Boismortier; Harpsichord lectr., Brabants Conserv., Tilburg, 1959-; Dept. Hd., ibid, 1972-. Recordings: Harpsichordist, Organist, Pachelbel, Magnificant-Fugues, Bach, Organ Works. Contbr. to: Mans & Melodie; Het Orgbel. Mgmt: Nederlands Impresariaat, Van Breestraat 77 Amsterdam, The Netherlands. Mbrships: Soc. of Dutch Musicians; Bach Soc.; KDOV; Soc. of Lectrs. aan van rijkswege erkende in stellingen voor, Muziekvakonderwijs, KNTV. Address: 10 Apennijnenlaan, Son, NB 4563, Netherlands.

DE LACOUR, Marcelle, b. 6 Nov. 1896, Besancon, Doubs, France. Harpsichordist; Honorary Professor. Educ: Studied Harpsichord w. Wanda Landowska. Career: Solo Harpsichordist, num. major fests., concerts thru'out Europe; Num. broadcasts for ORTF, BBC, Swiss Radio etc.; Transcriped for harpsichord num. 17 O 18 century music textbooks; Prof., Harpsichord (on creation of special class), Conserv. Nat. Sup. de Musique, Paris. Recordings w. Pathé Marconi. Mbr., French Musicol. Soc. Hons: More than 70 music writers have dedicated their work to her; Chevalier de Legion d'Honneur; Palmes Academiques, Cmndr. Nichan Iftikar, Tunisia, Address: 62 Boulevard Clincy, Paris 18 ème, France.

de la FUENTE, Gita, b. 4 Sept. 1921, London, UK. Singer. Educ: Acad. of Music, Marseille, France; GSM, London; studied w. Dino Gorgioli & Joseph Hyslop, London, Maestro Raffaele Tenagilia, Milan, Italy. m. Mortimer Fuber. Debut: Wigmore Hall, London. Career: Prin., Soprano, Carl Rosa Opera Co., Sadlers Wells Opera Co., Covent Gdn. Opera Co.; Guest Artist, Dutch Nat. Opera; recitals & concerts throughout UK, Switz., Greece; num. BBC broadcasts, 1948-; TV broadcasts, Malta, 10(970. Contbr. to Lady (mag.). Mbrships: ISM; Equity; Soc. Int. des Arts et Lettres, Switz. Hons. incl: Soprano Prize; Opera Prize. Hobbies: Cooking; Writing. Address: Castelnau, St. Mary St., Naxxav, Malta, e.

DELAGE, Roger, b. 4 1922, Vierzon, France. Professor of Chamber Music & Musical History. Educ: Nat. Sup. Conserv. of Music, Dip., Choral Dir., studies of harmony. m. Micheline Ansaloni, 4 c. Career: Cond.; Collegium Musicum, Strasbourg, ORTF & var. TV progs.; Num. conferences; Prof., Chamber Music & Music Hist., Nat. Conserv., Strasbourg Region. Compositions: Scherzo, violincello & piano; Pieces for piano, melodies & choir works; Fisch-Ton-Kan, (orchestration). Recordings: Migot, symph. for orch. of strings; Oratorio de Noel et Motet in Convertendo, Campra; Symphonic Périodique no 6, Ignance Pleyel. Publs: Emmanuel Chabrier in Histoire de la Musique, 1963; Correspondance inédite entre E Chabrier et F Mohl, Revue de Musicol., 1963: Emmanuel Chabrier est amil impressionnistes, L'Oeil, 1963; Emmanuel Chabrier en Espagne, (w. F Durif), Revue de Musicol., 1970; Fred Barlow, Marie Jaell, Charles Koechlin, La Musique en Alsace, 1970. Contbr. to: Musica; Ency. Universalis; Cahiers Alsaciens d'Archéologie, d'Art et d'Histoire. Mbrships: Cttee. mbr., AJAM; French Musicol Soc. Hobby: Tennis. Address: 6 Rue Geiler, 87000 Strasbourg, France.

DELANIAN, Zorick, b. Tauris, Iran. Violinist (Amateur). Educ: Am. Coll. of Tehran; Cert. of Proficiency in Engl., Cambridge, UK; pvte. study of violin w. Serge Houtcieff. m. Marion English, 1 s. Debut: Iran, 1929. Career: Num. pub. & pvte. recitals in Iran, 1931-; num. apps. (solo, trio, quartet), Classical Hour prog., Iranian TV & Radio, some pub. perfs. abroad, Ldr., Tehran Chamber Music Ensemble, 1976. Contbr. of articles on musical topics to local press. Mbrships: Hons. Mbr., Tehran Phil. Soc.; Tehran Club; Wellington Club, London, UK. Hon: MBE. Hobbies: Philately; Numismatics; Photography; Tegestology; Table Tennis; Snooker; Bridge; Chess. Address: c/o Tehran Club, Tehran Iran.

DELANO, Jack, b. 1 Aug. 1914, Kiev, USSR. Violinist. Educ: Dip., Pa. Acad. of Fine Arts; Settlement Music Schl., Phila., Pa.

m. Irene Delano, 1 s., 1 d. Comps. incl: La Bruja de Loiza, ballet suite (recorded); Sonata for Viola & Piano (recorded); 7 Duos in Canon Form (recorded); songs; choral, chmbr. & orch. works; arrs. & film music. Mbrships: ASCAP; Musical Soc. of Puerto Rico. Hons. incl: Puerto Rico Atheneum Prize (Comp.), 1959, 67 & 69; Prize, Inst. of Puerto Rican Culture, 1967. Hobbies: Photography; Drawing; Painting. Address: RFD 2, Box 8-BB, Rio Piedras, Puerto Rico 00982, USA.

DELAPIERRE, André William, b. 20 Jan. 1921, Geneva, Switz. Pianist; Composer; Piano Teacher. Educ: studied piano w. Hermann Klug & Alfred Cortot; Dip., SMPV, Zurich, Switz. m. Franccoise Coulon, 1 s. Career: Pianist, Radio Basle. Mbrships: Soc. of Swiss Musicians; Swiss Soc. of Musical Pedagogy; Soc. of Frederick Chopin, Warsaw. Recip. 1st Prize, Int. Competition, Vercelli, Italy, 1950; Dip.of Merit, Vercelli, 1952. Hobbies: collecting 1st eds. of books & music scores, antiques & musical manuscripts; Animals; Bicycle. Address: Schillerstr. 2, 4053 Basle, Switzerland.

DE LA PORTE, Elizabeth, b. 15 Sept. 1941, Johannesburg, South Africa. Harpsichordist. Educ: Vienna Acad. of Music; RCM, London; QPLM; UTLM (S Africa); ARCM (London). m. Paul Dawson-Bowling, 1 s. St. John's Smith Square & Purcell Room, London, 1972. Career: Solo Apps. & Broadcasts in Switzerland, Germany, Austria & S Africa; Apps. on BBC TV incl: Music from the Great Houses, 1974; Staff, RCM Jr. Dept., 1964-; Harpsichord Tutor, Morley Coll., London, 1967-74. Recordings incl: The Elizabethan de la Porte Collection; Bach French Overture, Chromatic Fantasy & Fugue & Italian Concerto. Hons. incl: Mozart Prize, RCM, 1965. Hobbies: Travel; Reading; Cooking; Family. Mgmt: Helen Jennings Concert Agcy., London, UK. Address: 87 Quentin Rd., London, SE13 5DG, UK. 3, 27.

DE LARROCHA, Alicia, b. 23 May 1923, Barcelona, Spain. Concert Pianist. Educ: studied w. Mas. Serracant, R Lamonte de Grignon, J Zamacois, Frank Marshall, m. Juan Torra, 1 s., 1 d. Debut: Barcelona, Spain at age 4. Career: Solo recitals & concerts w. major orchs. in Europe, USA, Can., Ctrl. & S Am., S Africa, New Zealand, Australia, Japan. Recordings: Hispavox, CBS, EMI, Decca. Mbrships: Dir., Academia Marshall, Barcelona; Bd. of Dirs., Música en Compostela; Pres., Int. Piano Lib. Hons: Harriet Cohen Int Music Award, 1956; Paderewski Memorial Medal, 1961; Grand Prix du Disque Academie Charles Cros, 1960; Edison Award, 1968; 1st Gold Medal Merito a la Vocacion, 1972; Decorated Spanish Orders of Civil Merit, 1962, and Isabel La Catolica, 1972; Grand Prix du Disque, Academie Charles Cros, 1974; Grammy Award, 1974; Musician of the Year, (USA), 1978; Edison Award (Amsterdam), 1978. Mgmt: USA, Columbia Artists Mgmt., Inc.; Spain, Vitoria, Madrid; UK, Ibbs & Tillett, London. 2, 27.

DELAVAN, E Macon, b. 7 Sept. 1932, San Antonio, Tex., USA. Professor of Music; Choral, Operatic Conductor. Educ: BMEd, SW Tex, Univ., 1955: MMus, Westminster Choir Coll., 1958; DME, Univ. of Okla., 1969. m. Marlene McKenzie, 1 s., 1 d. Career: World tour, as soloist, Westminster Choir, 1965; Africa tour 1958; Cond., Coll. Choir, Japanese tour, 1970, European tour, 1974; Prof. & Chmn., Music Dept., Grand Canyon Coll., Ariz.; Dir., Phoenix Symph. Chorale & Opera Chorus. Recordings: Choralaries of the Spirit. Publs: Singing Success Library, (voice lessons on cassette tapes), 1937. Mbrships: Life Mbr., Phi Mu Alpha Sinfonia; MENC; Am Musicol. Soc. Hons: Winner, Regional Metrop. Opera Auditions, 1963. Hobbies: Golf Swimming; Tennis; Sculpture. Address: 7519 N. 9th Place, Phoenix, AZ 85020, USA. 2, 12.

DELAVAN, Marlene Elizabeth McKenzie, b. 8 May 1932, Grapeland, Tex., USA. College Teacher; Singer. Educ: BMusEd, Southwest State Univ., San Marcos, Tex.; MMus, Westminster Choir Coll., Princeton, NJ; Doct. Studies, N Tex. State Univ., Denton. m. Dr. Erin Macon Delavan, 1 s., 1 d. Career: Opera roles w. San Diego, Seattle, Shreveport, Phoenix, Valley Opera Co., Marshall, Tex.; Has sung w. San Antonio Symph. Orch., Princeton, NJ, NY Phil., Johannesburg, S Africa, etc. Cons. ed. w. husband, Singing Success Library (cassettes). Mbrships: incl: Sigma Alpha Iota; Nat. Assn. of Tchrs. of Singing. Hobbies: incl: Sewing. Address: 7519 N 9th Pl., Phoenix, AZ, USA. 5.

de LAVEAUX, Teresa Maria, b. 20 Feb. 1940, Lukowa, Tarnów, Poland. Musicologist. Educ: Jagiellonian Univ., Carcow: Univ. of Warsaw; study in Venice; Master of Musicol. m. Wieslaw Brychcy. Career: Chief, Polish Musical Off., Int. Festival of Old Music, Bydgoszch, 1964-66; w. Radio Bydoszcz, 1966-70; w. TV Stn., Katowice, 1970- Contbr. to var. music jrnls., reviews & mags. Publs: Annals: Rocznik Bydgoski, 1971. Hobbies: Films; Travel; Theatre. Address: aleja Mireckiego 43/29, 41-200 Sosnowiec, Poland.

DELDERFIELD, George Edward, b. 25 Dec. 1919, Aston Clinton, Bucks., UK. Bass Singer; Organist; Teacher of Singing; Conductor. Educ: Pvte. Study of speech & elocution; studied singing under Norman Allin Cert. of Merit (Singing), RAM. m. Patricia Viola O'Henry, 2 d. Career incls: Num. concerts, UK; apps. w. leading orchs. & conds.; Broadcasts for BBC & Radio Levant; Organist, Westbourne Pk. Bapt. Ch., 1961-64; Cond. & Musical Dir., Chatsworth Christian Choir, 1962-70; Organist & Choirmaster, Queens Pk. United Reformed Ch., 1964-67, & Clapham United Reformed Ch., 1970-; Prin. Bass Choriste, Holy Trinity, Kensington, 1968-70; Dir., Dee Singers, 1970-. Former mbr., var. musical assns. Hons. incl: Frank Odell Cup, 1962. Hobbies: Writing; Motoring. Addresss: 3 Telferscot Rd., Balham, London SW12OHW, UK.

DE LEEUW, Paul, b. 13 Nov. 1927, Amsterdm, Netherlands. Conductor. Educ: Juilliard & Mannes Music Schls.; studies conducting w. Fritz Mahler, Fritz Stiedry, Jean Mordel, Carl Bamberger, Pierre Monteaux, George Szell. Career: Further study & work in German Opera Houses; Cond., sev. standard repertory operas in NY; Fndr., own opera co. which opened in 1963 W. Bach's cantata Phoebus & Pan; later prods. incl: Walküre; act 3 of Siegfried; immolation scene, Götterdammerung; Elektra; Rosenkavalier; last scene of Cappriccio; excerpts from L'Enfance du Christ & Fidelio.

De LEEUW, Ton, b. 16 Nov. 1926, Rotterdam, Holland. Composer; Educator. Educ: Musical Colls. in Holland & France; Study w. Jaap Kunst, Amsterdam. m. Arlette Reboul, 1952, 1 s., 3 d. Career: w. Radio Hilversum, 1954-; i/c annual radio progs. of Comtemporary Music., ibid. 1956-; Prof. of Composition, Conservs. of Amsterdam & Utretcht, 1959-; Lectr., Univ. of Amsterdam, 1972-. Compositions: Hiob (Radiophonic Oratoio), 1956; Mouvements Retrogrades, 1957; 1st String Quartet, 1958; Antiphonie (Chmbr. music & tape), 1960; Symphs. for Wind Instruments 1963; The Dream (opera), 1963; Men Go Their Ways (piano), 1964; 2nd String Quartet, 1965: Syntaxis I, 1966; Spatial Music I-IV, 1966-68: Litany of our Time, 1970. Publ: The Music of the 20th Century, 1964. Hons. incl: Prix Italia, 1956; Prix des Jeunnesses Musicales, 1961. Address: Costeruslaan 4, Hilversum, Netherlands.

de LERMA, Dominique-René, b. 8 Dec. 1928, Miami, Fla., USA. Musicologist. Educ: BM, Univ. of Miami; PhD., Ind. Univ.; Curtis Inst. of Music; Berkshire Music Ctr.; Univ. of Okla.; studied w. Marcel Tabuteau, Fernand Gillet, Albert Andraud, Joel Belov, Ben Storch. Career: Assoc. Prof. of Music, Univ. of Miami, Univ. of Okla., Ind. univ. Prof. of Music, Morgan State Univ. Recordings: Ed., Saint-Geoirges, Symph. No. /, Str. Quartet No. /, Scena from Ernestine. Publs: Reflectioins on Afro-American Music, 1973: Black Music in Our Culture, 1970; Charles Edward Ives, 1970; Ignor Stravinsky, 1974. Contbr. to: Previews, Choice; Notes; Jrnl. of Rsch. in Music Educ.; Canon; Music Review; Acta Mozartiana; Music Educators Jrnl.; AAMOA Reports; Black Perspective in Music Instrumentalist; Le Conservatoire; Umana, Mbrships: Afro-Am. Music Oppoprtunities Assn.; Assoc. Dir., ibid; Chief Cons., Black Comps. Series, Columbia Records; Bd. of Dir., Music Lib. Assn.; Am. Musicol. Soc. Advsry Bd; Dance Theatre of Harlem. Recip. num. hons. Hobbies: Cooking; Hiking., Address: Morgan State Univ., Music Dept., Baltimore, MD 212398, USA. 12, 15, 28, 30, 42, 139.

DELEVORYAS, Sonja Gisela Clara (Hornstein), b. 13 Sept. 1926, Hamburg, Germany. Performer on Viola & Viola d'Amore. Educ: N. Tex. State Univ., USA, 1944-46; BA, 1966, MA Libnship. 1971, San Jose State Univ., Calif.; studeid Violin w. father Max Hornstein & other masters; Viola w. Emanuel Vardi; Piano & Comp. w. Julius Hijman. separated, 1 s., 2 d. Career: Violinist & Violist w.Houston Symph., Okla. Symph., & San Jose, Santa Cruz, Fremont, Monterey & Vallejo orchs., Calif.; Viola d'amore player w. Pardo Players of Ancient Instruments, Castro Valley, Calif. Hobby: Music. Address: 1931 Rosswood Drive, San Jose, CA 95124, USA.

DELFRATI, Carlo, b. 14 Dec. 1938, Milan, Italy., Teacher of Music Pedagogy. Educ: Deg. in Lit.; Dips. in Choir Direction & Music Palaeoigraphy. m. Rita Ferri, 2 s., 2d. Career: Tchr., Music Educ., Secondary Schl., 1963; currently Tchr., A. Boito Conserv. of Music, Parma; Collaborator to Min. of Educ., 1969-; Cond., Italian Educl. Instns., 1970-; Dir., Int. Music Campus, Fermo; Fndr., mag. 'Musica Domani', ¢971; Cons., Centro di Sperimentazioine Didattica, Milan 1973-; has made TV schl. broadcasts. Publs: The Academic Madrigals of Adriano Bachierei, 1965; Music Education, 1969; The Horizons of Music, 1973; Creativity & Music Pedagogy, 1974. Contbr. essays to sev. books & articles to profl. jrnls. Mbrships: Fndr. & Pres., 1969-, Italian Soc. for Music Educ.; Bd of Dirs., Int. Soc. for Music Educ., 1970-74, Music Youth of Italy & Italian Music Coun. Address: Via M. Loria 60, 20144 Milan, Italy.

DE LIGT, Ben Nicolas, b. 28 Jan. 1939, Utrecht, Netherlands. Cellist; Viola da Gamba Player; Professor of Cello, Violo da Gamba & Chamber music. Educ: Amsterdam Conserv., cello w. Carel van Leeuwen Boomkamp; Tchng., Orchl. & Soloist Dip. m., Mary Macrow, 2 c. Career: 8 yrs. co-prin. cellist, Netherlands Chmbr. Orch. (Goldberg); 4 yrs. 1st prin. cellist, Utrecht Symph. Orch.; 9 yrs. Amati String Quartet; currently cellist, Amsterdam String Quartet; Prof. of Cello, Viola da Gamba & Chmbr. music, Groiningen Conserv.; Prod., radio prog., für Elise. Num. recordings w. Am ati String Quartet & Amsterdam String Quartet. Mbrships: Viola da Gamba Soc. Hons: Grand Prix, 5th Chmbr. Music Contest of Colmar, France, 1972. Hobbies: Cooking; Restoratioin of Antiques; Building; Youth Clubs Organization. Address: Oosterhoutlaan 27, Amstelveen, Netherlands.

DE LIGT, Thomas, b. 15 Oct. 19844, Amsterdam, Netherlands. Musician (Double Bass & Violone). Educ: Amsterdam Conserv. w. K de Ligt; Theory, NRU w. T Andriessen. m. Astrid Geiger, 2 s. Debut: 1964. Career: Omroep Orkest & Radio Filharmon. Orkest; 1st solo bass player; bass & violone progs. on radio; fndr., Dutch Double-Bass Quartet; bass player of Radio Wind Ensemble & Ensemble M; tchr. of jazz bass players. Comps: sev. arrs. Hobby: Gardening., Address: Spoorlaan 4a, Bosch & Duin, Netherlands.

DE LIS, Jehanne, b. 6 Dec. 1885, Hjoerring, Denmark. Concert Singer; Composer. Educ: Royal Danish Music Conserv.; Pvte. tutors, Paris, France, & London, UK., 1 s. Career: Concerts, Italy, USA, Denmark; Benefit concerts for French children esp. for bombed village Equay-Notre Dame, Normandy, 1942-50. Comps: Trois Chansons, 1946; Christmas Candle, 1961 (broadcast on Danish radio & put into miniature street organ invented by her); Mon petit coin, 1961: Vaaren paa rej, 1964. Recordings: Il pleat sur la route, 1940; Ici l'on peche, 1940. Mbr.,, KODA. Hons: Solistforbundet of 1921. Address: Christiansholmsverj 4 DK-2930 Klampengborg, Denmark.,

DELISA, Victor V, b. 31 Oct. 1924, Hartford, Conn., USA. Composer; Director-Owner, Lakeland Conservatory of Music & Arts. Educ: Piano, Julius Hartt Schl. of Music, 1942-46: Comp., Los Angeles Conserv. of Music & Arts, 1942-47; Comp. & Conducting, Hartford Schl. of Music, 1948-51: BS & MA, Tchrs. Coll, Columbia Univ., 1955-58; PhD, 1977. m. Emilia Delisa, 1 s., 1 d. Publs. incl: Num. symphonic works for piano & orch., violin & piano string ensemble; num. comps. for piano & for voice w. piano accompaniment; Musical scored 'Moses, Prince of Egypt'. Author of books of progressive piano pieces; progressive guitar pieces; progressive organ pieces. Hons: Best transcription of I Love You Truly, preserved in Hartt Coll. Lib., Conn.; Distinguished Music Schlr. Award; Mbrships. incl: Musicians Union; Am. Music Ctr.; ASCAP; United Poet Laureate Int. Address: Renee Gate, Rte 6, Main St., Laurie Rd., Peekskill, NY, NY 10566, USA.

de LISLE, Christiane, b. 14 July 19134, Haguenau, France. Organist. Educ: studied w. Albert Frommer, Cannes, Paulk Fauchet, Marcel Dupré, Louis Vierne, & Olivier Messiaen, Paris. m. Melchoir de Lisle, 4 children. Debut: 1927. Career: made 1st recordings for French radio, Paris, 1946; Asst. to Jean Langlais, Eglise Sainte-Clotilde, Paris, 1950-51; Olivier Messiaen, Eglise de la Trinité, Paris, 1950-63; Titular Organist, Eglise de Val-de-Groe, Paris, 1949-65; Titular Choir/Organist & Chapel Music Dir., Eglise Saint-Eustache, Paris, 1965-. num recordings. Publs; transls. into French opf Yehudi Menuhin's Violin in Six Lessons, Hans Fantel's Johann Strauss - Father & Sons, & Paul & Eva Badura-Dkoda's Mozart Interpretation. Contbr. to: LeGuide Musical (Music Critis & Mbr. of Ed. Bd., 1963-). Mbr.: French Soc. of Musicol. Address: 94 rue St. Denis, 75001 Paris, France.

de LISLE, Rae, b. 22 Dec. 1947, Wellington, NZ. Pianist., Educ: BA, Victoria Univ., NZ, 1969; LTCL 1966; LRSM, 1967; GSM. m. Bill McCarthy Debut: Wigmore Hall, London, 1975. Career: NZ Broadcasting Corp. broadcast, 1966-72; Promenade Concert, ibid., 1969; BBC Concert Hall broadcast, 1976; Radio NZ broadcasts, 1976-78; Soloist w. NZ Symph. Orch., 1977-78; NZ Recital tours, 1977-78: NZ TV, 1978. Recordings: Songs of Roger Quilter (w. Christopher Keyte), 1976. Mbr., ISM. Hons: Auckland Star Piano Concerto Prize, 1967; Victor Hoddy Mem. Prize, 1970; Sheriff's Piano Prize, 1972; Prizewinner, Stella Murray Mem. Competition, 1973; Hastings Concerto Competition, 1974. Address: 136 Cashmere Ave., Khandallah, Wellington 4 NZ.

DELLA CASA-DEBELJEVIC, Lisa, b. Burgdorf, Switzerland. Opera Singer (soprano). Educ: Berne Conserv. of Music. Debut: Zürich Opera, 1943. Career: Mbr., Vienna State Opera, 1947; Mbr., Metropol. Opera, NYC, 1953; performances in leading opera houses throughout the world, inclng: Salzburg; Munich; Bayreuth; London; Buenos Aries; New Orleans; Glyndebourne &

Edinburgh Festivals; Australia, etc. Num. recordings. Mbr: Lisa della Casa music club, NY. Hons: Kämmersingerin awards, Austria & Bavaria. Hobbies: Collecting antiques & pictures. Address: Krapfenwaldgasse 51, Vienna, Austria, & Schloss Gottlieben/Thg., Switzerland.

DELLER, Mark Damian, b. 27 Sept. 1938, St. Leonards-on-Sea, UK. Counter Tenor. Educ: Chorister, Canterbury Cathedral; Choral Schlr., St. John's Coll., Cambridge. m. Sheelagh Elizabeth Benson, 3 s. Career: Lay Vicar, Salisbury Cathedral, 19650-68; Fndr. & Dir., Guildhall Winter Concerts, 1962; Artistic Dir., 1st Fest. of the Arts, Salisbury, 1967; Vicar-Choral, St. Paul's Cathedral, 1969-73; Choral Cond., 1970-, currently of 2 choral socs. in Kent, Ashford & Folkstone & of Petersfield Musical Fest.; began recording w. father Alfred Deller in 1962; joined Deller Consort in early 1960s; has toured extensively in Europe & 3 times in USA, Can. & S. Am., both w. Dellar Consort & as Solo Singer. Recordings; num. as Soloist & w. Dellar Consort, Accademia Monteverdiana & other grps., on Vanguard, Harmonia Mundi, Argo & Nonesuch labels. Hobbies: Gardening; Watching Cricket (Kent Supporter), Walking. Address: 61 Oxenturn Rd., Wye, Ashford, Kent, UK.

DELLEY, József, b. 31 March 1937, Szirmabesenyö, Hungary. Pianist; Professor of Piano. Educ: Liszt Ferenc Musical Acad., 1962. m. Piroska Delley, 2 c. Debut: Prague, Czech., 1963. Career: Prin. Asst., Piano Fac., Liszt Ferenc Music Acad. Tchrs. Coll.; Radio apps. Mbr., S Hungarian Sect., Assn. of Hungarian Musicians. Hons: Medal of Merit in Socialist Culture, 1971; Excellent Worker of Educ., 1978. Hobby: Tourism. Address: 6725 Szeged. Bécsi krt. 8-16, Hungary.

DELLI, (Helga) Bertrun, b. 17 July 1928, Dresden, Germany. Music & Art Historian. Educ: State Acad. for Music & Theatre (Carl Maria von Weber Coll.), Dresden; PhD, Musicol., Free Univ., Berlin, 1957: Lang. Dips., 1967, '68; MSc (Lib. & information) Pratt Inst., NY, 1978. Career: Var. Ed. positions in music & art publs., Germany, 1957-, USA, 1960-; Tchng. positions, jnr. schls. & coll. level, in music & art hist., piano langs., Germany & USA, 2958-; Asst. Prof., Concordia Tchrs. Coll., Seward, Neb., 1972-73: Asst. Ed., Art Index, H W Wilson Co., NY, 1973-76; Ed., Biography Index, ibid, 1977-. Publs. incl: Dances from Igoo, 1968; Co-compiler, The Arts in America, a Bibliography, 1979. Mbrships: Am Musicol. Soc.; ALA; Int. Biographical Assn. Hons. incl: Clawson Mills Rsch. Fellowship, Metropolitan Museum of Art, 1969-70. Address: 408 W 34 St., NYC, NY 10001, USA. 27, 29.

DELLO JOIO, Norman, b. 24 Jan, 1913, NYC, USA. Organist; Composer. Educ: studied comp., Juilliard Grad. Schl., 3 yrs., comp. under Paul Hindemith, Yale Schl. of Music, m. Barbara Bolton, 2 s., 1 d. (by previous marriage). Career: on Fac., Sarah Lawrence Coll., sev. yrs.; Prof. of Comp., Manness Coll. of Music; currently Prof. of Music & Dean of Boston Univ. Schl. for the Arts; Cultural Exchange Prog. to Russia, Rumania, Bulgaria, US State Dept., 1964; Rsch. Advsry. Coun. Mbr., US Office of Educ., 1965; US Rep. to the Fest. of the Arts of this Century, Hawaii; Chmn., Policy Comm. for the Contemporary Music Prog., administered by the MENC; Has written TV scores for Columbia Broadcasting, Nat. Broadcasting & ABC. Compositions incl: (scores) Air Power; Here is New York; The Saintmakers's Christmas Eve; Time of Decision (series on Pres. Truman); (orchl.) Air for Strings; Antiphonal Fantasy, for organ, brass & strings; Concertante, for clarinet & orch.; Concert Music; Fantasy & Variations, for piano & orch.; (chorus) The Blue Bird, for SATB; Madrigal, for SATB & piano; Songs's End, for SSA & piano; num. works for voice & piano, band, piano music, opera, ballet chamber music, etc. Has been commissioned to write works by many orgs. Mbrships: Nat Inst. of Arts & Letters; Century Assn. Hons: Pulitzer Prize, 1957; Emmy Award (TV), 1964: Hon. degrees from sev. univs., etc. Address: Boston Univ., 855 Commonwealth, Boston, MA 02215, USA. 2.

DELLOW, Ronald Graeme, b. 29 Sept. 1924, Auckland, NZ. University Lecturer; Choral Conductor; Orgnist; Harpsichordist. Educ: MusB, Auckland Univ. Coll.; Assoc., RSCM; FRCO (CHM); LTCL. m. Jane Brown Currie Cowan, 1 s., 3 d. Career: Lectr., Dept. of Music, Auckland, Univ. Coll.; 1949; Adult Educ. Tutor, ibid, 1950-64; Ext. Lectr. in Music, Univ. of Auckland, 1964-; Organist & Choirmaster, Pitt St. Meth. Ch., Auckland, 1964-78. Compositions: Six Recorder Trios, 1971; Anthem, Let the Children Come to Me, 1972, Missa Brevis for Boys choir & organ, 1974; Jubilate for chorus & organ, 1977; Magnificat, 1978; Suite for 4 records, 1978. Mbrships: RSCM (Special Commissioner 1962-73); Auckland Festival Soc. (Chmn., Music Committee, 1972-73); Auckland Dorian Singer (Dpty. Cond. 1969-73); Auckland Organist Assn. (Pres., 2 terms); Soc. of Recorder Players, NZ (Musical Dir, 1954-73); Dolmetsch Fndn. (Gov. 1963-73). Hons: Auckland Centennial Music Scholar, 1943; Prize for Fantasia for Viols. Viola da

Gamba Soc., UK, 1958. Hobbies: Tape Recording; Singing. Address: 8 Lynch St., Point Chevalier, Auckland 2, NZ.

DEL MAR, Norman Rene, b. 31 July 1919. Conductor. Educ: Marlborough; Royal Coll. of Music. m. Pauline Mann, 2 s. Career: Asst. to Sir Thomas Beecham, Royal Phil. Orch., 1947; Prin. Cond., Engl. Opera Grp., 1949; Cond. & Prof. of Conducting, Guildhall Schl. of Music, 1953-60; Cond., Yorks Symph. Orch., 1954; BBC Scottish Orch., 1960-65; RCM, 1972-; RAM 1974-77; Prin. Cond., Acad. of BBC, 1974-77 Publs: Richard Strauss, 3 vols., 1962-72. Num. recordings Hons: CBE, 1975; Hon. DMus; Hon. DLitt. Hobbies: Writing Chamber Music. Address: Clarion Concert Agency, 64 Whitehall Pk., London N19, UK 1, 16, 23, 28.

DEL MAR, Pauline Elizabeth, b. 11 May 1926, London, UK. Cellist., Educ: RAM; LRAM (Cello perf.); ARCM (Cello perf.). m. R. H. Del Mar, 1 s., 1 d. Debut: Rudolf Steiner Hall, London. Career: Freelance orchl. player; String Quartet; Piano Trio; Cello Tchr. Mbrships: Solo Perfs. Sect., ISM; Musicians Union. Hobbies: Golf; Surfbathing. Address: 8 Campden Hill Gate, Duchess of Bedford's Walk, London W8, UK & Penmaen, Constantine Bay, Padstow, Cornwall, UK.

DEL MONACO, Mario, b. 1919, Italy. Singer. Educ: Scuola d'Arte, Pesaro. Debut: Madame Butterfly, Teatro Puccini, Milan, 1940. Career: apps. world wide, inclng: La Bohéme, La Scala, 1943: Royal Opera House, Covent Gdn., London, 1945; in Manon Lescaut, Met. Opera House, NYC, 1950; Otello, Teatro Colon, Buenon Aires, 1950; num. films: Arena d'Oro, 1955; Orfeo d'oro, 1957; Maschera d'Oro, 1958. 16.

De Los ANGELES, Victoria, b. 1 Nov. 1923, Barcelona, Spain. Opera Singer (soprano). Educ: Univ. & Conserv. of Barcelona. m. Enrique Magrina Mir, 1948, 2 s. Debut: Barcelona, 1945. Career incl: Opera roles at Paris & La Scala, Milan, 1949; Royal Opera House, Covent Garden, London, 1950; Metropol. Opera House, NY, USA, 1951; Vienna State Opera, 1957; num. concert tours & recordings. Hons: 1st Prize, Int. Competition, Geneva, 1947; Cross of the Order of Isabel the Catholic & num. other decorations. Mgmt: Van Wyck, 235-241 Regent St., London. Address: Ave. de la Victoria 57, Barcelona 17, Spain.

DE LOUSTAL, Geneviéve Marie-Louise Odette, b. 11 June 1918, Sceaux, Hauts de Seine, France. Founder-President, Association, Cultural Centre, Festival, & Artistic Meeting Centre section of Nuits de Sceaux. Educ: Conserv. Nat., Versailles; Dip. de l'École Marguerite Long. m. Maurice Croux, 3 children. Career incl: Prof., (pianist), l'École Marguerite Long-Jacques Thibaud; Prof., (music hist. & dance hist.), l'École de danse Nikitinia; Lectr., (music hist. & dance hist.), NBBS & USNA; Choral cond.; Prod. of artistic broadcasts on French & For. Radio & TV; Hist. Prep.-pres., Assn., Nuits de Sceaux, 1945-; Fndr., festival, Nuits de Sceaux, 1963-; Fndr., cultural ctr., Nuits de Sceaux, 1959—65; Fndr., ctr. for artistic meetings sect., Assn. Nuits de Sceaux, 1977-; Formerly, critic, Guide du Concert & of broadcasts on French Radio, (ORTF), asst., Unesco Fine Arts; mbr. protl. socs. Hons: Chevalier de l'Ordre des Arts et Lettres, 1958; Bronze medal, la Jeunesse et Sports, 1974; Chevalier de l'Ordre du Merite Agricole, 1976. Hobbies incl: Musical & histl. rsch; Violin; Folk music & dance; Nursery trees hist.-Artistic Initiation-Arts creation; Social action. Address: Le Val d'Aulnay, 62 rue Chateaubriand, 92290 Chatenay-Malabry, France.

DELROY, Albert, b. London, UK. Accordionist; Composer; Teacher. m. Mona Marion, 1 s. Career: Broadcaster of own ensembles, BBC, for 25 yrs.; Performances on 'Music For You', BBC TV, BBC Radio & ORTF. Radio, Paris, France; Var. film performances inclg. solo in 'Magic Christian' & appearances under batons of Henry Mancini, Dimitri Tiomkin, Maurice Jarre, Lennox Berkeley & Elizabeth Lutyens; Int. Adjudicator for World Accordian Festivals, Compositions: Var. Light Music; Solos & Studies for Accordian; Light orchestral background music for TV plays & films. Contbr. to Music Accord. Mbrships; Performing Right Soc.; Tchrs. Advsry. Coun., Brit. Coll. of Accordionists; Songwriters Guild of Gt. Britain; Mech. Copyright Protection Soc. Hons: Croix de Chevalier, Academie d'Expansion Philanthropique, Paris, 1948 & 1949; Dip. di Benemerenza Assn., Nat. Fisarmonicisti, Milano,1954. Address: 64 Tankerville Rd., Streatham, London SW16 5LP, UK.

DELVAUX, Albert, b. 31 May 1913, Leuven, Belgium, Composer. Educ: Royal Conserv. of Music, Liége, Belgium. m. Fernande Tassignon, 2 s., 1 d. Career: Tchr., Acad. of Tirlemont; Conserv. of Louvain (Harmony, solfeggio); Dir., Acad., St. Nicolas-Waes; Prof., Royal Conserv. of Music, Brussell. Compositions incl: Suite symphonique; Scherzo; Miniatures; Bagatelles; Concerto per violoncello e violinoi;

Concerto pour Bois et Cordes. Recordings: Esquisse; Sinfonia; Burlesque Trio; Sonata a quatro; Concerto pour bois et orchestre á cordes. Mbrships. Pres., Pro Arte. Hons: Queen Elisabeth, 1st Prize, Comp. for Orch., 3rd prize. Comp. for Chamber Music; Priz de la province de Brabant; Prix Neerlandia. Address: Koningin Astridlaan 43 St. Nicholas-Waes, Belgium.

DEL VESCOVO, Pierre Louis Emile, b. 1 June 1929, Nice, France. French Horn Player. Educ: Nat. Paris Conserv., 1949. Debut: Paris. Career: 1st Horn, Basel Symph., Orchestre de Chambre de Paris; Israel Phil.; Montreal Symph. Num. recordings, espec. Mozart concerti; Bach's Brandenburg Concerto No. 1, Brahms Trio. Hons: 1st Prize, Paris Conserv., 1949. Hobbies: Sailing; Skin diving; Water skiing; Motorcycling; Bicycling; French horn playing; Mechanics. Address: 3470 Ste. Famile St., Montreal, Canada H2X 2K8.

DE MACQ, René, b. 18 Nov. 1932, Brussels, Belgium. Professor of Flute. Educ: Royal Conserv. of Mons; Royal Conserv. of Gand. m. Yolande Uyttenhove, 2 children. Debut: 1948. Career: Concert & Recital appearances in Belgium, France, USA & Switzerland; Creator of num. contemporary Belgian works for flute; Prof. of Flute, Acads. of Music, Brussels, Etterbeek. Mbrships: AEMS. Hons: 1st Prize, solfeggio, Royal Conserv. of Mons: 1st Prize, flute, ibid; 1st Prize, Chmbr. Music, Royal Conserv. of Gand; Francois Aveau Prize, 1966. Address: 128 rue des Confédérés, 1040 Brussels, Belgium.

DE MAEYER, Jan Irma Maria, b. 1 Sept. 1949, Bornem, Belgium. Oboist; Professor (oboe & literature) at Conservatory of Antwerp. Educ: Licentiate in Classical Philol.; Cand. Ancient Hist.; Dip. Superieure, oboe & chmbr. music. m. Godelieve Verstraelen, 1 s, 1 d. Debut: Philharmony of Antwerp, 1974. Career: Prof., Oboe & Lit., Conserv. of Antwerp; Recitals on TV & Radio; 1st Oboe, Philharmonie van Antwerpen, 1974-78: Oboist, Phil. Orch. of Belgian Radio. Mbr. Int. Double Reed Soc. Hons: incl: Ann Rutzky Prize, 1974; 1st Prize, Concours Int. pour musique de Chambre - Colmar, 1976., Hobbies: Lit. (Poetry, Philos.; Hist.); Vegetable World. Address: Consciencestraat 66, B-1800 Vilvoorde, Belgium.

de MAJO, Cecilia, b. Caracas, Venezuela, Harpist. Educ: 1st Prize, Paris Conserv., 1947. m. Leo Algisi, 1 s. Career: 1st Harpist Solo, Orquesta Sinfónica Venezuela, 1947-57; Harpist, Collegium Musicum, Caracas; Fndr. & Dir., Caracas Harp. Ensemble; Judge, Paris Nat. Conser. of Music, 1975. Mbr., Am. Harp Soc. Hons: Boton Cuatricentenario, 1967; Orden 27 de Junio, 1974. Address: Av. Los Proceres No., 1 San Bernardino, Caracas 101, Venezuela.

DEMANT, Leo S, b. 17 May 1900, between Denmark & Riga. Conductor; Adjudicator; Accompanist; Teacher of Singing. Educ: Studied piano w. Bruno Eisner, Vienna, Austria & Artur Schnabel, Berlin Germany, Studied singing w. Louis Bachner, Berlin & NY, USA & Adele von Skilondz, Stockholm; Studied accompaniment w. Hans Schmidt (pupil of Brahms) Riga; Studied conducting w. Valery Berdjajeff, Riga & Issaye Dobrowen, Stockholm. Widower, 1 s. Career: Soloist & accomp. on world tours, 1920-; 1st Dir., Latvia Conserv., 1930-; Musical Dir., NSW State Conserv. Opera Schl., Aust., 1959-; Adjudicator, many musical competitions throughout Aust.; Snr. Examiner in piano & singing, AMEB; Has played w. famous orchs. under Bruno Walter, Herman Aberndroth, Lovro von Matacic, Thomas Jensen, Nicolas Slonimsky, Hugo Werner & Hidenmaro Konoje; Sev. broadcasts in series, 'Contemporary Music from Different Countries' also broadcasts w. ABC, Aust.; Coached opera at Berlin & Stockholm Opera Hs. (under Leo Blech), in Copenhagen (under Egisto Tango), In Glyndebourne (under Fritz Busch), in Paris (under Emil Cooper); One of the fndrs. & committee mbrs., Sydney Nat. Opera. Recordings: Australian Piano Music (Columbia), 1055. Hons: Prof. of Music, Univ. of Riga, 1940; MBE, 1978, Catherine St., St. Ives, NSW, 2075, Aust.

DEMARCHI, Elida Maria, b. 26 June 1945, Buenos Aires. Argentina Pianist; Music Teacher. Educ: Prof. of Music Degree, Manuel de Falla Municipal Conserv., Buenos Aires grad. courses in music educ. & Argentine Soc. of Music Educ. seminars; studied piano w. Vicenzo Scaramuzza & Celia Bronstein. Career: has given Solo Recitals, Buenos Aires; Concert App. w. orchs. in major Argentine cities; has made radio & TV broadcasts. Publs: Body Expression, 1st Level (co-author), 1973; Cajita de Sorpresas, (Surprise Box, 1st Level Music Educ.). Contbr to jrnls. Mbr: Argentine Soc. of Music Educ. Recip. of 1st Prize, Piano Concourse org. by Municipality of Moron, Buenos Aires. Hobbies: Playing Scrabble; Car Driving. Mgmt: Rudolfo Giannini, Juramento 4355/Chacabuco 409, Buenos Aires, Argentina. Address: Chacabuco 56, Ramos Mejia, Buenos Aires, Argentina.

de MAREZ OYENS, Gerrit H, b. 6 Sept. 1922, The Hague, Netherlands. Music Theory Tchr. Educ: Amsterdam Conserv. m. (1) Tera Wansink; (2) Donalda Knoops; 4 children. Debut: 1945. Career: Music Tchr., Organist, Cond., Hengelo, 1949-59; Dir., Acad. of Music, Organist, Hilversum, 1959-76; Tchr., Rotterdam Conserv., 1977-. Comps: chr. music; Christmas Oratorio; var. vocal works; organ & carillon works; chmbr. music. Address: Strausslaan 40, 3055 CV Rotterdam, Netherlands.

DE MENEZES BASTOS, Rafael José, b. 26 Dec. 1945, Salvador, Brazil. Musical Educator; Ethnomusicologist; Musicologist; Social-anthropologist. Educ: AB, Musicol. Univ. Brazil, 1968; MA Social Anthropol., ibid., 1976. m. Maria Luziza de Lavenére Bastos, 7 children. Publs: A Musicológica Kamayurá; para uma Antropologia da Comunicacao no Alto-Xingu, 1976. Contbr. to Revista Musical Chilena; Educacan, Brazil; Atualidade Indijena. Membrships: Soc. for Ethnomusicol. Inc.; Int. Musicol. Soc.; Int. Folk Music Coun.; Am. Musicol. Soc.; ISME. Hobby: Music. Address: Caixa Postal 15-2807, 70.000 Brasilia DF, Brazil.

DE MIDDELEER, Jean, b. 24 Feb. 1909, Brussels, Belgium. Professor; Director; Composer. Educ: Diplomes du Conservatoire Royal de Bruxelles de piano, orgue; Var. prizes. m. Paul Daloze. Career: Prof., Brussels Conserv., 1937; Concert tours; Dir., Nairobi Conserv., 1946-50; Prof., Comp., Royal Conserv. Mons; Dir., Music Acad. Tirlemont, 1953-. Comps. incl: De Congo Symfonie; Concerto 1958 for piano & orch.; Amusettess 19D65: Faune Baroque 1960; Angelus 1930; Rails 1952; Frisson d'eau vive 1960; La goutte de pluie 1963; Stemmingen 1965. Recordings: Congo Symphony; Les Amusettes. Contbr. as mbr. of Presse Musicale Belge. Mbrships: SABAM; Afiliée á la Confédération Int. des Auteurs et Comp. Hobby: Music. Address: Vieux Marché aux grains II, Brussels 1000, Belgium. 1.

DEMIEREE, Aline, b. 15 June 1930, Lausanne, Switzerland. Pianist; Organist; Professor of Piano. Educ: Ribaupierre Inst., Lausanne; Paris Conserv., France. m. Joseph Baruchet, 1 s., 2 d. Career: Concerts in Switzerland, France, Italy, Germany; Broadcasts, Swiss, French Radio & Swiss TV; Soloist & Accomp., Tibor Varge Fest.; Jury Mbr., Competitions & Conservs. Mbrships: Bd., Musical Review of French Switzerland; Assn. of Swiss Musicians; Soroptimst Club Int.; Lyceum Club Int. Hons: 1st Prizes, Barcelona Int. Competition, 1956, Swiss Lyceum, 1956; 1st Medal Geneva Int. Competitioin, 1956. Hobbies incl: Reading; Travel. Address: 55 rte. de Loëche, 1950 Sion, Switzerland.

DEMOS, Peter John, b. 29 May 1941, Jackson, Mich., USA. Professor; Conductor. Educ: BMus, Mich. State Univ., 1964; MMus, Western Mich. Univ., 1968; AMusD, Univ. of Mich., 1975. m. Zoe Eleades Demos, 1d. Career: Assoc. Prof. of Music & Cond. of the Wind Philharmonia, Westfield State Coll., Mass.; Guest Cond., Adjudicator & Clinician throughout New England, Mid-West & Canada; Perfs. w. Wind Philharmonia incl. Wash., DC, & The Bahamas. Publs: The Little-Known Carl Nielsen in Comparisoin to Well-Known Masters - An Analysis of Nielsen's Clarinet Concerto, Op. 57, 1971. Mbrships: Am. Symnph. Orch. League; Nat. Assn. of Coll. Wind & Percussion Instructors; Int. Clarinet Soc.; MENC; Coll. Band Dirs. Nat. Assn. Hons: Silver Medal, Washington DC, as cond. of Wind Philharmonia. Hobbies: Jogging; Swimming. Address: 8 Zephyr Dr., Westfield, MA 0 1085, USA.

DE MOURA CASTRO, Luiz Carlos, b. 16 Mar. 1941, Rio de Janeiro, Brazil. Concert Pianist; Associate Professor of Music. Educ: Grad., Acad. of Music Lorenzo Fernandez, 1963; Nat. Schl. of Music, Fed. Univ. of Rio de Janeiro, 1964: Cert of Studies, Acad. of Music Franz Liszt, Budapest, Hungary, 1965-66. m. Bridget, 3 children. Career: Soloist w. Brazilian Symph. Orch., Nat. Symph. of Rio de Janeiro, Dallas Symph. Orch., Ft. Worth Symph.; Concerts & Chmbr. Music Recitals in S & N Am., Lisbon, Milan, Madrid & Budapest; Assn. Prof. of Music, Tex. Christian Univ., Ft. Worth,; Assoc. Prof., Hartt Coll., Conn., 1978-; Fndr., Annual Course of Piano Interpretation, Gorizia, Italy, 1978. num. recordings. Mbrships: Pi Kappa Lambda; Nat. MTA; NGPT; Fndg. mbr. Bartok Ensemble, Geneva, 1978. Hons: Professorship, Acad. of Music Lorenzo Fernandez, 1973; Tchr. of the Yr., Ft. Worth MTA, 1973 & 76; var. prizes in Nat. Piano Competitions, Brazil, 1957-64; Mgmt: Sula Jaffé, Brazil. Address: Hartt Coll. of Music, 200 Bloomfield Ave., Hartford, CT. 06117, USA. 23.

DEMUS, Joerg, b. 1928, St. Poelten, Austria. Professor; Concert & Recording Pianist. Educ: Prof., MA, Humanistic Gymnasium, Vienna Acad.; Annual Vienna Music Fest. Piano Master Class; Annual Piano Courses at Mexico City. Comps: Piano Pieces; String Quartet (unpubl.): Introduction and

Tarantella for Piano Solo (recorded). Publs: Abenteuer der Interpretation, musical essays at Brockhaus/Wiesbaden (Bach, Schumann, Schubert, French Impressionists). Hobbies: Mushrooming; Collecting Antiques. Address: Doeblinger Haupstreasse 77a, Vienna 19, Austria.

DEN BOER, Jan, b. 4 Aug. 1932, The Hague, Netherlands, Arline Pilot. Educ: Pilot's Trng. Schl.; Piano tuition w. Willem Andriessen, & Jaap Spaanderman. m. Annegien Huzinga, 2 d. Comps: Chromatische Etudes voor Piano; Perseiden I voor Piano; Chant d'un Fantassin (voice & piano); Rondeaux Amoureux (voice & orch.); Farthing for the Irish Harp; Cirrus for Flutes. Mbrships: Dutch Comps. Assn.; Dutch Airline Pilots Assn. Hobbies: Lit.; Sailing; Astronomy; Oceanography. Address: Overcingelaan 2, Havelte, Netherlands.

DENCKER-JENSEN, Aksel Ingvard, b. Sept. 1914, Ollerup, Denmark. Concert pianist; Organist; Composer; Music Teacher. Educ: Det Kgl. danske Musikkonservatorium, 1938; Robert Casadesus, Paris, 1939; Cours d'Interprétation par Alfred Cortos w. Chopin, 1939; Victor Schilor, Copenhagen, 1941-42. m. Aase Nielsen, 2 c. Debut: Odd Fellow Palaeet, Copenhagen, 1939. Career: Piano recitals; Broadcasts; Lectr. on Music & History of Civilization; Tchr., Musikdramatisk Skole, Copenhagen, 1942-48; Den frie Laererskole, Ollerup, 1950-59; Organist, Ollerup Ch., 1950-78; Mgr., Svendborg Amts Museum, 1964-74; & lectr. in music, Tchr., Skaarup State Seminary, 1951-. Comps: Songs; Church Music. Publs: Seks Sange, 1948; Svendbord Amts Museum, 1908-68. Contbr. to newspapers. Mbrships: Solistforeningen of 1921; Seminariernes Musiklaererforening. Hobbies: Historical studies; Travel; Agriculture. Address: Staagerupvej 50, 5762 Vester Skerninge, Denmark.

DEN HERTOG, Gerard, b. 4 Jan. 1914, Bandung, Indonesia. Violinist. Educ: Degree BV, Gymnasium, The Hague, Netherlands; Studied w. Arthur Orobio de Castro & Oscar Back. m. Antonia Borst. Debut: Violin Recital, Breda, 1924. Career: Residentie Orch., The Hague, 1945-54; Condertgebouw Orch., Amsterdam, 1954-72; Ldr., Rogeri String Quartet, Amsterdam; String Quartet apps. on Dutch Radio; Recitals nationwide; Schl. Concerts; 2 Tours of GB inclng. concerts in Wigmore Hall, London, Publs: Regular translator for Dutch Ed. of the Reader's Digest: Articles & Books on music & hist. of art. Hobbies: Zoology. Address: Churchill-laan 163, I, Amsterdam 1010, The Netherlands.

DENIS, Valentin, b. 18 Sept. 1916, Louvain, Belgium. University Professor. Educ: Doct., Univ. of Louvain, 1945; Louvain Conserv. of Music. m. Anne-Marie Van Kerckhove, 2 d. Career incls: Prof., Univ. of Louvain; Fndr., Louvain Record Lib.; Mbr. of Bd., Belgian Record Lib.; Sec. Gen., Princess Marie-José Nat. Fndn., Brussels & Rome; Music Critic, Monitor, Louvain. Contbr. to num. profl. publs. & jrnls., Mbrships. incl: 1st Mbr., Academia Belgica, Rome, 1939; Bd., 1965-; Fndr., Int. Assn. of Music Libs., Luneburg, 1950; 1st Prize, Brussels, 1964. Address: Eburonenlaan 32, 3030 Heverlee (Louvain), Belgium. 19.

DENISON, John Law, b. 21 Jan. 1911. Reigate, UK. Musical Administrator. Educ: Brighton Coll.; RCM. m. Francoise Henriette nee Garrigues, 1 d. Career: played honr, BBC Symph., London Phil., City of Birmingham & other orchs., 1934-39; Served War of 1939-45; gazetted Somerset Light Infantry, 1940; DAA & QMG 214 Infantry Brigade & var. staff appts., 1941-45 (despatches); Asst. Dir., Music Dept., British Coun., 1946-48: Music Dir., Arts Coun. of GB, 1948-65; Gen. Mgr., Royal Festival Hall, 1965-71; Dir., South Bank Concert Halls, 1971-76. Contbr. to var. musical publs. & mags. Mbrships: The Royal Phil. Soc.; The Royal Soc. of Musicians of Chmn., Royal Concert Committee Chmn., Arts Educl. Shcls. Hons: MBE (Mil) 1945; CBE (Civil), 1960; FRCM, 1962; Hons. GSM, 1972; Hon. RAM, 1972, Commander Order of Golden Lion, Finland. Address: 49 Egerton Gdns., London SW3, UK.

DENIZ, Clare Frances, b. 7 April 1945, London, UK. Cellist. Educ: pvte. piano study from age 5; pvte. cello study from age 11; RAM; LRAM; further study w. Christopher Bunting & Jacqueline de Pré; master classes w. Paul Tortelier. Career: ldr., European Youth Orch. cellos while at schl.; former prin. cellist, Royal Ballet Orch.; & sub-prin. Engl. Nat. Opera; recitals, chmbr. music, in UK; toured Denmark; num apps. as continuo cellist; perfs. of specially written film scores; app. on TV; cellist-in-residence, Southhill Pk. Arts Ctr., Bracknell; cello tutor, Stowe & Leighton Park Schls. Contbr. to: Classical Music; Album Reviews. mbr., ISM. Hons: Jr. Exhibition to RAM after only / yrs. tuition. Hobbies: Walking; Yoga; The Countryside. Address: 31 Friday St., Henley-on-Thames, Oxon., UK.

DENMAN, John, b. 23 July 1933, London, UK. Clarinetist. Educ: Kneller Hall. m. Sonia Rees, 3 children. Career: Prin., Clarinet, Guilford Phil., Prof., TCM; Assoc. Prof. of Music & Prof of Clarinet, Tucson Symph. Recordings: Sonatas by Bax, Ireland, Hughes, Stanford, Reger, Mendelssohn; Concertos by Spohr (nos. 2 & 3) & Stamitz (no. 3); Quintes by Sphor & Reicher. Hobbies: Golf; Swimming; Tennis; Discovering neglected music. Mgmt: Astra Blair, Quinville House, Maulden, Beds., UK. Address: 17 Braebourne Rise, Beckenham, Kent, UK.

DENNING, Darryl, b. 29 May 1939, Palmdale, Calif., USA. Classical Guitarist. Educ: BA, Univ. of Calif., Santa Barbara, 1961; Grad. work, Univ. of Calif., 1962-64; studied classical guitar w. var. tchrs. Debut: (London) Wigmore Hall, 1975. Career: Prof. of Applied Music, Occidental Coll., Los Angeles, 1968-; Instructor of Music, Univ. of Calif., Ext., ibid., 1970-, & Calif. Tech., Pasadena, 1974-; Solo recitals; Soloist w. symph. orchs.; chmbr. music; Concert tours incl. Europe, 1971, Mexico, 1971-72, London series, 1975; Broadcasts, film & TV apps.; Community Concerts, 1977-78. Recordings: Music of Spain & S Am.; Miklos Rozsa. Mgmt: New Era Int. Concerts Ltd., 16 Lauriston Rd., London SW19 4TQ. Address: 6116 Glen Tower Dr., Los Angeles, CA 900928, USA. 4.

DENNISON, Peter John, b. 18 Aug. 1942. Wollongong, Austria. Professor of Music. Educ: BMus, Univ. Sydney, 1963 MA, DPhil, Univ. Oxford, 1970; FRCO, 1966. Career: Fellow & Dir. of Music, Clare Coll., Cambridge, UK, 1971-75; Cond.; Cambridge Phil. Orch. & Choir, 1971-75. Prof. of Music, Univ. of Melbourne, Aust., 1975-. Publs. incl: Humfrey, Complete Ch. Music, 1972; Ed., Locke: The Instrumental Music in the Tempest, 1976; Purcell Ode on St. Cecilia's Day 1692 (1978). Contbr. to Essays on English Music on Opera in Honour of Sir Jack Westrup, 1976. Contbr. to Musical Times Music & Letters. Mbrships: Royal Music Assn.; The Melbourne Club. Hons. incl: Organ Scholar, Univ. Sydney, 1960-63 Magdalen Coll., Oxford, 1964-66. Address: Fac. of Music, Univ of Melbourne, Parkville, Victoria 3052, Austria.

DEN OUDEN, Peter, b. 18 Aug. 1948, Buren, Netherlands. Organist; Pianist; Choir Conductor; Teacher; Church Musician. Educ: Conserv., Hiversum. m. Tanja Schipper. Debut: as Organist, Laren, 1964. Career: num. organ concerts, Netherlands & Germany; choir concerts in Netherlands, Germany & Israel; frequent TV & radio broadcasts, Netherlands. Comps: var. choral works. Recordings: organ recital (Bach, Pachelbel, Franck & Langlais) Mbrships: KNTV; Dutch Soc. of Organists; Dutch Soc. of Ch. Musicians. Hobbies: Music; Literature; Travel. Address: Kroos 28, Huizen (N-H), Netherlands.

DENTON, William Lewis, b. 25 July 1932, San Diego, Calif., USA. Managing Director of the National Symphony Orchestra. Educ: BA, San Diego State Univ., 1957. Mbrships: Metropolitan Club; on Bd. of Dirs., former Treas., Am Symph. Orch. League. Address: 819 C St. S E, Wash. DC 20003, USA.

de NYS, Carl Augustin Léon, b. 27 Mar. 1917, Eupen, Belgium. Musicologist; Artistic Director. Educ: Lic. in German Lang. & Lit.; Dip., Classics. Career: Prod., Radio & TV, France & Belgium; Artistic Dir., Var. record cos. & fests.; Music Bd. Mbr., Int. Wallonia Summer Schl.; Asst. Lectr., Lyon-St-Etienne Univ. Recordings (as artistic dir.); Polydor; Lumen; Schwann; Charlin; Vergars; Harmonia Mundi; Music in Wallonia. Publs. incl: The Ideal Record Library, 1960; Saint Thomas' Cantatas, 1957; Sinfonia Sacra, 1957; Organ Works of Wolhelm-Friedemann Bach, 1960. Contbr. to var. profl. publs. Mbrships. incl: French Musicol. Soc. Hons. incl: Kt. of Arts & Letters, 1975. Address: Centre Culturel de Valprivas, 43210 Bas-en-Basset, France.

DE OLIVEIRA, Babi (Idalba), b. 23 Nov. 1915, Bahia, Salvador, Brazil. Pianist; Composer. Educ: degree in Music, Bahia Conserv. w. Silvio D Froes & Luzia Bamboza; advanced study w. Maximilian Hellmann. div., 3 c. Debut: 1940 on radio. Career: over 50 concerts in Brasil; concerts & recitals in USA, Argentina, Mexico, Portugal & Italy; radio & TV apps. Comps: about 350, incl: A Meus Amigos; songs from Brazil; Inezita Barroso (all recorded). Recordings: 6 as pianist. Mbrships: Ordem dos Musicos do Brasil; Brasil/US Inst. Hons: Gold Medals, Milan, 1975, Venice, 1975, Bahia, 1976; Marble Plaque, Bahia, 1976. Hobbies: Comp; Study; Listening to Music. Mgmt: Daniel de Carvalho (SBAT). Address: Rua Alm, Goncalves 50, Apt. 301, Capacabana, Rio de Janeiro, Brazil 20000.

DE OLIVEIRA, Fernando Correa, b. 2 Nov. 1921, Porto, Portugal. Composer; Teacher; Pianist. m. (1) Maria Feliciana Correâ de Oliveira (dec.); (2) Teresa do Céu Corrâ de Oliveira, 2

s. Career: Public concerts w. chmbr. music & orch.; His opera 'The Slaker' presented on TV & Radio. Comps incl: 1 Symph.; 1 opera; works for string & full orch.; Place of Magic; 3 Lyrical Sonnets & 3 Metaphysical Sonnets (recorded); Peter Noster & Ave Maria; 20 Pieces in Symmetric Counterpoint; Trio (recorded). Author: Sound Symmetry (Portuguese & Engl.). Fndr. & Pres., Assn. Juventude Musical Portuguesa do Porto. Hobby: Flying (pilot). Address: Rua Nossa Senhora de Fátima 231, Porto, Portugal.

DE PASCHOAL, Glaucio Roberto, b. 26 Mar. 1942, San Paula, Brazil. Musician (Classical & Electric Spanish Guitar). m. Eliza Pontes de Paschoal, 2 d. Debut: Hallmark Hall, Vancouver, Can., 1969. Career: Perfs. w. Los Bravos (Italian Band) in Western Can.; Guitarist w. a Greek Band & soloist Harry Lemonopoulos, 1972-74; TV apps. in Vancouver, Toronto & num. cities in USA. Recordings w. Los Bravos & Harry Lemonopoulos. Mbrships: Am. Assn. of Musicians; Musicians Union of Vancouver. Hons: 2 Trophies in 1971. Hobbies: Swimming; Chess; Flying. Address: 3176 E 18th Ave., Vancouver, BC, Canada, V5M 2R5.,

DEPELSENAIRE, Jean-Marie, b. 6 May 1914, Maubeuge, France. Conductor; Pianist; Solo Singer; Conservatory Director. Educ: Lille Conserv. m Marthe Duhamel. Career: Dir., Gravelines Schl. of Music, 1948-54, Maubeuge Conserv., 1954-: Works played at Monte-Ceneri, Hilversum, radio Lille, Radio Brussels. Comps. incl: (publs) Impromptu, for trombone & piano; The 7 Last Words of Christ (oratorio); Concert suite, for alto saxophone & piano or orch.; Concertino for 3 Bassoons. Titular Mbr., Northern Acad. Hons: Gold Medal, Arras Acad. of Fine Arts; Order of the State, 1975; Chevalier du Mérite Culturel Monégasque, 1977. Hobby: Reading. Address: Résidence Le Cannes 9 Rue de Provence.

DE PEYER, Adrian Christopher, b. 9 Sept. 1933, London, UK. Concert & Operatic Tenor; Professor of Singing. Educ: Cambridge Univ.; MA (Cantab) Maths. & Music; Hon. FTCL. m. Theresa Rose Marie Smith, 2 s., 2d. Career: Prof. of Singing, TCL; Apps: Sadlers Wells-ENO: The Prince, Love of Three Oranges (Prokofiev); Oedipus, Oedipus Rex (Stravinsky); Pierre, War & Peace (Prokofiev); Marseille Opera; Royal Opera House 1972-76; Narraboth, Salome (R Strauss); Andres, Wozzeck (A Berg); & many more. Hobbies: Family; Chess. Address: Southlands, Warninglid, Sussex RH17 55N, UK.

DE PEYER, Gervase Alan, b. 11 Apr. 1926, London, UK. Solo Clarinettist; Conductor. Educ: Royal Coll. of Music; ARCM. m. (1) Sylvia Southcombe; (2) Susan Rosalind Daniel, 1 s., 2 d. Debut: Broadcast Mozart Concerto while at schl. Career: Fndr. Mbr., Melos Ensemble, London; Cond; Melos Sinfonia; 1st Clarinet, LSO, 1955-71; Dir., LSO Wind Ensemble; Assoc. Cond., Haydn Orch.; Num. TV documentaries & shows in Europe, USA & Japan; Regular broadcasts, concerts, recitals, talks quiz shows & Desert Island Discs. Compositions: Sev. arrangements for clarinet & piano. Recordings: Solo clarinettist, Cond. & w. Melos Ensemble, & Chmbr. Music Soc. of Lincoln Ctr., NYC. Hons: Plaque of Hon., for recording of Mozart concerto, Am. Acad. of Arts & Scis.; Grand Prix de Disque, Acad. Charles Gros, Paris; Hon LRAL. Hobbies incl: Sports; Good food; Sightseeing while Touring; Theatre Mgmt: Kazuko Hillyer Int., NYC, for USA & Far East. Address: 16 Langford Pl., London, NW8, UK. 13, 21.

DEPKAT, Gisela, b. 5 Sept. 1942, Königsberg, Germany. Cellist. Educ: Detmold Musikakademie, Germany, cello studies w. George Neikrug, 1962-65; Oberlin Coll. Conserv. Music, Ohio, USA, w. George Neikrug. Debut: NY Town Hall, 1966. Career: Recitals in NY, Amsterdam, London, Milan, Copenhagen, Paris, and in Can. & USA; apps. w. leading orchs; perfs. for CBC radio & TV, Radio Suisse Romande, Radio Moscow, RAI (Italy), WQXR (NY) & Iceland radio & TV; prof. of cello, McGill Univ., Montreal. sev. recordings. num. hons. & prizes incl: Silver Plaque winner, Gaspar Cassado Int. Cello Competition, 1969, '71; 1st prize, Nat. Instrumentalist Competition, Boston, USA, 1967; Dip. winner, Tchaikovsky Competition, Moscow, 1966; US rep., Jeunesses Musicales, Carnegie Hall, NY, 1967-69; 2 awards for Best Solo Recording of the Yr., 1977, 1979. Hobbies: Gymnastics; Cross Country Skiing. Address: 372 Erb. St. W, Waterloo, Ont. N2L 1W6, Canada.

DE PLACE, Adélaïde, b. 14 Apr. 1945, Paris, France. Musicologist; Music Teacher. Educ: Académie Marguerite Long, Paris (piano); Schola Cantorum, Paris (harpsichord); Conserv. Nat. Supérieur de Musique de Paris; dip., musicol., Paris; Doct. in musicol. & hist. of Music. Publs: Le Piano-forte en France de 1760 á 1812, 1975; Le Piano-forte á Paris entre 1760 et 1822, 1978. mbr., Société Francaise de Musicologie. Hobbies: Tennis; Dogs. Address: 24 Ave. Pierre 1er de Serbie, 75116 Paris, France.

DePRIEST, James, b. 21 Nov. 1936, Philadelphia, Pa., USA. Conductor. Educ: BS, MA, Univ. of Pa.; Study of Theory, Harmony, Composition, Orchestration w. Vincent Persichetti, Phila. Conserv. m. Betty Louise Childress, 2 d. Debut: NY Phil. Orch., 1969. Career: Asst. Cond. to Leonard Bernstein, NY Phil., 1965-66; Assoc. Cond., Nat. Symph., 1972-; Guest Cond., maj. US orchs. inclng. Phila. Orch.; Boston Symph., NY Phil., Chgo., Symph., Cleveland Orch.; Guest Cond., Europe, w. Rotterdam Phil., Radio symph. orchs. of Berlin, Munich, Stuttgart, Helsinki; Stockholm Phil., Amsterdam Phil., Prin. Guest Conductor, Nat. Symph. Wash. DC, 1975-76; Music Dir., Quebec Symph. Orch., 1976-. Recordings w. Stockholm Phil. Hons: 1st Prize, Mitroipoulis Int. Conds. Competition, 1964. Mgmt: Hurok Concerts, Inc., NYC; Interaurists, Europpe. Address: c/o Hurok Concerts, 1370 Ave. of the Americas, New York, NY 10019, USA. 2.

DePUE, Wallace Earl, b. 1 Oct. 1932, Columbus, Ohio, USA. Composer; University Professor. Educ: BMus & BMusEd, Capital Univ., 1956: MA, Ohio State Univ., 1957; PhD, Mich State Univ., 1966. m. Linda Elaine Kallman, 4 c. Comps. publd: Hosanna (dougle chorus-SATB/SATB); Separation (SATB a capella); Glory to God in the Highest (SATB a capella); Psalm I (mixed chorus, organ, assorted percussion). Comps. recorded Dr Jekyll & Mr Hyde (opera); Something Special (opera). Author: An Approach to Music Composition, 1957. Contbr. to jrnls. Mbrships: ASCAP; Nat. Opera Assn.; SPEBSQSA (Barbershop Quartet Assn.). Winner, nat. contest sponsored by Rochester Fest. of Relig. Arts, for Psalm 90 (SABT & viola), 1967. Hobbies: Mail Order Sales; Sports; Chess. Address: Coll. of Musical Arts. Bowling Gn. State Univ., Bowling Gn., Ohio, USA.

DE REEDE, Rien, b. 2 Mar. 1942, Leiden, Netherlands. Flautist. Educ: HBS-A dip.; Solo-Dip. cum laude, Conserv. of Tilburg; Dip. di Merito for chmbr. music, Acad. Chigiana, Siena. Career: Mbr., Concertgebouw-orch., Amsterdam; Mbr. Netherlands Wind Ensemble; TV recordings of concertos by Vivaldi, Mozart & Jolivet, also mod. chmbr. music; Concerts & radio recordings in most major European cities. Recordings: Kees van Baaren, Musica per flauto; Jon de Kruyf, Pas de Deux for flute & orch.; Enrique Razach, Imaginary Landscape; J S Bach, Experts h-moll suite. Recip. Johan Wagenaar Award for perfs. of Dutch music. Address: P C Hoofstraat 114 11, Amsterdam, Netherlands.

DERIETEANU, George, b. 8 May 1918, Bucharest, Romania. Composer; Conductor; Violinist; Teacher. Educ: Acad. of Music, Becharest, 1936-41: 1946-48; cert., ibid. m. Georgeta Baucila 1 d. Debut: (violin) w. Romanian Radio & TV Symph. Orch., 1940; (Cond.) w. Gurtg Artistic Ensemble Orch., Bucharest, 1949. Career: Asst. lectr. (cond.), Acad. of Music, Bucharest, 1949-50: Cond., Railwaymen's Choir, Bucharest, 1950-53; Hd., Documentation & cond. of Chmbr. Choir of Comps. Union, 1951-53; Prof., Musical Military Schl., 1957-57; Ed.-in-chief, Musical Publishing House, 1957-62; 46 documentaries on ethno-folklore for radio, TV & film. Comps: choral & vocal music for solo voices, male, female & mixed voices. Publs: (ed) Little Musical Dictionary, 1960; Opera Choirs, 3 vols., 1956, '62, '65; Famous Melodies from World Music, 1974. Hons: Romanian Comps. Union Prize, 1977; Order of Cultural Merit, 1969; Medal, 30 yrs. since the liberation of Romania, 1974. Address: Str. Luminei 7, 70252 Bucharest, Romania.

DERMOTA, Anton, b. 4 June 1910, Kropa, Yugoslavia. Concert Singer; Music; Music Educator. Educ: Dip., State Conserv., Ljubljana; .Vienna Acad. of Music; Vocal study w. Prof. Marie Rado, Vienna. m. Hilda, 3 c. Debut: Vienna State Opera, 1936. Career: incl. performances in opera & concert (lieder & oratorio) in num major opera houses & concert halls throughout the world; Prof., Acad. of Music, Vienna. Recordings: num complete opera & oratorio works. Recip. var. hons. in Austria & abroad. Hobby: Art Collecting. Address: Hagenberggasse 36, 1130 Vienna, Austria.

DERNESCH, Helga, b. 3 Feb. 1939, Vienna, Austria. Opera Singer. m., 2 children. Career: Bern, 1961-63; Wiesbaden, 1963-66; Cologne, 1966-69; opera & concert apps. throughout Europe & USA; regular apps. w. Bayreuth Fest., 1965-69, Salzburg Easter Fest., 1969-73; guest apps., Deutsche Oper Belin. Has made many recordings. Hobbies: Riding; Hunting; Lit. 16.

de ROET, Janette, b. 8 May 1938, Larchwood, Epsom, UK. Concert Pianist & Harpsichordist. Educ: Perf.'s LRAM. Debut: Wigmore Hall. Career: extensive tours in Europe & Scandinavia; 4 concert tours of Austria; apps. in USA & Can.; radio & TV broadcasts in UK, Denmark & Austria. Mbr., Perf.'s Sect., ISM. Recip. Assoc. Bd. Schlrship., RSM. Hobbies: Golf; Designing &

working tapestries; Knitting; Drawing & painting; Bird watching; Writing. Address: Larchwood, Longdown Rd., Epsom, Surrey, UK.

DEROO, Maurits Alfons, b. 4 Nov. 1902, Brugge, Belgium. Director; Professor. Educ: Conservatoire Royal de Musique, Bussels. m. Magdalena Borrey, 5 c. Career: Concerts (violin); Cond., choirs, orch.; Prof. violin, harmony, counterpoint, fugue, Conservatory of Music Bugge, 1926-46: Dir., ibid. 1946-68; Cond. of concerts. Comps: works for choirs, violin, piano, flute, etc.; Lessons for Musical Educ.; var. works in MS. Recordings incl: Lieder; violin; orch.; choirs. Mbrships: Sabam; Unie van Belgische Componisten. Hons: First Prize, Comp. of Flanders; Laureat de l'Academie d'Alsace (comp. choir), France; Officer, Order of Leopold II; Chevalier, Ordre de La Couronne; Lecturing. Address: Wserfstraat 72,8000 Brugge, Belgium.

DE ROOIJ, Dorthy, b. 21 Apr. 1946. Nuenen, The Netherlands. Organist. Educ: Gymnasium: Studied w. Albert de Klerk: Soloist Dip. 'cum summa laude': Prix d'Excellence, 1972; Studied w. Maurice Duruflé, Paris & Luigi Tagliavini, Bologna; Master courses w. Marie Claire Alain & Anton Heiller. Career: Many concerts in Europe; Many radio appearances and recitals; Prof. at the Conserv. at Zwolle. Recordings: on the organ at St. Bavo at Haarlem. Mbrships: Kon. Ned. Toonkunstenaarsvereniging. Hons: Prize of the City of Eindhoven, 1971. Hobbies: Arts; Philosophy. Address: Het Puyven 25, 5672 RA, Neunen N Br., Netherlands.

de ROOS, Robert, b. 10 Mar. 1907, The Hague, Holland. Composer. Educ: Dip., Royal Conserv., The Hague. m. Christa von Falkenhavn, 1 s. Career: Dutch for Serv., 1946-72. Compositions incl: 5 Etudes for piano & small orch.; Sonata for piano; String Quartet; Overture for a Tragi-Comedy; Concerti for piano, violin, viola, 2 flutes, etc.; var. orchl. & choral works, chmbr. music, one-act opera, etc. Recordings: Suggestioni -orch. (Bonemus Audio-visual series); Composizione per Orch. (Radio Nederland). Mbrship: Soc. of Dutch Composers. Hons. incl: Off., Order of Orange-Nassau; Off., Legion of Hon., France; Grad Off., Order of Francisco de Mirando, Venezuela; WSillem Pyper Prize (for 3rd string quartet). Hobby: Archaeol. Address: 12 Sonderdank Straat, The Hague, Holland.,

DERR, Emily, b. Cadillac, Mich., USA. Singer (Soprano); Teacher; Astrologer. Educ: BA, MMus, Mich. State Univ.; pvte. studies w. Samuel Margolis. Career: apps. incl. w. Boston Symph.-Tanglewood, 1968, Augsburg, Germany, 1970, Pottland Opera Assn., 1972, Los Angeles Opera Theatre, 1973, NYC Opera, 1974; roles incl. Mimi (La Boheme), Marguerite (Les Huguenots), Sophie (Der Rosenkavalier), etc.; Soprano Soloist, Robert Shaw Chorale; Tchr., Interlochen Music Schl.; Meadowbrook Schl. of Music (Rochester), & Oak Pk. Schl. System, all Mich. Recordings incl: The Medium (Menotti) w. Opera Soc. of Wash. Mbr., Sounds Out of Silent Spaces. Recip., var., awards & grants. Address: 8 Jones St., NY, NY 10014, USA.

DE RYKE, DeLores "Fiddling De", b. 10 Nov. 1929, Lincoln, Neb., USA. Musician (Violin, Fiddle, Piano, Autoharp). Educ: BSc, Univ. Neb.; Grad. work, Neb. Wesleyan Univ. & Univ. Neb., Lincoln; Pvte. studies. Debut: Dance recital at age of 4 yrs. Career: Tchr. of Music in public schls. & pvtely.; Personal apps. on radio & TV in Neb., Iowa, Kan., Colo. & NY; Instr., Traditional Fiddling Judging; Fiddling Nationally; Instr., Fiddling & Fiddling Judging & Appreciation, Southeast Community Coll., Neb. Num. recordings. Publs: incl: Fiddling De's Beginning Fiddlers Notebook, 1976; Complete Book of Fiddling, (in progress). Contbr. to profl. jrnls. Mbr. num. profl. orgs. Hons. incl: Fiddling contest awards. Hobbies: Embroidery; Sewing. Address: 61341 Morrill Ave., Lincoln, NB 68507, USA. 4, 5.

DESBY, Frank, b. 24 Feb. 1922. Cleveland, OH, USA. Conductor; Composer; Musicologist; Obist. Educ: BM, 1949., MMus, 1958, DMusA, 1974, Univ. of Southern Calif. m. Xenia Anton Desby (dec.), 2 s., 1 d. Career: Cond., Highland Pk., Symph., Calif.; Dir. of Music, St. Sophia Greek Orthodox Cathedral of Los Angeles; Prof. by Byzantine Music, Univ. of Southern Calif. Comps: Liturgical works and folk song arrs.; film scores, whole & part. Recordings (as Cond.): Treasures of Byzantine Music, w. Byzantine Choral; Divine Liturgy; Choral Fest. of Greek Folk Songs. Publs: incl: Choral Music to the Divine Liturgy, 1951; Services of Nativity, 1955; Resurrection Services of the Orthodox Church, 1959; Music Ed., Orthodox Observer. Mbrships: ASCAP; MENC; Am. Musicol. Soc.; Dept. of Worship & Arts, Nat. Coun. of Chs. Hons. incl: Archon Lampadarius of the Great Ch. Patriarchate of Constantinople, 1976. Hobby: Photography. Address: 6234 Scenic Ave., Hollywood, CA 90068, USA.

DE SIGNORI, Giocondo, b. 20 Sept. 1915, Massagno, Lugano, Switz. Violoncellist. Educ: Tchr., Dip., Music Conserv., Neuchâtel, Switz. Debut: Radio perf., Lugano. Career: Tonhalleorch., Zürich; Festival orch., Lucerne. Address: Ottenweg 16 Zürich, Switzerland.

DE SMET, Monique Henriette Mathilde Antoinette, b. 10 Dec. 1925, Ixelles, Brussels, Belgium. Professor; Administrator; Pianist. Educ. incls: Doct., archaeol. & hist. of art (musicol.), Cath. Univ. of Louvian, 1958; musical studies, Acad. Jean Absil, Brussels, 1948. Career incls: Prof., 1965-, Dir., Ctr. for Rsch. on Hist. of Contemp. Music, 1969-, fac. of philos. & letters, Cath Univ. of Louvain. Publs. incl: La Musique á la Cour de Guillaume V, Prince d'Orange (1748-1806), 1973. Author of articles & monographs. Mbr. profl. orgs. Recip. num. hons. Address: Ave. René Stevens 133, Brussell 1160, Belgium. 14.

DE SMET, Robin John, b. 11 Apr. 1935, Colindale, London, UK. Music Editor, Clarinettist, Teacher. Educ: Royal Military Schl. of Music, Kneller Hall; LTCL; ARCM; ALCM. m. Bernice Hoyle, 2 s, 1 d. Career: Var. radio & TV recordings. Compositions: Elegy for voice & string trio; A Jacobean Suite for string quartet. Publs: num. eds. of works by var. comp. Published music for the Viola da Gamba & other viols., 1971. Contbr. to: Living Music; Guitar Mag.; Music Industry; BMG Mag. Mbrships' ISM; Viola da Gamba Soc. of GB. Hobbies: Antique bottle collecting; Antiques. Address: 17 Sandfield Road, St. Albans, Herts., UK, 3, 28, 139.

DESMOND, Gary Christopher, b. 1 Apr. 1948, Knowle, Bristol, UK. Teacher; Organ Recitalist. Educ: RAM; GRSM; LRAM; ARCO. m. Beryl Margaret Newbury. Debut: Pershoe Abbey, Worcs. Career: Music Master, Bristol Grammar Schl.; Organist & Choirmaster, Bristol City Parish Ch.; var. TV & radio ch. serv. broadcasts. Recorded w. Bristol Phoenix Choir for Decca. Mbr., Pres., 1975-76: Bristol & Dist. Organists' Assn. Hobbies: Music; Motoring; Gardening. Address: 37 St. Ladoc Rd., Keynsham, Bristol BS18 2DR, UK.

DE SOLLIERS, Jean, b. 1 Mar. 1916, Oran, Algeria. Radio Producer for ORTF. Educ: Lic. & Dip., Philos., Sorbonne, Paris; Conserv., Nancy, France; Studied w. Lazare Levy, Paris. m. Mariette Reutter, 4 c. Career: Piano recitals & concerts; Prod., Org., Radio progs., musicals etc. for ORTF, France, 1946-. Contbr. to: Revue Musicale, Europe, Paris; Beiträge zur Musikwissenschaft, Sinn und Form, Berlin;var. Encys. Mbrships: French Soc. Musicol.; Dir. Ctte., Des Amis de Gabriel Faure; Soc. of Men of Letters; Acad. Charles Gras. Hobbies: Philosophy; Museums; Travel; The Old Testament. Address: 223 Blvd. Raspail, 75014 Paris, France.

DE SOUZA, Raimundo Nonato, b. 26 Feb. 1938, Januaria, Minas Gerais, Brazil. Violinist. m. Eber Oliveira de Souza, 2 s, 1 d. Career: Sololist w. Orquestra Sinfonica da PMMG; Spalla da Orquestra Sinfonica Municipal de Campinas; Prof. of violin at Universidade Estadual de Campinas (UNICAMP); mbr. chmbr. music ensembles. sev. recordings. Mbr. Ordem dos Musicos do Brasil. Hon: Trofeu, Personalidades 1977, from Jrnl., City News (Best musician of the Year). Hobbies: Aviation; Models. Address: Universidade Estaudual de Campinas (UNICAMP), Instituto de Artes, Dep. Musica, Campinas, SP Brazil.

DE SOUZA SALVADOR, Aecio, b. 10 Nov. 1906, Sao Paulo, Brazil. Musician; Pianist. Educ: Cert. in piano, Conserv. Musical de Sao Paulo; Cert. of Conserv. Paulista de Canto Orfeônico; Cert. Course. Conserv. Nacional Canto Orfeônico. m. Maria Zonotto Salvador, 3 c. Career: Tchr., Harmony & Instrumental Practise at Faculdade de Musica Santa Marcelina-Botucatu, SP. Mbr., Academia Botucatuense de Letras, Botucatu, SP. Address: Rua Cardose de Almeida no. 80, (c.e.p.) 18.600, Botucatu, E S Paulo, Brazil.

DESPIĆ, Dejan, b. 11 May 1930, Belgrade, Yugoslavia. Composer; Musicologist; Professor of Music Theory. Educ: Acad. of Music, Belgrade, 1955. m. Ljiljana Despić, 2 s. Debut: w. Three Preludes for piano, 1950. Career: Tchr., second. music schl. Mokranjac, Belgrade, 1956-; Lectr.- Prof., Fac. of Music, Belgrade, 1965-. Comps. incl: var. orchl. works inclng. a symph.; works for chmbr ensembles inclng. 2 str. quartets; var. piano works inclng. 2 sonatas; works for children., Publs: Harmonic analysis, 1968; A Theory of Tonality, 1971; Tone setting (Tonski slog) 4 books, 1973-75. Mbr., Assn. of Comps. of Serbia. Address: Čarli Čaplina 38,11000 Beograd, Yugoslavia.

DESPINS, Jean-Paul, b. 6 Jan. 1935, Quebec, PQ, Can. Music Teacher. Educ: BA, Univ. of Montreal; Dip., Advanced Study in Ancient Langs., Univ. of Laval; BMus, Univ. of

Montreal; M Musicol., McGill Univ.; Cert. in Gregorian Music, St-Benoit-Du-Lac. m. Claire Jodoin, 1 s. Career: Tchr. of German flute, schl. harmony & orch.; Num. chmbr. music concerts, live & radio, 1965-70; Tchr. of Musical Educ., Univ. Laval of Quebec. Comps. (publs.) incl: Suite in E Minor, for 4 flutes, 1965; 2 Melodies, for soprano voice, flute & harp, 1966: Triptych, for piano, 1968; Chorale, for full orch. or 4 flutes, 1975. Publs. incl: Lachrymosa from Hector Berlioz's Requiem (commentary), 1974. Mbr., Int. Soc. for Music Educ. Hobbies: incl: Sport; Athletics. Address: 976 F. Ave. Jean-Charles Cantin, Cap Rouge, Quebec, GOA 1KO, Canada.

DE STOUTZ, Edmond, b. 18 Dec. 1920, Zürich, Switz. Conductor. Educ: studied w. law at Zürich Univ.; studied cello piano & comp. at Zürich, Lausanne, Salzburg & Vienna. m. Marie-Louise de Chambrier, 1 d., 1 s. Debut: as cond. of Zürich Chamber Orch., Paris, 1951. Career: Fndr. of Zürich Chamber Orch., 1945; Fndr. of Zürich Concert Choir, 1960; num recordings, esp. w. Zürich Chamber Orch. Mbrships: Swiss Musicians Soc.; Rotary Int., Hon. Naegeli gold medal of the city of Zürich. Hobby: Painting. Address: Kreuzbühlstr. 36, 8008 Zürich, Switzerland.

DETONI, Dubravko, b. 22 Feb. 1937, Krizeci, Yugoslavia. Composer. Educ: Zagreb Acad. of Music; Chigiana Music Acad.; Warsaw Higher Schl. of Music. Career incls: Chmbr., Music Ed. & Prod., Zagreb Radio & TV; Fndr., ACEZANTEZ, ensemble of Zagreb Ctr. for New Tendencies. Comps. incl: Figures & Surfaces, 1968; Elucubrations, 1970; cyclusses: Monos, 1971-74; Graphics, 1968-74; Fable, 1973, de Música, 1973; Taboo, 1975. Num. recordings in Europe & Asia. Publs: Pahopticum Musicum, 1971. Author num. articles on problems of new music. Hons. incl: 1st Prize, Sixth Paris Biennale, 1969; Zagreb Music Critics' Award, 1968; Vladimir Nizor, 1971; 7 awards at Yugoslav Radio Music Festivals, 1968, 69 & 70. Address: Pantovcak 66, Zagreb, Yugloslavia.

DETREKÖY, Béla, b. 13 Feb. 1925, Budapest, Hungary. Concertmaster (Violin) Danish Radio. Educ: F Liszt Conserv. of Music, Budapest, 1935-44: Nat. Cert in Music Pedagogica, 1944. m. Tove Detreköy, 2 children. Debut: Copenhagen, 1947. Career: Mbr., Royal Danish Orch., 1953-67; Assoc. Prof., Western Wash. State Coll., USA, 1967-71; Soloist w. Scandinavian Orchs.; Artistic Ldr., Copenhagen Chmbr. Orch.; Soloist, Chmbr. Music Recitals in Hungary, Scandinavia, Switzerland, USA; Tchr. of violin, Fyns Musikkonserv., Odense, Denmark. Recordings incl: J M Leclair; Triosonata D Maj. Mbrships: Danish Music Pedagogic Soc.; Bd. Mbr., Danish Sect., ESTA; Danish Soloist League of 1921. Hons. incl: Wilhelm Hansen Prize for Perfs. 1959. Hobbies: Travel; Camping. Address: Halls Alle 1, 1802 Copenhagen V, Denmark.

DETTMER, Roger Christian, b. 2 Aug. 1927, Cincinnati, Ohio, USA. Author; Journalist. Educ: Univ. of Cinn., 1945-47; Columbia Univ., 1947; BA, Univ. of Mich., 1950; pvte. music study of piano, clarinet, trumpet & timpani; Composition & Theory w. Vittorio Giannini, NYC, 1950-52. Career: Asst. Mgr., Cinn. Symph. Orch., 1950-51; Music Writer, NY Herald-Tribune, 1951-53; Music & Theatre Ed., Chgo. Herald-Am. (later Chgo.'s Am., The Chgo. Am. & Chgo. Today.), 1953-74; Theatre Critic, Chgo. Tribune, 1974-75; Annotator, var. recordings cos. Publ: ed., Cincinnati Symphony Orchestra; History & Repertory, 1945. Contbr. to num. music jrnls., newspapers, etc. Mbrships. incl: Fndng. VP, Am. Music Critics Assn., 1955-; Nat., Acad. of Recording Arts & Scis. Co-recip., Assoc. Press Feature Div. Award, 1965. Hobbies incl: Astrol.; Cuisine. Mgmt: Randolph Herron, Beverly Hills, Calif. Address: 415 W Aldine Ave., Apt. 9-B, Chgo, IL 60657, USA. 2,8.

DEUTSCH, Herbert Arnold, b. 9 Feb. 1932, Baldwin, NY, USA. Composer/Performer of Electronic Synthesizers; Chmn., of Music, Hofstra Univ. Educ: BS (Educ.), Hofstra Univ.; BMus, MMus, Manhattan Schl. of Music. m. Margaret Ann, 1 s, 1 d. Career: Collaborated w. R A Moog on development of the Moog Synthesizer; Consultant to Norlin Music, Inc.; Concerts at Town Hall, Carnegie Recital Hall. Comps: 12 electronic works; Mutima, for chorus; Fantasia I on Es ist Geung, for band (recorded); Moon Ride, for band; Sonorities, for orch. Publs: Synthesis, an Introduction to History, Theory & Practice of Electronic Music. Contbr. to: Audio Engineering Soc. Jrnl.; Nat. Schl. Orch. Assn. Jrnl. Mbrships: ASCAP; Am Assn. of Univ. Profs.; Fndr., & co-dir., L I Comps. Alliance. Mgmt: Allied Promotions, Huntington, NY. Address: 19 Crossman Pl., Huntington, NY 11743, USA. 6.

DE VALE, Sue Carole, b. 30 Nov. 1942, Chgo., Ill., USA. Harpist; Ethonomusicologist; Organologist. Educ: BA,

Mundelein Coll., 1971; MM, 1972, PhD, 1977, Northwestern Univ. m. Donn Allen Carter, 2s. 1d. Debut: as Harp Soloist, Orch. Hall, Chgo., 1960. Career: Harpist w. Chgo. Symph Orch., Lyric Opera of Chgo., Michel Legrand, Henry Mancini, Sammy Davis, Jr., Tony Bennett, Lena Horne, Pearl Bailey et al.; Gamelan Prog. Dir., Field Museum of Nat. Hist., 1976-78 Curator for Ethnomusicol., ibid, 1978-; Tchr.,Harp. Ethnomusicol. & Music Hist., Valparaiso Univ., 1972, Northwestern Univ., 1972-76, Univ. of Wis.-Madison, 1976-77. Recordings & film soundtracks w. var. Am. grps. Publs: A Sundanese Gamelan: A Gestalt Approach to Organology, 1977. Contbr. to: Grove's; Field Museum Bulletin. Mbrships incl: Soc. for Ethnomusicol.; Int. Folk Music Coun.; Am. Musicol. Soc. Hons: Charles Seeger Award, 1976; Grants, Nat. Endowment for the Arts, 1976, Walter E Heller Fndn.,1977. Hobbies: Cooking; Needlework; Swimming. Address: 3750 N Lakeshore Dr., Chgo., IL 60613, USA.

DE VARON, Lorna Cooke, b. 17 Jan. 1921, Western Springs, Ill., USA. Choral Conductor. Educ: AB Wellesley Coll.; Am, Radcliffe-Harvard; pvte studies in voice, organ, cond., theory & comp. m. Jose de Varon, 2 d., 2 d. Career: Concerts, Jordan Hall, Boston, New England Conserv. of Music, Town Hall, 1949-; NYC; Concerts w. Boston Symph. Orch., Symph. Hall, Boston, Carnegie Hall, NYC, & Tanglewood, Mass., 1951-; Cultural Exchange Concert Tours, USSR & Spain, Europe & Ireland, France & Switz; TV apps. Recordings incl: Copland's Choral Works., Mbr., Pi Kappa Lambda. Contbr., to Notes, Wellesley Alumnae Mag. Recip., Var. hons. Hobby: Gardening. Address: 94 Lake View Ave., Cambridge, MA, USA. 5.

DE VASIONELLOS CORREA, Sergio, b. 16 July 1934, Sao Paulo, Brazil. College Professor. Educ: Prof. Music Educ., Santa Marcelina Music Coll.; Prof. Piano, Drama & Music, Conserv. Sao Paulo; Prof. Choral Singing, Choral Singing Conserv., Sao Paulo. m. Dina Irene Mazzucato, 3 children. Debut: Pianist, 1948; Comp., 1951. Career: Sev. apps.on radio & TV as pianist; Instr., Musical Educ. on TV; Prof., Musical Theory, sev., conserv. in Sao Paulo, 1955-. Compositions incl: Velha Modinha, 1974. Sev. Recorded works. Publs. incl: Introduction to Harmony, 1975. Contbr. to newspapers & profl. mags. Mbr. num. profl. orgs. Hons. incl: 1st Prize for Concertina, State Govt., 1974. Hobbies: Sports; Basketball; Football; Bowls. Address: Rua Barao de Goiana 76, Aeroporto de Congonhas, Sao Paulo, Brazil.

DEVÁTÝ, Antonin, b. 12 June 1903, Skutec, Czech. Music Director; Conductor; Composer; Professor. Educ: State Conserv., Prague. m., 1 s., 1 d. Career: Violinist, Czech., Switz., Germany, Film-Opera-Concert Orch., Prague, 1935-38; Cond., Radio Brno, 1938-50, Pilsen, 15960-63; Guest Cond., Hungary, Poland, German Dem. Repub., USSR; currently Prof., Conserv., Pilsen, Brno & Bratislava. Comps. incl: 3 song cyclese (Zamilovaný, Vzpominky, Matka); Tanzsuite; 2 quartets; 5 works for 5 accordions & percussion; concertos for violin, viola, trombone, 2 accordions; Fantasy for oboe; Contrasts for clarinette; Skici for chmbr. orch.; Heimatsgesänge for flute, viola & guitar. Publs: Dirigienlehre. Mbr., Czech. Union of Comps. Hons: Recognition for Disting. Serv., Pres. of CSSR, 1963; Artist of Merit, CSSR, 1975. Hobbies: Nature; Children; Youth. Address: Dvořákova 33, 32000 Pilsen, Czechoslovakia

DEVI, Susheela, b. 4 June 1930, Singapore, Violinist. Educ: RAM; ARCM. Debut: Victoria Mem. Hall, Singapore, 1952. Career: Sub-ldr., ENSA Symph. Orch., under Dr. Erik Chisholm, 1946; Recitalists on All-India Radio,1947, BBC Radio,1950, BBC-TV, 1951, Radio Malaya, 1952 & Aust. Broadcasting Co., 1959; Ldr., Singapore Symph. Orch., Chmbr. Ensemble, Radio Orch. & Musica Viva Players, 1952-61; Sub-ldr., London Cert Orch. & 1st Violin, Delos Quartet 1970-; currently Sub-prin., Engl. Nat. Opera Co. Orch. Hobbies: currently Sub-prin., Engl. Nat. Opera Co. Orch. Mbrships: ISM. Hobbies: Cooking; Badminton. Address: 23 WSoodbastwick Rd., London SE 26 5LG, UK.

DEVICH, Sandor, b. 19 Jan. 1935, Szeged, Hungary. Violinist; Prof. of Chamber Music; Member of Bartók String Quartet. Educ: Ferenc Liszt Acad. of Music, Budapest. m. Klára Körtvélyessy, 3 c. Career: over 2,000 apps. in all European countries, USA, Can., Mexico, Aust., NZ, Japan, Hong Kong, Singapore, Philippines; Fest. apps. at Salzburg (Helsinki), Spoleto, Montreal (EXPO 1967), Adelaide Ascona, Bregenz, Edinburgh, Lucerne, Menton, Schwetzingen, Wiener Festwochen, opening fest. of Sidney Opera House, Prague Spring. Recordings: all Bartók Quartets; Mozart & Beethoven Quartets; complete chmbr. music of Brahms. Puls: Bach, Sonatas & Partitas for violin solo, Pagauini, Barucaba Variatioins, 1980. Contbr. to: Muzsika (Budapest). Mbrships: Hungarian Musicians Assn.; Int. Kodály Soc. num. prizes &

awards for perfs. & recordings. Hobbies: Photography (colour slides); Collecting Antiques; Recordings; Miniature Books., Mgmt: Interkoncert, Budapest. Address: Ráday u. 32, 1092 Budapest, IX, Hungary.

DE VILLIERS, Dirk Izak Catoggio, b. 1 Nov. 1920, Simonstown, S Africa. Music Educator; Choral Conductor (Piano), Univ. S Africa; Pvte. Study w. Dean of Music, Cape Town Univ. m. Hendrika C Grobbelaar, 3 children. Debut: Solo Boy Soprano, Cape Town, 1928; Pianist, Simonstown, 1930; Organist, SABC, 1947; Choral Cond., Bloemfontein,1956. Career; Hd. of Music, Educ. Dept. of Province of Orange Free State, 1975-; Guest Lectr., Rider Univ., Lawrenceville, USA, 1975. Comps. incl: Over 100 Songs (Art & Folk); 120 Official Schl. Songs. Num. recordings. Contbr. to profl. mags. & newspapers. Mbr. of profl. orgs. Hobbies: Golf; Bridge; Reading. Address: PO Box 521, Bloemfontein 9300, Repub. of S Africa.

DEVIRIAN, Diana Lynn Armstrong, b. 4 Nov. 1944, Madison, Wis., USA. Harpist. Educ: BM, Univ. of Wis., 1967; Certs., Music Acad. of the W, Santa Barbara Calif. 1966 & 69; studied w. M Grandjany of the Juilliard Schl., NYC. m. Donald B Devirian. Debut: Madison, Wis. Career: educ. TV app., Madison, Wis., 1964; toured USA w. Wis. Harp Choir; perfs. w. Madison Symph., 1962-67; var. musicals, Calif., Wis & Ill.; Solo recital, Montecito, Calif., 1968; Harp Tchr., Santa Barbara, Calif., 1968-; Soloist, W Coast Symph., 1969; var. perfs. in Calif. Mbrships: Am. Harp Soc.; Sigma Alpha Iota. Hons. Harp Award, Madison Music Clin., Wis.,1961 0 62; Special Award, Harp, Music Acad. of W, 1966. Hobbies: Travel; Skiing; Art; Poetry. Address: 21727 Ulmus Dr., Woodland Hills, CA 91364, USA. 27.

DE VITO, Gioconda, b. 26 July 1907, Martina France, Apuila, Italy. Violinist. Educ: 1st Class Hons. in final exam., Conservatorio Rossini, Pesaro, 1921. m. David Bicknell. Debut, Martina Franca, 1971. Career: Prof. of Violin., Bari, 1925-34, Conservatorio in Santa Cecilia Rome, 1934-45, Accademia in Santa Cecilia, Rome, 1945-58; concerts in most European countries; tours in Aust., Argentina, USSR; Soloist, inaugural yr. of Edinburgh Fest., 1945, & Fest., 1945, & Fest. of Violin w. Yehudi Menuhin & Isaac Stern, 1955; Ret'd., 1962. Recordings for DGG & HMV. Hons: 1st Prize, Int. Competition, Vienna, 1932; Gold Medal for servs. to art, Italian Govt., 1957. Hobbies: Bird watching; Croquet. Address: Flint Cottage, Loudwater, Rickmansworth, Hertf, UK.

de VOLT, Artiss, b. Iowa City, IA, USA. Harpist; Musician Educ: Grad., New England Conserv. of Music, Boston; Studies w. Alfred Holy. m. Robert M. Zacharias., Debut: Steinert Hall, Boston, Mass Career: Town Hall recital, NYC; Kimball Hall recital, Chgo.; Soloist, Mozarteum Symph., Salzburg, Salzburg Fest., Austria & symphs. throughout the world; 5 harp fests. organised on Sea Is. & St. Simons Is.; Mbr., Disting Fac., Mozarteum Acad., Salzburg, many yrs.; Fac. Mbr. New England Conserv. & Coll. of Music, Boston Univ. 5 yrs.; Many radio perfs., Boston WBZ, WEEI. Contbr. to: Grove's Dictionary, int. harp mags. Mbrships: incl: Fndr., Mozart Soc., Sea Is., Ga; Mu Phi Epsilon; Int. Music Sorority; Pi Kappa Lambda; Nat. Music Fraternity. Address: Box 202, Sea Island, GA, USA. 4, 5.

DEVOLT, Charlotte, b. Iowa City, Iowa, USA. Violinist; Music Educator. Educ: MusB, Coe Coll., Cedar Rapids, Iowa; Dip., Longy Schl. of Music, Cambridge, Mass.; New England Conserv., Boston, Mass.; Boston Univ., Mass.; Univ. of Vienna, Austria. m. Joseph Denison Elder. Debut: Town Hall, NYC, USA. Career: Harp-Violin Recitals w. sister, Artiss deVolt, USA & abroad, 1927-; Instructor of Violin & Dir. of orch., Winthrop Coll.; Instructor of violin, Solfeggio, Pub. Schl. Music, Univ. & Vt.; Concertmaster, Vt., Symph., Orch.; Prof. of music & Dir of orch., Erskine Coll.; Hd., Music Dept., Lynchburg Coll. Mbrships: incl: Mozart Soc. of Glynn Co. Hobby: Geneal. Address: 114 Arthur J. Moore Dr., St. Simmons Island, GA 31522, USA. 5,3.

DE VRIES, Han Samuel, b. 31 Aug. 1941, The Hague, Netherlands. Oboist. Musical Educ: Royal Conserv., The Hague, 2 yrs.; Conserv., Amsterdam, 3 yrs.; Dips. in tching., orch. & solo. Career: 1st Oboe, Concertgebouw Orch., 1963-70: Solo Oboe, Netherlands Chmbr. Orch., 1970-74; 1st Oboe, Netherlands Wind Ensemble, 196 2-73; Oboe Tchr., Sweelink Conserv., Amsterdam, 1964- Oboe Tchr., Royal Conserv., The Havue, 1974-76 Oboist, Danzi Quintet, 1973-76 Num. radio & TV apps.,; Recitals; & solo apps. in Europe, N & S Am., Russia, Aust. & Japan. Recordings incl: Exclusive contract w. EMI; Bach oboe-oboe d'amore concertos w. Zagreb; Soloists; Mozart KV314, KV294B, w. Prague Chmbr. Orch.; Oboe; Oboe & organ sonatas by var. comps. Hons. incl: Prix d'Excellence, 1962. Edison Award for recording, 1974. Hobbies: Collecting

antique oboes & oboe music MSS. Mgmt: Sheldon Soffer, NY; Sogobunkasha Inc., Tokyo, Japan De Koos Concert Mgmt., 46 King's Rd., London SW10. Address: Vossiusstreaat 28, Amsterdam, Netherlands.

de VRIES, Leo Gerrit Herman, b. 27 Oct. 1924, Wassenaar, Netherlands. Violinist. Educ: Korinklÿk Conservatorium, The Hague. m. Dorothea Käthe Hoffmann. Career: Mbr., Groninger Orkest Vereeniging & Rotterdams Philharmonisch Orkest; Soloist in secular & ch. concerts. Comps. incl: chmbr. music Mbr., Koninklÿke Nederlandse Toonkunstleraas Vereniging. Recip. 1st Prize for Sexet. Address: Merelhoven 321, Capelle a/d Yssel, Netherlands.

DE VRIES ROBBÉ, Willem Arnold, b. 3 Dec. 1902, Amsterdam, The Netherlands. Composer; Teacher of Violin & Viola. Educ: Conserv., Amsterdam; studied violin & viola w. Herman Leydesdorff; comp. & theory w. Sem Dresden; pvtly. w. Sem Dresden. m. Anna Margaretha Bergmans, 2 s., 1 d. Debut: Serenade for Orch., dir. Willem van Otterloo, Tivoli Hall, Utrecht. Career: Tchr. of violin, viola & ensemble playing; Var. radio broadcasting of own orch. & chamber music; Perfs. for public (concerts). Compositions incl.: Butterflies for vibraphone solo; Poems (Emily Dickinson) for flute, vibraphone & voice; Sonatas for flute & harp, flute & guitar; Arbesques for solo harp; A Summer Day for violin & piano; Concerto pastorale per flauto e orchestra; Concertino for flute & string orch.; Concert for flute, harp & orch.; Rondeaux for flute, vibraphone & declamation (text Charles d'Orleans); Blackbirds for a flute player & a percussionist; Invention for pedal harp & harpsichord. Mbrships: GENECO (Soc. of Composers, Netherlands); KNTV. Address: Melkweg 5, Blaricum, The Netherlands.

de Waart, Edo, b. 1 June 1941, Amsterdam, Netherlands. Conductor.Educ: Amsterdam Music Lyceum. m. Roberta Alexander, 1 s., 1 d. Career: Asst. Cond., Concertgebouw Orch., Amsterdam, 1966; Permanent Cond., 1967, Musical Dir. & Prin. Cond., 1973-, Rotterdam Phil.; Prin. Guest Cond., San Fran. Symph. Orch., 1975-. Recip. 1st Prize, Dimitri Mitropoulos Competition, NY, 1964. 16.

DEXTER, Benning, b. 11 Mar. 1915, Oakland, Calif., USA. Pianist. Educ: Univ. Calif.; Stanford Univ.; Dip., Juilliard Grad. Schl.; MS, ibid. m. Elizabeth Brinkman, 1 d. Career: Solo recitals, var. colls. & univs.; Asstng. artist for string players inclng. Doktor, Houser, Jelinek, Mays, Mischakoff, Ross, & Totenberg; NBC Network Radio, Radio Tokyo, & Educl. TV apps.; Concert & recital premieres of music by Finney, C Jones, Milhaud & Wilson; Fac. Mbr., Univ. Mich., 1949-, 1949-; Prof. music, piano, ibid. 1958; Piano Dept. Chmn., 1961-73. Recordings: Tokyo. Publ: Editions of Piano Music (w. Joseph Brinkman), 1951, 59. Contbr. to jrnls. Mbrships: Pi Kappa Lambda; Bohemians. Hobbies: Tennis; Swimming. Address: 928 Aberdeen, Ann Arbor, MI 48104, USA.

DEXTER, Harold, b. 7 Oct. 1920, Leicester, UK. Organist; Teacher; Conductor. Educ: MusB, MA (Cantab); FRCO; ARCM; ADCM. m. Faith Grainger, 1 d. Career: Organist, Southwark Cathedral, 1956-68; Prof., GSM, 1956-; currently Hd. of General Musicianship Dept. Mbrships: Coun., RCO; past service on ISM & IAO Execs.; var. assns. w. RSCM. Hons: FGSM; FRSM. Hobbies: Gardening; Aquarium; Brewing. Address: 8 Prince Edward Rd., Billericay, Essex, UK.

DE YOUNG, Lynden E, b. 6 Mar. 1923, Chgo., Ill., USA. Composer; Professor; Jazz Trombonist. Educ: BMus, Roosevelt Univ., 1950: MMus, ibid., 1951; DMus, Northwestern Univ., 1966. m. June Hope De Young, 1 d., 1 s. Career: Fac., Roosevelt Univ., 1951-59; Assoc. Prof. of theory & comp., Schl. of Music, Northwestern Univ., 1966-; Chmn., Dept. of theory & comp., ibid., 1967-75. Comps. incl: Divertissement, for brass ensemble & percussion; Praise the Lord, for chorus & chamber ensemble; Homage to Dixieland, for wind & percussion ensemble; Chmbr. Music for alto saxophone & chmbr. ensemble; 6 Miniatures for piano & violin; Piano Music; Texture: organ, harp, celesta. Publs: Fugue, the Treatment of Thematic Materials (in Clavier), 1968. Mbrships: incl: Pi Kappa Lambda (past pres., Alpha Chapt.); AMS; ASUC; AAUP; Am Fed. of Musicians. Hons: Thor Johnson Brass Ensemble Award, 1951; NU grant for perf., 1977. Hobbies: Photography; Fishing; Playing jazz. Address: 664 Pine Court, Lake Bluff, Ill., USA. 29.

DEYTON, Camilla Hill, b. 23 Sep. 1952, Raleigh, NC, USA. Composer; Theorist. Educ: BMus, Converse Coll., Spartanburg, SC; MMus, Univ. of NC, Greensboro; Brevard Music Ctr.; Canon Music Camp. Career: now working as customer service mgr., Richway, working pvtely. on comp. & theory. Comps: Songs for Thursday; Songs for Monday; The Cusp; Remuda,

Op. 7 (all perf. at Converse Coll., 1974). Mbrships: Pi Kappa Lambda; League of Women Comps. Hon: Andante & Allegro for str. orch. perf. at Univ., of SC New Music Fest., 1974. Address: 6610, Apt. 5, Wisteria Dr., Charlotte, NC 28210, USA.

D'HAESE, Iwein Lydia Roeland, b. 4 Nov. 1932, Aalst, Belgium. Bassoon Player; Professor of Bassoon, Koninklijk Muzickconservatorium, Brussels. Educ: Dip. in bassoon, dip. in piano (le prÿs), chmbr. music (le prÿs), Koninklyk Vlaams Muziekconservatorium, Antwerp. Career: Soloist, Nat. Opera Brussels; TV & radio broadcasts; chmbr. musician; Prof., Koninkyk Muziekconservatorium, Brussels. Has made sev. recordings. Mbr. Rondo woodwind quartet (flute, clarinet, bassoon & horn). Recip. trophy, Belgian Comps. Union, 1969. Hobby: Cooking. Address: Bodegemstraat 91, 1740 Ternat, Belgium.

D'HOOGHE, Kamiel Frans Marie, b. 17 Nov. 1929, Beveren-Waas, Belgium. Organist; Director, Royal Conservatorie of Music, Brussels. Educ: Higher Cert. Organ w. highest distinction, Royal Flemish Conserv., Antwerp, 1954; 1st prize, Fugue, Royal Conserv., Ghent, 1956. m. Agnes Dumon, 3 s., 1 d. Debut: Organist, St. Salvator Cathedral, Bruges. Career: Dir., Royal Conserv. Music, Brussels; Recitalist, Europe, USA & Japan. Recordings. Mbr., Organ Sect, Koninklyke Commissie voor Monumenten & Landschappen. Hons: Laureat, Int. Bach Competitioin, Ghent, 1955; 1st Laureate Int Organ Competitioin, Munich, 1955; Bach Medal, Harriet Cohen Fndn., 1956. Address: Beiaardlaan No. 1 Grimbergen, Belgium.

DIAMOND, David Leo, b. 1915, Rochester NY, USA. Composer; Conductor; Lecturer. Educ: Eastman Schl. of Music; Cleveland Inst.; New Music Schl.; Dalcroze Inst.; Fontainebleau; pvte. study w. Roger Sessions. m. Nadio Boulanger in Paris. Career: w. Metropolitan Schl. of NY; Lectr., Harvard Seminar, Salzburg, Austria; Fulbright Prof., Rome, 1951; Chmn., Composition Dept., Manhattan Schl., NY, 1966; Slee Prof., Univ. of Buffalo, 1961 & 63; Tchr., Juilliard Schl of Music, 1973-. Comps. incl: 8 symphs.; 10 str. quartets; 3 violin concertos; piano concerto; cello concerto; This Sacred Ground for mixed chorus, soloist, orch. & children's chorus; Choral Symphony - To Music; Psalm for Orchestra; sev. ballets; music for The Tempest & Romeo & Juliet; sev. ballets; music for the Tempest & Romeo & Juliet; sev song cycles & miscellaneous songs; unaccompanied sonatas for var. instruments; miscellaneous a capella choral works; 75 songs, etc. Recip. of many awards inclng. Paderewski Prize; Prix de Rome. Hobbies incl: Cooking; Silent Films; Painting. Address: 249 Edgerton St., Rochester, NY 14607, USA. 3.

DIAMOND, Eileen, b. London, UK. Composer; Music Teacher. Educ: RCM; ALCM. Career: Composer of children's songs & musical stories; comp., ibid, for BBC TV children's progs.; Infant Schl. music tchr.; tchr. of piano & theory. Comps. incl: The Little Gingerbread Man, 1977; Find A Bin, 1978; The Toy Shop, 1978; Act One Sing Too (12 action songs for young children), 1979; Let's All Sing a Happy Song, 1980; Banding Together (songs w. percussion), 1980. Recording: Banding Together. Mbrships: Performing Right Soc.; ISM Songwriters Guild of GB. recip. 1st prize, piano comp., E London Music Fest., 1974. Hobby: Tennis. Address: 17 Haslemere Gdns., London N3, UK.

DIAZ, Alirio, b. 1923, Carora, Venezuela, Guitarist; Composer, Educ: Caracas Conserv.; Madrid Conserv.; studies w. Andres Segovia, Accademia Musicale Chigiana, Siena. Debut: Caracas, 1950. Career: tours of Austria, UK, France, Germany, Italy, Belgium, Spain, Israel & the Ams.; Asst. Prof. to Segovia, 1955-. Recip., Order del Maestro Libertador Andes Bello, Venzuela. Address: 30 Via Nobili, Rome, Italy. 2.

DIAZ, Justino, b. 29 Jan. 1940, San Juan, Puerto Rico. Operatic Bass. Educ: Univ. of Puerto Rico; New England Conserv. of Music. m. Anna Aragno, 1 d. Career incl: New England Opera Theatre, 1961; Am. Opera Soc., 1963-64; Ldng. Am. orchs. & operas. also at La Scala, Barcelona's Gran Teatro del Liceo & Teatro Colon, Buenos Aires; Salzburg, Spoleto & Casals Fests. Var. Recordings. Mbrships: Dutch Treat Club, NYC; Alpha Beta Chi. Hons. incl: Family of Man Citation, 1966; Handel Medallion, NYC, 1966. Address: Metrop. Opera Co., Lincoln Ctr., NY, NY 10023, USA. 2.

DI BELLO, Victor, b. 11 Feb. 1933, Toronto, Can. Conductor; Pianist; Administrator. Educ: Univ. of Toronto; Royal Conserv. of Music; Cond. studies w. Walter Sussikind; Berkshire Music Centre, Tanglewood. Debut: Toronto Symph. Orch., 1958. Career; Fndr. & Cond., Pro Arte Orch. or Toronto, 1950; Cond. & Music Dir., Hamilton Phil. Orch., 1958-62; apps. as Cond. w. Toronto Symph., Pro Arte & CBC Orchs., CBC Radio TV; Cond.,

annual perfs. of Messiah, Toronto & Stratford Fest. Theatre; Cond., staged prondns. of 18th Century chmbr. opera, Hart House Theatre, Univ. of Toronto; Music Administrator, 1962-67, Dir. of Music, 1968-69, Stratford Fest., Can.; Asst. Managing Dir., Cond., inaugural season Student Showcase Concerts, Second. Schls. w. new Pro Arte Orch., Toronto, 1979-80. Scholarship award, Kiwanis Music Fest., Toronto, 1948; Sibelius Centennial Medal, Sibelius Concert w. Pro Arte Orch., Toronto, 1965. Address: 1692 Danforth Ave., Toronto, Ont. M4C 1H8, Canada.

DiCHIERA, David, b. 8 Apr. 1935. McKeesport, Pa., USA. Impresario; Professor of Music; Composer. Educ: BA, MA, 1958, PhD, 1962, Univ. of Calif., Los Angeles; Naples Conserv. of Music, Italy. m. Karen VanderKlott, 2 d. Debut: Naples, 1959. Career. Gen. Dir. & Fndr., Mich. Opera Theatre; Artistic Dir. & Fndr., Music Hall Ctr. for the Performing Arts. Comps incl: Concerto, piano & orch.; Preludes (piano); Piano Sonata; Fantasy for 2 Pianos; Fantasy for Violin & Piano. Contbr. to: Musical encys.; num. profl. jrnls. Mbrships incl: Oplera Am. (Bd. of Dirs.); Mich. Arts Coun. (Advsry. Committee). Hons. incl: Fulbright Award. 1958; Cert. of Appreciation, City of Detroit, 1970. Hobbies: Collecting Art Glass; Tennis. Address: 5030 Chain Bridge Road., Bloomfield Hills, MI 48013, USA.

DICHLER-SEDLACEK, Erika, b. 23 June 1929, Vienna, Austria. Pianist; Composer. Educ: Univ. of Music, Vienna. m. Dr. Josef Dichler. Debut: 1950. Career: Approx. 1000 piano concerts, Austria & abroad; approx. 5000 radio & TV broadcasts. Comps: Skizzen (Sketches, 27 pieces); Minaturen (Miniatures, 26 pieces); Märchenbilder (Pictures out of Fairy Tales, 12 pieces) - all for piano. Sev. recordings. Publs: Leitfaden für den Klavierunterricht (Guide to the teaching of thepiano), 1971. Contbr. to var. mags. Mbrships: Pres., Vienna Belvedere, 1972-74; Bd. Mbr., Soroptimist Int.; Bd. Mbr., Künstler helfen Künstlern; Bd. Mbr., Beethoven-Gedenkstätte; Bachgemeinde; Mozartgemeinde; VÖSA; IMZ; IGNM; AKM; Isme; Austromachana, etc. Hons: Hon. Mbr., Klub der Wiener Muskerinnen. Hobbies: Art; Lit. Address: Gymnasiumstrasse 4, A-1180 Vienna XVIII, Austria. 27, 30.

DICK, Eleanor, b. 12 Apr. 1922, NYC, USA. Teacher of Piano & Theory; Adjudicator. Educ: BS, Brooklyn Coll.; Ms, Columbia Univ.; student of AK Virgil, Alexander Bartnowslay, Carl Friedbert & Josef Fidelman; Fac. Mbr. Am. Coll. of Musicians; Mastger class of Artur Schanabel; Grad. studies at Hunter Coll., CUNY. m. Franklin Dick, 3 s. 1 dec. Career: 30 yrs. tchng. experience presenting annual student recitals of solo & ensemble works at Carnegie Hall, NYC; Solo students presented in recital at Judson Hall, Town Hall & 'The Young American Artists' of the Municipal Broadcasting System, WNYC; Her musical transcriptions for one hand for handicapped students (Baroque-Contemporaty), played by students in recitals & competitions. Many students have won piano scholarships for colls. throughout the USA. Mbrships: Piano Guild Hall of Fame, NGPT; State & Nat. Fedn. of Music Clubs; Music Tchrs. Nat. Assn.; Piano Tchrs. Congress; Chmn. of Scholarship Awards & Auditions. Assoc. Music Tchrs. Leag e of NYC. Hobbies: Reading; Travel. Address: 530 Valley Rc, Upper Montclair, NJ 07043, USA.

DICKENSON, James William, b. 20 Oct. 1940, Grappenhall, UK. Pianist; Harpsichord Player; Teacher; Composer. Educ: LLB, Bristol Univ.; BMus, Manchester Univ.; postgrad. rsch. in Am. music, Keele Univ.; Royal Manchester Coll. of Music; ARCM; Debut: BBC Radio 3, 1972. Career: Harpsichord player w. Manchester Camerata Orch.; Extra-mural lectr., Univs. of Liverpool & Manchester; Examiner, Assoc. Bd. of Royal Schls. of Music. Comps: Suite for Orch. (1973); St. Patrick's Avowal, for double choir & organ, 1974; Part-songs, educl. music & modern jazz arrs. Mbrships: Royal Musical Assn.; ISM; Musicians' Union. Hobbies: Sailing; Cycling; Reading fiction; Modern jazz. Mgmt: Shelia Cooper Concert Artists, Ltd. Address: 7 Brook Ln., Chester CH2, 2AP, UK.

DICKERSON, Bernard Francis, b. Barnes, Surrey, UK. Singer (tenor). Debut: Maj. role in A Lesson in Love (Chabrier), St. Pancras Festival, 1961. Career: Perfs. incl: Glyndebourne Festival Opera; Royal Opera House, Covent Gdn.; Engl. Opera Grp.; Royal Opera, Ghent; Scottish Opera; New Opera, Co. Wexford Festival; Apps. in USA, Can., Aust., Europe, etc.; Apps. w. LPO Halle & City of Birmingham Orchs., Proms., TV Operas, Danish Radio, Aust. TV. Recordings: Les Contes d'Hoffmann; Manon Lescaut; Pilgrim's Progress; Sir John in Love; Serenade to Music; Monteverdi Madrigals. Hobbies: Food; Wine; Gardening Mgmt: Music Int.

DICKERSON, Charles L, b. 4 Mar. 1928, Tulsa, Okla., USA. Baritone; Dramatist; Teacher; Writer. Educ: BMus, Univ. Tulsa;

Current study, Southern Meth. Univ. m. Mary Leslie Dickerson, 2 d. Debut: Singer, NYC, 1946. Career: Toured w. The Great Mantell Troupe, 6 yrs.; Dramatist (40 yrs.) & Baritone (30 yrs.) on Radio, TV, Stage & Screen on Broadway & Hollywood; French Hornist w. Idaho Symph. 29 yrs. Var. recordings. Publs. incl: 2 Science Fiction Novels; 2 books of Poetry & Prose; Golden Anthology of Poetry, 1976; The Poems of Charles, 1976. Contbr. to num., mags. Mbrships: incl: Phi Mu Alpha Sinfonia. Hons: 2 scholarships to Univ. of Tulsa & Southern Meth. Univ. Hobbies: Boating; Racing; Tennis; Archery & Riflery; Gold & Silversmith., Address: 1531 S Gillette, Tulsa, OK 74104, USA.

DICKIE, Murray, b. 3 Apr. 1924, Scotland, UK. Opera Singer. Educ: music studies in Glasgow. Debut: London, 1947. Career: Opera performances at Covent Gdn.; La Scala, Milan; Metropol. Opera, NYC; Mbr., Vienna State Opera; Film Prod., Vienna. Address: Hasenauestra. 41. Vienna, Austria.

DICKIE, William Payne, b. 7 Sept. 1914, Belfast, UK. Theatrical Manager. Educ: Studied singing w. Prof. Stefan Pollmann, Vienna, Austria, Dino Borgioli, London, & Titta Ruffo, Florence, Italy. m. Mary Cecilia Denniss, 1 s., 1 d. Career: Prin. Baritone, New London Opera, Covent Garden Opera Guest Perf., Vienna State Opera, Sadlers Wells Opera, & Welsh Nat. Opera; app. by invitation, singing, aria, Largo Al Factotum, 60th Anniversary Henry Wood Promenade Concert, 1954. Recordings; Aria, Largo at Factotum; Aria, Bella Siccome un Angelo; Complete Operas, Rigoletto & La Traviata, Columbia La Scala Milan Series. Hon. Lt.-Col., mentioned in Dispatches. Mbrships: Coun. of Theatre Mgrs. Assn.; Green Room Club. Hobby: Golf. Address: 1 Holland House, Kingsgate Bay, Broadstairs, Kent, UK. 3.

DICKIESON, George William, b. 6 Feb. 1912, New York, NY, USA. Professor of Music. Educ: BMus., Schl. of Music, Salem Coll., 1934; MMus., Cinn. Conserv. of Music, Univ. of Cinn., 1940; Study of conducting, L'Ecole Monteaux, Me. m. Anna Bell, 1 d. Career: Former Cond., Greensboro (NC) Symph.; Cond. Univ. of NC Sinfonia; Prof., Music. Univ. of NC; & Chmn., Conducting Div., Schl. of Music; Violinist, Mbrships: Past Pres., NC String Tchrs. Assn.; Past Pres., NC Orch. Assn.; Co-Fndr., Past Sec., Greensboro Chmbr. Music Soc.; Participant, Orch. Symposium under Eugene Ormandy; Pi Kappa Lambda; Phi Mu Alfa Sinfonia Fraternity. Hons: Orpheus Award, 1977. Address: 3505 Greenwood Ter., Greensboro, NC 27510, USA.

DICKINSON, Dorothy Helen, b. 27 Aug. 1941, Pilling, Preston, UK. Dir. of Music. Educ: RCM; GRSM; LRAM; ARCM. Career: Dir. of Music, Lowther Coll., Abergele, N Wales; Dir. of Music, Downe House Schl., Newbury; Lectr. in Music, Kingston Polytechnic; Dir. of Music. Cheltenham Ladies Coll.; Examiner, Assoc. Bd. of Royal Schls. of Music. Recording; as cond. of semi-chorus in Elgar's The Apostles. Contbr. to Music Master Assn. Magazine. Mbr., ISM. Hobbies: Tennis; Driving, Antiques. Address: 1 Lawrence Close, Hambrook Pk., Charlton Kings, Cheltenham, UK.

DICKINSON, Meriel, b. 8 Apr. 1940, Lytham St. Annes, UK. Mezzo-Soprano. Educ: GRSM; ARMCM; Piano & Singing Perf.'s Dip. w. Hons., Vienna Acad., Austria. Debut: London, 1964. Career: Frequent radio progs.; 2 BBC TV documentary films; recital progs. w. comp. Peter Dickinson (brother) throughout Europe. Recordings; Contemp. Brit. Comps. (Crosse, Berkeley, Dickinson); Erik Satie Songs & Piano Music; Brecht-Weill series w. London Sinfonietta. Mbrships: Soc. for Promotion of New Music; Pk. Ln. Grp.; ISM. Recip. Countess of Munster Musical Trust Scholarship, 1964-66. Hobbies: Listening to jazz. Entertaining. Mgmt: Trio Mgmt., 5 Warwick Ln., St. John's Working Surrey, UK. Address: Flat 4, 14 Lancaster Gate, London, W2 3LH, UK. 4.

DICKINSON, Peter, b. 15 Nov. 1934, Lytham, Lacs., UK. Composer; Pianist; Professor of Music. Educ: Queens' Coll., Cambridge; MA (music); LRAM; ARCM (piano perf.); ARCO (Swayer Prize); FRCO; Juilliard Schl. of Music, NY. m. Bridget Jane Tomkinson, 2 s. Career: regular perfs. as Pianist, most w. sister Meriel Dickinson (mezzo), radio & TV in UK & abroad. Comps. incl: orchl. works; concertos; chmbr. music; choral works; keyboard music; ch. music. Works recorded; Winter Afternoons; Recorder Music; Extravaganzas. Has recorded on Argo & Unicorn labels. Ed: 20 British Composers, 1975. Contbr. to var. jrnls. Mbrships: incl: PRS; Comps. Guild; ISM; Royal Musical Assn. Recip. var. hons. Hobby: Books. Address: Music Dept., Keele Univ., Staffs. ST5 5BG, UK.

DICKREITER, Michael, b. 13 Apr. 1942, Koinstanz, German Fed. Repub. Editor. Educ: PhD. Musicol., Univ. of Heidelberg, 1971. m. Regine E. Soffner, 2 children. Career: Lectr., Univ.

Austral, Chile, 1968-70: Exhibitioner, Studienstiftung des deutschen Volkes, 1966-71. Publs: Der Musiktheoretiker Johannes Kepler, 1973; Musikinstruments, 1976 Der Klong der Musikinstrumente, 1977; Tonstudiotechnik, 1978. Contbr. to: Dur und Moll bei Johannes Kepler, 1971; var. book reviews. Mbrships: Soc. of Music Rsch., Germany; Union of German Sound Engrs. Address: Auf der Schanz 12, D 8500 Nuremberg, German Fed. Repub.

DICKSON, Hester Mary Campbell, b. 22 July 1924, Edinburgh, Scotland. Pianist. Educ: BMus, Edinburg Univ., 1945; LRAM, m. (1) Lawrence Pool (dec.), (2) George Martineau (dec.), 2 s. Debut: Lunch Hour Concert, Nat. Gall., Edinburgh, 1942., Career: Sonata recitals w. Joan Dickson, cellist, at home & abroad inclng. perfs. at Edinburgh Int. Fests. Concertos in Brit.; Accomp., Staff of RSAM. Recordings; Cesar Franck Sonata for cello & piano. Hobbies: Cooking; Dressmaking. Address: 2 Bellevue Terrace, Edinburgh EH7 4DU, UK.

DICKSON, Ivey, b. 1 Nov. 1919, Felton, UK. Pianist; Cellist; Violinist; Violist; Musical Director. Educ: FRAM; LRAM. m. John Victoir Stoddart. Debut: Wigmore Hall, London. Career: began piano aged 4, later playing violin, viola & cello; recitals throughout world; Pianist w. major symph. orchs. & at Promenade Concerts, London; toured W Indies, Africa & NZ as Examiner; Musical Dir., Nat. Youth Orch. of GB, 1966-. Recip., num. musical awards. Hobbies: Gardening; Photography. Address: 40 Avondale Ave., Worcester Pk., Surrey, UK. 3.

DICKSON, Joan, b. 21 Dec. 1921, Edinburgh, Scotland. Cellist; Teacher. Educ: LRAM; ARCM. Career: Solo Cellist w. major Brit. Orchs., London Proms, Cheltenham Festival, Edinburgh Festival, tours abroad; Prof. of Cello, RCM, London; Tchr. of Cello, RSAM, Glasgow; Short talks, BBC Radio. Recordings; Ian Hamilton Cello Sonata; Tam O'Bedlams Song; Cesar Franck Sonata. Contbr. to Inc. Soc. Musicians mags. Mbr., Inc. Soc. Musicians. Hons: FRCM; FRSAMD; Cobbett Gold Metal for servs. to Chamber Music. Hobbies: Gardening; Philately; Painting. Mgmt: Ingpen & Williams. Address: 4 Gt. Stuart St., Edinburgh EM3 6AW, UK. 3.

DICKSON, Katherine Joan Balfour, b. 21 Dec. 1921, Edinburgh, Scotland. Cellist (Performer & Teacher). Educ: LRAM; ARCM; Studied in Paris & Rome. Career: Solo cellist w. maj. Brit. Orchs.; Proms.; Edinburgh Festival; Cheltenham Festival; Tours abroad; Regular Broadcaster; TV apps.; Prof. of Cello, RCM. London & RSAM, Glasgow. Recordings: lain Hamilton cello sonata; Cesar Franck sonata; Tam o'Bedlams song w. Peter Pears. Contbr. to ISM Mag. & teaching jrnls.; (mbr. of coun. & vice-chmn.). Broadcasts talks. Mbrships: ISM; European String Tchrs, Assn. Hons. FRCM; FRSAMD; Cobbett Medal for Sevs. to Chmbr. Music. Hobbies: Gardening; Philately. Address: 4 Gt. Stuart St., Edinburgh EH3 6AW, Scotland, UK.

DIDRICKSON, Luther Norman, b. 19 July 1938, Chgo., Ill., USA. Professional Trumpeter; Trumpet Teacher. Educ: BMus Ed., 1960, MMus, 1961, Northwestern Univ.; postgrad. work in musicol., ibid., 1967-69. M. Sally B. Ritter. Career: Freelance soloist, Chgo. area. 1955-; freelance perfs. w. Chgo. Symph. Orch., Chgo. Lyric Opera, etc.; Mbr. & Soloist, Peninsula Music Fest., Wis., 1967-; Asst. Prof. Trumpet, Northwestern Univ., 1964; Lectr. in Brass, Ind. Univ., 1973- N. Pk. Coll., Chgo., 1975-; Fndr.-Dir., Brass Choir of N Shore, 1969-. Publs: Arr., Morales, O Mangum mysterium. Recordings incl: Janacek. Symphonietta, Mahler 2nd Symph. & Khatchaturian, Symph. 3, w. Chgo. Symph. Mbrships; Pi Kappa Lambda. Int. Trumpet Guild; Music Lib. Assn. Hobbies: Avid Photographer. Address: 2115 Ridge Ave., Evanston, IL 60201, USA.

DIEBEL, Wendel Hobard, b. 20 Feb. 1914, Des Moines, Iowa, USA. Professor of Piano & Theory. Educ: Drake Univ., Des Moines; Dips., Piano & Comp., Juilliard Grad. Schl. of Music. m. Thayer Hunter, 2 s. Career: Prof. Emeritus, Colo. State Univ., Comps. publd: Fantasy for Harp, Flute & Strings; Toccata for Solo Harp; Two Easy Etudes for Solo Harp; 12 Musical Clock Pieces for non-pedal harp - Haydn; Second harp part to Toccata for Solo Harp; 10 Bagatelles for Harp & Brass Quintet. Recordings; Books I & II Debussy Preludes. Mbrships: ASCAP; Am. Harp Soc.; MTNA; CSMTA; Fedn. of Music Clubs. Recip. Chales Lory Award for outstanding contbrns. in tchng. & scholarship. Hobbies: Gardening; Carpentry. Address: 1314 W Mtn. Ave., Ft. Collins, CO 80521, USA.

DIEDERICHS, Yann, b. 13 Mar. 1952. Lyon, France. Sound Engineer. Educ: BTS for sound engrng. w. specialisation; Paris Univ. III. Comps: Shrei, for solo male voice; Lied A, B, for chmbr. orch.; Kene, for clavichord; Fels, for solo flute;

Schiemm, for 2 instruments, percussion & soprano; Stream, for orch.; N.S.M., for choir. Address: 69 rue Dunois, F 75013 Paris, France.

DIEMENTE, Edward, b. 27 Feb. 1923, Cranston, RI, USA. Composer; Organist; Professor of Composition & Theory. Educ: Boston Univ.; BMus, Hartt Coll. of Music; MMus, Eastman Schl. of Music. m. Eleanor Marchesseault, 4 d., 1 s. Comps: Diminsions I, II, III, IV; Hosanna I, II, III; Celebration, Unvelopment; Design; Quartet, 1966; Quartet, 1967; Trio; Something Else; For Miles & Miles; 3-31-70; Response; Love Song for Autumn; Variations for Wind Quintet; For Lady Day; The Eagles Gather; Diary I; Diary II; Seven Things from the Box of Magic; Alleluia, 1973; 2 Pieces for Organ; Fanfare for organ; Mirrors, I-VI. Recording: Quartet 1966 recorded by Bertram Turesky Quartet; Diary, Part 2 by Trent Kynaston & David Fish. Contbr. to: Holy Cross Quarterly, Composer Mag.; Music & Artist. Mbr., ASCAP. Recip., ASCAP Award, 1973. Address: 72 Montclair Dr., W. Hartford, CT 06107, USA.

DIEMER, Emma Lou, b. 24 Nov. 1927. Kansas City, Mo., USA. Composer; Pianist; Organist; Teacher. Educ: BM, Yale Schl. of Music, 1949; MMus, ibid, 1950; Fulbright Schlr., composition & piano, Royal Conserv., Brussels, Belgium, 1952-53; studied composition, Berkshire Music Ctr., 1954 & 55; PhD., Eastman Schl. of Music, 1960. Career: Composer-in-Res., Arlington, Va., schls. under Form Fndn. grant, 1959-61; Composer-Cons., Arlington & Balt. Md., Schls. under Contempt. Music Prog. of MENC, 1964-65; Prof. of composition & theory, Univ. of Md., 1965-70, & Univ. of Calif., Santa Barbara, 1971-; organist, 1st Ch. of Christ Scientist, Santa Barbara, 1973-. Compositions publd: over 200 choral & instrumental works inclng. Symphonie Antique, Rondo Concertante, The Brass Menagerie, Fantasie for Organ, Seven Etudes for Piano, Anniversary Choruses. Compositions recorded: Toccata for Flute Choruses. Contbr. to jrnls. Mbrships; Am. Soc. of Univ. Composers; ASCAP; AGO; Mu Phi Epsilon. Recip. of many awards. Hobbies: Reading; Building. Address: Dept. of Music, Univ. of Calif., Santa Barbara, CA 93111, USA. 5.

DIETHELM, Caspar, b. 31 Mar. 1926, Lucerne, Switz. Composer; Estate Book Supervisor. Educ: Dip., theory of music, Acad. of Music, Lucerne. m. Brigette Ullrich, 3 children. Debut: Tonhalle Zürich, 1948. Career: Free-lance contbr. to radio; Prof., Hist. of Music, Lucerne Acad. of Music, 1963-; Mbr., Co. Coun. Obwalden, Pres. of Coun., 2972-73. Comps: 140 works inclng. symphs. concertos, cantatas, chmbr. music organ music, etc. Mbr., Swiss Comps. Assn. Recip. Creative Arts Award, Caton of Obwalden, 1969. Hobbies: Mineralog.; Archaeol.; Chess; Gardening; Politics Address: Bruenigstrassa 170, 6060 Sarnen, Switzerland.

DIETRICH, Karl, b. 9 July 1927, Wachstedt, Kreis Mühlhausen/Thüringen, Germany. Composer; Teacher. Educ: State Examination for music teachers. m. Gerdia Lins. 2d. Career: Tchr. of comp., Franz Liszt High Schl. for Music, Weimar. Comps: 3 Symphs.; Dramatic Scenes for 3 flutes & large orch.; piano Concerto; Symphonic choral works; Chmbr. music; songs; 2 concertos for string orch.; 3 Divertimenti for orch. mbr. profl. socs. Hons: Kunstpreis des FDGB, 1971; Kunstpreis der DDR for Dramatic Scenes, 1975. Address: zum Wilden Graben 24, 53 Weimaar, German Dem. Repub.

DIETRICH, Oskar, b. 16 Feb. 1888, Vienna, Austria., Composer; Author. Educ: DPh, Univ. of Vienna; pvte. study of Theory w. R. Braun, & of Instrumentatioin w. F. Schmidt. m. Ingeborg Kronberger. Compositions incl: (orch.) 2 Symphs.; Variations; Divertimento; (opera) Temptation; 3 pieces for chmbr. orch.; 6 str. quartets; (published) Lavendel - fuge für: Klavier (2 Häaden); Rapsodie Es-moll, (klavier, 2 Händen); Suite G-moll für Flöte (Geige) & Klavier; (recorded) Thema mit 9 Wandlungen für Grosses Orchester; Diptychon für Kammerochester; Fantasie für Kammerochester. Mbr., Austrian Soc. of Comtemporay Music (exec. committee). Hobbies: Literature; Gardening. Address: Bernardgasse 20, A-1070 Vienna, Austria.

DIGGS, Leonard Lee, b. 6 Apr. 1939, Colo. Springs, Colo., USA. Educator; Conductor; Performer (Bassoon). Educ: BMus, Univ. Colo., 1962; MMus, ibid., 1963; Doct. cand., 1970-72. m. Jane Elizabeth Weigand, 2 children. Career: incls: Instrumental music instructor, Jefferson Co. Schl. Dist. R-1, Colo., 1963-; Bassoon Instructor, Univ. Colo., Boulder, 1956-66; Musical Dir., Conductor. Golden Symph. Youth Orch., USA, 1967-; Supvsng. tchr., student tchrs. music, var. colls., Colo. & Ill., 1971-. Mbr. & Off., var. profl. orgs. Hons. incl: Bronze Medal, outstanding musical perf. as cond., Golden Symph. Youth Orch., Pavia, Italy, 1973. Hobbies: incl: Travel. Address: 6668 Vivian St., Arvada, CO 80004, USA.

DI GIROLAMO, Joseph, b. 5 Feb. 1942, Fossacasia, Chieti, Italy. Music Teacher (piano, clarinet, flute, trumpet, saxophone); Accomponist; Organist; Band Leader. Educ: studied accmp. pvtely.; studied arr. & comp. w. Gordon de Lamont. m. Maria, 3s., 1d. Recordings: Broken Home; We've Got the Blues; Oh, Donne mie Carissime & Mi'nsonnai (folksongs); Oh Giovanotto; Io Sono Angelina. Pres., Can Accordion Tchrs. Assn. Hobbies; Music; Comp.; Arr. Address: 67 Troutbrooke Dr., Downsview, Ont., Can.

DIGNEY, John Neil, b. 25 Aug. 1948, Stoke-on-Trent, UK. Orchestral Oboist. Educ: Royal Manchester Coll. of Music, 1967-71: GRSM, Manchester; ARMCM Perf's, Dip. Career: W Riding Wind Quintet, 1971-73: New English Chmbr. Ensemble, 1971-73; Sup-prin. Oboe, Bournemouth Symph. Orch., 1973-. Recordings: Num. symphonic works by Sibelius, Holst, Shostakovich, Nielsen, Franck, Borodin, etc., w. Bourenmouth Symph. Orch. Mbr., Musicians Union. Hons: Woodwind Scholarship, 1969-71, & Hiles Gold Medal for orchl. playing, 1971, Royal Manchester Coll. of Music. Hobbies: Sailing; Walking. Address: 10 Fernlea Ave., Fernwood, Wimborne, Dorset, UK.

DIJCK, Jeanette van, b. 29 Jan. 1925. Utercrht, Netherlands. Lyric Soprano. Educ: Tchrs. Degree, Royal Conserv. of Music, The Hague; studied Music Theory & Hist. w. H B Buys, Singing w. Johanna Zegers de Beijl. & Opera Acting w. Prof. L Wallerstein. m. T van Duijvendijk, 1 s., 1 d. Debut: Netherlands Opera, Amsterdam, 1957. Career: Has appeared in Concerts & Oratio w. Amsterdam Concertgebouw, The Hague Phil., Rotterdam Phil. & Gürzenich Orch., Cologne, Capella Coloniensis; Soporano w. Netherlands Opera Co., Amsterdam, repertoire of 30 parts inclng. Marzelline (Fidelio), Micaela (Carmen); Paminia (Magic Flute); Butterfly, Mimi (La Boheme); sang Fiordiligi (Costi fan Tutte) w. Opera Cologne, Germany; Solo Song Recitals, Netherlands, Germany, Belgium, UK; regular TV & Radio broadcasts. Recording: Haydn, Die Schöpfung, cond. G. Wand. Mbr., Soroptimists, The Hague. Hons: 2nd Prize, Geneva Int. Singing Contest, 1954; Grand Prix Nat. du Disque (for record Die Schöpfung), Paris, 1965. Hobbies: Music; Cooking; Ikebana; Embroidery. Mgmt: Interartists, The Hague, Address: Riouwstraat 88C, The Hague, Netherlands.

DILKES, Neville, b. 28 Aug. 1930, Derby, UK. Conductor. Educ: B'ham Cathedral; Netherlands Radio Union Int. Conds. course; FTCL (Perf.); FRCO m. Dorothy Pamela Walton, 4 d. Career: Fndr. Cond., Engl. Sinfonia; Guest Cond. & tours abroad Europe, USA, etc.; Broadcasts throughout Europe. Recordings: w. English Sinfonia & Philharnonia Orchs; English Music, Bax, Butterworth, Harty, Bridge Warlock, Leigh, Mooeran, Ireland. Mbrships: ISM; RCO; CGGB. First Recip., Watney Sargent Award for Cond., 1964-65, Hobbies: Sailing. Address: Easton Hall, Easton on the Hill, Stamford, Lincs., UK. 3.

DIMITROFF, Pashanko, b. 22 Mar. 1924, Stanimaka, Bulgaria. Double Bassist; Cellist. Educ: Barrister, Law Fac., Univ. of Sofia; LLD, Law Fac., Sorbonne, Paris; Acad. of Music, Sofia. m. Margaret Yetts Greenwood, 2 s. Career: Sofia Phil. Orch., Bulgaria: Vienna Symph. Orch., Austria; Orch. Pasdeloup, Paris, France; Orch. de Chambre, Louis de Fronment, Paris; LSO, UK. Hobbies: Cooking; Golf. Address: 82 The Avenue, London NW6, UK.

DIMSDALE, Verna Lorraine, b. 27 Mar. 1936, Sydney, Aust. Teacher; Musicologist. Educ: AMus A, NSW Conserv. Music, 1953; BA, Univ. Sydney, 1956; MA, ibid., 1959. DPhil, Lady Margaret Hall, Oxford, 1968. m. Nicholas Hampden Dimsdale. Contbr. to: Bulletin John Rylands Lib.; Lute Soc. Jrnl. Mbrships: Royal Musical Assn.; Lute Soc.; Univ. Women's Club. Hons: Busby Musical Schlrship., Univ. Sydney. 1953; Sydney Moss Traveling Schlrship., 1959-61. Hobbies: Opera; Recorder Playing. Address: 30 Blandford Ave., Oxford, UK.

DINN, Winifreda (Freda) Louise, b. 18 June 1910, Dulwich, London, UK. Lecturer; Teacher; Examiner; Performer on Violin, Viola, Recorders, Piano, Writer; Editor of Music; Festival Adjudicator. Educ: GRCM; ARCM (3 dips., violin tchrs., violin perfs., tchng. of musical appreciation, aural trng. & sightreading.) Career: Tchr., violin & viola, Fndr. & Cond., Jr. Exhibitioners' Orch., RCM, 1932-41: i/c Music, Mitcham Girls' Grammar Schl., Surrey, 1941-46: Lectr.-Sr. Lectr., Music, Froebel Coll. of Educ., Roehampton, 1946-61; Prof. of Recorder, RCM, 1967-71; Educ. Advsr. to Messrs. Schott & Co., 1964-. Comps. incl: Expert the Lord build the house (voice & piano); num. small works for recorders & strings; songs. Publs: The Observer's Book of Music, 1953; The Recorder in School, 1965; Early Music for Recorders; an introduction & guide to its interpretation & history, for amateurs, 1974. Contbr. to jrnls. Mbr. profl. orgs. Recip. prizes at RCM. Address: Sunnydene, 23 Old Farm Rd., Birchington-on-Sea, Kent CT7 9PH, UK. 3.

DINNEEN, Georgina L, b. 18 Jn. 1940, Exeter, UK. Music Therapist; Clarinettist; Lecturer. Educ: RAM; LRAM; clarinet & piano; BSc, Univ. of London; GSM. Career: radio & TV broadcasts; over 400 solo & chmbr. concerts; Clarinet Tutor, Dartington Coll. of Arts, RAM Jr. Exhibitioners; Rsch., psychol. of Infant & Remedial Music Ed.; currently Lectr., Dept. of Educ., NE London Polytechnic. Mbrships; ISM; NATFHE. Hobbies: Travel; Cooking; Fashion Design; Interior Decoration. Address: 37A Dartmouth Park Ave., London NW5, UK.

DISPA, Robert Francois Joseph Louis, b. 18 Sept. 1929, Brussels, Belgium. Cellist. Educ: Solo Dip., Koninklijk Conservatorium, Ghent. m. Jannie van Mever, 2 children. Career: Solo Cellist, Rotterdam Chmbr. Orch., 1956, Arnhem Symph. Orch., 1961, Overijssels Phil. Orch., 1965; regular perfs. w. wife in piano-cello duo; Tchr., Arnhem & Enschede Conservs. Comps: 3 str. quartets; Concerto for str. orch.; Requiem Music for orch.; etc. Mbr. Koninlijke Nederlandse Toonkunsternaars Vereniging. Hobby: Painting. Mgmt: Netherlands Impresariat. Address; Klaashuisstraat 18, Haaksbergen (O), Netherlands.

DI STEFANO, Giuseppe, b. 1921. Operatic Tenor. Debuts: in Manon, 1946; Berlin, 1966. Career: incls: apps. w. Metrop Opera, NYC, La Scala, Milan, Chgo. Lyric Opera: N Am. tour w. Viennese Opera Co., 1967. sev. Recordings. Address: Via Palatino 10, Milan, Italy, 2.

DITTRICH, Paul-Heinz, b. 4 Dec. 1930, Gornsdorf i/E, Germany, Composer. Educ: German High Schl. for Music, Leipzig; Dip., Meisterschüle, German Acad. of Arts, Berlin, 1958-60. m. Hedwig Kühl. Career: Prof., counterpoint, harmony & analysis, Hanns Eisler High Schl. for Music, Berlin. Comps. incl: Str. Quartet, 1971; Dialoge, for flute & double bass, 1974; Kammermusik II, 1975; Illuminations, for orch., 1976; Cantiis II, 1977; other chmbr., intrumental & vocal works. recording of own works. mbr. Composers Prof. of German Dem. Repub. Hons: Jury prize, Comps., UNESCO, Paris, 2976; Int. Competition, IGNM, Rome,1975; Premio di Trieste, 1976; Hanns Eisler prize, Radio-DDR, 1978. Address: K Marxst. 21, 1615 Zeuthen, German Dem. Repub.

DIVALL, Richard S, b. 9 Sept. 1945, Sydney, Aust. Opera Conductor. Debut: Sydney, Aust. Career: Prod., Aust. Broadcasting Commission, 1962-70; Musical Dir., Queensland Opera Co., 1971; Musical Dir., Vic. State Opera, 1972-; Assoc., Fac. of Music, Univ. of Melbourne; Artist in Residence, Queen's Coll., Univ. of Melbourne. num. recordings for ABC. Publs: Complete Works of Carl Linger, 1971; Symphonies, Cipriani Potter, Samuel Wesley, 1980; ed., works by Gluck, Rameau, Handel, Linger, Weley. Contbr. to profl. jrnls. Mbrships: Australian Club; Univ. House. Hons: Churchill Fellow, 1975; French Govt. Scholarship, 1973; Aust. Coun. Scholarship, 1979. Hobbies: Hist. & Histl. Cooking. Mgmt: Jennifer Eddy, 2 Dunlop Ave., Kew, Melbourne, Aust. Address: E Wing Flat, Queen's Coll., Univ. of Melbourne, Parkville, 3053 Australia.

DIX, Barbara, b. 23 Oct. 1944, Southport, UK. Contralto. Educ: Royal Manchester Coll. of Music. m. Alexander Abercrombie. Debut: Park Lane Grp. Concert, London, 1973. Career incls: Prin., Glyndebourn Fest. Opera & BBC Northern Singers, 1975. Mbrships: Equity; ISM. Hobbies: Cooking; Detective Stories. Address: Dormy House, Kent Rd., Birkdale, Southport, UK.

DJAKONOVSKI, Dragan, b. 11 Mar. 1931, Skopje, Yugoslavia. Conductor. m. Marija Djakonovska, 4 children. Debut: Radio TV Skopje, 1955. Career: Cond., Orch. of Radio TV Skopje, 1955-; Writer of music for theatrical drama, comps. & arrs. for fests. of popular music; Arr. of over 5,000 comps.; Comp. of about 100 works of popular & jazz-intrumental music, mainly recorded on radio & TV. Mbrships: Soc. of Comps. of Macedonia; Union of Yugoslav. Comps. Hons. incl: 1st Prize, Radio TV Skopje 1970, fest. of popular music; 3rd Prize, Skopje 71; 3rd Prize, Skopje 74. Hobbies: Precise mechanics; Electronics. Address: Naselba 11 Oktemvri, Prvomajska 2/11, stan 31, Skopje, Yugoslavia.

DOAMEKPOR, Cornelius Raymond Kwame, b. 11 Sept. 1937. Hedzranawo, Ghana. Teacher of Viola & Piano. Educ: Tchrs. Cert.; Music Educ. Dip., Ghana. m. Agnes Adzo Adadzie, 5 s., 1 d. Comps: Xixeame (The World) (2nd movement of this work recorded by Ghana Broadcasting Corp.) Mbr., Ghana Music Tchrs. Assn. Hobbies: Gardening; Animal Husbandry; Choral Singing. Address: PO Box 66, Denu, Volta Reg., Ghana.

DOBBS, Jack Percival Baker, b. 22 July 1922, Newport, Berkeley, Glos., UK. Director of Musical Studies. Educ: BA, Univ. of Wales; MEd, Univ. of Durham; MPhil., Univ. of London; LRAM; LTCL (CMT); FRSA; Dip. Ed. (Wales). m. Ruth Heaton, 2 s. Career: Music Master, var schls., County Music Advsr., Co. Durham; Fellow, Univ. of Durham Inst. of Educ.; Dir., Malayan Tchrs. Coll. Brinsford Lodge; Lectr., Univ. of London Inst. of Educ: Dir. of Musical Studies, Dartington Coll. of Arts; Chmn., Schls. Coun. Music Comm.; Advsr., Brit. Soc. for Music Therapy; Chmn., UK Coun. for Music Educ. Comps. incl: songs, hymn tunes, anthems, string suite. Publs: Oxford Schl. Music Books. Junior Series (w. R Fiske), 1954; Senoir Series, (w. Roger Fiske), 1956: Three Pioneers of Sight-Singing, 1960; The Slow Learner & Music, 1964; Ears & Eyes (w. M Lane & R Fiske), 1974. Contbr. to var. profl. jrnls. Mbrships: ISM; Int. Soc. for Music Educ.; Int. Folk Music Coun., etc. Hons: Hon. FTL, 1976. Address: Barton Farmhouse, Dartington Hall, Totnes, Devon, UK. 28, 29, 30.

DOBBS, Mattiwilda, b. USA. Opera Singer. Educ: Spelman Coll., Atlanta, Ga.; Columbia Univ.; Study w. Lotte Leonard, 1946-50: Mannes Music Schl. & Berkshire Music Ctr., 1948; w. Pierre Bernac, Paris, 1950-52. Career: Soloist, Mexico Univ. Festival, 1947; Concert tour, Holland France & Sweden, 1952; appeared in the Italian Girl in Algiers, La Scala, Milan, 1953; Appearances at Glyndebourne, UK, 1953, '54, '56, '61; Royal Opera House, Covent Gdn., London, 1954-56, 1959; San Fran. Opera, 1955. Metropol. Opera, NY, 1956-; Stockholm Royal Opera, 1957-; Hamburg State Opera, 1961-63; Prof. of Music, Univ. of Ga., 1976-. Concert perfs. in num. countries in Europe, Am., Austria, NZ, Israel, USSR. Hons: 1st Voice Prize, Int. Competition, Geneva, 1951; Order of the North Star, Sweden. Address: 130-26th St. NW, Apt. 802, Atlanta, GA 30309, USA.

DOBIAS, Charles, b. 6 Aug. 1923, Klatova Nova Ves, Czech. Violinist. Educ: BA, Univ. of Toronto; Artist dip., Conserv. of Music, Toronto. Debut: soloist in Mendelsshon's violin concerto w. Toronto Symph., 1946. Career: soloist, Czech., 1975; num. TV & radio apps., CBC; soloist in USA & Mexico; soloist & ldr., Edmonton Symph., 1969-71; soloist & ldr., Halifax Symph. 1960-61; soloist & ldr., Nat. Ballet Co. of Can., 1951-60; ldr., Pro Arte Chmbr. Orch., Toronto, 1961-70; now ldr., Royal Winnipeg Ballet & assoc. ldr., Winnipeg Symph. Hons: 2 Can. Coun. awards for study w. Josef Suk, Prague, 1973-74; Scholarship, Toronto Music Conserv., 1953; 3 gold medals at music fests., Can. exhibitions, Toronto. Hobbies: Languages; Travel. Address: 1219-90 Smith St., Winnipeg, Man. R3C 1J8, Canada.

DOBIAŠ, Václav, b. 22 Sept. 1909, Radcice, Czechoslovakia. Professor of Music. Educ: BA, Tchrs. Trng. Coll.; Dip., State Conserv., Prague; MA. Schl. of Arts, ibid. m. Jarmila Stranska, 2 s., 2 d. Debut: w. Chmbr. Symph./Czech Phil. Career: Prof., Acad. of Musical Arts, Prague; coop. w. Czechoslovak Radio, Czechoslovak Symph. Orchs. & TV, 1939-. Comps. incl: 2 Symphs.; Symphoniette; Sonata for Piano & String Orch. Piano Sonata; Wind Quintet; Overtures; 2 song cycles; cantatas; chmbr. comps., popular songs (all recorded except Symph. no. 1). Contbr. to: Hudebni rozhledy. Mbrships: Guild of Czech Comps. & Concert Artists; Czechslovak Coun. for Music. Hons: Smetana Prize, 1947; Int. Peace Prize, Warsaw, 1950: Czech State Prize, 1952, '56, '58; Nat. Artist, 1976. Address: Slavickova 13, 160 00 Prague 6, Bubenec, Czechoslovakia.

DOBLER, Charles (Jean-Theodore), b. 3 May 1923, Niedergoesgen, Kanton Solothurn, Switz. Pianist. Educ: Conserv. & Univ. of Basle; Educl. & Master Dips. m. Ursula Stephanie Weinand, 2 children. Debut: W. Tonhalle Orch. Base.,1949; Zürich, 1952. Career: Concerts as soloist, also w. orchs. in Switz., Germany, Netherlands, Spain; Radio & TV apps. in Europe, Asia, Aust., S Am. Num. recordings. Publs: Contemporary Swiss Piano Music, 1973. Contbr. to Schweizerishe Musikzeitung, Zürich. Mbr. num. profl. orgs. Recip. Grosser Kunstpreis, State of Solothurn, 1972. Hobbies: Travel, Swimming; Steam Locomotives. Mgmt: Konzertgesellschaft, Steinwiesstrasse 2,8032 Zürich. Address: Postfach 64, CH-4501 Solothurn, Switzerland.

DOBOS, Kálmán, b. 22 July 1931, Szolnok, Hungary. Composer; Pianist. Educ: Dip. Comp., Ferenc Liszt Acad. of Music, Budapest, 1959. m. Ilona Tóth, 7 children. Career: Radio & TV recordings at 51 broadcasting stns. in Europe, Africa & Asia. Comps. incl: Projecting I (orch.), 1973; Csango Songs from Moldavia, 1974; Hungarian Mass (mixed choir), 1974; Variations & Fugue on a Hungarian Song from 16th Century (organ), 1974; Projection II (percussion), 1975: Deák Ferenc (male choir), 1975: Missa, 1976; Rosary, 1979. num. radio TV recordings. Publs: János Viski, 1968. Mbrships: Union of Hungarian Musicians; Supporting Mbr., Jeunesse Musicale; Kidaly Soc.; Union of the Blind of Hungary. Address: Hegedüs Gyula u. 20, H-1136 Budapest, Hungary.

DOBOS, Viorel-Constantin, b. 14 April 1917, Iasi, Romania. Composer; Conductor. Educ: Grad., RAM, Bucharest. m. Gilda Dobos. Career: Cond.; Palladium Theatre, Bucharest 1945, Theatre of Army, Bucharest 1947-49; Cond., Artistic Dir., The Skylark Ensemble, Bucharest, 1949-57, 1964-68; Cond. & Dir., Musical Theatre of Galati, 1957-59; Cond. & Dir., Perinitza Ensemble, Bucharest, 1959-64; Tours, Hungary, Bulgaria, Poland, China, Mongolia, Korea, USSR, Vietman, Yugoslavia, Switz. & France. Comps. incl: Little Romanian Suite, for orch. or fanfare; A Bewitched Hammer (fairy-ballet); The Song of the Mountains (musical); A Wedding of Somes-Country (ballet); Festive Overture; Over Moldavian Plains, cantata; Pacala (ballet); Nausicaa (musical); The War of the Guitars (rock musical); Penes-Curcanul (symph. rock suite); Zamfira's Marriage (ballet); Tarsita & Rosiorul (musical); Madáme Sans-Gêne (musical); The Silver Hoff (musical); The Miracle of the Violina (rock musical). Mbr., Romanian Comps. Union. Hons: State Prize, 1953, RTV prizes, 1975: Merited MA, 1967. Hobby: Photography. Address: Brezoianu St. 51, b1.B, et.IV, ap.21, Bucharest I, 70711, Romania.,

DOBRÉE, Georgina, b. 8 Jan., 1930, London, UK. Clarinettist; Teacher; Editor; Adjudicator. Educ: RAM; LRAM, study w. Gaston Hamelin, Paris. Career: Soloist & mbr. of chmbr. ensembles in num. concerts & broadcasts in UK, Europe & USA; Lecture-recital tours; Prof., RAM, 1967-; Dir., Chantry Records Ltd. Recordings: works by Pert, Motler, Coleridge-Taylor, Stravinsky, Phillips Tate, Lytyens, Bennett, North etc. Publs: Ed., sonatas, concertos & chmbr. music inclng. clarinet. Mbrships: Royal Musical Assn.; Galpin Soc; Int. Clarinet Soc. (USA); CASS. Hons: French Govt. Scholarship; ARAM; 1st prize, Darmstadt, 1953. Hobby: Gardening. Address: 5 Wellfield Ave., Muswell Hill, London N10, 2EA, UK.

DOBROWOLSKA-GRUSZCZYNSKA, Maria Franciszka, b. 25 Feb. 1918. Singer; Actress; Professor. Educ: Conserv., Lwów, Dip.; Opera, 1947-63: Broadcasts w. Polish Radio, 1945-78: Apps. in Rumania, Yugoslavia, Bulgaria & Can.; Inst. P. Acad. Nauk, Warsaw, 1939-44; 10 yrs. w. Panstw. Opera, Warsaw. Recordings: 50 Songs, Karol Szymanowski. Mbrships: Spatif-zasp Polish Assn. of Theatre & Film Artists; SPAM Polish Musicians Assn.; WTM, Warsaw Music Soc. Hons: Medal of 10 Yrs. of Polish People, 1944-54; Medal of 1000 Yrs. of Poland, Hobbies: Improvisatioins on Piano. Address: Ozarów Maz. 05-850. Mickiewicza 51, Warsaw, Poland.

DOBROWOLSKI, Andrzej, b. 9 Sept. 1921, Lwow, USSR. Composer. Educ: Dip. in Theory of Music & Composition, State Coll. of Music, m. Irena 3 s., 1 d. Debut: Variations for Orch., 1949. Compositions; Woodwind Trio; Music for Tape No. 1; Music for String Orch. & 4 Grps. of Wind Instruments; Music for Tape & Oboe; Music for Strings, 2 Grps of Wind Instruments & Tape; Krabogapa; Music for Orch.; Amar -Music for Orch. No. 2; Music for Orch. No. 3; Music for Tape & Piano Solo. Recordings: works issued on Muza & Phillips Labels. Career: Prof. of Composition, State Coll. of Music, Warsaw. Publs: Methodology of Teaching Harmony, 1967; Schwirigkeiten der Formenlehre neuer Musick - Uberlegungen an einem Prak-tischen Beispiel, 1972; S for S (electronic), 1973; A-LA, music for orch., No. 4; Music for mixed choir, 2 grps. of wind instruments & percussion. Mbrships: Int. Soc. of Contemporary Music; Pres., Polish sect., ibid; Polish Composers Union; Prog. Comm. & Festival Comm., Warsaw Autumn Festival. Hons: Award, Min. of Culture, 1971; Award, Polish Composers Union, 19712. Hobbies: Mountaineering; Hiking. Address: 00-819 Warszawa, Zolta 75.m.30., Poland.

DOBRZYNSKI, Jerzy, b. 1 March 1936, Warsaw, Poland. Conductor. Educ: Warsaw Coll. of Music (organ), 1955-60; Warsaw Higher (Acad.) Schl. of Music, Dept. of Cond. w. Prof. S. Wislocki, 1960-65. M., 2 c. Debut: Concert w. Symph. Orch. of Nat. Phil. Hall, 1964. Career incl: Cond., Central Orch. of Polish Army, 1964, '67, '77; Int. Fest. of Contemporary Music, Warsaw, 1967; Choirs Cond. of Nat. Phil. of Music, 1964-. Recordings: Polish Radio & TV; TV, German Fed. Repub. Mbr., Assn. of Polish Musicians. Hobbies: Bicycling; Touring. Address: Solec 63A/39, 00-409 Warsaw, Poland.

DOBSON, Jean Gabrielle Austin, b. London, UK. Singer. Educ: Royal Manchester Coll. of Music; LRAM; ARAM, 1970. Debut: Wigmore Hall, 1952. Career: Recitals; Oratorio; Broadcasting; Tchr. of Singing; Prof., RAM. Mbr., ISM; RAM Club. Recip. Louisa Banerji & Grisi Prizes. Hobbies: Gardening; Art work w. threads & frabric. Address: 17 Wensleydale Gdns. Hampton, Middx TW12 2LU, UK. 27.

DOBSON, Michael, b. 10 Apr. 1923, Wavedon, UK. Conductor; Oboist. Educ: RAM & Pvte. study (oboe) w. Myrtil Morel, Paris; FRAM. m. Mary Thornbery, 1 s., 1 d. Career: has been Prin. Oboist, LPO, 1942-52, London Mozart Players,

London Chmbr. Orch. & Bath Fest., Orch. (now Menuhin Fest. Orch.); has appeared as soloist thru'out UK, & in France, Italy, Germany, Czechoslovakia, USA & Can.; Fndr. of Prin. Cond., Thames Chmbr. Orch.; gives regular concerts at Queen Elizabeth Hall, also does BBC broadcasts & provincial concerts; has appeared as Guest Cond., Engl., Wales, Scotland, Germany, Switz., Spain, Austria and USA. Has recorded. Hobbies: Fishing; Printing. Mgmt: The Thames Chamber Orch. Ltd., 3 Vineyard Row Hampton Wick, Kingston-upon-Thames, KT1 3EG, UK. 4.

DODERER, Gerhard, b. 25 March 1944, Kitzingen, Germany. Musicologist; Organist. Educ: Univ. studies to doct. degree; studied organ & harpsichord at Conserv. Würzburg; studies histl. keyboard instruments, Conserv. Lisbon, Portugal. m. Cremilde Rosado Fernandes Doderer. Career: Prof. of Organ & Organol., Nat. Conserv., Lisbon, Portugal, & Curator, Musical Instrument Collection, ibid. 19773-75; Prof. of Organ & Musicol., Hermann Zilcher Conserv., Würzburg, Bavaria, German Fed. Repub., 1975-78; Dir., ibid, 1978-. Recordings of Portugese & Italian organ music on historic organs of Coimbra & Lisbon, 1975. Publs: incl: Obras selectas para órgao (Portugaliae Musica vol. XXV), 1974: Orgelmusik & Orgelbau im Portugal des 17 Jahrhunderts, 1978. Contbr. to: Ars organi; Anales Lusitanae Musicae. Hobbies: Music; Iberian langs. Address: Heinrich-Zener-Str. 42, D-8700 Würzburg, German Fed. Repub. & Alameda DA Henriques, 48-5DT., Lisbon, Portugal.

DODGE, Charles, b. 5 June, 1942, Ames, Iowa, USA. Composer; (Computer Music, Computer Synthesized Speech & Vocal Sounds). Educ: BA, Univ. Iowa; MA, DMA, Columbia Univ.; Aspen Music Schl. Berks Music Ctr. (Tanglewood). m. Katharine Schlefer, 1 s., 1 d. Career: BBC Horizons Prog. The 3 Chord Trick, 1975; Var. commissions inclng: Nat. Endowment for the Arts, 1974, '75. Comps: Folia, 1965; Rota, 1966: Changes, 1969; Earth's Magnetic Field, 1970; Speech Songs, 1972; Extensions, 1973; The Story of Our Lives, 1974; in Celebration, 1975: Cascando Pres., 1979, Num. recordings. Contbr. to Music Jrnl. Mbrships: Pres., Am. Comps. Alliance, 1971-75; Am. Music Ctr., Recip. num Awsrd. Address: Music Dept., Brooklyn Coll., Brooklyn, NY 11210, USA. 2, 6.

DODGSON, Jolyon, b. 23 July1936, Hereford, UK. Singer Conductor; Arts Administrator. Educ: ARMCM. m. Prudence Singleton, twin d. Career: Freelance Solo Singer, 1956-; Fndr.-mbr., BBC Northern Singers, 1956; Vis. Mr. of Staff, Lancaster Univ. Music Dept., 1969-74: Dir., MacRobert Arts Ctr., Univ. of Stirling, 1974-; Chorusmaster/Cond., BBC Scottish Singers, 1975. Recordings: (w. BBC Northern Singers) Liszt, Via Crucis; Holst, Part Songs: Mendelssohn, Part Songs. Mbr., ISM. Hobbies: Cabinet-making; Picture Framing; Building; Preservation of Rural Life & Crafts. Mgmt: John Wright, Suite 500 Chesham House, 150 Regent St., London. Address: Gurnel Beck, Millside, Witherslack, Grange-over-Sands. Cumbria, UK.

DODS, Marcus, b. 19 Apr. 1918, Edinburgh, UK. Conductor. Educ: MA, MusB, King's Coll., Cambridge Univ.; RAM, London; FRAM. m. Deirdre E Lind, 4 c. Career: Cond. & Chorus Master, Sadler's Wells Opera, 1952-58; Prin. Cond., BBC Concert Orch.,1966-69; Films, musicals, operas, etc.; Musical Dir., London Concert Orch., 1972-. Recordings: Musicals; Film Scores. Mbrships: Savile Club; Brit. Acad. of Film & TV Art.; Musicians Union; ISM. Recip., DFC, 1944. Hobbies: Fishing; Golf; Flying. Mgmt: London Mgmt. Address: Fawley Lodge, Marlow Rd., Henley-on-Thames, Oxon, UK. 3

DOE, Paul Maurice, b. 8 Sept. 1931, Norwich, UK. Professor of Music. Educ: BA, Oxford, 1952; MA, 1956; LRAM (violin perf.), 1951. m. Olwen Margaret Jones, 2 s., 2 d. Career: Prof. of Music, Univ. of Exeter; Gen. Ed., Early English Church Music series. Publs: Ed., Early Tudor Magnificats, 1964; Tallis, 1968; Ed., Elizabethan Consort Music, I (Musica Britannica, Vol. 44), 1979. Contbr. to: Music & Letters; Proceedings of the Royal Musical Assn., etc. Mbrships: Coun., Royal Musical Assn., 1977-80; Ed. Committee, Musica Britannica. Hobbies: Bridge; Squash; Bookbinding. Address: Dept. of Music, Univ. of Exeter, Exeter EX4 4PD, UK.

DOGARU, Anton, b. 17 May 1945, Bucharest, Romania. Composer; Professor; Pianist. Educ: studied comp. at Conserv. C Panumbescu, Bucharest, 1962-68. m. Valerica Dogaru. Debut: (as comp.) Piano Sonata, Conserv., 1967. Career: works perf. on radio & TV, at the Phil. of Bucharest, 1965-79: Prof. of harmony & counterpoint. Comps: Triptique lirique for orch.; Triptique for chmbr. ensemble; Sonata for piano; 4 songs, for voice & piano; choral works, etc. Recordings; all the above comps. Publs: co-author, Romanian revues, Music & Romanian Literature. Contbr. to profl. jrnls. mbr., Union of

Romanian Comps. Hons: 2 nat. prizes for children's choirs. Address: str. V Stroiescu 19, 73236 Bucharest, Romania.

DOISY, Marcal, b. 9 Feb. 1916, Paris, France. Critic. m. Germaine Gerlin. Career: Critic, Belgian Radio & TV, 1954-; Ed., La Revue des Disques (monthly). Publs: l'Oeuvre de Richard Wagner, 1945: Musique et Drame, 1950; 8 other books on theatre & poetry. Contbr. to Revue des Disques, 1954-; Var. other mags. & reviews. Address: Ave. Franklin Roosevelt 182,1050 Brussels, Belgium. 1.

DOKTOR, Paul Karl, b. 28 Mar. 1919, Vienna, Austria. Concert Artist (viola). Educ: Dip., Vienna State Acad. of Music, 1938. Studied w. father, Kark Doktor. Career: w. Busch Chmbr. Or ch., tours to Belgium, UK & Switzerland; 2nd viola, Busch Quintet, London & Zürich; Solo violist, Collegium Musicum Zuerich, w. Paul Sachedr & Lucerne Symph Orch., 1940-47; Am. Debut, Wash. Lib. of Congress, 1948; num. appearances as soloist w. orchs., recitals & chmbr. music, USA, Salzburg & Edinburgh Festivals; Fndr., Rococo Ensemble; NY String Sextet & Paul Doktor String Trio (The New String Trio of NY); Tchr., Univ. of Mich., 1948-51: Fac., Manness Coll. of Music, 1952- NY Univ., 1968-, Juilliard Schl. & Phila. Musical Acad., 1971; Guest Prof., Inst. de Hautes Etudes Musicales, Montreux/Crans, Switzerland, 1973-; NC Schl. of the Arts, 1974-75. Recordings incl. var. sonatas & concertos by Brahms, Bach, Hindemith, Walton, etc. Publs: Collectioins of V iola Pieces; edits. of var. works for strings. Mbrships: Am. String Tchrs. Assn.; Bohemians, (NY Musicians Club), etc. Recip. Unanimous 1st Prize, Geneva Int. Music Comp., 1942. Mgmt: Colbert Artists Mgmt., NY. Address: 215 W 88th St., NY, NY 10024, USA. 3, 19, 28.

DOLAN, Diane Marie, b. 9 Sept. 1941, Boston, Mass., USA. Musicologist. Educ: BA, Boston Univ. Coll. of Liberal Arts, 1965; MA, Boston Univ. Grad. Schl., 1968; Doct., Centre d'Etudes Supéerieures de Civilisation Medievale, Poitiers, France, 1972. Publications: Le drame liturgique de Pâques en Normandie et en Angleterre au moyen âge; Publs. de l'Université de Poitiers, Lettres et Sciences Humaines XVI, 1975. Contbr. to profl. jrnls. inclng: Annals de Normandie, Caen, France. Mbrships: Medieval Acad. of Am.; Boston Athenaeum Lib.; Am. Musicol. Soc. Hobbies: Chmbr. Music; Equestrian Sports. Address: 29 Pembroke Rd., Weston, MA 02193, USA. 29.

DOLANSKA, Vera, b. 29 Nov. 1926, Trinec, Czech. Music Editor; Librarian. Educ: PhD, Charles Univ., Prgue. m. Josef Kalas. Career: w. music publng. house, 1950-; Chief Ed., musicol. ed., 1958-71; Chief Ed. of series Hudebni profily (Profiles in Music), Hudba v zrcadle doby (Music in the Mirror of Time), & Operni Libreta (Opera Librettl). Contbr. to: var. pub. & profl. jrnls. Hobbies: Music; Ballet; Literature. Address: V inohradska 125, Vinohrady, Prague 3, Czechoslovakia.

DOLLITZ, Grete Franke, b. 12 June 1924, Kalden Kirchen, Germany. Instructor in Classical Guitar. Educ: BA, Hunter Coll., NY; Univ. of NC; Univ. of Calif. Debut: Richmond, Va. Career: Prod., half hour Sunday guitar music prof. over Richmond's WFMV radio, 8 yrs.; Writer, prod. & engineer, Classical Guitar Music Prog., WRFK-FM, Richmond; Instructor in classical guitar, VCU, Richmond, Va.; VP & Organizer, Community Concert Series. Contbr. to: Creative Guitar Int. Mbrships: The Guitar Fndn. of Am.; Coll. Music Soc.; Amateur Chmbr. Music Soc.; Past Corres. & Pres. of Richmond Chapt., Am. Recorder Soc. Hobbies: Wild flowers; Conservation; Gardening; Sewing; Swimming. Address: 2305 Norman Ave., Richmond, VA 23228, USA.

DOLMETSCH, Carl Frederick, b. 23 Aug. 1911, Fantenay-sous-Bois, Paris, France. Recitalist, Chmn. & Managing Dir., Arnold Dolmetsch Ltd., musical instrument makers. Educ: studies w. Arnold Dolmetsch & Carl Fiesch. div., 2 s. (1 dec.), 2 d. Debut: 1st Haslemere Festival, 1925; Wigmore Hall, 1939. Career: 1st Concert Tour at age 8, 1st Broadcast at 14; toured USA 1935 & '6; Holland, 1946; Italy & Switz., 1947; Sweden, 1949: NZ, 1953: France, 1956; USA, 1957; Switz., Austria, Germany, Holland, 1958; Belgium, USA, 1959; Sweden, Austria, Germany, 1960; Australia, 1965; Columbia, 1966; France, Sweden, 1967; Alaska, Canada, 1969: Japan, 197 4; USA yrly. 19612-; yrly. Recital, Wigmore Hall, 1946-; Dir., Haslemere Fest of Early Music, 1940-. Publs: Recorder Tutors 1957 & 1977. num. eds. of 16th-18th century music. Contbr. to var. profl. jrnls. Mbr. num. profl. orgs. Hons: CBE, 1954: DLitt, 1960; FTCL, 1950; FLCM, 1963. Mgmt: Ibbs & Tillett, London. NY. Address: Jesses, Grayswood Road, Haslemere, Surrey GU27 2BS, UK. 1, 3, 21.

DOLMETSCH, Cécile, b. 22 Mar. 1904. Dorking, UK. Musician specialising in Early Music & Musical Instruments.

Educ: Studied w. her father. Arnold Dolmetsch; Studied singing w. Blanche Marchesi. m. C Leslie C Ward, 2 s., 2 d. Debut: Theatre des Bouffes-Parisiens, Paris, France. Career: Num. Concerts & Recitals; Radio & TV Perfs. Var. Recordings incl: History of Music, 1st Ed. Contbr. to: The strad; The Consort. Mbrships: VP, Viola da Gamba Soc.; Mbr., Dolmetsch Fndn. Hobbies: Tropical Birds; Painting. Mgmt: Chantry Records. Address: Chantry House, Gray's Close, Haslemere, Surrey GU27 2LJ, UK. 3, 30.

DOLMETSCH, Jeanne-Marie, b. 15 Aug. 1942, Hindhead, Surrey, UK. Concert Artist (Recorder, Treble viol & Violin); Teacher. Educ: RAM, violin & piano, 1961-64: LRAM (piano tchr.). Debut: Queen Elizabeth Hall, 1973. Career: Toured Am., France, Ireland & Sweden w. Dolmetsch Ensemble; Recorder soloist & Asst. Dir., Haslemere Festival; Bath Festival; English Bach Festival; num. broadcasts & TV progs. sev. Recordings. Mbrships: ISM. Hobbies: Painting; Gardening. Mgmt: Ibbs & Tillet. Address: Jesses, Grayswood Rd., Haslemere, Surrey, UK.

DOLMETSCH, Marguerite Mabel, b. 15 Aug. 1942, Hindhead, UK. Recorder & Viola da Gamba Player. Educ: LRAM. m. Brian E. Blood, 1 d. Career: Travelled widely w. the Dolmetsch Ensemble & the Dolmetsch Concertante, touring Am., France, Germany, Sweden, & performing at the 3 Choirs Fest., Bath Fest., & Haslemere Fest; Has also app. at Queen Elizabeth Hall Purcell Room, & Wigmore hall, & in broadcast & TV progs. in Brit. & Germany., Var. recordings. Hobbies: Gardening; Dressmaking. Cooking. Address: Heartsease, Grayswood Rd., Haslemere, Surrey, UK.

DOLMETSCH, Nathalie, b. 31 July 1905, Chgo, Ill., USA. Musician specialising on Viola da Gamba; Dancer; Writer. Educ: Studied ancient music w. father, Arnold Dolmetsch; ancient dance w. mother, Mabel Dolmetsch. m. George Henry Carley, 1 s., 2 d. Debut: Paris, 1911. Career: Prof., Viola da Gamba in num. concerts, on radio, stage & TV. Recordings incl: History of Music. Publs: Num. Eds. of Early Music; Twelve Lessons on the Viola da Gamba, 1948; The Viola da Gamba, Its History, Technique & Musical Resources, 1962; Ed., The Division Viol, by Christopher Simpson, 1667, 1955, & Lyr. Viol, 1682 Ed., 1962. Contbr. to: The Strad; Music & Letters; Viola da Gamba Soc. Bulletin; The Consort; Recorder & Music Mag. Mbrships: Pres., Viola da Gamba Soc.; Chmn., Dolmetsch Histl. Dance Soc.; Gamba Soc.; Chmn., Dolmetsch Histl. Dance Soc.; num. profl. orgs. Hobbies: Woodcarving; Writing. Address: Middlefield, Seavington St. Mary, Ilminster, Somerset, UK. 1, 27.

DOMAZLICKY, Frantisek, b. 13 May 1913, Prague, Czech. Composer; Musician (violin & viola). Educ: study of violin & composition, Acad. of the Arts of the Muses. m. Eva Ebel. Comps. incl: Overture piccola; Symph.; Suites; Concertos for violin, viola oboe, trombone, horn & bassoon; Concerto for wind octet; Symph. picture 'The Spring of the Chevalier d'Artagnan' for cello & orch.; song cycles; Concerto for Violin No. 2 op. 47; Concerto for Flute, op. 48; chmbr. music & num. smaller pieces. Recordings incl: Overture piccola; Horn concerto. Hobby: Riding. Mgmt: Music Ct., Besedni 3, 110 00 Praha 1. Address: 120 00 Praha 2, - Vinohrady, Budecska 39, Czech.

DOMBRECHT, Paulus Stephanus, b. 9 Oct. 1948, Geluwe, Belgium. Oboist; Teacher. Educ: Higher Dip., Royal Music Conserv., Brussels. m. Cristina de Aguiar, 2 c. Career: perfs. at concerts as oboist & chmbr. musician throughout Europe; regular recordings on oboe & baroque oboe for Belgian Radio; recordings for Bremen Radio, WDR, French & Dutch radios; mbr. Harmonia Mundi, Seon, Accent; tchr. for chamber music, Royal Brussels Conserv. & Lemmens Inst., Louvain. Recordings: Bach, Bradenburg Concerto No. 2; Telemann, Trio Sonatas; oboe sonatas. Hobbies: Dogs; Gardening. Address: Waverstr. 31, 9390 Moorsel-Aalst, Belgium.

DOMBROWSKI, Stanley, b. 7 May 1932, Greensburg, Pa., USA. Violinist. Educ: Bachelor's Degree, New England Conserv. of Music, Boston, 1954: Paris Conserv.; Berks. Music Ctr., Tanglewood, Mass., 1951-55. Studied w. R. Burgin, W Kroll, R Possett, J Calvert & I Markevitch. m. Vivienne Polson, 2 s. 1 d. Debut: Boston. Career: Num. sonata recitals & concerts of chmbr. music, NE USA & France; Mbr., Pitts. Symph., 1958-. Contbr. to Senza Sordino, Int. Conf. of Symph. & Opera Musicians. Mbrships: Sec.,Int. Conf. of Symph & Opera Musicians; Exec. Bd., Pitts. Musical Soc.; Pi Kappa Lambda; Kappa Gamma Psi; Leica Histl. Soc. Hons: George Whitefield Chadwick Gold Medal, 1954; Fulbright Scholarship, 1955-57. Hobbies incl: Photography; Tennis. Address: Heinz Hall for the Performing Arts, Pitts., PA 15222, USA.

DOMER, Jerry Lloyd, b. 3 Oct. 1938, Polson, Mont., USA. College Professor; Oboe Soloist. Educ: BMus, Univ. Mont.; MMus, Boston Univ.; Studied w. Ralph Gomerg, John Mack, Marc Kifschey. m. Joan Paula Gilbert, 1 s. Career: W US Army Band, 1962-65; 1st Oboe: Robert Shaw Chorale; Portland Symph. Orch.; Portland Opera Assn.; Amici della Musica Chmbr. Orch.; Amici Woodwind Quintet; Mont. Woodwind Quintet; Northwest Woodwind Quintet; Oboe Soloist at Anchorage Music Festival, Peter Britt Music Festival & throughout USA & Can.; Tchr., Coutenay Youth Music Ctr., BC, Can., 1967-. Recordings; CBC Broadcasts. Contbr. to The Cadenza. Mbrships. incl: Phi Mu Alpha Sinfonia; Pi Kappa Lambda. Hobbies: Outdoor Sports; Fishing; Hunting; Photography; Skiing. Address: 7859 Birch St., Vancouver, BC V69 4R8, Canada.

DOMINGO, Placido, b. Madrid, Spain., Operatic Tenor. Educ: Conserv., Mexico City. m. Marta Domingo, 3 s. Debut: 1961. Career: Convent Gdn.; Vienna & Hamburg State Operas; Nat. Hebrew Opera, Tel-Aviv; La Scala, Milan; Metrop. Opera, NYC; NYC Opera; San Fran. Opera; has sung ldng. roles in over 50 operas. Var. Recordings. Address: Metrop. Opera Co., Lincoln Ctr., NY, NY 10023, USA. 2.

DOMINIQUE, Carl-Axel Martinelli, b. 1 Sept. 1939, Uplands Bälinge, Sweden. Pianist; Flautist; Composer. Educ: Music Dir. Exam. (LRAM), Royal Acad., Stockholm, 1962; Piano (Soloist Dip.) & Flute Studies, ibid. m. Monica Dominique, 2 s. Debut: Swedish Radio, 1966. Career: Var. perfs. as soloist, & w. symph. ochs.; Co-Fndr. w. wife Monica Dominique of grp. Solar Plexus, 1971; Concert tours in Scandnavia & France, & sev. TV concerts. Compositions incl: Conderto Grosso for Solar Plexus & Symph. Orch. (recorded); Swedish Eurovision Song Contest Entry, 1973; theatre & TV music. Recordings: 4 Albums w. Solar Plexus; Satie & Ives, Piano Music, 1976. Publs: Book on Improvisation & Planning (w. M Dominique), 1976. Hobbies: Family Life; Nature. Address: Lännavägen 50, 14146 Huddinge, Sweden.

DOMMEL-DIÉNY, Amy, b. 21 June 1894, Beauvais, France. Musicologist; Professor of Music Writing & Harmonic Analysis. Educ: Schola Cantorum, Paris, 1911-21; Dips. in Harmony, Counterpoint & Gregorian Chant, ibid. m. Paul Dammel, 1 s., 1 d. Career: Asst. Prof., Sorbonne, Paris; Prof., Strasbourg Conserv., Conserv. of the 6th Dist., Paris, Fresnes Conserv., Annecy Int. Musicol. Ctr. Comps. (publs.) incl: The Story of my Dolls, duets for children; 2 Musical Plays, for children, etc. Ed., Harmonie Vivante, (Living Harmony), 6 parts, 18 vols., 1953-76. Contbr. to var. profl. jrnls. Mbrships. incl: French & Int. Musicol. Socs. Recip. 1st Int. Prize for comp. by a woman, Gedock Competition, Mannheim, Germany, 1950. Hobby: Collection of children's tales. Address: 4 rue Paul Couderc, Sceaux 92330, France.

DOMSAITIS, Adelheid Agathe Marie, (profl. name Adelheid Armhold), b. 4 Mar. 1900, Kiel, Germany. Concert & Oratorio Singer; Singing Teacher. Educ: Dips., piano & singing in German, Maria Ivogün Schl., in French Schl. of Singins w. Prof. Alexander de Rival, & in Italian Schl. of Singing w. Prof. Alexander Scareno. m. (1) Pranas Domsatis (dec.); (2) Kazys Zvironas. Debut: as concert singer, when aged 19. Career: made num. apps in Europe w. many noted conds. inclng: Furtwängler; Klemperer; Sir Henry Wood; Sir Adrian Boult; Mengelberg, etc.; Sr. Lectr. in singing, Univ. of Cape Town., 1949-. Publd. Singing, based on Irrefragable laws, 1963. Address: 25 Evergreen Ave., Newlands, 7700 Cape Town, S Africa.

DONATH, Helen, b. 10 July 1940, Corpus Christi, Tex., USA. Opera & Concert Soprano. Educ: Del Mar. Coll., Tex.; studied w. Paola Nivikova & Klaus Donath. m. Klaus Donath, 1 s. Debut: Cologne Opera House, 1962. Career: Hanover Opera House, 1963-68: Bayerische Staatsoper, Munich, 1968-72; guest apps., Vienna, Milan, San Fran., Lisbon, etc.; concerts in Europe & Am. Roles incl: Pamina, Magic Flute; Zerlina, Don Giovanni; Eva, Die Meistersinger; Sophie, Der Rosenkavalier. Has made many recordings. Hons: Pope Paul Medal; Salzburg 50 Year Anniversary Medal; Bratislava Fest. Award. Hobbies: Swimming, Filming. 16.

DONATO, Anthony, b. 8 Mar. 1909, Prague, Neb., USA. Educator; Composer; Violinist; Conductor. Educ: BMus, MMus, PhD, Eastman Schl. of Music; studied violin, comp., cond. m. Carolyn C Scott. Career: Hd., Violin Depts., Drake Univ., 1931-37, Iowa State Tchrs. Coll., 1937-39, & Univ. of Tex., 1939-47; Prof. Theory & Comp., Northwestern Univ., 1947-. Comps. incl: (orch.) Sinfonietta No. 2; Prairie Schooner; The Plains; (chmbr. music) 4 str. quartets; Sonata for Horn & Piano; (chorus & orch.) The Congo; num. choral works, songs, band, piano tchng. & instrumental pieces. Publ: Preparing Music

Manuscript, 1963. Contbr. to var., profl. jrnls. Mbr. profl. assns. Recip., num. awards & commissions. Address: School of Music, Northwestern Univ., Evanston, IL, USA. 2, 8.

DONINGTON, Margaret, b. 6 May 1909, Leeds, UK. Music Teacher; Player of the Recorder & the Viola da Gamba. Educ: studied w. Mrs. A Rudolph & Carl Dolmetsch; Cert., Soc. of Recorder Players. m. Oswald Byrom Powell (dec. 1967), 2 stepsons. Career: Adjudicator of recorder & other woodwinds, strings, etc.; played w. Dolmetsch Family, 1928-; Mbr. of Engl. Consors of Viols, 1931-57; Branch Tchr., EFDSS, 1932-39: Tchr. var. schls., inclng. Birmingham Schl. of Music. Recordings: The History of Music in Sound. Publs: Scales, Arpeggios & Exercise for the Recorder (w. Robert Donington), 1961. Mbrships: ISM; Gov. & Comm., Dolmetsch Fndn.; Brit. Fedn. of Music Fests.; Engl. Folk Dance & Song Soc.; Soc. of Recorder Players. Hobby: Bird Watching. Address: Little Hawsted, 58 Kiln Lane, Headington, Oxford OX3 8EY, UK, 4, 27.

DONINGTON, Robert, b. 4 Mar. 1907, Leeds, UK. Musician (Viol da Gamba); Musicologist Educ: BA Queen's College, Oxford; BLitt, ibid; studied w. Arnold Dolmetsch & Egon Wellesz. m. Gloria Rose. Career: Viol da Gamba & Violin, Haslemere Festival, 1930-; English Consort, 1935-39; BBC London Consort, 1950-60; formed Donington Consort, 1956; lectr., TCL, 1948; num. appts. as visiting lectr., visiting scholar in UK & USA; Prof. of Music, Univ. of Iowa, 1964. Publs: The Instruments of Music, 1949; Wagner's Ring, 1963; The Interpretation of Early Music, 1963; The Interpretation of Early Music, 1963; A Performer's Guide to Baroque Music, 1973; Words & Music in Opera, & Baroque Music, 1973; Words & Music in Opera, & Baroque String Playing, forthcoming. Contbr. to: Times Literary Supplement; num. musical & musicol. jrnls.; var. books. Mbrships: Fndr.-Mbr., Galpin Soc.; Vice-Chmn., Analytical Psychol. Club, London, 1963; Nat. Coun., Am Musicol. Soc., 1967-69, 1970-72. Recip. num. hons. Hobbies: Antique Clocks; Walking. Address: Dept. of Music, Kings Coll., Univ. of London, Strand, London WC2, UK. 3, 14.

DONNELLY, Malcolm Douglas, b. 8 Feb. 1943, Sydney, Aust. Opera Singer. Eudc: Sydney Conserv. & Opera Schl.; London Opera Ctr. m. Dolores Ryles. Debut: Aust. Opera, 1966. Career: Aust. Opera; Scottish Opera (in Scotland, England, Poland, Switz. & Germany); apps. at Edinburgh Fest., 1975, '76, Wexford Fest., 1977, '78, and Glyndebourne, 1979; roles incl. Macbeth, Simon Boccanegra, Rigoletto, Almaviva (Marriage of Figaro), Herode, Pizarro (Fidelio). Recordings: Songs by F G Scott; Antonio in Le Nozze di Figaro. Hons: Sydney Sun Aria competition, 1969; Aust. Opera Auditions scholarship, 1970. Hobbies: Philately; Squash; Gardening. Mgmt: Music Internatioinal, London. Address: 1 Clifton Rd., Giffnock, Glasgow G46 7QT, UK.

DONNER, Henrik Otto, b. 16 Nov. 1939, Tempere, Finland. Composer; Trumpet Player. Educ: studies at the Sibelius Acad., Helsinki, at electronic studios in Bilthoven, Munich & w. György Ligeti. m. Irina Martina Donner, 3d, 1s. Career: Chmn., State Music Bd., 1974-79; Hd. of Light Music & Entertainment Dept., Finnish Broadcasting Co. Comps. incl: Gilbert, a musical, 1965; Symph. 1, 1965; To Whom It May Concern, 1966; Esther (tape), 1963; Notte, for guitar, 1971; Etude for Summer Wind, a capella chorus, 1971; Str. Quartet 1, for baritone & str. quartet (text by Lenin), 1970; For Emmy 2, for chmbr. orch., 1963; Ideogramme 2, for chmbr. orch. & tape. Mbrships: Chmn., Soc. for Living Music, 1978-. Hobby: Boating. Address: Fabriksgatan 22 G 52,OO140 Helsinki 14, Finland.

DONOHOE, Peter Howard, b. 18 June 1953, Manchester, UK. Pianist; Chamber Musician; Conductor. Educ: Chetham's Schl. of Music; RMCM; ARCM; GRNCM; ARNCM; postgrad. study at Paris Conserv. Debut: Purcell Room, London, 1979. Career: Pianist & accomp., BBC, Manchester; num. broadcasts; approx. 80 concerts a yr. incl. apps. at Promenade Concert, Queen Elizabeth Hall, London, & abroad. Hons: Dayas Gold Medal, RMCM, 1976-77: 3rd prize, Brit. Liszt Competition, 1976; finalist, Bartok/Liszt Competition, Budapest, 1976. Mgmt: Ingpen & Williams, London. Address: Greenside, Way Gate, Rossall Beach, Gleveleys, Lancs. FY5 1JF, UK.

DONOHUE, Richard William, b. 19 June 1936, Cromwell, Conn., USA. Tenor; Pianist; Organist; Choral Director. Educ: BA, Wesleyan Univ., 1958; MM, Yale Univ., 1960. m. Lois Ann Franklin, 2 s., 2 d. Career: Exec. Dir., Fine Arts Fndn. of Conn.; Fac. Mbr., Wesleyan, Yale Univs; Holy Apostles Seminary; Fndr. & Pres., Richard Donohue Studio of Music, Cromwell; Dir. of Music, S. Congl. Ch., Hartford, Conn. Recordings: Luther Legacy. Mbrships: Phi Beta Kappa; Nat. Assn. of Tchrs. of Singing; MTNA; Conn. State Music Tchrs. Assn.; AGO. Hons: Most Valuable Mbr., Tanglewood Choir,

1956; High Distinction in Music, Wesleyan Univ., 1958. Hobbies: Carpentry; Farming; Am. social hist. Address: 14 Prospect Hill Rd., Cromwell, CT 06416, USA.

DOOLEY, Rosemary Margaret Stanton, b. 7 April 1947, Sandwich, Kent, UK. Editor. Educ: RAM; GRSM; LRAM (Piano). m. Jonathan Mark Dooley. Career: 5 yrs. tchng.; 4 yrs. copy editing for The New Grove; 2 yrs. freelance for Cambridge Univ. Press; Ed., music books, ibid, 1979-. Publs: (under maiden name, Wise) A Guide to Internatioinal Congress Reports in Musicology 1900-1975, 1979 (w. John Tyrrell). Mbrships: Am. Musicol Soc.; Asst. Treas.; Royal Musical Assn., 1977-; Music Lib. Assn. Hobbies: Skiing; Goat Keeping; Gardening. Address: College House, Braggs Lane, Wrestlingworth, Sandy, Beds. SG192ER, UK.

DOOLEY, William, b. 9 Sept. 1932, Modesto, Calif., USA. Opera-Concert Singer. Educ: BA, Univ. of Rochester, NY; BMus, Eastman Schl. of Music, Rochester, NY. m. Chardelle Hayward Dooley. Debut: Heidelberg, Germany, 1957. Career incls: Has sung w. maj. cos. in Austria, Denmark, Finland, France, Greece, W Germany, Japan, Mexico, Spain, USA. Recordings: Role of Telramund in Complete Lohengrin (Wagner). Hons: Kammersanger, Berling Senate; Kunstpreis, ibid; Best Singer. Théâtre des Nations, Paris; Citation for Outstanding Achievement in the Performing Arts, Univ. of Rochester Alumnus Award. Hobbies: Wood & leather work; Gardening; Landscaping. Mgmt: Columbia Artists Mgmt., 165 W 57th St., NY, NY 10019, USA. Address: PO Box 11, S Salem, NY 10590, USA.

DOPPELBAUER, Josef Friedrich, b. 5 Aug. 1918, Wels, Austria. Composer; Organist. Educ: Univ. of Graz; Musik-Akademie Graz, (composition, organ); Musik-Akademie Mozarteum, Salzburg. m. Margarete Stroh, 3 s. Career: Tchr. of music theory, Brucknerkonservatorium, Linz, 1957-50; Prof. for composition & organ, Musikakademie Mozarteum, Salzburg, 1960-. Comps. inc: Organ; chamber music; choral works; ch. music; symphs; concertos (organ & strings). Recordings: Toccatina for Organ (Psallite); Ornaments for Organ (Pelca); Trio for 2 Clarinets & Bassoon (Preiser); Frohlocket, Motet (Amadeo). Contbr. to: Singende Kirche, (Vienna); Musica Sacra, (Germany Vienna). Ratgeber, (Germany). Mbrships: Consociation Internationalis Musicae Sacrae, Rome. Hons: 1st prize for organ comp., Harlem, Holland, 1955, 1956; Gent, Belgium, 1958; Anton Brucknerpreis, 1972; Österreichischer Staatspreis 1967; Sylvesterorden, Vatikan, 1978. Address: A-5026 Salzburg, Josef Thorkstrasse 31, Austria.

DORATI, Antal, b. 9 Apr. 1906, Budapest, Hungary. Conductor; Composer. Educ: Franz Liszt Acad. of Music, Budapest; Univ. of Vienna., Career: Asst. Cond., Royal Opera, Budapest, 1924-28; 1st Cond., Opera House, Munster, 1929-32; Musical Dir., Ballet Russe de Monte Carlo, 1933-39; Ballet Theatre of NY, USA, 1939-41; New Opera Co., NY, 1942-43; Dallas Symph. Orch., 1945-49; Mpls. Symph., 1949-60; Chief Cond., BBC Symph. Orch. London, 1962-66; Stockholm Phil. Orch., 1966-; Musicl Dir., Wash. Nat. Symph. Orch., 1970; Guest Cond. of var. orchs. in USA & Europe & at num. festivals. Recordings made of over 200 works. Compositions incl: Concerto for cello & orch.; The Way of the Cross (cantata); Missa Brevis; Magdalena (ballet); Symph.; Octet for Strings; Largo Concertato (string orch.); Madrigal Suite (chorus & small orch.). Recip num. hons. & awrds incl. 2 Grand Prix du Disque. Mgmt: Ibbs & Tillet, London. Address: St. Adrian, Walchwil 6318, Zugersee, Switzerland.

DORFMAN, Joseph, b. 3 Aug. 1940, Odessa, USSR. Composer; Musicologist; Pianist. Educ: Dip., Odessa Conserv. (Acad. of Music); PhD, Moscow Gnessin Inst. m. Lily Dorfman, 1 d. Career: Israel Broadcasting Corp.; Belgium Radio & TV apps.; Apps. w. West Deutscher Rundfunk, Sender Freis Berlin & Nord Deutsche Rundfunk. Comps: Trio No. 2 in Memory of D. Shostakovich; Partita for a String Quartet; Piano Sonata No. 1; Kol Nidrei for Violin Solo; Looking at Silence, cello solo; Divertimente for String Orch.; Sic et Non for ensemble. Copntbr. to: Tel Aviv Univ. Periodical; Hindemith Jahrbuch. Mbrships: ACUM; Israel League of Comps. Hons: ACUM Prize for Trio No. 2, 1978. Hobbies: Photography. Mgmt: Jeunesse Musicale, Israel. Address: Korazim St., 13/4, Neve Sharet, Tel Aviv, Israel.

DORFMÜLLER, Kurt, b. 28 Apr. 1922, Munich, Germany. Musicologist; Librarian. Educ: Dr. phil.; trng. & state exam in lib. sci.; studied musicol., Univ. of Munich, 1946-52. m. Liselotte Laubmann, 2 s. Career: w. Bavarian State Lib., 1954-; Hd. of Music Collect., 1963: Hd. of Acquisitions Div., 1969-. Publs: Studien zur Lautenmusik in der ersten Hälfte des 16 Jahrhunderts, 1967; Beiträge zur Beethoven-Bibliographie, 1978. Contbr. to: Zeitschriften und Sammelbänden; Fontes

Artis Musicae. Mbrships. incl: Chmn. Classification Commn., Int., Assn. of Music Libs.; Chmn., Advsry. Rsch. Comm., Int. Inventory of Musical Sources. Hobby: Puns. Address: 8022 Grünwald, Gabriel-von-Seidl-Str. 39, German Fed. Repub.

DORIAN, Frederick Deutsch, b. 1 July 1902, Vienna, Austria. Musicologist. Educ: studied piano w. Edward Steuermann & comp. w. nton Webern; State Acad. of Music, Vienna; PhD, Univ. of Vienna, 1925. M. Sadie Pearlman. Career: Cond., Austria, Germany, USA; Music Critic, Morgenpost (Berlin) Neues Wiener Journal (Vienna), Paris Off. of Frankfurter Zeitung; Prof. of Music, Carnegie-Mellon Univ., 1936-72; Andrew Mellon Lectr. in Music, ibid., 1972-75; Prof. of Music Hist., Curtis Inst. of Music, Phila., currently. Publs: The History of Music in Performance, 1942; The Musical Workshop, 1947; Commitment to Culture, 1965. Mbrships: Am. Musicol. Soc.; Int. Musicol. Soc. Address: 4921 Forbes Ave., Pittsburgh, PA, USA. 2, 11, 14.

DORSAM, Paul, b. 25 Jan. 1941, Bayside, NYC, USA. Collge Professor; Conductor; Composer; Writer-Historian; Music Educator; Trumpeter. Educ: BMus (Trumpet), BMus (Educ), & MMus, New Engl. Conserv. of Music, Boston, Mass.; DMusA, Boston Univ.; pvte. lessons in trumpet, conducting & composition. m. Linda Kleppinger, (2nd wife). Career: Trumpeter, Vt. Phil. Orch., 1964-67; Cond., ibid, 1967-69; Trumpeter, Richmond Symph. Orch., 1973-. Compositions incl: Fanfare & Fugato for 5 trumpets & snare drum; 4 songs, Dust of Snow, Melville, O Most High & Barton River Falls; Sonata in E. Minor; Symphonies 1-4; Cello Sonata in F Major; Sunrise, Life-Dances, & Resurrection. Contbr. to jrnls. Mbrships: MENC; Am. Musicol. Soc.; Sinfonia; Coll. Music Soc.; Int. Trumpet Guild. Hobby: Model & Prototype Railroad. Address: 2162 E. Tremont Ct., Richmond, VA 23225, USA.

DORUZKA, Lubomir, b. 18 Mar. 1924, Prague, Czechoslovakia. Music Critic & Writer. Educ: Fac. of Arts, Charles Univ., Prague; PhD.m. Blazena Doruzkova, 1 s. Career: Ed., Jazz Monthly, 1947-48: Exec. Off., Czechoslovak Composers Assn., 1949-53; Hd., For. Contacts Dept., State Publishing house of Music, 1954-64; Ed.-in-Chief, Melodie Monthly, 1964-71; Dpty. Copyright & Licence Mgr., Supraphon, 1971-. Publs: Tvar Jazzu (The Face of Jazz), 1964; 1964; Tvar moderniho jazzu (The Face of Modern Jazz), 1970; Ceskoslovensky jazz (Czechoslovak Jazz) (w. Ivan Polednak), 1967. Contbr. to: Hudebni rozhledy; Melodie; Jazz Forum; Jazzforschung. Mbrships: VP, Int. Jazz Fedn.; Chmn., Comm. for Jazz, Czech Assn. of Composers & Performing Artists. Hobby: Gardening. Address: 14 Zeleny pruh, 14700 Prague 4 Branik, Czechoslovakia.

DORWARD, David Campbell, b. 7 Aug. 1933, Dunmdee, Scotland, UK. Music Producer. Educ: GRSM; LRAM; MA, St. Andrews. m. Janet Oxford, 2 d. Career: freelance & music publrng., 1961-62; BBC music producer, Edinburgh, 1962-. Compositions incl. 4 Concerti, 1 Symph., 3 Cantatas; 4 String Quartets, num. Chamber Pieces; var. songs, children's pieces, music for film, radio, TV. Mbrships: Comp. Guild of GB; ISM. Hons: Royal Phil. Soc. Prize, 1960; Patrons Fund Award, 1959; num. prizes & awards, RAM, 1958-60. Hobbies: Photography; Walking; Chess; Astronomy. Address: 10 Dean Park Cres., Edinburgh EH4 1PH, UK. 3, 28.

DOSSOR, Lance, b. 14 May 1916, Weston-super-Mare, UK. Concert Pianist; Teacher. Educ: RCM, London, m. Diana Levinson, 1 s., 2 d. Debut: Aeolian Hall, London, 1937. Career: Soloist for Royal Phil. Soc. & w. all major Engl. orchs.; toured Israel w. Israel Phil. Orch., 1950; solo, chmbr. & concerto broadcasts, BBC; Staff Mbr., RCM, 1946-53; Prin. Tchr. of Piano, Elder Conserv. of Music, Univ. of Adelaide, Aust., 1953-; perfs. w. Aust. & NZ orchs.; solo broadcasts, Aust. Broadcasting Commn. radio & TV. Mbrships: ISM; Royal Phil. Soc. Hons: Medal of the Worshipful Co. of Musicians, 1936; Franz Liszt Prize, Int. Pinoforte Competition, Vienna, 1936; Prizewinner, Chopin Concours, Warsaw, 1937, Ysaye Concours, Brussels, 1938. Hobbies: Golf; Walking. Address: 22 Regent St., Millswood, SA, Austria.

DOSTAL, Nico, b. 27 Nov. 1885, Korneburg, Austria. Composer. Educ: Akademie für Musik Komposition; Abteilung Kirchenmusik. m. Lillie Claus Sängerin, 1 s. Debut: as Organist, Messe Dom zu Linz, 1912; as Cond., Innsbruck, 1918. Career: 2 TV Personality Shows; Apps. on TV & Radio. Comps. incl: Clivia; Der Dritte Wunsch; Der Kurier der Königin; Die Flucht ins Glück; Die Grosse Tänzerin. Recordings: Clivia; Die Ungarische Hochzeit; Manina; Monika. Mbr. var. profl. orgs. Hons. incl: Ehrenkreuz für Wissenschaft und Kunst, Austria.1965; Das grosse Verdienstkreuz des Verdienstordens der BRD, 1972. Hobbies: Billiards; Reading. Address: 5020 Salzburg, Heinrich Wallmannweg 3, Austria.

DOUGHERTY, Christina Hosack, b. 2 June 1938, Pitts., Pa., USA. Singer; Voice Teacher. Educ: BM, Univ. of Mich. m. George H. Dougherty, 1 s., 2 d. Debut: Chgo. Symph. Career: apps. w. Chgo. & St. Louis Symphs., August Opera, Lyric Opera of Kansas City; broadcasts in Chgo. & St. Louis; currently Voice Tchr., St. Louis Univ.,Tchr., N Shore Music Ctr., Chgo., Singer, Bel Canto of Young Audiences, Inc.; Mgr., Dougherty-Mottl Concerts. Recordings: Beethoven's 9th Symph., Fritz Reiner cond. Mbrships: Nat. Assn. of Tchrs. of Singing; Ladies Friday Musical; AGMA (singers' union). Hobbies: Sailing; Cooking; Sewing. Address: 51 Kingsbury, St. Louis, MO 63113, USA.

DOUGLAS, Audrey, b. 21 Oct. 1926, Windsor, Ont., Can. Piano & Organ Teacher. Educ: ARCT. m. William K. Douglas (dec.). Debut: as organist, Toronto, 1956. Career: Organist in Sudbury, Gananoque; ch. organist in Toronto. Mbr., Can. Bureau for the Advancement of Music (piano tchr.).Hons: Tchr. of the Year, Ont. Conserv. of Music, 1976, '77. Address: 250 Scarlett Rd., Apt. 1903, Toronto, Ont. M6N 4X5, Canada.

DOUGLAS, Clive Martin, b. 27 July 1903, Rushworth, Victoria, Australia. Composer, Conductor. Educ: BMus, Univ. of Melbourne, 1934; DMus, ibid., 1958. m. Marjorie Eloise, nee Ellis, 1 d. Career: Staff Orch. Cond., Aust. Broadcasting Commission, 1936-66; Examiner, AMEB, 1953-66; Chief Study Tchr., Comp., Melbourne Univ. Conserv., 1958-66; Assoc. Cond., Sydney Symph. Orch., NSW, 1947-53; Res. & Assoc. Cond., Melbourne Symph. Orch., Victoria, 1953-66. Compositions: 5 Operas; 3 Symphs.; 2 Choral Wks. w. Orch.; 4 Symph. Suites for Documentary Film Scores; 2 Overtures; 6 Light Pieces for Orch; 15 Symph. Poems. Contbr. to var. mags. & profl. jrnls. Hons: ABC Comp. Competition Awards, 1933, 1935; ABC/APRA Comp. Awards,1950, 1951, 1956, 1965, 1954, 1970. Hobbies: Biographical & Historical Writings; Model Railways. Address: "Kelhead Brae", 283 Dendy St., Brighton East, 3187, Victoria, Australia. 3, 15.

DOUGLAS, James b. 4 July 1932, Dumbarton, UK. Composer; Accompanist; Teacher. Educ: LRAM; ARCM. m. Helen Torrance Fairweather, 2 s., 1 d. Debut: Wienersalle, Mozarteum, Salzburg (Accomp.); Wigmore Hall, London. Career: Apps., Austrian TV; Border TV, Scotland; Comps. perf. Edinburgh Int. & other Fests., BBC, UK & elsewhere; Comp., accomp., Music publisher; managing dir., Scotus Music Publications, Ltd. Comps. incl: The 7 Deadly Sins (mask); A Christmas Fable; 2 Antiphons; (vocal) Kingfisher Songs; (organ) De Profundis; (piano) Tabula Rasa; (Chmbr.) Oboe Sommerso; (Chmbr. orch.) Leonardo Sketches; (orchl.) Scenes from Beowulf; (choral/orchl.) Nox et Tenebrae. Contbr. to jrnls. Mbr. profl. orgs. Hobbies incl: Reading. Address: c/o Scotus Music Publicatioins, 28 Dalrymple Cres., Edinburgh, EH9 2NX, UK.

DOUGLAS, Nigel, b. Lenham, Kent, UK. Operatic Tenor. Educ: Magdalen Coll., Oxford; Musikakademie, Vienna, Austria. m. Alexandra Roper. Debut: Rodolpho in La Bohéme, Vienna Kammeroper, 1959. Career: Leading roles in opera houses & fests., Aldeburgh, Antwerp. Barcelona, Basel, Berne, Brussels, Covent Gdn., Edinburgh, Sadler's Wells; Scottish Opera, Venice, Vienna Voklsoper, Welsh Nat. Opera, Wexford, Zurich etc.; roles incl. Pete Grimes, Captain Vere (Billy Budd), Aschenbach (Death in Venice), Eisenskein (Fledermaus); Regular TV in UK & Europe; Frequent broadcasts talks, BBC Radio, on opera. Recordings: Opera & Operetta. Hobbies: Gardening; Fishing. Mgmt: Thea Dispecker (USA only). Address: 19 Wandle Rd., London SW17 7DL, UK.

DOUGLAS, Richard Roy, b. 12 Dec. 1907, Tunbridge Wells, UK. Composer, Music Editor; Pianist. Educ: self-taught. Career: Orch. Pianist w. LSO & other orchs.; composed music for films & BBC; helped Ralph Vaughan Williams prepare his works, 1944-58. Compositions: works for String Orch.; Chamber Music; Orchestration of Chopin's Les Sylphides. Publs: Working With RVW, 1972. Mbr. Comp. Guild of GB. Hobbies: motorcycling; Collecting Uniforms. Address: 3 Eden Road, Tunbridge Wells, Kent, UK. 3,14.

DOUGLAS TUTT, Jean Marjorie, b. Leatherhead Surrey, UK. Concert Pianist; Harpischordist; Accompanist. Educ: Jr. Exhib., Grad., GSM; AGSM; ARCM; further study w. Paul Hamburger & Cyril Smith. Career: Recitals in UK & abroad. Mbr., ISM. Hobbies: Walking; Riding. Address: Bannatyne, 55 Woodlands Rd., Little Bookham, Surrey, UK.

DOUGLASS, Robert Satterfield, b. 1 Apr. 1919, Senath, Mo., USA. Musicologist; Musician; Script Writer. Educ: BMus, N Tex. State Univ , 1948; MMus, ibid., 1951; PhD, ibid., 1963. M. Elaine Killen, 1 s., 1 d. Publs: Church Music Through The Ages, 1967; Mechanics of Research,1970. Contbr. to: Am. Choral Review; Opera News; Tex. Music Educator; The Student; The Illustrator; Am. Musical Digest. Mbrships: Phi Mu Alpha; Pi Kappa Lambda; Am. Musicol. Soc.; Music Critics Assn.; S Baptist Conf. of Ch. Musicians. Hobbies: Camping; Hunting; Tennis. Address: 5736 Wedgmont Circle, N Fort Worth, TX 76133, USA. 7.

DOUGLASS, Steven L, b. 30 Mar. 1945, Rochester, NY, USA. French Horn Player; Teacher. Educ: BMusEd, Wheaton Coll., Ill.; MMus, Eastman Schl. of Music. m. Eunice Anderson, 3 s. Career: 2nd Horn, Syracuse Symph., 1968-69; Instrumental Music Tchr., Penfield Ctrl. Schls., NY,1969-76; Special Instructor of Horn, Brockport State Univ., NY, 1971-76; Horn Player, Rochester Woodwind Quintet, 1972-76; Ensemble & Solo Apps., Rochester, Phil. Orch., Brockport Symph. Orch., Chuck Magione Orch., touring prods. of Coco, 1176, Fiddler on the Roof, Disney on Paraqde. Mbrships: NEA; NYSUT; MENC. Hobbies: Woodworking; Gardening; Cooking; Photography. Address: 33 Hilltop Dr., Penfield, NY 14526, USA.

DOUGLAS-WILLIAMS, Eiluned, b. 18 June 1919, Llanflyllin, Wales, UK. Professional Piano Accompanist. Educ: pvte; LRAM. m. Douglas Williams, 1 s. Career; Frequent radio & TV perfs. in Wales; accomp., Royal Nat. Eisteddfod of Wales, 1949-; accomp., Llangollen Int. Eisteddfod, 1959-60. Recordings; as accomp. to var. Welsh singers. Mbrships: ISM; Musicians' Union; Brit. Fed. of Music Fests.; hon. mbr., Druid Order (Welsh Gorsedd of Bards)., recip., Royal Silver Jubilee Medal, 1977. Hobbies: Knitting; Caravanning. Address: Pennant, Dolgellau, Gwynedd LL40 2YS, Wales, UK.

DOUKAN, Pierre, b.11 Oct. 1927, Paris, France. Concert Violinist; Professor. Educ: Conserv. Nat. Supérieur de Musique, Paris. Career: Concert tours, Europe, Africa, USA; apps. w. Int. Orchs. incl. Berlin, Chicago, Amsterdam, Geneva, Brussels, Paris, etc; Prof., Conserv. Nat. Supérieur de Musique, Paris. Recordings: Sonatas by Schumann, Fauré, Franck, Ravel, Grieg, Roussel; Vivaldi's Four Seasons. Publs: L'école du violon, 1979. Hons: var. acad. hons.; 3rd Prize Reine Elisabeth de Belgique, Brussels, 1955; Grand prix du disque, Paris, 1958; Commandeur de l'Ordre du merite et devouement francais, 1978. Hobby: Walking. Address: 14 rue de l' Echiquier, 175010 Paris, France.

DOULIEZ, Paul, b. 4 Apr. 1905, Hasselt, Belgium. Painist; Conductor; Composer; Author. Educ: Conserv., Antwerp; certificated prof. of music, 1931. m. Ursula von Jagow, 1 d. Debut: Nat. Inst. of Radio, Brussels. Career: pianist, 1931-33; cond., Omroep-Orkest, Nat. Inst. of Radio, Brussels, 1933-44; musical advsr., Europäische Bildungsgemeinschaft, Stuttgart, German Fed. Repub., 1955-. Comps. incl: (piano) Tarentella, 1922: Rhapsodie Fantastique, 1926; Sonata; Flemish Dances; Inventions; Suite (1952); Str. Quartet, 1942; sev. orchl. scores for radio & TV plays. Recordings: works by Chopin, Albeniz, Granados, Tchaikovsky, Rossini, etc. Publs: Zeven sleutels tot de toonkunst, 1942; biographies of Joh. Strauss (1952), Debussy (1953), Peter Benoit (1954); co-author, Das Buch der Lieder und Arien, 1956; Machorka (novel), 1979. Mbr. sev. profl. socs. Hobbies: Langs; Writing. Address: Haldenstr. 44 Schnait, 7056 Weinstadt, German Fed. Repub.

DOUVERE, André Alphonse Theophile, b. 4 July 1924, Ostend, Belgium. Musicians (Cello, Viola da Gamba, 13th Century Fiddle). Educ: Royal Conserv., Brussels; Hochschule für Musik, Berlin, Germany. m. Jacqueline Torney. Career: Solo per., Radio & TV, & at concerts thru'out Belgium & Europe; Mbr. of Chmbr. Music Grps., Trio or Ensemble Orpheus, Bella Arte Str. Quartet, Pro Musica Antiqua, dir. Safford Cape; Cello Soloist, Orch. de Chambre de Wallonie, (Ensemble D'Archets Eugene Ysaÿe) dir. Lola Bobsco; Cond. & Musical Dir., Musica Viva Chambr. Orch., (1960-63); Concert tours, Europe, Austria, Middle East, Far East, Can., Ctrl. Am., S Am., N Africa; Prof. for Cello & Viola da Gamba, Lemmens Inst., Louvain; Prof. for Chmbr. Music, var. summer courses, Germany & Yugoslavia. Recordings: Var. records w. Pro Musica Antiaqua & Trio Orpheus. Hobbies: Literature; Photography & Filming. Address: 296 Ave Brugmann (boite 15), B1180 Brussels, Belgium.

DO VALLE, Raul Thomas Oliveira, b. 27 Mar. 1936, Leme, Sao Paulo, Brazil. Teacher of Musical Compositions. Educ: BMusEd, 1972. m. Maria Delma Dutra do Valle, 3 s., 1 d. Debut: 1971 (as comp. & cond.). Career: Cond., Percussion Grp., Cecilica Meireles Room, Rio de Janeiro, 1975; Asst., Deleg. of Culture, Sao Paulo State, 1968-69. Comps. incl: Variations for Orch.; Divertimento for Clarinet & String Orch.; Divertimentos for Brass & Percussion; Sonatina for Flute & Piano. Mbrships. incl: Fndr. Mbr., Brazilian Assn. Hons. incl; Alberto Ginastera Award, Ctr. Int. de Percussion, Geneva, 1975. Hobbies incl: Gardening. Address: Rua Gen. Osorio 2093, Cambui, 13100 Campinas, Sao Paulo, Brazil.

DOWD, Charles, b. 4 Aug. 1948, Syracuse, NY, USA. Timpanist; Classical Percussioinist; Jazz Vibraphonist & Drummer; Profssor of Music. Eudc: BA, Calif. State Univ., San Jose, 1970; MA, Stanford Univ., 1971. Debut: San Francisco, Calif. Career: Freelance perf., San Francisco Symph., Cabrillo Music Fest., Nat. Symph., Juilliard Orch., RCA Studios, Calif. recordings ind.; Guest perf., Ore., Calif. & NY; Tchr., clinics, workshops; Prof., Univ. of Ore. Schl. of Music. Comps: 3 Canons for Percussioin Quartet. Publs: A Primer for the Rock Drummer, 1970; A Thesaurus for the Jazz-Rock Drummer, 1974. Mbrships. incl: 2nd VP, Ore. Chapt., Percussive Art Soc., 1975-76; Nat. Assn. of Coll. Wind & Percussion Instructors; MENC. Hobby: Sports. Address: 772 Larch St., Eugene, OR 97403, USA.

DOWD, Ronald, b. 23 Feb. 1914, Sydney, Austria. Operatic Tenor. m. Elsie Burnitt Crute, 1 s. Career incls: arrival in UK for Sadler's Wells, 1956; return to Aust. for Elizabethan Theatre Trust; rejoined Sadler's Wells, 1959-60; concert & opera apps.w. ldng. orgs. (inclng. Royal Opera House, Covent Gdn.) & conds., 1960-; tour of Europe w. Sadler's Wells, 1963-65; toured of Aust. & NZ for Aust. Broadcasting Commn. 1964; w. Aust. Opera Co., 1972-. Mbrships: Chmn., Opera Panel, Aust. Coun. for the Arts, 1973-. Hobbies: Numismatics; Squash. Address: 10 Marion Crescent, Lapstone, NSW, Austria 2773. 1.

DOWER, Catherine A, b. 19 May 1924, South Hadley, Mass., USA. Professor of Music History. Educ: AB, Hamline Univ.; MA, Smith Coll.; PhD, Cath. Univ. of Am.; Pius X Schl.of Liturgical Music. Publs. num. eds. inclng. eds. of Palestrina's Haec Dies & Regina Coeli, & Toccata for Organ (Matteoi Simonelli). Contbr. to: num profl. jrnls. inclng. Musart; Music Jrnl.; Grove's Dictionary; Die Musik in Geschichte & Gegenwart. Mbrships: Nat. Cath. Music Educators' Assn.; Am. Musicol. Soc., Coll. Music Soc.; Nat. Soc. for Lit. & the Arts; Ch. Music Assn. of Am.; Inst. Sacred Music Soc.; Music Soc. of Puerto Rico. Hons. incl: Prof. of the Yr. Award. AAUP, 1975. Address: 60 Madison Ave., Holyoke, MA 01040, USA. 23, 27, 29.

DOWNES, Edward Olin Davenport, b. 12 Aug. 1911, Boston, Mass., USA. Music Historian; Broadcaster; Critic. Educ. incl: Manhattan Schl. of Music; Univ. of Paris; PhD, Harvard Univ., 1958. Career incls: Asst. Music Critic, NY Post, 1936-38; Music Critic, Boston Evening Transcript, 1939-41; Lectr., Boston Mus. of Fine Arts, 1946-50 Wellesley Coll., 1948-49, Metrop. Mus. of Art, NYC, 1960-66; Prof. of Music Hist., Univ. of Minn., 1950-55, PhD Grad. Ctr., Queens Coll., CUNY, 1966-; Fac. Mbr., Master Classes, Bayreuth Fest., 1959-65; Quizmaster, Metrop. Opera broadcasts, 1958-; 1st Hearing series, WQXR, NYC, 1968-. Publs. incl; Transl., Verdi: The Man in His Letters, 1942; Adventures in Symphonic Music, 1943; CPE Bach's opera Temistocle (ed. w. H C Robbins Landon), 1965; NY Phil. Guide to the Symph., 1976. Mbrships: incl. Int., Italian & Belgian Musicol. Socs.; German Soc. for Music Rsch.; Am. Coun. of Learned Socs. Address: 1 W 72nd St., NY, NY 10023, USA. 2.

DOWNES, Ralph William b. 16 Aug. 1904, Derby, UK. Organist; Conductor; Organ Consultant. Educ: RCM, London; Schlr., Keble Coll., Oxford, BA, 1928, MA, 1931, BMus, 1933; ARCM, 1925, Pius X Schl. of Liturgical Music, NY, USA. m. Agnes Mary Rix, 1 s. Debut: London, 1925. Career: Asst. Organist. Southwark Cathedral, London, 1923-25; Dir. of Univ. Chapel Music, Princeton, NJ, USA, 1928-35; Organist, Brompton Oratory, London, 1936-; Prof. of Organ, RCM, 1954-74; has given recitals, esp. of 16th & 17th century music, on radio & TV; Recitalist, France, Italy, Belgium, Netherlands, Germany, Switz., Repub. of Ireland; Jury Mbr., competitions in Munich & Haarlem; designed many important organs, 1949-71, inclng. Royal Fest. Hall, London, Paisley Abbey & Gloucester Cathedral; has composed var. works for keyboard. Recordings: Bach, 18 Chorales & Klavierübung pt. 3; Franck & His Pupils; Widor, Bach, Couperin, Liszt, etc. Contbr. to var. jrnls. Mbrships: Royal Musical Assn., ISM; Gaplin Soc.; Musicians' Union. Hons: CBE; Hon. RAM; FRCO; FRCM; KSG. Hobbies: Nursing; Domestic chores. Address: 9 Elm Cres., Ealing, London W5 3JW, UK.

DOWNEY, James Cecil, b. 13 Feb. 1931, Grand Bay, Ala., USA. Professor; Musician. Educ: pvte, study of piano; BA, Wm. Carey Coll., Hattiesburg, Miss., 1958; MMus, Univ. of Southern Miss., Hattiesburg, 1963; PhD, Tulane Univ., New Oleans, La. m. Phyllis Barber Downey, 2 s., 2 d. Contbr. articles to var. musical publs. inclng. Grove's Dictionary. 6th ed.; Yearbook of Inter-Am. Inst. for Musical Rsch.; Ethnomusicol. Mbrships. incl: Mus. Folklore Soc.; Am. Musicol. Soc.; Soc. for Ethnomusicol.; Phi Mu Alpha Sinfonia; Pi Gamma Mu. Hons: Jaap Kunst Prize, Soc. for Ethnomusicol., 1964; Younger

Humanist Fellowship, Nat. Edowment for Humanities, 1971. Hobbies: Animal husbandry; Organic gardening; Woodworking. Address: Box 198 William Carey Coll., Hattiesburg, MS 39401, USA.

DOWNEY, John W, b. 5 Oct. 1927, Chgo, Ill., USA. Composer; Pianist; Conductor; Educator. Educ: BMus, De Paul Univ., 1949; MMus, Chgo. Musical Coll.. Roosevelt Univ., 1951; Prix de Comp., Paris Conserv., 1956; PhD, Sorbonne, 1956; studied w. Darius Malhaud. Comps. incl: What If? (recorded), A Dolphin (recorded), Symph. Modules, Almost 12, 1975-76; Cello Sonata (recorded), Pyramids, Jingalodeon, Agort (recorded), 1973-74; Eastlake Terrace (recorded), 1966; Song for Tuba (recorded), 1968. Publs: La Musique Populaire dans l'Oeuvre de Béla Barok, 1967. Contbr. to: Focus Mag.; var. recorded album notes. Mbrships. incl: ASCAP; Am. Soc. of Univ. Comps.; Pres., Wis. Contemp. Music Forum, 1970-. Recip., Num. commns. Hobby: Cycling. Address: 4413 N Prospect, Shorewood, WI 53211, USA. 4.

DRABKIN, William Morris, b. 9 Nov. 1947, NYC, USA. Musicologist; Editor. Educ: AB, Cornell Univ., 1969; MFA in Music, Princeton Univ., 1971; currently preparing PhD, ibid. Contbr. to: Musical Times; Prespectives of New Music; Grove's Dictionary of Music, 6th ed. Mbrships: Am. Musicol. Soc.; Royal Musical Assn. Hons: Fellowship for rsch. & study in Germany, DAAD, 1972-73. Hobbies: Chamber Music (Violin, Piano); Teaching the Piano; Archery; Swimming & other Sports. Address: 1027 Garrison Av., Teaneck NJ, USA.

DRAEGER, Walter, b. 14 Dec. 2888, Batzlow, Germany. Composer. Educ: PhD; Music studies, comp. widower, 1 s., dec. Comps. incl: Cane Songs, Lenau; Ana Kreonistic Rhapsody; Doris and Damon, Pastorales from gallant times; Symph. in D; Concerto for violoncello and orch.; Divertimento for violin and piano; I Str. Quartet A Minor; II Str. Quartet D Minor; Quintent for wind instruments. Recordings: var. Radio recordings. Mbrships: Assn. of German Comp., hon. mbr. Hons: Art Prize Halle, 1955; Art Prize Weimar, 1970; Merit Order GDR; Hon. Gold Medal Assn. of German Comp., GDR. Address; Tiefurter Allee 19, 53 Weimar, German Dem. Repub.

DRAGOUMIS, Markos Ph, b. 18 Dec. 1934, Athens, Greece. Musicologist. Educ: Athens Univ. Law Schl.; Piano, Athens Conserv.; Hist. of Music, Greek Conserv.; Byzantine Music, Piraeus Conserv.; Byzantine Musical Palaeography, Lincoln Coll., Oxford. m. Ada Cristou, 4 children. Career: Supvsr., Melpo Merlier Ctr. for Greek Folk Music Studies, 1960-; Dir. of Music, Athens Coll., 1964-; Lectr. in Hist. of Music, Athens Conserv., 1970-. Recordings: Ed. of 2 records containing Greek country folk music, etc. Publs: Rebetia, songs from old jrnls. Hobbies: Poetry; Lit. Address: 7 Corais St., Kiphissia, Nr. Athens, Greece.

DRAKE, Bryan Ernest Hare, b. 7 Oct. 1925, Dunedin, NZ. Singer (baritone). Educ: BA, Otago Univ., NZ; studied w. Ernest Drake, NZ & Dawson Freer, London; LRSM. m. Jean Margaret Keen, 2 s., 1 d. Debut: Escamillo, Carmen, 1948. Career: Creates roles in Britten's Billy Budd, Curlew River, Burning Fiery Furnace, Pridigal Son; TV apps., Billy Budd, Peter Grimes; Royal Opera; Engl. Nat. Opera; Engl. Opera Group; English Music Theatre; Welsh Nat. Opera; Prof., GSM. Recordings: Curlew River; Burning Fiery Furnace; Prodigal Son; Billy Budd; Rape of Lucretia. Hobbies: Gardening; Camping; Sailing. Address: 31 Wordsworth Walk, London NW11 6AL, UK.

DRAKE, George Warren James, b. 4 Aug. 1939, Aucklnd, NZ. Lecturer in Music & Musicologist. Educ: BA, 1961, MA, 1963, Univ. of Auckland, NZ; PhD, Univ. of Ill., 1972. m. Carla Maria Drake, 1 s., 1 d. Career: Sr. Lectr., Univ. of Auckland, NZ, Publs: The First Printed Books of Motets, Petrucci's Motetti a Numero Trentatre (Venice, 1502) & Motetti de Passioine, De Cruce, de Cruce, de Sacramento, de Beata Virgine et Huiusmodi (Venice, 1503): A Critical Study & Complete Edition, 1972. Address: c/o Conservatorium of Music, Univ. of Auckland, Private Bag, Auckland, NZ.

DRAKE, Susan, b. Cardiff, UK. Harp Soloist. Educ: LRAM; ARCM; studied w. Alwena Roberts, Gwendolen Mason,Marisa Robles. m. John Wilbraham. Debut: Wigmore Hall, London, 1969. Career: regular apps. at major music fests. & in London concert halls; radio & TV broadcasts, UK & France; Mbr., w. Wm. Bennet (flute) & Jan Schlapp (viola), of London Harp Trio, performing in UK & Europe. Recordings; Britten's Ceremony of Carlos. Publs: ed.; Stephen Dodgson's Ballade for harp & Duo for flute & harp, 1978. Mbr., Lansdowne Club. Recip., Nat. Fedn. of Music Socs. Award, 1969. Hobbies: Needlework; Swimming; Tailoring; Dressmaking. Mgmt: Helen Jennings Concert Agcy., 60 Paddington St., London W1M 3RR. Address: 14B Elizabeth Mews, London NW3 4TL, UK.

DRAPER, Glenn Wright, b. 18 July 1928 Roanoke, VA., USA. Professor; Director of Choral Music. Educ: BMus; MMus; Dr. of Humanities m. Lounelle, 2 s. Career: Tchr., 22 yrs.; Dir. Professional choir, 23 yrs.; 12 overseas tours w. choir; 6 Nat. TV shows w. choir. Recordings: (w. choir) 17 Albums. Mbrships: ACDA; Phi Mu Alpha; AGO; Phi Beta Psi; Rotary Club. Hons: 1st Place, Military Choirs, 1954-55. Address: 810 Crown Point Rd. W, Chattanooga, TN 37377, USA.

DRAZINIC, Ivan, b. 3 July, 1942, Lastovo, Yugoslavia. Conductor. (piano). Educ: Tchng. maj., Secondary Music Schl., Dubrovnik; Conducting maj., Acad., of Music, Beograd. m. Milica Jevtic Drazinic, 1 s. Debut: Concert w. Choir of Artistic Ensemble of Yugoslav Nat. Army, Belgrade, 1966. Career incls: Pianist, City Symph. Orch., Dubrovnik; Cond. & Artistic Mgr: Choir Abrasevic, Belgrade; Choir & Symph. Orch., Nat. Arnmy of Yugoslavia, 1965-; Cond. & Artistic Mgr., Choir Iva Lola Ribar, 1970-; Concerts, TV & radio apps. worldwide. Num recordings. Contbr. to Zvuk, Sarajevo; Pro Musica, Belgrade. Mbr. var. profl. orgs. Hons. incl: Silver Sword Decoration awarded by pres. Tito, 1971. Hobby: Collecting Records. Address: Jurija Gagarina 235/st. 86, 1100 Beograd, Yugoslavia.

DREGER, Alvin Brice, b. 6 June 1912, Huntsville, Ala., USA. Cellist. m. Patricia A Houston. Career: Fndr., 1954, Prin. Cellist, 1954-, Huntsville Symph.; String instrument repairer & appraiser. Mbrships; Bds. of Dirs., Huntsville Symph., Huntsville Youth orch., Huntsville Chmbr. Music Guild; Hunts ville Music Appreciation Grp. Hons: Plaque as fndr., personnel mgr., & libn., Huntsville Symph., 1965; Virginia Simms Award for artistic contbns. to Huntsville, 1971. Hobby: Collecting string instruments. Address: 610 Holmes Ave., Huntsville, AL 35801, USA.

DREIER, Per Erling, b. 25 Dec. 1929, Trondheim, Norway. Orchestral Conductor; Oboist; Pianist. Educ: Grad., Tech. Univ. of Norway, 1953 Royal Conserv. of Music, The Hague, Netherlands, RAM, London, UK, & Staatstheater, Württemberg, 1953-57; Cond. course, Netherlands Radio Union, 1954, 55. 1 s., 2 d. Debut: w. Trondheim Symph. Orch., 1953. Career: Chief Cond., Jutland Opera, Denmark, 1957-71; Chief Cond. & Artistic Dir., Aarhus Symph. Orch. 1957-73; num. apps. as Guest Cond., Europe & USA. Recordings: Grieg, Piano Concerto, w. Percy Grainger. Mbr., profl. assns., Norway. Hons. incl: Ricordi Prize, 1955; Arnold Bax Memorial Medal, 1958; Aarhus Fest. Artist, 1972. Hobbies: Fishing; Skiing. Mgmt: Impressario A/S, Oslo; Gosta Schwarck, Copenhagen. Address: Ladbyvej 12, 8270 Hojbjerg, Aarhus, Denmark.

DRESSKELL, Oleka Nadine, b. 13 June 1911, Groverhill, Ohio, USA. Professor of Piano & Organ. Educ: BS Bowling Green State Univ., Ohio. MA, Columbia Univ., NYC; also grad. work, Univ. of Wis. & Peabody Conserv., Balt. m. Miles A Dresskell, dec., 1 s., 1 d. Career: tours of USA & Europe as pianist, harpsichord player & organist. Contbr. to: Clavier; Am. Music Tchr.; Clarion; publs. of State Assns. of Music Tchrs., Ore., Minn., Va., Ariz., Mont. & Wyo. Mbrships: Pres., Music Tchrs. Nat. Assn. (Nat. pres., 1975-79); Mbr. of Treas., MTNA Schlrship, Fndn, Bd. of Trustees, former Div. & State (Ariz.) Pres.); Phi Sigma Mu; Delta Kappa Gamma; AGO. Hobbies: Collector of Music Boxes. Address: 328 E. Palmcroft Dr., Tempe. AZ 85282, USA.

DREW, David, b. London, UK, 1930. Music Publisher; Writer on Music; Editor. Educ: Cambridge Univ. m. Judith Sutherland. Career: Dir. of Publs., Boosey & Hawkes Music Publrs. Ltd.; Music Critic, New Statesman, 1959-67; Collaborator on prod. of works by Kurt Waill at Sadler's Wells, La Scala, Frankfurt, Gelsenkirchen, Holland, Berlin Festivals; Mbr. BBC Music Advsry. Committee, 1963-73; Dir., Gulbenkian Fndn. Mod. Music Recording Series, 1963-75; Mbr. Arts Coun. Music Panel, 19709-; Ed., Tempo, 1971-. Publs: Modern French Music (Routledge); Eds. of Waill's 2 Symphs. Berlin Requiem; Mahagonny (opera); num. articles & reviews; Ed. Uber Kurt Waill & Waill, Ausgewahlte Schriften. Address: 12 Favart Rd., London SW6 4AZ, UK.

DREW, James, b. 9 Feb. 1929, St. Paul, Minn., USA, Composer; Pianist. Educ: Cert., NY Schl of Music; MA Tulane Univ.; studied w. Wallingford Riegger, Edgard Varese. m. Gloria K. Drew, 1 s., 1 d. Career: Comp., Concert Hall, Theatre, Film, 1956-; Tchr., Comp.-in-Res., Northwestern Univ., 1964-66. Yale Univ., 1966-73, La State Univ., 1974-, Tanglewood, Lennox, Mass., summer 1973; Dir., Am. Music Theatre, 1975-; visting comp., Calif. State Univ. Fulkerton, 1976-77, Northridge, 1977-78; UCLA, 1977- 78; freelance comp., 1979-. Comp. incl: Lute in The Attic, soprano, chmbr. ensemble; Symphonies; Motet; October Lights, orch.; Violino

Grande Concerto; Persona Means Mascara, orch. & choir; Lux Incognitus, Str. Quartet; Violo Concerto; Chmbr. Symph.; Concerto, Small Percussion Orch.; W. Indian Lights, Mysterium opera; Concerto, 2 celli, chmbr. orch.; Songs of Death & Blue Light Dancing, soprano & chmbr. ensemble. Contbr. to: Yale Jrnl. of Music Theory; Sonada; Alea; The Black Perspective in Music; Webern Perspectives; Notations. Mbrships: Nat. Assn. for Am. Comps. & Conds.; Int. Webern Soc. Hons. incl: Gugenheim Fellowship, 1972-73; Panamerica Prize for Music, 1974; ASCAP Comp Award, 1974-75. Address: 412 Yorktown Dr.., Chapel Hill, NC 27514, USA. 2, 7.

DREYFUS, George, b. 22 July 1928, Weppertal. Germany. Composer. Educ: Vienna Acad. of Music. m. Dr. Kay, 1s., 1 d. Compositions: Opera - Grani Sands; The Gilt-Edged Kid; Orchestra - Symph. No. 1 & 2; Symphonie Contertante, 1977; Jingles... & More Jingles; Reflections in a Glasshouse; The Illusionist; MO; The Grand Aurora Sustralis Now Show; Chmbr. Music - Galgenlieder Songs Comic & Curious; Music in the Air; From within Looking out; The Seasons; Ned Kelly Ballads; Quintet after the Notebook of J.-G. Noverre; Sexted for Didjeridu & Wind Instruments; Old Melbourne; Music for young people - The Takeover; Song of the Maypole; The Adventures of Sebastian the Fox. Recordings: num. compositions recorded on lables of EMI, Festival, Philips, RCA, & World Record Club. Mbrships: Pres., ISCM, Melbourne, 1972-73. Hons: Prix de Rome, 1976; Henry Lawson Award for outstanding servs. to the arts, 1972. Hobbies: Swimming; Gardening. Address: 3 Grace ST., Camberwell, Vic. 3124, Australia.

DREYFUS, Huguette (Pauline), b. 30 Nov. 1928, Mulhouse, France, Harpsichordist. Educ: Dips., Piano, Harmony, Counterpoint, Ecole Normale de Musique, Paris; 1st mention, Harpsichord, 1st prizes, Aesthetics, Hist. of Music, Nat. Sup. Conserv. of Music, Paris; Adv. Studies, Harpsichord, Chigiana Acad., Siena, Italy. Career: Soloist, ORTF, & num. other Radio & TV networks in France, S Africa, German Fed. Repub., Belgium, Canada, Denmark, UK, Luxembourg, Portugal, Switzerland, USA; Prof., Harpsichord, Schola Cantorum, Paris; Prof., Harpsichord & Chamber Music, Summer Acad., St. Maximin, Provence; Hd., Complementary Course, Inst. of Musicol., Sorbonne. Num. Recordings incl: J S Bach, 6 French Suites, 6 English Syites; J Ph Rameau, Piéces de Clevecin; F Couperin, Piéces de Clavecin; D Scarletti, Anthologie chronologique de 70 Sonates; Carlos Seixas, 14 Sonatas pour Clavecin; Bela Bartok, Extraits de Mikrokosmos; Chamber Music, Jl S Bach, J M Leclair, J Haydn, J Ph Rameau, Vivaldi, Corelli, etc. Hons:1st Medal Harpsichord, Int. Comp., Geneva, 1958; Chevalier de l'Ordre Nat. du Merité, June 1973; Num. 'Grand Prix' for her recordings, Acad. du Disque Francais; Acad. Charles Cros. Mgmt: Admin. de Concerts Maurice et Yves Dandelot, 252, Faubourg Saint-Honoré, 75008 Paris. Address: 91 Quai d'Orsay, 75007 Paris, France.

DRIESCH, Kurt, b. 15 May 1904, Heidelberg, Germany. Composer. Educ: High Schls. for music in Leipzig, Cologne, Heidelberg, sudies in comp. m. Dora von Dosky, 2 d., 2 s. Comps: ca 80 works, incl. songs, ch. music, chmbr. music, film music, symphs., stage works, choral music; violin concerto; cello concerto, Divertimiento; 3 Reihen for orch.; 5 operas. num. hons. & awards. Hobbies: Philately; Gardening; French lang. Address: Thielenbrucher Allee 22, 5000 Cologne/Dellgrück 80, German Fed. Repub.

DROBACZNSKI, Ryszard, b. 16 July, 1923, Kamien, Chtm, Poland. Conductor. Educ: Higher Music Schl., Wroctaw. Career: Higher Music Schl., Wroctaw, Fac. of Music Ed., 1952; ibid, Fac. of Cond., 1954; Cond. of student choirs at Wroctaw, 1948-52; Cond. of Song & Dance Ensemble, Polish Army, Wroctaw, 1952-57; Cond. of Choir & Orch., K Conserv. of Watbrzych, 1957-77; Prof., Higher Music Schl., Worctaw. Recordings: Military Songs w. Military Choir & Orch., 1952-57. Contbr. to: Ruch Muzyezny; Poradnik Muzyezny. Mbrships: SPAM, Polish Musicians Union. Hons: Prize of Minister for Culture & Arts, 1977; Golden Cross of Merit, 1975; award, Meritorius Engagement in Culture, 1975. Hobbies: Philately; Photography; Tourism; Mushrooming. Address: 53-143 Wroctaw, ul Orla 8 m 4, Poland.

DROBNER, Mieczyslaw, b. 3 Nov. 1912, Cracow, Poland. Musicologist; Composer; Conductor. Educ: MPhilos. m. Eugenie Drobner, 2 s. Debut: 1931. Career: Rector, Musical Acad., Lodz, 1953-57; Dir. of the Opera in Lodz, 1954-56; Dir. of the Opera in Cracow, 1958-61; Prof., Musical Acad. Compositions: Concertino for piano; Children's songs; Choir music. Publs: Handbook of Musical Instruments, 1959 (4 edns.); Musical Acoustics, 1973. Mbrships: Polish Acoustical Soc.; Soc. of Polilsh Comps.; Polish Musicol. Soc. Address: Slowackiego 6, 30-037 Cracow, Poland.

DROSSIN, Julius, b. 17 May 1918, Phila., USA. University Professor; Composer; Cellist. Educ: BMus, Univ. of Pa.; MMus, PhD, Western Reserve Univ. m. (2) Barbara Wolpaw, 6 c. Comps: 5 Symphs.; 11 Quartets; 7 Sonatas; opera, Spinoza; Oratorio; Cantatas; num. songs & piano works. Recordings: Quartet No. 6 - Advent. Publs: Music in the Twentieth Century, 1980. Mbrships: Am. Musicol. Soc.; Am. Soc. of Univ. Comps.; Cleveland Comps. Guild (Pres., 1968-72); Am. Soc. for Jewish Music. Hobbies: Tennis; Bridge; Puzzles. Address: 24051 S Woodland, Shaker Heights, OH 44124, USA. 2.

DRUCE, Duncan, b. 23 May 1939, Nantwich, Cheshire, UK. Violinist; Violist; Violda Gamba; Composer. Educ: studied comp. w. Herbert Howells, & violin w. Antonio Brosa, RCM, 1 yr.; BA, MusB, King's Coll., Cambridge. m. Clare Katherine Spalding, 2d. Career: Lectr., Leeds Univ., 1 yr.; Music Prod., BBC Radio, London, 3 yrs.; Pt.-time Lectr., Univs. of E Anglia, Lancaster, London (Goldsmiths Coll.); lectr., Bretton Hall Coll., W. Yorks; Freelance Violinist w. an interest in baroque violin, playing w. Fires of London, 1967-77 (many tours abroad); Music Pty., Ars Nova, Kings Musick, Yorks. Baroque Soloist, & many London chmbr. orchs. Comps. incl: Tower of Needles; The Creator's Shadow; Images from Nature (song cycle); Whose Doing Is It? (narrator & orch.). Has made many recordings w. var. grps. Mbrships: Musicians Union; PRA. Hobby: Reading. Address: 9 Grange Dr., Emley, Huddersfield HD8 9SF, UK.

DRUCKER, Arno Paul, b. 25 Dec. 1933, Phila., Pa., USA. Pianist; College Teacher; Administrator. Educ: BMus, MMus, Eastman Schl. of Music, Univ. of Rochester; Music Acad. of the W, Calif.; Akademie fur Musik, Vienna, Austria; Mozrteum, Salzburg; Univ. of Mich.; D Musical Arts, Peabody Conserv., Balt., Md. m. Ruth Landes Drucker, 2 s. Career incls: Chmn., Applied Music Dept., & Asst. Prof., W Va Univ., 1959-67; Prof. & Hd., Music Dept., Essex Community Coll., 1968-; Concert tours of W Germany, Mexico, & USA as pianist of Am. Arts Trio; Piano Soloist w. Balt. Symph., Nat. Symph., Wash. DC; TV progs. Mbr., var. profl. socs. Hons: incl: US Fulbright Grant, 1955-56. Hobby: Photography; Musical Philately. Address: Glencliffe Circle, RFD 7, Balt., MD 21208, USA.

DRUIAN, Joseph, b. 27 Oct. 1916, Vologda, Russia. Violin Cellist. Educ: Grad., Curtis Inst. of Music, Phila., 1943. m. Yvonne de Rambouillet Kerensky. Career: Has concertized widely in USA w. his wife. (concert pianist) Yvonne Druian; Gave first perf. in Am. of Sonata No. 2 of Hector Villa-Lobos; Introduced for 1st time in Wash. & Phila., Zoltan Kodaly's Sonata for 'Cello Unaccompanied; Prin. Solo Cellist. Dallas Symph. Orch., 4 yrs.; currently w. Phila. Orch. & Instr., Princeton Univ., NJ & the Settlement Music Schl. in Phila. Address: 348 S. Smedley St., Philadelphia, PA 19103, USA.

DRUILHE, Paule, b. 5 Jan. 1908. Le Havre, France. Professor of History of Music. Educ: Cert. of Advanced Study in Music Hist., Sorbonne, Cert. of Aptitude in Music Educ. Comps. incl: 5 Progressive Dictations, 1970. Recordings: Documents for Music History. Publs: History of Music, 1949; Music Texts Explained, 1956; Monsigny, 1955; Picture Envy. (contng. author), 1959; Cictées Musicales. Contbr. to: French Musicol. Review; Music Educ.; Music Larousse; MGG; Groves; Annales Gronégasques. Mbrships: French Musicol. Soc.; Int. Musicol. Soc. Address: 4 bis rue Antoine Bourdelle, 75015 Paris, France.

DRUMMOND, John Richard Gray, b. 25 Nov. 1934, London, UK. Arts Administrator. Educ: Trinity Coll., Cambridge; MA (Cantab.). Career: BBC Radio & TV, 1958-78, as writer, dir., prod., & ed.; mbr., Music Panel, Arts Council, 1974-78; mbr., Dance Committee, ibid., 1974-; Dir., Edinburgh Int. Fest., 1978-. Mbr., Scottish Arts Club. Hobbies: Architecture; Conversation. Address: c/o Edinburgh Fest. Soc., 21 Market St., Edinburgh 1, Scotland, UK.

DRUMMOND, Philip John, b. 30 Apr. 1951, Sydney, Aust. Musicologist; Bibliographer; Computer Scientist. Educ: Newcastle Conserv. of Music; BSc (Hons), Univ. of NSW, 1974; doct. studies, CUNY Grad. Ctr., 1975-. Career: Computer Cons., 1972-75, & Tutor in Computer Sci., 1974-75, Univ. of NSW; Computer Cons., CUNY Grad. Ctr., 1975-; Computer Programmer; Répertoire Int. de Littérature Musicale, 1975-, & Répertoire Int. de la Littérature de l'Art, 1979-; Lectr. in Computer Sci., NY Univ., 1979-. Publs: Australian Directory of Music Research, 1978; Reference Manual for the RILM Automated Bibliographic System, 1976. Contbr. to: Computers & The Humanities; RILM Abstracts; Musicology; Computing reviews; conference papers. Mbrships: Am. Musicol. Soc.; Assn. for Computer Machinery; Assn. for Computers & the Humanities; Musicol. Soc. of Aust.; Int. Assn. of Music Libs.; Int., Computer Music Assn.; Aust. Soc. for

Music Educ. Hobbies: Swimming; Squash; Photography. Address: Music Dept., CUNY, 33 W 42nd St., New York, NY 10036, USA.

DRUMMOND, Pippa, b. 27 Feb. 1943, Bristol, UK. Music Historian; Flautist. Educ: BMus, MA, DPhil, St. Hugh's Coll., Univ. of Oxford. m. Andrew Drummond, 1 s. Career: Rsch. Fellow, St. Hugh's Coll., Oxford, 1965-71; Lectr. in Music, Sheffield Univ., 1971-77. Publs: The German Concerto; Five 18th century Studies, 1979. Contbr. to: Grove's Dict., 6th ed.; Musical Times; Music & Letters; Proceedings of the Royal Musical Assn. mbr. Royal Musical Assn. Hobbies: The Sea & Ships. Address: 268 Dobcroft Rd., Ecclesall, Sheffield S11 9LJ, UK.

DRUZINSKY, Edward, b. 16 June 1924, St. Louis, Mo., USA. Harpist. Educ: Washington St St. Louis; NY Univ.; Curtis Ints. of Music. m. Dorothy Siegel, 4 s. Career: 1st Harpist, Pitts. Symph. Orch., 1948-52; 1st Harpist, Detroit Symph. Orch.,1952-57; 1st Harpist, Chgo. Symph. Orch., 1957-; Prof. of Harp, Northwestern Univ. Recording: Ravel, Introduction & Allegro, w. Chgo. Symph. Orch. Jean Martinon. Address: 429 West Roslyn Pl., Chicago, IL 60614, USA.2.

DUARTE, John William, b. 2 Oct. 1919, Sheffield, UK. Composer; Teacher of Classical Guitar & Music; Concert, Record & Music Critic; Writer of Record & Concert Notes. Educ: BSc (tech) & AMCT, Manchester Univ. m. Dorothy Seddon, 2 s., 1 d. Has composer num. works & ed. many works for other composers; original works recorded incl: Catalan Folksong Variations op. 25; English Suite op. 31; Sonatinette op. 34; Six Friendships for two guitars; Sans Cesse op. 34; Prelude op. 13; Suite Piemontese op. 46; Going Dutch op. 36; Miniature Suite op. 6; Sonatina op 27; Danse Joyeuse; Sua Coas. Publs. incl: Guitar Accompaniement the Easy Way; The Young Person's Way to the Guitar; Foundations Studies in Classical Guitar Technique; The Guitarist's ABC of Music; The Guitar Fingerboard Teacher; Taking Care of Your Guitar; Studies in Apoyando. Contbr. to many jrnls. in field. Mbrships: Hon. Fellow, Soc. of Classic Guitary of NY; Hon. Mbr., Guitar Socs. of Swedon & Wellington; Composer's Guild; PRS; MCPS Hons: 1st Prize, Int. Composition Contest, 1958. Hobby: Golf. Address: 30 Rathcoole Gdns., London N8 9NB, UK.

DUBENOVA, Dagmar, b. 23 July 1940, Rajecke Teplice, Czechoslavakia. Pianist; Professor. Educ: Grad., Acad. of Music Arts; Postgrad. study, Akademie für Musik and Darstellende Kunst, Vienna. Career: Phil. concerts, grand piano concerts, radio, TV recordings; Perfs. in German Democratic Repub., Poland; Prof., Music Schl., Zilina. Recordings incl: Cajsovsky G dur Sonáta, Mjaskovskij, H dur Sonáta, Piano solo works of Chopin, Brahms, Liszt, Rachmaninov, Matzudzinsky, Shostakovich, num. others; Accompanist in cemballo recordings by var. soloists. Mbrships: Can., Concert Artist Sect. Hons: 1st Prize, Competition of Interpretation of Soviet Compositions, 1960; 2nd Prize, Czech. Acad. of Music Art Competition, 1961; 2nd Prize, Haydn Style Competition, 1958. Hobbies: Touring; Cooking; Reading; Theatre. Address: Gagarinova c. 405, Zilina, Czechoslovakia.

DUBLAC, Emilio Antonio, b. 15 July 1911, La Plata, Argentina. Composer; Teacher. Educ: studies in comp., piano, theory at Nat. Conserv. of Music Carlos Lopez Buchardo, Buenos Aires. Career: Prof., Superior Schl. of Music, Nat. Univ. of Cuyo, 1941-59; Prof., Superior Inst. of Music, Nat. Univ. of Litoral, 1960-73; Dir., ibid., 1964-73. Comps: works for orch., choir instr. & chmbr. music incl. Suite; Nativa; Sonata for piano & violin; 2 strg. quartets; Flor de Jarilla & Pajarin Carpintero, albums for equal voices; 2 pieces for clarinet & piano; num. songs. Publs: Analytical Study of Hindemith's Ludus Tonalis. Mbr., Argentinian Comps. Assn. num. nat., provincial, municipal & private org's. prizes. Address: Luis Maria Campos 1160 (90, A), Buenos Aires, Argentina.

du BOIS, Rob(ert) Louis, b. 28 May 1934, Amsterdam, Netherland. Composer; Pianist. Educ: Dr. in Law; studied piano w. T Hart Nibbrig. m. Vincentia van Waveren, 3 chilodren. Has publd. over 90 comps. (songs, vocal works, chmbr. music, ballet music, orchl. works, etc.) inclng: Pastorale VII. Works recorded incl: Summer Music for saxophone, violin & cello; Le Concerto pour Hrisande for piano & orch.; Quartet for oboe & str. trio; Pastorale VII. Contbr. to musical jrnls Mbrships: Legal Advsry., BUMA (Dutch performing rights soc.); Genootschap van Nederlandse Componisten. Recip. Visser Neeklandia Prize, 1965 & 69. Hobby: Etching. Address: Prof. J, Bronnerlaan 7, Haarlen, Netherlands.

DUBOSE, Charles Benjamin, b. 20 Aug. 1949, Greenville, SC, USA. Conductor; Trumpeter; Arranger; US Army Band Officer. Educ: BMus, Furman Univ., 1971; MFA, Univ. of Ga., 1974.

m. Maryellen Goldsmith DuBose. Career: Staff, Armed Forces Schl. of Music, 1975-76; Assoc. Bandmaster, US Army Band, 1976-; Dir., US Army Herald Trumpets. Comps: arrs. for symph. band of works incl. music by Debussy, Sibelius, Mahler & Prokofiev. Recordings w. US Army Herald Trumpets. Mbrships: Phi Mu Alpha Sinfonia; Phi Kappa Lambda; Phi Kappa Phi; Int. Trumpet Guild; Nat. Band Assn. Hon: Meritorious Service Medal (US Army). Hobbies: Golf; Collecting Books & Antique Brass Instruments; Military Miniatures. Address: The US Army Band, Ft. Myer, VA 22211, USA.

DUBOURG, Evelyne, b. 26 Mar. 1929, Paris, France. Pianist. Educ: Tchng. Dip. w. Dinu Lipatti, Geneva Conserv., Switzerland; Virtuosity Class, ibid.; Interpretation course, A Cortot & Nikita Magaloff. m. Andrej Lütschg, 2 children. Career: Recitals, major European cities inclng. Paris, Vienna, London, Munich; Perfs. as soloist w. Munich Phil., Phil. Orch. of Paris, Orch. de la Suisse Romande & other major orchs.; num. radio perfs. Recordings; A Skrjabin, 24 preludes op. 11, & 10 Sonatas; Robert Schumann, Sonata number 2 in G minor, op. 22, & Davidsbündlertänze op. 6; W Vogel, Complete Piano Works. Mbr., Swiss Tchrs. Union. Hons: Prix de Virtuosité, Geneva, 1952. Hobbies: Walks in the Woods. Mgmt: Konzertdirektion Klaus Menzel, Rennweg 15, 8001 Zürich. Address: Klusdörfli 6, CH-8032 Zürich, Switzerland.

DUBROVAY, László, b. 23 Mar. 1934, Budapest, Hungary. Composer. Educ: Dip., Franz Liszt Acad. of Music, Budapest. m. Zsuzsanna Kiss. Debut: Budapest, 1966. Comps. publd: 5 pezzi per fagotta e pianofore; 6 duo per violino & percussioni; Delivrance für orgel; Stighmen for soprano & piano; Quintetto per fiati; Quintetto per ottoni; Quartetto per archi (recorded); Magic Square for violin & dulcimer; Sequence for wind instrument & synthesizer. Mbr., Confedn. of Musical Artists, Budapest. Hons: 2nd Prizes, Int. Competitions of Comps., Steffin, Polsnd, 1973, Trieste, Italy, 1974. Address: Szakasits 54/a, H-1115 Budapest, Hungary.

DUCANDER, Sten Carl, pen name KOSTA, Ensio, b. 2 Mar. 1923, Helsinki, Finland. Music Producer; Composer. m. (2) Hedvig Suomi, 2 d, & 2 d. by 1st marriage. Career: Music Prod., YLE, Finnish Broadcasting Corp. Compositions: (recorded) Jazzonia, 1956; Suites 1 & 2 for Piano & Orch., 1960, 66; Capriccio Barbaro, 1958; Hibiscus, 1961; Serenade, 1961; Divertimento, 1966; Valse Lente & Triste, 196; 2 Arabesques for Strings, 1968; Svejk, symphonic march, 1974; 2 suites for piano & orch.;. Serenade for Horn & strgs.; Arabesque for Strings; Divertimento for small orch.; etc.; Arr., records of Finnish folk songs & light music. Hobby: Actively doing nothing. Address: Vuorimiehenkatu 21 A 4, 00140 Helsinki 14, Finland. 30.

DUCHAMP, Jean-Francois, b. 23 Mar. 1949, Lyon, France. Professor of Music; Organist. Educ: Cert. d'aptitude Pédagogique; 2 yrs. univ. Debut: 1974. Career: Prof. de musique (école); Prof. de Pédagogie Musicale, l'Institut de Musique Sacrée de Lyon; Dir., Petits Chanteurs de St. Bernard. Comps: Psalms. Recordings: Rondes et Comptines II; Les Metiers; religious motets. Contbr. to Choristes, bulletin of Assn. of Perfs. of Music. Mbrships: Exec. committee, APEMEC (Assn. of Professors of Music). Hobbies: Swimming; Skiing; Walking; Philately. Address: 3 Place St. Jean, 69005 Lyon, France.

DUCHOW, Marvin, b. 10 June 1914, Montreal, Can. Musicologist. Educ: MusB, McGill Univ., 1937; Dip. in Comp., Curtis Inst. of Music, Phila., USA, 1939; BA, NY Univ., 1942; MA (Musicol.), Eastman Schl. of Music, 1951. m. Rebecca Briansky, 2 s. Career: Asst.-Assoc. Prof. McGill Univ., 1946-58; Acting Dean, 1955-57, Dean, 1957-63, Fac. of Music, ibid.; Prof., Fac. of Music, ibid., 1958-. Comps: (choral) A Carol Choir, 1946; (piano) Chant Intime, 1950; Passacaglia, 1961; (organ) 7 Chorale Preludes in Traditional Style, 1970. Contbr. to: Jrnl., Can. Assn. Univ. Schls. of Music; Can. Music Jrnl.; MLA Notes: Music Scene. Mbr., Am. Musicol. Soc.; Can. Assn. Univ. Schls. of Music. Recip., Hon. MusD, Chgo. Conserv. Coll., 1960. Address: 7910 Westbrooke Rd., Côte St. Luc. Montreal, PQ, Canada.

DUCKWORTH, Manly, b. 26 Sept. 1906, Orlando, Fla., USA. Pianist; Music Critic. Educ: BMus, Rollins Coll.; studied w. James Friskin, Percy Grainger, Isidore Philipp, Ernst von Dohnanyi Mieczyslaw Horszowski. m. Louise Howes Duckworth, 1 d., 1 s. Career: Solo Piano Recitals, maj. cities, USA; TV, Radio Apps.; Solo, Chmbr. Musiuc Recitals, Clautauqua, NY Music Fest.; Lecture-Recitals, var. Colls. & Univs.; Music Critic, Orlando, Fla., Sentinel Star. Contbr. to Musical Am. Mbrships: Phi Kappa Lambda; VP, Xi Chap., ibid, Rollins Coll.; Music Critics Assn.; Assoc. Press. Hobbies: Gardening; Swimming. Address: 640 Lake Dot Circle, Orlando, FL 32801, USA.

DU CLOU, Adrienne Jeannette, b. 5 Feb. 1938, Delft, Netherlands. Professor of Music. Educ: Dip., Royal Conserv., the Hague. m. Levon van der Eijk, 2 children. Career: Prof. of Music, speacialising in the recorder & the intrepretation of baroque music, Conserv. for Music, Zwolle; Concerts w. harpsichord & sometimes w. organ on stage & radio. Hobbies: Lit.; Books on music. Address: Gender 16, Zwolle, Netherlands.

DUCLOUX, Walter Ernest, b. 17 Apr. 1913, Kriens, Lucerne, Switz. Symphony, Ballet & Opera Conductor; Opera Stage-Director. Educ: PhD, Univ. of Munich, 1935; Cond. Dip., Acad. of Vienna. m. Gina Rifino, 2 s., 1 d. Career: Guest Cond., Vienna, Prague, NY; Music Dir., Original Ballet Russe, 1948; Musical Dir., Voice of Am., 1950-53; Orch. & Opera Dir., Univ. of Calif., 1953-68 & Univ. of Tex., Austin, 1968-; Opera Expert., Met. Opera Radio Prog., 1948-74; Opera Dir., Metro-Goldwyn-Mayer & Paramount film studios. Recorded film score for Interrupted Melody (MGM, 1954). Publs. incl. Engl. transls. of operas; Hindemith's Mathis der Maler & Harmonie der Welt. Mbrships: incl: ASCAP; Ctrl. Opera Serv. of Nat. Coun., Met. Opera (Dir.); Nat. Opera Assn. Recip. decorations & awards. Hobbies incl: Mountaneering. Addres: 2 Wildwind Pt., Austin, TX 78746, USA. 3, 9.

DUCZMAL-JAROSZEWSKA, Agnieszka, b. 7 Jan. 1946. Krotoszyn, Poland. Orchestra Conductor. Educ: Dips. in Piano & Flute, Second Musical Schl.; Dip. in Conducting. State Higher Musical Schl., Poznan, 1971. m. Jozef Jaroszewski, 1 s. Debut: 1968. Career: Fndr., & Cond., Jeunesses Musicales, (chmbr. orch.) w. concerts throughout Poland, & apps. at many musical fests.; Recordings on Polish Radio & TV; Concerts in E Germany, Gulgaria & W Germany; Cond. of many symph. concerts & oratorio concerts w. var. Polish phil. orchs.; Comp. of Music for theatre.; Cond., St. Muniuszko Opera House, Poznan. Mbr., Assn. of Polish Artist-Musicians. Recip., var hons. Hobbies incl: Touring & sightseeing. Address: ul. Libelta 10 m 4, 61-700 Poznan, Poland.

DUDLEY, John Charles Eric, b. 1 July 1938, London, UK. Singer (tenor). Educ: Pvte. studies w. Julian Kimball, Alexander Young, Eduardo Asquez. m. Nancy Long, 2 s. Career: Soloist in concerts in major European Fests. & countries incl. Flanders, Belgium, Netherlands, Russia, Denmark, Switz., Portugal, Aust., Italy; TV apps., Paris, Brussels, Dublin, Spain; Radio broadcasts BBC, BRT, France, Germany, Austria, Spain, Czech. Recordings: (w. Brompton Oratory Choir, London), Dvorak Mass op. 86, 1974, Palestrina & Victoria, 1975, Carb Rutti, 1979: Huelgas Ensemble (Belgium), 6 records; Musica Reservata (London), 4 records; Consort of Music (London), 1 record. Mbr., Actors Equity. Hobbies: Cooking; Gardening; Swimming; Skiing. Address: Worcester House, 38 Alwyne Rd., Wimbledon, London SW19 7AE, UK.

DUDLEY, Raymond Coleman, b. 20 June 1931, Bowmanville, Ont., Can. Concert Pianist; Professor of Piano. Educ: Univ. of Toronto Royal Conserv.; ARCT; LRCT; RCAD. m. Frances Young, 1 s., 1 d. Debut: Toronto Symph., Wigmore Hall, Carnegie Hall. Career: 1st pianist to perf. complete cycle of Haydn sonatas, Purcell Room, London, 1968; annual concert tours, Europe, USA, Can.; Artist-in-Res., Prof., Ind. Univ. 1957-63, Fla. Southern Coll., 1963-64; Univ. of Cinn. Coll. Conserv., 1964-78; Univ. of SC, 1978-; Soloist, NY Phil., LPO, BBC & CBC Symphs., Cinn., Detroit, Vancourver, Toronto Orchs. Comps: A Coronation March. Recordings: Complete Haydn Sonatas. Mbrships: incl: Phi Mu Alpha; MTNA; SCMTA; Am. Fedn. of Musicians; Coll. Music Soc. Hons. incl: MTNA Artist of the Year, 1978. Hobbies: Oil Painting; Swimming. Address: 57 Olde Springs Rd., Columbia, SC 29204, USA.

DUDMAN, Michael Philip, b. 2 Oct. 1938, Sydney, Aust. Cathedral Organist; Lecturer. Educ: Grad., NSW State Conserv. of Music & Univ. of New England; LittB (N E); FRCO; FTCL; DSCM; LMusA. m. Nicole Madeleine Dudman, 2 s. Career: Organist, Newcastle Cathedral & Univ.; Lectr., Newcastle Conserv.; recitals Westminster Abbey, King's Coll., Cambridge, Sydney Town Hall, Sydney Opera House, Sydney, Perth & Newcastle Univs.; concerto apps. w. Sydney Symph. Orch. Recordings: works by Widor, Liszt, Vierne & Laglais. Publs: Organs of the Hunter Valley, 1973; Organs of Western Australia, 1975; Titelouze, Hymnes de l'Eglise, 1978. Hons. incl: Vasanta Scholarship for overseas study, 1961. Hobby: Boating. Address: 44 Newcomen St., Newcastle, NSW 2300 Aust.

DUEHLMEIER, Susan Hunter, b. 15 Apr. 1949, Salt Lake City, Utah, USA. Concert Pianist; Teacher. Educ: BMus, Univ. of Utah, 1970; MMus, ibid., 1972. m. F Douglas Deuhlmeier, 1 s. Debut: w. Boston Symph. Orch., 1975. Career: apps. w. orch. in Salt Lake City, 1969-; solo perfs. in Arizona, Utah, Boston, etc.. 1972-; Dir., USO tour of Iceland, Greenland, Nfld.

& Labrador, in Walking Happy; Musical Dir., Lagoon Opera House, 4 seasons; tchng. posts at Univ. of Utah, Boston Univ.; now adjunct asst. prof. of piano, Univ. of Utah, & co-chmn. Summerarts Piano Fest., ibid. Mbrships incl: Nat. Fed. of Music Clubs; Utah Fed. of Music Clubs; Nat. Music Tchrs. Assn.; Utah Music Tchrs. Assn.; State Audition chmn.; Am. Musicol. Soc.; Coll. Music Soc.; Mu Phi Epsilon; Phi Kappa Phi. Hons: num. scholarships, awards & prizes. Address: 1926 Orchard Dr., Salt Lake City, UT 84106, USA.

DUERKSEN, George Louis, b. 29 Oct. 1934, St. Joseph, Mo., USA., University Professor; Department Chairman; Conductor; Pianist; Trombonist. Educ: BMusEd, Univ. of Kan., 1955; MMusEd, ibid, 1956; PhD, ibid, 1967; studied w. Clayton H. Krehbiel, Martha Boucher, Roy Johnson, G M Carney, John Hill. m. Patricia Gay Beers, 2 s., 1 d. Career: Public Schl. Music Tchr., 1955-56, 1959-64; Asst. Prof. of Music, Dir., Psychol. of Music Laboratory, Mich. State Univ., 1964-69; Prof., Chmn., Dept. of Music Educ. & Music Therapy, Univ. of Kan., 1969-. Music Therapist, Borocourt Hosp., Reading, Berks., 1976. Author, Teaching Instrumental Music, 1973. Contbr. to: Music in Therapy, Ed. E T Gaston, 1968; Jrnl. of Rsch. in Music Educ.; The Music Educators Jrnl.;. Jrnl. of Music Therapy; Kan. Music Review; Educl. Mag., State Dept. of Educ. of Victoria. Mbrships: Soc. for Rsch. in Music Educ.; MENC; Nat. Assn. for Music Therapy; Am. Psychol. Assn.; Soc for Ethnomusicol.; num. other Profl. Orgs. Recip. Fulbright Scholarship to Australia, 1956-57. Hobbies: Photography; Boating. Address: 2836 Maine Ct., Lawrence, KS 66044, USA.

DUFFUS, John L L, b. 12 Feb. 1946, Aberdeen, Scotland, UK. General Manager. Educ: MA, Univ. of Aberdeen. Career: Prog. Asst., BBC London, 1969-70; Personal Asst. to Gen. Administrator, Scottish Opera, 1971-73; Asst. Gen. Administrator, ibid, 1976-76; Technical Controller, ibid, 1977-78; Gen. Mgr., Hong Kong Phil., 1979-. Hobbies: Theatre; Opera; Swimming; Squash. Address: Hong Kong Philharmonic Soc., PO Box 3858, Hong Kong.

DUFFY, John, b. 23 June 1928, NYC, USA. Composer; Conductor; Pianist; Percussionist. Educ: Berkshire Music Ctr.; studied w. Aaron Copland, Henry Cowel & Luigi Dallapiccola. m. Dorothy Bottom, 2 children. Career: Comp./Cond./Music Dir., Am. Shakesheare Fest., Theatre of Lincoln Ctr., Tyronne Guthrie Theatre, ABC Orch. & TV Comps. incl: Clarinet Concerto; Concerto for Stan Getz & Concert Band; Songs from W B Yeats; The Days of Dylan Thomas; num. pieces of theatrical & incidental music. Contbr. to: Berkshire Bicentennial Commission, 1963; Duke Univ. Commission, 1969. Hobbies: Reading; Theatre; Walking; Bird Watching. Mgmt: Maura Music Inc., NYC. Address: 120 W 70 St., NY, NY 10023, USA.

DUFFY, Philip, b. 6 June 1954, Harrogate, UK. Teacher; Arranger. Educ: chorister, Ripon Cathedral; Workshop Coll.; Dip.Ed., Reading Univ.; GBSM; ABSM (piano tchng.), Birmingham Schl. of Music. Career: mbr. of staff, music dept., Hurstpierpoint Coll. Mbrships: Music Masters Assn.; ISM. Hobbies: Hill-walking; Antique; Var. crafts. Address: Hurstpierpoint Coll., Hassocks, W Sussex BN6 9JS, UK.

DUFFY, Philip Edmund, b. 21 Jan. 1943, Liverpool UK. Master of the Music, Liverpool; Metropolitan Cathedral. Educ: Studied Organ w. Noel Rawsthorne; studied Organ & Singing at Royal Manchester Coll. of Music; GRSM; ARCM; London Univ. Career: Master of the Music, Liverpool Metropolitan Cathedral, 1966-. Comps: Misc. Ch. music. Contbr. to: Music & Liturgy. Mbrships: ISM; Soc. of St. Gregory. Hobbies: Reading; Walking. Address: 53 Kundonald Rd., Liverpool L17 OAE, UK.

DUFFY, Terence, b. 12 Jan. 1940, Liverpool, UK. Cathedral Organist. Educ: ARCM. m. Moya Duffy. Recordings: Six Concertos for 2 organs - Soler. Contbr. to Ch. Music Mag. Mbr., ISM. Hobbies: Driving; Walking; Swimming. Address: 81 Abbeystead Rd., Liverpool L15 7JE, UK.

DUFOURCQ, Norbert, b. 21 Sept. 1904, St. Jean de Braye, Loiret, France. Musicologist; Organist. Educ: Sorbonee; Ecole Nat. des Chartes. m. Odette Latron, 1926, 1 s., 5 d. Career: Hist. Tchr., Coll. Stanislaus, Paris, 1935-45; Prof. of Hist. of Music & Musicol., Paris Conserv., 1941-; Organist, St.-Merry Ch., 1923-; Lectr., Jeunesss Musicales de France, 1942-61; Prof., Ecole Normale de Musique, Paris, 1958-63; Ed.-in-Chief, review L'Orgue Francais, 14e.-18e. siecles, 1934-35; Petite Histoire de la Musique en Europe, 1948; Bach, le Maitre de l'Orgue, 1948; La Musique Francaise, 1948, 2nd edit., 1970; Le Livre de l'Orgue Francaise, 4 vols., 1969-; Ed. & Contbr. to var. musical publs. Mbrships. incl: Sec.-Gen., VP, Soc. of Friends of Organ; Committee for Historic Organs. Hobbies: Archaeol.; Travel. Address: 14 rue Cassette, Paris 6e., France.

DUGGAN, Daniel Joseph, b. 28 Feb. 1949, Wash. DC, USA. Composer. BMus, 1971, MMus, 1976, Schl. of Music, Cath. Univ. of Am. Comps: Quartet for Brass & Piano, 1969; Introduction & Fugue (clarinet, viola, cello, piano), 1970; Drei Harfenspieler Lieder, 1970; The Memory of the Sun, 1970; Sinfonia (organ), 1972; Songs on Poems by Herman Hesse, 1973, & Rupert Brooke, 1974, O Edna St. Vincent Millay, 1974; Symphonic Ode: 1914 (after Siegfried Sasson), 1976. Mbrships: Phi Mu Alpha Sinfonia; Pi Kappa Lambda. Hons: Highest Scholastic Achievement Award, Eta Theta Chaps., Phi Mu Alpha Sinfonia, 1971. Hobbies: Reading Poetry; Outdoor Activities; Sports; Raising English Bulldogs. Address: 637 W Lynfield Drive. Rockville, MD 20850, USA.

DULACK, Henrik, b. 17 Apr. 1913, Heerde, Holland. Music School Director; Conductor. Educ: Conserv. Amsterdam; Mozarteum, Salzburg; Piano, Organ, Conduct Dips. m. Martha Klaaysen, 3 c. Debut: Organist, Epe, Holland; Cond., Groningen, Holland. Career: Concerts, Kampen, Winterwyk, Groningen, Almelo, Enschede, Deventer, Holland; Radio Perfs., Austria, Switzerland; Dir., Municipal Music Schl., Deventer; Cond. Musical Soc. Choirs, Almelo, Enschede, Chmbr. Orch., Deventer. Mbr. KNTV, Holland. Hobby: Sport. Address: 139 Ryksstzaatweg, Twello, Holland.

DUMICIC, Petar, b. 20 Dec. 1901, Prybram, Czechoslovakia. (Yugoslav citizen). Piano Professor. Educ: Conserv. of Musical Inst., Zagreb; Studies in Vienna, & at École Normale de Musique, Paris. m. Elizabeth Dumicic. Career: Solo concerts & piano recitals, Paris, 1926, Salzburg, Vienna, Bratislava & all major Yugoslav cities; Solo perfs. Radio Zagreb, 1926-, & Radios Vienna & Bratislava; Perf. in Italo-Yugoslav film, Night of a Butterfly; TV apps., Zagreb; Dir. & Prof., own music schl., Zagreb. Comps. incl: 3 Piano Sonatinas; Sonata for Violin & Piano; 6 Piano Preludes. Mbrships incl: Soc. of Music Tchrs. (Pres.); Assn. Croatian Comps. Hons: Decoration from Pres. Tito. Hobbies: Card Games; Dogs. Address: Rokov perivoj 6, Zagreb 41000, Yugoslavia.

DUMITRESCU, Iancu Ioan, b. 15 July 1944, Sibiu, Romania. Composer; Music Critic; Conductor; Pianist. Educ: studied Comp., musical educ: & piano, Bucharest High Schl. of Music; Int. Dirigentenkurs Sergiu Celibidache, Trier, German Fed. Repub. m. Cristina Angelescu-Dumitrescu. Career: Comps. perfd. in Fests.,I ge Biennale de Paris, Orléans, Bitthoven, Poitiers, Bucarest; Fndr./Ldr., Hyperion ensemble of new music. Comps. incl: Diachronmies II & III; Methamorphoses; Eco I & II; Apogeum; Reliefs, for 2 orchs & piano; Pasarea Maiastra; Le Jeu de la génése; Movemue II, III, IV, V; Movemur et sumus; Basoreliefs simphonique; Musiques pour Hyperion, Sursum corda II; Orion; Perspectives au Movemur; Infinitul Univers al Mioritzei-Orakorio; Melos infinit; Zenith etc. Recordings: Mutiple; Sev. radio recordings. Contbr. to: Saptamîna Culturala a Capitalei; Luceafarul; Română Literara. Mbrships: Romanian Comps. League; Sacem. Hons. Prize de Critique, Luceafarul, 1967; Priz pour Cantates, RTV Bucharest, 1977. Address: Dr. Draghiescu nr. 16, sector 6, 76224 Bucharest, România.

DUNBAR, Roslyn Frances Jessie, b. 9 Aug. 1937, Sydney, Aust. Singer; Singing Teacher. Educ: studied w. Helen Langston, Roland Foster & Elizabeth Todd, Aust.; European Tchrs. incl. Roy Henderson & Gustave Sacher (London), Rupert Gunlach (Munich), Frau Prosene (Vienna); LMusA. m. Clifford Rodney Wells. Debut: Radio app., Sydney, aged 12. Career: Theatre perfs. incl. Gilbert & Sullivan Opera season, Gueneuere (Camelot), Resi (The Great Waltz); Operatic roles incl. Zerlina (Don Giovanni), Despina (Cosi fan Tutte), Gilda (Rigoletto); Ldng. Prin., Thornhill's Annie, West End, London, 3 yrs.; Guest Artist, Sadler's Wells Opera; TV apps., Aust.; Concert perfs. w. num. Aust. Orchs. incl. Sydney & Victorian Symph. Orchs.; Concert apps., Europe & N Am.; currently Prof. of Singing, Conserv. of Music, Examiner, Aust. Music Exams. Bd. & Eisteddfod Adjudicator. Mbrships: Actors & Announcers Equity of Aust.; MTA of NSW; Nat. Lieder Soc.; Conservatorium Ex-Students Assn.; Adviser, Redlands Soc. of the Arts. Hons: Sun Aria, 1960. Hobbies: Body Surfing; Walking; Reading. Mgmt: Jun Evans Enterprises. Address: 10 Birkley Rd., Manly, NSW 2095, Aust.

DUNCAN, Andrew Christie, b. 9 Mar. 1929, Istanbul, Turkey. Music Director, Scottish Arts Council. Educ: RSAMD. m. Pamela Robertson, 2 d. mbr., ISM. Address: c/o Scottish Arts Council, 19 Charlotte Squre, Edinburgh, Scotland, UK.

DUNCAN, Charles F(reeman), Jr., b. 23 Mar. 1941, Savannah, Ga., USA. Guitarist (Performer & Teacher). Educ: BA, Yale Univ., 1961; MA, 1962, PhD, 1965, Emory Univ.; studied w. Aaron Shearer, Peabody Conserv., Balt., 1965-66; Dip., Segovia Master Class, Santiago de Compostela, Spain, 1970; studied w. Jose Thomas, Alicante, & w. John Durante,

London UK, 1974. m. Norma Stewart, 1 s., 1 d. Career: Var. concerts, Univs. of Mich., Ala., Emory, Ga. State & others, 1975-78; Mbr. Teaching Staff, Music Dept., Emory Univ., Atlanta, Ga., 1973-; fac., Mercer Univ., Atlanta. Publs: The Art of Classical Guitar Playing, 1979. Contbr. to Atlanta Jrnl.-Constitution (book reviews). Mbrships: Classic Guitar Soc. of Atlanta Inc. (Fndr. & Pres.); Nat. Assn. Music Tchrs.; AAUP. Hons: scholarship, Spanish Min. of Foreigh Affiars, 1970. Mgmt: Alkahest, Atlanta, Ga. Address: 155 Bolling Rd. NE, Atlanta, GA 30305, USA.

DUNCAN, Richard Lawrence, b. 13 June 1945, Demopolis, Ala., USA. Conductor; Pianist. Educ: BMus Piano, Fla. State Univ., 1967; Ma Musicol., Ind. Univ., 1972; DMus, Cond., ibid, 1979. m. Malda Barron. Hons: Warren D Allen Award, 1967; Woodrow Wilson Fellow, 1967-68. Address: Tulip Tree House 601 Bloomington, IN 47401, USA.

DUNCAN-SHORROCK, Sarah Esther Janina, b. 6 Aus. 1953, Blackburn, Lacs. Soprano singer; Flute & Recorder Player; Teacher. Educ: Northern Schl. of Music, Manchester; Manchester Schl. of Music; LCM; LLCM; TD; Conserv. of Berne, Switz.; (flute dip.) studied singing w. Arthur Reckless, Ellis Keeler, Isobel Baillie, flute w. James Galway. Career: vocal recitals specialising in oratorio & Viennese music; joint recitals, singing & flute/recorder, perfs. on local radio; Adjudicator; tchr., Oakhill Coll., Wiswell, Whalley, Queen Elizabeth Grammar Schl., Blackburn, & for Lancs. Educ. Authority. Mbrships: LCM Soc.; ISM. Hobbies: Travel; Driving; Reading. Address: Isola Bella, 22 Alice St., Oswaldtwistle, Lancs., BB5 3BL, UK.

DUNHAM, Meneve, b. 28 Dec. 1930, Dubuque, Iowa, USA. Musicologist; Administrator. Educ: BA, Clarke Coll., 1955; MMus, De Paul Univ., 1963; PhD, Univ. of Mich., 19069. Publs: Ed., Secular Cantatas of Antonio Vivaldi (2 vol.), 1979. Mbrships: Am. Musicol. Soc.; Phi Delta Kappa; Dir., Iowa Coll. Fndn. Hons: Am. Coun. on Educ: Fellow, 1971-72; Nat. Endowment for the Humantities Fellow, 1970. Address: 1550 Clarke Dr. Dubuque, IA 52001, USA.

DUNKELS, Alfreds, b. 14 June 1907, Daugavpils, Latvia. Concert & Orchestral Violinist; Music Teacher; Conductor. Educ: Univ. Latvia, Riga; Conserv. Latvia, Riga. m. Irena Springis. Career: Concert & radio perfs., Latvia; Violinist, Nat. Opera Orch., Riga; Concert & radio perfs., Sweden, 1944-; Concert tour w. pianist wife, Germany, 1957, USA & Canada, 1958; Permanent violin tchr. & youth orch. cond., Music Schl., Upsala; Violinist, Upsala Univ. Acad. Chapel. Address: Geijersgat. 1, S-752 26 Uppsala, Sweden.

DUNKERLEY, Patricia, b. 21 Apr. 1940, Sliema, Malta (Irish national). Flautist. Educ: ARCM, 1961; studied w. Ande Prieur, Dublin, Julius Baker, NY, Severino Gazzelloni, Rome. m. Alessandro Bonelli, Debut: Musical Assn. of Ireland, 1959. Career: Contemporary music reportoire specialist; Flautist, Radio Telefis Eireann Symph. Orch., 1961-72; Flute Soloist, New Irish Chmbr. Orch., 1965-72; Soloist, Dublin Fest. Contemp. Music, 1969, 74, 76, Orch. Michelangelo di Firenze tour of Am., 1971, Autuhno Jusicale Como, 1971-74, Bach. Fest. Killarney, 1971-76; 1st Flute & Soloist, Orch. da Camera dell'Angelicum, Milan, 1974-75; currently 1st Flute, Teatro G Verdi, Trieste; Mbr., Venetian Boroque Ensemble; Recitals, radio & TV broadcasts, Ireland, UK, Italy, USA, Netherlands, Can., Tunis, Zambia, Malta, Sicily. Recip. many hons. Address: S Marco 1960, Venezia, Italy.

DUNN, (Frank) Richard, b. 27 Feb. 1929, Birmingham, Ala., USA. Conductor; French Hornist. Educ: MA, Univ. of Calif.; Grad. cum laude in Cond.; Staatsakademie, Vienna, Austria. Debut: Vienna, 1956. Career: Cond., Santa Barbara Summer Symph., Walt Disney Prods. Ballet Spectacular, Concert Theater Assn., Oakland Symph. (Assoc.), San Fran. Chmbr. Opera; Hornist, San Fran. Symph. & Opera, Royal Ballet, NBC Opera, etc. Recordings: (as Cond.) Music for French Horn & Orch., Forest & Hunting Songs of The Romantic; (as soloist) Royal Music of Europe. Contbr. to: Mozart Jahrbuch, 1960-61; var. jrnls. Mbr. profl. assns. Hons: A Hertz Scholar, 1955-56; US State Dept. Specialist in Music, 1962. Hobbies: Anticlastic Tension Structures; Swimming. Address: 27 Skyline Circle, Santa Barbara, CA 94109, USA.

DUNN, Lester Lay, b. 25 Oct. 1912, Newburg, Okla., USA. Professor of Voice; Conductor; Tenor Soloist. Educ: BFA, Bethany Nazarene Coll., 1936; MMus, Univ. of Okla., 1941; extensive postgrad. & ext. studies. m. Cyrena Margaret Middleton, 2 s. Career incl: Music, Engl. & Speech Tchr., Pub. Schls., 1936-42; Bethany Nazarene Coll., 1942-; Chmn., Div. of Fine Arts, 20 yrs.; Staff, Wash. & Lee Univ., 1945; Min. of Music, Ch. of the Nazarene, 30 yrs.; tours w. A Capella Choir

as Dir. & Mgr., giving total of approx. 2000 concerts; radio & TV, 1928-65; Guest Soloist, Cond. & Adjudicator, 1936-68. Compositions: Songs. recordings: Soloist w. choir on recordings, 20 yrs. Publs: The Conductor in Action, 1967. Contbr. to: Okla. Musician. Mbrships: Kappa Delta Pi; State & Nat. Music Orgs.; Fellow, Nat. Assn. Tchrs. of Singing. Hons. incl: Hon. LLD. Hobbies: Athletics; Mechanics. Address: 7608 NW, 21st, Bethany, OK 73008, USA. 7. 11, 12.

DUNN, Michael Peter, b. 7 Mar. 1943, Sherbrooke, Can. Luthier. Educ: Served apprenticeship in workshops of George Bowden, Palma de Mallorca, Spain, under Maestros Orti & Ferer. 1 s. Career: Commissioned to construct sev. histl. instruments for Vancouver Soc. for Early Music, 1972-73; Commissioined to construct 2 baroque guitars for collectioin, Nat. Mus. of Man. Ottawa, 1973; Can. Coun. Grant to construct copy of Chittarone for 1st Maj. Exhib. of Contemporary Instrument Making in Can., Burnaby, BC, 1974; Artist-in-Res., BC Pavillion, World's Fair, Spokane, USA, 1974; Craftsman Rep. of BC, Craftsmen's Village, Olympic Games, Montreal, 1976. Address: Box 169, Gibsons, BC, VON 1VO, Canada.

DU PLESSIS, Christian, b. 2 July 1944, Vryheid, S Africa. Opera Singer (Baritone). Educ: Music study Univs. of Bloemfontein & Potchefstroom. Debut: Yamadori in Madame Butterfly, Johnnesburg, 1966. Career incl: appearances w. leading S African opera cos.; UK appearances w. London Opera Soc.; Brighton Festival; Prin. Baritone Engl. Nat. Opera; concert performances w. Bournemouth Sinfonietta, Halle Orch., Ulster Orch., & at Festivals at York, Bath & Queen's Univ., Belfast; Broadcasts on BBC, S African Broadcasting Corp., Spanish Nat. Radio & Radio Eire. Recordings incl. var. operatic roles. Mbrship: Equity, UK. Recip. Ernest Oppenheimer Bursary, 1968-71. Hobby: Art Collecting. Mgmt: Patric Schmid 'Opera Rara'. Address: c/o Ingpen & Williams Ltd., 14 Kensington Ct., London W8 5DN, UK.

DU PLESSIS, Hubert, b. 7 June 1922, Malmesbury, S Africa. Senoir Lecturer; Composer; Pianist; Harpsichordist. Educ: BA, Univ. of Stellenbosch; Music, ibid., & Univ. of Grahamstown; RAM, London, 3 yrs.; UTIM; UPLM; ARAM; BMus. Career: Num. piano recitals; sev. harpsichord & clavichord recitals; Many talks on music; Num. concerts apps. Comps. incl: Songs; Piano works; Choral & orchl. music; Chmbr. music; Incidental music; Publs. incl: Johann Sebastian Bach (in Afrikaans), 1960; Letters from William Henry Bell, 1973. Contbr. to: Eikestadnuus; Die Burger. Mbr. var. profl orgs. Hons: incl: Medal of Hon., S African Acad. of Arts & Scis., 1963. Hobbies incl: Keeping dogs & cats. Address: 14 Tinktinkie Ave., Stellenbosch, S Africa. 18.

du PLESSIS, Karl L, b. 13 Feb. 1932, Montreal, Canada. Pianist; Composer. Educ: Second. Schl. Dip., Univ. of Ottawa; Assoc., Royal Conserv. of Toronto; Juilliard Schl. of Music, NY. Debut: Ottawa, 1949. Career: recitals in Toronto, Montreal & Ottowa; TV & radio broadcasts for CBC; currently Comp. on staff, Nat. Film Bd. of Can. Comps. music scores for NFB films. Mbrships: FRSA; Musicians Guild of Montreal; Soc. General du Cinema et TV, PQ; Can. Assn. of Publrs., Authors & Comps. Hons. incl: 1st Prize, Can. Open Piano Competition, CNE, 1947. Hobby: Gardening. Address: 2106 Claremont Ave, Montreal, PQ, Canada.

DUPORT, Denise, b. 8 July 1938, Geneva, Switz. Pianist. Educ: Grad., Geneva Conserv.; Post degree work, Vienna Acad. (Richard Hauser), Sienna (Guido Agosti) & Venice (Carlo Zecchi). m. Dr. Maurice Cellich, 2 c. Debut: Piano duet w. Muriel Slatkine. Career: Recitals, Switz., France, Italy, Austria, Germany; Soloist, Orch. de la Suisse Romande; Perfs., Swiss Radios & TV, France-Musique, Österreichsicher Rundfunk. Recordings: Romantic music for two pianos, Chopin (Rondo), Schubert (Fantasy), Brahms (Waltes); Mozart-Concerti for 2 and 2 pianos; Stravinsky, Sonate, Concerto for 2 pianos, 3 & R easy pieces. Mbr., Assn. des musiciens Suisses. Hons: 1st Prize, Jeunesses Musicales Suisses; Top Prize, Vercelli competition. Address: Passeiry, 1249 Chancy, Switzerland.

DUPRÉ, Heather, b. 30 Mar. 1949, St. Helier, Jersey. Solo Pianist. Educ: LRAM; Recital Dip., RAM. Career: BBC Recital Broadcast; apps in Farfield Hall, Edinburgh Fringe Fest., Purcell Room, Wigmore Hall. Mbrships: ISM; RAM Club. Hons: Oliveria Prescott Prize for Comp., 1971, Alexander Roller Prize for Piano, & Walter MacFarren Prize for Piano & Gold Medal, 1972, all RAM. Hobbies: Painting; Writing poetry; Woodwork; Walking. Mgmt: H H H Concert Agyc., 5 Draycott Pl., London SW3, UK. Address: 23 Alma Square, St. Johns Wood, London NW8 9QA, UK.

Du PRE, Jacqueline, b. 26 Jan. 1945, Oxford, UK. 'Cellist. Educ: Hervert Wallen's London Cello Schl.; GSM; studied pvtely. w. William Pleeth, Mstislav Rostropovic (Moscow Conserv.), Paul Tortelier, & Pabla Casals. m. Daniel Barenboim., Debut: Wigmore Hall, 1961. Career: made 1st pub. app. at age 7; has played w. all major orchs. inclng. BBC Symph. & LSO; frequently apps. w. husband; broadcasts on TV & radio; has toured USSR, Europe, USA, Can. & Brit. Isles; made NY Debut, 1965; subject of feature film on BBC, 1967; currently tchng. in London. Recordings incl: Beethoven's Cello Sonatas 3 & 5 & Piano Trios 4, 5, 6 & 10; Boccerini's Concerto in B flat; 'Cello Concertos by Elgar, Franck, Haydn, Monn, Saint-Saens, etc. Hons. incl: Suggio 'Cello Award, 1955; Gold Medal, GSM, 1960; Queen's Prize, 1960; OBOE; Hon. RAM; FGSM; D.Vnis (Open Univ.). Mgmt: Harold Holt Ltd., 134 Wigmore St., London, W1, UK. Address: c/o Mgmt.

DUQUENNOIS, Francis, b. 2 Apr. 1915, Calais, France. Concert Pianist. Educ: Royal Conserv., Brussels, Belgium, 1933-34; studies w. Walter Gieseking, Hohe Musikschule, Saarbrücken, Germany, 1936-39; Inst. Lemmens, Malines, 1941. m. Claudia Doppagne. Debut: Belgian Radio, 1936. Career: Recitalist, Belgium, France, UK, Germany, etc., & apps. as soloist w. orch. on Belgian radio, 1950-65; Concerts & recital as mbr. of Duquennois-Doppagne Piano Duo throughout Europe, & in Israel, 1967-. Recordings: Mozart, Sonate pour deux pianos; Liszt, Concerto pathetique; Rchmaninoff, Fantaisis-Tableaux op. 5; works by Stehman, De Greef, Infante & Albeniz. Hons: Order of Leopold; num. prizes as student. Hobbies: Reading Swimming. Address: 6A Tervuurse Steenweg,3078 Everberg, Belgium.

DURAN, Elena, b. 21 Feb. 1949, Oakland, Calif., USA. Flautist; Writer; Researcher. Educ: Aspen Music Fest.; Master Classer, San Fran. Conserv.; Staatliche Hochschule für Musik, Freiburg, Germany, soloistin Klasse of Auréle Nicolet; Studies w. Rampal, Paris, James Galway, Berlin & Eastman Music Schl., Rochester, NYO, Darius Milhaud. Career: TV & radio apps., USA, Mexico, Yugoslavia, Belgium, Eire; Master Classes, Stratford upon Avon, Univ. of Mexico; Apps., UK music Fest.; Asst. to James Galway. Recordings: Music of Delius, Bournemouth Sinfonietta. Pubs: (in prep.): Playing the Flute; The Romantic Flute; The Classical Flute. Mbr., Musicians Union. Hons: Mills Coll., Hellman Music Award, 1971a; Aspen Music Fest. Scholarship, 1972. Hobbies: Mexican hist.; Physical Fitness; Travel; Reading. Mgmt: c/o London Artists, 73 Baker St., London, W1, UK. Address: c/o Mgmt.

DURAND, Marc (Joseph-Victor), b. 28 Aug. 1949, Saint-Samuel, PQ, Canada. Pianist. Accompanist; Teacher. Educu: BMus, MMus, Artist Dip., Ecole de Musique Vincent d'Indy, Montreal; MMus, Temple Univ., USA. Debut: Sarah Fischer Concert, Montreal, 1967; Carnegie Hall, NY, USA, 1976. Career: Soloist w. Quebec & CBC Symph. Orchs.; Num. recitals in Can., USA, Portugal & Switzerland; Guest Accomp., Montreal Int. Competition (voice), 1973: Num. radio & TV apps. in Can. & USA. Mbrships: Musicians Guild of Montreal; Leschetisky Assn. Inc.; NY Gen. Alumni Assn., Temple Univ. Hons. incl: 1st Prize, Leschetizky Piano Competition, NY, 1975. Hobbies: Travel; Cinema; Swimming. Address: 4854 Cote des Neiges, Apr. 1805, Montreal, PQ, Canada H3V G7. 4.

DÜRR, Alfred, b. 3 Mar. 1918, Berlin-Charlottenburg, Germany. Research worker in music. Educ: Dr. Phil., Univ. of Göttingen, 1950. m. Emmi Dolle, 2 s., 1 d. Career: Research woirker at Johann Sebastian Bach Inst., Göttingen, 1951-; Deputy Dir., ibid., 1962-; Publs incl: Studien über die frühen Kantanten J S Bach, 1951, 2nd. ed., 1977; Zur Chronologie der Leipzig Vokalwerke J S Bachs, 1957, 1976; Bach, Weinachts-Oratorium, 1967; Die Kantaten von J S Bach, 1971, 1975, 1979; Neue Bach-Ausgabe, Serie I, Bänd 1 (w. W Neumann), 2, 10, 12, ¢4 w. A Mendel), 15 (w. R Freeman & J Webster), 18 (w. L Treitler) 27, 35; Serie 2, Bände 3, 5, 5a, 6 (w. W Blankenburg); Serie V, Bände 7, 8; Ausserdem zahl reiche Aufsätze im Bach-Jahrbuch, mehrer Einzelausgaben ätterer Musik. Mbrships: Akademie der Wissenschaften, Göttingen. Address: Leipzigerstr. 20, 3406 Bovenden 1, German Fed. Repub.19.

DÜRR, Walther, b. 27 Apr. 1932, Berlin, Germany. Musicologist. Educ: Dr. Phil., Tübingen Univ. m. Vittoria, 2 c. Career: Lectr., Bologna Univ., 1957; Asst. at Tübingen Univ., 1962; hon. prof., ibid., 1977; Gen. Ed. (w. Arnold Feil & Christa Landon), Neue Schubert-Ausgabe; Confs. at the radio stns. Südwestfund & Deutsch Welle (Cologne). Publs: Studien zu Rhythmus und Metrum im Italienischen Madrigrl, insbesondere bei Luca Marenzio, 1956; Serie IV (Lieder) of the Neue Schubert-Ausgabe (Edited); Franz Schuberts Werke in Abschriften: Liederalben und Sammlungen, Kassel, 1975. Mbrships: Gesellschaft für Musikforschung; Int. Musicol. Soc. Contbr. to profl. publs. Address: Hausserstrasse 140, 74 Tübingen, German Fed. Repub.

DURRANT, James, b. 23 Nov. 1929, Bournemouth, Hants, UK. Music Educator; Violist. m. Dawn, 1 s. Career incl: Prin. Viola, Scottish Nat. Orch. 1957-64; Mbr., Scottish Piano Quartet & New Music Grp. of Scotland; Fndr. Mbr., Clarina Ensemble; Broadcaster in Concertos & solo Recitals of major works in viola repertoire; Solo Appearances at Wigmore Hall & Purcell Room; Sr. Lectr. of Music, Royal Scottish Acad. of Music, 1964-. Mbrships: Inc. Soc. of Musicians. Hobbies: Table Tennis: Cricket; Bookbinding; Clock Collecting. Address: 5 Rosslyn Terr., Glasgow G12 9NB, UK.1.

DURSTON, Roger Andrew Cadle, b. 7 May 1948, Croydon, Surrey, UK. Conductor; Double Bass Player. Educ: Cathedral Chorister, Wells Cathedral Schl.; Choral Scholar, King's Coll., Cambridge Univ., 1966-70; MA (Hons.) m. Angela East, 1 d. Debut: Purcell Room, Royal Fest. Hall, London, 1974. Career: Many Recordings & TV appearances as a Mbr. of Choir of King's Coll., Cambridge; Cond., London Baroque Soloist; Cond., Handel Sinfonia; Cond., London Boy Singers; Cond., Maidenhead Chamber Choir; Desborough Schl. Maidenhead). Mbrships: Royal Soc. of Musicians of GB; Musicians' Union. Hobbies: Theatre; Cinema. Mgmt: Ibbs & Tilletlt. Address: 2 High St., Sonning-on-Thames, Berks., RGH OUP, UK.

DURUFLÉ, Maurice, b. 11 Jan. 1902, France. Organist; Composer. Educ: Paris Conserv. Career: Organist, St.-Etienne-du-Mont; Asst. Prof., Conserv. of Paris, 1942; Prof. of Harmony, ibid, 1943-. Compositions incl: Organ works -Prelude, Adagio & Choral Varie sur le Veni Creator, 1929; Suite, 1933; Prelude & Fugue, 1942; Chmbr. Music - Trio pour Flute, Alto & Piano; 4 Motets, 1960; Orchl. works - 3 Dances, 1935; Andante & Scherzo, 1940; Requiem pour Solo, Choeurs Orch. & Organ Prize, Paris Conserv., 1922; Prize for Harmony, 1924; Prize for accompaniment, 1926; Prizes for Fugue & Composition, 1928; 'Amis de l'Orgue' Prize, 1930. Address: 6 Place du Pantheon, Paris 5e, France.

DUSEK, Milan, b. 26 May 1931, Ustlnad Orlicl Czech. Professor of Piano. Educ: Grad., Prague Conserv., 1956. m. Eva Freyová, 1 s., 1 d. Debut: w:>amateur orch. Ustlnad Orlicl, 1943. Career: approx. 800 pub. perfs. on radio & TV, records & in var. Czech. cities, 1953-; Choir Dir. & Music Tchr., Vysoké Mýto, 1956-58; Dir. of Sound Servs., Na zábradll Theatre, Prague, 1958-59; Prof. of Piano, State Conserv. of Music, Prague, 1959; Prof. of Piano, State Conserv. of Music, Prague, 1959-. Compositions: Základ hry na zobcové flétny (Elementary Text for Recorders), 1965; Klavlrnl doprovody k Houslové škole (of Cermák & Beran) (Piano Accompaniments for the Violin Text by Cermák & Beran), 1966; music for TV prog. Bajky (Fables), 1972; 15 additional smaller pieces either publd. or recorded. Recordings: 4 dics of baroque music; 120 pop pieces. Publs: Historicl Sketch of the Church Choir of Ustlnad Orlicl, 1966. Contbr. to: Zidovský věstnik (Jewish Bulletin); Vlasta. Mbrships: Protective Soc. of Comoposers (OSA(; Ed. Bd., News from Bertramka, Mozart Soc. Hobbies: Books: Old Music Manuscripst; Practical Mechanics. Address: Mahulenina 1857, 16200 Prague 6 Czech.

DUSSAUT, Thérèse, b. Versailles, France. Pianist. Educ: Conservatoire Nationale Supérieur de Musique de Paris; Staatliche Hochschule für Musik, Stuttgart. m. Claude Lemaréchal. Debut: aged 5 at Duchess de la Rochefouchault's; concerto, aged 12, w. Orch. of the Société des Concerts. Career incl: perfs. in most countries in the world incl. USA, USSR, Japan; world tour w. complete piano works of Ravel, 1975. Recordings: Haydn. Romantics, Russian, French (Ravel, Rameau) music. Publs: Transcriptions of instrumntal works of J-P Rameau. Mbrships: SACEM & other profl. soc. Hons: aged 17, 1st Int. prize, piano, Munich comptition; silver medal, Société Academique Arts, Sciences, Lettres, Hobbies: Hist.; Jigsaw Puzzles. Mgmt: Bureau de Concerts Marcel de Valmalète, 11, Ave. Delcassé, 75008 Paris. Address: 49 rue Erlanger, 75016 Paris, France.

DUSSOUIL, Jacques, b. 19 June 1933, Montmorillon,France. Organist. Educ: Dip. (organ), l'Institute Supérieur de Musique Sacreé de Paris, 1965. Career: recitals at Notre-Dame de Paris, Bordeaux, Chartres, Bourges, Liverpool, Blackburn, Bonn, Aachen, Düssldorf, etc; apps. on French radio. Recordings: works by Couperin & Bach. Contbr. of music criticism to Sud-Ouest. Address: 4 bis Ave. des Congrès, 17200 Royan, France.

DUSSOUIL, Jacques, b. 19 June 1933, Montmorillon, France. Organist. Educ: Dip. (organ), l'Institute Supérieur de Musique Sacreé de Paris, 1965. Career: recitals at Notre-Dame de Paris, Bordeaux, Chartres, Bourges, Liverpool, Blackburn, Bonn, Aachen, Düssldorf, etc; apps. on French radio. Recordings; works by Couperin & Bach. Contbr. of music criticism to Sud-Ouest. Address: 4 bis Ave. des Congrès, 17200 Royan, France.

DUTILLEUX, Henri, b. 22 Jan. 1916, Angers, France. Composer; Music Educator. Educ: Nat. Conserv. of Music, Paris. m. Genevieve Joy, 1946. Career: Dir., Serv. Creations Musicales, Radiodiffusion Francaise, 1945-63; Prof. of Composition, Ecole Normale de Musique, Paris, 1961-; Conserv, Nt. Superieure de Musique, Paris, 1970-. Compositions: Sonata for piano, 1948; 1st Symph., 1951; Le Loup (ballet) 1953; 2nd Symph. (Le Double), 1959; Cinq Metaboles, 1964; Cello Concerto; Tout un monde lointain, 1970. Mbrships: UNESCO Music Coun. Hons: 1st Grand Prix de Rome, 1938; Grand Prix du Disque, 1957, '58,'66, '68; Grand Prix du Counseil Gen. de la Seine, 1959; Grand Prix. Nat. de la Musique, 1968. Address: 12 rue St.-Louis en L'Ile, Paris, 4, France.

DU TOIT, Julius Ronald, b. 11 July 1934, Johannesburg, S Africa. Teacher (Piano, Organ, Harmony). Educ: BMus; Potcherfstroom Univ. Conserv., 1952-55: PULM. Career: Var. broadcasts as Boy Soprqano, 1940s; currently, Vice-Prin. & Hd. of Music Dept., Tech. Coll., Kroonstad. Mbrships: Coun., S African Soc. of Music Tchrs. (VP for Orange Free State, & Chmn., Kroonstad Ctr., 1974-76); Music Committee, Univ. of S Africa (Rep. of S African Soc. Music Tchrs.). Hons: Gold Medal, Nat. Eisteddfod, Johannesburg, 1940s. Hobbies: Tapestry Making; Reading; Amatuer Dramatics. Address: Technical College, Pvte. Bag X22, Kroonstad 19500, S Africa.

DVORACEK, Jiri, b. 8 June 1928, Vamberk, Czechoslavakia. Composer. Educ: State Music Conserv., Prague; Acad. of Arts, & Music, Prague. m. Jarmila Sirova, 1 s. Career: Acad. of Arts & Music, 1953-; Prof.'s Asst., 1960; Lectr., 1967. Num. compositions incl: Symphonic Suite for Large Orchestra, 1958; Concertante Suite for Large Orchestra, 1962; Ex Post, for piano & orch., 1963; Num. settings of poems, by Ho Chi Min, Frantisek Halas, Josef Hora, Langston Hughes, others; Quattro Episodi (sinfonietta), 1971; Dialogues, for flute & piano, 1973; Quintet for Brass. Mbrshihp: Guild of Czech Composers & Concert Artists. Hons: Vit Nejedly Prize, for choir cycle Mobilizace, 1967. Address: Krc, Antala Staska 1015/43 00 Prague, Czechoslovakia.

DVORAK, DeLyle Dennis, b. 13 Nov. 1941, Olivet, SD, USA. College Music Professor. Educ: BS, Univ. of SD, Springfield, 1962; MMus, Univ. of SD, Vermillion, 1965; Doct. study at UCLA, 1968, Mont. State Univ., 1971; EdD, Ariz. State Univ., 1973; Post Grad. Study, Fredonia State Univ., NY. m. Judith B. Dvorak nee Wenzel. Career: Band & Vocal Instr., Armour Public Schls., SD, 1962-64; Dept. Chmn. & Band Instructor, Chamberlain Public Schls., SD, 1964-66; Asst. Dir. of Bands & Brass/Perc., Minot State Coll., ND, 1966-67; Coord. of Music & Dir. of Bands, Palo Verde Unified Schl. Dist., Blythe, Calif., 1967-69; Teaching Assoc. in Music & Educ., Ariz. State Univ., Tempe, 1969-72; Dir. of Bands & Acting Chmn. of Fine Arts, William Penn Coll., Oskaloosa, Iowa, 1972-75; Asst. Dir. of Bands & Music Ed., Southwestern State Univ., 1975-. Publs: The Use of Filmstrip-Sound Materials in Instrument Repaid Instruction,1973: A Comparison & Evaluation of Marching Bands in Selected S. Dakota High Schools. Contbr. to: Ariz. Audiovisual Jrnl.; The Instrumentalist. Mbr. num. profl. orgs. inclng. Nat. Band Assoc., former Ariz. State Chmn.; Life mbr., MENC. Recip. num. hons. Hobbies: Photography; Record Listening; Reading; Travel; Golf; Bowling; Hunting. Address: 1222 Kaiser Rd., Weatherford, OK 74396, USA.

DWORKIND, Betty, b. 29 Jan. 1928, Copenhagen, Denmark. Pianist. Educ: Accademia di Santa Cecilia Corso Superiore (w. Carlo Zecchi), Rome, Italy; w. prof. dr. Edwin Fischer, Lucerne, Switzerland. m. Dr. jur. Ole Markussen. Debut: Copehangen, 1948. Career: Recitals all over Denmark, & in Sweden, Rome, London, Edinburgh, & Slazburg. Broadcasts for Radios Basel, Hamburg, Rome & Vienna; Broadcasts perfs. as Soloist w. Danish Radio Symph. Orch. & w. TV Prof., Copenhagen Tchrs. Coll. Mbrships: Danish Soloist Assn. of 1921; Danish MA Soc. Hons: Italian State Scholarship, 1953; Harriet Cohen Int. Piano Medal, 1960; var. Danish state awards. Mgmt: Wilhelm Hansen. Address: Somosevej 19, 2740 Skovlunde Copenhagen, Denmark.

DYER, Michael George, b. 2 May 1930, Sydney, Australia. Lecturer; Pianist; Organist; Conductor. Educ: Sydney Tchrs. Coll.; BA, MA cad., Sydney Univ.; Dip., State Conservatorium;

ARCO: ARCM: LRAM: student, RSCM, UK, 1959-60 m. Ruth Marjorie McGregor, 2 s. Career incls: broadcasts, choral & organ, BBC, 1960 & Aust. Broadcasting Commission 1956-75; Organ Tchr. & Examiner, State Conservatorium, 1965-;Dir. of Music Fndn., St. Philips Ch., Sydney, 1965-; Cond., Ten Centuries Consort, Sydney, 1967; Cond. in Sydney Town Hall Sydney Opera House, etc.; St. Lectr. in Music, Nepean Coll. of Adv. Educ., 1971-75. Contbr. to profl. jrnls. & newspapers. Mbr. profl. orgs. Hobbies: Collecting Aust. paintings & antique furniture; Ch. arch.; watching horse racing. Address: 24 Almora St., Balmoral Beach, NSW, Australia 1088.

DYKES BOWER, (Sir) John, b. 13 Aug. 1905, Glouycester, UK. Organist (retired). Educ: Cheltenham Coll.;. MA, MusB, Corpus Christi Coll., Cambridge; John Stewart of Rannoch Scholar in Sacred Music, 1922-28; Hon DMus (Oxon); Hon. RAM; FRCM; FRCO; FRSCM; FTCL. Career: Organist & Master of the Choir, Truro Cathedral, 1926-33; Organist, Durham Cathedral, 1933-36; Organist, St. Paul's Cathedral, 1936-67; Pres., RCO; Master of the Worshipful Co. of Musicians, 1967-68; ISM; Currently Hon. Sec., RCO. Hons: CVO, 1953; Kt., 1968. Address: 4 Z Artillery Mansions, London SW1H OHZ, UK. 1, 3.

DYSON, (Barbara) Ruth, b. 28 Mar. 1917, London, UK. Professor of Harpischord & Piano; Lectr. on History of Early Keyboard Instruments. Educ: ARCM. m. Edward Eastaway Thomas. Debut: Wigmore Hall, 1941. Career: Recitals & broadcasts in Amsterdam, Oslo, Stockholm, Copenhagen, Helsinki, Hamburg, etc.; Lecture tours for Brit. Coun.; Soloist w. Royal Phil., London Phil., BBC Welsh, London Studio Strings, London Mozart Players; Many world premieres on radio; Prof., RCM. London. Mbrships: ISM; Royal Musical Assn.; Galpin Soc. Contbr. to profl. jrnls. Hobbies incl: Reading. Address: The Shippen, Pilgrims' Way. Westhumble, Dorking, Surrey, RH5 6AW, UK. 27.

DZERZHINSKY, Ivan Ivanovich, b. 9 Apr. 1909, Tambov, Russia. Composer. Educ: Gnesin Inst., Moscow; Leningrad Conserv.; Study of piano w. Prof. B L Yavorsky; Study of composition w. Profs. M G Gnesin, P B Ryazanov, & B Asafyech. Compositions incl: Operas - Quiet Don, 1935; Virgin Soil Upturned, 1937; Days of Volochaevsk, 1939; Thunderstorm, 1940; Blood of the People, 1941; Nadezhda, Svetlova, 1942; Prince Lake, 1947; The Snow Storm, 1946; Far from Moscow, 1954; Symphonic poem, Ermah; 3 Piano Concertos; Piano cycles - Spring Suite & Russian Painters; Song cycles - First Love, 1943; The Flying Bird, 1945; Earth, 1949; To a Woman Friend, 1950; The New Village, 1950; The Northern Bojan, 1955; Leningrad, 1957; Operas - Destiny of a Man, 1961; The Whirlwind, 1965; Grigory Melexov, 1966. Mbrships: Bd., Union of Soviet Composers, 1936-48. Hons: State Prize, 1950; Order of Lenin, 1939. Address: Union Soviet Composers, RSFSR, 8/S10 Ul. Nezhdanovoy, Moscow, USSR.

DZIEWULSKA, Maria Amelia, b. 1 June 1909, Warsaw, Poland. Musician; Lecturer in Theory of Music; Composer. Educ: MA, Warsaw State Conserv., 1933. Career incls: Lectr., State Acad. of Music, Cracow, 1945-66; Dean, Dept. of Comp., Conducting & Theory of Music, ibid., 1950-66; Prof., State Acad. of Music, Warsaw, 1966-76; Prof. Emeritus, ibid., 1976-. Comps. (publs.) incl: Songs & Instrumental Music for Children, 5 vols.; Polish Folk Songs (for mixed choir); Instrumental music. Recordings: var. works performed by 'Con Moto ma Cantabile' ensemble. Publs. incl: Methods of Ear Training, 1948. Mbr. var. profl. orgs. Hons. incl: Polonia Restituta Cross, 1964; Min. of Culture & Arts Awards, 1965, 1971. Address: Korotynskiego 20 m 35, 02-123 Warsaw, Poland.

DZIKOWSKA-KAMASA, Barbara, b. 23 Feb. 1935, Warsaw, Poland. Singer (Mezzo-soprano). Educ: Master's Degree; Dip., Music Acad., Warsaw Phil. Hall, 1966. Career incl: Soloist, UK (London, Oxford), France (Paris), Italy & Germany; Fests. in France (Scaux), Poland; Warsaw TV & radio. Mbr., Polish Music Assn. Hons: 3rd Prize, Warsaw Mozart Competition, 1959. Hobbies: Gardening; Medicine; Psychology; Yoga. Mgmt: Pagart, Polish Artistic Agency, Warsaw. Address: Obróncόw 21, 03-933 Warsaw, Poland.

E

EACOTT, Kenneth Clifford, b. 23 July 1923, Esher, UK. Former Music Director; Composer. Educ: 8 yrs. study of piano & orchestration. div., 2d., 1s. Career: formerly musical dir. to Allan Jones & Harry Secombe, also num. touring revues, variety shows etc., for 7 yrs. after the war; semi-pro dance band pianist until 1974. Comps: Dance of the Asteroids; March of the Men of Mars; Andromeda Overture, etc.; num. orchl. comps. for revues, pantomimes etc.; some piano comps. Mbrships: hon. asst. cond., Portsmouth Light Orch. Hobbies: Music & Yachting. Address: Winton House 37 Beach Rd., Hayling Island, Hants., UK.

EADIE, Barbara Jean, b. 16 Aug. 1947, Cambridge, Mass., USA. Teacher & Performer (Flute, Piccolo). Educ:BMus, Hope Coll., 1970; MMus, Eastman Schl. Music, 1974. m. Thomas Gordon Eadie. Career: Flute Tchr., Brockport State Coll. Univ., 1971-74, Eastman Schl. Music, 1973-75, Camosun Coll. Vic., BC, 1976-78, Vic. Conserv. of Music, 1975-; Recitalist, Vic. BC, Rochester NY; Toured E BC as flute soloist w. Kootenay Chmbr. Orch., 1978; TV app. Mbrships: Local 247, Am. Fedn. Musicians; Sec., Vic. Branch, BC Registered Music Tchrs., 1977-79. Hons: BC Provincial Winner, Nat. Competitive Fest. of Music, 1977; Recip., Intermunicipal Medallion, City of Gtr. Vic., 1977. Hobbies: Swimming; Philately. Address: 495 Victoria Ave., BC V8S 4M8, Can. 4, 27, 29.

EADY, Rosemary, b. 26 July 1934, Northamptonshire, UK. Pianist; Professional Accompanist. Educ: LRAM in pianoforte perf. & tchng. m. John P T Eady (dec.), 1 s., 2 d. Career: Pianist, Midland Flute Trip; 2 pianos w. Helen Cleaver; Vinton/Eady Flute/Piano Duo; Dalby/Eady Cello/Piano Duo; concert work w. var. singers of lieder, chansons & songs of Benjamin Britten; Accomp., Pitsford Manor Concerts Trust, 1975-76. Contbr. to: Northampton Chronicle & Echo; Northamptonshire Past & Present. Mbrships: ISM; Coun., Northamptonshire Record Soc.; Country Landowners Assn. Coun., Royal Agri. Soc. of England. Hobbies: Local History; Bibliography; Fine Arts; Book Collecting; The Land. Address: Pytchley Lodge, Kettering, Northamptonshire, UK.

EAGLE, David W, b. 13 Aug. 1929, Crookston, Minn., USA. Musicologist; Flautist. Educ: BS, BA, Univ. of Minn.; PhD, ibid. m. Elaine Berge Eagle. Career: Recitals & lectures on Brit. & Am. flute music of early 19th century; flute instructor, Univ. of Minn.; record annotator for Quintessence & Vox records. Mbrships: Am. Musicol. Soc.; Coll. Music. Soc.; Soc. for Ethnomusicol.; Nat. Flute Assn. Address: 2904 W River Pkway., Mnpls., MN 55406, USA.

EAGLES, Moneta M, b. Concord, NSW, Australia. Composer. Educ: studied piano, organ, singing, comp., Sydney Conserv. of Music, 1943-50; L Mus, piano, RSM & Aust., 1955; DSCM (perfs. & tchrs.), piano, 1947; pvte. study of comp. w. Matyas Seiber, London, 1951. Debut: Piano Soloist w. Sydney Symph. Orch., 1949. Career: Piano Recitalist, Aust. Broadcasting Commission, 1946-61; Tchng. Staff, var. schls., 1946-57; Soloist w. Sydney Symph. Orch. for own comp. Diversions for piano & orch., 1954; Dir. of Music, Aust. C'wlth. Film Unit, 1957-64; Aust. Deleg., Edinburgh Fest., 1960. Comps. incl: scores for 21 documentary films; num. short orchl. & instrumental works; choral settings; etc. Mbrships. incl: Fellowship of Aust. Comps; APRA. Recip. num. hos. & awards for comps. Address: 9 Elms Rd., Mooroolbark, Vic. 3138, Aust.

EAKEN, John Reese, b. 13 Sept. 1949, Chambersburg, Pa., USA. Violinist; Professor in Strings. Educ: studied violin, Settlement Music Schl. & New Schl. of Music, Phila., 1960-69; BSM (applied music), Messiah Coll., 1972; M Mus (violin), Temple Univ., 1974. m. Dorcas Crone Eaken. Debut: as soloist, 1971. Career: Prof., Messiah Coll., Grantham, Pa.; Mbr., Harrisburg Symph. Orch.; Soloist w. Harrisburg Symph., three times, w. Potomac Symph., Hagerstown, Md., 1971, w. Ll Youth Symph., 1972; recitals, Messiah Coll., Temple Univ., Nat. Gall. of Art, Wash. DC, 1972. Hons: Eugene Ormandy Schlrship., 1968; Phila. Fndn. Schrlrship., 1969. Hobbies incl: Carpentry; Hunting; Fishing. Address: 612 Range End Rd., Dillsburg, PA 17019, USA.

EARL, David Thomas Nelson, b. 5 Oct. 1951, Stellenbosch, S Africa. Concert Pianist; Composer; Portrait Painter. Educ: Univ. S Africa Perfs. & Tchrs. Lic. Dips.; FTCL; LRSM. Debut:

Wigmore Hall, 1974. Career: Cape Town Symph. Orch.; Broadcasts on SABC & BBC; Many perfs. in GB, Italy, Austria & Spain. Comps: Piano Concerto; Mosaics (piano suite); var. chmbr. works. Mbr., Comps. Guild of GB. Hons. incl: Trinity Coll. Fndr's Schlrship., 1973; Gtr. London Coun's "Young Musician 75". Hobbies: Painting; Drawing; Writing; Tennis. Mgmt: Ibbs & Tillet. Address: 39 Tite St., London SW3 4JA, UK.

EARL, Donn L(ee), b. 19 Aug. 1917, Las Vegas, Nev., USA. Teacher; Conductor; Stage Director. Educ: BA, Brigham Young Univ., Provo, Utah; MA, ibid.; PhD, Ind. Univ. m. Ruth Lillian Moss, 4 s. Career: Choral Dir., Bern, Switzerland, 1937-39; Violinist, Grand Rapids Symph., USA, 1940; Instructor, Asst. Prof., Assoc. Prof., Prof. Music, Brigham Young Univ., 1946-; Artistic & Musical Dir., Utah Valley Opera Assn., 1959-63; Assoc. Cond., Utah Valley Symph., 1969-73; Guest cond., 1976. Publ: An Introduction to the Aural Skills of Musicians, 1975. Mbrships. incl: Pres., Local 272 Provo Federated Musicians, Am. Fedns. Musicians, 1967-. Hon: Ford Fndn. Schlrship., Cond., NYC Ctr. Opera Co., 1959. Hobbies incl: Geneal. Address: 2701 N 700 E, Provo, UT 84601M USA, é.

EARLS, Paul, b. 9 June 1934, Springfield, Mo., USA. Composer; Media Artist. Educ: B Mus, M Mus, PhD, Eastman Schl. of Music, Univ. of Rochester. m. Zeren Earls, 1 s. Career incl: Assoc. Prof. of Music, Duke Univ., 1965-72; Fellow, Ctr. for Adv. Visual Studies, 1970-, & Visiting Assoc. Prof., Lectr. in Humanities, 1972-74, both MIT; Lectr., Media & Performing Arts, Mass. Coll. of Art, 1972-; active as visual artist & comp.; media artist. Recent events incl: Sounding Space, Hayden Gall., Cambridge, Mass., 1972, & Vancouver Art Gall., BC, Can., 1973; Interactive Music & Light, Portland, Ore., 1975; Death of King Phillip (opera), Boston, 1976. Comps. incl: And On the 7th Day; Hugenot Variations; Brevis Mass; Dreamstage, 1977; Inside, 1976-77; Contbr. to profl. publs. Mbr., Broadcast Music Inc. Recip. var. awards. Hobby: Electronics. Address: 40 Massachusetts Ave., Cambridge, MA 02139, USA.

EAST, Angela, b. 15 Nov. 1949, New Maiden, UK. Cellist. Educ: RAM; LRAM, 1968. m. Roger A C Durston. Debut: Wigmore Hall, London, 1972. Career: solo perfs., Purcell Rm., Wigmore Hall, Edinburgh Fest. 'Fringe'; TV app., 1969; Mbr., Troika Trio, Cantus in Camera; formerly Vis. Tchr., Eton Coll.; Cellist w. London Mozart Players, London Bach Orch., New London Ensemble; Fndr., Mbr. & Mgr., London Baroque Soloists. Mbrships: ISM; Musicians Union. Hons. incl: Herbert Walenn Prizes, 1968; Suggia Award (RAM), Moir Carnegie Prize, J B MacEwen Prize, Sir Edward Cooper Prize, 1970. Hobbies: Chess; Cooking. Mgmt: London Baroque Soloists: Ibbs & Tillett, Peter Freeman, Music & Musicians Artist Mgmt. Address: 2 High St., Sonning-on-Thames, Reading, Berks., UK.

EAST, Leslie, b. 8 July 1949, Doncaster, Yorks., UK. Pianist; Conductor; Director of Music. Educ: BMus, MMus, King's Coll., Univ. of London, 1967-72. m. Lilija Zobens. Career: Vis. lectr. in music & music organizer, City Univ., London, 1973-75; Dir. of Music, GSM, 1975-. Publs: Thea Musgrave & Gordon Crosse, in Brit. Music Now, 1975. Contbr. to: Music & Musicians: Musical Times; Financial Times; Soundings. Mbrships: Royal Musical Assn.; Coun. & Exec. Committee, SPNM (chmn., 1979). Hons: FGSM, 1975. Hobbies: Sport; Food & Drink; Architecture. Address: GSM, Barbican, London EC2, UK.

EASTON, Robert, b. 8 June 1898, Sunderland, UK. Bass Singer. Educ: studied w. Bozzelli, Dinh Gilly, Plunket Greene. m. Madeline Ruby, 1 d. Career: almost every musical test, in England; BBC from 1924; Promenade Concert from 1926; Opera Covent Garden, 1934-39; Fest. Adjudications, 1937-. Sev. Recordings. Mbrships: ISM; Brit. Fedn. of Music Fests. Hobbies: Home; Golf; Billiards; Gardening. Address: Scotland Cottage, Scotland Ln., Haslemere, Surrey, UK.3.

EASTWOOD, Thomas Hugh, b. 12 Mar. 1922, Hawley, UK. Composer. Educ: Trinity Coll., Cambridge; studied w. Necil Kâzimakses, Ankara, Boris Blacher, Berlin, & Erwin Stein, London. m. Cristina Carneiro de Mendonça, 1 s. Comps: Christopher Sly (opera); The Rebel (opera for TV); sev. song cycles (Ronde des Saisons, Cantata Mariana, Solitudes); orch. works (Music to Celebrate, Hymn to Pan); guitar music (Ballade-Phantasy, Amphora, Sonate). Contbr. to: Music & Musicians; Musical Opinion. Mbrships. incl: Royal Phil. Soc.; Exec. Comm., Treas., Soc. for Promotion of New Music; Exec. Comm., Composers' Guild of GB. Recip. 1st Prize comp. Cheltenham Competitive Music Rest., 1949. Hobbies: Mod. langs.; travelling; astronomy. Address: Heath Close, Wootton Rivers, Marlborough, Wilts. WN8 4NQ, UK.3,4,28.

EATHORNE, Wendy, b. 25 Sept. 1939, Four Lanes, Cornwall, UK. Soprano Soloist. Educ: RAM, 1959-65; ARAM;

LRAM; ARCM. m. Geoffrey Pratley, 1 d. Career: num. concerts, opera perfs. (Glyndebourne, Engl. Nat., Welsh Nat. & Covent Gdn. Opera Cos.); num. radio & TV broadcasts. Var. Recordings. Mbr., ISM. Hobbies: Cooking; Dressmaking. Mgmt: Ibbs & Tillett. Address: 23 King Edwards Rd., Ruislip, Mdddx. HA4 7AQ, UK.

EATON, Darryl, b. 3 June 1940, Woodstock, Ont., Can. Composer; Trumpeter. Educ: BMus (comp.) Berklee Coll. of Music, Boston, Mass. m. Bernice Susan Soren, 1d. Career: trumpet soloist, RCAF, 1958-63; w. Stan Kenton & Buddy Rich, 1968-69; w. Phil Nimmons, Nimmons 'N' Nine Plus Six, 1974-. Comps: Dialogue for strs., 1974; Brass Quintet No. 1, 1976; Reflections for chmbr. orch., 1978. Recordings: w. Stan Kenton, Buddy Rich & Phil Nimmons; above comps. recorded for CBC by Vancouver Chmbr. Orch. & Can. Brass. mbr. Can. League of Comps. Address: Unit 125/2315 Bromsgrove Rd., Mississauga, Ont. L5J 4A6, Can.

EATON, David Hugh James, b. 25 July 1947, Southampton, UK. Flautist; Orchestral Musican. Educ: RCM; ARCM, 1969; Hochschule für Musik, Hamburg. m. Carol Overton, 1s. Career: Flautist, Bournemouth Sinfonietta, 1971-; Southern TV Music in Camera Series. Recordings: 26 as mbr. of Bournemouth Sinfonietta. Hobbies: Dinghy Sailing; Gardening; DIY. Address: 79 Hankinson Rd., Winton, Bournemouth, Dorset BH9 1HP, UK.

EATON, John C, b. 30 Mar. 1935, Bryn Mawr, Pa., USA. Composer; Electronic Music Performer; Pianist; Teacher. Educ: AB, MFA, Princeton Univ. m. Nelda Nelson Eaton, 1d. Career incls: Myshkin (opera), Pub. Broadcasting Corp., 1972, 74; The Lion & Androcles (opera), Cinn. Symph., 1974, Pub. Broadcasting Corp. TV, 1974; Prof. of Music, Ind. Univ., 1970-76. Comps. incl: (publs.) Song Cycle on Holy Sonnets of John Donne; Herakles; (recordings) Songs for RPB; Microtonal Fantasy; Electro-Vibrations; Concert Piece for Synket & Symph. Orch; Opera, Danton & Robespierre. Author, New Music Since 1950, 1976. Contbr. to Music Educators' Jrnl; Musical Courier. Mbr. var. profl. orgs. Recip. num. hons. Hobby: Cooking. Mgmt: Sheldon Soffer. Address: Schl. of Music., Indiana Univ., Bloomington, Ind., USA.2,L4.

EBADI, Ahmed, b. 4 Apr. 1904, Teheran, Iran. Sitarist. Educ: Studied w. Mirza Abdullah. m. Masume Ebadi. Debut: 1st Public App. in Iran. Career: Appts. in France, UK, Germany, Austria, Italy, Dubai, Iraq & India; Apps. w. Persian Opera & on Radio & TV. Recordings incl: Mahur, Sega & many ancient Iranian preludes; First person to write down this classical music. Contbr. to Keyhan, Etalat, Tamsha, Zan-e-Ruz, Etalat-e-haftazi, Javanan, Banuvan, Sefid-e-Siaha, etc. Hons: Two Medals presented by His Imperial Majesty of Iran: Homayun, 1966; Taj-in, 1974. Hobby: Collecting Old Musical Instruments. Address: Bldg. 4/21 Khiabane Kenndy, Yazde Gard 3 Avn., Teheran, Iran.

EBBAGE, David, b. 24 May, 1942, Bingley, Yorks., UK. Lec turer; Conductor; Pianist. Educ: B Mus, Dunelm; GTCL; LTCL (Mus Ed); LTCL (harpsichord). m. Avril Dean, 1 s., 2 d. Career incl: recitals as Pianist & Accomp., UK & abroad; profl. staff, TCM, 1965-; Lectr., Univ. of Salford, 1965-69; made 3 progs. (Music Making) for BBC, Leeds; Lectr., Scarborough Tech. Coll., 1972-75; Cond., Manchester Beethoven Soc., Bolton Chmbr. Orch., N Manchester Symph. Orch., Scarborough Symph. Orch. Comps: Essay for Orch.; Str. Quarter; Sonato for 4 Trombones; film music, In a strange place. Contbr. to : Southern Arts Mag. Mbrships: Composers Guild of GB; ISM; Royal Music Assn. Recip. Alec Rowley Mem. Prize, 1964. Hobbies: Swimming; Tennis. Address: 80 Filey Rd., Scarborough, Yorks., UK.3.

EBEN, Petr, b. 22 Jan. 1929, Zamberk, Czech. Composer; Pianist; Lecturer. Educ: Acad. of Music, Prague. m. Sárka Hurniková-Ebenová, 3 children. Debut: as Pianist, Prague, 1952; as Comp. Concert for organ & orch., Prague, 1954. Career: Music Dir., TV, Prague, 1954; Lectr., Inst. for Musicol., Charles' Univ., Prague, 1955-. Comps. incl: Sunday Music for organ; Concerto for piano & orch.; Apologia Sokratus (oratorio); Vox Clamatis for orch.; Maidens & Swallows for female choir; Unkind Songs; Vesperae for choir & organ; Pragensia (cantata); Greek Dictionary, cycle for female choir & harp; Nachtstunden, (Night Hours) symph. for wind quintet & chmbr. orch. Publs: Cteni a hra partitur (co-author). Contbr. to jrnls. Mbrships: Union of Composers, Prague; Chmn., Creative Sect., Czech. Music Soc. Hons: 1st Prize & Gold Medal for "6 Love Songs", Moscow, 1957; 2st Prize, for "The Loveers Magic Spell" (cantata), Jhilava VocaL Fest., 1959; 2st Prize, for "Ten Children's Duets", Jirkov, 1966; 2 prizes for "Laudes", 1965. Mgmt: Pragokoncert, Prague 1. Address: El. Peskove 11, 150 00 Prague 5, Czech.

EBENHÖH, Horst, b. 16 May 1930, Vienna, Austria. Professor. Educ: MA; Univ. of Vienna, Acad. of Music; Staatsprufung for piano. m. Edda Ebenhoh, 1 d., 1 s. Career: Former chmbr. music pianist; Dir., chmbr. orchs. Comps. incl: (Publs.): Klavierstücke op. 10; Minutenstucke fur Klavier, op. 283; Concerto for double percussion & orch; Einige Minuten fur Klaviertrio op. 321; Epigramme fur Chor nach Sinngedichten von G E Lessing, op. 232; Symphonie op. 34; Sultan zu verkaufen (scenic work). Mbr., Mng. Committee, Osterriechischer Kompanistenbund. Contbr. to musical jrnls. & mags. Hons. incl: Premio citta di Trieste, 1975. Hobby: Mountaineering. Address: Radeckgasse 2, A 1040 Wien, Austria.

EBERLY, John Wilgus, b. 26 May 1913, David City, Neb., USA. College Administrator; Pianist. Educ: BA., PhD., Ed. Psych., Univ. of Neb.; MA, Music Educ., NY Univ.; Study of piano w. Paul Reuter, Edwin Hughes, Maurice Dumesnil. m. Margaret Baker, 2 s. Career: Recitalist, w. wife, 2-piano & piano duets; Dean, Conserv. of Music, Flora Macdonald Coll., 1938-44; Chmn., Dept. of Music, Limestone Coll., 1944-49; Chmn., Dept. of Music, Tex. Woman's Univ., 1952-69; Dean, Coll. of Fine Arts, ibid., 1969-. Mbrships: Bd. of Dirs., MTNA; Past Pres., Tex. Music Tchrs. Assn.; Past Pres., Tex. Assn. of Music Schls. Hons: Pi Kappa Lambda. Hobbies: Reading; Travel. Address: 1918 Archer Trail, Denton, TX 76201, USA.7.

EBERT, Carl (Anton Charles), b. 20 Feb. 1887, Berlin, Germany (Citizen of USA). Actor; Opera Director. Educ: Max Reinhardt Schl. of Dramatic Art, Berlin. m. (1) Lucie Splisgarth, 1912 (div. 1923), 1 s., 1 d. (dec. 1946); (2) Gertrude Eck, 1924, 1 s., 2 d. Career incl: Actor, Max Reinhardt's Deutches Theater, Berlin, 1909-14Z: Schauspielhaus, FrankfurtMain, 1915-22; Staatstheater, Berlin, 1922-27; Tchr., Dir. & Prof., Schls. of Dramatic Art, Frankfurt & Berlin; Gen. Dir. & Prod., Hess Landestheater, 1927-31; Stadtsche Oper, Berlin, 1931-33; Actor & Prod., Switzerland & Austria, 1932-38; Artistic Dir. & Prod., Glyndebourne Opera, UK., 1934-59; Prof. & Hd., Opera Dept., Univ. of Southern Calif., USA., 1948-54; Artistic Dir. & Prod., Guild Opera Co., LA., 1950-; Gen. Dir. & Prod., Stadtische Oper, Berlin, 1954-61; Opera Dir. & Prod., Europe, UK & USA. Recip: num. hons. & decorations incl: CBE, 1960; Mus D Edinburgh Univ., 1954. Address: 809 Enchanted Way, Pacific Palisades, LA, CA, USA.

EBSWORTH, Phyllis, b. Krugers Dorp, S. Africa. Violist; Teacher; Lecturer. Educ: Editha Knocker Schl. of Violin Playing, London. Debut: Wigmore Hall. Career: Co-fndr., violist, Ebsworth Quartet; Concerts, UK & abroad; Violin, Viola Tchr; Chmbr. Music Coach; Dir., Hampstead String & Ensemble grp. Mbrships: Solo Viola Players Sect., ISM; European String Tchrs. Assn.; Viola rsch. Soc. Hobbies: Skitching & painting; Antique porcelain & pottery. Address: 14 Ornan Road, London NW3 4PX, UK.3,27.

EBY, Margarette Fink, b. 8 Feb. 1931, Detroit, Mich., USA. University Professor & Administrator. Educ: BA, 1955, MA, 1962, Wayne State Univ.; PhD, Univ. of Mich., 1971. m. Stewart Leon Eby, 2 s., 2 d. Career incls: Instr., Music Hist. & Theory, 1960-68. Detroit Bible Coll.; Music Tchr., Barton Jr. HS, Royal Oak, Mich., 1968-69; Assoc. Prof., Oakland Co. Community Coll., Farmington, Mich., 1970; Asst. Prof., Wayne State Univ., Detroit, 1971-72, Univ. of Mich.-Dearborn, 1972-75; Assoc. Prof. of Music Hist., 1975-, Chmn., Dept. of Humanities, 1975-, ibid. Contbr. to: Diapason. Mbrships. incl: Am. Musicol. Soc., AAUP; Vice-Chmn., Artistic Dir., Fair Lane Music Guild, 1972-. Recip., acad. awards. Hobbies: Travel; Gardening; Theatre; Chamber Music. Address: Univ. of Mich.-Dearborn, 4901 Evergreen Rd., Dearborn, MI 48128, USA. 11, 27.

ECKHARDT, Andreas, b. 6 Dec. 1943, Marienberg/Erzgebirge, Germany. Director of Production. Educ: State examinations for Arts & Higher Educ. (Music & History); Grad. (musicol.). m. Edda Lusse, 1s. Career: Director of Production, music publr. B. Schott's Söhne, Mainz. Publs: Männerchor; Organisation und Chorliteratur nach 1945, 1977. Contbr. to Musik und Bildung. Mbrships: Sec-Gen., Verbandes Deutscher Schulmusikerzieher. Address: Musikverlag B.Schott's Söhne, Weihergarten 5, 6500 Mainz, German Fed. Repub.

ECKLEBE, Alexander, b. 12 Jan. 1904, Cosel o/s, Germany. Composer. Educ: Univ. of Breslau; Konservatorium Breslau; Hochschule für Musick, Berlin. Career: Radio Berlin, 1930-50. Compositons: (operas) Genoveva; The Book of Love; The False Prince; Symph.; Overtures; Suites; Dances for orch.; 3 str. quartets; 3 string trios; Concertos & sonatas for piano, cello & trombone; Music for piano; Variations; Dances; Studies; Partita

& Fantasia for organ; Many cantatas & songs. Mbrships: Deutscher Komponistenverband; Künstlergilde; Eichendorff-Gesellschaft. Hons: Ehrengabe zum Johann-Wenzel-Stamitz Preis, 1967; Uberschlesischer Kulturpreis, 1978. Address: Mommsenstrasse 35, 1000 Berlin 12, German Fed. Repub.

ECKSTEIN, Pavel, b. 27 Apr. 1911, Opava, Czechoslovakia. Music Writer; Critic; Commentator; Organizer. Educ: PhD., Prague Univ. m. Anna Gerberova, 1 d. Career: Music Critic; Lectr., Germany, Holland, GB, USSR, Australia, USA; Gen. Sec., Int. Musical Fest. Prague Spring, 1948-52; Sec., Czech Composers Guild, 1952-71; Artistic Advsr., Nat. Theatre, Prague, 1969-. Publs: Daivd Oistrakh, 1958; Czecholovak Contemporary Opera, 1967. Contbr. to encys. & jrnls. in Czechoslovakia, GB, USA, Canada, Germany, Denmark, USSR. Hobbies: Reading; Theatre; Wandering. Address: Srobarova 23, 130 00 Prague 3, Czechoslovakia.

EDANDER, Gunnar, b. 3 Feb. 1942, Stockholm, Sweden. Composer. Career incls: currently comp., Young Klara, producing plays for adults & children; Tours, Norway, The Netherlands, Belgium, German Fed. Repub., Poland & Ven ezuela. Comps. incl: Music for 18 plays, Pocket-Theatre, Stockholm, 1968-71; Music to 22 plays, Young Klara group, City Theatre of Stockholm, 1971-; TV & Radio music. Recordings: 8 LP's incl. Love Performance, Gee Girls - Freedom is Near & Factory Girls. Publs: 6 Song Books. Hons: Prize, STIM, 1979. Address: Duvnäsgatan 12 8 tr, S 116 31 Stockholm, Sweden.

EDA-PIERRE, Christiane, b. Fort de France, Martinique. Lyric Artist. Educ: Dip., Conserv. Nat. Supèrieur de Musique, Paris (1st prize for singing, opera & opera-comique). m. Pierre Lacaze, 1s. Debut: Nice. Career: apps. in opera at NY, Chgo., San Francisco, Miami, Lisbon, Barcelona, Florence, Milan, Hamburg, Budapest, London & Wexford; num. TV & radio broadcasts in France & other countries. Recordings: in Barber of Seville (Rossini), Benvenuto Cellini & Beatrice & Benedict (Berlioz); oratorios; recital of 18th century airs. Hobby: Flowers. Address: 87 Blvd. St-Michel, 75005 Paris, France.

EDDLEMAN, G(eorge) David, b. 20 Aug. 1936, Winston-Salem, NC, USA. Educ: BSc, Appalachian State Univ., 1958; M Mus, Va. Commonwealth Univ., 1963; D Mus Arts, Boston Univ., 1971. m. Mirian Yanes. Career: Choral Dir., Savannah (Ga.) Public Schls., 1959-60; Morristown (NJ) Public Schls., 1963-67; Dir., Third Army Chorus, 1960-62; Teaching Assoc. in Theory, Boston Univ., 1968-72; Music Editor, Silver Burdett Co., Morristown, NY, 1972-. Comps. incl: Intimations; Reflections; The Innkeeper's Carol (choral); Alleluia; Sing, O Sing; String Quartets 1 & 2. Num. recordings. Publs: incl: Reading Rhythm (2 vols.); Playing the Recorder, 1974; New Music: Electronics, 1976. Contbr. to Pipeline. Mbr. num. profl. orgs. inclng: ASCAP. Hons: Boston Univ. Comp Awards, 1969, 70. Address: 12 James Ct., Rockaway, NY. 07866, USA.29

EDELMANN, Otto Karl, b. 5 Feb. 1917, Vienna, Austria. Operatic Singer. Educ: State Acad. of Music, Vienna. m. Ilse-Maria Straub, 2 s., 1 d. Career: opera apps., 1938; Vienna State Opera, 1948-; Salzburg Fest., 1948-; Permanent Mbr., Met. Opera, NYC, 1954-; participant in 1st Bayreuth Fest., 1951; noted interpreter of Sachs, Die Meistersinger. Hons. incl: Kt., Order of Dannebrog. Hobbies: Painting; Boxing. 16.

EDELMANN, Toni, b. 25 Oct. 1945, Hamina, Finland. Composer; Music Teacher. Educ: Final Exam. (Music Tchr.), Sibelius Acad., Helsinki. 1 s. Career: currently Music Tchr., Theatre Schl. of Finland. Comps: stage music for Faust, Gilgamest, Aniara (by Harry Martinsson), The Terrible Murder Lalli, The Fugitives (by Johannes Linnakoski); Five Love Songs (words by Marja-Leena Mikkola, recorded); many songs for mixed choir, soloists, etc. Mbrships: Org. for Writers & Culture Workers; Org. for Film & Light Music. Hons. incl: 1st Prize for stage music, Tampere Theatre Fest. Address: Kulmakatu 8 B25 00170, Helsinki 17, Finland.

EDEN, Conrad William, b. 4 May 1905, Lindford, UK. Organist. Educ: RCM; B Mus, St. John's Coll. Oxford; ARCO. m. Barbara Landemann, 1 s., 1 d. Career: Organist, St. Philip & St. James & Mbr., Music Staff, Dragon Schl., Oxford, 1926; Asst. Organist, 1927, Organist, 1933, Wells Cathedral; Organist, Durham Cathedral, 1936; War serv. w. Durham Light Infantry, 1939-45; Ret'd., 1974. Publs: The Organs of Durham Cathedral, 1970. Recordings: Schoenberg & Handel-Karg-Elert, EMI. Mbrships: Past Pres., Cathedral Organists' Assn.; ISM. Hons: Hon. FRCO, 1971: D Mus, 1973. Hobbies: Motoring; Antiques. Address: The Vale, Highmore Rd., Sherborne, Dorset DT9 4BT, UK.

EDER, Helmut, b. 26 Dec. 1916, Linz, Austria. Composer; Teacher. Educ: Bruckner Conserv., Linz; High Schl. for Music,

Munich (comp. w. Carl Orff, condng. w. Fritz Lehmann); High Schl. for Music, Stuttgart (comp. w. Joh.Nep. David). m. Erna Gresslehner, 1d, 1s. Career: Perfs. of own comps. at num. European fests. incl. Salzburg, Vienna, Prague, Zagreb, Carinthia; 3 TV operas; 2 TV ballets; many broadcast perfs.; Prof., comp., Mozarteum, Salzburg. Comps: 4 symphs.; 6 operas; 4 ballets; concertos for var. instruments & orch.; chmbr. music; (recorded) 3rd Symph.; Concerto a dodici; Wind Septet; Melodia-Ritmica; Sonatine for flute & piano; Wind quintet, Op. 2. Mbrships: Rotary; IGNM. Hons: Austrian State Prize, 1962; Anton Bruckner Prize, 1966; Merit Prize for music, Min. of Arts, 1972. Hobbies: Mountain climbing; Sailing. Address: Mörkweg 17, 5020 Salzburg, Austria

EDINGER, Christiane, b. 20 March 1945, Potsdam, Germany. Concert Violinist. Educ: Berlin Acad. of Music; Juilliard Schl. of Music, USA; studied w. Prof. Vittorio Brero, Nathan Milstein & Prof. Joseph Fuchs. Debut: Berlin Fest., 1962. Career: Guest soloist w. major European & Am. Orch. incl. Berlin, Leningrad, Munich Phil., BBC London, Vienna, Boston, Pitts. Symphs.; Recitals & concert tours throughout Europe, USA, S Am., India, Africa & USSR; Radio & Fest. apps. Recordings: All Bach sonatas & partitas for solo violin; solo pieces by Blacher, Linke, Maderna; Two Sonatas for Violin & Piano by G Fauré. Hons: Young Generation Arts Prize of Berlin, 1969; German Critics Prize, 1975. Hobbies incl: Painting; Chess; Cooking; Hiking. Mgmt: Thea Dispeker, NYC, USA; Konzertdirektion De Koos, Hamburg. Address: königin Luise str. 32, 1 Berlin 33, Fed. German Repub. 3, 16, 27.

EDLEFSEN, Blaine E., b. 24 Aug. 1930, Soda Springs, Idaho, USA. Professor of Music; Oboist; Composer, Editor & Arranger of Pedagogical Works for Oboe. Educ: BA, Brigham Young Univ., Provo, Uah, 1952; M Mus, Eastman Schl. of Music, Univ. of Rochester, NY, 1966; D Mus,ibid, 1966. m. Jean Harris, 3 s., 2 d. Career: Solo Engl. Horn & Asst. 1st Oboe, Utah Symph. Orch., Salt Lake City, 1953-59; Oboe Soloist, Paganini, Walden & other str. quartets; former Mbr., Eastman Wind Ensemble; Instructor in Music, Brigham Young Univ., 1953-61; currently Prof., Univ. of Ill., Urbana-Champaign, Solo Oboist in Ill. Woodwind Quintet & Springfield Symph. Orch. & Champaign-Urbana Symph. Orch., Recitalist & Clinician; composed & arr. 6 elementary oboe solos (Blaine Edlefsen Oboe Solo Series of The First Division Band Course), & collaborated on the Belwin Student Instrumental Course, Levels, 1, 11, & 111; made teaching film, Making the American Scrape Oboe Reed. Recordings: Oboe & Engl. Horn in Utah Symph. Orch. & Eastman Wind Ensemble. Mbrships: former Treas., Int. Double Reed Soc.; Phi Mu Alpha Sinfonia. Recip. of fellowships. Hobbies: Italic handwriting; Walking; Yoga. Address: Music Bldg., Univ. of Ill., Urbana, IL 61801, USA.

EDLUND, Mikael, b. 19 Jan. 1950, Tranas, Sweden. Composer. Educ: Musicol. at Univ. of Uppsala; comp. w. Ingvar Lidholm & Arne Mellnàs, Music High Schl. Stockholm. Career: works w. artists in dance, theatre, cinema, painting; prod. at Fylkingen, soc. for experimental music, giving concerts, recording etc. Comps: The Lost Jugglery, 1974-77; Leaves, 1977-79; Stardust, tape pieces for an intermedia work, 1976, etc. Mbrships: Froeningen Svenska Tonsättare; ISCM (Swedish sect.); Fylkingen Soc. Hon: represented Sweden w. The Lost Jugglery at ISCM Fest., 1978. Hobby: Cactaceous Plants. Address: Tomtebogatan 8, 1139 Stockholm, Sweden.

EDMONDS, Thomas James, b. 6 Apr. 1934, Peterborough, Aust. Singer (Lyric Tenor). Educ: BA, Adelaide Univ.; Dips. Secondary Educ. & Teaching; Vocal & Stage Trng., Elder Conserv., Adelaide, 6 yrs. m. Ruth I M Humphrey, 1s. Career: Prin. tenor roles w. Engl. Opera Grp., London, UK, State Opera, S Aust., Music Depts., Univs. of Sydney & Adelaide, etc.; Solo concert & guest apps. throughout Aust. & in UK in oratorio, serious & light music; Broadcasts, Aust. & UK; num. TV apps., Aust.; film roles. Recordings: 12 LP albums. Hons. incl: Adelaide Vocal Championship, 1967; Shell Aria Award, Canberra, 1969; about 40 1st Prizes for Eisteddfod perfs., Aust. Hobbies incl: Photography; Camping, Reading. Mgmt: (UK) Music & Musicians, Quinville House, Maulden, Bedford. Address: 6 Orvieto Rd., Seacliffe Pk., SA 5049, Aust.

EDMONDSON, John Baldwin, b. 3 Feb. 1933, Toledo, Ohio, USA. Composer; Arranger; Editor. Educ: BA, Univ. of Fla.; MMus in Comp., Univ. of Ky. m. Laura Backus Edmondson, 1 s., 1 d. Career: Tchr. Instrumental Music, pub. schls., Ky., 10 yrs.; Concurrently Freelance Comp. & Arr. for Schl. & Univ. Bands, recording, advertising & publ. firms; Educl. Ed., Hansen Publs., 1970-; var. appearances as guest cond. w. schl. bands. Compositions incl: (publd.) Pageantry Overture; Hymn & Postlude; Song for Winds; Fantasy on a Fanfare; num. comps. & arrs. in Fun-Way Band Book, The Fun-Way Bandsman, The Bacharach & David Fun-Way Concert Band Book; Fun-Way Band Method, 2 vols. (w. P. Yoder), 1973-74; over 100 band arrs. Mbr., ASCAP. Recip., ASCAP Popular Award, 1970-. Hobby: Tennis. Address: 20502 NW 2nd Ct., Miami, FL 33169, USA.

EDMUNDS, Christopher Montague, b. 26 Nov. 1899, Birmingham, Warwicks., UK. Composer. Educ: BMus, Birmingham Univ.; DMus, Manchester Univ. m. Ivy Kathleen Vaughan-Jones, 1 s., 1 d. Career: Lectr., Dir. of Opera, Birmingham Schl. of Music; Prin., ibid.; 1945-56; Mbr. Corp., Examiner, Trinity Coll. of Music. Comps. incl. Orchl., Operatic, Instrumental, Choral & Vocal Music. Publ: num. Hobbies: Gardening. Address: 247 Mereside Way N. Olton, Solihull, Warwicks., UK. 1, 3.

EDMUNDS, Janet Ward, b. 20 Nov. 1933, Banbury, Oxon., UK. Singer. Educ: RCM; ARCM (Piano & Singing); Nat. Schl. of Opera; Singing studies in Lucerne & Frankfurt; GRSM. m. David Byrt, 2 d. Debut: accomp. by Gerald Moore, Wigmore Hall, London, 1963. Career: apps. throughout UK & France, Germany & Switz. in recital, oratorio & opera; TV & radio broadcasts. Mbr., ISM. Hons. incl: Clara Butt Prize; Countess of Munster Award. Hobbies: Country Life; Languages. Mgmt: Ibbs & Tillett, London. Address: Lark Rise, Halse, Brackley, Northants., UK. 3.

EDWARDS, H. Neil, b. 12 Dec. 1931, Dalton, Ga., USA. Teacher; Conductor, Composer. Educ: BS Music Educ., M Mus Ed., Univ. of Ga.; postgrad. study in Value Theory, Fla. State Univ., 2 yrs.; Master Tchr. Cert. m. May Pittman Edwards, 2 s. Career: Dir. of Music, Pub. Schls., Lyons, Wayne Co., & Hawkinsville, Ga.; Chmn., Music Dept., Brewton Parker Coll., Mt. Vernon, Ga.; Acting Chmn., Music Dept. & Dir. of Instrumental Music & Music Educ., Ga. Southwestern Coll., Americus; TV apps., Ga. & Fla.; Guest Cond., Clinician & Music Cons. Comps. incl: Psalm 118 (SATB & Organ); It is Enough (SATB, Brass & Organ); Suite Religioso (Woodwind Ensemble); March Opus 2 (Band); Trombone-Piano Apogee; Fanfare & Chorale (Brass Ensemble). Recordings: On Campus; Sounds of the Southwestern Winds. Publs: Var. privately printed Monographs on Music Educ. Mbrships incl: Southeastern Comps. League, MENC; Coll. Band Dirs. Nat. Assn.; Nat. Band Assn.; Nat. Assn. Jazz Educators; Phi Kappa Phi; Phi Mu Alpha; Kappa Phi Kappa. Hobbies: Painting & Graphic Arts; Carpentry. Address: 3661 N Decatur Rd. Apt. E-5, Decatur, GA 30333, USA.

EDWARDS, John Vivian, b. 3 May 1945, Bristol, UK. Guitar Teacher & Performer. Educ: Spanish Guitar Ctr., Bristol; theory & harmony w. Teresa Babbage & Alistair Ross; guitar w. Thomas Hartman; master classes w. Emilio Pujol, Oscar Caceres & Alexandre Lagoya; LRAM; LTCL (perf.). m. Heide Mueller-Haas, 2 s. Debut: Wigmore Hall, London, 1975. Has recorded. Contbr. to : Jamaica Daily Gleaner; BMG; Guitar. Mbr., ISM. Recip. French Govt. Scholarship for Lagoya master class in Nice, 1973. Hobbies: Listening to music; Yoga; Reading. Mgmt: Helen Jennings Concert Agcy. Address: 73 Harcourt Rd., Redland, Bristol 6, UK.

EDWARDS, Morfen, b. 21 July 1938, Rhosllannechrugog, N Wales, UK. Harpist. Educ: Perf.'s & Tchr.'s Dips. (w. distinction), Royal Manchester Coll. of Music. Career: Work as Soloist, w. num. TV & Radio appearances; perfs. w. most Brit. Orchs., inclng. 8 yrs. w. Halle Orch., Light Music, inclng. BBC Northern Dance Orch., 2 yrs., & TV work; sev. concertos, esp. w. Bournemouth Sinfonieta; Prin. Harpist, Bournemouth Symph. Orch., 1971-. Recordings: All Bournemouth Symph. Orch. records, 1971-, inclng. as Soloist in Sibelius, Swan White Suite. Hobbies: Oil Painting; Driving. Mgmt: Bournemouth Symph. Orch. Address: 5 Glen Mews, 352 Poole Rd., Branksome, Poole, Dorset, UK.

EDWARDS, Nigel Rousseau, b. 11 May 1952, Brit. Mil. Hosp., Rinteln, Fed. German Repub. Director of Music; Freelance music journalist; Critic; Broadcaster, Organist; Pianist; Countertenor; Conductor. Educ: BA, Oxford Univ., 1973; MA, ibid., 1977; Music Educ. as pupil of Gordon Lawson & Colin Marston at Brighton Coll., Sussex. Career: Asst. Master, Lime House Schl., Dalston, Cumbria, 1973-74; Hd. Engl. & Choirmaster, Slindon Coll., Sussex, 1975; Dir. Music, Hillstone Schl., Malvern, 1976-. Recordings: Music from Malvern Coll. Chapel, 1978. Contbr. to: Malvern Gazette; Ledbury Reporter. Mbrships. incl: Incorp. Soc. of Musicians; Music Masters' Assn.; Aldwyn Consort of Voices; Langland Recorder Consort; Dir., Malvern Museum Soc. Ltd.; Conductor, Malvern Male Voice Choir. Hobbies: Photography; Local Hist.; Genealogy; Hymnology; Theology. Address: Hillstone Schl., Como Rd., Malvern, WR14 2HT, UK.

EDWARDS, Owain Tudor, b. 10 Nov. 1940, Ruabon, N Wales, UK. Reader in Music History. Educ: BMus, 1962, Univ.

of Wales; MMus, 1964, ibid; PhD, 1967, ibid; Accademia Musicale Chigiana, Siena, Italy, 1961. m. Grete Strand, 1 s, 2 d. Career: Fellow, Univ. of Wales, 1964; Asst. Lectr. in Music, Univ. Coll. of Wales, 1965; Lectr., ibid, 1967; Lectr. in Music, Open Univ., 1970-73, Univ. of Liverpool, 1973-74; Reader (Dosent), Music Hist., Norwegian State Acad. of Music, 1974-. Publs. incl: Joseph Parry, 1970; Beethoven, 1972; Romanticism in Music, 1972; Baroque Instrumental Music, 2 vols. & scores, 1974. Contbr. of num. articles to encys. & profl. jrnls. Mbr., profl. assns., Norway & UK. Hons: Var. awards, inclng. Nat. Coun. Music, Wales, 1960. Hobbies incl: Family; Playing Chmbr. Music; Skiing. Address: Solbakken, Sentralvn. 29, 1430 As, Norway. 29

EDWARDS, Ross, b. 23 Dec. 1943, Sydney, Australia. Composer. Educ: NSW State Conservatorium; M Mus, Univ. Adelaide. m. Helen Hopkins, 1 s. Career: ISCM Festival, Stockholm, 1966; ISCM Festival, Basel, 1970. Comps: Sextet, 1966; Sonata for 9 instruments, Querm Quaeritis (Childen's Nativity Play), 1967; String Quartet, 1968; Etude for Orch., 1969; Monos 1, cello solo, Monos 11, piano solo, 1970; Mboc for strings; Choros for piano & orch., 1972; Mountain Village in a Clearing Mist, for orch.; Antifon for Voices, brass ensemble, organ & percussion; 5 little piano pieces; The Tower of Remoteness, etc. Recording of Monos 11. Contbr. to Music Now; Aust. Contemporary Music Quarterly. Mbr. num. profl. orgs. Hobbies: Prospecting; Mountaineering. Address: 2 Diamond Rd., Pearl Beach 2256, Aust.

EDWARDS, Warwick Anthony, b. 22 Apr. 1944, Dewsbury, UK. University Lecturer; Performer on early instruments. Educ: King's Coll., Univ. of Cambridge; MusB, MA, PhD, m. Jacqueline Freeman, 2d. Career: Lectr., Glasgow Univ., 1971-; Dir., Scottish Early Music Consort, 1976-. Publs: (ed.) Music for Mixed Consort (Musica Britannica 40), 1977. Contbr. to : Grove's Dict., 6th ed.; Music & Letters; Proceedings of the Royal Musical Assn.; Early Music; The Consort; Brit. Book News. Hobby: Hill Walking. Address: 15 Falkland St., Glasgow G12 9PY, UK.

EDWINN, Edwin Frank, b. 1 May 1922, New York City, USA. Opera Singer; Music Historian & Teacher. Educ: Miami Conserv.; Mus B, Univ. of Miami; Juilliard Inst.; Acad. di Santa Cecilia, Rome; Am. Acad., Rome; PhD, Univ. of Rome. m. Jo Ann Lipinsky. Career: Opera & concert appearances, USA & Europe, incl: Rome & La Scala Operas; Maggio Musicale, Florence; Venice Music Festival; tours w. Rome Phil. Orch.; concerts at the Vatican; Carnegie Hall; approx. 400 concerts for Civic Music; Film work w. Rosselini & Di Sica, in Italy; Assoc. Prof. of Music, Univ. of N.C., Asheville; featured in TV series, Movin' On. Publ: Music in the Humanities, 1970. Mbrships. incl: Studio Int.; NEA; MENC; Southern Humanities Assn.; Am. Musicological Assn.; Soc. for Rsch. in Music Educ.; AAUP; Nat. Opera Assn.; Music Lib. Assn.; GO; NC Histl. Assn.; Asheville Buncombe Min.'s Fellowship; Assn. for Biblical Lit. Hobbies: Antique & exotic musical instruments; Tropical plants; fish & marine invertebrates. Address: The Manor Grounds, Asheville, NC 28801, USA.

EFFINGER, Cecil Stanley, b. 22 July 1914, Colo. Springs, Colo., USA. Composer. Educ: AB, Colo. Coll., 1935; studied violin, Dietrich, Colo. Springs, 1922-33; oboe, Andraud, Interlochen, 1931 & Debucher, LA, 1935; theory & comp., Boothroyd, Colo. Springs, 1934-35; comp., Wagenaar, Colo. Springs, 1938 & Boulanger, Fontainebleau, France, 1939. m. Corinne Lindberg, 1 s, 1 d. Career: Instr., Music, Colo. Schl. for the Blind, 1939-41, First Oboist, Denver Symph., 1937-41; Music Ed., Denver Post, 1946-48; Assoc. Prof., Music, Univ. of Colo., 1948-56; Prof., Music, Univ. of Colo., 1956-. Compositions incl. works for orch., band, chorus, organ; concerto for violin & chamber orch.; var. chamber music; opera (Pandora's Box, 1961 & Cyrano de Bergerac, 1965); oratorio (The Invisible Fire, 1957 & Paul of Tarsus, 1968); cantata (The St. Luke Christmas Story, 1953 & A Cantata for Easter, 1971). Inventor of the Musicwriter, 1955. Designer of the Tempowatch, 1969. Mbr. of var. profl. orgs. & Pres. of Music Print Corp., Boulder, Colo. Hons. incl: Stoval Prize, Comp., Am. Conserv., Fontainebleau, France, 1939; Naumburg Recording Award, Little Symph. No. 1, 1959; D Mus, Colo. Coll., 1959. Var. hobbies. Address: 2620 Lafayette Dr., Boulder, CO 80303, USA. 2, 9, 14.

EGBERTS, Sandrie, b. 8 Apr. 1929, Dedemsvaart, Netherlands. Drum Major, Royal Dutch Army; Freelance. Educ: Military Schls. of Music. m. Jenny Kremer, 2 s. Debut: 1951. Career: Drum Maj., Royal Dutch Army; Sev. broadcasts. Num. comps. for drum bands, drum & bugle bands etc. Recordings: Many of comps. Publs. incl: Methodical Instructin for March & Show; We Want to Know (co-author). Contbr. to: Royal Dutch Music Fedn. Mag.; Christian Music Mag. Mbrships. incl:

Advsry. Comm., Royal Dutch Music Fedn. Hons: Ridder van Oranje Nassau Medal of Hon., Netherlands; Bundesverdienstkreuz, W Germany; Order of Tudor Vladimirescu, Rumania. Hobbies incl: Flora & fauna. Address: Obrechtlaan 110 te, Assen, Netherlands.

EGER, Joseph, b. 9 July 1925, Hartford, Conn., USA. Music Director. Educ: Dip., Curtis Inst. of Music. Debut: French Horn Soloist, 1956, Cond., 1961, Town Hall, NYC. Career: has performed w. and/or conducted NY Phil., Los Angeles Phil., Israel Phil., Pitts. Symph., Am. Symph. Orch., Orch. Symp. de L'Etat (Greece), Haifa Symph., LPO, Royal Phil., New Philharmonia, etc.; currently Music Dir., Symph. for UN & UN Singers. Comps: Classical Heads (recorded album); Carolina (film score). Recordings incl: Around the Horn; 5 Bridges; var. classical works. Contbr. to: Cultures; Musical Am.; Musical Courier. Mbrships: Curtis Inst. Alumni; Symph. for UN. Recip., Awards from Mayor of NYC, 1973, 74 & 75. Hobbies: yoga; Religion; Politics. Address: 40 W 67th St., NY, NY 10023,USA.2.

EGGEBRECHT, Hans Heinrich, b. 5 Jan. 1919, Dresden, GDR. Professor. Educ: State Music Acad. Weimar; Univ. Jena; 1949 PhD Jena; 1955 Lectr.; 1961 Prof. Career: Asst. Humboldt Univ. Berlin; since 1951 Co-operator Pocket Dictionary of Musical Terms, Mainz Acad.; 1955, Lectr.; 1956-57, Lectr. Heidelberg Univ.; 1961, Full Prof. musicol., Freiburg Univ.; 1972-73, Vis. lectr. Bern Univ. Mbrships: Acad. for Sci. and Lit., Mainz. Publs. incl: Studies for Musical Terminology, 1955, 1968; Heinrich Schütz, Musicus Poeticus, 1959; The Organ Movement, 1967; Schütz and Religion, 1969. Contbr. to: var. profl. jrnls. Mbr., Akademie der Wissenschoften und der Literatur, Mainz. Address: Hanselhofstr. 5, 7815 Burg., Höfen, German Fed. Repub.

EGGEBRECHT, Jörg, b. 7 Nov. 1939, Berlin, Germany. Violoncellist and Barytonist. Educ: "Künstlerische Staatsprüfung", München; studied with Walter Reichardt, Maurice Eisenberg and 1964 & 65 w. Janos Starker, Bloomington, USA. m. Christine Eggebrecht - Korfes. Debut: Helmstedt, 1962, München, 1966. Career: Mbr. of Munich Phil. Orch. ("Münchner Philharmoniker") and Baryton-Player in the "Münchner Baryton Trio". Recordings: Trios for Baryton, Viola & Cello by J Haydn, played in sev. Radio Stns. & on TV. Hobbies: History, Philosophy, Literature, Politics. Address: 8 München 40, Herzogstr. 54, German Fed. Repub.

EGGINGTON, John, b. 29 May 1926, Melbourne, Australia. Orchestral Violinist; Organ Recitalist. m. Audrey Walklate, 2 d., 1 s. Career: Violinist, Melbourne Symph., Aust.; 1953-64, Halle Orch., Manchester, UK; Organ Recitalist, Aust., UK, France. Recordings: Organ, l'Oiseau-Lyre. Address: Heatherfield, Beswicks Lane, Alderley Edge, Cheshire, UK.

EGGLESTON, Anne E, b. 6 Sept. 1934, Ottawa, Ont., Can. Teacher; Composer. Educ: Assoc., Royal Conserv. of Music, Toronta, 1952; Dip. (comp.), Univ. of Toronto, 1956; MMus, Eastman Schl. of Music, 1958. Career: freelance composer & tchr. of piano, theory & comp. Comps: Armenian Lullaby; Jewish Lullaby; Norse Lullaby (recorded); 7 Variations for piano, 1977; Hurry, Hurry, Hurry, for piano, 1973. Mbrships: Can. League of Comps.; League of Women Comps., USA. Hons: Winner, CBC First Original Music Competition, Ottawa Radio, for Str. Quartet & Sonatine, 1964-65. Hobbies: Handicrafts; Yoga. Address: 234 Clemow Ave., Ottawa, Ont. K1S 2B6, Can.

EGILSON, Gunnar, b. 13 June 1927, Barcelona, Spain. Clarinettist; Teacher of Clarinet & Chamber Music. Educ: Reykjavik Conserv. of Music, 1945-47; Vermileya Acad. of Music, Calif., USA, 1947-48; Pvte. studies w. Frederick J Thurston, 1948-49, Bernard Walton, 1962, John McCaw, 1972. Career: Soloist w. Iceland Symph. Orch. & Concerts throughout Iceland & on Radio & TV; Recitals & Chamb. Music Appearances in Iceland, Sweden, Denmark, Germany, Switzerland, Belgium, France & UK; Prin. Clarinettist, Iceland Symph. Orch., 1958-; Tchr., Clarinet, Raykjavik Conserv. of Music, 1958-; Tchr. Chamb. Music, ibid., 1970-. Recordings: L'Histoire du Soldat, (Iceland); Intradakisum, (Sweden). Mbrships: Chrmn., Icelandic Musicians Union, 1955-60; Dir. Bd., Iceland Symph. Orch., 1958-; Chmn., Iceland Soloists Union, 1968-70; Musica Nova of Iceland, 1966-68. Hobbies: Chess; Philosophy. Address: Gardastraeti, 11, Reykjavik, Iceland.

EGK, Werner Joseph, b. 17 May 1901. Auchsesheim, Donauworfh, Bavaria. Composer. Educ: studied w. Anna Hirzel-Langenham, Carl Orff. m. Elisabeth Karl, 1 s., dec. Career: Cond., Prussian State Opera, Berlin, 1937-41; Dir., Prof., High Schl. for Music, W. Berlin, 1950-53; Permanent Guest Cond.,

Bavarian State Opera, Munich, 1951-71. Compositions: operas Die Zaubergeige, Peer Gynt, Columbus, Irische Legende, Der Revisor, Die Verlobung in San Domingo, Circe; ballets Joan von Zarissa, Abraxas, Die chinesische Nachtigall, Danza; num. Concert Works. Publs: Music-Wort-Bild, 1958; Die Zeit wartet nicht, 1973. Mbrships: Hon. Pres., German Comps. Grp.; Hon. Mbr., Supvsry. Bd., GEMA; Bavarian Acad. of the Fine Arts; Acad. of the Arts, W. Berlin; German Acad. of the Arts, E. Berlin; Rotary Club. Hons: Great DSC, German Fed. Repub. & Star; Baravian Order of Merit; Hon. Medal, City of Munich; Golden Broadcast Medal, German Fed. Repub.; Richard Strauss Medal. Address: Bachermer Weg, D8084 Inning/Ammersee, German Fed. Repub.

EGMOND, Max Rudolf van, b. 1 Feb. 1936, Semarang, Indonesia. Concert, Recital & Opera Singer (Baritone); Teacher of Singing Technique & Interpretation. Educ: Univ. of Utrecht, Netherlands; Pvt. studies of voice & interpretation. Debut: 1959. Career: Oratorios, Recitals & Operas, Europe, N & S Am.; Apps. in most leading fests. & music ctrs.; Regular broadcasts for radio & TV. Recordings incl: Schubert, Schwanengesans & Ravel, Don Quichotte; Baroque Songs; Arias by Bach, Handel, Telemann. Mbr., Royal Netherlands Musicians Soc. Hons. incl: Edison Award for gramophone recordings, Amsterdam, 1969 & 1971. Hobbies incl: Theatre. Mgmt: Ariette Drost; Prins Hendriklaan 13, Amsterdam, Netherlands. Address: Willemsparkweg 150-1, Amsterdam 1007, Netherlands, 3.

EGNER, Richard John, b. 29 Jan. 1924, St. Louis, Mo., USA. Pianist; Theorist; Composer. Educ: B Mus., St. Louis Inst. of Music; M Mus, Chgo. Musical Coll.; PhD, Univ. of Chgo. m. Helen Thomas Egner. Debut: Carnegie Hall, NY, 1949. Career: Piano soloist w. St. Louis Symph. Orch., Chgo. Symph., Cleveland Symph. Compositions (publs.): Sonata No. 3 for Piano; Symph. No. 4. Recordings: Echoes of Carnegie Hall; Becker (John) Sonata No. V. Publs: A Brief History of Musical Theory From Boethius to the Present, 1964; The Evolution of Polyphony From Antiquity to Bach, 1970. Contbr. to Music News Mag. Mbr. var. profl. orgs. Recip. Paderewski Gold Medal, 1951. Mgmt: Int. Artist Corp., NY, USA. Address: 216 Crosman Terrace, Rochester, NY 14620, USA.

EGNOT, Johnnye F., b. 12 Dec. 1943, Ft. Worth, Tex., USA. Organ Recitalist; Choir Director; Lecturer. Educ: BSc, Northwestern Univ., Evanston, Ill., USA; Am. Conserv. of Music, Chgo., Ill.; MMus, Perfs. Cert., Villa Schifanoia; Grad., Schl. of Fine Arts, Florence, Italy. Debut: for Soc. of Am. Musicians, Chgo., Ill.; 1970. Career: Organ Recitalist; Choir Dir.; Lectr. on early Italian organs & lit. Publs: preface to vol. of Pistoian organ music of 18th Century. Contbr. to: The Diapason. Mbrships: AGO. Hons: Young Artist Award (organ), Soc. of Am. Musicians, Chgo., 1970. Hobbies: Reading; Sewing. Address: c/o S Egnot, 3624 Lakeshore Dr., Newport, MI 48166, USA.

EHLE, Robert Cannon, b. 7 Nov. 1939, Lancaster, Pa., USA. Composer; Theorist; Performer on Electronic Instruments. Educ: Dip., Capitol Radio Engrng. Inst., 1968; Certs. in Electronics, Physics, Maths., AS Army Engr. & Security Schls.; B Mus., Eastman Schl. of Music, Rochester, NY, 1961; M Mus., N Tex. State Univ., 1965; PhD ibid, 1970. m. Linda Caudle, 1 s. Career: Tech. Writer; Recording Engr.; Techn.; Designer, Builder of Electronic Instruments; Rsch. Asst., N Tex. State Univ. Electronic Music Comp. Lab.; Asst. Prof. of Music, Schl. of Music, Univ. of Northern Colo., Greeley. Compositions: Five Pieces For Instruments with Prepared Electronics; Algorhythms, for amplified soprano & electronically prepared instruments; Soundpiece For Orchestra. Recordings: Prelude in 19 Tone Equal Temperament; Spiral of Archimedes; The Chinese Lute. Author, w. Merrill Ellis & Robert Moog, N Tex. State Univ. Electronic Music Composition Manual, 1965. Contbr. to num. profl. jrnls. Mbr. Audio Engrng. Soc. Named Dallas Symph. Orch. Rockefeller Fndn. Symposium Winner, 1965. Hobbies: Cycling; Hiking; Model Railroading. Address: 2107 26th Ave. Ct., Greeley, CO 80631, USA.

EHRENHAUS, Germán Hermann, b. 4 Mar. 1921, Düsseldorf, Germany. Instrumentalist (Oboe, Oboe d'Amore & Cor Anglais). Educ: Gymnasium zum heiligen Kreuz, Dresden, Germany; Akademisches Gymnasium, Neuland-Schule, Vienna, Austria; Coll. St. Michel, Fribourg, Switz.; Dip. (Prof. of Music), Conserv. Manuel de Falla, Buenos Aires, Argentina; studied oboe w. Edmond Gaspard. m. Leila Yaël, 1 s., 1 d. Debut: w. Municipal Symph. Orch., Buenos Aires, 1944. Career: 1st Oboe, Argentina's Radio Symph. Orch.; Nat. Symph. Orch. of Argentina; Symph. Orch. of Mendoza; Oboe Tchr., Music Schl., Cuyo Univ.; currently Coord. Solo-Oboist, Buenos Aires Phil. Orch., Teatro Colon; Co-Fndr., Musician's Summer Camp (Camping Musical Bariloche), 1947; Fndr., Camerata

Instrumental de Buenos Aires (double reed chmbr. grp.), 1960; Co-Fndr., Chmn., Ensemble Musical de Buenos Aires (coop. chmbr. orch. soc.), 1966. Has recorded w. the Nat. Symph. Orch., the Phil. Orch. of Buenos Aires, Camerata Instrumental & Ensemble Musical. Hons: Kt. of Schlaraffia Bonaerensis. Hobbies: Lit.; Mountaineering; Theatre. Address: Beruti 3846, 4B., Buenos Aires, Argentina.

EHRENSPERGER, Carlos, b. 14 Oct. 1911, Medellin, Colombia. Music Master of Piano & Singing. Educ: Univ. of Zürich, Switz.; Piano Dip., Conserv. of Winterthur, 1947. m. Henriette Ehrensperger-Bosshard, 2 d. Comps: Konig Drosselbart (song); Marquise von O (opera); Der Fall Dr. Mann (opera); Der grosse Tod (cycle of lieder for baritone & instruments); Der schwarze Tod tanzt mit (ballet); Sapphos Gesang (cantate for solos & choir); Fruhlingsfeier (cantate); Ermunterung (cantata); Veni creator spiritus (cantata). Mbr., Schweizerischer Tonkunstler-Verein. Recip., Carl Ernst-Kunstpreis for Music, 1953. Address: Wulflingerstr. 174, 8408 Winterthur, Switzerland.

EHRISMANN, Alfred, b. 16 May 1926, Winterthur, Switz. Pianist. Educ: Studied under Lazare-Lévi, Edwin Fischer & Alfred Cortot. Nat. Conserv. of Music; Dip., Winterthur Conserv. m. Adelheid Rohner, 4 children. Debut: Symph. Concert, Coll. of Music, Winterthur. Career: Chmbr. Musician & Soloist on European Continent. Mbrships: Union Swiss Musicians; Swiss MTA. Hobbies: Painting & Lit. Address: auf dem Morgen, 8620 Wetzikon, Zürich, Switz.

EHRLICH, David, b. 7 Jan. 1949, Bielsko, Poland. Violinist. Educ: Israeli Conserv.; Artist Dip., Tel Aviv Univ., 1972; pvte. study w. Prof. Ilona Feher; BA, MMus, N Ill. Univ.; postgrad. study, ibid. Career: concertmaster, soloist, Tel-Aviv Chmbr. Orch., 1968-72; soloist w. Israeli orchs.; concerts & recitals in NYC, Chgo., Boston, Balt., Tex., Idaho, Montana, Ark., Wis., Ind. & Va.; radio & TV apps. Israel & USA. Hons: Alexander Schneider Scholarship, 1964; Am.-Israel Cultural Fndn. Scholarship. 1969-72; 1st prize in chmbr. music, Israel, 1972; winner, Concerto Competiton, N Ill. Univ., 1973, '75; 2nd prize, Young Artists Competition, Springfield, Mo., 1973; Nat. Young Artists Winner, Nat. Fed. of Music Clubs, 1975. Mgmts: incl: Sound Rising Artistic Mgmt., Skokie, Ill., USA. Address: 5054 Olympia Court, Indpls., IN 46208, USA.

EHRLING, Sixten, b. 1918, Malmo, Sweden. Conductor. Educ: studied piano, also violin, cello & French horn; Royal Acad. of Music, Stockholm; conducting apprenticeship, Dresden Opera House. m. Gunnel Lindgren, 2 d. Career incls: w. Stockholm Royal Opera, 1940-60, becoming Chief Cond. & Music Dir., 1953; Guest Cond. 1961, 62, Music Dir. & Cond., 1963-73, Detroit Symph. Orch.; Fndr., Music Dir., Meadow Brook Music Fest., 1964; Cond., Met. Opera, NYC & Tchr., Juilliard Schl., 1973-; many guest apps., tours, etc. Hons. incl: Kt., Cmdr., Order of the White Rose, Finland (for championing works of Sibelius); sev. hon. degrees. Mgmt: Ibbs & Tillett, London, UK.

EHTEMAM, Mohammad, b. 18 Sept. 1948, Teheran, Iran. Clarinettist; Professor. Educ: Lic. degree in Music. Debut: as 1st Clarinet w. Teheran Opera Orch., 1966. Career: 1st Clarinettist, Teheran Symph. Orch.; Recital & Concert w. Symph. Orch. of Teheran; num. recitals for Jeunesse Musical, & Am. Soc., Teheran; Prof. of Clarinet, Teheran Conserv. Recordings: Works of Alireza Machayeki (modern music); much film music. Hobbies: Sports; Books; Good Films; Photography. Address: c/o Teheran Symphony Orchestra, Rudaki Hall, Arfa Ave., Teheran, Iran.

EICHBAUM, Heinrich Alexander, b. 23 Feb. 1914, Magdeburg, Germany. Consulting Insurance Adviser; Artist (Watercolours & Pastels); Art Critic; Sworn Translator. Educ: Dip., Ins. Sci.; Fellow, Soc. Sworn Translators & Interpreters; Cello, var. tutors inclng. Hermann Lenz, Walter Schilling, Emil Gmeindl; Music studies w. Fritz Busch. m. Dorothy Patricia Considine, 5 children. Contbr. to:Africa Verlag 'Der Kreis'; Critic, Windhoek Advt., Allgemeine Zeitung, & Suidwester. Mbrships: Exec. Comm., State Conserv. Music, Windhoek; Chmn., Cir. Promotion Arts & Sci., SW Africa Region; Pres., Shakespeare Soc.; Arts Assn. Hobbies: Musicol.; Chmbr. Music Playing; Hist.; Art; Writing; Reading. Address: PO Box 5106, Windhoek, SW Africa 9111. 28,29.

EICHER, Eugene Christian, b. 8 June 1927, Pitts., Pa., USA. Professor of Cello & Chamber Music. Educ: B Mus, Univ. of Tex. at El Paso; studied w. Gregor Piatigorsky, Curtis Inst. of Music, Phila. m. Lorraine Davis Eicher, 1 s., 1 d. Career: Solo Bach Suite Concerts, Vienna, Austria, & NYC; w. Melkus Str. Quartet, Cambridge, UK, NYC, Vienna & Innsbruck, Austria; w. Melkus Trio, Haydn. Conf. 1975, Wash. DC. Compositions:

Monteverdi Vespers for Chorus & Chmbr. Orch. Recordings: Gerschefski, Mountain Etude for Solo Cello, Piano Quintet, Str. Quartet. Publs: 6 Bach Suites, 1974. Mbrships: Arts & Letters; Kappa Lambda. Hons. incl: 1st Prize, Musicians Club, Pitts., Pa. Hobbies incl: Photography. Address: 386 Westview Drive, Athens, GA 30601, USA.

EICHINGER, Hans, b. 15 May 1902, Vienna, Austria. Conductor; Professor; Wiener Akademie für Musik & darstellende Kunst; Dip. in comp., Wiener Musikhochschule. m. Ilse Eichinger (Täubler), Career: Impresario, Baden Theatre, 1921-22; Violinist, Salzburger Festspiele, 1922; Institute, Wiener Staatsoper, 1922-27; Cond., Göteborg symph. orch., 1932; Cond., theatres in Marburg, Volksoper Hamburg & Baden, 1941-44; 150 recordings w. Stockholm Phil. Orch. & all Swedish radio orchs., 1946-65; 300 concerts w. Norrköping symph. orch., 1949-54; Music Dir., Katrineholm, Cond., symph. concerts, Dir., town music schl., Fndr. & Pres., chmbr. music soc., 1950-67; Guest Cond., Radio Vienna, 1958-64; Concerts w. orch. in Arkadenhof, Vienna town hall, 1965, 67; Guest Cond., radio orch., Athens, 1970-73; Guest Cond., Katrineholm, 1973. Comps. incl: Athen (rhapsody); Griechische Tänze; Romanze der Schnsucht; Eichinger-Tänze; Melancholie; Ausserhalb von Wien. Recordings: Erinnerrung; Am. Brillantengrund; Katrineholm; Es gibt eine Sehnsucht. Recip. of hons. Hobby: Theatre & concert visits. Address: Biondekgasse 10, 2500 Baden bei Wien, Austria.

EICHNER, Saul, b. 16 Oct. 1930, NYC, USA. Clarinettist. Educ: BM, 1951, MMus equivalent, 1960, Manhattan Schl. of Music. m. Carol Greenwald. Career: 1st Clarinettist, Fla. Symph. Orch., Boris Goldovsky Opera Theatre, NBC Opera Co., Aspen (Colo.) Music Fest., Mantovani Concert Orch.; var. Broadway theatre prods., NYC, & freelance musical ensembles; Prin. Clarin ttist, Radio City Music Hall Symph. Orch., currently. Hobby: Travel. Address: 150 Union Ave., Rutherford, NJ 07070, USA.

EINFELDT, Dieter, b. 11 Apr. 1935, Hamburg, German Fed. Repub. Conductor; Pianist; Organist; Teacher. Educ: Music Acad. Hamburg, State exam TD; 1949-62 Music tchr.; 1963 Hamburg Univ. m. Elisabeth-Charlotte Sabin, 1 s., 1 d. Career: Concert ldr.; Cond. Int. Orch. Course Youth and Music; Independent co-operator N German Radio, TV, 1965-69; Since 1972, tchr. Music Acad. Hamburg. Comps. incl: Symph; Operas; Ballet; Str. Quartet; Solo concertos for violin ,cello, organ, piano, oboe. Recordings: Str. Trio nr. 2, 1965; Loewe Ballads and Baluus Choirs, Mbrships: var. profl. orgs. Contbr. to: New Music Paper; Comp. about Comp. Hons: Prize Bavarian Art Acad., Mühchen, 1962; Prize Youth and Music, 1967; Kühlau Prize, Welzen, 1960. Hobbies: Mountain climbing; Lit. Address: 2071 Hoisdorf, Immenhagen 6, German Fed. Repub.

EISENMANN, Will, b. 3 Mar. 1906, Stuttgart, Germany. Composer; Professor of Music. Educ: Acad. of Music, Stuttgart; Ecole Normale de Musique, Paris. m. (1) Eva Westphal, 4 s. (2) Hanna Willi, 1 s. Career: Dramatist & Stage Mgr., State Operas, Stuttgart. Wiesbaden, Cologne; in Switz. 1935-; Fndr., Opera Schls., Zurich, 1947-50, Lucerne, 1952-; Commissioner, Cultural & Musical Exchange, German Fed. Repub. Switz. Comps. incl: (operas) King of the Dark Chamber; Bethsabé; (suite) 7 Pictures by Vincent Van Gogh; Gitanjali-songs w. orch. (recorded); Haiku 1 & 11; Wind Trio; Travermusik for orch., etc. Contbr. to musical jrnls. Mbr., profl. assns. Hons: Emil Hertzka Prize, Vienna, 1936. Hobbies incl: Collecting Antiques & Objets d'Art; Oriental Studies. Address: Chalet Alpina, 6103 Schwarzenberg/LU, Switz. 19,23,28.

EISENSTEIN, Alfred, b. 14 Nov. 1899, Brody, Poland (now USSR). Composer; Engineer; Pianist; Music Publisher. Educ. incl: studies in piano & music theory w. Prof. Anton Trost, Vienna; lifelong self-study of music. m. Mercedes Malespin Felix. Career: All-Eisenstein symph. concerts & ballet perfs. in Miami, 1972, '74; num. TV & radio perfs. Comps. incl: Romance & Souvenir for violin & roch.; Petite Suite for orch.; Tango of Love for orch.; Movements for str. orch.; songs. Recordings: a 2 LP record album containing perfs. of most of the works mentioned above. Contbr. to Civil Engineering Magazine. Mbrships: ASCAP; Profl. Engineers. Hons: ASCAP Standard Award prize for last 15 yrs.; num. interviews on TV. Hobbies: Charitable Concert Prods.; Surfing. Mgmt: Pops Music Publishing Co. Address: 18900 N E 14th Ave., N Miami Beach. FL 33179, USA. 7.

EISIKOVITS, Max, b. 8 Oct. 1908, Blaj, Romania. Composer; Professor; Musicologist. Educ: doct., Cluj Univ. Debut: Cluj, 1933. Career: collected Chassid folksongs, Maramures, Romania, 1938-39; Dir., Hungarian State Opera, Cluj, 1948-50; Rector, George Dima Conserv., Cluj, 1950-53. Comps. incl: chmbr. music; choral music, inclng. music for children's choirs; Opera; Songs. Publs: Horras & Madrigals, 1965; Vocal Polyphony of Renaissance, 1966; Baroque Polyphony, 1973; Introduction in the Vocal Polyphony of the 20th Century, 1976. Mbr., Romanian Composers' Union. Hons: State Prize, 1957; Award of Acad. of Romanian Socialist Repub., for musicol., 1975; Union of Romanian Comps. Prize, 1978. Address: Str. Voltaire No. 12, 3400 Cluj-Napoca, Romania.

EISMA, Will Leendert, b. 13 May 1929, Soengailiat, Holland. Violinist; Composer. Educ: Conserv. of Rotterdam; Comp., Accademia Santa Cecilia, Roma; Inst. for Sonology, Utrecht. m. Wilhelmina A. Reeser, 1 s., 1 d. Career: Violinist, Rotterdam Phil., 1953-59, Chmbr. Orch., Società Corelli, 1960-61, Chmbr. Orch., Radio Hilversum, 1961-; Mbr. electro-instrumental grp. ICE; Dir. of Studio for Electronic Music, Five Roses. Compositions: 3 Concerti for orch., 1 for 2 violins & orch.; Taurus, Volumina, for orch.; concerti for oboe, horn; Chmbr., Electronic Music.; Concerto for String Trio & Orchestra. Recordings: Donemus - Composers' Voice: Concerto for oboe, le Gibet. Mbr. Genootschap van Nederlandse Componisten. Hons: Béka Bartók Prize, Bloomington, USA, 1958; Visser Neerlandia Prize, 1963. Hobby: Photography. Address: 206 Oude Amersfoortsweg, Ilversum, Netherlands.

EJVIN PALTBO, Susanne, b. 8 Apr. 1942, Copenhagen, Denmark. Opera & Oratorio Singer (Mezzo Soprano). Educ: Studied Cello, Royal Danish Music Conserv., 3 yrs.; Opera Acad., Theatre Royal, Copenhagen. m. Prof. Dr. Henneke Gülzow. Debut: Marie, in Wozzeck (Alban Berg). Career: Serena in Porgy & Bess, Mercedes in Carmen, Pierrot Lunaire (Sch&nberg), all at Opera, Copenhagen; in Germany has sung in num. oratorios, given conerts w. symph. orchs., & perfs. of renaissance & baroque chmbr. music. Hons: Leonie Sonning Scholarship for Young Musicians, 1972. Address: 2308 Preetz, Klosterhof 12, German Fed. Repub.

EKWUEME, Lazarus Edward Nnanyelu, b. 28 Jan. 1936, Oko, Aguata, Nigeria. Professor of Music. Educ: Gov. Coll. Umuahia; BMus, MMus, RCM, London; MA, PhD, Yale Univ., USA; ARCM; AMus, TCL; LMus.TCL; LTCL; FTCL; LRAM; LGSM. m. Lucy Nnakwe Ekwueme, 1 s., 1 d. Career: Tchr., Lagos City Coll., Nigeria, 1958-60; Tchr., Ctrl. Tutorial Schl. for Young Musicians, London, 1963-64; RCM, Junior Dept., 1963-64; Lect. in Music, Univ. of Nigeria, 1964-66; stet Yale Univ., USA, 1968-70; Asst. Prof. of Music & Chmn. of Black/Hispanic Studies, State Univ. Coll., Oneonta, NY, 1973-74; Assoc. Prof., ibid, 1974-78; Prof. & Hd. of Music, Univ. of Lagos, Nigeria, 1978 ; Num. stage, film, TV & radio apps. Comps: Missa Africana, 1964; O Mary Dear Mother, 1967, Welcome, Umu Uwa Golibe, 1974; Nigerian Rhapsody for Strings; Flow Gently Sweet Niger; Psalm 23 (for Contralto & Orch.); Num. Anthems & Christmas Carols; Canticles; Solo Songs, etc. Contbr. to: African Music; The Black Perspective in Music; Journal of Black Studies; Journal of African Studies; Nigerian Music Review. Mbrships: Pres., Nat. Music Coun. of Nigeria; Soc. for Prom. of Igbo Lang. & Culture. Hons: Cond., Nigerian Nat. Choir for Festac 77. Hobbies: Drama; Karate. Address: Dept. of Music, Univ. of Lagos, Akoka, Lagos, Nigeria. 25,29.

ELDER, David George, b. 13 Jan. 1942, Hastings, Neb., USA. Violinist; Violist; Teacher. Educ: BM., Yankton Coll., SD., 1964; MMus, Univ. of Louisville, KY., 1966. m. Lelia Cecilia Elder, 1 d. Career: Violinist, Sioux City Symph., Iowa; violist, Sioux Falls Symph., SD.; in charge of strings-orch. program, Yankton public schls. Columnist in SD Musician. Mbrships: News Ed., SD String Tchrs. Assn.; Am. String Tchrs. Assn.; State Orchestra Chmn., SD. Music Tchrs. Assn.; Music Educators Nat. Conven.; Nat. Educ. Assn.; SD. Educ. Assn.; Yankton Educ. Assn. Hons: Grad. Playing Fellowship w. Univ. of Louisville & Louisville Orch., 1964. Hobbies: Bowling; Reading. Address: 2014 Walnut St., Yankton, SD 57078, USA.

ELDER, Mark Philip, b. 2 June 1947, Hexham, Northumberland, UK. Conductor. Educ: Univ. of Cambridge, 1966-69; BA, MA, ibid. Debut: Liverpool Conds. Seminar, Liverpool Phil., 1971. Career: Fest. Chorusmaster & Asst. Cond., Glyndebourne Opera, 1970, '71; Music staff, Royal Opera House, Covent Garden, 1970-71; Staff cond., Australian Opera, 1972-74; Assoc. Cond., Eng. Nat. Opera, 1974-; Musical Dir., ibid., 1980-; apps. as pianist, harpsichordist & cond. at Fests. in Wexford, Edinburgh, Bath, King's Lynn w. most major Brit. symph. orchs.; worked at Komische Oper in E Berlin 1977-78; num. broadcasts for BBC. Hobbies: Tennis; Wine; Theatre. Mgmt: Ingpen & Williams, London. Address: 14 Trinity Church Sq., London SE1, UK.

EL HABASHI, Nagi Ibrahim Ahmed, b. 6 Oct. 1936, Cairo, Egypt. Cellist. Educ: Arabic Conserv.; Accademia Santa Cecilia,

Roma; Acad. of Music, Berlin. m. Karin Mang-Habashi, 1 s. Career incls: tours of USSR, E Germany, Sweden, Czech., Norway, Belgium, Tunisia, Lebanon; radio broadcasts, Sweden, Norway, E Germany; TV broadcasts, Sweden & Egypt; Mbr., Swedish Broadcasting Orch., 1964-67, Stockholm Phil. Orch., 1967-. Comps: Canzone Orientale; Suite for Cello. Recordings: as Soloist w. Stockholm Phil. Orch. Hons. incl: 1st Prize, Classical Music, Competition of the Arabic World, 1955 & 1957-59. Hobbies: Photography; Philosophy. Address: Glömmingegränd 4, 16362 Spanga, Sweden.

ELIAS, Rosalind, b. 13 Mar. 1931, Lowell, Mass., USA. Operatic Mezzo-soprano. Educ: New England Conserv. of Music. Debuts: w. Boris Goldowsky, Boston, 1948; Metrop. Opera Co., NYC, 1954. Career incls: concert apps. & TV broadcasts; app. at San Carlo Opera, Naples, premiered role of Erika in Samuel Barber's Vanessa. Recordings: Columbia; RCA. Mbr., Sigma Alpha Iota. Address: 24 Park St., Lowell, MA 01852, USA.2.

ELIASON, Robert E, b. 28 Mar. 1933, Flint, Mich., USA. Music Curator; Tuba Player; Teacher. Educ: BMus, Univ. of Mich., 1955; MMus, Manhattan Schl. of Music, NYC, 1959; DMA, Univ. of Mo., 1968. m. Ellen I Easter, 1d.,2s. Career incl: Pub. Schl. tchr., 1957-58, 1960, 1969-70; Prin. Tuba, Kansas City Phil., 1960-69; Curator of Musical Instruments, Henry Ford Museum, Dearborn, Mich., 1971-. Recordings: Sousa Am. Bicentennial Collection; 19th century Am. Ballroom Music; Our Musical Past, 19th century band music. Publs: Keyed Bugles in the United States, 1972; Graves & Company, Musical Instrument Makers, 1975; Early Am. Brass Makers, 1979. Contbr. to num. profl. jrnls. Mbrships: Am. Musicol. Soc.; Am. Musical Instrument Soc. (Bd. of Dirs., prog. chmn., 1974, Treas., 1978-79). Hobby: Flying. Address: 549 N Melborn Ave., Dearborn, MI 48128, USA.

ELIASSON, Anders, b. 3 Apr. 1947, Borlänge, Sweden. Composer Educ: Studied comp. at Coll. of Music, Stockholm, w. Ingvar Lidholm. 1 d. Career: Num. radio apps.; works for TV, 1973, '78. Comps. incl: (orchl. music) Canti in Lontananza; (Chmbr. music) Disegno per Quartetto d'Archi; Disegno per Sestetto d'Ottoni; (Choral Music) Memet, for mixed chori (Electronic Music); In the Presence of Logus; (Ch. Opera) One of Us; Times, for soprano & chmbr. ensemble; Disegno per Quartetto d'Archi. Hons: Christ Johnson Prize for "Canti in Lontananza", 1977. Address: Strömkarlsvägen 86, 16138 Bromma, Sweden.

ELKUS, Jonathan, b. 8 Aug. 1931, San Francisco, Calif., USA. Composer; Conductor; Editor. Educ: BA, Univ. of Calif., Berkeley; MA., Stanford Univ.,; studied comp. w. Darius Milhaud, Leonard Rather & others. m. Marilyn McCormick, 1 s. Career: Comp.; Cond. Ed.; former Prof. of Music, Lehigh Univ; Vis. Lectr., Univ. of Calif. & Yale Coll., Yale Univ., 1977. Comps: operas The Outcasts of Poker Flat, Medea, The Mandarin, Helen in Egypt, Tom Sawyer, Treasure Island; chmbr. music; songs; Band comps.; Ragtimes. Author, Charles Ives & The American Band Tradition, 1974. Mbr. ASCAP; Sonneck Soc. Address: 8 Pearl St., Provincetown, MA 20657, USA. 6.

ELLA, István, b. 8 Jan. 1947, Veresegyház, Hungary. Organist; Choral & Orchestrtal Conductor. Educ: Béla Bartók Conserv., Budapest; Ferenc Liszt Acad., Budapest, 1967-71 (Dip. in organ & choral cond.); studied organ w. J E Köhler, orchl. cond. w. Olaf Koch; Dip., Orchl. Cond., Budapest, 1973. m. Katalin Bodonyi, 1 s. Career: Perfd. organ music for a film about Bach, Bach in Arnstadt; Organ music for TV film perfd. in Cathedral, Szeged. Recordings: Six fugues on the name BACH by Schumann; Choral-fantasie, Straf mich nicht in deinem Zorn; Works by Bach. Mbrships: Assn. of Hungarian Musicians. Hons: 4th Prize, 23rd Int. Spring Fest., Prague, 1971; 2nd Prize, 4th Int. Bach Competition, Leipzig, 1972; 1st Prize, 1st Int. Bruckner Competition, Linz, 1974; 1st Prize, Int. Organ Competition in Brugge, 1976. Hobby: Wine-making. Mgmt: Interkoncert Budapest. Address: Vásár ut 4, 1084 Budapest, Hungary.

ELLEFSON, Art, b. 17 April 1932, Moose Jaw, Sask., Can. Musician (alto, tenor, baritone saxophones; clarinet; bass clarient; flute; piccolo). Educ: Pvte. studies w. Gordon Delamont, Toronto, Can. m. Gloria Hodgkins, 1 d., 1 s. Career: Vic Lewis Orch., 1952-56; Freelance Soloist, 1956-59; John Dankworth Orch., 1959-66; BBC Radio Orch., 1966-69; Joe Wylie Orch., Bermuda, 1969-74; Phil Nimmons, Nimmons 'n Nine Plus Six, Toronto, Can., 1974-79; TV Special, Art Ellefson Quintette, 1979-; Num. Concerts & Jazz Fests., Europe, 1956-69. Num. recordings. Hobbies: Art; Woodwork. Address: 241 Wellington St. E, Barrie, Ont., Can.

ELLINGSON, Linda Jeanne, b. 26 Aug. 1947, Seattle, Wash., USA. Professional Singer; Private Teacher of Voice. Educ: BA Mus. Standard Tchng. Cert., Univ. of Wash.; Pacific Luth. Univ. m. Paul Gordon Ellingson. Career: has sung w. Portland, Seattle & Tacoma Opera Cos. Roles incl: Despina, Cosi Fan Tutte; Ann, Merry Wives of Windsor; Monica, The Medium; Lucy, The Telephone; Lauretta, Gianni Schicchi; Grethen, Student Prince; Juliet, Britten's Little Sweep. Mbrships: Tacoma Opera Soc.; Bus. & Profl. Women; NEA; Wash. Educ. Assn. Recip. Young Career Woman award, Wash. BPW, 1976. Hobbies: Gourmet cooking; Sports; Needlecraft. Address: 31012 29th Ave. SW, Federal Way, WA 98003,USA. 27.

ELLIOT, Willard Somers, b. 18 July 1926, Ft. Worth, Tex., USA. Bassoonist; Composer. Educ: B Mus, N Tex. State Coll.; Denton; M Mus, Eastman Schl. of Music, Rochester, NY. Career: Mbr., Houston Symph., Dallas Symph., Chgo. Symph.; Perf. own bassoon concerto w. Chgo. Symph., Ravinia Fest., 1965. Comps incl: Poem for Bassoon, String Quartet; Two Creole Songs for Oboe, Clarinet & Bassoon; Three Duets for flute, bassoon. Recordings incl: Frank Martin, Concerto for Seven Winds; Ravel, Alborado del Grazioso. Hons. incl: Koussevitzky Fndn. Award, 1959. Hobbies incl: Collecting fossi s. Address: 339 Custer, Evanston, IL 60202, USA.2,8.

ELLIOTT, Douglas Ferguson, b. 21 July 1916, Woodstock, Ont., Can. Organist; Pianist; Teacher; Adjudicator. Educ: studied piano w. Marie Thomson & Lubka Kolessa, organ w. Charles Peaker, & Comp. w. Healey Willan; Mus B, Univ. of Toronto; ACCO; Assoc., Toronto Conserv. of Music. m. Elizabeth Porter, 1 s., 1 d. Debut: Casavant Soc., Toronto. Career: Organ & Piano Recitalist, CAn. & USA, broadcasts on CBC; Organist & Choirmaster, Toronto chs.; Tchr., Examiner, Fac. of Music, Univ. of Toronto, Royal Conserv. of Music, Toronto; Fest. Adjudicator; Cond. for many perfs. of works inclng. Brahms Requiem, Bach Magnificat, Mozart Requiem, Handel Messiah, etc. Recorded Mozart Requiem. Contbr. to jrnls. Mbr., Examiner in Organ Playing & Theory, Councillor, Committee Chmn., Can. Coll. of Organist. Hobby: Landscape painting. Adress: 257 Belsize Dr., Toronto, Ont. M4S 1M5, Canada.

ELLIOTT, Graham John, b. 10 Nov. 1944, Abergavenny, UK. Cathedral Organist. Educ: RAM; St. George's Chapel, Windsor Castle; BMus, FRCO, FTCL, FLCM. Career: Sub-Organist, Llandaff Cathedral, 1966-70; Organist, St. Asaph Cathedral, 1970-; Dir. of Music, Lowther Coll., 1970-. Num. recordings as soloist & Accomp. Mbrships: Royal Acad. Club. Hobbies: Medieval & Victorian Architecture. Address: Bryn Siriol, St. Asaph, N. Wales, UK 30.

ELLIOTT, Paul Murray Christopher, b. 19 Mar. 1950, Macclesfield, UK. Tenor Singer. Educ: St. Paul's Cathedral Choir Schl., 1959-63; King's Schl., Canterbury (music scholar), 1964-69; Magdalen Coll., Oxford, 1969-72; MA (Oxon). Career: mbr., Deller Consort; fndr. mbr., London Early Music Group; Hilliard Ensemble; apps. w. Musica Reservata, The Consorte of Musicke, Pro Cantione Antiqua & Acad. of Ancient Music; num. solo apps.; tours of Europe, Am. & Aust. w. Deller Consort; singer & flautist, The New Excelsior Talking Machine. Recordings: works by Purcell, Bach, Handel; much early music. Mbrships: ISM; British Actors Equity. Hobbies: Current Affairs; Walking; Squash; Swimming; TV. Mgmt: Magenta Music, 33 Cholmeley Pk., London N6 5EL. Address: Little Green, 8 Park Ln., Selsey, Chichester, W. Susses PO20 OHD, UK.

ELLIOTT, Paula Kelch, b. 5 June 1938, Joliet, Ill., USA. Flautist; Orchestral & Chamber Music Performer. Educ: BM, Oberlin Coll. Conserv. of Music; MMus, New England Conserv. m. Thomas Charles Elliott. Career: Prin. Flautist, Royal Winnipeg Ballet, Can., 1962-64, St. Paul Chmbr. Orch., USA, 1968-69, Hamilton Phil. Orch., Can., 1969-; 2nd Flautist, 1964-65, Prin. Flautist, 1965-68, Winnipeg Symph. Orch.; currently Mbr., Sentiri Wind Quiteet, HPO Bach baroque ensemble & Lorcini-Elliott Duo. Address: RR No 1, Brantford, Ont., Canada.

ELLIOTT, Robert Conyers, b. Cheltenham, Glos., UK. Harpsichordist; Head of School of Keyboard Studies. Educ: RCM; Royal Manchester Coll. of Music. m. Honor Sheppard. Career: Organist & Choirmaster, St. Michael-le-Belfry, York, 1952-55; St. Michael's Spurriergate, York, 1955-67; Acomb Parish Ch., 1967; Has worked w. Deller Consort as harpsichordist & organist in num. European countries, USA, Can. & S Am.; Staff, Royal Manchester Coll.of Music, 1957-; Hd. of Schl. of Keyboard Studies, ibid (Royal Northern Coll. of Music, 1973-); Mbr., Bd. of Profs.; Examiner, Assoc. Bd., Royal Schls. of Music, 1962-. Comps: Piano Sonatina Op. 2; Fantasie for Pianoforte Duet; Three Lyric Pieces for Piano. Recordings:

As harpsichordist & organist, solo & continuo. Recip. Hon. FRMCM. Address: The Firs, 27 The Firs, Bowdon, Cheshire WA14 2TF, UK. 3.

ELLIOTT, Vernon Pelling, b. 27 July 1912, Croydon, Surrey, UK. Musician (Bassoon & Contra-Bassoon); Composer; Conductor. Educ: RCM, London; FTCL. m. Nora Jane Mukle, 2 d. Career: Prin. Bassoon, Bournemouth Orch., 1936; Sadlers Wells Opera & Ballet, 1938; Royal Opera, Covent Gdn., 1949; Engl. Opera Grp. & Aldeburgh Festival, 1954-60; Asst. Prin., Philharmonia, 1945-49; Sub-prin. & contra bassoon, New Philharmonia, 1954. Prof., Trinity Coll. of Music, London; Prof., NE Essex Tech. Coll. & Schl. of Art; Prof., London Coll. of Music. Compositions: Incidental Music for TV films Ivor the Engine; Pogles Wood; Clangers; Mermaids Pearls; Noggin the Nog; Pingwings; Double-bass solo, Odd Man Out. Recordings: Turn of the Screw opera (Britten); Contra-bassoon solo in Series instruments of the Orch. Recip. Edwin F. James Prize, 11936. Hobbies: Sailing; skiing; Riding; Beekeeping; Wine Making. Address: 3 Maxted Pk., Harrow, Middx., HA1 3BB, UK. 3.

ELLIS, Linus Marvin III, b. 17 Nov. 1943, Wilmington, Del., USA. Musicologist; Recitalist on Organ & Harpsichord; Teacher of Piano, Organ & Harpsichord. Educ: BS, MS, Juilliard Schl. of Music; PhD Cand., Cath. Univ. of Am. m. Ruth Elizabeth Hyde. Career: Over 200 organ & harpsichord recitals in USA & Europe; Instr. of Music & Chapel Orgnaist, St. Andrew's Schl., Middletown, Del., 1969-71; Asst. Prof. of Music, Salisbury State Coll., Md., 1971-74; Dir. The Ellis Studio, Salisburg, Md., 1974-; Musical Dir., The Salisbury Consort, 1976-; Mbrships: Int. Musicol. Soc.; Am. Musicol. Soc.; Coll. Music Soc.; AGO. Hons. incl: 1st Place AGO Reg. Playing Competition, Lancaster, Pa., 1967. Hobbies incl: Histl. preservation. Address: 200 E William St., Salisburg, MD 21801, USA.

ELLIS, Martin John, b. 23 Sept. 1943, London, UK. Teacher; Organ Recitalist; Accompanist (piano & organ); Conductor; Composer; Editor. Educ: RCM, London, 1961-65; ARCM (Organ Perf.); GRSM; FRCO; CHM (RCO). m. Miriam Ann Tuckwell. Career: Dir. of Music, Cargilfield Schl., Edinburgh, 1966-71; Dir. of Music, Dean Close Jr. Schl., Cheltenham, 1971-73; Asst. Dir. of Music, Taunton Schl., 1973-; Cond.; Wellington Choral Soc.; Examiner, Assn. Bd. of the RSM. Comps: Communion Service Series 3, 1976. Recordings: Music for the Bi-Centenary Exhib. of Sir Walter Scott, 1971; Organ & Choral Music from Taunton Schl., 1978. Publs: Ed., Church Choir Library, 4 Vols., 1978-81; History of the Organ in the Central Hall, Westminster, 1970; History of the Organ in the Chapel of Taunton School, 1977. Contbr. to: Musical Opinion; Methodist Recorder. Mbrships. incl: RCO; ISM; Methodist Ch. Music Soc.; Inc. Assn. of Organists. Hons: R.J. Pitcher Organ Scholarship (RCO), 1963. Hobbies: Philosophy; Theology; Railways. Address: 157 Staplegrove Rd., Taunton, Somerset, UK.

ELLIS, Merrill, b. 9 Dec. 1916, Cleburne, Tex., USA. Composer; Researcher & Performer in Electronic Media; Teacher. Educ: B Mus, M Mus, Univ. of Okla.; Univ. of Mo.; pvte. study of comp., Roy Harris, Spencer Norton, Charles Garland. m. Willa Naomi Wiggins, 3 s., 2 d. Career incls: Dir., Electronic Music Ctr., Prof. of Comp., N Tex. State Univ., Denton. Comps. incl: Kaleidoscope (orch., live synthesizer, soprano voice w. visual display); Dream of the Rode; A Dream Fantasy; Nostalgia (strings, percussion, electronic tape & theatrical events). Mbrships: ASCAP; AAUP; MENC; Music Tchrs. Nat. Assns. Recip. sev. commissions & rsch. grants, also ASCAP awards for contrbns. to serious music. Address: 909 Ave. E, Denton, TX 76201,USA.

ELLIS, Osian, b. 1928, Ffynnongroew, N Wales, UK. Solo Harpist; Singer. Educ: ARCM; FRAM.; D ,Mus. m. Rene Ellis Jones, 2 s. Career: has broadcast frequently on radio & TV & app. in recitals & concerts thru'out world; Mbr. of Melos Ensemble; Prin. Harpist, LSO; Organist, London Welsh Meth. Ch.; has made many apps. at recitals of poetry & music; has done much work w. Benjamin Britten since 1960, making 1st perfs. & recordings of many of his works (Britten wrote Harp Suite in C op. 83 for him); made film, The Harp, for Educl. Film Fndn. Recordings: many for Oiseau Lyre, Delyse & Argo labels, both as Solo Recitalist & w. LSO. Mbrships: Brit. Coun. Music Committee; Welsh Advsry. Committee, Hons. incl CBE; Grand Prix du Disque & Radio Critics Award (Paris) for recording of Handel Harp Concertos; Premier Prix, French Soc. of Authors & Eds. of Music, for Ravel's Introduction & Allegro, 1962. Adress: 90 Chandos Ave., London N20,UK.3.

ELLISON, Ebenezer Blay, b. 16 June 1943, Atuabo, Ghana. Music Teacher (Violin, Viola, Flute, Piano & Drums). Educ: Tchrs. Cert. A; Dip. Mus. Ed. m. Florence Ntow, 1 s., 1 d. Career: Music Tchr. Comps: Nyame ye Dan Wo (anthem);

Christmas Songs; Afe Fofor; Bronyia Ako Aprow; Patriotic Songs; Suzu Adwenlekpale; Arise. Mbr. Ghana Music Tchrs Assn. Hobbies: Reading; Instrumental Playing. Address: Foso Trng. Coll., Box 87, Assnin Foso, Ghana, W. Africa.

ELLISON, Maxine A, b. 3 Oct. 1952, Buffalo, NY, USA. Teacher; Violinist. Educ: BM, Perfs. Cert., NY State Univ. Coll. at Fredonia. m. Thomas W Ellison. Career: Concertmaster, Fredonia Coll. Symph. Orch.; 1st Violin, Schenectady Symph. Orch., Albany Symph. Orch. & Saratoga Performing Arts Ctr. Orch., NY. Mbrships. incl: Am. String Tchrs. Assn.; Kappa Delta Pi; NYSSMA; NYSUT. Hobby: Skiing. Address: 67 Hyde St., Saratoga Springs, NY 12866, USA.

ELLMERICH, Luis, b. 8 Apr. 1913, Vienna, Austria. Music Teacher; Pianist; Composer; Journalist. Educ: Studied Piano, Vienna; Dips. in Piano, Music Educ., Orch. Pianist & Cond., Acad. of Music, Sao Paulo, Brazil. m. Ciriaca Ellmerich. Debut: Buenos Aires, 1930. Career: Music Tchr., Municipal Schl. of Ballet, Sao Paulo; Piano Tchr., State Conserv., ibid.; Jrnlst., 1959-; Music Critic, Diário, Sao Paulo, 1964-; Prof., Conserv. Estadad, Sao Paulo & Escola Municipale de Balé. Compositions incl: (piano) 2 Prelúdios; Ritmost Musicais; Cancao das águas; Valsa Capr cho; (vocal) Trova brasileira; Evocacao paulista. Publs. incl: História da Música, 1962, 4th ed., 1977; História da Dança, 1962, 3rd ed. 1970; Manual da Balé, 1973. Mbr., var. cultural & musical orgs. Hon: Mencas honrosa, Pen Club, 1964. Hobbies: Lecture; Travel. Address: Travessa Humberto Primo 55, 04018 Sao Paulo, Brazil.

ELLOWAY, Julian Dominic, b. 28 July 1950, Oxford, UK. Music Publisher; Accompanist (piano, harpsichord, organ); Choral Conductor. Educ: BA, Sussex Univ., 1972; Darmstadt Ferienkürse für Neue Musik, 1965-68; studied piano w. Lucy Page, Oxford, & Paul Hamburger, London; GSM, 1969-78; LGSM (piano); studied organ w. John Birch, cond. w. Laszlo Heltay. m. Janet Elloway. Career: Freelance accomp. w. soloists & choirs incl Brighton Fest. Chorus; Repetiteur, Manuel Theatre, Malta, 1969; cond., Univ. of Sussex Choir, 1978-79; Assoc. cond., New Sussex Opera, 1979-80; Asst. Dir., Chapel Music, Sussex Univ., 1976-; Promotion Mgr., Faber Music Ltd. Publs: continuo realisations & eds. for Faber Music Ltd. Mbrships: Musicians' Union; Engl. Folk Dance & Song Soc. (mbr., editorial committee); ISM; Consumers' Assn.; Modern Churchman's Union. Hobbies: Motorcycling; Gardening; Langs. Address: 18 Elm Dr., Hove, Sussex BN3 7JJ, UK.

ELLOWAY, Kenneth Albert, b. 17 Jan. 1916, Weymouth, UK. Conductor; Music Educator. Educ: Royal Military Schl. of Music, Kneller Hall, 1936-38, 1942-45; ARCM (Band Cond), 1943; Hon. Grad., Kneller Hall, 1951. m. Eva M Elloway, 1 d., 1 d. Career: Bandmaster, Royal Artillery, 1949-55; Dir. of Music, Royal Canadian Artillery, 1955-65, Inspector of Bands, 1963-65; Cond., CBC Halifax (Can.) Chmbr. Orch., 1966-; Dir., Maritime Conserv. of Music, 1965-70; Music Fac., Dalhousie Univ., 1974-78; Supervisor of Music, Dartmouth City Schls., 1978-; Fndr.-Cond., Chebucto Orch. of Nova Scotia, 1974-. Comps: Works for Band & Choir. Mbr., profl. orgs. Hons: Can. Centennial Medal, 1967; Silver Medal, Worshipful Co. of Musicians, 1944. Hobbies: Record & Score collecting; Reading. Address: 4 Breeze Dr., Dartmouth, Nova Scotia, Can. B2X 2N9.

ELMS, Roderick James Charles, b. 18 Oct. 1951, Ilford, UK. Concert Pianist; Organist; Arranger. Educ: LGSM; RAM; LRAM; ARCO. Debut: GSM 1961. Career: Played Greig Concerto when 14; Appeared twice in the "Maltings" playing Tschaikovsky & Rachmaninov Concertos; Recitals & Conerts in all maj. concert halls of London & Home Cos. Played items w. Royal Marines Orch., Deal, Kent; Played on French Nat. Music Prog. (Radio), 1973. TV Debut, 1975; work on radio w. BBC Symph. Orch. . Comps: Trumper Fanfare Commissioned to commemorate Formation of London Borough of Redbridge. 1965-75, sev. recordings. Mbr., RCO. RAM Club, Recip., Kate Steel Prize for Piano, RAM. Hobbies: Photography; Electronics & Recording. Address: 34 Ridgeway Gdns., Redbridge, Essex G4 5HL,UK.

ELMSLY, John Anthony, b. 1 July 1952, Auckland, NZ. Composer; Harpsichordist; Flautist. Educ: BSc (Maths.); BMus, 1975, Vic. Univ. of Wellington; Royal Conserv. of Brussels; Royal Consrv. of Liège, Special Certs.; LTCL; studied w. David Farquhar, Victor Legley, Frederic Rzewski, Henri Pousseur. Career: Chmbr. music & electronic music broadcast by Radio NZ & RTB3 and BRT3, Belgium. Comps. incl: Three Pieces for Orch., 1977; Diamant (electroacoustic); Works for solo flute, violin, cello; other chmbr., choral, orchl. & electronic works. Mbrships: Australasian Perf. Rights Assn.; Comps. Assn. of NZ. Hons: First Prize in Comp., Royal Conserv. of Brussels, 1977. Address: Top Flat, 24 Kenwyn Rd., London SW4, UK.

ELROD, Elizabeth Louella, b. 23 Apr. 1935, Chattanooga, Tenn., USA. Educator; Ethnomusicologist; Singer; French Horn

Player. Educ: BA, Baylor Univ.; B Mus, Ca. State Univ.; MME, EdD, Univ. of Ga. Debut: Atlanta Symph., 1960. Career: Apps. on network TV, Films & Radio. var. recordings. Mbrships: Coll. Music Soc.; AACTE; AGVA; MENC. Publs: Music of the Sea Islands, 1975; If You Can't Sing, Blame Your Mother, 1975. Contbr. to: Human Behavior; Symposium; Red Book; Observer; NY Times; Chgo. Daily News. Hons. incl: Hon. D Mus, 1972; WGN Opera of the Air Winner, 1970. Hobbies: Sports; Numismatics. Mgmt: Irv Hinkle Assocs. Address: 9627 White Acre Rd. Bl, Columbia, MD 21045, USA.

ELSCHEK, Oskar, b. 16 June 1931, Bratislava, Czech. Musicologist. Educ: Fac. of Philos.,Komenskeho Univ., Bratislava, 1950-55. m. Alica Elschekova, 4 children. Career: w. Inst. of Musicol., Slovak Acad. of Scis., 1953-; currently Chief, Dept. of Ethnomusicol. ibid.; concurrently w. Union of Slovak Comps., 1963-71. Recordings: Supraphon. Publs: On Slovak Folk Music (w. A Elschekova), 1956; Introduction to the Study of Slovak Folk Music (w. A Elschekova), 1962; Systems of Graphical & Symbolic Signs ofr Typology of Aerophones, 1969; Ed.-in-Chief, Slovenska hudba (monthly), 1964-71. Mbrships. incl: Int. Musicol. Soc.; Soc. for Ethnomusicol.; Soc. for Music Rsch., Germany; Exec. Bd., Int. Folk Music Coun. Recip., musicol. & ethnol. prizes. Address: Beskydska 6, 80 100 Bratislava, Czechoslovakia.

ELSNER, Jürgen, b. 22 Apr. 1932, Finsterwalde, German Dem. Repub. Musicologist. Educ: Deutsche Hochschule für Musik, Berlin; Inst. of Musicol., Humboldt Univ., Berlin, 1950-55; Dip., 1958; Dr.Phil, 1964; Habil., 1970. Career: Sr. Asst. Musicol., Inst. of Musicol., Karl-Marx Univ., Leipzig, 1964-68; Asst. Musicol., 1958, Sr. Asst. Musicol., 1968-70, Inst. of Musicol., Lectr. in Music Ethnol., 1970-75, Hon. Prof. of Music Ethnol., 1975-, Dept. of Musicol., all Humboldt Univ. Publs. incl: der Begriff des maquam in Aegypten in neuerer Zeit, 1973. Contbr. to profl. jrnls. Mbrships: Union of Comps & Musicols. of GDR; Int. Soc. for Musicol.; Int. Folk Music Coun. Recip. Hanns Eisler Prize, Serv. Medal of GDR. Address: Humboldt Univ., Bereich Musikwissenschaft, 108 Berlin, Universitätstr.7, German Dem. Repub.

ELSTE, Rudolf Otto Martin, b. 11 Sept. 1952, Bremen, German Fed. Repub. Musicologist; Music Critic. Educ: Univ. of Cologne; Rheinische Musikschule, Cologne; King's Coll., Univ. of London (CAMS). Publs: Internationale Heinrich Schütz Diskographie 1928-1972, 1972; Verzeichnis deutschprachiger Muskisoziologie, 1975. Contbr. to musical publs. incl: Grove's Dictionary, 6th ed.; Rheinische Musiker; fono forum. Mbrships: Am. Musicol. Soc.; Gesellschaft für Musikforschung; Music Lib. Assn.; Assn. for Recorded Sound Collections. Hobbies: Films; Cooking. Address: Sielwall 62, . D-2800 Bremen 1, German Ged. Repub.

ELTON, Antony, b. 3 July 1935, Romford, UK. Composer; Lecturer; Pianist; Conductor; Administrator. Educ: Magdalen Coll. Choir, Oxford Univ., 1944-51; Monckton Schl., RAM; LRAM (piano); B Mus (Dunelm), Univ. of Durham (Ext.), 1968; M Mus, Univ. of Surrey, 1977. 2 s., 2 d. Career: RAF Music Servs., 1953-55; Radio perfs. as composer & accomp., NZ Broadcasting Commission, Pianist, NZ Ballet & Kerridge-Odeon Ballet, 1957-62; Pianist on tour, Australian Ballet, 1963-64; Broadcasts, composer & cond., Australian Broadcasting Commission, 1963-65; Lectr., Music Ctr., Durham Tech. Coll., 1968-72; Chmn., Dept. of Music, Univ. of Nigeria, 1973-76. Comps. incl: The Trojan Women, Santa Claus, The Minister of Justic (operas); At Music's Sacred Sound (cantata); Mass 1972 From Nigeria (Suite), 1974; The Senate Meets (comic opera), 1975; Prelude to Midsummer, etc.; Var. songs & partsongs. Mbrships: Perf. Right Soc.; Composers Guild of GB; Musicians Union, UK; Univ. of Nigeria Assn. of Univ. Tchrs.; Chief Patron, Univ. of Nigeria Music Assn. Hons: Monckton Scholarship, 1955-57; N Arts Commission, 1977. Hobbies: Poetry; Hiking; Astronomy; Architecture. Address: Toad House, 50 Middleham Rd., Durham, DHI, 5QH, UK. 3,4,28,29.

ELTON, Christopher Douglas, b. 28 Apr. 1944, Edinburgh, UK. Pianist; Cellist; Teacher; Examiner. Educ: RAM; Recital Dip., in piano & cello; ARAM; pvte. study w. Maria Curcio. m. Elizabeth Richardson, 2 d. Career: num. broadcasts & concert apps. as soloist & as pianist in ensembles; Prof. of piano, RAM; Examiner, Assoc. Bd. of Royal Schls. of Music; adjudicator in fests. & on TV in UK & Can. Mbrships: ISM; Nat. Assn. of Tchrs. in Further & Higher Educ.; Musicians' Union. Hons: Prizewinner, Concorso Busoni; Mozart Piano Concerto Competition; Queen's Prizes, etc. Hobbies: Hill Walking; Gardening. Address: 14 Park Dr., London NW11 7 SH.

ELVIN, René, b. 20 Oct. 1896, Paris, France. Journalist; Music Critic. Educ: PhD, Univ. of Zurich, Switzerland. m. Daphne Bland, 1 s., 1 d. Career: Num. broadcasts, lectures to

Univs., etc. Contbr. to: La Revue Musicale, Paris; Schweizerische Musikzeitung, Zurich; Musical Opinion, London; L'Ordre Professionel, Geneva; Fono Forum, Hamburg; Music & Musicians, London, etc. Mbr., Critics' Circle. Hobbies: Reading; Travel; Swimming. Address: Longheath, 114 Rd., Watford, Herts. WD1 3RP, UK.

ELYN, Mark Alvin, b. 4 Feb. 1932, Seattle, Wash., USA. Basso; Opera & Concert Singer. Educ: Seattle Univ., Univ. of Wash. Voice Study w. Robert Weede. m. Jaclyn Rendall Elyn. Debut: Seattle, Wash., 1954. Career: NYC Opera, San Francisco Opera, NBC Opera, Phila. Lyric Opera; Europe, 1961-69, Leading Bass, Cologne, Munich, Stuttgart, Hamburg, Vienna, Monte Carlo, Geneva, Barcelona, Bordeaux Opera, Salome, Wash. DC, Kennedy Ctr., Othello; Assoc. Prof., Univ. of Ill. Schl. of music. Recip., 1st Prize, Seattle Music & Art Fndn., 1955. Hobbies: Swimming; Art Collecting; Travel. Address: 2012 Vawter, Urbana, IL 61801, USA.

EMERSON, Gordon C., b. 16 Sept. 1931, Keene, NH., USA. Critic; Composer; Conductor; Percussionist. Educ: BA Univ. of New Hampshire, 1955; MA, Amherst & Smith Colls., 1958; M Mus Yale Univ. Schl. of Music, 1961. m. Emily E Nanny, 1 d. Career: Tympanist, Marlboro Music Fest., Vt., 1952-56; Tympanist & Prin. Percussionist, New Haven Symph. Orch. 1958-66; Cond. New Haven Brass Ensemble, 1964-66; Res. Composer-Music Dir., Long Wharf Theatre, New Haven, 1963-72; Music Dir., New Haven Civic Orch., 1969-; Chief Music Critic, New Haven Register, 1967-; Dir. of Music, Albertus Magnus Coll., New Haven, CT, 1976. Has composed & cond. music for documentaries, TV & radio commercials; has made educl. records for Crowell-Collier & recorded as Tympanist for Richard Donovan, Mass., on CRI. Compositions publs. incl. choral arrs. Compositions recorded: num. scored for legitimate theatre inclng. Volpone, Trojan Women, Glass Menagerie. Contbr. to: New Haven Register, regularly, 1967-. Mbrships: Bds. of Dirs., New Haven Arts Coun., Neighborhood Music Schl. of Choreo-Lyric Dance Co. Hons. incl: Horatio Parker Fellowship & Woods Chandler Prize 1962. Hobbies: Painting; Furniture Design. Address: 198 Lawrence St., New Haven, CT 06511, USA.

EMERSON, June, b. 24 June 1937, Finchley, UK. Specialist Supplier of Music for Wind Instruments; Music Publisher. Educ: Studied Bassoon w. Frank Rendell & William Waterhouse; LGSM (Bassoon Tchrs.). m. Geoffrey Emerson, 1 s., 1 d. Career: 1971-, Started business as specialist supplier of wind music & since built up extensive stock w. unique catalogue; w. Geoffrey Emerson launched Emerson Edition of music for wind, 1971; As well as specially commissioned music for young players, the edition also includes difficult works such as Gordon Jacob Saxophone Quartet, reprints of music otherwise unavailable & special arrs. for wind instruments of string chmbr. music. Hobbies: Chmbr. Music; Embroidery; Finding cheaper ways of doing things; Growing potatoes; Chickens. Address: Windmill Farm, Ampleforth, Yorks., UK.

EMERSON, Roy Kenneth, b. 8 Nov. 1940, Isleworth, Middx., UK. Harpsichordist; Organist; Classical Record Producer. Educ: GTCL; LTCL, Performer; LTCL, Schl. Music. m. Ronwen Nussey. Career: Librarian, Trinity Coll., 1961-66; Orchl. Mgr., ibid, 1961-67; Lectr., ibid, 1965-67; Freelance Recording Advsr. & Specialist Ed., 1968-; Music Staff, EMI Records, 1969-; Dir. of Music, St. Barnabas Ch., Hove, 1961-69, St. Mary Magdalene Munster Square, London, 1969-; The Rosary Church, London NW1. 1973-; Fndr. & Dir., Cavendish Consort, The Doyen Consort, London Student Singers. Contbr. to A Concise History of Music, eds. of 1966, 1972; The English Chamber Orchestra, A Pictorial Review; var. profl. jrnls. Mbrships: RCO; Pres., TCL Students Assn., 1962-63; Brighton & Dist. Organists' Assn.; Pres., ibid, 1971-72. Hons: Ricordi Conducting Prize, 1965; Kennedy Scott Choral Prize; 1963; Freeman of the City of London, 1968; Freeman of the Worshipful Co. of Goldsmiths, 1968. Hobbies: Photography; Wild life. Address: 80 Darwin Ct., Gloucester Ave., London, NW1, UK.

EMERY, Valérie, b. 26 July 1916, London, UK. Antiquarian Bookseller, (specialising in music & musical literature). Educ: in Folkestone, Florence & Berlin. m. Walter Emery (dec.). Career: worked for 8 1/2 yrs. w. Otto Haas, formerly owner of Leo Liepemannsohn Antiquariat of Berlin; established Alec Clunes Music Shop, 1955, & Travis & Emery w. husband, 1960; sole owner, 1974-. Mbrships: Royal Musical Assn.; Int. Musicol. Assn.; Brit. Mus. Soc.; Antiquarian Booksellers Assn. Hobbies: Needlework; Church Architecture. Address: 17 Cecil Ct., London WC2 4EZ, UK.

EMIG, Lois Irene (Myers), b. 12 Oct. 1925, Roseville, Ohio, USA. Composer. Educ: BS, Music Educ., Ohio State Univ.,

Columbus; Grad. Work, Comp., ibid; Music Educ., Queens Coll., NYC; Piano Pedagogy, Peabody Conserv. of Music, Balt., Md.; Permanent NY State Tchrs. Cert. m. Jack Wayne Emig, 1 s., 1 d. Career: Comp., Librettist, over 150 varied publd. works for choral grps.; Pvte. Tchr., Piano & Theory; Pub. Schl. Music Tchr., vocal & instrumental until 1965. Compositions (publd.) incl: (cantatas) Come to Bethlehem, 1954; The Greatest Blessing, 1957; The Herald Angels Sing, 1958; The Children's Alleluia, 1960; Beautiful Savior, 1962; A Song of Bethlehem, 1963; The Wonder of Easter, 1970; (musical prog.) Christmas Comes to Our School, 1961. Recordings incl: Pin a Star On a Twinkling Tree; He Took a Child; Soft is the Night; All My Heart This Night Rejoices; Come, Ye Blessed. Publs. incl: Let's Learn to Count, Books I & II, 1963; The Shepherd's Carol (cantata), 1966. Contbr. to: Choir Ldr.; Choir Herald; Purdue Choral Series, etc. Mbrships: ASCAP; Delta Omicron profl. music fraternity. Hons: 1st Prize, W Va. Women's Clubs anniversary song, 1954; Lorenz anniversary contests, 1954, 64. Hobby: Collecting Am. Art Pottery. Address: 82 Fletcher Ave., Valley Stream, NY 11580, USA. 5,6,27.

EMILSON, C Rudolph, b. 20 Sept. 1939, Hammondsport, NY, USA. Solo Tubist; College Professor; Conductor. Educ: BS Mus. Ed. State Univ. Coll., Fredonia, NY, 1961; MMus Perf, Ithaca Coll., 1967; Doct. studies, Ind. Univ. Career: 1st perfs. incl. Largo for Tuba & Piano (Walter S Hartley), Trio for Tuba & 2 Vibraharps (Charles Rulon), Concerto for Tuba & Orch (Theodore Frazeur). Comps. written for and dedicated to Rudolph Emilson incl: Bivalve Suite, Sonorities for Tuba & Piano & Concerto for Tuba & Percussion Orch. by Walter S Hartley; Concerto for Tuba & Orch. by Theodore Frazeur; Trio for Tuba & 2 Vibraharps by Charles Rulon. Mbrships. incL Pi Kappa Lambda; Kappa Gamma Psi; Musicians Local 108. 1st Recip. William J Bell Memorial Scholarship, Ind. Univ., 1972-73. Address: 50 Central Ave., Fredonia, NY 14063, USA.

EMILSSON, Gudmundur, b. 24 April 1951, Reykjavik, Iceland. Conductor; Author. Educ: Music Tchr. Dip., Reykjavik Coll.of Music, 1971; BA, Music Educ., Eastman Schl. of Music, Univ. of Rochester, NY, 1975; MA, Theory, ibid, 1979. m. Agusta G Emilsson. Career: Prod. of num.,programs on music in Iceland State Radio & TV, particularly on contemporary music in Iceland. Publs: Tónmennt handa Unglingaskólum (Text book in music for secondary schls.). Contbr. as critic to Morgunbladid, Reykjavik, 1973-79. Mbrships: Selection Committee for comps. perfd. during Nordic Music Days Fest. of Contemporary Music (Scandinavia, Helsinki, Finland), 1980. Hobbies: Photography; Chess. Address: Sogavegi 224, 108 Reykjavik, Iceland.

EMRYS-ROBERTS, Kenton, b. 16 Jan. 1923, Penarth, Glam., UK. Composer. Educ: RCM. m. Jennifer Ann Pettitt, 2 s., 1 d. Career: BBC Sound Music Dept.; BBC TV Music Dept.; Dir. for Music Progs., Assoc.-Rediffusion TV; Music Advsr., J Walter Thompson Co. Comps: film scores The World of Elida, The Natural Look, Starting from Scratch, A Matter of Consequence & Tai-Chee; TV scores You're on Your Own, State of Emergency, Poldark, Count Dracula & The Mill on the Floss. Hons: Ivor Novello Award, 1978. Address: The White House, Old Avenue, W Byfleet, Surrey KT14 6AE, UK.

ENFIELD, Patrick Keen b. 14 Mar. 1929, Maldon, UK. Composer. Compositions: Sonatina, Descants Delight, descant recorder & piano; The Sea-King, Sweet Suffolk Owl, The Old Man From Lee, unison songs; Girls In The Garden, Mrs. Peck-Pidgeon, Lady Anne, Food Out Of Doors, Jim At The Corner, The Maid Of Dunstable, Sailor Harry, Last Voyage, two-part songs; Christmas Eve, three-part song; The Vernal Shower, Break, Break, Break, Mariner's Song, four-part songs. Contbr. to The Recorder & Music Mag. Mbr. Performing Right Soc. Hon: Int. Congreee for Choral Song. Tours, 1977; var. commissions. Hobbies: E Anglia past & present, Politics. Address: Cranleigh, Freehold Rd., Ipswch IP4 5HL, UK 1.

ENGEL, Francis Werner, b. 8 June 1920, Thun, Switz. Musician; Pianist; Lecturer. Educ: Conservs. of Berne & Geneva; Lehrdip.; comp. studies w. Frank Martin. Career: Sr. Prof., piano, Royal Irish Acad., Dublin, 1948-54; Prof., piano, hist. of music & art, Biel Conserv.; Dir., Biel Conserv., 1965-73; num. lectures in var. countries; recitals & broadcasts. Hobbies: Travel; Regular visits to Asia. Address: Alpenstr. 62, 2502 Biel, Switz.

ENGEL, Karl Rudolf, b. 1 June 1923, Basel, Switzerland. Concert pianist; Prof. Educ: Conserv. Basel, soloist dip.; Tchr. Trng. Coll. Paris, lic. concert. 1 s., 1 d. Career: Soloist since 1952 in Belgium, Germany, France, UK, Italy, Austria, Switzerland; perf. of all piano sonatas by Mozart and Beethoven in cycles; song evenings w. a. o. D Fischer-Dieskau; chmbr.

music w. Casals. Recordings: R. Schumann; Piano works: W A Mozart: Piano concertoes; song cycles. Mgmt: Concert dir. H U Schmid, Schmiedstr. 8, Hanover. Mbrships: Rotary Club, Honover. Hons: 2nd Prize Concours Reine Elisabeth, 1952. Hobbies: Chess; Mountain Walking. Address: Kohnestr. 25, D3 Hanover 71, W Germany.

ENGEL, Lehman, b. 1910, Jackson, Miss., USA. Composer; Conductor. Educ: Univ. of Cinn. Conserv. of Music; Cinn. Coll. of Music; Univ. of Cinn.; Juilliard Grad. Schl. Career: Cond., musical show, inclng. Lil Abner, Fanny, Wonderful Town, also recordings of musical shows & operas; has done choral, madrigal & concert work thru'out USA. Compositions incl: music for stage, screen, radio & concert hall; 5 operas (Pierrot of the Mintue, The Soldier, Malady of Love, etc.); 2 symphs.; viola concerto; str. quartet; sonatas for solo for piano; miscellaneous choral works. Publs: Musical Shows; Planning & Producing; Music for Classical Tragedy; Renaissance to Baroque; Folksongs; Poor Wayfaring Stranger; The American Musical Theatre - A Consideration. Hons: 2 Mus D., Chgo. & Cinn.; LHD. Millsaps Coll.; Special Award of Merit, Hartford Conserv.; Antoinette Perry Award, 1950-53. Address: 350 E 54th St., NYC NY/10022, USA.3.

ENGEL, Paul, b. 27 June 1920, Littlehampton, UK. Teacher; Pianist; Organist; Horn Player; Orchestral & Choral Conductor; Composer; Opera Producer. Educ: RAM; ARAM; FTCL; LGSM. (Piano Tchr.); LTCL. (Orch. Cond.); L Mus. TCL; A Mus. LCM. m. Mary Grace Hannam, 1 s., 1 d. Career: Horn Player, Royal Liverpool Phil., 1943-46, BBC Welsh Orch., 1946-50; Worthing Municipal Orch., 1950-59; Cond., Littlehampton Phil. Soc., 1944-50; Fndr., Littlehampton Players Operatic Soc. & Musical Comedy Soc.; Organist, Choirmaster, Sacred Heart Ch., 1962-64; Cond., N. Staff. Grand Opera Club, 1965; Cond., St. Cecilia Choral Soc., 1966-69; Cond., N. Staffs Opera Soc., 1970; Music Master, St. Joseph's Coll., Stoke-on-Trent, 1960-72, Wolstanton Grammar Schl., 1972-73; Hd. Music, St. Aidan's Schl., Sunderland 1973-; Vis. Tutor, Sunderland Col. of Educ., 1974. Comps. Fantasia & Fugue on B.A.C.H. Mbrships: RAM Club; Music in Educ. Sect., ISM; Nat. Operatic & Dramatic Assn.; Gilbert & Sullivan Soc.; Assn. of Asst. Masters in Secondary Schls. Hobbies: Walking; Whist; Amateur movies. Address: 70 St. Barnabas, Burnmoor, Co.Durham DH4 6EU, UK. 28,29.

ENGEL, Yehuda, b. 25 Oct. 1924, Vienna, Austria. Teacher; Conductor, Composer; Musician (piano, organ, accordion, recorders, oboe). Educ: Music Acad., Jerusalem; Music tchr. Seminar, Oranim, Music Acad., Vienna. m. Shoshana Schwarzbart, 3 c. Debut: as cond., Kibbutz Michael & Oranim. Career: Kibbutz Symph. orch.; Kibbutz Youth Symph. orch.; Kibbutz Me'uhad Choir; Haifa Chmbr. Choir; Tchr., Seminar Choir. Comps: Elegy for violin (recorded); 2 Preludes for piano; Fantasia for harp; Sinfonietta; Serenade for strgs.; Divertimento; 23rd Psalm; choral works. Mbrships: Israel Comps. League; ACUM. Hons: 1st prize, Mikve-Israel Jubilee, 1944; Nissimov prize, 1957; 1st prize, Kibbutz Comps. Contest, 1968; ACUM prize, 1975; 1st prize, 10th Int. Choir Meeting, 1977. Hobbies: Carpentry; Swimming; Tennis; Bicycling. Address: Kibbutz Ma'agen-Michael, D N Menashe, Israel.

ENGELBRECHT, Eileen, b. 24 Mar. 1945, Hull, UK. Viola Player. Educ: B Mus., London; ARCM., Viola Performing & Teaching, Piano Teaching; LRAM., Viola Teaching. m. Paul Winch. Debut: Wigmore Hall, 1968. Career: Concerti, Recitals & Chamber Music for BBC, London & the provinces; Prin. viola, Wren Orch. & London Baroque Soloists; apps. w. London Sinfonietta & other ensembles. Mbr. ISM Hons: Tagore Gold Medal, 1966; Joint 1st Prize, BBC Viola Competition, 1968. Hobbies: Boating. Address: 31 Princes Ct., Wembley, Middx. HA9 7JJ UK.

ENGELMANN, Hans-Ulrich, b.8 Sept. 1921, Darmstadt, Germany. Professor. Educ: Dip., Comp.; PhD, 1952. m. Roma Engelmann. Debut: 1945. Career: Radio, Theatre Perfs., Comp., Cond., Lectr., Film, TV Apps., 1945-: Prof. of Comp., Hochschule fur Musik, Frankfurt a.M., 1969-; Compositions incl: (publd.) operas, Der Fall van Damm, Ophelia, Revue; Doctor Faustus, Lost Shadow; Cantata, The Wall; Orchl. & stage music, etc. Recordings incl: 99 Measures for Cembalo; Leopoldskron, for chmbr. orch.; Commedia Humana. Author, Bela Bartoks Mikrokosmos, 1953. Contbr. to Melos. Mbr., ISCM. Recip. num. hons. Hobbies: Tennis; General Sports; Skiing. Address: 15 Perk Rosenhéohe, Darmstadt, German Fed. Repub. 4,19.

ENGLANDER, Lester, b. 5 June 1911, Phila., Pa., USA. Baritone. Educ: BA, Univ. of Pa.; B Mus, Curtis Inst. of Music. Debut: as recitalist, Plays & Players, Phila., 1931; as Herald in Lohengrin, San Carlo Opera Co., 1933. Career: 30 yrs. of operatic & concert work under Mitropoulos, Stokowski, Reiner, Ormandy, Leinsdorf, Bernstein, in casts inclng. Martinelli, Peerce, Steber, Pinza, Traubel, Albanese & Castagna; Dir., Lester Englander Studio of Singing; Fac. Mbr., Curtis Inst., Bronx House Music Schl., NYC & Coll. of Music, Temple Univ., Phila.; Judge, Metropolitan Opera Auditions, 1976, '77, '79. Recordings: 1st ever recoring of Mozart Requiem, w. Phila. Orch. for RCA (78 rpm, later re-released on Camden LP as 'Warwick Orch.'). Mbrships: VP Curtis Inst. Alumni. Address: 1222 Spruce St., Philadelphia, PA 19107, USA.3.

ENGLER, Ole, b. 22 Aug. 1940, Copenhagen, Denmark. Solo Trombonist. Educ: grad., 1960; State exam., Music Educ., 1965; Cond. Course, State Conserv., 1966; Musical studies, Copenhagen Univ., 1967-72. Debut: 1962. Career: Soloist, Danish Radio, Tivoli Concert Hall; External Examiner, Min. of Educ., 1966; Trombone Tchr., Danish State Conserv., 1970. Recordings: sev. Scandinavian works for trombone & orch. w. Radio Symph. Orch. & Tivoli Symph. Orch. Contbr. to Dansk Mus. Tidsskrift. Mbrships: Int. Trombone Assn.; Danish Music Educators Assn. Address: Tulipanhaven 43, 2760 Malov, Denmark.

ENGLISH, Gerald, b. 6 Nov. 1925. Lyric Tenor. Educ: RCM. m. Jennifer Ryan, 2 s., 2 d. Career incls: tours of Europe & USA; apps. at Covent Gdn.; Sadler's Wells & Glyndebourne; Prof., RCM, 1960-. Recordings: for ldng. recording firms. Address: 63 Springfield Rd., London NW8, UK.1.

ENGVALL, Anna Elisabet, b. 7 Jan. 1907, Orebro, Sweden. Church Organist; Church Warden; Pianist. Educ: Juridicial exam., Uppsala Univ., 1931; Swedish Ch. Musicians Dip., 1960. m. John Engvall. Career: Ch. Musician, Värmskogs Ch., 1958-60, Stora Skarmnas Chapel, Karsbols Chapel, Rombottens Chapel, 1949-68, Österviks Chapel, Kristinehamn, 1968-73. Contbr. to sev. profl. publs. Mbrships: Swedish Musicians Union; Österviks Chapel Fndn.; Landsrönningens Antiquarian Fndn. (Chmn.); Värmskogs Antiquarian Assn. (Sec.); Vasa Orden of Am. Hons: Swedish Tourist Assn. Medal, 1958; Värmlands Touristtraffic Union Medal, 1959; Värmlands Home Dist. Union Medal, 1962. Hobbies: Flowers; Travelling. Address: Österviks kapell, S-681 00 Kristinehamn, Sweden. 4,27,29.

ENGVALL, John Alvar Åke, b. 29 May 1902, Kristinehamn, Sweden. Clergyman; Church Organist (Organ, Piano Psalmodicon). Educ: Phil. Cand. (Music Hist. & Theory), Uppsala Univ.; Theol. Cand., Lunds Univ.; Music exam.; Clergymen's exam. m. Anna Elisabet Ericsson. Career: Clergyman, Erikstad, 1939-44, Väse, 1945-47, Värmskog, 1948-68, Österviks Chapel, Kristinehamn, 1968-; Ch. Musician, ibid, 1974-. Publs: Värmskog I-III, 1951-56; Österviks Kapell, 1962; Sveriges odekyrkor, 1972. Contbr. ot num. profl. publs. Mbrships incl: Swedish Ch. Musicians Union; Assn. of Unison Song; Värmskogs & Högeruds Antiquarian Assn. (Chmn.); BOsterviks Chapel Fndn. (Chmn.); Societas Heraldica Scandinavica. Hons. incl: Swedish Tourist Assn. Medal, 1958; Medal, Order of N Star, 1967. Hobbies: Travel; Antiquities. Address: Österviks kapell, S 681 00 Kristinehamn, Sweden. 3,23,29.

ENRICO, Eugene Joseph, b. 25 July 1944, Red Lodge, Mont., USA. Musicologist. Educ: PhD, Univ. of Mich., 1970; Postdoctl. Rsch. Fellow, Smithsonian Instn., 1973. m. Sherry Lee Enrico. Career: Dir. of concerts broadcast nationally by Radio Smithsonian; Cond. or Perf. on Recorder, concerts in Wash. DC & Louisville, Ky. Publs: The Orchestra at San Petronio, 1976; The Trumpet Music of Giuseppe Torelli, 1977. Contbr. articles on music of wind instruments to Ency. Britannica, 15th ed. Mbrships: Am. Musicol. Soc.; Am. Musical Instrment Soc.; Coll. Music Soc. Hons. incl: Ford Fndn. Rackham Prize Fellow, 1968-70. Address: Schl. of Music, Univ. of Okla., Norman, OK 73019, USA.

ENRIQUEZ, Manuel, b. Ocotlan, Mexico. Composer; Educator. Educ: Juilliard Schl. of Music, NYC. Career: Concertmaster, Guadalajara Symph. Orch., 5 yrs.; participant in num. fests. inclng. Donaueschinger Fest., Germany, 1969, Autumn Fest., Warsaw, & Tanglewood (NJ) Fest., tours in Italy, France, Austria, Germany, The Netherlands, Switz., UK, Belgium & Poland, 1967-. currently Dir., Nat. Conserv. of Music, Mexico City. Compositions incl: Musica para Federico Silva (Music for F. Silva). Hons. incl: Guggenheim Fellowship, 1971; US State Dept. Fellowship, 1965; Sourazky Prize, 1972; Composition Prize, Tanglewood Fest., NJ.

ENTREMONT, Philippe, b. 7 June 1934, Rheims, France. Pianist. Educ: Paris Conservatorie. m. Andrée Ragot, 1 d., 1 s. Career: Concertizing for the last 22 yrs. all over the world;

Cond. & Musical Dir., Wiener Kammerorch., 1976-. Recordings on CBS. Pres., l'Academie Internationale de Musique Maurice Ravel. Hons: Queen Elizabeth of Belgium, 1952; Grand Prix Marguerite Long-Jacques Thibaud, 1953; Harriet Cohen Piano Medal, 1953; Grand Prix du Disque, 1967, '68, '69, '70; Edison Award, 1968; Nom. for Grammy Award, 1972; Chevalier de l'ordre National du Merité; Chevalier de la Legion d'Honneur, 1978. Hobby: Golf. Mgmt: Maurice Werner, 11 Avenue Delcasse, 75008, Paris, France. Address: 14 Rue d'Alger, 75001 Paris, France. 2.

EOSZE, László, b. 17 Nov. 1923, Budapest, Hungary. Art Director. Educ: PhD in Aesthetics & Literature. Div., 2 c. Career: Music Tchr. & Pianist; Concerts in Hungary & Europe, 1946-51. Publs: 14 books inclng. Kodály Zoltán élete és munkássága (Life & Work of ZK), 1956; Kodály Zoltán élete Képekben (k's life in Pictures), 1957; Az opera utja (History of Opera), 1960; Giuseppe Verdi, 1961; 2nd ed., 1966; enlarged, 1975; Zoltán Kodály, His Life & Work in Engl., 1962, German, 1964; Kodály Zoltán, 1967. Kodály. His Life in Pictures, 1971, Engl. & German. Richard Wagner, 1969; Richard Wagner. Eine Chronik seines Lebens und Schaffens, 1969; essays & articles in var. langs. Contbr. to num. profl.publs. Mbr., Soc. of Hungarian Musicians. Mgmt: Editio Musica Budapest. Address: Attila ut 133 1012 Budapest, Hungary.

EPPERLY, Glenn Barry, b. 29 Nov. 1944, Wichita, Kan., USA. Conductor; Arranger; Pianist. Educ: B Mus. Ed., Okla. State Univ., Stillwater, 1966; M Mus Ed., ibid, 1968; D Mus. Arts, Univ. of Southern Calif., LA, 1973. m. Alice Jane Riemer. Career: Prod., Arr. & Cond., Walt Disney Corp., 1969-71; Cond., The US Army Chmbr. Orch., 1971-. Recordings: The Singers of Stillwater (Choral Selections), 1968. Mbrships: Am. Symph. Orch. League; Am. Choral Dirs. Assn.; Music Educators Nat. Conf. Hons: Teaching Assistantships, Okla. State Univ., 1966-68 & Univ. of Southern Calif., 1970-71; Num. minor awards. Hobbies: Translating French Music History Books; Tennis; Sailing. Address: US Army Band, Bldg. T-71, Ft. Meyer, VA 22211, USA.

EPPERSON, Gordon, b. 18 Jan. 1921, Williston, Fla., USA. Cellist; Professor of Music. Educ: Mus B, Coll. Conserv. of Music, Univ. of Cinn., 1941; Mus M, Eastman Schl. of Music, 1949; Doct. Musical Arts, Boston Univ., 1960. m. Mary Elizabeth Pearson, 2 d. Debut: NYC, 1956; London, 1971. Concert tours, USA, Can. & Europe, 1952-; Soloist w. major orch.; num. perfs. for TV; Prof. of Music, Univ. of Ariz., Tucson; num. master classes all over the world; Prod., educl. video tapes. Recordings: Sonatas for Cello & Piano by Rachmaninoff, Muczynski, Barber & Martinu. Publs. incl: Manual of Essential Cello Technique; The Musical Symbol, 1967; Ed., Yampolsky, Violoncello Technique. Contbr. to: Ency. Britannica; profl. jrnls. Mbrships incl: Violoncello Soc., NYC. Hons: Spaulding Fellow, Boston Univ., 1958-59. Mgmt: New Era Int. Concerts, London. Address: 3248 N. Olsen Ave., Tucson, AZ 85719, USA.

EPPSTEIN, Hans, b. 25 Feb. 1911, Mannheim, Germany. Teacher, Musicology. Educ: PhD, Bern, 1934; PhD, Uppsala, 1966. m. Lilli Lipsky, 1 s. Career: Docent, Musicol., Uppsala Univ., Sweden. Publs: Nicolas Gombert als Motettenkomponist, 1935; Brahms, 1948; Sdien u..ber J S Bachs Sonaten für ein Melodieinstrument & obligates Cembalo, 1966; Heinrich Schütz, 1972. Contbr. to: Die Musikforschung; Svenskl tidskrift für musikforskning. Hobbies: Gardening; Wandering. Address: 21 Törnrosvagen, 182 75 Stocksund, Sweden.

EPSTEIN, David M., b. 3 Oct. 1930, NYC, USA. Composer; Conductor; Professor. Educ: A B Antioch Coll., 1952; Mus M., New Engl. Conserv. of Music, 1953; MFA Brandeis Univ., 1954; PhD, Princeton Univ., 1968. m. Anne Merrick, 2 d. Debut: Cleveland Orch., 1961; Career: Prof. of Music, MIT; Guest Cond., Bavarian Radio Symph., Berlin Radio Orch., Vienna Tonkunstlerorchester, Czech Radio Orch., RPO, etc. Israel Broadcasting Orch., Boston Symph. Chamber Players, NYC Ctr., etc. Music Dir., Cond., Harrisburg Symph. Orch. 1974-. Compositions incl: String Trio; Sonority - Variations for Orchestra; Fantasy Variations for Solo Viola or Violin; The Seasons; String Quartet, 1971; Concord Chorale, 1978. music for theatre, film & TV. Recordings incl: Bloch - Concerto Grosso for String Orch. & Piano Obbligato, Czech Radio Orch.; Music for Synthesizer & 6 Instruments. Publ: Beyond Orpheus, Studies in Musical Structure, 1979. Contbr. to var. profl. jrnls. Mbrships. incl: Am.Symph. Orch. League (chmn., Univ. Orch. sec., 1958-60); Am. Soc. Univ. Composers (Nat. Coun., 1968-70). Hons. incl: Arthur Shepherd Prize, 1965; Ford Fndn. Recording Grant, 1971&1976. Hobbies incl: Skiing; Sailing. Mgmt: Thea Dispeker Mgmt., 59 E 54th St., NY, NY 10022, USA. Address: 54 Turning Mill Rd., Lexington, MA 02173, USA. 2,24,28.

EPSTEIN, Dena J., b. 30 Nov. 1916, Milwaukee, Wis., USA. Music Librarian. Educ: BA Music, Univ. of Chgo., 1937; BS Lib. Sci., Univ. of Ill., 1939; MA, ibid., 1943. m. Morton B Epstein, 1 s., 1 d. Career: Cataloguer in Art & Music, Univ. of Ill., 1939-43; Sr. Music Libn., Newark, NJ. Pub. Lib., 1943-45; Music Cataloguer, & Reviser, Music Sect., Copyright Cataloguing Div., Lib. of Congress, 1946-48; Curator of Recordings & Asst. Music Libn., Univ. of Chgo., 1964-. Publs. incl: Music Publishing in Chicago before 1871, 1969; Sinful Tunes & Spirituals, Black Folk Music to the Civil War, 1977. Contbr. to profl. jrnls. Mbrships incl: Music Lib. Assn. (Pres.) Recip., var. grants. Hobbies: Singing; Playing Piano Duets; Cooking; Reading. Address: 5039 S. Ellis Ave., Chgo., IL 606L5, USA.

EPSTEIN, Eli K, b. 30 July 1958, Phila., Pa., USA. French Horn Player. Educ: Univ. of Pa.; Settlement Music Schl., Phila.; studies w. Anton Ryva, John Simonelli, Herbert Pierson. Debut: w. Phila. Orch., 1969. Career: Soloist w. Phila. Orch. 4 times; Mbr., Settlement Music Schl. Woodwind Quintet. Mbr., Int. Horn Soc. Hons: 1st recip., Anton Horner Mem. Scholarship, 1971 & 72; recip. grant for HS instrumentalist (given to Settlement Music Schl. by Ford Fndn.), 1971-75. Hobbies: Classical studies; Horticulture; Swimming. Address: 618 Spruce St., Philadelphia, PA 19106, USA.

ERB, Donald James, b. 17 Jan. 1927, Youngstown, Ohio, USA. Composer. Educ: BSc., Kent State Univ., 1950; MMus., Cleveland Inst. of Music, 1953; DMus, Ind. Univ., 1964. Compositions (publd) incl: Christmasmusic; New England's Prospect; Autumnmusic; Z Milosci Do Warszawy; Trio for Two; Sonneries for Brass Choir; Four for Percussion; The Purple-Roofed Ethical Suicide Parlor. Compositions Recorded: Sonata for Harpsichord & String Quartet; Three Pieces for Brass Quintet & Piano; Phantasma; String Trio; Diversion for Two; In No Strange Land; Reconnaissance; Symphony of Overtures; The Seventh Trumpet; concerto for Solo Percussionist & Orchestra; Basspiece; VII Miscellaneous; Harold's Trip to the Sky; Three Pieces for Brass Quintet & Piano. Contbr. to: Encyclopedia Britannica. Mbrships: Am. Music Ctr.; Broadcast Music, Inc.; Cleveland Composers Guild. Hons. incl: Cleveland Arts Prize, 1966; Rockefeller Fndn. Composer-in-Res., Dallas Symph. Orch., 1968-69. Address: 3968 Navahoe, Cleveland Hts., OH 44121, USA, 2.

ERBER, James Edwin, b. 14 Feb. 1951, London, UK. Composer; Editor. Educ: External Lic. in flute tchng., Trinity Coll., London; BA, MPhil, Univ. of Sussex; MA, Univ. of Nottingham. Career: Music Ed., Peters Edition Ltd., London, 1976-79; Freelance Ed. for sev. London music publrs., translator for sev. music publrs & BBC, 1979-; Dir., Gagliano Consort (baroque vocal & instrumental ensemble), 1977-. Comps: Seguente, for oboe & piano; Music for string orch.; Ed., Marco da Gagliano - Veni creator spiritus, Magnificat, La Dafne, Responsories for Holy Week; Ed., Carlo Wiseman, Trio for two flutes & cello - continuo realisation; Ed., G F Handel, Suite no. 3 in D minor, Suite no. 6 in F sharp minor. Publs. incl: Articles in Opera. Contbr. to: Time Out; The Consort; Sleeve notes to Transit, by Brian Ferneyhough. Mbrships: Royal Musical Assn.; Soc. for the Promotion of New Music. Hobbies: Reading; Walking; Cycling; Woodwork; Tearing apart the contemporary music establishment. Address: The Garden Flat, 49 Belsize Ave., London N13 4TL, UK.

ERBSE, Heimo, b. 27 Feb. 1924, Rudolstadt, Germany. Composer. Educ: Studied comp., conducting, opera directing & flute, Musikhochschule, Weimar & W Berlin. Debut: Berlin, German Fed. Repub., 1951. Compositions incl: Chmbr. music: Aphorismen, for flute, violin & piano, 1954; Drei Lieder (Eduard Mörike), for baritone & piano, 1959; Quartett, for woodwinds, 1961; Drei Studien, for flute & guitar, 1972; Nachklänge (Joseph von Eichendorff), song cycle, 1973: Choral music: DRei Chöre zu sechs Stimmen, 1971; Orchl. works: Sinfonie in vier Sätzen, 1963-64; Das Hohelied Salomo's (translation from Luther), 1968-69; For String & Wind Players, 1970-71; Zweite Sinfonie, 1969-70: Tripelkonzert, 1972-73; Stage works: Julietta (opera), 1956-57; Ruth (ballet), 1958; Der Herr in Grau (comic opera), 1965-66. Hons. incl: Beethoven Prize, Bonn, 1961: Appreciation award for msuic, Austrian Min. for Educ. & Art, 1973. Hobbies: Moutain climbing; Skiing; Sci. Address: Haus Neu Kamm, A 5660 Taxenbach-Eschenau, Austria.

ERDELYI, Miklós, b. 9 Feb. 1928, Budapest, Hungary. Conductor. Educ: Acad. of Music, Budapest. m. Katalin Miklos. Debut: Budapest Opera Comic. Career: Cond. of the State Opera House; Sev. concerts; Radio & TV appearances in Hungary & abroad (England, Italy, German Fed. Repub., Holland, USA, USSR, etc.); apps. at fests. in Ascona, Montreux, Athens. Recordings: Bartok: Four orch. pieces; Two portraits; II suite; many operas of Mozart, Verdi, Puccini; Pieces of Bach, Handel, etc. Publs: Schubert Biography, 1963.

Contbr. to New Hungarian Qtly. Hons: Merited Artist; Liszt Prize & Kossuth-Prize, 1975. Hobbies: Travel; Architecture. Address: Tétényi vt. 7a, 1115 Budapest, Hungary.

ERDMANN, Dietrich, b. 20 July, 1917, Bonn, Germany. Composer; Professor. Educ: High Schl. for Music, Berlin (comp., cond., cello). m. Gerti Erdmann, 2 d., 1 s. Debut: Berlin. Career: perfs. at concerts, fest., on radio in Germany & other countries, 1938-; High Schl. Prof. Comps. incl: works for orch., chmbr. music, songs, cantatas. var. recordings of own works. Mbrships: GEMA; VDMK; Comps. Soc.; Studio Neue Musik, Berlin. Address: Biesalskistr. 12, 1000 Berlin 37, German Fed. Repub.

ERDMANN, Gunther, b. 26 July 1939, Oberdorla bei Mühlhausen, Germany. Composer; Shoemaker. Educ: Dip. (choir direction, piano, comp.), Hochschule für Musik Hanns Eisler, Berlin, 1960-66. m. Brigitte Erdmann. Career: Dir., children's & youth ensembles at Haus der Jungen Talente, Berlin, 1965-; freelance composer, 1966-. Comps. incl: works for adult, youth & children's ensembles; film music; choral works; songs; music for TV & radio; orchl. & chmbr. music. num. recordings of own comps. Contbr. to Musik in der Schule. Mbrships: Candidate of the Central Committee of the Composers' Union; Chorausschusses der DDR. num hons. & prizes. Hobby: Painting. Address: Grünbergerstr. 8, 1034 Berlin, German Dem. Repub.

EREDE, Alberto, b. 8 Nov. 1908, Genoa, Italy. Conductor. Career: Guest Cond., Berlin Phil, Vienna Phil., Orchestre du Conservatoire, Orchestre Nat., Paris, New Philharmonia, London, Prague Phil., den Hague Residentie, Budapest Phil., Suisse Romande Orch., S. Cecilia Rome, NBC of Toscanini, NYC, State Opera, Vienna, German Opera, Berlin, Covent Garden, London, Colon Theatre, Buenos Aires, num. Fests.; Cond., La Scala, Milan, 6 seasons; Musical Dir., reorganized Radio-TV Turin Symph., 1945; Musical Dir., Cond., New London Opera Co.; Leading Cond., Italian Opera, Met. Opera, NYC; Gen. Music Dir., Deutsche Oper am Rhein, 5 yrs.; Cond. all Lohengrin Perfs., Bayreuth, 1968. Recordings: num., inclng. 14 full operas. Address: c/o S A Gorlinsky Ltd., 35 Dover St., London W1X 4NJ,UK.

ERHARDT, Ludwik Jerzy, b. 29 Apr. 1934, Koscieszki, Poland. Music Writer. Educ: Warsaw Univ. m. 1) Krystyna Meissner, 2) Anna Ciechanowicz. Career: Music Critic, Przeglad Kulturalny mag., 1954; Music Commentator of the Polish TV, 1958-70; Music Critic of the following mags. & newspapers: Przeglad Kulturalny, Express Wieczorny, Sztandar Mlodych, Kultura; Editl. Staff, music mag., Ruch Muzyczny, 1957-; Asst. Ed., ibid, 1961; Ed., 1969. Publs: Balety Strawinskiego (The Ballets of Stravinsky), 1962; Johannes Brahms, 1969; Papierowe Nosy (The Noses of Papers), essays, 1970; Ponizej Muzyki (Below Music), essays, 1972; Polish Music, 1974; Spotkania z Pendereckim (Encounters w. Penderecki), 1974; Igor Stravinsky - A Biography (in prep.). Mbr., Polish Comps. Union. Address: Izabelii 2/10, 01-738 Warsaw, Poland.

ERICKSON, Frank, b. 1 Sept. 1923, Spokane, Wash., USA. Composer of Band Music. Educ: B Mus., 1950, M Mus., 1951, Univ. of So. Calif. m. Mary McGroarty, 3 s. Comps: 100 publd. original works for concert band inclng. two symphs., a concerto for Alto Sax. & Band (dedicated to Sigurd Rascher) and a Double Concerto for Trumpet, Trombone & Band. Most popular works: Toccata for Band; Air for Band; Balladair; Fantasy for Band; Symphonette for Band; Lyric Overture Arietta for Winds & Festive Winds. Mbrships: ASCAP; Pi Kappa Lambda; Phi Mu Alpha; Am. Bandmasters Assn.; Phi Beta Mu. Hobby: Swimming. Address: 7404 Crisp, Raytown, MO 64133,USA.

ERICKSON, Gordon McVey, b. 30 July 1917, Bismarck, ND, USA. Percussionist; Musician. Educ: Univ. of ND, Grand Forks, 1935-42; BS, Black Hills State Coll., Spearfish, SD, 1961. Career: Tympanist, Grand Forks Symph. Orch., 1932-42; has made var. solo apps., also plays other percussion instruments (mallets, marimba, xylophone, etc.); has made local TV apps.; currently w. FargoMoorhead Symph. & Opera Co. orchs. Has collected & compiled Standard Repertoire manuscript I Ballet, II Opera (donated to Univ. of ND Music Dept., Grand Forks). Hobbies: Copying & Collecting Symphonic Music. Address: 356 7th Ave. S, Fargo, ND 58102, USA.

ERICKSON, Robert, b. 7 Mar. 1917, Marquette, Mich., USA. Composer. Educ. incl: pvte. study of piano, violin, music theory, canon & fugue & composition w. var. tchrs.; BA & MA, Hamline Univ., St. Paul, Minn. Compositions (recorded): Ricercar a 3 (for contrabass), 1969; Ricercar a 5 (for trombones), 1970; Oceans (for trumpet), 1972; The End of the Mime of Mick, Nick & the Maggies (Joyce) (for mixed chorus), 1974. Compositions (publd.), incl: Cradle (for 3 sets of tube

drums & instrumental ensemble), 1971; Summer Piece (for 2-channel tape); Second Cradle (for 4 sets of tube drums & instrumental ensemble), 1972; LOOPS for instruments (clarinet, trumpet, alto saxophone, bassoon, marimba & flute), 1972-73; Percussion LOOPS (solo percussion), 1973; Summer Music (for violin & tape), 1974. Publs: The Structure of Music -A Listener's Guide to Melody & Counterpoint, 1955 (paper ed., 1957); Sound Structure in Music, 1974. Contbr. to many profl. jrnls. Hons. incl: Mu Sigma Award (Marion Bauer Prize) for Str. Quartet No. 2, 1957; Fellow, Inst. for Creative Arts, Univ. of Calif., 1968. Address: 1849 Crest Dr., Encinitas, CA 92024,USA.

ERICSON, Barbro. Operatic Mezzosoprano. Debut: as Eboli in Don Carlos, Stockholm. Career: Prin. singer, Royal Opera, Stockholm; apps. at Metropolitan Opera, NY, Berlin, Paris, Bayreuth, Salzburg, Zürich, Barcelona & in Germany, France, Italy & Netherlands; roles incl. (Wagner) Brangäne, Fricka, Ortrud, Kundry, Erda, Waltraute, Venus; (Verdi) Amneris, Azucena, Eboli, Quickly, Ulrica; also Carmen, Marie (Wozzeck), Klytemnestra (Elektra) etc. Mgmt: Artistsekretariat Ulf Törnqvist, Norrtullsgatan 26, tr.4, 11345 Stockholm, Sweden. Address: c/o mgmt.

ERICSON, Eric Gustaf, b. 26 Oct. 1918, Sweden. Choral Conductor; Professor. m. Monica Ericson-Spangenberg, 4 c. Career: Organist, Choir Master & Leading Musician var. chs. since 1943; Lectr., Conservatoire of Music, Stockholm, 1953-; LMA, 1961; Titular Prof., 1968; Countless radio progs. worldwide; Toured USA w. OD & USSR w. Chmbr. Choir of Stockholm Conservatoire; Conducted Ingmar Bergman's prod. of The Magic Flute by Mozart for TV; Conducted at Festivals in Venice; Florence; Bratislava & Warsaw & ISCM World Festivals in Stockholm, Num. recordings. Publs. incl: Kordirigering w. G Ohlin & L Spangberg, 1974. Hons. incl: Deutscher Schallplatten Preis, 1973; The Edison Prize, Holland, 1972. Address: Tegnergatan 4, Box 45054, 10430 Stockholm, Sweden.

ERIKSEN, Jostein, b. 7 July 1926, Fluberg, Norway. Opera Singer. Educ: Music & Vocal studies, Conserv. of Music & State Theatre Schl., Norway & in var. European Centres. m., 1 c. Debut: Osla Domkirke, 1956. Career: Tenor Soloist, The Norwegian Opera, 1958-; Var. concert apps. on Radio & TV in Norway, Sweden & Denmark; Fest. apps. incl. Bergen Music Fest. Mbrships: Pres., Norwegian Opera Singers Assn., 1975; Norwegian Musicians Assn.; Int. Music Fedn.; Norwegian Vocal Artists Assn.; Artists Assn., Oslo. Address: 21B Jarun, 1342 Jar, Norway.

ERIKSEN, Richard Dahl, b. 1 Mar. 1918, Detroit, Mich., USA (Danish citizen). Violist. Educ: Royal Danish Conserv. of Music, Copenhagen, 1935-38; Dips. in Violin & Viola, 1942; studied w. René Benedetti, Paris, France, 1947. m. Grethe Krogh, 1 d. of former marriage. Career: Violin Player, Tivoli Concerthall Orch., Copenhagen, 1942-48; Violist, Danish Radio Symph. Orch., ibid, 1948-; Fndr., Musica Vitalis Str. Quartet, 1951-; Tchr., Musical Handwriting, Royal Danish Acad. of Music, Copenhagen, 1968-. Recordings incl: Str. Quartetes of Carl Nielsen & Vagn Holmboe. Address: Primulavej 13, 2720 Vanlose, Denmark.

ERIKSSON, Björn, b. 9 Apr. 1927, Bromma, Stockholm, Sweden. Chamber Musician; Viola & Violin Teacher. Educ: Studied Violin & Viola w. Prof. Tage Broström, Stockholm; Studied Viola, Royal Acad. of Music, Stockholm; studied Viola w. Prof. Frederick Riddle, London, UK. m. (Siv Maria) Birgitta Eriksson, 3 d. Career: Mbr., Stockholm Phil. Orch., 1950-71; Tchr., Täby Community Music Schl., 1971-. Mbrships: Viola Rsch. Soc.; ESTA. Hobby: Outdoor life around holiday mountain cabin in Northern Dalecarlia. Address: Runmästarvägen 24, S-18342 Täby, Sweden.

ERIKSSON, John M, b. 1 July 1923, Krylbo, Sweden. Trumpeter; Brass Teacher; Band Director. Educ: Royal High Schl. of Music. m. Gunnel Eriksson, 3 c. Debut: Norrkopius Symph. Career: Trumpet Soloist, Norrkopings Symph., 1946; III Trumpet, Cornet Soloist, Stockholm Phil., 1954; Trumpet Soloist, Musica Nova, 1963-72; Brass Tchr., Royal High Schl. of Music, & Music Educ. Inst., Stockholm; Ldr., Stockholms Brassens. Recordings: w. Stockholm Phil.; w. Musica Nova. Recip. Govt. Scholarship. 1970. Hobby: Sport. Mgmt: Stockholms Konsertforening. Address: 9 Toresjovagen, 13500 Tyreso, Sweden.

ERLING, Ole, b. 29 July 1938, Copenhagen, Denmark. Conductor; Organist; Music Producer. m. Annalise, 2 c. Debut: 1959. Career: Free lance organist; sev. apps., Danish Radio & TV; Music Prod., Gramophone records & duplicating systems for tapes & cassettes. Recordings: 8 long-playing albums; 28

music cassettes. Mbr., Int. Fedn. of Gramophone Prods. Hobbies: Sound & tapetechnics; Swimming. Address: Roerkaer no. 1, 2760 Masloev, Denmark.

ERMOLENKO, George, b. 19 Feb. 1925, Rostov on Don, USSR. Violinist. Educ: Musical Coll.; Moscow Conservatorium of Music. m. Ludmila Ermolenko, 1 s. Career: 1st Violin, Moscow Bolshoi Theatre Orch., 1950-61; 1st Violin, Moscow State Symph. Orch., 1961-75; 1st Violin, Str. Quartet of Moscow Symph. Orch., 1964-75. Recordings: Num. tapes of the Str. Quartet for radio transmission, USSR & abroad; Sonatas for Violin, Piano & other Chamber Ensembles. Hobbies: Chess; Swimming. Address: 8/5 - 11 Balfour St., Carlton, NSW 2218, Australia.

ERNESAKS, Gustav, b. 12 Dec. 1908, Perila, Estonia. Conductor; Composer; Teacher of Music. Educ: Dip., State Common Tech. High Schl. 1928; Tchrs. Dip., Tallinn Conserv., 1931; Comps. Dip., ibid., 1934. M. Stella M..erjam (dec.), 3 s. Career: Music Tchr., var. schls., 1931-; Lectr. & Tutor of Choral Cond., Tallinn State Conserv., 1935-; Chief Choirmaster, State Academic Male Choir of Estonia, 1944-; Prof., 1946. Comps. incl: (operas) Holy Lake, 1946; Stormy Coast, 1949; Hand-in-Hand, 1955; Baptism of Fire, 1957; Suitors from Mulgimaa, 1959; about 400 choral songs, (many recorded). Publ: Mouth Sings, Heart Worries. Mbr., profl. assns. Hons. incl: People's Artist, USSR, 1956; Lenin Prize, 1970; Order of Lenin, 1974. Hobbies: Literature; Sport; Chess. Address: 10 Oru St., 200010 Tallinn, Estonia, USSR.

ERNEST, David John, b. 16 May 1929, Chgo., Ill., USA. Music Department Chairman; Musician, Oboe, English Horn. Educ: BMEd., Chgo. Musical Coll., Ill.; MS., Univ. of Ill., Urbana; Sorbonne, Univ. of Paris, France; EdD., Univ. of Colo., Boulder. m. Prudence Ellene Michael, 4 s. Career: Soloist, Orchl. Perf., Tchr., 21 yrs.; Clinician, Adjudicator, var. Music Competitions. Compositions: Sonatine, oboe & string orch.; folk opera Ten Year Thunder; num. smaller works, arrs., transcriptions. Publs: Use of the Opaque Projector in Improving Error Recognition in Classes of Music Theory, 1967; Chmn., Dept. of Music & Prof., St. Cloud State Univ., 1963-. Contbr. to: Jrnl. of Rsch. in Music Educ.; Music Educators Jrnl.; Instrumentalist; Minneapolis Tribune; Gopher Music Notes. Mbrships: Chapt. Pres., Phi Delta Kappa; Charter Mbr., Phi Kappa Lambda; MENC; NEA; Phi Mu Alpha Sinfonia; Kappa Delta Pi; Galpin Soc.; num. other profl. orgs. Recip. num. hons. Hobbies: Numismatics; Philately; Fishing; Hunting. Address: Crest Rd., Rte. 5, St. Cloud, MN 56301, USA. 28.

ERNST, Robert, b. 9 June 1900, München, Germany. Comp. Educ: Pvte. study. widower, 1 d. Debut: concertoes. Career: Radio prod. Comp. incl: Songs, choirs (cycles); wind instruments; orch. and organ comp. Recordings: Tapes made in Austria, Germany, Holland. Mbrships: AKM, Austria, OGLM; OKB. Hons. incl: Silver Schubert Medal, Vienna Song Soc. 1944; Stimulation Prize, Austria 1960; Hon. mbr. Josef Weinheben Soc., Vienna. Address: Kupelwiesegasse 29/5, 1130 Vienna, Austria.

ERÖD, Iván, b. 2 Jan. 1936, Budapest, Hungary. Composer; Concert pianist; Professor of Theory & Compositon. Educ: Budapest Acad. of Music w. Ferenc Szabo (comp.), Pal Kadosa (piano): Vienna Acad. of Music w. Karl Schiske (comp.), Richard Hauser (piano) 1961; m. Marie-Luce Guy, 1 s., 2 d. Debut: Budapest, 1956 (both as comp. & pianist). Career: Prof. of Theory & Comp., Hochschule für Musik und Aarstellende Kunst, Graz, Austria. Concert, recordings & broadcasts in 20 countries. Comps: Die Seidenraupen (3 act opera), performed at Vienna Fest, 1968; Sonata für Orchester; 4 piano pieces; 4 pieces for Str. Quartet; 3 movements for violoncello & orch.; Ricercare ed Aria for wind quartet; Sonata for violin & piano; string quartet; Concerto for Violin & orch.; Concerto for piano & orch.; Sonata for Orch.; La doncella, el marinero y el estudiante (short opera); Recordings: 7 LPs w. Rudolf Schock , featuring Lider of Schubert, Schumann, Brahms, Dvorak, R Strauss, Pierrot Lunaire of Schonbérg. Mbrships: AKM; Austrian Comps. Assn.; Bd. mbr., Dramatic Writers & Comps. Assn.; Control Coun., Literar-Mechana; Austro-Mechana; Working Community of Austrian Music Tchrs. Hons: Bosendorfer Prize, 1961; Busoni Prize (Bolanno), 1962; Rome Fellowship, 1961; Fellowship of the Vienna Zentralsparkasse, 1964; Korner Prize, 1970; Austrian Staatpreis for Opera, 1970; Prize of the City of Vienna, 1974. Hobbies: Family; Theatre; Literature; Friends; Walking; Pipes; Gastronomy; Study & application of Scientology. Address: A-8043 Graz, Hans Friz-Weg 6, Austria.

EROS, Peter, b. 22 Sept. 1932, Budapest, Hungary. Symphony Conductor. Educ: Piano, compositon, orch. direction, Franz Liszt Music Acad., Budapest. m. Georgette Weiser, 2 c. Career: Assoc. Cond., Concertgebouw Orch.,

Amsterdam, 1960-65; Chief Cond., Malmo Symph., 1967-69; Music Dir., San Diego Symph. Orch., Calif., 1972-; Guest Cond. w. Chgo., Cleveland, San Fran., St. Louis, Denver, Rochester, Indpls., Dallas Symphs.; also NY Mozart Fest. & Bach Fest.; Concertgebouw Amsterdam; Rotterdam Phil.; RPO, London; Liverpool Phil.; Vienna Radio; Vienna Summer Fest.; Israel Fest.; Hamburg Symph.; Stuttgart Symph.; Madrid Nat. Orch.; Barcelona, Mex. City, Rio de Janeiro; 3 Australian Tours, 3 S African Tours, etc. Hons: Headline of the Yr., San Diego Press, 1973. Hobbies: Films; Reading; Gourmet Cooking. Mgmt: Herbert Barret Mgmt., NYC. Address: PO Bx 3175, San Diego, CA 92103 USA. 2,9.

ERRANTE, F Gerard, b. 11 Jan. 1941, NYC, USA. College Professor; Clarinettist. Educ: BA, Queens Coll., NYC, 1963; MMus, Univ. of Wis.-Madison, 1964; A MusD, Univ. of Mich., 1970. m. Barbara Edwards. Debut: as Solo Clarinettist w. Norfolk Symph. Orch., 1973. Career: Assoc. Prof. of Music, Norfolk State Coll., Va., 1970-; Prin. Clarinettist, Norfolk Symph. Orch., 1971-; Va. Opera Assn., 1974-; Assoc. Dir., Norfolk Chmbr. Consort, 1970-. Comps: Souvenirs de Nice for clarinet & piano, 1975. Recordings: The Dissolution of the Serial by Sydney Hodkinson, CRI SD-292. Publs: A Selective Clarinet Bibliography, 1973. Contbr. to profl. jrnls. Mbrships incl: SE Reg. Chmn., Int. Clarinet Soc.; Nat. Assn. of Coll. Wind & Percussion Instructors; MENC. Hons. incl: Tchr. of the yr., Norfolk State Coll., 1972-73. Hobbies: Swimming; Hiking; Cycling; Tennis. Address: 1444 Melrose Parkway, Norfolk, VA 23508,USA.7.

ERSÉUS, (Erik) Torsten (Eugen), b. 3 Sept. 1923, Grycksbo, Sweden. Educational Adviser in Music. Educ: Primary Schl. Tchrs. Exam, 1947; Music Tchrs. Exam, Music High Schl., 1964; music studies, Gothenberg Univ. m. Anita Erséus, 3 s., 1 d. Career: Primary Schl. Tchr., 1948-57; Educational Advsr. in Music, Borås Local Educ. Authority, 1957-64; Gothenburg Local Educ. Auth., 1964-; Publrs. & Ed., Musik & Skola Förlag Ab. Mölndal, 1957-75. Compositons: Choral music; educl. music (instrumental & vocal). Publs: Ed., Musik & Skola, 1957-66; Fackläraren (mag. for tchrs. in specialised subjects), 1972-. Mbrships: Bd., Nat. Swedish Assn. of Music Tchrs., & Swedish Union of Specialist Tchrs.; Swedish Union of Music Educ.; Scandinavian Union of Music Educ.; Int. Soc. of Music Educ. Hobby: Art (especially Drawing). Address: Lekevallsgatan 10, S-431 39 Möndal, Sweden.

ERSKINE, William Robin, b. 27 June 1943, Glasgow, UK. Teacher; Organist; Conductor; Composer. Educ: B Mus, Glasgow Univ.; ARCO, 1963; Acad. d'Orgue, St. Maximin, France, 1969. m. Marliese Häuber. Career incls: Tchr. Galsgow Schls., 1967-71. Paisley Grammar Schl. 1971-; Cond. The Albion Singers (BBC), 1963; Organist & Choirmaster, St. James' Ch., Paisley, 1966; Fndr. & Dir., Paisley Brass Ensemble, 1972-; num. recitals as organist & cond.; radio & TV apps. Comps. incl: Organ Preludes & Partita; Fugue for Brass Quintet, Fanfares for Brass & Organ. Recordings: 2 w. Glasgow Univ. Chapel Choir. Contbr. to Console. Mbr., profl. assn. Hons: Currie Kerr Prize for Organ, 1966; 1st Prize, Dr. W B Ross Memorial Trust Comp. Competiton, 1975. Hobbies incl: Walking. Address: 30 Gallowhill Rd., Paisley PA3 4TE,UK.

ESCALANTE, Eduardo Alberto, b. 14 Feb. 1937, Buenos Aires, Argentina. Composer; Director; Professor. Educ: Univ. of Music; Grad. in Piano; Bach., Comp. & Direction; pupil of Camargo Duarnieri. m. Marilena De Fino, 1 s. Career: Musical Dir., Man of La Mancha, 1973; Assessor, Folclore de Brasil, TV. Compositions incl: (published) Noctius; Invencao (flute & piano); Ciriri; Ponto de Oxala; La Chacerera (choral); Duas Miniaturas para Orquestra; (recorded) Invencao para Xilofono, agogô é ron-tons; Adágio (flute & viola); Embolada (chant & guitar). Contbr. to: Laqui; Journal da Música. Mbr., profl. assns. Hons: Prize, Comissao Estadual de Música de Sao Paulo, 1968; Finalist, Prize Silvio Romero, 1974. Mgmt: Folklore Ctr., SESC, Sao Paulo. Address: Rua Duerte da Costa 91, 05080 Sao Paulo, Brazil.

ESCALAS, Roman, b. 5 July 1945, Barcelona, Spain. Musician; Flautist; Musicologist. Educ: Bach. Superior; Prof. Superior of Flute. m. Esther Nolla. Career: Ldr., ARS Musicae de Barcelona; Concerts on Radio & TV in Spain, France, UK & USA; Tchr. of the ARS. Recordings w. ARS Musicae de Barcelona. Publs. incl: Técnica Básica Elemental. Flauta Dulce Soprano, 1970; Ejercicios y Estudios de Perfeccionamiento. Flauta Contralto, 1972; Metodo Escolar de Flauta Dulce Soprano, 1975. Contbr. to Anuario Musical Espanol, Barcelona. Mbrships: Int. Musicol. Soc.; Am. Recorder Soc. Hobbies: Reading; Chemistry; Instrument Making. Address: 61, Barcelona 17, Spain.

ESCHENBACH, Chirstoph, b. 20 Feb. 1940, Breslau, Silesia. Pianist; Conductor. Educ: Hochschule fuer Musik, Cologne &

Hamburg; Konzertpruefung. Career: concerts w. major orchs. throughout the world; radio & TV broadcasts in many countries. Recordings: exclusive contracts w. DGG (Polydor), 1966-76, & EMU, 1976-. Hons: Int. competition, Munich, 1962; Clara Haskil Int. competiton, Lucerne, 1965. Address: 2 Hamburg 13, Magdalenen Str. 64, German Fed. Repub.

ESCOBAR, Luis, b. 14 July 1925. Composer. Comps. incl: Symphs., Divertimenti, Concertos; 3 cantatas; 2 operas; 2 str. quartets; wind quintet; 2 sonatinas for piano; 3 ballets. num. recordings of own comps. Publs. incl: Cartilla Musical Escobar; Obres Polifonicas de Autores Colombianos; Aspectos de la Musica Colonial en Colombia; Quien fue Beethoven, Papa? Address: Carrera 1-77-24, Bogota, Colombia.

ESCOBAR, Maria Luisa, b. 8 Dec. 1910, Valencia, Venezuela. Composer; Writer; Pianist; Singer. Educ: studied piano & voice w. Prof. Roger Ducasse, Paris. m. J A Escobar Saluzzo, 2 s., 1 d. Debutr: Mus. Pedagog., Paris, 1937. Career: recital, Hall of the Ams., Panam. Union, Wash. DC., 1937, accomp. soprano Fedora Aleman in recital of own songs, Carnegie Hall, NYC, 1949; Soloist w. orch. under Antonini in perf. of own Concierto Sentimental for piano & orch., CBS NYC; radio & TV apps. Comps. incl: Nocturno; Dos Danzas Aborigeners venezolanas; Canto Caribe (recorded, ARCO 002, 1965); Canciones Sentimentales; Costa Montaña y Llano (recorded ARCO 001, 1957); Concierto Sentimentale (recorded w. 6 piano solo works, Polydor, 1969. Perf., ibid, Warsaw, Poland, 1969.) Contbr. to: nat. press; reviews; music jrnls. Mbrships. incl: Fndr. & Pres., Ateneo de Caracas, until 1943; Fndr. & Dir.-Gen., AVAC. (Venezuelan Assn. of Authors & Composers), until the present; Venezuelan Writers Assn. Recip. of 86 hons. Hobby: Musicotherapy. Address: Apartado Postal 10233, Caracas, Venezuela.

ESCOT, Pozzi, b. 1 Oct. 1933, Lima, Peru. Composer. Educ: BS, Juilliard Schl. of Music, 1956; Acad. of Music & Dramatic Art, Hamburg, 1957-61. div., 1 c. Comps. incl: 3 Poems of Rilke for string quartet & reciter, 1959; Differences Grp. I, for piano, 1961; Lementus for soprano, 2 violins, 2 cellos, piano, 3 percussionists, 1962; Cristos for 3 violins, alto flute, contrabassoon, percussion, 1963; Differences Grp. II, for piano, 1963; Visione for bass solo, flute, alto saxophone, soprano, ghost speaker, percussion, 1964; Sands for 9 basses, 17 violins, 5 saxophones, elec. guitar & 4 bass drums, 1965; Ainu for 20 solo singers, 1979-71; Fergus Are for organ, 1974-75. Publs: Sonic Design: The Nature of Sound & Music; Sonic Design; Practice & Problems. Contbr. to: Perspectives of New music, Bulletin of Music; Music in the Ams. Recip., num commns. & grants. Address: ° £ Avon Hill, Cambridge, MA, USA.

ESCUDIER, Monique, b. 16 Oct. 1940, Aurillac, France. Critic; Professor of History of Music. Educ: Conserv. de Paris, Paris-IV-Sorbonne. Career: Radio perfs., France; Prof. of Hist. of Music, Conserv. Régional de Rouen; Prof., Centre National de Télé-Enseignement, Vanves. Contbr. to: Grove's Dict., 6th Ed.; Dix-Huitiéme Siècle; Harmonie; Saisons de la Danse; record sleeves. Mbr., French Musicol. Soc. Address: 2, rue du Capitaine Guynemer, 78400 Chatou, France.

ESHPAI, Andrey Yakoulevitch, b. 15 May 1925, Kozmodemiansk, USSR. Composer; Pianist. Educ: Moscow Conserv. m. Alexandra Stempnevski, 2 s. Debut: 1947. Career: Regular TV & radio apps. Comps: 3 symphs., 1959, 62, 64; 2 piano concertos; violin concerto; symphonic dances; Hungarian Rhapsody; Concerto grosso; Lenin With Us (cantata); Kremlin's Bells (overture for orch.); chmbr. music; Angara (ballet for Bolshoi); music for 30 films. Mbrships: Sec., Union of Comps. of USSR; 1st Sec., Union of Comps. of RSFSR. Hons: Narodni Artist RSFSR; Zaslusmenni Deyatel Isskustv, RSFBR. Address: G-165, Studentcheskaya 44/28 R 12, Moscow, USSR.

ESPARZA, Elfego, b. 23 Aug. 1929, San Benito, Tex., USA. Opera Singer. Educ: Trinity Univ., San Antonio, Tex.; Royal Conserv. of Music, Brussels, Belgium; Akademie für Musik, Vienna. m. Karin Ehlers, 2 d. Debut: Seagle Colony, Schroon Lake, NY, 1949. Career: Guest Artist & Res. Artist, operas in Dusseldorf, Bremen, Hamburg State Opera, Bavarian State Opera, Vienna State Opera; Glyndebourne Opera; Scottish Opera; San Fran. Opera; Metropolitan Opera; Also in France, Italy, Holland, Spain, etc. Hobbies: Fishing; Swimming; Chess. Address: Hotel Stefano, Island of Elba, 57037 Portoferraio, Italy.

ESPINA, Noni, b. 29 July 1923, Ayuquitan, Neg. Or., Philippines. Singer (Concert Baritone); Teacher of Singing; University Professor; Choral Conductor; Composer; Musicologist; Lecturer. Educ. incls: BS (Educ.), Silliman Univ.; Master in Sacred Music, Voice, Schl. of Sacred Music, NY,

1950; PhD (Voice), ibid, 1962; MA (Voice), Ind. Univ., 1951; Juilliard Schl. of Music. Debut: As singer, Carnegie Hall, NYC, 1958. Career incls: Num. recitals & guest apps., 1950-; Concert tours, The Far East, 1965, '69; TV & radio apps., USA; Dir., num. choral orgs.; Lectr.; Dir. of Workshops & Musical Clinics; Vocal & Choral Adjudicator; Prof. of Music, Univ. of Colo., 1966-67, Jacksonville State Univ., 1967-71, Univ. of Redlands, 1971-72, NYC Univ., 1974-; Pvte. voice tchr., 25 yrs. Comps. incl: The Legend of Bakunawa (opera); Seashore (cycle of 8). Recordings: Hi-Fi in An Oriental Garden; His Real Presence. Publs: Reference books. Contbr. to profl. publs. Mbr., profl. orgs. Hons. incl: Hon. Citizen of New Orleans. Address: 1866 Cedar Ave., NY, NY 10453, USA. 7, 29.

ESSAH, Daniel Richard, b. 25 July 1930, Anum, Ghana. Music Teacher. Educ: Tchrs. Cert. A, 1951; Specialist Music Cert., Univ. of Sci. & Technol., Kumasi, Ghana, 1955; LRSM, 1964. m. Victoria Bowaa Essah, 3 s., 4 d. Career: Music Tchr., Adisadel Coll., Cape Coast, Achimota Schl., Latymer Upper Schl., London, UK & Radley Coll., Oxford; Piano Accomp. for violinists, Orchl. Arr. & Cond., Ghana TV; Schl. Song Writer; currently Asst. Headmaster, Accra HS. Mbr., Ghana Music Tchrs. Assn. Hobbies: Listening to mod. orchl. pieces & folk music. Address: Accra High School, PO Box 155, Accra, Ghana, W Africa.

ESSLINGER, Nell Daniel, b. 13 June 1903, Huntsville, Ala., USA. Singer; Choral Director; Voice Teacher. Educ: Vocal Cert., Agnes Scott Coll., Decatur, Ga.; BA, Univ. of Ala., 1954; MMus, Univ. of Ill., 1962; Num. pvte. tchrs. Debut: Carnegie Hall Chmbrs., NY, 1925. Career: Ch. & solo oratorio apps., Am.; Guest soloist, sev. Southern concert tours; Theatre apps., Adrienne, NY, Monte Carlo Operatic Quartet, Chgo., Roxy's Gang, NY; Radio perfs., USA; Dir. & Instr. in Voice, Koch Schl. of Music, Ohio, 1963-64; Voice tchr., Baldwin Wallace Coll., Ohio, 1965-66. Comps: Magnolia, Chorus for 4 female vaoice, 1975. Publs: Revised Notation, textbook, 1965; Song Lyrics, poetry & rhymes, 1975. Mbrships. incl: Life Mbr., The Huntsville Music Study Club; Alpha Epsilon Rho; Charter mbr., The Business & Profl. Women's Club, Rainsville, Ala., 1966. Hons. incl: 1st Place, Dixie Dist. students & artists contests, 1927; Award for Creative Achievement, Ga. Sci. & Technology Commission, 1968. Address: 1411 Hermitage Ave. S E, Huntsville, AL 35801, USA.

ESSWOOD, Paul Lawrence Vincent, b. 6 June 1942, West Bridgford, Notts., UK. Singer Counter-Tenor. Educ: ARCM. m. Mary Cantrill, 2 s. Debut: Messiah on BBC. Career: Apps. incl: Cavalli L'Frismena, Univ. Calif., USA; L'Erismena in Holland Fest. & Brussels; A Scarlatti's Il Tigrane in Basel & Naples; Handel's Ricardo Primo & Susarme in Gottingen: 3 Monteverdi operas in Vienna & Salzburg Fest.; Concert perfs. incl: Handel's Jeptha in Ceaserea, Jerusalem & Copenhagen; Messiah in Lucerne & Holland Fests; Penderecki's Paradise Lost (World Premiere, Chgo.); Co-fndr. of Pro Cantline Antiqua; Prof., RCM. Num. recordings. Mbr: ISM. Recip. Henry Blower Prize for Singing, 1964. Hobby: Aquariol. Mgmt: Ibbs & Tillet. Address: 6 Gowan Ave., London SW6 6RF, UK. 1,2.

ESTEBAN, Julio, b. 18 Mar. 1906, Shanghai, China. Professor of Music. Educ: B Mus., Conser. of Music, Univ. of Phillippines; M Mus., Escuela Municipal de Musica, Barcelona, Spain. m. Carmen Ramon, 3 s., 1 d. Career: Cons., Soloist & Accomp., Europe, USA & Far E; Perf. & Lectr., summer sessions of annual Int. Music Course, Santiago, Spain; Chmn., Curric. Committee, Bur. of Educ., Phillippines; Instr. in Music, San Juan de Letran Coll., Manila, 1925-28; Instr.-Assoc. Prof., Conserv. of Music, Univ. of Phillippines, 1925-47; Hd., Piano Dept., Phillippine Women's Univ., 1943-44; Dir., Conserv. of Music, Univ. of Santo Tomas, Manila, 1947-57; Fac. Mbr., Advanced Dept., Peabody Conserv. of Music, Balt., Md., USA, 1955-. Comps. incl: UN Hymn in the Phillippines; El Madrid de mis Amores (musical); arts songs; piano pieces; music for about 35 films. Publs: The Technical Exercises of Liszt, 1971; Etudes by Chopin, 1973. Contbr. to: Am. Music Tchr.; Clavier. Mbrships: Nat. Pres., Music Tchrs. Nat. Assn.; Past Pres., Md. State Music Tchrs. Assn.; V.P., Balt Music Tchrs. Assn.; Kappa Chapt., Phi Mu Alpha; Peabody Chapt., AAUP; Coll. Music Soc.; Am. Musicol. Soc. Recip. of many prizes inclng.: Kt. of the Order of Queen Isabella, Spain. Address: 1111 Park Ave., Baltimore, MD 21201, USA. 23.

ESTILL, Ann H. M., b. Wash. DC, USA. Associate Professor of Music; Coloratura Soprano. Educ: BMus, W Mich. Univ.; MA & Prof. Dips., Tchrs. Coll. Columbia Univ. Career: Num. recitals, NYC, Wash. DC & Atlants, Ga.; Radio & TV apps.; perf. over 60 oratorios w. St. Bartholomew's Ch. Chorus, NYC; Bernstein, Mass, Kennedy Center, Wash. DC, 1972; Scott Joplin's Treemonisha, Wolf Trap Farm for the Perf. Arts, Vienna, Va., 1972; Ethel Evans' Master Class for Singers, NYC; Researched

& Developed 2 Coll. Courses in progress at Jersey City State Coll. in African & Afro-Am. Classical Music; Assoc. Prof. of Music, Jersey City State Coll. Mbrships: Hon., Sigma Alpha Iota; Educ. hon., Phi Delta Kappa; Kappa Phi Methodist Wom's. Club. Hons: 4 yr. Citation, Kalamazoo Jr. Symph. (Violinist); SAI Dean's Honor Award. Hobbies: Sewing; Travel. Address: Jersey City State Coll., 2039 Kennedy Blvd., Jersey City, NJ 07305, USA. 27.

ESTRELLA, Arnaldo, b. 14 Mar. 1908, Rio de Janeiro, Brazil. Pianist. Educ: grad., Schl. of Music, Fed. Univ. of Rio de Janeiro. m. Mariuccia Lacovino. Debut: Rio de Janeiro, 1923. Career: recitals, apps. w. orchs. & radio broadcasts, Brazil, Uruguay, Argentina, Cuba, USA, Can., Angola, Algeria, Tunisia, Portugal, France, Switz., Belgium, Czech., Poland, Bulgaria, Romania, USSR, China; Pianist of Guanabara Quartet; former Prof., Univ. of Distrito Federal & Schl. of Music, Fed. Univ. of Rio de Janeiro. Recorded in Brazil & France. Publs: The String Quartets by Villa-Lobos, 1970. Contbr. to jrnls. Mbrships: Brazilian Acad. of Music; Musicians Soc. of Brazil. Recip. many hons. Mgmt: Maria Abreu Concerts, Rio de Janeiro. Address: Avenida Rui Barbosa, 60 ap. 1501, 20.000 Rio de Janeiro, Brazil.

ESZTENYI, Szabolcs László, b. 20 Dec. 1939, Budapest, Hungary. Composer; Pianist. Educ: BA in piano & comp., Warsaw Conserv. m. Teresa Roslon. Debut: as comp., 1971, Polish Radio, Warsaw. Career: apps. as Piano Soloist or in Piano Duets at fests. & w. orchs.; Asst. Tchr., comp. sect., Warsaw Conserv.; Piano-Improvising Tchr., Middle Schl. of Music No. 2, Warsaw. Comps. incl: Concerto for tape & piano; Concertino per due pianoforti soli; Motet for 3 actors; Intermezzo for 6 instruments. Contbr. to: Ruch Muzyczny. Recip. 1st Prize, Polish Piano Improvisation Competition, 1968. Address: ul. Targowa 44 M 35, 03-733 Warsaw, Poland.

ETHERDEN, Alan Bradley, b. 18 Apr. 1956, Coventry, UK. Pianist; Accompanist; Teacher. Educ: Coventry Schl. of Music (w. Vivian Langrish), 1972-74; RAM (w. Guy Jonson & John Streets); LRAM (Perf.), 1973; ARCM (piano tchr.), 1976; profl. cert., RAM, 1977. Debut: Town Hall, Birmingham, in Beethoven's 3rd Piano Concerto, 1978. Mbr., ISM. Hons: Scholarships to RAM from Leverhulme Trust, Spencer's Industrial Arts Trust, Sir Thomas White's Educational Fndn. Music Scholarship. Address: Hunters Moon, Paget's Ln., Bubbenhall, Coventry, UK.

ETLIK, Milan, b. 19 Mar. 1927, Nymburk, Czechoslovakia. Clarinettist. Educ: Prague Conserv., 1948; Dip., Acad. of Arts, Prague, 1953. Div., 2 d. Debut: 1948. Career: Mbr., Nat. Theatre Orch., Prague, to 1951; Soloist, w. concert tours throughout E & W Europe, & to Iran; Mbr., Prague Chmbr. Trio & Prague Wind Trio; Prof., Acad. of Arts; Mbr., Prague Chmbr. Ensemble of Profs. of Acad. of Arts; num. TV & Radio recordings of works of Czech & other comps. Recordings: Works of MyslivecVek, Kramár, Brahms, Bartók, Slavicky, Martinu & I. Krejcí. Publ: Etudes for Clarinet. Contbr. to Hudební rozhledy. Mbr., Guild of Czech Comps. & Concert Artists. Recip., Grand Prix de l'Acad. Charles Cross. Hobby: Tourism. Mgmt: Pragokoncert. Address: 110 00 Prague 1, Valentinská 1, Czechoslovakia.

ETTI, Karl, b. 26 Oct. 1912, Vienna, Austria. Orchestra & Choir Conductor; Music Professor; Composer. Educ: State Dips. in comp. orchl. conducting, piano playing & instrn. m. Gertrud Paulitsch. Debut: Cond., Vienna Boys' Choir. Career: Orch. Cond., German stages, 1938-45; since 1945, in Vienna; Cond., Vienna State Opera, 1945-47; Cond., ORF Symph. Orch. & Tonkuenstler Orch.; Cond., Wiener Männergesang-Verdein; Prof., HS of Music, Vienna. Comps. incl: 1 opera; 1 oratorio; 3 cantatas; 3 masses; num. orchl., choral, instrumental, chmbr. & vocal pieces. Recordings: piano concerto & num. choral works. Contbr. to: Osterreichische Musikzeitschrift; Der Komponist; Osterreichische Sänger-Zeitung. Mbrships: Austrian Composers Union; Wiener Männergesang; Austrian Soc. for Contemporary Music; Wiener Akademische Mozaart-Gemeinde. Hons. incl: Austrian State Prize, 1952; Preis der Ziehrer-Siftung, 1954; Kulturpreis von Niederösterreich, 1962; Förderungspreis der Gemeinde Wien, 1967; Valentin Becker Prize, 1972. Hobbies: Reading; Hiking; Swimming. Address: Gattringerstr. 40, A-2345 Brunn am Gebirge bei Wien, Austria.

ETTINGHAUSEN, Elizabeth S, b. 5 Aug. 1918, Vienna, Austria. Art Historian; Recorder Teacher. Educ: Univ. of Vienna; License degree, Univ. of Istanbul, Turkey, 1942; PhD, ibid, 1943; Jr Fellow, Dumbarton Oaks, Harvard Univ., 1943-45. m. Richard Ettinghausen, 2 s. Career: Singer, pvte. choral grps., Istanbul & Wash. DC until 1949; Player, 2-5 chmbr. grps., Fairfax Unitarian Ch., Oakton, Va., 1955-65; Singer, ibid, until

1965, & at Trinity Episcopal Ch., Princeton, N.J., 1969-; Chmbr., grp. recital, Salon Music Grp., Herndon, Va., 1965; Player, Trinity Episcopal Ch., Princeton, N.J., 1969-; Special Christmas season serv., St. John the Divine, NY., 1979, '71; Recorder Tchr., Green Hedges Schl., Vienna, Va., 1957-62, privately, 1969-. Mbrships: Am. Recorder Soc.; Treas., Princeton Chapt., ibid, 1969-70. Hobbies: Sports; Music; Reading; Photography. Address: 24 Armour Rd., Princeton, NJ 08540, USA. 2.

ETTLINGER, Yona, b. Munich (Possenhofer), Germany. Clarinettist; Conductor; Professor. Educ: studies w. Louis Cahuzac, Nadia Boulanger in France, Simon Bellison, Rosario Mazeo in USA, Tzwi Tzipin, Paul Ben Chaim in Israel. m. Miriam Irsai, 1 c. Career: Soloist of Israel Phil. Orch. for 15 yrs.; played w. Tel Aviv Str. Quartet, 1958-; condng., Israel Chamber Orch., Jerusalem Symph. orch., etc. Recordings: Brahms Clarinet Quintet & Clarinet sonatas; Mozart Clarinet Quintet. Publs: num. transcriptions for clarinet. Hons: FGSM. Address: 89 Priory Rd., London NW6, UK.

ETZKORN, Cleaon, b. 5 Jan. 1919, Highland, Ill., USA. Band Director; Instrumental Music Teacher; Performer on Baritone Euphonium & Trombone. Educ: B Mus Ed, 1941, M Mus Ed, 1952, Millikin Univ.; St. Louis Inst. of Music. m. LaVelle Turner, 1 d., 1 s. Career: Dir. of HS Band & Supvsr. of Instrumental Music, Edwardsville Schls., 1946-74; 1st Chair Baritone, Edwardsville Municipal Band, 1934-56; Dir., ibid., 1957-; Terry's Trombones, 1974-; Dir., Wood River Municipal Band, 1946-54. Comps: Partly in Eb Minor; Alpine Quartet. Mbr., num. profl. assns. Contbr. to profl. jrnls. Hons. incl: Goodwill Educl. Inspection Tour, 1959, 60, & 61. Hobbies incl: Family & friends. Address: 237 Gremer St., Edwardsville, IL 62025, USA.

ETZKORN, K Peter, b. 18 Apr. 1932, Karlsruhe, Germany. Sociologist/Anthropologist of Music; Ethnomusicologist. Educ: AB, Ohio State Univ., Columbus USA; AM, PhD, Princeton Univ.; studied Organ w. Walter Schwan, Anton Boellinger, Carl Weinrich; studied Musicol. w. August Herden & Arthur Mendel; studied Ethnomusicol. w. George Herzog. m. Hildegard Garve Etzkorn, 2 s. Career: Asst. Prof., Univ. of Calif., Santa Barbara, 1959-63; Assoc. Prof., Univ. of Nev., 1964-67; Prof., Univ. of W. Fla., Calif. State Univ., Northridge, Univ. of Mo.-St. Louis, 1969-. Publs: Music & Society, 1973. Contbr. to: Ethnomusicology; Kölner Zeitschrift für Soziologie & Sozialpsychologie; Social Forces; Jrnl. for Research in Music Education; Am. Sociological Review; Sociology & Social Research; Int. Folk Music Council Yearbook. Mbrships: Soc. for Ethnomusicol. (Coun. Mbr.); Assoc., Current Anthropol.; Fellow, Am. Anthropol. Assn., Am. Sociol. Assn.; Bd. of Dirs. & Pres., St. Louis New Music Circle; Chmn., Univ. Symposia, Bicentennial Horizons of Am. Music, 1976. Hons: Princeton Univ. Fellow: Haynes Fndn. Fellow. Hobbies: Tennis; Chamber Music. Fellow, Salzburg Seminar, Contemporary Am. Music, 1976. Address: 8042 Gannon, University City, MO 63130, USA, 2.

EUBANKS, Rachel Amelia, b. San Jose, Calif., USA. Executive Administrator; Educator. Educ: BA, Univ. of Calif., Berkeley; MA, Columbia Univ., NYC; Eastman Schl. of Music; Ohio State Univ.; UCLA; Univ. of Southern Calif. Career: Fndr., Eubanks Conserv. of Music & Arts, 1951; Pres. & Prof. of Theory, Comp. & Piano, ibid., currently; Former Chmn., Music Dept., Wilberforce Univ. Publs: Musicianship, Vols. I & II, 1976. Comps: Prelude for piano. Mbrships: MENC; Music Tchrs. Assn.; Alpha Mu. Hons: Mosenthal Fellow, 1946; Nat. Assn. of Negro Musicians Comp. Award, 1948; Phelan 3rd Hon. Mention in Comp. Hobbies: Travelling; Sewing. Address: 4928 Crenshaw Blvd., Los Angeles, CA 90043, USA. 5,23,27,29.

EULER, Josephine Mary, b. Wanstead, Essex, UK. Musician (viola); Teacher; Conductor. Educ: LRAM; Tchrs. Trng. Course; RAM, study w. Spencer Dyke, Bernard Shore & Eric Grant. Career incl: Tchr. of violin & piano, Putney Co. Schl., -1940; Pt.-time lectr., piano & strings, Southlands Trng. Coll., 1937-52; Violin Tchr., Princess Margaret Schl. (Dr. Barnardo's), 1953-58; Violin tchr., Claremont-Esher, 1958; Viola player (freelance) w. var. leading orchs., incl. LSO, Covent Gdn., BBC Orch., 1947-; Quartet recital at Cowdray Hall, 1952; Perfs. at var. music clubs; Current coach, Harrow Schls. Youth Orch.; Violin & Viola Tchr. (pt.-time), Watford Grammar Schl. for Bolys; Music Specialist (violin), Park H.S., Stanmore, Middx. Mbrships: ISM; Musicians Union; Viola Rsch. Soc. Hobbies: Stamp Collecting; Driving; Reading; Cooking. Address: 48 Meadow Rd., Pinner, Middx., UK.

EVANS, Anne. Operatic Soprano. Educ: RAM; Conserv. de Musique, Geneva. Debut: Mimi (La Boheme), 1968. Career:

Prin. soprano, Engl. Nat. Opera; apps. w. opera cos. of Rouen, Geneva & Dusseldorf; guest artist w. DeutscheOper am Rhein, Welsh Nat. Opera, Valencia opera (Spain), San Diego & San Francisco Operas (USA), Stuttgart Opera & Royal Opera House, Covent Garden; roles incl. Mimi & Musetta (La Boheme), Ramina (Zauberflöte), Tosca, Ilia (Idomeneo), Rosalinda (Fledermaus), Elsa (Lohengrin), Senta (Dutchman), Sieglinde (Walküre), Coutess (Figaro) & Donna Anna (Don Giovanni); concert apps. incl Verdi's Requiem & Britten's Spring Symph. Hons: Boise Fndrn. Music Award; Sir Thomas Beecham Operatic Scholarship. Mgmt: Trafalgar Perry Ltd., 4 Goodwin's Ct., St. Martin's Ln., London WC2N 4LL. Address: c/o mgmt.

EVANS, David Gruffydd, b. 8 May 1925, Treherbert, Wales, UK. Conductor; Repetiteur; Accompanist. Educ: AGSM in conducting, GSM, 1951; Dip. in conducting, State HS for Music, Hamburg, 1954. m. Maja Moebius, 1 s., 1 d. Career: Freelance orchl., choral & operatic Cond., Coach, Accomp., Germany, Wales, Repub. of Ireland; Staff Cond. Repetiteur, Welsh Nat. Opera, 1962-72; Cond., Repetiteur & Dpty. Chorus Master, Oldenburgisches Staatstheater, 1973-; num. conducting engagements w. BBC Cardiff & RTE Dublin. Mbrships: ISA; Guild for Promotion of Welsh Music; Genossenschaft Deutscher Bühnenangehöriger. Hobbies: Reading; Walking. Address: Heinrich-Schütte-Str. 29 Oldenburg, German Fed. Repub.

EVANS, Edgar, b. 9 June 1914, Cardiganshire, UK. Opera Singer. Educ: Pvte. Study w. Dawson Freer, London & Luigi Ricci, Rome Opera. m. Nan Walters, 1 s. Debut: London, 1947. Prof. of singing, RCM. Career: Prof. Mbr. & Prin. Tenor, Royal Opera House, 1946-; Num. Radio & TV Progs. Recordings: Tristan Und Isolde (HMV); Albert Herring (Decca). Mbrships: ISM. Hobbies: Reading; Motoring; Gardening. Address: The White House, 110 Preston Hill, Harrow, Middx. HA3 9SJ, UK. 3.

EVANS, (Sir) Geraint Llewellyn, b. 16 Feb. 1922, Pontypridd, Wales, UK. Opera Singer. Educ: GSM; FGSM, 1960. m. Brenda Evans Davies, 2 s. Debut: as Nightwatchman in Die Meistersinger, Royal Opera House, 1948. Career: has sung prin. roles w. ldng. opera houses, Europe & the Ams.; particularly known for his Mozartean roles & as Falstaff & Wozzeck; 1st perfs. incl: Pilgrims Progress(Walton), Gloriana, Billy Budd (Britten), The Rose Affair (Kaye), Beach of Falesa, Murder the Magician (Hoddinott); Dir., prods. of Peter Grimes, Le Nozze di Figaro, Falstaff & prods. for Harlech TV; Gov., London Opera Ctr.; Dir., Harlech TV; Trustee, Churchill Theatre Trust, Inc. Recordings incl· Falstaff; Peter Grimes; Cosi fan Tutt; Le Nozze di Figaro; Don Giovanni; Des Knaben Wunderhorn; Yeoman of the Guard; Mikado; Die Meistersinger; var. recitals. Hons. incL CBE, 1959; Kt. Bach., 1969; D Mus, Univ. of Wales, 1965, Univ. of Leicester, 1969. Address: 34 Birchwood Rd., Petts Wood, Kent BR5 1NZ, UK. 1,3,4.

EVANS, Graham Norman, b. 22 June 1938, Birmingham, UK. Clarinettist. Educ: Birmingham Schl. of Music; RCM, London. m. Carolyn Jane Murrill, 2 s., 1 d. Debut: Irish Guards Band, London. Career: Freelance Musician, London; BBC Music recitals; Schl. broadcasts; Mbr., Northern Sinfonia Orch. & Ensembles, 1968. Recordings w. Northern Sinfonia. Hobbies: Hill walking; Reading. Address: 37 Hawthorn Rd., Gosforth, Newcastle-upon-Tyne, NE3 4DE, UK.

EVANS, Mark, b. St. Louis, Missouri, USA. Composer; Conductor; Pianist; Organist; Playwright; Lyricist; Author. Educ: BMus (comp.) Calif. Inst. of the Arts; MA, Claremont Grad. Schl.; PhD, ibid.; studied comp. w. M Castelnuovo-Tedesco, Roy Harris, Ernest Kanitz & Aurelio de la Vega; cond. w. Fritz Zweig & Joseph Wagner; piano w. Helena Lewyn & Julia Bal de Zuniga. Career: active as comp.-cond. in musical theatre, films, TV & radio; lectr.; pianist-host-prod., radio show, Mark My Words; jazz soloist. Comps: stage musicals, films & TV scoring; choral, chmbr. & guitar music incl. jazz. Publs: Soundtrack: The Music of the Movies, 1975; Scott Joplin & the Ragtime Years, 1976; The Morality Gap, 1978; Pepito, 1979 (co-author) & Straight Shooting, 1980. Mbr. num. profl. orgs. Hons. incl. num. fellowships. Hobbies: Book collecting; Records; Langs.; Travel; Menus; Ballroom dancing. Address: c/o Am. Fed. of Musicians, Local 1 No. 47, 817 Vine St., Los Angeles, CA 90038, USA. 9.

EVANS, Wynford, b. 30 April 1946, Swansea, UK. Singer (Tenor). Educ: GSM, 1963-67. m. Judith Thomas, 1 s., 1 d. Career: Soloist w. num. orchs.; inclng. BBC Symph. at Promenade Concerts; Fest. incl. Bath, City of London, Cardiff, St. Albans; Operatic roles in Boris Godunov & Falstaff; Concerts, Holland, Sweden, Germany, France, Italy & Belgium; Tour of Yugoslavia, 1973, Romania, 1973, 74; frequent broadcasts for BBC. Recordings incl: Serenade to Music;

Pilgrims Progress; Schubert Mass; Rachmaninov Vespers. Hons. incl: Gold Medal, GSM; Winner, Young Welsh Singers Competition; Tenor Prize, s'Hertogenbosch Int. Competition, Netherlands, 1971. Hobbies: Golf; Rugby Union; Womens Hockey. Mgmt: AIM, 5 Regents Pk. Rd., London NW1. Address: 97 Gresham Rd., Staines, Middx., UK.

EVENS, Clifford Wallis, b. 19 Oct. 1921, Vancouver, BC, Can. Music Director & Conductor; Violinist. Educ: Studied Violin w. Josef Gingold; studied Cond. w. Hideo Saito & Kazuyoshi Akiyama at Toho Gakuen, Tokyo, Japan. m. Mary Edith Bucklin Hammond. Career: Former Violinist w. Toronto Symph. Orch. Ont.; Music Dir. & Cond., London Symph. Orch., London, Ont. Address: 112 Bloomfield Drive, London, Ont., Canada N6G 1P3.

EVERETT, Thomas G., b. 4 Dec. 1944, Phila., Pa., USA. Conductor; Educator; Writer; Bass Trombonist. Educ: BS Music, Ithaca Coll., 1966; MS Music, ibid, 1969; Eastman Schl. of Music. Career: Dir. of Bands, Harvard Univ., Cambridge, Mass.; Staff Mbr., New England Conserv., Boston, Mass.; Bass Trombone w. Boston Trombone Ensemble, Boston Ballet & Opera Orchs. Trombone Instr., Brown Univ., 1975-76. Compositions: Feowertig Nu (large grp. of instruments). Recordings: w. Zoom, Cantata Singers. Publ: Annotated Guide to Bass Trombone Literature, 1973. Assoc. Ed., The Composer Mag.; Trombone Ed., Brass World. Contbr. to: Instrumentalist; Music Jrnl.; Music Educators' Jrnl. Mbrships: Int. Trombone Assn. (Pres.); Soc. for Commissioning New Music; Phi Mu Alpha Sinfonia; Am. Fedn. Musicians; Coll. Band Dirs. Nat. Assn.; MENC. Hons: Selected to serve on Fac., Int. Trombone Workshop, Nashville, Tenn., 1972, 1973, 1974; num. Bass Trombone comps. written for his perf. Hobbies: Jazz Record Collecting; Baseball Fan. Address: 15 Chester St. Apt. 2, Cambridge, MA 02140, USA. 2.

EVJU, Helge, b. 7 Feb. 1942, Drammen, Norway. Pianist. Educ: Brandeis Univ., Mass., 2 yrs.; Oslo Univ. Exams. in Fine Arts & Music; studies w. num. pvte. tchrs. Debut: Drammen, 1959; Oslo, 1968. Career: Many concert tours as soloist é accomp.; Apps. w. Oslo & Bergen Symph. Orch., Norwegian Opera Orch., Drammen & Vestfold Orchs. & N Norwegian Symph. Orch.; sev. concerts on Norwegian radio; Finnish Nat. Radio, 1975; Concerts in Denmark, Netherlands & Prague, 1974. Hons: Coffey Award, Brandeis Univ., USA, 1962; 2nd Prize, Riefling Competition, 1969; Drammen Sparebank Special Achievement Prize, 1975. Hobbies: Drawing; Sketching; Outdoor Life; Skiing. Address: Hammerstadsgt. 2, Oslo 3, Norway.

EWART, John Graham, b. 28 Oct. 1949, Erith, Kent, UK. Orchestral Bassoon Player. Educ: RCM, 1968-72; ARCM; GRSM w. hons., 1972. Career: Freelance player, 1972-74; 2nd. bassoon, Bournemouth Sinfonietta, 1975-. Hobbies: Woodwork; Photography. Address: 10 Hungerford Rd., Bournemouth, Dorset, UK.

EWING, Maryhelen, b. 28 Oct. 1946, Tulsa, Okla., USA. Violist; Educator. Educ: BM, Violin, Juilliard Schl. of Music, 1968; MMus, Viola, Manhattan Schl. of Music, 1971. Career: Mbr., NJ Symph., 1969-71; Participant, Aspen Music Fest., summers, 1969-73; Mbr., Am. Symph. under Stokowski & Brooklyn Philharmonia, 1971-76; Mbr., Violin & Viola Fac., Manhattan Schl. of Music Prep. Div., 1972-; Prin. & Solo Violist, NY Pro Arte Chmbr. Orch., 1971-; Violist, Blue Hill String Quartet, 1975-. Recordings: w. NY Pro Arte Chmbr. Orch. for Radio Hamburg & Musical Heritage Soc. Mbr., Am. Fedn. of Musicians. Address: 210 W 70th St., NY, NY 10023, USA.

EYK, Tonny, b. 4 July 1940, The Hague, Netherlands. Conductor; Composer; Performer (piano, accordion, trombone). Educ: Royal Conserv., The Hague. m. Elisabeth J Vasbinder, 2 s. Debut: w. twin sister as Lew Deux Jeateux (accordion variety act), 1947. Career: Cond. (Band Ldr.), popular Dutch radio & TV progs. Comps. incl: film & TV music; Theme music. Recordings: As piano soloist, has made about 40 LPs. Hobbies: Painting; Cycle racing. Mgmt: Phonogram, Hilversum. Address: Prins Clauslaan 2, Badhoevedorp, 1171 LD Netherlands. 30.

EYRAMYA, Carmen Stanley, b. 17 Jan. 1936, Chicago, Ill., USA. Concert pianist; Opera singer; Educàtor. Educ: B Mus., Am. Conserv. of Music; N Western Univ. Schl. of Music; Juilliard Schl.; Boston Conserv.; Columbia Univ.; Hunter Coll.; pvte. study. m. Ben Eyramya, 1 s., 1 d. Career: Children's parts w. NY Metropol. Opera, 1942; NY City Ctr. Opera, Chgo. Opera; as child, leading roles w. All Children's Grand Opera of Chgo.; leading parts in Children's Grand Opera of Chgo.; leading parts in Children's Civic Theatre Prods. by Chgo. Drama League; TV apps. Stn. WBKB, WMAQ; Radio broadcasts, Univ.

of the Air, Stn. WILL.; Concerts apps. w. NY Choral Soc., Carnegie Hall. Teaches piano privately Winston Towers Complex, Cliffside Park, NJ. Contbr. of Music reviews to Star Publs. Mbrships. incl: Off., Chgo. Chapt., Mu Phi Epsilon; Fac., NGPT; Soc. of Am. Musicians; Chautaugua, NY Summer Choir. Chgo. Artists Assn.; Sec., Chgo. Women's Musical Club; Bd. of Dirs., Ill. Fedn. of Music Clubs, Hons. incl: Gold Medal, Chgo. land Music Festival Piano contests, 1953; All state winner, Nat. Fedn. Music Clubs Piano Comps., Ill., 1954. Am. Legion Award for Special Achievement. Address: 200 Winston Dr., Cliffside Pk., NJ 07010, USA.

EYSER, Eberhard, b. 1 Aug. 1932, Kwidzyn, Prussia. Composer; Violist. Educ: Akademie fur Musik & Theater, Hannover; Mozarteum, Salzburg; Accademia Chiggiana, Siena. Career: Violist, Royal Swedish Opera Orch. Comps: about 100 works incl. chmbr. & vocal music, orchl., electronic & computer music, chmbr. operas; operas incl. Molonn, 1970; Carmen 36, 1972; Dream of Man 1972; Last Voyage, 1973; King of Hearts, 1973; Aub Said, 1976; Quimeras, 1978; Summer's Day, 1979; The Unaccomplished Fly Flapp, 1979. Recordings: King of Hearts; Last Voyage; Water Music (electronic). Mbrships: FST; Fylkingen; ISCM; STIM. Hons: 1st Carl Maria Von Weber prize, Dresden, 1978. Address: Royal Opera, Box 16094, 10322 Stockholm, Sweden, 30.

EZRAHI, Yariv, b. 1 Jan. 1904, Jerusalem, Israel. Violinist; Composer. Educ: BA, Prof., Acad. of Music, Vienna. m. Hanna. Career: Dir., Ron-Shulamith Israeli Conserv., Tel-Aviv. Comps. incl: many songs; string pieces & ensemble works for young players; 3 suites for strings; Wilde Shepherd (violin w. piano accomp.). Contbr. to: Ydioth Aharonoth newspaper (music critic). Mbrships: Pres., Music Critics Assn.; Pres., Israeli Musicians & Music Tchrs. Hobby: Sports. Address: Ibn Gvirolstr., 103, Tel-Aviv 64046, Israel. 2.

F

FABER, Joachim, b. 17 Feb. 1913, Berlin, Germany. Composer; Conductor. Educ: studied w. H W V Waltershausen, asst. Kapellmeister. m. Anne Hebberling, 1 d., 1 s. Comps: Hermann Hesse Lieder (recorded), songs, music for radio, TV, theatre, ballet, & film. Recordings: Kulota story; chansons. Mbr., German Comps. Assn. Hons: Schwabinger Kunstpreis; Goldmedaille Bayerischer Rundfunk. Address: Beltweg 10, 8 Munich 40, German Fed. Repub.

FABIAN, Imre, b. 15 June, 1930, Mateszalka, Hungary. Musicologist; Music Critic; Editor. Educ: Ferenc Liszt Music Acad., Budapest. m. Maria Aczel, 1 d. Career: Music Critic, Hungarian Radio, wkly. mag. Film, Szinhaz, Muzsika, Moderator, monthly TV Prod., Hungary, 1964-70; Ed., Operwelt, 1971-. Publs: Richard Strauss, 1962; H. Berlioz, 1968; Szazdunk zeneje, 1961, 1967; Egyutt uj utakon, 1963; A 20, szazad zenefe, 1966; Dezso Ernster, 1969; Oper in Crisis? 1969; Ed., Jahrbuch der Opernwelt, 1977; Ring-Aspekte, 1976. Contbr. to: Osterreichische Musikzeitschrift; Neue Zeitschrift fur Musik; Melos; The New Hungarian Quarterly; The X World of Music; Tempo; The Musical Quarterly. Address: Tiestestrasse 25, D-3 Hannover, German Fed. Repub.30.

FABRICIUS, Jacob, b. 2 July 1949, Hviokildevej, Copenhagen, Denmark. Composer. Educ: 2 yrs. cello playing w. Erling Blondal Bengison. Debut: Royal Danish Music Conserv., Dec. 1970 (String Quarter No. 2). Career incls: Perfs. in D.U.T., Nikolaj Ch. Fuglsang, Danish Music Conserv., Denmarks Radio. Mbrships: CODA, Danish Comps. Soc. Hobbies: Cello playing; Editing Poetry. Address: Norrefarimagsgade 27A St., 1364 Copenhagen K, Denmark.

FAGIUS, Hans, b. 10 Apr. 1951, Norrköping, Sweden. Organist. Educ: Organist & Perf. Exam., 1973; Music Tchrs. Exam., 1976; Concert Dips. in Organ, 1974; studied w. Maurice Durufle, Paris. m. Karin Fagius. Career: concerts in Sweden, Finland, Norway, Denmark, Germn Fed. Repub. & Belgium; radio & TV broadcasts, Sweden, Finland, & Belgium. Recordings: Swedish & French organ music on Gammelstad ch. organ, BIS LP-7. Hons: 3rd Prize, 4th Int. JS Bach Competition, Leipzig, 1972; 2nd Prize, Scandinavian Music Competition for Organists, 1973. Address: Redaregatan 19, S-60365 Norrköping, Sweden.

FAHEY, Brian Michael, b. 25 Apr. 1919, Margate, Kent, UK. Composer; Arranger; Musical Director. m. Audrey Laurie Kathleen Watkins, 3s., 3d. Career: Prin. Cond., BBC Scottish Radio Orch., 1972-. Comps: Num. film scores; Instrumental & Orchl. Works; Songs; Signature Tunes, etc. Recording: Many w. own orch. & as accompanying orch. to maj. singers & artists. Address: Tigh Geal, Skelmorlie, Ayrshire, UK.

FAHEY, Patrick James (Rev), b. 6 May 1933, Yeppoon, Aust. Musical Director. Educ: BA, Villanova Univ., Pa., 1954; BD, Augustinian Theological Col., Wash., DC, 1958; STL, Pontifical Liturgical Inst., Rome, 1974; STD, ibid., 1976; MMus, Cath. Univ. of Am., 1959. Debut: (as organist) 1958. Career: Music Master, St. Augustine's Coll., Brookvale, Sydney, 1959-72; Fndng. Dir. of choir, ibid., 1959-72; Musical Dir., St. Stephen's Cathedral, Brisbane, 1977-80; Dir., Brisbane Liturgical Inst., 1977-80; Archdiocesan Co-ordinator of Liturgy & Music, Brisbane, 1977-80; lectr. in music, Banyo Regional Seminary, Qld; lectr., Liturgical Theology & Music, Athenaeum Augustinianum, Rome, 1980—. Sev. recordings. Publs: Ritualism, Liturgical Revision & Liturgical Theology in the Church of Ireland, 1842-77, 1976. Contbr. to Music Maker. Hobbies: Tennis; Squash. Address: Collegio Internazionale Agostiniano, Via Sant' Uffizio 25, 00193 Rome, Italy.

FAINI, Philip James, b. 13 Oct. 1931, Masontown, Pa., USA. Professor of Music in Percussion. Educ: B MUs, M Mus, additional study of percussion, theory & arranging, W Va. Univ. m. Doris Jeanne Netchi, 1s., 2d. Career incls: apps. w. symphs., on radio & TV broadcasts & films, as well as work w. var. name bands & singers. Comps. incl: Creation; Paradiddle Dandy; Bravura; Fuga V; Little G Minor Fugue; American Frontiers of Hope. Recordings: Protest in Percussion; Percussion on the Rocks. Mbrships: Phi Mu Alpha; NACWP; State Chmn., Percussive Arts Soc.; Chmn., Ethnomusicol. Comm. Recip. var. hons. inclng: 2st Place Award, 3rd Annual Comp. Symposium of Solo's & Ensembles. Hobbies: Golf;

Tennis; Flying. Address: 1056 Windsor Ave., Morgantown, WV 26505,USA.

FAIRHURST, Harold, b. 8 June 1903, London, UK. Violinist; Violist; Conductor; Lecturer; Teacher. Educ: TCL; w. Prof. Sevclk, Czech.; w. Eugene Ysaye, Belgium. m. Ria Boettcher. Debut: London Proms, 1923. Career incls: tour, S Africa, w. Carrie Tubb & Reginald Paul, 1924; Solo, BBC, 19215; 10 Wigmore Hall Recitals; Solo apps. throughout UK & Netherlands; Concertos w. prin. orchs.; Ldr., Bournemouth Municipal Orch., 1937-41; Soloist, Arts Coun. Concerts; Formed Trio w. Reginald Paul & John Moore; Prof. of Violin & Examiner, RAM; Ldr., Sev. London Ballet seasons; Fndn. Mbr., RPO; Lectr. in Music, Elder Conservatorium of Music, Univ. of Adelaide, SA; Sr. Lectr., ibid; Mbr., Elder String Quartet; Solo & Chmbr. Music apps., Aust.; num. broadcasts; Cond., Mbr., S A Symph. Orch., 5 yrs.; Examiner, Aust. Exams. Bd. Mbrships: Past Chief, Adelaide Savage Club; Hon. Life Mbr., ibid; SA MTA (Hon. Life Mbr.). Hobbies: Skindiving; Photography. Address: 85 Murray Dr., Riverglades, nr. Murray Bridge, SA, Aust.

FAIRHURST, Robin Angus, b. 3 June 1941, London, UK. Singer; Teacher; Musical Therapist; Conductor. Educ: FTCL.; Grad., Akademie für Musik & Darstellende Kunst, Vienna, Austria. m. Annemarie Steffens, 2 s. Debut: as boy soprano, 1953; as baritone, 1965. Career: (as boy soprano) Many BBC broadcasts; Chief Chorister, Temple Ch., London; Apps. w. EOG in Britten's "Let's Make an Opera" & "Turn of the Screw"; (as baritone) Engagements at Gelsenkirchen & Essen town operas; Lead in BBC TV opera "Some Place of Darkness" by Christopher Whelen; Tchr., Folkwangschule, Essen, & Univ. of Essen. Recordings: (as boy soprano) 2 solo discs & part of Johnny in Britten's "Let's Make an Opera"; (as baritone) Part of Adam in Decca recording of Haydn's "Creation". Mbrships: Schlaraffia; Templars Union; Genossenschaft Deutscher Bühnenangehörigen. Recip., 2nd Prize, Int. Singing Competition, Vienna, 1965. Hobbies: Chess; Football; Cooking; Composing. Mgmt; Basil Douglas Ltd., London, UK. Address: Hohe Kuppe 19, 4300 Essen 14, German Fed. Repub. 3.

FAIRLEY, E Lee, b. 4 Dec. 1917, Hannibal, NY, USA. Musicologist & Foreign Affairs Specialist in Cultural Programs. Educ: B Mus. Eastman Schl. of Music, Univ. of Rochester, NY, 1939; M Mus, ibid., 1941; Geo. Wash. Univ., 1942; African Studies Ctr., Boston Univ., Mass., 1964-66. m. Gisela Hensel, 1 s., 2 d. Career: w. Music Div., Lib. of Congress, Wash. DC., 1941-48; Music Advsr., Dept. of State, ibid., 1948-52; Prog. Annotator, Nat. Symph. Orch., Wash. DC., 1942-52; For. Serv. Off., Dept. of State, US Info. Agcy., 1952-75, w. overseas assignments in Paris, 1952-54, Bonn, 1955-57, Kampala, Uganda, 1960-65, & Rabat, Morocco, 1966-69; Cellist, Arlington Symph. Orch., Va., 1969-76; & Roanoke Symph. Orch., Va., 1971-76; Asst. Sec., Kindler Fndn., 1978-. Contbr. to: Notes; Musical Am.; Musical Quarterly; Int. Music Co. publs. Mbrships: Am. Musical. Soc.; Music Ed. of Notes, 1946-52, Music Lib. Assn.; Am. For Serv. Assn. Hobbies: Reading; Writing; Gardening; Photography; Craftwork. Address: 6134 Tompkins Dr, McLean, VA 22101,USA.

FAIRLEIGH, James Parkinson, b. 24 Aug. 1938, St. Joseph, Mo., USA. Musicologist; Pianist. Edus: BMus, Univ. of Mich., 1960; MMus, Univ. of Calif., 1965; PhD, Univ. of Mich., 1973. m. Marlene Alberta Paxson, 1 s., 1 d. Career: Solo piano recitals & accomp. for recitals, Calif., Ind., Mass., Mich., Mo., NY & RI; Duo piano recitals w. wife, Hanover Coll., RI Coll., Providence Coll. Guest soloist w. RI Coll. Orch. & RI Coll. Symph. Band; Pianist w. RI New Music Ensemble; Instructor, Music, Hanover Coll., Ind., 1965-68; Asst. Prof.-Assoc. Prof., Hanover Coll., 1968-75; Assoc. Prof., RI Coll., Providence, 1975-. Contbr. to jrnls. Mbr. profl. socs. Hons: Theodore Presser Schlrship., 1959-60; Horace H. Rackham Schlrships., 1970-72. Hobbies: Swimming; Waterskiing. Address: Dept. of Music, RI Coll., Providence, RI 02908, USA. 8.28.

FAIZI, Djaudat Kharisovich, b. 4 Jan. 1910, Orenburg, Russia. Composer. Educ: Kazan Univ.; Tatar Opera Studio, Moscow Conserv. Compositions: Bashmachki (slippers), 1942; Seagulls, 1944; On the Banks of the Volga, 1949 (all musical comedies); Undispatched Letters (opera), 1959; Over 150 songs, instrumental music & theatre music. Mbrships: Exec., Composers Union of Tatar SSR. Hons: Honoured Worker of Arts of Tatar SSR, 1944 & of RSFSR, 1957; Peoples Artist of Tatar SSR, 1964. Address: Composers Union of Tatar SSR, Kazan, USSR.

FAJARDO, Raoul J, b. 17 Feb. 1919, Santiago, Cuba. Professor of Physics; Flute Teacher; Ensemble Flautist. Educ:

BA, MA, Stanford Univ., 1951; Solfeggio, Conserv. Provincial, Santiago, Cuba; flute & music theory, Prof. Riso, Cuba; advanced flute, Calif. State Univ., Fuillerton, 1971. Career: Half-hour colour TV app., The Flute & Acoustic Resonance, Los Angeles, sponsored by Pasadena City Coll., 1974. Comps: On the Mountains (flute & harpsichord), 1974; Song of Light (voice & piano), 1974; Images of Spring (flute & violin), 1974; Voice of the Heart (solo flute), 1977. Publs: Romance of the Flute, 1976; The Art of Flute Expressiveness, 1977. Contbr. to var. jrnls. on flute acoustics. Mbrships: Sigma Delta Pi (Pres., Stanford Chapt., 1950); Nat. Flute Assn. (lectr., 1975). Hons: US patent on flute head joint redesign, 1977. Hobbies: Photography; Mountain Hiking; Swimming. Mgmt: c/o W T Armstrong Co., Inc., Elkhart, Ind. Address: PO Box 8711, San Marino, CA 91108, USA. 9.

FAKO, Nancy Jordan, b. 19 May 1942, White Plains, NY, USA. French Horn Player. Educ: B Mus, Ind. Univ., 1963; Mbr. Chgo. Civic Orch., trng. orch. of Chgo. Symph.; Orch. mbr. Pierre Montreaux' Domaine Schl. of Conds. m. Martin Fako, 4 d. Career: Apps. w. Fla. Symph. Orch.; Houston Symph. Orch.; Chgo. Cymph. Orch.; Lyric Opera Orch. of Chgo.; Former Mbr., Fac., Nat. Music Camp, Interlochen, Mich.; currently, Freelance artist & Tchr. Num. recordings w. Chgo. Symph. Orch. Publs: The Art of Brass Playing, Wind Music, 1962 (w. Philip Farkas). Contbr. to profl. jrnls. Mbrships: Advisory Council, Int. Horn Soc.; Mu Phi Epsilon. Hobbies: Foreign Langs; Travel; Corres. w. friends around the world. Playing Recorder in Baroque Ensembles. Address: 337 Ridge Ave., Elmhurst, IL 60126, USA.

FALKMAN, Carl Johan, b. Stockholm. Opera & Concert Baritone. Educ: Stockholm Opera Schl. Debut: Ferdinand in Werle's Tintomara, Stockholm. Career: Prin. Baritone, Royal Opera, Stockholm; roles incl. Masetto (Don Giovanni), Marcel (Boheme), Figaro (Barber), Harlequin (Ariadne), Orloffsky (Die Fledermaus); num. apps. on radio & TV; num. perfs. in concerts & oratorios. Mgmt: Artistsekretariat Ulf Törnqvist, Norrtullsgatan 26, tr.4, 11345 Stockholm, Sweden. Address: c/o mgmt.

FALKNER, (Sir) (Donald) Keith, b. 1 Mar. 1900, Sawston, Cambs., UK. Musician; Singer. Educ: Royal Coll. of Music, 1920-25; ARCM; FRCM. m. Christabel Fullard, 2 d. Debut: Promenade Concerts - 3 Choirs Festival, 1925. Career incl: Asst. Vicar Choral, Westminster Abbey, 1920, 0 St. Paul's Cathedral, 1921-26; Profl. Singer, 1925-40; Concert tours of Europe, USA, S Africa, NZ; Broadcasts on BBC Radio & TV; appeared in 3 Warner Bros. musicals; Music Off., Brit. Coun., Italy, 1946-50; Prof. of Music, Cornell Univ., USA, 1950-60; Dir., Royal Coll. of Music, 1960-74. Recordings: var. 78 rpm records, re-issued as LP in EMI Golden Voices Series, 1972. Mbrships: Coll. Music Soc., USA; Inc. Soc. of Musicians; Chmn., M.B.F. Royal Concert. Hons: KB, 1967; DMus (Oxon.), 1968. Hobbies: Golf; Gardening. Address: Low Cottages, Ilketshall St Margaret, Bungay, Suffolk, UK. 1.

FALLOWS, David, b. 20 Dec. 1945, Buxton, UK. Musicologist. Educ: BA, Jesus Coll., Cambridge; MMus, King's Coll., London; PhD, Univ. of Calif. at Berkeley. m. Paulène Oliver. Career: Lectr. in music, Univ. of Wis., Madison, 1973-74; lectr. in music, Univ. of Manchester, 1976-. Publs: scholarly articles in Revue de Musicologie, Rivista Italiana de Musicologia, Acta Musicologica, Proceedings of the Royal Musical Assn.; eds. of early music. Contbr. to Gramophone; Musical Times; review ed., Early Music. Recip. 1st Ingolf Dahl prize in musicol., 1971. Hobbies: Travel; Skiing. Address: 16 Brook's Rd., Manchester 16, UK.

FALTIN, Peter, b. 12 July 1939, Velicna, Czech. Musicologist. Educ: Univ. (Philosophy, Psychol., Musicol.); Dr.Phil., 1968; Dr. habil., 1976; Prof., 1977. m. Marta, 1 d. Publs: Igor Stravinsky, 1966; The Function of Sound in Music, 1967; Music & Ideology, 1969; Music & Understanding, 1973; The Phenomenology of Musical Form, 1979. Hobbies: Cinema; Lit.; Skiing. Address: Graf Skauffenberg Ring 26, 6380 Bad Hamburg, German Fed. Repub.

FALVY, Zoltan, b. 28 Aug. 1928, Budapest, Hungary. Musicologist. Educ: Grad., Hungarian Lit. & Linguistic, Hist., Univ. of Budapest; Doctor's degree, 1964; Grad. in comp., Conservatoire of Budapest, 1949. m. Eva Kardos, 1 s. Career: Asst. Dir., Inst. for Musicol., Budapest; Univ. Lectr., 1973. Publs: A Pray-kodex zenei paleográfiája, 1953; A gráci antifonárium, 1956; Drei Reimoffizien aus Ungarn und ihre Musik, 1968; Codex Albensis, 1963; A magyar zenetörténet Képeskönyve, 1960. Mng. Ed., Studia Musicologica. Mbrships: Inst. Assn. of Musical Instrument Coll.; Commission Internationale Mixte of RIDIM. Address: Institut for Musicol., Országház-u.9, H-1014 Budapest, Hungary.

FANELLI, Frances, b. 3 Nov. 1942, Phila., Pa., USA. Concert Pianist; Teacher of Piano. Educ: B Mus summa cum laude, Phila. Musical Acad.; postgrad. study w. Leon Fleisher. Debut: Town Hall, NYC, 1966. Career: apps. incl. Young Am. Artists Prog., WNYC Radio, Phila. Mus. of Art Concert Series, Studio Recital, WNYC TV, Portraits in Music, WRCV TV, Leschetizky Artist Recitals & w. Bucks Co., Wilmington & Lansdowne Symph. Orchs.; app. w. Phila. New Music Grp., Int. Fest., Barga, Italy. Mbrships: Leschetizky Assn.; Delta Omicron. Recip. of Town Hall Debut, Int. Leschetizky Assn. Competition. Hobbies: Reading; Writing Poetry; Gourmet Cooking; Gardening. Address: 7256 Spruce St, Upper Darby, PA 19082,USA.

FANNING, David John, b. 5 Mar. 1955, Reading, UK. Lecturer; Concert Pianist. Educ: MusB, Manchester Univ.; grad., RNCM. m. Hazel Atherton Ralphs. Career: Lectr., Manchester Univ. Contbr. to: The Guardian; Classical Music. Mbrships: Royal Musical Assn.; ISM; European Piano Tchrs. Assn. Hobbies: Languages; Table Tennis; Meccano Models. Address: 7 Richmond Rd., Fallowfield, Manchester 14, UK.

FANSELAU, Rainer, b. 8 May 1934, Berlin, Germany. Musicologist; Church Musician; Educator. Educ: State HS for Music, Berlin; Free Univ., Berlin; PhD, Univ. of Göttingen, 1973. m. Ruth Hoffmeister, 1 s. Career: Organist, Marienrode, 1948-54, Martin-Luther-Kirche, Hildesheim, 1960-61, Athanasius-Kirche, Hanover, 1962-; Music Educator, ibid., 1961-; Lectr., Musicol., Univ. of Göttingen, Didactics of Music, State HS for Music & Theatre, Hanover, 1974-. Publs: Die Orgel im Werk Edward Elgars, 1978. Mbrships. incl: Soc. for Music Rsch.; Soc. of Organ Lovers; Philol. Grp.; Elgar Soc. Hobbies: Cycling; Wandering. Address: Bodenstedtstr. 6, 3000 Hanover, German Fed. Repub. 4,28.

FANSHAWE, David Arthur, b. 19 Apr. 1942, Paignton, Devon, UK. Composer; Explorer; Conductor; Singer; Pianist; Lecturer; Author; Photographer. Educ: Film Ed., Film Prods. Guild; RCM. m. Judith Croasdell Fanshawe, 1 s., 1 d. Debut: Comp., Soloist, Queen Elizabeth Hall, London, 1970. Career: Comp., BBC, ITV, Brit. Film Inst., Documentaries; num. TV Apps., UK; Radio Apps. BBC 1,2,3, & 4, Capitol Radio, LBC, BBC World Service, BBC African Service, Radio Kuwait, Voice of Kenya, WQXR, NY, USA. Compositions: (publd.) African Sanctus (recorded); Salaams; Requiem For The Children of Aberfan; Triumph; Fantasy On Dover Castle; The Clown's Concerto; Mini-Serenade; The Strange Lady; Coloured Hats; Escapades for Piano; Early Potato Musicks; Symph. of the Arabian Gulf; Carols; Sing Alleluia; The Pensive Clown; (recorded) African Sanctus; Arabian Fantasy; Softly Softly Task Force; Three Men in a Boat. Contbr. to: Africana; Shell Mag.; E. African Standard. Mbr. num. Profl. Orgs. Recip. num. hons. Hobbies: Reading; Tennis; Cycling; Good Company. Mgmt: A.D. Peters Ltd., London, UK. Address: St. David's, 8 Firs Ave., E Sheen, London SW14 7NZ, UK.

FANTAPIÉ, Henri-Claude, b. 9 Sept. 1938, Nice, France. Musical Director; Composer. Educ. incls: studied musicol., Univ. of Paris Sorbonne; studied harmony, clarinet, counterpoint, chmbr. music, conducting, comp., etc. w. noted tchrs. Debut: 1960. Career: Fndr., 1964, Musical Dir., Les Solistes de Paris, giving concerts in UK, Germany, Madagascar, Ethiopia, Monaco, Belgium, etc., at fests. & on radio stns. in many countries. Comps. incl: 3 Errances (orchl.); 4 Miniatures (guitar); 2 pieces (contrabass & piano) Kuklos (violin & piano); Quintet (clarinet & strings); Aleatorica I (chmbr. orch.). Has made many recordings. Publs: Studies in Musicology & History of Music about Finnish Music & Finnish Composers, 1977/78. Hons: SACEM Comp. Prize (for Musique symphonique), 1970, 71; Acad. du Disque Français selection for 1973 (3 records of Villa Lobos works for voice & instruments). Address: 56, Rue Rouget de Lisle, f93160, Noisy Le Grand, France.

FARBER, Otto Leopold Friedrich, b. 5 Oct. 1902, Prag, Austria. Composer; Conductor; Professor. Educ: Music Acad., Prag. m. Jarosch-Farber, 1 s. Career: Conduc. Aachen, Berlin, Zürich, Vienna; num. perf. in Austria, Germany, Switz., Bulgaria; Prof., Acad. of Music, Vienna, 1956. Comps. incl: 2 Operas; 3 Symph.; Concertos for piano and orch., violin and orch., horn and orch., oboe and orch., flute and orch., 3 Suites for big orch.; Chmbr. music; Sonatas for str., flute, piano; Duos, Trios for str. and wind instruments; Quintet for wind instruments. Recordings: var. of own works. Mbrships: Austrian Soc. for Contemporary Music; Soc. for Music Theater. Hons: Music Prize Theodor Körner, 1965, 1968. Hobby: Inventions. Address: Brigittenaverlände 172/II/9, A-1200 Vienna, Austria.

FARIS, Alexander, b. 11 June 1921, Caledon, Northern Ireland. Composer; Conductor. Educ: MA, Oxon.; ARCM; studied w. Bernard Wagenaar. Career: Cond. Carl Rosa Opera

Co., 1949, Sadler's Wells Opera, 1960-69, Royal Ballet, 1960-61; Cond., Orchestrator, num. West End Musicals. Compositions; film scores Georgy Girl, The Quare Fellow, Rowlandson's England; operetta R Loves J; music for var. TV Series inclng. Upstairs, Downstairs. Recordings: Operetta, Orchl. recordings for HMV, World Record Club. Contbr. to: New Statesman; Observer; Opera; Composer. Named Fellow, C'wlth. Fund of NY. Hobby: Swimming. Address: 118D Regent's Park Rd., London NW1 8XL,UK.3.

FARISH, Margaret K, b. 17 May 1918, Omaha, Neb., USA. Editor; Violinist; Teacher. Educ: B Mus., Eastman Schl. of Music, Rochester, NY; M Mus., ibid. m. Philip Farish. Career: Violinist, var. Symphs., Str. Quartet; Tchr.; Assoc. w. Univ. of Ill. String Rsch. Project 1966-70. Publs: Ed., String Music in Print, 1st Ed., 1965. Supplement, 1968, 2nd Ed., 1973; Orch. Music in Print, 1979. Mbrships: Am. String Tchrs. Assn.; Sec 1976-78, Publ. Chmn. 1978-; MENC. Address: 925 Elmwood Ave., Evanston, IL 60202, USA.

FARISH, Stephen Thomas Jr, b. 5 May 1936, Columbia, Va., USA. Professor of Music; Singer; Conductor. Educ: BSc, E Car. Univ.; M Mus. & DMA, Univ. Ill. m. Anna Withers Montgomery, 1 s., 1 d. Debut: W NBC Symph. Orch., Chgo. Career: Prof. of Music, N Tex. State Univ.; Musical Dir., Denton Co. Music Assn. Inc., producing & directing a full season ranging from concert to oratorio to musical theatre; Apps. w. Ft. Worth Symph. Orch.; Tex. Boys Choir; Ft. Worth Opera Assn.; W Coast Symph.; Num. apps. as soloist & lectr. in S & SW USA. Mbrships. incl: Regional Auditions Chmn., Texoma Region, Nat. Assn. Tchrs. of Singing; Pi Kappa Lambda; Phi Kappa Phi; Phi Mu Alpha. Hobby: Bd. Mbr. Gtr. Denton Arts Coun. Address: 1900 Emerson, Denton, TX 76203, USA. 7.

FARKAS, Ferenc, b. 15 Dec. 1905, Nagykanizsa, Hungary. Composer; Professor of Composition. Educ: Grad., Acad. of Music, Budapest, 1928; Corso Superiore, Accad. Sta. Cecillia, Rome, study w. Respighi. 1929-31. m. Margit Kummer, 1 s. Debut: Concert of own works, Budapest, 1930. Career: Composer, Cond., film music, Vienna, 1932, Copenhagen, 1934-36; Prof. of Comp., Municipal Music Schl., Budapest, 1935-41; Conserv. in Kolozsvar, 1941-46; Dir., Conserv. in Szekesfehervar, 1946-49; Prof., Acad. of Music, Budapest, 1949-. Num. comps. incl: Operas & Ballets - The Magic Cupboard, The Sly Students, Panegyricus; Cantatas & Oratorios - Cantata Lirica, Cantus Pannonicus, Waiting for the Spring, Unfurled Flags; Aspirationes Principis; Num. orchl. works & concertos, & chmbr. music, 2 masses, other choral works & songs, many recorded. Mbrships: Mbr., Praesidium, Hungarian Union of Musicians; Nat. Choir Coun.; Chmn., Budapest Choir Coun. Hons: Franz Joseph Prize, 1934; Klebelsberg Prize, 1942; Kossuth Prize, 1950; Erkel Prize, 1960; Merited Artist, 1965; Honored Artist, 1970. Address: Magyajtai utca 12, H-1026 Budapest II, Hungary.

FARKAS, Philip Francis, b. 5 Mar. 1914, Chgo., Ill., USA. Horn Player; Professor of Music. Educ: Pvte. horn studies w. Louis Dufrasne; Music student, Chgo. Civic Orch. (trng. orch. of Chgo. Symph. Orch.). Hon. DMus, Eastern Mich. Univ., 1978. m. Margaret Groves, 4 d. Career: Solo horn w. Kan. City Phil., Chgo. Symph. Orch., Cleveland Orch. & Boston Symph. Orch.; Prof., Ind. Univ. Recordings: All Chgo. Symph. Orch. recordings of Artur Rodzinski, Raphael Kubelik & Fritz Reiner, until 1960. Publs: The Art of French Horn Playing, 1956; The Art of Brass Playing, 1962; A Photographic Study of 40 Virtuoso Horn Players' Embouchures, 1970. Mbrships: Am. Fedn. of Musicians; Phi Mu Alpha Sinfonia. Hobbies: Flying; Paddle Ball; Photography. Address: 5994 E State Rd. Bloomington, IN 47401, USA. 2;8.

FARLEY, Carole, b. 29 Nov. 1946, Le Mars, Iowa, USA. Soprano Singer. Educ: BM, Ind. Univ.; further studies in voice, piano & clarinet, Hochschule für Musik, Munich. m. Jose Serebrier, 1 d. Debut: Town Hall, NY, 1969. Career: has sung w. all major Am. symph. orchs. & in most European & S Am. countries; apps. w. Cologne Welsh Nat., Strasbourg, Lyon, NYC Ctr. & Met. Operas. Recorded Beethoven's 9th Symph. w. Antal Dorati & RPO. Mbr., AGMA. Hons incl: Alumnae of Yr., Ind. Univ., 1975. Mgmt: HUROK Concerts Inc. Address: 270 Riverside Dr., N.Y., NY 10025, USA.

FARMER, Virginia, b. 8 Feb. 1922, Brooklyn, NY, USA. Violinist; Educator. Educ: BMus (violin), Eastman Schl. of Music; MA (Music), Columbia Univ.; Dr.Mus.Arts (violin), Univ. of Ill. Career: mbr.; Buffalo, Balt. & Mpls. Symph. Orchs.; Am.; Florestan & Traldy String Quartets; Vi-Ro-Vi Trio; Performing Artist, Marlboro Music Festival 1957; currently Asst. Prof. of Violin, Univ. of Ill. Recordings w. Mpls. Symph. & Marlboro Festival Orch. Mbrships: Am. String Tchrs. Assn.; Past Sec., Pi Kappa Lambda; Am. Fedn. of Musicians. Hobbies:

Photography; Travel; Cooking. Mgmt: Agricola Bookings, Urbana, Ill. Address: 118 W Vermont, Urbana, IL 61801, USA.

FARNADI, Edith, b. Budapest, Hungary. Professor of Music; Pianist. Debut: solo pianist, age 9. Career: Recitalist & concert appearances throughout the world w. leading orchs. & conds.; Prof., Franz Liszt Acad.; Prof. (Master Class), Acad of Music, Graz, Austria. Num. recordings issued on Columbia, Westminster & Deutsche Grammophon labels. Hons: Franz Liszt Prize (twice won). Address: Vienna, Austria.

FARNCOMBE, Charles Frederick, b. 29 July 1919, London, UK. Conductor. Educ: BSc, London Univ., 1940; AMICE; RSCM; RAM; LRAM; FRAM; Chiugi Acad., Siena, Italy. m. Sally Mae Felps, 1 d. Career: MUsical Dir., Handel Opera Soc., 1955-; Musical Dir., Drottningholm Ct. Theatre, Stockholm, Sweden, 1969-. Recordings: Drottningholm Music (Roman); Great Handel Choruses. Mbrships: Royal Musical Assn.; ISM; Royal Soc. Musicians; Royal Swedish Acad. of Music. Hons: Augustus Manns Prize for Cond., RAM, 1952; CBE, 1977. Hobby: Cottage on Offa's Dyke. Address: 2 Westover Rd., London SW18 2RG, UK.

FARNON, Robert Joseph, b. 24 July 1917, Toronto, Ont., Can. Composer; Conductor. Educ: Broadus Farmer Schl. of Music. m. Patricia Mary Smith, 5 s., 2 d. Debut: Massey Hall, Toronto, 1941. Career: apps., Royal Fest. Hall, Royal Albert Hall, London, Phil. Hall, Liverpool, Massey Hall, Can., Carnegie Hall, NYC; broadcasts, BBC & CBC Radio & TV, ITV, Netherlands Radio & TV, Danish Radio & TV; 40 Film scores. Comps. incl: 2 symphs.; Rhapsody for Violin; Prelude & Dance for Harmonica; 2 orchl. tone poems; num. light orchl. works. Recordings: over 1000 singles, EPs & LPs. Over 100 orchl. & vocal works publd. Contbr. to: Can. Comp.; Crescendo; Bandsman. Mbrships: Song Writers Guild of GB; Variety Club of GB; Pres., Guernsey Softball Assn. Hons: Ivor Novello Awards, 1960, 66 & 72; J Lewis Gold Cup, Hollywood, 1959; Nordring Fest. Music Award, 1973. Address: La Falaise, St. Martins, Guernsey, Channel Islands.

FARQUHAR, David Andross, b. 5 Apr. 1928, Cambridge, NZ. Composer; Prof. of Music, Victoria Univ. of Wellington, NZ. Educ: GSM; comp. class Benjamin Frankel; BA; BMus. (NZ); MA (Cambridge). m. Raydia d'Elsa, 2 c. Compositions: Partita; Symphony. 1959; Three of a Kind; Three Pieces for Violin & Piano; Six Songs of Women; Three Scots Ballads; Ode for Piano; Anniversary Duets (first set); ..And One Makes Ten; Five Scenes (guitar); Ostinato, Capriccio & Epilogo (guitar); Concertino for piano & strings ; Evocation; 3 Pieces for Doublebass. Recordings: Partita; Symphony; Three of a Kind; Three Pieces for Violin & Piano; Three Scots Ballads; Ring Around the Moon Suite; Concertino for Piano & Strings; Evocation (orchl. violins). Pres., Composers' Assn. of NZ., 1974-75. Address: 15 Nottingham St., Wellington 5, NZ.

FARRAR, Carol Ann Reglin, b. 10 Oct. 1942, Waxahachie, Tex., USA. Educ: BA in Music, N. Tex. State Univ., 1964; grad. work in music, Yale Univ., 1964; MA in Musicol., The Am. Univ., Wash. D.C., 1966; PhD in Musicol., N. Tex. State Univ., 1978; studied flute w. George Morey, Julius Baker, Mark Thomas, etc. m. Charles Edwin Farrar, 3 s. Career: Taught music theory, Am. Univ., 1956-66; Music cataloger, Lib. of Congress, Wash. D.C., 1966-67; Flute Instr., N. Tex. State Univ., 1968-71; on Music Fac., El Centro, Mountian View & Dalls Bapt. Colls., Tex., 1969-. As flautist has perf. w. San Angelo Symph., Dallas Symph., Am. Wind Symph., Pitts., Pa., Fairfax Co. Symph., Va., E. Tex. Symph., Tyler, Richardson Symph. Orch., Denton, Tex.; serves as Flute Clinician for solo & ensemble contests. Publs: Michel Corrette & Flute-playing in the Eighteenth Century, 1970. Mbr., Am. Musicol. Soc. Hobby: Needlework. Address: 1219 E Marvin, Waxahachie, TX 75165, USA.

FARRAR, Ruth Price, b. 21 Oct. 1901, Broadland, SD, USA. Teacher of Piano & Organ. Educ: Huron Coll., 2 yrs.; MacPhail Schl., Mpls., 2 yrs.; Am. Conserv., Chgo.; Master Classes Markey, Mason, Broome, Pandet, Karl Ulrich Schnable, Wagness. m. John Edson Farrar, 1 s. Career: Interviews on tchng., var. radio stations. Comps: Elementary tchng. pieces; sev. original & arrs. for adult & children's classes, piano & organ. Publs: You Can Play - But First You Must Think, 1975. Contbr. to num. profl. publs. Mbr., num. profl. orgs. incl: Treas., Alumna Chapt., Seattle, Sigma Alpha Iota; Bd., Music Tchrs. Assn. of Calif. Hons incl: Num. prizes & awards, NGPT; Outstanding Contribution Plaque from Keyboard Industry, 1978; CALCO Award, Calif. Adult Educators, 1971. Hobbies: Camping; Travel; Photography; Working w. adult & children's music hobby groups. Address: Box 603, Mercer Island, WA 98040, USA.

FARRELL, Eileen, b. 1920, USA. Opera Singer. Career: made debut on Columbia Broadcasting Co., 1941, & had own prog. for 6 yrs.; made opera debut w. San Fran. Opera; tours throughout USA & abroad. 16.

FARRELL, Frances, F, b. 17 July 1947. Pt. Washington, NY, USA. Vocalist (dramatic soprano). Educ: Peabody Conserv. of Music, Balt., Md.; BS in Music Educ., Hofstra Univ., Hempstead, L.I., NY. m. Paul Jurkowski, 2 s. Career: Music Tchr. (K-12) at Pt. Wash. Pub. Schls., 1969; Music Dance Instr., Sands Pt. Country Day Schl. Acad., Pt. Wash., summers 1968-; Soloist at Christ Episcopal Ch., Manhasset & Community Synagogue, Sands Point, L.I., NY; Dramatic Soprano Soloist w. lead roles in sev. prodns. of the L.I. Opera Showcase inclng: 'Azucena' in Verdi's 'Il Trovator'; 'Marcellina' in Mozart's 'Marriage of Figaro'; 'Mamma Lucia' in 'Cavalieria Rusticana' & Interfaith Oratorio Soc. of L.I.'s perf. of Handel's 'Judas Maccabaeus', etc. Mbrships. incl: MENC; NEA; NY State Schl. Music Assn.; Pres., Parents Assn. of the Pre-Schl. Development Prog. Recip. var. hons. & awards. Hobbies: Swimming; Bowling. Address: 59 Hickory Rd., Pt. Washington, NY 11050, USA. 4,6.

FARRELL, Peter Snow, b. 13 Sept. 1924, Greensboro, NC, USA. Professor; Concert artist, cello & viola da gamba. Educ: MMus, Eastman Schl. of Music, Univ. of Rochester; Artists' Dip., ibid. m. Miriam, 2 s. Career: Solo & chmbr. music perfs. throughout USA & in UK, German Fed. Repub., Poland, France, & Hawaii; Appearances on major festivals; Specialization on perf. of contemporary music (cello) & Renaissance & Baroque Music (gamba); Former Prin. Cellist, Columbus Phil. Orch. & San Diego Symph. Orch.; Former Fac. mbr., Eastman Schl. of Music & Nat. Music Camp, Interlochen; Former Prof. of Music, Univ. of Ill., Urbana; Prof., Music Dept., Univ. of Calif., San Diego. Num. orchl. & chmbr. music recordings. Contbr. to: Am. String Tchr.; Jrnl. of the Viola da Gamba Soc. of Am. Mbr., Bd. of Dirs., Viola da Gamba Soc. of Am. Hobbies: Sailing; Hiking. Address: Univ. of Calif., San Diego, La Jolla, CA 92037, USA.

FARRELL, Susan Caust, b. 25 Dec. 1944, NYC, USA. Restorer of Antique Musical Instruments. Educ: BA, Goddard Coll., Plainfield, Vt., 1966. div. Career: Sr. Restorer, Musical Instruments, Metrop. Mus. of Art, NY; Keymaker for Friedrich Von Huene, Boston, Mass.; Cons., NY State Craftsmen Inc.; Restorer of woodwinds for var. US collects. Publs: Checklist of Recorders & Flageolets, 1976; Checklist of Flutes & Piccolos, 1976; Directory of Contemporary Am. Musical Instrument Makers (in process). Contbr. to: Jrnl. of Am. Musical Instrument Soc. Mbrships. incl: Galpin Soc.; Am. Musical Instrument Soc.; Am. Recorder Soc.; Guild of Am. Lutiers; Fellowship of Makers & Restorers of Histl. Instruments. Hobbies incl: Cabinetmaking; Astrology. Address: 17 High St., Belfast, Maine 04915, USA. 27.

FARRELL, Timothy Robert Warwick, b. 5 Oct. 1943, Cape Town, South Africa. Organist. Educ: Diocesan Coll., Cape Town; RCM, London; FRCO; ARCM (organ & piano perf.); also studied in Paris. m. Penelope Walmsley-Clark. Career: Asst. Organist, St. Paul's, Knightbridge, 1962-66; Asst. Organist, St. Paul's Cathedral, London, 1966-67; Sub-Organist, Westminster Abbey, 1967-74; Organist, Choirmaster & Comp. at HM Chapels Royal, St. James's Palace, 1974-; Organ Tutor, RSCM, Addington Palace, 1966-73; Regular broadcaster for BBC; Recitals in many parts of GB & abroad. Num. recordings. Recip., W T Best Meml. Scholarship, awarded by Worshipful Co. of Musicians. Hobbies: Golf; Walking; Fast cars; Sailing. Address: The Chapel Royal, St. James's Palace, London SW1, UK. 1,3.

FARRIER, Walter Halliday, Jr., b. 8 Feb. 1932, Newark, NJ, USA. University Professor; Tenor; Choral Director, Composer & Arranger; Woodwind Performer. Educ: BA, Yale Univ., 1954; BM, 1960, MM, 1965, Univ. of Southern Calif. m. Joan Carol Hiebel, 2 s. Career incls: Tenor Soloist, chs. in Maplewood, NJ, Los Angeles & Salem, Ore.; Mbr., Roger Wagner Chorale, 1961-62; Dir. of Choral Activities, Tex. Luth. Coll., 1962-67, Willamette Univ., Salem, Ore., 1967-; Chmn. of Music Dept., Willamette Univ., Salem, Ore., 1977-78. Comps: Livin' All of My Time, spiritual for SATB choir, 1972; Psalm 150 for SATB choir & 2 percussionists; var. arrs. for RCA Victor recordings. Mbrships. incl: Life, Am. Choral Dirs. Assn.; MENC; Nat. Assn. of Tchrs. of Singing. Recip., Alumni Award for Outstanding Achievement & Serv., Univ. of Southern Calif. Schl. of Music, 1961; Pi Kappa Lambda, 1961. Hobby: Carpentry. Address: 4432 Coloma Dr. SE, Salem, OR 97302, USA.9.

FARRINGTON, Michael James, b. 23 Mar. 1935, Hawick, Scotland, UK. Music Adviser; Teacher; Lecturer. Educ: choral exhibnr., Christ's Coll., Cambridge Univ.; Newland Park Coll., Bucks.; Hons. Cert., Oxford Inst. of Educ.; GSM; LRAM (perf.

accomp.); ARCM (tchr., piano). m. Josephine, 3 s. Career incls: Co. Area Advsr. for Music, Lancs., 1969; Advsr. for Music, Trafford Metrop. Borough. Dept., 1974; Vis. Lectr., Tutor, Cond., Repetiteur, Accomp., var. arts & music courses, summer schls., art fests., youth orchs.; Speaker to var. grps. Contbr. to: Spaces for Music - MANA, 1976. Mbrships: Exec., Music Advsrs. Nat. Assn.; Music Panel, N W Arts Assn.; ESTA. Hobbies incl: Theatre. Address: 114 Victoria Rd., Fulwood, Preston, Lancs., UK.3.

FASANG, Árpád, b. 29 June 1912, Cracow, Poland. Professor of Music. Educ: Dip., composing, organ playing, choir master, Musical Acad. m. Elisabeth Orbán, 3 s., 1 d. Career: Music Tchr.-Headmaster, Tchrs. Trng. Coll.; Musical Supvsr. of co. schls.; Headmaster, Schl. of Music; Dept. Ldr., artistic educ., Min. of Culture & Educ.; Chief Dept. Ldr., musical matters, Min. of Educ.; Headmaster, Conserv. in Budapest; Ret'd.; still active as Lectr. on musical matters, Organizer & Supvsr. of choral events. Comp., many choral works. Regularly records for Hungarian Radio. Author of songbooks for music tchrs. & elem. schls. & handbooks on music hist. Contbr. to profl. jrnls. Mbrships. incl: Liszt Ferenc Soc.; Hungarian Musical Assn. Hons incl: Order of Labour, 1st degree, gold medal, 1972. Hobbies incl: Gardening. Address: 1026 Budapest, Pasareti U. 1, Hungary.

FASSBAENDER, Brigitte, b. 3 July 1939, Berlin, Germany. Opera and concert singer, mezzo-soprano. Educ: Conserv. Nürnberg. Debut: München, 1961. Career: apps. in all leading opera houses. Recordings: var. operas, concerts, oratorios. Address: Agnesstr. 57, D 8000 München 40, German Fed. Repub.

FAULCON, Clarence August, II, b. 8 Aug. 1928, Phila., USA. Professor of Music & Music Education; Consultant; Musicologist; Linguistic Researcher; Electronic Music Methodologist; Pianist; Clarinettist. Educ: Phila. Musical Acad.; Phila. Conserv. Music; Univ. Pa.; BS; MS; Mus D. m. Jacqueline Frances Beach, 1 s. Career: Cond., Phila. Concert Orch. & 111th Regimental Combat Team Pa. Nat. Guard Concert Band; Piano soloist; Radio & TV apps.; YMCA State Song Ldr. Publ: Graduate Record Examination in Music, 1971. Contbr. to jrnls. Mbr. var. profl. orgs. Hobbies incl: Chess; Conservation; Gardening; Reading; Walking. Address: 4 Elkdale Rd., Lincoln Univ., PA 19352, USA.

FAULCON, Jacqueline Frances Beach, b. 8 Dec. 1934, New York City, USA. Concert Artist (Soprano); Pianist; Accompanist; College Voice Professor; College Music Education & Piano Professor; Middle School Music Teacher (Choral). Educ: BS, Piano, Music Educ., Music Supervision; MS, Piano, Voice, Music Educ. m. Clarence Augustus Faulcon II, 1 s. Career: Soloist w. num. orchs. inclng: Balt. Symph. Orch.; Newark Symph. Orch.; TV & Opera apps. Mbr. num. profl. orgs. inclng: Sigma Alpha Iota; Phi Beta Kappa; Mu Phi Alpha; Afro Am. Music Opportunities Assn. Recip. num. awards. Hobbies: Gourmet Cooking; Reading; Conservation; Gardening; Designing Clothes. Address: 4 Elkdale Rd., Lincoln Univ., PA 19352, USA.

FAULKNER, Helen, b. 1 Jan. 1953, Brighton, UK. Music Librarian; Lecturer. Educ: BMus, MMus (analysis), Goldsmith's Coll., Univ. of London. Career: Music Libn., Goldsmith's Coll., Univ. of London; Music Lectr., ibid. Publs: Bibliography of British Music since 1950, 1976. Contbr. to: Contact (reviews). Mbrships: Royal Musical Assn.; Int. Assn. of Music Libns. Hobbies: Theatre; Food; Hedonism. Address: 22 Conger's House, Bronze St., London SE8 3DT, UK.

FAUNCH, Paul, b. 25 Jan. 1933, Forest Gate, UK. Educationalist. Educ: BA, St. John's Coll., Durham; LTCL (TD); LTSC; LNCM. Career: Precentor, Guildford Cathedral, 1959-60; Prin., Tonic Sol-Fa Coll., London, 1967-71, Curwen Coll. of Music, 1972-; Dir. of Music, Buckingham Coll., Harrow, 1975-; currently Ed., Ecclesiol. Newsletter. Contbr. to: Ch. Times; Wellingburian; Bulletin of Curwen Int. Music Assn. (Ed., 1967-71). Mbrships. incl: Chmn., Ecclesiol. Soc., 1967-; Hon. Sec., Minor Canons Assn., 1975-; FSA (Scotland); FPhS, England. Hons. incl: Kt., St. John of Malta, 1971; sev. hon. degrees & fellowships. Address: 13 Hindes Rd., Harrow, Middx., UK. 3,28.

FAUST, Karl Richard Robert, b. 16 April 1929, Solingen, Germany. Musician (viola); Composer; Conductor. Educ: Pvte. studies. m. Dagmar F Witzel. Career: Musician & Comp., German radio - 1952; Cond., Musical Dir., Radio & TV, Brazil, -1962; Prod., classical records, Deutsche Grammophon/Polydor, -1977; Managing Dir., Polytel Music Prodns., TV/Film Div., Polygram Group. Comps: Chmbr. music, cantatas, orchl. & choral works. Contbr. to: Schriftenreihen, etc. Mbrships: Coun., Deutscher Musikrat, Deutsche Phonoakademie, etc. Hons: Prize for Comp., Solingen, 1951; Edison award, 1970; Sev. Brazilian Awards; Officer, Ordem do rio branco, 1972. Address: Moordamm 54, D-2081 Ellerbek, Germany.

FAUST, Randall Edward, b. 3 July 1947, Vermillion, SD, USA. Instructor of Horn & Music Theory. Educ: BSc Mus, Eastern Mich. Univ. MMus, Mankato State Univ.; further study, Interlochen Arts Acad., Univ. of IA, & Univ. of Mich. Interlochen. m. Sharon Kay Mole, 1 s. Career: Instr., Shenandoah Conserv. of Music, Winchester, Va. Comps. incl: Soliloquies, double concerto for solo tenor trombone, solo bass trombone & trombone octet; Gallery Music for Brass Quintet; Concerto for Brass Quintet; Percussion & Strings; Celebration for Horn & Organ; Sonata for Bass Trombone. Contbr. to Jrnl. of NACWPi; Int. Horn Soc.; Phi Mu Alpha Sinfonia. Hons: Winner, Instrumental Div., Minn. Fedn. of Music Clubs Comp. Contest, 1973, for Canzona for Str. Orch. Address: Shenandoah Coll. & Conserv. of Music, Winchester, VA 26001, USA.

FAVRE, Georges, b. 26 July 1905, Saintes, France. Educational Administrator; Composer. Educ: Doct. es Lettres; Laur., comp., cond., Nat. Sup. Conserv., Paris. Career: Gen. Inspector of public instruction, musical educ. Compositions: Publd., Balises; Contes d'Arvor, (piano); Poèmes Marins, (voice & piano); Cantate du jardin vert, (voice & orch.); Symphonia Brevis, (orch.); Sonate, (piano & Violas), etc. Guan, drama lyrics; La Mandragore, comedy lyrics. Pubs: Boieldieu, sa vie, son oeuvre, Paris, 1945; Musiciens Français modernes, 1953; Musiciens Français Contemporaines, 1956; Ecrits sur la Musique et l'Education Musicale, 1966; L'oeuvre de Paul Dukas, 1969; Correspondance de Paul Dukas, 1971; Histoire Musicale de la Principauté de Monaco, 1974; Ouvrages d'Histoire de la Musique et d'Esthetique Musicale. Contbr. to: Revue Française de Musicol. Mbrships: Alsace Acad.; Admin. Coun., French Soc. of Musicol. Hons: Chevalier de Légion d'Honneur; Commandeur de l'ordre des Palmes Académiques. Hobbies: Swimming; Sea Fishing; Cruising; Address: 40 Ave. Secrètan, Paris XIX, France.

FAVRE, Max, b. 31 Mar. 1921, Berne, Switzerland. Music Scholar & Writer; Professor of Piano. Educ: PhD, Musicol., Univ. Berne; Piano Dip., Conserv. of Florence, Italy. m. Stella Favre-Lingorow, 4 children. Career: Music Critic, Der Bund; Vice-Dir., Tchrs. Trng. Coll., Berne. Publs incl: Kirchenmusik in Okunemischer Jchau, 1963; Bericht uber den 3, Internationalen Kongress fur Kirchenmusik in Bern, 1973; Tendenzen und Verwirklichungen, 1975; Hermann Haller, 1975. Contbr. to Schweizerische Musikzeitung; Revue Musicale de Suisse Romande. Mbr. Swiss Soc. of Musicol.; Swiss Soc. of Musical Educ.; Soc. of Swiss Musicians. Hobbies: Alpinism; Skiing; Swimming; Gardening; Cooking. Address: CH 3074 Muri, Jagerstrasse 5, Switzerland.

FAZAL, Ruth, b. 13 Aug. 1952, Leicester, UK. Violinist; Guitarist; Singer. Educ: Dartington Coll. of Arts, 1968-70; GSM; AGSM; studied w. Nell Gotkovsky in Paris. m. Aziz Fazal. Career: Recitals in Toronto, Can.; Ldr., Cecilia Str. Quartet; TV apps. on 100 Huntly St. show, singing & playing guitar. Comps: 75 Religious songs for guitar & voice. Hons: French Govt. Scholarship; Birdie Warshaw violin prize, 1973. Hobbies: People; Singing; Animals. Address: 110 Erskine Ave., Apt. 309, Toronto, Ont. M4P 1Y4, Can.

FAZZARI, Hans (Giovanni), b. 5 Oct. 1932, Milan, Italy. Pianist; Composer; Professor of Music. Educ: Studied w. Carlo Zecchi; Dip., Conserv. Verdi, Milan; Autodidatta as Comp.; Studied law, Univ. Milan; Prof. Piano, Conserv. Verdi, Milan. Career: Pianist w. concerts in Europe, USA & S Am.; More than 100 TV & radio apps.; Concerts in Piccola Scala, Santa Ceilia, Rome & w. Radio Orch.; As Comp., perfs. in Europe, USA, S Am & Japan; Chmbr. music perfs. Comps. incl: Anacronism, 1968; So Long George, 1970. Num. recordings. Mbrships. incl: Pres., Serate Musicali, Milan; Mbr., Jury of Int. Prices Consigliere d'Amministrazione di Casa Verdi. Address: Via Settala 72, Milan, Italy.

FEAR, Margaret, b. Edgware, UK. Concert Pianist; Teacher. Educ: RAM; pvte. study w. Joseph Weingarten, Cyril Smith & Phyllis Sellick; LRAM; ARCM. Debut: Wigmore Hall, 1961. Career: many recitals, broadcasts, concertos w. sev. orchs. throughout country; Recitals, Purcell Room. Mbr., Solo Perfs. Sect., ISM. Hobbies: Walking; Swimming. Mgmt: Terry Slasberg Agency. Address: 36 Parkside Dr., Watford, Herts., UK. 3.

FEASEY, Norman Edward, b. 11 Nov. 1903, London, UK. Opera Advisor & Repetiteur; Teacher; Lecturer; Adjudicator. Educ: Westminster Schl.; RCM. m. Alice Helen Laurie. Career:

Choral Clerk, Westminster Abbey; Chief Repetiteur, Royal Opera House, Covent Garden, 1936-40; Chorus Master, Royal Opera Choir; Cond. & coach, Sadler's Wells Opera, 1940-44; Cond., Old Vic Co., 1944-46; Sr. Repetiteur & Advsr., Royal Opera House, 1946-; Tutor, London Opera Schl. & Ctr., 1956-78; Prof., RAM, 1977-; Lecturer; Broadcaster; Adjudicator. Publ: Engl. translation of Massenet's Manon. Recip., HonRAM, 1979. Hobbies: Reading; Photography. Address: 124 Queen's Gate, London SW7 5LJ, UK.

FEBBRAIO, Salvatore Michael Turlizzo, b. 30 Apr. 1935, Mt Vernon, NY, USA. Educator; Concert Artist; Administrator; Composer. Educ: Mus B; Mus M; Mus Ed M; PD; Juilliard Schl. of Music; Manhattan Schl. of Music; Fordham Univ.; NY Univ. m. Antoinette Aurichio Febbraio, 2 s. Debut: Town Hall, Phila., 1947. Career incl: num. concert radio & TV apps. as prodigy & later; apps. at Carnegie Hall, Town Hall, etc.; Fndr. & Exec. Dir. Febbraio Conserv. of Music, 1954-. Comps: num. orchl., chmbr. & instrumental works, in addition to num. popular & jazz comps. Publs. incl: Theory of Music, 1957; Essentials of Music, 1973; Jazz Improvisation, 1975. Mbr., num. profl. orgs. Recip., num. awards & citations in nat. perf. & comp. competitions. Hobbies: Reading; Tennis. Address: 49 Parkway E, Mt. Vernon, NY 10522, USA.

FECHT, Johanna - Lotte, b. 15 May, Frankfurt, Hessen/-Germany. Opera singer. Career: Permanent engagement in Nürnberg; Guest perfs. in Hamburg, Berlin, Stuttgart, Brussels, Dusseldorf, etc. Address: Hainstr. 25, 85 Nürnberg, German Fed. Repub.

FECZKO, Elżbieta Maria, b. 8 Sept, 1922, Olkusz, Poland. Pianist. Educ: MA, Instrumental Fac., Coll. of Music. Debut: Katowice, 1952. Career: Piano concerts as soloist w. Symph. Orchs., Opole & Nysa; Chmbr. music concerts; perfs. as Accomp.; Teaching, in coop. w. Pedagogic Ctr. of Art Teaching; Lectures & seminars in courses for Piano Tchrs. Contbr. to Ruch Muzyczny, 1964. Mbr., Assn. Polish Musicians (Chmn. arch. circle). Hons: Prize & Dip., Competition of Young Talents, Warsaw, 1934. Hobbies incl: Problems of Teaching Children; Travelling Abroad; Collecting folk ceramics and books on art. Address: Os. Szklane Domy 1/257, 31-972 Craców, Poland.

FEDELE, John Anthony, b. 1 Sept. 1947, Syracuse, Onondaga, USA. Trombonist. Educ: B Mus, Music Educ., Ithaca Coll.; M Sc, Music Educ., ibid. m. Leah Stephens. Career: Music Educator in Elementary & Secondary Public Schls. Mbrships: Music Educators Nat. Conf.; NEA; NY State Schl. Music Assn.; NY State United Tchrs.; Kappa Gamma Psi. Recip. Solvay-Geddes Kiwanis Award for Instrumental Music, 1965. Hobbies: Golf; Discography. Address: 221 Pelham Rd., DeWitt, NY 13214, USA.

FEDER, Franz Georg, b. 30 Nov. 1927, Bochum, Germany. Musicologist. Educ: Univs. of Tübingen, Göttingen, & Kiel; PhD Christian-Albrecht-Univ., Kiel. m. Marianne Lott, 3 children. Career: Asst. to Prof. Jens Peter Larsen, Dir., Joseph Haydn-Inst., Köln 1957-60; Dir., ibid., 1960-. Mbrships. incl: Gesellschaft für Musikforschung. Publs. incl: Ed., Joseph Haydn, Werke, (38 vols. & 28 commentaries), 1962-; Haydn-Studien, (3 vols.), 1965-; Geschichte der evangelischen Kirchenmusik, Part III, 1965. Contbr. to profl. jrnls. Address: 5 Köln 90 (Porz-Westhoven), Am Kielshof 2, German Fed. Repub.

FEDERHOFER, Hellmut, b. 6 Aug. 1911, Graz, Austria. Professor; Musicologist. Educ: Dip., Kappelmeister, Akad. für Musik und darstellende Kunst, Vienna, 1934; Dr. Phil., Univ. of Vienna, 1936. m. Renate Federhofer-Königs, 1d., 1s. Career: Lect., musicol., Univ. of Graz, 1944; Hd., Inst. of Musicol., Univ. of Graz, 1945-; Dir., Inst. of Musicol., Johannes Gutenberg Univ., Mainz, 1962-; Dir., Acta Musicologica, 1962-; Ed. of Musick Alter Meister & of Mainzer Studien zur Musikwissenschaaft. Publs: Beiträge zur musikalischen Gestaltanalyse, 1950; Musikpflege und Musiker am Grazer Habsburgerhof der Erzherzöge Karl und Ferd. von Innerösterreich, 1967; Neue Musik, 1977; Georg Muffat, an Essay on Thoroughbass, 1961. Contbr. of Ca. 250 articles to jrnls., dict., & Encys. Mbrships: Assn. of Eds. of Denkmäler der Tonkunst in Österreich; Central Inst. for Mozart Research. Hons: Goldmedaille Pro Musica Austriaca; Österr. Ehrenkreuz für Kunst und Wissenschaft. Address: Am Königsborn 18, 6500 Mainz 21, German Fed. Repub.

FEDERHOFER-KÖNIGS, Renate, b. 4 Jan. 1930, Cologne, Germany. Musicologist. Educ: Dr.Phil., Univ. of Cologne, 1957. m. Hellmut Federhofer, 1s., 1d. Publs: Johannes Oridryus und sein Musiktraktat, 1957; Wilhelm Joseph von Wasielewski im Spiegel seiner Korrespondenz, 1975. Contbr. to Kirchenmusikalisches Jahrbuch, 1958 ff. Address: Am. Königsborn 18, 6500 Mainz 21, German Fed. Repub.

FEDERL, Ekkehard Friedrich Thomas, b. 26 Feb. 1905, Landstrassen, Czech. Benedictine Monk; Music Teacher & Musicologist. Educ: State Exam. for Adv. Music Tchrs.; PhD, Musicol. Career: Tchr., Music Grammer Schl.; Priest, Prior of Schweiklberg Abbey, Bavaria, Germany. Author, dissertation; Spätmittelalterliche Choralpflege in Würzburg und in Mainfränkischen Klöstern & var. articles in jrnls. Contbr. to: Kataloge Bayerischer Musiksammlungen. Mbrships: Soc. Music Rsch.; Soc. Hist. of Bavarian Music; Inst. Contemp. & Expmtl. Music. Hobby: Hist. of Art. Address: D-8358 Schweiklberg, Post Vilshofen, German Fed. Repub.

FEDOR, Viliam, b. 3 Jan. 1913, Smolnik, Czechoslovakia. University Professor of Musical Education. Educ: Tchrs. Coll.; Studied comp. & cond., Conservatoire; PhD, Pedagogical Fac., Comenius Univ., Bratislava. m. Maria Durikova, 3 children. Debut: Cond., final concert of conservatoire students. Career: Cond., Women's Vocal Choir; Several radio apps.; Univ. Prof. of Musical Educ., Pedagogical Fac., Nitra. Publs. incl: Some basic relations of Music & Psychic State taking into consideration time factor, 1968; Basis of Musical Pedagogy, 1969; Choir Singing & Choir Conducting (w. J. Vrchotova), 1969; Programmed Textbook of Intonation & Hearing Analysis (w. Zd. Svabova), 1971. Psychology of Music, 1972, 1975; Guide to Listening to Records, 1976. Contbr. to: Musik in der Schule; Slovenska hudba, Hudobna vychova. Mbrships: Hd., Slovak Soc. for Musical Educ.; Int. Soc. for Musical Educ. Recip., Prize, for essay, Slovak Soc. for Musical Educ. Hobbies: Touring; Cooking. Address: Presovska 67, Bratislava, Czechoslovakia.

FEIDJE, Åsmund Ivar, b. 5 June 1948, Ringebu, Norway. Musician (guitar, bass-guitar, banjo & violin); Vocalist; Composer. Educ: Pvte. studies. m. Marit Ofstad. Career: Mbr., Symph. rock group Rain, 1967-; Mbrs. of group have been writing, arranging & playing theatre music for Nat. Theatre & Radio & TV Theatres, 1969-; Bass guitarist, violinist w. Terje Rypdal Ensemble, 1971-72. Comps. incl: Rivalen, 1970; The Taming of the Shrew, 1975; The Burning Court, 1975; CAMP, 1977; A Ballet on the Neutron Bomb, 1978. Recordings incl: Viser fra pendlerne; Jenteloven; CAMP, Janet Hay's Greatest Hits. Mbrships: Norsk Musikerforbund; TONO. Hons: H A Benneches Legat, 1976. Address: St. Olavs Gt. 10, Oslo I, Norway.

FEIGIN, Sara, b. 1 July 1928, Rega, Latvia, USSR. Pianist; Composer; Teacher. Educ: MA, Comp., Rega. m. Oscar Feigin, 2 d. Debut: Rega. Career: Perfs. on stage & TV; Radio Concerts for Youth Phil.; Ballets perfd. at Opera House of Rega; Headmistress, Holon Municipal Conserv. Comps.: Ballets; Concerts for Orch. & Voice, Violin, Clarinet, Piano. Recordings: sev. recordings in Rega & in Israel. Publs: Tokkata for piano and other instruments. Mbrships: Union of Comps. Recip., award for Russian Dances. Address: 1/57 Brazzaville St., Holon, Israel.

FEIN, David N, b. 1 Nov. 1953, New York, NY, USA. Instructor of Timpani & Percussion; Timpanist & Percussionist; Conductor. Educ: BMus, MMus, MMus, Juilliard Schl.; Grad., High Schl. of Music & Art; DMA. Career: Instr. of Timpani & Percussion, Juilliard Schl. Pre-Coll. Div., 1973-; Freelance Percussionist, Timpanist & Cond.; Percussionist w. NJ Symph. & Boston Symph. in Gurrelieder; Timpanist in World Premier of Antony & Cleopatra; Apps. w. maj. orchs. in USA. Publs: Checklist & Glossary of Percussive Instruments & Terms in English, German, Italian, & French, 1975. Mbr. num. profl. orgs. Hobbies: Bldg. & repairing Timpani & Percussive Instruments; Mfrg. Timpani Mallets & Sticks. Address: 100-21 Alcott Pl., Bronx, NY 10475, USA.

FEINSMITH, Marvin P, b. 4 Dec. 1932, NYC, USA. Composer; Bassoonist. Educ: Juilliard Schl. of Music; BM & MMus, Manhattan Schl. of Music; Mozarteum, Salzburg; DMA Cand., Univ. of Colo. m. Roberta Feinsmith, 3 s., 1 d. Career incls: 1st Bassoon, Indpls. Symph. Orch., 1956-59; Tchr., Ball State Tchrs. Coll., Muncie, Ind., 1956-59, Henry St. Settlement of NY, 1961-66, Denver Free Univ., 1973-74, Hillel Acad., 1975-76; Bassoonist, Symph. of the Air, 1959-63, Little Orch. Soc., 1959-68, 1979-72; Alternate 1st Bassoon, Israel Phil. Orch., 1968-70; Solo bassoon, Bernstein Mass, 1972; Asst. Prin. Bassoon, Denver Symph. Orch., 1972-; Bassoonist var. Broadway musicals & studio recordings. Comps. incl: film scores of: Two Wheeler, Sky Sailing & Molly Brown; Ethics of the Fathers, premiered 1975 by Denver Symph. Recordings incl: w. Israel Symph. Orch. under Zubin Mehta. Hobby: Cycling. Address: 34 Athena Rd., Rt. 4, Blackhawk, CO 80422, USA.

FEINTUCH, Gerald S, b. 28 Feb. 1942, NYC, USA. Conductor (SymphonicOperatic). Educ: BA, Music, Queens Coll., CUNY, 1964; MA (Comp. Musicol.)ibid, 1971; Cond. w. Maestros

Igor Markevitch, Monte Carlo, 1971-72, Herbert Blomstedt, Monte Carlo & Aspen, Colo., 1971-73, Kresimir Sipusch, Monte Carlo, 1971-72, Leonard Bernstein, Tanglewood, 1970, Leon Barzin, NYC, 1970-71, Dr. Richard Lert, Orkney Springs, Va., 1969. m. Sherry C Dobb. Career: Dir.-Cond., Ruffino Opera Assn., NYC, 1964-72; Guest Cond., Oratoria Soc. of NJ, 1966; Fac., Queens Coll., CUNY, 1970-71; Assoc. Cond., Ft. Wayne Phil. Orch., 1973-. Mbrships: Am. Symph. Orch. League; The Coll. Music Soc.; Am. Fed. Musicians. Hons: Prince Ranier III Prize, Monte Carlo, w. Stipend, 1971, '72; Full Scholarship, Aspen Music Fest., Colo., 1972,-'73 0 Berkshire Music Fest., Tanglewood, 1970. Hobbies: Photography; Gourmet Cooking. Address: 5626-4 Old Dover Blvd., Ft. Wayne, IN 46815, USA.

FEIST, Leonard, b. 12 Dec. 1910, Pelham, NY, USA. Music Publishing Executive. Educ: BA, Yale Univ.; Columbia Univ. Grad. Schl. m. Mary Regensburg, 2 d. Career: Sec., Leo Feist Inc., 1933-35; Pres., Mercury Century Music Publrs., 1937-55; Pres., Assoc. Music Publrs., 1956-65; Exec. VP, Nat. Music Publrs. Assn., 1966-77; Pres. ibid., 1977-. Mbrships: incl: Pres., 1971-75, Chmn. of Bd., 1975; Nat. Music Coun.; VP, 1973-78. Copyright Soc. of the USA; VP, 1970, Nat. Acad. of Popular Music; Hon. Profl. Mbr., Mu Phi Epsilon (Sinfonia). Contbr. to num. jrnls. Hobbies: Landscaping; Sculpting. Address: 49 E 86th St., NY, NY 10028, USA.2.

FELBERMAYER, Anny, b. Vienna, Austria. Opera Singer. Educ: HS for Music & Dramatic Art, Vienna. Career incl: Leading roles w. Vienna State Opera & var. other European opera houses. Mbr: 1949 Mozart Assn., Vienna. Hons: Cebotari Prize; Prizes at Int. Competitions at Geneva & Verviers. Address: Wilhelm Busch Gasse 32, Vienna, Austria.

FELCH-MONOKOSKI, Patricia, b. 14 Mar. 1947, Boston, Mass., USA. Music Librarian; Educator; Programme Annotator. Educ: Assoc. of Arts, Pine Manor Jr. Coll., Chestnut Hill, Mass.; BA, Univ. of Denver, Colo.; MA (librarianship), ibid.; MA (music hist. lit.) ibid. m. Stanley A Monokoski, 1 d. Career: Music Libn., Atlanta Public Lib. (Asst. Hd., Fine Arts Dept.), Atlanta, Ga., 1973-75; Asst. Music Libn. for Public Services, Northwestern Univ. Music Lib., Evanston, Ill., 1975-; Music Instructor, Waubonsee Coll., Sugar Grove, Ill., 1977-; Prog. notes annotator, Chgo. Symph. Orch. Allied Arts, 1978-. Contbr. to: Clavier; Music Lib. Assn., Notes (lib. jrnl.); Literary Jrnl. Mbrships: Music Lib. Assn.; Int. Assn. of Music Libs.; Coll. Music Soc. Hon: Beta Phi Mu. Hobbies: Tennis; Skiing; Gourmet Cooking. Address: 145 Chandler Ave., Elmhurst, IL 60126, USA.

FELD, Jindřich, b. 19 Feb. 1925, Prague, Czech. Composer; Music Teacher. Educ: Prague Conserv., 1945-48; Acad. of Music, Prague, 1948-52; PhD, Charles Univ., Prague. m. Helena Feldova, 1 d. Career: Composer; Music Tchr.; Vic. Composer-in-Res., Univ. of Adelaide, Aust., 1968-69; Prof., Conserv. of Prague, 1972-. Comps. recorded incl: Sonatina for 2 Violins, 1952-53; Concerto for Flute & Orch., 1954; Rhapsody for Violin & Orch., 1956; Concerto for Cello & Orch., 1958; 3 Frescoes for Grand Symph. Orch., 1963; Str. Quartet No. 4, 1965; Inventions for Mixed Chamber Choir, 1966; 1 Symph. for Grand Symph. Orch., 1966-67; Wind Quintet No. 2, 1968; Dramatic Fantasy for Grand Symph. Orch., 1968-69; Sonata for Piano, 1971-72; Concerto for Piano & Orch., 1973. Num. other symph., concerto, chmbr., vocal, stage & pedagogic works publd. Contbr. to: Hudebny Rozhledy (Musical Review), Prague. Mbr: Guild of Czech. Composers. Hons. Mbr., Assn. of Danish Accordionists. Recip. of var. prizes for comps. & State Prize, Czech., 1968. Hobbies: Violin & Viola; Tennis; Swimming; Skiing. Address: Procernická 513, 108 00 Prague 10 Malesice, Czech.

FELDBRILL, Victor, b. 4 Apr. 1924, Toronto, Ont., Can. Conductor; Musical Director. Educ: RAM; RCM; dip., violin & cond., Royal Conserv. of Music, Toronto; studied w. Pierre Monteux & Willem van Otterloo. m. Helen Ledermann, 2d. Debut: Toronto, 1942. Career incl: fndr., Toronto Chmbr. Players, 1952; guest cond., BBC London, 1960-; cond. & musical dir., Winnipeg Symph. Orch., 1958-68; cond. & music dir., Nat. Youth Orch. of Can., 1960, '61, '63, '64, '69, '75; Cond. in residence, Univ. of Toronto, 1972-; resident cond. Toronto Symph., 1973-77; Cond. & music dir., Toronto Symph. Youth Orch., 1974-78; guest cond., num. orchs. in Can. & abroad; has given premieres of num. Canadian works; many apps. on radio & TV. Mbrships: Am. Fed. of Musicians; Am. Symph. Orch. League (Bd. mbr., 1960-67). num. hons. Address: 170 Hillhurst Blvd., Toronto, Ont., Can.

FELDBUSCH, Eric, b. 2 Mar. 1922, Liège, Belgium. Academic Director; Composer; Conductor. Educ: Sup. Dip., w. supreme dist., Royal Conserv., Liège; studied violincello w. Maurice

Maréchal, Paris. m. Aline Navaux, 1 s. Career: Recitals thru'out Europe as soloist & w. Trio Reine Elisabeth Belgique; Prof., Violincello, Royal Conserv., Mons; Dir., ibid; Dir., Royal Conserv., Brussels. Compositions incl: 30 melodies; Mein Land; 3 Poèmes pour Quatuour vocal & piano duet; Sh'ma Israel pour cordes; Threne pour une enfance foudroyée; Concerto pour violon et orch., etc. Recordings: Sh'ma Israel, for str. orch.; Stances pour recitant et orch., 3 poèmes de Garcia Lorca; 2 Sonates de Vivaldi pour violoncelle et clavecin; Trio pour fluste, violon et Violoncelle; Melodies pour chant et piano. Mbrships: SABAM; Scis. & Arts Acad., Hainaut; Belgian Comps. Union. Hons: Pablo Casals prize, (violoncelle) Dip., hon., Int. Competition, Prague, 1950; Laur., (comp.), Royal Acad., Belgium, 1972. Hobbies: Photography; Painting. Address: rue Vergote, 29, Boîte postale 4, 1040 Brussels, Belgium.

FELDERHOF, Jan Reindert Adriaan, b. 25 Sept. 1907, Bussum, The Netherlands. Composer; Violinist; Conductor. Educ: Violin & Comp. Cert., Amsterdam Conserv.; Cert., Schl. Music, Utrecht Conserv. m. Petronella J Mulder, 2 s., 1 d. Career: Hd. Tchr., Amsterdam & Utrecht Conservs.; Dir. of the Rotterdam Conserv.; Adj. Dir. of the Amsterdam Conserv.; Tchr. at a Girls' HS & at the Folk Music Schl.; Cond. of many choirs & orchs.; Guest Cond., Broadcasting Orchs. & the Concertgebouw Orch.; Has given many radio violin recitals. Compositions incl: (for orch.) Sinfoniettas; Symphs.; Overture; Funeral Music (w. vocalising choir); Flute concerto; (choir & orch.) Complimento (string orch.); Amaggio (crch); Cantata 'To Whom Shall We Go' (w. vocal soloists); (piano) Facetten (w. vocal soloists); 4 Str. Quartets; 1 Brass Quartet; 2 Operas; chamber music, etc. Recordings: Concerto for flute & str. orch. Mbr., Soc. of Netherlands Comps. Hons: Kt. in the order of Oranje Nassau, 1970. Hobbies: Tennis; Bridge; Mountain sport. Address: Trisstraat 2, 1402 ER, Busssum, The Netherlands.

FELDMAN, Elliott David, b. 8 Mar. 1950, Toronto, Can. Composer; Performer; Arranger; Producer. Educ: studied clarinet w. Benny Arthur, comp. & arr. w. Dr W A McCauley, theory & harmony w. Little Jack Soberman. Debut: 1971. Career: performer on guitar, quarter-tone guitar, piano & clarinet; var. perfs. of own & other works in Toronto & w. E York Symph. Orch. Comps. incl: They Diviners, for symph. orch.; Ymageries Chantepleure & Ego Sum Erst, for 5 male voices; Sofa Back, instrumental (recorded); Coltone for violin & guitar; Two Bits for quarter-tone guitar; Quarter-tone Blues, for quarter-tone guitar & violin. Recordings: Hustlin' & Bustlin'; Without the Moon (Richard Strong). Mbrships: Dir., E Yorks Symph. Orch., publicity & promotion; Composers, Authors & Publishers Assn. of Can. Ltd.; AFM. Hobby: Perf. w. rock & roll quartet. Mgmt: Carol Sherman, Tough Mgmt., Toronto. Address: 114 Vaughan Rd., No. 24, Toronto, Ont. M6C 2M1, Can.

FELDMAN, Ludovic, b. 25 May 1893, Galatz, Romania. Composer. Educ: Bucharest Schl. of Music, 1910-11; Neues Wiener Konservatorium, 1911-13. m. Alice (dec.). Career incl: Violinist, Zagreb Opera, 19215-26; Romanian Opera Orch., Bucharest, 1926-40; Violin Solo, George Enescu Phil., ibid., 1945-53, Concerts in chmbr. music ensembles. Comps. incl: Symphonie concertante, 1971-72. Concertino (suite concertante), for chmbr ensemble, 1975; Episodes et Visions, for symph. orch., 1976; Quintet No. 2 for Violin, Clarinet, Viola, Cello & Piano, 1977; Improvisations, (trio for Violin, Viola & Piano), 1979; Pièce de Concert (for Orch. instruments), 1980. Contbr. to: Muzica. Hons. incl: Ordre de Travail, 1954; Maître émérite de l'art, 1957; Prix de l'Union des Compositeurs, 1969; Ordre du Mérite Culturel, 1969; Prix George Enescu de l'Académie de la République Socialiste de Roumanie, 1978. Address: str. Theodor Stefanescu 8, 70082, Bucharest IV, Romania.

FELDMAN, Myrna Herzog, b. 1 Dec. 1951, Rio de Janeiro, Brazil. Cello & Viola da Gamba Player; Music Critic; Viola da Gamba Teacher. Educ: BA, Fed. Univ. of Rio de Janeiro, 1973; Studied gamba w. Judith Davidoff, cello w. Ibere Gomes Grosso; Sev. music workshops, Brazil & USA; Musical theory cert., Brazilian Music Conservatory. m. Eliahu Feldman, 1 s. Career: Soloist, Brazilian Symph. Orch., 1972; Played in Kalenda Maya (early music), Pro-Arte String Orch.; Sev. concerts w. Pro-Arte Antigua, 1971; TV appearances w. Kalenda Maya & Youth Symph. Orch.; Music Critic, Aonde Vamos?, weekly mag. Mbr. of Guadro Cervantes, Baroque Grp., sev. TV appearances with the grp. Mbrships: Brazilian Rep., Viola da Gamba Soc. of Am.; Viola da Gamba Soc. of England; Am. Recorder Soc. Hons: Winner, Young Soloists of Brazilian Symph. Orch. competition, 1972; Winner, Villa-Lobos Soc. Contest, 1973. Hobbies incl: Tapestry; Poetry; Translating gamba methods of 17th century (Engl. & French). Address: R. Carvalho Azevedo 65201, Rio de Janeiro, GB ZC 20, Brazil.

FELDSHER, Howard M, b. 11 July 1936, Middletown, NY, USA. Educator; Composer; Author; Publisher. Educ: BS Mus. Ed., Ithaca Coll; MA Mus. & Mus. Ed., Columbia Univ.; Profl. Dip. (coll. tchng. & admin.), ibid; PhD cand., Univ. of Utah. m. Eileen Sinkowitz. Career: Instrumental Music Tchr.; Comp. of music used in educ.; Dir. of Publ., Aulos Music Publrs. Comps: Adagio & Allegro (bass clarinet & Piano); 2 Fugues (mixed clarinet quartet); Habanera (oboe or violin & piano); Calypso Song (alto sax & piano); Spanish Serenade (flute & piano); Little Suite for Brass (2 trumpets, 2 trombones); Excursion (trumpet & piano); The Lure of Latin (bass clef instrument & piano); My Love is Like a Red, Red Rose (SATB choir, a capella). Contbr. to profl. jrnls. Mbrships: ASCAP, MENC; Phi Mu Alpha Sinfonia; United Tchrs. Assn.; Pres., Orange County Music Educators. Recip., Rsch. Fellowship, Comp., Univ. of Utah, 1971-72. Hobbies: Travel; Photography. Address: PO Box 54, Montgomery, NY 12549, USA.

FELIX, Leonard (Lennie), b. 16 Aug. 1920, London, UK. Pianist. Educ: pvte. tuition followed by self-trng. Career: num. broadcasts on BBC radio & TV, usually w. own Trio; concerts at Fest. Hall, 1970 & Wigmore Hall, 1974; Extensive tours of Switzerland & Germany both as solo artist & w. Am. jazz soloists. Comp: Morning Stroll; Bubblin' Nova; Cat-Nap. Recordings incl: That Cat Felix; The Many Strides of Lennie Felix; In His Stride; Tribute to Louis Armstrong. Contbr. to: Crescendo; Jazz Jrnl. Mbrships: PRS; Songwriters Guild; Mech. Copyrights Soc. Recip. Melody Maker Piano Award, 1966. Hobbies: Golf; Swimming; Travel. Address: 233 Lauderdale Mansions, London W9, UK.

FELIX, Václav, b. 29 Mar. 1928, Prague, Czech. Composer; Musicologist; Educator. Educ: Grad., Musical Fac., Acad. of Musical Arts, Prague, 1953; PhD & Cand. of Sci., Charles Univ., Prague. m. Danuse Felixova, 1 s., 2 d. Career: Ed., Hudebni rozhledy, Prague, 1959-61; Asst., Musical Fac., 1951-54, Special Asst., 1960-73, Docent in Music Theory, 1973 . Acad. of Musical Arts, Prague. Comps. incl: Fantasy for clarinet & orch., 1959; Suite for strings, 1969; The Shy Casanova or What Matures Men (opera buffa), 1966; Wind Quintet, 1972; The Most Beautiful Country, 1973; The Living Land, 1973; Sonata Giocosa for Bassoon & Piano, 1974. Publs. incl: The Harmony of Smetana, 1959; The Tectonics of Vaclav Kalik, 1973; The Fundamental Harmonic Principles in the Music of Bohuslav Martinu, 1976. Contbr. to: Hudebni rozhledy; Zivá hudba. Mbrships. incl: Presidium, Ctrl. Committee, Union of Czech Comps. & Concert Artsit, 1971-; Ctrl. Committee, Czech Musical Soc., 1975. Hobby: Entomology. Address: Hribska 2, 100 00 Prague 10, Czech.

FELIX, Werner, b. 30 July 1927, Weissenfels, Germany. Professor of the History of Music; Musicological Secretary of the Bach Committee of the German Democratic Republic. Educ: Halle & Berlin Univs.; Weimar Coll. of Music; State exams, Music Pedagogy, 1951; promotion, 1956; Prof., 1959. m. Beate Riehmann, 2 children. Career: Lectr., Hist. of Music, 1952, also Rector, 1955-65, Coll. of Music, Weimar; Dir., Erfürt Conserv., 1953; Prof., 1966, Hon. Prof., 1974, currently also Hd. of Musicol. Dept., Coll. of Music, Leipzig. Publs. incl: Christoph Willibald Glück, 1965; Johann Sebastian Bach-Erbe und Gegenwart, 1975. Contbr. to profl. publs. Mrbships. incl: Ctrl. Committee, Union of Comps. & Musicols. of GDR; Pres., Chopin Soc. & Debussy Circle. Address: 7033 Leipzig, Otto-Schmiedt-Str. 2b, German Dem. Repub.

FELLEGI, Adam, b. 30 Dec. 1941, Budapest, Hungary. Pianist. Educ: MA, Franz Liszt Music Acad., Budapest; Master course for Young Pianists, Vienna, 1966. m. Esther Lázár, 1 s. Debut: Budapest, 1963. Career: Num. guest perfs., Austria, Czechoslovakia, German Dem. & Fed. Repubs., UK, Italy, Netherlands, USA; solo recitals & orchl. concerts, USSR; Special interest, 20th century & avant-garde music; Radio & TV perfs.; lectures. Recordings: Works of Schönberg, Berg, Bartok, Stravinsky & contemporary Hungarian comps. Hons: 1st Prize, Int. Cultural Ctr., Vienna, 1966; Special Prize for contemporary music, Budapest, 1966; A Rubinstein Prize, Int. Piano Competition, Brazil, 1974. Hobbies: Tourism; Alpinism. Mgmt: Interkoncert, Budapest; Ibbs & Tillet, London, UK. Address: Zichy Jeno utca 41, 1066 Budapest, Hungary.

FELLERER, Karl Gustav, b. 7 July 1902, Freising, Bavaria. Musicologist. Educ: PhD, Univ. of Munich; Univ. of Berlin; Ch. Music Schl., Regensburg; studied composition w. H K Schmid, Jos. Haas. m. Irmingard Hanses-Ketteler, 2 c. Career: Lectr., Musicol., Univ. of Münster; Prof., Univ. of Fribourg, Switzerland; Univ. of Cologne; Mbr. Acad. of the Scis., Düsseldorf, Brussels, Kopenhagen & London. Publs. incl: Ed., Das Musikwerk, 47 vols., 1952-74; Das Problem Neue Musik, 1967; Monodie & Polyphonie, 1972; Der Stilwandel in der abendländischen Musik um 1600, 1972; Geschichte der katholischen Kirchenmusik, 2 Vols., 1972, 1976; Max Bruch, 1974; Der Akademismus in der deutschen Musik des 19 Jahrunderts, 1976; Der futurismus in der italienischen Musik, Brüssel, 1977. Mbr. Int. Musicol. Soc.; Soc. for Music Rsch. Recip. Dr., Honoris Causa. Address: 17 Biggestr., 5 Cologne 41, German Fed. Repub.

FELLINGER, Imogen, b. 9 Sept. 1928, Munich, Germany. Musicologist. Educ: Univ. of Munich and Tübingen; PhD, Univ. of Tübingen, 1956. Career: Collaborator, Int. Inventory of Musical Sources, RISM, Research German Fed. Repub., 1957-62; Chmn., Rsch. Dept. for Bibliography, 19th Century Inst. of Musicol., Univ. of Colgne, 1963-70, Music Archive of the 19th Century, State Inst. for Music Rsch. Prussian Culture Collection Berlin, 1970-; Hd., Lib., ibid, 1971-; Scientific Councillor, 1974. Publs: Uber die Dynamik in der Musik von Johannes Brahms, 1961; Verzeichnis der Musikzeitschriften des 19. Jahrhunderts, 1968; Ed., Klavierstücke op. 118 & 119 von J Brahms 1974. Contbr. to: MGG; Riemann Musik Lexikon; Neue deutsche Biographie; Die Musikforschung; Studien zur rheinischen Musikgenchicte des 19. Jahrhunderts; Beiträge zur rheinischen Musikgeschichte;; Grove Dictionary of Music & Musicians; Fontes Artis musicae. Mbrships: Soc. for Music Rsch.; Int. Musicol. Soc.; Int. Assn. of Music Libs.; Study Team for Rhenish Music History; Mendelssohn Soc. Address: 34 Devrientweg, D-1 Berlin 45, German Fed. Repub. 27.

FELS-NOTH, Elena, b. 9 Nov. 1907, Milan, Italy. Music Educator; Opera & Concert Singer; Stage Director. Educ: Lyzeum, Philanthropin, Frankfurt am Main, Germany; Attended the opera Schl. & Dr. Hoch's Conserv., Frankfurt am Main; Prof. Emerita of Music, Univ. of Ill., 1976. m. Ernst Erich Noth (div.), 3 s., 1 d. Debut: Frankfurt am Main, 1931. Career: Opera Concerts in Germany, France, Switzerland, Holland & USA; Radio apps. in Marseille, Paris, Strasbourg, & many cities in USA; TV apps. in Norman,Okla. & Milwaukee, Wis.; Prof., Music, Univ. of Ill., USA. Publs: Notes without Music (w. Darius Milhaud), 1952. Contbr. to: Milwaukee Jrnl.; German-Am. Review; Books Abroad; Opera; Opera News. Mbrships: Pi Kappa Lmbda; Nat. Assn. of Tchrs. of Singing, Hon. Life Mbr., 1977; Ctrl. Opera Serv.; Fedn. of Music Clubs; Met. Opera Guild; Lyric Opera of Chgo. Guild; Soc. of Am. Musicians. Hons: Master of French Song; Winning Artist, Int. Singing Contest, Paris, France, 1937. Hobbies: Cooking; Gardening; Interior Decorating; Writing; Translating Opera. Address: 2317 E Wyoming Place, Milwaukee, WI 53202, USA. 2,5,8.

FENBY, Eric William, b. 22 Apr. 1906, Scarborough, Yorks., UK. Professor of Composition. Educ: Privately & largely self-taught in music; Amanuensis to Frederick Delius, 1928-34. m. Rowena Marshall, 1 s., 1 d. Debut: (as composer) Promenade Concerts. Career: Prof. of comp., Royal Acad. of Music. Compositions: Overture Rossini on Ilkla Moor; Ch. music; Arrangements of Delius works. Recordings: Delius Arrangements (Bournemouth Sinfonietta); Delius Violin Sonatas (w Yehudi Menuhin); The Delius Violin Sonatas (Ralph Holmes, violin, Eric Fenby, Piano). Publs: Delius As I Knew Him, 1936, revised ed. 1966; Delius (Great Composers Series), 1971; Menuhin's House of Music, 1969. Contbr. to: Music & Musicians; Books & Bookmen. Mbrships: Coun. mbr., Comps. Guild of GB; Former Chmn., ibid; Pres., Delius Soc.; Hon. mbr., Royal Acad. of Music. Hons: OBE; Award-winning script of A Song of Summer (TV documentary film directed by Ken Russell); Hon DMus (Jacksonville); Hon. D.Litt (Warwick & Bradford), 1978. Address: 35 Brookfield Mansions, Highgate West West Hill, London N6, UK. 1,3.

FENIGSTEIN, Victor, b. 19 Dec. 1924, Zürich, Switz. Piano Professor; Composer. Educ: Zürich Univ., 3 yrs.; Tchng. Dip. for Piano, Zürich Conserv.; violin & piano studies w. noted tchrs. m. Marianne Sigg, 2 d. Career: Concert Player until 1952; began receiving commissions for TV, theatre & film music in early 1960's; Prof., Conserv. of Music de la Ville de Luxembourg. Comps. incl: Three Events (piano & classical orch.); Trois Hommages (piano); Aus Deiner Jugend (7 melodies, mezzo & symph. orch.); etc. Mbr. profl. orgs. Recip. Chevalier de l'Ordre de Merite du Grand-Duche de Luxembourg, 1973. Address: 35A, Avenue Pasteur, Luxembourg (G-D).

FENLON, Iain Alexander, b. 26 Oct. 1949, Prestbury, Cheshire, UK. Musicologist. Educ: Mus B. Univ. of Reading, 1970; MA, Univ. of Birmingham, 1971; St. Catherine's Coll., Cambridge, 1971-75; PhD, Univ. of Cambridge, 1978. m. Sheila Margaret Hotton. Career: Hayward Fellow, Univ. of Birmingham, 1973-74; Ed., Grove's Dict. VI, 1974-75; Fellow, Harvard Coll., 1975-76; Fellow, King's Coll., Cambridge, 1975-. Mbrships: Am. Musicol. Soc.; Royal Musical Assn.; The Bibliographical Soc.; Società Italiana di Musicologia. Publs. incl: Jacques Arcadelt, Three Madrigals (ed.), 1975; Catalogue of

Printed Music & Music Manuscripts in the Library of the Barber Institute of Fine Arts, 1976. Contbr. to profl. jrnls. Address: King's Coll., Cambridge, UK.

FENNELLY, Brian, b. 14 Aug. 1937, Kingston, NY, USA. Composer; Theorist; Pianist. Educ: B Mechanical Engrng., Union Coll., Schenectady, NY, 1958; BA, ibid., 1963; MMus Schl. of Music, Yale Univ., 1965; PhD, Grad. Schl., ibid., 1968. m. Priscilla Proxmire Fennelly, 1 s. Career: USAF, 1958-61; Tchr., Union Coll. & Yale Univ. Fac., NY Univ., 1968-; Assoc. Prof., ibid.; Ed., Contemporary Music Newsletter, 1969-; Comp's forum, 1968; var. perfs., USA, & ISCM Int. Fest., 1973. Comps. incl: (publd.) Tesserae III, viola; Tesserae IV, contrabass trombone; Festive Psalm, narrator, choir, organ, tape; In Wildness...(orch.); Concert Piece (trumpet & orch.); Quintuplo (brass quintet & orch.); (recorded) Empirical Rag (brass quintet); Prelude & Elegy (brass quintet); Wind Quintet, Evanescences, instruments & tape. Contbr. to var. profl. jrnls. Mbr., num. socs. inclng. Pres., US section, ISCM, 1977. Address: RD2, Barton Hill Rd., Schohorie, NY 12157, USA.

FENNIMORE, Joseph, b. 16 Apr. 1940, NYC, USA. Composer. Educ: BMus, Eastman Schl. of Music; MSc, Juilliard Schl. of Music. Debut: piano recital, Metrop. Mus.'s Young Artists series, 1967. Career: Fndr. & Dir., Hear America First (concert series). Comps: Berlitz: Introduction to French (song cycle for soprano); The Cynic's Song; Bits & Pieces (piano suite). Mbrships: ASCAP; AFM Local 802; Am. Music Ctr.; Bd. Am. Comps.' Forum. Hons. incl: 1st Prize, piano, Internacional Concourso, Barcelona, 1969. Address: 463 W St., No. 105D, NY, NY 10014, USA.

FENSKE, David Edward, b. 26 June 1943, Sheboygan, Wis., USA. Music Librarian; Musicologist. Educ: BMus., Univ. of Wis., 1965; PhD., ibid, 1973. Career: Admin. Asst. & Asst. Music Libn., Univ. of Wis., 1967-71; Assoc. Music Libn. thru' Music Libn., Ind. Univ., 1971-. Author, Texture in the Chamber Music of Johannes Brahms, 1973; In Music East and West - Essays in Honor of Walter Kaufmann. Ed., Annotations, 1978-. Mbrships: Bd. of Dir., Music Lib. Assn.; Treas., Ind. Univ. Libns.' Assn., 1972-73; Pres., ibid, 1973-74; Am. Musicol. Soc. Address: 1640 Maplecrest Dr., Bloomington, IN 47401, USA.

FENWICK, Angela Mary, b. 9 Oct. 1940, Shotley Bridge, UK. Music Therapist; Organist & Choirmaster; Private Piano Teacher. Educ: BA, Durham Univ.; ARCO; LGSM (Singing Tchr.); ARCM (Piano Tchr.); LGSMT (Music Therapy). Career: Tchr., Organist, Chapelmaster, Queen Margaret's Schl., Escrick, York, 3 yrs.; Profl. Music Therapist, now tchr., music in special schools, Birmingham. area. Contbr. to profl. jrnls. inclng: Jrnl. of Brit. Soc. for Music Therapy; Nursing Times. Mbrships: Rep., Brit. Soc. for Music Therapy; ISM; Soc. for Psychol. of Music & Music in Educ. Hons: invited Lectr. at sev. int. music therapy congresses. Hobbies incl: House renovation; Antiques. Address: 7 Church Hill, Northfield, Birmingham B31 2JA, UK.

FERBER, Albert, b. 29 Mar. 1911, Lucerne, Switz. Pianist. Educ: Gymnasium, Lucerne. Debut: Lucerne, 1920. Career: Concertos, recitals, radio & TV perfs. in 41 countries. sev. recordings. Comps: Music for 2 films & 1 ballet. Address: 65 Cholmley Gdns., London NW6, UK.

FERENCSIK, Janos, b. 18 Jan. 1907, Hungary. Conductor. Educ: Budapest Conserv. Career: Musical Dir., Hungarian State Opera House; Musical Dir., Hungarian State Concert Orch.; Chief Cond., Budapest Phil. Orch., Asst., Bayreuth Festival, 1930-31; Guest Cond., Vienna Opera House, 1948-50; Concert perfs. in Austria, Belgium, Czechoslovakia, Finland, Germany, Roumania, UK, USA & USSR. Hons: Kossuth Prize, 1951, 1961; Eminent Artist Award. Address: Csopakyu. 12, Budapest, Hungary.

FERGUSON, Edwin Earle, b. 4 Aug. 1910, Brocket, ND, USA. Composer; Choral Conductor; Pianist; Retired Attorney. Educ: BS, Drake Univ., 1931; LLB., ibid 1934; at Drake Conserv., 1927-31; JSD., Yale Univ., 1937; pvte. study w. Meyer Kupferman. 1973-74. m. Alice Jewell Ferguson, 1 s., 1 d. Career: Profl. Pianist & Arr., Des Moines, Iowa, 1928-35: Accomp., Coach, Choral Cond., Comp., Wash. DC, 1938-; Dir. of Music, Chevy Chase United Meth. Chr., Md., 1960-; Lectr., Wesley Sem., Wash. DC, 1973; Speaker on Ch. Music, AGO & other grps. Comps: Over 90 publd. Sacred & secular works inclng. A Christman Exultation; Ye Followers of the Lamb; Easter Fanfare; A Woman Unashamed (song cycle); Three Idiomatic Exercises (piano, clarinet, violin); Recordings: The Confrontations of Judas (sacred opera); The Betrayal (Oratorio); Sorely Tried (musical play); The Ice Age & Volcanos (Smithsonian Instn. film scores). Mbrships: ASCAP; Am. Choral Conds. Assn.; AGO; Program Dir., Friday Morning Music Club, Wash. DC, 1977-; Rotary Int. Music Fellowship (VP for new music, 1976-). Recip. of ASCAP Standard Awards, 1977, 78, 79 & many other comp. awards. Hobby: Travel. Address: 5821 Osceola Rd., Bethesda, MD 20016, USA. 6,7.

FERGUSON, Howard, b. 21 Oct. 1908, Belfast, N Ireland. Musicologist; Composer; Pianist. Educ: RCM, London. Compositions: Chamber Music, Orchl., Vocal, Choral, mostly publd. by Boosey & Hawkes, London. Publs: Edns: Tisdall, Complete keyboard works, 1957; Purcell, Complete harpsichord works, I & II, 1964; Blow, Six Suites, 1965; Style & Interpretation, I-VI, 1963-69; Early French, Italian, German, English Keyboard Music, 2 vols. of each, 1966-69; Dagincour, Pièces de clavecin, 1969; (book) Keyboard Interpretation, 1975; Croft, Complete Harpsichord works I & II, 1974; Shubert, Complete Piano Sonatas, I, II, & III, 1978; Picchi, Complete Keyboard Works, 1979. Mbrships: Royal Musical Assn. Hons: hon. MusD, Queens Univ., Belfast, 1959; Cobbett Medal, 1966. Hobbies: Reading; Cooking. Address: 51 Barton Rd., Cambridge CB 3 9LG, UK. 14.

FERGUSON, Robert Stanley, b. 6 May 1948, London, UK. Pianist. Educ: studied piano w. Cyril Smith, RCM; ARCM; LRAM; LGSM. Debut: Royal Fest. Hall, 1973. Career: Piano Duo w. Christopher Kite, debuting at Wigmore Hall, 1973, also giving regular Purcell Room recitals 1974-79, including use of original early pianos; solo recital of 20th century music, Purcell Room, 1975. Mbrships: ISM; Musicians Union. Hons: Hopkinson Gold Medal, 1969, & Dannreuther Prize, 1970, both RCM. Hobbies: Geneal.; Tropical fish. Mgmt: Basil Douglas Ltd., 8 St. George's Terr., London NW1 8XJ, UK. Address: 52 Parkstone Ave., Hornchurch, Essex RM11 3LW, UK.

FERGUSON, Suzanne, b. 13 Aug. 1939, E Stroudsburg, Pa., USA. Associate Professor of English; Performer, Teacher, Recorder, Early Wind Instruments. Educ: BA, Converse Coll., 1960; MA, Vanderbilt Univ., 1961; PhD, Stanford Univ., 1966; Am. Recorder Soc. Teaching Cert., 1971. m. James Ferguson, 1 d. Career: Perfs. w. early music groups in Santa Barbara, Calif., & Columbus, Ohio; Cond. of Workshops in OH; Tchr., Ohio State Univ. Contbr. to Am. Recorder Mag. Mbrships: Phi Beta; Am. Recorder Soc., Past Pres., Columbus Chapt., ibid. Address: 33 Erie Rd., Columbus, OH, USA. 11.

FERNANDEZ, Oscar Rubens, b. 16 July 1939, Montevideo, Uruguay. University Professor; Violinist. Educ: MPsychol. & Humanities, Univ. of Montevideo; Dips., Philos., Sociol., ibid; MMus & Theory, Bach Conserv., Montevideo; Dips., Performing Arts, Appreciation of Music, ibid. m. Ninette Fernandez, 2 c. Deubt: Montevideo, age 11. Career: Concerts, Radio Apps., Buenos Aires, Montevideo, age 14; Solo Perfs., Mexico, Latin Am.; Concerts w. Nat. Symph. of Sto. Domingo; Concertmaster, Juventud Chmbr. Orch., age 16; Mbr. Nat. Symph., SODRE, age 17 &for 7 yrs.; Tech. Advsr., 1st Violin, Cuba Nat. Symph., 1960; Mbr. Nat. Symph., Mexico; Co-Concertmaster, Univ. of Veracruz Symph.; TV app., Frankfurt, Germany, 1973; 1st Violin, Cinn., Ohio, USA, Symph.; Lectr. Violin, Cinn. Coll.-Conserv. of Music; Tchr., Cond., Eastern Michigan Univ.; Prof., Univ. of Veracruz, 1976-; Asst. Concertmaster of Symph. Orch., ibid. Contbr. to num. newspapers, profl. jrnls. Mbrships: FUDEM, Uruguay; Cinn. Musicians Assn. Recip. num. Hons. Hobbies: Reading; Travel; Languages. Address: c/o Universidad de Veracruz-OSX, Nicolas Bravo No 11, Xalapa, Veracruz, Mexico.

FERNANDO, Sarathchandra Vichremadithya, b. 22 July 1937, Colombo, Sri Lanka. Organiser of Music, Sri Lanka Broadcasting Corporation. m. Manel Lakshmi Fernando, 2 c. Career: Regular Broadcasts (oboe & piano); Apps. as solo oboist w. orchs. & chmbr. ensembles in Sri Lanka; Cond., Colombo Sinfonietta; Assoc. Cond., Symph. Orch. of Colombo; Mbr., Panel of Examiners in Western Music, Dept. of Examinations, Min. of Educ., Sri Lanka. Comps. incl: Piano Pieces; Orch. Works inclng: Fantasia on a Folk Tune, 1973; Three Pieces for Strings, 1974; Chmbr. Music; Songs; music for films. Contbr. to var. mags. Recip. 1st Prize, Instrumental Sect., Festival of Music organised by CBC, 1967. Address: 63 Sangbo Mawatha, Borupone, Ratmalana, Sri Lanka.

FERNS, Martin Allen, b. 13 Sept. 1921, Portsmouth, UK. School Director of Music; Organist; Choir Trainer; Conductor. Educ: LTCh TCL. m. Mary Dorothy Harrop, 1 s., 1 d. Career: Dir. of Music, Lord Weymouth's Schl., Warminster, 1947-65, Scarborough Coll., 1966-70, & Reigate Grammar Schl., 1970-78; Warden, Royal Schl. of Ch. Music, 1979-. Cond., Trowbridge Phil. Soc., 1964-65; Cond., Dorking Madrigal Soc., 1975-; Special Commissioner, RSCM, 1971-. Contbr. to Music in Educ.; Chr. Music Quarterly. Mbr., ISM; RCO. Hobbies:

Reading; Watching Sport; Natural History. Address: Royal Schl. of Ch. Music, Addington Palace, Croydon CR9 5AD, UK.

FERNSTRÖM, Karl-Eric, b. 10 Dec. 1926, Norberg, Sweden. Musician (organ & accordion). m. Eyvor Elisabet, 5c. Career: Orch. musician (Fernströms Orkester) & tchr. for 40 yrs.; TV apps. in Sweden, Denmark, German Fed. Repub.; radio perfs. in Sweden, Finland, Norway, Denmark, & Iceland. Comps. about 80 published, of which 25 recorded. Recordings: 7 LPs. Publs: 5 books of comps. Contbr. to: Dragspels-Journalen; Trollhättan, Sweden. Mbr., SDR. Hobby: Fishing. Address: PL 2525, 77800 Norberg, Sweden.

FERRAND, Emma, b. 1 Oct. 1948, London, UK. Cellist. Educ: Int. Cello Ctr.; LRAM 1969; Recital Dip., RAM 1971; Study w. Pierre Fournier, Switzerland. m. Richard Deakin. Debut: Wigmore Hall, 1974. Career: Apps. on S Bank, Wigmore Hall inclng. concert for Kirckman Concert Soc.; Num. concerts, music socs. etc. throughout UK; BBC app. in Tortelier Master Class, 1974; Broadcasts for BBC Radio 3. Mbr. ISM. Winner, Nat. Fedn. of Music Socs. Award, 1974. Mgmt: John Wright. Address: The Homestead, Hartley Wintney, Nr Basingstoke, Hants., UK.

FERRARI-BARASSI, Elena b. 28 Dec. 1936, Milan, Italy. Musicologist. Educ: Letters Degree, Univ. Milan; Piano Dip., Conserv. of Milan; Dip. Scuola di Paleografia e Filologia Musicale, Cremona (Univ. of Pavia). m. Pietro Ferrari, 1 d. Career: Asst. in Hist. of Music, Univ. of Milan, 1961-70; Univ. of Pavia, 1970-; Tchr., Summer Course, Hist. of Music, Portland State Univ., USA, 1970; Lectr., Univ. Strasbourg, France, 1974; Prof. of Hist. of Medieval & Renaissance Musical Theory, Scuola di Paleografia e Filologia Musicale, Cremona (Univ. of Pavia), 1975-; Musicale, Cremona (Univ. of Pavia), 1975-78; Prof. of Hist. of Musical Instruments, ibid, 1978-. Publs. incl: Monteverdi, Madrigali A 5 Voci, Book 4, Vol. 5 in Monteverdi, Opera Omnia, 1974; Le Origini Del Melodrama; Storia Del L'Opera, 1977. Contbr. to profl. jrnls. Mbr. num. profl. orgs. Address: Via Ariberto 8, 20123 Milan, Italy.

FERRAS, Christian, b. 1933, Le Touquet, France. Violinist. Educ: Nice Conserv.; Paris Conserv. Career incl: num. recitals & concerts w. leading conds. & orchs. throughout world; played before Pope John, 1963; invited to play before Danish Royal Family at wedding of Princess Margrethe; apps. at major fests. inclng. Salzburg Easter Fest., Llandaff Fest. Records for DGG. Hons. incl: 1st Prize, violin, Paris Conserv., 1946; 1st prizes at many int. competitions; sev. times winner of French Acad.'s Prix du Disque. Mgmt: Ibbs & Tillet, London, UK.

FERRÉ, Susan Ingrid, b. 5 Sep. 1945, Boston, USA. Concert Organist; Composer; Harpsichord Player. Educ: BA, BMus, Tex. Christian Univ., 1968; Dip., Organ & Improvisation, Schola Cantorum, Paris, 1969; MMus, Eastman Schl. of Music, 1971; DMA, N Tex. State Univ., 1979. m. Robert Duane Ferré. Career incl: num. apps. in concerts, workshops & lecture-recitals in USA & W Europe incl. over 50 perfs. in France; Perf./Comp./Musical Dir., French Theatre Co., Avant-Quart, 1969-71, 1978-79; Tchng. Fellow, N Texas State Univ., 1974-76; Philos. & Eng. Instructor, Univ. of Paris, 1969-70; Fac. mbr., Choral Music Inst., Southwestern Univ., Texas, 1974. Fndr. & Musical Dir., Temple Choral Ensemble, Temple, Tex., 1973-75; Fac., Baroque Keyboard Workshop, N Tex. State Univ., 1979. sev. comps. for the Avant-Quart Co. Recording: Hommage à Jean Langlais. Contbr. to: The Diapason. Mbrships: AGO (sub-dean, chmn., Educ. Projects Committee & other offices at local level). Hons. incl: Pres., Phi Sigma Tau; Winner, AGO Student Competition, N Tex. region, 1968. Mgmt: Murtagh-McFarlane Artists Mgmt., Hackensack, NJ, USA. Address: 5426 W Ledbetter Dr., Dalls, TX 75236, USA.

FERREIRA, Carel Pieter, b. 7 May 1943, Humansdorp, S Africa. Tecaher. Educ: Music dip. (tchr.) Stellenbosch Univ.; Grade VIII (final), Univ. of S Africa; ATCL (singing). Career: Tchr. of piano, singing, classical guitar, harmony, Hist. of Music. Mbrships: Soc. of S African Music Tchrs. (Port Elizabeth Branch), 1967-79; sec., ibid., 1968-69; chmn., ibid., 1969-71. Hon. Bursary, Grade V (piano), Univ. of S Africa, 1959. Hobbies: Tennis; Wild Life; Travel. Address: Sydenham Primary Schl., Loch St., Port Elizabeth 6001, S Africa.

FERRIER, Garry, b. 11 June 1936, Kitchewsen, Ont., Can. Writer; Producer; Pianist. Educ: Toronto Conserv. of Music; Hamburg Conserv. of Music; Oscar Peterson Advanced Schl. of Contemporary Music. Career: Prod.-Writer, num. CBC TV music series; Jazz disc jockey; TV film writing in Hollywood; prod.-writer of Oscar Peterson, Very Special. num. Comps. Recordings: sev. singles. Contbr. to: Jazz World; Today; Los Angeles Times; NY Times; Toronto Globe & Mail. Mbrships:

ACTRA; ARTRA; Writers Guild of Am. Hobbies: Playing jazz piano & flute. Address: 969 Hilgard, Los Angeles, CA 90024, USA.

FESSEL, Erik Oskar, b. 17 Aug. 1933, Copenhagen, Denmark. Pianist. Educ: w. H Sigurdsson & A Skjold Rasmussen, Royal Danish Music Conserv., 1950-55; w. Hedy Salquin, Conserv. of Lucerne, Switz., 1963-66. Debut: Copenhagen, 1959. Career: concerts & radio broadcasts in Europe; Prof., trng. coll., Jelling, Conserv. of Jutland (Aarhus), 1970-72, & Conserv. of Odense, 1971-. Mbr., Assn. of Danish Soloists. Hobby: Painting. Address: Skibsholtvej 91, Assendrup, 8721 Daugard, Denmark.

FETSCH, Wolfgang, b. 8 Dec. 1923, Mannheim, Germany. Pianist; Professor of Piano. Educ: BM, MM, Univ. of Denver, USA; DMus, Ind. Univ. m. Nicholette Ganshaw, 1 s.,d. Career: recital tours, soloist w. orchs. in USA & Japan; radio & TV broadcasts; Asst. Prof., E Carolina Coll.; Assoc. Prof., Prof., Tex. Coll. of Arts & Inds.; currently Prof. of Piano & Chmn., Dept. of Applied Music, Conserv. of Music, Univ. of the Pacific, Calif. Mbr., Music Tchrs. Assn. of Calif. Contbng. Ed., Websters New World Dict. of the Am. Lang. Address: 7557 Andrea Ave., Stockton, CA, USA.

FEUER, Maria, b. 20 Aug. 1932, Budapest, Hungary. Musical Journalist. Educ: Dip., Pedagogical Acad.; Dip. Shcl. Music Teaching, 1953. m. Szilárd Molnár. Debut: Music Critic, 1958. Career: Collaborator at Hungarian Musical Monthly, Muzsika, 1958; Ed., ibid, 1968-; Ed-in-Chief, ibid, 1970-. Publs. incl: Rimsky Korsakof, monography, Gondolat, 1966; Who Needs Modern Music, lessons of an experimental concert & its sociological survey, 1970; In the Workshop of 88 Musicians, 1972; In the Workshop of 50 Musicians, 1976; Snapshot-Hungarian Composition, 1975-77, 1978. Mbrships: Union of Hungarian Musicians; Union of Hungarian Journalists; Int. Union of Journalists; Nat. Bd. of Jeunesses Musicales. Address: 1071 Budapest, Damjanich-u 52, Hungary. 1,2,4.

FEUERSTEIN, Robert, b. 12 Jan. 1949, Oradea, Romania. Classical Guitarist; Composer. Educ: Comp. studies w. Stepfen Foldy; Classical Guitar w. Menache Baquiche, Eli Kassner, & Alexandre Lagoya. m. Sarah Elizabeth Nitsch, 1 s. Career: Concerts, Romania, Israel, Can., USA, France; Radio & TV apps., Can. & Israel. Comps: Three Pieces for Guitar (recorded); Three Sonatas by R Straube (arr. for 2 guitars). Recordings: Transmutations. Mbrships: Toronto Guitar Soc. Mgmt: P N Fleishman Prodns. Inc., Toronto. Address: 835 Roselawn Ave., Ap. 502, Toronto, Ont., Can. M6B 1B5.

FIALA, George Joseph, b. 31 Mar. 1922, Kiev, Ukraine. Composer; Pianist; Organist; Radio Producer. Educ: Tchaikovsky State Conserv. of Music, Kiev; Acad. HS for Music, Berlin; Royal Conserv. of Music, Brussels. widowed. Comps. publd. incl: Montreal, Symphonic Suite for Orch.; Saxophone Quartet No. 2; 4 Russian Poems for Medium Voice & Piano; Pastoral & Allegretto (recorder quartet); Cantilena & Rondo (soprano recorder & piano); var. piano works. Comps. recorded: Concertino for piano, trumpet, timpani & str. orch.; Quartet No. 2 for saxes; Montreal, Symphonic Suite for Orch.; Woodwind Quintet; Sinfonietta Concertata for accordion, harpsichord & string orch. Mbrships: Can. League of Comps.; BMI of Can. Ltd.; Ukrainian Can. Arts Coun. Hobbies: Philately; Graphic Design. Address: 4100 Cote des Neiges No. 4, Montreal, PQ, Canada H3h 1W8.

FIAS, Gábor, b. 7 May 1941, Györ, Györ-Sopron, Hungary. Violinist. Educ: Dip., Acad. of Music. m. Erzsébet Szödy, 1d. Debut: as mbr. of Kodály Quartet, Vienna, 1966. Career: Mbr., Kodály Quartet; apps., Salzburg-Mozarteum, Tokyo-NHK, Sydney Opera House, London-Purcell Room, Paris-Grand Auditorium Radio France. Recordings: Ravel, Dvorak, Haydn - Trios; Kodály, String Quartets No. 1 & 2; over 20 works by contemporary comps. Mbr., Kodály Soc. Hons: 1st Prize, Leó Weiner Int. Music Competition, Budapest; 2nd Prize, Munich Int. Trio Competition; Ferenc Liszt Prize, 1970. Hobbies: Architecture; Excursions. Mgmt: Interkoncert, Budapest. Address: Varga Gyula András Park 16/a, Budapest, 1149, Hungary.

FIASCONARO, Gregorio, b. 5 Mar. 1915, Palermo, Italy. Singer; Director. Educ: Paganini Conserv.; S Cecilia & Centro Sperimentale, Rome. m. Mabel-Marie Brabant, 1s. Deubt: Germont (Traviata), Genoa. Career: apps. in Italy, UK, S Africa (Johannesburg, Cape Town, Durban); gave 1st perf. of Bartok's Duke Bluebeard's Castle in London & Glasgow; fndr., Opera Schl., Cape Town Univ.; has directed 72 operas; app. in film, The Winner; now dir., Univ. of Cape Town Opera Schl. Hons: Award of Merit, Cape Town Tercentenary Fndn., 1952; Needeberg Opera Prize, 1978. Hobbies: Painting; Cooking.

Address: 603 Devonshire Hill, Grotto Rd., Rondebosch, Cape Town, S Africa.

FICARELLI, Mario, b. 4 July 1937, Sao Paulo, Brazil. Pianist; Composer. Educ: Acad. Paulista de Musica; studied piano w. Alice Philips & comp. w. Olivier Toni. m. Ana Rita de Godoy, 5 c. Career: TV & Radio broadcasts. Publd. Comps: Maktub I, 1972, Maktub II (piano & violin), 1972, Maktub III, Piano (4 hands), 1978; Ensaio (mezzo soprano, double bass & cymbals), 1972; Zyklus (str. quartet), 1974; 6 Duets, for 2 Violins, 1976; Canzona, for violin & cello, 1978; Zyklus II (orch.); The Pit & the Pendulum, for 24 percussion instruments, 1969; etc. Var. recordings. Mbrships: Soc. Brasileira de Música Contemporânea. Hons. incl: 1st Prizes (2), Brazilian Concourse of Comp., 1974; Int. Tribune of Comps., Paris, 1975. Address: Rua Taperóa 45, 04571 Sao Paulo, SP, Brazil.

FICHER, Jacobo, b. 15 Jan. 1896, Odessa, Russia. Violinist; Orchestra Conductor; Composer. Educ: St. Petersburg Imperial Conserv., 1912-19. m. Ana Aronberg, 2 s. Debut: as Violin soloist, State of Leningrad Opera, 1919. Career incls: Became Cond., Argentine Music Gen. Assn. Symph. Orch., 1939; Fndr., Argentine League of Comps., 1949. Comps. incl: 1st Str. Quartet, 1929; Sulamita (symph. poem), 1931; 1st Sonata for Piano, 1943; Concerto for Violin & Orch., 1942; Asi Hablo Isaias (5th Symph.), 1948; Mirth Psalm (cantata), 1948; Saxophone Quartet, 1957; 7th Symph., 1960; Piano & Str. Quartet, 1961. Mbrships. incl: Nat. Acad. of Fine Arts, 1969. Recip. num. hons. for comps. Address: Viamonte 2534 3 , Buenos Aires, Argentina.

FIDDIAN, Ian Paull, b. 17 Aug. 1909, Adelaide, SA, Aust. Barrister & Solicitor; University Officer. Educ: studied law, Univ. of Melbourne. Career: Co-Fndr., Gilbert & Sullivan Soc. of Vic., 1935; Sec., Royal Melbourne Phi. Soc., 1936-46; Concert Mgr., Aust. Broadcasting Commn., 1938-46; Sec., Univ. of Melbourne Conservatorium of Music, 1946-74; Exec. Dir., Sidney Myer Music Bowl Trust, 1958-70. Hobbies: Reading; Tennis. Address: 107 Leopold St., S Yarra, Victoria 3141 Australia. 4,15.

FIEBIG, Kurt, b. 28 Feb. 1908, Berlin, Germany. Composer; Organist (also playing Piano & Cembalo); Choir Leader. Educ: studied piano w. Gertrud Wertheim & Rudloph Schmidt, organ w. Arnold Dreyer & composition w. Karol Rathaus & Franz Schreker; State Exam for Organists & Choir Dirs., Berlin, 1933. m. Dorothea Simke, 2 s. Career: Organist & Choir Leader, Berlin, 1926-36; Cathedral Organist, Quedlinburg, 1936-38; Dir., Ch. Music Schl., Halle, 1939-50; on Fac., 1951-, Lect. (Composition), 1960-, Hamburg Inst. of Music. Compositions: Markuspassion; Kantate ET UNAM SANCTAM; Missa secunda; Missa "media vita"; Paul-Gerhardt-Kantate; Concertino for Violin & String Orch.; Easter oratorio; Cantata "Wie nach einer Wasserquelle"; Concerto Cembalo & String Orch.; Works for Organ, Piano & Cembalo; Songs; Advent Oratorio. Publs: Psalmkantaten (Anthems) G F Handel, 1947; 73 73 Choral Preludes, 1952. Recip. of Mendelssohn Prize in composition, 1931. Hobbies: Literature; Theatre. Address: Görlitzer Str. 30, 2 Hamburg 70, German Fed. Repub. 19.

FIELD, Andrew, b. 5 Mar. 1922, Bromley, Kent, UK. Singer; Vocal Coach. m. Audrey Langford. Career: apps. in concerts, in oratorio & contemporary opera; voice coach, opera apprentice prog., Santa Fe, USA, 1970-; vocal fac., Manhattan Schl. of Music, NY, 1977-; vocal fac., Opera Schl. of Chgo; vocal fac., RNCM, UK, 1978-. Hobbies: Swimming; Reading; Gardening. Address: 55 Hayes Rd., Bromely, Kent BR2 9AE, UK.

FIELD, Christopher David Steadman, b. 27 Apr. 1938, Frimley, UK. University Lecturer; Violinist. Educ: New Coll., Oxford Univ.; MA; D Phil.; ARCM. Career: Lectr. in Music, 1964-; Sr. Lectr., 1976-, Univ. of St. Andrews; mbr. Scottish Early Music Consort; Violinist, Scottish Baroque Ensemble, 1970-75. Publs: Eds. of works by Dussek & Jenkins. Contbr. to: Music & Letters; Musical Times; Grove's Dictionary, 6th ed. Mbrships: Oxford Univ. Musical Club & Union (Pres., 1961-62); Governing Bd., RSAM. Address: Dept. of Music, The University, St. Andrews, Scotland, UK.

FIELD, Robin, b. 16 Sept. 1935, Redditch, UK. Composer. Educ: Private study in comp. w. H P Allen, Worcester, J Murray Brown, London & Durham & Thomas Pitfield, Manchester. m. Jean Wilson, 2 d. Comps. incl: choral & orchl. music, chamber music, songs & piano music & film scores. Mbrships: The Composers' Guild of GB; PRS. Hons: 1st Prize awarded for 'Fantasia on a theme of Guillaume de Machaut' for oboe & string orch., N-Western Arts Assn. competition for comps., 1971. Hobbies: Geology; Lapidary. Address: 4 Ellergreen, Burneside, Kendal, Cumbria LA9 5SD, UK.

FIELD-HYDE, Margaret, b. 4 May 1905, Cambridge, UK. Soprano; Lecturer; Adjudicator; Actress. Educ: studied w. father F C Field-Hyde; LRAM; ARCM; Hon. TSC; MRST; further studies in Germany; studied perf. of vocal music of 12th to 15th centuries w. Yves Tinayre. m. E V Sharples. Debut: in 1st stage revival of King Arthur (Purcell), 1928. Career incls: num. apps. in oratorio, opera & recitals, singing in most cathedrals in UK, in Albert Hall, Queens Hall & Royal Fest. Hall; was noted for singing of Purcell, Bach & Faure; Fndr. & Dir., The Golden Age Singers (quintet); toured in most European countries, N Africa, Can. & USA; app. at many fests., inclng. at Kings Lynn Fest. in presence of HM Queen Elizabeth, the Queen Mother & HRH Princess Margaret; has made many radio & TV broadcasts; has given poetry readings for BBC & Brit. Coun. Recordings; Lectr. on tchng. of solo singin, Inst. of Educ. of Univ. of London & Music Tchrs. Assn. Recordings incl: Ariel in the Tempest; Ariel in the Rape of the Lock; Venus & Adonis; A Garland for the Queen; num. records w. The Golden Age Singers. Mbrships: Royal Musical Assn.; ISM. Hobbies: Gardening; Painting; Sewing. Address: Bredon's Norton Croft, Bredon's Norton, Nr. Tewkesbury, Glos., UK. 3,14,27.

FIFIELD, Christopher George, b. 4 Sept. 1945, Croydon, UK. Conductor. Educ: Mus. B., Manchester Univ.; GRSM; ARMCM; ARCO Staatliche Hochschule fur Musik, Cologne, W Germany. m. Judith Weyman, 1 s. Career: Mbr., Music Staff, Glyndebourne Opera, 1971-72, 1977-78; Asst. Musical Dir., Cape Town Opera House, 1973 76; Mbr., Music Staff, Wexford Opera, 1977; Guest Cond., Cape Town Symph. Orch.; PACOFS Opera, 1978-79; Music Dir., London Contemporary Dance Theatre, 1976-, Guest Cond.,Festival Opera, 1978; BBC Radio & TV. Hobbies: Photography; Travel; Bridge. Address: 17 Falkland Park Ave., London SE 25, UK.

FIGATNER, Nancy, b. 2 May 1957, New York, NY, USA. Baroque Oboe & Recorder Player. Educ: Beloit Coll.; New England Conserv. of Music; Pvte. study mod. oboe, recorder, baroque oboe & violin. Career: Apps. in Recorder Quartet on Radio; 1st Oboist w. New Rochelle High Schl. Wind Ensemble; Oboe & Engl. Horn Player in NY All-State; Apps. w. var. small baroque orchs.; Baroque Oboe & Recorder in New England Conserv. of Music's Collegium Musicum. Recordings: All-State Music Festival of NY; New Rochelle High Schl. Wind Ensemble. Mbr. Am. Recorder Soc. Recip. New Rochelle Music Educators Award, 1974. Hobbies: Hiking; Sewing; Cooking; Bicycling; Art. Address: 254 Broadway, Cambridge MA 02139, USA. 4.

FIGLER, Byrnell Walter, b. 9 May 1927, St. Louis, Mo., USA. Pianist; Teacher. Educ: Wash. Univ., St. Louis; BMus, MMus, St. Louis Inst. of Music; Bavarian State Music Acad., Munich, German Fed. Repub. Career: Tchr., Univs. of Ill. & Ala.; Assoc. Prof. Piano, Ft. Hays Kan. State Coll.; 30 Concerts as Accomp. & Soloist, US Info. Ctr., German Fed. Repub., 1954-55; Solo recitals of Am. piano music, Portugal, Repub. of Ireland, France & Switzerland, 1971; Tours of USA, giving recitals on num. campuses; num. perfs., Europe & Am. Recordings: 2 Sonatas, Arthur Kurtz (for French Nat. Radio). Contbr. to Grand Cru (wine mag.). Mbrships: Pi Kappa Lambda; Phi Mu Alpha Sinfonia; MTNA; Coll. Music Soc. Recip., Fulbright Grant. Address: Fort Hays State Univ., Kan., USA.

FIGUEROA, José, b. 25 Mar. 1905, San Sebastian, Puerto Rico. Concert Violinist; Teacher. Educ: Royal Conserv., Madrid, Spain; License de Concert, Ecole Normale de Musique, Paris, France. Div., 2 s. Debut: San Juan, Puerto Rico. Career: Concert tours of Spain, France, Portugal, Switz., Austria, England, Poland, Morocco, USA, Mex., Ctrl. Am., Chile, Colombia, Venezuela, Ecuador, W. Indies, Argentina; Dean of Studies, Puerto Rico Conserv. of Music; Lectr., Univ. of Puerto Rico; Prof. of Violin, Ecole Normale de Musique, Paris, France; Tours w. the Figueroa Quintet. Var. recordings. Hons: Doctor Honoris Causa, bestowed by Pablo Casals & the Conservatory of Puerto Rico; Hon. Dip., Warsaw, Poland, Wieniawski Competition. Hobbies: Reading, Travelling. Address: 107 Tres Hermanos St., Santurce, Puerto Rico 00907.

FILIPPINI, Rocco b. 7 Sept. 1943, Lugano, Switz. Cellist. Educ: BA, Lugano; Dip., Conserv. of Geneva, Switz. m. Dr Giuseppina Boni, 1 c. Career: Apps. as soloist & as chmbr. musician in Europe, N & S Am., Japan, inc. fests. at Lucerne, Edinburgh, Vienna, Stresa, Milan (Scala), Helsinki, Spoleto & Marlboro (USA); Fndr., Trio di Milano; 1st Solo cellist of Virtuosi di Roma, Fest. Strings, Lucerne, Orch. di Santa Cecilia, Roma; cello fac., Milan Conserv. Hons: Winner, Geneva Int. Competition, 1964; Soloist's Prize, Soc. of Musicians, Switz.; Casals Prize, Budapest, 1968. Hobbies: Gen. Culture; Psychoanalysis; Mathematics. Address: 6951 Lugaggia, Ticino, Switzerland.

FILLER, Susan M, b. 18 July 1947, Gary, Ind., USA. Musicologist. Educ: BA (music), Univ. of Ill., Chgo., 1969; MM (music & lit.), Northwestern Univ., 1970; PhD, ibid., 1977. Career: contbr. of scholarly papers at meetings of Am. Musicol. Soc., Midwest chapt., & Nat. meetings, 1975, '78, '80; guest lectr. on coll. campuses, 1972, '79,'80. Publs: Dissertation on Editorial Problems in Symphonies of Gustav Mahler; a study of the sources of the 3rd & 10th symphonies, 1977. Contbr. to: Music Jrnl.; Jrnl. of the Can. Assn. of Univ. Schls. of Music; Ravinia Fest. prog. notes; Chgo. Symph. Orch. prog. notes. Mbrships: Am. Musicol. Soc.; Coll. Music Soc.; Int. Musicol. Soc.; Int. Gustav Mahler Soc. Hobbies: Writing; Plants; Zoos; Furniture Finishing; Walking. Address: 441 W Barry, Chgo., IL 60657, USA.

FINDLAY, Elsie, b. 25 Dec. 1902, Guildford, Surrey, UK. Oratorio & Concert Singer; Teacher. Educ: Sydney Conserv., Aust. m. Frederick Lawson (dec.), 3 d. Debut: Sydney Royal Phil. Soc. Career: Num. apps. w. disting. conds.; Regular recitals, Aust. Broadcasting Corp., throughout Aust. & NZ, Wigmore Hall, London, UK, etc.; Examiner, Aust. Music Exams. Bd. Recordings: EMI; Aust. Broadcasting Corp. Mbrships: Musical Assn. NSW; Musical Dir. & Pres., Josef Kretschmann Music Club; Adjudicator, competitions & Eisteddfods. Hobbies: Reading; Gardening; Travel. Address: 49A Towns Rd., Vaucluse, NSW 2030, Australia.

FINE, Vivian, b. 28 Sept. 1913, Chgo., Ill., USA. Composer; Pianist. Educ: pvte. study in comp. w. Ruth Crawford Seeger & Roger Sessions, & in piano w. Djane Lavoie-Herz & Abby Whiteside. m. Benjamin Karp, 2 d. Career: Concerts consisting solely of her works at NYC, Mills Coll., Univ. of Calif. at Berkeley, Calif. State Univ. at Hayward, SUNY at Albany. Compositions incl: 4 Songs, 1933; The Great Wall of China, 1947; String Quartet, 1957; Alcestis (ballet), 1960; Missa Brevis, 1972; Concerto for Piano Strings & Percussion, 1972; Teisho, 1975; Meeting for Equal Rights 1866, 1975; (recorded) Concertante for Piano & Orch.; Alcestis; Paean; Sinfonia & Fugato. Mbr., ASCAP. Recip. grants from var. fndns. Hobby: Walking. Address: R.D.1, N. Bennington, VT 05257, USA. 2.

FINK, Laure, b. Mattawa, Can. Pianist; Accompanist; Teacher. Educ: Lauréat, Music Schl. of Univ. of Montreal. Assoc., Royal Conserv. of Toronto; LGSM.; UK; BA., Univ. of Montreal. BMus. Career: has given solo recitals on CBC Radio & CKAC Radio (La Presse) & app. as accomp. on CBC Radio & TV; Lectr. & Accomp., concert tours, Jeunesses Musicales du Canada; has given Lieder & Chmbr. Music Recitals, Centre d'Art d'Orford & Camp Musical de Lanaudière; Fest. Adjudicator, 30 fests. in Can. Conservatoire de Musique de la Province de trois-rivieres, Quebec, 1975. Recordings: Accomp., La Voix d'Or du Quebec. Contbr. to: Can. Univ. Post; Opera News; Le Devoir. Mbrships: Dir., Thomas More Inst. for Adult Educ.; Sec.,Quebec Music Tchrs.' Assn. Hons. incl: Gold Medal, Music Schl., Univ. of Montreal, 1939. Hobbies: Hiking; Canoeing; Play-going. Address: 4815 Queen Mary Rd., Apt. D, Montreal PQ. H3W 1X1, Canada.

FINK, Lorraine, b. 1 Sept. 1931, Oakland, Calif., USA. Violinist; Teacher; Specialist in Suzuki Talent Education. Educ: BA Mus Ed, San Fran. State Univ.; MMus (violin perf.), W Va. Univ. m. Reginald H Fink, 1 s., 1 d. Career: Instrumental Music Tchr., San Fran. Pub. Schls.; 1st Violinist, Okla. City Symph.; on fac.,Ithaca Talent Educ. Schl., NY, & summer Suzuki Insts. in USA; Fndr.-Dir., Suzuki Assn. of Athens, Ohio; Suzuki Specialist, giving Seminar Workshops for Tchrs., students & parents, Scherl & Roth Inc., div. of C G Conn Ltd. Contbr. to: Am. Str. Tchr.; Notes-A-Tempo. Mbrships: Bd. of Dirs., Sec., Suzuki Assn. of Ams.; VP, Ohio Unit, Am. Str. Tchr. Assn. Address: 7 Briarwood Dr., Athens, OH 45701, USA.

FINK, Michael Armand, b. 15 Mar. 1939, Long Beach, Calif., USA. Musicologist; Composer; Classical Guitarist. Educ: BMus, 1960, PhD 1977, Univ. of Southern Calif.; MMus, New England Conserv. of Music, 1962. m. Jo Ann Brister, 1 s., 1 d. Career: Comp., commissioned choral works, major US colls. & univ.; Tchr. of theory, comp., classical guitar & musicol., conserv., coll. & univ. levels; Arr. & Prod., series of educl. musical recordings; currently Fac. Coord. for Musicol., Univ. of Tex. at San Antonio. Comps: publd. by Schirmer, Avant, Western Int. Mark Foster, Hinshaw; Te Deum for Tenor solo, mixed chorus & piano & Tell Out! (Magnificat) for soloists, mixed chorus & piano recorded by Reelsound. Publs: Musicology - Publications in Current Musicology. Contbr. to profl. publs. Mbrships incl: ASCAP; Am. Musicol. Soc.; Music Lib. Assn. Recip., acad., musical & mil. hons. Hobbies: Sailboat Racing; Lit. Address: Div. of Music, Univ. of Tex. at San Antonio, San Antonio, TX 78285, USA.

FINK, Reginald H., b. 20 June 1931, York, Pa., USA. Professor of Music Education; Trombone Player. Educ: B Mus, Eastmans Schl. Music, Univ. Rochester, 1953; M Mus Ed,

Univ. Okla., 1957; PhD, ibid., 1967. m. Lorraine J. Friedrichsen, 1 s., 1 d. Career: Bass trombonist, Okla. City Symph. Orch., 1953-55; Prin. trombonist, ibid., 1955-62; Prof. Music, WVa. Univ., 1962-67; Ithaca Coll., 1967-70; Ohio Univ., 1970-. Recording: Co-perf., Ithaca Brass Quintet (Mark Records), 1969. Publs. incl: Studies in Legato for Bass Trombone & Tuba, 1969; From Treble Clef to Bass Clef Baritone, 1972. Contbr. to profl. jrnls. Mbrships. incl: Life, MENC; Coll. Music Soc. Hobby: Aviation. Address: 7 Briarwood Dr., Athens, OH 45701, USA.

FINK, Robert Russell, b. 31 Jan. 1933, Belding, Mich., USA. Music Educator. Educ: B Mus, M Mus, PhD in Music Theory, Mich. State Univ. m. Ruth Joan Fink, 1 s., 1 d. Career: Chmn., Dept. of Music, Western Mich. Univ.; Dean, Coll. of Music, Univ. of Colo., Boulder. Comps: Modal Suite (trumpet, horn & trombone); Four Modes for Winds (flute, clarinet, horn & bassoon); Two Songs (mixed chorus). Publs: Directory of Michigan Orchestral Composers, 1967; Univ. of Mich. Composers, 1977; The Language of Twentieth Century Music, 1975; Contbr. to Jrnl. of Rsch. in Music Educ. Mbrships: Nat. Assn. Schls. of Music (Examiner & Regional VP); Mich. Orch. Assn. (Past-Pres.); Phi Mu Alpha Sinfonia (past Province Gov.); Am. Soc. Univ. Comps.; Am. Music Ctr.; MENC. Hobbies: Canoeing; Gardening; Fishing. Address: 643 Furman Way, Boulder, CO 80303, USA.

FINNEY, Ross Lee, b. 23 Dec. 1906, Wells, Minn., USA. Composer. Educ: BA, Carleton Coll.; studied w. Nadia Boulanger, Alban Berg & Roger Sessions. m. Gretchen Ludke, 2 s. Career: Prof. of Music & Comp. in Res., Univ. of Mich. Comps. incl: 4 Symphs.; 2 Violin & 2 Piano Concertos; Violin, Viola & Cello Sonatas; 8 str. quartets; num. choral & keyboard works; (stage work) Nun's Priest's Tale, 1965; many of works also recorded. Mbrships incl: Nat. Inst. Arts & Leters; Am. Acad. Arts & Scis. Hons. incl: Pulitzer Prize, 1937; Guggenheim Fellowships, 1937, 1947, Fulbright Award, 1955; Boston Symph. Prize, 1956; Brandeis Gold Medal, 1967. Hobby: Cooking. Address: 2015 Geddes Ave., Ann Arbor, MI 48L04, USA. 2.

FINNILÄ, Birgit, b. 20 Jan. 1931, Falkenberg, Sweden. Contralto Singer. Educ: Studied w. Ingalill Linden, Sweden, & Roy Henderson, London, UK. m. Allan Finnilä, 2 s., 3 d. Debut: Göteborg, 1963. Career: has sung w. most important orchs. & choral socs., Sweden, Scandinavia, Europe, USSR, USA, Aus., Asia, S Am.; many fest. apps.; roles incl: Orgeo (Gluck, Orgeo ed Euridice); Lucretia (Britten, Rape of Lucretia); Teodata (Handel, Flavio); Erda (Wagner, Rheingold & Siegfried); etc. Recordings: orchl. works by Bach, Telemann, Cimarosa, Bruckner, Handel, Mahler, Mozart, Wagner, Vivaldi; var. lieder progs. Recip. Grand Prix du Disque, Vivaldi's Juditha Triumphans (sang Juditha). Mgmt: Svensk Konsertdirektion AB, Junigatan 27, 415 15 Göteborg, Sweden.

FINSCHER, Ludwig, b. 14 Mar. 1930, Kassel, Germany. Professor of Musicology. Educ: Dr. Phil., Gottingen Univ., 1954. Career: Freelance music & theatre critic, 1956-60; Asst. in Musicol., Kiel & Saarbrucken Univs., 1960-67; Prof. of Musicol., Chmn., Musicological Inst. of Johann Wolfgang Goethe-Univ., FrankfurtMain, 1968-. Publs: Loyset Compere (c. 1450-1518). Life & Works, 1964; Studien zur Geschichte des Streichquartetts, Vol. 1, 1974; Ed., Loyset Compère, Opera Omnia, 1958-; Co-ed., Festschrift Walter Wiora, 1967; Co-ed., Hindemith-Gesamtausgabe. Contbr. to: Die Musik forschung; Archiv. fur Musikwissenschaft, etc. Mbrships: Pres., Gesellschaft fur Musikforschung, 1974-77; Pres., Int. Musicol. Soc., 1977-; Hon. Foreign Mbr., Royal Musical Assn., 1978. Hon: Prize, Philos.-Hist. Klasse der Akad. der Wissenschaften, Gottingen, 1968. Hobbies: Mountain climbing; Skiing. Address: D-6365 Rosbach 1, Gruner 18, German Fed. Repub.

FIRCA, Gheorghe Bujor, b. 15 Apr. 1935, Gradinari, Romania. Musicologist. Educ: Grad., Ciprian Porumbescu Conserv. of Music, Bucharest, 1959; Univ. of Saarbrücken. m. Clemansa Firca. Publs. incl: The Modal Bases of Diatonic Chromaticism, 1966; The Modal Concept in George Enescu's Music (French), 1968; Leos Janacek-Promoter of Contemporary Modal Thought (French), 1970; Der Beitrag des Tritonus zur Entwicklung konstructiver Prinzipien, 1970; Sturcture & Structuralism in Musical Research, 1973. Contbr. to: musicol. jrnls. Mbrships: Comps. Union of Romania, 1960-; Soc. for Music Rsch., Cassel, Germany, 1969-. Recip., Ciprian Porumbescu Prize, Romanian Acad., 1968. Address: Str. Dr. Kock nr. 5, Sector 6, 7000 Bucharest, PO 35, Romania.

FIRFOV, Živko, b. 24 Dec. 1907, Tito, Veles, Yugoslavia. Ethnomusicologist. Educ: B Mus, Stevan Mokranjac Coll. of Music, Belgrade, 1927-31; Musical Acad., Belgrade, 1937-38.

m. Danka Firfova, 1 s. Career incls: Collector & Arr., Macedonian folk songs, 1923-; Dir. & Cond., choirs in Belgrade & Skopje; Artistic Dir. of prize-winning cultural socs.; Artistic Advsr., TANEC; Music Tchr., Zemun, 1931-41; Folk music prod., Radio Skopje; Hd., Folk Music & Choreography Sect., 1950-65, & Dir., 1955-63, Folklore Inst., Peoples' Repub. of Macedonia. Publs. incl: Co-Ed., Makedonski Muzicki Folklor, I-II, 1953, 59. Contbr. to profl. jrnls. Mbrships incl. IFMC. Hons: Num. state awards; Folk dance grp., London, named after him. Address: ul. 955 br. 7, 91000 Skopje, Yugoslavia.

FIRKUSNY, Rudolf, b. 11 Feb. 1912, Napajedla, Czech. Pianist. Educ: Conserv. of Music, Coll. & Univ., Brno & Prague. m. Tatiana Nevolova, 1 s., 1 d. Debut: w. Czech Philharmonic Orch., Prague, 1922. Career: concert tours in Europe, USA, Australia, New Zealand, S. Am. & Israel. Comps: Piano Concerto; Str. Quartet; var. vocal & piano pieces. Recordings: DGG; RCA Victor; Columbia Records; Decca; Vox; etc. Mbr., Bohemians Club, NYC. Mgmt: Ronald A. Wilford, Columbia Artists Mgmt. Inc., NYC; Address: c/o Interartists, J. Beek, The Hague, The Netherlands. 2,28.

FIRTH, Everett Joseph, b. 2 June 1930, Winchester, Mass., USA. Solo Timpanist. Educ: BMus, New Engl. Conserv. of Music. m. Olga Kwasniak, 2 d. Career: Solo Timpanist, Boston Symph. Orch., Boston Pops Orch., Fac. Hd., Berkshire Music Ctr., New Engl. Conserv. Has recorded for RCA Victor, DGG & Mercury. Publd. about 30 works. Contbr. to profl. jrnls. Mbrships: Pi Kappa Lambda; Phi Mu Alpha Sinfonia. Hobbies: Collecting art & antiques; Skiing; Hunting; Fishing. Address: Pine Wood Rd., Dover, MA 02030, USA. 2,6.

FISCHBACH, Elis Beck, b. 8 Jan. 1921, Prague, Czechoslovakia. Cellist. Educ: Study of cello, Czechoslovakia, Israel & USA, w. Pravoslav Sadlo, Harry Son, Joseph Schuster, B. Vaska, A. Bass; Composition, w. Ben Chaim, Winthrop Seargeant, Karl Weigl; Ensemble & Orch. study w. Nat. Orchestral Assn., NYC, w. Leon Barzin. m. Rudy Fischbach (dec. 1968), 1 d. Debut: Prague, 1934. Career: Radio perf. of sonata series w. Charles Rosen, pianist, NYC; Soloist, WQXR Radio Orch.; 2 seasons w. Busch Chmbr. Players; 2 seasons w. NYC Symph.; 1st Cellist, Worcester (Mass.) Orch., 4 yrs.; Denver Symph., 15 yrs. Num. chmbr. music orchestral recordings. Mbrships: Vol. music tchr. & therapist, Nat. Asthma Ctr., Children's Asthma Inst. Hosp., Denver. Hons: Cert. of Merit, Nat. Orchestral Assn., 1945; Schlrships. for study of cello w. NY Phil. Symph. Orch., composition w. Seargeant & Weigl. Hobby: Working w. sick children. Address: 10600 Huron St., Apt. 104, Denver, CO 80234, USA.

FISCHBACH, Gerald Frederick, b. 24 Oct. 1942, Milwaukee, Wis., USA. Violinist. Educ: BFA, Univ. of Wis.-Milwaukee, 1964; M Mus, Univ. of Ill. at Urbana, 1965; D Musical Arts, Univ. of Iowa at Iowa City, 1972. m. Gail M Benge Fischbach, 1 d., 2 s. Career incl: Prof. of Music, Western Mich. Univ.; 1st Violinist, res. quartet, Dir., Hons. String Quartet Prog.; Num. concerts in US & abroad, inclng. recent perfs. in NYC, Montreal, Wash. DC, London, & Cambridge, UK, & Innsbruck, Austria; Coord., Int. String Workshop. Recordings: 5 Sonorous Inventions for Violin & Piano. Mbrships: Mich. Pres. & N Central Chairperson, Am. String Tchrs. Assn.; Strings Prog. Chairperson, Music Tchrs. Nat. Assn. Contbr. to The Am. String Tchr. Hobbies incl: Fishing. Address: 1209 Sheridan Dr., Kalamazoo, MI 49001, USA.

FISCHER, Annie, b. 1914, Hungary. Educ: Budapest Acad. of Music; studied w. Arnold Szekely & Erno von Dohnanyi. m. Aladar Toth (dec.). Debut: 1922. Career: num. concerts, tours, recordings, 1926-. Hons: 1st Prize, Int. Liszt Competition, Budapest, 1933; Kossuth Prizes, 1949, 55, 65; Hon Prof., Acad. of Music, Budapest, 1965; Eminent Artist; Red Banner Order of Labour, 1974. 16.

FISCHER, Edgar, b. 3 Mar. 1942, Santiago, Chile. Cellist. Educ: Bachelor, Inst. Nacional; Conserv. Nat. de Santiago; Escuela Moderna de Musica; Dip., Juilliard Schl. of Music, NYC, USA. m. Elba Fischer, 1 s., 1 d. Career: Recitals & chmbr. music concerts in USA, S Am. & Europe; Rep. of Chile, Image of Chile, Wash. DC, USA, 1963; Mbr., Trio Fischer, -1973; currently, Solo Cellist, Swiss Romande Orch.; Cello Tchr., Lausanne Conserv. Mbr., Assn. de Musiciens Suisse. Hons: Jeunesses Musicales, Berne, 1970; Concours Int., Geneva, 1967. Hobbies: Nordic Ski; Chess. Address: Le Cheminet 9, 1305 Penthalaz, Vaud, Switz.

FISCHER, Eduard, b. 24 Nov. 1930, Prague, Czechoslovakia. Conductor. Educ: Cond. Dip., Acad. of Arts, Prague, 1954. m. Ludmila Tomasova, 1 s., 1 d. Debut: Prague, 1954. Career: Music Dir., State Symph. Orch., Gott Waldov, 1958-68; Cond., Prague Chmbr. Soloists, 1964-; Chief Cond., State

Chmbr. Orch., Zilina, 1974-; Apps., music fests. inclng. Expo 67, Canada, Prague Spring Fest., Strassbourg. Recordings: Handel's Concerti Grossi Opus 6; Num. Czech contemp. composers. Hons: Int. Concours Award of Young Conds., Besançon, 1958. Hobby: Chess (listed chess player). Mgmt: Slovkoncert, Bratislava. Address: Sporilov 2503, 141 00 Prague 4, Czechoslovakia.

FISCHER, Ewald, b. 1 Sept. 1924, Pressnitz, USSR. Musician (Flute). Educ: Music High Schl., Leipzig; Masterclasses. Debut: 200th Birthday of Handel, Film made by DEFA, 1959. Career: TV apps. w. the Händelfestspielorch. Recordings: (w. Händelfestspielorch.), Poros, Imenev, Rademisto, Feuerwerksmusik. Mbrships: Union of Comps.; Musicians of the German Dem. Repub. Hons: Handel prize, 1956; Medal of Hon. of the VDK (Berlin State Opera), 1976. Mgmt: Landestheater Hall, Händelfestspielorch. Hobbies: Bicycling. Address: DDR 402 Halle, Heinrich Ram Str. 14, German Dem. Repub.

FISCHER, Klaus Peter, b. 16 Jan. 1937, Breslau, Silesia. Musicologist. Educ: PhD, Univ. of Cologne, 1970; Franz Liszt-Hochschule, Weimar, 1955-58; Studium der Schulmusik, 1958. Career: Stipendiat des Deutschen Historischen Insts. 1970-72; Stipendiat, Deutschen Forschungsgemeinschaft, 1972-. Mbr., Gesellschaft für Musikforschung. Contbr. to: Archiv für Musikwissenschaft; Analecta Musicologica; Grove's Dict. of Music & Musicians, 6th ed. Hobbies: Lit.; Chess. Address: Musikgeschichtliche Abteilung des Deutschen Historischen Insts., Via Aurelia Antica 391, 00165 Rome, Italy.

FISCHER, William S, b. 5 Mar. 1935, Shelby, Miss., USA. Musician (Woodwinds, Viola & Piano). Educ: BS Mus., Xavier Univ., La.; MA, Comp. & Theory, Colo. Coll., Akademie fur Musik und Darstellende Kunst, Vienna, Austria. m. Dlores Labrie, 4 children. Debut: w. Profl. Show Bands at age of 16 yrs. Career incls: Tchr., High Schl. & Coll.; Lectr: Univ. Mich.; Bucknell Univ.; Cond: Berlin Radio Orch.; Cologne Radio Orch.; Toronto Symph. Orch. CBS-TV. Comps. incl: A Quiet Movement for Orch.; Jesse (opera in 3 acts). All comps. recorded. Publs. incl: Gospel Spirit, 1974. Mbr. num. profl. orgs. Hons. incl: NYS Coun. of Arts Award, 1971. Hobbies: Sailing; Cooking; Skiing. Address: 1365 St Nicholas Ave., 13J, New York, NY 10033, USA. 2,4.

FISCHER-DIESKAU, Dietrich, b. 28 May 1925, Berlin, Germany. Concert & Operatic Baritone. Educ: studied w. Prof. Georg Walter & Prof. Hermann Weissenborn. m. (1) Cellistin Irmgard Poppen (dec.), 3 s.; (2) Ruth Leuwerik (div.); (3) Kristina Pugell. Career: 1st Lyric & Character Baritone, Berlin State Opera, 1948-; Mbr., Vienna State Opera Co., 1957-; apps. at major fests.; concert tours, Europe, USA, Asia. Num. recordings. Publs: Texte Deutscher Lieder; Auf den Spuren der Schubert-Lieder; Wagner und Nietzsche, der Mystagoge und sein Abtrünniger, 1974. Mbrships: Akad. der Künste; Int. Mahler-Gesellschaft, Vienna; German Sect., Int. Music Counc. Recip. many awards & hons. inclng: Grosses Verdienstkreuz des Verdienstordens der Bundesrepublik Deutschland, 1974. Hobby: Painting. 16.

FISCHER-DIESKAU, Klaus, b. 2 Jan. 1921, Berlin, Germany. Composer; Conductor; Organist. Educ: Dip., Ch. Music, State Acad. of Music, Berlin. m. Eleonore Schröder, 3 d. Debut: fndn. of Hugo Distler Choir, 1953. Career: num. perfs. w. Hugo Distler Choir, UK, 1956, 58, 74, & 76, Belgium, 1958 & 68, France, 1959, 62, 64, 65, 66, 76, Greece, 1966, Switz., 1969 & 71, Austria, 1970, Denmark, 1972 & 73; USA visiting prof., 1969; Switzerland, 1978; TV broadcasts, UK, Belgium & Germany. Comps: Sonata for 2 pianos, Op. 15; String Quartets, Op. 16, 17, & 62; Der Spielmann, songs w. instruments, Op. 22; Cantata, Komm. Trost der Nacht, Op. 22; Sonata for cello & piano, Op. 22; Quartet for recorders, Op. 40; Motets a capella, Op. 48; Die Auferstehung, oratorio, Op. 60; Cantional-motets, Op. 71. Recordings: Musicaphon; DGG; RB; Da Camera. Contbr. to Am. & German profl. publs. Mbr., European Fedn. of Youth Choirs. Recip., Medal, Min. of Pub. Educ., Belgium. Hobbies: Photography; Gadgetry; Ship Models. Address: Schützallee 116, D 1000 Berlin 37, German Fed. Repub. 4.

FISHBEIN, Robert Edward, b. 13 May 1933, NYC, USA. Violinist; Violist; Composer; Poet; Physician. Educ: Manhattan Schl. of MUsic; HS of Music & Art; Yale Schl. of Music; AB Harvard Coll., 1953; M.D., Yale Univ. Schl. of Med., 1957. div. Career: app. on Ted Mack's Original Amateur Hour playing musical glasses, 1951; wrote music & lyrics, Sr. Class Show, Yale Schl. of Med., 1957, On Call revue, Phila. Gen. Hosp., 1958; w. Doctor's Symph. Orch., 1959, Chmbr. Music Grp., Hastings-on-Hudson, 1964-68, Hudson Valley Symph.,

1967-68, Westchester Philharmonic & Orchl. Soc. of Westchester, 1966-68, Broadway Symph. Orch., 1968; apps. at Pennypoint, Goddard Coll. & Int. Str. Conf., 1968; Cammac, Quebec, Can., 1972; Composers' Conf., Johnson State Coll., Vt., 1974; Merrimack Valley Music Centre, New Hampshire, 1977; Balalaiker Symph. Orch., 1978. Compositions incl: num. vocal, instrumental, & chmbr. works; Saturday Night in Scollay Square, 1950; Board Stiff, 1957; On Call, 1958; transcriptions for viola. Mbrships: Amateur Chmbr. Music Players; Chmbr. Music Assocs.; Am. Str. Tchrs. Assn.; Pierian Sodality of 1808; Nat. Assn. for Am. Comps. & Cond. Hobbies: Musical Philately. Address: 888 Eighth Ave., NYC, NY, USA.

FISHER, Esther Frances Eveleigh. Pianist. Educ: Wellington, NZ; Studied at Paris Conservatoire. m. Sir John N Barran Bart, dec. Debut: London, 1923. Career: Prof., RCM; London, Harold Holt Celebrity Tour; Num. piano concerts & TV apps., BBC. Recordings: Victoria & Albert Recordings (Onyx Records). Mbrships: Solo Perfs. Sect., ISM; Brit. Inst. of Recorded Sound; Royal Phil. Soc. Hon: Hon. RCM. Hobbies: Reading; Art Galleries. Address: 2 Phillimore Place, London W8 7BU, UK.

FISHER, Jack Berry, b. 19 Sept. 1924, Dallas, Tex., USA. Organist. Educ: B Mus, Univ. of Tex., Austin; MSM, Union Theol. Sem., NYC; AAGO; Chmn., AGO. Career: Chmn., Organ Dept., Augsburg Coll., & Instr. St. Paul, Minn., MacPhail Coll. of Music, Mpls., Minn., 1955-60; Prof., Boston Univ., Mass., 1965-; Chmn., Music Dept., Bradford Coll., Mass., 1967-; Organist-Choirmaster, var. chs., currently (1968-) Union Ch., Waban, Mass.; has given many recitals. Contbr. to profl. jrnls. Mbrships. incl: Bd. of Trustees, Methuen Mem. Music Hall, Mass.; Charter Mbr., Boston Organ Club; Chartet Mbr., Diocesan Music Commissions; Past Dean, Minn. & Mass. Chapters, AGO; Organ Histl. Soc. Hobby: Travel. Address: 16 Carver St. No. 2, Boston, MA 02116, USA.

FISHER, John Henry, b. 7 June 1944, Jubbulpore, India. Administrative Director. Educ: MA, Trinity Coll., Cambridge; GSM (pt.-time, singing). m. Margaret Mary Fisher, 2 c. Career: Economist Intelligence Unit, 1965-66; British Broadcasting Corporation, 1967-76; Bath Fest. Soc., 1976- (Administrative Dir.). Contbr. to: Hi Fi News; Studio Sound; Video & Audio Visual Review; Video Yearbook. Hobbies: Singing (chmbr. choir); Writing; Photography. Address: c/o Bath Festival, Linley House, 1 Pierrepont Place, Bath BA1 1JL, UK.

FISHER, Judith Booth, b. 25 Apr. 1941, Dover, Ohio, USA. Professional Clarinetist; Conductor; Teacher. Educ: BS Music Educ., Ohio State Univ.; M Mus Ed., SUNY at Buffalo. m. Walter C. Fisher, Jr. Debut: w. Tuscarawas Co. Phil., aged 14. Career: Clarinet Soloist, Col. & profl. bands & orchs., Ohio; Prin. Clarinetist & Soloist w. Niagara Parks Band, Niagara Falls Phil., & Can. orchs., 1962-; Music Cons., to Niagara Falls Pub. Schls., 1966-; Band Dir., secondary level, Niagara Falls, w. 120 mbrs., 1972-; one of 1st female conds. in USA; Cond. of musicals, Shaw Theatre & Brock Univ., Can. Mbr., profl. assns. Hons. incl: Pres.'s Scholarship Meda., Ohio State Univ., 1961; var. scholarships. Hobbies: Travel in US & Europe. Address: 4642 Miller Rd., Niagara Falls, NY 14304, USA.

FISHER, Lawrence V, b. 20 Nov. 1923, Vinton, Iowa, USA. Professor of Violin & Chamber Music. Educ: BM., 1949, MM., 1950, Eastman Schl. of Music, Rochester Univ.; Study w. Elizabeth Green, Jacques Gordon, Andre de Ribaupierre, Ivan Galamian. m. Dayna Larason, 2 d. Career: Soloist, symph. orchs. & ensembles, 25 yrs.; Num. US tours as mbr. var. grps. inclng. Okla. String Quartet, 1954-67; Perf. w. Juilliard Quartet, w. mbrs. of Pro Arte Quartet, Alma Trio, Hungarian Quartet; Asst. Concertmaster, Okla. City Symph., 12 yrs.; Prof., Violin & Chmbr. Music & Mbr., Univ. String Quartet, Univ. of Alb., Canada, 1969-; Quartet perfs. Canada, CBC radio & TV, & at Fests., UK & Canada. Recordings: CBC Int. Serv. recordings of music by Coulthard, Maconchy, Debussy. Schubert. Hons: Outstanding Instrumentalist, HS Regional Music Contest, St. Paul, 1941; Perf.'s Cert., Eastman Schl. of Music, 1950. Hobbies: Writing fiction; Photography. Address: Dept. of Music, Univ. of Alb., Edmonton, Alb., Canada.

FISHER, Norma, b. 11 May 1940, London, UK. Concert Pianist. Educ: GSM. m. Barrington Saipe, 2 s. Debut: Wigmore Hall, 1956. Career: 1st Promenade Concert, 1963; perfs. in Germany, France, Austria, Italy, Belgium, Can., USA, Israel & throughout GB; frequent broadcasts, recitals, chmbr. & concerto perfs. Hons: 2nd Prize, Busoni Int. Piano Competition, Bolzano, Italy, 1961; Piano Prize (jointly w. Vladimir Ashkenazy), Harriet Cohen Int. Awards, 1963. Hobby: Reading. Mgmt: Ingpen & Williams. Address: 5 Lyndhurst Gdns., Finchley, London N3, UK. 3.

FISHER, Paul G, b. 30 June 1922, Reading, Pa., USA. Professor of Music; Conductor; French Horn. Educ: BS.,

Lebanon Valley Coll., 1947; MA., George Peabody Coll., 1948; MM., 1951, EdD., Music Educ., 1969, Univ. of Mich. m. Sara Amanda Schott, 1 s., 1 d. Career: Cond., Miss. Coll. Band, 1948-50: Hershey HS Band, 1951-66; Millersville State Coll. Band, 1966-; Asst. Cond., Harrisbrug (Pa.) Symph., 1970-; Cond. var. community & coll. choruses; 1st Horn, Harrisburg Symph., 1951-, Lancaster (Pa.) Symph., 1967-74; Millersville Coll. Community Orch., 1966-76; Cornet Soloist, var. bands; Recitalist, French horn, & Guest Cond.; Prof. of Music, Millersville State Coll.; Acting Chmn., Music Dept., 1973, Chmn., Music Dept., 1978. Publs: Music: A Dominant Force in the First Century of Lebanon Valley College, 1969. Contbr. to profl. jrnls. Mbrships: Past Pres., S. Dist., Pa. Music Educators Assn.; Past Pres., Pa. Collegiate Band Dirs. Assn.; Past Pres., Pa. Collegiate Choral Assn.; Pi Kappa Lambda. Hobbies: Sports; Travel. Address: 214 E. Charlotte St., Millersvile, PA 17551, USA. 6.

FISHER, Roger Anthony, b. 18 Sept. 1936, Woodford, Essex, UK. Organist; Pianist; Conductor. Educ: ARCM; MA, Christ Ch., Oxford; ATCL; FRCO. m. Susan Mary Green, 1 d. Career incls: recitals in major chs., cathedrals & halls in GB, France, Can. & USA; Asst. Organist, Hereford Cathedral & Lectr. in Music, Hereford Coll. of Educ., 1962; Organist & Master of Choristers, Chester Cathedral, 1967; Special Commnr., Royal Schl. of Ch. Music, 1970. Comps: Festival Te Deum commnd. for Chester Fest., 1973. Recordings: Decca; RCA; HMV; Guild; Vista. Contbr. to: Chester Fest. Serv. Books; Liverpool Echo. Mbrships: ISM; RCO. Recip., Geoffrey Tankard Prize, RCM, 1959. Hobbies incl: Organ Building & Design; Walking; Cycling; Railway History. Mgmt: Ibbs & Tillett. Address: 11 Abbey St., Chester, CH1 2JF, UK 4.

FISHER, Sylvia Gwendoline Victoria, b. Aust. Operatic Soprano. Educ: Conserv. of Music, Melbourne. m. Ubaldo Gardini. Career: Prin. soprano, Covent Garden; apps. at num. opera houses incl. in Italy & Germany; roles incl: Leonora (Fidelio), Sieglinde, Gutrune, Brunnhilde, Marschallin. Hons: Winner, Sun Aria Competition, Melbourne, 1936. Hobbies: Gardening; Rare Books on Singing. Address: 24 Dawson Pl., London W2, UK.

FISHER, Zeal Isay, b. 2 Dec. 1930, NY, USA. Teacher; Violist; Conductor; Composer. Educ: BS., Music Educ., Miami Univ., Ohio, 1952; Mus M., Ind. Univ., 1954; Grad. work in Educ. ibid, 1972-74; Studied viola w. Joseph Bein & David Dawson; Studied cond. w. Ernst Hoffman. m. Marilyn Ann Hershman, 1 s., 1 d. Career: Violist, South Bend String Quartet; Prin. Viola, South Bend & Elkhart Symph. Orhcs.; (Soloist in Hindemith's Schwanendreher). Cond., Presby Players (Theatre); Tchr., South Bend Schls. Comps: String Quartet; Woodwind Quintet; Chantecler (Operetta); The Far Princess (Opera); South Bend Bicentennial Pageant; Three Surrealistic Songs; Viola Fantasy. Recordings: South Bend Bicentennial Pageant. Mbrships: Pres., South Bend Chmbr. Music Soc.; Bd. of Dirs., Michiana Arts & Sci. Coun. Address: 2920 Kettering Dr., South Bend, IN 46635, USA.

FISHWICK, John Charles, b. 13 Sept. 1951, Wallasey, Ches., UK. Instrumentalist (bass trombone). Educ: The Nat. Youth Orch. of GB.; RCM; The Camel Laird's Brass Band. Career: Bass Trombone w. BBC Scottish Symph. Orch., 1971-. Recordings: w. BBC; SSO; Nat. Youth Orch. of GB. Mbrships: Musicians' Union. Platform (Glasgow); Glasgow Soc. of Musicians. Hobbies: Sea Angling; Camping; Reading; Jazz Music; Yoga. Address: 61 Cleveden Dr., Glasgow G12, UK.

FISKE, June, b. 2 Apr. 1941, Passaic, NJ, USA. Dramatic Coloratura Soprano. Educ: Grad., Bergen Coll. m. Joseph W Fiske, 1 s., 1 d. Debut: NJ Opera Fest., 1967. Career: Apps. w. opera cos. of Phila., Hartford, San Antonio, NY City; app. on TV as Violetta (La Traviata). Hons: Opera Am. Audience, Phila. Opera Grand Prize, 1975. Hobbies incl: Gourmet Cooking; Golf; Fly Fishing; Antiques. Address: 363 Crescent Dr., Franklin Lakes, NJ 074417, USA.

FISSINGER, Edwin Russell, b. 15 June 1920, Chgo., Ill., USA. Music Educator; Composer; Choral Conductor. Educ: B Mus, Am. Conserv., Chgo., DMA, Univ. Ill., Urbana. m. Cecile Patricia Monette, 1 s., 1 d. Career: TV & radio apps. w. Concert Choir & Chmbr. Choir, Univ. Ill., Chgo. Cir., 1962-67; Annual Concert Tours w. Concert Choir, ND State Univ. Fargo, (USA & Europe). Comps: Num. motets, masses, anthems & secular choral pieces. Recordings incl: Morning of Mist (ND State Choir), 1971; Witness (Warburg Coll. Choir), 1973. Publs. incl: Parkway Choral Series (ed.), 11964-73. Mbrships: Am. Choral Dirs. Assn.; MENC. Hons. incl: Religious Arts Award, anthem 'Long, Long Ago', 1953. Hobbies: Sport; Reading. Address: 57 15th Ave. N., Fargo, ND 58102, USA. 4,28.

FISTOULARI, Anatole, b. 20 Aug. 1907, Russia (British citizen). Conductor. Educ: Kiev, Berlin & Paris. Debut: Symph. Concert, Kiev, 1914. Career: Cond., leading orchs. in Russia; Concerts in W. Europe, 1920; Cond., Grand Opera Rousse, Paris, w. Chaliapin, 1931; Cond., Ballet de Monte Carlo, UK, USA, France & Italy w. Massine; Cond., Symph. Concerts w. LSO, 1942-; Prin. Cond., LPO, 1943-44; Fndr., London Int. Orch., 1946; num. perfs. in Europe, Israel, S. Africa & Am. Recordings of num. works. Address: 65 Redington Rd., London NW3, UK.

FITZGERALD, Ella, b. 25 April 1918, USA. Singer. Career incl: Singer w. Chick Webb Band, 1934-39; Toured w. Jazz at the Phil. Troupe, USA., Japan & Europe, 1948-; Film appearances, USA & abroad, 19556-; Toured w. An Evening of Jazz Troupe, Scandinavia & W. Europe, 1957. Hons. incl: Awards from var. musicians polls; Awards from Downbeat & Metronome mags.; Recording Artist on Decca label, 1936-55 & Verve label, 1956-. Address: c/o The Gale Agcy., 48 W. 48th St., NY, NY 10019, USA.

FITZGERALD, Robert Bernard, b. 26 April 1911, Martinsville, Ill., USA. Professor of Music; Composer; Lecturer. Educ: B Mus, Oberlin Coll., 1932; M Mus. Jordan Conserv., 1935. m. Ina Daw Fitzgerald, 1 s., 1 d. Career incls: Univ. of Texas, 1940-56; Prof. of Music, Dir. of Bands & Hd. of Music Dept., Univ. Ky., 1956-63; Dir. of Contemporary Music Project for Music Educators Nat. Conf., Wash. DC, 1963-65; Prof. of Music, Univ. Ky., 1965-76; Prof. Emeritus, 1976-. Comps. incl: more than 60 comps. & arrs. for solo brass instruments & ensembles, choral works & band arrs. inclng: Soliloquy, 1975; Chorale Fantasia, 1975; Celebration Suite, 1975; 4 Love Songs. Num. recordings. Contbr. to profl. jrnls. Mbrships. incl: Kappa Kappa Psi; Pi Kappa Lambda; Phi Mu Alpha; ASCAP. Hobbies: Fishing; Golf. Address: 2087 Old Nassau Rd., Lexington, KY 40504, USA.

FITZPATRICK, Horace Allgier, b. 24 April 1934, Louisville, Ky., USA. Organologist; Player, Maker & Restorer of Historic Wind Instruments. Educ: BA, Northwestern Univ.; B Mus, M Mus, Yale Univ.; D Phil, MA, Oxford Univ.; Dip., Vienna State Acad. of Music. m. Margaret Joy Merry, 1 s., 2 d. Debut: on natural horn, Wigmore Hall. Career incls: Lectr. in Music, St. Catharine's Coll., Oxford, 1965-70; estab. Bate Coll. of Historic Wind Instruments, Oxford; Prof. of Natural Horn & Co-Fndr. of Early Music Dept., Guildhall Schl. of Music & Drama, London; played valve horn w. var. int. chmbr., symph. & opera orchs. until 1964; plays natural horn w. own Baroque ensemble, Florilegium, w. Musica Antiqua, Amsterdam & also w. Capella Academica & Concentus Musicus, Vienna. Publs. incl: The Horn & Horn-Playing, 1680-1830, 1970. Contbr. to: Grove; MGG; Bordas; int. musical jrnls. Hons. incl: Gold Medal for Perf., Italian Min. of Culture. Mgmt: Spry Concert Mgmt., Bicester, UK.

FITZPATRICK, Noreen, b. 16 Aug. 1955, Glasgow, UK. Cellist. Educ: RCM, 1973-77; ARCM; MMus, New England Conserv., Boston, USA; pvte. study w. Pierre Fournier, Geneva. m. Phillip Alan Silver. Debut: Cheltenham Int. Fest., 1978. Career: mbr., Fitzpatrick/Silver duo w. husband; recitals & concerts in London, Cheltenham, Oxford, Cambridge, Glasgow, Boston & Harvard Univ. (USA); TV & radio perfs. mbr., ISM. Hons: Ivor James Concerto prize, RCM, 1975; Earl of Dalhousie Award, 1976. Hobbies: Cooking; Ancient Hist.; Psychol. Address: 4 May Terr., Galsgow G42 9XF, Scotland, UK.

FITZSIMMONS, Edith Dizon, b. 24 Aug. 1922, Roxas City, Philippines. Organist; Music Teacher (theory, piano, organ). Educ: Assoc. in Music (piano), Philippine Christian Coll., 1950; BA (English), Central Philippine Coll., 1946; BMus (theory), Philippine Women's Univ., 1958; Accreditation Course for Advanced Music Tchng., Univ. of Melbourne, 1979. m. (/) D Paulo Dizon (dec.), 4 s., 2 d. (2) Ray Fitszimmons. Career incls: Music Tchr., Philippine Women's Univ., 1958-61; Hd., Schl. of Music, Central Philippine Univ., 1963-66; Organist, Ellinwood Presby. Ch., Manila, 1954-56, Central Methodist Ch., Manila, 1956-61, St. James Old Cathedral, Melbourne, Aust., 1970-72; Staff Announcer, Prod. & Organist, DZFM Radio Manila, 1956-59; Prod. & Organist, Far East Broadcasting Corp., Random Reveries, 1959-61; Prod., TV Progs., Manila, 1958, 1959-61; Dir., Central Goulburn Valley Music Studio, Shepparton, Aust., 1973-79; Organ soloist, Aust. & Philippines. Contbr. to profl. publs. Mbr., num. profl. orgs. Hons: num. grants. Address: 62 Orr St., Shepparton, Vic., Australia.

FJELDSTAD, Oivin, b. 2 May 1903, Norway. Violinist; Conductor. Educ: Oslo Conserv., w. Gustav Fr. Lange; Leipzig Conserv., w. Walther Davisson; Berlin Conserv., w. Clemens Kraus. Debut: As violinist, 1921; As Cond., w. Oslo Phil. Orch.,

1931. Career: violinist, Oslo Phil. Orch., 1923-45; Chief Cond., Norwegian State Broadcasting, 1945-62; Norwegian State Opera Orch., 1958-59; Musical Dir. & Chief Cond., Oslo Phil. Orch., 1962-; Guest cond. in num. countries in Europe, USA, USSR, Israel, etc. Hons. incl: Kt., Order of St. Olav; Order of the Lion, Finland, Ordre de la Couronne; Order of Orange-Nassau, Holland; Golden Hon. Medal of Norwegian King; Hon. Medal of Norwegian Musicians; Arnold Schoenberg Dip., Salzburg, 1952. Address: Damfaret 59, Bryn-Oslo 6, Norway.

FLAGELLO, Nicolas Oreste, b. 15 March 1928, NYC, USA. Composer; Conductor; Performer on Piano, Violin & Viola. Educ: B Mus & M Mus, Manhattan Schl. of Music; Doct. in musical comp., Accademia i Santa Cecilia, Rome, Italy, 1956; studied comp. w. Vittorio Giannini & Ildebrando Pizzetti & conducting w. Dmitri Mitropoulos. m. (1) Dianne Danese, 2 s; (2) Maya Randolph. Comps. incl: 2 symphs.; concertos, 4 for piano & 2 for violin; 5 operas; Passion of Martin Luther King (oratorio); choral works; art songs; chmbr. music; sonatas; film scores. Sev. recordings. Mbrships: Pres., Am. Artists Ad Astra Inc.; Fndr., Musical Dir., Fest of Salerno; ASCAP; Bohemians; Kts. of Malta. Hons. incl: annual ASCAP award, 1961-; Kt. of Malta, 1966. Hobbies incl: Painting; Electronics; Cybernetics. Mgmt: Lyra Music, NYC. Address: 1385 York Ave., NY, NY 10021, USA. 2.

FLAHERTY, Patrick James, b. 14 Jan. 1954, Boise, Idaho, USA. Percussionist. Educ: B Mus, Boise State Univ., Boise, Idaho, 1977; M Mus, E Carolina Univ., Greenville, N Carolina, 1979. Contbr. to: The School Musician; NACWPI Jrnl.; Woodwind World; Brass & Percussion. Mbrships: Charter Pres., Lambda Delta Chapt., Phi Mu Alpha Sinfonia; Percussive Arts Soc.; MENC; NACWPI. Hons: Scholarships & Acad. awards; 1st Place, Keyboard Percussion, Percussive Arts Soc. Idaho Div., 1975; 1st Place, Northwest Div., MTNA Coll. Div. Auditions: Finalist, Nat. Competition, MTNA Nat. Div. Coll. Auditions; Grad. Tchng. Fellowship, E Carolina Univ., 1977-79. Hobbies: Outdoors; Photography; Woodworking; Cooking. Address: 1115 N Cole Rd., Boise, ID 83704, USA.

FLANIGAN, Laura Wilson, b. 29 Nov. 1926, Knoxville, Tenn., USA. Musician, Voice, Violin, Cello, Piano, Recorder. Educ: BSc., Ohio State Univ., Columbus, 1952; MA, Tchrs. Coll., Columbia Univ., NY, NYC; studied w. Ruth Geiger, Evalyn Steinbock, Philip Levin, Jeanne-Marie Widergren, Carole O'Hara, Dorothy Smith & Edith Eisler. m. George A. Flanigan. Career: Public Schl. Music Tchr., Voice, Recorder; App. on Ohio State Univ. Radio; Concerts in Ch.'s NYC; Estab. Recorder Prog. in Lakeland Ctrl. Schls., Shrub Oak, NY. Contbr. to The Am. Recorder. Mbrships: Am. Recorder Soc.; Am. String Tchrs. Assn.; MENC; Nat. Bd., Am. Youth Symph. & Chorus; Nat. Coun. of Negro Women; Fine Arts Dir., Sulfolk Br., ibid, Bay Shore, Long Island, NY. Hons: Scholarship, Ohio State Univ., 1949; NY State Tchrs. Grant, 1964; num. awards for Performing Grps., NY. State Schl. Music Assn. Competitions. Hobbies: Travel; Cycling; Reading; Writing. Address: 3992 Paulding Ave., Bronx, NY 10466, USA.

FLAY, Alfred Leonard, b. 26 Dec. 1905, Devizes, Wilts., UK. Retired Educator; Choirmaster & Organist. Educ: LRAM; FRSA; studied organ w. A E Howell; organ & comp. w. Percy Whitloch; organ & singing & class tchng. w. Canon N C Woods; singing, w. Herbert Smith, Winchester Cathedral. Career: Var. BBC Radio Broadcasts; Broadcasts of his comps. July 1944, in Junior Concert Hour from Irish TV, in Mar. 1966 on Western ITV from Southampton; Hd. of Arts Dept. (ic Music & Arts Depts.), Broadway Schl., Weymouth, Dorset, 1950-71; Many appts. as Choirmaster & Organist inclng. Holy Trinity, Weymouth, 1938-61 & St. Peter, Dorchester, Dorset, 1971-73; currently Freelance Organist. Compositions incl: Cantata 'Off the Ground' (De la Mare), 1964; Str. Orch. 'A British Heritage Suite', 1967; Voices, recorders & piano 'Follow Me', 1964; Organ, Two Chorale Preludes; 1961; Anthem, 'Forth In Thy Name', 1961; 'The Squirrel', 1961, etc. Var. book reviews for Organists' Review & Musical Opinion; Articles in var. profl. publs. Mbrships incl: Exec. Mbr., Inc. Assn. of Organists; Libs. Circulation Mgr., Organists' Review Mag. Address: Adelaide House, Longcroft Rd., Weymouth, Dorset DT4 ONY, UK. 3.

FLEECE, Marianne, b. Budapest, Hungary. Violinist. Educ: Tchrs. Dip., Liszt Ferenc Acad., Budapest; MA, State Univ. of Iowa, USA. m. Jeffrey Fleece, 1 s., 1 d. Career: Tutti, Soloist, Budapest Municipal Orch.; Asst. Concertmaster, Soloist, State Univ. of Iowa Orch.; Denver Symph. Orch.; Concertmaster, Soloist, Honolulu Symph. Orch., 1955-; Pvte. Tchr., Chmbr. Music, Solo Recitals; Represented State of Hawaii in 1971 World Symph.; Disneyworld, Fla.; Wash. DC & NY. Mbrships: Am. String Tchrs. Assn.; Am. Fed. of Musicians. Hobbies: TV; Bridge; Cooking; Reading. Address: 4623 Kilauea Ave., Honolulu, HI 96816, USA. 9, 27.

FLEISCHER, Gerda, b. 12 Mar. 1920, Bergen, Norway. Pianist; Soprano Singer. Educ: highest exams, piano playing & singing, Royal Danish Conserv.; further study in piano w. Anders Rachlev, & singing w. Margrethe Ernst. Debut: Copenhagen, 1946. Career: Recitals & broadcasts, Copenhagen, Oslo, Stockholm, Hilversum, Cologne, Salzburg, Vienna. Made 7 records for Philips inclng: Nielsen's Vocalise; Heise's Igennem Bogeskoven; Schubert's Nacht und Träume; Brahms' Wiegenlied & Der Jäger. Mbr.: Solisforeningen, Copenhagen. Hobbies: Lit.; Art. Address: Borupsalle 2, 2200 Copenhagen N, Denmark.

FLEISCHMANN, Aloys Georg, b. 1910, Munich, Germany. Composer; Conductor; Professor of Music. Educ: MA, Univ. Coll., Cork; Mus D., Nat. Univ. of Ireland; Mus D., Dublin Univ.; State Acad. of Music, Munich. m. Anne Madden, 2 s., 3 d. Career: Cond., Cork Symph. Orch., 1934-; Dir., Cork Int. Choral & Folk Dance Fest.; Prof. of Music, Univ. Coll., Cork. Comps: Overture, The Four Masters; Introduction & Funeral March, for large orch.; Song of the Provinces, for choir & orch. w. audience participation; Songs of Colmcille, for choir & chamber orch.; Clare's Dragoons, for baritone, war pipes, choir & orch.; 2 Song Cycles, for tenor & orch.; Cornucopia for horn & orch; 4 Song Cycles for voice & orch.; Sinfonia Votiva, for large orch.; Mass for Peace. Recording: Piano Suite. Publs: Music in Ireland - A Symposium, 1953. Contbr. to: Grove's Dict. & var. profl. jrnls. & Encys. Mbrships: Chmn., Cork Orch. Soc., 1948-; Chmn., Munster Br., Music Tchrs. Assn., 1937-; Off. of Merit, German Fed. Repub.; Royal Irish Acad.; Irish Nat. Commn. for UNESCO; Advsry. Committee for Cultural Relations, Dept. of Foreign Affairs. Hons: Freeman, City of Cork, 1978. Address: Glen House, Ballyvolane, Cork, Eire. 3.

FLEISCHMANN, Ernest Martin, b. 7 Dec. 1924, Frankfurt, Germany. Musical Administrator & Artistic Director. Educ: Univ. of Witwatersrand, S Africa; Mus B., Univ. of Cape Town; S African Coll. of Music. m. Elsa Leviseur, 1 s., 2 d. Debut: Cond., Johannesburg Symph. Orch., 1942. Career: Music Organiser, Van Riebeck Festival, Cape Town, 1952; Dir. of Music & Drama, Johannesburg Festival, 1956; Cond., S African Coll. of Music Choir, 1950-52; Labia Grand Opera Co., 1953-55; Asst. Cond., S African Nat. Opera, 1948-51; Cape Town Univ. Opera, 1950-54; Gen. Sec., London Symph. Orch., 1959-67; Dir. for Europe, CBS Records (Classical), 1967-69; Exec. Dir., Los Angeles Phil. Orch. & Hollywood Bowl, 1969-; French Govt. Commission on Reform of Paris Opera, 1967-1968. Mbrships: Young Musicians Fndn.; Chmn. Supervisory Bd. Address: 135 N Grand Ave., Los Angeles, CA 90012, USA. 3.

FLEISHER, Leon, b. 23 July 1928, San Fran., Calif., USA. Pianist; Conductor; Professor. Educ: studied w. Artur Schnabel. m. (1) Doroth Druzinsky, div., 1 s., 2 d.; (2) Risselle Rosenthal, 1 s., 1 d. Debut: as Pianist, San Fran., 1935; as Cond., w. NY Chmbr. Orch., 1970. Career: Concert Perf., Europe, USA, Can., Latin Am. etc.; since mid 1960's has been paralysed in right hand but still gives recitals of music for one handed pianists; Music Dir., Theatre Chmbr. Players, Wash. DC, 1968; Prof. of Piano, Peabody Conserv., Balt., 1959-; Dir., Walter W. Naumburg Fndn., 1965; has made many Guest Cond. apps.; Cond., Annapolis Symph., 1970-, and mostly Mozart Fest., NY Phil. Hall, 1970. Has made many recordings. Mbr: AAUP. Hons. incl: 1st Prize, Int. Queen Elisabeth Concourse, Belgium, 1952. Address: 1723 Park Ave., Baltimore, MD 21217, USA.

FLEMING, Amaryllis, b. London, UK. Cellist. Educ: RCM; w. Pierre Fournier & Pablo Casals. Debut: Wigmore Hall, Royal Albert Hall. Recordings: Complete Bach Suites (& some cello & piano works). Mbr., ISM; Prof., RCM. Hons: Queen's Prize, Munich Int. Comp. Hobby: Studying Bach. Address: 137 Old Church St., London SW3, UK.

FLEMING, Shirley Moragne, b. 2 Dec. 1930, NYC, USA. Editor; Critic. Educ: BA, MA (musicol.), Smith Coll. Career: Ed., Musical America mag., 1960-. Contbr. to: High Fidelity mag.; Musical Am. mag.; Arts & Leisure sect., NY Times; prog. annotator for RCA Records, Mercury, Decca, etc. Mbrships: Music Critics Assn.; Bd., Am. Music Ctr. Hobbies: Hiking; Reading. Address: 350 First Ave., NY, NY 10022, USA. 5.

FLEMING, Victor Albert, b. 29 May 1901, London, UK. Conductor; Violinist. Educ: Guildhall Schl. of Music; Birmingham Schl. of Music. m. Mary Theresa O'Flynn. Career: Carl Rosa Opera Co.; Welsh Nat. Opera Co.; Birmingham Choral Union; Coventry Philharmonic Soc.; Midland Symph. Orch.; over 100 broadcasts w. Victor Fleming Orch.; Portsmouth Grand Opera Co.; Isle of Wight Opera Co.; Guest Cond., main orchs. & USAF Band; currently Cond., Brit. Concert Orch. Mbrships: ISM; Worshipful Co. of Musicians; Savage Club; Fellow, Inst. Int. des Arts et des Lettres, Zürich. Hobbies:

Sailing; Swimming. Mgmt. Choveaux. Address: 'Honeythorne' Ventnor, Isle of Wight, UK. 4,21.

FLETCHER, Eric, b. 19 Dec. 1933, Westcliff, Essex, UK. Professor; Musicologist; Keyboard Player (organ, harpsichord, clavichord); Conductor. Educ: Pembroke Coll., Cambridge, UK; MA (Cantab.); MusB, (Cantab.); FRCO. Career: Cathedral Organist, Llandaff Cathedral; sub-organist, Peterborough Cathedral; Prof., GSM; sub-organist, Westminster Cathedral; Pres., Worldwide Music Publishers; Dir. of Ch. Music Ctr. & Early Music Ctr., NY; solo organ recitals, BBC radio & TV. Recordings w. Choir of King's Coll., Cambridge. Publs: Ed., Renaissance & Baroque Music. Mgmt: Worldwide Music Services, 59 Mayfield Ave., Southend-on-Sea, Essex, UK. Address: c/o Mgmt.

FLETCHER, Malcolm John, b. 11 Mar. 1955, Birmingham, UK. Professinal Pianist; Tenor Singer. Educ: Pupil of Mr. Else Cross, Mr. Henry Cummings & Mr. Rex Stephens, Royal Acad. Music, London, 1975-79; Lic., Royal Acad. Music in Singing & Piano Teaching; Profl. Cert., ibid. Debut: Royal Acad. Music, 1977. Career: Pvte. tchr., Birmingham. Mbrships: Incorp. Soc. of Musicians; Pvte. Tchrs.' Sect., ibid.; Royal Acad. Music Club. Hons: Charles Norman Prize, Royal Acad. Music; Birmingham Post Challenge Cup, 1975; Sev. cups at Midland Competitive Music Festivals. Hobbies: Building record lib.; Reading; Tennis; Watching cricket. Addres: 67 Sheldonfield Rd., Sheldon, Birmingham, B26 3RR, UK.

FLETCHER, Peter G, b. 9 Jan. 1936, Grimsby, UK. Conductor; Pianist; Music Educator. Educ: Organ Scholar, Jesus Coll., Cambridge, 1954-58; MA; BMus; FRCO; ARCM. Career: Organist, Beverley Minster & Music Adviser, E Riding of Yorks., 1962-66; Staff Inspector for Music, ILEA & Prin. Cond. of London Schls. Symph. Orch. 1966-73; Fndr., ILEA Music Centre, ILEA Centre for Young Musicians at Pimlico School & of the Music Bias Course, Pimlico Schl.; Prof., Chmn. of Music Dept. of Dalhousie Univ., Halifax, Nova Scotia, Can., 1973-76; Fndr. & Cond., Opera East; Prin. Music Adviser, Leics. Educ. Authority, Dir., Leics. Schls. Symph. Orch., 1976-. Recordings: Block Viola Suite & Suite Hebraque w. Daniel Daggers & the London Schls. Symph. Orch. Contbr. to: Educ.; Music in Educ. Hobbies: Photography; Hillwalking. Address: The School House, Thornton, Leics.,UK.

FLETCHER, Shane, b. 16 Jan. 1951, London, UK. Teacher; Critic. Educ: Brasenose Coll., Oxford; MA; Univ. of Durham, postgrad. cert. of Educ. Career: Dir. of Music, Latymer Upper Schl., London; Dir. of Music, St. Mary's Ch., Bourne St., London. Contbr. to: The Strad; Records & Recordings; Music & Musicians; Financial Times. Hobbies: Stage Plays; Films; Listening to Radio. Address: 15 Arundel Gdns., London W11 2LN, UK.

FLINDELL, Edwin Frederick, b. 27 Feb. 1926, San Antonio, Tex., USA. Music Professor; Organist; Pianist; Choral Conductor; Arranger; Musicologist; Lecturer. Educ: AB, Yale Coll., 1947; AM, Univ. Pa., 1957; PhD, ibid., 1959; Temple Univ.; Gottingen Univ.; Piano Tchr. Cert., Peabody Conserv., 1952. m. Ingrid Dieckmann, 2 s., 2 d. Career: Piano recitalist, 1935-; Choral Cond., 1958-; Lectr., 1964-; Prof., var. colls. & univs., USA, 1964-; Organist, Ev. Gymnasium zum Grauen Kloster, Berlin, German Fed. Repub., 1971-; Assoc. Prof., Dir., Collegium Musicum, Univ. of Nevada, 1978-. Comps: 5 Negro Spirituals arr. for 4 parts. Publ: The Achievement of the Notre Dame Schl. (microfilm), 1959; (transl.) 4 Cantatas by W. F. Bach. Contbr. to profl. pubs. Mbr. profl. orgs. Hons: Georg Leib Harrison Fellow, 1957-58; Fulbright Grantee, 1960-61; Humboldt Fellow, 1962-64. Hobbies: Swimming; Sailing. Address: Kaiserkorso 5, 1 Berlin 42, German Fed. Repub. 30.

FLOR, Samuel, b. Gurahumorului, Austria. Violinist; Violist; Teacher; Lecturer. Educ: Univ. Carolina, Romania; Royal Romanian Conserv.; Wiener Konservatorium, Vienna. m. Gertrude Flor, 1 d. Deubt: Soloist w. Filharmonic, Radio Romania. Career: Soloist w. Flor Quartet in concerts in Europe, Africa, Asia, S Am. & USA; Dir., Vt. Music & Arts Center; Dir. of educl. TV Series, When and How to Listen to Music. Comps. incl: The First String Orchestra, 1969; I Like to Play the Violin, Viola, Cello, Bass, 1973; The Positions for Violin & Viola; Scales for Violin & Viola. Mbrships: AAUP; MENC. Address: 1049 Holly Tree Rd., Abington, PA 19001, USA.

FLORCZAK, Kazimierz, b. 11 Aug. 1942, Zeronice, Poland. Violist; Pianist. Educ: MA (in music), Superior Schl. of Music. m. Ewa Walkowska. Career: w. Opera Orch., Wroclaw, Poland; currently w. Phil. Orch., Antwerp, & Mozart Orch. of Belgium. Comps: Shop with toys (ballet for children). Recordings w. orch. for radio & TV. Recip. Hon.-Dip. as Cond. of amateur orch., Wroclaw, Poland, 1968. Hobbies: Chess; Driving. Address: Otto Veniusstraat 27, 2000 Antwerp, Belgium.

FLORES REYES, Rene Augusto, b. 18 Feb. 1924, Quetzaltenango, Guatemala. Journalist; Music Critic. Educ: Nat. Conserv. of Music, Guatemala. m. Graciela Arenales de Flores, 4 c. Career incl: presenter, TV progs. Vida Cultural & Sala de Conciertos; var. radio progs.; Mgr. Ninos Cantores de Morelia, Mexico 1954-57. Contbr. to var. jrnls. & reviews in Ctrl. Am., Colombia, Argentina, etc. Mbrships: Assn. of Jrnlsts., Guatemala; Latin-Am. Assn. for Adv. of Jrnlsm., Bogota; Inter-Am. Assn. of Music Critics, Wash. DC, USA. Hons: 1st Prize, Bernal Diaz del Castilla, Assn. of Jrnlsts., Guatemala, 1975; 1st Prize 'Tricentenario', Univ. of San Carlos, Guatemala, 1976. Address: PO Box 1345, Guatemala City, Guatemala.

FLORIAN, Ion, b. 26 May 1929, Poenarii Burchii, Rumania. Musicologist. Educ: Town Conservs. of Ploiesti & Club, 1948-53; studied Museography, 1954-58. Publs. incl: (Folklore) A Dance Around the World: Perinita, 1968; Art of Miniature in Old Manuscripts, 1972; Manuscript of Greek Music of Iasi of the VIIIth Century, 1972; Mediaeval Musical Manuscripts in Rumanian Libraries, 1973; (Musicol.) The Union of the Rumanian Principalities & Music, 1967; Cemballo Diary of the Prince Brincoveanu 1763, 1968; Johann Strauss & Rumanian Music, 1970; Dimitrie Cantemir Prince of Universal Music, 1973; Vera Mora, Prague, 1974; A Famous Musician: Johannes Honterus, 475 from his birth, 1973; The Prescence of Women in Roumanian Music (in Braille), 1975; The Blind in Universal Music, 1975. (Musical Museography) Org. of 25 musical documentary exhibs. w. documents of personal coll.; Chinese Musical Engraving, 1971 - 130 yrs. from Antonin Dvorak's Brith, 1971. Mbrships: incl: Hon. Mbr., Fndr., Spolecnost Antonina Dvoraka v. Praze, 1970; Georg Friedrich Handel - Gesellschaft Halle, German Dem. Repub., 1972; Int. Musicol. Soc., Basle, Switz. Address: Str. Blocuri Nord N.5, Scora B.pt 28, Ploiesti, Rumania.

FLOROS, Constantin, b. 4 Jan. 1930, Saloniki, Greence. Professor. Educ: Dips. in comp. & cond., Acad. of Music, Vienna, 1953; Dr., Univ. of Vienna, 1955. m. Edeltraut Steinbacher. Career: Habilitation, Hamburg Univ., 1961; Prof. of Sci. of Music, ibid., 1967-; Ed., Hamburger Beitrage zur Musikwissenschaft, 1971-; Ed., Hamburger Jahrbuch fur Musikwissenschaft, 1975-. Comps: Zwei Tricinien, 1958; var. Lieder; comps. for chorus, piano and organ. Publs: Das mittelbyzantinische Kontakienrepertoire, 3 vols., 1961; Universale Neumenkunde, 3 vols., 1970; Die geistige Welt Gustav Mahlers, 1977; Mahler und die Symphonik des 19. Jahrhunderts in neuer Deutung, 1977; Beethovens Eroica und Prometheus-Musik, 1978; Mozart-Studien, 1979. Address: 6B Kanatatenweg, 2 Hamburg 74, German Fed. Repub.

FLOTHUIS, Marius Hendrikus, b. 30 Oct. 1914, Amsterdam, Netherlands. Composer; Musicologist. Educ: piano, state exam. minor degree, 1932-33; theory, state exam., major degree, 1937; studied musicol., Univ. of Utrecht; studied langs. & musicol., Doct in musicol., 1969, Univ. of Amsterdam. m. (1) 2 d.; (2) Rosa Voorzanger. Career incls: Prof. of Musicol., Univ. of Utrecht, 1974-. Over 70 Comps. Publs: Piano Music, 1958; Mozarts Bearbeitungen eigener und fremder Werke, 1969; Notes on Notes, 1974. Ed: Eduard van Beinum (w. K Ph Bernet Kempers),1959 ; Het Concertgebouworkest 75 jaar, 1963. Contbr. to var. publs. Mbrships: Zentralinstitut für Mozartforschung, Salzburg; Pres., Dutch Sect., Int. Gustav Mahler Soc. Recip. sev. comp. awards. Address: Quinten Massijsstraat 9, 1077 MC Amsterdam, Netherlands.

FLOUR, Mireille Juiliette Antoinett, b. 29 Apr. 1906, Marseille, France. Professor of Harp. Educ: Studied solfeggio & harp, Music Conserves. in Marseille & Paris. Debut: when aged 10, Marseille. Career: concerts in Paris, Brussels & Marseille; int. Radio & TV apps.; Fndr., Harp Quartet Mireille Flour; currently Prof., Music Conserv. of Brussels. Has made recordings for Alpha, Decca & Festival lables. Hobbies: Pholos.; Astrol. Address: 7 Ave. Georges Lecointe, 1180 Brussels, Belgium.

FLOYD, John Morrison, b. 19 Nov. 1950, Thomasville, NC, USA. Percussionist; University Teacher; Conductor. Educ: BMus, E Carolina Univ. Schl. of Music, 1973; MMus, Va. Commonwealth Univ., 1974; Doct. candidate, Eastman Schl. of Music. m. Beverly Rouse Floyd. Career: Asst. Prof., Va. Polytechnic & State Univ.; Principal Tympanist & Percussionist, Roanoke Symph.; Principal Percussionist, Richmond Symph. & Richmond Sinfonia; Instructor, Clarion State Coll. & Va. Commonwealth Univ. Comps: Theme & Variations for 4 Timpani; Mobile for Percussion Ensemble. Recording from E Carolina Univ. Contbr. to Notes from Va. Tech. Mbrships incl: Percussive Arts Soc.; Coll. Music Soc.; MENC; VMEA. Hons incl: Pi Kappa Lambda, 1973; Winner, E Carolina Univ. Concerto Audition, 1972; Award for Service at Va.

Commonwealth Univ. Schl. of Arts, 1974; Va. Commonwealth Univ. Leadership & Service Award, 1974; 2nd Prize (tied), Percussive Arts Soc. Int. Percussion Comp. Contest, 1976. Hobbies: Bike riding; mountain hiking. Address: Dept. of Perf. Arts & Communications, Va. Polytechnic Inst. & State Univ., Blacksburg, VA 24061, USA. 28,29.

FLOYD, Samuel A, Jr., b. 1 Feb. 1937. University Professor & Administrator. Educ: BS, Fla. A & M Univ., 1957; MME, 1965, PhD, 1969, Southern Ill. Univ., Carbondale. m., 1 s., 2 d. Career: Tchr., Smith-Brown HS, Arcadia, Fla., 1957-62; Instr. in Music & Asst. Dir. of Bands, Fla. A & M Univ., Tallahassee, 1962-64; Assoc. Prof. of Music, 1965-; Coord. of Grad. Studies, Schl. of Music, Southern Ill. Univ., Carbondale; Dir., Inst. for Afro-American Music, Fisk Univ. Publs: 99 Street Beats, Cadences & Exercises for Percussion, 1961; 101 Street Beats, Cadences & Exercises for Percussion, 1965; Contemporary Cadences & Cadences for Marching Percussion, 1975. Contbr. to: var. musical jrnls. Mbrships. incl: Coll. Music Soc.; MENC; Phi Delta Kappa. Address: Schl. of Music, Southern Ill. Univ., Carbondale, IL 62901, USA.

FLUCK, Alan Paul, b. 3 Feb. 1928, Pontypridd, Wales, UK. Administrator to Youth & Music. Educ: RCM, London. Career: Dir. of Music, Farnham Grammar Schl., 1951-71; Fndr. & Dir., Farnham Fests. of new music for young people; Music Dir., Farnham Maltings; Has commissioned over 40 works for children from Brit. Comps. Comps: many orchl. transcriptions; Love on the Dole (musical), 1971. Publs: The Sour Sweet Music, 1955; The Confident Young Musician, 1961; The World Orchestra of Jeunesses Musicales, 1975. Contbr. to profl. jrnls. Hobbies incl: Tennis. Mgmt: Jimmy Grafton, 10 Lesley Ct., 2333 Strutton Ground, London SW1P 2HZ, UK. Address: 8 Morley Rd., Farnham, Surrey, UK.

FLUEGEL, Neal L, b. 21 Mar. 1937, Freeport, Ill., USA. Associate Professor of Music. Educ: BA, Ariz. State Univ., Tempe; M Mus., Southern Ill. Univ., Carbondale; Univ. of Wis., Madison. m. Diane Hanson, 2 d. Career: Num. solo percussion & piano recitals, var. Univs.; Prin. Percussionist, Phoenix Symph., Southern Ill. Symph., Wis. Symph.; Timpanist, Terre Haute Symph.; Master of Ceremonies, daily TV Prog., 1971-72; num. Radio & TV apps.; Clinician throughout USA; Chmn., maj. Contemporary Music Fests.; Percussion Activities Chmn., Mid-East Instrumental Conf.; Asst. Prof. of Music, Ind. State Univ., Terre Haute; Ed., Percussionist; Asst. Ed., Percussive Notes. Contbr. to: Instrumentalist; Music Jrnl.; The Am. Music Tchr.; Image. Mbrships incl: Exec. Sec-Treas., Percussive Arts Soc.; Chmn., Brass, Woodwind & Percussion Div., Music Tchrs. Nat. Assn.; Life, Phi Mu Alpha Sinfonia; MENC; NACWPI; Am. Musicol. Soc.; Coll. Music Soc.; Ind. Music Educators Assn.; VP, E. Ctrl. Div. MTNA. Recip. var. Hons. Hobbies: Golf; Bowling; Fishing. Address: 130 Carol Dr., Terre Haute, IN 47805, USA. 8.

FLYNN, William George, b. 18 June 1917, Melbourne, Australia. Composer; Conductor; Arranger. Educ: studied w. Prof. Shoenberger, Sydney, & in USA. m. Gladys Irene Flynn, 3 s. Career: Cond., Arr., Aust. Army Band, WW II; Cond., Arr., all Aust. Nat. Radio Networks; devised, arranged & conducted musical TV prog. (93 episodes), Aust. Broadcasting Commn.; Music Dir., Toho Theatre on 3 tours of Aust. & NZ, Celebrity Theatre Circuit, Tivoli Australasian Theatre Circuit, Lord Mayors Command Perfs., all Aust. capitals, & Spotlight & W & G Record Cos. Comps: TV & film music; music for radio palys; works for light concert orch.; mood music. Num. recordings. Mbrships: Aust. Performing Right Assn.; Fndn. Mbr., Fellowship of Aust. Comps.; Life Mbr., Professional Musicians Union of Aust. Recip., 1st Prize, Light Comp. for Concert Orch., Aust. Broadcasting Comm./Aust. Perf. Right Assn., 1959. Hobbies: Golf; Motoring. Address: 397 Beach Rd., Beaumaris, Vic. 3193, Australia. 28,29,30.

FODI, John b. 22 March 1944, Nagyteval, Hungary. Composer; Pianist. Educ: BMus (Comp.); MMus (Comp.). m. Elizabeth, 1 d., 1 s. Career: Commissions from CBC Radio; Days Months & Years to Come, perfd. at 1976 ISCM, Boston. Comps. incl: Divisions IV for solo guitar; Concerto in 4 parts for free bass accordion. Recordings: Tapes for Can. Music Centre & CBC. Contbr. to: Array Newsletter. Mbrships: Can. League of Comps.; Past Pres., Sec./Treas., ARRAY; CAPAC; Can. Music Centre (affiliate). Hons: League of Comps. prizes, 1968, '70; CAPAC Prize, 1970; Woodrow Wilson Fellow, 1970; Hon. mention for Tettares, percussion Quartet in State Univ. of NY at Buffalo Competition, 1968. Hobbies: Reading Science Fiction; Speculating. Address: 14 Times Rd., Toronto, Ont. M6E 3B9, Can.

FOGELL, Martin Maurice, b. 3 Aug. 1929, Glasgow, UK. Conductor; Accompanist; Composer. Educ: RSAM, 1946-49;

pvte. study of Cond. w. Boult & Leitner, & of Piano w. Cyril Smith; ARCM (piano perf. & tchng.); LTCL (piano perf.); FTCL (comp.). m. Anne Goldwater, 1 s., 1 d. Debut: w. New London Orch., 1951. Career incls: guest Cond. w. var. orchs., UK & Netherlands, Italy & Czechslovakia, 1951-; Cond., Reading Symph. Orch., 1958-64, & Southern Sinfonia Orch., 1964-; Cond., Fogell Ensemble, 1954-60, Chelsea Choral Soc., 1954-59, & Caversham Singers, 1961-71; Music Dir. & Prin. Cond., London Students Opera Co., 1966-71; Cond., Wides & Runcorn Orpheus Choral Soc., 1975-; apps. as Accomp.; Comps. incl: The Grave-Digger (song) Piano Sonata; Prelude & Toccata (piano); Bass Concerto; Divertimento for Orch.; TV music Recordings; 3 Highland Sketches; Haydn & Romberg Symphs. Mbr., ISM (var. committees). Hons: Leverhulme Fndn. Grant, 1973; Barlow Cup for Comp., Chester, 1974. Var. hobbies. Address: 63 Lache Ln., Westminster Pk., Chester CH14 7LP, UK. 3.

FOLDES, Andor, b. 21 Dec. 1913, Budapest, Hungary. Concert Pianist; Conductor. Educ: Master's Dip., Franz Liszt Music Acad., Budapest, 1932; studied piano under Ernest von Dohnanyi. m. Lili Rendy. Debut: w. Hungarian Phil. Orch., Budapest, aged 8. Career: annual concert tours throughout Europe & USA; frequent tours of Far E inclng. Japan; tours of S Am.; regular TV apps.; num. concerts as Cond.-Pianist. Comps: cadenzas to most Mozart piano concertos. Recordings: DGG; EMI. Publs: Keys to the Keyboards, 1948; Is there a contemporary style of Beethoven-playing, 1963. Contbr. to Rdrs. Digest. Hons: Grands Prix du Disque for 4 Bartok records, Paris, 1956; Grand Cross, Order of Merit, German Fed. Repub., 1964; Silver Medal, City of Paris, 1969. Hobbies: Collecting Modern Art; Reading; Walking; Swimming. Mgmt: Ibbs & Tillett, London. Address: Herrliberg nr. Zürich, Switzerland. 2,3,21.

FOLDES, Imre, b. 8 Mar. 1934, Budapest, Hungary. Musicologist; Professor of History. Educ: Grad. in comp., Ferenc Liszt Acad. of Music, Budapest. m. Dr. Zsuzsa Vadász, 1 d. Career: Musicol., Prof. of Hist. of Music, Ferenc Liszt Acad. of Music, Dept. for Tchrs. Trng. Inst.; Educl. Lectr. on Music for the general public, radio, etc. Publs: Harmincasok, Beszélgetések magyar zeneszerzo..kkel (Generation of the Thirties - Talks w. Hungarian Composers), 1969; Life & Works of J S Bach, 1976; The Melody Dies Irae, 1977. Contbr. to: Az ének-zene tanitása; Muzsika; Parlando. Mbrships: Hungarian Musicians Assn.; Club 'Feszek'; Pres., Music Dept., Soc. for Propagating Scis. & Arts; Hungarian Ferenc Liszt Soc. Hons: Art Prize for Socialist Culture, 1974; Art Prize, Nat. Coun. of Trade Unions, 1975. Hobbies: Collecting gramophone-records; Hiking. Address: Kresz Géza utca 26, 1132 Budapest, Hungary.

FOLTS, Martha Neary, b. 7 Sept. 1940, Cleveland, Ohio, USA. Organ Recitalist. Educ: B Mus, Syracuse Univ.; M Mus, New Engl. Conserv. of Music, Boston; Int. Summer Acad. for Organist, Haarlem, Netherlands, 1970, 71, 73; summer study w. Anton Heiller, Wash. Univ., St. Louis, Mo. m. Stephen B Folts. Career: recitals throughout USA; radio recordings in sev. cities; Asst. Prof., Iowa State Univ., 1970-75; concert tour, Denmark, 1976; Guest Artist Nat. AGO convention, 1976. Comps: film score, Sideissue; Internal Organ (for AGO convention). Has recorded works by Ligeti, Bach & Schoenberg. Contbr. to The Diapason. Mbrships: Pi Kappa Lambda; Coll. Music Soc.; AGO; Pitts. Alliance of Comps. Recip. Iowa Arts Coun. grants. Address: 6337 Jackson St., Pittsburgh, PA 15206, USA. 2.

FOLTYN, Maria, b. 28 Jan. 1924, Radom, Poland. Singer; Opera Director. Educ: MA, State Higher Music Schl., Gdansk, 1949; MA Directing, State Higher Theatre Schl., Warsaw, 1970. div. Debut: Singer as Halka in Halka by Stanislaw Moniuszko w. State Opera, Warsaw. Career: As Singer apps. in maj. cities in Poland, USSR, Hungary, Germany, Italy, Can., USA & S Am.; Apps. on radio. Recordings in Poland & abroad. Contbr. to Ruch Muzyczny (Music Movement), Warsaw, Poland. Mbrships: Polish Soc. of Music Artist; Int. Theatre Inst. Hons. incl: Gold Medallion, Int. Competition, Vercelli, 1956; Prize of Warsaw Musical Assn., 1973; Min. of Foreign Affairs Annual Prize, 1974. Hobbies: Writing of Memoirs; Travel. Address: Swietokrzyska 3058, 00-116 Warszawa, Poland.

FONDA, Jean Pierre, b. 12 Dec. 1937, Boulogne sur Seine, Paris, France. Concert Pianist. Educ: Virtuosity Prize, Piano, Instrumentation, Geneva Conserv. Debut: Germany, 1958. Career: Concert tours in Europe, S Am., USA, Japan, Middle East, Turkey, etc.; TV in Paris, Munich; Maj. European Summer Festivals inclng: Lucerne, Montreaux, Edinburgh, Monte Carlo, etc. Comps: Cadenzas for Different Piano Concertos. Recordings: CBS; DGG; Concert Hall. Recip. Harriet Cohen Medal, London, 1968. Hobbies: Reading; Theatre; Films;

Collecting & Purchasing Autographs. Mgmt: Ingpen & Williams Ltd., 14 Kensington Ct., London W8, UK. Address: 20 Chateau Banquet, 1202 Geneva, Switz.

FONGAARD, Björn, b. 2 Mar. 1919. Composer. Educ. incls: Composer, Orch. Cond. Dip., Conserv. of Music, Oslo; studied comp. w. Bjarne Brustad, Sigurd Islandsmoen, Per Stenberg & Karl Andersen. m. Bertha Fongaard, 1 s., 5 d. Career: has given sev. perfs. of own music in concert halls, in films & on Norwegian art for Radio & Tv. Comps. incl: Sonata for piano opus 110 No. 1; Peintures for piano; Galaxy; Homo Sapiens; Space Concerto; Legende; Sinfonia per organo. num. recordings of own works. Author in field. Contbr. to jrnls. Mbrships incl: Soc. of Norwegian Composers. Hons. incl: Prizewinner, Int. Competition for organ composers, Stockholm, Sweden, 1973. Hobbies: Astronomy; Biology; Ecology. Address: Herslebsgt. 14, Oslo 5, Norway.

FONT, Nydia E, b. 21 July, 1927, San Juan, Puerto Rico. Professor; Pianist; Harpsichordist. Educ. incls: Dip. in Piano, 1949, Postgrad. Dip., 1951, Juilliard Schl. of Music; MMus, Univ. of Kan., 1968. m. Arturo Vera, Jr. (dec.), 1 s. Career: recital apps. throughout Puerto Rico, in USA & Dominican Repub.; TV broadcasts, San Juan, Puerto Rico; radio broadcasts, Montreal, Madrid & San Juan; Prof. of Piano, Conserv. of Music, Puerto Rico, 1960-67; Prof. of Music, Univ. of Puerto Rico, Rio Piedras, 1960-. Recordings: Inst. of Puerto Rican Culture. Mbrships: Ateneo Puertorriqueno; Am. Musicol. Soc.; Chmn., Recruiting Comm., Musical Soc. of Puerto Rico, 1975-76. Recip., Dip. as outstanding woman in music of Puerto Rico, Mayor of San Juan, 1975. Hobbies incl: Reading; Collecting Porcelain; Travel. Address: 553 Rosales St., Santurce, Puerto Rico, PR 00909.

FONTYN, Jacqueline, b. 27 Dec. 1930, Antwerp, Belgium. Composer; Professor of Composition. Educ: studied piano w. Ignace Bolotine & Marcel Maas; studied harmony, counterpoint, comp. etc. w. Marcel Quinet; studied in Paris & Vienna; Grand Prix de Rome, for comp. - dip. m. Camille Schmit, 2 c. Career: Prof. of Counterpoint, Conserv. Royal d'Anvers, 1963-70; Prof. of Comp., Conserv. Royal de Bruxelles, 1971-/ Jury Mbr. 'Concours de Composition'; Participant in many int. fests. Compositions incl: Galaxie, for chamber orch.; Pour 11 Archets, 1971; Evoluon, for orch.; Per Archi, for orch., 1973; Filigrane, for flute & harp, 1969; Strophes for violin & piano, 1970; Frises for big wind orch., 1975; Violin Concerto, 1975; Décors for symph. orch., 1977; Spirals for 2 pianos, 1971; Shadows for harpsichord, 1973; Intermezzo for harp, 1974; Harizons for string quartet, 1977. Recip. many hons. & awards. Address: Rue Leon Dekaise 6, B1342 Limelette, Belgium.

FORBES, Elliot, b. 30 Aug. 1917, Cambridge, Mass., USA. Professor of Music. Educ: BA, MA Harvard Univ. m. Kathleen Brooks Allen. Career: Asst. Prof. of Music, Princeton Univ., 1947-54; Assoc. Prof., ibid, 1954-58; Prof. of Music, Harvard Univ., 1958-61; Fanny Peabody Prof. of Music, ibid, 1961-; Cond. of the Harvard Glee Club & Radcliffe Choral Soc., 1958-70. Recordings: Harvard in Song; Songs of the World; Josquin des Prez, Missa Mater Patris et Filia & Motets on Carillon Records w. the Harvard Glee Club. Publs: Compiled & Edited, The Harvard Song Book, 1966; Ed. & Rev., Thayer's Life of Beethoven, 1964, 2nd edn., 1967; Ed., Ludwig van Beethoven, Symphony No. 5 in C Minor, 1971. Contbr. to profl. jrnls. Mbrships: Phi Beta Kappa; Am. Musicol. Soc.; Am. Acad. of Arts & Scis.; Int. Musicol. Soc.; Coll. Music Soc. Hobbies: Sailing. Address: 182 Brattle St., Cambridge, MA 02138, USA. 2.

FORBES, Janet, b. 1932, Grantham, UK. Flautist. Educ: RAM. m. Colin Bradbury. Career: has done much Solo & orchestral works; former Prin. Flute, Sadler's Wells Orch. Address: 56 Castlebar Rd., Ealing, London W5, UK. 3.

FORBES, Sebastian, b. 22 May 1941, Amersham, Bucks., UK. Composer; University Lecturer; Conductor. Educ: RAM, 1958-60; King's Coll., Cambridge Univ., 1960-64; MA Cantab.; Mus B. Cantab.; MusD, ibid.; LRAM; ARCO; ARCM. m. Hilary Spaight Taylor, 2 d. Career: Treble Soloist, 1953-56; Organist, Trinity Coll., Cambridge, 1968; Cond., Aeolian Singers, 1965-69; Seiriol Singers, 1969-72; BBC Producer, 1964-67; Univ. Lectr., Bangor, 1968-72, Surrey, 1972-; Prin. Commissions, Essay for Clarinet & Orch., Proms, 1970; Symphony, Edinburgh Fest., 1972, etc. Var. Orchl., Chamber, Vocal, Organ & Choral comps. Recordings: Treble; few minor records; Cond:Bach Motets, Aeolian Singers; Hermann Moby Dick; Comp: Str. Quartet No. 1. Var. publs. Mbrships: Composers' Guild of GB. Hons: McEwen Meml. Prize, 1962; Clements Meml. Prize, 1963; Radcliffe Music Award, 1969. Var. hobbies. Address: 72 Shepherd's Ln., Guildford, Surrey GU2 6SW, UK.

FORBES, Watson, b. 16 Nov. 1909, St. Andrews, Scotland, UK. Violist; Teacher. Educ: Studied w. Prof. Sevcik. m. (1) Mary Hunt, 2 s., (2) Jean Beckwith. Career: Mbr. Aeolian Str. Quartet, 1932-, London String Trio, 1944-, London Piano Quartet, 1952-; Prof. of Chmbr. Music, RAM, 1956-; Prof. of Viola, RAM, 1958-; Hd. of Music, BBC Scotland, 1964-72. Compositions incl: Arrs. & transcriptions for viola & piano, string trio, clarinet & piano, recorder & piano, cello & piano, violin & piano, trumpet & piano. Recordings: Decca; Brit. Coun.; Argo. Publs: Chamber Music Catalogue; Compiler, BBC History of Music in Scotland. Contbr. to: Musical Times; Strad; Groves Dictionary of Music & Musicians, 6th Ed. Mbrships: ISM; Warden, 1946-; Nat. Fedn. of Music Socs. Hons: FRAM; Hon. D Mus., Glasgow Univ., 1971; Cobbett Memorial Prize for Chmbr. Music, 1972; Sir James Caird Scholar for Scotland. Address: The Coach House, Great Wolford, Shipston-on-Stour, Warwickshire, CV36 5NQ, UK.

FORD, Anthony Dudley, b. 19 Sept. 1935, Birmingham, UK. Senior Lecturer in Music; Pianist; Harpsichordist; Conductor. Educ: BMus, Univ. of Birmingham, 1957. m. Diane Clare Anwyl, 1 s., 1 d. Career: Sr. Lectr. in Music, Univ. of Hull; Cond., Hull Bach Choir. Publs: Ed., Purcell - Fantasias and In Nomines; Ed., G Bononcini - Arias from the Vienna Operas; Ed., G Bononcini - Aeterna Fac. Contbr. to: Musical Times; Proceedings of the Royal Musical Assn.; Encyclopaedia Britannica. Life Mbr., Royal Musical Assn. Hons: Barber Post Grad. Scholarship, 1957. Hobbies: Transport; Photography. Address: Music Department, Univ. of Hull, Hull, Humberside, UK.

FORD, Charles, A, b. 13 June 1908, Niagara Falls, NY, USA. Musician (Tuba & String Bass); Sales Executive. Educ: Southwestern Univ., LA, Calif., 2 yrs.; special bus. courses at var. univs.; pvte. Tuba lessons from Jeroslav Cimera of Chgo. m. Mary K. Welrer Ford, 2 s. (1 dec.), 1 d. Career: Stage, Jan Garber Orch., 6 short films & 2 feature films at Universal, Hollywood; Yeast Foam & Burns & Allen Shows on Radio; TV Staff Musician, Stn. WSAZ-TV, Huntington, WVa.; We The People, & Educl. TV Progs. of Circus Music. Recordings w. Jan Garber Orch. on Brunswick, WOR Feature, Capitol, Okeh, Victor Coral Hit & Vocalion. Contbr to: The Music Jrnl.; Down Beat Namm Daily; The Schl. Musician, etc. Mbrships incl: Gold Card in Local 10, Chgo.; Local 59 Kenocha Fed. of Musicians; Sec., Treas., Music Industry Coun.; Music Educators Nat. Conf. Hons. incl: Award of Special Merit by Kenosha Band Boosters Org., 1972. Hobbies: Golf & Bowling. Address: 6820 49th Ave., Kenosha, WI 53140, USA.

FORD, Clifford Robert, b. 30 May 1947, Toronto, Ont., Can. Composer; Writer; Professor. Educ: BMus, Univ. of Toronto; McGill Univ. m. Elinore Marguerite Ford, 2 s. Publs: An Historical Survey of Music in Canada, 1980. Contbr. to: Contemporary Can. Comp., 1975; Ency. of Music in Can.; former ed. & contbr. to Array Newsletter. Mbrships: Can. League of Comps.; co-fndr., former pres., Array; co-fndr., 1st pres., Atlantic Can. Comps. Assn. Hons: Sir Ernest MacMillan Fellowship, 1970; Can. Coun. Arts Grants, 1971, '73. Address: Box 266, Greenwood Heights, RR1, Armdale, NS B3L 4J1, Can.

FORD, Denham Vincent, b. 31 Aug. 1921, London, UK. Concert Manager. m. Violet Elsie Ford. Career: Asst. Concert Dir., LPO, 1942-45; Sec., London Phil. Arts Club, 1942-45; Mgr., London Int. Orch., 1946; Orchl. Mgr., RPO, 1946-49; Personal Sec. to Sir Thomas Beecham, 1949-52; Asst. Mgr., Victoria Palace, 1954; Ed. Publsr., Sir Thomas Beecham Soc. Newsletter; London Ed. & contbr. to 'Le Grand Baton', jrnl. of the Sir Thomas Beecham Soc., publd. in USA; Opera Critic (casual), B'ham Post. Hon. Chmn., The Sir Thomas Beecham Soc. Hobbies: Music; Theatre; Music Hall; Steam Railways. Address: 46 Wellington Ave., Westcliff-on-Sea, Essex SSO 9XB, UK.

FORD, Peter Hilary, b. 15 Dec. 1931, Meriden, Conn., USA. Professor; Composer; Organist; Pianist. Educ: BMus, Yale Univ.; MMus, Converse Coll.; DMA, Stanford Univ.; studied philos. & French, Univ. of N Carolina. m. Sue Gettys, (dec.), 2 s. Career: Univ. & Coll. tchr., USA, 1965-78; piano & organ recitals; progs. of original comps. Comps. incl: 3 mini-operas (Buddha, Pot & Universitatis Shenanigansum); ch. music; music for organ; works for var. instruments; songs; suite for idiosyncratic orch. Publs: Techniques of Meaning, 1956. Mbrships: Southeastern Comps. League. Hons: Kellogg Fugue Prize, Yale Univ., 1953; Pi Kappa Lambda, Converse Coll., 1956; Humanities Award in Comp., Stanford Univ., 1964. Hobbies: Yoga; Hypnosis; Painting. Address: 16 Cecil St., Sumter, SC 29150, USA.

FORD, Richard, b. 19 May 1902, London, UK. Bass Baritone; Teacher. Educ: GSMD. m. Hilary E Traynier. Debut: Wigmore

Hall, 1924. Career: Vocalist; Prof. of Singing, Lectr., Adjudicator, Metro. Acad. of Music, 1936-40; Lay Clerk, St. Alban's Cathedral, 1938-40; Prin., Rickmansworth Schl. of Music, 1937-52; Prof. of Singing, GSMD, 1946-70; First broadcast 2LO, 1922; Has broadcast regularly for over 25 yrs.; Adjudicator of Fest. throughout GB & Canada. Hons: FGSM. Hobbies: Gardening; Cooking; Cycling. Address: Linden Lea, 26B Field Stile Rd., Southwold, Suffolk, UK. 3.

FORD, Wyn Kelson, b. 17 June 1927, Preston, Lancs., UK. Editor; Archivist. Educ: King's Coll., Univ. of London; TCm. m. Margaret Ann Rose. Career: freelance Music Critic, Worthing Herald, 1961-63; Tutor to occasional adult evening educ. classes, WEA etc. Publs: Music in England before 1800 - a select bibliography, 1967. Contbr. to num. musical & non-musical publs. inclng: Groves Dictionary of Music & Musicians, Supplementary Volume, 1961; Sussex Archaeol. Collects.; Jrnl. of Am. Musicol. Soc.; Musical Times; National Trust Year Book, 1978-79. Mbrships: Fellow Royal Histl. Soc.; Histl. Assn.; Assoc., Soc. of Archivists; Sussex Archaeol. Soc.; Life Mbr., Royal Musical Assn.; Sussex Record Soc.; Brit. Records Assn. Hobbies: Local Hist.; Histl. Rsch.; Engl. Archives; Music. Address: 48 Harlands Rd., Haywards Heath, W Sussex RH16 1LS, UK. 3.

FORDELL, Erik Fritiof, b. 2 July 1917, Karleby, Finalnd. Composer. Educ: Ch. Music Schl.; Sibelius Acad. High Schl.; studies in Berlin & Vienna. m. Anna-Lisa Fordell. Career: apps. on stage, TV & radio in Scandinavia. Comps. incl: 40 symphonies; chmbr. music; songs. Recordings: string & choir music. Contbr. to sev. Finnish newspapers. Mbrships: Finlands tonsättare r.f., TEOSTO. Hons: Sibelius Prize, Kulturfonden o.a. Hobbies: Lit.; Travel; Nature. Address: 67410 Vittsar, Karleby, Finland.

FOREMAN, Charles L., b. 11 May 1949, E Chicago, USA. Pianist; Assistant Professor. Educ: BMus, Ind. Univ., 1971; Artist Dip., Univ. of Toronto, 1972; MMus (perf. & Lit.), Univ. of Toronto, 1973; Am. Conserv., Chicago, 1964-67. Debut: w. Chicago Civic Orch., Orchestra Hall, Chicago, 1972. Career: apps. w. Chicago Civic Orch., Univ. of Toronto Orch., Denver Symph. Orch., Calgary Phil. Orch., etc.; Recitals, Toronto, Calgary, Chicago, San Diego; chmbr. music perfs., BC, Alta., Sask.; Instructor, Univ. of Calgary (Alta.), 1973-76; Asst. Prof., Dept. of Music, ibid, 1976-. Num. radio recordings. Hons: Can. Coun. Grants, 1974, '75; Belgian Radio Prize, Queen Elisabeth Competition, 1975; Cert. of Merit, Geneva Competition, 1974. Hobbies: Reading; Eastern religions; Recorder playing; Ragtime. Address: c/o Dept. of Music, Univ. of Calgary, Calgary, Alta. T2N 1N4, Can.

FORK, Günter, b. 17 Aug. 1930, Duisburg, German Fed. Repub. Composer; Conductor; Professor. Educ: Music Acad. Berlin, GDR, comp. 1951-1955. m. Gisela Fork, 2 c. Debut: comp., 1946; cond., 1947. Career: Choir, Orch. Cond. Wolfsburg, 1947-50, Dessau 1950-51 and 1954-56; Candidate Music Acad. Berlin 1954-55; Cond. Regional Theater Dessau 1956-59; Lectr. Music Acad. Lübeck 1959-73; Lectr. Music Acad. Cologne since 1972; Prof. 1974; Guest cond. var. orch. Comp. incl: Ballet, Theater music; orch. works; choir music; chmbr. music; songs; cantatas; organ concerto; schule des Partiturspiels. Mbrships: German Soc. of Comps. and GEMA. Hons: Award for Choir Comp., Weimar, 1952. Address: D 5206, Neunkirchen-Seelscheid 1, Eischeider Str. 22, German Fed. Repub.

FORMAN, Jeanne, b. 3 Mar. 1916, Los Angeles, Calif., USA. Piano-Theory Teacher. Educ: Bush Conserv.; De Paul Univ.; Redlands Univ.; UCLA; Seminars & Workshops; 3 yrs. coll. studies. Widow, 3 d. Career: 27 yrs. of pvte. tchng., prep. of students for coll. music majors; 3 yrs. of specialization in the tchng. of visually handicapped; Contracted as Instr. for the Assistance League of Santa Clara Co. (visually handicapped prog.) Comps. perf. at Univ. of Calif., Santa Barbara. Mbrships: Calif. Profl. Music Tchrs. Assn.; Music Tchrs. Assn.; NPG. Address: 1119 Alameda Padre Serra, Santa Barbara, CA 93105, USA.

FORONDA, Elena Isabel, b. 15 Jan. 1947, NYC, USA. Teacher of Music/Choral Music; Pianist. Educ: BS, 1969, MA, 1971, Hunter Coll., CUNY. Career: Mbr., Hunter Coll. Choirs; Tchr. of Music/Choral Music, NYC Pub. Schl. System; Piano duet, film, Morning Song. Mbrships: MENC; NY State Schl. Music Assn.; Amateur Chmbr. Music Players Inc., Vienna, Va.; Int. Platform Assn. Hons: Dist. Winner, Nat. Piano Playing Auditions, Nat. Guild of Piano Tchrs., 1965. Hobbies: Playing chmbr. music; Attending concerts; Plays; Visiting museums of art; Reading hist. books; crewel work; Travel. Address: 43 Kings Pl., Bkly., NY 11223, USA. 5,6,27.

FORRAI, Katalin, b. 25 Sept. 1926, Debrecen, Hungary. Music Teacher; Researcher. Educ: Trng. Dip., Tchrs. Coll. m. Laszio Vikar, 2 s., 1 d. Career: Music Tchr.; Choir Cond.; 264 Kindergarten broadcast progs.; 26 TV appearances; 2 films (dealing w. own activity); Elaboration of Music Tchng. Methodol. for pre-schl. age based upon the Kodaly concept; Prof. in the Kindergarten Tchrs. Coll., 1950-60; Supvsr. of Music Educ. & postgrad. courses at the Hungarian Pedagogical Inst., 1960-68; Rsch. of Early Childhood, 1968-. Four recordings of children's games, for kindergarten children. Publs: Music Methodology & Song Material for Kindergarten, 1951-, '57-, '74-; Children's Games Collection, 1952, '56; Children's Songs of the Neighbouring Peoples, 1965; European Children's Songs I & II, 1966. Contbr. to var. jrnls. Mbrships: Hungarian Union of Comps.; Franz Liszt Soc.; Hungarian Pedagogical Rsch. Soc.; Inst. Soc. of Music Educ. Recip., Prize of Master Tchng., 1963. Address: Bajcsyu ZS.60, 1054 Budapest, Hungary.

FORRAI, Miklós, b. 19 Oct. 1913, Magyarszék, Baranya, Hungary. Conductor; Chorus Master; Professor. Educ: studied under Zoltán Kodály, Artur Harmat, Lajor Bárdos, F. Liszt Acad. of Music, 1931-37; Chorus Master, ibid, 1934; Singing Master, 1935; Artist of Trumpet, 1937. m. Maria Gyurkovics, 2 d. Debut: as Chorus Master of the 'Forrai' Chamber Choir, 1936. Career: Ldr. of conert series 'Kis Filharmónia', org. for children, 1936-44; Chorus Master of 'Budapesti Kórus', 1948-78 (perf. num. oratorios by Hungarian & for comps.); Has taken part regularly in music progs. of the Hungarian Radio, 1936- & TV, 1958-, as cond., chorus master & referee; Prof., F. Liszt Acad. of Music, 1941-, Recordings incl: Cantata lyrica, 1960 & Cantus Pannonicus, 1961, F. Farkas; Missa Choralis, 1963; Liszt Requiem, 1976. Publs: incl: A karvezető (book for Chorus Masters), 1936, '41; Ot évszázető kórusa (Choral works of 500 yrs.), 1956; Ezer év kórusa (Choral works of 1000 yrs.). Enekgyakorlatok I (Singing Exercises), 1963; Deep River - negro spirituals, 1963. Co-Ed., musicological set of recordings Musica Hungarica, 1965, '67 & Musica Mundana, 1974, by Qualiton, Mbrships: Sec.-Gen., F Liszt Soc.; Presidium of KOTA, Hungarian Counc. of Choirs. Hons. incl: Liszt Prize, 1955; Merited Artist of the Hungarian People's Rep., 1963; Gold Medal of Order of Labour, 1973. Address: Budenz út 18, 1021 Budapest, Hungary. 30.

FORREST, Sidney, b. 21 Aug. 1918, NYC, NY, USA. Professor of Clarinet & Chamber Music. Educ: MA, Columbia Univ.; BA, Univ. of Miami; Juilliard Schl. of Music. m. Faith Marian, 1 d. Career: Former solo clarinet, Nat. Symph. Orch., Wash. DC; Former clarinet soloist, US Marine Band, Wash. DC; Clarinet soloist, recitalist; Prof. of Clarinet & Chmbr. Music, Peabody Conserv. of Music, Catholic Univ., Am. Univ.; Summers, Univ. of Mich. at Interlochen; Annual adjudicator Quebec Province (Can.) Conserv. Concours; Recitalist, lecturer, Int. Clarinet Soc., Denver, Colo., 1979. Comps: Nocturne No. 20, Chopin, arr. for clarinet & piano; Entrance March of the Boyards, arr. for clarinet & piano. Recordings: Mozart - Clarinet Quintet, Trio; Hindemith - Clarinet Sonata; A Berg - Vier Stücke; Weber - Grand Duo, Concertante Variations, op. 33; Brahms -Trio op. 114. Contbr. to: Bandwageon & Clarinet mags. Mbrships: Former Pres., Peabody Conserv. Chapt., AAUP; MTNA; NFMC; Galpin Soc. Hobbies: Photography; Stamps; Bicycling; Antiques. Address: Peabody Conserv. of Music, Baltimore, MD 21202, USA. 6.

FORRESTER, Maureen Katherine Stewart, b. 25 July 1930, Montreal, PQ, Canada. Contralto Singer. Educ: studies w. Bernard Diamant, Sally Martin & Frank Rowe. m. Eugene J Kash, 1 s., 3 d. Debut: Town Hall, NYC, 1956. Career incls: concerts w. ldng. Am. orchs. inclng. NY Phil.; apps. w. Am. Opera Soc.; title role in Orfeo, Toronto, Ont., 1961; apps. at Edinburgh, Montreux, Bournemouth, Berlin & Holland Fests., also Am. & Can., inclng. Empire State Fest., NY. Recordings: RCA. Address: 338 Roslyn St., Westmount, Montreal, PQ, Canada. 2.

FORSBERG, Roland, b. 18 Sept. 1939, Stockholm, Sweden. Director of Music; Organist. Educ: Prof. of Music, Royal Acad. of Music, Stockholm, 1961; Higher Organist Exam., 1963; Higher Cantor Exam., 1964; Dipl. Organist, 1968. m. Margaretha Widlund, 1 s., 1 d. Career: Dir. of Music, Norrmalm's Ch., Stockholm. Comps: Liten svit (organ), 1959; Passacaglia (organ), 1960; Verbum Christi (vocal), 1963; 12 Sacred Songs, 1964; Musica solenne (organ), 1965; Magnificat (vocal), 1966; Kristi himmelsfärd (organ), 1971; motets, cantatas, masses & other choral works. Recordings: Kärlekens musik (Proprius 7716); Tre orglar i Västervik (Proprius 7720); En gang blir allting stilla (Sirius LP 812). Contbr. to: Mixturen, Stockholm. Mbr: Samtida Musik, Stockholm. Hons: Swedish State Composer's Schlrship., 1970; Music Schlrship., Deverthska kulturstiftelsen, 1970;

Culture Schlrship., Ekerö Lions Club, 1971; Gustaf Aulén Prize, 1972; Composer's Schlrship., STIM, Stockholm, 1974. Address: Jaktstigen 9, 170 10 Ekerö, Sweden.

FORSBLOM, Enzio, b. 14 March 1920, Lohja, Finland. Organ Recitalist; Professor of Organ. Educ: PhD; Dip. Organ, Sibelius Acad. m. Ulpu Laikkala, 2 children. Debut: Helsinki, 1948. Career: Recitals in Sweden, Denmark, Norway, Germany, Holland, France, Italy, USSR & Czechoslovakia; Prof. of Organ, Sibelius Acad., Helsinki. Recordings incl: J S Bach Organ Works; J S Bach, The Art of Fugue. Publs: Studier over stiltrohet och subjektiritet: Interpretationen av J S Bach orgelkompositioner, 1957. Mbrships: Gesellschaft der Orgelfreunde, Germany; Det Danske Orgelselskab, Denmark; Organum-Seura, Finland. Recip. Harriet Cohen Bach Medal, 1959. Hobby: Lit. Mgmt: Musik-Fazer, Konsertdirektion, Helsinki. Address: Jlomaenpolku 7C, 00840 Helsinki 84, Finland.

FORSMAN, John Väinö, b. 11 Aug. 1924, Hämenlinna, Finland. Composer. Educ: Royal Conservs., Stockholm & Copenhagen; studied w. Paul Hindemith, Salzburg, Arthur Honegger, Paris & Luigi Dallapiccola, Florence. m. Maria Luisa Chavetz, 4 children. Debut: as Comp., Copenhagen, 1945. Comps. publd. incl: 5 piano sonatas; chmbr., orchl. & educl. music; A Symphonic Song. Comps. recorded: Romance for Oboe & Piano, TONO, Copenhagen; Christmas Oratorio for Children, Nordisk Polyphon, Copenhagen; Little Juan in Mexico, Philips, Mexico City & Cablevision, ibid. Contbr. to Scandinavian musical press. Hons. incl: Hugo Breitner Soc. Award, Vienna, 1956; Henry Bellamann Award, USA, 1964. Hobbies: Reading; Table Tennis; Chess. Address: Apartado Postal 4.004, Mexico City 4, DF, Mexico.

FORSTER, John Charles Stirling, b. 18 Mar. 1915, London, UK. Music Teacher (retired). Educ: MusD, Dunelm; FRCO; ARCM. m. Frances Mary Pink. Career: Asst. Organist, St. George's Chapel, Windsor, 1941-45; Dir. of Music, Reed's Schl., Cobham, 1950-58; staff, Yorks. Coll. of Music, 1966-77. Hobbies: Birdwatching; Crossword Puzzles. Address: Holly Bank, N Rigton, Leeds LS 17 ODE, UK.

FORSTER, Laura Kathleen, b. 28 Oct. 1902, Newcastle-On-Tyne, UK. Violinist; Music Educator. Educ: Violin Student, Royal Manchester Coll. of Music; Studied w. Dr. Adolph Brodsky & Carl Flesch; LRAM; ARMCM. Career: Solo Radio Engagements, 1930-31; Concerts, Manchester & Liverpool Dist.; Mbr., Manchester Women's String Orch.; Prof., Violin, Royal Northern Coll. of Music & Northern Schl. of Music. Mbrships: ISM. Hobbies: Gardening; Walking. Address: 11 Abingdon Rd., Bramhall, Cheshire, UK. 3.

FORSYTH, James Alexander, b. 12 Nov. 1939, Sydney, Aust. Organist; Lecturer. Educ: MMus, Univ. of Melbourne; Dip. Ed., Sydney Tchrs. Coll.; Accademia Musicale Chigiana, Siena, Italy. m. Suzanne Pemberton, 2 d. Career: public & broadcast recitals, Sydney & Melbourne; accomp., var. choirs; organist, Sydney Symph. Orch.; lectr., Catholic Tchrs. Coll., Sydney; Music Dir., St. Patrick's Ecclesiastical Coll., Manly, NSW; part-time lectr. & organ coach, NSW Conserv. of Music, Dept. of Organ & Ch. Music; mbr., The Indefinite Four (folk group). Comps: Alleluia Verse for Corpus Christi, for choir & organ; Fanfare & Interludes to Gonfalon Royal, for brass quintet (recorded). Recordings: Aust. Hymn Book; as accomp. to choir, Singers of David. mbr., Royal Schl. of Ch. Music, NSW branch. Hons: Vic. State Winner & Commonwealth finalist in ABC concerto & vocal competitions. Address: 6 Wallace Parade, Lindfield, NSW 2070, Aust.

FORSYTH, Malcolm Denis, b. 8 Dec. 1936, Pietermaritzburg, Repub. of S Africa. Composer; Trombonist; Conductor. Educ: Fac. of Music, Univ. of Capetown; BMus, MMus, DMus. m. Lesley Mary Eales, 1 d. Career: Prin. Trombonist, Edmonton Symph. Orch.; Cond. of num. perfs. of own orchl. works w. Edmonton Symph., Capetown Symph. & Capab Symph.; TV apps. w. The Malcolm Forsyth trombone ensemble, other solo & chmbr. groups. Comps. incl: 2 Symphs.; Music for Mouths, Marimba, Mbira & Roto-Toms; The Golyardes' Grounde (recorded); 2 Concerti Grossi for brass quintet & orch.; The Melancholy Clown; Aphorisms for Brass; Quartet '74 for trombones; Sagittarius (recorded); Viva Vivaldiev (recorded). Mbrships: Can. League of Comps.; Alberta Comps. Assn. Address: 11650 72 Ave., Edmonton, Alta., Can. T6G OC1.

FORTNER, Wolfgang, b. 12 Oct. 1907, Germany. Music Educator; Composer. Educ: Univ. of Leipzig; Leipzig Conserv. of Music. Career: Lectr., Evangelical Ch. Music Inst., Heidelberg, 1931-53; Prof. of Composition, NW. German State Acad. of Music, Detmold, 1954-57; State HS for Music, Freiburg, 1957-; Fndr. & Dir., Heidelberg Chmbr. Orch., 1935-41; Fndr.

& Dir., Musica Viva, Heidelberg, 1946, Freiburg, 1958, Munich, 1964. Compositions: Operas - Bluthochzeit, 1957; In seinem Garten leibt Don Perlimphin Belisa, 1962; Die weisse Rose (ballet), 1953; Due Pfingstgeschichte (cantata), 1963; Orchl. works - Capriccio, 1938; Sinfonie, 1947; Phantasie uber B-A-C-H, 1950; Impromptus, 1957; Triplum, etc. Address: Mühltalstrasse 122D, Heidelberg, W. Germany.

FORTUNATO, Andrew III, b. 25 Oct. 1951, Bay Shore, NY, USA. Teacher of Instrumental Music; Band Conductor & Director. Educ: B Mus; NY State Provisional Cert. to teach music; MS (Music Educ.). Career: Perfs. in band, orch., & chorus concerts, org. & marching band competitions, fests., & parades, musicals & stage bands; Cond., Bolton Ctrl. Schl. Band. Mbrships: MENC; NY State Schl. Music Assn.; Phi Mu Alpha Sinfonia (Asst. Historian & Warden). Recip., var. hons. Hobbies incl: Swimming; Snorkeling; Collecting coins. Address: 60 Chelsea Court Apt. 1, Bohemia, NY 11716, USA. 23,28,29.

FOSBY, Anders Julius, b. 25 Jan. 1905, Oslo, Norway. Military Musician (trombone, baritone contrabassoon). Educ: Military Schl. Music; Music Conserv., Oslo. m. Doris. Mbrships: Oslo Musikerforening; Norsk Musikerforbund. Hobbies: Working on landplace by Dröbak. Address: Trondheimsreien 70C, Oslo 5, Norway.

FOSS, Lukas, b. 15 Aug. 1922, Berlin, Germany. Composer; Conductor; Pianist; Educator. Educ: Dip., Curtis Inst. of Music. m. Cornelia Foss, 1 s., 1 d. Career incls: Dir., Ojai Fest., Calif., NY Phil. Summer Fest. Concerts, Lincoln Ctr., 2 yrs.; Fac. Mbr., Berkshire Music Ctr.; Prof. of Comp., UCLA, 10 yrs.; Music Dir., Buffalo Phil., 1963-70; currently Cond. & Music Advsr., Jerusalem Symph. & Brooklyn Philharmonia; guest apps. w. major US orch. & such others as the Berlin Phil., Israel Phil., Leningrad Phil. & Tokyo Phil. Comps: 75 publd.; approx. 12 recorded. Contbr. to var. mags., inclng. Source. num. hons. & awards. Hobby: Reading. Mgmt: Columbia Artists, Am.; Dispeker, Europe. Address: 1140 Fifth Ave., NYC, NY 10028, USA.

FOSTER, Anthony, b. 11 April, 1926, Gravesend, UK. Musician. Educ: studied piano w. Tracy Robson; organ w. John Cook & John Webster; comp./orchestration w. Gordon Jacob & Richard Arnell; LRAM; ARCO. m. Barbara Humphreys, 1 d. Career: Comp. music for BBC prods. & schls. fests.; var. works for orch.; choir, piano; music for children. Var. recordings for BBC. Publs: Sing It, Play It, 1976. Mbrships: Comps. Guild of GB. Hons: Life Mbr., Brighton Schls. Music & Drama Assn. 1977. Hobbies: Cinematography; Video Recording. Address: 1 Cawley Rd., Chichester, Sussex, UK. 28,29,30.

FOSTER, Beryl, b. 2 Sept. 1944, London, UK. Contralto Singer; Lecturer; Writer; Teacher. Educ: Schl. of Music, Colchester; BMus, London, 1969; LRAM, 1967; postgrad. student, RCM, 1969-72. m. Richard Watson. Career: specialist in Scandinavian song; concert & oratorio apps. throughout UK, 1973-: 1st Brit. perfs. of Robert Fleming's The Confession Stone, 1976, & of songs by Oistein Sommerfeldt, 1979. Publ: The Songs of Edvard Grieg (in prep.). Mbrships: ISM; Brit. Fed. of Music Fests. (adjudicator-mbr.); Soroptomist Int. recip., W European Rsch. Award from the British Acad., 1978. Hobbies incl: Dressmaking; Needlework; Reading; Crosswords. Address: 11 Burnham Road, St. Albans, Herts. AL1 4QN, UK.

FOSTER, Donald Herbert, b. 30 Apr. 1934, Detroit, Mich., USA. Professor of Musicology. Educ: BS, Wayne State Univ., Detroit, 1956; Mus M, 1959, PhD, 1967, Univ. of Mich. Career: Fac. Mbr., Olivet Coll., Olivet, Mich., 1960-67; Prof. of Musicol., Coll.-Conserv. of Music, Univ. of Cinn., Ohio, 1967-. Publs: Ed., L.-N. Clérambault, L'Histoire de la Femme Adultère, 1974; Ed., Clérambault, 2 Cantatas for Soprano & Instruments, 1976. Contbr. to: Recherches sur la musique classique française; Diapason; Acta Musicologica. Mbrships: Int. Musicol. Soc.; Am. Musicol. Soc. (Sec.-Treas., Mid-west chapt., 1975-77); Société Francaise D'Etude du XVIIIE Siècle; AAUP. Hons: Fulbright Scholar, Paris, 1962-63. Hobbies: Hiking; Travel. Address: 393 Amazon Ave., Cincinnatti, OH 45220, USA.

FOSTER, Dudley Edwards, Jr., b. 5 Oct. 1935, Orange, NJ, USA. Organist; Composer; Conductor; Musicologist. Educ: BA, MA, Univ. of Calif., Los Angeles; PhD candidate, Musicol., Univ. of Southern Calif.; FTCL (Organ). Career: Lectr. in Music, Immaculate Heart Coll., Los Angeles, 1960-62, & Calif. State Univ., ibid., 1968-71; Prof. of Music, Los Angeles Mission Coll., 1975-; Dir. of Music, First Luth. Ch. of Los Angeles, 1968-71, & St. Marth's Episc. Ch., W. Covina, Calif., 1975-; frequent apps. as organ recitalist & cond. Comps. incl: O Sacrum Convivium for Trumpet & Organ, 1973; Scherzo for

Trumpet & Piano, 1974; Introduction, Arioso & Fugue for Cello & Piano, 1975. Contbr. to Worship & Arts. Mbr., profl. assns. Address: 1631 N. Dillon St., Los Angeles, CA 90026, USA. 28.

FOSTER, Lawrence, b. 23 Oct. 1941, LA, Calif., USA. Conductor. Educ: studied cond. W. Fritz Zweig; close assn. w. Karl Boehm & Bruno Walter, & piano w. Joanna Graudan. m. Angela Suciu. Debut: 1960. Career: Cond. & Musical Dir., Young Musicians' Fndn. Debut Orch., 1960-64; Assoc. Cond., San Fran. Ballet, 1960-65, touring USA 3 times; Asst. Cond. to Zubin Mehta, LA Phil., 1965-68, touring world, 1967; Chief Guest Cond., RPO, 1969-74; Guest Cond., major orchs. in UK, Europe & USA; Music Dir., Houston Symph. Orch., 1971-78; Music Dir., Orch. Nat. of the Opera Monte Carlo, 1979-. Recordings: sev. records. Hons. incl: Koussevitsky Mem. Cond. Prize, & Eleanor R Crane Mem. Prize, Berkshire Fest., Tanglewood, Mass., 1966. Mgmt: Harrison/Parrott, 22 Hillgate St., London W8, UK. Address: c/o Mgmt.

FOSTER, Robert Estill, b. 21 Jan. 1939, Raymondville, Tex., USA. Conductor; Trumpet soloist & Clinician; Band Director; Teacher. Educ: B Mus., Univ. of Tex.; M Ed., Univ. of Houston; Profl. study in trumpet w. Frank Elsass & Armando Ghitalla. m. Rebecca Cox Foster, 1 d., 2 s. Composer of over 70 works for band. Num. educl. recordings. Author of Multiple Option Marching Techniques, 1974. Contbr. to: Instrumentalist; The School Musician. Mbrships: American Bandmasters Assoc.; MENC; KBA; TBA; Kappa Kappa Psi; Coll. Band Dirs. Nat. Assn.; Phi Mu Alpha. Hobbies: Perf.; Raising house plants & orchids. Address: Rt. 2, Lawrence, KS 66044, USA.

FOSTER, Robert Ivan, b. 14 July 1918, Moose Jaw, Sask., Can. Baritone. Educ: BA, Open Univ., UK, 1974; FTCL; FLCM; LRAM; LRSM; Assoc., Royal Conserv. of Music Toronto, Can.; ARCM; GSMD (CT); Perfs. Dip., Mozarteum, Salzburg. Debut: Toronto, Can. Career: Can. Opera Co., Toronto; Sadler's Wells Opera Co., London, UK; Onslo Records, ibid.; CBC; BBC; Arts Coun. of GB, 1955. Comps. (publs. & recordings): 4 Canadian Cowboy Songs, 1965. Recordings: Dominion Records, Can.; Onslo Records, London. Mbrships: ISM; Equity. Hons: Can. Rose Bowl, Toronto, 1947; Scholarships for study to NY, Toronto, London, Salzburg, 1945-55. Hobbies: Photography; Philately; Food. Mgmt: Onslo Concert Artistes' Bureau, 61 Kingswood Rd., London SW2. 4JN, UK. 3.

FOSTER, Thomas William, Jr., b. 30 Mar. 1922, Paterson NJ, USA. Musician, Trumpet, Violin, Bass Viol; Conductor. Educ: BS., Mansfield State Tchrs. Coll., Pa.; MA., NY Univ.; Siena Coll., New Paltz State Coll., studied w. Raymond Meyers. Jr., Bernard Mandelkern, Karl Rissland. m. Lorraine Day, 1 d., 1 s. Debut: Wilkes-Barre, Pa. Career: 1st Trumpet, Esquires Dance Band, Mansfield State Tchrs. Coll., Gen. MacArthurs HQ Dance & Show Band, Manila, Phillipines, Dutchess County Phil.; Hudson Valley Phil., Hudson Valley Theatre Orch.; 1st Trumpet, Cond., Pough. Local 238 Musicians Union Concert Band, Jazz Workshop Orch., Pough., NY; Cond., Concerts w. soloists James Burke, Robert Nagel, Warren Covington, "Doc" Severinsen, & others; Hd., Music Dept., Pine Plains Central Schl. System, NY.; Adjud., NY State Schl. Music Assn.; Dir., Presby. Ch. Choir, PP, NY; Perf., Hunter Mt. Bavarian Fest., 1975-78; Chief Adjud., Talent Search, Dutchess County Fair, 14 yrs. Recordings: Peter & The Wolf, Dutchess County Phil., w. var. name bands, 1940-47. Mbr., profl. orgs. Recip. var. hons. Hobbies: Sports; Sports Cars. Address: Poplar Ave., Pine Plains, NY 12567, USA.

FOTEK, Jan, b. 28 Nov. 1928, Czerwińsk on Vistula, Poland. Composer; Organist; Conductor. Educ: Conserv. of Music, Warsaw. m. Zofia Ostrowska, 2 s. Debut: as comp. w. Apostrophes, 1958. Career: apps. on radio, concerts & Great Theatre, Warsaw. Comps: Epitasis, Partita, Apostrophes, Hymne de St. Brigitte (all recorded); Vir Sapiens Dominabitur Astris; The Sea of Found Unity; Cantatina Coparnicana; Laudess; A Princess from the Woods. Mbrships: Assn. of Polish Comps.; Assn. of Authors & Stage Comps. Hons: Prize, Coun. of Ministers, for creative work for children & youth, 1973; Prize, Grzegorz Fitelberg competition, 1969; Feliks Nowowiejski prize for comp., 1979; Brother Albert Chmielowski prize for religious music, 1977. Address: 05892 Warsaw, Izabelin, Sierakowska 37, Poland.

FOU, Ts'ong, b. 10 March 1934, China. Pianist. Educ: studied in Shanghai & Warsaw. m. (1) Zamira Menuhin (dissolved); (2) Hijong Hyun. Debut: Shanghai, 1953. Career: concerts in Eastern Europe & USSR, 1953-59; 1st London app., 1959; concerts in Europe, N & S Ams., Aust., Far E. 16.

FOURIE, David Gerhardus, b. 25 Dec. 1944, Pretoria, S Africa. Lecturer. Educ: BA, THOD; ATCL; LTCL. m. Anne-Marie

Holtzhausen. Career: Lectr., Pretoria Tchrs. Trng. Coll.; Choirleader & Accomp.; Organist, 14 yrs. Recordings: 4 Choir Recitals, 1 Sacred Music Recital. Mbrships: S African Music Tchrs. Soc.; Pretoria Art Soc. Hobbies: Gardening; Art. Address: Martha Rd. 22, Eldoraigne Ext. 1, Verwoerdburg 0140, S Africa.

FOURNIER, Jean, b. 3 July 1911, Paris, France. Concert Violinist; Professor of Music. Educ: 1st Prize, violin, Nat. Sup. Conserv. of Music, Paris. m. Ginette Doyen, 1 s. Career: Concert violinist & Solo perf. w. maj. French & other orchs.; num. Tours, Europe, Africa, Asia, etc.; Prof., Nat. Sup. Conserv. of Music, Paris; Vis. Prof., (summer), Int. Acad., Mozarteum, Salzburg. Recordings: Westminster, NY; Vega, France; Nipon Westminster, Tokyo. Hons: Chevalier de la Légion d'Honneur, 1968; Chevalier de l'Ordre des Arts et Lettres, 1972. Address: 11 Ave. de Versailles, 75016 Paris, France. 3.

FOURNIER, Pierre Leon, b. 24 June 1906, Paris, France. Concert Cellist. Educ: Nat. Conserv. of Music, Paris. m. Lyda Antik, 1 s. Debut: Paris, 1928. Career: Tchr., Normal Schl. of Music, Paris, 1937-39, & Nat. Conserv. of Music, Paris, 1941-49; Soloist, major orchs. & important musical socs., Europe, USA, S Am., Far E, USSR, Japan, S Africa & NZ; has done many transcriptions (publd. by Int. Music Co., NYC). Recordings: num. for Decca, HMV, Columbia, RCA, DGG, Erato & others. Hons: Off., Legion of Hon. & Order of Arts & Letters, and Cmdr., Order of Merit, France; Cmdr., Order of Leopold II, Belgium; Kt. of Luxembourg w. crown; num. prizes for recordings, USA, France & Germany; Edison Prize, Netherlands. Address: 14 Chateau Banquet, Geneva, Switz.

FOUSE, Sarah Baird, b. 13 Oct. 1935, Gary, Ind., USA. Flute Instructor; Flautist. Educ: B Mus. in Wind Instruments, Univ. of Mich., 1958; M Mus. in Applied Music, Univ. of Ky., 1961. m. Claude Andrew Fouse. Career: Flute Instr., Univ. of Ky., 1958-67; Asst. Prof. of Music, Univ. of Fla., 1967-; Perf. mbr. of the Fla. Woodwind Quintet, the Fla. Baroque Ensemble, The Fla. Sinfonietta; frequent solo flute recitals. Recordings: Flute Contest Music, vol. 1, LP 1245, vol. II, LP 1707, Coronet Recording Co. Contbr. to: The Instrumentalist; The De Ford Digest. Publs: Ed., 18 Studies on Solos for Flute, G. Briccialdi, 1979; Ed., First Sonata for Flute, F. M. Veracini, 1979. Mbrships: Tau Beta Sigma; Mu Phi Epsilon; Delta Kappa Gamma; Fndr. & VP., Fla. Flute Club, Gainesville; Nat. Flute Assn. Hobbies: Gardening; Sewing; Cooking. Mgmt: Univ. of Fla., Gainesville. Address: 12832 SW 14th Ave., Gainesville, FL 32601, USA.

FOWKE, Philip Francis, b. 28 June 1950, Gerrards Cross, UK. Concert Pianist. Educ: scholarship, RAM, 1967-74; piano studies w. Gordon Green; LRAM (piano perf.); ARCM (piano perf.); Recital Dip. Debut: Wigmore Hall, 1974. Career: Recitals, Wigmore Hall, Fairfield Hall (Croydon), Royal Fest. Hall, Purcell Room; Bath Fest., Cheltenham Fest.; concertos, BBC Symph. Orch. & BBC Northern Symph. Orch.; radio broadcasts; tours in Germany, France (inclg. Paris Conserv.), & Denmark; apps. w. RPO; Promenade Concert perf. Recordings: Carnival of the Animals on EMI Classics for Pleasure label; solo recital on Gaudeamus Label. Mbr., ISM. Recip. many prizes & awards, inclng. Churchill Fellowship, 1976. Hobbies: Walking; Talking; Reading; Architecture. Mgmt: Ibbs & Tillet. Address: 4 Morton Terr., London SW1V, 2NT, UK.

FOWLER, Charles Bruner, b. 12 May 1931, Peekskill, NY, USA. Journalist; Consultant in the Arts. Educ: BS Mus Ed. SUNY; M Mus Ed. Northwestern Univ., Ill.; DMA, Boston Univ. Career incls: Music Cons. & Journalist, Walt Disney Prods., 1971-; Cons. & Journalist for var. educl. projects sponsored by Nat. Endowment for the Arts, JDR 3rd Fund & other agcys., 1971-; Educ. Ed., Musical America, 1974-. Publs: The Search for Musical Understanding (co-author), 1973; The Arts Process, Pa. State Dept. of Educ., 1973. Contbr. to profl. jrnls. Mbrships incl: Music Panel, DC Commn. on the Arts, 1974-; Music Critics Assn. Recip. num. awards inclng: Disting. Alumnus Citation, SUNY, 1972. Hobbies: Painting; Theatre. Address: 320 Second St. SE, Washington, DC 20003, USA.

FOWLER, Francis Norman, b. 3 Apr. 1930, Bridport, Dorset, UK. Organ Builder, Designer; Organist; Managing Director. Educ: Study of organ & piano w. Alex Stone; Fellow, Inc. Soc. of Organs Builders; Fellow, Inst. of Musical Instrument Technol. m. Margaret David. Career: Organist, var. churches inclng. St. Mary's Walditch, Dorset at age 14, St. Werburgh's, Bristol, St. Joseph's, Cardiff; Recitals at Gaumon State Theatre Kilburn, Granada, Harrow, ABC Theatre, Ipswich & Odeon, Bristol; Apprentice Organ Builder w. Hill Norman & Beard; Nat. Serv.; Returned to Hill Norman & Beard; W J W Walker & Sons Ltd., 15 yrs.; Rejoined Hill Norman & Beard, Mng. Dir., 1974-.

Contbr. to Jrnl. of Cinema Organ Soc. Mbrships: Mbr., Royal Coll. of Organists; Sec., Inst. of Musical Instrument Technol.; Lectr., Organ Building, Mid-Warwickshire Coll. of Further Educ.; Hon. Life Mbr., Leics. Organists Assn. Hons: Pres.'s Award Inc. Soc. of Organ Builders, 1969. Hobbies: Show jumping; Travel; Food & Cooking. Address: 20 Disraeli Rd., Ealing, London W5 5HP, UK.

FOWLER, Jennifer, b. 14 Apr. 1939, Bunbury, Western Aust. Composer. Educ: BA, Univ. of WA, 1961; Dip. of Educ., ibid, 1962; B Mus., 1968. m. Bruce Paterson, 2 s. Comps incl: Sculpture in Four Dimensions for orch., 1969; Chimes, Fractured for chmbr. ensemble, 1970; "Veni Sancte Spiritus -Veni Creator" for chmbr. choir, 1971; Look on This Oedipus for orch., 1973; Piece for an Opera House, for 2 pianos or piano & tape, 1973; Chant with Garlands, for orch., 1974; Voice of the Shades, for soprano, oboe or clarinet & violin, 1977; "Ring Out The Changes", for bells & string orch., 1978. Recordings: Australian Festival of Music, vol. 10. Mbr: Fellowship of Aust. Composers. Hons: Composition Prize, Int. Composers Competition, Acad. of Arts, Berlin, 1970, for The Hours of the Day for 4 mezzo sopranos, 2 clarinets & 2 oboes; Radcliffe Music Award, UK, 1971, for Ravelation for str. quintet; 1st Prize for chmbr. music, Int. Contest for Women Comps., Gedok, Mannheim, Germany, 1975. Address: 21 Deodar Rd., London SW15, UK.

FOWLES, Glenys Rae, b. Perth, WA, Australia. Opera Singer (lyric soprano). Educ: Pvte. music tutors; A Mus. A (piano performer's). m. Kevin Bleakley. Debut: w. Aust. Opera, Melbourne Season, 1969. Career incl: Res. Soprano, NYC Opera;apps. in UK w. Scottish Opera, Glyndebourne Festival, Convent Gdn., Engl. Nat. Opera & Aust. Opera; Oratorio performances, Aust. & UK; Gilbert & Sullivan operettas; Radio & TV broadcasts, UK & Aust.; roles incl. Susanna, Pamina, Constanza, Poppea, Marenka, Rosina, Juliette. Hons: Winner, Aust. Broadcasting Commn. Concerto & Vocal Comp., 1967; Schlrship. & Prizewinner, Metropol. Opera Auditions, 1968. Hobbies: Travel; Cooking; Fashions. Mgmt: Lies Askonas (Europe); Ludwig Lustig & Florian Ltd. (USA). Address: 225 W 70th St., Apt. 3E, NY, NY 10023, USA.

FOX, Alan Hugo, b. 1 Apr. 1934, Chgo., Ill., USA. Bassoon & Contrabassoon Manufacturer. Educ: BS, Chem. Engrng., Purdue Univ., 1955. m. Pamela A. Michne, 1 d. Career: 1st Lt., US Army Ordnance, 1955-57; Chem. Plant Planning & Constrn., 1957-60; VP in mfg., Fox Products Corp., 1960-69; Pres., ibid, 1969-; Made basic acoustical design of all Fox Bassoons & Contrabassoons currently in use in the world's major orchs. Mbrships: Charter Mbr., Int. Double Reed Soc. Contbr. to Instrumentalist Mag. 'Defining the Bassoon', 1968 & 'The Case for Plastics in Woodwind Instruments', 1971. Hobbies: Sailboat racing; Tennis. Address: T.No. 1, S Whitley, IN 46787, USA. 8,30.

FOX, John Victor, b. 25 Nov. 1929, Stoke-on-Trent, UK. Senior Inspector For Music. Educ: MA, Trinity Coll., Cambridge; LRAM; ARCM; LGSM. (2) Career: Hd. of Music, Elliott Schl., Putney, 1957-64; Asst. Music Advsr., Hants., 1964-69; Asst. Educ. Off., Croydon, 1969-71; Sr. Dist. Insp., Music, Manchester, 1971-. Comps: Prelude-Hymn-Allegro, for guitar; song cycle, Nature Studies; Guitar Grp. Material Mbrships: MANA; ISM; NAIEA. Recip. Alan Gray Prize, Cambridge, 1953. Hobby: Philately. Address: Educ. Office, Crown Square, Manchester M60 3BB, UK. 3.

FOX, Leland Stanford, b. 25 Jan. 1931, Worcester, Mass., USA. Singer; Conductor of Opera; Lecturer in Music History; Professor of Music. Educ: B Mus, 1956, M Mus, 1957, Baylor Univ.; PhD, Fla. State Univ., 1962. m. Wanda Nelson Fox, 1 d., 1 s. Career: Masque & Lyre Opera Co., NYC; Metropolitan Light Opera Co., NYC; Asolo Theatre, Fla.; Prof. of Music, Univ. of Miss. Mbrships: Bd. of Dirs., Ed. of publs., Nat. Opera Assn.; Ctrl. Opera Serv.; Royal Musical Assn. Publs. incl: Touring Opera: A Manual for Small Companies (ed.), 1975. Contbr. to Grove's Dictionary of Music & Musicians, 6th ed., & profl. jrnls. Hobbies incl: Reading. Address: 2206 Ch. St., Oxford, MS 38655, USA.

FRADKIN, Mark Grigoryevich, b. 4 May 1914, Vitebsk, Byelorussia, Russia. Composer. Educ: Leningrad Theatre Inst.; Byelorussian Conserv., Minsk. Compositions incl: Music for films - They Were the First; Good Luck!; Volunteers; First Day of Peace; Fores; Farewell; Dovesl; An Ordinary Incident; On a Business Mission; The Volga Flows; Last Harvest; In Performance of His Duties; If You Are Right; over 100 songs. Recip: Order of the Red Star, 1943. Address: Composers Union of RSFSR, 8-10 Nezhdanovoi ulitsa, Moscow, USSR.

FRAGER, Malcolm, b. 15 Jan. 1935, St. Louis, Mo., USA. Concert Pianist. Educ: pvte. studies w. Carl Madlinger,

1942-49; Tutoring Schl. of NY, 1949-55; Am. Conserv., Fontainebleu, France; BA., Columbia Univ. m. Morag Macpherson. Career: gave 1st pub. recital when aged 6; Soloist w. St. Louis Symph. when aged 10; app. in Town Hall, NYC, 1952, & Carnegie Hall, 1955 & 60; toured USSR, 1963 & Iceland, 1964, since touring thru'out world; Soloist, Berkshire Music Fest., USA, 1963-66. Hons. incl: 1st Int. Music Competition, Geneva, 1955; Michaels Mem. Music Award, Chgo., 1956; 1st Edgar M. Leventritt Int. Competition, 1959; 1st Queen Elisabeth of Belgium Contest, 1960; invited to perf. at White House by Pres. Eisenhower, 1960. Address: 155 W. 68th St., NYC, NY 10023, USA.

FRAJT, Ludmila, b. 31 Dec. 1919, Belgrade, Yugoslavia. Composer. Educ: univ. degree in music (comp.), Acad. of Music, Belgrade; course for new music, Darmstadt. widow. Career: Music Ed.-Dir.of Music Dept., Avala-Film, 1946-52; Music Ed.Dpty. Ed.-in-Chief of Music prog., Radio Belgrade, 1952-58; Sec., Music Committee, Yugoslav TV & Radio, 1958-72. Comps. recorded: Songs of Night & The Dirge; Farewell Songs; The Strange Piper; Twelve Months. Comps. publd. incl: Silver Sounds (str. quartet); A Prayer for Rain (women's choir a cappella); The Eclogue (chmbr. orch.). Mbr., Assn. of Comps. of Yugoslavia. Recip. many awards for comps. Hobby: Gardening. Address: Filipa Kljajića 40, YU-11000 Belgrade, Yugoslavia.

FRANCAIX, Jean, b. 23 May 1912, Le Mans, France. Composer. Educ: Le Mans & Paris Conservs.; studied pvtely. w. Nadia Boulanger. Career: became a publd. composer at age 9 with 1st piano suite; toured USA, 1938. Compositions incl: Eight Bagatelles; 2 Concertinas for piano & orch.; L'Apostrophe (opera).

FRANCESCATTI, Zino, b. 9 Aug. 1902, Marseilles, France. Concert Violinist. Educ: Pvte. music study. m. Yolande Potel de la Briere, 1930. Career incl: concert appearances w. leading orchs. throughout the world; Jurist in var. int. musical competitions; Hon. Mbr., Paris Conserv. Orch., Phila. Orch., USA, etc. Hons: Off., Legion d'Honneur; Cmndr., Ordre de Leopold de Belgique, 1967; Cmndr., Ordre des Arts & Lettres. Hobbies: Chess problems; Stamp collecting; Driving; Gardening. Address: 3 E 85th St. NY, NY 10028, USA.

FRANCHISENA, Cesar Mario, b. 3 Sept. 1923, Argentina. Composer; University Professor. Educ: Bach. m. Irma C Machado, 1 d. Debut: Buenos Aires. Career: Prof. of Harmony & Comp., Arts Coll., Nat. Univ. of Córdoba, Argentina. Comps: 34 works for var. instruments, soloists, instrumental grps. & symph. orch. Comps. recorded: Visiones Siderales for piano, Qualiton QI4001; Tres Momentos Mágicos; Intermezzo. Contbr. to profl. publs. Mbrships: Fndr. Mbr., Grp. of Latinam. Acoustics (GALA). Hons: Premio a la cultura de la Ciudad de Córdoba, 1978. Address: Avda Sagrada Familia 181, Bajo Palermo, Córdoba, Argentina.

FRANCIS, Alun, b. 29 Sept. 1943, Kidderminster, UK. Conductor; Composer. Educ: ARMCM. m. June Leslie Moore, 1 s., 1 d. Career: has conducted perfs. in London, Vienna, Munich, Milan, most major fests. & in over 20 countries. Comps: Orchestral; choral; chmbr. music. Recordings of works by Donizetti. Hons: Leon Grindon Prize for Comp., RMCM, 1962. Mgmt: London Artists, 73 Baker St., London W1, UK. Address: as mgmt.

FRANCIS, Hannah Mary, b. 11 Mar. 1945, London, UK. Singer (soprano). Educ: Scholarship to RCM, London; ARCM (perfs.) Hons. m. Miochael John Lankester. Career: Solo recitals throughout GB; Many broadcasts & TV apps. Perf. at Aldeburgh Fest. & all over the Continent; Profl. Harpist until 1972; Apps. w. English Nat. Opera; Prof. of Harp, Jr. Royal Coll. of Music. Mbrships: ISM; Noise Abatement Soc. Hons: Winner of Royal O'seas League Prize for the best UK Soloist; Winner of the Gtr. London Arts Assn. Award for 1969. Hobbies: Reading; Walking; Swimming; Tennis; Cooking. Mgmt: Ibbs & Tillet, 124 Wigmore St., London W1H OAX. Address: 21 Birchington Rd., London N8, UK.

FRANCIS, Harry, b. 2 May 1908, London, UK. Orchestral Percussionist & Arranger; Music Journalist, Critic and Consultant. Educ: Camden Inst. of Music. m. Winifred Chapman, 1 d. Career: began career as Orchl. Musician, 1926; held var. sr. positions as official in Musicians' Union, 1945-73; currently Music Jrnlst., Critic & Cons. Contbr. to: Crescendo. Mbrships: Hon. Treas., Theatres' Advsry. Coun.; Deleg., London Dist. Coun., Musicians' Union. Address: 9 Bedgebury Gdns., Wimbledon Pk., London SW19 6PH, UK. 3.

FRANCIS, Kenneth, b. 4 Feb. 1938, Tonypandy, Wales, UK. Operatic Bass. Educ: Civil Engrng., Glamorgan Coll. of Technol.; Coll. of Music & Drama, Cardiff; w. Redvers.

Llewelyn & Mme. Julia Hilger, Welsh Nat. Opera Co. Trng. Scheme; w. John Hargreaves. m. Jacqueline. Career: Prin. Bass, Performing Arts Coun., Transvaal, S Africa; Prin. Bass, 3 yrs., now Guest Artist, Sadlers Wells Opera; sings in major fests. & on radio & TV; tours in Yugoslavia & Austria. Roles incl: Angelotti, Tosca; Fasolt, Rheingold; Kaspar, Die Freishutz; Don Pasquale, Don Pasquale. Recip. Bronze Medal, Grand Prix du Concours Int. de Chant, Toulouse, 1969. Hobbies incl: Watercolour & oil painting. Address: 60 Rusper Ct., 325 Clapham Rd., Stockwell, London SW9, UK.

FRANCIS, Sarah Janet, b. London, UK. Oboist; Professor. Educ: ARCM; Studied in Paris, France. m. Michael D C Johnson, 2 d. Career: Regular broadcasts as soloist for BBC since aged 19; Prin. oboe, BBC Welsh Orch., 1962; Appearances, Cheltenham & Aldeburgh Festivals; Perf. in concerto, Promenade Concert, London, 1974; annual apps. at Royal Fest. & Queen Elisabeth Halls; Prof., Royal Coll. of Music; Mbr., London Harpsichord Ensemble; Sev. compositions written for Sarah Francis by Brit. composers. Recordings: 6 Metamorphoses, unaccompanied oboe, (Britten); Ariadne Concerto for oboe w. London Symph. Orch. (Crosse); Britten Phantasy Quartet w. Aeolian String Quartet; oboe sonatas by Bach, Handel, Telemann & Vivaldi. Mbr., ISM. Hons: Schlrship., Royal Coll. of Music, 1956; Wind Prize, ibid, 1960; Boise Fndn. Schlrship., 1960; French Govt. Schlrship. Hobbies: Reading; Walking. Address: 10 Avenue Rd., London N6 5DW, UK. 27.

FRANCK, Georges, b. 6 Sept. 1926, Herstal (Liège), Belgium. Musicologist. Educ: Piano & general branches, Conserv.; DPh (Musicol.), Paris. div. Career: Music critic, Belgian Periodicals & Newspapers, 1958-66; Lectr., Europe & S Am.; Adjudicator, some Int. Piano Contests; Advisor, var. foreign broadcasting stations; Freelance musicologist & tchr. Contbr. to: Journal des Jeunesses Musicales; Jrnl. des Beaux-Arts; Ruch Muzyczni (Poland); Current Musicol. (Univ. of Columbia); Piano Tchr.; Canto Gregoriano (Portugal); Musik und Bild (Germany); Rassegna Musicale Curci (Italy); Opera Jrnl. (Univ. of Miss.), etc. Hobby: Gastonomy. Address: rue du Trône 95, 1050 Brussels, Belgium.

FRANCKE, Donald Max, b. 26 Oct. 1929, London, UK. Singer. Educ: St. Catharine's Coll., Cambridge Univ.; ARCM. m. Margaret Rose Lindsay, 1 s., 1 d. Debut: W. New Opera Co., Sadlers Wells Theatre. Career: Regular Broadcasts for BBC Sound Opera & TV; Recitals w. Gerald Moore at Wigmore Hall; Intimate Opera Co.; Opera Players; Ed., RCM Mag., 1969-74; Scottish Nat. Opera; Phoenix Opera; New Opera Co.; Pk. Lane Opera Co.; Recitals w. John Ireland Soc. Comps. incl: Mass; Lux et Origo; Anthem & Songs. Recording w. Purcell Singers. Publs. incl: Ed., The Ways & Means of Vocal Expression, 1974. Contbr. to profl. jrnls. Mbr. num. profl. orgs. Hons. incl: Clara Butt Singing Prize, 1958; Tagore Gold Medal. Mgmt: Ibbs & Tillet. Address: Orama House, 263 Sheen Lane, London SW14 8RN, UK. 3.

FRANCO, Johan, b. 12 July 1908, Zaandam, Netherlands. Composer. Educ: The Hague First Coll.; Amsterdam Univ.; pvte. study w. Willem Pijper, 1928-33. m. Eloise Bauder Lavrischeff, 2 steps. Comps. publd. by Am. Comps. Alliance. Comps. recorded. incl: Symphony V, "The Cosmos"; Cantata, "As the Prophets Foretold"; Fantasy for cello & orch.; Dream Monologue for soprano & orch. Contbr. to jrnls. inclng: Musical Quarterly; Musical Am. Mbrships: Am. Comps. Alliance; BMI. Hons. incl: 1st Prize, Delius Composition Contest for Ode for male chorus & symph. band, 1972. Hobby: Stereo photography. Address: 403 Lake Dr., Virginia Beach, VA 23451, USA. 2,14.

FRANCY, Paul, b. 23 Oct. 1927, Vaux-sous-Chevremont, Belgium. Pianist; Conductor; Magazine Editor; Professor. Educ: Lic., Philos. & Letters; Dips., Piano, Solfeggio, Harmony, Fugue, Orchestration. m. Marcelle Soeur, 2 d. Debut: 1949. Career: var. Film Apps.; num. Radio & TV Perfs.; Concerts, Belgium, Europe; Ed.-in-Chief, Prologue. Compositions: musical Carnival; farces Les-Chevaliers De La Table Ronde, Alice in Wonderland; ballets Poker, Danses Barbares, Horace; var. orchl. & Jazz works. Publs: Le Particularisme Metaphysique Chez Shakespeare, 1949; Phonetique Analytique De L'Anglais Moderne, 1956; Les Recherches De Timbres Dans L'Orchestre De Jazz, 1957. Contbr. to Cles Pour La Musique. Mbrships: Soc. of Authors; Gen. Assn. of the Belgian Press. Hobbies: Collecting Books; Gardening; Fencing; Judo; Boating. Address: Residence Le Belvedere, 10 quai Van Beneden, B-4020 Liège, Belgium.

FRANDSEN, Per Kynne, b. 11 Apr. 1932, Copenhagen, Denmark. Organist; Choirmaster. Educ: Dips. as Organist (liturgical & recital). Tchr. of Organ, & Choirmaster; studied at Univ. & Conserv. in Aarhus, Royal Danish Conserv. of Music

(Copenhagen), Paris & other European ctrs. m. Inger Johanne Madsen, 3 children. Debut: Copenhagen, 1960. Career: Organist & Choirmaster, Custodian of Hist. Organ (Esaias Compenius 1610), Frederiksborg; has given recitals & made radio & TV apps. playing old & new organ music, Denmark, France, Netherlands, Germany, Sweden, Finland & Poland; Fndr. & Cond., Frederiksborg chmbr. Choir, 1963; Organ Tchr., Royal Danish Conserv. of Music, 1965-71; Organ Advsr. Has recorded on Compenius organ for Fona, Principal & RCA Victor. Mbrships: Co-Fndr. & Chmn., Danish Organ Soc., 1971-76; DOKS. Hons: French State Schlrship., 1959; Tipsmidlerne; Carlsbergs Mindelegat; Mbr. of the Jury, Grand Prix de Chartres, 1974. Address: Bogfinkevej 2, DK-3400 Hillerod, Denmark.

FRANJO, HRG, b. 21 Mar. 1933, Ivanec, Yugoslavia. Journalist & Editor. Educ: degree as tchr. of Russian, studies in music sect., Pedagogical Acad., Zagreb; Yugoslav lit. & Croation, Philos. fac., Univ. of Zagreb; music studies w. A Vidaković; degree as musical ed., radio stn. course. m. Marija, 2 d. Career: Jrnlst. & Musical Ed. Hungarian Newspaper Comps. incl: many popular melodies & songs, Osamljen lutam ulicom, Zelje, Znatizelja, Stari Foxtrot, etc.; choral works & arrs.; Sonatina for accordion; works & transcriptions for accordion orch. Publs: Melodika basova (for accordion beginners), 1970, 71, 72, 75; Harmonika (accordion), I (a primer), 1978. Contbr. to var. publs. & radio stns. Mbr., Soc. of Croatian Comps. Hobbies: Writing poetry & lyrics; Translating lyrics. Address: 42240 Ivanec, Gajeva ul. 14, Yugoslavia.

FRANK, Alan Clifford, b. 10 Oct. 1910, London, England. Music Publisher. m. Phyllis Tate, 2 children. Career: Hd., Music Dept., Oxford Univ. Press, 1954-75. Publs: Ed., The Year's Work in Music, 1947-51; The Playing of Chamber Music (w. Geo. Stratton), 1945, new ed., 1951; Modern British Composers, 1953. Contbr. to: Listener; Radio Times; Musical Times; BBC Progs; etc. Mbrships: Chmn., Performing Right Soc., 1975-78; Arts Coun. Music Panel, 1951-53 & 1965-70; BBC Music Advsry. Coun., 1953-57; Gov., British Inst. of Recorded Sound, 1972-78. Hobbies: Swimming; Looking at Buildings. Address: 12 Heath Hurst Rd., London NW3, UK.

FRANK, Claude, b. 24 Dec. 1925, Nuremberg, Germany. Musician; Pianist. Educ: Columbia Univ., 1942-44, 47-48; Piano study w. Artur Schnabel, 1941-44, 47-48, 51; comp. w. Paul Dessau, Normand Lockwood; cond. w. Serge Koussevitzky. m. Lillian Kallir, 1 d. Debut: Town Hall, NY., 1950. Career: Regular perf. w. maj. symph. orchs. on four continents; Recitals & Chamber Music at all music ctrs. & Fests.; Adj. Prof. of Mus., Yale Univ. Recordings: The Complete 32 Beethoven Piano Sonatas, RCA; Chamber Music of Mozart, Schubert, Brahms, RCA. Contbr. to: FM Mag., 1971; The Piano Qtly., 1974. Hons: EMMY Award nom. for TV Documentary on Beethoven, 1966. Hobbies: Some sports; Bridge. Mgmt: Columbia Artists Mgmt., NY. Address: 825 West End Ave., NY, NY 10025, USA. 3,14.

FRANK, Evelyn Lucy, b. 9 Mar. 1945, Mexico City, Mexico. Flautist. Educ: Concert Dip., North West German Music Acad., Detmold, 1966; Studied w. Prof. Dr. Hans-Peter Schmitz, Marcel Moyse, Aurele Nicolet. Career: Flautist, Solo Apps., UK, Solo Tours, Germany, Czechoslovakia; TV apps., Germany; Radio apps., UK, Czechoslovakia, Translator, Hans-Peter Schmitz, School of Fluteplaying, 1966. Hobbies: Photography; Drawing. Address: 46 Fortismere Ave., London N10, UK.

FRANKEN, Cootje, b. 19 Dec. 1913, Antwerp, Belgium. Music Librarian; Flautist; Music Copyist; Research Assistant. Educ: BA, Holland; Royal Conserv., The Hague; Dip. Profl. Flautist. m. Harold Franken. Debut: Diligentia, The Hague. Career: Specialist Chmbr. Music Presentations in num. Concert Halls; TV & radio apps. in var. countries inclng: Holland, Peru, Bolivia, Chile & Uruguay; Rsch. Asst., UCLA, USA, 1959-. Hobbies: Lit. in Dutch, Engl., French, German & Spanish. Address: Verdi 4339 Bis, Montevideo, Uruguay.

FRANKEN, Wim, b. 7 Jan. 1922, Assen, Netherlands. Composer; Pianist; Piano Teacher; Carilloneur. m. S H Gans, 3 c. Compositions incl: Chmbr. Music, sonatas, Serenade for flute, piano, double bass; 5 series of songs w. piano; choir, ballet, film music, inclng. Portret van Franz Hals; Orchl. Music Symphonietta, Rapsody on European Folksongs, Cirio, Concertino, Rapsodia Compestre; w. Violin Solo De Musica di Campanile, Suite from Moussorgsky, Pictures at an Exhibition, for carillon & brass band; electronic music. Monofrase, Trois Poems de Voyage. Recordings: Carillon Music; Arrs. of Folksongs. Mbrships: Genootschap van Nederlandes Componisten; Nederlandes Klokkenspiel Verenigin; Exec., ibid. Hons. Comp Prizes, 1st Roterdam, 1957, Petit & Fritsen, 1959, Concertgebouw Kammermusik, 1962. Address: 12 de Bosch Kemperlaan, Amersfoort, Netherlands.

FRANKENBERGER, Yoshiko Takagi, b. 15 March 1946, Tokyo, Japan. Vocalist; Voice & Piano Instructor. Educ: BMus, Coll. Conserv. of Music, Univ. of Cinn., 1969. m. Heinz D Frankenberger. Debut: Solo recording artist, Tokyo, Japan, 1952. Career: Educl. film, Red Carnations (Mother's Day), Japan, 1958; Voice & piano recitals, Dayton, Ohio, USA, & Tokyo, Japan; TV & radio apps., Japan & USA; Pt.-time Voice Instr., St. Joseph's Coll., Rensselaer, Ind., USA, 1972; Pvte. Voice & Piano Instr., Alvin, Tex., USA, 1973. Recordings: Over 250 (mostly educl.), 1952-70, incl. solo, Chuchan-ga Dobutsuen ni itta Ohanashi & Tokyo no Uta. Hons: Disting. Service Award, King Record Co. Ltd., Tokyo, Japan, 1963, '71; Japanese Poet Assn. Award, 1968. Hobbies: Comp.; African violets; Camping. Address: 110 E Wildwinn, Alvin, TX 77511, USA. 27.

FRANKFELDT, Chester, b. 7 Aug. 1942, NYC, USA. Mathematician; Computer Consultant; Pianist. Educ: studied piano, theory & harmony at NY Coll. of Music, & conducting pvtely. w. Dr. Irene Paulsen; BA, Univ. Coll. of Arts & Sci., NY Univ.; MS Grad. Schl. of Arts & Sci., Northwestern Univ.; grad. study in computer sci., Courant Inst. of Math. Scis., NY Univ. Career: Opera-Accomp.; Show Orchestrator & accomp., NY Univ.; Musical Dir.-Accomp., Antrim Playhouse, NY; Accomp., Westchester Opera, NY; Participant in Chmbr. Music Fests.; Participating Artist, Grp. 212 Intermedia Arts Ctr.; Mbr., NY Mensa Chmbr. Consort; app. as Accomp. w. Alice Dutcher (mezzo) & Moondog (composer, performing his music). Mbrships: Assn. for Computing Machinery; Chapt. Pres., Exec. VP & Bd. Mbr., Data Processing Mgmt. Assn.; Phi Beta Kappa; Tau Kappa Alpha; Mensa; Amateur Chmbr. Music Players. Hobbies: Folk Banjo-uke Playing; Camping; Sailing. Address: 350 Bleecker St., NYC, NY 10014, USA.

FRANKL, Peter, b. 2 Oct. 1935, Budapest, Hungary. Pianist. Educ: Franz Liszt Acad. of Music. m. Annie Feiner, 1 s., 1 d. Career: Appears regularly w. world famous orchs. & conds. in all 5 continents; Gives many solo recitals & chmbr. music concerts. Recordings: Complete Piano Music by Debussy & Schumann; Works by Mozart, Schubert, Chopin etc. Hons: 1st Prizes, Int. Competitions, Paris, 1957, Munich, 1957, Rio de Janeiro, 1959; Liszt Award for disting. Musicians, Budapest, 1958. Hon. Citizenship of Rio de Janeiro, 1960. Mgmt: Harrison Parrott Ltd. Address: 5 Gresham Gdns., London NW11 8NX, UK. 2,3.

FRANKLE, Hubert Axel Donato, b. 19 Jan. 1930, Geneva, Switzerland. Composer; Conductor; Opera Coach; Musician (Piano Accompanist. Harpsichord, Organ, Flute). Educ: Coll. Classique, Univ. of Geneva; Conserv. of Music, Geneva; Städtebudntheater, Biel-Solothurn, Switzerland; Studied Theory of Music Cond., var. instruments. div., 3 c. Debut: As comp., Radio Geneva w. songs, 1950; As cond., Geneva, 1951, Stadttheater, Solothrun, 1952. Career: Num. engagements incl. Städtebundtheater, Biel-Solothurn, 1952-57; Orch. Suisse Romande (Radio Geneva), for Geneva City, 1958-63; Stadttheatre, Basle, 1959; Opera Italiana (Milano), Musical Dir., European Tour, 1960; Chamber Orch. of the Quantz Coll., Baden-Baden, German Fed. Repub., 1963-65 (Inauguration); Osaka Phil. & Univ. Orchs., Japan; Fndr. & Musical Dir., Les Voix Unies, Choir Grp. of UN, 1967; Cerde Instrumental Int., & Musica Pro Pace, 1974. Var. appts. as Choir Dir. incl. Les Voix Unies, Choir Grp. of UN, 1967; Choeur lyrique de la Radio, Geneva, 1958-62; Tchr., Conserv. of Music, Geneva & Osaka Univ; Official Accomp., var. Concerts. Compositions incl: Divertissement, opus 5, pour Piano; L'Ode a L'OIT., Opus 8; Sonnerie de Cuivres, Geneva, 1970; Rhymes polychroiques, Ballet perf'd., Theatre Rose, Geneva. Num. Recordings. Contbr. to num. mags. in Geneva, UN Special, Union (ILO staff mag.). Mbrships: VP, 1973-74, Pres., 1974-75, Classe des Beaux Arts, Soc. des Arts, Geneva; Life mbr., committee, Soc. of Arts, Geneva; & Assn. Friends, Conserv., Geneva; SUIZA (Soc. Suisse des auteurs, compositeurs et editeurs); Union Suisse des Artistes Musiciens et VPOD; Assn. des Musiciens Suisses; Amateur Chamber Music Players Inc., NY. Hons: Prix Fernex, 1950; 1st Medal for Harmony; Medal, City of Kyoto, Japan, 1965. Hobbies: Astronomy; Philosophy; Psychology. Address: Rue des Artisans, 1229 Crans, Switzerland.

FRANKLIN, Alfred John, b. 2 Sept. 1929, Manchester, UK. Composer; Pianist; Teacher. Educ: Studied music privately, & at Coll. of Music. Career: Music Tchr.; Broadcasts of educl. music, Brass Band, Orchl. music & songs; Prod. of short documentary films, Educl. Visual Aids. Compositions: Peter Duck; Missee Lee; A Country Ramble; A Song of Manchester; In Derbyshire; Wonderful Wales, etc. Mbr., CGGB. Hobbies: Travel; Research in Folk & Rural Customs; Industrial & Historical Archaeology. Address: Tree Tops, 31 Crossefield Rd., Cheadle Hulme, Cheadle, Cheshire SK8 5PD, UK. 3.

FRANKS, Roderick, b. 31 May 1956, Shipley, W Yorks., UK. Principal Trumpeter. Educ: Huddersfield Schl. of Music; Post Grad., Royal Northern Coll. of Music. m. Dorothy Franks. Debut: The Maltings (Snape), Aldeburgh Fest. Career: Asst. Prin Cornet, Black Dyke Mills Band, 1973-76; Approx. 40 TV apps. in UK, 6 in Norway; Approx. 150 radio apps. as mbr. of Black Dyke Mills Band; Sev. broadcasts w. BBC Northern & Halle Orchs.; Prin. trumpet, Bergen Symph. Orch., Norway. Recordings: 10LP's. Mbrships: Pres., Brass Band Club of Norway; Soc. of Musicians (Norway). Hons: Hiles Gold Medal for Orchl. Playing, 1976-77, Royal Northern Coll. of Music. Hobbies: Skiing; Football; Squash. Address: c/o Bergen Symph. Orch., Lars Hillesgate 3A, 5000 Bergen, Norway.

FRANSMAN, Holger Alexander, b. 10 Feb. 1909, Helsinki, Finland. French Horn Player; Professor. Educ: Grad., Sibelius Acad., 1931. m. Karin Wahlroos, 1 d., 1 s. Debut: Soloist, Helsinki City Orch., 1940. Career: 1st Solo Horn Player, Helsinki City Orch., 1937-69; Tchr. of French Horn, Sibelius Acad., 1931-61; Sr. Tchr., ibid., 1961-69; Cond., Band., ibid., 1967-73; Soloist, symph. concerts, Finland, & chmbr. concerts, Finland & abroad; Comp. of many band arrs. Mbrships. incl: Govt., Union for Musicians, 1949-50, Chmn., Ctrl. Union of Wind Instrument Players. Hons. incl: Awards, Sibelius Acad. & City of Helsinki. Hobby: Numismatics. Address: Olavinlinnantie 4 A 28, 00900 Helsinki 90, Finland. 1, 28.

FRANZÉN, Olov Alfred, b. 22 Jan. 1946, Umea, Sweden. Composer; Cellist. Educ: Music High Schl., Stockholm, 1966-73. m. Ingeborg Axner-Franzén. Debut: as comp., Wind Quintet, Lund, 1963; as cellist, Köping, 1971. Career: Concerts in Europe, USA, Can.; perfs. on radio & TV; comps. played by num. orchs. in sev. countries & at ISCM, Reykjavik, 1973. Comps. incl: Beyond, 1973; Di Nuovo, 1974; The Vancouver Piece, 1975-76; Extension, 1977; Preludium, 1978. Recordings of new Swedish music. Mbrships: Harpans Kraft (group for new music), 1971-77; Soc. of Swedish Comps.; Fylkingen Soc., Stockholm; ISCM; Hobbies: Transcendental Meditation; Open-air life. Address: Grönkullarägen 2F, 87100 Härnösand, Sweden.

FRASER, Barbara, b. 12 Aug. 1933, Milwaukee, Wis., USA. Violinist. Educ: B. Mus., Wis. Conserv.; M. Mus., Eastman Schl. of Music. Career: Violinist, Rochester Phil.; Houston Symph.; Santa Fe Opera; Concertgebouwahest of Holland; Chgo. Symph. (current). Mbr: De Camerata Soc., Chgo. Recip. Performance Cert., Eastman Schl. of Music, 1955. Hobbies: Playing String Quartets; Raising parrots; Swimming. Address: 333 E Ont. St., Chgo., IL 60611, USA.

FRASER, Derek Peter, b. 5 Jan. 1929, Kingston, UK. University Lecturer. Educ: B Mus, London; LTCL; LRSM. m. Pamela Elizabeth Fraser, 1 s. Career: Pianist, Southern Africa, 1950s; Chmbr. & Concerto work in UK; Cond, Southern Africa, 1955-66, Vis. Cond., LSC mbrs., Engl. Symph. Orch., New Cantata Orch. of London; Fndr., New London Strings; Prof., TCM; Dir. of Music, Brunel Univ.; Sr. Lectr. in Music, Univ. of Nigeria. Comps: Elegy for Strings 1975; 12 Orchl. Pieces; mainly Educl Comps. Hobbies: Painting; Chess; Self-sufficiency. Address: Birdsong, Muckton Bottom, Louth, Lincs., UK.

FRASER, Norman George, b. 26 Nov. 1904, Valparaiso, Chile. Composer; Lecturer; Pianist. Educ: Music Educ. in London, Paris, Lausanne & Vienna. m. Janet Smith Fraser, 1 s. Career: Radio & Concert Work in Europe & S Am.; Brit. Coun. Lectures in many Univs.; Prof. of Music, Univ. of Chile, 1934. Compositions incl: Orchl., Chmbr., Choral, Solo Instrumental & Vocal publd. in Santiago, Buenos Aires, Paris & London. Many BBC Commercial Recordings. Publs: British Council Catalogue of British Music, 1946; UNESCO international Catalogue of recorded Folk Music, 1953. Contbr. to: Ency. Britannica; Musik in Geschichte und Gegenwart; Grove's Dictionary of Music & Musicians; Num. articles in music mags. in S Am., France & Brit. Mbrships: PRS. Hons: Tobias Matthay Silver Medal, 1925. Hobbies: Ethnomusicol; Walking; Eschatol. Address: 12 Corsica Rd., Seaford, Sussex BN25 1BB, UK.

FRASER, Shena Eleanor, b. 26 May 1910, Stirling, UK. Composer. Educ: ARCM. m. Laurence Beale Neame, dec., 3 s., 1d. Career: Piano recitals; Lectr.; Adult educ. tutor; Adjudicator. Compositions: Carillon (Christmas cantata); To Him Give Praise (choral suite); Child of Bliss (cycle of carols); Full Fathom Five (cantata); Carols for the Accompanist; Hornpipe & Jig for 2 Pianos; num. anthems, part-songs & instrumental pieces. Mbrships: CGGB. Hobbies: Reading; Walking. Address: The Coach House, The Oaks, Ospringe, Faversham, Kent ME13 0RR, UK.

FRAZEE, Jane, b. 16 July 1936, Cumberland, Wis., USA. Orff-Schulwerk Specialist. Educ: B Mus, Univ. of Wis.; MA, Univ. of Minn., Orff-Schulwerk study, Royal Conserv. of Music, Toronto, Can., & Orff Inst., Salzburg, Austria. m. James L Frazee. Career: on facs., Hamline Univ. & Macalester Coll., St. Paul, Minn.; Dir. of Orff Dev. Prog., Ind. Univ.; workshops for tchrs., & summer courses at other univs. throughout USA; Celebrations educl. TV series demonstrating Orff-Schulwerk, Univ. of Minn., 1973. Publs (ensembles for voices, recorders & Orff instruments); A Baker's Dozen, 1974; This is the Day, 1975; Strawberry Fair, 1977; American Folk Carols for Christmas. Contbr. to: Music Educl. Jrnl. Mbrships: Fndr., Minn. Chapt., Chmn., Higher Educ. Comm., Past Pres., Am. Orff-Schulwerk Assn.; MENC. Hobbies: Travel; Gardening; Cooking. Address: 24 S. St. Albans, St. Paul, MN 55102, USA. 27,29.

FRAZEUR, Theodore C, b. 20 Apr. 1929, Omaha, Neb., USA. Professor of Perucssion. Educ: B. Mus., Eastman Schl., Univ. of Rochester, 1952; M. Mus., ibid, 1956. m. Joyce S Frazeur, 1 s., 2 d. Career: TV & radio, Arthur Godfrey Show, w. Marimba Masters, 1955; Perf. Mbr. of the Omaha Symph. Orch., Erie Phil. Orch., Rochester Phil. Orch., Eastman Symph. Wind Ensemble; Mbr., Music Dept., SUNY at Fredonia, 17 yrs.; Prof. of Percussion; Ed., Music for Percussion, inc., NYC Compositions; Orchl. Music - poets In A Landscape, for chmbr. singers, percussion ensemble & harp; Chiastic, for string orch.; Uhuru, percussion ballet; Divertimento, for trombone & wind ensemble; Suite for Viola and Percussion Quartet; Suite for Orchestra; Allegro for Orchestra; Allegro Gioioso for Orchestra; Ballot, 'Four Beauties', Suite for Tuba & Orchestra; Film score, Spotlight on Fredonia, etc. Recordings: The Marimba Masters, Kendall Recording Corp.; The Percussionist, Mark Records; Some Music of Ted Frazeur. Contbr. to: The Percussionist; Mo. State Educators Jrnl., etc. Mbrships: Bd. Dirs., Percussive Arts Soc.; MENC; Chmn. for Percussion Music, NYSSMA, Manual of graded music lists. Hons: Perfs. Cert., Eastman Schl. of Music, 1956. Hobbies: Skiing; Trout Fishing. Address: 3 Westerly Dr., Fredonia, NY 14063, USA.

FRAZIER, Larry Richard, b. 5 Feb. 1947, Alexandria, La., USA. Vocalist. Basso; Assistant Professor of Music. Educ: B. Mus., La. State Univ., 1969; M. Mus., ibid, 1970; D. Mus., Fla. State Univ., 1976. Apprentice Artist, Santa Fe Opera, 1968; Fla. State Univ. m. Patricia A Kagan. Career: Leading Basso, Nat. Opera Co., 1970-71; Prin. Role, Elie Siegmeister, World Premier of The Plough & The Stars; maj. Opera, Solo Apps. w. San Antonio Symph., Shreveport Symph. Repertory Opera, Midland-Odessa Symph.; Asst. Prof., Tex. Tech. Univ., 1971-73, Tenn. Technol. Univ., 1973-. Mbrships: Nat. Assn. of Tchrs. of Singing; AGO; Phi Mu Alpha Sinfonia. Pk Kappa Lambda. Hons: Nat. Finalist, Artist Auditions, Nat. Assn. of Tchrs. of Singing, 1973; Nat. Finalist, Student Auditions, Nat. Fedn. of Music Clubs, 1967; Tex. State Winner, Oratorio Auditions, Nat. Fedn. of Music Clubs, 1973. Hobbies: Officiating at Sporting Events; Sailing; Golf; Showing & Breeding Engl. Bulldogs. Address: 800 E Spring St., Apt. H-10, Cookeville, TN 38501, USA.

FRCEK, Josef, b. 19 Mar. 1931, Prague, Czech. Composer; Trombonist. Educ: Grad., State Conserv. of Music, Prague, 1953; Dip., Dept. of Composition, Acad. of Musical Art, 1962. div., 1 d. Career: Mbr., Czech. Radio Symph. Orch., Tylovo Theatre Orch., & conductorless Chmbr. Orch., Prague; Prof., People's Conserv. of Prague. Compositions incl: 1st Str. Quartet (perf. Prague, 1950); 1st & 2nd Symph. Suites; Str. Quartets 3 & 4; Wind Quintet; var. arrs. of classical works for amateur chmbr. grps., radio & TV. Mbrships: Czech. Musicians Fund. Address: Chválova 1, Praha 3, Czech.

FREAS, Elizabeth H, b. 22 May 1943, Albany, NY, USA. Tympanist. Educ: Dip., New England Conserv. of Music, Boston, Mass., 1965. Career: Tympanist, Oklahoma City Symph. Orch., 1967-; Assoc. Prof. of Percussion, Oklahoma City Univ., 1971-. Mbr. Exec. Bd., Local 375, Am. Fedn. of Musicians. Address: Oklahoma City Symph. Orch., Civic Ctr. Music Hall, Oklahoma City, OK 73102, USA.

FRECCIA, Massimo, b. 19 Sept., Florence, Italy. Symphony Conductor. Educ: Conserv. Luigi Cherubini, Florence. m. Maria Luisa Azpiazu. Debut: w. Orchestra Santa Celia, Rome; Am. debut in 1938 at the Lewisjohn Stadium, NY cond. the NY Phil. Orch. Career: Musical Dir. & Cond. of the Havana Phil. Orch., 1939-43; Musical Dir. & Cond. of the New Orleans Symph. Orch., 1944-52; Musical Dir. & Cond. of the Balt. Symph. Orch., 1952-59; Chief Cond. of the Rome RAI Radiotelevisione Symph. Orch., 1959-65; Guest Cond., maj. symph. orchs. in USA, inclng. (7 consec. seasons) the NBC Symph. Orch. at invitation of Arturo Toscanini; Toured extensively in Aust. under sponsorship of Aust. Broadcasting Commission, 1963;

series of concerts in Tokyo, 1967; Toured S. Africa, 1968; Guest Cond. of London's maj. orchs. (London Phil., Royal Phil. & BBC Symph. Orch.); Has cond. in many European Fests. & cities. Recordings: on RCA Victor; Decca; EMI. Hons: Mus.D., Tulane Univ., New Orleans, La., 1950; Order of the Star of Italian Solidarity, 1957. Mgmt: Ibbs & Tillet, London, UK & Kozertdirektion, Munich, German Fed. Repub. Address: 25 Eaton Sq., London SW1, UK & Palo Laziale 00055, Rome, Italy. 2.

FREDERICK, Kurt, b. 4 Mar. 1907, Vienna, Austria. Professor Emeritus of Music. Educ: Grad., Violin & Comp., State Acad. of Music, Vienna; Grad., Cond., State Coll. of Music, ibid.; BS, Univ. of NM, USA; MMus, PhD, Univ. of Rochester. m. Gladys Morgan Miller, 1 s., 2 d. Career: Opera Coach & Cond., Free City of Danzig; 1st Violist, Orch. of the New Friends of Music, & Kolisch Quartet, USA, 1938-42; Fac. Mbr., Music Dept., Univ. of NM, Albuquerque, 1942-72; Prof. Emeritus, 1972-; Cond., Orch., Chmbr. Orch., Choral orgs., etc., Univ. of NM; Cond., Albuquerque Symph. Orch., Choral Assn., Opera Co., & Youth Symph., & Los Alamos Sinfonietta. World Premieres incl: Schoenberg, The Survivor of Warsaw; Krenek, 5th Symph. Mbrships: Bruckner Soc., NYC, Phi Kappa Phi. Address: 700 Griegos Rd., NW, Albuquerque, NM 87107, USA.

FREDRICKS, Richard, b. 15 Aug. 1933, Los Angeles, Calif., USA. Operatic & Concert Baritone. Educ: AS (Engrng.), El Camino Jr. Coll., Calif.; Music study, Univ. of Denver & w. pvte. tutors. m. Judith Pennebaker, 2 d. Debut: w. NYC Opera, 1960. Career incl: leading opera roles w. Metropol. Opera; NYC Opera; Opera Cos. of San Fran., New Orleans, Balt., Miami, Phila. Lyric, Houston, Ft. Worth, Hawaii, Memphis, Florentine Opera of Milwaukee, Newark, Phila. Grand; perfs. incl: Nottingham in Roberto Devereux, 1975; Germont in La Traviata, 1976; Concert performances w. leading Symph. Orchs. in USA, Can. & Israel; var. TV appearances incl. soloist w. Boston Pops Orch. & WNET Opera Theatre. Hobbies: Flying; Sailing; Running. Mgmt: Columbia Artists Mgmt. Address: c/o Edgar Vincent Assocs., 145 E 22nd St., No. 804, NY, NY 10022, USA.

FREDRIKSSON, Risto Lennart, b. 5 June 1941, Turku, Finland. Cellist. Educ: Sibelius Acad.; Music High Schl., Cologne, Germany. m. Ritva Forsstrom, 1 s., 2 d. Debut: Helsinki, 1967. Career: 2nd Solo Cellist, Orch. of Nat. Opera of Finland; Mbr., Suhonen Quartet & Helsinki Chmbr. Orch.; Recitals in Finland; Soloist w. Finnish Orchs.; Solo & Chmbr. Music, radio & TV; Also in Sweden, Germany & USSR. Recording: 4th Str. Quartet of Sallinen. Mbrships: Fedn. of Musicians, Finland. Administrative Body, Nat. Opera. Hobby: Sailing. Address: Maamonlahdentie 1 i 51, 00200 Helsinki 20, Finland.

FREED, Dorothy Whitson, b. 10 Feb. 1919, Dunedin, NZ. Reference Librarian; Composer. Educ: Mus B, Victoria Univ. of Wellington, 1958; Dip., NZ Lib. Schl., 1959. m. William Ian Freed (dec.), 1 s., 2 d. Career: Comp. of unpubld. music for local stage, choirs, small orchs. & chmbr. grps., 1959-; broadcasts incl. Radio NZ, Aust. Broadcasting Commn. & BBC; live perfs. of vocal & chmbr. works, NZ, Aust., UK & USA; Ref. Libn., Vic. Univ. of Welllington, 1968-. Comps. publs: Whence comes this rush of wings afar, carol for women's voices (in Second Treasury of Christmas Music, ed. Wm. L Reed, 1967) -recorded, Kiwi Records, 1969. Publs: Music for amateur choirs & orchestras in New Zealand, 1960. Contbr. to: Grove's Dict., 6th ed.; Directory of Music Rsch. Libs., in press; NZ Libs.; Continuo; Fontes artis musicae. Mbrships. incl: Full Comp. Mbr., Australasian Performing Right Assn., 1960-; Sec., Wellington Committee, Comps. Assn. of NZ, 1976-; Int. Assn. of Music Libs. Recip., prizes for comp. Address: 2B Gladstone Terr., Kelburn, Wellington 5, NZ.

FREEGARD, Michael J, b. 3 Mar. 1933, London, UK. Manager. Educ: Haileybury & ISC; Fellow, Inst. of Chartered Secs. & Admnstrs. Career: Asst. Sec., The Performing Right Soc. Ltd., London, 1964; Sec., ibid, 1966; Dpty. Gen. Mgr., ibid, 1968; Gen. Mgr., 1969-; Radio Apps., Lectures, UK, Commonwealth, USA. Contbr. to: Symposium on the Public Lending Right, 1971; num. profl. publs. Mbrships: Administrative Coun., Int. Confederation of Socs. of Authors & Comps., 1969-; Exec. Bureau, ibid, 1969-; Pres., Exec. Bureau, ibid, 1972-75; Brit. Copyright Coun.; Hons: Mbr. Royal Soc. of Musicians, 1975-; Order of Arts & Scis. (Egypt), 1976. Address: Gen. Mgr., The Performing Right Soc. Ltd., 29/33 Berners St., London W1P 4AA, UK.

FREEMAN, Elizabeth, b. 31 July 1951, Cleveland, Ohio, USA. Harpsichord Player. Educ: grad. prog., Juilliard Schl. of Music; BFA, Calif. Inst. of the Arts. m. Laurence Bergreen. Debut: London, 1977; NY, 1978. Career: perfs. as soloist throughout

USA, in London & Cambridge, UK. Hons: Juilliard Scholarship. Hobbies: Visual Art. Address: c/o Bergreen, 980 5th Ave., NY, NY 10021, USA.

FREEMAN, Isadore, b. 5 Sept. 1912, Paterson, NJ, USA. Musician; Pianist. Educ: BMus, Effa Ellis Perfield Schl. of Music, 1941; Pedagogical Dip., ibid; Courses at NY Coll. of Music; Cert. Affil. Oxford Piano Tchr.; Pvte. piano study w. Dr Clarence Adler of NY. m. Sara Levin. Career: Pianist, Instr., Lectr., Commentator, Chmbr. Music Perf., Cultural Prof. Cons.; Music Prof., Rutgers, NJ, Open Univ. Prog.; As pianist has appeared on Radio & Concert Platform as recitalist, accomp., ensemble perf. & lectr.; Conducts solo & grp. classes for children & adults in piano playing & music appreciation; Adjunct Prof. of Music, Kean Coll., Union, NJ; Dir., Cultural Progs. Inc.; Chmn., Federate Arts Coun. of Fair Lawn, 1965-79; Fair Lawn Summer Fest. of Music, 1971-79. Wrote weekly column for the Fair Lawn Beacon for sev. yrs. Mbrships: Past Pres., Rotary Club of Fair Lawn, 1953-54; Fndr. & Chmn., Flame Friends of the Living Arts & Music Enjoyment, 1961-71; Dir., Cultural Progs., Fair Lawn, 1961-76; Chmn., Fed. Arts Coun., Fair Lawn, 1968-75; Sec., Am. Fedn. of Musicians, Local 248, Paterson, NJ, 1974, 75, 76, 77. Hons. incl: Special Award for Cultural Activities in Community of Fair Lawn, 1969. Hobbies: Reading; Travel; Photography. Address: 13-08 Bellair Ave., Fair Lawn, NJ 07410, USA. 6, 28.

FREEMAN, Robert Bruce, b. 5 Aug. 1952, Toronto, Can. Organist & Choirmaster; Composer & Arranger; Lecturer; Pianist. Educ: Assoc. in Piano & Organ, Royal Conserv., Toronto; MusB, Univ. of Toronto; Proficiency Award, RCCO; MA, Univ. of Guelph. m. Hallie Freeman, 1 d. Career: Ch. Organist & Choirmaster, w. perf. for special sacred progs.; Org. & Cond., Massed Choirs; Organist, Knox Presby. Ch., Toronto; Organist & choirmaster, W. Ellesmere United Ch., Toronto. Comps: Choral arr. of Six Familiar Hymns; Festival Te Deum, Benedictus; Missa Brevis in B Flat; num. instrumental hymn tune descants; Fest. Organ & Brass. Recordings: Pvte. for interch. uses. Mbrships: MRCM; Royal Can. Coll. of Organists; Ontario Choral Fed. Contbr. to: AGO/RCCO Music; United Ch. Observer, etc. Hons: Winner, Organ & Choir competitions. Address: 68 Lionhead Trail, Scarborough, Ont. M1B2J6, Can.

FREEMAN, Robert Norman, b. 29 Aug. 1939, Vancouver, BC, Canada. Musicologist. Educ: BA, MA, PhD, UCLA, USA; Clarinet, Akademie für Musik und Darstellende Kunst, Vienna. m. Angelika Freeman, 2 d. Career: Fac., Dept. of Music, Univ. of Calif., Santa Barbarta. Publs: The Practice of Music at Melk Abbey in the Eighteenth Century (in preparation). Contbr. to Die Musikforschung; Opera Jrnl.; Groves Dictionary of Music; Notes. Mbrships: Int. Musicol. Soc.; Am. Musicol. Soc.; Am. Soc. for Eighteenth Century Studies; Int. Albrechtsberger-Gesellschaft. Hons: 1st Prize, Atwater Kent Awards, Musicol., UCLA, 1968; Fulbright Scholar, 1968-70. Address: 505 Hillgreen Dr., Beverly Hills, CA 90212, USA.

FREITAG, Erik, b. 1 Feb. 1940, Vienna, Austria. Composer; ViolinTeacher. Educ: Dip., Acad. of Music. m. Waltraud Freitag. Career: Composer; Violin Tchr., Conserv. of Vienna. Recordings: 3 Pieces for String Quartet; Divertimento for Wind Quintet; Limericks, 5 songs for medium voice & 6 instruments. Mbrships: Österreichischer Komponistenbund; Österreichische Gesellschaft für Zeitgenössische Musik; ISCM; Hons: Comp. Prize, Nord-Elbischetage, Hamburg, 1971; Prize, Austrian Ministry of Educ., 1975; Prize, City of Vienna, 1978. Address: Ruthnergasse 56/7/10, A1210 Vienna, Austria.

FRÉMAUX, Louis, b. 13 Aug. 1921, Aire sur Lys, France. Orchestral & Operatic Conductor. Educ: Nat. Conserv., Paris. Career: Chef d'orchestre permanent & Dir., l'Orchestre Nat. de L'Opéra de Monte Carlo, 1956-66; Dir., Orchestre de Lyon, 1968-71; Prin. Cond. & Musical Dir., City of Birmingham Symph. Orch. & Chorus, 1969-78; Chief Cond., Sydney Symph. Orch. (Aust.), 1979-. Num. recordings. Hons incl: Kt., Legion of Hon.; Order of Cultural Merit, Monaco; Hon. DMus, Univ. of Birmingham; Hon. RAM; Grands Prix du Disque (8 times); TMA Award (twice); Koussevitsky Award, 1973.

FRENCH, Patsy Ruth (Jones), b. 21 Jan. 1936, Muncie, Ind., USA. Public School Music Teacher (strings, orch.); Private Teacher for 15 yrs, teaching violin & viola. Educ: BSEduc., Ball State Univ., 1958; MAEduc., ibid, 1964; Licensed in State of Ind. as Tchr. & Supvsr. of Music. m. John R French, 1 s., 1 d. Career: Mbr., Muncie Symph. Orch., 4 yrs.; Indpls. Civic Orch., 11 yrs. (4 yrs. as Prin Violist); Indpls. Phil. (community orch.), 4 yrs.; Tchr. of Strings for Metropolitan Schl. Dist. of Perry Township, Ind.; organized 1st Perry Township Middle Schl. Symph. Mbrships: Am. String Tchrs. Assn.; MENC; Ind. Music Educators Assn.; Ind. Schl. Music Assn. Perf. Mbr. of Str. Quartet & community orchs.; 3 yrs. mbr. Bd. of Dirs., Indpls.

Phil. Orch.; 3 yrs. VP, ibid. Hobbies: Swimming; Camping. Address: 837 E Stop 11 Rd., Indianapolis, IN 46227, USA. 27.

FRENI, Mirella, b. Moderna, Italy. Opera Singer. Debut: 1955. Career: apps. at major opera houses throughout world inclng: La Scala, Milan; Royal Opera House, Covent Gdn.; Met. Opera, NYC; Vienna State Opera; fest. apps. inclng. Glyndebourne & Salzburg Fests. Roles incl: Nanetta, Falstaff; Mimi, La Bohème; Zerlina, Don Giovanni; Susanna, Adina, L'elisir d'amore; Violetta, La Traviata; Desdemona, Otello. Has recorded. 16.

FRERICHS, Doris Coulston, b. 20 Apr. 1911, Edgewater, NJ, USA. Pianist; Teacher; Composer. Educ: Grad., Post-Grad. Artist's Degree, Juilliard Schl. of Music. Debut: Town Hall, NYC, 1943; Europe, 1961. Career: Solo tours, USA; toured Europe, 1961; perfs. on Nat. Radio Networks; w. NY Phil. Septet; perf. in USSR, 1976; apps. w. orchs.; TV perf., World's Fair, 1965; on Piano Facs., Juilliard Schl. of Music, 1934-48; Co-operating Fac., Tchrs. Coll., Columbia Univ., 1948-55; Barrington Schl. for Girls, 1939-42. Comps: From My Jewel Box; A Royal Suite; Piano Compositions USA; The Land of Tempo-Marks. Mbrships: incl: Assoc. Music Tchrs. League; Fac., NGPT; also adjudicator, 1932-; Life Mbr., VP, 1975-; French Huguenot Histl. Soc. of New Paltz, NY; Nat. Chmn., Am. Coll. of Musicians, 1957-; Nat. Dir. of Music & Art Progs., People-to-People Int., 1977-. Recip. many hons. Address: 227 Claremont Rd., Ridgewood NJ 07450, USA. 5.

FRERSMILLAN, Carlos Adalberto, b. 11 Aug. 1938, Temperley, Provincia de Buenos Aires, Repub. of Argentina. Composer; Teacher; Bassoon & Contrabassoon Player. Educ: Grad., Manuel Belgrano Nat. Nautical Schl., 1961; Conserv. of Music, Buenos Aires; Superior Inst. of Music, Colon Theatre; Avellaneda's Schl. of Orchl. Practice. Career incls: Contrabassoon & Bassoon, Teatro Colon Permanent Orch., 1965-; Alternate 1st & 2nd Bassoon, Ensemble Musical de Buenos Aires, 1967-73; Sev. apps. on radio as chmbr. soloist. Comps: Pequena Pieza para Guitarra; Derivaciones, 2 movements for guitar. Hons: 2nd Prize, comp., Asociacion Guitarristica de Salta; Mention of Hon. & Silver Medal, SADIC. Hobbies: Photography; Films; High fidelity. Address: Teatro Colon, Cerrito 618, Buenos Aires, Argentina.

FREUD, Eli, b. Trieste, Austria (now Italy). Conductor; Organist; Oboist; Harpsichord Player; Director of Library. Educ: Dip., Acad. of Music, Vienna; pvte. studies in Prague & Jerusalem. m. Judith Steiner-Freud, 1 d., 1 d. Career: Oboist in Vienna, Prague radio, Jerusalem Symph. Orch.; Cond. & concert organist in Israel, Europe, USA; stage & radio apps.; Fndr. & Dir., Israel Bach Soc.; Dir., music lib., Israel Broadcasting Authority. Comps: orchestral & chmbr. music (recorded). Recordings: Israeli organ music; as cond. of choir & chmbr. orch. of Israel Bach Soc., Tabor, by Ben Zwi. Mbrships: Israel Comps. League. Hobbies: Journalism; Building musical instruments. Address: 6 Shatz St., Jerusalem, Israel.

FREUDENTHAL, Otto, b. 29 July 1934, Gothenburg, Sweden. Composer; Pianist; Violist. Educ: TCL, UK; studied piano w. Ilona Kabos. Debut: (as pianist) Wigmore Hall, London. Career: Recitals & Concerts in UK, Germany, Switzerland, Netherlands, Scandinavia; Broadcasts; Tchr., Royal Coll. of Music, Manchester; Asst. to Dr. Otto Klemperer to 1973. Comps: Chmbr. music for Oboe & Viola, Viola & Piano; Chmbr. opera; In Highgate Cemetery, for str. orch., etc. Hons. incl: Harriet Cohen Medal for interpretation of Beethoven. num. recordings. Publ: (essay) Music & Equity (w. Irene Lotz). Hobbies: Farming; Beekeeping. Address: Bäckfall, 590 41 Rimforsa, Sweden.

FREY, Lia, b. 12 Aug. 1949, Crosby, Minn., USA. Opera Singer (Spinto Soprano). Educ: BMus (opera), MMus (voice), Ind. Univ., Bloomington, Ind.; As recip. of German Govt. stipend, Folkwang Hochschule, Essen, Germany, 1971-72. m. Eugene Rabine. Debut: Municipal Theatre, Bern, Switz. Career: engagements in Switz. (Bern) & Germany (Flensburg, Nürnberg, & Hagen); Guest engagements, Bielefeld, Hagen, Osnabrück, Eutin Summer Fest. (Germany); Concerts & recitals, Germany & Switz. & in USA. Mbrships: Pi Kappa Lambda; Mu Phi Epsilon. Hons: Finalist, Metropolitan Opera Auditions, 1971. Hobbies: Photography; Handiwork (Sewing & Knitting); Cooking. Address: Berlinerstr. 102, 5800 Hagen 7, German Fed. Repub.

FREYHAN, Michael, b. 31 Aug. 1940, London, UK. Pianist; Violinist; Harpsichord & Viola Player. Educ: MA, King's Coll., Cambridge; LRAM. Debut: Wigmore Hall, London, 1963. Career: 3 yrs. Ldr., Nat. Youth Orch.; Recitals (chamber music) & broadcasts on radio & TV in Europe, USA, S America, Far East, Aust. & NZ; Solo apps. on BBC & at Royal Fest. Hall; formely repetiteur, Glyndebourne Opera & Tchr. at Reading Univ. & Summer Schls. in England, USA, Spain, & Aust.; currently tchr. at Birmingham Schl. of Music. Comps: Toy Symphony. Mbrships: ISM; Musicians Union; Hons: Major Scholarship in Music, King's Coll., Cambridge. Hobby: Travel. Address: 15 Chelmsford Square, London NW10 3AP, UK.

FRIAR, Ernest Richard, b. 21 Jan. 1939, St. Helens, Lancs., UK. Music Advisor. Educ: RMCM, 1957-60; GRSM; ARMCM. m. Christine A Banks, 1 s., 2 d. Hd. of Music Dept., Quarry Bank High Schl., Liverpool, 1960-67; Hd. of Music Dept., New Heys Comprehensive Schl. Liverpool, 1967-70; Deputy Dir., Holland, Lincs., Co. Music Schl. & asst. Co. Music Advsr., 1970-71; Co. Music Advsr., Holland, Lincs., & Dir., Holland Rural Music Schl., 1971-74; Music Advsr., London Borough of Enfield, 1975-. Contbr. to Junior Education Mags. Mbrships: Rural Music Schls. Assn.; Music Advsrs. Nat. Assn.; Enfield Schls. Music Assn. (VP, vice chmn., 1978-79, Chmn., 1979-80). Hobbies incl: choral training; Playing organ; Lit.; Gardening; Walking; Comp. Address: 7 Wood View, Cuffley, Herts. EN6 4RE, UK.

FRIBEC, Krešimir, b. 24 May 1908, Daruvar, Yugoslavia. Composer. m. Ljerka Jakovac. Career: Music Ed., Zagreb Radio & TV, 1943-64; Comp., 1955-. Comps incl: Vibrations, ballet, 1955; Lamento for Strings, 1967; Heliophony for orch., 1969; Lady Chatterley, ballet, 1970; Oceania for orch., 1970; Heretic, opera after the novel by I Supek, 1971; Medea, ballet, 1975. Comps. recorded: Vibrations; Lamento; Heliophony. Mgmt: ZAMP (Inst. for the Protection of Performing Rights), U1. 8. maja 37, YU 41000 Zabreg, Yugoslavia. Address: Duklijaninova 1l, Zagreb, Yugoslavia.

FRICK, Gottlob, b. 1906, Germany. Operatic Bass. Educ: studied w. Neudörfer-Opitz; Stuttgart Opera Chorus. Debut: Bayreuth Fest., 1930. Career: Coburg Opera, 1934; Freiburg-im-Breisgau & Königsberg Opera; Dresden Opera, 1940-50; W Berlin City Opera, 1950-; regular apps., Vienna & Bavarian State Operas; Guest Artist, Covent Gdn., London, & Met. Opera, NYC; noted for Wagnerian roles, Daland, Hermann, King Heinrich, King Mark, Pogner, Gurnemanz, Fasolt, Hunding, Hagen, etc.; Oratorio perfs. Hons: Verdienstkreuz, 1st class; Grosse Bundesverdienstkreuz; Österreichische Ehrenkreuz für Wissenschaft und Kunst, 1st class. 16.

FRICKER, Peter Racine, b. 5 Sept. 1920, London, UK. Composer. Educ: FRCO; ARCM. m. Helen Clench. Career: Dir. of Music, Morley Coll., London, 1953-64; Prof. of Music, RCM, 1955-64; Prof. of Music, Univ. of Calif., Santa Barbara, 1964-. Compositions incl: 5 Symphs.; Two Violin Concertos; Concertos for Piano, Viola; Five Concertantes; Oratorio, The Vision of Judgement; Magnificat; Chamber Music; Music for Piano, Organ, Chorus, Guitar, Music for Films & Radio. Contbr. to: The Listener; Soundings; The Sunday Times. Mbrships. Comps. Guild of Gt. Brit.; Royal Phil. Soc.; ISM; Am. Soc. Univ. Comps.; Coll. Music Soc., USA; Int. Soc. for Contemporary Music. Hons. incl: Clement's Prize, 1948; Koussevitsky Award, 1949; Collard Fellowship, 1955; Freedom City of London, 1958; Order of Merit, Fed. German Repub., 1965; Hon. Mbr., RAM, 1966. Hobby: Travel. Address: 5423 Throne Ct., Santa Barbara, CA 93111, USA. 1,2,3,9,14,16,21.

FRID, Geza, b. 25 Jan. 1904, Maramarossziget, Hungary. Composer; Pianist. Educ: studied w. Bartok, Kodaly. m. Ella Van Hall, 1 s. Career: Concert Tours, Perfs. in Italy, UK, Indonesia, Siam, Egypt, France, Israel, USSR. Turkey, Netherlands, Suriname, Dutch Antilles, Venezuela, USA & throughout Europe & S. Am., 1926-74; settled in Amsterdam, Holland, 1929; Temporary Cond., Radio Phil. Orch., Djakarta, Indonesia, 1948-49; Radio Perfs. in UK, all countries in Europe. Compositions incl: 4 Str. Quartets; opera parodistica, De Zwarte Bruid; Chamber music & Etudes Symphoniques; Concerti, 2 violins & orch.; piano & choir; Variations on a Dutch Folksong, orch. & choir; Paradou, symphonic fantasy; Suite for orch. Toccata for orchestra; Recip. num. hons. for comps. Address: 63 Van Eeghenstraat, Amsterdam, Netherlands.

FRIDMAN, Ruth, b. 8 May 1921, Mexico City, Mexico (Argentine Nat.). Musical Researcher. Educ: Manuel de Falla Municipal StateSchl., Buenos Aires, Argentina; Fac. of Philos. & Arts, ibid.; Piano studies, 1927-. m. J Niemetz, dec., 2 s. Career: Rsch. into vocal sonorous rhythms in babies; Pioneer in theatre classes for parents; Creator, class-show for parents "Let Us Sing With Mama", 1968. Comps. incl: 12 musical stories, 1966; Calesita de Canciones para jugar, 1976. Recordings incl: Let Us Sing With Mama, 1968. Publs. incl: Los comienzos de la conducta musical, 1974. Contbr. to: MEJ; JRME. Mbrships: ISME; OMEP. Hons incl: Hon. degree, Manuel de Falla Conserv.; Fulbright Grant, 1972. Hobby: Gardening. Address: Coronel Diaz 1564-60C, Buenos Aires 1425, Argentina.

FRIED, Miriam, b. 9 Sept. 1946, Satu Mare, Rumania. Violinist. Educ: Tchrs. Dip., Perf. Cert., Rubin Music Acad., Tel Aviv, Israel; w. Josef Gingold, Music Schl., Ind. Univ.; w. Ivan Galamian, Juilliard Schl. of Music, NYC. m. Paul Bliss. Career: has appeared w. major orchs. in USA & Europe, inclng. Boston, Phila., Chgo., LA & Cleveland orchs., LSO, RPO, New Philharmonia, LPO, Munich Phil., Frankfurt, Stuttgart & Hamburg orchs. Recordings: live perform of final round in Queen Elizabeth competition on Deutsche Gramoaphone; Chevalier St. George-Symphonie Concertante for 2 Violins & String Orchestra, on CBS. Hons: 1st Prize, Paganini Int. Competition, Italy, 1968; 1st Prize, Queen Elisabeth Competition, Brussels, 1971. Mgmt: Harold Shaw Inc., NY., Worldwide; Harold Holt Ltd., London. Address: 1885 Ganyard Rd., Akron, OH 44313, USA.

FRIEDLANDER, Annekate Emma, b. 24 May 1902, Berlin, Germany. Music Teacher; Pianist. Educ: Berlin Acad.; Amsterdam Conserv. (Dip.); Tchng. Dip., Music Sem., Cologne; LRAM. m. Prof. Hans F Friedlander, 1 d. Debut: Recital, Bechsteinsaal, Berlin. Career: Pvte. Tchr., Berlin; Music Tchr., Sutton Coldfield, UK, 1942-47, Friary Schl., Lichfield & Edgbaston HS., 1947-48, Portsmouth, HS for Girls, 1948-68; Broadcast, Berlin, 1938; Piano recitals in Germany, Holland & UK (specialist in Beethoven; performed cycle of all 32 sonatas on sev. occasions in Univ. Ext. Lectures, Portsmouth). Contbr. to: The Friend; Musical Interpretation; Mbrships: ISM; Pres., Portsmouth Music Club; Quaker Fellowship of Arts. Hobbies: Painting; Rug Making & other house crafts. Address: 12 Grove Rd., Havant, Hants, PO9 1AR, UK. 3,27.

FRIEDLER, Egon, b. 13 Aug. 1932, Vienna, Austria. Music Critic. Educ: Violin study, 7 yrs. m. Roje Etel Kanovich, 2 d. Career: Music Critic, El Pais newspaper, 1961-. Publs: Arnold Schoenberg, 1976. Contbr. to profl. publs. Mbr., Interamerican Music Critics Assn. Address: Solano Antuña 2749/101, Montevideo, Uruguay. 3,28.

FRIEDMAN, Viktor, b. 23 Sept. 1938, Moscow, USSR. Concert Pianist. Educ: Central Music Schl., Moscow Conserv.; Master's degree, 1962, PhD, 1965, ibid. Career: Concert pianist, perf. in solo recitals & w. orch., Am., Europe & Asia; Piano tchr., 19 yrs. Sev. recordings. Hons: Gold Medal, Moscow Conserv., 1962. Mgmt: Int. Concert Administration, Netherlands; de Valmalette, France; Columbia, USA. Address: 2101 Chestnut St., Apt. 622, Phila., PA 19103, USA.

FRIEDMANN, Moshe, b. 23 Sept. 1947, Oradea, Rumania. Cellist. Educ: Rubin Acad. Music, Jerusalem, Israel; Dip., solo studies, Conserv. Europeen de Music, Paris, France. m. Sarah Friedmann, 1 s. Career: Mbr., Israel Broadcasting Symph. Orch.; Apps., solo & chmbr. music concerts, Israel & France; Recorded Beethoven Sonatas, Israeli Radio. Hons: Norman Fndn. Musical Prizes, 1965-66, '67-68, '69-70; Schlrship., High Solo Studies, French Govt., 1975-76. Hobbies: Photography; Excursions. Address: 89 Rue Nollet, 75017 Paris, France.

FRIEMAN, Zbigniew, b. 8 Jan. 1927, Warsaw, Poland. Teacher; Viola Player; Performer of Chamber Music; Conductor. Educ: MA, Lodz Acad. of Music, 1954. m. Maria Frieman, 2 children. Debut: Perf., Chmbr. Music, Poznan, 1950; Soloist, Polish radio, 1951. Career: Soloist w. Polish Phil. Soc., radio & TV; Cond., Poland, Czechoslovakia, W & E Germany, Holland, Austria, Italy, France & Spain; Own chmbr. orch. Pro Muzica, Lodz; Dean, Instrumental Fac., Lodz Acad. of Music. Num. recordings. Mbr. Polish Assn. of Music Artist. Hons. incl: Gold Decoration, Polish Assn. of Music Artists; Gold Medal from Herbert von Karajan, 1970. Hobbies: Yachting; Line Fishing. Mgmt: Polish Artistic Agcy., Pagart, Warsaw. Address: 90 145 Lodz ul. Narutowicza 99 m 25, Poland.

FRIEMANN, Witold, b. 20 Aug. 1889, Konin, Poland. Composer; Pianist; Pedagogue. Educ: Dip. of Warsaw Conserv. m. Irena Lelewel, 1 s. Debut: Piano Recital in Leipzig. Kauthaus, 1914. Career: Prof., Cond. Class, Conservatoire, Polish Soc. of Music, Lwow, 1921-29; Dir. of the State Conservatoire in Katowice (& its Organiser); Mil. Schl. of Music, Katowice, 1929-33; Hd. of Music Sect., Polish Radio, Warsaw, 1934-39. Compositions: approx. 1200 inclng: 24 Concertos for var. solo instruments & symph. Orch.; 3 Operas - Gewont, Kasai, Polish Folk Mystery Play; 6 cantatas for soloist, choir & symph. orch.; Quartets, quintets; 3 symphs.; 5 Mazovia Suites for violin & combinations; approx. 600 comps. for piano solo; 80 works for violin, viola, cello (sonatas, suites); 350 songs (soloist w. piano accomp.); Choral & capella comps. w. piano accomp. Mbr., Polish Assn. of Authors & Comps. Hons: Prize, Min. of Culture & Art; Prize, Min. of Nt. Defense. Hobbies: Hunting; Horse-riding. Address: Laski Warszawskie 05-891, Zaklad dia Ociemnialych, Poland.

FRIEND, Lionel, b. 13 March, 1945, London, Uk. Conductor. Educ: RCM, London, 1963-67; London Opera Centre, 1967-68; ARCM; LRAM. m. Jane Hyland, 2 c. Debut: Welsh Nat. Opera, La Traviata, 1969. Career: Staff Cond., Glyndebourne Opera, Welsh Nat. Opera; Kapellmister, Staatstheater, Kassel, German Fed. Repub.; Staff Cond., English Nat. Opera; Guest apps., Hungarian Radio Symph. Orch., BBC Symph. Orch., other BBC orchs.; London Sinfonietta, Nash Ensemble, Melos Ensemble, etc. Recordings: Music of Anthony Payne. Hons: Var. Cond. prizes as student. Hobbies: Reading; Theatre. Address: 114 Abbeville Rd., London, SW4 9LU, UK.

FRIESER, Erika, b. 24 Sept. 1927, Aussig/Elbe, Czech. Pianist; Professor. Educ: Cologne Conserv.; Vienna Conserv.; Salzburg Mozarteum. Debut: Salzburg Fest. w. Vienna Phil., 1946. Career: Mbr., Vienna Trio, 1952-60; Duo w. cellist Gerhard Mantel, 1957-; Tours, S Am., USA, Japan, Near & Far East, most European countries; Apps. w. many famous conds. & orchs.; Prof. of Piano & chmbr. music, Salzburg Mozarteum. Recordings of works by Serge Rachmaninoff, Richard Strauss, Hans Pfitzner, Edvard Grieg, Felix Mendelssohn-Bartholdy, Max Reger. Hons: 1st Prize, Radio Frankfurt Competition, 1947. Address: Haus 188, A5322 Hof bei Salzburg, Austria.

FRISCHKNECHT, Hans Eugen, b. 8 May 1939, St. Gallen, Switz. Composer; Teacher; Organist; Harpsichord Player; Choirmaster. Educ: Berliner Hochschule für Musik; Paris Conserv. m. Eliane Kneuss. Debut: 1960. Career: Concerts in Switz., France, Netherlands, Belgium, Germany; Comps. also played in USA, Can. & Japan; Music Tchr., Lehrerinnenseminar, Bern; Organist, Johanneskirche, Bern; Choirmaster, IGNM-Vokalsolisten, Bern. Comps: Klaviermusik in 5 Teilen; 9 Stücke fur Tonband; Posaunen fur Stimme und Orgel. Contbr. to reviews. Mbrships: Neue Horizonte; Pres., IGNM, Sektion Bern; Pres., Musikpädagogische Vereinigung, Bern. Recip. 1st Prize for improvisation, Organ Competitions, St. Albans, 1971. Hobby: Skiing. Address: Kräyigenweg 93, 3074, Muri, Switz.

FRISS, Gabor, b. 28 June 1926, Budapest, Hungary. Professor; Conductor; Composer. Educ: Dip., Budapest Acad. of Music. m. Magda Klein. Career incls: Hd., Methodol. Fac., Tchrs. Trng. Inst., Budapest Acad. of Music, 1966-; Tchr. & Lectr.,var. instns., Benelux, Denmark & USA; concerts w. choir & orch. throughout Europe. Comps: A Story in the Forest; choral works; songs; accomps. Recordings: contemp. Danish & Hungarian works w. Danish Broadcst Choir; pre-classical works, ibid. Num. publs. inclng: Musical Education in Hungary, 1966; Methods for the Teaching of Music to Children, 1971; From So-Mi to Folksong, 1971; Pre-instrumental Music Education Method, 1971; From Folksong to World Music, 1976. Ed., Parlando educl. jrnl. Mbrships: Nat. Coun. of choirs; Assn. of Hungarian Musicians. Recip., num. musical & pedagog. hons. Hobbies: Collecting Folk Art & Music; Photography. Address: Damjanich ut. 14, 1071 Budapest, Hungary.

FRISTORP, Karl Göran, b. 26 May 1948, Skara, Sweden. Singer; Guitar Player. Educ: 5 yrs. guitar studies at Gothenburg Conserv. m. Ann-Charlotte, 1 d. Career: TV & radio perfs. throughout Europe; leading part in Leonard Bernstein's Mass, 1975. Recordings: 3 LPs of own comps.; 2 LPs of music to Swedish poets; 2 LPs w. other singers. Mbrships: STIM; SKAP. recip. SKAP Comps. Award, 1979. Hobbies: Food & Wine; Angling; Travel. Mgmt: Sonet Records, Sweden. Address: Stugvägen, 32, 16146, Sweden.

FRITSØ, Egil Gerhart, b. 27 Sept. 1941, Drammen, Norway. Percussionist. Educ: Pvte. studies w. Bobben Hagerup, Per-Erik Thorsen. m. Berit Fritso, 1 d., 1 s. Career: Musician lieutenant, Staff Band of the Norwegian Army, Oslo; Theatre, radio & TV apps. Hobby: Stamps. Address: Rosslyngveien 8E, 3408 Tranby, Norway.

FRITTER, Genevieve Davisson, b. 13 Dec. 1915, Clarksburg, W.Va., USA. Violinist; Composer. Educ: B Mus., Judson Coll.; grad. study, Birmingham Conserv., Ala.; Cinn. Conserv.; Juilliard Summer Schl. m. Charles Eldon Fritter, 2 d. Career: Violinist, w. ballet & opera orchs.; concerts at Kennedy Ctr. for Performing Arts, Wolf Trap Farm Pk. & Nat. Gall. of Art, Wash., DC area; Past Concertmaster, Nat. Ballet Orch.; Music Dir., Montgomery Ballet Co., Md., 12 yrs.; Lectr. on writing ballets for children. Compositions: Monotone, 1944; Judean Hills Are Holy, 1961; num. unpubl. works incl. chmbr. music & 6 ballets for children. Contbr. to: Mu Phi 'Triangle'. Mbrships: ASCAP; Mu Phi Epsilon; DC Fedn. of Musicians; Friday Morning Music Club of Wash., DC; Christ Cong. Ch. Hons: Composition Awards, Ala. Fedn. of Music Clubs, 1938, Nat. Comp., 1946; Outstanding Alumna Achievement Award, Judson Coll., 1966, etc. Hobbies: Sewing; Knitting; Travel. Address: 9012 Walden Rd., Silver Spring, MD 20901, USA.5.

FROBENIUS, Wolf, b. 1 June 1940, Speyer/Rhein, Germany. Musicologist. Educ: Studies in musicol., hist. of art & hist., Freiburg i. Br., Germany & Paris, France; PhD, Freiburg i. Br., 1968. Career: Staff Mbr., Handwörterbuch der musikalischen Terminologie, Akademie der Wissenschaften und der Literatur, Mainz, 1968-; Tchr., Univ. of Freiburg i. Br., 1971-. Publs: Johannes Boens Musica und seine Konsonanzenlehre, 1971. Contbr. to: Handwörterbuch der musikalischen Terminologie; Archiv für Musikwissenschaft; Grove's 6th Ed.; Die Musik in Geschichte und Gegenwart. Address: Britzinger Str. 68, D78 Freiburg i. Br., German Fed. Repub.

FROESE, Reinhard, b. 28 Nov. 1944, Mecklenburg, Graal Müritz, Germany. Musician & Teacher (Guitar & Vihuela). Educ: State Music Tchrs. Exam., 1970; Concert Exam, 1976; studied guitar w. Prof. Kersting & comp. w. Prof. Kelemen. m. Beate Froese, 1 s. Career: Dpty. Dir., Music Schl., Duisburg; Tchr., Music HS, Dortmund; Organizer, yrly. int. guitar seminar, Arbeitstage für Gitarre, Langwaden; Solo recitals throughout Europe; in duo w. Margaret Peckham, 1974-. Address: Grossenbaumer Allee 349, 41 Duisburg 28, German Fed. Repub.

FROHLICH, Willy, b. 20 June 1894, Strasbourg, France. Composer; Music Professor; Broadcaster. Educ: Strasbourg Univ.; High Conserv., Frankfurt; Studied Comp. w. Waldemar Baussnern, Cond. w. Fritz Bassermann & w. Prof. Moritz Bauer; Studied comp. w. Ewald Sträesser, cond. w. Erich Band, Stuttgart High School. Career: Musical Adviser, Stuttgart; Reviews for Radio & Daily Press, 1928-. Comps: Liederkreise nach Goethe, Holderlin, Morike, Binding, Morgenstern & CF Meyer; 6 Klaviersonaten; Sonaten f. Geiger, Viola, Violincello, Flöte, Saxophon & Klavier; Klaviertrio; 2 Klavier quintette; Str. Trio; 8 Str. Quartette; 3 Bläserquintette; Oktett f. Str. u Bläser; 3 Orgel Sonaten; 2 Orgel Konzerte; Choral f. Orgal; 13 Psalm f. 5 Stimmigen a Capella - Chor; 6 Symph. f. Orch.; Orch. Konzerte; 2 Saxophonkonserte; Klavierkonzert; Ballet Nansikaa. Address: Treitschkstr. 10, Stuttgart 75, German Fed. Repub.

FROHNE, Vincent Sauter, b. 26 Oct. 1936, La Porte, Ind., USA. Composer; Pianist; Professor of Music. Educ: B Mus, DePauw Univ., Ind.; M Mus, PhD, Eastman Schl. of Music; Hochschule fur Musik, Berlin; Techische Univ., Berlin; Goethe Institut; Aspen & Tanglewood Music Schl. m. Margaret Bourket, 2 d. Career incls: Fndr. Dir., Schiller Coll. Schl. of Music, Berlin, 1971-74; Prof. & Chmn. of Music for all Schiller Coll. Campuses; Coord., Comp. & Theory & Assoc. Prof. of Music., Univ. of Tulsa Schl. of Music, 1975-; Perfs. & broadcasts w. var. quartets & orchs. inclng: Indpls. Symph. Orch.; Berlin Phil. Orch. Comps. incl: Blake sons for soprano & orch, Op. 30. Var. recordings. Publs: Bote & Bock, Berlin. Mbr. profl. orgs. inclng: Fellow, Am. Acad. in Rome (FAAR); Pi Kappa Lambda; Phi Mu Alpha. Recip. num. grants & awards. Hobbies: Hi-Fi Equipment & Recording; Petrol-powered Model Airplanes. Address: 1515 E. 61st., Tulsa, OK 74136, USA.

FROMAGEOT, Henri Pierre-Marcel, b. 25 Jan. 1937, Paris, France. Biochemist; Flautist. Educ: Dip. Ingenieur chimiste, Ecole Nat. Supérieure Chimie, Paris, 1959; BS, Sorbonne, 1960; PhD, Cambridge Univ., UK, 1966; Rsch. Assoc., Rockefeller Univ., NYC, USA, 1966-69; Flute w. pvte. tutors inclng: René Le Roy, Julius Baker; Summer Schl. Music, Weikersheim an der Tauber, German Fed. Repub., 1951-57. m. Juana Zayas, 3 s. Career: Participant, num. concerts, Europe & US; Flautist, Cambridge Univ. Orch., 1964-66; Mbr., Schenectady Symph. Orch., 1970-; Biochem., Gen. Elec. Rsch. & Dev. Ctr., Schenectady, 1969-. Address: 1356 Valencia Rd., Schenectady, NY 12309, USA.

FROMME, Arnold, b. 2 Dec. 1925, Brooklyn, NY., USA. College Music Professor; Trombonist; Sackbutist. Educ: B Mus, M Mus, Manhattan Schl. of Music; PhD course, NY Univ.; studies at Juilliard, Paris Conserv. & other Schls. of Music. m. Catherine Thomasian Fromme, 1 s., 1 d. Career: Trombonist & Fndr., Am. Brass Quintet; Sackbutist, NY Pro Musica; Prin. Trombone, San Antonio, Tex., Symph., NYC Ballet Orch., Am. Ballet Theatre Orch.; freelance trombone work; Asst. Prof. Music, Jersey City State Coll. Compositions: 3 Short Studies for Brass Quintet. Recordings incl: 8 records w. NY Pro Musica; 10 records w. Am. Brass Quintet; num. as freelance. Publs: 6 Transcriptions of Early Music by G Gabrieli & others, 1961-69. Contbr. to profl. jrnls. VP, Am. Musical Instrument Soc.; Mbr., num. profl. assns. Address: 533 Cicilia Pl., Scotch Plains, NJ 07076, USA.

FROMMEL, Gerhard, b. 7 Aug. 1906, Karlsruhe, Germany. Composer; Teacher. Musical Educ: Hermann Grabner Musikhochschule, Leipzig; Master class Hans Pfitzner, Prussian Acad. of Arts; State exams. in comp. & theory of music. m. Gertrud Meuhaus, 2 s., 1 d. Career: Tchr., comp. & theory of music, Fokwangschule, Essen, 1929-32, Musikhochschule, Frankfurt am Main, 1933-44, Trossingen Hochschulinstitut für Musikerziehung, 1945-47, Musikhochschule, Heidelberg, 1947-56, Musikhochschule, Stuttgart, 1956-60; Prof., Staatliche Hochschule für Musik, Frankfurt am Main, 1960-. Compositions: 2 symphs.; Sev. orchl. works; Piano music; Chmbr. music; Vocal music; Ballets; Operas; Oratorios. Publs: Uber St. George in "Castrum Peregrini", Neue Klassik in der Musik; R. Wagner & der Geist der Antike. Mbrships: Süddeutscher Rundfunksrat, 1961-; Chmn., Baden-Württemberg sect., Deutscher Komponistenverband, 1961-. Hobbies: Poetry; Philos.; Langs. Address: Werderplatz 10, D 69 Heidelberg, German Fed. Repub.

FRONT, Theodore, b. 26 Nov. 1909, Darmstadt, Germany. Dealer in Musicological Literature. Educ: Conserv. of Music, Darmstadt; Univ. of Munich. m. Victoria Front. Career: Asst. Opera Stage Dir., Asst. to Carl Ebert, Städtische Oper, Berlin; Dealer in phonograph records & high fidelity components; founded present co., Theodore Front Musical Lit., 1961. Publs: 35 catalogues; Berlioz-Strauss, Treatise on Instrumentation (transl.). Mbrships: Am. Musicol. Soc.; Music Lib. Assn.; Int. Assn. of Music Libs.; Antiquarian Booksellers Assn. of Am.; Am. Booksellers Assn.; Soc. for Ethnomusicol.; Galpin Soc.; Royal Musical Assn. Hobbies: Music; Reading; Swimming; Hiking. Address: 1046 S Holt Ave., Los Angeles, CA 90035, USA.

FROSETH, James O, b. 14 Sept. 1936, Racine, Wis., USA. Professor of Music. Educ: B Mus, Univ. Mich., 1959; BS, Univ. Wis., 1965; PhD, Univ. Iowa, 1968. m. Martha Gail Millen Froseth, 2 s. Publs: The Inidivdualized Instructor (for winds & percussion), Books 1, 2, & 3, 1970, 1971, 1972, 1974; The Individualized Instructor (for soprano recorder), 1973; The First Individualized Concert Collection, 1974; The Individualized Instructor (for strings), Book One (w. Elizabeth A H Green & Robert Johnson), 1975; The Individualized Instructor, Supplementary, Books 1 & 2, 1972, 1973, 1975; The Individualized Instructor (Gen. music ed.) (w. Norma J Goecke), 1975; NABIM Recruiting Manual, 1974. Contbr. to Jrnl. Rsch. in Music Educ: Mbr., MENC. Address: Univ. Mich. Schl. Music, 2005 Baits Dr, Stearns Bldg., Ann Arbor, MI 48109, USA.

FROSETH, Nancy Ellen Aurora Thompson, b. 20 May 1936, Grand Forks, ND., USA. Musician (Recorders, Renaissance Reeds, Viola da Gamba). Educ: BA, Concordia Coll., Moorhead, Minn.; MS, Mus., Mankato State Coll., Minn.; Advanced study w. August Wenzinger & Hannelore Müller, Basel Schola Contorum, Switzerland. m. Kent Froseth Career: perfs. on WCCO TV & radio, & KSJN radio. Recordings: w. Concentus Musicus (Minn.); Spanish Music of the Goldn Age; Music from the Field of the Cloth of Gold; Music from the Royal Court of Cracow; w. Musica Antiqua; Music Antiqua Entertains. Mbrships incl: Mu Phi Epsilon; Schubert Club; Mpls. & St. Paul Musicians Unions. Hobby: Water Colours. Mgmt. Prog. Prods. Inc., Bud Goldstein. Address: 816 W. Arlington, St. Paul, MN 55117, USA.

FROST, Bobby Jean, b. 3 May 1932, Nashville, Tenn., USA. Musician (piano); Teacher. Educ: BMus, George Peabody Coll., Nashville. n. Lee E Frost, 2 d. Career: num. solo & orchl. apps. as concert pianist; commercial engagements as pianist/vocalist; theatrical engagements as music dir.; Piano instructor G Peabody Coll, 1959-60; Choral Dir., Pearl High, 1969-71; Music Dept. Chmn., Dir., McGavock Jazz-Rock Ensemble, McGavock Comprehensive High Schl., Nashville, 1971-; Music Dir., I Hear America Singing (TV), 1979; freelance clinician, composer & arr. sev. comps. var. recordings. Contbr. to The Instrumentalist. Mbrships incl: MENC (Sr. High General Music Committee); Nat. Assn. of Jazz Educators; AFM; Sigma Alpha Iota (past nat. chmn.); TMEA (Convention Chmn.); Tenn. Jazz & Blues Soc. (past sec.). Hons: Sigma Alpha Iota Sword of Honor, 1962, Rose of Honor, 1972. Hobbies: Bridge; Chess; Art. Address: 2137 June Fr., Nashville, TN 37214, USA.

FROST, Larry Stone, b. 18 May 1934, Neosho, Mo., USA. Orchestra Violist. Educ: BA, Univ. of Portland, Ore., 1956. m. Khaki Susanne Homesley Frost, 4 d., 2 s. Career: Ore. Symph., Portland; US 7th Army Symph., Germany; Kan. City Phil.; Dallas Symph. Orch.; Nat. Symph. Orch., Wash. DC; Prin. Violist, Perth Symph. Orch., WA, Aust., & Hobart Symph. Orch., Tasmania; TV & radio apps. for Aust. Broadcasting Commission in Perth & Hobart; Recordings of var. chmbr. music ensembles for Aust. Broadcasting Commission. Mbr., Am. Fedn. of Musicians. Hobbies: Children; Animals, esp. dogs & horses; Ch. work. Address: 101 Pecan St., Forreston, TX 76041, USA.

FROST, Ronald, b. 30 Mar. 1933, Bury, UK. Organist; Pianist; Choral Trainer. Educ: Royal Manchester Coll. of Music, 1951-55; ARCO, 1953; FRCO, 1955; B Mus, Dunelm, 1966.

m. Barbara Frost. Career: Staff, Royal Manchester Coll. of Music & Royal Northern Coll. of Music 1955-; Special Commnr. Guild Advsr., RSCM; Chorus Master & Organist, Halle Concerts Soc., 1972-; Dir. of Studies, Royal Manchester Coll. of Music, 1970-73; Sub-organist, Blackburn Cathedral, 1969-72. Mbr., RCO. Hons. incl: Limpus Prizes, RCO, 1953& 55; FRMCM, 1971; Hon. RSCM, 1973. Hobbies incl: Art. Address: 510 Holcombe Rd., Greenmont, Bury, BL4EJ, UK.3.

FROST, Thomas, b. 7 Mar. 1925, Vienna, Austria. Conductor; Writer; Director & Producer. Educ: Chattanooga Univ., Tenn., 1945-47; Yale Univ. Schl. of Music (studied comp. w. Paul Hindemith), 1947-51; studied cond. pvtely. w. Leon Barzin. m. Minnie von Selle, 1 s., 1 d. Debut: Cond. w. the Chattanooga Music Club, 1947. Career: Dir. of CBS Records, USA. Classical Dept.; Producer of Recordings; Cond. & Writer of Musical articles; Has produced recordings of: Isaac Stern, Rudolf Serkin, George Szell, Bruno Walter, Eugene Ormandy, Pablo Casals, etc. Compositions: Little Suite; Little Suite No. 2; other orchl. arrangements recorded by Eugene Ormandy. Contbr. to num. music mags. Mbrships: Hon. Mbr. of the Anton Bruckner Soc. of the USA: Bd., Carl Nielsen Soc. of the USA. Hons. incl: Three 'Grammys' from the Nat. Acad. of Recording Arts & Scis., 1963, '65, '66. Hobbies: Skiing; Mountain climbing, etc. Addres: 350 Central Park W, NY, NY 10025, USA.

FROUNBERG, Ivar, b. 12 April 1950, Copenhagen, Denmark. Composer; Organist. Educ: Dip., Organist & Choirleader, 1976; Comp. studies, 1972. Career: Organist, Kobenhavns Faengsler. Comps: Peripeti; Phantasia Dekadenz; Neuton-Triptique; Five eco's of a Sonata; Thrice-told Tunes; Faust-Variations I-VII. Contbr. to: Organistbladet. Mbr., committee of the Danish Sect. of ISCM. Hons: Dronning Ingrids romerske fond, 1977. Hobby: Hiking in the mountains of Norway & Greeland. Address: Melchiorsvej 1, DK-3450 Alleroed, Denmark

FRUGONI, Orazio, b. 28 Jan. 1921, Davos, Switz. Concert Pianist; Music Educator. Educ: M Mus., Giuseppe Verdi Conserv., Milan; Conserv. of Geneva; grad. studies, Chigiane Acad., Siena & St. Cecilia Acad., Rome. m. Janne Preston, 1 d. Debut: NY, 1947. Career: has given concerts thru'out world; Chmn., Music Dept., Villa Schifanoia Grad. Schl. of Fine Arts, Florence, 1967-; on Fac., Luigi Cherubini Conserv., Florence, 1972-; Mbr., Nat. Music Coun., Min. of Entertainment & Tourism, Rome, 1974-; Aidem, Press, 1975-; Prof. Luigi Cherubini Conserv. Has made num. recordings for Vox Prodns., inclng. concertos by Beethoven, Chopin, Khatchaturian, Kaio & Liszt. Contbr. to: Musical Am.; Musical Courier. Mbrships: Prefect, E. Florence Rotary Club; Chmn., Music Sect., Compagnia del Paiolo, Florence. Recip. of Prize of Virtuosity, Geneva, 1945. Hobby: Mod. Art. Address: 3 San Pietro, 1-53040 Cetona (Siena), Italy. 2,3,14,19,28.

FRUHBECK de BURGOS, Rafael, b. 15 Sept. 1933, Burgos, Spain. Conductor. Educ: Music Acads., Bilbao, Madrid & Munich; Univ. of Munich. m. Maria Carmen Martinez, 1959, 1 s., 1 d. Career: Chief Cond., Municipal Orch., Bilbao, 1958-62; Music Dir. & Chief Cond., Spanish Nat. Orch., Madrid, 1962-; Music Dir. & Chief Cond., Dusseldorf Symphoniker, 1966-; Hons: Gran Cruz al Merito Civil, Orden de Alfonso X; Orden de Isabel la Catolica. Mgmt: Wilfred Van Wyck Ltd., 80 Wigmore St., London W1H OBN. Address: Madrid 7, Reyes Magos 20, Spain.

FRUSCIANTE, John Augustus, b. 11 Jan. 1945, NYC, NY, USA. Artist Consultant; Master Pianist. Educ: B Mus, Juilliard Schl. of Music, 1967; MSc, ibid., 1968. Debut: Vienna, Austria, 1971. Career: Tours of USA, Canada & Europe; Orchl., radio & TV apps. in USA; Adjudicator, Texas Int. Piano Competition; Piano Instr., Univ. of Ariz., 1972-74. Mbrships: Southwest Pianists Fndn., Dir.; Am. Musicol. Soc. Hons: Dip. di Merito - "Ettore Pozzoli" Int. Piano Competition, Italy, 1971. Hobbies: Flying; Bicycling. Address: 9000 W Oakland Pk. Blvd., Sunrise, FL 33321, USA.

FRY, Christopher Charles, b. 11 May 1938, London, UK. Conductor. Educ: Royal Coll. of Music; ARCM; hon. FLCM. m. Natalie Usselmann, 4 d. Career: Cond., Stadttheater, Augsburg, W Germany, 1962-63; Staatsoper, Hamburg, 1963-64; Royal Ballet, Covent Gdn., 1965-67; Guest Cond., BBC & other Brit. Orchs., & in Scandinavia, Germany, Belgium & Holland; Prof., London Coll. of Music & Trinity Coll. of Music, London, 1969-. Address: 6 Westbury Ln., Buckhurst Hill, Essex, UK.

FRY, Stephen Michael, b. 5 Jan. 1941, Boise, Idaho, USA. Music Librarian. Educ: BA, Univ. of Calif., Riverside; MA, Clarement Grad. Schl.; MSLS, Univ. of Southern Calif. m. Frances W White, 2 s. Career: Music Lib., Univ. of Calif.,

Riverside, 1967-70; Music Libn. & Assoc. Prof. of Music, Ind. Univ. of Pa., 1970-72; Assoc. Music Libn., Northwestern Univ., 1972-75; Hd., Music Lib., UCLA, 1975-. Publs. incl: A Manual for the Classification & Cataloging of Bell & Carillon Literature, 1970, 2nd ed., 1974; The Life & Times of Sadakichi Hartmann, 1867-1944 (ed.), 1970. Contbr. articles & reviews to var. profl. jrnls. Ed: 1810 Overture; Music Reference Bulletin. Mbrships: Music Lib. Assn.; Am. Musicol. Soc.; Int. Assn. Music Libs.; Guild of Carilloneurs in N Am. Recip. acad. hons. Hobbies: Musical philately; Sports. Address: 4249 Coolidge Ave., Los Angeles, CA 90066, USA.

FRYDENLAND, Per Karsten, b. 8 Nov. 1943, Baerum, Norway. Tuba Player. Educ: Norges Musikkhogskole. m. Kari, 3 c. Career: Soloist w. The Baerum Symph. Orch.; Substitute Tuba Player, Norwegian Radio Orch. & Oslo Phil. Orch.; Freelance studio musician. Recordings: Knut Nystedt, Pia Memoria op. 65 Requiem for 9 Brass Instruments, 1978; Jan Garbarek, Dis (w. Norwegian Brass Sextet). Mbrships: Norwegian Musicians Assoc.; Tubists Univeral Brotherhood Assn. Hobbies: Painting/Drawing; Fishing; Old Cars; Winter Sports. Address: Loekebergv. 3B, 1344 Haslum, Norway.

FRYER, Jack, b. 19 Mar. 1929, Stamford, UK. Music Adviser. Educ: BA (music), Univ. of Durham. m. Kathleen Mary Holt, 1 s., 1 d. Career: Music Organizer, W Bromwich, 1961-66; Music Adviser, City of Salford, 1966-74; Sr. Music Adviser, ibid., 1974-. Mbrships: FRSA; ISM. Hobby: Private Flying. Address: 544 Manchester Rd., Hollins Gn., Rixton, nr. Warrington, Cheshire WA3 6JT, UK.

FRYER, Judith Anne, b. 20 Oct. 1935, NYC, USA. Professor of Music; Violist. Educ: B Mus, 1959, M Mus in viola, 1961, in music educ., 1963, Manhattan Schl. of Music, NYC; Profl. Dip., 1969, EdD, 1974, Columbia Univ. Tchrs. Coll. Career: num. perfs. as Soloist & as Violist in Fryer Sisters String Trio, concerts & broadcasts, NYC & area; String Specialist & Orchl. Cond., NYC pub. schls., 1963-69, Rye Co. Day Schl., Rye NY, 1969-71; Fac. Mbr., Mannes Coll. of Music, NYC, 1969-77; Rsch. Asst., Prof. of Music & Music Educ., NY Univ., NYC, 1977-; Adj. Asst. Prof., Fordham Univ., 1975-. Contbr. to: Opera Jrnl.; Index of Am. Doctl. Dissertations. Mbrships: Soc. for Rsch. in Music Educ., MENC; Kappa Delta Pi. Hons. incl: Harold Bauer Award, Manhattan Schl. of Music, 1961; 5 times Gold Medal Winner, Music Educ. League. Hobbies: World Travel; Water Sports. Address: Apt. 14H, 345 W 58th St., NY, NY 10019, USA. 27.

FUCHS, Jacob, b. 7 May 1923, NYC, USA. Tympanist. Educ: BA, Chem., NY Univ., 1944; MS, Chem., Univ. of Ill., 1947; PhD, Analytical Chem., ibid, 1950. m. Rose Lochansky, 1 s., 1 d. Career: w. NY Univ. Orch., 1940-44; NY Univ. Band, 1940-44; Sperry Symph. Orch., NY, 1942-44; Univ. of Ill. Bands, 1946-52; Phoenix Symph. Orch., 1952-. Mbr. of many sci. & profl. orgs. Hobby: Tennis. Address: 2035 College Ave., Tempe, AZ 85282, USA. 2,9.

FUCHS, Lillian F, b. New York, NY, USA. Violist; Teacher; Composer. Educ: Grad. Inst. of Musical Art. m. Ludwig Stein, 2 children. Career: Recitalist, Viola Soloist w. maj. orchs., USA & Europe, inclng. Aspen Fest. Orch., NY Phil. & Pablo Casals Fest.; Duos w. brother, violinist Joseph Fuchs; 1st to perform & record 6 Bach Suites for Viola Solo. Compositions incl. 12 Caprices, 16 Fantasy Etudes, 15 Characteristic Studies, Sonata Pastorale, & num. arrangements. Recordings incl. Mozart Duos for Violin, Viola; Beethoven String Trios, Flute Trios; Debussy's Sonata for Flute, Harp & Viola; Roussell's Trio for Cello, Viola & Flute. Hons: Silver Medal; Morris Loeb Mem. Prize & Isaac Newton Seligman Composition Award, 3 yrs. Mgmt: Albert Kay Mgmt. Address: 186 Pinehurst Ave., NY, NY 10033, USA.

FUCHS, Peter, b. 7 April 1933, Zürich, Switzerland. Musician, oboe. Educ: Nat. Conserv. Paris 1950-54. m. Doris Bättig, 1 s., 1 d. Career: Solo oboe player Tonhall Orch., Zürich; mbr. Stalder Quintet since 1955; Tchr. Conserv., Music Acad. Zürich since 1967; 1954-1957, solo oboe player City Orch. St. Gallen; 1957-70, solo oboe player Radio Orch. Beromünster, Zürich; 1970 Radio Symph. Basel. Recordings: R. Blum; A. Furer; Beethoven, Quintet in Es Major op. 16 for piano, oboe, clarinet, horn, bassoon; Viruose Windmusic. Mgmt: Concert Sox. Zürich (Stalter Quintet). Mbrships: Swiss Soc. for Musical Arts; Swiss Assn. for Musicologists. Hons: 2nd Prize Int. Music Competition, München 1957; 2nd Prize Int. Music Competition, Geneva 1959. Hobbies: Model building. Address: Buchenstr. 6, 4142 Münenstein, Switzerland.

FUCHS, Peter Paul, b. 30 Oct. 1916, Vienna, Austria. Conductor; Stage Director. Educ: Piano Tchrs. Dip., Austria; Cond. Dip., Acad. of Music, Vienna; studies of comp. & piano. m. Elissa M. Fuchs, 1 d. Debut: NYC, USA, 1941. Career:

Musical staff, Met. Opera, NYC, 10 yrs.; also w. San Fran. & other US Operas; Asst. to Bruno Walter & other Conds.; Prof., La. State Univ., 1950-; Music Dir., Baton Rouge Symph., 1960-; Greensboro Symph., NC, 1957-; Artistic Dir., Beaumont Civic Opera, 1962-; Guest Cond., var. European countries. Compositions incl: Serenade at Noon (opera). Publs: The Psychology of Conducting, 1969; The Music Theatre of Walter Felsenstein, 1975. Contbr. to music jrnls. Mbr., profl. assns. Hons: D Mus, Combs Coll., 1959. Address: 6776 Menlo Drive, Baton Rouge, LA 70808, USA.

FUCHSOVA, Liza b. 31 March 1913, Brno, Czech. Pianist. Educ: Conservs., Brno & Prague; Masterschl. for Pianists, Prague. Widow. Debut: Soloist w. Czech. Philharmonic Orch., Prague. Career: concerts throughout Europe; regular broadcasts on BBC Radio; sev. TV apps. Recordings: Smetana piano works, HMV; Dvorak chmbr. music, Vox & Decca. Hobbies: Walking; Mountaineering; Gardening. Address: 4 Gardiner Ave., London NW2 4AN, UK. 14.

FUGELLE, Jacquelyn, b. 9 Sept. 1952, Portsmouth, UK. Soprano Singer. Educ: GSM; AGSM (dip. & postdip.); Vienna Hochschule für Musik; study w. Paolo Silveri, Rome. m. George Frank Johnston, 2 d. Debut: Wigmore Hall, London, 1975. Career: extensive repertoire in oratorio, opera & recital; apps. in major concert halls & cathedrals in UK; Can. debut, 1977; perfs. in Germany, Austria, Italy, Netherlands & France; Dutch TV apps.; radio perfs. for BBC & Radio Cologne. Recordings: Joan Sutherland, Luciano Pavarotti, Jacquelyn Fugelle in Operatic Favourites. Mbrships: Equity; ISM. Hons: Silver medal, Worshipful Co. of Musicians, 1975; Ralph Vaughan Williams Scholarship, 1975; Martin Musical Scholarship, 1975; Countess of Munster Scholarship, 1977; RSA Scholarship, 1977; Greater London Arts Assn., Young Musician, 1976. Hobbies: Gardening; Geology; Genealogy. Mgmt: Ibbs & Tillett, London. Address: 93 Kingsley Rd., Southsea, Hants., PO4 8HL, UK.

FUGLESANG, Káre Halvard, b. 10 June 1921, Raelingen, Norway. Concertmaster; Violinist. Educ: Barratt-Dues Music Inst., Oslo; Juilliard Schl. of Music, NYC; Dartington Hall Summer Schl. of Music. m. Reidun Fuglesang, 1 child. Deubt: 23 Nov. 1940, Oslo. Career incls: Violinist, Oslo Phil. Orch., 1945-. w. 1 yr. leave as Concertmaster, Norwegian Opera Orch.; Conertmaster, Gothenburg Symph., Sweden, 1965-72; Norwegian Opera Orch., Oslo, 1975-; Concertmaster, Cond. & Tchr., Music Conserv., Kristiansand, Norway, 1972-73; num. perfs. as soloist & in Chmbr. grps. Mbr., Norsk Tonkunstlersamfund, Oslo. Mgmt: Norsk Musikkdireksjon, Oslo. Address: Elgfaret 4 D, Nesoddtangen, Postnr. 1450, Norway.

FUJIKAWA, Mayumi, b. 27 July 1946, Asahigawa City, Japan. Solo Violinist. Educ: Tokyo Conserv.; Antwerp Conserv., Netherlands. Career: Concerto apps. w. most major orchs., USA, E & W Europe, Israel, Japan, etc. Recordings: Mozart, Violin Concerti 3 & 5; Japan Phil. w. Paavo Berglund; Tchaikovsky & Bruch w. Rotterdam & Edo De Waart; Vioi i Recital; Beethoven Kreutzer, & Franck Sonatas w. Michael Roll. Hons: 2nd Prize, Tchaikovsky Competition, Moscow, 1970; 1st Prize, Vieuxtemps Competition, 1970. Hobbies incl: Chamber Music; Reading; Plays; Movies; Concerts; Being with Friends; Drawing. Mgmt: Harrison & Parrott, London, UK. Address: Flat 308 Nelson House, Dolphin Square, London SW1, UK.

FUJIWARA, Hamao, b. 12 July 1947, Kamakura, Kanagawa, Japan. Concert Violinist; Teacher. Educ: Post Grad. Dip., Juilliard Schl. m. Katsurako Mikami. Debut: Recital, Tokyo, 1961; NY, 1971. Career: Soloist w. major orchs. incl. Toronto, Vancouver, Rochester, Dallas, Musica Aeterna Orch., NY, etc. Solo recitals, sev. cities throughout USA & Japan. Recordings: Bartok - Violin Concerto; Italian Baroque Sonatas; Violin Encores; Beethoven, Fauré, Ravel & Debussy Sonatas. Hons incl: Winner, Nat. Music Competition, Japan, 1967; Paganini Int. Violin Competition, Geneva, 1969; Diploma d'Onore, Accademia Chigiana, Siena, 1969; Queen Elizabeth Music Competition, Brussels, 1971. Hobbies: Model trains; Railroad photography. Mgmt: Judd Concert Bureau, NY; Kambara Music Office, Tokyo. Address: 171 W 57th St., NY, NY 10019, USA.

FUKA, Václav, b. 7 Dec. 1933, Prague, Czechoslovakia. Contrabassist. Educ: State Conserv. of Music, Prague; Acad. o Musical Arts, Prague. m. Helena Hubikova, 1 s., 1 d. Career State Theatre Karlin, Prague; Orch. of Prague Symph Musicians; Czech Noneto, Chmbr. Ensemble of Czech Phil Orch. Appearances on radio w. Chmbr. Harmony, w. Prague Chmbr. Soloist, w. Czech Noneto, w. pianist Jir-l Hubicka Recordings: w. Czech Noneto, w. orchestra E. Hlobil, Concer for Contrabas Orch. Address: Navalech 24, 160 00 Prague 6 Czechoslovakia.

FUKUI, Naohiro, b. 28 July 1912, Tokyo, Japan. Music Educator. Educ: Tokyo Acad. of Music, 1933; State HS for Music, Berlin, Germany, 1937-39. m. Naoko Naokuni. Career: Violinist; Dir., Mussashino Acad. Musicae, 1962-. Mbrships: Pres., Japan Soc. for Music Educ., 1963; VP, Int. Soc. for Music Educ.; Exec. Committee, Int. Music Coun. Hons. incl: Off., Order of Arts & Letters, France, 1965; Cross of Hon. for Sci. & Art 1st Class, Austria; Smetana Medal, Czech., 1974; Order of Merit, German Fed. Repub., 1976. Address: 4-7-16 Mejiro, Toshima-ku, Tokyo, Japan.

FULD, James J, b. 16 Feb. 1916, NY, NY, USA. Lawyer; Musicologist. Educ: MA, Harvard Coll., 1937; LLB., Harvard Law Schl., 1940. m. Elaine Gerstley, 2 d., 1 s. Composer, I Talk About You. Publs: The Book of World-Famous Music - Classical, Popular & Folk, 6th Ed., 1971; American Popular Music 1875-1950, 1955; A Pictorial Bibliography of The First Editions Of Stephen C Foster, 1957. Contbr. to: Notes Mag.; Music & Letters. Mbrships: Int. Musicol. Soc.; Am. Musicol. Soc.; Music Lib. Assn. Address: Room 2100, 300 Park Ave., NY, NY 10022, USA.

FULIN, Angélique Jeanne Amélie, b. 20 Sept. 1927, Le Houga, France. Music Teacher. Educ: Bacc., scis.; Lic. ès Lettres, music hist., aesthetics, child psychol., pedagogy; studied solfège, piano, harmony, & analysis, Nat. Music Conserv., Lyon. m. Ernest Fulin, 1 d. Career: Tchr., Schl. & Conserv. Strasbourg, at l'Ecole Normale d'Institutrices, Seine; Rsch. Asst. studying musical intervals in the speech of children, CNRS; Hd., rsch., NRDP., (to change the musical expression & creativity of children); var. broadcasts of old music w. "La Ménestrandie," Participant, Congress of aesthetics, Amsterdam, 1964, Congress of ISME., Moscow, 1970. Recordings: Danceries de la Renaissance. Publs: La Ménestrandie - danses de la renaissance. Contbr. to: L'Education Musicale; Revue d'Esthetique; L'Education; Pedagogie Fonctionnelle; Dossiers Pedagogiques; Bull. de L'Assn. des Professeurs de Mathématique. Mbr., Nat. Music Commission Ligue Française de L'Enseignement et de L'Education Permanente. Hobby: Travel. Address: 1 Ave. Normandie Niemen, 93150 Le Blanc Mesnil, France.

FULLBROOK, Charles, b. 17 Feb. 1950, London, UK. Timpanist; Percussionist; Educ: RAM, 1968-71; LRAM (Tchrs.). m. Avis Ann Perthen. Career: Prin. Percussionist w. English Nat. Opera; Tchr. of Timpani & Percussion, Watford Schl. of Music; Freelance Musician. Mbr., The Royal Soc. of Musicians of Great Britain. Hons: LRAM, 1971; Hugh B Fitch Prize, 1970. Hobbies: Cookery; Swimming; Cinema; Tennis. Address: 5 Maxwelton Close, Mill Hill, London NW7 3NB, UK.

FULLER, Charles Oliver, b. 9 June 1916, Coeur d'Alene, Idaho, USA. Music Educator; Band, Orchestra Conductor. Educ: AA., Coeur d'Alene Jr. Coll. 1936; B Mus Ed , 1939, MM , 1947, Northwestern Univ.; Postgrad. study, Whitworth Coll., Wash. State Univ., Gonzaga Univ.; Trumpet, Violin study. m. Margaret Elizabeth Murphy, 1 s. Career: Band, Orch. Dir., pub. shcls., 34 yrs.; Hd. Dept. of Music, Lewis & Clark HS., Spokane, Wash., 29 yrs.; Lectr., Music Educ., Gonzaga Univ.; Retd., 1973; Studio work & composing for band. Compositions: Fuguing Tune for Band; Kingsgate March; Plymouth Town. Mbrships: Phi Mu Alpha Sinfonia; MENC; Wash. Music Educators Assn.; NEA. Hons: First Chair of Am. (outstanding bands of Am.); Order of Silver Horn. Hobbies: Antiques; Golf. Address: 226 W. Joseph, Spokane, WA 99208, USA.

FULLER, Frederick, b. 7 Nov. 1908, Kirkham, Lancs., UK. Concert Singer (Baritone). Educ: Cath. Coll., Preston; BA, Univ. of Liverpool; Sorbonne, Paris; Univ. of Munich; MA, Harvard Univ. m. Patricia Nicol, 4 d. Debut: Nat. Gall. Concerts, 1940 accomp. Gerald Moore). Career: Solo Recitalist; European countries, USA & S Am.; Radio & TV apps. throughout the world; Lectures & radio talks, BBC; master classes (Spanish, Portuguese & Latin Am. art song; German lieder). Num. recordings. Publs: Transl. of Roman Vlad; Stravinsky from

Italian. Mbr. ISM. Hobbies: Transl. of Musical Texts; Jogging. Mgmt: Ibbs & Tillett. Address: Manor Barn, Ratton Village, Eastbourne, E Sussex, UK.

FUNK, Heinrich, b. 23 May 1893, Meiningen, Germany. Composer; Educ: studied comp. w. Ph. Wolfrum & Hermann Poppen, Heidleberg; Otto Volkmann, Halle; ax Reger & Erwin Lendvai, Jena. m. Hildegard Fritsch. Career: Tchr., Conserv., Jena, 1919-22; Freelance music critic, 1922-55; independent comp. Comps. incl: orchl. works, chamber music, songs, works for solo instruments; stage works. Hons: Ehrennadel des Kommponistenverbands; Kunstpreis des Bezirks Gera; Verdienstmedaille der DDR. Address: Leninstr. 17, 69 Jena, German Dem. Repub.

FUNKHOUSER, Frederick A, b. 23 April 1905, Dayton, Ohio, USA. Violist. Educ: BA, Oberlin Coll.; B Mus, ibid.; Studied violin w. Andre Touret, Paris, France & Ottakar Sevcick, Pisek, Czechoslovakia. m. Mary LeRoy, 2 s. Career: Violist, Cleveland Orch., 1929-; Asst. Prin. Violist, ibid., 1946-. Participated in all recordings of Cleveland Orch. since 1929. Mbrships: Phi Beta Kappa; Pi Kappa Lambda. Hobbies: Hand Weaving; Bird Study. Address: 4046 Silsby Rd., Cleveland, OH, USA.

FURNESS, Alan, b. 11 June 1949, Whitstable, UK. Trumpet Player; Teacher; Composer; Conductor. Educ: RAM, 1968-71; LRAM; ARCM. m. Lesley Hobbs. Career: Trumpet Player, mainly in London; Tchr., Cond. & Comp.; Perfs., BBC & European Radio & TV; Formed Intrada Brass Quartet, 1972. Var. recordings w. orchl. & instrumental combinations inclng. works for Brass. Hobbies: Transcendental Meditation; Vegetarianism. Address: Ahimsa, 9 Haslemere Rd., Seasalter, Whitstable, Kent, UK.

FURRER, Walter, b. 28 July 1902, Plauen iVogtland, Germany. Composer. Educ: Ecole Normale de Musique, Paris. m. Margreth Vogt, 1 s., 1 d. Career: Singing Coach, Landestheater Gotha; Cond. & Theatre Dir., City Theatre, Berne, Switz.; Comp., Cond. & Dir. of Radio Berne Chmbr. Choir, radio studios, Berne, 1957-; Freelance Comp., 1973-. Comps. incl: Der Faun, opera in 2 acts, 1947; Tuef im Tal for mixed choir a capella; 3 Choruses for male choir a capella (Der Strom, Vision & Weltgebot); Fabrikgang for male choir a capella; Huetet des Licht for mixed choir a capella; Liebe for female choir a capella. Works recorded by: Radio Suisse Romande; Radio Studio Berne; Radio della Svizzera Italiana; Bavarian Broadcasting Co., Munich. Mbrships: Swiss Musicians Assn.; Swiss Profl. Conds. Assn. Swiss Prize for radio ballad Quatembernacht, Geneva, 1968. Address: Halen 39, 3037 Stuckishaus BE, Switzerland.

FURZE, Jessie, b. 4 Feb. 1903, Wallington, Surrey, UK. Pianist; Composer. Educ: RAM. m. Willem L F Nijhof (dec.). Career: Recitalist. inclng. BBC broadcasts & chamber music. Compositions which specialise in Educl. Music, incl. more than 250 short piano pieces & songs, also arrs. of Traditional Airs, inclng. Ten Little Ditties, In Time of Spring, Six Little Piano Pieces, Isle of Sark, Windmill Land, The Western Isles, Grandpapa's Diary, Scenes from Holland, Things I Remember, In My Country Garden & Graded Pieces for the Assoc. Bd.; Contbr. to: The Music Teacher. Mbr., ISM; Comps. Guild of GB. Hons: Elected Assoc., RAM; Alexander Roller Prize & Challen Gold Medal for Piano; Cuthbert Nunn Prize for comp. Address: 31 Bramley Hill, S. Croydon, Surrey, CR2 6NU, UK.

FUSSELL, John Michael, b. 15 May 1933, Luton, UK. Organist; Administrator. Educ: MA, Hertford Coll., Oxford Univ.; BMus, Univ. of London; FRCO; studied Organ w. var. tchrs. m. Elizabeth Stewart Broadley, 1 s., 1 d. Career: Dir. of Music & City Organist, Swansea; Dir., Swansea Fest. of Music & The Arts; Broadcasts for BBC & Belgian radio; Tchr.; Organ Recitalist; Tours, Belgium, Germany, France. Contbr. to: Guild for Promotion of Welsh Music; BBC Wales; Swansea Sound. Mbr., RCO. Hons: Sawyer Prize, RCO, 1962. Mgmt: Terry Slasberg Agency, London. Address: 114 Pennard Drive, Southgate, Swansea, W Glamorgan, UK.

G

GAARENSTROOM, Harry, b. 15 July 1918, Amsterdam, Netherlands. Composer; Arranger; Pianist; Radio Producer. Educ: Studied Psychol. & Philos., Nymegen; studied Music w. Tiggers, K Van de Griend & W F Strietman. m. Hertha C Seithen. Career: Pianist, Arr., Prod., Allied Forces Radio, Batavia, Indonesia, 1946; Pianist, Arr., Prod., Radio Djakarta, ibid., 1950; Comp., Arr., Exec. Prod., Music Dept., VARA Broadcasting Corp., Hilversum, Netherlands, 1958-. Compositions: Symphonic works: Full Midnight & More; Intrada alla Aram; Festival Overture; var. Background Scores & Signature Tunes for Radio Progs. Recording: Modern Indonesian Folk Music. Contbr. to VARA RadioTV Guide. Mbrships: BUMASTEMRA; Stichting Nederlandse Toonkunstenaars. Hobby: Riding. Address: Gysbrecht Van Amstelstraat 52, 1302 Hilversum, Netherlands.

GAARN-LARSEN, Hanna, b. 1 Mar. 1951, Aborg, Denmark. Violinist. Educ: Dip., Acad. of Music, Odense, Denmark, 1973; Acad. of Music, Prague. m. Jan Snábl, 1 c. Career: Violinist, Odense City Symph. Orch., 1974. Address: Solvaenget 2, 5653 Nr. Lyndelse, Denmark.

GABB, Harry, b. 5 Apr. 1909, Ilford, Essex, UK. Musician; Organ Recitalist. Educ: ARCO; FRCO; ARCM; Hon. FTCL. m. Helen Burnaford Mutton, 1 s. Career: Sub-Organist, Exeter Cathedral & St. Pauls' Organist, Llandaff Cathedral & Her Majesty's Chapels Royal; Sr. Organ Prof., TCL. Has made many recordings w. St. Paul's Cathedral Choir. Hons: MVO, 1961; CVO, 1974; Mus D., Lambeth (Cantab.). Hobby: Reading. Address: Littledene, 34 Windsor Rd., Chobham, Woking, Surrey.

GABER, George, b. 24 Feb. 1916, NYC, USA. Percussionist. Educ: New Schl. of Social Rsch.; Queens Coll., NYC; Juilliard & Manhattan Schls. of Music. m. Esther Gaber, 1 s., 1 d. Career: Ballet Russe de Monte Carlo Orch., Goldman Band, Pitts., Los ANgeles; NBC, ABC networks; Aspen, Balt., NY World's Fair Fests.; perfs., lectures, Cond., Judge, Can., Brazil, Iran, Japan, etc.; Prof. of Music, Ind. Univ. Recordings: MGM; RCA; Columbia; Decca; Capitol; Urania. Publs: var. eds. for Peters, Kerby, Shawnee. Mbrships: Am. Fedn. of Musicians; AAUP; Bohemians; Coll. Music Soc. Recip., Hon. Dips. w. Merit, G B Escola Imperio & Federacao das Escolas, Sao Paulo, Brazil. Hobbies: Photography; Racquet Ball. Address: 1909 Arden Dr., Bloomington, IN 47401, USA.

GABOLD, Ingolf Georg August, b. 31 Mar. 1942, Heidelberg, Germany. Composer. Educ: Dip., Conserv. of Music, Copenhagen; Dip., Music Conserv., Arhus. Compositions: (publd.) operas 7 Visions to Orpheus, Towards Aquarius; Atlantis, Fur louise, orch.; Visione, Written In Sand, chorus; (recorded) Your Sister's Drown'd. Recip. 1st Prize, Salzburg Operapreiss, 1971. Address: 26 Peder Skramsgade, 1054 Copenhagen K, Denmark.

GABOS, Gábor, b. 4 Jan. 1930, Budapest, Hungary. Pianist. Educ: Master's degree, perf. m. Ingeborg Sándor, 2 c. Debut: Budapest, 1952. Career: Fesitval Hall, London; Musikverein, Vienna; Chatelet, Paris; Palais des Beaux-Arts, Brussels; appearances in Italy, USSR, Japan, German Fed. Repub.; Sweden, Greece, Switz., Yugoslavia, Poland, S Am. Recordings: Hungaronton, Deutsche Grammophon; Pathé-Marconi, King Record, Tokyo, Japan. Hons: Hungarian Govt.'s Award 'Liszt Ferenc', 1959; 1st Prize of 'Liszt-Bartók, Int. Piano Competition, 1961; Top Award of the Japan Record Acad. for the complete Bartók Concertos, 1968; Merited Artist of the Hungarian People's Republic, 1977. Address: Nyul utca 10, 1026 Budapest, Hungary.

GABRYS, Ewa, b. 5 Nov. 1936, Cracow, Poland. Harpsichordist; Music Publisher. Educ: 3 dips., Higher Schl. of Music, Cracow. Debut: Pomaranczarnia, Warsaw, Polish Renaissance Harpsichord music, 1961. Career: perfs. at Herbert von Karajan's Fest., W Berlin, Fests. of Polish Piano & Harpsichord Playing at Supsk, Poland; perfs. at 'The Days of Organ Music', Cracow (harpsichord recitals), as a soloist & basso continuo w. Warsaw Chmbr. Music Orch. ''Con Moto Ma Cantabile'', also w. Avantgarde Music Ensemble, 'MW2', Cracow; Recitals on Polish TV & Radio. Comps: Miniatures for Harpsichord. Recordings: Basso continuo in XVII century Polish Instrumental Music, w. 'Con Moto Ma Cantabile'; Musica Antiqua Polonica. Publs: Realization of thorough - bass in A Vivaldi's Concerto B flat major for 4 violins, strings, Cracow, 1965; Realization of thorough-bass in GP Telemann's Polish Concerto G major for strings, Cracow,

1966; Realization of thorough-bass in A Vivaldi's Concerto C minor for 2 violins, strings, Cracow, 1967; Commentary on A Vivaldi's Concerto A minor for 2 violins, strings, Cracow, 1975; ed. Double Bass from A to Z. Cracow, 1974. Hons: 1st Prize (harpsichord) Old Music Competition, Lodz, Poland, 1964; 2nd prize (1st Prize not awarded) Competition for Young Comps., Warsaw, 1967; Special Commendation in Int. Gaudeamus Competition, Rotterdam, 1971. Hobbies: English lang.; Swimming. Address: U1. Prusa 15/7, 30-109 Cracow, Poland.

GADD, Jack Norman, b. 16 June 1931, New Plymouth, NZ. Percussionist. Educ: Registered Music Tchr., NZ. m. Fay B Walshaw, 1 d., 1 d. Career: Percussionist, NZ Symph. Orch., 25 yrs.; Prin. Percussionist, Regular Marimba Soloist, Radio NZ, 1966-; Radio & TV apps. w. Norman Gadd Percussion Ensemble; Schl. perfs. w. Percussion Quartette; Judge, NZ Brass Bands Assn. Drum Championships Comps: Night in the City; 4332; Tympanistic Tinamarre. Recordings: Percussion Parade; Music for Creative Dance; Creative Dance Sercies. Mbrships: Percussive Arts Soc.; Australasian Performing Rights Assn. Contbr. to var. jrnls. Hons: Winner, NZ Brass Bands Side Drum Championship, 1950. Hobbies incl: Table Tennis. Address: 5 Hollies Cres., Johnsonville, Wellington, NZ.

GADDARN, William James, b. 1924, Neyland, Pembrokeshire, UK. Musician. Educ: TCL. Career: Cond., London Orpheus Choir, 1952-; London Orpheus Orch., 1960; Dir., Opera Seria, 1962; Chorus Master, Royal Choral Soc., 1964-65; Cond., Ealing Choral Soc., 1968-; Musical Dir., Croydon Phil. Soc., 1973-; Prof. Staff Mbr., TCL, 1957-; Has worked w. BBC Chorus frequently, 1958-. Hons: GTCL; Hon. FTCL; LRAM; ARCM. Hobbies: Reading; Travel; Vintage Cars. Address: 2 Tenby Mansions, Nottingham St., London W1M 3RD, UK. 3.

GADE, Per, b. 26 May 1944, Aalborg, Denmark. Trombonist; Professor of Music. Educ: Royal Acad. of Music, Copenhagen; GSM, London. Debut: Royal Danish Conserv. of Music, 1974. Career: began as Jazz Trombonist; Solo Trombone w. Scandinavian Symph. Orch., 1973 & 74; participant in num. permiere perfs. of works by Scandinavian comps.; perfs. on radio & in solo, ensemble & orchl. concerts; Asst. Instructor, Trombone Class, Royal Danish Conserv. of Music, 1973-74; Prof. of Music, Sakuyo Coll. & Acad. of Music, Japan, 1978-. Publs: Scales & Arpeggios for Trombone or Baritone, 3 vols., 1978; Intonation & Lipflexibility; Embouchure & Breathtechnique. Contbr. to var. music mags. Mbrships: Int. Trombone Assn., Musicians Union, Denmark, Danish Music Pedagogue Assn., Japan. Recip. prizes from Royal Danish Conserv., 1973 & 74. Hobbies: International Cuisine; Reading; Travel; Collecting Art Objects; Philosophy. Mgmt: Ongaku Geijytsuka-Kyo Kai, Tokyo, Japan. Address: c/o Iwamoto, 3-2-12 Nishihara, Utsunomiya-shi, Japan, 320.

GADJIBEKOV, Sultan Ismail Ogly, b. 8 May 1918, Shusha, Azerbaizhan, USSR. Composer, Educator. Educ: Baku Conserv. Career: Vice-Chmn., Azerbaijan Composers Union, 1952; Prof., Baku Conserv., 1965-. Compositions incl: Gyzl-Gyul (musical comedy), 1940; Sonata for Piano, 1940; Six Preludes for Piano; Motherland (cantat), 1941; 1st Symph., 1944; Caravan (symphonic picture), 1945; 2nd Symph., 1946; Concerto for Violin & Orch., 1947; Gyulshen (ballet), 1950; Overture for Symph. Orch., 1956; music for theatre, etc. Hons: State Prize, 1952; Honoured Worker of Arts of Azerbaijan SSR, 1958; Red Banner of Labour, 1959; People's Artist of Azerbaijan SSR, 1960. Address: Azerbaijan Composers Union, 58 Ulitsa Nizami, Baku, USSR.

GAGNEBIN, Ruth, b. 5 Mar. 1921, Neuchatel, Switzerland. Pianist. Educ: Conserv. Geneva, concert dip. piano. m. Schmid. Career: Concert tours throughout Europe. Mbrships: AMS. Hobbies: Walking in the country side. Address: Marche-Neuf 23, CH-2500, Bienhe, Switzerland.

GAGNON, Paul-André, b. 2 Feb. 1947, Quebec, Can. Concert Guitarist. Educ: 4 yrs. at Univs. of Quebec & Montreal, masterclasses w. A Lagoya, N Yepes & L Brouner. m. Marie-José Gagnon, 1 d. Career: perfs. w. Montreal & Quebec Symphs., 15 yrs. old; Perf. in Buffalo, 16 yrs. old; num. apps. on radio & TV w. CBC Chmbr. Orch.; solo recital, Int. Fest., Toronto, 1975; mbr. of jury, Nat. Contest of CBC, 1979; asst. to A Lagoya at Orforc Music Fest. Mbrships: Am. Guild of Music; Acad. de Musique de Quebec; fac., Conserv. of Quebec. Hobbies: Skiing; Cinema Travel. Address: 61 Ave. de Troyes, Neufchatel, PQ, G2A 3S2, Can.

GAILLARD, Paul-André, b. 26 Apr. 1922, Veyraux Chillon, Montreux, Switzerland. Conductor; Composer; Violinist Musicologist. Educ: PhD, Univ. of Zürich; Dip. of Master in Musicol., ibid.; Dip. of Tchr. of Music, Zürich Conserv. m

Marie-Louise Boy de la Tour, 1 d. Debut: St. Gall, 1946. Career: Orch. & Choir Cond., Zürich, Lausanne & Geneva; has conducted in all European countries & the E; Prof., Lausanne Conserv. & Fed. Polytechnic Schl. Comp., var. works. Recordings incl: Decca; Concert-Hall; His Masters Voice. Author, var. publs. Conbtbr. to: Swiss Musical Review, etc. Mbrships. incl: Int. Soc. for Music Knowledge; Swiss Musicians Assn. Recip. Richard Wagner Gold Medal, Bayreuth, 1963. Hobby: Mountaineering. Address: Ave. du Général Guisan 33, 1009 Pully/Lausanne, Switzerland.

GAISBAUER, Dieter, b. 9 Nov. 1944, Vienna, Austria. College Teacher; Composer. Educ: Dip. (w. distinction), Comp., Coll. of Music & Performing Arts, Vienna. Studied under Karl Schiske & Erich Urbanner, ibid. m. Therese Falkner 1 d. Career: Tchr., Harmony, Counterpoint & Musical form, Coll. of Music of Performing Arts, Vienna. Comps: Prin. Work, Requiem & mixed choir, without orch.), 1972; sev. chmbr. music comps., songs & piano pieces. Pubs: author sev. articles specializing in Music Tchng. & Musical Sociology; bibliogl. appendix to: Neue musikalische Verhaltensweisen der Jugend (Kurt Blaukopf), 1973. Mbrships: Austrian Union of Composers; Int. Soc. Contemp. Music. Recip. prize for his comps., Vienna, 1972; Achievement Award for Comp. from the Austrian Fed. Min. of Educ. & Arts, 1977. Hobbies: Poetry; Animals; Nature. Address: A-1080 Vienna, Laudongasse 5420, Austria.

GAJDOV, Stefan, b. 8 June 1905, Titov Veles, Yugoslavia. Composer; Conductor; Pedagogue; Musical Writer. Educ: Musical Schl., Belgrade. m. Ljubica Vasiljevic, 1 s., 1 d. Debut: Titov Veles, 1923. Career: Music Tchr.; grammar schls.; Prof. of Music, Musical Schl., Skopje; Cond., Skopje Broadcasting Choir; Dir., Macedonia Nat. Opera; Dir., Music Schl., Skopje. 700 comps. incl: String Quartet in C minor; Fantasia (solo flute & symph. orch.); Toccata; 3 Inventions; Preludlum; Fuge; Concertino for string orch.; 22 solo songs w. Chmbr. music; music for 3 documentary films. Mbr., sev. music assns. Publs. incl: Solfeggio for Musical Schools, 1949. Contbr. to profl. jrnls. Recip., sev. hons. Hobbies incl: Reading. Address: Orce Nikolov 72, 11000 Skopje, Yugoslavia.

GAJEWSKI, Ferdinand John Vincent, b. 13 Feb. 1941, Plainfield, NJ, USA. Musicologist; Pianist. Educ: S.B., Juilliard Schl. of Music (piano under James Friskin); A.M., Harvard Univ., PhD., ibid. Career: Asst. Prof. of Music, Univ. of Tex., Austin. Publs: Pier Domenico Paradies - The Man & His Experiments in Sonata Form; The Work Sheets to Chopin's Violoncello Sonata Nieznane zrodto manginesowych notatek Chopina, 1977. Mbrships: Am. Musicol. Soc.; Polish Inst. of Arts & Scis. in Am; Towarzystwo im. Fryderyka Chopina, Warsaw. Address: Dept. of Music, Univ. of Tex. at Austin, Austin, TX 78712, USA.

GAL, Hans, b. 5 Aug. 1890, Brunn, Austria. Composer; Writer. Educ: PhD, Univ. of Vienna, 1913; Mus D, Univ. of Edinburgh, 1950. m. Hanna B Schick, 1 d. Debut: as Comp. & Pianist, 1910. Career: Lectr., Univ. of Vienna, 1919-28; Dir., Municipal Coll. of Music, Mainz, 1929-33; Cond., Vienna Concert Orch., Vienna Bach Soc., 1933-38; Lectr., Univ. of Edinburgh, 1945-65. Comps: 105 works publd. (4 operas, 2 oratorios, orchl., chmbr. music, piano works, choral works, pieces for string orch.). Publs. incl: The Golden Age of Vienna, 1948; Johannes Brahms, 1961; Richard Wagner, 1963; Franz Schubert, 1970, Drei Meister, Drei Welten, 1975. Mbrships: Brit. Pen. Right Soc.; ISM; Brit. Assn. of Univ. Tchrs.; Austrian Soc. for Contemp. Music. Hons. incl: OBE, 1964; Decoration of Hon. in Sci. & Art, 1st Class, Austria. Hobbies: Photography; Mountaineering. Address: 16 Blacket Pl., Edinburgh 9, UK.

GALBINSKI, Liviu, b. 9 June 1947, Constantza, Romania. Concert Pianist; Conductor; Piano & Music Teacher. Educ: grad., Telma Yelin Music Conserv., Tel-Aviv, Israel; grad., Rubin Acad. of Music, Tel Aviv, 1970; postgrad., GSM (piano & cond.), 1970. m. Jaffa, 1 s. Debut: Tel Aviv, 1968. Career: Concerts & recitals in Rumania, Israel, UK, Spain, France & Belgium. Comps: Songs. Mbrships: ISM;p EPTA. Hobbies: Cooking; Tennis; Fishing. Address: 74 Pennine Dr., London NW2 1NP, UK.

GALIMIR, Felix, b. 20 May 1910, Vienna, Austria. Violinist. Educ: Dip., Vienna Conserv.; studied w. Carl Flesch. m. Suzanne Hirsch. Debut: Vienna, 1928. Career: Fndr., Galimir String Quartet; concertized extensively in Europe until 1938; concerts & tchng. in USA, 1938-; Tchr., Marlboro Music Fest., Vt.; summers, 1953-, currently Juilliard Schl., NYC, Curtis Inst., Phila., Pa. & CCNY. Recordings: Vox; Columbia; RCA Victor; Marlboro Recording Soc. Recip. grand Prix du Disque, Paris, 1937. Mgmt: Frank Salomon, Assoc. Address: 225 E 74th, NY, NY 10021, USA. 2.

GALLAGHER, Jack, b. 27 June 1947, Forest Hills, NY, USA. Composer; Teacher of Music Theory, Composition & Trumpet.

Educ: BA, cum laude, Hofstra Univ., 1969; MFA (Comp.), Cornell Univ., 1975; Doct. study, Comp., Cornell Univ.; num. pvte. tchrs. m. April Lorenz Gallagher. Debut: Carnegie Recital Hall, NYC, 1978. Career: Assoc. Prin. Trumpet, Nat. Orchl. Assn., NYC, 1968-70; Solo Trumpet, Bach Cantata Series, Holy Trinity Lutheran Ch., NYC, 1969; Grad. Tchng. Asst., Cornell Univ., 1971-75; Co-Prin. Trumpet, Cornell Brass Quintet, 1974-75; Prin. & Solo Trumpet, Wooster Symph. Orch., 1977-; Instr. in Comp., Music Theory & Trumpet, The Coll. of Wooster, Wooster, Ohio, 1977-. Contbr. to: Pro Musica Sana. Mbrships: Am. Music Center; Broadcast Music Inc. Hons: Nat. Orchl. Assn. Accomplishment Award, 1969, '70; Am. Music Project Award, Winston-Salem, N Carolina, 1977. Hobbies: Films; Reading; Sports. Mgmt: Celia B Goodstein, Artist Rep., Linden Lane at Muttontown, E Norwich, NY 11732, USA.

GALLASCH, David Russel, b. 24 Sept. 1934, Hahndorf, SA, Aust. Pianist; Organist; Composer; Teacher. Educ: BMus, Assoc., Univ. of Adelaide; Mbr., RCO, London; LRAM. m. Ruth Thelma Gallasch, 1 s., 3 d. Career: Music Master, independent schls., currently w. St. Peters Coll. Preparatory Schl., SA; Organist & Choirmaster, Christ Ch., N Adelaide, SA. Comps: The Missus (opera); Sound & Image; Ruth (ch. opera); The Way of the Cross (audio-visual); Kamanka (opera). Contbr. to local mags. Mbrships: Pres., St. Peters & Payneham Lions Club, 1975-76; C'wlth. RSCM Summer Schl., Adelaide; Adelaide Organ Music Soc.; ASME; Ch. Music Soc., London, UK; Adelaide Savage Club. Recip. C'wlth. Govt. Assistance for Comp., 1974. Hobbies incl: Aleatoric music rsch. & perfs.; Youth music camps. Address: 71 N Terrace, Hackney, SA 5069, Australia.

GALLASCH, Florel Anne, b. 10 Jan. 1918, Broken Hill, NSW, Aust. Teacher of Piano & Theory; Examiner. Educ: LRSM, 1938. m. Egbert Sidney Victor Gallasch, 1 s., 1 d. Career incls: Tchr. of Piano & Theory; Examiner, AMEB, Univ. of Adelaide, 1968-. Mbrships: Coun., MTA, SA; Cou., AMEB, Univ. of Adelaide; Life Mbr., Organ Music Soc.; Aust. Soc. for Keyboard Music. Hons: Winner, num. prizes, Eisteddfods, 1930-36; Prize Winner, Final Grade Exam., 1935. Hobby: Pipe Organ. Address: 21 Dunrobin St., Black Forest, Adelaide, SA 5035, Aust.

GALLICO, Claudio, b. 4 Dec. 1929, Mantova, Italy. Musicologist; Orchestra Director. Educ: Laureato in Letters; Docent in Hist. of Music; Adv. Dips. in Pianoforte & Composition; Dip. in Musical Paleography. Debut as Cond., 1966. Career: Cond. at Festivals, on RAI (Italian Radio), & Channel 2, ORF-TV. Recordings incl: works by Monteverdi, Pergolesi & Asioli. Mbrships: Past Pres., Coun., Italian Musicol. Soc.; Coun., Virgilian Acad., Mantova; Cheubini Acad., Florence. Publs. incl: Un Canzoniere Musicale Italiano del Cinquecento, 1961; Un libro di Poesie per Musica dell'Epoca di Isabella D'Este, 1961; C. Monteverdi. Il Teatro, 1967; L. Viadana: Centro Concerti Ecclesiastici (ed.) 1964. Address: Via Bertani, 8, 46100 Mantova, Italy.

GALLIVER, David, b. Bristol, England. University Professor; Tenor Soloist. Educ: MA, New Coll., Oxford; ARMC. m. Gabrielle Galliver, 3 s. Debut: Oxford, 1947. Career: Concert Singer making num. apps. as Tenor Soloist w. leading choral & orchl. socs. in UK, Europe, Am., Asia, 1950-64; Lectr. in Music, Univ. of Adelaide, S Aust., 1964; Elder Prof. of Music, ibid., 1966-. Sev. recordings. Contbr. to: Rassegna di Studi Musicali (Florence). Miscellanea Musicologia; Studies in Music; IMS Congress Report; Aust. Jrnl. of Music Educ. Mbrships: Int. Musicol. Soc.; ISM; Int. Soc. for Rsch. in Singing. Hobbies: Gardening; Reading. Address: Dept. of Music, Univ. of Adelaide, S Aust. 3, 15.

GALLO, F Alberto, b. 17 Oct. 1932, Verona, Italy. Professor of History of Music, University of Bologna. Educ: LLD.; PhD. Publs. incl: Antonii Romani Opera, 1965; Mensurabilis musicae tractatuli, 1966; Franchini Gafurii Extractus parvus musice, 1969; Petrus Picardus Ars motettorum compilata brevier; 1971; Johannes Boen Ars musicae, 1972; La prima rappresentazione al Teatro Olimpico, 1973; Italian Sacred Music, 1976; Storia della musice: il Medioevo, 1977. Contbr. to: Acta musicologica; Annales musicologiques; Archiv für Musilwissenschaft; Die Musik in Geschichte und Gegenwart; Grove's Dictionary; Handwörterbuch der musikalischen Terminologie; Musica Disciplina; Quadrivium. Mbrships: Int., Italian & Am. Musicol. Socs.; Gesellschaft für Musikforschung. Recip. of Dent Medal, 1966. Address: L Alberti, 34, 40137, Bologna, Italy. 21.

GALLUZZO, Marino R, Jr., b. 20 Oct. 1951, Uniontown, Pa., USA. Saxophone Player; Teacher. Educ: BS (Music Educ.), Duquesne Univ., Pittsburgh, 1973; grad. study, ibid. & at Univ. of Mich. Debut: Pittsburgh. Career: num. apps. on sev. TV shows, perfs. on radio, CBC; mbr. Can. Saxophone Quartet; recitals & clinics in USA & throughout Can.; fac., Royal Hamilton Coll. of Music, Hamilton, Ont. sev. arrs. Recordings: Brodie Quartet in

Concert; Can. Saxophone Quartet. Mbrships: Toronto Musicians' Guild; Hamilton Musicians' Guild; N Am. Saxophone Alliance. Hon: winner, Pittsburgh Concert Soc. Competition, 1976. Hobbies: All sports; Cooking; Travel. Address: 100 Main St. E, Apt. 1308, Hamilton, Ont. L8N 3W7, Can.

GALPER, Avrahm, b. 16 Aug. 1921, Edmonton, Alta., Can. Co-Principal Clarinet. Educ: BMus, Univ. of Toronto. m. Charna, 5 c. Career: Co-Prin. Clarinet, Toronto Symph. Recordings: Bartok Contrasts; CAPAC recordings of Can. Clarinet Comps. Publs: Clarinet for Beginners, Books 1 & 2; Scales and Arpeggios. Contbr. to: B & H Woodwind Year Book; The Clarinet. Address: 679 Coldstream Av., Toronto, Ont., Can.

GALUN, Andrija, b. 19 Feb. 1945, Beograd, Yugoslavia. Composer; Organist; Theoretician; Pedagogue. Educ: Dip., Musical Acad., Beograd; M Musical Scis.; Dip., Summer Musical Courses, Sienna, Italy, Dir. Prof. Fernando Germani. m. Maria Loche, 1 s. Debut: Comp., Beograd, 1969; Organist, Beograd, 1970. Career incls: Asst., Fac. of Music Arts, Beograd; Prof., Secondary Musical Schl. Steven Mokranjac, Beograd; Comps. performed by Beograd Phil. Orch. in Yugoslavia & abroad; Organist, Yugoslavia & foreign countries. Comps. incl: Soanta for Organ, 1975; Music 68 (for orch.). Num. recordings. Publs: Les modes a transpositions limitees in harmonian style of O messinen. Contbr. to num. profl. publs. Mbrships: incl: Assn. of Yugoslav Comps. Hons. incl: Stevan Hristic Prize, 1969. Hobby: Undersea Fishing. Address: 11070 N Beograd, Jurija Gagarina 191/111, Yugoslavia.

GALWAY, James, b. 8 Dec. 1939, Belfast, Northern Ireland. Flautist. Educ: RCM; GSM; Conservatoire National Supérieure de Musique, Paris. m. Anna Christine Renngli, 1 s. by former marriage, 1 s., 2 d. Career: Wind Band of Royal Shakespeare Theatre, Stratford; Sadler's Wells Orch.; Royal Opera House Orch.; BBC Symph. Orch.; Prin. Flute, LSO & RPO; Prin. Solo Flute, Berlin Phil., 1969-75; Num. radio & TV apps. inclng. own shows on BBC. Comps: Var. arrs. for flute & roch. Recordings: Works by CPE Bach, JS Bach, Beethoven, Franck, Mozart, Prokoviev, Rodrigo, Reicha, Telemann & Vivaldi. Publs: Autobiography, 1978. Hons: OBE, 1978; Hon. Degrees, Open Univ. & Queen's Univ. Belfast, 1979; ISM Musician of the Yr., 1979. Hobbies: Music; Walking; Swimming; Films; Theatre; TV; Chess; Backgammon; Talking to people. Mgmt: London Artists, 73 Baker St., London W1, UK. Address: c/o Mgmt. 1, 16.

GAMBERINI, Leopoldo, b. 12 Mar. 1922, Como, Italy. Composer; Conductor; Musicologist; University Professor in the history of Music. Educ: Grad. Arts & Medicine; attended musical paleography Schl. Cremona; studied piano, violin, comp. & cond.; adv. courses. cond., comp., Mozarteum, Salzburg, Accad., Chigiana, Siena, & Vacanze Musicali, Venice; successful cand., exams, Conservs. of Genoa & Turin. m. Benini Graziella, 2 c. Debut: as Cond., Genoa, 1940, as Comp., Pesaro, 1948. Career: Cond., Radio Grp., "L Madrigalisti of Genoa"; Music Critic, 16 yrs., Il Nuovo Cittadino, Genoa; Fndr., Sound & Recording Studios; Consultant for Cybernetics & Music, Fac. of Physics, Genoa. Dir., Arts Dept., Fac. of Arts, Univ. of Siena, Arezzo; Prof. of Music Hist., ibid., & Fac. of Arts, Genoa. Compositions incl: Oratorio, Anna Franck; Cango Esoterico; Num. vocal-instrumental pieces inclng., 2 Quartetts, 1956; Il Cristo degle Abissi, 1956; Canto dello spazio, 1960; Prelude, for piano solo, 1961; Spiritual Poliptikon, 1967; Musica per Flauto e Orch. d'archi in sordina, 1969, (perfd. Italian Radio, Rome, 1974); var. works for the stage & films. Recordings: The Ancient Greek Chants, w. I Madregalisti di Genova, Angelicum, Milan. Publs: Genova nella vita musicale europea del 1800; Plutarco: De Musica; Ed., Modernità della musica greca nella tragedia, 1958; La parola e la musica nell'antichità, Florence, 1962; Religiosité dans la Messe en si min. de JS Bach, Genoa, 1960; La musica instrumentale a Genoa, 1974; Manuscripts, Genoa, 1967-70. Contbr. to num. reviews on ancient & modern music, var. profl. jrnls. Hon. mbr., French Assn., Royaume de la musique. Hons: Comp. prize, Int. Musical Content, "GB Viotti", Vercelli, 1952; 1st prize w. "I Madrigalisti di Genova", Int. Youth Music Fest., Neerpelt, Belgium, 1967 & 1970; Num. other medals. Address: Via Trieste, 8/13, Genova, Italy.

GAMBOLD, Geoffrey, b. 5 July 1930, Swansea, Wales, UK. Bassoonist. m. Constance Rimell, 3 d. Career: Prin. Bassoon, BBC Symph. Orch., 1959-. Hons: FRAM, 1974; Hon. RCM, 1970. Address: Fawley, The Avenue, Maidenhead, Berks., UK.

GAMMELTOFT-HANSEN, Bendt, b. 8 June 1932, Copenhagen, Denmakr. Organist; Carilloneur. Educ: MA, Music, Univ. of Copenhagen; Organ Dip, Royal Danish Acad. of Music; Carilloneur Diplomé d l'Etat, Carillon Pedagogue, France. m. Inger Bjerre Kjong, 1 s., 1 d. Career: Ch. Music Dir., Saint Nicolas' Ch., Svendborg, 1961; Rector, Preliminary Schl. of Carillon,

Aarhus, 1976. Publs: The Black Pot, 1974; Help, The Bishop Is There, 1975; Old Carillons in Copenhagen, 1976; Co-author, Choral Vignets I & II, 1978. Contbr. to Acta Campanologica. Mbrships: Guild of Carillonneurs of N Am.; Guilde De Carillonneurs de France; Dansk Klokkespiller Laug; Nederlandse Glockenspeler Vereniging; Exec. Committee, World Carillon Fedn. (European Sec.). Hons: Dip., Organ Improvisation, Graz, 1966. Hobbies: Stereo; Photography; Yachting. Address: Strandvej 13, DK 5700, Svendborg, Denmark.

GAMSON, Arnold, b. 30 Dec. 1926, Greenwich, Conn., USA. Conductor; Composer. Educ: MS, Juilliard Schl. of Music; Grad. studies, Musicol., CUNY. m. Annabella Gamson, 1 s., 1 d. Career: Musical Dir., Am. Opera Soc., 1951-62; Asst. Cond., NY Phil., 1961; Artistic Dir., Amici del'opera of Rome; Guest Cond. for TV The Voice of Firestone, Camera Three; Musical Dir., Caramoor Festival; Guest Cond., Teatro Bellas Artes, Mexico City; NY City Opera; Teatro Verdi in Trieste & Pergola in Florence; Former Musical Dir. Richmond Opera Co. Comps: Music for documentary films: Giacometti; There Must Be a Catch; The Name of the Game, etc. Num. recordings. Address: Hillandale Rd., Port Chester, NY 10573, USA.

GANGBAR, Lynne Carol, b. 20 May 1957, Toronto, Can. Classical Guitarist. Educ: Num. pvte. tchrs.; Orford Arts Centre, Quebec, Can. (w. Alexandre Lagoya); RCM, London; ARCM. Debut: Wigmore Hall, London, 1976. Career: Perfs. at num. Guitar Socs., USA, Can. & UK; Apps., Stratford Fest. Theatre, Town Hall of St. Lawrence Centre (Toronto), Emelin Theatre (NY); 2 perfs., 2nd Int. Guitar Fest., Toronto, 1978; Perfd. w. McMaster Symph. Orch., Hamilton, Ont., 1979; Recital at Hart House, Univ. of Toronto, 1979 (recorded); TV & Radio apps., UK, USA & Can.; Many perfs. as duo w. John Mills, recitals in UK & Can. Recordings incl: Guitar '75. Mbrships: Am. Fedn. of Musicians, USA & Can.; Toronto Guitar Soc. Hons. incl: Sev. First Awards, Kiwanas Music Fest. Assn.; 1st Place, Guitar, Int. Stepping Stone Class of the Can. Music Competitions, 1973; Recip., Scholarship by Alexandre Lagoya to study w. him; 2 Maximum Grants, Can. Govt., 1975-76, 1976-77; Exhibition scholarship, RCM; Jack Morrison Prize, ibid. Hobby: Psychology. Address: 32 Harrison Rd., Willowdale, Ont. M2L 1V4, Can.

GANGE, Kenneth Edward, b. 13 June 1939, Burry Port, Wales, UK. Schoolmaster (Music); Composer. Educ: Pvte. studies w. John Brydson; ARCM; AMusTCL; FVCM. m. Jacqueline Mary Perks, 2 d. Career: Schoomaster; Composer. Comps: Festive Suite (for recorders); Miniature Suite (piano); Wedding Music (organ); Var. pieces of Ch. Music and carols; Christmas Prelude (recorders & piano; Three Easy Pieces (violin & piano), etc. Contbr. to: Child Educ.; Music Tchr.; Welsh Music. Hons: 1st Prizes, Anthem for Christmas and Organ Solo, St. Peters Music Makers (Bexhill on Sea), 1978. Hobbies: Reading; Visiting ancient ruins and sites; Listening to radio. Address: 129 Dartmouth Ave., Cannock, Staffs. WS11 1EJ, UK.

GANGEMI, Charles David, b. 22 Dec. 1928, Phila., Pa., USA. Professor of Theory and Piano. Educ: BMus, 1951, MA, 1955, Univ. of Pa. Career: piano, lieder and contemp. chmbr. recitals, inclng. premier perfs. of Am. works in NYC, Princeton, Phial. & Wash. DC. Compositions (unpubld.): String Quartet; Shakespeare Songs; Paino Pieces. Mbrships: Am. Soc. of Univ. Comps.; Am. Musicol. Soc.; Pa. Music Tchrs. Assn.; Phi Mu Alpha. Hons: Hilda K Nitsche Prize, 1950, David Halstead Award, 1951, Univ. of Pa. Hobbies: Collecting recordings; Attending concerts & opera; Art. Address: Cambridge Hall Apts., Pembroke House A3, W Chester, PA 19308, USA.

GANGFLØT, Søren, b. 20 Apr. 1921, Onsoy, Norway. Organist; Pianist; Choral Director. Educ: Oslo Conserv. of Music; Study in Paris, Copenhagen, Haarlem & Amsterdam; Organist Dip., 1952. m. Bjorg Roed, 5 c. Career: as pianist, 1943; as organist, Oslo, 1946. Career incl: Radio broadcasts in France, Holland, Belgium, Denmark, Sweden, Finland & Norway; Organ recitalist in Germany, Holland, USA & Scandinavia; Organist & Choral Dir., Chs. of Krakeroy, Ptrs (Oslo) & Fredrikstad Cathedral. Compositions incl: Missa for 3 voices a capella; Sanctus for mixed chorus; 65 short chora preludes; 290 choral introductions; 4 motets, etc. Mbrships Soc. of Norwegian Organists; Soc. of Norwegian Musicians Hobbies: Reading; Dogs; Sport. Address: Glommens gt. 4 Fredrikstad, Norway.

GANSON, Paul, b. 18 Sept. 1941, Detroit, Mich., USA Bassoonist. Educ: BA, 1964, MA, 1968, Univ. of Mich. m Astrid Akmentins, 1 s. Career: Bassoonist, City of Belfast Orch. Toledo Orch., Dallas Symph. Orch., Detroit Symph. Orch.; Artis Tchr., Univ. of Windsor, dept. of Music, Can., 1974-; Vis Lectr. in Bassoon, Schl. of Music, Univ. of Mich., 1975. Made broadcasts recordings w. Northern Ireland BBC orch: Mozart Concerto No. 1 in B flat for bassoon & orch., Sonata for bassoon and cello. Contbr. to The Bulletin, Detroit Histl. Soc. Mbrships incl: Pres., Bd. of Trustees, Orch. Hall, Inc.; Charter Mbr., Int. Double Reed Soc.; Fndng. Admnstr., Detroit Symph. Youth Orch. Hobbies: Reading; Skiing. Address: 23225 Oak Ave., Dearborn, MI 48128, USA.

GANSZ, George Lewis, b. 5 Apr. 1924, Phila., Pa., USA. Music Director; Conductor; Arranger; Composer. Educ: BS, Temple Univ.; MS, Univ. of Pa.; LTCL; FTCL; orchl. cond. w. Pierre Monteux & Eugene Ormandy; studied w. E Power Biggs, Organ Inst.; NBC Inst. of Radio & TV. m. Martha Sealey Gansz, 2 c. Career: Cond., Comp. & Arr. w. var. colls. & univs., profl. orchs., Town Hall & Carnegie Hall, NYC & NBC & CBS radio networks; currently Music Dir., Va. Mil. Inst. Comps. publd. by Shawnee Press & J Fischer (Belwin). Contbr. to jrnl. of Am. Choral Dirs. Assn. Mbrships: Am. Symph. Orch. League; Coll. Band Dirs. Nat. Assn.; AGO; Coll. Music Soc.; Am. Choral Dirs. Assn.; AAUP. Recip. var. hons. Address: Va. Mil. Inst., Lexington, VA 24450, USA.

GANT, William Campbell, b. 24 Aug. 1916, Lincoln, Neb., USA. Pianist; Teacher. Educ: Dip., Yale Univ., New Haven, Conn., 1939; BM, ibid., 1941; MMus, ibid., 1946; Dip., Am. Schl. of Music, Fontainebleau, France, 1951; Dip., Nat. Conserv. of Music, Paris, France, 1953. Career: Instructor, Piano, Univ. of NC, 1941-42, Piano & Chmbr. Music, Yale Univ., 1946-51; Asst. Organist & Choir Master, Nat. Cathedral, Wash., DC, 1936-37; Prof. of Music, Univ. of Ark., 1953-. Recordings: Bach, Prelude & Fugue in A Minor; Beethoven, Sonata in E Flat Major, op. 81 a, Emperor Concerto; Franck, Prelude, Choral & Fugue; Paul Dukas, Sonata in E Flat Minor; Bach: Brandenburg Concerto Gross no. 5; Gershwin: Rhapsody in Blue. Contbr. to: Review; Perspective. Mbrships: Music Tchr. Nat. Assn.; Am. Music Ctr., NY; Ark. State MTA; Smithsonian Inst.; Phi Mu Alpha, AAUP. Hons: Premiere Medals, Solfegge, Sight Reading, Chmbr. Music, Fontainebleau, 1951; Bronze Plaque for Disting. Service to Music in Ark., 1961. Hobbies: Gardening; Walking; Hiking; Travel. Address: 1658 Hotz Dr., Fayetteville, AR 72701, USA. 7.

GANZ, P Felix, b. 23 Jan. 1922, Basel, Switzerland. Professor; Dean of Chicago Musical College, Roosevelt Univeristy. Educ: Univ. of Basel; Art Inst., Chgo., USA; Dip. in Piano, Konservatorium, Basel, 1946; MMus, Piano Chgo. Musical Coll., 1948; PhD, Music Hist., Northwestern Univ. Career: Piano Instr., Chgo. Musical Coll., 1947-54; Dir., Non-Credit Divs., ibid., 1949-54; Asst., Assoc. Prof., Piano, Roosevelt Univ., 1954-70; Dean, Chgo. Musical Coll. & Prof. of Piano, 1970-. Contbr. to US, Swiss Jrnls. Mbrships: Bd. Mbr., Soc. of Am. Musicians, Chgo.; Advsr., Contemp. Concerts, Chgo.; MENC; MTNA; Swiss Composers & Musicians League; Am. Musicol. Soc.; Bach Riemenschneider Inst.; Coll. Music Soc. Hobbies: Mountain climbing; Philately; Heraldic arts. Address: 430 S Michigan Ave., Chicago, IL 60605, USA. 2, 8.

GARABEDIAN, Edna, b. 28 May 1939, Fresno, Calif., USA. Opera Singer; Teacher. Educ: BA, Fresno State Coll., Calif.; Nat. Inst. of Opera, 2 yrs. m. Otis S Dugule Jr., 2 d. Debut: NY C Opera as Santuzza (Cavalleria Rusticana), 1964. Career: apps. w. NYC Opera, Kansas City Lyric Opera, Balt. Civic Opera, Fresno Opera Assn., Wash. Opera Soc., Chgo. Lyric Opera Co., Houston Grand Opera Co.; now w. State Theatre, Nürnberg; guest apps. Munich, Berlin, Düsseldorf, Augsburg, Hannover, Frankfurt & Stuttgart opera houses; perfs. also w. San Diego Opera Co., Fresno Grand Opera & in Sao Paulo, Brazil; num. concert apps.; var. teaching posts incl. Am. Univ., Washington, & Calif. State Univ.; pvte. teaching. Hons: num. grants & awards incl. Disting. Artists Award, NYC & 1st place, Am. Medallist, 4th Int. Tchaikovsky Competition, Moscow, USSR; app. in The Magic Flute at White House for late Pres. & Mrs. Kennedy. Address: 3338 Lowe Ave., Fresno, CA 93702, USA. 5.

GARANT, Serge, b. 22 Sept. 1929, Quebec City, P.Q., Can. Composer; Conductor; Teacher; Pianist. Educ: Piano w. S Lacharitté & Y Hubert; Comp. w. C Champagne & O Messiaen; Counterpoint w. J Binet & A Vaurabourg-Honegger. Debut: Concert of contemporary music, Montreal, 1954. Career: Clarinettist, w. Sherbrooke Symph. Orch., 1946-50; Arranger, Comp. & Pianist, CBC, 1957-67; Fndr. and Musical Dir., Société de Musique Contemporaine du Québec, 1966; Prof. and Sec. of Fac. of Music, Université de Montréal. Comps: Concerts sur terre, Cage d'oiseau, 1962; Variations, 1954; Asymétries, 1958-59; Jeu à auatre, 1968; Circuits II, 1972; Offrande III, 1971; Anerca, 1961; Phrases I, 1967; Chand d'amours, 1975 (all recorded). Contbr. to: Musique de notre siècle (texts), CBC-FM Weekly. Mbrships: Ligue Canadienne des Compositeurs. Hons: Jullliard Schl. Award, 1949; 1st Prize, Comp., Sherbrooke Youth Fest., 1950; Medal of Conseil Canadien de la Musique, 1971; Wm. Harold Moon Trophy (BMI), 1978. Hobbies: Art collection; French cuisine; Outdoor winter sports. Address: 2300 St. Mathieu, app. 911, Montreal, Québec, Can.

GARBELOTTO, Antonio, b. 9 Feb. 1906, Venice, Italy. Composer; Musicologist; Teacher of Organ. Educ: Dip., Composition, 1936, Organ, 1938, C Pollini Schl., Padua; studied w. Or. Ravanello & C Grassi. m., 1 s. Debut: perf. of Trittico Natalizio (Nativity Triptych), Sala della Ragione, Padua, 1937; Tchr. of Music Hist. & Libn., C Pollini Music Acad., Padua, 1945, V Bellini Conserv. of Music, Palermo, 1956-61; G Rossini Conserv. of Music, Pesaro, 1962-69, FE Dall' Abaco State Conserv. of Music, Adria Sect., 1979-. Compositions incl: Mondo Piccino (for str. orch.), 1938; 3 Pieces in Diverse Styles for Organ, 1942; Adagio for violin, cello & organ, 1945; Suite in the Antique Style (organ), 1950; Gesu di Nazareth (oratorio for boys' choir, baritone solo & piano), 19062; 15 Masses for 1-5 voices (w. organ & w. orch.); 12 Concert Pieces for Organ. Recordings incl: var. organ & choral works on disc & magnetic tape. Publs. incl: Alessandro Scarlatti, 1962; Gino Marinuzzi, 1965; var. bibliog. works. Contbr. to: Disionario Biografico degl' Italiani; Die Musik in geschichte und Gegenwart Ency.; Padova; Il Santo, Pauda. Mbr: Hon., Nobel Acad. Class, Acad. of Scis., Leters & Arts, Milan, 1972. Address: Via E Fermi 112, 47030 Gatteo, Italy.

GARBER, Herbert, b. 8 Dec. 1919, New York, NY, USA. Conductor; Violinist; Violist; Pianist; Teacher. Educ: BA, Wash. Sq. Coll. of Arts & Scis., NYU, 1946; Dip., Frank Damrosch Schl. of Music, 1933; Dip., Violin, Inst. of Musical Art, Juilliard Schl. of Music, 1938; MA, 1963, Profl. Dip., 1964, Tchrs. Coll., Columbia Univ.; EdD, ibid., 1971; Pvte. study, conducting w. Leon Barzin; Violin, w. Ronald Murat & w. Theodore & Alice Pashkus. m. Jeannette Hall, 2 d. Career: Violist, Ronald Murat Str. Quartet, 1940-43; Asst. Cond., NYC Ballet Co., 1951-52; Fac., Am. Theatre Wing, 1951-56; Asst. Cond., Hartford Symph., 1958-59; 2nd Violin, Hartford Str. Quartet, 1958-59; Assoc. Cond., Tulsa Phil. Orch., 1959-61; Dir., Chmbr. Music Prog., Tulsa schls., 1959-61; Fac. of Music, Wilkes Coll., 1965-; Guest Cond., Wilkes-Barre Phil., 1969, '70; Cond., var. musicals, Wilkes-Barre, 1966-74; Cello-piano sonata recitalist (pianist), w. Enzo Liva, 1968-74; Pvte. tchr., conducting. Mbrships: Am. Fedn. of Musicians; AAUP; Am. string Tchrs. Assn.; Nat. Schl. Orch. Assn.; Am. Symph. Orch. League; Alumni Assn., Juilliard. Hons. incl: Shlrships. & study grants, Frank Damrosch Schl. of Music, Inst. of Musical Art, Juilliard, Wash. Sq. Coll. & Tchrs. Coll., Columbia. Hobbies: Abstract sculpting; Photography; Tennis. Address: 64 Mallery Place, Wilkes-Barre, PA 18702, USA.

GARBER, Lloyd Elmer, b. 31 Oct. 1940, Middleton, NS, Canada. Guitarist; Composer; Author. Educ: Comp. credits, Berklee Coll. of Music, Boston, Mass., USA; Studied Lydian Chromatic Concept w. George Russell; Guitar w. Derek Bailey, Ike Isaacs & Wilburn Burchette. Career: Jazz Guitarist at clubs, studios & concerts; Ldr. var. grps. in Can. & USA, 1961-70; Solo concerts & workshops involving Guitar Energy Concepts (Avant Garde), 1971-76; Concerts, video-taping, recordings & composing, 1976-78. Comps. in Eds. of Guitar Energy; Auntie Nature. Recordings: Energy Patterns (solo guitar), 1976. Publs: Guitar Energy, Ed. 1, 1973; Guitar Energy, Ed. 2, 1975;' Guitar Energy, Ed. 3, 1976. Hobbies: Concerts; Travel; Reading; Wine Tasting. Address: Box 7020, Stn. A, Toronto, Canada M5W 1X7.

GARCIA NAVARRO, Luis Antonio, b. 30 Apr. 1941, Valencia, Spain. Conductor. Educ: Royal Conserv., Valencia; Madrid; Music Baad., Vienna. Career incls: Chief Cond., Symph. Orch., Valencia, 1970; Prin. Guest cond., N Phil. Orch. (Netherlands), perfs. w. Spanish Nat. Symph.; City of Barcelona Orch.; Engl. Bach Fest. Orch.; Het Residentie Orkest (Den Haag); Warshau Phil., etc. Num. apps. in Austria, Sweden, Portugal, France, Netherlands, England, Poland. Recordings: w. T Berganza, Placido Domingo etc. var. concertos w. N Yepes; London Symph. Orch. Hons. incl: 1st Prize, Int. Competition for cond., France, 1967. Address: Juan Llorens 20, Valencia, Spain.

GARDEN, Edward James Clarke, b. 28 Feb. 1930. Edinburgh, Scotland, UK. University Professor; Organist. Educ: LRAM; ARCM; FRCO; ARAM; B Mus & D Mus, Univ. Edinburgh. m. Jenett Farrer, 1 s., 1 d. Career: Music Staff, Clifton Coll., 1954-57; Dir. of Music, Loretto, 1957-66; Sr. Lectr. in Music, Organist & Glasgow Univ., 1966-75; Prof. of Music, Sheffield Univ., 1975-; Num. organ recitals, radio perfs. & lectures. Comps. incl: Carlos: Angel Voices Singing; Fairer than the Sun at Morning; 2 Sketches for clarinet & piano. Recordings incl: Organ soloist & Dir., Glasgow Univ. Chapel Choir. Publs. incl: Balakirev (Faber), 1967; Tchaikovsky (Dent), 1973. Mbr. ISM. Hons. incl: Henry Richards Organ Prize. Hobbies: Hill Walking; Reading. Address: Dept. of Music, Univ. of Sheffield, Sheffield S10 2TN, UK.

GARDIEN, Jacques, b. 19 Feb. 1909, Dole, France. Musicologist, Solicitor. Educ: studied law, (dio., scis., jury, dip., dip., sup. studies); Doct. és Lettres, Sorbonne, Paris; studies piano, solfège, organ & harmony, Conserv. m. Anne Bourgès, 3 s., 2 d. Career: Solicitor, Autun, Saône et Loire (hon.); In charge of course on hist. of music, Fac. des Lettres, Dijon; series of radio broadcasts on the hsit. of music (30), ORTF. Publs: L'Orgue et les Organistes en Bourgogne et en Fränche-Comte au 18 ème siècle, 1943; La Chanson Populaire Française, 1948; Jean-Philippe Rameau, 1949; Le Vin dans la chanson populaire bourguignonne, 1967. Contbr. to: L'Orgue; Bull. trimestriel des Amis de L'Orgue; France-Comté et Monts Jura; Echanges et Recherches; L'Organiste, etc. of the Organ; French Assn. for Teaching, etc. Hons: Acad., Mâcon, 1944; Assn. Acad. des Beaux-Aets, Kastner-Boursault triennial prize, 1943. Hobby: Sport. Address: 28 Rue du Pré de L'Etang, 94500 Champigny-sur-Marne, France.

GARDINER, John Eliot, b. 20 Apr. 1943, Shaftesbury, UK. Conductor. Educ: King's Coll., Cambridge 1961-65; MA (Cantab) in Hist.; King's Coll., London, 1965-66; Cert. of Advanced Studies in Music, 1966. Debut: Wigmore Hall, London, 1966. Career: Fndr., Monteverdi Choir, 1964, & Monteverdi Orch., 1978; youngest cond. of Promenade Concert, 1968; has cond. at Engl. Nat. Opera, Royal Opera House; concert revivals in London of major dramatic works of 17th & 18th centuries; world première of Rameau's Les Boréeades, 1975. num. recordings w. awards for early music & choral records. Publs: (ed) Claude le Jeune, Hélas! Mon Dieu, 1971. Contbr. to: The Listener; Music & Musicians. Mbr. ISM. Hons: Gollin Prize, 1964; French Govt. scholarship to study w. Nadai Boulanger. Hobbies: Pedigree Sheep Breeding; Organic Corn Growing in Dorset; Ecological Rehabilitation in Central Africa. Address: 3 Hauteville Ct. Gdns., Stamffor Brook Ave., London W6 0YF, UK. 1.

GARDINER, John Ernest, b. 6 Dec. 1928, Oxford, UK. Musician; Teacher; Organist. Educ: Schlr., Magdalen Coll. Schl., Oxford, 1939-47; Organ Exhibitioner, St. Peter's Coll., Oxford, 1949-53; MA; BMus (Oxon); FRCO; LRAM; Dip. Ed. (Oxon). Career: Dir. Music, Bloxham Schl., Banbury, 1953-62; Hurstpierpoint Coll., Sussex, 1962-64; Belmont Schl., Sussex, 1965-69; Brighton, Hove & Sussex Grammar Schl. (now VIth Form Coll.), 1969-; Examiner, Oxford Delegacy Local Exams. & Assoc. Bd., Royal Schls. Music; Organist & Choirmaster, Hove Parish Ch., 1973-78. Contbr., past music critic, Oxford Times, Banbury Advtsr. & Mid-Sussex Times; var. jrnls. Mbrships: Past Coun., ISM; Past Chmn., Mid-Sussex Arts Fest.; Past Chmn., Lewes Music Fest. Hobbies: Driving; Bridge; Squash. Address: Oak, 13 College Lane, Hurstpierpoint, Sussex BN6 9AB, UK. 3.

GARDINI, Ubaldo Graziano, b. 18 Dec. 1924, Poggio Renatico, Ferrara, Italy. Musician. Educ: Inst. Technico, Vincenzo Monti, Ferrara; A Marconi, Bologna, Letteratura Firenze; violin & viola studies w. Consolini, Barrera & Bruto Michelini; comp. w. Gilfredo Cattolica; singing & var. instruments; worked w. Mascagni. div., 1 s., 2 d. Career: perfs. w. & cond. var. orchs. & ensembles; broadcasts w. RAI; coach at Glyndebourne; res. coach at Covent Gdn.; tchng. at Nat. Opera Studio; concert coaching in NY. num. recordings. Contbr. to sev. Italian musical mags; exhibitions of paintings in Ferrara & in pvte. collections. Hobbies: Gen. Scientific Study; Literature; Art. Address: 86 Elm Grove Rd., Barnes, London, SW13, UK.

GARDNER, Gary David, b. 30 April 1949, Chgo., Ill., USA. Principal Hornist; Artist/Clinician. Educ: Kalamazoo Coll., Mich., 1971-72; Ambassador Coll., St. Albans, UK, 1968-71; Chgo. Musical Coll. of Roosevelt Univ., 1967-68; Studies w. Neill Sanders & Rudolph Macciocchi. m. Marcia Ellen Cvetan. Career incls: Prin. Hornist, Orquesta Sinfonica del Noroeste de Guadalajara, Mexico, 1972-73; Prin. horn, Savannah, Ga., Symph. Orch., 1973-78; currently Prin. horn, Jackson Symph. Orch. & Mbr., Jackson Symph. Woodwind Quintet; Artist/Clinician, Selmer Co. Contbr. to: The Horn Call. Mbrships: Exec. Bd., Savannah Fedn. of Musicians, Local 447-704; Am. Fedn. of Musicians; Int. Horn Soc., 1971-78. Hons: Prize winner, Rome Fest. Orch. Concerto Competition, 1977. Hobbies: Rebuilding histl. horns: Cross country running. Mgmt: The Selmer Co., Box 310, Elkhart, Ind., USA. Address: PO Box 4584, Jackson, MS 39216, USA.

GARDNER, John Linton, b. 2 Mar. 1917, Manchester, UK. Composer; Conductor; Pianist; Educator. Educ: BMus, Exeter Coll., Oxford Univ., 1939. m. Jane Abercrombie, 1 s., 2 d. Career incl: Dir. of Music, Repton Schl., 1939-40; RAF Serv., 1940-46; Music Staff, Royal Opera House, Covent Gdn., 1946-52; Tutor, Morley Coll., 1952-76; Dir. of Music, ibid., 1965-69; Prof. of Composition, Royal Acad. of Music, 1956-; Dir. of Music, St. Paul's Girls' Schl., 1962-75; Compositions incl: Symph.; 5 operas; 3 concertos; 7 cantatas; num. instrumental, choral, vocal & solo works, etc. Recordings incl: A Latter Day Athemian Speaks (Argo); Brass Quartet (Argo).

Contbr. to var. music jrnls. Mbrships: Exec. Dir., Performing Rights Soc.; Coun., CGGB. Hons: Gold Medal, Bax Soc., 1958; Hon. RAM, 1959; CBE, 1976. Hobbies: Eagrephily; Tesseraphily. Address: 10 Lynton Rd., New Malden, Surrey, UK. 1, 3, 14, 16.

GARDNER, Randy Clyburn, b. 2 June 1952, S Bend, Ind., USA. Horn Instructor; Horn Instructor. Educ: BMus, Ind. Univ. Schl. of Music, 1974. m. Barbara Bradford Gardener, 2 s. Career: 2nd Horn, Miami Phil., Fla., 1974-75, Phila. Orch., 1975-; Instructor of Horn, New Schl. of Music & Temple Univ. Recordings: as Mbr., Phila. Orch. Mbrships: Pi Kappa Lambda; Phi Mu Alpha Sinfonia; Int. Horn Soc. Hobbies: History; Sports; Reading; Theology. Address: 138 E St. Andrews Dr., Mt. Laurel, NJ 08054, USA.

GARDNER, Robert Neil, b. 27 Feb. 1922, Colchester, Essex, UK. Diplomat. Educ: Pvte. study of music; LRAM. m. Grace Rolleston, 1 s. Career incls: Prin. Cellist, Aspen Music Fest., Aspen, Colo., 1979-. Mbr., CGGB. Hons: Cheltenham Gold Cup for Comp., 1946; Hobby: Music. Address: 91 Bedford Gdns., London W8, UK. 3.

GARDNER, Samuel, b. 25 Aug. 1891, Elizabethgrad, Russia. Violinist; Teacher; Composer; Conductor. Educ: Artist Dip., Juilliard Schl. of Music. m. Henrietta Holtzman, 1 s., 1 d. Debut: as Violinist, NYC, 1913. Career: Tchr. of Violin, Juilliard Schl. of Music, 1924-41; concerts in USA; App. w. NY Philharmonic Orch., playing own Violin Concerto in E Minor, NYC, 1925; same w. Boston Symph. Orch., Providence, RI, 1925. Compositions: violin pieces; From the Cane Brake; Piano Quintet in F Minor; School of Violin Suty Based on Harmonic Thinking. Mbr: Bohemian Club, NYC. Recip. of Pulitzer Prize for 1st Str. Quartet, Columbia Univ., NYC. Address: 303 W 66 St., Apt. 15 GE, New York, NY 10023, USA.

GARFORTH, David, b. 9 May 1942, Harrogate, UK. Conductor. Educ: RMCM, 1960-64; Paris Conserv., 1965-68. Career: Tutor, RNCM, 1969-75; Prin. Cond., Tehran Opera House, 1975-76; Staff cond., Scottish Ballet, 1976-77; guest cond., BBC, City of Birmingham Symph. Orch., London Mozart Players, also in France, Germany, Bulgaria, Iran, Aust. & USA. Recording w. London Mozart Players, 1979. Hons: Silver medal, Ricordi Opera Prize, RMCM; Premier Prix, Paris Conserv., 1968; Silver medal for improvisation, Worshipful Co. of Musicians, London, 1968. Mgmt: Helen Jennings Concert Agency, 60 Paddington St., London W14 3RR, UK. Address: c/o mgmt.

GARLAND, Roger Kimberley, b. 29 Sept. 1945, Bristol, UK. Violinist. Educ: studied violin w. Ivey Dickson & Manoug Parikian; ARCM (perfs. & tchrs. dips.); LRAM (perfs. dip.); LGSM (perfs. & piano dips.); LRAM (tchrs. piano dip.); Mus B, MA, Fitzwilliam Coll., Cambridge. m. Viviane Ronchetti, 2 s. Debut: Wigmore Hall, 1973. Career: w. Nat. Youth Orch. of GB, Soloist on tour to Israel & Greece, 1963, Ldr. for 3 yrs.; Mbr.; Soloist in tours to S Am., 1972, Italy, 1975, Engl. Chmbr. Orch.; Mbr., Soloist in NZ & Aust., Mbr. of Octet since 1975, Acad. of St. Martin's-in-the-Fields, 1973-. Mbrships: ISM; Musicians Union. Hobbies: Squash; Tennis; Vintage cars. Mgmt: Marjorie Dutton, 27B Nottingham Pl., London NW1, UK. Address: 31 The Ridgeway, Kenton, Harrow, Middx., UK.

GARLICK, Antony, b. Dec. 1927, Sheffield, UK. Professor of Music, Organ, Piano, Harpsichord, Theory, History & Composition. Educ: RCM Maestro, Organ & Comp., Santa Cecilia Conserv., Rome; MusM, Musicol., Univ. of Toronto, Can.; Univ. of Va. m. Fiorella Tiade Missoni, 2 s. Career incls: Coll. Prof. Num. comps. incl: 57 Organ Preludes; Masquerade for band; 2 String Quartets; Pasticcio, for Orch.; Sinfonietta, Brass Choir. Mbrships: Coll. Music Soc.; Am. Musicol. Soc.; Neb. Educ. Assn.; Musical Heritage Soc. Hons: Nat. Endowment for the Humanities Award, 1976. Address: 602 Main St., Wayne, NB 68787, USA.

GAROFALO, Robert Joseph, b. 25 Jan. 1939, Scranton, Pa., USA. Music Educator; Trombonist; Conductor. Educ: Eastman Schll. of Music; Am. Symph. Orch. League E. Coast Cond. Inst., BS., Mansfield State Coll., Pa., 1960; MM., Cath. Univ. of Am., Wash., DC., 1963; PhD, ibid., 1969. m. Ann Marie Bowling, 1 s., 1 d. Career: Trombonist, USAF Band, Wash., DC; Music Educator, elem., second & univ. levels, pub. & pvte. schls.; currently Prof. of Music, Cath. Univ. of Am., Wash., DC. Comps: Publs: The Life & Works of Frederick Shepherd Converse 1871-1940, 1969; Blueprint for Band, 1976; Ensemble Sessions, 1979. Contbr. to Music Educators Jrnl.; Musart; Grove's Dictionary of Music & Musicians; Coun. for Rsch. in Music Educ. Bulletin & Jrnl; Instrumentalist; NH Quarter Notes. Mbrships: Pi Kappa Lambda, 1968; Phi Mu Alpha; MENC; State Chmn., DC., Coll. Band Dirs. Nat. Assn. Hobbies: Tennis; Archery; Woodcraft. Address: 6306 Pontiac St., Coll. Pk., MD 20740, USA.

GAROVI, Angelo, b. 25 Jan. 1944, Sarnen, Obwalden, Switz. Musicologist; Organist. Educ: PhD, Univ. Zürich & Bern, 1972; Organistenschule Luzern (Organ & Theory); w. Mauricio Kagel, Rheinische Musikschule, Cologne. m. Anne Marie von Moos, 2 c. Career: Editor, new music & Ch. music, Radio-Studio Bern. Contbr. to: Luzerner Zeitungen, as Music Critic. Mbr., Schweiz Tonkünstlerverein. Address: Aegertenstrasse 6, CH-3005 Bern, Switz.

GARRARD, Don, b. Vancouver, BC, Canada. Opera Singer. Educ: Royal Toronto Conserv. of Music; Acad. of the W, Santa Barbara, Calif.; Opera Schl., Milan. m. Margaret Gale, 1 d. Career: Prin. Soloist, Can. Opera Co., Sadler's Wells, 1961; solo apps. w. Welsh Nat. Opera & Scottish Opera; TV & cinema apps.; apps. in UK prods. of Il Trovatore, Eugene Onegin, Jeptha, Anna Bolena. Recordings incl: Roberto Devereux; Bruckner's Te Deum; The Rake's Progress. Address: 85 Morden Hill, London SE13, UK. 2.

GARRICK, Michael, b. 30 May 1933, Enfield, UK. Composer; Pianist; Organist; Electronic Keyboard Player; Teacher; Lyricist. Educ: BA (Hons.) London; Post Grad. Cert. in Educ.; Opern Fellowship to Berklee Coll. of Music, Boston, Mass. Career: Num. recitals in schls.; Tutor, Wavendon Allmusic Plan; Dir., WAP Jazz Course; as group leader, many BBC perfs. and tours, UK; First jazz musician to perform at St. Paul's, Coventry Cathedral and the Royal Fest. Hall, using pipe organs. Comps. incl: Jazz Praises, 1968; Mr. Smith's Apocalypse, 1969; Judas Kiss, 1971; The Hobbit Suite, 1973; Heavenly Bodies, 1974; Underground Streams, 1977. Recordings: Poetry & Jazz in Concert (4 vols.); October Woman; Promises; Black Marigolds; Heart is a Lotus; Home Stretch Blues; Troppo. Contbr. to: Jazz Now. Mbrships: Dir., Jazz Centre Soc., 1975-. Hobby: Sound recording. Address: 12 Castle St., Berkhamsted, Herts., UK.

GARRISS, Phyllis Weyer, b. 25 Dec. 1923, Hastings, Neb., USA. Music Educator; Musician (violin). Educ: AB, B Mus, Hastings Coll., 1945; M Mus, Eastman Schl. of Music, Univ. of Rochester, 1948; grad. studies in Switzerland, Aspen Inst. & Tchrs. Performance Inst., Oberlin, Ohio. m. William Philip Garriss, 1 s., 2 d. Career: Instr., Music Theory & Violin, DePauw Univ., Greencastle, Ind., 1948-51; Vis. Instr., violin, Ball State Univ., Summers 1951 & 53; Asst. Prof. of Music, Meredith Coll., Raleigh, NC, 1951; Vis. Instr., Appalachian State Cannon Music Camp, summers, 1971-; Mbr., TriCity Chmbr. Symph., 1951-, Roanoke Symph., 1954-64, & Duke Univ. Symph., 1954-. Contr. to Am. String Teacher. Mbrships. incl: Am. String Tchrs. Assn.; MENC; MTNA, AAUP; Mu Phi Epsilon; Pi Kappa Lambda. Hobbies: Cooking; Chamber Music. Address: 3400 Merriman Ave., Raleigh, NC 27607, USA. 7, 27, 29.

GARROTT, Alice, b. 13 July, 1948, Battle Ground, Ind., USA. Mezzo-soprano. Educ: BMus (voive), MMus (voice), Ind. Univ., Bloomington. Debut: PBS TV "Princess Bolokonsky", Myskin. Career: PBS TV, USA & Europe, Vera Boronnel, The Consul, 1977; PBS TV, USA, Old Baroness, Vanessa; Spoleto Fest., USA, 1977, '78. Recordings: Christopher Columbus, Queen Isabella, 1976. Mbrships: Delta Omicron. Hons: Metropolitan Opera Regional Audition Winner, 1971, '72, Northwest Ind. Region. Hobbies: Jazz Dancing; Studying acting. Mgmt: Ludwig Lustig & Florian, 111 W 57th St., NY 10019, USA. Address: 115 W 82nd St., Apt. 2R, NY, NY 10024.

GARSIDE, Patricia Ann, b. 3 Feb. 1834, Norfolk, Neb., USA. Flautist. Educ: BM, Calif. State Univ., LA.; Flute studies w. Roger S Stevens of the LA Phil. Orch., George Drexler, Los Angeles Phil. & Julius Baken, NY Phil. m. G Rodney Garside, 1 s., 1 d. Career: Prin. Flautist, Pasadena Symph. Orch. & Fest. Players of Calif.; Music Fac. USC; Calif. State Univ., LA; appears regularly on Getty Museum Chamber Music series. Mbrships: Musicians Union, Local 47, Los Angeles; Local 7, Orange County; Sigma Alpha Iota (SAI). Nat. Assoc., Coll. Wind & Percussion Instructors. Hons: Alumni Award for Music, Calif. State Univ., 1975; Sigma Alpha Iota Deans Honor Award, Calif. State Univ., 1975. Hobbies: Needlework; Gardening. Address: 2147 Gardi St., Bradbury, CA 91010, USA.

GARTENLAUB, Odette, b. 13 Mar. 1922, Paris, France. Pianist; Composer; Professor. Educ: Conserv. de Paris. m. Haultier Bernard, 1 d. Career: apps. as soloist on radio; concerts w. orch.; recitals; Prof., Conserv. Nat. Supérieur de Musique de Paris. Comps: Concerto for flute & orch.; Concerto for piano & orch.; chmbr. music; music for tchng. use. Hons: 1st prize, piano, harmony & fugue, Conserv. de Paris; 1st Grand Prix de Rome for comp. Address: 36 rue de la Tour Auvergne, 65009 Paris, France.

GARTRELL, Carol Ann, b. 24 Dec. 1952, Morley, Yorks., UK. Lecturer in Music. Educ: BMus, Univ. of Surrey, 1974;

Further Educ. Tchrs. Cert., 1979. m. Paul Gartrell, 1 d. Career: Archivist, Boosey & Hawkes Music Publishers Ltd., 1974-76; Lectr. in Music, Kingston Polytechnic (Gipsy Hill Ctr.), 1976-; Tutor, Open Univ., 1978-. Publs: Orchestral Catalogue - Agency Works, 1976; Introductory Notes for Series & Song Collections & Editorial Errata for many Boosey & Hawkes Publs. mbr., ISM. Hobbies: Rsch. for MPhil/PhD on: The Baryton, Its History & Music Reexamined. Address: 168 Argyle Ave., Hounslow, Middx., UK.

GARVELMANN, Donald M, b. 19 Feb. 1927, Stamford, Conn., USA. Music Editor & writer; Piano Teacher; Artistic Director. Educ: Keyboard studies w. Leroy Taylor, David Rabinowitz & Phillis Moss. Career: Radio progs. incl: the many transcriptions (piano, instrumental & orchestral) of Chopin's Minute Waltz, 1969; Special 3-hour prog. on composer K S Sorabji, 1970; Fndr., Artistic Dir., & Mgr., Music Treasure Publs. (devoted to making available neglected Romantic music). Publs: Ed.-annotator, Thirteen Transcriptions for Piano Solo of Chopin's Minute Waltz, 1969; Compiler-annonator, Youthful & Early Works of Alexander & Julian Scriabin, 1970; Annotator-Henry Herz. Op.60. Variations on non piu mesta from Rossini's La Cenerentola for piano solo, 1970. Contbr. to: Clavier. Hobbies: Swimming; Cycling; Hiking; Gardening; Painting. Address: 620 Ft. Washington Ave., Apt. 1-F, NY, NY 10040, USA.

GARVEY, David, b. Reading, Pa., USA. Pianist; Coach-Accompanist. Educ: Dip., Post-Grad. Dip., Juilliard Schl. of Music. Career: Assoc. Pianist w. many noted artists, USA, Can., Europe, Far E, Aust., etc; Pianist, Coach, Ivan Galamian's Summer Schl. for Strings, Meadowmount, also conducting Master Classes for singers & accomps., NYC, Univ. of Tex., Austin & var. other univs., for over 20 yrs. Has recorded for RCA Victor & other labels. Mbrships: Am. Matthay Soc.; NY Singing Tchrs. Assn. Hons: Rosenberg Award; Damrosch Prize. Hobbies: Walking; Reading; Theatre. Address: 303 W 66th St., Apt. E13A, NY, NY 10023, USA.

GARY, Marianne, b. 19 July 1903, Vienna, Austria. Professor; Composer. Educ: Univ. of Vienna & High Schl. for Music. Career: Tchr., grammar schl., Vienna; apps. on ORF (Austrian radio), 1977 & '78; Dr. Phil. Comps. incl: many songs for var. voices; duets; choir music; chamber music; comps. for full & str. orch.; Oratorio, Von Leid u. Heldentorn Ungenaneston, for soloists, choirs, organ & large orch., religious music. Mbrships: Austrian Comps. Assn.; Union of Friends of Chmbr. Music. Hobbies: Mountain walking; Listening to music; Lyric writing. Address: 1190 Vienna, Pfarrwiesung 23/521, Austria.

GASCOIGNE, Brian Alvery, b. 16 June 1943, Much Wenlock, Shrops., UK. Composer; Arranger; Pianist; Percussionist. Educ: BA, Univ. of Cambridge. Career: Film scores incl: Under Milk Wood, 1969; Malachi's Cove, 1972; Phase IV, 1974; Comps: (recorded) Emperor Nero Suite (guitar); (arr.) LP of Vivaldi, Bach, & Purcell. Recordings: 4 LP of Vivaldi, Bach, & Purcell. Recordings: 4 LPs w. Stomu Yamashta. Publ: Shusha's Book of Persian Folk Songs (Ed.), 1978. Hobbies: Theatre; Gardening. Address: 25 Parliament Hill, London NW3, UK.

GASSMANN, Frank Silver, b. 22 Dec. 1939, Winterthur, Switz. Violinist. Educ: Music. Acad., Winterthur, 7 yrs.; Music Acad., Geneva, Michel Schwalbé & Lorand Fenyres, 6 yrs.; Music Adac., Basle, Hansheinz Schneeberger, 1 yr. m. Roswitha Stolz, 1 c. Debut: Violin concerto by Bruch, Winterthur Stadtorchester, 1952. Career: Ldr., First Violin (Konzertmeister), Tonhalle und Theater Orchester, Zürich; serv. TV & Radio apps. during the past years (solo). Recordings: 4 recordings w. own Chamber Orch, The Baroque Strings, Zürich, & two as Soloist (Leclair, violin concerto F-dur); Vivaldi Double concerto for violin and villoncello B-Dur. Mbr., Schweiz. Musikverband. Hons: First prize, TV competition, 1956; Prix de virtuosité, Geneva, 1963. Hobbies: Sports; Travelling. Address: Opernhaus, 8000 Zürich, Switz.

GASTER, Adrian, b. 9 Feb. 1919, London, UK. Music Critic; Conductor; Pianist; Teacher; Writer; Research Worker; Editor. Educ: BA Hons., English, University Coll., London; Mus B, MA Christ's Coll., Cambridge; ARCM; Piano studies w. Hilda Bor. div. 2 s., 1 d. Career: Music Critic, Express & Star, Wolverhampton, 1949-57; Music Critic John o'London's, 1959-62; Fndr. & Cond., Wolverhampton Opera Club, 1952-57; Cond. perfs. of Carmen, Cav. Pag, La Traviata, Le Nozze di Figaro, etc. Hd., Music Dept., Burnham Grammar Schl., 1960-74; Rsch. worker, Melrose Press, 1975-; Ed., 8th - 9th Edition, Who's Who in Music and Musician's Directory; WEA Lectr., 1959-. Contbr. to Encyclopedia della Spettacolo; The Spectator; var. newspapers Prog. notes for Israel Phil. Orch., 1955. Hons: 1st Prize, Comp., Wolverhampton Music Fest., 1950, 1952. Hobbies: Playing chmbr. music; Chess; Reading. Address: Ty-Bach, Glynbrochan, Llanidloes, Powys SY18 6PL, UK.

GATES, Crawford Marion, b. 29 Dec. 1921, San Francisco, Calif., USA. Conductor; Composer. Educ: BA San Jose Coll.; MA, Brigham Young Univ.; PhD Music, Eastman Schl. of Music, Rochester Univ. m. Georgia Lauper, 2 s., 2 d. Debut: As Composer, Stanford Univ., 1938; Cond., Utah Symph., 1948. Career: Chmn., Dept. of Music & Cond., Symph., Orch. & Opera, Brigham Young Univ., 1960-66; Artist in Res. & Prof., Music, Beloit Coll., Wis., 1966-; Music Dir., Beloit Symph. Orch., 1966-; Music Dir., Quincy Symph. Orch., 1969-70; Music Dir., Rockford Symph. Orch., 1970-. Compositions inclk: Promised Valley (musical play) & 4 other stage works: 5 symphs., num. choral arrangements, 2 maj. choral works, Trumpet Concertino, Horn Sonata. Recordings: Symph. No. 2 recorded by Utah Symph.; Beloved Mormon Hymns (orch. setting). I Am Called By Thy Name; A New Commandment; To Obey is Better than Sacrifice. Publs: Catalog of Published American Choral Music, 1955, 2nd ed., 1969; Approx. 100 misc. choral works. Mbrships: Am. Symph. Orch. League; ASCAP; MENC; Nat. Fedn. of Music Clubs; Am. Fedn. of Musicians. Hons: 1st Prize, 1st Annual Max Wald Competition, NYC, 1955. Hobbies: Tennis; Reading. Address: 911 Park Ave., Beloit, WI 53511, USA. 1, 2, 8.

GATES, J Terry, b. 4 Oct. 1936, Aurora, Ill., USA. Administrator; Teacher; Conductor. Educ: BS, Northern Ill. Univ., DeKalb, 1958; Mus M., ibid., 1964; EdD., Univ. of Ill., Urbana, 1974; Studied doublebass viol w. Radivoj Lah, Chgo. Symph. Orch.; Studied tuba w. William Whybrew & Daniel Perantoni; Studied cond. w. Thor Johnson. m. Laurie, 1 s., 1 d. Career: Pub. schl. tchr., instrumental & gen. music, N. Ill., 1958-61 & 1962-64; Music Dept. Fac., Northern Ill. Univ. 1961-62 & 1964-68; Dir. of Music Placement, Univ. of Ill. Schl. of Music, 1968-72; Chmn., Music Dept. & Dir., Instrumental Music, Teach Composition, Orchestration & Conducting, Muskingum Coll., New Concord, Ohio, 1972-. Contbr. to The Ill. Music Educator. Mbrships: Music Educators Nat. Conf.; Ohio Music Educ. Assn.; Dist. Pres., State Bd., Mbr., Mag. Ed. & Chmn., State Student Mbrship., Ill. Music Educators Assn.; Pi Kappa Lambda; Phi Mu Alpha Sinfonia. Recip., Composition prize, Epsilon Rho Chapt., Phi Mu Alpha, 1962. Hobbies: Carpentry; Camping; Tennis; Painting. Address: 1 E. High St., New Concord, OH 43762, USA.

GATI, Laszlo, b. 25 Sept. 1925, Timisoara, Roumania. (Canadian Citizen). Conductor; Musician (violin & viola). Educ: Nat. Conserv. of Music (violin & condng.); Acad. of Music (composition). m. Agnes Keresztesi, 2 d. Career: Mbr., State Phil. Orch., Budapest, 1950; Hd., Symphonic Dept., Hungarian Radio, 1954-56; Fndr.-Music Dir., Montreal Chmbr. Orch., Can., 1959; Music Dir.-Cond., Victoria Symph. Orch., BC, 1967-; Artistic Exec. Dir., Victoria Symmer Festival, 1972-. Recordings: var. works for CBC. Contbr. to: Jeunesses Musicales. Mbrship: Ed., Assn. of Can. Orchs., 1972-. Hons: Prof. Zoltan Kodaly Acad. of Music; Hon. Citizen of City of Victoria. Hobbies: Flying; Swimming; Painting; Sport. Mgmt: Galacon Int., PO Box 5151, Victoria. Address: 591 Falkland Rd., Victoria, BC, Can. V8S 4L6.

GATTERMEYER, Heinrich, b. 9 July 1923, Sierning nr. Steyr, Austria. Composer; Professor. Educ: Vienna Univ.; Musical Acad., Vienna; Tchr. of Music, 1948; Reifepruefungsdiplom Komposition, 1950. m. Franziska Katzböck, 1 s., 3 d. Career: appointed Tchr. of Germanics, Vienna Univ., 1950; currently Prof., Hochschule für Musik, Vienna; TV musicals; Broadcast concerts; Dir., Vienna Schubertbundes. Comps. incl: 3 Oratorios, Intention 1 for large orch.; Piano concerto; Concerto Grosso I & II; Concertino da Camera; 7 Interludien (ballet); Skolion (chmbr.); Asinusrex (opera); 4 musicals; 4 masses; Guitar concerto; Serenade for string orch.; Partita atre for String Orch.; chmbr. works & songs. Mbrships. incl: Pres., Oesterr Gesellschaft für Zeitgenossische. Recip. var. hons. Hobbies: Painting; Skiing. Address: Guyzkowplatz 6/11/2, 1130 Vienna, Austria.

GATWOOD, Robin Frederick, b. 25 Mar. 1916, S Whitley, Ind., USA. Double Bassist; Baritone Horn Player. Educ: BS, 1938, MA, 1939, Peabody Coll., Nashville, Tenn.; EdD, NY Univ., 1960; Nashville Conserv. of Music. m. Mary Ann Bouchard, 2 s., 1 d. Career incls: Dir. of Instrumental Music, City Schl., High Point, NC, 1941-47; Prof. of Music, Lenoir Rhyne Coll., Hickory, NC; Double Bass w. symphs. in Dayton, Ohio, Nashville, Tenn., Greenville & Columbia, SC; Baritone w. Horn w. municipal bands in Dayton, Ohio, Greeville, SC & Nashville, Tenn. Mbr., var. socs. Hobby: Model railroading. Address: 1315 4th St. NW, Hickory, NC 28601, USA. 23.

GAUDIO, Jennie, see under WILKINSON, Jennie Gaudio.

GAUGGEL, George William, b. 26 Aug. 1912, Buffalo, NY, USa. Violist; Violinist. Educ: BA, Samford Univ.; BMus, MMus, Birmingham (Ala.) Conserv. of Music; Post Grad. study, State Univ. of Iowa; Berkshire Music Center, 1947; Peter Paul Prier Workshop in string instrument repair, Utah, 1977. m. Elizabeth Abby Higgins Gauggel, 3 s., 3 d. Career: Pvte. Instructor, viola & violin; Violist, Honolulu Symph. Orch. Mbrships: Am. String Tchrs. Assn. (Corresponding Sec., Hawaii Chapt.). Hons: Percy Goetschius Music Scholarship, 1939; Tchng. Fellowship, State Univ. of Iowa, 1946. Hobbies: Photography; Electronics; Chmbr. Music. Address: 3660 Puuku Mauka Dr., Honolulu, HI 96818, USA.

GAULT, Willis Manning, b. 10 June 1908, Showell, Md., USA. Violinist; Composer; Violin Maker & restorer & repairer. Educ: studied violin & harmony w. Anton Nimmerrichter, Anton kasper & Dudley Clark. m. Katherine Louise Armel, 2 s. Career: Played violin sev. yrs. in Glove Theatre, Berlin, Md.; For 20 yrs. org. & dir. chamber music, workshop in Wash. DC; Much solo work; Has made many violas, cellos, violins, lutes, wuintons, viola d'amores, bass viola da gambas, troubador harps; Prop., Gault Schl. of Bowed Instrument Making. Compositions: Fantasia No. 1 in D maj. for viola d'amore & orch.; Fantasia No. 2 in D minor for viola d'amore & orch.; Suite in A maj. for d'amore & och.; misc. other comps. for viola d'amore. Mbrships: Wash. Readers Club; Musicians, Amateur & Profl. 'Musical Director'. Recip. var. hons. & citations. Hobby: Chamber music. Address: 35A Ridge Rd., Greenbelt, Md., USA, 20770. 2.

GAVAZZENI, Gianandrea, b. 1919, Bergamo, Italy. Musician; Writer; Conductor. Educ: Milan Conserv. w. Renzo Lorenzoni; Study with Ildebrando Pizzetti & Mario Pilati. Career incl: Cond., 1940-; Assoc. w. La Scala, Milan, 1948-; Artistic Dir., ibid., 1966-68; num. int. festival perfs. w. La Scala Co., incl. Edinburgh, 1957, World Fair, Brussels, 1957, Expo 67 Montreal, Bolshoi & Kremlin Theatres, Moscow, 1964. Compositions incl: Concerto bergamasco (orch.); Paolo e Virginia (opera), 1935; Il furioso nell'isola di San Domingo (ballet), 1940; Il Canto di S. Alessandro; Candi d'operai lombardi (orch.); 3 Concerti di Cinquando (orch.); Cello & Violin Concertos; Piano pieces & songs. Publs. incl: studies of Donizetti Pizzetti, Mascagni & Mussorgsky; Guides to the opera of Mozart, Wagner, etc. Address: Via Porta Dipinta 5, Bergamo, Italy.

GAWRYLUK, Jerzy, b. 2 Feb. 1909, Brzesc, USSR. Flautist. Educ: MA, PWSM, Warsaw. m. Wiera Redzko. Debut: Warsaw, 1934. Career: major concerts in Poland & aborad; num. TV & radio broadcasts; concerts w. Polish Nat. Phil. Orch. (as Soloist); Prof. of Music, PSSM, Warsaw. Recordings: Muza label. Mbrships: Assn. of Polish Musical Artists; ZAIKS. Hons: Silver cross of Merit, Gold Cross of Merit & Cross of Polonia Restituta, Polish Coun. of State. Hobbies: Activities in the 7th-day Adventist Church. Address: ul. Armii Ludowej 7m. 96, 00-575 Warsaw, Poland.

GAY, Bram, b. 19 Sept. 1930, Treorchy, Wales, UK. Trumpeter; Orchestral Director. Educ: LRAM. m. Margaret Bywater, 3 s. Career: Prin. Trumpet, City of Birmingham Symph. Orch., 1953; Prin. Trumpet, Halle Orch., 1960; Fndr., Halle Brass Consort, 1961; Orchestral Dir., Royal Opera House, Covent Garden, 1974; Ed., Sounding Brass. num. recordings. Hobbies: Music; Photography. Address: c/o Royal Opera House, Covent Garden, London WC2E 7QA, UK.

GAY, George Errol, b. 8 Feb. 1941, Pouce Coupé, BC., Can. Conductor; Pianist; Trombone Player. Educ: Assoc. of Royal Conserv., Toronto, 1959; BMus, Univ. of BC, 1962; MA, Univ. of NC, Chapel Hill, 1966; DMA, Stanford Univ., 1969. m. Rebecca Ann Cooper, 2 d. Career: Trombonist, Vancouver Symph. Orch., 1960-62; Asst. Dir. of Band, Univ. of NC, 1962-64; Asst. Cond., Stanford Symph. Orch., 1964-66; Cond., St. Lawrence Chamber Orch., Canton, NY, 1968-70; Asst. Cond., Can. Opera (Touring) Co., 1970-72; Assoc. Cond., ibid., 1972-74; Asst. Cond. & Coach, Can. Opera Co., 1971-75; Assoc. chorus master, ibid., 1974-75; Mus. Dir., Can. Opera Co. on Tour, 1974-76; Assoc. Prof., Sul Ross State Univ., Alpine, Tex., 1976-; Fndr., Mus. Dir. & Cond., Big Bend Chamber Orch. & Chorus, Alpine, 1976-. Hons: Top of Graduating Class in Music, Special Prize, Univ. of BC, 1962; Can. Coun. Pre-Doctoral Grant, 1965. Hobbies: Golf; Tennis; Softball; Badminton; Hockey; Bridge; Railroading. Address: c/o Music Dept., Sul Ross State Univ., Alpine, TX 79830, USA.

GAYLER, Wolfgang, b. 19 Dec. 1934, Stuttgart, Germany. Conductor; Pianist. Educ: Musikwissenschaft, Geschichte -Staatsexamin, Universitat Freiburg i. Br.; Staatliche Hochschule für Musik in Stuttgart & Freiburg i. m. Lelia Doflein, 4 c. Debut: Stadt. Buhen, Freiburg. Career incls: apps., Freiburg, Nürnberg, Nancy, Frankfurt, Bayreuth Fest. Hons: Kvanichsteiner Musikpreis (piano), 1958. Hobbies: Botany; Foreign Languages. Mgmt: Muiktheater Nürnberg. Address: Beethoven Str. 16, D-8500 Nürnberg, German Fed. Repub.

GAYLORD, Monica, b. 6 Feb. 1948, NYC, USA. Concert Pianist. Educ: BMus, MMus, Perfs. Cert., Eastman Schl. of Music. Debut: NY Town Hall. Career: Num. solo concerts, Can., for the CBC, and in Europe; TV solos w. the Toronto Symph. & alone. Recordings: Monica Gaylord Plays Ben McPeek; The Toronto Baroque Trio. Hobby: Astrology. Mgmt: David Haber Artists Mgmt. Address: 318 Robert St., Toronto, Ont., Can.

GAZDER, Adi Jamshed, b. 13 Sept. 1930, Calcutta, India. Pianist & Accompanist; Music Critic. Educ: MBBS., Calcutta Univ., 1953; DCH., London, 1957; MRCP., Edinburgh, 1958; FRCP., Edinburgh, 1972; LTCP. (Perf.), 1948. Div. Career: Solo Pianist & Accomp., All India Radio, 1947-; Duo ptnrship w. Stanley Gnomes (violinist), 1960-70 & Beryl Burridge-Majumdar (cellist), 1959-73, on radio & concert platform; Concert apps. regularly both as soloist & chamber music perfs., 1947-; Accomp. for Erich Gruenberg for his All India Radio recital, 1964; Accomp. for Gwendolyn Geddes for her Calcutta concerts, 1969; Concert Tour as accomp. for Margharita Schack-Koellreutter, Calcutta, Lucknow, Bombay, Goa, 1968 & 69; Concert Tour w. Romy Kalb-Gundermann, featuring Lieder recitals, in Rourkela, Jamshedpur, etc. in 1973; Soloist, German Pediatricians Wrld., Nat.Bibliothek Auditorium, Vienna, 1971; concerto soloist w. Delhi Symph. Orch., 1973; Sonata Recitals w. Alexander Schneider, violinist, Delhi, 1974; Beethoven Sonata recital w. Thomas Brandis, Calcutta & Dacca. Prof. of Med. & Hd. of Dept. of Pediatrics, Calcutta Nat. Med. Coll. Music Critic, The Statesman, 1960-; var. articles in weekly mags. Lectures over All India Radio & var. cultural orgs. in Calcutta on musical subjects. Mbrships: Zonal Auditioning Bd. of All-India Radio; Jury, Beethoven All India Comp., 1970. Hons: Stenton-Dozey Gold Medal, 1948; Bhikaiji Palamkote Medal, 1949; Smetana Medal, Calcutta, 1974. Address: No. 99 Park St., Calcutta 700016, W Bengal, India.

GAZE COOPER, Walter Thomas, b. 11 June 1895, Long Eaton, UK. Pianist; Composer; Teacher; Conductor. Educ: Nottingham Univ. Coll.; RAM, London; LRAM (Piano perf.); Registered Tchr., TRC; MRST. m. Frances Lucy Kirkland, 1 d. Debut: (as comp.) Bournemouth Symph. Orch. Career: Var. of his works broadcast by BBC. Comps. incl: 9 Symphs.; 4 Piano Concertos; Concertos for Violin, viola, Oboe, Horn & Guitar; 7 Piano Sonatas; Sonatas for Flute & Piano, Clarinet & Piana, Violin & Piano, etcl.; Athene (1-act opera); Missa Brevis; num. works for piano & chmbr. combinations; Amorea (6 songs for contralto & str. quartet); My Grandchildren (orchl. suite). Mbr., PRS. Hobby: Oriental Art. Address: Resides nr. Nottingham, UK.

GAZZELLONI, Severino, b. 1920, Rome, Italy. Flautist. Career: Int. Concert Perf.; 1st Flute, Italian Radio & TV, Rome; has music written for him by noted contemp. composers inclng. Stravinsky, Boulez, Stockhausen; holds chairs in advanced flute studies at Holiday Course, Darmstadt, State Acad. of Music, Cologne (both German Fed. Repub.), Darlington Summer Schl. of Music, (UK), Kursus, Stockholm (Sweden), Jvanskula Conserv., Helsinki (Finland), Conserv. of St. Cecilia, Rome & Chigiana Acad., Siena (both Italy). Address: Via Tullio Martello 14, Rome, Italy, 3.

GEARY, Barbara Ann, b. 2 July 1935, Chgo., Ill., USA. Concert & Recital Pianist; Professor of Piano. Educ: BA, St. Mary's Coll., Notre Dame, Ind.; Middlebury Coll., Vt.; M Mus, Ind. Univ., Bloomington; Master classes w. Vlado Perlemutter, Paris. Debut: Wigmore Hall, London, UK, 1972. Career: Recitals & concerts, USA, England, France, Germany, Austria, Greece, Spain, Portugal, Scotland. Soloist w. Tulsa Phil. Orch. & Okla. City Symph. Orch.; Prof. of Piano, Ohio Univ., 1963-69, Univ. of NC, presently Okla. State Univ. Mbrships: Music Tchrs. Nat. Assn.; AAUP. Hobbies: Langs.; Teaching French to children; Environmental activist. Address: 2545 S. Birmingham Pl., Tulsa, OK 74114, USA.

GEBAUER, Victor Earl, b. 13 Oct. 1938, Christchurch, NZ. Dean of Chapel; Chairman of Fine Arts Division. Educ: AA, Concordia Coll., Milwaukee, Wis., 1958; BA, Concordia Sr. Coll., Ft. Wayne, Ind., 1960; M. Div., Concordia Seminary, St. Louis, Mo., 1964; PhD, Musicol., Univ. of Minn., 1976; Free Univ., Berlin, 1969-70; Univ. of Chgo., 1968. m. Marilyn Ruth Schrieber, 2 d., 2 s. Career: Dean of Chapel, Chmn., Fine Arts Div., Concordia Coll., St. Paul, Minn., 1977-79. Contbr. to: num. profl. publs. Mbrships: Am. Musicol. Soc.; Int. Heinrich Schütz Soc., etc. Address: Concordia Coll., Hamline & Marshall, St. Paul, MN 55104, USA. 23, 29.

GECK, Martin, b. 19 Mar. 1936, Witten, German Fed. Repub. Full Professor. Educ: 1962, PhD musicol.; 1975, Pvte. Lectr. musicol. Career: Full Prof. Music Educ., Dortmund Univ. Publs. incl: The Vocal Music of Dietrich Buxtehude and the early Period of Pietismus, Kassel, 1965; The Re-discovery of the St. Mathew Passion in the 19th Century, The Contemporary

Documents and their Meaning for the History of Thought, Regensburg, 1967; Nicolaus Bruhn, Life and Works, Cologne, 1968; The Portraits of Richard Wagner, Munich, 1970; Music Therapy as a Problem of Society, Stuttgart, 1973; Sequensen, 1976; Banjo, 1978. Contbr. to: num. profl. jrnls. Address: Königsteiner Str. 75, 432 Hattingen, German Fed. Repub.

GÉCZY, Joseph, b. 27 Mar. 1944, Galánta, Hungary. Composer; Arranger; Pianist; Record Producer. Educ: Dip., Univ. of Economics, Budapest. m. Eva Thalwieser. Career: TV & radio apps as pianist (jazz & pop) in Europe to 1969, in Canada, 1969-. Comps: score for film, It is True, Isn't It?, Budapest, 1963; num. pop. songs published & recorded in Hungary & Can. Hobbies: Sports; Fishing; Chess; Stamp Collecting. Address: Apt. 303, 10011 116th St., Edmonton, Alta. T5K 1VH, Can.

GEDDA, Nicolai, b. 11 July 1925. Operatic Tenor. Educ: Musical Acad., Stockholm, Sweden. Debut: Stockholm, 1952-; Salzburg Fest., 1957-59; Edinburgh Fest., 1958-59; Met. Opera, NYC, 1957-; has appeared in opera, concerts & recitals throughout world. Has made num. recordings. 16.

GEDGE, David Patrick, b. 12 Mar. 1939, London, UK. Organist & CHoirmaster; Teacher. Educ: Royal Academy of Music & Inst. of Educ. London Univ.; LRAM; GRSM (London); FRCO. m. Hazel Davies, 1 s., 1 d. Career: Chorister, Southwark Cathedral, 1947-59; Treble Soloist, 1st London perf. of Britten, St. Nicholas; Treble, Coronation Choir, 1953; Viola Player, London jr. Orch., London Schls. Symph. Orch.; Cond., Thomas Morley Chmbr. Orch., 1956-62; Organist & Choirmaster, St. Mary the Virgin, Primrose Hill, London, 1957-62, Selby Abbey, Yorks., 1962-66; Cond., Selby Choral Soc. & Sec., Selby Music Soc., 1964-66; Hd. of Music Dept., Selby HS, 1964-66; Organist & Choirmaster, Brecon Cathedral & St. Mary's Brecon. & Cond., Cathedral Singers, 1966-; Music Master, Builth Wells High Schl., 1966-; Cond. Gwent Chmbr. Orch., 1975-; Tours of S. Germany, Canada & USA w. Brecon Cathedral Choir; Tour of S Germany w. Cathedral Singers & Gwent Chamber Orch. Recordings: Christmas in Wales; Praise the Lord (19th Century Anthems). Publs: Ed., Pring, O Lord We Beseech Thee, 1973. Contbr. to: Yorkshire Post; Western Mail; Country Quest. Mbr., Cathedral Organist Assn. Recip., Turpin Prize, FRCO. Hobbies: Reading; Sport; Motoring. Address: Garth Cottage, Pendre Brecon, LD3 9EF, UK. 3.

GEE, Harry Raglan, b. 20 Feb. 1924, Minneapolis, Minn., USA. Professor of Clarinet & Saxophone; Soloist; Composer; Arranger; Writer. Educ: BA, Univ. Northern Colo.; Dip. Clarinet, Curtis Inst. of Music, Pa.; MMus, Univ. Denver; Post Grad. studies, Univs. of Minn. & Ind. m. Marie-Louise Saucourt, 1 s. Career: Vis. Prof., Woodwind Workshop, St. Mary's Coll., Trickenham; Instructor, Nat. Music Camp, Interlochen, Mich.; Prin. Clarinet & Saxophone Soloist, Therre Haute Symph.; Clarinettist, Denver Symph. Orch., Summer Series & Mpls. Summer Pops Orchs.; Prof. of Clarinet & Saxophone, Ind. State Univ. Comps. incl: Over 60 comps., arrs. & edited works for clarinet, saxophone, woodwind ensembles & band. Num. recordings. Contbr. to profl. mags.; Dept. Ed., Schl. Musician. Mbr. profl. orgs. Address: 419 S 32nd St., Terre Haute, IN 47803, USA.

GEERING, Arnold Felix Christoph, b. 14 May 1902, Basel, Switzerland. University Professor. Educ: High Schl. Music Tchr's Dip., Conserv. of Basel; PhD, Univ. of Basel, 1931; studied w. Alfredo Cairati. m. Genevieve Court, 3 c. Career: Concert Singer, 1925-40; Schl. Music Tchr., 1927-50; Tchr., Schola Cantorum Basiliensis, 1933-50; Lectr., Univ. of Basel, 1947-50; Prof. of Musicol., Univ. of Bern, 1950-72 (ret'd.); Guest Prof., UCLA, 1957-58. Publs: Die Vokalmusik in der Schwwizz z.z. der Reformation, 1933; Retrspektive Mehrstimmigkeit in den ma. Hansschriften des deutchen Sprachgebiets, 1952; Ed. Psalmen & geistliche Gesänge von J Wannenmacher & Cosmas Alder, 1933; Ed., Ludwig Senfl. Deutsche Lieder, Vols. I-V, 1939, 1940, 1949, 1960, 1961, Ein tütsche Musica 1491, 1964; Liederbud des Johannes Heer aus Glarus, 1967. Contbr. to num. profl. jrnls. Mbrships: Swiss Music Rsch. Soc.; Int. Musicol. Soc.; Sec., ibid., 1948-51; Swiss Soc. of Humanities; Pres., ibid., 1961-69; Rsch. Commission, ibid., 1956-69; var. other profl. orgs. Recip. var. hons. Address: Ave. Reller 36, CH-1804 Corsier sur Vevey, Switzerland.

GEESIN, Ron, b. 17 Dec. 1943, Stevenston, Scotland, UK. Composer; Performer (Voice, Fretted Strings, Keyboards, Percussion). m. Frances, 3 s. Career: Live perfs. incl. Royal Albert Hall & Purcell Room, London; Tours, Finland & Sweden, inclng. radio apps.; Subject, BBC 2 prog. One Man's Week; Radio perfs., UK. Comps. incl: (film music) Sunday, Bloody Sunday; The Body; Ghost Story; Clydescope; Blast Sam Smith-Genuine England; Shapes in the Wilderness (BBC); Leapfrog

(ITV). Recordings incl: Patruns; As He Stands; Music from the Body; Atom Heart Mother (arr. & comp. for Pink Floyd); Electrosound, 2 vols. Publ: Fallables. Mbrships: PRS; Mechanical Copyright Protection Soc. Hobbies incl: Gardening; Golf; Carpentry; Woodturning; Painting, Un-painting. Address: Headrest, Street End Lane, Broad Oak, Heathfield, Sussex TN21 8TU, UK.

GEFORS, Hans Gustaf, b. 8 Dec. 1952, Stockholm, Sweden. Composer; Editor; Writer. Educ: Acad. of Music, Stockholm, 1972; Jutland Conserv. of Music, Arhus, Denmark, 4 yrs.; dip., ibid., 1977. m. Anne Goodrich, 1 s. Debut: (as comp.) Copenhagen, 1972. Career: Free-lance comp.; co-ed., Dansk Musiktidskrift. Comps. incl: Reveille, 1975; La Boîte chinoise, for guitar, 1975; Sculpture in Motion, for organ, 1978; Me moriré en Paris, for baritone & instruments, 1979; La vie en beau, chmbr. opera, 1979. Recordings: La Petite Boîte chinoise; 4 songs about trusting. Contbr. to: Dansk Musiktidskrift; Nutida Musik; Tonfallet; Helsingborgs Dagblad; radio progs. Mbr., Swedish Soc. of Comps. Hobbies: Travel; Outdoor Life. Address: Stortorget 13, 25220 Helsingborg, Sweden.

GEHLING, Ronda, b. 21 Oct. 1921, Eudunda, S Australia Musician (piano). Educ: LRSM, BMus, Adelaide Univ. m. Dr. K V Sanderson, 3 s. Debut: Elder Hall, Adelaide Univ., 1939. Career: Broadcaster & Accompanist, Aust. Broadcasting Commn., 18 yrs. & later w. BBC; gave Aust. premiere of Bartok's 3rd Piano Concerto. Recordings: var. works for Aust. Broadcasting Commn. Mbrships: Inc. Soc. of Musicians. Hons. incl: LRSM Prize, 1938. Hobbies: Reading; Writing; Painting. Address: 36 Priory Ave., Bedford Park, London W. 4, UK.

GEIGER, Carroll C, b. 16 Oct. 1910, Gowanda, NY, USA. Music Educator; Director of Music. Educ: B Mus Ed., Eastman Schl. of Music, Rochester, NY, 1933; M Mus Ed., ibid., 1940; additional studies at SUNY, Buffalo & NY State Univ., Buffalo. m. Edith L Swedenborg, 3 s., 1 d. Career: Ensemble & solo (instmntl.) apps. over radio stns. WHAM & WHEG, Rochester, NY & WBEN, WGR, WKBW, WEBR & WBNY, Buffalo, NY; TV apps. on WBEN & WNED as a panelist, musician & demonstrational tchr.; Tchr., var. instruments, many yrs.; Cond. of var. orchs., 1931-43; Mbr., Buffalo Civic Orch.; Dir. of Music, Buffalo Pub. Schls., NY., 1951-75. Contbr. to var. music jrnls. Mbships: AFM; Nat., State & Co. Music Educators Assn.; Past Pres., Erie Co. Music Educators Assn. Hobby: Photography. Address: 6191 Ward Rd., PO Box 23, Orchard Pk., NY, USA.

GEIGER, Edith Lucile, b. 15 July 1911, Ashtabula, Ohio, USA. Piano Teacher; Retired Public School Music Teacher; Consultant. Educ: Studied piano w. Edgar Rose, Cecile Staub Genhart, trombone w. Emory Remington & organ w. Catherine Crozier, Eastman Schl. of Music; B Mus., ibid., 1934; art courses, State Univ. Coll., Buffalo.m. Carroll C Geiger, 4 c. Career: Piano Tchr. for 25 yrs.; Ch. Organist for many yrs.; Music Tchr. in pub. schls. sev. yrs.; Music Cons., Head Start, Buffalo Public Schls. & Early Push, ibid.; Music Demonstration Spkr., SUNY, Buffalo for Head Start orientation prog., 1966, & at NY State Western Zone, Tchrs. Conf., 1967 & 69; Gave many music workshops for tchrs., 1967-73; Spkr., on muci for young children, PTA meetings & Parent Coun. meetings; Guest on TV prog. to discuss & demonstrate creative music for young children, etc. illustrator & Music Cons. for Kenworthy Music Symbols Flash Cards. Mbr. sev. profl. orgs. One of 12 tchrs. hon. nationally by Columbia Univ. Rsch. Publs. The Exemplary Tchr. of the Disadvantaged: Two Views. Var. hobbies. Address: 6191 Ward Rd., N Boston, NY 14127, USA.

GEIGER, Emil, b. 14 Dec. 1908, Liestal, Basle, Switz. Wind Instrumentalist. Educ: Studied under Dr. Münch, Conserv. of Music & under Guarnieri, Alfredo Casella, Vito Frazzi, Acad. of Music, Siena, Italy; Dip., Orch. & Opera Cond. m. Helena Kammerer, 1 s., 1 d. Debut: 1933. Comps. incl: Pro Oemion (Goethe, Oratorio); Springbrunnen (Opera); Walpurgisnacht (Sumph. Poem); Hiob (Oratorio); Die Richterin (Opera); Eie Zwei Bru..der (Opera). Author var. publs., 1945-75. Mbrships: Union Swiss Musicians; Assn. Swiss Conds. Hobbies: Composing & Tchng. Music. Address: Klingentalstr. 89, CH-4057, Basle, Switz.

GEIGER, Hans, b. 3 Jan. 1920, Moson, Hungary. Violinist. Educ: studied w. W H Reed & Max Rostal, RCM. m. Johanna Angela Leichtle, 1 s. Career: Mbr., London Harpsichord Ensemble, London Soloists Ensemble, London Ensemble, Philharmonia Orch., 1949-63, LSO; Ldr., Engl. Opera Grp. Chmbr. Orch., 1949-53. Mbr: ISM. Address: 8 Tiverton Rd., London NW10 3HL, UK.

GEIGER, Loren Dennis, b. 23 Jan. 1946, Buffalo, NY, USA. m. Elaine Silvers. Public School Band Director & Instrumental Teacher; Professional Tuba Player. Educ: B Mus, 1968, M Mus,

1970, Eastman Schl. of Music. Debut: 20th Century Band. Career: Prin. Tuba w. Amherst Symph., Orchard Pk. Symph., Niagara Falls, Philharmonia Orch., Eastman Wind Ensemble, Minnewaska Symph. Orch., 20th Century Band & Clarence Pops Orch.; Clarence Symph., 1973-. Comps. incl: 12 military & circus band marches; 6 pieces for symph. orch.; num. arrs. Recordings w. Eastman Wind Ensemble. Publs: Notes on Early Band History in America, 1969; Ed., Boombah Herald; contbr. to profl. jrnls. Mbrships: incl: Pi Kappa Lambda; num. musical & circus assns. Hobbies incl: Photography; Raising Animals; Band Arranging. Address: Box 146, Orchard Park, NY 14127, USA. 28, 29.

GEIGER, Ruth, b. 30 Jan. 1923, Vienna, Austria. Pianist. Educ: studied in Vienna w. J Isserlis & Hans Gal; Hon. Dip., Juilliard Grad. Schl. NY (student of Josef Lhevinne); later studied w. Erns Rosenberg. Debut: Town Hall, NY, 1944. Career: Recitals & apps. w. orchs. in USA; also radio & TV in NY; Annual concert tours in Europe since 1957 - recitals, soloist w. orchs. inclng. Suisse Romande, New Philharmonia English Chamber Orch.; many radio apps. inclng. BBC series "My Favourite Concertos", Complete Schubert Sonatas taped for Radio Basel; Toured Sweden, Holland, Belgium, Switz., England, Italy, Austria; Master classes at Sussex Univ., UK, summer 1971, where perf chamber music w. Allegri Quartet; Tchng. in N. Recordings: Schubert Piano Music for Critics Choice Records. Hons: Naumburg Award NY, 1943; Finalist, Leventritt Contest, 1944 & Rachmaninoff Contest 1948. Hobbies: Photography; Literature; Nature. Mgmt: Jocelyn Goldsborough, Basil Douglas. Address: 160 W 73 St., NY, NY 10023, USA. 3.

GEIRINGER, Karl J, b. 26 Apr. 1899, Vienna, Austria. Professor of Musicology. Educ: musicol. studies, Vienna & Berlin; PhD, Univ. of Vienna, 1923. m. Irene Steckel, 2 s. Career: Curator, Gesellschaft der Musikfreunde, Vienna, 1930-38; Vis. Prof., RCM, UK, 1938-39; Prof., Boston Univ. Schl. of Fine & Applied Arts; Prof., ic grad. studies in music, Univ. of Calif., Santa Barbara. Publs: The Bach Family, 1954; Music of the Bach Family, 1955; Johann Sebastian Bach, 1966; Johannes Brahms, His Life & Work, 2nd ed. London, & NY, 1948; Joseph Haydn, 1946, 3rd ed. London & NY 1948; Joseph Haydn, 1946, 3rd ed., 1968; Musical Instruments, 1943, 2nd ed. 1945; Instruments in the History of Western Music, 1978. Mbrships: incl: Am. & Int. Musicol. Socs.; FAAAS. Hons. incl: Austrian Cross of Hon. 1st class, 1969. Address: 1823 Mira Vista Ave., Santa Barbara, CA 93103, USA. 2, 9.

GEISER, Brigitte, b. 12 June 1941, Langenthal, Switzerland. Musicologist. Educ: Univs. of Bern & Tübingen; PhD. Publs: Studien zur Frühgeschichte der Violine, 1974; Das Hackbrett, ein alpenländisches Musikinstrument (w. John Henry van der Meer & Karl-Heinz Schickhaus), 1957; Les instruments de musique dans la tradition populaire en Suisse, 1976; Das Alphorn in der Schweiz, 1976. Contbr. to: Glareana; Informationsbulletin des Schweizer Musikrat; Schweizer Volkskunde; Studia instrumentorum musicae popularis; Zuger Neujahrsblatt. Mbrship: Pres., Swiss Soc. of Folk Traditions, 1978. Address: Sonnenbergrain 6, Berne, Switz.

GEISER, Walther, b. 16 May 1897, Zofingen, Switz. Composer; Violinist; Educator; Choir Director. Educ: Music Acad., Basel; studied w. Ferruccio Busoni, Acad. of Art, Berlin. m. Hanna Moos, 1 s., 1 d. Career incls: Tchr., Basel Music Acad., 1924-62; Dir., Baseler Bachchors, 1954-72; Orchl. & quartet violist. Comps. incl: var. chmbr. works; concertos for violin, horn, organ, 2 violins & harpsichord (w. str. orch.), flute & piano; var. orchl. works, many vocal works. Mbr. Swiss Musicians Union. Recip. Comp.'s Prize of Swiss Musicians Union. Address: Tiefengrabenstr. 21, CH-4102 Binnigen, Switzerland.

GEISSLER, Walter Fritz, b. 16 Sept. 1921, Wurzen, Germany. Composer. Educ: Music Acad. Leipzig; Music Acad. Berlin. m. Mechtild Geissler, 1 d. Career: Prof. for comp. Comps. incl: Operas, The Broken King, Crazy Jourdain, The Shadow; 8 Symph.; 2 Oratoira; Cantatas; Vocal music; Chmbr. music. Recordings: Own symph., oratorium; Italian Comic Overture, Cheerful Suite for Wind Instruments. Mbrships: Art Acad. German Dem. Repub.; vice-pres. Assn. for Comps. and Musicologists German Dem. Repub. Hons: Art Prize Leipzig, 1960; Art Prize GDR, 1963; Nat. Prize, 1971. Hobbies: Sports; Wandering. Address: Kleinsaara 13, 6510 Saara Ortsteil, Germany.

GEITNER, Leopold, b. 18 Mar. 1898, Vienna, Austria. Conductor; Composer. Educ: TTD; pvte. music studies. m. Adele Geitner. Debut: 1914. Comps: Demon Dance; Concert, Les Adieux; Sssyrian Suite in 3 parts; Overture, Montezuma; Symph. Poem; Overture, Fantastique; Romantic Phantasy, Serenata Appassionata; Gypsy Rhapsody. Mbrships: Assn. for Comp., Austria; AKM; Austro-Mechana. Address: Gogolgasse 46, Vienna A 1130, Austria.

GELBLOOM, Gerald, b. 3 May 1926, Toronto, Can. Violinist; Teacher. Educ: AA, Univ. of Hartford; studied w. Mischa Mischakoff, Juilliard Schl. of Music, 1942-45; pvte. study w. Ivan Galamian. m. Mildred, 1 d. Debut: recital, Royal Conserv. of Toronto, 1934. Career: w. Cleveland Orch., 1947-49; Asst. Ldr., Balt. Symph., 1949-53; Concert Master, Hartford Symph., 1954-61; apps., Casals Fest., Puerto Rico, 1958-60; w. Boston Symph. Orch., 1961-; formerly on facs., Peabody Conserv., Adelphi Coll., Hartt Coll. of Music, Wesleyan (Conn.) Univ., Bennington Coll.; currently Violin Tchr., Boston Univ. Schl. of Music, & Artist-Tchr., Off. for the Arts, Harvard & Radcliffe. Hons. incl: 1st Prize Gold Medalist, Can. Nat. Exhib., 1933. Address: 16 Furber Ln., Newton Ctr., MA 02159, USA.

GELBRUN, Artur, b. 11 July 1913, Warsaw, Poland. Composer; Conductor. Educ: Dips., State Conserv., Wardaw, Santa Cecilia Acad., Rome, & Accademia Chigiana, Siena. m. Eugenie Marschak. Career: Orchl. Cond., Europe & Israel; Lectr., Acad. of Music, Art Dept., Univ. of Tel-Aviv, 1966-. Comps. incl: num. orchl. & chmbr. works; songs w. piano accomp.; choral works (a capella). Recordings: Everest Recordings: Ars NovaArs Antiqua. Mbrships: Exec., Comps. League of Israel; Mbr. of Soc., ACUM; Tel-Aviv Municipal Council for Music. Hons. incl: 1st Prizes, ACUM Comp. Competition, 1965, 68 & 71; 1 Prize, Israeli Broadcasting, 1973. Address: 3 Karnistr. Ramat-Aviv, Tel-Aviv 69025, Israel. 14.

GELIOT, Michael, b. 27 Sept. 1933, London, UK. Opera & Theatre Director. Educ: BA Cantab. m. Diana Geliot, 2 children. Debut: First London Prod., 1960, Sadlers Wells. Career: Many Opera prods. inclng: Royal Opera House; Munich Festival; Amsterdam; Geneva; Ottawa; Kassel; Scottish Opera; Barcelina; Lausanne; Zürich; Artistic Dir., Welsh Nat. Opera, 1969-. Publs: Transl. of Magic Flute, Mamagonny. Hons: Critics Prize, Barcelona, 1974; Prague Int. TV Music Prod. No 5 Papa Haydn: String Quartet Op. 54 No. 2. Hobbies: Cricket; Sailing; Walking; Chess. Mgmt. Harrison & Parrott. Address: 35 Westbourne Rd., Penarth, Glam., UK.

GELKER, Ellton Groth, b. 13 Mar. 1922, Copenhagen, Denmark. Flautist. Educ: Royal Conserv. of Music, Copenhagen, studied w. Prof. H Gilbert-Jespersen; studied in Rome w. Severino Gazzeloni. m. Else Freundlich, 2 d. Career: Mbr. of Band, Royal Guard, 1943-54; w. Danish Radio, 1954-; Solo Flutist, ibid., 1959-. Hobbies: Painting; Photography. Address: Havrevej 5, 2760 Malov, Denmark.

GELLER, Bernard, b. 12 Apr. 1948, Pully, Vaud, Switzerland. Association Secretary General. Educ: Lic. in Law, LLD, Univ. of Lausanne. m. Anne-Marie Dreyfuss. Career: Gen. Sec., Swiss Musicians' Assn., 1972-. Author, 75 Years of Action: History of the Swiss Musicians' Association, in Trends & Actions, 1975. Hons. incl: Fndn. Fluvet Prize, Fac. of Law, Univ. of Lausanne, 1969; Prize for form analysis, Assn. of Former Pupils of the Conserv., 1970; Swiss Centenary Prize, Fac. of Law, Lausanne, 1972. Address: 7 Ave. du Grammont, PO 160, 1000 Lausanne 13, Switz.

GELLHORN, Peter, b. 24 Oct. 1912, Breslau, Germany (now Poland). Conductor; Pianist; Composer. Educ: Univ. of Berlin; Passed final exams. as pianist & cond., both w. distinction, Music Acad., Berlin; Medal, Berlin Acad. of Arts. m. Olive Shirley Layton, 2 s., 2 d. Career: Musical Dir., Toynbee Hall, London, 1935-39; Asst. Cond., Sadlers Wells Opera, 1941-43; Cond., Royal Carl Rosa Opera, 1945-46; Cond. & Hd. of Music Staff, Royal Opera House, Covent Garden, 1947-53; Cond. & Chorus Master, Glyndebourne Fest. Opera, 1954-61; Dir., BBC Chorus, 1961-72; Rejoined Glyndebourne Staff, 1974; Co-Fndr. & Musical Dir., Opera Barga, Italy, 1967-69; While w. BBC, regular appearances as cond. in choral music concerts as well as each yr. at the Henry Wood Promenade Concerts; Frequent broadcasts as a pianist & accompanist; Musical Dir., Barnes Choir; Artistic Dir., The Opera Players Ltd.; Member of staff, London Opera Centre. Contbr. to music jrnls. Mbrships: ISM; Musicians Union; RPS; BBC Club; Pres., Twickenham Music Soc. Hobbies: Walking; Swimming; Theatre. Address: 33 Leinster Ave., East Sheen, London SW14 7JW, UK. 3.

GELLMAN, Steven D, b. 16 Sept. 1947, Toronto, Ont., Can. Composer; Pianist; Professor of Music. Educ: Juilliard Schl. of Music, NY; Conservatoire de Paris. m. Cheryl, 1 d., 1 s. Career: Soloist w. CBC Symph. Orch. in own Concerto for Piano & Orch., aged 16; Comps. perfd., USA, Can., France, etc.; currently Asst. Prof., Dept. of Comp. & Theory, Fac. of Music, Univ. of Ottawa. Comps. incl: (orchl.) Chori, 1976; Anima, Animus (orch.), 1976; Odyssey, 1971; Overture for Ottawa, 1972; Symph. in Two Movements, 1971 (recorded); Symph. No. 2, 1972; (Chmbr. Music) Mythos II, for flute & string quartet, 1968 (recorded); Soliloquy, cello solo, 1966; Wind Music, for Brass

Quintet, 1978; Deux Tapisseries, 1978; Dialogue for solo horn, 1978; (Piano) Melodic Suite, 1972; Sonata, 1964; Poème, 1976 (recorded); The Warrior, 1978 (recorded); Waves & Ripples, 1979. Mbrships: Can. League of Comps.; Can. Music Centre; PRO Can., etc. Hons: Premier Prix, Comp., Conservatoire de Paris; Winner, BMI Awards to Student Comps. Competition, 1963; 1st Prize, Comp., Aspen, Colo.; Award, Int. Rostrum of Comps., Paris, 1970 for Mythos II; num. commissions. Mgmt: PRO Can. Address: c/o Music Dept., Stewart St., Univ. of Ottawa, Ottawa, Ont., K1N 6N5, Can.

GELMETTI, Vittorio, b. 25 Apr. 1926, Milan, Italy. Composer; Conductor. m. Kamilla Nelly Gorska, 3 c. Debut: Comp., 1958; Cond., Circolo Toscanini, Torino, 1975. Career: Num. apps., var. fests., Italy, Poland & USA; Film, DesertoRosso; TV, Electronic & Computer Music, 1968; Tutto è Musica Prog. for musical education, 1978. Comps. incl: Non Otterrete Risposta (opera, text Corrado Costa), 1974-76; Come Se (orch.), 1974; Modus Sonandi (Trio), 1975; Apocryphe (guitar & orch.), 1978. Recordings incl: (Premier) L'Opera Abbandonata Tace e Volge la Cavità Verso L'Esterno, 1969; Ipotesi A, 1974. Contbng. musical ed., Marcatre, 1963-69; Mbr., Sindacato Musicisti Italiani. Hobby: Motoring. Address: Via Genova 2, 00061 Anguillara Sabazia, Rome, Italy.

GENA, Peter, b. 27 Apr. 1947, Buffalo, NY, USA. Composer; Assistant Professor. Educ: BA, SUNY, Buffalo, 1969; MA, ibid., 1971; PhD, 1975. m. Rhoda Lederman Gena. 1 d. Career: Pvte. piano Instr., pt.-time, 1965-72; Tchr., Informal course in Computer Music, Int. Darmstadt, German Fed. Repub., 1972; Rsch. & Tchng. Ast., SUNY, Buffalo, 1969-73; Dir., Electronic Music Studio, Instr. in Electronic Music, Brook Univ., St. Catherines, Ont., Canada, 1971-74; Coord., Computer Music Rsch., SUNY, Buffalo, NY. Asst. Prof., Schl. of Music, Northwestern Univ, Evanston. Lectr., Calif. State Univ., Fresno, Latest Appearance, Evenings for New Music, Albright-Knox Art Gall., Buffalo, NY, 1974. Compositions (unpubld.) incl: Homage to GK Zipf, 1971; EGERYA, 1972; Aleutian Lullabies, 1972; Scherzo, 1973; Schoenberg in Italy, 1973. Contbr. to: Musical Box Soc.; Musicol. Manual, Sunyab Press. Mbr., Coll. Music Soc. Recip. of hons. Hobbies: Computer programming; Electronic systems; Audiophile. Address: Schl. of Music, Northwestern Univ., Evanston, IL 60201, USA.

GENDRON, Maurice, b. 26 Dec. 1920, Nizza, France. Violoncellist. Educ: Grad., Conservs. of Nice & Paris. m. Monique Nerot, 1 s., 1 d. Career: premiered Prokofiev concerto w. LPO, 1945; concerts throughout Europe & N Cam., also Israel, Angola, S Africa, Canary Islands; apps. in USA, 1958-; TV Broadcasts, France & German Fed. Repub.; Tchr., Master Classes, Am. Conserv. at Fontainebleau; Prof., State Schl. of Music, Saarbrüken, German Fed. Repub.; fest. apps. throughout Western Europe; featured in film Maurice Gendron, Metamorphose of the Cello. Recordings: Epic; Philips. Recip., Grand Prix, Paris Conserv. Address: 5 Blvd. Magenta, Fontainebleau, France. 2.

GENTRY, Gerald Frank, b. 16 May 1927, Chelmsford, Essex, UK. Conductor; Adjudicator; Lecturer; Music Adviser. Educ: Mid-Essex Tech. Coll. & Schl. of Art; GSM, London. m. Muriel Delves. Debut: Holland Fest., Haarlem, 1954. Career: Dir. of Music, Beckenham Orchl. Soc. & BBC Scottish Choral Soc., 1954-56; Cond., BBC Midland Orch., 1956-58; Freelance Cond., 1959-65; Music Advsr., W Riding Educ. Dept., 1965-72. Doncaster Metropolitan Dist. Coun., 1972-; Cond. & Dir., Essex, N Ireland, Mid-Wales, Edinburgh, Cheshire, W Riding & Doncaster Dist. Youth Orchs. Hobbies incl: Photography; Mediaeval hist. Address: Tickhill Castle, Tickhill, S Yorks., UK.

GENTRY, Jacques, b. 16 Aug. 1921, Paris, France. Pianist; Piano Teacher; Guest Conductor. Professor at Conservatoire Royal de Musique de Bruxelles (Belgium). Educ: Conserv. Nat. Supérieur de Musique, paris; Tchrs. incl: Lazare-Levy, Charles Münch, Jacwues de la Presle, Norbert Dufourcq. m. Suzanne Leroy, Debut: w. Pasdeloup Orch., Paris, 1941. Career: Soloist & Chmbr. Music Perf.; Duo w. Violinist Lola Bobesco; Concert perfs. thru'out Europe, ilng. USSR, & in Asia, Africa & USA, 1973; Piano Tchr., Conserv. Royal de Musique de Mons, Belgium; currently acting Dir., ibid. Recordings: Chopin, Second Sonata; Liszt Sonata; Clementi's Sonatas; Mozart, Prelude & Fugue in C major & Fantasie & Sonata in C minor; Quintet, Third Piano Concerto; Fauré Sonata & Franck, Sonata (w. Lola bibesco); all the Mozart & Bach Sonatas for Radio-TV Belge. Hons: Chevalier, Ordre de la Couonne, Belgium; Musician of the yr., Manilla, Phillippines, 1951. Hobbies: Cinema & Photography of Birds & Wild Animals; Clay Pigeon Shooting; Glider Pilot. Address: Rue Gustave Huberti 15, 1030 Brussels, Belgium.

GENZMER, Harald, b. 9 Feb. 1909, Bremen, Germany. Composer. Educ: Hochschule für Musik, Berlin. m. Gisela Klein.

Career: Prof. for Comp., Hochschule für Musik, Munich. Compositions: Chamber Music, Choir Music; Compositions for Orchs. & for Chamber Orchs. Recordings: Elektonische Musik Trompete und Orgel; Zauberspiegel für Orchester; Jimenez-Kantate; Sonatina für Streicher, Introduktion und Adagio für Streicher. Mbrships: Akademie der Schönen Künste, Munich & Berlin. Address: Eisensteinstrasse 10, 8000 Munich 80, German Fed. Repub.

GEORGE, Alan Norman, b. 23 Dec. 1949, Newquay, Cornwall, UK. Violist. Educ: MA, King's Coll., Cambridge. m. Lesley Schatzberger. Debut: as mbr. of Fitzwilliam Quartet, Purcell Room, London, 1973. Career: Mbr. Fitzwilliam Quartet, Quartet-in-Res., Univ. of York, 1971-74, Univ. of Warwick, 1974-77, Univ. of York, 1977-; participant in 1st perfs. of Quartets, No. 2 by Sebastian Forbes, Edward Cowie David Blake, & Cuaderna by Bernand Rands, Clarinet Quintet by D Blake, also 1st Brit. perfs. of Shostakovich quartets 13, 14 & 15; Alfred Schnitke, Canon in memory of I.F. Stravinsky. Recordings: Shostakovich Quartets, Nos. 1-15; Franck, Quartet in D; Delius Quartet, Sibelius, Voces Intimae; Brahms Clarinet Quintet. Publs: Shostakovich Chamber Music. Hons. incl: Grand Prix du Disque, Paris, 1976; Gramophone Award for best chamber music record of the year, 1977. Hobbies: Cricket; Football; Walking; Collecting Records. Mgmt: Dr. G. de Koos & Co., London. Address: 2 Cat Lane, Bilbrough, York YO2 3PN, UK.

GEORGE, Graham Elias, b. 11 Apr. 1912, Norwich, UK. Church, School & University Musician (Composition & Analysis). Educ: Studied w. Alfred Whitehead, Montreal, 1933-36; BMus, 1936, DMus, 1939, Univ. of Toronto; ACCO, 1934, ARCO, 1935; FCCO, 1936. m. Tjos Coster, 4 s. Career: Ch. Musician, 1932; Schl. Musician, 1938-41; Can. Army Overseas, 1941-45; Queen's Univ., Kingston, Ont., 1946; Asst. Prof., ibid.; Prof. Emeritus, ibid., 1977-. Comps. incl: (Choral) Benedictus es, Domine, 1940; New Prince, New Pomp, 1962; In God's Commands, 1964; Fight the Good Fight, 1967; Office of Holy Communion BMI, 1964; (Organ) Two Preludes on The King's Majesty, 1963; Elegy for RVW, 1968; Two Wedding Preludes & Fugues, 1974. Publs: Tonality and Musical Structure, 1970; Twelve-note Tonal Counterpoint, 1976. Contbr. to num. profl. publs. Mbrships: Gen. Sec., Int. Folk Music Coun., 1969-; Pres., RCCO, 1972-74; Pres., Can. Folk Music Soc., 19655-68; AMS; CMS; CAUSM. Hons: FRCCO hon. causa, 1977; Prix Jean Lallemand (Montreal), 1938; CAPAC Prizes, 1943, '47. Hobbies: Marriage; Famiuly; Building things; Aesthetics; Comparative religion. Address: 151 Earl St., Kingston, Ont. K71 2H3, Can.

GEORGE, Lial-Gene Plowe, b. 25 Sept. 1918, Sioux City, Iowa, USA. Composer; Pianist; Teacher. Educ: BA, Univ. Okla., 1939; B Mus, 1940; Post grad., Northwestern Univ., 1950; Columbia Univ., 1963-65. m. Richard Painter George, 1 s., 1 d. Career: Pvte. piano tchr., Latin Am., 1947-52; Houston, Tex., 1955-60; '71-, NY, 1961-65; Adjudicator, Texas & La. Comps: Madrigals. Mbrships: Am. Music. Ctr.; Am. Musicol. Soc.; Sigma Alpha Iota; Tuesday Music Club (Pres., 1960). Hon: Comps. Award, Sigma Alpha Iota, Okla., 1969. Hobby: Geneal. Address: 2301 Reba Dr., Houston, TX 77019, USA. 5, 7, 27, 29.

GEORGE, Ronald Alan, b. 16 Aug. 1955, San Francisco, Calif., USA. French Horn Player. Educ: BMus (perf.), Univ. of Toronto; Folkwang Hochschule, Essen, German Fed. Repub. Career: Prin. horn, London Symph. Orch., London, Ont., Can. recip., Can. Coun. award for 1 yr. study in Germany w. Hermann Baumann, 1978-79. Hobbies: Racquet Sports. Address: 1223 Bracknell Cres., N Vancouver, BC V7R 1V4, Can.

GEORGE, Thom Ritter, b. 23 June 1942, Detroit, Mich., USA. Conductor; Composer. Educ: BMus, 1964, MMus, 1968, Eastman Schl. of Music; DMA, The Catholic Univ. of Am., 1970. m. Patricia Imogene Dengler George, 2 d. Career: Comps. perfd. by orchs. incl. Eastman Rochester, Houston, Memphis & Chgo. Symph. Orchs.; Comp.- Arr., US Navy Band, Wash., DC, 1966-70; Music Dir. & Cond., Quincy Symph. Orch., 1970-. Comp. of over 280 works incl: Proclamations (Band); Western Overture (Band); Flute Concerto; Bass Trombone Concerto; The People, Yes (Chorus & Orch.); 2 Piano Concertos; 3 Woodwind Quintets; 3 Brass Quintets; Six Rhymes From Mother Goose (Chorus); Six English Songs (Chorus); many sonatas and smaller works. Recordings: Tubasonatina; Six Rhymes From Mother Goose; Would I Might Go Far Over Sea; Proclamations. Mbrships: Am. Soc. of Comps., Author & Publs.; Am. Musicol. Soc.; Music Lib. Assn.; Am. Symph. Orch. League; Nat. Band Assn.; Phi Mu Alpha Sinfonia. Hons. incl: Edward B Benjamin Award, 1964; 2 Howard Hanson Prizes, 1965, '68; 7th Sigvald Thompson Award, 1975. Hobbies: Reading; Photography; Maths.; Art and Architecture. Address: 2125 Prairie Ave., Quincy, IL 62301, USA. 8.

GEORGE, Warren Edwin, b. 20 Mar. 1936, Abilene, Kans., USA. Music Educator. Educ: BMusEd., Univ. of Kans., Lawrence, 1958; MMus., Mich. State Univ., 1959; PhD, Univ. of Kans., 1969. m. Janet Kay Crawford, 2 s. Career: Dir. of Instrumental Music, Olathe Pub. Schls., Kans., 1960-63; Tchng. Asst., Univ. of Kans., Lawrence, 19643-64; Tchng. Asst. & Rsch. Asst., ibid., 1964-67; Admnstv. Asst. to Dept. Chmn., 1966; Asst. Prof. of Music, Univ. of Tex. at Austin, 1967-69; Asst. Prof., Music & Educ., ibid., 1969-71; Assoc. Prof., 1971-73; Dir., Student Tchng. & Supvsr. of Instrumental Student Tchrs., 1970-73; Co-ord. of Undergrad. Studies, Dept. of Music, 1971-73; Prof. of Music Educ., H d. of Music Educ. Dept., Pa. State Univ., 1973-77; Prof. of Music, Educ. Hd., Div. of Music, Coll. Conserv. of Music, Univ. of Cinn. Ed., Jrnl. of Band Rsch., 1974-. Contbr. to var. music & educl. jrnls. Mbrships. incl: Pi Kappa Lambda; Phi Kappa Phi; Phi Mu Alpha; Life Mbr., MENC; Ohio Music Educ. Assoc.; VP., Tex. Music Educators Assn., 1970-72. Recip., Outstanding Musician Award, Midwestern Music & Art Camp, Univ. of Kans., 1953. Var. hobbies. Address: 8818 Castleford, Cinn., OH 45242, USA.

GEORGESCU, Dan Corneliu, b. 1 Jan. 1938, Craiova, Romania. Composer; Ethnomusicologist; Researcher. Educ: Musical Acad. Ciprian Porumbescu, Bucharest, 1955-61. m. Libia Elena Georgescu. Debut: as Comp., 1967. Comps: Motive Maramamuresene for Orch., 1963 (recorded); Jocuri I, for Orch., 1963; Jocuri 3 for Orch., 1965; Jocuri 4 Colaje, for Orch., 1966; Alb-Negru, for Orch., 1967; Continuo, for Orch., 1968; Jocuri 6 Pianissimo, for Orch., 1972 (recorded). Publs: Antologia-Melodii de joc din Oltenia, 1968. Contbr. of num. articles to: Muzica; Revista de Etnografie si Folclor. Hons. incl: Prize of the Union of Romanian Comps. for orchl. music, 1969, '70, '78; Prize for Ethnomusicology, Union of Romanian Comps., 1969; George Enescu Prize, Acad. of Romania, 1974; Romanian Radio/TV Prize for opera music, 1974. Hobbies: Painting; Photography. Address: str. Aleea Compozitorilor nr. 4, Bloc F17, ap. 19, R - Bucharest 77358, Romania.

GEORGESCU, Remus, b. 23 Aug. 1932, Timisoara, Romania. Conductor; Composer. Educ: MA, Comp., 1956, MA, Cond., 1957, Acad. of Music, Bucharest. m. Clara Georgescu, 2 c. Debut: The Orch. of the Acad. of Music, Bucharest, 1956. Career: Recordings on Radio, TV; Cond., var. orchs. at home, and in Europe, USA. Comps: Concerto for String Orch.; The Second Suit for the Piano; Choral Works: Ballad for choir & orch.; Oratorio for soloists, choir & orch.; Exorcism, for flute & string orch. Recordings: Concerto for String Orch.; Ballad for choir & orch.; Oratorio for soloists, choir & orch. Contbr. to: Muzica, Bucharest. Mbr., Soc. of Comps., Romania. Hons: Order of Cultural Merit, 1967, '68; Nat. Prize for Comp., 1977; Prize of the Soc. of Comps., 1976, '77. Hobbies: Philately; Collecting maximum cards. Mgmt: ARIA, Bucharest. Address: Bd. Victoriei 58, 1900 Timisoara I, Romania.

GEORGIADIS, John, b. 17 July 1939, Rochford, UK. Conductor; Violinist. Educ: studied violin w. Vanna Brown, Joan Rochford-Davis, Frederick Grinke & Réné Benedetti; studied cond. w. Sergiu Celibidache. 2 s., 1 d. Career: ldr., City of Birmingham Symph. Orch., 1962-65; ldr., LSO, 1965-73, 1976-79. num. recordings as conductor, chmbr. musician & solo & orchl. violinist. Mbrships: ISM; Johann Strauss Soc.; Caravan Club. Hons: Dove Prize, Queens Prize & Gulbenkian Award, 1960. Hobbies: Motorcaravanning; Antiques; Squash; Golf; Mexicans. Address: 30 Church Ln., E Finchley, London N2 8DT, UK.

GERAEDTS, Jaap, b. 12 July 1924, The Hague, Netherlands. Composer; Flautist; Music Journalist & Author; Ulmpresario; Musical Director. Educ: Royal Conservs., The Hague & Brussels. Career: Comp., 1946-; Music Journalist, 1952-; Apps. on Radio, 1957-70; Organizer of Concerts on ships of Holland Am. Line, 1964-68; Musical Dir., Netherlands Chmbr. Orch., Amsterdam. Comps: Orchl., Chmbr. & Choral Music. Contbr. to Wkly. Haagse Post, 1952-58; The Hague daily paper, 1967-75; NCRV Broadcasting Co., 1957-70; Num. musical publishing papers in Holland. Recip. Visser-Neerlandia Prize for Comp., 1957, 63. Hobbies: Philos.; Yachting. Address: Zeekant 42, Scheveningen, The Netherlands.

GÉRARD, Yves René Jean, b. 6 Jan. 1932, Châlons-sur-Marne, France. Professor of Music History & Musicology. Educ: Lic. in Letters, Dip. of Advanced Study in Letters, Univ. of Nancy; Cert. in Musicol., Sorbonne, Paris; Nancy & Paris Music Conservs. Career incl: Researcher, CNRS, 1965-75. Prof. of Music Hist. & Musicol., Nat. Higher Conserv. of Music, Paris, 1975-; Assoc. Prof., Univ. Laval, PQ, Can. Publs: Thematic, Bibliographical & Critical Catalogue of the Works oif Boccherini, 1969; Quintetti con Chitarra Boccherini, 1975. Contbr. to var. profl. publs. Mbrships: Bd., French Musicol. Soc.; Int. & Am. Musicol. Socs. Address: Conservatoire National Supérieur de Musique, 14 Rue de Madrid, 75004 Paris, France.

GERBER, René, b. 29 June 1908, Travers, Neuchâtel, Switzerland. Composer. Educ: Univ. of Zürich; Dip., Zürich Conserv., 1933; Coll. of Music Educ., Paris, France. m. Ruth Matthey-Doret. Comps. incl: 3 Spanish Visions, for singer & instruments, 1973; Concertino, for clarinet & chmbr. orch., 1975; Concerto, for cor anglais & chmbr. orch., 1975-76; Concerto for 2 pianos & orch., 1977; Trois Poèmes de la Renaissance for singer & 3 instruments, 1977. Mbrships: Swiss Musicians Assn.; Pres., French Switzerland Commission, Swiss Soc. of Music Teaching; Friends of the Arts Soc., Neuchâtel; Int. Inst. of Community Serv. Hobbies: Collection of paintings; Chess; Reading. Address: Rue de Neuchâtel 22, 2022 Bevaix, Switz. 23, 28.

GERBRANDT, Carl J, b. 27 Oct. 1940, Meade, Kan., USA. Singer; Teacher. Educ: BME, Tabor Coll., Hillsboro, Kaqn., 1962; MME, Wichita State Univ., Kan., 1963; DMA, Peabody Conserv. Music, 1974; Nordwestdeutsche Musik Akad., Germany. m. Marilyn Gaye Friesen, 1 d. Debut: Ramphis, 'Aida', Wichita Symph. Orch., 1963. Career: Solo apps. w. Nat. Symph., Balt. Symph., Wichita Symph. & Phila. Chmbr. Orch.; Balt. & Wash. Civ. Opera Cos.; Chmbr. Opera Co. Balt.; Chmbr. Theatre Players Wash.; Harford Opera Theatre Assn.; Kennedy Ctr. Performing Arts; Gatlinburg Summer Music Fest.; Local educl. TV prods. Mbr. profl. orgs. Hons. incl: Finalist, Eastern Metrop. Opera Competitions, 1970. Hobbies: Woodwork; Tennis. Address: 3208 Guilford Ave., Baltimore, MD 21218, USA.

GERGELY, Jean G, b. 23 May 1911, Budapest, Hungary. Professor; Composer; Musicologist; Ethnomusicologist. Educ: Fac. of Letters, Budapest; Lic. in Letters, Paris; Dr. of Hungarian Linguistics, Paris, 1968; D Litt, Strasbourg, 1975; F Liszt Acad., Budapest, 1935; Dip., Gregorian Inst., Paris, 1945. m. Eliane Delage, 1 s., 1 d. Career incls: Nat. Schl. of Mod. Oriental Langs. (now Nat. Inst. of Oriental Langs. & Civilisations), Paris, 1949-. Comps: (publs): Sonata for piano, 1951; Popular Hungarian Medlodies, for voice & piano, 1953; Hungarian Music, 2nd Ed., 1976. Contbr. to num. publs. Publs. incl: Introduction to the Study of Music Folklkore, 1967. Mbr. var. profl. assns. Kt., Order of Acad. Palms, Paris. Hobbies incl: Linguistics. Address: 15 rue de la Planche, 75007 Paris, France.

GERHARDT, Walter, b. 1912, Vienna, Austria. Violinist; Viuolist; Professor. Educ: New Vienna Conserv.; State Acad. of Music, Vienna; studied composition w. Hindemith, Zürich Univ. Career: Ldr., Vienna Radio Symph., 1937-38; Prof., Ankara Conserv., Turkey, 1938-48; Prin. Viola, Zürich Radio Orch., 1948-56; Mbr., Pascal Str. Quartet, Paris, France, 1955-56; Ldr., S Aust. Symnph., Adelaide, 1966-59; Prof., GSM, UK; Hd., String Dept., Welsh Coll. of Music, Cardiff; Prin. Viola, Mehuhin Fest. Orch., 1960-. Recip. of Fritz-Kreisler Prize, Vienna, 1932. Hobbies: Collecting Instruments & Stamps. Address: 49 Windsor Rd., London W5, UK. 3.

GERHART, Martha, b. Rahway, NJ, USA. Coach/Accompanist; Assistant Conductor. Educ: BA, Middlebury (Vt.) Coll.; MMus, Univ. of Colo. Career: Opera Workshop Dir., Queens Coll.; NY; Opera Assn. Staff, Chautauqua, NY; Asst. Cond., NYC Opera Co., 1975-; Coach/Accomp. Publs: Vocal score, Leon Kirchner's opera, Lily, 1979. Address: 50 W 67th St., NY, NY 10023, USA.

GERIG, Reginald Roth, b. 20 Apr. 1919, Grabill, Ind., USA. College Professor; Church Organist. Educ: B Mus, Wheaton Coll., Ill., 1942; BS, Juilliard Schl. Music, 1948; MS, ibid., 1949. m. Irene Conrad Gerig, 1 s., 1 d. Career: Piano Fac., Eastman Schl. Music, Univ. Rochester, NY, 1950-52; Currently, Prof., piano & Chmn. Piano Dept., Conserv. Music, Wheaton Coll., Ill. & Organist, Coll. Ch., Wheaton. Comps: Piano Preludes on Hymns & Chorales (anthol. work by var. composers inclng. himself), 1959. Publ: Famous Pianist & Their Technique, 1974. Mbrships. incl: Wheaton Coll. Scholastic Hon. Committee (Chmn.); MTNA; Soc. of Am. Musicians; Ill. State Music Tchrs.; Am. Liszt Soc.; British Liszt Soc. Assn; Nat. Guild of Piano Tchrs. Hobbies: Reading; Philately. Address: 1328 Naperville Rd., Wheaton, IL 60187, USA.

GERLACH, Sonja, b. 15 Oct. 1936, Hannover, German Fed. Repub. Reader; Editor. Educ: Univ. Career: Asst. Master, Second. Schl. for Music & Maths.; Rdr., Joseph Haydn Inst., Köln, & G Henle Verlag, Duisburg. Mbr., Gesellschaft für Musikforschung. Ed. & co-ed., sev. vols. of Joseph Haydn Werke. Contbr. to Haydn-Studien. Address: Klarenbachstr. 196, Köln 41, German Fed. Repub.

GERLE, Robert, b. 1 Apr. 1924, Abbazia, Italy. Concert Violinist; Conductor. Educ: Artist Dip. (MMus), Franz Liszt Acad. of Music, Budapest; Tchrs. Dip. (MMusEd), Nemzeti Zenede, Budapest. m. Marilyn Neeley, 1 s. Debut: Soloist w. Budapest Symph., 1941. Career incls: Prof., Peabody Conserv., Balt.,

1955-68, Mannes Coll. of Music, NYC, 1959-70; Manhattan Schl. of Music, NYC, 1967-70; Prof., Artist-in-Res., Cond. of Orchs., Ohio State Univ., 1968-72; Prof., Cond. of Orchs. & Hd., Instrumental Program, Univ. of Md. Balt. County, 1972-; Prof., Catholic Univ. of Am., Wash., DC, 1973-; Cond., Catholic Univ. Orch., 1974-75; Cond., Friday Morning Music Club Orch., Wash., DC, 1976-; Guest Cond., num. orchs., USA & Brazil; Concert Tours, USA, Europe, S Am., S Africa; Soloist, BBC, Berlin Phil., LSO, Concerts Lamoureux, etc. Num. recordings. Contbr. to: MTNA Jrnl. (former string Ed.); ASTA Mag. Mbr., profl. orgs. Hons. incl: Emmy Awards, 1970, '71. Mgmt: Ibbs & Tillett, London. Address: 101 Birchwood Rd., Balt., MD 21228, USA.

GERMANI, Fernando, b. 5 Apr. 1906, Italy. Organist; Professor of Organ Playing. Educ: Rome Conservatory; Pontifical Inst. of Sacred Music. Career: Prof., Rome Conservatoire, Chigiana Music Acad., Siena, Curtis Inst., Phila., Pa., USA; Recitals, N & S Am., Australasia, S Africa, Europe. Publs: Revision of works of Girolamo Frescobaldi, 1936; A Method of Organ Playing, 1942. Hons: Cmdr., Order of St. Gregorius Magno; Cmdr., Order of St. Sylvester; Kt. Crown of Italy. 16.

GERMETEN, jr., Gunnar, b. 1 May 1947, Oslo, Norway. Composer. Educ: Oslo Conserv. (guitar, theory), 1968-72; State Music Acad., Oslo (comp.), 1971-74; Dip., ibid., 1974; Inst. for Sonology, 1975-76. Career: music for TV progs., films & theatre; interviews on radio & TV. Comps: Lyric Ragtimerock, for 4 pianos & strgs.; The Case of Janice, for large orch. & 2 soloists; AKT & AKT2 (recorded), for 6 players; Veins, for 4 violins; Skisse 1, for piano; Siokate, for 2 children's choirs, ballet dancer, 2 percussionists & tape. Contbr. to: Ballade; Nutida Musik. Mbrships: Soc. of Norwegian Comps.; NY Musikk. Hons. sev. scholarships, commissions & grants. Hobbies incl: Music; Norwegian Mountains; Trout Fishing; Hunting. Address: Asdalsveien 5, Oslo 11, Norway.

GERSCHEFSKI, Edwin, b. 10 June 1909, Meriden, Conn., USA. Composer; Pianist; Educator. Educ: PhB, Yale Univ., 1931; MusB, Yale Schl. of Music, 1931; Dip. in Perf. & Tchng., Matthay Pianoforte Schl., London, UK, 1932; Postgrad. study in piano w. Artur Schnabel, Como, Italy, 1935; comp. w. Joseph Schillinger, NYC, 1936-38. m. Ina Magnuson, 3 s., 2 d. Career: Chmn., Dept. of Music, Univ. of NM, 1959-60; Hd., Dept. of Music, Univ. of Ga., Athens, 1960-72; Prof. w. rsch. in musical cimp., ibid., 1972-; Featured comp.-lectr. at var. univs.; 10 concert tours as pianist sponsored by Assn. of Am. Colls., 22 States, 1943-52; Pianist in 'Scored for Three', 12 weeks series of trio progs., ecucl. TV, 1961; var. appearances on maj. radio & educl. TV networks; Res. Comp., The Jay Hambridge Fndn., 1963-70, etc. Compositions: works for orch., band, scores. Num. recordings as comp., pianist & speaker. Contbr. to profl. jrnls. Mbrships. incl: BMI; Phi Mu Alpha. Hons. incl: Gold Medal, Arnold Bax Soc., 19634. Address: 765 Riverhill Dr., Athens, GA 30606, USA. 2, 3, 7.

GERSON-KIWI, Edith, b. Berlin, Germany. Ethnomusicologist; Musicologist; Professor of Musicology. Educ: Stern Conserv., Belin; Pianist's State Dip., Leipzig Acad. of Music; PhD, Univ. Heidelberg. m. Kurt Gerson, 1 s. Career: Pianist & Piano Tchr.; Concert Harpsichordist; formerly Lectr. at Acad. of Music, Jerusalem & Tel Aviv; Prof. of Musicol., Univ. of Tel-Aviv, 1966-; Hd., Jerusalem Phono-Archives of Oriental & Jewish Music; Ed. of sev. edns. of ancient music. Recordings: The Folkmusic of Israel; Music of the Bible; Traditional Music of Israel (single play). Publs: The History of the Italian Madrigal; The Legacy of Jewish Music Through the Ages, 1963; The Doctrine of the Persian Dastgah-composition, 1963; Oriental Instruments in Israel. Contbr. to var. jrnls. & Co-Ed., Orbis Musicae (yearbook of Dept. of Musicol., Univ. of Tel-Aviv). Mbrships: Bd., Int. Soc. of Musicol., Bd., Int. Folk Music Coun. Address: 8 KKL St., Entrance 5, Jerusalem 92428, Israel.

GERTLER, André, b. 26 July 12907, Violinist. Educ: Franz Liszt Acad. of Music, Budapest. m. Diane Andersen. Career: Fndr.-ldr., Gertler Quartet, 1931-51; Soloist & recitalist in Europe, Am., Africa, Asia & Austrialia; num. sonata recitals w. Bartok; Prof., Cologne Acad. of Music, 1954-59; Prof. Hanover Acad. of Music, 1964-; Prof., Royal Conserv. of Music, Brussels. Num. recordings made. Publs: Transcritions of works by Bartok, Geza Frid, etc. Contbr. to: Revue Musicale; The Score. Hons: Kt. Order of Leopold & Order of the Crown, Belgium; Off., Order of Gustav, Vasa, Sweden; Order of the Flag, Hungary; Order of Merit, 1st Class, German Fed. Repub.; Hon. FRAM, London. Address: 28 ave. d'Overhem, Brussels 18, Belgium.

GERVERS, Hilda F, b. 28 Oct. 1909, London, UK. Musicologist; Pianist. Educ: RCM, London; ARCM; GRSM (London); MMus, Converse Coll., SC; PhD, NY Univ. m. H

Suilven Gervers, 2 s. Career: Dir. of Music, The Thomas Schl., Rowayton, Conn.; Rsch. Assoc., NY Bartok Archives; Adjunct Lectr., Brooklyn Coll. of CUNY. Contbr. to num. profl. publs. Mbrships: Am. Musicol. Soc.; Int. Assn. of Music Libs.; Int. Repertory of Musical Iconography; Music Lib. Assn.; Ga. Music Tchrs. Assn. (Past Pres.). Hons: Award, Am. Assn. of Univ. Women, Coll. Tchng. Program, 1964. Hobbies: Swimming; Country Dancing; Reading. Address: 242 Ancon Ave., Pelham, NY 108034, USA. 4.

GESSNER-ASTEN, Erika, b. 17 May 1928, Annaberg, Erzgebirge, Germany. Educator; Piano Instructor. Educ: Hochschule Fur Musik, Weimar; Conserv. Music John Perterson, Berlin; Tchrs. Cert. Musical Educ. (Piano), 1951; Free Univ. Berlin, 1951-57; PhD, 1960; Waldrof Tchr. Trng. Inst. Mercy Coll. Detroit, USA; Mich. State Cert. & Waldorf Dip. Elem. Educ., 1972. m. Dietrich V Asten. Career: Asst. to Prod., Music Progs., WGBH-TV, Boston, 1962-65; Music Dir., WUHY-FM Radio, Phila., 1965-67; Prog. Dir., WUHY-FM Radio, Phial., 1967-70. Publs. incl: Complete edition of S Scheidt's Works, Vol. XII, 1965. Contbr. to jrnls. Mbr. profl. orgs. Recip: Berlin Airlift Mem. Schlrship. Adv. Studies, NY Univ., NYC, 1961. Mem. Schlrships. Adv. Studies, NY Univ., NY C, 1961. Hobbies incl: Crafts; Sport. Address: 1678 N Forge Mountain Dr., Box 472, Valley Forge, PA 19481, USA.

GESZLER, György (George), b. 1 Feb. 1913, Budapest, Hungary. Composer; Pianist; Professor of Music. Educ: Comp. & Piano Dips., Liszt Ferenc Acad. of Music, Budapest, 1935-37. m. Mária (Mary) Timkó, 4 d. Career: HS Prof., Budapest, 1935-; has had 3 'Author's Nights'' in Vienna, 2 in 1957, also in 1960; works broadcast in Austria & Switz. Comps. incl: Guitar Trio; Largo & Allegro deciso for violin (or cello) & piano; Five Vasarely Paintings for 2 pianos & percussion; Knight St. George (orchl. overture); Variations for cello & orch.; var. piano pieces. Has transcribed works by Liszt, Schubert & Erkel for wind orchs. Mbrships: Hungarian Comps. Soc.; Artisjus. Hons. incl: Liszt Scholarship, 1935; Francis Joseph Prize, 1942. Address: H-1117 Budapest, Mészöly-utca 4, Hungary.

GETAN, Jesus, b. 9 Feb. 1916, Panama City, Panama. Violinist. Educ: Dips., Guanche Conserv. v. Carmen Getan, 1 s., 1 d. Debut: aged 12, w. havana Phil. under Pedro San Juan. Career incls: Concertmaster, Chmbr. Orch. of Havana; Havana Municipal Symph.; Radio & TV Orch.; 1st Violinist, Balt. Symph. Orch., Md.; gave world premier of Austian comp. Paul Csonka's 2nd Violin Concerto (dedicated to Jesus & Carmen Getan), 1950. Recordings: RCA & Montilla, Havana; w. Nat King Cole, Havana. Mbrships: Balt. Musicians' Assn.; Pro Arte Musical Soc. Hons: 1st Prize, Royal Conserv., Barcelona; Winner, Havana Phil. Violin Competition, 1942. Hobby: Billiards. Address: 6800 Liberty Rd., Baltimore, MD 21207, USA.

GEVERS, Frederick, b. 13 Mar. 1923, Antwerp, Belgium. Concert Pianist; Professor of Piano. Educ: studied w. Walter Rummel, Yves Nat., Paul Roes. Debut: Brussels Phil., 1946. Career: Concerts throughout Europe, Can., S Africa, Zaire, Egypt, USSR; Prof., Royal Music Conserv., Antwerp, 1959-. Recordings: Duchesne. Address: 61 bis Missemburglei, B 2520, Edegem, Belgium.

GEYMULLER, Marguerite-Camille-Louise de, b. 5 Mar. 1897, Le Havre, France. Pianist; Composer. Educ: Dip., Lausanne Conserv. 1919. m. (1) R H Bodmer, 3 s., (2) M A de Freudenreich, (3) H F Sarasin. Career: Comps. performed on Swiss Radio, 1942, 44, 50, Mozarteum, Salzburg, 1957, SAFFA Exhib., Zurich, 1958, Expo Exposition Nat., Lausanne, 1964, & 14 other concerts in Zurich, Basle, Berne, etc., mostly in Lyceum Clubs, also in larger halls. Comps: (publ.) 3 Liriche de Riccardo Bacchelli, 1939. Mbrships: Assn. des Musiciens Suisses; SUISA. Recip., num. letters & congratulations from outstanding musicians & personalities. Hobbies incl: Music. Address: 106 Engelgasse, CH 4052 Basle, Switz.

GHANDAR, Ann, b. 1 Nov. 1943, Adelaide, SA, Aust. Lecturer in Composition; Pianist; Composer. Educ: BA, Adelaide; MA, Aust. Nat. Univ.; BMus, Southampton; LMusA. m. Mostafá El Sayed Ghandar. Debut: as comp., Sonata for flute & piano, Southampton Univ., 1974. Career: Lectr., Univ. of New Engl., Armidale; perfs: Messiaen's Quatres Études Rhythmiques, Adelaide Fest. of Arts, 1972; Ives Concord Sonata, Southampton, 1973; Schoenberg's complete works for solo piano, Univ. of New Engl., 1975; Debussy's Études, Bks. I & II, Armidale, 1978. Comps: Sonata for flute & piano; Recollections of a Latvian Song. Contbr. to: Miscellanea Musicologica. Hobbies: Reading; Travel. Address: Music Dept., Univ. of New Engl., Armidale, NSW 2351, Australia.

GHECIU, Diamandi, b. 20 Apr. 1892, Bucharest, Romania. Composer. Educ: Grad., Univ. of Law, Bucharest; Pvte. music studies. m. Mariana Pencioiu, dec. Comps. (recorded): Suites for piano, Reflections, Children's Corner, Stray Thoughts; Three Books of lieder; String Quartet No. 3. Publs. (w. Dumitru Bughici): Forms and Genres of Instrumental Music, 1960; Musical Forms and Genres, 1962. Contbr. to: Music, Bucharest. Mbr., Comps. Soc. of Romania. Hons: Labour Order; Cultural Merit Order; Prize of Comps. Soc., 1972, '75. Address: 22 Apolodor St., 4th Floor, Flat 9, Bucharest, Romania.

GHERDJIKOW, Pavel Iwanow, b. 21 May 1938, Kardjali, Bulgaria. Vocalist. Educ: Music Acad., Sofia. m. Anna Gherdjikowa, 1 s. Debut: The Nat. Opera Theatre, Sofia, 1962. Career: Apps., Vienna, Salzburg, Moscow, Paris, Naples, Budapest, Warsaw, Berlin, Copenhagen, Brussels, Hague, Amsterdam, Belgrade, Athens, Glyndebourne Fest. Opera, Aust., Japan, etc.; currently vocalist, The Nat. Opera Theatre, Sofia; Tchr., Scenic Art, Music Acad., Sofia. Recordings inc: Arias from Mozart; Songs by Pipkow, Vladigerow, Goleminow; Italian Pre-Classic & Classic Songs; Harmonai Mundi, Rimski-Korsakow; Mozart & Salieri, opera. Contbr. to sev. profl. publs. Mbrships: Union of Bulgarian Musicians; Union of Bulgarian Comps. Hons: Prize, 1961; Prize e, Sofia Opera Singers, 1963; Prize, Erkel, 1965; People's Artist, Bulgaria, 1979.Hobbies: Cooking, Red Wines. Address: Dimitar Manow Str. B1. 15, Ap. 36, 1408 Sofia, Bulgaria.

GHERTOVICI, Adia, b. 19 Dec. 1919, Cetatea-Alba, Romania. Violinist; Violin Teacher. Educ: Grad., Bucharest Conserv. of Music. m. Jehudit Ghertovici, 2 d. Debut: Bucharest, aged 8. Career: Recitals & soloist w. orchs. in Romania & abroad; Tape recordings for Radio Broadcast Co., Bucharest, 1950-67. Comps: Hypostasis, 1975. Mbrships: Hon. Mbr., E Ysaye Fndn., Brussels; Am. Soc. for Lit. & Arts; Soc. of Am. Musicians; ASTA. Publs. incl: Revision of Paganini Caprices, Dont & Gavinies Studies, Tartini Sonata in G Minor, 1960-62. Contbr. to Muzica, Bucharest. Hons. incl: E Ysaye Medal & Dip., 1967. Hobbies incl: Movie pictures in mimo-choreograph manner on modern music. Address: 430 S Mich. Ave., Chgo., IL 60605, USA.

GHEZZO, Dinu Dumitru, b. 2 July 1941, Tulsa, Romania. Composer; Conductor of Contemporary Music; Lecturer on 20th Century & Romanian Music. Educ: MA, Music Tchng. & Conducting, 1964 & MA, Comp., 1966, Univ. of Bucharest Conserv. of Music; PhD, UCLA, 1973. Career: Perfs. of comps. in Europe & US; Radio broadcasts, recordings, publs.; Music Dir. & Cond., The New Repertory Ensemble of NY; Dir., Ctr. of Rsch. & Perf. of Romanian Music, Queens Coll., NY; Asst. Prof., ibid. Comps. incl: (publs.) Ritualen (prepared piano); Kanones (flutes, cello & harpsichord); Kanones II (flutes, clarinet, cello, double bass, 2 percussions); Music for Flute & Tape; Concertino for Clarinet & Symphony Wind Ensemble; Celebrations. Mbrships. incl: ASCAP; ISCM NY; Coll. Music Soc. Hons. incl: Gus Kahn Comp. Award, Los Angeles, 1972; ASCAP, 1976, 77, 78; CAPS, 1977. Hobbies incl: Tennis. Address: 61-04 171st St., Fresh Meadows, NY 11365, USA.

GHEZZO, Marta Elisabeth, b. 14 May 1940, Tinca, Romania. Professor; Conductor. Educ: BA, Lyceum No. 2, Tg-Mures; BFA, Schl. of Fine Arts, ibid., MA., Univ. of Bucharest, Conserv. of Music. m. Dinu D Ghezzo, 1 d. Career: Prof. of Theory, Solfege, Orch. Conducting, Schl. of Fine Arts, Constanza, Romania, 1964-70; Cond., City Symph. Orch., ibid., 1968-69; Asst. Prof., score reading, Univ. of Bucharest, 1969-70; Instr., Theory-Solfege-Dictation, Calif. Inst. of the Arts, Valencia, USA, 1970-; currently working for PhD, CUNY. Radio & TV broadcasts & recordings w. City Symph. Orch. & Orch. of Schl. of Fine Arts, Constanza. Publ: From Medieval Modes to Graphic Symbpls (in press). Mbrships: Coll. Music Soc., Dante Alighieri Soc. Hobbies: Rsch. into Romanian Folk Music; Travel. Address: Calif. Inst. of the Arts, Music Dept., 24700 McBean Pkwy., Valencia, CA 91355, USA.

GHIGLIERI, Sylvia Marie, b. 13 Mar. 1933, Stockton, Calif., USA. Pianist; Harpsichord Player. Educ. incls: BMus, Dominican Coll., San Rafael, Calif., 1954; Dip., Music Acad. of W, Santa Barbara, 1954; Dip., Conserv. Ecole des Beaux Arts, Fontainebleau, France, 1955; MMus, Univ. of Pacific, Stockton, 1960; Grad. study, Eastman Schl. of Music, 1969 & Northwestern Univ., 1971. Debut: as pianist, San Fran., 1954. Career: concerts and recitals in France, Italy, Switz., 1955. Calif., 1947-76; Piano soloist, Modesto & Stockton Symphs., 1950-69; harpsichord recitals, Calif., 1973-76; on fac., 1961-, Assoc. Prof., 1970-75, Prof., 1975-, Calif. State Coll., Stanislaus at Turlock. Mbr. profl. orgs. Hons. incL: 1st Prize for Three Irish Pieces for Piano, Mu Phi Epsilon Comp. Contest, 1959; Hon. Mention, Mu Phi Epsilon Comp. Contest, 1959. Address: Calif. State Coll., Stanislaus, 800 Monte Vista Ave., Turlock, CA 95380, USA. 5, 27, 29.

GHIRCOIASIU, Romeo, b. 22 Nov. 1919, Cluj, Romania. Musicologist; Pianist. Educ: Dr. Law, Scis.; Dr. State Sci; D Musicology; MA, Piano & Pedagogy. m. Tudora Pogangeanu, 2 c. Career: Asst., 1946-49; Chair of Gen. Sociology, Univ. Cluj; Asst. Lectr., Prof., 1949-; Chair of Musicology, Conserv. of Cluj; Chief of Prog. for DMusicol.; Congs. on Music Hist. at Romanian TV & Radio, 1960-. Comps. for piano & voice. Recording: Muresian's Romanian Concerto for piano & orch. Publs: Contributions to the Romanian History of Music, Bucaresti, Editura Muzicala, 1963. Contbr. to profl. jrnls. Mbrships. incl: VP, Union of Comps. & Musicologists of Romania. Recip. num. hons. Hobbies: Antiques; Travel. Address: 3400 Cluj-Napoca, Str. Rakoczi 25, Romania. 4.

GHOLMIEH, Walid, b. 14 Apr. 1938, Marjeyoun, Lebanon. Composer; Conductor; Musicologist. Educ: Music & Art Tchng. Ctr.; Nat. Conserv.; Wichita State Univ. Kan., USA. m. Elham Nadda. Career: Lectr. in Schls., Conservs. & Insts. Comps: Al Qitar Al Akhdar (1st Odyssey in hist. of Arabic music); Musical Studies; music for int. fest., Baalbeck & others; musical plays, folk music, prog. music, instrumental music, music for films & plays; 3 Symphs. Num. recordings. Contbr. to: Arab Acad. of Music; Lebanese mags. & jrnls. Mbrships: Arab Acad. of Music; Int. Musicol. Soc.; SACEM; BIEM; Shocker Club, Wichita State Univ. recip. grant at Wichita State Univ., 1974. Hobbies: Reading; Technical Essays on Sound. Address: Sabbah Bldng. behing Banco di Roma, Hamra, Beirut, Lebanon.

GHOSH, Nikhiljyoti, b. 2 Jan. 1919, Barisal, E Bengal, India. Educator; Composer; Tabla Player. Educ: vocal music studied w. Shri Bipin Chatterjee, Shri Jnan Prakash Ghosh, Shri Feroze Nizami; Table studied w. Ustad Ahmed Jan Thirakwa, Ustad Amir Hussain Khan, Shri Jnan Prakash Ghosh. m. Usha Nayampalli, 3 c. Debut: Aged 8 in Barisal. Career: 1st broadcast as solo vocalist, All-India Radio, 1938; solo tabla & accomp. in concert halls, fests., radio & TV, worldwide, 1944-; Fndr. & Dir. Sangit Mahabharati, Acad. of rsch. & educ. in performing arts; Sponsor & Chief Ed., A Concise Ency., of Music, Dance & Drama in India. Num. recordings. Publs: Fundamentals of Raga & Tala with a New System of Notation (transl. into Marathi, Gujarati, Bengali & Hindi). Contbr. to: Jrnl. of the Indian Musicol. Soc., Baroda; Ramakrishna Mission, Inst. of Culture, Calcutta, Innuscia, Calcutta. Many comps. for films, dance, ballet, radio etc. Hobbies: Collecting rare music; Reading; Gardening. Address: Sangit Mahabharati, A/6, 10th Rd., Juhu Scheme, Vile Parle (West), Bombay 400 056, India. 28.

GHYOROS, Julien J C, b. 18 Nov. 1922, Liege, Belgium. Orchestra Conductor. Educ: Conservatoires Royaux de Musique de Liege et Brussels; Boursier de l'UNESCO a Glyndbourne, UK; Boursier de l'Academia Chigiana, Siena, Italy. m. Nora Van Moerbeke, 2 s., 1 d. Debut: Liege, 1960. Career: Cond., Liege Orch., 1960-63; First Cond., Royal Opera of Liege, 1963-65; Guest Cond., Belgian Radio & TV Orchs.; Guest Cond. in Liege, Antwerp, Brussels, Athens, Karlovy-Vary & Festival des Ardennes Francaises; also in Germany; Prof. of Orch. Cond. & Perm. Dir. & Cond. of the Brussels Youth Orch.; Perm. Cond. at the Fest. of Huy, Belgium; Kapelmeister, Colonster, Domaine Universitaire of Liege. Musical Dir., & permanent cond., Orch. of the Young musicians of Queen Elisabeth, Brussels. Compositions: American Rhapsody (Yankee) for Orch.; Balder 72 for Orch., Sonate d'Irchonwelz for piano; Conte a l'Enfant au Berceau for violin & piano. Recordings: The Sonate & Conte; Reflects; 7 pieces for piano solo. Mbrships: Sabam; Union des Compositeurs. Hons: Prize of the City of oLiege. Hobby: Swimming. Address: Rue Franklin 34, B 1040 Brussels, Belgium.

GIBBINS, Clarence Wingfield Mingay, b. 26 Sept. 1916, Ladysmith, Natal, S Africa. Teacher; Church Organist; Choirmaster. Educ: MA (classics); FTCL (harmony & comp.); LTCL (recorder); LTCL (class music). m. Ruth Daphne Reynolds. Career: Lectr., Nuttall Training Coll., Natal, 1939-50; Headmaster, S Rhodesian Govt., 1951-60; Educ. Off., ibid., 1961-63; retired 1964, now pvte. tchr. in Cape Town. Publs: School Method for African Schools, 1946; An African Song Book, 1946; (co-author) Songs at School, 1960. Contbnr. to TCL Bulletin. Mbrships: S African Soc. of Music Tchrs.; Cape Guild of Organists; Royal Schl. of Ch. Music; Cape Recorded Guild. Hons: 1st prize for Christmas Carol, Cape Town Phil. Choir competition, 1977. Hobbikkes: Baroque music; Photography. Address: 26 Cornwall Rd., Lakeside, Cape Town 7945, S Africa.

GIBBS, Alan (Trevor), b. 21 Apr. 1932, Chipping Norton, Oxon, UK. Teacher; Composer; Conductor; Organist; Educ: Privately w. Edwin Rose & Matyas Seiber (comp.); John Webster & Conrad Eden (organ); John McKinnell (piano); BA, BMus, Univ. of Durham; FRCO;p Dip. Educ. Durham; FRCO. m. Vivienne Whysall, 1 s. Career: Hd. of Music, Archbishop Tenison's

Grammar Schl., 1957-. Compositions incl: (publd.); O Ye Children; Thy Word is Truth; 4 Communion Services; Evening Canticles for Trebles; (recorded) Organ Sonata 2, 1970; God Hath Spoken (anthem); (performed) Organ Sonata 1 (Nuremburg Int. Organ Week & BBC); Viewpoints for Organ (BBC); Four Motets (McNaughten Concert & BBC); The Life of Music (Durham Cathedral); 5 Elizabethan Songs (BBC).Contbr. to: Musical Times; Musical Opinion; Music Teacher. Mbr., Royal Musical Assn. Recip., Pears Scholarship in Music, Durham Univ., 1950. Hobbies: Art; Architecture; Chess; Swimming. Address: 8 St. Margaret's Drive, Twickenham, Middx., TW1 1QN, UK.

GIBBS, Geoffrey David, b. 29 Mar. 1940, Copiague, NY, USA. Composer; College Teacher; Baritone Soloist. Educ: Studied piano privately w. Gladys M Gehrig & comp. w. Elie Siegmeister; BMus., Eastman Schl. of Music, Univ. of Rochester, 1962; MMus., ibid., 1963; DMus Arts, ibid., 1974; Studied comp. w. Bernard Rogers & Howard Hanson, electronic comp. w. Wayne Barlow & voice w. Julius Huehn & Yi-Kwei Sze. m. Sona Aronian, 1 d. Career: Lect.-recitals on Modern Art Song, New England, 1970-71; Major perfs. of original comps. inclng. Symph. No. 2 by Univ. of RI Symph. Orch., 1972, Icon; Igor Stravinsky by Jacksonville Univ. Orch., Fla., 1972 & Capers for 2 pianos, Montevideo, Uruguay, 1974; Instr.-Asst. Prof. of Music, Univ. of RI Kingston, 1965-; Dir., Electronic Music Studio, ibid. Compositions: Praise Ye the Lord (anthem), 1970; Pastorale for Violincellor or Bassoon & Piano, 1971. Contbr. to Kinsman. Mbrships: Am. Soc. of Univ. Comps.; Am. Music Ctr.; Pi Kappa Lambda; RI Music Educators Assn.; MENC; AAUP. Recip. of hons. Hobbies incl: Painting & illustrating; Arch. Address: Dept. of Music, Univ. of RI., Kingston, RI 02881, USA.

GIBBS, Ronald A, b. 29 Mar. 1945, Hendersonville, NC, USA. Percussionist; Teacher; Composer. Educ: BMus, MS, Juilliard Schl. of Music. m. Linda M Gibbs, 2 d. Career: Freelance perf. w. NY orchs. & chmbr. grps.; perfs. in Broadway shows (Man of La Mancha, Irene, Cry for Us All, Candide, etc.); has given premiere perfs. of works by contemp. comps.; Tchr., Horance Mann Schl., Riverdale Country Schl., Jersey City State Coll. Sev. unpubld. comps. Hons: scholarship, Juilliard Schl., 1965-70; Award, Nat. Orch. Assn., 1969. Hobby: Cabinet making. Address: 3658 Waldo Ave., Bronx, NY 10463, USA.

GIBSON, (Sir) Alexander Drummond, b. 11 Feb. 1926, Motherwell, Scotland, UK. Orchestral Conductor. Educ: Glasgow Univ.; RCM; Mozarteum, Salzburg, Austria; Acad. Chigiano, Siena, Italy; LRAM; ARCM; ARCO. m. Ann Veronica Waggett, 3 s., 1 d. Career: Repetiteur & Asst. Cond., 1951-52, Staff Cond., 1954-57, Musical Dir., 1957-59, all Sadler's Wells; Asst. Cond., BBC Scottish Orch., Glasgow, 1952-54; Prin. Cond. & Musical Dir., Scottish Nat. Orch., 1959-; Artistic Dir., Scottish Opera, 1962-. Has made num. albums, RCA, EMI, Decca, Philips, CRD. Mbr., Garrick & Oriental Clubs. Hons: CBE, 1967; LLD, 1968; Hon. RAM, 1969; St. Mungo Prize, 1970; D Mus, Glasgow, 1972; Musician of Yr., ISM, 1976; Kt. Bachelor, 1977. Mgmt: Harold Holt Ltd. Address: 15 Cleveden Gdns., Glasgow G12 OPU, UK. 1, 3, 14.

GIBSON, Maude Virginia Janie Phelps, b. 16 Apr. 1909, Lipsie Lake, Spooner, Wis., USA. Piano Teacher; Vocalist. Educ: Pvte. & Conserv., study in music, voice & dance. m. Clelland Albert Gibson, 3 s., 1 d. Career: Cinema pianist, 4 yrs.; Orch. pianist & stage accompanist; Pvte. Music Tchr.; Perfs. to local Schl., Ch. & Soc. orgs. Mbrships. incl: Pres., 1974-, fmr. stet Sherwood Tchrs. Seminar Club, Chgo., Ill. NGPT; Nat. Guild of Piano Tchrs. Tchrs. Div., Am. Coll. of Musicians; Pres., Duluth, MTA, 1957-58; Elder, Minn. Soc. of Mayflower Descendants; Minn. Pres., Daughters of Founders & Patriots of Am.; Historian, Minn. Daughters of Am. Colonists; DAR; Order of Eastern Star; Choir, Duluth Cong. Ch. Hobbies: Writing; Composing for children; Illustrating; Photography; Dancing; Crafts. Address: 2124 Ed 5th St., Duluth, MN 55812, USA.

GIBSON, William McHargue, b. 30 Nov. 1916, Marlow, Okla., USA. Symphony Trombonist. Educ: Okal. State Univ., 2 yrs.; Dip., Curtis Inst. of Music, Phils. m. Frances Barbour, 2 s. Career incls: Prin. Trombone, Pitts. Symph., 1948-55, Boston Symph., 1955-75; Mbr., ibid., 1975-; Mbr., Boston Symph., Chmbr. Players, 1965-75; Tchr. of Trombone, New England Conserv. of Music, Boston, 1955-; Lectr.on trombone related instruments; sev. recordings. Contbr. to Nat. Schl. Orch. Assn. Bulletin. Hobbies incl: Expmtl. Brass Instruments; Trout fishing. Address: 342 Hillcrest Rd., Needham, MA 02192, USA.

GIDEON, Miriam, b. 23 Oct. 1906, Greeley, Colo., USA. Composer. Educ: BA., Boston Univ.; MA., Columbia Univ.; Dr. of Sacred Music, Jewish Theol. Sem. of Am. m. Frederic Ewen, Career: Instructor, Dept. of Music, Brooklyn Coll., 1944-54; Prof. of Music, Jewish Theol. Sem., 1955-; CUNY, 1971-;

Compositions incl: (orch.); Symphonia Brevis; Lyric Piece for String Orch. (chamber works); 2 Str. Quartets; Cello Sonata; Clarinet Suite; Woodwind quartet; (vocal music); sev. cycles for solo voice & chamber grps. & for solo voice & piano; 2 sacred servs., (piano); 7 suites for piano solo; sonatina for 2 pianos; Songs of Youth O madness (Hölderlin) for voice & orch. Works performed by London, Prague, Tokyo & Zurich Symph. Orchs. Mbrships: Bd. Govs., Am. Music Ctr., Am. Composers Alliance, League of Composers, Int. Soc. for Contemporary Music. Hons: Bloch Prize for choral work, 1948; Nat. Fedn. Music Clubs & ASCAP Award for contbn. to Symphonic Music, 1969; Nat. Endowment of the Arts Grant for work for orch. & voice, 1974; Elected to: Am. Acad. & Inst. of Arts & Letters, 1975. Address: 410 Central Pk., W., NY, NY 10025, USA. 2, 4, 5.

GIEBEL, Agnes, b. 1921, Heerlen, Germany. Soprano. Educ: Folkwang Acad. of Music, Essen. m. Herbert Kanders, 1 s., 2 d. Debut: 1940. Career: weekly broadcasts, RIAS Berlin, 1950; concert apps., London, Vienna, Paris, Rome, Zurich, Berlin, etc., 1950-; num. fest. apps. Address: Bachemer Str. 84, 5 Klolin-Lindenthal, German Fed. Repub. 2.

GIEBLER, Albert Cornelius, b. 17 Aug. 1921, Hays, Kan., USA. Professor of Music; Musicologist. Educ: AA, St. Joseph's Jr. Coll., 1941; BMus, Ft. Hays, Kan. State Coll., 1946; MMus, 1950, PhD, Musicol., 1957, Univ. of Mich. m. Florence Higgins, 1 s., 1d. Career: Supvsr. of Music, Qunter High Schl., Kan., 1946-48; Prof. of Music, 1957-, & Chmn., Music Dept., 1968-, Univ. of R.I. Publ: The Masses of Hohann Caspar Kerll (1627-1693), 1957. Contbr. to: Recent Researches in Music of the Baroque Era, 1967; Grove's Dictionary, 6th ed.; profl. jrnls. Mbrships. incl: RIMEA; Nat. MTA (Chmn. Winds & Percussion Div., 1968-70); R.I. MTA (Pres., 1965-69, 72-74). Recip., Fellowship & Grants, Univ. of R.I.; Meritorirue Service Award, ibid., 1978. Hobbies: Personal Professional Library; Photography. Address: Pine Hill Rd. Rt. 5, Wakefield, RI 02879, USA.

GIELEN, Michael Andreas, b. 20 July, 1927, Dresden, Germany. Pianist; Conductor; Composer. Educ: Univ. of Buenos Aires, Argentina; Study of composition w. E Leuchter & J Polnauer. m. Helga Augsten, 1957, 1 s., 1 d. Career: Pianist, Buenos Aires; Music Staff, Teatro Colon, 1947-51; w. Vienna State Opera, 1951-60; Permanent Cond., ibid., 1954-60; 1st Cond., Royal Swedish Opera, Stockholm, 1960-65; Cond. & composer in Cologne, Germany, 1965-69; Musical Dir., Nat. Orch. of Belgium, 1969-72; Musical Dir., Netherlands Opera, 1972-. Address: Ave. Massenet 25, 1190 Brussels, Belgium.

GIERSTER, Hans, b. 12 Jan. 1925, Germany. Musical Director. Educ: Music HS., Munich; Mozarteum, Salzburg. Career: Musical Dir., Freiburg-im-Breisgau Municipal Theatres; Gen. Musical Dir., Municipal Theatres; Nuremberg, 1956-; Musical btheatre, 1971-; Guest Cond., State Operas of Hamburg, Munich & Vienna; Guest appearances at Festivals incl: Munich, 1964; Edinburgh (w. Bavarian State Opera, Cosi Fan Tutte), 1965; Glyndebourne (The Magic Fluge), 1966; Zurich, 1971; Vienna, 1972; Concert perfs. w. Phil. Orchs. of Bamberg, Berlin, Munich, Vienna, London, Mexico City, etc. Address: Stadtische Buhnen, Nurnberg-Furth, 8500 Nuremberg, Lessingstrasse 1, W Germany.

GIFFORD, Anthea, b. 17 Feb. 1949, Bristol, UK. Classical Guitarist. Educ: RCM; Accademia Musicale Chigiana, Siena, Italy. m. John Trusler, 1 s., 1 d. Debut: Purcell Room, London. Career: Solo recitals; recitals w. Amici String Quartet, Chilingirian String Quartet, Cummings String Trio; BBC broadcasts w. Amici, Neil Jenkins, Keith Swallow, Alexander Young; Prin. 3 times for classical guitar programme; solo recitals in Purcell Room, Wigmore Hall, Fairfield Hall; Concerto, Elizabeth Hall. Recordings: Peter Katin presents Young Artists from Croydon Arts Festival. Mbr. ISM. Recip. Young Musician Award, Gtr. London Arts Assn., 1972. Hobbies: Painting; Drawing; Gardening. Mgmt: Barbara Graham Mgmt., 35 Northwick Pk. Rd., Harrow, Middx, UK. Address: 24 Donovan Avenue, Muswell Hill, London N10, UK. 2.

GIFFORD, Gerald Michael, b. 12 Jan. 1949, Cambridge, UK. Director of Music; Professor; Lecturer; Organ & Harpsichord Recitalist. Educ: RCM BMus (Dunelm); GRSM; FRCO; ARCM; MA (Cantab). Career: Organ & Harpsichord Recitalist; Broadcaster; Prof., RCM; Fellow & Dir. of Music, Wolfson Coll., Cambridge; Lectr., Ball State Univ., Muncie, Indiana. Recordings: Polydor & Saga Labels w. Ely Cathedral Choir, Bath Univ. Recordings (Harpsichord); Crescent & CRD Labels (Organ); Hexham Abbey, Framlingham Parish Ch., var. harpsichords. Publs. incl: Italian Music at the Fitzwilliam Musuem, 1976. Contbr. to: Grove's Dictionary of Music; Dictionary of Composers. Mbr. profl. orgs. Hons: Cambridge Fest. Comps. Prize, 1967;

Grad. & Tankard Harpsichord Prizes, RCM, 1972. Hobby: Travel. Mgmt: Ibbs & Tillett, Wigmore St., London, UK. Address: 17 Crowlands, Cottenham, Cambridge CB4 4TE, UK. 4, 29.

GIFFORD, Helen Margaret, b. 5 Sept. 1935, Melbourne, Aust. Composer. Educ: BMus., Melbourne Univ. Conserv., 1958. Comps. incl: Chimaera, Imperium, orch.; Canzone, chmbr. orch.; As Dew in Aprille, Red Autumn In Valvins, soprano & piano; Vigil SSATB, choir; The Glass Castle, soprano & SSATB choir; Bird Calls From An Old Land, soprano & female choir; percussion; Fantasy, flute & piano; Septet, flute, oboe, bassoon, violin, viola, cello, harpsichord; Skiagram, flute, viola, vibraphone; Lyric, flute, clarinet, cello; Str. Quartet; Fable, harp; Myriad, 3 flutes, 4 percussion, piano & celesta; Sonnet, flute, guitar, harpsichord; Military Overture, clarinet, bassoon, cornet, bass trombone, violin, double bass, percussion; Of Old Angkor, horn & marimba; Company of Brass, brass ensemble; The Wanderer, Images for Christmas, speaker & instrumental ensembles; Regarding Faustus, solo tenor voice & chmbr. ensemble, 1978. var. piano music; var. stage music. Recip. var. hons. Hobbies: Travel in Asia; Theatre. Address: Flat 3, 4 Studley Ave., Kew, Victoria 3101, Aust.

GIGNAC, Marguerite, b. 17 July 1928, Windsor, Ont., Can. Opera & Concert Singer; Professor of Voice. Educ: Assoc. Degree & Artist's Dip., Royal Conserv. of Music, Toronto; Grad. Dip., Grad. Schl. of Fine Arts, Florence, Italy. m. William S Hedges, 3 d. Debut: Toronto Opera Fest. Career: ldng. Roles, Toronto Opera Fest., Montreal Fest., Vancouver Fest., San Fran. Opera, CBC Opera (Toronto), CBC TV Opera (Montreal); num. concert tours & guest apps. Can., USA, France, Italy; Fac. Mbr., Aspen Fest., 1971-74. Recordings: Angelicum, Milan; RCA Victor, Paris. Mbrships: Mu Phi Epsilon; Chmn., Contest Materials List for Voice, Minn. Music Tchrs. Assn.; Nat. Assn. Tchrs. of Singing; AAUP. Hons. incl: 1st Prize, Singing Stars of Tomorrow, Toronto, 1952; Finalist, Metrop. Opera Auditions, 1959. Hobbies: Swimming; Travel; Cinema. Address: 2090 Lincoln Ave., St. Paul, MN 55105, USA.

GILBERT, Anthony, b. 26 July 1934, London, UK. Composer. Educ: Studied w. Matyas Sieber, Anthony Milner, Alexander Goehr at Morley Coll., London. Comps. incl: Orch: Sinfonia; Symph.; Ghost & Dream Dancing; Crow-cry; Chmbr: 9 or 10 Osannas; Brighton Piece; String Quartet w. Piano Pieces; Vocal: Inscapes; Love Poems; Instrumental: 2 Piano Sonata; Spell Respell; The Incredible Flute Music, etc.; Dramatic: The Scene-Machine; The Chakravaka Bird. Hobbies: Walking; Swimming; Art Galleries. Address: 52 Hague Bar, New Mills, Stockport SK12 3AT, UK. 3, 14.

GILBERT, Goeffrey Winzer, b. 28 May 1914, Liverpool, UK. Flautist; Teacher; Conductor. Educ: Royal Manchester Coll. of Music. m. Marjorie Johnston, 1 s., 1 d. Debut: Prin. Flute, Halle Orch., 1930. Career: LPO, 1936-39, 1945; BBC Symph. Orch., 1948-52; RPO, 1957-63; Prof. of Flute, TCL, 1947-65, GSM, 1948-69, Royal Manchester Coll. of Music, 1959-69; Cond. in Res., Summer Orch., Stetson Univ., Fla., USA, 1966-; Prof. of Flute, Dir. Instrumental Studies, Cond., Stetson Orch. & Keenan Chair for Disting. Profs., ibid., 1969-. Mbrships: Omicron Delta Kappa; Pi Kappa Lambda. Hons: FTCL; FRMCM; FGSM. Hobbies: Electronics; Cars; Golf. Address: 422 E Oakdale Ave., DeLand, FL 32720, USA.

GILBERT, Kenneth, b. 1931, Montreal, PQ, Can. Harpsichordist; Organist; Musicologist. Educ: Montreal Conserv. of Music; advanced studies in organ w. G Litaize, & in harpsichord w. R Gerlin, both Paris. Career: Harpsichord Instr., Montreal Conserv., 1967-; Lectr. in Music, McGill Univ., Montreal, 1964-; Assoc. Prof. in Music, Univ. of Ottawa, Ont. & Laval Univ., Quebec, 1969-; Vis. Prof. of Harpsichord, Royal Flemish Conserv., Antwerp, 1971. Recordings: Complete Harpsichord Works of Francois Couperin (16 discs, Harmonia Mundi); Organ Works of Clerambault (Oryx). Publs: Complete Harpsichord Works of Francois Couperan, 4 vols., 1969-; Complete Keyboard Works of Domenico Scarlatti, 11 vols., 1971-. Hons: Prix d'Europe, PQ.; Can. Coun. Sr. Arts Fellowships, 1968; Int. Calouste Gulbenkian Fndn. Award, 1970. Mgmt: Wilfrid Van Wyck Concert Mgmt. Ltd., 80 Wigmore St., London W1, UK. 3.

GILELS, Emil Grigorevich, b. 19 Oct. 1916, Odessa, Russia. Pianist. Educ: Odessa Musical & Dramatic Inst.; Moscow Conserv. Career: Prof., Moscow Conserv. in late 1930s & 1954-; European Concert Tours, 1945-; N Am. Tours, 1955, 1960. Hons: 1st Prize All-Russia Music Competition, 1933; People's Artist of USSR; State Prize, 1946; Lenin Prize, 1962; Orders of Lenin & Red Banner of Labour; Badge of Hon.; Gold Medal, Brussels, 1972. Address: MoscowState Conserv., U1. Herzena 13, Moscow, USSR.

GILES, Allan Ronald, b. 11 Mar. 1945, Adelaide, S Aust. Music Librarian. Educ: BMus (Adelaide); Assoc., Lib. Assn. of Aut. m. Judith Anne Cox, 1 s., 1 d. Career: State Lib. of SA, 1963-73; Educ. Dept. of SA, Music Branch, 1974-; Ed., Continuo, 1979-. Contbr. to: Continuo; programme notes for Fest. Theatre. Mbrships: Int. Assn. of Music Libns., Aust. & NZ Branch. Hobbies: Reading; Gardening. Address: 6 Silverdale Crescent, Bellevue Heights, SA 5050, Aust.

GILES, Paul W, b. 2 Sept. 1903, Dexter, Maine, USA. Retired Army Bandsman; Flutist; Piccolo Player. Career: Played w. some of the best bands in Maine, 1920s; Bandsman, US Army, 1931-55; Cond., own band, Dexter, Maine, 1955-. Mbrships: Life, Nat. Band Assn.; Past Chmn., State of Maine, ibid.; Masons; Odd Fellows; Am. Legion. Hobby: Fishing. Address: 79 Maple St., Dexter, ME 04930, USA.

GILFILLAN, Frank Allen, b. 20 Dec. 1921, Liverpool, UK. Cost Accountant; Semi-professional Pianist & Organist. m. Ann Vickers, 1 s. 1 d. Career: Guest perfs. on theatre organs, 1938-post WW II; currently mainly charity perfs. & some profl. apps. illustrated talks on music, harmonic theory, organ hist. & construction; index of·11,000 organs maintained until 1963. Publs: Kendal to Anywhere; Point-to-Point Guide to Lakeland; series of brochures for Lancastria Theatre Organ Trust, 1976-; 2 musical books in preparation. Contbr. to: Musical Opinion; The Organ. Mbrships: Organ Club, London; Lancastria Theatre Organ Trust. Hobbies: Music; Printing; Travel in Britain. Address: 14 Warwick Drive, Endmoor, Kendal, Cumbria LA8 OEE, UK.

GILL, Dominic, b. 8 June 12941, London, UK. Teacher; Writer; Music Critc. Educ: BA (Oxon); LRAM. m. Elizabeth, 1 s., 1 d. Contrib. to: Financial Times. Address: 82 Carlton Hill, London NW8 OER, UK.

GILL, Richard Thomas, b. 30 Nov. 1927, Long Branch, NJ, USA. Singer (bass). Educ: AB, Harvard Coll., 1948; Henry Fellowship, Jesus Coll., Oxford Univ., UK, 1948-49; PhD (Econs.), Harvard Univ., 1956; Vocal study w. Herbert Mayer, NYC. m. Elizabeth Bjornson, 3 s. Debut: w. Opera Co. of Boston, 1970. Career incl: major operatic roles w. NYC Opera, 1971-; NY Metropol. Opera, 1973-76 inclng. Magic Flute, Boris Godunov, Romeo & Juliet; Turandot, etc.; appeared at Edinburgh Festival, 1976, Holland Festival, 1977. Publs: 7 books on econs. Mbrships: Bd. Govs.; Am. Guild of Musical Artists; Am.Econ. Assn. Hons: Phi Beta Kappa; Atlantic Monthly Short Story Prize, 1954. Hobby: Tennis. Mgmt: Thea Dispeker, NYC. Address: Box 111, Chocorua, NH 03817, USA.

GILLARD, David Owen, b. 8 Feb. 1947, Croydon, UK. Opera & Ballet Critic; Freelance Writer on the Arts. Career: Critic for the London Daily Mail, 1971-; Formerly film & theatre critic, London Daily Sketch. Publs: Beryl Grey, A Biography, 1977. Contbr. to: Radio Times. Mbr., The Critics' Circle. Hobbies: Hiking; Amateur dramatics; Swimming. Address: 4 Green Ct., 27 Beckenham Grove, Shortlands, Bromley Kent BR2 OJN, UK.

GILLEN, Gerard Thomas Mary, b. 16 Aug. 1942. University Lecturer in Music; Concert Organist; Adjudicator; Examiner. Educ: B Mus., Univ. Coll., Dublin, 1965; MA, ibid., 1966; B Litt., Queens Coll., Oxford, 1970; studied under Flor Peeters, Organ, Royal Flemish Conservatoire of Music, Antwerp, 1963-64, '66-67. m. Patricia Nolan, 2 s. Debut: 1st official recital Dublin, 1964. Career: Organ recitals in Ireland, UK., Belgium, Germany, Scandinavia, Poland, USA & Canada; Radio appearances on RTE., BBC Radios, CBC, BRT, NDR; Organist at St. Mary's Ch., Dublin, 1961-; Lectr. in Music, Univ. Coll., Dublin, 1969-; Chmn., Dublin Diocesan Commn. on Sacred Music, 1972-; Titular organist, Metropolitan Pro-Cath., Dublin, 1976-; Cond., Univ. Madrigal Singers, 1972-74. Recordings: Buxtehude & JG Walther on the Chapel Organ of Trinity Coll., Dublin, NIR; Bach & César Franck on St. Audeon's Dublin, IFD. Contbr. to var. jrnls.; Mbr., profl. orgs. Hons. incl: Premier Prix avec grande distinction, Antwerp, 1964; Prix d'Excellence, Antwerp, 1967; 3rd Laureat of Bruges Int. Organ Comm., 1964. Hobbies: Theatre; Reading, etc. Address: 1 Southwood Pk., Blackrock, Dublin, Eire.

GILLESPIE, Don C, b. 25 Aug. 1936, Metter, Ga., USA. Musicologist; Editor. Educ: BA (piano), Univ. of Ga.; Vienna Acad. of Music, Vienna, Austria, 1958-59; MA (musicolo.), Univ. of Ga.; PhD, musicol., Univ. of NC at Chapel Hill. Career incls: Pvte. piano tchr., Metter, Ga., 1963-64; Instructor in piano, Univ. of Ga., 1965-66; Asst., Music Lib., ibid.; 1965; Rsch. Asst., Univ. of NC at Chapel Hill, 1968-69; Corresponding Ed., Current Musicology, 1968-70; Ed. Committee, Ed., Rep., C F Peters Corp., 1970-. Publs: Ed., Henry Cowell, 2 Rhythm-Harmony Quartets 11915-19). Contbr. to: num. profl. publs. Mbrships: Am. Musicol. Soc.; The Sonneck Soc.; Bd. of Dirs., The Percy Grainger Lib. Soc.; The

Delius Soc.; Educl. Committee, Committee on Choral Ed. Standards, Music Publrs. Assn.; Int. Mahler Soc.; Phi Beta Kappa; Phi Kappa Phi. Hons. incl: NDEA Fellowship, Univ. of NC, 1968-70. Address: 260 Sixth Ave. Apt. 32, NY, NY 10014, USA.

GILLESPIE, James Ernest Jr., b. 30 Nov. 1940, Tazewell, Va., USA. Associate Professor of Music; Clarinettist. Educ: BS, Mus Ed., Concord Coll., 1962; MMus, Ind. Univ., 1963; DM, ibid., 1969. m. Cheryl Hopkins Gillespie. Career: Fac. Mbr: Concord Coll., Ind. State Univ.; Univ. of Redlands; Northeast La. Univ.; Clarinettist, Contemporary Wind Quintet; Solo clarient, Monroe Symph. Orch. Faculty mbr., Univ. of Denver, 1976-. Publs: The Reed Trio: An Annotated Bibliography of Original Published Works, 1971; Solos for Unaccompanied Clarinet: An Annotated Bibliography of Published Works, 1973. Contbr. to The Clarinet, The Schl. Musician; Instrumentalist; Woodwind World; NACWPI Jrnl. Mbrships: incl: Review Ed., The Clarinet; Phi Mus Alpha. Address: Schl. of Music, NLU, Monroe, LA 71201, USA.

GILLESPIE, Rhondda Marie, b. 3 Aug. 1941, Sydney, Australia. Concert Pianist. Educ: NSW Conserv. of Music; pvte. studies w. Louis Kentner & Denis Matthews. m. Denby Richards. Career: 1st broadcast, Aust., aged 8; 1st pub. recital aged 12; apps. w. major orchs. & in recital, UK, 1962-, & in Netherlands, Scandinavia, Germany, Iran, Egypt, USA & Aust.; radio & TV broadcasts. Recordings: Philips; EMI; Argo; Vesta. Recip., Aust. Broadcasting Corp. Concerto Competition Prize, aged 18. Hobbies: Exotic Cooking; Golf; Languages; 1st Edition Liszt. Mtmg: Alex Aaron, Zwaluwenweg 11, Blaricum, Netherlands. Address: Hill House, Hasketon, Suffolk IP13, 6J4, UK.

GILLETTE, John Carroll, b. 16 May 1941, Girard, Kan., USA. College Teacher of Bassoon. Educ: BS, MS, both music educ., Kan. State Coll., Pitts., Kan.; D Mus, Ind. Univ., Bloomington. m. Linda Moulton, 2 s. Career: study, Tanglewood & Montreux Conducting Camp; 1st Bassoon, Erie Phil. Orch.; Mbr., Fredonai Woodwind Quintet; Tchr., SUNY Fredonia. Mbrships: MENC; NACWPI; Int. Double Reed Soc.; Phi Mu Alpha Sinfonia; Am. Fedn. of Musicians. Hobbies: Reading; Woodworking. Address. 56 Curtis Pl., Fredonia, NY 14063, USA.

GILLIAM, Roger Wayne, b. 22 Nov. 1948, Rangeley, Colo., USA. Private Teacher of Trumpet; Freelance Trumpet Player. Educ: B Mus., Southern Meth. Univ., Tex.; M Mus, Hartt Coll. of Music, Univ. of Hartford, Conn. m. Margaret R. Gilliam, 1 s. Comps: Variations on Eight Notes (Brass Quintet); Three Episodes for Brass (Brass Quintet), Three Movements for Horns (French Horn Trio). Mbr. Phi Mu Alpha Sinfonia. Hobbies: Audio Components; Golf; Tennis. Address: 26 Midfield Dr., Apt. 4, Waterbury, CT 06705, USA.

GILLIES, Anne Lorne, b. 21 Oct. 1944, Stirling, Scotland, UK. Soprano. Educ: MA, Edinburgh Univ.; PGCE, London Univ.; LRAM. m. Neil Fraser, 1 s. Career: began as Gaelic & Scots Folk-Singer w. apps. throughout UK and sev. apps. at Edinburgh Int. Fest.; since classical trng. has branched out into lieder, operatic arias, operettas & musicals; num. apps. on TV on BBC Scotland, BB1 & BBC2, 1970-; frequent concert & cabaret apps. Recordings: There Was A Girl, Phonogram. Mbrships: Equity; ISM. Recip., Awared for Most Promising Newcomer on Radio TV, Radio Inds. Club, Scotland, 1975. Hobby: Writing, esp. in Gaelic. Address: 74 Terregles Ave., Glasgow, G41 4LX, UK.

GILLINGHAM, Diana, b. 1 Dec. 1932, W Wickham, Kent, UK. Mezzo-Soprano singer. Educ: pvte. study in Switz. & London; ARCM (singing perf.). m. Harold Wells, 2 s. Debut: Royal Fest. Hall, 1959. Career: recital debut at Wigmore Hall, 1961; Recitals & Oratorio perfs. throughout UK, also Germany & Switzerland (also broadcast); Prof. of Singing, Blackheath Conserv., 1964-64. Recorded Le Nozze di Figaro w. Phil. Concert Soc. under Carlo Maria Giulini. Mbr., ISM. Hobbies: Gardening; Riding; Crossword puzzles. Mgmt: Ibbs & Tillet. Address: Beech House, Hollowell, Northampton, UK. 3.

GILLIS, Verna, b. 14 June 1942, NYC, USA. Ethnomusicologist; Vocalist. Educ: MA, Goddard Coll., 1974; PhD, Union Grad. Schl., 1976. m. Bradford Graves, 1965. Career: Chmn., Music Committee, Int. Women's Arts Fest.; Prod., Concerts & progs. for radio stn. WBAI, NYC; Tchr., Brooklyn Coll., New Schl. of Liberal Arts, CUNY. Rerdings: Vocalist on Brown Rice - Don Cherry, EMI; Compiler of ethnomusicol. recordings issued by Folkways & Lyrichord. Address: 799 Greenwich St., NY, NY 10014, USA.

GILLMAN, Robert Edward, b. 4 June 1943, St. Albans, UK. Music Teacher; Recitalist; Accompanist. Educ: MMus, Royal Coll. of Music; FRCO (CHM); Assoc., Royal Coll. of Music. m. Vivien Jean Blythin, 2 s., 1 d. Debut: 1967. Career: Pvte.

teaching prac. until 1974; Organist, Master of Song Schl., Newark Parish Ch., 1974-; Asst. Dir. of Music, Stamford HS, 1979-; Major recitals & perfs. incl: Nottingham, York Minster, Stamford, Edinburgh, Southwell Minster, Newark, 1967-. Mbrships: Royal Coll. Organists; Incorp. Soc. of Musicians; Newark Music Club (Committee mbr., Prog. planning); Incorp. Assn. of Organists. Recip. Pauer Prize, Royal Coll. of Music, 1967. Hobbies: Winemaking; Walking; Camping. Address: TheSong Schl., Ch. St., Newark, Notts., UK.

GILLMOR, Alan Murray, b. 10 Oct. 1938, Fort Frances, Ont., Canada. Musicologist (Piano & clarint). Educ: B Mus, Univ. of Mich., 1963; MA, ibid., 1964; PhD, Univ. of Toronto, 1972. m. Susan Gay Leonard, 1 s., 1d. Career: Lectr., McGill Univ., Montreal, 1970-71; Chmn. & Assoc. Prof., Carleton Univ., Ottawa, 1971-. Publs: Erik Satie & the Concept of the Avant-Garde, 1972; author of radio documentaries on Erik Satie & John Cage for Canadian Broadcasting Corp.; Music Critic, The Ottawa Citizen, 1971-; Prog. Annotator, Nat. Arts Ctr. Orch., Ottawa; Contbr. to: Canadian Music; Ency. Int. Mbrsh ips: Am. Musicological Soc.; Canadian Assn. of Univ. Schls. of Music; Delius Soic. Hons: Canada Coun. Grants, 1965-66, 1969-70. Hobbies: Philately; Travel. Address: 25 Wendover Ave., Ottawa, Ont., Canada K1S 4Z5.

GILLON, Baruch (Gorlatshikov), b. 7 Sept. 1901, Ekaterinoslav, Russia. Producer; Impresario. Educ: Mines Engrng. Coll., 1919-1921; Inst. Social & Econ. Scis., 1921-22. m. Bela Finkelstein, 2 c. Career: Fndr. & Dir., Int. Concert Office, Tel Aviv, 1924-27; Mgr., Palestine Opera, 1924-26; Co-fndr. &. Co-Dir., Palestine Symph. Orch., 1924-25; Co-fndr., Palestine Oratorio Soc., 1926; Co-Dir., ibid., 1929-49; Mng. Dir., Hamatate Theatre, Tel Aviv, 1929-49; Prin., B Gillon Impresario Ltd., Tel Aviv, 1927-; participated in War of Liberation, 1948, Sue Campaign, 1956, & 6 day war, 1967. Contbr. to local jrnls. Mbrships: Hagana, 1923-; Israeli Assn. of Impresarios (chmn., 1960-73); Int. Theatrical Inst. Hons: Sign of Hagana, Sign of Erect.; Dist. Citizen of Tel Aviv Award, 1977. Address: 14 A D Gordon St., Tel Aviv, Israel. 30.

GILMAN, Irvin Edward, b. 28 Mar. 1926, Phila., Pa., USA. Flautist; Educator; Clarinetist; Saxophonist. Educ: B Mus, Oberlin Coll. Conserv., 1953; M Mus, Manhattan Schl. of Music, 1954. m. Elinor Goldberg (div.), 1 d. Career: Asst. Prin. Flute, Detroit Symph. Orch., 1956-68; Prin. Flute, Albany Symph. Orch., 1969-; Assoc. Prof. Flute, SUNY, Albany, 1968-. Many recordings w. Detroit Symph. Orch., (Mercury Records & Motown Records). Publs: The Still Surface Breaks (poetry), 1959; The Craft & Art of Playing the Flute, 1976; Contbr. to: The Instrumentalist. Mbrships: Am. Fedn. of Musicians; Nat. Flute Assn. Address: PAC-1400 Washington Ave., Albany, NY 12222, USA.

GINASTERO, Alberto E, b. 11 Apr. 1916, Argentina. Composer. Educ: Nat. Conserv. of Music & Arts, Escenico. Career: Dir., Inst. Torcuato di Tella, Ctr. Latino-am. de Altos Estudios Musicales. Compositions incl: Ollantay (symphonic poem), 1948; Music for film Cabailito Criollo, 1954; Variaciones concertantes, 1957; Obertura para el Fausto Criollo (orch.); 2 Symphs.; Panambi (ballet); Estancia (ballet); Don Rodrigo (opera); Bomarzo (opera), 1967. Address: Inst. Torcuato de Tella, Ventro Latinoamericano de Altos Estudíos Musicales, Florida 936, Buenos Aires.

GINN, Sophie, b. 29 Oct. 1933, NYC, USA. Singer; Voice Professor Educ: BS, MS, Juilliard Schl. of Music. m. Paul Paster, 1 s. Debut: Town Hall, NYC, 1958. Career: Mbr., NYC Opera Co.; sev. apps. w. Goldman Band, Guggenheim Mem. Concerts, Ctrl. Pk.; Soloist w. Camarata Singers, on Nat. TV & w. Oakdale (Conn.) Musical Theatre; concert & opera apps. throughout USA. Contbr. to: Fine Arts Mag. Mbrships. incl: Mu Phi Epsilon; Nat. Assn. of Tchrs. of Singing; Ctrl. Opera Serv. Recip., num. musical awards & schlrships. Hobbies: Reading; Painting. Address: 519 Karen Dr., Berea, OH 44107, USA. 5, 8, 23.

GINSBURG, Gerald M, b. 7 July 1932, Lincoln, Neb., USA. Composer; Pianist; Teacher; Lecturer; Critic; Editor. Educ: B Mus, Oberlin Conserv. of Music; M Mus, Manhattan Schl. of Music, Debut: The Music of Poetry, Carnegie Recital Hall, 1974. Career: Tchr., Columbia Grammar & Preparatory Schl., Third St. Music Schl. Settlement; Bi-Centennial Parade of Am. Music, Kennedy Ctr., Wash., DC, 1976; The World is a Beautiful Place...(theatre piece), Alice Tully Hall, 1977; Concerts of comps., Nat. Arts Club & Liederkranz, NYC. Comps., over 200 songs to 20th Century poetry. Contbr. to: Music Jrnl. (music critic); 1975 Artist Directory of Music Jrl. (ed.). Mbrships: ASCAP; The Bohemians; Musicians Club of NY. Recip. var. hons. Address: One Sheridan Sq. Apt. 7C, NY, NY 10014, USA.

GINZBURG, Dov, b. 8 Feb. 1906, Warsaw, Poland. Pianist; Percussionist; Composer. Educ: Warsaw Conserv. m. Hadasa, 1 d. Debut: w. Warsaw Phil. Career: currently w. Israel Phil. Orch.; broadcasts for Radio Warsaw & Radio Israel; currently tchng. music. Comps. incl: Fantasy (quintet w. woodwinds & horn); Sonatina (flute, viola & guitar); Fantasia Concertante (5 woodwinds, trumpet, percussion, strings); Quartette (violin, viola, cello & horn); Little Trio (violin, horn, piano); Fantasia (symph.); Concertino (symph.); Imagination (symph. orch.); Capricio (percussion); Prelude (percussion). Mbr., League of Comps. in Israel. Address: Ben-Yehuda St. 177, Tel-Aviv 63-471, Israel.

GIPPS, Bryan, b. 15 June 1910, Bexhill-on-Sea, UK. Conductor; Violinist. Educ: RAM; ARAM; LRAM; certs. RAM. m. Judy Hollis, 1 s., 1 s. by previous marriage. Career: formerly prin. 2nd violin, RPO, ldr. & cond., Ballet Rambert, str. tchr., Westminster Abbey Choir Schl.; now cond., Greenwich Symph. Orch., Ashford Symph. Orch., South Eastern Sinfonia, Kent Singers; freelance cond. (incl. BBC). Comps. incl: Lullalby for orch.; German Folk Song for orch.; French Folk Song for small orch. recip., Waley Prize, RAM. Hobbies: Local Hist.; Antiquarian Books & Music; Genealogy; Engl. Hist. Address: Egerton House, Egerton, Kednt, UK.

GIPPS, Ruth, b. 20 Feb. 1921, Bexhill-on-Sea, UK. Composer & Conductor; Formerly Concert Pianist & Oboist. Educ: Bexhill Schl. of Music; RCM; ARCM (Piano Perf.), 1936; B Mus, (Dunelm), 1941; D Mus. (Dunelm), 1948. m. Robert Baker, 1 s. Debut: Concerto engagements from age 10. Career: Solo Pianist & Freelance Oboist until 1952; Chorus Master, City of Birmingham Choir, 1948-50; Cond., London Repertoire Orch., 1955-; Cond., London Chanticleer Orch., 1961-; Prof., RCM, 1967-77; Prin. Lectr. in Music, Kingston Polytechnic, 1977-. Compositions incl: The Cat, Opus 32, Contralto & Baritone soli, double chorus & orch.; Goblin Market, Opus 40, Two soprano soli, female voice chorus & string orch.; Magnificat & Nunc Dimittis, Opus 55, 5-part chours & organ; Seascape, Opus 53, Tone poem for ten wind instruments; 4 symphs. & 5 concertos. Contbr. to var. profl. jrnls. Mbrships: Chmn., Composers Guild of GB, 1967; Pres., Hastings Musical Fest., 1960-; Parton, Crusade Against all Cruelty to Animals. Hons: Cobbett Prize, 1957; Hon. RAM, 1966; FRCM, 1972. Hobbies: Photography. Address: Allfarthings, Hermitage Rd., Kenley, Surrey CR2 5EB, UK. 3, 14, 27.

GIRARD, Philippe Jean, b. 11 July 1949, Doix, Vendée, France. Musician. Career: Radio & TV broadcasts, France; Dir. of Chorale, Les Chanteurs a la Croix d'Aunis, la Rochelle. Recordings: 2 LP's. Address: 43 Avenue Guiton, 17000 La Rochelle, France.

GIRAUD, Claude, b. 11 July 1923, Clamart, France. Producer. Educ: Law Univ. m. Liane Daydé, 1 s. Career: Office, Productions Claude Giraud, 1942-; Prod., Classical & Folkloric Ballets. Mbrships: Sec., General du Syndicat Nat. des Directeurs de Tournées Theatrales; Assn. Europienne des Directeurs de Concerts et Spectacles. Address: 252 Faubourg Saint Honore, 75008 Paris, France.

GIROUX, Paul Henry, b. 24 May 1916, Humboldt, Ariz, USA. Teacher; Musician (flute); Conductor. Educ: BA, Ariz. State Coll., Flagstaff; BS (Psychol.), Univ. of Wash.; MA (music educ.), ibid.; grad study, ibid., & at Eastman Schl. of Music. m. Florence Carroll, 1 d. Career incl: w. Radio KTAR, Phoenix, Arix., 1939-50; Choirmaster, Cantor & Tchr., Phoenix, 1939-50; Grad. Asst., Univ. of Wash., Seattle, 1950-53; Pub. Schl. Tchr., Olympia, Wash., 1953-55; Hd., Music Dept. & Chmn., Arts Div., Everett Community Coll., Wash., 1955-78; Cond., Everett Symph. Orch., 1955-65; Choirmaster, Trinity Episc. Ch., 1963-72; Flute soloist, Everett Community Band, 1960-78; Cantor, St. Aidans Episc. Ch. Ret'd., 1978. current Mbrships. incl: MENC; Nat. MTA; NEA; Phi Delta Kappa. Hons. incl: Theodore Presser Followship, 1952-53. Hobbies: Behavioral Sci.; People. Address: 1750 S. Desert Vista Dr., Tucson, AZ 85710, USA.

GIRVOEANU, Aurel, b. 24 Sept. 1916, Girov-Neamt, Romania. Composer; Pianist; Conductor. Educ: Egizio Massini Conserv. m. Marilena Giroveanu, 2 children. Debut: Pianist, Romanian Broadcasting Co., 1945; Career: Pianist & Cond. in concerts & shows for Radio Romania, 1946-52. Comps. incl: Operettas; Golden Apple, 1970; Musicals; Movies; One, Two, Three, 1974; Musical Shows; Silver Wedding, 1974; Light Music; I'll Never Grow Old, 1976; Choruses; Country, My Ancestors' Home, 1976; Music for children & schl. children. Num. recordings. Publs. incl: Chosen Tunes vol. 1, 1964. Mbr. var. profl. orgs. Hons. incl: Cultural Merit Medal. Hobby: Flower Growing. Address: 25 Pitar Mos St., PO 25, 7000 Bucharest, Romania.

GISCA, Nicolae, b. 30 Sept. 1942, Tibirica, Romania. Conductor (Choir & Orchestra); Professor. Educ: Dip., Music conserv. George Enescu, Iasi. m. Elena Gisca, 1 d. Debut: w. Conserv. Chmbr. Orch., 1967. Career: Cond. of Conserv. Symph. & Chmbr. orchs.; cond. of Conserv. Choir & Chmbr. Choir, Cantores Amicitiae; Symph. & vocal symph. concerts w. Phil. Orch., Botosani & Bacau; apps. in Romania, Austria & German Fed. Repub. TV apps.; Prof. of condng. & orchestration, G. Enescu Music Conserv. Comps. incl: arrs. of folk songs for Cantores Amicitiae Choir. Publs: Choir collection for mixed voices, 1978; Year Book of Conserv. G Enescu, 1960-70. Contbr. to: Musicology Writing, Iasi. Hobbies: Travelling. Address: Str. Vasili Lupu Nr. 134, B1 P7 Sc A et. 4 ap 1, 6600 Iasi, Romania.

GISTELINCK, Elias, b. 27 May 1935, BeverenLeie, Belgium. Composer; Chief Producer Belgian Radio. Educ: Conserv., Brussels & Paris. m. Lucy Feron, 2 s., 1 d. Career: Trumpet Player, night clubs & jazz grps.; Classical Trumpet Player, Nat. Orch. & Radio Orch.; Engr., Radio; Created Jazz Sect., Belgian Radio; Chief Prod., Belgian Radio. Comps; Chmbr. music; Symph. music; Ballet; Jazz. Recordings: Per Che (homage to Che Guevara); Ndesse or Blues on Poems of Leopold Sedar Senghor. Hons. Prix de la Rai; Italia Prize, 1969; Koopal Prize; Prize of Belgian Comps. Guild; Prize of Belgian Musical Critics; Prize of Belgian Min. of Culture. Hobbies: Lit.; Writing poetry; Karate. Address: Zuidlaan 1, 1990 Hoeilaart, Belgium.

GITLIS, Ivry, b. 1922, Haifa, Palestine. Solo Violinist. Educ: Nat. Conserv. of Music, Paris; studied w. Georges Enesco, Carl Flesch, Jacques Thibaud. m. Paule Deglon. Career: solo apps. w. ldng. orchs. of UK & Europe; concerto sonata & contemp. chmbr. perfs. Address: co Rerdings Div., Dover Publs. Inc., 180 Varick St., NY, NY 10014, USA. 2.

GITTINGS, John William, b. 8 July 1940, New Castle, Pa., USA. Choral Director; Vocalist; Teacher; Educational Representative. Educ: BA (voice), Univ. of Calif., 1963; MA (choral music & voice), Calif. State Coll., Fullerton, 1969. Career: Dir. & Prod., Community prods. of The World of Carl Sandburg, Amahl & the Night Visitors, HMS Pianoforte, The Marriage of Figaro. Mbrships: Pi Kappa Lambda; Am. Choral Dirs. Assn.; Am. Choral Fndn.; Choral Cond. Guild; Am. Musicol. Soc.; Music Lib. Assn. Hobbies: Gardening; Tropical Fish. Address: c/o 915 First Ave., Spokane, WA 99204, USA.

GIULEANU, Victor, b. 11 Nov. 1914, Stroesti-Vilcea, Romania. Professor of Music Theory. Educ: Grad., Fac. of Law, Bucharest; Dip., State Acad. of Music, Bucharest; Qualified Prof., Music Theory; Choir Cond.; Musicol.; D Musicol., 1976; m. Miseta Giuleanu. Career: Cond., Ciocirlia State Ensemble; Dean of Fac. of Cond. & Comp.1960-62. Chancellor 1962-72 Acad of Music, Bucharest; Hd., Dept. of Music Theory, Cond. & Pedagogy, ibid. Tape recordings of Ciocirlia choirs & of Romanian Broadcasting & TV perfs. (as cond.). Publs: Books in Romanian inclng. Treatiste of Music Theoty, 2 vols., 1962; Musical Rhythm, 2 vols., 1969; Fundamental Principles in the Theory of Music, 2 vols., 1974; The Byzantine Melody. Contbr. to musical reviews. Mbrships: Bd. of Dirs., Int. Soc. of Music Educators; Union of the Comps. & Musicologists of the S.R. of Romania. Hons: 1 Prize, Min. of Educ., 1964; Ordinul Muncü 3rd Class, 1958; Meritul Cultural 3rd Class, 1970; Steaua Românei 3rd Class, 1971; Rameau Medal, Dijon, France, 1974; Acad. of The S.R. of Romania, 1975. Address: 534 Brezoianu, Bucharest VII, Romania.

GIULINI, Carlo Maria, b. 9 May 1914, Italy. Conductor. Educ: Acad. Santa Cecilia, Rome. Debut: Rome, 1944. Career: Dir. Italian Radio Orch.; Prin. Cond., La Scala, Milan, 1953-55; Cond., Philharmonia Orch., London; Edinburgh Festival, 1965. Address: Via Jacopo da Ponte 49, Rome, Italy.

GIURANNA, Bruno, b. 6 Apr. 1933, Milan, Italy. Musician (viola); Educator. Educ: Music Conservs. of Santa Cecilia, Rome, & S Pietro a Maiella, Naples. Career: Fndr. Mbr., I Musici, 1951-61; Prof., Conserv. G Verdi, Milan, 1961-65; Conserv. S Cecilia, Rome, 1965-72; Prof., Acad. Chigiana, 1966-72; Prof., NW German Music Acad., Detmold, 1969-72; Jurist, Int. Music Competitions, Munich, 1961-62, '67, '69, 0 Geneva, 1968; Soloist at Festivals incl. Edinburgh, Holland; Concert soloist w. leading orchs. incl. Berlin Phil., Amsterdam Concertgebouw, Teatro all Scala, Milan Recordings: Sinfonia Concertante, Mozart; Viola d'Amore Concerti, Vivaldi. Recip: Premio Diapason, 1968. Address: Via Misurina 71, 00135 Rome, Italy.

GJÖNNAESS, Sunniva, b. 12 May 1934, Oslo, Norway. Musician (Oboe & Cor Anglais). Educ: studied w. Tom Klausen, Oslo, Evelyn Rothwell & Janet Craxton, UK, Mogen Steen-Andreassen & Age Voss, Copenhagen. Debut: Soloist in Haydn Oboe Concerto w. Oslo Phil. Orch., 1956. Career: Solo-Oboist, Sjoellands Symph. Orch., Copenhagen; has given concerts & recitals in Oslo, Arhus & Copenhagen; has broadcast for Norwegian & Danish radio stns. Hons: Danish Music Critical honour prize, 1977. Hobbies: Reading; Gardening; Skiing; Gymnastics; Swimming; Biking; Walking; People. Address: Albrobakken 5, 2730 Herlev, Denmark.

GLAŇCOVÁ-KRUPIČKOVÁ, Eva, b. 21 Apr. 1926, Minichovo Hradiste, Czech. Pianist; Teacher. Educ: Dip., Musical Conserv., Prague, 1947; Dip., Acad. of Musical Arts, 1951. m. Svatopluk Krupicka, 1 s. Debut: B Smetana Mem. Concert, 1944. Career: recitals of int. & Czech. works; concerto perfs. w. orch., Prague & other cities, Czech.; w. chmbr. grps.; accomp.; num. broadcasts, Czech. & German Fed. Repub.; Accomp., num. int. competitions; Asst. Prof., Musical Fac., Acad. of Musical Arts, Prague; Mbr., V Kaprálová Trio, 1974-. Recordings: V Kalabis' Sonata for cello & piano. Mbr: Concert Artists Sect., Union of Czech. Composers. Recip. of 3rd Prize, Prague Springtime Int. Competition, 1949. Address: Rimska 17, 120 00 Prague 2, Czech.

GLANZ, Elemer, b. 11 June 1924, Matranovak, Hungary. Violinist. Educ: Dip. of Virtuosity of Violin, Franz Lizst Musik Akad., Budapest. m. Resi Messinger, 1 d. Debut: Budapest, age 14. Career: Solo orch. appearances, radio, Caracas, Venezuela; Concert Master of Zürcher Chamber Orchester, Switz., 1960-64; Concert Master. Tonhalle Orch., Zürich, 1964-. Recordings: w. Orch. Sinfonica Venezuela, Caracas, Khachaturian Violin Concerto; w. Trio 'Pro Musica Kürich', Haydn 0 Mozart 0 Mersson Trios. Address: Klosnbachstr. 88, 8032 Zürich, Switzerland.

GLASER, Ernst, b. 24 Feb. 1904, Hamburg, Germany. Violinist; Conductor; Teacher. Educ: Music Acad. of Berlin; Studied w. Carl Flesch. m. (1) Kari Aarvold, 2 d., (2) Christine Brinck-Johnsen, 1 s., 1 d. Debut: 1925. Career: concert tours, Germany, Italy, 1925-26; Concertmaster, Bremen Phil. Orch., 1926-28, Oslo Phil. Orch., 1928-59; Dir., Bergen Music Conserv., 1969-71; Civic Music Dir., Alesund, 1971-76; Tchr., Norway Music High Schl., 1976-77; Guest Cond., Norway Opera, 1978-79. Contbr. to Norwegian newspapers. Mbrships. incl: Norwegian Sect.,ISCM; Norsk Tonekunstnersamfunn, 1929-; Norwegian Music Tchrs. Assn. Hons. incl: Golden Medal, King Olav, V, 1958. Hobbies: Old Testament History; Languages. Address: Uranienborg Terrasse 8, Oslo 3, Norway.

GLASER, Werner Wolf, b. 14 Apr. 1910, Cologne, Germany. Composer; Pianist; Conductor. Educ: studied at univ.; pupil of Abendroth, Dahmen, Jarnach & Hindemith. m. Reée Glaser, 3 c. Debut: Pianist, 1918. Career: Cond., Opera of Chemnitz, 1929-31; Tchr. in Denmark; Tchr., Vá .steras, Sweden, 1945-; Comp.; Critic; Soloist; var. pros. at the Swedish Broadcasting Serv.; series of recitals, confs., etc.; V.-Dir., Town Music Schl., Västeras Comps. 8 symphs., 5 operas, str. quartets, chmbr. music, 2 ballets, cantatas, work for solo instruments, concertos, etc. Stage work perf. at Stockholm, Gothenburg, Västeras. Publs: Trumma och triangel, 1946; Den sköna leken, 1947; Poems 1-7, 1959-77. Contbr. to var. mags.; Music Critic, Vestmanlands Läns Tidning. Mbr. Bd., Swedish Soc. of Composers. Hons: Culture Prize, Västeras (twice); Winner of Concurrences, Kiruna, Norrköping. Hobbies: Lyrics; Art. Address: Djäknegatan 16, 722 15 Västeras, Sweden.

GLASS, Jerome, b. 13 Nov. 1920, Minersville, Pa., USA. Conductor; Teacher; Performer on Woodwind Instruments. Educ: BS, NY Univ.; MMus, Univ. of Southern Calif.; studied composition w. Mario Castelnuovo-Tedesco & Ingolf Dahl. m. Sylvya Leon, 1 s., 2 d. Career: currently Cond., Seattle Phil. Orch. & Assoc. Prof. of Music, Western Wash. State Coll. Mbrships: Am. Symph. Orch. League; MENC. Hobbies: Carpentry & Cabinetry; Physical Fitness; Reading; Crossword Puzzles. Address: 720 11th St. No. 3, Bellingham, WA 98225, USA.

GLASSER, Stanley, b. 28 Feb. 1926, Johannesburg, South Africa. Composer; University Lecturer. Educ: B Comm, Witwatersrand Univ., 1949; BA (Music), King's Coll., Cambridge, UK, 1958; MA, ibid., 1962; Study of Comp. w. Matyas Seiber. m. (1) Mona Vida Schwartz, 1 s., 1 d. (2) Elizabeth marianne Aylwin, 2 s. Career: Lectr. & Asst. Dir., Fac. of Music, Cape Town Univ., 1959-62; Tutor, Extra-Mural Studies Dept., London Univ., UK, 1963-68; Lectr., Music Dept., Goldsmiths' Coll., ibid., 1966-69; Music Dir., Dept of Adult Studies, ibid., 1967-69; Hd. of Music, Goldsmiths' Coll., 1969-. Mbrships. incl: Chmn., Comps. Guild of GB, 1975. Comm. Mbr., Int. Folk Music Coun. Comps. incl. var. orchl. instrumental choral works. Hons: Royal Phil. Soc. Prizeman, 1952; George Richards Prize, King's Coll., Cambridge, 1958. Address: Head of Music, Univ. of London Goldsmiths' Coll., Lewisham Way, London SE14 6NW, UK.

GLAZER, David, b. 7 may 1913, Milwaukee, Wis., USA. Clarinettist. Educ: BMus, Univ. of Wis.; Clarinet study w. Victor Polatschek, Boston; Berkshire Music Center, summers, 1940-42. m. Mia Helen Deutsch. Career: Cleveland Symph. Orch., 1946-51; NY Woodwind Quintet, 1951-; Soloist w. BBC, Orchs. of Hamburg, Frankfurt, Copenhagen, Baden-Baden, Tokyo. Comps: Ed. of Rossini, Introduction & Variations for concert band & piano reduction. Recordings: All clarinet sonatas & chmbr. works of Brahms, w. Beethoven Trio; Weber - Concerto No. 1, Quintet w. Strings & Concertino; F Krommer Concerto in E flat; Schuber, Octet; Beethoven, Septet; Num. quintets for winds. Contbr. to: Woodwind Mag.; Music Jrnl. Mbr., Bohemians (Musicians Club) of NY. Hobbies: Outdoor activities. Address: 25 Central Park W, NY, NY 10023, USA. 2.

GLAZER, Frank, b. 19 Feb. 1915, Chester, Wis., USA. Pianist. Educ: Studied Piano w. Artur Schnabel, Arnold Schoenberg & other tchrs.; studied Piano Technol., Piano Crafts Dept., NY Trade Schl. m. Ruth Gevalt. Debut: Town Hall, NYC, 1936. Career: Soloist w. world's leading orchs., inclng. NY Phil., Chgo. Symph., Orch. de la Suisse Romande; Recital Tours, USA, Europe, Near East, S Am.; Guest Artist, leading US Chmbr. Ensembles; Mbr., Eastman Quartet; Num. radio & TV apps., USA & abroad; large repertoire of lectures on Piano Music & Piano Technique; Prof. of Piano, Eastman Schl. of Music. Compositions: Num. songs publd. by Broadcast Music Inc. Recordings incl: A Schubert Album; The Eager Piano (musical excerpts); An Ives Album of Chamber Music; Frank Glazer Plays American Music; Dvorak's Piano Quintet; Beethoven & Mozart Piano Quintets; Piano Music of Erik Satie, 3 vols. Mbrships: Bohemians, NYC; Am. Fedn. Musicians. Hons. incl: Civic Music Medal, Milwaukee, 1932; MA, Spencerian Coll., 1955; Award for Disting. Perfs. of Chmbr. Music, Univ. of Wis.-Milwaukee, 1955-64; Paderewski Centenary Medal, London, 1966. Mgmt: Herbert Barrett Mgmt., NYC. Address: Eastman Schl. of Music, 26 Gibbs St., Rochester, NY 14604, USA. 2.

GLEASON, Harold, b. 26 Apr. 1892, Jefferson, OH, USA. Musicologist; Author; Organist. Educ: MM, Eastman Schl. of Music, Univ. of Rochester. m. Catharine Croziet, 4 children by previous marriage. Career incls: Organist, num. chs. in Calif. & NY; Hd. Organ Dept., 1921-53, Prof. of Musicol., 1932-55, of Music Lit., 1939-55, Grad. Dept., Eastman Schl. of Music; Dir., Grad. Studies, ibid., 1953-55. Recip., Hon. Mus D, MacMurray Coll., Jacksonville, Ill., 1952. Hobbies: Travel; Photography. Address: Apt. 104, 16450 Caminito Vecinos, San Diego, CA 92128, USA.

GLEAVES, Ian Beresford, b. 19 July 1937, Stoke on Trent, UK. Lecturer in Music; Composer. Educ: Royal Manchester Coll. of Music, 1954-58; BMus., Dunelm; ARCM; LRAM; L Mus TCL., m. Linda Mae Goddard. Career: Music Master, Knypersley Hall Schl., 1959-61; Dormston Sec. Schl., 1959-61; King Edward VI Gram. Schl., Lichfield, 1963-65; Lectr. in Music, Birmingham Univ. Extra Mural Dept., N Staffs WEA. Piano Tchng. & Perfs. Compositions: Violin Concerto; Tudor Suite for small orch.; Clarinet Quintet; Wind Quintet; Str., Quartets; Trios for var. instruments; sonatas for var. instruments; Divertimento for str. orch.; Variations on a theme of Scriabin for lge. orch.; var. piano pieces inclng., suite, 3 sonatinas & 24 preludes; Song cycle. Apotheosis of the Rose; num. other songs. Hons: Edward Hecht Prize for comp.; RMCM; Mrs. Leo Grindon Prize, ibid. Hobbies: Walking; Cycling; Food; Wine. Address: 35 Queensbille, Stafford, ST17 4NJ, UK. 3.

GLEICH, Clemens Chr. J von, b. 17 June 1930, Essen, Germany. Musicologist. Educ: State Dip., Piano, The Hague, 1952; Dr degree in Musicol., State Univ. of Utrecht, 1964. m. Maria Vonk, 3 c. Career: Lectr., Univ. of Groningen; Teacher; Music Critic, Cooperator of radio & TV; Hd. of the Music Dept., Gemeentemuseum, The Hague, 1964-. Publs: Die sinfonischen Werke von Alexander Skrjabin, Bilthoven, 1963; Die Bedeutung der Allegemeinen Musikalischen Zeitung, Amsterdam, 1969; Schönberg-Webern-Berg (Catalogue, The Hague), 1969; Edition of the Pianoconcerto in A major by Anton Stamitz, The Hague, 1969. Contbr. to: Encyclopedia 'Die Musick in Geschichte und Gegenwart'; Grove's Dictionary of Music & Musicians, etc. Hobbies: Chess; Sailing. Address: Breitnerlaan 77, The Hague, The Netherlands.

GLICK, David Alan, b. 6 Jan. 1946, Pitts.,Pa., USA. Musician (Clarinettist; Specialist in Early Clarinets). Educ: BFA, Carneige-Mellon Univ., Pitts., Pa., 1968; M Mus, Manhattan Schl. of Music, 1971; doct. studies, Eastman Schl. of Music. Debut: Munich, 1973. Career: Concerts, Stuttgart, German Fed. Repub. & Hague, Netherlands, 1975; Broadcast recordings, Radio Corps. of Munich, Stuttgart, Cologne, Frankfurt & W Berlin, 1976; Concerts, Holland & Germany, 1976. Recordings: Mozart, Clarinet Concerto, & Weber, Concertino 1973. Contbr. to Woodwind World. Mbrships: Am. Musical Instrument Soc.;

MENC. Hons: 1st Prize, Int. Clarinet Competition, Munich, 1973; A M Gannett Veterans Scholarship, 1973. Hobbies: Art History. Address: 1775 Stone Rd., Apt. 1, Rochester, NY 14615, USA.

GLICK, Jacob, b. 29 Jan. 1926, Phila., Pa., USA. Violinist; Viola d'Amore Player; Mandolinist; Educator. Educ: New Schl. of Music, Phila.; Peabody Conserv., Baltimore, M. m. Lilo Kantorowicz Glick, 2 d. Debut: Carnegie Recital Hall, NYC, 1962. Career incls: perf. of Hindemith's Schwanendreher Concerto w. Clarion Orch., Avery Fisher Hall, Lincoln Ctr., 1965; Soloist in Vivaldi Concerto for Mandolines, NY Phil. under Bruno Maderna, 1972; perf. of Schoenberg's Serenade w. Boulez, Philharmonic Rug Concert, 1974; Fac., Bennington Coll., Vt., 1969; Lecture-recital, 5th Int. Viola Congress, Eastman Schl. of Music, Rochester, NY, 1977. Comps: Mandolinear. Recordings: w. Contemp. Quartet & Beaux Arts Quartet, CRI; Nonesuch; VoxCandide; Marlboro Record Soc. Contbr. to: Contemp. Music Newsletter; record album notes. Mbrships: Dir., Chmbr. Music Ctr., Johnson State Coll., Vt., 1976, '77; Contemp. Chmbr. Ensemble, 1961. Hobbies: Bookbinding; Legerdemain & Prestidigitation. Address: Bennington Coll., Bennington, VT 05201, USA.

GLIGO, Nikša, b. 6 Apr. 1946, Split, Yugoslavia. Musicologist. Educ: BA, Comparative Lit.; BA, Musicol. Career: Dire. of Music Dept., Student Ctr. of Zagreb Univ.; Artistic Dir., Zagreb Biennale of Contemporary Music. Publs: The Time of Music, 1976; The Extended Music (in preparation). Contbr. to Melos, Zeitschrift fur Musiktheorie; Teka; Pitanja, Radio Zagreb, III prog. Mbrships: Union of Croatian Comps.; Am. Musicol. Soc. Hons: Prize of Skoi for Music Criticism, 1970. Hobbies: Skiing; Sailing; Tennis; Photography. Address: Amruseva 19, YR-41000 Zagreb, Yugoslavia.

GLOCK, (Sir) William Frederick, b. 3 May 1908, London, UK. Musician; Music Critic; Administrator. Educ: Gonville & Caius Coll., Cambridge Univ.; pupil of Artur Schnabel, Berlin. m. Anne Balfour Geoffroy-Dechaume, 1952. Career: Music Critic, Daily Telegraph, 1934, The Observer, 1934-45, New Statesman, 1958-59; Serv. w. RAF, WWII, 1941-46; Dir., Summer Schl. of Music, Bryanston, 1948-52; Dartington Hall, Devon, 1933-; Fndr. & Ed., The Score, 1949-61; Controller of Music, BBC, 1959-72; Dir., Bath Festival, 1975-; Chmn., London Orch. Concert Board, 1975-; Chmn., Brit. Sect., ISMC, 1954-58. Mbrships: Bd. of Dirs., Royal Opera House', Covent Gdn., 1968-72; Hon., Royal Phil. Soc.; Arts Coun. of Gt. Britain, 1971-75. Hons: Kt.; CBE; DMus, Nottingham Univ.; Dr. of Univ. of York; Albert Medal, Royal Soc. of Arts, 1971. Address: Sudbury House, Faringdon, Oxon., UK.

GLODEANU, Liviu, b. 6 Aug. 1938, Cluj, Rumania. Composer. Educ: Conserv. Cluj, 1955-57; Conserv. Bucharest, 1957-61. m. Florica, 2 c. Debut: 1958. Career: Prof. of Music, Schl. of Arts, Bucharest, 1961-63; In charge of Rsch., Inst. of Folklore of Bucharest, 1961-62; Musical Sec., Phil. 'George Enescu', 1963-71; Inspector, Musical Sect., Coun. of Socialist Cultural Educ., 1971; Comps., for stage, TV, radio & films. Compositions incl: Zamolxis (opera); Suite for Children's chorus, wind instr. & perf.; Ulysees (ballet); Symph. movement; Flute Concerto; Study for children's Chorus & perc.; Incentions for wind quintet & perf.; Symphs. of wind instruments; Socle pour le temp, cantata. Var. recordings. Contbr. to profl. publs. Mbrships: Rumanian Union of Comps. Hons: Prize, Rumanian Union of Comps., 1968, '69, '71; Order 'Meritul Cultural'. Address: Calea Victorei 214, Bucharest, Rumania.

GLOOR, Elisabeth, b. 26 July 1915, Langenthal, Switzerland. Violin player., Conserv. Basel. Career: Concert Studies, Lausanne, London; Solo concertos w. orch. Switzerland; Concertow w. piano Spain, portugal, Germany, Sweden, Italy; Mbr. Trio Pro Musica; Var. radio recordings. Mbrships: Swiss Soc. for Music Pedagogues (SMPV); Swiss Musical Art Assn.; European Str. Tchr. Assn. (ESTA); Zonta Club, Basel, Hobbies: Wandering; Reading. Address: Gartenstr. 11, 4908 Langenthal, Switzerland.

GLORIEUX, François, b. 27 Aug. 1932, Kortrijk, Belgium. Pianist; Composer; Professor; Conductor; Recording Executive. Educ: Royal Music Acad. of Ghent; Paris. Career incls: num. concert tours in N & S Am., Europe, Africa & the Middle E; radio & TV broadcasts; Pres., Panoramic Records Co.; Guest Prof., Yale Univ., USA; Master Class, Antwerp Royal Music Acad. Comps: Movements for piano brass & percussion; Manhattan for piano & large symph. orch.; about 20 works for percussion ensemble; piano music, lieder; songs; musicals; stage & film music. Recordings: Panoramic Records: EMI-HMV; Musica Magna. Recip., Harriet Cohen Int. Music Award, London. Mgmt: Int. Concertbureau G Arien, Antwerp. Address: Frankrijklei 54-56 (B.1), B-2000 Antwerp, Belgium.

GLOSSOP, David William, b. 8 Dec. 1951, Derby, UK. Musician; Teacher (oboe). Educ: RAM; FTCL (oboe perfs.); LRAM (oboe perf., tchrs.); ARCM (oboe perfs.); LTCL (Oboe perf.). m. Roselinde Mary Bowker. Career: Played on German radio, perfs. of Solo Oboe, Chamber & Orchestral music; Oboist, Fndr., Lindum Wind Quintet; Sr. Woodwind Tchr., Wigan Metropolitan Borough Educ. Dept.; Oboe Tchr., Schl. of Music, Huddersfield Polytechnic; Oboist, Rosevaad Duo. Mbrships: Solo Perfs., Pvte. & Educl. Sects., ISM; Methodist Ch. Music Soc. Hons: Winner, Open Woodwind Competition (Mrs. Sunderland), Huddersfield. Hobbies: Sports; Ch. Life activities for Methodist Ch. Address: 4 Ash Grove, Standish, nr. Wigan, Lancs. WN6 ODZ, UK.

GLOSSOP, Peter, b. 6 July 1928, Sheffield, UK. Opera Singer. m. Joyce Blackham. Debut: Sadlers Wells Opera, 1952. Career: Sadlers Wells, 1952-62; Covent Gdn. Opera House, 1962-65; Freelance (all major opera houses of the world), 1965-. Recordings: Othello; Roberto Devereaux; Dido & Aeneas; Rigoletto; Il Trovatore; Billy Budd; Merrie England. Hons: Gold Medal, Young Opera Singers' Competition, Sofia, Bulgaria, 1961; Verdi Gold Medal, Parma, Italy, 1964; Best Perf. Medal, Barcelona, 1968; Mus D, Sheffield Univ., 1970. Hobbies: Squash Racquets; New Orleans Jazz Mgmt: S A Gorlinsky. Address: Kenlade, 11 The Bishop's Ave., London N2, UK.

GLOVER, Betty S, b. 24 Jan. 1923, Hudson, Ill., USA. Musician, Bass Trombone, Euphonium; Conductor. Educ: B Mus., Conserv. of Music, Cinn., Ohio; M Mus., ibid. div. Career: Prin. Trombone, Kan. City Phil., 1944-48, Columbus, Ohio, Phil., 1948-49; Dir. of Band, Instructor of Brasses, Otterbein Coll., 1950-52; Bass Trombone, Cinn. Symph., 1952-; Instructor, Trombone, Coll.-Conserv. of Music, Univ. of Cinn., 1952-72; Cond., Brass Choir, Adjunct Assoc. Prof., ibid., 1969-. Recordings: w. Cinn. Symph., 1952-. Mbrships: Sigma Alpha Iota; Pi Kappa Lambda. Hobby: Showing Dogs - Bouvier des Flandres. Address: 8791 Cottonwood Dr., Cinn., OH 45231, USA.

GLOVER, Felix Kwadwo Mukeli, b. 21 Une 1946, Toklokpo nr. Sogakope, Ghana. Music Teacher; Violinist. Educ: Cert. A Tchr.. Mt. Mary Coll.. Somanya. 1965: Music Educ. Dip. (main instrument, violin), Specialist Trng. Coll., Winneba, 1971. m. Christiana Tsali, 2 s., 2 d. Debut: as comp., God Has Not Forgotten Me, 1972. Career: Tchr., Presby Secondary School, Abetifi, 1971-74. Dist. Music Organizer, Ketu Dist., Volta Reg. Comp. or Arr. of about 15 works. Mbrships: Music Tchrs. Assn., Ghana; Fndr. Mbr., Denu Mawuli Singers. Address: Ghana Educ. Serv., PO Box 43, Denu, Ghana.

GLOVER, Jane Alison, b. 13 May 1949, Helmsley, York., UK. Conductor; Musicologist. Educ: BA, St. Hugh's Coll., Oxford, 1971; DPhil., Oxford, 1976. Debut: Wexford Fest. Opera, 1975. Career: Wexford Fest. Opera; BBC Radio & TV; English Bach Fest.; Musical Dir.; Musical nel Chiostro, Italy; Glyndebourne Fest. Opera. Publs: Cavalli, 1978. Contbr. to: Musical Times; Music & Letters; Early Music; The Listener. Mbrships: Royal Musical Assn.; PRS. Recip., Stephen Arlen Bursary, 1975. Hobbies: Crosswords; Piano duets; Theatregoing. Mgmt: Trafalgar Perry. Address: 33 Sinclair Gardens, London W14, UK. 29.

GLOVER, Lawrence, b. 7 Feb. 1931, Belfast, N Ireland. Pianist. Educ: ARMCM (Tchr. & Perf.); Hon. FRMCM. m. Mabel Kinghorn, 1 s., 1 d. Career: Solo, Concerto, Chmbr. Music recitals & broadcasts; Sr. Lectr., RSAMD; Inventor of visual aid musical board game, Con Moto, 1978. Mbr., ISM. Hobby: Golf. Address: 6 Devonshire Tce., Glasgow, G12 OXF, UK.

GLYDE, Judith Pamela, b. 15 Oct. 1944, Toronto, Ont., Canada. Artist in Residence; Cellist. Educ: Univ. of Chattanooga; BM, Hartt Coll. of Music, Hartford Univ., 1966; MMus, Manhattan Schl. of Music, 1969; Postgrad. study in quartet perf., SUNY, Binghamton. m. Eric Lewis. Career: Cellist, Chattanooga Symph., 1962-64; Hartford Symph., 1964-67; Prin. cellist, NY Opera Orch., 1967-69; Radio City Music Hall; Pro Arte Chmbr. Orch.; Cellist, Manhattan Str. Quartet, 1970-; Quartet in Res., Corfu Music Fest., Greece; Artist in Res., Cornell Univ., 1971-72, Grinnell Coll., 1972-; Educl. TV apps. Mbrships: Chmn., Music Dept., Grinnell Coll., 1974-75; Coll. Music Soc.; AAUP; Am. Fedn. of Musicians; Alpha Lambda Delta. Hons: NY State Arts Coun. Grant; Tchng. Fellowship, SUNY; Iowa State Arts Coun. Grant; Award, Concerto Competition, 1969; Finalist, Naumberg Chmbr. Music Award, 1974. Hobbies: Cooking; Reading. Mgmt: Thea Dispeker, NYC. Address: 1589 Sylvan Rd., Mohegan Lake, NY 10547, USA.

GNAM, Adrian, b. 4 Sept. 1940, NYC, USA. Conductor; Performer on oboe, oboe d'amore & English horn. Educ: B Mus., Coll.-Conserv. of Music, Cinn., 1961; BS, Univ. of Cinn. Coll.-Conserv. of Music, 1962; MMus., ibid., 1962; DMus Arts, Univ. of Cinn., in progress; Perf.'s Cert. in oboe & English horn, Coll.-Conserv. of Music. m. Sarah Young Gurley, 1 s. Career: Music Dir. & Cond., Ohio Univ. Symph. & Chmbr. Orchs.; Cond. & Prin. Oboe, Eastern Music Fest., Greensboro, NC; Oboist, Heritage Chmr. Quartet & Chmbr. Arts Ensemble; Ensembles-in-Res., Coll.-Conserv. of Univ. of Cinn.; Oboe Soloist, Tanglewood, Eastern Music Fest., Carnegie Hall, Carnegie Recital Hall, Town Hall, Kennedy Ctr.; Guest Cond., E Ctrl. Regional Ohio All-State Orch., 1971 & '73; Guest Cond., S Ctrl. Regional Ohio All-State Orch., 1972; Guest Cond., Ohio String Tchrs.' Assn. Orch.; Former Prin. Oboe, Am. Symph. & Cleveland Orch. Recordings w. Heritage Chmbr. Quartet, Cleveland Orch. & Ohio Univ. Symph. Orch. Mbrships: Am. Symph. Orch. & Ohio Univ. Symph. Orch. Mbrships: Am. Symph. Orch. League; Pi Kappa Lambda; Phi Mu Alpha Sinfonia; Local 1, 802 & 179, Am. Fedn. of Musicians; Ohio Music Educators Assn.; MENC; Bd. of Dirs., Eastern Music Fest. Hobbies: Photography; Golf. Mgmt: Int. Artists Alliance. Address: 28 Beechwood Estates, Athens, OH 45701, USA.

GNEUSS, Helmut Walter Georg, b. 29 Oct. 1927, Berlin, Germany. University Professor; Hymnologist. Educ: Free Univ., W Berlin, 1948-53; Rsch. Student, St. John's Coll., Cambridge, 1953-55. Career: Lektor, Durham Univ., 1955-56; Asst. Lectr., Lectr., Free Univ., Berlin, 1956-62; Lectr., Heidelberg Univ., 1962-65; Prof., Univ. of Munich, 1965-; Vis. Professiorial Fellow, Emmanuel Coll., Cambridge, 1970; Vis. Prof., Univ. of NC, Chapel Hill, USA, 1974. Publs: Hymnar und Hymnen im englischen Mittelalter, 1968; Latin Hymns in MEdieval England: The State of Scholarship, in RH. Robbins Festschrift, London, 1973. Contbr. & Ed., Anglia; Zeitschrift für englische Philologie, etc. Mbrships: Bayerische Akademie der Wissenschaften; Henry Bradshaw Soc.; Early English Text Soc.; Cambridge Bibliographical Soc. Address: Schellingstrasse 3, D-8 Munich 40, German Fed. Repub.

GOBBI, Tito, b. 24 Oct. 1915, Bassano del Grappa, Vicenza, Italy. Operatic Baritone. Educ: Padua Univ. m. Matilde de Rensis, 1 d. Debut: in La Traviata, Rome, 1938. Career: opera apps. in major theatres throughout world; Prod. sev. operas inclng. Simon Boccanegra, Covent Gdn., London, 1965; sev. films; Lectures & master classes, UK, USA, Italy, Portugal. Hobbies: Reading; Painting; Driving; Boating. 16.

GODFREY, Peter David Hensman, b. 3 April 1922, Bluntisham, Huntingdon, UK. Pianist; Organist; Conductor; Teacher; Professor; Dean. Educ: Chorister, King's Coll. Cambridge; Choral Scholar, ibid., MA, BMus; FRCO; ARCM; RCM; Hon. FRSCM. m. Sheila Margaret McNeile, 4 d. Career: Asst. Dir., M Uppingham Schl., Marlborough Coll.; Dir. of Music, Marlborough Coll.; Lectr., Univ. of Auckland, NZ; Prof. & Dean of Fac. of Music, ibid.; Dir. of Music, Auckland Cathedral; Cond., Auckland Dorian Choir; Cond., Auckland Symphonia. Recordings: Music of the Church's Year; Music of the Eucharist; Five Centuries of Sacred Music; NZ Choral Music. Hons: MBE, 1978; Hon. FRSCM, 1973. Hobby: Gardening. Address: University of Auckland, Auckland, NZ. 17.

GODIN, Imrich Karol, b. 17 July 1907, Vráble, Czech. Opera Singer (tenor); Senior Lecturer at the Academy of Fine Arts in Bratislava. Educ: Agricultural Univ.; Acad. in Rome, Milan & Vienna; studied w. Ricardo Stacciari m. Edita György, 3 c. Debut: State Opera House, Vienna, 1935. Career: State Opera House, Vienna; Opera Houses in Munich & Stuttgart. Recordings for Supraphon Prague, Electrola Geselschaft m.b.H., Berlin. Publs: Hlasová vychova (Vocal Education), 1959; Technika spevu (The Technique of Singing), 1971; Divadelne masky (Masks in Theatre), 1964. Mbr., Comps. Union of Czech. Recip. Hon. Mentions for work in vocal pedagogical activity. Hobbies: Gardening; Cars. Address: Holleho 13, Bratislava, Czech.

GODSKE, Poul, b. 6 May 1929, Tommelrup, Denmark. Arranger; Conductor; Bandleader. Educ: Pvte. studies. m. Jytte, 1 d. Career: 1952. Career: Dance music, clubs & restaurants; Theatre, 1964-; Num. radio & TV shors, Scandinavia & Germany; Arr./Cond. for EMI Denmark, 1967-. Comps: Popular songs; Music for vaudeville & revue; The Good Doctor (Danish version); Music for films. Num. recordings. Mbrships: Koda; Danish Soc. of Bandleaders; Danish Songwriter's Guild. Hons: Danish Jazz Musician of the Year, 1959. Hobbies: Music; Books. Address: 20 Hojager, DK 2670 Greve Strand, Denmark.

GODSON, Daphne, b. Edinburgh, Scotland, UK. Violinist. Educ: LRAM (Violin Perf.); Premier Prize in Violin & Chmbr. Music, Brussels Conserv. Career: Solo Violinist Tchr. & Chmbr. Music Player; Tchr., RSAM; Mbr., Bernicia Ensemble; Prin. 2nd Violin, Scottish Baroque Ensemble; Prin. 2nd Violin, Scottish Baroque

Ensemble & Scottish Chmbr. Orch. Recordings: Rameau, Pièces de Clavecin w. Bernicia Ensemble; History of Scottish Music - 18th Century. Mbrships: ISM; ESTA. Hons: Medal of Belgian Govt.; 1st Prize, Darmstadt; Finalist Wieniawski Int. Violin Competition. Hobbies: Hill-walking; Reading; Growing Things in Pots. Address: 7 Scotland St., Edinburgh EH3 6PP, UK. 4.

GODWIN, Joscelyn Roland Jasber Chloestro, b. 16 Jan. 1945, Kelmscott, Oxon, UK. Musicologist; Educator. Educ: Magdalene Coll., Cambridge Univ.; BA, 1965; Mus B, 1966; MA, 1970; PhD, Cornell Univ., USA, 1969; FRCO, 1966. m. Sharyn Cook. Career: Instr., Cleveland State Univ., 1969-71; Assoc. Prof., Colgate Univ., 1971-. Comps: Publs: Ed., Henry Cowell, New Musical Resources, 1969; Ed., A Scarlatti, Marco Attilio Regolo, 1975; Schirmer Scores, 1975; Robert Fludd, Hermetic Philosopher, 1978. Contbr. to var. profl. jrnls. Mbrships: Am. Musicol. Soc.; RCO. Hons: Abngdon Prize, Camgridge Univ., 1966; Harding Prize, RCO, 1966. Hobbies: Philosophy; Religion; Bio-dynamic Gardening. Address: Dragon Acres, Earlville, NY 13332, USA.

GODZISZEWSKI, Jerzy, b. 24 April 1935, Wilno, USSR. Pianist. Educ: Dip., MA, Superior Music Schl., Warsaw; Piano master classes w. Arturo Benedetti Michelangeli, Italy. Debut: w. Phil. Orch., Cracow, 1949. Career: Regular apps. in concert halls & num. fests., Poland; Recordings for Polish Radio & TV; Concerts, Czech., Bulgaria, Romania, German Dem. Repub., Italy, Austria, France, Sweden & Norway; Piano duet w. Alicja Mukusek; Piano Tchr., Wroclaw, 1967-77, Superior Music Schl., Bydgoszcz. Recordings: Songs by C Debussy; Piano works by A Skriabin & S Prokofiev. Mbrships: Polish Musicians Assn.; Fr. Chopin Soc. (TIFC). Hons: Distinction, 6th Chopin Int. Piano Competition, Warsaw, 1960. Mgmt: Pagart, Warsaw. Address: ul. Zamojskiego 17m4, 85-063 Bydgoszcz, Poland.

GOEBELS, Franzpeter, b. 5 Mar. 1920, Mülheim-Rhur, Germany. Pianist; Harpsichordist; Professor. Educ: Univs. of Cologne & Berlin. m. Gertraud Kockler, 1 s., 1 d. Debut, 1940. Career: Solo Pianist, Deutschanlandsender, Berlin; Docent; Robert Schumann Konservatorium, Dusseldorf; Prof., Hochschule fur Musik, Detmold. Comps. (pseudonym& Angfied Traudger): Dependances for harpsichord & strings, 1970, BVK; Vyrd-Boogy for harpsichord BVK, 1971; Bach: Goldberg Variations for harpsichord & strings. Recordings incl: Bach, 6 Sonatas; Bach, Concertos for harpsichord. Publs: Das Sammelsurium, 1968; Handbuch der Pianistik, 1973. Contbr. to: Melos; Musica; Musick & Bildung. Mbrships: VDMK; Hon. Prof., Univ. of Barcelona; IAM. Recip., Ruhr Preis fur Kunst & Wissenschaft, 1969. Hobbies: MSS; Sculpture; Modern Graphics. Address: Fromhauser Str. 9, (Privatzufahrt: Clara-Schumann Weg), Postfach 4023, D493 Detmold 14, German Fed. Repub.

GOEDECKE, David Stewart, b. 3 Dec. 1929, Walla Walla, Wash., USA. Professor of Music; Trumpet Artist-Instructor. Educ: BA, MA, Music, Wash. State Univ., Pullman; Doct. studies Univ. of Ore., Eugene; studied Trumpet, Bands & Cond., & Music Theory, Hist. & Educ. w. var. masters. m. Ellita Shaffer Goedecke, 1 s., 1 d. Career: Res. Artist, Trumpet & Solo & Ensemble Recitals, Univ. of the Pacific; Trumpet Recitals, Trumpet Soloist w. Wash. State Univ. Band, Univ. of Ore. Band, num. High Schl. & Coll. Bands; profl. Trumpet in Symph. Orchs., Show & Dance Orchs., States of Wash., Ore. & Calif.; Adjudicator of var. bands in Wash., Ore., Calif. & Nevada; Cond. of Select, Massed & All-State Hon. Bands. Recordings incl: Band records, Univ. of Pacific, 1970-75. Publs: A Study Guide for Teaching the History of Western Music in Secondary School Band Class, 1976. Mbrships: MENC; Coll. Band Dirs.; Nat. Assn.; Am. Schl. Band Dirs. Assn.; NACWPI; Phi Mu Alpha Sinfonia; Pi Kappa Lambda; Am. Fedn. Musicians. Hon: Outstanding Music Educator in Am., Schl. Musician Mag., Mar. 1966. Hobbies: Swimming; Cross-country Skiing. Address: 3436 W Swain Rd., Stockton, CA 95207, USA. 9.

GOEDICKE, Kurt-Hans, b. 17 Feb. 1935, Berlin, Germany. Timpanist; Percussionist; Pianist. Educ: Grad., Acad. of Music, W Berlin. m. Angela Willman. Debut: Soloist, opening of New Concert Hall, Acad. of Music, Berlin. Career: Prin. Timpanist, Radio Eireann Symph. Orch., 1954-; Prof. for Timpani & Percussion, Royal Irish Acad. of Music; Prin. Timpanist, LSO, 1964-; apps. as Prin. Timpanist w. several European orchs. Mbrships: incl: Nat. Trust. Hobby: Literature. Address: 390 Harlyn Dr., Pinner, Middx. HA5 2DF, UK. 3.

GOEHR, Alexander, b. 10 Aug. 1932, Berlin, Germany. Musician; Composer. Educ: Royal Manchester Coll. Music; w. O Messiaen, Parisk Conserv., France; pvte. study w. Yvonne Loriod. m. (1) Audrey Baker, 3 d., (2) Anthea Staunton, 1 s. Career: Classes, Morley Coll., London; appt. w. BBC; Com.-in-Res., New England Conserv., Boston, USA, 1968-69; Assoc. Prof. Music, Yale Univ., 1969-70; Prof. W. Riding Chair of Music, Univ. of

Leeds, UK, 1971-76; Prof. of Music, Cambridge Univ., 1976-. Comps. incl: Little Symphony; Piano Trio; Arden Must Die (opera); Quartet; Romanza; Naboth's Vineyard; Shadowplay 2; Sonata about Jerusalem; Metamorphosis Dance. Mbrships: Fellowm, Trinity Hall, Cambridge. Hons: FRMCM; Churchill Fellow, 1968; DMus, Southampton Univ., FRAM. Address: Fac. of Music, Univ. of Cambridge, Cambridge, UK.

GOEMANNE, Noel, b. 10 Dec. 1926, Poperinge, W. Flanders, Belgium. Now US Citizen. Composer; Organist; Choral Conductor; Teacher. Educ: Grad. w. Dip. of Laureate, Lemmens Inst., Mechelen, Belgium; studied w. Flor Peeters, Staf Nees, marinus DeJong, Jules Van Nuffel; postgrad. study, Conservatoire Royale, Liege. m. Janine Marloye, 3 c. Career: Regular piano recitals over radio stn. NAMUR (Belgian Nat. Radio Br.); TV appearances as Choral Cond. on KDFW (CBS Affil.), Dallas, Tex., USA, & interviewed on music on KDFW; appeared as Organist, Choral cond., guest cond. of his own works, lectures-demonstration, in N Am., Europe & the Philippines. Compositions incl: over 100 anthems, motets, hymns & arrangements of hymns, sev. organ works, piano comps. & secular choral music. Prin. works: Missa Internationalis; Missa Hosanna; Ode to St. Cecilia; Credo, written for 6th Int. Cong. of Sacred Music; The Walk, choral drama, etc. Mbrships: VP., Ch. Music; The Walk, choral drama, etc. Mbrships: VP, Ch. Music Assn. of Am., 1968-72; currently on Bd. Dirs., ibid.; ASCAP; AGO; ACDA. Var. compositions selected to be premiered in Europe, USA, etc. Recip., Award for Outstanding Work & Contbrn. to Sacred Music, Inst. of Sacred Music, Manila, Philippines; Pro Ecclesia et Pontifice Medal from Pope Paul VI, 1977; sev. ASCAP awards. Address: 3523 Woodleigh Dr., Dallas, TX 75229, USA.

GOEMANS, Pieter Willem, b. 6 June 1925, Istanbul, Turkey. Composer; Lyricist; Television & Film Director. Educ: law studies, Amsterdam & Utrecht Univs.; studied violin & piano. married, 1 s., 2 d. Career incls: Pres., R & R Geluidsdragers B V (records & recordings, audio-viusal prods.). Hundreds of comps. inclng. Aan De Amsterdamse Grachten; You're Closer to Me. Mbrships: Bds., BUMA, BUMA Fndn., STEMRA; Pres., WTL (Dutch Songwriters' Guild); BUMA Deleg. in Bd. of CONAMUS (Propaganda committee for light music). Hons. incl: 3 times Nat. Winner, Eurovision Song Contest. Hobbies: Music; Golf; Chess. Address: Puttensestraat 13, Amstelveen, Netherlands.

GOERTZ, Harald, b. 31 Oct. 1924, Vienna, Austria. Conductor; Pianist; Manager. Educ: PhD, Univ. of Vienna, 1947; advanced studied of piano w. Wüher, & conducting w. Reichwein, Krips & Swarowsky, all at Acad. of Music, Vienna. m. Carola Renner, 1 s., 1 d. Career: Asst. to von Karajan, Scala di Milano, Lucerne, etc., Cond., Vienna Boys' Choir, 1947-48 & State Opera, Ankara, Turkey, 1948-50; Music Dir., opera & concerts, Ulm, Germany, 1955-63; Guest Cond., Stuttgart Opera, Vienna Volksoper, Berlin Phil., etc., Tchr., Acad. for Music, Stuttgart & Salzburg Mozarteum; Prof., Ldr. of Opera Workshop & Seminars for Interpretation, Acad. for Music, Vienna, on staff, Vienna Opera; Pres., Austrian Soc. of Music, 1963-; Writer & Commentator, weekly music info. prog., Austrian TV, 1972-. Publs: Ed., Osterreichisches Musikhandbuch; Dictionary of Contemporary Austrian Comps. Contbr. to var. mags. Recip. of OBE; Bundesrerdienst-Kreuz. Hobbies: Lit.; Arch.; Archaeol. Address: Wiedner Hauptstrasse 40, 1040 Vienna, Austria.

GOETHALS, Lucien Gustave Georges, b. 26 June 1931, Gent, Belgium. Producer; Artistic Director; Professor of Analysis. Educ: Royal Conserv., Ghent. m. Maria De Wandelaeir, 1 s. Career: Prod., Ille Prog. BRT; Artistic Dir., Inst. of Psychoacustica & Electronic Music, Univ. of Ghent; Prof. of Analysis, Royal Conserv. of Ghent. Comps. incl: Soliloquios, for violin, 1970; Llanto por Salvador Allende, for trombone, 1973; Entreuxis, for chmbr. orch., 1968; Studie VII B (electroacoustical), 1973. Var. recordings. Publs: incl: Basiselementen van de Elektronische Muziek, 1964. Contbr. to: Yang; Gamma; ed. Bd., Interface. Mbr. Spectra Grp. Hons: incl: Provincial Comp. Prize, 1960. Hobbies: Lit.; Philos. Address: Verschansingsstraat 32, 9910 Mariakèrke, Belgium. 19.

GOEYVAERTS-FALK, Karel August, b. 8 June 1923, Antwerp, Belgium. Radio Producer; Professor. Educ: Harmony counterpoint, hist. of music, piano, piano accomp., Kon. VI, Muziekconservatorium, Antwerp; Musical analysis, comp., Martenot Waves, Conservatoire National, Paris. m. Iolanda Massara. Career: Producer, Inst. of Psychoacoustic & Electronic Music, Belgian Radio & TV, Ghent, 1970; Lectr. at Univ. of Montreal, Univ. of Montreal, Univ. of Toronto, York Univ., 1974, Lectr., New Univ. of Lisbon, Portugal, 1975. Compositions incl: Sonata for two pianos, 1950-51; Piece for piano & tape, 1964; Piece for three, flute, violin, piano, 1960; Goathemala, for voice & flute,,1966; Piano Quartet (w. tape), 1972; Belise dans un jardin, for 24 voices & 6 instruments; electronic works; Pour que les fruitsmûrissent cet été, 1975 (for ancient instruments); Ach Golgatha! (for harp, organ & percussion). Recording: Goathemala, 1971; To bet on 8 horses, 1973. Contbr. to var. jrnls. Hobbies: Motorcycling; Sailing. Address: Avenue des Eperviers 121, 1150 Brussels, Belgium. 3.

GOFF, Martyn, b. 7 June 1923, London, UK. Director of the National Book League. Educ: Clifton Coll.; Fellowship of the Int. Inst. of Arts. Publs: A Short Guide to Long Play, 1955; A Further Guide to Long Play, 1956; LP Collecting, 1958; Record Choice, 1974. Contbr. to Musical Times. Hons: OBE, 1977. Hobbies: Travelling; Fast cars; Collecting pictures & sculptures. Address: Tedworth House, Tedworth Sq., Chelsea, London SW3 4DU, UK. 1.

GOILAV, Florenza, b. 19 Oct. 1933, Bucharest, Roumania. Violinist. Educ: Univ. of Music, Bucharest; Dip. Solo Violinist. m. Yoan Goilav, 2 d. Career: 1st Violinist, Phil. Orch. of Bucharest, 1955; Solo Violinist, Phil. of Ploesti, Roumania, 1958; 2nd Prime Violinist, Chmbr. Orch. Ramat Gan, Israel, 1961; Currently Violinist, Piano Quartet Ensemble Faure; Solo apps. in Europe, S & Am. & Israel. Num. radio apps. Recordings w. Yoan Goilav & Ensemble Faure. Mbr. Schweizerischer Musiker-Berband. Hons: Prize Winner, Nat. Competition of Roumania, 1961, 66. Hobbies: Interior Decorating; Psychol. Mgmt: Harriet R Schmidt-Heider, Rosentalstrasse 23, CH 8400 Winterthur, Switzerland. Address: St. Georgenstrasse 19, CH 8400 Winterthur, Switzerland.

GOILAV, Yoan, b. 18 Mar. 1933, Botosani, Romania. Double Bassist. Educ: Univ. of Music, Conserv. C Porumbescu, Bucharest (recip., Scholarship of the Repub.). m. Florenza Goilav, 2 d. Mbr., Buahrest Phil. Orch., 1956; Solo Bassist, Ploesti Phil., 1958-61, Chmbr. Orch. Ramat Gan, Israel, 1961-63 & City Symph. Orch., Winterthur, Switzerland, 1963-; Prof., Double Bass, Conserv. Schaffhausen, Switzerland; Solo apps., Romania, Israel, Switzerland, Germany & on radio; Mbr., piano quintet, Ensemble Fauré. Recordings: Der virtuose Kontrabass; Musik für Kontrabass; Music by Bottesini & Schubert (1977). Contbr. to profl. publ. Mbr., profl. assn., Switzerland. Hobby: Chess. Mgmt: Harriet R Schmidt-Heider, Rosentalstr. 23, Wintherthur. Address: St. Georgenstr. 19, CH-8400 Winterthur, Switzerland.

GOLABOVSKI, Sotir, b. 30 Oct. 1937, Struga, Yugoslavia. Composer; Musical Writer. Educ: Univ. of Phils., Ljubljana; MA, Akademiya za Glasbo, Ljubljana. m. Stevka Golabovska, 2 s. Career: Works performed in all maj. ctrs. in Yugoslavia, France, W Germany, Italy, USSR, USA, Can., Czechoslovakia, Tunis, etc.; Art Mgr., Festival Struga's Autumn (musical). Compositions incl: Divertimento for Symph. Orch.; Adante for Symph. Orch.; Camera Comps: Sonatina No. 1; Arabesque & Suite for Piano. Publs: Collaborator on Muzicka Enciklopediya; Monographycs for Prilep, Debar & Ohrid. Contbr. to profl. mags. Mbr. Musical Assn. of Yugoslavia. Hobby: Photography. Address: Karpos III, Zgrada II, (Rumunska) Stan 11, 9100 Skopye, Yugoslavia.

GOLAN, Orit (Svetlana Levin), b. 22 May 12946, Vilnus, USSR. Musicologist; Critic; Teacher. Educ: Vilnus Musical Coll., 1964-68; MA Music, Vilnus State Conserv., 1969, 5 yrs.; MA, postgrad. course, Leningrad State Conserv., 2 yrs., 1971. m. Matiyaho Golan, 1 s. Career: Tchr. of Theory, Vilnus Musical Coll., 1968-71; Lectr., Znaniye Soc., Lithuania, 1968-71; Music critic & reporter, var. jrnls., USSR, 1968-71; Lectr., Jersaelm Acad. of Music, Israel, 1972-73; Tchr., Conservs. of Tel-Aviv, Holon & Gyvatayim, 1972-; Series of Musical reviews for Kol Israel (radio), 1972; Music critic, Nasha Strana (Russian lang. newspaper), 1972-; Author of musicol. rsch. articles. Mbr., profl. assns. Hobby: Modern Theatre. Address: 31/30 Maimon Str., Bat Yam, Israel.

GOLAN, Ron, b. 16 Aug. 1924, Gladbach, Germany. Viola Soloist. Educ: Conserv., Jerusalem; Acad. of Music, Jerusalem; master course w. William Primrose. m. Gabrielle Kochmann, 3 children. Debut: soloist w. Middle E Allied Forces, 1941. Career: Soloist, Israel Phil. Orch., Orch. de la Suisse Romande, all major European concert orgs. Has recorded for all major European radio stns. Mbrships: Geneva Conserv. of Music; Instrumentarium chamber ensemble, Geneva; Orch. de la Suisse Romande; CIEM, Geneva. Mgmt: Caecilia, Geneva. Address: 9 ave. du Lignon, Geneva, Switzerland.

GOLANI-ERDESZ, Rivka, b. 22 Mar. 1946, Tel-Aviv, Israel. Violinist. Educ: studied w. Oedoen Partos; grad. (advanced solo perfs. degree), Tel-Aviv Acad. of Music. m. Otto Erdesz, 1 s. Debut: Carnegie Recital Hall, 1979. num. perfs. w. orch., Israel & N Am.; recitals in Israel, Can., Germany, Netherlands, USA, UK; prin. viola, orchs. in Israel, incl. Tel-Aviv Chmbr. Orch.; prin. viola tchr., Univ. of Toronto, Royal Conserv. of Music. num. recordings for CBC & CJRT; num. recordings for Israeli & Can.

radio. Hons: 1st prize, viola competition, Tel-Aviv Univ.; represented Israel at Int. Music Course, Queekhoven, Netherlands & selected to give solo concerts w. Netherlands Fest. Hobbies: Mathematics; Painting; Photography. Address: 34 Roselawn Ave., Totonto, Ont. M4R 1E4, Can.

GOLD, Ernest, b. 13 July 1921, Vienna, Austria. Composer; Conductor. Educ: Vienna Conserv.; State Acad. of Music, Vienna; studied Cond., Nat. Orchl. Assn.; pvte. study w. Otto Cesana, Leon Barzin, George Antheil. m. Jan K Gold, 1 s., 2 d. Career: Musical Dir., Santa Barbara Symph., Calif., 1958-60; Cond., Santa Barbara Symph., Calif., 1958-60; Cond., Santa Barbara Civic Opera Assn., Broadway musicals, var. Community orchs.; Fndr., Sr. Citizens' Orch., LA, Calif. Compositions incl: 2 Symphs.; Piano Concerto, Chamber & Vocal Music; Choral Comps. Symph. for 5 Instruments; Introduction & Fugue, Gavotte & March; 3 Miniatures for the Piano; A Song Cycle, Songs of Love & Parting; About 75 Film Scores inclng. On the Beach, 1959, Exodus, 1960, It's A Mad, Mad, Mad, Mad, Mad World, 1963, The Secret of Santa Vittoria, 1969; Broadway Musical, I'm Solomon, 1968; num. popular songs, 19039-45. Recordings: Num. recordings of film soundtracks. Contbr. to profl. jrnls. & to daily press. Mbr., num. profl. assns. Hons: incl: Academy Award (Oscar) for Exodus; 5 Acad. Award Nominations; Fold Record (Exodus); 2 Grammy Awards (Exodus); Golden Globe Award. Hobbies: Tennis; Kite Building. Mgmt: Robert Light, 333 S Beverly Dr., Beverly Hills, CA 90212, USA. Address: 500 Paseo Miramar, Pacific Palisades, CA 90272, USA.

GOLD, Morton, b. 6 Oct. 1933, NYC, NY, USA. Professor of Music; Composer; Conductor; Pianist. Educ: MusB, Boston Univ., 1953; MAT, Harvard Univ. Grad. Schl. of Educ., 1954; DMA, Boston Univ., 1960. m. Esther Miriam Morse, 2 d., 1 s. Career incls: Organist & Choir Dir., Temple Emanu-el, Providence, RI, 1961-64; Assoc. prof. of Music, Nasson Coll., 1964-; Cond. of orch. & concert band, Amherst Summer Music Ctr., Raymond, Maine, 1969-75. Comps. incl: Havdalah; Proverbs of the Sages; Prayer of Micah; Piano Concerto. Recordings incl: Haggadah. Mbrships. incl: ASCAP; Coll. Music Soc. Address: 16 Bradeen St., Springvale, ME 04083, USA.

GOLDBERG, Irwin Steven, b. 12 Mar. 1949, Brooklyn, NY, USA. Pianist; Choral Director; Educator. Educ: B Mus, Ithaca Coll., 1971; MS in Music, Syracuse Univ., 1976. m. Ellen Beth Hillman. Career: Music Dir., musical theatre prods.; Ldr., MOSS soc. orch., Ctrl. NY area; Dir., fest. choruses, NY; Dir., Eagle Hill Chorale, Hd., Music Dept., Eagle Hill Schl., Manlius, NY. Recordings: Eagle Hill Chorale, MARK MC-5313. Mbrships. incl: MENC; Am. Choral Dirs. Assn.; Am. Fedn. of Musicians. Hons: Winner, Stars of Tomorrow, Allentown, Pa., 1966. Hobbies: Photography; Stereophonic Equipment; Antique phonographs & music boxes; Skiing. Mgmt: Valex Agcy., Box 241, Ithaca, NY 14850, USA. Address: 4624 Glencliffe Rd., Manlius, NY 13104, USA.

GOLDBERG, Louise, b. 12 April 1937, Chgo., Ill., USA. Musicologist; Music Librarian. Educ: BA, Smith Coll., 1958; MA, Univ. of Chgo., 1961; PhD (Musicol.), Univ. of Rochester, 1974. Career: Fac., New Trier Township High Schl., Winnetka, Ill., 1961-67; Fac., Hobart & William Smith Colls., Geneva, NY, 1971-74; Staff, Sibley Music Library, Eastman Schl. of Music, Rochester, NY, 1971- (Hd., Reference & Rare Books). Publs: J A Amon, Viola Concerto; A Huberty, 9 sonatas for viola d'amore. Mbrships: AMS; MLA; IAML; Am. Viola Soc.; Viola d'amore Soc. of Am. Address: 72 Clintwood Court, Rochester, NY 14620, USA.

GOLDBERG, Szymon, b. 1 June 1909, Wloclawek, Poland. Concert Violinist. Educ. incls: studied w. Carl Flesch, Berlin. m. Maria Manasee. Debut: 1919. Career: Dresden Phil. Orch., 1925, Berlin Phil. Orch., 1929; Mbr. of trio w. E Feurermann & Paul Hindemith, 1930-34; USA, 1934; duo w. Lili Kraus, 1935-40; Concert Violinist, 1955-; Mbr., Fest. Quartet; Cond., Musical Dir., Netherlands Chmbr. Orch. Mgmt: Columbia Artists Mgmt., 165 W 57th St., NY, NY 10019, USA. 2.

GOLDBERGER, David, b. 25 July 1925, Memphis, Tenn., USA. Pianist; Editor; Teacher; Author. Educ: BA, SUNY, 1975; MA, Tchrs. Coll., Columbia Univ., 1976; EdD, Tchrs. Coll., Columbia Univ., 1978. 2 Dips. Univ. Nacional de Mexico, studied Piano w. Artur Schnavel, Karl Ulrich Schnabel, Egon Petri, Leonard Shure; studied Theory at Mannes Coll. of Music & Conserv. Nat. paris, France. m. Helen Rothenberg (dec.). Debut: NYC recital debut, 1960. Career: Appearances in recital, chamber music & w. orch., USA, France, Italy & Mexico; Radio & TV appearances in NYC, Phila., Memphis & Mexico City; participated in Artur Schnabel's Master Classes, Univ. of Mich.; Fac. Mbr., Mannes Coll. of Music, 1955-. Recordings:

Sonatinas of Beethoven & Clementi; Piano works of Mozart; Piano works of Beethoven; CMP Piano Library, I & II; Schubert Piano Works. Publs. incl: CMP Piano Library, 23 vols. (mostly w. Poldi Zeitlin), 1961-74; Russian Music for the Young Pianist, 6 vols., 1967-69. Contbr. to: The Piano Teacher: The Musical Leader; Piano Guild NOtes. Mbrships: Nat. Guild of Piano Tchrs.; NY State Music Congress; Former VP, Artur Schnabel Memorial Committee. Hons: Hall of Fame, Nat. Guild of Piano Tchrs. Hobbies: Politics (elected to Democratic Co. Committee, NY Co.); Photography; Travel; Languages. Address: 375 Riverside Dr., NY, NY 10025, USA.

GOLDBLATT, Rose, b. 28 Aug. 1913, Montreal, Can. Copncert Pianist; Professor. Educ: Pvte. study w. Stanley Gardner, Montreal, & Egon Petri, NY; RCM. m. Henry Finkel, 1 s., 1 d. Debut: London, 1935. Career: num. concerts in USA & Can.; radio broadcasts on CBC networks, also WNYC & WXQR; TV apps. on major CBC network progs.; Prof. of Music, McGill Univ.; Co-ordinator & examiner, ibid.; music examination across Can. new works by Can. Comps. introduced at concerts & broadcasts. Recordings: Comps. by Can. comps. for CBC. Mbrships: Quebec MTA; Fndn. mbr. & dir., Can. Fed., MTA; Hons: Ladies Morning Musical Club scholarships; Strathcona; Montreal scholarship to RCM; scholarship to study w. Egon Petri. Hobbies: Literature; Travel; Geology. Address: 342 Elm Ave., Westmount, Quebec, Can. H3Z 1Z5.

GOLDING, Robin Mavesyn, b. 4 June 1928, London, UK. Administrator; Freelance Writer. Educ: MA, Christ Church, Oxford. m. (1) Claire Simpson, 1 d., (2) Felicity Lott. Career: Freelance Writer on Musical Subjects; Libn., Boyd Neel Orch., 1953-56; Admin. Asst., RAM, 1961-65; Registrat, RAM, 1966-. Publs: Ed., Musical Performance in the times of Mozart & Beethoven by Fritz Rothschild, 1961; Ed., History of the Piano by Ernest Closson, 1973. Contbr. to: Music & Musicians; Records & Recording: Musical Times, etc. Mbrships: Royal Musical Assn. Hons: Hon. ARAM, 1965; Hon. RCM, 1971; Hon. RAM, 1976. Hobbies: Venice; Claret; Carpentry. Address: 80 Princedale Rd., London W11, UK. 3.

GOLDMAN, Richard Franko, b. 7 Dec. 1910, New York, NY, USA. Conductor; Composer; Critic; Educator. Educ: AB, Columbia Coll.; Pvte. study w. Pietro Floidia, Wallingford Riegger, Ralph Leopold & Clarence Adler. m. Alexandra Rienzi, 1 s. Career: Assoc. Cond., The Goldman Band, 1937-56; Cond. & Musical Dir., 1956-; Dir., Peabody Conserv. of Music, 1968-; Pres., Peabody Inst., 1969-; Comps. incl: about 50 published works. Recordings w. Goldman Band. Contbr. to var. anthologies, Oxford History of Music, var. scholarly & profl. periodicals. Mbrships: Chmn., Assn. of Independent Colls. of Music, 1970-73. Hons. incl: Deems Taylor Award for Disting. Critical Writing, 1975. Address: Peabody Inst., 1 East Mt., Vernon Pl., Baltimore, MD 21202, USA. 2.

GOLDMANN, Helmut, b. 3 March 1929, Nuremberg, Germany. Broadcasting Executive; University Teacher; Conductor. Educ: Civic Conserv., Nuremberg; PhD, Univ. of Erlangen, 1956. m. Hanna Fuchs. Career: Cond. & Musical; Dir. Titular, Guadajajara Symph. Orch., Mexico, 1957-65; Titular Prof., Univ. og Guadajara, 1957-65; TV concerts w. Guadajara Chmbr. Orch.; Prog. Prod. Bavarian Radio Studio, Nuremberg, 1967-; Lectr., Erlangen-Nuremberg Univ., 1974-. Recordings: num. tapes for Bavarian Radio; Symphonische Folklore w. Siegfried Behreud & Nuremberg Symph. Orch. Mbrships: Soc. for Music Rsch., Kassel; RFFU. Contbr. to var. newspapers. Hobbies: Photography; Model Railroads. Address: Ziegenstr. 36, 8500 Nürnberg - Mögeldorf, German Fed. Repub.

GOLDOVSKY, Boris, b. 7 June 1908, Moscow, Russia. Pianist; Conductor; Stage Director; Opera Producer; Writer; Lecturer; Radio Commentator. Educ: Grad., E Dohnanyi's Master Class, Franz Liszt Acad., Budapest; Grad. in conducting (studied w. F Reiner), Curtis Inst. of Music, Phila., Pa., USA. m. Margaret Codd, 1 s., 1 d. Debut: as Pianist w. Berlin Bhil., 1921. Career: has made extensive tours of USA as Pianist & Lectr.; has done intermission broadcasts for Met. Opera, NYC, 1945-. Publs: Accents on Opera, 1953; Bringing Opera to Life, 1968; Bringing Soprano Arias to Life, 1973. Contbr. to var. jrnls. Mbrships: Fellow Am. Acad. Arts & Scis. Hons: D Mus., Bates Coll. & Cleveland Inst. of Music; DRA., Northwestern Univ. Evanston., Ill.; Peabody Award for excellence in broadcasting. Mgmt: Herbert Barrett, NY. Address: 183 Clinton Rd., Brookline, MA 02146, USA. 2.

GOLDSCHMIDT, Harry, b. 17 June 1910, Basel, Switz. Musicologist. Educ: Basel Univ. & Conserv.; musical studies w. F Weingarter, Basel, H Scherchen, Königsbert & K Nef. Handschin, Berlin; Prof. Dr Phil. m. Anna Goldschmidt, 1 s. Career incls: Mgr., a wokrers coir, Basel, also Music Critic for var. newspapers & mags., 1945-; Lectr., Hist. of Music, E Brlin Music Coll.,

1950-55; China, 1955-56; Freelance Musicol., Guest Lectr., Humboldt Univ., Berlin, 1956-; Dir., Ctrl. Inst. for Musicol., 1960-65. Contbr. to publs. in field. Hons: Nationalpreis, German Dem. Repub. Address: Gregoroviusweg 26, 1157 Berlin-Karlshorst, German Dem. Repub.

GOLDSTEIN, Malcolm, b. 27 Mar. 1936, Bklyn., NY, USA. Composer; Violinist; Teacher. Educ: BA, 1956, MA, 1960, Columbia Univ. 2 children. Career incls: Co-Fndr., Dir., Tone Roads (concerts of 20th century music); Violinist & Electronic Music Engr, Judson Dance Theatre & Merce Cunningham Dance Co.; Co-Fndr. & Dir., New Roots in music & dance; Columbia-Princeton Electronic Music Studio, Tchr. at var. schls.; Dir., New Music Ensemble & Collegium Musicum, Dartmouth Coll.; Cond.; Asst. Prof. of Music Bowdoin Coll., Brunswick, Maine. Comps. incl: Illuminations from Fantastic Gardens; death; act or fact of dying; Yosha's Morming Song; upon the string, within the bow...breathing. Contbr. to profl. books & jrnls. Recip. acad. hons. Address: Sheffield, CT 05866, USA.

GOLSTEIN, Marvin Allan, b. 1 June 1950, Columbus, Ohio, USA. Rock & Roll Musician; French Hornist; Keyboard Player. Educ: BA, MA, Fla. State Univ.; Tel Aviv Univ. Schl. of Music; Mozarteum, Salzburg, Austria (1 semester). m. Lenae L Robison. Career: var. apps. w. schl. orchs. on French Horn; Profl. experience on Keyboard instruments w. rock; Perfs. w. Munich Phil., Webster Symphonette, Brahms Trio. Var. comps. Mbr. Int. Horn Soc. Hons: Music Scholarship, Tel Aviv Univ., 1968; Music Scholarship, Fla. State Univ., 1969-72. Hobbies: Weight-lifting; Tennis; Wiffle Ball; Mgmt: West Mgmt: Seattle, Wash., USA. Address: 649 E Coll. Ave., Tallahassee, FL 32301, USA.

GOLDSTEIN, Michael, b. 8 Nov. 1917, Odessa, USSR. University Teacher; Violin Soloist; Composer. Educ: Studied Conserv. Odessa (Stoljarski), 1921; Conserv. Moscow (Hampolski, Mjaskovski), 1930-36. div., 1 d. Debut: Violin soloist, Odessa, 1922. Career: Concerts in all major Russian & European cities, 1934-; Num. TV & Radio perfs. Compositions: 4 Symphs.; 1 Piano Concerto; 4 violin sonatas; 3 string Quartets; 2 cello sonatas; 1 ballet; Scenic & Screen Music; Songs; Chamber Music (publd. under pseudonym Mychajlo Mychajlowsky in var. Cities). Recordings: 55 in USSR, 6 in German Fed Repub. Publs: Notizen von Musikern; Michail Ignatieff and Balalaica, 1978. Contbr. to: Riemann's Annual & other Int. Mags. Mbrships: GEMA. Hons: 3 prizes, Russian Comps. competition, 1962; Given sev. Professorships inclng. Rubin Acad. of Music, Jerusalem, 1967, Menuhin Schl., London, 1968, Music High Schl., Hamburg, 1969. Hobby: Collecting old Music Manuscrpits. Address: D-2000 Hamburg 50, Griegstr. 1016, German Fed. Repub. 19.

GOLDSTONE, Anthony Keith, b. 25 July 1944, Liverpool, UK. Pianist. Educ: Royal Manchester Coll. of Music; GRSM; ARMCM. Debut: London recital debut, Purcell Room, 1968. Career: Perf. in Germany, Austria, Hungary, Greece, Holland, Belgium, Spain, Eire, USA. (debut 1968), Canada, S Africa; S Am. tour, 1974; Frequent broadcaster; Henry Wood Promenade Concert debut, 1971; Edinburgh Fest. debut, 1973. Recordings: Five records/cassettes of solo works of Schubert, Schumann & Chopin, ORYX. Mbr., ISM. Hons: Munich & Vienna Pianoforte Comps., 1967; Calouste Gulbenkian Fndn. Fellowship, 1968; FRMCM, 1973. Mgmt: London Artists Ltd., 124 Wigmore St., London W1H 0AX. Address: 289 Leagrave High St., Leagrave, Beds. LU4 ONB, UK.

GOLDTHORPE (John) Michael, b. 7 Feb. 1942, City of York, UK. Tenor. Educ: MA, Trinity Coll., Cambridge; Cert. of Educ., King's Coll., London; GSM. m. Gilliam Emily Kinver, 2 s., 2 d. Debut: w. Pk. Lane Grp., Purcell Room, 1970. Career: Apps. w. Intimate Opera & in concerts in GB from Channel Islands to Outer Hebrides; Regular perfs. in London & all maj. concert halls; Guest artist in Germany, Reykjavik, Paris, Granada; Erg. Bach Fest. & Rotterdam. Recordings w. CBS, RTF, BBC & Hilversuin. Mbrships: ISM; Brit. Actors Equity Assn., Byron Soc. Hons: Mirsky Memorial Prize for Lieder, GSM, 1966; Selected by Gtr. London Arts Assn., 1972 & ISM, 1973 for their Young Musicians Series. Hobbies: Langs.; Gardening; Brewing. Address: 25 Vaughan Rd., Long Ditton, Surrrey KT7 OUF, UK.

GOLL, Gertrude, b. Buffalo, NY, USA. Music Teacher; Choral Director. Educ: Univ. Buffalo Music Schl. Career: Dir. of 100-voice choruses w. repertoire in 6 langs., incl. num. TV appearances, notably in original musical 'Our American Heritage'; perfs. to var. local orgs.; appearances at Music Festivals, 1951, '52, '60, '65; Cond., Music Tchrs. Orientation Prog.; 1959; Dir., Gilbert & Sullivan operettas, Buffalo Community Ctr.; Guest Dir., musical in Chattanooga; Critic Music Tchr., 1957-64. Contbr. to: Teaching Elementary Music Without a Supervisor, 1958; Tchr. Opera Study Guide; Music Curric.; Youth Guide to

Phil. Concerts. Mbrships: MENC; chmn., Youth Guides to Phil. Concerts, 1967-68; Committee, ibid., 1957-58; Music Textbook Committee, 1958, 1961. Hons: Teacher Freedoms Fndn. Medal, 1968. Hobbies: Travel; Theatre; Reading; Indoor gardening. Address: 1290 Delaward Ave., Buffalo, NY 14209, USA.

GOLLAND, John, b. 13 Sept. 1942, Aston-under-Lyne, Lancs., UK. Composer; Conductor; Pianist. Educ: LRAM; BBCM. Comps: Five & Threes; Wind Quintet; Relay; Concerto for piano & brass band; Deva; Sounds I for band; Mancunia; Diversions; Epic Theme; In Celebration; Lesser Thorns; Band Kraft. Contbr. to: Composer; Brit. Bandsman; Brit. Mouthpiece. Mbrships: CGGB. Address: 35 Lismore Rd., Dukinfield, Cheshire SK16 4AZ, UK.

GÖLLNER, Marie Louise (nee Martinez), b. 27 June 1932, Ft. Collins, Colo., USA. University Professor of Music History. Educ: BA, Vassar Coll., 1953; Eastman Schl. of Music, 1953-54; Univ. of Heidelberg, Germany, 1954-56; PhD, 1962, Dr phil. habil, 1975, Univ. of Munich. m. Theodor Göllner, 1 s., 1 d. Career: Rsch. Asst., Bavarian State Lib., Munich, 1964-67, 69-70; Lectr., Coll. of Creative Studies, Univ. of Calif. Santa Barbara, 1968; Asst. Prof.-Prof., of UCLA, 1970-; Chmn., Dept. of Music, ibid., 1976-. Publs. incl: Rules for Cataloging Music Manuscripts, 1975; Die Musikhandschriften der Bayerischen Staatsbibliothek Müchen, 1979. Contbr. to profl. publs. Mbrships. incl: Int. Assn. of Music Libs.; Am. Musicol. Soc.; Mediaeval Acad. of Am. Address: 817 Knapp Dr., Santa Barbara, CA 93108, USA. 27, 29.

GÖLLNER, Theodor, b. 25 Nov. 1929, Bielefeld, W. Germany. Musicologist; Administrator. Educ: PhD., Univ. of Heidelberg, 1957; Phil. Habil., Univ. of Munich, 1967. m. Marie Louise Martinez, 1 s., 1 d. Career: Lectr., Univ. of Munich, 1958; Asst., ibid, 1962, Assoc. Prof., 1967; Vis. Assoc. Prof., Univ. of Calif., Santa Barbara, USA, 1967, Assoc. Prof., 1968, Prof., 1971; Chair in Musicol. & Dir., Inst. of Musicol., Univ. of Munich, Germany, 1973; Dean, Div. of Hist. & Fine Arts, Univ. of Munich, 1975-77. Publs: Formen früher Mehrstimmigkeit, 1961; Die mehstimmingen liturgischen Lesungen, 2 vols., 1969; Ed., Münchner veröffentlichungen zur Musikgeschichte, 1977-. Contbr. to var. publs. Mbrships: Int. Musicol. Soc.; Am. Musicol. Soc.; Gesellschaft für Musikforschung; Gesellschaft für Bayerische Musikgeschichte. Address: Musikwiss. Instr., Univ. of Munich, 8 Munich 22, Geschw. Scholl Platz 1, German Fed. Repub. 16.

GOLOS, Jerzy Stanislaw, b. 27 July 1931, Warsaw, Poland. Musicologist; Organologist; Slavic Philologist. Educ: BSc, Columbia Univ., 1954; MA (Musicol.), ibid., 1958; PhD (Musicol.), Warsaw Univ., 1961; MA (Polish Philology), ibid., 1962; Dr. habil. (Hist. of Technology), Polish Acad. of Arts & Scis., Warsaw, 1971. Career: Instr. in Russian, Brooklyn Coll., NY, 1962-64; Rsch. Asst., Inst. of Musicol., Warsaw Univ., 1965-67; Rsch. Assoc. & instr., Graduate Centre City Univ. of NY & Rsch. Center for Musical Iconography; Ed., RIdIM/RCMI Newsletter, 1973-76; Special Cons., Repertoire Int. de Litterature Musicale, 1973-; Chief Cons., Organology, Histl. Monuments Documentation Centre, Warsaw, 1976-; Asst. Prof., Musicol., Acad. of Catholic Theology, 1977-. Publs. incl: An Outline of the History of Organ-Building in Poland (in Polish), 1966; 2 vols. in Antiquitates Musicae in Polonia series, 1967; Polish Organ & Organ Music (in Polish), 1972; 4 vols. in the Corpus of Early Keyboard Music Series, 1965, 67. Contbr. to profl. publs. Mbr., profl. orgs. Hons: Fellow, Nat. Endowment for Humanities. Address: ul. Navielaka 2 m. 37, 00-743 Warsaw, Poland. 30.

GOLTZ, Christel, b. 8 July, Dortmund, Germany. Singer, Soprano. Educ: studies singing w. F Leeb, Munich. m. Theodor Schenk. Debut: Furth, 1935. Career: Dresden State Opera 1936/1950; Berlin Stat Opera, 1947; Covent Gdn., 1951; app. in Vienna, Munich, overseas.

GOMBERG, Harold, b. 30 Nov. 1916, Malden, Mass., USA. Oboist. Educ: Grad., Curtis Inst. of Music, Phila., Pa., USA. m. Margaret Brill, 1 d., 1 s. Career: at 17, solo oboist, Nat. Symph., Wash. Toronto, Symph., 1 yr. St. Louis Symph. Orch., 4 yrs.; NY Phil. Orch., currently: Hd., Oboe Dept., Juilliard Schl. of Music & Manhattan Schl. of Music, NYC. Recordings: The Baroque Oboe; The Art of Harold Gomberg; Six Metamorphoses After Ovid. Hobby: Painting (3 one-man shows). Address: 165 W 66 St., NY, NY, USA.

GOMBERT, Karl E, b. 14 Aug. 1933, Ft. Wayne, Ind., USA. College Music Professor; Plays trumpet, French horn, violin. Educ: BS Ball State Univ., Muncie, Ind., 1955; MA, Mich. State Univ., E Lansing, 1962; DA, Ball State Univ., 1977. m. Shirley J Gobert, 1 s., 1 d. Co-Author, Toward A Musical Classroom, 1969. Contbr. to Instrumentalist. Mbrships: MENC;

Phi Mu Alpha Sinfonia; Am. Musicol. Soc. Recip., Fellowship, Ball State Univ., 1972-73. Hobbies: Golf; Tennis; Canoeing. Address: PO Box 348, Edinboro, PA 16412, USA.

GOMEZ, Victor E, b. 7 Nov. 1930, Niagara Falls, NY, USA. Violinist; Teacher. Educ: SUNY; Syracuse Univ.; BS (Music);MMus. Career: Tchr.; Violinist w. Niagara Falls Phil. Orch., Erie Phil. (pa), Buffalo Orch., Utica Symph. (NY), Boston Pops Orch., & Syrcuse Symph. Mbrships. incl: NY State String Musicians Assn.; Music Educators Nat. Conf.; Am. Fedn. of Musicians; NEA. Hobbies: Golf; Walking; Antiques; Sports. Address: 7221 Coleman Mills Rd., Rome, NY, USA.

GOMEZ, William Arthur, b. 7 Sept. 1939, Gibraltar. Classical Concert Guitarist. Educ: Madrid Conserv., 1 yr.; Pvte. Music study w. Narciso Yepes & Quintin Esquembre. m. Olga Patricia Llufrio, 1 s., 1 d. Debut: Theatre Royal, Gibraltar; UK Debut: Wigmore Hall, London. Career: Broadcasts on Spanish TV; ITV (London); BBC Radio; Radio Nacional Spain; Soloist w. London Bach Orch.; Ulster Orch.; Engl. Sinfonia; Northern Sinfonia; Madrid Symph. Orch.; Recordings: Guitar recitals (Ace of Diamonds & decca labels); 35 recordings for BBC Radio; 10 recordings for Radio Nacional, Spain. Mbrships: VP, St. Bernards Cath. & Soc. Club. Hons: 1st Prize (Composition), Gibraltar Song Festival, 1968, '71, '73; 2nd Prize, ibid., 19069. Hobbies: Song Writing; Chess; Pistol Shooting. Mgmt: Ibbs & Tillet, London. Address: 10 City Mill Lane, Gibraltar. 3, 28.

GOMEZ MARTINEZ, Miguel A, b. 17 Sept. 1949, Granada, Spain. Conductor. Educ: Piano Dip.; Comp. Dip.; Chorus Cond. Dip.; Orch. Cond. Dip.; sev. violin courses. Debut: Trovatore, Municipal Theater Luzern, 1972. Career: deutsche Oper W Berlin; Staatsoper Hamburg, Bayerische Staatsoper; Nationaltheater Munich; Royal Opera House, Covent Garden, London; Staatsoper Vienna; Grand Theatre Geneva; Opera National Paris; Orchestra Philharmonia Hungarica; Orquesta Nacional de España; Radio Symphonie-Orchester Berlin; Orquesta de la Radio-Television Espanola; Symphonie-Orchester des Westdeutschen Rundunf (Cologne); Orchestra Sinfonica del Teatro Reale, San Carlo (Naples); Magyar allami Hangversenyzenekar (State Phil. Orch., Hungary), Budapest; TV & Radio apps. Hons: Prize of the Ministerium für Wissenschaft and Forschug of Austria, 1971; Special Prize of the Orch. Radio Symph. of Copenhagen, Nicolai Malko Competition for Young Conds., 1971. Hobbies: Reading; Photography. Mgmt: Martin Taubman. Address: Menéndez Pelayo 101, Madrid 7, Spain.

GOMM, Elizabeth, b. 12 Mar. 1951, Henley-on-Thames, UK. Music Teacher. Educ: GGSM; LRAM. m. Duncan Dwinell. Career: Comps. performed on BBC. Comps: Agnus Dei; Moonraking for solo violin; Clytemnestra s Argument for women s choir; Four Songs for tenor & piano. Hons: Young Musicians Comp. Prize, Gtr. London Arts Coun., 1974. Address: 4 Chapel View, Ightham, Sevenoaks, Kent, UK.

GONDA, János, b. 11 Jan. 1932, Budapest, Hungary. Pianist; Composer; Music Educator. Educ: Dip. of Musicol. & Piano, Ferenc Liszt Music acad. m. Olga Tóth, 1 s. Debut: Hall of Music Acad., Budapest, 1961. Career: Worked to establish modern jazz as a popular art form in Hungary in early 1960s, incl. own jazz band, recording 1st Hungarian modern jazz LP, arr. & ldr. of Jazz progs. for Radio & TV; Dir., concerts, festivals & studio recordings: Co-fndr. & Prin. Jazz Fac., Bela Bartok Conserv., 1965-; Toured Australia, 1965, 1972; appeared at Jazz Festivals in Belgium, Yugoslavia, Poland, etc. Composition incl: symph. jazz - Orchestral Improvisations in 7 Movements, 1967; Australian Concerto, 1971; dance compositions for Pecs Ballet Ensemble - Rondo & Divertimento, 1964; Blues, 1965; Chairs, 1967; Roaring, 1968; African Oratory, 1978; Music for sev. films. Recordings incl: var. Modern Jazz LP Albums; Rhapsody in Blue (Qualiton); Shaman Song (Pepita). Publ: Jazz-History, Theory, Practice, 2nd ed.; 1979; VP, Int. Jazz Fedn., 1972; Mbr. of Presidency, Hungarian Comps. Union. Recip: Erkel Prize, 1974. Mgmt: Interkoncert. Address: 1121 Budapest, Remete út. 12, Hungary. 30.

GONTIJO, Flavio, b. 3 July 1948, Minas Gerais, Belo Horizonte, Brazil. Concert Violinist; Violin Teacher; Composer. Educ: 3rd Yr. Student in Music, Univ. of Brasilia; studies of Violin, Comp., Cond. Musica Antiqua, Chmbr. Music, Singing, Vocal Technique. Debut: Belo Horizonte, 1961. Career: Concerts in Minas Gerais, Rio de Janeiro, Teresopolis, Brasilia, & Buenos Aires, Argentina; TV apps. Bracil. Comps: (choral) Ave Maria, 1968; Requiem para um Boi, 1971; (chmbr. orch.) O Vento, 1969; (Violin & piano) Poema da areia, 1972; Christe Dona Nobis Pacem, 1975. Mbr., profl. assns., Brazil. Recip. var. awards for violin & comp., inclng. Finalist, 1st & 2nd Nat. Comp. Contest 12975 & 1976. Hobbies: Swimming; Chess; Motorcycle Races. Address: SQS 411 Bloco B apt. 108, Brasilia DF (70.000), Brazil.

GONZALEZ, Dalmacio, b. 12 May 1946, Olot, Gerona, Spain. Tenor. Educ: studied voice & lang. w. Gilbert Price, Barcelona; operatic repertory w. Arleen Augur, Salzburg; Lieder & other art songs w. Anton Dermota, Barcelona. m. Montserrat Pares, 2 s., 1 s. Career: Voice Tchr., 10 yrs.; Apps. as Ugo in Donizetti's Parisina, Barcelona & Nice; Radio & TV apps., Italy; num. recitals & oratorios, incl. works of Bach, Schubert, Strauss & Britten; Operatic roles incl. Nemorini (L'Elisir d'Amore), The Count (The Barber of Seville), The Duke (Rigoletto), Alfredo (La Traviata), Don Ottavio (Don Giovanni), Ernesto (Don Pasquale); Apps., Metropolitan Opera & NYC Opera. Mgmt: Columbia Artists Mgmt. Inc., 165 W 57th St., NY, NY 10019, USA. Address: c/o Mgmt.

GONZALEZ GARCIA, Pablo, b. 15 June 1932, Madrid, Spain. Violinist. Educ: Royal Conserv. of Music, Madrid, prof. of educ.; Int. Conserv. of Music, Paris, w. George Enescu, Maurice Crutz & Rene Benedetti. m. 1 s. Debut: Madrid, 1950. Career: TV & radio apps. in Madrid, Paris & Buenos Aires. Recordings: 3 of Baroque music. Contbr. to Georama (Argentina). Mbrships. incl: Consejo Diretivo Confederación Argentina Trabajadores Espectaculo; Directivo Asociación Profesorado Orquestal Argentino; selection OEA panel for scholarships for chmbr. music courses, Siena, 1975. Hons: num. awards during violin courses, Madrid; 1st Accesit, 1958, & 3rd medal, 1959 in chmbr. music, Paris. Hobbies: Aviation; Yachting; Drawing; Handicrafts. Address: via Brasil No. 405 Apt. 16, Panamá 7, Panamá.

GONZALEZ-ZULETA, Fabio, b. 2 Nov. 1920, Bogota, Colombia. Composer; Organist. Educ: Los Angeles Schl. of Music, USA, 1929; Organist degree, 1944, Comp. degree, 1945, Nat. Conserv., Nat. Univ. of Colombia, Bogota. m. Ines González de González, 2 s., 2 d. Career incls: Prof., 1943-Sec., 1952-57, Dir., 1957-67, Nat. Conserv. of Bogota; Asst. Dean Schl. of Arts, Nat. Univ. of Colombia, 1967-71; Dir., 1973-74, Prof. & Dir. of Fine Arts, 1974-; INSE (Inst. of Higher Educ., Univ. Level). Comps. incl: 8 symphs.; var. other orchl. works inclng. works for chorus & orch.; Chmbr. music ?; ballets; songs; incidental music for plays; Electronic essay (electronic music). Contbr. to profl. jrnls. Mbr. nat. & int. orgs. Recip. many awards & hons. Mgmt: Peer Int. Corp., NY. Address: Calle 100 No. 9A-95, Apto. 402, Bogota, Colombia.

GOOD, Anny Ida, b. 12 June 1920, BucksKt., St. Gall, Switz. Concert Singer; Singing Teacher. Educ: Zürich Conserv.; Summer Schl. Mozarteum, Salzburg; Studied langs., Brussels, London & Turing. Career: Concerts, Switz., Germany, Austria; Broadcasts. Recordings: LP w. orch. & choir (Columbia); singles w. var. instruments, Columbia & Philips. Mbrships: Swiss Musicians Union; Swiss Music Tchrs. Assn.; Swiss lyceum (women's) club. Hobbies: Reading; Travel; Needlework. Address: Stussistrasse 90, 8057 Zürich, Switz.

GOOD, Ronald, b. 15 Dec. 1910, London, UK. Violinist. Educ: GSM; studied w. Max Rostal & Sascha Lasserson. m. Mary McLeod, 2 s. Debut: BBC solo broadcast. Career: Queens Hall Orch., 1929; BBC Symph. Orch., 1930-39; RAF Radar Operator, 1942-46; Sub. Ldr., LSO, 1948-52; Ldr., Western Phil., 1952-56, Leighton Lucas Orch., 1952-65; Philharmonia Orch., 1956-72; tchng. in Cornwall, 1972-. Recip., Gold Medal, London Music Fest., 1928. Hobbies: Golf & Gardening. Address: 'Spray', Porthcothan Bay, Padstow, Cornwall, UK. 3.

GOODE, Daniel, b. 24 Jan. 1936, NYC, USA. Composer; Clarinettist; Electronic Performer. Educ: BA, Oberlin Coll., 1957; MA, Columbia Univ., 1962; further study w. var. tchrs. Career incls: Perf. & Cond., new music inclng. sev. premieres of new works, USA & E Can.; Tchr., Univ. of Minn., 1964-67; Livingston Coll. Rutgers Univ., 1971-77; Dir. & Fndr., Electronic Music Studio of Rutgers Univ.; Fndr., Neshanic Group for Music, 1975; Mbr., perf. orgs. Son of Lion Gamelan & Sounds Out of Silent Spaces; Music Cons., NY State Coun. on the Arts, 1977, '78. Comps. incl: Circular Thoughts for solo clarinet (recorded); Two Thrushes, for two woodwinds; Chord Progression; Paths, for piano. Contbr. to Ear Mag. Recip. var. hons. Address: Box 268A, Main Rd., Neshanic, NJ 08853, USA.

GOODFRIEND, James, b. 29 June 1932, Bronx, NY, USA. Music Critic. Educ: BA (Music), NY Univ. m. Carol Hodgdon Goodfriend, 2 d. Career: Music Educ., Stereo Review. Publs: Guide to Classical Music, 1979. Contbr. to: Stereo Review; NY Times; Muscial America, etc. Mbrships: Music Critics Assn.; Nat. Assn. of Recording Arts & Scis.; ASCAP. Hobby: Collecting Art. Address: 309 West 104th St., Apt. 2C, NYC, NY 10025, USA.

GOODKIND, Herbert Knowlton, b. 30 April 1905, NYC, USA. Violinist. Educ: Cornell Univ. & pvtly. m. (1) Mabel Goldhammer, 2 s., (2) Virginia Haggett, 1 s., 1 d. Publs:

Cumulative index to the Musical Quarterly, 1915-1964, (1965); Violin Iconography of Antonio Stradivari 1644-1737 (1972); Stradivari Colour Print (1972). Contbr. to The Violin Makers Jrnl. Mbrships: Am. Musicol. Soc.; VP & Advertising Manager, Jrnl. of the Violin Soc. of Am. Hons: Medal of Hon. from the Eugen Ysaye Fndn., Brussels, Belgium, 1974. Hobbies: Str. Quartet playing - entertainment ensemble for senior citizens; Violin Collecting (connoisseur); Water Kyak Boating; collecting & indexing Violin Literature. Mgmt: Goodkind & Chapman Violins, Inc., 1879 Palmer Ave., Larchmont, NY 10538, USA. Address: Helena Ave., Larchmont, NY 10538, USA.

GOODMAN, A Harold, b. 14 July 1924, Solomon, Ariz., USA. Professor of Music; Conductor; Violinist; Administrator. Educ: BA, Univ. of Ariz., 1947; MMus., Univ. of Southern Calif., 1951; EdD, ibid., 1960. m. Naomi Foster Goodman, 2 s., 1 d. Career: Music Supvsr., Snowflake Union High Schl., Ariz., 1947-50, Tucson Public Schls., 1950-52; Choir Dir., LDS Ch., Tucson & Flagstaff, 1950-60; Cond., Tucson Symph., 1951-52, Northern Ariz. Symph., 1954-58; Asst. Prof. of Music, ibid., 1958-60; Assoc. prof. of Music, 1960, Chmn., Music Educ., 1960-66, Prof. of Music, 1963, Chmn., Music Dept., 1966-74, Chmn., Lyceum Progs., 1968-74, Chmn., Fac. Advsry. Coun., ibid., 1970-71, Brigham Young Univ.; Toured Europe w. A Capella Choir, ibid., 1970. Fndn., Cond., 1960-65, Utah Valley Youth Symph.; Cond., Music Dir., Utah Valley Symph., 1961-66. Publs: We Can Become Perfect, 1974, Music Administration in Higher Hearing, 1976. Contbr. to var. profl. jrnls. Mbr. Off., num. profi. orgs. Recip. num. Hons. Hobbies: Sports; Hunting; Fishing. Address: 725 E Stadium Dr., Provo, UT 84601, USA.

GOODMAN, Alfred Grant, b. 1 Mar. 1920, Berlin, Germany. Composer; Musicologist. Educ: BS, Columbia Coll., NY; MA, Comp., Musicol., etc., Columbia Univ.; PhD, Technische Universitet, Berlin. m. Renate Goodman, 1 s. Career: Ed., Westminster Records, NY; Comp., Movietone, NY; Music Ed., Bavarian Broadcasting Serv., 1971-; Lectr., State Coll. of Music, Munich, 1976-. Compositions: Psalm XII, Mercury Music, NY; The Audition, Opera in one act (Schott); Pro Memoria for Orch.; Chamber works: Songs; Choral comps.; TV & Film scores; orchl. works; TV music. Publs: Musikim Blut; Lexikon: Musik von A-Z; Die Amerikanischen Schuler Franz Liszts (Diss.). Mbrships: Deutsche Musik Forschung; Dramatiker Union (Beirat); Am. Guild of Authors & Composers. Hons: Ernest Bloch Award, NY, 1949; Prize for Oper, The Audition, Univ. of Ohio, 1954. Hobbies: Walking, Reading. Address: Clemens Krauss Str. 22, 8 Munich 60, German Fed. Repub.

GOODMAN, Bernard Maurice, b. 12 June 1914, Cleveland, Ohio, USA. Conductor; Violinist; Professor of Music. Educ: BS, Western Reserve Univ.; Cleveland Inst. of Music; Pvte. study w. Joseph Fuchs, Carlton Cooley, Arthur Shepherd, George Szell. m. Margaret Carfray (dec.), 1 s. Debut: as mbr. of Walden String Quartet, Cleveland, 1934. Career: Mbr., Cleveland Orch., 1936-46; Asst. Prof., Music, & Artist in Res., Cornell Univ., 1946-47; Prof. of Music & Artist in Res., Univ. of Ill., 1947-74; Cond., Univ. of Ill. Symph. Orch., 1950-74; Cond., Champaign-Urbana Symph., 1960-74; Cond., Bloomington-Normal Symph., 1971-74; Mbr., Walden String Quartet, 1934-74, incl. tours in USA & W Europe, major Music Fest. concerts; Cond., Univ. of Ill. Symph. Orch., tour of Latin Am., 1964. Recordings; Music by Walter Piston, Robert Palmer, Martinu, Kodaly, Szymanowski, Elliot Carter & Charles Ives, (w. Walden String Quartet). Mbr., Phi Mu Alpha Sinfonia. Hons: Kulas Fndn. Fellowship, 1960. Address: Pemaquid Pt., New Harbor, ME 04554, USA. 2, 8.

GOODMAN, Wallace Richard, b. 7 Aug. 1942, Buffalo, NY, USA. Instrumental Music Teacher. Educ: BSc, State Univ. Coll. of NY, Fredonia; MSc, Ithaca Coll.; Secondary & Total Schl. Supvsr's Lic., NY State Dept. of Educ. m. Christine Struzik Goodman, 3 s. Career: Public Schl. Instrumental Music Tchr., Lancaster Ctrl. Schl., Williamsville Ctrl. Schl., & presently Niagara-Wheatfield Ctrl. Chl. Mbrships: VP, Niagara Counry Music Educators Assn.; MENC; NY State schl. Music Assn.; NY State Tchrs. Assn.; Nat. Band Assn.; Niagara-Wheatfield Tchrs. Assn.; Phi Delta Kappa; Am. Fedn. of Musicians, Local 106; Niagara Falls Phil. Orch.; Cond., Sanborn Fire Co. Band; Cond., Niagara Falls Am. Fedn. of Musicians Concert Band; Bd. of Dir., Am. Youth Symph.; Music Schl. Dir., Kenan Ctr. Hons: Outstanding Your Educator Award, 1967; Medal of Hon., Mid-west Band & Orch. Clinic, 1971. Address: 2722 Maple Rd., Wilson, NY 14172, USA.

GOODWIN, Andrew John, b. 11 Nov. 1947, Hillingdon, Middx., UK. Cathedral Organist; Recitalist; Teacher. Educ: BA, Univ. of Liverpool; MA, Univ. Coll. of N Wales, Bangor; FRCO. m. Diana Jane Guest. Career: num. recitals inclng. St. George's Hall, Liverpool; Radio & TV broadcasts as Soloist & w. Bangor

Cathedral Choir; pt.-time Organ Tutor, Univ. Coll. of N Wales; Examiner to Assoc. Bd., Royal Schls. of Music, 1978-. Author, The Anthems of Maurice Greene, 1972. Mbr., ISM. Hobby: Railways. Address: 34 Ffordd Gwenllian, Llanfairpwll, Anglesey LL61 5QD, UK.

GOODWIN, Peter Anthony, b. 15 Apr. 1945, London, UK. Trombone & Sackbut Player; Professor. Educ: RCM, 1965-68. m. Carole Goodwin, 2 s., 1 s. Career: Freelance player in London, 1968-73; mbr., Philharmonia Orch., 1973-; Dir., ibid., 1975-; fndr. Equale Brass, 1974; Prof. of Trombone, RCM. Recordings: sev. Renaissance works w. Early Music Consort of London; Music for His Majesty's Sackbuts. Mbrships: Int. Trombone Assn.; Musicians' Union. Hobbies: Cooking; Chess; Swimming. Mgmt: Clarion Concert Agency, London. Address: 11 Highlands Gdns., Ilford, Essex, UK.

GOORHUIS, Rob, b. 25 Mar. 1948, Amsterdam, Netherlands. Composer; Conductor; Organist. Educ: Organ solo-playing cum laude; Highest Dip., choir cond.; Music Theory; Orch. cond. w. Paul Hupperts. div. Debut: Cathedral, Breda. Career: Concert tours, France & Italy; Comps. perf., St. Bravo Ch., Haarlem & Oude Kerk, Amsterdam. Comps: Danses Dydactyles for Organ (Pedal Solo); Concertino for Fanfare; Sev. ch. musical works. Mbrships: KNTV; KDOV. Recip: Citta di Morciano Prize, playing Italian organ music, 1976. Hobbies: Building Harpsichords; Chess. Address: Otselaan 28, Werkhoven, Netherlands.

GOOSSEN, Jacob Frederic, b. 30 July 1927, St. Cloud, Minn., USA. Composer; Professor, Educ: BA, Univ. of Minn., 1949; MA, ibid., 1950; PhD, 1954; pvte. study w. Melville Smith (counterpoint) & Arthur Shepherd (comp.) m. Shirley Reed. Publs: Six Chorales for Organ; Equali for Four Trombones; Death, Be Not Proud; American Meditations; Hodie (all for chorus); Temple Music for Violin & Piano; Clausulae for Violin & Piano. Let Us Now Praise Famous Men, 1975. All works publd. by Peer-int. Corp., NY & Hamburg; Clausulae & Temple Music (violin & piano). Contbr. to Musical Qtly.; Notes; Jrnl. of th Am. Lib. Assn. Mbrships: Am. Composers Alliance; Past Pres., Southeastern US Composers League. Hobbies: Modern European History; History of WWII. Address: 3125-4th Ct. East, Tuscaloosa, AL 35401, USA.

GOOSSENS, Marie Henriette, b. 11 Aug. 1894. London, UK. Musician (harp). Educ: RCM. m. Frederick Laurence (dec.), 2 s., 2 d. Debut: Liverpool Phil. Hall, 1910. Career: Prin. Harp, Covent Gdn. Opera; Diaghilev Ballet Seasons; Prin. Harp., Queen's Hall Orch., 1920-30, LPO, 1932-39, LSO, 1940-59; Freelance appearances in films. Radio & TV: London Mozart Players, 1972-, etc. Compositions: Music for Radio Serial Mrs. Dale's Diary (BBC); 14 Tunes for Celtic Harp (arr.). Recordings: Minuet, Nocturne & Impromptu by Derrick Mason; Le Cygne (Pavlova's Ballet Music); Fairy Song (Rutland Boughton). Mbrships: UK Harpists Assn.; chmn., Clarsach Soc. (London). Hons: Exhibitioner, RCM, 1912; Hon. ARCM, 1964. Hobby: Serendipity. Address: 15 Marlbourough Mansions, Cannon Hill, London NW6 1JP, UK. 27.

GOOSSENS, Sidonie, b. 19 Oct. 1899, Liscard, Cheshire, UK. Harpist. Educ: RCM. m. Norman K Millar. Career: Prin. Harpist, BBC Symph. Orch., 1930-, Prof. of Harp., GSM, 1960-. Hons: MBE, 1974, FGSM. Address: Woodstock Farm, Gadbook, Betchworth RH3 7AH, UK.

GORANSSON, Harald, b. 5 May 1917, Norrköping, Sweden. Professor of Music, Royal Academy of Music, Stockholm. Educ: Royal Acad. of Music, Stockholm, & Uppsala Univ., 1935-44; further studies in Europe & Uppsala Univ., 1935-44; further studies in Europe & USA. m. Anna-Lisa Ttjernström, 1 s., 1 d. Career: Has given piano & organ concerts on Radio Sweden; has made radio & TV apps. Recordings: series of choral & organ works for Kyrkoton. Publs: Lyssnarens harmonilära, 1950; Koralmusik, 1957; Psalm och Koral, 1958; Koralmusik II, 1960; Tillägg till Den svenska Koralboken, 1963; Kanonmusik, 1964; Koralmusik III, 1964; 17 psalmer, 1965; Ny mässmusik, 1967; Tillägg till Den svenska mässboken, 1968; Tillsammans, 1970; Attentat mot kyrkomusiken, 1971; Mera tillsammans, 1972; Musiken i "Svensk gudstjänst i dag", 1974; Psalmer och visor, 1974; Gudstjänstordning för Svenska Kyrkan, 1976. Contbr. to sev. mags. Mbrships: Royal Acad. of Music; Bd. of Dirs., Ecclesia Cantans; Ctrl. Bd., Northern Ch. Music Coun.; Bd., Swedish Guild of Organists; Commissions on Liturgy O Hymnody of Ch. of Sweden. Hobby: Sailing. Address: Frimuravägen 2, S-181 41 Lidingö, Sweden.

GORDON, David Alex, b. 20 June, 1933, Kansas City, Mo., USA. College Teacher; Composer; Theorist; French Horn Player. Educ: BMus., Yale Univ., 1955; MA, UCLA, 1957;

PhD, Eastman Schl. of Music, Univ. of Rochester, 1961. Career: Asst. Prof. of Music, Miss. State Coll. for Women, 1961-64; Lectr. in Music, Univ. of Calif. at Santa Barbara, 1964-65 & 1974; Assoc. Prof. of Composition, Univ. of Mo. at Kansas City, 1965-70; Assoc. Prof. of Theory, Univ. of Wyo., 1970-74. Compositions incl: Bali for Percussion (publd.). 1965; Niagara (orchl. tone poem), 1969; Trio for Violin, viola & cello, 1970; Lento for Orch., 1971; Canticle of the Sun for chorus, organ & brass, 1972; Trio for violin, cello & piano, 1974. Publs: Music Theory 301f & 301g. (Univ. of Wyo. corres. courses), 1970-71. Mbrships: Pi Kappa Lambda; Am. Fedn. of Musicians; ASCAP. Recip. of acad. fellowships. Hobbies: Skiing; Tennis. Address: 204A Oceano, Santa Barbara, Calif., USA. 8.

GORDON, Jerry Lee, b. 15 Sept. 1938, Greenville, Ohio, USA. Tenor; Assistant Professor of Voice. Educ: BSc, 1960; MM, 1967, DMA, 1973. Coll.-Conserv. of Music, Univ. of Cincinnati. m. Cornelia Conn, 1 s. Career: Symph. Soloist, Cincinnati, Atlanta, Honolulu, Ft. Smith (Ark.), Dayton (OH); Operatic Soloist, Cincinnati, Honolulu. Recordings: Light in the Wilderness w. Dave Brubeck & Cincinnati Symph., Decca. Mbrships: Nat. Assn. of Tchrs. of Singing; Phi Mu Alpha Sinfonia; Patron, Delta Omicron. Hons: Gorno Mem. Prize in Voice, 1961; Baur Mem. Prize in Voice, 1967. Hobby: Sports. Address: 2601 Rockview, Waco, TX 76710, USA. 7.

GORDON, Nathan, b. NYC, USA. Violinist; Conductor; Teacher of Viola. Educ: Fellowship in Violin & Fellowship in Viola, Juilliard Schl. of Music (Grad. w. a Cert. for both instruments). m. Marjorie Gordon, 2 c. Debut: Concert as Solo Violist, Town Hall, NYC Career: Has perf. w. NBC, Pitts., Detroit & Chautauqua Symphs. as First Viola; Chamber Music w. Kroll Quartet & Budapest Quartet as well as NBC Quartet, etc.; int. Artist; Fndr. of Gateway to Music (Pitts.). Excursions in Music (Detroit); w. Detroit Women's Symph. for 10 yrs. as Cond.; on. Facs. of Dalcroze Schl. of Music, Univ. of Mich., Wayne State Univ., Interlochen Arts Acad. & Nat. Music Camp, Meadow Brook Schl. of Music, Carnegie Inst. of Pitts., Duquesne Univ.; currently Solo Viola w. Detroit Symph. Orch.; Cond. of Dearborn Orch.; Coordinator of Excursions in Music; Fac. of Wayne State Univ. Detroit. Has recorded w. many major orchs. Mbrships: Am. Fed. Musicians (locals 802, 5, 60); Mich. Orch. Assn.; State String Chmn., Mich. Music Tchrs. Assn. Hobbies: Tennis; Swimming, etc. Mgmt: Lee Jon Assocs., 18662 Fairfield Ave., Detroit, MI 48221, USA. 16.

GORDON, Peter Jon, b. 6 Feb. 1946, NYC, USA. French Horn Player. Educ: BMus, Ind. Univ., 1967. Debut: Recital w. parents Detroit, 1972. Career incl: Mbr. of Orch. for num. touring Opera & Ballet Cos.; 2nd Horn, Met. Opera Orch., 1971, 72, 73; Chmb. musician w. var. grps., NYC & Portland, Orc.; Mbr.; New Amsterdam Ensemble, NYC, 1971-76; currently 2nd Horn, Boston Symph. Orch.; Mbr., var. contemporary orchs. & grps. inclng. Joel Kaye's Neophonic orch., 1972-76, & Gil Evans Orch. 1974-76; perfs. in other grps. w. major artists. Recordings (as grp. mbr.) incl: Gil Evans plays Jimi Hendrix; Phil Woods Album. Mbrships: incl: Phi Eta Sigma; Phi Mu Alpha Sinfonia. Hobbies: Photography; Table Tennis; Yoga. Mgmt: Leejon Assoc., Detroit. Address: 300 Riverside Drive, NY, USA.

GORDON, Stewart Lynell, b. 28 Aug. 1930, Olathe, Kan., USA. Pianist; University Professor & Administrator. Educ: Dip., State Conserv. of the Saar; BA, 1953, MA, 1954, Univ. of Kan.; D Mus A, Univ. of Rochester, 1965. Career: tour of USA, Middle E, Can. & Europe; Fndr., currently Dir., Univ. of Md. Int. Piano & Fest. & Competition; Chmn., Piano Div., Univ. of Md., 1965-. Recordings: Schubert Sonata Op. 143& German Dances; Schumann Sonata Op. 11; complete Rakhmaninov Preludes. Mbrships: Phi Beta Kappa; Phi Kappa Lambda; Music Tchrs. Nat. Assn.; Keyboard Ed., Am. Music Tchr. Hobby: Bulldogs. Address: Music Dept., Univ. of Md., College Park, MD 20742, USA.

GOREN, Eli Alexander, b. 23 Jan. 1923, Vienna, Austria. Violinist; Violist; Teacher; Conductor. Educ: Grad., Jerusalem Acad. of Music. m. Doreen Stanfield, 1 s., 1 d. Debut: Vienna, Austria, 1931. Career: Ldr., London Mozart Players, 1952-59, BBC Symph. Orch., 1968-; Mbr., Melos Ensemble, 1951-56; Soloist & Ldr., Allegri Quartet, 1953-77; Prof., RNCM, GSM; Dir. & Cond.; num. concerts, TV & radio apps. Num. recordings as Ldr. of Allegri Quartet, Melos Ensemble, etc. Contbr. to: British Book News. Mbr., ISM. Recip. FGSM, 1971. Address: 11 Lyndhurst Gdns., Finchley, London N3 1TA, UK. 14.

GORNER, Hans-Georg, b. 23 Apr. 1908, Niederschönhausen, Berlin, Germany. University Professor; Composer; Organist. Educ: Berlin Music Inst.; Berlin Univ. m. Lili

Groeck. Debut: Organist, St. Marien Ch., Berlin, 1932. Career incl: Schl. music tchr.; Choir ldr., Organist, St. Nicolai Ch.; City Ch. Music Dir. for Berlin Provost; Choir Dir. Deutschlandsender Radio Stn.; Prof. of Composition, State Inst. of Music, HaleSaale; currently Prof., Humboldt Univ., Berlin. Compositions incl: Great Mass for soli, choir & orch.; 2 symphs.; piano concerto; violin concerto; 4 orchl. suites, etc. Recordings of var. works on Eterna label. Mbrship: Composer's Soc., Berlin. Hons. incl: Fritz-Reuter Prize, 1956; Pestalozzi Medal, 1963. Address: Keleine Homeyer-Str. 6, DDR 111 Berlin, German Dem. Repub.

GORR, Rita. Operatic Mezzo-soprano. Debuts: as Frika, Die Walküre, Theatre Royal, Antwerp, 1949; as Amneris, Aida, Metrop. Opera, NYC, 1962. Career incl: app. as Frika, Die Walküre, Bayreuth Fest., Covent Gdn.; Lyric Opera, Chgo. Recordings: EMI; RCA; Epic Mgmt: S A Gorlinsky Ltd., 35 Dover St., London W1, UK. 2.

GORSKI, Paul S, b. 9 Aug. 1941, Chicago, Ill., USA. Violinist; Concertmaster. Educ: BA, 1965, MMus, 1966, Univ. of Ill.; Study w. Paul Rolland, Roman Totenberg. m. Letia Ferlen, 1 s. Career: Staff, Univ. of Ill., 1965; Asst. Concertmaster/Concertmaster, Santa Fe Opera, 1963-; Asst. Concertmaster, New Orleans Phil., 1967-73, Assoc. Concertmaster, 1973-; Concertmaster, NC Symph. Address: Rt. 8, Box 207, Raleigh, NC 27612, USA. 2.

GORTON, James Allen, b. 13 Feb. 1947, Corpus Christi, Texas, USA. Oboist; Associate Principal Oboe. Educ: BM, Eastman Schl. of Music, Univ. of Rochester, NY, 1969; Perfs. Cert., ibid. Pvte. oboe study w. Charles Morris, Louis Rosenblatt, John deLancie, Robert Sprenkle. m. Karen McDaniel, 1 d., 1 s. Career: 2nd oboe, Rochester Phil. Orch., 1966-69; 1st oboe, Rochester Chmbr. Orch., 1967-69; Mbr., Mid-Am. Woodwind Quintet, 1969-71; New Pitts. Quintet, 1972-; Assoc. Prin. Oboe, Pitts. Symph. Orch., 1971-; Prin. Oboe, Pittsburgh Opera-Ballet Orch., 1971-; Fac., Carnegie-Mellon Univ., Pitts., Pa., 1973-76; Fac., Carlow Coll., Pitts., Pa., 1971-. Hons: Rochester Nat. Scholar, 1965-69. Address: 1288 Girard Rd., Pitts., Pa 15227, USA. 2.

GORTON, Thomas Arthur, b. 12 Mar. 1910, Oneida, NY., USA. Composer; Conductor; Pianist. Educ: BM, 1932, MM, 1935, PhD, 1947, Eastman Schl. of Music, Univ. of Rochester, m. Catherine Urlass, 1 d. Career: Instr., Muic, Riverside Jr. Coll., 1935-37; Chmn., Piano Dept., Memphis Coll. of Music, 1937-38; Asst. Prof., Music Univ. of Tex., 1938-46; Dir., Schl. of Music, Ohio Univ., 1947-50; Dean, Schl. of Fine Arts, Univ. of Kan., 1950-75; Prof. of Music History, 1975-77; Dean & Prof. Emeritus, 1977-; Piano Soloist Rochester Civic Orch., Houston Symph., St. Louis Symph. Compositions: Concertino for Piano & Orch., Symph. No. 1, Legend of Sleepy Hollow (symph. suite). Variations & Fugue on a Welsh Tune. Mbrships: Past Pres., Past Commn. on Curricula Chmn. & Cons., Nat. Assn. of Schls. of Music; Past Chmn., Music Execs. in State Univs.; Int. Coun. of Fine Arts Deans. Hobbies: Genealogy; Chess; Bridge. Address: 831 Ill. Ave., Lawrence, KS, USA. 2.

GORTVA, Iren, b. 3 May 1939, Csanadapaca, Hungary. Opera Singer; Soloist. Educ: Conserv. div., 1 d. Debut: Verdi's Masked Ball, Ulrica, 1971. Career: Counod - Faust (Marta); Verdi - Trovatore (Azucena); Nicolai - The Merry Wives of Windsor (Mrs. Reich); on stage, Verdi - Falstaff (Quickly); on TV & Radio, Mozart - Figaro's Marriage (Marcellina); on TV, Puccini - Il Trittico, Kodaly - Székely Fonó (Housewife), Tchaikovsky - Onegin (Olga). Hobbies: Sun bathing; Pop music. Address: Nemzeti Szinhaz, Dea'k Ferenc u. 12, Szeged, Hungary.

GORVIN, Carl, b. 15 June 1912, Hermannstadt, Translyvania. Conductor. Educ: studied music & jurisprudence, Bucharest; Lic. of law. m. Edith Janura, 3 s., 1 d. Debut: 1934. Career: Musical Dir., Deutsches Landestheater in Rumänien; Conductor, var. theatres, Germany; Conductor, Deutsche Staatsoper Berlin & Gen. Musical Dir., Kaiserslautern; Prof., Hd., opera dept., Staatliche Hochschule für Musik & Theater, Hanover, 1968-; Guest Conductor, var. orchs.; Num. radio broadcasts. Recordings, particularly of old music, Archivproduktion, Deutsche Grammophone Gesellschaft. Recip., Grand Prix de Disque, 1956. Address: Wöhlerstr. 9, 3 Hanover, German Fed. Repub.

GÓRZYNSKI, Zdzislaw, b. 23 Sept. 1895, Cracow, Poland. Conductor. Educ: Cracow Conserv.; Hochschule für Musik, Vienna, Austria. m. Irena Lorenc-Gorzynska, 1 d. Debut: Cracow. Career: Concerts & Opera stages in Paris, Berlin, Dresden, Leipzig, Moscow, Kiev, Amsterdam, The Hague, Belgrade, Zagreb, Vienna, Warsaw, Prague, Budapest & Sofia; Biographical film, Polish TV; prog. on Polish radio. Compositions: Songs & small pieces. Recordings: Il Trovatore; Faust (Verdi); La Boheme; Waltzes by Johann Strauss, Waldteufel, Sibelius & Lehar; Polish operas. Mbr. of var. profl. assns. Hons. incl: Gold Cross, & num. other medals of Polish People's Repub. Hobby: Record Collecting. Address: Elektoralna 4/6 m. 18, Warsaw, Poland.

GOSLICH, Siegfried, b. 7 Nov. 1911, Stettin, Germany. Conductor; Educ: Akademisches Gymnasium, Vienna; PhD, Univ. & State Music Inst., Berlin. m. Dr. Maria Ottich, 3 s. Career: Radio Stn. Music Dir., Weimar, 1945-48; Hd. Cond. of Radio Bremen, 1948-; Dir., Music Dept., Bayerischer Rundfunk, Munich, 1961-; Guest Dir. in var. countries; Prof. of State Music Inst., Munich, 1964; Chmn. of Audio-Grp., Internationales Musikzentrum, Vienna. Recordings: Orbis, Publs: Geschichte der deutschen romantischen Opera, 1937, '74; Funkprogramm und Musica viva, 1961; Musik im Rundfund, 1971; Technik des Dirigierens, 1975; Ed. (w. others) 50 Jahre Musik im Hörfunk, Wien, 1973; Contbr. to: Die Musik in Geschichte und Gegenwart; Riemann, Musiklexikon; Grove's Dictionary. Mbrships: ISMC; Gesellschaft für Musikforschung. Groves Dictionary of Music & Musicians. Hobbies: Acoustics; Electronic Music. Address: Johann Biersack-Str., 8133 Feldafing 1Obb., German Fed. Repub. 23, 30.

GOSSETT, Philip, b. 27 Sept. 1941, Musicologist. Educ: BA, Amherst Coll., 1963; MFA, 1965, PhD, 1970, Princeton Univ. m., 2 c. Career: Asst. in Instruction, Princeton Univ., 1964-65; Asst. Prof., 1968-73, Assoc. Prof., 1973-77, Prof., 1977-, Univ. of Chgo., Vis. Assoc. Prof., Columbia Univ., Spring, 1975. Publs. incl: Treatise on Harmony by Jean-Phillipe Rameau (transl.), 1971. Contbr. to: musicol. jrnls.; musical encys. (Grove's, Ricordi). Mbrships. incl: Bd. of Dirs., 1974-76, Ed. Bd., Jrnl., 1972-, Am. Musicol. Soc.; Ed. Bd., 19th Century Music, 1977-; Ed. Bd., Opera Omnia di Gioachino Rossini; Ed. Bd., The Works of Guiseppe Verdi. Int. Musicol. Soc. Hons: acad. awards; Alfred Einstein Award, Am. Musicol. Soc., 1969. Address: 5509 S Kenwood Ave., Chicago, IL 60637, USA.

GOSTOMSKI, Henryk, b. 4 Dec. 1929, Sierakowice, Poland. Conductor. Educ: Cond. Dip., Higher Schl. of Music. m., 3 children. Debut: 1955. Career: Cond. at num. concert halls; Prof., Higher Schl. of Music; Dean of Music Tchng. Mbr., Assn. of Polish Musicians. Hobbies: Sport; Cars. Address: 80-410 Gdansk, Baczynskiego St. 2 m 45, Poland. 3.

GOTKOVSKY, Nell, b. France. Violinist. Educ: Conserv. nat. Superieur de Paris. m. Daniel Odier. Debut: London. Career: apps. w. major orchs. throughout the world; duo w. brother Ivar Gotkovsky (piano). Recorded for RCA. Address: 9 Grande rue, 78610 Auffargis, France.

GOTOVAC, Jakov, b. 11 Oct. 1895, Split, Yugoslavia. Composer; Conductor. Educ: Univ. of Zagreb (law), 1914-19; music study in Split, Vienna 1920-21. m. Katja Mitrović (dec.), 1 s., 2 d. Debut: w. mixed choir, Split, 1918. Career: Opera Cond., Croatian Nat. Theatre Zagreb, 1923-58. Compositions: opera - Dubravka; Morano; Ero the Joker; Kamenik (The Quarry); Petar Svacić; Dalmaro; Mila Gijsalića; Gjerdan (The Necklace); Stanac; 6 Symphonic Works inclng: Symphonic Reel; Oraci (The Ploughmen); Guslar (The National Bard); var. choral & vocal works, etc. Mbrship: Assn. of Croatian Composers, Zagreb. Recip. var. hons. Address: Pierottijeva 4/11, 41000 Zagreb, Yugoslavia.

GOTTHOFFER, Catherine Johnk, b. 12 Apr. 1923, Kowa, Kan., USA. Harpist; Educator. Educ: Dip. in Harp., Juilliard Schl. Music. m. Robert Gotthoffer, 1 s., 1 d. Career: Solo Harpist, Dallas Symph. Orch. & Metro-Goldwyn-Mayer Studios Orch.; Recoreings, cinema & TV films; Solo Perfs., Musical Arts Soc., la Jolla, Ojai Festival, Music Guild Series, Monday Evening Concerts, Calif. Chamber Symph. & the Inglewood Burbank, Highland Park, Santa Monica & Downey Symph. Orch.; Fac. Calif., Inst. Arts. Pres., Am. Harp Soc. Hobbies: Sailing; Golf. Address: 43748 N Waddington Ave., Lancalster, CA 93534, USA.

GOTTI, Tito, b. 6 July 1927, Bologna, Italy. Orchestral Conductor; Musicologist; Teacher. Educ: Dips. in Piano, Conserv., Milan, 1956; Choral Music & Choir Condng., Conserv. Bologna, 1956; Orchl. Condng., Hochschule für Music, Vienna, 1960; Conserv. Bologna (Comp.), 1961. m. Brigitte Pasquet. Debut: Teator Commuale, Bologna, 1960. Career: Cond. of operas by Gluck, Verdi, Maderna, Belli, Gabrielli, Rossini, Gretry, Weill; Apps. in Italy, Switz., France, Poland, Czech. & Germany; Broacasts with Radio Televisone Italiana; Radio Svizzera Italiana & Radio Suisse Romande. Tchr., choral comp. & cond., Bologna Conserv., 1961-. Comps: Transcriptions of Bolognese Baroque music. Recordings incl: Les Grandes Heures de S. Petronio de Bologna; 6 Concertos Italiens pour Trompette & Orch.; Paer, Concerto per organo & orch; Colonna, Masses, Pslams. Publs. incl: Guida all'analisi della polifonie vocale, 1962; Spiriti della musica in Emilia e Romagna in L'Emilia-Romagna, 1974. Contbr. to: Nuova Rivista Musicale Italiana Quaderni dell'Instituto de Studi Verdiani; Educazione Musicale. Hobbies: Railways; Visual Arts. Address: Via Sabbioni 1, 40136 Bologna, Italy.

GOTTLIEB, Jay Mitchell, b. 23 Oct. 1948, Brooklyn, NY, USA. Pianist; Composer. Educ. incls: BA, Hunter Coll., CUNY, 1970; MA, Harvard Univ., 1972; Dartmouth Coll., Juilliard Schl.; Chatham Square Music Schl.; Cert., Conserv. of Music, Fontainebleau, France. Debut: NY, 1966. Career: TV & radio apps., USA, Italy, France; Soloist w. Boston Symph., Orch. della RAI (Turin), Ars Nova & Itinéraire (Paris); ORTF (Paris); Chmbr. Music Recitals & Concerts, USA, Bermuda, France; Fac. Mbr., Hunter Coll., CUNY, 1970, Harvard Univ., 1971-75. Comps: Synchronisms for Two Percussionists & Tape; Sonata for Violin & Piano. Recordings: Trois Chants de Médée; Trois Contes de l'honorable fleur; Armande Altai. Publs: Ed., Appello, 1978. Mbrships: ASCAP; Phi Beta Kappa. Recip. num. hons. Hobbies: Theatre; Cinema; Dance; Reading; Art Exhibitions; Travel. Mgmt: Gilles Daziano, American Embassy, Paris. Address: 484 W 43rd St., Apt. 3M, NY, NY 10036, USA. 29.

GOTTSCHALK, Arthur William, b. 14 Mar. 1952, San Diego, Calif., USA. Composer; Professor. Educ: BMus, MA, DMA, Univ. of Mich. Career: Prof. of Music & Co-Dir., Electronic Music Studio, Rice Univ. Comps. incl: Children of the Night (Wind Quintet); Phases (Flute duet); Variants II (Flute); Night Play (2 amplified basses, 2 percussion); Substructures (Tuba Ensemble); Roulades (Symph. Band); Night Flight (Piano); Communiqué (Orch.); Dark Songs (mezzo-soprano & Chamber Orch.); Symph. for Wind & Percussion. Recording: Substructures. Contbr. to Ann Arbor Art Fare Mag. Mbrships: ASCAP; Am. Soc. of Univ. Comps.; num. hons. Hobbies: Playing Trombone; Community Orchs.; Jazz Bands. Address: 7702 Marinette Rd., Houston, TX 77074, USA.

GOUBAULT, Christian, b. 21 Feb. 1938, Thouars, France. Professor; Music Critic. Educ: Dr., Univ. of Paris. m. Michelle Damestoy, 2 s. Career: Prof., École Normale de Rouen; Music Critic, Figaro-Paris Normandie, 1970-. Publs: La Décentralisation de l'art lyrique (1830-1900), 1976; Boieldieu et la Musique à Rouen au XIXe siecle, 1978; La Musique, le public et les acteurs au Théâtre des Arts de Rouen (1770-1914), 1979. Contbr. to: Le Figaro-Paris-Normandie; Bulletin des Amis de Flaubert; Musiciens et Musique en Normandie. Mbrships: Sociète Française de Musicologie; Société des Amis de Flaubert; Association Internationale des Docteurs de l'Université de Paris. Hobby: Travel. Address: 5, rue des Canadiens, 76420 Bihorel, France.

GOÜIN, Isabel, b. 8 Mar. 1904, Paris, France. Librarian; Curator. Educ: studied piano, harmony, counterpoint & fuque, partly at Conserv. Nat. Supérieur de Musique de Paris. m. Henri Goüin (dec.), 2 d. Career: fndr. w. husband of the Fondation Royaumont pour le progrès des Sciences de l'homme, 1964; now hon. pres., ibid.; Curator, Bibliothéque musicale François Lang (Abbaye de Royaumont), Fnded. by her brother, the pianist Francois Lang. Mbrships: Int. Assn. of Musical Libs.; Société française de Musicologie; Assn. des Amis de l'Orgue. Hobby: Music. Address: Abbaye de Royaumont, 95270 Asnieres-sur-Oise, France; 148 bis, rue de Longchamp, 75116 Paris, France.

GOUIN, Pierre, b. 22 May 1947, Pierreville, PQ., Canada. Composer; Arranger; Pianist; Conductor; Teacher. Educ: BA, Univ. Laval; Mus M, Univ. of Montreal; Electronic music study, McGill Univ. Former cond. Shakespearian Festival Theatre, Stratford, Ont. Compositions: Mobile 1970; Monochromie, 1971; Phoebe, 1973; Galapagos, 1974; David & Goliath, 1974. Mbrship: Assoc., Canadian Assn. of Publrs. Authors & Composers. Contbr. to: Le Musicien Educateur (publ. of Fedn. of Assns. of Music Educators of Quebec). Recip. Canadian Music Prize, Fndn. des Amis de l'Art, Montreal, 1970. Hobby: Photography. Address: 4096 Ave. Laval, Montreal, PQ., Canada.

GOULD, Coral Lydia, b. 7 July 1937, Burton upon Trent, UK. Teacher of Music (solo singing); Conductor; Soprano. Educ: Birmingham Coll. of Educ.; LRAM; LTCL; ARCM. m. John Gould. Career: Secondary Schl. Tchr., Schl. of St. Malry & St. Anne, Abbots Bromley; Cond., Musical Dir., of Amateur Operatics, Burton/Derby; Cond., Coral Gould Singers; Radio app. Contbr. to: Burton Daily Mail. Mbrships: ISM Committee, Derby Centre; BFMF Accomp. Mbr. Hons: w. Coral Gould Singers, Best Choral Entry Derby Music Fest., 1977, '78, joint 79, Leamington Brownhills & Burton Music est., 1979. Hobby: Cookery. Address: Warren Farm Grange, Walton upon Trent, nr. Burton upon Trent DE12 8NB, UK.

GOULD, Eleanor Diane, b. Brooklyn, NY, USA. Violist; Teacher; Contralto. Educ: B Mus, Univ. of Ill.; MFA, Carnegie-

Mellon Univ., DMA, cand., Univ. of Cinn.-Coll.-Conserv. of Music; Mannes Coll. of Music; Mozarteum, Salzburg, Austria. Career: Violist w. Halifax Symph., Atlanta Symph., Cinn. Symph.; Asst. Prof. of Music, Northern Mich. Univ., Berea Coll., LI. Univ., Brooklyn, Music Schl.; Var. freelance orchl. & small ensemble perf.; Cond., Berea Coll. Orch. & Berea Youth Orch.; Ch. choir perf. & direction. Mbrships: AMS; CMS; ASTA; ASOL; ACMP; AF. of M. Hobbies: Chamber Music. Address: 18 West 70 St., NY, NY 10023, USA.

GOULD, Glenn, b. 1932, Canada. Pianist. Educ: Toronto Royal Conserv. Debut: USA, 1955. Career: European Tour, 1957; 1st N Am. pianist invited to tour USSR; wide repertoire from 16th Century keyboard music to modern jazz.

GOULD, James F, b. 5 Apr. 1917, Ark. City, Kans., USA. University Professor; Professional Performer on Trombone & Viola. Educ: B Mus., Wichita (Kans.) State Univ.; M Mus. & DMA., Univ. of So. Calif. m. Imogene Gifford, 1 s., 1 d. Career: Radio studio musician, 3 yrs.; Soloist & Perf., 4 yrs. during WWII, w. US Army Band, Wash., DC.; Prin. Trombone, Wichita Symph. (While tchng. at Wichita State Univ.), 18 yrs.; Prin. Viola, Flagstaff Symph., 8 yrs.; Mbr., N Ariz. Univ. Fac. Str. Quartet; Has served as both Prin. Trombone & Assoc. Prin. Violist, Flagstaff Summer Fest. Orch. (Izler Trombone & Music Hist. & Lit., N. Ariz. Univ., 1966-. Contbr. to var. music jrnls. Mbrships: MENC; NACWPI; Ariz. Music Educators. Hons: Naftzger Award, Wichita, Kans., 1945; Conn (Instr. Co.) 'Album of Stars'. Hobbies: Cabinetry; Italian cooking; Landscaping. Address: 3703 N. Grandview Dr., Flagstaff, AZ 86001, USA.

GOULD, John Leslie, b. 6 Sept. 1940, London, UK. Musician (Violin & Viola). Educ: Dip. in Music, Sydney Conservatorium, Aust. m. Jonty Whitehead. Debut: Wigmore Hall, London, UK. Career: Soloist & Chmbr. Music Perf., Aust. Broadcasting Commission; Prin. Viola, London Symph. Orch.; Mbr., Carl Pini Str. Quartet. w. Carl Pini Quartet. Hobbies: Sport; Chess; Gardening. Address: 2 Protea Ave., Coronmandel Valley, S Australia.

GOULD, Morton, b. 10 Dec. 1913, Richmond Hill, NY, USA. Composer; Conductor; Pianist. Educ: studied piano w. Joseph Kardos & Abby Whiteside, Inst. of Musical Art; studied theory & composition w. Dr. Vincent Jones. m. Shirley Bank, 2 s., 2 d. Career: has made radio & TV broadcasts, films & recordings; Guest Cond. or Soloist w. symph. orchs. thru'out USA & abroad. Compositions incl: Spirituals for Orchestra; Interplay; Latin American Symphonette; Fall River Legend; American Salute; Venice, Vivaldi Galley, Jekyll & Hyde Variations; Soundings; music for TV & film; ballets; musical comedy. Recordings have been made of most works by num. conds., perfs. & orchs.; has recorded as Cond. & Soloist. Mbrships: Bd. of Dirs., ASCAP; Am. Symph. Orch. League; Am. Music Center. Recip. of num. awards inclng. Grammy for Best Classical Recording, as Cond., Chgo. Symph., 1966. Hobby: Model Railroading. Address: c/o G Schirmer, Music Publrs., NY, USA. 2, 4.

GOULD, Murray Joseph, b. 4 June 1932, Paris, France. Violinist; Music Theorist. Educ: BMus, 1956, MMus, 1958, Manhattan Schl. of Music; Grad. studies, Queens Coll., CUNY, 1963-66; PhD, NY Univ., 1973. m. child. Career incls: Instructor in Music, Univ. Coll. & Rsch. Assoc., Inst. for Computer Rsch. in Humanities, NY Univ., 1968-70; Asst. Prof. Music, Univ. of Md., 1970-76; num. perfs. as orchl. violinist & chmbr. musician, 1957-68; perfs. w. Md. Trio & Chmbr. Ensemble, 1970-76. Comps. incL: Solo Sonata for Flute, 1975. Publs. incl: Schenker's Theory in the World of Teacher & Student, 1975; Ed., Contemporary Music Newsletter. Contbr. to books & profl. jrnls. Mbr. profl. assns. Recip., var. grants & awards. Address: 12101 Dove Circle, Laurel, MD 20810, USA.

GOULD, Peter Philip William, b. 12 May 1948, Swinton, Lancs., UK. Musical Director; Organist; Composer. Educ: Royal Manchester Coll. of Music (now Royal Northern Coll. of Music); ARMCM. m. Gillian Sandra Gould, 1 d. Career: Accomp., cabaret & Theate shows throughout GB; Ldr., Darren Gould Trio, res. grp.; Gallop Inn, Harrogate, Yorks; Freelance comp. & promotion; Accomp. & Musical Dir. of Salford's 1st Pub. Theatre. Recordings: Accomp. on demonstration tapes. Mbrships: ISM; Musicians Union. Hons: Edward Hecht Prize for Comp., 1969; Mrs. Leo Grinden Prize for Comp., 1970. Hobby: Yoga; Reading Sci. fiction. Address: 81 Partington Lane, Swinton, Manchester, M27 3NS UK.

GOULD, Raymond, b. 14 May 1922, Hull, Yorks., UK. Concert Pianist & Organist; Organist & Choirmaster; Teacher; Composer; Arranger. Educ: ARCM., 1946; Lic., Royal Conserv. of Music, Toronto, Ont., Can., & Univ. of Toronto Dip., 1950; ACCO., 1958; FRCCO., 1959; m. Marion G C Gould, 2 s., 1 d. Career: App. on Pick The Stars, Can. TV; Piano

Broadcasts on CBC Radio, & CKEY Radio, Toronto. Compositions: Listen Here, We Are Alive & Well; Let Us Sing Noel; The Holy Star; 4 Original Canadian Carols; 4 More Original Canadian Carols; Live Live; Praise the Master of the Universe; Hymn to the Universe; My Canada; Christmas is Here Again (also recorded). Recordings: Dubois, The Seven Last Words of Christ; A Christmas Wish. Mbrships: Toronto Musicians' Assn.; Royal Can. Coll. of Organists. Hons: Winner, Etobicoke Song Competition, 1967; Listen Here, We Are Alive & Well chosen as all-Can. Theme Song, United Ch. of Can. Address: 10 Mitre Pl., Weston, Ont., Can. M9R 3C4.

GOULD, Ronald John, b. 6 May 1911, Sutton Coldfield, Warwicks., UK. Musician; Violist. Educ: Studied Chmbr. Music w. Johann Hock; Viola w. Lena Wood; Birmingham Schl. of Music; LRAM; ARCM. m. Isabell agould, 1 s., 1 d. Career: W. City of Birmingham Symph. Orch., 1946-56; BBC Northern Symph. Orch., 1956-66; Tchr. many yrs. in Manchester, Midlands & Yorks; Presently on staff of Huddersfield Polytechnic & N Yorks. Educ. Auth. Mbr. ISM. Address: 12 Fell View, Embsay, Nr. Skipton BD23 6RY, Yorks., UK.

GOURLAY, Ian, b. Wishaw, Lanrks., UK. Composer; Arranger; Musical Director. Educ: Wishaw HS. m. Doris Anderson, 1 s., 1 d. Career: Approx. 4000 broadcasts as saxophonist, clarinetist, vocalist, dpty. cond., BBC Scottish Variety Orch.; After 1961, Composer, Arranger, Music Assoc.; Musical Dir., num. radio, TV shows. Compositions incl: As Long as the Sun Shines; Para Handy Polka; Marching thro the Heather, The Gathering of the Clans; My Song; The Royal Mile; Var. signature tunes for radio & TV; Scores for 4 consecutive Glasgow Citizens Theatre Pantomimes. Recordings: As Mus. Dir., num., LPS & singles, w. singers inclng. Alas dair Gillies, Moira Anderson, Bill McCue, Helen McArthur, etc. Address: Dorian, 4a Dundonald Rd., Glasgow, UK. 3.

GOVICH, Bruce Michael, b. 15 Oct. 1930, Lorain, Ohio, USA. Associate Professor. Educ: BMus. Ed., Baldwin-Wallace Conserv., Berea, Ohio, 1956-; M Mus. in Voice, Univ. of Ill., Urbana, Ill., 1958; DMA, ibid., 1967; additional study at Tex. Christian Univ. w. Artur Faguy-Coté; Voice w. Clenn Schnittke, Thomas Bellovich, Burton Garlinghouse, Bruce Foote; Opera w. Ludwig Zirner, Hans Buech; Accomp. & style w. George Reeves. m. Marilyn Sue Green, 3 s. Debut: Severence Hall, Cleveland, Ohio. Career: Lake Erie Opera Theatre, Cleveland Orch. Many radio & TV Appearances as individual solist. Recordings: appears on a number of Univ. of Ill. Recordings inclng. premiers of Meyerowitz 'Esther' & Krenek's 'Belltower', Contbr. to Am. Music Tchr., Mbr., profl. orgs. Hons: incl: Opera Award, Univ. of Ill, 1957; Grad. Fellowships in Voice & Choral Music, ibid., 1957-59; perfs. Hons. Award, 1960; Pi Kappa Lambda, 1959. Hobbies: Philatelics; Athletics, etc. Address: 410 East Keith, Norman, OK 73069, USA.

GOWER, Christopher Stainton, b. 15 Mar. 1939, High Wycombe, UK. Cathedral Organist. Educ: MA, Magdalen Coll., Oxford; FRCO; Coll. of Ch. Musicians, Wash., DC, USA, 1965. m. Sylvia Marina Trude, 1 d., 1 s. Career: Asst. Organist, Exeter Cathedral, 1961-69; Lectr., Univ. of Exeter, 1967-69; Organist & Master of Choristers, Portsmouth Cathedral, 1969-77; Master of the Music, Peterborough Cathedral, 1977-. Recordings: Tomkims Ch. Music w. Magdalen College Choir, Oxford & other ch. music w. Exeter Cath. Choir & Portsmouth Cath. Choir. Mbrships: RCO; Royal Musician Assn.; ISM; Ch. Music Soc. Hons: Mackinnon Organ Schlrship., Magdalen Coll., Oxford; RH. Lane Mem. Schlrship., Coll. of Ch. Musicians, Wash., DC., USA, 1965. Hobbies: Railway & Cricketing hist. Address: The Norman Hall Precincts, Peterborough, PE 1 1XX, UK.

GRABIE, Monica Helen, b. 4 Apr. 1950, New York, NY, USA. Musicologist. Educ: BA, French & Music; MA, Univ. m. Michael Cohn, 1 c. Career: Piano Recital, Radio Stn. WNYC, USA, 1969. Publs: Thematic Catalogue of the Published & Unpublished Works of Erik Satie (in progress). Contbr. to Current Musicol. Mbrships: Am. Musicol. Soc.; Phi Beta Kappa; Pi Delta Phi; Pi Kappa Lambda. Hobbies: Boating; Fishing; Sewing. Address: 392 Ft. Washington Ave., New York, NY 10033, USA.

GRABS, Manfred, b. 26 Feb. 1938, Meissen, Germany. Musicologist; Composer. Educ: Dip. Musicol.; studies comp. Career: Radio prod. on Musicol., GDR; Dir. Music Archives Art Acad. GDR; Ed. dir. Hans Eisler Publ. Company. Comps. incl: Piano concerto after Scarlatti, 1972; Two Intermezzi for Wind Quintet, 1976; Kerkaporta, Recital after St. Zweig and A. Rimbaud, 1976; Song cycles after texts by Lessing, Heine, Hoffmann w. Fallersleben, Kahlau w. o.; Choir music; Chmbr. music; Piano music. Mbrships: Assn. for Comp. and Musicologists, GDR. Publs: Complete Ed. of Hans Eisler's Works; Hans Eisler: material for the Dialetics of Music, re-ed., 1973; Problems of the

Eisler Editions, 1976. Contbr. to: var. profl. jrnls. Address: Wendenschlosstr. 454, DDR-117 Berlin, German Dem. Repub.

GRADENWITZ, Peter Werner Emanuel, b. 24 Jan. 1910, Berlin, Germany. Musicologist. Educ: Studies at Univs. of Berlin, Freiburg/Br., Prague & London Polytechnic; PhD (musicology) German Univ. of Prague; comp. studies w. Julius Weismann, Joseph Rufer. etc. m. Ursula Mayer-Reinach, 1 d. Career: Lectr. at European and Am. Univs.; Lectr. in musicology, Tel Aviv Univ., 1968-76; Fndr. & Ed.-Dir. of Israeli Music Pubs. Ltd. Comps. incl: symph. & chmbr. music; ed. of newly discovered works by Salomone Rossi, Johann Stamitz, Karl Stamitz, Anton Stamitz, Franz Schubert. Publs. incl: Johann Stamitz, Das Leben, 1936; Johann Stamitz, Life & Works, 1979; The music of Israel, 1949, ibid. 2nd ed., 1979; Music & Musicians in Israel, 1978. Mbrships: Int. Musicol. Soc.; Israeli Sect. of Int. Music Coun. Hons: Int. Critics' Prize, Salzburg, 1971; Golden Insignia of Salzburg, 1978. Hobbies: Mountain tours. Address: PO Box 6011, Tel Aviv, 61060, Israel.

GRAEME, Peter, b. 17 Apr. 1921, Petersfield, UK. Freelance Player & Teacher of the Oboe. Educ: Studied w. Leon Goossens; Open Schlrship., RCM, 1938. m. Inge Anderl, 1 s., 3 d. Career incls: 1st Oboe, Boyd Neel's Philomusica, Goldsbrough Chmbr. Orch., Engl. Chmbr. Orch. (current); Mbr., Melos Ensemble of London; Prof., RCM, 1949-; Tchr., Ropyal Northern Coll. of Music, 1974-. Recordings incl: num. records w. Engl. Chmbr. Orch. inclng. Holst, Fugal Concerto for Flute & Oboe; sev. records w. Melos Ensemble. Mbrships: Musicians Union; ISM. Hons. incl: Hon. ARCM, 1959. Address: 85 Elgin Cres., London W11 2JF, UK.

GRAF, Erich Louis, b. 11 Apr. 1948, Ann Arbor, Mich., USA. Concert Flautist; Teacher. Educ: Univ. Mich., 1966-67; Summer Fest., Nice, France, 1968-69; BS, Juilliard, M Mus, ibid., 1974. Debut: Recital, NY Flute Club, 1973. Career incls: Flautist, Aeolian Chmbr. Players, 1969-; Graf-Whiteside Flute Duo; Solo Flautist, Erick Hawkins Dance Co., 1974-; Solo Flautist, Stamford Symph. Orch., 1975-; Pvte. tchr.; Adj. fac. mbr., Bowdoin Coll., 1975-. Recordings incl: Voice of the Whale; Night of the Four Moons. Hobbies: Reading & Writing Poetry; Swimming. Mgmt: for Aeolian Chmbr. Players; Hally Beall Mgmt: for Graf-Whiteside Flute Duo: Alpert & Lichtenstein Mgmt. Address: 210 W 70th St. 311, NY, NY 10023, USA.

GRAF, Peter-Lukas, b. 5 Jan. 1929, Schlieren-Zürich, Switz. Flautist; Conductor. Educ: 1st Prize for Flute & Dip. for Conducting, Nat. Conserv., Paris, France. m. Agnette Schüler. Career: 1st Flautist, Winterthur Symph. Orch., & Swiss Fest. Orch., Lucerne, 1950-56; Cond., Opera House, Lucerne, 1961-66; Prof., Acad. of Music, Basel, 1973; has made concert apps. in Europe, S Am., Japan, Aust., USSR, & Iarael. Recordings: for Concert Hall Soc. (NY), Columbia, Disco (Zurich), Armida (Lucerne) & Claves (Thun). Hons: 1st Prize, Int. Music Award, Munich, 1953; Bablock Prize, H Cohen Music Award, London, 1958. Mgmt: Sec. Ursula Pfaehler, OB. Wart 150, CH-3600 Thun, Switz. Address: St. Alban-Rheinweg 76, CH-4052, Switz.

GRAF, Walter, b. 20 June 1903, St. Pölten, Lower Austria. Musicologist. Educ: Univ. of Vienna; Schl. of Music, Ludwak, Vienna. m. Dr. med. Margarete Holzen, 3 s., (1 dec.). Career: Lectr. on Comparative Musicol., Univ. of Vienna, 1952; Dir. Phonogram Archives, Acad. of Scis., 1957-71; Prof. of Comparative Musicol., Univ. of Vienna, 1963-73; Exec. Chmn., Commission for Sound Research, Austrian Acad. Sciences, 1972-. Over 1090 publs. Mbrships: Austrian Acad. of Scis. (Corres. Mbr., 1962; Chmn. of Committee for Sound Rsch.); Soc. for Publ. of Old Austrian Musical Works (VP to 1974); Österreich, Volksliedwerk (Sci. Commission). Hons: Cross 1st Class for Sci. & Art, 1968; Ehrenmedaille der Bundeshaupstadt Wien in Godl, 1978. Address: Linzerstrasse 412/8/6, Vienna A 1140, Austria. 30.

GRAFFMAN, Gary, b. 14 Oct. 1928, NYC, USa. Pianist. Educ: Curtis Inst. of Music, Phila.; Columbia Univ.; studied w. Vladimir Horowitz, NYC & Rudolf Serkin, Vt.m. Naomi Helfman. Debut: Soloist w. Phila. Symphonette, 1936. Career: Recitalist in major concert halls; has app. & recorded w. major orchs. thru'out world; tours incl. S. Am., India, Hong Kong, Aust., Africa, USSR & Japan; sometime Tchr., Phila. Musical Acad.; Jude for Leventritt Award competitions. Recordings incl: Beethoven's Piano Concerto No. 3 in C minor; Brahms' Piano Concerto No. 1 in D minor; The Virtuoso Liszt; Prokofiev's Piano Sonata No. 1 in D minor. Recip. of many hons. & awards inclng: Leventritt Award, 1949; Winner, 1st regular competition of Rachmaninoff Contests & Special Award from Rachmaninoff Fund, 1948. Mgmt: Arthur Judson Mgmt. Inc., 119 W. 57th St., NYC, NY 10019, USA.

GRAHAM, Alasdair, b. 19 Apr. 1934, Glasgow, Scotland, UK. Pianist; Teacher; Professor at Royal College of Music. Educ: B Mus. Edinburgh Univ.; LRAM; Dip., Vienna State Acad.; Hon. RCM. Debut: Wigmore Hall, 1958. Career: Apps. on TV & Radio; Tours incl: UK, Europe, India, Turkey & Aust. Rerdings: Schubert Sonata in B flat. Contbr. to Music & Musicians. Hon: Represented Scotland at Festival of Britain, 1951; hon. RCM, 1972. Harriet Cohen Commonwealth Medal, 1963. Address: 4 Camden Rd., London NW1, UK. 3.

GRAHAM, Colin, b. 22 Sept. 1931, Hove, Sussex, UK. Stage Director; Set & Lighting Designer; Artistic Director; Author. Educ: Pvte. study; Dip., RADA, London. Debut: Dir., Noye's Fludde, Engl. Opera Group, Aldeburgh Fest., 1958. Career: Artistic Dir., Engl. Opera Group, 1963-75; Artistic Dir., Aldeburgh Fest., 1969-; Artistic Dir., Engl. Music Theatre, 1975-; Dir. of Prodns., Engl. Nat. Opera, 1978-. Publs. incl: Libretti for the Golden Vanity (Britten); Penny for a Song (Bennett); New version of King Arthur (Purcell); Operetta, Not In Front of the Waiter, 1965. Contbr. to: Opera; Musical Times; The Oepras of Benjamin Britten. Hons: Orpheus Award, 1972; Churchill Fellowship, 1975. Hobbies: Motor cycles; Weight training; Rex Stout's Detection. Mgmt: London Mgmt. Address: c/o Engl. Nat. Opera, London Coliseum Theatre, London WC2, UK. 1, 13, 29.

GRAHAM, William Allen, b. 15 Mar. 1946, Pitts., Pa., USA. University Professor. Educ: BA in Music, 1968, MA in Educ., 1969, Stanford Univ.; D Musical Arts in Choral Cond., ibid., 1975. Career: Jr. High Schl. Tchr., Sunnyvale Schl. Dist., Calif., 1969-72; Chmbr. choir participant (Fellowship), Aspen Choral Inst., 1974, 75; Asst. Cond., Stanford Univ. Memorial Ch. Choir, 1973-75; currently Asst. Prof., Choral Music, Choral Cond., etc., Univ. of Tex. at Dallas. Mbrships: Am. Choral Dirs. Assn.; Tex. Music Educators Assn.; Coll. Music Soc.; Am. Musicol. Soc. Hons. incl: Outstanding Young Tchr., Sunnyvale, Calif., 1971. Hobbies: Musical Theatre Director; Swimming; Hiking; Reading. Address: co Univ. of Texas/Dallas, PO Box 688, Richardson, TX 75080, USA.

GRAHAM-JONES, Ian, b. 6 Sept. 1937, London, UK. Lecturer in Music. Educ: B Mus, London; RAM; LRAM; ARCM; Univ. London Inst. of Educ. m. Jean L McRea, 3 c. Career: Mbr., Engl. Consort of Viols., 1958-60; Music Tchr., Isle of Ely Educ. Comm., 1960-63; Dir., Cornwall Rural Music Schl., 1963-72; Dir., St. Mylor Festival of Music, 1964-71; Examiner, Assoc. Bd., 1972-76; Lectr., Dept. of Music, Chichester Coll. of Further Educ., 1972-; Tutor in Music & Cons. on reaarder for Open Univ. Contbr. to Making Music. Mbrshins; ISM; Viola de Gamba Soc. Hons. incl: Peter Latham Prize for Musicol., RAM, 1959. Hobbies: Sailing; Walking. Address: The Tilings, Creek End, Fishbourne, Chichester, Sussex, UK.

GRAHN, Ulf, b. 17 Jan. 1942, Solna, Sweden. Composer. Educ: Violin pedagog degree, Stockholms Musikpedagogiska Inst., 1968; MMus, Cath. Univ of Am.; studies in violin, viola, recorder, piano; comp. studies w. Hans Eklund. m. Barbro Elsa Margareta Dahlman. Debut: as a comp. w. the piece Pour Quatre on Swedish Radio, 1967. Career: Comps. for all medias; Fndr., Pres. & Music Dir., Contemporary Music Forum, Wash., DC; Lectr., Radio & Univs., USA; Works perfd. throughout world. Comps. incl: Snapshots for Piano (recorded); To Barbro; Alone for Flute; Pace, for flute & tape; Beautivul Thoughts, for cello; Hommage à Charles Ives for strings; Ancient Music, for piano & orch.; Concertino for piano & str. orch. Quartet No. 2, Musik fur oboe solo, etc. Num. recordings. Var. contbns. to jrnls. Mbr., profl. orgs., Sweden & USA. Hons: Pres., Wolf Trap Farm Park, 1976, '77; Swedish Inst. Athens, 1979; Grants from Swedish Govt.; Fndn. Sweden-Finland Prize, Stockholm Organ Days, 1973. Hobby: Photography. Address: Hagtornstunet 2, S181 48 Lidingo, Sweden.

GRALINSKI, Waldemar Jerzy, b. 11 Apr. 1946, Lódz, Poland. Violinst; Chamber Music Performer Teacher. Educ: Dip. w. mark of preferance-MA, Lódz Acad.of Music, 1969. M. Renata Gralinski (Nowak), 1 s. Debut: as soloist, 1969. Career: Asst. Lectr., 1972, Lectr., 1976, Lódz Acad.; concerts & fests., Poland, Czech., Netherlands, E & W Germany, Italy, Austria, Spain, France, Hungary, Switz. Has recorded for radio & TV. Mbr., Polish Assn. of Music Artists. Hons. incl: Gold Medal, Herbert von Karajan Fndn., 1970. Hobbies: Making string instruments; Photography. Address: ul Marchleskiego 76/20, Lódz, Poland.

GRAMENZ, Francis L, b. 5 Dec. 1944, Independence, Iowa, USA. Music Librarian. Educ: BMus (piano), Drake Univ.; MA (Musicology), Boston Univ.; MLS, Simmons Coll.; PhD program in Musicology, Boston Univ., in progress. m. Sarah Henn Gramenz. Career: Lectr. in Music History & Piano, Emmanuel Coll., 1973-76; Music Bibliographer, Mugar Memorial Library, Boston

Univ., 1973-78; Hd., Music Lib., Mugar Memorial Lib., ibid., 1979-. Publs: Telemann: 36 Fantaisies; Program Notes. Mbrships: Am. Musicol. Soc.; Mediaeval Acad. of Am.; Music Library Assn.; Int. Assn. of Music Libraries; Delta Phi Alpha; Beta Phi Mu. Address: 1401 Walnut St., Newton, MA 02161, USA.

GRANAT, Juan Wolfgang, b. 29 Nov. 1918, Karlsruhe, Germany. Viola Player. Educ: pvte. w. Rudolf Zwinkel. Dip., Master Schl. of Svecik & Marteau, Munich, Herma Studeny. Career: Prin. violist, Swiss Italian Broadcasting Orch.; Violist, Quartetto Monteceneri, 1939-40; Prin. violist sev. major Argentine Symph. Orchs., 1940-45; Prin. Violist, Havanna Phil. Orch. Violist, Cuban Chamber Music Soc., Havana, 1946-53 & Guest Artist, 1955, '57 & '58; Prin. Violist, Pro Arte Opera, Havana & Ballet Alicia Alonson, 1946-53; Prof. of Violin. Conservatorio Levy, Havana, & Nat. Conserv. of Mantanzas, Cuba, 1946-53; Violist, Mnpls. Symph., USA, 1954-56, Phila. Orch., 1956-, Robin Hood Dell Orch., 1958-; Prin. Violist, Reading Symph. & Lancaster Symph., 1965-, etc. Var. non commercial tapes & records of viola recitals. Records w. Phila. Orch. Mbrships: Viola Rsch. Soc.; Am. Fed. of Musicians, local 802 & 77. Hons: First Latin Am. Perf. of William Walton's Viola Concerto w. the Cordoba Symph., Argentina, TTeodoro Fuchs cond.; 1945; NY Madrigal Soc's Annual Town Hall Debut Award, 1957, etc. Address: 4738 Osage Ave., Philadelphia, PA 19143, USA.

GRANDI, Hans, b. 21 July 1904, Berlin, Germany. Musikpädagoge; Musicologist. Educ: Humboldt Univ. Berlin, 1931-3, 1947-9; PhD, dissertation - The Music in the Novels of Thomas Mann, 1952. m. Katharine Franke. Career: tchr; lectr; music advr.; Fndr., Ctrl. Symph. Concert for the Young in Berlin, 1956; music planner for Min. of Educ.; maker of educ. films & records; lectr. at num. educ. insts. Recordings: Records for schls: "Der Freischütz", 1968; "Lieder Instrumentalstücke", 1972; "Operette u. Musical", 1975; films: "Shostokovich 7th symph.", 1975; "The symph. orch.", 1975. Publs. incl: "Thomas Mann Musiziert"; Lehrbuch Musik, Klassen 1112. Contbr. to num. profl. jrnls. Hons: Hon. tchr. of the people, 1955; DDR service medal, 1970; Pin of hon., comp. union of German Dem. Repub., 1972; Dr. Theodor-Neubauer medal, 1974. Address: 1034 Berlin, Karl-Marx-Alee 139, German Dem. Repub.

GRANT, Clifford Scantlebury, b. Sydney, NSW, Aust. Upera Singer (Bass Batitone). Educ: Sydney Conservatoire. m. Jeanette Earle, 1 s., 2 d. Debut: da Sylva in Ernani, Sadlers Wells, 1966. Career: leading roles, Oedipus Rex, Peter Grimes, Magic Flute, Mma. Butterfly, Barber of Seville, Don Giovanni, Coronation of Poppea, Meistersingers, etc.; has appeared w. Engl. Nat. Opera & at Covent Gdn.; Guest apps. at Glyndebourne & W. Welsh Nat. Opera, also yearly in San Fran., 1966-; apps. w. all major Brit. orchs. Recordings: Marriage of Figaro; The Apostles (Elgar); Rhinegold; Rigoletto; Les Huguenots; Tosca; Don Giovanni. Hobbies: Oil painting; Breeding fish. Address: 45 Oakleigh Gdns., Whetstone, London N20, UK.

GRANT, William Parks, b. 4 Jan. 1910, Cleveland, Ohio, USA. Retired University Professor; Composer; Writer on Music; Music Editor. Educ: Dip. in Music Theory, Capital Univ., 1930; BMus, ibid., 1932; MA, Ohio State Univ., 1933; PhD, Eastman Schl. of Music, Univ. of Rochester, 1948. m. (1) Esther Folsom (dec.); (2) Paulette Deeson, 3 stepchildren. Career: Tchr. & Prof. of Music, 1934-51 & '53-74; Music Libn., 1951-52; Music Authenticator & Advsr. for New Standard Ency., 1957-; Ed. for Int. Gustav Mahler Soc., Vienna, 196566, 1970, '72-73. Comps. (publd.); Symphopny No. 2; Double-bass Concerto; 3 Night Poems for Str. Quartet; Poem for Str. Orch.; A Pennsylvania Dutch Tale; Looking Across; When Icicles Hang by the Wall; (recorded) Excursions; Laconic Suite; Brevities; Essay for Horn & Organ; Prelude and Canonic Piece Publs: Handbook of Music Terms, 1967; Music for Elementary Tchrs., 1951 & '60. Contbr. to var. jrnls. Mbrships. incl: Am. Composers Alliance; Southeastern Comps. League; Am. Music Ctr. Hons. incl: Educational TV Prize, 1970. Hobbies: Railroads; Mysterious Phenomena. Address: 1720 Garfield Ave., Oxford, MS 38655, USA. 11, 28, 29.

GRANT, Willis, b. 1907, Bolton, UK. Pianist; Organist. Educ: DMus (Dunelm); FRCO; ARCM. m. Grace Winifred Baker. Career incls: Asst. Organist, Lincoln Cathedral & Music Master, S Pk. HS, 1931-36; Organist & Master of Choristers, Birmingham Cathedral, 1936-58; Dir. of Music, King Edward's Schl., Birmingham, 1948-58; Stanley Hugh Badock Prof. of Music, 1958-72, Emeritus, 1972-, Bristol Univ. Publs: An Album of Songs for Baritone, 1951; Music in Education - Colston Rsch. Ed., 1963. Mbrships. incl: elected Hon. Mbr., RAM, 1969; Pres., Bristol Bach Choir, 1967-, ISM, 1974-75; Chmn., Bristol Opera Co., 1970-. Hobbies: Photography; Gardening. Address: The Old Rectory, Compton Martin nr. Bristol, UK. 1.

GRAPPELLI, Stephane, b. Jan. 1908, Paris, France. Jazz Violinist. Career: perfs. in France & worldwide; num. apps. on radio & TV; duos w. Django Reinhardt, Yehudi Menuhin, Johnny Ethridge, etc.; apps. w. num. jazz groups & bands.

GRASSI, Paulo. Theatre Director. Career: Dir., Teatro Piccolo, Milan, Italy, 1946-72; Supt., La Scala, Milan, 1972-76. 16.

GRAU, Irene Rosenberg, b. 12 Oct. 1927, NYC, USA. Pianist; 1 s., 1 d. Career: Prof. of Music, Miss. Univ. for Women. Compositions: "Hymn of Praise"; "Passacaglia & Fugue for Strings", "Hear Us, O Lord, from Heav'n They Dwelling Place"; "Unto Thee Do We Cry". Publs: A Comparison Three Methods for Improving Intonation in the Performance of Instrumental Music, 1963. Contbr. to: The Instrumentalist; Miss. Educl. Advance; Tenn. Musician; Ed.; Miss. Notes. Mbrships: Phi Delta Kappa; Lambda Delta Sigma; ASCAP; Am. String Tchrs. Assn.; Coll. Music Soc.; Nat. Schl. Orch. Assn.; MENC; Miss. Music Educators Assn. Hons: Graceland Coll. Silver Seal in Music, 1936; Lamoni-Graceland Orchl. Award, 1936; F E Olds & Son Schlrship. in Music Award, 1963; Grants for composing music from Miss. Univ. for Women, 1965-. Hobbies: Photography; Woodworking; Ceramics; Gardening; Travel. Address: PO Box 2363, Columbus, MS 39701, USA. 7, 23, 28.

GRAUBART, Michael, b. 26 Nov. 1930, Vienna, Austria. Composer; Conductor; Teacher; Ex-flautist; Director of Music. Educ: BSc, Univ. of Manchester, UK, 1952; Pvte. studies w. Mátyás Seiber (theory, comp.), Geoffrey Gilbert (flute), Lawrence Leonard (conducting). m. Ellen Barbour Graubart (Clark), 2 d., 1 s. Debut: London, 1953. Career: Free-lance flute player, 1953-57; Conductor, var. amateur orchs. & choirs & occasional profl. orchs. inclng. Ars Nova Chmbr. Orch., 1953-; Musical Dir., Focus Opera Group; Tchr. & Conductor, Morley Coll., 1966-; Dir. of Music, ibid, 1969-; Lectr. to aesthetics seminars; Ed., var. old works for perf. inclng. Monteverdi's "Orfeo" & works by Dufay & Pergolesi. Compositions performed incl: Deciensions (for 10 players); Aria for Orch.; Improvization on a Chord (electronic tape); Metabola (4 playser & electronic tape); Cantata, Untergang; Quasi una Sonata; Mosaic-Chiasmus (solo piano). Contbr. to: Tempo; Lute Soc. Jrnl.; Times Literary Supplement. Solo Performers' Sect., ISM; Soc. for the promotion of New Music; Musicians Union, Composers Guild of Gt. Britain (Treasurer); Co-Vice-Chmn., Music Panel, Greater London Arts Assn. Hobbies: Hill & mtn. walking; Sailing. Address: 95 Leconfield Rd., London, NG 2SD, UK. 3.

GRAVES, Mel, b. 6 Nov. 1946, Parkersburg, W Va., USA. Composer; Performer (Contravass, Electric Bass, etc.); Teacher. Educ: BMus, San Fran. Conserv. of Music; MMus, Univ. of Calif., San Diego. m. Susann Simpson Graves. Career incls: Jazz perfs. w. Denny Zeitlin, Jerry Hahn & other major artists; player w. San Diego Symph. & La Jolla Chmbr. Symph.; Ctr. for Music Experiment Improvisation Grp.; Comp.-in-Res., Chmbr. Music Northwest, 1976. Comps. incl: Vertical Horizons, 1973; Sea Oracle, 1974; Sceptre, 1975; Illusions: Plateau, 1976. Recordings incl. jazz, documentaries & film scores. Publ: Some Electronic Timbral Modification Extensions for Contrabass & Electric Bass, 1976. Mbr., profl. assns. Recip., num. grants & scholarships. Mgmt: Seesaw Music, NYC. Address: 8528A Via Mallorca, La Jolla, CA 92037, USA.

GRAVES, William Lester, Jr., b. 26 Aug. 1915, Terry, Miss., USA. University Professor. Educ: Dip. in Pub. Schl. Music, Graceland Coll.; BSEd, NW Mo State Coll.; MMEd, Drake Univ.; EdD, Univ. of Colo.; Studied violin w. Joseph Anthony, Frank Noyes & Forest Schultz; Studied comp. w. Francis Pyle & Cecil Effinger. m. Kathlyn Earlita Cato, 1 s., 1 d. Career: Prof. of Music, Miss. Univ. for Women. Compositions: 'Hymn of Praise'; 'Passacaglia & Fugue for Strings'; 'Hear Us, O Lord, from Heav'n They Dwelling Place'; 'Unto Thee Do We Cry'. Publs: A Comparison of Three Methods for Improving Intonation in the Performance of Instrumental Music, 1963. Contbr. to: The Instrumentalist; Miss. Educl. Advance; Tenn. Musician; Ed., Miss. Notes, 1966-74. Mbrships: Phi Delta Kappa; Lambda Delta Sigma; ASCAP; Coll. Music Soc.; MENC; Miss. Music Educators Assn.; Am. Symph. Orch. League. Hons: Graceland Coll. Silver Seal in Music, 1936; Lamoni-Graceland Orchl. Award, 1936; F E Olds & Son Scholarship in Music Award, 1963; Grants for comp. music from Miss. Univ. for Women, 1965-70, '72; Hobbies: Photography; Woodworking; Ceramics; Gardening; Travel. Address: 1421 College St., Columbus, MS 39701, USA. 4, 7, 23, 28, 29.

GRAY, George Branson, b. 9 July 1945, Winfield, Kan., USA. Pianist; Conductor; Opera Coach; Chorus Master. Educ: B Mus (piano), Ind. Univ., 1967; MMus (accompanying & condng.), Univ. of Cinn., 1969. Debut (as Cond.): NYC Opera, 1974. Career: Asst. Cond., Cinn. Opera, 1970-74; Asst. cond., NYC Opera, 1972-74; Chorus Master & mbr., Condng.

Staff, ibid., 1974-. Address: 170 W 74th St., Apt. 204, NY, NY 10023, USA.

GRAY, George Charles, b. 7 Oct. 1897, Nuffield nr. Redhill, Surrey, UK. Organist, Conductor, Lecturer. Educ: Articled pupil of Sir Edward Bairstow, York Minister; FRCO; B Mus (Durham); Hon. M Mus. (Leicester); D Mus. (Lambeth degree); FRSCM. m. Gladys Gofton, dec., 2 s., 2 d. (1 dec.). Career incls: Organist & Master of the Music, Leicester Cath., 1931-69; Cond., Leiscester Bach Choir, 1931-69; Lectr. in Singing, Univ. Coll., Leicester, 1931-58; Extra Mural Lectr., Vaughan Coll., Leicester, 1931-51; Sr. Lectr. in Music, Leicester Coll. of Educ., 1946-; has made many radio broacasts in cathedral servs. organ recitals & choral progs. by Leicester Bach Choir, also a small number of TV broadcasts. Recordings: Music for Christmas (organ solo, Leicester Bach Choir & Leicester Cathedral Choir). Publs: Church Choir Training, 1935. Contbr. of occasional articles to jrnls. Mbrships: former mbr. of Coun. & Exec., ISM: Pres.; Cathedral Organists Assn., 1968-70; Leicester Rotary Club. Hons: FRCO Lafontaine Prize, 1920; Worshipful Co. of Musicians Silver Medal, 1922. Hobby: Watching Cricket. Address: 8 Knighton Court, Leicester LE2 1ZB, UK. 1, 3.

GRAY, Stephen, b. 1923, Guildford, Surrey, UK. General Manager & Secretary, Royal Liverpool Philharmonic Society. Educ: Trinity Coll. Oxford. m. Frances Burn, 1 s., 1 d. Career: Fndr., Chelsea Opera Grp., 1950; Gen. Mgr. & Sec., LPO, 1957-59; Gen. Mgr., Philharmonia Orch., 1959-64; Gen. Mgr., Sec. Royal Liverpool Phil. Soc., 1964-. Hobbies: Reading; Walking. Address: 4 South Bank, Birkenhead, Merseyside, LR3 5UP, UK. 3.

GRBA, Nedeljko, b. 30 June 1929, Karlovac, Yugoslavia. Writer & Editor; Violinist. Educ: Studied aesthetics; studied Violin w. Vaclav Kubicek. Career: Music Ed., Operatic Music, Radio Belgrade; prepares Radio opera series. Contbr. to: Borba & Dnevik daily papers; Pro Musica; other musical jrnls. Mbrships: Serbian Soc. of Comps. & Musical Authors; Yogoslav Assn. of Comps. & Musical Authors. Hons: Prizes, Radio Novi Sad, 1959, 1961 & Radio Belgrade 1972, 1974; Yugoslav Prize in Ohrid. Hobbies: Records; Swimming. Address: Knexa Danila 55A, Belgrade, Yugoslavia.

GREAGER, Richard C, b. 5 Nov. 1946, Christchurch, NZ. Operatic Tenor. Educ: Univ. of Melbourne Conserv. of Music. m. June Rosemary Greager. Debut: as Gaston in La Traviata, Royal Opera House, Loneon, 1974. Career incls: began singing (oratorio, recitals & opera) in NZ, 1965; sang w. Victorian Opera Co., Melbourne, Aust., 1968; in UK, 1973-; w. Royal Opera House, Covent Gdn., London, 1973-74; Prin. Tenor, Scottish Opera, 1974-. Mbr., Brit. Equity. Hons. incl: Melbourne Sun Aria Prize, 1969; Canberra Shell Aria Prize, 1970; Sydney Sun Aria Prize, 1971; Royal Overseas League Music Prize, London, 1973. Hobbies: Hillwalking; Rock Climbing; Geology; Mineralogy; Skindiving; Reading. Address: 5 Netherblane, Blanefield, Stirlingshire G63 9JW, UK.

GREAVES, Terence, b. 16 Nov. 1933, Hodthrope, Derbyshire, UK. Composer; Pianist (Duo & Ensemble). Educ: Kreble Coll., Oxford Univ., 1957-61; MA, B Mus; Fellow, Royal Northern Coll. Music; LRAM; ARCM, Hon. ABSM. m. Sheila Nichols, 3 d. Lectr., 1962-66, Grad. Tutor, 1966-70, Dir. of Studies, 1970-73, Birmingham Schl. of Music; Tutor, Extra-Mural Dept., Birmingham Univ., 1962-67; Dean of Dev. & Assoc. Hd., Schl. of Comp. & Perf., Royal Northern Coll. of Music, 1973-. Comps: Num. educl. comps. Hobbies: Badminton; Tennis; Hill-walking. Address: 85 Broad Walk, Wilmslow, Cheshire, UK.

GREBE, Maria Ester, b. 11 July 1928, Arica, Chile. Musicologist; Ethnomusicologist. Educ: BA, Univ. of Scholar, UCLA, USA, 1965-66, Ind. Univ., Bloomington, 1967. m. Juan Marconi, 12 s., 1 d. Career incls: Prof. of Musical Analysis, Univ. of Chile, Santiago, 1957-; Prof. of Anthropol., Schl. of Med., ibid., 1970-; Prof. of Methodol., Dept. of Anthropol., 1974-; Prof. of Ethnomusicol., Dept. of Music, 1973-. Author, The Chilean Folk Verse: A Study in Musical Archaism, 1967. Contbr. to num. profl. jrnls. Mbr. var. profl. orgs. Hons: Fulbright Grant, 1965-66; Guggenheim Grant, 1966-67. Address: Av. El Cerro 1983 (P de Valdivia Nortre), Santiago, Chile. 27.

GRECH, Pawlu, b. 20 Feb. 1938, Malta. Composer; Conductor; Teacher. Educ: St. Augustine's Coll., Valletta; Piano Dip., Conservatorio St. Cecilia, Rome, 1962; Cond., RAM, London. Career: Cond., ECO, BBC broadcast; Tchr., Music Theory & Pianoforte, Chelsea-Westminster Inst., London. Comps. incl: Tre Canti (soprano & piano); Musica (soprano, percussion cellos, double basses); Quattro Pezzi (8 instruments); Quaderno I & II (piano); Differentiations (string orch.); Tetrad I (string quartet);

Rhapsoïda (piano); Duo I (violin & piano). Mbr. ISM. Recip. Ricordi Prize for Conducting, 1965. Hobbies: Painting; Swimming. Address: 54 Canterbury Ct., South Acre, Hendon, London NW9, UK.

GREDLER, Ake Samuel, b. 15 Aug. 1929, Lund, Sweden. Music Director; Organ, Piano & Violin. Educ: Dips. as Organist, Cantor, Music Tchr. Orch. Cond.; Royal Swedish Music HS; summer conducting courses, Acad. Musicale, Chigiana, Siena. m. Inger Fristrom, 2 d. Debut: w. Symph. Orch. of Helsingborg, 1961. Career: Choirmaster, Cathedral of Stockholm, 1959-64; Choir & Orch. Cond., freelance, 1964-67; Choirmaster, Kungsholm Ch., Stockholm, 1967-72, Sta. Clara Ch., 1972-; Symph. concerts in Helsingborg, Norrkoping & other cities, 1961-; app. on Swedish Radio & TV, 1958-. Publ: A Summer Day with CM Bellman, arr. for wind septet & male choir, 1971. Hons: Golden plaque, Stockholm Male Singers, 1969; 1st Prize, Comp. for male choirs, Stockholm, 1968. Hobbies: Photography; Caravanning. Address: Fornbyvagen 21, 4 str., S-163 70 Spanga, Sweden.

GREEN, Douglass Marshall, b. 22 July 1926, Rangoon, Burma. Music Educator. Educ: BMus, Univ. of Redlands, Calif., USA, 1949; MMus, ibid., 1951; PhD (musicology) Boston Univ., 1958. m. Marguita Dubach, 1 s., 2 d. Career incl: Music Fac., Univ. of Calif., Santa Barbara; Prof., Eastman Schl. of Music, Univ. of Rochester, NY; Prof., Univ. of Texas at Austin (current). Comps: 4 Conversations for 4 Clarinets; Missa Brevis; 6 Preludes on Medieval Hymns for Organ. Publs: Form in Tonal Music, 1965, 1979; Harmony Through Counterpoint, 1970; Performances and Structure, 1978; var. eds. of 18t Century music. Contbr. to: var. profl. jrnls. Mbrships: Am. Musicol. Soc.; Coll. Music Soc.; Exec. Board, Soc. for Music Theory. Hobby: Lit. Address: 5600 Ridge Oak Dr., Austin, TX 78731, USA. 9.

GREEN, Gordon, b. 6 Aug. 1905, Barnsley, UK. Pianist; Teacher of Piano. Educ: Royal Manchester Coll. of Music; pvte. study w. Egon Petri. m. Dorothy Simpson, 1 s. Career: Pianist; Lectr. & Tchr.; Prof. of Piano, Royal Manchester Coll. of Music (now Royal Northern Coll. of Music), 1945; Prof. of Piano, RAM, 1962. Publs: Liszt, a selection, 1973. Contbr. to var. musical mags. ISM, Warden, Solo Performers' Section, 1968. Hons: FRMCM, 1954; Hon. RAM, 1964; Hon. MA, Liverpool Univ., 1972. Hobby: Reading. Address: 5 N Villas, Camden Sq., London NW1 9BJ, UK. 3.

GREEN, Jonathan D, b. 4 May 1945, NYC, NY, USA. Operatic Tenor. Educ: BA, Middlebury Coll.; Manhattan Schl. of Music; Yale Univ. m. Charlene A Green, 1 s. Debut: NY City Opera, 1977. Career: Prin., tenor, NY City Opera; apps. w. Central City Opera, Cinn. Opera, St. Paul Opera Assn., Milwaukee Opera under the Stars. Hons: var. scholarships; winner, NY Liederkranz Competition, 1975. Mgmt: Martha Munro, Lombardo/Munro Assocs., NYC. Address: 34 W 75th St., NYC, NY 10023, USA.

GREEN, Roger, b. 12 Jan. 1945, Bristol, UK. Pianist; Musicologist. Educ: Queen's Coll., Oxford; MA (Oxon.); Studied w. Peter Katin, Guido Agosti, Paul Badura-Skoda & Karl Engel. Debut: Purcell Room, London, 1967. Career: 3 recitals in Purcell Room & 1 in Wigmore Hall; has given sev. recitals on radio & TV; is working on a book on Michael Haydn. Contbr. to Grove's Dictionary of Music & Musicians, 6th ed. Mbrships: Royal Musical Assn.; ISM. Hobbies: Philos.; Gastronomy; For. Travel Mgmt: Basil Douglas Ltd. Address: 31 Greencroft Gdns., Hampstead, London NW6, UK. 3.

GREENAWALT, Terrence Lee, b. 5 Aug. 1936, Hamburg, Pa., USA. College Professor; Pianist; Bass Trombonist. Educ: BS, State Coll., W Chester, Pa., 1958; MA, Eastman Schl. of Music, Rochester, NY, 1962; PhD, ibid., 1972. m. Carol June Smith, 2 d. Career: num. solo piano recitals & duo piano recitals w. wife; Bass Trombonist, Fifth Army Band, Evanston (Ill.) Symph. Orch.; Asst. Prof., Univ. of Bridgeport, Conn., 1963-; Chmn., Theory Dept., currently Bass Trombonist, Gtr. Bridgeport Symph. Orch. Contbr. to: Bridgeport Post. Mbrships: Nat. Slavic Hon. Soc.; Friars Club; Phi Mu Alpha; Am. Fedn. of Musicians; MENC; Conn. Music Educators Assn. Hobbies: Sports; Model Train Collecting. Address: 64 Shawnee Rd., Trumbull, CT 06611, USA.

GREENBERG, Marvin, b. 24 June 1936, NYC, USA. Music Educator. Educ: BA in Music Educ., NY Univ., 1957; MA & EdD in Music Educ., Columbia Univ., NY, 1958, '62; studied piano at Juilliard Schl. of Music, 1955-59; Music Tchng. Cert., NY & Hawaii. Career: Assoc. Prof. of Educ., Curric. Rsch. & Dev. Grp., Univ. of Hawaii; Prof. of Educ. Publs. incl: Music Handbook for the Elementary School, 1972; Head Start Music Curriculum (Music for the Pre-Schooler), 1971; Your Children Need Music -

A Guide for Parents & Teachers (1979); many articles. Mbrships incl: MENC; Soc. for Rsch. in Music Educ.; Coun. for Rsch. in Music Educ. Hons: Outstanding Young Educator of Hawaii Finalist, 1967; Sev. US Govt. Rsch. Grants, etc. Hobbies: Gardening; Stamps, etc. Address: 1765 Ala Moana Blvd. No. 994, Honolulu, HI 96815, USA. 9.

GREENBERG, Roger D, b. 7 Apr. 1944, Pottsville, Pa., USA. Concert Saxophonist; Lecturer in Music. Educ: B Mus, Juilliard Schl. of Music, NYC; M Mus, Univ. of Southern Calif. m. Sylvia Greenfield. Career: Soloist, World Saxophone Congress, Bordeaux, France, 1974; apps. w. Los Angeles Saxophone Quartet, Los Angeles Phil. Orch., 20th Century Fox Studio Orch., Calif. Wind Symph.; Warner Bros. Studio Orch.; Solo & Chmbr. Music recitals; Lectr., Calif. State Univs., Fullerton & Long Beach. Recordings: J S Bach, The Art of the Fugue, w. Los Angeles Saxophone Quartet; The Westwood Wind Quintet Plays Music by Cortes, Chavez, Revueltas & Ginastera. Mbrships: World Saxophone Congress (former Regional Coord.); Juilliard Alumni Assn. (Advsry. Bd.). Address: 4122 Laconcetta Dr., Yorba Linda, CA 92686, USA.

GREENE, Allen Walker, b. 21 Aug. 1921, Passaic, NJ, USA. Professor of Music History & Literature; Freelance harpsichordist. Educ: BA, Harvard Univ., 1942; MA, Denver Univ., 1953; Further grad. study, Harvard Univ., 1962-63; Berkshire Music Ctr., Tanglewood, 1941, '46; Instrumental study, Longy Schl. of Music, Cambridge, Mass., 1938-42, New England Conservatory, 1941-42. m. Lenore Hays, 1 s. Career: Mbr., Denver, Colo.; Freelance harpsichordist. Mbrships: Am. Musicological Sco.; Coll. Music Soc. Hobbies: Mountain climbing; Backpacking. Address: 1744 S Humboldt St., Denver, CO 80210, USA. 9.

GREENE, Gordon K, b. 27 Dec. 1927, Cardston, Alta., Canada. University Professor. Educ: A Mus in Piano; MA in Philos (Aesthetics), Univ. of Alta.; PhD in Musicol., Ind. Univ. Career: Music Historian specializing in Mediaeval & Renaissance; Choral Cond.; Radio host of classical progs.; Music Critic; Symph. prog. annotator; Contbr. to Jrnl. of Aesthetics & Art Criticism. Mbrships: Int. Musicol. Soc.; Am. Musicol. Soc.; Am. Soc. for Aesthetics; Mediaeval Acad. of Am. Recip., Canada Coun. Fellowship, 1972-73. Address: Fac. of Music, Wilfred Laurier Univ., Waterloo, Ont., Canada.

GREENE, Thomas Enoch, b. 13 Sept. 1935, Providence, RI, USA. Professor of Music. Educ: BMus, New England Conserv. of Music, Boston, Mass.; MMus, Univ. of Conn. m. Barbara Anne Martinelli, 2 s., 3 d. Career: Var. TV appearances, Channels 10 & 36, Providence; TV Series, 'Lute, Vihuela & Guitar', 1971; Prof. of Lute, Viheuela & Guitar, Brown Univ., RI Coll.; Music Dept. Hd., Warwick Pub. Schl. System, RI. Compositions: Guitar duets, transcriptions from lute tablature of Greensleeves; La Rosignoll; Flatt Pavane; Queens Treble; Queen Elizabeth's Galliard; (solo); Etude in three dimensions; A method for scale practice. Contbr. to: The Am. String Tchr. Mbrships: Am. Fedn. of Musicians; Lute Socs. of Am. & England; Soc. of the Classic Guitar; Pres. Prog. Chmn., Guitar Guild of RI; chmn., Music comm. for RI 76. Hobbies: Amateur Histn.; Maap collector. Address: 119 Olney Ave., N Providence, RI 02911, USA.

GREENFIELD, Bruce Henry, b. 23 Nov. 1948, Lower Hutt, Wellington, New Zealand. Pianist; Accompanist. Educ: BMus, Comp. & Perf., Vic. Univ., Wellington; LTCL. m. J H McLeod. Carer incls: Musical Dir., NZ Ballet Co., 1971-72; Dir., New Opera Quintet, 1973-75; Musical Advsr. to Music Fedn. of NZ, 1974-75; Mbr., Gagliano Trio, 1975-; Nat. Solo Artist & Accomp., Radio NZ; Execultant Piano Tutor, Wellington Polytechnic Schl. of Music; Nat. Tours as accomp. Comps. incl: several for unaccompanied choir; Songs for viola, piano & voice; Setting for NZ Liturgy Serv. Hobbies: Yoga; Cooking; Reading; Films; Cards; Billiards; Meditation. Mgmt: Music Fedn. of NZ Inc. Address: 487 Karaka Bay Rd., Wellington 3, New Zealand.

GREENING, Anthony John, b. 10 Dec. 1940, Santa Barbara, Calif., USA. Musicologist; Editor; Professor; Organist; Choir-Trainer. Educ: BMus, London Univ.; RCM; FRCO (ChM); ADCM; ARCM (Op. Pft.). m. Patricia Coltman, 1 d. Debut: Music in Our Time, organ recital, 1963. Career: Organist, Ely Cathedral, 1964; Rsch. Scholar, 1968; Tutor, RSCM, 1972; Professor, GSM, 1974; Dir. of Music, Nashdom Abbey. Comps: Sacred choral music of Amner; TCM revisions for OUP; hymnals & office books; Sacred choral music. Recordings: Works of Amner; Organ music. Publs: The Organs & Organists of Ely Cathedral, 1969. Contbr. to: MGG; Musical Times; Grove's 6th Ed. Mbrships: ISM; RCO; Soc. of St. Gregory. Hons: Tovey Memorial Rsch., scholar (Oxford), 1968. Mgmt: Bermudamusik, 2 Bolton Rd., Harrow, Middx., UK. Address: c/o Guildhall Schl. of Music, Barbican, London, EC2, UK.

GREENING, Richard George, b. 17 Nov. 1927, Sunningwell, Berks., UK. Organist & Choirmaster; Lecturer. Educ: BA, New College, Oxford Univ., 1951; B Mus, ibid., 1952; MA, ibid., 1955; FRCO, 1952. m. 1955, Audrey Joyce Pollard, 2 s. Career: Organist, St. Giles Ch., Oxford, & Vis. Music Master, var. Schls., 1950-55; Asst. Organist, St. George's CHapel, Windsor, Organist, Royal Chapel, Windsor Great Park & Dir. of Music, St. George's Schl., Windsor Castle, 1955-59; Organist & Choirmaster, Lichfield Cathedral, 1959-77; Fndr. & Cond., Lichfield Cathedral Special Shoir (Choral Soc.); Prin. Lectr., Schl. of Music, City of Birmingham Polytechnic; Recordings: Ascensiontide Evensong; Lichfield Cathedral Choristets Sing Christmas Carols. Publ: The Organs of Lichfield Cathedral, 1974. Contbr. to: Musical Times; The Organ. Mbr., Lunar Soc., Lichfield. Hons: ABSM; Harding Prize, RCO, 1952; High Constable of Lichfield, 1974-75. Hobbies: Steam Railways; Church Architecture; Organs; Travel; Books. Address: 110 Russell Bank Rd., Four Oaks, Sutton Coldfield, West Midlands, B74 4RJ, UK.

GREENSMITH, John Brian, b. 12 April 1929, Bournemouth, UK. Cellist; Orchestral Manager and Administrator. Educ: Birmingham Schl. of Music; GSM; LTCL; ARCM. m. Magdalen Aurelia Green, 3 s. Career: Bournemouth Municipal Orch., 1952-53; Prin., BBC, Glasgow, 1956-63; Instrumental Tchr., WRCC, 1963-74; Vis. Tutor, Bretton Hall, 1965-; Co-Ord. for Instrumental Music, Barnsley MBC, 1974-; Freelance w. leading Orchs.; Orchl. Mgr., Yorkshire Concert Orch., 1965-72, Yorkshire Sinfonia, 1972-75; Gen. Mgr., Yorkshire Phil. Orchs., 1975-. Var. recordings. Mbrships: Musicians Union (N E Dist. Coun. Mbr. & Conference Delegate); NUT. Hobbies: Game Fishing; Mountain Walking; Gardening. Address: Torridon House, 104 Bradford Rd., Wrenthorpe, Wakefield, UK.

GREENWOOD, Barrie Leck, b. 5 Oct. 1934, Invercargill, NZ. Choral Singer. Educ: Pvte. Piano Tuition; 22 yrs. Choral Singing. m. Susan Nichol. Career: Active Mbr., Choir of Royal Christchurch Musical Soc., 1954-; S Brighton Choral Soc., 1959-62; Adelaide Harmony CHoir & Phil. Choir, Aust., 1962; Travelling Chorus, NZ Opera Co., 1964, '65; Choir, Oxford Terrace Baptist Ch., Christchurch, 1963-70; Choir, Cathedral of Blessed Sacrament, Christchurch, 1975-77. Contbr. to Studies in Music (Nedlands, Western Aust.), Vol. 7, 1973. Mbr. NZ Div.; Aust.-NZ Br., Int. Assn. of Music Libs.; Court Star of Canterbury; Ancient Order of Foresters, 1959-. Recip. 2 Grant-in-aid, Am. Philos. Soc., Phila., 1972, '73. Hobbies: Choral Singing; Musicol.; Hist.; Hist. of Music; Thinking; Reading. Address: PO Box 2316, Christchurch 1, NZ. 4, 28, 29.

GREER, David Clive, b. 8 May 1937, London, UK. Musicologist. Educ: MA, Oxford Univ. m. Patricia Regan, 2 s., 1 d. Career: Lectr. in Music, Univ. of Birmingham, 1963-72; Prof. of Music, The Queen's Univ., Belfast, 1972-. Publs: John Adson, Three Courtly Masquing Ayres (1963); English Madrigal Verse (3rd Ed., 1967); English Lute Songs (9 vols., 1967-71); Monteverdi, Three Sinfonias (1968); G Gabrieli, Canzon quarti toni, (1968); Alison, Campion etc., Twenty Songs (1969); Hamilton Harty, His Life and Music (1979); Lute Songs From Manuscripts (2 vols., 1979). Contbr. to profl. publs. Mbrships: Mbr. of Coun., Ed. of Proceedings, Royal Musical Assn.; ISM; Lute Soc. Hobbies: Reading; Squash. Address: Dept. of Music, The Queen's Univ., Belfast BT7 1NN, N Ireland. 3.

GREER, Linda, b. 28 Jan. 1939, Pitts., Pa., USA. Pianist; Teacher. Educ: Univ. of Pitts., Pa.; Doct. Studies, Okla. State Univ.; BS, Juilliard Schl. of Performing Arts, 1962; MS, ibid., 1963; Aspen Schl. of Music, Aspen, Colo.; Pvte. study. m. Juan A Morales, Jr. Career: Recital & ensemble perfs. in 10 states; Soloist, Liszt Piano Concerto No. 1, W Okla. City Symph.; Soloist in Cesar Franck Symphonic Variations w. Wheeling Symph. Orch., W Va.; Soloist in Bach Concerto in D minor w. chmbr. grp. from Wheeling Symph. Orch.; Soloist in Schumann Piano Concerto w. Independence Symph. Orch., Mo.; Soloist in Beethoven Piano Concerto No. 3 w. Okla. State Univ. Orch.; Num. local TV & radio apps.; Asst. Prof. of Music, Okla. State Univ. for 8 yrs.; Lectures & workshops on teaching of piano. Judge for student auditions, Music Tchrs. Nat. Assn. Recip., var. schlrships. & awards. Hobbies: Cooking; Reading; Interested in giving benefit perfs. for charity; Children. Address: Apt. 147, 2507 N Wilburn Ave., Bethany, OK 73008, USA.

GREER, Thomas Henry, b. 24 July 1916, Gustine, Tex., USA. Violinist; Violist; Trumpeter; Musicologist; Conductor; Director of Chamber Music. Educ. incls: BS, McMurry Coll., Abilene, Tex.; MMus, Southern Meth. Univ., Dallas; PhD, N Tex. State Univ., Denton. m. Bette V Van Der Heydt, 2 d. Career: Concert apps. on violin & viola; perfs. as trumpeter w. jazz orchs.; Tchr., Public Schls., Colls. & Univs.; Cond., 6th Army Group Band, ETO; Cond. of Symphs., Chmbr. groups; TV apps.; Comp. Contbr. to var. publs. Mbrships: Pi Kappa Lambda; Alpha Chi; Phi Mu Alpha. Hons. incl: Disting. Alumnus Award, McMurry Coll., 1975. Hobbies: Rebuilding violins; Independent Rsch.; Writing. Address: 6900 Hart Lane, Apt. B, Austin, tX 78731, USA. 7.

GREGOR, Bohumil, b. 14 July 1926, Praha, Czechoslovakia. Conductor. Educ: State Conserv., Prague. m. Blanka Gregorova. Debut: Prague. Career: Opera Cond. in Prague & Brno; Chief Cond. & Hd. of Opera, State Theatre, Ostrave; Chief Cond., Nat. Theatre, Prague; Long term cond. in Stockholm, Hamburg & Holland. Recordings incl: Complete works of Janaceks Janufa: From the House of the Deadl; The Makropoulos Affair; The Cunning Little Vixen (Suprahon & EMI). Hobby: Mini Railways. Mgmt: Nat. Theatre, Prague; Nederlands Opera Amsterdam. Address: Praha 5, Janáckovo nabrezi 7, Czech.

GREGOR, Josef, b. 8 Aug. 1940, Rákosliget, Hungary. Bass singer. Educ: Acad. of Music; Master of perf. m. Elisabeth Belle, 2 c. Debut: as Sarastro in The Magic Flute. Career: bass parts in major oratorios & operas; TV apps. in Falstaff, Fidelio etc. & in portrait films. Recordings: Liszt oratorios, masses & choral works; 2 Haydn operas; Kodaly Te Deum & Missa Brevis; Mozart Requiem, Magic Flute & Concert arias. Hons: Ferenc Liszt prize, 1st grade; Honoured Master of People's Repub. of Hungary, etc. Hobbies: Car Driving; Cats. Mgmts: Nat. Opera House, Budapest; Nat. Theatre of Szeged. Address: Lugas u. 7 B, 6723 Szeged, Hungary.

GREGOR, Vladimir, b. 10 Dec. 1916, Olomour, Czech. Musicologist; Critic; Educator. Educ: PhD; Scientarium candidatus. m. Bozena Gregorová, 2 s. Career: Lectr., Pedagogical Fac., Ostrava. Publs: Mudebnívlastiveda Olomouckého kraje, 1956; Ceská detská písen umelá, 1959; Delnické pevecké spolky na Ostravsku a v jinych prumys slovych stredisclch ceskych zemi, 1961; Ceská a slovenská hudebne dramatická tvorba pro deti, 1966; Vladimlr Ambros, 1969; Dejiny hudebni vychovy v ceskych zemlch a na Slovensku, 1973; Cs. Spolecnost pro hud. výchovu, 1974; Rudolf Kubin, 1975. Contbr. to: Hudebni rozhledy; Opus Musicum; Slezsky sbornik; rev. Ostrava; Otázky divadla a filmu; Cesky lid. Mbr. Czech. Soc. for Music Educ. Address: Sokolovská 1135, 708 00 Ostrava-Poruba, Czech.

GREGORC, Janez, b. 20 June 1934, Ljubljana, Yugoslávia. Jazz composer. Educ: High Schl. of Music & Acad. of Music, Ljubljana; Beklee Coll. of Music, Boston. m. Marija, 1 s. Comps: Swamp, soppramette; The Barbed Wire (Ballet); Film music; Cartoon music. Recordings: Collage; Landluber; Tarsua Vala; Ikona; Croquis. Mbrships: Assoc. of Slovene Comps. (Brd. of Managers); Jazz Research, Graz, Austria. Hons: Prize for Arr., Youth Fest., Helsinki, 1962, Slovene Pop Music Contest, 1973 & '78; Film Music Prize (Telematerija), 1975. Hobbies: Skiing. Mgmt: RTV, Ljubljana. Address: Cesta 27, Aprila 57, 61000 Ljubljana, Yugoslavia.

GREGORC, Joža, b. 24 Jan. 1914, Pula Yugoslavia. Professor at University of Maribor; Conductor; Composer. Educ: Dip., Solo Singing, State Conserv. & Acad. of Music, Ljubljana; Pvte. studies. m. Vlasta Rau d., 1 d. Career incls: Cond: Chorus & Orch., Glasbena Matica & Municipal Band, 1945-50; Orch. & Chmbr. Chborus, Radio Maribor, 1950-51; Dir., Theatre of Ptuk, 1953-58; Dir., Phil. at Maribor, 1958-63; Prof., Music Dept., Pedagogical Acad., Maribor, 1964-. Comps. incl: Brodnik, cantata for baritone, men's & mixed chorus & symph. orch.; Mixed chorus; Fant, Sopet & Markjo Skace. Num. recordings. Contbr. of reviews of concerts, operas etc. to profl. jrnls. Mbr. num. orgs. Recip. var. hons. & musical prizes. Hobbies: Paintings & Architecture; Swimming; Car Driving. Address: Askerceva 4, 62000 Maribor, Yugoslavia.

GREGORIAN, Henry, b. 14 May 1924, Tabriz, Iran. Violinist. Educ: grad., Tehran Conserv., 1945; Dip., Longy Schl. of Music, Cambridge, Mass., 1952; BMus, MMus, Boston Univ., 1953. div., 3 c. Career: 1st violinist, Minnesota Orch., 1955-; soloist w. Boston Pops, Boston Civic Orch., Minnesota Orch., Tehran Symph., etc.; num. solo recitals. Address: c/o Minnesota Orch., 1111 Nicollet Mall, Mpls., MN 55403, USA.

GREGORIAN, Rouben, b. 23 Sept. 1915, Tifliz, Russia. Violinist; Conductor; Teacher. Educ: Armenian Ctrl. Coll., Tabirz, Iran; Tehran Conserv. Music, Iran; Comp. class, Ecole Normal Musique, Paris, Franc; Orch. Direction class, Nat. Conserv. Musique, Paris. Career incls: Choral Dir., Boston Conserv. Chorus, 1952-; Instr., violin, Boston Conserv., 1953-; Instr., Chmbr. Music, ibid., 1954-; Cond., Boston Conserv. Orch., 1955-; Fndr. & 1st Violinist, Komitas String Quartet, Boston, 1953-; Dir., Komitas Choral Soc., 1955-. Publs. incl: Iranian Folk Songs (2 vols.). Recordings incl: Sharagans

(Armenian Christmas Carols). Mbr. profl. orgs. Hons. incl: Decorated twice, Govt. Iran, Min. Educ. Address: 67 Betts Rd., Belmont, MA 02178, USA.

GREGORY, Barbara Elizabeth, b. 21 Aug. 1921, Mitcham, Surrey, UK. Teacher. Educ: qualified tchr. w. dip. for tchng. maladjusted children. Career: Full time Tchr., inclng. music tchng. & appreciation w. maladjusted & educationally sub-normal children aged 11-16; Fndr.-Sec., Tilford Bach Fest. & Tilford Bach Soc., 1952, currently Organiser of Tilford Bach Fest., also associated w. Bach in London proj. organized by Tilford Bach Fest. Choir & Orch. Contbr. to: Musical Times; Musical Opinion; Surrey Life; Special Educ. Hobbies: Natural Hist.; Arch.; Reading. Address: Ling Lea, Frensham, Farnham, Surrey GU10 3A2, UK.

GREGSON, Edward, b. 23 July 1945, Sunderland, UK. Senior Lecturer in Music. Educ: LRAM, 1966; GRSM, 1967; BMus, Univ. of London. m. Susan Carole Smith, 2 s. Comps. recorded: Brass Quintet (Pye), 1967; 3,Dance Espidoes for Brass Octet & Percussion (Decca); Essay for Brass Band (Granada); The Plantagenets, Symph. Study (Decca & RCA); Concerto Grosso for Brass Band (Pye); Preude & Capriccio for Cornet & Band (RCA); March Prelude (Decca); Connotations for Brass Band (RCA); Prelude for an Occasion (Decca, Pye). Ed., Sounding Brass. Vice Chmn., Comps. Guild of GB. Recip., Frederick Corder Mem. Prize, RAM, 1967. Hobbies: Tennis; Squash; Watching Football. Address: 54 Lower Gravel Rd., Bromley Common, Kent BR2 8LJ, UK. 3, 30.

GRGIĆ, Marijan, b. 19 Apr. 1929, Letina, Sisak, Yugoslavia. Musicologist; Art Historian. Educ: Acad. Dip. in Divinity, STL, Dip. in Musicol., PhD, Zagreb; MA, London. Career: Choir-master & Organist, Theol. Coll., Zagreb, 1948; Organist, Cathedral, Zadar, 1952; Curator, Permanent Exhib. of Ch. Art, Zadar, 1970-; Lectr. in Musicol., Fac. of Arts, Zadar Univ. of Split, 1973. Contbr. articles on ch. music to profl. publs. Mbrships: Prog. Committee, Music Evenings in St. Donat's Zadar; Permanent Contbr., Yugoslav Acad. of Scis. & Arts, Zagreb. Address: Put Dikla 72 d, 57000 Zadar, Yugoslavia.

GRIBENSKI, Jean François, b. 5 Aug. 1944, Castelmoron sLot, Lot-en-Garonne, France. Musicologist. Educ: Lic. in Hist., Sorbonne, 1966; Study of Music Hist. & Musicol., ibid., 1963-67. m. Monique Bonenfant, 2 c. Career: Asst., Music Hist., Univ. of Paris-Sorbonne, 1970-; Mbr., Ed. Committee, RILM Abstracts, 1970. Acta Musicologia, 1972-; Ed.-in-Chief, Revue de Musicologie, 1974-. Publs: Dictionnaire de la Musique (Contbng. author), 1970; Die Musik in Geschichte und Gegenwart (contbng. author), 1972; French dissertations in Music; an annotated bibliography, 1976. Contbr. to Musicol. Review. Mbrships. inali Franah & Int. Musicol. Soc. Address: 9 Impasse des Champs Fleuris, 92320 Châtillon, France.

GRIER, Hugh Christopher, b. 4 Dec. 1922, Derby, UK. Music Critic; Lecturer. Educ: MA, King's Coll., Cambridge; MusB; Hon. RCM. m. Mary Elisabeth Martin, 1 s. Career: Music Off., Brit. Coun., Scandinavia, 1947-49; Music Critic, The Scotsman, 1949-63; Freelance, 1970-; Prof., RCM; Broadcaster. Contbr: Daily Telegraphy; Music & Musicians; Music Critic, The Evening Standard. Mbrships: ISM; Inst. of Journalists. Hobbies: Skiing; Tennis; Reading. Address: 20 Redington Rd., London NW3, UK.

GRIEVE, Alexander John, b. 3 July 1923, Melbourne, Vic., Aust. Musician (Double Horn, Descant Horn, Hand-Horn). Educ: Melbourne Univ. Conserv., Aust. m. Judith Grieve, 1 s., 1 d. Debut: Horn soloist, Hobart, Tas., Aust., 1950. Career: Soloist, Melbourne & Adelaide Symph. Orchs.; Perfs. in Los Angeles, Chicago & San Fran., 1971; Mbr., Melbourne Sextet; Tchr., Melbourne Univ. Conserv., sev. Melbourne schls., & Melba Conserv., Melbourne. Num. recordings, Aust. & USA. Publs: The Horn Call; The Brass World. Brass Ed., JAMM. Mbrships: Vic. Artists Soc.; Inst. of Music Tchrs.; Int. Horn Soc. Address: 3 Parring Rd., Balwyn, Vic. 3103, Aust.

GRIFFEL, Kay, b. Eldora, Iowa, USA. Opera Singer. Educ: BA Mus, NW Univ., Evanston, Ill.; Berlin Schl. of Music. m. Prof. Exkart Sellheim. Debut: Chgo. Lyric Opera. Career: Chgo.; Berlin E & W), Munich, Karlsruhe, Rome, Stuttgart, Hamburg, Salzburg Fest., Glyndebourne Opera, Orange, Brussels, Bremen, New York City; W German Radio; RAI-Italy; S TV England; Cologne Opera, W Germany. Recordings: Janacek, Diary of one who vanished; Orff, De Temporum Fine Della Comedia. Mgmt: Schulz, Munich; ngpen and Williams, London. Address: Taunusstr. 10, 5303 Rösberg, German Fed. Repub.

GRIFFEL, L Michael, b. 12 Nov. 1942, New York City, USA. Musicologist; Educator; Pianist. Educ: BA, Yale Coll., 1963; MS, Juilliard Schl. of Music, 1966; MA, Columbia Univ., 1968; PhD, ibid., 1975; Piano studies, NY Coll. of

Music, Yale Schl. of Music & Juilliard Schl. m. Margaret Ross, 1 s. Career: Solo & Chamber Music apps. in NY, New Haven, Lenox, Hartford, Princeton, etc.; Radio perfs., WNYC & WFUV-FM, NY; Instr. of Music, Hunter Coll., CUNY, 1971-75; Asst. Prof. of Music, ibid., 1975-77; Assoc. prof., ibid., 1978-; Asst. Prof. of Music, Grad. Schl. & Univ. Center, CUNY, 1977; Assoc. Prof., ibid., 1978-; Assoc. Ed., Current Musicol., 1966-70; Ed.-in-Chief, 1970-72. Publs: Assoc. Ed., Performance Practice, A Bibliography, 1971; Teaching Music, in Scholars Who Teach, 1978. Contbr. to var. profl. publs. Mbrships. incl: Am. Musicol. Soc. (Coun., 1969-71); Int. Musicol. Soc.; Coll. Music Soc: Hons. incl: Clarence Barker Fellow, Columbia Univ., 1969-70. Address: 3135 Johnson Ave., Apt. 9E, Bronx, NY 10463, USA.

GRIFFETT, James Kenneth George, b. 30 April 1939, Stevenage, UK. Concert & Opera Singer (tenor). Educ: RCM. m. Catherine M Scott, 1 s., 1 d. Career: Tenor Soloist, Westminster Cathedral Choir, -1974; Fndr., Pro Cantione Antiqua (soloist voice ensemble); Num. fest. apps.; Radio perfs., Europe. Recordings: Monteverdi Vespers 1610; Haydn English Songs; Lute Songs; Gilbert & Sullivan; Folk Songs; Gregorian Chant; arias by Gounod & Franck; Works by Purcell, etc. Contbr. to: Musical Times; Classical Music; Hi-Fi News; Record Review. Mbr., Equity. Hobbies: Horse Riding; Wine making; Reading; Collecting 78 rpm discs. Mgmt: Concert Directory Int., Lyndhurst, Denton Rd., Ben Rhydding, Ilkley, Yorks. LS29 8QR, UK.

GRIFFIN, Harvi Alonzo, b.14 Dec. 1936, Detroit, Mich., USA. Concert harpist; Vocalist. Educ: Mich. State Univ.; Study w. Lucille Lawrence Mannes Schl. of Music, NYC & Eileen Malone, Eastman Schl. of Music, Rochester, NY. Debut: Detroit Irst. of Arts, 1965. Career: TV apps. in USA incl. Ed Sullivan Schow, Dinah Shore Show; Sev. perfs. for Am. Presidents at the White House, Wash.; Perf. for Grand Duchess Charlotte of Luxembourg on US visit. Comps: Arrs. of Handel, Harp Concerto, Bb Major; Handel, Harmonious Blacksmith; Debussey, Clair de Lune; Salzedo, Petite Valse, Chanson dans la nuit, Rhumba. Recordings: The Harp & Voice of Harvi Griffin; The 2 Sides of Harvi Griffin. Mbrships: Am. harp Soc. Hons: Final Concert at Am. Harp Soc. Coven., Albuquerque, New Mexico, 26 June, 1976. Hobbies: Downhill Skiing; Riding. Mgmt: Claude P Schrantz, 8702 Smith St., Bay City, Mich., 48706, USA. Address: As Mgmt.

GRIFFIN, Judson, b. 7 Sept. 1951, Lewes, Delaware, USA. Violist. Educ: BMus, Eastman Schl. of Music; MMus, DMA, The Juilliard Schl. Career: Mbr., Strawbery Banke Piano Quartet, Portsmouth, NH, 1970, '71; Mbr., Rochester Phil. Orch., 1970-73; num. concerto, recital & chmbr. music apps.; Freelance musicians, NYC, 1973-77; Asst. Prof., Schl. of Music, Univ. of NC at Greensboro, 1977-79; Prin. Viola, Aspen Chmbr. Symph., 1977-; Fac., Aspen Music Schl., 1979-. Recordings: w. Light Fantastic Players & Contemporary Chmbr. Ensemble. Contbr. to: Notes. Mbrships: Am. Fedn. of Musicians; Music Lib. Assn.; Am. Musicol. Soc.; Am. Music Center; Am. Viola Soc. Hons: Winner, Juilliard viola competition, 1976; Winner, Aspen viola competition, 1977; Recip., William J Henderson Award, Juilliard, 1976; Recip., Floyd Corbin Award, Dixie Club of NY, 1975; Contestant, Wm. Primrose Int. Viola Competition, 1979. Address: 230 Riverside Dr., Apt. 18N, NY, NY 10025, USA.

GRIFFITHS, Ann, b. Caerffili, Glam., UK. Harpist. Educ: Nat. Higher Conserv. of Music, Paris; Univ. Coll., Cardiff. m. Dr Lloyd Davis, 2 s. Career: Soloist & Freelance Orchestral Player; Fndr. & Dir., Ysgol Y Delyn (holiday harp courses), 1961-; w. Royal Opera House, Covent Gdn., 1959-50; has toured as Soloist in Spain, Iceland, & USA; is only Professional Triple Harp Player in world. Recordings: recital of harp music by Grandjany, Caplet, Suddek, Alvars, Templeton, Mortari, Rubbra & Walters (CFP156). Publs: Beginners Harp Method, 1967. Contbr. articles on harp & related subjects to var. jrnls. Mbrships: Royal MNusical Assn.; Galpin Soc.; UK Harp Assn. Hobbies: Collecting Harpiana; Cooking. Address: Pantybeiliau, Gilwern, Abergavenny, Mon., Wales, UK. 3.

GRIFFITHS, Chris M, b. 12 March 1948, Purley, Surrey, UK. Musician (Horn, French Horn & Wagner Tuba). Educ: study of Horn w. Barry Tuckwell, RAM; GRSM; LRAM. m. Angela Turner, 1 s., 1 d. Career: BBC Training Orch., 1970; Co-Prin. 3rd Horn, BBC Scottish Symph. Orch., 1972-75; Prin. Horn, Scottish Chmbr. Orch., 1975-; Mbr., Amphion Wind Quintet; Regular Freelance work for Scottish TV & Scottish Opera; Prof. of Horn, RSAM Jr. Dept., 1972. Mbrships: Hon. Mbr., Siskin Soc.; Scottish Phil. Club. Hobbies: Mountain walking; Heath Robinson inventions; Tomato cultivation. Address: 175 Queen Victoria Dr., Glasgow G14 9BP, UK. 3.

GRIFFITHS, David John, b. 23 Aug. 1950, Auckland, NZ. Composer. Educ: hon. Mmus, Auckland Univ.; GSM. Career:

recip. many commns. from amateur & semi-profl. choirs, orchs., etc. Comps: mainly choral music, inclng. carols, introits, anthems, 2 settings for new liturgy for both Anglican & Cath. servs.; major works: Five Credo Extracts; Improperia; O Magnum Mysterium; Salve Regina. Comps. Recorded: Five Credo's Comps. Publd: Dormi Jesu, 1972; Praise the Lord, 1973; Dean on the Tree, 1974. Recip. John Cowie Reid Mem., 1972. Hobbies: Singing; Model making. Address: 12 George St., Mt. Albert, Auckland, New Zealand.

GRIFFITHS, David Maurice, b. 25 Aug. 1907, Aberystwyth, UK. Music Teacher & Adjudicator. Educ: MA, Hertford Coll., Oxford; pupil of Vaughan Williams, RCM. London; ARCM. m. Joyce B McGlashan, 2 s., 3 d. Career: Dir. of Music, Durham Schl., 1932-43; Merchiston Castle Schl., Edínburgh, 1944-48; Concerts Organiser, Scottish Arts Coun., 1948-52; Mbr. of Panel of Examiners, TCL; Fest. Adjudicator (experience includes 3 tours of Canada). Comps: Anthem for Female Voices, Banks: Two Piano Duets, Curwen & Elkin. Contbr. to: Scotsman & BBC Scotland (music criticism). Hons. Sec., Scottish Area Coun., Brit. Fedn. of Music Fests. Hons: Signor Foli Exhbn., 1931 & Ernest Farrar Prize, 1932, comp., RCM. Hobbies: Gardening; Grandchildren. Address: Whiteways, Goslawdales, Selkirk TD7 4EP, UK. 3.

GRIFFITHS, Gwyneth, b. 19 Sept. 1943, Welwyn Garden City, Herts., UK. Singer (Contralto). Educ: GSM, London, UK; AGSM Singing & Piano; Pvte. studies w. Roy Henderson & Paul Hamburger. m. J Martin Heraud. Career: Has sung w. most leading choirs & orchs. in London & UK; Brazil, Germany, Holland, Belgium, Switz. Mbr. ISM. Hons: Kathleen Ferrier Memorial Scholarship, 1968; Leverhulme Scholarship for study in Germany, 1970; Finalist in Hertogenbosch Vocalist Concours, 1974. Hobbies: Driving; Sunbathing. Mgmt: Ibbs & Tillett. Address: 21 Langside Crescent, Southgate, London N14, UK.

GRIFFITHS, Paul (Anthony), b. 24 Nov. 1947, Bridgend, Glam., Wales, UK. Critic & Writer on Music. Educ: BA, MSc, Lincoln Coll., Oxford. m. Rachel Griffiths, 1 s. Career: Area Ed., 20th Century Music, Grove's Dictionary (6th Ed.), 1973-76. Publs: A Concise History of Modern Music, 1978; Boulez, 1978; A Guide to Electronic Music, 1979. Contbr. to Times; Musical Times. Hobbies: Theatre; TV; Pets (Bulldog & Cat). Address: Darville Cottage, Lower Heyford, Oxford, UK.

GRIGGS, (Ruby) Frances, b. London, UK. Teacher of Music & Singing. Educ: pvte. & at TCL & Goldsmith's Coll., London; LRAM; ARCM. Careeer incl: Hd. of Music, Welling Girls' Schl., 10 yrs.; Dir. of Music, Greenwich Girls' Schl., 4 yrs.; Cond., Falconwood Jr. Choir, London Choral Singers, Streatham Ladies' Choir, 1948-58; Fndr., Cavendish Singers, 1950; Tutor, LCC Evening Insts.; Contralto, St. Columba's Ch., Pont St., 1946-47 & St. Michael's Chester Sq., 1953-64; Fndr. mbr., Coun. of Bermondsey Music Fest.; vis. tchr., Hereford/Worcester Co. Coun. LEA, 1971-76; pvte. tchr., 1976-. Comps: A Carol Pageant; var. arrs., songs & carols. Mbrships: ISM; MTA; Assn. of Tchrs. of Singing. Address: 34 Hampton St., Hereford, HR1 2RA, UK. 3.

GRIGORIU, Theodor, b. 25 July 1926, Galati, Romania. Composer. Educ: studied arch.; studied w. Michael Jora, Conserv. of Bucharest, & A I Khachaturian, Conserv. of Moscow. m. Antoaneta Dinora. Career: Violinist, 1932-; Comps., 1943-, Comps. incl: Concerto for double chmbr. orch. & oboe; Cosmical Dream (orchl. poem); Homage to Enescu; Infinite Melodie; Suite for Quartet; 8 lieder; music for 16 Romanian films; theatre music; Canti per Europe; etc. Contbr. to Music (mag. of Romanian Comps. Soc.) Mbr., Sec., Romanian Comps. Soc. Hons: 3 Prizes of Romanian Comps. Soc., State Prize. Hobby: Painting. Address: Str. Pictor Rosenthal No. 2, Bucharest, Romania.

GRILLER, Sidney Aaron, b. 10 Jan. 1911, London, UK. Leader, Griller String Quartet. Educ: Royal Acad. of Music. m. Honor Elizabeth Linton, 1 s., 1 d. Career: World-wide Concerts; Lectr. in Music, Univ. of Calif., Berkeley, 1950-63; Prof. of Music, Dublin, 1963-73; Prof., Music, Royal Acad. of Music, London, 1964-. Recordings on HMV, Decca, Columbia, Vanguard. Hons: CBE; FRAM; Worshipfull Co. of Musicians; Cobbett Medal for Chamber Music. Hobby: Painting. Address: 63 Marloes Rd., London W8 6LE, UK. 3, 4, 19.

GRILLO, Joann, b. 14 May 1939, NYC, USA. Mezzo-soprano. Educ: BS, Hunter Coll., 1976; Pvte. study, Lorenzo Anselmi, Daniel Ferro & Joan Dornemann. m. Richard Kness, 1 s. Career: Leading Mezzo-soprano, Metropolitan Opera; Res. Artist, ibid., 1963-; Roles incl. Santuzza (Cavalleria Rusticana), Neocle (Siege of Corinth), Laura (La Gioconda); Vienna Staatsoper Debut, Carmen, 1978. Hobbies: Egyptology; Cooking; Travel. Mgmt: Joseph Scuro Assocs., 111 W 57 St., NYC, NY 10019, USA. Address: Metropolitan Opera, Lincoln Center, NY, NY 10023, USA. 5.

GRIMES, J Scott, b. 4 July 1949, Indpls., Ind., USA. Harpist. Educ: studied w. Nicanor Zabaleta (Spain) Susann McDonald (Calif.) Gerard Devos (France) Ann Mason Stockton (Calif.) & Mildred Dilling (NYC); Univ. studies at Culver Military Acad. (Ind.), Ind. Univ. (Bloomington), Univ. of Kansas (Lawrence), Butler Univ. (Indpls.) & Univ. of Calif. (Los Angeles). Career: soloist & orchestral performer; lectr. at annual Int. Jazz Harp Fest., Santa Barbara, Calif.; formerly prin. harpist, Seattle Phil. Orch., Seattle, Wash. Mbrships: Patron mbr., Am. Harp Soc.; Am. Musicol. Soc.; AF of M, Los Angeles & Seattle. Hobbies: Water Sports; Backpacking. Address: 1610 Argyle Ave., Suite 102, Hollywood, CA 90028, USA.

GRIMS-LAND, Ebbe Bertil Vilhelm, b. 11 June 1915, Malmo, Stockholm, Sweden. Composer; Chamber Musician (viola, Mandolin). m. Vera Linnea Annerstedt, 2 s. Career: Viola w. Swedish Radio Symph. Orch., 1943-74; Gitarr-Kammartrion, 1955-; Tonkonstars-trion, 1970-; Soloist on radio & TV. Comps. incl: Concertino (mand. & 10 instruments); Train-Suite (Piccolo, Mandolin, Marimba); Sinfonietta, Carl von Linne, Music-serial story for solo instruments; Konnexion (Marimba & Orch.); Montafoni (D trumpet & orch.); Consideration (mixed choir & 3 instruments); Songs (soprano, flute, guitar). Contbr. to Musikern. Mbr. num. profl. orgs. inclng: The Soc. of Swedish Comps. Recip. Culture Prize of City of Stockholm, 1974; Stim-composer Prize, 1976; Konstnärsnämnden, 1977, 78. Address: Stim. Box 5091, S-10242 Stockholm 5, Sweden.

GRINDE, Nils, b. 8 Jan. 1927, Enebakk, Norway. Musicologist; Organist. Educ: Cand. Mag., Musicol., Univ. of Oslo, 1953; Higher exam. in organ, Oslo Music Conserv., 1959. Kirsti Wilhelmsen. Career: currently Dosent in Musicol., Univ. of Oslo. Publs. incl: The Halfdan Kjerulf Bibliography, 1956; Hafdan Kjerulf's Piano Music, 1961; Textbook in Counterpoint in the Style of Bach, 1966; History of Norwegian Music, 1971; Norwegian Music. An Anthology, 1974; Ed., Studia Musicologica Norwegica vol 2-4 (1976-78); Ed., Halfdan Kjimlf-Collected Songs, vol. 1-2, (1978). Contbr. to: Grove's Dict., 6th ed.; Sohlmans Musiklexikon, 2nd ed. Address: Slemdalsverin 91b, Oslo 3, Norway.

GRINDEA, Carola, b. Piatra N, Romania. Pianist; Piano Teacher. Educ: Lic., Bucharest Univ.; Dip., Acad. of Music, Bucharest; studies w. Constanta Erbiceanu, Tobias Matthay, George Enescu. m. Miron Grindea, 1 d. Career: Solo recitalist & Chamber musiciansapps. on BBC & in other European countries; Lectures on music educ. on TV & radio & in music colls. in UK, USA & Can.; Piano Prof., GSN. Publs: Rumanian Dances (co-author), 1952; The First Ten Lessons, 1964; We Make Our Own Music (recorded as audio-visual unit), 1972; Tensions in the Performance of Music - A Symposium, 1978; The Adult Beginner (cassette), 1976. Mbrships: ISM; Fndr. & Organising Sec, European Piano Tchrs. Assoc. Hons: 1st Prize, Piano & Chamber Music, Acad. of Music, Bucharest. Hobbies: Conversation; People. Address: 28 Emperor's Gate, London SW7 4HS, UK.

GRINDEA, Nadia-Myra, b. 28 Oct. 1943, London, UK. Pianist; Teacher. Educ: RAM & London Univ.; ARCM; GRSM; B Mus, London. m. Dr. Michael Lasserson, 2 s., 1 d. Career: Fndr. Young People's Music Club; Solo Piano & Chmbr. Music recitals concerto perfs.; Mbr., Studio 3 Trio w. Kathleen Moy (flute) & Christine Geer (oboe). Contbr. to Music & Musicians. Recip. Manns Mem. Prize, RAM. Address: 74 Dovercourt Rd., London SE22 UK.

GRINHAUZ, Berta C R, b. 18 Mar. 1940, Buenos Aires Argentina. Pianist. Educ: Study w. Teodoro Fuchs, Tino Rossetti & Bertia Sujowolski (Argentina); w. Alfonso Montecino (piano) Janos Starker & William Primrose (Chmbr. Music), Ind. Univ. USA. m. Luis Grinhauz, 1 s. Career: Recitals, Chmbr. Music Radio & TV apps. in Argentina, USA & Canada. Recordings issued by CBC (Montreal). Mbrship: Am. Fedn. of Musicians. Hons: 1s Prize, Direccion Gen. de Cultura, Buenos Aires, 1963; Trave Grant, Mozarteum Argentino, 1968; Bianco y Marfil, Buenos Aires, 1964. Hobbies: Gardening; Tapestry; Needlepoint Address: 5694 Merrimac Rd., Cote St., Luc., PQ Canada.

GRINHAUZ, Luis, b. 27 Jan. 1942, Concordia, E R Argentina. Violinist; Teacher. Educ: Prof. of Music, Municipa Conserv. of Music, Buenos Aires, 1966; Perf. Cert., Ind. Univ. USA, 1969. m. Berta Clara Rosendhl, 1 s. Career: Recitals concerts, radio & TV apps.; Lectr. in Argentina, Chile, Mexico USA, Can.; Asst. Concertmaster, Montreal Symph. Orch.; Mbr. McGill Chmbr. Orch. Musica Camerata Mtl.; Fac. Mbr., Ind Univ.; Interlochen Arts Acad., USA; Ecole Normal de Musique Montreal. Recordings: CBS Radio. Mbr. Am. Fedn. of Musicians Hons. incl; Aspen Musical Festival, 1970; CBS Festival, 1972 Hobbies: Photography; Lit.; Skiing; Wines. Address: 569 Merrimac Rd., Cote St. Luc, PQ, Canada H4W 156. 4.

GRINKE, Frederick, b. 8 Aug. 1911, Winnipeg, Can. Violinist; Teacher. Educ: studied w. John Waterhouse, Winnipeg, Can.; studied w. Rowsby Woof, Adolf Busch & Carl Flesch, RAM; FRAM. m. Doronty Sheldon, 1 s. Career: Chmbr. Music & solo apps., UK, Europe, Am., Aust. & NZ; has had works written for him by noted comps. inclng. Vaughan Williams, Lennon Berkeley, Rubbra; has acted as Juror, num. int. violin competitions; Prof., Royal Acad. of Music; currently devoting time to tchng. Recordings: as Soloist & Chmbr. Music Player. Hons: CBE, 1979. Address: Frog's Hall, Braiseworth, Eye, Suffolk, UK. 1, 2, 19.

GRIPPE, Ragnar, b. 15 Oct. 1951, Stockholm, Sweden. Composer; Cellist. Educ. incl: Stockholm Univ. (musicol.), 1966-75; Music Conserv., Stockholm (cello); Groupe de Recherches Musicales, Paris. Career: radio commissions Swedish Broadcasting Corp., 1975; Stockholm Opera Ballet (Waiting Lounge), 1977; La Scala Bicentennial, Omaggio a Picasso, 1977; feature films, 1978-79, incl: The Emperor's Sleep of Death; Situation I (TV). Comps: in addition to above, Shandar, 1978; Cri, 1975; electronic music. Recordings incl: Ragnar Grippe Electronic Comps., 1977. Publs: Musiques Electroacoustiques, 1977; Neue Zeitschrift für Musik, 1979; Tonfallet, 1976, etc. Contbr. to: Vogue (French ed.); Nutida Musik (Sweden); Musiques France, etc. Mgmt: martin Engström, Organisation Int. Opera et Concert, Paris. Address: 79 rue St. Louis en l'Ile, 75004 Paris, France.

GRIST, Reri, b. New York City, USA. Singer. Educ: BA (Music), Queens Coll., CUNY; pvte. vocal coaching w. Claire Gelda. m. Ulf Thomson, 1 c. Career: appeared in mal. Broadway shows inclng. West Side Story; regular appearances w. major opera houses inclng. Vienna State, Royal Opera House Covent Gdn., Metropol. Opera NYC, San Fran., La Scala Milan, Munich State, Chgo., Buenos Aires, etc., Festival appearances incl: Salzburg, Munich, Glyndebourne & Holland. Appearances in var. operatic films for TV. Recordings incl: works by Mozart, Strauss, Verdi, etc. on EMI, RCA Victor, Columbia, etc. Recip. var. hons. & awards. Hobbies: Walking; Skiing; Cooking. Mgmt: Ronald Wilford, Columbia Artists Mgmt. & Rudolph Raab. Address: Vievigplaz 11, 8 Munich 21, German Fed. Repub.

GROBE, Donald Roth, b. 16 Dec. 1929, Ottawa, Ill., USA. Opera & Concert Singer. Educ: B Mus, Chgo. Musical Coll.; Mannes Coll. of Music, NYC; Aspen, Colo.; studied voice w. Robert Long, Martial Singher, Robert Weedie, Frau Prof. V. Winterfeldt. m. Carol Jean Pritchett, 2 s., 1 d. Debut: Chgo., 1953. Career: NY, 1953-56; Lyric Tenor, Sädt Bübven, Krefeld-München-Gladbach, 1956-57; Tenor, Landestheater Hannover, 1957-60, Cologne, 1959-60; Deutsche Oper Berlin, 1960-; Guest concerts, Hamburg, Munich, Vienna. Recordings incl: Lulu (Berg); Der junge Lord (Henze); Das Rheingold (Wagner); Fiedelio (Beethoven); Trionti (Orff); Cardilla (Hindemith). Mbr., Phi Mu Alpha Sinfonia. Hons. incl: Kammaersänger, Deutsche Oper Berlin, 1970. Hobbies: Photography; Gardening. Mgmt: Adler, Berlin Robert Schulz, Opera, Germany; Thea Dispeker, USA. Address: Ahrenshooper Zelle 68, 1000 Berlin 38, Germany.

GROCOCK, Robert, b. 1 Nov. 1925, New Haven, Conn., USA. Musician (Trumpeter, Conductor); College Professor. Educ: BM Music Educ. & Perf.'s Cert. in Trumpet, Eastman Schl. of Music, 1948; pvte. study w. Harry Glanz, NYC, 1949, 1950; MM, Eastman Schl. of Music, 1950; post-graduate study Ind. Univ. m. Dorothea Roberts Letzler Grocock, 1 s., 1 d. Career: Played w. Rochester, NY Phil. & Civic Orchs., Chgo. Symph. Orch.; Freelance Perf., Radio, TV, Opera, Ballet; Recitalist; Clinician; Adjudicator; Cond. Recording: w. Chgo. Symph., 1951-52. Publ: Advanced Methof for Trumpet, 1968. Contbr. to: NACWPI Bulletin; Holton Fanfare; Instrumentalist. Mbrships: NACWPI (Pres., 1962-64); MENC; AAUP; Am. Fedn. Musicians; Pi Kappa Lambda; Int. Trumpet Guild. Hobbies: Golf; Tennis; Cooking. Address: 720 Terrace Ln., Greencastle, IN 46135, USA. 8.

GRODNER, Murray, b. 23 Aug. 1922, NYC, USA. Bassist; Professor of Music. Educ: BM, 1954, MM, 1955, Manhattan Schl. of Music. m. Leah Grodner, 1 s., 1 d. Career: Mbr., Ballet Theatre Orch., 1941, 52, 53, Ballet Russe Orch., 1942, Pittsburgh Symph. Orch. (Asst. Prin.), 1942, 1946-48, Houston Symph. Orch. (Prin.), 1948-51, NBC Symph. Orch. under Toscanini, 1951-54; Tchr., Ind. Univ., 1955-. Recordings: w. NBC & Pitts. Symphs., RCA; w. Berkshire Quartet, Vox; w. Baroque Chmbr. Players, Coronet Records. Publs: Comprehensive Catalog of Available Literature for the Double Bass, 1958, 64, 74; An Organized Method of String Playing (Double Bass Vol.), forthcoming. Contbr. to profl. & pedagogical publs. Mbrships: Bd. of Dirs., Int. Soc. of Bassists; Am. String Tchrs. Assn. Hobbies: Home Design; Travel. Address: 2611 Fairoaks Lane, Bloomington, IN 47401, USA.

GRØN, Chr. Ancher, b. 10 Apr. 1943, Copenhagen, Denmark. Saxophonist. Educ: Avantgarde-jazz Flautist and conductor until 1965 when he devoted himself to the classical saxophone; Highest Dip., Royal Danish Acad. of Music, Copenhagen, 1973, (State Music Tchrs. Dip., s.p. 1972); pvte. study, w. Daniel Deffayet, Paris, 1973-75. Career: Radio & Concert apps. in Denmark, Sweden & Norway, 1968-; Saxophonist, DUT (Danish Sect., Int. Soc. of Contemporary Music), 1971-; Soloist, Royal Acad. Orch., 1972 & 73; Soloist, Danish Radio Symph. Orch., 1973-; Solo-saxophonist, Royal Opera, Copenhagen, 1974-, Recitals in France (Paris, etc.), 1974. World Saxophone Congress (Bordeaux), 1974; Soloist, Swedish Radio Symph. Orch., Stockholm, .1975; columnist, Danish radio. Publ: Teaching Saxophone, 1'972. Contbr. to: Bulletin de AsSaFra, Paris. Mbrships: The World Saxophone Congress; Assn. des Saxophonistes de France, Danish Soloists Assn. of 1921, Copenhagen; Danish State Music Tchrs. Assn. Hons: Works for saxophone dedicated to him by var. comps. in Denmark & Sweden; Grant from Nordic State Coop. for Music (NOMUS) to commission the Nilsson Saxophone Concerto. Address: Danas Plads 18, 1915 Copenhagen V. Denmark.

GROOM, Lester Herbert, b. 19 Jan. 1929, Chgo., Ill., USA. Organist; Educator; Composer. Educ: B Mus, Wheaton˝Coll., Ill., 1951; Mus M, Northwestern Univ., Evanston, Ill., 1952; AAGO (by exam.), 1954; pvte. study of comp. m. Myrtle Vera Jacobson, 1 s., 2 d. Career: Fac. Mbr., Moody Bible Inst., 1953-55, Blue Mtn. Coll., 1957-62, Baker Univ. 1962-67; Fac. Mbr., Evergreen Conf. Schl. of Ch. Music, Colo., 1965-, (Press., Evergreen Conf., 1973-); Assoc. Prof. Music, Seattle Pacific Coll., Wash., 1969-; organ recitals through out USA. Comps. incl: 24 Psalm Voluntaries; Gothic Fanfare; organ works & anthems. Contbr. to profl. jrnls. Mbr., AGO (Former Miss. State Chmn.); MTNA. Hobbies: Collecting Records; Photography. Address: 10629 NE 26th St., Bellevue, WA 98004, USA. 4.

GROPPENBERGER, Walter, b. 10 Nov. 1938, Vienna, Austria. Pianist; College Lecturer; Conductor. Educ: Boys Choir, Vienna, 1946-48; Concert Dip., Town Conserv. of Vienna, 1958; Studied under Prof. Bruno Seidlhofer, 1961-66. m., 1 d. Career: Lectr., Piano, Coll. of Music, Graz; Mbr., Concert Orch., Vienna, Paris, Brussels; Piano & Chmbr. Music perfs. for TV & Radio. Hons: designation as Ausserordentlichen Hochschulprofessor for Piano by the Federal President of Austria, 1975. Address: A-8184 Anger 1255, Styria/Steiermark, Austria.

GROSCHEL, Ernst Ludwig Sr., b. 12 Aug. 1896. Composer; Conductor; Pianist. Educ: Manualo Sexencises Fortepiano 'Dupont' and Konservatorium Nurnberg. m. Emma Herold, 2 s. Debut: Bad Reichenhall, 1922. Career: Cure Orch., radio appearances in France, Austria, Italy, USA, Switz., Poland, Argentina, Germany, UK. Compositions publd. by: Bosworth & Co. London; Sikorski, Hamburg; Franz Zorn, Nurnberg; Willi Martin, Nurnberg. Recordings on Electrola, Decca. Publs: Frank Altmann: Tonkunsterlexikon. Mbr., Deutscher Komponistenverband. Mgmt: GEMA. Address: Rankestrasse 30, 8500 Nurnberg, German Fed. Repub.

GROSS, Eric, b. 16 Sept. 1926, Vienna, Austria. Associate Professor of Music; Composer; Conductor. Educ: MA (Hons.). M.Litt., Aberdeen; LMusTCL; FTCL.; D Mus, Aberdeen. m. Pamela M Davies. Career: Perf., Arr., Cond., Light Music, UK, Ceylon; Accomp., Radio Ceylon, BBC, 1960-74; Tchr., Conserv., Sydney; Lectr., Sr. Lectr., ibid., 1971; Assoc. Prof., ibid., 1973, Univ. of Sydney; Cond., Pro Musica Orch. & Choir; Cond., St. Andrew's Cathedral Choral Soc., Sydney, 1964-69; Guest Cond., Conserv., Newcastle, NSW, etc. Num. publd. Compositions incl: Orchl., Concert French Mood, 1966; Fanfopus, 1973; Cantatas, Sunset, Moon, Dreams, 1972; Other Choral Music, Bring us in Good Ale, 1967; Psalms, 122, 130, 1972; Chamb. & Instrumental Music; Rondino Pastorale, 1962; Interlude for 6 Horns, 1965; Wedding March for Organ, 1967; Solo Voice, 3 Burns Settings, for soprano & piano, 1967; Stage works, The Amorous Judge, (1 Act Opera); The Ugly Duckling, (Pantomime); TV & Film Music, The Big Nine, Wait for Tormorrow, 1970; Psalmody (1975); 6 Miniatures for Brass Trio; The Grand Adventure (1977); Num. Scores for the Aust. Commonwealth Film Unit, & many other comps. Contbr. to: Cannon; Aust. Jrnl. of Music Educ.; Point & Counterpoint: The Aust. Composer, etc. Mbrships. incl: Fellowship, Aust. Comps., (Pres., 1976-78); Aust. Soc. for Music Educ. Recip., Albert H Maggs Award for Comp., 1976. Hobbies: Squash; Table Tennis; Soccer; Stamp Collecting. Address: Dept. of Music, c/o Univ. od Sydney, NSW, Australia 2006.

GROSS, Marcel, b. 2 July 1924, Czernowitz, Roumania (USSR). Viola & Viola d'Amore Player. Educ: Studied Violin & Viola w. Prof. Krämer, Musikverein, Czernowitz; Violin & Viola, Prof.

Avakian Royal Acad., Bucharest. m. Gaby Yvonne Tomiteanu. Debut: Solo Viola, Mozart's Symphonia Concertante, Roumanian Radio Symph. Orch. Career: Mbr., Roumanian Radio String Quartet, 1949-; Ldr., Viola Sect., Roumanian Radio Symph. Orch., 1951-; Roumanian State Opera, 1957-58, Asst. Ldr., Viola Sect., Kol Israel Symph., 1960-62; Ramat Gan Ch-O; Ldr., Viola Sect., Stadtorchester Winterthur-CH, 1962-; Mbr., Winterthur Streich Quartett; Tchr., Winterthur Music Schl. & Conserv. Num. recordings. Hons. incl: II Prize, G Enescu Festival, 1958. Hobbies: Music; Lit.; Arts; Working w. hands; Walking. Address: Tellstrasse 43, CH-8400 Winterthur, Switzerland.

GROSS, Zygmunt, b. 11 June 1903, Vienna, Austria. Composer. Educ: PhD, (Law, Philos. & Music), Jagiellonian Univ., Cracow, Poland; studied Comp. m. Hanna Szumanska, 1 s. Comps. 30 Preludes for Pianoforte (some recorded); Sonata Op. 14 no. 2. Contbr. to: publs. of Polish Acad. of Sci. Mbrships: Polish Comps.' Union; Polish Philosophical Soc.; Polish Sociol. Soc. Address: 84-31 62 Drive Apt. V-34, Middle Village, NY 11379, USA.

GROSSE, Erwin G Friedrich, b. 4 Dec. 1904, Hannover, German Fed. Repub. Pianist; Harpsichordist; Violinist; Violist. Educ: Studies of piano, harpsichord, violin, viol., conducting & comp. m. Ursula Meusel, 2 d. Career: Cond., Opera House Hannover; Tchr. of violin, viol, piano, harpsichord, & Cond. of Orch., Acad. of Music, Karlsruhe; Soloist on piano & harpsichord; Free Comp. 3 Concerts w. double bass, trumpet & saxophone; Comps. incl: Chmbr. music; Music for Orch.; Music for voice; Jeanine (Opera); Revelation of St. John, (oratoio); 3 pieces for drums. Mbr., German Fed. Repub. Comps. publs: story einer musikalischen Entwicklung 1904-1974, 1974. Hons: 1st Prize, Western German Publrs. of Music, Berlin, 1960. Hobby: Lit. Address: 7505 Ettlingen, Vordersteig 7a, German Fed. Repub.

GRØTHE, Anders. b. 4 Nov. 1944, Sor-Trondelag, Norway. Musician; Teacher. Educ: Masters Degree; Comp. Dip., Norwegian State Conserv.; Trossingen, German Fed. Repub. Comps: Norwegian Miniature Suite for Accordion; Romance & Rondo for Accordion & String Orch.; Grolsch per Orchestra; Tre Nocturner for Accordion; Forstyrrelser for Accordion & String Quartet; Pa Lopende Band for piano. Address: Hoffsbakken 1, Oslo 2, Norway.

GROUT, Donald Jay, b. 28 Sept. 1902, Rock Rapids, Iowa, USA. Professor of Musicology. Educ: AB (Phil.), Syracuse Univ., 1923; AM, 1932, PhD, 1939, Harvard Univ. m. Margaret Dunn Grout, 1 d. Career: Vis. Lectr. in Hist. of Music, Mills Coll., 1935-36; Asst. in Music & Tutor, Div. of Music, Harvard Univ., 1936-39; Instructor in Music & Tutor, Div. of Music, ibid., 1940-42; Assoc. Prof. of Music Lit., The Univ. of Texas, 1942-45; Prof. of Music, Cornell Univ., 1945-62; Chmn., Dept. of Music, ibid., 1947-51, 1953-58; Fndn. Prof. of Musicol., ibid., 1962-70; Prof. emeritus, ibid., 1970-; Bloch Prof. of Music, Univ. of Calif., Berkeley, Calif., 1975-76. Publs: A Short History of Opera, 2 vols., 1947, 2nd Ed., 1965, Japanese Ed., 1960; A History of Western Music, 1960, 3rd Ed., 1978; The Operas of Alessandro Scarlatti, 4 vols. Contbr. to num. profl. publs. Mbr., num. profl. orgs. Hons. incl: Archibald Thompson Davison Medal for Musicol., London, 1962; George Arents Pioneer Medal for Excellence in Music, Syracuse Univ., 1965. Address: Cloudbank, R.D. 3, Skaneateles, NY 13152, USA. 2.

GROV, Magne, b. 13 Mar. 1938, Naustdal, Sunnfjord, Norway. Composer. Educ: Bergen Conserv.; Oslo Conserv.; w. Lennox Berkeley, London. m. Britt Karin Grov, 1 d., 1 s. Debut: Norwegian Broadcasting System, 1969. Radio & concert perf. Comps. Ballade for strings, piano & Harp; Concerto for piano & orch.; suite for chmbr. orch.; Trio for flute, oboe and clarinet; Piano comps: Sonatina; Fantasy; Four Norwegian Folk Tunes; Organ & choral works; Voice & piano works. Recip: Var. grants; State Grant, 1975, 78; Prizewinner, Opening of Oslo Concert Hall, 1977. Mbrships: Soc. Norwegian Composers; Norwegian Soc. Musicians. Address: Nordbyringen 9A, 2050 Jessheim, Norway.

GROVÉ, Stefans, b. 23 July 1922, Bethlehem, S Africa. University Lecturer; Composer. Educ: perfs. & tchrs. licentiate dips., Univ. of S Africa; Perfs. dip. (piano), Univ. of Cape Town; MA, Harvard Univ. m. Catherine Alison Marguard, 5 c. Career: works perf. in S Africa, Austria, Germany, UK, Scotland, Israel, USA & Aust.; lectr., Peabody Conserv., Balt., USA, 1956-72. Comps. incl: Sinfonia Concertante; Psalm 54 for mezzo, flute & harp; Chorale prelude on Psalm 42; Easter music for SATB, Instrumental ensemble & organ. Recordings; 3 Inventions; orchl. & chmbr. works by S African Broadcasting Commission. Publs: Ed.; orchl. score, Bruch's newly discovered Concerto for 2 pianos, Op. 88, 1972. Contbr. to: Musicus; Lantern; Ars Nova; Standpunte.

Hons: N Calif. Harpists Assn., 1952; G Arthur Knight prize & Bohemian Club prize, Harvard. Hobbies: Photography; Carpentry; Calligraphy. Address: Music Dept., Univ. of Pretoria, Pretoria 0002, S Africa. 14.

GROVEN, Sigmund, b. 16 March, 1946, Heddal (Telemark), Norway. Harmonica soloist; Composer. Educ: BA, Univ. of Oslo, 1969; Studies w. Tommy Reilly. Debut: Norwegian radio, 1965. Career: Concerts, radio & TV apps. in Norway, Sweden, Denmark, Germany, Switz., Netherlands, UK; Soloist w. Orchs. (incl. Norwegian Radio Orch.); Apps. w. String Quartets in Norway, Sweden, Netherlands, UK; 14 major tours throughout Norway for Rikskonsertene; Played for films; Wrote & introduced TV series teaching harmonica in Norway (w. Tommy Reilly). Comps. incl: Music for radio, TV & films; Songs, instrumental pieces incl. Sa spiller vi harmonica (recorded), Blow Silver Wind & Motlys. Recordings incl: Num. solo LP's; Music for Two Harmonicas, Tommy Reilly Plays Fried Walter, w. Tommy Reilly; Musikk for en lang natt, w. Ketil Björnstad, etc. Publs: Tommy Reilly Harmonica Course, Norwegian version, 1971. Mbrships: Norwegian Musicians Union; TONO. Hons: 2nd Prize, Int. Harmonica Competition, Fedn. Int. de l'Harmonica, Germany, 1967; Scholarship Fund for Perf. Artists, Oslo, 1977. Hobbies: Broadcasting; Photography. Address: Rute 15/26, 3670 Notodden, Norway.

GROVER, Cyril Russell, b. 16 Jan. 1941, Dufftown, Scotland, UK. Freelance Teacher; Conductor; Performer (organ, Piano, Harpsichord). Educ: RCM, 1959-62; GRSM; ARCO; ARCM; LRAM; pvte. study piano & organ. m. Jennifer Ann Stephenson, 1 s., 1 d. Career: Lectr., Rhodesian Coll. of Music, Rhodesia, 1964-68; Cond., Salisbury Choral Soc., 1967-69; Cond. & Musical Dir., Salisbury City Orch., 1969-; Organist, Cathedral of St. Mary & All Saints, Salisbury, 1970-; Own Schl. of Music; Radio & TV work, inclng. 2 series, Rhodesia. Recordings: Elgar, Dream of Gerontius; Vaughan Williams, Sea Symphony. Hobbies: Photography; Gardening; Squash. Address: 49 Pendennis Rd., Mt. Pleasant, Salisbury, Rhodesia, 18.

GROVER, Paul Barton, b. 17 Dec. 1908, Ellsworth, Kan., USA. Music Educator. Educ: AB, Kan. Wesleyan Univ.; M Mus Ed, Kan. Univ.; EdD, Univ. of Ill.; Cleveland Orch. Cond.'s Workshops, W. Szell, 1954-55; Phila. Orch. Cond.'s Symposium, w. Ormandy, 1955. m. Ethel Wildermuth, 1 s., 3 d. Career incl: Prof. of Music, Northeastern Okla. State Univ., -1974; Cond., Northeastern Okla. Symph.; currently pvte. tchr. of orchl. instruments. Mbrships: Phi Mu Alpha Sinfonia; MTNA; Oka. MTA; Pi Gamma Mu. Hobbies: Theatre (acting & dir.); Bird Watching; Travel. Address: 710 Janet St., Talequah, OK 74464, USA.

GROVES, (Sir) Charles Barnard, b. 10 Mar. 1915, London, UK. Orchestral Conductor. Educ: RCM, London; ARCO. m. Hilary Barchard, 1 s., 2 d. Career: BBC Northern Symph. Orch., 1944-51; Bournemouth Symph. Orch., 1951-61; Welsh Nat. Opera Co., 1961-63; Royal Liverpool Phil. Orch., 1963-77; Assoc. Cond., Royal Phil. Orch., 1967-; Dir. of Music, English Nat. Opera Co., 1977-; Cond. of orchs. all over the world; broadcasts on TV and radio. Recordings on EMI. Mbrships: Pres., Nat. Fed. of Music Socs., 1972-; Pres., ISM, 1972. Hons. incl: OBE, 1958; CBE, 1968; Kt. Bach., 1973; FRCM, 1956; RAM, 1967; MusD, Liverpool, 1970; FRNCM, 1974; FTCL, 1974; GSM, 1974; Dr., Open Univ., 1978. Hobbies: English Lit; Cigars; Wine. Mgmt: Ingpen & Williams, 14 Kensington Ct., London W8. Address: 12 Camden Sq., London NW1 9UY, UK. 1, 16.

GROVES, John Phillip, b. 6 Sept. 1949, Horsham, UK. Singer; Teacher; Conductor. Educ: Cert. of Educ., Borough Rd. Coll. of Educ.; ALCM. Debut: Adeline Genee Theatre, E Grinstead, 1971. Career: Dir. of Music, Prior's Field Schl., Godalming, 1974-; Cond., Horsham District Youth Orch. & Choir, 1978-; Opera apps. incl: Gemini Opera & Gilbert & Sullivan for All; Recitals, concerts & oratorios, London, Sussex & Surrey. Mbrships: Oxford & Cambridge Music Club. Hobbies: Drama; Music. Address: 10 Bilbets, Rushams Rd., Horsham, Sussex, UK. 3.

GROWIEC, Michalina Izabela, b. 19 Apr. 1933, Jedlicze, Krosno, Poland. Singer. Educ: Ceramics Engr.; MA in music; Dip., Acad. Musicale Chigiana; XV Int. Musikseminar der DDR. m. Jerzy Growiec, 2 s. Debut: 1962. Career: stage perfs., Silesian Opera, Bytom, Poland; var. perfs. w. phil. orchs., Poland & Bulgaria, also Bayreuth Fest. Orch.; TV & radio broadcasts, Poland & German Dem. Repub.; apps. at concerts of Jeunesse Musicales de Pologne & concerts in USA; Dean, Vocal Fac., Conserv. of Katowice, Poland. Mbr., Assn. of Polish Musicians. Hobby: Collecting old porcelain. Address: 40-007 Katowice, ul. Bankowa 34-142, Poland.

GRUBER, Gernot, b. 17 Nov. 1939, Bruck, Austria. Musicologist; Lectr. Educ: Univ. Graz, 1964, PhD. Career:

1964, Asst. Graz Univ., 1970, Scholarship Alexander Humbolt Org., Mainz Univ.; 1973, Lectr. musicol., Vienna Univ., 1975-76, Vis. Prof. Salzburg Univ. Mbrships: Pres. sci. bd., European Liszt Centre. Publs: Contributions to the History and Composition Technique of the Perodie Magnificat, Graz, 1964; W A Mozart's Zauberflöte, in New Mozart-ed., Kassel, 1970; Lodovico Tacconi as Theoretical Musician, Vienna, 1973. Contbr. to: var. profl. jrnls. Address: Rukerlberggasse 16, A-8010 Graz, Austria.

GRUBICH, Joachim Antoni, b. 16 Jan. 1935, Chelmno, Poland. Organist; Recitalist. Educ: MA; Dip. w. distinction in Organ perf., State Coll. of Music Cracow. m. Ewa Czernek, 2 s. Debutr: Int. Music Competition, Geneva, 1962. Career: Recitals & concerts in most European countries inclng. UK, Netherlands, Switzerland, Italy, & USSR; num. apps. in int. fests.; Radio recordings in Poland & num. other countries; apps. on Polish TV; Prof. in Organ Playing, State Coll. of Music, Wardaw & Cracow. Recordings: 11 LPs for Muza (some also issued abroad). Publ: Edition of Old Polish Organ Music, 1968. Contbr. to PWM Cracow. Mbr., Assn. of Polish Musicians. Hons: Golden Disc, Polish Recording Co., 1972. Hobbies: Photography; Travel. Address: ul. Chopina 107, 30-047 Cracow, Poland.

GRUHN, Nora, b. 6 mar. 1905, London, IK. Former Opera Singer; Singing Teacher; Music Therapist. Educ: RCM. m. Sydney Mitchell (dec.), 2 s. (dec.), 1 d. Career: Prin. Soprano, Royal Opera, Covent Gdn., Cologne Opera House, Sadlers Wells; Many radio apps.; TV Music & the Mind; Mag., Bristol; Film, Conquest of the Air. Recordings: The Woodbird in Siegfried w. Lauritz Melchior, EMI. Contbr. to: RCM Mag.; Brit. Soc. of Music Therapy Conf. Publs. Mbrships: ISM; Committee, Brit. Soc. of Music Therapy; Soroptimists, Croydon. Hobbies: Psychol.; Bird watching. Address: Warblers Hatch, Beech Rd., Merstham, Surrey, UK. 3, 4, 27.

GRUMIAUX, Arthur, b. 1921, Belgium. Violinist. Career incl: Perfs. at int. music festivals at Glyndebourne, Salzburg, Lucerne, Aix-en-Provence, Strasbourg & Vienna; Soloist w. many leading Duropean orch.; Concert tours of Am., Japan & Middle E.; Wide repertoire of classical works, noted particularly for interpretation of Mozart; Also performed many works of modern composers incl. Bartok, Berk, Stravinsky & Walton. Recordings of var. works issued on Phillips Label. Hons. incl: sev. Grand Prix du Disque; Critics awards, Germany & Italy. Address: co Ibbs & Tillett, London, UK.

GRÜMMER, Elisabeth, b. 1921, Germany. Operatic Soprano. Educ: Drama Schl., Meiningen; music studies, Aachen. Career: Stadttheater, Aachen, 1941; Städtische Oper, Duisburg, 1941; Staatsoper, Berlin, 1948; Deutsche Oper, Berlin, 1961-; many apps. in opera houses of other countries; Prof., Staatliche Hochschule für Musik und Darstellende Kunst, Berlin. Hons: Berliner Kunstpreis, 1965; Kammersängerin. 16.

GRUMMITT, Margaret Halliday, b. 27 Mar. 1905, Anerley, London, UK. Pianist. Educ: Brighton Schl. of Music;o ARAM, 1935; studied w. Isidor Philipp. Debut: Wigmore Hall, 1936. Career: num. Violin & Piano Sonata Broadcasts, BBC, 1925-45; freelance Piano Soloist, Chmbr. Musician, Accomp.; Official Accomp., Brighton Competitive Musical Fest., 1946-72, & var. other fests. Mbrships: Solo Perfs., Sect., ISM; Accomp., Brit. Fedn. of Music Fests.; RAM Club; Sussex Musicians Club; Pres., ibid., 1945-47. Hons: Blakiston Memorial Prize; Nicholls Prize; Roller Prize; Potter Exhib., RAM, 1924-27. Address: 12 Eaton Grove, Hove, E Sussex BN3 3PH, UK. 3, 27, 29.

GRUNDSTAD, Aage, b. 26 May 1923, Vefsn, Norway. Accordion player. m. Astrid, 2 c. Debut: Radio Norway, 1946. Career: TV apps., Germany, Scotland, USA, Can., Japan, Korea, Iran, France & Scandinavia; Music & song Tchr., Veit vet Musikkskole, 1967; Accordion Tchr., Baerum Comm. Music Schl. Comps: Accordion book Vols. 1 & 2 for group, 1965; Finger-practise (10 lessons), 1965; Accordion Album, 1978. Recordings: Oldtime Dances from Norway; Norwegian Folkdances. Contbr. to: Trekkspill Nytt Mag., 1971-. Mbrships: Norwegian Accordionist's Assn.; Norwegian Music Assn.; TONO Int. Music Assn. Hobbies: Open Air Living; Travelling. Address: Riiser-Larsensvei 10, 1320 Stabekk, Norway.

GRUNENWALD, Jean Jacques, b. 2 Feb. 1911, Cran Gévriex, Haute Savoie, France. Organist; Composer. Educ: Bacc., Maths & Philos.; Conserv. Nat. Sup. de Musique, (2 1st prizes); Ecole des Beaux Arts, Paris; Grand Prix de Rome, for Musical Comp. m. Sonia Virenque, 1 s. Career: Num. concert tours w. the organ; Organist, St. Sulpice, Paris. Compositions incl: Oeuvres pour piano, orgue, clavecin; 2 concertos for piano & orch.; OPuverture pour un Drame Sacré, De Profoundis; Sazdanapale, Opera in 3 acts. Recordings: Intégrale de l'Oeuvre d'orgue de J S Bach; Intégrale C Franck; Intégrale Grigny. Mbr., Comm., Min., Organs of France. Hons: Grand Prix du Conseil Général de la Seine, 1962; Grand Prix Nat. du Disque, 1962; Chevalier de la Légion d'Honneur; Off. de l'ordre des Arts et des Lettres; Off. de l'Ordre Nat. du Mérite. Hobbies: Modern Art; Painting. Address: 9 Rue Dupont des Loges. 75007 Paris, France.

GRUNEWALD, William P, b. 16 June 1907, Cedar Rapids, IA, USA. Violinist. Educ: BA, Coe Coll.; MA, Univ. of IA. m. Rosemary Jacobi, 2 d. Career: Mbr., Violin Sect., Cedar Rapids Symph. Orch., 45 yrs.; Dir., 1st Luth. S S Orch., 5 yrs. Mbrships: Phi Mu Alpha Sinfonia; Am. Fedn. of Musicians; Order of Artus, Univ. of IA. Hobbies: Philately; Musical Memorabilia. Address: 1103 Harold Dr. SE, Cedar Rapids, IA 52403, USA.

GRÜNFARB, Josef Mendel, b. 27 Aug. 1920, Stockholm, Sweden. Violinist. Educ: RCM. Stockholm; Studied w. Ernst Glaser, Oslo; Tibor Varga, London. m. Gertrud Meyer, 2 d. Debut: Stockholm, 1932. Career: Apps. as soloist w. all maj. orchs. in Scandinavia; 1st Violinist & Ldr., Stockholm Phil. Orch., 1943-61; Formed Grunfarb Quartett, 1951; Ldr., Swedish Broadcasting Symph. Orch., 1961-64; Ldr., Royal Opera Orch., 1964-; Tchr. & Prof., Violin & Chmbr. Music, RCM, Stockholm, 1965-. Mbr. Royal Swedish Acad. of Music, 1967. Hons: Jenny Lind, 1945; Swedish State's Artist Scholar (twice), 1965-66. Hobby: Photography. Address: Vanadisplan 3, S-113 31 Stockholm, Sweden. 1.

GRUNTH, Lars, b. 23 Oct. 1938, Copenhagen, Denmark. Violist. Educ: Copenhagen Univ.; studied w. Esther Skorpik, Slavko Skorpik, Julius Koppel, Mihhail Vaiman. m. Annette Heine, 1 d. Debut: Tivoli Concert Hall, 1962. Career: Mbr. Tivoli Concert Hall Orch., Zealand Symph., 1962-; Prin. Viola, ibid., 1965-; Vice-Chmn., Artistic Committee, ibid., 1972; Chmn., ibid., 1973-; Soloist, ibid & other orchs.; num. Perfs., Denmark & abroad w. var. Chmbr. orchs. & ensembles; Co-Fndr., Chmbr. Ensemble Musica Danica; Tchr., instructor of Chmbr. Music, Mbrships: Copenhagen Chmbr. Music Soc.; Chmn., Fredensborg-Humlebaek Music Soc. Hobbies: Literature; Wine. Address: 420 Boserupvej, 3050 Humlebaek, Denmark.

GRUPPE, Paulo Mesdag, b. 1 Sept. 1891, Rochester, NY, USA. Violoncellist. Educ: Royal Conserv., The Hague, Netherlands; Nat. Conserv., Paris, France. m. Camille Plasschaert Gruppe, 2 s. Debut: The Hague, 1907. Career incls: Cello Soloist, St. Louis, Seattle & Chgo. Symph., 1910; Tours of England, USA, France; Apps. w. maj. orchs. in US; 1st all exclusive cello recital, US tour, 1910. Mbr., Tollefson Trio NY, Letz Quartet, NY Pascal Quartet, Paris, France. Recordings: Solo Cello, 1909. Mbr., Am. String Tchrs. Assn. Publs: A Reasonable & Practical Approach to the Cello, 1964. Contbr. to Am. String Tchrs. Mag. Hobbies: Art of painting. Address: 20 Livingston St., New Haven, CT 06511, USA.

GRUSON, Sheila, b. 21 Mar. 1951, Tel-Aviv, Israel. Stage Director. Educ: BA, Harvard Univ., 1972. Career: Gärtnerplatztheater, Munich; Asst. to Everding, Götz Friedrich, Hamburg Staatsoper, Hamburg, San Fran. Opera. Hobbies: Music; Riding; Yachting; Flying. Address: c/o Sydney Gruson, NY Times, 229 W 43rd St., NY, NY 10024, USA.

GRUSZCZYNSKI, Ryszard, b. 1 June 1916, Warsaw, Poland. Baritone. Educ: MA; Conserv. of Warsaw. Career: since 1933 has given num. concerts in Poland & abroad inclng. concert at UN, NYC, 1946, apps. w. Beniamino Gigli, Stockholm, & w. Lili Pons, USA; has made num. radio & TV broadcasts; film, The Song in the Dark. Recorded in USA for Dana Music Co. & in Poland for Muza label. Mbr., Polish Soc. of Musical Artists. Hons. incl: Decorations, for war activities, 1946, for artistic activities, 1947, '55, '61, '67, '68, '73; Hon. Citizen, Warsaw, Cracow, Radom. Hobbies: Singing; Lit.; Poetry. Address: Mokotowska 26 m. 34, 00-561 Warsaw, Poland.

GRUYS, Hans (Johanna Dorothea), b. 18 Nov. 1903, Ginneken-Bavel, The Netherlands. Concert Singer & Violinist. Educ: studied violin under tuition of André Spoor, Royal Conserv. of Music, The Hague; Dip. as Soloist & Tchr. of Violin; educ. as singer by Jacoba Dresden-Dhont & Jacques van Kempen, Amsterdam; Dip., Royal Neth. Soc. of Musicians (KNTV) as soloist & tchr. of singing. m. Jacob Van Lier. Career: Num. first perfs. as concert singer, often w. the comps., such as Stravinsky, Apostel, Aubert, Milhaud, etc.; Num. concert tours in Holland & abroad; Soloist w. Concertgebouw Orch. of Amsterdam & other symph. orchs. in Holland; Over 100 concerts for 'les jeunesses musicales' in Holland, also in Aust. & Indonesia; Radio recitals in Holland & elsewhere. Mbrships: Bd. Mbr., Netherlands Fndn. for Music Therapy; Royal Netherlands Co. of Musicians. Var. hobbies. Address: Wielingenstraat 42, Amsterdam 10, The Netherlands. 19.

GUADAGNINI, Ernest Richard, b. 22 May 1945, Queens, NY, USA. Musician (Saxophone, Clarinet, Flute); Music Educator. Educ: US Navy Band, 1963-67; BMus & MMus, Juilliard Schl. of Music; Profl. Study Plan, ibid., 1 yr.; studied Theory, Solfedge & instruments w. var. tchrs. m. Karen Scheirer; Saxophone & clarinet w. Joseph Allard; Flute w. Julius Baker; Jazz w. Phil Woods; Theory w. Hall Overton; Solfedge w. Mme. Longy. Debut: w. Juilliard Orch., Alice Tulley Hall. Career: Num.apps. w. var. orchs.; Mbr. Nat. Orch. (Solo Saxophonist), 1970-75; Guy Lombardo Orch., 1975; Paul Lavalle Band of Am., 1975-76; Paul Lavalle Chmbr. Music Soc. of Lower Basin Street, 1977-78; Guy Lombardo Orch., 1978-79; num. TV apps. & radio broadcasts. Mbr., Juilliard Schl., 1970-76; Marion R Steckler Prize for Grad. Study, ibid., 1974-75. Hobby: Photography. Address: 319 Fairview Ave., Paramus, NJ 07652, USA.

GUADAGNO, Anton, b. 2 May 1925, Castellammare del Golfo, Trapani, Italy. Conductor. Educ: Grad., Conservatory Vincenzo Bellini; Deg. Cond., Deg. Comp., Conservatory Santa Cecilia (Rome); Postgrad. Cond., Academia Mozarteum. m. Dolores Guidone, 1 s. Compositions: Hymn for Holy Infancy, Vatican, Holy Yr. 1950. Recordings on Angel Records, RCA, Victor, London Decca Records & EMI. Hons: 1st Prize cond., Academia Mozarteum, 1948; Silver Medal, Lima, Peru, 1953; Gold Medal, Mex., 1957; Order of Cavalier, Italian Govt., 1965; Gold Medal, Chile, 1970; Gold Medal, Spain, 1971; Critics Award, Chile, 1970; Grand Prix du Disc Paris, 1973. Mgmt: Hurok Concerts, Inc., USA. Address: 9 Peach Orchard Dr., E Brunswick, NJ, USA.

GUALILLO, Nicholas D, b. 19 April 1903, Utica, NY, USA. Composer; Conductor; Opera Coach; Educator. Educ: MusB (Coll. of Fine Arts), MusM, PhD, Syracuse Univ.; Dip., New England Conserv. of Music; studied comp. w. Dr. William Berwald. m. Meta Dinger, 1 s. Career incls: Dir., Manhattan Grand Opera Co.; Dir., Syracuse Conserv. of Music; Cond., Syracuse Symph. Orch.;o Dir., Inter-City Opera Fund Inc.; Exec. Dir., League of Independent Cultural & Educl. Orgs., Inc. Comps. incl: Overture to Shakespeare's Macbeth; Journeys of a Hero (symphonic poem); 2 Symphs; Str. Quartet; The Phantom Princess (opera trilogy), 1976. Mbr., profl. & alumni assns. Hons. incl: Munson-Williams-Proctor Fellowship, 1937. Hobbies incl: Prospecting; Mineral Research. Address: PO Box 494, Syracuse, NY 13201, USA. 3, 4, 12, 28.

GUARINO, Piero, b. 20 June 1919, Alexandria, Egypt. Pianist; Conductor; Composer; Director of Conservatorio di Musica A Boito, Parma, Italy. Educ: Piano Dip., Lic. of Harmony & Counterpoint. Conserv., Athens; Dip. Piano, Accademia of S Cecilia, Rome, Italy. m. Magendanz Donna Ruth, 4 c. Debut: Concert Pianist, 1940; Cond., 1946. Career: Piano Recitals, Chmbr. Music & Conducting in num. countries; TV & radio apps. Comps. incl: Divertimento for violoncello; Omaggia a Clementi for piccola orch.; Songs: Piano pieces. Num. recordings. Contbr. to profl. jrnls. Mbrships: Societa Italiana di Musicologia; Rotary Int.; Associazione Direttori Conservatori di Musica. Hons. incl: Concorso nazionale di composizione, 1944. Address: Conservatorio de Musica A Boito, via del Conservatorio 27, Parma, Italy.

GUBBY, Roy, b. 15 Mar. 1911, London, UK. Composer. Educ: Bournemouth Conserv. of Music. div., 1 s. Debut: Bournemouth Symph. Orch., 1932. (Guest Cond.). Career incls: own Light Radio Orch., Buckingham Palace Gdn. Parties, 1955-58; Dpty. Ldr., Majorcan Symph. Orch., Palma di Mallorca, 1955-56; Num. BBC broadcasts as cond., violinist & raconteur. Comps. incl: The Great Panathenaeae; Baroque Suite on Five Movements; num. light orch. pieces; The Wimborne Christmas Pageant 1978; The First Christmas; Settings of Psalm 139. Recordings incl: Les Images Musicales; Music Mosaic; Merrily for Christmas. Mbrships. incl: Performing Rights Soc. Contbr. to profl. jrnls. Hons. incl: Gold Medal, 1933. Hobbies incl: Painting. Address: 17 Brunstead Rd., Branksome, Poole, Dorset, UK. 3.

GUDBRANDSEN, Håkon Roald, b. 3 May 1931, Bergen, Norway. Violinist. Educ: Acad. of Music, Bergen, 1941-47; Royal Acad. of Music, Copenhagen; Pvte. studies w. Prof. Emil Telmanyi, Prof. Jean Fournier & Prof. E Mainardi m. Malfrid Margrethe, 1 s., 1 d. Debut: Recital, Oslo, 1953. Career: Mbr. of Music Soc., Harmonien's Symph. Orch., Bergen, 1957-; Concertmaster, ibid., 1965-; Ldr., Harmonien String Quartet, 1970-; Ldr., Chmbr. Orch., Musica Maria; Soloist, Norwegian Orchs.; sev. apps., Swedish & Danish Broadcasting. Hobbies: Painting; Reading; Chess; Chmbr. music. Address: Fredlundveien 4, 5032 Minde, Norway.

GUDEL, Joachim, b. 16 Aug. 1927, Torun, Poland. Concert Pianist; Musicologist. Educ: PhD, Jagiellonian Univ., Cracow; State HS of Music, Cracow. m. Elzbieta Jacunska, 1 s., 1 d.

Debut: Cracow, 1953. Career: radio broadcasts; film scores; concerts in Poland & abroad; recitals of piano sonatas by Haydn, Mozart & Beethoven; Tchr., HS for Music, Gdansk. Publs: Ornamentation in Bach's Keyboard Works, 1968. Contbr. to profl. jrnls. Mbr., Polish Assn. of Music Artists (SPAM). Recip. Azsluzony Dzialacz Kultury, 1975. Hobbies: Keyboard instruments; Photography; Hist.; Lit. Address: ul. Piecewska 28A 25, 80288 Gdansk, Poland.

GUDGER, William Dillard, b. 3 June 1947, Asheville, NC, USA. Musicologist; Organist. Educ: BA, m c 1, Duke Univ.; MPhil, MA, PhD, Yale Univ. Career: Tchr. at Eastman Schl. of Music, Duke Univ., Ariz. State Univ. & Coll. of Charleston; artist-in-residence, Univ. of Calif., Davis. Publs: Ed., Habermann Mass, 1974. Contbr. to: The Diapason; MLA Notes; Current Musicol.; Am. Harp Jrnl. Mbrships: Am. Musicol. Soc.; Int. Musicol. Soc.; Music Lib. Assn.; Organ Historical Soc.; Am. Guild of Organists; Am. Soc. for 18th Century studies. Hons: Phi Beta Kappa, 1968. Address: Dept. of Fine Arts, The Coll. of Charleston, Charleston, SC 29401, USA.

GUDMUNDSEN-HOLMGREEN, Pelle, b. 21 Nov. 1932, Copenhagen, Denmark. Composer. Educ: studied Music Theory & Hist., Royal Danish Music Conserv., 1953-58. m. Gunvor Kaarsberg, 2 c. Career: works have been played at Scandinavian Music Days, Royal Danish Ballet & Music Fest., ISCM etc., on Danish TV, on radio throughout world; Music for plays & film scores. Comps. (publd.) incl: Solo for electric guitar, 1972; Mirror II (orch.), 1973; Songs Without (mezzo soprano, piano), 1976; Passacaglia (quintet), 1977. Comps. (recorded & publd.) incl: Chronos (for Chmbr. Orch.), 1962; Terrace in 5 Stages (for Wind Quintet), 1970; Tricolore IV (orch.), 1979; Recycling (Septet), 1975. Contbr. to: Danish Music Review. Mbrships: Danish Sect., ISCM. Address: Eggersvej 29, 2900 Hellerup, Denmark.

GUEDEN, Hilde, b. Vienna, Austria. Lyric & Coloratura Soprano. Educ: Acad. of Music, Vienna; dramatic studies, Max Reinhardt. m. Robert Josef, 2 d. Debut: Zürich State Opera, 1939. Career incls: Munich State Opera, 1941; Royal Opera, Rome, 1942; La Scala, 1946; Salzburg Fests., 1946-; Metrop. Opera, NYC, 1951; Vienna State Opera, 1955; TV broadcasts, UK; tours of Europe; concerts w. Chgo. & Phila. Orchs. Recordings: Decca. Mbrships: Royal Naval Assn.; Sigma Alpha Iota. Hons. incl: Grand Cross of Sci. & Art, Austrian Repub., 1950; Kammersängerin, Austria, 1950; Silver Rose, Vienna Phil. Orch., 1959; Le Discobole, Acad. du Disque Francais, 1961; Cross of the Order of Dannebrog, Denmark. Address: co Metrop. Opera Co., Lincoln Ctr., NY, NY 10023, USA. 2.

GUENTHER, Eileen Morris, b. 20 Jan. 1948, Leavenworth, Kan., USA. Musical Director & Educator. Educ: BA, Univ. of Kan., 1970; BMus (organ), ibid., 1970; MA, Cath. Univ. of Am., 1973; Dr. Mus. Arts, ibid., 1973. m. Roy James Guenther. Career. incl: Solo recitalist & concert appearances w. orchs. & brass ensembles, Wash., DC. NY & Midwest states, Broadcaster, Radio Stn. WGMS-AM-FM: Prod., weekly organ music prog. The Royal Instrument, ibid.; Min. of Music, Foundry United Meth. Ch., Wash., DC; Mbr. Music Fac., the Holton-Arms Schl., Bethesda, Md. Recordings: Litanies. Contbr. to: The Diapason; Grove's Dict.; 6th Ed.; Music Mag. Mbrships. incl: Phi Beta Kappa; Pi Kappa Lambda; Am. Guild of Organists; Am. Musicol. Soc.; Am. Choral Dirs. Assn. Hons. incl: 1st Place, Nat. Organ Comps., Ft. Lauderdale, Fla., 1973. Address: 221 W Cameron Rd., Falls Church, VA 22046, USA. 4.

GUERRA VICENTE, Jose, b. 12 March 1907, Almofala, Portugal. Concert Cellist. Educ: Dip., Nat. Schl. of Music, Univ. of Brazil. m. Giselda Guerra Vicenta, 2 s. Career: Apps. on Radios Guanabara, Jornal do Brasil & Nacional; Cellist, Sinfônica, Municipal Theatre, Rio de Janeriro: Prof. of Harmony & Morphol., Inst. Villa-Lobos. Comps. incl: Noturno (Violin & Piano): Danca (Piano solo); Resignaçao (Piano solo); Toccata (Piano solo); 2nd Suite (Piano solo); 4 Peças (Piano solo): Miragem (Small Orch.) Recordings incl: Valsa Seresteira (Violin solo); 1st Suite (Cello & Piano). Publs: Cadências, sua origem e evoluçao, 1960. Mbrships: Int. Soc. of Contemporary Music; Brazilian Soc. of Contemporary Music. Hons: Sinfonia Brasllia Prize, 1960; Abertura Sinfônica Prize, 1968. Hobby: Football. Address: Rua Almirante Alexandrino 4025, (Santa Teresa), Rio de Janeiro 20.000, Estado do Rio de Janeiro, Brazil.

GUERRANT, Mary Thorington, b. 7 May 1925, Taft, Tex., USA. Pianist; Composer; Piano & Comp. Teacher. Educ: AB, Austin Coll., Sherman, Tex.; MMus (Applied Piano). Tex; PhD in Fine Arts (Music, basic area), Tex. Tech. Univ., Lubbock. m. W B Guerrant, Jr., 1 s. Career: Instructor of Piano, Austin Coll., 1957-58; Solo piano recitals given at Austin Coll., 1957-58; Solo piano recitals given at Austin Coll., Tex. Tech.

Univ., Dallas-Ft. Worth area. Assoc. Prof., Comp. & Piano, Tunghai Univ., Taichung, Taiwan, 1976-77. Compositions: Pecos Ruins, Woodwind octet, perf. at Tex. Tech Univ., 1974 as part of the 23rd Annual Symposium of Contemp. Music; The Shepherd (chmbr. opera). Mbrships: Nat. Cert. Mbr. (as Tchr. of Piano). Music Tchrs. Nat. Assn.; Am. Coll. Musicians (a Div. of NGPT); Adjudicator, NGPT, 1966-. Hobbies: Backpacking; Foreign travel; Languages. Address: 3301-24th St., Lubbock, TX 79410, USA.

GUEST, Alison Anne, b. 2 Oct. 1946, Aberdeen, Scotland, UK. Lecturer; Teacher; Musicologist. Educ: MA, 1968, PhD, 1971, Aberdeen Univ. m. David H Guest, 1 s. Career: Tchr. of Music, 1972-77; Tutor, Open Univ. Music Courses, 1974-. Publs. (as Ed.): Wagenseil Sinfonia, 1972; Hoffmeister Clarinet Concerto, 1973; Viola Concerto, 1973. Hons: Carnegie Travelling Scholarship, 1966; British Coun./Hungarian Govt. Scholarship, 1970. Hobbies: Reading; Embroidery; Swimming. Address: 8 Woodhall Grove, Colinton, Edinburgh, EH13 OHR, UK.

GUEST, Douglas (Albert), b. 9 May 1916, Mortomley, Yorks., UK. Organist; Master of the Choristers & Director of Music of Westminster Abbey. Educ: RCM, London; King's Coll., Cambridge (Organ Scholar); Univ. Scholar in Music, Cambridge; CVO, MA; MusB (Cantab.); FRCM; Hon. RAM; Hon. FRCO; Hon. FRSCM. m. Peggie Florentia Falconer, 2 d. Career: Dir. of Music Uppingham Schl., 1945-50; Organist of Salisbury Cathedral, 1950-57; Organist of Worcester Cathedral & Cond. of Three Choirs Fest., 1957-63; Dir. of Music, Westminster Abbey, 1963-; Prof., RCM, 1963-. Compositions: Missa Brevis, 1957. Sev. recordings w. the choir of Westminster Abbey. Mbrships: Hon., Royal Soc. of Musicians, etc. Hobbies: Golf; Fly fishing. Address: 8 The Little Cloister, Westminster Abbey, London SW1P 3PL, UK. 1, 3, 16.

GUEST, George Howell, b. 9 Feb. 1924, Bangor, Wales, UK. Conductor; Organist; Lecturer. Educ: MA; MusD; FRCO; FRSCM. m. Nancy Mary Talbot, 1 s., 1 d. Career: Fellow & Organist, St. John's Coll., Cambridge; Univ. Lectr. in Music; Organist to the Univ. Recordings: Some 65 records, mostly for Argo Records Ltd., featuring St. John's Coll. Choir & occasionally, the Acad. of St. Martin-in-the-Fields. Contbr. to Musical Times. Recip., John Stewart of Rannoch Scholarship in Sacred Music, 1948. Hobby: The Welsh Languages. Address: St. John's Coll., Cambridge Univ., UK. 1, 3.

GUETTLER, Knut Arne, b. 31 Jan. 1943, Oslo, Norway. Bass Player. Educ: pvte. study w. Henrick Lindemann & Gary Karr (Univ. of Wis., USA). div., 1 d. Career: Soloist, Co-Prin. Bass until 1974, Oslo Phil.; sev. solo perfs. on Norwegian Broadcasting; Prof. of Bass, Norwegian State Acad. of Music, 1973-. Comp. music for films, radio plays, TV ballets, etc. Contbr. to Bass sound post. Mbr., Bd. of Advsrs., Int. Soc. of Bassists. Hobbies: Sound engrng.; Photography. Address: Eilins V.20, 1342 Jar, Norway.

GUI, Vittorio, b. 14 Sept. 1885, Italy. Conductor; Composer. Educ: Santa Cecilia Conserv., Rome. Career: Cond., Teatro Adriano, 1970; Soc. del Concerti Sinfonici, Milan, 1924; Teatro di Torino, Turin, 1925-27; Fndr., Orch. Stabile, Florence, 1928; Cond., ibid., 1928-43; Guest Cond. in Rome, Naples, Milan, Lisbon, Leningrad, Moscow, Londdon, Edinburgh & Glyndebourne; Artistic Counsellor & Dir. of Music, Glyndebourne Festival Opera, 1960-. Hons. incl: Gold Medal for Culture, Italy, 1957; num. for decorations. Address: Villa S Maurizio, Fiesole, Italy.

GUICHARD, Leon, b. 1 March 1899, Lyon, France. Retired University Professor. Educ: D Litt., Sorbonne, Paris. m. Marie Jose de Mulatier, 2 d. Career incl: Dir., Grenoble Univ. Choir, 1945-61; Publs. incl: La Musique & Les Lettres au Temps du Romantisme, 1955; La Musique & Les Lettres au Temps du Wagnerisme, 1963; Les Soirees de l'Orchestre (Berlioz), 1969; A Travers Chants (Berlioz), 1971. Mbrships: Revue de Musicologie. Hon: Int. Trophy for Choir Music, w. Grenoble Univ. Choir, Llangollen Eisteddfodd, 1950. Address: Le Prieure, 73610 Lepin le Lac, France. 19.

GUIDI-DREI, Claudio Cafiero, b. 17 Aug. 1927, Buenos Aires, Argentina. Composer; Orchestra Director. Educ: Nat. Conserv. of Music & Dramatic Art; Rossini Conserv., Pesaro, Italy, 1956; Comp. Dip., Academia Chigiana, 1955; Studied viola & comp. w. many maestros. 1 s. Debut: Dir. of Orch., Buenos Aires, 1957. Career: Asst. to Alfredo Bonnaccorsi, Rossini Conserv. Pesaro, Italy; Chief of Studies, Argentine Theater, la Plata, 1960-62, 1964-66 & 1969; Artistic Counsellor & Artistic Dir., ibid., 1972-73; Substitute Prof. thru' Dir. of Studies, Colon Theatre, Buenos Aires; In charge of Broadcasting & Cultural Ext. Off., Min. of Educ., Buenos Aires Province,

1970-71; Orch. Dir., Nat. Broadcast, Buenos Aires, La Plata, Bahla Bianca, Cordoba & Tucumain Orchs.; Opera & Ballet Dir., La Plata Theater; Artistic Dir., Colon Theatyre, Buenos Aires. Comps. recorded incl: "Medea" (opera); "Miniaturas" for orch. & string quartet; "Concierto Bizzaro" for viola & orch; Canciones (soprano & percussion), 1975. Publs: Ton-Kunstler Lexikon (2nd part) w. Frank Altmann, 1971. Mbrships: Composer Assn. of Argentina; 2nd Liric Theater of Argentina. Recip., Nat. Prize (Fando Nacional Pelas Artes), 1978. Hobbies: Art Books. Address: Chacabuco 337, Banfield, Buenos Aires, Argentina.

GUIGNARD, (Paul) Eric, b. 31 Jan. 1913, Aarau, Switzerland. Cellist. Educ: Lehrdiplom., Schweizerischen Musikpaedagogischen Verbandes, 1935. m. Doris Froebel, 5 c. Debut: Stefi Geyer String Quartet, 1941. Career: Mbr., Tonhalle Orch., Zürich, 1951-78; Radio broadcasts w. Spira Trio, Zürich, Munich, Hamburg; 1st Perf. in Switzerland of Shostakovitch's Cello Concerto No. 1 w. Tonhalle Orch.; Mbr., Collegium Musicum Zürich, chamber orch., 1941-71. Comps: 32 Duos for Cello, 1971; 20 small Pieces for cello & piano, 1978; Swiss Folk Dances for Flute or violin & violoncello, 1975. Composer. Duos mit Violoncello, 1971. Mbrships: Mgr., Swiss Festival Orch., Lucerne, 1955-73. Hon. Mbr., Collegium Musicum Zurich. Hobby: Reading. Address: Scheuchzerstr. 24/III, CH-8006, Zürich, Switzerland.

GUILLAUME, Edith, b. 14 June 1943, Bergerac, France. Opera & Concert Singer. Educ: Soloist Dip., Royal Danish Coll. of Music, Copenhagen; pvte. study, Copenhagen & Paris. m. Niels Hvass, 2 children. Debut: (opera), Thérèse, Dream of Thérèse, Jutland Opera. Career incls: Concerts as recitalist & mbr. of Danish Baroque Ensemble; duo w. guitarist Ingolf Olsen (have had works written for their repertoire by var. contemp. comps.); concerts in Netherlands, Sweden, Denmark, Germany, Norway, Iceland, Finland, France, UK; radio & TV broadcasts, Netherlands, Sweden, Denmark, Germany. Has recorded Danish songs. Hons. incl: Critics' Prize of Hon., 1970; Tagea Brandt Memorial Fund, 1977. Mgmt: Wilhern Hansen, Gothersgade, Copenhagen, Denmark. Address: Ellebakken 2, 2900 Hellerup, Copenhagen, Denmark. 30.

GULDA, Friedrich, b. 16 May 1930, Vienna, Austria. Pianist; Composer. Educ: HS for Music & Dramatic Art, Vienna. m. Paolo Loew. Career: Recitals & concerts w. leading orchs. in Austria, other European countries & USA. Compositions: Galgenlieder for baritone & orch., 1951; Music for piano & band; Music for 4 soloists & band; num. jazz compositions. Num. recordings issued on Decca label. Recip: 1st Prize for piano, Geneva Int. Competition, 1946. Hobbies: Chess; Record Collecting. Address: Schottengasse 7, Vienna, Austria.

GULLEY, John, b. 23 Jan. 1934, Exeter, UK. Lecturer; Conductor; Adjudicator; Examiner. Educ: LLB, King's Coll., Univ. of London; RCM, London; Dip. Educ., Reading Univ. m. Jean Earl, 2 s. Career: Former freelance Horn Player; Sr. Lectr., Schl. of Music, The Polytechnic, Huddersfield, 1962-; Cond., Polytechnic Orch. & choral soc.; Colne Valley Male Voice Choir; Radio, TV & Recording; Adjudicator; Examiner, Assoc. Bd., Royal Schls. of Music. Recordings: Colne Valley Male Voice Choir. Mbrships: Adjudicator, Nat. Fedn. of Music Fest; Nat. Assn. of Tchrs. in Further & Higher Educ. Hobbies: Reading; Walking; Caravanning; Painting. Address: 42 Gledholt Rd., Huddersfield, UK.

GULLI, Franco, b. 1 Sept. 1926, Trieste, Italy. Concert Violinist. Educ: B Humanities; Artist Dip. in Violin. m. Enrica Cavallo. Debut: 1932. Career: Worldwide apps. w. maj. orchs. inclng. Chgo., Mpsl., Cleveland, Pitts., Ottawa, etc.; Chmbr. music activity w. wife & w. Trio Italiano D'Archi; Master Classes, Accademia Chigiana, Siena, Italy, 1964-72; Prof. Music Conserv., Lucerne, Switz., 1971-72; Prof. of Music, Ind. Univ., Bloomington, 1972-. Recordings incl: complete sonatas by Beethoven; Paganini's Concerto No. 5; Mendelssohn Sonata in F. Mbrships. incl: Accademia Nazionale Santa Cecilia, Rome, Italy. Hons. incl: Premio dell'Accademia Chigiana, Siena. Mgmt: Columbia Artists. Mgmt: NY. Address: 1000 S Ballantine Rd., Bloomington, IL 47401, USA.

GULYAS, Gyorgy, b. 1 Apr. 1916, Korostarcsa, Hungary. Conductor; Professor; Music Academy Director in Debrecen. Educ: Comp., Cond., Prof. of Music, Acad. of Music, Budapest. m. Eva Manya, 3 c. Debut: Bekes, 1938. Career: Fndr. of 1st Hungarian Musical Element, Hungary, 1938; TV apps., UK, France, W Germany, Hungary, USA; Radio Apps., UK, France, W Germany, E Germany, Austria, Finland; tours of Italy, France, Switzerland, W & E Germany, USSR, Austria, Poland, Bulgarfa, USA; var. Fest. Apps.; Prof., Dir., Franz Liszt Acad. of Music. Recordings: UK, USA, Hungary. Contbr. to: Nepmuveles; Prlando; Elet es Irodalom. Mbrships: Fndr. Mbr., Soc. of Hungarian Comps.; Fndr. Mbr., Liszt Ferenc Soc.; Jury, Arezzo,

Llangollen, Debrecen Int. Choral Fests. Hons: Liszt Ferenc Prize, 1st Degree, 1959; Artist of Merit, Hungarian People's Repub., 1st Prize, Llangollen., 1958; 1st & 2nd Prizes, Arezzo, 1959. Hobbies: Mountaineering; Travel; Motoring; Reading. Mgmt: Interkoncert 1, Vorosmarti ter, Budapest, Hungary. Address: 8 Blahane u., 4024 Debrecen, Hungary.

GUMMESSON, Thord Erik, b. 19 May 1930, Uppsala, Sweden. Music Teacher. Educ: Grad., Tchrs. Trng. Coll., Uppsala, 1956; Commercial subjects tchr., Stockholm, 1962. m. Berit Margareta, 1 s., 1 d. Career incls: Music Tchr., comprehensive schl., 9 yrs.; Ldr. Stockholm Youth Chorale, touring USA, 1964; Prod. & Ldr., special progs. children's music, Swedish radio; Sev. TV progs. w. children's grps. Comps: about 50 children's songs & 20 Swedish hit songs. Recordings: 25 singles; 1 LP children's songs, 1968. Publs. incl: Rytm-Mattan (Patterns for Rhythm), 1972; Nu-musik, 1M, 2M & 3M, 1973-76. Contbr. to profl. jrnls. Mbr., profl. orgs. Hons: Cultural prize, 1971; SKAP stipend, educl. music, 1975. Hobbies: Travel; Composing. Address: Blaklintstigen 3, 134700 Vasterhaninge, Sweden.

GÜMPEL, Karl-Werner, b. 6 Jan. 1930, Duderstadt, Germany. Professor of Musicology. Educ: Univ. of Göttingen; PhD, Univ. of Freiburg i. Br., 1955. m. Isolde Ambs, 2 d., 1 s. Career: Rsch. Asst., German Rsch. Union, 1955-57; Asst. Prof. of Musicol., Univ. of Freiburg i. Br., 1958-69; Rsch. Fellow, Görresgesellschaft, 1962-63; Assoc. Prof. of Musicol., Univ. of Louisville, Ky., USA, 1969-74; Prof. ibid., 1974-; Chmn., ibid., 1974-75. Publs: Die Musiktraktate Conrads von Zabern, 1956; Hugo Spechtshart von Reutlingen; Flores musicae, 1958. Zur Frühgeschichte der vulgärsprachlichen spanischen und Katalanischen Musiktheorie, 1968. Contbr. to num. profl. jrnls. Mbrships: Int. Musicol. Soc.; Am. Musicol. Soc.; German Soc. for Music Rsch. Outstanding Educator of Am., 1974. Hobbies: Art History; Photography; Hiking. Address: 1803 Devondale Dr., Louisville, KY 40222, USA.

GUNDERSHEIMER, Muriel Blumberg, b. 5 Dec. 1924, Chgo., Ill., USA. Harpist. Educ: Eastman Schl. of Music, Univ. of Rochester; B Mus, Northwestern Univ.; Nat. Music Camp, Interlochen, Mich. m. Allen Gundersheimer, 3 c. Career: Was Harpist w. Waukegan, Ill. Phil., Chgo. Civic Orch., Tucson, Ariz., Symph.; Guest w. Charleston, Wheeling, etc.; Solo progs. for UNICEF, etc.; Currently Harpist, Columbus Symph., Mbrships: Sigma Alpha Iota; Past Pres., voung Assocs. of Columbus' Symph.; Past Pres., Bexley Unit of Columbus' Symph.; Bd. Mbr., Columbus Women's Music Club. Hons: named one of ten outstanding women of Columbus, Columbus Citizen Jrnl., 1953; one of six outstanding women for civic & community servs.; City Panhellenic Assn., 1964; Angel of the Yr., Coun. of Jewish Women, 1970. Hobbies: Entertaining hospitals, etc. Address: 2671 Bryden Rd., Columbus, OH 43209, USA.

GUNDRY, Inglis, b. 8 May 1905, Wimbledon, UK. Composer; Lecturer. Educ: MA, Balliol Coll., Oxford Univ.; Barrister-at-law; ARCM. m. Nina Peggy Maggs, 2 d. Career: Instructor-Lieut., Educ. Dept., Admiralty, 1944; Lectr. on Music to WEA & London, Surrey & Cambridge Univs., 1946-. Comps. incl: (operas) The Partisans, 1946; The 3 Wise Men, 1967 (excerpts recorded); The Prisoner Paul, 1970 (excerpts recorded); 5 Bells for Chorus & Orch.; 3 Song Cycles (recorded); In Those 12 Days, harp variations (Recorded); Sing From the Cradle to the Grave; First Will & Testament, for male voices. Publs. incl: Opera in a Nutshell, 1945; The Naval Song Book, 1945; Canow Kernow (songs & dances from Cornwall), 1967. Contbr. to profl. jrnls. Mbr., profl. assns. Hons. incl: Winner, Morley Coll. Opera Competition, 1963. Hobbies: Pastel Painting; Gardening. Address: 11 Winterstoke Gdns., Mill Hill, London NW7 2RA, UK. 3.

GUNNARSSON, Bengt-Ove, b. 17 Dec. 19409, Varberg, Sweden. Music Teacher; Woodwind Instrumentalist (esp. Clarinet); Ensemble Leader. Educ: Music Tchr. Exam.; Clarinet tchrs. exam., Gothenburg; Studied in Stockholm & Vienna. m. Monica Elmquist Gunnarsson. Career: Communal Music Dir., Kungsbacka Music Schl., 1966-75; Tchr. & musician, esp. clarinet concerts, 1975-; Orgnsr., music courses & helped estab. sev. orchs. inclng. Chmbr. Orch., Gothenburg, 1975; Clarinet Concerts, Sweden, Norway, Denmark & USA; 2nd instrument, Flute. Hobbies incl: Nature Conservancy; Walking. Address: Koberg Pl. 4006, 434 00 Kungsbacka, Sweden.

GUNNERFELDT, Louise Ulla, b. 17 Mar. 1917, Helsinki, Finland. Violinist. Educ: Helsinki, State Univ., E Lansing, Mich., USA; Dip., Sibelius Acad., Helsinki, Finland; Dip., Konservatorium der Reichshaupstadt, Berlin, Germany; Study w. Prof. Nauwinck, Paris, France. m. Lennart U. Gunnerfeldt, 1 d. Debut: Sibelius Acad. Concert Hall, Helsinki, Finland, 1941. Career: Solo & orch. work, Finland, Sweden & USA; Solo performances on radio in

Finland & on TV in USA. Hobbies: Travel; Reading. Address: 3411 Oakcliff Lane, Lansing, MI 48917, USA.

GUNOVSKY, Vilém (stage name of Vilem Gundel), b. 29 Oct. 1912, Pula, Yugoslavia. Composer. Educ: Degree, HS of Econs. m. Vera Cermak. Compositions: more than 30 popular works, inclng. Tango-habanera, Romantic Waltz, Goodnight Waltz, Your Ship is Not Coming Back & With the Left Marching On. Hons: 1st Prize, ESTA Gramophone Co. Competition, 1940; musical prize, 1957. Hobby: Painting. Mgmt: Osautor, Prague. Address: Vilem Gundel, SNB 99, Prague 10, Czech.

GUNTER-McCOY, Jane Hutton, b. 9 Feb. 1938, Kingston, NY, USA. Dramatic Soprano. Educ: BMus, Eastman Schl. Music, Univ. Rochester, NY; MMus, Ind. Univ. Schl. Music, Bloomington; DMA cand., ibid. m. Seth T McCoy. Career: Soloist, Robert Shaw Chorale, touring Can., Europe, S Am., USSR; Schola Cantorum NY, USA & Europe; Amor Artis Chorale & Orch.; NY Phil.; Musica Aeterna & Musica Sacra, NY; w. Am. Ballet Theatre; w. Wagner & Beethoven Socs., NYC. Park Ave. Christian Ch., NYC; Opera tours w. Boris Goldovsky Opera Co.; Chmbr. Music Soc., Lincoln Center, NYC; Canta Herbraica of NY: Guest soloist, Riverside Ch., NYC; num. oratorio & rectial perfs. Recordings: w. Robert Shaw Chorale & Amor Artis Chorale & Orch. Mbrships. incl: VP, Chap., Sigma Alpha Iota. Hon: Solo Recital, Concert Artists Guild NY. Hobbies incl: Collecting Records. Address: 334 W 86th St., Apt. 2B, NY, NY 10024, USA.

GÜNTHER, Ulrich, b. 19 Sept. 19234, Magdeburg, Germany. University Professor. Educ: studied pedagogy, hist. & relig. pedagogy, Celle, FrankfurtM & Erlangen; 1st & 2nd Tchr. qualifying exams.; State exams.; 2nd Stage State exams; Dr. phil.; studied schl. music, Music Coll., FrankfurtM; studied musicol., Frankfurt Univ. & Erlangen-Nürnberg. Career: Dean, Fac. of Communication/Aesthetics, Univ. Oldenburg, 1974-77; Pres., Soc. for Music Pedagogy Rsch., 1971-77. var. publs. Contbr. to publs. in field. Mbrships. incl: Union of German Schl. Music Tchr.; German Soc. for Educ.; Soc. for Music Rsch. Address: Husbrok 4, D-2900 Oldenburg, German Fed. Repub. 30.

GUPTA, Shyamal, b. 3 Dec. 1922, Calcutta, India. Composer of Songs; Writer of Stories & Scenarios. Educ: BSc. m. Sandhya Mukherjee, 1 d. Career: comp. songs for over 500 films; wrote scripts, etc., for All India Radio. Comps: a collect. of lyrical songs; over 1000 songs recorded by ldng. perfs. of India. Publs: 3 novels (2 made into films). Mbrships: Audition Bd., All India Radio. Recip., Film Jrnlsts. Award, 1973. Hobbies: Reading; Travel. Address: 146/D/613 Lake Gnds., Calcutta 700 045, India.

GÜRTLER, Friedrich, b. 15 Apr. 1933, Dresden, Germany. Pianist. Educ: Dip., Royal Danish Conserv. of Music, 1956; further studies w. Edwin Fischer, Paul Badura-Skoda & Alfred Brendel. m. Birfit Kleist Gürtler, 2 d. Career: has appeared as Soloist, Chmbr. Musician & Accomp., Scandinavia, Berlin, Vienna, Brussels, London, Glasgow, Berlin, Vienna, Brussels, London, Glasgow, Birmingham, etc. on BBC radio & TV; has appeared w. many well-known artists, inclng Boris Christoff, Wolfgang Schneiderhan, I. Seefried, Michel Rabin, Ernst Hfliger, Thomas Hemsley, Norma Procter, Alfred Brendel & Janet Baker; Lectr., Royal Danish Conserv. Recordings: sev. of Danish vocal & chmbr. music. Mbr: Soloist foreningen af 1921, Dansk Musik poedagogisk forening. Hobbies: Gardening. Address: Dalgas Blvd. 168, DK 2000, Copenhagen F., Denmark.

GURTNER, Heinrich, b. 15 Oct. 1924, Wattenwil, Switz. Organist. Educ: Dips. for organ & piano, Conserv., Berne; studies s. Maurice Duruflé, Paris & Adriaan Engels, The Hague. m. Eugenie Tenger, 4 c. Career: Organist, Berne Cathedral; Tchr., Berne Conserv.; Int. concert work. Recordings: Bach Trio Sonatas; Mendelssohn Organ Works. Mbrships: Schweizerischer Tonkünstlerverein; Schweizerischer Musikpädagogischer Verband. Hons: City of Berne Music Prize, 1974. Address: Kräyigenweg 41, Muri/Berne, Switz.

GUSCHLBAUER, Theodor, b. 1939, Vienna, Austria. Conductor. Educ: Perf.'s Dip., conducting, piano & cello, Music Acad., Vienna; took courses w. Matacic, & von Karajan. Career: Cond., Vienna Baroque Ensemble, 1961-69, Nat. Theatre, Salzburg, 1966-68, & Lyon Opera,m 1968-; Dir., Lyon Opera, 1971-. Recordings: Sev. w. Bamberg Symph. Orch., Bournemouth Sinfonietta, Gulbenkian Chmbr., Orch., New Philharmonia, Salzburg Chmbr. Orch. & Vienna Baroque Ensemble. Hons: 3 Grand Prix du Disque, 1966 & 69. Hobbies: Langs.; Athletics. Address: Oelzeltgasse 411, A-1030 Vienna 3, Austria. 3.

GUSH, Jacqueline, b. 26 July 1936, Luanshya, Zambia. Orchestral Musician (Percussion). Educ: LRSM Perf.'s Dip. (Piano);

LRAM Tchrs.'s Dip. (Piano); studied piano w. Eileen Reynolds, Rhodesian Coll. of Music, 1954-57, & Frederick Jackson, RAM, 1957-60; studied percussion w. Charles Donaldson. Career: Freelance to 1962; 2nd Percussion, 1962-66, Prin. Percussion, 1966-, Bournemouth Symph. Orch. Recordings: All Bournemouth Symph. Orch. records w. percussion, 1962-. Hobbies: Cage Birds; Reading Military History; Gardening; Arranging & Playing Music of the Baroque Period on the Vibraphone. Address: 28 Wroxham Rd., Poole, Dorset, BH12 1HA, UK.

GUSSET, Monique L, b. 6 Jan. 1928, Montreal, PQ, Can. Pianist; Harpsichord Player. Educ: Grad., Conserv. of Music & Dramatic Arts. of PQ. m. Georges Gusset (dec.), 2 d. Debut: as accomp., Montreal. Career: Accomp., Montreal Choir, 1955-56; apps. w. Atlantic Symph.; regular Accomp., CBC chmbr. music, radio & TV, Nova Music; sev. prods., Neptune Theatre; Jeunesse Musicale tour of BC; toured USA w. Gary Carr (double bass). He has recorded for CBC (w. orch.). Mbr., Am. Fedn. of Musicians. Recip. Chmbr. Music Prize & Solfege Medal, Conserv. Hobbies: Handicrafts; Sewing; Collecting antiques. Address: PO Box 224 Armdale, NS B3L 4K1, Canada.

GUSTAFSON, Dwight, b. 30 Apr. 1930, Seattle, Wash., USA. University Dean. Educ: BA, Bob Jones Univ., 1952; MA, ibid., 1954; DMus, Fla. State Univ., 1967; cond. studies w. Izler Solomon & Richard Burgin; voice w. Grace Levinson & Elena Nikolaidi; comp. w. John Boda & Carlisle Floyd. m. Gwendolyn A Adams, 1 s., 3 d. Career: Dean, Schl. of Fine Arts, Bob Jones Univ., 1954-; Cond. of Bob Jones Univ. Orch. & Concert Chorale; Dir., Bob Jones Univ. Opera Assn.; Guest Cond. for all-state & fest. concerts; Bass soloist w. local & regl. opera & choral orgs. Compositions: five scores for educl. & religious films; a number of shorter choral & instrumental works in the catalogs of five US publsrs. Mbrships: Pi Kappa Lambda; Southeastern Composers League; Music Educators Nat. Conf.; Am. Choral Directors Assn. Hons. incl: 1st prize, Erskine Coll. Anthem Competition, 1965; LLD honoris causa, Tenn. Temple Schls.; Graduate fellowship, Fla. State Univ., 1966. Address: 111 Stadium View Dr., Greenville, SC 29614, USA. 2.

GUSTAFSSON, Kaj-Erik, b. 27 Nov. 1942, Lovisa, Finland. Organist; Conductor. m. Anna-Leena Marzukka, 1 s., 2 d. Debut: (organ) 1969. Career: Prod. w. E Cederlo..f, series educl. progs., Finnish radio, 1970-74; Lectr., Sibelius Akademien. Comps: Motet for Chmbr. Choir, 'Räds ej bekänna'; Song for Bora stift, 'Hemma i kyrkan'. Recordings: Organ & choir for Finnish radio; Choir Music from Finland w. Chorus Sanctae Ceciliae. Publ: Kyrkokörernas repertoar XVIII (Christmas Music), 1970. Hon: Prize, Conducting choirs, IX Ch. Music Fest., Helsinki, 1975. Hobby: Lit. Address: Sökögränd 8 A 8, 02360 Esbo 36, Finland.

GUSTAVSON, Corliss Ann, b. 26 Mar. 1951, Brisbane, Aust. Pianist; Piano Teacher. Educ: BMus, Univ. of Qld., 1973; LMusA. Career: regular concerts (solo & chmbr. music) in Brisbane; app. w. Qld. Symph. Orch.; part-time accomp., Qld. Conserv. of Music; tchr., piano & music hist., tertiary insts.; Eisteddfod adjudicator. Publ: A Pianistic Survey of Selected Editions of Beethoven's Sonata No. 32 in C minor, Op.111, 1976; Pianists of Australia, 1977. Contbr. to Aust. Jrnl. of Music Educ. Hobbies: Reading; Squash; Horse Riding. Address: Unit 5, 89 Whitmore St., Taringa, Brisbane 4068, Aust.

GUSTIN, Lyell, b. 31 May 1895, Fitch Bay, PQ., Can. Piano Teacher. Educ: Stanstead Coll., PQ.; studied w. Blanche St. John-Baker, Saskatoon, Jeannette Durno, Chgo., Madeley Richardson, NY. Career: Tchr., Summer Schls., Royal Conserv. of Music, Toronto, 1950 & 1968; Lectr. in Music, Univ. of Sask., 1950-51, Regina Conserv. of Music, Sask., 1936-42; Examiner, Royal Conserv. of Music, Toronto, 1944-70. Mbrships: Dir., Leschetizky Assn.of Am. & Huguenot Soc. of Can.; Musical Art Club (Saskatoon); Reg. Music Tchrs. Hons: Hon. Pres., Can. Fedn. of Music Tchrs., 1971; Can. Music Coun. Award, 1973; Hon. Fellow, Trinity Coll. of Music, 1978. Address: 512 Tenth St., Saskatoon, Sask., Canada. 3.

GUTHRIE, John, b. 24 Feb. 1912, Lyttleton, New Zealand. Composer. Educ: Christ's Coll., Christchurch, NZ; MB. chB., Edinburgh Univ., Scotland, UK, 1937. m. Vivian Mairi Duncan, 1 d. Career: Comps. performed at Univ. of Glasgow, 1965, 1974. & on BBC Scotland. Contbr. to: The Lancet; The Proceedings of the 6th Int. Congress on Malaria & Tropical Medicine; Blackwood's Mag.; The Scotsman. Mbr. CGGB. Mentioned in Despatches. RAFVR, 2nd World War. Hobbies: Writing; Reading; Swimming; Walking. Address: PO Box 236 Girne, Kibris, via Mersin 10, Turkey. 3.

GUTIÉRREZ, Horacio, b. 28 Aug. 1948, Havana, Cuba. Concert Pianist. Educ: Studied w. Sergei Tarnowsky, Los Angeles,

Calif., USA, 5 yrs.; Juilliard Schl. of Music, NYC, 1967-70. m. Patricia Asher Gutiérrez. Debut: Havana Symph. Orch., aged 11. Career: Played w. most maj. symph. orchs. inclng. NY, Phila., Boston, Chgo., Cleveland, ; LPO; LSO; RPO; Orch. de Paris; Recitals in most maj. cities; App. on Andre Previn's Music Night progs., BBC TV. Recordings: Tchaikowsky's 1st Piano Concerto; Liszt's 1st Piano Concerto; Schumann Concerto; Greig Concerto. Recip., 2nd Prize (Silver Medal), Tchaikowsky Competition, 1970. Hobbies incl: Reading. Mgmt: Columbia Artists Mgmt. Inc., 165 W57 St., NYC, NY 10019, USA. Address: 257 Ctrl. Pk. W., No. 11-B, NY, NY 10024, USA.

GUY, Barry John, b. 22 Apr. 1947, Lewisham, London, UK. Musician (Double Bass; Violone); Composer. Educ: AGSM. Career incls: Freelance bassist; Prin. Orch. St. Johns Smith Square; Monteverdi Orch.; Richard Hickox Orch.; Duo w. soprano Jane Manning; Artistic Dir., London Jazz comps. Orch.; Plays w. inmprovisation grps., Howard Riley, Tony Oxley & Iskra 1903; also w. London Contemporary Dance Theatre. Comps. incl: (recorded) Play (1977); EOS for Double Bass & Orch., 1977; Detairs, 1978; Hold Hands and Sing, 1978. Recordings: w. improvisation grps. & London Jazz Composers Orch. Mbr. profl. orgs. Hons: Radcliffe Award 1st Prize, 1973. Hobbies incl: Painting. Mgmt: Clarion Concert Agcy. Ltd., 64 Whitehall Pk., London N19 3TN. Address: 6 Hassendean Rd., Blackheath, London SE3 8TS, UK. 3, 30.

GUYONNET, Jacques, b. 20 March 1933, Geneva, Switz. Composer; Conductor. Educ: Maturite Classique, Geneva Univ.; Lettres Anciennes, Conserv. of Geneva; comp. & conducting w. Pierre Boulez. m. Genevieve Calame. Career: Fndr., 1958, Chief Cond., 1960-, Studio de Musique Contemporaine; broadcasting, 1959-; made 3 TV films w. Stuttgart Philharmony; concert tours, Switz., France, USA, Netherlands, Yugoslavia, Brazil; Tchr., Zürich Conserv.; currently Artistic Dir., Artistic Rsch. Team Geneva Educ. Bd. Comps. incl: Polyphonies I, II, III; Mondades I, II, II; The Approach to the Hidden Man I & II, Publs. incl: Structure & Communication, 1963; D'Est en ouest, 1966. Mbr., Chmn., 1976-, Int. Soc. for Contemp. Music. Address: 7 BD Jacques Dalcroze, 1204 Geneva, Switzerland.

GWILT, George, b. 11 Nov. 1927, Edinburgh, UK. Actuary; Flute, Alto Flute, Piccolo Player. Educ: MA., St. John's Coll., Cambridge Univ.; Self taught Flautist. m. 3 s. Career: Mbr., Reid Orch., 1945-; Fndr., Edinburgh Wind Quintet, 1957; Broacasts in Scotland. Mbrships: Fellow, Fac. of Actuaries; Fellow, Brit. Computer Soc. Hobbies: Film Making; Walking. Address: 39 Oxgangs Rd., Edinburgh EH»10 7BE, UK.

GYARFAS, Ibolyka, b. 5 May 1904, Budapest, Hungary. Violinst. Educ: studied w. Jeno Hubay. Hungarian Acad. of Music. Debut, 11 Nov. 1911. Career: created a sensation in Berlin, UK & Belgium when began to give concerts at age of 7 (1911-12), at this time played before mbrs. of Engl., Russian & Belgian Royal families; became 1st woman violinist accorded privelege of playing on Paganini's violin (before a select audience). Geneva, 1914; returned to studies in Budapest during war yrs., reappearing as Concert Perf., Germany 1916; has since made many apps. (sometimes giving as many as 60 concerts in Germany alond during a single season); played before Czar Ferdinand & the Duke & Duchess oc Coburg-Gotha, 1918; Guest Soloist under Furtwangler, mannheim, Respighi, Budapest, Nedbal, Vienna, & many other noted conds.; played Bruch Concerto in hon. of composer's 80th birthday, Danzig; Franz Ries composed La Capricciosa for her; has made radio & TV broadcasts; has done some pvte. tchng. Recorded for DGG, Odeon & Vox. Recip. of many hons. inclng: Guarnerius del Gesu violin, presented in Berlin; Red Cross Medal. Hobbies: Reading; Crochet & Knitting. Address: 269 Arlington Ave., Apt. 1, Ottawa, Ont., K1R 5T1, Canada.

GYÁRTÓ, Stefan, b. 24 Mar. 1940, Troy, NY, USA. Conductor; Pianist. Educ: BMus, Eastman Schl. of Music, Univ. of Rochester; MMus, ibid.; DMA, Univ. of Mo., 1970; perfs. cert. (piano), Eastman Schl. of Music. Career: Cond. of opera, Univ. of Toronto, Pittsburgh & NY City Opera; cond. in Basle, Heidelberg; now cond., Hamburgische Staatsoper. Mbrships: Pi Kappa Lambda; Phi Mu Alpha. Address: Am. Langenzug 21/21, 2000 Hamburg 76, German Fed. Repub.

GYIMESI, Kálmán, b. 13 May 1933, Csenger, Hungary. Opera Singer. Educ: Franz Liszt Conserv., Budapest. m. Ágota Bajthay Horváth, 1 c. Debut: title role, Verdi's Rigoletto, 1960. Career: Leading baritone roles of Verdi, Mozart and Puccini operas; Von Einem - Danton's Tod, (title role), Der Besuch von Einem Alten Damen, III; Hindemith - Mathis der Maler (title role); Prokofyev - The Love for Three Oranges, Verlobung in Kloster; Gotovac - Ero; Zikker - Beg Bajazid; Egk - Peer Gynt (title role); Vántus - Golden Coffin, The Three Wanderer; Tschaikovsky - Onegin (title role), Pique Dame; Erkel - Hunyadi, Bán Bánk, etc. Hons: Juhász

Prize, 1962; Liszt Prize, 1969. Hobbies: Angling; Hunting; Chess. Mgmt: Interconcert, Budapest. Address: Szilléri sor 1, 6723 Szeged, Hungary.

GYÖNGY, Paul, b. 19 Oct. 1902, Vienna, Austria, Composer; Pianist. Educ: Pvte. study of Piano, Harmony, Form & Comp. w. Prof. A Schiffer of Music Acad., Budapest. m. Maria Harsányi (dec.). Debuty: Première of first Operetta Budapest, 1932. Career: Composed Operettas, musical comedies, var. film scores, songs & instrumental pieces; Radio portraits broadcast in 1963, 1971, 1975, TV portrait 1972; Asst. Gen. Mgr., Hungarian Film Industries, Ltd., 1945-46; Dir., Hungarian Soc. of Comps. & Authors, 1947-52; Dir., Hungarian Musical Fund, to 1968; Assoc. Dir., Chief Music Sect., Artistic Fndn. of Hungarian Peoples Repub., 1968-. Compositions (publd.) Excerpts of all operettas & comedies; (recorded) about 100 records inclng. LP w. 18 evergreens, 1973. Contbr. to: Billboard; Music Week, UK; Der Musikmarkt. W. Germany. Mbrships: Assn. of Hungarian Musicians; Union of Artistic Workers; Artistic Fndn.; Artisjus, Hungary; Bur. pour la Protection des Droits d'Auteurs; Liszt Ferenc Soc. Hon: Order of Laboru, Golden Class. Hobby: Collecting Old Silver, China & Glass. Address: 1016 Budapest, Derékutca 6, Hungary.

GYSELYNCK, Franklin Benjamin, b. 26 April 1950, Ghent, Belgium. Professor of Harmony & Analysis. Educ: Harmony, Counterpoint, Fugue, Comp., Brussels; Comp., Chapelle Musicale Queen Elisabeth, Waterloo. m. Jenny Spanoghe. Debut: Brussels, 1974. Career: TV & radio interviews, Belgium & Monaco; Prof. of Harmony & Counterpoint Analysis, Royal Music Schl.

(Conserv.), Brussels. Comps. incl: Ballad for Violin & Piano (recorded); Los Alturas de Macchu-Picchu, for voices, choir & large symph. orch. Recordings: Allegretto Grazioso for Flute & Piano; First String Quartet; Three Songs, for voice & chmbr. orch.; 2nd String Quartet; Lacrimosa, for piano. Mbrships: SABAM; CEBEDEM. Hons: Prize, Royal Acad. of Arts & Scis., for String Quartet No. 1, 1974; Prize of SABAM, Queen Elisabeth Concours for Violin for Ballad for Violin & Piano, 1976; Prize Oscar Espla, for Los Alturas de Macchu-Picchu, Spain, 1978; Prize of Monaco for 2nd String Quartet, 1979; ISCM Festival, 1980. Address: 7 Koning Boudewŷnlaan, 9820-St. Denijs-Westrem, Belgium.

GYULAI-GAAL, János, b. 28 April, 1924, Budapest, Hungary. Composer; Conductor. Educ: Graduate; studied at Fac. of Piano & Violin, Ferenc Liszt Acad. of Music, Budapest. m. Martha Gyulai-Gaál, 1 s. Debut: w. Hungarian State Symph. Orch., 1943. Career: Repétiteur, Operetta Theatre, ibid., 1957-58; Prog. Planner, Hungarian Radio, 1959-; Guest Perfs; Brussels TV, Belgium, 1956; OIRT. Fest., 1960; Radio Munich, Germany, 1965, 1967, 1969; Radio Berlin, ibid., 1968; Radio Brno, Czechoslovakia, 1971. Comps. incl: (publd.) Three in Paris; Visit to India; Five-minute Rhapsody; An Evening in the French Quarter, arr. w. Peggy Coolidge; March of the Twenty Years Old; (recorded) Music for Miller, Death of a Salesman; var. songs. Music for 12 Feature Films, full-length cartoon & 60-minute TV Ballet. Mbrships: Artistic Fund of Hungarian Peoples Repub.; Hungarian Music Assn. Hons: Jeno Hubay Prize, 1941; 3rd Prize, Concours de Musique Symphonique Legère, Belgian Radio, 1956; Ferenc Lerkel Prize, 1967. Hobby: History of the Primitive Ages. Address: 1029 Budapest, Budaliget, Honfoglalás u. 28, Hungary.

H

HA, Jae Eun, b. 16 Sept. 1937, Seoul, Korea. Composer; Educator; Performer. Educ: B Th., Hankuk Theol. Sem., Seoul, 1960; BM, Univ. of Tenn., Knoxville, 1968; MM, ibid, 1969; D Musical Arts, Cleveland Inst. of Music, Ohio, 1974. m. I Hui Yim. Debut: Knoxville, Tenn. Career: Assoc. Prof., Chmn. of Div. of Theory & Comp., Miss. Valley State Univ., Itta Bena; played w. Knoxville Symph. Orch., Tenn., 1968-70, & Univ. Circle Orch., Cleveland, Ohio, 1973; perf., WUOT FM radio, Knoxville; Seoul Phil. Orch., 1975. Comps. incl: Sanjo for Solo Flute; Symph. No. 1 & 2; Three abstractions for Tuba. Recordings: Three pieces for Tuba, 1978. Mbrships: ASCAP; Pi Kappa Lambda; Southeastern Comps. League; Am. Soc. for Univ. Comps.; Nat. Assn. of Comps., USA. Hons: Nat. Endowment for the Arts; Teaching Fellow, Cleveland Inst. of Music; Knoxville Symph. Scholarships. Hobbies: Ping Pong; Swimming; Travelling. Mgmt: Rapsodia Concert Mgmt., Chicago, Ill. 60654. Address: 203 W. Jefferson St., Greenwood, MS 38930, USA. 7,29.

HAACK, Helmut Bernhard, b. 14 Feb. 1931, Duesseldorf, Germany. Musicologist. Educ: PhD, Munich, 1964. Career: Collaborator, Editing Redactor, Riemann Musiklexikon; Personal Asst. to Ed., H H Eggebrecht, ibid, 1964-69; 1st Dir., Hindemith Inst., Mainz, (now located in Frankfurt), 1969-73; Music Critic, Mainz, & freelance rschr., perf. prac. as documented on histl. records, 1973-74; Collaborator, Inst. üer Auffüehrungspraxis, & Tchr., Hochschule füer Musik & Darstellende Kunst, Graz, Austria, 1974-. Publs. incl: Anfaenge des Generalbass-Satzes, 2 vols., 1974. Contbr. to profl. publs. Mbr. profl. orgs. Hobby: Collecting histl. records. Address: Lucolf-Krehl-Str. 17, D-6900 Heidelberg, German Fed. Repub.

HAAGER, Maximilian Ludwig Michael, b. 18 May 1905, Goerz, Italy. Composer; Teacher; Professor; Musician, Cello, Violin, Piano, Organ, Flute, Oboe. Educ: Educ. Inst., Linz; PhD, Univ. of Vienna, 1932; Univ. of Graz; Acad. of Music & performing Arts, Vienna. m. Karoline Adam, 3 c. Career: Prof., Acad. of Music & performing Arts, Graz. Compositions incl: Chmbr. Music; Songs; var. works for string orch.; 6 Symphs.; var. orchl. works; 'Ballade vom Brennesselbusch', soloists, choir, small orch.; Spiel Musik for woodwinds; Sonata, violin solo; Partitas, violin & piano, guitar; 3 operas; Toccata & Fugue for organ; Sonata for piano. Publs: Tanz-& Frstmusik aus Osterreich, 1928; Jodlerbuch, 1934;Die instrumentale Volksmusik Im Salzkammergut, 1979. Mbr. AKM. Recip. num. Hons. for Comp. Hobbies: Mountaineering; Photography. Address: Märiatrosterstrasse 113, A-8043 Graz, Austria.

HAAHTI, Marjatta, b. 3 Mar. 1938, Helsinki, Finland. Harpist. Educ: Piano Educ. Cert., Sibelius Acad., Helsinki; studied w. Pierre Hamet. m. Heikki Haahti, 2 c. Debut: Jyvaskyla, 1968. Career: Recitalist, Finland, 1968-; Soloist w. orch., ibid, 1969-; Duo Concerts, Harp & Flute, Finland & Sweden, 1972-; Apps. in France, Halland, Sweden; TV, Radio, Solo & Chmbr. Music perfs., Finland, 1966-. Mbr. Int. Assn. of Harpists & Friends of the Harp. Named Music Debutante Of The Yr., Finland, 1968. Hobbies: Swimming; Literatur. Address: Jtäkangastie 8.C.19., 90500, Oulu 50, Finland.

HAASE, Hans b. 12 May 1929, Neumünster, Germany. Librarian, critic, musicologist. Educ: PhD, 1960; Libn. exan. 1969. m. Renate Ahrens, 2 s., 2 d. Career: Asst., music inst., Kiel univ. 1956-60; ed. asst., 'Musik in Geschichte und Gegenwart', 1954-8; J S Bach inst., Göttingen, 1964-5; Libn., Herzog August Lib., Volfenbüttel, from 1969. Publs: 'Jobst vom Brandt 1517-70', 1967: Heinrich Schütz und seinen Bexiehungen zum Wolfenbüttler Hof, 1972; Hans Albrecht in memoriam (ed. w. W Brennecke), 1962. Contbr. to: Die Musikforschung; Die Musik in Geschichte und Gegen Wart; Groves dictionary of music & musicians; Wolfenbüttler Beiträge; Aus den Schätzen der Herzog-August Bibliothek. Hobbies: reading; walking. Address: D-3340 Wolfenbüttel, Bernardusring 32, German Fed. Repub.

HAASNOOT, Leendert, b. 25 Nov. 1917, Katwyk, Netherlands. Master of Music Training College; Instructor Solfège; Vocalist. Educ: Tchrs. Cert.; Masters Degree, Musicol., Leiden Univ.; Candidate Dr's Degree, Amsterdam Univ. m. A M Nieuwenhuis, 3 children. Career: Dir., Choral Soc.; Master, Music Trng. Coll., The Hague. publs: Peter Hellendaal: Life and Works. Mbreships: Nederlandse Vereniging voor Muziekgeschiedenis. Address: 25 Merelstraat, 2225 PS Katwijk ZH, Netherlands.

HABA, Alois, b. 21 June, 1893, Vizovice, Czechoslovakia. Composer; Educator. Educ: Conservs. of Prague, Vienna & Berlin. Career: Prof., Acad. of Music & Dramatic Arts, Prague, 1945-51. Compositions incl: Cesta Zivota; Fantaisie Symphonique; Operas -- Matha; Nova seme; Prijd Kralovstvi Tve. Author of sev. music books. Mbrships: Preparatory Committee, Union of Czech Composers & Performing Artists, 1970-; Czech. Acad. & Inst. Soc. for Contemporary Music. Hons: Honoured Artist, 1963; Order of the Repub., 1968. Address: co U druzstva Prace 59, Prague 4, Podoli, Czechoslovakia.

HABERL. Ferdinand, b. 15 Mar. 1906, Lintach, Oberfalz, Bavaria. Music Institute President. Educ: Univ. of Munich; Pontifical Inst. of Sacred Music, Rome; Magister, Gregorian Chant. ibid; Magister, Sacred Comp., ibid; Dr. of Sacred Comp.; PhD. Career: Dir., Ch. Music Schl., Regensburg, 1939-70; Pres., Pontifical Inst. of Sacred Music, Rome, Italy, 1970-. Publs: Joannis Cavacli, Magnificat omnitonum, 1581, 1965; Das Gradulé Romanum, Erster Band, 1976; Il canto gregoriano dell' Introito e del communio, 1977; Il canto responsorale del graduale, 1979. Contbr. to: MGG; Musica Sacra CVO; The New Cath. Ency.; Grove's Dictionary of Music & Musicians; Brockhauslexicon fur Theologie & Kirche. Mbrships: Cecilian Soc. of the German-Speaking Lands; Int. Sacred Music Soc., Rome; Int. Soc. for Copyright Reform; Italian Musicol. Soc.; Antiquae Musicae Italicae Studiosi. Hons: Culture Prize, E. Bavaria, 1962; Nordgau Medal of Hon., 1966; Lasso Medal, 1970; Prelato d'Onore, 1971; Bavarian Order of Merit, 1972; Accademico Filarmonico di Bologna, 1975. Address: 250 via Nomentana, J-00162 Rome, Italy. 19.

HABIG, Dorothy Kathryn, b. 8 Oct. 1945, Newark, NJ, USA. Musician (French horn, piano, organ); Music Teacher. Educ: B Mus, Manhattan Schl. Music, NYC; M Mus. Ed., ibid.; var. pvte. tutors. Career incl: Organist & Choir Dir., Holy Trinity Ch., Hackensack, NJ, 1967-68; Hornist, Title III Woodwind Quintet, Bergen Co. Schl. System, 1966-67; Asst. Prin. Horn, NJ Stmph., 1969-71; Solo Horn, Radio Orch, Basel, Switz. 1972-73; Asst. Prin. Horn, Stuttgarter Phil., 1974-76; Piano & Horn Instructor, Backnange Jugendmusik-hochschule, Germany, 1975-76; 3rd Horn, Phil. Staatsorchester, Hamburg Staatsoper. Mbr. profl. orgs. Recip;. var. schlrships. Hobbies: Swimming; Sewing. Address: 7302 Ostfildern 4, Hohenheimer Str. L8, German Fed. Repub.

HACHÉ, Reginald W J, b. 26 Nov. 1932, Waterville, Maine, USA. Concet Pianist; Composer; Professor of Music. Educ: BMus, MMus, D Arts, New England Conserv. of Music; Postgrad. work at TCL. m. Maxine Baron Haché, 4 s. Debut: Boston, USA. Career: boston Pops Soloist, 10 yrs.; Radio perfs., Cambridge, Mass., & TV apps. Boston, Cambridge, Phila., USA; Tours of US & Europe as soloist & ambassador for US 7th Army Symph.; Kaleidoscope (ballet); Concerto for piano & orch.; Fantasy 1984 (piano solo); Suite for Piano; Background music for radio prodn. of Treasure Island. Recordings: Contemporary Music for gymnastic competitions; Double Concertos, Poulenc; Mendelssohn, Bach, Mozaart, Gershwin (w. Boston Pops). publs: Piano Class Methods for Laboratory, Books I-IV. Mbrships. incl: MTA (Pres., Boston chapt.). Hons: Winner, var. perf. & comp. competitions. Hobby: Golf. Address: 68 Fordville Rd., Duxbury, MA 02332, USA.

HACKER, Alan Ray, b. 30 Sept. 1938. Clarinettist. Educ: RAM; FRAM. m. Anna Maria Sroka, 1959, 2 d. Career: Joined LPO, 1958; Prof., RAM, 1960-; founded, w. H Birtwistle & S Pruslin, Pierrot Players, 1965;Fndr., Matrix, 1971; Mbr., Fires of Londorn, Fndr., The Music Party, 1972; Sir Robert Mayer Lectr., Leeds Univ., 1972-73; has premiered works of Boulez, Stockhausen, Maxwell Davies, Goehr, Birtwistle & Feldman. Publs: Ed., Mozart Concerto & Quintet (for clarinet); Ed., reconstructed Mozart Concerto, 1973. Hobby: Bar Billiards. Address: 15 Fox Hill, London SE19 2UX, UK. 1.

HADARI, Omri, b. 10 Sep. 1941, Petach-Tikva, Israel. conductor. Educ: Tel Aviv Music Coll.; GSM. m. Osnat, 1 d., 1s. Debut: London, 1974. Career: Perfs. as cond. w. Nat. Dutch Ballet, Victorian Opera Co., RPO; City of Birmingham Symph. Orch., New Symph. Orch., English Symph., Holon Chmbr. Orch., Beer-Sheva Orch. Hons: Dr Leo Kestenberg Prize (1st), Israel, 1969; Conducting Prize, GSM, 1974; Capsalic Cup for Cond., 1974. Hobbies: Sports; Politics. Mgmt: Victor Hochhauser, London. Address: 36 Brookside Rd., London, NW11, UK.

HADDON, Peggy Ann, b. 23 Mar. 1931, Johannesburg, S Africa. Pianist. Educ: LRAM; LRSM; UPLM; UTLM; LTCL. m. Neville John Richardson, 2 d. Debut: Johannesburg. Career: regular broadcasts, S African Broadcasting Corp., 1943-; concerts in Germany & UK; Sr. Music Lectr. in piano,

Witwatersand Univ., 1969-. Recordings incl: 3 educl. LPs 'Let Us Hear'; works by Bach., Beethovan, Brahms, Dohnanyi, Harvey. Mbr., S African Soc. of Music Tchrs. Hobbies: Flower arranging; Tennis. Address: 34 Bath Ave., Parkwood, Johannesburg, S Africa.

HADELICH DE FERREIRA, Valeska, b. 24 April 1943, Stuttgart, Germany. Violinist; Professor. Educ: Hochschule für Musik, Belin; Hochschule für Musikerziehung, Trossingen, Germany. m. Paulo Affonso de Moura Ferreira, 1 d, 1 s. Career: Mbr., String Quartet of the Univ. of Brasília; many Europian and Am tours, incl. concerts in Autumn of Warsaw, Interamerican Fest. of Wash., May Fest. of Wiesbaden, Fest. de Arte Bahia, Fest. de Inverno de Campos do Jordao, Fest. Int. de Música de Curtiba; Prof., Arts Dept., Univ. of Brasília. Sev. recordings. Mbrships: Ordem dos Músicos do Brasil;; Brasília country Club. Hons: Troféu Joao de Barro, 1966; Melhor conjunto Instrumental de 1973, Da Apca. Hobbies: Painting; Gardening. Address: Bloco B. Apto. 506, Superquadrasul 105, 70 000 Brasília, Brazil.

HADIDIAN, Eileen, b. 9 June 1948, Beirut, Lebanon. Musicologist; Baroque Flautist. Educ: BMus, Am. Univ. of Beirut, 1972; DMA, Stanford Univ., 1979; Dip., early music, Longy Schl. of Music, Cambridge, Mass.; Baroque & Boehm flute w. Janet See, San Francisco & Frances Blaisdell, Stanford Univ.; recorder workshops w. Edgar Hunt; Oberlin Baroque Inst., 1978. Career: Baroque flautist, San Francisco Bay area; fac., East Bay Ctr. for the Performing Arts, Richmond; fac., Mills Coll., Extension prog., Oakland, Calif. Publ: ed. & transl. of Antoine Mahaut: A New Method for learning to play the Transverse Flute (1759), 1980. Mbrships: Bd. Dirs., San Francisco Early Music Soc.; concert mgr. for the Soc.'s concert series. Hons: Univ. Honors Student, Am. Univ. of Beirut, 1969-72; Grad. Fellowship, Stanford Univ., 1976-79. Hobbies: Langs.; Travel; Hiking; Balkan folk dance. Address: 2642 Derby St., Apt. 2, Berkely, CA 94705, USA.

HADJINIKOS, George, b. 3 May 1927, Volos, Greece. Concert Pianist; Conductor; Lecturer; Teacher. Educ: Athens Univ.; Dip., Athens Conserv.; Mozarteum, Salzburg; study in Germany & France. m. Mattina Crithary, 1 s. Career: Concert soloist in Europe, India, etc. inclng. sev. world premières; appeared w. Berlin Phil., BBC; ORTF France; Suisse Romande; Halle Orch.; Radio Orch., Vienna etc.; cond., London Bach Festival Ensemble; Northern Sinfonia; Athens Radio; Swedish Radio Orch., etc; Tchr., Royal Northern coll. of Music; Lectr. in var. countries. Helped Ed., The Complete Works by Nikos Skalkottas. Contbr. to: The Listener; Greek periodicals, inc. Hobbies: Reading; Country walks; Swimming. Address: 59 Ashley Rd., Altrincham, Cheshire, UK, & Aghia Pelaghia, Kythera, Greece. 3.

HADL, Vitězslav, b.5 May 1945, Prague, Czechoslovakia Composer; Pianist; Organist. Educ: Absolutorium, State conserv., Prague. m. Helena Jungmann, 1 s. Career: has composed music for film (Jak Utopit Dr mrácka), & radio (Na Lvy Dáme Zlatou, Maminko), & scene music for TV braadcast; many works have been recorded. Mbr: OSA; Prague, SCSKU. Hons: Has twice received 1st Prize, Pisnicky Pro Hvezdu. Hobbies: Home Film Making; Pipe Smoking; Fishing. Address: Solidarita A 531, 100 00 Prague 10, Czechoslovaki.

HADRABA, Josef, b. 8 May 1903, Vienna, Austria. Trombonist. Educ: Acad. for Music & performing Arts, Vienna. m. 1) Lydia Orinskaja (dec.); 2) Friederika Zimmerer. Career: Toured as soloist, 1924; mbr. Vienna State Opera Orch., 1929; mbr., Vienna Phil. Orch., 1930; lectr., Acad. for Music & Performing Arts, Vienna, 1936-38, 1947-; mbr., Hofmusikkapelle, Vienna, 1938; 1dr., Trompeterchor, Vienna, 1945. Comps. incl: 70 trombone solos; 30 Fanfares & Chorales for wind; 60 trombone quartets; over 70 songs; works for string & wind orch.; Jazz ballet, Professor Bumba. Publs: 10 vols, Unterrichtsmaterial für Posaune and Horn, 1941-75. Mbrships: Mgmt. Bd., Vienna State Opera Orch., 1945-46, & Vienna Phil. Orch. Hons: Nicolai Medal, 1942; Vienna Phil. Ring, 1955; Vienna State Opera Orch. Ring, 1967; Hon. silver medal of Bundes Haupstadt, Vienna, 1978. Hobbies: Reading; Study. Address: Alsestr. 27/II/2/12, 1080 Vienna, Austria.

HADRYS, Stefan, b. 23 July 1929, Katowice, Poland. Trumpeter; Musicologist; Teacher. Educ: Master in philos. & musicol., Univ. of Poznan, 1954; M Mus, 1960, docent (rdr.), 1969, HS of Music, Warsaw; studied w. Prof. L Vaillant, Paris Conserv., 1965. m. Aniela Hadrys, 1 d. Debut: w. Poznń Phil., 1950. Career: 1st Trumpet, chmbr. music soloist, Warsaw Phil.; has played for TV, radio & film; has given 1st perfs. of contemp. Polish Trumpet works, but specializes in Baroque music, esp. works written for high trumpets; Hd., Brass & Wind

Dept., High Schl. of Music, Warsaw. Comps: First Exercises for Trumpet, 1973; Daily Exercises for Trumpet, 1976; piano transcriptions of trumpet concertos. Author: The Modern Methods of Trumpet Playing, 1977; History of Trumpet, 1974. Contbr. to: Jazz. Mbrships: VP, Music Tchrs. Sect., Int. Trumpet Guild; Polish Musicians Assn. Recip. sev. awards. Hobbies indl: Film & Photography. Mgmt: PAGART, 00-078 Warsaw, Plac Zwyci,stwa 9, Poland. Address: Ciasna 15-44, 00232 Warsaw, Poland.

HAEBLER, Ingrid, b. 20 June 1929, Vienna, Austria. Concert Pianist. Educ: Dips., High Schls. for Music, Vienna, Salzburg & Geneva, Career: Concert Tours, all Europe, Australia, USA, Canada, S. Africa & Japan; Feature Artist at Num. Fests. inclng. Salzburg, Edinburgh, Wiesbaden, Bath, The Holland Fest. & The Prague Spring Fest.; Apps. w. Best Renown Orch. such as The Concertgebouw Orch., Amsterdam, LSO, RPO, Vienna Phil. Orch., Berlin Phil. Orch., Boston Symph. Ordh., The Lanoureux Orch. Paris, The Brussels, Stockholm & Warsaw Phil. Orchs. Recordings incl: All Mozaart concerrtos & Mozart & Schubert Sonatas; Beethoven's Second & Fourth Piano Concertos; Schumann Piano Concerto & Symphonic Variations by Cesar Franck. Hons: 1st Prize, Int. Competiotion, Munich, Germany & Int. Schubert Competition, Geneva, 1954; Beethoven Medal, Harriet Cohen Fndn., 1957; Grand Prix du Disque, Paris, 1958; Puthon Prize, Salzburg Fest.; Mozart Medal, Vienna, 1971. Mgmt: Klaus Menzel, Zürich, Switzerland. Address: 5412 St. Jakob am Thurn, Post Puch Bei Hallein, Land Salzburg, Austria.

HAEFLIGER, Ernst, b. 6 July 1921, Davos, Switz. Lyric Tenor. Educ: Music Acad., Zürich. m. Anna Hadorn, 2 s., 1 d. Concert debut: 1943; Operatic Debut: 1949. Career: European concert tours, 1945-; N Am. debut, Vancouver Fest., 1959; Ldng. Lyric Tenor, Deutsche Oper, Berlin, 1952-; Fest. apps., Glyndebourne, Salzburg, Munich, Lucerne, Aix-en-Provence. Recordings: DGG; Columbia. Hons. incl: German Critics' Prize, 1955; Chapell Gold Medal, 1956. Address: Konzertgesellschaft Zürich, Steinweisstr. 2, Aürich 7, Switz. 2.

HAENCHEN, Hartmut, b. 1943, Dresden, German Dem. Repub. Conductor. Educ: High Schl. for Music, Dresden, 1960-66; studies w. Werner Matschke, Prof. Rudolf Neuhaus & Prof. Horst Förster; study course w. Leningrad Philharmonic, 1973; master classes w. Prof Helmut Koch & prof. Fritz Höf, Berlin, 1964-. Career: Dir., Robert Franz Singacad., Halle; cond., State Symph. Orch., Halle; 1st. Kapellmeister, State Theatre, Zwickau; Asst. Cond., Dresden Phil., 1973-76; perm. guest cond., State Opera, Dresden, 1974-; Dir., Staatskapelle, Mecklenburg, 1976-; Music Dir., State Theatre, Schwrin, 1976-; num. guest apps., inc. Tokyo, 1975 & Barcelona Mod. Music Fest., 1975. Hons: 1st. prize, Carl Maria von Weber Competition, 1971. Address: 27 Schwerin, Waldschulweg 1, German Dem. Repub.

HAENDEL, Ida, b. 1924, Poland, Violinist. Educ: Study of violin w. Flesch & Enesco. Debut: Queen's Hall, London, age 13. Career: Num. concert appearances, noted for brilliant technique.

HAENFLEIN, Robert Henriques, b. 2 May 1924, Hamburg, German Fed. Repub. (Swedish nationality) Violinist; Composer; Conductor; Author. Educ: RAM, Stockholm. Debut: Vienna Bradcasting Corp., 1937. Career: Violinist, Gothenburg Symph. Orch., Sweden, 1946; Soloist & Bandldr., Swedish, Danish & Italian Broadcasting & TV, 1947-65; Violinequilibrist, China Variety, 1956; Cond. & Ldr., Hofors Symph. Orch., & Stage Mgr., Operett Theatr, 1965-. comps. incl: 12 virtuos solos for violin & piano; concerto in C for viola & orch.; Swedish Rondo for flute & orch.; 2 musicals. Recordings. incl: The Magic Violin of Robert Haenflein. Mbrships: STIM; SKAP. publs. incl: Piano School, 1974. Recip., var. hons. Hobby: Kaligraphy. Address: Centralgatan 29, 813 00 Hofors, Sweden.

HAENTJES, Werner, b. 16 Dec. 1923, Cologne, Germany. Composer. Educ: Musikhochschule, Cologne, 1939-41. m. Johanna Hock, 2 s, 2 d. Debut: Stadtishe Buhnen Bielefeld, 1946. Career: Co-operation w. var. TV & broadcasting stns. in Germany & theatres in Cologne, Dusseldorf, Hambrug & Zürich; Music Dir., Stadtische Theatre, Cologne. Compositions: 2 operas for theatr, Cologne 1964, Cologne, 1966; Opera for TV 'Leonce & Lena', 1963; Opera Goldspur, 1975-76. works for orch. & choir, chamber music, works for soloists. Mbrships: Musikakademie Vercelli; Vorstand Deutscher Komponistenverband. Hons: Kulturkreis im Bundesverband der deutschen Industrie, 1957. Address: P Humburgstr. 62, 5 Cologne 60 German Fed. Repub.

HAFFORD, Mary Gale, b. 6 Apr. 1902, Dallas, Tex., USA. Violinist, Teacher. Educ: Artist's Dip., Cinn.. Conserv. of Mus., 1922. Tutors: Ysaÿe, Auer, Enesco, Galaminan. m. Dr. Clinton

S Hafford, 2 d. Debut: Town Hall, NYC., 1930. Career: Toured USA, solo recitals: Orch. Appearances w. F Reiner, W Hendi, Nat'l Orch. Ass'n, Oratorio Soc., NYC, etc.; specialized in Amer. Contemp. Chmbr. Mus. & 1st perf. Mus. Dir.-Violinist, Intimate Concerts Ass'n, 1952-66; cond. Chmbr. Mus. Soc. & Youth Orchs. Weekly broadcasts, NY Stns.; Fac. NY Coll. of Mus., 16 yrs., Manhattan Schl. of Mus., 1968-69; Tchr. of Zuzuki Method. Cond., Sun City Sinfonietta, 1974. contbr. to num. jrnls. Mbrships: int. Mu Phi Epsilon; Violin Tchrs. Guild, NYC.; Alliance Francaise, etc. Recip., Belgian Medaille d'Honeur at Recital, Hommage á E Ysaÿe, Ariz., 1972. Address: 10820 Caron Dr., Sun City, AZ 85351, USA.

HAGAN, Paul Wandel, b. 18 Nov. 1930, Grandview, Ind., USA. Music Teacher; Organist; College Professor; Concert Artist; Composer. Educ: B Mus Ed, Univ. Evansville, Ind.; MS, Ind. State Univ. Career: Music Prof., Ind. Univ. Regional Campus, Ft. Wayne, Ind,; Organist, St Joseph Ch., Ft. Wayne; Engl. Prof., St Francis Coll., Ft. Wayne; Recitals, Europe & UK. Comps: Life of Christ in sound; Sketches of Paris Churches; 3 Petite Elegies, Psalm Chorale Preludes, 11 vols.; Scottish Suite; Monastic Suite; Grecian Suite; Liturgical Prayers; Swedish Suite. Mbrships: AGO; Phi Delta Kappa. Hon: Nominated for Hon. D Mus, Univ. Evansville, 1972. Hobbies incl: Theatre. Address: 533 Kinnaird, Ft. Wayne, IN, USA. 2, 8.

HAGE, (Rev.) Louis, b. 1 May 1938, Bteddine El Lokche, Lebanon. Priest; Educator. Educ: Higher Studies Dip., Paris, France, 1971; D Mus, Sorbonne, Paris, France, 1970; Licence of Theology, Rome, 1967. Career: Prof., Musicol., Inst. of Musicol., Univ. of the Holy Spirit, Kaslik, Lebanon, 1970-, Dir., 1970-, Dir. of Choir, 1970-; Lectr., Music, Num. Univs. in Europe & USA; Num. TV Progs., Lebanon; Apps. on Radio Progs. in Lebanon, Paris, Vatican. Compositions: Arr. of Old Syriac Melodies Publd. & Recorded w. Texts in Arabic. Recordings: 16 records w. choir of Univ. of the Holy Spirit, 1971-73. 5 cassettes of rel. music. Publs. incl: Le Chant de l'Eglise Maronite, 1972; Musique Occidentale et Orientale, French Ed., 1973, Arabic Ed.; 1974; Le piano chahine, un piano occidental-oriental, 1974; Maronite Music, 1978. Mbrships: Int. Musicol. Soc. Hobbies: Recordings; Reading. Address: Inst. of Musicol., Univ. of the Holy Spirit, Kaslik, Lebanon.

HAGEGAARD, Erland Boerje, b. 27 Feb. 1944, Aruika, Sweden. Opera singer. Educ: Music Schl. Ingesund; Royal acad. of music, Stockholm; coll. of music & drama, Vierna. m. Anne Terelius. Debut: Stockholm, 1965. Career: Volksoper, Vienna; opera house, Frankfurt; State opera, Hamburg; TV app. in Xerxes & Bocoaccio, Germany & Denmark. Recordings: 'Opera-Lieder'. Mbrships: Peterson-Berger-Sällskapet, Stockholm. Hons: 3 Christina Nilsson Schlrships: Fröding Schlrship; Wermlandsstidningens cultural Schlrship. Address: 2081 EllerbeckHamburg, Birkenau 5, German Fed. Repub.

HAGERUP DULL, Edvard, b. 10 June, 1922, Borgon, Norway. Composer; Pianist. Educ: Matric. Degree, Oslo Univ.; Dip. Organ, Oslo conserv., 1947; Conserv. Nat. Superieur de Musique, Paris, (w. Darius Milhaude, Charles Koechlin & Jean Rivier); Hochschule für Musik, Berlin, w. Josef Rufer & Boris Blacher. m. Anna Kvarme, 2 children. Debut: Phil. Orch. of Paris. Career: Perfs. in more than 25 countries. Cmps incl: 5 Symphs., ballets, 2 operas, Orch. & Chmbr. Music works, sev. commissioned by French radio, TV & Min. of Culture. Num. recordings. Contbr. to Musique et Instruments, Paris. Publs: Catalogue of Musical Works. Mbr. Soc. of Comps., Oslo; L'Union Natinale des Comps. de Musique, Paris. Hons. incl: Prix de Composition Musicale, Conserv. Nat. Superieur de Musique, Paris, 1952; German State, French State & Norwegian Scholarships. Hobbies: Lit., Art; Hist. Address: 14 re de Lozere, 91400 Orsay, France. 30.

HAGER-ZIMMERMANN, Hilde, b. 17 April 1907, Rosenthal, Böhmen, Austria. Housewife. Educ: Tchr. Trng. Coll.; Brucknerkonservatorium, Lina. Musikhochschule, Vienna.mD. med. Hager, 3 d. Debut: as organist in early youth; as comp., 1959. Comps: over 1,000 songs & instrumental works of which half have already been publd.; chmbr. works; songs w. accomp. Works recorded: Frühlingsgeschenk; Meditation. Mbrships: Comps. Union; Authors Soc. Recip., Cultural prize of the City of Passau. hobbies: Philosophy; Flowers. Address: Ferihumerstr. 344020 Linz A Austria.

HAGGART, Margaret, b. 11 Dec., Melbourne, Australia. Operatic Soprano. Educ: Studied singing w. Antonio Moretti-Pananti, Melbourne Univ. Conservatorium. m. Michael Foudy, 1 d. Debut: WNO, Cardiff, Wales, 1972. Career: Res. Prin. Soprano, Engl. Nat. Opera, 4 yrs.; Guest Prin. Soprano, WNO, Engl. Nat. Opera N, Vic. State Opera; Major roles, BBC TV & Proms., Aust. Broadcasting Commission; Opera Concert, Camden Fest. Hons: Sydney 'Sun' Aria, 1970. Hobbies:

Horseriding; Cooking. Address: 2 Nascot Lodge, 90 Langley Rd., Watford, Herts., UK.

HAGGER, Roger Watson, b. 18 July 1925, Sandwich, Kent, UK. Bassoonist. Educ: TCL; London Univ. m. Joyce Hagger, 1 d. Career: Music Dir., Radio SEAC, Ceylon, WW II; w. Int. Ballet, Martha Graham Dance Co.; Prin. Bassoon, Royal Opera House, Covent Gdn., 1954-. Mbrships: Automobile Assn.; Inst. of Adv. Motorists; Co. of Veteran Motorists. Hobbies: Horses; Photography; Motoring; Model Engineering. Address: 20 Mandeville Dr., Ditton Hill, Surbiton, Surrey, UK.

HAGGH, Raymond Herbert, b. 4 Sept. 1920, Chicago, Ill., USA. Professor of Music Theory & Musicology; Associate Dean of College of Arts & Sciences, 1973-77; Dir., Schl. of Music, 1977-. Educ: B Mus, M Mus, Northwestern Univ.; PhD, Ind. Univ.; Post-Grad., Univ. of Cologne; Fellow, Fund for Advancement of Educ., Harvard Univ., 1955-56. m. Hilde Wentzlaff-Eggebert Haggh, 2 d. Comps: Many misc. comps. (chmbr., orchl. & choral music), 1947-63. Publs. History of Music Theory Books I & II by Hugo Riemann, Transl., commentary & preface by Raymond Haggh, 1962. contbr. to profl. jrnls. Mbrships. incl: Pi Kappa Lambda. Hons. incl: Woods Fellowhip, 1968-69. Hobbies: Reading. Address: 4708 Kirkwood Dr., Lincoln, NE 68516, USA.

HAHN, Gunnar A, b. 16 March 1908, Stockholm, Sweden. Composer; Arranger of Folk Music; Performer (Piano, Accordion). Educ: Grad. in Organ, Piano & Harmony, Stockholm Conserv. of Music, 1930; piano studies w. Simone Barere, 1930-32. m. Elsa Edström, 2 s. Debut: Stockholm, 1932, London & NYC, 1950. Career: Piano tours, Scandinavia, as Accomp., Soloist & Orchl. Soloist, 1934-50; Arr. & Ldr., own radio quartet, 1936-47, & own folk dance ensemble, 1947-; num. radio perfs., inclng. guest apps. abroad; TV perfs., 1949-. Comps. incl: Suite gothique, 1949; Swedish suite, 1965; 4 Suites for str. quartet, 1973; num. folk songs. Recordings: Num. Folk songs, dances & ballads. Hon. Mbr., Swedish Soloists Union. Recip., var. bursaries. Address: Storforsplan 5, S 123 47 Farsta, Sweden.

HAIEN, Jeannette, b. Dayton, Ohio, USA. Musician; Concert Pianist; Teacher. Educ: Piano study w. Artur Schnabel & Leonard Shure; BA, MA, Univ. Mich. m. Ernest S Ballard Jr., 1 d. Career: Annual solo recitals, chmbr.-music concerts & orchl. apps., USA & Europe; Asia, 1971, '73; Ctrl. & S. Am., 1975; TV & radio apps., world capitals; Prof. Piano, Mannes Coll. Music, NYC; Master Classes, var. musical institutions, USA, Holland, Portugal, Phillippines, Malaysia, Burma & India. Recordings: Mozart's Concerto K.451 w. Nat. Gall. Orch. (WCFM); All Kabalevsky Record (WCFM). Mbr., Cosmopolitan Club, NYC. Address: 120 E 75 St., NY, NY 10021, USA.

HAILPARN, Lydia Rosen, b. 6 April 1938, NY, NY, USA. Pianist; University Music Department Chairman. Educ: BS., Juilliard Schl. of Music; MS., ibid; MA, Columbia Univ., PhD., ibid; EdD., ibid; Dip., Conservs. of Music of Paris, Fontainebleu, France. div., 2 d. Debut: Town Hall, NYC, Age 10. Career: num. Concerts, East Coast, & Calif., USA, France, Holland, UK; Soloist, Chgo. Symph., NY. Symph. Children's concerts: num. Radio, TV Apps.; Chmn., Music Dept., Drew Univ., Madison, NJ.; Fndr., Ed., Dissonance. Composer, Songs My Children Love. Author, Contemporary Dutch Keyboard Music, 1960. Contbr. to: Drew Univ. Mag.; Music Review; Clavier; Choral Jrnl., Univ. of S Fla.; Music Jrnl.; Women's League Outlook. Mbrships: Phi Beta Kappa; Pi Lambda Theta; Mu Phi Epsilon; Am. Musicol. Soc.; Int. Musicol. Soc.; Coll. Music Soc.; Soc. for Ethnomusicol. Recip. num. Hons Inclng: Winner of Nat. Endowment for the Humnanities Award, 1975. Hobbies: Swimming; Boating; Art; Theatre; Travel; Gourmet Restaurants. Address: 8 Donald Ct., Wayne, NJ 07470, USA. 5.

HAIPUS, Eino, b. 30 Jan. 1910, Oulu, Finland. Violinist; Conductor. Educ: Violin studies, & Dip. Comps., Sibelius Acad.; cond. Cert., Mozarteum. Salzburg. m. Elsa Hikka Karjalainen, 1 d. Debut: Helsinki. Career: (radio) violin, viola, cond. perfs.; (TV), cond. of Finnish TV Vaasa, Operas Gipsybaron Pohjalaiset, Nabucco, Il Tabarro & Aida; Cond. concerts in Finland, Sweden, Estland & Germany. Mgr.., Music Inst. Compositions: String Quartet in D Maj., etc. Recordings: Tulindberg: violin concerto (orch. accompaniment). Mbrships: Pres., Vaasa Southern Rotary Club, 1962-63; Hon. Mbr., Pohjan Miehet, male choir. Hons: Rafael Ahlstrom Fond, 1944; Leo & Regina Wainstein Fond, 1952; Fond of Finnish Culture, 1960 & '68. Hobbies: Tennis; Tourism. Mgmt: Kuula Inst. Address: Kirkkopuistikko 22 A 10, 65100 Vaasa 10, Finland.

HAIR, Graham Barry, b. 27 Feb. 1943, Geelong, Vic., Aust. Composer; Pianist; Lecturer. Educ: Mus. Bac., Melbourne Univ.; MMus, ibid.; PhD, Sheffield Univ., UK. m. Greta Mary Larsen.

Career: Lectr. in music, LaTrobe Univ., Vic. Contbr. of articles on Milton Babbitt to Perspectives of New Music. Comps: Monody for solo voice, 1976. Mbrships: Comps., Guild of Aust.; Musicol. Soc. of Aust. (Pres., Vic. Chapt.). Hons: commonwealth UK award, 1967-70; Maggs award for comp., Melbourne Univ., 1973; Aust. Coun. grant for study at Princeton Univ., USA, 1974-75. Address: c/o Music Dept., Univ. of LaTrobe, Bundoora, Vic., 3083, Aust.

HAIR, Harriet Inez, b. 28 June 1935, Spartanburg, SC, USA. Associate Professor of Music Education. Educ: BA., Mt. Holyoke Coll.; MAT., Harvard Grad. Schl. of Educ.; M Mus., Converse Coll., EdD., Tchrs. Coll., Columbia Univ.; Studies in theory w. Nadia Boulanger, 1955-56. Contbr. to: SC Music News (Book Review Ed., 1966-68); Jrnl. of Rsch. in Music Educ., 1973, 1977; Ga. Music News (Student News Column, 1973-75). Mbrships: Pi Kappa Lambda; Delta Kappa Gamma; MENC; State Student Advsr., Ga. Music Educators Assn.; Bd. mbr., ibid; Nat. Coun. of State Student Advsrs., MENC. Hons: Harry Robert Wilson Schlrship., Columbia Univ., 1969-70; Edna McGuire Boyd Schlrship. (Int. Schlrship. of Delta Kappa Gamma), 1969, Hobbies: Travel; Needlework. Address: 33 N. Stratford Dr., Athens, GA 30601, USA.

HAITINK, Bernard, b. 1929, Amsterdam, Holland. Conductor. Career incl: Cond., Netherlands Radio Phil. Orch., 1955-61; regular guest Cond., Concertgebouw Orch., Amsterdam. 1956-61; Jt. Cond., ibid; now Musical Dir.; dond. of Concertgebouw Orch. at festivals incl. Osaka, 1962, Wiener Festwochen, 1962, Edinburgh, 1963, Berliner Festwochen, 1963; Prin. Cond. & Artistic Advsr., LPO, 1967-70; Artistic Dir., ibid. 1970-; Toured USA, with LPO; Guest cond., Halle Orch., London; Berlin Phil. Orch.; Los Angeles Phil. Orch., USA. Recording issued on Philips label. Mbrship: Hon., Int. Gustav Mahler soc. Hons: Gold Medal, 1970; Bruckner Medal of Hon., Breuckner Soc., 1970; Chevalier, Ordre des Arts & Lettres. Address: London Phil, Orch., 53 Welbeck St., London W1M 7HE, UK.

HAJDU, Julia, b. 8 Sept. 1925, Budapest, Hungary. Composer; Pianist. Educ: Piano Tchr's Dip., Hungarian Acad. of Music; Course in composing w. György Ranki. m. Stephen Pajor. Debut: Hungarian Radio, 1948. apps. on TV & Radio, 1948. apps. on TV & Radio. Comp: 14 operettas; 6 musicals; sev. revue, vaudeville & TV shows: 4 suites; 180 songs; 80 chansons. Over 100 recordings. Author Editions Musical (Zenemükiado), Budapest. Mbrships: Mars (now Artissus); Soc. of Artists of the Hungarian Repub.; Soc. of Musical Artists of the Hungarian Repub.; Soc. of Musical Artists. Hons: 1st Prize, song festival of Radio Budapest, 1948; 1st Prize, folk song festival, 1950; Special Prize, Hungarian Repub., 1952; Var. prizes, Hungarian radio & TV; 1st femal stage-composer in Hungary. Hobbies: Reading; Langs. Address: Pozsonyi ut 7, 1137 Budapest, XIII, Hungary.

HAJDU, Loránt, b. 12 Aug. 1937, Bucharest, Romania. Professor of Piano; Composer. Educ: studied horn, piano & comp., Conserv. of Music, Budapest; Grad., Acad. of Music, Budapest, 1965. m. Matild Varga, 1 d. Debut: perf. awarded comp. on piano, Geneva, 1967. Career: Piano perfs.; var. comps. perfd. on radio, TV, etc. Comps: Ten easy piano pieces, 1972; Pieces for Violin & Piano, 1969; Fanfar, for horn & piano, 1972; incidental music to radio-plays & films. Hons: Reine Marie José prize, 1966, Geneva, Switz. Hobbies: Photography. Address: Hársmajor u. 17, 1118 Budapest XI, Hungary.

HAJDU, Mihály, b. 30 Jan. 1909, Oroshaza, Hungary. Composer; Professor. Educ: Dip., Comp. w. Zoltan Kodaly, piano w. Istvan Thoman, Acad. of Music. m. Irene Bonis, 1 d. Career: Prof., HS of Music, Budapest, 1941-49, Conserv. Bela Bartok, 1949-60, Acad. of Music Ferenc Liszt, 1961-. Comps. incl: Kadar Kata (opera); piano pieces; songs w. piano accomp.; Hungarian shepherd songs for flute & piano; Capriccioall'ongarese for clarinet & orch.; Concerto for cello & str. orch.; Hungarian children's songs (pieces for cello). Mbrships: Assn. of Hungarian Musicians; Legal Aid Bur. ('Artisjus'). Hons. incl: Gold Degree Medal of Merit, Hungarian govt., 1960; Prize of the Public, Hungarian Radio, 1975. Hobbies: Gardening; Excursions; Touring by car. Address: Bécsi ut 88, 1034 Budapest, Hungary.

HÁJEK, Aleš, b. 17 July 1937, Náchod, Czech. Composer. Educ: Comp. Dip., Janackova Music Acad., Brno. Is. Debut: Brno, 1962. Career: Tchr., Music, Hradec Kralove Gymnasium; Num. Radio Apps. & Concerts. Comps: Short Notes for Piano, 1972; Fables for Piano, 1971; Changes for Violin & Piano, 1973; (Orchl. Comps.) First Symph., 1964; Introspekce, 1969; Three Symphonic Pictures, 1971; Five Pieces for Orch., 1971; Extrospekce, 1973; Concert for Violoncello & Orch.,

1973; 3rd String Quartet; 1975; Concert for Chmbr. Orch., 1975; Dialogues for Bassoon & Harp; Concert for Bassoon & String Orch., 1978; Feminine Choruses - Sing About Woman, 1978. Mbrships: OSA. Hons: Special Prize, Radio Competition, 1973. Address: Osvoboditely 288, 549 41 Cerveny Kostelec. Czech.

HALA, Vlastimil, b. 7 July 1924, Sous-Most, Czech. Composer; Arranger; Trumpet Player; Musical Director. Educ: Commercial Acad., Prague, Czech., 1943; Pvte. studies in Counterpoint, Forms, Comp., Theory of Music & Hist. of Music w. Prof. J Stanislav, Jan Rychlik & J Feld. m. Perla Havlová, 2 s. Career: Musical Dir., Czech. Radio, Prague; Musical Comedies incl. Lemonade Joe, Lady on the Tracks; Music for TV series Mr. Tau. Comps: Jazz Suite; The Feelings; New Synthesis, Blue Effect Blues; TV Suite; Rondo-Blues; Confrontation, A Concerto for Harp & Marimba. Recordings incl. many songs, orch. pieces, jazz & pop music; LP - Portrait of a Composer - Simple Recipe. Publs: Arranging Jazz & Pop Music, 1978-79. Contbr. to: Hudebni Rozhledy; Melodie. Mbrships. incl: Vice Chmn. & Chmn. of Jazz Subcommission, Guild of Czech. Comps. & Concert Artists; Gen. Sec., OSA. Hons: Best Film Music, 1964; Best Film Songs, 1965; Bronze Medal, Decin Song Fest., 1976; Gold Medal, Decin Song Fest. Hobbies: Music; Film; Touring. Address: Zabadilova 13, Prague 6 - Dejvice, Czech.

HALACZ, Bogna, b. 29 Dec. 1934, Milolow, Poland. Pianist. Educ: High Schl. of Music, Cracow; Int. Masters Course, Belgium & Italy. m. Wiktor Weinbaum. Debut: Piano Recital, Cracow, 1959. Career: Perf. of Chopin's Works in TV Film, German Fed. Repub & German Democratic Repub.; Recitals as soloist & accomp. in Poland, Hungary, Belgium, Rumania & German Fed. Repub.; concert recitals in num. countries. Contbr. to Ruch Muzyczny, Poland; Profl. Musicians, Warsaw; Frederic Chopin Soc., Warsaw. Hobbies: Records; Collecting Perfume Samples & Postcards; Theatre; Films. Mgmt: Polish Artistic Agcy., Pagart, Warszawa, Poland. Address: 00-264 Warszawa, Piekarska 56, Poland.

HALAHAN, Guy Frederick Crosby, b. 21 Feb. 1917, London, UK. Composer; Double-Bass. Educ: MA., Cambridge Univ. Compositions; Operas; Elanda & Eclipse, 1957; The Spur of the Moment (BBC TV), 1959; They Smile When They Sleep, 1963; Ballet Tenement 14, 1952; Sinfonia Concertante (Clarinet & Orch.); Songs From the Madhouse (Baritone & Orch.); Concertino (Trombone & Str.) Contbr. to Music Review, etc. Mbrships: RAC; ISM; Composers Guild. Hons: Salzburg 1960. Hobbies: Ocean-Sailing; Golf; Fruit-machines. Address: 21 Court Close, Liphook, Hants., UK. 3.

HALASZ, Michael, b. 21 May 1938, Lkausenburg, Romania. Conductor; Bassoonist; Composer. Educ: Tchrs. Dip., Bassoonist, Budapest & Zürich; Grad. as Cond., Music Acad., Essen, German Fed. Repub. m. Gertraud Kiefel. Debut: Gelsenkirchen, German Fed. Repub., 1970. Career: Bassoon Player, Phil. Hungarica, 1957-65; Theatr work, Gelsenkirchen, 1968-70, Gärtnerplatz Theatre, Munich, 1972-75, Städische Bühnen, Frankfurt, 1975-77; Concerts, Berlin, 1973, Solingen, 1974. Compositions: (radio recording) Woodwind Trio. Recordings: Chmbr. Orch., J C Bach, J Haydn; 2 Woodwind quintet records. Hons: 1st Prize w. Woodwind quintet, Geneva, 1962. Mgmt: Zentrale Bühnen Vermittlung, Frankfurt. Address: 6000 Frankfurt 70, Letzter Hasenpfad 13, German Fed. Repub.

HALDEMANN-GERSTER, Rita, b. 14 Apr. 1925, Gelterkinden, Switz. Pianist. Educ: Studied music w. Paul Baumgartner, Basle; Tchrs. Dip., 1951, Solosits Dip., 1953; studied chmbr. music w. var. masters inclng. Pablo Casals. m. Hugo Haldemann (flute), 1 s. Career: Asst. to Sandor Vegh, advanced music courses, many yrs.; Solo apps., Switz., Germany, France & Denmark; Sev. tours of Italy as accomp.; frequent apps. as radio accomp.; specialist in contemporary music, & in publicising works of Swiss comps. Mbrships: Swiss Music Tchrs. Assn.; Swiss Musicians Union; Contemporary Concert Pianists, Germany. Hobbies: Travelling; Pictorial Art. Address: Unterer Rebbergweg 132, 4153 Reinach, Switz.

HALE, Ralph G, b. 28 May 1923, Scott, Miss., USA Band Director; Teacher. Educ: Univ. of Ark., Monticello; Delta State Univ.; Cinn. Conserv. of Music; Memphis State Univ. Recordings: Christian Brothers High Schl. Band, Historical Performances. Publs: Scale Exercises, an instruction book, 1961. Contbr. to: Instrumentalist; Schl. Musician: Holton Fanfare; Bandwagon; Tenn. Musicians Mag. Mbrships: Am. Bandmasters Anns.; Am. Schl. Band Dirs. Assn.; Nat. Band Assn.; Tenn. Bandmasters Assn. (past pres.); Nat. Catholic Bandmasters Assn.; Phi Beta Mu (past VP); AFM. Hons: Doct. of Music; Christian Brothers High Schl. Hall of Fame, 1968; MAC award for Tenn., 1977; Tenn. Bandmasters Hall of Fame,

1978. Hobbies: Travel; Tennis. Address: 4904 Greenway Ave., Memphis, TN 38117, USA.

HALE, Robert, b. 22 Aug. 1933, Kerrville, Tex., USA. Opera Singer. Educ: BMus. Ed., Bethany Nazarene; MMus. Ed., Univ. of Okla.; Artistic Dip., New England Conserv.; grad. study, Univs. of Boston, San Francisco & Northwestern. m. Inga Nielsen, 3 s. Debut: in La Boheme, NYC Opera, 1967. Career: Apps. with Opera Cos. of NYC. San Diego, Phila. Lyric, San Antonio, Mobile, Hamburg; Symph. Orch. apps. w. Chgo., Boston & Montreal Symphs.; Fest. apps. at Wolf Trap, Tanglewood, Lausanne & Bordeaux. Recordings: 15 albums. Mbrships: Phi Mu Alpha Sinfonia; Mu Phi Epsilon; Am. Guild of Musical Artists. Hons. incl: Singer of the Year, Nat. Assn. of Tchrs. of Singing, 1963. Hobbies: Photography; Antique cars. Mgmt: Herbert Barrett, NYC. Address: 5009 New Ranch Rd., El Cajon, CA 92020, USA.

HALEK, Vaclav, b. 17 Mar. 1937, Prague, Czecholslovakia. Composer; Pianist. Educ: Studied Comp., Prague Conserv. & Prague Acad. of Fine Arts. m. Jane Halkova. Career: Free Lance Comp. of State, Film & TV Music. Compositions: Concerto No. 1 for Piano & Orch., 1957; Symph. in C Maj., 1961; Concerto No. 2 for Piano & Orch., 1968; Str. Quartet No. 2, 1969; Num. Folk songs; Battle for Peace, a composition for Organ & Str. Orch.; Concerto for Violin, Piano & Orch.; Concerto for Trombone & Orch. Recordings: Vesele vanocni hody & 10 Czech & Moravian Christmas Carols (Discant Recordings); Vanocni prosba & Gloria, narodil se Kristus Pan (Supraphon Recordings). Mbrships: Assn. for Protection of Authors' Rights, Prague. Hons: 3rd Prize, Young Comps. Competition, Prague, 1955; competition of Children's Choir Comps., Jirkov, 1968 & '74. Hobbies: Chess. Address: Pomoranská 482, 180 00 Prague 8-Traja, Czechoslovakia.

HALEN, Walter J., b.17 Mar. 1930, Hamilton, Ohio, USA. University Professor; Composer; Conductor; Performer (Violin, Viola). Educ: B Mus, Miami Univ., Ohio, 1952; MFA, Ohio Univ., Athens, 1953; PhD, Ohio State Univ., 1969; sutdies of Violin, Viola, Comp., var. masters. m. Thalia Sims Halen, 2 s. Career: Tchr., Pub. Schls., Bellevue, Ohio; Drury Coll., Springfield; Mo.; OH.; Assoc. Prof. Music, Central Mo. State Univ.; former mbr. var. orchs. 7 concertmaster, Springfield Symph. Comps. incl: Meditation for Oboe, Prepared Piano & Percussion, 1973; Suite in C; Suite for Violin & Viola; Settings of Yankee Doodle & a Free Americay. Contbr. to profl. jrnls. Mbrships. incl: Am. Str. Tchrs. Assn. (Mo. State Pres., 1973 75). Hons. Incl: Disting. Tchrs. Award, MTNA, 1974. Address: Rt. 5 Green Acres, Warrensburg, MO 64093, USA.

HALEY, Elizabeth, b. 24 April 1952, Houston, Texas, USA. Opera and Concert Singer; Lyric Coloratura Soprano. Educ: BMus, N Texas State Univ.; 2 yrs. Post Grad. study, Juilliard Schl. of Music, NY; Pvte. studies w. Luigi Ricci, Rome, Italy. m. John Haley. Debut: as Adele, new prodn. of Die Fledermaus, NYC Opera, 1974. Career: Perfs. w. NYC Opera, NY, LA, Wash. DC as Adele (Debut), Olympia (Tales of Hoffmann), Rosina (Barbiere de Siviglia), Baby Doe (The Ballad of Baby Doe), Soprano solo (Carmina Burana), Mabel (Pirates of Penzance); Perfs. w. NY Phil., Dallas Symph., Milwaukee Symph & Johann Strauss Ensemble of the Vienna Symph. Hons: Dallas Morning News G B Dealey Award, 1968; Scholarships, Am. Opera Center, Juilliard Schl., 1970-71; Nat. Opera Inst. Grants & Sullivan Fndn. Grants, 1975-76. Address: 310 W 106th St., Apt. ZD, NY, NY 10025, USA.

HALEY, Johnetta Randolph, b. 19 Mar. 1923, Alton, Ill., USA. Pianist; Voice Teacher; Choral Director; Music Educator. Educ: Mus M, S. Ill. Univ.; BSME Lincoln Univ.; Piano studies w. Martha Ayres & Thomasina Green; Voice studies w. O. Anderson Fuller. M. David Haley, 1 s., 1 d. Debut: Lincoln Univ., 1945. Career: Music Educator, Elementary Specialist, Jr. High Schl.; Vocal, Univ. Music Educator. Contbr. to: The Ivy Leaf Magazine; Proud Magazine. Hons. incl: Mu Phi Epsilon; Pi Kappa Lambda; Service to Music Award, Mo. Music Educators. Hobbies: Community Service. Address: 7326 Stanford, St. Louis, MO 63130, USA. 5, 8, 23

HALFFTER, Cristobal, b. 24 Mar. 1930, Madrid, Spain. Conductor; Composer. Educ: studies w. Conrado del Campo & Alexander Tansman. m. Maria Manuela Caro, 2 s., 1 d. Career: Cond., Manuel de Falla Orch.; Radio Nacional d'Espana, 1952-; tchr., comp. & form, Royal Conserv., Madrid, 1960-66 (dir., 1964-66); cond., num. orchs. in Spain & abroad; freelance comp. Comps. incl: orchestral words, electronic works, chmbr. works, concertos, cantatas, etc. Address: Bola 2, Madrid 13, Spain.

HALFORD, Margery, b. 9 June 1927, Reisterstown, USA. Music Teacher; Harpsichordist; Writer; Music Editor. Educ:

Cert. Tchr., piano & harpsichord, Music Tchrs. Nat. Assn.; Peabody Conserv. Music, Balt., Md. m. Richard James Halford, 1 d. Career: Tchr., piano harpsichord, comp. & theory. Publs. incl: Couperin, Francois, l'Art de Toucher le Clavecin (French & Engl.), 1974; Scarlatti, Domenico -An Introduction to his Keyboard Works, 1974; Greig, Edvard - an Introduction to his Piano Words, 1975. Contbr. to profl. jrnls. Mbrships. incl: Am. Musicol. Soc.; Music Tchrs. Nat. Assn.; Tex. Music Tchrs. Assn.; Fndng. Mbr., past Prog. Coord. & Pres., Houston Harpsichord Soc. Hobbies incl: Writing; Chess. Address: 1641 Marshall, Houston, TX 77006, USA.

HALL, Graeme Edison, b. 22 Mar. 1937, Melbourne, Australia. Director of Music (Piano, Organ, Harpsichord). Educ: Scotch Coll., Melbourne; Univ. Melbourne; B Mus; B Ed. m. Joan Catherine Mackerras, 4 s. Career: Dir. of Music, Sydney Grammer Schl., 1962; Dir. of Music, Thorpe Grammer Schl., Norwich, UK, 1968-75; Dir. of Music, Woodbridge Schl., Suffolk. MBR. Nat. Coun., ISM. Hobby: Antique Furniture. Address: Hazeldell, Elton Pk., Sproughton, Ipswich, UK.

HALL, John Joseph Michael, b. 22 Aug. 1943, Haywards Heath, UK. Composer. Educ: RAM, London. Career: (as actor): Leading roles in London Prods. of 'Little Eyolf', 'Mbr. of the Wedding', 'Gt. Expectations' & 'Auntie Mame', Many film & TV apps.; Prof. of Harmony, Counterpoint & Comp., RAM. comps. incl: Oboe Sonata Op. 19; Organ Concerto Op. 14; Piano Trio Op. 16; Symphonic Study or Orch. Op. 37; Those Dancing Days are Gone (Yeats) Op. 32; Trio No. 3 Op. 38. Mbr., Comps. Guild of GB. Recip., num. prizes inclng. Ivor Novello Award, 1975. Hobbies: Tennis; Cooking. Address: 47 New England Rd., Haywards Heath, Sussex, RH16 3LE, UK.

HALL, Kristina Scholder, b. 15 May 1951, Pierre, SD, USA. Violinist; Concertmaster. Educ: Univ. of Houston, Tex.; Peabody Conserv. of Music, Balt., Md.; New Schl. of Music, Phila., Pa.; Fellowship., Cath. Univ. of Am., Wash. DC. Debut: Sacramento, Calif., .1964. Career: Mbr., Christmas String Seminar, Carnegie Hall, NY, 1970; Recital, Fine Arts Ctr., as Concertmaster, Colo. Springs Symph., 1975; 1st Violin, Marandtha String Quartet, w. TV & local radio apps., Houston, Tex., 1972; 1st Violin, Colo. Springs Symph. Piano Trio, 1975-; Vis. Artist, Univ. of Southern Colo., Pueblo, Colo. Mbrships. incl: New Orleans Phil. Orch.; Phila. Musicians Union. Recip., sev. schlrships. & merit certs. Hobbies incl: Ballet lessons. Address: 2517 E Boulder, Colo. Springs, CO 80909, USA.

HALL, Peter, b. 22 Nov. 1930, Suffold, UK. Theatre, Film & Opera Director; Producer; Manager. Educ: MA, St. Catherine's Coll., Cambridge. Career incls: over 70 major theatre prods., London, Stratford-upon-Avon & NYC; opera at Covent Gdn., Sadlers Wells & Gydebourne; 8 films since 1967; Dir., Oxford Playhouse, 1954-55, Arts Theatre, London, 1955-57; Mgn. Dir., Royal Shakespeare Co., 1960-68; cons. Dir., ibid., 1968-; Dir. Designate, 1972, Dir., 1973-. Nat. Theatre; Assoc. Prof. of Drama, Warwick Univ. Opera prods. incl: Moses & Aaron, Royal Opera House, 1965; Cavlll's La Caliste, Glyndebourne, 1970; The Knot Garden (Michael Tippett), Royal Opera House, 1970; Eugene Onegin, ibid., 1971; Tristan & Isolde, Covent Gdn., 1971; Il Ritorno d'Ulisse (Monteverdi), Glyndebourne, 1972; Marrigae of Figaro, ibid., 1973. Hons. incl: Docts., Univs. of York, Reading & Liverpool; CBE, 1963. Address: The Wall House, Mongewall Pk., Wallingford, Oxon., UK.

HALL, Thomas Munroe, b. 1 Sept. 1943, Tallahassee, Fla., USA. Musician (Violinist). Educ: B Mus., Fla. State Univ., 1964; M Mus., ibid, 1966. Career. w. musical orgs: Fla. Symph. Orch., Orlando, 1962-64; Richmond (Va.) Symph. Orch., 1966-69; US Army Band, Wash. DC., 1966-69; Cinn. Symph. Orch., 1969-70; Chgo. Symph. Orch., 1970-; Meridian String Quartet, 1969-; Contemporary Arts Quartet, 1975-. Hons: Disting. Grad., Fla. State Univ. Hobbies: Collecting Art, Minerals, stamps & coins. Address: 2800 Lake Shore Dr., Chgo., IL 60657, USA. 2.

HALLER, Hermann, b. 9 June 1914, Burgdorf, Switz. Composer; Professor of Piano; Pianist. Educ: BA; Dips. for Piano & Comp., Zürich Conserv.; studied Comp. w. Nadia Boulanger, Paris, & Piano w. C Marek, Zürich. m. Margret Huber, 2 d. Comps. incl: Works for organ; Variations for Orch.; Exoratio, for alto & strings; Ed è subito sera (Quasimodo) w. Orch.; 2nd Concerto for piano (recorded); Trio for violin, cello & piano; 3 Nocturnes for viola & piano; Herbst (Morgenstern) for alto & piano; 2 Str. Quartets; Concerto per Archi; Per la Camerata (16 strings); 2 Concertos (piano & orch); Symph.; 5 Lieder for deep voice & orch.; Hiob (oratorio); (recorded) Elegia variata (piano). Publs: Harmonie-Lehre, 1949. Mbrships. incl: Swiss Comps. Assn. (Pres. 1968-73). Hons. incl: Musikpreis der Stadt Zürich, 1976. Address: Alte Landstrase 84a, CH 8700 Küsnacht-Zürich, Switz.

HALLIN, Margareta. Coloratura & Lyric Soprano. Debut: Rosina in The Barber of Seville, Stockholm. Career: Prin. soprano, Royal Opera, Stockholm; apps. in Rome, Florence, Vienna, Hamburg, Munich, Glyndebourne, Copenhagen, Moscow, Leningrad etc.; roles incl. Manon, Queen of the Night, Olympia, Butterfly, Violetta, Ann Trulove (Rake's Progress), Tosca, Leonora (Il Trovatore), Aida, Ariadne; lieder recitals, oratorio & concert perfs. Mgmt: Artistsekretariat Ulf Törnqvist, Norrtullsgatan 26, tr.4, 11345 Stockholm, Sweden. Address: c/o mgmt.

HALLMAN, Ludlow B., III, b. 1 Aug. 1941. Dayton Ohio, USA. Conductor; Singer. Educ: B Mus., Oberlin Coll., 1963; M Mus., So. Ill. Univ., 1965; Kapellmeister Dip., Mozarteum, Salzburg, Austria, 1970. m. Mary Mayall Hallman. Career: Appearances w. Santa Fe Opera, St Louis Symph., Bongor Symph., Portland (Me.) Symph., Salzburg Fest., Mozart Opera Salzburg; Musical Dir. & Cond., Salzburg Baroque Ensemble, Univ. of Maine at Orono Opera Theatre, UMO Orch., UMO Oratorio Soc. Mbrships: Nat. Assn. of Tchrs. of Singing; Nat. Opera Assn.; Am. Symph. Orch. League. Hons: Winner, Young Artist Comps. of the St. Louis Symph. Orch., 1965; Abgangs Prize from Austrian Govt., 1967; John Haskall Fellowship, 1966. Address: Star Rt., Forest Ave., Orono, ME 04473, USA. 6.

HALLNAS, Eyvind Johan, b. 30 Apr. 1937. Goteborg, Sweden. Organist. Educ: Student Exam.; Goteborg Music Conserv., 1964-67. m. Margareta, 2 d. Career: Dir. of Music & Organist, Kristina Ch., Sala, 1968-; has composed works for organ, piano, solo singer, choir recorder ensemble, etc.; Cantata for bassoon, soprano, choir & organ perf. over radio, 1972; Jubilate Cantata for choir, trumpet & strings perf. at Sala, 1974; Sinfonio da chiesa, 1977-78; Concertino for piccolo & strgs., 1978. Hobbies: Football; Philately; Drawing. Address: Vasby gat. 22, 73300 Sala, Sweden.

HALLNAS, Hilding, b. 24 May 1903, Halmstad, Sweden. Composer Director of Music. Educ: Kgl. Music Conserv., Stockholm; Studied organ in Paris (1929) & comp. in Leipzig (1930). m. Gun Holmquist, 3 children. Career: Music Dir. in Stromstad; Organist in Jonkoping, 1932; Organist & Tchr. in Goteborg, 1933. Comps: 100 songs for 1 voice & piano and guitar; 2 violin concertos; 2 flute concertos; 1 oboe & 1 viola concerto; 7 symph.; 2 ballets; 1 mass for choir, wind instruments & organ; 2 sonatas for violin & piano; 2 sonatas for organ; Musica dolorosa - 15 pieces for organ etc.; sonata for viola & piano; 1 Trippelconcert for violin, clarinet & piano; Musica magica, for cello & piano; 3 String Quartets; 6 piano trios; 3 sonatas for piano; 3 Rhapsodies for different instruments; about 40 pieces for guitar; 1 trio for flute, guitar & viola; 1 Quintet for violin, viola, cello, doublebass & piano. Var. recordings. Publs: A systematic List of Hilding Hallnas Compositions (by S. Gulich & C. Carisson), 1968; Hilding Hallnas Songs: Mbrships: Royal Acad.; Swedish Comps.; ISCM. Recip. var. hons. Address: Skeppargatan 13, 114 52 Stockholm, Sweden.

HALPIN, Patricia, b. 15 June 1935, Sydney, Aust. Music Publishe; Author. Edu: Studies w. Arthur E Holley; NSW Conserv. of Music, Alexander Sverjensky; A Mus A, 1950; L Mus A, 1953; DSCM Tchr., 1956; DSCM, Performer, 1957; A Mus A Theory, 1960. Career: Many broadcasts as solo pianist for Aust. Broadcasting Commission & commercial stations, 1951-; TV apps. as pianist; Many concert apps. as solo pianist, w. orch., as accomp. & w. chmbr. grps. Cond.; choral & orchl. grps. Ownerfndr., Opheus Publs., musical educ. works, Examiner, AMEB; Staff Mbr., NSW Conserv. of Music. Publd. num. text-books on music theoretical subjects (Allan & Co., & Orpheus Publs.). Hons: As a student, many prizes in Eisteddfods; Var. Mbr., var. profl. orgs. scholarships awards by Federated. Music Clubs & NSW State Conserv.; Frank Shirley Prize on graduation from NSW State Conserv. as most disting. student of year, 1957. Hobbies: Conchology; Lapidary; Genealogy; Reading; Hancrafts; Walking; Genealogy; Reading; Handcrafts; Walking; Comparative religions. Address: 4 Lilli Pilli Point Rd., Lilli Pilli, NSW, 2229 Aust. 23,27,29,30.

HALSEY, Louis Arthur Owen, b. 19 Mar. 1929, London, UK. Conductor; Music Producer; Lecturer. Educ: MA, B Mus, King's Coll., Cambridge. m. Evelyn Elisabeth Calder, 2 s. Career: Fndr. Cond., Elizabethan Singers, 1953-66, Louis Halsey Singers, 1967-, Thames Chmbr. Choir, 1964-, Louis Halsey Baroque Orch., 1976-. Music Prod., BBC London, 1963-; Artistic Dir., Thames Concerts Soc; Lectr., Canford Summer Schl. of Music, 1974-; workshops & seminars in USA, Canada & UK. Recordings: L'Oiseau-Lyre; Argo; Pye; Unicorn. Publs. Jt. Ed., Sing Nowell; 51 Carols New & Arranged, 1963. Contbr. to: Musical Times: Music in Educ. Mbr., ISM. Hobby: Gardening. Address: 4 Revell Rd., Kingston-upon-Thames, Surrey KT1 3SN, UK.

HAMBRAEUS, Bengt, b. 29 Jan. 1928, Stockholm, Sweden. Composer; Musicologist; Organist; Professor. Educ: BA Uppsala Univ., Sweden, 1950; PhD, ibid, 1956; studied organ w. Alf Linder. m. Enid Odenäs, 1 s., 1 d. Debut: 1948. Career: Lib., Asst., Inst. for Musicol., Upsala Univ., 1948-56; Staff Mbr., Music Dept., Swedish Broadcasting Corp., 1957-72, Prog. Prod., 1957-64, Hd., Chmbr. Music Div., 1965-68, Hd. of Prod., 1968-72; Prof., Fac. of Music, McGill Univ., Montreal, Can., 1972-; num. radio lectures, organ recitals, Sweden & abroad. Comps. (publd.) incl: Pianissimo, String orch.; Invocation, wind orch. & percussion; Continuo for organ & orch.; num. Chmbr., Organ, Choral, Electronic works; (recorded) Transfiguration; Fresque Sonore; Rota II; Tetragon; Constellations II; Rencontres; Nebulosa. Publs: codes Carminum Galicorum; Une etede sur le volume VH 87 de la Bibliotheque d' Upsala, 1961; Om Notskrifter, 1971. Contbr. to num. profl. Encys & jrnls. Mbr. var. Swedish & Can. profl. orgs. Recip. var. hons. Hobbies: Lit.; Gardening. Address: RR1 Apple Hill, Ont. KOC No. 1BO, Can. 19.

HAMBURG, Otto, b. 5 Apr. 1924, Stettin, Germany. Professor; Conductor. Educ: Dip. (hist. of music & cond.), Amsterdam Conserv.; studied cond. w. Paul van Kempen, Willem van Otterloo & Ferdinand Leitner. m. M T E van Marissing, 4 d. Debut: 1953, as cond. in broadcast concert. Career: Prof., hist. of music, Conservs. in Utrecht & Groningen; lectures on radio on Opera; cond., major Dutch orchs. Publs: Music History in Example (in Dutch, Geman & Engl.); translator & reviser of Sachs: Our Musical Heritage; Gräter Konzertführer Neue Musik, 1962; Stage-Musik hören, verstehen, erleben, 1966. Mbrships: Int. Gesellschaft für Musikwissenschaft; Dutch Soc. of Profl. Music Tchrs. (co-fndr. & 1st chmn.). Hobbies: Aviation. Address: Bussumergrintweg 5, 1217 BM Hilversum, Netherlands.

HAMBURGER, Klára, b. 29 Sept. 1934, Budapest, Hungary. Musicologist. Educ: Study of Piano, Béla Bátok Conserv., 1949-53; Dip., Misicol., Liszt Ferenc High Schl. for Music, 1961. m. Iván Kertész, 1 d. Career: Mbr., Lib. of Acad. of Scis., 1959-61; Misic Dept., Nat. Széchényi Lib., 1961-66; Ed., Music Books, Gondolat Publrs., Budapest; Radio, TV Lectr. on Liszt. Publs. incl: Liszt Ferenc, 1966; Kókai Rezsö, 1968; Franz Liszt, rev., enlarged German Ed., 1973; Prefaces to scores of Liszt publs. Contbr. to profl. jrnls. Mbrships: Assn. of Hungarian Musicians; Fndn. mbr., Hungarian Liszt Soc. Hobby: Family music. Address: Deres u. 12., H-1124, Budapest, Hungary.

HAMBURGER, Paul, b. 3 Sept. 1920, Vienna, Austria. Accompanist; Educator; Writer. Educ: Vienna State Acad., Austria; ARCM, London, UK. m. Clare Walmesley. Career: Freelance Accomp. & Chmbr. Music Player; Mbr., Engl. Opera Grp., 1953-56; Mbr., Glyndebourne Opera, 1956-62; Part Time Staff Accomp., BBC, 1962-. Recordings: w. var. singers inclng. April Cantelo, Bernadette Greevy, Benvenuto Duo, Heather Harper & cellist Marius May. Publs: Transl. of Bruno Walter's Music & Music Making, 1961 & Hans Hollander's Leos Janacek, 1963. Contbr. to: A Britten Symposium 1954; A Mozart Companion, 1956; A Chopen Symposium, 1966; Music Survey; Music Review; Tempo; Music & Musicians. Mbrships: ISM; Soc. for the Promotion of New Music. Address: Flat 1, 11 Netherhall Gdns., London NW3, UK.

HAMER, Joseph, b. 3 Oct. 1925, Eselborn, Luxembourg. Director. Educ: Conserv. Royal of Brussels. m. Allice Hamer Michels, 1 d. Debut: Radio Tele Luxembourg (Orch.). Career: Orch. of Radio Luxembourg, 1949; Dir., Philharmone of Diekirch, 1955; Dir., Conserv. of Luxembourg, 1965. Recordings: w. the students' orch. and the choir of the Conserv. Contbr. to newspapers and reviews. Mbr., Assn. Wuropeenne des conservatoires et Musikhochschulen. Hobbies: Volleyball; Photography; Painting. Address: 42a, rue Charlemagne, Luxembourg.

HAMES, Richard David, b. 1945, Chelwood Gate, Sussex, UK. Composer. Educ: RCM; studied w. Messiaen & Nadia Boulanger, Paris Conserv.; Univ. of Southhampton; w. Goffredo Petrassi, Accademia de Santa Cecilia, Rome. Career: Dir. of Music, Caldicott Schl., 1966-67; Personal Asst. to Peter Maxwell Davies & Pierrot Players, 1968-69; Lord Attlee Fellow & Comp. in Res., Sevenoaks Schl., Kent, 1969; Lectr. in Comp., Dartington Coll. of Arts & Dir., Dartington Sound Rsch. Studio, 1973-76; Dir., Contemporary Music Studies The Vic. Coll. of the Arts, Melbourne, Aust., 1976-; Fndr./Dir., Vic. Time Machine. Comps. incl: Monody for St. Michael (organ); Melencolia for orch., 1970; Alba for flute & ensemble, 1973; Monody after Dufay for two ensembles, 1977; Veni Sancte Spiritus for amplified trombone, 1978. Mbrships: CGGB; PRS; GEMA. Recip. of sev. prizes. Mgmt: Hans Wewerka, Edition Modern, Elizabethstrasse 38, 8000 Munich 40, German Fed. Repub. Address: c/o Mgmt.

HAMILL, Paul Robert, b. 10 June 1930, Tobyhanna, Pa., USA. Editor; Composer; Organist. Educ: B Mus., Boston Univ. Col. of Music; MA, Wesleyan Univ., Conn.; ChM, AGO. M. Elinor Smith Hamill, 1 s, 1 d. Career: Dir. of USN Chapel Choir, Bainbridge, Md., 1952-54; Instr., Woodmere Acad., NY, 1957-64; Instr., Adelphi Univ., NY, 1960-65; Music Ed., Am. Book Co., NY, 1965-70; Exec. Ed., ibid, 1970-72; Asst. Editl. Dir., 1972-75; Ed. Dir., 1975-. Compositions: (choral works) The Strife is O'er; Behold, I Build an House; Tenebrae; Resurrection Carol; Now Thank We All Our God; O Little Star of Bethlehem; A Candlelight Carol Service; Lenten Devotion; Lord Jesus, Think On Me; Olove, How Deep, etc.; (organ works) Choral Prelude on 'Foundation'; Aria da Chiesa, Antiphon I & II, etc. Ed. of var. music projs. inclng: Music for Young Americans (9 books), 1966; New Dimensions in Music (10 books), 1970. Mbrships. incl: AGO; Am. Musicol, Soc.; MENC; Williams Club. Address: 230 Mosher Ave., Woodmere, NY 11598, USA.

HAMILTON, Christina Dee, b. 30 Nov. 1935, Bloomfield, Ind., USA. Teacher; Voice, Piano, Flute, Violin. Educ: BS, Miami Univ., Oxford, Ohio; MS Ind. Univ. Bloomington. div. Career:Public Schl. Tchr. of Vocal & Instrumental Music for 20 yrs; Pvte. Tchr. Piano, Flute, Violin; Local Educl. TV perfs. w. children. Mbrships: MENC; NEA; Ind. State Tchrs. Assn.; Monroe County Educl. Assn.; Ind. Music Educators Assn.; Hobbies: Sewing; Writing; Dancing & Travelling. Address: 516 N Fess Ave., Bloomington, 47401 IN, USA. 27.

HAMILTON, David, b. 18 Jan. 1935, NYC, USA. Writer; Editor. Educ: AB, 1956, MFA, 1960, Princeton Univ.; MA, Harvard Univ., 1960. Career: Music Ed., WW Norton & Co Inc., NYC, 1968-74; Music Critic, The Nation, 1968-. Contbr. to: New Yorker (Guest Music Critic, 1974); High Fidelity (contributing Ed.); Musical Newsletter (Assoc. Ed.); NY Times; Opera News: Perspectives of New Music, etc. Mbrships: Am. Musicol. Soc.; Music Lib. Assn.; Am. Music Ctr. (Bd. of Dir.); Music Critics Assn. Hons: ASCAP-Deems Taylor Award, 1975. Address: 91 Central Park W, NY, NY 10023, USA. 2.

HAMILTON, David John Loudon, b. 17 May 1937, Edinburgh, UK. Clarinettest; Conductor. Educ: RCM, 1962-65; ARCM, 1963; Regent St. Polytechnic, London (pt.-time), 1965-67; Mbr., Inst. of Linquists, 1966. m. Kathleen Margaret Bailey, 2 s, 1 d. Career: Freelance Clarinettist, Specialist in full clarinet family, i.e. piccolo clarinet, basset clarinet, basset horn, bass clarinet, contrabass clarinet, etc.; Mbr., Music Staff Surrey Educ. Dept., 1972-, Hd. of Woodwind, 1974-. Mbrships: ISM; Galpin Soc.; Int. Clarinet Soc. Hobbies: Language & Languages. Address: 48 St. James's Ave., Hampton Hill, Middx. TW12 1HN, UK.

HAMILTON, Henry (Harry) Speirs, b. 2 Sept. 1921, Toronto, Ont., Can. Conductor; Teacher; Arranger. Educ: Harmony, Theory & Comp., Royal Conserv. of Music, Toronto; Trumpet study w. Edward Smeal. m. Hazel Lorraine McCliggott, 3d. Debut: Radio Station CFCA, aged 10 yrs. Career: Radio apps. w. Art Hallman Orch., Mart Kenny Orch., Pat Riccio Vocal Group, Cal Jackson Orch., Los Cubanos & Latin Am. Serenade; Dir., Mason Schl. of Music, 8 yrs.; Dir., Ont. Youth Music Camp, 5 yrs.; Tchr., classroom music, Toronto Bd. of Educ. (band), 8 yrs.; French Horn, Toronto Symph. Proms, TV, radio & concerts; hd. of Music, Dept. of Georgetown Dist. High Schl. Comps: Shalinlor March; num. arrs. Recordings: Chicho Valle y Los Cubanos. Mbrships: Toronto Musicians Assn.; Past Mbr., Bd. of Dirs., Can. Bandmasters Assn. Hons: Gold medal, Harmonica under 12 yrs., 1933, Silver medal, Harmonica under 16, 1934, Silver medal. Piano Accordion Open, 1938, Can. Nat. Exhibition. Hobby: Writing short stories & poetry. Address: 8 Abner Place, Weston, Ont. M6R 3L9, Can.

HAMILTON, Iain Ellis, b. 6 June 1922, Glasgow, UK. composer; Educator. Educ: B Mus, London Univ.; FRAM Career incls: Lectr., Morley Coll., 1952-59 & Univ. of London, 1955-60; Mary Duke Biddle Prof., Duke Univ., NC USA, 1961-71; Prof. of Music, Lehman Coll., CUNY. Compositions incl: Agamemnon (opera); Royal Hunt of the Sun (opera); Pharalie (opera) Alastor for symph.; voyage for horn & orch.; Eupitaph for This World & Time for 3 choruses & 2 organs; Circus for 2 trumpets & orch.; many chmbr. works; Sinfonia for 2 orch.; Scottish Dances; many choral works. Mbrships. incl: Chmn., Composers Guild, 1958, ICA Music sect., 1958-60, & Music for Today, 1959-61; Dir., Am. Music Ctr., 1971; ISM; Int. Webern Soc. Hons. inch: D Mus, Glasgow Univ.; Arnold Bax Gold Medal. Address: 40 Park Ave., NYC, NY 10016, USA.

HAMILTON, Jerald, b. 19 Mar. 1927, Wichita, Kan., USA. professor of Music; Teacher; Organ Recitalist; Church Musician. Educ: B Mus, Univ. of Kan., 1948; M Mus, ibid, 1950. m. Phyllis Jean Searle, 3 d. Debut: Hoch Auditorium,

Univ. of Kan., 1948. Career: Fac. Mbr., Washburn Univ., Topeka, Kan., 1949-59, Ohio Univ., Athens, 1959-60, Univ. of Tex., 1960-63, Episc. Theol. Sem., Austin, Tex., 1961-63; Prof. of Music, Univ. of Ill., Urbana, 1963-; Organist, Choirmaster, Grace Episc. Cathedral, Topeka, 1949-59, St. David's Ch., Austin, 1960-63, Chapel of St. John the Divine, Champaign, Ill., 1963-; Organ Concerts, throughout USA. Mbrships: Coll. Music Soc.; AGO; Pi Kappa Lambda; Omicron Delta Kappa; Phi Mu Alpha. Recip. Fulbright Scholarship to France, study w. Andre Marchal, 1954-55. Hobbies: Gardening; Equitation. Address: RR1 Sidney, IL 61877, USA. 2,4,12.

HAMM, Michael Edward, b. 11 Feb. 1934, W Kirby, UK. Conductor. Educ: Studied w. Norman Del Mar, GSM; AGSM; ARCM; LTCL; Brussels Conserv., Belgium; Accademia di Santa Cecilia, Rome, Italy. Career: Broadcasts w. BBC Northern Symph. Orch., & BBC Scottish Symph. Orch; Musical Dir., West End Musicals; Cond., Southend Symph. Orch., Southend Mozart Orch., Southend Fest. Chorus, & Southend Bach Choir. Mbr., ISM (Solo Perfs. sect.). Hons: Ricordi Prize for Conds., 1957. Hobbies: Stamp Collecting; Theatre. Address: 156A North Rd., Westcliff-on-Sea, Essex, UK.

HAMMER, Erik, b. 4 Oct. 1945, Odense, Denmark. Baritone Singer. Educ: Dipl. Exam, Det Fynske Muskkonservatorium, 1968. m. Marianne Hansen, 1 d. Debut: Ben in Menotti's The Telephone, Odense Theatre, 1973. Career: concerts in Austria & Germany; Danish radio & TV broadcasts; studies Salzburg, Stuttgart(Prof. Hetty Plümacher), & Stockholm (Prof. Torsten Föllinger). Mbr., Danish Music Tchrs. Soc. hobbies: Travel; Orchids; Music. Address: Hannerupgaardsvej 38, 5230 Odense, Denmark.

HAMMER, Jane Amelia Ross, b. 9 Apr. 1916, Charlotte, NC, USA. Violinist; Educator (Philosophy). Educ: BA, MA, Univ. of NC; Grad., Radcliffe Coll.; New England Conserv. m. Philip G Hammer, 3 s. Musical career: Charter Mbr., & Mbr., Symph. Str. Quarter, NC Symph. Orch. 1936; Violinist, Atlanta Symph., 1947-52; Violinist, Thursday Morning Music Club, Atlanta, 1946-61; Friday Morning Music Club; Mbr., Fndn. Bd. of Trustees, ibid. Hobbies: Sports; Gardening. Address: 5152 Manning Pl. NW, Washington, DC 20016, USA. 5, 21.

HAMMOND, Arthur, b. 9 Dec. 1904, Sheffield, UK. Musical Director (Opera). Educ: B Engrng. (Civil), Sheffield Univ., 1925; pvte. study of music. Debut: Carl Rosa Opera, Theatre Royal, Glasgow, 1928. Career incls: Chorus Master, 1927, cond., 1928-32, Carl Rosa Opera; cond., Dublin Opera Seasons, 1936-47; cond., Covent Garden English Opera Co., 1936 & 1938; Music Dir. & Prin. cond., 1948-57, Music Dir. Final Season, 1960, Carl Rosa Opera; cond., Opera Seasons, Belfast & Glasgow, 1960-63; coénd., Israel Nat. Opera, Tel Aviv, 1963-65; vis. prof., Wayne State Univ., Mich., USA, 1966-67; Pt.-time mbr., Opera Staff, Royal Manchester (Royal Northern) coll. of Music, 1969-73; Musical cons., Royal Opera House, Covent Garden, 1973-. Contbr. to profl. publs. Mbr., ISM. Address: co Royal Opera House, London WC2, UK.

HAMMOND, Joan, b. 24 May 1912, Christchurch, NZ. Singer. Debut: London, Messiah, 1938; Operatic debut, Vienna, Austria, 1939. Career: Guest Artiste; Royal Opera House, covent Garden, UK; Vienna State Opera; Bolshoi, Moscow, USSR; Marinsky, Leningrad; Liceo, Barcelona, Spain; NYC Ctr.; Netherlands Opera; Elizabethan Theatre, Aust.; Sadler's Wells, London, UK; Hd. of Vocal Studies, Vic. Coll. of the ARts. Recordings: Num. records for HMV. Publs: A Voice, a Life (autobiog.), 1970. Mbr., var. golf & yacht clubs. Hons: Sir Charles Santley Award, 1970; OBE, 1953; CBE, 1963; CMG, 1972; DBE, 1974. Hobbies: Reading; Gardening; Writing; Yachting; Golf. Address: Pvt. Bag 101, Geelong Mail Ctr., Vic. 3221, Australia 1, 15, 16, 27.

HAMMOND-STROUD, Derek, b. 10 Jan. 1929, London, UK. Concert & Operatic Baritone. Educ: studied w. Elena Gerhardt & Gerhard Hüsch, TCM. Career: Guest Artist w. num. opera cos.; prin. Baritone, Engl. Nat. Opera, 1961-71, Royal Opera Covent Gdn., 1971-; broadcasts on BBC & European radio; opera & recital apps., Netherlands, Denmark, Iceland, Germany, Austria, Spain, USA. Has recorded for HMV, RCA, Célèbre. Mbr., ISM. Hon. RAM. Hobbies: Chess; Badminton; Philos. Mgmt: Ibbs & Tillett. Address: 18 Sutton Rd., Muswell Hill, London N 10 1HE, UK. 28.

HAMPE, Michael, b. 3 June 1935, Heidelberg, Germany. Intendant. Educ: Arbitur; D Phil.; Actor's Dip.; Cello, Syracuse Schl. of Music & Musikhochschule Munich. Career: Intendant, Oper der Stadt Koln. Contbr. to: Opernwelt; Theater heut; Neue Zürcher Zeitung. Address: Oper der Stadt Köln, Cologne, German Fed. Repub.

HAMPTON, Ian, b. 13 Mar. 1935, London, UK. Cellist. Educ: ARCM. m. Judith Fraser, 2 s. Career: Edinburgh Str. Quartet, 1959-65; Prin. Cellist, Vancouver Symph., 1967-73, CBC Chmbr. Orch., 1966-, Purcell Quartet, 1966. Recordings: M. Schafer Quartet; Mozart Quintets; 2 Haydn Quartets; Schafer; Pentland; Prevost; Freedman. Mbrships: ISM; Pres., Vancouver Cello Club. Address: 17-1460 Esquimalt Ave., W Vancouver, BC, Can.

HAMVAS, Lewis, b. 10 Nov. 1919, Budapest, Hungary. College Professor; Pianist; Composer. Educ: courses, CCNY & Univ. of Mich.; BS, 1948, MS, 1949, Juilliard Schl. of Music; pvte. study w. Leo Weiner, Lehmann Engel, Egon Petri. m. Carol Eschliman, 4 s., 1 d. Career: Solo & cnmbr. music recitals, USA & India; Soloist w. Louisville Phill., Calcutta Symph., Lewis & Clark Symphonette; Tchr., Yankton Coll., SD. Comps: Psalm 66 (3 part choir & organ); unpubld. solo, chmbr. music, choral & orchl. works. Contbr. to: Am. Music Tchr.; Mbrships: Music Tchrs. Nat.f Assn.; VP, SD Music Tchrs. Assn., 1971-. Hons. incl: commission from SD All State HS Orch. & chorus, 1972. Hobbies: Gardening; Reading; Chess; Bridge. Address: 609 Douglas, Yankton, SD 57078, USA.

HANCOCK, Gerre, b. Lubbock, Tex., USA. Organis; Master of the Choir Faculty, The Juilliard Schl., NYC. Educ: B Mus., Univ. of Tes., Austin; M Sacred Mus., Union Theol. Sem., NYC; studied organ w. E. Wm. Doty, Robert Baker & Marie-Clarie Alain. m. Judith Duffield Eckerman, 2d. Career: organist & Master of the Choir, St. Thomas Ch., NYC, 1971-. Compositions: Out of the Deep; In Thanksgiving; A song to the Lamb; Air for Organ; Fantasia on 'Divinum Mysterium'. Recordings: The Plum Line & the City; Improvisation. Mbrships: Fellow, AGO; St. Wilfred's Club, NY; Phi Mu Alpha Sinfonia. hobby: Golf. Mgmt: Murtagh/McFarlane Concert Mgmt., Hackensack, NJ, USA. Address: 1W 53rd St., NYC, NY 10019, USA.

HAND, Colin, b. 2 June 1929, Winterton, Lincs., UK. Composer; College Lecturer. Educ: Mus. B, Trinity Coll., Dublin; FTCL m. Margaret Hadley. Career: Teaching Appts. in Lincs., Coll. of Further Educ. Compositions incl: (publd.) cantata, in The Beginning; Variations & Fugue, for orch.; Stabat Mater, choir & orch.; Discussions, violin & cello; Str. Quartet; Guitar Sonatina; Sonata Piccola, Recorder Sonatina, Fenland Suite, Divertimento, var. others, for recorder: Fest. Overture; Fanfare for A Fest.; Symphony for Strings. num study materials, partsongs, anthems; (recorded) Petite Suite Champetre, recorder & Piano; Plaint, recorder & Piano; Plaint, recorder & harpischord. Publs: John Traverner, His Life and Music, 1978. Contbr. to: Choir Mag.; The Comp.; Recorder & Music Mag. Mbrships: CGGB. Address: 33 Kingsway, Boston, Lincs., UK.3.

HAND, Frederic W, b. 15 Sept. 1947, Brooklyn, NY, USA. Guitarist; Composer; Teacher. Educ: B Mus, Mannes Coll. of Music; High Schl. of Music & Art, NYC; studies w. Julian Bream, UK, 1971. Debut: NYC, 1951. Career: Annual tours of USAw. perfs. in colls. & Univs., 1967-; num. radio & TV appearances; European tour, 1972; Fac. Mbr., Mannes Coll. of Music & SUNY. Compositions: Homage (Elegy for Dr. Martin Luther King, Jr., Adagio for Ralph Vaughn Williams, & A Dance for John Dowland); 4 Excursions for Guitar & Flute. (also recorded); Five studies for solo guitar (recorded). Mbr., ASCAP. Hons: Fulbright Scholar, 1971. Hobbies: Tennis. Mgmt: Charles Hamlen, 22 W79 St. 3, NYC, NY 10024, USA. Address: RR 3 24 Vine Rd., Rocky Point, NY 11778, USA.

HANDEL, Darrell D, b. 23 Aut. 1933, Lodi, Calif., USA. Professor of Music Theory & Composition. Educ: BM Univ. of Pacific, Stocton, Calif., 1956; M Mus, Rochester, 1969; PhD, ibid., 1969. m. Lynn, 4 children. Compositions: Variations for Brass Ensemble; Suzanne's Animal Music for harp; Three Balloons for Harp. Publs: Britten's Use of the Passacaglia, Tempo, 1970. Mbrships: ASCAP; AM. Musicol., Soc. Recip. of schlrships & fellowships. Address: 198 Lafayette Circle, Cincinnati, OH 45220, USA.

HANDFORD, Maurice, b. 29 Apr. 1929, Salisbury, UK. Conductor. Educ: RAM; FRAM. m. Daphne V Smith. Debut: w. Halle Orch. Career: Assoc. Cond., Halle Orch., 1960-71; Staff Cond., City of Birmingham Orch.; Cond., Liverpool Welsh Choral Soc; Musical Advsr., Brighouse Band; Prin. Cond., Calgary Phil., Filharmonic de Stadt, Cluj, Romania; Guest Cond., UK, Filharmonic de Stadt, Cluj, Romania; Guest Cond., UK, Can., USA, S Africa, France, Romania, Yugoslavia, Hungary, S Am., etc. Recordings: var. Mbrships: Hon. Life, Am. Fedn. of Musicians. Recip., Arnold Bax Mem. Medal. Address: Old Manor House, Codford St. Peter, Warminster, UK.

HANDLEY, Vernon George, b. 11 Nov. 1930, Enfield, UK. conductor. Educ: BA, Balliol Coll., Oxford; GSM. m. (1) Barbara

Black, 2 s. (1 dec.), 1 d; (2) Victoria Parry-Jones, 1 d. Debut: Bournemouth Symph. Orch., 1961. Career: cond., Oxford Univ. Music Club & Union, 1953-54; Dir., OUDS, 1953-54; cond., Tonbridge Phil. Soc., 1958-61, Hatfield Schl. of Music & Drama, 1959-62; Prof., RCM, for 1st Orch. & Cond., 1966-72, for Choral Class, 1969-72; Guest Cond., many orchs. in UK; cond., LSO in Int. Series, London, 1971; Toured Germany, 1965, '66, S. Africa, 1975; cond., var. Fests. & Proms in UK; Musical Dir., Guildford Phil. Orch. & Phil. & Proteus Choirs, 1962-. Recordings incl. many records w. LPO, Guildford Phil. Orch., RPO, RLPO, LSO, Philharmoria, etc. Hons: Classics Club Award, 1962; VW Trust Award, 1962; Cabot Fndn. Award, 1962; Hon. RCM, 1970; FRCM, 1972; Bax Medal Int. Music Awards, 1963; Cond. of the Year (CGGB), 1974. Mgmt: Tower Music, London. Address: Rosewood, Hewlsfield, Glos., UK. 30.

HANDZEL, Leon, b. 16 May 1921, Wapienica, Poland. Musicologist; Phoniatrician. Educ: Dip., piano & theory, Inst. of Music; PhD in musicol; MD in phoniatrics. m. Barbara Weiss. Career incl: Prof. of phoniatrics, Med. Schl., Wroclaw, 1957-; currently Dir., Dept. of phoniatrics; studies on acoustic structure of speech & voice; musical components of speech, physiology & pathology of the singing voice, introduction of computer technique in the study of voice microstructure; cons., opera & theatre staff in Wroclaw. Comps. incl: secular & sacred choral music; chmbr. music; theatr music; concertos. Publs: monograph on life & work of 16th century composer S B Madelka; contrb. of num. articles on musicol., phonetics, acoustics, phoniatrics & oto-laryngol. Mbrships. incl: presidium, VP and Pres., Polish Phoniatric Soc.; 1952-75; consulting Committee, Prisidium of Union of Europeazn Phoniatricians, 1976-; Organiser, Wroclaw Dept., Union of Polish Comps. Address: skr.p. nr. 76, ul, Siemienskiego 17/14, 50950 Wroclaw, Poland.

HAN-GORSKI, Adam, b. Lvov, Russia. Violinist; Concertmaster. Educ: BA, Acad. of Music Tel-Aviv; Master Class- U.S.C.; Pvte. studies. m. Barbara, 1 d. Debut: Katowice, Poland, 1948. Career: TV & film, Poland, USA; Radio, Poland, German Fed. Repub., Austria, Portugal; Major recitals, NY, London, Vienna, Mexico city, La, etc.; Concertmaster, Vienna Radio Symph. Orch. Mbr., Musicians Union. Hons: Prix Suisse, 1970. Hobbies: Languages; Photography. Mgmt: Echo Concerts, Fraümünsterpost 8022 Zürich. Address: Anton Baumgartnerstr. 44/A6/032, 1233 Vienna, Austria, 16.

HANISCH, Eduard, b. 2 Aug. 1908, Steinau, (now) Poland. Comp; Ed. Educ: Autodidact. Career: Independent comp.; Free Radio contbr.; Music ed. Radio Hanover. Comp. incl.: Orch. music; concertoes; Secular sacred vocal music; Chmbr. music; Radio Secular and sacred vocal music; Chmbr. music; Radio plays; Theater music. Recordings: many Radio recordings of own music. Mbrships: Artists Guild, Esslingen am Neckar; German Soc. for New Music. Publs.: Self description, in: Contemporary Composers from Schlesweg, vol. 2, 1976. Hons: Johann Wenzel-Stamitz Prize, 1970. Hobbies: Tape recording; Hobby film; Wandering; Hill walking; Nature observing. Address: Rodewaldstr 6, 3 Hanover 61, German Fed. Repub.

HANKINSON, Michael Neville, b. 23 Jan. 1946, Maghull, Liverpool, UK. Organist; Composer; conductor. Educ: TCL; FTCL LTCL (Mus Ed.). m. Kay Connett. Comps: Num. Film scores; works for organ & brass for 1300th Anniversary Serv., hereford, 1976; Cantata, Christus Vincit; With a Little Help From My Friends, ballet score; Ceremonial music for Hereford Cath., 1976. Recordings: Tchaikovsky, Francesca da Rimini, Von Einem, Phila. Symph. w. Nurnberg Symph. Orch; songs I Love w. Mimi Coertse. Mbrships: CGGB; S African Soc. Music Tchrs. Hobbies: Reading; Electronics. Mgmt: vista Music Co., 22 Grove Road Gardens, Johannesburg, S Africa. Address: as above.

HANKS, Thompson Willis, Jr., b. 3 July 1941, Beaumont, Tex., USA. Freelance Tuba Player. Educ: Lamar State Coll. of Techno., Beaumont, Tex., Eastman Schl. of Music; pvte. studies w. Arnold Jacobs. m. Shirley Lynn Bender. Career: Solo tuba w. San Antonio Symph., Mpls. Symph., NYC Ballet & Chautauqua Symph. Orch.; Fndg. mbr., Nedw England conserv. of Music, Boston, Manhattan Schl. of Music, Yale Univ. Schl. of Music & Hartt Coll. of Music. Recordings: Num. records w. NY Brass Quintet, and as freelance perf., NYC. Mbr., Tubists Universal Brotherhood Assn. Hons: Donald Swann Award, Tanglewood, Mass., 1964. Hobbies: Backpacking; woodcraft; Sailing; Scuba diving. Address: 820 West End Ave., NY, NY 10025, USA.

HANLY, Brian Vaughan, b. 3 Sept. 1940, Perth, WA, Aust. Violinist. Educ: Perf.'s Dip., 1960, Tchr.'s Dip., 1961, Aust. Music Exams. Bd. Career Incls. Soloist w. symph. orchs. of

Sydney, Melbourne, Perth & Hobart; num. TV & radio broadcasts, Aust. Broadcasting Commn.; in USA, 1965-, concertizing as Soloist & Chmbr. musician; Violinist, Western Arts Trio, touring throughout world; prof. of Violin, Univ. of Wyo. Recorded trios of Walter Piston, Earnest Bloch, Joseph Schwantner & James Hopkins, etc., w. Wester Arts Trio. Recip. var. hon. & awards. Mgmt: Int. Artists Agcy., San Fran., Pietro Menci, Dir. Address: Dept. of Music, Univ. of Wyo., Box 3037, Univ. Stn., Laramie, WY 82071, USA.

HANNA, Betty Joy, b. 3 Feb. 1934, Newcastle, Aust. Teacher: Lecturer; Examiner. Educ: Dip., NSW Conserv. of Music, Sydney, Aust.; DSCM Performers Dip.; DSCM Tchrs. Dip.; L Mus A, Performers Dip.; A Mus A Performers Dip. div. 1 s, 2 d. Career: Solo pianist & accomp. at num. concerts; Duo pianist; Radio apps., 1951-53; Ch. organist; Lectr. in Musicianship, Aural & Harmony, Conserv. of Music; Tchr., Piano, Harmony, Theory Aural Musicianship; Examiner, AMEB, Piano & Theory. Publs: Musicianship--Grades I-VII, Theory-- Grades IV-VI, 1974. Comps: Sev. relig. works for ch. choirs. Recordings: Saint-Saens Piano Concerto in G Minor, w. NSW Conservatorium Orch. Contbr. to: Key Vive; Musical Assn. Quarterly Notes. Mbr., The Musical Assn. of NSW; Aust. Coll. of Educ. Hons: Medal for Theory, TCL, 1945: Many eisteddfod 1st & 2nd prizes; Lieder 1st prizes, 1950-53; Highest marks in Aust., L Mus A (Piano), 1953; Highest No. of Distinction DSCM 4 yr. Dip. Course. Hobbies: Sewing; Gardening; Address: 8 Mistletoe St., Loftus Heights, NSW, 2232, Aust.

HANNA, James R, b. 15 Oct. 1922, Siloam Springs, Ark., USA. Professor; Violist. Educ: B Mus. 1948, M Mus, 1949, Northwestern Univ. m. Margie O. Owen, 1 s., 1 d. Career: Porf. of Theory & Comp., Univ. of Southwestern La., Lafayette; Violist. Comps. incl: Elegy for Chamber Orch.; Fugue & Chorale for 4 Percussionists; Song of the Redwood Tree. Contbr. to: Dictionary of 20th Century Music; Profl. jrnls. Mbrships: Southeastern Comps. League (Sec.); Nat. MTA; Viola- Forschungsgesellschaft; Am. Symph. Orch. League; pi Kappa Lambda; Phi Mu Alpha Sinfonia. Hons: Winner, La. Fedn. Music Clubs Comp. Contest, 1954, 56, 58, 64; Award Comp., La. Coun. Music & performing Arts, 1968. Hobbies: Philatelics; Photography; Western US History. Address: 523 Taft St., Lafayette, LA 70501, USA. ª.

HANNA, Nabil Iskandar, b. 12 Sept. 1934, Suez, Egypt. Assistant Professor of Music. Educ: Dip., music theory, Nat. High Conserv. Music, Cairo, 1965; MA, UCLA, USA, 1971; PhD, ibid., 1972. m. Dora-Jean, 1 s., 1 d. Contbr. to Ethnomusicol Mbr., AAUP. Hons: Cert. Hon., Late pres. Nasser, Egypt, 1965; Fulbright-Hayes Doct. Rsch. Abroad Fellowship, 1972. Hobbies: Fishing; Gardening; Reading. Address: co Am. Embassy, Port-au-Prince, Haiti.

HANNAN, Michael Francis, b. 19 Nov. 1949, Waratah, NSW, Aust. Keyboard performer; Writer; Educator. Educ: BA, Univ. of Sydney; PhD, ibid. Career: Tchng. at Univ. of NSW, 1975-76, Univ. of Sydney, 1977-79. Comps: Fortune Pieces for piano, 1978; Price Milburn (NZ), 1979; Garland for small orch., 1979; Love Thoughts for piano strings, shakuhachi & voice, 1978. Recording: The Piano Music of Peter Sculthorpe. Publs: num. articles on Aust. contemporary comps. & Afro-Am. music. Contbr. to Aust. Playboy. mbr., Musicol. Soc. of Aust. Hon: Frank Albert Prize, 1970. Hobbies: Surfing; Asian Cooking; Wine; Watercolour Painting; Collage; Collecting Australiana. Address: 17 The Drive, Stanwell Park, 2509 Aust.

HANNER, Barry Neil, b. 20 Feb., 1936, Stinesville, Ind., USA. Opera singer; Voice teacher. Educ: BA, Curtis Inst. of Music, Phila., 1961. m. Helga Schweitzer, 1s., 1d. Debut: Bad. Staatstheater, Karlsruhe, 1962. Career: Opera & concert apps. in Vienna, Berlin, Munich, Cologne, Frankfurt, Stuttgart & Nuremberg etc.; Dean of Opera Dept., Fach Acad. of Music, Nuremberg. Address: Dörlbach-Austr. 26, 8501 Burgthann, German Fed. Repub.

HANNESSON, Thorsteinn, b. 19 Mar. 1917, Siglufjordur, Iceland. Opera Singer; Radio Director of Music. Educ: 4 yrs. RCM (singing). m. Kristin Palsdottir, 2s., 1d. Debut: Royal Opera House, Covent Garden, as Radames, 1948. Career: Prin. tenor, Covent Garden, for 6 yrs.; guest apps., Corc Opera Co., Royal Opera, Amsterdam, Sadlers Wells & Icelandic Nat. Theatre. 11 yrs. Purchasing Mgr., Icelandic State Wine, Spirits & Tobacco Authority; apps. in Icelandic Musical Life as perf. & adminstr., 1954-; w. Iceland Broadcasting Service, 1969-; Dep. Dir. of Music, ibid., 1969-75; Dir. of Music, ibid., 1975. mbr., Fed. of Icelandic Artists. Address: Tverbrekka 4/801, 200 Kopavogur, Iceland. 19.

HANOUSEK, Vladimir, b. 2 May 1907, Przemysl, Poland. Primary Violinist. Educ: Violin Dept., prague Conservatory of

Music, Czechoslovakia, 1924-28; comp. Dept., ibid, 1926-28; Studied w. Josef Suk & Karel Hoffmann, Masters' comp, Shcl. Dip., 1928-30; Masters' Violin Schl. Dip., 1928-31. m. Jarmila Bulanova, 2 s. Career: Solo violinist, esp. in Czechoslovak Broadcasting, Prague, 1928-. Perf., 1st violin concerto by Karel Szymanowsky w. Czech Phil. Orch., Prague. 1930; Pianist, K. Szymanowsky's 'Myths' for violin & piano, Prague, 1935; Mbr.. chmbr. ensembles; Primarius, New Czech Quartet, until 1960; Artistic Ldr., Prague Chmbr. Orch., until 1966; Tours in Poland, 1949, German Democratic Repub. & Austria, 1956, Italy, 1957-58. Compositions incl: Mascaron, scherzo for symph. orch.; Passion Improvisation, for viol & symph. orch.; Drama's Exodus, music to poem by J. Orten for symph. orch.; Messa dei Morti, for speaker, solo soprano, alto, tenor & baritone, mixed & recital chorus & symph. orch.; Dies Irae, scenic rhapsody; Intermezza, for piano solo. Mbrships: Union of Czechoslovak Comps., until 1968; Protective Union of Authors, Prague, 1932-. Recip. of hons. Address: W Picka 96, 10100 Prague 10, Vinohrady, Czechoslovakia.

HANSELL, Kathleen Amy Kuzmick, b. 21 Sept. 1941, Bridgeport, Conn., USA. Musicologist; Organist; Harpsichordist. Educ: BA, Wellesley Coll., Mass., 1963; M Mus, Univ., of Ill., Urbana, 1969; PhD Cand., Univ. of Calif., Berkeley; studied piano, organ & harpsichord w. pvte. tchrs. m. Sven H Hansell, 1 s., 1 d. Career: Instructor in music hist by corres., Univ. of Ill., 1967-68; Organist, Luth. Ch. of Good Shepherd, Sacramento, Calif., 1969-71, Gloria Dei Luth. Ch., Iowa City, Iowa, 1973-74; Instructor in musicol. & Harpsichordist, Grinnell Coll., Iowa, 1976-. Contbr. to profl. publs. inclng. Grove's Dictionary, 6th ed. Mbrships: Am., Italian & Int. Musicol. Socs. Recip. var. hon. Address: 1126 Pickard St., Iowa City, IA 52240, USA.

HANSELL, Sven Hostrup, b. 23 Oct. 1934, NYC, USA. Professor of Musicology & Harpsichord. Educ: BA, Univ. of Ps., 1956; AM, Harvard Univ., 1958; PhD, Univ. of Ill., 1966. m. Kathleen Hansell, 1 d., 1 s. Career: Prof., Univ. of Calif., Davis., Univ. of Ill., & Univ. of Iowa; cond. of choral grps.; Apps. as harpsichordist & organist throughout Calif. & on Univ. campuses in USA. Mbrships. incl: AMS; IMS. Publs.; A Provisional List of Electronic Music Compositions, 1966; Works for Solo Voice of JA Hasse, 1968; J A Hsse, cantates pour une voix de femme & orchestra (ed), 1968; The Madrigals of Antonio Lotti (ed). Contbr. to profl. jrnls. Hons. incl: Fellowship, Univ. of Iowa, 1974. Address: 1126 Pickard St., Iowa City, IA 52240 USA.

HANSEN, Hanne Wilhelm, b. 23 Jan. 1927, Copenhagen, Denmark. Music Publisher; Concert & Theatre Agent. mbr., Bd., Association Europénne des Directeurs de Concerts et Spectacles. Hobbies: Music; Art. Address: 9-11 Gothersgade, 1123 Copenhagen K, Denmark.

HANSEN, Ove Verner, b. 20 July 1932, Helsingr, Denmark. Opera Singer. m. Birthe Bruun, 1 d. Debut: Theatre Royal, Copenhagen, 1964. Career: Opera Singer (bass buffo) at Theatre Royal, Copenhagen; Roles incl: Osmin, Bey Mustafa, Leporello, Falstaff, Bottom, Baculus, Fiesco, Lodovico, Don Alfonso; num. Film apps; Radio & TV perfs.; Concerts in Stockholm, Oslo, Helsinki, Reykjavik, & in Germany, Holland & Italy. Recordings: 8 records of Danish songs & ballads. Mbr., Danish Actors Assn. Hons: Helge Nissions Mindelegat, 1966. Hobbies: Fishing; Cooking. Mgmt: Theatre Royal, Copenhagen. Address: Jollen 41 Snekkersten, Denmark.

HANSEN, Peter, b. 15 Aug. 1917, The Hague, The Netherlands. Pianist; Administrator. Educ: Studied piano w. cor De Groot, Royal Conserv., The Hague, 1936-41; Degree C1, ibid, 1939; Degree C2, 1941; Studied w. Jaap Spaanderman, Amsterdam, 1950-60. m. Adriana Cornelia Den Dulk, 2 s. Debut: The Hague, 1940. Career: 2 pianocencertos, Hague Philharmony, conducted by Louis Stotijn & Willem van Otterloo, 1953 & 1956; Pianocencertos w. sev. orchs. incldg. Groningen, Enschede & Arnhem orchs.; Accompanist to many violinists incldg. Herman Krebbers, Theo Olof, William Noske, Thomas Magyar & Herman Salomon; Mgr., De Zingende Zolder, The Hague 1952-; Pres., Music Commn., The Hague's Art Soc. for Youth; Mgr., The School Concert, The Hague, covering 75 schls.; 3000 schl. concerts all over The Netherlands for The School Concert, Amsterdam, 1958-. Royal Conservatory of Music, The Hague, 1965. Mbr., Royal Netherlands Musicians Soc. Hobbies: Nature Warden; Ornithol; Presbyter, Netherlands Reformed Ch. Address: Jozef Israelslaan 34, The Hague, The Netherlands.

HANSEN, Poul Erik, b. 15 Nov. 1945, Odense, Denmark, Teacher; Singer. Educ: Music, Aarhus Univ., 2 yrs.; Dip., Tchng. voice, Jutland Acad. Music, Aarhus. m. Kirsten Simonsen Hansen. Career: Broadcast app. inlb Nrholm's opera

'Den Unge Park', Danish Radio; Sev. apps. in concerts; Dir., La Serva Padrone & HMS Pinafore, Aarhus Opera Grp.; Lectr., N. Norwegian Acad. Music, Tromso, 1975-78; Tchr., Norges Musikpaedagogisk Forening. Hobby: Photography. Address: Digerudveien 40, Kongsvinger, Norway.

HANSHUMAKER, James Richard, b. 8 Apr. 1931, Lima, OH, USA. Professor of Music Education; Bassoonist. Educ: BS (Educ.), 1949, MA, 1953, Phd, 1961, OH State Univ.; Cleveland Inst. of Music. Career: was Profl. Bassoonist; Tchr. & cond., Pub. Schls.; Univ. of Southern Miss.; curently Prof. & Chmn., Music Educ., Univ. of Southern Calif.; Host, TV series The Lively Arts, Los Angeles, 1973; created 5 music educ. films for Churchill Films, Inc., 1968-72. Contbr. to: MENC Jrnl.; Jrnl. of Am. Psychol. Assn.; Jrnl. of Rsch. in Music Educ. Mbrships: MENC; Ed. Bd., Jrnl., Soc. for Rsch. Coun. Hons. incl: Outstanding Music Fac. Mbr., 1973. Address: 6614 Cahuenga Terrace, Los Angeles, CA 90068, USA.9.

HANSLER, George E, b. 27 Oct. 1921, Mpls., Minn., USA. Teacher; Conductor. Educ: BS, Univ. Wis.; MA, Tchrs. Coll., Columbia Univ.; PhD, NY Ulniv.; Post-doct. work, summer conducting course, w. Erich Leinsdorf, Mozarteum, Salzburg, Austria, 1959. Career: Prof. Music, Jersey City State Coll., Jersey City, NJ. Contbr. to: Living Monument--the Casals Festiveal in Puerto Rico, Musical Am. Vol., No.8, 1961. Mbrships: Am. choral Dirs. Assn; Nat. Assn. Tchrs. Singing; MENC. Hobbies: Gardening; Swimming. Address: 2039 Kennedy Blvd., Jersey City, NJ 07305, USA.

HANSLI, Asbjorn, b. 13 Sept. L944, Vinje, Telemark, Norway. Concert Singer; Baritone. Educ: Tchr. Trng. Coll., 1968; voice, Choral Conducting, Oslo Musikkonservatorium. m. Aud-Kari Hansli, 2 children. Debut: Oslo, 1969. Career: Recitals, Norway, Sweden, UK & USA; Appd. w. Symph. Orch., Norway, Finland & Denmark, Bergen Int. Fest. & Helsingfors Fest.; Guest Prof., Calif. State Univ. Mbrships: Norsk Tonekunstnersamfund; Oslo Muslkklereforening. Hons: 1st Prize, Scandinavian Singing Contest, 1967; Hon. Prize, 'Familien' weekly mag., 1968. Hobby: Flying (Pilot). Address: Micheletsve, 16, 1324 Lysaker, Norway.

HANSON, Howard, b. 28 Oct. 1896, Wahoo, Neb. USA. misic Teacher; composer; conductor. Educ: Luther Coll. cnserv.; Univ. of Neb.; Inst. of Musical Art, NY; N. Western Univ., Ill. m. Margeret Elisabeth Nelson, 1946. Career: Prof. of Music & Dean of Conserv. of Fine Arts, Coll. of the Pacific, 1919-21; Fellow, Am. Acad., Rome, Italy, 1921-24; Dir. Eastmen Schl. of Music, Univ. of Rocheste, NY, 1924-64; Dir. Inst. of Am. Music., ibid, 1964-; Guest Cond., num. Am Inst. of Am. Music., ibid, 1964-; Guest Cond., num. Am & for. orchs. Compositions incl: 6 Symphs.; Elegy in Memory of Sege Koussevitsky; Mosaics; Summer Seascape; Concerto for Organ, Strings & Harp; The Cherubic Hymn; Merry Mount (opera); var. chmbr. music pieces, piano music & sorigs. Publ. Harmonic Materials of Modern Music. Mbrships: Fellow, Swedish Royal Acad. of Music; Nat. Inst. of Arts & Letters. Hons. incl: num. Hon. Doctorates; Pulitzer Prize; Freedom Award, etc. Hobbies: Swimming; Boating. Address: 362 Oakdale Dr., Rochester, NY 14618, USA.

HANSON, John R., b. 14 Feb. 1936, Jamestown, NY, USA. Teacher, Music Theory. Educ: BM, MA, PhD, Eastman Schl. of Music, Univ. of Rochester. m. Patricia Selover, 1 s., 1 d. Career: Tchr., Univ. of Kan., Carroll Coll.; Tchr., Theory Dept., Eastman Schl. of Music; currently Tchr., SUNY at Binghamton. Compositions: Oblation, (Sop., Alto, Tenor, Bass & Trumpet). Publs: Music Fundamentals Workbook, 1979. Mbrships: Pres., Music Theory Soc. of NY. State. Hons: US Govt. Grant 1968-69. Hobbies: Tennis, Bicycling. Address: 77 Eastland Ave., Rochester, NY 14618, USA.

HARAPAT, Jindrich, b. 26 Nov. 1895, Litomysl, Czechoslovakia. Composer. Educ: Pvte. study w. J Cyril Sychra. m. Herma Dubcova, 1 s. Debut: Avezzano, Italy, 1918. Career: Musicmaster; Bandmaster; dir. of Municipal Admin., & cond., Orch. Assn.; Zelezny Brod; Ed. in Chief, Music Dept. DILIA (Theatrical & Lit. Agcy.), Prague. Compositions incl: 7 operattas, 12 plays w. songs for children, num. program & dance music compositions, choral works, songs; Travicka zelena, mil. march. Mbrships. incl: Authors Assn. for Protection of Rights for Musical Works; Union of Czech Composers. Hons: Hon. Appreciation, Union of Czech Composers, 1970; Num. composition prizes. Address: Klobucnicka 11, 140 00, Prague £, Czech.

HARBO, Erik, b. 12 May 1937, Ride, Fovling, Denmark. Opera Singer (Tenor). Educ: Royal Danish Music Acad., 1965; Opera Schl., Royal Theatre, Copenhagen, 1967. m. Bente Harbo, 3 children. Debut: Royal Theatre, Copenhagen, 1966.

Career: Sev. concerts & recitals, Danish TV & Radio; Num. concerts, Denmark, Sweden & Germany; Maj. roles incl: Capt. in 'Wozzeck'; Sporting life, 'Porgy & Bess'; Flute, 'A Midsummer Night's Dream'; Rane Jonson, 'Drot og Marsk'; Masino, 'Der Gestiefelte Kater', Bonn, 1975. Recordings: Danish songs & ballads. Mbr. profl. orgs. Hon: 1st Prize, Young Scandinavian Singers Competition, 1971. Hobbies incl: Photography; Travel. Mgmt: Royal Theatre, Copenhagen. Address: Herringlose, 3670 Vekso, Osterbo 5, Denmark.

HARDIN, Burton Ervin, b. 21 Aug. 1936, Lincoln, Neb., USA. Professor; Composer; Musician; French & Natural Horn Soloist. Educ: B Mus Ed.; M Mus.; DMA. m. Barbara Gene Ducker Hardin, 1 s. Career: num. apps. as French Horn Soloist, & cond., throughout USA. Comps incl: num. comps. for band, orch., chmbr. music, Recordings incl: Burt Hardin Plays It All (Horne Quartets, Quintets, Sextets); Columbus, OH, Vocal Music w. Horns, featuring Burt Hardin. Author, A Comparison of Two Methods of Arriving At The Most Suitable Thicknesses of Violin Plates, 1969. Contbr. to: The Instrumentalist; The Strad; Jrnl., NACWPI. Mbrships: NACWPI; Int. Horn Soc.; Coll. Music Soc.; Historian, Phi Mu Alpha; Fac. Advsr., ibid; Kappa Kappa Psi; MENC. Hons: Comp. Prize, Am. Schl. Band Dirs. Assn., 1974; Comp. Prize, Sigma Alpha Iota, 1968; Cert. of Esteem, Dept. of Defense, 1956. Hobbies: Violin Making; Golf; Flying. Mgmt: King Musical, 33999 Curtis Blvd., Eastlake, Ohio, USA. Address: 1068 S 7th St., Charleston, IL 61920, USA.

HARDING, John Phillips, b. 8 Nov. 1950, Newcastle, NSW, Aust. Violinist. Educ: Sydney Conservatorium High Schl. Career: Concertmaster, Aust. Elizabethan Trust Orch.; Ldr., Fidelio Str. Quartet; Asst. Concertmaster, Rochester Phil. Orch., NY, USA; currently Met. Opera Orch., NYC; apps. throughout Aust. & Far East w. Robert Pilker Chmbr. Orch.; Solos in USA w. Rochester Phil. & Rochester Chmbr. Orch. Hons: Albert Spalding Prize, Tanglewood, 1974. Address: 1340 Highland Ave., Rochester, NY 14620, USA.

HARDISON, Clifton James, b. 28 May 1958, Norgolk, Va., USA. Percussionist; Timpanist. Educ: Student, Juilliard Schl. of Music, 1976. Debut: As solo percussionist w. Va. Opera Assn. 1975-76. Career: Prin. Percussionist & Timpanist, Tidewater Youth Symph., Norfolk, 1973, 74, 75, 76; Participant, Eastern Music Fest., Greensboro, NC, summers 1975, 76 (TV app. 1976); Va. All-State Band Percussionist, 1975; 1st Chairs w. All Va. Band, & All Va. State Orch., 1976. Recordings incl: M Gould, American Salute for Orch.; Tchaikovsky, Symph. No. 6 in B Minor; Berlioz, Harold in Italy. Mbrships: Local 125, AFM; Percussive Arts Soc. of Am. Recip., var. scholarships & medals for solo perf. Hobbies: Tennis; Listening to recordings; Fishing. Address: 1313 Dartmouth Circle, Virginia Beach, VA 23462, USA.

HARDOUIN, Pierre Jean, b. 9 Aug. 1914, Paris, France. Musicologist; Organist. Educ: studied w. A. Pirro, P M Masson, P Brunold. m. Jeanine Lassaslle, 2 children. Career: Prof. Publs. incl: Legrand Orgue de St. Gervais a Paris, 1975; Le Grand Orgue de St. Nicolas des champs, 1975; Le Grand Orgue de St. Germain des Prés, 1978. Contbr. to: L'Orgue; Recherches; Renaissance del'Orgue; Connaissance d l'orgue; Acta musicologica; Organ Yearbook; Glapin Soc. Jrnl.; Tribune de l'Orgue; Revue Musicale. Mbrships: VP, French Assn. for the preservation of old organs; French Musicol. Soc. Hobbies: Making Harpsichords; Genealogy. Address: 15 Ave. de Quincy, F 77150, Combslavill, France.

HARE, Robert Yates, b. 14 June 1921, McGrann, Pa., USA. Musician, French Horn; Conductor. Educ: BM, Detroit Inst. of Musical Art, Univ. of Detroit; MA, Wayne State Univ., PhD, Univ. of Iowa. m. Constance Rutherford, 1 s., 2 d. Debut: Carnegie Hall, Pittsburgh, Age 19. Career: French Horn, Buffalo Phil., Pittsburgh, Indpls.; San Antonio Symphs., Pittsburgh, Cinn., Phil. La Scala Opera co.'s; Orchestrator, San Antonio Symph.; Tchr., Marietta Coll., Ohio, Del Mar Coll., Corpus Christi, Tex.; Prof., Band Cond., Grad. Advsr., Dir. of Theses, Chmn., Grad. Studies in Music,San Jose Coll., Calif., 1956-65; Prof. of Music History & Lit., Dean, Schl. of Music, Eastern Ill. Univ., Charleston, 1965-74; Cond., Univ. Symph., ibid. 1969-72; Dir., Schl. of Music, Ohio State Univ., 1974-. num. recordings. Contbr. to: Coonchord; Instrumentalist; Ill. Jrnl. of Music. Mbr., Off., num. Profl. Orgs. Hobbies: History; Philosophy; 18th Century English Literature; Theatre; Art; Linguistics; Archaeology; Acoustics; Cybernetics. Address: 2494 Farleigh Rd., Columbus, OH 43221, USA. 2, 8, 11, 12, 13, 15.

HAREWOOD, The Earl of (George Henry Hubert Lascelles), b. 7 Feb. 1923, London, UK. Musical Administrator. Educ: King's Coll., Cambridge Univ. m. (1) Maria Donata Stein, 1949 (div.

1967); (2) Patricia Tuckwell, 1967, 4 s. Career incl: Bd. of Dirs., Royal Opera House, Covent Gdn., 1951-53, 1969-72; Admin. Exec., ibid. 1953-60; Dir.-Gen., Leeds Musical Festival, 1958-74; Artistic Dir., Edinburgh Int. Festival, 1961-65; Chmn. British Coun. Music Advsry Committee, 1956-66; Arts Coun. Music Panel, 1966-76; Gen. Advsry Coun., BBC, 1969-77; Man. Dir., Sadlers Wells Opera, 1972. Mngng. Dir. Engl. Nat. Opera, 1972-. Publs: Ed., Opera, 1950-53; Ed. Kobbe's Complete Opera Book, 1954, 1973. Hons: Hon. LLD, Leeds & Aberdeen; Hon. D Mus., Hull Austrian Gt. Silver Medal of Hon., 1959. Mgmt: Ingpen & Williams. Hobbies: Painting; Sculpture; Opera; Theatre; Assoc. Football. Address: Harewood House, Leeds, Yorks, UK.

HARGAN, Alison Douglas, b. 26 Jan. 1943, Rotherham, UK. Lyric Soprano. Educ: Northern Schl. of Music, 1960-67; London Opera Ctr., 1967-69; ARCM; LRAM; GNSM. m. Jim Dening, 1 s., 1 d. Debut: Wigmore, 1967. Career: debut w. Royal Opera Covent Gdn. (as Flower Maiden, Parsifal), 1971; debut w. Welsh Nat. Opera (as Pamina, Magic Flute), 1971; Mbr., Engl. Music Theatre, 1976. Recorded as Flower Maiden, Parsifal (Solti & Vienna Phil., Decca). Mbr., ISM. Hons: Percival Operatic Prize & Stuyvesant Scholarship, both 1967. Mgmt: Lies Askonas. Address: Little Hertfordshire House, Coleshill, Amersham, Bucks, UK.

HARGREAVES, Walter Barrow, b. 27 Apr. 1907, Glasgow, Scotland, UK. Professor of Music (French Horn & Cornet). Educ: Grad., Athenaeum now Scottish Acad.; FTCL (Cond.); LTCL (Perf.); BBCM (Bandmaster). m. Cath erine Pollock Hamilton, 1 s. Career: Prin. Trumpet: NSO; Reid Symph. Orch.; Lectr. in Brass, Edinburgh Univ.; Band Cond. on regular broadcasts & TV 1946-. Comps. incl: Caprice & Variations for Band. Recordings: Cond., Brighouse & Rastrick Band; Cond., Stanshawe (Bristol) Band. Publs: Book on Teaching (appearing 1977). Contbr. to Sounding Brass; Britt. Bandsman; Brass Band Review. Hobby: Lawn Bowls. Address: 14 Archery Square, Walmer, Deal, Kent, UK. 3.

HARICH-SCHNEIDER, Eta (Margaretha), b. 16 Nov. 1897, Berlin, Germany. Harpsichordist; Musicologist; Japanologist. Educ: studies in musicol., piano & comp., Berlin Univ.; MA, New Schl. for Soc. Rsch. & Columbia Univ., NY, 1955. m. Dr Walther Harich, dec., 2 d, dec. 1931 Debut: Piano Recital, Sing-Akademie, Berlin, 1924. Career: Concert tours in Germany, UK, France, Scandinavia, Italy, 1924-40; Many radio apps. UFA Film 'The Harpsichord' (Das Cembalo), 1940, EHS. in the leading role; Var. scripts & musical arrangements; Yearly concert tours to Japan, USA, Europe; Prof., Berlin Schl. of Music, 1932-40, Vienna Schl. of Music, 1955-67; Guest Prof. at Sorbonne, London Univ., Chgo. Univ., Tokyo Univ., etc., Many guest lectures; Tchr. of the Imperial Musicians, Tokyo, Japan, 1946-49. Recordings: 2 for HMV, 1939-40; series of 12 for Polydor, Japan, 1952; num. others. Publs. incl: The Harpsichord, Darenreiter, 1954, '60, '73; The Medieval Court Songs of Japan, 1965: A History of Japanese Music, 1973; Charaktere und Katastrophen, 1978. Contbr. to schol. reviews & newspapers. Mbrships incl: Gesellschaft fur Natur und Volkerkunde Ostasiens; Asiatic Soc. of Japan. Hons. incl: Grand Prix due Disque, Paris, 1965; Cross of Hon., Austria, 1966; Gt. Cross of Hon. of German Fed. Repub., 1973; Imperial Order of the Holy Crown, Japan, 1977. Address: Lerchenfelderstrasse 85, A 1070 Vienna VII, Austria. 3, 19, 27.

HARITUN, Rosalie Ann, b. 30 May 1938, Johnson City, NY, USA. professor of Music Education; Clarinetist. Educ: BMusEd, Baldwin-Wallace Conserv. of Music, 1960; MS, Univ. of Ill., 1961; Profl. Dip., 1966, Ed D, 1968, post-doctl. study, 1971, Columbia Univ. Career: Instrumental Music Tchr., elem., 1961-63, Jr. HS, 1963-65, Patchoque, Li, NY; Instr. of Music Educ., Temple Univ., Phila., Pa., 1968-71; Asst. Prof., E Carolina Univ., Greenville, NC, 1972-. Contbr. to NC Music Educators Jrnl; The Schl. Musician. Mbrships: Pi Kappa Lambda (Pres., Beta Zeta Chapt., E Carolina Univ., 1977-); Sigma Alpha Iota (Fac. Advisor, Beta Psi Chapt., E Carolina Univ., Pres., Alpha Theta Chapt., Columbia Univ., 1966-68; MENC; Tau Beta Sigma. Hobbies: Long distance seimming; Reading. Address: 206 N Oak St., Apt. 8, Grenville, NC 27834, USA. 7, 27.

HARKER, Clifford, b. Newcastle upon Tyne, UK. Organist; Master O The Choristers. Educ: B Mus.; Hon. M Mus.; FRCO.; ARCM. Career: Organist & Master Of The Choristers, Bristol Cathedral; Cond., Bristol Choral Soc., Bristol Cathedral Special Choir & Orch., Bath Choral & Orchl. Soc. Composer, Organ & Ch. Music. Mbr. ISM. Address: The Cathedral, Bristol, UK.

HARLEY, Alexander Medard, b. 17 Dec. 1894, Budapest, Hungary. Music Educator; Violinist; Violist. Educ: BMus, MMus,

Northwestern Univ., Evanston, Ill.; postgrad., Chgo. Conserv., Bush Conserv. of Chgo. & Univ. of S Calif., Los Angeles. m. Frances M Mikkelson. Career: Dir. of Music in var. chls. in Ill.; Chmn., Music Dept., Maine Jr. Coll., Park Ridge, Ill.; choral dir., Mundelein Coll., Chgo.; choir dir., Ravenswood Meth. Ch. & Wooley Memorial Meth. Ch., Chgo, St. Luke's Lutheran Ch., Park Ridge; fndr., cond., Park Plaines Symph. Orch. (now Northwest Symph.). Contbr. to: The School Musician; Music Supervisors Jrnl.; Educational Screen; Ed., The Scroll, Ill. ASTA Jrnl. Mbrships incl: fndr., hon. life Pres., Modern Music Masters Int. Honor Soc.; Am. Str. Tchrs. Assn. (Pres., Ill. Unit); chmn., Nat. Coun. of Music Educators Clubs; MENC; chmn., Ill. Jr. Coll. Assn.; Phi Mu Alpha Sinfonia. num. hons. & prizes. Hobbies: Reading; Fishing; Travel; Photography; Giving Travelogues. Address: 1416 Garden St., Park Ridge, IL 60068, USA. 8, 12.

HARLEY, Frances Marjorie, b. 24 Sep. 1914, Park Ridge, Ill., USA. Music Educator (composition, voice, piano). Educ: BMus, Mundelein Coll., Chgo.; MMus, Am. Conserv., Chgo.; postgrad., Univ. of S Calif., Los Angeles. m. Alexander M Harley. Career: Choir Dir., St. Luke's Ch., Park Ridge; Dir., Park Ridge Men's Chorus; Dir., 20th Century Jr. Women's Club Chorus, Park Ridge; Dir., Music Dept., Park Ridge Schl. for Girls; pvte. tchr. in voice, piano & theory; 2 yrs. as vocal soloist on seekly radio prog., Chgo. Comps: 38 choral comps. & arrs. Contbr. to num. profl. jrnls; contributing ed., Who's Who Among Am. High Schl. Students. Mbrships: co-fndr. & exec. sec. emeritus, Modern Music Masters Int. Honor Soc.; MENC; ASTA. sev. awards & scholarships. Hobbies: World Travel; Photography; Giving Travelogues; Cooking; Fishing. Address: 1416 Garden St., Park Ridge, Il 60068, USA.

HARLING, Jean M., b. 27 July 1923, Detroit, Mich., USA. Flautist. Educ: BS, Wayne Univ.; studies w. John Wummer. m. Thomas Edwin Harling, 1 s. Career: Flautist, Buffalo Phil., 1946-58; Prin. Flautist, Honolulu Symph., 1958-; Flute Instructor, Punahou Music Schl., 1958-63; Lectr. in Flute, Univ. of Hawaii, 1963-. Mbrships: Nat. Flute Assn.; Bd. of Dirs., Ensemble Players Guild; Mu Phi Epsilon. Hobbies: Reading; Cooling. Address: 11 Aimikana St., Kailua, HI 96734, USA. 5.

HARMAN, Bernard Albert, b. 17 July 1919. Professor of Music. Educ: GSM; London Coll. of Music. m. Josephine Harman, 2 s. Career: Civil Servant to 1939; Band of the Life Guards, 1946-62; Timpanist & Percussionist, then Orch. Dir., Royal Opera House Orch., 1962-72; Prof., RCM, 1968, Royal Mil. Schl. of Music, Kneller Hall, 1969-; Dir., Symphonic Wind Band, London Coll. of Music. Trustee, London Orchl. Assn.; Hon. RCM.; Hon. FLCM. Address: 10 St. Andrews Ave, Windsor, Berks., UK.

HARMAN, Dave Rex, b. 9 Nov. 1948, Redding, Calif., USA. Clarinettist; Conductor; Educator. Educ: DMusA, Eastman Schl., Univ. of Rochester, NY; studied w. Ulysse Delecluse, Paris Conserv.; BA, MA, Calif. State Univ., Sacramento. m. Mary Ann Mastrovich Harman. Career: Frequent solo clarinet recitals, Fndn. Des Etats-Unis, Paris, St. Martin's-in-the-Fields, London, Rice, Louisville, Georgia Univs. Recording: Berg Kammerkonzert. Contbr. to: Am. Music Tchr.; Woodwind World. Mbrships: Coll. Music Soc.; Am. Symph. Orch. League; Am. Fedn. of Musicians. Hons: French Govt. Scholar, 1971-72. Hobbies: Camping; Languages. Address: 1621 Leesdale Ct., Ft. Collins, CO 80521, USA.

HARMAN, Richard Alexander, b. 19 Nov. 1917, Gooty, Madras State, India. University Professor. Educ: B Mus.; ARCM.; GRSM. m. Jan Elizabeth, 2 s., 2 d. Career: Dir. of Music, Durham Schl., Durhan City, UK, 1943-49; Lectr. thru Sr. Lectr., Durham Univ., 1949-66; Prof., Univ. of Wash., Seattle, USA, 1966-. Publs: Ed. & annotated. A Plain and Easy Introduction to Practical Music by Thomas Morley, (1597), 1952, 2nd. ed. 1962; Ed., Luca Marenzio's madrigals from Musica Transalpina (1588-97), 1956; Ed. & translator, Palestrina: Ten Four-Part Motets for the Church's Year, 1963; A Catalogue of the Printed Music and Books on Music in Durham Cathedral Library, 1969; Preface, Index & corrections to The Interpretation of the Music of the 17th. & 18th. Centuries by Arnold Dolmetsch, 1969; Ed. & translator, popular Italian Madrigals of the 16th. Century; Ed. & translator. Comparative Italian Madrigal Settings (in preparation). Contbr. to: Man and His Music, Volumes I & II, 195859; The Pelican History of Music Volume II, 1963; Audio & Record Review; Die Musik in Geschichte und Gegenwart; Ency. Americana; Ency. of Worl Biog. Mbrships: Royal Musical Assn.; Am. Musicological Soc. Hobbies: Gardening; Sport. Address: Music Schl., Univ. of Wash., Seattle, WA 98105, USA. 3, 14.

HARMON, Thomas F, b. 28 Feb. 1939, Springfield, Ill., USA. Organist. Educ: AB, PhD, Wash. Univ.; St. Louis, Mo.; MA,

STANFORD Univ.; Organ study w. Howard Kelsey, H. Nanney, Anton Heiller; Harpsichord study w. Putnam Aldrich. m. Edwina Sue Snow. Career: Univ. Organist, Univ. of Calif., Los Angeles; Organist, Los Angeles Master Chorale & Los Angeles Chmbr. Orch.; frequent apps., Music Ctr., Hollywood Bowl; app. in film, Discovering Jazz; Recital tours, Austria & Italy, 1973, UK & N. Europe, 1976; Ch. organist. Recordings: Am. Organ Music of 3 Centuries; Fest. of Early Latin Am. M usic; Latin Am. Musical Treas. Publs: The Registration of J.S. Bach's Organ Works. Contbr. to profl. jrnls. Mbrships incl: AGO (Dean, Los Angeles chapt.). Hobbies incl: Skiing; Swimming. Address: 15945 Miami Way, Pacific Palisades, CA 90272, USA.

HARMS, Benjamin William, b. 17 May 1942, Detroit, Mich., USA. Percussionist; Performer on Viola da Gamba & Renaissance Winds. Educ: AB, Univ. of Cincinnati, 1963; Artists Dip., Curtis Inst. of Music, 1966; MA, Queens Coll., NYC, 1973. m. Lucy Bardo. Career: Percussionist w. sev. ensembles in NYC, inclng. Steve Reich grp. & Metrop. Opera, 1966-; Fndng. Mbr., NY Renaissance Band, 1973-. Publs: The Fife Instructor, 1975 (publd. w. recording Spirit of '76) Mbrships: Am. Musicol. Soc.; Music Lib. Assn.; Coll. Music Soc. Hobbies: Hiking; Camping. Address: Apt. 95, 55 W 95th St., NY, NY 10025, USA.

HARMS, Molly, b. 2 Sept. 1913, Brighton, Sussex, UK. Violinist; Pianist. Educ: ARCM, violin; ARCM, piano. Career: played w. London Symph., Covent Gdn., Sadlers Wells (sub-ldr.), & Northern Ireland Orchs; broadcast solos & some of own arrs. for children for 2 violins; w. BBC Symph. Orch., inclng. tours abroad, for 15 yrs. Mbr.; ISM; Musicians Union. Recip. scholarship to RCM, 1931. Address: 108 College Rd., Bexhill, Sussex TN40 1TW, UK.

HARNER, Martin W, b. 26 Oct. 1920, St. Joseph, Mich., USA. Music Educator; Administrator; Performer (Viola, Violin). Educ: Juilliard Schl. of Music, summer 1947; BS Music & Music Educ., 1948, MA Music & Music Educ., 1949, Ed D Music Pedagogy, 1975, Columbia Univ.; studied Horn & Violin w. var. tchrs. m. Marjorie Helen Feeke. Career: Pub. Schl. Music Tchr.; currently Dir., Music Educ., Lakeland Schl. Dist., Shrub Oak, NY.; Gen. Mgr., Northern Westchester Symph. Orch. Assn.; Prin., ibid; num. single profl. perfs. on Viola & Violin. Mbrships. incl: MENC; NY State Schl. Music Assn.; Phi Mu Alpha Sinfonia; Local 398, Am. Fedn. Musicians. Hobbies: Chamber Music; Photography. Address: RD2, Armstrong St., Peekskill, NY 10566, USA.

HARNESS, William Edward, b. 26 Nov. 1940, Pendleton, Ore., USA. Operatic & Concert Tenor. Educ: trng., San Fran Merola Opera, 2 yrs., Seattle Opera, 1 yr.; vocal study w. Mary Curtis Verna; opera coaches, Otto Guth, Luigi Ricci, Robert De Ceunynck. m. Marie, 5 children. Debut: 1973. Career: many recitals & apps. w. orchs., leading roles w. Boston, Ft. Worth, Houston, Memphis, Seattle & NYC Operas, also San Fran. Opera & Spring Opera. Recip. grants & awards inclng: Florence Bruce Award, San Fran. Opera Audition; Enrico Caruso Centennial, Kurt Adler & Rev. Dibble Awards. Hobby: Cycling. Mgmt: Columbia Artists, NY. Address: 152 Gray St., Teaneck, NJ 0766, USA. 2,3.

HARNONCOURT, Nikolaus, b. Dec. 1929, Berlin, Germany. Conductor; Musicologist. Educ: Acad. of Music, Vienna. m. Alice Hoffelner, 3 s., 1 d. Career: Mbr., Vienna Symph. Orch., 1952-69; Fndr.-Mbr., Concentus Musicus of Vienna, 1954-69, reviving perf. techniques; Ed. of performance eds. of histl. operas. Publs. incl: new scores of Monteverdi operas Poppea & Il Returno d'Ulisse; new edns. of Bach choral works w. orchl. accomp. Recip., num. critical awards for recordings of pre-classical music. Address: 38 Piaristengasse, A-1080 Vienna, Austria. 2.

HARPER, (Don) William Donald, b. 18 March 1921, Melbourne, Aust. Violinist; Violist; Composer. Educ: Melbourne Conserv.; Sydney Conserv.; studied w. Reginald Bradley, Sascha Lsserson, Ray Hanson. m. Gloria Thompson, 2 s, 1 d. Career: Orch. Ldr., Soloist, Aust., -1955; moved to UK, 1955; BBC Radio Series; num. radio, TV apps., UK, Aust. Comps. incl: num. TV Themes; Champion House; World of Sport; Cheeky Bird; The Quiet One; Don't Panic; Fiddle Chop; many children's hymns. Recordings: LPs incl. Homo Electronicus; Don Harper On The Fiddle; Combo; Songs From Alice; Make Rhythm. Contbr. to: Melody Maker. Mbrships: Musicians Union; Concert Artists Assn.; PRS; MCPs. Hobbies: Walking; Old Furniture; Photography; Travel. Address: Orchard Cottage, 71 London Rd., Shenley, Herts., WD7 9BW, UK. 3, 30.

HARPER, Edward James, b. 17 Mar. 1941, Taunton, UK. Lecturer; Composer; Conductor; Pianist. Educ: MA, B Mus, Christ Ch., Oxford; ARCM; LRAM. m. Penelope Harper. Career incls: Lectr. on Fac. of Music, Edinburgh Univ.; Dir., New Music Grp. of Scotland. Comps. incl: Bartok Games for orch. (recorded), 1972; Ricercari in memoriam Luigi Dallapiccola for chmbr. ensemble, 1975; Fantasias I (for chmbr. orch.) & II (for 11 solo strings), 1976. Recip;., Cobbett Chmbr. Music Prize, RCM, 1964. Hobbies: Cricket; Football; Squash. Address: 1 Bellevue Crescent, Edinburgh EH3 6ND, UK.

HARPER, Heather, b. 8 May 1930, UK. Opera & Concert Singer (soprano). Educ: FTCL; LTCL. m. Eduard J Benarroch. Career incl: Perfs. at London Promenade Concerts, 1957-; Appeared at leading music festivals throughout the world; Concert tours of USA., Middle E. & Asia; Noted for Soprano role in Britten's War Requiem, perfs. in U.K., Europe & Australia; Leading roles in Opera at covent Gdn., Glyndebourne, Sadler's Wells & Bayreuth. Hons: CBE, 1965; Hon. D Mus, Queens Univ. Belfast, 1968; Hon. RAM, 1972; Hon. VP, Belfast Youth orch., 1974. Address: 15 Lancaster Grove, Hampstead, London N.W.3, UK.

HARPER, James Cunningham, Sr., b. 17 Feb. 1893, Lenoir, NC., USA. Flutist; Teacher; Director of High School Bands. Educ: BS., LHD., Davidson Coll., NC; M A, Univ. of NC, Chapel Hill; Grad. study. Columbia Univ., Lenoir-Rhyne Coll., Hickory, NC., & Appalachian State Univ., Boone, NC.; studied Violin at Davenport Coll., Lenoir & Columbia Univ., & w. var. tchrs., Nat. Music Camp, Interlochen. Mich. m. Charlotte Critz (dec.), 2 s., 2 d. Career: Played, var. Orchs.; Fndr. & Dir., Lenoir High Schl. Band, 1924-58; Tchr., Lenoir High Schl., 1958-. Composition: Fencing Master March. Recordings: Records of Band Selections, RCA Victor & other Cos. Contbr. num. articles to profl. jrnls.; Mbr.; Advsry. Bd. School Musician. Mbrships. incl: Lenoir Country Club; Phi Mu Alpha Sinfonia; Trustee, Caldwell Memorial Hosp.; Am. Legion; Am. Bandmasters' Assn. (Pres. 1956, Chmn. of Bd. 1957, Hon. Life Pres., 1976). Hons. incl: Mbr., US Army Band, Wash. D.C.; Goldman Award, Am. Schl. Band Dirs. Assn.; Mac Award, Montgomery, Ala., 1960; LA, Dysart Award of Citizenship, 1962. Hobbies: Travel; Motoring; Playing w. Grandchildren. Address: 203 Norwood St. S.W., Lenoir, NC 28645, USA. 7.

HARPER, Margaret Pease, b. 22 July 1911, St. Paul, Minn., USA. Pianist; Teacher. Educ: Cert., Am. Conserv.; BA, Univ. of Ariz., 1933; MA, Univ. of Chgo., 1938. m. Ples Harper, 1 s., 1 d. Career incls: Accomp. to father, concert & oratorio singer Rollin Pease, 1928 on; Piano Tchr., Canyon Tex., 1946-70; Fndr. & Publicist, theatre for histl. musical drama, Tex. Panhandle, Heritage Fndn. Inc. Publs: Meet Some Musical Terms, 1959; Thundering Sounds of the West, Histl. drama, 1965; They Came From Spain, histl. drama, 1971. Mbrships: Advsr., Tex. Comm. of Arts & Humanities, 1974-; Pres., Canyon Fine Arts Club, 1975-76. Hons: Governor's Award for Tex. Tourism, 1974; Trustees Award-Nat. Cowboy Hall of Fame, 1976. Hobbies: Travel; Music, Reading. Address: 2523 Fifth Ave., Canyon, TX 79015, USA. 5.

HARPHAM, James Stanley Medcalf, b. 6 Aug. 1940, Lincoln, UK. Composer; Musician (Piano, Spinet, Recorder, Flute, Douce.). Educ: BA., Oxon. m. Brigid Harpham. Debut: 1962, film score, The Saturday Men. Career: TV, Radio Perfs. w. own Medieval Group, The Wooden O. Compositions incl: over 50 film scores; over 100 Radio, TV, Cinema Commercial scores; Allegro in Jazz, for orch. Recordings: The Wooden O, A Handful of Pleasant Delites; over 150 tracks for Studio G; Allegro in Jazz. Mbrships: Performing Right Soc.; Mechanical Copyright Protection Soc.; Musicians' Union; British Acad. of Film & TV Arts. Recip. Mrs. Tinkler Memorial Prize, 1956, 1958; Arts Coun. Award, 1978. Hobbies: Badminton; Making Harps, Lute, etc. Address: 34 Rylett Rd., London W12, UK.

HARRAN, Don, b. 22 April 1936, Cambridge, Mass., USA. Musicologist. Educ: BA., Yale Univ., 1957; MA., Univ. of Calif., Berkeley, 1959; PhD., ibid, 1963. m. Aya Arnon Harrán, 1 s., 1 d. Career: Chmn., Musicol. Dept., Hebrew Univ., Jerusalem, Israel. Publs: Verdelot & The Early Madrigal, 1963; Das Atlantisbuch der Musik, Ed. & transl. into Hebrew, 1969; Musicology: Areas and Aims (in Hebrew) 1975; The Anthologies of Black Note Madrigals, 5 vols. in 6. Contbr. to profl. publs. Mbrships: Chmn., Israel Musicol. Soc.; Renaissance Soc. of Am.; Phi Beta Kappa; Am. Musicol. Soc; Int. Musicol. Soc. Recip. var. grants, and fellowships; Tovey Memorial Prize, 1977. Address: 24 Ha'Reches St., Savyon, Israel. 14,28,30.

HARRELL, Lynn, b. 11 Jan. 1944, NYC, USA. Cellist. Educ: Juilliard Schl.; Curtis Inst.; Master Classes w. Piatigorsky & Casals. Debut: Carnegie Hall, 1963. Career: Prin. Cellist, Cleveland Orch., 1965-71; Soloist w. major Am. & European orchs., 1971-; Fac. Mbr., Juilliard Schl. of Music, NY. Many recordings incl: Dvorak Cello concerto in B Minor w. LSO under

James Levine; Chmbr. Music recordings w. James Levine. Hons. incl: Avery Fisher Award, 1975. Hobbies: Tennis; Fishing; Chess. Mgmt: Columbia Artists Mgmt., 165 W 57th St., NY, NY 10019, USA; (Europe) Harold Holt Ltd., London. Address: cĊo Columbia Artists. 2, 14.

HARREX, Patrick, b. 26 Sept. 1946, London, UK. Composer; Violinist. Educ: BA, Univ. of York, 1968; studied comp. w. Olivier Messiaen, Paris Conserv., & pvtely w. Gilbert Amy, Paris, 1968-69. m. Alexandra Margaret Burton, 1 s. Comps: Sonata for Voice, flute & percission (publd. by Schott); Narnian Suite (recorded w. Argo); Passages III for saxophone (p;ubld. by Dorn Prods.). Mbrships: Comps. Guild of GB; Inst. of Chartered Accts. in Engl. & Wales. Hons: 1st Prize, BBC Comps. Competition, & French Govt. Scholarship, 1968. Hobbies: Gardening; Painting. Address: 132 Beaconsfield Villas, Brighton BN1 GHE, UK.

HARRHY, John Douglas, b. 18 Sept. 1919, Pontypool, Mon., UK. Educator; Organist; Pianist; Composer; conductor. Educ: BA., Univ. Coll. of Wales, Aberystwyth, 1948; Pt-time Student, Comp & Theory, Univ. Coll. of Cardiff, 1945-46, TCL, 1950-51, Battersea Coll. of Advanced Technol., 1950-51. m. Mary Tudor Morgan, 1 d. Career: Organist & Choirmaster, Var. Chs., 1938-74; Accomp. to disting. soloists, mixed male & mixed schl. choirs; Dir. of Music, C. Grammar Schl. for Boys, Bromley, Kent, 1948-57; Hd. Music Dept., Sedgehill Mixed Comprehensive Schl., London, 1957-67; Chief Examiner, M usic, Metrop. Regional Exams. Bd., 1966-72, 1978-, SE Regional Exams. Bd., 1971-77; NW Regional Exams. Bd., 1971-77, 1978-; Sr. Lectr., Music, Southlands Coll. of Educ., Wimbledon, London, 1967-; Vis. Examiner in music, Assoc. Examining Bd., for A & O Levels, 1975-; Musical Dir., St. Augustine's Singers & Orch., 1977-. Comps: Comp. of many pieces for CSE Exams., 1964-. Mbrships: Asst. Masters' Assn., 1948-; Nat. Assn. of Tchrs. in Further & Higher Educ. Hobbies: Gardening; Motoring; Tape Recording. Address: 56 Siward Rd., Bromley, Kent BR2 9JZ, UK. 3.

HARRIES, Kenneth Clive, b. 5 June 1951, Slough, Berks., UK. Assistant Director of Music, Millfield School, Street, Somerset; Professional Singer (Counter Tenor); Adjudicator. Educ: King's Coll., Cambridge: MA Mus.; Cert. Ed. (Mus); FRCO; LRAM; ARCM; Career: TV & radio broadcasts in England, Europe, W Africa & Can. w King's Coll. Choir; Cond., Clive Harries Singers & orch.; Adjudicator, Brit. Fedn. of Music Festivals; Adjudicator, many maj. Brit. Festivals;; Profl. Singer (Counter Tenor Soloist) w. var. orchs. & choirs; Mbr., Co. Music Committee, Somerset. Num. recordings w. King's Coll. Choir & Wells Cathedral Choir. Mbrships: RCO; Oxford & Cambridge Club. Recip. Open Choral Scholarship, King's coll., Cambridge, 1969. Hobbies: Chess; Bridge; Golf; Squash. Address: Etonhurst House, Millfield Schl., Ashcott, Nr. Bridgwater, Somerset, UK.

HARRINGTON, Grace, b. 17 June 1927, Englewood, NJ., USA. Pianist. Educ: Postgrad. Dip., 1948, B Mus. 1966, Juilliard Schl. of Music; M Mus Ed. Manhattan Schl. of Music, 1974; permanent tchng. cert., NY State. m. Calvin J Heusser (div.), 1 s, 1 d. Debut: Town Hall, NYC. Career: Tchr., Piano Fac., Julliard Preparatory Div., 1952-62, Dwight Schl., 8 yrs., & currently at Marymount Coll., NY; pvte. studio; Fulbright Lectr., Univ. of Santiago, Chille, 1963; Solo & chmbr. tours. USA, Europe, S. Am.; orchl. perfs. throughout USA; Recital, Alice Tully Hall, NYC, 1975. Mbr., AAUP. Hons: incl: Walter Damrosch Award. 1948; Morris Loeb Prize, 1948; M B Rockefeller Grant, 1958. Hobbies: Swimming; Hiking; Reading; Cycling. Mgmt: Judith Liegner. Address: 4 Lucille Blvd., New City, NY 10956, USA.

HARRINGTON, Helmi Hanni Strahl, b. 22 May 1945, Bad Worishhofen, Germany. Musicologist; Concert Pianist; Accompanist; Accordionist; Organ Teacher. Educ: BM, Univ. of Houston, Texas, USa, 1967; MM, ibid., 1968; PhD, Univ. of Texas, Dean's Lists; Performers Certs., 1966. Piano studies w. Prof. Blaise Montandon & Prof. Albert Hirsh; Musicol. studies w. Dr Albert Feil, Dr John W Grubbs & prof. Prof. Gilbert L Blount; Musical entertainer's techniques w. mother, Mrs Hanni Strahl. Career: Local TV, radio apps., 1955-68; Interview on Westdeutscher Lundfunk, Stuttgart; Univ. dptl. asst., tchng. asst., rsch. assoc. in NDEA-funded computer programming of 14th century anon. manuscripts; Author; Ed.; Critic. Publs: Hugo Herrmann; The Man & His Music, 1968; 1977; Hugo Herrmann Biografie, 1976. Contbr. to Biog. & analytical articles publd. in Musik in Geschichte und Gegenwart; Baker's Biog. Dict. of Musicians; Schwabishe Sangerzeitung Harmonika Revue; Der Volksmusiklehrer; Lied und Chor; Sammelband d. Universitat Stuttgart. Mbrships: Hugo-Herrmann-Freundeskreis; Am. Musicol. Soc.; Phi Beta; Phi Theta Kappa Fraternities. Hons: Chopin Prize, Texas 1964; Deutscher

Akademischer Austauschdienst, 1970-72. Hobbies: Austin Community YWCA (Bd. of Dirs.); Charitable, social & youth work; Wood carving. Address: 3107 Hemphill Park, Austin, TX 78705, USA.

HARRIS, Alice Eaton, b. 5 Aug. 1924, Milwaukee, Wis., USA. Pianist; Harpsichordist; Clavichordist; Fortepianist; Educator. Educ: Profl. Artist's Cert., Westchester Conserv. of Music; BA, Barnard Coll. m. David H Harris, 1 d. Debut: solo piano recital, NY Times Hall, 1945. Career: solo piano recitals, Carnegie Recital Hall & Town Hall, NYC; Solo Harpsichordist w. Westchester Chmbr. Music Soc.; apps. as Harpsichordist w. Westchester Symph. Orch.; num. solo & chmbr. music perfs. as keyboard player; Fac. Mbr., Westchester Conserv. of Music, 1944-; Tchr. of Music Theory, Scarsdale Alternative HS. Mbrships: incl: Am. Mudicol. Soc.; Libn., Music Tchrs. Coun. of Westchester; Sec., Bd., Music Educators League of Westchester. Hobby: Travel. Address: 58 Brite Ave., Scarsdale, NY 10583, USA. 5.

HARRIS, Carl Gordon, Jr., b. 14 Jan. 1935, Fayette, Mo., USA. Professor of Music; Chairman, Dept. of Music; Director of Choral Activities. Educ: AB, Philander Smith Coll., Little Rock. Ark.; AM Univ. of Mo. at Columbia; Vienna State Acad. of Music; DMusA, Conserv. of Music, Univ. of Mo. at Kansas city. Career: currently Dir. of Choral Activities & Prof. of Music, Va., State Univ., Petersburg. Recordings: as Cond., w. Va. State Univ. Concert Choir - The Undine Smith Moore Song Book (1974). Contbr. to: Choral Jrnl.; Mo. Jrnl. of Rsch. in Music Educ.; Chant Choral. Mbrships. incl: Phi Mu Alpha Sinfonia; Alpha Kappa Mu; Am. Choral Dir. Assn.; Choral Conds. Guild of Am.;. AGO. Hobbies: Continuo Playing; Antique Keyboard Instruments; Operatic Record Collecting. Address: Box 7, Va. State Coll., Petersburg, VA 23803, USA. 7.

HARRIS, Catharine Elizabeth, b. 19 May 1949, Birmingham, UK. Orchestral Musician (Viola & Violin); Music Teacher. Educ: ARCM (piano tchrs. dip.); GRSM (at RCM); Dip Ed, Newton Park Coll., Bath. m. Chris J Harris. Debut: piano solo, Wycombe Abbey, 1963. Career: Piano Soloist & Orchl. Violist, 1964-67; Orchl. Violist, 1967-; Tchr. of theory, piano, violin, viola. Hobbies: Numismatics; Gardening; Naturalist. Address: 9 pankhurst Cres., Stevenage, Herts SG2 0QB, UK.

HARRIS, Donald, b. 7 April 1931, St. Paul, Minn., USA. Composer; Administrator. Educ: B Mus, 1952; M Mus, 1954, Univ. of Mich. 2 s. Career incls: Asst. to Pres. for Acad. Affairs, 1967-71, VP, 1971-74, Exec. VP, 1974-, New England Conserv. of Music; Comp. in Residence, Prof. of Music & Chmn., Dept. of Comp. and Theory, Hartt Coll. of Music, 1978-. Comps. incl: Piano sonata, 1956; Symph. in Two Movements, 1961; String Quartet, 1966; Ludus I, 1966; Ludus II, 1973; On Variations, 1976; For the Night to Wear; Charmes; num. commissions. num. recordings sev. scholarships & grants. Contbr. to profl. jrnls. Hons. incl: ASCAP Awards, 1973-74 & 1974-75. Address: 74 Union Pl., 414 Hartford, CT06103, USA.

HARRIS, Ellen T., b. 4 Dec. 1945, Paterson, NJ, USA. Assistant Professor of Music. Educ: AB, Brown Univ., 1967; MA, 1970, PhD, 1976, Univ. of Chicago. m. John T Harris, 2 d. Career: Asst. Prof. of Music, Columbia Univ. Publs: Handel and the Pastoral Tradition, 1980. Contbr. to: Jrnl. of the Am. Musicol. Soc.; Musical Quarterly; Notes. Mbr., Am. Musicol. Soc. Hons: Marion Hassenfield premium in music, Brown Univ., 1965-66; Elijah Benjamin Andrews Scholar, Brown Univ., 1966-67; Marc Perry Galler Prize, Univ. of Chicago, 1976; Nat. Endowment for the Humanities summer stipend for musicol. research, 1978; Columbia Univ. Coun. for Rsch. in the Humanities Rsch. Grant, 1978, '79. Hobbies: Perf. as soprano soloist; Taking voice lessons. Address: 560 Riverside Drive, Apt. 21M, NY, NY 10027, USA.

HARRIS, Floyd Olin, b. 30 Nov. 1913, Wichita, Kansas, USA. Director of Bands & Ensembles. Educ: BS, McPherson Coll., Kansas; Grad. work at Univ. of Northern Colo., Univ. of Neb., Univ. of Denver & Colo. Univ. m. Marilee McLaughlin, 2 s, 1 d. Career: 41 yrs. of experience as tchr. of instrumental & vocal music in the publ. schls. in Kansas & Colo.; 13 yrs. of experience as Dir. of Adult & Jr. Choirs in ch. work. Comps. incl: 60 instrumental solos & ensembles for schls.; 13 secular & sacred choral octavos; 7 children's songs; 5 Choral & Instrumental Books. Publs: (jr. choir books) The Cherubim Collection, 1955; Marching Forward, 1957; The 20 and 1, 1960; Lidwig Collection of Floyd O Harris Clarinet Solos, 1972. Contbr. to: Tchr.; Wee Wisdom. Address: 3032 S Ivan Way, Denver, CO 80227, USA. 9, 28, 29.

HARRIS, Rex, b. 18 Dec. 1904, Crayford, Kent, UK. Ophthalmic Optician; Author; Broadcaster; Journalist. Educ:

Colfe's & London Refraction Hosp. m. Mary St. Leger-Chambers, 2 s. Career: Lectr. on Jazz Music, Num. Co. Educl. Authborities, Schls. & Univ.; Regular broadcaster on Jazz Music, Num. Co. Educl. Authorities, Schls. & Univ.; Regular broadcaster on Jazz, over 20 yrs.; Chmn., Selection Comm., Jazz book Club; Fndr. Mbr., Past Chmn., Nat Fedn. of Jazz Orgs. Composition; Rex Marks the White Spot. Recording: The Story of Jazz. Publs: Jazz, 1952, 5 eds.; Recorded Jazz, 1957; The Story of Jazz, 1954; Enjoying Jazz, 1962, 2 eds.; Contbr., The Decca Book of Jazz. Contbr., num. UK, US jrnls. Mbrship: Savage Club. Hons: Freeman, City of London. Hobbies: Gardening; Amateur dramatics; Astronomy. Address: Mary Croft, Valley Rd., Rickmansworth, Herts. WD3 4DT, UK. 3.

HARRIS, Robert A., b. 8 May 1928, Rich Hill, Mo., USA. Musician (Piano & Organ); Professor of Piano & Music History. Educ: BMus, MSEd, Pitts. (Ks.) State Univ.; Post-grad., Aspen Music Schl., Colo.; Piano pupil of Rosina Levinne; Cert., Piano, Music Tchrs. Nat. Assn. & Mo. State Bd. Educ.; Cert. Dir. Music, United Meth. Ch. Career: Prof., Piano & Music Hist., Mo. Southern State Coll., Joplin, Mo.; Organist, 1st United Meth. Ch., Carthage, Mo. Mbrships: Nat. Fedn. Music Clubs; Music Tchrs. Nat. Assn.; Mo. Music Tchrs. Assn.; Am. Music Scholarship. Assn.; Fellowship United Meth. Musicians. Hobby: Tape Recording. Address: 1344 S Main St., Carthage, MO 64836, USA. 8, 28, 29.

HARRIS, Russell G (ingrich), b. 3 Aug. 1914, Graymont, Ill., USA. Music Educator; Composer; Pianist. Educ: BMus, Knox Coll.; MMus, Univ. of Mich.; Univ. of S Calif.; Mills Coll.; studied comp. w. Ernst Krenek, Darius Milhaud, Ernst Toch, Egon Wellesz, Bela Rozsa & Healey Willan. m. Dorothy L Stephenson (div.), 1d. Career: Music educator, 1935-79, at Baylor Univ., Upper Iowa Univ., Hamline Univ. (chmn. of music dept.); apps. on TV (harpsichord & clavichord); soloist (hurdy-gurdy) w. St. Paul's Chmbr. & Minn. orchs.; comps. perf. in Europe & USA. Comps: over 150 works in all instrumental & vocal media. Recordings: Tarye No Longer; It was beginning winter; The Moon is Hiding. Publs: article on Ockeghem & Dufay Masses in Hamline Studies in Musicology. Contbr. to: St. Paul's Pioneer-Dispatch; Prog. Notes for St. Paul's Chmbr. Orch. Mbrships: Am. Musicol Soc.; MTNA; for organ, nat. competition, 1935. songs perf. ISCM, NYC, 1941. Address: 1815 Englewood Ave., St. Paul's, MN 55104, USA. 8, 11.

HARRIS, Stanley James Philip, b. 21 Feb. 1909, Seven Kings, Essex, UK. Organ Builder. Educ: Bus. Trng. Coll.; London Chmbr. Comm. (distinction). m. Kate Irene Dando, 1 d. Career: Civ. Serv. w. War Dept. & War Damage Commn., Joined Robert Slater & Son, 1951; Prin., ibid., 1952-; Num. commns., var. chs., colls. & residences inclng. Dora Cohen Hall, Lady Spencer Churchill Coll., Wheatley, Oxon. Contbr. to: Musical Opinion; Pamphlets. Mbr., Inst. Musical Instrument Technol., London. Recip. Hon. Mention, Sumner's The Organ, 3rd ed. Hobbies: Organ Playing; Organ Publs. Address: 2 The Drummonds, Knighton Lane, Buckhurst Hill, Essex 1G9 5HG, UK.

HARRIS, William Lewarne Capes, b. 23 May 1929, Birkenhead, UK. Composer; Pianist; Conductor. Educ: Comp. & piano, RCM, 1950-52; ARCM. div., 2 s, 1 d. Career: Broadcast Suite for Viola & Piano, BBC 3rd Prog., 1953; Music Tchr., Schls. in Kent, 1955-58; Recitals of works, London, 1959, '61, '73, Twickenham & Richmond, 1975; cond., 1 st perfs. of Inglis Gundry's operas, The Prisoner Paul, 1970, & The Three Wise Men, 1972. Comps. incl: Suite for Viola & Piano; Cantata de Femmina; countess Cathleen· (opera); 2 song cycles; The Woman on the Hill (Chmbr. Opera), 1977; Chansons de Baudelaire, 1978. Recordings: Cond. & Pianist, var. works of I Gundry, 1975. Contbr. to newspapers & mags. Mbrships. incl: CGGB. Hons. incl: Lionel Tertis Prize 1952. Hobbies: Folklore; Swimming; Walking. Address: 26 Park Ct., Park Hall Rd., London SE21 8DZ, UK.

HARRISON, Derek Birch, b. 12 May 1947, Bath, Somerset, UK. Singer (counter-tenor); Musical Director; Musician (organ & Harpsichord). Educ: MA, St. Edmund Hall, Oxford Univ., FRCO; Music Tchrs. Cert., London Univ. m. Rosemary Anne Stanser. Career: Chorister, Salisbury Cathedral; Mbr., Clerkes of Oxenford, Musica Deo Sacra; Dpty. Lay Clerk, St Paul's Cathedral, London; Counter-tenor soloist & rebec player w. St. George's Canzona; Mbr., St. George's Baroque Ensemble; Musical Dir. & Fndr., Patchwork Concerts for children; Musical Dir., de Merc Chmbr. Choir; Musical Dir., Hertford Choral Soc.; Var. recordings made as counter-tenor soloist w. St. George's Canzona (Argo, EMI, Oryz labels, etc.) Mbrship: Inc. Soc. of Musicians. Hobbies: Golf; Computer Sci. Address: 71 Finchmoor, Harlow, Essex, UK.

HARRISON, E Earnest, b. 13 July 1918, Moberly, Mo., USA. College Professor; Orchestral Soloist on Oboe, English Horn &

Obo d'Amore. Educ: Moberly Jr. Coll.; B Mus, (1942), M Mus. (1946). & Perfs. Cert., Eastman Schl. of Music, Univ. of Rochester. m. Phyllis Hunter, 2 s., 3 d. Career: w. All. Am. Youth Orch. (under Stokowski), Rochester Phil., Houston Symph., San Antonio Symph., Nat. Symph., Wash. Choral Soc., Nat. Gall. Orch., & Wash. Opera Soc.; has made radio & TV apps. on CBS & NBC; player w. Nat. Capitol Woodwind Quintet, Timm Woodwind Quintet of LA. State Univ. & Baroque Ensemble; Prof., Schl of Music, La. State Univ., Baton Rouge; Cons. w. Dr. Everett Tim on his book 'The Woodwinds'. Sev. recordings. Publs: The Story of the Oboe & English Horn, 1973; Ed. Sonata in A major by Telemann, 1971. Contbr. to: Woodwind World; Brass & Percussion. Mbrships: NACWAPI; Int. Double Reed Soc.; MENC; Am. Fedn. of Musicians; Phi Mu Alpha Sinfonia; Pi Kappa Lambda. Hobbies: Photography; Swimming; Fishing. Address: 2053 Tamarix St., Baton Rouge, LA 70808, USA.

HARRISON, Francis Llewelyn, b. 29 Sept. 1905, Dublin, Ireland. Musicologist. Educ: Royal Irish Acad. of Music, Dublin; Mus B, Trinity Coll., Dublin Univ., 1926; Mus D, ibid, 1929; MA Oxford Univ.; D Mus ibid, 1952. m. Joan Harrison-Rimmer. Career: Prof. of Music, Queen's Univ., Kingston, Ont., Can., 1935, Colgate Univ., Hamilton, NY, USA, 1946, Wash. Univ., St. Louis, 1947; Lectr., History of Music, Oxford Univ., 1952; Sr., Lectr., 1956, Rdr., 1962-70, ibid; Sr. Rsch. Fellow, Jesus Coll., Oxford, 1965-70; Prof. of Ethnomusicol. Univ. of Amsterdam, 1970-76; Prof. Emeritus, ibid., 1976; Vis. Mbr., Inst. for Advanced Study, Princeton, Univ., 1957; Vis. Prof., var. Univs. & Coll., USA, 1958-72. Recordings: Medieval English Lyrics; Richard Davy, Passion According to St. Matthew; Eton Choir book, Record 2; Now Make We Merthe. Publs: The Eton Choirbook, 3 vols., 1956-61; w. J A Westrup, Collins Music Encyclopedia, 1956; Music in Medieval Britan, 1958, 1963; William Munday, Latin Antiphons & Psalms, 1963; w. M Hood, C Palisca, Musicology, 1963; w. Joan Rimmer, European Musical Instruments, 1964; 14th-Century Motets of French Provenance, 1969; Now Make We Merthe; Medieval & Renaissance Carols, 1968; Time, Place & Music, & w. E. Dobson, Medieval English Songs, 1974. Contbr. to var. profl. jrnls. Mbr. num. profl. orgs. Named Fellow, Brit. Acad., 1965. Hobbies: Travel; Eating; Model Railways. Address: 83 A Kloveniersburgwal, Amsterdam-C, Holland. 1.

HARRISON, Jay Smolens, b. 25 Jan. 1927, New York City, USA. Music Critic; Musicologist; Teacher. Educ: NY Univ. Career: Instr. of Music, NY Univ., 1948-55; Asst. Prof., ibid, 1955-56; Guest Critic, NY Hearld Times, 1948-52 Assoc. Critic, 1952; Music Ed., 1952-60; Ed., Music Mag., 1960-61; Dir., Readers Digest Music Ins., 1961-63; Scriptwriter for Radio & TV, 1954-; Assoc. prod., Metropol, Opera broadcasts, 1954-; Ed. in Chief, Musical America, 1963-64; Advsr. to NY State Coun. on the Arts, 1962-; Mbr., US Nat. Coun. on the Arts & Govt., 1955-; Permanent Panellist, Metropol. Opera Quiz radio broadcasts, 1958-72; Dir., Editorial Servs., Columbia Records, 1964-67; Assoc. prof. Queen's Coll., CUNY, 1958-72. Hobby - Playwriting. Address: 741 W. End Ave., NY, NY 10025, USA.

HARRISON, Pamela, b. 28 Nov. 1915, Orpington, Kent, UK. Composer; Accompanist. Educ: ARCM (Perf.'s Piano). m. Harvey Phillips (separated), 2 s. Debut: Wigmore Hall, London. Comps. incl: (published) A Suite for Tomothy; A Present for Paul; Piano Anderida (6 pieces for piano solo); Drifting Away (Clarinet & Piano); Sonnet for Cello & Piano; Lament for Viola & Piano; (recorded from broadcasts Sonatas for Cello & Piano, Clarinet & Piano, & Viola & Piano; Conertante for Piano & String. Orch.; Piano Trio; Quintet for Clarinet & Str. Quartet; var. song cycles. Mbrships: CGGB; ISM; Monumental Brass Soc.; Royal Horticultural Soc.; Sherborne Art Club. Hobbies: Painting; Gardening. Address: The Old Toll House, Yarlington, Wincanton, Somerset, UK.

HARRISON, Ronald Derwyn, b. 21 Oct. 1932, Hamilton, Ont., Can. Composer of Film Music; Pianist; Organist; Synthesizer. Educ: Royal Conserv. of Music, Hamilton, Toronto, Ont.; Eastman Schl. of Music, Rochester, NY; studied 10 yrs. w. Gordon Delament, NY. m. Jean Harrison, 1 s., 2 d. Debut: comp. for 10 Centuries concert, Univ. of Toronto, 1964. Career: Comps. for Int. TV Films & series incl. To the Wild Country; Matt & Jenny; The Canadian ·Establishment; Audubon WildLife Theatre; Adventures in Rainbow Country & Wings in the Wilderness; Feature & TV films distributed to 60 countries. Recordings: Moods of the Wild (own comps.); Portage - Bondfield Dickson. Mbrships: Can. Guild of Film Comps.; CAPAC. Hobbies: Sailing; Tennis. Address: 6 Oriole Gdns., Toronto, Ont. M4V 1V7, Can.

HARRISON, Sidney, b. May 1903, London, UK. Concert Pianist; Teacher; Broadcaster; Writer. Educ: GSMD, London;

FGSM; Hon. RAM. m. Phyllis S Graham, 1 d. Debut: early 1920's. Career: Hundreds of radio broadcasts & TV appearances at home & abroad (inclng. Aust., NZ., Canada); Gave the first ever TV piano lesson, 1950; Prof., RAM, London; Many engagements for lecture-recitals, master classes, etc. Publs: Music for the Multitude, 1939; Beginning to Play the Piano (TV lessons, 1950; Teacher Never Told Me, 1961; The Music Makers, 1962; The Young Person's Guide to Playing the Piano, 1966; Grand Piano (in prep.) Mbrships: ISM; Brit. Fedn. of Comp Musical Fests. Hobbies: Travel; Reading; Gardening. Mgmt: Ibbs & Tillett. Address: 57 Harlington Rd. London W4, 3TS, UK.

HARRISS, Donald Steven, b. 10 Sept. 1948, St. Louis, Mo., USA. Keyboardist (including synthesizers). Educ: 15 yrs. classical piano study; Training in Harpsichord, Pipe Organ & electronic synthesis. m. Sandra Harriss, 1d. Career incls: Wrote scores for stage plays - Cuchulainn, San Fran., 1969, The Bacchae, San Fran., 1968, Hosea, Palo Alto, 1978; Num. radio apps. Recordings: Stay With Me; Under The Influence. Mbrships: ASCAP (CAPAC); Can. Fedn. of Musicians. Hobby: Sailplane Flying. Address: 2430 Agnes Way, Palo Alto, CA 94303, USA.

HARRISS, Elaine Atkins, b. 20 Oct. 1945, Springfield, Tenn., USA. Pianist; Flautist; Educator. Educ: BMusEd, George Peabody Coll., 1966; MMusEd, ibid, 1967; Specialist in Educ., George Peabody Coll., 1968; Cand., Philos., Univ. of Mich. m. Ernest Charles Harriss, 1 s. Career: Prin. Flautist, Jackson (Tenn.) Symph.; Flautist, Univ. Trio; Instructor & Staff Accomp., Univ. of Tenn. at Martin; Recitalist (piano, flute); Piano soloist w. Jackson Symph.; Fac. mbr., Sewanee Summer Music Center. Mbrships. incl: Province VP, Sigma Alpha Iota; MENC; Nat. Flute Assn.; Music Tchrs. Nat. Assn. (Local Sec.ÇTreas.); Phi Delta Kappa. Hons. incl: Algernon Sidney Sullivan Award; Sigma Alpha Iota Leadership Award. Address: Route No. 4, Mimosa Drive, Martin, Tenn., USA.

HARROD, Sheila Georgina, b. 27 Jan. 1944, Swindon, Wilts., UK Music School Principal. Educ: LTCL. m. Christopher Leslie Harrod. Career: Prin., Kentwood Schl. of Music, Swindon; Tutor in voice prod., pianoforte & theory; Cond., Kentwood Choir, incl. appearances on BBC Radio & TV, tours of Calif., Germany and Norway. Contbr. to local newspapers. Hons: Many prizes in Music Festivals, Swindon, Bath, Bristol, Basingstoke, Devizes, Oxford, Cheltenham, London & Bournemouth; Swindon Champion Singer, 1967. Hobbies: Good eating; Keeping fit. Address: 48 Collett Ave., Swindon, Wilts., UK. 3

HARRON, LeRoy Peter, b. 12 May 1908, Clear Springs, Tex., USA. Violinist; Violist; String Bass Player. Educ: BA & MA, Univ. of Southern Calif. m. Wilva Edith Deskins, 1 s., 1 d. Career: played w. orchs. & ensembles, Developer, Harron String Instrument Bows & Conductors Batons, other items of musical merchandise marketed. Contbr. to pamphlets & trade mags. Hobbies: Playing duets; Trout fishing. Address. 29705 109th Ave. SE, Auburn, WA 98002, USA.

HART, Dunstan, b. 24 Feb. 1903, Croydon, UK. Operatic Baritone. Educ: Open Schlrship., Singing, RMC; ARCM; LRAM. m. Doris Mary Ingrams, 1 s., 1 d. Debut: Royal Albert Hall Ballad, Concerts. Career: Glyndebourne Opera Co., 1940; Tours, S Africa, Aust., Spain; London musicals, Wigmore Hall recitals, radio & TV concerts & opera. Recording: The Dancing Years. Mbrship: Savage Club. Hobbies: Bowls; Gardening; Motoring. Address:

HART, Leen't, b. 39 Apr. 1920, Delft, Netherlands. Composer; Carillonneur; Organist; Director; Writer. Educ: State Dip., Organ, 1941; Final Dip., Carillon, Mechelen, Belgium, 1950. m. Maria L Dorland, 1 s., 2 d. Debut: Carillon, Delft, 1938; Organ, ibid, 1939. Career: City Carillonneur, Delft, 1943-, Leiden, 1952, Amersfoort, 1953, Rotterdam, 1956; Organist, Delft, 1938-; Dir. Netherlands Carillon Schl., Amersfoort, 1953; Radio & TV apps, The Netherlands, Belgium, Switz., Germany, Denmark, Sweden, Brazil, USA, Spain, Aust. & Canada. Comps. incl: Laren Suite, 1970; Ann Arbor Suite, 1974; Springfield Suite; Dorische Suite; Dorishche Toccata; Preludes, Etudes, etc. Var. recordings. Publs. incl: Campanalogie, 1968; Improvisation (carillon), 1975; Handbook for the Carillonneur, 1977. Contbr. to: Organist en Eredienst; Klok en Klepel. Mbrships. incl: Hon. Mbr., GCNA; KNTV; GENECO. Hons. incl: 1st Prize, Int. Carillon Contest, Ireland, 1958; Kt. Order of Oranje, Nassau, 1975; Leuve-penning Medal, Rotterdam, 1975; Gold Medal, Barcelona, Spain, 1976. Hobbies: Photography; Travel. Address: Hooglandseweg 18, 3864 PV Nijkerkerveen, The Netherlands.

HART, Perry, b. 30 June 1928, Byron Bay, Aust. Violinist. Educ: Sydney Conservatorium of Music; pvte. study w.

Szymon Goldberg. m. Ronald La Fontaine, 1 s. Debut: Amsterdam, Netherlands. Career: Solo Tours, Aust. (for Aust. Broadcasting Commissioon) & Indonesia; Solo apps., Netherlands & UK; Tours w. piano & str. trios & London Oboe Quartet, Europe & Israel; Prof., GSM. Has recorded w. Oromonte Piano Trio & London Oboe Quartet. Mbrships: ISM; European Str. Tchrs. Assn. Hobbies: Gardening; Reading; Needlework. Address: 50 Suffolk Rd., Barnes, London SW13,UK.

HART, William Sebastion, b. 1920, Baltimore Md., USA. Symphony Orchestra Conductor; Educator; Lecturer. Educ: Peabody Conserv. of Music; John s Hopkins Univ.; Golden State Univ.; Allen Univ.; St. Mary's Coll., Univ. of Tex., gaining PhD; D Mus; LHD LL D. m. Regina Litsch. Career: Musical Dir., Gettysburg Sump. Orch. Inc., 1958-. Compositions: for Solo Percussions Music. Mbrships. incl: Am. Musicological Sco. Hobbies: Pol. Sci., Languages; Public Speaking; Theatre; Intelligent Discussion. Address: 1800 Cromwell Bridge Rd., Baltimore, MD 21234, USA.2.

HARTINGER, Albert F., b. 13 July 1946, Seekirchen, Salzburg, Austria. Singer (baritone). Educ: Abitur; Doct. (Educ.ÇPsychol.); Voice & opera, Mozarteum, Salzburg; Grad., authentic interpretation of baroque music, music educ. m. Heather G Woodall, 3 c. Career: Concerts, Austria, Germany, Italy; TV & radio recordings (oratorios, cantatas & lieder), Austria & Germany; Mbr., Salzburg Baroque Ensemble; Art Dir., Salzburger Bach-Gesellschaft. Hons: Winner, Mozart Competition, Mozarteum, 1970. Hobbies: Mountaineering; Skiing; Model railways. Address: Mölckhofgasse 3a, A-5020 Salzburg, Austria.

HARTLEY, Keith, b. 6 Oct. 1947, Huddersfield, UK. Musician (Double Bass). Educ: Royal Manchester Coll. of Music; GRSM; ARMCM (Tchrs. & perf.); Dip. in Educ. Career: BBC Northern Orch., 1970-72; BBC Concert Orch., 1972-74; RPO, 1974-; Formed The Forellen Ensemble form mbrs. of the RPO, 1977. Hons: Hiles Gold Medal, RMCM, 1969. Address: 18 Rosecroft Gdn., London NW2, UK.

HARTLEY, Walter Sinclair, b. 21 Feb., 1927, Wash. DC, USA. Composer; Pianist; Educator. Educ: B Mus., Eastman Schl. Music, Univ. of Rochester NY, 1950; M Mus., Grad. Schl., Univ. of Rochester 1951; PhD in Music, ibid, 1953. m. Sandra Mount, 2 d. Career: Tchr., Nat. Music Camp, Interlochen, Mich., 1956-64; Assoc. Prof. of Music, SUNY, Fredonia, NY., 1969; Prof., ibid, 1974. Comps: over 120 publd. works, mostly instrumental works, inclng. Sonata for Tuba & Piano, 1967; Metamorphoses for Clarinet & Piano, 1975; Octet for Saxophones, 1975. Contbr. to: Jrnl. Band Rsch.; Instrumentalist; World Saxophone Congress Newsletter. Mbrships: ASCAP; Coll. Music Soc.; MENC; AAUP. Hons: GC Conn Brass Music Award for Sinfonia No. 3 for brass choir, 1964; SUNY Rsch. Grants in Comp., 1970, '71, '74. Hobby: Reading. Address: 60 Maple Ave., Fredonia NY 14063, USA.

HARTMAN, Vernon, b. 12 July 1952, Dallas, Tex., USA. Opera Singer. Educ: N Tex. State Univ.; Dip., Acad. of Vocal Arts, Phila. Debut: Fort Worth Opera, 1974. Career: Leading Baritone, NY City Opera; apps. at Spoleto Fest., Dallas Civic Opera, Western Opera Theater, A solo Opera, State Opera of Conn., Opera co. of Phila., Shreveport Opera, Wilmington Opera, Chautaugua Opera, Pittsburgh Opera, Charlotte Opera, Dayton Phil., Opera Midwest, Balt. Symph.; roles incl.; Almaviva (Marriage of Figaro), Figaro (Barber of Seville), Bretigny (Manon), Silvio (Pagliacci), Louis (The Wandering Scholar), Iago (Otello), Valentin (Faust); apps. on film, TV & Radio. Hobbies: Athletics; Cooking. Mgmt: LowÇBenson, NY. Address: 32201 Delaire Landing Rd., Phila., PA 19114, USA.

HARTWELL, Hugh Kenneth, b. 18 Jan. 1945, Hamilton, Ont., Can. Composer; Theorist; Professor. Educ: BMus, McGill Univ.; MA, PhD, Univ. of Pa. m. Elizabeth Irwin. Career: Asst. Prof., Kirkland Coll., Clinton, NY, 1971-76; Asst. Prof., McMaster Univ., 1976-79; Assoc. Prof., ibid., 1979-. Comps: Soul Piece for 6 or 7 Players, 1969; Matinee d'Ivresse, 1971; Septet, 1971; Resta di darmi noia...1978; Waltz Inventions, 1979; Acitore; How to Play Winning Bridge; 3 x 3 - an epigram; Piece for Piano. Sev. radio recordings. Mbr., Can. League of Comps. Hons. incl: num. commissions & grants; Can. Coun. Doct. Fellowship, 1968-71; Univ. of Pa. Tchng. Fellowship, 1968-71; David Halstead Prize, 1969; Helen Nitche Prize in Comps., 1970. Address: 1966 Main Street West, Hamilton, Ont., Can.

HARTWIG, Dieter, b. 18 July 1934, Dresden, Germany. Musicologist (piano, organ). Educ: Dip. music, Leipzig univ., 1959; PhD, Leipzig, 1963; Habilitation, 1970. m. Urte Petzoldt, 1 s. Career; music prod., Saxony regional theatre,

Dresden, 1960-5; chief prod. deputy arts dir., Dresden Philharmonie, from 1965; also pt.-time lectr., Dresden. Publs: incl: Rudolf Wagner-Régeny-Der Opernkomponist, 1965; Die Dresdner Philharmonie 1870-1970, 1970; Fidelio F. Finke-Leben u. Werk, 1970; Kurt Masür für Sie portraitiert, 1976. Contbr. to num. profl. jrnls. Mbrships: comps. & musicians union of German Dem. Repub.; Kulturbund der D D R; Dresden Intelligensia club. Hons: Anderson-Nexö art prize, Dresden, 1974. Address: 8051 Dresden, Neubühlauerstr. 19, German Dem. Repub.

HARTZELL, Marjorie, b. 1 May 1938, Plainfield, NJ, USA. Harpist. Educ: B Mus & Perf's Cert., Eastman Schl. of Music. m. Karl Drew Hartzell, Jr., 1 d. Career: Prin. Harp, Buffalo Phil. Orch., NY, 1960-66; Prin. Harp, Albany Symph Orch., NY, 1967-; Lake George Opera Fest., NY, 1970-. Mbrships: Am. Harp Soc. Recip. Fulbright Grant, 1966-67. Address: 10 Glenwood St., Albany, NY 12203, USA.

HARUTUNIAN, John Martin, b. 29 Aug. 1948, Watertown, Mass., USA. Graduate Student in Musicology. Educ: B Mus, Wheaton Coll., Ill., 1969; Grad. Study, Harvard Univ., 1969-70; MA, Univ. of Pa., 1975; PhD candidate, UCLA. Debut: Soloist Boston Pops Orch., 1965. Career: Performed own comp., Fantasy-Govotte, Youth Concerts, w. Boston Symph Orch., 1966. Mbr., Am. Musicol. Soc. Recip. Paderewski Medal, 1966. Hobby: Collecting recordings of Arturo Toscanini. Address: 355 Newtonville Ave., Newtonville, MA 02160, USA.

HARVERSON, Alan, b. Ireland. Organist; Harpsichordist. Edu: RAM. Career: recitals & broadcasts, Germany, Netherlands, Sweden, Denmark, Belgiuim & GB; Harpsichordist, London Concertante; Assoc. & Prof. of Organ, RAM. Recordings: sev. LPs of music by Bach & early composers. Recip of RAM Prizes for Organ, Piano. Mgmt: Ibbs & Tillett, London. Address: 34 Park Farm Cl., London N2 OPU, UK.

HARVEY, Anthony Keith, b. 13 Apr. 1938, Waterloo, UK. Cellist. Edu: RAM; ARAM. m. Meralyn Knight, 2 s. Debut: London, 1959. Career: Prin. Cellist, LPO, Engl. Chmbr. Orch.; num. radio & TV broadcasts. Recordings: quartets by Dvorak, Schubert, Borodin, Shostakovitch, Brahms, Mozart, Beethoven, Wm. Alwyn, Mendelssohn; sinfonia concertantes by Haydn & J C Bach. Hobbies: Swimming; Antiques; Collecting Books & 78rpm Records; Theatre; Cimema. Mgmt: Harold Holt Ltd. Address: 23 St. John's Wood Terrace, London NW8, UK.

HARVEY, Arthur Wallace, b. 20 May 1939, Boston, Mass., USA. Tenor Soloist; conductor; Lecturer; Organist; University Professor Educ: BS, Gordon Coll., Wenham, Mass., 1959; Boston Univ., Mass., 1965; DMA, Temple Univ., Phila., Pa., 1974. Career: Tchr., Maine, NB, Can., Pa., NJ, RI, Ky.; Sacred concerts in 22 States & 4 Can. Provinces; Apps. on TV & Radio in 8 States; Extensive workshop experience in Ch. Music, Creative Tchng., Orff Schulwerk, & Creative Movement. Mbrships. incl: Music Educators Nat. Conf.; Ky. Music Educators Assn. Contbr. to profl. publs. Hobbies incl: Travel. Address: Susan Dr., Hillcrest R9, Richmond, KY 40475, USA.

HARVEY, Bobby, b. 3 Feb. 1935, Milngavie, Scotland, UK. Scottish Fiddler. Educ: Royal Scottish Acad., Glasgow. m. Cathie Symington, 1 s, 1 d. Debut: BBC Hootenanny Shows. Career: Apps., many series of Scottish TV & BBC & Grampian TV shows. Recordings: Aye on the Fiddle; Sailing up the Clyde; backing on many recordings of Will Starr, Andy Stewart, Calum Kennedy, etc. Mbrships: Glasgow Soc. of Musicians; Glasgow Press Club. Hons: Scottish Fiddle Champion, 1962, '63; Judge of Scottish Championship, 1977; Judge of Golden Fiddle Awards, 1979. Hobbies: Golf; Sailing; Football. Address: 66 Braefoot Ave., Milngavie, Scotland, UK.

HARVEY, Dorothy Fay (née Wood), b. 23 July 1935, Mansfield, UK. Teacher of Piano & Percussion. Educ: studied piano w. Edwin Benbow, RCM, 1955-58; pvte. piano study w. Nellie Houseley; ARCM. m. Paul Harvey; /d. Career: Percussionist, Scottish Nat. Orch., Ballet Rambert, Etc.; Pripatetic Tchr., Borough of Richmond upon Thames; Prof. of Pianoforte, Royal Mil. Schl. of Music, Kneller Hall, 1974-. Recip. Major Co. Award (Notts) to RCM, 1955. Hobby: Painting. Address: 36 Alton Gdns., Twickenham, Middx., UK.

HARVEY, Jean, b. 2 Jan. 1932, Glasgow, Scotland, UK. Concert Artist (violin & piano); Professor of Piano, Violin & Chamber Music. Edu: RAM, London; FRAM. Debut: Dual concerto perfs., Promenade Concerts, 1954. Career: Prof. of piano, violin & chmbr. music, RAM, London; Broadcaster; Examiner; Adjudicator. Mbr., ISM. Hons: Worshipful Musicians of London Silver Medal, 1953. Hobbies: Gardening; Cinema; Reading. Address: Kittswood, Three Gates Lane, Haslemere, Surrey, UK. 27.

HARVEY, Jonathan Dean, b. 3 May 1939, Sutton Coldfield, UK. Senior Lecturer in Music. Educ: MA, St. John's Coll., Cambridge; Mus, D ibid; PhD, Glasgow Univ.; studies w. Erwin Stein, Hans Keller. m. Rosaleen Marie Harvey, 1 d., 1 s. Career: Harkness Fellow, Princeton Univ., 1969-70; Sr. Lectr. in Music, Southampton Univ.; Rdr. in Music, Univ. of Sussex. Compositions: Symphony; Benedictus; Persephone Dream, for orch.; Cantatas I-VII; Inner Light 1-3, instruments & tape; var. shorter pieces. Author, The Music of Stockhausen: An introduction, 1974. Contbr. to: Music Review; Perspectives of New Music; Tempo; Musical Times; Times Lit. Supp. Music & Letters. Mbrships: Brit. Sect., ISCM Committee; Exec. Committee, SPNM; CGGB; Music Panel, Southern Arts Assn.; Assn. of Univ. Tchrs Recip. Clements Memorial Prize, 1963. Hobbies: Tennis, Skiing. Mgmt: Novello & Co, Faber Music. Address: 35 Houndean Rise, Lewes, Sussex, UK.3.

HARVEY, Marion Bradley, b. 3 Sept. 1916, Phila., Pa., USA. Singer; Teacher of Singing. Educ: incls: Dip. & Post-grad. Dif., Juilliard Schl. of Music; B Mus, MA, Univ. of Pa.; pvte. study w. noted tchrs. m. Burlingame Harvey, 2 children. Debut: as Clarina, Rossini's La Cambiale di Matrimonio, NYC, 1939. Career incls: var. roles w. Gotham Opera Co., NYC, inclng. Madama Rosa, Donizetti's Il Campanelo di Notte; Esmeralda, Dvorak's The Bartered Bride, Wilmington Opera Soc.; Lieder Recitals; Mbr.; Philomel Trio (voice, flute, piano); Voice fac., Phila. Conserv. of Music, 1946-62, Phila. Coll. of the Performing Arts & Wilmington Music Schl., 1962-. Mbrships. incl: Nat. Assn. Tchrs of Singing; Am. Musicol. Soc. Recip. var. hons. Address: 2414 Knowles Rd., Wilmington, DE 19810, USA.

HARVEY, Paul Milton, b. 14 June 1935, Sheffield, UK. Clarienettist; Saxophonist; Composer. Educ: LRAM; ARCM; RCM. m. Dorothy Fay Wood, 1 d. Career: SNO; Bournemouth Symph. Orch.; Prof. of Clarinet, TCM; currently, Prof. of Clarinet, Royal Mil. Schl. of Music, Kneller Hall, & Ldr., London Saxophone Quartet. Comps: Clarinet Concerto; 3 Saxophone Concertinos; Chester Saxophone Series; many other Works for clarinet & saxophone. Recordings: London Saxophone Quartet. Publs: The Clarinettist's Bedside Book, 1978. Contbr. to profl. publs. Mbrships: VP, Clarinet & Saxophone Soc. of GB; Int. Clarinet Soc.; N Am. Saxophone Alliance; Comps. Guild. Recip., var. hons. Hobbies: Eating; Sleeping. Mgmt: Barbara Graham Mgmt. Address: 36 Alton Gdns., Twickenham, Middlesex, UK.

HARVEY, Trevor, b. 30 May, 1911, Freshwater, Isle of Wight, UK. Orchestral Conductor; Critic of Classical Gramophone Records. Educ: Heberden Organ Schlr., Brasenose Coll., Oxford; BA B Mus, Oxon. Career: has made sev. records; regular aps. on BBC Radio 3, both as Cond. & Critic; does reviews for Gramohone (as TH). Mbrships: ISM; Royal Phil. Soc. Hobbies: Ciné-filming (Collect, dating 1936-); Backgammon. Address: 1A Charlwood Place, London SW1V 2LX, UK.

HARVEY, Violet Mabel. Music Educator. Educ: A Mus., TCL, UK. m. Walter Harry Harvey, 1 s. Career: Local Rep., TCL; Tchr., Eastbourne Ctr. & Hastings Ctr. Mbrships: ISM; Advsry. Coun., Hastings Music Fest. Hons: Special Cert. of Merit Pianoforte & Theory of Music, TCL. Hobbies: Stamp Collecting; Motoring; Bridge. Address: Quarry Cottage, Mt. Pleasant Cres., Hastings, Sussex TN 34 3SG, UK. 16

HARWOOD, Elizabeth Jean, b. 27 May 1938. Opera & Concert Singer, Educ: RMCM; FRMCM; GRSM; LRAM. m. Julian Adam Christopher Royle, 1s. Career: prin. roles at Glyndebourne, Sadler's Wells, Covent Garden, Scottish Opera; apps. at Salzburg & La Scala; tour of Aust., 1965. num. recordings of opera & oratorio. Hons: Kathleen Ferrier Memorial Scholarship, 1960; joint winner, Verdi Competition, Busetto, Italy, 1965. Hobbies: Swimming; Horse Riding. Address: Masonetts, Fryerning, Ingatestone, Essex, UK.

HAS, Stanislaw, b. 27 Mar. 1914, Cracow, Poland. Composer. Educ: Law degree, Jagiellonian Univ.; Acad. of Music (Panstwowa Wyzsza Szkola Muzyczna). m. Anna Bakowska, 1 s., 1 d. Debut: Warsaw Opera. Career incls: Var. appearances on Polish radio & TV. Compositionsl: Comic Overture; Parantelle for piano & orch; Concertino for clarinet & orch.; Magic Shoes, ballet; 2 mIniatures for Hautboy & orch.; Songs for voice & piano; Songs for choir a capella; Concertino for bassoon & piano, etc. Recordings: approx. 250 works form The Classical to the contemporary music. Mbr: Assn. of Polish comps. Hons: Prize for song 'In The Town of Dreams' Competition in Vienna, 1959. Hobby: Gardening. Mgmt: PRTV Polish Radio & TV. Address: Zloty Róg 29, Cracow 30095, Poland.

HASA, Jaroslav, b. 26 Feb. 1908, Wien, Austria. Violoncellist. Educ: Conserv., Vienna; L'Ecole Normal, Paris;

Studied w. Hugo Recker, Paul Grummer, A Walter (Casals-Alexanian). m. Magdalene Riedl, 3 children. Debut: W. Prague Broadcasting Orch. Career: W. Czechoslovak String Quartet, 1946-64; Concertmaster, Symphonic Orch., Malmo, Sweden; Soloist w. apps. in Czechoslovakia, Germany, Austria, Sweden, etc., 1964-70. Recordings: String Quartets (Supraphon); Soloist Concertos (Supraphon). Mbr. Musical Sect., Union of Czech Comps. Recip. Czechchoslovak Prize for Outstanding Work, 1969. Hobbies: Nature; Woodworking. Address: Cerrmakova 8, 12000 Prague 2, CSSR.

HÁSEK, Josef Václav, b. 12 Sept. 1903, Tuhan, Czech. Composer; Civil Servant. Educ: State Music Educ. Exam., prague Conserv. of Music, 1935; pvte. studies w. Oldricha Filipovského (piano) & Karel Janeek (harmony), Pilsen & Jaroslav Ridkho (harmony, counterpoint & comp.), Prague. m. Johanna Kovaríková, 1 s., 2 d. Career: Composer; Music Tchr.; External Reader in Music, Leisure & Culture Gdns., Hradec Kralove; Pianist; Violinist; Violist; Bassist; Flautist; Oboist; Organist; Dirigent; Pedagog. Compositions incl: 125 opus nos., of which 40 are publd.; Suite of 3 works recorded by Supraphon; 30 canonical works. Mbrships: Full Mbr., Ochrannéo Union of Comps., 1936-. Hons: var. dips. from music contests: 1st degree Hon. Mention, Min. of Machine Tool Inds., 1954. Hobby: Mycology. Address: Klumparova 606, Hrdec Králové 1, Czech.

HASELAUER, Elisabeth, b. 14 June 1939, Linz, Austria. Professor; Musical Sociologist. Educ: Dr. Phil., Univ. of Vienna; Hochschule für Musik, Vienna; dips., piano & organ. Career: organ recitals, radio & TV recordings in most European countries, 1967-72; rsch. in musical sociol., 1972-; prof. of piano, Hochschule für Musik and darstellende Kunst, Vienna. Recordings: 1st series of Musical Sociol. Publs: Musiksoziologische Studie nach Emile Durkheim, 1977; Handbuch der Musiksoziologie, 1980; Ed., Fragmente als Beiträge zur Musiksoziologie, 1977-; Ed., Komponieren heute, 1979. Contbr. to ORF; Der Komponist; Muzikerziehung; talks on musical sociol. Mbrships: Hud. of Music Sociol. working group, Bd. mbr., Osterreichischer Komponistenbund; Bd. mbr., Verein zur Unterstützung der Osterreichischen Gegenwartsmusik. Hobbies: all kinds of writing; Organ; Books. **Address:** Weihburggasse 18/48, 1010 Vienna, Austria.

HASELBACH, Josef, b. 14 June 1936, Switz. Composer; Teacher of Theory of Music. Educ: Musikakademie Zürich; Univ. of Zürich: Musikakademie Basel. m. Brigitte Haselbach-Peyer. Career: Perfs. of comps. in concert halls, & radio stns., in Europe & USA; Ballets, TV, Switz., Can., France, Belgium. Comps. incl: Moving Theater, for 5 dancers, 3 tape; TREMA, for violoncello & small orch.; Ausbruch & Einkehr, for 2 mixed chorus, baritone & small orch; Fragen an die Nacht, for String Quintet. Mbrships: incl: Assn. of Swill Musicians. Recip., var. hons. Hobbies incl: Music. Address: Schützenstr. 11, CH-8702 Zollikon, Switzerland.

HASHIMOTO, Eiji, b. 7 Aug. 1931, Tokyo, Japan. Harpsichordist; Educ: B M Organ, Tokyo Univ. of Arts., 1954., Composition & Musicol., Univ. of Chgo., USA. 1959; MMus Harpsichord, Yale Univ. Schl. of Music, 1962. m. Ruth Anne Laves, 1 s., 2 d. Debut: Tokyo, age 7. Career: Recitals in maj. cities, inclng. Amsterdam, Berlin, Tehran, London, Milan, Paris, Washington, NY, Caracas, Tokyo. Harpsichordist in Res. & Assoc. Prof., Harpsichord. Coll.-conserv. of Music. Univ. of Cinn., 1968-. Recordings: 4 Solo harpsichord albums; Other Baroque, contemp. chmbr. music. Publs: 100 Selected Sonatas by D. Scarlattie (ed) 3 vols., 1974. Mgmt: Int. Concert Administratie, Amsterdam. Address: 8966 Farmedge Lane, Cincinnati, OH 45231 USA.

HASLAM, David P, b. 12 Feb. 1940, Loughborough, UK. Conductor; Flautist; Composer. Educ: RAM, 3yrs.; LRAM. sep. 2d., 2s. Career: 1st flute, Scottish Nat. Orch., 1959-61; 1st flute & Assoc. Artistic Dir., Northern Sinfonia, 1961-81. Comps: Juanita The Spanish Lobster; Cooey Louis The Racing Pigeon; Daggerlengro the Gypsy; M4;Lollopanlog the Racehorse. Recordings: (as cond.) Juanita The Spanish Lobster; Peter & the Wolf; Songs of Alex Glasgow; (as flautist) Bach, Brandenburg concertos Nos. 2, 4, 5. Hobbies: Reading; Walking. Address: 20 Armstrong Ave., Heaton, Newcastlr-on-Tyne NE6, UK.

HASLUM, Bengt Sirgurd, b. 23 Oct. 1923, Gudmundra, Sweden. Radio Producer; Music Journalist; Lyric Writer; Composer. Educ: BA, Stockholm, 1948. m. Margit Sporrong, 2 d. Career incls: Own progs., records. operettas, Film music etc., Swedish Broadcasting Co., 1961-; Apps., Light musical progs., TV; Writer & Transl., many lyrics for popular songs; Transl., adaptor, operattas for Swedish theatres. Compositions: Children's songs; Ballads. Publs: Svensk Popularmusik (ed.). 1967-70, Operett och musical, 1971. Contbr. to jrnls. Mbr.,

Stim & Skap. Hons: SKAP Premium, 1972. Hobbies: Tennis; Travel. Address: Grevgatan 70, 114 59 Stockholm, Sweden.

HASSELMANN, Ronald Henry, b. 3 Mar. 1933, Chicago, Ill., USA. Musician (Trumpet); Instructor of Trumpet. Educ: B Mus. Ed., Northwestern Univ., 1954; MMus. Ed., ibid, 1957. m. Marilyn Dykes Hasselmann, 3 c. Career: 1st Trumpet, Lyric Opera Orch., Chgo., 1957; 3rd & Asst. 1st Trumpet, Lyric Opera Orch., 1958-; instr. of Trumpet, St. Olaf Coll., Northfield, Minn., 1968- & Univ. of Minn., 1970- . Hobbies: Backpacking; Cross country skiing; Scuba Diving. Address: 4928-5th Ave. S, Minneapolis, MN, USA.

HASTINGS, Baird, b. 14 May, 1919, NYC, USA. Conductor; Flutist; Lecturer; Writer. Educ: AM, Harvard Univ., 1939; Cert., Paris Conserv., 1946; Cert. Fulbright Fellow, 1949-50, Tanglewood, USA, 1957; Dip., Salzburg, Austria, 1961; MA Queen's Coll., NY., 1966; PhD, Sussex Coll., 1976. m. Lily Hastings. Career: Cond., Mozart Fest. Orch 1960-; Musical Advsr., Eglevsky Ballet, 1964-; Cond. Trinity Coll., 1965-70; Guest Cond., Dessoff Choirs Holyoke, Hartford Symph., Am. Symph., Tufts., Harvard, etc.; Staff, Juilliard Schl., 1973-. Recordings: Educo (Mozart) & Vocarium VM 1000 (Sammartini. Martin, Corrette, Mozart). Publs: Sonata From in Classic Orchestra, 1966; Treasury of Opera Libretti, 1967. Contbr. of approx. 300 reviews, articles, transl, in var. profl. publs. Mbrships: Musicians Union; Am. Musicol. Soc.; AAUP. Hobby: Collecting prints & drawings. Address: 33 Greenwich Ave., NY, NY 10014, USA.6.

HATCH, Donald J, b. 29 Jan. 1919, Little Rock, Ill., USA. French Horn Player & Teacher; Educational Representative for Music Store. Educ: BS in Music Educ., Univ. of Ill. m. Betty M Hatch, 1 s.; 1 d. Career: Prin. Horn, Aurora Civic Orch., Chgo. Businessmen's Symph., currently Quincy Conserv. & SE IA Comminity Coll.; Solo Recitalist & Mbr., Quincy Symph. Woodwind Quintet. Mbrships: Fndr., Quincy Horn Club; Int., Horn Soc.; Phi Mu Alpha; Am. Fedn. of Musicians. Address: 1807 Grove Ave., Quincy, IL 62301, USA.

HATCHER, Paula Braniff, b. 10 Feb. 1947, Santa Monica, Calif., USA. Flautist; Performer on Recorder; Music Educator. Educ: BMA, MMA Peabody Conserv. of Music. m. Daniel Franko Goldman. Career: Am. & Int. tours, 1968-; Mbr., NY Camerata, 1971-76; commissioned, perfd. works by George Crumb, Richard Rodney Bennett, John Harbison; subject of two USIA films, 1975; Mbr., Half & Half, 1968-; Mbr., Pro Musica Rara, 1971-; Perf. on Renaissance & Baroque instruments; Occasional Mbr., Charlie Byrd Trio, 1976-; Ldr., Paula Hatcher Jazz Quartet, 1971-; Radio & TV apps, USA; Fac. Mbr., Peabody Conserv. of Music, 1972-. Recordings: Trios for Flute, Cello and Piano; Charlie Byrd - a Direct Disc Recording. Hons: Peabody Alumni Award, 1969. Hobby: Growing Pumpkins. Address: cÇo Peabody Conserv. of Music, 1 E Mt. Vernon Place, Balt., MD 21202, USA.

HATFIELD. Lenore Sherman, b 26 June 1935, Garden City, Kan., USA. Violinist. Educ: B Mus, Eastman Schl. Music, 1957; M Mus, Univ. Mich., 1958; Doct. study, Univ. Southern Calif. m. Frank Michael Hatfield, 1 s., 1 d. Career: (past) Mbr. Indpls. Symph., Rochester Phil., Cinn. Symph.; Currently Asst. Concertmaster, Aspen Fest. Orch.; Violin recitalist; TV & radio apps. Mbrships: Pres., Sigma Alpha Iota; MacDowell Soc. Hons. incl: Coleman Chmbr. Music Award, 1960; Sword of Hon., 1960; Rose of Hon., 1972. Mgmt: Alfred C Myers. Address: 2736 Turnkey Ct., Cinn. OH 45226, USA.

HATFIELD, Michael, b. 1 Oct. 1936, Evansville, Ind., USA. Musician; Teacher (French Horn). Educ: BS, Ind. Univ., 1958; Perf.'s Cert., ibid., 1958. m. Lenore Sherman Hatfield, 1 s, 1 d. Career: Prin. Horn, Cinn. Symph. Orch., 1961-; Co-Prin. Horn, Aspen Fest. Orch., 1974-; Faculty, Aspen Music Fest., 1974-; Faculty Adj. Prof. of Music, Coll.-Conserv. of Univ. of Cinn., 1961-. Recordings w. Cinn. Symph. Orch. Mbr., MacDowell Soc. Address: 7368 Quail Hollow Rd., Cinn., OH 45243, USA. 3, 8.

HATTON, Rachel Lenora, b. 28 Oct. 1933, Pueblo, Colo., USA. Soprano; Violinist; Organist; Teacher. Educ: BS Music Educ., & Dip. Voice, Violin & Piano, Coll. of Mt. St. Joseph on the Ohio, Ohio, 1955; Masters degree, Colo. Coll., 1971; pvte studies. Debut: Colo. Springs Opera, 1957. Career: Soprano Soloist, Colo. Springs Opera, Chorale Soc. & Colo. Springs Music Theater; Violinst w. Pueblo Symph., Colo. Springs Symph. & Colo. Springs Community Orch., Vocal Music Tchr., Madison Elementary Schl.; Dir., Madison Musicmakers (children's chorus); Organist; St. Paul's Cath. Ch., Broadmoor, 1955-70. Mbr., var. musical assns. Recip., var. scholarships & awards. Hobbies incl: French Antiques; Chinese Porcelain; Paintings. Address: 1203 La Veta Way, Colo. Springs, CO 80906, USA. 4, 27.

HATZINASSIOS, George, b. 19 Jan. 1945, Thessaloniki, Greece. Composer; Conductor; Instrumentalist (Piano, Organ, Accordian). Educ: Dip., piano, Conserv. Greece; Conserv., Paris, France. 1 d. Debut: 1963. Career: Concerts, many countries; Orch. Dir., Nat. Radio-TV (ERT). Comps: Music scores, 14 films & 4 theatre shows. Recordings: 8 LPs. Mbrships: PRS; BRITICO. Hons: Prizes, Song Fest., 1972, '73; Prizes, Instrumentation, 1972, '73; Gold Record for 'Diadromi'. Hobbies: Football; Fishing. Address: Grammou 36, Papagou, Athens, Greece.

HAUFLER, August Otto, b. 22 May 1944, San Antonio, Tex., USA. Music Educator; Oboist. Educ: B Mus, Tex. A & I Univ., Tex., 1966. m. Janet Lee Smith, 1 s. Career: Band Dir., Thomas Nelson Page Middle Schl., San Antonio; Prin. Oboist w. the 149th Armoured Div. Band, Tex. Army Nat. Guard; Appeared w. the Tex. A & I Univ. Fac. Woodwind Quintet as an undergrad. on local TV. Mbrships: Tex. Music Educators Assn.; Int. Double Reed Soc.; Am. Redn. of Tchrs. Hobbies: Tennis; Listening to short-wave radio. Address: 6842 Blue Lake, San Antonio, TX 78244, USA. 4, 28, 29.

HAUG, Halvor, b. 20 Feb. 1952, Trondheim, Norway. Composer. Educ: Degree, schl. music tchr., Conserv. of Music, Veitvet, Oslo, 1970-73; Sibelius Acad. (comp.), Helsinki, 1973-74; studied w. Kolbjrn Ofstad, Oslo, 1974-75, & Robert Simpson, London, 1978. Career: perfs. in Norway w. major orchs. incl. Oslo Phil.; num. radio & TV perfs. in Norway. Comps. incl: (orch.) Symphonic Picture, 1976; Symphonic Contours, 1977; Silence for strng. orch., 1977; Miniature Concerto for horn & small orch., 1978; (instrumenta) Sonatina for violin & piano (recorded), 1973; Three Upshots for guitar, 1973-74; Duetto Bramoso for violin & guitar, 1976; Fantasia for oboe, 1977; Symphony for Five, for flute, clarinet, horn, guitar & piano, 1979. Mbrships: Soc. of Norwegian Comps; Ny Musikk (ISCM Norway). Hobbies: Bird Watching; Fishing. Address 2743 Harestua, Norway.

HAUG, Leonard H, b. 18 Sept. 1910, Eau Claire, Wis., USA. University Professor & Administrator. Educ: B Mus, 1934, MA, 1935, Univ. of Wis. m. Irene D Robbins, 2 d. Career: Tchr., pub. schls., Fall River, Wis., 1935-38; Asst. Band Dir., Univ. of Wis., 1935-38; Asst. Band Dir., 1938-45, Instr., 1938-41, Asst. Prof., 194145, Dir. of Bands, 1945-62, Assoc. Prof., 1945-52, Prof., 1952-, Assoc., Dir., Schl. of Music, 1962-71, Asst. Dean, Coll. of Fine Arts, 1971-77; Prof. Emeritus of Music, Univ. of Okla. 1977-. Mbrships. incl: Am. Bandmasters Assn.; Exec. Comm., John Philip Sousa Mem. Inc.,; Vice-Chmn., John Philip Sousa Hall of Fame Committee. Recip., Hall of Fame, Okla. Bandmasters Assn.; 1970. Hobbies: Fishing; Photography; Cabinetmaking; Travel. Address: 1521 S Pickard. Norman, OK 73069, USA. 125.

HAUGAN, Paul, b. 28 March 1945, Oslo, Norway. Percussionist. Educ: Pvte. studies. Debut: 1962. Career: Dance musician, 15 yrs. apps. in hotels, restaurants & on cruise ships; Studio musician. Mbrships: Norwegian Musicians Union. Hobbies: Photography; Football. Mgmt: Norwegian Musician Agency, Oslo, Norway. Address: Norobergvn. 25, Oslo 8, Norway.

HAUKSSON, Thorsteinn, b. 4 Aug. 1949, Rekjavík, Iceland. Composer. Educ: Bus. Dip., Commercial Coll. of Iceland, 1969; Soloist Cert., Reykjavík Coll. of Music, 1974; M Mus, Univ. of Ill., 1977. m. Bergljöt Jonsdóttir, 1 child. Career: Music Dir., music schl., Olafsvík, Iceland, 1974-75. Comps. incl: Humma? for 2 sopranos & bass (recorded by Swedish radio, 1974); Taijahñ for children's choir, contralto & woodwinds)recorded by finnish radio, 1975); Mosaic for string quartet & wind quintet. Address: Vogaland 7, 108 Reykjavík, Iceland.

HAUPT, Albrecht Otto Thorolf, b. 7 Dec. 1929, Bonn, Germany. Conductor of choir & orchestra; Organist. Educ: Abitur, Humanistisches Gymnasium; Univ. Jena (Hist. of Arts and Music); High Schl. for Music, Leipzig; Staatsexamen, High Schl. for Sacred Music EsslingenÇStuttgart. m. Eva Maria Jätzold, 3 c. Debut: Stuttgart. Career: Dir. of Sacred Music, Radio Stuttgart and Sudwestfunk TV Stuttgart; Concert tours, foreign countries; Bezirkskantor of Ulm; Cond., Ulmerkantorei; Organist. Recordings: Janacek; R Keiser Markuspassion; Haydn Schöpfung, Motets and Madrigals; Mendelssohn, etc. Contbr. to mags. of Sacred Music. Mbrships: Arbeitskreis für Musik in der Jugend. Hons: KMD, 1965. Hobby: Hist. of Art. Address: Susoweg 7, 7900 Ulm, German Fed. Repub.

HAUPT, Walter, b. 28 Feb. 1935, Munich, Germany. Composer; Conductor; Stage Director. Educ: Conserv.; Schl. for Dramatic Art; Univ. Career: currently Hd., Expmtl. Theatre, Bavarian State Opera, Munich; apps. as Cond., Munich & Melbourne; TV broadcasts in Germany; radio broadcasts,

Germany, Italy, USA, etc. Comps. incl: Apeiron, 1960; Sümtome, 1970; Die Puppe, 1971; Laser, 1972; Sensus, 1973; Kontemplation, 1974; Reziprok, 1975; Moira, 1976; Rilke, 1977; Zofen, 1977; Münchner Stadtbespielung, 1978. Hons: Festspielpreis, 1971; Föderungspreis für Musik, Minich, 1974. Mgmt: Bayer, Staatsoper, Brieffach, 8000 Müchen 1, German Fed. Repub.

HAUSE, James B, b. 5 Apr. 1929, Waltz, Mich., USA. Music Educator; Clarinetist. Educ: Mus B, Univ. of Mich., Ann Arbor, 1951; Mus M ibid, 1952; Ed D, 1969. m. Mary Ann Hoy, 3 s., 1 d. Career: Dir. of Instrumental Music, Quincy Community Schls., Mich., 1954-58; Mbr., Hillsdale Symph. Orch. (Clarinet), ibid, 1955-58; Instr. - Prof. of Music, Western Mich. Univ., Kalamazoo, 1958-71; Mbr. Kalamazoo Symph. Orch. (Clarinet), ibid, 1958-70; Asst. Chmn., Dept. of Music, Western Mich. Univ., 1967-71; Hd., Dept. of Music, Eastern Mich. Univ., Ypsilanti, 1971-. Compiler & Ed., A Handbook for Teachers of Bank & Orchestra Instruments, 1967. Contbr to MSBOA Jrnl. Mbrships: Mich. Acad. Si., Arts & Letters (chmn., music sect., 1971-74); Hon. Mbr., Mich. Schl. Band & Orch. Assn. (dist. VI Pres., 1957-58; State 2nd. VP, 1961-62); Music Educators Nat. Conf.; Mich. Music Educators Assn.; AAUP; Pi Kappa Lambda; Kappa Kappa Psi; Am. Schl. Band Dir. Assn. Hobbies incl: Fishing; Golf. Address: 1049 Louise, Ypsilanti, MI 48197, USA.8.

HAUSNER, Henry H., b. 1 June 1901, Vienna, Austria. musicologist. Educ: Dr. Eng.; Dip. Eng. m. Ada Hausner. Publs: Franz X Suessmayr, 1964. Contbr. to: Mozarteum Mitteilunge; Music Jrnl. Mbrships: Am. Musicol. Soc.; Mozarteum, Salzburg, Austria. Hon: Prof. (hc). Address: 67 Red Brook Rd., Kings Point, NY 11024, USA. 2.

HAUTVAST, Willy, b. 31 Aug. 1932, Maastricht, Holland. Composer; Clarinettist; Pianist. Educ: Conserv. of Music. m. Janssen W., 2 c. Comps: Evolution Overture; Fest. Suite; Funny Fantasy; Playful Interlude; Music to Relax; Musique à la Carte; Theme Varié; Suite Fantasque. Mbrships: BVO. Comps. Sect. Hons: 1st Prize, Competition for Comps., 1970. Address: Graafseweg 397, 6532 ZP Nÿmegen, Holland.

HAUTZIG, Walter, b. 28 Sept. 1921, Vienna, Austria. Pianist. Educ: State Acad. of Music, Vienna; Conserv., Jerusalem; Curtis Inst. of Music, Phila. m. Esther Hautzig, 1 s., 1 d. Debut: Town Hall, NY, USA, 1943. Career: Recitalist & Soloist w. maj. orchs. on 4 continents; Prof. of Piano, Peabody Conserv. of Music, Balt., USA. Recordings: Victor; Monitor; Vox; Gemini; Haydn Soc.; Turnabout; Solsgirth Cassettes; Musical Heritage Soc. Contbr. to: Am. Record Guide. Mbrships: AAUP; Curtis Alumni Assn. Hons: Award, Phila. Music Club, 1941; Endowment Award, NY Town Hall, 1943. Hobbies: Swimming; Hiking; Ping Pong; Photography. Mgmt: Eric Semon Assocs. Inc., 111 W 57 St., NY, USA; Dougas Gray, Solsgirth, Kirkintilloch, Glasgow, UK. Address: 505 West End Ave., New York, NY 10024, USA. 6.

HAUXVELL, John, b. 7 July 1925, Otahuhu, Auckland, NZ. Operatic Baritone; Teacher of Voice; Opera Producer. Educ: St. Stephens Coll., NZ; w. Prof. E Herbert-Caesari; RAM. m. Anthea Slatter, 2 s., 2 d. Debut: As Marcel in La Boheme, Dublin Grand Opera, Gaity Theatre, 1958. Career: Prin. Baritone, Sadlers Wells Opera Co.; Welsh Nat. Opera Co., Engl. Opera Grp. & Guest w. for. cos.; Extensive Radio, TV & Concert workl Currently, Singing Tchr. & Opera Prod., Royal Scottish Acad. Music & Drama. Recordings: Die Fledermaus w. Vienna Phil. Orch. & Chorus & Famous Operettas (RCA Victor); William Walton's Troilus & Cressida & R Strauss' Capriccio (Columbia). Hobbies incl: Collecting old vocal recordings. Address: 275 Nithsdale Rd., Dumbreck. Scotland, UK.

HAVAS, Kato, b. 5 Nov. 1920, Hungary. Violinist; Teacher of Violin; Lecturer. Educ: Music Acad., Budapest. 3 children. Debut: Concert at Carnegie Hall, 1939. Career: Dir., Annual Summer Schl. for Strings, Digby Stuart Coll., Univ. of London; Dir., Annual Spring Violin Course, Higham Hall, Cumbria; Fndr. & Dir., Purbeck Fest. of Music & Roehmpton Music Fest.; Annual Am. lecture tours. Publs. incl: The Violin and I, 1968; Stage Fright: Its Causes and Cures, 1974. Mbrships: Hon. Mbr., Isaye Fndn., Belgium. Hobbies: Theatre. Address: 15 Rocks Lane, Barnes, London SW 13 0DB, UK.

HAVELAAR, Charles Eduard, b. 12 Apr. 1908, Rheden, Holland. Flautist; Teacher. Educ: Univ. of Amsterdam; Univ. of Utrecht; Govt. Examination, Flute; Gehrels-Cert, Elementary Music Educ. m. Catherina Renske Lampe, 1 s. 1 d. Career: Tchr., Volksmuziekschool, Amsterdam, 1939-45; Mbr. Radio Chmbr. Orch., 1945, Utrecht, Symph., 1946-73, Nos Jungit Musica quartet, 1946-58. Publs: Ed., Bodino Sonata, 1960, corette Sonata, 1967. contbr. to Mens en Melodie. Mbrships: Raad voor de Kunst, 1957-64; Mgmt., Utrecht Symph.,

1946-73, Nos Jungit Musica quartet, 1946-58. Publs: Ed., Bodino Sonata, 1960, corette Sonata, 1967. Contbr. to Mens en Melodie. Mbrships: Raad voor de Kunst, 1957-64; Mgmt., Utrecht Symph., 1954-69; Provincial Utrechts genootschap; Pres., Orkestenverbond, 1960-68. Address: 45 Kromme Nieuwegracht, Utrecht, Netherlands.

HAVERGAL, Henry MacLeod, b. 21 Feb. 1902, Evesham, UK. Musical Educator. Educ: BA, 1924, MA, 1927, St. Johns Coll., Oxford; B Mus, Univ. of Edinburgh, 1931. m. (1) Hyacinth Chitty; (2) Nina Davidson; 2 s. Career: Dir. of Music, Fettes Coll., Edinburgh, 1924-33; Haileybury Coll., 1934-36, Harrow Schl., 1937-45; Winchester Coll., 1946-53; Prin., Royal Scottish Acad. of Music & Drama, 1953-69 (Ret'd); Dir., Jamaica Schl. of Music, 1973-75. Comps., var. minor works, most ch. music. Mbr., ISM, Pres., 1949. Hons: D Mus, Edinburgh, 1958; OBE, 1964; LLD, Glasgow, 1969; FRCM, 1969 FRSAMD, 1971. Hobbies: Fishing; Carpentry. Address: 2 Bellevue Terr., Edinburgh, EH7 4DU, UK. 1, 3.

HAVLICEK, Franz Frantisek, b. 3 Jan. 1921, Karlovy Vary, (Carlsbad) Czechoslovakia. Composer; Pianist. Educ: Studied piano & comp. w. Dip., Acad. of Musical Scis., Prague, Czechoslovakia; Studied comp. w. Dip., High Schl. of Musical Scis., Vienna, Austria. Debut: Concert, Carlsbad & Marienbad, Czechoslovakia, 1928. Career: European Tour as Pianist, vis. most Capitals, 1941-46; Var. Perfs., CS Radio & TV; His compositions have also been broadcast insev. Radio Stns. Europe & USA. Compositions: solo works for piano; chamber music; songs; concertos for piano & orch.; rhapsodies & fantasies for piano & orch.; impressions; orchl. music; music for solo instruments; film music, light music, etc. Approx. 800 recordings, inclng., Supraphon, Artia, Panton, etc. Mbrships: ZSS, Soc. of Czechoslovak Comps.; SOZA, Soc. for the jprotection of Comps.; OSVU, Soc. of perf. Artists, Czechoslovakia. Hobbies: Painting; Sculpture. Address: 801 00 Bratislava 1, Jelenia 5, Czechoslovakia.

HAVLIKOVÁ, Klára, b. 15 Oct. 1931, Martin, Czech. Concert Pianist. Educ: High Level Degree, Acad. of Drama, Arts & Music, Bratislava. m. Frantisek Bartosek, 1 s. Debut: Prague 1956. Career: Solo Pianist, Slovak Phil. Orch., 1973-; Played w. sev. other Czech. & foreign orchs.; Tours incl. USSR, Germany, Austria, Italy, Spain, Sweden, Bulgaria, Hungary, Switz., Iran, Cuba, Japan; Radio & TV apps. in Czech., Poland, USSR, Austria, Sweden, Hungary, Finland, Yugoslavia, Greece, Switz. Recordings: Shostakovitch: 24 preludes; Hindemith: 3rd Sonata; Hindemith: 4 Temperamente; Greig: Sonata e-mol; Brahms: 3 repsodions; Stravinsky: Capricco; All Works of Eugen Suchon for piano. Mbrships: Committee Mbr., Concert Sect., Union of Slovak Comps. Hons: Merit Artist, Czechoslovak Socialist Repub., 1974, 1966, 1972; Prize of F. Kafenda. Hobbies: Foreign Languages; Handicrafts. Address: 801 00 Bratislava, Szabova 16, Czech.

HAVLU, Ivo T. b, 11 Mar. 1923, Prague, Czech. Librettist; Lyricist; Translator. Educ: Fac. of Law, Charles Univ., Prague. m. Atya Fierlinger, 1 d. Librettos incl: Night Is My Day; A Little Night Music; A Jug & Handle; Over the Border of Ordinary Days; The Revolt of Angels; Giannina Mia. Translator of librettos inclng: The Good Soldier Schweik, The Gondoliers, The Yeoman of the Guard, Kiss Me Kate, Can-Can, Zorba, The Pajama Game, Man of La Mancha, Cabaret, Chicago, Two Gentlemen of Verona & Promisis Promises. Author, num. popular songs & children's songs, recorded & broadcast. Mbrships: Exec. Comm., Cir. of Lyricists & Librettists, Guild of Czech Composers & Concert Artists, Prague; Subcomm. for musicals, ibid; Creative Bd., Authors Assn. for Protection of Rights on Musical Works, Prague. Address: Podbelohorska 2773/F1, 150 00 Prague 5, Czech.

HAWEL, Jan Wincenty, b. 10 July 1936, Pszow, Poland. Composer; Conductor; Teacher. Educ: Dip., Teaching Dept., Music Coll., Katowice, 1960; Comp. Dip., 1964; Cond. Dip. 1967. m. Jolanta Zajax, 1 d. Career: Tchr., Music Coll., Katowice. Comps: (published) Nocturne for Men's Choir; (published & recorded) Sinfonietta (mixed a cappella choir); Contrast for Orch.; Studium (organ); (recorded) quartetto d'archi No. 2; chmbr. music. Mbr., Polish Comps. Assn. Hons. incl: 2nd Prize, Polish Comps. Competition, 1965; 2nd Prize, Comps. Competition, Miedzyzdroje, 1969; 2nd Prize, G Fitelberg Competition, 1972; 1st Prize, Comps. Competition, Opole, 1973; 3rd Prize, 2nd Competition for Piano Comp., Stupsk, 1975. Address: 40-686 Katowice 8, ul. Zurawia 43 m. 4, Poland.

HAWES, Jack Richards, b. 18 May 1916, Ipswich, Suffolk, UK. Composer. Educ: Studied cello, Ipswich Conserv. of Music; Studied w. Dr. George Gray & Alfred Earnshaw. Comps. incl: Magnificat & Nunc Dimittis (choir & organ); Burlesque &

Pastorale (piano); Nocturne (piano); Three Whimsical Pieces (piano); Psalm Trilogy (unaccomp. female voices); Toccata (piano); Carol - Christ is Born; Pieces of Eight (Woodwind Octet); Three Commands (Brass Band); Concertino Lirico (flute & strings); Fest. Pieces (Brass Septet & percussion); Pieces for organ, 20 solo songs, carols, choral & orchl. works & misc. items. Contbr. Freelance Music Critic, The Evening Star Ipswich. Mbrships: CGGB; PRS. Hons incl: First Award for Comp., Suffolk Music Fest., 1953, '55 & '59. Hobbies: Swimming; Gardening; Reading; Motoring. Address: 29 Lynwood Ave., Felixstowe, Suffolk IP11 9HS, UK. 3,4,29.

HAWKEY, William Richard, b. 19 Jan. 1932, Timaru, NZ. Principal Lecturer in Performing Arts. Educ: B Mus, Univ. of Canterbury; FTCL, organ; LRSM, London, pianoforte teaching; LTCL, pianoforte teaching, choral conducting & organisation; L Mus TCL. m. Ruth Mary Hosking, 2 s., 2 d. Career: Rdr., Music, Univ. of Canterbury; Prin. Lectr., Performing Arts. Torrens Coll. of Advanced Educ., Adelaide, SA, 1976-; Musical Dir. & Chief Cond., Christchurch Harmonic Soc. Inc.; Nat. Accomp., Radio NZ; Nat. Comm., 1969, 1974. Compositions incl: Sweet Sleep (carol); Lullaby (carol). Recordings: 7 LPs conducterd by self. Contbr. to Christchurch Press. Mbr. many profl. orgs. Hons. incl: MBE, 1974. Hobbies incl: Fishing; Squash. Address: Univ. of Canterbury, Pvte. Bag, Christchurch, NZ. 17.

HAWKINS, Brian, b. 13 Oct. 1936, York, UK. Viola Player; Professor. Educ: St. Peter's York; RCM, London; ARCM. m. Mavis E. Spreadborough, 1 s., 1 d. Career: Prof. of Viola & Chamber Music, RCM, London; Mbr. London Virtuosi; London Oboe Quartet; Vesuvius Ensemble; Nash Ensemble; HawkinsConstable Duo; Fndr. Mbr. & Prin., Viola. London Sinfonietta, 1968-72; Edinburgh Quartet, 1960-65; Martin Quartet. 1965-68; Engl. Chambr Orch., 1966-71. Recordings: w. London Virtuosi, Vesuvius & Nash Ensembles. Mbr., ISM. Hons: Silver Medal of the Most Worshipful Co. of Musicians, 1961. Hobbies: Painting; Photography; Mah Jong. Address: 48 Combemartin Rd., London SW18 5PR, UK. 3.

HAWKRIDGE, Douglas Leighton, b. 20 Nov. 1907, Dirby, UK. Organist. Educ: Derby Schl, Assoc. Bd. Exhibitioner, piano, RAM; FRAM; FRCO; LRAM (Pfte. Perf.). m, G M Dudden. Career: Organist & Choirmaster, Ilford Parish Ch., 1928-31, St. Philip's Ch., Kensington, 1931-54, St. Columba's Ch. of Scotland, 1954-63, St. James Ch., Sussex Gdns. London, 1963-77; Examiner, Assoc. Bd., Royal Schls. of Music, 1945-. Mbrships: Coun., RCO, 1948-; Pres., London Assn. of Organists, 1966-68. Hobby: Photography. Address: 8 Elmwood Ave., Kenton, Harrow, Middx. HA3 8AH, UK.

HAWRYLUK, Brian Douglas, b. 25 Oct. 1955, Toronto, Ont., Can. Musician (Piano, Accordion, Guitar, Clarinets); composer. Educ: BA (Political Sci.); Grade II theory, Royal Conserv. of Music; Grade X Accordion Cert.; Recording courses, George Brown Coll., Toronto. Career: engagements w. Toeronto Harbour band. Comp: You are the Dancer. Recording. w. Lady Godiva Memorial Band, Univ. of Toronto Album. Mbrships: Toronto Musicians Assn. Hon: 1st place, Kiwanis Fest. w. Martingrove Collegiate Senior Band, 1972. Hobbies incl: Recording; Audio; Weight Training; Reading. Address: 20 Decarie Circle, Islington, Ont. M9B 3H8, Can.

HAWTHORNE-BAKER, Allan, b. 21 March 1909, Coventry, UK. Composer; Organist; Pianist. Educ: Tech. Coll., Coventry; B Mus. Dunelm; FTCL (Pft Sgp); FRCO.; D Mus Lond.; M Mus (Hon); RCM, London. m. Lillian Eleanor Keuneman. Career: Sub-Organist. Coventry Cathedral, 1934-39; Organist & Choirmaster, Nuneaton Parish Ch., 1939-56; Fndr., St. Nichlas Choral Soc., Nuneaton, 1946; Con. 1946-56; Prof. of Comp. & Theory, B'ham Schl. of Music, 1947-64; Trinity Coll. of Music, London, 1963-64; Examiner, 1953-64; Adjudicator; Toured India, Pakistan & Ceylon examining, 1959. Compositions: Three Symph.; Viola Concerto; Three Str. Quartets; Oboe Quintet; Comic Opera (Tom Thumb); Behold the Bridegroom Cometh (cantata); Amoretti (tenor & orch.); Overtures & tone-poems for orch.; Music for brass band & brass ensemble; Madrigals, part-songs, solo songs, anthems, etc. Mbrships: ISM (Coun. Mbr.); Inc. Assn. Organists; CGGB. Hobbies: Reading; Heraldry; Wine Making. Address: 9 Leveson Cres., Balsall Common, Nr. Coventry. Warwicks., UK, 3.

HAYASHI, Nakako, b. 28 Sept. 1932, Osaka, Japan. Concert Electric Organist. Educ: M Lit., Kwanseigakuin Univ.; Kobejogakuin Coll., Fac. of Music, Piano Dept.; Electric organ studies w. Shinji Suzuki, 1965-; Debut: Piano Concert Mainichi Hall, Osaka, 1963. Career incls: Brazilian music recital sponsored by Deutsche-stiftung, Berlin, 1970; Venezuelan music recital sponsored by Norway-Yamaha, 1972; Am. music concert sponsored by Art-Fest., Nishinomiya City, 1973;

Goodwill concert, Spokane YMCA, USA, 1975; All-Japanese music prog. boradcast from KOHO, Hawaii, USA, 1976; Pipe-organ recital by Albeniz, Greig prog., The Evangelist, USA, 1976; Friendship recital, St. Louis, USA, 1978. Comps: Leroy Anderson Classic album for Organ, 1977. Publs. incl: Overture from O Guarany (arr. for electric organ) 1967. Contbr. to: The Mainichi Newspaper, Osaka. Mbrships: Toyo-Ongakugakukai, Tokyo, Japan; Soc. for Ethnomusicol., USA; The Soc. for Asian Music, USA. Hobby: Noh Play. Mgmt: Kajimoto Concert Mgmt. Co. Ltd., 44 Dojimakitamachi K;taku Osaka. Address: 2-12 Futabacho Imazu Nishinomiya City Hyogo pref. Japan. 1, 30.

HAYASHI, Tetsuya, b. 24 Aug. 1946, Tokyo, Japan. Solo Violist. Educ: Aichi Prifectural Univ. of Fine Arts; Univ. of Tex.; Sah Fran. State Univ.; Staatliche Hochschule für Musik, Freiburg im Breisgau; violin studies w. Prof. Andor Toth, Prof. Mischa Mischakov, Robert Man; viola studies w. Prof. Ulrich Koch. m. Michiko Tanaka. Debut: w. Japan Phil., Tokyo. Career: Former mbr., 1st violin sect., Buffalo Phil. Orch., Vic. Symph. Orch. (BC) & San Antonio Symph. Orch.; Concerts, Berlin, Paris, Frankfurt, Hamburg, Brussels, Stuttgart, etc., as solo violist w. The Stuttgart Chmbr. Orch.; Apps., num. cities in S Germany playing viola concerts. Recordings: as solo violist of Stuttgart Chmbr. Orch. Hobbies: Harpsichord building; Travel. Address: D-7250 Leonbert-Warmbronn, Asternstr. 10, German Fed. Repub.

HAYES, Deborah, b. 13 Dec. 1939, Miami, Fla., USA. Musicologist; Violinist; Music Teacher. Educ: AB Oberlin Coll.; AM, Stanford Univ.; PhD., ibid. Career: Musicologist; Tchr. of Music History, Lit., & Theory; Violinist. Translator, introduction, notes & index, Harmonic Generation, by JP Rameau, 1974, Dissertation on the Different Methods of Accompaniment, by JP Rameau; Co-Ed., Musicology at Colorado, 1978. Contbr. to: Choral Jrnl.; Jrnl. of the Am. Musicological Soc.; Boulder Daily Camer. Mbrships: Am. Musicological Soc.; Coll. Music Soc. AAUP. Hobby: Politics. Address: 3290 Darley Ave., Boulder, CO, 80303, USA.

HAYES, Paul Ignatius, b. 27 May 1951, Dublin, Repub. of Ireland. Composer; Part-time Music Teacher. Univ. Coll., Dublin; Educ: Royal Irish Acad. of Music; Lic., London Coll. of Music. Comps: Construction Work for clarinet, cello & piano; Players 2 for tape & film; ELM for flute, clarinet, percussion & sound effects; Protean Echoes for solo piano; Stern for string quartet; Coda for organ; Sturm und Drang for piano, violin, trumpet, double bass, percussion & female reciter; Oboes & Other Woodwinds for 2 oboes, flute, clarinet & bassoon; Extraneous for 2 stereo tape recorders; var. songs in different styles. Mbr., Assn. of Young Irish Comps. Hobbies: Swimming; Reading. Address: 2 Royal Marine Rd., Dun Laoghaire, Co. Dublin, Repub. of Ireland.

HAYMAN, Richard Perry, b. 29 July 1951, Sandia, NM, USA. Composer; Performer on Various Instruments & Mixed Media. Educ: studied philos. & humanities, Columbia Univ.; comp., theory, w. Philip Corner & John Cage; electronic music w. Vladimir Ussachévsky, Gordon Mumma, David Tudor; Indian music w. Ravi Shankar; piano w. Grete Sultan: flute w. Eleanor Laurence. Career: Mastering Engr., Sterling Sound Studios; Ch. Pipe Organ Renovator; Ear Plug Peddler, NY subways; Sleep Lab. Experimenter, Montefiore Med. Ctr.; Audio Rschr., ZBS Media Fndn. Residency. Comps. incl: Musique injouable; BLOW (flute); Enlightened Speaker; dat (14 voices); it is not here (light & tone). Co-Ed., Ear Mag., 1975-. Publs: Dreamsound Pillow Notes, 1976. Contbr. to jrnls. Hobby: Gardening. Address: 326 Spring St., NY, NY 10013, USA.

HAYMAN, Terence Raymond, b. 31 Dec. 1942, Wellington, NZ. Licensed Customs Agent; Composer; Record Producer; Actor; Artist Manager. Career: Prod., Decca Records, London; publisher, Palace Music Ltd., London; small acting parts, TV & films; sev. recorded comps. mbrships: Fellow, NZ Soc. of Customs Agents, Inc.; Comps. Assn. of NZ; Australiasian Performing Right Assn. Hobby: Music. Address: PO Box 37339, Auckland, NZ.

HAYNES, Eugene, b. E St. Louis, Ill., USA. Pianist; Composer; Educator. Educ: Dip. & Post Grad. Dip., Juilliard Schl. of Music; Studies w. Nadia Boulanger & Isador Philipp. Debut: Carnegie Hall, NYC, 1958. Career: Concert tour of Scandinavia & Germany, 1956-57; European tour of Zurich Amsterdam, London, Vienna, Stockholm, 1964; Apps. on TV; Soloist w. Indpls., Okla. City & Detroit Symph. Orchs. Comps. incl: String Quartet, Song Cycle, Symph. & Fantasy for Piano & Orch; Rhapsody on a Gospel Song (concerto for piano & orch.), 1978. Contbr. to Music Jrnl. Mbrships: Am. Music Ctr. Inc.; Nat. Acad. of TV Arts & Scis.; Am. Fedn. of TV & Radio Artists. Hons. incl: Maurice Loeb Prize for overall excellence in grad. studies, Juilliard Schl. of Music; Elected to Nat. Acad. of Arts &

Scis., 1975; Moton Fellowship. Address: 710 State St., Jefferson City, MO 65101, USA. 8.

HAYS, Doris, b. 6 Aug. 1941, Chattanooga, Tenn., USA. Pianist; Composer. Educ: B Mus, Cadek Conserv.-Univ. of Chattanooga; M Mus, Univ. of Wish.; Concert Artist Dip., Munich Hochschule für Musik. Career: Soloist, Residence Orch., The Hague; num. radio concerts, Netherlands, Germany, Italy, Yugoslavia; extensive apps., Am. univ. campuses; premiered Am. piano works, Como Fest., Arte Viva Piano Series-Trieste, Gaudeamus Comps. Week-Netherlands; Tchr., Univ. of Wis., Queens Coll. CUNY; Artist-in-Res., Ga. Coun. for Arts, 1975-76. Comps. incl: Schevenigen Beach (flute quintet); If for 2 pianos & 2-4 tapes; Duet for Pianist & Audience; Juncture Dance & 18 other comps. for Small ensemble of young players; Arabella Rag & 22 other electronic music works. Has made var. recordings. Contbr. to jrnls. Mbrships: ASCAP; League of Women comps. Recip. sev. awards. Address 697 West End Ave., Penthouse B, NYC, NY 10025, USA.

HAYS, William Paul, b. 11 Feb. 1929, Westville, Okla., USA. Organist; Musicologist; Professor. Educ: BM, Univ. of Ark., 1950; MM. w. Distinction, Ind. Univ., 1952; DSM, Union Theol. Sem., 1970; Organ tchrs. incl. Kenneth Osborne, Oswald Ragatz, Andre Marchal, Jean Langlais. m. Dorothea Richter, 1 d. Career: OrganistChoirmaster, churches Okla., Ark. & NY. 1952-68; Asst. Prof., Music, Hendrix Coll., 1952-53, Assoc. Prof., Organ, Union Coll., Ky., 1954-66; Lectr., Histl., Musicol., Union Theol. Sem., 1970-72; Assoc. Prof., Organ, Westminster Choir Coll., 1972-; Continuo Organist, Bach Cantata Series, Holy Trinity Luth Ch., NYC, 1970-; Organ recitals. E. USA. Recording: The Choir & Organs of St. Thomas Church, NYC. Publs: 20th-Century Views of Music History. 1972; Contbr. to profl. jrnls. & Grove's Dictionary. Mbrships: Exec. Coun., NYC Chapt., AGO; VP, NJ, MTNA; Pres., Eastern Div., MTNA; Am. Musicol. Soc.; Music Lib. Assn.; Past Ky. State Comm. Mbr., Past Union Coll. Chapt. Pres., AAUP. Hobby: Breeder, cattery owner, Manx Cats. Address: 335 Halsey Ave., W Hempstead, NY 11552, USA. 29.

HAYWARD, Marie, b. Norwich, UK. Soprano. Educ: LRMA; Dip., RAM; Vienna; Rome. m. Michael Segal. Career: Royal Opera House, Covent Gdn.; Engl. Nat. Opera; Germany - Kiel Opera; Scottish Opera; Glyndebourne; Engl. Opera Grp.; concerts & broadcasts, UK & Europe. Recordings: Serenade to Music; Pilgrim's Progress. Mbr., ISM. Hons: 2nd Prize, Int. Concours, Netherlands, 1964; Medal of Distinction, Geneva, 1966. Hobbies: Dogs; Cooking; Golf; Swimming; Walking; Theatre. Mgmt: Music & Musicians Artists Mgmt. Address: 26 Long Lane, Church End, Finchley, London N3, UK. 3, 27.

HAYWOOD, Charles, b. 20 Dec. 1904, Grodno, Russia. Ethnomusicologist; Concert & Opera Artist; Tenor. Educ: BSc, CCNY, 1926; Artist Dip., Inst. Musical ARt, NY, 1930; Dip., Juilliard Grad. Schl., 1935; MA, Columbia Univ., 1940; PhD, ibid., 1949. m. Frances Dillon (dec.), 1 s. Debut: Conce .., Aeolian Hall, NY, 1925; Opera, Chautauqua Opera Co., N , 1932. Career incls: Prof. Music, Queens Coll., CUNY, 1939-74; Lectr. & Vis. Prof., var. colls. & univs.; Vis. Prof., Univs. of Harvard, Minnesota, Ind. & Calif.; Concert apps.; Lecture-recitals, US & abroad. Recordings: A Folk Song Recital (Capitol). Publs. incl: A Bibliography of North America Folk Lore & Folk Song, 1961; Folk Songs of the World, 1967. Contbr. to jrnls. Mbr. profl. orgs. Recip. num. fellowships & awards. Hobbies incl: Musical Philately. Address: 145 E 92nd St., NY., NY 10028, USA. 2, 14, 28.

HAZZARD, Claire Hatsue Sakai, b. 5 Jan. 1951, Honolulu, HI, USA. Violinist. Educ: BA. m. Don Philip Hazzard. Career: Violinist, Don Ho Show, 3 1/2 yrs.; currently Violinist w. Honolulu Symph. Mbrships: Am. String Tchrs. Assn.; Musicians' Assn. of HI; var. acad. hon. socs. Hons. incl: 4 Gold Medals, solo & ensemble competitions, Honolulu, 1966-68; Concertmistress, HI Youth Symph., 1967-68, Univ. of HI Orch., 1972. Hobbies: Reading; Chamber Music; Jazz. Address: 2825 S King St., No. 1901, Honolulu, HI 96826, USA.

HAZZARD, Peter Peabody, b. 31 Jan. 1949, Poughkeepsi, NY, USA. Composer; Teacher; Conductor. Educ: Boston Univ., 1966-68; B Mus, Berklee Coll. of Music, 1971; pvte. study in comp. w. John A Bavicchi. div., 1 s., 1 d. (2) Katherine Beers Hazzard. Career: Tchr., comp., cond., hist. of music, Berklee Coll. of Music, 1971-; Chmn., Music History & Analysis Dept., ibid; Cond., Berklee Symph. Band; Asst. Cond., Arlington (Mass.) Phil. Orch.; works have been performed throughout E USA O Luxembourg. Comps. incl: A Praise Book (chorus, brass, percussion); Weird Sisters for 7 percussionists; soundtrack for 'Laughing Till It Hurt': The Death of Faust (chorus & band);

Sonata for clarinet & marimba; Sonata for unaccompanied clarinet; Concerto for clarinet & band; Saxophone Quartet. Mbrships: ASCAP; Harvard Musical Assn. Hobbies incl: Photography; Tennis; Darts. Address: 20 Myrtle St., Winchester, MA 01890, USA.

HEADINGTON, Christopher John Magenis, b. 28 April 1930, London, UK. Composer; Pianist; Broadcaster; Writer on Music. Educ: BMus, Dunelm; LRAM (piano tchr.); ARAM; ARCM (piano perf.). Career: Solo Recitalist, UK & abroad; frequent speaker on musical subjects, BBC Radio 3. Comps. incl: Five Preludes for Piano; Toccata for Piano; 2 piano sonatas; Violin Concerto; 2 string quartets; Piano Quartet; song cycles; choral music. Recordings: Soloist in Thirty-Nine Steps Piano Concerto (Ed Welch), 1978. Publs: The Orchestra & its Instruments, 1965; The Songs in Franz Liszt, The Man & his Music, 1970; The Bodley Head History of Western Music, 1974; Chapters on Debussy, Holst, Rachmaninov, Ravel, Shostakovich, Szymanowski, Vaughan Williams, in A Dictionary of Composers, 1977. Contbr. to var. musical publs.; Record Critic, Country Life mag. Mbrships. incl: Exec. Committee, CGGB; ISM. Hons: Arts Coun. Bursary for Comp., 1978. Hobbies incl: Aviation; Skiing. Address: Old Quarry House, 1 Beckley Ct., Beckley, Oxford OX3 9UB, UK. 3, 16.

HEALD-SMITH, Geoffrey, b. 30 March 1930, Mexborough, UK. Conductor; Music Adviser; Pianist. Educ: RCM; ARCM; LRAM; GRSM (London); pvte. study of cond. w. Lawrence Leonard. m. Janet Elizabeth Harrison, 1 s., 1 d. Career: Music Master, Ainthorpe High Schl., & Hessle High Schl.; Music Advsr., City of Hull, 1966-; TV & radio apps.; Guest Cond., UK & abroad, inclng. Siegerland Orch., Germany, Stavanger Symph., Norway, Yorks. Orch., R. T. E. Orch. (Dublin); Own Concert Orch. Recordings: German, Bantock. Publ: Co-Ed., A Word About Music in School, 1973. Mbrships: Musicians Union; Fndr., Soc. to record previously unrecorded works of English comps. Hobbies: Model Railways; Boating. Mgmt: Choveaux Mbmt. Address: Con Brio, 4 Tremayne Ave., Brough, Humberside HU15 1BL, UK. 3,4.

HEALEY, Derek Edward, b. 2 May 1936, Wargrave, Berks., UK. University Professor; Composer. Educ: RCM; ARCM (Organ & Piano Tchng.); ARCO; FRCO; BMus (Durham); DMus, Toronto; Accademia Chigiana, Siena, Italy. m. Olive May Smith, 1 d. Career: Comps. perfd. on BBC, CBC, at Cheltenham, Cookham, Guelph, Vancouver & Victoria Fests.; Lectr., Univ. of Vic., Can.; Vis. Lectr., Univ. of Toronto, Can.; Assoc. Prof., Univ. of Guelph, Can. & Univ. of Oregon, USA. Comps. incl: (recorded) Arctic Images, for orch.; Concerto for organ strings & timpani; Primrose in Paradise for orch.; Seabird Island, opera; Six Canadian Folk Songs; num. choral, organ & chmbr. works. Mbrships: CGGB. Hons: (prizes) Cobbett (Ex Aequo), 1956; Sullivan, 1956; Farrar, 1957; FM Napolitano, 1962. Hobbies: Gardening; Coin collecting. Mgmt: PROC. Address: Schl. of Music, Univ. of Oregon, Eugene, OR 97403, USA. 2, 3, 28.

HEARD, Alan, b. 7 Feb. 1942, Halifax, Can. Composer; Professor of Theory & Composition. Educ: BMus, McGill Univ., 1962; MFA, Princeton Univ., 1964; studies w. Boris Blacher, Hochschule für Music, Berlin, 1964-65. m. Ann Mackidd. Career: Asst. Prof., McGill Univ., 1967-72; Assoc. Prof., Kirkland Coll., NY, 1972-75; Assoc. Prof., Univ. of W Ont., 1975-. Comps. incl: Music for Brass, 1979; Sonata for Organ, 1978; Sinfonia nello Stile Antico, 1977; Double, for Harp & String Quartet, 1976; Timai, for 10 instruments, 1974; Prelude, for String Quartet, 1974; Voices, for Soprano & 4 instruments (recorded); Variations for Two Flutes & Two Horns (Berandol 1771, 1979); Variations for String Quartet (Berandol 1779, 1979), etc. Mbrships: Can. League of Comps.; Can. Music Centre; Comps., Authors & Publrs. Assn. of Can.; Can. Assn. of Univ. Schls. of Music; Coll. Music Soc. Hons: Anthony Amor Prize, 1959; Leutenant Governor's Bronze Medal, 1962; Harold H Helm Scholarship, 1962-64; Can. Coun. Scholarship, 1964-65; Hon. Mention, Arbury Orch. Competition, 1979. Address: R.R. No. 2, Ailsa Craig, Ontario N0M 1A0, Can.

HEARD, Gordon, b. Birmingham, UK. Educationalist; Conductor; Administrator; Composer; Flautist. Educ: MA (ed.) M Mus, (RCM); B Mus, (Lon). m. Noreen Heard. 2 d. Career: BBC, 1953-64; subsequently Music Advsr., Northamptonshire. Comps: Sinfonietta; Educl. works. Recordings: Flute Concerto by Nielsen. Publs: Play the Flute. Hobbies: Golf. Address: 80 St. Georges Ave., Northampton, UK.

HEARD, Thomas, b. 25 Sept. 1952, Belton, USA. Musician (horn); Music Instructor. Educ: BA (Econs); B Mus (lit. & Horn). Career: Horn, All-State Orch. of Tex., 1970-71; 3rd horn, Southwest Symph., under Raymond Schroeder, 3 yrs.; 1st horn, ibid., 4 yrs. Mbrships# Int. Horn Soc.; Tex. Music Educators Assn. Hobbies: Restoration of early Am. Violins &

Brass Instruments. Address: Box 410, Georgetown, TX 78626, USA.

HEATH, (Rt. Hon.) Edward R G, b. 9 July 1916, St. Peters-in-Thanet, Kent, UK. Member of Parliament; Musician (Piano; Organ; Voice; Conductor). Educ: MA, Balliol Coll., Oxford Univ. (Organ Scholar); D C L, ibid, 1971. Career incls: Prime Minister, 1970-74; Mbr., RCM, 1961-70; Chmn., London Symph. Orch. Trust, 1963-70; Hon. Mbr., London Symph. Orch., 1974; Mbr. trust, ibid, 1976-. Recordings: Elgar, Cockaigne, w. LSO; Robert Meyer Concert, BBC, 1973, Publs. incl: Music - A Joy for Life, 1976; Carols - The Joy of Christmas, 1977. Hons: FRCO; FRCM. Hobbies: Sailing; Music. Address: House of Commons, London SW1A 0AA, UK.

HEATH-DAVIES, Valerie, b. Neath, Glams., UK. Singer. Educ: Cardiff Coll. of Music; RAM; LRAM; Acad. of Music, Vienna. Debut: Wigmore Hall, 1967. Career: concerts & opera; apps. at Fest., Queen Elizabeth & Albert Halls, London; Sadlers Wells; TV & radio; major halls in Vienna; more recently, perfs. in Madame Butterfly, Turandot, Nabucco, Cosi fan Tutte & Don Giovanni; Voice Tchr. Mbr., ISM. Hobbies: Gardening; Reading; Crosswords. Address: 25 Old Fold View, Arkley, Barnet, Herts., UK.

HEATH-GRACIE, George Handel. Organist. Educ: BMus (Dunelm); FRCO. m. Marjory Josephine Knight. Career incl: Organist & Master of the Choristers, Derby Cathedral, 1933-57; Fndr., cond., Derby Bach Choir, 1935; Diocesan Choirmaster, 1936-57; Special Commissioner, RSCM, 1951-; num. broadcasts; examiner for Assoc. Bd.; lectr., adjudicator; num. recitals & concerts in UK, Can., USA, Asia, W Indies, S Am. & NA. Comps: var. items of ch. music. Contbr. to musical jrnls. Address: Shorms, Stockland, Honiton, Devon EX14 9DQ, UK.

HEATON, Eloise, b. 1 June 1909, Baldwinsville, NY, USA. Music Instructor. Educ: BMus, Coll. of Fine Arts, Syracuse Univ., 1933; MA (Musicol.), 1960; cert. in choir training, Royal Conserv. of Music, Toronto, 1950; studied comp. w. William Berwald & Quincy Porter. m. Charles Heaton. Career: radio app., Today's Woman, Syracuse, 1945; Itawamba Junior Coll., Fulton, Miss., 1950; N W Junior Coll., Senatobia, Miss., 1954-55. Mbrships: MTNA; MENC; Am. Musicol. Soc.; Int. Musicol. Soc.; Comps., Authors & Artists of Am. Address: 135 Kensington Place, Syracuse, NY 13210, USA.

HEBERT, Ronald A., b. 30 Aug. 1946, Yonkers, NY, USA. Orchestra Director. Educ: BS in Mus Ed. State Univ. Coll., Potsdam, NY (Crane Schl. of Music), 1968; MS in Mus Ed., ibid, 1971; Saratoga-Potsdam Choral Inst., 1971. m. Irene Haskins, 2 s. Career: Cond. & Music Dir. for sev. community & schl. prodns. incl: Man of La Mancha, Camelot, 1776, Mame, Fiorello, No No Nanaette, also for Utica presentation of Rock Operas Joseph & the Amazing Technicolor Dreamcoat & Truth of Truths; Violinist in Gtr. Utica Opera Guild Orch. & Con Amore Orch.; Tenor in Temple Emmanuel & Grace Ch. Choirs; Grad. Asst., Crane Schl. of Music, 1970-71 & Saratoga-Potsdam Choral Inst., 1971; Cond., Oneida Co. Elem. Orch., 1074; Music Dir. & Cond., Greater Utica Opera Guild. Comps: Revolution - A Theatre Piece, 1976; Adaptation of Truth of Truth (Ray Ruffin), both recorded. Mbrships: Music Educs. Nat. Conf.; NY State Schl. Music Assn.; Pres., Greater Utica Opera Guild; Am. String Tchrs. Assn. Address: 106 Proctor Blvd., Utica, NY 13501, USA.

HECHT, Ruth, b. 20 June 1929, Breslau, Germany. Pianist. Educ: Mus Bac, Melbourne. m. Michael McIntyre, 2 s, 1 d. Debut: Pianist w. De Freville Trio, 1976. Career: Pianist w. De Freville Trio (Michael McIntyre, violin & Christopher van Kampen, cello), Purcell Room, London, UK, 1976. Mbr., Solo Perfs. Sect., Inc. Soc. of Musicians. Hons: Homewood Scholar, 1946-48. Hobbies: Gardening; Walking; Needlework; Musical Instrument Making. Address: 51 De Freville Ave., Cambridge, UK.

HECK, Thomas F, b. 10 July 1943, Washington, DC, USA. Musicologist. Educ: BA in Music, Univ. of Notre Dame, Ind., 1965; PhD in Music Hist., Yale Univ., 1970. m. Anne Elizabeth Goodrich, 1 s., 1 d. Career: Asst. Prof. of Music, Case Western Reserve Univ., 1971-74; Asst. Prof. of Music, John Carroll Univ., 1974-75; Music critic Los Angeles Times, 1976-77; Hd., Music Library, Ohio State Univ., 1978-. Lectr. on music printing. & hist. of the guitar; throughout USA. Publ: Critical Edit. of Selected Works for Solo Guitar by Mauro Giuliani, 1973. Contbr. to Jrnl. of Am. Musicological Soc.; Current Musicol.; MLA Notes; Grove's Dictionary; Guitar Review; Il Fronimo; Jrl. of Lute Soc. of Am. Mbrships: Int. & Am. Musicological Soc.; Music Lib. Assn.; Lute Soc. of Am.; Fndr. & Archivist, Guitar Fndn. of Am., 1973-; Chmn., Guitar

Committee, Am. String Tchrs. Assn., 1972-74. Recip: Fulbright Schlrship. to Vienna, 1968-69. Hobbies: Photography; Old instruments; Sailing. Address: Music Library, Ohio State Univ., Columbus, OH 43210, USA.

HECKMANN, Harald, b. 6 Dec. 1924, Germany. Musicologist. Educ: Musicology, Freiburg im Br. (w. Wilibald Gurlitt & Hermann Zenck), 1944-52. Career: Asst. to W Gurlitt, Freiburg im Br., 1950-54; Dir., Deutsches Musikgeschichtliches Archiv Kassel, 1971; on Bd. Dirs., Deutsches Rundfunkarchiv, Franfurt a M., AIBM, Gen. Sec., 1957-74; Pres., ibid., 1974; hon. mbr., ibid., 1974-76; Sec., RISM; VP, RILM; Co-Prs., RIdIM; Mbr., Musikgeschichtliche Kommission; Sec., Kuratorium Internationale Schubert-Gesellschaft; Exec. Comm. Mbr., Gesellschaft für Musikforschung, 1968-74; Ed., Documenta Musicologica, & Catalogus Musicus, 1961-72. Publs: Deutsches Musikgeschichtliches Archiv, Katalog der Filmsammlung, 1955; W.A. Mozart, Thamos, König in Agypten, Chöre und Zwischenaktmusiken, 1956; W. A. Mozart, Musik zu Pantomimen und Balletten, 1963; Chr. W. Cluck, La rencontre imprévue, Edn. und Kritischer Bericht, 1964; Elektronische Datenverarbeitung in der Musikwissenschaft, 1967; Address: 6242 Kronbert/Taunus, Albanusstrasse 6, German Fed. Repub.

HECL, Jan, b. 29 May 1929, Svebohov, Czechoslovakia. Flautist; Professor. Educ: prague Conserv., 1955; Acad. of Musical Arts, Prague, 1960. Career: Concert perfs., films, TV, radio; Mbr., Prague Woodwind Quintet. Var. recordings. Mbrship: Guild of Czech Composers & Concert Artists. Hons: 1st Prize, Competition, Prague Spring, 1959. Mgmt: Pragokoncert, Prague. Address: Janouskova 1, Prague 6, Czech.

HEDGES, Anthony John, b. 5 Mar. 1931, Bicester, UK. Senior Lecturer in Music; Composer; Pianist. Educ: B Mus, Keble Coll., Oxford; MA, ibid; LRAM. m. Delia Joy Marsden, 2 d., 2 s. Career: Pianist, Arr., Royal Signals Band, 1955-57; Tchr., Lectr., Royal Scottish Acad. of Music, 1957-62; Lectr., Univ. of Hull, 1962-; Reader in Comp., ibid, 1978; Sr. Lectr. in Music, ibid, 1967-. Comps. incl: 28 Orchl.; 11 Choral works; 10 pieces of Chmbr. Music; 2 operas; var. collections ed. music; 13 ANthems; 21 Partsongs; Ballet; Stage Incidental Music, Songs; filmscore; TV music. Contbr. to: Yorks. Post; The Guardian; The Scotsman; The Glasgow Herald; Musical Times; Current Musicol.; Comp. Mbrships incl: CGGB; Exec. Committee, ibid, 1968-71; Chmn., ibid, 1972; Joint Chmn., ibid, 1973; Coun., Ctrl. Music Library; Coun., SPNM; Music Bd., Nat. Coun. for Academic Awards, 1973-76; Music Panel, Lincs. & Humberside, 1973-78. Address: 13 Norfolk St., Beverly, Humberside HU17 7DN, UK. 1, 3, 19.

HEDSTROM, Ruth Elaine, b. 30 Oct. 1925, Honolulu, Hawaii, USA. String Teacher; Violinist. Educ: BA (Music Educ.), Univ. of Neb., Omaha, 1947; Ill. Ctrl. Coll.; Violin study w. Samuel F Thomas & Richard E Duncan. m. Richard M Hedstrom (dec. 1971), 3 s. Career: Violinist w. Neb. Women's Symph., 1945, Southern Idaho Symph., 1947-48, Rapid City Symph. 1948-51, Gary Symph., 1957, Peoria Symph., 1951-; Knox-Galesburg Symph., 1974-78; Peoria Symph. Chmbr. Orch.; Preoria Civic Opera Orch., 1975-; String Tchr., Acad. of Our Lady, Peoria, 1967-70, & Roanoke-Benson Unit Dist. 60, 1971-72; Pvte. violin tchr., current. Mbrships: Am. String Tchrs. Assn.; Peoria Fedn. of Musicians. Hons. incl: WH Schmoeller Music Schlrship, 1944. Hobbies: Art; Photography; Sewing; Gardening. Address: 113 Crestwood Dr., E Peoria, IL 61611, USA. 138.

HEDWALL, Lennart, b. 16 Sept. 1932, Goteborg, Sweden. Composer; Conductor; Critic; Pianist; Organist. Educ: Royal Conserv., Stockholm, & in Paris, Vienna, Darmstadt (comp.); studied w. Karl-Birger Blomdahl. m. Ingegerd H Hedwall, 4 c. Debut: Swedish Radio, 1950. Career: Cond., Riksteatern, 1958-60, Stora Teatern, 1962-65, Göteborg, Royal Opera, Stockholm, 1967-68, Orbro Chmbr. & Symph. Orch., 1968-74, Radio, TV, Concerts, Sweden; Guest Cond., Finland, Holland, Norway, Czechoslovakia. Comps. incl: (publd.) Oboe, Cello Concerti; Mr. Sleeman Comes (Opera); num. works for String Orch.; Cmbr. Music for var. ensembles; Piano, Organ works; Songs; Cantatas; Stage music; revisions of older Swedish works; (recorded) Solo, Choral Songs; Canzona per orch. d'archi. Recordings: as Cond., Orebro Chmbr. Orch. Publs: Svensk Kyrkomusik Under 1900-Talet, 1966; Antecningar Kring Peterson-Bergers Pianosviter, 1967; Hugo Alfven, 1973 Operett och musical, 1976. Contbr. to Dagens Nyheter. Mbr. Bd., Soc. of Swedish Comps., 1969-. Hons: Recip. Scholarships, Stockholm City, 1961, 1971, Swedish State, 1966-67, 1972, 1975-76, 1978; Birger Sjoberg Prize, 1975. Hobbies: Literature; Theater. Address: 37 Mardvagen, 16137 Bromma, Sweden.

HEENAN, Ashley David Joseph, b. 11 Sept. 1925, Wellington, NZ. Composer; Conductor; Lecturer; Broadcaster. Educ: Vic. Univ., Wellington; RCM, London: Dip. Music & BMus, Vic. Univ., Wellington, NZ. m. Glenda Anne Craven. Career incls: Musical Dir., Schola Musica, of NZ Symph. Orch., 1961-; NZ Youth Orch., 1965-75; Musical Advsr. & Orch. Coord., QE II Arts Coun., 1964-65; Musical Dir., NZ Ballet Trust, 1966-68. Comps. incl: Film Scores: Moana Roa; Rotorua Symph.; Radio Drama: Jack Winters Dream; Incidental music: War & Peace; Scottish Dances for Orch.; A College Overture; Maori Suite (Soloists, chorus & orch.); Sea Songs (baritone & orch.); Var. vocal & instrumental works; arrs. & transcriptions of traditional Maori music. Num. recordings. Publs. incl: The Schola Musica, 1974; The NZ Symph. Orch., 1971. Contbr. to Challenges in Music Educ., 1974 (UNESCO). Mbr., profl. orgs. Hons. incl: UNESCO Music Fellowship, 1962-63. Hobbies: Croquet; Pvte. Aviation Hist. Address: 11 Kiwi St., Alicetown, Wellington, NZ. 4, 17, 23, 28, 29.

HEERKENS, Adrianus (Ad) Ludovicus Cornelis Donatus, b. 10 Feb. 1913, Tilburg, Netherlands. Music Educator; Author of Music Pedagogical Books, Articles etc. Educ: Degree, Amsterdam Conserv. m. Wilhelmina V Hooff, 5 children. Career: Hd. Music Dept., Social-Cultural Acad., De Kopse Hof, Nijmegen; Coord., KASP courses for Min. of Culture, Recreation & Social Welfare; Mbr., Commission for Curriculum Dev. in Music, Min. of Sci. & Educ.; Author & comp. of folk & children's songs. Num. recordings. Publs. incl: Muziak in Dienstverband, 1976. Contbr. to profl. jrnls. Mbrships. incl: Royal Netherlands Musicians Union. Hons: Kt., Order of Oranje Nassau. Hobbies: Photography; Writing; Lit. Address: Molenaarschoek ; Bunnik, Holland.

HEESCHEN, Barbara Ann Stuhlmacher, b. 22 Dec. 1931, Gary, Ind., USA. Pianist; Folk Singer; Teacher; Choral Director. Educ: BA, Hanover Coll., Ind., 1953; MMus, Ctrl. Mich. Univ., 1977; Cert. Tchr., MMTA; Dips., NGPT; Dips., Am. Coll. of Mujsicians. m. Jerry P Heeschen, 3 s. Career: Num. TV apps.; Dir., Youth Choir, Memorial Presby. Ch., Midland, Mich., 1963-; Music Instructor, Acad. of Music, Delta Coll., Mich., 1975-76; Piano Tchr., 1961-; Mbr., Canyona di Musica Chmbr. Choir. Recordings: Choir & musical records; Folksong & harpsichord tapes for radio. Contbr. to Midland Daily News (Music Critic). Mbrships: Nat. MTA; Asst. Coord. of Student Activities Mich. MTA; Midland MTA (VP, Student Activities Chmn.); NGPT (Bd. of Adjudicators). Hons: DAR Citizenship Award, 1949; Nat. Hon. Soc., 1949; Hanover Coll. Alumni Award, 1953. Hobbies: Violets; Knitting. Address: 4426 Gladding Ct., Midland, MI 48640, USA. 5, 27.

HEFNER, Sharon Ann, b. 25 Sept. 1952, Lake Jackson, Tex., USA. Musicologist; Pianist. Educ: BMus, 1974, MA, 1976, Eastman Schl. of Music, Univ. of Rochester. Career: Micrographics Specialist, Sibley Music Lib., Eastman Schl. of Music. Mbrships: Am. Musicol. Soc.; Nat. Micrographics Soc. hons: Nat. Merit Schlr., 1971-74; Grad. Awards, 1974 & 75, Grad. Asstship., 1975, Eastman Schl. of Music. Hobby: Ballet. Address: 424 University Ave., Box 139, Rochester, NJ 14607, USA.

HEFT, David Yule Marchbank, b. 25 July 1943, Edinburgh, Scotland. Musician (pianoforte & organ). Educ: ALCM; LLCM. Debut: Edinburgh, Scotland. Career: Tchng., Perfng. & Choir Training. Mbrships: Edinburgh Soc. of Musicians; ISM; Musicians Union; Glasgow Soc. of Musicians; Edinburgh Soc. of Organists. Hobbies: Hi-Fi; Fishing. Address: 13 Glengyle Terrace, Edinburgh, EH3 9LN, Scotland, UK.

HEGDAL, Magne Gunnar, b. 27 Dec. 1944, Gjerdrum, Norway. Composer; Pianist; Critic. Educ: Dip., comp., Conserv. Oslo, 1972. m. Therese Hauge, 3 children. Debut: Piano, 1969. Career: Num. perfs., piano, chmbr., vocal & orchl. works, all Scandinavian countries, UK, Germany, USA & Vienna, Austria; Occasional radio & TV apps., pianist & comp. Comps: Herbarium (piano); 3 Prunes; Piece for 2 pianos. Recordings: Sinfonia; 5 Studies for Organ; Herbarium & Toccata. Contbr., reviews, to Norsk Musikktidskrift, 1974-75; Int. Music Guide; sev. books & mags; Critic in Dagbladet, Oslo. Mbr. of Bd., Soc. Norwegian Comps. Hobbies: Painting; Woodcarving; Gothic Arch. Address: Frogner Terr. 7, Oslo 2, Norway, 4.

HEGEDUS, Margit Franciska, b. 22 Nov. 1922, Budapest, Hungary. Violinist; Teacher of Violin; Performer. Educ: studied w. mother (former pupil of Ysaye), father Ferenc Hegedus, Max Rostal & Phillip Newman. Career: toured Brit. Isles giving recitals; broadcasts for BBC; currently Tchr., RAM Jr. Exhibners., Westminster Schl. & N London Music Ctr. Mbr: ISM. Recip. Hon. ARAM., 1969. Hobbies: Reading; Writing; Listening to music. Address: 8, Kensington Place, London W8 7PT, UK. 3.

HEGEDUS, Olga, b. 18 Oct. 1920, London, UK. Cellist. Educ: London Violoncello Schl.; pvte. study w. Pierre Fournier. Career: Solo recitals; Many BBC perfs. w. Trios, Chmbr. Ensembles, etc.; Co-Prin. cellist, Engl. Chmbr. Orch.; TV apps. & world tours. Recordings: Art of Fugue, Bach, & Musical Offering w. Tilford Fest. Ensemble: The Curlew, Warlock, w. Haffner Ensemble; Vivaldi Motets w. Teresa Berganza & Engl. Chmbr. Orch. Contbr. to: A Pictorial Review. Mbrships: ISM, London Violoncello Club. Hobbies: Reading; Swimming. Address: 8 Kensington Pl., London W8, UK.

HEGER, Jiri, b. 11 Jan. 1947, Hradec Králové, Czech Violist. Educ: Dip., Prague Conserv., 1968, Prague Acad. of Music, 1972. Debut: Rudolfinum Hall, Prague, 1963. Career incls: Soloist, Pragoconcert (Ctrl. Czech. Agcy.), 1965-; Mbr., Czech. Radio Symph. Orch., 1966-68, Skvor Quartet, 1968-73; Concertmaster, Viola Sect., Czech. Ctrl. Army Orch., 1973-74; Soloist, Collegium Musa Pragensis, 1972-75; Mbr., Tehran Symph. Orch., 1975-; Soloist, Tehran Phil. Orch. & Jeunesses Musicales d'Iran, 1975-; 1st Concertmaster, Viola sect., Tehran Symph. Orch., 1976-. Recordings: w. Skvor Quartet, Panton Records. Mbrships: Elected, Young Soloist Sect., Czech. Comps. Fedn. Recip. num. awards as soloist & chmbr. musician. Mgmt: Pragoconcert. Address: Belehradska 47/1402, 120 00 Prague 2, Czechoslovakia.

HEGER, Theodore Ernest, b. 27 Feb. 1907, St. Paul, Minn., USA. Musicologist. Educ: BA, Univ. of Minn.; MMus, Univ. of Mich. m. Dorothy J Heger, 1 s., 1 d. Career: Chmn., Music Dept., Mesabi State Coll., Virginia, Minn., 1929-45; Prof. of Music (Music Hist. Musicol.), Univ. of Mich., 1945-76 (Prof. Emeritus). Mbrships: Am. Musicol. Soc.; Pi Kappa Lambda; Pres., Chi Chapt., ibid., 3 terms; AAUP. Publs: Music of the Classic Period, 1969. The Symjphony & the Symphonic Poem (w. Earl V Moore), 6th ed. 1974. Contbr. to profl. jrnls. Address: 1502 Golden Ave., Ann Arbor, MI 48104, USA.

HEGIERSKI, Kathleen, b. 6 June 1947, Batavia, NY, USA. Opera Singer. Educ: BA (Music), Rosary Hill Coll., Buffalo, NY; MMus, Manhattan Schl. of Music, NYC: Ctr. Lyrique Int., Geneva, Switzerland. m. Louis Salemno. Debut: Geneva Opera House, 1972. Career incl: broadcasts w. Radio Suisse Romande, Geneva, 1971-72; The Ballad of Baby Does, NYC Opera, on Pub. Broadcasting System, 1976. Currently Soloist w. NYC Opera. Hons: Kirsten Flagstad Mem. Grant, 1972; William Matheus Sullivan Fndn. Grant, 1971-76; Minna Kaufmann Ruud Mem. Grant, 1973. Mbr: Am. Guild of Musical Artists. Address: 160 W. End Ave., Apt. 17M, NY, NY 10023, USA.

HEIBERG, Harold, b. 6 Feb. 1922, Twin Valley, Minn., USA. Pianist: Vocal Coach. Educ: BMus, St. Olaf Coll., 1943; MA, Columbia Tchrs. Coll., 1949; Piano Study w. Karl Ulrich Schnabel & Leonard Shure; Voice Study w. Gerhard Huesch & Cornelius Reid. m. Eva Margrethe Lundberg. Debut: Tully Hall, NY, 1971. Career: Solo Recitals in Germany, Austria, UK, France, Italy, Switzerland, Norway & USA: Apps. w. Ensemble w. Voice, Violin & Cello, Germany, Austria & USA; Fac. Mbr., N Tex. State Univ. & Vocal Inst., Graz, Austria. Publs: Translator of Parts of over a hundred Choral Works inclng. Dvorak; Songs of Nature, Respighi: Laud to the Nativity, Shostakovich: Execution of Stephan Schenker: Der Freie Satz (w. Ernst Oster). Mbrships: Pi Kappa Lambda: Music Tchrs. Nat. Assn.; Tex. MTA: Luth. Soc. for Worship, Music & The Arts. Hons: Disting, Alumnus Award, St. Olaf Coll., 1974. Hobbies: Gardening. Address: 2111 N Locust, Denton, TX 76201, USA.

HEICHELMANN, Palle, b. 19 Aug. 1935. Violinist. Educ: Royal Danish Conserv. of Music, Copenhagen; Juilliard Schl. of Music, NYC, USA; Rimsky Korsakoff Conserv., Leningrad, USSR. m. Anette Amand, 1 s., 1 d. Debut: Copenhagen, 1959. Career: About 2000 apps. in Europe, USA & USSR w. Danish Quartet. Recordings w. Valois & Fona. Recip., Prize of Honour, Danish State Cultural Fund, 1968. Address: Akavcievej 30, 2830 Virum, Denmark.

HEICKING, Wolfram, b. 19 May 1927, Leipzig, German Dem. Repub. Composer; Professor of Music. Educ: Music Acad. Leipzig; State exam, 1951; Prof. Comp. m. Lieselotte Heicking, 1 s., 1 d. Career: Comp. for film, TV; Stage msic; Chmbr. music; Symph. music; pop music. Comp. incl: Concertino for Clarinet, Piano and Orch.; 2 sonatas for Piano; TV Ballet; Contrasts: 30 Songs; Musical: The World is Round. Mbrships: Chmn., Assn. of Comp. and Musicologists German Dem. Repub.; Dist. Soc. Berlin. Hons: Art Prize German Dem. Repub., 1973; Art Prize FDGB (Union of the GDR); Patriotic Merit Order in gold. Address: Gündelfinger Str. 32, 1157 Berlin, German Dem. Repub.

HEIFETZ, Daniel, b. 20 Nov. 1948, Kansas City, Mo., USA. Concert Violinist. Educ: Dip., Beverley Hills High Schl.; Calif. Inst. of the Arts; Dip., Curtis Inst. of Music w. Efrem Zimbalist & Ivan

Galamian. m. Janne Freeman, 1 d. Debut: Avery Fisher Hall, Lincoln Center, NYC, 1970. Career: Concert tours, USA, Can., Europe & S Am., Unaccompanied violin recital, CBS TV; app., CBC TV (Can.); Bd. of Govs., Inst. for Humane Resource Dev., Phila., Pa.; Violin fac., Peabody Conserv. of Music; Bd. of Advsrs. Nat. Cathedral Choral Soc., Wash., DC. Mbr., The Bohemians. Hons: 1st Prize, Merriweather-Post Competition, Wash., DC, 1969; 4th Prize, Int. Tchaikovsky Competition, Moscow, USSR, 1978. Hobbies: Skiing; Horseback riding. Mgmt: Columbia Artists Mgmt. Inc., NY. Address: 390 Riverside Dr., NY, NY 10025, USA.

HEIFETZ, Jascha, b. 2 Feb. 1901, Russia (Citizen of USA). Violinist. Educ: Petrograd Conserv. of Music. Debut: age 7. Career: Concert perfs. in Russia, Germany, Austro-Hungary, Scandinavia & USA, 1917; UK; toured Australia & NZ, 1921; Far E, 1923; World tour, 1925-27, and subsequent regular appearances in many countries; Commissioned works from var. leading composers, incl. William Walton's Violin Concerto. Mbrships: 1st VP, Guild of Musical Artists; Hon., Soc. of Concerts, Paris; Assn. des Anciens Eleves du Conserv.; Cir. Int. de la Jeunesse Artistique; Hon. VP, Mark Twain Soc.; Hon. Pres., Musicians Fund of Am. Recip: Legion d'Honneur. Address: Beverly Crest, Beverly Hills, CA, USA.

HEILBRON, Annette Marian, b. London, UK. Harpsichordist; Organist; Pianist. Educ: BMus, Goldsmith's Coll., Univ. of London; LRAM; ARCM; AGSM; studied at GSM & w. Harold Craxton, Celia Bizony. Career: Harpsichordist, Helicon Ensemble; App., Belgian TV; num. Recitals, UK; Accomp.; Continuo Player; Tchr., Piano, Harpsichord. Mbr. ISM. Hobbies: Reading; Theatre; Cooking; Dressmaking. Address: 25 Ave. Mansions, Funchley Rd., London NW3 7AX, UK.

HEILMANN, Harald Arthur, b. 9 Apr. 1924, Aue, Saxony, Germany. Composer. Educ: Dip. in Music Theory, Leipzig Music HS. m. Hildegard Leuckfeld, 1 d. Career: Lectr., German Acad. of Music, Berlin, 1951; Acad. of Music, Stuttgart, 1969; Acad. of Music, Karlsruhe, 1971. Compositions incl: Symph.; Concerto for piano & orch.; Concerto for Trombone, Cor Anglais & Orch.; Concerto for Harp, Cello & String; Intro., Passacaglia & Fugue for Orch.; Der Sundenfall (oratorio); Mass for Soprano, Choir & Brass; Sonatas for var. instruments. Recordings: Mass (Euromaster); Sonata I for Violin & Piano (Collosseum). Contbr. to var. music jrnls. Mbrships: Gema; German Composer's Union. Addrss: D-6931 Brombach, German Fed. Repub.

HEILMANN, Ingeborg, b. 22 Feb. 1903, Allingabro, Denmark. Music Librarian. Educ: Cand. Phil., Univ. Copenhagen; Italian, Spanish & Russian, Univ. of Arhus. m. Johan Christian Heilmann. Career: Libn., State & Univ. Lib., Arhus, 1923-71; Music Libn., ibid., 1928-71; Ret'd., 1971. Publs: Jt. Ed., Statsbibliotekets Fagkatalog over danske Musikalier I, 1932; Statsbibliotekets Fagkatalog over undenlandske Musikalier I-IV, 2 Ed., 19512-60. Contbr. to Forestry bibliography of Oppermann & Grundtvig Oph., 1931-35. Mbrships: incl: Int. Assn. of Music Libs. Recip. F M II Medal, Order of Merit, 1971. Hobbies: Prehist., Danish & Foriegn; Gemmol. Address: Enebaervej 11, 8240 Risskov, Denmark.

HEILNER, Irwin, b. 14 May 1908, NY, NY, USA. Composer; Piano Teacher; Librarian. Educ: BS, Tchrs. Coll. Columbia Univ.; MA, ibld.; MS, Columbia Univ.; studled w. Rubin Goldmark, Nadia Boulanger, Roger Sessions. m. Florence Kronhaus, 1 s., 1 d. Career: Prin. Libn., Passaic Public Lib., NJ; Music Critic, Jewish Currents Mag. Compositions incl: (publd.) The Traveler; The Tide Rises: The Wild Anemone; Boogie Woogie Rhapsody.Recordings: Chinese Songs, Comps. Recordings Inc. Mbr. Am. Comps. Alliance; Am. Music Centre. Recip. Honorable Mention, for Suite For Harp & Chmbr. Orch., Northern Calif. Harpists Assn. 1950. Hobbies: Folk Dancing; Travelling; Reading. Address: 101 Dawson Ave., Clifton, NJ 07012, USA.

HEIM, Elsbeth, b. 27 June 1917, St. Gallen, Switz. Pianist. Educ: Dip., Conserv. of Music, Lausanne. m. Werner Heim, 2 children. Career: 4 concert tours across USA; apps. in Budapest, Helsinki, Rome, Liège, Austria, Germany, Switz.; Specialist in contemp. piano music, giving num. 1st pers. (concert & radio). Recordings: Jecklin Disco, Switz.; Disque Duchesne, Belgium; Preis der Stadt St. Gallen, 1977. Mbr., Lyceum Club. Recip., title Artista Europea, Rome, 1973. Address: CH 9000 St. Gallen, Notkerstr. 19, Switz.

HEIM, Leo Edward, b. 22 Sept. 1913, Chandler, Ind., USA. Pianist; Teacher; Organist. Educ: Northwestern Univ.; BM, MM, Am. Conserv. of Music. m. Margaret Borchers. Career: Many yrs. as solo pianist in recital & w. orchs.; Ensemble Pianist; Accompanist for instrumentalists & singers; Mbr., Piano Fac., Am. Conserv. of Music, 1935-; Dean, 1957; Pres., 1971-. Mbrships: Chmn., Standards Commn., Phi Mu Alpha Sinfonia;

Soc. of Am. Musicians; AGO; Pres., Cliff Dwellers Club; Univ. Club, Chgo. Hobbies: Travel; Gardening; Theater. Address: 515 Vine Ave., Park Ridge, IL 60068, USA. 8.

HEIM, Norman Michael, b. 30 Sept. 1929, Chgo., Ill., USA. University Professor; Clarinettist; Conductor; Composer; Writer. Educ: BMus, Univ. of Evansville, 1951; MMus, Univ. of Rochester, Eastman Schl. of Music; DMA, ibid. m. Catherine Lou Tiemann, 2 d. Career: Clarinet soloist & chmbr. musician for 28 yrs.; Fndr. & clarinettist, Md. Woodwind Quintet; Fac., Univ. of Evansville & Ctrl. Missouri Coll.; Prof., Univ. of Md., 1960-; Comps. incl: Suite for unacc. clarinet, 1972; A Carol for Jesus, 1975; Preludium & Canzona for clarinet choir, 1974; Sonata for Clarinet & Piano, 1976; Suite for Horn Trio, 1978; other choral & instrumental works. Publs. incl: A Handbook for Clarinet Performance, 1970; The Clarinet Instructor, 1968; Development of the Clarinet Altissimo Register, 1976; Style Studies for Clarinet, 1978. Contbr. to num. profl. jrnls. mbr. profl. socs. Hons: Eli Lilly Fndn. Grant, 1959-60; Rsch. grant, Univ. of Md. Hobbies: Gardening; Composing; Travel. Address: Music Dept., Univ. of Md., Coll. Park, MD 20742, USA. 28.

HEIM, Werner, b. 28 Mar. 1909, St. Gallen, Switz. Conductor. Educ: Univ. Zürich, Berlin; Conserv. Zürich, dip. piano, dip. theory; Music Acad. Berlin, schl. of cond. m. Elsbeth Heim-Bernegger, 2 s. Career: Oratorium singer, baritone; Cond. Switz., Berlin, Vienna, Cologne. Milan;o Fndr. St. Gallen Chmbr. Orch., many first perf.; Num. prod. Radio Zürich, Radio Lugano, Radio Cologne WDR. Recordings: Ernest Blod, Avodath Hakodesch. Mbrships: Swiss Musical Art Soc.; Swiss Org. for Music Pedagogues. Contbr. to: var. newspapers. Hons: Prize St. Gallen, 1963; Prize Bd. of Citizens, St. Gallen, 1969. Address: Notkerstr. 19, CH 9000 St. Gallen, Switz.

HEINEKEN, Mary Francesca, b. 14 Apr. 1922, Amsterdam, Netherlands. Singer. Educ: Conserv., Rotterdam; Pvte. studies w. M Dresden. Dhout & Noemie Peringian. Debut: 1957. Career: Apps. in Holland, Spain & France; w. Nederlands Kodaly Koor for 8 yrs. Contbr. to Mens en Melodie. Hobbies: Mountain Walking; Cross Country Skiing. Address: Tavealey, 7499 Feldis, Switzerland.

HEINER, Brita, b. 20 Feb. 1915, Malmo, Sweden. Opera Singer; Professor of Singing. Educ: Conserv. of Music Copenhagen, 1934-37; Royal Acad. of Music, Stockholm, 1937-40; Royal Opera Acad. of singing, 1943-45; pvte. study in Italy & Sweden. m. (1) Gunnar MacDowall, 1 s.; (2) Gunnar Hagglund. Concert Debut: 1941. Opera Debut: as Olympia-Antonia-Guiletta, Tales of Hoffman, 1953. Career: Oscars Theatre Operetta, Stockholm, 1943-44; w. Swedish Broadcasting, 1938-; TV apps., Sweden, Rome, Can., Monte Carlo. Recordings incl: Three Waltzes, J Strauss; Swedish Folksongs. Contbr. music criticism to jrnls. Mbr., Swedish Confedn. of Singing. Hons: incl Le Fleur de Lis, Pro Patria. Hobbies: Reading; Writing. Address: Klittervagen 26, 32070 Halmstad, Sweden.

HEININEN, Paavo Johannes, b. 13 Jan. 1938, Helsinki, Finland. Composer. Teacher. Educ: BA, Helsinki Univ., 1959; comp., piano & cond., Sibelius Acad., 1957-60; Dip. in Comp., ibid., 1960; further studies in Cologne, 1960-61 & Juilliard Schl. of Music, NY, 1961-62. m. Anja Anneli Sipolainen, 3 c. Career: Pianist, Finnish Nat. Opera, 1960-61; Lectr. on Theoretical Subjects, Sibelius Acad., 1962-63; Chief Instr. of Theoretical Subjects, Turku Acad. of Music, Inst. of Theoretical Subjects, Turku Acad. of Music, 1963-66; Tchr. of Comp., Lectr. on the Theory of Music & on the Hist. of New Music, Sibelius Acad., 1966-. Compositions incl: Choral Works, Solo songs, Chamber works, Orchl. works, Solo works w. Orch. & Instrumental solo works. Contbr. of essays on Finnish composers to the mag. Musikki, Helsinki. Address: Pöytäalhontie 81, 04400 Järvenpää, Finland.

HEINIÖ, Mikko Kyösti, b. 18 May 1948, Tampere, Finland. Composer; Music Teacher. Educ: MA, Musicol., Helsinki Univ., 1972; Cert. for comp., Sibelius Acad., 1975; studied comp., Hochschule der Künste, Belin, 1975-77; Dip. in comp., Sibelius Acad., 1977; Lic. in Philos. (Musicology) Helsinki Univ., 1978. Career: Tchr., Espoo Music Inst., 1971-75, Helsinki Univ., 1977; perfs. in Ung Nordisk Music Fest., 1973-78, ISCM, 1978. Comps. incl: 2 Piano Concertos; 2 Song Cycles for Voice & Symph. Orch.; Tredicia for orch.; Bassoon Concerto; Akása for 6 trombones; Quattrofonia for flute, oboe, bassoon & harpsichord; Notturno di fiordo for flute & harp; Lindgreniana for oboe; Drei finnische Volkslieder for choir; songs; piano pieces. Mbrships: Bd. of Dirs., Soc. of Finnish Comp; Chmn., Soc. for publ. of Finnish Music. Hons: 1st Prize, Competition for Young Comps., 1972. Hobbies: Lit.; Philos. Address: Kuhatie 4 B 8, Espoo 17, Finland.

HEINITZ, Thomas, b. 12 Aug. 1921, Berlin, Germany. Audio Engineering Consultant; Musical Journalist; Record

Reviewer. Educ: BSc, (Eng.) London Univ. m. Viva S Eckert, 1 s., 2 d. Career: Cond., Chmbr. Orch., 1944-47; Ed., 'Critique', 1943-55; London Music Coirres., 'Saturday Review', USA, 1948-71; Record Reviewer', 'Records & Recording', 1958-; Opera & Concert Critic, Classical Music Weekly, 1977-; Tech. Dir., Gramophone Exchange, 1943-55; Own Studio, 'Music in the Home', 1956-. Contbr. to num. jrnls. inclng: Observer, Homes & Gardens, etc. Hobby: Tennis. Address: 35 Moscow Rd., London W2, UK. 3.

HEINLEIN, Federico A, b. 25 Jan. 1912, Berlin, Germany. University Lecturer; Composer; Music Critic. Educ: Study of Harmony, Counterpoint & Composition, Sternsches Konservatorium, Berlin; Music History w. Arnold Schering; Musicol., w. Friedrich Blume, Berlin Univ.; Composition w. Nadia Boulanger. m. Inés Santander. Career: Lectr., Music Fac., Chilean State Univ.; Music Critic, El Mercurio (in Spanish), Condor (German). Compositions: Sinfonietta (orch.), 1954; String Quartet; Tripartita for wind quintet; A capella work, songs for voice & piano. Recordings: Tripartita; Num. tape recordings. Contbr. to Revista Musical Chilean & Chilean newspapers. Mbrships: Chmn., Chilean Arts Critics Circle; 1st VP, Interamerican Assn. of Music Critics; Chilean Nat. Assn. of Composers; Chilean Schl. of Jrnlsts. Hons: 1st Prize, Composer's Contest, Vina del Mar, Chile, 1946; Sev. other composition awards. Hobbies: Nature; Languages. Address: Holanda 434 Dep. 61, Santiago 9, Chile.

HEINRICH, Siegfried, b. 10 Jan. 1935, Dresden, German Dem. Repub. Conductor. Educ: 1954-61 studies Dresden, Frankfurt. Debut: 1945, Dresden. Career: 1957, Cond. Chmbr. Orch., Frankfurt; since 1961 artistic Dir. Hersfeld Festival Concerts; Lectr. Music Acad. Kassel; Cond. Radio Symph. Orch. Prag, Frankfurt, Hanover, Luxemburg, ORTF (France), Budapest, Venice, Stuttgart; Concert tours throughout Europe, Japan; New interpretations of Bach - The Art of the Fugue, Händel - Messiah, Monteverdi - Maria vesper. Mgmt: Concert Dir. Robert Kollitsch, Geisbergstr. 40, Berlin 30. Address: Am. Hopfengarten 5, 6430 Bad Hersfeld, German Fed. Repub.

HEINY, Margaret Harris, b. 16 Oct. 1911, Amarillo, Tex., USA. Concert Pianist & Organist. Educ: Teaching Certs., St. Louis Inst. of Music & Sherwood Music Schl., Chgo. m. Roy Wendell Heiny. Career: Tchr., organ & piano, 30 yrs.; Organist, 1st Ch. of Christ Scientist, Amarillo; Organ & Piano concerts. Compositions (publs.): My Eyes are Unto Thee (song), 1975; Devotional (organ solo), 1975. Mbrships: Pres., Amarillo MTA, 3 yrs.; Dean, Amarillo Guild of Organists, 2 yrs.; Am. Coll. of Musicians; Pres., local music club, 3 yrs. Hobbies: Reading; Walking; Romping w. German shepherd Dog; People. Address: 1503 Travis, Amarillo, TX 79102, USA. 5.

HEINZE, (Sir) Bernard Thomas, b. 1 July 1894, Shepparton, Vic., Australia. University Professor; Conductor. Educ: MA, Univ. of Melbourne; RCM; Schola Cantorium, Paris; FRCM. m. Valerie Antonia Hennessy, 1932, 3 s. Career: Acad. Staff, Univ. of Melbourne, 1924-; Ormond Prof. of Music, ibid., 1925-; Dir.-Gen. of Music, Australian Broadcasting Commn. 1929-32; Cond., Royal Melbourne Phil. Soc., 1928-; Melbourne Symph. Orch., 1933-46; Cond., Vic. Symph Orch., current; Dir., State Conserv. of NSW 1957-66; Cond. Australian Broadcasting Commn. Mbrships: Chmn. Commonwealth Assistance to Australian Composers, 1967-; Music Advsry. Committee, Australian Coun. for the Arts, 1969 Hons: Kt.; Off., Order of the Crown, Belgium; LLD, Univ. of BC Canada; DMus, Univ. of WA. Hobbies: Golf; Philately; Antique furniture. Address: 101 Victoria Rd., Bellevue Hill, Sydney NSW, Australia.

HEISE, Michael, b. 22 July 1940, Berlin, Germany Conductor; Pianist. Educ: Abitur, Freie Universität, Berlin Cond., Pianist Dip., High Schl., Berlin. m. Angelika Nosky, 2 c Debut: Deutsche Oper Berlin. Career: apps. as Cond., Berlin Mannheim, Braunschweig; Concerts as pianist, Germany, USSR Romania. Hons: Stairway Concours Berlin, 3rd Prize, 1954 Hobbies: Sport; Chess. Mgmt: Zellermayer, Munich. Address Wiesenerstr. 37, 1000 Berlin 42, German Fed. Repub.

HEISS, John Carter, b. 23 Oct. 1938, NYC, NY, USA Composer; Flute Player; Teacher; occasional Conductor. Educ: BA Lehigh Univ., 1960; MFA, Princeton Univ., 1967. m. Arlene Tubio Heiss, 1 d., 1 s. Career incls: num. perfs. in concert, or radio, TV & recordings as perfd. & cond. inclng: Prin. Flute, Bostor Musica Viva, 1969-74; Fac., New England Conserv., 1967- Comps. incl: Four Short Pieces for Piano; Four Movements fo Three Flutes; Inventions, Contours & Colors; Quartet, for flute clarinet, cello & piano, 1971; Songs of Nature, 1975; Flut Concerto, 1977. Mbrships. incl: ASCAP; Am. Fedn. o Musicians. Contbr. to profl. jrnls. Hons. incl: Nat. Endowment fo the Arts grants, 1974 & '75; Award - Nat. Inst. of Arts & Letters

1973; Grant - Guggenheim Fndn., 1978. Hobbies incl: Sailing. Address: 61 Hancock St. Auburndale, MA 02166, USA.

HEISTØ, Karin, b. 21 Aug. 1954, Oslo, Norway. Flautist. Educ: Instrumental main study, Norwegian State Acad. of Music, Oslo, Norway, 1 d. Career: Norwegian Broadcasting Corp. Youth Orch., 1969-75; Jeunesses Musicales World Orch., 1974-; Soloist, Oslo Phil. Orch., The University's Aula, Oslo (radio apps.), 1976; Soloist, Norwegian Radio Orch., Oslo, TV, 1977; Norwegian Opera Orch. Address: Ekebergveien 212, Oslo 11, Norway.

HEISTØ STRAND, Rigmor, b. 28 Mar. 1951, Oslo, Norway. Solo Horn Player. Educ: Pvte. studies, Oslo; w. Prof. Hermann Baumann, Folkwang-Hochschule, Essen, Germany. m. Morten Strand, 2 d. Debut: Oslo, 1972. Career: Sev. concerts, Norway & Germany; Radio & TV apps.; Solo horn, Norwegian Radio Orch., Oslo. Address: Lindbäckveien 36, Oslo 11, Norway.

HEITZ, Klaus, b. 13 Sept. 1941, St. Gallen, Switz. Cellist. Educ: student of A Navarra, J Hubeau, J Calvet, Paris Conserv. & of P Casals at the Accademia Chigiana, Siena, Italy; Licence de concert, Ecole Normale de Musique, Paris. m. Martine-Christine Goimbault, 1 d. Debut: Paris, 1963. Career: First Solo Cellist w. The Festival Strings, Lucerne & Paris Chmbr. Orch., 1966-70, & w. the Kolner Rundfunk Sinfonie-Orchester, 1969-; Prof., Musikhochschule Rheinland, 1973-; Solo apps. in Europe & USA at Marlboro, Tanglewood, Salzburg & Montreaux Fests. Recordings: for 'Da Camera' in Germany & for 'Calliope' in France. Mbrships: Deutsche Orchester Vereinigung; Schweizerischer Tonkunstlerverein; Int. Gesellschaft für Neue Musik. Hons: 3 first prizes at the Paris Conserv., 1961, '64; Gregor Piatigorsky Prize, Tanglewood Fest., Mass. Mgmt: Konzertgesellschaft Zürich, Switz. & West-deutsche Konzertdirektion, Cologne. Address: Bachemer Str. 96 B, 5 Cologne 41, German Fed. Repub.

HELANDER, Gunvor Hedda Kristina, b. 12 April 1941, Borga/Porvoo, Finland. Organist; Music Secretary. Educ: Dip. Organ, 1963; Studies in Denmark w. Dr. Finn Videro, Holland w. Prof. Anton Heiller. Debut: Helsinki, 1963. Career: Organ concerts in Filand, Sweden, Norway, Denmark, Iceland, German Fed. Repub. & Namibia; Cond., mission choir, Furahachoir; Radio progs., Finland, Denmark, Iceland; TV progs., Finland; Music Sec., Finnish Missionary Soc. Recordings: Gavan fran ovan; Fran Advent till jul; Mission och musik med Furahakören. Publs: Me, kaukana ja lähellä, songbook w. mission songs, 1976. Hobbies: Mission work. Address: Tähtitorninkatu 18, 00140 Helsinki 14, Finland.

HELDT, Gerhard Alfred, b. 16 Apr. 1943, Colmar, Alsace, France. Assistant Musical Theoretician. Educ: Univ. of Cologne, 1962-63, 67-72; Dr phil, 1973; pvte. study of violin, 1950-63; studied schl. music, State HS for Music, Cologne, 1963-67. m. Brigitte Rosenthal. Career: Tchr., Music & German, State Gymnasium, Friedrich Wilhelm, Cologne, 1969-72, Asst. Musical Theoretician, Musicol. Inst., Univ. of Cologne, 1973-. Ed. & Author in field. Mbrships: Gesellschaft für Musikforschung; Viola Forschungs Gesellschaft; Arbeitsgemeinschaft für rheinische Musikgeschichte; Verein der Freunde und Förderer der Universität zu Köln. Hobbies: Mng. Pro Music Orch., Cologne; Orchl. & str. quartet violist; Gardening; Car constrn. Address: 500 Cologne 41; Sigmaringerstr. 11, German Fed. Repub.

HELFFER, Claude, b. 18 June 1922, Paris, France. Pianist. Educ: Pvte. studies w. Robert Casadescus. m. Mireille de Nervo, 2 s., 2 d. Debut: 1st Recital, 1948. Career: Num. apps. as soloist & w. Orchs. in France, Europe, USA & USSR; Played w. var. conds. inclng. Boulez, Van Otterloo, Maderna, Gielen, Martinon, Prête etc.; Played in London Proms Concerts; summer Masterclasses, Aspen, Colo., 1974, 77. Recordings: Schönberg, Ravel, Debussy, Boulez, Bartok. Publs: 26 Emissions a l'ORFT sur la Musique contemporaine, 1973. Mgmt: Konzert direktion de Koos - Laren (NH) The Netherlands. Address: 6 Rue Mignet, Paris 16, France.

HELFFER, Mireille, b. 6 Jan. 1928, Boulogne-Billancourt, France. Ethnomusicologist. Educ: Licence-ès-lettres; Doct. en Ethnomusicologie. m. Claude Helffer, 4 c. Career: Ch. de recherche, CNRS; Chide mission, Mussee Guimet. Publs: Les Chants dans lj'épopée tibetaine de Ge-sar, 1977. Contbr. to profl. jrnls. Mbrships: Société Asiatique; Soc. for Ethnomusicol.; Soc. for Asian music; Int. Folk Music Coun.; Société de Musicologie. Address: 6 rue Mignet, 75016 Paris, France.

HELGER, Lutz, b. 29 Mar. 1913, Cologne, Germany. Composer; Conductor. Educ: State Acad. of Music, Munich. m. Elfie Kröner. Career: Has worked in theatres in Mannheim, Konstanz, MünsterW. & Munich; Broadcasts on nearly every radio

station, German Fed. Repub.; Comp. of music for sev. films. Compositions: num. works, publd. & recorded, incl: Münchner Bilderbogen; Morning Melody; suites; chmbr. music; songs. Recordings: Philips; Ariola; Polydor; Metronome; etc. Contbr. to Int. Podium (German Musicians Union). Mbr., German Musicians Union (Pres.). Hobbies: Cooking (Pres. of Amateur Cookery Club). Address: Winterstr. 3, 801 Baldham/Munich, German Fed. Repub. 19.

HELLDEN, Daniel, b. 29 Dec. 1917, Göteborg, Sweden. Composer; Teacher of Music. Educ: Organist Ex., 1938; Cantor Ex., 1940; Music Tchr. Ex., 1941; Studies in comp. & cond., Stockholm, 1938-41 & Salzburg, Munich 1956-57. m. 1) Britta Brodén, 4 c., 2) Bodil Asmussen, 2 c. Career: Tchr. of Music & Organist at sev. places, 1942-69; Cond. of orchs., 1947-55; Cond. Lidingö Chmbr. Choir, 1948-; Tchr. of Music Educ., Conserv. of Music, Stockholm; Schl. music progs. on Radio & TV, 1958-; Courses in Music Educ. for Tchrs. in Scandinavia, Canada, USA, 1957-, in choir dance, 1970-. Comps. incl: for string orch.; string trio; recorders; film music; Samothrake, for solo, choir & orch.; 12 studies in piano; Sonatina rapsodica for piano; Choir music, etc. Recordings incl: Taxelina och nägra till (songs for children). Publs: Swedish edn. of Orff-Schulwek (Music for Children I & II), 1957; Method of Music Educaction 1-6, 1961-74; Choir Dances I-V, 1970-76; Choir Plays 1-4, 1977-78; Cantata I for Choir & Str. Orch., 1978; etc. Recip., Culture Prize, of Lidingö, 1969. Hobby: Yachting. Address: Tunavägen 8, 18162, Lidingö, Sweden.

HELLER, Jack Joseph, b. 30 Nov. 1932, New Orleans, La., USA. College Professor. Educ: Dip. in Violin, Juilliard Schl. of Music, 1952; MMus, Univ. of Mich., 1958; PhD, Univ. of Iowa, 1962. m. Judith Ann Krawetz, 2 s., 1 d. Debut: Soloist, New Orleans Symph., 1947. Career: Asst. Concertmaster, New Orleans Opera, 1947-49; Freelance Violinist, NYC (Radio, TV, Chamber Grps.), 1950-52. '55; Concertmaster, Toledo Symph. Orch., 1955-58; Grad. Asst., Univ. of Iowa (Dir., String Prog., Elem. & HS), 1958-60; Fac., Univ. of Conn., 1960-; Cond. & Music Dir., Manchester, Conn., Symph. Orch. & Chorale. Publs: Computer Analysis of the Auditory Characteristics of Musical Performance, 1972; Graphic Representation of Musical Concepts; A Computer Assisted Instructional System, 1971, etc. Mbrships: Sec., Rsch. Coun., Music Educators Nat. Conf., 1968-74; Am. Educl. Rsch. Assn., etc. Hons: Post-doctoral Fellow, Ohio State Univ. Ctr. for Expmtl. Rsch. in the Arts, 1966-67. Address: 60 Farmstead Rd., Storrs. CT 06268, USA. 6.

HELLER, John Henry, Jr., b. 22 Feb. 1945, Phila., Pa., USA. Assistant Professor of Music History. Educ: BMus & BMusEd, Phila. Musical Acad., 1968; MMus, Temple Univ., 1970; D Musical Arts, 1976. Debut (as Comp.): Phila., 1960s. Career: Tchr., Phila. Community Coll., Temple Univ., Phila. Musical Acad., West Chester State Coll. & Trenton State Coll.; presently Asst. Prof. Music Hist. & Theory, Va. C'wlth. Univ. Comps: Str. Quartet No. 1, 1965; Symph. Concerto for Bass Clarinet & Chmbr. Orch., 1966 (both published 1969). Mbr., profl. assns. Hons: Creative Accomplishment Award in Comps., 1966; Pre-doct. Fellowship, 1971. Hobbies: Solving puzzles; Reading in Fields of Psychology & Medicine. Address: 1434 Clarkson Rd. Apt. H, Richmond, VA 23224, USA.

HELLER, Richard, b. 30 Dec. 1919, Buxton, UK. Retired Violinist, Impresario & Businessman. Educ: pvte. study w. Leonard Hirsch & Rowsey Woof; Gold, Silver & Bronze Medallist, RAM, 1936-40. 1 d. Career: Violinist, Scottish Orch., 1940-41, LPO, 1 yr., freelance playing under noted conds.; Ldr., orch. accompanying Sadlers Wells Ballet, 1941; Soloist, Mozart's Symphonia Concertante, 500th concert of Grupo Filarmonico, Mahon, Menorca, 1975; Impresario, presenting num. soloists, ballet troupes, opera grps., inclng. Karl Ulrich Schnabel, & Tito Gobbi; formed Soc. w. Terry-Thomas for promotion of Sunday Shows; ran schl. of dancing; Businessman, var. enterprises (travel agcy., employment agcy. chain, property development, etc.), 1953-. Recip. var. music fest. prizes. Addressw: Obispo Severo 7-2°°, Villacarlos, Menorca, Spain.

HELLER, Richard (Rainer), b. 19 Apr. 1954, Vienna, Austria. Composer. Educ: Hochschule für Musik und Darstellende Kunst, Vienna; Dip., comp., ibid., 1979; final examination, comp. for Audio-visual media, ibid., 1978; final examination, cultural mgmt., ibid., 1979. Career: num. perfs. of own works in Vienna; also in Istanbul, Ankara, Cairo, Dahran; many commissions. Comps. incl: Elegy for mixed chorus to texts of Rainer Maria Rilke; Assoziationsmusik, for clarinets; Kontake, for 2 clarinets; Klavierstuck, 1976; Quartet for 2 trumpets, flugelhorn & trombone; 3 songs for soprano & piano; Nocturne (chmbr. ensemble); Konzentrationen (3 percussionsts). Contbr. to Jrnl. of Austrian Comps. Soc. Mbrships: Österreichischer Komponistenbund; Österreichische Gesellschaft für

Zeitgenössische Musik; ISCM, Austrian sect. Hons. incl. Theodor Körner prize, 1978. Hobbies: Photography; Mathematics. Address: Ausstellungsstr. 21/20, 1020 Vienna, Austria.

HELLESNES-HUKVARI, Astrid, b. 15 Dec. 1937, Oslo, Norway. Singer (contralto). Educ: Mozarteum, Salzburg; Vienna Acad. of Music & Performing Arts. m., 1 d. Debut: w. Musikverein, Vienna (contralto part in Beethoven's 9th Symph.). Career incl: concert appearances in Chgo. & Milwaukke, USA; Innsbruck & Vienna Festivals; Radio & TV broadcasts from Vienna inclng. Haydn's St. Cecilia Mass & Charpantier's Te Deum; Soloist w. Norwegian Opera, 1965-; appearances at Bergen & Northern Norway Festivals. Var. recordings made in Vienna. Mbrships: Norwegian Opera Singers Union; Norwegian Musical Artists Union; Norwegian Musical Union. Address: Oskar Bratensvei 30, 1412 Sofiemyr, Norway.

HELLEWELL, David Walter, b. 27 Oct. 1932, Morley, Yorks., UK. Composer; Musical Director; Conductor; Educator. m. Monica Smedley. Career: Formed Apollo Contemporary Music ensemble, 1969; Dir. & Cond., ibid; Radio broadcasts as Cond. of contemporary music. Compositions incl: Metamusic (flute & piano); Continuum Electronicum (tape & instruments); Synergy (ensemble, piano & percussion); Serraphoenum (ensemble & Indian tabla); Virtexia (ensemble); Cronos-Dynamikos (cimbalom & ensemble); Music (3 orch. & percussion); Mythologies (narrator, synthesizer & chmbr. orch.); str. quartets; chamber music; jazz. Author, The New Music; An Introduction & General Suvey for the non-Specialist, 1973. Mbrships: CGGB. Recip., Arts Coun. Bursary for rsch. in electronic music techniques, 1973. Hobbies: Gardening; Cultural hist., esp. pre-Renaissance; Art; Architecture; Sci.; Philos.; Theatre. Address: 57 Lansdowne Rd., Bournemouth, Dorset BH1 1RN, UK.

HELLIER, Harry Clifford, b. Bristol, UK. Pianist; Composer. Educ: RAM. m. Edith Leila Webb, 1 s., 1 d. Debut: Accompanist to Maurice Chevalier, 1931. Career: Recitalist; Broadcaster, BBC; Pianist in occasional films. Compositions: Lunch Hour (piano); num. unpubl. compositions broadcast, incl: The Harbour Tavern; An English Rhapsody; Sonata for Violin; English Harbour; Theatreland Waltz; The Land - The Sea & the Dream; 4 miniatures for violin, cello & piano; Cello Solo; Watercolour Landscape for cello & piano. Hobbies: Travel; Philately; Gardening. Address: Lamorna, Knowle Grove, Virginia Water, Surrey, UK. 3.

HELLIWELL, Clifton, b. 23 Sept. 1907, Farnworth, Lancs., UK. Pianist. Educ: Assoc., Royal Manchester Coll. of Music; Fellow, ibid. m. Jessica Mountfort, 1 s., 2 d. Career: BBC Music Staff, 1929-61; Tutorial Staff, Royal Manchester Coll. of Music, 1961-72; Hd., Schl. of Keyboard Studies, Royal Nothern Coll. of Music, 1972-78. Mbr., ISM. Recip., Chappell Gold Medal, 1927; Fellow, Royal Nothern Coll. of Music. Hobby: Photography. Address: 5 Yew Tree Rd., Plumley, nr. Knutsford, Cheshire WA16 OUQ, UK. 3.

HELMAN, Zofia, b. 8 Mar. 1937, Radom, Poland; Musicologist. Educ: studied Musicol., Warsaw Univ., 1954-59; Dr. of Musicol., 1967. m. Andrzej Bednarczyk. Career: Lectr., Inst. of Musicol., Warsaw Univ., 1959-. Publs: approx. 20 articles about the 19th & 20th century music, particularly about Karol Szymanowski; Edition: K Szymanowski; Stabat Mater, Score Cracow, 1965; Krol Roger, Score Cracow, 1973; Veni Creator, Litania, Demeter, Agawe, in press. Mbr: Int. Musicological Soc. Address: Chlodna 11 m. 1501, 00-891 Warsaw, Poland.

HELMER, Erik Axel, b. 18 Sept. 1925, Stockholm, Sweden. Musicologist. Educ: Univ. studies in Lund & Uppsala; Fil.kand., 1953; Fil.Lic., 1958; PhD & Docent, 1973; piano studies in Copenhagen, 1948-49 (J Fernström). m. Sigrid Schlegel, 2 d. Career: Dir., Swedish Music Hist. Archive, Stockholm, 1965-; Lectures on radio; Var. apps. as Accompanist in Concerts & Radio, all in Sweden. Publs: Svensk solosang 1850-1890, 1) En Genrehistorisk Studie, 2) Sangförteckning, Stockholm, 1972. Var. articles & reviews in Swedish jrnls. VP, Swedish Soc. of Musicol. Address: Liljestigen 1, 182 32 Danderyd, Sweden.

HELMICK, Carl N, Jr., b. 18 Oct. 1937, Riverside, Calif., USA. Physicist; Amateur Performer on Viola da Gamba, 'Cello & Tenor Violin. Educ: BA, Univ. of Calif., Riverside, 1960; MS, Univ. of Ariz., 1964. Contbr. to: Jrnl. of Viola da Gamba Soc. of Am.; Catgut Acoustical Soc. Newsletter. Mbrships: Perf. Mbr., Univ. of Ariz., Collegium Musicum, Tucson, 1964-70; Viola da Gamba Soc. of Am.; Catgut Acoustical Soc.; Dolmetsch Fndn., UK; Galpin Soç., UK; Viola da Gamba Soc., UK; Am. Musical Instrument Soc.; Int. Heinrich Schütz Soc., Germany; Am. Phys. Soc. Hobby: Early music & musical instruments, especially bowed strings & keyboard instruments. Address: 240 W Iowa Ave., Ridgecrest, CA 93555, USA.

HELTAY, Laszlo Istvan, b. 5 Jan. 1930, Budapest, Hungary. Conductor. Educ: MA, Franz Liszt Acad. of Music, Budapest;

BLitt, Oxford. Career: Dir. of Music, Merton Coll., Oxford, 1960-64; Assoc. Cond., NZ Broadcasting Corporation Symph. Orch., 1964-65; Musical Dir., NZ Opera Co., 1964-66; Cond., Phoenix Opera Co., London, 1967-69, 1973; Cond., Collegium Musicum of London, 1970-, Brighton Fest. Chorus, 1968-, Chorus of the Acad. of St. Martin in the Fields, 1975-; Freelance Cond. of Orchs. & Opera. Sev. recordings. Hobbies: Chess; Skiing; Tennis. Address: 44 Pattison Rd., London NW2 2HJ, UK. 3.

HELWEG, Per, b. 7 Jan. 1924, Copenhagen, Denmark. Opera Singer; Musical Adviser. Educ: Conserv. of Copenhagen; Studies w. George Jouatte, Paris; Einar Nörby, Copenhagen. m. Lisbeth Helweg, 2 d., 1 s. Debut: Paris, 1948; Copenhagen, 1949. Career: Roles incl. Sharpless (Madame Butterfly); Don Juan, Count almaviva (Noce de Figaro); Aeneas (Dido & Aeneas); Junius (The Rape of Lucrecia); Ceprano (Rigoletto); Schaunard (la Bohème). Contbr. to: Danish Musical Review; Teostory (helsini). Mbrships: Bd., Soc. of Young Musicians (Det unge Tonekunstnerselkab); Soc. for Publ. of a Danish Anthol. of Music (on records); Music Advsr. Danish Authors Soc (KODA). Address: Classens gade 54, 2100 Copenhagen, Denmark.

HEMBERG, (Bengt Sven) Eskil, b. 19 Jan. 1938, Stockholm, Sweden. Composer; Conductor. Educ: Music Tchrs. Degree, Dip. in Solo Organ, Orch. Cond. Class, Royal Coll. of Music, Stockholm, 1957-64. m. Birgit Sofia Ohlson, 2 s., 1 d. Debut: as Cond. at Llangollen, Wales, 1961. Career: Exec. Pror., Swedish Broadcasting Corp., 1963-70 (Hd. of Choral Dept.); Planning Mgr. at The Inst. for Nat. Concerts, 1970-; Pres., Swedish Composers Assn., 1971- Cond., Stockholm Univ. Chorus, 1959- Num. tours all over the world. Compositions: Choral works, solo concerts, organ music, opera Love (Stockholm Opera 1973). Recordings: Cond. of Stockholm Univ. Chorus on Philips, FABO, etc. (6 LP); Music of Eskil Hemberg on EMI, FABO & Swedish Soc. Discofil (3 LP). Mbrships: Swedish Roayl Acad. of Music. Hons: Stockholm City Arts Grant, 1970; Gustaf Aulen Prize, 1970; Swedish State Composers Grant, 1972 & '73; The Music Assn. of Stockholm Prize, 1974; 2nd & 4th prize in Llangollen Int. Award. Address: Floravägen 3, S-131 41 Nacka, Sweden.

HEMMINGS, Peter William, b. 10 Apr. 1934, Enfield, Middx., UK. Opera Company General Administrator. Educ: MA (Hons) in Classics, Choral Exhbnr., Gonville & Caius Coll., Cambridge Univ. m. Jane Kearnes, 5 c. Career: Admin. Asst., Harold Holt Ltd., 1957-58; Repertory & Planning Mgr., Sadler's Wells Opera, 1959-65; Gen. Mgr., New Opera Co., 1957-65; Gen. Admnstr., Scottish Opera, 1962-. Hobby: Railways. Address: 61 Hamilton Dr., Glasgow, G12 8DP, UK. 3.

HEMON, Sedje, b. Rotterdam, Netherlands. Composer of Classic & Folk Music; Teacher of Panpipes; Professor of Integration Painting Music Dance. Educ: Conserv. Amsterdam. div. Career: TV & radio apps. about paintings, music, etc. Europe & other countries, 1955-; Made film about Integration; Broadcasts in 4 langs. Comps. incl; Orchestre Symphonique; Never Again an Auschwitz; Suite in Four Movements; Solos for organ, piano, panflute, etc. Recordings: 4 records & many tapes. Mbrships: incl. Org. of Dutch Comps. Contbr. to radio mags. Hobby: Collecting 1900-1930 records. Address: Loosduinsekade 180, The Hague, Netherlands.

HEMPFLING, Volker Wolfgang, b. 26 Jan. 1944, FrankenholzSaar, W Germany. Cathedral organist; choirmaster. Educ: Music Acad., Cologne, ch. musician exam; Dip. organ, voice, cond. Career: 1964, Ch. musician, Cologne; 1968, fndr. the Kölner Konditorei; 1972, Cathedral organist, choirmaster, Altenberg; 1976, Regional Supvsr. of ch. music; Concert tours through Europe; App. w. W German Radio; Live broadcasts, a.o. concert for 300th anniversary of the death of Heinrich Schütz. Recordings: Willi Burkhard; Cantata The Flood; Psalm Motets, 1975; Choir music in Altenberg Cathedral, Renaissance and Romantic Period, 1976. Mbrships: Soc. of Evangelic Ch. Musicians in the Rhine Dist. Hobbies: Swimming; Boating; Mountain climbing; Gardening. Address: 5071 Altenberg Feld, German Fed. Repub.

HEMSLEY, Thomas Jeffrey, b. 12 Apr. 1927, Coalville, UK. Baritone. Educ: MA, Brasenose Coll., Oxford. m. Gwenllian James, 3 s. Career: Glyndebourne since 1953; Prin. Baritone, Stadttheater Aachen, 1953-56, Deutsche Opoer am Rhein, 1957-63, Opernhaus Zürich, 1963-67; Freelance, 1967-; Bayreuth Fest., 1968-70; Scottish Opera, Covent Gdn., Engl. Nat. Opera; Welsh Nat. Opera; concerts throughout Europe; frequent broadcasts; Specialist in German lieder; Master Classes, inclng. TV in UK & Denmark. Recordings: Dido & Aaneas (Purcell); Alceste (Gluck); Midsummer Night's Dream (Britten); Saul (Handel); Savitri (holst); Knot Garden (Tippett); German lieder (for Ensayo); Bach cantatas. Mbrships: Hon. RAM, 1974; ISM;

Equity; United Oxford & Cambridge Club. Hobby: Gardening. Mgmt: Harold Holt Ltd. Address: 10 Denewood Rd., London N6, UK.

HENAHAN, Donal J, b. 28 Feb. 1921, Cleveland, Ohio, USA. Music Critic. Educ: Kent & Ohio Univs.; BA, Northwestern Univ.; grad. study, Univ. of Chgo. & Chgo. Schl. of Music; pvte. piano & guitar study. Career: Music reviewer & writer, Chgo. Daily News, 1948-58; Music Critic, ibid., 1958-67; Music Critic, NY Times, 1967-. Contbr. to num. music jrnls. & mags. inclng: Musical Quarterly; Gramophone; Stereo Review; High Fidelity, etc. Mbrships: Centry Club, NYC; Arts Club, Chgo. Address: c/o NY Times, 229 W 43rd St., NY, NY 10036, USA. 2, 6.

HENDERSON, Carlesta Elliott, b. 8 Mar. 1925, Norfolk, Va., USA. Professor of Music. Educ: BMus, Howard Univ.; MMus, Profl. Dip. & EdD, Tchrs. Coll., Columbia Univ. div., 1 s., 1 d. Career: Tchr. & Supvsr. of music in pub. elem., second. & collegiate educl. insts.; Lectr., seminars, workshops & music clins.; Vocal Recitalist; Prof. of Music w. specialty in voice & tchr. trng. Mbrships: incl: Phi Delta Kappa; Kappa Delta Pi; Pi Lambda Theate; MENC; Alpha Kappa Alpha; Black Educators Alliance. Recip., acad. schlrship. & fellowship. Hobbies: Swimming; Tennis; Reading; Painting. Address: 792 Columbus Ave. (4-0), NY, NY 10025, USA.

HENDERSON, Ian H, b. 28 Jan. 1925, Hamilton, UK. Music Teacher (piano, harpsichord, clavichord). Educ: AB., ED Mus B., Ed Mus M., Oberlin Coll. & Conserv.; PhD, Syracuse Univ. m. Rita H Henderson, 3 c. Career: Tchr., Brockport Coll., SUNY, 1948-54, 1965-; Dean of Fine Arts, & Acting Pres., ibid., (1973); Syracuse Univ., 1957-65; Piano, Harpsichord recitals, 1947-; Ch. Organist & Choir Dir., var. churches, 1940-65. Pub. Is: Music & The Electronic Medium (co-author), 1973, Contbr. of chapt. to Review of Educational Research, 1967. Mbrships: MENC; Phi Mu Alpha; Pi Kappa Lambda; Phi Mu Epsilon. Hons: Grant, Nat. Endowment for the Humanities, 1973. Address: 4039 N Lake Rd., Brockport, NY 14420, USA. 2.

HENDERSON, Roy Galbraith, b. 4 July 1899, Edinburgh, UK. Baritone; Teacher. Educ: RAM; FRAM. m. Bertha Collin Smyth, 1 s., 2 d. Debut: Queen's Hall, London, 1925. Career: 1st Broadcast, 1924; Num. concert apps.; Covent Garden Opera, 1928-29; Glyndebourne, from 1st night, 1934, -40; Apps., all Brit. fests. Contemp. Music fest., Amsterdam, Edinbugh Fests., 1947-48; Mbr., int. juries, Holland, Switzerland, Pain; Master Classes, Toronto, Rotterdam; Ret'd., 1952, Tchr., Prof., Singing, RAM, 1940-74; Cond., choirs in Nottingham, Huddersfield, Bournemouth. Num. recordings inclng. Marriage of Figaro, Glyndebourne, 1934. num. recordings. Publs: Contbr. to kathleen Ferrier 'A Memoir', ed. by Neville Cardus, 1954; The Voice, ed. K. Falkner. Contbr. to profl. jrnls. Mbrships: Past Warden, Solo Perfs. Sect., ISM; Past Mbr., Arts Coun. Music Panel & BBC Music Panel. Hons: Worshipful Co. of Musicians Medal, 1925; Charles Stantley Medal, 1956; CBE, 1970. Hobbies: Trout fishing; Gardening; Watching cricket. Address: 85 Belsize Park Gardens, Hampstead, London NW3 4NJ, UK. 1, 3, 14, 28.

HENDL, Walter, b. 12 Jan. 1917, W NY, NJ, USA. Conductor; Pianist; Composer. Educ: piano study w. Clarence Adler, 1934-37; piano w. David Saperton, cond. w. Fritz Reiner, Curtis Inst. of Music, 1937-41. m. Barbara Heisley, 1 d. by former marriage. Career: Asst. cond. & pianist, NY Phil. Symph. orch., 1945-49; Musical Dir., Dallas Symph. Orch., 1949-58; Assoc. cond., Chgo. Symph. Orch., 1958-64; Musical Dir., Chautauqua (NY) Symph. Orch., 1953-72; Dir., Eastman Schl. of Music, 1964-72; Orchestral Dir., Erie (Pa.) Phil., 1976-. Address: c/o Erie Philharmonic, 409 G Daniel Baldwin Bldg., Erie, PA 16501, USA.

HENDRIE, Gerald Mills, b. 28 Oct. 1935, Westcliff-on-Sea, UK. University Professor. Educ: Fndn. Scholar (piano), RCM, 1952-54; Organ Scholar, subsequently Rsch. Student, Selwyn Coll., Cambridge Univ., 1954-61; MA; MusB; PhD; FRCO; ARCM. m. Dinah Barsham, 2 s. Career: Prof. of Music, Open Univ., 1969-; formerly Prof. of Music, Univ. of Victoria, BC, Canada, 1967-69; Lectr. in the Hist. of Music, Manchester Univ., 1963-67; Hd. of Music, Homerton Coll., Cambridge, 1962-63; Univ., Supvsr. in Music, Cambridge. Compositions: Two carols, as I outrode that Enderis Night, & Sweet Was the Song the Virgin Sang; Magnificat & Nunc Dimittis for New Coll., Oxford (MS), Magnificat & Nune Dimitis for St. John's Coll., Canmbridge; Ave. Verum Corpus; The Precas & Responses for St. John's Coll., Cambridge. Recording: Bach Organ Music, w. Geraint Jones; Renaissance Music (Harpsichord). Publs. incl: Orlando Gibbons, Keyboard Music, Musica Birtannia vol. XX 1962, 2nd rev. 1967; John Coprario; Funeral Teares., Songs of Mourning; The Masque of Squires (Ed. w. Thurston Dart); Introduction of Music

(w. D Barsham); Case study; Mendelssohn's Rediscovery of Bach; Renaissance Music (w. D Barsham); Harmony; An Approach to Harmonic & Stylistic Analysis. Many articles. Address: The Open Univ., Milton Keynes, MK7 6AA, UK.

HENDRIX, Richard, b. 15 May 1958, Martinsville, Ind., USA. Concert Violinist. Educ: studies at Ind. Univ. & w. James Buswell, Taduez Wronski, Franco Gulli & Daniel Guilet. Career: Recitals & concerts in USA; competitor, Int. Competition, Concert Artists Guild, 1979 (2nd place); Competitor, Int. Paganini Competition, 1979. Mbr. AFM. Hons: Violin award, Matinee Musical Performance, 1976. Address: 824 W 54th St., Indpls., IN 46208, USA.

HENIGNBAUM, John, b. 16 Sept. 1922, Bettendorf, Iowa, USA. Musician (French Horn). Educ: BA, Ogelthorpe Univ., Atlanga, Ga.; Study of horn w. Philip Farkas; Chgo. Civic Trng. Orch., 4 yrs. Career: French horn. Milwaukee Symph. & Chgo. Symph.; Prin. Horn, Atlanta Symph., 19612-; Mbr., Wind Quintet, ibid.; Appearances on Network TV in NBC Today Show. Address: 13 Pine Cir. NE, Atlanta, GA 30305, USA.

HENKIN, Daniel J, b. USA. Corporation Chairman. Educ: Kansas City Conserv. of Music, 4 yrs.; Degree in Advertising, Univ. of Mo. Debut: w. Kansas City Concert Band (clarinet), aged 15. Career incls: 1st Clarinettist, Ctr. Symph., Kansas City Conserv. Symph., Univ. of Mo. Band & Orch., & Burrall Symph.; Ldr., own dance band; Dir., Japan Air Command Band, USAF; Dir. of Advertising, Leblanc Corp., 1954-61; Dir. Advertising & Sales Promotion, Conn Corp., 1961-70; Pres. & Chmn. of Bd., Gemeinhardt Corp., Elkhart, Ind. (leading manufacturer of flutes & piccolos), 1970-. Hons. incl: Voted one of Top Ten Young Men in Music Ind.; Mbr., Woodwind World Hall of Fame; Awards from Int. Coun. Indl. Eds., NY Univ., & other bodies. Addrss: 1449 Greenleaf Blvd., Elkhart, IN 46514, USA.

HENNENBERG, Fritz, b. 11 June 1932, DöbelnSachsen, German Dem. Repub. Musicologist. Educ: Music Acad. Dresden; Karl Marx Univ. Leipzig, PhD. m. Roswitha Trexler, 1 d. Career: 1956-59 Conserv. Halle; 1958-63 Rsch. Art Acad. German Dem. Repub.; 1972 Chief Music Advsr., Gewandhaus Orch. since 1974 Chief Music Advsr., Radio Symph. Orch., Leipzig; Lectureconcert tours abroad; since 1973 piano Accomp. to singer Roswitha Trexler. Publs. incl: The Gewandhaus Orchestra in Leipzig, 1962; DessauBrecht, Musical Works, 1963; Paul Dessau, a biography, 1965; Wolfgang Amadeus Mozart, 1970; Ed., Paul Dessau: Notebook for Notes, 1974; Ed., Witold Lutotawski: Talks, 1976; The Cantatas of Gottfried Heinrich Stölzel, 1976. Contbr. to: var. profl. jrnls. Address: Zum Harfenacker 2, 7035 Leipzig, German Dem. Repub.

HENNIG, Dennis John, b. 28 Feb. 1951, Melbourne, Aust. Lecturer; Pianist. Educ: BMus, Melbourne Univ., 1973; BPhil, Oxford, 1975. Career: recitals & lecture recitals in Vic., Oxford, Canberra & Sydney, specialising in contemporary Aust. music; perfs. w. major contemporary ensembles incl. ASCM & ISCM; competitor in var. int. competitions incl. Van Cliburn & Tchaikovsky; now lectr., NSW State Conserv. of Music, 1979-. Recordings: Felix Werder's Banker; Donald Hollier's 12 Sonnets. Mbr. Musicol. Soc. of Aust. Hons: Allan award (piano), 1970; Aust. Musicians' Overseas Scholarship, 1973. Hobbies: Skiing; Malacol. Address: NSW State Conserv. of Music, Macquarie St., Sydney 2000, Aust.

HENNING, Cosmo Grenville, b. 20 April 1932, Uitenhage, S Africa. Musicologist; Cultural Historian. Educ: incls: LTCL (piano), 1952; LMusTCL, 1954; FTCL, 1954; ATCL (organ); Int. BMus, London, 1954; BMus, UNISA, 1958; MMus, 1964, PhD, 1971, Univ. of Pretoria. m. Joyce Roebuck, 3 s., 1 d. Career incls: Schl. Tchr., UK, Cape Province, Natal, 1955-61; Lectr., Trng. Coll., Graaff Reinet, 1963-67, & Univ. of Pretoria, 1968, 69, 71, 73; Asst.-Sr. Rschr., S African Music Ency., 1970-74; Hd., Nat. Documentation Ctr. for Music, 1974-, both of Human Scis. Rsch. Coun.; currently Organist & Choirmaster, Bklyn. Meth. Ch., Pretoria. Publs. incl: Four South African Composers; Graaff-Reinet, A Cultural History, 1786-1886. Contbr. num. articles to musical publs. Mbr. profl. orgs. Address: 42 van Wouw St., Groenkloof, Pretoria, S Africa. 29.

HENNING, Roslyn Brogue (composes as BROGUE, Roslyn), b. 16 Feb. 1919, Chgo., Ill., USA. Professor of Music; Composer; Concert Harpsichordist. Educ: Wilson & Tomlinson Schls. of Music, Ill., 1923-30; AB, Univ. of Chgo.; AM, 1943, PhD, 1947, Radcliffe Coll. m. Ervin Henning (div., 1 s., 1d.). Debut: Chgo., 1923. Career: Pvte. studio & perfs. in Boston & NYC, 1947-52; num. radio perfs., 1958-62; concert apps. Boston, Cambridge, Mass., & NYC. Comps. incl: 5 Songs of Courtly Love; A Valediction: Of Weeping; Wuintet for Woodwinds; Equipoise, I & II. Contbr. to: Schwobel, Ranaissance

Men & Ideas, 1971; var. jrnls. Mbr., profl. assns. Hons. incl: Comp. Prize, Brookline Lib. Music Assn., 1965. Hobbies incl: Breeding Himalayan Cats. Address: 28 Bromfield Rd., Somerville, MA 02144, USA. 5, 6.

HENNINGER, Jacqueline Pates, b. 18 Nov. 1946, Richmond, Va., USA. Harpist; Pianist. Educ: BMus, Oberlin Conserv. of Music; MMus, Boston Univ. m. William B Henninger, Jr. Career: Harp & Piano Instructor, Stephens Coll., Columbia, Mos., 1971-72; Prin. Harpist, Richmond Symph., Richmond, Va., 1973-76; Dir. of largest public schl. harp program, in USA, Richmond, Va., 1973-76; solo perfs. w. Richmond Sinfonia, Midland (Mich.) Symph. Orch. & Traverse City (Mich.) Symph. Orch.; currently Tchr. & Free-lance Harpist, Toronto. Mbrships: VP, Toronto Chapter, Am. Harp Soc. Address: 1031 Royal York Rd., Toronto, Ont. M8X 2G5, Can.

HENNY, Jeanne Katherine, b. 11 Mar. 1952, Birmingham, UK. Co-Director; Teacher of French Song. Educ: BA, London; Tchng. Degree in Drama, Goldsmiths Coll., London; Hon. RCM. Career: Co-Dir., Mayer-Lismann Opera Workshop; Tchr. of French Song, RCM. Hobby: Bridge. Address: 47 Beaufort Mansions, Beaufort St., London, SW 3, UK.

HENRIKSEN, Elvi, b. 6 June 1916, Birkenwerder, nr. Berlin, Germany. Pianist. Educ: Concert preparation w. Alexander Stoffregen, 1940-45; Theory & Comp. w. Svend Erik Tarp. m. Niels Björn Larsen, 1 d. Debut: Soloist, Tivoli Concerthall, Copenhagen, 1929 (age 13). Career: European tour; Soloist & Musical Advsr., The Royal Theatre, Copenhagen, 1950-; Tchr., ballet-children in music & rhythmics, The Royal Danish Ballet, 1960-. Contbr. to: Takt og Tone. Mbrships: Det unge Tonekunstnerselskab; Dansk Musikforbund. Hons: Den Kulturelle Pris (Culture Prize), 1972. Address: Egernvej 12, 2000 Copenhagen F, Denmark.

HENROTTE, Gayle Allen, b. 20 Nov. 1935, Long Beach, Calif., USA. Musicologist; Music Librarian. Educ: AB, Vassar Coll., 1958; MA, 1961, PhD, 1967, Univ. of NC at Chapel Hill. Studied Piano, Organ & Viola w. var. tchrs. Career: Instr. of Music, Rosary Coll., River Forest, Ill., 1965-66, & Miss. State Coll. for Women, 1966-67; Asst. Prof. Music & Music Libn., Miss. Univ. for Women, Columbus, 1967-76; Assoc. Prof. Music & Music Libn., Mississipopi Univ. for Women, Columbus, 1976-. Contbr. to: Groves Dictionary of Music & Musicians, 6th ed. Mbrships. incl: Int. Musicol. Soc.; Hons. incl: Rotary Int. Fndn. Fellowship, 1961-62. Hobbies: Theolog. studies: Biblical archaeology; Language study; Cooking. Address: 1023 College St., Columbus, MS 39701, USA.

HENRY, James Donald, b. 14 Aug. 1933, Kingsport, Tenn., USA. Professor of Music; Musician, Clarinet, Bassoon, Saxophone. Educ: BS in MusEd., W Ky., Univ., 1956; MMus, Woodwinds, Ind. Univ., 1960. m., 1 s., 1 d. Career: Instr., 4th Army Band Tchng. Unit, 1956-58; Grad. Asst. in Bands, Ind. Univ., 1959-60; Prof., Woodwinds, Music Lit., Marching Band, Duke Univ., 1960-; Instr., Bassoon, Univ. of NC, Greensboro, 1970-71. Recording: Drei Morgenstern Lieder by matyas Seiber (sop. & clarinet). Mbrships: Coll. Band Dirs. Nat. Assn.; MENC. Hobbies: Tennis, Gardening. Address: Box 6695 Coll. Stn., Duke Univ., Durham, NC 27708, USA. 28.

HENRY, Jean-Claude, b. 30 Dec. 1934, Paris, France. Professor; Organist. Educ: Conserv. Nat. Supérieur de Paris. m. Cotron (dec.), 2 c. Career: Prof. of Counterpoint, Conserv. Nat. Supérieur de Paris; Organist, St. Pierre de Neuilly; organ concerts & recitals in France, Switz., Italy & Germany. Comps. incl: (organ) Quatre Pièces Breves; Office de Sexagesime; Chacone; Thalle; Symphonie Concertante for organ & orch.; Mouvement pour tuba & piano; Symph. for strgs., etc. Hons: 1st prize, harmony, counterpoint, fugue, organ, improvisation, philosophie de la musicque (Messiaen class), Conserv. Nat. Supérieur de Paris; Grand Prix de Rome for comp. Address: 2 Villa des Couronnes, 92400 Courvevoie, France.

HENSCHEN, Dorothy Adele Dregalla, b. 26 Aug. 1921, Cleveland, Ohio, USA. Harpist. Educ: BMus, Piano & Harp, Oberlin Coll., Ohio; Salzebo Harp Colony, Camden, Maine. m. Charles K Henschen, 3 s. Career: Asst. Prof. in Harp, Univ. Tex., 1944-49; Harpist w. Symph. Orchs. inclng: Austin, Waco, San Antonio & Corpus Christi; Asst. Prof., Harp & Piano, Mt. Union Coll., Ohio, 1949-; 1st Harpist, Canton & Akron, Ohio, Symph. Orchs.; Harp parts for Kenley Players, Warren & Dayton, Ohio; Front Row Theater, Cleveland, Ohio & var. engagements as called upon. Mbr. Am. harp Soc. Hobby: Tennis. Address: 1001 Overlook Dr., Alliance, OH 44601, USA.

HENZE, Hans Werner, b. 1 July 1926, Gütersloh, Westfalia, Germany. Composer; Conductor. Educ: State Music Schl., Brunswick; studied w. Wolfgang Fortner, Inst. of Ch. Music, Heidelberg. Career: Repetiteur, Bielefeld Municipal Theatre,

1945; Musical Collaborator, Heinz Hilpert, Deutsche Theatre, konstanzBodensee, 1948; Artistic Dir. & Cond., ballet of State Theatre, Wiesbaden, 1950; gave Masterclasses in composition, Mozarteum, Salzburg, 1962-66; Tchr. & Rsch., Havana, Cuba, 1969-70; has composed operas, radio operas, ballets, incidental music, works for full & chmbr. orchs., ballet suites, solo concertos, works for full & chmbr. orchs., ballet suites, solo concertos, works for voice & orch., choral works, solo antatas, works for voice & piano, & works for solo instruments. Composition recorded incl: scenes from Elegy for Young Lovers (opera); The Young Lord (opera); 5 Symphonies; Sinfonia No. 6 for 2 chmbr. orchs.; Ondine, First Suite (from the ballet for orch.); Fantasia for Strings; ode to the Westwind for 'cello & orch., based on poem by Shelley; The Raft of Medusa; El Cimarrón; We Come to the River. Publs. incl: Undine, Diary of a Ballet, 1958; Essays, A Collection of Lectures & Articles from the years, 1952-62, 1964; El Cimmarrón. A Work Report (w. Hans Magnus Enzensberger), 1971; Musik und Politik, 1976. Hons. incl: DMus, Univ. of Edinburgh, 1971. Mgmt: Sheldon Soffer, 130 W. 56th St., New York, USA; Michael G Vyner, 11 Hinde St., London W1, UK. Address: La Leprara, Via del Fontanile, 1-00047 Marino/Roma, Italy.

HERBERT, James Wesley, b. 18 Dec. 1939, Omaha, Neb., USA. University Band Conductor. Educ: BMusEd, Univ. of Neb., 1963; trombone study w. Emory Remington & Keith Brown; MMus, (cond. w. Jonel Perlea) Manhattan Schl. of Music, 1964; MA, profl. dip., Columbia Univ., 1966. Career: profl. trombonist, NYC, incl. solo trombonist, Fred Waring's Pennsylvanians, Paul Lavalle's Cities Service Band of Am.; mbr., Radio City Music Hall Symph. Orch.; Broadway shows, name bands; NY chmbr. orchl. perfs., TV & radio broadcasts, recordings; current perfs. in Phila. & NY; Dir. of Bands, Temple Univ., Phila., Pa.; past fndr. & dir., Wagner Coll. Bands, NYC; pvte. teaching of trombone, NY & Phila. Recordings w. NY Symph., etc. Mbrships. incl: AFM; Phi Mu Alpha; Gamma Lambda; Kappa Kappa Psi. Address: 520 Barbara Dr., Norristown, PA 19403, USA.

HERBERT, Nuala, b. 28 Nov. 1935, Dublin, Repub. of Ireland. Harpist; Pianist. Educ: Jr. & Sr. Tchng. Certs., Univ. Coll. Dublin; RCM, London; Hochschule für Musik, Munich; Conservatorio di Santa Cecilia, Rome; Accademia Chigiana, Siena. Debut: Radio Eireann, Dublin. Career: Mozart Concerto for Bicentenary Concert, Univ. Coll. Dublin, 1956; Purcell Room, London, UK, 1968; Solo broadcasts on Radio Telefis Eireann, Ireland, Radio Vaticano, Rome, BBC, London & Provinces & Edinburgh Fest.; Recordings w. Engl. Chmbr. Orch., LSO, LPO, New Philharmonia Orch. MBr., ISM. Recip., num. schlrships., cups & prizes. Hobbies: Art Collect. (furniture); Sport. Address: 48 S Hill Pk., Hampstead, London NW3, UK.

HERBIG, Gunther, b. 30 Nov. 1931, Ustinad Labem, Czech. Conductor. Educ: State Exam., State Acad. for Music, Weimar. m. Jutta Czapski, 1 s., 1 d. Debut: German Nat. Theatre, Weimar. Career: Music Dir., Potsdam; Cond., Berlin Symph. Orch.; Gen. Music Dir. & Prin. Cond., Dresden Phil. Orch.; Gen. Music Dir. & Prin. Cond., Berlin Symph. Orch. Recordings: about 35 LPs w. Eterna inclng. works by Haydn, Mozart, Beethoven, Brahms, Mendelssohn, etc. Mbr., Comps. Soc. of German Dem. Repub. Hons: Fontane Prize, 1965; Art Prize of German Dem. Repub., 1974; Nat. Prize of GDR, 1977. Hobbies: Lit.; Chess; Nature. Address: Hoffmannstr. 13, 1193 Berlin, German Dem. Repub.

HERMAN, Vasile, b. 10 June 1929, Satu Mare, Romania. Composer. Educ: Dip. of Comp., 1957, Dr. Musicol., 1974, High Schl.; Dip. of Tchr. in Music, 1954. m. Titina Herman, 2 c. Career: TV & radio apps. Comps: Double Concerto; Symph.; Poliphony; Concert of Strings; Chmbr. works, Melopee, Variante, Epsidi. Recordings: Cantilations; Rimes nostalgiques. Publs: Form and Style in the Contemporary Romanian Music, 1977. Contbr. to: Muzica; Steaua; Tribuna; Utunk (Romania). Mbr., Comps. Union of Romania. Hons: Prize of the Comps. Union, Romania. Hobbies: Numismatics; Nat. Hist. Address: str. Jozsa Bela nr. 33 ap. 4., 3400 Cluj-Napoca, Romania.

HERMAN, Witold Walenty, b. 14 Feb. 1932, Torun, Poland. Cellist; Violoncellist. Educ: Dip., Szymanowski Conserv., Torun, 1950; MA, Acad. of Music. Cracow, 1956; Dip, Ecola Normale de Musique, Paris, 1960. m. Catherine Bromboszcz, 1 s., 1 d. Debut: Phil., Cracow, 1954. Career: Concerts & recitals in Poland & other European countries; Prof. of summer acad., Franz Liszt Akademie fur Musik, Weimar, 1972; Cello Tchr., Prof. of Acad. of Music, Cracow. Num. recordings w. Radio Symph. Orch. in Katowice & Cracow, & Radio Symph. Orch. of Radio Luxembourg. Mbr. Musical Socs. in Poland. Hons. incl: Special Prize, Polish Min. of Culture & Arts, 1972; Golden Cross of Merit of the Polish Govt., 1977. Hobbies: Philos.; Sociol.;

HERMANNS, Alfred, b. 31 Jan. 1919, Phila., Pa., USA. Organ Teacher; Arranger; Author. Educ: BMus, 1941, MMUs, 1942, Temple Univ., Phila. m. June Nelson, 3 s. Career: Tchr.; var. engagements as organist. Comps: Num. organ solo arrs. Publs: Organizing Books 1 & 2, Supplementary Books 1-4; Al Hermanns Organ Series Books 1-4, etc. Contbr. to: Keyboard World. Mbrships: Am. Fedn. of Musicians. Address: 1398 Temple St., Clearwater, FL 33516, USA.

HERMANS, Nico, b. 28 June 1919, Maastricht, Netherlands. Conductor; Composer; Cello Player. Educ: study of Law; City Conserv., Dips. for cond., cello & Comp., Royal Danish Conserv., Copenhagen. m. Hanne Garnaes, 1 s., 1 d. Debut: (as comp.) Oslo, 1947; (as Cond. & Cellist) Maastricht, 1948. Career: Cello player, Utrecht Symph. Orch.; Cond., Maastricht City Orch., Dutch Nat. Youth Orch., Amsterdam Symph. Orch. "Con Brio", Symph. Orch. of Nat. Fedn. of Amateur Symph. Orchs. & Capella Majellana, Utrecht. Comps: Orchl. works & chmbr. music; (recorded) Christus vincit (motet) Capella Majellana. Mbr., Royal Dutch Union of Musicians. Hons: Music Prize, City of Amsterdam, 1970; Kt. of St. Silvester, Rome (for work as cond. of Cath. Ch. music), 1976. Hobby; History Address: Peltlaan 147, Utrecht, Netherlands.

HERMANSON, Åke Oscar Werner, b. 16 June 1923. Mollosund, Bohuslan, Sweden. Composer; Pianist; Organist. Educ: studied w. Hilding Rosenberg, Knut Back, Alf Linder. m. Britt Hermanson, 1 d. Debut: Sveriges Radio. Career: Chmn., Soc. of Swedish Comps., 1969-71; Bd. Mbr., ibid., 1967-71; Bd. Mbr., STIM, 1969-71. Comps. incl: (publd.) Nenia Bahusiensis, children's choir; Symph. No. 1; In sono per 4; Prelude & Fugue, organ; Lyrisk metamorfos, str. quartet; (recorded) Suoni d'un Flauto; Alarme per corno; Appell I-IV; Invoco; In nuce; Ultima; Symphony No. 2; Flauto D'Inverno. Contbr. to: Konsertnytt; Nutida Musik. Mbrships: Kungl Musikaliska Akademien; Soc. of Swedish Comps.; Int. Music Bureau, ibid; Swedish Sect., ISCM. Hobby: Sailing. Address: "Vindila", Djupvik, S-130 54 Dalaro, Sweden.

HERNADI, Lajos, b. 13 Mar. 1906, Budapest, Hungary. Pianist; Professor. Educ: Artist's Dip., F. Liszt Acad. of Music, 1927; Studied under Bela Bartok, Artur Schnabel (Berlin) & E.v. Dohnanyi. m. Susan Furedy, 3 s. Debut: Budapest, 1929. Career: Perf. in Budapest, Vienna, Moscow, Leningrad, Warsaw, Berlin, Stuttgart, Amsterdam, London (1930), Paris, Milan, Rome, Bucharest, Sofia, Ankara, Cairo, Alexandria, Beyrouth (1956-57); Prof., Feranc Liszt Acad. of Music. Compositions: A few cadenzas to Concerto's of Mozart; some transcription (not publd.). Recordigns: (Beethoven) Sonata Pathetique, Sonata F-major op. 102; (Schumann) Concerto A-minor; (Liszt) Venezia e Napoli, Rhapsodies Nr. 2, 9 & 15; (Bartok) Sonata, 15 Hungarian Peasant songs, Sonatina, 6 Rumanian Dances; (Leo Weiner) Concertino. Publs: Bela Bartok, pianist, teacher, 1968; Chopin's Piano Style; Anticipation; Problems of polyphonic piano playing; Sev. instructive edns. of Bach, Handel, Haydn, Mozart, Czerny, etc. Mbr., Union of Hungarian Musicians. Hons: Merited Artist of the Hungarian People's Rep., 1953; Kossuth Prize, 1956. Hobbies: Reading; Recording music; Swimming in the open air. Address: Hegedus Gyula u. 8 Budapest 1136, Hungary.

HERR, Joyce Elaine Dissinger, b. 17 Nov. 1933, E Drumore Township, Lancaster Co., Pa., USA. School Vocal & Instrumental Music Teacher; Private Teacher of Woodwind Instruments & Piano. Educ: BS, Music Educ., Lebanon Valley Coll., Pa.; MA, Music Educ, Univ. Wyo.; Post Grad., Univ. of Wyo. m. James R Herr, 1 s. Career: Tchr., Vocal Music, Wrightsville & Canadochly Valley Elementary Ctrs. of Eastern York Schl. Dist.; Tchr., Theory & Ctrs. of Eastern York Schl. Dist.; Tchr., Theory & Comp., Univ. Wyo. Summer Vand Camp; Dir., var. Ch. Choirs, Brass Choirs; Choruses & Bands; Tchr. at own studio. Comps. incl: Arrs. of vocal & instrumental music for pupils. Publs: A Survey of Community Music Activities in York County, Pa. Contbr. to newspapers & profl. mags. Mbrships. incl: Delta Kappa Gamma. Hobbies: Gardening; Culinary Arts; Travel; Fishing. Address: 241 Maple St., Wrightsville, PA 17368, USA.

HERREN, Lloyd K, b. 18 Jan. 1922, Crescent, Okla., USA. College Music Teacher, Administrator; Conductor; Singer; Violist. Educ: Bs., George Peabody Coll., Nashville, Tenn.; MMus, ibid; EdD, Univ. of Tex., Austin. m. Mary Elizabeth Grisham, 1 d., 1 s. Career: Violist, Nashville Symph., Tenn., Community Arts Symph., Denver, Colo.; Asst. Prof., Supvsr. of Music, Northeastern State Coll., Tahlequah, Okla.; Assoc. Prof., Choral Dir., Tex. A & I Univ., Kingsville; Chmn., Div. of Music, Prof. of Music, Ft. Hays Kan. State Coll.; Chmn., Div. of Humanities, & Dept. of Music, Metropolitan State Coll., Denver; Dir. num. Ch.

Music Progs. Author, A Study of The Administration of Student-Teaching Courses for Music Education Majors in Texas Schools & Colleges, 1955. Contbr. to KMTA & KMEA Jrnl. Mbr., Officer, num. profl. orgs. Hons: Elected Marshall of The Commencement; Elected Mbr., Presidential Selection Committee. Hobbies: Fishing; Camping; Back-Packing. Address: 9873 W Hawaii Dr., Lakewood, CO 80226, USA.

HERRERA, Rufo, b. 1933, Córdoba, Argentina. Composer; Musician (Cello; Piano). Educ: Studies w. var. masters, Argentina & Brazil. Debut: Sao Paulo, 1967. Career: TV & Radio apps., Argentina, Chile, Bolivia & Brazil, 1955-. Compositions: (publs.) Estandos (piano) 1970; Engramas, 1973; (recorded) Los Tangos de Vanguardia, 1967; Enantiodroma, 1970; Engramas, 1971. Contbr. of interviews to mags. & newspapers. Mbrships: Musicians Syndicate, Argentina; Musicians Soc., Brazil; Brazilian Soc. Theatre Authors; Int. Soc. for Contemporary Music; Bahia Comps. (UFBA). Hons. incl: Prize, Rio de Janeiro Music Fest., 1969; Prize, Goethe Inst., 1972; Special Prize Comp., EMAC-UFBA, 1975. Hobbies: Horsemanship. Address: Escola de Música e Artes Cênicas de UFBA, Salvador, Bahia, Brazil.

HERRICK, Christopher, b. 23 May 1942, Bletchley, Bucks., UK. Organist; Harpsichordist; Conductor. Educ: MA, Exeter Coll., Oxford; FRCO. m. Brenda Garton, 2 children. Career: Sub-organist, Westminster Abbey; Cond., Twickenham Choral Soc. & Bd. of Trade Choir; Recitals & broadcasts on organ & harpsichord. Recordings: Vista; L'Oiseau-Lyre. Mbrships: Musicians Union; ISM. Hobbies: Reading; Walking. Mgmt: John Wright. Address: 61 Burlington Ave., Kew Gardens, Richmond, Surrey, UK.

HERSCHMANN, Heinz, b. 15 Apr. 1924, Vienna, Austria. Composer; Pianist; Conductor. Educ: LRAM., ARCM. m. Isobel Ann Stein, 2 s. Career: Co-repetitor, Metropolitan Ballet, Stadsteater, Malmo, 1947-48; Piano Soloist, Revues, Spa Orchs ; Cond. Musical Shows, Music Dir., Assoc. Arts Schl , 1949-59; Dir., Apollo Sound Recording Co., & Publrs. Obelisk Musick, Melo-Musick, Adastra-Musik. Compositions: (recorded) Suite of Moods; Countryman in the City; Joy of Life; Launceston Serenade; Marlowes; Meditations for Brass; Punchinello; Cradle-Serenade; Fleurette; Reflections: Prosit; Galleon; Solemn Dignity; Palaver; Majestic Interlude; Agile; Gyroscope; film score Changing Cities. Mbrships: CGGB; Musicians Union. Hobbies: Chess; Reading; Motorcycling. Address: 32 Ellerdale Rd., London NW3 6BB, UK. 3.

HERTEL, Hanns, b. 5 Feb. 1896, Lössnitz, Germany. Composer. Educ: Univ., Conserv. Leipzig, 1 d. Career: Organist; Music tchr.; Cond.; Comp. Comps. incl: (Opera) Die gute Hansi; Der lange Magister; Der Pferdeschwanz ist ab; Happy-End zu dritt; (Orchl.) Fahrt ins Weekend; Im Atelier; Erzgebirgs-Suite. Mbrships: Dramatiker-Union; Deutscher Komponisten-Verband; Gema (Berlin). Address: Willestrasse 3, 23 Kiel, German Fed. Repub.

HERTZ (HERZ), Talmon, b. 19 Feb. 1933, Tel-Aviv, Israel. Professor of Music; Concert Cellist. Educ: BMusEd., Music Trng. Tchrs. Coll., Tel-Aviv; BMus., Israel Acad. of Music, Tel-Aviv; MMus., Manhattan Schl. of Music, NYC, USA. m. Ena Palnick, 2 s. Career: 1st Cellist, Ramat Gan Chmbr. Orch., 1955-57; Cond., Inbal Dance Grp., World Tour, 1957-58; Mbr., Pitts. Symph. orch., 1960-61; Prin. Cellist, Calgary Phil., 1962-74; Prof. of Music, Univ. of Calgary, 1962-; Chmn., Applied Div., Dept. of Music, ibid., 1974-; Soloist, num. concert stages inclng. Carnegie Hall, Wigmore Hall, Place des Arts (Montreal), Nat. Art Gall. (Ottawa), Rome, Switz.; Pain; has app. w. sev. chmbr. music ensembles. Recordings: for CBC, Radio Suisse - Romande, Kol Israel, Radio Sudwestfunk, & Radio Norway. Mbrships: Can. Music Coun.; Can. Assn. of Univ. Tchrs.; Can. String Tchrs. Assn.; Am. Fedn. of Musicians. Recip. of sev. prizes & hons. inclng. Canadian Coun. Commn. of cello concerto. Hobbies: Art Collecting; Interior Decorating; Golf; Tennis. Address: 3405-13th St. S.W. Calgary, Alta. T2T 3P9, Canada. 21, 28.

HERZ, Gerhard W, b. 24 Sept. 1911, Düsseldorf, Germany. Musicologist. Educ: Univ. of Freiburg, 1930-31; Univ. of Vienna, summer, 1931; Univ. of Berlin, fall 1931 - spring 1933; PhD, Univ. of Zürich, 1934. m. Mary Jo Fink. Career: music Critic, Düssedorf & Florence (Italy), 1935-36; Instr. Music Hist. - Assoc. Prof., Univ. of Louisville, 1938-45; Prof., Music Hist., ibid., 1946-; Chmn., Dept. of Music Univ., 1945-46; Vis. Prof. of Music, Univ. of Chgo., summer 1965; Disting. Lectr., Univ. of Louisville, 1977-78. Publs: Joh. Seb. Bach im Zeitalter des Rationalismus und der Frühromantik, 1935, 2nd printing, 1936; Bach - Cantata No. 4, Christ lag in Todesbanden, 1967; Bach - Cantata No. 140, Wachet auf, ruft uns die Stimme, 1972. Contbr. to many books & jrnls. in field. Mbrships: Chmn., S.-Ctrl. Chapt., 1965-66 & 73-74, Am. Musicol. Soc.; Int. Musicol. Soc.; Coll. Music Soc.; Gesellschaft fuer Musikforschung; Chmn., Exec.

Committee, Am. Chapt., 1972-74. Neue Bach Gesellschaft; Trustee, 1946-, Pres., 1966-68 & 69-70, Chmn., Artists & Programme Committee, 1970-, Louisville Phil. Soc.; Bd. of Dirs., 1963-, Louisville Bach Soc. Address: 729 Middle Way, Louisville, KY 40206, USA. 2.

HESBERT, René-Jean, b. 22 Jan. 1899, Sorel-Moussel, Eure-et-Loire, France. Benedictine monk in Solesmes. Educ: Paris Univ., Sornbonne, Lic. Sci. Debut: Solesmes Abbey. Comps. incl: Gregorian Structures, 6 French comps. on the structural line of 6 Gregorian comps., Paris, 1957; The Mystery of Christ, series of 5 introits of the Liturgical Cycle, Saint-Wandrille, 1972. Recordings: all own works. Mbrships: Henry Bradshaw Soc., vice-pres.; Plainsong and Medieval Music Soc., vice-pres. Publs. incl: Corpus Antiphonalium Officii vol. IIV, 1963-70; The Problem of Christ's Transfixion the following Traditions: Biblical, Patristic, Iconographic, Liturgical and Musical, Tournai, Desclée, 1940. Contbr. to: Num. profl. jrnls. Address: Abbey Saint -Wandrille, Seine-maritime, 76490 Caudebecen-Caux.

HESCHKE, Richard J, b. 7 Oct. 1939, Sheboygan, Wis., USA. Professor; Organ Recitalist. Educ: Eastman Schl. of Music, Univ. of Rochester, NY; MMus, DMA, in Ch. music w. organ major; perf.'s cert. in Organ. Career: Recitals in major cities in USA inclng. NY, Chgo., Miami, Buffalo, Cleveland, etc., & for state, regional & nat. conventions of AGO; formerly on facs., Eastman Schl. of Music, La. State Univ. & Univ. of Iowa; now Assoc. Prof. of organ, Concordia Coll., Bronxville, NY. sev. recordings. Publs: choral music reviewer for ChurchMusic mag., 1967-72. Mbrships: AGO (served as chapt. Dean in sev. states); MTNA (competition judge in var. states & regions); Hymn Soc. of Am.; Coll. Music Soc.; Am. Musicol. Soc. Hons: Pi Kappa Lambda. Mgmt: Phillip Truckenbrod/ Arts Image Ltd. Address: 220 Midland Ave., Tuckahoe, NY 10707, USA.

HESFORD, Michael Bryan, b. 19 July 1930, Eccles, Lancs., UK. Organist; Church Music Director; Composer; Examiner. Educ: LTSC; Dip., Music Educ., TSC; LRAM; ARCM; BA; MA; PhD; DMus., Geneva Theol. Coll., Ind., USA; Studied w. W H Selby, Marcel Dupré, max Drischner. m. Maureen Judith Newton, 1 d. Debut: Copenhagen Cathedral, Denmark, 1955. Career: TV Perfs., Cond., BBC & ITV; num. Organ Recitals, Denmark, E & W Germany, Spain, UK; Broadcasts, Spain, USA, France, Czech., Hungary, Silesia, Norway; World premiere of Flor Peeters' organ music for Belgium radio; Ed., Musical Opinion & The Organ. Comps. incl: var. Carols, Ch. Music; Organ Partita on a Theme of Bartok; Rottenbucher-Fantasie, Introduktion, Passacaglia & Choral on BACH organ; Variationen zum Jubilaums fest. der DDR. Recordings: Bach, Pieces From the Anna Magdelena Notebook; The Choir of Christ Coll., Brecon; Organ Music On The Organ of Melton Mowbray Parish Ch. Publs: The Organ Music of Max Drischner, 1955; Complete Organ Works, 1974; The Organ Works of Flor Peeters, 1978. Contbr. to var. profl. jrnls. Mbrships: Fellow, Gesellschaft der Orgelfreunde; DDR Travel Club; Cathedral Organists Assn. Named Titular Organist, Rottenbuch Abbey, Germany, 1973. Address: Adagio, 6 Richmond Dr., Melton Mowbray, Leics., UK. 3.

HESKES, Irene, b. 15 June 1928, NYC, USA. Soprano; Musical Consultant. Educ: BA, NY. Univ.; Music Educators Cert., Schl. of Sacred Music of the Hebrew Union Coll., Jewish Inst. of Religion, NYC; Cert., Arts Admin. Inst. of Harvard Univ.; musical studies at Juilliard, NYC & Eastman, Rochester, NY.; cantorial-Jewish liturgical studies, Cantor's Inst. of the Jewish Theol. Sem. of Am. NYC. m. Jacob Heskes, 1 s., 1 d. Career: Lecture-recital apps. in USA & Canada; Some radio & TV (minor stns.); Dir. of the Nat. Jewish Music Coun. of the Nat. Jewish Welfare Bd.; Music Cons. & featured Lectr. at the Theodor Herzl Inst. of the Jewish Agency of Am. Publs: Rev. edn. by Irene Heskes of Jews in Music, by Artur Holde, 1974, Ernest Bloch: Creative Spirit (w. Suzzane Bloch), 1976; Israeli Music; A Program Aid, 1978; Jewish Music Programs-Sampling & How to Commission New Works, 1978; etc. Contbr. to num. Jewish jrnls. & the Ency. Judaica. Mbrships: Phi Beta Kappa; Am. Musicol. Soc.; Int. Musicol. Soc. Mgmt: Jewish Ctr. Lectr. Bur. of the Nat. Jewish Welfare Bd. Address: 90-15 68th Ave., Forest Hills, NY 11375, USA.

HESS, Andrea (Megaery), b. 7 May, London, UK. Cellist. Educ: RAM, recital dip.; Nordwestdeutsche Musikakademie, Detmold, German Fed. Repub. Debut: Wigmore Hall, London, 1979. Career: num. perfs. as soloist & as mbr. of sev. chmbr. ensembles in London, throughout UK, Europe & Can. mbr., ISM. Hons: Muir Carnegie Dip. prize, 1974; Harold Craxton prize for chmbr. music, 1974; Benjamin Dale Award, 1975; Countess of Munster Trust Scholarship, 1975. Hobbies: Cinema; Reading; Philos.; Cooking; People; Travel. Mgmt: Blythe & Hackel Ltd., 6 Firsby Rd., London N16. Address: 81 Lacy Rd., Putney, London SW15, UK.

HESS, Jürgen, b. 5 Dec. 1923, Hamburg, Germany. Violinist. Educ: Pvte. studies as a child; Studied violin w. Jadviga

Elsner-Frommer; ARCM. m. Gabrielle Anne Barnard, 5 c. Career: Concertos & recitals, London, Switz. & Netherlands; Perfd. w. Boyd Neel Orch., Haydn Orch., London Mozart Players, Jacques & Leppard Orchs., London Chmbr. Orch., etc.; Fndr., London cantata Ensemble; Ldr., Leppard Chmbr. Ensemble, Delphos & Nash Ensembles, Guarnerius String Quintet; Mbr., Prometheus & Melos Ensembles; Mbr., RPO, 1956 (Co-Ldr. of Orch. under Rudolf Kempe); Fndn. Mbr., Delme String Quartet & Tononi Piano Trio, 1964; Sub Ldr., English Chmbr. Orch., 1969, sev. world tours; Ldr., London Bach & English Baroque Orchs.; Staff Mbr., RSAMD; Formed Hess Family Ensemble, 1976. Contbr. to: BBC Spare Time for Music. Hobbies: Philos.; People; Table Tennis; Stamps. Address: 14 Rosslyn tce., Horslethill Rd., Glasgow G12 9NA, UK.

HESSE, Axel Ernst, b. 16 July 1935, Berlin, Germany. Musicologist. Educ: Dipl. phil., 1961, Dr phil, 1971, Humboldt Univ., Berlin; student, Inst. of Musicol., Karl Marx Univ., Leipzig, 1962; postgrad. study in Cuba, 1963-65; studies w. noted tchrs. m. Flora, 2 children. Career: Asst., Leipzig Univ., 1968; Oberassistent, Dept. of Musicol., Humboldt Univ., 1970; asst. prof., ethnomusicology, ibid.; Vis. prof., ethnomusicology, peru, 1978; specialist in Latin Am. & German folk music. Contbr. to publs. in field. Mbrships: Sec., Arbeitskreis Muskethnol. of Verband der Kompositen und Musikwissenschaftler der DDR; Bd. of Dirs., Nat. Comm. for GDR, Int. Folk Music Coun. Address: Akazienallee 4, 115 Berlin, German Dem. Repub.

HESSE, Marjorie Anne, b. 13 Nov. 1911, Brisbane, Australia. Lecturer in Music; Pianist; Composer; Examiner in Music. Educ: BA, Univ. Sydney; DSCM (Sydney Conservatorium); LRAM; LMusA. m. Tiborn Kereny, 1944-58. Debut: Sydney, 1932. Career: Lectr. in Music, Sydney Conservatorium of Music; Lectr., Piano Studies, Music Dept., Univ. Sydney; As pianist toured Aust. & num. countries; Adjudicator & Examiner for Aust. Music Examinations Bd.; Concert Soloist w. orchs. in Aust. & NZ. Comps. incl: The Ballerina, 1971; Children's Suites; Piano Music; Songs. Mbr. num. profl. orgs. Hons. incl: MBE, 1975. Hobbies: Photography; Reading; Films. Address: 4 Cowdroy Ave., Cammeray, Sydney, NSW 2062, Australia.

HESSE-BUKOWSKA, Barbara, b. 8 Feb. 1930, Lodz, Poland. Pianist. Educ: MA in Music; Dip. w. highest hons. div., 1 s. Career: Concert tours, all 5 continents; Film, TV & radio recordings; Prof. of Piano, Warsaw Acad. of Music. Recordings for Musa, Lumen, Chant du Mode., Deutsche Grammophon Gessellschaft & Westminster. Mbr., F. Chopin Soc., Warsaw. Hons: 2nd Prize, Int. Chopin Competition, 1949; Chopin Prize, M. Long-Jacques Thibaud Int. Competition, 1953; Harriet Cohen Piano Medal, 1962. Hobbies: Archives; Architecture. Mgmt: Pagart. Address: ul. Wielicka 54, Warsaw, Poland.

HESSENBERG, Kurt, b. 17 Aug. 1908, Frankfurt am Main, Germany. Composer; Professor of Compositions. Educ: pvte. lessons in piano, -1927; Landes-Konservatorium, Leipzig, w. Günter Raphael (comp.) & Robert Teichmüller (Piano), 1927-31. m. Gisela Volhard, 2 c. Career: Tchr. for Comp., Dr. Hochs Konservatorium Frankfurt am Main, 1933; Tchr. at the Hochschule für Musik, Frankfurt am Main, 1938; Prof., ibid., 1953. Compositions: For Orch: 3 symphs., 2 concertos, Regnart-Variationen, & other comps., also for solo instrument w. orch. Chamber Music: 5 Str. Quartets, 2 Str. Trios & other comps. Piano & Organ Comps: Lieder w. piano & w. other instruments, also w. orch, e.g. Lieder eines Lumpen. For Choir; Fiedellieder, Psalmen-Triptychon, Von Wesen und Vergehan, etc. Var. recordings. Mbr., Deutscher Komponisten-Verband. Hons: Robert-Schumann-Preis der Stadt Dusseldorf, 1951; Goethe-Plakette der Stadt Frankfurt am Main, 1973. Address: Fuchsohl 76, 6 Frankfurt am Main 50, German Fed. Repub.

HETTEMA, Gerhardus Johannes, b. 15 May 1941, Leeuwarden, Netherlands. Orchestra Leader; Violinist. Educ: studied w. Herman Krebbers, Music Lyceum. Amsterdam, 1958-63; Solo (Concert) Dip., ibid., 1963. m. Elisabeth Gout. 4 children. Debut: Canada, 1959. Career: 1st Violin, Concertgebouw Orch., Amsterdam, 1963-65; Ldr., Zürich Chmbr. Orch., Switzerland, 1965-67; Ldr., South-West Radio Orch., Baden-Baden, Germany, 1967-69; Ldr., Rotterdam Phil., 1969-; num. radio apps. w. orch. & ensembles; Netherland String Trio, concerto Rotterdam. Contbr. to Das Orchester; The Stasd Andante II, 2925 AA Krimpen a/d ljssel, Netherlands. Hon. Prix d'Excellence, 1966. Hobbies: Walking; Filming & Travelling. Address: Adante II, 29255 AA Krimpen a/d ljssel, Netherlands.

HETTRICK, William Eugene, b. 15 Nov. 1939, Toledo, Ohio, USA. Musicologist; College Teacher; Director of Collegium Musicum. Educ: BMus, MA, Univ. of Mich.: study at Univ. of Munich, Germany; PhD, Univ. of Mich. m. Jane Schatkin

Hettrick. Career: currently Assoc. Prof., Music Dept., Hofstra Univ., Hempstead, NY; Tchng. Dean, Coll. of Lib. Studies, ibid. Publs: The Thorough-Bass in the Works of Gregor Aichinger 1564-1628, 1968; The Cantiones Ecclesiasticae (1607) of Gregor Aichinger; critical edn. w. commentary, 1972; The Rosetum Marianum of Bernhard Klingenstein (1604), critical edn., 1977. num. smaller edns. of instrumental & vocal music of the late Renaissance. Contbr. to profl. publs. Mbrships: Am. Musicol. Soc.: Gesellschaft für Bayerische Musikgeschichte; Am. Musical Instrument Soc., etc. Hons. incl: Stanley Medal, Univ. of Mich. Schl. of Music, 1962; Phi Beta Kappa; Pi Kappa Lambda; var. fellowships. Address: 863 Duncan Dr., Westbury, NY 11590, USA.

HEULYN, Meinir, b. 9 Mar. 1948, Newport, Gwent, UK. Harpist. Educ: BMus, Cardiff Univ. Coll.; Conservatorio di Musica, Genova, Italy. m. Brian Raby. Career: Prin. Harp, Welsh Philharmonia; Music club recitals throughout Brit. of both harp & harp & flute; Major exponent of traditional Welsh music; Harp Tutor, Coll. of Music & Drama, Cardiff. Publs: Telyn Y Werin, 1975. Hons. incl: 1st Prize for Harp Solo, Caerwys 400th Centenary Eisteddfod. Hobbies incl: Dressmaking. Address: 50 Edward VII Ave., Newport, Gwent, UK.

HEUSSENSTAMM, George, b. 24 July 1926, Los Angeles, Calif., USA. Composer; Concert Manager. Educ: studied violin & clarinet; self-taught pianist: music theory, LA City Coll., 1946-48, LA State Coll., 1961-63, & pvtely. w. Leonard Stein, 1961-63. m. Mary McManus. Career: formerly mbr. of Committee for Encounters (avant-garde concerts), Pasadena, & Music Critic, Pasadena Star-News; Profl. Music Copyist; Tutor; Lectr.; Mgr., Coleman Chmbr. Music Assn., 1971-; on music theory fac., Calif. State Coll., Dominguez Hills, 1976-. Over 50 pubbld. comps. for instrumental ensembles, a cappella choruses, etc. Recorded comps: Our Soul Waits for the Lord & My Soul is Exceeding Sorrowful (a cappella choir); Seven Etudes, Op. 17 (oboe, clarinet, bassoon); Set for Double Reeds, Op. 39; Tetralogue, Op. 36 (4 clarinets & percussion); Tubafour, Op. 30 (4 tubas). Contbr. to jrnls. Mbrships. incli: ASCP; Western Alliance of Certs Admnstrs. Recip. many hons. Address: 5013 Lowell Ave., La Crescenta, CA 91214, USA. 9.

HEUSSNER, Horst, b. 10 July 1926, Kassel, Germany. Professor of Musicology. Educ: PhD, Marburg, 1956. m. Ingeborg Skuthaus. Career: Lctr., Marburg & Giessen Univ., 1957-72; music reporter for var. jrnls.; evening class lectr., 1958-61; Prof. of musicoloigy, Marburg, from 1972. Publs: (w. I Schultz) Collectio Musica, in Catalogus Musicus VI, 1973. Contbr. to: Die Musikforschung; Neue Zeitschrift für Musik; Musica; Mozart Jahrbuch; Neue deutsche Biographie; Musik in Geschichte und Gegenwart; Riemann-Musiklexikon; Sohlmans Musiklexikon. Ed., Catalogus musicus. Mbrships: Int. Soc. of Musicologists; Soc. for Music Rsch. Hobbies: Travel. Address: 355 Marbury/Lahn, In der Badestube 29, German Fed. Repub.

HEWITT-JONES, Tony, b. 27 Jan. 1926, Ealing, UK. Composer; Conductor; Accompanist (piano, organ, harpsichord). Educ: MA, Christ Ch., Oxford Univ.; studied w. Bernard Rose, Herbert Sumsion, Nadia Boulanger; ARCO. m. Anita Lawson, 1 s., 1 d. Career: Dir. of Music, Dean Close Jr. Schl., Cheltenham, 1953-57; Asst. Co. Music Advsr., Gloucs., 1958-77; Freelance, 1977-. Num. choral works, inclng. Seven Sea Poems, Te Deum, The Divine Image; Wind Quintet; Capriccio for Clarinet & Piano; Sinfonietta for Strings; Whit Sunday Processional for organ. Mbrships: CGGB; ISM; RCO. Recip., Limpus & Read Prizes, 1957. Hobbies: Reading; Walking; Conviviality; Railways; Languages; Scrabble. Address: 6 Tivoli Rd., Cheltenham GL50 2TG, UK. 3.

HEWSON, David Graham, b. 27 Nov. 1953, Clapham, UK. Composer; Music Teacher; Lecturer. Educ: BEd.; studied comp. w. Richard Arnell & Robert Long. Debut: Commissioned to write Oboe Concerto for Stockwell Coll. Career: Composed Electronic Music for the Black Panther (feature film), 1978. Comps. (recorded): Mood and Mode (Electronically Produced). Mbrships: PRS; CGGB. Address: 145 Silverdale, Sydenham, London SE26, UK.

HEYDE, Norma, b. 31 Dec. 1927, Herrin, Ill., USA. Singer; Teacher of Voice. Educ: BMus, MMus, Univ. of Mich.; Certs. in Voice & Oratorio, Mozarteum, Salzburg, Austria. m. Dr. John B Heyde. Debut: Ann Arbor, Mich., 1950. Career incls: Soprano Soloist in recital, concert & oratorio w. var. orchs. inclng. Phila Orch., Nat. Gallery Orch., Wash., DC, Madison, Wis., Symph., York Symph. of Pa., Northern Va. Choral Soc. & Orch.; CBS Messiah perf.: Artist, num. Coll. & Univ. choral perfs.; Asst. Prof. Music, Salisbury State Coll., Md.; Assoc. Prof. Music, Salisbury State Coll., Md. Recordings: Soloist, Handel, Judas Maccabaeus, & Mendelssohn, Elijah: Soloist & Dir., Saint-

Saens, Christmas Oratorio. Mbrships. incl: Phi Kappa Phi; Pi Kappa Lambda; Mu Phi Epsilon, MENC. Recip., var. scholarships, Univ. of Mich. Address: 508 Kings Highway, Millford, DE, USA. 5. 29.

HEYMAN, Alan Charles, b. 16 Mar. 1931, NYC, USA. Ethnomusicologist; Performer on Traditional Korean Instruments; Specialist in Asian Music & Dance. Educ: BA, Univ. of Colo.: Nat. Classical Music Inst. of Korea, Seoul: Korean Traditional Musical Arts Conserv., Seoul. Career: num. broadcast perfs., Korea; perfs. & lectrs. given throughout USA, & in Korea & Japan; Fndr., Dir., Perf., Sahm-Chun-Li Dancers & Musicians of Korea Co. in US inclng. 2 perfs. at Phil. Hall, Lincoln Ctr., NYC: Dir., perfs. of Nat. Classical Music Inst. of Korea, Iran, France, German Fed. Repub. & Switz. Comps. incl: 14 documentary, 4 feature film scores. Contbr. to: Dance Perspectives; Essays in Asian Music & Theatre, 1972; Dict. de la Musique, 1976; Musical Jrnl.; etc. Mbrships. incl: Soc. for Ethnomusicol.; Soc. for Asian Music; Pres., Int. Culture Assn. Recip., awards for film scores, Aust. & Korea. Hobby: Philately. Address: Apt. 5, 1st Floor, Ra-dong, Tong-Myung Yun-Rip Apts., 192-5, Teungchon-dong, Kangsuh-ku, Seoul, Korea.

HEYWORTH, Peter Lawrence Frederick, b. 3 June 1921, NY, USA. Music Critic. Educ: Balliol Coll., Oxford. Career: Music Critic, The Observer, 1955-. Publs: Berlioz, Romantic & Classic Writings by Ernest Newman (ed.), 1972; Conversations With Klemperer, 1973. Contbr. to The New York Times. Address: 32 Bryanston Sq., London W1, UK. 1.

HICK, Susan Elizabeth, b. 24 Feb. 1949, Dudley, Worcs., UK. Music Teacher. Educ: Grad., London Coll. of Music; Lic., ibid. for flute; Assoc., ibid. for singing. Career: Tchr. of Flute & Piano, St. Helen's Schl., Abingdon, Summer Fields Schl., Oxford, and St. Mary's Schl., Wantage. Contbr. to: Musical Times; Classical Music. Hobbies: Walking; Gardening; Playing oboe. Address: 57 Virginia Way, Abingdon, Oxfordshire, UK.

HICKEN, Kenneth Lambert, b. 4 Apr. 1934, Lethbridge, Alta., Can. Associate Professor of Music, Univ. of Lethbridge. Educ: BSc, Univ. of Alta., 1959; AMus & BMus, ibid., 1962; MA, Brigham Young Univ., Provo, Utah, 1964; PhD, ibid., 1970. m. Alice Ruth Jensen, 4 s., 2 d. Career: Assoc. Prof. of Music; Paper at 1st Int. Schoenberg Congress, Vienna, 1974; Compositions: Str. Quartet No 1; musical spoofs; sacred songs. Contbr. to: Musicol. Annual, Ljublijana. Mbr: Int. Schoenberg Soc. Hons: Canada Coun. Awards, 1964-65, 65-66, 69 & 73; 1st Prize, Chmbr. Music, Alta. Centennial Competition, 1967. Hobbies: Church Work; Family Activities; Travel; Performing as a Musical Humorist. Address: 1054 Lakeview Dr., Lethbridge, Alta., Can.

HICKMANN, Ellen, b. 28 July 1934, Flensburg, German Fed. Repub. Musicologist. Educ: Hochschule für Musik, Hamburg; Acad. of Music & Performing Arts, Vienna, Austria; Hamburg & Vienna Univs.; State Tchrs. Lics., 1962, 1975; PhD Musicol., 1971. m. Prof. Hans Hickmann (dec. 1968), 1 s., 1 d. Career: Asst. to husband; Ed. & author of sleeve notes, 1968-70, Record Prod., 1970-74, Polydor, Hamburg; Tchr., Gymnasium, Eppendorf, & Tchr., Hamburg Voelkerkunde museum, 1974-. Publ: Musica Instrumentalis, 1971. Contbr. to: Ency. des Musiques Sacrées, 1968: Lexikon der Ägyptologie, 1972-; Musikforschung. Mbr., profl. assns. Hons. incl; (for records) Orpeées d'or; Edison Prize; Grammy nominee, 1974. Address: D-2000 Hamburg 52, Quellental 50, German Fed. Repub.

HICKOX, Richard Sidney, b. 5 Mar. 1948, Stokenchurch, Bucks., UK. Conductor; Organist. Educ: RAM, 1966-67; Organ Scholar, Queen's Coll., Cambridge Univ., 1967-70; MA; FRCO (CHM); LRAM. m. Frances Sheldon-Williams. Debut: (as cond.) London, 1971. Career: Musical Dir. The Richard Hickox Singers & Orch.; Dir., London Symph. Chorus; Organist, St. Margaret's Ch., Westminster & Dir., St. Margaret's, Westminster Singers; Musical Dir., Bradford Fest. Choral Soc.; Artistic Dir., Woodburn, St. Endellion & Christ Church, Spitalfields Fests.; Over 50 broadcasts for BBC; apps. w. his Singers & Orch. at Proms & num. Brit. & foreign Fests.; Guest Cond., LSP, RPO, Bournemouth Symph. Orch. & Sinfonietta, Royal Liverpool Phil. Radio Kammererkest & other major orchs. Recordings: Bach, Short Masses in G minor & G major; Finzi (2 records); Rubbra, Masses; Medieval English Christmas Music (2 records.). Hobbies: Watching Football & Tennis. Mgmt: Ibbs & Tillett, London. Address: 1 c Morpeth Tce., London, SW1, UK.

HICKS, David, b. 6 March 1937, Phila., Pa., USA. Opera Director (Producer) and Singer; Teacher of Opera Acting; Lighting Designer. Educ: BS, Music, Temple Univ., Pa., 1959. Debut: (Singer) Pa. Lyric Opera, 1961; (Dir.) NYC Opera, 1967. Career: Sang 50 supporting roles (baritone) w. NYC Opera & 20 other Am. Cos.; Dir., 22 major operas w. 20 Am. Cos. incl.

NYC Opera, Baltimore, Pitts., Pa., Cinn., Kansas City, Ft. Worth, Memphis, Seattle, Honolulu, San Fran. (Western Opera Theatre), Charlotte, Palm Beach, & sev. summer fests.; Stage Dir. & Instructor in Operatic Acting, Acad. of Vocal Arts, Pa., 1973-77; currently on acting Fac., Am. Opera Center, Juilliard Schl., NY. Mgmt: Ludwig Lustig & Florian Ltd., 111 W 57th St., NY, NY 10019, USA. Address: 18 W 75th St., NY, NY 10023, USA.

HIGBEE, Dale (Strohe), b. 14 June 1925, Proctor, Vt., USA. Clinical Psychologist; Flutist & Recorder Player; Record & Book Reviewer. Educ: AB, Harvard, 1949; PhD in Clinical Psychol., Univ. of Tex., 1954; Pvte. flute study w. Georges Laurent, 1945-47; flute study w. Arthur Lora, Juilliard, summer 1947; Master class in flute w. Marcel Moyse, 1970. Div., 1 d. (2) m. Anne Dwyer Higbee. Career: Flautist in Vt. State Symph., Columbia, SC Symph., Charlotte Opera Orch. NC, Charlotte Symphonette, Charlotte Oratorio Orch. NC, Western Piedmond Symph. NC; Flautist & Recorder Player in Charlotte Camerata NC & var. chmbr. music grps.; Psychol. Intern, Western Psych. Inst., Univ. of Pitts.; Clin. Psychol., SC State Hosp., 1954-55; VA Hosp., Salisbury, NC, 1955-; Record & Book Review Ed., The Am. Recorder, 1967-. Publs: A Survey of Music Instrument Collection in the US and Can., Ann Arbour, Mich. Contbr. to: var. profl. mags. & jrnls. Mbrships: Gov., Dolmetsch Fndn., 1963-; Gov. Bd., Am. Musical Instrument Soc., 1972-75; Bd. Dirs., Am. Recorder Soc., 1963-65; Am. Musicol. Soc., etc. Hobby: Collecting Antique flutes, recorders & flageolets. Address: 412 S Ellis St., Salisbury, NC 28144, USA.

HIGGINS, Cathy Eisenberg, b. 9 Jan. 1948, Reading, Pa., USA. Instrumental Music Teacher: Monroe County French Horn Adjudicator; Professional French Hornist. Educ, 15 yrs. pvte. French Horn lessons w. Clarence Mayer, David Gray, John Covert, Barry Tuckwell, etc.; BMus & MS, Ithaca Coll. Schl. of Mus. m. James F Higgins. Career: Has taught coll. music theory, solfeggio & dictation & perf. French Horn w. the Utica & Cornell Symphs., the Fla. Int. Fest. Inst. Orch. w. the London Symph., Schl. Band of Am. European Concert Tour, & the Ithaca Coll. Concert Band & Orch. Recordings: Six Pieces for Four Horns, on Recital Music for French Horn, Mark Records; The Hunt, The Dancers, and Night by Nicolas Tcherepnine. Mbrships: Pi Kappa Lambda; Warden-Libn., Mu Phi Epsilon; Schl. Band of m. Alumni Assn.; MENC, etc. Recip. var. hons. inclng: John Phillip Sousa Award, 1966; Outstanding Brass Instrumentalist, 1966. Hobbies: Camping; Bicycling; Skiing; Sewing; Reading. Address: 1968 Lehigh Stn. Rd., Henrietta, NY 14467, USA. 29.

HIGGINS, Elliot Lloyd, b. 13 Mar. 1941, Albuquerque, NM, USA. Composer; Conductor; Producer; Musician, French Horn; Administrator. Educ: Bachelor of Univ. Studies, Univ. of NM, studied w. Robert McBride, Ingoll Dahl. m. Roxanne Bates, m. Betsy Hamrah, 1 s., 1 d. Debut: Albuquerque, NM; 1962. Career: Mgr., Symph. Orchs., 5 yrs.; Prin. Horn, Ventura County Symph., Santa Barbara Symph., Calif., Ft. Wayne, Ind. Symph., & Birmingham, Ala.; Horn, & Prod., Neo Mobicentric Ensemble, Cleveland, Ohio; Asst. Dir., Hummingbird Music Camp; Lay Min. of the arts, Unitarian-Universalist Ch.; Cond., Opus I Chmbr. Orch., Cleveland, Ohio. Comps. incl: var. Theatre, Ballet music. Contbr. to: Thunderbird Literary Mag.; Percussive Arts Mag. Mbrships: Int. Horn Soc.; Unitarian Universalist Worship Arts Clearing House; Religious Arts Guild. Recip. Comp. Award, The Unitarian-Universalist. Hobbies: Mycology; Fly Fishing; Canoeing. Address: 12932 Clifton Blvd., Lakewood, OH 44107, USA.

HIGGINS, Francis Edward (Frank), b. 23 June 1915, Benalla, Vic., Aust. Music Educator; Flautist & Recorder Player. Educ: Melbourne Tchrs. Coll.; Mus. Bach. (Melb.); Dip. Ed. (Melb.); TPTC; STPC; MACE. m. Ellen Veronica Roche, 2 s., 1 d. Career: Hdmaster., Boomahnoomoonah & Detpa State Schls., Specialist Music Tchr., 1946-56; Lectr. in Music, Melbourne Tchrs. Coll., 1956-60; Hd. of Music Dept., State Coll. of Vic., Burwood, 1960-; Sr. Tutor on Recorders, Coun. of Adult Educ., for over 10 yrs. Publs: Music Education in the Primary School, 1964; Progressive Recorder Method for Descants & Tenors, 1960; Recorder Trios for Descant & Treble, 1962; Progressive Recorder Method for Trebles, 1964; 16 German Folk Tunes for Recorders & Percussion, 1971. Contbr. to: Vic. Educl. Mag.; Canon; ASME Jrnl. Mbrships: VP, Vic. Chapt., Aust. Soc. of Music Educ. Hobbies: Ancient Instruments; Fishing; Australiana. Address: 32 Hutchinson St., Bentleigh, Victoria 3204, Australia. 4.

HIGGS, Timothy John, b. 8 March 1951, Edenbridge, Kent, UK. Composer. Educ: RCM; Pvte. study w. Gordon Jacob. m. Jane Thornton, 1 s. Comps: (operas) Ptishfahtushamun; Thomas Bullen; The Buzgloak Child; Mass for Chorus, Soloist & Orch.; Variations for oboe, harp, strings & percussion; Anthem,

Let the Souls of the Saints. Mbr., CGGB. Hons: Octavia Travel Scholarship, 1973. Hobbies: Walking; Swimming. Address: 21 Remington St., Islington, London N1, UK.

HIGHAM. John. b. 17 Feb. 1940, Blackpool, UK. Concert Agent & Manager; Pianist. Educ: Liverpool Matthay Schl. of Music; RAM; ARCM. m. Anthea Fry, 2 s. Debut: Wigmore Hall, London, 1962. Career: sev. BBC broadcasts; concerts as soloist & chmbr. musician throughout UK; Mng. Dir., New Era Int. Concerts Ltd., 1969-; Fndr., Young Musicians Series, London, 1970. Hons: Prizewinner, Geneva Int. Piano Competition & Silver Medal, Royal Amateur Orchl. Soc., 1960. Hobbies: Travel; Weighligting; Tennis; Cooking. Address: 16 Lauriston Rd., London SW19 4 TQ, UK. 3.

HIGUET, Nestor Gustave Ghislain, b. 3 June 1903, Manage, Hainaut, Belgium. Double-Bass Teacher. Educ: piano, Conserv. de la Louviere, Hainaut, 1918; full studies inclng. Virtuosity Prize for double-bass (superior dip.), Royal Conserv. of Brussels. m. Simonne Avet-Foray, 3 s., 1 d. Career incls: 1st solo Double-Bass Player, many places in Belgium, 1930-45; num. recitals w. piano & concert perfs. w. orch., Belgium & abroad; Mbr., Theatre Royal de la Monnaie (opera) orch., Brussels, 1930-53; Tchr., Royal Conserv. of Brussels. Comps. incl: Fantaisie pour contrebasse et piano; Suite Enfantine (piano & small orch.). Sev. recordings. Contbr. to jrnls. Mbrships: incl: Sabam Comps. Assn. Many hons. inclng: Off., Order of Couronne; Kt., Order of Leopold. Hobbies incl: Writing poetry. Address: Ave. Docteur Decroly 24, B-1180 Brussels, Belgium.

HILDEBRAND, John G, b. 26 Mar. 1942, Boston, Mass., USA. Bass-Trombonist; Tubist; Scientist; University Teacher. Educ: AB, Harvard Univ., 1964; PhD, Rockefeller Univ., 1969. Career: Freelance bass-trombonist, symphs., opera & brass ensembles, Boston & NYC; Mbr., Boston Civ. Symph., Newton Symph., Emmanuel Music, Cantata Singers Orchs.; Dir.-Mbr., Cambridge Symphonic Brass Ensemble; Sci. Fac., Harvard Univ. Mbr., Worcester (Mass.) Symph. Orch., Boston Brass Ensemble, Castle Hill Fest. Orch. Recordings w. MIT Symph. Orch. Contbr., Reviews, Int. Trombone Assn. Publs. Mbrships: Int. Trombone Assn.; Tubists Universal Brotherhood Assn.: Local 9-535 Am. Fedn. Musicians; Am. Musical Inst. Soc.; Am. Symph. Orch. League; Sec., Pierian Sodality 1808, Harvard Univ., 1962-63. Hobbies incl: Natural Hist. Address: 14 Fernald Dr., Cambridge, MA 02138, USA.

HILEY, David, b. 5 Sept. 1947, Littleborough, UK. Lecturer in Music. Educ: BA, Oxon. m. Ann Fahrni, 2 d. Career: Lecturer in Music, Royal Holloway Coll., Univ. of London; Sub-Ed., Grove's Dictionary, 6th Ed. Publs: Ed., Journal of the Plainsong & Mediaeval Musical Society. Contbr. to: Musical Times; Music & Letters; Jrnl. of Ecclesiastical Hist. Mbrships: Treas., Plainsong & Mediaeval Music Soc. Address: 46 Bond Street, Englefield Green, Engham, Surrey TW20 0PY, UK.

HILFRED, Borge, b. 16 Apr. 1918, Silkeborg, Denmark. Violinist. Educ: Dip., Royal Danish Acad. of Music, Copenhagen. m. Karen Hilfred, 1 s., 1 d. Debut: Copenhagen, 1948. Career: Perfs. as soloist, chmbr. musician & ensemble ldr. in concerts & radio prods., Denmark, Sweden, Norway, Iceland, Austria, Switz. & S Africa; Perfs. w. trio & orch. at hotels & restautants; Master course, Lucerne, Switz., Wolfgant Schneiderhau; Bartok seminar, Budapest, Hungary, 1968. Recordings: Odeon. Mbrships: Danish Soloist Soc.; Danish Musicians Soc. Hobbies: Amateur Radio; Sailing sports.

HILL, Anthony Nicholas Finch, b. 26 Oct. 1936, Jordans, Bucks., UK. Horn Player. Educ: RCM, 1954-55, 1957-59; ARCM. m. Gwendoline Mary Gale, 3 c. Career: 1st Horn, Sadler's Wells, 1960-61; 3rd Horn, BBC Concert Orch., 1961-62; 3rd Horn, LPO, 1962-66; 1st Horn, Bournemouth Symph. Orch., 1966-68; BBC Symph. Orch., 1970-77; Freelance, 1977-. Arrangements incl. pieces for 8 horn & bass guitar. Mbr., Savage Club. Hobbies: Motor cars; Eating and Drinking. Address: Penny Cottage, 46 Green End St., Aston Clinton, Aylesbury, Bucks., HP22 5JE, UK.

HILL, Catharine Charlotte Benita, b. 7 Oct. 1951, London, UK. Flautist; Teacher. Educ: Oxford Music Schl., 1966-70; RMCM w. Trevor Wye, 1970-73; RNCM w. Trevor Wye (2 post grad. years), 1973-75; master classes w. Marcel Moyse & William Bennett (on summer courses); GRSM; ARMCM (tchrs.); ARNCM (perf.). Career: Tchr., Chetham's Schl. & RNCM, Manchester; freelance player in London; asst. tchr., Int. Summer Schl., Ramsgate; mbr., Guildford Phil. Orch.; mbr., Int. Musicians Seminar, 1978. Mbrships: Musicians' Union; ISM. recip., scholarship for further study at RNCM, 1973. Hobbies: Walking; Sewing; Travel; Theatre; Reading. Address: 27 Rivermead Ct., Ranelagh Gdns., London, SW6, UK.

HILL, Cecil, b. 30 Aug. 1936, Rochdale, UK. University Professor (organ, harpsichord). Educ: RMCM; PhD, Univ. of St. Andrews; BMus, (Durham); FRCO; ARMCM. m. Doreen Edith Cropper, 2 s., 1 d. Career: Music Master, West End Boys CS Schl., Aston-under-Lyne, Lancs., 1959-61; Demonstrator, Dept. of Music, Univ. of St. Andrews, 1961-64; Lectr., ibid., 1954-70; Asst. Prof., Univ. of Calif., Santa Barbara, 1970-71; Fndn. Sr. Lectr. & Hd. of Dept. of Music, Univ. of New England, Armidale, NSW, Aust., 1971-76; Assoc. Prof. & Hd., ibid., 1977-. Publs: Sir William Leighton, The Tears or Lamentations of a Sorrowful Soul 1614; Early English Ch. Music, Vol. XI, 1970; Ferdinand Ries: A Thematic Catalogue. Contbr. to var. profl. jrnls. Mbrships: RCO; Royal Musical Assn.; Int. Musicol. Soc.; Musicol. Soc. of Aust. Address: Dept. of Music, Univ. of New England, Armidale, NSW 2351, Australia. 28.

HILL, Charles Bud, b. 12 July 1929, London, Ont., Can. Music Educator; Composer; Arranger; Trombonist. Educ: BA, Vic. Coll., Toronto, 1950; MEd, Univ. of Toronto, 1977; Assoc. of the Royal Conserv., Toronto, 1961; MMus, Univ. of Toronto, 1972. m. Eleanor M Hill. Career: Profl. trombonist, 1947-67 (toured UK, France, Belgium, Germany, 1952-54; trombonist w. Vic Lewis, Freddie Randall, Roy Fox & Teddy Foster); High Schl. music tchr., 1954-, at N Bay, Oakville, Toronto & Richmond Hill. Comps: Ode to Canada, for chorus & orch., 1967; Rondo Semplice, for Clarinet & piano, 1968; Idyll, for trombone & piano, 1968; Northern Dance, for trombone & piano, 1969; Labourers' Song, for trombone & piano, 1969; num. arrs. Mbrships: AFM; Can. Music Educators Assn.; Ont. Music Educators Assn. Hobby: Electronic Music. Address: 8 Brooke Ave., Toronto, Ont. M5N 2J6, Can.

HILL, Eric James, b. 10 Apr. 1942, London, UK. Solo Guitarist (Classical). Educ: BSc, Leeds Univ.; Advanced guitar tuition w. Julian Bream; postgrad. study of Jazz Guitar, York Univ. m. Rhona Hill, 1 s., 1 d. Debut: Wigmore Hall, 1970. Career: Frequent TV apps., BBC, Granada, Yorks. & ORTS; Frequent radio perfs., Recitals at Wigmore Hall & sev. fests. inclng. harrogate, Aldeburgh, York & Newcastle. Comps: Solo improvisations, Music Till Mignight, BBC Radio. Recordings: The Classical Guitar; The Virtuoso Guitar. Contbr. to Guitar Mag. Mbrships: Musicians Union; ISM. Hons: Prize, Int. Guitar Competition, ORTF, Paris, 1970. Hobbies: Improvision Jazz; Reading; Cars. Mgmt: Basil Douglas Ltd. Address: 31 Huntington Rd., Yorks, UK.

HILL, Jenny, b. 20 June 1944, London, UK. Lyric Soprano. m. Dimitrios Raftopoulos, 2 d. Educ: nat. Schl. of Opera; London Opera Centre. Career: Sadlers Wells Opera Co., 1964, Hansel & Gretel, Kristina in Makropoulos Case British Prem. etc. English Opera Group; Lucia in The Rape of Lucretia, London & Russia, Titania in Midsummer Night's Dream, London & Canada Expo 67. Pretty Polly in Punch & Jody, World Prem. Aldeburgh & Edinburgh Festivals, 1968. Repertory Operas perfd; Traviata, Sonnambula, Lucia, Rigoletto, Marriage of Figaro, Magic Flute. In the concert field num. appearances incl: Down by the Greenwood Side, World Pre. Brighton Festival, 1969. A Mother Goose Primer, w. Pierrot Players; Petrassi's Magnigficat w. Giulina both British orems. at the RFH, 1972, City of London Fest. opening-concert B Minor Mass with Giulini at St. Pauls, London. Opening concert English Bach Fest., Blenheim Palace. Perfs. on Radio-TV incl: Sappho, The Findings, The Stag King, Down by the Greenwood Side. Also num. song recitals of classical & Avandgarde music. Recordings: Rape of Lucretia, St. John Passion, Schumann's "Faust" (Decca). Mbrships: ISM; Assn. for Tchrs. of Singing. Hons: Leverhulme Schlrship., 1960-63; Calouste Gulbenkian Fndn. Mus. Fellowship, 1969. Address: 5 Oaklands Grove, London W12, 9 Petalodos St., Ekali, Athens, Greece.

HILL, John Walter, b. 7 Dec. 1942, Chicago, Ill., USA. Professor of Music History. Educ: AB, Univ. of Chgo., 1963; MA, 1966, PhD, 1972, Harvard Univ. m. Ann B Hill, 2 s. Career: Assoc. Prof. of Music, Univ. of Ill. Contbr. to var. profl. jrnls.; Grove's Dictionary. Mbrships: Am. Musicol. Soc., Coun. Mbr., 1970-77, Chmn., Mid-Atlantic Chapter, 1972-73; Società Italiana di Musicologia. Hons: Fulbright Grant, 1968-69; Am. Philos. Soc. Grant, 1974; Am. Coun. of Learned Socs. Fellowship, 1976-77. Address: 407 W Pennsylvania Ave., Urbana, IL 61801, USA.

HILL, Malcolm John, b. 2 April 1944, London, UK. Concert Organist; Professor of Music; Composer; Conductor; Choirmaster. Educ: RAM, 1961-69; PhD, MMus, RCM; BMus (Dunelm); ARAM; Archbishop's Dip. in Ch. Music; FRCO (CHM); RAM Recital Dip. m. Katharine Tylko. Career: Concert Organist, specializing in improvisation; Prof. of Music, RAM; Composer; Cond. of Triptych Singers; Organist, Choirmaster, Churchwarden, Holy Trinity Ch., Kensington Gore, London;

Rschr. into works of Karol Szymanowski; Examiner, Assoc. Bd., Royal Schls. of Music. Mbr., Am. Musicol. Soc. Hons: Finalist, Int. Organ Improvisation Fests., Nürnberg, Haarlem; 12 prizes & exhibitions at RAM. Hobbies: Books; History. Mgmt: Hylko Co. Ltd., 8 Woodstone Ave., Stoneleigh, Epsom, Surrey. Address: 34a Wellington Rd., Bush Hill Pk., Enfield, Middx. EN1 2PF, UK.

HILL, Margaret Shirley (Sister M Mildred OP), b. 22 July 1930, Sydney, NSW, Aust. Music Teacher. Educ. incl: Dip. of Tchng., Dominician Trng. Coll., Maitland; Sydney Conservatorium; LMus A & T Mus A, Aust. Music Exams. Bd.; LTCL (CMT class music tchng.); Liszt Acad., Hungary, 1973. Career: Tchr., piano, violin, cello, singing, comp., elective & cultural classes, orch., choir, NSW & Vic.; Lectr. in Music, Qld., NSW, SA & ACT. Comps. incl: Mass of St. Dominic; Palm Sunday Mass; Prayers of the Ark. Author: Listen, books 1, 2, 3, 4 (for second. schls.), 1968. Mbrships: incl: Pres., Cath. Music Tchrs. Assn. of NSW; Sr. Vice-Chmn., NSW Chapt., also on Nat. Coun., 1976, Aust. Soc. for Music Educ; Music Exams. Advsry. Bd. of NSW; Coun., Musical Assn. of NSW. Hobbies incl: Carpentry; Upholstery; Embroidery. Address: Dominican Convent, Moss Vale, NSW, Aust.

HILL, Martyn Geoffrey, b. 14 Sept. 1944, Rochester, Kent, UK. Singer (Tenor). Educ: Kings Coll., Cambridge Univ., ARCM; Studied w. Audrey Langford. m. Marleen Marie J B De Maesschalck. Career: Concert, Opera & Recital apps. throughout the world; Apps. at most major Brit. Fests.; BBC radio & TV. Recordings: 30 inclng. Charpentier's Louise; Shostakovich's Katerina Ismailova; Handel (Acis & Galatea); num. recital records. Mgmt: Ibbs & Tillett, London. Address: 5 Durham Ave., Bromley, Kent, UK.

HILL, Robert Leslie, b. 21 Nov. 1945, Enfield, England, UK. Clarinettist. Educ: Jr. Exhibnr., RAM. m. Patricia Margaret Gregory, 1 s. Career: Freelance Clarinettist; Co-Prin., Clarinet, RPO, 1970-72; Prin. Clarinet, LPO, 1972-. Hons: George VI Scholarship to RAM, 1963; N London Orchl. Prize, 1964; Geoffrey Hawkes Clarinet Prize, RAM, 1966; John Solomon Wind Prize, RAM, 1966; ARCM, 1964; ARAM, 1973. Hobby: Lepidoptery. Address: 35 Oakwood Pk. Rd., Southgate, London N14, UK.

HILL, (Stephen) Jackson, b. 23 May 1941, Birmingham, Ala., USA. Composer; Conductor; Violinist; University Professor. Educ: BA Univ. of NC at Chapel Hill, 1963; MA, ibid., 1966; PhD, 1970; studied w. Iain Hamilton, 1964-66. m. Martha Gibbs Hill, 1 s. Career: Composer since age 13; num. works performed by age 18; works performed throughout eastern US & Western Europe, inclng. orchl. performances in 7 cities; Fac. Mbr., Bucknell Univ., Lewisburg, Pa., 1968-; Guest Composer, Duke Univ., 1968, Univ. of NC, 1973; Cond., Bucknell Symph., 1969-; Guest Cond., Susquehanna Valley Symph., 1969; num. recitals as violinist, violist, pianist & organist. Compositions: 60 works available, inclng. Variations for Orch., 1964, Paganini Set (orchl.), 1973; Synchrony for 6 or 7 players, 1967; 4 Studies for violin & piano, 1964, 3 Fantasie for Piano, 1966; Dark Litany (organ & electronic tape), 1973, Death Cycle for Soprano & Str. quartet, 1964, Agnus Dei, 1971; Missa Brevis, 1974, Parados I (ballet, tape), 1968, Epirrhematic Zyzygy for 114 Fizzing Alka-Seltzer Tablets, 1965. Publs: The Collection of Musical Instruments, 1975. Contbr. to: NOTES. Mbrships: incl: Am. Soc. of Univ. Composers; Am. Music Ctr.; Am. Musicol. Soc.; ASCAP. Recip. of num. composition prizes & var. acad. hons. Hobbies: Book Collecting; Shortwave Radio; Boating. Mgmt. (UK): R Morris Young, 72 Clark Rd., Wolverhampton WV3 9PA, UK. Address: 336 N 3rd St., Lewisburg, PA 17837, USA.

HILL, Terry S, b. 13 Apr. 1946, Provo, Utah, USA. String Educator; Violist; Conductor; Adjudicator; Clinician. Educ: BMus, MA, Brigham Young Univ. Debut: as soloist, Mormon Youth Symph., 1974. Career: Prin. Viola, Mormon Youth Symph., BYU Phil., Idylwild-Isomata Orch., Utah All-State Orch. Utah Valley Youth Symph.; Asst. Cond., Mormon Youth Symph., Salt Lake Chmbr. Orch.; Asst. Audio Dir., sev. TV specials for Pub. Broadcasting Serv.; Cond. Utah Valley Youth Symph.; Provo HS Orch.; Guest Clinician, sev. summer progs.; Orch. VP, Utah Music Educ. Assn. Publs: A Comprehensive Analysis of Selected Orch. Music Lists, 1976. Contbr. to Utah Music Educators Mag.; Critic, Local newspaper. Mbrships: Pi Kappa Lambda; Pres., Bd. Mbr., Utah Valley & Utah Valley Youth Symphs. Recip. Outstanding music educ. major award, BYU, 1969. Hobbies: Photography; Hi-fi; Tennis; Travel. Address: 1495 N 300 W, Provo, UT 84601, USA.

HILLEN, Kees, b. 25 Jan. 1946, Amsterdam, Holland. Musicologist; Head of Radio Music. Educ: Degree, Musicol., Univ. of Utrecht. m. Bartje Nauta, 1 d., 1 s. Career: Music Dept., Radio VARA, Hilversum, 1973-; Hd. of Music, ibid.,

1976-. Contbr. to var. mags. Hobbies: Gypsy music; Sauna; Sports. Address: Valeriusstraat 115 hs, Amsterdam, The Netherlands.

HILLER, Lejaren (Arthur), b. 23 Feb. 1924, NYC, USA. Composer. Educ: BA, 1944, MA, 1946, PhD, 1947, Princeton Univ., MMus, Univ. of Ill., 1958. m. Elizabeth Halsey, 1 s., 1 d. Career: Prof. of Music & Dir. of Expmntl. Music Studio, Univ. of Ill., 1958-68; Fulbright Lectr., Music to Poland, 1973-74; currently Frederick B Slee Prof. of Comp. & Co-Dir. of Ctr. of the Creative & Performing Arts, SUNY, Buffalo. Comps. publd. & recorded incl: An Avalanche..., 1971; Quartet No. 5 for Strings, 1973; Sonata No. 3 for Violin & Piano, 1975; Quartet No. 6 for Strings, 1975; Malta for Tuba & Tape, 1978; Appalachian Ballads for voice & guitar, 1977; Jesse James for vocal quartet & piano, 1977. Publs: Experimental Music (w. Leonard Isaacson), 1959; Informationstheorie und Computermusik, 1964. Contbr. to musical & sci. jrnls. Mbrshipos: ASCAP; Am. Soc. of Univ. Comps.; Am. Music Ctr. Hobbies: Woodwork; Photography; Travel. Address: Dept. of Music, SUNY, Buffalo, NY 14214, USA. 2, 6, 16, 30.

HILLER, Roger Lewis, b. 26 Feb. 1933, NYC, USA. Clarinettist. Educ: summers, Tanglewood & Chautauqua Music Schls.; BSc Mus, Juilliard Schl. of Music, 1954; studied w. Daniel Bonade & Robert McGinnis. m. Margaret E Goranson, 1 s., 1 d. Career: US Military Acad. W Pt., 1954-56; Prin. Clarinet, Houston Symph. Orch., 1956-59, Metrop. Opera Orch., 1959-, Chautauqua Symph. Orch., summers, 1960-; Tchr., pvtely., at NY Univ., at Chautauqua Music Schl.; Chmbr. musician; has made TV broadcasts. Has recorded w. concert orchs. Hobbies: Language study; Tennis. Address: 73-24 194th St., Flushing, NY 11366, USA.

HILLIARD, Thomas Lee, b. 20 Jan. 1930, Detroit, Mich., USA. Musician (Saxophone, Woodwinds); Composer; Director. Educ: BA Music Educ., Northeastern Ill. State Univ.; Grad. studies in comp., DePaul Univ. m. Darleen Cowles, 1 s., 1 d. Career: Player w. Bands of Tex Baneke, Buddy Morrow, Billy May, etc.; broadcasts for major networks; Dir., Metropolitan Jazz Octet & Jazz Ensembles, DePaul Univ. Comps. incl: Stonehenge; Ballad of Emmett Hardy; Grand Junction's Functions; Jivaro; Service I; Service II; Air for Squared Circle; City of Angels; Levi Lullaby; Kettlehead; Show Me A Rose. Recordings: The Legend of Bix; Riptide. Mbr., profl. assns. Hons: Comp./Fellowship Grant, Nat. Endowment for the Arts, 1975. Hobbies: Poetry; Theatre; Film; Art. Address: 1222 W Altgeld, Chicago, IL 60614, USA. 4.

HILLIER, Helen, b. 17 Feb. 1937, London, UK. Dramatic Soprano; Teacher of Singing. Educ: Studied w. Harold Phillips, Maestro Rodolpho Mele & Mary Cornish. m. Kenneth Putt, 1 s., 1d. Debut: Wigmore Hall, London. Career: Apps. incl: Royal Albert Hall; St. Margaret's Westminster & other London Concert Halls; Prin. Soprano, Sadlers Wells Opera Co., 10 yrs., Apps. on BBC TV & Radio Shows. Mbr. ISM; Equity. Hobbies: Theatre; Concerts; Paintings; Archaeol. Address: 440 Streatham High Rd., London SW16 3PX, UK.

HILLIER, Marion Lucy, b. 20 Apr. 1932, London, UK. Violinist; Teacher; Performer. Educ: RAM; GRSM; ARCM; LRAM. m. Noel Terence Broome, 2 d., 1 s. Career: Halle Orch.; BBC Revue; Sub-leader, Northern Sinfonia Chmbr. Orch.; Ldr., Profl. string quartet for many yrs.; Regular sonata recitals w. Alison Gordon (piano); Also solo recitals & tchng. Mbrships: ISM; European String Tchrs. Assn. Hobbies: Hill Walking; Badminton; Sewing. Address: 15 Tynedale Terrace, Benton, Newcastle-on-Tyne, NER 8AY, UK.

HILLMER, Leann, b. 10 Nov. 1942, Lincoln Co., Kansas, USA. Vocal Coach; Chorusmaster. Educ: BMus, MMus, Univ. of Kansas; Mannes Schl. of Music; studies w. Roy H Johnson, John Goldmark, Evelyn Swarthout, Paul Berl, Robert Baustian, Luigi Ricci & Jani Strasser. Career: Opera Theatre of N Va.; Wash. Opera; Omaha Opera; Kansas City Lyric Theatre; Santa Fe Opera; NYC Opera (Asst. Chorusmaster); Metropolitan Opera Studio (Assoc. Music Dir.); Minnesota Opera Studio (Music Dir.); Minnesota Opera Co. (Asst. Music Dir.); Dir., Opera Workshop, Univ. of Kansas; Staff Accomp., Am. Univ.; Coach, Lieder Program, Tanglewood Fest. Mbr., Mu Phi Epsilon. Hons: Winston Churchill Travelling Fellowship, ESU, 1974. Hobbies: Tennis; Sailing; Cooking. Address: 235 W 75th St., NY, NY 10023, USA.

HILLMON, Betty Jean, b. 23 Mar. 1945, Kinder, La., USA. Music Educator; Cellist; Folk Song Consultant. Educ: BA, San Jose State Univ. MA, Fresno State Univ.; Kodaly Teaching Cert., Liszt Acad. of Music Kodaly Musical Trng. Inst.; pvte. study of Cello. Career: Documentary Film, Conn. Coun. of the Arts; Cello recitals, Boston, Calif. & Miscolc, Hungary; Folk

song rsch., Afro-Am. songs; Mbr., Fresno Symph. Orch.; Mbr., Festive Arts Str. Quartet; Soloist, San Jose State Univ. Orch., 1968. Mbrships: Mu Phi Epsilon; Alpha Kappa Alpha; Music Educators Nat. Assn.; Am. Str. Tchrs. Assn. Hons: incl: Congress of Strings, 1968; Nat. Endowment for the Arts Fellowship. Hobbies: Tennis; Plays; Travel. Address: 1082 Commonwealth Ave. 502, Boston, MA 02215, USA.

HILLS, Charles Walter, b. 19 Oct. 1922, Northville, Mich., USA. Music Educator; Instrumental Teacher (Clarinet & Saxophone); Band Director. Educ: BMus Ed, MMus Ed, Univ. of Mich. m. Virginia C Tomion, 2 s. Career: Tchr., Instrumental Music, Pub. Schls., Fowlerville, Mich., 15 yrs., & Ann Arbor, Mich., 11 yrs.; Adjudicator & Clinician, Band & Orch., Solo & Ensemble Fests., 20 yrs.; Concert Band Dir., Youth Music Prof., Mich. State Univ., 6 summers; Dir., Bands & Ensembles, other summer music camps, etc.; Assoc. Dir., Youth for Understanding Wind Ensemble, Tour of Chile, 1972. Mbr., var. profl. assns. Hons: Band Tchr. of Yr., State of Mich., 1971-72; Cond., Honors Band, Mich. Youth Arts Fest., 1971. Hobbies: Golf; Sailing; Tennis. Address: 2416 Essex Rd., Ann Arbor, MI, USA.

HILTON, Janet Lesley, b. 1 Jan. 1945, Liverpool, UK. Clarinettist. Educ: Assoc., Royal Manchester Coll. of Music; Vienna Conserv. m. David Vivian Richardson, 1 s. Career: frequent broadcasts (concerto, chmbr. & recital), BBC, 1965-; recitals at fests. inclng. Bath, Cheltenham, Harrogate & Wexford & for music clubs; Staff, Royal Scottish Acad. of Music, 1973-; Prin. Clarinet, Scottish Chmbr. Orch., 1973-; Mbr., New Music Grp. of Scotland; 1st perfs. of John McCabe clarinet concerto & concerto no. 2 (Edward Cowie). Mbrships: ISM; Musicians Union. Hons. incl: Nat. Fedn. of Music Socs. Award for Young Artists, 1965; Hiles Gold Medal, Royal Manchester Coll. of Music. Hobbies: Cooking; Literature. Mgmt: Ingpen & Williams Ltd., 14 Kensington Ct., London W8. Address: Braehead, Blanefield, Glasgow G63 9AP, UK.

HILTON, Lewis Booth, b. 21 Nov. 1920, Bulyea, Sask., Canad. Professor of Music. Educ: BA, Univ. of Northern Iowa, USA, 1942; MA, Columbia Univ., NY, 1946; EdD, ibid., 1951. m. Jean Hilton Comps: Polarities for Brass Quintet. Author of the Woodwinds; Learning to Teach through Playing, 1971; Allegro & Minuet for 2 Flutes, by Beethoven, 1976; Allegro & Minuet for 2 Clarinets by Beethoven, 1976; From Bass to Tenor Cleft for the Bassoon, 1978. Contbr. to: Music Educators Jrnl.; Mo. Jrnl. of Rsch. in Music Educ. (Ed.); Bulletin for Coun. of Rsch. in Music Educ.; Tchrs. Coll. Record; Schl. & Soc. Schl. Activities; Instrumentalist. Mbrships: Int. Soc. for Music Educ.; Phi Mu Alpha Sinfonia; Bd. mbr., Young Audiences; Bd. mbr., Community Music Schl., St. Louis; MENC; Hon. mbr., Music Masters, 1962. Hobby: Musical Instruments of Pre-Cortesian Mexico. Address: 1335 Purdue, University City, MO 63130, USA. 8.

HILTON, Ruth B, b. 9 Oct. 1926, Detroit, Mich., USA. Music Librarian. Educ: BA, Cornell Univ., 1947; MLS, Syracuse Univ., 1967. Career: Asst. Music Libn., Cornell Univ., 1958-68; Music Libn., NY Univ., 1968-. Publs: An index to early music in selected anthologies, 1978. Contbr. to: Notes; Grove's Dict., 6th Ed.; RILM abstracts; var. informal ed. & cons. work, etc. Mbrships: Treas. & Bd. Mbr., Music Libn. Assn., 1969-75; Coun., 1970-77, Sec./Treas. & Bd. Mbr., 1975-77, Nat. Lib. Assns.; Int. Assn. of Music Libs.; Am. Musicol. Soc.; Am. Music Center; Sonneck Soc. Address: Music Lib., NY Univ., 70 Washington Square S, NY, NY 10012, USA.

HILTY, Everett Jay, b. 2 Apr. 1910, NY, NY, USA. Professor of Organ & Church Music. Educ: Univ. of Miami, Fla., BMus, Univ. of Mich., 1934; MMus, Univ. of Colo., 1939; Union Theol. Sem. Schl. of Sacred Music, 1946-47, 1956-57. m. Rose Elizabeth Vann, 2 s. Career incls: Organist, var. Ch.'s 1928-42, Hotel Pancost, Miami Beach, 1934, Denver Symph., Colo., 1936-42, Radio, WGAM, WIOD, Miami, 1930-35; KLZ, KOA, Denver, 1935-39; Organist & Choirmaster, 1st Congregational Ch., Boulder, Colo., 1943-68; Min. of Music Emeritus, ibid., 1968-p; Official Carilloneur, Winter Olympics, Squaw Valley, Calif., 1960; Dean, Denver Coll. of Music, 1935-37; Fac. Mbr., Univ. of Colo., 1940-; Prof., Hd. Div. of Organ & Ch. Music, ibid., 1951-; Prof. Emeritus, ibid., 1978-; Vis. Lectr., Union Theol. Sem., NYC, 1956-57. Compositions: num. Choral & Organ. Recordings: Maas-Rowe Symphonic Carillon, Inc.; Principles of Organ Playing. Publs: Principles of Organ Playing, 1971; How to Play the Symphonic Carillon, 1974. Choral Music for Worship, 1974. Contbr. to num. profl. jrnls. Mbrships: AGO; Regional Chmn., ibid., 1958-73; State Chmn., ibid., 1978-; Music Tchrs. Nat. Assn.; AAUP; Pi Kappa Lambda; Phi Mu Alpha; Alpha Chi Rho; Rotary. Recip. num. hons. Hobbies: Gardening; Bowling. Address: 2241 4th St., Boulder, CO 80302, USA. 9, 28.

HINDAR, Johannes, b. 30 April 1917, Sel, Norway. Violist. Educ: studied w. Hugo Kram, Istvan Opolyi. m. Solveig Hindar, 2 c. Career: Hindar Str. Quartet; Concerts in Scandinavia, Hungary, Czechoslovakia, Austria, Belgium; var. Radio & TV Apps. in Europe. Recordings: Str. Quartets, Grieg, G Minor, F Major, Egge, No. 1, Nystedt, No. 4, Svendsen, A Minor; Svendsen Str. Quintet, Str. Octet; Sinding, Piano Quintet; Monrad Johansen, Flute Quintet; Mozart, Oboe Quartet, F Major, Flute Quartet, D Major. Recip. Spelmannsprisen, 1973. Hobbies: Fly-Fishing; Cross-Country Skiing. Address: 76 Elgefaret, 1347 Hosle, Norway.

HINDEN, Jonathan, b. 12 Jan. 1938, Tel Aviv, Israel. Conductor; Pianist; Harpsichord Player. Educ: BA, Trinity Coll., Cambridge; ARCM (piano perf.); LRAm (piano tchr.). m. Jacqueline Froom, 1 d. Career: Music Staff, Glyndebourne (now prin. coach), 1966-; Kent Opera (now chorus master, Hd. of music staff & prin. keyboard player), 1969-. Recordings: (harpsichord) Cavalli's L'Ormindo & La Calisto, Monteverdi's Ritorno d'Ulisse & Madrigals; (piano) Frank Bridge songs. Mbr., ISM. Hobbies: Yoga; Bridge. Address: 5 Harrington Rd., Brighton, E Sussex BN1 6RE, UK.

HINDERMANN, Walter F(elix), b. 8 Apr. 1931, Zürich, Switz. Director of Church Music; Musicologist. Educ: BA, Zürich Cantonal Schl.; Conserv. of Music, Zürich; Schola Cantorum Basiliensis; studied cond. & comp. abroad. m. Feodora Schaub, 2 d. Debut: 7th Int. Bach Fest., 1962. Career: Dir. of Ch. Music, Dübendorf-Zürich & Winterthur; Theorie-tchr., Conserv. of Schaffhausen; Fndr., Dir. & Harpsichordist, Zürich Bach Circle; Comps. incl: Cantata on Psalm 5; minor pieces of ch. music. Recordings: Has recorded & publd. sev. important reconstructions of works of Bach. Publs. incl: Wiedergewonnene Schwesterwerke der Brandenburgischen Konzerte J S Bach, 1970; Die Nachösterlichen Kantaten des Bachschen Choral-kantaten jahrgangs, 1975; Die Oratorien J S Bach, 1980. Contbr. to profl. jrnls. Mbr., Schweiz. Musikpädag, Verband; Schweiz. Tonkünstlerverein. Recip., var. musical prizes. Hobbies incl: Reading; Sports. Address: La Comacina, Dino over Lugano, Ticino, Switz.

HINDLE, Alan James, b. 24 Nov. 1937, Preston, Lancs., UK. Music Inspector. Educ: RMCM; GRSM; ARMCM; Manchester Univ.; ARCO. m. Betty. Career: Music Tchr., Nottingham Schls.; Principal, S Notts. Music Schl.; former Asst. Music Adviser; LEA Music Instpector, Notts. Mbrships: NAIEA; MANA. Hobby: Photography. Address: 113 Nottingham Rd., Nuthall, Nottingham, Notts., UK.

HIND O'MALLEY, Pamela, b. 27 Feb. 1923, London, UK. Cellist; Pianist. Educ: ARCM (perf.); studied 'cello w. Ivor James & Pablo Casals, piano w. Lillian Gaskell & Kathleen Long, & composition w. Herbert Howells. m. Raymond O'Malley, 2 s., 1 d. Debut: 'Cello Recital, Wigmore Hall, 1963. Career: Cello Soloist & Ensemble Player, London & elsewhere, 1945-67; began giving Solo Recitals playing both piano & 'cello, 1967-, apps. incl. Wigmore Hall, 1970; Tchr. of 'cello & piano, Cambridge; Pt.-time 'Cello Tchr., Kings Coll. Schl.; Pt.-time Ensemble Coach, Cambridge Univ. Music Soc. Contbr. to RCM Mag. Mbrships: Committees for building a hall in Cambridge; Int. 'Cello Ctr.; London Violoncello Club; Cambridge Univ. Music Soc. Hobbies: Walking; Reading; Gardening. Address: 8 Hills Ave., Cambridge, CB1 4XA, UK. 3, 27.

HINDSLEY, Mark Hubert, b. 18 Oct. 1905, Union City, Ind., USA. Conductor; Educator. Educ: AB, AM, DMus, Ind. Univ.; Met. Schl. of Music, Indpls., Ind.; Sherwood Schl. of Music, Chgo., Ill.; Nat. Music Camp, Interlochen, Mich.; Univ. Ill.; Pvte. studies. m. Helena Alberts, 2 s., 1 d. Career incls: Asst. Dir. of Band, Assoc. to Assoc. Prof. of Music, 1934-48, Dir. of Bands, Prof. of Music, 1948-70, Univ. of Ill.; Music Off., USAF Trng. Command, Cond., Biarritz Am. Univ., France; Guest cond., Tchr., adjudicator in USA & Can. Num. recordings. Publs. incl: Mark Hindsley Band Method, 1940. Contbr. to profl. jrnls. & books. Mbrships. incl: Pes., Am. Bandmasters Assn., 1957-58; Pres., 1947, Coll. Band Dirs. Nat. Assn.; MENC. Recip. num. awards. Hobbies: Golf; Lawnwork; Sports Watching; Photography. Address: 1 Montclair Rd., Urbana, IL 61801, USA.3, 4, 8, 28, 29.

HINES, Jerome, b. 8 Nov. 1921, Hollywood, Calif., USA. Opera & Concert Singer. Educ: BA, Chemistry & Maths. m. Lucia Evangelista, 4 s. Debut: Civic Light Opera Co., LA, Calif. Career: Metropolitan Opera, La Scala, Bayreuth, Bolshoi, Kirov, Teatro Colon, etc.; Sev. TV apps. Comps: I Am The Way (Opera on Jesus Christ). Var. Recordings. Contbr. to: Musical Am.; Opera Can.; Maths. Mag. Mbrships: 1st VP, AGMA. Hons: Caruso Award, 1946; Bliss Award, 1950. Hobbies: Scuba Diving; Composing; Math Rsch. Address: 370 N Wyoming Ave., S Orange, NJ, USA.

HINES, Robert S, b. 30 Sept. 1926, Kingston, NY, USA. Music Educator; Conductor; Writer; Arranger; Editor. Educ: BS, Juilliard Schl., 1952; MMus, Univ. of Mich., 1956. Comps: over 100 choral eds. & arrs. Publs: The Composer's Point of View: Essays on 20th Century Choral Music, 1963; The Orchestral Composer's Point of View, 1970; Singer's Manual of Latrin Diction & Phonetics, 1975; Aural Training (w. Allen R Trubitt), 1976. Contbr. to: Choral Jrnl. Mbrships. incl: Am. Choral Dirs. Assn. HI State Pres., 1974-; MENC; Coll. Music Soc. Hobby: Travel. Address: 555 Univ. Ave., 3500 Honolulu, HI 96826, USA. 9.

HINGLEY, Herbert Barrie, b. 4 Mar. 1938, Selby, UK. Director of Music. Educ: BMus (London); LRAM; ARCM. m. Winifred Dorothy, 2 s. Career: Royal Air Force, 1956-; Dir. of Music, Band of RAF Germany, Midland Band RAF; Dir. of Music, RAF Schl. of Music, 1973-. Comps: The Foss Way; Glorious Service; Hall Porta Moenia Vira; The Newcomers. Recordings: Flying High; Flying Festival; In Step With The Shows; Passing Out Parade. Hons: MBE; The Cassel Bronze Medal, 1958. Address: 12 Birch Crescent, Uxbridge, Middx., UK.

HINKLE, Ellen Clair Fuqua, b. Deland, Fla., USA. Musician & Teacher (Flute). Educ: BMusEd, Fla. State Univ.; study w. Patricia Stenberg & Albert Tipton; grad. study at N Tex. Univ.; study w. George Morey. m. Winson C Hinkle. Career: Prin. Flautist, Wichita Falls Symph. Orch., Tex.; 2nd Flautist, Greeley Phil. Orch., Colo.; Instructor of Flute, Midwestern Univ., Wichita Falls, Tex., 1971-73; Grad. Asst. in Flute, N Tex. State Univ., 1972-73. Flute Instr. Rollins Coll., Schl. of Creative Arts., Flautist, Bach. Fest. Orch., Winter Pk., Fla. Mbrships: Nat. Assn. of Coll. Wind & Percussion Tchrs.; Tau Beta Sigma. Hobbies: Knitting; Needlepoint. Address: 1444 Chilean Ln., Winter Pk., FL 32789, USA.

HINLOPEN, Francina, b. 9 Aug. 1908, Amsterdam, Netherlands. Harpist; Composer; Poet. Educ: State Examination, The Hague; Harp study w. Rosa Spier; Comp. & Theory w. Prof. Anthon van der Horst, C van Erven Dorens. Debut: 1938. Career: 1st Solo Harpist, var. provincial orchs., Netherlands; introduced Harp as prin. instrument in chs.; TV and radio apps. w. own comps.; Organist, Clemens Ch., Hilversum. Comps. incl: Missa Sacra for solo voice & harp; 3 works for choir & harp; harp solos; Sonatine for organ; Fantasy for harp & flute; Praeludium & Fuga for 4 trombones, 4 horns & harp; Fantasy for string orch.; Missa Antiphonalis. Publs: A Bundle of Poems, 1967; The History of the Harp & Its Significance in the Worship of Israel, 1971. Hons: Town of Hilversum Prize; Silver Medal of Arts, Scis. & Letters, Paris, 1975. Mbr., profl. orgs. Hobbies: Rowing; Sailing; Golf. Address: 273 Diependaalselaan, Hilversum, 1215 KE, Netherlands.

HINREINER, Ernst, b. 1 Jan. 1920, Salzburg, Austria. Conductor of Choir & Orchestra; Chief Producer of Music; Professor of Music. Educ: studied piano, organ, French horn, cond., Univ. of Music & Dramatic Arts, Mozarteum, Salzburg; Final exams. in organ & cond., 1946, 1947. m. Friedolinde Gaschnig, 2 d. Career: Chief Prod. of music, Radio ORF Studio, Salzburg, 1946-; Fndr., Salzburger Rundfunk-und Mozarteumbhor, 1951; Fndr., Salzburger Mozartchor, 1966; Ldr. of concerts Gang durch den Advent, 1963; Concerts, Austria, Germany, Italy, Switz.; Prof. of Music, Mozarteum. Recordings: Musica sacra (Mozart, Haydn, etc.). Mbr., Schlaraffia Juvania. Hons: Mozart medal, 1956; title Prof., 1964; Ring der Stadt Salzburg, 1970; Goldene Ehrenzeichen für Verdienste um die Republik Österreich, 1979. Address: Anton Hochmuthstr. 4, 5020 Salzburg, Austria. 30.

HINTERHOFER, Grete, b. 18 July 1899, Wels, Upper Austria. Pianist. Educ: State Cert.; studied w. Emil von Sauer. Career: Recitals in Austria, Germany, Hungary, Holland; Soloist under Richard Strauss, Eugen Jochum, Franz Schalk; Prof. Acad. of Music, Vienna, 1927-; Sr. Prof., ibid., 1964-; Guest Prof., Univ. of Nagoya, Japan, 1966-67. Recip. DSC for Arts & Science, 1959. Hobby: Travel. Address: 64/14 Klosternenburgerstr., 1200 Vienna, Austria.

HINTON, Dallas Edward, b. 12 April 1946, Hammersmith, London, UK. Instrumentalist; Composer; Arranger; Teacher; Piano Technician. Educ: Cert., Berklee Schl. of Music, Boston, Mass., USA, 1967-; BEd (Secondary), 1979. m. Ardith J Hinton. Career: And Now, Noel Coward, World Premiere; Extensive Night Club Experience; Played w. Vancouver Symph.; Accomp., Ford & Hines, Bill Cosby, Harry Belafonte; Played 'Theatre in the Park' for sev. yrs.; Pvte. Music Tchr., 10 yrs.; Arr. & Comps. for var. local grps. & singes. Contbr. to: The Resonator. Mbrships: Musicians Union; W Coast Autosport Club. Hobbies: Car Rallies; Camping; Chess; Judo; Aikido; Breeding Bulldogs. Address: 2110 W 45th Ave., Vancouver, BC. V6M 2J1, Canada.

HINTON-BRAATEN, Kathleen, b. 15 Sept. 1941, Ventura, Calif., USA. Violinist; Writer. Educ: Oberlin Coll. Conserv. of Music, Ohio; Calif. State Univ., San Fran., Northridge, Fullerton; Univ. of Md./Coll. Park. m. Richard E Braaten, 1 s., 1 step-daughter. Career: Violinist, Nat. Symph. Orch., Wash., DC, 10 Yrs.; Former Asst. personnel mgr.; ibid; Cinn. Symph. Orch.; San Antonio Symph.; Co-Fndr., 20th Century Consort, Music in Maine String Quartet (Title III programs). Recordings: w. Nat. Symph. Orch. Contbr. to: NY Times; Christian Science Monitor; Wash. Post mag.; Accent Mag.; New Mexico mag., etc. Hobbies: Reading; Tennis; Travel. Address: 4813 S 28th St., Arlington, VA 22206, USA.

HIRSCH, Leonard, b. 19 Dec. 1902, Dublin, Ireland. Music Educator; Conductor. Educ: Royal Manchester Coll. of Music, w. Adolph Brodsky, m. Anne Richardson. Debut: Dublin. Career incl: Halle Orch., 192137; Ldr. & occasional cond., BBC Empire Orch., 1937-39; Toured Am. w. RAF Symph. Orch., during WWII; Ldr., Philharmonia Orch., 1941; Hirsch String Quartet re-established 1944; Assoc. w. Nat. Youth Orch., 1948-66; Cond., Hirsch Chmbr. Players, 1961-; 1st Musical Dir., BBC Trng. Orch., 1966-69; Chief Music Cons., Co. of Herts., 1964-; Prof., RCM. Recordings incl: Bartok Quartet No. 1; Bloch No. 2 (string quartet); Hugo Wolf Serenade. Contbr. to book, Sir Hamilton Harty, 1978. Hons: Fellow, Royal Manchester Coll. of Music; FRCM. Hobbies: Gardening; Travel. Address: Loughrigg, 51 Church Rd., Sneyd Park, Bristol BS9 1QT, UK.

HIRSH, Albert, b. 1 July 1915, Chgo., Ill., USA. Pianist; Professor of Piano. Educ: Studied pvtly. under Djane Lavoie-Herz. m. Mildred Rigby Wile, 3 c. Debut: Town Hall, NYC, 1934. Career: Concert Tours throughout USA, Canada, Latin Am., Europe, 1932-. as Soloist & in Chamber Music; Toured w. many of the world's leading artists; Prof., Univ. of Houston, 1950-. Recordings: Works for Violin & Piano w. Wolfgang Schneiderhan, for Deutsche Grammophon. Mbrships: Phi Mu Alpha; Patron, Phi Beta; AAUP; Tex. Assn. of Coll. Tchrs. Hobbies: Philately; Gardening; Mountain Climbing. Address: 5711 Jackwood St., Houston, TX 77096, USA.

HIRSHHORN, Philipp, b. 11 June 1946, Riga, USSR. Violinist. Educ: Conservs. of Riga & Leningrad. Debut: 1967. Career: Violinist w. major European Orchs. inclng: Berlin Phil., Berlin Radio Orch.; Vienna Symph.; London Symph.; Royal Phil.; concert tours of Israel, Holland, Scandinavia, France, Germany, Belgium, Spain, Portugal, Italy, Switzerland, UK, USA, S Africa & Japan. Recordings: Paganini Violin Concerto (DGG label). Recip: 1st Prize, Queen Elizabeth Competition, Brussels, 1967. Mgmt: Harrison-Parrott Ltd., 22 Hillgate St., London W8 7SR, UK.

HIRT, Franz Josef, b. 7 Feb. 1899, Lucerne, Switz. Concert Pianist; Professor. Educ: Dip., Conserv.; study of piano w. his mother, Egon Petri, Alfred Cortot & Felix von Weingartner. m. Zilla Elisabeth Kaser, 1 s., 1 d. Career: Concert tours throughout Europe & Africa; Tournées w. Maurice Ravel, Hans Pfitzner, Arthur Honegger & Paul Hindemith; Prof., Concert Classes, Berne Conserv. Recordings: Num. records for Electrola, His Masters Voice & Polydor. Publs: Meisterwerke des Klavierbaus, 1955; Stringed Keyboard Instruments, 1968. Mbrships. incl: Swiss Musicians Union. Hons. incl: Off., Légion d'Honneur, 1957; Music Prize, City of Berne, 1970; Prize, BAT. Fndrn., 1972. Address: Alpeneggstrasse 14, 3001 Berne, Switz. 14, 19.

HIRTE, Klaus, b. 28 Dec. 1937, Berlin, Germany. Kammersänger. Educ: w. Prof. Hans Hager (voice) Stuttgart Acad. of Music, 5 yrs. m. Alice Knorr, 2 s., 1 d. Debut: Staatsoper Stuttgart, 1964. Career: Num. fest. apps. incl. Bayreuth & Salzburg; num. guest apps., Chgo., Portland (Ore.), State Opera Vienna, Hamburg, Frankfurt, Nuremberg, Basle, Versailles, Brighton, San Antonio Texas, Venice, Lisbon, Paris, etc.; Guest contract w. Munich State Opera; Character baritone, Württ. State Opera, 1964; num. radio apps. Recordings: Meistersinger; Schweigsame Frau; Hoffmans Erzählungen; Wiener Blut, etc. Hons. incl: Hon. Pin in Gold of Paratrooper Div.; Max Reinhardt Plaque, Salzburg Fest. Hobbies incl: Jazz Music. Address: Waldburgstrasse 156, 7000 Stuttgart 80, German Fed. Repub.

HIRTZEL, Robert Lewis, b. 25 Dec. 1913, Rainier, Ore., USA Musician (Violin, Viola, Cello); Music Educator. Educ: Pacific Coll., 1940-42; BA, Univ. of Ore., 1948; MMusEd., Univ. of Portland, 1953; Holder Standard Gen. Teaching Cert.; pvte. study w. Franck Eichenlaub, Wme. Davenport-Engberg, Alfred Keller. m. 1) Mildred Boyes (dec.) 2) Mary T Adams, 2 s., 2 d. Career: Violin Tchr. Pacific Coll. (now George Fox Coll.), 1940-42; String Tchr., Pub. Schls., Vancouver, Wash., 1942-; Vis. Fac. Mbr., Univ. of Ore., 1945-; Adjudicator, num. music festivals; Gives workshops on the Application of

Neurophysiology to Playing Skills. Contbr. to Wash. State String Tchrs. Bulletin. Mbrships: Am. String Tchrs. Assn. (Pres. Wash. Chapt., 1960-62); MENC; Music Tchrs. (Nat. Assn). Hobbies incl: Violin Bows; Chinese Art. Address: 123 W 37th St., Vancouver, WA 98660, USA. 4.

HISCOTT, James Michael, b. 4 Dec. 1948, St. Catharines, Ont., Can. Composer; Radio Producer; Pianist; Organist. Educ: BSc, Brock Univ., St. Catharines, 1970; MSc, Univ. of Toronto, 1971; BFA, York Univ., Toronto, 1976; pvte. studies w. Samuel Dolin, Toronto. Career: now radio music prod., CBC. Comps. incl: 4 Pieces for str. orch., 1972; Quintet for Woodwinds, 1973; Planes, for orch., 1973; 4 Terrains, for solo piano, 1974; Moss Growing on Ruins, for instrumental ensemble, 1974; Trio, for flute, cello & piano, 1975; Ceremony, for instrumental ensemble, 1975; Memories of the Forgotten Stream, for flute, oboe, guitar, cello & piano, 1975-76; Waterwheel, for guitar & piano, 1977; Midnight Strut, for alto saxophone, 1978; The Curtain's Graceful Fall, for accordion & 5 synthesizers, 1978. Mbrships: Can. League of Comps.; Can. Music Ctr.; AFM; Performing Rights Org. of Can.; Nat. Radio Producers. Hons: BMI Canada Ltd Centennial Scholarship, 1974-77; Creative Arts Award from Can. Fed. of Univ. Women, 1977. Hobbies: Travel; Photography; Hist.; Film. Address: 9715 77th Ave., Edmonton, Alta., T6E 1M2, Can.

HISLOP, Joseph Dewar, b. 5 Apr. 1884, Edinburgh, Scotland, UK. Operatic Tenor; Teacher. Educ: Royal Schl. of Opera, Stockholm. m. (1) Karin Askland, 1 s.; 2 d. (2) Nancy Passmore. Debut: in title role, Gounod's Faust, Royal Opera, Stockholm. Career: prin. operatic tenor roles, French & Italian repertoire, ldng. opera houses in Europe, the Ams.; tour of Aust., NZ & S Africa; Prin. Tchr. of Singing (Solo Class), Royal Acad. of Music, Stockholm, 1936Ñ48; Advsr. on Singing, Govent Gdn. & Sadlers Wells, 1948-52, GSM, 1952-64. Recordings: HMV. Hons: Litteris et Artibus Gold Medal, Sweden, 1922; Kt. of the Vasa, Sweden, 1928; Kt. of the Dannebrog, Denmark, 1927; FGSM, 1953. Hobby: Painting. Address: Berryside Farm, by Leven, Fife, Scotland, UK.

HITCHCOCK, H Wiley, b. 28 Sept. 1923, Detroit, Mich., USA. Musicologist; Professor. Educ: AB, Dartmouth Coll., 1944; MMus, 1947, PhD, 1954, Univ. of Mich. m. Janet Cox-Rearick, 1 s., 1 d. Career: Teaching positions: Univ. of Mich., 1947-61; Hunter Coll., CUNY, 1961-71 (Chmn. of Dept., 1962-67); Vis. Prof., NY Univ., 1963-68; Brooklyn Coll., CUNY, 1971-; Fndng. Dir., Inst. for Studies in Am. Music, ibid., 1971-. Publs: Music in the United States, 1969, 2nd ed. 1974; Ives, 1976; Ed., Prentice-Hall History of Music Series, 11 vols., 1964-; Ed., Giulio Caccini, Le Nuove Musiche, 1970, & Nuove Musiche & Nuova Maniera de Scriverle, 1979; Ed., An Ives Celebration, 1977. Contbr. to profl. jrnls. Mbrships. incl: Am. Musicol. Soc. (Bd. of Dirs.); Music Lib. Assn. (Pres.). Recip. var. Fellowships. Address: 1192 Park Ave., NY, NY 10028, USA. 2.

HITE, David Leroy, b. 25 Sept. 1923, New Straitsville, Ohio, USA. Clarinetist; Manufacturer of David Hite clarinet mouthpiece. Educ: BA, Ohio State Univ., 1953; MMus, ibid., 1970. m. Rosemary Ann Curtin Hite, (div.), 2 s. Career: w. Columbus Phil. Orch., 1941-42; 595th Army Air Force Band, 1942-46; Columbus Phil. Orch., 1946-49; Prof. Music, Conserv. Music, Capital Univ., Columbus, 1955-78. Comps. incl: Melodious & Progressive Studies for Clarinet, Books I & II. Recordings incl: David Hite Plays the Clarinet, Vols. I & II, 1969. Contbr. to Selmer Bandwagon Mag. Mbr. var. profl. orgs. Address: PO Box 09747, Columbus, OH 43209, USA.

HIXON, Donald L, b. 9 Aug. 1942, Columbus, Ohio, USA. Fine Arts Librarian. Educ: AB, Calif. State Univ., Long Beach, 1965; MS, UCLA, 1967; MA, Calif. State Univ., Long Beach, 1967. Career: Ref. Libn., Univ. of Calif., Irvine, 1967-74; Fine Arts Libn., ibid., 1974-. Publs: Music in Early America, 1970; Women in Music: A Bibliography, 1975; Nineteenth-century American drama-a finding list, 1977. Mbrships: Int. Assn. of Music Libs.; Music Lib. Assn.; Am. Musicol. Soc.; Int. Musicol. Soc. Address: 9392 Mayrene Dr., Garden Grove, CA 92641, USA.

HJELMBORG, Bjørn, b. 25 Jan. 1911, Copenhagen, Denmark. Professor; Organist & Cantor. Educ: Dips. in Music Hist. & Theory, 1933, Organ, 1934, Sol-fa, 1939, Royal Danish Music Conserv.; MA (musicol.), Copenhagen Univ., 1944. m. Ingrid Hjelmborg, 3 s. Career: Ch. concerts, 1935-; Organist & Cantor, Hoite Ch., 1940-; Tchr., 1942-48; Prof. Music Hist. & Theory, 1949-; Coun. Mbr., 1949-75, Royal Danish Music Conserv.; num. radio perfs., 1946-60. Comps: Von Himmel Hoch (cantata); Maria's Uro (ch. play); chmbr. music; motets, songs & carols. Publs. incl: Musik-orientering,

1948, 4th revised ed. 1971; Om den venezianske arie indtil 1650, 1965; Aspects of the Aria in the Early Operas of Fr. Cavalli, 1962. Mbrships: Danish Soc. Musicol. (Bd., 1954-73); Accademia di Danimarca, Rome (Bd.). Address: Kastanievej 43, 2840 Holte, Denmark.

HLAVÁČ, Miroslav, Ing., b. 23 Oct. 1923, Protivín, S Bohemia. (Czech.). Composer. Educ: Civil Engrng. Coll., Prague; Municipal Schl. of Music, Pilsen; Studied comp. w. Borivoj Mikoda, Jaroslav Rídký & Klement Slavický. m. Kvetoslava Zsárková, 1 d. Debut: Pastorale for flute & piano on radio, 1945. Career: Almost all comps. performed on radio & TV and in concerts. Comps. incl: Inultus (opera); The Sorcerer's Apprentice (ballet); Atlantiana, Nocturne by the Fountain (electronic ballets); Symphony; Sinfonietta epitaffica; Partita; (concerto for violin & orch.; Musica Diafonica, for bass clarinet, piano, stereo tape). Mbr., Union of Czech. Comps. & Concert Artists. Publs: M Hlaváč's musical Dramatic Works, 1973. Hons. incl: Prize of Czech. Music Soc., 1976; Prize in great jubilee artistic contest for the anniversary of Czech., 1960; Czech. music fund prize, 1972. Hobby: Touring. Address: Zelenecská 26, 19400 Praha 9, Hloubetin, Czech.

HLAWICZKA, Karol, b. 14 Feb. 1894, Ustron, Cieszyn, Poland. Musicologist; Pianist; Organist; Educator. Educ: Studied Law at Univ.; Dip. of Music, Warsaw Conserv., 1932. m. Emily Rakjowska, 1 d. Debut: (as Pianist), Cieszyn, 1912. Career: Music Tchr., Tchrs. Sem., Pedagogical Coll., Silesian Univ. Comps: Piano Concerto in D minor; Polish Dances for Piano. Publs. incl: Chopin, Master of Rhythmic Shaping, 1960; Polonaises from the Collections of Anne Marie de Saxem I-III, 1967-71; Outline of the History of the Polonaise until the Beginning of the 19th Century, 1968. Mbrships: Hymnological Soc.; Soc. of Polish Comps. Hons: Kt. Cross, Polonica Restituta; Medal of Towazystwo im. F Chopina. Address: Cieszyn, 22 Lipca 2/2B, 43-403, Poland.

HLOBIL, Emil, b. 11 Oct. 1901, Veseli, Czech. Composer; Professor of Composition. Educ: Fac. of Philos., Univ. of Prague; studied comps. w. Josef Suk. Conserv. of Prague. m. Marie Hlobilova, 2 children. Debut: as comp., String Quintet (w. 2 violas), Prague, 1926. Career: Prof., Grammar Schl., 1925, Conserv. Prague, 1941, Acad. of Music & Dramatic Arts, Prague, 1958-. Comps. incl: 7 symphs.; 5 str. quartets; concertos for violin, clarinet, organ & accordion; many chmbr. works; var. orchl. works; operas of Anna Karenina (Tolstoy), & Bourgeois gentilhomme (Moliere); ballet, Beauty & the Beast. Recip. Deserving Artist, 1971. Address: Stresovicka 62, 16200 Prague 6, Czechoslovakia.

HO, Edward, b. 27 Sept. 1939, Hong KJong. Lecturer; Pianist. Educ: BA (Geography & Geology), Hong Kong; BMus, MMus, DMus (Durham); FTCL; LMusTCL, LTCL, LRSM, TCL, RSCM. m. Maria Leung, 2 c. Career: Programme Asst., BBC; Lectr. & Chmn. of Music Dept., the Chinese Univ. of Hong Kong; established the Music Dept. for the Uni. of Singapore: TV & Radio apps., Far East; Choral & Orchl. Cond.; Solo & ensemble pianist; currently Prin. Lectr., Gipsy Hill Music Centre, Kingston Polytechnic, Kingston upon Thames, Surrey. Contbr. to: The Musical Times. Mbrships: CGGB; ISM. Hons: Univ. Degree Scholarship, TCL, 1963; Fellowship, Univ. of Edinburgh, 1964. Hobbies: Cooking; Motoring; Bridge; Table-tennis; Soccer. Address: 5 Wallace Fields, Epsom, Surrey, UK.

HOARE, William Acton, b. 5 Sept. 1928, Tavistock, UK. Musician (double bass). Educ: Royal Mil. Schl. of Music; RCM, London; Exhbn. & Fndn. Scholarship. m. Jean Hoare, 1 s., 1 d. Debut: w. RPO, cond., Beecham. Career: Twenty yrs. as BBC Staff Musician - BBC Midland Light Orch., BBC Scottish Symph. Orch.; Dir., Novar Chamber Ensemble, Glasgow. Recordings: w. Delphos Chamber Grp., B'ham. Mbrships: B'ham. Soc. of Musicians; Glasgow Soc. of Musicians. Hons: First double bass prize, RMSM, 1950. Hobbies: Bridge; Horse racing; Home Beer brewing. Address: 53 Lauderdale Gdns., Glasgow G12 GQT, UK.

HOBBS, Allen (Alain), b. 10 May 1937, Denver, Colo., USA. Organist; Improviser. Educ: pupil of André Marchaql, Jean Langlais & Marcel Dupré in Paris. Career: Organist of the Cathedral (Denver), 1953-71; Organist, Notre Dame Ch. (Denver), 1972-; int. reputation as tchr. of improvisation & score reading. Life mbr., Société Française de Musicologie, 1968. Hobby: Musicol. (specialist in the hist. of music tchng). Address: 1985 S Depew St., NO. 6, Denvr, CO 80227, USA.

HOBBS, Oliver P, b. 1 Jan. 1907, Lawrence, Kans., USA. High School Band & Orchestra Director; Trombonist, Baritone. Educ: BMusEd., Univ. of Kans., grad. work at Univ. of Kans. & Fla. State Univ. m. Beryl L Montgomery, 2 s., 3 d. Career: Dir. of the HS Band & Orch. & Instrumental Music Supvsr. in the Lawrence, Kans. Pub. Schls., 10 yrs.; Band & OPrch. Dir., Leon HS, Tallahassee, Fla., 1950-; Served as Clinician & Adjudicator in Music Fests. in Fla., Ga., Ala., 35 yrs.; Dir., Fla. All-State Band at the conven. of the Fla. Music Educators Assn., 1964-73; Dir., Ga. All-State Band at the Ga. Tchrs. Assn. Conven., Atlanta, GA., 1965, & Ga. All-State Jr. Band, 1971. Recordings: many of Leon HS Band & Fla. State Music Camp Bands. Mbrships: MENC; FMEA; ASBDA; FBA; Former Pres., Fla. Band Masters Assn.; First Pres., Fla. Omega Chapt., Phi Beta Mu. Hons. incl: Disting Musicianship Cit., Fla. State Univ., 1963. Address: PO Box 891, Tallahassee, FL 32303, USA.

HOBCROFT, Rex Kelvin, b. 12 May 1925, Renmark, SA, Australia. Music Conservatorium Director. Educ: Dip. Mus., Univ. of Melbourne. m. Perpetua, 4 children. Career: Dir., Tasmanian Conservatorium of Music, 1964-71; Hd., Music Dept., Univ. of Tasmania, 1961-70; Hd., Keyboard Dept., Qld. State Conservatotium of Music, 1957-61; Dpty. Dir.-Dir., Australian Comps. Seminars, 1963 & 65; Cond., Premiere, 3 Australian Operas, Australian Opera Seminar, 1965; Dir., NSW State Conservatorium of Music, Sydney, currently. Mbrships: Bd. Dir. Australian Opera; Exec. mbr., Australian Music Exams. Bd.; Competition, 1977, '81; Pres., Fed. Music Clubs of Aust. Recip., Churchill Fellowship, 1968. Hobbies: Reading; Film making. Address: c/o NSW State Conservatorium of Music, Macquarie St., Sydney, NSW 2000, Australia. 15.

HOBSON, Ann Stephens, b. 6 Nov. 1943, Philadelphia, Pa., USA. Harpist. Educ: Phila. Musical Acad., 1961-64; BM, Cleveland Inst. of Music, 1964-66; Marlboro Music Fest., 1966 & 67. Career: Fac. Ambler Music Fest., 1968 & 69; Fac., New England Conserv., 1971-; Soloist, Boston Symph., Boston Pops., Wash. Nat. Symph., Ricmond (VA) Symph., Wichita Symph. etc. Recordings: Debussy Trio. Hobbies: Tennis; Bridge; Cooking; Classical Guitar. Mgmt: Boston Concert Artists. Address: Symphony Hall, Boston, MA 02115, USA. 27.

HOBSON, Bruce, b. 16 Aug. 1943, Hartford, Conn., USA. Piano Teacher; Composer; College Instructor. Educ: BA, Columbia Coll., NYC, 1965; MMus, New England Conserv. of Music, Boston, 1967; Columbia Univ. Schl. of the Arts, NYC, 1969-72. m. Lynda Hobson. Career: Teaching Fellow, Univ. of Mich. & Columbis Univ.; Instructor, Southern Vt. Coll., Bennington; Piano Tchr.; perfs. at Donnell Lib. Comps. Forum, Columbia Comps., ISCM & Comps. Guild for Perf. Comps. incl: Three (for 2 solo trumpets & orch.); 2 Movements for Piano; Concerto for 3 Groups; Three Portraits (for baritone voice & piano); Quintet 1970; Concerto for Woodwinds; Sonata for 2 Pianos, 1971; Trio, 1966. Mbr., Comps. Guild for Perf. (Bd. of Dirs.). Hons: Fellowship, Comps. Conf., Johnson Coll., Vt.; selected to represent Vt. at Bicentennial Concert, Wash., DC, 1976. Address: Crow Hill Rd., Arlington, VT 05250, USA.

HOCH, Francesco, b. 14 Feb. 1943, Lugano, Switz. Professor of Music. Educ: G Verdi Conserv., Milan; Course in Comp. Padua & Darmstadt, Germany. m. Beatrice, 1 d. Career: Appt. incl: Prof. of Music, Lugano, Switz.; Asst., courses in comp, Chigiana Acad., Siena, 1974; Invited to Int. Lab., Venice Biennial, 1975; Comps. incl: Prove concertanti, for orch., 1970 (chosen to represent Switz. in Int. Comps. Tribune, Paris, 1973); L'oggetto disincantato (13 instruments), 1974; Transparenza per nuovi elementí, 1976. Contbr. to: Riviste Musicale Swizzera. Mbrships. incl: Assn. of Swiss Musicians; Swiss Soc. of Learning; Fndr., Assn. OGGI musica, Lugano, Switz. Publ: Schweizer Komponisten unserer Zeit, 1974. Hons: Premio Angelicum, Milan, 1975; Pro Arte, Berna, 1976; Invitato Fest. Pontino, Rome, 1976. Address: via Campagna 19, 6952 Canobbia, Switz.

HOCHHEIMER, Laura, b. 18 Apr. 1933, Worms, Germany. Violinist; Music Educator. Educ: BMus, Eastman Schl. of Music, USA, 1955; MFA, Ohio Univ., 1957; PhD, Music Educ., Ind. Univ., 1973. Career incls: Asst. Prof. Music Educ., W Liberty State Coll., WVa., 1968-70; Towson State Coll., Md., 1971-73, Cinn. Coll.-Conserv. of Music, 1973-, Univ. of British Columbia, Vancouver, BC; Assoc. Prof., Music Educ., James Madison Univ. Publs: A Sourcebook for Elementary Schl. Music, 1978. Contbr. to profl. jrnls. Mbrships. incl: MENC; Am. Orff-Schulwerk Assn. Hons. incl: Fulbright Scholar, Austria, 1966-67; var. other awards. Hobbies incl: Playing Chmbr. Music; Writing. Address: Music Dept., James Madison Univ., Harrisonburg, VA 22807, USA.

HODDINOTT, Alun, b. 11 Aug. 1929, Bargoed, Glam., Walews. Composer; Professor of Music. Educ: BMus, Univ. Coll., Cardiff, 1949; DMus, ibid., 1960. m. Beti Rhiannon Huws, 1 s. Career: Lectr., Welsh Nat. Coll. of Music & Drama, 1951-59; Lectr., Univ. Coll., Cardiff, 1959-65; Reader in Music, ibid., 1965-67; Prof. of Music, ibid., 1967-; Artistic Dir., Cardiff Fest. of Music. Comps: The Beach of Falesa (opera); The Tree of Life (oratorio); 5 symphs. (2nd, 3rd & 5th recorded); 11 Concertos (those for clarinet, harp, piano & horn reco·ded); Variants (recorded); Floriture; 4 Sinfoniettas; Welsh Dances (recorded); 6 Sonatas for Piano (2, 3, 6 recorded); o 4 Violin Sonatas (recorded); Sonatas for harp, cello, clarinet, horn, organ; 2 Sonatas for cello & piano; Passaggio for orch.; Dulcia Inventutis; Voyagers for baritone solo, male voices & orch.; Sonatina fro 2 pianos; Operas, The Rajah's Diamond & What the Old Man Does is Always Right. Contbr. to: Musical Times; Tempo; Music & Musicians. Mbrships: Athenaeum; BBC Advisory Committee. Hons: Walford Davies Prize, 1954; Arnold Bax Medal, 1957; Hon. RAM, 1971. Address: Maesawelon, Mill Rd., Lisvane, Cardiff, UK. 1, 3, 21.

HODELL, Ake, b. 1919, Author; Producer of Text-Sound Compositions. Educ. incls: Training as fighter pilot. Career: during 1950's publs. lyric poetry, moving in the 1960's into ''picture-sound-poems'' w. ethical & political overtones, using concrete poety & collage (has prod. a series of books in this style); became known as Reader, & since 1967 has produced a series of textsound compositions incl: Structure III (based on airplane sounds), 1967; USS Pacific Ocan (radio play), 1968; where is Eldridge Cleaver? (using Black Panther calls & slogans), 1970; Mr. Smith in Rhodesia, 1970; The Way to Nepal.

HODGES, Anthony Thomas, b. 24 May 1934, London, UK. Music Librarian. Educ: FTCL; GTCL; ARCM; ALA. m. Jacqueline Margaret Lawson, 2 s., 1 s. Career: Ctrl. Band, RAF, 1952-57; toured Far East, 1954-56; Islington Public Libs., 1963-65; Westminster City Libs., 1966-67; Music Libn., Luton Public Libs., 1967-79; Music Libn., Liverpool City Libs., 1969-73; Libn., RNCM, Manchester, 1973-; fndr., ed., Sound Recordings Group Newsletter; Ed., Audiovisual Librarian. Contbr. to: Brio; Fontis Artis Musicae. Mbrships: Int. Assn. of Music Libs. (Pres., Commission for conservs. of music); Lib. Assn. Hon: FRNCM, 1978. Hobbies: Reading; Swimming; Writing novels; Playing Chamber music. Address: 23 Charnville Rd., Gatley, Cheshire SK8 4HE, UK.

HODGES, William Kennedy, b. 25 July 1951, Miami, Fla., USA. Music Autographer; Professional Percussionist; Studio Percussionist. Educ: BA, Music Educ., Brigham Young Univ., 1974. m. Nannette N Hodges, 2 d. Career: Instructor, percussion, Prin. Percussionist, Utah Valley Symph., 1969-77; Music Reprod. Co., 1972-; Percussionist, Osmond TV Studios, incl. network TV pers. w. Osmond family, Roy Clark & others; perf. w. Utah Symph. Orch., 1977-. Comps. incl: An American Portrait (TV theme); Elegy, for Engl. horn & vibraphone. Recordings incl: The Osmonds - Live, Donny & Marie, Goin' Coconuts; Osmond Brothers, Stepping Out. Mbr. profl. orgs. Hons: Award Musicianship, percussion perf. & ensemble perf., Brigham Young Univ., 1973, '74, '75. Hobbies incl: Travel. Address: PO Box 381, Orem, UT 84057, USA.

HODGSON, Alfreda, b. Morecambe, UK. Concert & Opera Singer. Educ; pvte. study of cello; grad., winning highest singing award, Northern Schl. of Music, 1961. m., 2 d. Debut: concert w. Royal Liverpool Phil. orch., 1961; opera, Ulrica, Verdi's Masked Ball, English Nat. Opera, 1974. Career incls: frequent apps. w. Halle Orch., Scottish Nat. Orch., sev. London Orchs.'s tour of Scandinavia, 1973; tours to USA, Venezuela, Israel; apps. in Rome, Madrid, Paris, Toronto, etc. Recordings incl: St. John Passion; Purcell's The Fairy Queen; Monteverdi Madrigals; Pilgrims Progress; Das Lied vonder Erde. Mgmt: Harold Holt Ltd., 122 Wigmore St., London W1H 0DJ, UK.

HODINAŘOVA, Elvira, b. 6 Jan. 1927, Olomouc, Czechoslovakia. Pianist. Educ: Dip. w. distinction, Stáni Konzervator Hudby, Prague, 1949; Dip. w. distinction, Akademia Muzickych Umeni, Prague, 1953; Chopin Scholarship, Poland, 1953-54. m. Adolf Wladyslaw Malinowski, 1 s. Debut: Olomouc (Piano Concerto A-Major, Mozart), 1939. Career: Cooperation w. Polish Radio since 1954; approx. 400 solo recorgings of chmbr. music, also as accomp.; Soloist w. Panstwowa Filharmonia Baltycka, Gdansk, Poland; Cooperation w. Polish TV; Cooperation w. Radio in Czech., E & W Germany, France, Spain, Italy, Switz., Holland, USSR, Bulgaria. Recordings: 2 Supraphon records; piano recitals. Contbr. to: Jazz, in Poland. Mbrships: Stowarzyszenie Polskich Artystów Muzykop. Hons: 1st Prize, young Musicianś Competition, Prague, 1952. Hobbies: Country Life. Mgmt: Pagart, Plac Zwyciestwa 9, Warsaw, Poland. Address: ul. Chlebnicka 2728 m3, 80-830 Gdansk, Poland.

HODKINSON, Sydney Phillip, b. 17 Jan. 1934, Winnipeg, Man., Can. Educator; Composer. Educ. incls: BMus, 1957, MMus, 1958, Eastman Schl. of Music; DMusA, Univ. of Mich., 1968; studied w. noted tchrs. m. Elizabeth J Deischer, 3 s. Career incls: tchr., Univ. of Va., 1958-63, Ohio Univ., 1963-68; Tchr., Cond. for Rockerfeller New Music Proj., Univ. of Mich.,

1968-73; Artist-in-Res., Mpls.-st. Paul, Minn, 1970-72; Asoc. Prof., Conducting & Ensembles, Eastman Schl. of Music, Univ. of Rochester, 1972-; Profl. Clarinetist; Cond. Num. comps. inclng: Vox Populous (active oratorio); Contemporary Primer (band); Daydream (chorus, speaker, instruments); Pillar (winds & percussion); November Voices (voice), speaker, small ensemble); Cortege (dirge for band). Mbr. profl. orgs. Recip. many hons. & commissions. Address: 18 Timber Ln., Fairport, NY, USA.

HOECKELE, Andrew L, b. 1 Oct. 1942, Glendale, NY, USA. Choral Director; Theory & Harmony Instructor; Piano Instructor. Educ: BS & MA in Sec. Schl. Music, NY. Univ., Schl. of Educ.; voice, piano & theory. Brooklyn Conserv. of Music: ballet & dance w. Patricia Bowman & June Taylor. m. Barbara Casella Hoeckele. Career: Maj. roles in summer stock of 'Oklahoma' & 'The Mikado'; Dir. of amateur prodns. of 'Camelot', 'Bye, Bye, Birdie' & 'Olivier'; Choral Dir., New Hyde Park Meml. HS & Centereach HS, LI, NY; Baritone in Collegiate Chorale, Abraham, Kapan San Marco Choristers, Atlanta Symph. Orch. Chorus (Cond. Robert Shaw, 1974-79), Ralph Hunter. Mbrships. incl: Phi Mu Alpha; Beta Epsilon Chapt. Histn.; NY State Schl. Music Assn.; MENC. Hons. incl: Generoso Pope Meml. Scholarship, 1960; NYSSMA Choral Competition 'A' rating, 1965 & 72. Hobbies: Bowling; Golf, etc. Address: 5606 Noblett Rd., Stone Mountain, GA 30087, USA.

HOEG, Michael Erling, b. 11 Dec. 1948, Hitchin, UK. Cathedral Organist. Educ: RAM, London; London Univ.; FRCO (ChM); GRSM (Lond.); LRAM. Career: Organist & master of the Choristers, Londonderry Cathedral, 1972. Mbr., RCO; Cathedral Organists Assn. Hons: Stewart 0 Prout Prize, Univ. of Dublin, 1977. Address: 4 St. Columb's Ct., Londonderry, UK.

HOELTZEL, (Hans) Michael, b. 22 Apr. 1936, Tubingen, Germany. Horn Soloist; Conductor; Professor of Horn. Educ: State Acad. of Music, Stuttgart; Mozarteum, Salzburg. m. Ingeborg-Johanna Spiess, 2 s. Career: Salzburg Camerata Academica; Bamberger Symph.; Munich Phil.; Instructor in Horn, Mozarteum, Salzburg; Prof. of Horn & Chmbr. Music, Acad. of Music, Detmold; Vis. Prof. of Music, Ind. Univ., Bloomington; Guest Cond., Camerata Academica & NWD Phil. Orch.; Musical Dir., Philharmonia da Camera. Recordings: 4 Horn Concertos & Concert-Rondo (Mozart), as Soloist & Cond., Camerata Academica. Contbr. to: Brass Bulletin; Horn Call. Mbrships: VP, Int. Horn Soc.; Schlaraffia. Recip., Medal, Int. Music Compeition, Geneva, 1965. Hobbies: Hunting; Fine Arts. Address: Brokhauser Strasse 76, D-4930, Detmold, German Fed. Repub.

HOENGEN, Elisabeth, b. Gevelsburg, Germany. Opera Singer. Educ: Acad. of Music, Berlin. Career incl: mbr. of Opera Cos., Wuppertal Opera House, 1933; Dusseldorf Opera House, 1935; State Opera, Dresden, 1940; Vienna State Opera, 1943-. Hobbies: Painting; Flowers; Animals; Philately. Address: Zuckerkandlgasse 28, Vienna, Austria.

HOENICH, Richard S, b. 15 May 1955, Montreal, Canada. Musician (Bassoon). Educ: McGill Univ., Montreal; BMus, Curtis Inst. of Music, 1977. Debut: Pianist, Montreal Symph. Orch., 1970; Bassoonist, Montreal Symph. Orch., 1974. Career: Sev. solo apps. in Can. w. Can. Orchs.; Solo recitals in num. Can. Ctrs.; Mbr., Nat. Youth Orch. of Can., 1970-75. Recordings: As mbr. of 1973 World Youth Orch. recorded as prin. bassoon in Mabler Symph. No. 1; Recordings for nat. radio & TV (CBC). Hons: Can. Coun. awards, 1974, 75; Num. competition prizes w. scholarships & bursaries as pianist & bassoonist. Hobbies: Amateur Magician; Fine Arts; Travel. Address: 840 Brunet St., St. Laurent, Quebec, Canada.

HOENIG, Lawrence Martin, b. 20 Dec. 1942, New York, NY, USA. Choral Conductor; Lyric Tenor. Educ: AB, Columbia Coll.; MA, Univ. of Pa.; BM, Phila. Musical Acad.; Grad. study, Temple Univ. m. Carolyn Mather, 1 s. Career: Soloist w. Pa. Orch., Am. Soc. of Ancient Instruments, Concerto Soloists of Phila., Mendelssohn Club of Phila., num. others; Perfs., Europe, USSR; Cond., Phila. Musical Acad. Choir & Chmbr. Choir; Germantown Friends Schl. Chorus. Recordings: Stravinsky's Les Noces; Gershwin's Of Thee I Sing. Mbrship: Am. Choral Fndn. Hobby: Travel. Address: 414 E Allens Lane, Philadelphia, PA 19119, USA.

HOEY, Juliet Therese, b. 8 Oct. 1937, Gympie, Aust. Pianist & Accompanist; Church Musician; Cello Teacher; Class Music Teacher; Piano Examiner. Educ: BA, Univ. of Qld., 1959; Dip. Mus, Qld. Conserv., 1972; FTCL (Piano); LMus (Piano); Master Classes (piano) w. Kenneth van Barthold, London, 1970; var. pvte. tchrs., piano & cello; Studied singing, Conserv. m. Denis Hoey, 4 s. Debut: Piano duo recitals w. husband, Brisbane, 1966; Workshops, Aust. House, 1968-70. Career: Piano Tchr., 1962-; Ch. Musician, 1971-; Class Music Tchr., 1975-; Pt.-time cello tchr., Educ. Dept.; Writer, sev. libretti for operas incl. The Loaded Dog. Cointbr. to: Catholic Leader; Courier Mail;

Sunday Mail; Baby Talk. Mbrships: Kodaly Assn. of Aust.; Bach Soc.; MTA; Royal Schl. of Ch. Music. Hons: Trinity Coll. Prize, Brisbane, 1964. Hobbies: Reading; Writing; Cycling; Swimming; Bushwalking; Talking; Praying. Address: 21 Normanton St., Stafford Heights, Brisbane, Qld. 4053, Aust.

HOFF, Brynjar, b. 1 Oct. 1940, Trondheim, Norway. Oboist. Educ: Studies in Oslo, Stockholm, Leningrad & London. Debut: Oslo Phil., 1958. Career: Prin. Oboist, Trondheim Symph. Orch., 1955-58, Norwegian Oper Orch., 1959-65, Oslo Phil., 1965-; Soloist Engagements w. all Norwegian orchs., chmbr. ensembles, radio, TV, major conds., 1960-. Recordings: Contemporary Norwegian Music for Wind Quintets; Mozart Oboe-Quartet F Major K 370; Mozart: Oboe-Quartet F Major, Allessandro Besozzi; Sonata in C Major, JB Loeillet. Three Romances, B Bartok; Three Folksongs, S. Berge. Mbrships: Norsk Tonekunstnersamfunn; Kunstnerforeningen "Blom''. Hons: Dr. Forsberg's Legate, 1969; 1st Prize, serious recording in Norway, Mozart Quartet, 1974. Hobbies: Reading World Travel. Address: Tyristubbveien 13, Oslo 6, Norway.

HOFFER-V WINTERFIELD, Linde, b. 5 Sept. 1919, Sylt, Westerland, Germany. High School Professor; Composer. Educ: Conserv., Berlin; Pvte. Music Tchrs. Exam, Violoncello & Flute, 1940. m. Paul Höffer, 2 c. Career: Var. concerts & courses; Prof., High Schl. for Music, Berlin. Compositions incl: Hohe Schule des Blockflötenspiels, 1955; Blockflötenstudien; Bach, Handel, Telemann, 1959; Der Neue Weg, 1964, 21 Lektionen, 1967, Klingende Flotenfilel 1968 (these 3 trans., French); Studienbuch für Jeanette, 1969; Flötenfibel für Fortgeschrittenen, 1971. Recordings: Die Blockflöte Nr. 2 & Nr. 5 Publs: Handbuch der Blockflötenliteratur, 1959. Address: Westendallee 986 1 Berlin 19, German Fed. Repub.

HOFFERT, Paul, b. 1943, Brooklyn, NY, USA. Composer; Performer. Educ: Comps. & orchestration, 1957-63; Univ. of Toronto (BSc) 1961-66. Career incl: Dir. of Contemporary Music, Blue Mountain Schl. of Music, 1975; Cons., Ont. Arts Coun., 1976; guest lectr., Fanshaw Coll., London, Ont. & York Univ., Toronto, Ont., 1977, Univ. of Guelph, 1979; 1st VP, Acad. of Can. Cinema, 1979; fndr., Lighthouse, 1968; num. perfs. at fests., etc. Comps. incl: Democratic Concerto for Jazz Quartet & Orch., 1967; Concerto for Contemporary Flute, 1975; Concerto for Violin, 1976; Electric Str. Quartet 1977; theatrical music incl. Marat Sade, 1969, Prometheus Bound, 1971; Caucasian Chalk Circle, 1976; Ballet music; num. film scores; music for TV series. sev. recordings incl. 9 albums w. Lighthouse. Hons: Special jury prize, Cannes Film Fest., 1970; Juno awards for best Van. group, 1972, '73, '74, Can. film awards, 1977; 10 certs. of merit for most performed songs, BMIC. Address: 73 Brookview Dr., Toronto, Ont. M6A 2K5, Can.

HOFFMAN, Alfred, b. 3 Aug. 1929, Bucharest, Romania. Musicologist; Music Critic. Educ: studied piano and musicol. Bucharest Conserv., 1949-54; Dip. in Musicol. m. Adriana Palade. Career: Permanent music critic, România Liberá (daily), 1951-; Contemporanul (weekly), 1957-; România Literará (weekly), 1976-; Muzica (review), 1951-; frequent apps. in music criticism broadcasts on radio & TV; Prin. Rsch. Wkr., Arts History Inst., Romanian Acad. Scis., 1960-75. & Romanian Opera, Bucharest, 1975-; juror Prix Mondial du Disque, Montreux, 1976, & Int. Record Critics' Award, W. Berlin, 1977, Salzburg, 1978, Gstaad, 1979. Publs: Drumul Operei (The Road of the Opera), 1960; Repere Muzicale (Landmarks in Music), 1974; co-author, George Enescu (monograph), 1971. Contbr. to profl. jrnls. Mbrships. incl: Romanian Union of Comps. Recip. sev. decorations and awards. Address: Bulevardul Republicii 86, App. 19, Et. 3, R-70312 Bucharest, Of. Post. 20, Sect. 3, Romania.

HOFFMAN, Grace, b. Cleveland, Ohio, USA. Opera, Oratorio & Concert Singer (mezzo-soprano). Educ: Western Reserve Univ.; Manhattan Schl. of Music, NY; Fulbright Scholar, study in Italy. Career: Appeared at Maggio Musicale, Florence; Guest Artist & Late mbr., Zürich Opera, 2 yrs.; Debut at La Scala, Milan as Fricak in Die Walkure; w. Stuttgart Opera; perfs. at Edinburgh & Bayreuth Festivals; Guest appearances in leading roles, Teatro Colon, Buenos Aires, San Fran. Opera, roles, Teatro Colon, Buenos Aires, San Fran. Opera, Chgo. Lyric Opera, Covent Gdn., Metropol. Opera NY., Vienna Opera, etc.; Num. Oratorio & Concert appearances in major European music ctrs. Hobby: Interior furnishing. Address: c/o Staatsoper, Postfach 982, 7 Stuttgart, Germany.

HOFFMAN, Irwin, b. 26 Nov. 1924, NYC, USA. Symphony Conductor; Violinist. Educ: Juilliard Schl. of Music. m. Esther Glazer Hoffman, 3 s., 1 d. Career: Cond., Vancouver Symph., BC, 1952-64; Assoc. Cond. & Acting Music Dir., Chgo. Symph., 1964-70; Music Dir., Fla. Gulf Coast Symph., 1968-; Chef Permanent, Belgian Radio & TV Symph., 1972-; Guest Cond., var. ldng. orchs., Europe, N Am., Israel, S Am.

Recordings: DGG. Mgmt: Harold Shaw Concerts, NYC. Address: 1901 Brightwaters Blvd., St. Petersburg, FL, USA. 2, 7, 8.

HOFFMAN, Jan, b. 11 June 1906, Cracow, Poland. Pianist; Professor. Educ: Dip. w. highest hons., Cracow Conserv., 1928; Pupil & asst. to Egon Petri, Berlin, 1928-31. widower, 2 d. Debut: Vienna, 1924. Career: Tchr., 1928-, currently Prof., Vice-Rector, Higher Schl. of Music; concerts throughout Europe as Soloist, ensemble player & Cond.; Mbr. of Jury, many int. competitions; summer courses, Finland. Recordings for Poslie Nagrania & Polish Radio. Ed. num. musical publs. Author, School of Sight Reading, 1949. Mbrships: Chopin Soc., Warsaw; Soc. of Polish Artists. Hons. incl: Cmdr.'s & Off.'s Crosses, Polania Restitua. Hobbies: Arts; Lit.; Sport. Address: Dzierzynskiego 19A6, 30-048 Cracow, Poland.

HOFFMAN, Ludwig, b. 11 Jan. 1925, Berlin, Germany. Concert Pianist; Professor. Educ: Acads. Vienna & Berlin; Grad., Acad., Cologne. Debut: Cologne, 1933. Career: Prof., Hochschule für Musik, Munich. num. recordings. Publs: Moderne Klaviertechnik. Mbrships: Juries of all nat. competitions & of ARD-Munich Int. Competition; Juries of competitions in Warsaw, Versailles, Sydney, Budapest etc.; Chopin Competition; DAAD. Recip. Liszt prize, Weimar, 1948. Hobby; Chevalier du Tastevin. Mgmt: Konzertdirektion Drissen, Mainz. Address: Walleitnerstr. 3, 8022 Grünwald bei München, German Fed. Repub.

HOFFMAN, Stanley, b. 8 Dec. 1929, Balt., Md., USA. Violinist; Violist. Educ: BS, Juilliard Schl. of Music, 1959; pvte. studies w. var. masters. Debut: Carnegie Recital Hall, NYC, 1962. Career: Violinist, NY Phil., 1961-64; Violinist & Dir., Sal Segno Ensemble, 1966-; Violist, Wagner Coll. Str.-Quartet-in-Res., 1970-. Recordings: Vocal Chmbr. Music Vol. I, Sudan Reid-Par, Vol. II, Elinor amlen & Rose Macdonald, Vol. III (projected), Carol Lurie. Mbrships: Am. Fedn. Musicians, Local 802; Bohemians Club, NYC; Nat. Assn. Am. Comps. & Conds. Hons: Invited by Soviet-lativian Committee of Cultural Rels. to premiere Dr. G Ponés Violin Concerto, Riga, 1971. Mgmt: Norman Seaman. Address: 350 Richmond Terrace Apt. 4J, Staten Island, NY 10301, USA.

HOFFMAN, Theodore, b. 18 Oct. 1925, Palo Alto, Calif., USA. Composer; Professor. Educ: AB, Stanford Univ.; MA, Mills Coll.; PhD, Univ. of the Pacific; grad. study, Univ. of Ill. m. Nancy Maguire Hoffman, 2 s., 2 d. Career: Music Supvsr., KTTV Hollywood, 1951-52; Music Fac., Univ. of Ill., 1953-54; Music Dir., WILL-TV (Educl. TV), 1954-56; Music Dir., WGBH-TV & FM, Boston, 1956-57; Fac., San Francisco State, 1957-59; Music Chmn., San Benito Coll., 1959-61; Music Dir., Perry-Mansfield Schl. of Theater & Dance, Colo., Summer, 1961; Fac., Univ. of S. Fla., 1962-. Contbr. to: 'Variations on Jesu Meine Freude'; Jrnl. of Band Rsch. Mbrships: Am. Soc. of Univ. Composers, 1967-71; Southeastern Composers League, 1968-72. Hons: Heller Scholarship, Mills Coll., 1952; Southwestern Band Dirs. Award, 1965, etc. Hobbies: Golf; Bridge. Address: Rte. 8, Box 1378, Lutz, FL, USA.

HOFFMANN, Bruno, b. 15 Sept. 1913, Stuttgart, Germany. Concert Soloist on Glass Harp. Educ: Dipl. Eng; study of piano, organ & glass harp. m. Marianne, Arzt, 2 s., 1 d. Debut: London 1938. Career: has given concerts, made radio & TV broadcasts & appeared in films on 4 continents. Comps: for glass harp solo w. piano & w. orch. has recorded for Archiv, DGG, Philips, Supraphon, Fono & Vox labels. Contbr. to: MGG. Address: 64 Thueringer-Wald-Strasse, D-7 Stuttgart 30, German Fed. Repub.

HOFFMANN, Richard, b. 20 Apr. 1925, Vienna, Austria. Composer. Educ: pvte. study of music, 1930-; BMus, Univ. of NZ, Auckland, NZ, 1945; studied Comp. w. Arnold Schoenberg, Los Angeles, USA, 1947-51. m. Joan Alfhild, 2 s., 1 d. Debut: (as Comp.) Vienna, 1935. Career incls: Amanuensis to Schoenberg, 1947-51; Prof. in Com. & Theory, 1954-, Oberlin Coll. Comps. incl: Piano Concerto Cello Concerto, Orchestra Piece, 1961; Music for Strings; String Trio; 4 String Quartets; Changes for Chimes; Deca dance; In Memoriam Patris, 1976; Soufflent, 1976. Publs: Co-Ed., Schoenberg Gesamtausgabe, 1961. Mbr., Am. Soc. Univ. Comps. Hons. incl: Huntington Hartford Prize, 1949; Award, Nat. Inst. of Arts & Letters, 1966; Guggenheim Fellow, 1970-71, 1977-78; Nat. Endowment for the Arts, 1977, 1978.

HOFFMANN-ERBRECHT, Lothar, b. 2 Mar. 1925, StrehlenSchlesien, Germany. Professor. Educ: Grad. Acad. of Music, Weimar, 1949; PhD, Univ. of Jena, 1951; Habilitation, Dept. of Musicol., Univ. of Frankfurt, 1961. m . Margarete Fischer, 2 d. Career: Prof. of Musicol., Univ. of Frankfurt a.M. Publs. incl: Deutsche & italienische Klaviermusik zur

Bachzeit, 1954; Thomas Stoltzer. Leben & Schaffen, 1964; Heinrich Finck, Ausgewählte Werke, I-II; Beethoven, Klaviersonaten (w. Cl. Arrau). Contbr. to: profl. jrnls. Mbrships: Soc. for Music Rsch.; Int. Musicol. Soc. Address: 9 Amselweg, D-6070 Langen-Oberlinden, German Fed. Repub.

HOFMAN, Shlomo, b. 24 Apr. 1909, Warsaw, Poland. Musicologist; Composer; Conductor; Educator. Educ: Grad., State Music Conserv., Warsaw, 1933 & 1934; Conserv. Nat. de Musique, Paris, 1937-38; Gregorian Inst., Paris, 1947-49; Doct., Sorbonne, Paris, 1949. m. Cyla Pelzmann, 2 d. Career incls: Lectr. on Methodol. of Music Educ., Hebrew Univ., Jerusalem, Israel, 1950-53; Tchr. of Music & Methodol. of Music Educ., State Sem. for Arab Tchrs., Jaffa & Haifa, 1954-67; Tchr. of Hist. of Music, israel Acad. of Music, Tel Aviv Univ., 1954-. Composer of sev. works, mainly for voice. Mbr., sev. musical socs. Publs. incl: L'Oeuvre de Clavecin de Francois Coperin, 1961; Migra'ey Musica (Multilingual ed.), 1974. Recip., sev. awards & grants. Address: 67 Gordon St., Tel-Aviv 64388, Israel.

HOFMAN, Srdjan, b. 4 Oct. 1944, Glina, Yugoslavia. Composer. Educ: Violin Dip., Music Schl.; Dip. in Comp., Music Acad., Belgrade; Masters degree, Comp., ibid.; courses in comp. & orchestration, Darmstadt, Stuttgart & Cologne. m. Mirjana Veselnovic-Hofman, 2 c. Debut: 1966. Career: Prof. of Harmony & Counterpoint, Josip Slavenski Music Schl., Belgrade, 1969-74; Docent for Comp. & Orchestration, Music Acad., Belgrade. Comps: incl: (recorded) Variations for Flute, Viola & Piano; Str. Quartet; Movimento energico (symph. orch.); Simfonija: Zakonika posledovanije (clarinet & 2 string sextets); Concerto dinamico (symph. orch.). Recordings: Episodi Concertanti per violino e orch., 1978. Mbrships: Pres., Assn. of Servian Comps. Hons: Octover Prize for Students, 1969; Prize, Assn. of Serbian Comps., 1974. Hobby: Sailing. Address: Vojvode Sime Popovića 8, Belgrade, Yugoslavia.

HOFMANN, Hermann Wolfgang, b. Karlsruhe, Germany. Conductor; Composer. Educ: studied w. Kurt Stiehler, Rudolf Kempe, Dr. Reinhart Oppel. m. Erna Zehner, 2 c. Debut: Gewandhaus Orch., 1940. Career: Concertmaster, Kaiserslautern, Darmstadt, Mozarteum Orch., Salzburg, 1955-59; Musical Dir., Palatinate Chmbr. Orch., Mannheim-Ludwigshafen, 1959-; Guest, Saar Broadcasting, 1966-71. Compositions incl: Operas; Ballets; Symphs.; Solo Concerti; Chmbr. Music; Christmas Oratorio; Requiem. Recordings: DGG; da camera; Camerata; RBM. Author, Goldender Schnitt & Komposition. Mbr. Kiwanis Club, Mannheim Ludwigshafen. Recip. Peter Cornelius Plaque. Address 13 Hebelstr., Mannheim, GErman Fed. Repub.

HOFSTETTER, Igo, b. 1 June 1926, Linz, Austria. Composer; Professor of Music. Educ: Grad., Bruckner Conserv., Linz; studied w. Prof. F H Klein, GMD, Ludwig Leschetitzky. m. Hermine Hostetter, 1 s. Career: Radio apps., Austria, Germany, Belgium, France, Holland, Sweden, Czech., Poland, 1945-; Work w. ORF (Austrian State Radio), 1965-. Comps: incl: (publd.) operettas Roulette der Herzen, Alles spricht von Charpillon, Schach dem Boss, Ligh Music: (recorded) Die Bimmel-Bammel-, Bummelbahn; Moldau-Polka; Obersöterreicher-Marsch. Mbrships: Austrian Comps. Grp.; AKM; Austro-Mechana; Bd., Int. Soc. for Operetta, Musical & Light Music. Hobbies: Photography; Cinema. Address: 20/IX Rilkestrasse, A-4020 Linz/Donau, Austria.

HOGG, Merle E, b. 25 Aug. 1922, Lincoln, Kan., USA. Professor of Music; Trombonist. Educ: BS, Emporia Kan. State Coll., 1948; MFA, Univ. of Iowa, 1952; PhD., ibid. 1954; Am. Conserv. Fontainebleau, France, summer 1960. m. Mary Jean Gladfelter, 3 d. Career: Prof. of Music, San Diego State Univ.; Trombonist, San Diego Symph. Orch., 1964-. Comps: Concerto for Brass; Invention for Brass Quintet; 3 Short Pieces for Brass Trio; Sonatina for Tuba & Piano; Suite for Band; Variations for Brass Trio; 3 Studies for Euphonium & Piano 1974; Etude I for Tuba & Piano, 1974; Interludes for Symh. Brass, 1974; Toccata for Brass Quartet; Sonata for Brass Choir; Variations for Bassoon & Piano; Concerto for trombone & chmbr. orch. Mbrships: Music Educators Nat. Assn.; Nat. Assn. of Jazz Educators; Nat. Assn. of Coll. Wind & Percussion instrs. Hons: Johnson Brass Comp. Awards, 2nd Prize, 1953; Grad. Fellowship, Univ. of Iowa, 1953; Rsch. Fellowship, Univ. of Calif., San Diego, 1974. Address: 5688 Campanile Way, San Diego, CA 92115, USA.

HOGWOOD, Christopher Jarvis, b. 10 Sept. 1941, Nottingham, UK. Musicologist; Keyboard Player; Writer; Broadcaster. Educ: Cambridge Univ.; Charles Univ.; Prague; BA; MA. Recordings: L'Oiseau Lyre Florilegium series, etc. Publs: Music at Court, 1977; The Trio Sonata, 1979; Haydn's Visits to England, 1980. Contbr. to: Grove's Dict., 6th Ed. Address: 2 Claremont, Hills Rd., Cambridge CB2 IPA, UK.

HOHENSEE, Wolfgang Johann August, b. 3 Jan. 1927, Berlin, Germany. Composer. Educ: Abitur, Real-Gymnasium, 1947; Univ. (Humboldt) Berlin and Heidelberg, 1947-51; Hochschule für Musick, Berlin (Charlottenburg), 1946-50. m. Kaete H Pick, 1 s., 1 d. Career: Cond., Dt. Nationaltheater, Weimar, 1951-57; Prof. of Comp., Hochschule für Musik Hanns Eisler, Berlin, 1957-. Comps: 3 Symphs.; 2 piano concertos; 2 string quartets; chmbr. music especially for wind instruments; songs; 4 cantatas (Der Schäfervom Hohen Venn, Sturmvogel, etc.); 5 ballets (König Drosselbart, Sklaven, etc.); music for approx. 70 films. Contbr. to: Konzertführer. Mbr., Verband der Komponisten und Musikwissenschaftler der DDR. Hobbies: Physics; Sailing. Address: Rudolf-Grosse-Str. 33/10-34, 1157 Berlin, German Dem. Repub.

HOING, Clifford Alfred, b. 21 Nov. 1903, High Wycombe, Bucks., UK. Luthier: Specialist in Violas. Educ: High Wycombe Tech. Schl. Publs: Hoing Technique of Viola Making with working drawings, 1972. Contbr. to; The Woodworker; num. musical mags. Hons: Dip., The Hague, 1949, Fest. of Britain, 1951, Bournmouth (tie for 1st pl.), 1951; Dip. Hon. Ascoli Piceno Italy & Special Silver Medal for Viola of Outstanding Artistic Character; Hoing viola made record price for mod. Engl. instrument, f1,300, Phillips, London, 1974. Hobbies: Oil Painting; Restoring Old Oil Paintings; FRSA. Address: 137 W Wycombe Rd., High Wycombe, Bucks., UK.

HOKE, Hans Gunter, b. 12 June 1928, Meissen, Germany. Musicologist. Concert Pianist. Educ: Dr. phil., Univ. of Halle, 1974; Dr.sc.phil., ibid., 1975; Music HS of Leipzig, Dresden & Berlin. m. Ruth, 1 s., 2 d. Career: Cyclic performances of Bach's Welltempered Clavier, Art of Fugue, Goldberg Variations, Inventions & Sinfonias, etc.; Musicol. Advsr. of Beethoven Complete Ed. & J S Bach Ed. (Eterna); Mbr., Ed. Staff, Beitrage zur Musikwissenschaft. Contbr. to: Die Musik in Geschichte & Gegenwart, etc. Mbr., E Germann Union of Composers & Musicologists. Recip: Banner der Arbeit Award, 1971. Hobbies: Old prints; Gardening. Address: Huettendorfer Weg 9, GDR-1183 Berlin.

HOL, Dirk, b. 2 Nov. 1907, Dordrecht, Holland. Conductor; Composer; Violinist. Educ: State Examination, Violin; var. Architecture Dips. m. Johanna-Cornelia Colijn, 4 c. Career: Cond., Dordrecht Chmbr. Orch., & Ch. Choir, Radio App., 1971; Violinist; Composer. Compositions incl: Concerto, oboe & orch.; Concert Piece, trumpet & Chmbr. orch.; Kleine danssuite; Morceau, guitar & collo; Dans bij het draaiorgel; Gloria, choir & ORch.; Old French Songs, oboe, english rn, orch.; Fests. choir & orch.; Quintet, flute, oboe, violin, alto, cello; Pslam 100, choir, flute, organ; Divertimento, flute solo; Just a Moment, guitar & cello; Sonate, guitar; St. Nicolaasliederen, choir, piano, percussion, 2 oboes, bassoon; Entre de boeuf et l'ane gris, choir; var. Arcs. Recordings: w. Dubbeldams Ch. Choir. Mbr. Register of Dutch Musicians. Address: 79 Heysterbachstr., Dordrecht, Holland.

HOLASEK, Ladislav, b. 23 Dec. 1929, Rikincice, Czech. Conductor. Educ: examen, piano & conducting, Conserv.: univ. degree in piano & conducting. m. Eugenia Stacha, 1 s., 1 d. Career: Chief Cond., opera choir, slovak Nat. Theatre, Bratislava; Cond., Slovak Madrigalists choir; film, TV & radio apps. Has made 6 LP records w. Slovak Madrigalists Choir & Collegium musicum chmbr. orch. Mbr., Assn. of Slovak Music Compositors. Recip. Fritz Kaffenda Prize for Interpretation. Hobby: Motor cars. Address: Pupavova 36, 81600 Bratislava, Czechoslovakia.

HOLCOMB, Bruce Ring, b. 14 Sept. 1926, Conneaut, Ohio, USA. Orchestral Musician; Teacher (Tuba, Ophicleide, Double Bass). Educ: BMus, Perfs. Cert. (Tuba), Eastman Schl. of Music, Rochester, NY; Reifeprüfung, Double Bass, Hochschule für Musik Mozarteum, Salzburg. m. Ester Ingrid Toiviainen, 2 s. Career: Vancouver Symph. Orch., Ottawa Phil. Orch., Montreal Symph. Orch., Mozarteum-Orchester, Salzburg; Tchr. of Tuba, Hochschule Mozarteum, Salzburg. Publs: Die Verbesserung der Stimmung der Ventilblasinstrumente. Contbr. to num. profl. publs. Hobbies: Railway and music instrument hist. & technology. Address: Wilhelm-Erben-Strasse 7/12, A-5020 Salzburg, Austria.

HOLD, Trevor, b. 21 Sept. 1939, Northampton, UK. Music Tutor. Educ: BMus, MA, Univ. of Nottingham. m. Susan Turner, 2 c. Career: Music Master, Market Harborough GS, 1962-63; Asst. Lectr. in Music, UCW Aberystwyth, 1963-65; Lectr. in Music, Univ. of Liverpool, 1965-70; Music Tutor, Dept. of Adult Educ., Univ. of Leicester, 1970-. Comps: The Unreturning Spring (song cycle); Kemp's Nine Daies Wonder (piano suite), etc. Publs: The Walled-In Garden, a study of the songs of Roger Quilter, 1978. Contbr. to: Music & Letters; Music Review; Composer. Mbrships: AUT; CGGB. Hons: Clemens Memorial Prize, 1965; Royal Amateur Orchl. Soc. Prize, 1968. Hobbies: Ornithology; Walking; Lit. Address: Dovecote House, Wadenhoe, Oundle, Peterborough PE8 5SU, UK. 3.

HOLDEN, Poppy, b. 15 Feb. 1948, Torquay, Devonshire, UK. Singer. Educ: Univ. of York: ARCM Dip. m. Jonathan Lloyd, 1 s. Career: Singer of contemporary music w. conds. Bruno Maderna, Gunther Schuller, Yehudi Menuhin; concerts in Queen Elizabeth Hall, London, & Tanglewood, USA; perfs. w. Netherlands Opera; Concert tours, Mediterranean, & USA, Spring 1975; Parts writtent for her by Maderna in Satyricon & Mellers in White Bird Blues (premiere Toronto, 1975); dedicatee, Knussen, 2nd Symph.; has worked w. Musica Reservata, the Consort of Musicke, own group, Hortus Musarum. Has recorded for Decca. Mbr., Musicians Union. Hons: Dans Price Prize, 1968; Pownall Prize, 1968. Address: 21 St. Paul's Square, York, UK.

HOLDEN, Randall LeConte (Jr.), b. 4 Dec. 1943, Bronxville, NY, USA. Academic Administrator; Opera Production Manager; Consultant. Educ: BA, Colby Coll., Maine, 1965; MA, Univ. of Conn., 1967; MMus, Univ. of Wash., 1969; DMA, ibid., 1971. m. Pamela Harris Holden. Career: Asst. Stage Mgr., Seattle Opera, Wash., 1967-70; Stage Mgr. for Seattle Opera in Phoenix, Ariz., 1971-73 & for San Diego Opera in Phoenix, 1973-74; Asst. Prof. of Music, Ariz. State Univ., Temple, 1971-; Asst. Dean, Coll. of Fine Arts, ibid., 1971-; Opera Prodn. Mgr., Phoenix Symph., Ariz., 1974-; Cons., Tucson Opera Co., 1974-. Publs: From Plymouth to Woodstock: The American Musical Experience, 1975. Mbrships: Regl. Dpty. Gov. for Southwest USA, Nat. Opera Assn.; Met. Opera Guild. Hobbies: Camping; Bridge; Swimming; Tennis. etc. Address: 1121 E. Watson Dr., Tempe, AZ 85283, USA.

HOLDEN, Thomas Lee, b. 21 Dec. 1926, Wilson, NC, USA. Musician (Horn; Natural Horn). Educ: Artists Dip., Curtis Inst. Music. m. Carol D Holden, 3 d. Career: Solo Hornist w. Denver Coll. Symph. ORch., 1946-53; Prof. Music, Univ. Ill., 1953-; App., Marleboro Music Fest., 1964; Natural Horn Soloist w. Concentius Musicus, Vienna, 1966. Recordings: Das Alte Werke series w. Concentus Musicus Vienna. Address: 2015 Cureton Dr., Urbana, IL 61801, USA.

HOLDER, Alison Joyce, b. 20 July 1917, Adelaide, SA, Aust. Pianist; Teacher of Piano. Educ: BMus, Adelaide Univ.; Study leave, UK, inclng. accomp. studies w. Paul Hamburger, 1950-51. Career: Accomp. for leading singers & instrumentalist, Coach & Repetiteur, num. opea prods.; Tchr. & Lectr., Dept. of Music, Univ. of Adelaide, 1945-; Adjudicator, music fests.; Examiner, Aust. Music Exams. Bd. Mbrships: SA Music Tchrs. Assn. (Coun.); Advsry. Committee on Theory of Music. Hobbies: Nature Photography; Gardening; Reading. Address: 47 Linden Ave., Hazelwood Pk., 5066, Australia.

HOLDER, Henry Richard, b. 18 Nov. 1924. Concert Artist (Violin & Piano); Music Teacher. Educ: BA, Brooklyn Coll.; MA, Hunter Coll.; Profl. Dip., Columbia Univ. Specialist in MusEd.; Dip., NY, Coll. of Music. Debut: Carnegie & Town Hall in var. Ensembles. Career. Has played piano recitalts of contemporary & classical music on FM Stns. WNYC, WKCR, WFUU & WRVR in NYC for many yrs.; served 28 yrs. in NYC Schl. System as Instrumental Music Tchr.; piano recitalist, Brooklyn Museum. A number of his piano compositions has been recorded on Stns. WNYC & WKCR, FM. Publs: Symphony in Hunter College Library - Violin Concerto in Hunter College Library. Mbrships: local 802, Musicians Union AFL-CIO, US. Hobbies: Winter bathing; Bicycle Riding; Karate. Address: 176 Hastings St., Manhattan Beach, Brooklyn, NY 11235, USA.

HOLDSWORTH, Frank, b. 10 Aug. 1930, Manchester, UK. Orchestral Clarinettist; Clarinet Teacher. Educ: Royal Northern Coll. Music, Manchester; LRAM; Clarinet Performer's Dip. Career: Bass Clarint, Halle Orch., Manchester, 1955-60; 2nd, Eb & Bass Clarinet, BBC Scottish Symph. Orch., 1960-63; Co-Prin. & Bass Clarinet, Bournemouth Symph. Orch., 1963-70; Prin. Clarinet, Bournemouth Sinfonietta, 1970-; Clarinet mouthpiece specialist & cons.; Developed 'Holdsworth' mouthpiece, 1971. Recordings: many w. above orchs. Co-author w. Patrick Dingle, Introduction to the Clarinet, 1978. Contbr. to Woodwind World, 1974. Hons. incl: Wind Prize, Royal Northern Coll. Music. Hobbies: Swimming; Cricket; Golf. Address: halumeau, 10 Aston Mead, St. Catharines Hill, Christchurch, Dorset, UK.

HOLECEK, Josef, b. 28 Oct. 1939, Prague, Czech. (Swedish national). Guitarist; Teachr of Classic Guitar; Composer; Editor. Educ: Dip., Conserv. of Music, Prague, 1965; Dip. Guitar, Akademie dür Musik und Darstellende Kunst, Wien, 1967. Career: Soloist & Chmbr. Musician w. Concerts, Radio & TV recordings in Europe, USA, Aust.; Hd. of Guitar Dept., Gothenburg Univ., Sweden. Publ. Comps: Ministudies for Guitar; Guitar Moods; Nevergreens; Guitar Jokes; Easy & Various; Guitars Together; Six Aquarelles; Swedish Romance; Temolo Pieces. Recordings incl: Works by B Britten & M Castelnuovo-Tedesco. Publs: Guitar method, Lar dig spela gitarr, 1975; Guitar method, Gitarrdags, 1979. Hons: Finalist, Concours Int. de

Guitare, organised by ORTF, Paris, 1966; Artist Award, Royal Swedish Acad. of Music, 1977. Address: Ovre Besvarsgatan 13, S-411 29 Goteborg, Sweden. 24, 28, 30.

HOLL, John William, b. 20 Feb. 1928, Danville, Ill., USA. Engineer; Musician (Clarinet, Saxophone, Flute). Educ: BS, MS, Univ. of Ill.; PhD, Pa. State Univ.; Chmbr. Music Ctr., Bennington, Vt., 8 yrs.; Pvte. study w. W B Holl, R Willaman, R Gorman, S Runyon, W Thomas, S Toulson. m. Antoinette Fillhouer, 2 s., 5 d. Career: Mbr., Randy Brooks Orch., 1945; Univ. of Ill. Band & Orch., 1945-49; Pa. State Orch., 1950-54; Symph. & Municipal Band, Lincoln, Neb., 1959-63; State Coll. Music Guild & Symph., Pa., 1963-. Recordings: Randy Brooks Orch. w. Ella Fitzgerald. Mbrships: Am. Fedn. of Musicians locals; Past Pres., State Coll. Music Guild; Phi Mu Alpha Sinfonia. Address: 1108 Mayberry Lane, State Coll., PA 16801, USA. 6.

HOLLAND, Dulcie Sybil, b. 5 Jan. 1913, Sydney Aust. Composer; Pianist; Lecturer; Adjudicator; Examiner, Australian Music Examinations Board. Educ: Shirley Coll.; NSW State Conservatorium; RCM, London; DSCM (Tchr's. Dip.); LRSM.; A Mus A; AM, 1977; Mbr., Inst. of Music Tchrs., 1978. m. Alan Bellhouse, 1 s., 1 d. Career: has made broadcast & concert apps., 1935-. Organist, St. Lukes Ch., NSW, 1975-. Compositions incl: many songs & pieces for piano, solo or w. other instruments. Recordings: Symphony for Pleasure; Ballad for Clarinet & Piano; 40 film scores. Publs: A History of Music, Senior School Harmony & From Beethoven to Brahms, all w. Alan Bellhouse, 1970; Dulcie Holland Musicianship, Grades I-VIII, 1972. Mbrships: Sec., Fellowship of Aust. Composers, 1970-; Coun., Aust. Soc. for Music Educ., 1972-73; Fine Arts Chmn., Bus. & Profl. Women's Clubs, 1962-66. Recip. sev. awards. Address: 67 Kameruka Rd., Northbridge, NSW 2068, Australia. 4, 29, 30.

HOLLAND, Jacynth, b London, UK. Musician (violin & viola). Educ: Royal Coll. of Music; ARCM (violin performer's). m. Antony Cleminson, 1 s., 1 d. Career: Violin, Birmingham Symph. Orch., 1945-50; Viola, Covent Gdn., 1969-71; Prin. Viola, BBC Concert Orch., 1973-. Hobbies: Reading; Travel; Chmbr. Music; Langs.; Arch. Address: 27 Upper Montagu St., London W.1, UK.

HOLLAND, James, b. 12 Feb. 1933, London, UK. Percussionist. Educ: LTCL. m. Rita Silke, 1 s., 1 d. Career: Prin. Percussion, LPO, 1957-62, LSO, 1967-72, London Sinfonietta, 1970-, BBC Symph. Orch., 1972-; Mbr., London Percussion Ensemble. Recordings: Bartok Sonata for 2 pianos & percussion (w. John Ogden, Brenda Locas & Eden Tamir); w. all above grps. Publs: Percussion (Menuhin Music Guides series), 1978. Mbr., ISM. Address: Stonelea, Village Rd., Coleshill, Amersham, Bucks., UK.

HOLLAND, Jon Burnett, b. 19 Mar. 1949, Rock Island, Ill., USA. Musicologist; Organist. Educ: BSc (secondary music educ.), S Ore. Coll., 1971; MA (music hist.), Univ. of Ore., 1978. m. Heather Lynne Hinchliff. Career: Organist, Zion Lutheran Ch., Medford, Ore.; organist & choirmaster, All Saints Anglican Ch. & Third Ave. United Ch., Saskatoon, Sask., Can.; Organist & choirmaster, First Presbyterian Ch., Cottage Grove, Ore.; Lectr., Univ. of Sask.; broadcast concert, Saskatoon radio. Mbrships: Royal Can. Coll. of Organists (chmn., Saskatoon Ctr., 1976-77); Am. Musicol. Soc. Address: 1720 Garfield St., Eugene, OR 97402, USA.

HOLLAND, Wilfrid Marshall, b. 27 June 1920, Hull, Yorks, UK. Teacher of Piano & Harpsichord. Educ: MA, Mus B, Cantab.; ARCO. m. Elizabeth Carroll Hele. Career: Dir. Music, Dover Coll., 1950-60; Cond., Dover Choral & Orchl. Socs., 1950-60; Dir. Music Canberra Grammar Schl., 1960-62; Examiner. Aust. Music Exams. Bd.; Cond., Canberra Choral Soc., 1960-70. Comps: (Anthem) Preserve Us O Lord; Part Songs: Wit & Beauty; Epitaph; Songs of Fancy & Fortune; Three Biblical Poems; Let's Sing a Carol. Hobby: Culinary Arts. Address: 85 Endeavour St., Red Hill, ACT 2603, Australia.

HOLLIER, Donald Russell, b. 7 May 1934, Sydney, Aust. Performer; Composer; Lecturer. Educ: BMus, DMus, London; DSCM (Dip. Tchng. & Perf.), Sydney Conserv., Aust. m. Sharman Ellen Pretty, 1 d. Debut: Sydney, 1955. Career: Apps. w. Sydney Symph., Qld. Symph., Canberra Symph.; 4 Aust. concert tours. Comps: Musicks Empire (baritone & orch.); Variations for Violin & Piano; 4 Dryden Songs for Baritone & Piano. Recordings: Magnificat (Clow); Dimensions for Piano (Sibsky); Piano Concerto (Benjamin); Dryden Songs (Hollier). Mbrships: Comps. Guild; Fellowship of Aust. Comps. Hons: Frank Shirley Memorial Prize, 1957; Churchill Fellowship, 1974; Maggs Award, 1975. Address: 13 Raoul Pl., Lyons, A.C.T., Aust.

HOLLIGER, Hans, b. 1939, Langenthal, Switz. Oboist; Composer. Educ: studied oboe w. Emile Cassagnaud & comp. w.

Pierre Boulez. Career: apps. in Japan, USA, Aust., Israel, etc. & at all major European fests. Comps. incl: Der magische Tänzer; Trio; Siebengesang; Wind Quartet; Dona nobis pacem; Pneuma; Pslam; Cariophonie; Kreis; Str. Quartet; Aternbogen. Has recorded for Philips, DGG & other cos. Recip. sev. prizes & awards. 16.

HOLLIMAN, Jamesetta, b. 17 Nov. 1938, Balt., Md., USA. Concert Pianist; Lecturer; Musicologist. Educ: BMus, Oberlin Coll., Ohio; MS, Juilliard Schl. of Music; PhD, NY Univ., Mozarteum, Salzburg, Austria. div. 1 s. Career: Concerts throughout USA as Recitalist, & orchl. Soloist w. Am. Symph., Brooklyn Phil., Symph. of the New World, etc.; Lecture-demonstration-recitals at NY & Johns Hopkins Univs. & on radio, Balt.; Repertoire incls. works of Max Reger, & var. black comps.; Chmn., Humanities Div. & Assoc. Prof. Music, Medgar Evers Coll., CUNY. Mbrships. incl: Afro-Am. Music Opportunities Assn.; MENC. Hons. incl. Concert Artist Guild Award, 1973; Outstanding Woman of Yr., Balt. Chapt., Alpha Kappa Alpha, 1975. Hobby: Reading. Address: 1627 N Bond St., Balt., MD 21213, USA.

HOLLINGSWORTH, Samuel H, Jr., b. 29 June 1922, Birmingham, Alabama, USA. Principal Bassist. Educ: studied w. Frederick Zimmermann, Juilliard Schl. of Music, NYC. m. Elizabeth Malezi-Hollingsworth, 1 d., 1 s. Career: Prin. Bassist, Nashville Symph., 1947-66, Chmbr. Symph. of Phila., 1966-68, Dallas Symph., 1968-70, Pitts. Symph., 1970-. Recordings: Gunther Schuller Bass Quartet; Dallas Symph., Donald Johanos, Cond. Address: 4403 Centre Ave., Apt. C6, Pitts., PA 15213, USA. 2.

HOLLINRAKE, Roger Barker, b. 2 June 1929, Auckland, NZ. Musical Scholar. Educ: Bernard Hale Organ Schlr., MA, MusB, Peterhouse, Cambridge Univ., UK; Fellow, Harvard Univ., USA, 1951-52; MA, DPhil. Merton Coll., Oxrord Univ., UK; Michael Foster Mem. Scholar, Heidelberg Univ., 1961-62; studied comp. w. Aaron Copland, Berkshire Music Ctr., USA; studied organ w. Fernando Germani, Rome (Italian Govt. schlrship.). Contbr. to: Music & Letters: Oxford German Studies; Nietzsche-Studien; Wagner Soc. Yrbook. Mbrships: Royal Musical Assn.; Int. Musicol. Soc.; Schopenhauer Gesellschaft e. V. Address: Flat 1, 6 Crick Rd., Oxford OX2 6QJ, UK.

HOLLISTER, Jane Love, b. 2 Nov. 1952, San Fran., Calif., USA. Symphony Violinist. Educ: BMus, Hartt Coll. of Music, Conn., 1975. Career: Violinist w. Hartford Symph. Orch., 1973-. Mbr., Alpha Chi (Charter mbr., Beta chapt., Univ. of Hartford). Hobbies: Sewing; Outdoor Activities; Reading. Address: 63 Milton St., W, Hartford, CT, USA.

HOLLOWAY, Clyde, b. 5 Sept. 1936, Clarksville, Tex., USA. Concert Organist; Teacher. Educ: BMus; MMus; SMD; AAGO. Career: Prof. of Music, Ind. Univ., 1965-. Mbrships: AGO; Phi Beta Kappa; Pi Kappa Lambda; St. Wilfrid. Hons: Fulbright Scholar, 1959-60; winner, Nat. Playing Competition, AGO, 1964. Mgmt: Lilian Murtagh Concert Mgmt., USA. Address: 2305 E Second St., Bloomington, IN 47401, USA.

HOLLOWAY, David, b. 12 Nov. 1942, Grandview, Mo., USA. Singer. Singer (Baritone). Educ: BM, MMus, Univ. Kan.; Santa Fe Opera Apprentice Prog.; Merola Opera Prog. of San Francisco Opera; Met. Opera Studio; Pvte. study w. Luigi Ricci, Rome, Italy. m. Deborah Seabury, 1 s. Debut: Belcore, l'Elisir d'Amore, Kan. City Lyric Theater, 1968. Career incls: Apps. w. maj. USA opera cos. inclng: Met. Opera; Apps. at Nat. Arts Ctr., Ottawa, Can. & Tanglewood Festival. Recordings: The Taming of the Shrew (CRI); Songs by Frederick Rzewski (Desto); Songs by Vally Weigle. Num. hons. inclng: Hi Fidelity Award, 1971. Hobbies: Camping; Fishing; Sailing; Motorcycling; Piano. Mgmt: Columbia Artists; Matthew Epstein. Address: c/o Epstein, Columbia Artists Mgmt., 165 W 57th St., New York, NY 10019, USA.

HOLLWEG, Werner Friedrich, b. 13 Sept. 1936, Solingen, W Germany. Opera & Concert Singer. Educ: Grad., Acad. of Music, Detmold, N W Germany. m. Constance Daucha, 2 c. Debut: Vienna Kammeroper, 1962. Career: Opera engagements in Brlin, Munich, Hamburg & Cologne; Concerts throughout the world; Regular apps. at Festivals in Salzburg, Vienna, Edinburgh, Munich & Berlin. Num. recordings. Hobbies: Sailing; Photography; Elec. Engrng. Address: D-565 Solingen, Eichenstrasse 71, W Germany.

HOLM, Peder, b. 30 Sept. 1926, Copenhagen, Denmark. Director of Academy of Music, Esbjerg; Conductor of Vestjysk Symfoniorkester, Esberg. Educ: studied piano, violin, theory, Royal Danish Acad. of Music, 1945-47. Compositions: approx. 50 in three groups, 1) music for profl. musicians, 2) music for amateurs & children, 3) group 1 & 2 in combination. Recordings: Pezzo concertante, 1964. w. the Danish Radio

Symph. Orch. (Holm cond.); String Quartet, 1967, The Danish Str. Quartet. Address: Skovbakken 34, 6700 Esberg, Denmark.

HOLMAN, Peter Kenneth, b. 19 Oct. 1946, Hillingdon, Middx., UK. Musician; Writer; Lecturer. Educ: BMus, MMus, London Univ. m. Therese Patricia Rimes, 2 d. Career incl: Fndr., specialist early music grp. Ars Nova; recitals throughout GB & Broadcasts on BBC Radio 3; Rschr. & writer on 17th Century Music; Lectr., NE Essex Tech. Coll.; Prof., Royal Acad. of Music; Editorial Advrs., Macmillans & Longmans. Publs: Ed. & intro. to Thomas Campion: Lord Hays Masque (1607) & Lord Somerset's Masque (1614), 1974. Contbr. to: Early Music & Musicians; The Consort, etc. Mbrships: Royal Musical Assn.; Inc. Soc. of Musicians; Viola da Gamba Soc.; Lute Soc. Hobbies: Steam Engines; Travel; Lit. Address: The White House, Leewick Ln., St. Osyth, Essex, UK.

HOLMBOE, Vagn, b. 20 Dec. 1909, Horsens, Jutland, Denmark. Composer. Educ: Dip., Royal Conserv., Copenhagen, 1929. m. Meta May Graf, 2 c. Career: Music Tchr., Inst. for Blinds, Copenhagen, 1940-49; Tchr., Royal Conserv. Copenhagen, 1950-55; Prof., ibid., 1955-65; Music Critic, Politiken, Copenhagen, 1947-55. Comps: Ten Symphs., 7, 8, 10, recorded; Fifteen String Quartets - publd., 1-11 recorded; Orchl. & Chmbr. Music - some recordings; Choirs. Ballets, Operas, etc. Publs: Mellemspil (interlude), Wilh Hansen, Copenhagen, 1961. Mbrships: Kung Musikaliska Akademien, Stockholm, 1957; Composers Guild, 1933-; on Bd., ibid., 1942-73. Recip., many prizes & awards. Address: Holmboevej 6, Ramlose, 3200 Helsinge, DK Denmark. 4, 19, 30.

HOLMES, Ralph, b. 1 April 1937, Penge, Kent, UK. Violinist. Educ: RAM London w. David Martin; w. George Enescu, Paris; w. Ivan Galamian, NY. m. Jeannette Ashby, 1 s. Debut: Mendelssohn Violin Concerto w. RPO, London, 1951. Career: Sev. first perfs.; Violin & Piano Duo w. Denis Matthews, 1964-72; w. Holmes Piano Trio, 1972-76; Mbr. of Jury, City of Glasgow Competition for Junior Violinists, 1975, John Players Int. Conds. Award, Bournemouth, 1976, Carl Flesch Int. Violin Competition, London, 1978; Frequent broadcasts & much solo playing, UK & abroad. Recordings: Sonatas for violin & piano, Delius; Hommage to Kreisler; Bartok/Reger/Prokofiev for solo violin; Vivaldi Seasons; Harty Violin Concerto; Tchaikovsky Violin Concerto. Mbr., ISM; RAM Club. Hons: Arnold Bax Memorial Medal, Harriet Cohen Int. Music Awards, 1955; Marguerite Long - Jacques Thibaud, Paris, 1957; Grand Prix, George Enescu Int. Competition, Bucharest, 1958; ARAM, 1958; B J Dale Award, 1965; FRAM, 1965. Address: 107 Foxgrove Rd., Beckenham, Kent BR3 2DA, UK. 3.

HOLMQUIST, Nils-Gustaf, b. 15 July 1906, Stockholm, Sweden. Author. Educ: Cond. & Comp., Hochschule für Musik, Berlin; Organ w. Albert Schweitzer; Cond. course, Lausanne, Switzerland w. W Furtwängler. m. Nancy Carlsson-Wennlund, 2 s. Career: Musician; Jrnlst.; Chief Ed.; Theatre Mgr., Prod. & Dir.; Prod. & Dir. about 500 films & 1200 Radio & TV progs.; Cond., Breslau Opera, Hoftheater, Bad Salzbrunn, Grand Theatre, Gothenburg, etc. Compositions incl: To a Wild Rose; The Girl in the Rain; Tango Harmony; Springtime; Pass für Anetta; Flikan fran Paris; Carina mia bella (all recorded). Contbr. to: Swedish jrnls. & newspapers. Mbr./, profl. assns. Hons: 1st Prize, Comp., 1930; Recip. 12 Orders of Chivalry. Hobbies: Music; Sport; Gardening. Address: Finca Limonero 1, Alfaz del Pi, Alicante, Spain.

HOLNTHANER, Eduard, b. 6 June 1944, Zwischenwassern, Althofen, Austria. Musician (Trumpet); Teacher. Educ: Dip., Classical & Jazz Trumpet, HS Music Gras, Austria. m. Ivana, 1 child. Career: Trumpet Soloist, Orf Big-Band, Vienna; RTV Orch., Ljubljana, Yugoslavia; Currently, Tchr., Jazz Trumpet, HS Music, Graz, Austria. Comps: num. jazz pieces & songs. Recordings: w. Orf, Vienna, & RTV, Ljubljana, Yugoslavia, & for Helidon Records. Mbr., Int. Sco. Jazz Rsch. Hobby: Rally Driving. Address: YU-62314 ZG, Polskava, Yugoslavia.

HOLOMAN, Dallas Kern, b. 8 Sept. 1947, Raleigh, NC., USA. Musicologist; Conductor. Educ: BA magna cum laude, Duke Univ., 1969; MFA, 1971, PhD, 1974, Princeton Univ. m. Elizabeth R Holoman. Career: Vis. Instructor of Music, Westminster Choir Coll., 1972; Fulbright-Hays Fellow, Paris, France, 1972-73; Asst. Prof. of Music, Univ. of Calif., Davis, 1975-; Dir., Early Music Ensemble, ibid.; Cond., Univ. of Calif. at Davis Symph. Orch. Publs: Ed., Berlioz, Roméo & Juliette (New Berlioz Ed.), forthcoming. Contbr. to: Acta Musicologica; Coll. Music Symposium; Early Music; Jrnl. of the Am. Musicolog. Soc.; other profl. jrnls. Mbrships: Am. Musicol. Soc.; Music Lib. Assn.; Assn. Nat. Hector Berlioz; Phi Beta Kappa. Hons: Woodrow Wilson Fellow, 1969-70. Address: 203 Aurora Ave., Davis, CA 95616, USA.

HOLROYD, John Dudley, b. 19 April 19343, Halifax, UK. Organist & Master of Choristers; Senior Lecturer in Music. Educ: FRCO (CHM); ARCM; ADCM; MusB, Trinity Coll., Dublin. m. Dorothy Mary Cockroft, 2 s. Career: Organist & Choirmaster, Halifax, Leeds, Hastings, High Wycombe, Bath; Hd. of Music, Aylesbury Grammar Schl.; Organist & Master of the Choristers, Bath Abbey, 1967-; Currently Sr. Lectr. in Music, Bath Coll. of Higher Educ.; Fndr. & Cond., Wessex Chmbr. Choir; Organ recitalist. Comps: Arr. of Carols (recorded). Recordings: A Festival of Carols from Bath Abbey; Music from Bath Abbey. Mbrships: RCO; RSCM. Hobbies: Fishing; Motoring. Address: 4 Ivy Bank Pk., Entry Hill, Bath, UK. 16.

HOLSCHNEIDER, Andreas Georg, b. 6 April 1931, Freiburg, German Fed. Repub. Musicologist. Educ: Freiburg, Musikhochschule, 1950-55; Tubingen & Heidelberg Univs.; PhD, Tubingen, 1960. Career: Asst., Sem. of Musicol., Hamburg Univ., 1961-67; Habil., Univ. Lectr., 1967; Prof. of Musicol. ibid., 1971; Hd., Archiv Produktion, Deutsche Grammophon Geslellschaft (Polydor), 1970-. Comps. incl: Die Gorgan von Winchester, 1968; Mozarts Arrangements of Works by Handel, Neue Mozart Ausgabe (Int. Stiftung Mozarteum), 1960. Mbrships: Int. Gesellschaft für Musikwissenschaft; Gesellschaft für Musikforschung; Plainsong & Medieval Music Soc., London, Joachim Jungins Gesellschaft der Wissenschaften, Hamburg. Contbr. to profl. publs. Address: 2 Hamburg-52 Müllenhoffweg 7, German Fed. Repub.

HOLST, Henry, b. 25 July 1899, Copenhagen, Denmark. Violinist. Educ: Royal Conservatoire, Copenhagen; Studied w. Prof. Willy Hess, Berlin; Hon. RCM, London. m. Else Werner, 2 c. Debut: Copenhagen, 1919. Career: Ldr., Berlin Phil. Orch., 1923-31; Prof., Royal MC Coll. of Music, 1931; Prof., RCM, London, 1946-56; Performed Sibelius Concerto w. Furtwangler & Sir Thomas Beecham; 1st European perf. of William Walton's Concerto, Royal Albert Hall, conducted by comp.; perfs. w. most loading orchs. in England, Guest Prof., Tokyo Univ. of Arts, 1961-63; Tchr. of Violin; Pres., Danish Sect., ESTA. Hons. Kt. of Order of Dannebrog, 1st Grads. Hobbies: Lit.; Memoirs; Motoring; Architecture. Address: Schimmelmannsvej 43, 2920 Charlottenlund, Denmark.

HOLST, Imogen Clare, b. 12 Apr. 1907, Richmond, Surrey, UK. Conductor; Lecturer & Writer on Music. Educ: Comp., RCM; ARCM (piano perf.). Recordings (as Cond.) of music og G Holst incl: Savitri; Rig Veda (III); Lyric Movement; Fugal Concerto; Double Concerto; 2 Songs without Words; St. Paul's Suite. Publs. incl: Gustav Holst: A Biography, 1938, 69; The Music of Gustav Holst, 1951, 68; Ed. Henry Purcell; Essays on his Music, 1959; Tune, 1962; An ABC of Music, 1963; Britten, 1966; Byrd, 1972; Holst, 1972; Conducting a Choir, 1973; Holst, 1974; A Thematic Catalogue of Gustav Holst's Music, 1974. Mbr., Royal Musical Assn. Hons: FRCM, 1966; Doct. Essex Univ., 1968; DLitt, Exeter Univ., 1969; RAM, 1970; CBE, 1975. Hobby: Walking. Address: 9 Church Walk, Aldeburgh, Suffolk 1P 15 5DU, UK. 1.

HOLSTEIN, Jean-Paul, b. 6 Nov. 1939, Angoulême, France. Composer; Professor. Educ: Dr. Musicol., Paris IV/Sorbonne, 1978; Conserv. Nat. Supérieur de Musique, Paris. m. Aline Charpentier, 2 s. Career incl: Fndr., Dir., l'École municipale de Musique du Raincy, 1967-73; Hd. of course for analysis & writing, Univ. of Paris/Sorbonne, 1969-; Prof. of analysis, Conserv. Nat. Supérieur de Musique, Paris, 1973-78; Prof. of counterpoint, ibid., 1978-. Comps. incl: symph. music, choral & instrumental works, chmbr. music. Recordings: La Guitare au XX siècle. Publs: Le Renouveau de la Symphonie française, 1870-1900; sev. pedagogic books. Mbrships: SACEM; Union Nat. des Compositeurs. Hons. incl: sev. 1st prizes, Conserv. Nat. Superieure de Paris; Chevalier du Mérite Cultural et Artistique. Hobby: Reading. Address: 68 rue Jouffroy, 75017 Paris, France.

HOLT, Anthony Edward, b. 6 Nov. 1940. Henley, UK. Singer (Baritone). Educ: Brighton Coll. & Christ Church, Oxford; MA, Oxon. m. Janette Buque, 1 d., 1 s. Career: Boy treble in Coronation, 1953; BBC Chorus, 1969; St. Paul's Cathedral Choir, 1970; 1st Baritone w. King's Singers, 1970-. Recordings (w. King's Singers) incl: French Collection; Madrigal Collection; Contemporary Collection; Concert Collection; Tallis Lamentations; Encore; Out of the Blue; Keep on Changing; Noël Coward & Flanders & Swain; Swing; Tempus Fugit; Lollipops; 18th Anniversary Concert; The King's Singers Collection; By Appointment; Captain Noah and His Floating Zoo; Deck the Hall; German & Spanish Madrigals; Requiem for Father Malachy; Medieval Scottish Music. Mbr., Soc. of Crudgemen. Hons: Best Classical record & Best Artist in any Category, Germany, 1977; Best Early Music Record, USA, 1974; German Folk Songs & Early Music Prizes, Germany, 1979. Hobbies: Reading; Travel; Sport; Ornithology. Address: 2 Grimwade Ave., Croydon, Surrey, CR0 5DG, UK.

HOLT, Carol Rosemary Smedley, b. 28 Dec. 1939, Birmingham, UK. Accompanist; Pianist; Harpsichord player; Organist. Educ: Grad., Birmingham Schl. of Music; Lic., Royal Acad. of Music; Assoc., Birmingham Schl. of Music; Cert. piano tchr. m. James Arthur Philip Holt, 1 s., 2 d. Contbr. to: Malvern Gazette. Mbr., Conductor, The Cradley Singers Choral Soc. Hons: J H Dowler Schlrship., 1959; Clarence Raybould Prize for Piano playing & accompaniment; Mervyn Cox Prize, 1959; Sydney & Eva Mary Grew Schlrship., 1960; St. Clare Barfield Rosebowl for accompaniment, 1961. Hobbies: Gardening; Needlework; Swimming; Cycling; Letter writing. Address: Dunhampstead Manor, Nr. Droitwich, Worcs., UK.

HOLTEN, Bo, b. 22 Oct. 1948, Rudköbing, Denmark. Composer; Music Critic; Editor. Educ: studied musicol., Univ. of Copenhagen. 2 c. Comps: Orchl. music, choral music, var. chmbr. music & songs; 1 opera. Recordings: Choral works; Choral arrs. of folksongs. Contbr. to: Weekendavisen; Danish Musicol. Jrnl. (ed.). Mbrships: Danish Comps. Soc.; Danish Journalist's Union. Address: Marstrandsgade 28, DK2100 Copenhagen Ö, Denmark.

HOLTZ, Josef, b. 1 Dec. 1930, Kreuzlingen, Switz. Conductor; Concert Organist; Composer; Music Teacher. Educ: State Dip., Organ Counterpoint & Composition, Zürich Acad. of Music; Concert Dip., Organ & Cond. Dip., ibid., Licensed, 1950. m. Annemarie Codoni, 3 s., 1 d. Debut: Organ & Choral Concert, Switz. Career: Cond., SBV; Concert Organist, SMPV; 30 perfs. on Radio Zürich & 4 TV perfs.; Music Tchr. Comps: publd. by Hug & Co., Zürich; Pelikan Verlag, ibid. & Lucerne Verlag. Author, num. publs. on organ-building, reviews on concerts & comps., Contbr. to Thurgau Newspapers. Mbr., Swiss Soc. Musical Rsch. Hobby: Organ-building (over 30 projs. in Switz. & Germany). Address: Tannenstrasse 13, CH-8500, Frauenfeld, Switz.

HULTZENDORFF, Virginia Sheffield, b. 23 Dec. 1914, Hazen, Ark., USA. Instructor of Piano, Organ & Theory; Church Organist. Educ: Grad., St. Louis Inst. of Music, Mo.; Wash. Univ.; BMus, LA State Univ., Baton Rouge; MM, Northwestern Univ., Evanston, Ill.; Pupil of Gottfried Galston, Mme. Schaffner, Prof. C Liddle, Van Horne. Career incls: Instr. of Piano, & Theory; Prof. in Carlisle Public Schls. & Ark.; Organist 1st Bapt. Ch., Hazen, Ark., 17 yrs.; formerly on Fac., Lander Coll., Greenwood SC & Sullins Coll., Bristol, Va.; num. recital apps., & on radio & TV. Mbrships. incl: Ark. State & Nat. MTA; Nat. Piano Tchrs. Guild of Am. Fac., & num. other profl. organizations. Recip. Cert. of Profl. Advancement, ASMTA. Hobbies incl: Concerts; Plays. Address: PO Box 352, Hazen, AR 72064, USA. 16, 27.

HOLTZMAN, Julie, b. 13 July 1945, Montreal, PQ., Can. Concert Pianist; Teacher. Educ: studied Psych. & Lit., McGill Univ. & Sir George Wms. Coll.; Grad., (premier prix), Conserv. of Music & Dramatic Arts, Montreal, Juilliard Schl., NY; studied piano w. Germaine Malepart, Rosina Lhevinne, & Dorothy Taubman & Chmbr. music w. Claus Adnam; studied w. Louis Bailly of Flonzaley Quartet & w. Ernst oster, NY. Debut: London, 1970. Career: gave world premiere of unpubld. Concerto in C. op. 14, by Franz Xavier Mozart, Queen Elizabeth Hall, London. w. Neville Dilkes & ENgl. Sinfonia Orch., 1970 (holds exclusive perf. rights to present ed. of piece), & Am. premiere of same piece, along w. world premiere F X Mozart's solo piece (unpubld., but recorded) "Quatre Polonaises Melancoliques" op. 22, w. Lukas Foss & Bklyn. Philharmonia, NYC, 1974; Can. premiere of Concerto in C, w. Alexander Brott Cond., live concert in Montreal, televised by Radio-Can. French TV, July 1974; has given concerts in USA, Can., Mexico & Europe; has performed on CBC, BBC & RTB (Belgian radio), WNYC radio & TV, WBAI & WQXR. Has made sev. recordings for Radio-Can. Int. Serv. Contbr. to profl. publs. Recip. num. prizes, schlrships., etc. Hobbies: Nature; Langs.; Writing; Theatre; Travel. Address: 205 W 57th St. (The Osborne), NYC, NY 10019, USA.

HOLTZWART, Fritz, b. 12 Jan. 1892, Liverpool, UK. Conductor; Composer. Musical Educ: studied w. Prof. Ivan Knorr, Prof. Bernhard Sekles, Prof. Fritz Bassermann (Gen. music Dir., Karl Schuricht), Dr. Hoch'sches Konservatorium, Debut: 1909. Career: Theatre conductor, var. places incing. Bamberg, Würzburg, Heidelberg & Ulm, 11 yrs.; Composer & Guest Conductor, 1928-; w. Frankfurt radio, 1938-. Compositions incl: Orchl. suites; 4 symphs.; choral works; songs; Halla (opera). Mbrships: Deutscher Musikverband; Komponistenverband, Berlin. Recip., Schubert Prize for Comp., Vienna, 1928. Hobby: Painting. Address: Eschersheimerlandstr. 276 pt., Frankfurt am Main, German Fed. Repub.

HOLZER, Gerhard, b. 15 Apr. 1932, Buenos Aires, Argentina (Swiss citizen). Composer; Graphic Artist. Educ: Studied theory w. Prof. Sandor Veress, Berne, comp. w. Prof. K Lechner, German Fed. Repub. m. Heidi Holzer-Saxer. Career: Comps.

performed on TV & radio, Switzerland, German Fed. Repub., Romania; art exhibs., Switzerland & German Fed. Repub., Romania; art exhibs., Switzerland & German Fed. Repub. Compositions incl: Exégèses pour Piano & Cordes; Begnunen (choir); MIssa pro defunctis; Chaka II (soprano, choir, orch., ballet); Concertos; piano pieces. Mbr., Swiss Musicians Unin. Hons: 2nd Prize, Pforzheim Chmbr. Orch., 1970; 1st Prize, Prince Pierre of Monaco Fndn., 1971; 2nd Prize, Swiss BAT, 1974; 3rd Prize, Opera & Ballet Competition, Geneva, 1975. Address: Jurablickstrasse 14, CH 3028 Spiegel-Bern, Switzerland.

HOLZKNECHT, Václav, b. 2 May 1904, Prague, Czech. Musician (piano); Writer. Educ: Fac. of Law, Univ. of Prague; Dip., Prague Conserv. Debut: w. Czech. Phil., 1928. Career: Concert Pianist; Prof. of Piano, Prague Conserv., 1942-46; Artistic Dir., ibid., 1946-70; Ldr. of Opera, Nat. Theatre, Prague, 1970-73; Critic; Writer. Publs: A Dvorák, 1955; J Jezek & the Liberated Theatre, 1957; Debussy, 1958; Ravel, 1967; Schubert, 1972; Isa Krejcí, 1976. Contbr. to Hudebni Rozhledy; Gramo review. Mbrships: Czech. Union of Comps. & Musical Performers; Czech. Union of Actors. Hons: Order of Labour, 1964; Distinction for Outstanding Work, 1961; Golden Prize of Panton, 1973; Prize of Nejedlý, 1978. Hobbies: Lit., Plastic Arts. Address: Prague 1, Staré Mesto, Siroka 10, Czech.

HOMS OLLER, Joaquin, b. 21 Aug. 1906, Barcelona, Spain. Composer; Violoncellist; Engineer. Educ: Grad. Ind. Engr., 1929; Prof., Violoncello; Studied w. Roberto Gerhard. m. Pietat Fornesa Alvina, 1 c. Comps. incl: 125 works until 1976 (83 instrumental & 42 vocal works). Recordings incl: A monographic record w. 3 Impromptus; Soloquin 1, String Trio & Wind Quintet. Publs: Spanish transl. of Tonality, Atonality, Partonality of Rudolph Reti w. original introduction. Contbr. of reviews to newspapers & jrnls. Mbrships: Pres., Catalan Comps. Assn., 1975-76. Hons. incl: Music Prize, City of Barcelona for Comp. Presencies for orch., 1967. Address: Calle San Mario 4, Atico 2a, Barcelona 6, Spain.

HONEGGER, Henri Charles, b. 10 June 1904, Geneva, Switz. Cellist. Educ: Cello studied, Geneva; Leipzig (w. Julius Klengel); Ecole Normale, Paris, w. Diran Alexanian & Pablo Casals. m. Claire Pallard, 1 s., 1 d. Career: Soloist w. major European Orchs., N & S Am. & Japanese Orchs.; Gave 1st perf. of entire set of Bach's Suites in NY, 1950, Leipzig, 1952, China (1st western musician invited to give concerts in Peking, Shanghai, etc.); TV apps., Tokyo, Hong Kong, Singapore, etc.; Num. fest. apps. Num. recordings. Hobbies: Mountaineering; Skiing. Mgmt: Basil Doublas Ltd., 8 St. George's Tce., London NW1 8XJ, UK. Address: 21 Chemin de Conches, CH 1231 Conches, Switz.

HONEGGER, Marc, b. 17 May 1926, Paris, France. Musicologist. Educ: Lic. in Letters, Sorbonne, 1950; DLitt, ibid., 1970. m. Geneviève Weltz, 4 s., 1 d. Career: Asst., Paris Musicol. Inst., 1954; Asst. Lectr., Musicol. Inst., Strasbourg Univ., 1958; Lectr., Univ. of Strasbourg II, 1970; Titular Prof., ibid., 1972. Recordings incl: The Tournai Mass; Renaissance Polyphonies. Publs. incl: The Sacred Songs of Didier Lupi II and the Beginnings of Protestant Music in 16th Century France, 1970; Dictionnaire de la Musique, 4 volumes, 1970-76. Contbr. to var. profl. jrnls. & publs. Mbrships. incl: Pres., French Musicol. Soc. Hobby: Walking. Address: 4 rue Blessig, 67000 Strasbourg, France.

HONES, Julia Anne, b. 15 March 1944, Sidcup, Kent, UK. Clarinet & Other Woodwind Teacher; Musician (Clarinet & Bass Clarinet). Educ: Roedean Schl. London Univ., 1964-65; RAM, 1965-68; w. Alan Hacker; ALCM (Clarinet). m. Michael Bell, 2 d. Career: Mbr., London Jr. & Sr. Orchs.; Edinburgh Rehearsal Orch., Carnegie Fest. Orch.; Freelance player, Lewisham Concert Band, Dartford Symph. Orch.; Peripatetic Woodwind Tchr., ILEA & Bexley Borough; Woodwing & Clarinet Choirs, Bexley Music Schl.; Own Clarinet Choir (Clarinetics); 40 pvte. pupils. Recordings w. Royal Choral Soc., 1963-68. Mbrships: ISM; CASS. Hons: Clarinetics, winner of num. competitions, etc. Hobbies: Choral singing; Travel; Good Food. Address: 490 Hurst Rd., Bexley, Kent, UK.

HONEY, Albert Edward, b. 29 April 1919, Torquay, Devon, UK. Lecturer in Music; Military Band Director; Composer; Arranger (Flute). Educ: TCM, London; Dip., Conservatoire Nat. de Musique, Paris; LRAM; ARCM; LGSM; MMus, 1970; PhD, Rhodes Univ., S Africa, 1973. m. Jean Enid Farr, 2 s., 1 d. Career: Prin. Flute, Band of Royal Dragons, 1941-45; Band of H M Coldstream Guards, 1945-49; Scottish Nat. Orch., Glasgow, 1951-54; BBC Revenue Orch., 1954-64; Lectr., Dept. of Music, Rhodes Univ., S Africa, 1967; Bandmaster, Prince Alfred's Guard, S Africa Defence Force, Pt. Elizabeth. Recip. Silver Medal (Tchr's. Flute) LGSM, 1961.

Hobbies: Comp. & Arranging; Numismatics. Address: "Quavers", France St., Grahamstown 6140, S Africa. 3.

HONG, Yat-Lam, b. 22 Aug. 1940, Shanghai, China. Piano Technician. Educ: BMus, Ind. Univ., USA, 1965; MMus, ibid., 1967. m. Barbara Jean Blanchard, 3 c. Career: Music Instructor, Piedmont Coll., Demorest, Ga., 1967-69; Piano techn., Ind. Univ., Bloomington, 1971-73; Piano techn., Western Mich. Univ., Kalamazoo, 1973-; Tech. Ed., The Piano Technician's Journal, 1977-78; Registered Craftsman Mbr., Piano Techns. Guild. Hons: Guest pianist, Am. Liszt Soc. Fest., Provo, Utah, 1968. Hobbies: Playing piano transcriptions of operatic & orchl. lit.; Jogging. Address: 2904 Grace Rd., Kalamazoo, MI 49007, USA.

HONINGH, P, b. 10 June 1935, Winkel (NH), Netherlands. Clarinettist. Educ: Dip., Amsterdam Conserv., m. H C Helman, 1 c. Debut: 1957. Career: Concertgebouw Orch., 1961; mbr., Danzi Quintet, 1962-78; tchr., The Hague Conserv. & Sweelinck Conserv., Amsterdam. Recordings: Beethoven, Brahms, Ries Trios; Reich Clarinet Quintet; num. recordings w. Danzi Quintet. Hobby: Playing Old Clarinets. Address: Anna van Buren Laan 38, 2012 SM Haarlem, Netherlands.

HONKANEN, Antero Terho, b. 3 Apri. 1941, Kesälahti, Finland. Music Recording Tone Man; Electronic Composer. Educ: Studied electronic music, Finland, Holland & Sweden, 7 yrs. m. Seija I Miettinen, 1 s., 1 d. Debut: Finland, 1966. Career: Perfs. of music in radio concerts, 1966, 67, 68, Paris Biennale, 1973, Denmark, 1974, Paris Fest., Int. Soc. Contemporary Music, 1975. Compositions incl: (electronic) Japanese Cherrytree; The Milky Way; LSDF; Strontium; Meteor; Romeo & Julia (TV film), 1972; Midnight; Nightmare; Something About Freedom (TV documentary), 1974-75; Convent in a Whirling Snowstorm; Killmoney; (recorded) Ode to Marilyn, 1974. Mbrships incl: Finnish Soc. of Comps. Hobbies incl: Painting in Oils; 8 mm Film Making. Address: Laajaniityntie 10 D 48, 01620, Vantaa, 62, Finland.

HOOD, Alexander, b. 25 May 1930, Glasgow, UK. Tenor; Actor. Educ: RSAM. m. Elizabeth Gracie, 2 s., 1 d. Debut: As Singer, Scottish Light Orch. Career: Created tenor role in La Mere Coupable, Bath; 1st Tenor Solo, Brit. premiere, Alfano's Rissurezione; sang Canio, Calaf, Florestan, Cavaradossi & many other roles in the UK & on Continent; Pantomime, shows, concerts. Hons: Ayrshire Music Fest., Lanark Music Fest., 1956. Hobbies incl: Golf; Philosophy; Driving; Teaching; singing. Address: 23 Harrow View Rd., London W5, UK. 3.

HOOD, Ann Neville, b. 23 May 1940, Middleton, Manchester, UK. Principal of Solo Singer. Educ: LRAM. Debut: Royal Opera House, Covent Gdn. Career: Prin. Soprano, D'oyly Carte Opera Co.; Prin. Soprano, Engl. Nat. Opera. Recordings of Gilberg & Sullivan Operas w. D'Oyly Carte. Hobbies: Reading; Gardening; Sport. Mgmt: Music Int. Address: 23 Buntingford Rd., Buckeridge, Herts. SG11 1RT, UK.

HOOD, Burrel Samuel III, b. 14 Dec. 1943, Hattiesburg, Miss., USA. Professor of Music Education (Brass). Educ: BSc, Instrumental Music Educ.; MMus Educ.; EdD. m. Billie Lane Williams Hood, 1 d. Career: Dir. of Bands & Chmn. of Music Dept., Phila. City Schls., Miss.; Ch. Music Dir.; Teaching Asst., Brass & Music Educ.; prof. of Music educ. (Brass & Methods of Teaching), Miss. State Univ.; Festival Adjudicator. Contbr. to Jrnl. of Rsch. in Music Educ.; Miss Music Educators Jrnl. Mbrships. incl: Music Educators Nat. Conf.; Nat. Assn. of Coll. Wind & Percussion Instructors; Phi Kappa Phi; Phi Mu Alpha Sinfonia; Miss. Alliance for Arts Educ.; Miss., Music Educators Assn.; Phi Delta Kappa. Hons. incl: 1st Chair Scholarship, Miss. State Univ., 1963-66. Hobby: Barbershop Quartet. Address: 411 Myrtle St., Starkville, MS 39759, USA.

HOOD, Marguerite Vivian, b. Drayton, ND, USA. Professor of Music. Educ: BA, Jamestown Coll., ND, MMus, Univ. of Southern Calif.; DMus, Jamestown, Piano Dip., ibid., Northwestern Univ. Chgo. Musical Coll.; MMusEd, Univ. of Southern Calif. Career: State Music Supvsr., Mont.; Prof., Mont. State Univ., Univ. of Southern Calif., Univ. of Mich., Univ. of Cinn.; Guest Prof., Columbia Univ.; Univ.'s of Colo., Tex., Mo.; Westminster Choir Coll.; Prof. of Music Emeritus, Schl. of Music, Univ. of Mich., Ann Arbor; Choral Cond., Ann Arbor May Fest., 1943-58; Speaker at num. Confs. Publs: Singing Days, 1936; On Wings of Song, 1944; Learning Music Through Rhythm, 1948; Let's Sing, 1952; Kindergarten Music Book, 1958; Art Songs for Treble Voices, 1967; Teaching Rhythm & Using Classroom Instruments in School, 1972. Contbr. to bar. Music Educ. Books, num. profl. mags. & jrnls. Mbrships: MENC; Past Pres., ibid.; Past Chmn., Ed. Bd., Music Educators Jrnl., ibid.; Past Chmn., Commission on Accreditation of Tchr. EWduc., ibid.; Past

Chmn., Committee on Int. Rels., ibid.; Bd. of Dirs., Int. Soc. for Music educ., 1972-. Recip. var. Hons inclng: Hon. Mbr., Int. Soc. for Music Educ., 1974. Hobbies: Travel; Record Collecting; Cooking. Address: 1540 Packard St., Ann Arbor, MI 48104, USA.

HOOD, Walton Donnie, III, b. 15 Nov. 1933, Houston, Tex., USA. French Horn Player; Band Director. Educ: BMus, MMus, Univ. of Tex. at Austin. Career: Prin. French Horn, Austin Symph., 1955-56; Band Dir., Lake Jackson Jr. High Schl., Tex., 1958-65; Band Dir., Angleton High Schl., Tex., 1965-. Mbrships: Tex. Music Educators; Tex. Bandmasters Assn.; UIL Music Advsry. Sub-Committee; Phi Beta Mu; Phi Mu Alpha Sinfonia. Address: 6 Pine Pl., Angleton, TX 77515, USA.

HOOGENAKKER, Virginia Ruth, b. 8 Apr. 1921, Des Moines, Iowa, USA. Violinist. Educ: BMus, Belhaven Coll.; MMUs, Chgo. Musical Coll. Career: Chmn., Dept. of Music, Belhaven Coll., Jackson, Miss.; Chmn., Div. of Fine Arts & Assoc. Prof. of Violin & Music Theory, ibid.; Prin. 2nd Violin, Jackson Symph. Orch.; Musical Dir., Ascension Luth. Ch. Contbr. to Jrnl. of Ch. Music. Mbrships: Nat. VP, Mu Phi Epsilon, 1962-68; Provincial Gov., ibid., 1962-68; Pres., Miss. Music Tchrs. Assn., 1973-74; Bd., ibid., 1966-76; Worship & Music Comm., Southeastern Synod, Luth. Ch. in Am. Hon: Alumnus of Yr., Belhaven Coll., 1963. Hobby: Gardening. Address: 2020 Plantation Blvd., Jackson, MS 39211, USA. 5, 7.

HOOGERWERF, Frank W, b. 24 June 1946, The Netherlands. Musicologist; Assistant Professor of Music. Educ: BA, Calvin Coll., Grand Rapids, 1969; MMus, Univ. of Mich., 1970; PhD, musicol., ibid., 1974. m. Sharon Scripps Hoogerwerf. Career: Tchng. Fellow, Univ. of Mich., 1972-74; Asst. Prof. of M usic, Emory Univ., 1974-79; Assoc. Fac., Emory Univ. Grad. Inst. of the Liberal Arts, 1978-79; Departmental Lib. Rep., 1974-79; Fac. Supervisor, Music Dept. Listening Lab.; Co-ordinator, concerts, lecture series, profl. meetings; Reviewer, Nat. Endowment for the Arts; Adjudicator, Atlanta Symph. Young People's Artist Competitions. Contbr. to profl. publs. Mbrships. incl: Am. Musicol. Soc. (Chmn., S Central Chapt., 1978-79); Coll. Music Soc.; Sonneck Soc.; Music Lib. Assn.; Vereniging voor Nederlandse Muziekgeschiedenis. Hons. incl: Ford Fndn. Grants, 1972-74; Emory Fac. Rsch. Grants, 1976-77, 78-79; Ga. Coun. for the Humanities Grant, 1977. Address: 1293 Willivee Dr., Decatur, GA 30033, USA.

HOOKE, Wayne Raymond, b. 5 Jan. 1941, Melbourne, Australia. Double Bassist. Educ: Cert. of Adv. Studies, Montreal Conserv., Can. m., 3 c. Career: Kingston & Quebec Symphs., Can.; Melbourne Symph., Aust.; CBC & Aust. Broadcasting Commn. TV; Solo Bassist, Lee Grands Ballets Can.; Prin. Double Bass, Tas. Symph. Aust. Recordings: Aust. Broadcasting Commn. Hobbies: Walking; Reading. Address: c/o Aust. Broadcasting Commn., Box 205B, Hobart, Tas. 7001, Australia.

HOOKER, Ian Anthony, b. 18 Aug. 1948, Pinner, Middx., UK. Director of Music; Conductor. Educ: Beckwith Schlr., Royal Coll. of Music; Grad., ibid.; Assoc., ibid. for piano perf.; Coll. of St. Mark & St. John, Chelsea, London; Cert. Educ., ibid. Career: Dir. of Music, Dr. Challoner's Grammar Schl., 1971-; Conductor, Bucks. Youth Choir w. tour of Brittany; Challoner's Boys Choir in BBC prod. of Opera Hansel & Gretel. Recordings: The Golden Vanity by Benjamin Britten; Litanies a la Vierge Noire by Francis Poulenc. Contbr. to: Times Educational Supplement. Mbrships: Incorp. Soc. of Musicians; Asst. Masters & Mistresses Assn. Recip. Fndn. Schlrship., 1967. Hobbies: Theatre; Books. Address: 1 Outfield Cottages, Bowstring Lane, Chalfont St. Giles, Bukcks., UK.

HOOPER, William Loyd, b. 16 Sept. 1931, Sedalia, Mo., USA. Professor. Educ: Dip. in Music, Southwest Bapt. Coll., Bolivar, Mo., 1951; BA, Wm. Jewell Coll., Liberty, Mo., 1953; MA, Univ. of Iowa City, 1956; PhD, Geo. Peabody Coll. for Tchrs., Nashville, Tenn., 1966; student of Humphrey Searle, RCM, London, 1969-70. m. Doris J Wallace, 1 s., 1 d. Career: Prof. of Voice & Dir. of Choral Activities, Southwest Bapt. Coll., 1956-60; Prof. of Music Theory, New Orleans Bapt. Sem., 1962-; Dean, ibid., 1964-74; currently Hd. of Music, Newstead Wood Schl. for Girls, Orpington, Kent. Compositions: Jubilee, cantata for SATB & instruments; Litany of Praise, cantata for two equal voices & organ; Sing Joyfully, coll. of easy hymn-anthem arrangements; My Soul Waiteth in Silence, SATB anthem; over 30 other ch. anthems. Publs: Church Music in Transition, 1963; Music Fundamentals, 1967. Mbrships: Am. Soc. Univ. Comps.; Soc. for Promotion of New Music, UK; MENC. etc. Hons: First Prize, New Times Comp. Competition, 1972 & Delius Comp. Competitions, 1973. Address: 16 Greenway, Chislehurst, Kent BR7 6JE, UK. 23, 29.

HOPE, Eric, b. Warwick, UK. Concert Pianist. Educ: Pvte. music study in London w. Kathleen Arnold, Solomon & Reizenstein; in Vienna w. Joseforvicz; ARCM Debut: Royal Albert Hall Promenade Concert w. BBC Symph. Orch. & Sir Adrian Boult. Career incl: Concert perfs. throughout Europe; num. apps. at Royal Fest. Hall, Dubrovnik Int. Festival & w. all leading orchs., in UK; Num. radio & TV broadcast perfs.; Prof., LCM, 1960-; Prof., RAM, 1973-. Comps: Transcription for piano of Handel's Arrival of the Queen of Sheba (Hinrichsen). Recordings incl: Mozart Sonatas (Decca label) & Beethoven Sonatas (Delyse label). Publs: A Handbook of Piano Playing, 1954; Basic Piano Exercises, 19623; Aids to Technique, 1965; Contbr. to The Music Tchr. Mbrships: RAM: Hons: Hon. FLCM, 1963; Hon. ARAM, 1974; Hon. RAM, 1978. Hobbies: Langs.; Visiting Art Galls.; Travel. Address: 6 East Heath Rd., Hampstead, London NW3 1BN, UK. 1.

HOPFMÜLLER, Martin Christian, b. 4 July 1929, Munich, German Fed. Repub. Music School Professor; Organist; Choir Conductor; Hymnologist; Composer; Lecturer. Educ: Dip., Evangelical Ch. Music, Stuttgart Music Schl., 1952. m. Elisabeth Rudolph, 3 s. Career: Lectr., Evangelical Ch. Music, Vienna Univ. Contrbr. to: Der Kirchenmusiker; Gottesdienst und Kirchenmusik. Mbrships: Int. Arbeitskreis für Musik, Kassel; Int. Heinrich-Schultz-Gesellschaft; Arbeitsgemeinschaft der Musikerzieher Österreichs; Int. Arbeitsgemeinschaft für Hymnologie. Hobbies: Gliding & power pilot & instruction; Renaissance music (playing viols & recorders). Address: 7432 Oberschützen 275, Austria. 28, 30.

HOPKINS, Antony, b. 21 Mar. 1921. Musician; Author. Educ: RCM. London, UK. m. Alison Purves, 1947. Career: Lectr., RCM, 15 yrs.; Gresham Prof. of Music, City Univ., London; Cond., Norwich Phil. Soc.; Dir., Intimate Opera Co., 1952-64. Compositions incl: (operas) Lady Rohesia; Three's Company; Hands Across the Sky; Dr. Musikus: Ten O'Clock Call; The Man from Tuscany; (ballets) Etude; Cafe des Sports; (works for young people) A Time for Growing; Rich Man, Poor Man, Beggar Man, Saint; 3 Piano sonatas; Num. scores fo incidental music inclng. Oepidus, The Love of Four Colonels, Cast a Dark Shadow. Hons: Chappell Gold Medal at RCM, 1943; Italia Prize for radio prog., 1951 & '57; Medal, City of Tokyo for servs. to music, 1973. CBE, 1976. Address: Woodyard, Ashridge, Berkhamsted, Herts., UK. 1, 3, 14.

HOPKINS, John Raymond, b. 19 July 1927, Preston near Hull, UK. Conductor. Educ: Cello student, RMCM; ARMCM; FRMCM. m. Ann Rosemary Blamey, 5 d. Career: Asst. Cond., BBC Northern Orch., 1952-57; Cond., Nat. Orch. NZ, Musical Dir., NZ Opera Co., 1957-63; Dir. of Music, Aust. Broadcasting Commission, 1963-73; Dean, Schl. of M usic, The Vic. Coll. of the Arts, Melbourne, Aust., 1973-; Guest Cond. throughout the world. Recordings: w. Sydney Symph, Orch., Melbourne Symph. Orch., NZ Symph. Orch., Moscow Symph. Orch., etc. Hons: OBe, 1970; Queen's Silver Jubilee Medal. Hoby: Gardening. Address: The Victorian Coll. of the Arts, 234 St. Kilda Rd., Melbourne, Vic. 3004, Aust.

HOPKINS, Zuilmah Bland, b. 11 Apr. 1925, Dublin, Eire. Soprano Singer; Teacher. Educ: Won Scholarships, Piano & Singing w. Percy Whitehead, Alexandra Coll., Dublin; ARCM; studied w. Louise Trenton & Lady Hamilton Harty (London), Dr. John Hutchinson (Newcastle). m. James Winterschladen, 2 s., 2 d. Debut: Radio Eireann, 1946. Career: 2 seasons w. Glyndebourne Opera; Arts Coun. Opera for All; perfs. w. Opera Nova & Palatine Opera (incl. Medea, by Cherubini); oratorio & recital work in UK & Eire; apps. on radio & TV in UK, Eire & Switz.; vis. singing lectr., Tchrs. Traning Coll., Middlesborough Polytechnic; pvte. tchr. Mbrships: ISM; Northern Arts Music Panel. Hobbies: Theatre; Art; Animal & Wildlife Conservation; Cookery. Mgmt: Ibbs & Tillett, London. Address: The Manor House, GT. Ayton, Middlesborough, Cleveland, UK.

HOPPIN, Richard Hallowell, b. 22 Feb. 1913, Northfield, Minn., USA. University Professor. Educ: AB, Carleton Coll., Northfield, Minn., 1936; MA, Harvard Univ., 1938; PhD, ibid., 1952; Ecole Normale de Musique, Paris, 1933-35. m. Jean Rice. Career: Asst. Prof. of Piano & Hist., Mt. Union Coll., Alliance, Ohio, 1938-42; Teaching Asst., Harvard Univ., 1946-49; Asst. to Assoc. Prof. of Music Hist., Ohio State Univ., Columbus, 1961-. Publs: The Cypriot-French Repertory of the Manuscript Torino, Biblioteca Nazionale, J.11.9, in 4 volumes, 1960-63; Cypriot Plainchant of the Manuscript Torino, Biblioteca Nazionale, J.11.9, 1968; Mediaeval Music, 1978; Anthology of Mediaeval Music, 1978-. Contbr. to; The Musical Quarterly; Musica Disciplina; Revue belge de musicol.; Grove's Dictionary of Music & Musicians. Mbrships: Editl. Bd. of Jrnl., Am. Musicol. Soc.; Int. Musicol. Soc.; Renaissance Soc. of Am. Hons: Fulbright Rsch. Grant, 1954-55; Guggenheim Fellow, 1959-60; Dr. of Humane Letters (Honorary), Carleton

College, 1977. Hobbies: Gardening; Travel. Address: 331 Brevoort Rd., Columbus, OH 43214, USA. 11.

HOPWOOD, Barbara Helen, b. 21 June 1951, Epsom, Surrey, UK. Guitarist. Educ: studied w. John Prior & John Mills; ALCM (guitar), 1974. m. Ken Bates. Debut: London, 1970. Career: Tutor, Sutton Coll. of Liberal Arts, 1973-; pvte. guitar tchr., 1970-; guitar recitals, Europe Gallery, Whitehall House, etc. mbr., ISM. Address: 61 Stag Leys, Ashtead, Surrey, UK.

HORA, Jan, b. 7 Dec. 1936, Prague, Czechoslovakia. Organist. Educ: Music Conserv., Prague; Acad. of Music, Prague; High Schl. of Music, Weimar. m., 2 d. Debut: 1955. Career: Organist, New Town Hall, Prague; Piano Accompanist. Prof., Prague Music Conserv.; High Schl. of Music, Prague, 1977; Concerts, E, W Germany, Belgium, Holland, Switzerland, Austria, Sweden, Denmark, Poland. USSR. Recordings: Brahms, organ works; Prague organs; organ recitals. Hons: Hon. Dips., Int. Competitions, Munich, 1957, Prague, 1958; 3rd prizes, Int. Bach. Competitions, Ghent, 1958, Leipzig, 1964. Hobbies: Fine Arts; Architecture. Address: Sluknovska 321, 190 00 Prague 9, Czechoslovakia.

HORAK, Jaroslav, b. 8 April 1914, Krosna, Zitomir, Ruddia, Czech. Musician; Violinist opra-viola da Gamba; Recorder; Viola d'Amore. Educ: Music Conserv., Prague, study w. Prof. Bedrich Voldan. m. Helena Komstova, 1 s., 1d. Debut: w. Czech Phil., 1939. Career: Violin, Czech. Phil. Orch.; Viola da Gamba, Recorders, Pro Arte Antiqua; Mbr., Viola d'Amore Trio; Duo, w. Frantisek Posta (contra-bass); Num. apps., radio, TV, and tours of Europe, USA, Can., Aust., NZ, Japan, India, China; Prof., Old Instments & Viola, Prague Conserv., 1953-. Num. recordings. Hons: Deserving Mbr., Czech. Phil. Orch., 1971. Hobby: Photography. Address: Matousova 10, 150 000 Prague 5 Smichov, Czech.

HORÁK, Josef, b. 24 Mar. 1931, Znojmo, Czech. Concert Artist; Music Educator. Educ: Attended State High Schl. for Musical & Dramatical Arts. m. Elfrida Horáková. Career: Clarinetist, Czech. Radio Symph. Orch. & State Phil., Brno; Concert Soloist; Prof., State Music High Schl., Prague; Chmbr. Music Lectr., Biberach, W Grmany; Mbr., Chmbr. Music Ensemble Due Boemi Di Praga w. Emma Kovárnová. Prague, 1963-: Concerts in Europe & Africa; TV Progs. in Czech. & W Germanyh; Radio Progs., many countries of Europe; Discovered a new solo instrument--the bass clarinet, 1955. Recordings: Due Boemi di Praga (Panton); At the New Ways (Supraphon); Bass Clarinet, the New Solo Instrument (Corona); The Bass Clarinet Plays Paganini; Due Boemi & Inspiration. Mbrships: Union of Czech. Comps. & Interpreters; Hon. Mbr., Jeunesses Musicales de Suisse. Hons: Gold Medal, 1958; Prize, L Janacek Competition, 1959; Hi-Fi Fest., Paris, 1965, Czech Music Fndn., 1967. Address: Ovenecká 36, 170 21 Prague 7, Czech. 14.

HORAN, Albert Henry, b. 25 Sept. 1932, Newark, NJ, USA. Recorder Artist; Vocalist. Educ: BS & MBA Seton Hall Univ.; attended Seton Hall Univ. Schl. of Law; studied recorder w. Kenneth Wollitz & Philip Newman, & voice w. Marl Rhone. Career: Recorder Perfs. (solo & w. var. early music grps.) thru'out NJ & Metrop. NY area; Vocal & Recorder Soloist, Lutnia Choir. Asst. to local music grps. as lead tenor. Mbrships: Lutnia Choir; Am. Recorder Soc. Recip. of Griffith Music Fndn. Award. Hobbies: Collecting Recorders, Early Musical Instruments & Early Music Compositions; Chess; Go; Decoupage. Address: 205 Richelieu Terr., Newark, NJ 07106, USA. 6.

HOREIN, Kathleen Marie, b. 17 Jan. 1952, Indpls., Ind., USA. Oboist; Music Teacher. Educ: BS (music educ.) Ball State Univ., Muncie, Ind., 1974; studied oboe w. Warren Sutherland, Judith Pence, Eric Barr, Ralph Strobel, Joseph Turner. m. Timothy D Horein. Career: perfs. w. Brevard Music Ctr. Orch., Brevard, NC, 1973; Harrisburg Symph. Orch., Pa.; York Symph., Pa.; Lancaster Symph. Orch., Pa.; York Symph., Pa.; Lancaster Symph. Orch., Pa.; Lancaster Opera Workshop Orch., Pa.; Midwest Chmbr. Ensemble; Capital Woodwind Quintet; Ionian Woodwind Quintet; general freelancing. Mbrships: Pi Kappa Lambda; Am. Musicol. Soc.; Int. Double Reed Soc.; Sigma Alpha Iota (VP, coll. chapt.). sev. colls & soc. awards. Address: RD No. 2, N View Dr., Ephrata, PA 17522, USA.

HORN, Lois Burley, b. 8 Sept. 1928, Syracuse, NY, USA. Lecturer in Piano; Concert Pianist; Teacher. Educ: BMus, Syracuse Univ.; MMus, Mich. State Univ.; Aspen Schl. of Music; Summer; pvte. study w. Leon Fleisher, 1956-. m. Allen F Horn, 2 s., 1 d. Career: Lectr. in Piano, Cazenovia Coll., NY.; Tchr. of Piano to gifted & handicapped students. Mbrships. incl: Sigma Alpha Iota (province VP, 12 yrs.); Civic Morning Musical Inc., Syracuse (Bd. of Dirs. 15 yrs.); NY State Assn. Music Tchrs. (Past Pres.); Eltinge Guild of Pianist (past pres.); Pro Arte; Bd. of Dirs., NY Fedn. of Music Clubs. Hons. incl: Tuition Scholarship,

1946-50; Crouse Award for Keyboard Excellence, 1975. Hobby: Gardening. Mgmt: Chambers Artists Mgmt. Address: 3978 Pompey Ctr. Rd., Manlius, NY 13104, USA. 4.

HORNE, Marilyn, b. 16 Jan. 1934, Bradford, Pa., USA. Mezzo-Soprano. Educ: studied w. William Vennard, Univ. of Southern Calif. m. Henry Lewis, 1 d. Career: apps. w. sev. German opera cos., 1956; San Fran. Opera, 1960; has also appeared at Covent Gd., London, Chgo. Lyric Opera, La Scala, Milan, Met. Opera, NYC, etc. Roles incl: Eboli, Don Carlo; Marie, Wozzeck; Amneris, Aida; Carmen; Rosins, Barber of Seville; Fides, Le Prophète; Mignon. Hobby: Needlepoint. 16.

HORNE, Richard Sherman, b. 2 May 1930, Sabraton, WVa., USA. Violinist; Instrumental Teacher; Retired US Air Force Bandsman; French horn player. Educ: WVa. Univ., 1948-51; Pvte. study w. James Werner, 1937-48, & Prof. Kenneth Wood. m. Leona Cheuvront Horne, 1 s., 2 d. Career: Violin, French horn & vocal soloist, USAF, 1951-73; Played & sang, Berlin Stadium, 1964; Assoc. Concertmaster, Colo. Springs Symph., 1973; Concertmaster. Colo. Springs Choral Orch. & Colo. Coll. Choral Orch.; Cond., Mgr., Colo. Springs Community Orch. Libn., Colo. Springs Symph.; 1st Violinist & Ldr., string quartet. The Modern Strings; Concertmaster, Summer Opera Festival Orch. Mbr., Local 154, Am. Fedn. of Musicians. Recip., Schlrship.; violin, WVa. Univ. Hobbies: Modern railroading; Golf; Bowling; Swimming; Hiking. Address: 2219 Clarkson Dr., Colo. Springs, CO 80909, USA.

HOROVITZ, Joseph, b. 1926, Vienna, Austria. Composer; Conductor. Educ: MusB, MA, New Coll., Oxford; RCM. m. Anna Landau, 2 d. Career: Dir. of Music, Bristol Old Vic., 1950-51, & Ballet Russe, 1952; Asst. Dir., Intimate Opera Co., 1952-63; Asst. Cond., Glyndebourne Opera, 1956; Prof. of Composition, RCM, 1961-. Compositions incl: 2 one-act operas; 11 ballets; concerts for violin, clarinet, trumpet, etc.; Goldoni Overture; ballet suites; chmbr. music for wind & strings; Fantasia on Theme of Couperin for strings; educational music for orch., recorders, etc.; Much incidental music for radio, film, theatre & TV; many reconstructions of 18th century operas. Hons: Hon. ARCM; C'wlth. Medal for composition, 1959. Address: 7 Dawson Place, London W2, UK. 3.

HOROWITZ, Norman, b. 1 May 1932, New York, NY, USa. Concert Pianist. Educ: Acad. & Musical Studies, NY. Career: Duo Pianists, Stecher & Horowitz, 1951-; Co-Dir., Stecher & Horowitz Schl. of the Arts, 1960-; Ed. Cons., G Schirmer Inc., 1975-. Comps: Learning to Play, Books 1-4, 1963; Playing to Learn, Books 1-4, 1965; Rock With Jazz, Books 1-5, 1969; We Wish you a Merry Christmas, Books 1-2, 1971; In The Spirit of '76, 1973; The Pleasure of Your Company, Books 1-5, 1974; Num. Piano Solos. Recordings of Duo Piano Recital, Stecher & Horowitz. Mbr. Music Tchrs. Nat. Assn. Mgmt: Columbia Artists Mgmt., Inc., New York, NY. Address: 74 Maple Ave., Cedarhurst, NY 11516, USA.

HOROWITZ, Vladimir, b. 1 Oct. 1904, Russia. Pianist. Educ: studied w. Felix Blumenfeld & Sergei Tarnowsky. m. Wanda Toscanini, 1 d. Debut: 1917; USA. w. NY Phil. Orch., 1928. Career incls: num. apps. as Soloist w. leading orchs. inclng: NY Symph. Orch.; Phila. Orch.; NBC Symph. Orch. Many recordings. Hosn: 12 Grammy awards for best classical perf.; Prix du Disque, 1970, 71; Royal Phil. Soc. Gold Medal, 1972. Hobby: Collecting Americana inclng. antique Am. furniture. 16.

HORROD, Norman, b. 27 June 1936, London, UK. Composer; Horn Player. Educ: FTCL, 1958. Debut: London, 1958. Career: Prin. Horn to Northern Sinfonia (Fndr. mbr.), Netherlands Radio Phil., Netherlands Chmbr. orch., Overijsels Phil. Orch. Welsh Phil. Welsh Nat. Opera (Fndr. mbr.); Soloist, Nothern Sinfonia, Welsh Phil., Netherlands Radio, BBC, etc. Comps: Concerto for Horn & Chmbr. Orch.; Trio for Horn, Trombone & Bassoon; Duo for 2 Horns; Scherzo for 3 Horns; Prelude & Aubade, Wind Quintet. Hobby: Painting. Address: 33 Canada Rd., Cardiff, UK.

HORSLEY, Colin, b. 23 Apr. 1920, Wanganui, NZ. Pianist. Educ: RCM; Hon. ARCM, 1959; FRCM, 1973. Debut: at Hallé Concerts, Manchester, 1943, on invitation of Sir John Barbirolli. Career incls: solo apps. w. all ldng. UK orchs.; tours Netherlands, Belgium, France, Spain, Scandinavia, Malta, Malaya Ceylon, Aust. & NZ; frequent broadcasts; num. fest. apps inclng. Aix-en-Provence, Brit. Music Fests. in Fest., Palermo Recordings: HMVEMI. Recip., OBE, 1963. Hobby: Gardening Address: Tawsden Manor, Brenchley, Kent, UK. 1.

HORTIN, Christopher, b. 14 May 1934, London, UK Horn Player. Educ: BMus, Durham Univ.; RAM; LRAM. m. Rita Mays, 2 s. Career: Luxemburg Radio Symph. orch., 1957-61

Canford Summer Schl. of Music Organiser, 1964; Bournemouth Sinfonietta, 1968-. Hobbies: Mediaeval Chs.; Winemaking. Address: 15 St. Luke's Rd., Bournemouth, UK.

HORTON, John William, b. 22 Oct. 1905, Nottingham, UK. Educ: BA, London Univ.; BMus, Durham Univ.; FRCO; ARCM. m. Olwen Morfydd Griffiths, 1 s., 2 d. Career: Tchr., 1925-37; BBC Prog. Asst., 1937-47; HM Insp. of Schls., 1947-67; Staff Inst. of Music, 1959-67. Pt.-time Lectr., Author, etc., 1967-. Publs: Geig (Master Musicians Series), 1974, Grig (Great Lives Series), 1950; Scandinavian Music; A Short History, 1963; Brahms Orchestral Music, 1968; Mendelssohn Chamber Music, 1972; Music in English Primary Education, 1972; Cesar Franck, 1948; The Music Group (6 books), 1969-72; The Wayfarer's Part Song Book, 1946; Monteverdi, 1975; A Book of Early Music, 1978; Songs, Signs & Stories (3 books), 1979; & num. educl. publs. Contbr. to: Musical Times; Music in Educ.; Music Tchr., etc. Address: The Cottag, Burland Rd., Brentwood, Essex, UK.

HORTON, William Lamar, b. 26 Aug. 1935, Rock Hill, SC, USA. Professor of Voice. Educ: BA in Music, Furman Univ.; MSM, D Musical Arts, Southern Bapt. Theol. Sem.; post-doct. studies, Univ. of Mich., & Acad. des Arts Musicaux, Paris, France. m. Peggy Ann Small, 3 s., 1 d. Career: Frequent Soloist, Clinician & Adjudicator for var. choral fests. & clinics; currently Prof. of Music, Okla. Bapt. Univ., Shawnee. Comps. incl: Song of the Lamb; Salvation to Our God; Praise to the Lord the Almighty. Publs: Introduction to Singing, 1968; Score Reading, Pts. I-III w. cassette tapes, 1975. Cont;br. to var. profl. jrnls. Mbr., profl. assns. Hons. incl: Gov.'s Citation, Okla. Musician of Yr., 1975; Okla. Arts & Humanities Coun., 1977-80. Hobbies: Bridge; Swimming; Writing. Address: 18 Mojave Drive, Shawnee, OK 74801, USA.

HORUSITZKY, Zoltán, b. 18 July 1903, Pápa, Hungary. Composer; Professor. Educ: Fac. of Law, Budapest (Dr's degree 1972); Dip. of Comp. & piano Tchng., F Liszt Music Acad. m. Katalin Rácz, 1 s., 1 d. Debut: First Concert, 1925; First maj. comp. perf. in Budapest in 1932; 'Fekete hold ejszakajan'. Career: Prof. of Piano, F Liszt Music Acad., Budapest. Comps. incl: Bathory Zsigmond, 3 act Hungarian histl. opera, first perf. in Greiz, DDR, 1957, in Budapest, 1960 & radio version in Budapest in 1955; 6th String Quartet, 1976; Concerto for piano & chamber orch., 1978; Les Rêveries du Promeneur, for piano, 1976; Hivas, for tenor, choir & piano, 1976. sev. works of chamber music five string-quartette two piano concertos, one violin concert, suites for orch., cantatas, songs; Three Shakespeare-Sonnets; Songs for Chinese verse; Comps. for piano Exercises poétiques; Sonate 'The Mountain'; Sonata for two piano Sonata for Alto & piano; Choral works, etc. Recordings: Shakespeare Sonnets & songs for Chinese verses. Contbr. to articles & papers to var. periodicals. Former Ed. of 'A zene'. REcip., F Erkel Prize, 1955. Address: Gellért tér 3, 1111 Budapest XI, Hungary.

HORVATH, Janet, b. 13 July 1952, Toronto, Can. Cellist. Educ: BMus, Univ. of Toronto; MMus, Ind. Univ.; student of Vladimir Orloff & Janos Starker. Career: Assoc. Prin. Cellist, ndpls. Symph. Orch., 1977-79; Assoc. Prin. Cellist, Minn. Orch., 1979-80; Participating Artist, Marlboro Music Fest., 1979; Touring artist for 1979 Music from Marlboro concert our of E USA, inclng. Lincoln Centre; Prin. Cellist, Aspen Chmbr. Symph., 1977; Soloist w. Indpls. Symph., Bayreuth Fest. Youth orch., in tour of S France; Can. radio recitals; Mbr., Prevcil Piano Trio (touring chmbr. group); Radio tapings for USA radio. Hons: Finalist, Munich Int. cello-piano duo competition, 1978; Can. Govt. Awards. Hobbies: Reading; Cooking. Address: 7156 Knobwood Drive, Apt. H, Indianapolis, IN 46260, USA.

HORVATH, Jeno, b. 28 May 1914, dec. 19 Aug. 1973, Budapest, Hungary. Composer; Conductor of Orchestra; Pianist. Educ: Acad. of Music. m. Ibolya Harza, 1 s., 1 d. Comps: 19 operettas inclng: Boronkay's Sisters, 1942; Katalinkis, 1948; Marriage by 3, 1948; The Rape of Sabine Women, 1948; Girls on the Danube; Spring Vaise, 1957; The Love Sets In, 1960; Fall in Love With Me, 1961; Sev. hundred pieces of dance & film music; Budapest Concertino for piano & orch.; Perpetuum Mobile for violin & orch.; Spring Valse for violin & orch., In a Teahouse (symphonic character piece); Concertino for vibrophon & orch. Address: Mrs. Jeno Horvath, H-1122 Budapest, Biro u. 27, Hungary.

HORVATH, Josef Maria, b. 20 Dec. 1931, Pécs, Hungary. Composer; Pianist. Educ: Hochschule für Musik; Dip., Liszt-erence Hochschule, Budapest; Dip., Hochschule Mozarteum, Salzburg. Career: Concert tours in European countries; Performing given up in favour of composing; Now occasional performances. Compositions: (publd.) 4 Lieder nach Hölderlin, for soprano & 4 instruments, 1958; Die Blinde, nach Rilke, for mezzo-soprano, 2 speakers & 4 instruments, 1959; 8 Ungarische

Volksliedbearbeitungen, for voice & piano, 1964; Redundanz 1, 2, 3, for wind woctet & string quaertet, 1966-68; Tombeau de Gigue, for orch., 1971; Melencolia I, for violin & orch., 1971; 6 Ansichten eines Gegenstandes, 1971; 8 Ungarische Volksliedbearbeitungen; prigines for chmbr. ensemble, 1975; Sothies I for chamber ensemble, 1977. Hons. incl: 1st Prize, comp. competition, Int. Jeunesses Musicales, Montreal, 1967; Körner Prize, Vienna, 1968; Staatlicher Förderungspreis, Vienna, 1974. Address: Schwarzenbergpromenade 41, A-5026 Salzburg, Austria.

HORVIT, Michael Miller, b. 22 June 1932, Brooklyn, NY, USA. Composer. Educ: BMus, MMus, Yale Univ.; DMA, Boston Univ. m. Nancy Harris Horvit, 2 s. Career: Trombonist, New Haven Symph. Orch., Conn., 1952-56; Assoc. prof., Southern Conn. State Coll., 1959-66; Prof. & Hd., Theory-Comp. Dept., Univ. of Houston, Tex., 1966-; Music Dir., Temple Emanu El, Houston, 1967-. Comps. incl: Antiphon I, for Saxophone & Electronic Tape; Antiphon II, for Clarinet & Electronic Tape (recorded); Antiphon III, for Piano & Electronic Tape; Antiphon IV, for Marimba & Electronic Tape; The Gardens of Hieronymus B (orch.); Tomo (opera); Adventure in Space (opera); Interplay for percussion quartet; Moonscape (ballet); sev. liturgical works for SATB choir & organ, etc. Recordings: Concert Music for Band No. II. Publs: The Techniques & Materials of Tonal Music with an Introduction to Twentieth Century Techniques (co-author); Music for Analysis (co-author), 1978. Mbrships. incl: Am. Assn. of Univ. Comps.; Am. Fedn. of Musicians; Coll. Music Soc.; Am. Music Center. Recip., musical awards & commissions. Hobby: Boating. Address: Schl. of Music, Univ. of Houston, Houston, TX 77004, USA. 7.

HOSE, Anthony, b. 24 May 1944, London, UK. Conductor; Accompanist. Educ: RCM; ARCM. m. Moira Griffiths, 1 c. Career: Glyndebourne Fest. Opera; Bremen Opera; Royal Oper House, Covent Gdn.; Welsh Nat. Opera (currently Hd. of Music); Accomp., La Scala; BBC; Musical Dir., Musica Fest. Recip., Countess of Munster Award, 1966 & 67. Hobbies: Good Food & Wine; Football. Address: 24 Victoria Pk. Rd., E, Cardiff CF5 1EG, UK. 30.

HOSHI, Akira, b. 25 Feb. 1931, Seoul, Korea (Japanese nationality). University Professor. Educ: Grad., Lit. Dept., Nagoya Univ., 1954; Grad., Music Dept., Tokyo Univ. of Arts, 1965; MA, ibid., 1967. Career: Prof., Utsunomiya Univ. Publs: The History & Appreciation of Japanese Music, 1971; Co-Ed., Japanese Music & its Outskirts: Essays in Celebration of Professor Eishi Kikkawa's 61st Birthday, 1973. Mbrships: Int. Musicol. Soc.; Japanese Musicol. Soc. Address: 149-28 Miyukigahara-machi Utsunomiya City, Tochigi-ken 320, Japan. 4.

HOSHINO, Hiroshi, b. 15 July 1932, Kyoto, Japan. Musicologist. Educ: Tokyo Nat. Univ. of Fine Arts & Music, 1958. m. Kazuko Hoshino, 2 s., 1 d. Career: Asst. Prof., 1965-70, Prof. of Musicol., 1971, Ueno Gakuen Coll. Tokyo. Publs: incl; Japanese ed. of K H Wörner's Geschichte der Musik, 1962. Contbr. to; Jrnl. of Japanese Musicol. Soc.; profl. publs. Mbrships: Japanese Musicol. Soc.; Soc. for Music Rsch., German Fed. Repub. Address: Suzuki-cho 2-722-41, Kodairashi, Tokyo, Japan.

HOSIER, John, b. 18 Nov. 1928, London, UK. Principal, GSM. Educ: St. John's Coll., Cambridge; MA; FGSM; FRSA. Career: Music Prod., BBC radio for schls., 1953-59; Prod., Sr. Music Prod., Exec. Prod., BBC TV (pioneering TV music progs. for schls.; Staff Inspector for Music & Dir., Ctr. for Young Musicians, ILEA, 1973-76; currently Prin., GSM, London. Comps: much music for film, radio & TV. Publs: Books, music & song arrs. Contbr. to profl. jrnls. Mbrships: Exec. Committee, ISM; V Chmn., UK Coun. for Music Educ.; Gulbenkian Committee enquiring into training of musicians. Address: Guildhall School of Music & Drama, Barbican, London EC2Y 8DT, UK. 1.

HOSSACK, Donna, b. 7 Apr. 1931, Toronto, Can. Harp & Recorder Player; Teacher. Educ: Orff Tchrs. Cert., Univ. of Toronto, 1969; Dip. in Adult Educ., Univ. of BC, 1974, 1 s., 1 d. Career: Prin. Harp, Toronto Symph. Orchs., 1953-59; CBC Symph., 1954-62, Vancouver Symph. Orch., 1962-64; currently Harpist, TV, radio, films, Early & New Music Grps.; Tchr., Orff-Schulwerk & Harp, Univ. of BC; Harp Tchr., Community Music Ctr., Vancouver. Recording: (w. CBC Symph.) Stravinsky, Sermon, Narrative & Prayer; Weinzweig, Wine of Peace. Contbr. to profl. jrnls. Mbrships. incl: Music for Children; Carl Orff Canada (Bd. of Dirs., 1974, VP 1976); Vancouver New Music Soc. (Bd. of Dirs., 1976). Hons: Harp Scholarship, Royal Conserv. of Music, Toronto, 1950. Address: 3993 W 21st Ave., Vancouver, BC V6S 1H7, Can.

HOSTIKKA, Pertti Antero, b. 2 Feb. 1936, Ylamma, Finland. Trombonist. Educ: Music Schl., Finnish Army; Sibelius

Acad., Helsinki. m. Tuuia Kautto, 2 c. Career: Trombonist, Army Orch., 1950-63; 1st trombonist, Finnish Nat. Opera Orch., 1963-; 1st trombonist, Royal Oper House, Stockholm, 1970-71; 1st trombonist, Summer Opera Fest. Orch., Savonlinna, 1967-; Trombonist, Chmbr. Orch., Finnish Org. JSCM, 1975-; Soloist, Helsinki City Orch. Concert, 1973; Tchr., trombone. Recordings: sev. for Finnish Radio Corp. Mbr., Profl. Soc. Finnsih Musicians. Hons: 1st prize, trombone Army Competition, 1973. Address: Kristianinkatu 16 A 8, SF-00170 Helsinki, Finland.

HOTCHKIS, John, b. 22 Nov. 1916, Taunton, UK. Composer; Conductor. Educ: Organ Scholar, Selwyn Coll., Cambridge. Comps. incl: over 150 radio & TV drama & documentary scores; over 25 TV prods. incl. Orwell 1984; over 20 films incl. Man on the Beach, Velvet House, A Wedding; 25 stage prods. in London & NY incl. Shakespeare, Moliere, moden Engl. & French plays; Son et Lumiere, UK, France, Middle East, USA; Fanfares, other ceremonial music, consecration of Coventry Cathedral, 1962, for Feast of Reconciliation, ibid., 1966 & for Fanfare for Europe, ibid., 1973; var. music for Balt. Cathedral, 1970-79, S Va., 1976, Lincoln, Neb., 1977-79; Visions of St. Bede, for voices a cappella; Overture, Fantasia, for oboe & orch.; instrumental & chmbr. music; James Joyce Song Cycle; Pslam 23; The Bell Song. Mbrships. incl: Trustee & Dir., Ballet Rambert & Mercury Theatre Trust. Hobbies: Archery; Falconry; Deer-stalking; Country & Field Sports. Address: Stede Court, Biddenden, Ashford, Kent TN27 8JG, UK. 14, 23, 28, 29, 30.

HOTTER, Hans, b. 19 Jan. 1909, Germany. Concert & Opera Singer. Debut: concert, 1929; opera, 1930. Career: Mbr., Vienna, Hamburg, & Munich Oper Cos.; concerts & operas, Europe, USA, Aust.; Participant in Salzburg, Bayreuth & Edinburgh Fests.; noted for interpretation of Wagnerian roles; Ret'd., 1972. Has recorded. 16.

HOUGH, Charles Wayne, b. 28 Apr. 1933, Westchester, Pa., USA. Lyric Tenor. Educ: BA, Eastern Coll., Pa.; MRE, Eastern Sem., Pa.; MCh. Music, Southwestern Bapt. Sem., Tex. 3 d. Career: Soloist, Oratorio & Opera in USA; Mbr., Southern Bapt. Radio-TV Choir; Schutzfest, Schluchtern, W Germany, 1973; Mbr., Music Fac., Univ. of SD, 5 yrs.; Mbr., Music Fac., E Wash. State Coll., Cheney, 1971-; Chaplain, Wash. Air Nat. Guard, Spokane. Contbr. of reviews to Choice Mag. Mbr. num. profl. orgs. inclng: Phi Mu Alpha Sinfonia. Hons. incl: Winner, Men's Div., Voice Contest, Bob Jones Univ., 1952. Hobbies: Auto Mechanics; Hunting (Bow & Gun); Rsch. in Psychology of Music (Singing). Address: 522 Irene Pl., Cheney, WA 99004, USA.

HOUSE, Robert William, b. 28 Nov. 1920, Bristow, Okla., USA. Music Educator & Cellist. Educ: BFA, Okla. State Univ., 1941; MMus, Eastman Schl. of Music, 1942; EdD, Univ. of Ill. 1954. m. Esther Hawkins, 3 s., 1 d. Career: Asst. Prof. of Band, Cello & Wind Instruments, Neb. State Coll., Kearney, 1946-55; Prin. Cellist, Kearney Symph., 1946-55; Prof. of Orch., Cello, Music Educ. & Chmn. of Music Dept., Univ. of Minn., Duluth, 1955-67; Prin. Cellist, Duluth Symph., 1955-67; Dir., Schl. of Music, So. Ill. Univ., Carbondale, 1967-. Publs: co-auth., Foundations & Principles of Music Education, 1958, rev. 1972; Instrumental Music for Today's Schools, 1965; Administration in Music Education, 1973. Contbr. to profl. jrnls. inclng. The Illinois Music Educator, 1975. Mbrships. incl: Pres.-Elect, MENC, No. Ctrl. Div., 1974-76, Pres., 1976-78; Chmn., Music Educ. Rsch. Coun., 1958-60; Editl. Bd., Jrnl. of Rsch. in Music Educ., 1958-70; Publs. Planning Comm., MENC, 1972-78. Address: RR8, Box 143, Carbondale, IL 62901, USA. 2, 3, 8, 11, 12.

HOUSER, Roy, b. 11 Feb. 1920, Centerville, Iowa, USA. Woodwinds Player. Educ: BM, Eastman Schl. of Music, Rochester, NY; MA, Columbia Univ., NYC; ABD, Univ. of Ill., Urbana. m. Kathryn Irene Houser, 1 s. Debut: Columbus, Ohio, 1937. Career incls: Prof., Ind. Univ., Bloomington, 1948-68, Univ. of Dubuque, Iowa, 1969-71; Duluth Symph., Minn., 1971-73; Prof., Univ. of Colo., Boulder, 1973-74, Eastern Ky. Univ., Richmond; Solo perfs. w. num. orchs. Recordings: Serenade for Bassoon & String Trio by B Heiden; Berkshire Quartet. Redwood Label. Mbrships. incl: Galpin Soc.; Int. Double Soc. Publs: Catalogue of Woodwind Chamber Music, 2nd ed., 1973. Contbr. to profl. jrnls. Recip., sev. hons. Hobbies incl: Restoration of early musical instruments. Mgmt: Colbert Artist Mgmt. Address: 111 W 57th St., NY, NY 10019, USA.

HOUSEWRIGHT, Wiley Lee, b. 17 Oct. 1913, Wylie, Tex., USA. Music Educator; Music Administrator. Educ: AB, N Tex. Univ., 1934; MMus, Columbia Univ., NYC, 1938; EdD, NY Univ., 1943. m. Lucilla Gumm. Career: Dir. of Music, pub. schls., Tex. & NY, 1934-42; Lectr. in Music, NY Univ.,

1942-43; Asst. Prof., Univ. of Tex., 1946-47; Univ. of Mich., summer, Prof. Music Educ., 1960; Prof., Fla. State Univ., 1947 66; Dean, Schl. of Music, Fla. State Univ., 1966-. Publs: Birchard Music Series (w. Karl Ernst & Rose marie Grentzer), vols. I, II, III, IV, V & VI. Chmn., Editl. Bd., Music Educators Jrnl., 1957 66; Editl. Assoc., Jrnl. of Rsch. in Music Educ., 1953-62; Book Reviews, Jrnl. of Rsch. in Music Educ., etc.; Ed., The School Director, 1955-57. Mbrships. incl: Pres., MENC, 1968-70; Am. Musicol. Soc. Hons. incl: Disting. Prof., Fla. State Univ., 1961-62; Cons., US Dept. of State, 1958-; US nat. Commn. for UNESCO, 1958-. Address: 515 South Ride, Tallahassee, FL 32303, USA. 2, 11.

HOUSTON, Patricia Alice, b. 6 Sept. 1942, Sheffield, Ala., USA. Flautist. Educ: BMus, New Engl. Conserv. of Music, Boston, 1964; grad. study, Ind. Univ. Schl. of Music & Aspen Music Fest. m. Alvin B Dreger. Career: has played flute w. Birmingham (Ala.) Symph., Birmingham (Ala.) Pops Orch., Ind. Univ. Opera Orch., & New Engl. Conserv. Orch.; currently 1st Flute, Huntsville Symph. Orch. Mbrships: Huntsville Chmbr. Music Guild; Bd., Am. Youth Orch. Assn. Hobbies: Gardening; Ping-pong. Address: 610 Holmes Ave., Huntsville, AL 35801, USA.

HOUSTON, Roxane Mary, b. London, UK. Lyric Soprano. Educ: LRAM. m. Joseph Graham Senior, 1 s., 1 d. Debut: Glyndebourne Fest. Opera, Sussex. Career: began w. apps. at Glyndebourne & Edinburgh Fest.; later branched into oratorio, orchl. concerts & recitals; num. apps. as soloist w. var. chmbr. ensembles inclng. Grosvenor Ensemble & Divertimenti of London; freelance concert work, UK & abroad; perfs. on radio & TV & for Ballet Rambert; specialises in French repertoire. Mbr., Solo Perf. Sect., ISM. Hobbies: Writing; Swimming. Address: 34 Chelwood Gdns., Kew Gdns., Richmond, Surrey TW9 4JQ, UK. 27.

HOUTMANN, Jacques, b. 27 Mar. 1935, Mirecourt, France. Conductor. Educ: 1st Prizes, violin & chmbr. music, Dips., harmony, horn, percussion, Conserv. Nancy; Lic. in conducting, Ecole Normale de Musique, Paris, Santa Cecilia, Rome, Italy. m. Yolaine Gérard, 2 d. Career: Cond. w. many orchs. in Europe & USA; Cond., Lyon Phil., 4 yrs.; Asst. cond., NY Phil., 1965-66; currently Music Dir., Richmond Symph.; apps. at Belgrad, Aix-en-Provence & Besançon FEsts., also in S Am. & Czech. Recordings: Gossec, 3 symphs. & Grande Messe des Morts; Gretry, Panurge (opera). Hons: 1st prizes, Int. Competition for Conds., Bescançon, 1961 & Int. Competition for Conds. Dimitri Mitropoulos, NY, 1964; DFA, Univ. of Richmond, Va., 1976. Hobbies: Astronomy; Mountain Climbing. Mgmt: Herbert Barrett. Address: 5303 Toddsbury Rd., Richmond, VA 23226, USA.

HOVE, Michael Østergärd, b. 26 May 1950, Arhus, Denmark. Saxophonist (soprano, alto, tenor & baritone); Flautist; Clarinettist. Educ: The Royal Danish Conserv. of Music. m. Lene Tiemroth Hove. Debut: Montmartre Jazz Club, Copenhagen. Career: Num. jazz club apps., Denmark, Sweden, Germany, 1967-; Regular apps. on Danish Radio w. freelance bands; Mbr., Danish Radio Jazz Group, 1971-. Comps: Summer Dream; Tri-Talk. Recordings: Music Train, 1969; Music Book, 1970; The Forgotten Art, 1977. Mbrships: Copenhagen Musicians Union; Danish Jazz Musicians Union. Address: Peter Fabersgade 24 2200-N, Denmark. 3.

HOVHANESS, Alan, b. 8 Mar. 1911, Somerville, Mass. USA. Composer. Comps., about 150 publd. comps. Comps recorded: Avak the Healer; Armenian Rhapsody nos. 1, 2, 3 Ldy of Light Magnificat; God Created Great Whales; St. Vartar Symphony; Fra Angelico; Symphonies 4, 6, 11, 15, 19, 20 21, 23, 24, 25, 26, 27, 28; Mysterious Mountain Meditation on Orpheus; Fantasy on Japanese Woodprints. Hons DMus, Univ. of Rochester, & Bates Coll., Me. 2, 14.

HOWARD, Ann, b. 22 July 1936, Norwood, London, UK Opera Singer (Mezzo-Soprano). Educ: studied w. Topliss Green & Rodolfa Lhombino; special grant, Royal Opera Hs. Covent Garden to study w. Modesti, Paris, France. m. Keith Giles, 1 d. Debut: a Czipra, Gyspy Baron, Sadler's Wells Opera, 1964. Career: ir var. shows; chorus, Royal Opera House, Covent Gdn.; Prin. Salder's Wells; Freelance apps. w. Scottish Opera, Welsh Nat Opera, Royal Opera House, Santa Fe Fest. Opera, Canadian Opera Co., New Opera Co. taking many leading roles inclng: Carmen Anneris, Frieka, Btangaene, Dalila, Azucena, Cassandra, Grande Duchesse, Héélene. App., Verdi Requiem, Royal Choral Soc. 1975; Apps. in France, Can. & USA; regular broadcasts, BBC radio & TV, Scottish TV. Has made many recordings for EMI Hobbies: Gardening; Cooking. Mgmt: Stafford Law Assocs Address: -5 Catherine Rd., Surbiton, Surey, UK.

HOWARD, Dean Clinton, b. 17 Nov. 1918, Cleveland Ohio, USA. Professor of Music. Educ: BSM, Baldwin Wallac Coll., 1941; MMus, Univ. of Mich., 1942. m. Patricia Joa

Smith, 3 s. Career: Fac. Mbr., Buena Vista Coll., 1947; Bradley Univ., 1948-, Prof. of Music, Music Theory, Counterpoint, Comp.; State Univ. of NY, summers, 1954, '58; Clarinetist, Peoria Symph. Orch., 1971-76, Bradley Community Chorus & Orch., Peoria Municipal Band, etc.; Dir. Adult Choir, Forrest Hill United Methodist Ch. of Peoria. Comps. incl: An Illinois Symph., 1967; Perspectives for Orch., 1972; Three Miniatures; Proud Heritage; O Sacred Banquet, Motet; Chmbr. Music, Choral Music, Sonatas, Electronic Music. Mbrships: Danforth Sr. Assocs.; AAUP; Am. Soc. of Univ. Comps.; Phi Kappa Phi; Phi Mu Alpha Sinfonia. Hons: Putnam Award for Excellence in Tchng., 1962; Baldwin Wallace Coll. Conservatory of Music Achievement Award, 1976; num. comp. awards. Hobby: Watercolour painting. Address: 1814 Bradley Ave., Peoria, IL 61606, USA. 2, 8.

HOWARD, Gaynor Margaret, b. 31 Oct. 1932, Neath, W Glamorgan, UK. Teacher of Schl. Music & Pianoforte & Cello. Educ: Grad., Royal Schl. of Music; Assoc., Royal Coll. of Music; Lic. Royal Acad. of Music. m. Francis William Howard, 1 s., 1 d. Career: Music Mistress, Abhergavenny HS for Girls, 1953-56; Hd. of Music, Cardiff HS for Girls, 1957-63; Dir. of Music, Howells' Schl., Llandaff, Cardiff, 1970. Compositions: Adam lay y-bounden; var. carol arrangements. Recordings: Carols at Llandaff. Contbr. to: Set to Music. Mbrships: Incorp. Soc. of Musicians; Asst. Masters & Mistresses Assn.; Guild for Promotion of Welsh Music. Hons: Piano exhib. at Royal Coll. of Music, 1951-53. Hobbies: Antiquarian interests; Music. Address: 63 St. Michael's Rd., Llandaff, Cardiff, CF5 2AN, UK. 3.

HOWARD, George Sallade, b. 24 Feb. 1903, Reamstown, Pa., USA. Band & Orchestra Conductor. Educ: Hon. Grad., Ithaca Coll.; BA, Ohio Wesleyan Univ., 1930; MA, NY Univ., 1937; Grad., Ithaca Conserv.; BMus, MMus, DMus, Chgo. Conserv. m. Sadako Takenouchi. Carrer: Clarinet Soloist. Patrick Conway Band, 6 Seasons; Dir. of Music, Pa. State Tchrs. Coll., Mansfield, Pa.; Dir., Band Orch. & Chorus Schl., The Pa. State Univ.; Dir. & Cmdng. Officer, USAF Band & Orch., 21 yrs.--toured 57 countries; Dir., Met. Police Band, Wash., DC, 10 yrs.; Originiated idea of using music as a crime deterrant. Compositions: Alfalfa Club March (recorded by Royal Marine Band, UK); 94 marches & songs published & recorded; var. other recordings inclng. 10 marches rec. in Jan. Publs: The Big Serenade, 1962; 10 Minute Self Instructor for Pocket Instruments; Perfecting the Musical Marching Unit, 1974. Publs: The Big Serenade, 1962; Perfecting the Marching Band, 1974. Contbr. to var. music jrnls. Mbrships: incl: Past Pres., Am. Bandmasters Assn.; Nat. Band Assn.; Pres., John Philip Sousa Meml., Inc. (Chmn. of Bd.). Hons: Legion of Merit, 1945 & w. Cluster, 1960; Cmdr., Order of Nonsaraphon Cambodia; Guarde Republique Medal. Hobbies: guest cond.; Training dogs; Travelling. Address: Air Force Village, 4917 Ravenswood Dr., San Antonio, TX 78227, USA. 2, 12.

HOWARD, Joseph, b. 17 July 1912, Chgo., Ill., USA. Dental Director. Educ: BA, Fisk Univ.; DDS, Univ. of Ill.; MPA, Univ. of Southern Calif. m. Tommye R Howard, 2 s., 1 d. Publs: Drums in the Americas, 1967; Instruments in Central America, 1970. Contbr. to: The Artesia, 1969. Mbrships: Soc. of Ethnomusicol.; Am. Musical Instrument Soc. Hobby: Collecting Percussion Instruments. Address: 1728 Victoria Ave., Los Angeles, CA 90019, USA. 9.

HOWARD, Joseph A, b. 23 Jan. 1928, Cleveland, Ohio, USA. Pianist; Professor of Music. Educ: Ba, Western Reserve Univ.; MA, Kent State Univ.; PhD, Case-Western Reserve Univ.; pvte. piano study w. Leonard Shure, Elliot Ebberhard & France Bolton Kortheurer. m. Joan Baker Howard, 2 s. Career: Musical Dir., WEWS TV; Staff Pianist, WTAM-WNBK Radio-TV; Apps. as piano soloist w. Cleveland Orch., etc.; Prof. of Music, Cyahoga Community Coll.; Hd. of Jazz Studies, Cleveland Music Schl. Settlement. Comps: Scores for soundtracks of Dateline, Ohio & Climate of Learning; Score for Defense Dept. Film, History of Photography. Recordings: Jazz Highway Twenty; Swinging Close In With Joe Howard & Friends; Pianist, Cleveland Orch. Recording of Carmina Burana. Mbrships: Music Tchrs. Nat. Assn.; Am. Assn. of Univ. Profs.; ASCAP; Am. Musicol. Soc. Hons: Fulbright-Hays Award, 1978-79; Sr. Lectr. to Univ. of the Philippines. Hobbies: Reading; Chess; Collecting stamps and records; Gardening. Address: 34480 Sherwood Dr., Solon, OH 44139, USA.

HOWARD, Leslie John, b. 29 Apr. 1948, Melbourne, Aust. Pianist; Composer. Educ: AMusA, 1962; LMus, 1966; BA, 1969; MA, 1973, Monash Univ.; piano studies w. June McLean, Donald Britton & Michael Brimer (Aust.), Guido Agosti (Italy) & Noretta Conci (London). Debut: Melbourne, 1967; London, 1975. Career: On staff, Monash Univ., 1970-73; Concertos w. var. orchs. in Aust., England & on continent; regular broadcasts as pianist as musicol. for BBC, ABC, RAI & var. American networks; Telecasts in Aust., Italy and Philippines. Comps: Fruits of the Earth (ballet); Hreidar the Fool (opera);

Sinfonia con contrabbasso; Sonatas for Violin, clarinet, percussion, double bass, horn and piano, piano solo; Canzona for brass ensemble; songs, etc. Recordings: Complete keyboard works of Percy Grainger; works by Glazunov, Liszt, Mozart etc. Mbrships: Liszt Soc.; Grainger Soc. Hons: Diploma d'Onore, Siena, 1972, Naples, 1976. Hobbies: Literature; Languages; Bridge; Shooker; Swimming. Mgmt: Trafalgar Perry. Address: 128 Norbury Cres., Norbury, London SW16 4JZ, UK. 30.

HOWARD, Michael Stockwin, b. 14 Sept. 1922, London, UK. Director of Music; Conductor. Educ: RAm & pvtely. m. Janet Margaret Cazenove. Career: fndr., Renaissance Soc. & Cond.; Renaissance Singers, 1944-64; Organist & master of the Choristers, Ely Cathedral, 1953-58; freelance organist, harpsichordist, cond., broadcaster & writer. Recordings incl: works by Tallis, Byrd, Palestrina. Publ: The Private Inferno, 1974. Contbr. to: Musical Times; The Listener, etc. Hons: Prix Musicale de Radio Brno, 1967; G Charpentier Grand Prix du Disque, 1975. Hobbies: Steam Railway Traction; Village Fairgrounds. Mgmt: Ann Manly Concert Mgmt., London. Address: 50 Church Sq., Rye, E Sussex, UK.

HOWARD, Patricia, b. 18 Oct. 1937, Birmingham, UK. Writer; Teacher. Educ: BA, MA, Lady Margaret Hall, Oxford Univ., 1959; PhD, Univ. of Surrey, 1974. m. David Louis Howard, 2 d. Career: Freelance writer, esp. on opera; Critic; Broadcaster; Tchr., esp. of Continuo playing & Accomp.; Tutor in Tchr., esp. of Continuo playing & Accomp.; Tutor in Music, Open Univ. Publs: Gluck & the Birth of Modern Opera, 1963; The Operas of Benjamin Britten: an Introduction, 1969. Contbr. to: Musical Times; Listener; Music & Letters; Gramophone. Mbr., Royal Musical Assn. Hons: Susette Taylor Travelling Fellowship, 1971. Leverhulme Research Grant, 1976. Hobbies: Gardening; Reading; Crossword puzzles. Address: Stepping Stones, Wonham Way, Gomshall, Surrey, UK.

HOWARD, Ray Reid, b. 26 April 1948, Norton, Kansas, USA. Assistant Professor. Educ: Dalcroze Schl. of Music, NYC, 1970; BA, N Texas State Univ. (Denton), 1972; MA, Stephen F Austin State Univ. (Nacogdoches), 1976; DMA Cand., Univ. of Southern Calif. (LA), 1980. m. Krisie Ione Van Zant, 2 s., 1 d. Debut: Alice Tully Hall, Lincoln Center, 1976. Career: Brooklyn Acad. of Music, 1975; Alice Tully Hall, 1976; Nat. NBC TV, 1978. Mbrships: Am. Musicol. Soc.; AGO; Am. Choral Dirs. Assn.; Am. Choral Fndn.; MENC; NGPT; Pi Kappa Lambda; Hymn Soc. of Am. Hons: Pi Kappa Lambda, 1976. Hobbies: Landscaping; Tennis; Beach Activities. Address: 1821 Meridian, South Pasadena, CA 91030, USA.

HOWARD, Ruth, b. 1 Jan. 1907, Antonienhutte, Germany. Concert Singer; Concert Pianist; Teacher, Voice & Piano. Educ: Dip., Lib. Schl., Breslau, Germany; Univ. of Breslau; Silesian Conserv., Breslau; Summa cum laude Dip. m. Arthur Edward Howard, 1 s. Debut: Breslau. Career: Soloist, Berlin Kulturbund Opera; Regular soloist, Radio Breslau; Voice & Piano Concerts, Berlin, Breslau, Frankfurt, other German cities & in Seattle, Wash., USA & US cities; TV paps. Tchng. career: Prof. Music, NW Coll., USA, Puget Sound Coll., Shoreline Community Coll.; Tchr., pvte. master classes in voice, piano. Mbrships: Musicians Soc., Breslau; Past Mbr., Ladies Musical Club, Seattle. Num. hons. from above colls. Address: 116 NW 79th St., Seattle, WA 98117, USA.

HOWARD, Samuel Eugene, b. 18 May 1937, Birmingham, Ala., USA. Duo-Pianist; Adjunct Professor of Music. m. Delores Hodgens, 1 d. Educ: BMus, Birmingham Southern Coll.; Postgrad. Artists Dip., Juilliard Schl. of Music; Studies at Aspen Schl. of Music; Studies w. Rosina Lhevinne, Ilona Kabos, Vronsky & Babin, European Debut: Geneva, Munich, Berlin, Stockholm, Amsterdam, London, 1965. Am. Debut: NYC, 1966. Career: Concerts in duet (Hodgens & Howard) throughout Europe, USA & Can.; Radio & TV apps. locally & abroad; Roster of Artists, BBC, London. Recording: Music for 2 Piano Encores (Mastercraft). Hons: Rosina Lhevinne Scholarship Student, 1959-61; Rockefeller Grant for European Debuts, 1965; Rockefeller Grant for NYC debut, 1966. Mgmt: Columbia Artist Mgmt. Address: 4220 Kennesaw Drive, Mountain Brook, AL 35213, USA.

HOWARD, Wayne, b. 7 Sept. 1942, Grenada, Miss., USA. Musicologist. Educ: BA (Maths.), Belhaven Coll., 1964; BMus, ibid., 1964; MMus (musicol.), Indiana Univ., 1967; PhD (musicol., ibid., 1975. Career: Tchr., Musicology, Kent State Univ., 1973-76; currently pvte. rschr. Publs: Samavedic Chant, 1977. Contbr. to: Agni - The Vedic Ritual of the Fire Altar; Music East and West; Essays in Honor of Walter Kaufmann; Encyclopedia articles on Arabian music, Indian Music. Mbrships: Am. Musicol. Soc.; Am. Oriental Soc.; Assoc. for Asian Studies; Soc. for Ethnomusicology. Hons: Bd. of Trustees Award (Belhaven Coll.), 1964. Hobbies: Jogging; Bicycling. Address: 315 Shirley Ave., Winona, MS 38967, USA.

HOWARTH, Elgar, b. 4 Nov. 1935. Brass Player; Conductor. Educ: MusB, Manchester Univ.; RMCM; ARCM; FRMCM. m. Mary Bridget Neary, 1 s., 2 d. Career: mbr., Royal Opera House, Covent Garden Orch., 1958-63; mbr., RPO, 1963-69; mbr., London Sinfonietta, 1968-71; mbr., Philip Jones Brass Ensemble, 1965-76; freelance cond., 1970-; Musical Dir., Grimethorpe Colliery Brass Band, 1972-76. Comps: mainly for brass instruments. Mgmt: Allied Artists, 36 Beauchamp Place, London SW13 1NV, UK. Address: c/o mgmt.

HOWAT, Audrey Miner, b. 20 Dec. 1903, Oxford, NS, Can. Accompanist; Teacher of Piano. Educ: Pvte. studies w. Llaina Hewson Donkin & David Renfrew Howat; Studied w. Dr. J Noel Brunton, Mt. Allison Univ., Sackville, NB. m. David Renfrew Howat (dec.), 1 d. Career: Tchr. & Supvsr. of Piano Classes, Can. Bureau for the Advancement of Music, 1955-. Mbr., NS Registered MTA. Hobby: Collecting Can. Lit. Address: 6249 Coburg Rd., Halifax, Nova Scotia, B3H 2A2, Can.

HOWE, Hubert S, Jr., b. 21 Dec. 1942, Portland, Oregon, USA. College Professor; Composer; Writer. Educ: AB, Princeton Univ., 1964; MFA, Princeton Univ., 1967; PhD, Musical Comp., ibid., 1972. m. Stefanie Howe. Comps: Freeze (electronic), 1972; Scherzo (orch.), 1975. Publs: Electronic Music Synthesis, 1975. Contbr. to: Perspectives of New Music; Proceedings of the Am. Soc. of Univ. Comps.; BYTE; Interface, etc. Mbrships: League of Comps. - ISCM, US Sect. (Pres., 1971-76); Am. Comps. Alliance; Am. Soc. of Univ. Comps.; Am. Music Center. Hobby: Personal computing. Address: 14 Lexington Rd., New City, NY 10956, USA.

HOWE, James Hakin, b. 11 Nov. 1917, Penshaw, Durham, UK. Conductor; Composer; Arranger; Musician (Trumpet & Piano). Educ: Royal Military Schl. of Music; LRAM; ARCM. Career: Bandmaster, Argyll & Sutherland Highlanders, 1949-59; Musical Dir., HM Scots Guards, 1959-74; Sr. Dir. of Music, Household Div., 1970-74; Guest Cond., BBC Symph. Orchs. Comps: Marches; Light Music. Num. recordings. Contbr. to Brit. Bandsman; Brit. Mouthpiece. Recip. MBE, 1971. Hobby: Gardening. Address: "Castleton'', Hookwood Pk., Limpsfield, Oxted, Surrey, UK.

HOWELL, Almonte Charles, Jr., b. 2 May 1925. Richmond, Va., USA. Musicologist; Organist; Bassoonist. Educ: AB Univ. of NC, 1946; PhD, ibid., 1953; MA, Harvard Univ., 1947. m. Kathryn Norman, 2 c. Career: Asst. Prof., Southwestern Univ., Memphis, Tenn., 1954-56; Asst. Prof.-Prof., Univ. of Ky., 1956-67; Rsch. Prof., Univ. of Ga., 1967-. Publs: Five French Baroque Organ Masses, 1961; Nine Seventeenth-Century Organ Transcriptions from the Operas of Lully, 1963; Seis Fugas de Juan Sessé, 1976. Contbr. to profl. publs. Mbrships: Am. Musicol. Soc.; Music Lib. Assn.; Pi Kappa Lambda; Phi Mu Alpha Sinfonia. Hons: Fulbright Student Grant, Grance, 1950-51; Fulbright Rsch. Grant, Spain, 1962-63. Hobbies: Mycology; Photography. Address: Dept. of Music, Univ. of Ga., Athens, GA 30602, USA. 2.

HOWELL, Henry William, b. 13 June 1936, Birmingham, UK. Singer (tenor). Educ: Dip., Electrical Engineering, Qld.; Dip., Fine Arts, Melbourne; studied singing, Qld. Conserv. of Music w. James Christiansen & Peter Martin; pvte. studies w. Roy Henderson, London. m. (1) Dolores Tansey, 1 d. (2) Diana Margaret Lawson. Debut: Royal Albert Hall, 1974. Career: Res. Tenor to Aust. Broadcasting Commission, Qld., radio & TV; First Prin. Tnor, Qld. Opera, 1967-73; Radio & TV Opera Artist, BBC; Prin. Tenor, Engl. Nat. Opera. Recordings: 6 LP recordings of Gelineau Psalms, 1967. Publs: With a Mile and a Song, a brief hist. of Qld. Opera. Contbr. to: Qld. Cultural Diary. Mbrships: British Actors Equity; ISM; Qld. Justices' Assn. Hons: ABC Concerto and Vocal Contest, 1962; NY Metropolitan Auditions, Qld., 1964, '66, '67. Mgmt: Basil Douglas Ltd., 8 St. Georges Tce., London NW1 8XJ, UK. Address: 31 Anthony Rd., Greenford Middlesex, UB6 8HF, UK.

HOWELL, Ronald Thomas, b. 24 Jan. 1942, Oklahoma, USA. Music Educator; Clarinettist. Educ: BM, Okla. City Univ., 1964; MME, Univ. of Okla., 1968; DME, ibid., 1976. m. Margaret Jean Graham, 1 s., 1 d. Career: Band Dir., Harrah, Okla., 1963-69; Music Instructor, Bethel Coll., N Newton, Kansas, 1970-72; Chmn., Inst. Music, Okla. Baptist Univ., 1972-; Perfs. in Okla. Symph. Orch., Lyric Theatre of Okla. Orch. Contbr. to: Woodwind Review; NACWPI Jrnl. Mbrships: MENC; Okla. Music Educs. Assn.; Nat. Assn. of Coll. Wind and Percussion Instructors; Coll. Band Dirs. Nat. Assn.; Am. Fedn. of Musicians; Kappa Kappa Psi. Hons: Outstanding Young Men of Am., 1977. Hobbies: Music; Photography. Address: 21 Birdie Land, Shawnee, Okla., USA. 7.

HOWELLS, Anne Elizabeth, b. 12 Jan. 1941, Southport, Lancs., UK. Opera & Concert Singer. Educ: Royal Manchester Coll. of Music. m. Ryland Davies. Debut: Flora, La Travista, Royal Opera House Covent Garden, 1967. Career: Glyndebourne chorus, 1964-67; under contract, 1969-71, now Guest Artist, Royal Opera House Covent Garden; apps. as Guest Artist w. Scottish Opera, Engl. Nat. Opera, in Chgo., at Me. Opera NYC, in Wexford, Geneva, Paris Opera, Royal opera Milan; recitals, Salzburg, Marseille, Nankes, Amsterdam, Naples, Brussels, Wexford, Toronto (Can.). Many roles inclng: Dorabella, Cosi Fan Tutte; Rosina, Barber of Seville; Cherubino, Marriage of Figaro; Poppaea, L'Incoronazione di Poppaea; Melisande, Pelleas & Melisande; Octavian, Der Rosenkavalier. Recordings: Scenes & Areas (Nicholas Maw); Der Rosenkavalier (Annina); L'Ormindo (Erisbe); Trojans (Ascanius); Parsifal (Flower Maiden). Recip. Fellowship, Royal Manchester Coll. of Music. Mgmt: Artists Int. Mgmt., 5 Regents Park Rd., London, NW1 7TL, UK. 1, 3.

HOWELLS, Herbert Norman, b. 17 Oct. 1892, Lydney, Glos., UK. Music Educator; Composer. Educ: RCM; FRCM; FRCO; DMus, Oxford Univ. m. Dorothy Eveline Goozee, 12920, 1 s. (dec.), 1 d. Career: Prof., RCM; Dir. of Music, St. Paul's Girls Schl., 1936-62; First John Collard Fellow, 1931; King Edward Prof. of Music, Univ. of London, 1954-64. Compositions incl: Sir Patrick Spens (Chorus & Orch.); Requiem (unacc. choir & soloists); Sine Nomine; Procession; Punch's Minuet (all orchl.); Pageantry (suite for brass band); Minuet (all orch.); Pageantry (suite ;for brass band); Hymnus Paradisis (soloists, chorus & orch.); Concertos for piano & cello; Music for a Prince (orch.); An English Mass; Stabat Mater (tenor solo, chorus & orch.); The Coventry Mass. Mbrships. incl: Press., ISM, 1952; Master, Worshipful Co. of Musicians, 1959. Hons. incl: CBE; CH, 1972; DMus, Cambridge Univ., 1961; Fellow, St. John's Coll., ibid., 1966. Address: 3 Beverly Close, Barnes, Loneon SW13, UK.

HOWES, Robert Frederick, b. 11 Feb. 1947, Melton-Mowbray, UK. Musician; Musical Director; Record Producer; Professor. Educ: RAM. m. Barbara Courtney-King. Career: Prof., GSM; Musical Dir., Engl. Chorale, & Engl. Rock Choir & on BBC TV progs.; Record Producer; Mbr., London Mozart Players, London Chmbr. Orch., etc. Comp. songs inclng: Wondourous Birth; Travelling; Escape away to Freedom; Why does the Wind Blow; Riv, Riv; Heavy Load; Music Factory; Certain People. Recording: Countdown to Christmas & Nationwide Carol Allums (Engl. Chorale). Recip. Samuel Prize for percussion, RAM, 1968. Hobbies: Squash; Ecology; Music. Mgmt: Chorale Music Prodns., London. Address: Claytiles, Threehouseholds, Chalfont St., Giles, Bucks., UK.

HOWLETT, Neil Baillie, b. Mitcham, UK. Opera & Concert Singer (Baritone). Educ: MA (Cantab.); St. Pauls Cathedral Choir Schl.; Kings Coll., Cambridge; Hochschule für Musik, Stuttgart. m. Elizabeth Robson, 2 d. Career: Major roles w. Sadlers Wells, Engl. Opera Group, Royal Opera House, Covent Garden, Hamburg, Bremen, Nantes, Bordeaux, Toulouse, Nice, Marseille; Currently Prin. Baritone, Engl. Nat. Opera, London; Has sung most major baritone roles; Sang title role in permiere of Toussaint (Blake); Apps., most major fests.; Recitalist; Teacher; Regular broadcaster; Prof., GSM. Hons: Kathleen Ferrier Memorial Prize. Hobbies: Sports; Jogging; Cycling; Langs.; Reading; Host.; Theatre. Mgmt: Ingpen & Williams, Ltd. Address: 42 Inner Park Rd., London SW19, UK.

HOY, Bonnee L, b. 27 Aug. 1936, Jenkintown, Pa., USA. Composer. Educ: Pvte. Instrn. in flute, clarinet, cello & organ, 1951-p65; Pvte. Instrn. in piano w. Florenga Decimo Levengood. Mme. Gaby Casadesus; Phila., Musical Acad., 1948-49; Fontainebleau Conserv. of Music, 1961; BMus, Phila. Musical Acad., 1954-58 & 1960-62; Grad. studies, Temple Univ. Grad. Schl. of Music, 1967-68. Career: 4 1-Comp. concerts, USA, 1970, 1972, 1973, 1975; Many concerts of major works, Pa., 1958-; Var. apps. inclng. Inaugural concert, Nat. Assn. of Am. Comps. & Conds., New Schl. of Music, Phila., Pa., 1975; Guest Speaker, Phila. Orch. Celebrity Luncheon Series, 1976; Pvte. instr. in piano, 1954-; Piano Fac., Phila. Musical Acad., 1962-64; Pvte. instrn., in piano & comp., 1966-; Fac., Settlement Music Schl. & pvte. students by arr., 1966-73; Music Cons., WUHY-FM Prog. Series on poetry & the Arts, 1973; Artistic Dir., Phila. Contemporary Music Committee, 1972-74; Bd. of Dirs., Nat. Assn. of Am. Comps. & Conds., Phila. Chant, 1975-, Comps. incl: (recorded) Verlaine Songs, 1972; Demazia Quintet, 1973; Lament for Solo Violin, 1947; (publd.) Circus Music I, 1975. Recordings incl: Hoy Plays Hoy Music for Voice: Tribe to Violette de Mazia (all Encore). Mbrships: Phila. Contemporary Music Committee, Artistic Dir., Nat. Assn. of Am. Comps. & Conds.; League of Women Comps. Hons: GB Viotti Int. Competition, Vercelli Italy, Dip. of Merit, 1974; Esther Cowen Hood Memorial Scholarship Award, 1960-61, 1961-62; Winner, Phila. Orch. Sr. &

Children's Auditions, 1956, 1949; New Century Club Scholarship Award, 1954; Gold & Silver Medals in Piano, Phila.Music Acad., 1956, 1949; Collectiong of Hoy manuscripts & comps. in Bala Cynwyd Lib., Bala Cynwyd, Pa. Hobbies: Camping; Birdwatching; Reading; Ceramic Sculpture; Sports; Candlemaking.

HOYEM, Nell Marie, b. 2 Sept. 1906, Solddiers Grove, Wis., USA. Music Educator. Educ: MA, 1957, PhD, 1967, Univ. of Minn.; BA, St. Olaf Coll., Northfield, Minn., 1927. Cáreer: Dir. of High Schl. Vocal Music, Morris, 1948-59, Mayville, ND, 1947-48, Spring Valley, Minn., 19309-47; Elementary & Secondary Supervisor of Music, Wilson Campas Schl., Mankato State Coll., 1959-66; Prof. of Music, Mankato State Univ., 1966-75; Prof. Emerita, Guest Lectr., ibid., 1976-79. Publs: Mankato Symph. Orch. Notes. Mbrships. incl: MENC; Minn. Music Educs. Assn. (VP, Gen. Music, 1971-73); Am. Musicol. Soc.; NEA. Hons: Hon. Life Mbr., Minn. Educ. Assn., 1975; Outstanding Educs. of Am., 1975. Hobbies: Concerts; Writing; Sports. Address: 416 Holly Lane No. 15, Mankato, MN 56001, USA.

HOYLE, Ted, b. 17 Aug. 1942, Huntsville, Ala., USA. Cellist. Educ: BMus, Eastman Schl. of Music; MMus, Yale Univ.; Studied w. Andre Navarra, Ecole Normale de Musique, Paris, France. Career: Cellist, Kohon Quartet; Prof., music, Kean Coll., NJ; Cellist, Performing Arts Trio, ibid. Recordings: Num. recordings w. Kohon Quartet inclng: String Quartets by Walter Piston, Peter Mennin, Charles Ives, William Schuman, Aaron Copland, Julia Smith, Roger Sessions & Penderecki. Mbrships: Violoncello Soc., Am. String Tchrs. Assn. Hobbies: Swimming; Reading. Address: 276 Riverside Dr., NY, NY 10025, USA.

HRISANIDIS (HRISANIDE), Alexandre Demetre, b. 15 June 1936, Petrila, Roumania. Composer; Piano soloist; Professor of Music. Ecuc. incls: Dips., Comp., 1959, Piano Soloist, 1964, Univ. of Bucharest-Roumania, Conserv. of Music "Ciorian Porumbescu"; Pvte. studies w. Nadia Boulanger, Paris, Am. Conserv., Fontainebleau, Debut: Roumania, 1956. Career: Piano Soloist, pub. concerts & recitals, radio recordings, TV broadcasts, Belgium, France, German Fed. Repub., W Berlin, Netherlands, Roumania, USSR, Spain, Sweden, Switz., USA, Yugoslavia & Greece. Num. comps. for piano, chmbr. ensembles, orchs., choruses, musicians & tape etc. inclng: Desseins Espagnols (piano), 1971; MP5-Musique Pour Cinq, 1966, I-RO-LA-HAI (voice & chmbr. orch., 1971; CORI (electronic music), 1972; Sonnets, 1973. Soloist on Recordings for Electrecord & Radio Nederland. Ed: Neue Rumänische Klaviermusik, 2 vols. Mbr. Profl. Orgs. Recip. sev. awards for comps. Address: Prof J Bronnerlaan 7, 2012 Haarlem, 1 Netherlands.

HRISTIĆ, Zoran, b. 30 July 1938, Belgrade, Yugoslavia. Composer. Educ: Dip. (comp.), Acad. of Musical Arts, Belgrade. m. Radmila, 2 s. Debut: Belgrade, 1958. Career: Comp., Chmbr. music, 2 TV Ballets, 1 stage Ballet, music for 30 films, approx. 100 stage music, sev. TV serials, Childrens TV musicals. Comps: 8 Vocal/Instrumental Comps. (Cantatas & Oratoriums). Mbr., Comps. Soc. of Yugoslavia. Hons: 1st Prize for Dip. Work, 1963; 1st Prize, Chmbr. music of Yugoslavia, 1967; 1st Prize for Film Music, 1967, '69; State Prize for ballet, Darinka's Bistoval, 1975. Address: 53 Gospodaras Jevrema, 11000 Belgrade, Yugoslavia.

HROVATIN, Radoslav, b. 8 Feb. 1908, Ptuj, Yugoslavia. Professor of Music; Composer; Ethnomusicologist. Educ: DpH, Univ. of Prague, Czechoslovakia, 1939; Dip., Conserv. of Ljubljana, Yugoslavia, 1935, Conserv. of Prague, 1938. m. Lidija Hrovatin, 1 d. Career incls: Prof. of Hist. of Music of Folk Music, Acad. of Music, Ljubljana, 1946-53, HS of Music, ibid., 1953-63, Instn. for Music & Ballet Instruction, ibid., 1963-. Comps. incl: (piano) Domaci plesi (Country Dances), 1943; (chorus) Zdravljice (Toast, for youth chorus), 1957. Recordings: Slovenian Folk Songs, suznji (Stand up, Slaves), 1976. Contbr. to profl. jrnls. Recip. var. hons. Hobbies incls: Learning for Langs. Address: Rozna dolina C V31, 61000 Ljubljana, Yugoslavia.

HRUBY, Frank M, b. 29 June 1918, Emporia, Kan., USA. Music Critic; Conductor. Educ: BMus, MMus, Eastman Schl. of Music Univ. of Rochester. m. Pollee Phipps, 4 s., 1 d. Career: Dir., Singers Club of Cleveland, 1956-65; Hd. of composition & Theory, Miss. Southern Coll., 1946-48, Chmn., Music & Arts Dept., Univ. Schl., Cleveland, Ohio, 1948-75; Music Dir. Cain Park Theater, Cleveland Hts., 1946-56. Compositions: 3 Musicals for children; var. works for students, HS glee clubs & Choruses; string quartets, etc. Contbr. to: Cleveland Press (current music critic), Cleveland Corresp., Musical Am. Mbrship: Recording Sec., Music Critics Assn. of AM. Hobbies: Carpentry. Address: 2350 Beachwood Blvd., Cleveland, OH 44122, USA. 2, 8.

HRUBÝ, Stanislav, b. 7 Apr. 1932, Srbice, Czech. Musician (flute, violin, piano etc.); Composer; Arranger; Song Collector. Educ: Bedrich Smetana Music Schl., Plzen; Prague Cons. of Music. Debut: Prague, 1953. Career: Flautist, Prague Chamber Orch., Prague Symph. Orch., Moravian Phil. Orch., Prague Radio Orch. Comps: Lullaby for Flute & Harp; Slow waltz, waltz & Polka for dance orchestra. Publs: Jindrich Jindrich: Chod Song-Book. Hobbies: Working in home and country house. Mgmt: Pragokoncert, Maltézské, nám. 1, Prague 1. Address: Na úlehli 7, 145 00 Prague-Michele, Czech.

HSU, Dolores Menstell, b. 4 Nov. 1930, Portland, Ore., USA. Music Educator; Administrator. Educ: BA Lewis & Clark Coll.; Piano Dip., Mozarteum, Salzburg, Austria; Grad. Study, Musicol. Univ. of Vienna, Austria; PhD, Univ. of Southern Calif., USA. m. Immanuel C Hsu, 1 s. Career: Prof. of Music, Hist. & Chmn. of Grad. Studies in Music. Univ. of Calif., Santa Barbara. Contbr. to: Music Review; Musical Quarterly; Yale Jrnl. of Music Theory; Piano Tchr.; Piano Quarterly; Festschriften; 19th Century music (Ed. Bd.). Mbrships: Am. Musicol. Soc.; Coll. Music Soc.; Am. Soc. of Eastern Arts; Mu Phi Epsilon; Soc. for Ethnomusicology. Hons: Fulbright Fellowship to Austria, 1952-54; AAUW Fellowship, 1957-58; Humanities Inst. Grant, Univ. of Calif., 1968; Disting. Alumni Achievment Award, Lewis & Clark Coll., 1969; Fulbright Rsch. Fellowship, 1973; Outstanding Educators of Am. Award, 1973. Hobbies: Gardening; Hiking. Address: 1415 Dover Rd., Santa Barbara, CA 93103, USA. 2, 5.

HSU, John Tseng-Hsin, b. 21 Apr. 1931, Swatow, China. Old Dominion Foundation Professor of Humanities & Music, Cornell University; Viola da Gamba Recitalist; Cellist, Amandé Trio. Educ: BMus, 1953, MMus, 1955, New Engl. Conserv. of Music, Boston. m. Martha J Russell. Career: perfs. throughout Am. & Europe; Solo viola da gamba progs., BBC London, radio stns. in Germany, Netherlands, Belgium, Switz. Recordings: Pièces de Viole by Antoine Forqueray & Louis de Caix d'Horvelois, 1966; Three Viola da Gamba Sonatas by J S Bach, 1971; Five Viola da Gamba Suites by Antoine Forqueray, 1972; 5 discs, Pièces de Viole by Marin Marias, 1973-77; Pièces de viole by Marais, Jacques Mordl & Charles Dollé, 1978. Hons: DMus, New Engl. Conserv. of Music, 1971; Hon. Mbr., Riemenschneider Bach Inst., Berea, Ohio, 1975. Mgmt: Lynn Glaser & Assoc., 3514 Dwight Way, Berkeley, CA 94704, USA. Address: 601 Highland Rd., Ithaca, NY 14850, USA. 2.

HSU, Wen-ying (Miss), b. 2 May 1909, Shanghai, China. (USA citizen) Pianist; Composer; Musicologist; Professor. Educ: Yenching Univ., Peiping, 1930-33; BS, Geo. Peabody Coll., Tenn., USA, 1955; MMus, New Engl. Conserv., Boston, Mass., 1959; studies w. Dr. John Vincent Jr., UCLA, 1963-64, & Ingolf Dahl, Univ. of Southern Calif., 1965-66. m. Ginpoh King (div.), 2 s., 1 d. Comps. incl: Sky Maidens Dance Suite for Orch.; Piano Sonata, No. 1, 1972; Dreams of Longing (female chorus), 1974; Sound of Autumn (piano pieces, intermediate), 1974; Violin Pieces (for beginners), 1974. Works have been broadcast in USA & Taiwan. Contbr. to: Chinese Culture Quarterly. Mbrships. incl: NACUSA; Nat. League of Am. Penwomen; Am. Musicol. Soc.; Soc. of Ethnomusicol; Int. Musicol. Soc.; Sigma Alpha Iota. Recip. many prizes & awards for comps. & poetry. Hobbies: Writing poetry; Cooking. Address: 114 S New Hampshire Ave. No. 101, Los Angeles, CA 90004, USA.

HUBAD, Samo, b. 17 July 1917, Ljubljana, Yugoslavia. Conductor (Piano). Educ: BA Jurisprudence; MA, Acad. of Music, Ljubljana; Dip. Cond., 1941; Mozarteum, Salzburg, 1948. m. Dana Kutin. Debut: Opera House, Ljubljana, 1943. Career: Cond., Opera House, Ljubljana, 1941-56; Slovens Phil. Orch., 1948-66; Zagreb Phil., 1956-58; Zagreb Opera, 1958-64; Cond. in Chief, RTV Symphonic Orch., Ljubljana, 1966-. Num. recordings. Mbrships: Pres., Union of Yugoslav Musical Artists. Hons: Prize of Yugoslav Govt., 1948; 3 Slovens Nat. Prizes; 3 Prizes of Yugoslav RTV for best recordings of Yugoslav Comps. Address: Ciril Metodov Trg 18, 61000 Ljubljana, Yugoslavia.

HUBER, Horst, b. 22 Mar. 1933, Munich, German Fed. Repub. Percussionist. Educ: Dip., Schl. of Music, Munich, 1948-52; Acad. of Music, Munich, 1952-56. div., 1 d. Career: Prin. Percussionist, Bavarian Radio Symph. Orch., 1955-. Has recorded for DGG, Philips, EMI, Polydor Int., Teldec, Harmonia Mundi & Electrola. Mbr., Musician's Union (DOV). Recip. Prize of Bavarian Govt., 1951. Hobbies: Lit.; Painting; Arch.; Collecting graphic art; Travel; Fishing. Address: Gruenwalderstr. 34, 8 Munich 90, German Fed. Repub.

HUBER, John Elwyn, b. 15 Dec. 1940, Hays, Kan., USA. Associate Professor in Music. Educ: BMus (Music Educ.), Ft. Hays Kan. State Coll., 1962; MMus (Music Theory), Univ. of Mich.,

1967; PhD in progress, ibid. m. Barbara Jane Krehbiel, 1 d. Career: Piano Instructor, Colby Pub. Schls., Kan., 1962-65; Assoc. Prof. in Music (Theory & Piano), Ft. Hays Kan. State Coll., Hays, Kan., 1967-. Mbrships: MENC; Nat. MTA; Kan. MTA; Kan. Music Educators Assn. Hobbies: Skiing; Gardening. Address: Ft. Hays State Univ., Hays, KS 67601, USA.

HUBER, Klaus, b. 30 Nov. 1924, Berne, Switzerland. Composer; Professor of Composition. Educ: Cert., Tchrs. Trng. Coll., Zürich; Conserv., ibid.; Musikhochschule, W Berlin. m. Susanne Bitter, 3 s., 2 d. Debut: Netherlands, 1955. Career: Dir., master class Comp., Music Acad., Basle, 1964-72; Prof. of Comp., & Dir., Inst. of New Music Hochschule für Musik, Freiburg, German Fed. Repub., 1973-; Frequent premieres & perfs. of works, Int. Soc. Contemporary Music Fests., 1958-, & other fests. of New Music. Compositions incl: Tenebrae; Turnus; (recorded) Tempora; Inwendig voller Figur. Mbr., profl. assns. Hons. incl: Music Prize, Canton of Berne, 1968; Beethoven Prize City of Bonn, 1970; Prize, Assn. of Swiss Musicians, 1975. Hobby: Camping. Address: CH-4418 Reigoldswil, Switzerland.

HUBER, Paul, b. 17 Feb. 1918, Kirchberg, St. Gallen, Switzerland. Music Teacher. Educ: Dips. for Schl. Singing, Piano, Organ & Counterpoint, Zürich Conserv.; studies w. Nadia Boulanger, Paris. m. Hedy Gähwiler, 2 s., 1 d. Career: Organist & M usic Dir., Ch. of St. Nikolaus, Wil, St. Gallen; var. stage, radio & TV perfs. Comps: (published) About 3000 works inclng. Der verlorene Sohn (perf. in Hereford, UK), Requiem, Das Schaufenster (opera), Corpus Christi Mysticum; 2 Violin Concertos; 1 Symph; (recorded) Miserere mei; Carmen Saeculare; Missa in C (recorded); Ring des Jahres; Negro spirituals. Mbr., var. profl. assns. Hons. incl: Comps. prizes, 1966; Stephan Jaeggi Prize. Hobbies: Long Walks in the Country; Composing. Address: Goethestr. 74, 9008 St. Gallen, S.witzerland.

HUBER, Walter Simon, b. 6 May 1898, Basel, Switzerland. Comp.; Cond.; Organist. Educ: TDD Bern, 19125-17; Conserv. Bern, 1919-21; Univ. Bern, 1918-20; Music Acad. Munich, 1921-28; Univ. Basel Zürich; DPh, 1956. m. Christiane Mayer, 2 d., 4 s. Career: Tchr. Basel, 1934-41; Tchr., Küsnacht-Zürich, 1941-65; Musical Dir., organist Bern, Basel. Comp. incl: Swiss Folk songs; Choirworks; Cantatas for solo, choir, orch.; Musicals; Operas. Mbrships: Swiss section Int. Heinrich Schütz Soc. Publs. incl: Dissertation, Black Symbolism in Heinrich Schütz. Contbr. to var. profl. jrnls. Hons: 2nd Prize Choir Contest, 1948. Hobbies: Writing poetry; Travelling. Address: Alte Landstr. 92, CH/8700 Küsnacht, Zřuich, Switzerland.

HUBERT, Marcel, b. 17 Aug. 1906, Lille, France. Concert Artist (Cello). Educ: Studied w. Andre Hekking at Paris Conservatoire. m. Elke-Gerhild Pany. Educ: W. Colonne Orch., Paris, France. Career: At 11 yrs. of age, made concert tour of 17 engagements; Recitals in Carnegie & Town Hall, NYC, USA; Toured from coast to coast in USA & Can.; Soloist w. major European Orchs. inclng: Phila. Orch.; Minneapolis Symph.; Guest on Bing Crosby's radio prog.; Apps. w. Lily Pons & Yvonne Hubert. Num. recordings. Hons. incl: 1st Prize of Paris Conservatoire. Hobbies: Tennis; Reading. Address: 140 W 69th St., New York, NY 10023, USA. 4.

HUDECEK, Václav, b. 7 June 1952, Rozmitál, Czech. Violinist. Educ: Acad. of Music, Prague; pvte. study w. David Oistrakh, 4 yrs. m. Eva Trejtnarová. Debut: w. RPO, London, 1967. Career: Concerts & fest. apps. throughout the world. Num. recordings. Mbr., Czech. Union of Concert Artists & Comps. Recip. Golden Prize for Panton recording of Dvorak Violin Concerto. Hobbies: Photography; Filming. Mgmt: Pragokoncert, Maltezske Nam 1, Prague 1, Czech. Address: Torunska 329, Prague 8, Czech.

HUDES, Eric Aubrey, b. 2 May 1920, London, England. Composer. m. Joan Hayto, 2 c. Career: composition of incidental music for all Theatre Union prodns., 1940-43, for BBC radio features, 1940-43; compositins of ballets for Art of Movement Studio, 1946-47; chmbr. music perf. in London (Wigmore Hall, Arts Coun., SPNM, etc.) & in many provincial cities. Compositions incl: Variations for Piano; 4 Fragments from Holderlin's Madness (song cycle); Partita for Piano Duet; Sappho Fragments (voice & piano); Fantasis Sopra Frammenti di Saffo (cello & piano); Pentaptych (Grass quintet); Sonata (Fluto & piano). Mbrships: Composers' Guild of Gt. Brit.; Soc. for Promotion of New Music; Coun., E Anglian New Music Soc.; Assn. for Brit. Music. Recip. of 1st Prize, Soc. for Modern Music Competition, 1969. Hobbies: Cooking; Chinese Pottery. Mgmt: Thames Publng., 14 Barlby Rd., London W10, UK. Address: Paigles, Perry Green, Bradwell, Braintree, Essex CM7 8ES, UK.

HUDEZ, Karl, b. 21 Jan. 1904, Salzburg, Austria. Musical Director. Educ: Mozarteum, Salzburg; State Acad. of Music, Vienna. m. Gusti Petyrek. Career: Max Reinhardt Prods., 1924-38; Salzburg Fest., 1928-60; Musical Dir., State Opera, Vienna, 1945-53; Dramatic Advsr., Musical Dir., Vienna People's Opera, 1938-44; Dir. of Studies, State Opera, Vienna, 1953-68; Dir., Conserv. Opera Schl., Vienna & var. Summer Courses inclng. SavonLinna, Finland. Compositions incl: ballet Daphnis & Chloe; Lieder; Stage Works. Recordings: Salzburg, Everyman; Lied Recital (Piano Accomp.). Mbrships: Hon. Pres. Austrian-Finnish Soc. Hons: Kt., 1st Class, Cross of the Golden Lion, Finland; Hon. Cross, Litteris & Artibus, Rep. of Austria, Golden Sign of Hon., 1976. Hobbies: Photography; Books. Address: 4 Michael Wengerg, 2380 Perchtoldsdorf, Austria.

HUDSON, Barton, b. 20 July 1936, Memphis, Tenn., USA. Musicologist. Educ: BMus, Midwestern Univ.; MMUs, PhD, Ind. Univ.; Dip., Staatliche Hochschule für Musik, Freiburg i. Br., German Fed. Repub. m. Elizabeth K Hudson, 1 d. Career: Prof. of Music, W Va. Univ. Publs. incl: G Salvatore, Collected Keyboard Works, 1964; B Storace, Selva di varie compositioni, 1965; S A de Heredia, Drei Magnificat, 1968; Antoine Brumel, Collected Works, 6 vols., 1969-73; Thomas Crecquillon, Collected Works, vols. 1-4, 1974-75; S A de Heredia, Magnificats (complete), 3 vols., 1975; Hayne van Ghizeghem, collected works, 1977. Contbr. to profl. jrnls. Mbr., profl. assns. Recip., var. scholarships & grants. Address: 473 Devon Rd., Morgantown, WV 26505, USA.

HUDSON, Derek Colbourne, b. 23 May 1934, Hove, Sussex, UK. Conductor. Educ: GSM; ARCM; pvte. studies. w. Ernest Ansermet. m. Jill Angela Froom, 2 d. Debut: Wigmore Hall, London, 1964. Career: Asst. Musical Dir., Chichester Fest. Theatre, 1963, 64, 66; Musical Dir., Ctr. 42, & London Dance Theatre, 1964; Cond., Royal Ballet, 1965; Concerts w. LPO, RPO, Engl. Chmbr. Orch. & Tonkünstler Orch.; Musical Dir., Cape Town Symphj. Orch., S Africa, 1967-72; Musical Dir., Bulawayo Phil. Orch., Rhodesia, 1974-; sev. broadcasts. Comps: Bachelor's Fare, 1964; (recorded) Incidental Music, The Story of the Passion, 1961. Recordings: Fauré, Requiem; Soldier's Tale (film). Hobbies: Bridge; Squash; Reading. Address: 3 Tait Rd., Hillside, Bulawayo, Rhodesia 3.

HUDSON, Frederick, b. 16 Jan. 1913, Gateshead Co. Durham, UK. Musicologist. Educ: FRCO, 1939; BMus, Univ. of durham, 1941; DMus, ibid., 1950. m. Mildred Hepplewhite, 2 s. Career: Organist & Choirmaster, Alnwick Parish Ch., Northumberland, 1941-48; Dir. of Music, Hexham Abbey, 1948-49; Lectr. in Music, Univ. of Newcastle upon Tyne, 1949-70; Reader in Music, ibid., 1960-64; Vis. Prof. of Music, Univ. of Cinn., Ohio, USA, 1967-68; Lecture-tour, N Am. Univ. Schls. of Music, 1974. Publs: var. original text & critical editions. Contbr. to var. profl. jrnls. Mbrships: Handel-Gesellschaft (Coun. & Editl. Panel, Hallische Handel-Ausgabe); Neue Bach-Gesellschaft; Int. Musicol. Soc.; Int. Heinrich Schutz Soc.; Royal Musical Assn.; RCO; Inc. Soc. Musicians; Past Pres., Newcastle upon Tyne Soc. Organists; Handel Avsry. Committee, Novello, London. Hobbies: Photography; Reading; Travel. Address: 12 Claremont St., Newcastle upon Tyne, NE2 4AH, UK. 3, 14, 28.

HUDSON, Paul, b. 24 June 1945, Barnsley, Yorks., UK. Opera Singer. Educ: studied singing, piano & viola, Huddersfield Music Schl.; RCM; London Opera Ctr.; ARCM; ALCM. Career: has performed w. most major Brit. orchs.; tours of France & Norway; regular broadcasts for BBC; apps. w. Welsh & Engl. Nat. Operas; Bass Soloist, Royal Opera House, 1969- (over 300 perfs.). Recordings: Le Nozze di Figaro; Sherrill Milnes LP; Die Feen; Rienzi; Creation; Verdi Requiem; Bach Magnificat; Les Noces. Mbr., Savage Club. Hons: Scholarships; Dr Saleeby Prize for Basses, 1967. Hobbies: Photography; Rough shooting. Address: 26 Firlands, Ellesmere Rd., Weybridge, Surrey, UK.

HUDSON, Richard Albert, b. 19 Mar. 1924, Alma, Mich., USA. University Professor; Musicologist. Educ: BS, Calif. Inst. of Technol., 1944; BMus, Oberlin Coll., 1949; MMus, Syracuse Univ., 1951; PhD, UCLA, 1967. Career: Assoc. Prof. of Organ & Theory, Converse Coll., Spartanburg, SC, 1949-50; Instructor, Organ & Theory Oberlin Coll., 1953-55; Tchr., UCLA, 1967-, presently Prof. of Music. Compositions: Trios for Organ, Vols. I, II; Postlude on Macht Hoch dic Tür, organ; Suite of Organ Carols, 1976. Contbr. to: The Diapason; Jrnl. of the Am. Musicol. Soc.; Acta Musicologica; Musica Disciplina; Jrnl. of the Lute Soc. of Am.; The Musical Quarterly; The Music Review. Hons: Fulbright Scholarship to Holland, 1952-53; Am. Coun. of Learned Socs. Fellowship, 1973-74. Address: 14934 Dickens St., Apt. 9, Sherman Oaks, CA 91403, USA.

HUDY, Wolfgang, b. 26 May 1928, HalleSaale, German Dem. Repub. Composer; Pianist. Educ: Music Acad. Leipzig; Music

Acad. Halle; Conserv. Halle and Quedlinburg. m. Ilse-Maria Geissler. Career: Piano tchr., Brugstadt; Ballet repetitor Weimar; Musical Dir. satirical cabaret "Kiebitzensteiner", Halle. Comps. incl: Ballet music, Two Found the Road, The Cold Heart, Annos, The Laughing Mask, The Frog King; Orch. works; Oratorium; Solo concerto for oboe; Cabaret songs. Mbrships: Assn. for Comp. and Musicologists, GDR. Hons: Händel Prize, dist. Halle, 1964. Address: Wilhelm-Külz Str. 2, HalleSaale, German Dem. Repub.

HUEBER, Kurt Anton, b. 9 July 1928, Salzburg, Austria. Composer. Educ: Dip., piano & conducting, Musikhochschule Mozarteum, Salzburg, 1948. Career: Section Ldr., Konservatorium der Stadt Wien; Works performed in concedrt & on radio. Comps. incl: Scenic music for stage, Linz, 1958-60; 1st Opera 'Schwarz Auf Weiss', compd. for Austrian TV, 1968; Symchromie I, 1970; Symchromie II, 1972; Formant spectrale for string orch., 1974. Recordings: Glockenspektren, for pipebells & piano; Iris, for piano & percussion. Contbr. to profl. publs. Mbr. var. orgs. Hons: Förderungspreis der Stadt Wien for music, 1967. Hobbies: Maths.; Physics; Swimming; Travel. Address: Paradisgasse 14, A1190 Vienna, Austria.

HUG, Theo, b. 12 Nov. 1906, Bern, Switz. Violinist; Konzertmeister; Quartettist; Professor; Conductor. Educ: Konservatorium Bern; study w. M Hewitt, Georges Enesco, Paris. m. Ruth Kaiser, 3 d. Career: Violinist; Konzertmeister; Quartettist; Conductor; Prof., Konservatorium Bern. Recordings: Othmar Schock, Elegie op.36; Richard Sturzenegger, Fresko; Jean Daetwyler, Concerto pour cordes et percussion. Publs: Bogentechnik - Praktische Studien für jegen Tag. Mbrships: Schweizerischer Tonkünstlerverein; Schweiz. Musikpädagogischer Verband; Schweiz. Musikforschende Gesellschaft; Pres., ESTA (European String Tchrs. Assn.). Hobbies: Travel; Sport; Photography. Address: Innerberg, CH 3044 Saeriswil, Switz.

HUGGLER, John Stillman, b. 30 Aug. 1928, Rochester, NY, USA. Composer. Educ: BM, Univ. of Rochester, NY. m. Mardean Butler, 3 c. Career: 2nd Clarinet, Okla. City Symph., 1952-56; jazz Pianist; Assoc. Prof., Univ. of Mass., Boston; Vis. Prof., MIT, 1965-66, Brandeis Univ., 1968, Harvard Univ., 1974. Comps. (publd.) incl: Ecce Homo, Sculptures, Elegy to the Memory of Lorca, Music in 2 Parts, for orch.; 4 Concerti: Divertimento for viola & orch.; Sinfonia for 13 Instruments; 7 Songs; 5 Str. Quartets; 3 Str. Quintets; 3 Brass Quintets; Sonata, 7 Bagatelles, for piano; Duo for trombone & piano; Bitterenüsse, poems of Paul Celan, soprano & 5 instruments. var. Chmbr. Music; (recorded) Brass Quintets Nos. 1 & II. Mbrships: Am. Comps. Alliance; BMI. Hons: Guggenheim Fellow, 1962, 1969; Com.-in-Res., Boston Symph., 1964-65; Horblit Award, 1968. Address: 94 Crest Rd., Wellesley, MA 02181, USA.

HUGHES, Andrew, b. 3 Aug. 1937, London, UK. University Professor. Educ: BA, Worcester Coll., Oxford, 1959; MA & DPhil, ibid., 1962. m. Diane M J Rycroft, 1 d. Career: on Facs. of Queen's Univ., Belfast; Univ. of Ill.; Univ. of NC at Chapel Hill; currently Prof. of Musicol., Univ. of Toronto., Musical Prodns. under his direction & edited; Filius Getronis (12 C), 1972; The Coronation Serv. & Mass for Henry V of England, 1973; Officium Nocte Resurrectionis (14 C), 1974. Publs: The Old Hall Manuscript (in collab. w. M Bent), 3 vols., 1969-73; Fifteen Century Liturgical Music: Antiphons for Holy Week & Easter, 1968; Manuscript Accidentals: Ficta in Focus, 1972; A Bibliography of Medieval Music: The Sixth Liberal Art, 1974. Contbr. to profl. jrnls. Mbrships: Mbr.-at-Large, Am. Musicol. Soc., 1972-73; Royal Musical Assn.; Int. Musicol. Soc.; Mediaeval Acad. of Am. Hons: John Guggenheim Fndn., 1973-74, etc. Hobbies: Computer building & programming. Address: Apt. 120, 49 Thorncliffe Pk. Dr., Toronto M4H 1J6, Ont., Canada.

HUGHES, Anthony George, b. 6 July 1928, Dublin, Repub. of ireland. University Professor of Music; Pianist; Organist; Conductor. Educ: LRIAM, 1947; BMus, Univ. Coll. Dublin, 1949; DMus, ibid., 1955. m. Nuala Mullen, 1 s., 3 d. Debut: Radio Telefis Eireann Symph. Orch., 1947. Career: Piano recitals in Europe, England & Ireland; Lectured extensively for Foras Eireann (Shaw Trust); Prof. of Pianoforte, RIAM, 1948-58; Asst. Lectr., Univ. Coll., Dublin, 1955; Prof. of Music, ibid., 1958-. Mbrships. incl: Int. Musicol. Soc.; Nat. Lib. of Ireland, Trustee, 1971-; Royal Musical Assn.; Dublin Grand Opera Soc., Pres., 1967-. Contbr. to Grove's Dict. of Music & Musicians. Recip., Arnold Bax Medal, 1956. Address: 14 Brighton Rd., Dublin 6, Repub. of Ireland.

HUGHES, Charles William, b. 20 Feb. 1900, Portsmouth, RI, USA. Musicologist; Educator; Organist. Educ: BS, 1923, MA, 1924, Tchrs. Coll., PhD, 1933, all Columbia Univ.; studied organ w. Seth Bingham, comp. w Percy Goetschius, Seth Bingham & Paul Dukas, theory & counterpoint w. Nadia Boulanger

& viola de gamba w. Rudolph Dolmetsch. m. Fannie L Hughes. Career: Instr., Music Dept., Hunter Coll., 1927; Asst. Prof., 1935; Assoc. Prof., 1948; Lehann Coll. Prof., 1969. Publs. incl: The Human Side of Music, 1948; American Hymns, Old & New, forthcoming. Contbr. to jrnls. Mbrships. incl: Am. Musicol. Soc. Hobbies: Gardening; Collecting old tools. Address: 28 Ralph Ave., White Plains, NY 10606, USA. 11, 12.

HUGHES, Martin Glyn, b. 23 March 1950, Hemel Hempstead, UK. Concert Pianist. Educ: Salisbury Choir Schl.; Bryanston Schl.; Conservatoire National Supérieure de Musique, Paris (w. Yvonne Lefebure); Tchaikovsky Conserv., Moscow (w. Lev Oborin). Debut: Wigmore Hall, 1972. Career: Soloist & recitalist, UK & abroad; London apps. incl. Queen Elizabeth Hall recitals, 3 seasons; Broadcasts, BBC, French & German radios; Featured on BBC TV, Making a Name, playing Chopin piano concerto w. LPO; Prom debut, 1972; Perfd. complete cycle of Beethoven Sonatas, 1979. Publs: (translation) Russian School of Piano Playing, 1977. Mbr., ISM. Hons: Martin Musical Fund, 1967; Frenchy Govt. Scholar, 1968; British Coun. Scholarship, 1970; Marguerite Long Int. Competition Bronze Medal, 1969; Maria Canals Int. Competition (2nd Prize), 1970. Hobbies: Fine Wine & Cuisine. Addrss: c/o Surrey Univ. Music Dept., Guildford, Surrey, UK.

HUGHES, Martin John, b. 24 May 1951, Hornchurch, UK. Violinist. Educ: RCM, 1969-74; ARCM; GRSM. m. Jill Whitehead, 2 c. Debut: Wigmore Hall, London, 1974. Career: num. concerto & recital apps. in UK; Prin. 2nd Violin, Northern Sinfonia. Hons: Ian Stoutzker prize, RCM, 1972. Hobby: Cricket. Address: 17 Alexandra Terrace, Hexham, Northumberland, UK.

HUGHES, Stacy, b. 30 June 1930, NY, NY, USA. Music Educator; Pianist; Clinician; Consultant. Educ: BA, MA, CCNY; BM, MM, Manhattan Schl. of Music; Doct. Candidate, Columbia Univ.; studied Cond. w. Pierre Monteux, William Revelli, Freddie Fennell, Izler Solomon; studied Comp. w. V Giannini, Howard Murphy; Mc Hose, Darius Milhaud; Educl. trng. w. V Jones, Gladys Tipton. m. Norman Hughes, 2 s. Career: Supvsr. of Music, NYC; Fndr. & Dir., Boys Club Band, NYC, & St. John's Univ. Band; Prof., Fine Arts Dept., Pace Univ.; Fac. Mbr., Manhattan Schl. of Music, 1973-, & NY Coll. of Music; Supvsr., Title One ESEA Music Prog.; Cons., NY State Narcotics Hosps. Music Prog.; Esducl. Advsr., Met. Opera; Choral Cons., Franco-Colombo publs.; Exec. Dir. La Puma Opera Workshops. Compositions: Settings for Shakespearian Sonnets; small musical comedies. Fndr., music mag. Changing Tones & contbr. num. articles to other profl. jrnls. Mbrships: NYC Music Tchrs. Assn. (Past Pres.); Bohemian Club. Hons. incl: NY State Rep., Committee No. 5 MENC, Chgo. 1970; Specialist, Mass State Humanities Prog. Hobbies: Coins; Stamps. Address: 11 Alden Rd., Larchmont, NY 10538, USA.

HUGHES, Trevor John, b. 28 Aug. 1953, King's Lynn, UK. Accompanist; Organist; Teacher. Educ: RCM, 1971-75; GRSM; ARCM (organ perf.); MTC, London Univ. Inst. of Educ., 1975-76. m. Marilyn Jane Hughes, 1 s. Career: Organist, St. Anne's Ch., S Lambeth, 1971-75; organist, St. David's Ch., Newtown, Powys, 1977-; freelance accomp. incl. Purcell Room, Wigmore Hall, radio, Int. competitions incl. Geneva & Amsterdam. Mbrships: ISM; RCO. Hobby: Cycling. Address: Rhosymedre, Dolerw Dr., Newton, Powys, Wales, UK.

HUGH-JONES, Elaine, b. London, UK. Accompanist; Teacher; Composer. Educ: studied w. Julius Isserlis, Dr. F W Wadeley & Lennox Berkeley; LRAM; ARCM. Career: Accomp. for BBC Midland Region, 1956-; Dir. of Music, Derby HS, 1949, Notre Dame Grammar Schl., Blackburn, 1952, & Kidderminster HS, 1955; Accomp., Malvern Girls' Coll., 1963-. Compositions: Sweet Was the Song the Virgin Sung; The Son of God Is Born for All; Chanticleer: Torches; Setting of Magnificat & Nunc Dimittis (perf. in Coventry Cathedral, Mar. 1974). Mbrships: ISM; AAM. Mgmt: Ibbs & Tillett. Address: 95, Church Rd., Malvern Links, Worcs., UK. 4, 138.

HUGLO, Michel, b. 14 Dec. 1921, Lille, France. Director of Research. Educ: Doct., (3 cycle), classical studies: Musicol.; studied piano. m. Martha Morel. Career: Dir., Rsch., CNRS ic of Musical Paleography, Ecole Pratique des Hautes Etude, Paris. Recordings: Ghant Gregorien collection, Harmonia Mund, CBS. Publs: Fonti e paleografia del Canto ambrosiano, 1957; Les tonaires, Paris, 1971. Contbr. to; Revue de Musicol.; Scirptotium, Brussels; RILM, New York. VP, French Musicol. Soc., 1974. Hobby: Gardening. Address: Parc Montaigne, 5 Square Gay-Lussac, 78330 Fontenay-Le-Fleury, France.

HUJSAK, (Ruth) Joy Detenbeck, b. 13 May 1924, Buffalo, NY, USA. Musician (harp, Piano, Organ) Performer; Teacher. Educ: Pvte. Organ study w. Catherine Crozier, Harold Gleason; BMus, Eastman Schl. of Music, 1945; Lamont Schl. of Music,

Univ. of Denver, Colo.; Schmitz Schl. of Piano, San Francisco, Calif., summers 1947, 1948, 1950; pvte. Piano study w. E Robert Schmitz, Leo Smit; pvte. study of Harp w. Marjorie Call. m. Edward Josef Hujsak, 2 s. Career incls: Pianist, Miss. State Coll. for Women, Columbus, 1946-47; Pvte. Piano Studio, Buffalo, NY, & Concert perfs. as Piano Soloist & Accompanist, 1947-53; pvte. Piano & Harp Instructor, & freelance Concert Perf., Calif., 1959-68; Instructor of Harp & Piano, Univ. of Calif. Ext., San Diego, 1968-; Instructor of Harp, San Diego State Univ., 1970-. Univ. of San Diego, 1976-, Point Loma Coll., 1977-; VP, Plektron Corp., 1971-; CME Fellow, Ctr. for Music Experiment, Univ. of Calif., San Diego, 1974; Harpist, La Jolla Presby. Ch. Comps: Var. pieces for Harp. Mbr., var. profl. orgs. Recip., Scholarship, Schmitz Schl. of Piano, 1948. Hobbies: Gourmet Cooking; Reading; Swimming. Address: 8732 Nottingham Pl., La Jolla, CA 92037, USA. 2, 4, 29.

HUKVARY, Eugene, b. 11 Feb. 1908, Torokbalint, Hungary. Conductor; Composer; Professor. m., 3 s. Debut: Budapest. Career: Theatre & Concert Cond., Budapest, pecs, Szeged, Debrecen, Hungary, Chgo., Detroit, Cleveland, USA. Comps: Harp solos; Violin piano duets; Voice & piano duets; String quartet; Saxophone trios; Flute duos, etc. Recordings: Hungarian Children Songs. Mbrships. incl: Am. Musicol. Soc.; Hungarian Radio-Chgo.: Chgo. Fedn. of Musicians. Publs: Relative Solmization--Music Shorthand. Address: 2248 W Leland, Chgo., IL 60625, USA.

HULA, Zdenek, b. 12 May 1901, St. Anthony, Austria. Composer; Music Theorist; Professor at Prague Conservatoire. Educ: Prague Conservatoire. Compositons incl: Light Music; The Little Soldier, 1925; Hunting Song, 1927; The Slavonic Capriccio, 1932; The Slovakian Country, 1934; The Blue Flower, 1937; Serious Music: Love Songs, Czech & Moravian nat. poetry, 1970; Etudes for string chmbr. orch., 1972; String Quartet, 1973; Trio Divertimento for violin, quitar & accordian, 1974. Publications: Harmony (2 volumes), 1956; Counterpoint (2 volumes), 1958. Mbr. Union of Czech. Comps., Prague. Hons. incl: Cert. of Merit, Zaslouzily umelec, 1972. Address: Zitomirska Str. 46, 101 00 Praha 10, Czechoslovakia.

HULTBERG, Warren Earle, b. 3 July 1921, Gt. Falls, Mont., USA. Musicologist. Educ: BA, Univ. Nev., 1957; MA, Univ. Southern Calif., 1959; PHD, ibid., 1964. m. Mary Lou Hendricks. Career: Over 20 yrs. as profl. musician; Owner-Mgr., Music Studio, Reno, Nev.; Lectr. in Piano & Music Hist., Univ. Southern Calif., 1959-63; SUNY, 1963; Prof., ibid., 1969; Acting Dean of Grad. Studies, ibid., 1975-. Publs. incl: Diego Pisador's Libro de Musica de Vihuela in Festival Essays for Pauline Alderman, 1976; Transcription of Tablature to Standard Notation in the Computer & Music, 1970, 71. Mbrships. incl: Am. Musicol. Soc.; Music Educators Nat. Conf.; Am. Fedn. of Musicians; Coll. Music Soc.; Phi Delta Kappa; Am. Lute Soc.; Am. Lute Seminars (Bd. of Dirs.). Hobbies: Study; Photography. Address: 72 Leroy St., Potsdam, NY 13676, USA. 6.

HUMPHREYS, Carey, b. 3 Mar. 1922, Truro, Cornwall, UK. Lecturer in Music. Educ: RAM; postgrad. work, Univ. of Edinburgh; MMus, RCM; BMus, Univ. of London; FRCO; GRSM (London); LRAM; ARCM. m. Joan Elsie Brading, 1 s. Career: Dir. of Music, Eltham Coll., London, 1950-55; Hd. of Music, Northern Grammar Schl., Portsmouth, 1955-58, & Fareham Grammar Schl., Hants., 1958-64; Sr. Lectr., Padgate Coll. of Educ., Lancs., 1964-67; Prin. Lectr. in Music & Hd. of Dept., Bognor Regis Coll. of Educ., Sussex, 1967-; Solo Organist; Continuo Player; Choral & orchl. Cond.; Accomp.; pvte. teaching. Mbrships: ISM; Assn. Tchrs. in Colls. & Depts. of Educ.; RCO Organ Club. Hobbies: Electronics; Acoustics; Walking. Address: 101 Selangor Ave., Emsworth, Hants. PO10 7LS, UK. 3.

HUMPHREYS, Garry Paul, b. 22 Feb. 1946, Nottingham, UK. Baritone Singer; Lecturer; Writer; Librarian. Educ: ALA, North-Western Polytechnic Schl. of Librarianship, London; pvte. singing w. Norman Platt, Nigel Rogers & John Carol Case. m. Janet Zimmermann. Career: profl. chorister & soloist in concerts, recitals & broadcasts; song recitals w. Patricia Williams; anthology entertainments w. Hardwick Players, etc. Publs: books on Arthur Somervell & Rudolf Kempe in prep. Contbr. of record sleeve & prog. notes. Mbrships: ISM; committee mbr., Elgar Soc. (London branch). Hons: FRSA. Hobbies: Listening to Music; Books; Theatre; People & Places. Address: 4 Hill Ct., Stanhope Rd., London N6 5AP, UK.

HUNDZIAK, Andrzej, b. 11 Mar. 1927, Krosniewice, Poland. Composer. Educ: Secondary Theory, State High Schl. of Music, Lodz; Studied Comp., State High Schl. of Music, Katowice; Supplementary Study w. Nadia Boulanger, Paris, France. m. Wieslawa Jarmurzynska, 2 c. Debut: Lodz, 1960. Career: Dir., Music Lyceum, Lodz. Compositions: Variations for Trumpet &

Piano, 1965; Lyrics for Soprano & 10 instruments, 1967; Concertino for Piano, Children's Choir & Percussion Instruments, 1972; Symph. Music; Chmbr. Music; Music for TV, Stage & Film Publs: Training in Solfége (2 parts). Mbrships: Union of Polish Comps. Hons: Spring of Arts Medal, Lodz; Gold Cross of Merit. Prin., Fedn. of Assns. of Culture, 1976. Hobby: Photography. Address: 90 303 Lodz, Brézna 10 ul. 41, Poland.

HUNGERFORD, Bruce, b. 24 Nov. 1922, Korunburra, Vic., Australia. Concert pianist. Educ: Melbourne Univ.; pvte. study w. Roy Shepherd & Ignaz Friedman, study w. Ernest Hutcheson, Juilliard Grad. Schl., NY, USA, 1945-47; study w. pvte. tutors incl. Dame Myra Hess & Carl Friedberg. Debut: NY, 1951. Career incl: European Tour, 1958; Pianist-in-Residence, Bayreuth Festival Master Classes, 1959-67; Prof. of Piano, The Mannes Coll. of Music, NYC, 1972-. Recordings: 1st Complete Recording of piano works of Richard Wagner (at invitation of Wagner family), 1960; 32 sonatas of Beethoven (Vanguard label); Wrote & recorded 17-part audiovisual lecture series, The Heritage of Ancient Egypt, 1971. Mbrships: Am. Soc. of Vertebrate Palaeontol.; Fellow, Am. Rsch. Ctr. in Egypt, 1967-68. Hobbies: Egyptol.; Paleontol. Address: 230 Pelham Rd., New Rochelle, NY 10805, USA. 3, 15.

HUNSBERGER, Donald, b. 1932, Souderton, Pa., USA. Educator; Conductor; Arranger. Educ. incls: studied trombone w. Frederick Stoll; BMus, MMus, DMusA, Eastman Schl. fo Music. Career incls: Bass Trombonist, Trombone Soloist, occasional Guest Cond., 1st full-time Staff Arr., US Marine Band, Wash., DC; Tchr., theory, lower brass, ensemble, crane Dept., of Music, SUC, Potsdam; currently Co-Chmn., Dept. of Conducting & Ensembles, & Cond., Eastman Wind Ensemble & Eastman Symph. Band, Eastman Schl. of Music, Num. arrs. inclng: Shostakovitch's Festive Overture for concert band; J S Bach's Passacaglia & Fugue in C minor for large symphonic wind ensemble. Mbrships. incl; MENC; ASCAP; Advsr., Young Audiences of Rochester prog. Address: Univ. of Rochester, Eastman Schl. of Music, Rochester, NY 14604, USA.

HUNT, Alexandra, b. Omaha, Neb., USA. Opera & Concert Singer (Soprano). Educ: Sorbonne Univ., Paris, France; BA, Vassar Coll., USA; BS, Juilliard Schl. of Music. Debut: Marie in Wozzeck, La Scala Milan. Career: Leading roles, USA & Europe inclng. title roles in Lulu, Katya Kabanova Jenufa & Tosca, also Curley's Wife in Floyd, Of Mice & Men; Soloist in Handel, Solomon, Gothenburg, Sweden, & in Penderecki, Passion According to St. Luke, w. Phila. Orch. & w. Dallas Symph.; Soloist w. Cleveland Orch., & w. Rome Symph. Orch., Italy. Recordings: Songs of Carpenter, Griffe & MacDowell. Mgmt: Courtenay Artists, Inc., A11 E 53, NY, NY 10022, USA. Address: 170 W. 74th St., NY, NY 10023, USA.

HUNT, Brian William, b. 18 Mar. 1950, Leeds, UK. Music Teacher. Educ: BEd, York Ripon & St. John Coll.; Cert. Educ., Leeds; Assoc., Royal Coll. of Music; BMus cand., Goldsmith's Coll., London. Career: Hd. of Music, Norton Comprehensive Schl., Cleveland, 1973-77; Hd. of Music, Sandon Choirmaster, St. Andrew's Sandon, 1978-. Comprehensive Schl., Chelmsford, Essex, 1977-; Mbrships: Incorp. Soc. of Musicians; Asst. Masters & Mistresses Assn. Hobbies: Philately; Walking; Cricket; Golf. Address: 2 Elizabeth Way, Hatfield Peverel, Chelmsford, Essex, CM3 2RU, UK.

HUNT, Donald Frederick, b. 26 July 1930, Gloucester, UK. Conductor; Organist. Educ: DMus(hc), Leeds; FRCO (chm.); FRCO; ARCM; Studied w. Dr. Herbert Sumsion. m. Josephine Benbow, 2 s., 2 d. Career: Asst. Organist, Cloucester Cathedral, 1948-54; Organist, St. John's Ch., Torquay, 1954-57; Dir. of Music, Leeds Parish Ch., 1957-74; Chorus Dir., Leeds Fest., 1964-74; Master of the Choristers & Organist, Worcester Cathedral, 1975-; Cond., Halifax Choral Soc., Worcester Fest. Choral Soc.; Three Choirs Fest. Comps: Missa Brevis; Missa Leodiensis; Magnificat & Nunc Dimittis; Te Deum; Music of the Spheres, chorus & orch.; Invitation to Music, solo, choir, chamber orch.; organ sonata; carols, motets. Recordings: The Organ of Leeds Parish Ch.; Recital from Leeds Town Hall; Organ Music of Elgar on the organ of Worcester Cathedral; num. recordings w. Leeds Parish Ch. Choir, Leeds Phil. Soc.; Halifax Choral Soc.; Worcester Cathedral Choir. Hobbies: Gardening; Reading; Sport. Address: 13 College Green, Worcester WR1 2LH, UK.

HUNT, Edgar Hubert, b. 28 June 1909, Clifton, Bristol, UK. Professor. Educ: FTCL; LRAM; MRST. m. Elizabeth W Hunt (dec.), 1 d. Career: Music publng.; Tchng.; Orgnsr., Summer Schls. for Recorder Players; Prof. & Dept. Head, Renaissance & Baroque Music, TCL. Comps: many eds. recorder music. Publs: The Recorder & its Music, 1962; The English Harpsichord Mag. (ed.), 1973-; Recorder & Music (ed.), 1974-. Mbrships: Fndr. Mbr., Chmn. Galpin Soc.; Life, Royal Musical Assn.; Mus. Dir., Soc. Recorder Players; ISM. Address: Rose Cottage, 8 Bois Lane, Chesham Bois, Bucks HP6 6BP, UK.

HUNT, Enid Clara, b. 8 July 1911, Clifton, Bristol, UK. Teacher (piano, violin, organ, recorder, theory, harmony). Educ: studied w. Marion Glass (piano) & Dr. Hubert Hunt (violin & organ); LRAM; ARCO; LTCL; BA, Open Univ., 1975. Career: Music Mistress, Collegiate Schl. of Winterbourne, Bristol, 1942-; Lectr. (recorder tchng. & playing) for Glos. Educ. Committee, 1958-74; Organist, Bristol Children's Hospital, 1960-77; vis. violin tchr., Red Maids Schl., Bristol, 1969-; Adjudicator, recorder classes, Bristol Baptist Eisteddfod, 1955-76. Mbrships. incl: ISM; fndr., hon. sec., hon. cond., Bristol Branch, Soc. of Recorder Players; Galpin Soc.; Engl. Folk Dance & Song Soc. Hon: Life mbr., Bristol Music Club, 1977. Hobby: Gardening. Address: 13 Clare Rd., Cotham, Bristol BS6 5TB, UK. 27, 29.

HUNT, Gordon, b. 20 Nov. 1950, Hillingdon, UK. Musician (oboe). Educ: Jr. Exhibitioners' Course, RAM; RCM, London. Career: Prin. Oboe, BBC Welsh Symph. Orch.; currently Prin. Oboe, Philharmonia Orch., London; plays frequent concertos w. Philharmonia & other in UK. Hobby: Ornithology. Address: 39 Sydenham Rise, Forest Hill, London SE23 3XL, UK.

HUNT, Jno Leland, b. 17 May 1947, Cedar Rapids, Iowa, USa. Musicologist. Educ: Univ. of Iowa, 1965-67; BMus Perf. (Clarinet), N Tex. State Univ., 1969; PhD Musicol., Univ. of Mich., 1973. m. Teresa Gioia, 1 d. Career: Mbr., Ft. Worth, Tex., Symph., 1969-70; Instructor, St. Olaf Coll., 1973-74; Asst. Prof., Carnegie-Mellon Univ., 1975-. Publ: Giovanni Paisiello: His Life as an Opera Composer, 1975. Contbr. to: Musical Quarterly; Opera Jrnl.; Notes; Jrnl. of Am. Musicol. Soc.; Choral Review. Mbrships: Am. Musical Soc.; Coll. Music Soc.; Am. Assn. of Univ. Profs., Pi Kappa Lambda; Phi Mu Alpha Sinfonia (Pres., Gamma Theata Chapt., N Tex., 1969). Hons: Rackham Prize Fellowship, 1971-73. Hobby: Tennis. Address: 322 Woodside Rd., Forest Hills, PA 15221, USA.

HUNT, Reginald Heber, b. 16 June 1891, Wolverhampton, UK. Organist; Director of Music; Lecturer in Music. Educ: DMus (London); FRCO; FLCm. m. 1) Lillian Blanceh Shinton, dec., 2) Mary Elizabeth Abbott, 1 s., 1d. Career: Organist, var. London chs.; Dir. of Music, Grammar Schls., 1927-52; Lectr. in Music, Coll. of St Mark & St. John, 1933-39; Dir., LCM, 1954-64; Chmn. of Corp., LCM, 1964-; Mbr. of Senate, Univ. of London, 1951-64; Moderator in Music, GCE, London, 1950-63. Comps. incl: The Wondrous Cross; This Blessed Christmastide; Fun With Tunes; More Fun with Tunes; Fantasy on a Ground for Organ; Fantasy on 'O Quanta Qualia' for organ; 6 pieces for organ; ch. & schl. music; exam. pieces for piaon, recorder, trumpet & clarinet. Publs. incl: First & Second Harmony Book(s), 1962 & 65; Extemporization for Music Students, 1968; Transportation for Music Studentsk, 1969; Harmony at the Keyboard, 1970. Mbrships: RCO; RAC; Worshipful Co. of Musicians. Address: 2 Oyster Band, Three Beachs, Paignton, Devon TQ4 6NL, UK. 1, 3, 19.

HUNTER, Francis John, b. 2 Sept. 1946, Horsham, Sussex, UK. Oboist. Educ: BA, Magdalen Coll., Oxford; MA, Oxford. Freiburg-Breisgau Conserv., W. Germany; studied w. Neil Black, Janet Craxton, Heinz Hillinger. m. Pamela May Johnson, 2 s. Career: Co-Prin. Oboe, Nat. Youth Orch. of GB, 2 yrs.; BBC Trng. Orch., Bristol, 1 yr.; Solo Oboist, Tonhalle Orch., Zürich, Switzerland, 1972; Oboe Prof., Zürich Conserv. of Music; Radio Perfs., Switzerland; Mbr. Pro Arte Wind Quntet, Zürich. Hobbies: Photography; Visual Arts; Reading; Indoor Gardening; Swimming; Tennis. Address: Stettbachstrasse 12, 8702, Zollikon, Switz.

HUNTER, Hilda, b. 6 Dec. 1919, Blackheath, Staffs., UK. Lectuer; Examiner. Educ: Univ. of Birmingham; MA (Wales); MSc, Aston in Birmingham; BA, Birmingham; FTCL; LRAM; ARCM. Career: Tchr. of Oboe, Birmingham Schl. of Music, 1944-52; tchr., piano & woodwind, & lib., music dept., Univ. Coll. of Wales, Aberystwyth, 1955-60; now Sr. lectr., Wolverhamton Polytechnic & Examiner for TCL. Comps: miscellaneous works for recorders. Publs: The Grammar of Music, 1952; Taching the Recorder, 1977; (co-author) Music for Today's Children, 1974. Hons: Barber scholarship in music to Birmingham Univ., 1945. Hobbies: Swimming; Gardening; Caravanning. Address: 13 Brook Rd., Pontesbury, Shrewsbury, Salop., UK.

HUNTER, Ian Timothy, b. 8 July 1942, York, UK. Director of Music; Singer. Educ: TCL; GTCL. Career: Vicar-Choral, St. Paul's Cathedral, 1964-75; Dir., Sunday Evening Choir SPC, 1968-70; Dir., Cunningham Singers, 1965-72; Dir. of Music, Colet Court, St. Paul's Preparatory Schl., 1974-; Dir., Colet Court Boys' Choir. Comps: Carol, Hodie Christus; Music for Percussion. Recordings: (w. Colet Court Boys' Choir) Prefabulous Animiles; Sing for Christmas. Publ: (arr.) Colet Court Carols, 1979. Mbrships: ISM; Equity. Hobbies: Photography; Stage Lighting; Steam Railways. Address: Colet Ct., St. Paul's Schl., Lonsdale Rd., London SW13 9JT, UK.

HUNTER, Rita, b. 15 Aug. 1933, Wallasey, Cheshire, UK. Prima Donna. Educ: music study w. Edwin Francis, Liverpool; Clive Carey; Eva Turner; Redvers Llewellyn. m. John Darnley, 1 d. Debut: w. Sadlers Wells. Career incl: leading operatic roles in UK, Germany, USA, Portugal, France, etc.; TV appearances incl. Rolf Harris Show & Russell Harty Show. Recordings incl: var. Wagnerian opera roles (EMI Label). Mbrships: Caravan Club; White Elephant Club; Royal Nat. Rose Soc. Hons: Hon. DLit, Warwick Univ., 1978; Hon. RAM, 1978. Hobbies: Sewing; Oil painting; Gardening. Mgmt: Stafford Law, Weybridge, UK. Address: The Cornerways, 70 Embercourt Rd., Thames Ditton, Surrey, UK.

HUNTER, Virginia, b. 4 July 1924, Edgemont, SD, USA. Lyric Soprano; Choral Director. Educ: BA, Univ. of Wash., Seattle; Paris Conserv., France; Licence de Concert, Ecole Normale, Paris. m. Dr. Dale S Hunter, 2 s., 1 d. Career: Interpreter, French & German Art Songs; Young Artist Auditions, NY, Columbus, Ohio; Yehudi Menuhin Fest., Gstaad, Switzerland; Bach Fest., Seattle, Wash.; Fest. de St. Hubert, Belgium; Own Radio Prog., KISW, Seattle, 2 yrs.; Summer Concert Series, Abbaye de Royaumont, France; Radio, Suddeutsches Rundfunk, Dir. of Music, Am. Ch.'s in Mannheim, Wiesbaden, Karlsruhe, Teaching Fac., Ch. Music Inst., Berchtesgaden, 1963-76; Fac., Music-Seminar Guntzel, Wiesbaden, Germany, 1970-73. Recordings: Soprano Soloist, Mozart, Requiem; Choir Dir., Revelation Generation. Mbrships: Mu Phi Epsilon; Tonkuństler Verband, Germany; Wagner Verband, Germany, Recip. num. hons. Hobbies: Skiing; Sewing & Needlecraft; Reading. Address: 8 Lessingstr., 7501 Eggenstein, Karlsruhe, German Fed. Repub.

HUNZIKER, Dominique, b. 9 Jan. 1944, Zurich, Switz. Flautist. Educ: Univ. of Zürich, 1 yr.; Dip., Bern Conserv.; master courses w. Marcel Moyse, Boswil & J-P Rampal, Nice. m. Anne Utagawa, 1 s. Career: Concerts as soloist throughout Switz., & Germany & in Pairs, Lyons, London, Salzburg & Japan. Radio perfs., Zürich, Basel, Geneva & Lugano; dedicatee, num. works of Swioo & German compo. Recordings: Jecklin, Zürich; Ariola-Eurodisc, Germany. Mbrships: Assn. of Swiss Musicians; Swiss Soc. of Music Tchng. Hong: Werkjahr desaarg. Kuratoriums, 1974; Jubilee Award, Swiss Bank Assn., 1975. Hobbies: Cooking; Drawing; Painting; Design. Address: Ochsengässli 9, 5000 Aarau, Switz.

HUOT, Guy Eugène, b. 21 Mar. 1943, Ottawa, Ont., Can. Music Administrator; Critic; Broadcaster; Organist. Educ: BA (French Lit.); pvte. musical studies. Career: Sec.-Gen., Can. Music Council; past Music Adminstr., Nat. Arts Centre; past Hd. of Music, Can. Coun. for the Arts, Ottawa; regular host for Radio-Canada's Augré de la fantaisie. Publs: Ed. & writer of all news & editorials of Musicanada. Contbr. to: Le Droit; Ottawa Revue; Sovietskaya Entsiklope-dia; Nat. Arts Ctr. concert & opera prog. notes. Mbrships: Sec., Can. Sect., ISCM; Advsry. Bd., Assoc. of Can. Orchs.; Hon. Mbr., Bd. of Ottawa Choral Soc. Hobbies: Art; Antiques; Travel. Address: 524 Clarence, Ottawa, Ont. K1N 5S2, Can. 2.

HURD, Michael John, b. 19 Dec. 1928, Gloucester, UK. Composer; Author. Educ: MA, Pembroke Coll., Oxford. Compositons incl: choral works. Canticles of the Virgin Mary, Missa Brevis, A Song For St. Cecilia, Charms & Ceremonies, Flower Songs, The Phoenix & The Turtle; operas, The Widow of Ephesus; cantatas, Johan-Man Jazz, Swingin' Samson, Hip-Hip Horatio; Dance Diversions, Choral; Music Praise; This Day to Man; Shepherd's Calendar. Publs: The Composer, 1968; Benjamin Britten, 1967; Immortal Hour, 1962; Young Person's Guides to Concerts, 1962; Opera, 1963; English Music, 1965; Sailors' Songs & Shanties, 1965; Soldier's Songs & Marches, 1966; Elgar, 1969; Vaughan Williams, 1970; Mendelssohn, 1970; Outline History of European Music, 1969; The Ordeal of Ivor Gurney, 1978. Contbr. to: Music in Educ.; Musical Times. Address: 4 Church St., West Liss, Hants., UK. 3, 28.

HURFORD, Peter John, b. 22 Nov. 1930, Minehead, UK. Organist & Church Musician. Educ: RCM (Open Fndn. Scholar), 1948-49; MA, Music & Law, Jesus Coll., Cambridge Univ., 1952 (Organ Scholar); MusB (Cantab); FRCO; ARCM. m. Patricia M Matthews, 2 s., 1 d. Debut: Royal Fest. Hall, 1957. Career: Concert tours since 1958 in USA & Canad, Aust., NZ, Japan, E & W Europe; TV apps. in UK, Aust. & Japan; Complete organ works of Bach for BBC radio, 1978-79; visiting prof., Univ. of Cincinnati, 1967-68, Univ. of W Ont., 1976-77; Master of Music, St. Albans Cathedral, 1958-78; Cond., St. Albans Bach Choir, 1958-78; Fndr. & artistic dir., Int. Organ Fest., 1963. Comps. incl: (Organ) Two Dialogues; Passingala; Bristol Suite; 5 Chorale Preludes; Suite, Laudate Dominum; (choral) Litany to the Holy Spirit; Magnificat & Nunc Dimittis in G; ibid., in A; The Communion Service, Series III. Num. recordings esp. of J S Bach; currently recording complete organ works of Bach for Argo. Mbrships: ISM; Coun. Mbr., Royal Coll. of Organists;

Cathedral Organists Assn. Hons: Laureate at the Concours International d'Execution Musicale, 1950, 55; Hon. Fellow, Royal Schl. of Ch. Music. Hobbies: Walking; Silence. Mgmt: North America: Murtagh/McFarlane Artists Mgmt; World except N Am: Van Walsum Mgmt: Address: Genesta, St. Bernard's Road, St. Albans, Herts, UK. 1, 2.

HURNEY, Kate (Claire), b. 14 Sept. 1941, Quincy, Mass., USa. Lyric Coloratura Soprano. Educ: BA, Tufts Univ.; Columbia Univ.; New England Conserv.; Juilliard Schl.; Manhattan Schl.; Accademia Chigiana; Int. Opernstudio, Zurich; Dalcroze Schl. m. Robert J Braveman, 1 s., 1 d. Debut: Carnegie Hall, Am. Opera Soc. Career incls: apps. w. Houston, Miami & Buffalo Symphs., Nat. Orch., Santo Domingo, Sudwest Funk; extensive chmbr. music & recital work; Am. Opera Soc.; Houston Grand Opera; Boston Opera; Dallas Civic Opera; Opera Rara, London; Theatre Monnaie Brussels; Zurich Opera; Freiburg Opera, Germany; New Opera Theatre, Brooklyn Academy; 2 yrs.; San Juan, Guggenheim Mus. (Virgil Thompson); Co-Fndr., Pub. Opera Theatre, 1972. Recordings: Decca. Mbrships: Am. Inst. of Verdi Studies; AGMA; Equity; Poseidon. Recip., var. musical hons. Hobbies incl: Travel; Cookery; Plants. Mgmt: M. Novarro, 46 Oakdale Rd., Stamford, CT 06906, USA. Address: Apt. 10B, 235 W 76 St., NY, NY 10023, USA.

HURNÍK, Ilja, b. 25 Nov. 1922, Ostrava, Czech. Composer; Pianist; Writer. Educ: Music Acad., Prague. m. Jane Hurnik-Roubal, 1 s. Debut: Prague, 1942. Career: concerts in Czech., German Dem. Repub., German Fed. Repub., France, UK, Cuba, USSR, etc.; Prof., Conserv. in Prague & Acad. in Bratislava. Comps: operas, Lady Killrs & Diogenes; cantatas, Maryka, Ezop, Noah & Pastorella; concertos for piano, oboe, flute; etc. Recordings: Debussy, Préludes, Images, Estampes, Childrens Corner & Arabesques; Ravel, Valses novles et sentimentales. Publs: Trumpeters of Jericho, 1965; Geese of Capitol, 1969; The Travel with the Butterfly, 1970; The musical Sherlock, 1972. Contbr. to profl. jrnls. Address: Na'rodni 35, 11000 Prague 1, Czech.

HURSEY, John Richard, b. 11 Feb. 1944, Carshalton, Surrey, UK. Orchestral Player (Cello & Celeste). Educ: RAM; LRAM (Piano Perfs.); LRAM (Cello Tchrs.). Career: City of Birmingham Symph. Orch.; Sadlers Wells Opera Orch.; Bournemouth Symph. Orch.; BBC Symph. Orch.; Freelance Cellist. Recordings: mostly w. City of Birmingham Symph. Orch. & Bournemouth Symph. Orch. Recip., acad. hons. Hobbies: Conservation; Natural Hist.; Cycling; Swimming; Painting (watercolours). Address: 34 Mount Park, Carshalton, Surrey, UK.

HURST, George, b. 20 May 1926. Conductor. Educ: Royal Conserv., Toronto, Can. Career incls: Cond., York Symph. Orch., Pa., 1950-55, concurrently Peabody Conserv. Orch., 1952-55; Asst. Cond., LPO, 1955-57, touring USSR 1956; Assoc. Cond., 1957, Prin. Cond., 1958-68, BBC Northern Symph. Orch.; Artistic Advsr., Bournemouth Symph. Orch., 1969-. Comps: vocal & piano works publd. in Can. Recip., 1st Prize, Comp., Can. Assn. of Publrs., Authors & Comps., 1945. Hobbies: Chess; Riding; Yachting. Address: 21 Oslo Ct., London NW8, UK. 1.

HURWITZ, Emanuel, b. 7 May 1919, London, UK. Musician (violin). Educ: Royal Acad. of Music. m. Kay, 1 s., 1 d. Career: Ldr., Aeolian String Quartet; Ldr., Melos Ensemble, 1956-74; Engl. Chmbr. Orch.; 1947-69; New Phil. Orcn., 1969-71. Recordings incl: Brandenburg Concerti, Hanel's Concerto Grosso, etc., w. Engl. Chmbr. Orch.; Schubert Octet, Trout Quintet, Mozart & Brahms Clarinet Quintets, etc.; Complete Haydn, Ravel, Debussy & Late Beethoven String Quartets. Mbr., ISM. Hons: Gold Medal, Worshipful Co. of Musicians, 1967; CBE, 1978. Hobbies: Collecting books & antique bows for string instruments; Photography. Address: 25 Dollis Ave., London N3 1DA, UK.

HURWITZ, Robert Irving, b. 7 Nov. 1939, NY, NY, USA. Assoc. Professor; Violist. Educ: AB, Brooklyn Coll., 1961; MMus, 1965; PhD, 1970, Ind. Univ. m. M Virginia Leonard, 3 d. Career: Tchng. Asst., Ind. Univ. Schl. of Music, 1962-65; Instructor, Univ. of Ore. Schl. of Music, 1965-68; Asst. Prof., ibid., 1969-71; Assoc. Prof., ibid., 1971; Prin. violist, Eugene Symph. Orch. Contb. to Symposium (jrnl. of Coll. Music Soc.). Mbrships: Am. Musicol. Soc.; Soc. for Music Theory; Coll. Music Soc. Hons: Fulbright Exchange Professorship to UK, 1969-70. Hobbies: Photography; Carpentry; Breadmaking. Address: 2908 Wash. St., Eugene, OR 97405, USA.

HUSA, Karel, b. 7 Aug. 1921, Prague, Czechoslovakia. Composer; Conductor; Educator. Educ: Dips., Comp. & Cond., Prague Conserv., 1941-45; Dips., Comp., Prague Acad., 1945-46; Comp. & Cond. at the Ecole normale de Paris (License); comp. w. Arthur Honegger & Nadia Boulanger; Cond. w.

J Fournet, Andre Cluytens; Cond. at the Paris Nat. Conserv. w. Mr. E Bigot (Dip. 1st Prize). m. Simone Pérault, 4 d. Debut: Prague Symph. Orch., 1945. Career: Cond., Radio Prague, 1945-46; Jury Mbr., Paris Nat. Conserv., 1952-53 & Fontainebleau Schl. of Music & Fine Arts, 1953; Cond. of the Conti Soli Orch. Paris (Recordings of Brahms Bartok), 1953-54; Asst. Prof., Cornell Univ. Music Dept., USA, 1954-57; Assoc. Prof., ibid., 1957-61; Prof., 1961-; Dir., Univ. Orchs.; Cond., Ithaca Chamber Orch., 1954-; Guest cond. w. many European orchs. as well as orchs. in the USA. Compositions: num. works for Orch., Chamber Music, Chorus & Orch., etc. Many recordings as Cond. Mbr. & Hon. Mbr. many profl. orgs. Var. commissions & scholarships. Hons. incl: Lili Boulanger Prize, Boston, 1950; Pulitzer Prize for Str. Quartet No. 3, 1969; Assoc. Mbr., Royal Belgian Acad. of Arts & Scis., Guggenheim Fellowship, 1964; Kappa Alpha Professorship in Music (endowed, named chair at Cornell Univ.). Address:333 The Parkway, Ithaca, NY 14850, USA.

HÜSCHEN, Heinrich, b. 2 Mar. 1915, Moers, Germany. University Professor. Educ: Univs. & Music Acadsa., Cologne & Berlin. m. Waldine Rosemeyer, 1 s. Career: Asst., 1948, Lectr., 1955, Asst. Prof., 1961, Full Prof., 1970, Univ. of Cologne; Full Prof., Univ. of MarburgLahn, 1964; Lectr., Cologne Music Acad., 1971; Dir., Musicol. Inst., Univ. of Cologne, 1970-. Publs. incl: Die Motett, 1974; var. musicol. works on medieval & renaissance periods. Contbr. to: Die Musik in Geschichte und Gegenwart. Mbrships: Soc. for Music Rsch.; Int. Soc. for Musicol.; German Commn. for Music Hist., Kassell; Joseph-Haydn-Inst., Cologne. Hons. incl: Dent Medal, Royal Soc. of Musicol., UK, 1968. Address: Elisabethstr. 5, D 497 Bad Oeynhausen, German Fed. Repub.

HUSEBY, Gerardo Victor, b. 23 Jan. 1943, Buenos Aires, Argentina. Musicologist; Critic; Performer of Early Music. Educ: Tchr's Dip., Argentina; Cert. of Proficiency in Engl., Univ. of Cambridge; Degree (Lic.) in Musicol., Fac. of Music, Cath. Univ. of Argentina. div., 1 d. Career: recitals as Ldr., Ars Rediviva (early music grp.), 1965-; Fndr. Critic, Tribuna Musical, Buenos Aires. Hobby: Collecting musical instruments. Address: Dean Funes 173, 1876 Bernal, Argentina.

HUSELTON, Marion Jackson, b. 23 July 1950, Memphis, Tenn., USA. Harpist. Educ: Dip., Tchrs. Cert., Sherwood Music Schl., Chgo., Ill., 1968; BA, Stephens Coll., Columbia, Mo., 1972; MA, Memphis State Univ., Tenn., 1974. m. James Michael Huselton. Career: Harpist w. var. orchs., Chmbr. Grps., Cologne-Bonn area, Germany, 1972-73; Free-lance Harpist, var. orchs., recording studios, Soloist, Tri-State area, USA; Grad. Teaching Asst., Memphis State Univ. Harp. Inst., ibid., Harpist w. Memphis Symph. Orch. Hons: Fulbright Scholar in Harp, to Cologne, Germany, 1972-73; Winner, 1974 Concerto Auditions, Memphis, Tenn. Address: 176 N. Holmes St., Memphis, TN 38111, USA.

HUSMANN, Heinrich, b. 16 Dec. 1908, Cologne, Germany. Professor of Musicology. Educ: studied maths., philos. & psychol., Berlin & Göttingen; studied musicol. Göttingen & Berlin; recip. of degree, 1932. Career: Asst., Musicol. Inst. Leipzig Univ.; qualified, 1941; Dir., Musicol. Inst., Hamburg Univ., 1949; Professorial Chairs for Musicol., Hamburg Univ., 1958, & Göttingen Univ., 1960. Publs. incl: Einführung in die Musikwissenschaft, 1958, 2nd ed., 1975; Die Melodien der Jakobitischen Kirche, 1969; Ein Syromelkitisches Tropologion mit altbyzantinisher Notation, 1975. Address: Kurze Geismarstr. 40, D-3400 Göttingen, German Fed. Repub.

HUSSELS, Helga, b. 15 Jan. 1930, Berlin, Germany. Violinist. Educ: Music HS, Berlin; Mozarteum, Salzburg; NWD Music Acad., Detmold. m. Otto Gmelin, 1 s. Career: Radio, TV & Solo Concerts, Germany, Austria, Switzedrland, Italy, Spain, Yugoslavia, Czech., Spain, Belgium, Netherlands, Ireland, Sweden & Finland. Mgmt: Henrik F Lodding, Junigatan 27, Goteborg. Address: Rosengatan 2A, S-413 10 Goteborg, Sweden.

HUSTIS, James Humphrey III, b. 30 June 1924, NYC, USA. Trumpeter; Conductor; Educator; Critic. Educ: BS, 1950, MS, 1953, Juilliard Schl. of Music; Nat. Music Camp. Interlochen, Mich., 1940; Berks. Music Schl., Tanglewood, Mass., 1948; Aspen Music Schl., Colo., 1959. m. Karola Muller Hustis, 2 s., 1 d. Career incls: Hd., Brass Dept., Morningside Coll. Conserv. of Music, Iowa, Dir., Siouxland Youth Symph. Orch., Dir. of Band, Morningside Coll., Prin. Trumpet, Sioux City Symph. Orch., 1955-62; Dir. of Bands, Univ. of Richmond, Va., 1st Trumpet, Richmond Symph. Orch., 1962-69; Dean, Peabody Conserv. of Music, Balt., Md., 1969-78. Recordings w. var. grps. Contbr. to Richmond Times Dispatch, Va. Mbr. var. profl. orgs. Hobbies: Hiking; Swimming. Address: 5407 Springlake Way, Balt., MD 21212, USA.

HUSTON, Thomas Scott, Jr., b. 10 Oct. 1916, Tacoma, Wash., USA. University Professor. Educ: BMus; Eastman Schl. of Music, Rochester, NY, 1941; MMus, ibid., 1942; PhD, 1952. m. Natalie Maser, 2 s., 3 d. Career: Tchr. Univ. of Redlands, Calif., 1946-47, Kearney State Tchrs. Coll., Neb., 1947-50, Eastman Schl. of Music, 1950-52. Cinn Conserv. of Music, 1952-55, Coll.-Conserv. of Music, Cinn., 1955-; Prof. of Comp., Univ. of Cinn.; Guest Cond., var. Orchs., Band & Choirs. Comps. incl: over 50 works for voice, instumental & orchl.; The Christ Child (vocal solo & organ), 1958; Symph. no. III, the Four Phantasms, 1964; Phenomena (Baroque quintet), 1967; Penta-Tholoi (solo piano), 1968; Sounds at Night (Brass Choir), 1971; Symph. No. IV (String Orch.), 1972; Symph. No. V (The Human Condition), 1975; Tamar Monodrama for soprano & piano, 1974; Eleataron (viola & piano), 1975; Symph. No. V (The Human Condition), 1975. Mbrships: Broadcast Music, Inc.; Am. Music Ctr.; AAUP; Univ. Composers Alliance. Recip. var. Awards for composition, etc. Hobbies incl: Photography; Swimming. Address: Coll.-Conserv. of Music, Univ. of Cinn., OH 45221, USS. 2, 8.

HUSZTI, Joseph Bela, b. 27 Sept. 1936, Lorain, Ohio, USA. Conductor; Professor; Voice Teacher. Educ: BMus, MMus, Schl. of Music, Northwestern Univ.; Oberlin Conserv.; Univ. of S Calif.; Occidental Coll. m. Melinda Murray, 1 d. Career: Dir. of Choral Activities, Bakersfield Coll., Calif., 1959-66; Dir. of Choral & Voice, Univ. of Del., Newark, 1966-72; Dir. of Choral Activities, Boston Univ., Mass., 1972-77; Dir. & Hd. of Young Vocalists Prog., Tanglewood, Lenox, Mass., 1972-77; Dir. of Choral & Voice, Univ. of Calif., 1977-; Choir tours, USA & Europe; Adjudicator, Clinician in 30 States & in Europe; Adjudicator, Clinician in 30 states & in Europe. Publs: Chorhythmics, 1975; In Search of Answers, 1977. Mbrships. incl: Life Mbr., Am. Choral Dirs. Assn.; Life Mbr., Coll. Music Soc.; MENC. Contbr. to progl. jrnls. Recip., sev. hons. Hobbies incl: Travel; Sports; Chmbr. music. Address: Univ. of Calif., Music Dept., Schl. of Fine Arts, Irvine, CA 92717, USA. 6, 28.

HUTCHESON, Jere Trent, b. 16 Sept. 1938, Marietta, Ga., USA. Composer; Professor of Music. Educ: BMus, Stetson Univ.; MMus, La. State Univ.; PhD, Mich. State Univ.; Berkshire Music Ctr. m. Virginia Bagby Hutcheson, 1 d. Comps. incl: Passacaglia for band; 3 things for Dr. Seuss; Shadows of Floating Life; Wonder Music I, II III, IV & V; Sensations; Transitions; Construction Set; Wonder Music IV; Colossus; 3 Pictures of Satan; Electrons; Fantaisie-Impromptu, (rec); Noctures of the Inferno (rec.); Passing, Passing, Passing; Patterns; Cosmic Suite. Publs: Music for the High School Chorus, 1967; Musical Form & Analysis, A Programmed Course, 2 vols., 1972. Mbr. ASCAP. Hons: Recip. yrly. ASCAP awards; Named Distinguished Composer of the Year, NMTA, 1976; Rockefeller Grant, 1977; National Endowment for the Arts Grant, 1978; Guggenheim Fellowship, 1979. Address: 6064 Abbott Rd., E Lansing, MI 48823, USA.

HUTCHINGS, Arthur James Bramwell, b. 14 July 1905, Sunbury, UK. Professor. Educ: BA, BMus, PhD (London); Hon RAM; FTCL; FRSM; Prof. Emeritus, Durham & Exeter. m. Marie Constance Haverson (dec.), 1 d. Career: Frequent broadcasts, BBC; Prof. (Hd. of Dept.), Univ. of Durham, 1947-68, Univ. of Exeter, 1968-70. Comps: Operetta, The Plumber's Arms; Cantata, Heart's Desire; Orchl. Variations; Suite for strings; Sev. Ch. Anthems & Liturgical music, incl. Mass for Double Choir. Publs: 13 books. Contbr. to profl. publs. Mbrships: Chmn., Gov. Bd., TCL; Ed., The English Hymnal. Hobbies incl: Wine; Women; Song; Opposing planning committees and people who ruin the countryside; Swimming. Address: 8 Rosemary Lane, Colytoh, Devon, UK.

HUTCHINSON, Lucie M (KA Sister Clare Lucille), b. 24 Mar. 1918, Portland, Ore., USA. Musicologist; Pianist. Educ: BMus, Marylhurst Coll., Ore., 1946; MMus, Univ. of Southern Calif., LA, 1957; PhD, Ind. Univ., Bloomington, 1969; Piano Tchng. Cert., Ore. & Wash. Career: Tchr. of Piano, elem. & second. schls., Ore. & Wash.; Prof. of Music Hist., Marylhurst Coll., Ore., & Ft. Wright Coll., Spokane, Wash.; Adjudicator of piano students, state, city & parochial schls., Ore. Publs: The Musical & Literary Manuscripts of Ferdinand Praeger, 1968; A Critical Analysis of Eight Piano Sonatas by contemporary Composers, 1958. Mbrships: Am. Musicol. Soc.; Ore. Music Tchrs. Assn. Recip. of fellowships & grants. Hobbies: Reading; Beach-combing. Address: Marylhurst, OR 97036, USA.

HUTCHISON, Warner, b. 15 Dec. 1930, Denver, Colo., USA. Composer; French Hornist; Author. Educ: BS Mus, SW Bapt. Theol. Sem., Ft. Worth, Tex., 1954; MusM, N Tex. State Univ. Schl. of Music, 1956; PhD, ibid., 1971; Studied in Comp. w. Samuel Adler, Wayne Barlow & Kent Kennan (Eastman Schl. of Music), Roy Harris, (Ind. Univ.) Career: Mbr. var. Grad. facs., Univs.; Lectr., Avant Garde Music & New Musical Notation; Assoc.

Prof., Music, Comp., & Dir., Elec. Music Lab., NM State Univ. Num. Compositions incl: The Sacrilege of Alan Kent for Orch., Baritone & Tape; Dirge & Hosanna for Band; Psalm 135 for Chorus & Organ; Prairie Sketch for Orch.; Homage to Jackson Pollock; Monday Music for solo Piano & Synthesizer; Ceremonies, Ballet for Oboe, Interior & Piano & Tape. Recordings: sev. on Crest Label. Contbr. to Nu-Mus West. Mbrships: ASCAP; Am. Soc. of Uni. Comps. (Exec. committee, Ed., Proceedings Jrnl.); Phi Mu Alpha; Pi Kappa Lambda. Hons: NM Fine Arts Commission, 1969; MacDowell Colony Fellowship, 1973, '74; Rsch. Grants, NM State Univ., 1972, '73; ASCAP Standard Awards, 1974. Address: PO Box 3174, Univ. Park Stn., Las Cruces, NM 88001, USA. 8.

HÜTTEL, Walter Oskar, b. 13 Feb. 1920, Glauchau, Germany. Composer; Musicologist. Educ: Coll. of Music, Leipzig (ch. music, comp.); Martin- Luther Univ. Halle-Wittenberg; PhD, Berlin, 1957; Dr. Sc. Phil., Berlin, 1977. m. Dora Elizabeth Schneider, 1 s. Career: Lectr. at var. colls. of music, 1951-6; Lectr., inst. of educ., Karl-Marx-Stadt, 1956-66; Schl. of music, Jütenborg, from 1968. Comps. incl: Missa brevis; Der Pslam 23; Philotas-Overtüre; Singonische Burleske; Intrada; Fantasie (clarinet & piano); Glauchauer Klavierbuch; Preciosa (after CM von Weber). Publs. incl: Das deutsche Volkslied im 17. Jahrhundert; 1957; Musikgeschichte von Glauchau; Gesanbücher und Liederdichtung im chemals schönburgischen Hoheitsgebiet, 1977. Mbrships: New Bach Soc.; comps. & musicians union of German Dem. Repub. Hons: Pestalozzi medal. Address: 961 Glauchau, Külstr. 55, German Dem. Repub.

HUYBERS, Bernard M, b. 24 July 19822, Rotterdam, Netherlands. Composer; Music Theorist; Schoolmusician; Choir Director; Theologian. Educ: Lic. Phil. & Theol.; State Cert. Music Theory, 1951; Cert. Schl. Music, Amsterdam Conserv., 1960. Career incls: Choirmaster, St. Dominic, Amsterdam, 1966-74; Pastor, ibid., 1966-; Prof. of Liturgy, Amsterdam Conserv., 1963-; Nederlands Instituut voor Katholieke Kerkmuziek, Utrecht, 1969-; Conserv. Vereniging Muzieklyceum, Amsterdam, 1975-; Guest Lectr. num. countries. Comps. incl: Settings for 40 Psalms; 200 other liturgical works. Recordings: 14 inclng: When From Our Exile. Publs. incl: Musik in der Gottesdienstlichen Versammlung, 1974. Contbr. to profl. jrnls. Mbrships. incl: IAH; SWVL; UL. Hobby: Music Sociol. Address: Valeriusstraat 245, II, Amsterdam, Holland.

HUYS, Bernard, b. 7 Sept. 1934, Hulste, Belgium. Musicologist; Professor of Music. Educ: LLD; Lic. Hist. of Art & Archaeol. (Musicol.); Studied piano & hist. of music, Royal Conserv., Ghent. m. Marie-Louise Garré, 1 c. Career: Hd. of Music Dept., Royal Lib. of Belgium; Prof. of Music, Hoger St. Lukasinstituut, Brussels. Publs. incl: Belgische en buitenlandse muziekbibliotheken, 1966; Bibliografie van de werken van Antointe Auda, 1879-1964, 1967; De Afdellng Muziek (van de Koninklijke Bibliotheek, 1969); Muziekdocumenten, 1969; Twee huldemotetten ter gelegenheid van Blijde Intreden te Antwerpen door Plantijn gedrukt, 1969; Jacques Champion de Chambonnières, humanist, klavecinist en komponist, 1972; Catalogue des impromés musicaux du XVIIIe siècle. Fondgs général/Catalogus van de muziekdrukken van de 18de eeuw. Algemnene verzameling. Koninklijke Bibliotheek Albert I (Brussels), 1974. Contbr. to var. jrnls. Mbrships. incl: Exec. Comm., AIBM; Editl. Comm., Catalogus musicus; Pres., Belgian Comm., RILM. Address: Kasteelstraat 5, 1750 Schepdaal, Belgium.

HUYS, Johan, b. 23 Apr. 1942, Ghent, Belgium. Harpsichord Teacher. Educ: 1st Prize for Piano & Organ, Ghent Conserv.; Higher Dip., Chmbr. Music, Brussels Conserv. m. Hilde Dombrecht, 2 c. Debut: Ghent. Career: Harpsichord Tchr., Ghent Conserv.; Recitals & Chmbr. Music concerts, Belgium, Netherlands, Gemrany, UK, France & Spain; Radio apps., Belgium & German Fed. Repub.; Harpsichordist, Parnassus Ensemble for Baroque Music w. original instruments, & Enteuxis Ensemble for Modern Music. Recordings: For Decca, w. Belgian Chmbr. Orch.; for Alpha, as Harpsichord & Piano soloist w. R Jacobs (countertenor). Hons: prizewinner, Int. Organ Competition, Prague, 1966. Hobbies: Literature; Science Fiction. Address: Tielstraat 20, 8080 Ruiselede, Belgium.

HYDE, Miriam, b. 15 Jan. 1913, Adelaide, SA. Composer; Pianist. Educ: BMus, Adelaide Univ.; LAB; ARCM (Piano & Comp.); LRAM. m. Marcus Bruce Edwards, 1 d., 1 s. Career: Perf. own 2 concertos w. LPO, LSO, BBC & in Aust. w. Sir Malcolm Sargent, Schneevoigt, Dr. Edgar Bainton, Sir Bernard Heinze, etc. Comps. incl: Piano Course (w. Warren Thomson) I-III; Sight Reading Adventures, Grades I-VIII; Venetian Lullaby (duet), 1948; Lullaby for Christine, 1952; Sunrise by the Sea (song), 1954; Winter Willow Music (song), 1955; Humoresque (piano), 1974; Study in Blue, White and Gold (piano), 1974; Reflected Reeds (piano); Serenade (violin solo); Nightfall and Merrymaking (oboe & piano); Beside the Stream (flute & piano); The Little Juggler (flute & piano); Six Carols; 2 Concertos; Overtures; Songs. Recordings incl: sev. piano works recorded by Walter Gieseking. Contbr. to: var. Music Tchrs. Assns. of Aust. Mbr., num. profl. orgs. Hons. incl: num. comp. prizes. Hobbies: Writing; Scrabble; Gardening. Address: 12 Kelso St., Enfield, NSW 2136, Aust. 3, 15, 21, 23, 27, 29, 30.

HYDE-SMITH, Christopher, b. 11 Mar. 1935, Cairo, Egypt. Flautist (solo & chamber music). Educ: RCM, London. m. Marisa Robles, 1 s., 1 d. Debut: Royal Festival Hall, 1961. Career: Mbr. of Robles Trio, Allegri-Robles Ensemble, Camden Wind Quintet, London Mozart Players; many flute & harp recitals w. wife. Apps. in Holland, Switz., Italy, Germany, Spain, Portugal, Scandinavia, USSR, N & S America; Prof., RCM; Dir., Stowe Summer School, Haydn-Mozart Soc.; Dedicatee of works by Alwyn, Dodgson, Horovitz, Mathias & Rawsthorne. num. recordings. Mgmt: Ibbs & Tillett. Address: 38 Luttrell Avenue, London SW15 6PE, UK. 30.

HYLIN, Birgitta Charlotta Kristina, b. 24 July 1915, Stockholm, Sweden. Artist; Composer; Poet; Translator; Guitarist; Pianist. Educ: pvte. study of piano, also at piano schl. Wohlfart, Stockholm. m. Gosta Hylin (div.), 2 d. Career: has sung own songs on radio, 1941-; Specialist in Faroese folk-lore, on TV prof. Hylands Hörna, 1970, also on radio; concert tours of Sweden & Faroe Islands; radio apps., Finland & Sweden. Comps. recorded: Sommardansen; Den Rätte; Om du bara höll mig; En söndagsvisa. Mbrships: STIM; SKAP; Visans Vänner; Samfundet för Visforskning; Samfundet Sverige-Färöarna. Recip. var. hons., incl: Silver Plate of Hon., from Visans Vänner, 1978. Hobbies incl: Skating; Skiing; Mountain climbing. Address: Infanterigatan 23, S-17159 Solna, Sweden.

HYLTON, Brent Eugene, b. 20 July 1948, Battle Creek, Mich., USA. Concert Organist; Choral Conductor; Church Musician; Teacher. Educ: BMus, Eastman Schl. of Music; MMus, Organ Perf., Syracuse Univ.; D Musical Arts (in progress), ibid. m. Marilyn Jean Flink. Career: Organist & Choirmaster, Hendricks Chapel, & Instr. in Organ, Schl. of Music, Syracuse Univ.; Organ & choral concerts (with Hendricks Chapel Choir) throughout USA & Europe. Mbrships. incl: AGO; Coll. Music Soc.; AAUP; Phi Mu Alpha Sinfonia.

Hons: Chosen to represent NY State in Wash., DC, & USA in Europe for Bicentennial w. Hendricks Chepel Choir. Hobbies: Harpsichord Building; All Types of Sport. Address: 848 Sumner Ave., Syracuse, NY 13210, USA.

HYNES, Elizabeth, b. 30 Apr. 1947, Flint, Mich., USA. Singer. Educ: BMus, Ind. Univ., Bloomington. Debut: NYC Opera, 1976. Career: operatic perfs. w. NYC Opera, Opera Soc. of Wash., DC, Ft. Worth Opera Assn., Ambler Music Fest., Chautauqua Opera Assn., Colo. Springs Opera Fest.; concert apps. w. Nat. Symph. of Wash., DC, Pitts. & St. Louis Symphs. Hons: Wm. Matheus Sullivan Musical Fndn. Award, 1975; Nat. Opera Inst. Grant, 1976. Hobbies: Plants; Travel; Sno-shoeing. Mgmt: Columbia Artists Mgmt., c/o Nell Walter. Address: 160 W 71st St., 11C, NY, NY 10023, USA.

HYSON, Winifred P, b. 21 Feb. 1925, Schenectady, NY, USA. Composer; Teacher (piano, comp., theory). Educ: BA, Radcliffe Coll. (Physics); studies. w. Evelyn Swarthout & Roy Hamlin Johnson (piano), Esther Williamson Ballou & Lloyd Ultan (theory & comp.). m. Charles D Hyson, 2 s., 1 d. Comps: Suite for Young Orch.; (for piano duet) Fantasy on 3 English Folk Songs; 8 Light-Hearted Variations on The Jolly Miller; A Western Summer; Our British Cousins. Mbrships: Chmn., Comps. Group, Friday Morning Music Club of Wash.; VP, Dir. of Music Theory Prog., Md. State Music Tchrs. Assn.; League of Women Comps.; Mu Phi Epsilon; ASCAP. num. hons., prizes & commissions. Contbr. to Am. Music Tchr. Address: 7407 Honeywell Lane, Bethesda, MD 20014, USA.

HYTINKOSKI, Antero Juhani, b. 11 Dec. 1914, Helsinki, Finland. Percussionist; Teacher. Educ: Studied Percussion w. Johan Jaala, 1929-38; pvte. study of music theory & hist. Career: Percussionist, Turku Symph. Orch., 1934-77; Mbr., var. ensembles w. apps. in recording studios, films, radio & TV; War Serv., 1939-40; Army Entertainment Corps, 1940-45; Pvte. Tchr. of Percussion, 1945-; Tchr. of Percussion, Peoples Conserv., Turku, 1964-70, & Music Inst. of Turku, 1969-. Comps. about 100 pieces of light music, music for plays, & solos for wind & percussion instruments. (some publd. USA); Pieces for Percussion (publd. at own expense), 1972. Contbr. to: Muusikkolehti. Mbrships. incl: Soc. of Finnish Musicians; Copyright Bureau of Finnish Comps. Hobbies: Golf; Sailing; Collecting books on percussion. Address: Puimalankuja 4C13, 20720 Turku 72, Finland.

I

IANCULESCU, Magda, b. 30 March 1929, Iassy, Romania. Singer; Dramatic Soprano. Educ: w. Prof. Livia Vrabiescu, Conserv., Bucharest. m. Ing. Mircea Ionescu-Muscel. Debut: Rosina, Barbiere di Seviglia, Bucharest, 1952. Career: Romanian Opera, Bucharest, 1952-; Prof. (voice), Conserv. Bucharest, 1963-. Recordings: Rigoletto (Gilda); Barbiere di Seviglia (Rosina); Operatic Airs. Hons: Merited Artist, Repub. of Romania & Laureate of Int. Contests Bucharest, 1953, Prague, 1954 & Warsaw, 1955. Hobbies: Pictures; Animal protection. Mgmt: ARIA, Bucharest. Address: Str. Grigore Mora 12, Sector 1, Bucharest RS, Romania.

IANNACCONE, Anthony, b. 14 Oct. 1943, Brooklyn, NY, USA. Composer. Educ: B Mus, M Mus, PhD, Eastman Schl. of Music. m. Judith Trostle Iannaccone, 1 d. Comps: Rituals for Violin & Piano; Bicinia for Flute & Alto Saxophone; Parodies for Woodwind Quintet; Remembrance for Viola & Piano; Sonatine for Trumpet & Tuba; Night Song; The Prince of Peace; 3 Mythical Sketches; Lysistrata (full orch.); Str. Quartet no. 1; Solomon's Canticle (SATB); (recorded) Chamber Music of Anthony Iannaccone (4 works); Hades & 3 Mythical Sketches. Address: Music Dept., Eastern Michigan Univ., Ypsilanti, MI 48197, USA.

IBBOTT, Daphne, b. 29 April 1918, London, UK. Pianist. Educ: RAM; LRAM; ARAM. m. (1) Rev. John Frost (dec.), (2) Wilfred Smith, 2 d. Career: Specialist in chmbr. music & accomp.; Conducts Master Classes for accompanists; Adjudicator. Recordings: Vaughan Williams music w. Jean Stewart, (viola); Songs by Elgar, Warlock, Gurney, Britten & Quilter w. var. artists; Voice of the Violin, w. Derek Cullier, Somervell's Maud & Butterworth's Shropshire Lad w. John Carol Case; Spanish Dances by Sarasate & Wieniawski Comps. w. Campoli. Address: 15 Castelnau, Barnes, London SW13, UK. 3.

IDE, Geneva Evelyn, b. 14 Jan. 1922, Portland, Ore., USA. Piano Instructor; Pianist; Violinist; Elementary Teacher; Accompanist. Educ: B Mus, Univ. Ore., 1952; M Mus, Lewis & Clark Coll., 1958; Doct. work, Univ. Southern Calif., 1963-66. Div., 1 s. Career: Num. solo concerts, W & Mid-W; Soloist, num. orchs.; Radio & TV apps.; Piano & Violin instructor, Chgo. Jewish People's Inst., Portland Schl. Music, St. Helen's Hall, Lewis & Clark Coll., Calif. Luth. Coll., Citrus Coll. & Los Angeles City Schls. Recording: Echoes from Morningside, w. A Capella Choir, 1966. Mbr., Ore. Fedn. Music Clubs. Hons incl: 1st prizes, all divs., Ore. Fedn. Music Clubs contests, state & dist. Hobbies incl: Dancing; Sewing. Address: 8830 Manzanar Ave., Downey, CA 90240, USA.

IDZIOR, Wladyslaw Piotr, b. 25 June 1932, Leszno, Poland. Music Critic; Lecturer. Educ: Grad., Piano & Theory, Secondary Music Schl., Ostrow Wielkopolski; Law Grad., Univ. of Wroclaw. m. Alicya Przybylak, 1 s. Debut: Participant, Young Pianists Contest, Przemysl, 1945. Career: co-organizer, jazz fests. in Poland & Polish Radio, TV progs. on music & jazz musicians; Co-fndr., Polish Jazz Soc. Recordings: Var. musical plays for Polish Radio. Contbr. to Jazz monthly mag. & Jazz Forum, mag. of Int. Jazz Fedn. Mbrships: Chmn., Ct. of Arbitration, Polish Jazz Soc.; Cons. to musical publr., & Mbr., Critics Sec., Polish Jazz Fedn.; Hon. Mbr., jazz clubs in Warsaw, Wroclaw & Geiwice; Mbr., Critics' Section, Int. Jazz Fedn.; Mbr., Soc. of Popularising Sci. Hons: 2nd Prize, Young Pianists Contest, Przemysi, 1945. Hobbies: Jazz; Modern Ballet; Theatre; Literature; Touring; Sports. Address: 57-540 Ladek Zdroj, ul. Paderewskiego 6, Poland. 2.

IGNATIUS, Anja, b. 2 July 1911, Tampere, Finland. Concert Violinist; Professor of Violin. Educ: Nat. Conserv. of Paris, 1924-28; Studies w. Prof. Otakar Sevcik, Pisek, Czech., 1928-29, Carl Flesch, Berlin, 1929-31. m. Kaarle Veikko Hirvensalo (dec.), 4 c. Debut: 1926. Career: Concert tours, most European countries, 1930-; Soloist w. all major European Orchs.; Boston Symph. Orch., 1938; 1st Violin, Helsinki Quartet, 1953-61; Prof. of Violin, Sibelius Acad. Recordings: Sibelius Violin Concerto; recordings for Finnish Broadcasting Co. Mbrships: ESTA; Finnish Soloists' Assn.; Cremona Fndn. (Bd. of Dirs.); Int. Zonta Club. Hons. incl: Silver Meda., Int. Violin Competition, Vienna, 1932; Hon. Prize of Finnish Cultural Fndn., 1948; Hon. Prize of Helander Fndn., 1977; Hon. Prize of State Bd. of Music, 1978. Hobbies: Country life; Cooking; Mushroom hunting; Reading. Address: Sibeliuksenkatu 11 A 15, 00250 Helsinki 25, Finland.

IGNATOWICZ, Ewa, b. 10 June 1941, Warsaw, Poland. Opera Singer. Educ: MA, Warsaw Conserv.; Profl. Dip. in psychol. m., 1 c. Debut: 1970. Career: Soloist, Warsaw Dist. Opera Co., 1970-72, Warsaw Operetta, 1972-74, Warsaw Chmbr. Opera, 1974-. Recordings: Polski Nagrania label. Mbrships: Polish Musicians Assn. (SPAM). Hobby: Housekeeping. Mgmt: Pagart, Warsaw. Address: Apt. 115, Broniewskiego 20, Warsaw, Poland.

ILES, Edna, b. Birmingham, UK. Concert Pianist. Educ: Studied w. Russian comp. Nicolas Medtner for sev. yrs. in UK. Career: Recognized leading exponent of Medtner's music; played all 3 Medtner concertos w. LSO, Albert Hall, London, 1946; further perfs. of these works incl. 1st broadcast of Number 1 w. City of Birmingham Symph., 1947; Soloist w. Philharmonia Orch., 1st provincial tour, 1949; Bloch's Concerto Symphonique in London & Bournemouth w. Bournemouth Symph. Orch., 1956; 1st perf., 1958, 1st broadcast, 1969, Alan Bush, Variations, Nocturne & Finale on an English Seasong; apps. w. most major orchs., & num. recitals, UK & Europe. Recordings: Medtner's works (broadcast, USSR). Mbr., ISM. Address: 86 Grange Rd., Olton, Solihull, W Midlands B91 1DA, UK.

ILIFF, James Frederick, b. 4 Jan. 1923, Wolverhampton, UK. Composer; Teacher of Composition & Harmony. Educ: studied under William Alwyn at RAM; B Mus, London; FRAM. m. (1) Elsbeth Henne, (2) Mary Makinson. Career: Pianist, Glyndebourne Opera, 1946-47, Univ. of London Class Music Tutor, 1947-58 & '66-; Pianist, English Opera Grp., 1949-50; Prof. of Comp. & Harmony, RAM, 1957-. Compositions: Str. Quartet, 2 Pieces (clarinet & piano); Oboe Sonata; Piano Sonata; Ending to unfinished fugue in the 'Art of Fugue'; Landscape (orch.); Syzygy, oboe & piano; Trio for organ. Contbr. to Composer. Mbrships: CGGB; Soc. for Promotion of New Music; Botanical Soc. of the Brit. Isles. Address: Eithin Tewion, Cilycwm, Llandovery, Dyfed, Wales, UK. 3.

ILIFFE, Barrie John b. 1925, Westcliff, Essex, UK. Head of Music, British Council. m. Caroline Mary Fairfax-Jones, 3 d. Career: Concerts Mgr., Liverpool Phil., 1951-55; Orchestral Mgr., Philharmonia, 1955-56; Mgr., Cape Town Orch., 1956-58; Concerts Mgr., Philharmonia, 1958-60; Mgr., London Mozart Players, 1961-63; Gen. Mgr., New Philharmonia, 1964-65; Hd. of Music, Brit. Coun., 1966-. Hobbies: Canal cruising; Print collecting. Address: 29 Murray Mews, London NW1, UK. 3.

ILLEK, Karel, b. 12 April 1936, Znojme, Czechoslovakia. Double-Bass Player. Educ: Brno Conserv.; Acad. of Music, Bratislava. m. Eva Medilková, 1 d. Debut: Bratislava, 1969. Career: Mbr., Slovak Phil. Orch.; has made sev. TV & radio broadcasts as Soloist or Mbr. of var. Chmbr. Orchs., Bratislava; Prof., Acad. of Music, Bratislava. Mbr: Profl. Musicians Sec., Union of Slovak Composers. Hobbies: Swimming; Drawing. Address: St. Majora 4, Bratislava, Czechoslovakia.

ILLING, Robert Henry, b. 16 Aug. 1917, London, UK. Musicologist; Organist; Harpsichordist. Educ: MA, Mus B, Cambridge Univ.; MA, Oxford Univ.; PhD, Nottingham Univ., & Univ. of Adelaide, Aust. m. Margaret Jane, 1 d. Career: Dir. of Music, Kings Coll. Schl., Wimbledon; Lectr. in Maths., Kesteven Coll. of Educ.; Warden, Oxford Polytechnic; Hd., Discipline of Musicol., Flinders Univ. of SA. Comps. incl: Mass; settings of folk melodies; num. eds. of early music. Publs. incl: Est-Barley-Ravenscroft, 1969; Est's Psalter, I & II, 1969, 71; The Periods of Musical History, 1975; On the Inability to Sing in Tune, 1975; Handel's Solo Cantatas, 1975; Early Handel in Australia, 1977 (w. Betty Kinnear). Contbr. to var. profl. jrnls. Hons. incl: Awards, Aust. Rsch. Grants Committee, 1969-78; var. univ. scholarships & prizes. Address: 12 Vine Lane, Glen Osmond, SA 5064, Australia.

ILLING, Rosamund Elizabeth Anne, b. 23 March 1953, Exmouth, UK. Soprano. Educ: BMus, Univ. of Adelaide. Career: Governess in Britten's Turn of the Screw, London, 1978; Soloist Mbr. of Schutz Choir of London. Hons: Var. prizes; Elder Scholar, Univ. of Adelaide; Major awards from Aust. Broadcasting Commission, 1976, & S Aust. Govt., 1977; Gold Medallist, Aldeburgh Fest., UK, 1978. Mgmt: Ibbs & Tillett, London. Address: 12 Vine Lane, Glen Osmond, S Australia.

IMMELMAN, Niel, b. 13 Aug. 1944, Bloemfontein, S Africa. Concert Pianist. Educ: studied w. Cyril Smith, RCM; pvte. study w. Ilona Kabos & Maria Curcio. Debut: w. London Phil. Orch, 1969. Career: concerts at Royal Fest. Hall, Albert Hall, Amsterdam Concertgebouw; concert tours, Netherlands, Italy, Greece, Cyprus, Ctrl. & Southern Africa, France & USA; TV & radio apps.; num. countries. Recip. Chappell Gold Medal (top piano prize), RCM. Hobbies: Collecting records; Cycling. Address: 21 Cardigan Rd., Richmond, Surrey, UK.

INBAL, Eliahu, b. 16 Feb. 1936, Jerusalem, Israel. Conductor. Educ: Dip., Violin, Jerusalem Conserv.; Study of Cond., Conserv. Nat. of Paris, Hilversum, & Siena. m. Helga Fritzsche, 1 s., 1 d. Career: Chief Cond., Frankfurt Radio Symph. Orch., Guest Cond., num. orchs. inclng: La Scala, Milan; Santa Cecilia & Radio Symph. of Rome; London, Paris, Munich, Berlin, Vienna, Hamburg, NY, Chgo., Toronto, Stockholm, Budapest; Tours w. Israel Phil. in USA and Australia; Apps. at Salzburg, Lucerne, Berlin & Holland Fests. Recordings: (as Cond. w. New Philharmonia, London) complete Schumann works for orch.; Debussy, w. Concertgebouw, Amsterdam; Complete Chopin works for piano & orch., w. LPO & Claude Arrau; Complete piano, orch. works of Tchaikovsky, w. Concerto Winderstein, Munich; Bartok, orchl. works op. 5, op. 10 & op. 12; Saint-Saens, Symphs. 1 & 2, w. Frankfurt Radio Symph. Orch. Hons: 1st Prize, Guido Cantelli Int. Competition for Conds., 1963. Hobbies: Hi-fi; Photography. Mgmt: Concerto Winderstein Munich. Address: Hessicher Rundfunk, Bertramstr. 8, 6000 Frankfurt, German Fed. Repub. 2,3,28.

INCERTI, Bruno, b. 10 Aug. 1910, Zürich, Switz. Violinist. Educ: Dip. Virtuos, Liceo Musicale Bologna, 1928; Dip., composing, ibid., 1928. m. Dora Zehnder. Career: Ldr., Radio Orch., Zürich; Ldr., Opera House, Zürich; Ldr., Chmbr. Orch. 'Vivaldi Players'; Ldr., Piano Trio Zürich. Comps. Concertino for violin & chmbr. orch.; Concert for 2 violins & orch.; Concert for violin & violoncello & orch.; Fantasie for violin; Music for ballet 'Pinocchio', 'Searcher of Vivaldi'. Mbr., Schweiz, Tonkunstlerverband. Hons: Prizes, City Zürich. Hobby: Model Railways. Address: Viktoriastr. 43, 8057 Zürich, Switz.

IND, Peter Vincent, b. 20 July 1928, Uxbridge, Middlesex, UK. Bass Violinist; Pianist; Composer; Jazz Improviser; Teacher. Educ: Trinity Coll. Music, London. m. Barbara Anne Schiffmacher, 2 d. Career incls: Emigrated to USA, 1951; Played & recorded w. Lennie Tristano, Lee Konitz, Buddy Rich, & other noted jazzmen; Freelance musician, Big Sur, Calif., 1963-66; Returned to England, 1966; Freelance musician & tchr.; Thames documentary film on his music & cosmic viewpoint, 1974. Comp. of var. jazz works. Recordings incl: Lee Konitz Quartet; Looking Out; Peter Ind Sextet. Mbrships. incl: Musicians' Union; PRS. Contbr. to var. profl. publs. Hobbies incl: Painting. Address: 207 Amyand Pk. Rd., Twickenham TW1 3HN, UK.

INGALL, Susan Marjory, b. 2 Aug. 1953, Crook, Cumbria, UK. Teacher of Clarinet & Piano. Educ: 2 yrs. tchr. trng. course, Christ Coll., Liverpool; LGSM, Piano, Mabel Fletcher Coll., ibid. Mbr., Incorp. Soc. of Musicians. Hobbies: Reading; Cooking; Travel. Address: Croft End Gillingate, Kendal, Cumbria, UK.

INGEBRIGTSEN, Stein, b. 23 Aug. 1945, Namsos, Norway. Singer; Musician (guitar, flute). Educ: Pvte. studies. m. Inger Lindegaard Ingebrigtsen, 1 s., 1 d. Career: Radio & TV apps. in Norway, Sweden, Germany; Film & theatre apps. Comps: Ettertanker, 1975: Disco Girl, 1977. Recordings: 4 LP's, Norway; 2 LP's, Sweden; 4 Duet LP's w. Inger Lise Rypdal, Sweden & Norway; num. single records. Mbrships: Den Norske Musikerforeningen. Hons: The Silver Microphone, 1972; 12 record awards. Hobbies: Reading; Writing Song Lyrics; Skiing; Gardening. Address: Maltrostvegen 7, 1404 Siggerud, Norway.

INGRAM, Reginald William, b. 3 Oct. 1930, Coventry, UK. Professor. Educ: BA (Engl. lang & lit.), Birmingham Univ., 1952; MA, ibid., 1953; PhD, London Univ., 1955. m. Doreen D, 2 s. Debut: accomp. at lieder recital, Univ. of Chgo., 1961. Career: Prof. of English, Univ. of BC, Vancouver. Publs: John Marston, 1978; Shakespeare, 1971; num. articles for scholarly jrnls. Contbr. to: Music & Letters; Musical Quarterly; Music & Musicians; Studies in English Literature; Shakespeare Yearbook; Anglia; Renaissance Drama. Mbrships: Royal Musical Assn.; Brit. Music Soc. Hobbies: Avoiding Gardening; Listening to Music on Record. Address: 3861 W 12th Ave., Vancouver, BC V6R 2N9, Can. 11,12.

INGRAM, Robert James, b. 1 June 1937, Perth, WA. Violinist. Educ: studied w. Cyril Philips, Vaughan Hanly, Florent Hoogstoel, Ernest Llewelyn, Jean Fournier, Eric Gruenberg. m. Beverly, 2 s., 1 d. Career: Study & Freelance orchl. work, London, 1959-64; Sydney Symph. Orch., 1965; Fndr. Mbr. (2nd Violin), Sydney String Quartet, 1966; Ldr., Pikler Chmbr. Orch., 1969; Concert Master, Elizabethan Sydney Orch., 1973-77; currently Ldr., Aust. Chmbr. Orch.; num. broadcasts, Aust. Broadcasting Commission. Recordings: Orchestral; Sydney String Quartet; Aust. Chmbr. Orch. Hons: AMEB Gold Medal & Scholarship, 1954; Philomusica Scholarship, 1959; MBE, 1979. Hobbies: Golf; Swimming; Reading. Address: c/o Dr. R M Powrie, Fairlight Crescent, Fairlight NSW 20 94, Aust.

INNES, Audrey Muriel, b. 29 Sept. 1936, Edinburgh, UK. Pianist; Harpsichord Player; Teacher of Music. Educ: B Mus, Edinburgh Univ.; Reifeprüfung, piano as concert study, Vienna Staatsakademie; LRAM (Tchr.). m. Ronald Mackie, 1 s., 2 d. Debut: Edinburgh Univ. Concert series. Career: Solo recitalist & concerto soloist w. SNO, BBC Symph. Orch., Edinburgh Symph. Orch., Perth Symph. Orch.; Radio & TV Broadcasts; Mbr., Bernicia Ensemble & Pegasus Piano Trio. Recorded Pièces de Clavecin en Concert (Rameau) w. Bernicia Ensemble. Mbrships: Exec. Coun., Edinburgh Competitive Fest.; EPTA; ISM. Hobbies incl: Painting; Yoga. Address: 7 Cobden Rd., Edinburgh EH9 2BJ, UK. 27.

INNISS, Josephine Consola, b. Chgo., Ill., USA. Pianist; Organist. Educ: Tchrs. Cert., Chgo. Conserv. of Music, 1931; Bachelor & Master degrees, ibid; postgrad. work at Sherwood Schl. of Music; Master Class in Piano w. Dr. Leo Podolsky & the late Moritz Rosenthal; Cert., Baldwin Piano Co. of Baldwin Organ Tchr. Workshop, etc. Debut: Recital at Kimball Hall Concert Hall, 1927. Career: Piano accomp. for the Pace Jubilee Singers; Victor Recording Artist; Perf. over Radio WGN, WMAQ & WLS; Selected by the late Carl R. Diton to appear on NBC as perf. artist in Boston, Mass., 1938; appeared w. the Mid-Southside Symph. Orch. under dir. of late Dr. E J Robinson, playing the Emperor Concerto in E Flat by Beethoven; Apps. in leading musical ctrs. in USA. Music Critic for The Met. Post. Mbrships incl: Nat. Dir., Jr. Div., Nat. Assn. of Negro Musicians; Bd. Dirs., Chgo. Music Assn. Many hons. & awards. Address: 1748 West Steuben St., Chgo., IL 60643, USA.

INOUE, Michi, b. 23 Dec. 1946, Tokyo, Japan. Conductor. Educ: Toho Gakuen Acad. of Music (BA, Cond.). m. Tamayo (Kuroda). Debut: La Scala, Milan, 1971. Career: Assoc. Cond., Tokyo Metropolitan Symph. Orch.; Chief Guest Cond., NZ Symph. Orch., 1976-80; TV & radio apps., Japan. Recordings: (w. Mozarteum Orch., Salzburg), Mozart - Symphs. No. 29 & 40; Schubert, Symph. No. 8; Mendelssohn, Symph. No. 8. Hons: 1st Prize, Guido Cantelli Competition, Scala, Milan, 1971; 1st Place, Celibidache Training Course, Bologna, 1972. Hobbies: Skiing; Sky Diving; Gardening. Mgmt: Harrison/Parrott, 22 Hillgate St., London W8 7SR, UK. Address: c/o Mgmt.

INWOOD, Mary Ruth Brink Berger, b. 27 July 1928, Boston, Mass., USA. Composer; Teacher (Piano). Educ: Yale Schl. of Music, 1946-47; BA, Queens Coll., 1975; MA, ibid., 1979. m. (1) Rev. Charles P. Berger (dec.), 1 d., 2 s.; (2) Rev. Jay M. Inwood (div.), 2 s. Career: Pvte. Tchr. of Piano & Theory. Comps. incl: 3 Movements for Brass Sextet, 1975; String Quartet No. 3, 1976; Cheerful and Tender Songs. Mbrships incl: ASCAP. Hons: Prizes in Comp., Queens Coll., 1972-76; Nominated to enter Charles Ives Fellowship Competition & Competition of Assn. of Univ. Comps., 1975. Hobbies: Ancient History; Poetry; Visual Arts. Address: 166 Congress St., Brooklyn, NY 11201, USA.

IONEL, Dumitru, b. 8 July 1915, Fumureni, Valcea, Romania. Tubist. Educ: Grad., Conservatorium of Bucharest. m. Maria Ionel, 1 s. Debut: W. Phil. Orch. Geroge Enescu, Bucharest. Career: Soloist, Symph. Orchs., Brussels, Berlin, Warsaw, Teheran Symph. Orch., Teheran, Iran. Comps. incl: Polka (Tubadiabolica) (tuba & piano), 1941; Praeludium (tuba & orch.), 1946; Humoreska (tuba & piano), 1950; Concert for Tuba & Orch., 1952; Conzertstuck (tuba & strings), 1957; Fantasie Nocturne (tuba & orch.), 1959; Romanian Dance (tuba & piano), 1974; Concert No. 2 (tuba & orch.), 1975; 4 Methods for Tuba; Rondo for Tuba & Piano; "Godzilla", poem for Tuba & Piano. Num. recordings. Mbr. Tubist Assn. of Montreal. Address: Str. Gradinari N-57 Sect. IV, Bucharest, Romania.

IONESCU, Liviu, b. 2 Nov. 1928, Bucharest, Romania. Compoers; Conductor. Educ: studied w. George Georgescu, Constantin Silvestri, Paul Constantinescu, Theodor Rogalski, Ciprian Porumbescu Conserv., Bucharest. m. Tilde Urseanu. Debut: as Comp., 1949; as Cond., 1954. Career incls: Cond., Symph. Orch. for Movies Dept., Bucharest, Ciocîrlia Symph. Orch.; Artistic Dir. of Musical Orchs. & Recordings & Cond. of Studio Symph. Orch., Romanian Radio-TV, 1962-. Comps. incl: symphonic works; vocal & symphonic works; operas, ballets; chmbr. music; choral works. Jt. Author: The History of Ballet, 1967. Mbr., Romanian Comps. Union. Hons: Order of Cultural Merit; Work Medal; Medal for 25th Anniversary of Liberation. Address: Strada Ceaikovski 13, Floreasca, Bucharest, Romania.

IORDACHESCU, Dan, b. 2 June 1934, Iassy, Romania. Baritone Singer. Educ: Fac. of Law; Grad., Acad. of Music, Bucharest, 1956; Grad., Schola Cantorum, Paris, France; Grad., Mozarteum, Salzburg, Austria. m. Irina Iordachescu, 2 d.

Career: Opera Singer, 1956-, currently w. State Opera House Bucharest; leading roles in opera & concert apps. throughout Europe, Can., USA, S Am. & N Africa. Recordings: Lieutenant Kije (Prokofiev); Don Carlos; Forza del Destino; Ottava Simfonia (Mahler); var. recordings of opera arias. Hons. incl: var. decorations & title of Disting. Artist, Romania; prizes in int. contests & fests. Address: cal. Serban Voda nr. 46, of. p. 53, Bucharest, Romania.

IRANYI, Gabriel, b. 6 June 1946, Cluj, Romania. Composer; Lecturer; Pianist. Educ: Grad. as pianist, Schl. of Music, Cluj, Romania, 1965; MA, Comp., George Dima High Schl. of Music, Cluj, Romania; Comp. studies w. Sigismund Todutza. m. Elena, 1 s. Comps: Segments, for piano; Alternances, for solo percussion; Solstice, for clarinet, electronic clarinet, violin & cello; Fusions for violin, cello & piano; Group, for mixed choir & percussion; Arteres du Temps, for piano & orch.; The Flux of Memory, for percussion; Prayer, for 6 instruments; Song of Degrees, for chmbr. ensemble. Recordings: 2 String Quartets; Song Cycles; Terra Mater for mixed choir a cappella; Realm for soprano & chamber orch.; De Profundis for piano. Mbrships: Israel Comps. League; Acum Ltd. Hons. incl: 1st Prize, Spring in Cluj Contest for Young Comps., Romania, 1968, '69, '70; Prize winner, Comp. Contest of the Int. Fndn. Gaudeamus, Bilthoven, Netherlands, 1979; 2nd Prize, Artur Rubinstein Competition, Tel Aviv, 1979. Hobbies: Tennis; Chess. Address: 13/22 Corazim St., Neve-Sharet, Tel Aviv, Israel.

IRELAND, Patrick, b. 20 Nov. 1923, Helston, Cornwall, UK. Violist. Educ: Wellington Coll.; Worcester Coll., Oxford; ARCM; M Mus, Hull Univ. m. Peggy Gray, 4 children. Career: Viola, Allegri String Quartet. Recordings: W. Allegri String Quartet; Bach Brandenburg Concertos w. Menuhin & Bath Festival Orch. Mbr. ISM. Hobbies: Bird Watching; Antique Clocks & Musical Boxes; Carpentry. Address: 93 Corringham Rd., London NW11, UK.

IRMEN, Hans-Josef, b. 13 April 1938, Mönchengladbach, Germany. Music Educator. Educ: Musikhochschule Cologne, State Exam. for Higher Schl. Music; PhD, Univ. of Cologne, 1969. Career: Hd., Int. music couse Kloster Steinfeld, Prof. Tchrs. Trng. Coll. Rhineland; Cond. of Chorus & Orch. Bachverein Düsseldorf. Recordings: J Chr. Bach, Dies irae. Publs. incl: G J Rheinberger, 1970; L Cherubini, 1972; E Humperdinck, 1975; Ed., Beiträge zür Musik-reflexion 1974-. Mbrships: Vorsitzender der Arbeitsgemeinschaft für rheinische Musikgeschichte. Hobby: Riding. Address: Virnich 4, D5352 Zülpich, German Fed. Repub.

IRONS, Jack, b. 24 Aug. 1937, London, UK. Opera Singer (tenor). Educ: BEduc, London Univ.; AGSM Guildhall Schl. of Music, London. m. Anne Pashley, 1 s., 1 d. Debut: in Rape of Lucretia, w. Engl. Opera Grp., 1964. Career incl: Prin. Tenor, Royal Opera House, Covent Gdn.; Engl. Opera Grp.; Welsh Nat. Opera; New Opera; Kent Opera; Yorks. Opera, etc.; appeared in 5 TV operas; Festival appearances incl: City of London, Aldeburgh, Bath, Edinburgh, Schwetzingen; Ghent, etc.; Prof. of Singing, Guildhall Schl. of Music, 1975-. Recording: Soloist w. Schutz Choir (Argo label). Hobbies: Wine; Landscape Gardening. Address: 289 Goldhawk Rd., London W 12, UK.

IRVINE, Daryl, b. 25 Aug. 1932, Toronto, Ont., Can. Pianist; Organist; Harpsichordist. Educ: ARCT, LRCT, ARCM, LRSM, Piano ARCT, ARCM, Organ; RCM; Royal Conserv. of Music, Toronto, Can. Hanover Music Acad., German Fed. Repub.; Zermatt Summer Schl., Switzerland. m. R Gordon Condie. Career: Radio Apps., Can., Switzerland; TV Apps., Can.; Recitals, Concerts w. Orch., UK, German Fed. Repub., Holland, Switzerland, France, USA, Can. Recordings: num., CBC. Mbrships: Music Convener, Heliconian Club; Royal Conserv. of Music Alumnae; Bd. of Examiners, Royal Conserv. of Music. Hons: Music Scholarship, Assoc. Bd., Royal Schls. of Music, 1953; Ellen Marie Curtis Prize, 1958; Dannreuther Prize, 1959; Hanover Chmbr. Music Prize, 1st and 2nd, 1960; 2 Scholarships Can. Coun. Hobbies: Dress Designing; Fishing; Gardening; Reading; Dogs; Cooking; Collecting Miniatures; Needlework, esp. Petit Point and Tapestry. Mgmt: Condie Concert Mgmt., Toronto, Ont., Can. Address: 107 McAllister Rd., Downsview, Ont. M3H 2N5, Can.

IRVINE, Demar Buel, b. 25 May 1908, Modesto, Calif., USA. Musicologist. Educ: AB, Univ. of Calif., 1929; AM ibid, 1931; PhD, Harvard Univ., 1937; Pvte. study, Vienna, Austria, Schola Cantorum, Paris, France & Stern Conserv., Berlin, Germany, 1931-34. m. Greta Eickenscheidt. Career: Instructor, Music Univ. of Wash., Seattle, USA, 1937-38; Asst. Prof., 1938-47; Assoc. Prof., 1947-60; Prof., 1960-68; Prof. Emeritus, 1978-; Acting Dir., Schl. of Music, 1962-63. Publs: Ed., Anton von Webern; Perspectives, 1966; Writing About Music, 2nd ed. 1968; Massenet: A Chronicle of His Life and Times, 1974.

Mbrships: Am. Musicol. Soc. Hons: George Ladd Prix de Paris, 1931-33. Address: 4904 NE 60th St., Seattle, WA 98115, USA. 11.

IRWIN, Jack H, b. 18 Dec. 1925, Jeannette, Pa., USA. Clarinet & Saxophone Player; Teacher. Educ: BMus Ed., Oklahoma Univ.; MMus Ed., ibid. m. Gwendolyn Erickson Irwin, 8 c. Career: Music Educ., Konawa, Okla., 1950; Central High, Okla. City, 1951-57; Midwest City Schls., 1957-59; El Paso, Tex., 1959-60: Alamagordo, New Mex., 1960-62; Jeannette, Pa., 1965-66; Hempfield Schls., Pa., 1966-; Marching Band Dir., Calif. State Coll. Band, 1979. Mbrships: Pa. Music Educators (Pres., Western 1st, 1970-72); Past Pres., PMEA, Great Lakes Judging Assn.; Nat. Music Educators, 1950-; ASBDA, 1973-; Phi Mu Alpha; Kappa Kappa Psi. Hobby: Candle Making. Address: RD6, Box 54, Greensburg, PA 15601, USA.

IRWIN, Phyllis Ann, b. 24 Mar. 1929, Manhattan, Kan., USA. Professor of Music; Conductor-pianist. Educ: BS, M Ed, Univ. of Houston; EdD, Columbia Univ.; Vienna State Acad. of Music & Dramatic Arts, Austria, 1947-48; Mozarteum, Salzburg, summer 1960; Piano study w. Friedrich Wührer, Patricio Gutierrez, Albert Hirsh. Career: Pianist (Accompanist & Soloist), Houston, Tex., Charlotte, NC, NYC, San Diego, Calif., Fresno, Calif.; Choral Cond., Festival & Honor Choirs, Houston, Tex., Lousiville, Ky., Fresno, Hanford, Madera & Turlock, Calif.; Writer & TV Tchr., series of 12 video-taped Music Lessons, Exploring Music, broadcast in Fresno Co. Schls., 1968-72; Asst. VP for Acad. Affairs, Calif. State Univ., Fresno. Contbr. to: Newsletter, Calif. Music Educators Assn. Ctrl. Sect.; Allegro; Calif. Music Educators Assn. News; Music Educators Jrnl. Mbrships: MENC; Sigma Alpha Iota; Nat. Assn. of Women Deans, Admnstrs. & Counselors; Calif. Music Educators Assn.; AUW. Hobbies: Horseback riding; Photography; Travel. Address: 6012 N Harrison, Fresno, CA 93711, USA.

ISAAC, Cecil, b. 30 Oct. 1930, Indpls., Ind., USA. Conductor; Historian & Professor of Music. Educ: BA, Oberlin Coll.; B Mus Ed, Oberlin Conserv.; MA, M Phil, Columbia Univ. Career: Cond., Collegium, 1959-61, Lectr., 1959-62; Columbia Univ.; Asst. Prof., 1962-69, Assoc. Prof., 1970-76, Prof. of Music, 1976-, Austin Coll., Sherman, Tex.; Cond., Sherman Symph., 1966-. Contbr. to: Musical Quarterly; MLA Notes; Lib. Jrnl.; Piano Quarterly; Music Educators Jrnl.; Choice. Mbrships: Am. Musicol. Soc.; Am. Symph. Orch. League. Address: Box 1592, Music Dept., Austin Coll., Sherman, TX 75090, USA.

ISAACS, John Kenneth, b. 23 July 1936, Teynham, Kent, UK. Musical Instrument Maker, Lutes & Early Instruments; Musician; Viols; Recorders. Educ: MA Cantab., Magdalene Coll., Cambridge Univ. m. Phillis Jane Bird, 1 d. Career: Mbr., Jaye Consort, 1960-70, Ely Consort, 1962-71; Campian Consort, 1970-75; Cambridge Consort of Violins, 1975-; Num. radio, concert & TV apps.; Lectr. in Early Fretted Instruments, London Coll. of Furniture, Dept. of Musical Instrument Technology. Num. records incl: Music of the Court Homes & Cities of England; The Music of Orlando Gibbons; Medieval Music; Thomas Weelkes; An Elizabethan Evening; Homage to Shakespeare. Hobby: Food. Address: 18 Barton Rd., Ely, Cambs. CB7 4DE, UK. 28,30.

ISAACS, Kelly, b. 31 Aug. 1922, Rangoon, Burma. Violinist. Educ: Univ. Coll., Rangoon; LRAM; studied w. Max Rostal, Alfreo Campoli. m. Isabel Stewart, 2 d. Career: Mbr. Peter Gibbs Str. Quartet, 1949-53, London Harpsichord Ensemble, 1956-58; Formed Duo w. Maisie Balch, 1953; Wigmore Hall Recitals & Broadcasts; Ldr., Tilford Fest. Orch., 1961-67. Mbrships: Royal Soc. of Musicians; ISM. Recip. Assoc. Bd. Scholarship to RAM. Hobbies: Swimming; Gardening. Address: 84 Sutton Rd., London NW1 HB, UK. 3.

ISACSON, Einar, b. 26 Mar. 1942, Vittangi, Kiruna, Sweden. Organist; Conductor. Educ: Organist, Precentor & Music Tchr. Adv. Exams, Royal Conserv., Stockholm; Master courses, organ & choir conducting, Sweden & Finland. Debut: Organist, 1962; Cond., Lulea Chmbr. Choir, 1966. Career: Organ concerts, Sweden, Finland & Denmark; Choir concerts, Sweden, Norway, Finland, UK, Russia, Czech., Italy, Holland, Belgium & Austria; TV & Radio apps.; Cond., Lulea Chmbr. Choir; Organist & Choir Cond., Ornaset's Parish, Lulea. Comps. incl: Acclamatio for Organ. Recordings incl: Einar Isacson plays at the historical Organ in Overtornea. Mbr., Swedish Masonic Soc. Freemasons. Hons. incl: Var. schlrships, 1970, '74. Hobbies: Music; Skiing. Address: Hallbruksgatan 17, 951 41 Lulea, Sweden.

ISADOR, Michael, b. 17 Sept. 1939, Phila., Pa., USA. Pianist. Educ: BA, Univ. of Calif., Berkeley; Paris Consrev., France, 1960; Juilliard Schl. of Music, NYC; study w. Ilona Kabos,

London, 1962-65. Debut: w. Phila. Orch., 1951. Career: Tchng. Facs., Univ. of Calif. & San Fran. Conserv., 1965-68; Univ. of Cape Town, S Africa, 1969-71; Solo recitalist in Europe & Am.; Pianist in chmbr. music ensembles & accompanist to Henryk Szeryng, Ida Haendel, Zara Nelsova, Symon Goldberg, etc., 1971-. Recordings: Faure & Debussy Sonatas, w. Maurice Hasson (Music for Pleasure); Selected Kreisler pieces w. Rodney Friend (Music for Pleasure). Mgmt: De Koos, London. Address: 79 Addison Way, London NW 11, UK.

ISENBERGH, Max, b. 28 Aug. 1913, Albany, NY, USA. Clarinettist. Educ: AB, Cornell Univ., 1934; AM, JD, LL M, Harvard Univ., 1942, '38, '39; Clarinet studies w. Peter Schmidt, 1925-26 & Ralph MacLean, Phila., 1946; Orchl. repertoire studies w. George Bailley, Ithaca, 1930-33. m. Pearl Evans, 2 s., 1 d. Career: Recitalist, soloist w. orch. & participant in chamber music grps. in Wash., Paris & NY, 1954-; one season (1947-48) w. Arlington (Va.) Symph. Orch.; Radio appearances, Wash., Paris, NY, 1957-69. Mbrships: Cosmos Club, Wash. DC; AFM; Pres., Wash. Chamber Music Soc., 1964. Hons: Hinckley Music Award, Cornell Univ., 1931; Rockefeller Pub. Serv. Award, 1954. Hobbies: Tennis. Address: 2216 Massachusetts Ave. NW, Wash, DC 20008, USA. 2.

ISEPP, Martin Johannes Sebastian, b. 30 Sept. 1930, Vienna, Austria. Pianist; Harpsichordist. Educ: Lincoln Coll., Oxford; ARCM. m. Rose Henrietta Harris, 2 s. Career incls: Music Staff, 1957-, Chief Coach, 1973-, Glyndebourne Fest. Opera; BBC Listening Panel, 1972-; Fac. Mbr., Juilliard Schl. of Music, NYC, 1973-76; Accomp. to Ldng. artists, inclng: Janet Baker, John Shirley-Quirk, Elisabeth Schwarzkopf, Elisabeth Söderström, Jessye Norman, Anne Howells, Shiela Armstrong & Hans Hotter. Recordings: as accomp. & continuo player -Westminster, RCA, Saga, Argo, Unicorn. Mbr., Committee, Anglo-Austrian Music Soc., London. Recip., Carroll Donner Stuchell Medal for accomp., Harriet Cohen Int. Music Fndn., 1965. Hobbies: Swimming; Walking; Gastronomy. Mgmt: HHH Concert Agcy., 5 Draycott Pl., London SW3. Address: 37A Steeles Rd., London NW3 4RG, UK. 3.

ISHERWOOD, Cherry Joan M. Pianist; Freelance Orchestral Harpist. Educ: Attended RAM; LRAM; ARCM. m. Henry Datyner (dec.), 1 s., 2 d. Career: Regular Broadcast Apps. w. Henry Datyner, 1950's; Harpist, LPO, LSO, RPO; Tours abroad w. all 4 orchs.; Former, Prof., Piano, GSM, London. Mbrships: ISM; UK Harpists Assn. Hons: Elizabeth Stokes Scholar; Chappell Gold Medal for Piano; Julia Laney Prize for Harp; ARAM. Hobbies: Theatre; Concerts; Reading. Address: 33A Corfton Rd., Ealing, London W5 2HP, UK. 3.

ÍSLÓFSSON, Páll, b. 1893. Organist; Composer. Educ: studied music, inclng. organ w. K Straube, Leipzig, 1913-18; studied w. Joseph Bonnet, Paris, 1925. Career: Asst. & Substitute Organist, St. Thomas Ch., Leipzig, 1917-19; Dir., Reykjavik Schl. of Music, Iceland, 1930-57; Organist, Reykjavik Cathedral, 1939-68; Hd. of Music, Iceland State Broadcasting Serv., 1930-59. Compositions incl: sev. short capricious pieces for piano; Variations on a Theme by his father, for piano; Little Preludes & Choral Preludes for organ; Introduction & Passacaglia for organ (also in orchestral version); Festive Overture for orch.; March for orch.; University Cantata; many solo songs w. piano accomp., songs for mixed choirs & for male choirs. Recordings incl: Althing Festival Cantata. Address: c/o Islenzk Tonverkamidstöd Laufasveg 40, Reykjavik, Iceland.

ISMAGILOV, Zagir Garipovich, b. 8 Jan. 1917, Verkhnee Sermenevo, Bushkirian, USSR. Composer. Educ: Moscow Conserv. Compositions incl: Lenin Cantata, 1950; Symphonic Overture, 1951; Vocal-Choreographic Suite, 1953; Salavat Yulalev (opera), 1954; Kodasa, 1959; var. vocal & instrumental works. Mbrships: Exec., USSR Composers Union; Chmn., Bashkir Br., ibid. Hons: Honoured Worker of Arts of RSFSR, 1955; People's Artist, ibid, 1968; People's Artist of Bashkir SSR, 1963; Red Banner of Labour etc. Address: Bashkir Sect., RSFSR Composers Union, Ufa, USSR.

ISOIR, André Jean Mark, b. 20 July 1935, St. Dizin, France. Organist. Educ: Autodidact, César Franck Schl; Nat. Conserv. m. Anie Kergomard, 1 d., 2 s. Debut: 1955. Career: Concerts; Recordings. Comps: Variations on a Huguenot Psalm, manuscript. Recordings: 24 Records of French music. Mbrships: Mbr. Commission for Hist. Monuments; Organist St. Germain des Prés, Paris. Contbr. to: AFSOA Review (Organ experts). Hons: 1st Prize Nat. Conserv., 1960; 1st Prize St. Albans, 1965; 1st Haarlem, 1966-68; 1st Prize for Comp., Friends of the Organ. Hobbies: Instrument making. Address: 51 Résidence d'Estienne d'Oross, 91120 Palaiseau, France.

ISOZ, Etienne, b. 22 Dec. 1905, Budapest, Hungary. Composer; Professor. Educ: Comp. studies, Nat. Conserv., Budapest; Univ. Franz Liszt (music); Royal Conserv. di Musica St. Cecilia, Rome. div. Career: Prof., Nat. Conserv., Budapest, 1939; Gym. of Music, 1946-; returned to Switz., 1950. Comps: Symphonic Poems; ballets; scherzos for orch.; concertos for piano, horn, cor des Alpes (cow-herd's horn), oboe and for horn and organ horn & harps, horn and piano; cor des Alpes & organ; flute & harps; flute à bec & harps; suite for oboe or cor anglais & harps; toccatta for organ; paino pieces; lieder on Italian, French & German texts. Mbr., Suisa, AMS. Hons: Prize of Nat. Conserv.; Prix de Rome. Hobby: Watches. Address: Rue de Geneve 89, 1004 Lausanne, Switz.

ISRAELIEVITCH, Jacques, b. 6 May 1948, Cannes, France. Violinist; Conductor. Educ: Nat. Conserv., Paris; Ecole Normale de Musique, Paris; Ind. Univ., USA. m. Gail Bass Israelievitch. Debut: aged 11, concert at Theatre des Champs Elysées broadcast on French Nat. TV & Radio. Career: concerts in Western Europe, Japan, Greece & N Am.; Asst. Concertmaster, Chgo. Symph. Orch., 1972-78; Concertmaster, St Louis Symph., 1978-; Artist in Residence, Webster Coll., 1978. Recordings: Orion Records. Mbrships: Pres., Camerata Soc. of Chgo.; Art Club of Chgo. Hons. incl: Prize, Paganini Competition, Genoa; Official Soloist, ORTF; Alumnus of the Year, Ind. Univ. Hobbies: Art; Wines; Reading. Address: c/o St. Louis Symph. Orch., 718 Grand Blvd., St. Louis, MO 63103, USA.

ISSELL, Robert, b. 7 Dec. 1938, Auckland, NZ. Violinist. m. Eske Hos, 1 s., 2 d. Career: Ldr., Symphonia of Auckland & Auckland Radio Orchs.; Soloist; Concert apps.; Radio & TV Recitals; Mbr., New Music Grp. & var. chmbr. ensembles; App., Nat. Film Unit Documentary, 'Arts in NZ'. Recordings: Chmbr. Music, Reed-Pacific & Pye labels. Contbr. to Record Mags. Hobbies: Boating; Light-Tackle Game Fishing; Hi-Fi. Address: 29 McDowell Cres., Birkenhead, Auckland, NZ.

ISTRATE, Mircea, b. 27 Sept. 1929, Cluj, Romania. Composer; Piano Teacher. Educ: Cluj Music Acad. (piano); Bucharest Conserv. (comp.); Tchr. I degree, ibid. div., 1 d. Career: Tchr., piano & chmbr. music, Cluj Music Acad., 1950-53; Piano Tchr., Schl. of Arts, Bucharest, 1959. Comps: Evocation, 1960; Sur un e plage japonaise, 1961; Sonata for flute & piano, 1954; Sonata for oboe & piano, 1962; film music. Recordings: Stereophonic music for 2 string orchs.; Burlesque, chmbr. concerto. Mbrships: Union of Romanian Comps. Hons: Nat. Comp. Competition, Bucharest, 1955, '57; Prize for film music "Pélikan blanc", Mamaia, 1966. Hobbies: Fishing; Ceramics. Address: str. Prundului 27 bl. I sc. III et I, ap. 32, Bucharest 6, Romania.

ITO, Yoshio, b. 1 July 1904, Tokyo, Japan. Pianist. Educ: Staatliche Univ, Berlin, Germany; Sternsches Conserv. of Music, Berlin. m. Mitsu Ito, 1 s. Debut: Tokyo, 1928. Career: Piano recitals, broadcasts, lectures; Prof., Musashino Academia Musicae. Comp: School song, 5th Momoi Elementary Schl., Suginamiku. Publs: Textbook of Harmony in Questions & Answers, 1940; Introduction to Elementary Pianoforte Playing, 1941; Musical Form, 1959; Pianoforte Works of Ludwig van Beethoven, 1962. Contbr. to: Ongaku no tomo; Lesson on tomo (both Tokyo). Mbr., Japanese Musicol. Soc. Address: Izumi 2-20-15, Suginami-ku, Tokyo, Japan.

ITURBI, Jose, b. 28 Nov. 1895, Valencia, Spain. Pianist; Conductor; Composer. Educ: Valencia Conserv. of Music; Grad. w. highest hons., Conserv. of Music, Paris, France, 1913. m. Maria Giner (dec.), 1 d. (dec.). Career: Café Perf. & Pvte. Tchr., Zürich, Switzerland; Prof. of Piano Virtuosity, Geneva Conserv.; Concert Artist, w tours throughout Europe, Middle & Far East, Africa, USSR & S Am.; US Debut, 1929; Cond., 29 Concerts, Mexico City, 1933; Cond. & Music Dir., Rochester Phil., NY, USA 1935-43; Perfs. as Cond. w. all major orchs. of world; Permanent Cond., Valencia Orch., Spain. Comps. incl: Seguidillas (orch.); Soliloquy (orch.); Fantasia (piano & orch.); var. piano pieces, recordings incl: Polonaise in A Flat; Clair de Lune (both golden discs). Hons. incl: French Legion of Hon.; Gold Medal of Labour, Spain, 1968; Quevedo Gold Medal for Arts, 1972; Grand Cross of Isable the Catholic, 1975. Address: 915 N Bedford Drive, Beverly Hills, CA 90210, USA. 2.

IVALDI, Christian, b. 2 Sept. 1938, Paris, France. Pianist; Teacher. Educ: Paris Conserv. Debut: 1959. Career: Chmbr. music & contemporary music apps.; Accomp. for singers; Concerts, radio & TV apps. w. most world famous artists in Europe, USA, Can., N Africa & Iran; Tchr. for sight-reading at Paris Conserv. Num. recordings incl. works by: Schubert, Mozart, Mendelssohn, Milhaud, Weber, Beethoven, Boulez, Webern, Couperin, Debussy, Britten, Bartok, etc.; Piano works;

Chmbr. music; Lieder. Hons: Grand prix du disque Charles Cros, 1966, '69, '70; Prix des disquaires de France, 1978. Address: 19 rue Rousselet, 75007, Paris, France.

IVERSEN, Carl Morten, b. 1 May 1948, Oslo, Norway. Musician. (Bass). Educ: Bach. Business Admin., S Colo. State Coll., 1972; pvte. studies, piano & violin; Bass studies w. Dave Holland, 1978. Career: Freelance musician w. emphasis on jazz, Oslo area, 1973-; Theatre, studio, recording & TV apps. w. many Norwegian folksingers. Comps: sev. comps. publd., 1 recorded by Lars Klevstrand. Recordings: Per Husby Septet, Peacemaker; Guttorm Guttormsen Quartet, Soturnudi. Publs: Ed. & staff mbr., Jazz Nytt (Jazz News), 1972-75; A report on the Norwegian broadcasting. systems (state controlled) treatment of Norwegian jazz, 1973 (w. Per Ottersen & S Kristiansen). Contbr. to: Jazz Nytt; Var Musikk. Mbrships: Bd., Norwegian Musicians Union; Past Pres., Norwegian Jazz Fedn. Hons: Norwegian Creative Artists Fund Scholarship, 1968; Norwegian Silver Record. Hobbies: Music; Theatre; Art; Cooking; Photography. Address: Uelandsgate 36, Oslo 4, Norway.

IVERSEN, Einar, b. 27 July 1930, Mandal, Norway. Musician (piano, flute). Educ: studied piano, flute & harmony w. pvte. tchrs.; studied choir cond. at Conserv. m. Sissel Mantor, 2 c. Career: Var. jazz groups in Norway & Sweden; Accomp., num. musicians, incl. Coleman Hawkins, Dexter Gordon, Tubby Hayes, Putte Wickman, singer Monica Zetterlund & entertainer Povel Ramel; Studio musician, Oslo; Own TV program; Tchr., jazz piano, summer schls.; Pianist, flautist, arr. & cond., Det Norske Teatret. Recordings: w. own trio, Me and My Piano, 1976; w. Bjarne Nerem, Everything Happens To Me, 1976. Mbrships: Norwegian Musicians Union. Hons: The Buddy Statuette, 1958, for Best Jazz Musician of the Year, Jazz in Norway, 1975. Hobbies: Tennis; Skiing; Gardening. Address: Marienlundun 10D, Oslo 11, Norway.

IVEY, Jean Elchelberger, b. 3 July 1023, Washington, DC, USA. Composer; Pianist. Educ: AB, Trinity Coll.; M Mus, Piano, Peabody Conserv., M Mus., Composition, Eastman Schl. of Music, Rochester Univ.; Mus.Doc., Mus D., Composition. Univ. of Toronto. m. Dr. Frederick M Ivey. Career: concerts, USA, Mexico, Europe in 1950's; Mbr., Composition Fac. & Fndr., Dir., Electronic Music Studio, Peabody Conserv., Balt., 1969-. Num. compositions incl: Forms in Motion; Tribute; Martin Luther King; Ode for Orchestra; Testament of Eve, Monodrama for mezzo, orch & tape; Chmbr. music incl: Hera, Hung from the Sky; Anthems, choral works, Sonatina for Unaccompanied Clarinet; Electronic music incl: Pinball; Cortege for Charles Kent. Recordings: Music by Jean Eichelberger Ivey; Pinball;

Hera, Hung from the Sky; Cortege for Charles Kent, others. Contbr. to Electronic Music: A Listener's Guide by Elliott Schwartz, 1973 & to num. profl. jrnls. Mbrships incl: ASCAP; Bd. of Dirs., US Sect., Int. Soc. for Contemp. Music; Am. Soc. of Univ. Composers., Am. Music Ctr.; Past Coun. Mbr., Coll. Music Soc.; Sigma Alpha Iota. Hons: Mexican concert tour, sponsored by US Embassy, 1956; ASCAP Awards, 1972-; Martha Baird Rockefeller Fund Grant, 1973; Peabody Conserv. Disting. Alumni Award, 1975. Address: Comp. Fac., Peabody Conserv., Baltimore, MD 21202, USA. 5,6,14,27.

IWAKI, Hiroyuki, b. 6 Sept. 1932, Tokyo, Japan. Conductor. Educ: Art Univ. of Tokyo. m. Kaori Kimura. Debut: Tokyo, 1956. Career: apps. w. num. ldng. orchs., USA, Europe, USSR; Chief Cond., Melbourne Symph., Aust.; Music Dir. & Cond., NHK Symph., Japan. Recordings incl: the 9 Beethoven symphs. Hobbies: Baseball; Fishing. Mgmt: Interartists, Netherlands; Columbia Artists, USA. Address: c/o Interartists, Koninginnegracht 82, The Hague, Netherlands.

IWANEJKO, Maria Wanda, b. 12 Aug. 1921, Chrzanow, Poland. Concert Pianist; Musicologist. Educ: MPh (musicol.), Jagiellonian Univ.; MA (piano), Nat. Conserv. of Music. m. Marian Iwanjko, 2 s., 1 d. Debut: premiered Michal Spisak's 1st Piano Concerto, Lodz, Poland, 1956. Career: Recitals & concerts in Polish cities, also London & The Hague; Piano Soloist, Cracow Phil.; gave 1st perfs. of works by many Polish & for. contemp. comps., 1955-71. Author: Maria Szymanowska, the First Polish (Woman) Pianist & Composer. Contbr. to jrnls. Mbrships. incl: Coun., Musical Soc., Cracow; Polish Musical Artists' Assn. Hobbies: Floriculture; Collecting for-portery. Address: ul Worcella 98, Cracow, Poland.

IWANOW, Wladimir, b. 21 June 1957, Sofia, Bulgaria. Lutenist; Guitarist; Musicology Student. Educ. pvte. studies w. Prof. Kurt Weinhoppel, Munich. sev. comps. Mbrships: Am. Musicol. Soc.; Verein zur Erhaltung und Förderung alter Musik e.v.; Capella Monacensis. Hobby: Filming Address: Weitlstr 141, Munich, German Fed. Repub.

IZQUIERDO, Juan Pablo, b. 1935, Chile. Conductor. Educ: Grad., comp., Univ. of Chile; Music Acad. of Vienna (comp. & cond.); studied w. Hermann Scherchen. Career incls: Tours, Latin Am., Europe; Asst. Cond., NY Phil. Orch.; Res. Cond., Indiana Univ., 2 yrs.; Chief Cond., Gulbenkian Orch., Lisbon, 1976-77 seasons; Music Dir., Testimonium Fest., Israel. Hons: Nat. Critics Prize; Mitropoulos Int. Competition for Conds., 1966; "The Most Outstanding Cond. of an Israeli Work", Ministry of Culture & Arts, Israel. Address: 55 Redington Rd., London NW3, UK.

J

JACCOTTET, Christiane, b. 18 May 1937, Lausanne, Switz. Harpsichordist; Professor. Educ: Piano Dip., La Chaux-de-Fonds, 1954; Harpsichord Matriculation, Vienna Acad., 1957; 2nd Prize, Harpsichord, 1st Prize, Basso continuo, Bruges, 1965. m. Pierre Jaccottet, 1 s. Debut: Switz. Career: apps. as Soloist, w. orchs. & in chmbr. ensembles, Switz, Italy, France, Austria, Germany, UK, Spain & Portugal; toured in USA, 1970; broadcasts on Swiss radio stns.; Prof., Conserv. of Geneva. Recordings incl: J S Bach, Goldberg Variations & Brandenburg Concertoes; Couperin; Frank Martin's Harpsichord Concerto; Sweelinck. Mbr., Assn. of Swiss Musicians. Recip. sev. recording awards. Hobby: Building Harpsichords. Address: Le Monteiller, CH-1812 Rivaz, Switz.

JACHINO, Carlo, b. 1887, Sanremo, Italy. Educator; Composer. Educ: Music Schl., Lucca; Univ. of Pida; studied w. H Rieman, Leipzig. m. Valentina Luisa Mori, 1 s. Career: Prof. of Composition, Conservs. in Parma, Naples & Rome, 1930-50; Dir. of Naples Conserv., 1951-53; Dir. of Nat. Conserv., Bogota, Colombia, 1953-57. Compositions incl: Giocondo e il suo Re (opera in 3 acts) I due Nasi (opera in 1 act); Fantasia del Rosso e Nero for orch.; Sonata Drammatica for violin & orch.; Preludio di Festa; concertos for piano (2) & cello; L'Ora inquieta for strings; Holy Prayer to the Virgin Mary for strings & soprano; trios, quintets; songs, etc. Publs: Gli Strumenti d'orchestra; Technica Dodecafona; Critical Essays on Lohengrin & Salome. Recip. of sev. prizes. Address: 171 Via Flaminia, Rome, Italy. 3.

JACKSON, Barbara Ann Garvey, b. 27 Sept. 1929, Normal, Ill., USA. Teacher. Educ: B Mus., Univ. of Ill.; MM, Rochester Univ., PhD., Stanford Univ. m. Kern C. Jackson, 4 stepsons. Career: Univ. Prof. Publs: incl: Practical Beginning Theory (co-author), 1963, 3rd ed. 1974; Songs of the Minnesingers (co-author), 1963; Ed., The Sonatas of Giovanni Antonio Piani, 1974. Contbr. to jrnls. Mbrships: Am. Musicol. Soc.; Past Mbr., Publs. Comm., Am. String Tchrs. Assn.; Viola da Gamba Soc.; Past Nat. Coun. Mbr., Coll. Music Soc.; MTNA; Hon. Mbr., Sigma Alpha Iota. Hobbies: Wildflower photography; Camping; Cooking. Address: 235 Baxter Lane, Fayetteville, AR 72701, USA. 5,27.

JACKSON, Francis Alan, b. 2 Oct. 1917, Malton Yorks., UK. Organist & Choirmaster. Educ: study w. Sir Edward Bairstow; FRCO, 1937; D Mus., Durham Univ., 1957. m. Priscilla Procter, 2 s., 1 d. Career: Organist, Malton Parish Ch., 1933-40; WW II Serv., 9th Lancers, 1940-46; Master of the Music, York Minster, 1946-; Organ recitalist throughout UK, incl: Royal Festival Hall, Westminster Abbey, St. Paul's; Recitals in Switzerland, Paris, Denmark, Bermuda; 6 tours of USA & Canada. Compositions: 2 organ sonatas; Monodramas -Daniel in Babylon, & A Time of Fire (speaker, choir & organ), words by John Stuart Anderson; Symph. in D Minor (Orch.); Variations on a Theme by Vaughan Williams, 1960; Overture Brigantia, 1972; var. organ pieces, anthems, canticle & communion settings. Recordings: num. organ works for EMI, Alpha, Abbey, Polydor, Canon, etc. Mbrships: RCO, 1935-; Pres., ibid, 1972-74; Past Pres., inc. Assn. of Organists. Hons: Fellow, RSCM,1963; Fellow, Westminster Choir Coll., Princeton, NJ, 1970. Hobby: Gardening. Address: 1 Minster Ct., York, YO1 2JJ, UK.

JACKSON, Geoffrey William, b. 20 Aug. 1939, Glossop, UK. Tutor; Baritone. Educ: Mus B, Manchester, 1961; GRSM; ARMCM., 1961. m. Josephine M Taylor. Career: Sr. Tutor w. responsibility for Historical Studies, Royal Northern Coll. of Music; Solo baritone - many engagements in North of England. Mbr., ISM. Hobbies: Comp. Electronic music. Address: 19 Churwell Ave., Heaton Mersey, Stockport, Ches., UK. 3.

JACKSON, Hanley, b. 6 July 1939, Bryan, Tex., USA. Professor of Music Composition. Educ: BA, Calif. State Univ., Northridge; MA, Calif. State Univ., Long Beach. m. Lee Jackson. Career: Prof. of Music Composition, Kan. State Univ., Manhattan. Compositions: "A Child's Ghetto" (for chorus & tape); "Tangents III" (for band & tape); "Tangents IV" (for piano & tape); "Tangents V" (for chorus & tape); Cradle Hymn & Hodie (for chorus & tape); Vignettes of the Plains (choir & tape); Day Hours of Darkness (choir & audience). Author, Music Listening, A Syllabus, 1974. Contbr. to The Instrumentalist. Mbrships: ASCAP; Am. Soc. of Univ. Composers; Am. Fedn. of Musicians. Hons: Cecilia Buck Award, 1963; Esther Tou Newman Award, 1968. Hobbies: Hunting; Photography. Address: Music Dept., Kan. State Univ., Manhattan, KS 66506, USA.

JACKSON, Harold, b. Haworth, Yorks., UK. Trumpeter (Classical). Educ: LRAM; ARCM. Career: Solo Cornet, Black Kike Mills Band, aged 14; Later w. RAF Ctrl. Band; Prin. Trumpet, Philharmonia Orch.; Royal Phil. Orch. under Sir Thomas Beecham. Mbr., ISM. Address: 83 Rosemary Ave., Hounslow W, Middlesex, 7W4 7JW, UK.

JACKSON, Henry, b. 5 May 1909, Amarillo, Tex., USA. Pianist; Coach; Accompanist. Educ: Am. Conserv., Chgo., piano w. Earl Blair; Berlin, Piano w. Georg Bertram; Vienna, Piano w. Julius Isserlis, Comp. w. Franz Schmidt. Career: Soloist, Wiener Symphoniker, NYC Symph., Chgo. Symph., LA Phil.; Tours w. Christa Ludwig, Bido Sayao, Carol Neblett, Nadine Conner, Georges Thill, etc.; Assoc. Prof. of Music, Calif. State Univ., LA; Dir., Opera Workshop, 1964-76. Recordings: All the songs of Chopin, w. Doda Conrad; Messien, Chants de Terre et de Ciel, w. Janet Fairbank. Mbr., Phi Mu Alpha. Hobbies: Travel; Cooking. Address: 3001 Norwood Pl., Alhambra, CA 91803, USA.

JACKSON, Paul Joseph, b. 14 Aug. 1927, Crystal Falls, Mich., USA. Educator-Administrator; Pianist; Musicologist. Educ: BM, Lawrence Coll.; MMus, Univ. of Mich.; PhD, Stanford Univ.; DFA, Lawrence Univ.; Acad. of Music, Vienna. m. Leland Page Jackson. Career: Concert Accomp., Metrop. & NYC Opera artists, 1953-64; Asst. Mgr., House Mgr., Ctrl. City, Colo. Opera & Drama Fests., summers, 1954-64; Fac. Mbr., Wm Woods Coll., 1950-53, 1954-56; Asst. to the Dir., Stanford Univ. Opera Prods., 1959-62; Dean, Coll. of Fine Arts, Prof. of Music, Drake Univ., 1964-. Contbr. to: Grove's Dict., 6th ed.; Opera News. Mbrships. incl: Commn. on Undergrad. Curric., Nat. Assn. of Schls. of Music, 1974-77; Am. Musicol. Soc.; Int. Coun. of Fine Arts Deans. Address: Drake Univ., Des Moines, IA 50311, USA.

JACKSON, Raymond T, b. 11 Dec. 1933, Providence, RI, USA. Concert Pianist; Organist; College Professor. Educ: B Mus, New England Conserv. Music, Boston, 1955; BS, Juilliard Schl. of Music, 1957; MS, ibid., 1959; DMA, 1973. m. Annette Barnhill Jackson, 1 d. Debut: Town Hall, NY, 1959. Career: Recitals & Soloist w. orchs., USA, Europe & S Am. Publ: The Piano Music of Black Americans; The Piano Music of Black Composers. Mbrships: Hon., Chopin Club, Providence, RI; Pi Kappa Lambda. Hons. incl: Prize winner, Marguerite Long Int. Piano Competition, Paris, 1965; Prize winner, 4th Int. Piano Competition, Rio de Janeiro, 1965; Rhode Island Heritage Hall of Fame, 1966. Hobby: Tennis. Address: 224 Midland Ave., Tuckahoe, NY 10707, USA.

JACKSON, Richard, b. 15 Feb. 1936, New Orleans, La., USA. Music Librarian. Educ: BMus, Loyola Univ.; MA, Tulane Univ.; MSLS, Pratt Inst. Career: Hd., Americana Collection, NY Public Lib. Publs: incl: Popular Songs of 19th Century America, 1976; The Stephen Foster Songbook, 1974; Piano Music of Louis Moreau Gottschalk, 1973; United States Music: Sources of Bibliography & Collective Biography, 1973; num. articles for encys. etc. Contbr. to: Lib. Jrnl.; Notes: New World Records (notes). Mbrships: Music Lib. Assn.; Am. Musicol. Soc.; Sonneck Soc.; Am. Music Ctr. Hobbies: Films; Reading. Address: 111 Amsterdam Ave., NY, NY 10023, USA.

JACKSON, Richard, b. 16 July 1949, Penzance, Cornwall, UK. Singer (baritone). Educ: MA, modern langs., King's Coll. Cambridge; 2 yrs. Post Grad. study, GSM, London; 1 yr., London Opera Centre. Career: Var. operas, concerts & recitals, UK, Europe, USA. Mgmt: Ibbs & Tillett. Address: 16 Rodenhurst Rd., London, SW4, UK.

JACOB, Gordon Percival Steven, b. 5 July 1895, London, UK. Composer. Educ: Dulwich Coll.; DMus, RCM. m. Margaret S H Gray, 1 s., 1 d. Career: Appearances as conductor, mainly of own works; Prof., Royal Coll. of Music, 1924-69; Examiner to many univs. Composer of many orchl. chmbr., choral works, also orchestrations & arrangements & compositions for wind orch., mil. band, brass band. Some works recorded. Publs: Orchestral Technique, 1931; How to read a score, 1944; The Composer & His Art, 1954. Contbr. to: Chamber's Ency.; Grove's Dict.; Var. musical mags. Mbr., ISM. Hons: John Collard Fellowship, 1943-46; Cobbett Medal for Chmbr. Music, 1949; CBE, 1968; FRCM; Hon. RAM. Hobbies: Reading; Crossword puzzles. Address: 1 Audley Rd., Saffron Walden, Essex, CB11 3HW, UK. 1,3,14.

JACOBI, Erwin R, b. 21 Sept. 1909, Strasbourg, France, dec. 2 Feb. 1979. Musicologist. Educ: Technische Hochschulen, Munich & Berlin-Charlottenburg; Dip.-Ingenieur, 1933; studied harpsichord w. Frank Pelleg, Wanda Landowska & Eduard Müller; studied musicol. & music theory w. P. Ben-Haim, Kurt Sachs, Paul Hindemith & E.E. Cherbuliez; Dr. Phil., Zürich Univ., 1957. Div., 1 d. Career: Lectr., Zürich Univ., 1961; Vis. Prof., Univ. of Iowa, 1970-71 & Ind Ind. Univ., 1971-72; lectures on

Radio Beromünster, on Congresses of Int. Musicol. Soc., etc. Publs. incl: Die Entwicklund der Musiktheorie in England nach der Zeit von Jean-Phillipe Rameau; (C.P.E. Bach) Doppelkonzert in Es-dur für Cembalo, Fortepiano und Orchester (1788), 1958; (J-Ph. Rameau) Pièces de Clavecin (1706, 1724, ca. 1728, 1741, 1747), 1958, 1961; (J.B. Boismortier) Pièces de Clavecin (1736) 1960, rev. eds., 1964, 1971; (G. Tartini) Traité des agréments de la Musique, 1961; (D.G. Türk) Klavierschule (1789), 1962, 2nd ed., 1967; (J-Ph. Rameau) Complete Theoretical Writing (1722-64), Vols. 1-6, 1967-72; Albert Schweitzer und die Musik, 1975; (A. Schweitzer) Zur Diskussion 8uber Orgelbau (1914), 1977; Musikwissenschaftliche Arbeiten im Anhang; Veröffentlichungen zur Biographie Albert Schweitzers, 1979. Mbr. sev. profl. orgs. Hons: Chevalier l'Ordre des Arts et des Lettres, 1975. Hobbies: First & rare eds. of Music, Music Books, etc. Address: Riedgrabenweg 29, 8050 Zürich, Switz. 14,19,28.

JACOBI, Roger Edgar, b. 7 Apr. 1924, Saginaw, Mich., USA. Arts Centre President; Professor of Music. Educ: B Mus., Schl. of Music, Univ. of Mich., 1948; MMus, ibid, 1959. m. Mary Jane Stephans, 1 s., 1 d. Career: Dir., Summer Music Prog., Recreation Dept., Ann Arbor Pub. Schls., summer 1952; Prog. Dir., Nat. Music Camp, Interlochen, Mich., summers 1953, '54, '55; Sec. & Dir. of Personnel, Nat. Music Camp, Interlochen, Mich., 1956-59; Fac. Mbr., ibid, summers, 1957-65; Music Co-ord., Ann Arbor Pub. Schls. pt, 1959-68; Assoc. Dean, Schl. of Music, Univ. of Mich., 1971; Lectr., Schl. of Educ., ibid, 1959-71; Prof. of Music (currently); Pres., Interlochen Ctr. for the Arts (Nat. Music Camp/Interlochen Arts Acad.), Interlochen, Mich. Publs: co-author, Teaching Band Instruments to Beginners, 1966; Contbr. of material to var. profl. publs. Producer of film, 'Let's Make Music', 1966. Mbrships incl: AFM; MENC; Nat. Assn. of Jazz Educators; Hon. Mbr., Phi Mu Alpha. Hons: Hon. Fine Arts Award, Mich. Acad. of Sci., Arts & Leters, 1973; Hon. Alumnus, Arthur Hill HS, 1972. Var. hobbies. Address: Interlochen Ctr. for the Arts, Interlochen, MI 49643, USA.

JACOBS, Arthur David, b. 14 June 1922, Manchester, UK. Music Critic; Editor; Lecturer. Educ: MA, Merton Coll., Oxford. m. Betty Upton Hughes, 2 s. Career: Prof., RAM, 1964 79; Hd. of Music Dept., Huddersfield Polytechnic, 1979-; George A Miller Centennial Lectr., Univ. of Ill., USA, 1967; Vis. Prof., Lectr., Univ. of Calif., LA & Santa Barbara; Temple Univ., Phila., Univ. of Victoria, BC, Can., Banff, Alta., Schl. of Fine Arts; Univ. of Wester Ont.; Vis. Fellow, Wolfson Coll., Oxford, 1979; Dpty. Ed., Opera, 1962-71; Record Reviewer, Sunday Times, 1968-; & Columnist, Hi-Fi News & Record Review, 1964-; Ed. Brit. Music Yearbook, 1971-75; Librettist, Nicholas Maw, One Man Show; Trans. var. Operas. Publs: Gilbert & Sullivan, 1951; A New Dictionary of Music, 1958, Spanish, Swedish Eds.; A Short History of Western Music, 1972; The Brit. Music Yearbook, 1972-73, 1973-74; Music Education Handbook, 1976, Eds.; 1975, 1976 W Stanley Sadie, The Pan Book of Opera, 1966. 2 Eds. in USA under different titles. Contbr. to: Musical Times; Music & Leters; num. Newspapers & jrnls., UK, Can., USA. Mbr. Royal Musical Assn.; Critics' Circle; Nat. Union of jrnlists. Recip. num. Hons. Hobbies: Swimming; Skiing; Puns; Theatre. Address: Music Dept., Polytechnic, Huddersfield HD1 3DH, UK.

JACOBS, Charles Gilbert, b. 26 Mar. 1934, Weehawken, NJ, USA. Musicologist; Choral Director; Organist. Educ: PhD, NY Univ., 1962; Peabody Conserv. of Music. Debut: Town Hall, NY 1950. Career: Asst. Prof., McGill Univ., 1969-70; Lectr., CUNY, York Campus, 1968; Acting Asst. Prof., Hunter Campus, CUNY, 1969-70; currently Prof. of Music, Kingsborough Campus & Graduate Schl., CUNY. Publs. incl: Luis de Milán: El Maestro, 1971; Antonio Valente: Intavolatura; Cabezón: Works; Miguel de Fuenllana: Orphenica Lyra. Contbr. to jrnls. & mags. Mbrships. incl: Int. Musicol. Soc.; Royal Musical Soc.; Am. Musicol. Soc. Recip., num. grants & fellowships. Address: 22-73rd St., N Bergen, NJ 07047, USA.

JACOBS, Harry M, b. 23 Aug. 1917, Chicago, Ill., USA. Music Director & Educator; Musician (French horn, Violin, Viola). Educ: B Mus., Eastman Schl. of Music, Univ. of Rochester; M Mus., N Western Univ.; Cert., Nat. Orchl. Assn. m. Vola O'Connor, 3 s., 2 d. Career: Chgo. Symph.; Mpls. Symph.; New Orleans Symph.; San Diego Symph.; Chgo. Symph. Woodwind Quintet; Guest Cond., Lugano, Switzerland; Flensburg, Germany; Charleston, Columbia, USA; Music Dir., & Fndr., Augusta Symph. Orch., 1954-; Dir. of Fine Arts Activities, Augusta Coll.; Recip. Gov's Award for Arts, 1974. Prof. of Music., ibid. Mbrships: AAUP; Torch Int.; Pi Kappa Lambda; Ga. Arts Commn., 1966. Hon. Life Hon. Mbr., Augusta Music Club, 1960; Recip. Gov's Award for Arts, 1974. Hobbies: Chmbr. Music; Unique Instruments; Water Sports. Address: 1903 Valley Spring Rd., Augusta, GA 30904, USA.

JACOBS, René, b. 30 Oct. 1946, Ghent, Belgium. Singer (Countertenor). Educ: Licentiaat Klassieke Filologie, Univ. Ghent; Solo singing w. Louis Devos (Brussels) & Lucie Frateur (The Hague). m. Suzy Depoorter, 4 c. Career: Recitals, Europe, Can., USA, Mexico, Philippines; Perfs. of authentic Baroque Operas & Oratorios, Cond. Gustav Leonhardt, Nikolaus Harnoncourt, Alan Curtis; Specialist in Händel-Opera; Tchr., Perf. practice of baroque singing, Schola Cantorum Basel (Switz.), Int. Sommerakademie für Alte Musik, Innsbruck, (Austria); Aston Magna Acad. for Baroque Music, Mass., USA. Recordings: Das Alte Werk; Seon; Handel-Admeto; Handel-Partenope; Concerto Vocale. Hobbies: Films; Detective Novels; Translating Greek, Latin & Italian poetry into Dutch verse. Mgmt: Concert Directie De Koos, Laren (Netherlands); Lee McRae, Berkeley, Calif. (USA). Address: Langenakkerlaan 34, 9130 Lochristi, Belgium.

JACOBS, Robert Louis, b. 2 Dec. 1904, Melbourne, Aust. Writer & Lecturer on Music. Educ: BA, Balliol Coll., Oxford Univ.; LRAM; pvte. studies of music, Vienna & Berlin. m. Isabel Sara Pyke, 1 s. Career: Extra-mural Lectr., Musical Appreciation, London Univ., 1947-72. Publs: Wagner, 1935, revised 1965, 74; Harmony for the Listener, 1958 (as Understanding Harmony, 1971, 77); Transl., Wagner Writes from Paris (w. G. Skelton), UK & USA, 1973; Three Essays by Wagner (Music of the Future; On Conducting; On Performing Beethoven's 9th), 1979. Contbr. to: Sargent, Outline of Music, 1962. Sadlers Wells Opera Books; Di Gaetani; Penetrating Wagner's Ring, an Anthology, 1979; BBC radio; profl. jrnls. Hobbies: Reading; Gardening. Address: 27 Asmuns Hill, London NW 11, UK.

JACOBS, Thomas, b. 19 Jan. 1954, Cinn., OH, USA. Orchestral Bassist. Educ: Oberlin Coll. Conserv. of Music, 1972-73; BM, Univ. of Louisville Schl. of Music, 1976; Univ. of Victoria Schl. of Music. m. Idalynn Besser Jacobs. Career: Louisville Orch., 1973-77; Ky. Operas Assn. Orch., 1973-77; Louisville Bach Soc. Orch., 1975-77; Victoria Symph., 1977-79; Birmingham Symph., 1979. Hobby: Travel. Address: 2907 13th Ave. S, Apt. A-1, Birmingham, AL 35205, USA.

JACOBS, Wesley D, B. 30 Nov. 1946, Independence, Mo, USA. Tubist. Educ: Univ. of Calif., Long Beach; Juilliard Schl. of Music; Music Acad. of W Calif.; Nat. Orch. Assn., NYC. Career: Tubist, most major record, TV & motion picture cos. in Hollywood; San Fran. Opera Orch.; Detroit Symph. Orch. Recordings: Num., incl. all Detroit Symph. records since 1970. Publs: 2052 Fingerings for Tuba, 1977. Hobby: Designing & improving tubas. Address: 2118 Babcock Dr., Troy, MI 48084, USA. 3.

JACOBSEN, Erwin, b. 9 March 1926, Flensborg, Sauth-Scleswig, Germany. Oboe Soloist. Educ: Royal Danish Music Conserv. m. Sonja Jacobsen, 3 d. Debut: Copenhagen, 1945. Career: Radio, TV apps. as Soloist & Chmbr. Musician; Royal Danish Theatre, Copenhagen, 1946-. Recordings: Chmbr. Music by Finn Hoffding, Ebbe Hamerik. Hons: Silver Medal, Int. Competition, Rumania, 1953; Danish Cross, Order of Chivalry, 1972. Hobbies: Fishing; Badminton; Sports. Address: 78 I Randklove Alle, 2770 Kastrup, Copenhagen, Denmark.

JACOBSON, Harvey, b. 24 Aug. 1936, Everett, Mass., USA. Concert Pianist; Teacher of Piano & Theory. Educ. incls: BA, Boston Univ.; B Mus, Va. C'wlth. Univ.; M Mus, Univ. of NC; D Mus A, Univ. of Md.; Cert. Music Therapist (registered), Univ. of Kan. Debut: Carnegie Recital Hall, NYC, 1975. Career incls: TV apps. as soloist & Accomp.; Soloist apps. at num. univs.; live & radio lecture-recitals on Edward Alexander MacDowell; Instr., NC Schl. of Arts, 1967-70; currently Asst. Dir., Potomac Conserv. of Music, Md. Mbrships. incl: Nat. Assn. for Music Therapy; Phi Mus Alpha Sinfonia. Recip. var. hons. Hobby: Record collecting. Mgmt: Int. Artists Alliance; Community Concerts Inc., Columbia Artists Mgmt. Address: Oakton Apts. No. 203, 1904 Fox St., Adelphi, MD 20783, USA.

JACOBY, Hanoch, b. 2 March 1909, Koenigsberg, Germany. Composer; Violist; Violinist. Educ: Univ., Berlin, 1927-28; studied comp. w. Hindemith, & viola w. Bohnke, Mahlke & Wolfsthal, State HS for Music, Berlin, 1927-30. m. Alice Kanel, 4 children. Career: Mbr., Orch. of Südwestdeutsche Rundfunk, Frankfurt, 1930-33, & var. chmbr. ensembles; Tchr. & Dir., Acad. of Music, Jerusalem, Israel, 1934-58; Mbr., Israel Phil. Orch., 1958-74; Artist in Res., Technion, Haifa, 1974-75. Comps. incl: 3 symphs.; Partita Concertata; Mutatio (orchl.); Concertino for solo viola & orch.; Cantata for soloist, choir & orch.; 2 str. quartets; Wind Quintet; Theme & variations for piano trio; etc. Recip. Engel Prize, Tel-Aviv, 1951. Hobby: Painting. Address: 10 Oliphantstr., Tel-Aviv, Israel.

JACOBY, (James) Richard, b. 12 Dec. 1940, Memphis, Tenn., USA. Pianist. Educ: Cert., Southwestern Univ.,

Memphis, Tenn., 1958; Tchr. Cert., DeShazo Coll. of Music, 1962. Career: Performed throughout SE USA; App on WKNO TV Stn.; Active concert artist; Pvte. piano tchr.; Former Assoc. Tchr., DeShazo Coll. of Music; Tchr., Shelby Co. Schls. Systems; Tchr., sev. music studios throughout Memphis. Mbrships. incl: Beethoven Club of Memphis; White Stn. Masonic Lodge; Memphis Chapt., Order of Demolays. Hons. incl: 1st Place, Martin Jr. Coll., 1959-60. Address: 1587 Oakwood Dr., Memphis, TN 38116, USA.

JACOBY, Robert John, b. 8 April 1940, Sussex, UK. Violinist. Educ: GSM; RCM (Violin & Cond.); MA; FLCM; LRAM; ARCM. m. Elisabeth Duddridge, 1 s., 1 d. Debut: Wigmore Hall, London, 1962. Career: 1st Solo app. aged 6; Played 3 concertos in 1 concert, London, aged 11; Ldr., Westphalian Symph. Orch., 1963-64; Fndr.-Cond., Oakwood Orchl. Soc., 1964-66; Ldr., Res. Str. Quartet, Univ. Coll. of Wales, Aberystwyth, 1967-; Fndr.-Cond., Philomusica of Aberystwyth, 1971-; Broadcasts on radio & TV inclng. 1st broadcast perfs. of concertos by Stamitz & David Harries. Hons: Stoutzker Violin Prize, 1963; 1st Prize, Cardiff Int. Violin Competition, 1966. Hobbies: Antiquarian subjects; Tennis; Walking. Address: Dept. of Music, University Coll. of Wales, Aberystwyth, UK. 3,28.

JACOMET, Johann Georg, b. 4 June 1946, Chur, Graubuenden, Switz. Concert Pianist & Organist (Blind). Educ: Concert Pianist Dip., G. Verdi Conserv. of Music, Milan, Italy; Concert Organist Dip., Conserv. of Zürich; studied Piano w. W Rehbrg, A Mozzati, C Vidusso, Organ w. B Billeter. Career: Prof. of Piano at Zürich High Schl. & Advanced Students Scwyz Music High Schl. Apps. on radio, TV & in concert in Milan, Padua, Munich, Basel, Zürich, Lucerne & num. other European cities. Repertoire: From Baroque to modern, esp. Bach, Scarlatti, Debussy & Ravel. Dedicatee of music by G Giuffrè & C Babic. Mbr., Assn. of Swiss Musicians. Hons: Prizes, Assn. of Swiss Musicians, 1965, 66, 67; Dip. of Hon., Int. Pianists Competition, Enna, Sicily. Hobbies: Philosophy; Languages; Comparative Religion. Address: Via Zurigo 46, CH 6900 Lugano, Switz.

JACQUES, Janet Elizabeth, b. 23 Sept. 1943, Birkenhead, UK. Opera Singer. Educ: ARMCM, 1965; Acad. of Music & Drama, Vienna, Austria, 1968; pvte. study, UK & Europe. Career incl: Mezzo-Soprano, concerts & oratorios, N. of England; Mbr., Sadler's Wells chorus, 1966-68; German debut as Sara in Roberto Devereux, Bonn, 1969, followed by other mezzo roles; Became Soprano, 1971, & has sung major roles in Switzerland, Austria, NYC, Rome & UK, 1971-; Concert tour of Austria, Germany & Switzerland, 1975-; Latest apps. in Macbeth, London, & Salome, Heidelberg, 1976; num. concerts & recitals, UK. Hons. incl: Frankenstein Scholarship, 1968. Hobbies incl: European Languages; German & Austrian History; Foreign Films. Mgmt: Allied Artists, 36 Beauchamp Pl., London SW3. Address: 2 Brookfield Hansions, Highgate W. Hill, London N6, UK.

JACQUOT, Jean, b. 27 March 1909, Le Havre, France. Musicologist. Educ: Dr. Lettres, Lyons Univ. m. Freda Phillips. Career: Musicologist, Centre National de la Recherche Scientifique, Paris. Publs: Ed. & Contbr., Le Luth et sa Musique, 1959; Ed. & Contbr., Les Fêtes de la Renaissance, 3 vols., 1956, 1960, 1975; Ed. & Contbr., Les Voies de la Création Théâtrale, vol. 6, 1978; Co-Ed., Corpus des Luthistes Français; Co-Ed., ' Thomas Mace: Musick's Monument, 1966, etc. Contbr. to profl. publs. Address: 107 Avenue de Choisy, 7501 3, Paris, France.

JAEGER, Ina Claire Burlingham, b. 18 July 1929, Ashtabula, Ohio, USA. Violinist; Teacher, Department of Music, University of Florida. Educ: B Mus. & M Mus., Eastman Schl. of Music, Univ. of Rochester, NY. m. Marc J Jaeger, 2 s., 1 d. Career: Violinist, Rochester & New Orleans Phil. Orchs. & Fla. Str. Quartet; Assoc. Prof., Dept. of Music, Univ. of Fla., Gainesville. Recordings: Faculty Showcase Album, Dedication 1972. Publs: Fundamentals of Music Theory, Syllabus & Assignments, 1973; Basic Elements in Music Theory - A Modular Program of Instruction, 1974. Mbrships: MENC; Fla. Music Educators Assn.; Fla. Orch. Assn.; Sigma Alpha Iota. Recip. of acad. grants. Hobbies: Gardening; Swimming; Travelling; Reading. Address: 519 N.W. 19th St., Gainesville, FL 32603, USA. 125.

JAEGER, Patricia Paul, b. 10 May 1930, Athens, Tenn., USA. Performer; Teacher (violin, viola & harp); Distributor of Wilfred Smith Harps (London). Educ: Staatliche Hochschule für Musik, Munich, Germany; B Mus., Eastman Schl. of Music, Rochester, NY., USA; M Mus, ibid. m. Reinhard Friedrich Jaeger, 2 s. Career: Asst. Prof., Drury Coll., Springfield, Mo., Concert Mistress, Springfield Symph., 1st Violin, Springfield Chmbr.

Music Soc., num. Solo perfs., radio, TV apps., 1953-55; Pvte. violin, viola tchr., 1967-; 1st Chair Violin, N Seattle Community Coll. Chmbr. Orch., 1971-72; Guest Lectr., Ind. State Univ. Harp Workshop. Contbr. to: Folk Harp Jrnl.; Am. String Tchrs. mag. Mbr., profl. orgs. Recip. George Eastman Hon. Scholarship, 1950: US Delegate, Am. String tchrs. Assn. to Europe & Soviet Union, 1976; Am. Minstrel Harp Soc. Award Trophy, 1975. Address: 1235 N.E. 95th St., Seattle, WA 98115, USA.

JÄGEL, Frederick, b. 10 June 1897, Brooklyn, NY, USA. Operatic Tenor; Teacher of Singing. Educ: pvte. studies, voice, music, acting & langs.; Hon. DMus, New Engl. Conserv. of Music. m. (1) Nancy Weir, (2) Virginia Barret. 2 s. Debut: Livorno, Italy, 1923. Career: Leading Tenor, Metropolitan Opera, NYC, 24 yrs., Colon Theatre, Buenos Aires, 15 yrs.; Cinn. Opera; San Fran. & Chgo. Opera Cos.; repertoire incl. all Verdi, Puccini, some Wagner; apps. w. all major symphs. in USA; Hd., Vocal Dept., New Engl. Conserv. of Music; currently Tchr.of Singing. Recordings: Excerpts from Wagner's Siegfried; Sacred Soli. Mbrships. incl: Am. Acad. Tchrs. of Singing; Nat. Acad. Tchrs. of Singing. Recip. DMus, New Engl. Conserv. of Music, Boston. Address: 327 20th Ave., San Fran., CA 94121, USA.

JAGER, Robert Edward, b. 25 Aug. 1939, Binghamton, NY, USA. Conductor; Composer. Educ: B Mus Ed, M Mus Ed, Univ. of Mich. m. Joan Lucille Jager, 1 s., 1 d. Career: Num. apps. throughout USA as Guest Cond., Comp. & Clinician, High Schls. & Univs.; Guest Cond., Japan, 1975, 76; Dir. of Comp. & theory, Tenn. Technol. Univ. Compositions incl: Symph. for Band, 1965; Sinfonietta for Band, 1973; The War Prayer for Orch., 1975; Variations on a Motive by Wagner, 1975; 3 Japanese Prints for Band, 1976; Aberrations for 2 Clarinets & Percussion, 1976. Contbr. to Instrumentalist. Mbr., profl. assn. Hons. incl: Ostwald Award, Am. Bandmasters Assn., 1964, 68, 72; Pitts. Bicentennial Comp. Award, 1975. Hobby: Photography. Address: Rt. 9 Box 42, Cookeville, TN 38501, USA.

JAHN, Theodore L, b. 12 June 1939, Spokane, Wash., USA. Professor of Clarinet. Educ: BMus, Oberlin Coll., 1961; MA, Ohio State Univ., 1964: DMus, Ind. Univ., 1975. m. Mary Leglar. Career: Tchr., Bemidji State Coll., Minn., 1964-67; Prof. of Clarinet, Dept. of Music, Univ. of Ga., 1967-; Mbr., Univ. of Ga. Woodwind Quintet. Mbrships: Int. Clarinet Soc.; MENC; NACWPI. Address: Dept. of Music, Univ. of Ga., Athens, GA 30602, USA.

JAHNS-GAEHTGENS, Renate Ursula Theophile, b. 22 Sept. 1927, Hamburg, German Fed. Repub. Violinist; Choir singer, soprano; Teacher. Educ: Pvte. music tchr. m. Werner Jahns, 1 s. Debut: Hamburg, Bonn. Career: Tchr. Claersches Conserv., Hamburg; Niederdeutsches Chmbr. Orch.; First violinist Altona Chmbr. Orch., Hamburg Chmbr. Orch., Radelow Chmbr. Orch., Wurnbert Symph. Orch.; Beethoven Concert Hall Orch., Bonn. Hons: Musical Contest Germany, 1944, Mecklenburg, 1st Prize soloist, 1st Prize Gaehtgens-Quartet. Hobbies: Riding; Reading; Travelling to Places with Archeological Interest. Address: Rheinanstr. 75, Bonn-Benel 53, German Fed. Repub.

JAKEY, Lauren Ray, b. 10 July 1937, Yakima, Wash., USA. Violinist; Teacher; Conductor. Educ: BM, Oberlin Conserv.; MMus, Peabody Conserv.; DM, Ind. Univ.; Pvte. violin studies. m. Patricia C O Jakey, 1 s., 1 d. Career incls: Concertmaster, 7th Army Symph., 1960-62; 1st Violinist, Balt. Symph., 1962-64; Concertmaster: Santa Clara Phil., 1969-70; San Jose Symph. Orch., 1971-76; Prog. Dir., San Jose Chmbr. Players, 1974-76. Recordings incl: Suite (Violin), Lou Harrison & Richard Dee, Tape of the Month. Mbrships: Am. String Tchrs. Assn.; MENC. Hons. incl: Fellowship to attend 3rd Annual Pablo Cassals Festival, San Juan, Puerto Rico, 1959. Hobbies: Sailing; Photography; Travel; Wine Tasting. Address: 3230 Verdaul Way, San Jose, CA 98117, USA.

JAKOB, Friedrich, b. 7 Nov. 1932, Zürich, Switzerland. Musicologist; Organ Builder; Organist; Contrabassist. Educ: PhD, Univ. of Zürich; Dip., Organist; Dip., Organ Tchr.; Dip. Music Theory Tchr.; Conserv., Zürich; Music Acad., Zürich. m. Barbara Jakob-Baumann, 2 d., 1 s. Publs: Der Orgelbau im Kanton Zürich, 1969-71; Die Orgel, 1969. Contbr. to: Musik in Geschichte & Gegenwart; Grove's Dict., 6th ed. Mbrships: Int. Soc. of Organ Builders; Pres., Gen. Music Assn., Zürich; Int. Musicol. Soc. Hobbies: Gardening; Family. Address: Bergstrasse 268 CH 8707, Uetikon am See, Switzerland.

JAKOBY, Richard Matthias, b. 11 Sept. 1929, Dreis, Kr Wittlich, Germany. Educ: musicol., music educ., Romance langs., philos. & psychol., Mainz, 1949-54; Doct., 1955. m. Irmgard Mohr, 2 s., 1 d. Career: tchng. posts, Acad. of Music,

Coll. of Adult Educ. & Mainz Conserv., Mainz, 1954-64; Prof., Hanover, 1964; Prin., State Acad. of Music & Drama, Hanover, 1969-. Author of about 200 publs. in musicol., music educ., cultural-pol. affairs, etc. Contbr. to jrnls. Chmn., German Music Coun., 1973-. Hons: Gutenberg Prize, 1952; Prin., Soc. of Music & Music Culture, 1974-76. Hobbies: Sport; Archaeol. Address: 3 Hanover, Ostfeldstr. 61, German Fed. Repub.

JAKUBOWSKA, Wanda, b. 28 May 1930, Kalinowa, Poland. Singer. Educ: M Mus, Govtl. Higher Schl. of Music (univ. level), Poznan. m., 1 s. Career: permanent engagement, Poznan Opera; perfs., Music Theatre, Poznan; Guest perfs., sev. operas & music theatres in Poland; apps. w. Poznan Opera ensemble, Gt. Theatre, Moscow, 1953, Italian towns, 1976; has given recitals, made opera & music theatre perfs., & broadcast on radio & TV in var. other Eastern European countries. Recordings: Polish songs; Beethoven's Ah, Perfidia. Mbrships: SPAM, Assn. of Polish Musicians; SPATIF, Assn. of Polish Theatre & Film Artists; Trade Union of Culture Workers. Hobbies: Gardening; Sun; Swimming. Address: ul. Senatorska 41, 60-326 Poznan, Poland.

JAMBOR, Agi, b. 4 Feb. 1909, Budapest, Hungary. Musician (Piano, Harpsichord, Marimba). Educ: MA, Royal Acad., Budapest. m. I Patai, 1 s. (dec.). Debut: Budapest. Career: Concertized around World w. Ormandy & Mengelberg. Recordings: Capitol Records. Publ: 12 Sonatas of Conrado F Hurlebusch (ed.), 1963. Mbrships: Bryn Mawr Coll.; Univ. Pa. Mus.; Int. Ethnomusicol. Soc. Hons: Brahms Prize, Berlin, 1928; Chopin Prize, Warsaw, 1937. Address: 103 Pine Tree Rd., Radnor, PA 19087, USA. 2.

JAMERSON, Thomas, b. 3 July 1942, New Orleans, La., USA. Baritone (Opera, Recital & Concert). Educ: MMus, La. State Univ. m. Madeline Mines, 2 c. Debut: w. Metropolitan Opera Nat. Co. Career: NYC Opera, 1969- (over 21 leading roles); Apps. w. opera cos. of Balt., Boston, Ft. Worth, Central City, Phila., Santa Fe, Metropolitan Opera Nat. Co., Am. Nat. Opera Co.; Artpark & Wolf Trap Perf. Art Centers; Perfs. w. Israel Phil.,St. Louis Symph., Hartford Symph. Recordings: La Traviata; The Merry Widow. Hons: Finalist, Metropolitan Opera Nat. Coun. Auditions. Hobby: Electronics. Mgmt: Ludwig Lustig & Florian. Address: 201 W 70th St., Apt. 15C, NY, NY 10023, USA.

JAMES, Benjamin Phillip, b. 26 Oct. 1940, Pender, Neb., USA. Composer; Conductor; Baritone; Instructor. Educ: BFA, Univ. of SD; MA, Comp. & Voice, Lamont Schl. of Music, Univ. of Denver; Univ. of Minn.; W Bank Schl. of Music. 1 s. Career: Guest Cond., Boulder Civic Orch. & Opera; Comps. Instr. & Opera Coach, Jamestown Coll., ND; Cond., Music Coord., Mpls. Children's Theatre Co.; Comp., Cond., Chimera Theatre, St. Paul; Music Dir., Mpls. Inst. of Art; Music Dir., Comp., Theatre of Involvement; Coord., Perf. Arts Learning Ctr.; Cond., 3M Workers Choirs; Comp., Cricket Theatre; Instructor, Twin City Inst. for Talented Youth. Comps. incl: 11 in a Row (song cycle); Ezra's Pound Cake; Molly, Rhonda, 20 other musicals for teenagers; Travelog formats; Comic Strip Operas. Recordings incl: Incidental music for As You Like It, Waiting for Godot, 60 other shows; Commercials; Whiskey; Opera, Headcheese, Lykos, etc. Contbr. to mags., newspapers. Sev. hons. & awards. Mbrships: NEA; Minn. Educ. Assn.; Nat. Comps. Assn.; Minn. Comps. Forum. Hobbies incl: Speaker & sound designing for theatre; Billiards; Writing poetry; Origami; Plants. Address: 941 Portland, St. Paul, MN 55104, USA. 4.

JAMES, Carolyne, b. 27 April 1945, Wheatland, Wyoming, USA. Dramatic Mezzo Soprano. Educ: BMus, Univ. of Wyoming; MMus, Ind. Univ. Debut: St. Paul Opera, 1970. Career: St. Paul Opera; Houston Grand Opera; NYC Opera debut 1973; Opera Co. of Boston debut, 1973; Premiere perfs. Captain Jinks, Thea Musgrave's A Christmas Carol, The Sweet Bye and Bye (Mother Rainey), Kansas City Lyric; Central City Opera; Lake George Opera; Cinn. Opera; Minn. Opera; Metropolitan Opera Studio; NY Oratorio Soc.; Indpls. Symph.; Evansville Symph.; Chautauqua Symph.; Tulsa Opera; Opera Theatre of St. Louis; Netherlands Opera, Dallas Opera Co. etc. Recordings: Jack Beeson's The Swet Bye and Bye; Jack Beeson's Captain Jinks. Hons: Nt. Fndn. of Music Clubs Young Artist, 1971; Martha Baird Rockefeller Grant; Metropolitan Opera Assn. Grant: Lillian Garabedian Award; Corbett Fndn. Grant Mgmt: 165 W 57th St., NYC, NY 10019, USA. Address: c/o Mgmt.

JAMES, Donald William, b. 19 May 1935, Portsmouth, UK. University Lecturer; Examiner; Broadcaster; Conductor; Adjudicator. Educ: BA & MA, Gonville & Caius Coll., Cambridge; Postgrad. Cert. in Educ., Inst. of Educ., Univ. of London; FRCO; LRAM (Piano Tchr.); ARCM (Singing Tchr.). m. Lorna Constance Dunford, 4 s. Career: Dir. of Music, The Edinburgh Acad., 1960-65; Producer of Music Talks, BBC

London, 1965-68; Lectr. in Music, Univ. of Exeter, 1968-. Comps: Carols; Editions of Spanish Cathedral Music; arrangements of folk songs. Recordings: (as cond.) Monteverdi Vespers (1973), Bach B minor Mass; (organ) Monteverdi Schütz & Purcell for Treble, 1978; Folksongs, 1979. Contbr. to: Music & Musicians; Musical Times; Organists' Review. Hons: Choral Scholar, Gonville & Caius Coll., Cambridge, 1954-57. Address: Neadon Farm, Bridford, Exeter, Devon, UK.

JAMES, Ifor, b. 30 Aug. 1931, Carlisle, UK. Horn Player; Conductor. Educ: Hon. RAM. m. Helen Hames. Career: Radio, GB & abroad; TV; Recitals; Concertos; Chamber Music. Comps: (horn & piano) Windmills of Amsterdam; Rondo; Repetition Waltz. Recordings: Brahms Trio; Mozart Quintet; Mozart Sinfonia Concertante; Solo recital records; Philip Jones Brass Ensemble records. Author, Practice Method, 1976. Contbr. to sev. jrnls. Mbr., ISM. Hobby: Pen drawing. Mgmt: Barbara Graham Mgmt. Address: Pinnacles, Cutlèrs Green, Thaxted, Essex, UK. 3.

JAMES, Peter Haydn, b. 17 Oct. 1940, Melbourne, Asut. Educ: B Mus, 1963, PhD, 1967, Univ. Coll., Cardiff, UK; Cert. Ed., Univ. of Bristol, 1964. m. Angela Heather James, 1 d., 1 s. Career: Vicar Choral, Lichfield Cathedral, 1968-74; Dir. of Studies, Birmingham Schl. of Music, 1974-; Chorus Master, CBSO Chorus, Birmingham, 1975-76. Mbrships: Royal Musical Assn.; ISM. Publs: Ed. of Tomkin's Know You Not, 1972. Contbr. to num. articles & music criticisms to Western Mail of Wales, 1964-67, & to Soundings, 1972. Hobbies: Cookery; Sport. Address: 41 Burton Old Rd., Lichfield, Staffs., UK.

JAMES, Vincent, b. 20 Nov. 1932, Thornton Heath, Surrey, UK. Organist; Choral & Orchestral Conductor; Teacher. Educ: TCM, London, 1950-54; LTCL (TTD); GTCL. m. Judith Anne Buxton, 2 s., 3 d. Career: Singing Mbr., Oriana Madrigal Soc., 1953-63; Libn., ibid, 1959-63; Organist, Choirmaster, Brixton Parish Ch., London, 1955 59; St. Thomas-on-The-Bourne, Farnham Surrey, 1959-64; Dir. of Music, Weydon Co. Schl. 1959-64; Fndr. Mbr., Farnham Fest., 1961; Organist, Choirmaster, Christ Ch., Wanganui, NZ., 1964-71; Music Master, St. George's Prep. Schl., Wanganui, 1965-70; Cond., Wanganui Orch. Soc., 1969-71: Master of the Music, St. John's Cath., Napier, 1971-76: Cond., Onona Singers, Napier, 1974, Concord String Ensemble, Napier, 1974, Schola Sacra-Choir & Orch., Wanganui, 1976. Var. choral music comps. Mbrships: RCO; RSCM. Hobbies: Reading; Tennis. Address: PO Box 593, Napier, NZ.

JAMES, Warren E, b. 20 Oct. 1922, Xenia, OH, USA. Flautist; Sociologist. Educ: BS, MA, PhD, Ohio State Univ.; pvte. music study w. Robert Cavally, Hall Overton & Phil Sunkel; Berklee Schl. of Music; Ali Akbar Coll. of Music. m. (2) Claire Jackson, 2 s.; (3) Martha Boulton. Career: Owner & Perf., sev. musical establishments, 1960-65; Owner, NADA Records 1972 ; Concert w Nexus, York Univ., Toronto, 1975; Workshops in improvised music, 1976-78; Perf., Miami Valley Music Fest., 1978. Comps. incl: Latino; Circles; Electric Wham; Electric Bam; Summer Rain. Recordings: Intersections, 1973. Contbr. to Metronome Jazz Yearbook, 1957. Mbrships. incl: Soc. for Ethnomusicol.; N Central Sociological Assn. Hobbies: Painting; Audio Recording. Address: 251 Whitehall Dr., Yellow Springs, OH 45387, USA. 8,28.

JAMES, William Garnet, b. 28 Aug. 1892, Ballarat, Vic., Aust. Solo Pianist; Composer. Educ: Dip. of Music, Melbourne Univ. Conserv. of Music; studied piano & comp. w. Arthur DeGreef, Brussels, Belgium. m. Saffo Arnau, dec., 2 c. Debut: Queen's Hall, London; Promenade Concerts - Sir Henry Wood. Career: Solo Pianist, Promenade Concerts, Royal Albert Hall, Int. Celebrity Tours of England, Ballad Concerts, Queen's Hall, Royal Albert Hall, London; Recital tours, Aust.; Dir. of Music, Aust. Broadcasting Commn., 1937-57. Has had over 100 compositions publd. inclng: Songs; Piano works; Orchl. comps.; 3 vols. Australian Christmas Carols; Ballet. Var. recordings & publs. Hons: OBE, 1960. Address: 12 MacLeav St., Potts Point, Sydney, NSW 2011, Australia.

JAMESON, R Philip, b. 7 Dec. 1941, Wooster, Ohio, USA. Trombonist; Music Educator. Educ: BM, MS, Juilliard Schl.; MEd, EEd, Tchrs. Coll., Columbia Univ. m. Patricia West Jameson, 3 d. Career: Mbr. & 1st Trombonist, Am. Wind Symph. Orch., NYC Ballet, Band of Am., Radio City Music Hall Orch., Musica Aetema Orch., Am. Symph. Orch., Martha Graham & Jose Limon Dance Cos.; Recordings for NET progs., RCA, DECCA, MGM, & Columbia records; currently, Assoc. Prof., Univ. of Ga.; Num. transcriptions & arrs. for trombone ensembles & brass ensembles. Mbr., sev. music assns. Hons. incl: Naumburg Prize, Juilliard Schl., 1965; Fromme Fndn. Award Boston, 1962; Moss Fellowship, Columbia Univ. 1974; Fulbright Prof. to Korea, 1978. Address: Dept. of Music, Univ. of Ga., Athens, GA 30601, USA.

JAMIESON, Nannie Hamilton, b. Edinburgh, UK. Viola Player. Educ: ARCM; FGSM; Studied w. Prof. Donald Tovey, Edinburgh; w. Prof. Carl Flesch & Prof. Max Rostal, Hochschule für Musik, Berlin. Career: Mbr., The Robert Masters Quartet for 25 yrs.; Fndr. Mbr., Menuhin Fest. Orch.; Prof. of Violin & Viola, GSM, London. Recordings: Fauré Piano Quartets, C minor op. 15 & G minor op. 45; Walton Piano Quartet. Mbrships: ISM; Org., ESTA, GB. Hobbies: Motoring; Foreign Travel. Address: 5 Neville Ave., New Malden, Surrey, KT3 4SN, UK. 3.

JANACEK, Bedrich, b. 18 May 1920, Prague, Czech. Organist; Teacher. Educ: Organ Soloist Exam., State Conserv., Prague, 1942; Dip., Master Class for Organ, ibid, 1946; Choirmaster degree, High Schl. of Music, Stockholm, 1961. m. Elisabet Wentz. Debut: Prague, 1938. Career: Concerts in Europe, BBC radio & TV, USA; Soloist w. orchs. under Nicolai Malko, Fritz Rieger, Rafael Kubelik, others; Tchr., organ perf., State Conserv., Prague, 1946-48; Swedish res., 1948-; Organist, Cathedral Parish, Lund (asst. organist, Lund Cathedral & organist at annex h.). Comps: 2 Choral Preludes; 3 Chorales for Passion Time; Partita & Ricercare; num. Choral Preludes; comps. & arrs. for Mixed Choir & Orch. Recordings of organ & concerted music by Bach, Rosenberg, Thyrestam, L. Janacek & Bedrich Janacek, etc. Address: Kyrkogatan 17, S 222 22 Lund, Sweden.

JANIAK, Bronislaus (Barney), b. 5 May 1916, Wyandotte, Mich., USA. Music Educator. Educ: Northwestern Univ., Chgo.; Jacksonville Univ., Fla.; LaSalle Univ., Chgo.; Clarke Conserv., Phila.; Berger Schl. of Music, Grand Rapids. Debut: Grand Rapids, Mich. & Chgo., Ill. Career: Orch. Musician, DuPage Symph., Albany; Columbus Symph., Grand Rapids, Stetson Symph. Orch of DeLand, etc. Compositions: Song of Ceylon - Western Song; By a Sylphan Waterfall; Juba Dance - When Skies Are Blue Again; String Quartets (1 & 2); var. other works & chmbr. music. Contbr. to: DuPage Jrnl.; Glen Elly News. Bd. Mbr., ACMP (Vienna, Va.). Hons: 3 Music Scholarships. Hobbies: Gardening; Reading. Address: 1434 SE 9th Ave., Ocala, FL 32670, USA. 8,28.

JANIEC, Henry, b. 21 Nov. 1929, Passaic, NJ, USA. Conductor; Musical Administrator; Pianist. Educ: B Mus Ed, Oberlin Conserv., 1952; M Mus Ed, ibid, 1953. m. Janice Hudson, 2 d. Career: Musical Dir. & Cond., Spartanburg Symph., Charlotte Symph., Chautauqua Student & Spartanburg City Schl. Orchs.; Musical Dir. & Cond., Charlotte Opera Assn. & Chautauqua Opera Co.; Artistic Dir., Brevard Music Ctr. Contbr. to: Musical Am.; Schl. Musician; Var. newspaper reviews; Radio & TV commentator. Mbrships: SC Arts Commn.; SC Arts Fndn.; Prog. Chmn., Spartanburg Music Fndn.; Delta Omicron; Pi Kappa Lambda; Am. Symph. Orch. League; MENC. Hons: Doctorate, Wofford Coll.; SC Gov's Award; Delta Omicron Nat. Patron; Presidential Citation, Nat. Fedn. of Music Clubs; Kiwanis Man of Yr. Hobbies: Sports. Address: 113 Beechwood Drive, Spartanburg, SC 29302, USA.

JANIGRO, Antonio, b. 21 Jan. 1918, Milan, Italy. Conductor; Violoncellist. Educ: Milan Conserv.; Licence de Concert, Ecole Normale de Musique, Paris, 1935. m. Neda Cihlar, 2 children. Career incls: Concert Cellist, 1933-; num. int. fest. apps., 1938-; adv. cello class, Zagreb Conserv., 1939-53; Cond., Zagreb Radio-TV Orch., 1954-64; Fndr. & Cond., I Solisti di Zagreb, 1954-67; Cond., Angelicum Orch., Milan, 1965-67; adv. cello class, Robt. Schumann Conserv., Düsseldorf, 1965-; Permanent Cond., Chmbr. Orch. of the Saar, 1968-. Recordings: Vanguard; RCA; Westminster; Amadeo. Hons. incl: Kt. of Order of Merit, Repub. of Italy, 1966. Address: 11 Piazza Erculea, Milan, Italy. 2.

JANIS, Byron, b. 24 Mar. 1928, Pa., USA. Concert Pianist. Educ: studied w. Adele Marcus & Vladimir Horowitz; Chatham Square Music Schl. m. (1) June Dickson-Wright, div., 1 s., (2) Maria Veronica Cooper. Debut: w. Pitts. Symph. Orch., 1944. Career: Soloist w. NBC Symph. Orch., 1944; toured USA, 1944-47, & S Am., 1948; debut as Recitalist, Carnegie Hall, 1948; made European debut w. Amsterdam Concertgebouw, 1952; toured Russia, 1960 & 62, app. w. Moscow Phil. Orch., 1962; has app. w. Boston Symph., Phil. Orch., Indpls. Symph. Orch., etc. Recordings incl: Liszt's Piano Concerti 1 & 2; Rachmaninov's Piano Concerto 3. Hons. incl: Kt. of Arts & Letters, France, 1965. Mgmt: Hurok Entertainments, 1370 Ave. of the Americas, NYC, NY 10019, USA.

JANKOWSKI, Loretta Patricia, b. 20 Oct. 1950, Newark, NJ, USA. Composer; College Instructor. Educ: B Mus, Eastman Schl. of Music; M Mus, Univ. of Mich.; PhD, Eastman Schl.; studied comp., UK & Poland. Career: Instructor of comp. & theory, Univ. of N Ill., 1977-78; Asst. Prof., comp. & theory, Calif. State Univ., 1979-80; Works often commissioned &

performed, 1974-. Comps. incl: Flute Sextet, 1972; Strephenade, 1973; Todesband, 1973; Demeanour, 1974; No Time to Mourn, 1975; Or, 1976; Next to of Course God, 1976; Lustrations, 1978. Mbrships: League of Women Comps.; Leschetizky Soc. Hons: 2nd Runner-up, ABA-Ostwald Band Comp. Contest, 1975; Winner, ABA-Ostwald Band Comp. Contest, 1976. var. high schl. awards. Hobby: Reading. Address: 291 Ravenswood, Mountainside, NJ 07092, USA.

JANOVICKY, Karel, b. 18 Feb. 1930, Czech. Composer; Pianist; Broadcaster. Educ: Realne gymnasium; Surrey Coll. of Music; pvtly w. Jan Sedivka (chamber music) & Matyas Seiber (comp.); MMus, RCM; LRAM; ARCM; L Mus, TCL. m. Sylva Simsova, 1 s., 1 d. Debut: Wigmore Hall, London, 1956. Compositions in MS; Concerto for organ, brass, timpani & strings; Capriccio & Passacaglia for orch.; many orchl. & chamber works, documentary film scores, incidental music. Mbr., CGGB. Hons: 1st prize, Shakespeare Comp.; Bournemouth Symph. Orch., 1957 for Variations Op. 17; Sonata for two violins & piano Op. 8, on Recommended List of the Soc. for the Promotion of New Music, London. Hobbies: Arts & films; Photography; Gardening, etc. Address: 18 Muswell Ave., London N10 2EG, UK. 3.

JANOWITZ, Gundula, b. 2 Aug. 1937, Berlin, Germany. Opera Singer. Educ: Acad. of Music & Performing Arts, Graz, Austria. m. Wolfgang Zörner, 1 d. Debut: w. Vienna State Opera. Career: Mbr., Vienna State Opera & Deutsche Opera, Berlin; apps. w. Met. Opera, NYC, Teatro Colon, Buenos Aires. Grand Opera, Paris; concerts throughout world; participant in Bayreuth, Aix en Provence, Glyndebourne, Spoleto, Salzburg & Munich Fest. Has recorded for DGG & EMI. Hobby: Modern lit. 16.

JANSEN, Alexander C B, b. 11 Sept. 1936, Voorburg, Holland. Musicologist. Educ: Drs. of Musicol., Univ. of Amsterdam, 1968. m. H J Grandean, 1 s., 1 d. Career: Musicological Cooperator, NOS, record lib., Broadcasting Fndn., Hilversum; Designer, system to classify items recorded on tape, discs, etc., 1974. Publs: Het Leven van Hendrik Anders (Ms.), 1965; Leos Janacek - Zapisnik zmizeleho (Hetdagboek van een verdwenen man - Een Inleiding), 1968; Contbr. to: Ouverture; Collection of songs popular c. 1900 in Amsterdam (Ms.). Mbrships: Int. Musicol. Soc.; Vereiging voor Nederlandse Muziekgeschiedenis. Hobbies: Linguistics; Philos.; Children. Address: Braam 28, Huizen (NH), The Netherlands.

JANSEN, Guy Elwyn, B. 27 May 1935, Carterton, NZ. Music Educator; Choral conductor; Arranger; Music Administrator. Educ: MA, BMus, Dip.Ed., Vic. Univ. of Wellington; Dip. tchng., Wellington Tchrs. Coll.; LRSM; FTCL. m. Judith Mary Rolls, 1 d., 2 s. Career: Sr. lectr. in music, Christchurch Tchrs. Coll., 1969-74; Educ. Off., Music Dept. of Educ., 1975-; cond. of choirs on TV; num. radio interviews; Dir., Festival Singers of Wellington; Dir., Nat. Youth Choir of NZ. Comps: Festive Sounds, 20 choral arrs. Recordings: w. Celebration Singers & Festival Singers. Publs: Ed., Looking at Music Education, 1969; Ed., Sound & Sense, 1972-76; Ed., Workbook for UE, 1973-74; Festive Sounds, 1979. Contbr. to: Challenges in Music Educ.; PPTA Jrnl. Mbrships: incl: Int. Soc. for Music Educ.; Aust. & NZ Hist. of Educ. Soc. Hobbies: Church Music; Rugby football; Native gardening; Family evenings. Address: 3 Kowhai St., Linden, Wellington, NZ.

JANSEN, Jojannes Felix Johanna Maria, b. 31 July 1923, Tilburg, Netherlands. Conductor; High School Music Teacher. Educ: Dips., schl. music & cond., "Small" Dip., organ, Conserv. m. Maria W A van Lierop, 3 children. Debut: as cond., Tilburg. Career: Cond. for var. choirs & orchs.; as Opera Cond. has given pers. of major operas inclng. Aida w. a chorus of 500, noted Italian soloists & live animals, 1972; cond. num. oratorios. Contbr. to: Koor & kunstleven; Mens en Melodie. Mbr., Rotary Tilburg. Hons: Concours of conds., Besancon, France, 1953; Van Lanschot prize, Tilburg, 1972. Hobbies: Gardening; Tennis. Address: Brakel 13, Riel N B, Netherlands.

JANSEN, Rudolf, b. 19 Jan. 1940, Arnhem, Holland. Pianist. Educ: Prix d'Excellence, Amsterdam Conserv.; Study w. Nelly Wagenaar. m. Margreet Honig, 2 children. Career: Soloist; Accompanist for num. famous artist in Europe, USA, Mexico, W. Africa, UK; Num. radio, TV apps.; Holland, BBC London, Germany, France, Sweden, Switzerland, USA. Var. recordings as accomp., chmbr. music & w. singers.; mbr. KNTV, Netherlands. Hons: Toonkunst Jubilee Prize, Holland, 1965; Silver Vriendenkrans Concertgebouw, Amsterdam, 1966; Edison Award, for recording w. Han de Vries, 1974. Hobbies: Table tennis; Chess; Bridge; Stamp collecting. Mgmt: Nederlands Impresariaat, Amsterdam. Address: Stadhouderskade, 150, Amsterdam, The Netherlands.

JANSONS, Andrejs, b. 2 Oct. 1938, Riga, Latvia. Oboist; Teacher; Conductor; Composer. Educ: BSc, Juilliard Schl. of Music, 1960; MMus, Manhattan Schl. of Music, 1973; Benedetto Marcello Conserv., Venice, Italy, 1958. m. Astrida Ribenieks, 1 s., 1 d. Career: Oboist, Balt. Symph. Orch., Pitts. Symph., Phoenix Woodwind Quintet; Music Dir., Latvian Folk Ensemble, Latvian Choir of NY; Guest Cond., Youth Fest. Chorus in Montreal., Manhattan Chorus & Orch.; Ballet perfs., Toronto & NY; Artist in Res., Bloomfield Coll. Comps. incl: 2 musicals; Suite of Old Lettish Dances; Arrs. Old Am. Works for woodwind quintet; 10 Latvian Folk Dances for voices & small orch. Recordings incl: Latvian Folk Ensemble, I & II; Behold a Bright Star; Ars Antiqua. Publs: The Art of Kokle Playing, I & II, 1965, 1978. Contbr. to: Int. Coun. on Folk Music Jrnl.; Ethnomusicology. Address: 73 Glenwood Ave., Leonia, NJ 07605, USA.

JANSSENS, Robert, b. 27 July 1939, Brussels, Belgium. Conductor; Composer; Teacher. Educ: Dips. w. many prizes at Conserv., Liege & Brussels, 1958-77. m. Dominique Vandermoere, 2 d. Career: tchr. in Brussels, 1958-62; Prof. of Music, ENCB, 1962-76: 1st horn, Centre Lyrique de Wallonia, 1968-75; Prof. of horn, Acad. of Music, Brussels, 1971-75; Deputy Dir., ibid., 1975-; Prof. of harmony, Conserv. of Brussels, 1978-; Cond., Centre Lyrique de Wallonia, RTB. & Orch. Symphonique de Liege, 1973-; cond. at fests. Comps: Concertos for violin, piano, horn; 4 Etudes for large symph. orch.; 4 Impromptus for piano, etc. num. prizes & awards. Hobbies: Yachting. Address: Vandervekenstraat 7, 1920 Diegem, Belgium.

JANSSON, Henrik Daniel Johannes, b. 20 Mar. 1916, Gothenburg, Sweden. Organist; Choirmaster. Educ: Royal Acad. of Music, Stockholm. m. Mildred, 2 d. Career: Organist & Choirmaster, Solleftea, 1942-45; Organist & Choirmaster, Sala, 1945-59; Organist & Choirmaster, St. Andrews Ch., Malmo, 1959-67; Organist & Choirmaster, Cathedral, Gothenburg, 1968 ; Sev. organ recitals & choir concerts for Radio & TV. Publs: ABC of Church Music, 1957; Ed., Special Choral Preludes, 1960; List of choir and organ chorals, 1964. Contbr. to: Arbetet; Var. musical mags. Mbrships: Royal Acad. of Music, Stockholm; Swedish Sect., ISCM; Assn. of Swedish Comps. Hons: Prize of Arts, Malmo, 1966; Estate Prize of Arts, 1971; Local Ch. Authorities of Gothenburg Prize of Arts, 1976; Bohus Country Coun., Prize of Arts, 1977. Address: Box 5265, S-402 25 Gothenburg, Sweden.

JANTARSKI, George, b. 13 July 1905, Veliko-Tarnovo, Bulgaria. Musicologist; Orchestral Musician (Violin & Viola). Educ: DPh, Karel Univ.; Dip., Lib. Inst.; Dip. in Comp., Prague Conserv. & Musical Acad., Czechoslovakia. m. Julia, 1 s., 1 d. Career: Libn., Slavonic Lib., Prague; Ed. & Fndr., 1934, Edition of Bulgarian Music; participant, var. World Congresses. Compositions: Songs. Publs. incl: (in Czech) Bulgarian Folk Music Instruments, 1976; var. lang. books & works on comp.; (in Bulgarian) Founders of New Bulgarian Music, 1976; Melodica of Bulgarian Folk Music, 1978; Bulgarian-Czech Lexicon, A-L. Contbr. to var. music encys. Mbrships. incl: Union of Czech Comps.; Bulgarian Military Hist. Soc. (Archivist). Address: 18a, Stefan Karadja Str., Sofia, Bulgaria.

JANZER, Georges, b. 15 Sept. 1914, Budapest, Hungary. Violist. Educ: studied violin w. Oscar Studer, Franz Liszt Acad., Budapest; Dip. of virtuosity w. distinction, Geneva, 1934. m. Eva Czako, 1 s. Career: num. Solo concerts & radio braodcasts, 1934-; Concertmaster, Budapest Symph. Orch.; Fndng. Mbr. (1940) & Violist, Vegh Quartet, concertizing w. them in Europe, N & S Am., Can., Japan, Aust., NZ., & S Africa; Mbr.; Grumiaux Trio., 1946-; Tchr. of Viol. Music Acad., Hannover, 1960-63, & Düsseldorf, 1963-; Prof., Ind. Univ., Bloomington, Ind., USA, 1972-. Recordings: sev. w. Vegh Quartet on DGG, Decca, Columbia & Discophiles Français labels, 1943-55, also re-recording of 6 Bartok quartets & all Beethoven quartets for Valois (Teldec), 1971; sev. w. Grumiaux Trio on Philips, inclng. Mozart's 4 flute quartets, & trios by Haydn & Schubert. Hons. incl: w. Vegh Quartet, Grand Prix de Disque for Mozart Quintet with clarinet, & Grand Prix de Disque, Paris, & Deutscher Grosser Schallplattenpreis, Berlin for Bartok quartets; w. Grumiaux Trio, Grand Prix for Mozart Divertimento, & Best Chmbr. Music Recording of Yr., USA, for 5 Beethoven String Trios. Hobbies: Photog.; Maths. Address: 1901 Ruby Lane, Bloomington, IN 47401, USA.

JARL, Birger Charles, b. 25 Dec. 1923, Stockholm, Sweden. Musician (Trombone). Educ: Soloist Class, RAM, Stockholm; Musical Trng. w. Military Bands of Army, Navy & Air Force. 2 d. Debut: 1940. Career: Cond. & Musical Ldr., Gothenburg Symphonic Band; Regional Music Auth., Uddevalla; Chief Cond. for RSAO (The Swedish Nat. Assn. of Amateur Bands); Cond., Home Guard Band, Gothenburg. Contbr. to RSAO's Band Mag.

Musikant. Mbrships: Assn. of Regional Musicians; Swedish Nat. Assn. of Amateur Bands; Nat. Band Assn., USA. Hobby: Band Music. Address: Stenasvagen 14, 45100 Uddevalla, Sweden.

JARMAN, Christopher John Bailey, b. 7 June 1945, Wellington, NZ. Piano tuner & technician. Educ: LRSM (Comp., Carillineur, Pianoforte Tuner & Technician, Pianist). Career: Broadcasts. Comps: (pianoforte) Resolution; Retrospection; Joie de Vivre; Comma of Pythagoras; (Carols) Little Child - Holy Child; Carol & The Kauri; Bell-bird from a Forest Tree; (Orchl.) Hommage à l'Elgar; First Light (180th Meridian). Recordings: Classical Pianoforte, Christopher Jarman, NZ Comp. & Pianist. Publs: Music in book, Tomorrow Comes The Song. Contbr. to: Annibal. Mbrships: Comps. Assn. of NZ; Reg. Music Tchrs. Assn. Hons: Orchestration, Hommage à l'Elgar accepted for broadcast by Aust. Broadcasting Commission. Address: 254 The Parade, Island Bay, Wellington 2, NZ.

JARRATT, Howard Marrug, b. 27 Jan. 1912, Colman, SD., USA. Singer (Tenor); Orchestral Manager. Educ: BMus, St. Olaf Coll., Northfield, Minn.; MMus, Am. Conserv. of Music, Chgo., Ill.; Doct. studies, Tchrs. Coll., Columbia Univ.; pvte. study of Voice. m. Stephanie Lanier Smith Jarratt, 1 s., 3 d. Career: Choir Dir. Soloist, var. Chs., 1935-50; Asst. Prof. Voice & Hd. Voice Dept., Ohio Wesleyan Univ., Delaware, 1937-44; Instructor Voice, Union Theol. Sem., NYC, 1951-60; Lead Tenor, Lemonade Opera Co., 1949; num. Concert Tours as Soloist, 1950-61; Leading Roles, Summer Musical Stock, 1950-58; Leading Roles, Met. Opera Touring Co., 1951-52; Leading Role, My Darlin' Aida, Broadway, 1952-53; Managing Dir. Entertainment, Gen. Electric Hd. Opera Dept., Southern Meth. Univ., Dallas, Tex., 1960-64; Promotion & Sales Mgr., Dallas Symph. Orch., ibid, 1964-68; Gen. Mgr., Dallas Symph. Assn. Inc., 1968-71; Exec. Dir. & Gen. Mgr., Kansas City Phil., Mo., 1971-75; Dir. of Development, Ill. Coll., Jacksonville, Ill., 1975-. Mbrships: Phi Mu Alpha Sinfonia; Pi Kappa Lambda; Am. Guild Musical Artist. Hobbies incl: Tennis; Bird-watching; Carpentry; Antique Collecting. Address: 233 Finley, Jacksonville, IL 62650, USA.

JARVIS, Edward Keith, b. 13 Mar. 1939, Swindon, UK. Organist; Lecturer in Music. Educ: MA., Balliol Coll., Oxford Univ., LRAM., ARCM., FRCO. m. Janet Keeton, 1 s. Career: Formerly Music Tchr. at schls. in Swindon, & Teignmouth, Devon; Lectr. in Music, Schl. of Music, Huddersfield, 1966-. (Organ, History, Harmony/Counterpoint, Gen. Musicianship); Snr. Lectr., Schl. of Music, Huddersfield Polytechnic, 1976; sev. BBC Organ Broadcasts (Huddersfield Town Hall, Huddersfield Polytechnic, Univs. of York & Keele); Organ Recitalist. Hons: ARCO. (Sawyer Prize). Hobbies: Construction & Design of Organs; Sound Recording & Reproduction. Address: 'The Woodlands', Thong Ln., Netherthong, Huddersfield, UK.

JARVIS, Roger Stanley, b. 20 Mar. 1943, Southend-on-Sea, Essex, UK. Music Adviser; Recorder Player; Organist; Conductor. Educ: BMus, Univ. of London, 1965; RAM, 1962-66; GRSM; LRAM (Organ tchr.); LTCL (recorder perf.). m. Margaret Jarvis, 1 s., 1 d. Career: pt.-time Tchr., London & home cos., 1963-67; Lectr., City of Belfast Schl. of Music, 1967-71; Dpty. Music Advsr., Southern Educ. & Lib. Bd., Northern Ireland, 1971-; recorder recitals; apps., BBC & Ulster Orch.; Cond., Portadown Phil. Soc. Comps: An Irish Folk Suite (orch.); Two Preludes & Fugues by Bach (arr. for recorders); A Voluntary by Greene (arr. for recorders). Mbrships: ISM; Nat. Assn. Inspectors & Educl. Advsrs.; Adjudicator, Brit. Fedn. of Music Fests. Recip. 1 FCCU prizes for comp., 1964. Hobby: Angling. Address: 111 Drumglass, Tullygally, Craigavon BT65 5BB, Ireland, UK.

JEANS, Susi, b. 25 Jan. 1911, Vienna, Austria. Concert Organist, Harpsichordist, Clavichordist; Musicologist. Educ: Dip., Akademie für Musik und Darstellende Kunst, Vienna; Study w. Karl Straube, Kirchenmusikalische Inst., Leipzig; Pvte. study w. Marie Widor, Paris. m. Sir James Jeans (dec. 1946), 2 s., 1 d. Debut: Vienna, 1929. Career: Concert Tours, Master Classes & Seminars, UK, Europe, USA & W. Australia; Staff Mbr., Dept. of Music, Boulder Univ., USA, 1967. Recordings for DGG. Contbr. to encys. & jrnls. Mbrships. incl: Royal Musical Assn.; Galpin Soc.; IMS. Hons: Hon. Fellow, Royal Coll. of Organists. Hobbies: Mountaineering; Skiing; Gardening. Mgmt: Ibbs & Tillet, London. Address: Cleveland Lodge, Dorking, Surrey RH5 6BT, UK. 14,27,29.

JEBSON, Peter Frederick, b. 19 Mar. 1950, Blackburn, UK. Schoolmaster; Broadcasting & Recording Theatre Organist; Organist & Choirmaster. Educ: Northern Schl. of Music, Manchester, 1969-72; awarded GNSM., 1972; St. Martin's Coll., Lancaster, 1972-73; Awarded 'Post Grad. Cert. in Educ.'

by Univ. of Lancaster; Organ tuition at the Univ. of Salford. Debut: Gaumont Cinema, Manchester, 1971. Career: sponsored by the Lancastrian Theatre Organ Trust; Played the organs at the Odeon & Gaumont theatres before films; Var. concerts for num. organ socs.; LP recordings produced by LTOT & broadcasts for Radio Two's 'The Organist Entertains', & for local radio stns; BBC TV, Songs of Praise; Organist & Choirmaster, Lytham Parish Ch.; Schoolmaster, Lytham Hall Prk County Primary Schl.; Res. Organist, Blackpool Cliffs Hotel. Compositions: Suite for Oboe & Piano, 1970. Recordings: Double Touch Vol. 2, 'Side by Side'; A Spotlight on Faces of the Future; Nights of Gladness at the Cliffs, Blackpool. Mbr., Profl. Assn. of Tchrs. Address: 93 Cornwall Ave., Blackpool, Lancs. FY2 9QP, UK.

JEDRZYKIEWICZ, Zofia, b. 25 Jan. 1923, Tarnow, Poland. Solo Singer. Educ: Nat. Higher Schl. of Music; Conserv. Debut: Krakow Opera, 1955. Career: Perfs. of recitals, Krakow Radio Broadcasting, 1951-55; sev. phil. concerts of Polish & Italian Old Masters music, Krakow, Czestochowa, Rzeszow; Concerts of old ch. music w. ortans; Soprano Soloist, Krakow Opera, 1955-63; Tchr. of Emission, Nat. Higher Schl. of Music, Krakow, 1959-; Recitals, San Fran., Calif., USA, 1961. Mbrships: Assn. of Polish Music Artist; Trade Union of Polish Schlrs. Hobby: Tourism. Address: Os. Bronowice bl. IVm. 30, 30-091 Krakow, Poland.

JEFFERSON, Meriel Kathleen, Pianist; Teacher; Writer. Educ: RCM, London; Postgrad. studies, Paris, France; ARCM; LRAM; Grsm. Career: Tchr., Jr. Dept., RCM; Prof., GSM; Accomp.; Engagements for Arts Coun.; TV apps., chidlren's progs.; Radio broadcasts; Lectures on teaching of grp. piano work, London, Cambridge, Jerusalem, Berlin & Cape Town & Cinn., USA. Contbr. to: Argosy; Adelphi Mag.; Manchester Guardian; Times Educl. Supplement. Hobbies: Languages; Travelling; Theatre; Ballet; Cinema; Cooking. Address: 78 Coleherne Ct., Old Brompton Rd., London SW5 OEE, UK.

JEFFREY, Walter Roy, b. 19 Nov. 1921, Kitchener, Ont., Can. French Horn Player. Educ: Royal Conserv. of Music, Toronto; Halifax Conserv. of Music. m. Gladys E Jeffrey, 1 s., 1 d. Career: prin. horn, horn player in num. orchs. & bands; apps. on radio & TV; cond. sev. orchs. & bands in N & S Am., Europe, India, Australasia, Egypt.; pvte. tchr., also tchng. posts w. Royal Can. Naval Schl. of Music, Toronto, & Royal Can. Army Summer Band Schl.; num. arrs. Mbrships: Toronto Musicians Assn.; AFM. hons incl. doct in music, Univ. of London, UK, 1973. Address: 918 Eglinton Ave. E, Toronto, Ont. M4G 2L3, Can.

JEHAN, Marie-Thérèse, b. 8 July 1944, St. Gildas-des-Bois, Loire-Atlantique, France. Organist. Educ: Nat. Higher Conserv. of Music, Paris. Debut: 1957. Career: Titular Organist, GO de St. Clément de Nantes; Concerts in Belgium, Germany, Switzerland; Soloist, French Radio. Hons: 1st Prize, Organ, Gil Graven Nat. Competition, 1964; Roger Ducasse Prize, 1964; 1st Prize, Organ Nat. Higher Conserv. of Music, Paris, 1973; Laureate, Vocation Family, 1974. Hobby: Painting. Address: 98 rue du Commandant Gâté, 44600 St. Nazaire, France.

JELINEK, Jerone, b. 23 Mar. 1931, Detroit, Mich., USA. Cellist. Educ: BMus, 1952, MMus, 1953, Univ. of Mich.; Fulbright Scholar, RAM, London, UK, 1956-57; ARAM, 1968. m. Frances L. Jelinek, 1 s., 2 d. Debut: London, UK, 1968. Career: Cellist, Detroit Symph. Orch., 1951-53; Prof. of Music, Univ. of Ore., 1957-61; Prof. of Music, & Cellist, Stanley Quartet, Univ. of Mich., 1961-; Perfs. as recitalist & soloist w. orch., Europe, Can. & USA. Recordings: Finney, Sonata in C, & Fantasy for Solo Cello; Bassett, Music for Cello & Piano (Jelinek-Gurt Duo). Publs: Fundamentals of Elementary Violoncello Technique, 1964. Hons: Stanley Medal, Univ. of Mich., 1952; Harriet Cohen Int. Music Award, 1958. Hobby: Tennis. Address: 2637 Essex Rd., Ann Arbor, MI 48104, USA.

JELINEK, Stanislav, b. 25 Mar. 1945, Prague, Czechoslovakia. Professor of Musical Theory & Aesthetics; Organist; Pianist. Educ: Acad. of Music. m. Marcela Krylova. Debut: Sonata for piano & violin, Prague, 1961. Career: Suite for orch. on radio. Compositions incl: Festival Overture. Contbr. of articles on aesthetics of music to review Dechovy Orchestr. Brass Orch. Hobbies: Lit.; Painting. Address: Na Brehu 1, 190 00 Prague 9, Czechoslovakia.

JELINKOVA-KURKOVA, Danuše, b. 19 Apr. 1931, Prague, Czechoslovakia. Piano Teacher. Educ: Prague Conserv.; Acad. of Musical Arts, Prague. m. Mudr. Jaroslav Kurka, 1 s., 1 d. Debut: 1943. Career: Many solo concerts every yr., Czechoslovakia; Radio perfs., 1960-61; Piano tchr., Conserv. Zilina, Czechoslovakia. Hobbies: Mountain Travelling; Foreign Languages. Address: Zilina 010 01, Vléince H2/30, Czech.

JELONEK, Leon, b. 16 Mar. 1916, Czestochowa, Poland. Educator; Violinist; Conductor. Educ: Pedagogical Coll.; theory of comp. conducting, 1954, Docent, State Conserv. m. Barbara Wozniak, 1 s., 1 d. Debut: w. State Silesian Phil. Orch., Katowice. Career: has made radio & TV recordings; currently Dir., Dept. of Musical Educ., Pedagogical Univ. Rschr. & author of publs. on musical abilities of children. Contbr. to Musical Movement. Mbr., Polish Musical Artists Assn. Hons: Min. of Culture & Art Award, 1970; Sec. of State for Higher Educ. & Technol. Award, 1972-73; People's Coun. Award, 1976. Hobbies: Tourism; Driving. Address: 42-200 Czestowchowa, ul. Palczynskiego 5456 m 7, Poland.

JENEY, Zoltán, b. 4 March 1943, Szolnok, Hungary. Composer. Educ: Comp. w. Zoltán Pongrácz (Zoltán Kodály Conserv., Debrecen, 1957-61), Ferenc Farkas (Acad. of Music, Budapest, 1961-66) & Goffredo Petrassi (Accademia Nazionale di Santa Cecilia, Rome, Corso di Perfezionamento di Composizione, 1967-68). m. Dr. Katalin Pik. Career: Fndr., Comp. & Perf., New Music Studio, Hungarian Youth Art Ensemble. Comps. recorded incl: Solitude, for female choir; Alef-Hommage à Schönberg for Orch,; Round, for piano, harp & harpsichord, or two prepared pianos; Orfeusz Kertje (Garden of Orpheus), for 8 instruments; Százéves átlag (Hundred Years' Average) for string quintet & 2 sine-wave generators; impho 102/6, for 6 metal percussion instruments tuned to different pitches; Soliloquim No. 1, for solo flute; End Game, for piano; music for films, film (directed), Round. Mbrships: Assn. of Hungarian Musicians; Artist's Club, Fészek. Hons: Prize, Lajos Kassák from Magyar Mühely, Paris, 1979. Hobby: Music. Address: Lejtö u.45, 1124 Budapest, Hungary.

JENKINS, John, b. 11 June 1942, Neath, Wales, UK. Music Advisor. Educ: BA (Music), Univ. of Cardiff; Music Tchrs. Cert., Inst. of Educ., Univ. of London; RCM; ARCM; LTCL; FTCL. m. Wendy Shepard, 1 s., 1 d. Career: Music tchr., Neath Boys Grammar Schl., 1964-74; Music Adv., W Glamorgan, 1974-. Recordings: 3 w. Youth Orch. Mbrships: NAIEA; Welsh Music Advs. Panel. W Wales Arts' Assn. Hons: John Edwards Memorial Award; 3 Prince of Wales awards during Silver Jubilee (w. youth orch.). Hobbies: Fishing; Reading; Sport. Address: 272 Neath Rd., Briton Ferry, W Galmorgan, Wales, UK.

JENKINS, Laurence L, b. 5 Oct. 1939, Clarksdale, Miss., USA. Conductor; Organist; Music Educator; Music Journalist. Educ: B Mus, Union Univ., Jackson, Tenn.; MA, Music Educ., George Peabody Coll., Nashville, Tenn.; Performer's Cert., Sherwood Music Schl., Chgo., Ill. Career: Conductor & Fndr., Finchley Chmbr. Choir, London, 1972-78; Conductor & Fndr., Sine Nomine Singers, London, 1978-; Music tchr., Am. Schl., London; Music Critic, The Diapason, 1972-. Contbr. to: L'Orgue, Paris; var. newspapers in USA. Mbrships: Phi Mu Alpha Sinfonia; Royal Coll. of Organists; Incorp. Soc. Musicians. Recip. fellowships to George Peabody Coll., 1966-68 & Univ. Mich., 1975. Hobbies: Skiing; Tennis; Swimming. Mgmt: LJ Concert Mgmt. Address: 68 Kellet Rd., London, SW2 1ED, UK.

JENKINS, Merril, b. 22 June 1945, Hafodyrynys, UK. Opera & Concert singer (soprano). Educ: Dip. in Educ., London Univ.; Trinity Coll. of Music, London; Grad., Vienna Acad. of Music; Chigiana Acad., Siena, Italy; GTCL; FTCL; LRAM. Debut: Queen Elizabeth Hall. m. Stephen Rose. Career incl: performances in Vienna, Siena, Geneva & Aix-en-Provence, num. concerts in GB; appearances on TV & Radio; Guest appearances w. Engl. Nat. Opera. Address: "Llys Cerdd", Hafodyrynys, Newport, NP1 5BE, UK.

JENKINS, Neil, b. 9 April 1945, St. Leonards-on-Sea, Sussex, UK. Concert & Opera Singer & Recitalist (Tenor). Educ: Choral Scholar, King's Coll., Cambridge Univ., 1963-66; MA; RCM, London, 1966-68. m. Sandra Ann Wilkes, 1 s. Debut: Purcell Room, London, 1967. Career: Guest Soloist w. Israel Chamber Orch., 1968-69; Mbr. of Deller Consort, 1967-76; Guest Soloist w. London Bach Soc. on tours of USA in 1971 & '73; Reg. apps. on BBC RAdio 3 w. large London Choirs & choral socs.; Apps. at 1968 & '76 Israel Fest.; 1969 Madrid Opera Fest.; Festival du Marais, Paris, Holland Fest.; Three Choirs Fest, 1974; Florence Fest., 1978; Aldeburgh Fest., 1975-77, etc.; Tours incl. Australia & NZ, 1973; Iceland, 1972 & '73; France, 1974; Denmark, 1974, Holland, 1979; Frequent concerts in Europe; Operatic Roles inlc: Don Ottavio, Ferrando & Ulysses for Kent Opera; Fenton in Falstaff for BBC TV; Inkslinger in Paul Bunyan for Engl. Music Theatre; specialises in oratorio, particularly Baroque music. Comps. incl: On a Journey, 5 poems set to music. Recordings incl: Acis & Galatea, Handel; Odes & Fairy Queen, Purcell; Wedding Anthem, Handel; St. Matthew Passion, Bach. Mbr. ISM; Brit.

Actors Equity Assn. Hons: Tankard Lieder Prize; Clara Butt Award; Nat. Fedn. of Music Socs. Award for Male Singers. Hobbies: Visiting ancient monuments; 18th Century Music Rsch., etc. Mgmt: Ibbs & Tillett, London. Address: 17 Birchwood Grove, Hampton, Middx., UK. 2,30.

JENKINS, Newell, b. 8 Feb. 1915, New Haven, Conn., USA. Conductor; Musicologist. Educ: Orchesterschule d. Sächsische Staatskapelle; Freiburg Musikseminar, Freiburg i.B., Germany; B Mus, Yale Univ., 1941. Debut: Freiburg, 1936. Career: Fndr. & Dir., Piccola Accademia Musicale, Italy, 1952; Fndr. & Dir., Clarion Music Soc., 1956; Prof., NY Univ.; Guest Prof., Univ. of Calif., Irvine; Dir., Castelfrance Fest. Recordings: Over 50 records, mainly of Italian comps. Publ: Thematic Catalogue of the Works of GB Sammartini, 1976. Contbr. to musical publs. Mbrships incl: Dir., Am. Musicol. Soc. Hons. incl: 2nd Annual NYC Handel Award, 1959; Cavaliere of Italian Repub., Order of Merit, 1967. Mgmt: (Europe) Nils Wallin, Château-Périgord, Monte Carlo. Address: Box 191, Hillsdale, NY 12529, USA.

JENKINS, Terry, b. 9 Oct. 1941, Hertford, UK. Operatic Tenor. Educ: BSc, Univ. Coll., London, 1964; GSM; London Opera Ctr. m. Pamela Ann Jenkins, 1 s., 1 d. Debut: Opera for All, 1966-67. Career: Basilica Opera & Glyndebourne Touring Opera, 1969-71; Glyndebourne Fest. Opera, 1970-72; Sadlers Wells Opera, 1972-74; Engl. Nat. Opera, 1974-; Covent Gdn. Opera, 1976, '77; Vienna Fest. w. Engl. Nat. Opera, 1975; ATV & BBC concert & broadcast apps., 1972; BBC Promenade Concerts, 1974-. Recordings: Justice Shallow in Vaughan Williams, Sir John in Love. Hobby: D-I-Y. Mgmt: Music Int., Ardilaun Rd., London, N5, UK. Address: 9 West End Ave., Pinner, Middx., UK.

JENKS, William Elliott, b. 27 Sept. 1946, Batavia, NY, USA. Assistant Principal Cello; Conductor. Educ: BA, Dickinson Coll., Carlisle, Pa., 1968; MA, Case Western Reserve Univ., Cleveland, Ohio, 1976; Studied cello w. Ronald Leonard, Ernst Silberstein, Robert Newkirk; Studied cond. w. G Wallace Woodworth, Thomas Briccetti, Marcel Dick, Luis Herrera de la Fuente. m. Ann B Gerzeny. Career: Asst. Prin. Cellist, Okla. Symph. Orch., 1975-; Fndr./Cond., Chmbr. Orch. of Okla. City, 1976-. Mbrships: AF of M Local 375; ISCOM. Hobbies: Reading; Collecting Antique Am. Decorative Arts. Address: 524 N W 20th St., Okla. City, OK 73103, USA.

JENKYNS, Peter Thomas Hewitt, b. 18 Sept. 1921, Birmingham, UK. Conductor; Composer; Lecturer; Adjudicator. Educ: LRAM; ARCM. m. Joyce J Mulrenan, 1 s., 2 d. Career: Prin. Lectr. in Music, Putteridge Bury Coll. of Educ., Luton, Beds.; Fest. Adjudicator & Cond. (competitive fests. & schls. fests.); Former Cond., St. Albans Operatic Soc. Comps. incl: (songs for children) Bessie The Black Cat; The Tiger; The Wizard; The Owls; The Bats; Snakes; Little Spanish Town; The Chimpanzee; Two Contrasted Part Songs; Carol of the Bells; How Still the Night; Fancy Fair, 8 songs for young children; Rumba, for voice & recorders; The Crocodile. Unpublished works: Europa, concert overture (commnd. for perf. in Luton by the Youth Orch. of Luton, UK, Eskilstuna, Sweden & Wolfsburg, Germany, 1972); Rhapsody for Harmonica & Piano, & Sonata for Harmonica & Piano, commnd. by Douglas Tate. Mbrships: Pres., St. Alban's Music Fest., 1974-. Address: 41 West St., Lilley, Luton, Beds., UK.

JENNER, Robert William, b. 5 Dec. 1937, Tonbridge, England, UK. Orchestral Trumpeter. Educ: GSM, London. m. Rosemary Moody, 3 c. Career: Prin. Trumpet, Scottish Nat. Orch., 1961-; Teaching Staff, Royal Scottish Acad. of Music, Glasgow; Organizing Sec., Antonine Brass Ensemble, Glasgow. Address: 8 Fraser Ave., Newton Mearns, Glasgow G77 6HW, UK.

JENNINGS, John Michael, b. 27 Aug. 1944, Christchurch, NZ. Lecturer in Music History & Theory; Occasional Recitalist on Piano, Harpsichord & Organ. Educ: Mus B, (Hons.) Univ. of Canterbury, Christchurch, 1966; M Mus, Univ. of Sydney, Aust., 1969; LRSM, 1963; LTCL, 1965. m. Cynthia Margaret Bensemann, 1 s., 1 d. Career: Asst. Lectr., Univ. of Canterbury, 1967-68; Lectr., ibid, 1969-77; Snr. Lectr., ibid, 1978-; Organist & choirmaster, var. chs.; Asst. to Organist & Master of the Choristers, Christchurch Cathedral, 1969-72. Comps: Abstract One, for piano. Contbr. to profl. publs. Ed., Music Education for the Very Young Child, 1975; The Music Teaching Profession in New Zealand, 1978. Mbrships: Pres., Christchurch Soc. for Contemporary Music, 1974-76 (Sec., 1968-71); Pres., Assn. of Friends of Christchurch Coll., 1972; Sec., Christchurch Soc. of Registered Music Tchrs. of NZ. Recip., sev. prizes & scholarships. Hobbies: Railways; NZ Hist. Address: Schl. of Music, Univ. of Canterbury, Christchurch, New Zealand. 30.

JENNY, Markus, b. 1 June 1924, Stein, Kt. St. Gallen, Switz. Minister; Lecturer; Professor. Educ: D Theol., Univ. of Basel; Habilitation, Theol., Univ. of Zürich; Schola Cantorum, Basel; Hon. Prof., Zürich, 1973. m. Marguerite Loeliger, 5 s., 2 d. Comps: var. songs, some texts, melodies & setting of Ch. hymns. Recordings: sev. in "Neues Singen in der Kirche". Publs: Geschichte des deutsch-schweiz. ev. Gesangbuches im 16. Jh., 1962; Zwinglis Stellung zur Musik im Gottesdienst, 1966; Die Zukunft des evangelischen Kirchengesanges, 1971. Contbr. to: Musik in Geschichte und Gegenwart; Musik und Gottesdienst; Der evangelische Kirchenchor; Zwingliana; Musik und Kirche; Musik und Altar; Jahrbuch fur Liturgik und Hymnologie; Neue Zürcher Zeitung. Mbrships: Chmn. Int. Hymnology STudy Grp.; Ctrl. Bd. of Dirs., Swiss Fedn. of Ch. Singers. Hobby: Collecting hymn books. Address: Pfarrhaus, 60 Unterdorf, CH-2514 Ligerz, Switz.

JENS, Eleonore Henriëtte (Elly), b. 28 July 1925, Arnhem, Netherlands. Concert Singer; Music Teacher. Educ: Tchr. & Soloist Dip. for Piano; Tchr. & Soloist Dip. for Singing; Dip. for Prix d'Excellence for Singing. Debut: As accomp. 1951, as singer 1956. Career: Singer in num. Oratorio Concerts & in Lieder Recitals for Soc. of Friends of the Lied; Radio Broadcasts; Tchr., Sweelinck Conserv., Amsterdam; Pvte. singing tchr. Mbrships: Royal Dutch Musical Soc. (KNTV); Landelijke Vereniging van Docenten van het Muziekvakonderwijs; Soroptomist Club. Hons: Prix d'Excellence, 1968; Jubilee Prize, Soc. for Promotion of Music, 1970. Hobbies: Reading; Thinking; Studying Nature & Art. Address: Jan Steenlaan ,; 2102 BG Heemstede, Netherlands.

JENSEN, Authur, b. 13 Mar. 1925, Logan, Utah, USA. Oboist. Educ: Univ. of Calif., Berkeley; Conservs. at San Fran., Basel & Lausanne. m. Johanna Menzel, 1 d. Career: Prof. of Oboe, Mozarteum Int. Summer Acad. & Musikhochschule Mozarteum, Salzburg, 1952-; twice Soloist, Salzburg Fest. under Bernhard Paumgartner; European tours as Soloist w. Camerata Academica; twice Jury Mbr., Int. Music Competition, Munich. Recordings; Club Français du Disque; DGG. Publs. incl: Ein Praktischer Beitrag zur Musikalischen Intonationslehre, 1975. Hons: 2 reg. & 1 nat. 1st prizes for trumpet solo, US HS music competition, 1940 & 41. Hobbies: Musicology; Aquatic Sports; Tennis. Address: Nissenstr. 16 A-5020 Salzburg, Austria.

JENSEN, Herluf, b. 22 Jan. 1919, Frederiksberg, Denmark. Music Teacher. Educ: Tchrs. exam.; State-tested Music Educator in solfege & cond. (choirs & bands). m. Else Kragelund, 1 s., 1 d. Career: currently Organiser of Danish music course for children & young people. Contbr. of articles on music & music educ. to Dansk Amatormusik & other Danish jrnls. Mbr., Danish Amateur Music Union (Committee). Address: Gordonhaven 8, DK 8370 Hadsten, Denmark.

JENTSCH, Walter, b. 11 Sept. 1900, Langenbielau, Germany. High School Lecturer; Composer; Pianist. Educ: studied Music Schls.,Univ. of Breslau, Vienna, Berlin; pvte. studies completed at State Acad. for Music & Representational Arts, Vienna; Dip., comp. & piano teaching. m. Leonie Kabella. Debut: Pianist, Opera House, Königsberg. Career: Comp., Reinhard-Robert-Barnowsky Theatre, Berlin; Concert Tours (pianist) throughout Europe; Music Ldr., German Overseas Radio; Lectr., comp. & theory, Stern'schen Conserv. & High Schl. for Music, Berlin. Compositions incl: Die Liebe der Donna Ines, Opera; K1. Kammermusik f. Bläser u. Klavier op. 5; Konzertante Serenade f. orch. op. 8; Str. Quartet op. 35; Fünf Stücke f. Blockflöte u. Klv. op. 49; Musik f. Cello-Solo op. 53; Vier Lieder f. Ges. u. Klav. op. 54; Impressionen f. Gitarre op. 57, & var. others. Mbrships: German Comps. Grp.; GEMA. Hons: Johann Wenzel Stamitz Prize for Music, 1969; Künstergilde, 1969. Address: Reichstr. 1, 1 Berlin 19, German Fed. Repub.

JEPSON, Beryl, b. 5 Feb. 1920, Bury St. Edmunds, Suffolk, UK. Teacher. Educ: LRAM, 1948. m. Fearnley Stewart Jepson, 1 d. Career: apps. at Suffolk Fests.; Bromley & Cheltenham (duets w. Audrie Goulty), 1949; Adelphi Theatre, London; pvte. tchr., piano, theory, aural. Contbr. to Music Tchr. mbr., ISM. Hons: 1st., solo & duet, Suffolk Fest., 1938; 1st., duet, 2 pianos, Bromley, Kent, 1948; cup, 2 pianos, Cheltenham, 1949. Hobbies: Knitting; Embroidery. Address: 10 Guildhall St., Bury St. Edmunds, Suffolk, UK.

JERITZA, Maria, b. 1887, Czechoslovakia. Opera Singer (Soprano). Debut: Vienna, 1912. Career: popular performer in Vienna for many years, noted for roles of Turandot & Tosca; Perf. at Covent Gdn., 1925.

JERNDORFF, Klaus, b. 16 Sept. 1932, Copenhagen, Denmark. Pianist; Organist. Educ: Piano Dip., 1953, Piano

Tchrs. Exam., 1954, Ch. music Exam. (Organ), 1970, Organ Tchrs. Exam., 1971, Solfége Tchrs. Exam., 1973, Royal Danish Conserv. of Music; studied w. Nadia Boulanger, Paris, 1955-58; Piano, Keyboard, Harmony, Counterpoint & Cond., Écoles d'art Améericaines, 1957; Organ & Comp., ibid, 1978. m. Birgitte Greve, 1 s. Debut: Copenhagen, 1955. Career: Concerts as Piano Soloist & Chmbr. Music perf., classical & contemporary music, Danish Radio, 1955, Odd Fellows Concerthall, Copenhagen, 1958-, & Danish Socs. of Chmbr. Music; Organist, Ansgarkirken, Copenhagen, 1971-. Mbr., var. profl. assns. Hons. incl: Bursaries, French State 1955, '56; Kunstkritikernes Aerslegat, 1955. Address: Dag Hammarskjölds allé 31, 4.tv., DK 2100 Copenhagen, Denmark. 4.

JERNIGAN, Malcolm Lathon, b. 30 July 1937, Goldthwaite, Tex., USA. University Professor; Pianist; Conductor. Educ: B Mus, 1959, M Mus, 1962, Southern Meth. Univ., Dallas, Tex.; doct. candidate, Univ. of Tex.; Grad., Sherwood Schl. of Music, Chgo.; studied Piano & Cond. w. var. masters. m. Linda L Dorough, 1 d. Career: Music Instructor, Pub. Schls., Dallas, 1961-68; Cond., All-City Youth Orch., ibid., 1963-68; Tchng. Asst. & Asst. Cond., Orch. & Opera Theatre, Univ. of Tex., 1968-71; Prof., Music Theory & Comp., Univ. of N Iowa, Cedar Falls, 1971-; Cond., Waterloo/Cedar Falls Symph. Orch., 1972-74. Mbrships incl: Pi Kappa Lambda; Phi Mu Alpha Sinfonia. Hons: Most Outstanding Educator, 1968. Hobbies: Sailing; Photography. Address: 1223 W 22nd St., Cedar Falls, IA, USA.

JESSETT, Michael Peter, b. 7 Feb. 1931, Christchurch, New Zealand. Composer; Music Teacher; Musician. Career incl: performer in Variety & Review, Recitals & Concerts; Edinburgh Festival, 1965; Own series, teaching guitar, BBC Radio 4, 1971-73; about 100 progs. in BBC schls, series as composer & performer; Artistic Dir., The Elizabethan Rooms, 1971; Prof. of Guitar, Royal Coll. of Music, 1964-; Organising Tutor of Guitar, Barry Summer Schl., Wales, 1969-; Music Examiner & Adjudicator. Compositions incl. num. works for Radio & TV Series, theatre & films; some 20 pieces for solo guitar. Var. recordings made on EMI label & 5 LPs 'Guitar School' for BBC. Publs. incl: Guitar School, 3 vols., 1971. Mbrships. incl: Songwriters Guild; CGGB; Performing Rights Soc. Recip: Hon. RCM. Address: 19 Courtfield Rd., London SW7, UK.

JESSNER, Irene, b. 28 Aug. 1901, Vienna, Austria. Singer; Educ: Conserv. of Music, Vienna. m. Arthur de Noeby. Debut: Teplitz Schonau, Czechoslovakia. Career: Leading Soprano, Met. Opera, NYC, 16 yrs.; Prof. of Voice, Univ. of Toronto, Can., 1952-. Recordings on RCA Victor. Address: 400 Walmer Rd., (West Tower), 1611 Toronto, Ont., Canada M5P 2X7. 2.

JEURISSEN, Herman G A, b. 27 Dec. 1952, Wychen, Holland. Horn Player. Educ: Soloists Dip., 1976, Prix d'Excellence, 1978, Brabants Conserv., Tilburg. m. Stans Boomgaard, 1 c. Debut: (as soloist) w. Netherlands Students Orch., 1975. Career: Co-ord. 1st Hornist, Utrecht Symph. Orch., 1975-78; Prin. Horn, The Hague Phil. Orch., 1978-; Solo & concerto TV apps. w. The Hague Phil. Orch., Utrecht Symph. Orch., Brabants Orkest, Radio Orchs. Comps: Reconstruction of 5th Horn Concerto (K370b, 371), Mozart; Completion of a fragment of a horn concerto in E major (K494a), Mozart. Contbr. to: Mens en Melodie; Horn Call. Address: Jacob Mosselstraat 58, The Hague, Netherlands.

JEWEL, Ian Douglas, b. 23 Jan. 1944, Ilford, Essex, UK. Violist. Educ: RCM; ARCM. m. Carol Slater, 1 s. Career: Mbr., Gabrieli String Quartet; Recordings: w. Gabrieli String Quartet; Brahms Songs w. Bernadette Greevy & Paul Hamburger. Mbr., ISM. Hobbies: Reading; Listening to Jazz; Collecting Antiques. Mgmt: Harold Holt Ltd. Address: 242 Willesden Lane, London NW2, UK.

JEZ, Jakob, b. 23 Nov. 1928, Bostanj, Yugoslavia. Composer; Professor of Pedagogical Academy; Editor. Educ: Acad. of Music, Ljubljana. m. Olga Jez, 1 child. Career: Ed., Slovene Review for Music. Educ: GRLICA, 1968-. Comps. incl: Cantatas; Do Fraig Amors for double mixed chorus, mandolin, lute, guitar & percussion; Electronic Music; The Star's Look II; Orchl.; Concertino semplice for viol. & strings; Chmbr.; Pastoral Inventions for viol. & piano; Piano; 2 suites; Vocal & Choral Music. Contbr. to GRLICA. Mbr. of Soc. of Slovene Comps. Hons: Radio Yugoslavia Prize, 1968. Preseren Fond Prize, 1969; 10 other prizes. Hobby: Nature. Mgmt: Musikverlage Hans Gerig, Cologne, Drususgasse 7-11. Address: Rutarjeva 5, 61000 Ljubljana, Yugoslavai.

JEZEWSKI, Zbigniew, b. 25 Feb. 1921, Krakow, Poland. Pianist; Composer. Educ: Dip. Piano Studies, Cracow

Conservatoire, 1946. m. Izabela Jezewska, 1 s. Debut: Cracow Phil., 1946. Career: Apps. w. Polish Phil. Orchs.; Soloist & in chmbr. music concerts on Polish Radio & TV; Asst. Prof., Cracow Conservatoire. Comps. incl: Music for dramatic & puppet theatres, films, radio, theatre & TV; Easy pieces for children. Num. recordings. Contbr. to Polish Music Eds. Mbrships: Assn. of Polish Music Artists; Assn. of Polish Authors & Comps. Hons. incl: 1st Prize for Music in Puppet Theatres Competitions, Opole, Poland, 1967; Num. prizes at Polish pianistic competitions. Hobby: Spinning. Address: Dtuga str. 34, Krakow, Poland.

JÍLEK, František, b. 22 May 1913, Brno, Czech. Conductor; Pianist; Composer. Educ: Conserv. of Music; Masterschl. of Music. m. Lenka Jilková, 1 d. Debut: Nat. Theatre, Brno. Career: Nat. Theatre, Ostrava; State Theatre, Brno; guest apps., Prague, Helsinki, Oslo, Ankara, Leipzig, Linz, Florence, Maggio Fiorentino, Perugia, Barcelona; apps. w. ldng. Czech. symph. orchs.; Prof. of Cond., Janacek Acad. of Musical Arts; currently Dir. of Opera, Chief Cond., State Theatre, Brno. Recordings: Works by Martinu, Smetana, Janacek & Fibich; scenes from Czech. operas & from Der Rosenkavalier. Contbr. of instrumental revisions to Janacek operas to Janácek Annual. Mbrships: Assn. of Czech. Comps.; Assn.of Czech. Theatre Artists. Hons. incl: Artist of Merit; Leos Janácek Prize; Bedrich Smetana Prize. Address: Tábor 426, Brno, Czechslovakia.

JINDRAK, Jindřich, b. 4 Nov. 1931, Stratkonice, Czech. Singer (Baritone); Teacher of Voice. Educ: Tchrs. Trng. Coll.; Acad. of Arts, Prague. m. Jana Procházková, 2 d. Debut: Operetta Theatre, Prague, 1956. Career: Num. roles from Czech & world opera repertoire; concerts, recitals of oratorio, cantatas & songs; radio & TV recordings; Docent, Acad. of Arts, Prague. Recordings incl: Dvorák, Biblical Songs (or ch.), & Song Cycles (LP); Martinu, Highland Songs; V J Tomasek, Goethe Songs; num. records of complete Czech opera & modern Czech music. Mbr., Czech profl. assn. Hons. incl: Smetana Medal, 1974; Supraphon Prize for Best Vocal Recording, 1975; Prize, Min. of Culture, 1976. Hobbies: Nature; Folk Instruments. Mgmt: Nat. Theatre, Prague. Address: Prague 4, Jeremenkova 72896, Czech.

JIRA, Milan, b. 7 Apr. 1935, Prague, Czech. Composer; Pianist. Educ: Studied Piano & Cond., Prague Conserv.; Studied comp., Acad. of Musical Arts, Prague. m. Milena Strunecká, 1 s. Career: Co-répétiteur, Opera; Music Drama Critic; Radio Prod.; Tchr.,Popular Conserv.; Prof., Prague Conserv. Comps: TV Opera; 5th Symph.; Piano Concerto; Symph. for Strings; 5 Impromptus for String Quartet; songs; comps. for Theatres & Puppet Theatres. Recording: Chansons. Recip. 2nd Prize, Music Fest., Piestany, 1978. Address: Spirkova 522, 140 00 Prague 4, Czech. 2.

JIRÁSEK, Ivo, b. 16 July 1920, Prague, Czech. Conductor; Composer; Director of Music Studio, Prague. Educ: Dip., Acad. of Music, Prague. m. Vedulka Matouskavá-Jirásková, 2 s. Career: Cond.; Composer; Dir. of Music Studio, Prague. Comps: 4 Studies for String Quartet; Stabat Mater, for soli, chorus & orch.; Serenades for Chmbr. Ensemble; Other chmbr., orchl. comps.; 5 Operas, 2 Cantatas. Recordings: Chmbr. & symphonic music. Contbr. to music reviews. Mbrships: Ctrl. Comm., Assn. of Czech Comps. Hons: Musical Prize, Province of Ostrava, 1962; Musical Prize, City of Ostrava, 1957, etc. Hobbies: Alpinism; Skiing. Address: Na úlehli 7/1257, 145 00 Praha 4 - Michle, Czech.

JIROUŠEK, Miroslav Václav, b. 25 Oct. 1903, Jindrichuv, Hradec, Czech. Retired Lecturer; Prof. of Mathematics; Pianist; Violoncellist. Educ: Secondary Schl. Tchrs. Dip., Fac. of Sci., Charles Univ., Prague, 1929; Paed. Dr., Palacký Univ., Olomouc, 1951; State Conserv. of Music, Prague (comp. & conducting). m. Marie Chmelová, 1 s. Career: Secondary Schl. Tchr., 1929-70; Lectr., Fac. of Sci., Palacký Univ., Olomouc, 1954-70; Collector of folk songs, Olomouc Dist. Comps: Songs from the Haňa (w. Oldrich Sirovátka), 1954; Hanácké písmicky (for children or womens choir, op. 16), 1943. Contbr. to jrnls. & mags. Mbrships: Copyright Authors Assn.; Former mbr., Union of Czechoslovak Comps.; Hon. mbr., Nesvera Choir, Olomous, 1971. Recip., Meritorious Tchr. Award, 1968. Address: Polská 63, 777 00 Olomouc, Czech.

JOACHIM, Heinrich, b. 26 Oct. 1910, Berlin, Germany. Concert Cellist; Teacher of Cello & Chamber Music. Educ: Pvte. study of Cello; Hochschule fur Musik, & Univ., Berlin. widower, 2 s., 2 d. Debut: Berlin, 1927. Career: Num. tours of Europe as recitalist & soloist w. orch.; Dir., Nat. Conserv., Guatemala; weekly chmbr. music prof., Guatemala Nat. Radio; Ldr., Cello sect., NYC Symph. w. Leonard Bernstein; Cellist, NY Phil.; 1st Cellist, Balt. Symph.; currently Soloist & Chmbr. musician, extensive concerts Am. continent. Recordings for Decca &

Vox. Mbr., Local 802, AFM., Recip., Dip. of Hon., Dip. of Merit, Guatemala Univ., etc. Hobbies: Records; Hiking. Mgmt: Norman Seaman, NYC. Address: 211 W St., White Plains, NY 10605, USA.

JOACHIM, Otto, b. 13 Oct. 1910, Düsseldorf, Germany. Composer; Violist; Violinist; Gambist. Educ: Concordia Schl., Düsseldorf; Buths-Neitzel Conserv., Düsseldorf; Rheinische Musik Schule, Cologne. separated, 1 s. Career: CBC, soloist, Montreal Str. Quartet, L'Ensemble des Instruments Anciens de Montreal; 1st violist, Montreal Symph. Comps. incl: Concertante No. 2 for str. quartet & str. orch., 1961; Contrastes, for orch., 1967; Nonet, 1960; Kinderspiel, for violin, cello, piano, speaker, 1969; Night Music, for flute (alto flute) & guitar, 1978; 4 Intermezzi, for flute & guitar, 1978; Requiem, for violin or viola or cello, 1977; Fantasia for Organ, 1961; 12 Twelve-Tone Pieces for Children, 1961; Psalm, for choir, 1960; 5.9, for 4 channel tape, 1971. Mbrships: Can. League of Comps. (past VP & Treas.); Exec., Can. Music Ctr. recip. Grand Prix Paul Gilson. Hobbies: Musical Electronics; Constructing replicas of ancient instruments; Painting. Address: 7810 Wavell Rd., Côte St-Luc (Montreal) H4W, 1L7, Can. 2.

JOCHUM, Eugen, b. 1 Nov. 1902, Babenhausen, Bayern. Conductor (Organ, Piano). Educ: Conserv., Augsburg; Musical Acad., Munich. m. Maria Montz, 2 children. Debut: W. Munich Phil. Orch., 1926. Career incls: Cond. in Kiel, Mannheim Opera, Duisburg, Berlin, 1932-; Civic Opera; Guest Cond., Berlin Phil., 1932-; Tours of Europe & USA; State Opera & Phil. Orch., Hamburg, 1934-39; Fndr. & Chief Cond., Bavarian Radio Orch.; Guest Cond. worldwide; Festivals in Bayreuth, Salzburg, Lucerne & Edinburgh. Num. recordings. Mbr. profl. orgs. Hons. incl: Brahms Medaille, 1938; Cond. Laureate, LSO; Goldenes Grammophon, 1972. Hobbies: Hist.; Philos.; Archaeology; Swimming; Mountains; Walking. Mgmt: Christian Lange, Sperbergwg 18, 8033 Krailling, Germany. Address: 8 Munchen 19, Brunhildenstr. 2, Germany. 2.

JOCHUM, Veronica, b. Berlin, Germany. Concert Pianist. Educ: grad., Staatliche Musikhochschule, Munich; Konzert-Reifeprüfung, 1955; Concert dip., 1957; studied w. Eliza Hansen, Maria Landes-Hindemith, Edwin Fischer, Josef Benvenuti & Rudolf Serkin. m. Wilhelm Viggo von Moltke. Debut: soloist w. Munich Phil., 1954. Career: Concerts in about 40 countries on 4 continents, recitals or as soloist w. leading orchs. incl: LSO, LPO, Berlin Phil., Boston Symph., Concertgebouw, Jerusalem Symph.; Prof., New England Conserv., Boston. num. recordings. Mgmts: Matthews/Napal Ltd., NY; Christian Lange,Munich. Address: 14 Gray Gdns. W, Cambridge, MA 02138, USA. 2,5,6,27.

JOELSON, Elliott W, b. 21 July 1905, Ashland, Wis., USA. Violinist; Violist. Educ: studied violin w. Serge Korgueff, Inst. of Musical Arts, NYC, 1027 20; B Mus, 1922, M Mus, 1962, MacPhail Coll. of Music, Mpls., Minn. m. Bernadette E Dauplaise, 1 d. Career: Staff Violinist, Arr., WEBC Radio stn., 1933-39; Instr., Univ. of Wis., Superior; Charter Mbr., Duluth Symph. & Symph. Str. Quartet, also on symph. Bd. of Dirs.; Guest Lectr., Art of Violin Playing; Adjudicator & Clinician, num. music contests; Cond., Duluth Civic HS Symph. Orch. for many yrs. Recordings: Elliott Joelson's String Ensemble. Author: Violin Vibrato: Its History, Literature & Significance in String Tone Production, 1962. Mbrships: incl: ASTA; Nat. Music Educators. Hobby: Duplicate bridge. Address: 1015 N 14th Ave. E, Duluth, MN 55805, USA.

JOERNS, Helge O L, b. 18 Mar. 1941, Mannheim, Germany. Harpsichord Player; Composer. Educ: Musikakadamie, Detmold; Technische Univ., Berlin; Dip., Tonmeister. m. Gabriele Schreckenbach, 2 s. Career: Tonmeister, RIAS, Berlin; Prof. of Comp., Bischöflichen Kirchenmusikschule, Berlin. Comps: Orchestral & chmbr. music, opera, Ballet, ch. music, choral & electronic music. Recording: Helge Joerns, Miscellaneous Works. Hons: Rome prize, Prucel prize, etc. Hobby: Riding. Address: Nicolaistr. 49-51, 1000 Berlin 46, German Fed. Repub.

JOHANNESEN, Grant, b. 30 July 1921, Salt Lake City, Utah, USA. Musician (Piano). Educ: B Mus, McCave Schl. of Music, Salt Lake City, Utah; HHD, Univ. Utah; D Mus, Cleveland Inst. of Music. 1 child. Debut: W NY Phil. (George Szell), 1950. Career: Concerts throut world for 30 yrs.; 3 tours of Soviet Union, 1 as soloist w. Cleveland Orch.; 3 tours as soloist w. NY Phil.; Apps. at all maj. music festivals; Aspen Festival, 6 yrs.; Currently Dir., Cleveland Inst. of Music. Comps: Improvisation over a Mormon Hymn (Oxford Univ. Press). Recordings: Over 50 inclng: Chopin, complete Polonaises; HMV w. LSO. Mgmt: Harold Shaw. Address: 10 Park Ave. 16 H, New York, NY, USA.

JOHANNSSON, Magnus Blöndal, b. 8 Sept. 1925, Skalar, Iceland. Conductor; Composer. Educ: Reykjavik Schl. of Music, 1935-37, 1939-45; Juilliard Schl. of Music, NY, USA, 1947-53. (studying piano, comp. & cond. w. J Carlson, M Bauer, L Teicher, R Ferrante). m. Sigridur Josteinsdorit, 3 s (former marriage). Debut: As cond., 1963. Career: Staff Mbr., Iceland State Broadcasting Serv., 1956-76; Cond. Iceland Nat. Theatre, 1965-72. Comps: Many comps. commissioned for radio, TV, film & concerts, also Kantata, 1954; 2 Sonatas for piano, Samstirni (tape), 1960; Punktar (orch. & tape), 1961; Sonorities I, 1961; Sequence (ballet) for Iceland Fest., 1970; Sonorities III (Iceland Fest.), 1972; Birth of an Island (film music), 1964; Sequel to Surtsey, 1965; The Other Iceland (BBC), 1973; Vestnammaeyjar, 1974. Publs: Bibliog., Dictionary of 20th Century Music, 1974; Tempo (Winter 1965-66); 4-5; Aurelio de la Vega "Regarding Electronic Music". Mbrships: Iceland Comps. Soc. Hons: Price of Honour Iceland State Comps. Fund, 1967; Gold Award, Trento; 1st Prize, Edinburgh Film Fest., UK (for 3rd ed. of Birth of an Island); Iran Gold Award, 1975 (for Birth of an Island). Hobbies: Flying. Address: Solheimar 23, Reykjavik, Iceland.

JOHANSEN, Gunnar, b. 21 Jan. 1906, Copenhagen, Denmark. Concert Pianist; ARtist in Residence. Educ: Studied w. Victor Schioler, Lamond, Edwin Fischer & Egon Petri, Berlin. m. Lorraine Johnson Johansen. Debut: Aged 12, Danish Orch. Career: 1st Perf., Busoni - Chopin Variations, 1924; 1st Perf., Palmgren Concerto, Paris, 1928; Debut, San Fran., 1929; NBC weekly recitals, 1930-35; 1st Perf., Ravel Concert - LA Symph., 1933; 1st Perf., Rachmaninoff 4th (after Rachmaninoff's own), 1934; 12 Historical Recitals, Europe & Am. Recordings: Complete J S Bach Clavier Works; Complete Franz Liszt Piano Works; Complete F Busoni Piano Works. Mbrships: Liszt Soc., Uk & Am.; Leonardo Acad. of Arts & Sci.; Bohemian Club. Hons: Citation for distinguished Univ. service, Wis. Acad. Scis., Arts & Letters, 1976. Hobbies: Science; Flying; Wood sawing & splitting. Address: Blue Mounds, Wisconsin, USA.

JOHANSÉN, Per, b. 19 July 1939, Vejerslev, Denmark. Opera Singer (Bass); Organist. Educ: Dip., Organ & Cond., Royal Danish Music Acad., 1962; Dip., Royal Opera Acad., 1970. m. Lone Mulvad, 2 s. Debut: Title-part in Wozzeck, 1971. Career: Organist, 1966; Opera Singer, Theatre Royal, Copenhagen, 1971-; Roles in Boris Godunov, Salome, Prince Igor, Simone Boccanegra, Katherine Asmajlowa, The Magic Flute & other operas; Concerts, Italy & Germany; Lieder - & Oratorio singer. Recordings of modern music. Mbrships: Danish Singing Soc.; Danish Soc. Organists. Hons: Hon. Prize, Danish Music Critics, 1975. Address: Lejrevej 5, 2700 Bronshoj, Denmark.

JOHANSSON, Bengt Viktor, b. 2 Oct. 1914, Helsinki, Finland. Composer. Educ: Cello Dip., Sibelius Acad.; Comp. Dip., ibid. m. Liisa Rahola. Comps. incl: (publd) opera The Castle; Requiem, baritone, 2 choirs, 2 string orchs., timpani; choir madrigals & lieds; (recorded) The Tomb At Akr Caar, baritone & choir; Triptych, soprano, baritone, choir; 3 Classic Madrigals, choir; Vesper Music, baritone, choir, organ; 3 Chansons, baritone & piano; Na Audiart choir; Venus & Adonis; Come into the yard of meditation, Canto baritone & piano. Mbr. Bd., Soc. of Finnish Comps. Hons: Pro Finlandia Medal, 1969; 1st Prize, S lo Voice Competiton, 1973; var. Prizes for Comp. Hobby: Cine-Photography. Address: 13 A 18 Tunturikatu, SF-00100 Helsinki 10, Finland. 19.

JOHANSSON, Björn Emanuel, b. 9 Mar. 1913, Smögen, Gothenburg, Sweden. Composer; Critic; College Teacher. Educ: Matriculation exam, 1934; BA, B Relig., Univ. of Lund, Sweden, 1937, '42; Theory of Music, Comp., The Royal Univ. of Music, Copenhagen, Denmark; Theory & comp., La Schola Cantorum, Paris, 1946-47; French Scholarships. m. Gunnel Kahlefeldt, 1 s., 1 d. Debut: the second symph., Gothenburg, 1948. Career: Many of his symphonic works, songs & chamber music have been perf. in Scandinavian countries, in Italy, on the Swedish broadcasting network, on the continent & in NY; Debater, Swedish TV. Comps. incl: Nevskij Prospect (orch.) Colloquio sensitivo (harp, clarinet, cello); Caractère (orch.); Hommage à Francois Villon (voice, flute, harp, cello); Songs, Ballads for choir; Music for stage-plays; Contbr. of num. articles to newspapers. Mbrships: The Order of Rosencreuz; STIM, Stockholm; The Spark, Gothenburg. Hons: Many scholarships from the Royal Swedish Acad. of Music, Stockholm; Prize of Hon., Town of Gothenburg, Sweden, 1965. Address: Doktor Forselius gata 20, 413 26 Gothenburg, Sweden.

JOHANSSON, Gunde, b. 18 Oct. 1922, Lindfors, Sweden. Singer; Poet. Educ: Studies of Hist. of Lit., Hist. of Relig. & Lang. at Univs. Gothenburg & Stockholm; fil. kand. degree; Grad., composition, SKAP, 1951. m. Ingrid, 1 d. Career: Work for Radio Sweden, 1951-. Num. compositions incl: Torparvisan; Hejaha; Visan till Jenny; Jul i stoga; Knotige broder; Du bortkomne broder; Viasn om oss sjalva; Rallarvisa; Dauktramparvals; Sommarhambo. 5 recordings. Mbrships: STIM; SKAP. Recip. SKAP Schlrship. for composition, 1965. Hobbies: Poetry; Music. Address: Motjarnshyttans herrgard, 68300 Hagfors, Sweden.

JOHN, Patricia Spaulding, b. 16 July 1916, Canton, Ill, USA. Harpist; Composer. Educ: BA, William March Rice Univ., 1941; Curtis Inst. of Music; Mills Coll., Calif.; studied w. Carlos Salzedo, Anna Louise David. m. Frank Geoffrey Keightley, 2 d. Career: Harpist, Springfield, Ill. Civic Symph., 1947, Galveston, Tex. Civic Symph., 1952, Houston, Tex. Symph., 1956; Pvte. Tchr., 1950-52, 1975. num. Solo Recitals, USA, Brit. W. Indies, England & Netherlands. Comps. for harp, Sea Change, Mnemosyne, Aprille, Henriette, Americana (1978), Tachystos; Let's Play (harp) series Clown Dance, Arithmetic & Canoe. Contbr. to: Am. Harp Jrnl.; UK Newsletter. Mbrships: Life, Am. Harp Soc.; PR Dir., Gtr. NYC, ibid, 1969; Ed., Harpists in NYC, ibid, 1969; Fndr., Houston Chapter, ibid; Assn. Int. des Harpistes, Paris, France; Musicians Club of NYC, 1967-72; Nat. Assn. for Am. Comps. & Conds., NYC, 1969-71; Galveston Musical Club; Pres., ibid, 1952; Pres., San Jacinto Chapt., Am. Harp. Soc., Houston, Tex., 1975-76. Address: 1414 Milford, Houston, TX 77006, USA. 27.

JOHNSEN, Hallvard, b. 27 June 1916, Hamburg, Germany. Composer; Flautist; Educator. Educ: studied flute, comp. & cond., Music Conserv., Oslo, 1930-41; flute studies, 1942-45, comp. studies, 1956, w. Vagn Holmboe, Copenhagen. m. Bjorg Johnsen, 4 d. Debut: as comp. & flautist, Oslo, 1942. Career: Flautist, Nat. Theatre Orch., Oslo; Solo Flautist, Military Band in Oslo, 1947-72; num. concerts, stage & radio; Master in music theory & flute, music schl. outside Oslo. Comps: 12 Symphs.; 1 opera; 4 cantatas; 6 concertos; quartets; 2 quintets; 2 overtures; chmbr. music works; piano pieces; songs; 1 oratorio. Recordings: 3 Symph.; 2 Violin Concertos; 2 Brass Quintets. Mbr., Norwegian Comps. Assn. Hobbies: Skiing; Walking in the mountains. Address: Krumveien 2, 1344 Haslum Norway.

JOHNSON, Bengt Emil, b. 1936. Author; Composer. Career: on staff, Swedish Radio, 1966-, currently Cons. to Music Dept.; Ed., Nutida Musik (periodical); moved from written poetry to compositions based on sound, working exclusively w. taped text-sound compositions since 1965. Compositions incl: "Semikolon; Äventyr pa vägen" (Semicolon; Adventures en route); "11967- New drag-leases with the wide world, visits, adventures, easings, etc.;" 21967 (while); " -(bland)-" (Among); "21969-For Abraham Jaboksson, en route" (w. texts by poet C J L Almquist); "61970-Homage to Mr. Miller" (Henry "41970 Jakter (Hunts)" (on poem fragments by painter CArl Fredrik Hil); sev. instrumental works during early 1960's. Publs: 4 collects. of poems, 1963-66.

JOHNSON, Bruce Christopher, b. 27 Aug. 1953, Phila., Pa., USA. Musicologist; Organist; Composer; Music Bibliographer. Educ: BMus, Coll. of Wooster, 1975; MSLS, Case Western Reserve Univ.; MA (musicol.), ibid.; service player cert., AGO. m. Holly Anne Wright. Career: Asst. in Musicol., Case Western Reserve Univ., 1975-77; Instructor, Cleveland Music Settlement, 1976-77; Music Bibliographer, Univ. of Fla., 1977-78; Asst. in Musicol., Northwestern Univ., 1978-. Comps: Brass Quartet, Op. 1; 3 Brief Sketches on Well-known Places, Op. 2. Mbrships: Am. Musicol. Soc.; Neuen Bach-Gesellschaft; AGO; Galpin Soc.; Coll. Music Soc.; Music Lib. Assn. Hons: Edward H Reuss Memorial Prize, 1970; Beta Phi Mu, 1977. Hobbies: Scouting; Sailing; Photography; Scuba diving. Address: 7601 N Sheridan Rd., Chgo., IL 60626, USA.

JOHNSON, Calvert, b. 15 Nov. 1949, Takoma Pk., Md., USA. University Professor; Organist. Educ: BA (music), Kalamazoo Coll.; DMus, MMus, Northwestern Univ. (organ); Toulouse Conserv. (Premier Prix, organ). Career: Prof. of organ, piano, music theory, Northeastern Okla. State Univ.; organist, Grace Episcopal Ch., Muskogee, Okla.; perfs. at 8th Int. Organ Fest., Morelia, Mexico, Kennedy Ctr., Wash., DC, Arkansas Day, USAF Acad., Kalamazoo Bach Fest.; recorded concerts for Radio-France; lectures & recitals in USA, Europe & Latin Am. Contbr. to: The Diapason; The Am. Organist; Orgues Meridionales. Mbrships: Am. Musicol. Soc.; AGO (sub-dean, Tulsa, 1979-80); Am. Assn. of Univ. Profs.; MTNA; Coll. Music Soc. Hons: French Govt. Fellowship, 1974-75; Phi Beta Kappa; Pi Kappa Lambda. Address: 317 W Morgan, Tahlequah, OK 74464, USA.

JOHNSON, Celeste Jean Everson, b, 27 July 1953, Oakland, Calif., USA. Harpist; Music Educator. Educ: BA, San Fran. State Univ.; Secondary Tchng. Dip. in Music, ibid, 1976; MA, ibid,

1978. m. Mark Louis Johnson. Career: tour w. Calif. Youth Symph.; Aust., 1969; tour w. Montgomery Co. Youth Orch., Louisville, Ky., & w. Walter Johnson HS (Bethesda, Md.), Boston, Mass., 1970; has perfd. w. Peninsula Symph. & Master Sinfonia of Los Altos, Calif., Loring Male Chorus of San Fran.; TV apps.; Perf. w. Schola Cantorum & Santa Clara Chorale; Guest Perfs. w. choruses, orch., receptions & chs. in Bay Area, Calif.; app. at Mu Phi Epsilon Nat. Conven., Palm Springs, Calif., 1974. Mbrships: Pres., Treas. & Histn., Epsilon Omega Chapt. & Mbr., Palo Alto Alum Chapt., Mu Phi Epsilon; Am. Harp. Soc. Recip. of num. scholarships. Hobbies incl: Spoon Collecting; Sewing; Model & Steam Railroading. Address: 2500 Medallion Dr., No. 183, Union City, CA 94587, USA.

JOHNSON, David Charles, b. 27 Oct. 1942, Edinburgh, Scotland, UK. Composer; Musical Historian; Performer, voice, cello, recorder. Educ: MA (Aberdeen); BA (Cambridge); PhD (Cambridge). m., 1 s. Career: Compiled and directed Mr. Topham's Diary, Edinburgh Fest., 1975; Radio Forth/Edinburgh Fest., Fringe Music Award for opera premiere, 1978; Mgr., Hill Square Consort. Comps: Trio for Recorders; Thomas the Rhymer (opera score). Publs: Music & Society in Lowland Scotland in the 18th Century. Contbr. to: Musical Times; Glasgow Herald; Opera Int.; Early Music. Hobby: Housework. Address: 1 Hill Square, Edinburgh 8, UK.

JOHNSON, Grace Gray, b. 22 Apr. 1924, Jacksonville, Fla., USA. Concert Piano Accompanist; Teacher. Educ: BM, Howard Univ., 1947; MA, Columbia Univ., 1952; DMA, Boston Univ., 1964. Career: Accompanist, Louisa Vaughn Jones, Lillian Evanti, concerts in USA, UK, 1943-47; Pt.-time Tchr., Am. Schl. of Music, Wash., DC, 1943-47; Prog. Dir., Int. House, NYC, 1951-52; Asst. Prof., Dept. of Music, Fla. A & M Univ., 1947-50, 1952-59; Prof., 1969-; Counselor & Tchng. Asst., Schl. of Fine & Applied Arts, Boston Univ., 1964-69. Num. mbrships. incl: Fndr., Fla. A & M Univ. Student Chapt., MENC; Mbr., Pres. Coun. for the Arts; Adjudicator, Guggenheim Assn., & Int. Music Competiton; Adjudicator & Cons., Tanglewood Music Fests.; Cons., New England Opera Guild; Coll. Music Soc.; Am. Musicol. Soc.; Nat. Assn. of Tchr. Educ; MTNA; Am. Guidance Org.; Phi Kappa Lambda; Pi Lambda Thets; Vice Chmn. of Bd. of Dir., Kt. Womens Bank of Fla. Hons: Selected for Int. Rsch. Seminar as one of 100 outstanding music educators, MENC, Chgo., 1970. Hobbies: Gardening; Interior decorating; Tennis; Flower arranging; Sewing; Skiing. Address: 1601 Hernando Dr., Tallahassee, FL 32304, USA. 125.

JOHNSON, Graham Rhodes, b. 10 July 1950, Bulawayo, Rhodesia. Concert Accompanist. Educ: RAM. Debut: Purcell Room, London, 1972. Career: Artistic Dir., The Songmakers' Almanac, 1976-; recitals w. Elizabeth Schwarzkopf, Victoria de los Angeles (USA tour, 1977), Peter Pears, Jessye Norman, Jill Gomez, Sarah Walker, Felicity Lott, Ann Murray, Richard Jackson. Recordings: w. Janet Baker; w. Martyn Hill. Contbr. to: Times Literary Supplement. Hons: ARAM, 1976. Hobby: Book Collecting. Address: 83 Fordwych Rd., London NW2, UK. 1.

JOHNSON, Guy, b. 8 Nov. 1933, Marinette, Wis., USA. Piano Department Head. Educ: BFA, Wis. State Coll., Milwaukee, 1955; MM, Ind. Univ., 1956; studied w. Irma Schenuit Hall, Katherine Bacon, Ozan Marsh, Dr. Bela Nagy, Rudolf Ganz, Gyorgy Sandor, Edith Oppens, William Masselos. Debut: Athenaeum Hall, Milwaukee, 1955; Fullerton Hall, Chgo., Ill., 1959. Career: Hd., Piano Dept., Drury Coll., Springfield, Mo., 1956-57; Luther Coll., Decorah, Iowa, 1959-68; Friends Univ., Wichita, Kan., 1968-; Perf., Soloist w. var. Symphs., USA; var. Solo Recitals; num. Chmbr. Perfs.; Accomp. var. artists; Adjudicator. Mbrships: Bd. Nam. Mta; Adjudicator, NGPT. Hons: Rotary, Piano Study, 1948; Wis. Fedn. of Music Clubs Scholarship, 1955; Milwaukee Tchrs. Assn., 1951; Milwaukee State Coll., 1951; Teaching Asst. Ind. Univ., 1955-56, 1957-59; Waukesha Symph. Auditions, 1951. Address: Friends Univ., 2100 Univ., Wichita, KS 67213, USA. 4,29.

JOHNSON, JOHN (Simon) Bird, b. 24 June 1934, Penrith, UK. Conductor; Chorus Master; University Director of Music. Educ: Durham Univ.; Reading Univ.; BA; ARCM; ARCO. m. Ann Hall, 2 s., 1 d. Career: Dir. of Music, King's Schl., Macclesfield, 1961-64, Brunel Univ., 1974-; Lectr. in Music (Educ.), Reading Univ., 1964-73; Fndr. & Cond., Reading Bach Choir, 1966-73; Chorus Master & Guest Cond. for Yehudi Menuhin at Windsor Fest., 1971-72; Assoc. Chorus Master, New Philharmonia Chorus, 1975-. Mbr., ISM. Hobby: Fell Walking. Address: 106 Redhatch Dr., Earley, Reading RG6 2QR, UK.

JOHNSON, Joseph Alan, b. 5 Nov. 1948, Salt Lake City, Utah, USA. Bass Trombonist; Teacher. Educ: B Mus (Educ.),

Brigham Young Univ., 1971; M Mus (Trombone), Univ. of Southern Calif., 1974. m. Betty E Johnson, 2 s. Career: Former Bass Trombonist, Santa Barbara Symph. & other orchs.; Bass Trombonist w. Pasadena Symph. Orch., Fine Arts Brass Quintet, Los Angeles Civic Light Opera Assn.; Perfs. &/or records w. num. orchs. & chmbr. orchs.; film & commercial work; Trombone Instr., Occidental Coll., & Pasadena City Coll. Conserv. Recordings incl: Mozart, Dominican Vespers; Music of Am. Comps.; Music of Virgil Thompson; Respighi, Ancient Airs & Dances. Mbr., var. profl. assns. Hons: Brass Chmbr. Music Award, Univ. of Southern Calif., 1973. Address: 2021 S Stoneman Ave., Alhambra, CA 91801, USA.

JOHNSON, La Rue, b. 3 Dec. 1908, Sedalia, Mo., USA. Teacher of Piano. Educ: Assoc. in Music, Stephens Coll., Columbia, Mo., 1928; B Mus, 1931, B Pub. Schl. Music, 1933, M Mus, 1948, Southern Meth. Univ., Tex.; Cert. Lib. Serv., Columbia Univ., 1947; pvte. study of Piano Chmbr. music, Juilliard Schl. of Music, NY. Career: Former Instructor of Piano, Southern Meth. Univ.; now pvte. Tchr. of Piano; Broadcasts, Mo. & Tex.; Recitals, Mo., Tex. & NY. Contbr. to: Concert prog. notes, Dallas, Tex., 1956-62, & Pretoria, S Africa, 1967; var. newspapers. Mbrships incl: Mu Phi Epsilon (Pres., Mu Chi chapt., 1930-31); Pro Musica (Chmn., 1962-64). Recip., Mu Phi Epsilon Award for Outstanding Music Student 1931. Hobbies: Reading; Travel; Watching Tennis Matches; Mountain Hiking. Address: 4524 Belclaire Ave., Dallas, TX 75205, USA.

JOHNSON, Lockrem Harold, b. 15 Mar. 1924, Davenport, Iowa, USA. Composer; Conductor; Pianist; Music Publisher; Teacher. Educ: Univ. of Wash., Seattle. Career: Radio Commentator, 1966-68; Cond., Orchestrator, Operas, Musical Comedies; Assoc., Univ. of Wash. Schl. of Music, 1947-49; Pianist, Seattle Symph., 1948-51; Music Dir., Eleanor King Dance Co., 1948-51; Educ. Dir., Mercury Music Corp., 1951-54; Hd., Orch. Dept., C F Peters Corp., 1954-58, NYC; Pres., Dow Music Publrs. Inc., 1957-62; Plant Mgr., Music Typographers, Oyster Bay, NY, 1961-62; Dir., Music Dept., Cornish Schl., Seattle, 1962-69; Pres., Puget Music Publs., Inc., 1970-. Comps: 3 Sonatas, Recercare, Chaconne, 24 Preludes, 2 Sonatinas, piano; 3 Sonatas, 6 Easy Pieces, violin & piano; 2 Sonatas, cello & piano; Sonata, 7 Preludes, guitar; Symph.; ballet She; opera A Letter To Emily; Choral Suite; Sonatina, trumpet & piano; 5 Song Cycles; incidental music. Mbr., Off., var. Profl. Orgs. Contbr. to var. profl. jrnls. Recip. var. Hons. for Comp. Hobbies: Gardening; Chess; Table Tennis. Address: 18456 40th Pl. NE, Seattle, WA 98155, USA.

JOHNSON, Regena Fix, b. 2 Apr. 1911, Shenandoah, Va., USA. Teacher of Voice, Piano & Organ. Educ: Univ. Cinn., Ohio; Madison Coll., Va.; B Mus, Cinn. Conserv. of Music; Cert. Tchr., Music Tchrs. Nat. Assn. m. Albert Dunston Johnson. Career: Pvte. Music Tchr.; Tchr. of Music, Pvte. & Public Schls. Va.; Soloist, var. occasions; Ch. Music Dir., Windsor Baptist Ch., 1940-; Singer, wkly. radio prog. on WSVA, Harrisburg, Va. Mbrships: Delta Kappa Gamma; Delta Chapt., Phi Beta; Music Tchrs. Nat. Assn.; Chmn., Eastern Dist., Va. Music Tchrs. Assn.; VP, Tidewater Music Tchrs. Forum; Va. Fedn. of Women's Clubs; Windsor Woman's Club. Hobbies: Reading; Civic Activities; Knitting. Address: P.O. Box 325, Windsor, VA 23487, USA. 5.

JOHNSON, Robert Sherlaw, b. 21 May 1932, Sunderland, UK. University Lecturer in Music; Composer; Pianist. Educ: BA, BMus, Univ. of Durham; MA (Oxon.); DMus (Leeds); ARAM; ARCM; LRAM; RAM, London. m. Rachael M Clarke, 3 s., 2 d. Career: Lectr. in Music, Leeds, then York; Univ. Lectr., Oxford & Fellow of Worcester Coll.; Concert Pianist & Comp., sev. BBC invitation concerts & other recitals. Comps. incl: 3 piano sonatas; Str. Quartet Nos. 1 & 2; Sonata for flute & cello; Triptych; Var. songs & choral works; Anslorum Feriae; Opera, The Lambton Worm. Many recordings. Publs: Messiaen, 1975. Mbrship: Vice Chmn., CGGB. Recip., Radcliffe Music Award for Comp., 1969. Address: Malton Croft, Woodlands Rise, Stonesfield, Oxon. OX7 2PL, UK. 3.

JOHNSON, Stuart, b. 8 May 1936, Chesterton, Staffs., UK. Musical Adviser; Composer. Educ: Cert. in Educ., St. Peter's Coll. of Educ., Birmingham; LGSM; LTCL. Comps: Kaleidoscope; Northumbrian Suite; A Circus Suite; A March Overture; Cantata, David & Goliath; Preliminary Band Book; Intermediate Band Books I & II; Progressive Band Book; Sinfonietta for Wind Orch.; A Second Band Book; A Third Band Book; Ceramic City Festival; Contrasts in Brass; Intermediate Horn Book; Festival Suite; French Folk Song Suite; Two Choral Preludes; Sinfonia for Brass. Contbr. to: Sounding Brass; The Trumpeter. Hobby: Badminton. Address: Mill Cottages, Teddesley Rd., Penkridge, Staffs., UK.

JOHNSON, Theodore Oliver Jr., b. 9 Oct. 1929, Elkhart, Ind., USA. University Professor of Music Theory, Viola & Violin. Educ: BM, 1951, MM, 1952, DMA, 1959, Univ. of Mich. m. Carol A Johnson, 2 d., 1 s. Career: Former Concertmaster, Lansing, Mich. Symph. Orch., & Grand Rapids Symph. Orch.; Recitalist & Chmbr. Musician; Violist, Beaumont String Quartet; Choir Dir., Bethel Bapt. Ch., Lansing, Mich.; Prof., Mich. State Univ. Comps: Here on the Cross He Lies (motet); Trust in the Lord with all your Heart (motet). Mbrships: Pi Kappa Lambda; Phi Kappa Phi; Phi Eta Sigma; Phi Mu Alpha Sinfonia. Hons: Stanley Medal, Univ. of Mich. Schl. of Music, 1951; Fulbright Award, Munich, Germany, 1956. Address: 651 Hillcrest Ave., E Lansing, MI 48823, USA. 8.

JOHNSON, Thomas Arnold, b. 1908, Neston, Wirral, Cheshire, UK. Music Teacher; Composer; Journalist; Arranger. Educ: LRAM; ARMCM; FRMCM. Career: Cinema Pianist; Soloist on BBC broadcasts, also participant in many Music Mag. broadcasts devoted to neglected composers. Compositions incl: over 200 educl. works, mainly piano solos, duets, duo piano pieces & studies; has arr. many works for solo piano, duo piano, or piano & another instrument. Publs: many teaching books; Musical Art Forms for Students; The Principles of Pianoforte Pedalling; Historical Facts by H J Taylor (revised ed.). Mbr: ISM. Hobbies: Reading; Collecting Silent Film Material & Complete Works of Minor Composers. Address: 18 Raby Park Rd., Neston, Wirral, Cheshire L64 9SP, UK. 3.

JOHNSON-HAMILTON, Joyce, b. 7 July 1938, Lincoln, Neb., USA. Conductor; Trumpet Soloist; Orchestral Trumpeter. Educ: B Mus. Ed., M Mus, Univ. of Neb.; 4 yrs. doctoral study, Stanford Univ.; Studied cond. w. Richard Lert, Sandor Salgo, George Cleve, Denis De Coteau; Studied trumpet w. Robert Nagel, Bernard Adelstein. m. Douglas H Hamilton, 2 s. Career: Asst. Cond., Oakland Symph. (4 seasons); Cond., San Jose Dance Theatre, Oakland Ballet, San Jose Symph. Children's Concerts; Fndr. & Music Dir., Sinfonia of N Calif.; San Jose State Univ. Orch.; Solo trumpet concerto perfs. w. Oakland Symph., San Jose Symph., Ore. Symph., Sinfonia of N Calif., Calif. Bach Soc.; Recitals & lecture demonstrations; Prin. trumpet w. Ore. Symph., Oakland Symph., San Jose Symph., Cabrillo Fest. Orch.; Asst. Prin. trumpet, San Fran. Symph.; Mbr., Aspen Fest. Orch.; Tchr., Stanford Univ., San Jose State Univ. Recordings: Music Makers. Contbr. to: Notes. Mbrships: Conds. Guild; Int. Trumpet Guild; Mu Phi Epsilon. Mgmt: Florence Kashiar. Hobbies: Collecting rare books on music; Gardening; Hiking. Address: 2 Bassett Lane, Atherton, CA 94025, USA.

JOHNSSON, Bengt Gustaf, b. 17 July 1921, Copenhagen, Danmark. Professor; Pianist; Organist. Educ: Musicol., Univ. of Copenhagen; MA, ibid, 1947; Piano studies w. Georg Vasarhelyi, Walter Gieseking; Degree as Organist & Ch. Musician, 1945, Royal Acad. of Music, Copenhagen. m. Esther Paustian, 2 d. Debut. Copenhagen, 1944. Career: Concert tours & broadcasts, Scandinavia, German Fed. Repub., Switz., France, Netherlands; Recitals, ibid; USA tour, 1964; Organist, Danish Broadcasting, 1949-70; Tchr., Royal Acad., Copenhagen, 1958-61; Prof., Royal Acad. of Music, Arhus, Jutland; Num. masterclasses. Recordings incl: N W Gade, Piano Music; Rissager, Complete Piano Works; Chmbr. music of Beethoven, Brahms, Busoni. Publs. incl: History of the Danish School Music until 1739, 1973; Ed., Hans Mikkelsen Ravn; Heptachordum Danicum 1646, Facs. & transl. w. histl. comments & studies in sources, 1977. Contbr. to mags. Mbr., Danish Soc. for Soloists. Hons: Hon. mbr., German-Arbeitskreis für Schulmusik und allgemeine Musikpädagogik, 1971; Prize of hon., Danish Soc. of Comps., 1971; Medal, Sibelius Acad. Address: Dronning Margrethesvej 81, Arhus N 8200 DK, Denmark.

JOHNSTON, Albert Richard, b. 7 May 1917, Chicago, Ill., USA. Professor of Music; Lecturer in Music Theory & Composition; Composer. Educ: BMus, Northwestern Univ., Evanston, Ill.; MMus, PhD, Rochester Univ., Rochester, NY; Pvte. studies w. Nadia Boulanger. m. Yvonne Jeanne-Marie Guiguet, 2 d., 1 s. Career: Prof., Univ. of Toronto, 1947-68; Dean, Fac. of Fine Arts, Univ. of Calgary, 1968-73; Prof. of Music, ibid, 1973-; num. broadcasts as commentator, host, cond. (choral), arr. & comp., Can. Broadcasting Corp. Comps: Symph.; String Quartet; Portraits, var. for Orch.; Suite for Bassoon & Piano (recorded); Trio (piano, violin, cello); Duo Concertante, for violin & piano; Irish Book for Soprano & Piano; Recordings: Folk Songs of Can. I & II (1954-1969); Folk Songs of Quebec, 1956; North American Children's Folk Songs, 1980; Songs for Today (Ed. in Chief), 9 Vols., 1960-70. Contbr. to: Perf. Arts in Can.; Musicanada. Mbrships: Can. League of Comps.; Alta. Comps. Assn.; Int. Soc. for Music Educ.; Int. Folk Music Soc.; Can. Music Coun.; Can. Music

Centre; Can. Nat. Youth Orch. Assn. Hons: Commissions as comp. from Can. Coun. & Can. Broadcasting Corp. Hobbies: Stamps; Travel; Talk. Address: Dept. of Music, Univ. of Calgary, Calgary, Alberta, Can. T2N 1N4.

JOHNSTON, Alison Aileen Annie, b. 13 Sept. 1916, London, UK. Freelance Musician; Piano soloist; Accompanist; Repetiteur Organist; Composer. Educ: Studied privately w. Maurice Cole; w. Kendall Taylor, RCM.; ARCM (performers' Piano). m. A.W. Johnston (dec.), 1 s., 1 d. Career: Concerts w. Cecil Aronowitz, Wilfred Brown, Tessa Robbins, Anna Shuttleworth, Douglas Heffer, Christopher Catchpole, Esther Salaman, John Brearley, Stephen Johnston, Finzi Orch.; Solo piano recitals; organ recitals; lecture recitals, WEA courses. Comps: Viola sonatina; Songs commissioned Roger Kidd; Piano bagatelles; Educational Music (Bassoon pieces, clarinet pieces, piano pieces, various trios for strings & recorders. Original learning methods for piano & organ, also method for learning tenor clef on cello). Mbr., ISM. Hobbies incl: Reading; Writing (incl. diary); Painting; Family music at home and w. friends; being hospitable. Address: Old Brewery, Marnhull, Sturminster Newton, Dorset DT10 1NJ, UK.

JOHNSTON, Benjamin Burwell, Jr., b. 15 Mar. 1926, Macon, Ga., USA. Composer; Professor of Music. Educ: BA, Coll. of Wm. & Mary; M Mus, Cinn. Conserv. of Music; MA, Mills Coll. m. Betty Ruth Hall, 2 s., 1 d. Compositions incl: Celebration (piano), Nine Variations, String Quartets, 2, 3 & 4; One man, A Sea Dirge; Compositions recorded incl: String Quartet No. 2, Carmilla (opera), Mass, Knocking Piece (2 percussionists & piano). Contbr. to music jrnls. Mbrships. incl: ASCAP; Exec. Bd., ASUC; Soc. des Auteurs & Compositeurs Dramatiques. Hons: Guggenheim Fellowship; Nat. Endowment for Arts Grant; Assoc. Mbr., Ctr. for Advanced Studies, Univ. of Ill. Hobbies: Karate; Choir singing. Address: 1403 W. Church St., Champaign, IL 61820, USA. 2,8.

JOHNSTON, David, b. London, UK. Tenor. Educ: studied singing w. Eric Greene & Alexander Young. m. Helen Drew, 2 s. Career: Freelance Tenor, Glyndebourne; app. w. Welsh Nat. Opera & at Aldeburgh, Bath & Three Choirs Fest.; regular Concert Perf., thru'out GB; app. at Holland Fest.; recital tours, Rhodesia & S. Africa; Evangelist in Bach Passions, Elgar's Gerontius, & Verdi's Requiem. Recordings: Messiah; Songs by Peter Warlock, Ivor Gurney, Quilter & Britten & Frank Bridge. Prof.; RCM, London. Mbrships: ISM; Brit. Actor's Equity. Hobbies: Poetry; Railways; Good Beer. Address: 161 Sheen Rd., Richmong, Surrey, UK.

JOHNSTON, Thomas Hamilton, b. 29 Dec. 1928, Motherwell, Scotland, UK. Principal Lecturer in Music, Aberdeen College of Education. Educ: B Mus, MA, Glasgow Univ.; Royal Scottish Acad. of Music & Drama; LRAM (piano perf.); LTCL (recorder tchr.); Tchr.'s Qualification (Second) in Music, Jordanhill Coll. of Educ. Career: sev. broadcasts w. Aberdeen Recorder Consort. Comps: Arrangements of Christmas Carols; Arrangements of Folk Songs; Scottish Country Dances for Recorder Quintet; Mary's Bairn (original carol for soloist & choir). Mbrships: ISM; Dir., N-E Music Schl. Hobbies: Golf; Tennis. Address: 4 Baillieswells Cres., Bieldside, Aberdeen, UK.

JOHNSTONE, Harry Diack, b. 29 Apr. 1935, Vancouver, BC, Can. University Lecturer. Educ: RCM, 1954-57; ARCM; FRCO; FTCL; Mus B., Trinity Coll., Dublin, Ireland, 1957; BA, Oxford Univ., 1960; MA, D Phil, ibid, 1968. m. Jill Margaret Saunders, 1 s., 1 d. Career: Lectr. in Music, Univ. of Reading. Compositions: I Sing of a Maiden That is Makeles (motet), 1957; Asst. Organist, New Coll., Oxford, 1960-61; Asst. Lectr. in Music (1963), Lectr., (1965), Snr. Lectr. (1970), Univ. of Reading. Ed., Var. works, mainly 18th century Engl. music. Contbr. to: Musical Times; Music & Letters; Proceedings of Royal Musical Assn.; Organists' Review-Groves; Mbrships: Royal Musical Assn.; RCO; Am. Musicol. Soc. Recip., Colles Memorial Essay Prize, RCM, 1957. Address: Corner Cottage, Sulhamstead, Reading, Berks. RG7 4BS, UK. 3,28,30.

JOHNSTONE, Maurice, b. 28 July 1900, Manchester, UK. Music Adminstrator; Composer. Educ: RMCM; RCM, (FRMCM, 1955). m. Marguerite Barker, 1 s., 2 d. Career: Freelance, 1923-32; Sec. & Asst. to Sir Thomas Beecham Bart, 1932-35; Music Staff, BBC, 1935-60. Hd., Sound Music Progs., 1953-60. Comps: Tarm Hows; Rhapsody for Orch.; Dover Beach for baritone solo & orch.; Transcriptions & Arrs.; Five original works for brass band; Two marches for brass band (recorded). Hobbies: Gardening. Address: 66 W. Common, Harpenden, Herts., UK. 3.

JOINER, Thomas Witherington, b. 26 April 1954, Columbus, Georgia, USA. Orchestral Musician; Associate Principal Second Violin. Educ: BMus, Violin Perf., Furman Univ., Greenville, SC, 1976; MCM, Musicol., Southern Baptist Theological Seminary, Louisville, Kentucky, 1978. m. Georgia Bunting Joiner, 2 s. Career: Greenville Symph.; Charlotte Symph.; Aspen Music Fest. Orch.; Louisville Orch.; Indianapolis Symph. (Assoc. Prin. Second Violin). Mbrships: Pi Kappa Lambda; Phi Mu Alpha; Am. Fedn. of Musicians; Am. Symph. Orch. League. Hons: Mattie Hipp Cunningham Award for excellence in the Arts, Furman Univ., 1975. Hobbies: Records; Tropical Fish; Bridge; Softball. Address: 5332 N Delaware, Indpls., IN 46220, USA.

JOKINEN, Urpo Oskari, b. 6 Feb. 1920, Hollola, Finland. Music Educator. Educ: TD, 1946; Music Tchrs. Dip., 1961; Univ. of Jyvaskyla; Sibelius Acad., pvte. studies. m. Marjatta Snellman, 4 c. Debut: Choir, Orch. Dir., 1945; Comp., 1950. Career: Dir., var. Choirs, Schl. Orchs.; Province Music Tchr.; Dir., Tchr., num. Music Courses; mbr. num. Curriculum Committees; Ed., Rondo. Compositions in cl: 4 Cantatas; num. Folksongs, choir & accomp.; Children's Choir, Schl. Orch. works; Children's Opera. Recordings: Children's Songs; Prize Comp. from Radio Contest; Finnish Military Marches. Publs. (in Finnish): Mixed choir songs, vols. 158-160, 1960; Songbook for Institute, 1961; Singing Youth, 1962; Singing Congress, 1967. Contbr. to num. mags. & newspapers. Mbrships: Music Tchrs. Union, Finland; Activities Dir., ibid, 1970-; Schl. Music Tchrs. Assn., Middle Org. Aklava; VP, Pres., ibid. Recip. Order of the Knights of the Finnish Lion, 1973. Hobbies: Fishing; Motoring. Address: 9.A.7 Luotsikatu, SF-00160 Helsinki 16, Finland.

JOLY, Simon, b. 14 Oct. 1952, Exmouth, Devon, UK. Conductor; Repetiteur. Educ: Corpus Christi Coll., Cambridge; BA, MA (Cantab.); ARCO; FRCO. Career: Music staff, Welsh Nat. Opera, 1974-78; cond., Barber of Seville, 1978; asst. chorus master, Engl. Nat. Opera, 1978-79; Assoc. chorus master, ibid., 1979-80. Hobbies: Food; Cinema. Address: 58 Fairview Rd., S Tottenham, London N15 6LJ, UK.

JOLY BRAGA SANTOS, José Manuel, b. 14 May 1924, Lisbon, Portugal. Composer; Conductor. Educ: Nat. Conserv. of Music, Lisbon. m. Maria Joeé de Mello Falcao Trigoso, 2 d. Debut: Cond., Sao Carlos Theatre, Lisbon, 1950; Comp., 1942. Comps. incl: 6 Symph.; Nocturne; Elegy to Vianna da Motta; Concerto in D (String Orch.); Variations on an Alentejano Theme; Symph. Overture III; Merope (opera); Concerto for Viola & Orch.; 3 Symphonic Sketches; Requiem; D Garcia (cantata); Choral Comps. on Castilian Classics, chorus a capella; Variations for Orch.; Aria II, cello & piano. Recordings incl: 4th & 5th Symphs.; Sounds of Portugal; Symphonic Overture No. 3; 3 Symphonic Sketches; Nocturne for violin & piano. Contbr. to profl. publs. Mbrships: Sec., APEM; Fndr. Mbr., Portugese Musical Youth; Sec., Nat. Coun. of Music. Hons: Donemus, 1962; Tribune Internationale des Compositeurs, UNESCO, 1966. Mgmt: Santos Beirao, Lda., Rua 1 de Dezembro 2, Lisbon 2, Portugal. Address: Avenida dos Estados Unidos da America, 101 32 Esq. Lisbon 1700, Portugal. 14.

JONÁK, Zdenek, b. 25 Feb. 1917, Prague, Czech. Composer; Chief Music Director, Radio Prague. Educ: studied comp. at Prague Conserv. & Prague Conserv. Master Schl. m. Dagmar Joank, 2 s. Career: Mbr., Music Dept., Radio Prague. Comps. incl: Chamber Symphony; Symphonic Variations; Symphonic Overture; 2 str. quartets; Sonata for cello & piano; Trumpet Concerto; Concerto for brass orch.; num. suites, dances, marches, songs. Contbr. to profl. mags. Mbr., Czech Comp. Soc. Recip. num. prizes. Address: U Spolecenské Zahrady 12, Prague 4, Czechoslovakia.

JONES, Alan Wynne, b. 11 Apr. 1942, Bangor, Wales, UK. Music Adviser. Educ: BA, Music, Univ. Coll., Cardiff; M Ed, Univ. Coll., Aberystwyth. m. Ann Williams, 2 s., 1 d. Career: Hd. of Music Dept., Pool Hayes Comprehensive Schl. Willenhall, Staffs., 1964-65; Hd. of Music Dept., Newtown High Schl., Montgomeryshire, 1965-67; Co. Music Organiser, Cardiganshire, 1967-74; now Music Advsr., Dyfed Co. Coun. Mbrships: Music Panel, W. Wales Assn. for the Arts; Welsh Music Advsrs. Assn. Hons: Morfudd Owen Prize, Univ. Coll., Cardiff, 1963. Hobbies: Reading; Walking. Address: Cemlyn, 35 Maes Ceiro, Bow Street, Dyfed, UK.

JONES, Andrew Vernon, b. 9 Sept. 1947, London, UK. Musicologist; Violinist; Organist; Pianist; Viola Player. Educ: Organ Schlr., St. Peter's Coll., Oxford, 1968-71; BA, ibid, 1971; Cert. Ed., St. Catharine's Coll., Cambridge, 1972. MA Oxon, 1975; RCM, 1965-68; ARCM; ARCO; GRSM. m. Gabrielle Mary McGrath, 2 s. Career: Jr. Lectr., music, Magdalen Coll., Oxford, 1973-75; Snr. Schlrship., St. Peters Coll., Oxford, 1974-75; Burton Sr. Schlrship., Oriel Coll., Oxford, 1975-76; Univ. Asst. Lectr. Music & Fellow, Selwyn Coll., Cambridge, 1976-. Mbrships: Royal Musical Assn.; RCO.

Hons: Sullivan Prize, Comp. & Ella Lord Gilbert Prize, Comp., RCM, 1968. Hobbies: Walking; Gardening. Address: Selwyn Coll., Cambridge, UK.

JONES, (Rev. Dr.) Arthur Morris, b. 4 June 1899, London, UK. Priest; Lecturer in African Music. Educ: MA, D Litt. Oxford Univ.; Dip Ed, London Univ. m. Nora Margaret. Career: Warden, St. Mark's Coll., Mapanza, Zambia, 1929-50; broadcast on African Music, Lusaka, 1947; Lectr., Schl. of Oriental & African Studies, Univ. of London, 1952-66; var. radio lectures, TV demonstrations, etc., BBC. Recording: Theory of African Music. Publs. incl: Studies in African Music, 2 vols., 1959; Africa & Indonesia, 1964, enlarged ed., 1971. Contbr. to encys. & jrnls. Mbrships. incl: African Music Soc., Johannesburg; Int. African Inst. Hobbies: The organ; Wood & metal work. Address: 52 Warwick Rd., St. Albans, Herts., UK.

JONES, Bertram Llywelyn, b. 2 Mar. 1897, E Grinstead, Sussex, UK. Professor of Piano. Educ: Lic., Royal Acad. Music, London; Lic., Trinity Coll. Music, ibid. m. Marion Barry-Vanston. Career: Prof., Piano, Bertram Jones Pianoforte Schl., Belfast, N Ireland; Former organist & choirmaster at Carrickfergus Presby. Ch. & Windsor Ch., Belfast. Mbr., Incorp. Soc. of Musicians. Hobbies: Motoring; Golf; Swimming; Walking. Address: 5 Mount Pleasant, Stranmillis, Belfast, N Ireland, BT9 5DS, UK.

JONES, Bronwen Dilys, b. 28 Apr. 1927, Northampton, UK. Pianist. Educ: B Mus; LRAM, LGSM & LTCL, 1940 (youngest ever to gain these dips. tog.); Tobias Matthay Schl.; Studied w. Louis Kentner. m. Derrick George Buttifant, 2 d. Debut: Northampton, UK, aged 5 yrs. Career: Promenade Concerts; Apps. w. all major Brit. orchs.; Toured Europe; many concerts & broadcasts; Toured USA when aged 12. Hobbies: Gardening; Reading. Address: 73 Sparrow Farm Rd., Stoneleigh, Epsom, Surrey, UK. 3.

JONES, Daniel Jenkyn, b. 7 Dec. 1912, Pembroke, UK. Composer & Conductor. Educ: MA, D Mus, Hon. D L.itt., Swansea Univ. Coll.; ARAM, RAM, London. m. Irene P Goodchild, 1 s., 1 d. Compositions incl: 9 symphs.; Violin Concerto; many other orchl. & chamber works; operas 'The Knife' & 'Orestes'; oratorio 'St. Peter'; Cantatas. Recordings: Symph. No. 6, Pye; Cantata 'The Country Beyond the Stars', EMI; Symph. No. 4, EMI; Symph. No 7, EMI; String Trio 1970, EMI; Str. Quartet 1957, EMI; Kettledrum Sonata, 1947, EMI. Mbrships: PRS; Mechanical Copyright Protection Soc.; CGGB. Hons: 1st Prize, Royal Phil. Soc., 1947; Oliveira Prescott Prize, 1936; Hon. Fellow, Inst. of Arts & Letters, 1963; OBE, 1968, etc. Hobbies: Languages; Chess. Address: 63 Southward Ln., Newton, Mumbles, Swansea, UK. 2,3,14.

JONES, David Hugh, b. 15 Dec. 1932, Leeds, UK. County Music Adviser. Educ: B Mus; Manchester Univ.; London Univ. m. Mary Catherine, 1 s., 1 d. Dpty. Clr. of Music, S Hackney Schl.,London; Asst. Music Org., Lancs. Ed. Cttee.; Coun. Music Advsr., Warwicks LEA. Compositions: Sev. works for Orch. & Voices; Var. Musicals, Vocal Pieces & Instrumental Works for children. Publs: Rhymes & Chimes, 1971. Hobbies: Badminton; Gardening; Political Biography. Address: 30 Rogers Lane, Ettington, Stratford on Avon, Warwicks, UK. 3.

JONES, Della, b. 13 Apr. 1946, Neath, Glam., UK. Opera Singer. Educ: Royal Coll. of Music, 1964-69; GRSM, 1967; ARCM, 1966; LRAM, 1966. Operatic debut: Grand Theatre, Geneva, 1970, in Boris Goudonov. Career incl: Leading roles at Grand Theatre, Geneva, 1970-71; w. Oxford Opera Co., 1972; Engl. Nat. Opera Co., 1973-76; Engl. Music Theatre Co., 1976. Title role in Cenerentola, Radio Telefis Eirann, 1975; var. opera roles, BBC Radio, 1974-. Recordings incl: Opera of Rossini & Handel, in Switzerland, 1970-71. Hons. incl: Tagore Gold Medal for Outstanding Musician of the Yr., 1969; Kathleen Ferrier Mem. Schlrship., 1969. Hobbies incl: Reading; Indoor plants. Mgmt: Music Int., 13 Ardilaun Rd., London N5. Address: 33 Chaffinch Ave., Shirley, Croydon, Surrey, UK.

JONES, Eric, b. 10 Sept. 1948, Pontarddulais, Swansea, Wales, UK. Teacher. Educ: BMus, Univ. Coll., Cardiff; LTCL (piano tchr.); FTCL (comp.). m. Gwen Owen, 1 d. Career: Hd., Music Dept., Mynyddbach Comprehensive Schl., Swansea; accomp., Pontarddulais Male Choir; adjudicator & cond.; Welsh fests. mbr., ISM. recip., Colman Prize, 1972. Address: Glasfryn, 27 Woodlands, Gowerton, Swansea, W Glamorgan, UK.

JONES, George Morton, b. 8 Jan. 1929, Evergreen, Ala., USA. Clarinet Performer & Teacher; Musicologist. Educ: B Mus & Perf.'s Cert. in Clarinet, 1951, M Mus, 1953, Eastman Schl. of Music, Univ. of Rochester; PhD, NY Univ., 1972. m. Arlene

Gerstenberger, 1 s., 1 d. Debut: NYC. Career: Clarinetist, Rochester Phil., Civic & Pops Orchs., 1951-54, Princeton Symph., 1954-65, Trenton (NJ) Symph., 1960-65, Princeton Collegium Musicum, 1969-76, Douglass Coll. Woodwind Quintet, 1969-76; Dir., Douglass Coll. Clarinet Ensemble, 1956-76; on Music Dept. Fac., Douglass Coll., 1954-; Clarinetist, Tanglewood Yaddo Fests., 1952; Prin. Clarinet, Nat. Opera Orch., 1978. Contbr. to Musik in Geschichte und Gegenwart; The Clarinet. Address: 130 Shady Brook Ln., Princeton, NJ 08540, USA.

JONES, George Thaddeus, b. 6 Nov. 1917, Asheville, NC, US. Composer; Author; Theorist. Educ: AB Univ. of NC, 1938; MA, Eastman Schl. of Music, Univ. of Rochester, 1942; PhD., ibid, 1950. m. Mary Peres Jones, 2 d. Career incl: Prof. of Music, The Cath. Univ. of Am. Comps. incl: 2 operas; 2 symphs.; chmbr. & vocal music. Publs: Music Composition, 1963; Symbols Used in Music Analysis, 1964; Music Theory, 1974. Mbrships: ASCAP; Am. Musicological Soc. Hons: Fulbright Rsch. Grant, Italy, 1953-54; US State Dept. Cultural Exchange to Romania, 1967-68. Hobby: Photography. Address: 6012 84th Ave., New Carrollton, MD 20784, USA.

JONES, Geraint Iwan, b. 16 May 1917, Porth, Wales,UK. Conductor; Organist; Harpsichordist. Educ: FRAM. m. (1) MA Kemp (2) Winifred Roberts, 1 d. Debut: Nat. Gall. Concerts, 1941. Career: 16 recitals of complete organ works of London, 1945-46; Musical Dir., Mermaid Theatre, 1950-53; Fndr., Geraint Jones Singers & Orch., 1951; Num. tours of Europe & USA; Dir., Lake Dist. Festival, 1960-; Salisbury Festival, 1973-; Frequent apps. at Promenade Concerts; Sonata recitals w. violinist wife, Winifred Roberts, Prof. RAM; Num. broadcasts as soloist & cond. Var. recordings inclng. on historic organs for BBC since 1949. Recip. Grande Prix du Disque, 1959 & 66. Hobbies: Antiques; Photography; Reading. Address: The Long House, Arkley Land, Barnet, Herts., UK. 1, 21.

JONES, Gwendolyn K, b. 12 Apr. 1948, Tulsa, Okla, USA. Professional Mezzo Soprano. Educ: B Mus, Okla City Univ., 1971. m. John R Miller. Career: San Fran. Opera, 1971-74; San Fran. Spring Opera Theater, 1971, 72, 74, 76; Carnegie Hall Debut w. Chgo. Symph., 1973; San Diego Opera, 1970; Phila. Lyric Opera, 1973; Tucson Opera Co., 1975; Apps. w. Miami Phil. Orch., 1973, Chgo. Symph. Orch., 1973, Okla. City Symph., 1970 & 73; Affiliate Artist, Sponsored by Sears Roebuck & Nat. Endowment for the Arts, Tucson, Ariz. Opera Co., 1975-76. Mbr., Alpha Zeta Chapt., Sigma Alpha Iota. Recip., num. hons. Hobbies incl: Cooking. Address: Address: 1459 Green St., San Fran., CA 94109, USA.

JONES, Gwyneth, b. 7 Nov. 1936, Pontnewynydd, Wales, UK. Opera Singer. Educ: RCM; Chigiana Acad., Siena; Int. Opera Studio Zurich. m. Till Haberfeld. Career: Mbr., Royal Opera House, Covent Gdn., & State Opera, Vienna; has made Guest Apps. w. La Scala, Milan, Bayreuth Fest., Rome Opera Co., German Opera, Berlin, Bavarian State Opera, Munich, Colon Theatre, Buenos Aires, opera house in Paris, NYC, Tokyo, Zurich, Geneva, Hamburg, San Fran., & Chgo.; roles incl. Leonora (Trovatore), Desdemona, Fidelio, Aida, Marschallia, Salome, Sieglinde, Brunnhilde, Kundry. Recordings incl: Mahler's 8th Symphony; Mendelssohn's Elijah; Strauss's Rosenkavalier & Saloma; Verdi's Otello; Wagner's Gotterdammerung, Der fliegende Hollander, Lohengrin & Parsifal; also several recital & opera excerpt records. Hons: CBE; Dr.l.c., Univ. of Wales; Kammersängerin, Austria & Bavaria. Address: PO Box 380, 8040 Zürich, Switzerland 3.

JONES, Harold Ian, b. 10 March 1942, Diego Martin, Trinidad. Economist; Steelband Musician (Soprano & Alto Steelpan). Educ: BA, MA Econ.; Pvte. guitar & piano studies. Debut: Trinidad & Tobago Steelband Music Fest., 1962. Career: Played w. Invaders & Starlift Steelbands, Trinidad; led Queen's Univ. Steelband, Kingston, Int., 1965-71; Musical Dir., Trinbyrds Steelband, Toronto, Ont., 1975-; Steelband Instructor, Georges Vanier Secondary Schl., N York Bd. of Educ., Toronto, 1977-; Lead soprano player, Trinbyrds Steelband, 1975-. Comps: Comp., arr. & prod. music for Poetry & Pan; Arr., Trinbago Bound. Recordings: First Flight. Mbr., Am. Fedn. of Musicians. Hobbies: Soccer; Tennis; Music listening; TV sports; Reading. Address: 115 Tyndall Ave., Apt. 705, Toronto, Ont. M6K 2G3, Can.

JONES, J Earl, b. 6 Dec. 1939, Berea, Ky., USA. Trumpeter; Recorder; Tenor Recitalist; Counter-tenor; Krumhorn, Cornetto, Cornamusa, Kortholt, Oriental Shawm, & Crumhorn Player. Educ: BS, M Mus, Miami Univ., Oxford, Ohio; Paris Am. Acad., France; Berks. Music Ctr., Lenox, Mass. Career: Trumpet Recitalist; Instrumental Music Tchr., Middletown Pub. Schls.,

Miami Univ., Ohio; Pvte. Trumpet Tchr. Mbrships incl: Am. Musicol. Soc.; Royal Musical Assn.; Dolmetsch Fndn.; MENC; Friends of Netherlands Music; Samfundet, Denmark. Hobbies: Record Collecting; Travel; Reading; English & Bulgarian culture. Address: 867 S Main St., Monore, OH 45050, USA.

JONES, Jeanne Nannette, b. 4 June 1948, Lake City, Fla., USA. Violinist; Music Educator. Educ: BM, Jacksonville Univ., Fla.; BME, ibid; MMus, Coll. Conserv. of Music, Univ. of Cinn., Ohio; Brevard Music Ctr., NC; Am. String Tchrs. Assn. Workshop, Austria, 1972; Kato Havas Summer Violin Schl., UK, 1973; Rome Fest. Orch. Summer Inst., Italy, 1974. Debut: Jacksonville, Fla., 1964. Career: Prin. 2nd Violin, Jacksonville Symph.; Orch. Instructor, Duval County Schls., Fla. Mbrships: Pres., Beta Beta Chapt., Pres., Jacksonville Alumni. Mu Phi Epsilon; Pi Kappa Lambda; Green Key Hon. Ldrship. Soc.; Jacksonville Univ.; MENC; Am. String Tchrs. Assn.; Nat. Schl. Orch. Assn.; Fla. Music Educators Assn.; Fla. Orch. Assn.; Am. Fedn. of Musicians, Delta Kappa Gamma. Hons: Jacksonville Univ. Presidential Scholarship, 1965-69; Mu Phi Epsilon Chapt. Scholastic Award, 1968; Univ. of Cinn. Grad. Asst. in Strings, 1969-71. Hobbies: Reading; Macrame; Swimming; Tennis. Address: 4770 Apache Ave., Jacksonville, FL 32210, USA.

JONES, Jonathan Barrie, b. 23 Apr. 1946, Prestwich, UK. University Research Fellow in Music; Pianist. Educ: Mus B, 1969, MA, 1972, PhD, 1974, Downing Coll., Univ. of Cambridge; ARCO, ARCM, Royal Northern Coll. of Music. Career: Organ Scholar, Downing Coll., Cambridge, 1965-68; Supvsr. in Music, ibid., 1970-73; Rsch. Asst. in Music, Open Univ., 1972-75; Rsch. Fellow in Music, ibid., 1976-. Mbrships incl: Life, Royal Musical Assn.; Life, Downing Coll. Assn.; The Cambridge Soc. Publs: From Classical to Romantic Keyboard Music, 1974; Tonality and Modulation, 1978; Debussy, 1979. Hons: Limpus Prize, ARCO, 1964; Distinction in Mus B, 1969. Hobbies: Travel; Good food & its preparation; Railway holidays. Address: 46 Western Dr., Hanslope, Milton Keynes, Bucks. MK19 7LD, UK.

JONES, Jonathan James Hellyer, b. 1 June 1951, Tanworth-in-Arden, Warwicks., UK. Organist; Harpsichordist; Pianist; Teacher. Educ: ARCM, 1970; BA, St. Johns Coll., Cambridge Univ., 1973; FRCO, 1973. widower. Career: Apps. on BBC radio & TV; has sung w. Cambridge Univ. Musical Soc. Chorus & Cambridge Univ. Chamber Choir. Recitals, London & Cambridge; Asst. Organist, Emmanuel Coll. Chapel Cambridge, 2 yrs. Recordings as Chorister w. St. John's Coll. Choir Cambridge. Mbr., Cambridge Union Soc. Hons: John Stewart of Rannoch Scholarship in Sacred Music, 1972; Brian Runnett Prize for Organ Playing, 1972. Hobbies incl: Travel; Theatre; Foreign Cuisine; Renaissance & Baroque Music. Address: 22 Covent Garden, Cambridge, UK.

JONES, Joyce Gilstrap, b. 13 Feb. 1933, Taylor, Tex., USA. Concert Organist. Educ: B Mus., Univ. of Tex., 1952; M Mus., ibid, 1953; DMA., 1970; MSM, S Western Bapt. Theol. Sem., 1957. m. Lt.-Col. RC Jones, 1 s., 2 d. debut: Dallas Symph. Orch., 1958. Career: Organ concerts throughout USA, Canada & Europe, 1959-; Only woman organist playing for Community Concert Assn.; Organist in Residence & Chmn. of Organ Dept., Baylor Univ., Waco, Tex. Recordings: Joyce Jones Plays the Tuffati Organ at Baylor University; American Beauties; And Give Him Praise. Publs: The Joyce Jones Collection - Hymn Preludes; Joyce Jones Pedal Technique (2 vol.). Contbr. to: Jrnl. of Ch. Music. Mbrships: Fellow, AGO; Pi Kappa Lambda; Mu Phi Epsilon. Hons: 1st Prize, GB Dealey Ward, 1958; 1st place, organ div., Nat. Fedn. of Music Clubs Student Auditions, 1953. Hobbies: Gardening; Collecting antiques; Sewing; Cooking. Mgmt: Roberta Bailey Artists Int., Boston, USA. Address: 3525 Carondolet, Waco, TX 76710, USA. 3,5.

JONES, Kelsey, b. 17 June 1922, S Norwalk, Conn., USA. Composer; Harpsichord Player; Teacher. Educ: B Mus, Mt. Allison Univ., 1946; B Mus, 1947, D Mus, 1951, Univ. of Toronto, Can. m. Rosabelle Jones. Career: Dept. of Music Theory, Mt. Allison Univ., 1947-48; Cond., Saint John's Symph. Orch., 1950-54; Prof., Fac. of Music, McGill Univ. (current). Comps. publd: Miramichi Ballas (symphonie); Quintet for Winds; Sonata da Camera (flute, oboe, harpsichord); Five Limericks (chorus); Rondo for Solo Flute; Nonsense Songs (chorus). Other works incl. chmbr. oper Sam Slick. Mbr., Can. League of Comps. Hobby: Gardening. Address: Cook's Lines, Athelstan, PQ, Canada.

JONES, Kenneth Victor, b. 14 May 1924, Bletchley, Bucks., UK. Composer; Conductor; Professor. Educ: Queen's Coll., Oxford; RCM; Hon. ARCM; ARCO. m. Annemarie C. Heine, 1 d., 1 s. Debut: Royal Festival Hall, London. Career: Asst. Organist, Choirmaster, St. Michael's Coll., Tenbury, 1941;

RAF, 1942-47; Asst. Cond., London Symphonic Players, 1952, Redhill & Reigate Choral Soc., 1956-64, Hill Singers, Wimbledon, 1954-60; Prof., RCM, 1958; Cond., Wimbledon Symph., 1961-70; Fndr., ibid; Pres., ibid, 1970-; Cond., Sinfonia of London, 1966-70; Fndr., Mbr., Gov.,Rokeby Educl. Trust, 1966-; Vis. Tutor, Univ. of Sussex, 1971-73. Compositions incl: 2 Sinfoniettas; 4 Sonatas; 2 Wind Quintets; Str. Quartet; 4 works for orch.; 6 song cycles, collections; 2 brass works; 3 Concerti; 2 Cantatas; 44 piano works; 24 works for violin, viola & cello & piano; about 74 film, play, TV scores; 2 ensembles; var. Ch. music; Dialysis; Remembrancer of an Inward Eye. Recordings: Dialysis Chorale, Ceremony & Toccata; Organ Sonata No. 1; Publs: num. books publd. by RSM; J & W Chester/Wilhelm Hansen. Mbr., Off., num. profl. orgs. Recip. RPS Prize, 1950. Address: Hickwells, Cinderhill, Chailey, nr. Lewes, Sx., UK. 3.

JONES, Martin Edwin Mervyn, b. 4 Feb. 1940, Witney, UK. Concert Pianist. Educ: RAM; Chigiana Acad., Siena, Italy; LRAM; Hon. ARAM; ARCO; ARCM. m. Patricia Strong, 2 s. Debut: Queen Elizabeth Hall, 1969. Career: frequent radio broadcasts; concert apps., USA, France, Belgiu, Germany, Italy, etc.; Pianist-in-Res., Cardiff Univ. Recordings incl: piano music of Szymanowski, Busoni & Rawsthorne (on Argo); Williamsons Sinfonie Concertante (EMI); Hoddinott's Piano Concerto (Decca); also chmbr. music by Kodaly, Delius, Prokofiev, Hindemith, Copeland, Ives, Strauss & Reger. Hons. incl: Dame Myra Hess Trust Award, 1968. H bbies: Model making; Home decorating. Mgmt: Ibbs & Tillett, London. Address: 11 Llwyn-y-Grant Rd., Penylan, Cardiff CF3 7ET, UK. 3.

JONES, Mary Olwen, b. 18 Oct. 1937, Hamilton, Vic., Aust. Horn Player; Teacher of Horn. Educ: B Mus, Melbourne Univ. (Tchr, Roy White). 1960; Horn studies w. Philip Farkas, Ind Univ., USA, 1972. Career: Horn Player w. Aust. Broadcasting Commission's Symph. Orchs. in Sydney, Melbourne, Adelaide & Hobart, 1958-65; Prin. Horn, Qld. Symph. Orch., Brisbane, 1966-; Mbr., Aulos Wind Quintet, ibid., 1967-; Tchr. of Horn, Qld. Conserv. of Music & Univ. of Queensland; Horn Tutor, Qld. Youth Orch., & Nat. Music Camp Assn., 1967-76; Horn tchr., Qld. Univ., 1976-. Recordings: as Mbr. of var. orchs., and as Soloist in concerti, solo recitals & Chmbr. music (Aust. Broadcasting commission studio recordings). Mbr., Int. Horn Soc. Hobbies: Gardening; Reading; Stamp Collecting. Address: 52 Wongabel St., Kenmore, Qld. 4069, Australia.

JONES, Patricia Collins, b. 27 July 1943, Lebanon, Pa., USA. Musicologist; Pianist. Educ: New England Conserv. of Music, 1961-64; B Mus Piano, Juilliard Schl. of Music, 1966; MFA, Ohio Univ., 1968; PhD studies, Rutgers Univ., 1972-. m. Richard E. Jones. Career incls: Instructor in Music Theory & Piano, Univ. of NC, 1970-72; Instructor in music theory & rsch. asst., Rutgers Univ., 1973-75; Instr. in music, Open Univ., Prof., ibid., 1975-76. Soloist w. orch., Solo recitals, Chmbr. music perfs. Publs. incl: An Introduction to the Fundamentals of Music (textbook), 1975. Contbr. to musical publs. Mbr., profl. assns. Recip., var. Fellowships, Assistantships & Scholarships. Hobbies: Cooking. Address: 9028 N 75th St., Milwaukee, WI 53223, USA.

JONES, Philip, b. 12 March 1928, Bath, UK. Trumpet Player; Director. Educ: RCM. m. Ursula Strebi. Career: Prin. Trumpet, all major London orchs.; Fndr., Dir., Philip Jones Brass Ensemble, 1951; Hd., Schl. of Wind & Percussion, Royal Northern Coll. of Music, 1975-77. Approx. 30 recordings w. Philip Jones Brass Ensemble. Co-Ed., Just Brass. Hons: OBE; FRNCM; ARCM. Hobbies: History; Mountain Walking; Skiing. Mgmt: Ursula Strebi, 14 Hamilton Tce., London NW8, UK. Address: c/o Mgmt.

JONES, Philip, b. 4 June 1933, Aberdare, S Wales, UK. Oboist. Educ: RCM; Paris Conserv. Career incls: Mbr., Mabillon Trio, 1957-66, Venturi Ensemble, 1965-70; Prin. Oboist, Sadler's Wells, 1963-69, BBC Welsh Orch.; Oboe Tutor, Cardiff Univ., 1964-69; Oboe Tutor & Chmbr. Music Coach, Royal Northern Coll. of Music, 1974-75; num. solo & chmbr. perfs. & broadcasts throughout UK & abroad. Hobbies: Reading; Poetry; Theatre; Films; Paintings; Food & Wine France; Golf. Address: 20 Nassau St., London, W1, UK.

JONES, Ralph, b. 9 July 1951, Phila., Pa., USA. Composer & Performer (electronic instruments). Educ: BA, State Univ. of NY, Buffalo, 1973; MA, SUNYAB, 1976; pvte. studies w. Julius Eastman, Jacob Druckman, Lejaren Hiller (comp.), Robert A Moog (electronics design), & Vasulkas (video). Career: Grad. Fellow, Ctr. of Creative & Performing Arts, Buffalo, 1973-75, Dir. of Research Design, Media Study, Buffalo, 1975-77,

Instructor, NY State Summer Schl. of Arts, 1976-78; Perfs. in Tanglewood, NH, Buffalo, Darmstadt, Paris & NY; Exhibitions in Buffalo, Brooklyn & Paris. Comps. incl: Circuitree, 1974; Chants Home-Passage, 1977; Star Networks at the Singing Point, 1978 (all electronic). Publs: (in press) On the Development of a Transposing Microphone for Airborne Ultrasound. Mbrships: Am. Music Ctr.; Fdnr. mbr., Composers inside Electronics. sev. grants. Address: 2001 Pierce St., No. 65, San Francisco, CA 94115, USA.

JONES, Richard Elfyn, b. 11 April 1944, Merionethshire, Wales, UK. Conductor; Composer; Organist; University Lecturer. Educ: Univ. of Wales, Bangor; King's Coll., Cambridge; BA; MMus; PhD; FRCO. m. Gill Owens. Career: Musical Dir., Cardiff Polyphonic Choir, 1977-; Welsh Vocal Ensemble. Comps: Choral and Instrumental music. Recordings: The Voluntaries of John Stanley. Hons: Limpus Prize, FRCO, 1967. Address: 41 Dorchester Ave., Penylan, Cardiff, UK.

JONES, Robert Milton, b. 5 Feb. 1944, Dallas, Tex., USA. Music Librarian; Oboist. Educ: BMus.Ed., Tex. Christian Univ., Fort Worth, Tex., 1967; MLS, N Texas State Univ., Denton, Tex., 1970. Career: Hd., Music Acquisitions Division, Music Lib., Univ. of Ill., Urbana, 1971-78; Hd., Music Bibliographic Rsch. Unit, Univ. Libs., ibid., 1978-. Publs: Study Scores & Performing eds. of Wind Chamber Music, 1974; Study Scores & Performing eds. of Percussion Music, 1974. Contbr. to: Notes, jrnl. of Music Lib. Assn.; Popular Music, A Survey of Books, Folios & Periodicals, w. index to recently reviewed recordings; Choice; Lib Jrnl Mbrships: Internationalen Vereinigung der Musikbibliotheken; Music Lib. Assn.; Am. Lib. Assn.; Am. Musicol. Assn.; Soc. for Ethnomusicol. Hobbies: Antiques; Art Nouveau; Glass; Pottery; Paperweights. Address: 902 West Nevada, Urbana, IL 61801, USA.

JONES, Roland Leo, b. 16 Dec. 1932, Ann Arbor, Mich., USA. Performer & Teacher of Violin & Viola. Educ: BMus, Univ. of Mich.; 5 yrs. study in NYC at Columbia Univ. & pvtely.; 3 yrs. w. Nat. Orch. Assn. Trng. Orch.; summers at Interlochen Music Camp, Meadowmount Music Schl. & Tanglewood Music Schl. m. Carol Anne Day. Career: Soloist w. Ann Arbor Civic Symph., 1951 & '53; Violinist, Denver Symph. Orch., 1960-74; Jackson Hole, Wyo., Fine Arts Fest., 1964-65; Tours throughout USA & Can.; Fndr. & 1st Violinist, Highland Chmbr. Players, 1978-79. Recordings: w. orch., Milena by Alberto Ginastera & Concerto No. 2 of Chopin. Mbrships: Colo. MTA; MTNA; Musicians Soc. of Denver Inc.; Denver Art Museum. Recip. scholarships to Interlochen Nat. Music Camp & Tanglewood Music Schl. Hobbies: Painting in oils, pastels, ink. Address: 3004 S Kearney, Denver, CO 80222, USA.

JONES, Timothy Russell Hellyer, b. 3 Apr. 1956, Tanworth-in-Arden, UK. Baritone Singer; Teacher of Singing, Piano, Flute & Bassoon. Educ: St. John's Coll. Choir Schl.; BA, St. John's Coll., Cambridge, 1977; Cert. Educ., 1978; Assoc., Royal Coll. Music, 1975. Debut: Royal Albert Hall, London, 1979. Career: Lay-clerk, Worcester Cathedral, 1978-; Music tchr., King's Schl., Worcester, 1978 & Malvern Girls' Coll., 1979. Recordings b. St. John's Coll. Choir & Worcester Cathedral Choir. Mbr., Incorp. Soc. of Musicians. Hobbies: Opera; Watching cricket; Home-brewing. Address: 3 Coll. Precincts, Worcester, WR1 2LG, UK.

JONES, Thomas Gwynn, b. 15 Jan. 1921, Tregarth, Bangor, Gwynedd, UK. Headmaster. Educ: BA, Univ. Coll. of N Wales; LTCL; LLCM. m. Bronwen M. Owen, 2 d. Career: Headmaster, Ysgol Bod Alaw, Colwyn Bay, Clwyd; apps. on TV & radio as singer, Accomp., Quizmaster & Presenter; Music Adjudicator, Nat. Eisteddfod of Wales, Tees-Side Int. Eisteddfod, Scottish Nat. Mod., Irish Oireachtas, etc.; Cond., singing fests., Wales, Engl., USA, Argentina; Music Examiner, Nat. Eisteddfod of Wales Exams. Comps. recorded incl: Diolch i'r lôr; Children's Songs; Two Carols. Mbrships. incl: Pres., Cymdeithas Cerdd Cant Cymru, 1976-77. Hons. incl: Grand Swordbearer, Gorsedd of Bards, Nat. Eisteddfod, 1967-. Hobbies: Crosswords; Ornithol. Address: Drws-y-Nant, Llanfairfechan, Gwynedd LL33 OSE UK.

JONES, Trevor Alan, b. 18 Dec. 1932, Sydney, NSW, Aust. Professor of Music; Ethnomusicologist; Composer; Performer (bassoon, harpsichord, recorder, didjeridu). Educ: BA, Sydney Univ., 1954; MA, ibid., 1959; L Mus, NSW Conserv. Music; Harvard Univ., USA; King's Coll., Cambridge; UK; RCM, London. m. Ann Leah Isaac, 2 s., 2 d. Career incls: Fndn. Prof., Music & Chmn., Dept. Music, Monash Univ., Clayton Vic., 1965-. Compositions incl: (recorded) Cantata Zoologica. Recordings incl: The Art of the Didjeridu. Publs. incl: Arnhem Land Music (w. AP Elkin), 1958. Contbr. to profl. publs. Mbr. var. orgs. Hons. incl: Univ. Medal, Music, Univ. Sydney, 1953. Hobbies incl: Reading. Address: 5 Williamson St., Berwick, Vic. 3806, Aust. 15, 14.

JONES, William John, b. 30 Nov. 1926, Pontiac, Mich., USA. Music Historian-Teacher; Flutist, Techer; Piccolo, Alto Flute. Educ: AB Taylor Univ., BSED., MA., Wayne Univ.; PhD., Northwestern Univ.; Pvte. study of flute w. August Witteborg, Otto Krueger, Arla Kluge. m. Virginia Ann Lee, 5 d. Career: Flutist w. Roanoke, Va., Battle Creek, Mich., Pontiac, Mich. & Mobile, Ala., orchs.; Prof., Music, Univ. of S Ala. Contbr. to profl. jrnls. Mbrships: Am. Fedn. of Musicians; AAUP; MENC; MTNA; Coll. Music Soc.; Phi Mu Alpha Sinfonia. Hons: Nat. Hon. Soc.; Cum Laude grad., Taylor Univ. Hobbies: Stamps; Electronics; Golf. Address: 309 Judson Dr., Mobile AL 36608, USA. 7.

JONES, Wynford Lyn, b. 11 Oct. 1948, Merthyr Tydfil, UK. Teacher. Educ: BA, Music, Univ. Leeds; Grad. Cert., Educ.; ARCM. m. Julie Avril Fellingham, 1 s. Career: Began tchrng., Wakefield, Yorks.; Cond., small grp. singers, Radio Leeds, 1973; Cond., Wakefield Youth Choir; Dpty. Cond., Dowlais Male Voice Choir, 1975, making cond. debut w. them, Luxembourg Cathedral during tour, May 1975; sev. concerts & on BBC Wales TV, Nov. 1975; Musical Dir., Dowlais Male Voice Choir, 1977; has cond. over 70 concerts incl. 2 apps. at Royal Albert Hall; Cond., Wales' 1st Royal Gala Concert; app. French TV, 1978. Recording w. Dowlais MVC, 1978, 1976. Mbr., ISM. Hon: Winner, Radio Leeds Christmas Carol Comp., 1969. Hobbies: Watching Rugby; Boxing referee. Address: 3 Sycamore Close, Landare Pk., Aberdare, Glam., UK. 4,30.

JONSON, Guy, b. London, UK. Pianist. Educ: Tobias Matthay Pianoforte Schl.; RAM; LRAM (Perf's Dip.); ARAM, 1936; FRAM, 1955. m. Patricia Burrell, 2 d. Career: Num. solo recitals, Wigmore Hall, London & Provincial music socs.; BBC, CBC Broadcasts; Instrumental Adjudicator, all prin. music fests., GB & Eire, & Federated Can. Fests., 1954, '60, '63; External Examiner, RSAM, Royal Irish Acad. of Music, Royal Manchester Coll. of Music; Prof., Tobias Matthay Pfte. Schl., 1937-40; Prof., RAM, 1946-; Tutor, 1968-; Examiner, Assoc. Bd. of the RSM, 1946-; Overseas tours, Brit. W Indies, 1952, S Africa, 1955, Malta, 1969. Publs: Musical Initiative Tests for Teachers Diploma Exams, 1958. Mbrships: Coun. Mbr., ISM, 1968-71; Past Pres., Sec., 1969-, RAM Club. Hons: Num. competitive prizes, RAM, inclng. Walter Macfarren Gold Medal; Ada Lewis Schol., RAM, 1930-35; Mbr., Royal Phil. Soc., 1947. Hobbies: Oriental philosophies; Photography. Address: 18 Bracknell Gardens, London NW3 7EB, UK. 3, 30.

JORDA, Enrique, b. 24 Mar. 1911, San Sebastian, Spain. Orchestra Conductor. Educ: Colegio Santa Maria, San Sebastian; Ctrl. Univ., Madrid; Sorbonne Univ., Paris; studied w. Paul Le Flem, Marcel Dupre. m. Audrey D Blaes, 2 d. Debut: Paris Symph., 1938. Career: Cond., Madrid Symph., 1940-45, Capetown Symph., 1948-54, San Francisco Symph., 1954-63, Antwerp Phil. Compositions: Ballets; Choral Music. Recordings: Decca; Columbia; Vox; Polydor; RCA Victor; Comps. Recordings: Hispavox. Author, El Director de Orquesta Ante la Partituro, 1969. Contbr. to La Vanguardia, Barcelona. Hons: Prize Conde de Caratgena, Acad. of Fine Arts, Madrid, 1941: Comendador of the Order Alfonso el Sabio, 1958. Hobby: Reading. Mgmt: Charles Kiesgen, 252 Faubourg, Saint-Honore, Paris. Address: 47 Rue Sellaer, 1910 Melsbroek, Brussels, Belgium.

JORDAN, Armin, b. 1932, Lucerne, Switz. Conductor. Educ: Univ. & Conserv. of Fribourg, Switz. m. Kathe Herkner, 2 c. Career: Artistic Dir., Orchestre de Chambre de Lausanne; Musical Dir., Basler Orchester-Gesellschaft, Basel. Recordings w. Orchestre de Chambre de Lausanne & Orchestre de Monte Carlo. Address: Chapfstrasse 53, CH 8126 Zumikon, Switz.

JORDAN, David, b. 8 Dec. 1930, Stockport, England. Conductor; Director of Opera. Educ: FRMCM; studied w. Iso Elinson & Sir John Barbirolli. m. Eleanor Bettye Cox, 1 s., 2 d. Career: Staff Cond., Royal Manchester Coll. of Music Symph. Orch., Chamber Orch. & Opera, 1959-72: Staff cond. & Dir. of opera, Royal Northern Coll. of Music, 1972-; conducted in Austria, Germany, Aust., Denmark, etc. Recordings: w. coll. orchs. & operas, for BBC. Hons. Ricordi Prize (conducting), 1956; Royal Manchester Instn. Medal (conducting), 1958; FRNCM, 1978. Hobbies: Gardening; Ornithology; Travel. Address: 52 Stockport Rd., Hyde, Cheshire SK 14 5QG, UK. 3.

JORDAN, John William, b. 24 Nov. 1941, Birmingham, UK. Master of the Music, Chelmsford Cathedral; Examiner. Educ: Organ Schlr., Emmanuel Coll., Cambridge, 1959; BA, 1962; MusB, 1963; MA, 1966; FRCO, 1961. Career: Master of the Music, Chelmsford Cathedral, 1965-; Examiner, RSM, 1971-. Mbrships: Pres., Inc. Assn. Organists, 1975-77; Special Commnr., RSCM; Life, RCO. Hons: Reade & Limpus prizes, RCO, 1961. Address: 56 Queens Rd., Chelmsford, Essex, CH2 6HG, UK.

JORDAN, Robert, b. 25 June 1944, Reading, UK. Bassoonist. Educ: BA, St. Edmund Hall, Oxford Univ., 1967; Royal Acad. of Music, 1957-62; BBC Trng. Orch., 1967-69. Career: Fndr. Mbr., Athena Ensemble, 1969-; Co-prin. Bassoon, Sadlers Wells Orch. (now Engl. Nat. Opera Orch.), 1969-; Prin. Bassoon, Richard Hickox Orch., 1971-; freelance musician w. var. major orchs. & chmbr. grps.; frequent broadcasts, especially w. Athena Ensemble. Num. recordings issued. Address: 58 Deangarden Rise, High Wycombe, Bucks, UK.

JORDANS, Hein Jacobus Maria, b. 24 Sept. 1914, Venlo, Limburg, The Netherlands. Conductor. Educ: Conserv. Amsterdam; Musikakademie Salzburg. m. (1) Jacqueline Dassen, 3 c. (2) Antoinette Cooymans, 4 c. Career: Second Cond., Arnhem Orch.; First Cond., Maastricht Orch.; Second Cond., Concertgebouworkest, Amsterdam; First Cond., Het Brabants Orkest, s-Hertogenbosch; First Cond., Overijssels Phil. Orkest Enschede. Recordings: cond. Het Brabants Orkest, J Chr. Bach, Sinfonia; Dvorak, 9th Symph.; Beethoven, 3rd Symph. 'Eroica'; Brahms & Bruch, Violin concerto (soloist Herman Krebbers); Tchaikowski, 1st Piano concerto; Rachmaninoff, 2nd piano concerto (soloist Jacques Klein). Mbrships: Culturele Raad Noord-Brabant; Provinciaal Genootschap voor Kunsten en Wetenschappen Noord-Brabant. Hons: Provincial Prize of Music, Noord-Brabant, 1955; Kt. Order of Orange Nassau, 1960; Kt. Crown Order of Belgium, 1965. Hobby: Golf. Address: Abelenlaan 5, St. Michielsgestel, The Netherlands.

JORDANS, Wieke Maria Hubert, b. 6 May 1922, Venlo, Holland. Conductor. Educ: Piano & Organ, Conserv., Amsterdam; Conducting, Mozarteum, Salzburg. m. H C Peddemors, 4 children. Debut: 1947. Career: Cond.; Venlona, Koninklyk s'Hertogenbosch' Mannenkoor, Venlose Oratorium Vareniging; Amsterdams Studentenorkest; Tegels Symphonie-Orkest, Almalo's Mannenkoor; Kerkkoor HL. Familierkerk; Frequent Cond.; Mozarteum Orch., Salzburg, Austria; Brabants Orch.; Limburg Symph. Orch. Num. unpublished comps. Mbr. Koninklyke Toonkunstenaars Vereniging. Address: Goltziusstraat 13, Venlo, Holland.

JØRGENSEN, Jesper, b. 16 July 1946, Copenhagen, Denmark. Oboe & Viola Player; Conductor. Educ: Studied viola w. var. tchrs.; studied oboe w. Paul Tofte-Hausen; Cond. studies, Royal Acad. of Music, Copenhagen, w. Arne Hammelboe; Music Science, Univ. of Copenhagen. Career: Solo oboe player & Asst. Cond., Tivoli Light Orch.; Num. concerts, Denmark & Sweden (Chmbr. Music, Ch. Music) & as Cond. of own Orch.; Studio host & Prod. of Chmbr. Music, Radio Denmark. Comp. & Arr. of film music. Sev. recordings. Mbrships: Center of Historical Music; Danish Organ Soc. Hobbies: Ornithology; Photography. Address: Mosevej 51 -Agerup, 4000 Roskilde, Denmark.

JØRGENSEN, Poul, b. 26 Oct. 1934, Copenhagen, Denmark. Conductor. Educ: Musicol., Univ. of Copenhagen; Royal Acad. of Music, Copenhagen. m. Marianne Jorgensen, 1 d. Debut: Copenhagen, 1959. Career: Asst. Permanent Cond., Royal Opera, Copenhagen; Royal Cond., 1964; Guest Cond. w. major European orchs. Contbr. on musico-pol. subjects to Danish reviews. Chmn., Danish State Music Coun. Hons: Awards at Besançon, 1959, & Stockholm, 1964; Kt. of the Dannebroz. Hobbies: Cooking; Gardening. Mgmt: Royal Opera House, Copenhagen. Address: Aurikelvej 18, 2500 Copenhagen, Denmark.

JORYSZ, Walter, b. 1 May 1919, Breslau, Germany. Violinist. Educ: landesmusikschule, Schlesien; studies w. Prof. Szephazy, Max Rostal; LLCM (VT). m. Elizabeth Mary Scarr, 1 s. Career: Prof., RNCM, City of Leeds Coll. of Music; ldr., Manchester Sinfonia, Sheffield Bach Players; Recitalist. Contbr. to The Strad. Mbrships: ISM; ESTA. Hobbies: Fellwalking; Photography; Motoring. Address: 88 Beckett's Park Dr., Leeds LS6 3PL, UK.

JOSEF, Ladislav, b. 12 Oct. 1907, Novy Bydzov, Hradec Králové, Czech. Violinist; Teacher; Headmaster. Educ: Prague Conserv.; State Examination for Conductors. m. Vera Svobodová, 2 s. Career: Tchr., Music Schl., 1932; Headmaster, 1958; Prof., Realue Gymnasium, Kolln; Concert Master, later Cond., Filharmonie Kolln. Comps: Koncertino F dur, for violin; Trifles, for violin; Polka, for 2 violins & piano; Drobnosti, for violin & piano; Lyricky fragments, for violin & piano; Allegro schersando, for violin & piano. Mbr., Union of Czech. Comps. Recip. 3rd Prize in comps. competition for 30th Anniversary of Liberation, CSR, 1975. Hobbies: Bicycling; Forest walking; Reading. Address: Brízách 793, 28000 Kolín II, Czech.

JOSEPH, Harold, b. Ootacamund, S India. Orchestral Conductor; Pianist. Educ: LTCL; ARCM. m. Iris Yasmin, 1 d.

Career: Asst.Dir., 1951-56, Dir., 1958-62, Mil. Schl. of Music, India; Dir. of Music, Army HQ, New Delhi, 1962; Fndr., Delhi Symph. Orch., 1964. Compositions incl: marches & programme music based on indigenous & original material. Recordings: Martial Music of the Indian Army. Contbr. to: Illustrated Weekly (India); Schl. Musician (USA); etc. Mbrships: Mng. Comm., Delhi Symph. Soc. & Delhi Music Soc.; Gandharva Maha Mahavidalya. Recip. of Padma Shri, Govt. of India. Hobbies: Tennis; Reading. Address: 86 Rabinder Nagar, New Delhi 3, India.

JOSEPH, Ota, b. 23 Dec. 1937, Aitutaki, Arutanga, Cook Islands. Musician (Cook Islands wooden drums, kettle drums, bass drum). Educ: pvte. studies m. Ngatangatapuapii Rongokea, 5 c. Career: Stage fests.; Dir./Prod., Cook Islands Nat. Arts Theatre Co. Sev. recordings. Mbr., Cook Islands Nat. Cultural Arts Coun. Hobbies: Dancing; Tennis; Cricket. Address: PO Box 98, Rarotonga, Cook Islands.

JOSEPH, Ronald A Peter, b. 4 July 1954, Diego Martin, Trinidad. Conductor; Music Director; College Principal. Educ: ATCL; LTCL; BA, BSc, MA, MSc, CUNY, USA. Career: Cond. & Dir. of Music, Caribbean Symph. Steel Orch., w. apps. in NYC, & in var. chs., Barbados, Trinidad, Can. & USA; Winner, Can. Music Fest.; Cond., NY Symphonic Orch.; Sessions' recitals, Metropolitan Mus.; NYC. Comps: People's Mass of St. Joseph; Chants for Te Deum, Magnificat, Nunc Dimittis & var. psalms; New arrs. for How Great Thou Art; Sing Gloria, Lord of our Life, Lord Who Shall Abide in thy Tabernacle (Anthem). Recordings w. Caribbean Symph. Steel Orch. & St. Marys Choir. Publs: The Art of Steel Drum Playing. Contbr. to: Musical Chords Int. Mbr., profl. orgs. Hons: Duke of Edinburgh Gold Award, 1973; Dean's Award for Best Music Student, CUNY, 1976. Mgmt: Ronmusic Int. Address: 3058 N Olive Ave., Altadena, CA 91009, USA.

JOSEPH, Samuel, b. 19 Mar. 1937, Guindy, Madras, India. Former Violinist; Film Arranger, Composer & Conductor. Educ: BA, Madras Univ.; studies in S Indian Classical Music (w. Sri G Lalgudi Jeyaraman) & Western Music. m. Violet, 2 s., 1 d. Career: Music Dir., composing music for 10 films; Arr. & Cond. of music for about 250 films. Has made pvte. recordings of relig. songs. Former Mbr., Madras Orchl. Assn. Hons: Best Solo Violinist, Intercollegiate Musical Competition, Madras, 1958; Best Music Dir. Award, Malayalam Film for the yr., 1974 (Cine Rekha Film Soc.) Hobbies: Listening to recorded music; Singing. Address: Flat No. 9-19 Motilal St., T Nagar, Madras 17, S India, India.

JOSEPHS, Norman Arthur, b. 20 June 1943, Coleford, Glos., UK. Lecturer in Music; Violinist. Educ: Birmingham Univ.; Lincoln Coll., Oxford Univ.; BMus; MA. Career: Lectr. in Music, Univ. of Keele. Contbr. to: Musical Opinion; Popular Music and Soc.; Contact; Grove's Dict., 6th ed. Mbrships: Royal Musical Assn.; ISM; Viola da Gamba Soc. of Great Britain. Hons: Barber Scholarships in Music, 1962, '67; Fellow of the Salzburg Seminar, 1976. Hobbies: Golf; Football. Address: Music Dept., Univ. of Keele, Staffs. ST5 5BG, UK.

JOSEPHS, Wilfred, b. 24 July 1927, Newcastle upon Tyne, UK. Composer. Educ: BDS (Dunelm); GSM; w. Maitre Max Deutsch, Paris, France; DMus, Newcastle Univ., 1978. m. Valerie Gloria Wisbey, 2 d. Comps. incl: Byrdsong; Aeroplanes & Angels, songbook; Solo Oboe Piece; Doubles: The 4 Horsemen of the Apocalypse; 8 Symphs.; Concertos for Piano, 2 violins, 4 pianos, clarinet, cello, viola, oboe, guitar, harp & harpsichord, etc.; 3 String Quartets, etc. Recordings incl: The Film & TV Music of Wilfred Josephs. Hons. incl: Harriet Cohen Medal, 1959; 1st Prize, Int. Jeunesses Musicales for 'The Ants', Majorca, 1963; 1st Prize, 1st Int. Comp. Competition, La Scala & City of Milan for 'Requiem', 1963. Mgmt. (films & TV): London Mgmt.; Regent House, 235 Regent St., London W1. Address: c/o London Mgmt., Regent House, 235 Regent St., London W1, UK. 3.

JOSEPHSON, David, b. 15 April 1942, Montreal, Can. Musicologist. Educ: BA, Columbia Coll., NYC; MA & PhD, Columbia Univ., NYC. m. Sheila Bloom Josephson. Career: Asst. Cond., Columbia Univ. Orch., 1964-65; Cond. & Musical Dir., Columbia Univ. Bands, 1967-70; Assoc. Ed., Current Musicol., 1966-68; Dir., Early Music Grp., Brown Univ., 1972-; Asst. Prof. of Music, ibid, 1972-. Contbr. to: Grove's Dictionary of Music & Musicians; Current Musicol.; Tempo; Studies in Music; Notes of the Music Lib. Assn.; Am. Choral Review. Mbrships: Am. & Int. Musicol. Socs.; Am. Soc. for 18th Century Studies; Renaissance Soc. of Am.; Royal Musical Assn.; Grainger Lib. Soc. Recip. of Can. Coun. Fellowship, 1967-68; Howard Fellowship, 1977-78. Address: Dept. of Music, Brown Univ., Providence, RI 02912, USA.

JOSEPHSON, Kenneth George, b. 22 Feb. 1926, Holyoke, Mass., USA. Associate Professor of Music Theory & Composition; Cellist. Educ: BS, Columbia Univ., 1950; MA (Comp. & Cello), Eastman Schl. of Music, 1956; postgrad. study w. Alvin Etler, Smith Coll. m. Lynn Hodges Josephson, 1 s. Career: Asst. Prof. Music Theory & Comp.; Shorter Coll.; Prin. Cellist, Chattanooga Symph.; Prod.-Dir., original operetta The Night Within, Educl. TV, Rome, Ga., 1974. Comps: Concert Piece for four U.U. Recordings; Concert piece for Bass & String Quartet w. Tenn. Chmbr. Players. Mbr., Brass Trio; Ga. Comps. Assn.; Joseph Page String Trio (cellist). Hon: Fatman Award for Original Comps., Smith Coll., 1953. Hobbies: Antiques; Oriental Rugs; Golf; Tennis. Address: 26 Pine Valley Rd., Rome, GA, USA.

JOSHI, Dhruva Tara, b. 1 Oct. 1915, Lucknow, India. Music Educator. Educ: music study w. leading Indian musicians. Debut: All-India Music Conf., Lucknow, 1936. Career incl: Broadcaster on all major radio stns. in India, & also abroad; retired Prin., Coll. of Music & Dance & Prof. & Hd., Dept. of Classical Music, Vilua-Bharat. Mbrships. incl: Nat. Acad. of Music & Drama; Uttar Pradesh; M Mus. Hobbies: Reading; Writing. Address: 383 Nayagavn, Lucknow, Uttar Pradesh, India.

JOUBERT, Duxie Anna Maria, b. 30 Nov. 1919, Calvinia, S Africa. Pianoforte Teacher; Organ teacher. Educ: Higher Dip. for Executants, Univ. of Stellenbosch; Lic.Tchr.'s Dips. in Pianoforte & Organ, & in Harmony & Counterpoint, Univ. of S Africa; Perfs. Lic. Dip. in Pianoforte & Organ. m. T G Joubert, 2 d. Career: Pianoforte & organ tchr.; Organist, Dutch Reformed Ch., Waterkloof, Pretoria, Music Tchr. & Examiner of Music, Univ. of S Africa. Mbrships: S African MTA; Pact Subscription Concerts; Pretoria Musical Soc. Hons. incl: Stipendium for best student, Conservatorium of Music, Stellenbosch Univ., 1940. Hobbies: Music; Reading. Address: 294 Milner St., Waterkloof, Pretoria 0181, S Africa.

JOUBERT, Hendrik Johannes (Hennie), b. 27 Dec. 1926, Belville, S Africa. Music Examinations Director; Concert Pianist; Organist. Educ: B Mus, Stellenbosch Univ.; LRAM; ARCM; LTCL; UPLM, Piano & Organ, & UTLM, Piano, Univ. of S Africa. Career: Regular perfs. as soloist & accomp., radio & TV; Accomp. for leading singers on concert tours; Dir., Music Exams, Univ. of S Africa; Organist, Dutch Reformed Ch., SE Pretoria; Mbr. of Jury, 5th Int. Piano Competition, Montevideo, Uruguay, 1978. Comps: 3 Christmas Carols (choir); Psalm 130 for female voice & organ; educl. piano music. Publs: Handbook on Music Theory, to be publd. Ed., Musicus; Music Critic, Hoofstad (newspaper). Mbr., Nederburg Opera Prize Committee. Recip., var. scholarships. Hobbies: Travel; Home Sound Movies. Address: 330 Derrick Ave., Waterkloof Ridge, Pretoria, Repub. of S Africa.

JOUBERT, John Pierre Herman, b. 20 March 1927, Cape Town, S Africa. Composer; University Lecturer. Educ: BMus (Dunelm); RAM, London; FRAM. m. Florence Mary Litherland, 1 s., 1 d. Career: Lectr. in Music, Hull Univ., 1950-62; Lectr., (now Reader) in Music, Univ. of Birmingham, 1962-. Comps: num. works in all forms & media, publd., broadcast & recorded. Mbr., CGGB. Hobby: Reading. Address: 63 School Rd., Moseley, Birmingham B13 9TF, UK. 3.

JOUBERT, Molly, b. 4 Dec. 1925, Johannesburg, S Afica. Dramatic Soprano; Pianist. Educ: FTCL (perfs.); LTCL (perfs.); ATCL (tchrs.). Debut: City Hall, Johannesburg. Career: Leading player; Mikado; Gondoliers; German, Tom Jones; Verdi, Aida; Elijah; Slomon; Soloist in Saul w. Johannesburg Symph. Orch.; appeared in Afrikaans film, Bou van'n Nasie; Radio broadcast as Soloist, Hymn of Priase, Lohengrin, Cond. Herman Herz. Contbr. to: S African Musical Ency.; History of S African Music (for archives). Mbrships: Johannesburg Phil. Soc. (VP & former Chmn.); Musical Rep., Exec. of Johannesburg Coun. of Adult Educ; S African Music Tchrs. Soc.; Braamfontein Recreation Soc. Hons: Winner, Gold & Silver Medals, Nat. Eisteddfod of S Africa & Afrikaans Eisteddfod of S Africa. Hobbies: Swimming; Gardening; Reading; Sewing; Record playing; Vocal Adjudications, especially Choirs. Address: 16 First Ave., Parys, 9585, O.F.S., S Africa.

JOVANOVIĆ, Vladimir, b. 25 April 1937, Ljubljana, Yugoslavia. Professor of Music (Solfege). Educ: Theory of Music, 1959, Cond., 1969, Undergrad. of Comp., Acad. of Music. Debut: 1963. Career: Radio apps.; Cond., Accordion Orch., Abrasevic; Female Chmbr. Choir; Mbr., Radio Belgrade Choir, 1965-75. Publs: Musical Writer - Solfege I-II, III, IV, 1972, V & VI, 1973; Exercises in all Diatonic Scales I, II, 1978; Alterations and Modulation. Mbrships: Extraordinary mbr., Assn. of Comps. of Serbia; Assn. of Music Tchrs. Hons: 2nd Prize, May Fest. of Students, 1965 (String Quartet). Hobbies:

Chess; Swimming. Address: Dure Strugara 9, 11000 Belgrade, Yugoslavia.

JOYCE, Eileen, b. Zeehan, Tasmania. Concert Pianist. Educ: Leipzig Conserv.; Studied in Germany under Teichmuller & Schnable. Debut: Promenade Concerts under Sir Henry Wood. m. 1st (husband killed in 1939-45 war), 1 s, 2) Christopher Mann. Career: Num. concert tours all over the world inclng: Berlin Phil. Orch.; Conserv. & Nat. Orchs., France; Concertgebouw Orch., Amsterdam; La Scala Orch., Italy; Philadelphia Orch., Carnegie Hall, NY. Has contributed to num. sound tracks of films inclng: The Seventh Veil, Brief Encounter, Man of Two Worlds, Girl in a Million. Hons. incl: D Mus, Cantab, 1971. Address: Chartwell FArm, Westerham, Kent, UK. 1.

JOYCE, Robert Henry, b. 20 Oct. 1927, Tynemouth, UK. Lecturer in Music; Organist. Educ: MA, B Mus, Corpus Christi Coll., Cambridge; RCM; ARCM; ADCM; FRCO (CHM). m. Mary Kelly. Career: Organist/Choirmaster, St. Matthew's, Northampton, 1950-58, Llandaff Cathedral, 1958-73; Lectr., Welsh Coll. of Music & Drama, 1974-; Examiner, RCO & Assoc. Bd. Recordings: EMI; Delysé; Ryemuse; Qualiton. Mbrships: RCO Coun.; ISM. Address: 99 Celyn Ave., Lakeside, Cardiff CF2 6EL, UK. 3.

JUAREZ, Manuel, b. 22 April 1937, Cordoba, Argentina. Pianist; Composer. Educ: Studied piano w. Ruwin Erlich, comp. w. Honorio Siccardi & Guillermo Graetzer. m. Julia Javkin, 2 s. Career: perfs. of symphonic & chmbr. works in major concert halls in Argentina, also on channels 7 & 11, Buenos Aires. Comps. incl: music for stage perfs. of Lysistrata & Nosotros No Usamos Frac (Carneiro); Despiazamientos. Mbrships: Hd., Dept. of Symphonic & Chmbr. Music, SADAIC (Argentina Soc. of Authors & Comps.); Musical Advsr., Fondo Nacionalbe las Artes; Pres., SIGLO XX; Fndr., 1957, Young Comps. Assn. of Argentina Bd. of Argentine Comp. United. Recip. Nat. Awards for comps., 1971, 72. Address: Nogoya 3477, Buenos Aires, Argentina.

JUDD, James, b. 30 Oct. 1949, Hertford, UK. Conductor. Educ: TCL; London Opera Centre. m. Susan Judd. Career: Cond. Asst. to Maazel, Cleveland Orch., 1973-75; Assoc. Cond. to Abbado, ECYO, 1978-. Recordings: Donizetti Arias/Opera Rara, Philharmonia Orch. Hobbies: Music; Tennis; Cricket; Food; Books. Mgmt: Allied Artists. Address: 4 Cholmeley Court, Southwood Lane, Highgate, London N6, UK.

JUDD, Margaret Evelyn, b. Brackley, Northants., UK. Composer. Educ: RAM, London; FRCO; FTCL; ARCM; LRAM; MRST. Num. comps. publd. for Pianoforte by Bosworth Curwen, Augener, & The Royal Schls. of Music - also songs 'To Daffodils' (3 part); Two Broadcasts, There's a Charm in Spring (2 part) & The Babe He Lay Asleeping (Unison song). Recordings: To Daffodils, BBC. Mbrships: Composers Guild of GB; RCO; ISM; PRS; London Assn. of Organists; Songwriters Guild; Int. Soc. for Music Educ; The RAM Club; The Music Club of London. Recip. many 1st prizes, cups & trophies for comp. at Musical Fests. Hobbies: Gardening; Cycling; Flower Arranging. Address: The Elms, Brackley, Northants, UK. 3.

JUHASZ, Elöd, b. 4 May 1938, Budapest, Hungary. Musicologist; Musical Critic; Musical Editor. Educ: Disting. Dip. of the Acad. of Music, Musicol. Fac., 1961; Dr. of Aesthetics at the Eötvéos Loránd Univ., Budapest, 1974. m. Zsuzsanna Mák, 3 d. Career: Var. radio, TV lectures, series; Musical Ed., Radio Budapest. Publs: Gershwin, 1964; American Variations, 1969; Bernstein Story, 1972, '73. Contbr. to: var. Newspapers. Mbrships: Hungarian Musicians Assn.; Art Fndn. of the Hungarian People's Rep. Recip. Ford Fndn. Scholarship, USA, 1966-67. Hobbies: Travelling; Photography. Address: Zajzon u.4, 1112 Budapest XI, Hungary.

JUHOS, Joseph Frank, b. 21 April 1935, Cluj, Romania. Flautist; Professor of Flute. Educ: Artist & Prof. Flute Dip., Liszt Ferenc Acad. Music, Budapest, Hungary, 1961. Debut: Budapest, Hungary. Career incls: 1st flute, Hungarian State Opera Budapest; 1st flute, Budapest Phil. Soc. Orch.; Mbr., Woodwind Quintet, Hungarian Opera, Budapester Nonet; Asst. Prof., flute, Liszt Ferenc Acad. Music; Fac., Conserv., State Music Schl., Hamburg, Germany, 1967-68; Cleveland Inst. of Music, Ohio, USA, 1969-; Instructor, Cuyahoga Community Coll., Cleveland; Mbr., Cleveland Baroque Soloists; concerts, TV & radio apps. Recordings: w. Phil. Soc. Orch. & State Opera Orch., Budapest; WCLV & WNYC, Cleveland. Hobbies: Art; Sport. Address: 13531 Detroit Ave. 9-A, Cleveland OH 44107, USA.

JULIAN, Joseph, b. 22 Jan. 1948, Los Angeles, Calif., USA. Composer. Educ: BA, MA, PhD, Univ. of Calif. m. Catherine Fairbairn. Career incls: Mbr., San Diego Symph., Los Angeles

Monday Evening Concerts, orchs. for films, TV & recording studios; var. tchng. positions inclng: Lectr., Palomar Coll., 1972-74; Univ. of Calif. San Diego, 1974-76. Comps. incl: Wave/Canon for trumpet & live electronica; Graphic I for undetermined instrumentation; Cloud Motion for flute & tape; Concerto for Flutes & Chamber Orchestra; Between: 8 Poems for instruments, dancer, tape & projections. Recordings incl: Don Ellis Orchestra Underground; Spaceship Earth; Open Loop. Publs. incl: Anthology of Improvisational Exercises. Recip. var. commissions & awards. Address: 255 Hill St., Solana Beach, CA 92075, USA.

JUNGK, Klaus, b. 1916, Stettin (Szczecin), Germany. Sound Engineer; Composer; Author. Educ: Loewe Conserv., Stettin; Griedrich Wilhelms Univ., Berlin; Dr. Phil. m. Jutta Loffler, 1 s. Career: Hd. of Dept. of Serious Music, Radio Free Berlin. Compositions incl: solo & chmbr. music works; var. orchestral works; film music; The Birds (ballet pantomime, after Aristophanes & Goethe). Publ: Musik im technischen Zeitalter. Contbr. of articles on musik to var. jrnls., TV & radio broadcasts, etc. Mbrships: Int. Music Ctr., Vienna; Int. Music Lib. Assn. Address: Kaiserstühlstrasse 29, 1 Berlin 38, German Fed. Repub. 3.

JURAITIS, Algis, b. 27 July 1928, Kaunas, Lithuania, USSR. Conductor. Educ: piano study, The Conserv. of Vilnius; cond. study, The Conserv. of Moscow. 1 d., 1 s. Debut: Vilnius Opera Theatre, Halka (Monjushko). Career: Eugene Onegin; The Queen of Spades; Prince Igor; Boris Godunov; Othello; Tosca; La Boheme; Madame Butterfly; Rigoletto; La Traviata; Un Ballo in Maschera; Cavallerio Rusticana; Pagliacci; The Swan Lake; Nutcracker; Giselle; The Spartacus; Ivan the Terrible; Romeo & Juliet; The Sacred Spring; Radio & phil. apps. incl. all symphs. by Beethoven, all symphs. by Brahms, Mozart, Haydn, Schumann, Schubert, Liszt, Wagner, R Strauss, Mahler, Sibelius, Stravinski, Prokofiev, Shostakovitch, Khachaturian, Ovchinnikov, Tchaikovsky, Musorgski, Borodin, Rimski-Korsakov, Balakirev, Glinka, Rubinstein, Arenski, Gretchaninov, Glazunov, Rachmaninov, Skriabin. Recordings of most of the above. Contbr. to: profl. publs. Hons: People's Artist; The State Prize of 1977; The Santa Cecilia Conds. Competition Prize Winner, Rome. Hobby: Collecting books. Address: The Bolshoi Theatre, Moscow, USSR.

JÜRGENS, Jürgen, b. 5 Oct. 1925, Frankfurt/Main, Germany. Conductor; Director. Educ: Music Gymnasium, Frankfurt, w. Kurt Thomas; Musikhochschule Freiburg/Breisgau, w. Konrad Lechner. Career: Cond., Monteverdi-Choir, Hamburg; Dir., Akademische Musikpflege, Univ. of Hamburg. Recordings: w. Monteverdi Choir. Publs: Monteverdi - Marien - Vesper; Domenico Scarlatti - Stabat Mater. Mbrships: Gema; GVL; VDOK. Hons: Brahms-Medaille der Freien und Hansestadt Hamburg; 13 Schallplattenpreise; 24 Wettbewerbspreise. Hobby: Writing Poetry. Mgmt: Konzertdirektion Kollitsch, 1000 Berlin 30, Geisbergstr. 40. Address: Oderfelder Strasse 11, 2000 Hamburg 13, German Fed. Repub.

JURINAC, Sena (Srebrenka), b. 24 Oct. 1921, Travnik, Yugoslavia. Operatic Soprano. Educ: Musical Acad., Zagreb. m. Josef Lederle. Debut: as Mimi in La Bohème, Zagreb Nat. Theatre, 1942. Career: Mbr., Vienna State Opera, 1944-;

Guest apps. throughout the world at ldng. opera houses & fests. Recordings incl: Fidelio (Furtwangler, Knappertsbusch); Le Nozze di Figaro (Karajan, Böhm); Don Giovanni (Fricsay); Idomeneo (Busch, Pritchard); Rosenkavalier (Kleiber). Hons. incl: Austrian Kammersangerin Award; Mozart Medal; Order of Merit, Repub. of Austria; Ring of Hon., Vienna State Opera; Mbr. of Hon., ibid. Hobbies: Antiques; Gardening. Address: Staatsoper, Vienna I, Austria. 1,2,5.

JURRES, Andre Georges, b. 23 April 1912, Amsterdam, Netherlands. Pianist; Piano Teacher; Lecturer. Educ: Grad., Amsterdam Conserv., 1936. m. Theresa van den Heuvel, 1 s., 1 d. Career: Tchr., Conservs. of Amsterdam, Rotterdam, Utrecht; num. lectures, articles, Radio Apps.; lecture tour, USA, 1965; Wkly. Reviewer, Radio Hilversum, 1959-; Artistic Dir., Documentation In The Netherlands For Music Fndn., Amsterdam, 1950; Gen. Dir., ibid, 1952-; Dir., Eduard van Beinum Fndn., Breukelen, Holland, 1974-. Mbrships: Pres., Int. Soc. for Contemporary Music, 1969-75; Bd., Int. Assn. of Music Libraries; Pres., ibid, 1965-68; Bd., Int. Music Coun.; Sec.-Gen., ibid, 1962-69; Bd., Nat. Committee, Netherlands, ibid; Bd., Nat. UNESCO Commission; Bd., Arts Coun., City of Amsterdam; Bd., Prince Bernhard Fund; Bd., Soc. for Netherlands Musical History; Bd., Gaudeamus Fndn.; Bd., Amsterdam Conserv. Hons: Jan van Gilse Prize, 1964; Kt., Order of Orange Nassau. Hobby: Travel. Address: Queekhoven Hs., Zandpad 39, Breukelen, Netherlands.

JUST, Helen, b. 31 Dec. 1903, Bristol, UK. Cellist. Educ: RCM; ARCM; FRCM. m. Ivor James, 1 d. Debut: Wigmore Hall, London. Career: Cellist in English Str. Quartet, 1955-73; Broadcast as Soloist (Sonata work); Concert work in provinces; ESQ. regular broadcasting; Many first perfs. of new works; Appeared at Cheltenham, Edinburgh, Aldeburgh Fests., etc.; Associated w. Hans Killen in lecture recitals & broadcasts. Mbrships: ISM; SWM. Recip. var. prizes. Hobbies: Gardening; Archaeol. Address: 65 Clarendon Rd., London W. 11, UK.

JUSTUS, William, b. 12 Nov. 1936, Kansas City, Mo., USA. Operatic Baritone. Educ: B Mus, Ctrl. Coll., Fayette, Mo. m. Barbara J Adams. Debut: Figaro in Barber of Seville, Kan. City Lyric Theatre. Career: operatic roles w. leading opera cos. in Europe & USA, inclng. Zurich, Dusseldorf, Berlin, NYC, Metropol. Opera, Boston, New Orleans, San Fran., etc.; concerts w. major symph. orchs. Recording: Brubeck's The Light in the Wilderness (Decca). Hon: Winner, Am. Opera Auditions 1963. Hobby: Crossword Puzzles. Mgmt: Hans J Hoffman, NYC. Address: 136 Seventh Ave., Westwood NJ, USA.

JUTILA, Unto Väinö, b. 5 Dec. 1944, Kalajoki, Finland. Accordion Artist; Pianist; Organist. Debut: Town Hall, Oulu, 1954. Career: Radio apps., 1956-; TV apps., 1963-; Stage Accompanist, USA & Canada, 1975; Tchr., Accordion. Comps: Kalajoki-Valssi Ym. Unto Jutilan Savellyksia (Album) 1973; Rhapsody for Accordion, 1974; Accordion Concerto in F, 1975. Recordings: Kalajoen Markkinoilla, LP, 1972. Mbrships: Film & Entertainment Composers Assn.; Finnish Musicians Assn.; Finnish Accordion Assn.; Recip: Hon. Prize, Accordion, Finnish Championship, 1963. Hobby: Photography. Address: 85100 Kalajoki, 1 KP, Finland.

K

KABALEVSKY, Dimitri Borisovich, b. 30 Dec. 1904, St. Petersburg,Russia. Composer. Educ: Scriabin Music Schl. Moscow; Moscow Conserv. Career: Tchr., children's Schl. & Scriabin Music Schl.; Prof. of Composition, Moscow Conserv. Compositions incl: sev. symphs.; Poem of Struggle; Requiem for Lenin; sev. Concertos; Colas Breugnon (opera); The Comedians for orch.; Sonata No. 3 for piano; Great Motherland (cantata); Under Fire (opera); Film music for Sister, Volnitsa, 18th Year & Gloomy Morning; Lenintsy (cantata); Sonata for 'cello & piano; Requiem (oratorio). Mbrships: Pres., Organizing Committee, Union of Soviet Composers; World Peace Coun., 1955. Hons. incl: Stalin Prize, 1946; State Prizes, 1946, 49 & 51; RSFSR State Prize, 1966; Badge of Hon., 1940; Red Banner of Labour, 1966. Address: c/o Union of Soviet Composers, 710 Nezhdanova St., Moscow, USSR.

KABALEWSKI, Wladyslaw, b. 28 Aug. 1919, Warsaw, Poland. Conductor; Composer; Violinist. Educ: State Coll. of Music, Warsaw; studied w. Erich Leinsdorf, Vienna; Dips. in conducting comp. & theory, Warsaw Acad. of Music. m. Teresa-Krystyna Boczkowska, 1 s., 1 d. Debut: as Violinist, 1945; as Comp., 1948; as Cond., 1951, State Phil. Soc., Warsaw. Career incls: Music Dir. & Prin. Cond., Chmbr. Opera Soc. at State Nat. Phil., Warsaw, 1963-65, State Musical Theatre & Operetta, Lublin, 1965-71; Conducting Prof. & Cond. of Symph. Orch., Warsaw Acad. of Music, 1966-; Cond., State Symph. Orch., Bialystok, 1972-74. Orchl. comps. incl: Old Polish Dances; Concerto Overture; Joc (Romanian dance); Poem (violin & orch.). Comp. of var. chmbr. & choral works. Mbrships: Dpty. Chmn., then Sec., Serious Music Sect., Assn. of Comps. & Theatrical Authors (ZAIKS). Recip., var. state hons. Hobbies: Motoring; Collecting Classical Records. Address: ul. Filtrowa 64 m47, 02-057 Warsaw 65, Poland.

KABELÁČ, Miloslav, b. 1 Aug. 1908, Prague, Czechoslovakia. Composer. Educ: studied comp. under Prof. K B Jirak & cond. under Prof. P Dedecek, Prague Conserv. of Music, 1928-32; Piano Master Class w. Prof. V Kurz, 1931-34. m. Berta Rixová, 1 d. Career: Cond. & Sound Dir., Radio Prague, 1932-41; Hd. of The Dept. of Music Prodn., ibid, 1945-57; Prof. of Comp., Prague Conserv., 1958-62. Compositions incl: (orchl.) Symph. No 1 in D, for strings & perc., 1941-42; Symph. No. 2 in C, for large orch., 1942-46; Symph. No. 3 in F for organ, brass instruments & Timpani, 1948-57; Symph. No. 4 in A 'Camerata', 1954-58; Symph. No. 5 in B Minor 'Dramatica', for soprano without text, & orch., 1960; Symph. No. 8 'Antiphonies' for soprano solo, mixed choir, perc. & organ, 1970; Overture No. 2 for large orch., 1947; The Mystery of Time, Passacaglia for large orch., 1953-57; Hamlet Improvization, for large orch., 1962-63; Reflections, Nine Miniatures for Orch., 1963-64 (for piano) Seven Pieces, 1944-47; Eight Preludes, 1955-56; (for organ) 2 Fantasies; Four Preludes, 1963. Hons. incl: State Prize, 1965; Artist of Merit, 1967. Address: Pisecka 20, 13000 Prague 3, Czechoslovakia. 3.

KACHER, Delton, b. 28 Dec. 1937, E Chgo., Ind., USA. Guitarist; Composer; Director. Educ: Ind. Univ.; Univ.of Pittsburgh; studies w. father. m. Eiko Kacher, 1 s. Debut: Chgo. TV. Career: Own radio show, age 16; apps., Midwest States of Am.; Mbr., Three Suns, 1959; Hit records, Japan; played w. Ray Conniff Orch. & Billy Vaughn Orch.; Music Dir., BBC TV special, Our Town. Comps: NBC Nightly News Theme; Chico and the Man, TV; music for Our Town, TV special. Recordings: NBC TV Nightly News Theme. Contbr. to: Songwriters Mag.; Billboard. Mbrships: Am. Fend. of Musicians Local 47; AFTRA; ASCAP. Hobby: Designing Guitars. Address: 5203 Sunset Blvd., Hollywood, CA 90027, USA.

KACZYNSKI, Adam, b. 13 Oct. 1933, Warsaw, Poland. Pianist; Composer; Assistant Professor; Ensemble Founder & Director. Educ: Dip., BA, State Acad. of Music, Krakow. Career: Asst. Prof., State Acad. of Music, Krakow; Fndr. & Dir., Ensemble MW 2, w. num. perfs. on TV, fests. & concerts, Poland & abroad. Comps. incl: Concert for Jazz Orch., 1962; Choices, for 3 pianos, electronic piano, celeste, harpsichord & choir, 1975; music for theatre & films. Recordings: Polish Avant-Garde Music (w. ensemble). Mbrships: Polish Artist Musicians Assn.; Polish Authors Assn. Hons. incl: Int. Competition for Young Performers of Contemp. Music Prize, Utrecht, Holland, 1965; Polish Comps. Assn. Medal, 1973; Pierre Schaeffer Prize, 1970; Fulbright Grant, 1974-75; Paderewdki Prize, Polish Arts Club, Rochester, USA, 1975.

Hobby: Painting. Address: 30-051 Krakow, Urzednicza 10 m. 10, Poland.

KACZYNSKI, Tadeusz, b. 18 Feb. 1932, Warsaw, Poland. Music Critic. Educ: MA, Music Inst. of Jagiellonian Univ., Cracow. m. Elzbieta Kaczynska. Career: Participant in radio & TV progs. about music; Var. music essays, articles, comments in many Polish & Foreign mags., especially about contemporary music. Publs: Dzieje Sceniczne Halki (Theatrical Hist.of 'Halka', opera by St. Monivszko), 1967; Rozmowy z Witoldem Lutoslawskim, 1973 (Interviews w. Witold Lutoskawski). Contbr. to daily mag. 'Sztandar Mlodyeh' etc. Mbrships: Soc. of Polish Comps.; Soc. of Polish Artist Musicians; Hons: Prize for best article about The Fest. of Contemp. Music, Warsaw Autumn, 1965, '66; Prize for best article about Fest 'Jazz Jamboree'; Prize for best publ. of Yr., 1970. Hobby: Sailing. Address: Al Niepodleglosci 67m. 247, 02-626, Warsaw, Poland.

KADLUBISKI, Jan Konrad, b. 12 Jan. 1931, Warsaw, Poland. Pianist. Educ: Law Fac., Univ. of Warsaw; MA, State High Schl. of Music, Warsaw, 1956; Acad. of Music & Performing Arts, Vienna, Austria, 1961; Accademia Chigiana, Siena, Italy, 1966-68. m. Anna Sikora-Kadlubiska, 1 s., 1 d. Debut: Warsaw, 1955. Career: Num. piano recitals & symph. concerts, Poland, Austria, Italy, German Dem. Repub.; num. radio & TV recordings; Role of Liszt & recordings of his music, French-Polish TV serial, Life of Balzac; now Soloist, Nat. Phil., Warsaw; Piano Tchr., State High Schl. of Music, ibid. Mbr., Polish Soc. Musical Artists. Hons: 5th Prize, 5th Int. Piano Competition, Warsaw, 1955. Hobbies: All Activities of Mankind. Address: ul. Jzabelli 29, 01-738 Warsaw, Poland.

KADOSA, Pal, b. 6 Sept. 1903, Levice, Czechoslovakia. Composer; Pianist. Educ: Study w. Zolton Kodaly & Arnold Szekely at Budapest Acad. of Music. Career: Tchr. Fodor Music Schl., 1927-43; Goldmark Music Schl., 1944; Prof. Budapest Acad. of Music, 1945-; Dirs.' Coun., ibid. Compositions incl. works for orch., symphs., string quartets, violin & piano concertos, cantatas, choral works, Huszti Kaland (opera). Mbrships: Bd. & Acting Chmn., Fedn. of Hungarian Musicians; Pres , Nat. Copyright Off.; Hon., RAM, London, 1967; Corresp. Mbr., German Acad. of Arts, 1970. Hons: Eminent Artist of Hungarian People's Repub., 1963; Labour Order of Merit, 1970. Hobbies: Art Collector; Gothic arts. Address: Hungarian Acad. of Music, Liszt Ferenc Place 8, Budapest VI, Hungary.

KAEGI, Werner, b. 17 June 1926, Uznach, Switz. Composer; Researcher. Educ: studied at Univs. in Zurich, Basel & Heidelberg; PhD, 1952; studied clarinet, piano & counterpoint, Gonserv., Zurich, 1937-48; studied comp. w. Louis Aubert, Paris, 1949-53, & Paul Hindemith, Univ. of Zurich, 1953-56. m. Regine Veronika Steiner, 1 s., 2 d. Career: many fest. perfs.; TV film on electronic music, 1968; electronic music for Swiss pavilion, Expo Osaka, 1970; Collaborator, Radio Suisse Romande, Geneva, 1963-71; Assoc. Prof., Inst. of Sonology, Utrecht Univ., 1971-. Comps. incl: Miniaturen für oboe, fagott und cembalo; Kyoto (violin, viola, cello, flute, clarinet, bassclarinet, piano, percussion & magnetic tape, recorded). Publs. incl: Vom Sinuston zur elektronischen Musik, 1970. Contbr. to jrnls. Address: Inst. of Sonol., Utrecht State Univ., 14-16 Plompetorengracht, NL 30 Utrecht, Netherlands.

KAELIN, Pierre, b. 12 May 1913, Estavayer-le-Lac, Switzerland. Teacher; Choir Conductor; Composer; Priest. Educ: Theol. Study; Dip., Cesar Franck Schl., Paris; Dip., Gregorian Inst., ibid. Debut: Swiss Radio, 1932. Career incl: Precentor, Fribourg Cathedral, 1949-; Dir. St. Nicolas Choir, Chanson de Fribourg, Fribourg Cathedral Symph. Choir, Fribourg Little Singers; Regular broadcasts, Swiss TV & Radio. Comps. incl: (oratorios) Votre Monde Seigneur; La Joie Partagée Le Jeu du noir et du Blanc; Terre de Gruyère. Recordings incl: Sir Francis (oratorio); ISCHA (opera) Popular Songs & Choirs. Publs: The Choir Conductor, 1949; Choral Art, 1974; Gregorian Practice, 1949. Mbr. var. profl. orgs. Recip. Italia Prize, 1954. Address: 1 Rue Mon-Foyer, 1700 Fribourg, Switzerland.

KAEMPER, Dietrich, b. 29 June 1936, Melle, Germany. Professor of Musicology. Educ: Dr. Phil.,Univ. Koln, 1963; Acad. Lectr. (Habilitation), ibid., 1967. m. Gisela Duis, 2 children. Career: Dir., Dept. of Rheinische Musikgeschichte, Univ. of Koln, 1965-68; Acad. Lectr., ibid., 1967; Prof., ibid. 1970. Publs: Franz Wuellner, 1953; Richard Strauss und Franz Wullner imm Briefwechsel, 1963; Max Bruch-Studien, 1970; Studien zur Instrumentalen Ensemblemusik des 16. Jahrhunderts in Italien, 1970; Studi sul'Insieme Strumentale in Italia nel XVI Secolo (It. transl., 1976). Contbr. to profl. jrnls. Mbrships: Int. Musicol. Soc.; Gesellschaft fur Musikforschung. Address: Sperlingsweg 41, D-5021 Koenigsdorf, Germany.

KAHN, David E, b. 23 Jan. 1932, Bklyn., NY, USA. Ethnomusicologist. Educ. incls: BA, NM Highland Univ., 1969; MA cand., Calif. State Univ., Los Angeles; pvte. study of violin, oboe, guitar, flute & banjo. m. Jane Boyd Kahn (separated), 2 d. Career: Folk Music Prog., 17 stns., 1966-68, KPFK, 1969-70; translating Dagueno (native Am. Indians) songs. Contbr. to var. publs. on Am. folk music; profl. meetings; radio progs. Mbrships: Fellow Royal Anthropol. Soc. of GB & Ireland; Ethnomusicol. Soc.; Am. Folklore Soc.; Med. Anthropol. Soc. Hobbies; Chess; Track; Skiing. Address: 16271 Chipper Lane, Huntington Beach, CA 92649, USA.

KAINZ, Walter, b. 21 Feb. 1907, Dobl, Austria. Professor. Educ: Trng. Coll. Career: Radio apps., songs, chmbr. music, symphs. & violin concerts; Concert Hall apps., Graz, Vienna & Paris. Comps: Songs; Sonaten for piano, for flute & piano, for saxophone & piano, for 2 violins & piano; Music for wind instruments; choral music. Publ: Compendium for the Cymbal, 1951, '54, '73. Mbrships: Osterreichischer Komponistenbund; Steirischer Tonkunstlerbund. Hond: Joseph Marx Prize. Hobbies incl: Investigation of the Styrian Dialect; Mod. Art. Address: A 8561 Soding 122, Austria.

KAISERMAN, David Norman, b. 15 July 1937, Cleveland, Ohio, USA. Pianist. Educ: BS, The Juilliard Schl., NYC, 1959; MS, ibid, 1960; DMA, in prof., Univ. of Iowa. m. Sonia Uvezian. Debut: Town Hall, NYC, 1963. Career: Artist-in-Res.,Hd., Piano Dept., Univ. of Puget Sound; NY solo recitals in Town Hall, Judson Hall, Carnegie Recital Hall, Colony Club, etc.; Radio appearances; Many solo recitals; Chamber music concets; Appearances w. orch.; radio & TV broadcasts in Midwest & Northwest. Contbr. to music jrnls. Mbrships: Local 802, Am. Fedn. of Musicians; Music Tchrs. Nat. Assn.; NGPT (Fac. Mbe.), etc. Hons. incl: Josephine Fry Bi-Annual Award of the Piano Tchrs. Congress of NY, 1963; Grand Prize, Tchr. Div. of Int. Piano Recording Comp., sponsored by NGPT, 1973. Address: Schl. of Music; Univ. of Puget Sound, Tacoma, WA 98416, USA.

KAKALA, Sòfele, B. 21 Mar. 1916, Lapaha, Tonga. Composer; Conductor; Teacher. Educ: Sydney Conserv. of Music; studied comp. w. Hopcroft & Peter Crowe. m. Susana Lupe. Career: Perfs. of own works at num. public functions incl. opening of Radio Tonga, 1961, Coronation of King Taufa'ahau IV, 1967 & Independence celebrations, 1970; radio talks on music, 1973-75; Lectr. in music, Tonga Teachers Training Coll. Comps: num. songs incl. Ko E Fai'anga Tukuhua (Si'a Finesola Song); masses, hymns & motets incl Diocese Mass & Mass for the Dedication of Tonga's 1st Basilica, 1980. Recordings: The Music of Tonga, 1972; num. for Radio Tonga. Mbrships: Tonga Music Tchrs. Assn.; Chmn., Music Fest. organizing committee. Hons: var. prizes in choir competitions; num. annual music fest. awards. Hobbies: Farming; Boxing. Address: Tchrs. Training Coll., PO Box 123, Nuku'alofa, Tonga.

KALABIS, Viktor, b. 27 Feb. 1923, Cerveny Kostelec, Czech. Composer. Educ: Charles Univ., 1945-49; Conserv. of Music, Prague, 1945-48; Acad. of Musical Arts, Prague, 1948-52. m. Zuzana Ruzickova. Compositions publd: Concerto for Cello & Orch.; 6 Canonic Inventions for Harpsichord; 5 Romantic Lovesongs for Higher Voice & Orch.; Symph. No. 1; Sonata for Violin & Harpsichord. Compositions recorded & pubd: tr. Quartet No. 2; Symph. 2-4; Accenti; Piano Concerto; Violin Concerto; Concert for Orch.; Sonata for violoncello & Piano; Sonata for Trombone & Piano; Sonata for Clarinette & Piano; Sonata for Horn & Piano; Chmbr. Music for strings; Symph. variations for orch.; Little chmbr. music for wind quintet; Three Pieces for flute solo; concert for trumpet; concert for harpsichord & strings. Mbr., Czech. Composers Guild. Hons: 1st Prize of the 20th Anniversary of CSSR. Critics Prize, 1967; State Prize, 1969. Hobbies: Motoring; Travel. Mgmt: Czech. Info. Music Ctr., Besedni 3, Prague 1. Address: Slezska 107, 130 00 Prague 3, Czech.

KALAMUNIAK, Helen Maria, b. 18 Feb. 1951, Nottingham, UK. Musician (classical guitar). Educ: Royal Coll. of Music; LRAM. m. Charles Ramirez. Debut: Wigmore Hall, 1975. Hon: Guitar Prize, Royal Coll. of Music, 1972. Address: 61B Cromwell Rd., London SW7, UK.

KALETSKY, J, b. 11 June 1911, Augustow, Poland. Concert Pianist; Professor. Educ: Grad. w. Hon., Chopin Inst., Warsaw; MA, Warsaw Univ. m. E Kaletsky, 2 s. Debut: Warsaw. Career: app. at Int. Chopin Fest., Duszuiki, Poland; broadcasts in Warsaw, Moscow, Melbourne. Recordings: Maliszewski's Piano Concerto. w. Polisti Badice Orch. Publ: Polish Folklore, 1956; num. essays, reports & articles. Mbrships: ISM; Inst. of Linguists, London. Recip. Golden Medal, Chopin Inst., Warsaw, 1934. Hobbies: Travel; Swimming. Address: 39 Ashley Gardens, London SW1, UK.

KALF, Karl Walter, b. 6 Aug. 1946, Westzaan, Netherlands. Trumpet Player; Arranger; Composer; Teacher. Educ: MD in chem.; dipl. D, Conserv.; pvte. lessons in studio playing. m. Marjon R Verkerk, 2 s. Career: apps. w. Dutch grps. Dizzy Man's Band, Golden Earring & Houseband, has played on major stages throughout the world inclng. Concertgebouw, Amsterdam, Maquis, London, l'Olympia, Paris, Winterland, San Fran. Comps: Red light district; Embryo; I'll kill you. Has made num. singles & 4 LPs. Mbrships: NTB; Herengracht, Amsterdam. Hobbies: Yoga; Film. Address: Dorpsstraat 8, 1536 AG Marken Binnen, Netherlands.

KALICHSTEIN, Joseph, b. 15 Jan. 1946, Tel Aviv, Israel. Pianist. Educ: BSc, MSc, Juilliard Schl., NYC, USA. m. Rowain, 2 s. Debut: NYC, 1967. Career incl: CBC TV, German & French TV; Perfs. w. Cleveland Orch., Boston Symph., London Symph., Berlin Phil., NY Phil., ECO, Israel Phil., Chicago Symph., etc., under leading conds. Recordings incl: Var. works of Mendelssohn inclng. 1st Piano Concerto, w. London Symph. Orch. under Previn; num. works of Chopin, Bartok, Prokofieff & Brahms. Hons: 1st Prize, Leventritt Int. Competitions, 1969; Edward Steuermann Mem. Prize, 1969. Hobbies incl: Reading. Mgmt: Harrison-Parrott (UK). Address: 588 Bloomfield Ave., W Candwell, NJ 07006, USA.

KALLIR, Lilian, b. Prague, Czechoslovakia. Concert Pianist. Educ: Mannes Schl. of Music, NYC, USA; Tanglewood. m. Claude Frank, 1 d. Debut: Recital, Town Hall, NYC, age 17. Career incl: Concert tours in USA, Europe, S Am., etc., w. major orchs. inclng. NY Phil., Boston Symph., Berlin Phil., London Philharmonia, Royal Phil., Concertgebouw of Amsterdam, Swiss Romande Orch., etc. Recordings: complete works of Chopin (RCA-Victor). Contbr. to var. musical publs. Mbrships: Hon., Sigma Alpha Iota. Hons: Winner, Nat. Music League Awards; Am. Artists Award. Mgmt: Columbia Artists Mgmt., 165 W 57th St., NY, NY, USA. 5.

KALLMANN, Helmut, b. 7 Aug. 1922, Berlin, Germany. Music Librarian; Historian. Educ: BMus, 1949, LLD, 1971, Univ. of Toronto; Royal Conserv. of Music, Toronto (piano). m. Ruth Singer, 1 step-daughter. Career: Music Library, Can. Broadcasting Corp. Toronto, 1950-70; Supervisor, ibid, 1962-; Chief, Music Division, Nat. Lib. of Can., Ottawa, 1970-. Publs: Catalogue of Canadian Composers, 1952; A History of Music in Canada 1534-1914, 1960. Contb. to: Can. Music Jrnl.; The Can. Music Book; The Can. Comp.; Opera Can.; num. Dicts. & Encys. Mbrships: Can. Delegate, Int. Assn. of Music Libs., 1959-71; Chmn., 1957-58, 1967-68, Can. Music Lib. Assn.; VP, 1971-76, Can. Music Coun.; Can. Folk Music Soc.; Bibliographical Soc. of Can. Hons: Can. Music Coun. Medal, 1977. Hobbies: Music; Travel. Address: 38 Foothills Drive, Nepean, Ont., Can. K2H 6K3. 2,14,29.

KALMAN, Charles Emmerich, b. 17 Nov. 1929, Vienna, Austria. Composer; Pianist; Lyricist. Educ: Grad. Columbia Univ., NY, NY, USA, 1952; Conserv. of Paris. m. Gerda Margarete Elizabeth Trettin. Debut: Columbia Univ. Caree . own Show, Austrian TV; num. TV Apps., Perfs., thru'out Europe & USA. Compositions incl: (publd.) Musicals Wir Reisen Um Die Welt, Rendezvous Mit Dem Leben, Alfie, Antonia, Mrs. Warren's Profession; ballet Hot Shoes; num. Concert Pieces, Instrumental Works, Songs; (recorded) Globe Trotter Suite. Recordings: London, Decca, Polydor, Raphael, Pathe Marconi, Phillips, Week-End, Mozart. Contbr. to Opera Guide mag., NY; num. others. Mbrships: GEMA; German Comps. League. Hons: Musical Prize, for Ricky Starr in Leeds, Wiesbaden Filmstelle; Hon. Mbr., IGOMU. Hobbies: Swimming; Chinese Restaurants & Food. Address: 56 Maximilianstrasse, 8 Munich 22, German Fed. Repub.

KALMANOFF, Martin, b. 24 May 1920, Brooklyn, NY, USA. Organist; Composer; Pianist; Director; Librettist; Author; Lecturer; Publisher. Educ: BA (cum laude), Harvard Univ.; MA. Career: has had 10 operas perf. w. orch. inclng. two he cond. w. mbrs. of the Detroit Symph. Orch; his music has been sung by George London, Gladys Swarthout, Licia Albanese, etc.; 'Young Tom Edison' perf. at Phil. Hall, NYC & Town Hall; Cond. Doretta Morrow, Bob Goulet, Gordon MacRae, Genevieve, Theodor Uppman (Met. Opera); His 'Mod Traviata' heard by 10 million CBS-TV listeners; Wrote original musical 'The Fourposter'. Compositions incl: (operas) Opera, Opera; The Great Stone Face; Photograph-1920; The Victory at Masada; (songs) The Lord is My Shepherd; The Lion & The Lamb; The Way of Life (cantata for voice & 2 instruments); etc. Recordings: Lamento di Puccini, words by Giacomo Puccini, sung by Miklos Gafni w. Hungarian Phil. Orch. under Zolton Rozsnyai & also The Lord is My Shepherd; 200 recordings of popular songs by popular artists. Contbr. to music jrnls. Mbrships. incl: ASCAP; Ctrl. Opera Serv. Hons. Won the $1,000 Robert Merrill Contest for best one-act opera, 1950,

Musical Give Me Liberty, performed on Broadway & now on 6 mnth tour. Address: Apt. 14P, 392 Ctrl. Park W., NY, NY 10025, USA. 2,3,6.

KALNINS, Janis, b. 3 Nov. 1904, Pernu, Estonia. Composer; Conductor; Organist; Educator. Educ: Latvian Conserv. Riga. m. Hermine Kalnins. Career incls: Cond. num. orchs. inclng: Latvian State Opera Orch.; Latvian State Nat. Drama Theatre Orch.; Fredericton, NB, Can. Civic Orch.; NB Symph. Orch.; Guest Cond., Baltic States; Cleveland, Milwaukee & Chgo., USA; Toronto, Montreal, Vancouver, Can.; Guest Cond., Royal Opera HS., Stockholm, Sweden. Comps. incl: Two Latvian Peasant Dances; 3 operas, 3 symphs.; 2 ballets, violin concerto, symph poems. Contbr. to num. mags. Mbr. CAPAC, Toronto, Can. Hons incl: 1st Prize for Song The Brids Lullaby from CBC Montreal, 1952; Gustav Wasa Order, Stockholm, Sweden. Hobbies: Fishing; Hunting; Target Practice. Address: PO Box 571, Fredericton, NB, Canada E3B 5A6.

KAMASA, Stefan, b. 18 July 1930, Bielsk, Podlaski, Poland. Violist. Educ: State Music Acad., Poznan; Warsaw Music Acad.; Paris Conserv.; MA. m. Barbara Dzikowska, 1 s. Debut: W. Phil. Orch., Poznan, 1950. Career incl: Soloist in num. countries in Europe, Ctrl., N & S Am.; Chmbr. Music performer, Europe, Am. & Japan w. Warsaw Quintet; Radio & TV appearances in UK., Germany, Japan, France, Switzerland & Poland, Salzburg Fest., 1976; Prof., Warsaw Music Acad. Recordings incl: num. works on Muza label of Bach, Brahms, Mozart, Franck, Dvorak, Schumann, Shostakowitch, etc. Publs: Arrs. of var. works by Polish & classical composers for viola, piano, strings, etc. Contbr. to var. music publs. Mbrships: SPAM (Polish Music Assn.); SPAL (Polish Assn. of Violin Makers). Hons: 1st Prize, Warsaw Viola Comp., 1957; Orpheo & Critics Prizes, Int. Music Festival 'Warsaw Autumn', 1970. Hobbies: Filming; Football. Mgmt: Pagart, Polish Artistic Agcy., Warsaw; Ibbs & Tillet, London. Address: Ul. Obronców 21, 03-933 Warsaw, Poland.

KAMENIKOVA, Valentina, b. 20 Dec. 1930, Odessa, USSR. Pianist; Professor of Acad. of Music & Arts, Prague. Educ: Musical High Schl., Odessa; Acad. of Musical Arts, ibid. div., 2 children. Debut: Odessa. Career: Recitals & apps. w. orchs., & TV perfs., Czechoslovakia, German Dem. Repub., USSR, German Fed. Repub., England, Belgium, France, etc. Recordings: Works by Tchaikovsky, Rachmaninoff, Chopin, Beethoven, Mozart, Haydn & Liszt for Supraphon. Mbr., Czech Union of Comps. & Soloists. Hons: Grand Prize, Supraphon, 1973; Wiener Flötenuhr Prize, Mozartgemeinde, Vienna, 1975. Address: Cechovo Namestl 9, 101 00 Prague 10, Czechoslovakia.

KAMILAROV, Emil, b. 15 April 1928, Toulouse, France. Violinist. Educ: Bulgarian State Conserv.; Leningrad State Conserv. m Dina Schneidermani, 1 s. Career: 1st Place and laureat at many int. competitions, incl. Jan Kubelik, 1949 (Prague), H Wienjawsky (Poznan), 1952, Arigo Serato (Rome), 1954, Jacques Tibeaut (Paris), 1959, N Paganini - Grand Prix (Geneva), 1961, Dimitroff Prize, Bulgaria; Popular Artist of Bulgaria, 1978-; Prof., State Conserv., 1961-; Concerts worldwide. Recordings incl: Paganini Violin Concertos No. 1 & 2; Wienjawsky Violin Concertos No. 1 & 2, etc. Publs: About the Left Hand Technics of the Violinist, 1954. Mbrships: Jury, many competitions; Ysaye Soc. (Belgium). Address: ul Petko Enev 47A, 1126 Sofia, Bulgaria.

KAMU, Okko, b. 7 Mar. 1946, Helsinki Finland. Orchestral Conductor. Educ: Violin (Vaino Arjava), 1949; studied violin & chamber music w. Onni Suhonen, piano & theoretical subjects, Sibelius Acad., 1952-67. m. Arja Nieminen, 1 s., 2 d. Debut: as violinist in early 1950's, as chamber musician (str. quartet), 1965, as cond., 1968-69. Career: 2nd Ldr. of Violino 2do of the Helsinki Phil. Orch., 1965-66; 1st Concert Master, Finnish Nat. Opera's Orch., 1966-69; 3rd Cond., ibid., 1968-69; Guest Cond., Royal Swedish Opera, 1969-70; Cond. & later Chief Cond., Radio Symph. Orch., Finland, 1970-77; Chief Cond. & Musical Dir., Oslo Phil., Norway, 1975-; guest cond., major symph. orchs. in Europe, USA, Japan, Aust. Comps: Film music; songs for children (recorded). Many recordings. Mbrships: Nötön Savustajat; RFYC; Koholmin Kämärät. Recip., Herbert von Karajan Prize, 1969. Hobbies: the Sea. Mgmt: Svensk Konsertdirecktion AB; Pears-Phipps Mgmt., London, etc. Address: Rakennusmestarintie 8, 00680 Helsinki 68, Finland.

KANAZAWA, Masakata, b. 6 Jan. 1934, Tokyo, Japan. Musicologist. Educ: BA, Int. Christian Univ., Tokyo, 1957; AM, 1961, PhD, 1966, Harvard Univ., USA. m. Chizuko Yasukawa, 1 c. Career: Teacher Fellow & Tutor in Music, Harvard Coll., 1963-66; Lectr. in Music, Int. Christian Univ., Tokyo, Japan, 1966-; Fellow in Music, Harvard Univ. Ctr. for Italian

Renaissance Studies, Florence, Italy, 1970-71; Vis. Prof., var. colls., USA. Publs: Ed., The Complete Works of Anthony Holborne, vol. 1, 1967, vol. II, 1973, vol. III in progress; Ed., Antonii Janue opera omnia, 1974; Ed., The Musical MS Montecassino 871 (w. I Pope), 1978. Contbr. to musicol. ref. books & jrnls. Mbrships incl: Am. & Japanese Musicol. Socs.; Int. Musicol. Soc. Hons: John K Paine Fellowship, 1962. Hobbies: Theatre; Travel. Address: 2-2-7 Nishikata, Bunkyo, Tokyo 113, Japan. 14.

KANIEWSKI, Jan, b. 1 Jan. 1931, Niechcice, Poland. Conductor. Educ: Nat. Acad. of Music, Warsaw. m. 2 children. Debut: Symphonic concert, Olsztyn, Poland, 1956. Career: Cond. choirs (a capella) and symph. orchs. in Poland; Asst. Headmaster, Fr. Chopin Second. Schl., 1968-72; Headmaster, music tchr.' extra-mural studies, Acad. of Music, 1972-75; currently Dean, Pedagogic Fac., ibid. Comps: works for choirs & orchl. socs. Mbrships: Polish Soc. of Musical Artist; Heunesses Musicales. Contbr. to: Guide of Music; var. newspapers & musical jrnls. Recip., 3rd Degree Prize, Min. of Culture & Art, 1973 & 75. Hobbies: Sport; Sightseeing. Address: Grzybowska St. 30/1427, 00-863 Warsaw, Poland.

KANITZ, Eernest, b. 9 Apr. 1894, Vienna, Austria. Composer; Conductor. Educ: Dr. jur., Univ. of Vienna, 1918. Pvte. study of Composition w. Franz Schreker, 1914-20. m., 1 s., 2 d. Career: Num. perfs., 1918-; Fndr., Cond., Vienna Women's Chmbr. Chorus. Compositions incl: Sonata Californiana for Alto Saxophone & Piano; Sinfonia Seria; Second Symph.; Sinfonia Concertante, (violin, piano & orch.), Ballet Music for Women's Voices & Orchestra; Concerto for Bassoon & Orchestra; Notturno for Flute, Violin & Viola. Mbrships: ASCAP; Bd. Mbr., Nat. Assn. for Am. Composers & Conds. Hobbies: Touring. Address: 6206 Murietta Ave., Van Nuys, CA 91401, USA.

KANN, Hans, b. 14 Feb. 1927, Vienna, Austria. Concert Pianist; Composer; Professor Piano. Educ: Vienna Music Academy. m. Kue Hee Ha, 1 d. Debut: Brahsmsaal, Vienna, 1946. Career: Num. concert apps. all over the world. Comps: (for piano) Sonatina; Abschnitt; 10 Stücke ohne Bassschlüssel; & Concertino; chmbr. music; music for ORF & ZDF TV & others; expmtl. music. Recordings: 94 recordings for num. cos. inclng. EMI (Toshiba); Musical Heritage Soc.; Vox; RCA; JVC. Publs. incl: Fingerübungen (Finger exercises). Contbr. to: Österr. Musikzeitung; Gendai Ongaku (Tokyo). Mbr. var. profl. orgs. Hons incl: Silver Medal, Concours, Geneva, 1948; Körnerpreis, 1962, 1964. Hobby: Collecting antiques. Address: Sonnenfelsgasse 11/7, Vienna 1010, Austria.

KANNGIESSER, Claus Dietmar, b. 13 Mar. 1945, Berne, German Fed. Repub. Cellist; Teacher. Educ: Artist Dip., Hamburg; Postgrad. Dip., Juilliard Schl. of Music, NYC. m. Nerine Barrett, 1 d. Career: Solo cello recitals in Europe & USA; Prof., Conserv., Saarbrücken. Hons: 2nd Prize, Munich Radio Competition; 1st Prize, Int. Rostrum of Young Interpreters, Paris. Hobby: Sport. Mgmt: Dr. Goette, Hamburg. Address: Aubachweg 9, 6631¢, Bedersdorf üb. Saarlouis, German Fed. Repub. 3.

KANSKI, Jozef Celestyn, b. 21 Oct. 1928, Warsaw, Poland. Pianist; Musicologist; Music Critic. Educ: MA, Univ. of Warsaw; Piano Dip.; Acad. of Music, Warsaw. m. Teresa Grabowska, 1 d. Debut: Bydgoszcz, Poland, 1961. Career: num. Perfs., inclng. w. Nat. Phil., Warsaw; Co-Ed., Ruch Muzyczny; Ind., Opera Dept., Polish Radio; num. Radio Apps. Publs: Ludomir Rozycki, 1955; Przewodnik operowy, 1963, 1967, 1973; Gwiazdy operowej sceny, 1974; Ludomir Rozycki's Symphonic Poems, 1971. Contbr. to: Annales Chopin; The Stars of The Polish Opera; Trybuna Ludu; Opera, London. Mbrships: Musicol. Sect., Union of Polish Comps.; Fr. Chopin Soc.; Bd., Soc. of Polish Musicians; Ctr. of Int. Music Studies, Rome, Italy. Hobbies: Record Collecting; Swimming; Tennis; Skiing; Driving. Address: 8 m. 14 ul Perzynskiego, 01-872 Warsaw, Poland.

KANTOR, Eva Ida, b. Baden, near Vienna, Austria. Guitarist; Guitar Teacher (Guitar, Laud, Piano). Educ: Grad. Dip. & Tchr's. Dip., State Acad. of Music, Vienna. Career: For 10 yrs. held courses for adults; Introduction to Music through the Guitar at Collegium Musicum of Buenos Aires; Currently fulltime tchr. of guitar to adults, children & cases of special educ. Publs: La Guitarra Cantora, 1969; A Jugary Cantar con Guitarra I w. V H de Galaza, 1970; A Jugary Cantar con Guitarra, II & III, 1974. Mbrships: Bd. Mbr. & Recording Sec., Argentina Soc. for Music Therapy; Argentina Soc. for Music Educ. Hobbies: Plants; Animals; Outdoors. Address: Adolfo Alsina 865, 1638 Vicente Lopez, Prov. de Buenos Aires, Argentina, S America.

KANTOROW, Jean-Jacques Alain, b. 1945, Cannes, France. Concert Violinist. Educ: Nice Conserv.; Nat. Higher Conserv. of

Music, Paris. Recordings incl: Mozart's Violin Concerti 3 & 4. Recip. of many awards inclng: 1st Prizes, Nat. Higher Conserv. of Music, Paris, 1960 & 63; Carl Flesch Gold Medal, 1962; 1st Prize, Paganini, 1964; Best Violinist Prize, Geneva, 1965. Hobbies: Lectures; Sports. Address: Point d'Or, Avenue du Roi Albert 1st, Cimiez, 06-Nice, France. 3.

KAPLAN, Althea E., b. 6 Aug. 1935, Crestline, Ohio, USA. Professor & Director of Music. Educ: B Mus., Ohio Wesleyan Univ., 1957; M Mus., Eastman Schl. of Music, 1958; PhD, study, ibid. m . Sheldon R Kaplan, 1 d. Career: Pub. Schl. Tchr., 1958-64; Ed., Dover Publs., 1964-66; Ed., Univ. of Miami, 1966-68; Prof., Miami-Dade Community Coll. N., & Prof. of Flute, Barry Coll., 1968-. Fndr., Miami Flute Club; Dir., Miami-Dade Electronic Music Workshop. Mbrships: Pi Kappa Lambda; Kappa Delta Pi; Mu Phi Epsilon (Pres., Miami Alumnae, Dist. Dir.); MENC; Fla. Music Educators Assn.; Fla. Coll. Music Educators Assn.; Nat. Assn. of Coll. Wind & Percussion Instrs.; Nat. Flute Assn. Contbr. of num. articles to Am. Educator Ency. Awards: 3rd Place, Nat. Composition Contest. Hobbies: Reading; Sewing; Travel. Address: 14415 N Kendall Dr., 409 Miami, FL 33186, USA.

KAPLAN, Barbara Connally, b. 19 Aug. 1923, La Grange, Ga., USA. University Professor. Educ: BA, Agnes Scott Coll., 1944; MA, Eastman Schl. Music, 1946; PhD, Fla. State Univ., 1966; Kodaly concept, Franz Liszt Acad., Budapest, Hungary, 1974, 1977; MA Lib. Sci., Univ. S Fla., 1977. m. Max Kaplan, 1 s., 1 d. Career: w. Chautauqua Opera Co., 1943-44; Recitals & Oratorio, USA, 1942-; TV concerts, KLRN TV, Austin, Tex.; Lyric Theatre, Tampa, Fla., 1960-62. Author, cons., recording singer, filmstrip, Stephen Foster: His Life & Melodies, 1972. Publs. incl: New Dimensions in Music (co-author); Harp Album Repertoire Primer, 1976 (co-author). Contbr. to profl. jrnls. Mbr. Profl. orgs. Hons. incl: Phi Beta Kappa; Pi Kappa Lambda; Int. Fellowship, Delta Kappa Gamma, 1967-68. Hobbies: Swimming; Travel. Address: Summit Lane Rt. 3 Box 81A, Auburn, AL 36830, USA. 27.

KAPLAN, Benjamin, b. 23 Sept. 1929, London, UK. Pianist; Teacher. Educ: LGSM; studied w. Franz Reizenstein & Louis Kenther. m. Naomi Reuben, 1 s., 1 d. Career: perfs. for BBC radio, Hessischer Rundfunk & ORF Studio Tirol. Mbr: ISM. Hons: Lady Mayoress Prize, GSM, 1948; Jt. 2nd Prize, Franz Liszt Competition, London, 1961. Hobbies: Bridge; Chess; Gardening. Address: 64, Addison Way, Hampstead Gdn. Suburb, London NW11 6QS, UK. 4.

KAPLAN, Lois Jay, b. 6 Feb. 1932, Chgo., Ill., USA. Composer; Music Director; Lecturer; Critic; Conductor; Instrumentalist; Writer; Sculptor. Educ. incl: BMus, De Paul Univ.; MSci., Univ. of Wis.; MArts, Jacksonville State Univ.; postgrad. studies for PhD, Fla. State Univ.; comp. w. Alexander Tcherepnin; cond. w. Paul Stassevitch. Career incl: Profl. trombonist, 14 yrs.; pvte. tchr., 12 yrs.; tech. dir., music dir., stage mgr., Univ. Theatre, Univ. of Chgo.; band dir., art tchr., Chgo. public schls., 1956-62; cond., De Paul Univ. Stadium Band, 1954-58. Comps: Pallas Athena (song & march); Salute to the Citizen Soldiers; This Indeed We'll Defend. Mbrships. incl: Pres., Tri-Arts Club, Chgo.; Ala. Coun. of the Arts & Humanities. Hobbies incl: Chess; Photography; Sailing; Riding; Backpacking; Travel; Gourmet Cooking. Address: 616 Lenwood Dr., Anniston, AL 36201, USA.

KAPP, Dorothy Louise, b. 14 Aug. 1910, Evansville, Ind., USA. Organist; Pianist; Teacher, Organ, Piano, Voice. Educ: Grad., Sherwood Music Schl., Chgo., Ill.; Univ. of Evansville, Ind. m. Louis Kapp, 1 s., 1 d. Career: Summer Stock, 1930's; Silent Film Organist & Pianist; Radio Perf., 25 yrs.; Ch. Organist & Choir Dir., 40 yrs.; Dir., World's Largest Organ Concert, 1966-67; Judge, Nat. Music Fests., Ind. State Univ., 1971-73; Tchr. of Blind; Tchr. & Music Dir., Nursery Schl. Singing Sabenko Music House, Tallahassee, Fla. Contbr. to: Piano Guild Notes; Modern Keyboard; Nat. Ret'd. Tchrs. Assn. Jrnl.; Keyboard Arts. Mbrships: Sec., Phi Club; Fndr., Pres., Lincoln Trail Organ Club; Nat. Fedn. of Music Clubs; Am. Coll. of Musicians; Organ & Piano Tchrs. Assn.; Int. Platform Assn.; Nat. Ret'd Tchrs. Assn.; VP, 8th Dist., Ind. Fedn. of Music Clubs. Recip. var. Hons. Hobbies: Walking; Fishing; Grandchildren. Address: 819 Reuben St., Tell City, IN 47586, USA. 4,27,29.

KAPP, Eugen Arturovich, b. 28 May 1908, Astrakhan, Russia. Composer. Educ: Leningrad Conserv. Career: Prof., Tallin Conserv. Compositions incl: Trio for Piano, 1930; The Avenger (symphonic poem), 1931; Concerto for Strings, 1935; Sonata No. 1 for Violin & Piano, 1936; Kalevipoeg (Overture - The Son of Kalev), 1938; Symph. No. 1, 1939; Sonata No. 2 for Violin & Piano, 1943; Fires of Vengeance (opera), 1944; Kalevipoeg (ballet), 1947; Sonata for Cello & Piano, 1948; Tallin Scenes, 1949; Bard of Freedom, 1950; Symph. No. 2, 1954; Overture on Finnish Themes, 1957; Leningrad Suite, 1957; Winter's Tale (opera), 1958; Children's Day (cycle of children's songs), 1958. Mbrship: Chmn., Estonian Composers Union. Hons: Peoples Artist of Estonia & USSR; State Prizes, 1946, '52; Order of Lenin, 1950: Order of Red Banner of Labour (twice). Address: Estonian Composers Union, Blvd. Estonia 4, Tallin, USSR.

KAPPEL, Ulla, b. 2 June 1936, Munster, Westfalia, Germany. Harpsichorsist; Pianist. Educ: Dip., Piano, Royal Conserv. of Music, Copenhagen, 1959; Dip., Music Teaching, ibid, 1961; Dip.,Harpsichord, ibid, 1961; Schola Cantorum Basilienses; studied w. A van de Wiele, E Muller, A Wenzinger, W Neininger. m. Jens Julius Kappel, 3 s. Debut: Copenhagen. Career: Concerts throughout Europe & USA; Radio, TV Perfs., Denmark, Austria; Tchr., Royal Conserv. of Music, Copenhagen, 1968-74. Contbr. to Dansk Musiktidsskrift. Mbr. Music Tchrs. Assn. Recip. 1st Prize, Jean-Claude Zehnder, Liechtenstein, 1972. Hobbies: Swimming; Yachting; Gardening. Mgmt: Jens Julius Kappel, 4 Hovmosevej, Gadevang, 3400 Hillerod, Denmark. Address: 4 Hovmosevej, Gadevang, 3400 Hillerod, Denmark.

KAPR, Jan, b. 12 Mar. 1914, Prague, Czech. Composer; Teacher; Pianist. Educ: Dip., Conserv. of Music, Prague, 1938; Dip., Master's Schl. (now Acad. of Music), Prague, 1940. m. Libuse Tomásková, 2 d. Career: Music Dir., Radio Prague, 1939-46; Ed.-in-Chief, nat. Music Publng. house 'ORBIS', 1950-53; Lectr. in Composition, Janacek Acad. of Music, Brno, 1961-70; artistic collaboration w. radio, theatre & film. Compositions publd. & recorded incl: Home (two cycles of pieces for piano), 1954; Str. Quartet No. 3, 1955; Fantasia for Violin & Piano, 1958; Str. Quartet w. Baritone Solo, 1965; Dialogues for Flute & Harp, 1977; Opportunities for piano solo, 1976; Symph. No. 8 (choir & orch.), 1977; Sonatina, 1977; Musica per Mila, Soprano & chmbr. orch., 1977; 3 Exercises, wind instrument & piano, 1978. Works recorded by Cz.BC.; Supraphon; Rec.Ed. Serenus; W German Broadcasting. Publs: Konstantly (constants), 1967. Contbr. to: Hudebni rozhledy; Tempo; Slovenská Hudba. Mbrships: var. exec. offs., Czech. Composers Guild; OSA (Protective Union of Authors). Hons. incl: Czech. State Prize, 1953; Artist of Merit, 1964; Unesco Prize, Paris 1968; Prize of the Czech. Guild of Composers, 1968; Prize of Czech. Music Critics, 1969. Hobbies: Chess; Table Tennis; Creative Arts. Address: Cerchovská 6, 1200 00 Prague 2, Czech. 30.

KARAI, József, b. 8 nov. 1927, Budapest, Hungary. Composer; Pianist. Educ: Acad. of Music, Budapest, 1947-54; comp. & 3 yrs. conductor's trng. m. Katalin Kertesz. Debut: 1950. Comps: Approx. 200 works for chorus, for children, female mixed & male choruses, mainly on the basis of modern 20th Century Hungarian poets poems, i.e. Ady, Attila József, Radnóti, Weöres, etc., but also on the basis of Love by R Browning; Folk song arrs. mainly Hungarian, but alos the Twelve Spirituals, & Three English Folk Songs. works are publd. by Editio Musica Budapest, & 35 by other publsrs; 3 children's choruses by Edition Tonos Darmstadt, A Day in a Childs Life by General Music Publng. Co., NY; Works for flute, trumpet, horn, piano , songs, partita for organ, str. quartet; works for orch. Recordings: 14 choruses. Broadcast of Hungarian Radio, Budapest. Mbr., Assn. of Hungarian Musicians. Recip., Erkel Prize, 1972. Hobbies: Drawing; Collecting car & train models, etc. Address: Gyöztes-u. 19, 1151 Budapest, Hungary.

KARAJAN, Herbert von, b. 5 Apr. 1908, Austria. Conductor. Educ: Mozarteum, Salzburg; Vienna Univ. & Conserv. Career: Musical Dir., Ulm, Germany; Opera & Gen. Music Dir., Aachen; Kapellmeister, Berlin State Opera; Cond., Berlin Phil. Orch.; Dir., Berlin Staatskapell, 1941-45; Concert tours in Europe, USA & Far E., 1945-; Artistic Dir., Berlin Phil. Orch., 1955-56; Vienna State Opera, 1956-64; Bd. of Dirs., Salzburg Festival, 1965-; Dir., Gesellschaft der Musikfreunde, Vienna; Guest cond. at Salzburg & Lucerne Festivals, Mozart Ring, 1957. Hons: Cmndr. 1st Class, Order of White Rose, Finland; Prix France-Allemagne, 1970. Address: c/o Vienna State Opera, Vienna, Austria.

KARAMANUK, Sirvart, b. 1 Dec. 1916, Istanbul, Turkey. Composer; Pianist. Educ: Istanbul Conserv.; special studies w. Lazar Levy. m. Kevork Karamanuk. Debut: Theatre Français, Istanbul. Career: Perfs. of comps. in N & S Am., Europe, Middle East, USSR. Comps: (publd.) series of songs for solo voice & piano, USA & USSR; (recorded) Achtamar; Tjar dari; Admiration. Contbr. to: Kulis; Shoghagat; Marmara. Mbr., Sacred Music Committee of the Armenian Patriarchate of Istanbul. Hobbies: Oil painting; Needlepoint; Social work. Address: 269/3 Halaskar gazi Cad., Sisli, Istanbul, Turkey.

KARASEK, Jiří, b. 6 July 1925, Brno, Czech. Conductor; Pianist. Educ: Pvte. Schl. of Prof. B Liska, Pizen. m. Dagmar Pistorová, 1 d. Debut: State Theatre, Brno, 1953. Career: State Theatre, Brno, 1950-56, 1966-; JK Tyl Theatre, Pizen, 1956-62; O Stibor Theatre, Olomouc, 1962-66. Comps: Stage Comps.: Incidental Music. Mbr: Union of Dramatic Artists. Recip. of Prize of the Czech Lit. Fund, 1968. Hobbies: Dogs; Swimming. Address: Vychodilova 16, 616 00 Brno 16, Czech.

KARASIK, Gita, b. 14 Dec. 1949, San Fran., Calif., USA. Concert Pianist. Educ: San Fran. Conserv. of Music; Aspen, Colo., Music Fest.; studied Piano w. Mme. Rosina Lhevinne & Karl Schnabel, 1955-. m. Lee Evan Caplin. Debut: NYC, 1969. Career: incls. apps. w. San Fran. Symph., 1958, 69, 72, 74, Los Angeles Phil., 1971, St. Louis Symph., 1975, 74, Boston Pops Orch., 1975, Indpls. Symph., 1976, & other major orchs.; Tours of Latin Am. & W Indies, 1972, the Far East, 1977, 78; Phillips Collection, Wash. DC, 1977; Featured artist w. Pro Musicis Fndn., NYC. Recording: Phillips Collection Recital, 1977. Hons. incl: Oakland, Calif., Symph. Award, 1962; Kimber Award, 1966; San Fran. Symph. Fndn. Prize, 1970; Winner, Young Concert Artists Int. Auditions, 1970; Ford Fndn. Artists Award (concerto commissioned), 1973; Rockefeller Artists Grant, 1976. Mgmt: Tornay Mgmt. Inc., 1995 Broadway, NYC 10023, USA. Address: 3223 Adams Mill Rd., NW, Wash. DC 20010, USA.

KARAYEV, Kara Abulfas ogly, b. 5 Feb. 1918, Baku, Azerbaizhan. Composer. Educ: Moscow Conserv. Compositions incl: Song of the Heart (Cantata for choir, symph. orch. & dance grp.), 1937; Azerbaijan Suite for Symph. Orch., 1939; 1st Symph., 1944; Veten (opera), 1945; 2nd Symph., 1946; Leili & Medjun (Symphonic poem), 1947; Seven Beauties (ballet), 1952; Albanian Rhapsody, 1952; Choreographic Sketches for Symph. Orch., 1953; Viet-Nam (Symphonic Suite), 1955; Prelude for Piano, 1957; Thunder Path (ballet), 1957; Three Nocturnes for Jazz Band, 1958; Sonata for Violin & Piano, 1960; Incidental music for plays - Masquerade, The Dancing Teacher, Othello, A Winter's Tale, The Crank, An Optimistic Tragedy; Film music for Story of Caspian Oil Workers. Mbrships: CPSU; Chmn., Azerbaizhan Composers Union; Sec., Soviet Composers Union. Azerbaizhan Acad. of Scis. Hons: State Prizes, 1946, 1948; People's Artist of the USSR, 1959; Lenin Prize, 1967; Order of Red Banner of Labour. Address: Azerbaizhan Composers Union, Ulitsa Nizami 58, Baku, USSR.

KARBOWSKA, Helena, b. 24 Dec. 1906, Warszawa, Poland. Artistic Vocalist; Operatic Singer. Educ: Studied w. Prof. Jul Marso, Warsaw & Profs. Maria & Sophia Kozeowski. Debut: In Cavaleria Rusticana w. Warsov Opera, 1926. Career: Apps. incl: Carmen (Bizet) w. Katowice Opera; Faust (Gounod); Butterfly (Puccini); Oratorium (Tosca); Stabat Mater (Rossini); Requiem (Verdi). Solo Vocalist, Nat. Phil., Warszawa, 1955-68. Contbr. to Ruch Muzyczny. Mbrships. incl: Dir., Concert Musicians Trade Union, Moscow, 1946-49; Assn. of Polish Artists & Musicians; Trade Union Workers of Culture & Art. Hons. incl: Annual Award of Bd. Mgmt., Polish Assn. of Artists & Musicians, 1971. Address: Arabska 3 m 76, 03-980 Warszawa, Poland.

KARBUSICKY, Vladimir, b. 9 Apr. 1925, Velim, Kolin, Czech. Musicologist; Lecturer. Educ: PhD., Charles Univ., Prague, 1953; Candidatus Scientiarum, ibid., 1959. m. Maria Karbusicky, 2 d., 1 s. Career: Lectr., Charles Univ., 1964-; Music tchr., Pädagogische Hochschule, Cologne, 1975-76; Prof., Systematic Musicol., Univ. of Hamburg, 1976-; Mbr., Acad. of Scis., Prague, 1968; Mbr., Inst. for Musical Folklore, Neuss, 1968-74. Publs. incl: Untersuchung zur Musikalität der Gegenwart, w. J Kasan, Vol. 1, 1964, 1969, Vol. 2, 1969; Beethovens Brief, An die Unsterbliche Geliebte, und sein musikalisches Werk, 1968, 1977; Wiederspiegelungstheorie und Strukturalismus, 1973; Musikwerk und Gesellschaft, 1977; Gustav Mahler und sein Umwelt, 1978; Einführung in die Systematische Musikwissenschaft, 1979. Contbr. to num. profil. jrnls. Mbrships: Soc. for Music Rsch.; Int. Musicol. Soc. Recip. num. hons. Address: 25 Lehmkuhlskamp, 2110 Buchholz, German Fed. Repub.

KARDONNE, Rick, b. 30 Mar. 1947, NY, NY, USA. Composer; Lyricist; Orchestrator; Pianist; Musical Director. Educ: BA, Hiram Coll., Hiram, Ohio; pvte. studies in piano & theory; grad. studies, McGill Univ., Montreal. m. Eda Golub. Career: 4 original stage musicals prod., Orang-Utang (Toronto, 1974), Frontenac Revue (Quebec, 1974), Olympian Follies (Montreal, 1975), 1999 (Toronto, 1978); comps. perf. in Can., Israel, UK. Comps: as above, also co-comp., Sweet Reason; film score credits, How Things Have Changed & Rip-Off; comp.-lyricist, As in Days Gone By; mus. dir. num. concerts & shows; song, Hit the Nail Right on the Head. Publ:

(co-author) Portrait of a Pianist (Sheila Henig). Contbr. to: Can. Jewish News, 1972-; The Chronicle-Review (Toronto), Mbrships: Am. Guild of Authors & Comps.; The Dramatic Guild; ASCAP; Am. Mechanical Rights Assn.; AFM. Hobbies incl: Swimming; Tennis. Address: 1050 Yonge St., Apt. 33A, Toronto, Ont., M4W 2L1, Can.

KARDOS, Dezider, b. 1914, Nadlice, Slovakia. Professor of Composition. Educ: Conserv. of music, Bratislava; Master Schl. of Composition, Prague. m. Maria Hisemova, 1 s., 1 d. Career: Hd. of Music Dept., Presov Broadcasting Stn., 1939-45; Chief of Musical Broadcasts, Kosice, 1945-51; Ldr., of Dept. for Folk Art, Bratislava Broadcasting Stn., 1951; Dir. of Slovak Philharmony, Bratislava, 1952-55. Compositions incl: On My Native Land (2nd symph.); Piccola (4th symph.); Elavazioni per organo da cencerto; The Heroic Ballad for string orch.; East Slovakian Overture; Suite from Rainbow Over Slovakia (film); Preludium quasi una fantasia for organ & str. quartet; Greeting to the Great Land, cantata for mixed choir & orch. Mbr: Union of Slovak Composers, Bratislava (Chmn. 1955-63). Hons: Laureate, State Prize; Czech. Prize for Peace. Hobby: Motoring. Address: Rubinsteinova 12, Bratislava, Czechoslovakia. 3.

KARKOFF, Maurice Ingvar, b. 17 Mar. 1927, Stockholm, Sweden. Composer. Educ: Matric, 1947; studied comp. (L E Larsson), theory; piano & cond., RAM 1945, '48-53; studied w. Karl Birger Blomdahl, Erland von Koch, J. Jersild (Instrumentation), V. Holmboe, A. Jolivet, N. Boulanger, U. Boscovitj, M. Deutsch, W. Vogel, H. Holewa, Ivo Petric. Career: Asst. Music Critic, Stockholms-Tidningen, 1962-66; Hi-Fi Music, 1978-; Tchr. of Theory & Comp., Music Inst., Stockholm, 1965-. Comps. incl: Concerto for violin, op. 22, 1956; 11 solo concertos; Piano sonata no.1, op. 19, 1956; Symph. no. 3, op. 38, 1958 (8 symphs.); Textum for strings, op. 87, 1967; Monopartita for piano, op. 99, 1969; Sonata for 6 brass players, op. 105, 1970; In the Beginning for mixed choir, op. 107, 1970-71; Chamberopera; Gränskibbutzen, op. 115. Recordings incl: Characters for woodwind quintet, trombone, euphonium & percussion, op. 118, 1973-74; Caprice, 7 Pezzi, 6 Kinesiskaimpressioner vision; Chamber concerto no. 2, op. 120. Mbr: Swedish Soc. for Comps.; Swedish Soc. Discofil; Royal Swedish Musical Acad., 1977. Hons: Christ. Johnsons Prize, Royal Musical Acad., Stockholm, 1964; Stockholm's Hon. Prize, 1976. Hobbies: Photography. Address: Stramaljvägen 4, 161 50 Bromma, Sweden.

KARKOSCHKA, Erhard, b. 6 Mar. 1923, Mahr. Ostrau, Czech. Composer. Educ: Konzertreife-Pruefungen, Musikhochschule; D Musicol. m. Rothraut Leiter Karkkoschka, 4 c. Career: Prof., Univ. of Hohenheim, 1948-68, Musikhochschule, Stuttgart, 1958-; Mbr. Exec. Bd., Institut Fur Neuemusik und Musikerziehung, Darmstadt, 1964-72. Pres., Gesellschaft für Neue Musik, 1974-. Comps: 50, for orch., ensembles, chorus, Chmbr. Music, scenic works, Electronic Music, for orch. & audience; multimed projects. Recordings: Ad Hoc 1; Antinomie for Winds; 4 Tasks for 5 Players; Desiderato Dei, for organ. Publs: Das Schriftbild Der Neuen Musik, 1965; Notation in New Music, 1972, Japanese translation, 1977; Analyse Neuer Musik, 1976. Hons: Prize, Nat. Olympic Committee, 1955; Prize, City of Stuttgart, 1957; Johann-Wenzel-Stamitz Prize, Kunstle-Gilde Esslingen, 1971. Address: 45 Nellinger, 7 Stuttgart 75, German Fed. Repub.

KARLSEN, Rolf Kåre, b. 26 June 1911, Oslo, Norway. Cathedral Organist. Educ: Latin-artium, 1930, Organisteksamen, 1931; Studies in London, Basel (Schola Cantorum), Copenhagen (Finn Vider), Belgium. m. Ruth Waaler, 2 s., 1 d. Debut: Organ, 1933, Piano, 1935, Harpsichord, 1945, Cond. of Choir & Orch., 1945, Oslo. Career: Cond., Norwegian Broadcasting Chmbr. choir, 1946-73; Ldr., Collegium Musicum, Oslo. Comps: Works for organ, choir, orch. & piano. Recordings: Sowerby - Classic Concerto for organ & string orch.; Grieg - 4 Salmer (chamberchoir). Mbrships: Ridder avl kalsse av St. Olavs Orden; Ehrenmitglied Int. Heinrich Schütz-Gesellschaft; Norges Organistforbund; Oslo Organist-forening. Address: Finnhaugveien 32, Oslo 7, Norway.

KARLSKOV, Poul, b. 16 Nov. 1927, Skaelskoer, Denmark. Opera Singer (Tenor). Educ: Royal Danish Music Conserv.; Opera Acad., Copenhagen. m. Hanne Karlskov, 2 s. Debut: Pedrillo, Die Entfuhrung aus dem Serail, Royal Theatre, Copenhagen, 1964. Career: Schuisky, 'Boris Godunow'; Cassio, 'Othello'; Goro, 'Butterfly'; Bardolph, 'Falstaff'; Tinca, 'Il Tabarro'; Spoletta, 'Tosca'; Sellem, 'The Rakes Progress'; Armand Brissard, 'Der Graf von Luxemburg'. Hobby: Radio 'Ham'. Mgmt: Royal Theatre, Copenhagen. Address: Bastkaer 7, 2760 Malov, Denmark.

KAROLAK, Marek, b. 25 Apr. 1954, Lódz, Poland. Bassoonist. State Phil. of Lodz. Educ: State Schl. of Music,

Lódz, Poland. Comps: Variations (5 wind instruments, harp & litle orch.), 1972; Episodes (little orch.); 3 Comps. (capella chorus); Evening Songs (capella chorus); 4 Preludes (mezzosoprano & percussion), 1973; Cadenze (percussionist), 1974; Canzona (flute, harp & 4 instruments); Cappriccio (oboe & 2 instruments), 1975; Profile of a White Lady (mezzosoprano & piano); Poems chosen from Jrnls. (coloratura soprano & 4 instruments); Serenade (tenor, 2 oboes & contralto Saxophone); Concerto 5a 3/piano, 9 wind instruments & 2 celli, 1976; Concerto grosso (8 wind instruments, violin & cello), 1978; Small comps. for different instruments. Publs: Sinfonietta by Leos Janacek (in Polish manuscript). Recip. Reward of Bd. of Union of Polish Comps. Address: ul. Norwida 3/5 m 93, 94-024 Lódz, Poland.

KÁROLYI, Pal, b. 9 June 1934. Composer. Educ: Liszt Ferenc Acad. of Music, Budapest. m. Edith Kiraly, 2 d. Career: works have been played in Europe, USA & Can. and at num. fests. Comps. incl: (publd) Five piano pieces, comp. in 1963; 24 piano pieces, 1964; Toccata Furiosa, 1966; Accenti, 1969; Four Studies, 1972; Triphtongus 1 & 2, 1968, 70; Four Pieces for Dulcimer, 1966; Meditazione per Clarinetto e Pianoforte, 1967; Contorni per Fagotto e Pianoforte, 1970; Incanto for Divided Chorus, 1973; Motivo per viola, 1973; Triphtongus 3a - Conclusio for organ & horn, 1975; Rondo for 2 Dulcimers, 1975. Recordings incl: num. records (String Quartet No. 2, var. radio recordings). Mbr., Assn. of Hungarian Musicians. Recip., 3rd Prize, Comp. competition org. in hon. of 200th Anniversary of the Harmonien Orch., Bergen, 1965. Address: Kölcsey Ferenc utca 17, H-2600 Vác, Hungary. 30.

KARP, Natalla, b. 1915, Krakow, Poland. Pianist. Educ: Studied w. Artur Schnabel, Berlin, Edward Steuerman & Zbigniew Drzewiecki. m. Dr. J Karp, 2 d. Debut: w. Berlin Phil. Orch., Berlin, 1930. Career: Num. concerts, London, UK & on Continent; Broadcasts for BBC & continental stns. Recordings: Alpha Piano Trio; Tchaikovsky Trio; Chopin Recital. Mbr., ISM. Hobby: Theatre. Mgmt: Basil Douglas, London, UK. Address: 8 Langland Gardens, London NW3, UK. 14.

KÁRPÁTI, János, b. 11 July 1932, Budapest, Hungary. Musicologist; Lecturer; Librarian. Educ: PhD, Eötvös Loránd Univ., Budapest; Dip., fac. of musicol., Ferenc Liszt Acad., Budapest; candidate in musicol. (CSc), Hungarian Acad. of Scis. Career: folk music rsch. in MOrocco, 1957-58; recording prod., Hungaroton, 1959-61; libn., Ferenc Liszt Acad. of Music, Budapest, 1961-; lectr., ibid. Publs: D Scarlatti, 1959; A Schönberg, 1963; Muzsikáló zenetörténet, Vols. II, IV, 1965, '73; Bartók String Quartets, 1975; Bartók kamarezenéje, 1976. Contbr. to: Muzsika; Magyar Zene; Studia Musicologica; Élet és Irodalom; Fontes Artis Musicae. Mbrships: chmn., Hungarian Nat. Committee, Int. Assn. of Music Libs.; Assn. of Hungarian Musicians. recip., Erkel Prize, 1971. Address: Mester u. 77, 1095 Budapest IX, Hungary.

KARR, Gary Michael, b. 20 Nov. 1941, Los Angeles, Calif., USA. Concert Artist & Teacher of the Doluble Bass. Educ. incl: B Mus, Juilliard Schl., 1965. Debut: Town Hall Recital, NYC, 1962. Career incl: many solo apps. inclng. premiere perfs. of Hans Werner Henze Concerto, 1969, Paul Ramsier Divertimento Concertante, 1965, & Alexander Brott Profundum Praedictum, 1964; num. recitals, Can., USA, Mexico, Europe; formed Karr-Lewis Duo (David Harmon Lewis, keyboards), 1971, num. recitals, Can. & USA, perfs. & workshops, Switz. & UK. Has made many recordings. Contbr. to jrnls. Mbrships: Phi Mu Alpha Sinfonia; Fndr.-Pres., Int. Inst. for String Bass, 1967-74. Recip. var. hons. Hobbies: Antiques; Gardening. Mgmt: Mariedi Anders Mgmt. Inc.; Address: PO Box 3365 S Postal Stn., Halifax, NS, Canada B3J 3J1.

KARSON, Burton Lewis, b. 10 Nov. 1934, Los Angeles, Calif., USA. Professor; Pianist; Harpsichordist; Organist; Conductor. Educ: BA, MA, DMA, Univ. of Southern Calif., 1956, 1959, 1964 respectively; Calif. State tchng. credentials, ibid. Career: public perfs., radio & TV apps. as boy soprano, pianist, harpsicordist; lectr. for LA Symph. previews in LA Music Ctr. & in S Calif.; Cond., S Calif. Lutheran Chorale; Organist & choirmaster, St. Joachim's Ch., Costa Mesa, Calif.; Prof. of Music, Calif. State Univ., Fullerton. Publs: Ed., Festival Essays for Pauline Alderman, 1976. Contbr. to: LA Times; Musical Quarterly; Performing Arts. Mbrships: Am. Musicol. Soc.; AGO; Phi Mu Alpha Sinfonia; Bd. of Dirs., Univ. of Southern Calif. Friends of Music; Fndr., Orange Co. Music Ctr. Hobbies: Running; Foreign Travel. Address: 404 De Sola Terr., Corona del Mar, CA 92625, USA. 9.

KASILAG, Lucrecia Roces, b. 31 Aug. 1918, San Fernando, La Union, Philippines. Composer; Music Educator; Administrator. Educ: BA, Philippine Women's Univ., 1936; Music Tchrs. Dip., St. Scholastica's Coll., 1939; B Mus,

Philippine Women's Univ., 1949; M Mus, Eastman Schl. Music, Univ. Rochester, 1950; D Mus (h.c.), Centro Escolar Univ., 1975. Career: Dean, Coll. Music & Fine Arts, Philippine Women's Univ., 1953-77; Dir., Perf. Arts, Cultural Ctr. Philippines, 1969-; Pres., ibid, 1976-. Comps. incl: Burlesque; 5 Philippine Folk Songs; Variations on Walay Angay; Philippine Scenes for Orch.; De Profundis, for mixed chorus & orch. Contbr. to var. jrnls. Mbr. & off. holder var. profl. orgs. inclng: Pres., Nat. Music Coun. of the Philippines. Hons. incl: Republic of China Ministry of Educ. Cert. of Merit & Gold Medallion Award, 1976; Dama de la Orden de Alfonso X el Sabio Spanish Govt. Award, 1977. Hobbies: Reading; Writing. Address: 1340 Perdigon, Paco, Manila, Philippines. 14, 27, 30.

KASLIK, Vaclav, b. 28 Sept. 1917, Policna, Czechoslovakia. Composer; Conductor. Educ: Charles Univ., Prague; Prague Conserv.; Conds. Master Schl., ibid. m. Rdzena Studesova, 1942, 3 s. Appts: Cond., EF Burian Theatre, Prague, 1940-41; Asst. Dir., Nat. Theatre, ibid, 1941-43; Chief of Opera Ensemble, Opera of May 5th, 1945-48; Cond., Smetana Theatre, Prague, 1952-62; Guest Cond., Munich, 1969, Covent Gdn., London, 1969, La Scala, Milan, 1969; Concert tours of NY, Leningrad; Moscow, Vienna, Munich. Compositions: Operas - Robbers' Ballad, 1944; Calvary, 1950; Krakatit, 1960; Ballets - Don Juan, 1939; Janosik, 1951; Prague Carnival, 1952. Hons: Klement Gottwald State Prize, 1956; Honoured Artist of Czech SSR, 1958. Address: Strutkova 10, Prague II, Czechoslovakia.

KASLOW, David Martin, b. 12 May 1943, Bklyn., NY, USA. French Hornist; Professor of Horn. Educ: BM, MM, Manhattan Schl. of Music. m. Judith Kaslow, 1 s., 1 d. Debut: Soloist, Bklyn. Symph., 1950. Career: Solo Horn, Halifax (NS) Symph., Nat. Ballet of Can., Aspen Fest. Chmbr. Orch.; Mbr., Wash. (DC) Nat. Symph. Orch.; Bklyn. Philharmonia; Tours w. world's leading ballet cos.; Mbr., NH Music Fest. Orch., Ctrl. City Opera Orch.; Apps. on ABC TV specials; Prof. of Horn, Univ. of Denver. Comp. of incidental music for Coriolanus. Mbrships: Int. Horn Soc.; AAUP; Mensa Soc.; Court of Last Resort. Hobbies: Walking; Reading. Mgmt: Young Audiences Inc. Address: 365 S Williams, Denver, CO, USA.

KASSLER, Jamie Croy, b. Neenah, Wis., USA. Musicologist. Educ: BMus, Univ. of Wis., 1964; MA, 1967, PhD, 1971, Columbia Univ. m. Michael Kassler. Career: Ed., Current Musicology, 1965-66; Post Doct. Rsch. Fellow, Dept. of Music, Univ. of Sydney, 1975-77; Rsch. Fellow, Schl. of History & Philosophy of Science, Univ. of New South Wales, 1979-. Publs: The Science of Music in Britain, 1714-1830: A Catalogue of Writings, Lectures & Inventions, 2 vols., 1979. Contbr. to: Current Musicology; Musical Quarterly; Jrnl. of the Am. Musicol. Soc.; Notes; Studies in Music; Grove's Dict., 6th Ed. Committee, Musicol. Soc. of Aust.; Am. Musicol. Soc.; Australasian Assn. of History & Philosophy of Science. Hons: 1st Prize, Comp., State of Wisconsin, for String Quartet No. 1, 1959; Fac. Scholar, Columbia Univ., 1966-67. Address: 9 Queens Ave., McMahons Point, NSW 2060, Aust.

KASTNER, Macário Santiago, b. 15 Oct. 1908, London, UK. Professor of Music; Musicologist. Educ: Studied Piano, Clavichord, Harpsichord, Musicol., etc., var. tchrs., Amsterdam, Leipzig, Barcelona. Debut: Barcelona, 1947. Career: Tchr., Nat. Conserv., Lisbon, Portugal, 1947-; Mbr. Musicol. Commission, Gulbenkian Fndn.; Courses, concerts, lectures, TV & radio apps., num. European countries. Recording: Monumentos Históricos de la Música Espanola. Publs: Author & Ed., num. musicol. & histl. musical works. Contbr. to: European music ref. books; Yrbook, Spanish Musicol. Inst.; other profl. jrnls. Mbrships: Int. Musicol. Soc.; San Fernando Royal Acad. Fine Arts, Madrid (corres.), 1965. Hobbies: Reading; Travel. Address: Ave. de Berna 4 2 E, Lisbon 1, Portugal.

KASTU, Matti, b. Turku, Finland. Operatic Tenor. Educ: Royal Opera, Stockholm. Debut: 1973, Stockholm. Career: Prin. Tenor, Royal Opera, Stockholm; apps. in Vienna, San Francisco, Munich, Düsseldorf, Frankfurt, Geneva, Rome, Berlin & in France; roles incl. Rodolfo (Boheme), Bacchus (Ariadne), Manrico (Il Trovatore), Walter (Die Meistersinger), Erik (Dutchman), Parsifal, Florestan (Fidelio). Recording: Die Ägyptische Helena. Mgmt: Artistsekretariat Ulf Törnqvist, Norrtullsgatan 26, tr. 4, 11345 Stockholm, Sweden. Address: c/o mgmt.

KATAHN, Enid, b. 10 Apr. 1932, Pittsburgh, Pa., USA. Concert Pianist; Assistant Professor of Music. Educ: Prep. Div., Juilliard Schl. of Music; Juilliard Coll.; B Mus, Hartt Coll., Conn. M Mus, George Peabody Coll., Tenn. m. Martin Katahn, 2 children. Debut: Town Hall, NYC, 1961. Career: European Tour, 1962; MC & Perf., Hill Hall Presents for Educl. TV, NC

Num. apps. in solo recital, as solist w. orch. & w. num. chmbr. grps.; Background music for film, Dear Dead Delilah; Artist-Tchr., Blair Schl. of Music, Nashville, Tenn. Mbr. Music Tchrs. Nat. Assn. Mgmt: Alkahest Agcy Inc., PO Box 12403, Northside Stn., Atlanta, GA 30355; Ozark Attractions, PO Box 7, Mountain View, Arkansas 72560, USA; New Era Int. Concerts Ltd., 16 Lauriston Rd., London SW19 4TQ, UK. Address: 4607 Belmont Pk. Terrace, Nashville, TN 37215, USA.

KATAJA, Lassi Pellervo, b. 30 July 1940, Ilmajoki, Finland. Conductor. Educ: Philos. Magister, Helsinki Univ.; Dip. in Cond. of Orch., & Theory of Music, Sibelius Acad. m. Aira Juntunen. Debut: Cond., Lahti City Orch. Career: Cond., Lahti City Orch. in concerts; Lahti Opera. Lahti Ch. Orch. (also in Radio); Sibelius Acad. Symph. Orch. (also in Radio); Kotka City Orch., Kotka Opera; Tchr. in Lahti & Kotka; Summer Univ. in Seinajoki, 1970-71. Cond., Rovaniemi Orch., 1975-; Cond. Orch. concerts var. places in N Finland & Sweden. Compositions: Chamber Music Trepezzi (perf. in Helsinki); Aleatroische Studien (in Helsinki) & Trondheim, Norway; Trapetz for Piano, in Helsinki & Stockholm; Scene music. Musical Ed., Finnish Radio, 1965, Lahti Regl. Radio, 1969-71; Ed. & Critic, var. newspapers. Mbrships: Govt. Union of Finnish Music Tchrs., etc. Address: Keskitie 1B, 100 Rovaniemi 10, Finland.

KATANYAN, Aram, b. 10 March 1926, Yerevan, Armenia, USSR. Conductor. Educ: Pianoforte & Theoretical Facs., Musical Coll.; Grad., Conserv. Cond. Fac. m. Berko Marina. Debut: Yerevan, USSR, 1949. Career: Cond., many operas inclng. "Tannhauser", "Oedipus Rex", "Consul", "West-Side Story", "Aida", "Othello", & "Almast"; Cond., "Swan Lake", "Raimonda", "Spartak", "Bolero" ballets; "Norma", "Immortality". Cond., 35 operas & ballets & nearly 100 symph. progs. inclng. classical & modern music; 12 Films; Many Radio performances; Chief Cond., Spendiarov Opera & Ballet Theatre, Yerevan; Chief Cond., Yerevan Opera & Ballet Theatre, 1974-. Recordings: Alicia Terzyan Concerto for Violin & Orch., Argentina, 1972. Mbr., Soviet Theatrical Soc. Hons: Actor of Armenian Repub., 1961; Wkr. of Arts, 1965. Hobbies: Caulking; Wood Carving. Address: Nalbandyan St. No. 25/14, Apartment 3, Yerevan-1, USSR.

KATES, Stephen Edward, b. 7 May 1943, NYC, NY, USA. Concert Cellist. Educ: Dip., Juilliard Schl. of Music, 1969; Master Classes w. Gregor Piatigorsky, Univ. of S Calif., 1964-67. Debut: NYC, 1963. Career: Concerts w. NY Philharmonic, Chicago Symph., Boston Symph., Phila. Orch., Detroit Symph., Cinn. Symph.; Recitals, Hong Kong, Tokyo, Taiwan, Italy, Austria, Hungary, Can., Moscow; Prof. of Cello, Ohio State Univ., 1969-72; currently Instructor of Cello, Peabody Conserv. of the John Hopkins Univ., 1974-. Num. recordings. Hons: Silver Medal, 3rd Int. Tchaikovsky Competition, Moscow, USSR; Ford Fndn. Grant, 1971; Young Musicians Fndn. Debut Award; San Fran. Symph. Fndn. Award; Piatigorsky Bi-annual Award of the NY Violoncello Soc. Hobbies: Photography; Coin collection. Address: 838 West End Avenue, NY, NY 10025, USA.

KATIMS, Milton, b. NYC, USA. Conductor; Violist. Educ: BA, Columbia Univ.; majored music. m. Virginia Peterson, 1 s., 1 d. Debut: Guest Cond., NBC Symph., 1947; as Violist, NY, 1940. Career: First desk violist w. Toscanini NBC Symph., 1943-54; Fac., Juilliard Schl. of Music, 1946-54; Cond., NBC, 1947-54; Music Dir., Cond. Seattle Symph., 1954-76; Artistic Dir., Univ. of Houston Schl. of Music; Guest Cond., major orchs. in USA & abroad. Cond. & viola Soloist, TV Special "Mozart in Seattle." Recordings as cond.: RCA, Columbia & Vox records w. Seattle Symph.; as violist w. Casals, Stern, NY Quartet (Columbia & Mercury); Viola Quintets w. Budapest Str. Quartet (Columbia). Publs: 25 Transcriptions & Edns. for Viola, Int. Music Co., 1940-70. Contbr. to profl. jrnls. Hons. incl: Columbia Univ. Medal of Excellence; Seattle Man of the Yr., 1966; 3 hon. doctorates of music; Alice M Ditson Award, 1967. Hobbies: Tennis; Ping-pong; Chess. Mgmt: Maxim Gershunoff, 502 Park Ave., NY 10022, USA. Address: Schl. of Music, Univ. of Houston, Houston, TX 77004, USA. 2,9,14.

KATIN, Peter Roy, b. 14 Nov. 1930, London, UK. Concert Pianist. Educ: Westminster Abbey; ARCM; LRAM. m. Eva Zweig, 2 s. Debut: Wigmore Hall, London, 1948. Career: Tours incl: UK, E & W Europe, Turkey, E & S Africa, Aust., NZ, India, Can. & USA; Leading Chopin Interpreter; Disting. player of romantic & impressionist comps.; visiting Prof., Western Ont. Univ., 1978-. Recordings of works by Chopin, Rachmaninov, Schumann, Khachaturyan, Liszt, Mendelssohn, Tschaikovsky. Var. mixed recitals. Publs: Book on Chopin (in preparation); Mbrships: ISM; Napoleon Club; Wig & Pen Club. Recip. Eric Brough Memorial Prize, 1944; Chopin Arts Award, NY, 1977. Hobbies: Fishing; Writing; Photography; Record Collecting;

Tape Recording. Mgmt: Raymond Gubbay Ltd., 125 Tottenham Ct. Rd., London W1P 9HN; Direction Arts, Toronto, Can. Address: c/o Raymond Gubbay Ltd.

KATLEWICZ, Jerzy, b. 2 April 1927, Bochnia, Poland. Conductor. Educ: MA, High Schl. of Music, Cracow, 1952. m. Irena Augustyn, 2 d. Career: Artistic Dir. & First Cond., Cracow Opera, 1952; Cond. Cracow Phil. Orch.; Dir., 1st Cond., Artistic Dir., Poznán Phil. Orch., 1958, Baltic Phil. Orch. & Opera, Gdaňsk, 1961; Dir., First Cond. & Artistic Dir., Nat. Cracow Philharmonia of Karol Szymanowski, 1968-. Compositions incl: Theatre Music. Recordings: Six records w. Nat. Philharmonia Orch., Warsaw; Two records w. Polish Radio Orch., Warsaw. Mbrships: Union of Polish Artist & Musicians. Hons: The Gold Cross of Merit, 1956; First Prize, Cond's Competition, Besanson, 1955; The Bachelor's Cross of Polonia Restituta, 1959; Culture & Art Winner, Prize of the Min. of Poland, 1967; Artistic Prize of Cracow, 1972; Medal of Polish Comps. Soc.; 1974; Officers Cross of Polonia Restituta, 1977. Hobbies: Literature; Theatre; Collecting. Address: ul. Stawkowska 24a3, Cracow, Poland.

KATTERJOHN, Arthur David, b. 8 Dec. 1929, Chgo., Ill., USA. Professor of Music; Conductor; Instructor in Trumpet. Educ: B Mus., Univ. of Mich., 1951; M Mus., ibid, 1952; Cert. of Advanced Study, Northern Ill. Univ., 1974. m. Rosemary Katterjohn, 3 s., 1 d. Career: Band Cond., Saline Area Schls., Mich., 1951-64; Joliet (Ill.) Township HS W., 1964-68; Cond., Symph. Orch. & Concert Band, Instructor in Trumpet & Orchestration, Wheaton (Ill.) Coll., 1968-78; Cond. of Bands, Nat. Music Camp, Interlochen, Mich., 1964-78. Recordings: w. Wheaton Coll. Concert Band & Symph. Orch. for Wheaton Coll., 1964. Mbrships: Coll. Band Dirs. Nat. Assn.; Exec. Sec., Fellowship of Christian Musicians; MENC. Hobby: Sailing. Address: 220 E. Union, Wheaton, IL 60187, USA.

KATUNDA, Eunice do Monte Lima, b. 14 March 1915, Rio de Janeiro , Brazil. Pianist; Composer. Educ: Pvte. studies w. Marietta Lion, Oscar Guanabarino, Furio Franceschini, H J Koellreutter & Hermann Scherchen. m. Omar Catunda (div. 1963), 2 children. Deubt: Pianist, child prodigy of 12, Rio de Janeiro, 1927, Comp., 1946. Career: Pianist, Argentinian debut, 1944; Italian debut, 1948; NYC debut, 1968; As Comp: Songs to Death, Orch. Switzerland Broadcast, 1948; Quintet, Brussels, 1950; Four Moments of Rilke, String Orch., 1958. Tape recordings for Min. of Educ. Broadcasts, Rio de Janeiro. Contbr. to profl. jrnls. Mbr. var. profl. orgs. Hons. incl: Best Broadcasting Concert Pianist of Yr. 1956, Sao Paulo. Hobbies: Painting; Psychol. Address: Rua Ministro Jesuino Cardoso 737, Sao Paulo 04544, Brazil.

KATZ, Dorothy, b. 19 Aug. 1924, Chgo., Ill., USA. French Horn Player & Teacher. Educ: Ball State Tchrs. Coll.; Ind. Northwestern Univ. m. William Katz, 2 d. Career incls: 3rd Horn, Indpls. Symph. Orch., 1944-46; Solo Horn, Columbus Phil. Orch., 5 yrs.; & Mutual Broadcasting System, Columbus, Ohio; New Orleans Pops Orch.; Chgo. Chmbr. Orch.; Aeolian Woodwind Ensemble, Chgo.; Freelance artist w. Lyric Opera, Grant Park Symph., Chgo. Symph. Orch. & City Symph., all Chgo.; Tchr. of French Horn, var. High Schls., Ill.; Teaching Assoc., French Horn, Northwestern Univ. Recording: Tschaikovsky Symphs. I & II, w. Indpls. Symph. Mbrships: Chgo. Fedn. Musicians; Int. Horn Soc. Hobbies: Conducting Student Ensembles; Motoring Trips in USA. Address: 6239 N. Fairfield Ave., Chgo., IL 60659, USA.

KATZ, Israel J, b. 21 July 1930, NY, NY, USA. Ethnomusicologist. Educ: BA, UCLA, 1956; PhD, ibid, 1967. m. Marcia T Merchasin, 2 d. Career: Asst. Prof., Fac. of Music, McGill Univ., Montreal, Can., 1968-69; Assoc. Prof., Dept. of Music, Columbia Univ., NY, 1969-75; Ed., Ethnomusicol., 1970-72; Book Review Ed., Yearbook of the Int. Folk Music Coun., 1971-76; Ed., ibid., 1977-; Co-Ed., Musica Judaica, 1975-; Tutor in Ethnomusicol., Int. Coll., Los Angeles, Calif., 1976-; Mbr., Graduate Faculty, CUNY, 1977-; Assoc. Prof., Chmn., Dept. of Fine/Perf. Arts, York Coll., CUNY, 1977-. Publs. incl: Judeo-Spanish Traditional Ballads from Jerusalem; An Ethnomusicological Study, 1972-75, 2 vols.; Critical Ed., Kurt Schindler, Folk Music & Poetry of Spain & Portugal. Contbr. to num. profl. jrnls. Mbr., profl. orgs. Recip. num. hons. incl: Can. Coun. Award, Guggenheim Fellowship, Ford Fndn., etc. Hobby: Hiking. Address: 415 W 115th St., NY, NY 10025, USA. 6, 29.

KATZ, Martha Strongin, b. 10 March 1943, NYC, USA. Musician (Viola); Music Educator. Educ: Curtis Inst. of Music; Juilliard Schl. of Music; Manhattan Schl. of Music; Univ. of Southern Calif. m. Paul Katz. Debut: New Schl. of NY, 1970. Career: Violist, Cleveland String Quartet; Took part in "Music from Marlboro" tours; Soloist w. num. orchs incl. Orch. de

Suisse-Romande; Artist-in-Residence & Assoc. Prof., SUNY, Buffalo. Recordings: Complete String Quartets of Brahms; Quartet No. 14 in D Minor (Schubert); Adagio & Fugue in C Minor (Mozart), on RCA label. Hons: Highest Award, 1968 Geneva Int. Viola Competiton; Max Reger Award, 1968; Int. Prize-Winner, Munich Competition, 1965; Grp. of the Month Award (The Cleveland Quartet), High Fidelity & Musical Am. mag. 1973; Best record of the yr. award, Time & Stereo Review mags. Mgmt: Kazuko Hillyer Ind., Inc., NYC. Address: 2884 Main St., Buffalo, NY 14214, USA.

KATZ, Paul, b. 2 Nov. 1907, NYC, USA. Violinist; Conductor; Teacher. Educ: B Mus, Cleveland Inst. of Music; D Mus, Univ. of Dayton & Ctrl. State Univ.; studied Violin & Theory w. var. tchrs. m. Phyllis Margolis, 1 child. Career: Cond., Dayton Phil. Orch., 1933-75; Violinist, Cleveland & Cinn. Symph. Orch., Cond., Cinn. Conserv. of Music, 1945-57; Fac. mbr., Cinn. Coll. Conserv. of Music, Wright State Univ., Univ. of Dayton, Antioch Coll.; Radio series w. Dayton Phil. Comps: (unpubld.) Symph.; Quartet; Songs. Hobbies: Sailing; Gardening; Bicycling. Address: 5100 Aquilla Dr., Dayton, OH 45415 USA. 2, 8.

KATZ, Paul, b. 16 Nov. 1941, Los Angeles, Calif, USA. Musician (cello); Music Educator. Educ: B Mus, Univ. of Southern Calif., 1962; M Mus, Manhattan Schl. of Music, 1964; Study of cello & chmbr. music w. var. leading tutors. m. Martha Strongin. Career incl: Perf. for Violoncello Soc. of NY., 1964; Marlboro Music Fest., 1968-69; Artist in Res., Assoc. Prof. of Music, State Univ. of NY, Buffalo, NY, 1970-75; Artist in Res., Assoc. Prof. of Music, Eastman Schl. of Music, Rochester, NY, 1976-. Cellist, Cleveland String Quartet; num. broadcasts in chmbr. music & as soloist on radio & TV throughout USA. Recordings: Complete String Quartets of Brahms; Quartet No. 14 in D Minor (Schubert); Adagio & Fugue in C Minor (Mozart) on RCA label; Haydn Quartets op. 64, No. 5 & op. 76, No. 2; Schubert Octet w. Tuckshell Wind Quintet Samuel Barber & Charles Ives Quartets. Hons: Selected nationally to perform in Pablo Casals Master Class, Berkeley, Calif., 1962; Prizewinner w. Univ. of Southern Calif. Quartet in Int. String Quartet Competition, Munich, 1965; Prize w. Toledo Quartet, Geneva Competition, 1966; Grp. of the Month Award to Cleveland Quartet, High Fidelity & Musical Am. mag., 1973. Mgmt: Kazuko Hillyer Int., Inc., NY. Address: 2884 Main St., Buffalo, NY 14214, USA.

KATZENELLENBOGEN, Elisabeth, b. 7 Dec. 1904, Zurich, Switz. Musician; Pianist; Teacher; Specialist on CPE Bach's Keyboard works. Educ: Tchr.'s & Concert Dips., Zurich Conserv. m. Adolf Katzenellenbogen, 1 d., 1 s. Debut: Leipzig. Career: Piano Fac., Schl. of Music, Winterthur, Switz., 1935-41; Prof. of Music, Vassar Coll., Poughkeepsie, NY, USA, 1943-58; Adj. Prof. of Music, Goucher Coll., Towson, Md., 1958-59; Piano Fac., Peabody Conserv. of Music, Balt., Md., 1961-; Regular piano recitals; Fndr., Arlington Jr. Concert Series, Poughkeepsie, NY, 1954; Guest Lectr., Dartington's Summer Schl. of Music, 1973. Recordings incl: The Six Essay Sonatas by CPE BAch. Mbr., var. music assns. Hobbies: Gardening. Address: 310 Broxton Rd., Balt., MD 21212, USA.

KAUFFMAN, Robert Allen, b. 14 June 1929, Newton, Kan., USA. Ethnomusicologist. Educ: BM, Bethany Coll., 1951; MMus, Ind. Univ., 1952; PhD, UCLA, 1971. m. 3 s., 1 d. Career: Asst. Prof., Unaiv. of Wash., Seattle, 1968-74. Publs: Multipart Relationships in the Shona Music of Rhodesia, 1971; An Ethnomusicological Perspective upon Western Music, 1974; Contbr. to profl. jrnls. Mbrships: Coun. Mbr., Soc. for Ethnomusicol.; Am. Musicol. Soc.; Int. Folk Music Coun.; African Music Soc.; African Studies Assn., Phi Mu Alpha Sinfonia. Address: Schl. of Music, DN-10 Ethnomusicol., Univ. of Wash., Seattle, WA 98195, USA.

KAUFMANN, Armin, b. 30 Oct. 1902, Ne-Itzkany, Bukovina, now Romania. Composer. Educ: Hochschule für Musik und Darstellende Kunst, Vienna; studied theory w. Josef Marx, Vienna. m. Maria Markwart, 1 s., 2 d. Comps. (publ. & recorded) incl: Music for Trumpet & Str. orch., Op. 38; Symphony No. 1, Op. 65; Symphony No. 2, Op. 74; Concerto for Tárogate & Chmbr. orch., Op. 91; Sonatine for trumpet, oboe & piano, Op. 53; Trio for violin, viola & cello, Op. 60; Trio for viola d'amore, double bass & piano, Op. 71; Rhapsody for Guitar, Op. 97; Der Krach im Ofen (schl. opera), Op. 72; Quartet No. 6, Op. 81; 4 pieces for piano, Op. 79; num. other comps. for instrumental & vocal ensembles. Hons. incl: Vienna City Prize, 1941, '66; State Prize, 1950; Dr. Theodor Koerner Prize, 1954; Ehrenmedaille der Bundeshauptstadt Wien in Gold, 1978. Address: Strohgasse 9/12, 1030 Vienna, Austria.

KAUFMANN, Dieter, b. 22 April 1941, Vienna, Austria. Composer; Teacher of electro-acoustic music. Educ: Grad.,

Univ. of Vienna; Tchng. exam. in musical educ., state exam. for violoncello, dip. in comp., Musikhochschule, Vienna; Conservatoire Nat. Superieure de Musique, Paris, France, & Groupe de Recherches, ORTF, Paris. m. Gunda König, 1 d., 1 s. Career: Commissions for Austrian radio & TV, for Warsaw harvest season, music report for Styrian harvest season, Donaueschingen & for Nürnberg Musiktheater. Comps. incl: (publd) Warten auf Musik, ballet; Concertomobil, for orch., solo violin & tape recorders; Papa for mixed chorus & 2 tape recorders; Volksoper (Musicktheater für ein Opernhaus); num. electro-acoustic comps. on tape recorder. Recordings: Jeunesses Musicales. Publs: Articles in Österreichische Musikzeitschrift & Melos; Radio broadcasts on Austrian radio. Mbrships: Austrian Sect., Int. Soc. for New Music. Recip. of hons. Mgmt: Edition Reimers, Fack 30 S-16115 Bromma, Stockholm, Sweden. Address: Tuchlauben 18/15, A-1010 Vienna, Austria.

KAUFMANN, Helen Loeb, b. 2 Feb. 1887, NYC, USA. Writer on Music; Violinist. Educ: AB, Barnard Coll.; pvte. study of violin. m. Mortimer J Kaufmann, 2 s., 1 d. Career incls: Sec., Soc. for Publn. of Am. Music, 1943-46; Prog. Annotator Ny Phil. Young People's Concerts, 1950-53; Dir., Music Dept., Am. Coun. for Emigrés in the Professions, 1950-. Publs. incl: From Jehovah to Jazz, the Story of Music in America; The Listener's Dictionary of Musical Terms; The Story of Mozart; The Story of Beethoven; The Story of Haydn; Anvil Chorus, The Story of Edward MacDowell; Seesaw, the Life & Loves of Hector Berlioz; The Story of Verdi; The Story of Sergei Prokofiev; Five Famous Operas & their Backgrounds. Hobbies: Playing str. quartets; Gardening; Cooking; Reading. Address: 59 W 12th St., NY., NY 10011, USA. 3.

KAULILI, Alvina Nye, b. 20 Oct. 1918, Honolulu, Hawaii, USA. Music Educator (retired); Choral & Music Director. Educ: B Mus, New England Conserv. of Music, 1942; MA, Tchrs. Coll. Columbia Univ., 1958; Specialist Dip., Music & Music Educ., ibid, 1962. m. Lordie Olinoikalani Kaulili. Career: Music Educator, 1942-74; Music Dir., Honolulu Community Theatre, 1956-72, Chinese Drama Group; Dir., Honolulu Police Choral Group, 1958-73; Music Dir., McKinley Theatre Group, 1958-74. Comps: Lei of Friendship. Mbrships. incl: Mu Phi Epsilon; Delta Kappa Gamma; Phi Lambda Theta; Epsilon Sigma Alpha. Hons: Tchr. of Yr., 1955. Address: 3817 Kaimuki Ave., Honolulu, HI 96816, USA.

KAUSHIK, Jagphool, b., 12 Oct. 1924, Rohtak, Haryana, India. Composer; Violinist; Pianist; Tabla Player. Educ: studied Indian classical music w. Ustad Ali Akber Khan. m. Kaushalya Rani, 4 s. Debut: Music Dir. for film Shehar Aur Sapna, 1964. Career: num. stage perfs. throughout India; num. violin recitals, All-India Radio; Composer for feature films, documentaries & TV. Has recorded over 30 discs. Mbrships: Cine Music Dir.'s Assn., Bombay; Indian PRS. Hons. incl: Disting. Serv. in Music, Govt. of Haryana, 1970; Best Nat. Integration Song Award, Ctrl. Govt. of India, 1970. Hobby: Sports. Address: 18/852 Punjabi Colony, Sion-Loliwada, Bombay 400 037, India.

KAVAFIAN, Ani, b. 10 May 1948, Istanbul, Turkey. Concert Violinist. Educ: BM & MS, Juilliard Schl. of Music, NYC, USA. Debut: Carnegie Recital Hall, NYC, 1971. Career incls: Soloist w. var. orchs. inclng: Detroit Symph.; Nat. Symph., Wash. DC; Boston Pops, etc.; Solo Recitals in NYC; Apps. in Mostly Mozart Festival & Great Performers Series, Lincoln Ctr.; Premiered a Sonata by Karel Husa at Alice Tully Hall, 1974; Apps. at Music Festivals in Spolato, Italy, Marlboro, Vt., & Aldeburgh, UK. Recording of Brandenburg Concerto w. Anthony Newmann. Hons. incl: Prize Winner, Naumburg Competition, 1975; Avery Fisher Prize, 1976. Hobby: Tennis. Mgmt: Young Concert Artists Inc., NYC. Address: 140 Riverside Dr., Apt. 14N, New York, NY 10024, USA.

KAWAKAMI, Genichi, b. 30 Jan. 1912, Kobe prefecture, Japan. Chairman of Board of Directors; President. Career: Employee, Nippon Gakki Co., 1937-; Pres., ibid, 1950; Established Yamaha Motor Co. Ltd., 1955; Pres., ibid, 1955; Exec. Dir. & Pres., Naka Nippon Kanko Kaihatsu Co. Ltd., 1962; Established Yamaha Music Fndn., 1966; Pres., ibid, 1966-; Chmn., Bd. of Dirs., Nippon Gakki, 1977-. Publs: Arranging Popular Music - A Practical Guide, 1975; In the Beginning was the Song, 1977; Basic Principles for Composition & Performance, 1978. Hons: Award for Outstanding Contributions to Popular Music, Int. Fedn. of Fest. Orgs., 1973, '77. Address: 434, 5000 Uchino, Hamakita-city, Japan.

KAWASAKI, Masaru, b. 19 April 1924, Tokyo, Japan. Composer. Educ: Dip., Tokyo Acad. of Music. m. Tasko Kawasaki, 2 s. Career: Dir., Tokyo Symphonic Band; 1st Perf. of Comps. at Festriche Musiktage Uster, Switzerland, 1971,

74. Comps: The Fountain of Hawk (opera for young persons); Essay on a Day (flute & piano); WARABE-UTA (symphonic band); Fantasy for Symphonic Band; The Sketch of Pastoral Scenery (band); March Forward for Peace; Ray of Hope (march). Recordings of WARABE-UTA; Ray of Hope (march). Publs: Instrumentation and Arrangement for Wind Ensemble. Contbr. to Band Jrnl., Tokyo. Mbr. num. profl. orgs. Hons. incl: Comp. Prize at Arts Festival, Japan. Hobby: Gardening. Address: 4-2-38 Hamatake, Chigasaki-shi, Kanagawa-ken, Japan 253. 3.

KAY, Don, b. 25 Jan. 1933, Smithton, Tasmania, Aust. Educ: B Mus., Dip. Ed., Melbourne, Aust.; Studied Comp.w . Malcom Williamson London. m. Grace Kay, 1 s., 2 d. Career: Tchr., Boy's Schl., London, 1959-64; Var. Broadcasts & Perfs. on ABC; Comp. & perf. for Children's Theatre. Comp: Four Australian Folk Songs for unaccompanied SSA choir. Songs of Come & Gone, A Choral Suite; Rapunzel, an Opera for Children's Theatre. Recordings: Dance Movement for Small Orch.; Instrumental Music & Songs for A Puppet Prod. of Hansel & Gretel. Contbr. to: The Tasmanian Teacher. Mbrships: . Nat. Exec., Aust. Soc. of Educ. through the Arts; Tasmanian Exec., Aust. Soc. of Music Educ. (Tasmanian Chapt.); Tasmanian Rep., Fellowship of Aust. Comps. Hobbies: Walking; Reading; Films; Theatre. Address: 21 Jenkins St., Taroona, Tas. 7006, Aust.

KAY, Ulysses, b. 7 Jan. 1917, Tucson, Ariz., USA. Composer; University Professor. Educ: B Mus., Univ. of Ariz., 1938; M Mus., Eastman Schl. of Music, Univ. of Rochester, NY., 1940; Yale Univ.; Columbia Univ. m. Barbara Harrison Kay, 3 d. Career: Currently Disting. Prof. of Music, Herbert H. Lehman Coll., CUNY. Compositions (all recorded): Serenade for Orch.; Markings (for orch.); 5 Portraits for Violin & Piano; Choral Triptych; Round Dance & Polka; Sinfonia in E; Umbrian Scene; Fantasy Variations. Mbrships: Phi Mu Alpha; US Musicians' Union; Dir., Corp. of Yaddo; Bd. Mbr., Composers' Forum, NYC. Hons. incl: Am. Acad. of Arts & Letters Award, 1947; Prix de Rome, 1949-50; hon. docts., Lincoln Coll., Lincoln, Ill., 1963, Ill. Wesleyan Univ., 1966, Bucknell Univ., 1969, Univ. of Ariz., 1969; Hon. D Mus, Dickinson Coll., 1978. Hobbies: Reading, Swimming. Address: 1271 Alicia Ave., Teaneck, NJ 07666, USA. 2,3.

KAYE, Bernard Louis, b. 12 Sept. 1927, New Haven, Conn., USA. Plastic Surgeon; Musician (Clarinet, Saxophone, Flute). Educ: BA., Yale Univ., 1949; DMD., Harvard Schl. of Dental Med., 1953; MD., Harvard Med. Schl., 1955; Pvte. music educ. on var. instruments. m. Joyce Bailey Kaye, 1 s., 1 d. Career: Yale Univ. Symph.; Yale Univ. Marching & Concert Bands; New Haven Symph.; Univ. of Kan. Symph.; Prin. Saxophonist, Jacksonville Symph.; 1st Saxophonist, Starlight Symphonette; Soloist in Duke Ellington's "Celebration" (Sax. solo specially writtten for him by Ellington); Kennedy Ctr. for Performing Arts. Wash. DC.; Carnegie Hall, NY. Soloist, Jacksonville Symph., 1976. Recordings: Num. nat. issues, incl. works w. Jacksonville Symph.; w. Connie Haynes & Jim Newton, Contbr. to var. med. jrnls. Mbrships: incl: Bd. of Dirs., Jacksonville Symph. Orch.; Bd. of Dirs., ic ops., WJCT Radio. Hobbies: Travel; Bagpipes; Automobiles. Address: 702 Laurette Howard Building, Jacksonville, FL 32207, USA.

KAYE, Buddy, b. NYC, USA. Lyricist; Publisher; Producer. Educ: Pvte. study of saxophone. m. Lillian Kipp, 2 s., 1 d. Career: MGM Records - Buddy Kaye Quintet; Record Prod., Concept LPs. Comps: Lyricist for about 500 published/recorded songs inclng. million sellers, Quiet Nights, A - You're Adorable, Full Moon & Empty Arms, Till the End of Time, Speedy Gonzales, & Brit. Gold Records The Next Time, Boys Cry, In the Middle of Nowhere, Little by Little, & Christmas Alphabet. TV themes incl: I Dream of Jeannie, Richard the Lionheart. Film songs incl: The Trouble with Girls, Not as a Stranger, Twist Around the Clock, Change of Habit, etc. Publs: The Gift of Acabar, 1978 (co-author); The Complete Songwriter, 1979. Mbrships. incl: ASCAP; Acad. Motion Picture Arts & Scis. Hons: Recip. Grammy Award as Prod. of Little Prince LP, Starring Richard Burton, 1976. Hobby: Teaching. Address: c/o ASCAP, 6430 Sunset Blvd., Hollywood, CA 90028, USA.

KAYE, Michael, b. 27 Feb. 1925, London, UK. Orchestra Manager. m. Faye Kaye, 1 d. Career incls: Pub. Rels Dir., Carreras Rothmans Ltd.; Dir., Peter Stuyvesant Fndn.; Gen. Admstr., Rupert Fndn.; Mng. Dir., LSO, 1976-. Hobbies: Photography; Clarinet. Address: 19-25 Argyll St., London W1, UK.

KAYSER, Audun, b. 29 Apr. 1946, Bergen, Norway. Pianist; Manager. Educ: Examen Artium, 1965; Hochschule für Musik, Vienna, 1966-72; Géza Andás Masterclass, Zürich, 1974. m. Dagmar Kayser. Debut: Oslo, 1969. Career: concerts in

Scandinavian countries, Austria, German Fed. Repub.; sev. broadcasts for Norwegian Radio & TV; Manager, Edv. Greig's home, Troldhaugen, 1978-. Recordings: A Concert in Edv. Greig's Home. Hons: 1st Prize, Scandinavian Piano contest, Gothenburg, 1965. Hobbies: Reading; Fishing. Mgmt: Impresario, Tollbugaten 3, Oslo, Norway. Address: Nipedalen 165, N-5031 Laksevag, Norway.

KAYSER, Leif, b. 13 June 1919, Copenhagen, Denmark. Composer; Music Teacher. Educ: Philos. & Theol. studies, Rome, Ordained Roman Cath. Priest, 1949; Royal Danish Conserv. of Music; Pvte. study w. leading tutors in Stockholm & Paris. Debut: as composer, Gothenburg, 1939; as pianist, Copenhagen, 1941; as Cond., Gothenburg, 1941. Career incl: Organ & piano recitalist & broadcaster, Denmark & abroad; Tchr., Royal Danish Conserv. of Music. Compositions incl: 5 Symphs.; Christmas Oratorio & Te Deum for Chorus & Orch.; var. orchl. & concert band works, chmbr. music & choral works; Horn concerto; Hymn settings; Film music. Mbrships: Danish Composers' Soc. Address: Holmestien 16, DK-2720 Vanlose, Denmark. 21, 134.

KEANE, David R., b. 15 Nov. 1943, Akron, Ohio, USA. Composer; Double Bassist; Teacher. Educ: B Mus, Ohio State Univ., 1965; BSc, ibid, 1965; MMus, 1967. m. Barbara Lorraine Siennicki. Career: Bassist, Columbus & Vancouver Symph. Orchs.; Prin. Bassist, Kingston Symph. Orch.; Cond., Kingston Chmbr. Orch. & Camerata; Assoc. Prof., music comp., Queen's Univ.; Dir., Queen's Electronic Music Studios; Writer & prod. of TV musical specials & incidental music for radio. Comps. incl: Carpophagous Canon 4; Round Dance; Nocturne; Sur le Pont; Tenebrae. Publs. incl: Techniques of 20th Century Comp., 1972; Techniques of Tape Music Comp., 1979. Contbr. to jrnls. Mbr. profl. orgs. Recip. Canada Coun. Grant, 1973, '77, '78; Ont. Arts Coun. Grant, 1978; Queens Grant, 1976. Address: Queen's Univ. Music Dept., Kingston, Ontario, Can.

KEARNS, William Kay, b. 17 Jan. 1928, Wilmington, Ohio, USA. Music Teacher; Musicologist; Musician, French Horn. Educ: BMusEd., Ohio State Univ., 1952; MA, ibid, 1954; PhD, Univ. of Ill., 1965. m. Sophia Coumanter Kearns, 1 s., 1 d. Career: Tchr. Music History & Lit., & French Horn, Columbus, Ohio, Public Schls., 1952, Friends Univ., Wichita, Kan., 1952-53, Ohio State Univ., Columbus, 1953-65, Bemidji State Coll., Minn., 1965, Univ. of Colo., 1965-; French Horn, Wichita Symph., 1952-53, Springfield, Ohio Symph., 1953-62, Wheeling, W. Va. Symph., 1954-58. Columbus Symph., 1953-65; Music Critic, Boulder, Colo., Camera. Co-Author, A Resource Book For Music Appreciation, 1969; Author, Folk Music of Colo. & the United States, 1977. Contbr. to num. profl. jrnls. Mbrships: Am. Musicol. Soc.; Coll. Music Soc.; MENC; Am. Folklore Soc. Recip. var. Fellowships. Hobbies: Reading; Gardening; Hiking; Camping. Address: 2065 King Ave., Boulder, CO 80302, USA.

KEATS, Donald H. (Howard), b. 27 May 1929, NYC, USA. Composer; Professor. Educ: MusB, Yale Univ. Schl. of Music; Yale Univ. Grad. Schl.; MA., Columbia Univ. Grad. Schl.; PhD., Univ. of Minn.; Fulbright Scholar, Staatliche Hochschule fur Musik, Hamburg, Germany, 2 yrs. Guggenheim Fellow, Europe, 2 yrs. Vis. Prof. of Music, Univ. of Denver, Colo., USA, 1975-. m. Eleanor Steinholz, 1 s., 2 d. Career: Prof. of Music, Antioch Coll., Yellow Springs, Ohio, 1957-; Pianist, particularly in connection with his own music; Concerts in London, Tel Aviv, Jerusalem, etc. Comps: 1st Symph.; An Elegaic Symph. (Symph. No. 2); Str. Quartet No. 1; Str. Quartet No. 2; Piano Sonata; A Ballet, "The New Work"; The Hollow Men (T.S.Eliot) for chorus & instruments; Anyone Lived in a Pretty How Town (E.E. Cummings) for SSATBB; The Naming of Cats (T.S. Eliot) for chorus & piano; "A Love Triptych" (W.B. Yeats), for voice & piano, etc. Recordings incl: Str. Quartet No. 2, by the Beaux Arts Quartet; Str. Quartet No. 1, Antioch Str. Quartet; Piano Sonata, Walter Anderson. Contbr. of book reviews to profl. jrnls. Mbrships: ASCAP; Coll. Music Soc. Recip. var. hons., fellowships, awards. Address: 4785 Meredith Rd., Yellow Springs, OH 45387, USA. 2.

KEBEDE, Ashenafi, b. 7 May 1938, Bulga, Shoa, Ethiopia. Ethnomusicologist; Composer; Poet; Teacher; Musician; Piano, Japanese Koto, Indonesian Gambang. Educ: BA., Univ. of Rochester, USA, 1962; MA., 1969, PhD., Ethnomusicol., Wesleyan Univ. m. Susan Mietkiewicz, 3 children. Career: Music Specialist, Ethiopia, 1962-64; Prin. Fndr., Dir., Yared Schl. of Music, Ethiopia, 1964-68; Adjunct Lect. in Music, ibid, 1968-70; Asst. Prof., Music & Dir., Prog. of World Music, Queens Coll., CUNY, 1970-; Guest Cond., Hungarian State String Orch., Budapest, 1967; Chmn., Teheran Int. Conf. of Music Educ. in Countries of the Orient, UNESCO, 1967. Compositions: Koturasia, for koto, violin & clarinet; Soliloquy

Eyeye, Soliloquy Mot. for voice, flute & koto. Recordings w. Hungarian Orch. of own compositions; An Anthology of the Worlds Music; Music of Ethiopia. Publs. incl: Yemuzika Seqasiw (Rudiments of Music), in Amharic, 1956; Booklets, articles & rsch. papers; Confession (novel), 1964. Mbrships. incl: Soc. for Ethnomusicol.; AAUP; NY State United Tchrs. Inc.; Doct. Fac., Grad. Ctr., CUNY; Pres., Ethiopia, 1950; ACLS Traud Grant; Queens Coll. Travel Grant, 1976. Hobbies incl: Reading; Writing; Recording; Tennis; Travel; Photography; Community affairs. Address: 98-15 Horace Harding Expressway No. 7-L, Corona, NY 11368, USA.

KECSKEMÉTI, István, b. 21 Dec. 1920, Budapest, Hungary. Musicologist. Educ: Doctor's degree in Econs., Fac. of Econs., Polytechnic Univ., Budapest; Grad. in piano, 1943 & in musicol. w. a diss. on Mozart's Salzburg piano concerts, 1957, Acad. of Music. Career: Rsch. Contbr., 1957, & Head of the Music Div., Nat. Széchényi Lib., Budapest, 1966-. Publs: Var. contbrns. to profl. publs. on Mozart, Süssmayr, Schubert, Chopin, Liszt, Debussy, Kodály; Ed. of unpublished musical autographs of Johann Joseph Fux, FX. Süssmayr, F. Schubert & F. Liszt. Recip. 2nd Prize in Int. Musicol. Competition in Warsaw with his Volkstum & Europäertum in Chopin's Mazurkas, 1960. Erkel-Prize, 1976. Address: PO Box 14, H-1400 Budapest, Hungary.

KEE, Piet, b. 30 Aug. 1927, Zaandam, The Netherlands. Organist; Composer. Educ: studied w. father, Cor Kee; organ w. Dr. Anthon van der Horst, Conserv. of Amsterdam; Final cert. 'cum laude', ibid, 1948; Prix d'excellence. m. Freya Lemaire, 2 c. Debut: Zaandam, 1941. Career: Organist of the Schnitgerorgan, St. Laurens Ch., Alkmaar & Municipal Organist of St. Bavo Ch., Haarlem; Prof. of Organ, Sweelinck Conserv., Amsterdam; Prof. at Int. Summer Acad. at Haarlem; Many concert tours in Europe & Am. Comps: Tryptich on Psalm 86, 1960; Two Organ Works, 1962; Variations on a Carol, 1954; Four Manualpieces, 1966; Music & Space for 2 Organs & 5 Brasswinds; Intrada for 2 organs; Choral music & chmbr. music; Valerius Gedencklanck, 1976. Recordings: Baroque Music & Works by Distler, Reger, etc.; Reihe; Das alte Werk; Bach's Organ Works; Porträt of St. Bavo; Romantic & modern music; The Organs of Alkmaar. CNR Mbr., KNTV, Holland. Hons: Jubilee Award of the Soc. for the Promotion of Musical Art, 1953; First Prize, Int. Improvisation Contest at Haarlem, 'The Silver Tulip', 1953, '54, '55; Bach Medal, Harriet Cohen Fndn., London, 1960. Hobbies: Ornithol.; Hist. Mgmt: Ibbs & Tillet, London, & Lilian Murtagh, USA. Address: Vaumontlaan 14, Heemstede, The Netherlands. 3.

KEECH, Diana, b. 29 May 1945, Kingston-upon-Hull, Yorks., UK. Peripatetic Woodwind Teacher of Oboe, Cor Anglais, Flute, Clarinet & Bassoon. Educ: Cert. Ed., Bretton Hall, Wakefield, 1967; GRSM; ARCM Pianoforte Tchng., 1965, Oboe Tchng., 1966. Debut: Scarborough Orchl. Soc., 1974. Career: Pvte. Oboe Tchr.; Snr. Peripatetic Woodwind Tchr., Hull Educ. Auth.; Mbr., Hull Phil. Orch. Mbrships: Musicians' Union; ISM; Hull Phil. Soc.; Committee Mbr., Yorks. & N Humberside Br., Royal Scottish Country Dance Soc.; Committee Mbr., Hull Music Fest. Soc. Hobbies: Collecting Postcards; Scottish Country Dancing; Conducting; Playing for amateur shows. Address: 33 Burniston Rd., Bricknell Ave., Hull, HU5 4JX, UK.

KEEFER, Anne-Elise, b. 19 April 1954, Toronto, Ont., Can. Solo Performer (flute, piccolo, alto flute, baroque flute). Educ: BMus, MMus (Music Perf.); ARCT; Royal Conserv. of Music. Debut: Paris, France, 1978. Career: Num. solo recitals, Toronto, Hamilton, Oslo, Paris, Sweden, Rome, London. Mbr., E York Symph. Orch., Toronto, 1971-73; Univ. of Toronto Symph. & Opera Orchs., 1972-75; Nat. Youth Orch. of Can., 1973-78; Soloist, Oslo Phil. Orch.; Zagreb Radio Orch., 1980; perf., Radio Zagreb concerts; perf., Marlboro Fest., Vermont, 1975; Baroque flute perf., Schloss Ambras, Innsbruck; Radio, TV engagement, Roving, Yugoslavia, 1979; Pvte. flute tchr. on staff of Bishop Strachen Girls' Schl., Toronto, 1973-74; Foss Music Schl., Oslo, 1980; Fac. flute tchr., Toronto Music Camp, 1977; Pvte. self-employed flute tchr., Toronto 1972-77, Oslo 1977-80; num. radio apps. Mbrships: Toronto Musicians' Assn.; The Nat. Flute Assn. Hons: Num. Acad. Awards, Scholarships & Grants; Winner, 1st Category, Ancona Int. Flute Competition, 1979. Address: Apt. 1012, Bjerke Studenthjem, Trondheimsveien 271, Oslo 5, Norway.

KEEFFE, Bernard, b. 1 April 1925, London, UK. Conductor; Professor. Educ: BA, Clare Coll., Cambridge; Hon. FTCL. m. Denise Jeanne Walker, 1 s., 1 d. Career: Cond. w. ldng. orchs.; num. TV apps. as commentator & cond.; Chief Cond., Bournemouth Municipal Choir; Prof. of Cond., TCL; Freelance Cond., Broadcaster, radio & TV. Recordings: as cond., Song recital by Janet Baker; as transl., The Diary of one who Disappeared (Janacek). Contbr. to: BBC Music Weekly; Music

Now; Hi-Fi News. Mbrships: Coun., Exec. Committee (former Warden, Solo Perfs. Sect.), ISM. Mgmt: Ibbs & Tillett. Address: 153 Honor Oak Rd., London SE23 3RN, UK.

KEENAN, Larry William, b. 14 Feb. 1941, Indpls. Ind., USA. University Professor; Pianist; Organist; Composer. Educ: B Mus, Univ. of Louisville, 1965; MMus, Ind. Univ., 1967; course work completed, D Musical Arts, Univ. of Cinn. m. Jo-Anne Ray Keenan, 2 s. Career incls: Assoc. Music Dir. & Organist, Stephen Foster Drama Assn., 1962-; Asst. Prof. keyboard, Morehead State Univ., Ky., 1967-; Min. of Music, 1st Presby. Ch., Ashland, Ky., 1969-75. Compositions: Spatials; Song of Silent Words; Trio in Blue; Moonwinds; Joyful Noise. Mbrships incl: Ky. Music Tchrs. Assn. (Pres., 2 yrs.) Recip. num. prizes & awards inclng. 1st Prize, US Grand Final, Yamaha Electone Fest., 1975. Hobbies: Table Tennis; Folk Dancing. Address: Rt. 6, M.S.U. Ct. 12, U.S. 60 E., Morehead, KY 40351, USA.

KEENE, James Allen, b. 27 Oct. 1932, Detroit, Mich., USA. Professor of Music; Violinist; Violist. Educ: BM, Eastman Schl. of Music, Rochester Univ.; MMEd, Wayne State Univ.; PhD, Univ. of Mich. m. 2 d. Career: Recitalist, violin & viola, solo & chmbr. music apps., NY., Mich., Mont., Vt. & Pa.; Prof. & Chmn., Music Dept., Mansfield State Coll. Publs: History of Music Education in Vermont, 1770-1900, 1969. Contbr. to musical jrnls. Mbrships: MENC; Am. String Tchrs. Assn.; Coll. Music Soc.; Pa. Music Educators Assn. Address: 37 Pearl St., Wellsboro, PA, USA.

KEENLYSIDE, Raymond, b. 9 May 1928, Southsea, Hants., UK. Violinist. Educ: Trinity Coll. of Music, London; LTCL (TTD). 2 s., 1 d. Career: Prin., chmbr. orchs. inclng. Boyd Neel, Philomusica, Engl. Chmbr., Acad. of St. Martins; Mbr., London Harpsichord Ensemble, 1959-62; Aeolian String Quartet, 1962-; Martin String Quartet, 1957-62; Fndr. Mbr., Acad. of St. Martins in the Fields; Prof., RCM. Recordings: Complete Mozart String Quintets & Haydn string quartets; late Beethoven Quartets; works by Debussy, Ravel, Schubert, Mozart, Elgar, Vaughan Williams, num. others, all w. Aeolian String Quartet. Contbr. to Daily Telegraph Mag. Hons: MA, Newcastle Univ., 1970. Hobbies: Fly fishing; Sailing; Reading; Collecting antique pottery; Beekeeping. Mgmt: Ibbs & Tillett, London. Address: 100 Westbourne Pk. Rd., London W12, UK. 3.

KEHLER, George Bela, b. 11 July 1919, Szod-Szodliget, Hungary. Professor of Piano; Concert Pianist. Educ: BA, Jr. Coll. at Vac, Hungary, 1937; B Mus., Ferenc Liszt, Royal Hungarian State Conserv. of Music, Budapest, 1941; MMus & Prof. of Music Dip., ibid, 1944; PhD., Univ. of Budapest, 1941; also studied in Germany, Austria, Switz., Italy under Edwin Fisher, Carl A. Martienssen, Franz Ledwinka, Erno Daniel, Kela Boszormenyi-Nagy & Wilhelm Kempff. m. Rachel A. Eatherly, 1 s. Career: Tchng. Asst., Ferenc Liszt Conserv. of Music, Budapest; Pvte. tchng. in Austria & Germany; Bethany Coll., Lindsborg, Kans., USA; Guest Instr., Ill. Wesleyan Univ., Bloomington, Kilgore Coll., Tex., Tex Lutheran Coll. & E. Tenn. State Univ.; Soloist w. Budapest Symph. Orch., The Mozarteum Orch. in Gt. Concert Hall, Salzburg, Marshall Symph. Orch., Tex., etc.; Solo recitals in Budapest, Vienna, Salzburg, sev. cities in Kan., Ill. & Tx.; Concert tour in Mex.; app. at Wigmore Hall, London; Yearly recitals in NY., 1961-; Soloist, Liszt Fest., Louisville, Ky. 1970. Recordings: Beethoven Sonatas, Liszt, Schumann, Chopin. Comps., LP's, Dombay Records. Publ: A History of the Piano. Mbr., var. profl. orgs. Recip., var. scholarships. Hobbies: Travel; Gardening. Address: 1408 Ridgecrest Rd., Johnson City, TN 37601, USA.

KEHLER, Linda Doreen, b. 26 May 1947, Winnipeg, Canada. Performer - Soprano; Private Music Teacher (Singing, Piano, Theory); Organist & Choir Director; Accompanist. Educ: B Mus; ARCT (Singing Perfs.); ARCT (Singing Tchrs.); ARCT (Piano Tchrs.); LMM (Singing). m. Clifford Edwin Kehler, 1 s., 1 d. Career: Apps., Theatre Ctr., CBC; Guest w. var. Oratorio Grps.; Festival Opera Co.; Man. Opera Assn.; Hollow Mug at Int. Inn; Num. roles w. Rainbow Stage Inc.; WPG Phil. Choir Symph. Contbr. to AGO; Can. Music Tchr.; Opera News. Mbrships: Man. Registered Music Tchrs. Assn. Inc.; Royal Can. Coll. of Organists; Musicians Union. Recip. W H Anderson Memorial Trophy, 1965. Hobbies: Aquariums; Camping; Interior Decorating. Address: 801 Niagara St., Winnipeg, Manitoba, Canada R3N OW2.

KEHLER, Sonja, b. Haldensleben, Germany. Actress. Educ: Dip. in Acting, Leipzig Theatre HS. Career incl: leading roles in plays of Brecht, Shaw, Shakespeare, Gorki, etc.; TV appearances as actress & singer of pol. songs, E Germany, Denmark, Austria, Portugal; many radio broadcasts; Tchr. of singing for actors; Denmark & E Germany; Concert singer, 197-. works of Brecht to music of Eisler, Dessan & Will &

contemporary chmbr. music composers, in Europe & Africa. Recordings incl: Sonja Kehler sings Hanns Eisler (Eterna & Songbird labels). Mbrships: E German Union of Composers & Musicians; E German Union of Theatre Artists. Mgmt: Kunstler-Agentur, DDR. Address: Talstr. 2s, 110 Berlin, German Dem. Repub.

KEHRER, Ewald Willy, b. 26 Apr. 1902, Dresden, Germany. Composer; Condutor; Pianist; Teacher. Educ: Dresdener Musikschule, 1918-23. m. Alice Karl, 1 s., 2 d. Debut: Dresden, 1925. Career: Concerts & recitals w. Dresden Staatskapelle & Dresden Phil.; num. perfs. of own comps.; apps. on radio. Comps. incl: Symphonic works, operas, ballets, oratorios, chamber music, airs, cycles of songs. sev. recordings of own comps. Publs. on piano technique & improvisation; articles on musical subjects. Mbr., Verbandes der Komponisten und Musikwissenschafttler der DDR. Hons: Medaillen für ausgezeichnete Leistungen 1954, '67, '69, '71, '72. Hobbies: Lit.; Formative Arts. Address: Hübnerstr. 12, 8027 Dresden, German Dem. Repub.

KEIJZER, Arie Johannes, b. 6 June 1932, Nieuwe Tonge, Holland, Netherlands. Organist. Educ: final cert., prix d'excellence for organ, Rotterdam Conserv., 1964. m. Christina Hovius, 1 child. Career: Prin. Organ Tchr., Rotterdam Conserv.; expert in field of organ bldg.; Organist, Concert Hall (De Doelen), Rotterdam; Cathedral Organist, Dordrecht; many perfs. in Netherlands & abroad. Comps: 5 Inventions for organ; Prelude for organ; Veni Creator Spiritus for orch., choir & organ. Recordings: St. Bavochurch in Haarlem; Frobenius-Organ in Oude Tonge; Organ Concert-Hall De Doelen in Rotterdam (2 records). Contbr. to jrnls. Mbrships: NOV; KNTV. Hons: Winner, Nat. Organ Competition, Bolsward, 1963, & Int. Organ Improvisation Competition, Haarlem, 1964. Address: BInnenKalkhaven 45 in Dordrecht, Netherlands.

KEILLOR, Elaine, b. 2 Sept. 1939, London, Ont. Can. Concert Pianist; Musicologist. Educ: BA, York Univ. & Univ. of Toronto; MA, Univ. of Toronto; PhD, ibid., 1976; Assoc. degree, Royal Conserv. of Music, Toronto, 1951 (youngest ever recip.). m. Vernon McCaw. Career: Recitals as Pianist throughout Can. & in USA, UK, Belgium, Germany & USSR; Perfs. w. orchs. in USA, Can. & Germany; Apps. on radio & TV progs., CBC & NBC. Contbr. to: Can. Music Book; Ency. of Music in Can. Mbrships: Am. Musicol. Soc.; Can. Assn. of Univ. Schls. of Music. Hons: Chappell Medal, 1958; Can. Coun. Doct. Fellowship, 1973. Hobbies: Swimming; Gardening. Mgmt: Mabel H. Laine, Suite 340 151 Bloor St. W., Toronto. Address: Carleton Univ., Dept. of Music, Ottawa K1S 5BG, Can. 27, 29

KEITH, Janice Gail, b. 1 June, 1951, Chgo., Ill., USA. Musicologist. Educ: BA, Sweet Briar Coll., 1973; MMus, 1974, PhD, 1978, Northwestern Univ. Career: Rsch. worker, special field; Medieval Music. Publs: HNH Records, rsch. & commentary for reproduction of European discs in Am., incl. Requiem (Ockeghem), Roman de Fauvel, René Clemencic et ses flûtes. Contbr. of prog. notes for Ravinia Fest. (Chgo. Symph. Orch.), 1978. Mbrships: Am. Musicol. Soc.; Société Int. Arthurienne. Hobbies: Swimming; Sewing; Tennis; Horseback Riding. Address: 1119 Golf View Ln., Glenview, IL 60025, USA.

KELDORFER, Robert, b. 10 Aug. 1901, Vienna, Austria. Conductor; Pianist; Organist. Educ: Akademie fur Müsik und darstellende Kunst, Vienna (comp., piano). m. 1) Felicitas Moser, 1 d.; 2) Maria Schober, 1 d. Career: Dir. of Music, Biesko, Poland, 1925-30; Dir., Bruckner Conserv., Linz, Austria, 1930-39; Dir., Kärtner Landeskonserv., 1941-66. Conps. incl: 2 operas, cantatas, choral music a cappella & w. orch., concertos, songs, chmbr. music. Publs: Aussprache im Gesang, 1955. Mbrships: Gesellschaft d. Autoren, Komponisten und Muikverleger, Vienna; Genossenschaft dramatischer Schriftsteller und Komponisten; Arbeitsgemeinschaft der Muzikerzieher, Austria; Steirischeh Tonkünstlerbund. Hons: Prof., h.c., 1934; Regierungsrat, 1951; Hofrat, 1966; Ehrenkreuz für Wissenschaft und Kunst, 1st class, 1972. Hobbies: Composition; Manuscript collecting. Address: Wulfengasse 9, 9020 Klagenfurt, Austria.

KELL, Sally, b. Phoenix, Ariz., USA. Performer (cello, viol, Baryton, early wind instruments). Educ: BA., Mills Coll., 1957; studied w. Nikolai Graudan, Gabor Rejto, Music Acad. of the West, Santa Barbara, 1950, '51, '53. m. Peter R. Ballinger, 2 s. Debut: 1953. Career: Prin. Cellist, Oakland Symph., Carmel Bach Fest., Cabrillo Music, Fest., San Francisco Ballet; Asst. Cond. of Oakland Symph. Youth Orch.; Mbr., sev. chamber grps.; Fac., MIlls Coll., Calif. Sate Coll., Sonoma; Perf. world premiere of Cello Concerto by Andrew Imbrie, commissioned by & w. Oakland Symph. Orch., 1973. Recordings: L'Incoronazione di Poppea, Monteverdi (Cambridge) Continue

cellist; L'Erismena, Cavalli (Vox) Continuo cellist. Mbrships: Pres., Calif. Cello Club 1957; Phi Beta Kappa, 1957. Hobbies: Reading; Travel. Address: 963 Peralta Ave., Albany, CA 94706, USA.

KELLAR, Allan Dean, b. 26 Jan. 1934, Danville, Iowa, USA. Professor of Music; Choral Director; Singer (Baritone). Educ: BA., Grinnell Coll.; MA., PhD., Univ. of Iowa. m. Linda Bricker, 2 d. Career: Choral Dir., Univ. of Iowa Laboratory Schl., 1963-65; Chmn., Music Dept. & Dir. of Choral Activities, Coe Coll., Cedar Rapids, Iowa, 1965-. Recordings Choral Music at Coe, 4 vols. Publ: The Hamburg Bach; Carl Philipp Emanuel Bach as Choral Composer, 1970. Contbr. to Iowa Music Educator Mag. Mbrships: Am. Choral Dirs. Assn.; MENC; Bd. of Dirs., Iowa Music Educators Assn.; Phi Beta Kappa; Pi Kappa Lambda. Hons: Pearl M. Taylor Assoc. Prof. of Music, Coe Coll., 1971. Hobbies: Skiing; Tennis; Reading; Travel; Photography. Address: 254 Brentwood Circle NE, Cedar Rapids, IA 52402, USA.

KELLEHER, Frank, b. 5 Aug. 1937, Cardiff, Wales, UK. Clarinettist; Lecturer. Educ: BMus, (London); FTCL; LRAM. m. Mary Rees. Career: Tutor, Monmouthshire Educ. Comm., 1960-68; Fndr., Monmouthshire Schls. Orch., 1964; Univ. Coll. of Wales, Cardiff, 1968-73; Sr. Lectr. Hd. of Wind Studies, Welsh Coll. of Music & Drama, 1973-; Woodwind coach, Nat. Youth Orch. of Wales, 1960-65; Univ. of Southern Calif., USA, 1964. Mbrships: Venturi Ensemble, 1966-70; Conductor, S Glamorgan Youth Orch., 1977-; Bd. of Govs., Welsh Coll. of Music & Drama, 1978; ISM (Nat. Coun.); Galpin Soc. Recip. Sir Charles Harris Prize, Univ. of London, 1968. Hobbies: Reading; Travel; Gardening. Address: 35 Palace Rd., Llandaff, Cardiff, Wales, UK.

KELLER, Alfred, b. 5 Jan. 1907, Rorschach, Switz. Director; Composer; Teacher. Educ: Zurich Conserv., 1925-27; Masterclass for Comp., Arnold Schoenberg, Prussian Acad. of Arts, Berlin, 1927-30. m. Hedy Züllig, 2 s., 1 d. Career: Dir. for choir & orch., Pianist; Comp., pvte. Tutor, 1931-46; Piano Tchr., St. Gallens Tchng. Seminar, Rorschach, 1946-72; Prof., 1956-. Comps. incl: Flageolett for piano; 3 Klavierstu..re; Choralvorspiel und Phantasie für Orgel. Recordings: Passacaglia for str. orch. Mbrships: Swiss Musicians Union; Ortsgruppe St. Gallen der IGNM; Schweiz. Berfdirigenten-Verband. Recip. anerkannungspreis der Stadt St. Gallen, 1954; Anerkennungspreis der Schweiz. Stiftung 'Pro-Arte', 1976; Kulturpreis der Stadt Rorschach, 1977. Address: Haldenstr. 8, CH-9400 Rorschach, Switz.

KELLER, Hans, b. 11 Mar. 1919, Vienna, Austria. Music critic. Educ: Vienna, violin studies; autodidact; LRAM, 1943. Career: was prisoner, escape to England; Violin player var. orch.; viola player Adler, Huttenbach Quartets; Musical advsr. British Film Inst.; 1949, joint ed. Music Survey; 1948, Naturalized British citizen; since 1949 BBC Music Division. Contbr. to var profl. jrnls. in England, Austria, Switz., USA. Address: 3 Frognal Gardens, London, NW. 3.

KELLER, Heinrich, b. 14 Nov. 1940, Winterthur, Switz. Solo Flutist; Teacher for Flute; Composer. Educ: Conserv. Music, Zurich, 1961-65; Flute dip., 1965; Composing w. Rudolf Kelterborn. m. Brigitta Steinbrecher, 2 s. Career: Solo flutist, Musikkollegium Winterthur; Tchr., flute, Conserv. Music, ibid.; Radio & TV apps., Switz.; Soloist, Switz., Austria, Germany and UK. Comps. incl: 'Reduction' for flute, cello & harpsichord, 1974; Refrains for flute, harp, celesta & percussion, 1975. Recordings incl: Flute Music of 18th Century, Rimaphon RILP. Mbr. profl. orgs. Hons. incl: Tonhalle Gesellschaft, Zurich for string quartet comp., 1974. Hobby: Lit. Address: Grüzenstrasse 14, CH 8400 Winterthur, Switz.

KELLER, Marjorie Murray, b. 9 May 1904, MacMinnville, Tenn., USA. Music Administrator; Violinist; Conductor; Lecturer. Educ: BS, Univ. Cinn., 1938; Mus M, Cinn. Conserv. Music, 1944; Post grad. study, Juilliard Schl. Music; Conducting w. W Herrman & D Johanos; Profl. workshop, TV prod., NY Univ. m. Henry Charles Keller, 1 d. Career incls: Dir., Creative Arts, Dallas Independent Schl. Dist. Tex., 1944-74; Co-prod. w. Dallas Symph. Orch., 40 tchng. films, 1971-74. Publs: Easy Steps to the Orchestra, I & II, 1950. Contbr. to profl. jrnls. Mbr. var. profl. orgs. Hons. incl: Disting. Alumna Award, Univ. Cinn. Coll.-Conserv. Music, 1974. Hobbies incl: Photography; Swimming. Address: PO Box 181, Edinburg Rural Stn., Northville, NY 12134, USA. 4.

KELLER, Peter, b. 5 Nov. 1944, Thalwil, Zürich, Switzerland. Musicologist. Educ: PhD., Univ. of Zürich. Contbr. to: Grove's Dictionary of Music & Musicians, 6th Ed.; Musica Disciplana; Handwortenbuch der musikalischen Terminologie, Freiburg, 1972. Mbrships: Int. Musicol. Soc.; Swiss Music Rsch. Soc.;

German Soc. for Music Rsch. Address: 31 Bielstrasse, CH-4153 Reinach, Switzerland.

KELLERMAN, Wolfgang, b. 8 Mar. 1925, Leipzig, Germany. Violinist. Educ: Awarded scholarship to RAM, London; studied at RAM w. Arthur Catterall & Prof. Max Rostal. m. Barbara Phyllis Pentith, 1 s., 1 d. Career: Recitals & solo perfs. at the Royal Fest. Hall Recital Room, Wigmore Hall & Music Clubs & Socs.; Mbr. of Yehudi Menuhin Chamber Orch., LPO & sev. other ensembles. Hobbies: Travel; Architecture; Photography; Reading; Chess. Address: 20 Glenwood Grove, Kingsbury, London NW9, UK.

KELLING, Hajo, b. 4 Oct. 1907, Essen, Germany. Director of Studies; Choir-Master. Educ: Studied at Hochschule für Musik, Cologne, & at Univs. of Bonn & Cologne, 1928-33; State exams, Berlin, 1932. m. (1) Katharina Ulbricht, (2) Katharina Rohde, 4 children. Debut: Remscheid, 1932. Career: Conducting in Remscheid, Solingen, Wuppertal, Essen, Stuttgart, Cologne; Performances of comps. in Germany & abroad (Melbourne, Switz., Austria, Italy, France); Dir. of choirs in Remscheid & Wuppertal. Comps. incl: Choral works; Orchl. works; Music for youth; Opera, Das Triptychon von den Hellingen Drei Königen; Oratorio, Vom enigen Werden. Works recorded. Author of Portraits in Lied & Chor, 1965, musica sacra, 1960, '67. Mbrships: Deutscher Komponistenverband; GEMA. Hons: 1st Prize, Sängerspruch für den DSB, Stuttgart, 1956; Orlando di Lasso Medal, 1971. Address: Albrecht-haer-Str. 31, 563 Remscheid-Lennep, German Fed. Repub.

KELLY, Danis, b. 17 May 1946, Temple, Tex., USA. Harapist. Educ: Curtis Inst.; BM, Cleveland Inst.; Grad., Interlochen Arts Acad. m. Timothy H Stroud. Career: Prin. Harpist, Milwaukee Symph. Orch., 1969-, Santa Fe Opera Co., 1973-. Recordings: w. Milwaukee Symph. Mbrships: Pi Kappa Lambda; Am. Harp Soc. Hons. incl: 1st Prize, Am. Harp Soc. Contest, Chgo., 1963. Address: 5515 N Dexter Ave., Milwaukee, WI 53209, USA.

KELLY, Denise Maria Ann, b. 24 Apr. 1954, Belfast, N Ireland, UK. Harpist; Composer; Teacher. Educ: B Mus, Trinity Coll., Univ. of Dublin; Univ. Coll. Dublin; Royal Irish Acad. of Music, Dublin; GSM; Conserv. of Music, Brussels; LGSM. Career: Solo, chmbr. & orchl. harpist; Tchr. of Concert Harp, Schl. of Music, Cork & Royal Irish Acàd. of Music, Dublin. Comps: Helas Mon Dieu, 1974; Metaphyscycle, 1976; Journey of a Soul, 1978; From Beginning to End, 1978. Recordings: sev. radio recordings. Mbrships: Music Assn. of Ireland; Irish Comps. Assn.; Performing Rights Soc. Hons: 2 Gold Medals, for Irish Hapr & Concert Harp, Dublin Féis Ceoil; Alexander Grosz Mem. Prize for Comp., GSM. Hobbies: Reading; Swimming. Address: 9 Adair, Sandymount Ave., Ballsbridge, Dublin 4, Eire.

KELLY, Mary Elizabeth, b. 14 May 1915, Olney, Ill., USA. Violinist. Educ: B Mus, M Mus, Coll. of Music, Cinn., Ohio. m. Robert Kelly, 3 s. Career: Concertmaster, Morton Franklin's All-Girl Orch.; Notes of Grace, Cinn., Ohio, 1939; Asst. Concertmaster, Champaign-Urbana Symph., Ill., 1960-; 1st Violinist, Memphis Symph., Tenn., 1963-75; Asst. Concertmaster, Springfield, Ill., Symph., 1966-; 1st Violinist, Kankakee, Ill., Symph., 1968-; Soloist w. Springfield Symph., 1973. Mbrships: Mu Phi Epsilon (Past-Pres., Treas., Correspondence Sec., Urbana-Champaign Alumnae Chapt.); Tuesday Morning Musical Club (Past Pres.). Hobbies: Hiking; Photography. Address: 807 S Urbana Ave., Urbana, IL 61801, USA.

KELLY, Robert, b. 26 Sept. 1916, Clarksburg, W Va., USA. Composer; Violinist; Violist; University of Ill. Professor Emeritus of Composition. Educ: B Mus, Curtis Inst. of Music, Phila., Pa.; M Mus, Eastman Schl. of Music, Rochester, NY; studied violin, Cinn. Coll. of Music & Juilliard Schl. of Music, NYC. m. Mary E Kelly, 3 s. Career: perfs. w. major orchs. Comps. incl: 3 Symphs.; 2 Operas; Concerti for violin, violin & cello, cello, & viola; num. chmbr. works, songs, works for chorus, percussion, etc. Recording of own comps., Symph. No. 2. Publs: Theme & Variations, 1969; Aural & Visual Recognition, 1970. Mbr. profl. orgs. Recip., var. hons. Hobbies: Hiking; Photography. Mgmt: Broadcast Music Inc., 40 W 57th St., NY, NY 10019, USA. Address: 807 S Urbana Ave., Urbana, IL 61801, USA.

KELSEY, Xenophon, b. 20 Apr. 1949, Ormskirk, Lancs., UK. Conductor; Pianist; Horn & Double Bass Player. Educ: Grad Dip., 1967-70, Post-grad. conducting course, 1970-71, Northern Schl. of Music. Career: Dir., Northern Schl. of Music Wind Ensemble, 1968-73; Northern Pro Arte Ensemble, 1970-; Stockport Youth Orch., 1975-; Cond., Northwest Phil. Orch., 1970-74; UMIST Orch., 1972-74; Edge Hill Coll. of Educ. Orch., 1973-74; var. freelance engagements; broadcasts on

BBC Radio Manchester, Radio 4 & BBC TV 1 w. Northern Schl. of Music Wind Ensemble. Mbrships: Committee, Manchester Br., ISM; Musicians Union. Recip. Stewart MacPherson Mem. Prize for Musicianship, Northern Schl. of Music, 1970. Address: Ashley House, Ure Bank, Ripon, Yorks, HG4 1JG, UK.

KELTERBORN, Rudolf, b. 3 Sept. 1931, Basel, Switz. Composer; Conductor; Professor of Musical Theory & Composition. Educ: Dips., theory & conducting. Music Acad., Basel, 1953; studied composition w. Blacher & Fortner, Salzburg & Detmold & conducting. w. Markeritch. m. Erika Kelterborn-Salathé, 2 children. Career: Tchr. & Cond., Basel, 1956-60; Prof. of Compositon, NW German Music Acad., Detmold, 1960-68; Prof., Music HS, Zürich, 1968-75: Hd., Music Dept., Swiss Radio, 1975; Ed., Swiss Music Review, 1968-75; active Cond.; compositions have been performed in Europe, USA & Japan. Compositions incl: 3 symphs.; 2 operas; 4 str. quartets; a ballet; var. works for orch.; concertos for var. solo instruments; cantatas; chmbr. music; piano & organ works. Has made sev. recording for Musicaphon-Baerenreiter. Publs: Stilistische Mannigfaltgheit in der zeitgenössischen Musik, 1958; Etüden zur harmonielehre, 1967. Contbr. to profl. jrnls. Mbrships: VP, Assn. of Swiss Composers & Interpreters. Hons: Bernhard Sprengel Prize of German Ind., 1962; Conrad Ferdinand Meyer Prize, 1971; Zürcher Radio Prize, 1973. Hobbies: Contemp. Arts & Lit.; Moutain Touring. Address: Unterer Batterieweg 152, CH-4059 Basle, Switz.

KELYNACK, Hilary Clifton, b. 31 May 1915, Beeston, Notts., UK. Lecturer; Administrator; Conductor; Pianist; Organist. Educ: MA, Mus B, St. John's Coll., Cambridge Univ.; GSM; FRCO. m. Grace Edith Fisher, 1 s., 1 d. Career: Acting Organist & Choirmaster, St. John's Coll., Cambridge, 1936-38; Organist & Choirmaster, Jesus Coll., ibid., 1938-39; Dir. of Music, Monkton Combe Schl., 1943-48; Music Master, Oundle Schl., 1948-52; Dir. of Music, Stowe Schl., 1952-60, & Hertford Grammar Schl., 1960-66; Lectr., Balls Park Coll. of Educ., Hertford, 1966-71; Prin. Lectr., & Hd., Music Dept., ibid., 1971-. Comps: Chelsea Miniatures; Signs to Sounds. Mbr., ISM. Hons: Turpin Prize, FTCL. Hobby: Gardening. Address: 5 Millfield, Wadesmill, Ware, Herts., UK. 4.

KEMP, Anthony Eric, b. 2 Jan. 1934, Tanga, Tanganyika. University Lecturer; Organist. Educ: Kent Coll., Canterbury; Coll. of S Mark & S John, Univ. of London; Univ. of Sussex; MA; DPhil; Acad. Dip. Educ.; TCL; FTCL; LTCL; LMusTCL. m. Valerie Francis, 1 d., 1 s. Career: Hd., Music Dept., Forest Hill Schl., London, 1958; Sr. Lectr. in Music, Brighton Coll. of Educ., 1964; Prin. Lectr. & Dir. of Music, Coll. of S Mark & S John, 1972; now Lectr. in Music Educ., Univ. of Reading Schl. of Educ.; various posts as organist & choirmaster, now at All Saints Ch., Wokingham; Dir. of Music, Univ. of Sussex Chapel, 1966-70. Publs: Chief Reviewer, Handbook for Music Teachers, 1964, '68; Fun to Make Music, 1975 (Norwegian ed., 1976). Mbrships: Brit. Psychological Soc.; sec., Soc. for Rsch. in Psychol. of Music & Music Educ; ISM; Plainsong & Medieval Music Soc. Address: 18 Blagrove Land, Wokingham, Berks. RG11 4BA, UK.

KEMP, Dorothy Elizabeth Walter, b. 23 Nov. 1926, Cincinnati, Ohio, USA. French Hornist; Pianist; Composer; Arranger; Accordionist; Conductor. Educ: BS, Univ. of Cinn., 1948; Coll. of Music of Cinn.; MA E Ky. Univ., 1949; Postgrad. courses, Univs. of W Ky. Cinn. & Miami, between 1949 & 1974. m. David H Kemp. Debut: Cond., Crosley Band, Fountain Sq., Cincinnati, June 3, 1973; French Horn soloist w. Concert Band, Coll. of Music, Cinn., 1948. Career: Freelance French Hornist w. Cinn. Symph. Orch., Shubert & Taft Theatres & City Park Concerts; Prof. of Horn, Music, Theory, Arr. & Music Educ., Appalachian State Univ., Boone, NC., 1950-54; Music Ed. Asst., Willis Music Co., 1959-62; Mt. Healthy, OH Pub. Schls., 1963-67; Newport, Ky., Pub. Schls., 1967. Comps: Easter Fanfares I & II. Recordings: Horn Quartet Selections (on tape), 1976. Publs: Christmas in Brass, 1959; 4 Brass for Christmas, 1960; Easter in Brass, 1962; The Groundhog Rock, song for schl. children, 1980. Contbr. to The Instrumentalist. Mbrships: Am. Fedn. of Musicians; Phi Beta Nat. Music Fraternity; Int. Horn Soc. Hons: Partial Scholarship for French Horn, Coll. of Music, Cinn., 1944-48; (towards BS in Educ.); Scholarship for MA, E Ky. Univ., 1948-49. Hobbies: Colour Photography; Reading; Collecting sheet music novelties; Collecting good 'out of print' concert band music; Arr. for Brass Ensemble & Symph. Band. Address: 4559 Hamilton Ave., Cincinnati, OH 45223, USA.

KEMP, Malcolm David, b. 19 Feb. 1948, Brighton, UK. Organist; Choir trainer; Conductor; Teacher of Music. Educ: ARCM (Organ Teaching); L Mus TCL; ARCO (CHM); FVCM (Organ Perf.). Career: Organist, Ch. of the Good Shepherd, Brighton; Tchr. of Music; Choir trainer & Cond. Mbrships:

Brighton & Dist. Organists Assn. (Past Pres.); RSCM (personal mbr.); ISM (Assoc.); Trinity Coll. Guild. Hobbies: Theology; Photography; The Arts; Good Food. Address: 39 Bear Rd., Brighton, E Sussex BN2 4DA, UK.

KEMP, Walter Herbert, b. 16 Nov. 1938, Montreal, Canada. Musicologist; Conductor; Pianist; Organist; Administrator. Educ: B Mus, Univ. of Toronto, 1959; M Mus, ibid, 1961; AM, Harvard Univ., 1963; D Phil., Oxford Univ., UK, 1972; FRCCO; ARCT; Studied organ w. Eric Rollinson, comp. w. John Weinzweig & Leon Kirchner, musicol. w. Nino Pirotta & Frank Harrison. m. Valda A Svenne, 1 s., 2 d. Career: Cond., Univ. of Toronto Chorus, 1959-61, Hart House Glee Club, 1962-63; Kitchener-Waterloo Phil. Choir, 1966-72; Fndr., Chmn., Music Dept., Waterloo, Luth. Univ. (now Wilfrid Laurier Univ.), Waterloo, Ont.; Dir., Univ. Choir, ibid; Pres., RCCO, 1974-76; Chmn., Music Dept., Dalhousie Univ., Halifax, Nova Scotia, 1977-; Dir., Dalhousie Chorale, 1977-. Compositions: Five Poems of William Blake; Five Latvian Piano Pieces; Latvian Boat Song; Four Latvian Folk Songs. Contbr. to var. profl. publs. Mbrships. incl: RCO; Royal Musical Assn.; Am. Musicological Assn. Hons. incl: Golden Jubilee Prize, RCCO, 1961. Address: c/o Dept. of Music, Dalhousie Univ., Halifax, Nova Scotia, Can.

KEMPFF, Wilhelm Walter Friedrich, b. 25 Nov. 1895. Pianist; Composer. Educ: Berlin Univ. & Conservatoire. Career: Prof. & Dir., Stuttgart Staatliche Hochschule für Musik, 1924-29; world-wide concert tours as Pianist. Comps. incl: 2 symphs.; 4 operas; piano concertos; chmbr. music; vocal & choral works. Publs: Unter dem Zimbelstern; Das Werden eines Musikers (autobiog.). Mbr., Prussian Acad. of Arts. Hons: Mendelssohn Prize; Artibus et Litteris Medal.

KENDELL, Iain, b. 13 June 1931, Greenford, Middx., UK. Lecturer; Composer of Music; Pianist. Educ: GRSM; FTCL; LRAM; ARCM. Debut: Musikhalle, Hamburg, 1952. Career: Freelance Musician, 1952-62; Music Master, Bishop's Stortford HS for Boys, 1962-65; St. Lectr., Digby Stuart Coll. of Educ., London, 1965-; Deputy Dir., Shcls. Coun. Rsch. & Dev. Prof. 'Music Education of Young Children' at Reading Univ., 1974-78. Comps: Music for Strings; Sonata for Strings; 'Episode' for Clarinet & Piano; 'Hymn of Light'; 'Mass of the Earth'; Spring Cantata, etc. Originator & Ed. of 'Junior Music' series; 'Beginning Music' series (all w. J & W Chester Ltd.); Time for Music, 1977. Recordings: Shepherds Tale; Sir Geoffrey's Book. Publs: A Music Desk Book for the Class Teacher, 1973. Contbr. to The Chesterian Mag. Hons: Harriet Cohan Piano Medal, 1958. Hobbies: Walking; Photography; The 18th Century. Address: 24 Cranes Pk. Ave., Surbiton, Surrey, UK.

KENDRICK, James Michael, b. 14 Aug. 1952, Flushing, NY, USA. Oboist; English Horn Player; Music Publisher. Educ: BMus, Manhattan Schl. of Music, 1975; MMus, 1976, Juilliard Schl. Career incls: Prin. Oboe & Soloist, Municipal Concerts Orch., 1975-; Brooklyn Philharmonia, 1976-; Music for Westchester Symph., 1976-; Houston Grand Opera, Porgy & Bess, 1976, '77; Operations Mgr., European Am. Music Dist. Corp., Clifton, NJ, 1977-. Var. recordings. Publs: Indexes, Ruth Dana Collection of first & early editions of Franz Liszt's piano music, 13 vols., 1976. Mbr., Am. Fedn. of Musicians. Hobbies: Collecting records & books; Railroad Hist. Address: PO Box 3001, Clifton, NJ 07012, USA.

KENDRICK, Virginia, b. 8 Apr. 1910, Mpls., Minn., USA. Pianist; Organist; Composer. Educ: Univ. of Minn., 1928-33. m. W Dudley Kendrick, 3 s., 2 d. Career: Pianist, Andahazy Ballet Co., Mpls., 1958-76; Organ Music Dept., Schmitt Music Co., Mpls., 1958-76; Organist, 1st Ch. of Christ Scientist, Excelsior, Minn., 1962-75. Comps. incl: (songs) Little Miss Whuffit, 1962; Green is the Willow, 1965; White Sky, 1967; Music is Beauty, 1969; Jade Summer, 1971; Before the World Was, 1974; Hear My Cry, O God, 1975; I Will Lift Up Mine Eyes Unto the Hills, 1976; In This Soft Velvet Night, 1977; Two Songs for Voice & Piano, 1976; The Lord God Omnipotent, 1978; Lo, I Am With You Always Unto the End of the World, 1978. Mbrships: AGO; Nat. Fedn. Music Clubs; League of Women Comps.; Sigma Kappa; Mu Phi Epsilon. Address: 5800 Echo Rd., Shorewood, MN 55331, USA. 5,27.

KENINS, Talivaldis, b. 1919, Latvia. Professor of Composition; Composer. Educ: B. ès Lettres, Fac. des Lettres, Univ. of Grenoble, France, 1939; Studies in piano & comp. w. Joseph Wihtol, State Conservatory of Music of Latvia, Riga, 1940-44; Conservatoire Nat. Superieur de Musique, w. Tony Aubin, Simone Pie Caussade, Oliver Messiaen, Paris, France, 1945-50; Dip. in analysis & aesthetics, Premier Prix Dip. in Comp., ibid. Career: Inst., Fac. of Music, Univ. of Toronto, Canada, 1952; Sessional Lectr., ibid, 1953; Full-time Lectr., 1956; Asst. Prof., 1962; Assoc. Prof., 1967; Prof. of Comp.,

1973; Lectr., Schola Cantorum, Toronto; Instr., special courses, Royal Conservatory of Music; Music commentator, Radio Canada; Adjudicator for several Canadian music competitions & festivals; Guest Lectr., var. univs.; Comp.-in-Res., Kalamazoo Coll., Mich. Composer of orchl. works, works for orch. w. soloist(s), works for chorus w. orch. or instrumental accompaniment, choral works, chmbr. music, keyboard works, educl. piano music. Var. works commissioned. Mbrships: Comps., Authors & Publns. Assn. of Canada Ltd.; Canadian League of Comps.; Int. Soc. of Contemporary Music; Affiliate, Canadian Music Ctr.; Pres., Canadian League of Comps. Recip. of num. hons. inclng. Sr. Music Award, Can. Coun., 1971, '78. Address: 73 Parkview Ave., Willowdale, Ont., M2N 3Y3, Can.

KENNEDY, Gilbert Young, b. 11 Mar. 1916, Liverpool, England. Composer; Organ & Harpsichord Recitalist. Educ: B Sc, Liverpool Univ.; PhD, Sheffield Univ.; Fellow, Tonic Sol-Fa Coll. (Curwen Coll.). m. Margaret Sewell. Debut: organ recital, Liverpool. Career: has given organ recitals throughout Britain & in France, Switz. & Brazil; Music Advsr., Playhouse Theatre, Sheffield, 1955-68. Compositions: incidental music to most of Shakespeare's plays; Duchess of Malfi; Oedipus Rex; Sergeant Musgrave's Dance; The Shaghraun; music for 3 successive Shakespeare prodns. (w. Colin George), Ludlow Fest., 1964-66; Royal Masque 'The Birth of Steel' (w. Wm. Empson) command. by Sheffield Univ. 1954; Fantasia on 'Personent Hodie' for chorus & full orch.; music for film 'O Rei das Amazonas' (Brazil); music for prodns. of the Manchester Youth Theatre; 25 Shakespeare Songs; music for the plays of Allan Cullen; R Brooke's 'The Dead' (setting for male choir). Mbrships: FRSA; Exec. Coun., Curwen Inst. Hobby: Gardening. Address: Bryneglwys, Penrhos, Llanymynech, Powys SY22 6QE, UK. 3.

KENNEDY, Josepha, b. 21 Mar. 1928, Elmira, NY, USA. College Professor; Private Voice Teacher. Educ: BS, Nazareth Coll. of Rochester; BA, ibid; MS, ibid; MA, Columbia Univ.; PhD., ibid. Recordings: Four Shakespeare Songs. Author, Paraliturgical Music in Italy, 1600-1650, 1969. Contbr. to: Saturday Review; Renascence; Clavier; Music Jrnl.; Sisters Today; Grove's Dictionary of Music & Musicians. Mbrships: Int Musicol. Soc.; Am. Musicol. Soc.; Nat. Assn. of Tchrs. of Singin; AAUP. Named Clarence Barker Fellow, Columbia Univ., 1966-69. Hobbies: Light Reading; Cooking; Sewing. Address: Nazareth Coll. of Rochester, 4245 East Ave., Rochester, NY 14610, USA.

KENNEDY, Michael, b. 19 Feb. 1926, Manchester, England. Journalist & Critic. m. Eslyn Durdle. Publs: The Hallé Tradition, 1960; The Works of Ralph Vaughan Williams, 1964; Portrait of Elgar, 1968; Barbirolli, 1971; Elgar Orchestral Works, 1970; History of the Royal Manchester College of Music, 1971; Autobiography of Charles Hallé, 1972. Mahler, 1974. Richard Strauss, 1976. Contbr. to: Musical Times; Music & Letters; Hallé; Listener; BBC scripts; etc. Recip. of Hon. RMCM., 1972 & Hon. MA, 1975. Hobbies: Cricket; Reading. Address: 3 Moorwood Dr., Sale, Cheshire, UK. 1, 3.

KENNEDY-KOCH, Valentine Charles, b. 3 June 1913, Frankfurt/Main, Germany. Musician (Bassoon, Contra Bassoon). Educ: Studied piano w. Else Krauss & Franz Osborne, Berlin; RCM, London, UK; ARCM. m. Marjorie Georgiana Broderick, 2 d. Career: W. LPO, 1946-; has recorded w. LPO & London Baroque Ensemble. Recordings incl: Mozart, E Flat Serenade for Wind; Arnell, Serenade for Wind. Mbr., Musicians Union. Hons: Hetty Waley Cohen Memorial Prize, 1938; Woodhouse Prize, 1939. Hobbies: Listening to records of famous singers. Address: 35 Byron Rd., N. Wembley, Middx. HA0 3PA, UK.

KENNESON, Claude, b. 11 Apr. 1935, Port Arthur, Tex., USA. Cellist. Educ: B Mus, M Mus, Univ. of Tex. m. Carolyn (div.) 1 s., 1 d. Career: Recitalist in N. Am., Pupil of Horace Britt. UK. & Europe; past Musical Dir., Royal Winnipeg Ballet; Co-Fndr., Corydon String Trio & Univ. of Alta. String Quartet; currently Prof., Univ. of Alta, Dir., Banff Cello Inst. Recordings: String Quartets by Elizabeth Maconchy (no. 10) & Jean Coulthard (No. 2), comps. for Alta. String Quartet; Quartets by Schubert & Debussy (all Canadian Broadcasting Corp.). Publs: A Cellist's Guide to the New Approach, 1974; A Bibliography of Cello Ensemble Music, 1974. Contbr. to: Am. String Tchrs. Assn. Jrnl.; The Strad. Mbrship.; Pres., Soc. for Talent Educ., Edmonton. Hons: Competitor Pablo Casals Int. Comps., 1959; Canada Coun. Grant, 1968. Address: Suite 1006, 11111 87th Ave., Edmonton, Alta., Canada.

KENNY, Yvonne Denise, b. 25 Nov. 1950, Sydney, NSW, Australia. Opera Singer (soprano). Educ: BSc (Biochem.), Sydney Univ.; Vocal study, Sydney Conserv., 5 yrs.; Schl. of

Opera, ibid., 2 yrs.; Schl. of La Scala, Milan, Italy, 1 yr. Debut: in Donizetti's Rosmonda d'Inghilterra, Queen Elizabeth Hall, London, 1975. Career: Mbr. of Co. of Royal Opera House, Covent Gdn.; appearances Scottish Opera & Engl. Nat. Opera; Recitalist w. Geoffrey Parsons for BBC. Recording: Donizetti's Rosmonda d'Inghilterra. Hons: ¢st Prize, Kathleen Ferrier Mem. Award, 1975. Hobbies: Tennis; Squash; Swimming; Tapestry. Mgmt: Lies Askonas. Address: 3/106 Fordwych Rd., London, NW2, UK.

KENSINGER, Donald Carey, b. 23 Sept. 1937, Bluefield, W. Va., USA. Music Educator; Choral Director; Performer (Piano, Organ, Harpsichord). Educ: BS in Music Educ., Concord Coll., Athens, W. Va.; MS in Music Educ., Radford Coll., Va.; Westminster Choir Coll., Princeton, NJ; Coll. Conserv. of Music, Cinn., Ohio; Mich. State Univ. Career incls: Dir., Bluefield High Schl. A Capella Choir & Madrigal Singers, 1961-70; Guest Dir., Music Fests, W. Va. & Va.; Music Fac. Mbr., Concord Coll., 1970-75 & Bluefield State Coll., 1975-; Recitalist; Choir & Music Theatre Dir.; Min. of Music, 1st Presby. Ch., Bluefield. Mbrships incl: Chmn., Fine Arts Commission, City of Bluefield; Nat. Democratic Committee; Mercer Co. Assn. Class Room Tchrs. (VP, 1970). Address: 530 Cumberland Rd., Bluefield, WV 24701, USA.

KENSWIL, Atma, b. 29 Apr. 1892, Paramaribo, Surinam. Composer. Educ: Studied piano at Conservatoire Utrecht; comp. w. Leo Weiner & piano w. Laszioffy at Liszt Acad., Budapest; comp. w. de la Presle & piano w. Lazare Levy, Paris Conserv. Debut: Haarlem (w. piano). Comps: Lentelicht (song); Preludium Pacis, (piano); Meditation Symphonic (orchl. mdsic in chorus). Publs: Lentelicht, 1946; Preludium Pacis, 1946; Meditation Symphonic, 1946; Per Tenebras ad Lucem, 1952; Wyzang v. Tagore I & II; Kerstmeditátie (chorus & piano); Poeme d'une flut Orientale piano; Phantasie Orientale (orch.); Fuga (4st), etc. Mbrships: NTB Mgmt: Donemus doc in Netherlands for music; Buma and Donemus & Stemra, Amsterdam. Address: Ommershoflaan 35A, Bung. 'Melotinto', Oosterbeek, The Netherlands.

KENT (Sister) Benen, (formerly Margaret Agnes Kent), b. 1 Nov. 1917, Tilden, Neb., USA. Music Instructor (piano, voice, theory, violin, organ). Educ: BSE, MA., Coll. of St. Teresa at Winona, Minn.; MMus., Ind. Univ. at Bloomington, Ind.; Dip. in piano, Conserv. of St. Cecilia, Winona, Minn. Mbr. of Franciscan Order. Career: Has taught in Minn., Neb., Ill. in HS., Elem. Schl., Conservs. & pvte. studios; Org., family Orch.; Has served as Choral Instr. in grade & HS's; Dir. orchs. & bands; Trained ch. organists, etc. Var. unpubld. comps. for piano, solo voice, & chorus. Contbr. of reviews to newspapers. Mbrships: Soc. of Am. Musicians; Am. String Tchr. Assn.; Am. Coll. of Musicians; Music Tchrs. Nat. Assn. (cert.); Nat. Assn. of Organ Tchrs.; APTA; Minn. Music Tchrs. Assn. (master cert.); NGPT; Rochester Symph. Orch. Hons: Admittance into SAM, 1960; TPI Orch. at Oberlin SS, 1970. Var. hobbies. Address: Assisi Heights, Rochester, MN 55901, USA. 27.

KENT, Christopher John, b. 12 Aug. 1949, London, UK. Musicologist; Organist; Teacher. Educ: Mus B, Univ. of Manchester; M Mus, King's Coll., London; PhD, ibid, ARMCM; FRCO. m. Angela Thomas. Career: Asst. Music Master, City of London Schl. for Girls, 1975-. Mbr., Royal Musical Assn. Contbr. to Musical Times; Yrbook of Br. Inst. of Organ Studies; Proceedings of the Royal Musical Assn. Hons: Hilda Margaret Watts Prize, 1973; Louise Dyer Award, 1975. Hobbies: Railways; Natural Hist. Address: 5 Drury Rd., W Harrow, Middlesex HA1 4BY, UK.

KENT, Flora, b. Oldham, UK. Concert Accompanist (piano). Musical Educ: Royal Manchester Coll. of Music; Studied w. Gerald Moore, London; ARMCM. (performers' & tchrs.'); ATCL. Career: Official Accompanist, Royal Manchester Coll. of Music, 1942-45; Halle Orch., 1944-46; London Choral Soc., 1947-50; Toured England at all major music clubs playing for famous artists inclng. Campoli; Toured Spain w. Campoli, 1953; Currently accompanist for Roy Henderson's tchng. & pt.-time music tchr., George Eliot Schl. Hobby: Tennis. Address: 17 Lanark Rd., MaidaVale, London, W9, UK. 3.

KENT, Richard Layton, b. 23 Jan. 1916, Harris, Mo., USA. Professor of Music; Composer. Educ: BME, Drake Univ., 1940; MMus, New Engl. Conserv. of Music, 1947; MusAD, Boston Univ., 1961; Grad. courses, Harvard Univ. m. Lillian L Wallace, 1 s. Career: Prof. of Music, 1947-, Chmn., Fine Arts Dept., 1961-75, Mass. State Coll., Fitchburg. Comps: 80 publd. incl: Colonial Spring; New England, March and April (SATB a cap.); The Thing About Cats (SATB acc.); Four Housman Songs (SSA a cap.); Alleluia (SATB a cap.). Publs: Ed., Windows of Song, 1968. Mbrships: Am. Choral Dirs. Assn.; Am. Musicol. Soc.; Int. Musicol. Soc.; Coll Music Soc.; MENC; Am. Assn. of Univ.

Profs. Hons: Sibelius Medal, Helsinki Univ., 1963; Lowell. Mason Award, MMEA, 1978. Hobbies: Golf; Travel. Address: 1171 Main St., Leominster, MA 01453, USA. 4,29.

KENTISH, John. Tenor Singer. Educ: Rugby Schl. & Oriel Coll., Oxford. m. Joan Valerie Howard, 1 s., 3 d. Career: Formerly Prin. singer, Sadler's Wells Opera Co., & Glyndebourne Festival Opera; Dir. of Studies, London Opera Centre. Mbr., Savile Club. Hobby: cottage in Denbighshire. Address: 13 Woodlands Rd., London SW13 OJZ, UK.

KENTNER, Louis Philip, b. 19 July 1905, Karwin, Silesia, Austro-Hungarian Empire. Concert Pianist. Educ: Liszt Acad. of Music, Budapest. m. Griselda Gould. Debut: Budapest, 1918. Career: Toured USA, USSR, S. Africa, Australia, Far East & throughout Europe; num. TV Apps., UK; num. Orchl., Chmbr. Music Perfs. Compositions: 3 Sonatinas, piano; The Piano, 1976. Recordings: Columbia; HMV; Saga; Vox. Contbr. to Franz Liszt, Pres., Liszt Soc. Recip. Hon. RAM., 1970; CBE, 1978. Hobbies: Reading; Chess. Mgmt: Harold Holt Ltd.; Concert Direktig De Koos. Address: 1 Mallord St., London SW3 6DT, UK. 1,2,

KENTON, Stan(ley) Newcomb, b. 19 Feb. 1912, Wichita, Kan., USA. Orchestral Leader; Pianist. div., 1 s., 2 d. Career: has app. in all media, inclng. concerts & road tours, for over 30 yrs. Comps: over 100 publd. & recorded. Recordings: has made 57 albums w. Capitol Records, 9 w. Creative World Records, & sev. w. other companies such as Decca & London. Contbr. to var. musical publs. Hons: DHL., Drury Coll., Mo.; D Mus., Villanova Univ., Pa.; 2 Grammy Awards, 1961 & 62; in Down Beat Jazz Hall of Fame; Hon. DMus, Univ. of Redlands, Calif.; var. hons. in jazz polls. Mgmt: Kentonia, Inc., 1012 S. Robertson Blvd., Los Angeles, CA 90035, USA. 2,16.

KENYON, Nicholas Roger, b. 23 Feb. 1951, Altrincham, UK. Writer. Educ: BA (Modern Hist.), Balliol Coll., Oxford. m. Marie-Ghislaine Latham-Koenig, 1 d. Career incls: English Bach Fest., 1973-75; Scriptwriter BBC Music Div., 1975-79; Freelance Music Critic, Financial Times, Sunday Times, Observer, The Early Music Gazette (Ed.) etc., 1975-79; Broadcaster, BBC music progs.; Music Critic, The New Yorker, 1979-. Publs: Ed., Sing the Mass; Mozart; The BBC Symphony Orchestra 1930-80. Mbr., Critics Circle (Music Sect.). Address: c/o The New Yorker, 23 W 43rd St., NY, NY 10036, USA.

KEÖNCH, Boldizsár, b. 16 Mar. 1938, Budapest, Hungary. Concert Singer; Singing Teacher. Educ: dip. (piano & solfege tchr.) Bela Bartok Conserv., Budapest, 1964; dip. (concert singer & singing tchr.), Ferenc Liszt Acad. of Music, Budapest, 1971. m. Katalin Bojta, 2 d., 1 s. Career: num. perfs. in Europe & Aust. Recordings: Bach, St. John Passion; Charpentier, Te Deum; Liszt, Der Gang um Mitternacht; Stravinsky; Renard; works by Kodály, Gy. Kósa & T Vujicić. Hons: Medal for social culture, 1979. Hobbies: Photography; Languages. Mgmt: Interkoncert, Budapest. Address: Greguss u. 5.1.2, 1123 Budapest, Hungary.

KEPLINGER, Lorraine Joyce, b. 9 Apr. 1931, Lena, Ill., USA. Private Instructor (Band, Mallet Keyboard & some Stringed Instruments); Performer (Organ, Harp, Trumpet, French Horn, Accordion, Piano & Vocal). Educ: Ill. Wesleyan Univ. Schl. of Music, Bloomington; Kent State Univ., Tuscarawas Co. Br., New Philadelphia, Ohio. m. Richard Alan Keplinger, 3 d. Career: Owner & Operator, Gospel Book & Music Co., New Philadelphia, Ohio. Hobbies: Sewing; Knitting; Crocheting; Painting; Swimming. Address: 144 3rd St. SW, New Philadelphia, OH 44663, USA. 5, 27.

KEREK, Ferenc, b. 31 Oct. 1948, Makó, Hungary. Pianist. Educ: BA; Special course on theory of music; Acad. Ferenc Liszt, Budapest. m. Eva Fekete. Career: Sev. Radio apps.; Concerts, German Fed. Repub., Yugoslavia, Bulgaria, Italy, Poland. Recordings as choral accomp. Mbrships: FÉSZEK; Hungarian Artists; Hungarian Musicians Coun.; Soc. Liszt Ferenc. Hons: 1st Prize Concours Debussy, 1976. Hobbies: Making amateur films; Tourism. Address: 6726 Szeged, Vedred u. 26 A.3, Hungary.

KEREN, Zvi, b. 18 Aug. 1917, NY, USA. Musicologist; Composer; Arranger; Pianist. Educ: BS, NY Univ.; MA, Columbia Univ.; PhD., London Univ.; pupil of Joseph Schillinger, 1938-41 & authorized by him to teach his method; studied piano w. Paolo Gallico & Nadia Reisenberg. m. Renate Koplowitz, 3 c. Career: Assoc. Prof. in Musicol., Bar-ilan Univ.; Arranger & Orchestrator for radio progs. Publs: The Sources & Stylistic Development of Israeli Art Music, 1975. Mbrships: Chmn., Israel Arrangers' Union, 1962-72; Israel Musicol. Soc. Hobbies: Jewish studies; Playing & listening to Jazz. Address: 8 Derech Hatayasim, Tel-Aviv, Israel.

KERENYI, Nicholas George, b. 7 Feb. 1913, Budapest, Hungary. Opera Singer (Tenor); Professor of Singing. Educ: Music Conserv.; studied w. Isa Alden, Aureliano Pertile & Prof. L Szamosi of Budapest Conserv. & Acad. of Music, Vienna. m. Margaret Kéry, (Prof. of Singing), 2 s., 1 d. Debut: 1931. Career: Opera, Concert & Radio singer, Hungary, Italy & Switzerland, 1931-40; wounded in action WWII; Prof. of Singing, Budapest Conserv. & High Schl. & Tchrs. Sem., 1945-; State insp. of Singing Repertoire; 20 operatic parts; 40 Cantatas & Oratorios; over 3000 songs in 12 languages. Publs. incl: The New Routes of Hungarian Singing Pedagogy, 1948; Basis & Practice of Voice Developing, 1950, 9th ed. 1959; Art & Pedagogy of Singing, 1959, 2nd ed. 1966; Basic Science of the Pedagogy of Singing, 1961; A Hundred-coloured Bunch, Folk-songs of 100 Nations, 1966; Singing School, 3 vols. (w. M Kéry), 1967, 4th ed. 1978. Contbr. to profl. jrnls. Mbrships: Soc. of Hungarian Musicians; Soc. of Phonetics; Soc. of Music Tchrs. Hons: Title, Honoured Professor; Order of Merit, Labour; Order of Merit, Culture. Address: 1132 Budapest XIII, Váci ut 46B, Hungary.

KERMAN, Joseph Wilfred, b. 3 April 1924, London, UK. Musicologist; Critic; Professor of Music. Educ: BA, NY Univ.; PhD, Princeton, NJ, 1951. m. Vivian Shaviro, 1 d., 2 s. Career: Dir. of Grad. Studies, Westminster Choir Coll., Princeton, NJ, 1949-51; Vis. Fellow, All Souls Coll., Oxford, 1966; Music Fac., Univ. of Calif. at Berkeley, 1951-71; Dept. Chmn., ibid, 1960-63; Prof. of Music, ibid, 1974-; Heather Prof., music, Oxford, 1972-74. Publs. incl: Opera as Drama, 1956; The Elizabethan Madrigal, 1962; The Bethoven Quartets, 1967; Ludwig van Beethoven Autograph Miscellany, 1786-99 (Kafka Sketchbook), 2 vols., 1970; The Masses and Motets of Wm. Byrd, 1980; Ed., California Studies in 19th Century Music. Contbr. to profl. publs. Hons: Num. Fellowships; Hon. FRAM; Hon. DHL Fairfield Univ., 1970. Address: Music Dept., Univ. Calif., Berkeley, CA 94720, USA.

KERR, Harrison, b. 13 Oct. 1897, Cleveland, Ohio, USA. Composer; Educator. Educ: Prin. pvte. studies in US in organ, harmony & counterpoint w. Vincent Percy; piano & comp. w. James Hotchkiss Rogers; piano w. Claus Wolfram; organ w. E A Tattersall; comp. w. Nadia Boulanger in France; piano w. Isidor Phillip; Fountainbleau Cons. Dip. m. Jeanne McHugh. Career: Num. Radio & TV apps. Dir. of Music, Greenbrier Coll., Lewisburg, W Va.; Dir. of Music, Chase Schl., Brooklyn, NY.; Ed. of Trend; Chief of Music & Art Unit of Reorientation, Br. of US Army; Dean, Coll. of Fine Arts, Univ. of Okla; Comp.-in-Res. & Prof. of Music, Univ. of Okla. Comps. incl: Trio for clarinet, violoncello & piano, 19349; Study for violoncello unaccompanied, 1941; Str. Quartet, 1942; Suite for Flute & Piano, 1943; Symph. No. 1, 1946; Piano Sonata No. 2, 1947; Six Songs to Poems by Adelaide Crapsey, 1952; Frontier Day, 1958; Variations on a Theme from 'The Tower of Kel' for guitar, 1972; Sonata for violin & piano, 1973. Var. Recordings. Contbr. to mags, newspapers, reviews, etc. Mbrships incl: Sec., Am. Composers Alliance; Ex. Sec., Am. Music Ctr.; Exec. Bd., Nat. Music Coun. Recip., Fellowship, Huntington Hartford Fndn., 1960. Hobbies: Photography; Travel. Address: 1014 Louisiana St., Norman, OK 73069, USA. 1,3,7,14.

KERSENBAUM, Sylvia Haydée, b. 27 Dec. 1944, Buenos Aires, Argentina. Pianist. Educ: Dip., Piano & Composition, Buenos Aires Nat. Conserv. Debut: Buenos Aires, age 8. Career: Apps. w. maj. European & world orchs., inclng. Orch. Nat. de ORTF, Paris, RPO, London, Munich Phil., San Fran. Symph., Japan Phil., LSO, Orch. de la Suisse Romande, Symph. Orch., Bonn.; Recitals, Vienna, Paris, London, NY, Tokyo; Fests. & recordings for BBC, RAI, RIAS. Recordings. incl. Chopin sonatas, etudes, Tchaikowsky's Concerto Opus 44 in C, & works by Liszt & Brahms; Franck Symphonic Variations; Weber, Sonatas. Mbr., Am. Liszt Soc. Hons: 1st Prize, Buenos Aires Conserv., 1958; Dip. di Merito, Accad. Chigiana, Siena, 1967; 1st Prize, Argentine Broadcasting, 1960. Mgmt: Wilfred Van Wyck (UK). Address: 92 New Kings Rd., London SW6, UK.

KERSLAKE, Barbara, b. 26 Oct. 1913, Halifax, Yorks., UK. Solo Pianist & Accompanist. Educ: ARCM; TD; LRAM; RCM. m. John Perry, 2 s. Career: Recitals, Wigmore Hall, London; Soloist w. Jacques Orch. & others; Toured throughout WWII for ENSA & Arts Coun.; Staff mbr., Yehudi Menuhin Schl.; Examiner, RSM Associated Bd., 1964-. Hons: Chapple Gold Medal, RCM; Leverhulme Schlrship., 1936. Hobbies: Theatre; Art Exhibs. Address: Flat 3, 12 Kensington Pk. Gdns., London W11, UK.

KESHNER, Joyce Grove, b. 24 May 1927, New Haven, Conn., USA. Conductor; Vocal Teacher; Pianist; Composer; Musicologist; Lecturer. Educ: BS in Educ., Southern Conn. State Coll., 1948; Studied Piano at Juilliard Schl. of Music & Mannes Coll. of Music; MA in Comp., CUNY, 1972; Westminster Choir Coll., 1974; studied piano, cond., comp. &

voice w. num. pvte. tchrs. m. Murray Keshner, 1 s., 1 d. Debut: (as Cond.) New Haven, Conn., 1946. Career: Artist-Affiliate w. Ramapo Coll., NJ, 1973-76; Cond., Music Program, Temple B'nai Jacob, New Haven, Conn., 1946-48; Cond., Chorus, Jewish Commnity Centre, Paramus, NJ, 1957-60; Tchr., piano, voice, theory, cond., 1960-; Cond., Paramus Chorale, 1963-66; Cond. & Music Dir., Ars Music Chorale & Orch., 1966-; Guest Cond., Brockport Symph. Orch., NY & Summit Chorale, 1977. Comps. incl: String Quartet, 1971; Piece for Solo Bassoon; Waiting Born (flute, voice & piano); Monophonic Piece for Bassoon; Lord What is Manı, (Baritone, chorus & small orch.). Recordings: Handel - Joshua; I Know I Love You; A Joyful Noise. Mbr., num. profl. orgs. Recip., num. hons. Hobbies: Swimming; Musicological Rsch.; Travel. Address: 794 Wynetta Pl., Paramus, NJ 07652, USA.

KESSLER, Jerome, b. 13 Aug. 1942, Ithaca, NY., USA. Musician (cellist & conductor); Attorney. Educ: AB., Columbia Coll., 1963; LLB., UCLA Schl. of Law, 1966; studied cello w. Lillian Rehberg Goodman, Laszlo Varga, Leonard Rose & Joseph Schuster; studied chamber music w. William Kroll, Joseph Fuchs & Lillian Fuchs; studied cond. w. Richard Karp & Pierre Monteaux. Career: Active in the orchs. of the motion picture, TV & recording inds.; Fndr.-Mbr., Beverly Hills Trio, with which he has appeared in num. concerts in S. Calif.; Fdnr., Cond. of the Cello Octet, I Cellisti; Cond., Hollywood Chmbr. Orch.; Fndr.-Mbr., Los Angeles Cello Quartet. Recordings: as cellist; Corelli sonatas for violin, harpsichord & cello; Suite for multiple celli, Everest Records; St. Saens Sonata in C Minor (Op. 32) & Faure Sonata in G Minor (Op. 117) for cello & piano (Orion Master Recordings); as cond. & cellist: Introducing I Cellisti (Orion Master Recordings). Mbrships: Violoncello Soc., Inc. of NY; LA. Copyright Soc. Hobbies: Photography; Travel. Address: 1777 Vine St., Los Angeles, CA 90028, USA.

KESSLER, Martha, b. 9 April 1930, Timisoara, Romania. Concert Singer (Contralto). Educ: Music Acad., Cluj, Romania. m. Dr. Klaus Kessler, 1 s. Debut: Mozart's Requiem, Temesvar, 1952. Career: Num. concerts, mainly Oratorios & Lieder; Soloist, Phil. State Orch. of Bucharest, 1957-. Recordings: Beethoven 9 Symph.; Bach Cantata No. 20, O Ewigkeit; Schumann Liederkreis op. 39; Brahms, Vier ernste Gesänge op. 121; Paul Constaniescu, Byzantine Oratorio. Hons: Hons. Dip. of Vienna, Geneva, 1959; Berlin Competitions, 1960. Mgmt: ARIA, Bucharest. Address: Strada Izvor 49, 70642 Bucharest VI, Romania.

KESSLER, Minuetta, b. Gomel, Russia. Concert Pianist; Composer; Teacher. Educ: Juilliard Schl. of Music, piano dip., 1934; post grad. dip., artist & tchr., ibid, 1936; pvte. scholarship w. Ernest Hutcheson & Ania Dorfman. m. Myer Michael Kessler, 1 s., 1 d. Debut: Town Hall, NYC, 1945. Career: 2nd Town Hall Concert, 1946; soloist w. Symph. Orchs. in USA & Can.; num. radio broadcasts. Comps. incl: Confirmation Prayer; Hear My Prayer; Peace & Brotherhood Through Music (cantata); Victory Hora (Engl. & Hebrew); Etude Brilliante for piano. Author: Piano Is My Name, 1975; Staftonia, 1960. Contbr. to var. publs. Mbr., profl. orgs. Recip. var. hons. Address: 30 Hurley St., Belmont, MA 02178, USA. 5, 6, 23.

KESSNER, Daniel Aaron, b. 3 June 1946, Los Angeles, Calif., USA. Composer; Professor; Conductor; Clarinetist. Educ: AB, UCLA, 1967; MA, ibid, 1968; PhD, 1971. m. Dolly Eugenio Kessner, 2 s. Comps. incl: Ensembles for violin, clarinet & harp, 1968; Equali I, for flute quartet & str. quartet, 1968-69; Madrigals, for 16 voices & organ, 1970; rev. version for chorus, winds & brass, 1972; Strata, for orch., 1971; Wind Sculptures, for symph. band, 1973; Array, for 2, 3 & 4 guitars, 1973; Six Aphorisms (clarinet & guitar), 1975; Trio (violin, guitar, cello), 1976. Recordings: The Contemporary Soprano. Mbrships: Nat. Pres., Nat. Assn. for Am. Comps. & Conds., 1977-78; Nat. Vice-Pres., ibid, 1978-80; Los Angeles Chapter Pres., ibid, 1976-. Queen Marie-Jose Composition Prize, Geneva, 1972; Calif. State Univ. Northridge Pres. Club Faculty Prize for Creative Achievement, 1975; num. commissions & grants. Address: 10955 Cozycroft AVe., Chatsworth, CA 91311, USA. 9, 23, 28, 29.

KESZEI, János, b. 1 June 1936, Kispest, Budapest, Hungary. Timpanist; Percussionist. Educ: pvte. studies. m. Marie Walshe, 1 d., 1 s. Career: BBC Symph. Orch.; Freelance percussionist, 1978; Timpani Professor, RCM, 1978-. Recordings: Strav. - Les Noces; Gurrelieder; Mahler 8 & 5; Berlioz - Bevenuto Cellini; Sibelius 1; John McCabe - Notturni ed Alba, Symph. 2, etc. Hobbies: Tape recording; Hi-Fi; Home brewing; Cars; Photography. Address: 295 West End Rd., Ruislip, Middx. HA4 6QS, UK.

KESZKOWSKI, Henryk, b. 29 Oct. 1927, Bydgoszcz, Poland. Solo Violinist; Educator. Educ: Dip. w. distinction, under Prof. Z

Jahnke, Conserv. Poznan; studied w. Prof. T Wronski, Conserv. Warsaw. 1 d. Debut: Soloist w. Poznan Phil Orch., 1952. Career: Soloist w. orchs., Recitalist, throughout Poland, also Belgium, Switz., Germany, UK, China; TV & Radio broadcasts, Poland, Belgium, China; Tchr., Conservs. in Warsaw & Lodz. Comp. cadenzas for Mozart Violin Concerto in G (KV 216). Recorded for Polish Radio-Warsaw; BRT-Brussels. Mbr., SPAM (Polish Musicians Soc.). Hons: Winner, PWM-Edition Competition for cadenzas for Mozart Violin Concerto in G, 1969. Hobby: Yachting. Address: Hoza 29 m 76, 00521 Warsaw, Poland.

KETCHAM, Charles, b. 31 Oct. 1942, San Diego, Calif., USA. Conductor. Educ: San Diego State Coll.; Eastman Schl. of Music; Vienna Acad. of Music, Austria. m. Linda D, 3 children. Career: Music Dir., Am. Opera Workshop, Vienna, 1969-70; Asst. Conductor, Gulbenkian Orch., Lisbon, Portugal, 1970-73; Asst. Conductor, San Diego Symph., 1973-; Guest Conductor, var. orchs. inclng. ORTF Radio Orch. of France, Lille, Seville Phil., Spain, Radio Orchs. of Holland 0 Rochester Phil.; Conductor, Exxon Affiliate Artists, 1973. Recip., Fulbright Schlrshp., 1969-70. Address: 3450 Anguin Dr., San Diego, CA 92123, USA.

KETELAARS, Leo Anton, b. 23 Dec. 1913, Maasniel, Netherlands. Concert & Oratorio Singer; Lecturer in Voice Ensemble, Uaastricht Conservatory. Educ: Conserv., Aachen; Dip., Singing, Organ & Chorus Cond. m. Justine Kocks, 1 d. Debut: Singer, Classical Songs, Radio Hilversum. Career: Violinist; Municipal Orch., Aachen; As baritone in oratorios. num. concerts at home & abroad; Radio concerts & TV apps. Comps. incl: 4 folk songs for solo or chorus (recorded). Num. recordings as soloist & w. men's chorus. Contbr. to Samenklank; Essays in German & Dutch newspapers. Mbr. KNTV (Royal Musicians Club). Recip. Golden Plateau, 1st Prize of Union Bel Canto, Den Haag, 1949. Hobby: Currently writing essay about formation of the voice. Address: Adelberstraat 39, Vaals, Netherlands.

KETOLA, Jouko Michael, b. 30 Jan. 1939, Ilmajoki, Finland. Teacher. Educ: Cert., Klemetti Coll., Orivesi; Cert., Tchrs. Coll. Helsinki. m. Kirsti Kaarina Kajander, 2 c. Career: Cond., Male Voice Choir, Virrat, tours to Sweden, 1964, Austria, 1972; Cond., Jussi Singers of Finland, 1968-, tours to USA, Can., 1968, 1973; Hdmaster., Music Coll. of Virrat, 1972-. Recording: Sibelius, Kullervo Symph., UK. Contbr. to var. profl. jrnls., Virrat. Mbrships: Tchrs. Alliance of Finland; Lions Club, Virrat; Pohjola-Norden, Virrat. Hons: 2nd Prize, Academic Singing Competition, Turku, 1961; 1st Prize Finnish Tchrs. Colls. Singing Competition, Raahe, 1962. Hobby: Travel. Address: Hyttystie 9 IY 65210 Vaasa 21, Finland.

KEYS, Ivor Christopher Banfield, b. 1919, Littlehampton, UK. Professor of Music; Organist. Educ: RCM; MA., D Mus., Oxford; FRCO. m. Margaret Anne Layzell, 2 s., 2 d. Career: Asst. Organist, Christ Ch., Oxford, 1938-40 & 46-47; Dir. of Music, Queen's Coll., Belfast, Headington Schl., Oxford, 1946-47; Lectr. in Music, 1947; Reader ibid, 1950; Sir Hamilton Harty Prof. of Music, 1951; Prof. of Music, Nottingham Univ., 1954-68, & Birmingham Univ., 1968-; Conductor. Compositions incl: Concerto for clarinet & strings; Sonata for 'cello & piano; The Wheel of the Year (choral song-cycle w. chmbr. orch.); Prayer for Pentacostal Fire; Anthem for Advent; A Garland of Carols for chorus & orch.; The Road to the Stable for unison voice & piano. Publs: The Texture of Music, Purcell to Brahms; History of German Music; Brahms Chmbr. Music; contributions to Psalm Praise. Contbr. reviews to jrnls. Hons: CBE; Hon. RAM; Hon. D Mus., Queen's Univ., Belfast. Hobbies: Bridge; Watching cricket. Address: 6 Eastern Rd., Selly Park, Birmingham 29, UK. 3.

KEYS, Robert, b. 30 Jan. 1914, Scholar Green, Cheshire, UK. Assistant Head of Music Staff, Royal Opera House, Covent Garden. Educ: ARMCM; FRMCM. Widower, 1s., 1d. Debut: Solo pianist & broadcaster, 1930-; Repetiteur, Engl. Opera Grp., 1948-53; Royal Opera House, Covent Gdn., 1953-72; Sr. Repetiteur, ibid., 1972-74; Asst. Hd. of Music Staff, ibid., 1974-; Light orch. cond., 1943-. Comps: piano & orch. pieces for light orch. opera transls. Recordings: Prince of the Pagodas. Mbrships. incl: Donizetti Soc. Publs: Biography of William Baines (w. Roger Carpenter), 1976. Contbr. to musical jrnls. Hons. incl: Halle Scholarship, 1934. Hobbies incl: Railway matters & records. Address: 10 Lawrie Pk. Gdns., Sydenham, London SE26, UK.

KEYTE, Christopher Charles, b. 11 Sept. 1935, Shorne, Kent, UK. Bass-Baritone. Educ: Choral Scholar, King's Coll., Cambridge. m. June Margaret Keyte. Career: Oratorio, concert & recital apps.; Fndr., Mbr., Purcell Consort of Voices, 1963-75. Recordings incl: Monteverdi songs, Sacred

Concertos, etc.; Purcell Anthems, Indian Queen; Haydn & Schubert Masses; Vaughan Williams Serenade to Music, Pilgrims Progress; Songs by Quilter & Gurney. Mbrships: ISM; Royal Phil. Soc. Hobbies: Opera; Athletics; Theatre. Mgmt: Ibbs & Tillett. Address: 20 Brycedale Cres., Southgate, London N14 7EY, UK. 3.

KHACHATURIAN, Margaret Miles, b. 10 Dec. 1929, Mason City, Iowa, USA. Cellist; Pianist. Educ: Interlochen Nat. Music Camp, 1945 & 46; Baldwin Wallace Coll., 1947, 48; Eastman Schl. of Music, 1948; B Mus., Univ. of Ill., 1951; M Mus., Chgo. Musical Coll., 1953. m. Narbey Khachaturian, 3 s., 1 d. Career: broadcasts on WILL Radio, Univ. of Ill. & radio stns. in Ohio & Mass.; symph. perfs. under Benjamin Britten, Pablo Casals, Georges Enesco, Rafael Kubelik, Igor Stravinsky, Duke Ellington, Leopold Stokowski & Bernard Goodman; has played w. Cleveland Woman's Symph. & Memphis Symph.; currently w. Champaign, Urbana, Springfield & Kankokee Symphs., Ill.; has taught & performed in num. states in the USA & in Kanpur, Uttar Pradesh, India. Recordings incl: WILL Radio, Univ. of Ill.; Lib. of Congress. Contbr. to Triangle. Mbrships: Var. exec. offs., Tuesday Morning Musical Club, Champaign-Urbana, Ill.; Champaign-Urbana Music Tchrs. Assn. Hons. incl: Schlrships. to Baldwin Wallace Coll. & Univ. of Ill.; Grad. Schlrship., Chgo. Musical Coll. Hobbies: Reading; Gardening; Travel. Address: 207 S Adams, Philo, IL 61864, USA.

KHACHATURYAN, Karen Surenovich, b. 19 Sept. 1920, Moscow, USSR. Composer. Educ: Moscow Conserv. Compositions incl: Sonata for Violin & Piano, 1947; Sinfonietta, 1949; By the Lonely Willow (cantata), 1950; Youth Overture, 1951; Symph. No. 1, 1954; A Simple Girl (operetta), 1959; Friendship (overture for symph. orch.), 1961; Sonata for Cello & Piano, 1962; Incidental music for cartoon films. Mbrships: Exec. Committee, Soviet Composers Union. Address: RSFSR Composers Union, 8-10 Ulitsa Nezhdanovoi, Moscow, USSR.

KHADEM-MISSAGH, Bijan, b. 26 Oct. 1948, Teheran, Iran. Violinist; Composer; Conductor. Educ: Univ., Vienna, Austria; Dip. w. distinction, Acad. of Music, Vienna, 1971. m. Shirin Nooreyezdan. Debut: as Soloist w. orch., aged 13. Career: Concert tours, inclng. radio & TV apps., & Fests throughout Europe & in Asia; Fndr., Eurasia Quartet, 1969-75; Fndr., Tonkünstler Chmbr. Orch., Vienna, 1974 (cond. & soloist); Fdnr., The Dawnbreakers, Austrian Baha'i singing grp., 1970. Comps: Instrumental & Vocal Works. Recordings: Works by Vitali, Paganini, Debussy, Szymanovsky, & other comps. Dawnbreakers LP, 1976. Publ: Lieder-Book of Songs, 1976. Mbr., AKM, Vienna. Hons: Grand Prix & 1st Prize, Int. Chmbr. Music Competition, Colmar, France, 1971. Address: Worthgasse 2/8, A 2500 Baden, Austria.

KHALE, Shrinivas Vinayak, b. 30 April 1926, Bombay, India. Composer of Light Music. Educ: Studied Classical Music w. Shri Madhusudan Joshi & Ustad Faiyaz Khan Saheb. m. Surekha S Khale, 3 d. Career: Num. radio broadcasts, Bombay; recent TV interview; currently Recording Off., Gramaphone Co. of India Ltd. (EMI); Music Dir., num. leading Marathi films & dramas. Comps: (recorded) num. works sung by leading playback singers inclng. Lata Mangeshkar; LP record, Sant Tukaram; radio recordings, var. langs., Bombay. Contbr. to regional lang. publs. Mbrships incl: Trustee, Acad. of Fine Arts & Crafts, Chembur, Bombay. Hons: Book published in his honour; JP & Special Exec. Magistrate, Govt. of Maharashtra. Hobby: Cricket. Address: 5 Sahakar Nagar, Bldg. 8/147, Shell Colony Rd., Chembur, Bombay 400 071, India.

KHAN, Hidayat I, b. 6 Aug. 1917, London, UK. Composer. Educ: Ecole Normale de Musique, Paris. m. w. children. Debut: as Comp. on Dutch Radio. Career: concert org. by UNESCO, Netherlands, 1969; 1st perf. of Gandhi Symph.; radio perfs. in Paris, Belgium, German Fed. Repub., Netherlands, Madrid, Helsinki, Dublin, Prague, Rome. Los Angeles, Seattle. Comps. incl: Gandhi Symph.; Zikar Symph.; La Monotonia, Suite Symphonique; Message Symph.; Va. Symph. Poem; Ballet Rituel; Poeme en fa; Quartet opus 45; Royal Legend Symph.; Concerto for string orch. opus 48; sev. choral comps. Mbr., Gema, German Fed. Repub. Publr: Annie Bank, 13 Anna Vondelstraat, Amsterdam. Address: Postfach 70 09 22, 8000 Munich 70, German Fed. Repub.

KHORRAM, Homayoon, b. 30 June 1930, Boushehr, Iran. Composer; Violinist. Educ: Private studies w. Iranian musicians eg. Abol Hassan Saba, Ruhollah Khaleghi & Freidoon Farzaneh. m. Farzaneh Chizari. Career: Radio & TV apps., 1928; Cond., Iranian Nat. Radio & TV Orch.; Lectr. & Instr., Nat. Iranian Music Schl. Comps: More than 200 songs, melodies & musical pieces in field of Iranian classical music w. different arrs. solo, chmbr. & large orchl. perfs. Recordings: Over 100. Publs:

National Iranian Musical Progressions. Contbr. to var. profl. jrnls. Mbrships: Sec., Iranian Syndicate of Musicians; Bd. of Dirs., Film Comps. Assn.; Sci & Social Rsch. Soc.; Rotary Club; Lions Club. Hons: Royal Medal of Homayoon, 1970. Hobbies: Reading; Sports. Address: No. 12 Babak Alley, Sab't St. (Tajrish), Tehran, Iran 19.

KHRENNIKOV, Tikhon Nikolayevich, b. 10 June 1913, Elets, Lipetsk region, Russia. Composer. Educ: Moscow Conserv. Compositions incl: 5 Pieces for Piano, 1933; 3 Pieces for Piano, 1935; Suite for Orch. from Music for Much Ado About Nothing; In the Storm (opera), 1939; 2nd Symph., 1941; Incidental music for play Long Ago, 1942; Frol Skobeyev (opera), 1950; Mother (opera), 1956; Concerto for Violin & Orch., 1959; A Hundred Devils & One Girl (operetta), 1961; White Nights (operetta), 1967; Mbrships: Gen. Sec., Soviet Composers Union, 1948-57; 1st Sec., ibid, 1957; Dpty. to USSR Supreme Soviet; CPSU., 1947-. Hons: State Prizes, 1942, '46, '51, '67; People's Artist of the RSFSR, 1955, USSR, 1963; Order of Lenin, 1963; Red Banner of Labour, 1967. Address: Composers Union of USSR; 8-10 Ulitsa Nezhdanovoi, Moscow, USSR.

KICKLIGHTER, Hampton, b. 17 May 1940, Hawkinsville, Ga., USA. Choral Conductor; Teacher. Educ: Mars Hill Coll., NC; BSc, Music Educ., EdS, Ga. Southern Coll.; MA, Appalachian State Univ., NC; further study, Univ. of Iowa. m. Donovan Ward, 1 s., 1 d. Career: Tchr., Public Schls.; Vis. Instructor, Ga. Southern Coll.; Pt-time Instructor, Middle Ga. Coll.; currently Dir. of Choral Activities, Carrollton, Ga., City Schls.; Mbr., Atlanta Ga. Symph. Orch. Chorus, 1973-78; Music Dir., Ga. Youth Chorale, 1st European Tour, 1978. Comps: Arrs. of choral works for young choirs containing boys changing voices; Introit & Kyrie (Requiem) Faureé; English Street Cry; Deutsch Messe (Schubert). Mbr., num. profl. orgs. inclng. Life Mbr., Ga. Pres. 1973-77, Am. Choral Dirs. Assn. Address: 113 W Allison Circle, Carrollton, GA 30117, USA.

KIDDELL, Sidney George, b. 18 May 1908, Enfield, Middx., UK. Organist. Educ: Enfield Licensed Reader, Ch. of England. m. Christine Henderson, 1 s (adopted). Publ: Ed., JH Arnold, Plainsong Accompaniment, 3rd ed., 1975, Ed., The Gregorian (jrnl. of the Gregorian Assn.). Mbrships: RSCM; Plainsong & Mediaeval Music Soc. (Sec.-Treas.); Gregorian Assn. Hobbies: Liturgy; Hymnology; Hymnody. Address: The Church Lodge, Wimborne St. Giles, Wimborne, Dorset, UK.

KIEFER, Bruno, b. 9 Apr. 1923, Baden-Baden, Germany. Professor; Flautist. Educ: degree in phys., Engrng. Schl.; degree in flute, comp. studies, Inst. of Arts, Fed. Univ. of Rio Grade do Sul. m. (1) 1 s., 1 d.; (2) Nidia Beatriz da Costa Nunes, 1 d. Career: 2nd Flute, Symph. Orch. of Porto Alegre, 2 yrs.; Flautist w. chmbr. grps.; Lectr. on musical subjects; Prof. of Maths., Schl. of Phillos., until 1969; Prof., Hist. of Music, Inst. of Arts, 1969-. Comps. incl: incidental music for theatre; Sonata No. 1 (piano); Madrigals Gauchos Vo. 1 (chmbr. chorus); Cantico; Cantata do Encontrol, Cantico, Testemunho (chmbr. chorus); etc. Recordings: No Cimo das Copas (cantata, mezzo-soprano & woodwind quintet). Publs. incl: Elements da Linguagem Musical, 2nd ed., 1973; Historia da Música Brasileira, Vol. 1, 1976. Mbr., Brazilian Soc. for Contemp. Music. Recip. var. awards. Address: rua Demétrio Ribeiro, 997-apto. 307, 90 000 Porto Alegre - RS, Brazil.

KIELLAND, Olav, b. 16 Aug. 1901, Trondheim, Norway. Conductor; Composer; Pianist. Educ: Piano & music theory, 1914-19; architecture, Tech. HS of Norway, 1919-21; Leipzig Conserv. & HS of Music, 1921-23 (Cond. & opera, Otto Lohse, Comp., Stephan Krehl). m. Agnes Konow Söeberg, 4 d. Debut: As cond., 1923. Career: Cond., Göteborg Opera House, 6 yrs.; Artistic Dir. & Perm. Cond., Oslo Phil. Soc., 1931-45; reorganized Trondheim Symph. Orch., 1945-47; Artistic Dir. & Cond.,Harmonien, Bergen; organized Iceland Symph. Orch., Reykjavik, 1952-55; Guest Cond. w. many orchs., Europe, USA, Scandinavia. Comps. incl: 4 Symphs.; 2 Concertos (violin, piano); Concerto Grosso Norvegese; 2 Symph. Suites; 2 Overtures; Incidental Music to "Brand" (Ibsen); String Quartet op. 22; Villarkorn, 20 piano pieces op. 13. Num. recordings. Mbr., Soc. of Norwegian Comps. Hons. incl: King's Gold Medal for Musical Merit; State Salary of Art, 1960-; sev. comp. awards. Hobbies: Books; Listening to the voices of unspoiled nature. Address: 3800 Bö, Norway.

KIENITZ, Marianne, b. 3 Jan. 1947, Nyborg, Denmark. Violinist. Educ: Dip., Acad. of Music, Odense Denmark; Acad. of Music, Prague, Czechslovakia, 2 yrs.; Dip. in pedagory, Acad. of Music, Odense. Career: Mbr., Symphoniorch. of Odense, 1973-. Hobbies: Weaving; Sports; Reading. Address: Vestergade 513 5000 Odense, Denmark.

KIESER, Karen Ann, b. 19 Feb. 1948, Sutton Coldfield, UK. Pianist; Writer; Broadcaster. Educ: BMus (piano perf. & lit.), Univ. of Toronto, 1970; MMus (perf. & lit.), ibid., 1971; MArts (musicol.), ibid., 1973. m. Larry E Lake. Career: Pianist specialising in contemporary repertoire; premieres of num. comps. by e.g. James Montgomery, Larry Lake, David Grimes, David Jaeger; Can. premiere of Krenek's Tape & Double, 1975; tours as soloist w. Can. Electronic Ensemble (Can., 1977-78, Europe, 1979); apps. as soloist & in chmbr. music on CBC radio network; as broadcaster, host of network CBC radio progs., incl. 2 nat. music series, 1973-76; now CBC staff exec. prod. of daily nat. music prog. from Ottawa. Recording: soloist in Piano Quintet by Can. Electronic Ensemble. Contbr. to profl. jrnls. on Can. & contemporary music. Mbrships: Nat. Radio Producers' Assn. of Can.; Bd. of Dirs., Nat. Youth Orch. of Can. Hons: sev. Fellowships. Hobbies: Reading; Films. Address: 15 Dundonald St., Apt. 1402, Toronto M4Y 1K4, Can.

KIILERICH, Jens Ole, b. 12 Feb. 1946, Copenhagen, Denmark. Tuba Player. Educ: pvte. study. w. Erik Aakerwall & Joergen Voigt Arnsted. m. Vivi Jessen, 1 c. Debut: Nesa Concert Band, 1965. Career: Cirkus Buster Stage Band; Tivoli's Concert Band; The Broadcasting Pops Orch.; Arhus By-Orkester; Soenderjyllands Symph. Orch.; The Broadcasting Symph. Orch.; Aalborg Symph. Orch.; Tchr., Nordjyak Musikkonservatorium; Dir., Vester Mariendal Skoleorkester; Dir., Aalborg Politi-Orkester. Recordings: Nesa Concert Band, Vols. I & II. Mbrships: Past Pres., Den Danske Tubaklub; TUBA. Hobby: Badminton. Address: Jens Bangs Vej 5, 9400 Norresundby, Denmark.

KIKKAWA, Eishi, b. 13 Feb. 1909, Kannabe-Cho, Hiroshima-Ken, Japan. Musicologist. Educ: B Lit. Tokyo Univ. m. Setsuko Kikkawa, 5 s., 1 d. Career: Lectr., Tokyo, Tokyo Arts & Ochanomizu Women's Univs.; Prof., Musashino Academia Musicae, Tokyo Arts Univ.; Commentator on traditional Japanese music, NHK-FM, Tokyo. Publs: Character of Japanese Music, 1948; Appreciaiton of Japanese Music, 1952; A Biography of Miyagi Michio, 1962; A History of Japanese Music, 1965. Contbr. to var. publs. Mbrships: Dir., Soc. of Rsch. for Asiatic Music, Japanese Song & Ballad; Pres., Socs. of Gidayu Music & Biwa Music. Recip. Prize of Broadcasting Culture, NHK & Purple Ribbon Medal, 1972. Hobbies: Gathering stones; Photography; Travel; Theatre. Address: 11 Shinanomachi, Shinjuku-ku, Tokyo, 160 Japan.

KILBURN, Paul, b. 7 Feb. 1936, Toronto, Ont. Can. Composer; Pianist; Teacher. Educ: Royal Conserv. of Music, Toronto (violin, piano), 1942-54; BMus, Univ. of Toronto (comp.), 1958. m. Myrla A Lantz (div.) 3 s., 1 d. Debut: Toronto, 1959. Career: apps. in public & on CBC radio in perfs. of avant-garde music (mixed media presentations). Comps: Five Piano Pieces, 1970; Sonata for Piano, 1971; Reflections on Ice, 1971; Trio for piano, 1971. Recordings: own comps. for CBC. Address: Apt. 2, 879 Sheppard Ave. W, Downsview, Ont. M3H, 2T4, Can.

KILIAN, Ivan Edward George, b. 28 July 1934, Cape Town, S Africa. Organist; Pianist; Educator; Adjudicator (Organ & Choral). Educ: RSCM; LRAM; ARCM; FTCL; LRSM; LTCL (CMT). Career: Dir. Music, St. Andrew's Schl., Bloemfontein, 1959-61; Dir., Music, St. Andrew's Coll., Grahamstown, 1961-71; Lansdowne HS, Cape Town, 1971-72; Hd. Music, Bergvliet HS, Cape Town, 1973-77; Sans Souci Girls' HS, Cape Town, 1978-; Cond., Kenilworth Choral Soc. Contbr. reviews to S African Music Tchr. Mag. Mbrships: Pres., S African Soc., Music Tchrs. 1976; Int. Soc. Music Educ.; RCO; ISM; Cape Guild Organists. Hobbies: Travel; Reading. Mgmt: S African Music Tchr. Mag. Address: 4 Mortimer Pk., Mortimer Rd., Wynberg, Cape Town, S Africa 7800.

KILLEBREW, Gwendolyn, b. Phila., Pa., USA. Vocal Musician (opera, concert). Educ: BSc, Temple Univ., Phila., Pa.; Dip., MMus, Juilliard Schl. of Music. Career: Opera apps. Metropolitan Opera, Boston Opera, NYC Opera, Staastheater am Gärtnerplatz (Munich), Wash. DC Opera Co., Salzburg Fest., Geneva Opera, Bordeaux, Nice, Split Yugoslavia summer fest., Santa Fe Opera, La Fenice Opera, San Diego Opera, Opera Stichting (Amsterdam), Deutsche Oper am Rhein, Wolf Trap Summer Fest., Nederlandse Operastichting, Bayreuth Fest., Zürich Opera; tours, Europe & USA; Apps. w. num. orchs. Recordings: Handel, (Tamerlano); Haydn; Orlando Paladino; Puccini; Edgar; Andre Chenier; Mascagni. Hons: Outstanding Musician, Temple Univ., 1971. Hobbies incl: Creative Cooking; Walking; Modern Dance. Mgmt: CAMI, c/o Epstein, 165 W 57th St., NY, USA. Address: Cecilienallee 51/E.R., 4000 Duesseldorf 30, German Fed. Repub. 2.

KILLGROVE, William Taliaferro, b. 21 Oct. 1895, Kan. City, Kan., USA. Organist; Trumpeter; Choral, Band & Orchestra

Conductor; Composer; Arranger. Educ: Dip. in Music Educ., Syracuse Conserv.; Univ. of Southern Calif., Los Angeles; Queen's Coll., Charlotte, NC. m. Arllys Bernadette Killgrove, 1 d., 1 s. Career: Cond., Los Angeles City Band, Killgrove's Radio Symph. Cal-Tech Band, var. opera cos. Organist & Choir Dir., 1st Presby. Los Angeles, Hollywood, St. Andrew's Episcopal Cathedral, Honolulu. Comps: Dawning (musical play); extensive educl. materials for piano & accordion; num. anthems. Active mbr., music socs. Publs. incl: Finger Frolics, 1975. Recip., var. hons. Hobbies incl: Chess. Address: 155 Rancho San Luis Rey, 200 N El Camino Real, Oceanside, CA 92054, USA.

KIM, Byong-kon, b. 28 May 1929, Taegu, Korea. Associate Professor of Music; Composer. Educ: Kyungpuk Nat. Univ., Taegu, 1954; B Mus., Chosun Univ., 1961; M Mus., Ind. Univ. Bloomington, USA, 1964; D Mus, ibid, 1968. m. Setsuko Komoda, 6 children. Career: Assoc. Prof. Music, Calif. State Univ., LA; perfs. of works in num. places inclng. NYC, Boston, LA, Rochester, NY, Seoul & Pusan, Korea, Hong Kong, & Bangkok; Guest Cond., Seoul Phil. Orch., Korea; comps. broadcast in USA & Korea. Compositions incl: (publd.) Concertino for Percussion, 1964; Str. Quartet, 1965; Symphony, 1968; (other) Essay for Brass & Percussion, 1963; Symphonic Poem, Nak-Dong-Kang, 1964; Four Short Pieces for Piano, 1972. Contbr. to Ethnomusicology. Mbrships: Nat. Assn. Am. Comps. & Cond. (VP, LA Chapt. 1970-75); Contemporary Music Project (Prog. Hd., Eastern Region, 1967-68); Pi Kappa Lambda. Hon: John Edward Fellowship, Ind. Univ., 1965-66. Hobby: Photography. Address: 30458 Via Victoria, Palos Verdes Peninsula, CA 90274, USA. 2.

KIM, Dong Jin, b. 22 March 1913, Anju Town, Pyangannando, Korea. Composer. Educ: Grad. (Lit.), Sungsil Coll., Korea, 1936; Bachelor Degree (violin), Japan Advanced Music Schl.; studied violin, piano, harmonics, counterpoint & Comp. w. Dwight R Malsbary, 1929-36. m. Bo Lim Lee, 2 s., 1 d. Career: 1st Violinist & in charge of comp., Shinkyung Orch., 1939; Prof., Coll. of Music, Suk Myung Women's Univ., 1952; Prof., Surabul Art Coll., 1953; Prof., Music Coll. of Kyung Hee Univ., 1963-. Comps. incl: (symphonic poem) The Impression of a Ceremonial Music; The Song of Yang San; A Funeral Song; An Oriental Suite; (Symph.) The Song for My Fatherland; The Road to Triumph; The Fatherland; Kyung Hee; Parade of our Country; Praying of our Country; (opera) Shim Chung Jun; Chun Hyang Jun; (Art songs) Spring Has Come; Magnolia, etc. Mbrships: Assn. of Korean Comps.; First Art Acad. Hons: Prize, Ministry of Cultural Information, 1960; Film Music Prize, Pusan Il Bo Newspaper, 1962, '70; Cultural Prize, Seoul City, 1976; Grand Prize, 1967. Hobby: Sports. Address: Nu Sang-Dong 16 1, Chong-Ro-Ku, Seoul, S Korea.

KIMBELL, David Rodney Bertram, b. 26 June 1939, Gillingham, Kent, UK. University Professor. Educ: MA, DPhil., Worcester Coll., Oxford; LRAM. m. Ingrid Else Emilie Lübbe, 2 d., 1 s. Career: Lectr. in Music, Univ. of Edinburgh, 1965-78; Prof. of Music, Univ. of St. Andrews, 1979-. Contbr. to: Music & Letters; Händel-Jahrbuch; Hallische Händel-Ausgabe. Mbr., Royal Musical Assn.; Hobbies: Miscellaneous Sports; German Lit. Address: 13 Irvine Crescent, St. Andrews, Fife, UK.

KIMBELL, Michael Alexander, b. 15 Mar. 1946, Glen Cove, NY, USA. Composer; Teacher; Clarinettist. Educ: BA (music), Haverford Coll., 1967'; MFA (Composition), Cornell Univ., 1970; DMA, ibid, 1973; Clarinet study w. Donald Montanaro. m. Edith Maria Guenther, 1 s. Career: Tchr. of Theory, Univ. of Sask., Saskatoon, summer 1970; Johnson State Coll., Vt., 1971-75; Conserv., Univ. of the Pacific, Stockton, Calif., 1975-; occasional clarinet recitalist. Compositions: 3 Lieder; 5 Dialogues for 2 Clarinets; Woodwind Quintet; wandrers Sturmlied, for baritone solo, chorus & orch., to text of Goethe. Publs: Ed. & contbr., Vt. Music Educators News, 1974-75. Mbrships: Am. Musicol. Soc., Coll. Music Soc. Recip. var. acad. grants & awards. Address: 2930 Prentiss Ct., Stockton, CA 95207, USA.

KIMBROUGH, Steven, b. 17 Dec. 1936, Athens, Ala., USA. Opera & Concert Baritone. Educ: BA, Birmingham Southern Coll.; BD, Duke Univ.; PhD, Princeton Theol. Sem.; Birmingham Conserv. of Music. m. Sarah Ann Robinson, 4 s. Debut: As Marcello, La Bohème, Mantova, Italy. Career: has appeared w. cos. in Germany, UK, Italy, etc. inclng: Theater den Stadt Bonn; London Opera Soc.; Theatre Municipal, Luxembourg; Le Grand Théatre, Geneva; San Fran. Opera. Transl: The Old Testament as the Book of Christ (Martin Kuske), 1976. Contbr. to relig. jrnls. Mbrships: Am. Acad. of Relig.; Soc. of Biblical Lit. Hons. incl: Hoernle Vocal Award, Liederkranz Fndn., NYC. Hobbies: Tennis; Squash. Mgmt: Lustig & Florian, USA; Marguerita Stafford, England. Address: Kolumbusring 21, 5300 Bonn-Bad Godesberg, German Fed. Repub.

KIMMEL, William Breyfogel, b. 23 Oct. 1908, Dayton, Ohio, USA. Musicologist; Professor. Educ: BA, N Ctrl. Coll., 1931; MM, 1935, PhD, 1942, Eastman Schl. of Music, Rochester Univ. Career: Prof., Music, Mich. State Univ., 1935-47; Prof., Music, Hunter Coll., CUNY, 1948-; Compositions: The Divine Mystery (oratorio w. G Jones); Short Communion Service in A w Gloria; Short Communion Service No. 2. Publs: Dimensions of Faith (w G Clive), 1960; Truth & Symbol (w W Klubach, J Wilde), 1959; The Search for Being (w J Wilde), 1962. Contbr. to profl. jrnls. Mbrships: Am. Music Soc.; Music Library Assn. Hobbies: Photography; Travel. Address: 400 Ctrl. Park W, New York, NY 10025, USA.

KINASZ-MIKOLAJCZAK, Bozena Anna, b. 21 Feb. 1927, Budzanow, Poland. Singer. Educ: MA, Acad. of Music, Warsaw; solo vocal class. m. Mikolajczak Stefan, 1 s. Debut: Tatiana in Eugene Onegin. Career: Soloist w. Gt. Theatre of Opera, Warsaw, 1965-; Soloist w. Wuppertalen Bühnen, German Fed. Repub., 1973 & '74; guest perfs. & concerts in Dusseldorf, Dortmund, Hamburg, Haag, Basel, Ghent, Moscow, Leningrad, Tbilisi, Amsterdam, Brussels; many apps. on Pol. TV & radio. Recordings: Boris Godunov, Mussorgski (cond. Semkow); Beethoven's IX, (cond. Wislocki). Mbrships: Polish Musicians' Soc. (SPAM). Hons: 1st Prize, Int. Vocal Competition, Holland, 1964. Hobbies: Gardening; Tennis. Address: 02-132 Warsaw, ul. Baleya 1 m 7, Poland.

KINDERMANN, Juergen, b. 14 June 1931, Zinnowiz, Germany. Musicologist. Educ: Kiel Univ., PhD. m. Dr. Ilse Indermann-Korthaus, 1 d. Mbrships: Soc. for Music Rsch.; German Soc. for Documentation. Publs: Thematical-chronological Catalogue of the Works of Ferrucio Busonis, Studies in Music History of the 19th Century, vol. 19; Eds: Annaberg Choirbooks, German Music Heritage, vol. 72, 73; Hector Berlioz Requiem, complete ed. of Musical Works, vol. 10; ETA Hoffmann, undine, selected Musical Works, vol. 23; Johannes Nucius, selected motets, German Music Heritage, Special set vol. 5 Contbr. ot: Music in Past and Present, ench.; Sohlmans Musica; Music and Church. Address: D3500 Kassel, Schéone Aussicht 2, German Fed. Repub.

KING, Alexander Hyatt, b. 18 July 1911, Beckenham, Kent, UK. Music Librarian. Educ: BA, King's Coll., Cambridge Univ. m. Evelyn Mary Davies, 2 s. Career: Dept. of Printed Books, Brit. Mus., 1934; Superintendant, Music Room, ibid, 1944-73; Music Libn., Ref. Div., Brit. Lib., 1973-76. Publs. incl: Mozart in Retrospect, 1955 & later eds.; Some British Collectors of Music c. 1600-c. 1950, 1963; Mozart Chamber Music, 1968; 400 Years of Music Printing, 1964; Handel & His Autographs, 1967; Mozart Wind & String Concertos, 1978. Mbrships: Royal Musical Assn. (Pres., 1974-78); Royal Phil. Soc. (Hon. Libn., 1970-); Int. Assn. Music Libs. (Pres., 1955-59); Brit. Inst. Recorded Sound (Chmn., exec. committee, 1951-62); Brit. Union Catalogue of Early Music (Hon. Sec., 1948-57). Address: 29 Lauradale Rd., London N2 9LT, UK. 14.

KING, Carlton W III, b. 28 Dec. 1947, Milford, Del., USA. Teacher & Performer (Recorder, renaissance winds & theory). Educ: BMus, (Theory & Comp.), E Carolina Univ., Greenville, NC; MMus, musicol., Univ. of Md. m. Janet Frances Gromfine King. Career: Mbr., Band of Musick, (Colonial Williamsburg), A Newe Jewell, Smith/King Duo; 3 yrs. playing French Horn & Organ w. US Army; Co-fndr., Music Dir., The Collegium Musicum, E Carolina Univ.; Past Tchr., Univ. of Md.; Dir., Kynge's Consort; Fac. Mbr., Selma M Levine Schl. of Music, Wash. DC; Recorder Instructor, Georgetown Univ.; Freelance music critic. Mbrships: Am. Fedn. of Musicians; Am. Recorder Soc.; Viola da Gamba Soc.; Am. Musicol. Soc. Mgmt: Am. Chmbr. Concerts. Address: 3 Riverview Court, Apt. 103, Laurel, MD 20810, USA.

KING, (Catherine) Mary, b. 16 June 1952, Tonbridge Wells, UK. Mezzo-soprano Singer. Educ: BA, Birmingham Univ.; cert. in Educ., St. Anne's Coll., Oxford; postgrad. cert., GSM. Career: Apps. w. Ballet Rambert in Pierrot Lunaire & Ancient Voices of Children; chorus & understudies, Glyndebourne Fest. Opera & Touring Opera; Baba the Turk in Rake's Progress w. Glyndebourne Touring Opera, 1980; Purcell Room debut, 1979; num. recital & oratorio perfs. in UK, Italy, Fance, Denmark. Hons: Kathleen Ferrier finalist, 1978; Park Lane Group Young Musicians & 20th century music, 1978; Glyndebourne Touring Award, 1978; Miriam Licette prize for French song, 1979. Hobbies: Reading; Writing; Sewing. Address: 75 Solent Rd., W Hampstead, London NW6, UK.

KING, Constance Audrey, LRAM, ARCM. b. Basingstoke. Educ: Roy. Acad. of Music. m. Valentine Homer Tyler (dec.). Prof: Music Mistress. Career: Pft.; Theory of Music; Diploma Coaching. Comps: My Little Garden Plot; Country Miniatures.

Hobbies: Theatre, Walking, Reading, Swimming. Mbrships: RAM; Chopin Soc.; ISM; Alkan Soc. Address: Homer, 64 Hengistbury Road, Southbourne-on-Sea, Bournemouth BH64 DJ, UK.

KING, James Ambros, b. 22 May 1925, Dodge City, Kan., USA. Tenor. Educ: B Mus, La. State Univ., 1950; MA, Univ. of Kansas City, Mo., 1952. m. (2) Marieluise Nagel, 3 s., 1 d. Career: Mbr., Deutsche Oper, Berlin, 1962-; Metrop. Opera debut, 1966; guest artist, Vienna, Bayreuth, Salzburg Fest., Covent Gdn., Munich. Recordings: London/Decca; EMIHMV. Address: Gabriel-Max-Str. 27, Munich, German Fed. Repub. 2.

KING, John Reymes, b. 2 July 1910, Hinckley, Leics., UK. Organist; Professor of Music. Educ: MA, Cambridge, 1934; Mus B, ibid, 1935; ARCM; FRCO; PhD, Univ. of Toronto, Can., 1950. m. Isobel R Cole, 1 s. Career: Prof. of music, Hd., Dept. of Art-Drama-Music, Univ. of Alta., Can., 1945-48; Prof. of Music, Dir., Grad. Studies in Music, Chmn., Div. of Music, Western Reserve Univ., Cleveland, Ohio, USA, 1948-56; Prof. of Music, Dir., Grad. Studies in Music, Univ. of Mass., Amherst, 1956; Vis. Prof., Queen's Univ., Ont., Can., 1948, Boston Univ., USA, 1956-57; Organ Recital Tours, Pacific, 1964, Europe, 1964, 1965, 1967, 1971, 1972, 1974; Nat. Radio Network Apps., Can., New Zealand, Aust., Switzerland, Holland. Composer, var. choral works. Recordings: Byrd Keyboard Works; harpsichord accomp., choral works, Allegro Records, NY, USA. Mbrships: Am. Musical Soc.; Am. Soc. for Aesthetics; RCO; Royal Can. Coll. of Organists; AGO. Hobby: Travel. Address: Avallon, Tamarind Vale, Warwick 7-27, Bermuda.

KING, Malcolm, b. 6 Feb. 1943, Malden, Surrey, UK. Opera & Concert Singer (Bass). Educ: BA, Lincoln Coll., Oxford. m. Hilary Diana Speight, 1 s., 1 d. Career incl: Scottish Opera & Opera for All Tour, 1967-68; Camden Fest., annually 1971-75; apps. w. Engl. Opera Grp., Kent Opera, Covent Gdn., Engl. Nat. Opera, Paris Opera; apps. in Angers, France, Netherlands (TV), Belgium. Hobbies: Literature; Fine Arts; Carpentry. Mgmt: Harrison/Parrott Ltd. Address: 4 Green Lanes, Newington Green, London N16, UK.

KING, Priscilla Tien-Tak, b. 20 Dec. 1948, Shanghai, China. Piano Teacher; Accompanist; Recitalist. Educ: Dip., Hong Kong Music Inst., 1965; Preparatory Div., Juilliard Schl. of Music, NYC, USA, 1965-67; BMus, Oberlin Coll. Conserv. of Music, Ohio, 1971; MMus, Univ. of Tex. at Austin, 1973. Debut: Hong Kong, 1961. Career: Solo recitals & concerts w. Hong Kong Phil. Orch., 1961-65; Solo recital, Singapore, 1964; Concert w. Am. Symph. Orch., 1968; & num. other concerts, USA, 1965-73; Radio & TV progs., USA & Hong Kong; Apps. in over 60 concerts & fests., 1973-; Tchng. Asst., Music Dept., Univ. of Tex. at Austin, USA, 1971-73; Fac. of Music, Chinese Univ. of Hong Kong, 1973-; Hong Kong Bapt. Coll., 1975-; Hong Kong Music Inst., 1976-; Hong Kong Conserv. of Music, 1978-. Mbr., Pi Kappa Lambda. Winner, num. Young Artist Competitions, USA. Hobbies incl: Reading; Concerts. Address: 510 Madeira Dr. NE, Calgary, Alta. T2A 4M8, Canada.

KING, Stanley, b. 30 July 1930, Bushey, Herts., UK. Concert Organist. Educ: pvte.; TCL (harpsichord). m. Elizabeth Dagger. Career: Organist. Bushey Parish Ch., 1951-55; Resident organist & musical dir., Borough of Folkestone, 1962-70; organist, St. Augustine's, Folkestone, 1968-70; staff organist, Hammond Organ Co., 1971-74; staff organist, Wurlitzer, Can., 1976-78. Recordings: All You Need to do is Play the Hammond; 29 Hammond Hits; A Touch of King. Mbrships: Royal Can. Coll. of Organists; AFM; Am. Theatre Organ Soc. Hobbies: Golf; Cooking. Mgmt: organ-King Productions. Address: Suite 1009, 5754 Yonge St., Willowdale, Ont., Can.

KING, Thea, b. 26 Dec. 1925, Hitchin, Herts., UK. Clarinetist. Educ: ARCM; FRCM. m. Frederick John Thurston (dec.). Career: Portia Wind Ensemble, 1954-68; Prin. Clarinet, London Mozart Players, 1956-; Engl. Chmbr. Orch., 1964-; Mbr., Vesuvius & Melos Ensembles; Prof., Clarinet, RCM, 1961-; Tutor, clarinet, Nat. Youth Orch., 1956-; Frequent broadcaster & soloist. Recordings incl: Mozart Clarinet Concerto, Quintet & Sinfonia Concertant; John Ireland Fantasy Sonata; Alan Rawsthorne Quartet; Herbert Howells Rhapsodic Quintet. Publs: Clarinet solos. Mbrships: ISM; Royal Soc. Musicians; RCM Union. Recip: Tagore Gold Medal, RCM, 1946. Hobby: Painting. Address: 16 Milverton Rd., London NW6 7AS, UK. 3,14,27.

KINGMA, Stanley George, b. 9 June 1937, Lafayette, Ind., USA. Choral Director. Educ: BS, Purdue Univ., 1959; Anderson Coll.; studies w. Robert Shaw, 1964. m. Marilyn Kay Myers, 2 s., 1 d. Career: Full-time Profl. Cond., 1964-; White House app.

w. Va. Tech. Varsity Glee Club; 40-60 musical perfs. each season, 1968-; currently Dir., the New Virginians; TV apps.; coast-to-coast tour, 1977. Comps: Man (multi-media choral-instrumental-visual prodn.), recorded 1970. Recordings: w. Va. Tech. Varisty Glee Club & New Virginians, incl. "Coast to Coast", 1977. Mbrships. incl: Am. Choral Dirs. Assn.; Va. Music Educators Assn.; Nat. Fedn. of Music Clubs. Recip., 2nd Pl. Nat. Prize w. Va. Tech. Varsity Glee Club, Fred Waring Choral Competition, 1965. Hobbies: Photography; Woodworking. Address: 1307 Greenwood Dr., Vineland, NJ 08360, USA. 2,4,7.

KINGSFORD, Charles, b. 16 Aug. 1907, Brooklyn, NY, USA. Composer; Pianist; Concert Accompanist; Music Therapist; Pedagogue; Voice Coach. Educ: CCNY; Tchr. Coll., Columbia Univ.; Grad. Schl. of Juilliard Musical Fndn. Debut: Concert Accomp., Town Hall, NYC for Rawn Spearman recital. Career: Comp. of Art Songs performed by notable singers inclng: Marian Anderson, Rise Stevens, Gladys Swarthout, William Warfield, etc. on concert stage, radio & TV; Music Cons., Educ. Publs., Apple-Century-Croft, 1973. Comps. incl: Broadway plays; Boy Meets Girl; Goodbye My Fancy; 26 Art Songs. Mbrships: ASCAP; Juilliard Alumni; Nat. Assn. for Music Therapy; Assn. Music Tchrs. League of NY; NY Singing Tchrs. Assn. Hobby: Photography. Address: 150 W 57th St., New York, NY, USA. 4.

KINGSLEY, Colin, b. 15 Apr. 1925, London, UK. University Lecturer; Concert Pianist. Educ: B Mus, Cantab, 1946; D Mus, Edinburgh Univ., 1968; ARCM. m. Dorothy Jean Nicholls, 2 s., 2 d. Debut: BBC, 1948. Career incls: W Indies Recital Tour, 1947-48; Solo Pianist, Royal Ballet, 2 yrs.; BBC concerts, London & Edinburgh; Pianist, Univ. Coll. of Wales, 1963-64; Lectr., Univ. of Edinburgh, 1964; Sr. Lectr., ibid., 1971. Recordings: Sonatas by John White. Mbrships: ISM; Chmn., Edinburgh Chopin Circle; Edinburgh Soc. of Musicians. Hons. incl: Guest of Hon., Chopin Int. Piano Competition, Warsaw, 1975. Hobbies: Golf; Squash. Mgmt: Terry Slasberg Agcy., 3 The Lodge, Richmond Way, London W12. Address: 16 Lauder Rd., Edinburgh EH9 2EL, UK.

KINGSLEY, Margaret, b. 20 Feb. 1939, Pool, Cornwall, UK. Opera Singer. Educ: Royal Coll. of Music; ARCM; LRAM. m. W A Newcombe. Debut w. Opera for All. Career incl: regular appearances w. Glyndebourne Opera, Engl. Nat. Opera, Scottish Opera, Royal Opera House Covent Gdn., etc.; prin. roles in major opera houses of Paris, Munich, Hamburg, Vienna, Naples & in USA; Concert appearances w. leading Brit. Orchs. & on BBC TV; Prof. of singing, RCM. Hobbies: Gardening; Cooking; Walking. Address: "Dormers", Wildwood Close, E Horsley, Leatherhead, Surrey, KT24 5EP, UK. 2.

KINGSWOOD, Peter John, b. 20 May 1934, Tunbridge Wells, UK. Teacher; Viola & Violin; Violist. Educ: studied w. Frederick Riddle, RCM; ARCM. m. Sylvia Mary Latchford, 1 s., 1 d. Career: RPO under Beecham; City of Birmingham Symph. Orch.; violist, res. Ensemble, Univ. Coll. of Wales, 1963-; broadcasts & TV apps.; regular coll. & music club concerts. Contbr. to: Strad Mag.; Western Mail (music reviews). Mbr., ISM; ESTA; Viola Rsch. Soc.; Chmn., Aberystwyth Music Club. Hobbies: Mountain walking; Writing. Address: Melindwr, 4 Trefor Rd., Aberystwyth, UK.

KINSEY, Tony, b. 11 Oct. 1930, Birmingham, UK. Musician; Percussionist; Composer. Educ: Studied comp. w. William Russo; USA: Percussion w. William West, USA. m. Patricia Doreen Kinsey, 1 d. Career: Extensive TV & radio work; Comp. MD, That's Life TV Show, 3 yrs.; Comp. w. Marty Feldman of musical Wam Bam Thank You Mam. Comps. incl: River Thames Suite; Work for Double String Quartet & Jazz Quintet; Num. TV commercials. Recordings: 5 LP's on Decca; 2 EP's on EMI. Hobbies: Golf; Reading; Sailing. Address: 5 The Pennards, Sunbury-on-Thames, Middx., UK.

KINTON, Leslie Wayne, b. 18 Feb. 1951, Toronto, Ont., Can. Pianist; Teacher. Educ: studied piano w. Pierre Souvairan, Jeaneane Dowis & Karl Ulrich Schnabel; comp. w. Samuel Dolin. m. Barbara J Black, 1 d. Career: as mbr. of Anagnoson & Kinton duo piano team, toured Europe, & N Am.; recordings for BBC, Swiss radio, Hilversum radio, CBC radio & TV; on piano fac., Royal Conserv. of Music, Toronto. Address: 300 Robert St., Toronto, Ont., M5S 2K8, Can.

KINZL, Franz, b. 2 July 1895, Mettmach, Austria. Composer. Educ: Tchrs. Acad., Linz; Music Schl., Linz; Conds. exam., Music Acad., Vienna, 1924. m. Irma Nessmayr, 1 d. Career: Musician (most instruments) & Cond., var. orchs.; Choir master, var. Austrian choirs; Music critic; Organiser, num. competitions & comp. contests. Comps. incl: Symph. in A sharp; 4 symphonic works; Die Jubilarin (opera); works for brass bands; (recorded) Divertimento. Publ: Irrlicht (novel, as T Franklin), 1947. Contbr. to Tagebuch-Wien & other papers & jrnls. (over 1000 articles). Mbr., var. Austrian musical socs. Hons: Stelzhamerpreis, 1952; Prof. h.c., 1965; Brucknerpreis, 1970. Hobbies: Literature; Painting (watercolour). Address: Flaviastrasse 9, A-4650 Lambach, Austria.

KIØNIG, Carl Jørgen, b. 9 March, 1949, Oslo, Norway. Percussionist. Educ: Degrees in Philos., Theatre Hist., Lit., Oslo Univ. m. Janine E Strand, 1 s. Career: Sev. TV & stage apps., inclng. The Rival (TV), Taming of the Shrew, Camp, Bacchai, Your Won Thing, Alice in the Underworld, Catalina; Comp. in collaboration w. Rain (musical group); Mbr., Rain. Comps: Mehitabel (ballet); The Last Race (Radio-theatre); In Collaboration with Rain; The Burning Court; Report to the Commissioner (Radio-theatre); Oedipus; Taming of the Shrew; Camp (Theatre prodn.); The Rival; Successful live for Three (TV-drama). Recordings: Camp; The Rival. Contbr. to: Decibel. Mbrships: Oslo Dept. of Norwegian Music Sco.; Norwegian Dept. of ICM. Hons: Benneches Scholarship. Address: Gml Drammens v. 160L, 1310-Blommenholm, Norway.

KIORPES, George Anthony, b. 24 Sept. 1931, Yonkers, NY, USA. Teacher; Pianist; Organist & Choir Director. Educ: Grad., Peabody Conserv. Preparatory Dept.; BMus., Peabody Conserv. of Music, 1954; MMus & Artist Dip., ibid, 1955; 1975 Doct. Musical Arts, Boston Univ. m. Suzanne Tetu, 2 s. Career: Instructor, Peabody Conserv. Preparatory Dept., 1953-55; Asst. Prof., Greensboro Coll., 1955-65; Dir. of Music, 1st Moravian Ch., Greensboro, 1961-; Assoc. Prof., Univ. of NC at Greensboro, 1965-; Piano Concerts thru'out USA. Publs: The Performance of Ornaments in the Works of Chopin, DMA Dissertation, Boston Univ., 2 vols. (Ann Arbor; Univ. Microfilms), 1975. Mbrships: MTNA; Nat. Fedn. Music Clubs, N.C. Music Tchrs. Assn.; Pi Kappa Lambda (VP, Tau Chapt.). Hons: May G Evans Scholarship, 1949; Paul Thomas Prize (piano), 1952; Bach-Horstmeier Scholarship, 1953. Hobbies: Reading; Bridge; Chess; Athletics. Address: 3917 Madison Ave., Greensboro, NC 27410, USA.

KIPNIS, Igor, b. 27 Sept. 1930, Berlin, Germany (derivative US citizenship). Harpsichordist. Educ: Dip., Westport Schl. of Music, Conn., 1948; AB, Harvard Univ., 1952. m. Judith Robison, 1 s. Debut: NYC, 1959. Career: Concerts & recitals throughout USA & Can., 1962-; extensive tours abroad, 1967-; Fac., Berkshire Music Ctr., Tanglewood, 1964-67; Prof. of Fine Arts, Fairfield Univ., Conn., 1971-75; Artist-in-Res., ibid, 1975-77; Early Music Inst., Indpls., summers, 1974-. Recordings: 35 solo LPs for major cos. Publs. incl: A First Harpsichord Book, 1970; Ed., Dussek, The Sufferings of the Queen of France, 1975; Telemann: Overture in E Flat, 1977. Author, Harpsichord & Clavichord, 1980. Contbr. to profl. jrnls. Mbr., profl. assns. Hons. incl: Nominee for Grammy Awards, 1964, '71, '72, '77; Deutsche Schallplatten Prize, 1969; Record of Yr. Award, Stereo Review, 1971, '72, '75; Hon. Phi Beta Kappa, 1977. Hobbies: Photography; Record Collecting. Mgmt: Am. Int. Artists, NY. Address: 20 Drummer Lane RD. 2, W Redding, CT 06896, USA.

KIRÁLY, István József, b. 9 Oct. 1939, Szombathely, Hungary. French Horn Player & Teacher. Educ: Horn tchrs. dip., Györ branch of Ferenc Liszt Music Acad., Budapest, 1964. m. (1) Maria Kiraly; (2) Maria Homor, 4 c. Debut: Budapest, 1965. Career: 1st horn, Györ Phil. Orch., 1961-64; 2nd horn, Nat. Theatre Orch., Szeged, 1965-69; 1st horn, Szeged Symph. Orch., 1969-; horn tchr., Szeged branch, Ferenc Liszt Music Acad., Budapest. Hons: Outstanding Musician title, 1976. Hobbies: Numismatics; Handicrafts; Electric railway modelling. Address: Szucs u. 3/b, 6721 Szeged, Hungary.

KIRBY, F(rank) E(ugene), b. 6 Apr. 1928, NYC, USA. Historian of Music. Educ: BA, Colo Coll., 1950; PhD, Yale Univ., 1957. m. Emily Baruch, 4 children. Publs: Transl. Hanns Neupert's Harpsichord Manual, 1961; A Short History of Keyboard Music, 1966; An Introduction to Western Music, - Bach, Beethoven, Wagner, Stravinsky, 1970. Contbr. to: Musical Quarterly; Music & Letters; Jrnl. of Am. Musicol. Soc.; Notes - Quarterly; Encyclopaedia Britannica, 15th ed. Mbrships: Am. & Int. Musicol. Soc.; Deutsche Gesellschaft fuer Musikforschung; AAUP. Recip. of Forschungsstipendium der Alexander von Humboldt-Stiftung, 1966. Hobbies: Hiking; Cycling. Address: Dept. of Music, Lake Forest Coll., Lake Forest, IL 60045, USA. 13.

KIRCHMEYER, Helmut Franz Maria, b. 30 June 1930, Düsseldorf, German Fed. Repub. Musicologist. Educ: Cologne Univ., musicol., phil., German philol., law; Bonn Univ., ch. hist.; 1954 PhD; Robert Schumann Conserv. Düsseldorf. m. Dr. Eva Maria Berke, 3 d., 1 s. Career: Epert G MA; Music critic; Radio co-operator; 1960 Lectr. musicol. TH Aachen; 1961 Lectr.

Librarian's Inst. Cologne; 1972 Dir. Schumann Conserv. Düsseldorf; 1973 Dean Schumann Inst. Düsseldorf. Publs. incl: Igor Strawinski - Contemporary History in the Description of Personalities, 1958; Liturgy at the Cross Roads, 1962; Wagner Documents 1842-1845, 1967 and 1846-1850, 1968; Wagner in Dresden, 1972; Strawinski's Russian Ballets, 1974. Hons: Richard Wagner Meda., Beirut, 1975. Hobbies: Dendrology. Address: Breitestr. 70, 404 Neuss, German Fed. Repub.

KIRCHNER, Leon, b. 24 Jan. 1919, NY, USA. Composer; Pianist; Professor. Educ: LA City Coll.; UCLA; BA, Univ. of Calif., Berkeley, 1940. m. Gertrude Schoenberg, 1 s., 1 d. Career: Tchr., San Fran. Conserv., 1946-47 & Berkshire Music Ctr., 1959-60; Lectr., Univ. of Southern Calif., 1950-54; Luther Bursie Marchant Prof. of Music, Mills Coll., Calif., 1954-59; Prof. of Music, Harvard Univ., 1961-66; Walter Bigelow Rosen Prof. of Music, ibid, 1966-; Cond. & Soloist, NY Phil.; has app. as Soloist at fests., etc. Compositions incl: Duo for violin & piano; Piano Sonata; Little Suite for Piano; sev. concertos; sev. quartets. Mbrships: AAAS; Nat. Inst. Arts & Letters. Hons. incl: NY Music Critics Circle Awards for str. quartets, No. 1, 1950, & No. 2, 1960; Pulitzer Prize in Music for Str. Quartet No. 3 (electronic music), 1967. Address: Harvard Univ., Music Bldg., 8 Hilliard ST., Cambridge, MA 02138, USA.

KIRCULESCU, Nicola, b. 10 Jan. 1910, Bucarest, Romania. Composer. Educ: Law Univ., Bucarest; Doct., Law, Paris; Wiener Conservatorium. m. Marietta. Debut: 1940. Comps: Over 500 light musical pieces; 4 symph. pieces (2 w. piano solo, one w. flute solo); 4 operettas; 32 musical reviews. Over 50 recordings. Contbr. to var. papers & special reviews. Mbr. Committee, Romanian Comps. Union. Hons: State Prizes, 1951; Merited Artist, 1962; Work Order, 1964; Cultural Merit, 1973. Hobbies: Boxing; Swimming; Skiing. Address: str. Batistei No. ii Etj. II ap. 4, Bucarest I, Romania.

KIREILIS, Ramon John, b. 25 June 1940, Urbana, Ill., USA. Clarinet Teacher. Educ: BME, MMus, N Tex. State Univ.; DMA, Univ. Mich. Career: Radio & TV apps.; Soloist & Lectr., Int. Clarinet Clinics, 1968-79; Guest soloist, Arapahoe Symph. Orch., 1974-; Prague Radio Symph. Orch., 1979; Solo clarinet, Colo. Springs Symph. Orch., 1972-79; Solo clarinet, Central City Opera Orch., 1974-79; European recital tour, 1978. Recordings: Bliss & Coleridge Clarinet Quintets, 1979. Publs: Learning Unlimited, 1974. Contbr. to: Instrumentalist; Clarinet. Mbrships. incl: Admin. Dir., Int. Clarinet Congress, 1967-79. Hobbies: Chess; Sailing. Address: 1728 S Ivy, Denver CO 80224, USA. 9.

KIRK, Colleen Jean, b. 7 Sept. 1918, Champaign, Ill., USA. Professor of Music; Choral Conductor (Voice). Educ: BS & MS, Music Educ., Univ. Ill.; EdD, Music Educ., Columbia Univ. Career incls: Prof. of Educ. & Music, Univ. Ill., 1945-70; Dir. of Music, Wesley Meth. Ch., Urbana, Ill., 1947-70; Prof. of Music, Fla. State Univ., Tallahassee, 1970-; Apps. in 15 states as guest cond., adjudicator of music competitons & fests.; Workshop Clinician in Vocal, Choral & Gen. Music; Speaker & Panel Mbr. at Profl. Mtgs. Publs. incl: Modern Methods in Elementary Education, 1959 (co-author). Contbr. to the Choral Jrnl. Mbr. num. profl. orgs. inclng: Am. Choral Dirs. Assn. (S Div. Pres., 1971-75); MENC; Am. Assn. of Univ. Profs.; Pi Kappa Lambda; Kappa Delta Pi. Address: 2028 Wildridge Drive, Tallahassee, FL 32303, USA. 4,5,

KIRK, Elise Kuhl, b. 14 Feb. 1932, Chgo., Ill., USA. Musicologist; Pianist; Lecturer. Educ: BMus, 1953, MMus, 1954, Univ. of Mich.; PhD, Catholic Univ. of Am., 1977; studies in musicol. w. Kurt von Fischer, Univ. of Zürich, 1961-63; studies (piano) w. Claudio Arrau, Aspen Inst. of Music, 1953. m. Robert L Kirk, 3 c. career: Adjunct Lectr., Baruch Coll., CUNY, 1972-77; Vis. Prof., Catholic Univ. of Am., summers 1976, '77; Adjunct Prof. of Music, Univ. of Dallas, 1978-. Publs: Ed., Dallas Civic Opera mag., 1978-. Contbr. to: Am. Music Tchr.; Notes; Musical Quarterly; Current Musicol.; Symposium; Grove's Dict., 6th Ed.; Opera News; Dallas Civic Opera Mag. Mbrships: Am. Musicol. Soc.; Int. Musicol. Soc.; Coll. Music Soc.; Sigma Alpha Iota; Bd. of Dirs., Gifted Students Inst. Hons. incl: Smithsonian Inst. Fellowship, Am. Coun. of Learned Socs.; appointed by Pres. Carter to Advisory Coun. for John F Kennedy Ctr. for the Performing Arts, Wash., DC, 1979. Address: 6516 Forest Creek Dr., Dallas, TX 75230, USA.

KIRKBY-MASON, Barbara, b. 7 Mar. 1910, London, UK. Pianist; Teacher; Lecturer; Adjudicator. Educ: RAm; FRAM; Hon. FTCL; LRAM; Later studied w. Harold Samuel. 2 s. Career: Piano Soloist, BBC, Radio Eirrean; UK Lecture Tours for Piano Pub. Assn.; Lecturer, MTA & ISM etc.; Music tours overseas for recitals, lectures, broadcasts, etc. Publs: Modern Piano Course (in 24 books); Adult Piano Course, 2 vols.; Growing Up Series; Jamaican Folksongs (arr. for solo piano & duet); It's Time for Music; Piano-Group For Children; First, Second & Third Collections (3 books); A Mood Sequence (in Progress). Contbr. to Assoc. Bd. Exam. Notes, The Music Teacher. Mbrships: Warden, Pvte. Tchrs. Sect., ISM; Performing Rights Soc.; Int. Soc. for Music Educ.; RAM Club; Musician Mbr. for Ctrl. London, Soroptomists Int. Recip. of Sterndale Bennett Prize, RAM, 1929. Hobbies: Walking; Gardening. Address: Flat 5, 6 Weymouth Mews, London W1N 3FS, UK. 3, 4, 27.

KIRKENDALE, (John) Warren, b. 14 Aug. 1932, Toronto, Can. Music Historian. Educ: BA, Univ. of Toronto, 1955; PhD, Univ. of Vienna, 1961. m. Ursula Kirkendale, 3 d. Career incls: Asst. Prof., Univ. of Southern Calif., 1963-67; Assoc. Prof., 1967-75; Prof. of Musicol., 1975-, Duke Univ., Durham, NC. Publs: Fugue & Fugato in der Kammermusik des Rokoko & der Klassik, 1966; L'Aria di Fiorenza, id est Il Ballo de Granduca, 1972; Madrigali a diversi linguaggi, 1975; Fugue & Fugato in Rococo & Classical Chmbr. Music, 1979. Contbr. to num. profl. jrnls. & dictionaries. Mbrships. incl: Int., Italian & Am. Musicol. Socs.; Ges. f. Musikforschung. Hons. incl: Election as mbr., Gesellschaft zur Herausgabe von Denmälern der Tonkunst in Österreich, 1966; Fellow of Nat. Endowment for the Humanities, 1970, and Am. Coun. of Learned Socs., 1974. Hobbies: Art History; Lit. History; Mountaineering. Address: Dept. of Music, Duke Univ., Durham, NC 27708, USA. 4, 14, 29.

KIRKPATRICK, Gary, b. 10 Aug 1941, Manhattan, Kan., USA. Pianist. Educ: B Mus., Eastman Schl. of Music, Rochester, NY; Artist's Dip., Acad. for Music & Dramatic Arts, Vienna, Austria. m. Ekla Gurova. Debut, NYC, 7 Apr. 1973. Career: has concertized in Europe, Near E., Ctrl. Am., Russia, USA & Can.; has perf. w. var. chmbr. music grps., USA & abroad; has made TV & radio broadcasts; Adjudicator; has presented num. lectures & master classes; Vis. Lectr., Univ. of Kan., Lawrence, 1967-69; Artist Tchr., Interlochen Ctr. for the Arts, Mich., 1969-73; currently on Music Fac., Wm. Paterson Coll., NY. Has recorded for Musical Heritage Soc. Hons. incl: Winner, Stepanov Piano Competition, Vienna, 1964, & Int. Piano Competition, Jean, Spain, 1966. Address: Box 598, Hewitt, NJ 07421, USA.

KIRKPATRICK, Ralph, b. 10 June 1911, Mass., USA. Harpsichordist; Clavichordist; Pianist. Educ: BA, Harvard Univ., 1931; studied w. Nadia Boulanger, Wanda Landowska, Arnold Dolmetsch & Gunther Ramin. Debut: Cambridge, Mass., 1930. Career incls: has app. at major concert & recital halls throughout world; is noted for perfs. of Bach & Scarlatti; on Fac., Mozarteum Acad., Salzburg, Austria, 1933-34; Dir., Williamsburg, Va. Fest., 1938-46; Ernest Bloch Prof. of Music, Univ. of Calif., 1964; Instr. in Harpsichord, 1940; Prof. of Music, Yale Univ., 1965-76. Has made num. recordings inclng: Sixty Sonatas by Scarlatti & Complete Clavier Works of J S Bach. Publs: (as Ed.) Bach's Goldberg Variations, 1938; 60 Scarlatti Sonatas, 1953; Domenico Scarlatti: Complete Keyboard Works in Facsimile, 1972. Contbr. to profl. jrnls. Mbrships: Fellow, AAAS; Am. Philos. Soc. Hons incl: Guggenheim Fellow, 1937-38; Order of Merit, Italian Repub.; Hon. Doctorates, Oberlin & Rochester Univs. Address: Old Quarry, Guilford, CT 06437, USA. 2, 14, 30.

KIRSCH, Winfried, b. 10 April 1931, Dresden, Germany. Musicologist & Choir Conductor. Educ: Pianist, Choir-cond., Musicol., Univ. of FrankfurtM.; PhD, 1958; Habilitation, 1971. m. 2 c. Career: Prof., Musicol., Univ. of FrankfurtM, 1971-; Tchr. of the Highschool for Music, 1962-76 & Dr. Hochs Consrev., FrankfurtM. Publs. incl: Studien zum Vokalstil der mittleren und späten Schaffensperiode Anton Bruckners, 1958; Die Quellen der mehrstimmigen Magnificat - und Te Deum - Vertonungen bis zur Mitte des 16 Jahrhunderts, 1966; Die Motetten des Andreas de Silva. Studien zur Geschichte der Motette im 16 Jahrhundert, 1971, '77. Contbr. to many profl. publs. Edns: Johannes Hahnel (Galliculus) und anonyme Meister; Drei Weihnachtsmagnificat zu 4 Stimmen, 1961; Drei Te Deum-Kompositionen des 16. Jahrhunderts zu 4-5 Stimmen, 1967; Andreas de Silva, Collected works, vols. I-III, 1970-; Paul Hindemith. Konzert fur Violoncello und Orchester in Es-Dur op. 3., 1977, etc. Address: Senckenberganlage 24, D6000 FrankfurtU, German Fed. Repub.

KIRSCHBAUM, Bernard, b. 2 Oct. 1910, San Diego, Calif., USA. Concert Pianist; Accompanist; Chamber Musician; Teacher; Lecturer; Author. Educ: BSc, 1943, MA Mus & Mus Ed, 1945, Columbia Univ.; Tchrs. & Artist's Dips., Juilliard Schl. m. Fannie Kirschbaum. Debut: San Diego, Calif. Career incls: Dir. of Music, summer camps, 1935-55; concerts, chmbr. music, solo recitals, accomp., 1940-70; duo-piano fac.

recitals, LI Inst. of Music, 1963-67; Prod., all Gilbert & Sullivan operettas & sev. musicals; on Keyboard Artists prog., WNYC Radio, 1970; World Program Dir. for Music & Perf. Arts of Who's Who Biographees, NY, 1977-80. Contbr. to profl. jrnls. Mbrships: Prog. Chmn., Piano Tchrs. Congress of NY, 1975-79; 1st VP, Assn. of Piano Tchrs. of KI, 1974-77; Pres., ibid, 1977-79; Audition Judge, NGPT, 1950-76; Bd., Leschetizky Assn. Inc., 1970-77. Recip. var. hons. Address: 78-18 165th St., Flushing, NY 11366, USA.

KIRSHBAUM, Thomas M., b. 8 Feb. 1928, Chgo., Ill., USA. Conductor; Pianist; University Professor. Educ: B Mus, Music Hist., Univ. of Mich., 1960; M Mus, Piano, Yale Univ., 1963; studied w. Rudolf Kempe, Germany, 1964; DMA in Cond., Univ. of Southern Calif., 1967. m. Julia Kauffman, 2 s. Career: Fndr. & Cond., Yale Repertory Symph., 1961-63; Cond. & Music Dir., Flagstaff Symph., Ariz., 1966-; Asst. Prof.-Assoc. Prof. Music, Northern Ariz. Univ., 1966-; Cond., Am. Premier of Strauss, Des Esels Schatten, 1970. Recordings: (w. Flagstaff Symph. & Oratorio Soc.) Strauss, Rosenkavalier Suite; Kodaly, Psalmus Hungaricus, 1973. Hons: Jr. & Sr. Scholastic Hons., Univ. of Mich., 1958-60; Fulbright Grant, 1964; Outstanding DMA. Recip., Univ. of Southern Calif. Alumni Assn., 1967. Hobbies: Aviation; Skiing; Sailing. Address: PO Box 122, Flagstaff, AZ 86001, USA.

KIRWAN, Anne Lindsey, b. 21 Dec. 1938, Aldershot, UK. Teacher of Piano & Harmony; Musicologist. Educ: RCM, 1955-59; BMus (Lond.); ARCM (piano perf.); LRAM (schl. music); PhD, Nottingham Univ., 1978. Career: Music tchr. & housemistress, Benenden Schl., Cranbrook, Kent, 1959-70; Rsch. student, part-time lectr., Nottingham Univ. Music Dept., 1970-77; sub-ed., Grove's Dict., 6th ed., 1974-77. Publs: The Music of Lincoln Cathedral, 1973. Contbr. of over 30 articles Grove's Dict., 6th ed. recip., Order of Independence, Hashemite Kingdom of Jordan, 1969. Hobbies: Travel; Walking; var. sports; Decorating. Address: 15 Fishpond Dr., The Park, Nottingham NG7 1DG, UK.

KIS, Istvan, b. 16 Mar. 1920, Tiszakarad, Hungary. Conductor; Chorus Master. Educ: Prof. of Music & Singing, Acad. of Music, Budapest. m Judit Janoky, / s., 1 d. Debut: 1943. Career: Tchr., 1949-57. Vice-Cond., 1957-58, 1st Cond., Chorus Master, 1958-, Hungarian Army's Ensemble; Ldr. of top amateur choirs; Sev. TV & radio apps. Recordings incl: Works by Franz Liszt; Franz Liszt; Choral Works II. Mbrships: Ldr., Coun. of Choirs, Budapest; Presidency, Nat. Coun. of Choirs. Hons. incl: Charles Cros Grand Prize, French Acad. of Gramophone Records; Int. Grand Prize, Franz Liszt Soc.; II Degrees, Franz Liszt Prize, 1971. Hobby: Stereo; Photography. Address: 1146 Budapest, Izso utca 6, Hungary.

KISER, Stephen Andrew, b. 25 July 1951, Auburn, Alabama, USA. Violist. Educ: BMus, Ariz. State Univ.; MMus, Univ. of Ill.; DMus Cand., Ind. Univ. Career: Phoenix Symph., 1972-73, 1975-76; Champaign-Urbana Symph., 1973-75; Springfield Symph., 1973-75; Gard. Tchng. Assistantship in Viola, Univ. of Ill., 1973-75; Assoc. Instructorship, Viola, Ind. Univ., 1976-; Prin. Violist, Thunder Bay Symph., Ont., Can., 1978-; Asst. Prin., ASU Symph. Orch., 1969-73; Prin., Univ. of Ill. Symph. Orch., 1973-75; Grad. String Quartet, Univ. of Ill., 1973-74; Asst. Prin., Ind. Univ. Symph. Orch. IV, 1976; Prin., ibid, 1977. Mbrships. incl: Viola Rsch. Soc.; Phi Kappa Phi; Nat. Hon. Soc. Hons: Num. scholarships. Address: 418 S Woodlawn, Bloomington, IN 47401, USA.

KISER, Wieslaw Maria, b. 20 July 1937, Poznán, Poland. Conductor; Critic; Composer. Educ: High Schol. of Music, Poznán. Debut: as comp., Poznán, 1959, as cond., Poznán, 1963. Career: Over 500 Concerts, Poland, Bulgaria, Finland, Germany, USSR, Czech.; Film, Poland, Finland, USSR; TV & radio, Poland, Finland, USSR, Germany; Artistic Manager, The Boy's Choir of Gniezno, Poland - The Thrushes. Comps. Approx. 70 Choral comps. Publs: Organization and education of children's choirs, 1971; Aerials of Poznán, 1975; The selected problems of music history, 1969. Contbr. to: The West Newspaper. Mbr., Polish Musicians Assn. Hons: Dip. of Honour, Polish Ministry of Art, 1970. Hobby: Working with youth. Address: u. Szelagowska 12, 61-626 Poznán, Poland.

KISHIBE, Shigeo, b. 16 June 1912, Tokyo, Japan. Emeritus Professor, University of Tokyo. Educ: PhD., Musicol. & Hist., Univ. of Tokyo. m. Yori Kishibe, 3 children. Career: Prof., Musicol. & Asian Hist. of Music, Univ. of Tokyo, 1949-73 (Emeritus Prof. 1973-); Lectr., Music Dept., Tokyo Univ. of Arts, 1949-; Lectr., Univ. of Calif. & Harvard Univ., USA, 1957-58; Vis. Prof., Univ. of Wash. & Stanford Univ., USA, 1962-63; Vis. Prof., Univ. of Hawaii, USA, 1973. Publs: (in Engl.) The Traditional Music of Hapan, 1969; The Traditional Music of Japan, 1972; Music of Japan, 1973; (in Japanese)

Todai Ongaku no Rekishiteki Kenkyu (A Historical Study of the Music in the T'ang Dynasty), 2 vols., 1961-62. Contbr. to musical books & jrnls. Hon: Award, Japanese Acad. of Sci., 1961. Hobby: Travel. Address: 2-36-18, Uehara, Shibuya, Tokyo, Japan.

KISIELEWSKI, Stefan, b. 7 Mar. 1911, Warsaw, Poland. Composer; Critic; Pianist. Educ: Dips. in Theory, 1934, Comp. & Piano, 1937, Warsaw Conserv. of Music. m. Lidia Hintz, 2 s., 1 d. Career incls: Prof., High Schl. of Music, Cracow, 1945-49; Ed., Puch Muzyczny (wkly.), 1945-50; Music Ed., WAIF, 1965-68; Critic, Tygodnik Powysechny (Cath. wkly.), Cracow. Comps. incl: (orchl.) Perpetuum Mobile, 1955; Sport Signals, 1966; 4 Symph.; 3 Ballets; Concert for Chmbr. Orch.; Cosmos I; Works for piano, chmbr. music, music for films, theatre, etc. sev. recordings. Publs: 6 books on musical subjects (in Polish), 1953-74. Contbr. to music & Cath. mags. Mbr., profl. assns. Hons. incl: Cracow Music Award, 1956; Polonia Restituta, 1957; Jurzykowski Fndn. Award, NYC, 1973. Hobbies: Bicycle; Cinema. Address: A1. l Armii WP. 16 m. 11, 00-582 Warsaw, Poland. 4, 14.

KISS, Gyula, b. 11 June 1944, Budapest, Hungary. Pianist. Educ: Ferenc Liszt Music Acad., Budapest. Career: TV & radio apps., Singapore, Aust., Japan, USA, UK, Germany, etc. 1970-. Recordings: 10 LPs, incl. Liszt's E flat major concerto, A major; Totentans, Sonata in A minor, Funerailles, Valses oublies; Mozart's C minor piano concerto, KV 491, D major, KV 537; Brahms' Chmbr. Works. Hons: Liszt State Prize, 1968, '69, '70; First Prize, Taormina, 1966; Budapest Liszt Concours, 1966; Piano Competition of the Budapest Radio & TV. Hobby: Making ceramics. Mgmt: Interkoncert, Budapest. Address: Manyecske u. 5, 1112 Budapest, Hungary.

KISS, Janos. Composer; Conductor; Music Director; Educator. Career incl: Judge, Int. Harp Competition, Univ. of Hartford, Conn., 1969; Co-fndr., Cond. & Musical Dir., W Suburban Phil. Orch., 1969-; Tchr. of Brasses, Cleveland Music Schl. Settlement, 1964-79; Chmn. of Music Dept., St. Luke Schl., Ohio, 1966-70; Orch. Dir., Comp.-in-Res. & Instrumental Tchr., W Reserve Acad., Hudson, Ohio, 1967-72; Comp.-in-Res. & Instrumental Tchr., St. Edward HS, Lakewood, Ohio, 1968-74; Comp.-in-Res., Luth. HS W, Rocky River, Ohio, 1973-76; Chmn., Dept. of Music, Holy Family Schl., Parma, Ohio, 1974-; num. radio broadcasts as Cond., w. W Suburban Phil. Orch. Comps. incl: Spring - At Last! (harp ensemble); Ballet for Harps; On the Wing (flute & guitar); In Homage; Rhapsody for Cimbalom & Orch.; South Dakota for harp ensemble; Sinfonia Atlantis, etc. Address: 229 Bradley Rd., Bay Village, OH 44140, USA.

KISSAUN, Maryann, b. Valletta, Malta. Pianist; Teacher. Educ: Brit. Co. Scholar, Assoc. Bd. Scholar, RCM, London; LRSM; ARCM; later studied w. Peter Katin & Peter Feuchtwanger. Debut: Purcell Room, London, 1969. Career: Pvte. Music Tchr., Malta & in Grammar Schls., until 1952; Concert Pianist, touring Europe, Brit. Isles, S Am. & N Africa & making num. radio & TV broadcasts throughout world; Adjudicator, nat. competitions for pianists, Malta, until 1968; Pvte. Tchr., London, 1969-; formed violin & piano duo w. Ivan Smith, 1971; Music Critic, Sunday Times of Malta, until 1966; Prof., LCM. Mbrships: ISM; Fedn. of Music Fests. & Music Tchrs. Assn.; LSO Club. Hons. incl: Prize, Beethoven Sect., London Music Fest. Competition, 1949. Hobbies: Travel; Interior Design. Mgmt: Ruth Ticher Concert Mgmt. Address: 3 Greycoat Gardens, Greycoat Place, London SW1P 2QA, UK. 2, 3, 27, 29, 30.

KITCHEN, Dorothy Ellen Johnson, b. 27 Aug. 1937, Dayton, Ohio, USA. Violinist; Conductor of Youth Orchestras; String School Director; Associate Concertmistress. Educ: BA, Western Reserve Univ.; MA, Brandeis Univ.; Eastman Schl. of Music; Longy Schl. of Music. m. Joseph Weston Kitchen Jr., 1 d., 1 s. Career: Recitals in Dayton, Ohio, Boston, Mass.; Durham, NC, Southern Pines, NC & Raleigh, NC; Dir., Duke Univ. String Schl., Durham, NC; Assoc. Concertmistress, Greensboro, NC Orch. Mbrships: MENC; NCMTA; ASTA. Hons. incl: Soloist, Holy Trinity Phil., Port-au-Prince, Haiti, 1974. Hobbies incl: Reading. Address: 1600 Del. Ave., Durham, NC 27705, USA.

KITCHINER, John, b. 2 Dec. 1933. Opera, Concert & Oratorio Singer. Educ: Nat. Schl. of Opera; London Opera Ctr. Debut: Glyndebourne Opera, in Marriage of Figaro. Career: Opera singer w. Engl. Opera Grp., Glyndebourne Opera, Scottish Opera, Welsh Nat. Opera, Sadlers Wells, Royal Opera Covent Gdn.; var. Radio & TV appearances w. Engl. Nat. Opera; Recitalist & Oratorio soloist. Recording: Wuthering Heights (Herrman). Hobbies: Carpentry; Gardening; Swimming. Mgmt: Stafford Law Assocs., 14A Station Ave., Walton on Thames,

Surrey KT12 1PE. Address: 52 Highams Rd., Hockley, Essex, UK.

KITCHING, Colin, b. 19 Sept. 1941, Redhill, UK. Violist. Educ: Schumann Conservatorium, Düsseldorf, 1961; RCM, 1961-65; ARCM, ARAM; Ind. Univ., USA, 1965-69. Career: Prin. Viola, Scottish Opera, 1972, Prin. Viola, Royal Liverpool Phil. Orch., 1972-75; Fndr., mgr., Kent Opera Orch., 1971; Prin. viola, Richard Hickox Orch. & Engl. Bach Fest. Baroque Orch. Num. orchl. recordings. Recip. Worshipful Co. of Musicians Medal, 1964. Hobbies: Theatre; Countryside. Address: The Old School, Fawley, Wantage, Oxon., UK.

KITE, Christopher James, b. 5 Nov. 1947, London, UK. Harpsichordist; Specialist in Early Piano; Educator. Educ: MA, Univ. of Oxford; ARCM. Debut: Wigmore Hall, 1972. Career: Debut of Christopher Kite/Robert Ferguson piano duo, Wigmore Hall, 1973 & duo-recital series, Purcell Room, London, 1974- (featuring use of original early pianos); Dir. of Keyboard Dept., Int. Barockensemble-Kurse, Schloss Ebenthal, Austria, annually 1974-; Dir., Askrigg Summer Acad. for Baroque Music, Yorks., UK, 1977; solo apps., harpsichord & early piano, Germany, Austria, Switz., Italy, France, Belgium, Yugoslavia; Prof. of Harpsichord, GSM; Broadcasts for BBC TV & radio. Mbr., ISM; EPTA. Publs: Ed., Scarlatti Sonatas (2 vols.), 1978; Ed., Handel The Eight Great Suites, 1978. Contbr. to profl. jrnls. Hons: Raymond Russell Mem. Prize, 1972; Bruges Int. Harpsichord Competition, 1977. Mgmt: Basil Douglas Ltd; Hanover Mgmt. Address: 111 Fernside Rd., London SW12 8LH, UK. 30.

KITE-POWELL, Jeffery Thomas, b. 24 June 1941, Miami, Fla., USA. Musicologist; Teacher; Choral Conductor. Educ: BMus, Coll.-Conserv. of Cinn., Ohio, 1963; BSc (music educ.), Univ. of Cinn., 1964; MA (musicol.), Univ. of NM, Albuquerque, 1969; PhD (musicol.) Univ. of Hamburg, German Fed. Repub., 1976. m. Helga Anna Minna Kite-Powell, 3 c. Publs: Hymnen für Orgel aus der Visby (Petri) Orgeltablatur, 1978; The Visby (Petri) Organ Tablature - Investigation & Critical Edition, 1979; Magnifikats für Orgel aus der Visby (Petri) Orgeltablatur, 1979; Hamburgische Kirchenmusik im Reformationszeitalter (unpub. PhD dissertation by Hugo Leichsenring), 1979; Kyrie und Sequenzen für Orgel aus der Visby (Petri) Orgeltablatur, 1980. Contbr. to Grove's Dict., 6th Ed. Hobbies: Photography; Skin & Scuba Diving; Reading. Address: 8600 S W 126 Terr., Miami, FL 33156, USA.

KITTO, Ann, b. 26 Dec. 19 , Leipzig, Germany. Pianist; Lecturer in Byzantine Music. Educ: RAM, London, LRAM. m. HDF. Kitto, 1 s., 1 d. Debut: Wigmore Hall, London. Career: Recitals; Lectures on Byzantine Music; Progs. of unpublished 17th Century str. music by Italian comps. & concerto perf., Glasgow; Prog. on Greek music, Radio Bristol; Lectures in USA & at Athens, ISM, Bristol, Glasgow, Edinburgh, & Hampstead Music Ctr. Recip., Gold Medal, Greek Red Cross. Hobby: Cooking. Address: 9 Southfield Rd., Bristol 6, UK.

KLACKENBERG, Ivanka Teodossieva, b. 6 Oct. 1942, G. Orjachoviza, Bulgaria. Musicologist; Piano Teacher. Educ: Dip. Musikwissenschaftler, Leipzig, 1966; Fil. kand., Stockholm, 1969. m. Viggo Klackenberg, 2c. Career: Musicologist; Piano Tchr.; Staff, RISM, Sweden & Sohlmans Musiklexikon. Hobby: Philos. Address: Scheelegatan 15, 112 28 Stockholm, Sweden.

KLATZOW, Peter James Leonard, b. 14 July 1945, Springs, Transvaal, S Africa. Composer; Lecturer. Educ: St. Martins Schl., Rosettenville (piano); RCM, London; studied w. Nadia Boulanger, Paris. Career incls: Lectr. in Piano, Harmony & Comp., Rhodesian Coll. of Music, Salisbury, 1966-68; Cond., Salisbury Municipal Orch., 1966-68; TV series, 1966-68; Music Prod., SABC Johannesburg, 1969; Lectr. in Comp., Univ. of Cape Town, 1973. num. commissions. Comps. incl: Nagstuk, for orch., 1966 (recorded); In Memorium N P van Wyk Louw, for soprano & string orch., 1970; Interactions I, for piano, percussion & chmbr. orch., 1971 (recorded); Phoenix, for orch., 1972; Time Structure I for piano, 1973; Night Magic II, for violin, horn & piano, 1977. Mbrships: Fndr. & Organizer, Univ. of Cape Town Contemporary Music Soc., 1975. Recip., num. comp. prizes. Address: Coll. of Music, Univ. of Cape Town, University Private Bag, Rondebosch, Cape. 14

KLAUS, Kenneth Blanchard, b. 11 Nov. 1923, Earlville, Iowa, USA. Composer; Violinist; Violist; Author; University Professor; Conductor. Educ: Prof. Cert., Meteorology, Univ. of Chgo.; MFA., Univ. of Iowa; PhD., ibid; studied w. Cecil Burleigh, Louis Krasner, Emil Cooper. m. Marian Ida Fyler Klaus, 2 s. Career: Prin. Viola, Assoc. Cond., Baton Rouge Symph.; Prof. of Music, La. State Univ., 1950-; Alumni Prof., ibid, 1966. Author, The Romantic Period in Music, 1970. Contbr. to: Ency. Americana; Music Ed. Jrnl. Mbrships: Am. Soc. of Univ. Comps.;

Schoenberg Soc.; Berg Soc.; Webern Soc.; Am. Musicol. Soc.; Am. String Tchrs. Assn.; Past Pres., State Chapt., ibid; Pi Kappa Lambda; Phi Kappa Phi; Omicron Delta Kappa; Delta Phi Alpha. Hobbies: Camping; Power Boating; Fishing; Movie Photography. Address: 1523 Leycester Dr., Baton Rouge, LA 70808, USA. 7, 12, 28.

KLEBE, Giselher, b. 28 June 1925, Mannheim, Germany. Composer. Educ: Berlin Conserv.; study w. Boris Blacher. m. Lore Schiller, 1946, 2 d. Career incl: Prof. of Composition & Theory of Music, NW German Music Acad., Detmold, 1957-. Compositions incl: Operas - Die Rauber, 1957; Die todlichen Wunsche, 1959; Die Ermordung Casars, 1959; Alkmene, 1961; Figaro laast sich scheiden, 1963; Jakobowsky & der Oberts, 1965; Das Mrchen von der Schonen Lilie, 1969; Ballets - Signale, 1955; Menagerie, 1958; Das Testament, 1970; Orchl. works - Zwitschermaschine, 1950; Deux Noctures, 1952; Adagio & Fuge (on theme from Wagner's Walkure), 1962; Dritte Sinfonie, 1967; Herzchhage (for Beat Bank & Symph. Orch.); Num. chmbr. music works, instrumental pieces & songs. Mbrships: Acads. of Arts, Berlin & Hamburg. Address: Quellenstrasse 30, 4931 Pivitsheide V.L., W Germany.

KLECKI, Paul, b. 21 Mar. 1900, Poland (Swiss Citizen). Conductor. Educ: Warsaw Conserv.; Berlin Acad. of Music. Career: Tchr. of Composition, Scuola Superiora di Musica, Milan, 1935; Prin. Cond., Kharkov Phil. Orch., 1937; Red Cross worker, Geneva, WWII. Dir., Lucerne Festival, Lausanne Composition Master Classes, 1944-45; Guest Cond., Vienna & Salzburg Festivals & of leading orchs. in Europe, USA, Israel, Australis & A Am.. 1945-; I a Scala inaugural concorto, 1946; Musical Dir., Suisse Romande Orch., 1967-; Hon. Prof., Lausanne Conserv. Compositions incl: 3 Symphs.; Sinfonieta for Strings; Violin Concerto; Piano Concerto; 3 String Quartets; Concerto w. Ordenburg Phil. Orch., 1919. Career: Asst., Phonogramm-Archiv, Berlin Univ., 1926-33; Transcribed & Analysed var. Field Recordings for N. Western & Columbia Univs., w. Grants from Carnegie & Rockefeller Fndns.; Prague, 1933-38; Lived in Brussels, 1938-51; Music Therapist, St. Albans Naval Hosp., NY, 1952-66; Tchr., Ethnomusicology & Musical Acoustics, Univ. of Toronto, 1966-. Comps. incl: Concortino (Sopr., Str. Quartet, Piano), 1956; Hatikvah (Str. Quartet), 1960; Encounterpoint (Organ & Str. Quartet), 1973; 6 Settings of French Folksongs (Voice, Flute, Piano), 1969; Sonata (Piano), 1966, & many others. Recordings: Music for Dance Rhythms (Folkways Records). Publs: Studeis in Ethnomusicology, 2 vols., 1961, 1965. Contbr. to num. jrnls. inclng: Ethnomusicology; Jrnl. of Am. Musicological Soc.; Musical Quarterly; The Record Changer; Yearbook of the Int. Folk Music Coun.; Anthropos; Encyclopedia Int. & Britannica. Mbrships: Co-Fndr. & Former Pres., Soc. for Ethnomusicol.; Int. Folk Music Coun.; Can. Music Centre. Address: 87 Blantyre Ave., Scarborough, Ont., MIN 2R6, Canada.

KLECZKOWSKA-POSPIECH, Danuta, b. 13 July 1939, Wilno, USSR. Musician (harpsichord, piano). Educ: Music Lyceum, Warsaw; harpsichord & piano studies, Lodz Conserv. Acad. of Music, Poland; studied w. E Altberg, Aimée van de Wiele (Paris), Hans Pischner (Weimar). m. Wlodzimierz Pospiech, 1 s., 1 d. Debut: 1960. Career: (harpsichord) TV & radio apps.; Concerts w. Chmbr. Orchs., solo concerts & concerts w. orchs., Poland & abroad; Prof. of piano & harpsichord, Conserv., Warsaw, 1978-. Recordings: Ancient harpsichord music. Mbr., Soc. of Polish Musicians Artists SPAM, Warsaw. Hons: 1st Prize, Harpsichord, Polish Competition of Ancient Music in Lodz, 1960. Address: ul. Wukiennicza 5 m 64, 91-851 Lodz, Poland.

KLEIN, Edward Arthur, b. 24 Jan. 1940, Boston, Mass., USA. Cellist; Bass Gambist; Chamber Music Coach; String Instrument Repairer. Educ: BA., Swarthmore Coll., 1966; Study w. Jacobus Cornelius Langendoen, Zara Nelsova; Greenwood, 1953-54; Tanglewood, 1956-57; Instrument Repair Trng. w. Adolph Primavera. m. Sally Vexler, 2 d. Career: Cellist, Mass. All-State Orchs., 1954-58; Mbr., US Naval Acad. B and Cello, oboe, baritone horn & string bass; Wide theatre experience, inclng. Gilbert & Sullivan; Solo recitals; Cellist, Swarthmore Coll. Orch.; Bass Gambist, Am. Soc. of Ancient Instruments; Chmbr. Music Coach, Swarthmore Coll. Mbrships: Viola da Gamba Soc. of Am.; Brit. Viola da Gamba Soc.; Am. Recorded Soc.; Int. Harpsichord Soc.; Amateur Chmbr. Music Players. Address: 409 Woodward Rd., Moylan, PA 19065, USA.

KLEIN, Elisabeth, b. 23 July 1911, Hungary. Pianist. Educ: Grad. w. distinction, Liszt Acad. of Music, Budapest; studied w. Béla Bartok. m. Rear-Admiral Jorgen Petersen, 2 s. Debut: Copenhagen, Denmark, 1946. Career: Concerts & lectures, Denmark, Norway, Sweden, Hungary, Germany, Austria, USA,

UK & Middle East. w. repertoire of classical works & modern Scandinavian music; dedicatee, num. works; Radio & TV perfs.; Teaching appts., Royal Danish Conserv., Copenhagen, & Acad. of Music, Oslo, Norway. Recordings incl: All Bartok's works, Danish Radio; works by Poulenc, Norholm, Norgard, Fongaard. Hons: Danish Radio Music Prize, 1966. Address: Iranvej 2, 2300 Copenhagen, Denmark.

KLEIN, Kenneth, b. 5 Sept. 1939, Los Angeles, Calif, USA. Orchestral Conductor. Educ: BMus, Univ. of Southern Calif.; Pvte. cond. study w. Fritz Zweig, 8 yrs.; Studied w. Dr. Richard Lert, Inst. of Am. Symph. Orch. League; w. Isler Solomon, Aspen Fest, 1961 & Bayreuth Fest. Master Classes, 1966; Studied w. Nadia Boulanger, 1966. Debuts: LA, 1961; Paris 1974; Moscow, 1974; Vienna, 1975; Geneva, 1977; NYC, Carnegie Hall, 1977; Casals Fest.; Puerto Rico, 1977; Rome, 1979. Career: Music Dir., Guadalajara Symph., 1961-; Fndr.-Cond., Westside Symph. Orch., LA, 1963-68; Guest cond. apps., USSR, Rumania, Sweden, German Fed. Repub.; Buenos Aires; Mexico City; Houston Symph. & Ore. Symph.; 7 concerts w. PR Symph. by invitation of Pablo Casals; Tour as guest cond. w. Stuttgart Ballet, 1971; Artistic Dir., Homage to Pablo Casals, Guadalajara, 1975. Recordings: Mexican Contemporary Music; Chavez Symph. No. 1, 1979. Mbrships: Phi Kappa Lambda; Phi Kappa Phi. Hons: Coleman Chmbr. Music Award, Univ. of Southern Calif. String Quartet, 1962; String Dept. Award, Univ. of Southern Calif. Schl. of Music, 1962. Mgmt: Harold Shaw, Peter Gravina (Personal), USA; Konzertagentur Baron, Austria. Address: 716 Alta Drive, Beverly Hills, CA 90210, USA.

KLEIN, Lothar, b. 27 Jan. 1932, Hannover, Germany. Composer. Educ: Hochschule für Musik, Berlin; Free Univ., Berlin; PhD, Univ. of Minn. m. Marjories Johnson, 2 s. Career: Comp. of Symphonic, stage & film music; Works perfd. by Ancerl, Barbirolli, Dorati, Szell & Andrew Davis. Comps: 3 Symphs.; 2 Concertos for Violin & Cello; Paganini Collage, The Philosopher in the Kitchen (Alto & Orch.); Slices of Time for Trumpet & Strings; Musica Antiqua for Consort & Orch.; Dance Moods for Clarinet & Orch.; chmbr. music. Recordings: Musique a Go-Go, for Orch.; Janizary Music, for Wind Orch.; Exchanges, for Saxophone. Contbr. to: Music Educs. Jrnl.; The Comp.; var. musicol. publs. Mbr., ASCAP. Hons: Golden Reel Award, Am. Academy Film Science, 1955; Rockefeller Fndn. New Music Prize, 1967; McDowell Fellow, 1971; Fulbright Fellow, 1969. Address: Grad. Dept. of Music, Univ. of Toronto, Toronto, Can. 1, 29.

KLEIN, Mitchell Sardou, b. 13 Aug. 1947, NYC, USA. Conductor; Cellist; Teacher. Educ: BA, Brandeis Univ., 1968; BA Music, Coll. of Notre Dame, Belmont, Calif., 1972; MA, Calif. State Univ., Hayward, 1976; studied cello w. Irving M Klein, cond. w. var. masters. Career: Cond. w. var. orchs. inclng: Young People's Symph. Orch. (40th season), San Fran. Bay area, Calif. Music Ctr. Orch., Berkeley Promenade Orch. Youth Concerts, Coll. of Notre Dame Orch.; Fac. mbr., Coll. of Notre Dame, & Calif. Music Ctr., Los Altos; nat. TV apps.; radio perfs., San Fran.; Newspaper music critic, 1968-70. Mbrships incl: Conds. Guild; Am. Symph. Orch. League. Hobbies: Photography; Athletics; Stereophonic Sound Equipment. Address: 266 Lenox Ave., Oakland, CA 94610, USA.

KLEIN, Peter, b. 1930, Ceará, Brazil. Concert Pianist. Educ: Brazilian Conserv. of Music, Rio de Janeiro; studied w. William Kapell, NY & Bruno Seidhofer, Vienna. m. 1 d. Career: Soloist w. major orchs. of world, having perf. in 25 countries; Tchr., Music Schl., Univ. of Brazil; Superintendant Dir., Brazilian Symph. Orch. Hons: 1st Prize, Geneva Int. Competition, 1953; Paderewsky Medal, London; Cmdr., Nat. Order of Merit, Brazil; Kt. of Isabel the Catholic, Spain. Address: Paula Freitas 20, Rio de Janeiro, Brazil. 3.

KLEINSASSER, Jerome Stewart, b. 28 Mar. 1939, St. Paul, Minn., USA. College Professor; Musicologist; Choral Director. Educ: BSc, Univ. of Minn.; MA, ibid.; PhD, ibid. Publs: Ed., Henry Purcell's Magnificat, 1975: Mbrships: Am. Musicol. Soc.; Am. Choral Fndn. Hobbies: Book & Record Collecting; Running. Address: 3812 Amberwood Ln., Bakersfield, CA 93309, USA.

KLEMPERER, Regina Mushabac, b. 10 Sept. 1949, NYC, USA. Cellist. Educ: Juilliard Schl., Studied w. Leonard Rose, Preparatory Div., 1961-67; B Mus, 1971, M Mus & Perf. Cert., 1973, Ind. Univ.; studied cello & chmbr. music w. Janos Starker & other masters. Career: Teaching Asst. to Starker, Ind. Univ., 1971-73; Asst. Prof., Univ. of Ky., 1973-75; Baldwin-Wallace Coll., Berea, Ohio, 1975-; Prin. cellist, var. orchs., inclng. Ind. Univ. Phil., 1971-73, Lexington Phil., 1973-75, Ohio Chmbr. Players, currently. Solo perfs. w. var. orchs., 1973-; Mbr., Concord Trio, 1973-75; Mbr., Elysian Trio currently; num. chmbr. music recitals inclng. Tv perfs., Sao Paulo, Brazil, 1973. Hons. incl: Winner, Abraham & Strauss Competition, 1967; Schiffer Award, Ind. Univ., 1973. Address: 11 Strathallan Pk., Rochester, NY 14607, USA.

KLEPPER, Walter Mihai, b. 27 July 1929, Lugoj, Romania. Composer. Educ: Grad. Dip. in Comp., Conserv. Ciprian Porumbescu, Bucharest. m. (1) Hildegard Klepper, 1s, 2d; (2) Alina Cristina Klepper. Career: Lecturer on Harmony & Counterpoint, Conservs. in Bucharest & Brasov; Artistic Mgr., Opera Romana, Bucharest; Comp., 1973-. Comps. incl: (chmbr. music) Sonata for piano; Sonata duo, for flute & viola; Sonatina for violin & piano; Three Movements, for organ; Three poems for soprano & chmbr. orch., Remember; Sonatina for cello & piano; (Symph. Music) 2 Symphs. for large orch.; Symphonic Tryptich, Impressions from Reshitza, Concertino for wind instruments, piano-celesta & percussion; 2 Cantatas for Chorus & large orch.; Songs of Hiroshima; Divertimento for Strings & timpani; Season of Beauty; Chorus music, etc. (all recorded). Mbr., Union of Romanian Comps. Hons: The Romanian Union of Comps. Prize for Comp., 1977. Address: str. Brezoianu 10, Sc.A, ap. 14, 70624 Bucharest, Romania.

KLEVE, Endre, b. 2 Oct. 1949, Lillehammer, Norway. Violinist. Educ: Examen Artium, Oslo, 1968; Violin Studies w. Aruid Fladmoe & Prof. André Gertler, Brussels Conserv., 1968-73; Diplôme Superieur avec la plus Grande Distinction, Violin & Chmbr. Music. m. Djanati Shahrzad. Debut: Brussels, 1977; Oslo, 1972. Career: Soloist w. Symph. Orchs. in Oslo, Bergen, Trondheim & Oslo Radio; Brussels Conserv. Orch.; L'Orchestre Nat. de Belgique; Amsterdam Chmbr. Orch.; Portugal Radio Orch.; Sev. radio & TV apps., Scandinavia, Belgium, Netherlands; Concertmaster, Theatre de la Monnaie, Opera Nat. de Belgique, 1975-; Asst. Prof. of Violin, Brussels Conserv., 1977-; Mbr., Ensemble Musique Nouvelle, Liège; Formed String Quartet, 'Le Quatuor Grieg De Bruxelles', 1976. Address: 44 rue Capouillet, 1060 Brussels, Belgium.

KLIEN, Walter, b. 27 Nov. 1928, Graz, Austria. Concert Pianist. Educ: Study in FrankfurtMain, Vienna & Graz. Career: Worldwide concert tours w. maj. orchs.; Fest. apps., Vienna, Salzburg, Israel, Edinburgh, Marlboro, USA, Lucerne, Bregenz, Prague, Berlin, Bonn, Dubrovnik, Athens. Num. recordings inclng. 1st complete set of solo works by Brahms; Complete colo Mozart works, complete Schubert sonatas. Hons: Prizes, Int. Piano Competitions, Bolzano, 1952, Paris, 1953, Vienna, 1953; Viener Flötenuhr, Best Mozart Record of Year, 1970. Mgmt: Harold Holt Ltd., London. Address: Singerstr. 27, 1010 Viennas, Austria.

KLIMA, Stanislav Václav, b. 13 March 1927, Prague, Czechoslovakia. Official. Educ: Georgetown Univ., Wash. DC, USA; JD, Charles Univ., Prague, Czechoslovakia, 1951. m. Eva Dobiásová, 2 d. Career: Writer of articles on music hist. for newspapers & mags., 1952-; Music hist. progs. for Prague Radio & Music Theatre. Publs: Josef Slafik, 1806-33, 1956; Jan Václav Hugo Vorlsek, 1791-1825, 1966; Muzikantské historky (Stories & Anecdotes about Musicians), 1970. Contbr. to num. musical jrnls. & dictionaries, inclng. Hudebni rozhledy, Opus Musicum, Monthly Musical Record, Musical Times, etc. Hobbies: Philately; Photography; Travel. Address: Moldavská 9, 101 00 Prague 10, Vrsovice, Czechoslovakia.

KLIMISCH, (Sister) Mary Jane, b. 22 Aug. 1920, Utica, SD, USA. Musicologist; Keyboard Performer. Educ: BA, St. Mary-of-the-Woods Coll., Ind.; M Mus Ed. Am. Conserv., Chgo.; PhD, Wash. Univ., St. Louis; studied Gregorian chant under Dom Desrocquettes & Dom Gajard of Solesmes. Career incls: Dir. of Sacred Music Resource Ctr. (Gregorian chant collect.). Comps: Mass to honor Joan of Arc; Threnody (voices & electronic sound sources). Contbr. to: AGO Quarterly; Caecilia mag. Mbrships: Am. Musicol. Soc.; Sub-Dean-Dean, AGO; 1st VP, Delta Kappa Gamma; Moderator, Delta Mu Theta. Recip. var. hons. Hobbies: Reading; Writing; Calligraphy. Address: Mt. Marty Coll., Yankton, SD 57078, USA. 5.

KLIMO, Stefan b. 1 Nov. 1919, Zvolen, Czechoslovakia. Artistic Director. Educ: LLD; studied w. Prof. Jelinek; Acad. of Music. m. Maria Bobokova, 2 s., 1 d. Debut: Cond., Tatran Choir. Career: Perfs. in USA, Switzerland, Italy, W Germany, UK, USSR, Yugoslavia, Rumania, Czechoslovakia; Artistic Dir., Lucnica Ensemble; Artistic Mgr., Cond., Lucnica Choir. Compositions: The Hay-Making Songs, women's choir; Songs From East Slovakia, choir; Pasture Songs, solo & women's choir; At Dawn, choir; Songs From Liptow Region, men's choir. Recordings: Ravel, Monteverdi, Palestrina, Festa, Schubert, Hassler, Morley, Dvorak, Eben, Suchon, Cikker, Mikula, Kardos, Hrusovsky, Moyzes. Contbr. to: Musical Life; Rhythm. Mbrships: Assn. of Slovak Comps.; Hd., Concert Artists Dept., Slovak Musical Fund; Dpty., Slovak Concert Artists; Mbr. Ed.

Staff, Opus & Slovkoncert, Musical Dept., Min. of Culture, Singing Advsry. Dept. Hons: Artist of Merit, Czech Govt.; World Fest. Laureate, Moscow; Special Cond.'s Prize, Song Contest, Arezzo, 1967; Fritz Kafenda's Prize, 1968. Hobbies: Automobiles; Travel. Mgmt: Min. of Culture. Address: 56 Astrova, Bratislava, Travniky, Czechoslovakia.

KLINDA, Ferdinand, b. 12 Mar. 1929, Kosice Czech. Concert Organist; Professor. Educ: Med.Dr., Univ. of Bratislava, 1952; dip., Conserv. of Bratislava, 1950; concert dip., Acad. of Music, Bratislava, 1954; studies in Prague & Weimar. m. Luba Klindová, 2d. Career: 8 concert tours in USSR; recitals in all European capitals; concert tours & master classes in USA; perfs. at fests. incl. Rome, Paris, Vienna, Prague, Helsinki, Budapest, Zürich, Leipzig, Moscow & Leningrad; orchl. concerts w. ldng. conds. incl. K Ancerl, H Adler, S Baudo, E Bour, A Dorati, G Rozhdestvensky. Recordings: works by Bach, Liszt, Franck, Messiaen, Haydn, old Czech. & Slovak masters, contemporary Czech. comps., etc. Publs: Slovak Organ Music, I, 1957, II, 1964; Organ Interpretation, I & II, 1980. Contbr. to Musik und Kirche. mbr., Int. Bachgesellschaft. Hons: Czech. State Prize, 1971; Merited Artist of Czech., 1978. Hobby: Medicine. Mgmt. Slovkoncert, Bratislava. Address: Langsfeldova 23, 80900 Bratislava, Czech.

KLING, Paul, b. 28 March 1929, Opava, Czechoslovakia. Violinist. Educ: Brno State Conserv.; Prague Acad. of Music; Artist Dip. m. Taka Shimazaki, 1 d. Debut: Soloist w. Vienna Symph., 1935. Career: Concert Violinist. Prague, Vienna, Tokyo, Paris, London, NY etc.; Concertmaster, Vienna, Tokyo, Louisville; Prof., Univ. of Arts, Tokyo, Kunitachi Univ., Tokyo, Univ. of Louisville, Univ. of Victoria. Recordings: Beethoven Sonatas 4 & 5; Britten, Martin & Blackwood Violin Concertos. Mbrships: Am. String Tchrs. Assn.; AAUP; Am. Fedn. of Musicians; Hon. Life mbr., NHK Symph., Tokyo, 1955. Hons: Prof., Kunitachi Univ., Tokyo; Imperial Award for Cultural Merits, Tokyo, Col. of Commonwealth, Ky., 1969. Hobby: Travel. Address: Univ. of Victoria, B.C., V8W Y2Y, Can. 7.

KLING, Taka Shimazaki, b. 1 Aug. 1936, Kyoto, Japan. Harpist. Educ: B Mus., B Mus Ed., M Mus., M Mus Ed., Tokyo Univ. of Arts; Artist Dip., Vienna State Acad. m. Paul Kling, 1 d. Career: Harpist, NHK Symph. (Tokyo), Louisville Orch. (Princ.); Recitals, Radio, TV, Japan, Austria, USA; Tchr., Tokyo Univ. of Arts, Univ. of Louisville. Recordings: Marcel Grandjany; Aria in Classic Style. Mbr. & past Chapt. Pres., Am. Harp Soc. Address: c/o Univ. of Victoria, B.C., V8W YTY, Can.

KLINKO, Albert, b. 18 July 1924, Jaszbereny, Hungary. Horn Player. Educ: Franz Liszt Acad. of Music, Budapest, 1940-48; studied w. Mason Jones, USA, 1953-56. m. Hedwig Jud Klinko, 1 s. Debut: Horn Soloist, Budapest Concert Orch., 1944. Career incls: Solo Horn, Budapest Opera & Phil. Orch., 1945-48, Tonhalle Orch., 1948-52; 1 season as 1st Horn, Denver Symph. Orch.; 2 yrs. in NYC w. NYC Opera, Symph. of the Air & RCA Victor Orch.; Solo Horn, Winterthurer Stadtorchester, Switz., 1956-. Recordings: Mozart Sinfonia concertante in E flat, KV 297b. Mbr. & Contbr., Int. Horn Soc. Recip., 1st Prize, Hungarian Nat. Competition for Int. Concours, Geneva, 1948. Hobbies: Oil Painting; Haute Cuisine. Address: Palm Str. 24, 8400 Winterthur, Switz.

KLINKON, Ervin O, b. 24 July 1933, Bozen, Italy. Associate Professor of Music; Cellist; Conductor. Educ: Hochschule für Music, Freiburg, Germany; Mannes Coll. of Music, NY; BM, Univ. of Houston; MM, Cath. Univ., Wash. DC. m. Sarah C Klinkon, 1 s., 1 d. Career: Mbr., Houston Symph.; Prin. Cellist, Nat. Gall. Orch., & Filene Ctr. Orch.; Solo & Chmbr. concerts, Germany & USA; Tchr., Geo. Wash. & Am. Univs.; Currently, Montgomery Coll. Mbrships: MENC; ASTA; MSTA; Phi Kappa Phi. Publs: Harmony & Workbook, 1975. Hobbies: Camping; Sailing. Address: 5206 Locust Ave., Bethesda, MD 20014, USA.

KLIPPSTATTER, Kurt, b. 17 Dec. 1934, Graz, Austria. Conductor. Educ: matura, humanistic gymnasium; studied violin, viola, piano, conducting, accomp. & theory. m. Mignon Dunn. Debut: Graz. Career: Coach & Cond., Graz, Vienna, Dortmund, Pforzheim, Saarbrüken, Düsseldorf; Cond., Krefeld, Vienna; Res. Cond.; Memphis Opera Theatre, 1972-, also Artistic Dir., 1974-; Music Dir., Ark. Symph. Soc.; Cond., Memphis State Univ. Hobby: Music. Address: 6605 Granada Dr., Little Rock, AR 72205, USA. 2.

KLOBUCAR, Andelko, b. 11 July 1931, Zagreb, Croatia, Yugoslavia. Composer; Organist. Educ: Dip., Musical Acad., Zagreb, 1956; Studies in Paris & Salzburg. Debut: Zagreb, 1956. Career incls: Docent, Musical Acad., Zagreb, 1959-; Chief Organist, Zagreb Cathedral; Solo concerts in Yugoslavia & abroad inclng: Westminster Cathedral, London. Comps. incl:

Symphony, 1966; Music for Strings, 1967; Two Sonatas for viola & piano, 1972, 73; 2 Sonatas for Organ, 1966, 69; Film music & choir music. Num. recordings inclng: Anthology of Croatian Music. Publs: Franjo Dugan: Life and Work, 1969. Contbr. to St. Cecilija (review for ch. music), Zagreb. Mbr. num. profl. orgs. Hons. incl: Zagreb Film Award, 1968; Micka Trinina Award, 1970. Hobby: Watercolour Painting. Address: Vlaska 72c, Zagreb, Yugoslavia.

KLOOS, Diet, b. 9 May 1929, Dordrecht, Netherlands. Singer (Contralto). Educ: Royal Conserv. of Music, The Hague; studied w. Charles Panzera, Paris; summercourse w. Giorgio Favaretto, Siena. m. Jan Kloos, dec. Debut: Arnhem, 1953. Career: apps. as contralto, singing lieder, concerts & oratorios, Germany, Netherlands, France, Belgium; Tchr., Brabants Conserv. for Music, Tilburg, 1961-. Sev. recordings. Recip. sev. acad. awards; Prize, Int. Concours Verviers, 1954. Address: 18 Lievershil, 3332 RJ Zwinjndrecht, Netherlands.

KLOP, Hendrik Teunis, b. 5 June 1946, Hardinxveld-Giessendam, Netherlands. Organist; Pianist; Oboist; Conductor; Composer; Painter. Educ: Solo Dip. w. distinction, Conserv., Rotterdam; studied w. Jean Langlais, Schola Cantorum, Paris. m. Rita Schneiter. Debut: Sint Laurenskerk in Rotterdam, 1969. Career: Organ recitals in churches & concert halls (mostly De Doelen, Rotterdam); Recital for Dutch TV; Radio recitals, AVRO & NCRV, broadcasting cos. Recordings: sev. Recently made recordings on the Cavaillé-Coll organ of Saint-Clotilde in Paris w. unknown comps. of Franck, Pierné, Tournemire & Langlais. Mbr., KNTV., Amsterdam. Hons: Prix de virtuosité pour interprétation et improvisation, Paris 1971; Prix d'excellence, Rotterdam, 1972. Hobbies: Interpreting French Organ Music; Modern Painting. Address: Peulenlaan 214, Hardinxveld-Giessendam, The Netherlands.

KLOPFENSTEIN, René, b. 15 Aug. 1927, Lausanne, Switzerland. Conductor; Festival Music Director. Educ: Lic. philos., Univ. of Basle; Mozarteum, Salzburg, Austria (1st Prize for Cond.); Paris Conserv., France. m. Nicole Hirsch, 2 children. Career: Debut: w. var. orchs. age 20. Career: Concert Agent & Gen. Sec., Schola Cantorum, Paris; Artistic Dir., Philips Records, 10 yrs.; Comeback as Cond. w. Concerts Lamoureux Orch., Paris, 1967; Dir., Montreux-Vevey Music Fest., Switzerland, 1968-; Concerts in Latin Am., Europe, Japan, USSR, etc.; Cond. w. num. major orchs. Recordings incl: Works by Mozart, Haydn, Arne, CPE Bach, Lalo, C Ferras, Mendelssohn. Hons: Grand Prix du Disque, Paris; Off. of Cultural Merit. Hobbies: Cooking; Gardening. Address: Villa Fidelio, CH.1823 Glion, Switzerland.

KLOTMAN, Robert Howard, b. 22 Nov. 1918, Cleveland, Ohio, USA. Music Educator; Violinist. Educ: BS, Ohio Northern Univ.; MMus, Western Reserve Univ.; EdD, Tchrs. Coll., Columbia Univ. m. Phyllis Rauch Klotman, 1 d., 1 s. Career incls: Dir. of Music Educ., Akron, Ohio Public Schls., 1959-64; Detroit, Mich. Pub. Schls., 1964-69; Chmn., Music Educ. Dept., Prof. of Music, Ind. Univ. Schl. of Music, Bloomington, 1969-; Cond., var. orchs. inclng. All-State Orchs. in Mich., Utah, Ga., Tex., Ohio, Minn., etc. Comps: String Music For Young People; Renaissance Suite; Gymnopedie, Satie-Klotman; Birchard Orch. Folio; Jesu, Joy of Man's Desiring, Bach. Publs. incl: Learning To Teach Through Playing; String Techniques & Pedagogy (w. Ernest Harris), 1971; School Music Administrator & Supervisor; Action With Strings; The Encyclopedia of Education. Contbr. to musical jrnls. Mbrships. incl: MENC (Pres., 1976-78, VP, 1978-); ASCAP; Phi Mu Alpha Sinfonia. Recip. of hons. Address: 2740 Spicewood Lane, Bloomington, IN 47401, USA. 2, 4, 289

KLOTZ, Hans, b. 25 Oct. 1900, Offenbach (Main), Germany. Professor. Educ: Dr.phil., Univ. of Frankfurt am Main, 1927; Grad., Landeskonservatorium, Leipzig, 1929. m. Anneliese Hartenfels, 3 d. Career: Organist, Evangelische Hauptkirche, Aachen, 1928; Ch. music Dir., Flensburg St. Nikolai, 1946; Prof., Staatliche Hochschule für Musick, Cologne, 1954. Compositions: Alma Redemptoris Mater; 16 Vorspiele zu evangelischen Kirchenliedern; Prelude a l'Introit "dicit Dominus Ego" Recording Wachet auf.; ruft uns die Stimme, by Max Reger. Publs: Über die Orgelkunst der Gotik, der Renaissance & des Barock, 1934, new ed. 1975, Das Buch von der Orgel, 1938, 8th ed. 1972. Contbr. to num. profl. publs. Mbr., num. profl. orgs. Address: Klarenbachstr. 190, D 5000 Cologne 41, German Fed. Repub. 14.

KLUG, Heinrich, b. 4 May 1935, Dresden, Germany. Solo Cellist. Educ: Studied cello & conducting, Hochschule für Musik, Dresden & Cologne. m. Barbara Klug, 1 s., 1 d. Career: Solo Cellist, Chmbr. Orch. of the Rhine, 1959; 1st Solo Cellist, Wuppertal Orch. & Lectr., Bergisches Landeskonservatorium, 1960-63; 1st Solo Cellist, Munich Phil. Orch., 1963-; Cello

concerts & recitals in all large German towns. Author of ed. of cello music (works by Franz Schubert, Franz Danzi & Anton Filtz). Address: Gautingerstr. 2, 8035 Buchendorf/Mü, German Fed. Repub.

KLUPAK, Jaroslav, b. 26 May 1920, Prague, Czech. Composer. Educ: Dip., Conserv. of Music, Prague. m. Lydia Pesek. Career: Musical Dir., Czech. Radio Stn.; Composer. Compositions incl: 1st Str. Quartet; Dramatic Overture for Large Symph. Orch.; Sonatina for Piano; Philosophical Sketches for Piano; Asteroids Suite for Winds & Percussion; 'The Seconds' Suite for piano & violin solo w. str. chmbr. orch.; Reincarnation for 2 accordions, chmbr. orch. & percussion; Symfoniette for 20 winds, piano & drums; Panychida 218 for Str. Orch.; Atlantis Symph. (orch., choir & female voice); 7 Found Songs (from Carl Sandburg) for lower voice & piano. Mbrships: Composer's Rights Assn. (OSA); Union of Czech. Composers, until 1969; Am. Accordion Musicol. Soc. for Rsch. & Seminars. Hons: Award, Czech. Musical Fund, 1966 & 68. Hobbies: Aviation History; Aircraft Modelling. Address: Jiráskovo Namesti 26, 301 54 Pizen 1, Czech.

KLUSAK, Jan-Filip, b. 18 Apr. 1934, Prague, Czechoslovakia. Composer. Educ: Acad. of Music & Dramatic Arts, Prague; studied comp. w. Jaroslav Ridky & Pavel Borkovec, 1953-57. 1 s. Compositions incl: (publd.) Four Small Vocal Exercises, 1960; 1-4-3-2-5-6-7-10-9-8-11 for Flute, 1965; Rondo for Piano, 1967; (publd. & recorded) Pictures for 12 Wind Instruments, 1960; 1st Invention for Chamber Orchestra, 1961; 2nd String Quartet, 1961-62; Variations on Theme by Gustav Mahler for Orchestra, 1960-62; Sonata for Violin & Wind Instrument, 1965-65. Contbr. to: Hudebni Rozhledy, 1962, 1965; Konfrontace, 1969; Opus Musicum, 1971, 1973. Mbrships: Union of Czechoslovak Comps., 1959-69; Umelecká Beseda, 1968-72. Hons: Prize (for comp.) Troisième Biennale, Paris, France, 1963. Hobbies: Astrology; Actor in 6 Czech Films, & in Jára Cimrman's Theater, Prague. Address: Blanická 26, 120 00 Prague 2, Czechoslovakia.

KLYMSHYN, Eugene John, b. 5 Mar. 1945, NY, NY, USA. Organist; Teacher, Lavelle School for the Blind. Educ: BA, Adelphi Univ., Garden City, NY; Courses in Musicol., Queens Coll., Flushing, NY; studied Piano w. Florence Halpin & George Bennette, Theory w. Gerard Gabrielli, & Organ w. Herbert Seversten & Frances Mains. Career: Tchr. of Piano, Organ, Recorder, Theory, Music History, Piano Tuning, Lavelle Schl. for the Blind, NY; Organist, St. Philip Neri Cath. ch., ibid; Asst. Accomp., Welch Chorale; apps. w. Chorale in num. Chs., NY area, inclng. St. Patrick's Cathedral. Mbrships: MENC; Am. Theatre Organ Soc.; Welch Chorale, St. Philip Neri Ch. Hons: Piano Award & Student of the Yr., 1960, Piano Award, 1961, Piano & Clarinet Award, 1961, Klopfer Award, 1964, Lighthouse Music Schl., NY Assn. for the Blind; Local Award 1961 & Dist. Award 1963, for Piano, NFSM. Hobbies: Collecting Antique Chime Clocks; Collecting Acoustical 78 rpm Recordings & Acoustical Phonographs & Music Boxes; Restoring Harmoniums; Railroad & Subway trips w. a Railroad Club. Address: 770-4E 221 St., Bronx, NY 10467, USA.

KMENTT, Waldemar, b. 2 Feb. 1929, Vienna, Austria. Lyric Tenor. Educ: Acad. of Music & Dramatic Art, Vienna. m. Rosemarie Rainer, 1 d. Career: Mbr., Vienna State Opera, 1951-; apps. at Salzburg Fests., 1956-; guest artist, Europe, Latin Am. & the Far E. Recordings: Decca. Hons. incl: Kammersänger, Austria, 1962-. Address: 36 Johann Straussgasse, Vienna 4, Austria. 2.

KNAPP, Alexander Victor, b. 13 May, 1945, London, UK. Lecturer. Educ: BA, MusB, MA, Selwyn Coll., CAmbridge; Dept. of Ethnomusicol., Jewish Theol. Sem. of Am., NYC; ARCM; LRAM. m. Caroline Mary Robinson, 1 d. Debut: Wigmore Hall, London, 1975. Career: Asst. Dir. of Studies, RCM, London; Vist. Lectr. in Jewish Music, Leo Baeck Coll., London; BBC Racio 3 Illustrated talk, Bloch, A Reassessment, 1977. Recordings: Cantor Naftali Herstik (Hear O Israel); Cantor Johnny Gluck. Contbr. to var. profl. jrnls. Mbrships incl: Staff Rep. in UK, Ernest Bloch Soc.; Royal Musical Assn.; Soc. for Ethnomusicol., Jewish Theol. Sem. NYC, 1968-69; Winston Churchill Travelling Fellowship in Religious Art, 1976. Hobbies: Chess; Table Tennis. Address: 15 Sutherland Grove, London, SW18 5PS, UK.

KNAPP, Peter, b. 4 Aug. 1947, Aylesbury, UK. Singer (Baritone). Educ: Pvte. studies w. Tito Gobbi, etc. Debut: as Count, Le Nozze di Figaro, Glyndebourne Tour, 1973. Career: Kent Opera; Engl. Nat. Opera; BBC TV; Num. BBC Radio recitals; Concert & Opera apps. abroad; Dir. of the Singers Company. Recordings: Monteverdi Vespers; da Falla, Master Peter. Hons: Winner of First Benson & Hedges Gold Award. Hobby: Sport. Address: 52 Randolph Ave., London W9, UK.

KNAPTON, Frederick William, b. 28 Mar. 1931, Bath, Somerset, UK. Pipe Organ Builder. Educ: Secondary technical. m. Margaret Eileen Haylock, 2 s., 1 d. Career: Apprenticeship, Wm. Hill & Son, & Norman & Beard Ltd., 5 yrs.; Air Frame Mechanic, RAF, 2 yrs.; London staff of Rushworth & Dreaper, 2 yrs.; Ont. & Northern NY Rep., Wm. Hill & Son & Norman & Beard Ltd., 1959-; Formed own co. & became concessionaire to Hill, Norman & Beard Ltd., 1974. Mbrships: Pres., 1975-76, Royal Canadian AF Assn., 416 Kingston; Dir., Assoc. Canadian Travellers Kingston Club; RCCO, Kingston, Ont., Chapt.; St. Lawrence River Chapt., AGO. Hobbies: General music interests; Electronics; Radio & TV; Wine making. Address: 36 Morden Crescent, Amherstview, Ont. K7N 1K2, Can.

KNAUS, Hans Herwig, b. 21 Sept. 1929, St. VeitGlan, Kärnten, Austria. Professor of Music. Educ: Tchr's Qualification, 1958, Dr Phil, 1959, Vienna Univ.; Dip., Acad. of Music, Vienna, 1954. m. Margarete Knaus, 2 d. Career: Insp. of Music Educ., 1976. Contbr. to Publs. in field. Mbrships: Soc. for Music Rsch.; Austrian Soc. for Music Rsch.; City Schls. Coun., Bd. of Govs., Vienna; Hist. Club, Kärnten. Hons. incl: Theodor Körnerpreiis, 1969 & 72. Hobbies: Mtn. climbing; Swimming; Reading; Cooking. Address: Theresianumg 8/18, Vienna 1040, Austria.

KNECHTEL, (Alban) Baird, b. 22 May 1937, Hanover, Ont., Can. Teacher; Violist. Educ: BMus, Univ. of Toronto, 1959; MMus, Eastman Schl. of Music, Rochester, NY, 1970; ARCT (viola), 1963. m. Maria Eugenia Kohut, 2 d. Career: mbr., solo viola, TV apps. w. Chmbr. Players of Toronto; Hd. of Music, Emery Collegiate Inst. (N York Bd. of Educ.), 1967-79; Hd. of Music Dept., Northview Heights Secondary Schl., N York, 1979-; viola player, var. orchs. & ensembles. Comps: 27 Etudes for Strings, 1978. Recordings: for CBC w. Chmbr. Players of Toronto. Contbr. to Recorder Mag.; Notes Mag. Mbrships: Ont. Music Educators Assn. (past pres.); Int. Viola Rsch. Soc. (Can. rep.); Toronto Musicians Assn.; Can. & Am. Str. Tchrs. Assns.; Int. Soc. for Music Educ. Hons: Special Dip., ARCT; Pi Kappa Lambda; Hilroy Award for Innovative Tchng. in the Humanities, 1970. Hobbies incl: Furniture Making; Model Airplane Building & Flying; Stamp Collecting; Photography. Address: 103 North Dr., Islington, Ont. M9A 4R5, Can.

KNEPLER, Georg, b. 21 Dec. 1906, Wien, Osterreich. Musicologist. Educ: Dr. Phil., Univ. Vienna; Studied piano w. Eduard Steuermann; Comp. w. Hans Gal. m. Florence Wiles, 1 s. Career: Dir., Hochschule fur Musik, German Democratic Repub., 1949-59; Dir., Inst. of Musicol., Humboldt Univ., Berlin, German Democratic Repub., 1959-70; Ed.-in-Chief, Beitrage zur Musikwissenschaft Quarterly, 1960-. Publs. incl: Musikgeschichte des 19. Jahrhunderts, 2 vols., Henschelverlag, 1961; Geschichte als Weg zum Musiverständnis, Leipzig, 1977. Reden, Referate, Versuche, Kritiken (Collected Essays), Berlin, 1977 (in print); Var. other essays. Mbr. Acad. of Sci. of GDR. Recip. Nat. Prize of German Democratic Repub., 1962. Address: Strasse 901, Nr. 8. DDR - 118 Berlin, German Democratic Repub.

KNEPPER, Noah Allen, b. 14 Nov. 1921, Columbus, Ohio, USA. Professor of Woodwind Instrument; Professional Orchestra Performer; Musician (Oboe; Bassoon; Clarinet; Saxophone; Flute). Educ: B Mus, Univ. Mich., 1947; M Mus, ibid., 1948. m. Dorothy Bosscawen Knepper, 2 s., 1 d. Career: Woodwind Prof., var. univs., currently, Tex. Christian Univ., Ft. Worth, 1968-. Recordings: Films, film strips & commercial 'jingles'. Contbr. to: Instrumentalist Mag.; Schl. Musician; Woodwind Mag. Mbrships: Treas., Int. Double Reed Soc.; Int. Clarinet Soc.; Nat. Assn. Coll. Wind & Percussion Instructors. Address: 3408 Westcliff Rd. S., Ft. Worth, TX 76109, USA.

KNESS, Richard M, b. 23 July 1937, Rockford, Ill., USA. Dramatic Tenor & Heldentenor. Educ: BA, San Diego State Univ.; Studied w. Prof. Clemens Kaiser-Breme, Essen, Fed. Repub. Germany; Martial Singher, Phila., Pa.; Frederick Wilkerson, Wash. DC; Mme. Marinka Gurewich, NYC; Daniel Ferro, Prof. of Music, Manhattan & Juilliard Schls. m. Joann Grillo, 3 children. Debut: Duca di Mantova (Rigoletto), St. Louis Opera, Mo., USA, 1966. Career: Res. Mbr., NYC Opera. Recordings incl: Beethoven 9th Symph., Pitts. Symph. Mbrships: NYC Athletic Club; Lions Int. Recip. Grammy Award for Best Classical Recording, 1967. Hobbies: Cooking; Making Jewelry; Archaeol.; Travel. Mgmt: Schulz Agcy., Munich, Germany. Address: Metropolitan Opera, NY, NY 10023, USA.

KNFUSSLIN, Fritz, b. 25 Apr. 1917, Basel, Switzerland. Cond.; Music tchr.; Music publr. Educ: read Law, Econs.; pvte. music studies. Career: 1941 Cond. Basel Orch. Soc., var. choirs; Cond. tours through Europe; since 1946 Cond., Music tchr. Delsberg, Pruntrut. Publs. incl: Re-ed. Albinoni, Concerti a clinque, op 5, nr. 5; Rosetti, Wind Quintet in ES major; L

Mozart, Trumpet Concerto in D major; W A Mozart, Aria; Ombra Felice, KV 255; Schubert, Slave Regina, for soprano and str., op 153. Hobbies: Bringing back to life music works from the 18th Century. Address: Amselstr. 43, CH-4059 Basel, Switzerland.

KNIEBUSCH, Carol Lee, b. 15 Aug. 1938, Woodstock, Ill., USA. Flute Professor. Educ: BMus Ed., Ill. Wesleyan Univ., 1960; MMus, Ind. Univ., 1962; Pvte. study w. Marcel Moyse, Samuel Baron & James Pellerite, John Krell, Harry Houdeshel & Britton Johnson; Master classes w. James Galway & William Bennett. Career: Instr., Univ. of BC, 1962-66; Flautist, Vancouver Symph. Orch., 1964-66; Flautist, Baltimore Symph. Orch., 1966-69; Flute Prof., James Madison Univ. Comps: Ed., Flute Concerto in D Major (F J Haydn) & Two Concert Duets for Two Flutes & Piano (E Koehler). Publs: Analysis of Major Orchestra Master Contracts, 1972; Analysis of Metropolitan Orchestra Contracts, 1972. Contbr. to: The School Musician (permanent Flute Ed.); The Nat. Flute Assn. Newsletter; Woodwind World; Notes. Mbrships: Nat. Flute Assn.; Am. Fedn. of Musicians; Delta Omicron; Music Tchrs. Nat. Assn.; Nat. Theory Soc.; NACWPI; Coll. Music Soc.; Women Band Dirs. Nat. Assn. Hobby: Breeding & showing pekingese dogs. Address: Music Dept., James Madison Univ., Harrisonburg, VA 22807, USA.

KNIETER, Gerard L, b. 2 June 1931, Brooklyn, NY, USA. Professor of Music Education; Conductor; Clarinettist. Educ: BS, MA, NY Univ.; EdD, Columbia Univ.; Studied clarinet w. Leon Russianoff; studied Cond. w. Norvel Church, Harry Wilson, Luther Goodhart. m. Barbara C Cashetta. Career: Prof. of Music Educ., & Chmn., Dept. of Music Educ., Temple Univ., Phila., Pa.; Mbr., Ed. Committee, Jrnl. of Rsch. in Music Educ.; Ed. Cons., Jrnl. of Aesthetic Educ.; Mbr., Bd. of Dirs., Theodore Presser Co., & Initial Teaching Alphabet Fndn. Contbr. to: Towards an Aesthetic Education, ed. Reimer, 1972; National Dance Education Conference, ed. Chapman, 1973; Ency. of Educ., Vol. VI; Tchrs. Coll. Record; Music Educators Jrnl. Mbrships: Soc. for Ethnomusicol.; Assn. for Supervision & Curriculum Dev.; Coll. Music Soc.; MENC; AAUP. Recip., Arch. Award, NY Univ. Address: 853 Goshen Rd., Newtown Square, PA 19073, USA. 2.

KNIGHT, Brenda Mary, b. 13 Dec. 1926, London, UK. Music Teacher. Educ: RCM, London; GRSM; ARCO; LRAM; ARCM (pianoforte & clarinet). Career: Piano Mistress, Sydenham High Schl., 1946-51; Music Mistress, St. James' Schl., W Malvern, 1951-54; Dir. of Music, St. Audries Schl. W Quantoxhead, 1954-. Mbrships: ISM; Assn. of Asst. Masters & Mistresses; St. John Ambulance (Div. Supt. & Bandmaster). Hons: Serving Sister Venerable Order St. John of Jerusalem, 1977. Hobbies: Gardening; Lapidary. Address: Ivy Cottage, Sampford Brett, Taunton, Somerset, UK. 27.

KNIGHT, Gerald Hocken, b. 1908, Cornwall, UK. Church Musician. Educ: Mus B., Ma, Peterhouse, Cambridge; Royal Schl. of Engl. Ch. Music; RCM; ADCM. Career: Organist & Choirmaster, St. Augustine's Ch., Queen's Gate, 1931-37, & Canterbury Cathedral, 1937-52; Dir., Royal Schl. of Ch. Music, 1952-72. Publs: Hymns Ancient & Modern (revised ed., jt. music ed.); Manual of Plainsong (revised psalter); Treasury of English Church Music, 5 vols.; Revised Parish Psalter (ed); accomps. for unison hymn-singing. Hons: CBE; FRCO; FRSCM; 1 Fellow, Westminster Choir, Coll., Princeton, NY, USA. Mbr: Athenaeum Club; Hon. Fellow, St. Michael's Choir, Tenbury. Address: 18 Warrington Cres., London W9 1EL, UK. 3.

KNIGHT, Janice Mary, b. 17 Apr. 1947, Crewkerne, Somerset, UK. Oboist. Educ: RAm, London; GRSM; LRAM. m. Stephen Block. Debut: W. Sartori String Quartet, Purcell Room, 1972; W. Kathleen Kennedy, piano, Wigmore Hall, 1973. Career: Freelance oboist (orchl.) w. an interest in solo work & chmbr. music; Recitals & Concerts in London & Far East; Solo apps., UK & Europe. Mbrships: ISM; Musicians Union. Hobbies: Gardening; Reading; Cookery. Address: 31 Petworth Rd., Finchley, London N12 9HE, UK.

KNIGHT, Mark, b. 29 Mar. 1916, Gunnislake, Cornwall, UK. Organist & Choirmaster; Bass Singer; Teacher. Educ: ARCO (CHM). m. Anne Morris. Career: Organist & Choirmaster, num. Chs., currently Royal Garrison Ch., Woolwich; Pvte. Tchr., Organ. Contbr. to: Musical Opinion; Organists Review. Mbrships: Brit. Horological Inst.; Chmn., Electronic Organ Constructers' Soc.; Organ Club; Amateur Entomologists' Soc. Hobbies: Electronics; Entomol.; Horol. Address: Royal Garrison Ch., Royal Mil. Acad., Woolwich, London SE18, UK.

KNIGHT, Mark Anthony, b. 24 April 1941, Kidderminster, Worcs., UK. Musician (violinist, violist); Teacher; Conductor. Educ: GSM, London; AGSM, 1963. m. Patricia Richards, 1 d.,

1 s. Career: Ldr., New Cantata Orch. of London, 1963-67; Cond., Wells Cathedral Schl. Chmbr. Orch. - many broadcasts & TV apps.; Concerts, Bath Fest., 1977-78, St. John's, Smith Square, London, 1978, '79; Wigmore Hall, 1976, '77, etc.; currently Prin. Specialist String Tchr., Wells Cathedral Schl. & Prof. of Violin & Viola, GSM, London. Mbrships: European String Tchrs. Assn.; ISM; Musicians Union; Nat. Assn. of Tchrs. In Further & Higher Educ. Hons: Anonymous Donation of Violin, 1967. Hobbies: Squash; Steam Locomotives & Railway Preservation. Address: 17 Clements Close, Wells, Somerset, UK.

KNIGHT, Norman James Clode, b. 9 June 1931, London, UK. Flautist. Educ: RAM; FRAM; ARAM. Career: Prof., RAM, 1953-; Prof., Nat. Youth Orch.; Mbr., Engl. Chmbr. Orch., 1954-73, EOG, 1954-, Philharmonia Orch., etc.; Mbr., var. chmbr. grps. Recordings: Arthur Bliss's Pastoral; the Brandenburgs (under Benjamin Britten). Mbrships: Royal Soc. of Musicians; RAM Club; ISM. Hobbies: Music; Life; Champagne. Mgmt: Basil Douglas Ltd., London. Address: Savage Club, 9 Fitzmaurice Pl., Berkeley Sq., London W1, UK. 2.

KNIGHT, Paul William, b. 23 Feb. 1954, Stockport, Cheshire, UK. Concert Pianist; Accompanist; Composer; Specialist in Lecture-Recitals. Educ: Chetham's Hospital Schl. of Music; Colchester Inst. (w. Peter Element); RCM; BA; ARCM; LRAM. Career: Recital tours in UK & Europe; played young Handel in "Handel's Resurrection" & Jerome Kern in a London revue. Comps: music for plays, TV, broadcast to Am. radio. Mbrships: ISM; Fellow of the Coll. of Psychic Studies. Hons: Canon Jack Award, 1974; Stephens Award, 1975. Hobbies: Psychic Rsch.; Theatre; Tennis; Swimming. Address: 10 Birchway Ave., Layton, Blackpool, Lancs., UK.

KNUDSEN, Ebbe, b. 29 Oct. 1925, Roskilde, Denmark. Musicologist; Lecturer. Educ: MA, Univ. of Copenhagen; Royal Danish Conserv. of Music. m. Gunhild Deckert Knudsen (div.), 1 s. Career: Fndr., The Danish Renaissance Chapel, 1960; concerts, Scandinavia, France, Germany; Radio apps.; Tchr., Royal Danish Conserv., 1964-; Sr. Lectr., ibid, 1966-. Publs: Hvad skal vi vide om musik, 1972. Contbr. to: Musik; Ed., mag. of the Soc. of Danish Soloists. Mbrships incl: Danish Soc. of Musicol.; Solistforeningen of 1921; Dansk selskab for musikforsking; Dansk musikpaedagogisk forening. Hobbies: Farming; Swimming; Reading. Address: Lune, Syvhojvej 4, Moseby, D4871 Horbelev, Denmark.

KNUDSEN, Gunnar, b. 30 July 1907, Drammen, Norway. Violinist; Conductor. Educ: Oslo Conserv.; Staatliche Akademische Hochschule für Musik, Berlin; pvte. study w. Gustav Havemann, Berlin. m. Judith Fjeld Torgersen, 1 s., 1 d. Debut: Oslo, 1928. Career: Mbr., Oslo Phil., -1938; War-time prisoner; Musical ldr. & Cond., Stavanger City Orch., -1941; Debut, Town Hall, NY, 1947; toured USA, solo recitals, 3 yrs.; Violin concertos w. Symph. Orchs., Scandinavia, USA; Recitals & radio perfs., Europe; Toured Nordic countries, giving lectures on great musicians & other musical topics, 10 yrs. Comps (recorded): Norwegian Rhapsody; Noveletta. Recordings: Works by Edv. Grieg, Sigurd Lie, Catharanus Elling, Johan Halvorsen, Paradis, Gabriel Fauré, Grieg-Flesch, Gunnar Gjerstrom, Gunnar Knudsen, Geirr Tveit, Henri Eccles, Max Reger, Serge Prokofieff, Charles Haubiel. Mbrships: Norwegian Soc. of Soloists; Norwegian Assn. of Artists; Oslo Rotary Club. Hons: Prize of the City of Oslo, 1973. Hobbies: Skiing; Mountain Walking; Travelling. Address: Wilhelm Faerdens vei 4A, Oslo 3, Norway.

KNUDSEN, Lennart Nordløf, b. 2 Sept. 1913, Oslo, Norway. Organist; Bassoonist. Educ: Music Conserv., Oslo, Stockholm & Juilliard Schl. of Music, NY. 3 c. m. (3) Birgit Gjernes, 1 c. Debut: Oslo, 1935. Career: Cond., Bergen Phil. Orch., 1940; Bassoonist, ibid, 1943; TV progs. & regular concerts, Norwegian Broadcasting (Cond.); Dir. of Music Lib., ibid, 1963; Tonmeister, ibid, 1970-. Contbr. to: Dagbladet; Aftenposten. Hons: Mbr. of Jury, Int. Bach Competition, Leipzig, 1968. Hobbies: Music; Housebuilding. Address: New Terrasse 24, 1360 Nesbru, Norway.

KNUSSEN, Oliver, b. 12 June 1952, Glasgow, UK. Composer. Educ: pvte. study w. John Lambert; studied w. Gunther Schuller, Tanglewood. m. Susan Freedman. Comps: 3 symphs.; Pantomime for nonet; Masks for solo flute; Fire-capriccio for flute quartet; Concerto for Orchestra; Choral for wind orch.; Pooh-songs; Rosary Songs; Océan de Terre for soprano & ensemble; Puzzle Music for ensemble; Trumpets for soprano & 3 clarinets; Ophelia Dances for chmbr. ensemble; Cat's Cradle for chmbr. ensemble; Chiara for female voices & orch. (publr., G Schirmer Inc.). Contbr. to Tempo Mag. Hons. incl: Comp-in-Res., Fla. Int. Fest., 1969; Kousseritzky Centennial Commission, 1974. Com-in-Res., Aspen Festival,

1979. Address: Cholesbury Rd. Nursery, Tring, Herts HP23 6PD, UK.

KOBELT, Johannes, b. 15 Dec. 1945, Weinfelden, Switz. Cellist. Educ: 5 yrs. study, degree, Zürich Conserv.; 3 yrs. adv. study w. var. tchrs., Zürich. m. Katharina Gubler. Career: Cellist, Chmbr. Orch., Cologne, Germany, City Orch. St. Gallen, Switz., Musikkollegium Winterhur, Switz., Tonhalleorchester Zürich; Fndr., Quartett Johannes Kobelt, 1973; sev. radio broadcasts & TV apps. Comps., some Swiss folk music. Recording: Quartett Johannes Kobelt (LP). Mbr., Assn. of Swiss Musicians. Hobbies incl: Folk music; Jazz. Mgmt:WITKA Winterther Theater-und Konzertagentur, 8400 Winterthur, Switz. Address: 8 Alpenblickstr., 8630 Rüti/ZH, Switzerland.

KOBYLAŃSKA, Krystyna, b. 6 Aug. 1925, Brzesc, Poland. Musicologist; Chopin-scholar; Museum Curator. Educ: Warsaw Adv. Schl. of Music; Warsaw Univ. Career: Curator, Chopin Mus., Warsaw, 1951-66. Publs: Chopin - The Poet's Inspiration, 1949; Chopin in His Own Land, 1955, 56; Chopin's Correspondence with His Own Family, 1972; Catalogue of Manuscripts of Chopin's Works, 1977; Chopin's Correspondence with George Sand & Her Children, in press; Chopin's Letters, in press. Contbr. to profl. jrnls. Mbrships. incl: Musicol. Sect., Polish Comps.' Union; ZAIKS Authors Assn.; Warsaw Music Soc.; Chopin Soc. Hons: VP, Chopin Circle Edinburgh; Golden Decoration of Town of Palma & Silver Decoration of Spanish Writers in Palma, Mallorca. Hobby: Travel. Address: Gornoslaska St. 16/38, 00.432 Warsaw, Poland.

KOCH, Frederick, b. 4 Apr. 1923, Cleveland, Ohio, USA. Composer-Pianist. Educ: B Mus, Cleveland Inst. of Music, 1949; MA, Case-Western Reserve Univ., 1950; D Mus A, Eastman Schl. of Music, 1970. m. Joyce Lillian Rowbotham, 1 d. Debut: piano recital, Lakewood, Ohio, 1950. Comps. incl: Trio of Praise (med. voice, viola, piano); String Quartet no. 2 w. voice; Sound Particles for piano, percussion, reciter; 1212 for two pianos; Five songs for prepared piano & voice; Monadnock Cadenzas & variations for 8 instruments, voice, tape; Concertino for Saxophone (orch. or band); Hexadic dance for harp; 5 Sacred Songs; etc. Publs: Reflections on Composing with four American Composers, 1976. Contbr. to jrnls. Mbrships. incl: Am. Music Ctr.; Am. Soc. of Univ. Comps.; Cleveland Comps. Guild; ASCAP. Recip. var. prizes. Hobbies: Swimming; Photography. Mgmt: Ron Henry, Cleveland. Address: 2249 Valleyview Dr., Rocky River, OH 44116, USA.

KOCH, Peter Maria, b. 7 Oct. 1925, Osnabrück, Germany. Headmaster; Advisor for music-educational questions. Educ: Philosophy & German Lit., Univ. of Münster/Westphalia; Studied music tchng. for secondary schls., violin tchng., comp. & cond., Acad. of Music, Berlin & Stuttgart/Troosingen. Career: Headmaster, Advsr. for music-educl. questions, Lower Saxon Admin.; Fndr. & Organizer, Nat. Youth Orch. of the Fed. Repub. of Germany; Fndr., Lower Saxon Youth Symph. Orch. Comps: Violine und Klavier Kleine Stücke Zeitgenöss; Komponisten. Publs. incl: Blattlesen in der Schule-Die nü-Methode, 1972; Co-Ed., Musik um uns (Schoolbook for secondary schls.), 11-13, 1976; Ed., Musik im kommunalen Kreislauf, 1973; Musik hören - Musik sehen, 2, 1974; Schulorchester, 2, 1974; Schulchor, 3, 1975; Methoden der Musikerschliessung, 4, 1977. Contbr. to num. profl. publs. Mbrships: Vice-Chmn., Assn. of Music Tchrs. of the Fed. Repub. of Germany; Rotary Club Osnabrück; Int. Soc. of Music Educ. Hobbies: Chmbr. music; Hiking; Skiing. Address: Corsikas Kamp 35, D-4500 Osnabrück, German Fed. Repub.

KOCH, Rainer, b. 6 Apr. 1933, München, W. Germany. Educ: Univ. München, PhB; Music Acad. München State exam. m. Arntrud Koch-Hiller, 2 children. Career: 1961-64 Hanover cond. NiederSachsen Symph. Orch.; 1965-70 Essen cond. Operahouse; since 1970 Cond. Opera Cologne; since 1972 Cond. Bavarian Phil.; Visiting cond. Hons: Bavarian State Scholarship; Cultural Scholarship Soc. of German Industry; Richard Strauss Scholarship. Address: Maybachstr. 15a, 4300 Essen, W. Germany.

KOCHAN, Gunter, b. 2 Oct. 1930, Luckau, Germany. Composer; Professor. Educ: Art Acad., Berlin, GDR. 2 c. Career: Prof., Hochschule für Musik Hanns Eisler, Berlin, GDR. Comps. incl: Cello concerto, 1976; Das Friedensfest, oratorio, 1977-78; 7 Miniaturen fur 4 Tuben, 1977; 3 Symphs.; Concertos for piano, violin, viola, cello; chamber music; operas; cantatas. Recordings: Piano concerto 1958; Concerto for orch., 1962; Cantata, Ashes from Birkenau, 1965; 2nd Symph., 1969; 3rd Symph., 1972; Viola Concerto, 1974; Lines for a Str. Quartet, 1961; Deutsche Volkslieder, for voice & piano, 1975. Mbrships: Bd. of Dirs., Assn. of Comps., GDR. Hons: State Prize, GDR, 1959, '64; Goethe Prize, 1973; Art

Prize FDGB, 1965, '75; 1st prize for comp., LA, USA, 1978. Address: Veltener Str. 13, 1406 Hohen Neuendorf, German Dem. Repub.

KOCI, Akil, b. 1 Sept. 1936, Prizren, Yugoslavia. Editor-in-Chief of Music Department of Radio-television Prishtina; Professor of Music at the Prishtina Academy. Educ: Music Acad., Sarajevo; State HS for Music & performing Arts, Stuttgart; Music Acad., Skopje; specialized studies, Cologne, Nürnberg. m. Xhejlana, 3 children. Compositions: 9 works for mixed choir; 6 works for vocal soloist; 32 instrumental works inclng. works for solo instruments, small ensembles, concertos, film & stage music, etc. Publs. incl: Zvuk; Fjala; Rilindja; Nota; Perparimi; Stremljenja; Pro musica. Mbrships: Soc. of Comps. of Kosova; SOKOJ; Serbian Folklore Soc. Recip. Dec. & Nov. Prizes. Address: Ramiza Sadika 12, Pritina, Yugoslavia.

KOCI, Přemysl, b. 1 June 1917, Rychvald Czechoslovakia. Singer (Baritone); Opera Producer; Professor of Music. Educ: pvte. study w. Prof. Rudolph Vasek. m. Milena Koci. Debut: Opera House, Ostrava, 1939. Career: Opera Singer, Ostrava, 1939-49, Prague, 1949; Prof., Prague Music Acad., 1963-; Gen. Mgr., Nat. Theatre, Prague, 1969-; Opera Prod. at home & abroad, 1969-. Recordings: Num. operatic roles in complete recordings for Supraphon inclng. works by Janácek, Smetana, Dvorák. Publ: Základy pevecké techniky (Basic Voice Technique, 1970). Hons: Worker's Order of Merit, 1958; Artist of Merit, 1963. Hobbies: Dogs; Cooking. Mgmt: Nat. Theatre, Prague. Address: Prague 1, Krocínova 5, Czechoslovakia.

KOCK, Virginia Downman, b. 2 Mar. 1935, New Orleans, La., USA. Associate Professor of Music; Specialist in Medieval-Renaissance Music & 18th Century Music. Educ: B Mus, BSM, Manhattanville Coll., Purchase, NY; MA, PhD, Tulane Univ. Career: Instr., Tulane Univ., 2 yrs.; Assoc. Prof., Univ. of New Orleans, 8 yrs. Mbrships: Am. Musicol. Soc.; Music Lib. Assn.; AAUP; Ch. Music Assn. of Am.; Bd., New Orleans Phil. Symph. Soc., New Orleans Friends of Music; Appointee, Histl. Dists. & Landmarks Commission, City of New Orleans. Contbr. to Grove's Dict., 6th ed. Hobbies: Needlepoint; MS printing; Reading. Address: 2525 St. Charles Ave., New Orleands, LA 70130, USA.

KOCSIS, Zoltán, b. 30 May 1952, Budapest, Hungary. Pianist. Educ: Studied comp. & piano, Béla Bartók Conserv., Budapest, 1963-; Ferenc Liszt Acad. of Music, ibid., 1968-. Debut: Budapest, 1970. Career: Concert, radio & TV apps. Hundary; Guest perfs., many European countries, & in USA & USSR; Soloist w. Amsterdam Phil., Berlin Phil., RPO & other major orchs.; tour of Japan, 1975. Recordings: Works by J S Bach, Beethoven, Bartók, Pál Kadosa; (w. D Ránki) works by Mozart, Ravel, Brahms & Bartók for 2 Pianos. Hons: 1st Prize, Hungarian Radio Beethoven Competition, 1970; Youngest-ever recip., Liszt Prize, 1973; Kossuth prize, 1978. Hobby: Collecting records. Mgmt: Int. Concert Mgmt., Budapest. Address: Hevesi Gyula utca 33, Budapest XV, Hungary.

KOEHNE, Graeme John, b. 3 Aug. 1956, Adelaide, Aust. Composer; Tutor (Piano & Composition). Educ: BMus, Adelaide Univ. Career: Comp.; Tutor in Piano & Comp., Univ. of New England, Armidale, NSW, Aust. Mbrships: ISCM (SA); Musicol. Soc. of Aust. Hons: Dr. Ruby Davy Prize for Comp., 1974; Sydney Youth Rostrum Scholarship, 1975; H Brewster-Jones Prize for Comp., 1975; Alex Burnard Scholarship for Comp., 1976. Hobby: Tennis. Address: 63 Arthur St., Tranmere, SA 5073, Aust.

KOELLREUTTER, Hans-Joachim, b. 2 Sept. 1915, Freiburg i. Br., Germany. Composer. Educ: Staatliche Ákademische Hochschule für Musik, Berlin; Conservatoire de Musique,Geneva. m. Margarita Schack, 3 children. Career incls: Dir., German Cultural Inst., New Delhi, Rep. for India & Ceylon, Goethe Inst., 1964-69; Dir. (Fndr.), Delhi Schl. of Music, 1966-69; Dir., German Cultural Inst., Tokyo, Rep. for Japan; Goethe Inst., 1969-75; Dir., German Cultural Inst. Rio de Janeiro, 1975-. Num. comps. & recordings. Music Critic, Diarios Associados, Sao Paulo, 1954-57. Mbrships: incl: Advsry. Bd., nat. Ctr. for Performing Arts, Bombay, 1967. Recip. num. hons inclng: Brazilian Govt. Award Cruzeiro do Sul, 1969. Address: Instituto Cultural Brasil-Alemanha, rua Graca Aranha, 416 9 andar, Rio de Janeiro, Brazil.

KOELZ, Ernst, b. 26 Jan. 1929, Vienna, Austria. Composer; Musician, Recorder; Professor. Educ: Conserv. of the City of Vienna; studied w. H U Staeps. m. Else Krempl, 1 s. Debut: Austrian Radio, 1947. Career: incidental Radio, stage & film music, Austrian Radio, TV, Stadttheater, Klagenfurt, Theater an der Wien, Volkstheater, Burgtheater, Vienna, Theater am Neumarkt, Thomas-Koerfer Film Prod., Zürich; num. Concerts. Recordings: Amadeo; Preiserrecords; Musical Heritage Soc.

Mbrships: AKM; Austro-Mechana; IGNM; OGZM. Hons: Vienna Art Fndn. Prize, 1962; Theodor Körner Prize, 1964; Förderungspreis, City of Vienna, 1965. Hobby: Collecting Antiques. Address: 3-7/1/26 Magdalenenstr., A-1060 Vienna, Austria.

KOENIG, Fernand, b. 16 Dec. 1922, Goekelsmühle, G-D of Luxembourg. Manager; Concert singer (baritone-bass). Educ: BSc; Grad Engineer; Singing, piano, virtuosity dip. in singing, Conserv. of Luxembourg; pvte. studies w. Charles Panzera, Paris & Arne Sunnegarth, Stockholm. m. Lydie Theisen, 1 d. Career: Fests. of Salzburg, Nuremberg, etc.; Soloist, major radio stations, Europe & USA; Concerts, London, Edinburgh, Dublin, Moscow, Leningrad, NY, Wash., Paris, Berlin, Madrid, Frankfurt, Stuttgart, etc.; Manager,Luxembourg Music & Open Air Theater Fest. Comps: Five Luxembourg Folk Songs (recorded). Recordings: Matthaüspassion; Die Winterreise; Il Maestro di Capella (Cimarosa); Liebeslieder (Beethoven); 4 Cantatas of J S Bach; Schulmeister by Telemann. Hons: High decorations of Belgium, Netherlands, Germany & Luxembourg. Hobbies: Astronomy; Geodesy. Mgmt: Choveaux, UK; Dietrich, Frankfurt; Vitoria, Madrid. Address: 17 rue des Pêcheurs, Wiltz, Gran-Duchy of Luxembourg. 19.

KOETSIER, Jan, b. 13 Aug. 1911, Amsterdam, Netherlands. Composer; Conductor. Educ: Acad. of Music, Berlin. m. Margarete Trampe. Debut: as comp. & cond., Concertgebouw, Amsterdam, 1937. Career: 2nd Cond., Concertgebouworkest, 1942-48; Cond., Residentieorkest, The Hague, 1949-50; Tchr., Royal Conserv., The Hague, 1949-50; Cond., Symphonieorchester des Bayerischen Rundfunks, Munich, 1950-66; Prof., Musikhochschule, Munich, 1966-76. Comps: 3 Symphs.; Orchl. works; The Man Lot, Cantata for soli, men's choir & orch.; opera, Frans Hals; chmbr. music; var. solo concertos w. orch.; piano music; Lieder. Recordings: Petite Suite; Brass Quintet; Partita for English horn & organ; Concerto for trumpet, trombone & orch. Mgmt: Donemus, Paulus Potterstraat 14, Amsterdam, Netherlands. Address: Florianhaus, Untgerkagn, 8251 Heldenstein, German Fed. Repub.

KOFSKY, Nathaniel Myer, b. 15 Dec. 1908, London, UK. Violinist; Conductor; Director. Educ: finished violin studies w. Prof. Carl Flesch. m. Cynthia Ryan, 1 d. Debut: Johannesburg, 1930. Career incls: Lectr. in violin & chmbr. music, Univ. of Capetown, 1946-51; Dir., Kenya Conserv. of Music, Nairobi, & Cond., Nairobi Orch., 1951-; Prin. Classical Concert (Weekly), Voice of Kenya, Nairobi, 1956-. Recip. OBE & Hon. RCC for servs. to music in Africa. Hobbies: Safari in Africa. Address: Kenya Conservatoire of Music, PO Box 41343, Nairobi, Kenya. 3.

KOGAN, Leonid Borisovich, b. 14 Oct. 1924, Dnepropetrovsk, Ukraine. Violinist. Educ: studied w. Abram Yampolsky, Moscow Conserv. Career: Prof., Moscow Conserv.; num. world tours. Hons: Honoured Artist of RSFSR, 1955; People's Artist of USSR; Lenin Prize, 1965. 16.

KOGAN, Nathan, b. 28 Sept. 1906, NYC, USA. Violoncellist; Conductor. Educ: BS, NY Univ., LL B., Las Schl., ibid. m. Edith R Kogan, 1 d. Career: Mbr. of the York Trio, a regular feature of Radio Stn. WEAF; Asst. Cond. of the Nat. Orchl. Soc.; Prin. Cellist of the Scranton Symph. & of the Ridgefield Symphonette. Mbrships: Pres., Chamber Music Assocs.; Treas., Violoncello Soc. (as well as a Trustee); The Bohemians. Hobbies: Law; Literature; Tennis. Address: 2 Tudor City Pl., NY, NY 10017, USA.

KOGAN, Peter Henry, b. 19 Apr. 1945, Yonkers, NY, USA. Percussionist; Timpanist. Educ: Cert. d'Etude de Timbales, Geneva Conserv., Switzerland, 1963; Juilliard Schl. of Music; B Mus, 1968, M Mus, 1972, Cleveland Inst. of Music; Aspen Schl. of Music, summers 1962, 64, 65; pvte. study. Career: Perfs. w. Grp. for Contemporary Music at Columbia Univ., & the Contemporary Music Ensemble of Rutgers Univ., 1965; Mbr., Cleveland Orch., 1969-72; Tchr. of Timpani & Percussion, Oberlin Coll. Conserv. of Music, Ohio, 1971-72; Prin. Percussion & Assoc. Prin. Timpani, Pitts. Symph. Orch., 1972-77; perfs. w. blues artists incl. Lightnin' Hopkins, Floyd Jones, NYC, 1978. Mbr., Pi Kappa Lambda. Hons: Winner, Annual Concerto Competition, Cleveland Inst. of Music, 1969. Hobbies: Cooking. Address: Apt. 1231, 2350 Broadway, NYC, NY 10024, USA.

KOHL, Richard McClure, b. 13 Oct. 1940, Colo. Springs, Colo., USA. Vocalist; Trumpet; Educator. Educ: AA., Northeastern Jr. Coll.; BA., Colo. State Coll.; Grad. work, Univ. of Northern Colo., Univ. of Denver, Oberlin Conserv. Music, Colo. Univ. m. Janet D Kibben, 2 s. Debut: Ctrl. City Opera Co., 3 yrs.; Pub. Schl. Music Educator, 16 yrs., Longmont Symph.,

6 yrs.; Longmont Community Choir, 3 yrs.; Dir., ibid, 1 yr. Recordings: Mozart: Requiem; Giannini; Christmas Canticle. Mbrships: MENC; Colo. Educ. Assn.; Am. Guild Music Artists; Fac. Rep.; St. Vrain Valley Tchrs. Assn. Recip., Rockefeller Fndn. Grant, Tchrs. Perf. Inst. Hobbies: Hunting; Fishing; Carpentry; Model Ship Bldg.; Collecting coins & antique instruments. Address: 1085 6th. St. Ct., Berthoud, CO 80513, USA.

KOHLER, Irene, b. London, Uk. Concert Pianist. Educ: B Mus; Hon. FTCL; GRSM; LRAM; RCM; ARCM; FRSA; pvte. studies w. Eduard Steuermann & Egon Wellesz, Vienna, Austria. m. Harry Waters. Debut: London, 1934. Career: num. radio broadcasts, UK, 1932-, Netherlands, 1937-, Europe & Aust., 1950-, also NZ, S Africa, Rhodesia, India, Singapore, Malaya, Hong Kong, Can., USA; app. in sev. films. Recordings: Albeniz Iberia (complete piano works); Prokofiev; Berg's Sonata for piano; Liszt's Malediction for piano & strings. Mbrships. incl: RCM Union; TCM Guild; ISM. Hons. incl: Challen Gold Medal, 1930; Silver Medal, Int. Piano Competition, Vienna, 1933. Hobbies: Travel; Reading; Cooking. Address: 28 Castelnau, Barnes, London SW13 9RU, UK. 1, 3, 14.

KÖHLER, Johannes, b. 24 June 1910, Milan, Italy. Organist; Professor. Educ: Gymnasium Abitur Univ. Halle & Berlin, 1917-1929; studied ch. & schl. music, 1929-33; Dip., organ & Master of Organ, 1933. m. Hannelor Wiczand, 2 c. Debut: Berlin. Career: Organist of Ch. St. Paul, Berlin, 1933-34; Prof. of Organ, Franz Liszt Acad., Weimar & Organist, Ch. of St. Peter & Paul, Weimar, 1934-75. Recordings: J S Bach, Organs of Silbermann; Bach, Kunst der Fuge; Organ concerts of Händel. Publs: Essay on Albert Schweitzer and the organ, 1965; The Musicians in 1000 Years of the Church at Weimar, 1975. Mbrships: J S Bach Komitee of German Dem. Repub.; Neue Bachgesellschaft Leipzig; Curator of Bach House in Eischoch. Hons: Nationalpreis of German Dem. Repub., 1955; Prize of Art of Town of Weimar, 1972. Hobby: Free Improvisations. Address: Humboldtstr. 58, 53 Weimar, German Dem. Repub.

KÖHLER, Karl-Heinz Helmut, b. 24 Oct. 1928, Blankenhain Thüringen, Germany. Scientific Librarian. Educ: Dr Phil; Dips., tchng. violin, musicol. & degree of sci. libn., Music Acad. Career: Dir., Music Dept., Deutsche Staatsbibliothek, 1956-. Publs: Felix Mendelssohn Bartholdy, 1972; Ed., Ludwig van Beethoven's Konversationsheften, 1968-; Griesinger: Joseph Haydn, 1975; Works of Felix Mendelssohn; Works of Joseph Haydn; Facsimiles Works of J S Bach. Contbr. to Profl. Publs. Mbrships: Pres., DDR Grp., Int. Soc. of Music Libs.; Music Coun. of DDR; Ctrl. Inst. for Mozart Rsch., Salzburg; Direktorium, Bach Soc.; Int. Musicol. Soc. Address: Beutsche Staatsbibliothek, Musikabteilung, 1086 Berlin, Unter den Linden 8, German Dem. Repub.

KÖHLER, Siegfried H, b 2 Mar. 1927, Meissen, Germany. Composer; Musicologist; Educator. Educ: Leipsig Univ.; Dr Phil, 1955; Dr Sc Phil, 1974; Coll. for Music, Dresden. m. Eva Schüttoff, 3 d. Career: Comp.; Dir.; Musical Arr.; Prof. of Comp., Rector, Carl Maria von Weber Coll. for Music, Dresden, 1968-; has performed own comps. in concerts & on TV. Comps. incl: 3 Symphs.; Reich des Menschen (oratorio); Wirunsere Zeit (oratorio); Johannes Bobrowski Choirbook; Chmbr. music; songs; film music; etc. Sev. recordings. Contbr. to & Mbr. of ed. staff, Musikwissenschaft, Berlin. Mbrships. incl: Union of Comps. & Musicols. of GDR. Recip. Kunstpreis der DDR. Address: Schevenstr. 2517-15005, DDR-8054 Dresden, German Dem. Repub.

KÖHLER, Volkmar, b. 20 May 1930, Hannover, Germany. Musicologist. Educ: Univ. of Göttingen; Dr Phil, 1956; studied violin, piano & organ w. Prof. W Lauboek, Hannover, & comp. w. Kurt von Wolfurth. m. Margret Solle, 2 children. Publs: Heinrich Marschners Bühenwerke, 1956; Helmut Jörns und seine Kompositionen, 1968; Studien zu Orlando di Lassos Prophetiae Sibyllarum, 1952. Contbr. to jrnls. Mbr. German Assn. for Music Rsch., Kassel. Hobby: Hist. of sea travel; Motor boating. Address: Schulenburgallee 110, 3180 Wolfsburg, German Fed. Repub.

KOHLRUSCH, Aram Clemens Ohannes, b. 28 Apr. 1922, Berlin, Germany. Conductor; Composer; Violinist. Educ: Conserv. Klindworth-Scharwenka, Berlin; Conserv. Ribeaupierre, Lausanne; Conserv. Musique Lausanne; Conserv. Nat. Superieur Musique, Paris; Cond. dip., 1950. m. Inger Barbro Dalenius, 2 s., 1 d. Debut: Radio Sottens, 1951. Career incls: Violinist, var. theatres, Berlin & Lausanne; Cond., num. orchs. inclng. Gavleborgs Radioorkester, Sweden. Comps. incl: Soli & Choir; Violin Concerto; Viola Concerto; String quintet Op. 3 Nr. 2. Recordings: Roulette label. Mbr. profl. orgs. Hobbies incl: Chess; Physics. Address: Kornvägen 8, 33030 Gnosjö, Sweden.

KOHOUT, Antonin, b. 12 Dec. 1919, Lubna, Czechoslovakia. Violoncellist. Educ: Grad., Conserv. of Music, Prague; Dip, Acad. of Musical Arts, Prague. Career: Fndr. Mbr., Smetana Quartet, 1945-; Num. Czech, German, Engl., USA, Japan recordings; Docent in Acad. of Musical Arts, Prague. Mbrship: Union of Czech Comps. & Concert Artists. Mgmt: Prasokoneers, Prague; Czech. Philharmonie, Prague. Address: Kosire 407/3, Prague 5, Czechoslovakia.

KOHOUTEK, Ctirad, b. 18 Mar. 1929, Zabreh na Morave, Czechoslovakia. Composer. Educ: Conserv. of Brno; Grad. Comp., Acad of Music, Brno; PhD, Palacky Univ., Olomouc. m. Jarmila Kohoutkova, 3 children. Career: Asst. Cond., Brno Symph. Orch., 1951; Dir., Ostrava Symph. Orch.; Rdt., Janacek's Acad. of Musical Arts, Brno; Apps. in most important musical ctrs. of Europe & USA. Comps: Solemn Prologue for Orch., 1971; O Panton Celebrations of Light (cycle of 3 symphonic pictures for orch.). Hons. incl: 2 regional Leos Janacek Prizes, 1962, 1975; Music Critic's Prize 9th Int. Contest, Paris, 1967. Address: 602 00 Brno, Capkova 22, Czechoslovakia.

KOHUT, Daniel L, b. 7 July 1935, Seymour, Tex., USA. Professor of Music. Educ: BM, N Tex. State Univ.; MMus, DMA, Eastman Schl. of Music, Rochester Univ. m. Maryann Pickett, 1 s., 1 d. Career: Instrumental Tchr., Brighton & Penfield (NY) pub. schls., 5 yrs.; Music Prof., Ithaca Coll., 3 yrs.; Asst. Dean, Coll. of Fine & Applied Arts & Chmn., Music Educ. Div., Univ. of Ill.; Prof., Music, ibid. Compositions: Arrs., for schl. orch. Sinfonia & Galliard, Sailor's Song. Recordings: 8 records w. Eastman Wind Ensemble. Publs: Instrumental Music Pedagogy, 1973. Contbr. to profl. jrnls. Mbrships: MENC; Ill Music Educators Assn.; Coll. Band Dirs. Nat. Assn. Hobbies: Fishing; Woodworking. Address: 607 S Ridgeway Ave., Champaign, IL 61820, USA. 8.

KOIZUMI, Fumio, b. 4 Apr. 1927, Shinagawa, Tokyo, Japan. BA, Univ. of Tokyo, 1951; Ctrl. Coll. of Karnataka Music, Madras, India, 1957-58; Bhatekhande Coll. of Hindustani Music, Lucknow, 1958-59. m. Mieko Kako Koizumi, 1 d. Career: Regular apps. on TV & radio of Japan Broadcasting Corp. as commentator on Japanese & ethnic music, 1959-. Recordings: Song of the Nile, 1964. Mbrships: Soc. for Ethnomusicol.; Dir., Soc. for Rsch. in Asiatic Music; Dir., Japanese Musicol. Soc. Publs: A Study of Japanese Traditional Music, 1958; A Study of Children's own Songs, 1969. Hobbies: Swimming; Horse-riding. Address: 1-43 Sakuradai, Nerima-ku, Tokyo, Japan.

KOIZUMI, Isao, b. 3 Nov. 1907, Osaka, Japan. Conductor; Editor; Composer. Educ: Grad., Osaka Univ. of Commerce in Economics; Organ & Comp. study w. Dr. Toraji Onaka. m. Tomi Kuginuki, 1s., 3d. Career: Lectr. of Economics, Osaka Univ. of Commerce, -1941; Organist & choir Dir., United States-Far East Air Force Chapel Center, Tokyo, 1951-72; Cond., Tokyo Choral Soc., 1950-; Music Ed., Sambika hymnal, United Ch. of Christ in Japan, 1951-; Music Ed., Kodomo-Sambika hymnal, Ch. Schl. of the United Ch. of Christ in Japan. Comps: Songs for Children, Vol. I (1926), Vol. II (1943); Songs of Bible Story (1960); Favourite Sacred Songs Old & New (1979); Choral Preludes for Organ, Vols. I & II (1951). Publs: The Pronunciation of Choral Latin, 1965; Handbook to the Hymnal, 1955; Japanese Transl. of Adam Carse's The Orchestra in the XVIIIth Century, 1957. Contbr. to profl. publs. Mbrships: Dir., Christian Music Seminary, Tokyo; Inspector, Japanese Musicol. Soc.; Am. Musicol. Soc.; Int. Musicol. Soc. Address: 16-9, 1 chome, Kamitakada, Nakano-ku, Tokyo 164, Japan.

KOIZUMI, Kazuhiro, b. 16 Oct. 1949, Kyoto, Japan. Conductor. Educ: Tokyo Univ. of Arts, Japan; Hochschule für Musik, Berlin. m. Masami Koizumi. Debut: w. Tokyo Metropolitan Orch., Tokyo Japan, 1970. Career: Berlin Phil. Orch., 1975, '76; Vienna Phil. Orch., Salzburg Fest., 1976; Hamburg Staatsoper, 1975, '76, '77; Orch. Nat. of France; Philharmonia Hungarica, 1975, '77, '78; num. concerts incl. w. Rubinstein, Rostropovitch; TV apps., 1975, '76; w. Chgo. Symph. Orch., Ravinia Fest., 1978; Gen. Music Dir., New Japan Phil. Orch., 1975-; w. Boston Symph. Orch., Tanglewood Fest., 1979. Recordings: Rachmaninov Paganini Variationen; Dohnanyi, Variationen über ein Kinderlied; Lalo, Konzert für Violin Russe; Lalo, Konzert für Violin in F. Hons: French Grand Prix du Disque; 1st Prize of 2nd Minon Int. Cond. Concours, 1970; 1st Prize of 3rd Karajan Int. Cond. Concours, 1973. Address: Langenscheidt str. 1, 1000 Berlin 62, German Fed. Repub. 3.

KOJIAN, Miran, b. 3 June 1942, Beirut, Lebanon. Violinist. Educ: Grad., Paris Nat. Conserv., 1956; Grad., Curtis Inst. of Music, Phila., Pa., 1963; MMus, Catholic Univ. of Am., Wash. DC, 1964; studied w. Ivan Galamian, 5 yrs., Lynn Talluel, 2 yrs., Jascha Heifetz, 1 yr., Henryk Szeryng, 2 yrs. Career: Num. radio & TV apps., USA & Europe; Cleveland Orch., 1965-67; Concertmaster, Kansas City Phil., 1967-69; Concertmaster, Nat. Symph., Wash. DC, 1969-; Prof. of Violin, Catholic Univ., Wash. DC, 1969-. Hons: 1st Prize, Paris Nat. Conserv., 1956; Hobbies: Boating; Fishing. Address: 3119 N 8th St., Arlington, VA 22201, USA.

KOK, Ronald, B. 24 Jan. 1944, Hilversum, Netherlands. Composer; Performer (Viola; Bass Trombone). Educ: Conserv. Dip. for Trombone. m. Madelon Michel, 3 children. Career: w. Radio Phil. Orch., Hilversum. Comps. incl: Wolfpack (4 French Horns). Mbr., ANOUK. Hobbies: Chess; Sailing. Address: Valken Hoflaan 2, Hilversum, Netherlands.

KOKAS, Klára, b. 24 Apr. 1929, Szany, Hungary. Educator. Educ: Masters, studied w. Zoltán Kodály, Liszt Acad., Hungary; PhD in pedagogy-psychol. div., 2 children. Career incls: Music Tchr. & Choir Cond. in second schl., establng. music courses at Kindergarten & elementary schl. Levels, Szombathely, Hungary, 1950's; Prof., Tchr. Trng. Coll., 1960-66; Rsch. Dir., Cons., Kodály Musical Trng. Inst., Wellesley, Mass., USA, 1970-72; Lectr., Zoltan Kodály Pedagogical Inst. of Music; Kecskemet, 1974; many experiments in musical pedagogy, Hungary & USA; lectures in USA & Aust. Publs: Developing abilities with Music Education, 1972. Mbr., Soc. of Music Artist, Budapest. Address: Petzvál u 22d, Budapest 1115, Hungary.

KOKKONEN, Joonas, b. 13 Nov. 1921, Iisalmi, Finland. Composer; Professor. Educ: MA, Helsinki Univ.; Dip., Sibelius Acad., Helsinki. m. Maija Heljo, 5 children. Debut: as Pianist, 1950; as Comp., 1953. Career: Tchr., 1948-59, Prof. of Comp., 1959-63, Sibelius Acad.; Mbr., Finnish Acad., 1963-; apps. as Pianist in concerts of own music, as Soloist in orchl. concerts & as Chmbr. Musician. Comps. incl: The Last Temptations (opera to Libretto by Lauri Kokkonen); orchl. works inclng. 4 symphs; Concerto for cello & orch.; chmbr. & choral works; solo songs; solo instrumental pieces. Contbr. to Ilta-Sanomat, 1947-57; Uusi Suomi, 1957-63. Mbrships: Soc. of Finish Comps.; Pres., Comps. Copyright Bur. TEOSTO, 1968-; Nordic Comps. Coun.; Royal Swedish Acad. of Music, 1972; Corres., Arts Acad., German Dem. Repub., 1975-. Hons: Wihuri Int. Prize, 1961; Music Prize, Nordic Coun., 1968; Wihuri Sibelius Prize, 1973. Address: Vanhakylä 04400 Järvenpää, Finland. 19.

KOKORNIAK, Dobromila, b. 7 May 1944, Poznan, Poland. Opera Singer (Mezzosoprano). Educ: MA, Econ. Geog.; MA, Opera Singing, Higher Musical Schl., Poznan. m. Andrzej Rozmarynowiez, 1 d. Debut: Poznan Opera House in Rigoletto. Career: Apps. in USSR & German Dem. Repub., Soloist, Wroclaw Opera House, 1971-76. Repertoire incls: Bizet, Carmen; Verdi, Amneris in Aida, Eboli in Don Carlos, Azucena in Trovatore, & Magdalena in Rigoletto; Britten, Florence in Albert Herring; Musorgski, Marina in Borys Godunov; Moniussko, Czesnikowa in Straszny Dwór; Gluck, Orpheus in Orpheus. Recordings, Radio recordings of Polish music. Mbr., Soc. of Polish Theatre & Film Artists. Address: 60-732 Poznan, Rynek Lazarski 11 m 12, Poland.

KOLAFA, Jiří, b. 26 Feb. 1930, Jicin, Czechoslovakia. Composer; Performer(Piano, Harpsichord). Educ: Grad., State Conserv., Prague; Grad., Acad. of Music, Prague. m. Vera Cihulova, 1 s. Debut: Song Cycle, 1950. Career: Perf. of Chmbr. Music in Czechoslovakia & abroad inclng: Germany, Denmark; External Rdr. in Music, Acad. of Dramatic Art, Prague. Comps: About 200 comps. for theatre & film inclng: Pinocchio, ballet & pantomime; Serious Music; Panychida; La Follia e Danza; Passacaglia, etc. Recordings as mbr. of chmbr. ensemble. Mgmt: OSA, Union Protecting Authors Rights, Prague. Dilia Theatre Agcy., Prague; Pragokoncert. Address: Cistpvicka 20, 16300 Praha 6, Czechoslovakia.

KOLAR, Henry, b. 1 Dec. 1923, Chicago, Ill., USA. Violinist; Conductor; Composer; University Professor. Educ: B Mus., DePaul Univ., Chgo., 1948; M Mus., North Western Univ., 1949; DMA, Univ. of Colo., 1970; Acad. of Music, Vienna, Austria, 1961-62; Univ. of Southern Calif. m. Aileen Kayser, 2 s., 2 d. Debut: Recital, N. Western Univ., 1949. Career: Concertmaster, San Diego Symph.; Sherwood Hall Orch.; El Paso Symphonette; Mbr., Modern Arts Quartet; Violinist; Alcala Trio (Res. Chmbr. Grp., Univ. of San Diego); Past Cond., MessColl. Orch., San Diego Youth Symph., La Jolla Civic Orch.; Cond., Univ. of San Diego Symph.; Guest Cond., var. Music Festivals, SW States. Compositions incl: Rhapsody for cello & piano; Andante for Strings; Little Suite Antique; from Etude to Concert; 2 String Quartets, etc. Mbrships: Am. String Tchrs. Assn.; MENC. Hobbies: Tennis; Chmbr. Music. Address: 4715 Glacier Ave., San Diego, CA 92120, USA.

KOLAR, Walter William, b. 8 Nov. 1922, Ambridge, Pa., USA. Performer & Teacher of Tambura; Conductor of Tambura Orchestras. Educ: BS & MEd., Duquesne Univ., Pitts., Pa. m. Jennie I Peternac, dec., 1 s. Career: active as Perf., Music Arr.; Composer, Tchr., Cond. & Writer for about 35 yrs.; for past 25 yrs. has toured thru'out most of world w. Duquesne Univ. Tamburitzans as Ldr., Dir (Artistic & Mgmt.). Prod., Cond., etc.; Dir., Duquesne Univ. Tamburitzans Inst. of Folk Arts; has composed over 100 works & arr. over 1,000, about 50 works having been recorded. Recordings incl: 25 of Duquesne Univ. Tamburitzans on Du-Tam Recording Co. Publs: Tamburitza Instruction, Books I (2954, revised, 1960) & II (1963); History of the Tambura, 1974. Contbr. to jrnls. Mbrships incl: Bds., Pa. Coun. on Arts & Am. Assn. of Dance Cos.; Soc. of Ethnomusicol.; MENC; Fretted Instrument Guild of Am. Hobbewish Assn., Delhi (Pres.). Hobbies: Reading; Art; Social Welfare; Religion. Address: 74 Babar Rd., N Delhi 110001, India.

KOLASINSKI, Jerzy, b. 20 Feb. 1906. Pilica, Poland. Composer; Teacher. Educ: Grad., Univ. of Warsaw, 1930: Dip., State Musical Conserv., Warsaw, 1930. m. Hildegarda Kolasinski, 1 s., 1 d. Career: perfs. of compositions on radio & in concert-halls. 1929-; Insp. of Artistic Schls. & Chief, Music Educ. Dept., Min. of Culture & Art. 1950-51; Chief, Music Educ. Dept., Pedagogical Ctr. of Artistic Educ., Warsaw, 1952-66; currently Prof., Conserv. & var. levels of music schl. compositions: 151 works. 53 publd. inclng: Folk Songs from Chelm; Oh, My Earth (mixed choir); Amber Tears (mixed choir); Lublin's Folk Songs (Soprano & String orch.); Love Folk Songs (tenor & orch.); Rustic Overture (symph. orch.); Autumn Songs (mezzosoprano & str. orch.); Waltz Capriccio (str. quintet); Melodie (str. quintet); Funny Folk Songs (choir & orch.). Publs: Instrumental Band Groups, 1972. Contbr. to: profl. publs. Mbrships: Union of Polish Composers: Soc. of Authors. Hons: Artistic Prize. Town of Lublin, 1948; Golden Merit Cross, 1955; Polonia Restitutaz, 1964. Hobbies: Philately; Photography. Address: ul. Sapiezynska 1 m25,00-215 Warsaw, Poland.

KOLBE, Grethe, b. 10 Dec. 1910, Kobenhavn, Denmark. Conductor. Educ: Royal Acad. of Music. Copenhagen. Debut: 1931. Career: Free Lance Cond., Opera, Popular Symphonic Music Concerts; Staff Cond., Denmark Radio Concert Orch., 1951-, num. public concerts, Radio, TV Studio Perfs.; Guest Cond., all important European Broadcasting orgs., Int. Fests. of Light Music. London, 1956-, 58-60, Munich, 1963-65-67. Address: 8 Falkoner alle, DK 2000 Kobenhavn F, Denmark.

KOLBE-DOBROWOLNY, Elfriede Else Johanna, b. 15 Mar. 1902, Graz, Austria. Pianist. Educ: Vienna Conserv.; studied w. Emily Sauer, Isidor Philipp, Carl Friedberg, Frida Kvast-Hodsapp. m. Dr. Robert William Kolbe. Debut: Berlin Symph. Career: Soloist, Berlin Phil. & var. orchs.; Piano Recitalist, Radio Berlin, Swedish Broadcasting Co., Stockholm; Concert Tours, Sweden; Prod., Swedish Inst. for Nat. Concerts; Chmbr. Music w. Kolbe Trio. Recording: duo-pianist, w. Brian Wilson, Fermat. Mbrships: Vice Chmn., Swedish Piano Tchrs. Assn., 1974-; Sec. Gen., ibid, 1968-74; Bd., IMC; Bd., Swedish MTA; Vice-Sec., ibid; Chmn., Editorial Grp., ibid. Address: 10/V Vattugatan, 11152 Stockholm, Sweden.

KOLET, Ezra, b. 6 Jan. 1914, Calcutta, India. Retired Civil Servant, Government of India; Violinist. Educ: Studied w. num. profl. violinists. m. Ruth Kolet, 3 s., 2 d. Career: Fndr.-amr., Delhi Symph. Soc. & Delhi Symph. Orch., 1965; played Bach's Double Violin Concerto w. Delhi Symph. Orch., 1971. Contbr. to Hindustan Times (music reviews). Mbrships: Delhi Symph. Soc. (Soc.); Jewish Assn., Delhi (Pres.). Hobbies: Reading; Art; Social Welfare; Religion. Address: 74 Babar Rd., N Delhi 110001, India.

KOLINSKI, Mieczyslaw, b. 5 Sept. 1901, Warsaw, Poland. Composer; Ethnomusicologist. Educ: PhD., Berlin Univ., 1930; Studied Musicol. w EM van Hornbostel, H Abert & A Schering, Psychol. w. W Koehier & Anthropol. w R Thurnwald, ibid; studied Comp. w P Juon & Piano w L Kreutzer, Hochschule Fur Music, Berlin. debut: Tchaikovsky's 1st Piano Concerto w. Oldenburg Phil. Orch., 1919. Career: Asst., Phonogramm-Archiv. Berlin Univ., 1926-33; Transcribed & Analysed var. Field Recordings for N Western & Columbia Univs., w. Grants from Carnegie & Rockefeller Fndns., Prague, 1933-38; Live in Brussels, 1938-51; Music Therapist, St. Albans Naval Hosp., NY, 1952-66; Tchr., Ethnomusicology & Musical Acoustics, Univ.of Toronto, 1966-. Compositions: Du Ru Bu (Ballet), 1931; Railroad Fantasy (Ballet), 1935; Man & His Shadows (Ballet), 1948; Prelude (orch.), 1958; Dance Fantasy (str. Orch.), 1968; Dahomey Suite (solo w Orch.), 1953; Lyric Sextet (Voice w Instrumental Ensemble), 1929; Concertino (Sopr., Str. Quartet, Piano), 1956; Hatikvah (Str. Quartet),

1960; Encounterpoint (organ & Str. Quartet), 1975; 29 Folksong Settings (Voice, Flute, Piano), 1969; Sonata (Piano), 1966 & many others. Recordings: Music for Dance Rythms (Folkways Records); Dahomey Suite (Folkways Records). Publs: Studies in Ethnomusicology, 2 vols., 1961, 1965. Contbr. to num. jrnls. inclng: Ethnomusicology; Jrnl. of Am. Musicological Soc.; Musical Quarterly; The Record Changer; Yearbook of the Int. Folk Music Coun.; Anthropos; Encyclopedias Int. & Britannica. Mbrships: Co-Fndr. & Former Pres., Soc. for Ethnomusicol., Int. Folk Music Coun.; Can. Music Centre. Address: 87 Blantyre Ave., Scarborough, Ont., MIN 2R6, Canada.

KOLJONEN, John Albert, b. 26 Aug. 1943, Williamston, Mich., USA. Clarinettist. Educ: BM Artist's Dip., Curtis Inst., Univ. of Pa.; Study w Anthony Gigliotti. m. Kyung Sook Lee, 1 d. Career: Prin. Clarinettist, maj. orchs. inclng. Am. Symph. Orch., Royal Ballet, Bolshoi Ballet, D'Oyly Carte Opera, Phila. Lyric Opera, & Hong Kong Phil.; Perfs. w Beaus-Arts & Lennox String Quartets; Recitalist, USA, Europe, Asia, on radio & TV & at Marlboro & Interlochen Music Fests.; Fac. Mbr., Phila. Musical Acad., Chinese Univ., Hong Kong. Orchestral & chmbr. music recordings on maj. labels. Contbr. to Music Jrnl. Mbrships: Chmn., Exec. Bd., Musicians Insurance Trust; Phila. Musical Soc.; NY Denver Musicians Assns. Hons: Grants, Phila. Fndn., 1965, Music Perf. Trust Funds of Recordings Inds., 1966, Hoover Fndn., 1967, Barra Fndn., 1969. Hobbies: Hiking; Fishing; Shooting; Scuba diving. Mgmt: Independent Concert Artist, Inc., Phila. Address: Greenview, Gdns., G Bldg. 6/Floor, 125 Robinson Rd.,Hong Kong. 3, 6, 21.

KOLLO, René, b. 20 Nov. 1937, Berlin, Germany. Opera singer (tenor). Educ: studied w. Elsa Varena, Berlin. div., 1 d. Debut: Braunschweig State Theatre, 1965. Career: Opera houses, Germany, Covent Garden, Scala, Paris, Metropolitan NY; TV shows; Films; Wagner Fest., Bayreuth, 10 yrs. Comps: 2 Songs. Num. recordings. Mgmt: Marguerite Werner-Kollo, Hofweg 6, 2000 Hamburg 76, German Fed. Repub. Address: c/o Mgmt.

KOMIAZYK, Magdalena, b. 2 Oct. 1945, Gdansk, Poland. Pianist; Composere. Educ: Wyjsza Szkota Muzyczua, Warsaw, 1972. m. Danila Alberti. Debut: As comp., Kracow, 1971; As pianist, Warsaw, 1973. Career: Tours as Concert Pianist & Pedagogue. Address: 37100 Verona, via Vicoletto Circola 3, Italy.

KOMLOS, Katalin, b. 1 Feb. 1945, Hidegség, Hungary. Musicologist. Educ: Dip., Franz Liszt Acad. of Music, Budapest. Career: musical Lectures, Radio Budapest; currently Asst. Prof., Liszt Acad. of Music, Budapest. Publs: 150 American Folk Songs, 1974. Contbr. to: Muzsika; musical reviews. Hobby: Travel. Address: Szatmár u. 53, 1142 Budapest, Hungary.

KONDEK, Patricia Lee, b. 2 Apr. 1939, New Kensington, Pa., USA. Music Copyist; Arranger. Educ: W Liberty State Coll.; Ind. State Tchrs. Coll.; pvte. study in voice & piano & arranging under Albert Lee Bryan, Sherwood Music Schl., Chog. (Dip.). m. Robert Josslyn Leonard, dec. Career: Music Copying for many recording, night club & personalities; Asst. Copyist, Broadway Show 'Seesaw', 1972-73. Mbrships: Musicians Local 802, NYC; Am. Soc. of Music Copyists (E Coast Chpt.), Exec. Comm. Mbr., 1974-76. Hobbies: Concerts; Ballet; Reading, etc. Address: 14 West 69th St. (Apt. 3), NY, NY 10023, USA.

KONDOROSSY, K. Elizabeth Davis, b. 23 Dec. 1910, East Canton, Ohio, USA. Teacher of Music to Handicapped Children; Organist; Pianist; Teacher of Organ & Piano. Educ: BA, Oberlin Coll.; EdM, Kent State Univ.; Special Educ. degree, ibid. m. Leslie Kondorossy. Debut: Piano accomp., Severance Chamber Music Hall, Cleveland. Career: Lectr., Organ Soloist, Piano Accomp., Dir. of Children's Chorus, WCLV Fine Arts Radio Stn., Cleveland; Lectr., Int. Soc. for Music Educ. Conf., Budapest, Hungary, 1964; Ch. Organist, 1st Hungarian Reformed Ch., 1948-; Apps. on radio, Cleveland & in Tokyo, Japan (piano) & Budapest, Hungary. Publs: Kalamona & the Four Winds, libretto, opera-oratorio for children's voices (under ps. Shawn Hall). Contbr. to Music Educ. Jrnl.; Parlando in Hungary. Mbr., sev. profl. orgs. Hons: Martha Holden Jennings Scholar Award, 1967 & Grant for perf. of Kalamona & the Four Winds; Wallstreet Jrnl. Newspaper Fund Award to Univ. of Mich.; Tchr. of the Yr. Award, Cleveland Coun. for Exceptional Children, 1979. Hobbies: Collecting Stamps; Travelling. Address: 14443 East Carroll Blvd., University Heights, OH 44118, USA. 5, 8, 27.

KONDOROSSY, Leslie, b. 25 June 1915, Bratislava, CSSR. Composer; Conductor; Music Teacher; Music Writer. Educ: Studied Music, Franz Liszt Acad. of Music, Budapest, Hungary; Music Educ. Sci., Western Reserve Univ., Cleveland, Ohio,

USA; Japanese theatre & music, Sophia Univ., Tokyo, Japan. m. K. Elizabeth Davis. Career incls: Cantor, a Reformed Ch., Hungary, 1932-37; Violinist in var. orchs., 1939-42; Fndr. of a musical & Lit. mag., 1951-42; Organizer & Cond., Budapest Little Symph. Orch., 1943-44; Composer, Tchr. of a RC Choir, & Cantor, Protestant Parish, Regensburg, Germany, 1945-51; Music Tchr., Cultural Arts Bur., Cleveland, USA, 1954-; Pvte. Tchr. & Chorus Dir., Opera of the Air radio prog., Stn. WSRS, Cleveland, 1955-56; Rep. abroad for Radio WCLV Fine Arts Stn., Cleveland, 1966-70. Commissions incl: New Dreams for Old, Ch. of the Master Bapt. 100 Yr. Anniversary, 1959; David Son of Jesse, The Oratorio Fund, 1967; Ode to the Loyalty of First, 1st Hungarian Reformed Ch. 80 Yr. Anniversary, 1971. Mbr., many profl. orgs. Publs: incl: Ammophila Arundinacea, piano work, 1973; Meditation for Organ, 1973; Harpsichord Trio, 1974; Two Religious Solos for Voice, 1978; Two Pieces for Organ, 1978. Hons. incl: Decoration Medal, Hungarian World Fed., Budapest, 1968; Martha Holden Jennings Fndn. (w wife), 1970. Address: 14443 East Carroll Blvd., University Heights, OH 44118, USA. 4, 8, 29.

KONDRACKI, Michael, b. 5 Oct. 1902, Poltava, Ukraine. Composer; Pianist. Musical Educ: Dip. Grand Prix, student of Karol Szymanowski, Warsaw Conservatory of Music, 1927; studied w Paul Dukas, P Vidal & Nadia Boulanger, Ecole Normale de Musique, Paris, France, 1928-33. m. Longina Turkowska Kassern. Compositions: Soldiers Marching, 1932; Little Mountaineer Symph. for 16 instruments, 1934; Opera "Popieliny", 1st perf., Warsaw, 1934; Ballet "Cracow Tale" staged at World Exhibition, Paris, 1937, & at World's Fair Hall of Music (choreography of Bronislawa Nijnska), NY, 1939; var. unpubld. comps. in MSS. Hons: Prize for Partita for small orch., comp. of Young Polish Composers Assn. Paris, 1928; Prize for Little Highlanders Symph., Polish Acad. of Sci., Cracow, 1934; 1st Olympic Grand Prix for Soldiers Marching, LA, USA, 1932; Medaille d'Or for Cracow Tale, Paris, 1937. Hobbies: Classical arts; Folklore of var. nations. Adress: 9 Ellwood St., Glen Cove, NY, NY 11542, USA. 2, 14.

KONDRASHIN, Kirill Petrovich, b. 21 Feb. 1914, Moscow, Russia. Conductor. Educ: Moscow Conserv. Career: Asst. Cond., Nemirovich-Damcenko Musical Theatre, Moscow, 1934-37; Cond., Maly Opera Theatre, Leningrad, 1938-42; Cond. Bolshoi Theatre, Moscow, 1943-56; Cond., All-Russia Symph. Orch. Touring Concert Co., 1956-60; Chief Cond., Moscow Phil. Orch., 1960-76; Prof., Moscow Conserv., 1976-. Hons: State Prize, 1948, 1949; People's Artist of USSR; M. Glinka State Prize, 1969. Address: Karietny Riad 5/10, Apt. 95, Moscow, USSR.

KONGSHAUG, Jan Erik, b. 4 July 1944, Trondheim, Norway. Recording Engineer; El. Bass Guitarist. Educ: Trondheim Tech. Schl. - Electronics, 1967. m. Kirsten Helene Kongshaug, 3 c. Career: Recording Engineer, Arne Bendiksen Studio, 1967-74, Talent Studios, 1975- (Oslo, Norway); Freelance Studio Musician; Played in Jazz Fests., Norway & France. Recordings: 7 Albums w. Sven Nyhus' Kvartett; Feelin' Allright & Night Sounds, w. Frode Thingnaes (trombone); Studio musician, over 100 other records. Address: Sondre Husebytun 34B, 7078 Saupstad, Norway.

KONÍČEK, Zdenek, b. 7 Oct. 1918, Bugojno, Yugoslavia. Cellist; Professor. Educ: AM (pol. econ.); Dip., Conserv. of Music. m. Ludmila Koniková, 1 s., 1 d. Career: Prin. Cellist, Prague Symph. Orch. until 1960; Fndr., Prague Quartet, 1955, touring extensively in Europe, S Am , USA, Can., Japan, NZ, Aust., India, USSR, etc.; Fndr., Czech Quartet, 1968, touring Europe, USA, Can., NZ, making TV & radio broadcasts, was res. ensemble, Univ. of Canterbury, Christchurch, NZ, 1968-72, then at McMaster Univ. Hamilton, Can. until 1973; Prof., McMaster Univ., 1972-. Has made many recordings w. Prague Quartet for Supraphon. Author, Cello Method Book, forthcoming. Address: 1868 Main St. W. Apt. 911, Hamilton, Ont. L8S 1J1, Canada.

KONITZKY, Sally White, b. 13 March 1928, East Aurora, NY, USA. Organist; Harpsichordist; Teacher of Piano. Educ: AA Stephens Coll., 1949; Adv. study, Organ, New England Conserv., 1960-64 & Harpsichord, Boston Univ., 1964-65; Orff-Kodály Course, Lesley Coll., 1967; Kodály Summer Course, Univ. of Bridgeport, 1971. Div., 2 c. Career: Organist at Christian Sci. Ch., 1944-46, Newtonville Swedenborgian Ch., 1959-71, Cambridge Swedenborgian Ch., 1973-; Accomp., Cambridge Chorale, 1960-69; Instructor, Perry Schl., 1968-71; Organ Recital, Kresge & MIT, 1964. Perf., Early Music Concerts at: Gardner Mus., Boston; Old N. Ch., Boston; MIT Chapel,Cambridge; First Ch. Congl., Cambridge; Busch Reisinger Mus., Cambridge; St. Andrew's Ch., Wellesley. Mbrships: NEPTA (Corres. Sec., 1977-); VP., Peabody Schl. PTA, Cambridge, 1966-68; Nat. Hon. Soc.,

1945. Hobbies: Drawing; Gardening. Address: 26 Whittier St., Cambridge, MA, USA. 5, 27.

KONJOVIC, Peter, b. 5 May 1883, Yugoslav citizen. Composer; Conductor. Educ: Prague Conserv. Career: Dir., Nat. Theatre. Novi Sad & Osijek; Dir., Min. of Pub. Instrn. & Zagreb Opera; Dir. Inst. of Musicol. & Sec. to Dept. for Arts & Music, Serbian Acad. of Scis.; Rector & Prof., Acad. of Music, Belgrade. Compositions incl: Operas - Vilin Veo-Zenidba Miloseva; Knezod Zete; Kostana; Majika Jugovica - La Patrie; Seljaci (folk opera); Moja Zemija; Makar Chudra (symphonic poem for orch.); Sonata for Violin & Piano; Capriccio Adriatico (concerto for violin & orch.); num. arrs. of folk songs for voice & piano; Liturgical & other choral works; Var. Chmbr. music items. incl: 2 string quartets. Mbrships: Past Pres., Yugoslav Sect., Int. Soc. for Contemporary Music; Soc. of Friends of Slavic Music; Fellow, Serbian Acad. of Scis. & Arts. Publs: Personalities in Theatre & Music; Serbian & Slav Music; Stevan Mokranjac - a Musical Portrait. Address: Prvog maja 32III, Belgrade, Yugoslavia.

KONO, Toshihiko, b. 8 Nov. 1930, Ashiya, Japan. Cellist. Educ: Kyoto Univ., Japan; Mannes Coll. of Music, NY, USA; Stanford Univ., Calif.; Berkshire Music Ctr., Tanglewood. m. Libby Kono, 2 d. Debut: Kyoto, 1957, USA, 1966. Career: Recital, TV, radio & fest. apps. in Japan & USA; Asst. Prin., Kyoto Symph.; Asst., Prin. New Orleans Phil.; Participant in 'Saudi Casals' in NY, 1970; Prin., Westchester Phil.; Am. Symph. (Leopold Stokowski), 1968-; Soloist w. Am. Chamber Orch. & Rochester Baroque Sinfonia, 1974. Mbr., Associated Musicians of Gr. NY., local 802 (AF. of M.); Nat. Soc. of Lit. & Arts; Bd. Dirs., Am. Symph. Hons: Fromm Fellowship in Tangleood. Address: 220 W 107th St., NY, NY 10025, USA. 28.

KONOLD, Wulf, b. 29 June 1946, Langenau/ulm, W Germany. Musicologist; Composer. Educ: Christian Albrechts Univ., Kiel, 1966-74; Musikhochschule, Lüeck, 1968-72; PhD, 1974. Career: Rsch. asst., Univ. of Kiel, 1974; Hd. of Dept. of serious music, Saarland Radio, 1975-76; freelance, 1976-77; Hd. of Drama, Musiktheaters Nürnberg, 1978-. Comps. incl: 5 Stücke für streichquartett, 1972; Inventionen for 7 solo players & strgs., 1975; Floors I & VI, 1973; Canzona, Improvvisazione e Toccata for solo flute, 1978. Publs: Weltliche Kantaten im 20. Jahrhundert, 1975; (ed) Beethoven, 5 Sinfonie (w. commentary), 1979; Das Streichquartet von den Aufängen bis Schubert, 1980; Deutsche Oper - einst und jetzt, 1979. Contbr. to num. profl. jrnls. Mbr., Gesellschaft für Musikforschung. Pommelsbrunnerstr. 24, 8500 Nürnberg, German Fed. Repub.

KONOWITZ, Bert, b. 22 Feb. 1931, Bronx, NY, USA. Music Educator; Composer; Conductor; Pianist. Educ: BA, Queens Coll., NY; Profl. Dip., MA & EdD Tchrs. Coll., Columbia Univ. m. Joan Konowitz, 3 c. Career: Prof. of Music; toured USA & Can., demonstrations, workshops & seminars. Comps. incl: Jazz for Piano, Bks. I & II; Lazy Daze (piano); Blue-Note Boogie; Jazz Spooks; The Complete Rock Piano Method; (vocal) Zodiac; Growing Up Free; We Care About Each Other (vocal); Cantus Firmus; The Last Word. Recordings: The Complete Rock Piano Method. Publs. incl: The Bert Konowitz Vocal Improvisation Method, 1971; Music improvisation as a Classroom Method, 1973. Contbr. to var. music jrnls. Mbrships incl: Am. Fed. Musicians; Nat. Assn. of Jazz Educators; MENC Chmn., Committee on Uses of Improvisation in Music Educ. Recip. var. hons. inclng. Raymond Burrow's Award, 1968. Address: 12 Hemlock Dr., Syosset, NY 11791, USA.

KONT, Paul, b. 19 Aug. 1920, Vienna, Austria. Composer; Conductor; Pianist; Writer; Professor, Music Academy of Vienna. Educ: violin & piano, Conserv. of Vienna; comp. & conducting dips., Music Acad. of Vienna. / s. Debut: Vienna Concerthouse, 1947. Career: perfs. & talks in most European & Am. countries; oepras, Austria (also TV), E & W Germany, Netherlands, (TV) & Switz. (TV). Publs. Comps. incl: piano music; chmbr. music; orchsl. works; operas (Lysistrate;Inzwischen); oratorios; ballet music. Comps. Recorded: Sieben Sonaten (piano); Der Raucher (str. orch.); Drei Ernste Stücke (str. orch.); Partita in D (str. orch.); Concerto und Concertino (str. orch.); Kassation (orch.); Klaviertrio, 1964. Author: Antianorganikum-Beobachtungen zur Neuen Musik, 1967. Contbr. to jrnls. Mbrships. incl: Couns., Authors Soc., Dramatic Authors Soc. & ISCM. Hons. incl: Grosser Preis der Stadt Wien, 1975; Österreichischer Staats-Wurdigungspreis, 1976. Address: Geusaugasse 47, A-1030, Vienna, Austria.

KONTARSKY, Aloys, b. 1931, Iserlohn, Germany. Pianist. Mgmt: Dr. R Goette, 42 Worburgstr., Hamburg, German Fed. Repub. Address: c/o Time Records Inc., 2 W 45th St., NY, NY 10036, USA. 2.

KOOIMAN, Elly, b. 24 June 1945, Amsterdam, Netherlands. Organist. Educ: Concert Dip., Conserv. Muzieklyceum, Amsterdam, 1969; High Schl. of Music, Vienna, 1972; Study w. Piet Kee, Marie-Claire Alain, Paris, Anton Heiller, Vienna. Career: Concerts in Holland, Denmark, Germany, Switz., Italy, Austria, France, Spain, & USA: Radio & TV apps.,Holland, Switz.; Prof. of Organ, Churchmusic Schl., Utrecht. Num. recordings: KNTV; NOV. Hons: 2nd Prize, Int. Organ Contest, Kiel, 1972; Prix d'Excellence of the Conserv. Amsterdam, 1972; 1st Prize, Int. Organ Contest, Bologna, 1973. Address: Weerdsweg 144, 7412 W X Deventer, Netherlands.

KOOKE, Simon Petrus Johannus, b. 13 Aug. 1915, Rottedam, Netherlands. Violinist. Educ: Conserv. of Rotterdam. m. Francoise Victorina Troupin, 2 children. Debut: Rotterdam, 1937. Career: Ldr., Haarlem Orch., 1941-42, Opera Orch., 1942-45, Brabants Orkest, 1945-49, Het Gelders Orkest, 1949-73; Soloist w. all major Dutch orchs.; many radio broadcasts; currently main Violin Tchr., Sweelinck Conserv., Amsterdam. Hobby: Architecture of old Italian violins. Address: Apeldoornse weg 218 Arnhem, Netherlands.

KOONTS, Cortlandt Morper, b. 7 March 1927, Gainesville, Fla., USA. Pianist; Organist. Educ: B Mus, M Mus, Fla. State Univ., Tallahassee. m. J. Calvin Koonts, 2 d. Career: Piano & Organ Recitals, southeast USA; Tchr. of Piano & Organ, Belmont Coll., Nashville, Tenn., Lander Coll., Greenwood, SC., & Erskine Coll., Due West, SC.; Organist, Assoc. Reformed Presby. Ch., Due West, Abbeville Presby. Ch., SC., & 1st Luth. Ch., Nashville. Contbr. to: Am. Music Tchr.; Assoc. Reformed Presby. Mbrships: Nat. MTA; SC. MTA (Treas., 2 yrs.); AGO (Dean, Greenwood Chapt., 2 yrs.); Pi Kappa Lambda; Sigma Alpha Iota (Recip., Sword of Hon.). Hobbies: Rose Gardening; Sewing. Address: PO Box 163, Due West, SC 29639, USA.

KOOPMAN, Ton, b. 2 Oct. 1944, Zwolle, Netherlands. Harpsichordist; Organist. Educ: B Musicol., Univ. of Amsterdam; Solo Degree Organ, 1969, Harpsichord, 1970, Amsterdam Conserv. m. Tini Mathot. Career: Ldr., Musica da Camera, & Musica Antiqua; num. concerts as soloist & in ensembles, Netherlands & abroad; Tchr., Conservs.of Rotterdam & Amsterdam; Num. apps. on radio & TV. Recordings incl: JP Sweetinch; Complete Keyboard Works; G Ricchi; Harp works; Italian Love Songs; Lecons de Tenebres; Spanish 17th Century Baroque Music. Ed., P Hellendaal's Cello Sonatas. Contbr. to profl. jrnls. Hons. incl: 1st Prize, Bruges Harpsichord Contest, 1968; Prix d'Excellence, Organ, 1972; Prix d'Excellence, harpsichord, 1974. Hobbies incl: Art; Hist. Address: 2e Anjeliersdwarsstraat 20, Amsterdam, Netherlands.

KOOS, Joseph, b. 19 March 1936, Budapest, Hungary. Cellist. Educ: AGSM. m. Leonora Kozuszek, 2 c. Debut: as soloist in Haydn's Symph. Concertante, Albert Hall, 1963. Career: Apps. w. major London Orchs.; Prin. Cello, Bournemoluth Symph. Orch., 11 yrs. Hobbies: Yoga; Philosophy; Teaching. Address: 9 Linwood Rd., Bournemouth, Dorset, UK.

KOOTZ, Günter, b. 7 Feb. 1919, Görlitz, Germany. Pianist; Professor. Educ: pvte. studies; Hochschule für Musick, Leipzig. m. Eva Kootz, 2 c. Debut: Dresden, 1946. Career: Concerts in Germany, Poland, Czech., Bulgaria, Romania, Yugoslavia, USSR, Finland, UK, Austria, Cuba, China; Prof., Hochschule für Musik, Leipzig. Recordings: Beethoven - Chorfantasie, Variations, Saint Liche Trios; Brahms - Violin Sonatas; Stravinsky, Duo; Kurz - Klavierkonzert. Hons: Franz Liszt Prize, Weimar, 1948; Bach Prize, Kunstpreis, National-preis, 1950, Mgmt: Kunsteragentur der DDR, Berlin. Address: Taro Str. 8-143, 701 Leipzig, German Dem. Repub.

KOPECNY, Frantisek, b. 13 March 1915, Castkovice, Czech. Cellist. Educ: Conserv. of Music, Brno; Acad. of Music, Prague. m. Marketa Gottlieb, 1 d. Debut: Brno, 1941. Career: Viennese Radio Symph. Orch., 1942-45; Czech. Radio Symph. Orch., 1945-56; State Phil. Orch., Brno, 1956-62; Prof., Conserv. of Music, Brno, 1960-66; Solocellist, Arhus Symph. Orch., Denmark, 1966-75; frequent solo apps.; recordings w. Czech. & Danish radio; Lectr., Int. Interpretation Summer Schl., Janacek's Acad. of Music, 1972, '73, '74. Recordings: Jan Novak, Capriccio, 1961. Mbr., Union of Czech. Comps. Recip., Prize for interpretation of L Janacek's work. Hobby: Gardening. Address: 61600 Brno, El. Machove 31, Czech.

KOPLEFF, Florence, b. 2 May 1924, NYC, USA. Singer. Debut: Concert Oratorio, 1946, Recital, 1954. Career: Soloist w. leading orchs. of USA, (Boston, NYC, Chgo., Atlanta, etc.); Extensive solo recitals & oratorio perfs.; Nat. & Int. tours as soloist w. Robert Shaw Chorale; participant, major music fests.;

currently Artist-in-Res., Music Dept., Ga. State Univ., Atlanta. Recordings incl: Berlioz, L'enfance du Christ, w. Boston Symph.; Beethoven, 9th Symph., w. Chgo. Symph.; Mahler, 2nd Symph. & Milhaud, Pacem in Terris, w. Salt Lake City Symph.; records w. Robert Shaw Chorale. Life Mbr., AGMA. Hobbies: Cooking & Baking; Needlepoint; Gardening. Mgmt: Walter A Gould, NYC. Address: 1945 Dellwood Drive NW, Atlanta, GA 30309, USA.

KOPP, Frederick Edward, b. 21 March 1914, Hamilton, Ill., USA. Composer; Conductor. Educ: AB, Carthage Coll.; AM, Univ. of Iowa; PhD, Eastman Schl. of Music, Univ. of Rochester; studies w. Pierre Monteux, Gustav Strube & Louis Hasselmanns. m. Kathryne L McNew, 3 s., 1 d. Career incls: Cond., Baton Rouge Civic Symph., motion picture & recording studios in Hollywood, Univ. of Ga. Symph. Choral Union & Univ. Symph. at Calif. State Univ., Los Angeles; Assoc. Prof., Univ. of Ga.; Asst. Prof., Calif. State Univ., Los Angeles. Comps. incl: 2 symphs.; 2 orchl. suites; oratorio; cantata; Dance Mass in Latin-Am. Rythms; 112 small works for chorus; 50 songs; Pepito (light opera for children), 1976; Musical comedy-melodrama, That Woman's Gotta Hang!! Publs. incl: Arthur Foote, American Composer & Theorist, 1957; The History & Literature of American Music, 1962. Mbrships. incl: ASCAP; Phi Mu Alpha; Am. Fedn. of Musicians; Comps. & Lyricists Guild of Am. Hobbies: Fishing; Camping; Woodworking. Address: 402 E Lime Ave., Monrovia, CA 91016, USA.

KOPPEL, Herman David, b. 1 Oct. 1908, Copenhagen, Denmark. Pianist; Composer. Educ: Royal Acad. of Music, Copenhagen. m. Edel Vibeke Clausen Bruun, 2 s., 2 d. Debut: 1930. Career: Prof., Piano Class, Royal Acad. of Music, Copenhagen, 1954-; Concerts, Scandinavia, N Europe, USSR, Australia. Comps. incl: 7 Symphs.; 5 Piano Concertos; 5 Str. Quartets; Opera; Oratorios; Concertos for cello, clarinet, flute, etc.; Songs; Piano pieces; Film & theatre music, num. works recorded. Address: Hojbjerg Vang 47, 2840 Holte, Denmark.

KOPPEL, Julius, b. 15 Sept. 1910, Copenhagen, Denmark. Orchestra Leader (Violin, Viola); Professor. Educ: Conserv., Copenhagen; studies in Prague, Budapest & Vienna. m. Elsemarie Brüun, 1 d. Debut: 1936. Career: Ldr. of Royal Orch., Copenhagen; Viola Player & Ldr., Koppel Quartet; Concerts in most European countries; Copenhagen. Recordings: Holmboe, Quartets III, IV & VI; Koppel Quartet & Piano Quintet; Mozart, Clarinet Quintet; Haydn Quartets; Mozart, Symph. Concertante for Violin, Viola & Orch. (w. E. Brüun); Bach, Double Concerto (w. E. Brüun). Mbrships: Chmbr. Music Soc. (Chmn.); Chmbr. Music of Hindesgave Castle. Address: Ved Volden 12, Copenhagen 1425 K, Denmark.

KOPROWSKI, Peter Paul, b. 24 Aug 1947, Lodz, Poland. Composer; Pianist; Teacher. Educ: Dip., Schl. of Music, Lodz, 1966; MA, Higher Schl. of Music, Cracow, 1969; DMus, Univ. of Toronto, 1977; studies w. Nadia Boulanger, 1971. m. Eva M Koprowski. Career: perfs. of own works on radio, TV & concert hall in Can., UK, USA, Europe, Israel, Aust., Japan; num. commissions in Poland, UK & Canada. Comps. incl: (stage) The Workshop, for 7 performers; Collage, for magnetic tape; Mahler, for magnetic tape; (Orchl.) In Memoriam Karol Szymanowski, Op. 20; Symph., Op. 36; Concerto for Youth Wind Symph. Orch., Op. 44; Concerto Grosso, Op. 35; Burlesque for violin & Orch., Op. 39; Symph. Grotesque, for children's choir & orch., Op. 22; (Choral) Biblical Cantata, Op. 18; Psalm 42, Op. 31; (instrumental) Percussion Quartet, Op. 32; String Quartet, Op. 30; Canzona for 13 Soloists, Op. 40; num. other orchl. choral & instrumental works; works for piano, violin, cello & organ; electronic works. num. recordings of own works. mbr. profl. socs. num. hons. & awards. Hobbies incl: Swimming; Skiing; Theatre. Address: c/o Can. Music Ctr., 1263 Bay St., Toronto MSR 2Cl, Can.

KOPSTEIN, David Mark, b. 10 Dec. 1946, Bronx, NY, USA. Music Educator; Professional Trumpet Player. Educ: Univ. of Hartford; B Mus, Hartt Coll. of Music, Hartford; MS, LI Univ., Greenvale, NY. Career: Lincoln Ctr.; Carnegie Hall; Mbr., Am. Concert Band, Oceanside Symph., Merrick Symph. Contbr. to: Schl. Music News; Music Educators Jrnl.; The Instrumentalist. Mbrships: Phi Mu Alpha Sinfonia; Am. Concert Band Soc.; Merrick Symph.; Am. Fedn. of Musicians Local 802; MENC; Nassau Music Educators Assn. Hobbies: Golf; Tennis; Paddleball; Bowling; Skiing. Address: 125 Hempstead Gdns. Dr., W Hempstead, NY, NY 11552, USA. 4.

KOPTAGEL, Yuksel, b. 27 Oct. 1931, Istanbul, Turkey. Pianist; Composer. Educ: Conserv. Real Madrid; Conserv. de Paris; Schola Cantorum, Ecole Superieur de Musique, ibid; study w. pvte. tutors. m. Danyal Kerven. Debut: Istanbul, age 4. Career: Soloist w. leading orchs., concert, TV & radio perfs.

in most European countries, India, Pakistan, Japan, etc. Comps. incl: Tamzara; Toccata; Danse Rustique; When We Two Parted; Deux Chansons du Pecheur Japonais; Zwei Spanische Lieder; Fossil Suite; Fossil fur Klavier; Tamzara fur Guitarre. Recordings of var. comps. issued on Phillips & Eternaschallplatten Berlin labels. Mbrships: Soc. of Authors, Composers & Editors of Music, Paris; Young Musicians of France, etc. Recip. var. awards for comps. Hobbies: Photography; Filming; Recording; Animals. Address: Cumhuriyet Cadd. 327/8, Harbiye - Istanbul, Turkey.

KOPYTMAN, Mark, b. 6 Dec. 1929, Kamenetz-Podolski, USSR. Composer; Pianist; Educator. Educ: MD, Tchernovitz, USSR, 1952; M Mus, Lwov Acad. of Music, 1955; D Mus, Moscow Acad. of Music, 1958. Career: Tchr. of theory & comp., USSR State Acad. of Music, 1955-72; Rubin Acad. of Music, Jerusalem, Israel, 1972-; Chmn., Theory Dept., ibid, 1974-75; Chmn., Theory & Comp. Dept., ibid., 1957-; Prof., ibid. Comps. incl: Kasa Mare (opera), 1966; Songs of Kodr (oratorio), 1965; Lamentation (flute), 1973; Voices (voice, flute & orch.), 1974-75; Monodrama (ballet), 1975; chmbr. music for var. instruments; music for choir a'cappella, film & drama. Publs: Choral Composition, 1971. Mbr., profl. assns. Recip., var. prizes. Address: 4 Tchernichkovsky St., Jerusalem, Israel.

KORČAK, Friedrich, b. 21 Feb. 1926, Vienna, Austria. University Professor. Educ: Cons., 1940-47; Acad. of Music & Dramatic Arts, 1947-51; Univ. of Vienna, 1945-52; Dr phil (musicol.); State Dip. for violin & voice trng.; Lehramtsprüfung, musical educ. m. Hertha Riedl, 1 s., 2 d. Career: Prof. of Music, Graz, 1947-51; Rector, Acad. for Music & Dramatic Arts, 1971; Mgr., Assn. of Austrian Music Educators, (AGMO), 1963. Publs: Luigi Tomasini, fürstl. esterhazyscher Konzertmeister unter Joseph Haydn, 1952; Musikerziehung in der Lehrerbildung, 1968; Musikerziehung als Anliegan der Pädagogischen Akademie, 1969. Contbr. to periodicals. Mbrships: Chmn., AGMO; Austrian Soc. for Musicol. Address: Vogelweiderstr. 39, Graz, Austria.

KORCHINSKA, Maria, b. 17 Feb. 1895, Moscow, Russia. Harpist. Educ: Moscow Conserv. m. Count Konstantine Benckendorff, dec., 1 s., 1 d. Career: Perf. & Tchr., Moscow Conserv., 1918-26; app. in films, concerts & on TV, UK, 1926-. Recordings: Harp & Viola Sonata by Arnold Bax (dedicated to her); Handel Concerto; Benjamin Britten's Ceremony of Carols. Contbr. to var. reviews. Mbrships: Chmn., Harp Assn.; Musicians Union. Recip. of 1st Gold Medal given to harpist, Moscow Conserv., 1911. Address: 36 Greville Rd., London NW6 5JL, UK.

KORECKA-SOSZKOWSKA, Maria-Jadwiga, b. 15 Oct. 1943, Lwów, Poland. Pianist. Educ: Dip., Hons., State High Schl of Music, Cracow, 1967; 1st Prize, Mastercourse for Modern Piano Technique, Switzerland; Dip., State High Schl. of Music, Vienna, Austria, 1976. m. Jan-Julian Soszkowski. Debut: Opole, 1959. Career: Annual symph. concerts & piano recitals, Poland; Concerts in Austria, Bulgaria, Czechoslovakia, German Dem. Repub., German Fed. Repub. & Switzerland; Repertoire of 11 symph. concerts & 18 piano recitals. Recordings: Sev. for Polish radio & TV. Contbr. to Polish Music Mag., 1974. Mbrships: Soc. Polish Artists of Music; Chopin Soc. Hons: 2nd Prize, Paderewski Competition, 1961; 1st Prize, Int. Mastercourse for Spanish Music, 1978. Hobbies: Musicology; Family; Tourism. Address: ul. Belska 6 m. 26, 02-638 Warsaw, Poland.

KORFF-KAWECKA, Helena, b. 10 Nov. 1907, Warsaw, Poland. Opera Singer; Soloist. Educ: Soloist Dip.(w. distinction), Warsaw Conserv., 1934. m. Zygmunt Kawecki (dec.), 1 d. Career: Prin., Warsaw Opera House & other leading opera houses, Poland; Num. radio apps. w. Phil. Orch.; Recitals; Guest apps. w. Polish Musical Centre; Pedagogical work w. musical centres. Recordings: Sev. light music records. Mbrships: Christian Assn. Pax; Warsaw Musical Soc., (Bd. of Dirs.,Organizing Sec.). Hons: Num. Prizes, Dips., etc. Hobbies: Pedagogics; Benefit Concert Perfs. Address: ul. Natolinska 3.m. 25, Warsaw, Poland.

KORN, Peter Jona, b. 30 Mar. 1922, Berlin, Germany. Composer; Conductor; Writer; Conservatory Director. Educ: Berlin HS for Music, 1932-33; Jerusalem Conserv., 1936-38; UCLA, 1941-42; Univ. of Southern Calif., 1946-47; studied comp. w. Edmund Rubbra, London, 1934-36, Stefan Wolpe, Jerusalem, 1936-38, Arnold Schoenberg, 1941-42, Ernst Toch, Hanns Eisler & Miklos Rozsa, 1946-47, all Los Angeles. m. Barbara Sheldon, 1 s., 1 d. Career incls: Guest Cond. w. many orchs., concerts & radio. Comps. incl: works for full, chmbr. & str. orchs. & chmbr. ensembles; song cycles; choral works; etc. Publs: A propos Zwangsjacke, 1959; Musikalische

Umweltverschmutzung, 1975. Contbr. to books & jrnls. Mbr. profl. orgs. Recip. many hons. Address: Mozartring 10, D-8011 Baldham nr. Munich, German Fed. Repub.

KORN, Richard (Kaye), b. 24 Aug. 1908, NYC, USA. Conductor; Clarinetist. Educ: BA, Princeton Univ., 1928; Juilliard Grad. Schl., 1937-39; Nat. Orchl. Assn., 1936-39; Tanglewood, 1940-41. m. Peggy Lashanska Rosenbaum Lehman, 2 d. Debut: NY Stadium Concerts, 1946. Career:, Mus. Dir., Orch. of Am., NY, 1959-65, Baton Rouge Symph., La., 1950-51, original Ballet Russe, 1947-48, Robin Hood Dell (Phila.) Children's Concerts, 1958; Apps. w. NBC Symph., 1951-53, London Symph., 1950, Paris Conservatoire, 1949-50, ABC Orch., Tokyo, 1957, etc. Compositions: Arniana, orch. suite of music of Thos. Arne; Many Me's orch. ballet suite; Hebraic Sketch. Recordings: Brahms Serenade in A; Mozart Serenade K.375; 3 records of histl. & contemporary Am. music; The Mikado (w. Martyn Green). Author of Orchestral Accents, 1956, 2nd ed., 1971. Mbrships: Pres., Soc. for Publs. of Am. Music, 1956-62; Bd. mbr., Nat. Music Coun., 1955-62; Exec. Comm., Friends of Music at Yale, 1960-70; Dir., The Bohemians, 1961-72; Bd. mbr., Musicians' Fndn., 1971-; Fellow, World Acad. of Arts & Scis.; Century Assn. Recip. of ons. Hobbies: Astonomy; Golf; Travel; Photography. Address: 898 Park Ave., NY, NY 10021, USA. 2.

KORNHAUSER, Bronia, b. 14 Feb. 1950, Tel Aviv, Israel. Ethnomusicologist; Gamelan Player. Educ: BA, Monash Univ., Vic., Aust., 1971; Master's Preliminary, ibid., 1973; Dip., Educ., ibid., 1977; MA, ibid., 1977. m. William Philip Kornhauser, 1 s. Career: Tutor & lectr. in Western & non-Western music; part-time lectr. on world music at Vic. Coll. of Arts; stage & TV perfs. as mbr. of Gamelan orch.; radio progs. in Java on Kroncong music. Publs: In Defence of Kroncong, 1978; Kroncong Music in Java, 1977. Mbrships: Int. Folk Music Coun.; Aust. Musicol. Soc.; Indonesian Arts Soc.; Aust. Indonesian Assn.; Monash Gamelan Soc. Hobbies: Tapestry; Dress Designing; Jigsaw Puzzles. Address: 5 Hillside Ave., Caulfield, Vic. 3162, Aust.

KORTE, Karl, b. 25 Aug. 1928, Ossining, NY, USA. Composer. Widower, 1 s., 1 d. Comps. incl: Symphony 2 & 3; Mass for Youth, chorus, orch., keybd.; Concerto for Piano & Wind; Libera me, chorus & orch.; Pale is the Good Prince, Oratorio, 2 pianos, 4 percussion; String Quartet 2; Matrix, woodwind quintet, piano, percussion; Dialogue, alto sax & tape; Remembrances, flute & tape; Facets, sax quartet; Psalm XIII, chorus & tape. Mbrships. incl: ASCAP; Am. Soc. Univ. Composers. Hons: Num. fellowships & awards; Priz du Govt. Belge (Gold Medal), Queen Elizabeth Int. Competition, 1970. Hobby: Sailing. Address: c/o Dept. Music, Univ. Tex., Austin, TX 78712, USA. 14.

KORTE, Oldřich Frantisek, b. 26 Apr. 1926, Sal, Czechoslovakia. Composer; Pianist; Music Critic; Writer; Actor. Educ: Prague Conserv. 1943-49. m. (3) div., 1 s. Debut: as composer/pianist, 1933; as symphonic composer, 1949; as film actor, 1956. Career: as Pianist & Actor, of Laterna Magica (expmntl. theatre), 1959-, has made over 3000 apps. on 4 continents, w. tours longer than 6 months in German Fed. Repub., USSR, Mexico, Argentina, inclng., Expo 67, Montreal, Can.; Artistic Ledr. of Chorea Bohemica (music-dance-theatre), Prague, 1972-; also assoc. w. Nat. Theatre. Compositions publd. incl: Excursion, cycle of instructive pieces for piano; Pirates from Fortunia, musical for children. Compositions publd. & recorded incl: Symphonietta for large orch.; Story of the Flutes, both played by Czech. Phil. Orch.; 1949, Orch. Suisse Romande, 1969; Sonata for Piano; Troubadour Songs. Publs: The Walking Legends (essays), 1970; The Chamber Essays (cycle of 9 TV progs., also broadcast on Czech. TV), 1974; Philosophical Dialogues for violin & piano; Pirates from Fortunia. Contbr. to var. mags. Mbrships: Authors' Org. (OSA), Syndicate of Czech. Composers. Recip. of 1st Special Prize for Piano Fantasy, played by Maurizio Pollini at competition in Bolzano, Italy, 1956. Hobby: Motoring. Address: Marikova 7, 160 00 Prague 6-Petriny, Czechoslovakia.

KORY, Agnes, b. 13 Dec. 1944, Budapest, Hungary. Cellist; Teacher. Educ: Final Cert., Bela Bartok Conservatoire, Budapest; Recital Dip., RAM, London. Career: Prin. Cellist, Royal Ballet Orch., 1970-72; Mbr. Engl. Nat. Opera, 1974-; Prin. Cellist, London Soloist's Ensemble, 1977-78; mbr. of ILEA Music Panel, 1977-; Solo Recitals; Purcell Room, London; Merton Coll., Oxford; Univ. Glasgow; Trinity & All Saints Colls., Leeds, Harrogate Fests. & Paris; Fndr. & Dir., Merle Ensemble, 1975. Contbr. to: The Strad; Music Teacher. Mbr. Musicians' Union; ISM; European String Teachers Assn. Hons. incl: RAM; H. Walenn Prize for scale-playing, 1966; H. Walenn Prize for the perf. of a solo Bach suite, 1968; John B. McEvevon Prize

(ensemble), 1969; Sir Edward Cooper Prize (Ensemble playing), 1969. Address: 6 Frognal Ct., Finchley Rd., London, NW3, UK.

KOS, Koraljka, b. 12 May 1934, Zagreb, Yugoslavia. Musicologist; Teacher. Educ: Acad. of Music, Zagreb; PhD, Musicol., Philos. Fac., Ljubljana. 1 d. Career: Prof., Musicol. Dept., Music Acad., Zagreb; Sci. study grant, Germany (Humboldt-Stiftung), 1973-74. Publs: Musikinstrumente im mittelalterlichen Kroatien, 1972; Num. musicol. studies. Contbr., & Ed. Bd. Mbr., Arti Musices, Zagreb. Mbrships: Union of Croatian Composers; Mbr., Int. Commn. Mixte. for Int. Musicol. Soc., of Int. Repertory of Musical Iconog. Hobby: Mountaineering. Address: Zelenjak 20, YU-41000 Zagreb, Yugoslavia.

KOSAKOFF, Gabriel, b. 24 Dec. 1926, NYC, USA. Music Educator; Conductor. Educ: BA, MA, NY Univ.; Mannis Coll. of Music; Manhattan Schl. of Music; Queens Coll. m. Carol Lenhoff, 1 s., 1 d. Career incls: Asst. Prin., Supvsn.-Music, LaGuardia HS of Music & the Arts; Music Educ. Depts., NY Univ., NY Coll. of Music & Manhattan Schl. of Music; Cond., NYC All-City HS Band, City Coll. Band, CCNY; Long Island Univ. Band; Guest Cond. & Adjudicator; Exec. Bd., NY State Schl. Music Assn. Contbr. to: Instrumentalist; Music Educs. Jrnl. Mbrships. incl: MENC; NYSSMA; United Fedn. of Musicians; Coun. for Specialized HSs; Coun. of Supvsrs. & Admnstrs. Hons. incl: Citation of Hon., Mayor Beame of NYC, 1979. Address: 160 W 96th St., NY, NY 10025, USA.

KOS-ANATOLSKYI, Anatol Ossypovych, b. 1 Dec. 1909, Kolomyya, Ukraine. Composer; Music Educator. Educ: LLm, Lviv Univ., 1931; Lviv Conserv., 1934. m. Nadiya Opryshko, 3 children. Career incl: Lectr., Lviv State Conserv., 1954-; Prof., ibid, 1973-. Compositions incl: Fiery Dawn (opera), 1959; Ballets - Dovbush's Kerchief, 1951; Jay's Wing, 1957; Oryssia, 1964; Spring Tempests (Musical Comedy), 1960; Concerto for Harp & Orch., 1954; 2 Concertos for Piano & Orch., 1955, 1962; Transcarpathian Rhapsody for Violin & Orch., 1955; Immortal Testament (cantata), 1964; From Niagara to Dnipro (oratorio), 1970; var. choral works, songs, etc. Num. works recorded. Publs: Monograph on S Ludkevych, 1951; contbr. to var. music jrnls., etc. Mbrships. incl: Chmn., Lviv Br., Ukrainian Composers Union; Mgmt. Exec., Composers Unions of Ukraine & USSR. Hons. incl: Order of Lenin, 1960; People's Artist of Ukraine, 1969. Hobbies: Linguistics; Football. Address: Flat 5, hlibiv Ul, 15, Lviv-5, 290005, Ukraine, USSR.

KOSCH, Franz, b. 1894, Steyr, Austria. Professor of Sacred Music. Educ: PhilD, Fac. of Catholic Theol. & Philos., Univ. of Vienna. Career: Music Tchr., Episcopal Sem. of Coll. of Hollabrunn, 1919-27; Prof., Sems. for Priests, Vienna, 1925-; Prof., Acad. of Music, Vienna, 1933-60; Hd., Dept. of Sacred Music, ibid, 1938-60; Advsr. on Musical Educ., Fedn. Min. of Educ., 1953-; Lectr. in Sacred Music, Univ. of Vienna, 1958-65. Compositions incl: liturgical motets; accomps., for Gregorian chants. Publs: eds of ch. music; Schubert's Salve Regina; Fl. L Gassmann Kirchenwerke; Sunol Gregorianischer Choral. Contbr. articles, essays & criticisms to the newspapers, jrnls., etc. Mbrships. incl: Fndr. & sometime Hd., Vienna Diocesan Commission for Sacred Music; Bd. of Dir., Vienna Soc. of Music Lovers. Recip. of many prizes. Address: Josefstadterstrasse 52/10, 1080 Vienna VIII Austria. 3.

KOSCHMIEDER, Erwin, b. 31 Aug. 1895, Liegnitz, Germany. Professor of Slavonic Languages. Educ: Doct. Breslau Univ.; 1975, Doct. Ukranian Free Univ., München. m. Annemarie Roth, 2 d., 1 s. Career: 1926, Lectr. Breslau Univ.; 1930, Assoc. Prof., 1938, full Prof. Wilna Univ.; 1939, Münich Univ. Publs. incl: Sopila, A Wind Instrument of Folk Music of the Island of Krk, Etnografia Polska 3, 1960; Old Russian Church Songs as Linguistic Material, Zbirnyk prysvjac, Paris, München, 1961; w. J V Gardner, A Handwritten Textbook on the Old Russian Neumen Scrip. Contbr. to var. profl. jrnls. Mbrships: var. profl. orgs. Hons. incl: Hohenzollern House Order; Bavarian Order of Merit, 1966. Hobbies: Music, flute, organ, piano; sports, tennis. Address: Beethovenstrasse 42, D-8011 Vaterstetten, Germany.

KOSEV, Atanas Nedialkov, b. 10 March 1934, Rousse, Bulgaria. Composer; Pianist. Educ: Comp. & Cond., Bulgarian State Conserv., Sofia. m. Radina Vulova, 1 s., 1 d. Debut: As comp. of theatrical music, Rousse, 1951; as cond. of the Youth Symphonic Orch., Rousse. Career: Ed., Bulgarian Nat. Radio & TV. Comps: More than 400 children's & popular songs; music for 30 theatrical perfs. & 10 films; musicals, Little Red Riding Hood, Doctor, The Millionaire, A Pleasant Day, Illumination of the Pose; Children's Suite for piano; Sonatina & Goke; Symphony 1300; Concerto for Piano & Orch.; Symphonic Poem, Strashitza; Symphonic Picture, Autumn Pastels; Cantata for Mixed Choir & Percussions. Mbr., Assn. of Bulgarian Comps. Hons: Prize of Sofia, 1968; The Golden Orpheus, 1972, ;74, '76, '77. Hobbies: Swimming; Tennis. Address: Kvartal Lagera, Block 33, Sofia 1612, Bulgaria.

KOSEWSKI, Mieczyslaw, b. 24 Mar. 1908, Warsaw, Poland. Conductor; Teacher; Manager of Brass Orchestras. Educ: MA (cond., trumpet & piano), Warsaw Schl. of Music, 1934. m. Irena Nizinska, 1 s., 1 d. Career incl: Cond., brass orchs., 1926-39; tchr. of music, 1934-39; fndr., chmn., Polish Assn. of Brass Orchs., 1949-50; Dir., Polish Assn. of Chorus & Brass Orchs., Warsaw, 1950-72; organizer, chmn. of jury, 12 nat. fests. of Russian music for brass orchs., Katowice, 1949-74; chief inspector, Brass Orchs., Assn. of Auxiliary/Voluntary Fire Brigades in Poland, organizer of fests., chmn. of jury, 5 nat. fests. of fire brigades brass orchs., 1933-39, 1946-78. Contbr. to sev. profl. jrnls. Mbrships: Democratic Party, 1945-78 (hon. mbr., 1973); Cultural Workers Trade Union; mbr., presidium, Assn. of Musicians in Poland. num. hons., prizes & awards. Hobby: Mountain Hiking. Address: ul. Ordona 12a m.44, 40164 Katowice, Poland.

KOSLER, Miroslav, b. 25 July 1931, Prague, Czechoslovakia. Conductor; Choirmaster. Educ: Grad. State Acad. of Music, Prague, 1962. m. Eva Reimoser, 1 d. Debut: Prague. Career: Cond., Czech choirs, tours of France, UK, USSR, Poland, Bulgaria, Hungary, Italy, E, W Germany, Austria, Spain, Rumania; Dir., Prague Male Choir, Symph. Orch. FOK; Jury Mbr., Int. choir competitions, W Germany, Italy, Bulgaria & Czechoslovakia. Hons: Cond., prizewinning choirs, Paris, 1956, Moscow, 1957, Bucharest, 1953, Spittal, 1967, Arezzo, 1965, Gorizia, 1969, Prague, 1965. Hobby: Hunting. Address: Marie Pujmanové 882, Prague 4 - Podoli, Czechoslovakia.

KOSLER, Zdenek, b. 25 Mar. 1928, Praha, Czechoslovakia. Orchestra Conductor. Educ: Cond., Acad. of Arts, Praha. m. Jana Koslerova. Debut: Opera, Nat. Theater, Praha, 1951. Career: Nat. Theater, Praha, 1948; Opera Dir., Opera House Olomouc, 1958; State Opera, Ostrava, 1962; Permanent Cond., Prague Symph. Orch., 1966; Gen. Music Dir., Komische Opera, Berlin, 1967; Permanent Cond., Czech Phil., Prague, 1971; Chief Cond., Opera of Slovak Nat. Theater, Bratislava, 1971. Num. recordings. Hons. incl: Prizes at Int. Conds. Competitions: State Title, Deserving Artist of the CSSR, 1975. Mgmt: Pragokoncert, Praha; Concerto C W Winderstein, Munchen; Kazuko Hillyar, NY; Nihon Denpa News, Tokyo; A Raab, Wien. Address: 160 00 Praha 6, Nad Sarkou 35, Czechoslovakia.

KOSMALA, Jerzy S., b. 15 Apr. 1931, Krakow, Poland. Violist. Educ: B Mus, M Mus, Krakow Schl. of Music; M Mus, Eastman Schl. of Music, Rochester, NY, USA; Mus D, Ind. Univ. m. Anna, 3 children. Career: Viola soloist in concerts in Europe & N Am.; Violist w. Krakow String Quartet, Polish String Quartet, Eastman String Quartet; Fac., Krakow Schl. of Music, Ind. Univ., Peabody Coll. & Univ. of S Fla.; Prin. Violist w. major orchs. in Poland & USA; TV & radio broadcasts, Europe & USA. Recordings (for Polish Radio) Mozart - Sinfonia Concertante; Bloch - Suite Hebraique; J C Bach - Concerto in C Minor; Telemann - Suite in D Major. Publs: Ed., Carl Stamitz viola concertos; var. transcriptions for viola & piano. Hons: 1st Prize, All-Poland Viola Comps., Warsaw, 1956; 3rd Prize, Int. Young Comp., Moscow, 1956. Address: 116 Hamilton Ave., Akron, OH 44304, USA.

KOSOWICZ, Francis John, b. 20 July 1946, Lowell, Mass., USA. Concert organist; Pianist; Harpsichordist. Educ: incl: Iona Coll.; Manhattanville Coll., Pius X Schl. of Liturgical Music; Univ. of Mass.; Amherst Coll.; studies w. Edgar Hilliar, Richard Casper, Charles A McGrail, E Power Biggs & others. m. Silvana Marisa Renata Anita Bruna Maria-Silvia Cenci. Debut: St. Catherine's Ch. Graniteville, Mass. Career: Organist, St. Catherine's Ch., Graniteville; Chapel of Peace, Kings Point, Bermuda; Holy Trinity Chapel, Gia Le, Vietnam; num. solo recitals, Mexico, USA & Bermuda. Comps: Wedding; Imperial Suit. Publs: Book of Worship for United States Forces, 1974. Contbr. to: The Diapason; Music Mag.; Jrnl. of the Am. Musicol. Soc.; Audubon; Smithsonian; Spectrum. Mbrships: AGO; Royal Can. Coll. of Organists; Am. Musicol. Soc.; Roane Arts & Humanities Coun. (fndr.) Hobbies: Gourmet Cooking; Writing Poetry; Raising Parrots & Birds. Address: Silfran, Box 13-C Harmony Route, Spencer, WV 25276, USA. 6.

KOSTER, Dijck (Anna Marijke), b. 13 Apr. 1923, Utrecht, Holland. Musician (violoncello, modern & baroque cello). Educ: Solo Dip. of the Royal Conserv. od The Hague, 1947 (class of Mr Max Orobio de Castro); studies in Paris w. Paul Bazelaire & Paul Tortellier, 1948-52. Career: 1st Cellist, Amsterdam Phil. Orch., 1954-60; Mbr. of the Concertgebouw Orkest, Amsterdam, 1963-; Mbr., Leonhardt-Consort, Baroque-grp., 1955-, chamber music, trio quartet, recitals. Recordings as

mbr. of the Concertgebouw Orkest (Philips) & Leonhardt-Consort (Teldec.).

KOSTER, Ernst, b. 8 Oct. 1904, Hamburg Germany. Composer; Violin Teacher; Music Critic. Educ: Violin w. concert master Bornemann, City Orch., Wuppertal, 1926-30; Gesterkamp, Phil. Orch., Hamburg, 1930-32. m. Grete Weltzien. Career: Composer; Freelance contbr. to radio, 1931-. Compositions incl: Chmbr. music: Diverse Divertimenti; Trios (strings, flutes); Schl. opera, 'The Village Wedding'; 'Mother Careys House'; Chmbr. Opera, 'New Shore'; 'Jeri & Bately'; Cantatas: 'Dark Voices'; 'Little Black Passion' (also recorded); Jardins au Printemps. Contbr. to profl. jrnls. Mbr., Hamburg State Youth Music Schl., 1958-76. Hobby: String quartet. Address: Volksdorfer Grenzweg 46a, 2000 Hamburg 67, German Fed. Repub.

KOSTIĆ, Dušan, b. 23 Jan. 1925, Zagreb, Yugoslavia. Composer; Professor. Educ: Degree of magistracy, comp.; Orch. Cond. w. Hermann Scherchen; Piano studies; I degree, law; II degree, Philos. m. Slobodanka. Debut: as comp., 1952. Career: Prof., grammar schl. for music, 1952; Redactor for music, Radio Beograd, 1956; Fac., Musical Art, Beograd, 1962. Comps. incl: Sonatina for bassoon & piano, 1953; Seven Hippopotamic studies for piano, 1977; Four and a half lumps for piano, Suite, 1977; Songs for childrens choir a cappella & w. piano accomp., 1978; (recorded) I Symphonie in Sol; II Symphonie; cantatas - Brod (Ship), Otadzbina (Fatherland), Kragujevac; Jokes of Backa, female choir; III Quartetto per archi; Cod-liver oil, children's choir & piano. Contbr. to: Politika; Zvuk. Mbrships: Union of Serbian Comps.; Jeunesses Musicales. Hobbies: Painting; Cooking; Travelling. Address: Steve Todorovića 35/XI, 11030 Belgrade, Yugoslavia.

KOSTIĆ, Vojislav, b. 21 Sept. 1931, Belgrade, Yugoslavia. Composer. Educ: Acad. of Music, Belgrade. div. Comps: 2 Ballets, several musicals, much chamber music (Sonata for violin & piano, Wind Quintet, Jazz Suite etc.); vocal-instrumental works (Cantata, Arches of Shade); almost 300 works for the theatre, films, radio & TV. Recordings: 19 LPs of own comps. Contbr. to profl. jrnls. in Yugoslavia & other countries. Mbr. num. profl. socs.; Gen. Sec., Union of Yugoslav Comps., 1966-75; VP, Union of Film & TV workers of Serbia, 1978-; Hons: Awarded over 20 prizes in Yugoslavia & abroad for comps., film & stage music; Order of Labour with Golden Wreath, Yugoslavia; Richard Strauss medal, German Fed. Repub. Hobbies: Cooking; Farming. Address: Kićevska 1/I, 11000 Belgrade, Yugoslavia.

KOSTOHRYZ, Milan, b. 1 June 1911, Kostelec nOrl., Czech. Professor of Clarinet. Educ: Ing. Dr., Agriculture; Studied Clarinet & Comp., Conserv., Prague. m. Jarmila Venturová, 1 s., 2 d. Career: Public & Radio concerts as Solo & Chmbr. clarinettist; Prof. of Clarinet, Conserv. of Prague, Mbr., Nat. Theatre, Prague. Recordings: Num. recordings in Czech. & abroad as Soloist & w. Chmbr. Ensembles & Orchs. Contbr. to: Hudebni Rozhledy; The Clarinet Mbr., Svaz c. skladatelu a Koncert umeulcu. Hon: Deserving Artist of CSSR. Hobby: Folk Music. Mgmt: Pragokoncert. Address: U smaltovny 22A, 17000 Prague 7, Czech.

KOSZEWSKI, Andrzej, b. 26 July 1922, Poznán, Poland. Composer; Musicologist. Educ: study of musicol., Poznán Univ. w. Adolf Chybinski (Dip. 1950); studies in comp. & theory of music, State Higher Schls. in Poznán (w. Stefan B Poradowski, Dips. 1948 & '53); w. Tadeusz Szeligowski, Warsaw (Dip. 1958). m. Krystyna Jankowska, 1 d. I chr. of Comp. & Theory of Music as Prof. at State Higher Schl. of Music in Poznán. His choral works are perf. at num. int. fests. & competitions in Europe & Am. Comps. incl: (orchl.) Sinfonietta, 1956; (for piano) Przystroje, 1970; 3 Sonatinas, 1978; (for mixed chorus a cappella) Muzyka Fa-Re-Mi-Do-Sl, 1960; Tryptyk Wielkopolski (Great Poland Triptych), 1963; La Espero (The Hope), 1963; Nicolao Copernico Dedicatum, 1966; Gry (Games), 1968; BA-NO-SCHE-RO, 1971-72, 3 Kole,dy, 1975; Prologues, 1975; Da Fischiare, 1973; Canzone e Danza, 1974. Var. recordings. Author of many publs. dealing w. Chopinology & Musical Educ. Contbr. to many profl. publs. Mbrships: Polish Comps. Union, sections of Comps. & Musicols.; Chopin Soc. in Warsaw. Hons: Prize of Min. of Culture & Arts in Poland, 1967, '73, '77; Artistic Prize of the City of Poznán, 1968. Address: ul. Poznanska 37 m. 9, 60-850 Poznán, Poland. 30.

KOSZUT, Urszula, b. 13 Dec., Psyczyna, Poland. Opera Singer. Educ: Magister, High Schl. for Music, Katowice, Poland. m. Gerhard Girst, 1 d. Debut: Stuttgart, 1967, in Lucia di Lammermoor. Career: Apps. in operas by Bellini (Norma), Donizetti (inclng. Don Pasquale), Gounod (inclng. Romeo & Juliette), Hindemith (Mathis der Maler), Mozart (Queen Konstanza, Donna Anna, Fiordeligi), Puccini, Strauss, Verdi & others; concert apps. as soloist in works by Beethoven, Bach,

Brahms, Handel, Haydn, Mozart, Mahler, etc. Recordings: in Symphony No. 9 (Beethoven); Mass in A Flat (Schubert); Mathis der Maler (Hindemith); Don Giovanni (Mozart), etc. Mgmt: Agentur Stoll (Schulz), Munich. Address: Lilienstr.26, 6670 St. Ingbert, German Fed. Repub.

KOTH, Erika, b. 14 Sept. Darmstadt, Germany. Opera Singer. Educ: Hessische Musikschule, Darmstadt. m. Ernst Dorn. Recordings: Bei Emi-Elektrola, Grammophon, Eurodisc. Publs: Herzlichst Erika Koth, Justus von Liebig; Verlag, Darmstadt. Hons: Bayerischer Verdienstorden; Bundesverdienstkreuz Mozartmedaille; Heinrich von Merck Preis. Hobby: Collecting Antiques. Address: 8011 Baldham, Erika Kothstr.6, Germany.

KOTLER, Marcie Susan Laitman, b. 21 Dec. 1941, NYC, USA. College Piano & Theory Instructor; Pianist; Lecturer in Musicology. Educ: Preparatory Divs., Manhattan & Juilliard Schls. of Music; Ecole des Beaux Arts, Fontainebleau, France, 1959; AB, Vassar Coll., USA, 1962; Grad. studies, Columbia Univ., 1963, & Manhattan Schl. of Music, 1962-67; MA, NY Univ., 1967. m. Morris N Kotler, MD, 1 s., 1 d. Career: Asst. Music Ed., HiFi/Stereo Review, 1962-63; Fac. mbr., Northeastern Christian Jr. Coll., Villanova, Pa.; num. community concerts & lectures. Mbrships: incl: Musical Coterie, Wayne, Pa. Hons: NY All-State Music Fest. Awards, 1954-58; var. scholarships & awards, NY State, 1958-64. Hobbies incl: Gardening; Sewing. Address: 2200 N Stone Ridge Lane, Villanova, PA 19085, USA.

KOTSARENKO, Anna, b. Crimea, Russia. Classical Guitarist; Teacher & Lecture-Recitalist. Educ: BFA in Music, Univ. of Pa., USA; Cert., Accademia Musicale Chigiana, Siena, Italy (master class of Andres Segovia, 1956). Career: Instructor of Classical Guitar, Temple Univ., Combs Coll. of Music, Phila., & Rutgers Univ., Camden, NJ.; Lecture-recital, The Guitar through the Ages. Mbrships: Phila. Classical Guitar Soc. (Fndg. Mbr.); Haddonfield Classical Guitar Soc., NJ. Hobby: Pastry-baking. Address: 2836 Benson St., Camden, NY 08105, USA.

KOTTICK, Edward Leon, b. 16 June 1930, Jersey City, NJ., USA. Musicologist. Educ: BA., NY Univ., Wash. Sq., NYC, 1953; MA., Tulane Univ., New Orleans, La., 1959; PhD., Univ. of NC., 1962. m. Gloria Astor, 2 d. Career: (Tchng.) Asst. Prof., Alma Coll., Mich., 1962-65; Vis. Lectr., Univ. of Kans., Lawrence, 1965-66; Assoc. Prof., Univ. of Mo., St. Louis, 1967-68; Assoc. Prof., Univ. of Iowa, 1968-75; Prof., 1976-. (Perf.) Trombonist w. Gershwin Concert Orch., 1953; Cond., Signal Schl. Band, 1953-55; Trombonist, New Orleans Phil. & New Orleans Opera Co., 1955-59; Cond. of Orch. & Band, Alma Coll., 1962-65; Cond., Univ. Chamber Orc. Orch., Univ. of Mo., St. Louis, 1967; Musical Dir., Collegium Musicum, Univ. of Iowa & Mbr. of the Fac. Baroque Trio (recorder), 1969-74; Arr. for band, Henry Purcell, Two Trumpet Tunes & Ayre, 1959. Publs: (books) The Unica in the Chansonnier Cordiforme, No. 42 of Corpus Mensurabilis Musicae, 1967; Tone & Intonation on the Recorder, 1974; The Collegium: A Handbook, 1977; many articles & papers. Mbrships: incl: var. offices, Am. Musicol. Soc.; Am. Musical Instrument Soc.; Galpin Soc.; Coll. Music Soc.; Lute Soc. of Am. Hobbies: Builing harpsichords, lutes, guitars, citterns. Address: 2001 Muscatine, Iowa City, IA 52240, USA.

KOUDELKA, George John, b. 27 Feb. 1945, Hallettsville, Tex., USA. Educator; Percussionist; Director of Bands. Educ: B Mus Ed., Southwest Tex. State Univ., 1968; M Ed., Prarie View A & M Univ., 1972; all level tchrs. cert. Career: Profl. percussionist w. radio dance orchs., 1955-80; Instructor in Percussion, Southwest Tex. State Univ., 1967-69; currently Dir. of Bands, Flatonia Pub. Schls., Tex., 1969-; perf. at US Pres. Inaugural, Wash. DC, 1965. Comps: incl: School Bell March, 1971; Flatonia Centennial March, 1973; Downtown Polka, 1976; var. organ comps. Recordings: Presidents' Marches, w. SWTSU Concert BAnd, 1965; J Holub Orch., Polkas & Waltzes, 1968; w. Donnie Wavra Orch., 1976, Musically Yours. Publs: Outline History of the United States, 1976. Contbr. to newspapers. Mbr., profil. assns. Hons: SWTSU Music Dept. Award, 1967. Hobbies: Stamp Collecting; Drawing. Address: P O Box 165, Flatonia, TX 78941, USA.

KOVACEVIC, Kresimir, b. 16 Sept. 1913, Zagreb Yugoslavia. Musicologist. Educ: PHD, Fac. of Philos.; studied comp., Acad. of Music. m. Bozena Kovacevic, 1 s., 1 d. Career: fac. mbr., Dean of Music, Acad., Zagreb; Music Critic, Borba (newspaper). Publs: Croatian Composers & Their Works, 1960; The Musical Creation in Croatia 1945-65, 1966; The History of Croatian Music of the Twentieth Century, 1967. Ed.-in-Chief: Muzicka enciklopedija, 2nd ed., 3 vols., 1971, 74, 76; Arti Musices, 1973-. Mbr., Pres., Union of Croatian Comps. Address: Savska 3, YU-41000 Zagreb, Yugoslavia.

KOVACH, Andor Andràs, b. 21 Apr. 1915, Szaszvaros, Transylvania, Hungary. Composer; Conductor; Professor; Organist; Pianist. Educ: baccalaureat, Liszt Ferenc State Music Acad., Budapest; Master's Degree (dip.) in comp., Zoltan Kodaly; pvte. studies, Bela Bartok; Prof. of music & tchng. & orch. conducting degrees under Clemens Krauss. m. Agnes Fazekas. Career: Cond., orchs. & choirs, Hungary & abroad; Prof., State Conserv., Saarbrucken, Germany; Fndr., Perm. Cond., Museo de Arte Symph. Orch., Sao Paulo, Brazil & Jeunesses Musicales State Symph. Orch., Brussels, Belgium; currently Comp., Prof. of comp., musical analysis & orch., Cantonal Conserv. of Music, Lausanne, Switz. Comps: 5 operas inclng. Medea (opera, text: Anouilh), Thieves Ball (Anouilh), 4 symphs.; many orchl. works; Chmbr. music, etc. Mbr. profil. orgs. Recip. many commissions for comps. Hobbies incl: Reading about psychol. Address: 29 de la Sallaz, 1010 Lausanne, Switz. 28.

KOVACS, Denes, b. 18 Apr. 1930, Vac, Hungary. Violinist. Educ: Budapest Acad. of Music, w. Ede Zathureczky. m. Adrienne Izsof, 1955, 1 s., 1 d. Career: 1st Violin, Budapest State Opera, 1951-60; Leading Violin Prof., Budapest Music Acad., 1957-; Dir., ibid, 1967-; Rector, Ferenc Liszt Acad. of Music, 1971-; Concert tours throughout Europe, & in China & Japan. Hons. Kossuth Prize, 1963; Eminent Artist Award, 1970. Address: Budapest III, Frankel Leo utca 21-23, Hungary.

KOVALENKO, Oleg Ivanovitch, b. 7 July 1936, Kiev, Ukraine, USSR. Conductor. Educ: BA., Univ. of Calif., 1959; MA, Stanford Univ., 1960. m. Dr. Susan, 1 d. Career: Asst. Cond., St. Louis Symph., 1963-66; Assoc. Cond., Indpls. Symph., 1972-; Guest Cond., Chgo. Symph., Dallas Symph. & Balt. Symph., Assoc. Cond., Indpls. Symph., 1972-75; Res. Cond. ibid, 1975-. Recip: Fellowship for European study (w. Rafael Kubelik, Numich), Ella Lyman Cabot Trust, Boston, 1962. Hobbies: Photography; Deep-sea fishing; Swimming. Mgmt. M. Bichurin Concerts Corp., Indpls. Address: 1032 Timberlane Dr., Indpls., IN 46260, USA.

KOVARICEK, Frantisek, b. 17 May 1924, Litetiny, Bohemia, Czechoslovakia. Composer. Educ: Conserv. of Music, Prague; Acad. of Musical Arts, Prague. m. Vera Fruhaufova. Compositions incl: Overture for Large Orchestra, 1951; Mourning Music for Large Orchestra; Concerto for Clarinet & Orchestra; Serenade for Nonet; The Golden Wave of June (song cycle) The Stolen Moon (lyric-comic opera); Capriccio for Chamber Orchestra, 1974. Mbrship: Guild of Czech Composers; Chmn. of Bd., Czech Jeunesses Musicales. Hobby: Touring. Address: Na Hroude 71, Prague 10, Czechoslovakia.

KOVÁRNOVÁ, Emma, b. 20 Aug. 1930, Prague, Czechoslovakia. Concert Pianist; Music Educator. Educ: Attended State Music High Schl., Prague & Acad. of Music Arts, Prague. Debut: Prague, 1951. Career: TV Music Dramaturg, Prague; mbr. Film Symph. Orch.; Concert Soloist & Chmbr. Interpreter; Chmbr. Music Lect., Biberach, W. Germany; Prof., State Music High Schl., Prague, Czechoslovakia; Concert Trips in Europe & Africa; Mbr., Due Boemi Di Praga Chmbr. Ensemble w. Josef Horak, Prague; Num. Radio & TV Progs. in Europe. Recordings: Due Boemi di Praga; At the New Ways; Bass Clarinet; The New Dolo Instrument; Horak plays the bass clarinet of Paginini; Duo Boemi & Inspiration. Mbrships: Union of Czech Comps. & Interpreters; Hon. Mbr., Jeunesses Musicales de Suisse, 1968. Hons: Prize, Czech Music Fndn., 1967. Address: Bubenska 39, 170 00 Prague 7, Czechoslovakia.

KOVÁTS, Barna, b. 24 Aug. 1920, Budapest, Hungary. Composer. Educator. Educ: Pvte. study of guitar w. Mme. M Varga, Hungary; studied comps. w. Dr. Lajtha & Szervansky, Conserv. of Budapest. widower. Debut: Radio Budapest, 1938. Career: Soloist, Hungarian Radio, Hungarian Nat. Theatre; Hd., Guitar Dept., Ctr. of Capital Music Schl. Assn.; Cons. & Music Arr., State Puppet Theatre; num. concerts, Hungary, later France, S Am., Austria & other European countries, also TV & radio broadcasts; Hd., Dept. for Guitar & Lute, HS of Music Mozarteum, Salzburg, 1961-. Comps. incl: Petite suite No. 2 pour guitare; Trois mouvements pour guitare; Minutenstücke 1-bis 6. Has recorded for MHV, Erato & DÖK. Ed. many musical publs. for var. cos. Address: Michael-Filzgasse 13, A-5020 Salzburg, Austria.

KOWALOWSKI, Zenon Eugenieusz, b. 20 Mar. 1939, Niala Podlaska, Poland. Composer. Educ: Krakow Conserv.; Wyzsza Schl. of Music, Krakow; MA., 1962. m. Miroslawa Sagan, 1 s., 1 d. Debut: Czestochowa. Career: Comp., var. TV, Theatre Music. Compositions incl (publd.) Songs for Children; (recorded) Prescoes, 2 clarinets; Piano Miniatures; Lyrical Essays; Canto, children's symph.; scores for 26 Cartoon Films. Mbrships: Assn. of Polish Comps.; Assn. of Authors & Comps.

of Light Music. Recip. Distinction, Competition of Young Comps., Warsaw, 1964. Hobby: Motoring. Address: 25 m. 34 Ul Chrobrego, 40-030 Katowice, Poland.

KOZDERKOVÁ, Jarmila, b. 10 Mar. 1934, Brnenské Ivanovice, Czech. Pianist. Educ: State Conserv. of Music, Prague; studied piano w. Ilona Stepanova-Kurzová & Chmbr. music w. Ladislav Cerny, Acad. of Musical Arts, Prague. div. Debut: Prague. Career: since 1965 has given concerts in London, Paris, Brussels, Vienna, Prague, Norway, Sweden, USSR, Bulgaria, Yugoslvia, German Dem. & Fed. Repubs., Helsinki & Amsterdam; has app. on TV in Prague, & made radio broadcasts in Prague, Hilversum, Brussels, Oslo, Helsinki, German Fed. & Dem. Repubs. & on BBc; as well as concerts has made apps. as Recitalist & Chmbr. Duo Perf.; has app. at Prague Spring Fests.; Lectr. of piano, Acad. of Music, Prague. Recordings: sev. w. Supraphon, Panton, & Qualiton labels. Hons. incl: w. Violist Peter Messieurer, top prize given (2nd Prize, Leo Weiner Award) at Budapest Competition of Chmbr. Music Duos, 1963; 1st Prize for best interpretation of 20th century music, Prague, 1964; 1st Prize & Special Award for best interpretation of Jancek's Sonata for Violin & Piano, Prague Spring Fest., 1964. Hobbies: Lit.; Nature; Antiques. Mgmt: Pragokoncert, Prague. Address: U Laboratore 12, 162 00 Prague 6, Czech.

KOZIEL, Yola, b. 25 May 1934, Pinctow, Radou, Poland. Concert singer, opera singer; Music pedagogue. Educ: Tchr. Trng. Coll. Berlin GDR; State exam, 1952; Music Acad. Hans Eisler GDR, State exam, 1957. m. 1 d. Debut: Child pianist. Career: 1949 Songevenings; Num. perf. Concert Halls, TV; 1957 Tatjana, Eugen Onegin; 1957-59, Opera House Karl Marx Stadt; 1959-61, Opera House Potsdam; since 1961 German State Opera, Berlin. Recordings: Many modern comps., Hans Eisler, Werzlau, Schostakowitsch, Mbrships: Assn. for Comp. and Musicologist, GDR. Hons: Gold Medal, Toulouse, 1959, 1957. Hobbies: Singing; Pedagogy; Lit.; Modern music; Nature; Wandering; Swimming. Address: 108 Unter Den Linden, German State Opera, Berlin, German Dem. Repub.

KOZUBEC, Lidia, b. 19 Jan. 1927, Poznán, Poland. Pianist; Musicologist. Educ: MA, High Schl. of Music, Katowice; M Phil., Cracow Univ.; High Schl. for Music, Warsaw; studied w. A B Michelangeli, Arezzo, Italy. Debut: Katowice, 1949. Career: recitalist & soloist w. orchs. in Poland, Austria, Belgium, Bulgaria, Denmark, Finland, France, German Democratic Repub., Italy, Norway, Romania, Switz., Czech., USSR, & Nigeria; apps. on radio & TV & at fests.; Tchr., High Schl. of Music, Warsaw. Recordings of Polish piano music. Publs: Michelangeli as man, artist & pedagogue (in preparation). Contbr. to Ruch Muzyczny & other profl. jrnls. Mbrships: SPAM (Chairwoman, High Schl. of Music, Warsaw). Hons: Golden Cross of Merit, 1977. Hobbies: Art; Archaeology; Travel; Photography; Films. Address: Al. Waszyngtona 116/98, 04074 Warsaw, Poland.

KRABER, Karl, b. 10 May 1935, New York, NY, USA. Flutist. Educ: BA, Harvard Coll.; Tanglewood; Marlboro; Santa Cecilia Conserv., Rome; Studied flute w. Moyse & Rampal. m. Joan Kalisch, 2 d. Debut: Rome, 1960; New York, 1971. Career: 600 concerts w. Dorian Quintet; 40 recitals; 30 apps. w. Italian Chmbr. Orchs. in Europe; 4 successful NY recitals; Mbr., NY Chmbr. Soloists; Fac., Brooklyn Coll. & Mannes Coll. of Music. Recordings w. Dorian Wing Quintet. Mbr. Bd. Dirs., NY Flute Club. Address: 160 W 87th St., New York, NY 10024, USA.

KRADER, Barbara Lattimer, b. 15 Jan. 1922, Columbus, Ohio, USA. Ethnomusicologist. Educ: AM (music) Vassar Coll., 1942; studies w. Ernst Krenek & George Dickinson; AM (Russian lang. & lit.), Columbia Univ., 1948; PhD (Slavic langs. & lit.), Radcliffe Coll., 1955. m. Lawrence Krader. Career: sub-ed. for E Europe, Grove's Dict., 6th ed. Contbr. to: Ethnomusicology; Jrnl. of the Int. Folk Music Coun.; Yearbook of the Int. Folk Music Coun.; Grove's Dict., 6th ed. Mbrships: Int. Folk Music Coun. (exec. sec., 1965-66); Soc. for Ethnomusicol. (Pres., 1971-73). Hons: Phi Beta Kappa, Radcliffe Coll., 1956. Address: Grainauerstr. 19, 1000 Berlin 30, German Fed. Repub. 14, 27.

KRAFT, Leo, b. 24 July 1922, NYC, USA. Composer. Educ: BA, Queens Coll., NYC, 1945; MFA, Princeton Univ., 1947. m. Amy Lager, 2 s. Career: Prof. of Music, Queens Coll., CUNY, 1947-. Comps. incl: A proverb of Solomon (chorus & orch.), 1953; Variations for Orch., 1958; String Quartet 2, 1959; 4 English Love Songs, 1961; 5 Pieces for clarinet & piano, 1962; 3 Pieces for orch., 1963; Night Piece for orch., 1965; Concerto for 13 players, 1966; Concerto for cello, winds & percussion, 1969; Spring in the Harbour, for soprano, cello, flute & piano, 1969. Publs: A New Approach to Sight Singing (w. others), 1960; A New Approach to Ear Training - Melody, 1967.

Mbrships. incl: Nat. Assn. of Am. Comps. & Conds.; Bd. of Dirs., Am. Music Ctr.; ASCAP. Address: 9 Dunster Rd., Gt. Neck, NY 11021, USA. 2.

KRAGERUP, Peder Emil, b. 18 Aug. 1948, Holbaek, Denmark. Pianist; Conductor; Composer; Arranger. Educ: Music studies, Univ. of Copenhagen. m. Jill Susanne, 1 d. Debut: (as cond.) Hair, 1971. Career: Cond., Danish Radio Big Band, Danish Radio Light Orch., Norwegian Radio Light Orch., BBC North Light Orch. (Glasgow); Cond., Own orch., Tivoli Gdns., Copenhagen (summer); Musical Dir., Hair, Jesus Christ Superstar, Godspell (Denmark & Sweden); Musical Dir., Two Gentlemen of Verona, Denmark. Comps: Songs for Danish vocal group, Flair, recorded 1975 & '76. Arr., sev. records w. num. Danish artists. Mbrships: Danish Assn. of Authors & Comps. Hobbies: Skiing; Transcendental Meditation. Address: Rygards Alle 29, DK-2900 Hellerup, Denmark.

KRAMER, Jonathan, b. 7 Dec. 1942, Hartford, Conn., USA. Composer; Professor; Theorist. Educ: AB, Harvard Univ., 1965; MA, Univ. Calif., Berkeley, 1967; PhD, ibid, 1969; Post-Doctoral study at Schl. of Criticism & Theory, 1976. m. Norma F. Berson, 1 s., 1 d. Career: Prog. Annotator, San Fran. Symph. Orch., 1967-70; Lectr., music, Univ. Calif., Berkeley, 1969-70; Asst. Prof., music theory, Oberlin Conserv., 1970-71; Asst. Prof., Theory of Music & Dir. Undergrad Comp., Yale Univ., 1971-78; Assoc. Prof., Music Comp. & Theory, Coll.-Conserv. of Music, Univ. of Cinn., 1978-. Comps. incl: The Canons of Blackearth (percussion & tape), 1972-73; Renascence (clarinet & electronics), 1974. Contbr. to: Dictionary of Twentieth Century Music, 1974, profl. jrnls. Mbr. var. orgs. Hons. incl: Morse Fellowship, 1975-76; Comps. Forum, 1978; Special Commendation, ISCM, 1976. Hobbies incl: Abstract photography; Gourmet cooking. Address: College-Conservatory of Music, Univ. of Cinn., Cinn., OH 45221, USA.

KRAMPEROVA, Jindra, b. 28 Sept. 1940, Prague, Czechoslovakia. Pianist. Educ: Prague Acad. of Music; Postgrad. studies, Moscow Conserv., USSR. m. Vit Micka. Debut: Recital when aged 12, Prague. Career: Concerts in German Dem. Repub. German Fed. Repub., Switz., Spain, USSR, Poland, Bulgaria, Cuba & Hungary; Many radio perfs.; Asst., Prague Acad. of Music. Recordings: Beethoven Sonatas & Rondos; Preludes & Fugues by D Shostakovitsch & O Flosman. Radio recordings in Czechoslovakia, German Fed. Repub. & Switz. Hons: State Figure Skating Champion, 1956-59; Winner, Smetana Competition, 1963. Mgmt: Pragokoncert. Address: Holeckova 19, 150 00 Prague 5, Czechoslovakia.

KRANER, Johannes Günther, b. 12 July 1930, Gera, Germany. Music Director; Organist; Conductor. Educ: Hochschule für Musik, Berlin; Freie Univ., Berlin. 2 s. Career: Dir. of Music, Paul-Gerhardt-Ch., Berlin-Schöneberg; Organist, Cond., Alt-Schéoneberger Kantorei; organ recitals and broadcasts in many countries of Europe & in USA; choral concerts & broadcasts. Publs: Ed., 10 Motetten von Andreas Hammerschmidt, 1975. Contbr. to Muisk in Geschichte und begenwart & Grove's Dict., 6th ed. Hobby: Climbing mountains. Address: Rothenburgstr. 22a, D1000 Berlin 4/, German Fed. Repub.

KRANERT, Veda Proctor, b. Jackson Co., Ala., USA. Piano Teacher. Educ: BMus, Chicago Musical Coll.; tchrs. cert., ibid. m LeRoy William Kranert. Career: tchr. N E Ala. & Tenn. Schls. over 35 yrs.; num. pvte. pupils; former harpist, Huntsville Symph. Orch.; adjudicator. Mbrships: Past Pres., Ala. Fed. of Music Clubs; organiser & ldr., Jr. Music Clubs; Huntsville Orch. Guild; Sigma Alpha Iota. Hons: State Rep., Nat. Bd. of Dirs., Nat. Fed. of Music Clubs. Hobbies: Travel; Antiques. Address: 1119 Locust Ave., S E, Huntsville, AL 35801, USA.

KRAPF, Gerhard W., b. 12 Dec. 1924, Meissenheim, Germany. Organist; Composer. Educ: Musikhochschule, Karlsruhe, 1950; MMus, Univ. Redlands, USA, 1951; AAGO. m. Trudl Lichti, 1 s., 3 d. Career: Prof., Univs. of Wyoming, Iowa; currently Prof. of Organ & Ch. Music, Univ. of Alberta, Can. Comps. incl: (organ) Little Organ Psalter, 1971; Fantasia on O Jesus Christ, to Thee May Hymns be Rising; Three Tryptichs; (choral) Cantata, From Heaven Above. Recordings: The Tracker Organ at Iowa, 1973. Publs. incl: Organ Improvisation: A Practical Approach to Chorale Elaborations for the Service, 1967. Contbr. to profl. publs. Mbr. var. orgs. Hobby: Lit. Address: 11704. -43 Ave., Edmonton, Alberta, Can. T6J 0Y7.

KRARUP, Gunnar, b. 5 May 1943, Roskilde, Denmark. Violinist. Educ: Dip., Royal Danish Music Conserv., 1966; Phila. Musical Acad., USA, 1968-69. m. Vibeke Krarup, 2 d.

Career: w. Irish Radio Orch., Dublin, 1966-67, Royal Danish Orch., 1967-68, & Siaelland Symph. Orch., 1969-74; Alternating Ldr., Arhus Byorkester, 1974-; Mbr., Arhus Chmbr. Orch., 1974-, Arhus Str. Quartet, 1976-. Hobby: Sailing. Address: N W Gadesvej 8, 8000 Arhus, Denmark.

KRARUP, Vibeke, b. 14 Nov. 1944, Hellerup, Denmark. Violinist; Violist. Educ: dip., Royal Danish Music Conserv., 1966; Phila. Musical Acad., USA, 1968-69. m. Gunnar Krarup, 2 d. Career: Violinist w. Irish Radio Orch., 1966-67, Royal Danish Orch., 1967-68, Siaelland Symph. Orch., 1969-74, & Arhus Byorkester, 1974-; 1st Viola Player, Arhus Byorkester, 1975-; Mbr., Arhus Chmbr. Orch., 1974-, Arhus Str. Quartet, 1976-. Hobby: Sailing. Address: N W Gadesvej 8, 8000 Arhus C, Denmark.

KRATOCHWIL, Heinrich, b. 23 Feb. 1933, Vienna, Austria. Teacher (Composition); Composer; Author. Educ: Music Tchrs. Dip., 1955, Dip. for Comp., 1961, Acad. for Music, Vienna. m. Gertrud Perchter, 3 c. Career: Tchr. in Gymnasium, 1955-73; Tchr., Acad. for Music, 1962- (Extraordinarius, 1975-). Comps: Concerto for viola & orch op. 67; Concerto for Trumpet & Orch. op. 88; Concerto for Percussion & Orch. op. 107; Night Songs for Choir, Contrabass & Percussion op. 50; num. pieces for choir. Contbr. to: Österreichische Musikzeitschrift; Musikerziehung. Mbr. of Leading Comm. of Österreichischer Komponistenbund. Hons: Theodor Körner - Preis, 1966; Foerderungspreis Stadt Wien, 1968; 1st Prize, The Modern Religious Song, 1969; 1st Prize of Österreichischer Sängerbund (Mass), 1978. Hobby: Sports. Address: Franz Grassler - G.22, A 1238 Vienna, Austria.

KRAUS, Detlef, b. 30 Nov. 1919, Hamburg, Germany. Pianist. Educ: studied w. F. Gebhard, W. Kempff & R. Koscalsky. m. Charlotte M. Poel, 2 s., 1 d. Debut: Hamburg, 1936. Career: has given concerts & made radio & TV broadcasts in over 40 countries, inclng. USA, Can., S Africa & Japan; is revising Viennese "Urtext" Ed. for publn. Num. recordings. Mbr: Rotary. Recip. of Cultural Prize of City of Kiel, 1961 & Brahms Prize Hamburg, 1975. Mgmt: M. Drissen, Mainz; Grevesmühl, Bremerhaven; Raymond Weiss, NY. Address: 62, Mintropstr., Essen 16, German Fed. Repub. 19.

KRAUS, Lili, b. Budapest, Hungary. Concert Pianist. Educ: Study w. Kodaly & Bartok, Royal Acad. of Music, Bucharest; Vienna Conserv. of Music; Pvte. study w. Arthur Schnabel. m. Dr. Otto Mandl (dec.), 1 s., 1 d. Career: Soloist w. European orchs., 1926-; Tours of Europe, N & S Am., Asia, 1949-; Tours of Australia, NZ, Japan, 1971-; Lectr., var. univs., USA & Europe; First to perform in NYC complete Mozart Piano Concerti (9 Town Hall concerts, 1966-67); Annual USA tours. Num. recordings incl. complete Mozart Piano Concerti; 1st recordings of other Mozart works; 1st recording of complete Mozart Piano Sonatas; Premier perf. & recording of Schubert Grazer Fantasie; Num. other works. Publs: The Complete Original Cadenzas by W.A. Mozart for His Solo Piano Concertos with Supplementary Cadenzas by Beethoven & Kraus. Mbrships: Artist-in-Res., Tex. Christian Univ.; Hon. Mbr., Calif. Music Tchrs. Assn., Sigma Alpha Iota. Hons: MusD., Roosevelt Univ., 1969; DMus, Williams Coll., 1975; Austrian Cross of Honour for Sci. & Art (1st class), 1978. Mgmt: Columbia ARtists Mgmt., Inc. Address: c/o Alix B. Williamson, 1860 Broadway, New York, NY 10023, USA.

KRAUS, Otakar, b. 1909, Prague, Czechoslovakia. Opera Singer. Educ: Pvtely., Prague & Milan. m. Maria Graf, 1 s. Career: Prin. Baritone, Nat. Opera House, Bratislava, then Opera House, Brno, State Opera House, Prague, Royal Opera House, Covent Gdn.; apps. w. Carl Rosa Opera, Engl. Opera Grp., at Bayreuth, Vienna State Opera, Aldeburgh, Venice, Glyndebourne, La Scala (Milan), Munich, Nederlandsche Opera, Amsterdam. Recip., OBE, 1973. Address: 223 Hamlet Gdns., London W6, UK. 1.

KRAUSE, Lloyd Thomas, b. 23 Feb. 1920, Chisholm, Minn., USA. Cellist; Trombonist. Educ: Dip., USN Schl. of Music, 1939; BA, San Diego State Coll., 1948; Profl. Teaching Cert., Univ. of Hawaii, 1962. m. Erma Lois Privat, 1 d., 2 s. Debut: Chisholm, Minn., Age 13. Career: Cellist, Honolulu Symph., 1939-43, 1948-49, San Diego Symph., 1945-48; Musician, USN, 1938-45; Music Tchr., Terr. Dept. Pub. Instruction & State Dept. of Educ., 1948-62; Mgr., Honolulu Pops Orch., 1949-58; Gen. Mgr., Civic Light Opera Assn., 1952-55; Libn., Honolulu Symph., 1950-62; Bandmaster, Royal Hawaiian Band, 1963-68; Arr., Honolulu Symph., 1969-. Compositions: (publd.) Quartet for Trombones; Pacific Frontiers Concert March; Str. Quartet; Brass Quintet; num. Marches; Musical, "Marry an American", 1960; (recorded) Pacific Folksong Medley; num. scores for TV. Life Mbr., Musicians Assn. of Hawaii. Hobbies: Gardening; Community Service. Address: 3479 Harding Ave., Honolulu, HI 96816, USA.

KRAUSE, Robert James, b. 1 July 1943, Milwaukee, Wis., USA. Oboist; Teacher; Assistant Professor of Music. Educ: BMus, Univ. Miami; MMus, ibid; DMusA, 1979. Career: Oboe, Miami Phil., Roswell Symph., Natchitoches-Northwestern Symph.; currently Prin. Oboist, Amarillo Symph., Tex.; Music Tchr., Eastern NM Univ., Northwestern State Univ. La. & currently Asst. Prof. of Music, W Tex. State Univ., Canyon, Tex.; Instructor of Oboe, Nat. Music Camp, Interlochen, Mich. Contbr. to: NACWPI Jrnl. Mbrships: Fac. Advsr., Phi Mu Alpha Sinfonia. Hons: Pi Kappa Lambda; Am. Guild Musical Artists Award, Most Outstanding Sr., Univ. Miami, 1965. Hobbies incl: Cooking. Address: 522 12th Ave., Canyon, TX 79015, USA. 4, 16.

KRAUSE, Sharon, b. 30 Oct. 1955, Chilliwack, BC, Can. Pianist. Educ: BMus (piano perf.), Univ. of BC, Vancouver, 1977; ARCT (piano perf.), Royal Conserv. of Music, Toronto, 1970; studied w. Robert Silverman, Can., Ivan Moravec, Czech., also studied w. Adele Marcus, Guido Agosti & Maria Curcio. Debut: Vancouver, 1969. Career: num. apps. w. orchs. & in recital, Can. & Europe, incl. w. Vancouver Symph. Orch.; num. perfs. for CBC radio & TV networks incl. perfs. w. Vancouver Symph., Edmonton Symph. & Winnipeg (CBC) orchs. Hons: num. prizes & awards incl. 1st prize, CBC Talent Fest., 1976; sev. scholarships. Mgmt: Mabel Laine, Toronto. Address: 92 Kenwood Ave., Toronto, Ont. M6C 2S2, Can.

KRAUSE-GRAUMNITZ, Heinz, b. 11 May 1911, Dresden, German Dem. Repub. Composer; Teacher. Educ: PhD, 1935, Univ. Leipzig; Conserv. Leipzig. m. Annerose Mann, 1 s. Career: Tchr. Conserv. Dresden, 1938; Musical Dir. var. theatres; Lectr. Drama Acad. Leipzig, 1953; Dir. Conserv. Rostok. Comps. incl: Brecht Cantata; To Posterity; Christmas Cantata, 1959; Brecht-cycle, 1965; Piano Quartet for young people, 1966. Mbrships: Assn. of Comp. and Muisicologists GDR (UDK). Publs. incl: Johann Beer, Leipzig, 1935; The Mad Monologue, Berlin, 1960; Richard Wagner's Wesendonk Songs, Leipzig, 1962; The Nature of Opera, Berlin, 1969; Heinrich Schütz, Leipzig, 1972. Hons: Johannes R Becher Medal, 1966; Art Prize, GDR, 1970. Hobbies: Music. Address: Schönbachstr. 20, 7027 Leipzig, German Dem. Repub.

KRAUSHAAR, Keith Conrad Francis, b. 1 Sept. 1928, Hendon, Middx., UK. Clerk BBC Music Library. Educ: Studied Singing, GSM, 1956-59. Career: Clerk, BBC Music Lib., 1961-; apps. in Music & Poetry progs., St. Martin-in-the-Fields, London; Co-author, features on comps. inclng: Constanza's Genius, 1974; The Life & Times of Henry Purcell, 1976; The Tragedy of Bizet & Carmen, 1976. Publs: (as Francis Conrad) Biography of Ethel Smyth, to appear 1977. Mbrships: Players Theatre; King's Head Theatre Club. Hobbies: Going to theatre, operas & concerts; Writing poetry & comedy sketches; Collecting theatre progs.; Watching cricket. Address: 13 Lambolle Rd., London NW3, UK.

KRAUTWURST, Franz, b. 7 Aug. 1923, Munich, Germany. Professor of Musicology. Educ: Trapp'sches Konservatorium der Musik, Munich, 1940-42; Univ. of Munich, 1946-48; PhD, Univ. of Erlangen, 1950. m. Roswitha Strathmann, 2 s., 2 d. Career: Asst.-Rdr.-Prof. of Musicol., Inst. of Musicol., Univ. of Erlangen, 1950-; Lehrbeauftragter, Univ. of Augsburg, 1976- (Zusätzlich). Publs: Untersuchungen zum Sonatensatztypus Beethovens, durchgeführt am I. Satz der 1. Symphonie, 1950; Die Heilsbronner Chorbücher der Unversitätsbibliothek Erlangen, 1956, 2nd ed., 1967; Das Schrifttum zur Musikgeschichte der Stadt Nürnberg, 1964; Armin Knab, 1973. Contbr. to var. musical publs. incl. Grove's Dict., 6th ed. Mbr. profl. orgs. Recip. Wissenschaftlicher Förderungspreis der Stadt Nürnberg, 1961. Hobby: Collecting musical instruments. Address: 18 Im Herrengarten, D-8520 Erlangen-Buchenhof, German Fed. Repub. 3, 14.

KRAVITZ, Ellen King, b. 25 May 1929, Fords, NJ, USA. Musicologist; Professor. Educ: BA, Georgian Court Coll., Lakewood, NJ, 1964; MM, Univ. of S Calif., 1966; PhD, ibid, 1970. m. Hilard L Kravitz, 3 step children. Career incls: Full Prof. of Music Hist., Calif. State Univ., LA, 1967-; Rsch. in musicol. & related arts; Dir., exhib of Schoenberg's art, music, etc. during Schoenberg Centennial Celebration, USC, 1974. Publs. incl: A Correlation of Concepts Found in German Expressionist Art, Music & Literature, 1970; Ed., Jrnl. of the Arnold Schoenberg Inst., Vol. I, No. 3, Vol. II, No. 3; Catalog of Schoenberg's Paintins, Drawings & Sketches. Mbrships: Am. Musicol. Soc.; Pi Kappa Lambda; Mu Phi Epsilon; MENC; Fndr., Friends of Music, Calif. Sate Univ., LA, 1976. Hons: Outstanding Master's Thesis Award, Univ. of S Calif., 1966. Hobbies: Theatre; Travel; Interior Decorating. Address: 402 Doheny Rd., Beverly Hills, CA 90210, USA. 4, 9.

KRAWCOWNA de BARBARO, Ludmila, b. 18 Aug. 1939, Gdynia, Poland. Singer. Educ: MA, Higher Music Schl. m. Marek de Barbaro. Debut: Warsaw Operetta. Career: Soloist, operetta, recordings w. Polish Radio & TV Orch.; TV broadcasts, chmbr. concerts & recitals. Mbr., Assn. of Polish Musical Artists. Hons: Prize, Polish Ministry of Culture & Arts, 1962; Prize, Cultural Ministry, Lithuanian Soviet Socialist Repub., 1968. Hobbies: Knitting; Gardening. Address: Miedziana 16 m. 17, Warsaw 00809, Poland.

KRAYK, Stefan, b. 19 Aug. 1914, Warsaw, Poland. Concert Violinist; Professor of Music. Educ: Sorbonne, Paris, France; Ecole Normale de Musique, Paris; RAM, London. m. Judith Ann Krayk, 1 s. Debut: Warsaw Phil., 1936. Career: Soloist, Warsaw Phil., BBC Symph., UK, Symph. de la reine Elisabeth of Belgium, Chgo. Symph., & others; Concertmaster & Soloist, Bear Valley Symph.; Cond.'s Workshop Symph., Asilomar, Calif., Santa Barbara Symph. (also Fndr.); Violinist, Paganini Quartet, Fine Arts Trio, Musica Mundi Quartet; Univ. of Calif., Santa Monica; recitals, concerto perfs. in Europe & USA. Recordings w. Paganini Quartet & Fine Arts Trio. Mbrships. incl: MENC, Past Pres., CMEA, ASTA. Publs: The Violin Guide, 1963. Contbr. to musical jrnls. Hons. incl: Award, Queen Elisabeth of Belgium, 1937. Hobbies incl: Tennis; Skiing. Address: 245 G Chateaux Elise, Santa Barbara, CA 93109, USA.

KRČMÉRY-VRTELOVÁ, Jela, b. 7 Jan. 1924, Martin, Czech. Mezzo soprano. Educ: Conserv. of Bratislava; Accademia di Sant Cecilia, Rome. m. Albin Vrtel, 3 c. Debut: Slovak Nat. Theatre. Career: has sung in Carmen (Bizet); The Snow White (Rimsky-Korsakov); Orpheus (Gluck); Verdi's Requiem; Beethoven 9th Symph.; var. concerts in Rome; Mezzo soprano, Slovak Nat. Theatre; has worked as librettist w. E Suchon, T Andrasovan, M Korinek, J Meier, J Zimmer, B Urbanec. Publs: has transl. many musical & dramatic works of Mozart, Gluck, Handel, Beethoven, Debussy, Verdi, Ravel, Orff, Britten, Bartok, Hindemith, Honneger, etc. Contbr. to profl. publs. incl. Ed., Javisko. The Stage. Mbrships: Czech. Writers Union; Union of the Czech. Dramatic Artists. Hons: Meritorious Worker of Culture. Hobby: Grandsons. Address: Frana Krála 21, Bratislava, Czech. 27.

KREBBERS, Herman Albertus, b. 18 June 1923, Kengelo (Ov), The Netherlands. Violinist. Educ: studied w. Prof. Oskar Back, Amsterdam Music Lyceum. m. A. Torlau, / s., 1 d. Career: First pub. appearance at age 9; Soloist w. Amsterdam Concertgebouw, at 12 yrs.; Concert tours throughout Germany, Switz., Poland, Finland, Norway, Sweden, Austria, England, France, Belgium, Portugal, 1945-; Appeared at Carnegie Hall, NY; Referred to as 'Il Paganini' in Italy; Tchr., Violin Class, Amsterdam Music Lyceum. Recordings: Bach, Concerto for 2 violins & strings in D minor w. Theo Olof & the Hague Phil. Orch.; Badings, Concerto for 2 violins & orch. w. Theo Olof & the Hague Phil. Orch.; Beethoven, Concerto in D maj. w. the Hague Phil. Orch.; Brahms, Concerto in D Maj. w. the Brabant Orch.; Bruch, Concerto No. 1 in G minor, w. Brabant Orch.; Paganini, Concerto No. 1 in D Maj. w. Die Wiener Symphoniker; Haydn, Concerto in G maj., Concerto in C maj., w. Amsterdam Chamber Orch., etc. Hons. incl: Prix d'Excellence, Amsterdam Music Lyceum, 1940; Kt., Oranje Nassau Order; many first prizes from int. competitons. Address: Capittenweg 22B, Blaricum, The Netherlands.

KREBS, Helmut, b. 8 Oct. 1913, Dortmund, Germany. Singer. Educ: Dortmund Conserv.; Univ. of Berlin. Career: Volksoper Berlin, 1937-41; Municipal Opera House, Berlin, 1947-; Prof. of Vocal Music, Acad. of Music, Berlin, 1957-63; Prof., Acad. of Music, Frankfurt, 1963; Comp. of orchl., operatic, chmbr., choral & vocal works publd. by Bote & Bock, Astoria Verlag; concert & broadcast perfs. Hons. incl: Kammersänger, Berlin, 1963. Address: 11 Im Dol Berlin 33 (Dahlem), German Fed. Repub. 2.

KREBS, Lottie. Concert Pianist. Educ: studied w. Profs. Eduard Erdmann & Willi Rehberg, HS for Music, Cologne. m. E W Krebs, 1 s. Career: Solo Recitalist; Chmbr. Music Player; Lectr. on Music; Tchr. of Interpretation. Mbr: Solo Perfs. Sect., ISM. Hobbies: Bird Watching; Collecting Antiques & Pictures; Travelling. Address: 44 Russell Hill, Purley, Surrey, UK. 4.

KREDBA, Oldrich, b. 24 Sept. 1904, Prague, Czechoslovakia. Professor of piano, harpsichord, hist. & lit. of piano. Educ: Dip. (piano), Master's Schl., Prague Conservatory, 1928; PhD., Caroline Univ., Prague, 1939. Debut: 1928. Career: Solo pianist & harpsichordist; Co-player w. instrumentalists & singers; Chmbr. music player; Work w. Prague Radio, 1930-; Prof., Prague Conservatory. Recordings incl. harpsichord music by old Czech masters. Publs: Critical evaluation of the Piano trio by Smetana, 1944; Revision of the Edition of all Piano sonatas by W A Mozart, 1952; Ceske sonatiny revision, 1954; JS Bach: Francouzske suity a partity - revision, 1950, '53; 150

Anniversary of Prague Conservatory (Piano Sect.), 1961. Contbr. to jrnls. Mbrships: Sect. of Concert Musicians, Czechoslovak Union of Comps. & Musicians, until 1970; Mozart Soc., Prague; Dvorak Soc., Prague. Hons: Silver Cross, Poland, 1933; Award for eminent work, 1964. Hobby: Verse writing. Address: Bubenecska 33, 16000 Prague 7, Czechoslovakia.

KREK, Uroš, b. 21 May 1922, Ljubljana, Slovenija. Composer. Educ: Musical High Schl. Acad. m. Lilijana Pauer. Debut: 1st Perfs. of Comps. in Ljubljana, 1945. Career: Perfs. of Comps. on concert stage, radio & TV, films. Comps. incl: Concerto for Violin & Orch.; Concerto for French Horn & Orch.; Concerto for Piccolo & Orch.; Sonata for 2 Violins; Five Songs for Voice & Piano; Mouvements concertants; Inventiones ferales, for violin & strings; Symph. for strings; Duo for violin & cello; La Journee d'un Bouffon, for Brass Quintet. Num. recordings. Mbrships: Union of Slovene Comps.; Union of Yugoslav Comps. Hons. incl: Yugoslav RTV Awards, 1968, 71, 72, 74 & 75; Zupancic Prize, 1978. Hobby: Mountaineering. Address: Vegova 8, Ljubljana, Yugoslavia.

KRENEK, Ernst, b. 23 Aug. 1900, Vienna, Austria. Composer; Writer. Educ: Univ. Vienna; Acad. Music, Vienna; Acad. Music, Berlin, Germany. m. Gladys Nordenstrom. Career: Asst. to Dir., Staatstheater Kassel, Germany; Prof. Music, Vassar Coll., Poughkeepsie, NY, USA; Prof. Music & Dean, Schl. Fine Arts, Hamline Univ., St. Paul, Minn. Comps: 220 works. Recordings: Over 20. Publs. incl: Tonal Counterpoint, 1958; Modal Counterpoint, 1959; Horizons Circled, 1974. Mbrships. incl: Nat. Inst. Arts; ISCM; MTNA; Akademie der Kunste, Berlin; PEN, Vienna. Hons. incl: Cross of Merit, Austria, 1960, & German Fed. Repub., 1965; Order Hon., Arts & Sci., Austria, 1975. Address: c/o BMI, West 57th St., NY, NY 10019, USA.

KREUTZ, Arthur, b. LaCrosse, Wis., USA. Composer; Conductor; Violinist. Educ: BS., BM, Univ. of Wis.; MA, Columbia Univ.; Royal Conserv., Ghent, Belgium; studied Comp. w. Roy Harris, Cecil Burleigh. m. Zoë Lund Kreutz. Career: Fac. Mbr., Univ. of Tex., 1942-44, Tchrs. Coll., Columbia, 1946, Univ. of Wis., 1947, Brooklyn Coll., 1947, Univ. of Miss., 1952; Guest Cond., NY Phil. Symph., Mar. 1945; Carnegie Pops, June 1946. Comps. (commissioned works) Litany of Washington St. (Martha Graham), 1942; Music for Hamlet, Elsinor, Denmark, 1949; Acres of Sky (Univ. of Ark.), 1950; Dixieland Concerto (Little Orch. Soc.), 1950; University Greys (Univ. of Miss.), 1954 (also publd.); Anniversary Album (Int. Rotary), 1955; Galorie Vivante, 1957; Violin Concerto (Sinfonia Fndn.), 1964 (publd.); Winter of the Blue Snow; Mosquito Serenade; Study in Jazz; Rob. Burns Songs; Symphonic Blues; Sourwood Mountain. Hons incl: Premier Prix Violin, Royal Conserv., Ghent; Prix de Rome in Comps., 1940; Guggenheim Fellowship, 1944-45; BMI-ACA Award, 1945; Sinfonia Award, 1950. Address: Route 6, Box 198A, Oxford, MS 38655, USA.

KRIGBAUM, Charles Russell, b. 31 Mar. 1929, Seattle, Wash., USA. Professor of Music; Organist. Educ: BA, 1950, MFA, 1952, Princeton Univ.; pvte. study w. Weinrich & Marchal; Helmut Walcha. Hochschule für Musik, Frankfurt am Main, 2 yrs. (Fulbright Grant); Organ Inst. Andover, Mass., 1950; Studied Choral & Orchl. Cond., Tanglewood, 1951, 52. m. Virginia Lee Crist, 1 s., 2 d. Career: Prof. of Music & Univ. Organist, Yale Univ. Recordings: R. Donovan, Antiphon & Chorale for organ solo; (as cond.) Donovan, Magnificat & Mass; Messiaen, Organ Works (4 records); JS. Bach, The Art of Fugue (2 records). Contbr. to profl. publs. Mbrships. incl: Phi Beta Kappa; AGO. Recip., var. fellowships & grants. Hobbies incl: Sports; Photography of Organ Cases. Address: 10 Mansfield Rd., N. Haven, CT 06473, USA.

KRIPS, Henry Joseph, b. 1912, Vienna, Austria. Conductor. Educ: Vienna Univ. & Conserv. m. Luise Deutsche, 2 s. Career: Res. Cond., S Australian Symph. Orch., 1949-, touring Europe yearly; Guest Cond., leading Brit. orchs.; has conducted sev. opera seasons at Sadlers Wells; active in biennial Adelaide Fest. of Arts. Recordings: 6 LPs w. LPO for EMI label. Recip. of Professorship, Austrian Govt., 1967. Address: c/o Australian Broadcasting Commission, Hindmarsh Square, Adelaide, Australia. 3.

KRIST, Joachim Oswald Paulus, b. 16 June 1948, Ried Innkreis, Austria. Composer; Violist. Educ: State Music Acads., Munich & Cologne, German Fed. Repub.; R Strauss Conserv., Munich. m. Ursula Schmidt. Career: Dir., Youth Acad., Munich 1966-70; Personal Asst. to K Stockhausen, 1970-76; Mbr.; Stockhausen & Oeldorf Grps.; Concert tours & Fest. apps., USA, Can., Europe & Iran. Comps. incl: Moresca, 1967; Duo für einen Pianisten, 1968; Zeremonie, 1970; Passus, 1970-72; Am. Tisch (musical theatre), 1975; Kreuzwege. Recordings: Works of Stockhausen; own comps. Publs: Ed., var. works of Stockhausen, 1975-76. Contbr. to profl. publs. Mbr., profl. assns. Hobbies: Cars; Wine; Music. Mgmt: Allied Artists Agcy., 36 Beauchamp Pl., London SW3. Address: 5073 Kürten, 8000 Munich 70, Murnauer Str. 234, German Fed. Repub.

KŘIVINKA, Gustav, b. 24 April 1928, Doubravice, Czech. Composer; Television Director. Educ: HS of Music; MA Mus, Mus Sc violin, Dip. Mus, Leos Janacek Acad., 1956. m. Jaroslava Rosenkranzová, 1 s., 1 d. Debut: as violinist, 1945; as comp., 1948. Career: Violinist, 1945-50; Comp. for radio, 1948-75; Comp.-Dir., TV Brno (current). Comps. incl: The Way of Man (cantata), 1972; Sonatas 2 & 3 for solo violin, 1975; Sonata for solo cello, 1975; many other orchl., chmbr. of choral works; music for films, radio & TV. Contbr. to var. newspapers & weeklies. Mbrships: Soc. of Czech. Comps.; OSA (Assn. for protection of musical authors rights). Hons. incl: GD CsTV Prize for musical arr. & direction, 1974. Hobbies: Fishing; Motoring; Touring. Address: Skrivanova 12, 602 Brno, Czechoslovakia.

KRIZEK, Jiri, b. 30 May 1942, Prague, Czechoslovakia. Composer; Pianist; Educator. Educ: Dip., State Conserv., Prague; Cert., Acad. of Santa Cecilia, Rome, Italy; Accademia Chigiana, Siena. m. Dr. Ludmila Dyr, 1 s. Career: Writer of Ballet & Stage Music for var. theatres, Czechoslovakia, Italy & German Fed. Repub.; TV Music, ibid; Pianist-Accomp., Teatro dell'Opera, Rome & Staatstheater, Darmstadt. Comps: Suite for 3 Instruments; Str. Quartet; Symphonic Poem for Human Voice & Orch.; Variations for Organ. Publs: Musicol. works about Altieri & Cavalli. Mbr., Assn. Czech Authors. Hons: Prize, Int. Music Fest., Venice, 1969. Hobbies: Chess; Golf. Address: Wacholderweg 8, 5205 Sankt Augustin 1, Bonn, German Fed. Repub.

KROES, Henk, b. 13 May 1916, Amsterdam, Netherlands. Bass-Baritone. Educ: Conserv.; studied w. Aaltje Noordwier-Reddingius, Gerard Souzay. Debut: Enkhuizen Toonkunst, 1946. Career: Num. Radio, TV Concerts; Oratorio; Songs; Opera; Passions; Bass, Amsterdam Vocal Quartet, 1946-; Concerts in Germany, Gelgium, UK, Israel. Mbr. Kon. Ned. Toonkunst. Ver. Hobbies: Philately; Colour Photography; World Travel. Address: Westhouder Frankeweg 34/1, Amsterdam 0, Netherlands.

KROG, Erling, b. 21 March 1938, Copenhagen, Denmark. Music Master. Educ: MA, Univ. of Copenhagen. m. Ida Krog, 3 c. Debut: The Music Reviewer's Prize, Copenhagen, 1966. Career: Cond., sev. operas, Students' Opera of Copenhagen; Volunteer service, Symph. Orch. of S Jutland, 1976; Tchr., Univ. of Copenhagen (Cond.), 1964-77; Music Master, Kildegaard Gymnasium, Copenhagen. Recordings: C E F Weyse, Sovedrikken (The Sleeping Potion), ballad opera, 1965; Song record w. Zahles Girls Choir, 1968. Publs: Textbook in Cond., Vejledning i Direktion, 1978. Address: Stubmarken 16, 2860 Soborg, Denmark.

KROG, Karin, b. 15 May 1937, Oslo, Norway. Singer. Educ: Vocal studies w. Anne Brown, 1962-69, Ivo Knesevic, 1970-73. m. Johs Bergh, 2 d. Career: Concerts, fests., radio, TV, jazzclubs throughout Europe; Toured USA, 1967, '70, & '72; Toured Japan 1971 & '75; Var. comps. Hons: Jazz Vocal Record of the Yr., Japan, 1971 & '77; winner var. jazz critic polls, incl. Down Beat, 1969. Hobbies: Skiing. Address: Nobelsgt. 35, Oslo 2, Norway. 2, 5.

KROGH, Grethe, b. 7 Nov. 1928, Viborg, Denmark. Professor of Organ. Educ: Dips. in Organ, Piano, Harpsichord, Royal Acad. of Music, 1951; studied w. Andre Marchal. m. Richard Dahl Eriksen. Debut: Copenhagen, 1953. Career: num. Concerts throughout Europe, Russia & USA. Organist Holmens Ch., Copenhagen, 1964-69; Prof. of Organ, Chmn., Organ Dept., Royal Danish Acad. Copenhagen, 1969-. Recordings incl: Carl Nielsen, Organ Works. Hons: Prize, Copenhagen Music Critics, 1968; Tagea Brandt Prize of Hon., 1972. Hobbies: Literature; Swimming; ballet. Address: 13 Primulavej, 2720 Vanlose, Denmark.

KROLICK, Edward John, b. 1 Aug. 1923, Rochester, NY, USA. Professor of Music; Double Bass; Educ: BM., 1948, MM., 1951, Eastman Schl. of Music, Rochester Univ.; M Mus. Ed., Univ. of Ill., 1956. m. Bettye A Maxwell, 2 s., 2 d. Career: Double Bass Sect., Rochester Phil., 4 yrs.; San Antonio (Tex.) Symph., 2 yrs.; Memphis (Tenn.) Symph., 8 yrs.; Prin. Double Bass, Champaign-Urbana (Ill.) Symph., 14 yrs.; Prof. of Music, Univ. of Ill. Publs: Prelude to String Playing - Double Bass (co-author). Contbr. to profl. jrnls. Mbrships: Am. String Tchrs. Assn.; Int. Soc. of Bassists; Phi Kappa Lambda. Hobbies: Reading; Camping. Address: 602 Ventura, Champaign, IL, USA.

KROMBHOLC, Jaroslav, b. 30 Jan. 1918, Prague, Czechoslovakia. Conductor. Educ: Prague Conserv.; Charles Univ., ibid. Career: Guest Cond., Prague Nat. Theatre & Czech. Phil. Orch., 1940; Cond., Prague Nat. Theatre, 1949-62; 1st Cond., ibid, 1963-68; Hd., Prague Nat. Theatre Opera, 1968-70; Chief Cond., Nat. Theatre Opera, 1970-; Presented operas in Vienna, 1947, Budapest, 1949; London, 1967, Warsaw, 1969, Naples, 1968, etc.; Toured USSR w. Nat. Theatre, 1955; Guest cond., Rumania, France, Denmark, Bulgaria, S Am., Poland, Uk, etc. Mbrships: Bd. of Trustees, Prague Nat. Theatre Opera House, 1945-49. Hons: State Prize, 1949, 1955; Honoured Artist, 1958; Nat. Artist, 1966. Address: Nat. Theatre, Divadelni 6, Prague, Czechoslovakia.

KROPFINGER, Klaus, b. 27 May 1930, GeraThür, Germany. Professor of Musicology. Educ: Dip., Musical Acad., Weimar, 1956; Grad., Univ. of Bonn, 1971. m. Helga von Kuegelgen, 1 d. Career: Metal Worker, 1949-51; Contbr. to the Complete Ed. of Beethoven's Comps., 1962-68; Prof. of Musicol., Freie Univ., Berlin, 1973-. Mbrships. incl: Int. Musicol. Soc.; Gesellschaft für Musiforschung. Publs. incl: L V Beethoven, Ballettmusik (ed.), 1970; Wagner und Beethoven, Regensburg, 1975. Contbr. to sev. books. Hobbies incl: Yoga; Walking tours; Swimming; Hist. of art. Address: 1 Berlin 62 (W), Hewaldstr. 10, German Fed. Repub.

KROSS, Siegfried, b. 24 Aug. 1930, Wuppertal, Germany. Professor of Musicology. Educ: Studied musicol., Freiburg im Breisgau & Bonn; Dr. Phil., 1957. m. Dorothee Brand, 2 children. Career: Asst., Beethoven Archives, Bonn, 1954, Univ. of Bonn, 1960; Lectr., ibid, 1966; Prof., ibid, 1970. Publs: Die Chorwerke von J Brahms, 1958, 2nd edit. 1963; Das Instrumentalkonzert bei Telemann, 1969; Ed., Beethoven, Diabelli-Variationen op. 120, 1961; Ed., Beethoven Klavierquintett & Klavierquartette, 1964; Ed., Telemann, 12 Violinkonzerte, 1973; Co-ed., Colloquium Amicorum, 1967; Ed., Max Reger in siner Zeit, 1973; Ed., Dokumentation zur Geschichte des deutschen Liedes, 1973, '76, '77; Ed., Briefe Robert und Clara Shumanns, 1978; Ed., Telemann, 12 Instrumentalkonzerte, 1980. Contbr. to jrnls. incl: Die Musikforschung. Address: Ippendorfer Allee 5, D-5300 Bonn, German Fed. Repub.

KRPAN, Vladimir, b. 11 Jan. 1938, Zelina, Yugoslavia. Concert Pianist; Professor of Piano. Educ: Dip., Zagreb Acad.; Dip., Academia di Santa Cecilia, Rome; Dip., Academia Chigiana, Sienna. m. Erika Jirku Krpan, 1 d. Debut: Sienna, 1960. Career: Prof. of piano, Zagreb Music Acad.; Skopje Music Acad.; TRU Zagreb; Apps. as concert pianist at festivals in Yugoslavia & abroad; Tchr.; summer courses, Int. Comp of Jeunesse Musicale, Groznjan, Istria. Recordings of classical & contemporary repertoire. Mbrships: Union of Musical Artists, Zagreb; Union of Musical Tchrs., Zagreb; Assn. of Croatian Music Pedagogues; Croatian Musicians Assn. Recip. hons. inclng: Prize of SR of Croatia, Vladimir Nazor, 1974. Hobbies: Sport; Photography. Address: Basaricekova 3, 41000 Zagreb, Yugoslavia.

KRUEGER, George F., b. 1 May 1907, Richmond, Ind., USA. Professor Emeritus of Choral Music. Educ: Westminster Choir Coll., Princeton, NJ; B Mus, Ithaca Conserv. of Music, NY, 1930; Mus M, Cleveland Inst. of Music, Oh, 1938. m. Elizabeth Cecil Krueger, 2 s., 2 d (1 dec.). Career: Chmn., Choral Dept., 1948-74, Admnstv. Asst. to Dean, 1955-73, now Prof. Emeritus, Schl. of Music, Ind. Univ.; Cond. of Choruses, touring Europe, Far E, USA; Guest Choral Cond., 35 states; Adjudicator, Int. fests. of music; Bass-Baritone Soloist, oratorio & concerts on radio & TV, w. Phila. Orch. under Stowkowski, & Oakland Symph.; Bass Soloist, Parsifal, Boris Goudenov, Ind. Univ. Contbr. to books & jrnls. Mbr. num. musical orgs. Recip. var. hons. Hobbies incl: Gardening; Fishing. Address: Upper Flanders, Box 128, Rte. 11 Bloomington, IN 47401, USA.

KRUGER, Natalie Wyatt, b. 29 Jan. 1934, Medfore, Mass., USA. Flautist. Educ: AB, Oberlin Coll.; M Mus, New England Conserv. Music. m. Harry Kruger, 1 s., 2 d. Career: Flautist w. Atlanta Symph., Toledo Orch., Columbus Symph., Ga.; Mbr., Atlanta Woodwind Quartet, Toledo Orch. Woodwind Quartet, Ohio; Concert Ensemble (trio, soprano, flute & piano); Flute Instructor, Columbus Coll., Ga.; Dir., Columbus Coll. Flute Ensemble, Flute Quartet & Recorder Consort. Contbr. to: The Instrumentalist. Mbr. profl. orgs. Hons: Schlrship winner, Pi Kappa Lambda, New England Conserv. Hobbies incl: Sewing. Address: 3484 Melrose Dr., Columbus, GA 31906, USA.

KRUGER, Rudolf, b. Berlin, Germany. Conductor. Educ: Dip., State Acad. of Music, Vienna, Austria; Studies of violin, piano, theory, comp. & cond. w. leading tutors in Europe & USA. m. Ruth Elizabeth, 1 s., 1 d. Career: Asst. Cond., Southern Symph.

Orch. & Columbia Choral Soc., SC, USA, 1939-42; Asst. Cond., New Orleans Symph. Orch. & Cond., Popular & Young People's Concerts, ibid, 1942-45; US Army, 1945-46; Cond., Mid-west Tour, Chgo. Light Opera Co., 1946; Musical Dir., Jackson Opera Guild, Miss., 1948-51; Musical Dir., Mobile Opera Guild, Ala., 1949-55; Musical Dir., New Orleans Light Opera Co., 1950; 1st Cond., Crescent City Concert Assn., New Orleans, 1954; Musical Dir. & Cond., Ft. Worth Opera Assn., 1955-58; Musical Dir. & Gen. Mgr., ibid, 1958-; Res. Music Dir., Ft. Worth Symph. Orch., 1963-65; Musical Dir., Ft. Worth Ballet Assn., 1965-66; Guest Cond.,v ar. orchs. in USA, Germany, Iran. Mbrships: Am. Fedn. of Musicians; Rotary Club. Hobby: Swimming. Address: Ft. Worth Opera Assn., 3505 W Lancaster, Ft. Worth, TX 76107, USA. 2.

KRÜGER, Walther, b. 25 Sept. 1902, Hamburg, Germany. Musicologist; Pianist. Educ: Dr phil, Univ. of Berlin, 1930; Habilitation (Musicol.), Univ. of Halle, 1956. M. Hildegard Schmersow, 3 children. Career: Lectr.; Music Tchr. at Gymnasium; Music Critic; Writer. Publs. incl: Die authentische Klangform des primitiven Organum, 1958; Karlheinz Stockhausen. Allmacht und Ohnmacht in der Neuesten Musik, 1974; Das Gorgonenhaupt. Zukunftsvisionen in der modernen bildenden Kunst, Musik, Literatur, 1972. Contbr. to profl. jrnls. Mbr., Gesellschaft für Musikforschung. Address: Kéornerstr. 3, D-2407 Bad Schwartau, German Fed. Repub.

KRUSE, Bjørn Howard, b. 14 Aug. 1946, London, UK. Composer; Teacher. Educ: Univ. of Calif. at Los Angeles, 1967-68; MMus (clarinet), Norwegian State Acad. of Music, 1975; Dip. (comp.), ibid., 1977. m. Gro Shetelig Kruse, 2 d. Career: Tchr. of theory, Norwegian State Acad. of Music. Comps. incl: Statement, for saxophone quartet, 1973Z; Janicke's Dance, for wind quintet, 1975; 3 movements, for double bass & piano, 1976; Claws, for jazz orch., 1977; Exit, for orch., 1978; Suoni della Voce, for mixed choir, 1978; A Chess Game, opera comique for orch. & 6 soloists, 1979; Move the Motion, for flute, clarinet, violin, cello, piano & percussion, 1979. Publ: Practical Arranging, 1978. mbr., Ny Musikk (Norwegian Contemporary Music Soc.); Soc. of Norwegian Comps. Hons: sev. works perf. at UNM fests in Scandinavia; 2nd & 3rd prizes in nat. contests. Hobby: Playing jazz. Address: Tormods vei 3, Oslo 11, Norway.

KRUSE, Harald, b. 12 Sept. 1923, Bremen, Germany. Composer; Conductor. Educ: Gymnasium Bremen Abitur. m. Ingeborg Eckert. Debut: as Cond: Mainz, 1958. Comps: Concerto for 4 orchs.; 2 Operas; 5 Symphs.; 5 Ballets; 3 String Quartets; Incidental Music; Orchl. & Chmbr. Music; Lieder; Ch. Music. Recordings: Radio Bremen; Sudwestfunk; Suddeutscher Rundf; Swiss Radio. Mbrships: Deutscher Komponisten Verband; GEMA. Address: Mozartstr. 20, 28 Bremen, Germany.

KRUSE, Philip Antony, b. 13 May 1949, Trondheim, Norway. Music Publisher; Artist. Educ: Music Coll.; Tchrs. Coll. m. Anita Wenche, 2 d. Career: many apps. w. Bendik Singers, inclng. Eurovision Song Contest, Luxembourg, 1973, & Brighton, 1974; Publng. Dir., Frost Music A/S, Norway. Comp. of about 300 works of popular music, childrens music & choir & orch. music. Mbr., NOPA. Hons: Co-Writer, Norwegian Eurovision Song Contest Entry, 1974 & 76; var. domestic hons. Hobbies: Reading; Decorating. Address: Liljev 1E, Oslo 5, Norway.

KRUTZFELDT, Werner J M., b. 27 Sept. 1928, Kiel, Germany. Composer; Musicologist. Educ: Dr. Phil., Univ. of Hamburg; Hochschule fur Musik, Hamburg. m. Hildegard Junker, 2 c. Career: Dozent fur Musiktheorie, 1954, Promotion, 1960, Prof. for Comp., Hochschule fur Musik, Hamburg. Comps: Zahlreich. Publs: Didaktik der Musik, 1967, 1969, '70; Die Wertproblematik in der Musididatkik, 1973; Musikpädagogik im Drahtverhau, 1973; Musik aktnell, 1971; Musik in der Gesantschule, 1974. Contbr. to profl. publs. Mbrships: Fed. Chmn. of Arbeitskreis für Schulmusik und allgemeine Musikpädagogik; Chmn., Landesmusikrat Hamburg. Recip., Bach-Preis-Stipendium, Hamburg, 1960. Address: Rögenfeld 42a, 2000 Hamburg 67, German Fed. Repub.

KRZEMINSKI, Franciszek, b. 15 Sept. 1925, Pila, Woj Poznan, Poland. Musician; Teacher of Music. Educ: Pedagogical Lyceum; Musical Conserv. m. Regina Padyjasek, 2 s. Debut: Philharmonic Hall, Kerecin. Career: Played w. Orch. Wind Quintet; Ret'd Recorded for TV & radio broadcasts. Mbr., Musicians Soc. Hons: Decoration for meritorious work, Lublin Dist.; Monetary awards from Min. of Culture. Hobbies: Gardening; Nature walks; Football. Address: ul. Balladyny 8/4, Lublin 20-601, Poland.

KRZYWICKI, Jan, b. 15 April 1948, Phila., Pa., USA. Composer; Teacher; Pianist. Educ: Phila. Musical Acad.,

1962-66; Juilliard Schl. of Music, 1966-68; Fontainebleu, summer 1967; Aspen Music Fest., summer 1968; B Mus, Univ. of Kan., 1971; M Mus, Phila. Musical Acad., 1975. Career: Instructor of Theory & Ear Trng., Phila. Musical Acad., 1972-. Comps. incl: Continuum (ballet, premiered by Pa. Ballet Co., 1976); Four Songs; Toccata for Piano; Motet Passionale (chorus & orch.); Sonata for Double Bass & Piano; Pastorale (baritone horn & wind ensemble); Snow Night for Marimba & piano, 1977; Poem for unaccomp. boys & mens voices, 1977. Hobbies: Reading; Sports; Ethol. Address: 1221 Spruce St., Philadelphia, PA 19107, USA.

KTENAVEAS, Takis, b. 19 June 1934, Kalamata, Greece. Violinist. Educ: Conserv. of Athens, 1951-58; Further study in Vienna & NY. m. Elli Schabmann, 1 d. Debut: Vienna. Career: Apps. w. orch. inclng: Berlin Symph.; Vienna Tonkunstler; Greek State; Czech. Phil.; Recitals in most European countries; Festivals incl: Yehudi Menuhin Festival, Switzerland; own festival in Kalamata, 1976; Recordings for German, Greek, USSR, Italian, Swedish & Danish Radio Stns.; Master Classes several countries; Prof., Conserv. of Vienna, 1968-. Contbr. to profl. mags. Recip. Dimitri Mitropoulos Prize, Athens, 1960. Hobbies: Motoring; Swimming. Address: Columbusgasse 105/12, A 1100 Vienna, Austria.

KUBELIK, Rafael, b. 1914, Bychory, Bohemia. Conductor; Composer. Educ: Prague Conserv. m. (1) Ludmila Bertlova, 1 s., (2) Elsie Morison. Career: Cond., Czech. Phil. Soc., 1936-39; Music Dir., Brno Opera, 1939-41, Czech. Phil. Orch., 1942-48, Chgo. Symph. Orch., 1950-53, Royal Opera House, Covent Gdn., 1955-58, & Bavarian Radio Symph. Orch., 1961-; Guest Cond. w. leading orchs. & at major fests. thru'out world. Compositions incl: 2 symphs. w. chorus; 4 str. quartets; concertos; 1 cantata; songs; instrumental pieces. Mgmt: Harold Holdt Ltd., Wigmore St., London, UK; Jacques Leiser, 52 Rue de Rome, Paris 8e, France. 3.

KUBEY, Arthur, b. 27 Feb. 1918, Paterson, NJ, USA. Bassoonist. Educ: Ernest Williams Music Schl.; studies w. Simon Kovar. m. Erika Kutzine Kubey, 1 s., 1 d. Career: Prin. Bassoonist, Pitts. Symph.; Tchr. of Bassoon & Woodwind Ensemble, Carnegie-Mellon Univ., Pitts., Pa. Hobby: Fishing. Address: 5283 Forbes Ave., Pittsburgh, PA 15217, USA.

KUBIAK-WOJTASZEK, Teresa Janina, b. 26 Dec. 1937, Lodz, Poland. Principal Opera & Concert Singer. Educ: Dip., Gymnasium, Poland, 1955; BA, HS of Music, Lodz; MA, Acad. of Music, Lodz, Poland. m. Janusz Kubiak, 2 d. Debut: Carmen, Bizet, Grand Teater, Lodz, 1964. Career: Apps., San Fran. Opera, Lyric Opera of Chgo., Houston Grand Opera, Teatro La Fenice, Glyndebourne Fest. Opera, Royal Opera House, Covent Garden, Vienna State Opera, Prague Nat. Theater, Metropolitan Opera, num. other European & USA Cos.; TV apps.; Perfd. w. Munich Phil., Warsaw Phil., etc.; sev. Fest. apps. Recordings: La Calisto (Cavalli); Glagolitic Mass (Janacek); Eugene Onegin (Tchaikovsky); Famous Polish Singers, vol. II. Hons incl: Special Award, Polish Musician Assn., Lodz, Poland, 1974; First Class Award, Ministry of Art & Culture, Warsaw, 1974; Cross of Knight, Polish Govt., 1975. Mgmt: Columbia Artists Mgmt. inc., 165 W 57th St., NYC, NY 10019, USA. Address: 195 Gates Ave., Montclair, NJ 07042, USA. 5.

KUBIK, Gerhard, b. 10 Dec. 1934, Vienna, Austria. Ethnologist & Ethnomusicologist; Musician. Educ: PhD, Univ. of Vienna, 1971; musical studies w. Evaristo Muyinda, Uganda, 1959-60, 61-62, 68. Career: Singer & Clarientist, Kachamba Brothers' Band (Malawian Kwela jazz band), on TV in Nairobi, Kampala (E Africa), Austria & S-W Germany, 1972, concert tours, Venezuela, Brazil, Ghana, Togo, Nigeria, Cameroon, Zaire, Zambia, S Africa, Madagascar, Tanzania & Kenya, 1974. Recorded LPs w. same band, 1972. Publs. incl: Mehrstimmigkeitt und Tonsysteme in Zentral - und Ostafrika, 1968; Musica traditional e aculturada dos 'Kung' de Angola, 1970; Theory of African Music - 9 essays, 1979. Contbr. to jrnls. Mbr., African Music Soc. Address: Inst. of Ethnol., Univ. of Vienna, Universitätstr. 7, A-1010 Vienna, Austria.

KUBIN-VALIC, Valeria, b. 10 Jan. 1938, Sarajevo, Yugoslavia. Concert Pianist; Professor of Piano. Educ: Dip., Music Conserv.; Dip., Music Acad. m. Mario Valic, 2 d. Debut: Sarajevo, 1946. Career: Concert tours, TV & radio apps. in Yugoslavia, Austria, USSR, Italy, Czech. etc. Hons: Wettbewerb für junge Künstler, Zagreb, 1956, 3rd prize; Ljubljana, 1957, 1st prize. Hobby: Painting. Mgmt: Konzertdirection Sarajevo, Linz, Zagreb. Address: Waldmullergang 8b/13, 4020 Linz-Donau, Austria.

KUBIZEK, Augustin, b. 15 Oct. 1918, Vienna, Austria. Professor of Music; Composer. Educ: Tchrs. Trng. Coll., 5 yrs.; State Dips. in Singing, Choral & Orchl. Cond., & Comp., Acad.

of Music, Vienna (studied w. J N David & P Hindemith). m. Elizabeth Lewinsky, 2 s., 2 d. Career: Prof., Acad. of Music, Vienna, 1956, Univ. Prof., 1973-; Fndn. & Cond., Wiener Schütz Kantorei (a cappella chmbr. choir), 1965. Compositions incl: Sacred Choral Works inclng. Missa Brevis, 1953 & Neue Messe, 1970; Secular Choral Works inclng. Kranz des Jahres, 1956; Mundus Cantat (folk-songs for Choir), 1970-72; Orchl. Works inclng. Concerto for Clarinet & Orch., 1977; Works for Solo Voice & Instruments, inclng. Marienlob (Cantata for Soprano, Flute, Clarinet, 'Cello), 1967; Chmbr. Music inclng. Der Kleine Tastenbezwinger, 1970; Concertos; Works for Choir & Orch.; num. works recorded on disc & radio. Contbr. to profl. jrnls. inclng. Der Komponist. Mbrships incl: Assn. of Austrian Comps; Austrian Soc. for Contemporary Music. Hons. incl: T Körners Stiftingsfond Award, 1958, 1967; Concours de Comp., ORTF, 1962; Grand Music Award of Vienna, 1973. Address: Schönburgstr. 13/27, 1040 Vienna, Austria.

KUBIZEK, Karl Maria, b. 11 May 1925, Eferding, Austria. Professor of Music; Composer; Clarinettist. Educ: Tchr. Trng. Coll.; Coll. for Music & Interpretive Art, Vienna; Grad., Music Acad.; Bruckner Conserv.; Dip., Vienna Music Acad., 1959. m. Mathilde Pfanner, 2 s. Debut: Linz, 1942. Career: clarinet concerts, Austria, Germany, Netherlands, Italy, Turkey, Iran, Lebanon, Syria, Egypt; var. radio broadcasts. Comps. incl: small suites, variations, 10 pieces & sonatinas (all for recorder); Sonata for oboe & piano (recorded); Clarinet quintet (recorded); Konzertante Sinfonie for Clarinet & Strings; Wind Quintet; Trio Concertante for clarinet, cello & piano. Contbr. to Musikerziehung. Mbrships: Soc. of Authors, Comps. & Music Publs.; Austrian Comps. Soc.; Austro-Mechana; Innviertler-Kunstlergilde; AGMOE. Hons: 1st Prize, Music Competition, Prague, 1943; Mozart Soc. Prize, Vienna, 1951; Comp. Prize, Youth Culture Week, Innsbruck, 1955. Hobbies: Painting; Drawing. Address: Grünbergerstr. 20, A-4540 Bad Hall, Austria.

KUCERA, Vaclav, b. 29 Apr. 1929, Czech. Composer; Musicologist. Educ: Univ. Carolina, Prague, 1948-51; State Conserv., Moscow, 1951-56; PhD., 1966; CSc in artistic scis., 1965. m. Marie Jerieova, 1951, 2 s. Career: Hd., Dept. of For. Music, Czech. radio, Prague, 1956-59; Hd., Dept. for Study of Contemporary Music, Guild of Czech Comps., 1959-62; Hd., Dept. of Musical Aesthetics, Inst. of Musicol., Czech Acad of Scis., 1962-69; Gen. Sec., Guild of Czech Comps. & Concert Artists, Prague, 1969-; External Docent, Acad. of ARts, ibid., 1972-. Comps. incl: Dramas for 9 instruments, 1961; Symph. for large orch., 1962; The Pied Piper, stereoconcertino for flute & 2 chmbr. orchs., 1964; Diario, homage to Che Guevara, concert-cycle for solo guitar, 1971; Lidice, radio musical-dramatic fesco, 1972. Num. recordings. Publs: Books on Modern Soviet Music & Moussorgski. Mbrships. incl: Czech. Musical Coun.; Prague Spring Festival Committee. Hons. incl: Prix d'Italia for Lidice, 1973. Address: Jizni II., 778, 141 00 Prague 4, Czech.

KUCHLER, Kenneth Grant, b. 27 Mar. 1922, Ogden, Utah, USA. Violinist; Music Educator. Educ: BS, Univ. of Utah, 1943; MS, ibid, 1951; Univ. of Calif., Berkeley, 1943-44; violin student of Toscha Seidel. Debut: w. US Army, 1943-46. Career: Staff Musician, KSL Radio, Salt Lake City, Utah, 1946-48; Dir. of String Studies, Ogden City Schl. System, 1948-54; Concertmaster, Utah Symph. Orch., Salt Lake City, 1946-; Chmn., Dept. of Music, Westminster Coll., 1954-; Music Dir. & Cond., Westminster Coll. Community Symph. Orch., 1954-; currently Music Dir., Westminster Coll. Early Instrument Consort; First Violinist, Peninsula Fest. Orch., Fish Creek, Wis., summers, 1962-; European tour w. Utah Symph., 1966; S. Am. tour, ibid, 1971; Tour of Gt. Britain w. Utah Symph. Orch., 1975, Europe, 1977. Recordings: w. Utah Symph. Orch. for Vanguard, Westminster & Vox as Concertmaster & Assoc. Mandolin. Publs: Play Folk Tunes & Hymns as You Learn the Recorder, 1965; United States Patent, Wrist Support During Violin Playing, 1956. Mbr., var. profl. orgs. Hobby: Early instrument research. Address: 304 S 12th E St., Salt Lake City, UT 84102, USA.

KUCINSKI, Leo, b. 28 June 1904, Warsaw, Poland. Musician (Violinist); Symphony Orchestra Conductor. Educ: Mus B, Mus D, Morningside Coll., Sioux City, Iowa, USA; Grad. Schl., Juilliard Schl. of Music; Oberlin Coll., Ohio. m. Irene Kucinski, 1 d. Career: Dir., Okoboji Summer Music Camp, 1930-52; Cond., Lincoln Symph., Neb., 1934-42; Cond., Sioux Falls Symph. SD, 1959-72; currently Cond., Symph. Orch., Sioux City, Iowa & Dir., Municipal Band, ibid; num. Guest apps. as Cond. & Violin Soloist. Recording w. Monahan Post Band for RCA Victor. Publ: Brahms Studies. Mbrships: Am. Symph. Orch. League (VP, 1947-48); Phi Mu Alpha. Hons: Proclaimed Outstanding Musician of Iowa by Governor Ray; Concertmaster Chair established in his name, Sioux Falls Symph. Orch. Hobbies: Chess; Bridge. Address: 219 Cook Dr., Sioux City, IA, USA. 4.

KUCKERTZ, Josef, b. 24 Nov. 1930, Würselen/Aachen, Germany. Musicologist; Ethnomusicologist. Educ: Choral Cond. Dip., Rheinische Musikschule Köln, 1957; PhD, Univ. of Cologne, 1962; Habilitation, Univ. of Cologne, 1967. m. Regina Bittermann, 4 c. Career: Profl of Musicology/Ethnomusicology, Univ. of Cologne, 1970-. Publs: Gestaltvariation in den von Bartók gesammelten rumänischen Colinden, 1963; Form und Melodiebildung der karnatischen Musik Südindiens - im Umkreis der vorderorientalischen und der nordindischen Kunstmusik, 2 vols., 1970; (w. M T Massoudieh); Musik in Busehr, Süd-Iran, 2 vols., 1976. Contbr. to profl. publs. Mbrships: Gesellschaft für Musikforschung; Soc. for Ethnomusicology, USA; Indian Musicological Soc. (Baroda,India). Address: Wittelsbacherstr. 112, 5040 Brühl, German Fed. Repub.

KUDYK, Jan, b. 10 May 1942, Cracow, Poland. Trumpeter; Leader of Jazz Band Ball Orchestra. Educ: MA, Jagiellonian Univ., Cracow, 1967; MA, Music Acad., Cracow, 1972. m. Elzbieta, 2 s., 1 d. Debut: Jazz Fest., Cracow, 1963. Career: has made concert, radio & TV apps., Poland, Austria, Belgium, Czech., Switz., Denmark, France, Netherlands, Yugoslavia, Germany, Sweden, Hungary & USSR. Comps. Recorded: Komplet; Ixi zamiast Dixi, Potwor; Grzecznosc; Zawrot Glowy. Has made both single & LP records w. Jazz Band Orch. Mbr: Polish Jazz Soc. Address: ul. Altanowa 18/3, 30 132 Kraków, Poland.

KUEBLER, David, b. 23 July 1947, Detroit, Mich., USA. Opera Singer (tenor). Educ: BA, Engl. Lit.; pvte. voice study w. Thomas Peck, Chgo., Audrey Langford, London. m. Elinore R McDaniels, 1 d. Career: Annelise Rothenberger TV program, Germany, 1975; Glyndebourne, Cosi fan Tutti, 1976; Cologne Opera, Falstaff, 1976; Vienna State Opera, Magic Flute, 1977; Wash. Opera, Wash. DC, Magic Flute, 1977; Mbr., Cologne Opera Ensemble, 1976-. Recordings: Mozart's Mitridate, Re Di Ponto. Hons: WGN Contest, Chgo., Ill. Hobbies: Running; Reading. Mgmt: Columbia Artists Mgmt., NY; Harrison/Parrott, Ltd., London; Dr. Rudolf Raab, Vienna. Address: Bunzlauerstrasse 5, 5 Köln 40, German Fed. Repub.

KUECK, Rudolf, Hermann, b. 10 March 1931, Wachtendonk, Germany. Tech. Dir. Educ: Acad. of Admin. m. Melitta Kunz. Career: 1954-58 City theater Krefeld-Mönchen Gladbach; 1958-60 Asst. tech. dir.; 1960-65 Tech. chief insp. Bad State Theater Karlsruhe; 1965-68 Tech. dir. Theater Kiel; since 1968 Tech. Dir., German Opera, Berlin West; Cons. for light and sound tech., New Opera, Cairo. Mbrships: var. profl. orgs. Publs. incl: Theater Technic 1976, Prag Quadrienale; Ana Desighn 1976, ITI Congres, St. Louis, USA. Contbr. to: var. prof. jrnls. Hobbies: Photography; Watersport; Travelling; Reading. Address: Knesebeckstr. 22, 1000 Berlin 12, Germany.

KUEHN, David Laurance, b. 26 Oct. 1940, San Marcos, Tex., USA. Professor of Tuba & Euphonium, N. Tex. State Univ., Denton. Educ: B Mus, N. Tex. State Univ.; MS, Univ. of Ill.; DMA, Eastman Schl. of Music; Fulbright Scholar, London, 1964-65; LGSM; ARCM. m. Susan Travis, 1 s., 1 d. Publs: 60 Musical Studies for Tuba, Books 1 & 2, & 28 Advanced Studies for Tuba, 1972 (both transcribed by D Kuehn). Contbr. to: The Instrumentalist; The Schl. Musician; The Southwestern Musician; The Wis. Schl. Musician; The NACWPI. Jrnl.; The Conductor. Mbrships: Nat. Assn. of Coll. Wind & Percussion Instructors, USA; N. Am. Chapt., Tubists Universal Brotherhood Assn. Address: 2913 Bristol Dr., Denton, TX, USA.

KUEN, Otto Ludwig, b. 20 May 1910, Munich, Germany. College Teacher. Educ: PhD. m. Rosa Kuen, 4 s. Debut: Bayrischer Rundfunk (Radio Munich). Compositions: Lieder der Weissblauen Drehorgel Der Isarnöck (Musical). Recordings: 7 Lieder der Weissblauen Drehorgel. Member, Deutscher Kompanisten-Verband. Hobby: Writing stories. Address: Bergmannstrasse 66, 8 Munich 2, German Fed. Repub.

KUERTI, Anton Emil, b. 21 July 1938, Vienna, Austria. Pianist; Composer. Educ: BM, Cleveland Inst. of Music, USA; Dip, Curtis Inst. of Music. m. Kristine Bogyo, 1 child. Debut: Soloist w. NY Phil., 1957. Career: Apps. w. maj. orchs in USA, Can., GB, Belgium, Germany, Italy, USSR, Czechoslovakia, Spain, etc.; Radio & TV apps. on CBC, BBC, Dutch, German & Polish Radio Stns.; Series of radio progs. discussing & performing 32 Beethoven Sonatas on CBC; Perf. of complete Beethoven Sonata cycles, NY, Toronto, Montreal, etc. Comps. incl: Violin Sonata, String Quartets, var. piano works. Num. recordings incl. Complete Beethoven Sonatas. Contbr. to Clavier Mag. & Piano Technicians Jrnl. Recip. Leventritt Award, 1957. Hobbies: Hiking; Skiing; Politics; Sci.; Lit. Mgmt: Jacques Leiser, 155 W 68th St., New York, NY 10023, USA. Address: 20 Linden St., Toronto, Ont. M4Y 1V6, Canada.

KUETEMAN, John-Anne, b, 5 Jan. 1918, Guthrie, Okla., USA. Teacher of Stringed Instruments; Orchestra Director; Private Teacher of Violin & Viola, String Quartet & String Quintet; Research Teacher. Educ: BA, Violin & Viola, Univ. Okla.; Studied w. Woolf & Carpenter; Vocal study w. Barre Hill. m. Herman F Kueteman, 3 children. Career: W. Okla. Symph., 11 seasons; Fine Arts String Quartet, 4 seasons; Community String Quartet, 15 seasons; Instructor, Strings & Orch., Okla. Schls., 15 yrs; Counselor & Prescriptive Tchr. of Children w. Learning Disabilities, 9 yrs. Mbr. num. profl. orgs. Hobbies: Travel; Oil & Tole Painting; Macrame; Antique Collecting; Archaeology; Geneology. Address: 516 Northwest 17th St., Okla. City, OK 73103, USA.

KUJALA, Walfrid Eugene, b. 19 Feb. 1925, Warren, Ohio, USA. Musician (flute & piccolo); Teacher. Educ: B Mus, M Mus, Eastman Schl. of Music; Rochester NY. m. Alice Pillischer, 2 s., 1 d. Career: Flautist & piccolist w. Rochester Phil. Orch., 1948-54, Chgo. Symph. Orch., 1954-; Fac. Eastman Schl. of Music, 1950-54; Prof. of Flute, N. Western Univ. Schl. of Music, 1962-; Solo & chmbr. music appearances throughout USA & Canada. Recordings: var. wors w. Chgo. Symph. Orch. under leading conds. incl. Barenboim, Solti, Stravinsky, etc. Publ: The Flutist's Progress, 1970; Contbg. Ed., The Instrumentalist, 1971-. Mbrships: VP, Nat. Flute Assn. Address: 1261 Ash St., Winnetka, IL 60093, USA. 8.

KULLMAN, Charles, b. New Haven, Conn., USA. Concert & Opera Tenor. Educ: BS, Yale Univ., 1924; Juilliard Music Schl.; Am. Conserv., Fontainebleau, France. m. Lisa Demander, 1 d. Debut: Concert, NYC, 1924. Career: Soloist, Yale Glee Club's European Tour, 1928; Asst. Prof., Music, Smith Coll., 1928-29; Mbr., Am. Opera Co., Chgo. Civic Light Opera Co.; Leading Tenor, Met. Opera Co.; apps. in Berlin, Vienna, Salzburg, San Fran., Buenos Aires, Rio de Janiero; radio & TV broadcasts; num. concerts; starred in film, Song of Scheherazade, 1941; Prof. of voice, Ind. Univ., 1957. Mbrships: incl. Met. Opera Assn.; Alpha Sigma Phi; Bohemian Club, San Fran. Address: 26 Chapman Ave., Madison, CT 06443, USA. 2.

KUMMEL, Werner Friedrich, b. 17 Oct. 1936, Zürich, Switz. Professor. Educ: Univ. Marburg, Kiel, Göttingen. Hist., Musical, Classical Philol., PhD, Lectr. m. Ute Rössiger. Career: Prof. for the Hist. of Medicine, Frankfurt Univ., 1973, Mainz Univ., 1976. Mbrships: Soc. for Music Rsch.; German Soc. for the Hist. of Medicine, Natural Hist. & Technol.; Int. Soc. for the Hist. of Medicine; Int. Soc. for the Hist. of Pharmacy. Publs: History and Music History, 1976; Music and Medicine, 1967. Contbr. to: Music Rsch.; Analecta Musicologica; Acta Musicologica; Italian Music Review; Jrnl. for Medical Hist. Hobbies: Violin, Chamber music. Address: Grosse Hohl 33, D-6501 Wackernheim, German Fed. Repub.

KUNAD, Rainer, b. 24 Oct. 1936, Chemnitz, Germany. Composer; Professor. Educ: HS for Music, Leipzig. m. Steffi, 4 c. Career incl: Tchr., music theory. Robt. Schumann Conserv., Zwickau; Composer of theatre Music for State Theatre, Dresden. Compositions incl: concerti for piano & organ; Antiphonie for 2 orchs.; Quadrophonie for 4 orchs.; Scene concertante for orch.; String quartet; opera - Maitre Pathelin, Sabellicus, Litanische Claviere, & Vincent van Gogh; ballet - Wir ober nennenlibe lebendigen Frieden. Contbr. to: Theater der Zeit; Musik & Gesellschaft. Mbr: Acad. of Arts of German Dem. Repub.; Soc. of Comps. of German Dem. Repub. Hons. incl: Hann-Eisler Prize, 1973; Nat. Prize of German Dem. Repub., 1975. Hobbies: Gardening; Swimming; Winter Sports. Mgmt: Henschelverlag, Berlin; Deutscher Verlag für Musik, Leipzig. Address: Sierksstr. 23, 8054 Dresden, German Dem. Repub. 2, 30.

KUNERT, Kurt, b. 12 July 1911, Stettin, Germany. Composer; flautist. Educ: Music schl. Anklam; Loewe Conserv. Stettin; Leipzig Conserv. m. Iris Renner, 2 s., 3 d. Debut: Stettin, 1929. Career: flautist, Deutsche Musikbühne, Berlin; solo flute, Städtische Bühne, Erfurt; lectr., Erfurt Conserv., Weimar Conserv., & Berlin Adv. Coll. of Music; ldr. Erfurt Chmbr. Music Soc. Comps. incl: Concert for flute & orch., 1954; concerto for orch., 1956; Sinfonietta, 1960; Festliches Vorspiel, 1963; Unsere Stadt, 1969; Concerto for alto flute, harp & chmbr. orch., 1974; Konzert für grosses Orchester, 1976. Publs. incl: Musikschaffende in Thüringen. Mbrships: mbr. ctrl. committee of Berlin; comps. & musicians union of German Dem. Repub. Hons: Kulturpreis, Erfurt, 1972. Address: 5034 Erfurt, Burg-Gleichenweg 27, German Dem. Repub.

KUNINSKA-OPACKA, Maria, b. 30 Mar. 1918, Rzgów, Poland. Opera & Concert Singer. Educ: Violin w. Prof. Irena Dubiska, Lodz & Warsaw Acad. of Music, 1937-46; Dip., MA, Katowice Acad. of Music, 1947-51; singing classes w. Prof.

Stefan Belina-Skupiewski. m. Bronislaw Opacki, 1 s., 1 d. Debut: w. State Opera, Silesia-Katowice, 1948. Career: Var. stage apps. incl: Margherite & Siebel in Faust, Antonia in The Tales of Hoffmann, Lisa in The Queen of Spades, Tatiana in Eugene Onegin, Cio-Cio-San in Madame Butterfly, Pamina in The Magic Flute; num. radio apps.; tchr. of singing, Warsaw, 1962; Assoc. Prof. of Singing, Lodz Acad. of Music, 1965; Dean of Vocal Dept., Warsaw Acad. of Music, 1969-72; Kenya Conserv. of Music, Nairobi, 1973-77. Recordings: Orpheus & Eurydice; Stabat Mater; Wedding Suite; Songs by Stanislaw Moniuszko. Mbrships: Polish Musicians' Soc.; Chmn., Soloist & Conds. Sect., Nairobi Music Soc. Hons: Golden Badge of Polish Musicians' Soc., 1965. Hobbies: Classical Lit.; Travelling. Address: Obozowa 91 m 9, 01-433 Warsaw. Poland.

KUNZ, Erich. b. 20 May 1909. Opera Singer. Educ: HS for Music, Vienna, Austria. Career: w. Vienna State Opera, 1941-; apps. at all leading opera houses & fests. Hons: Mozart Medal; Verdienstkreuz 1st Class for Arts & Scis.; Hons. Mbr., Vienna State Opera; Gold Medal of Hon. for servs. to Vienna. 16.

KUNZ, Ludvik, b. 26 Aug. 1914, Osicko, Kromeriz, Czechoslovakia. Head of Ethnographic Institut of Moravian Museum. Educ: Univ. M doc. DPh. m. Zora Kunzova, 1 child. Career: Lectr. on radio about instrumental folk music; Mbr. of Grp. studying instrumental folk music at Int. Folk music Coun. Publs: Dis Volksmusikinstrumente der Tshecholslowakei; Handbuch der europaischen Volksmusikinstrumente, 1974; 42 Studies of instrumental folk music. Address: Etnograficky ustav MM, Gagarinova 1, Brno, Czechoslovakia.

KUNZOVA-MISIKOVA, Viera, b. 6 Aug. 1942, Bratislava, Czech. Pianist. Educ: Grad., Conserv., Bratislava, 1961; Grad., Music Acad., ibid, 1965; studied w. Prof. A Kafendova. m. Petr. Kunz. Career: Asst., Music Acad., Bratislava, 1965-. Chief Repetitor, Theater der Altmark, Stendal, German Fed. Repub., 1973-. Solo, Chmbr. Music Concerts, Czechoslovakia & W Germany; var. TV & Radio Apps. Mbr. Union of Slovak Comps., Concert Artists Sect. Hobbies: Literature; Travel; Photography. Address: 1 Inovecka, 80100 Bratislava, Czech.

KUO, Chang-yang, b. 13 June 1934, Taichung, Taiwan. Repub. of China. Professor of Musicology & Piano. Educ: MA Mus, Univ. of Hawaii; PhD, Coll. of Chinese Culture. m. Lin Li-chu, 1 s., 1 d. Career: Dean & Prof. of Music, Coll. of Chinese Culture, 1972-73; Pres., Hwa Kang Scholar's Soc., 1974-75; Prof., Grad. Div. of Arts, Coll. of Chinese Culture & Taipei Jr. Normal Coll. Comps: Brilliance in the Past; Song of Yeh-Liw. Recordings: piano accomp. for 15 Chinese art songs. Publs: Chinese Art Song: A Melodic Analysis, 1972; Analysis of Chinese Folk Song Melodies, 1975. Contbr. to profl. jrnls. Mbrships: Dir., Rsch. Sect., Chinese Classical Music Assn., Taipei; Soc. for Ethnomusicol., USA; Nat. Music Coun. of China, Taipei; Int. Soc. for Music Educ.; Sec. Gen., 2nd Asian Pacific Music Conf. Recip. var. hons. inclng: JCI Ten Outstanding Young Men, 1973. Hobbies: Playing music; Sight-seeing. Address: 6-1 Lane 84, Ta-tung Rd., Shihlin, Taipei, Taiwan. 28, 30.

KUOSMA, Kauko Einari, b. 14 Jan. 1926, Viipuri, Finland. Pianist; Lecturer of Piano & Piano Pedagogy. Educ: Dip., Sibelius Acad., 1949, Conserv. of Paris, 1953; studies in Vienna. m. Arja Anna Kristiina Yli-Paavola, 1 s. Debut: Solo recital, Helsinki, 1949. Career: Piano recitals, Soloist w. orchs., & Accomp., 1948-; Tchr. of Piano, Sibelius Acad., 1954-; lectr., 1965-. Comps: Trio for Violin, Cello & Piano, 1951; String Quartet, 1952; Pièce pour Piano, 1979. Recordings: Music of Diktonius, 1976. Mbrships. incl: Pres., Finnish Soloists Assn., 1967-77; Finnish State Music Commission, 1971-73; Finnish Music Coun., 1974-75; Union of Musicians Socs. in Finland, 1976-; Assn. of Pianopedagogues, 1976-. Contbr. to radio, TV & musical mags. Hons. incl: Martin Wegelius Medal, Sibelius Acad., 1976; Pro Musica, MTA, 1975; Janacek, 1979. Address: Pohjoisniementie 3A, 00200 Helsinki 20, Finland.

KURAU, Warren Peter, b. 16 Aug. 1952, Torrington, Conn., USA. Performer (Horn); Teacher (Horn); Assistant Professor of Music. Educ: B Mus, Eastman Schl. Music; Performer's Cert., Horn, 1974; Cert. Adv. Studies, GSM, 1975; ARCM, 1975; MA, Univ. of Conn., 1978. Career: Solo horn w. Torrington Civ. Symph.; Eastman Schl. Symph. Orch.; Eastman Phil.; Eastman Wind Ensemble; Colo. Phil. Orch.; GSM Orch.; Syracuse Symph.; St. Louis Symph.; Rochester Phil. Orch.; London Florilegium; Rochester Chmbr. Orch.; Yale Summer Schl. Orch.; Mo. Arts Woodwind Quintet; Mo. Symph. Soc. Chmbr. Orch. Mbrships. incl: Mo. Music Educators Assn.; Int. Horn Soc.; Pi Kappa Lambda; MENC; Conn. Music Educators Assn.; Conn. Horn Assn. Hons. incl: Int. Telephone & Telegraph Int. Fellowship, UK, 1974-75; 3rd Place, Heldenleben Int. Horn

Competition, 1978; Recip., Univ. of Mo. Fac. Quality Improvement Grant, 1978. Hobbies incl: Hiking; Nordic Skiing; Bicycling; Woodworking. Address: 50 Travis St., Torrington, CT 06790, USA.

KURKIEWICZ, Ludwik, b. 24 July 1906, Poznań, Poland. Clarinettist; Professor. Educ: State Higher Schl. of Music; Conserv. of Music. 1 s. Debut: Paris, 1936-37. Career: num. concert & radio perfs.; Prof. & vice-rector, Conserv. of Music, Warsaw. Comps: Etude for Clarinet. Recordings: num. sonatas & concertos. Mbrships: VP, SPAM, Warsaw. Hobbies: Collecting old instruments. Address: ul. Kopernika 6, 00367 Warsaw, Poland.

KURMIS, Guna Astrid, b. 20 Mar. 1926, Riga, Latvia. Pianist; Teacher. Educ: Dip., Latvian State Conserv., 1944; Dip., Univ. of Stockholm, 1947; Studied w. Prof. Edwin Fischer, Prof. Gottfrid Boon. m. Edgar Ernstson, 1 d. Debut: Riga, 1943. Career: Soloist, Stockholm Phil.; Recitalist, Sweden, Denmark, W Germany, USA, Latvia. Mbrships: Dpty. Bd. Mbr., Swedish Piano Tchrs. Assn.; MTA of Calif., Inc., USA. Hobby: Reading. Address: 11 Foreningesvagen, 19143 Sollentuna, Sweden.

KURTZ, Efrem, b. 7 Nov. 1900, St. Petersburg, Russia (Citizen of USA). Conductor. Educ: St. Petersburg Conserv.; Stern Conserv., Berlin. m. Elaine Shaffer, 1955. Career: Cond., Berlin Phil. Orch., 1921-24; Musical Dir., Stuttgart Phil., 1924-33; Guest Cond., NY Phil., NBC Symph., San Fran., Cleveland & Chgo. Symphs., USA, 1933-54; Musical Dir., Kan. City Symph. Orch., 1941-46; Houston Symph. Orch., 1948-54; Guest cond. of major orchs. in Europe, Japan, Australia, Israel & N Am.; Perfs. at num. Int. Festivals. Hons: Cmdr., Order of Merit, Italy; Medal of Hon., Bruckner Soc. of Am.; Golden Disc for sales of 3 million recordings w. NY Phil., from Columbia Records Inc. Hobbies: Drawing; Collecting paintings, stamps & Histl. Letters. Address: 3780 Gstaad, Switzerland.

KURTZ, S James, b. 8 Feb. 1934, Newark, NJ, USA. Clarinetist; Composer; Teacher; Musical Director. Educ: BA, Wash. Sq. Coll., NY Univ., 1955; MA, Grad. Schl. of Arts & Sci., NY Univ., 1960; PhD, Univ. of Iowa, 1971; clarinet study w. Simeon Bellison, comp. w. Philip James. m. Elaine Rosenow, 2 s. Career: Clarinetist, w. The Little Orch., Firestone TV Orch., Symph. of the Air. Metropol. Mus. Orch., NYC, 1953-65; var. work w. ballet, films, recordings, etc.; Solo & Chmbr. music concerts; Dir., Figaro Chmbr. Concerts; Mannes Coll. of Music Fac.; Prof. of Music, Instrumental Coordinator, Madison Coll., Harrisonburg, Va., 1965-; Concerts & recitals, mbr., Chmbr. Arts wind quintet, ibid. Comps. incl: Suite for 3 Clarinets; 3 Impressions for 2 Clarinets; Fantasy for Unaccompanied Clarinet; Notturno for Clarinet or Flute & Piano. Publ: Edit. of Carl Stamitz' Quartet for Clarinet & Strings. Hons. incl: Winner, Marion Bauer Composer's Contest, 1956. Address: Music Dept., Madison Coll., Harrisonburg, VA 22807, USA.

KURYLEWICZ, Andrzej Roman, b. 24 Sept. 1932, Lwow, Poland. Composer; Pianist; Trombonist. Educ: Schl. of Music, Lwow; Dip., Conserv., Krakow (piano & comp.) m. Wanda Warska, 1 d. Debut: Krakow, 1955. Career: Bandleader, Soloist, Cond., Comp., w. perfs. throughout most of Europe, Can., Cuba; var. Film, Theater Perfs. Comps: Concerto on Baroque Themes; Rondo T; Oberek; Interferences; Rotation; Requiem for ZC; 12 plus 8; Oscillaziones; Schema Quattro per Quattro per Archi Tromboni e Batteria; Adagio da Dramma; Screenplay for orch.& 2 tape recorders; Psalm 60; Polish Year - 12 Songs; Liebe - 6 songs; Three Romantic Songs (after Pushkin); 6 PLays to Warm up for Piano Solo; Scores for over 40 films, 30 plays; var. Radio, TV music. Recordings: 11 LP's. Mbrships: Polish Comps. Union; Polish Artists-Musicians Assn. Hons: Silver Cross of Merit; The State Prize of Warsaw City. Hobby: Collecting Swords & Army Badges. Address: 13 Brodzinskiego, 01-557 Warsaw, Poland. 4, 28, 29, 30.

KURZBACH, Paul Johannes, b. 13 Dec. 1902, Hohndorf, Kr. Glauchau, Germany. Composer; Conductor. Educ: Tchr. Trng. Coll.; Music Acad. Leipzig; studies w. Carl Orff. m. Gertrud Kurzbach-Boenig. Comps: Operas, Hist. of Susanna, 1948, Thomas Münzner, 1955, Thyl Claes, 1958; 7 Serenades for Orch.; Concertos for harpsichord, piano, violin; Cantatas for solo, choir, orch.; Songs; Choir music; Chmbr. music. Mbrships: Vice-Pres. Assn. for Comp.and Musicologists, German Dem. Repub. Hons: Patriotic Merit Order, bronze, silver, gold; Art Prize FDGB. Address: Hüttenberg 15, 90 Karl Marx Stadt, German Dem. Repub.

KUSHNER, David Zakeri, b. 22 Dec. 1935, Ellenville, NY, USA. Musicologist; Educator; Lecturer; Lecture-Recitalist (piano). Educ: B Mus, Boston Univ.; M Mus, Univ. Cinn.; PhD, Univ. Mich. m. Rebecca Ann Stefan, 4 s. Career incl: Prof. of

Music on Doctoral Rsch. Fac.; Chmn., Musicology Fac.; Coord., Grad Studies in music, Univ. Fla.; Lectr. on coll. & univ. campuses & to profl. orgs. in USA & Europe; Vis. Prof. of Music, Florence Study Center, Italy, 1975; Apps. on radio & TV as lectr., pianist & panelist. Publs. incl: Bloch & His Music, 1973. Contbr. to profl. jrnls. Mbrships. incl: Phi Mu Alpha Sinfonia; Am. Musicol. Soc.; Music Tchrs. Nat. Assn.; Pi Kappa Lambda. Recip. rsch. grants & awards. Hobbies: Travel; Gardening; Pool. Address: 2215 NW 21st Ave., Gainesvile, FL 32605, USA. 2, 7, 28.

KÜTHEN, Hans-Werner, b. 26 Aug. 1938, Cologne, Germany. Editor, Beethoven-Archiv., Bonn. Educ: studied musicol., Bonn Univ., Civico Museo Bibliografico Musicale, Bologna. m. Annette Magdalena Leinen, 1 s. Publs. on Beethoven: Kammermusik mit Bläsern; Complete edn., Ouverturen und Wellingtons Sieg, 1974; Klavierkonzerte I. Contbr. to profl.publs. Mbr., Gesellschaft für Musikforschung. Hobbies: Drawing & painting; Pianoforte playing; Politics; Family. Address: Königstr. 8, D-5300 Bonn 1, German Fed. Repub.

KUTTNER, Fritz A(lexander), b. 8 Jan. 1903, Posen, Germany (now Poland). Musicologist. Educ: PhD, Berlin State Acad. of Political Econ., 1932; studied harmony, counterpoint, comp. & cond. w. var. masters. m. Ruth M. Wertheim. Career: Assoc. & Guest Prof. (Theory, & Hist. of Chinese music), St. John 's Univ., Shanghai, China, Grad. Schl., Asia Inst., NYC, USA & Pace Univ., NYC; Rsch. in above fields. Contbr. to: Musik in Geschichte & Gegenwart; Riemanns Musik Lexikon; Ency. des Musiques Sacrées; Harvard Dictionary of Music; High Fidelity Mag.; Stereo Review; Ethnomusicol.; num. musicol. jrnls. Mbrships incl: Am. Musicol. Soc.; Int. Musicol. Soc. Recip. num. rsch. grants. Hobbies: Musical Archaeology; Psychology & Physiology of Hearing. Address: 309 W 104th St., Apt. 3-C, NY, NY 10025, USA. 6, 11.

KUUSISTO, Iikka Taneli, b. 26 Apr. 1933, Helsinki, Finland. Conductor; Composer. Educ: Dip., Precentor-Organist, 1954 & Music Tchr., 1958; studied comp. w. Aare Merikanto & Nils-Eric Fougstedt, Sibelius Acad.; studied at the Schl. of Sacred Music & Union Theol. Sem., NY, under Seth Bingham, 1958-59; studied in Germany, 1960 & Vienna, 1961. m. Marja-Lisa Hänninen, 3 c. Debut: as Cond., 1955, as Comp., 1956. Career: Asst. Hd. of Music Sect., Finnish Broadcasting Co.; Choral Dir., Finnish Nat. Opera; currently Musical Dir.,Helsinki City Theatre & Cond. of the Radio Symph. Chorus; Messias, 1962; Missa Solemnis, 1969; over 100 TV progs. at Finnish Broadcasting Co.; Weekly Radio progs. Compositions incl: Moo min-opera for children; Stage works; Choral works; solo songs; Jazz comps.; var. recordings w. Radio Symph. Orch.; Suomi-Finland; Songs of Oskar Merikanto; Our Most Beautiful Songs. Mbrships: Composers of Finland; Bd. Mbr., Finnish Light & Film Music Composers. Hons: World Coun. of Churches Scholarship, 1958; Scholarship of the Finnish State, 1968. Hobby: Seafaring. Address: Pohjoinen Hesperiankatu 3 b 13, 00260 Helsinki 26, Finland.

KUZELL, Christopher, b. 22 July 1927, San Bernardino, Calif., USA. College Teacher; Composer; Violinist; Violist; Conductor. Educ: AA, LA City Coll.; BA, MA, Calif. State Univ., LA; Grad. work, ibid., & at Univ. of Southern Calif.; studied Violin w. ER Heifetz, P. Meremblum, Eudice Shapiro; studied Viola w. Sanford Schonbach; studied Comp. w. E. Krenek, R. Cortes; studied Cond. w. Lauris Jones, D. Lewis. m. Joy Lee Miller, 1 d. Career: Former Mbr., Indpls. Symph. Orch.; Broadcasts, gramophone records, film recording & TV work; Dir., Instrumental Music, Allan Hancock Coll., Santa Maria, Calif. Compositions: Six Little Pieces for the Marimba; Sonata for Marimba Solo. Mbrships: Locals 47 & 305, Am. Fedn. Musicians. Music Assn. Calif. Community Colls.; Southern Calif. Schl. Band & Orch. Assn. Hobbies: Gardening; Travel; Chamber Music; Stamp Collecting. Address: 907 E. El Camino, Santa Maria, CA 93454, USA.

KUZMANOVIC, Milorad, b. 1 Oct. 1932, Beograd, Yugoslavia. Composer. Educ: Acad. of Music. m. Miroslava Kuzmanovic. Comps: Requiem for those we love (cantata); Triptych for two choruses; Eve, War (orthodox requiem); Kolo quasi una toccata, Adagio & Allegro (Folk dance for mixed chorus); Space by the language of permanence retold (symph. orch.); Spectra (double bass); Two miniatures for soprano & double bass; Six pieces for vocal sextet & rhythm section; Scenic music; Music for cartoons; Arrangements. Mbr., Assn. of Comps. of Serbia. Hons. incl: 1st Prize, Yugoslav Radio & TV Competition, Ohrid, 1972. Hobby: Angling. Address: Sindjeliceva 9, 11000 Beograd, Yugoslavia.

KVAM, Oddvar S(chirmer), b. 26 Sept. 1927, Oslo, Norway. Composer. Educ: LLB, Oslo Univ.; MCL, NY Univ.; Oslo Music

Conserv.; pvte. studies w. Norwegian & other comps. m. Marit Hoem, 1 s. Comps: Opening, for orch.; sev. other orchl. works; Legend, for strngs.; Cantata for male chorus & orch.; Piano concerto; 4 Str. Quartets; 4 Piano comps. & num. choral songs. Recordings: 3 Centrifuges for wind quintet; sev. choral works. Mbrships: vice-chmn., Norwegian Comps. Assn.; chmn., New Music Assn. Hons: 1st Prize, comp. for male chorus & orch., 1967; 2 prizes, comps. for orch., 1977; choral comps. prizes. Hobbies: European handball; Bridge. Address: Breidablikkv. 12E, Oslo 11, Norway.

KVANDAL, (David) Johan (Jacob), b. 8 Sept. 1919, Oslo, Norway. Composer; Organist. Educ: Conserv., Oslo; w. Joseph Marx, Hochschule fur Musik, Vienna & w. Nadia Boulanger, Paris. m. Lilleba Lund, 2 children. Career: Pianist, Organist, Norwegian & Swedish Radio; Appd. in Norwegian TV Prog. Compositions incl: Antagonia (2 string orchs. & percussion) Op. 38; Norwegian Medieval Songs Op. 40; Quartet for Flute & Strings Op. 42; Recordings incl: Vakn op du Som Sover; Symphonic Epos Op. 21. Music Critic, Aftenposten, Oslo, 1973-. Mbr. Profl. orgs. Hobby: Mountain walking. Address: Box 122, 1312 Slependen, Norway.

KVAPIL, Radoslav, b. 15 Mar. 1934, Brno, Czech. Pianist. Educ: L. Janácek Musical Acad. & Brno Musical Acad. m. Eva Kvapilova, 1 s. Debut: Brno, 1954. Career: apps. & tours, 25 countries; has made broadcast recordings for European stns. Recordings incl: complete piano works of Dvorak, Janacek & Vorisek; Smetana's complete polka cycle; num. works by contemp. Czech. comps. Contbr. to musical jrnls. Mbrships: Czech. Music Soc.; ISME. Hons. 1st Prize, Janacek Competition, Brno, 1958; 1st Prize, Int. Record Competition, Brno Radio, 1968. Hobby: Chess. Address: Kladská 5, 120 00 Prague 2, Czech. 14, 30.

KVECH, Otomar, b. 25 May 1950, Praha, CSSR. Composer. Educ: Music Conserv.; Acad. of Music Arts. m. Miluska Wagnerova, 1 d. Debut: Symph. for organ & orch., Prag, Dvorak's Hall. Comps: When the Way Has Vanished (cycle of songs) (recorded); Moments for Akordeon Mbr. Organisation of Czech Comps. & Concert Artists. Hons: Best Estimated Chmbr. Comp. in Competition of Young Comps., 1973; Best Valued Comp. of Young Comps., 1975. Hobby: Elec. Engines. Address: Engelsova Nabrezi 34, 12800 Prague 2, Czech.

KVĚTON, Jiří, b. 27 Dec. 1947, Gottwaldov, Czech. Violinist. Educ: State Conserv., Brno; violin study w. Prof. Bruno Hycka. m. Eva Kvetonová, 3 c. Debut: State Phil. Brno, 1971. Career: Concerts w. Czech. Chamber Soloists & Phil. Brno, Europe, USA, Can.; TV & radio perfs. Recordings. Hobby: Tourism. Mgmt: Pragonkoncert Praha, Maltézské nám. 1. Address: Letovická 22, 62100 Brno, Czech.

KWASNICKA, Ursula, b. 14 Feb. 1943, Szczurowice, Poland. Harpist. Educ: Dip. in Piano & Harp, State Schl. of Music, Bytom, Poland, 1961; B Mus., Manhattan Schl. of Music, NYC; M Mus., ibid; studied w. Marcel Grandjany & Pierre Jamet. Debut: Carnegie Hall, NYC, 1968; Salle Cortot, Paris, 1971. Career: Solo Recital Tours, E Coast of USA, 1966. W. Coast of USA, 1968; Recitals in Poland, 1971; Soloist, Syracuse Symph. Orch. Recordings: Recitals taped by French Nat. Radio, Polish Nat. Radio. Num. recitals in NYC & TV appearances. Mbr., Am. Harp Soc. Hons: Harold Bauer Award, Manhattan

Schl. of Music, 1966; 1st Prize, Am. Harp Solo Contest, LA, 1966; 5th Prize, 4th Int. Harp Contest, Israel, 1970. Hobbies: Travel; Books; Swimming; Ice Skating. Address: 106 Edtim Road, Syracuse, NY 13206, USA.

KWIATKOWSKI, Ryszard, b. 27 June 1931, Jaranowo, Kujawy, Poland. Composer. Educ: Studied comp. w. Tadeusz Szeligowski, State Acad. of Music, Warsaw, & completed the course w. Witold Rudzinski; studied comp. w. Goffredo Petrassi in Rome. Compositions: (for orch.) Shapes: The Baltic Impression. 4 Lyrics; Polyphonic Music; Apotheosis; The Lights; 1 str. Quartet; 11 str. Quartet; Quartet for Percussion Instruments; Baltic Wave Song for cl. & pf.; Pictures from the Moon, for piano; Sea Wind Song, for violin & piano; Musica de salą svedese, for fl., oboe, cl. & fg., etc., (Recorded) Polyphonic music for orch. Mbr., Assn. of Polish Comps. Playing w. Jazz Life Groupe, 1975-. Hons: Awards in competitions for comps., 1960, '63, '66, '68, '69, '71, '73; Prize, 1960, '70; First prize in Buffalo, NYC for percussion quartet, 1968. Address: Powstancow 22/761 31-422 Krakow, Poland.

KYMLICKA, Milan, b. 15 May 1936, Louny, Czech. Composer. Educ: Conserv. of Music, Prague, 1952-57; Acad. of Music, Prague, 1957-58. m. Marie Markova, 2 c. Career: original music scores for films, Wedding in White, Reincarnation, Paul Bernard (TV). Comps: Two Dances; Four Instructional Pieces for Piano; Lazy Stream; Theme from Reincarnation. Recordings: New for Now (Two Dances); Four Pieces for Piano. Mbrships: CAPAC. Hons: State Comp. Award, 1965; 1st prize, popular song competition, 1968. Address: 223 Soudan Ave., Toronto, Ont. M4S 1W2, Can.

KYNASTON, Nicolas, b. 10 Dec. 1941, Morebath, UK. Organist. Educ: Accademia Musicale Chigiana, Siena; Conservatorio Santa Caecilia, Rome; RCM, London; ARCM. m. Judith Felicity Heron, 4 c. Debut: Royal Fest. Hall, 1966. Career: Organist, Westminster Cathedral, 1961-71; Freelance recitalist, 1971-; Recital tours, Europe, N Am., Africa & Asia; Radio, TV, films & recordings; Artistic Dir., J W Walker and Sons, Organ Builders. Recordings: 18 records. Contbr. to: Music and Musicians; Music Mag (USA); Organ Club Jrnl.; Ars Organi (Germany). Mbrships: Hon. Mbr., Organ Club. Hons: Hon. FRCO, 1976; EMI sales award, 1973; Music Trades Assn. Record Award, 1976; Deutscher Schallplattenpreis, 1978. Hobbies: Walking; Pubs; Churches. Mgmt: Ibbs & Tillett (UK); Arts Image (N Am.); Charles Finch (Far East); Stichting Tot Bevordering Der Orgelkunst (Netherlands); Michael Tramnitz (German Fed. Repub.). Address: The Old Vicarage, Wiggenhall Saint Peter, King's Lynn, Norfolk, PE34 3HF, UK.

KYZLINK, Jan, b. 6 July 1930, Olomucany, Czech. Operatic Soloist; Teacher of Singing. Educ: Prague Conserv.; Music Dept., Prague Univ. m. Anna Kyzlinkova, 2 children. Debut: Theatre of F X Salda. Career: Soloist, State State Theatre Ostrava, also in many chmbr. music concerts, oratorios. Cantatas: Guest Artist, Slovac Nat. Opera Bratislava & State Theatre Olomouc; Tchr. of Singing, State Conserv., Ostrava. Recordings incl: Heptameron (cantata by S Havelka); num. tapes for radio & TV broadcasts. Mbrships: Assn. of Czech. Comps. & Concert Artists; Assn. of Czech Dramatic Artists; Czech Music Soc. Recip. sev. hons. Hobbies: Dog; Car; Country cottage. Address: 70100 Ostrava 1, Revolucni 5, Czechoslovakia.

L

LAADE, Wolfgang Karl, b. 13 Jan. 1925. Zeitz, Germany. Ethnomusicologist; Anthropologist. Educ: Music Acads., Leipzig & W Berlin; Civc Conserv., W Berlin: Doct., Univ. of W Berlin, 1960. m. Dagmar Diedrich. Career incls: Bassist, Spree City Stompers jazz band, Berlin, 1952-58; Asst., Anthropol. Dept., Univ. of W Berlin, 1952-58; Asst., Anthropol. Dept., Univ. of W Berlin, 1958-62; Rsch. Fellow, Aust. Inst. of Aboriginal Studies, 1963-66; German Rsch. Fndn., 1967-70; Lectr., Univ. of Heidelberg, 1967-70; Prof. of Ethnomusicol., Dept. of Anthropol., Univ. of Zürich, 1970-. Recordings: Folkways; Ariola; Albatros. Publs: num. works on ethnomusicol. subjects, inclng: Neue Musik in Afrika, Asien & Ozeanien, 1971; Gegenwartsfragen d. Musik in Afrika, Asien & Ozeanien, 1971; Gegenwartsfragen d. Musik in Afrika u. Asien (Bibliography), 1971; Klangdokumente histor. Tasteninstrumente (Diskogrpahy), 1972. Mbrships. incl: Soc. for Ethnomusicol.; Int. Folk Music Coun.; African Music Soc.; Int. Soc. for Jazz Research, Indian Musicol. Soc. Address: c/o Ethnologisches Seminar, Univ. of Zürich, Rämistrasse 44, CH8001 Zürich, Switz.

LaBARRE, Kenneth Archer, b. 23 Dec. 1915. Uniontown, Pa., USA. Commercial Artist; Technical Illustrtor; Painter; Commercial Photographer; Amateur Musician, Playing Recorders, Lute, Guitar & Kortholts. Educ: Md. Inst. of Art; musical studies w. pvte. tchrs. & at seminars. m. Dina Montagna, 2 s., 2 d. Contbr. to: Am. Recorder (currently Art Dir.); designer, The First Book of Tablature (stanley Buetens, musical ed.), 1964. Mbrships: Organizer & Fndng. Pres., Pres., 1966-69, Lute Soc. of Am., Inc.; Past Pres., N. Jersey Chapt., Am. Recorder Soc., 1965-67, 73-. Hobbies incl: Astronomy; Bonsai; Sculpture. Address: 38 Crane St., Caldwell, NJ 07006, USA.

LABELLE, Nicole, b. 2 June 1946. Montreal, Can. Assistant Professor in Musicology. Educ: BMus, MMus (piano, organ); Doct., Univ. of Paris - Sorbonne. Career: Asst. Prof. in Musicol., Dept. of Music, Univ. of Ottawa, Can. Publs: Les différents styles de la musique religieuse en France: le psaume de 1539 á 1572, 1980; Inst. of Mediaeval Music, Da la stylistique du Psautier Huguenot entre 1546 et 1572, Univ. of Ottawa Quarterly, 1980. Contbr. of Concert Notes to Nat. Arts Center, Ottawa, Can. Mbrships: French Musicol. Soc.; ACEUM. Hons: Scholarship of France, 1974-76. Hobbies: Swimming; Reading. Address: 400 Slater apt. 315, Ottawa, Ont. K1R 7S7, Can.

LABHART, Walter, b. 22 Dec. 1944. Buchs AG, Switz. Author; Programme Producer; Art Critic. Educ: pvte. studies in Piano, Cembalo, Organ; comp. w. Alois Hába. m. Dora Kieser, 1s. Career: writer & ed. on music; ed., of instrumental music of 19th & 2&th centuries; Prog. prod., Swiss TV, Zürich, 1972; Music Ed., Swiss Music Archives, Zürich, 1973. Comps: chmbr. music, vocal & orchl. works. Publs: incl: Peter Mieg, 1976; Wladimir Vogel, Schriften und Aufzeichnungen über Musik, 1977; Chronologisch-systematishes Verseichnis der Musikalischen Werke von Maurice Ravel (w. Bibliography), 1976; Schweizer komponisten unserer zeik, 1975. Contbr. to num. jrnls. and mags. Mbrships: Schweizerischer Tonkünstlerverein; Int. Gesellscchaft für Neue Musik. Hobbies: Architectural Hist.; Collecting musical autographs & first eds. of 19th or 20th century. Address: Wolfgalgen, 36, 5304 Endingen, Switz.

LABOUNSKY, Ann, b. 9 Aug. 1939. New York City, USA. Organist: Associate Professor. Educ: B Mus, Eastman Schl. of Music, Rochester; M Mus, Univ. of Mich.; Dip., Schola Cantorum, Paris: Dip. in Tchng., Ecole Normale, Paris. m. Lewis M Steel, Jr., 1 s., 2 d. Career: Recitals in Scotland, Germany, USA, France & Holland; broadcasts on French Nat. Radio; Assoc. Prof. in Organ, Duquesne Univ. Schl. of Music, Pitts., Pa.; Hd. of Organ Dept. & Sacred Music Degree programs, ibid. Recordings issued on Mercury label. Mbrships: Phi Kappa Phi; AGO. Recip. Jt. 1st Place award, AGO Nat. Improvisation Contest, 1966; Winner, Soissons Concours. Address: 988 Norwood Ave., Pitts., PA 15202, USA.

LABUNSKI, Wiktor, b. 1895. St. Petersburg, Russia. Professor of Music; Concert Pianist; Teacher; Conserv.; pvte. studies in Russia & Poland. m. Wanda Mlynarski, dec. 2 s. Debut: St. Petersburg, 1913. Career: app. as Concert Pianist in Europe inclng. Brit. Isles, & in Am.; Soloist w. major orchs.; Guest Cond. w. many orchs.; Cond., Warsaw Symph., 1934-35; Prof. of Music, Conserv. of Music, Krakow, Poland, 1919-28, & Conserv. of Music, Nashville, Tenn., 1928-31; Dir., Memphis Coll. of Music, 1931-34 & 35-37, & Conserv. of Music, Kansas City, 1937; Dir., ibid., 1937-58; Prof. Emeritus, 1937-; has made many apps. as Lectr. on subjects related to piano playing, piano tchng. & musical appreciation. Compositions incl: Symph. in G minor; Piano Concerto; Concerto for 2 Pianos & Orchestra; Concertino for piano & orch.; Variations for piano and orch.; var. piano pieces. Contbr. of articles to mags. Address: 5801 Grand Ave., Kansas City, MO, USA. 3.

LACERDA, Osvaldo (Costa de), b. 23 Mar. 1927. São Paulo, Brazil. Composer; Music Teacher. Educ: Law, Univ. São Paulo; w. Mozart Camargo Guarnieri, 1952-62; Comp. w. Aaron Copland & Vittorio Giannini. Comps. incl: Suite 'Piratininga' Overture no. 1 (orch.); 4 Modal Pieces (sting orch.); Suite 'Guanabara' (symph. band); Proverbs (chorus & orch.); (recorded) Etudes ns. 6 & 7 (for piano), Clara Sverner, RCA Victor. Publs. incl: Regras de Grafia Musical, 1975. Contbr. to Música. Mbrships. incl: Fellow, John Simon Guggenheim Mem. Fndn. Hons. incl: Best Chmbr. Work, Trio for violin, violoncello & piano, Assn. Paulista de Críticos Teatrais, 1970. Hobby: Photography. Address: Rua Santarém 269 01251 São Paulo, SP, Brazil.

LACHERT, Hanna Katarzyna, b. 25 Nov. 1944. Podkowa, Warsaw. Poland. Violinist. Educ: Dip., Lyceum of Music, Warsaw, 1963; MA., Acad. of Music, ibid., 1967; Hochschule fur Musik, Hannover, Germany, 1967-68; Premier Prix, Conserv. Royal de la Musique in Brussels, Belgium, 1968-69; MA., Univ. of Conn., USA. 1971. Career: Recitals, soloist w. Orchs., Radio & TV Broadcasting, in Poland, Finland, Yugoslavia. Germany, UK., Italy & Belgium - 1970; & in USA. & Mexico, 1970-. Mbr., NY Phil., 1972-. Recordings: Szymanowski & Bartok (Telarc Records). Mgmt: Inversion, Music & Art Co., 421 W 57th St., NYC 10019, USA.

LACHOUT, Karel, b. 30 Apr. 1929. Ethnomusicologist; Composer. Educ: Mus D, Univ. of Prague, Czech., 1953. Career incls: Redacteur of Music Dept., Prague, 1953-79; Ethnomusicol., specialising in Latin Am. Music & folklore; composer. Mbrships. incl: League of Composers Rights, Prague, 1954-. Publs. incl: 'The World Sings', 1957; 'Music of Chile', 1976; 'Music of Cuba', 1979. 'Lexicon of Latin American ed. music', 1980. Creative work incls: var. musical compositions for orch. & piano incl. 'Such is Cuba', 1962; var. pieces for dance; light music. Hons. incl: Award, Czech. Music Fund, for 'The World Sings', 1957; Award for activity in propagation of music of Chile & other Latin Am. in Radio Prague Progs., 1977. Address: Viklefova 11, Prague 3, Czech.

LACK, Edwin Arthur, b. 5 Feb. 1934. Newport Pagnell, Bucks., UK. Teacher; Musicologist. Educ: Grad. cert. in Educ., Leeds Univ.; BMus, ibid.; Rsch. into Burgundian Court music, ibid. Career: Music master, Ashton County Secondary Schl.; Hd. of Music, Castleford High Schl.; continuing resch.; apps. as cond., var. choral socs. & as accomp. mbr. Royal Musical Assn. recip. Discount Snowden prize, 1956. Hobbies: Scuba diving & water sports; Fell walking; travel; Madrigal singing; Chmbr. music; opera. Address: 5 Anneslay Rd., Newport Pagnell, Bucks, UK.

LA COUR, Niels, b. 14 Nov. 1944. Copenhagen, Denmark. Composer. Educ: Dip., Royal Danish Conserv., 1969; studied comp. in Rome, 1975. Career: Tch., theory, Royal Danish Conserv. Comps: 6 str. quartets; 2 wind quintets, 3 symph. pieces; organ music; choral music; chmbr. music; 3 intermezzi & De Profundis for organ; 5 motets. Recorded: Str. Quartet No. 2; Wind Quintet No. 1; Archetypon for organ. mbr. Danish Comps. Soc. recip., 3 yr. State Art Foundation Prize, 1973. Address: Broholmsalle 6B, 2920 Charlottenlund, Denmark.

LAFFITTE, Frank, b. 17 June 1901. Bromley, Kent, UK. Concert & Broadcast Pianist; Teacher. Educ: 1st Piano lessons w. his mother, piano, Marmaduke Barton, violin, John Saunders, harmony & form, Dr. H Robinson, all GSM; piano w. Katherine Goodson & Edith Haymann, London. Debut: Queens Hall, London, 1920. Career incls: num. concerts, UK & Europe; apps. w. major orchs. under leading conds.; regular BBC broadcasts, 1925-66, also broadcast from Paris, Oslo, Brussels & Copenhagen; toured in USA & acclaimed one of the best interpreters of Debussy specialist in Schumann & Debussy; gave 1st perfs. of many works inclng. piano concertos of Albert Coates & Averil Coleridge Taylor; Prof., TCL, 1942-46, GSM, 1944-67. Recorded for Duo-Art Recordings. Hons: Gold Medallsit, GSM, 1918, FGSM, 1950; Hon. Assoc., Player Piano Group, UK, 1977; Hon. Mbr., Amica Int., USA, 1977.

Hobbies: House plants; Dogs; Cats; Model railways. Address: 19 Boxwell Rd., Berkhamsted, Herts, UK. 4, 23, 28.

LA FOSSE, Leopold, b. 3 Apr. 1928. Springfield, Mass., USA. Concert Violinist; Artist-Teacher of Violin. Educ: New England Conserv. of Music; Univ. Tex.; Trinity Univ.; Pvte. Violin studied w. Emanuel Ondricek & Richard Burgin, Boston; Raphael Bronstein, NYC. m. Marsha J LaFosse, 1 child. Debut: NYC, 1967; of Music, Univ. Iowa, 1972-; Num. solo apps. in recital & w. symph. orchs.; BBC radio recitals; Fac. mbr. & soloist, Haydnfest, 1976, Eisenstadt, Austria; Former Concertmaster, San Antonio; Dallas; Austin; Aspen Festival Orch. & Nat. Antonio; Dallas; Austin; Aspen Festival Orch. & Nat. Symph. of Peru. Contbr. to Instrumentalist. Mbrships: MENC; Am. String Tchrs. Assn. Hobbies: Art (Painting). Addess: Schl. of Music, Univ. of Iowa, Iowa City, IA 52242, USA.

LAGACE, Bernard, b. 21 Nov. 1930. St. Hyacinthe, PQ, Canada. Organist; Harpsichordist; Professor of Organ. Educ: Pvte. studies w. Andre Marchel, Paris; Anto Heiller, Vienna; BA, Montreal Univ. m. Mireille Lagace, 4 children. Debut: Bach's Claviernbung Pt. III, St. Eustache, Paris, 1955. Career: Prof. of Organ, Montreal Conserv. of Music, 1957-; Num. concerts & festivals in Can.; USA & Europe; Judge; Int. Competition; Lectures; Master classes; Cond., Choate Music Seminars, Wallingford, Conn., USA. Recordings incl: Bach's Art of Fugue; Pachelbal Organ Works. Hobbies: Lit.; Fine Arts (collector of abstract paintings). Address: 3783 Northcliffe Ave., Montreal, Canada.

LAGESEN, Ruth, b. 10 Aug. 1914. Valdres, Norway. Concert Pianist; Orchestral & Choral Conductor. Debut: w. Oslo Phil. Orch., Oslo, 1935. Career incls: Cond., Oslo Phil., Bergen Symph. Orch. & Trondheim Chmbr. Orch.; Guest cond., Radio Chorus, Denmark; Lectr., Summer Schl. Music, Dartington Hall, 1971; Masterclasses, Univ. Georgetown & Southwestern Univ., USA, autumn 1971; Lectr. on Grieg's music, Hoehschule für Musik und clarstellende Kunst, Vienna, 1974. Num. radio & TV apps. incln. BBC series-' Music of may Lands'; Performed Grieg Recitals, Grieg's Home, Int. Fest., Bergen; Concert Tour, black & white S Africa, 1973-74. Recordings: 3 LPs, Grieg's piano music. Mbr., Norwegian Art-Music Soc. Recip. schlrships. Hobbies incl: Painting. Mgmt: as Impressario, Tolbodgaten 3, Oslo 1; Ibbs & Tillet, Wigmore St., London W 1 Addess: Dronning Asasvei 8, 3100 Tonsberg, Norway.

LAGGER, Peter, b. 7 Sept. 1930. St. Gallen, Switzerland. Opera & Concert Singer. Educ: Univs. of Zurich & Vienna; Piano dip., Zurich Conserv.; Dips. in Lieder, Oratorio & Opera, Acad. of Music & Performing Arts, Vienna. m. Liva psachayan, 2 c. Career: leading operatic roles in W Berlin, Vienna, Munich, Hamburg, Milan, San Fran. & NYC Opera Houses; Festival appearances at Salzburg, Edinburgh, Glyndebourne, Aix-en-Provence, Lucerne & Tanglewood; TV appearance in Eugene Onegin, Tales of Hoffmann, Marriage of Figaro. Recordings of var. operas, lieder, etc. Mbr: Swiss Musicians Union. Hons: Critic's Award, Spain; 1968; Kammersanger, Berlin Senate, 1970. Hobbies: Painting; Hist.; Langs. Mountaineering. Mgmt: S A Gorlinsky, London: Thea Dispeker, NYC; Robt. Schultz, Munich. Address: Rauscheneralle 4, 1 Berlin, 19, German Fed. Repub.

LAINE, Cleo, b. 28 Oct. 1927. Singer. m. 1) George Langridge, 1s.; 2) John Philip William Dankworth, 1s., 1 d. Career: apps. as soloist & with Dankworth Orch. in UK, USA etc.; ldng. role, Seven Deadly Sins, Edinburgh Fest. & Sadler's Wells; num. apps. w. symph. orchs. in Walton's Facade; Julie in Showboat, 1971; num. apps. on TV. num. recordings. Hons: Melody Maker & New Musical Express Top Girl Singer Award, 1956; Moscow Arts Theatre Award, 1958; Top place in Int. Critics Poll by Am. Jazz mag., Downbeat, 1965; Woman of the Yr., 9th Annual Golden Feather Award, 1973; Edison Award, 1974. Hobby: Painting. Mgmt: Int. Artists Representation, Regent House, 233 Regent St., London, WC1, UK. Address: c/o mgmt.

LAING, Alan, b. 16 Sept. 1944. Glasgow, Scotland, UK. Lecturer. Educ: BMus, PhD, Univ. of Edinburgh; LRAM. Career: Dir. of Music, Univ. of Kent, 1968-78; Lectr., Music Dept., Univ. of Hull, 1978-. Recordings: as comp. & cond. Address: Music Dept., Univ. of Hull, Hull, UK.

LAIRES, Janet Lockhart, b. 22 Sept. 1938. Lampasas, Tex., USA. Pianist. Educ: Univ. of Tex.; Okla. Coll. of Liberal Arts; B Mus, Piano; Piano study w. Stanley Fletcher, John Goldmark, Fernando Laires, Tibor Yusti. m. Dennis B Prat, 1 s., 1 d. Career: Piano perfs. USA; Official Hostess, 5th Inter Am. Fest. of the World, Okla. Pres., Am. Artist, Int. Mbrships: Sigma Alpha Iota; Nat. Music Tchrs. Assn.; Chmn., SW Okla. area, NGPT; Judge.

Mgmt: Am. Artist, Int. 8403 Shoal Creek Blvd., Austin, TX 78758, USA. Am. Coll. of Musicians. Hobby: Sailing. Address: 203 Bowman Ave., Austin TX 78703, USA. 2.

LAKATOS, Stefan István, b. 26 Feb. 1895. Zorlentul-Mare, Caras-Severin, Romania. Musicologist. Educ: Music study, Blaj, Cluj Budapest; Dip. Construction Engr., Budapest Polytechnic, 1922; Doct., Fac. of Philos., Univ. of Cluj, 1946. Career incls: Prof. of Violin, Hungarian Conserv., Cluj, 1919-23; Prof., Music Hist., Cluj Conserv., 1949-63; Hd. of Rsch., Inst. of Art Hist., Cluj, 1955-68; Fndr. & Dir., Quatuor Lakatos, chmbr. music ensemble, 1920-40. Publs. incl: Samuel Brassai & Music, 1941; Studies in Music History, 1971; The Hungarian Lyric Theatre in Cluj (1793-1973). Contbr. to var. profl. jrnls. Mbrships. incl: Antonin Dvorak Soc., Prague, 1957. Recip., Order of Work, 1957. Address: Str. Gutinului 9, Cluj-Napoca, Romania.

LAKE, Ian Thomson, b. 26 Jan. 1935. Quorn, Leics., UK. Pianist; Composer. Educ: Performers' ARCM. div. 3 children. Debut: w. Hallé Orch., cond. Barbirolli, Royal Festival Hall, London, 1961. Career: Num. solo recitals & apps. w. maj. Brit. orchs.; Tours Africa, 1971; Far E & Middle E, 1974; W Indies & Ctrl. Am., 1976; Malta & Cypres, 1977, '79; TV & Radio perfs.; Prof., piano, RCM, 1967-. Compositions incl: Music for Young Pianists 3 vols., UK & USA; Classics for the Young Pianist, 3 vols.; Water Music for Brass Quintet (recorded). sev. recordings. Contbr. to The Composer. Mbrships: ISM; RCM Union. Associated Rediffusion Prize, 1961. Hobbies incl: Reading. Address: 95 Offord Rd., Islington, London N1 1PG, UK. 3.

LAKE, Larry Ellsworth, b. 2 July 1943. Greenville, Pa., USA. Composer; Trumpeter; Broadcaster; Freelance Record Producer. Educ: BMus, Univ. of Miami, 1966; MEd, ibid., 1968; MMus, ibid., 1970; doct. studies, Univ. of Toronto, 1970-72. m. Karen Ann Kieser. Career: comps. perf. throughout Can. & Europe, and broadcast in Can., Sweden, W Germany, Belgium, France, Italy & Yugoslavia. Comps. incl: FACE for piano, 4 synthesisers & tape, 1975; Ricercar for trombone & tape, 1977; Options for bass clarinet & symthesisers, 1978; Hommage, tape, 1978; The Devil in the Desert for soprano & electronics, 1979. Recordings: Canadian Electronic Ensemble. Contbr. to MusiCanada. Mbrships: Gen.mgr., fndr.mbr., Can. Electronics Ensemble, Toronto, Can. Address: 15 Dundonald St., Apt. 1402, Toronto, Ont., Can.

LAKE, Leslie John Frederick, b. 6 Sept. 1944. Northampton, UK. Musician (Trombone & Euphonium). Educ: Guidhall Schl. of Music. m. Rosamund Lea, 2 s., 1 d. Career: Mbr., Sadlers Wells & Engl. Nat. Opera Co. Orchs., 1966-; Fndr., The Locke Brass Consort, 1966-; Recording: Contrasts in Brass, Vols. 1 & 2; Jubilant Brass Panoply. Contbr. to: Sounding Brass. Mbrship: Wagner Soc. Hobby: Badminton. Mgmt: HHH Ltd., Concert Agcy., 5 Draycott Pl., London SW3. Addess: 55 Heather Rd., Grove Pk., London SE 12, UK.

LALANDI, Lina. Athens, Greece. Artistic Director; Harpsichordist; Clavichord Specialist. Musical Educ: Grad. w. hons. in keyboard,, Athens Conservatory; Studied harpsichord & clavichord, UK. Debut: Royal Festival Hall, London, 1954. Career: Concert, TV & radio perfs. in UK, France, Switzerland, Germany & Greece; Fndr., Engl. Bach Festival Trust; 1962; Dir., Engl. Bach Festival, 1963-. Occasstional contbns. to musical mags. & articles in prog. books of Engl. Bach Festival. Recip. OBE, 1975. Hobbies: Cats; Cooking. Address: 15 S. Eaton Place, London, SW1W 9ER, UK. 14.

LAMA, Lina, b. 20 Apr. 1932. Ravenna, Italy. Concert Violist; Professor of Viola. Educ: Univ; Dips. in violin and viola; Dip. in piano and composition. Debut: Teatro S. Carlo, Naples. Career: Prof., Conservatorio di Musica S. Cecilia, Rome, 1959-; Apps. on BBC, London and Italian TV; Radio Concerts in Germany, Belgium, Italy, Israel, Hungary, Greece, Finland; Concerts throughout Europe under the best Italian and foreign Maestri. At Teatro San Carlo, Naples, in Italy of "Sonata per la Gran Viola" by Paganini; Tchr., viola, Conserv. of S. Cecilia, Rome. Recip., sev. concert prizes, Italy. Hobby: Painting. Address: Via Ugo de Carolis 31, 00136, Rome, Italy.

LaMARCHINA, Robert A, b. 3 Sept. 1928. NYC, USA. Music Director & Conductor; Solo Cellist. Educ: Paris Conservatoire dde Musique; Curtis Inst. Debut: Solo cellist w. St. Louis Symph. under Vladimir Golschmann at age of 8 yrs. Career incls: Cond. & Music Dir. Young Musicians Fndn., LA., 1952-53; Solo cellist, Chgo. Symph. under Fritz Reiner, 1960; Cond., Met. Opera Co., also conducted "La Traviata" at Spoleto Festival (Two Worlds) & "The Medium", NY Ctr., 1963; Music Dir. & Cond., Met. Opera Nat. Co., 1964-66; Artistic & Music Dir., Honolulu Symph. Soc. & Hawaii Opera

Theatre, 1967-; Cond., num. symph. orchs. & operas, inclng. NY Phil., Nat. Symph., St. Louis Symph., Chgo. Symph., Radio Italiana, Zürich Symph., Vancouver Opera Assn., Fujiwara Opera Inst. Mgmt: Herbert Barrett Mgmt., 1860 Broadway, NY, NY 10023, USA. Address: Suite 303, 1000 Bishop St., Honolulu, HI 96813, USA. 9.

LA MARIANA, Angelo, b. 15 Nov. 1914. LI, NY, USA. College Professor; Orchestra Conductor, Violist. Educ: BS in Music, NY Univ. Schl. of Educ. & Fine Arts, 1936; M Mus., NY Univ. Grad. Schl., 1938; D Mus., Columbia Univ., 1954; grad. work at var. univs. m. Winifred Collins, 1d. Career: Assoc. Prof., Western Mich., Univ., 1949-55; Prof. of Music, State Univ. Coll. of Arts & Sci., Plattsburgh, NY, 1955-; summer session at Cath. Univ. Wash. DC, Univ. of Vt. & Eastman Schl. of Music, etc.; Violist, NBC Symph. under Toscanini; Soloed & perf. w. str. quartets & Chmbr. ensembles in the NE & Mid-W USA; Fndr. & Cond., The Plattsburgh Coll. Community Orch. & the Clinton Co. Jr. Symph.; Violist, Western Mich. Univ. Str. Quartet, etc. Ed. of String Column 'The School Musician, Director & Teacher' Publs: Music Education, 1954; Chamber Music for Festival Use, 1960, etc. Mbr. of sev. profl. orgs. Hons: Am. Guest Cond., French Radio Diffusion Orch., Concerts Cologne Symph. & Orch. of Paris. Address: 5 West Ct. St., Plattsburgh, NY 12901, USA.

LAMAS, Dulce Martins, b. 4 July 1919. Rio de Janeiro, Brazil. Musicologist; Educator. Educ: Maestro, Tchr. of Piano, Schl. of Music, Fed. Univ. of Brazil, 1944-45; Grad. in Social Sciences, Fac. of Philos., Brazil Univ. 1963. m. Manuel José Lamas (dec.) Career: Musical Folklore Master, Schl. of Music, Fed. Univ. of Brazil, Rio de Janeiro, 1958; Master in Harmony & morphology, ibid, 1960; Prof. of Hist. of Music, Brezilian Conserv. of Music. Comps: Angelus (voice & piano); A Cruz na Estrada (vioce & piano); Toada (violin & piano); Nocturno (piano); Variacoes (violin & piano); etc. Publs: Some Rules of Harmony, 1959; Pastorinhas, Pastoris, 1978. Contbr. to: Anuary of Tulane Univ.; Int. Folk Music Coun. Jrnl.; Literatura popular em verso. Mbrships: Int. Music Coun. (UNESCO); Liaison Officer, Int. Folk Music Coun.; Coun. Music & Sound Fund, Vieira Fazenda. Hons: Sylvio Romero Medal, 1957. Hobby: Arts History. Address: Rua da Glória, 122 ap. 601, 20.241 - Rio de Janeiro, Brazil. 29.

LAMB, Anthony Stuart, b. 4 Jan. 1947. Woodford, UK. Clarinettist. Educ: RCM; ARCM. m. Philippa Carpenter-Jacobs, 1s. Debut: w. chmbr. ensemble Capricorn, Wigmore Hall, London, 1974. Career: Prin. Clarinet, Royal Ballet Orch., 1970-73; Fndr. Mbr., Capricon (violin, clarinet, cello, piano), 1963, many broadcasts & concerts; Clarinettist w. Apollo Contemp. Music, London Sinfonietta & other London orchs.; Co-prin. clarinet w. Engl. Nat. Opera Orch., 1976-; sev. BBC Broadcasts; Freelance Clarinettist w. most major Brit. orchs. Mbr., Musicians Union. Hobby: Tennis. Address: 22 Munster Rd., Teddingtom, Middx. TW11 9LL, UK.

LAMB, Gordon Howard, b. 6 Nov. 1934. Eldora, la., USA. Choral Conductor. Educ: B Mus. Ed., Simpson Coll.; M Mus., Univ. of Neb.; PhD for Music, Univ. of Iowa. m. Nancy Painter Lamb, 3 s. Career: Choral Cond., pub. schls. in la., 1957-68; at Wis. State Univ., 1969-70; Univ. of Tex. at Austin, 1970-74; Dir., of the Div. of Music, Univ. of Tex. at Austin, 1970-74; Dir. of the Div. of Music, Univ. of Tex. at San Antonio, 1974-. Compositions (publd.): Three Choral Vignettes; Hodie Christus Natus Est, for mixed choir; Aleatory Psalm; Sit Down, Lord; O Leave Your Sheep; Magnificat in Primi Toni, by Palestrina, edited. Publs: Guide for the Beginning Choral Director, edited, 1973; Choral Techniques, 1974; Choral Dircetor's Guide to Repertoire for Mixed Choir: An Annotated Bibliography, 1974; Ed. of the Gordon Lamb Conductors Choral Series, containing choral works of Am. comps. Contbr. of articles to mags. & jrnls. Mbrships. incl: Chmn., Nat. Comm. on HS Choral Music & State Pres. of la., Am. Choral Directors Assn.; Chmn. of Choral Affairs, la. Music Educators Assn. Ed. Bd., The Choral Jrnl. Recip., ISEA Rsch. Grant, 1969. Hobbies: Editing Music; Fishing; Golf. Address: Div. of Music, Univ. of Tex. at San Antonio, San Antonio, TX 78284, USA.

LAMBERT, Marcel Amedee, b. 7 Aug. 1934. San Fran., USA. Co-Principal French Horn. Educ: Studies w. Pierre Lambert; Dip., Nat. Conserv. of Lima, Peru. m. Elsa, 2 d. 1 s. Debut: Lima Orch., 1953. Career: Soloist, in Chmbr. music & broadcasts, Peru, 1953-63; Co-Prin. French Horn, NZ Symph. Orch., 1965-; Soloist, num. chmbr. music apps., NZ; Toured NZ as mbr., NZ Music Fed. Recordings: w. NZ Broadcasting Corp. Mbr., NZ Fed. of Music. Hobbies: Tennis; Radio control model planes. Address: 19 Lyndfield Lane, Newlands, Wellington 4, NZ.

LAMBERT, Patricia Davis, b. 21 Feb. 1945. Brooklyn, NY., USA. Musician (flute & recorder); Music Teacher. Educ: BA,

Plymouth State Coll., Univ. of NH.; Pvte. study w. Bernard Goldberg. 1 s. Career incl: TV apps. w. The Renaissance Consort, recorder ensemble WTAV, Altoona; Flutist, Altoona Symph.; Tchr. of Flute & Recorder, The Music Academy State Coll.; PA. Mbrships: Am. Recorder Soc.; Nat., Flute Assn. Hobbies: Riding; Guitar; Bicycling; Gardening. Address: RD1, Warriors Mark, PA, 16877 USA.

LAMBERT, Victor, b. 8 Aug. 1917. Kent, UK. Teacher; Conductor; Organist. Educ: London Univ.; L Mus TCL. m. Mary Stansfield, 1 s., 1 d. Career: Asst. Organist, Royal Garrison Ch., Sheerness, 1933; Organist, All Hallows, Southwark, & St. Barnabeas, Pimlico, London, 1942; Organist, Llandaff Cathedral; Musical Dir., ST. Andres's Singers, Kingston, Jamaica; Cond., Capella Singers; Adjudicator, Jamaica Schl. Music & Univ. Coll. W Indies; Broadcasts, Radio Jamaica; Organist & Choirmaster, St. John's Farnham Common, UK, 1961; Dir. Music, All Sts. Maidenhead, 1975; Pvte. tchr., piano, organ, violin, theroy. Comps. incl: Introits for the Proprer of the Mass. Recordings; Carols, Univ. Coll. Jamaica. Mbrs. profl. orgs. Address: Orchard Cottage, Farnham Common, Bucks, UK. 3.

LAMBRO, Phillip, b. 2 Sept. 1935. Wellesley Hills, Mass., USA. Composer; Conductor. Conductor; Pianist. Educ: The Music Acad. of the West, Calif. w. Donald Pond & Gyorgy Sandor. Career: Has comp. & cond. music for sev. motion pictures inclng. 'Energy on the Move', documentary, for which he cond. mbrs. of the NY Phil.; His music has been per f. by Leopold Stokowski, The Phil. Orch., Balt. Symph. Orch., Indpls. Symph., Miami Symph., Okla. City. Symph. & others in Europe, S. Am. & the Orient. World Premiere by Rochester Phil. Orch. of Two Pictures, 1976. Comps. incl: Miraflores for String Orch.; Dance-Barbaro for Percussion; Two Pictures for Solo Percussionist & Orch.; Four Songs for Soprano & Orch.; Toccata for Piano; Toccata for Guita; Music for Wind, Brass & Percussion. Recordings: Structures, for String Orch. & Music, for Wind Brass & Percussion & a work by Ramiro Cortes, Meditation for String Orch. & work by Robert Lombardo, Largo, for String Orch., cond. the US Int. Orch. Hons: Musical score for documentary film 'Mineral King', named by Nat. Bd. of Review as the Best Music for a Documentary Film in 1972. Address: 1888 Century Park East (Suite 10), Century City, CA 90067, USA.

LAMIGEON, Louise, b. 21 June 1915. Edgware, Middlesex, UK. Educator. Educ: GRSM; ARCM (violion tchng.). Career: Tchr., chief music mistress, var. schls.; Staff Herts. Rural Music Schl.; Prof., ic schl. music, Royal Manchester Coll. of Music, 1955-70; Examineer, Assoc. Bd. Royal Schls. Music, 1959-70; Extra-mural lectr., Univ. Manchester; Adjudicator, Musical Fests.; External examiner, music dips., Colchester, 1970. Mbrships: ISM; Soc. Music Therapy. Address: Via del Cavalcavia 8, 00042 Anzio, Rome, Italy. 1.

LAMKIN, Michael Deane, b. 7 July 1945. Kansas City, Kan., USA. Musiocologist; Conductor; Educator; Bass Singer. Educ: B Mus Educ., Baylor Univ., Waco, Tex., USA, 1967; M Mus., ibid., 1970 Am. Inst. of Musical Studies, FreiburgBreisgau, W Germany; Am. Inst. of Musical Studies, Graz, Austria; PhD Univ. of Iowa, Iowa City, Iowa. m. Kathleen Joyce Plainview, Tex., William Penn Coll., Oskaloosa, Iowa, Univ. of Iowa, Am. Inst. of Musical Studies, Graz, Austria, Martin Coll., in Pulaski, Tenn., Univ. of N Ala., Florence, Ala., The Claremont Colls., Scripps Coll., Claremont, Calif., Vocal recitals throughout the Midwest, Southwest & S. USA; Cond. in perfs. throughout USA & Austria. Contbr. to: profl. publs. Mbrships: Am. Musicol. Sco.; Coll. Music Soc. Hons: Acad. & Perf. Scholarships, Baylor Univ., 1963-67; Highest Redinger Music Schl. Grad., Baylor Univ., 1967; Francis Redinger Sudy Scholarship Grac Austria; Am. Inst. of Musical Studies Grant, 1971; Travel; History; Cooking; Book Collecting; Films; Riding. Address: 408 S Indian Hill, Apt. 51, Claremont, CA 91711, USA.

LAMM, Robert Carson, b. 9 April, 1922. New Albany, Ind., USA. University Professor; Musical (Organ, Piano, Trombone). Educ: BM, Univ. of Louisville, Ky., 1947; M M, Univ. of Ariz., 1948; PhD, Ind. Univ. m. Kathryn S Kuehnl, 2 s., 1 d. Career: Dir., Ctr. for the Humanities, & Prof., of Humanities, Ariz. State Unvi., Tempe. Compositions: Tramway (trombone & piano). Publs: Music Theory in Outline Form (w. E Putnik), 2nd ed. 1965; The Search for Personal Freedom, 2 vols., (w. Cross & Turk), 5th ed., 1977. Mbrships: AGO (Dean, Southern Ariz. Chapt.); Nat. Assn. for Humanities Educ. Hobbies: Golf; Tennis; Swimming. Address: 8211 E Desert Cove, Scottsdale, AZ 85260, USA. 2, 11.

LAMMEL, Inge, b. 8 May 1924. Berlin, Germany. Musicologist. Educ: PhD in musicol. 2c. Career: Hd, Workers' Song Archives at Acad. of Arts, German Dem. Repub. for 25

yrs. Publs. incl: DAs Arbeiterlied, 1970, '75; Kampfgefährte - unser Lied, 1978. Contbr. to: Beiträge zur Musikwissenschaft; Musik in der Schule; Musik und Gesellschaft; Volksmusik, etc. Mbrships: Verband der Komponisten und Musikwissenschaftler der DDR; IFMC; Int. Gesellschaft für Musikwissenschaft. Hons: Hanns-Eisler prize, 1971. Hobbies: Books; Records. Address: Wisbyerstr. 59, 1071 Berlin, German Dem. Repub.

LA MONTAINE, John, b. 17 March 1920. Oak Park, Ill., USA. Composer. Educ: BM, Eastman Schl. of Music, 1942; Juilliard Schl., NYC; studies w. Nadia Boulanger. Career incls: Celestist & Pianist, NBC Symph. under Arturo Toscanini, 1950-54; Comp-in-Res., Am. Acad., Rome, 1962; Vis. Prof. of Comp., var. univs. inclng. Eastman Schl. of Music, Rochester Univ., NY. Comps: orchl., choral, vocal works; 5 operatic works; works for ensemble, piano, organ, string orch. Comps. recorded: Concerto for Piano & Orch., Op. 9, CRI; Birds of Paradise, for piano & orch., ERA; Music for the Dance, Incantation for Jazz Band, Fredonia Discs; The Nine Lessons of Christmas, Op. 44, Fredonia Discs; Music for Young People (piano) Fredonia Discs. Mbr., ASCAP. Hons. incl: Pultizer Prize, 1959; var. commns. (inclng. inauguration of Pres. J F Kennedy). Address: 3947 Fredonia Dr., Hollywood, CA 90068, USA.

LAMOTHE, Donat Romeo, b. 14 Oct. 1935. Keene, NH., USA. Teacher; Musicologist; Performer on Historical Instrumenta; Roman Catholic Priest. Educ: AB., Assumption Coll., 1957; MA., Relig. studies, St. John's Univ., Collegeville, Minn., 1969; Precentor's Cert., Assumption Coll. (Gregorian Plain song), 1955; Diplôme du 2 degré. Institut Saint-Grégoire-le-Grand, Lyons, France (plain song), 1960; M Mus., Musicol., Boston Univ. Schl. of Fine & Applied Arts, 1973. Ordained 1962. Mbr. of Relig. Order, Augustinians of the Assumption. Career: Fndr.-Dir., Salisbury Consort, perf. grp. of early music (medieval & renaissance) on histl. instruments, 1965- (num. perfs. in New England area); Fac. Mbr., Assumption Coll., Worcester, Mass., 1963-. Publs: Music in Early Spanish Drama, 1973. Mbrships: AGO; Am. Recorder Soc.; Ch. Music Assn. of Am.; Comps. Forum for Catholic Worship. Hobbies: Collector of ethnic & antique musical instruments: Stained glass designer & craftsman. Address: 500 Salisbury St., Worcester MA 01609, USA.

LAMOUTTE, Sylvia Maria, b. 29 Nov. 1935. Santurce, Puerto, Rico, USA. Pianist; Piano Teacher; Arranger; Publisher. Educ: Univ. of Puerto Rico, 1953-54; BMus, New Engl. Conserv. of Music, Boston, Mass., 1958; MMus, ibid., 1960. Career: Perfs. at concerts, fests., radio & TV in Puerto Rico; perfs. on radio, Domenican Repub.; recitals at Boston & Cambridge, Mass., USA; piano tchr., New Engl. Conserv. of Music, 1959-60 pvte. piano tchr. in Puerto Rico, 1960-79; lectr. Comps: Danza, Olas del Caribe; Danza, Amor Ausente; Danza, Brisas de Borinquen. Publs: num. compilations, adaptions & arrs. of Puertorican folk & traditional music, 1964-78 (approx. 30 vols); Libreta de Teoría Básica, 1973; Biografías Cortes de Compositores Puertorriqueños, 1971. mbr. num profl. socs. Hons: Pro Arte Musical de Puerto Rico medal; Walter W Naumburg Scholarship 1959-60; Hon. mbr., Pi Kappa Lambda. Hobbies: Reading; Embroidery; Crocket. Address: 267 San Jorge St., Apt. 12C, Santurce, PR 00912, USA.

LAMPRECHT, Christian Engelbertus, b. 1 Oct. 1927. Bloemfontein, S Africa. Organist; Composer; Collector of South African Folk Music. Educ: B Mus, Tchrs. Dip., Univ. of Stellenbosch; M Mus, Univ. of Pretoria, Lic. Dips. (perfs.) in piano, organ & singing, Univ. of S Africa. m. Elizabeth du Toit, 2 s., 1 d. Career: Univ. ofS Africa. m. Elizabeth du Toit, 2 s., 1 d. Career: Jr. Lectr., Univ. of Stellenbosch; Organist & Music Tchr., Boksburg; Insp. of Music, Transvaal Educ. Dept.; Chief Cultural Off., Dept. of Nat. Educ., 1968; on radio & TV progs. Comps. incl: Boerfess for orch., choir & concertina (recorded); Wie het ek buiten U (12 sacred comps.); Verbly jul in die Here (cantata) Trio for flute, violin & cello. Recordings: Kolperd en ander leidjies uit Suid-Afrika. Author: Dit kom van ver af-Volksliedjies Uit die volksmond, 1975. Mbr., Music Commission, FAK. Address: 222 Nicolson St., Brooklyn 0181, Pretoria, S Africa.

LAMPREY, Audrey Hardy, b. 6 March 1945. Almond, NY., USA. French Horn Performer & Teacher. Educ: B Mus, Eastman Schl. of Music; M Mus, Bowling Green State Univ., Ohio m. William H Lamprey, 1 d. Career: Pt.-time Instr. of Brass, Heidelberg Coll., Tiffin, Ohio, 5 yrs.; currently 1st Horn, Kokomo (Ind.), Symph., Mbr., Kokomo Bras Quintet, Pvte. Tchr. of French Horn. Mbrships: Int. Horn Soc.; Am. Fedn. of Musicians. Recip. 1st Prize, brass div., solo competition, Bowling Green State Univ., 1970. Hobbies: Philately; Tennis; Tropical fish. Address: 1904 Greytwig Dr., Kokomo, IN 46901, USA.

LANCELOT, James Bennett, b. 2 Dec. 1952. Orpington, Kent, UK. Organist. Educ: BA, 1974, B Mus, 1975, MA, 1978, King's Coll., Cambridge Univ.; ARCO, 1968; FRCO, 1969; CHM (RCO), 1971; ARCM Pianoforte, 1971. Debut: Queen Elizabeth Hall, London, 1975. Career incls: Num. radio & TV perfs., & concerts w. choir of King's Coll., Cambridge (UK, Europe & Can) & w. Winchester Cathedral Choir (UK, Can., USA & France); num. solo recitals & perfs., UK, inclng. var. Fests.; Recitals tour of NZ, 1978; Asst. Organist, Hampstead Parish Ch. & St. Clement Danes, London, 1974-75; Sub-Organist, Winchester Cathedral, 1975-. Recordings incl: w. choir of King's Coll.; (harpsichord) Haydn, Creation: (organ) Handel, Messiah, Chandos Anthems: Monteverdi Vespers; Venetian Fest. Music; Anthems from King's Blow, Coronation Anthems: Bernstein, Chichester Psalms; w. choir of Winchester Cathedral; Golden Hour; Coronation Music. Mbr., RCO. Recip., var. music prizes. Hobbies incl: Railways; Photography. Address: 8b The Close, Winchester, Hanks., UK. 4.

LANCEN, Jean-Serge, Mathieu-Pierre, b. Nov. 1922. Paris, France. Composer; Pianist. Educ: Conserv. Nat. Supérieur de Musique, Paris. m. Raphaële Hélńon. Compositions incl: Printaniéres for flute or vioce & piano, 1953; Concerto for harmonica & orch., 1954; Les Prix (ballet), 1954; Monologues for flute solo, 1957; Concert á six for 6 clarinets, 1961: Concerto da camera for flute & string orch., 1962; Concerto for string double bass & string orch., 1962; Sinfonietta for orch., 1970; Poéme Oecoménique for soloists, chorus, organ & orch., 1975; Croquis for double bass & piano, 1978. Comps. recorded: Manhattan Symph.; Festival á Kerkrade; Parade Concerto; Le Mont-Saint-Michel: Hymne á la Musique; Rhapsodie sur des Thrŕes Bretons; Cape Kennedy; Concerto for double bass, etc. Mbrships: SA CEM; Union Nationale des Compositeurs de Musique. Hons. incl: Prize of Rome for Comp., 1950; Prize, Communaute Radiophonique de Langue Française, 1966, '69; Grand Prix de la Musique Symphonique Légeŕe de la SACEM, 1974; Prize of European Broadcastins Union, 1977. Address: 65 rue, La., Fontaine, 75016 Paris, France.

LANCHBERY, John, b. 1923. London, UK. Conductor. Educ: FRAM. m. Elaine Fifield, div., 1 d. Career: Cond., Sadler's Wells Theatre Ballet, 1951-60; Prin. Cond., Royal Ballet, 1960-. Compositions incl: Pleasuredrome; House of Birds; La Fille mal Guradée; The Dream; Don Quixote; Giselle; Tales of Beatrix Potter; La Sylphide. Mbrships: Garrick Club; Petit Francais; Composers' Guild of GB. Recip. of Bolshoi Theatre Medal. Address. 11 Marlborough St., Lodnon SW3, UK. 3.

LAND, Boukje, b. 7 June 1923. Wageinigen, Netherlands. Concerto Pianist; Cellist; Professor. Educ: Dip. Piano-Collo, Amsterdam Conservatorium. Debut: Concertgebouw, Amsterdam. Career: Piano-duets (1 & 2 pianos, with & without orch.) w. sister Debora, in Europe & Indonesia, inclng. TV & radio appearances. Prof., Muzieklyceum, Amsterdam. Recordings: Edition Denemus: A Voormolen - Concerto, 2 pianos & orch. Mbr., Nederlandse Toonkunstenaars Raad. Hons: Rient van Santenprijs, 1949. Hobbies: Music; Lit.: Travelling. Mgmt: Nederlands Impresariaat, Amsterdam; Nic. Choveaux, London. Address: Jac. Obrechtstraat 63, Amsterdam (2), Netherlands.

LANDAU, Anneliese, b. 5 Mar. 1903. Halle a/S, Germany. Musicologist. Edud: Univs. of Halle a/S & Berlin; PhD, Univ. of Berlin, 1930. Career: Ed., Musikalische Zeitschriftenschau, 1930-35; Broadcasts in Leipzing, Berlin, NY; TV app., Los Angeles; Music Dir., Jewish Centers Assn., Los Angeles, 1944-68; Asst. Prof. in music, Calif. State Univ., Northridge, 1962-63; Instructor, Adult Schls. in Los Angeles. Publs: Conradin Kreutzer, 1930, '72; The Contribution of Jewish Composers to the Music of the Modern World, 1946, '66; The Lied, the Unfolding of its style, 1979; Music Ed., Lexikon des Judentums. Contbr. to: Zeitschrift für Musikwissenschaft; Die Musik; Musical Courier; The Etude; Los Angeles Times, etc. Mbrships: Am. Musicol. Soc.; Mendelssohn-Gesellschaft, Berlin & Zurich. Address: 386 S Burnside Ave., 6-F, Los Angeles, CA 90036, USA.

LANDAU, Siegfried, b. 4 Sept. 1921. Berlin, Germany. Conductor. Conductor. Educ: Stern & Klindworth-Scharwenka Conservs., Berlin; LGSM (comp.), UK; Cond. Dip., Mannes Coll., NY, USA. m. Irene Gabriel, 2 s. Career: Cond., Bklyn., Philharmonica, 1954-71; Mlusic Westchester, 1961-. Westphalian Symph. Orch., Germany, 1973-75. Comps: Friday Eve Service; choruses; The Sons of Aaron (opera); 4 ballets. Has made many recordings for Vox-Candide & Turnabout labels. Mbrships: ASCAP; Am. Musicol. Soc.; Nat. Jewish Music Coun. Hons. incl: Fellow, Jewish Acad. of Arts & Sci., 1971. Hobbies: Reading; Travel. Address: 26 Ogden Rd., Scarsdale, NY 10583, USA. 2, 6.

LANDAU, Victor, b. 18 June 1916. Brooklyn, NY, USA. Professor of Music; Conductor; Pianist; Composer; Author. Educ: BSS; CCNY, 1936; AM., 1938, PhD., 1957, NY Univ. m. 2 s. Career: Pianist., chmbr. music progs., WNYC radio & at colls.; Cond., Band & Light Opera Guild. Brooklyn Coll., Band, New Paltz Coll., SUNY; Prof., Music, New Paltz Compositions: Educl. music. Recording: Adagio for Strings. Contbr. to profl. jrnls. & newspapers. Mbrships: Am. Musicol. Soc.; Composition, Westminister Choir, 1938; Summer Rsch. Fellowship, SUNY, 1959, '62, '63. Hobbies: Art; Drama. Address: 5 Lincoln Place, New Paltz, NY 12561, USA.

LANDON, Eleanor Mary, b. 13 Feb. 1933. Mary Tavy, Tavistock, Devon, UK. Concert Singer (soprano). Educ: Dartington Hall Music Schl. (piano, clarinet, musicianship); studied singing w. Evelyn Langstone, Eric Greene & Pierre Bernac. Debut: London recitals, 1956. Career: Recitals; solo perfs. in oratorio, etc. mbr., ISM. Hobbies: Gardeining; Riding. Address: St. Joseph's, Horndon, Peter Tavy, Tavistock, Devon, UK.

LANDON, Howard Chandler Robbins, b. 6 Mar. 1926. Boston, Mass., USA. Musicologist. Educ: BMus, Boston Univ., 1947. m. Else Radant. Career: BBC radio & TV, 1954-; Guest tchr., Brit. & Am. Univs., 1969-; Hon. Professorial Fellow, Univ. Coll., Cardiff, 1972-; currently John Bird Prof. of Music, ibid.; prod. of num. recordings for Haydn Soc., Vox lib. of Recorded Masterpieces. Publs: The Symphonies of Joseph Haydn, 1955; Collected Correspondence & London Notebooks of Haydn, 1959; Essays on Viennese Classical Style, 1970; Beethoven, 1970; Haydn: Chronical & Works (4 out of 5 vols. now publ.); Ed., all Haydn's symphs. & other works by Haydn, Mozart, etc. Mbrships. incl: Pres., Int. Joseph Haydn Stiftung Eisenstadt. Hons: DMus, Boston Univ., 1969; DMus, Queen's Coll., Belfast, 1974. Hobbies: Cooking; Walking; Swimming. Address: Anton Frankgasse 3, 1180 Vienna, Austria.

LANDOWSKI, Marcel Francois Paul, b. 18 Feb. 1915. France. Composer. Educ: Nat. Conserv. of Music, Paris. Career: Dir., Conserv. of Boulogne-sur-Seine, 1960-65; Dir., of Music., Comedie Francaise, Paris, 1962-; Insp.-Gen. of Musical Studies, 1964; Dir. of Music, 1966-70; Dir. of Mlusic, Lyrical Arts & Dance, Min. of Cultural Affairs, 1970-. Compositions incl: Rythmas du Monde (oratorio); Jean de la Peur (Symph.); Le Rire de Nils Halerius; Le Fou; Le ventriloque; Les Adieux (opera); 2 cantatas; Chmbr. Bergerac, Comedie Francaise. Hons: Chevalier, Legion d'Honneur; Croix de Guerre. Address: 10 rue Max-Blondat, 92 Boulogne-sur-Seine, Seine, France.

LANDRE, Guillaume (Louise Frederic), b. 24 Feb. 1905. Holland. Educ: LLD., Univ. of Utrecht; Study of composition w. Willem Pyper. Career Tchr., Amsterdam, 1930-47; Gen. Sec., Arts Coun. 1947-57; Pres., Music Dept., ibid., 1957-. Composition: Symph. No. 1, 1933, No. 2, 1941, No. 3, 1951, No. 4, 1954; Concerto for Clarinet & Orch., 1957; Permutazioni sinfoniche, 1957; Anagrams for Orch., 1960; Variazioni senza Tema per orch., 1967; 4 String Quartets; 2 Wind Quartets; Jean Levecq (opera), 1966. Mbrships: Hon. Life Pres., Netherlands Composers Guild, 1961; Hon. Life Pres., 2nd Fedn. of Cont. Int. of Socs. of Authors & Composers, 1964; Artistic Bd., Socs. of Authors & Composers, 1964; Aristic Bd., Concertgebouw Orch.; VP., Netherlands Opera Fndn. Hons: Of., Order of Orange-Nassau; Off., Order of Polar Star., Sweden; Sweelinck Music Prize. Address: Molenweg 34, Amstelveen, Holland.

LANDRY, John F., b. 5 Nov. 1952. Yonkers, NY., USA. Composer; Teacher; Guitarist; Conductor. Educ: B Mus Ed, Manhattanville Coll., Purchase, NY; Geo. Wash. Univ., Wash. DC; Hoff-Barthelson Music Schl., Scarsdale, NY.; NY State Tchrs. Cert. Debut: (as Cond.) Manhattanville Coll. Career: Perfs. as Cond. & or Guitarist, NYC, Wash. DC, Boston, Ela. & Ore.; Fac. mbr., Greenwich Country Day Schl., Conn., & Hoff-Barthelson Music Schl.; Workshops in NYC, Boston, Ore. & Maine. Comps. incl: Orch. Pieces no. 1, Synisms for Orchestra; Trio for Flute Clarinet & Piano; Quintet for Guitar Solos & Duets; Original Songs. Contbr. to musical jrnls. Mbr., profl. assns. Hobbies incl: Painting; Writing Poetry. Address: 92 Brite Ave., Scarsdale, NY 10583, USA.

LANDSHOFF, Werner, b. 23 April 1905. Berlin, Germany. Cellist. Educ: Stern Conserv., Berlin; Ecole Normale de Musique, Paris. m. Zelda Landshoff, 1 d. Career: Soloist, concerts in Berlin, Paris, USA: Mbr., & Dir., USO Unit touring Pacific Theatre; Assoc. Prof. of Music, Univ. of Okla., Norman; Fndr. & Dir. of Music, Louis Braille Fndn. for Blin Musicians, NY; Tchr., Music Schl. of Light, NY; Asst. to Diran Alexanian, Ecole Normale, Paris, & pvtely in NY. Has recorded for Pro Musica, paris, & Allegro, NY. Mbr., Musicians Union, NY. Address: 75 Hinesburg Rd., Apt. 10, S Burlington, VT 05401, USA.

LANDY, Tonny (Tonny Landy Nuppenau), b. 30 July, 1937. Copenhagne, Denmark. Lyric Tenor; Opera & Concert Singer. Educ: Royal Danish Conserv.; studied singing in Copenhagen, Rome, Munich. m. Tove Hyldgaard, 2c. Debut: Alfredo (Traviata), Copenhagen, 1966: apps. in Scandinvavia, Germany, Italy, France, Czech., USSR, UK & USA; recital & concert apps.; broadcasts on radio & TV; roles incl. Arturo (Puritani), Berlioz's Faust, Nemorino (L'Elisir d'Amore), Gounod's Faust, Ferrando (Cosi fan Tutte), Rudolf (la Boheme), Almava (Barber of Seville), Lensky (Eugen Onegin), Duke (Rigoletto), Walther (Tannhäuser). num. recordings. Hon: Ridder of Dannerbrog. Address: Eivindsvej 37, 2920 Charlottenlund, Denmark.

LANE, Andrew Robert, b. 24 Aug. 1955. Bangor, Wales. Musician (flute, alto flute & piccolo). Educ: LRAM. Career: D'Oyly Carte Opera Co. Orch.; Max Jaffa Orch, Scarborough; City of Birmingham Symph. Orch. Address: 98 Sandford Rd., Moseley, Birmingham B13 9BT, UK.

LANE, George Bertram, b. 10 June 1943. Ft. Benning, Ga., USA. College Music Teacher, Trombone. Educ: BM, N Tex. State Univ., 1964; MS, in Music, Kan. State Tchrs. Coll., 1967; DMA, Univ. of Tex., Austin, 1975. m. Constance Grambling. Career: Mbr., Music Facs., Abilene Christian Coll., Univ. of Tex. at Austin, Univ. of SC; Pres., Broad River Press. Publs: Concise Daily Routine for Trombone, 1970; The Trombone in the Middle Ages & Renaissance, 1976; Co-ed., Sonata a Tre, by JJ Fux, 1974. Contbr. to: Jrnl. of Nat. Assn. of Coll. Wind & Percussion Instructors: Instrumentalist. Mbrships: Pres., SC Music Tchrs. Assn.; Am. Fed. of Musicians, Am. Assn. of Univ. Profs., Music Library Assn. Address: 2014 Mary Hill Dr., Columbia, SC 29210, USA. 7.

LANE, Philip Thomas, b. 7 May 1950. Cheltenham, Glos., UK. Composer; Arranger; Pianist; Organist; Teacher. Educ: B Mus, Birmingham Univ. Career: Radio app. & talks on Lord Berners. Comps. incl: Diversion (melody instrument & piano); Little Suite (orch.); Cotswold Dances (orch.); Suite of Cotswold Folkdances (orch.); Celebration Overture (orch.); Divertimento (wind band); A Spring Overture (brass band); Concertino (brass band). Recordings: Prestbury Park; Joy to the World; Robin & the Greenwood Gang. Mbrships: CGGB; RCO. Hons: Eric Sanders Memorial Prize, 1970; Ipswich Orch. Soc. Comp. Prize, 1977. Hobbies: Cricket; Cinema; Theatre. Address: 104 Nettleton Rd., Cheltenham, Glos. GL51 6NS, UK.

LANE, Richard Bamford, b. 11 Dec. 1933. Paterson, NJ, USA. Composer; Teacher of Piano & Compostition. Educ: B Mus, 1955, M Mus, 1956, Eastman Schl. of Music. Career: Comp., Tchr., Comp.-in-Res., schl. systems of Rochester, NY & Lexington, KY. Comps. publd: Four Songs (texts by Mark Van Doren) for Mezzo-soprano & orch.; trios; duets; chmbr. works; piano solos & duets; songs; band music; orchl. works. Comps. recorded: Four Songs; Song for Cornet; Flute Sonata. Mbrships: ASCAP; Bohemians; Phi Mu Alpha Sinfonia. Hons. incl: Eastman Schl. Recording & Publ. Award, 1956. Hobbies: Swimming; Walking. Address: 173 Lexington Ave., Paterson, NJ 07502, USA.

LANERI, Roberto, b . 25 Mar. 1945. Arzignano, Italy. Performer on Clarinet, Saxophone, Bass Clarinet; Vocalist; Composer; Teacher. Educ: philos., Rome Univ.; BA, MA (comp.), SUNY Buffalo; Dip. in Clarinet, St. Cecilia Conserv., Rome; PhD, Univ. of Calif. San Diego. Career incls: Clarinettist-Comp., Creative & Performing Arts Ctr., Buffalo, 1970-72; Comp., Co. of Man (dance grp.); Mbr., Sem. Ensemble, 1970-72; Fndr., Vocal Improvisation & Meditation Grp. Prima Materia. Comps. incl: Entropic Islands for clarinet & self-prepared tape; L'Arte del Violino for concert violinist, amplified violin, speaker (or tape), 2 piano, 2 percussionists & girls. Recordings: 11 Bestiario (w. Maria Monti); Todo Modo (w. Mingus). Contbr. to jrnls. Mbr., ASCAP. Hobbies: Photography; Tennis. Address: Lungotevere Navi 22, 00196 Rome, Italy.

LANG, Istvan, b. 1 Mar. 1933. Budapest, Hungary. Composer. Educ: Esthetics degree from univ.; Composer's degree. m. Csilla Fülöp, 1 s. Career: Lectr., Budapest Music HS.; Musical Advisor, Hungarian State Puppet Theatre. Many comps. edited by Edition Musica, Budapest together w. Boosey & Hawkes; & recorded by Hungaroton, Budapest. Mbrships: Gen. Sect. & Mbr., of the Presidency, Assn. of Hungarian Musicians. Recip., Erkel Prize, 1968 & 1975. Address: Mártirou útja 20, 1027 Budapest, Hungary. 30.

LANG, Paul Henry, b. 28 Aug. 1901. Hungary (Citizen of USA). Musicologist. Educ: Budapest Royal Acad. of Music; Univs. of Heidelberg; Paris; & Cornell, USA. Career: Asst. Prof. of Music, Vassar Coll., USA., 1930-31; Assoc. Prof. of Music, Wells Coll., 1931-33; Prof. of Musicol., Columbia Univ.,

1933-; Music Critic, NY Herald Tribune, 1954-66; Ed., The Musical Quarterly. Publ: Music in Western Civilisation, 1941. Mbrships: Fellow, Am. Acad. of Arts & Scis.; Pres., Int. Musicological Soc.; Musicological Socs. of France, Belgium & Holland. Address: 33 Aldridge Rd., Chappaqua, NY, USA.

LANG, Rosemary Rita, b. 29 April 1920. Weisburg, Ind., USA. Musician, Clarinet, Saxophone, Oboe, English Horn; Composer; Arranger; Teacher; Ensemble Director. Educ: B Mus, Ed. Jordan Coll. of Music, Butler Univ., Indpls., Ind.; M Mus, ibid. Career: Solo Alto Saxophone, Bass Clarinet, Clarinet, other Woodwinds, Indpls. Symph.; Mbr. var. Pit & Theatre Orchs., Midwest USA; Chamber Musician; Recitalist; Tchr. of Woodwinds, Dir. Woodwind Ensembles, Jordan Coll. of Music; Woodwind Repair Expert. Compositions: Rhapsody, Opus in Ebony, clarinet choir; Nocture, Tarantelle, Humoreske, clarinet quartet; Chorale, Scherzo, Flute Quartet; 4 Pieces, Woodwind Quintet; Concert Piece, solo bass clarinet; Great Music Of Jerome Kern, arr. for symphonic band. Publs: Saxophone; Beginning Studies In The Altissimo Register, 1972; Principles Of The Saxophone, 1974; Woodwind Class Method, 1974. Contbr. to: NACWPI Jrnl.; Instrumentalist Mag.; Woodwind Anthol. Mbrships: Mu Phi Epsilon; Am. Fedn. of Musicians, Local 3; Indpls. Matinee Musicale. Hobbies: Travel; Photography; Needlework; Leathercraft. Address: 821 N Temple Ave., Indpls., IN 466201, USA.

LANG, Siegfried, b. 3 Aug. 1919. Millstatt, Austria. Composer; Writer; Touring Pianist & Bandleader. Educ: Conserv.; studied composition w. Prof. Uhl, Vienna Music Acad. m. Brunhilde, 2 d. Career: has long been active, first as a Bandmaster, then as Solo Entertainer, in Austria & abroad, is currently touring as Entertainer, occasionally w. a small band; has worked in radio as both a Solo Perf. & Prod.; Writer on musical subjects. Compositions incl: Edelsteine-Walzer; Wiener Tradition; Strassenkameradschaft; Mein liebes Pötzleinsdorf; Ulrichsbert-Polka; Vision im Zwielicht; Alles Schöne; Leute von heute. Publs: Almanach der Osterreichischen Unterhaltungskomponisten des 20. Jahrhunderts, 1974. Contbr. to jrnls. Mbrships: Bd. of Dirs., Austrian Composers Guild; Robrt Posch Soc.; Full Mbr. (Fellow), AKM, Vienna. Hons: Robert Stolz Medal, 1968; Hut Von Lieben Augustin, 1970. Address: Potzleinsdorferstrasse 194/8/3, A-1180 Vienna, Austria.

LANG-BECK, Ivana, b. 15 Nov. 1912. Zagreb, Yugoslavia. Professor of Piano; Composer. Educ: Dip., Music Acad., Zagreb. m. Mariyan Beck (div.), 1 d. Debut: As Comp., Radio Zagreb, 1941. Caree: Prof. of Piano & Comp., V Lisinski Music Schl., Zagreb, 35 yrs.; Concert of own comps., 1974. Num. comps. Recordings: Ivana Lang: Toccatina for Harp; Play Rajka Dobronic-Mazzoni. Publs: Music Enciklopedie, 1963; Dr. Kresimir Kovacic; Music Development in Croatia 1945-1965 (1966); Andreis-Cvetko-Buric-Klajn: Historical Development of Music Culture in Yugoslavia, 1962; Truda Reich: Meeting With Contemporary Composers of Yugoslavia, 1972; Josep Andreis: History of Music, IV, 1974. Mbrships: Soc. of Comps. of Croatia & Yugoslavia; Soc. of Pedagogues of Croatia. Hons: 1nd Prize Radio Zagreb Comp. Competition, 1948; Acknowledgement & Prize, City of Zagreb, 1977. Hobby: Painting. Address: Klaiceva 58, 41 000 Zagreb, Yugoslavia.

LANGBEIN, Brenton James, b. 21 Jan. 1928. Gawler, S Aust. Musician (violin). Educ: Conservatorium Adelaide, SA; pvte. studies w. Cassals, Grümmer, Morawec in Europe. Debut: Recital in Adelaide age 13; as Soloist w. Orch. at age 15. Career: Fndr. of the chmbr. music grp. 'Die Kammermusiker', Zürich; World premiere & recording of Henze Concerto No. 2; Konzermeister of Collegium Musicum Zürich; Tchr. at Basel Acad.; Apps. at Edinburgh Fest., 1961, '62, '67, '73; Fndr. & Cond. of Youth Orch. 'Die Orchesterschule der Kammer Musiker'. 1961-. Recordings: Die Kammermusiker Zürich (Pelca); H W Henze Violin Concerto No. 2 (Decca). Hobbies: Film; Theatre; Travel. Mgmt: Ingpen & Williams, London. Address: Dreikonigstr. 37, 8002 Zürich, Switz.

LANGBERG, Peter, b. 21 Aug. 1945. Nykobing, Denmark. Pianist; Organist; Harpsichordist; Music Teacher; Choir Director. Educ: Dip., Organ, 1968; Dip., Music Tchr., 1971; Dip., Piano, 1972; Dip., Choir Dir., 1974. m. Lisbeth Nielsen, 1 c. Debut: Copenhagen, 1970. Career: Concerts in Denmark, France, Holland, USA, Can.; var. TV Perfs., Denmark, Recip. Scholarship. Royal Danish Music Conserv., 1969. Address: 148 Koigevej, 2630 Taastrup, Denmark.

LANGDON, John David, b. 29 May 1943. Minehead, Somerset, UK. Organist; Music Lecturer. Educ: King's Coll., Cambridge Univ.; New Coll., Oxford Univ.; MA; Mus B; FRCO. Career: Lectr. in Music, Royal Scottish Acad. of Music, Glasgow. Recordings: w. King's Coll. Chapel Choir, Cambridge,

w. Clement Dane's Chorale, London; w. Paisley Abbey Choir. Publs: Var. Anthems of Christopher Tye. 1969-; Contbr. to Musical Times. Mbr., ISM. Recip., Stewart of Rannoch Scholarship in Sacred Music. Hobby: Swimming. Address: 1058 Cathcart Rd., Glasgow, G42 9XW, Scotland, UK. 3.

LANGDON, Michael, b. 12 Nov. 1920. Wolverhampton, Staffs., UK. Opera Singer. Educ: GSM; Trained w. Joseph Yates, Walsall; Samuel Worthington, London; Alfred Jerger, Vienna; Maria Carpi, Geneva & Otaker Kraus, London. m. Vera Laura Duffield, 2 d. Debut: Royal Opera House, 1950. Career: Appointed Prin., Royal Opera House, 195; Royal Command perfs. at regular intervals in Royal Opera House at His Majestry's Theatre, Aberdeen before Queen Mother; 1st in app., 1961; Singer all leading opera houses worldwide. Num. recordings. Mbrships: Savage Club; Pres., Wolverhampton Orpheus Choir. Recip. CBE, 1973; Hon. GSM, 1973. Hobbies: Assn. Football; Reading Sci. Fiction. Mgmt: John Coast. Address: 34 Warnham Ct., Grand Ave., Hove, Sussex, UK, 3, 4, 16, 30.

LANGE, Helmut Karl Heinz, b. 16 Mar. 1928. Würzburg, Germany. Music College Director; Concert Pianist; Musicologist. Educ: Bavarian State Conserv. of Music; Univ. Career: Piano Tchr., Hanover Music Coll., 1966-70; Dir. of Schwäbisch Hall Music Coll., 1970-; Acad. Tchr. for Musicology; Fachakademie für Musik, Würzburg, 1978-; Comps: Floh-Walzer (1) 2-handed piano, 1976. Publs: Lehrbuch des Klavierstimmens, 1977; Hilfstafeln für Tonbestimmungen, 1977; Tabellenwerk musikalischer Temperaturen, 1978; Toulogarithmen, 1978. Contbr. to German musicol. & organol. jrnls. Mbr: Soc. for Music Rsch., Cassel. Hobbies: Gardening; Photography. Address: Schaalhofweg 265, D-7176 Braunbach am Kocher, German Fed. Repub. 23, 28, 29, 30.

LANGER, Hans-Klaus, b. 6 Dec. 1903. Tost, Germany. Composer; Conductor. Educ: State music tchrs.' exams., Conservatory, BeuthenGleiwitz; Master class for comp. w. Prof. Franz Schreker, Hochschule für Musik, Berlin, m. Elfriede Langer (Rück), 1 s. Career: Concert, radio & stage perfs. of own & other works in Berlin, Breslau, Baden-Baden, Budapest, Dortmund, Frankfurt am Main, Hanover, Colgne, Leipzig, Munich, Nürnberg, Prague, Vienna. Post 1946 Compositions (1920-43 comps. lost, WWII) incl: Der Heuchler (opera); Der Psycghotherapeut (opera); Grand Hotel (ballet); Plaisanterie amoureuse (ballet); Strassen-Serenade (ballet); Sinfonia tragica '72 (orchl. work); Impromptu '72 (orchl. work); Damals wie heute (opera); Dep letzte Weg (ballet); Sinfonia piccola '74 (orchl.); collage (orchl.); Kaleidoskop (orchl.); Works for solo instruments & orch.; Oratorios; Chmbr. music; Piano music Num. radio Recordings. Mbrships: Deutscher Komponisten Verband; GEMA; Künstlergilde; Dramatiker Union. Hons: Beethoven Schlrship., Berlin, 1932: Johann Wenzel Stamitz Prize, Künstlergilde, 1969. Address: Bundesallee 196, 1 Berlin 31, German Fed. Repub.

LANGFORD, Anthony, b. 15 Nov. 1942. Bradford, UK. Senior Lecturer; Organist. Educ: ARCO; BA, PhD, Reading Univ. m. Angela Victoria Wright, 2 d. Career: frequent broadcasts as organist-accomp., BBC; Fndr. & Cond.; Leeds Bach Choir; Sr. Lectr., City of Leeds Coll. of Music, 1968-; Dir. of Music, Selby Abbey, 1977-. Recordings: principally w. Leeds Parish Ch. Choir, Abbey Records & Windmill Records. Publs: incl: Ed., Adrian Batten's Third Service. Recip., Limpus Prize, RCO, 1964. Hobbies: Fell Walking; Travel. Address: 22 The Drive, Bardsey, Leeds LS17 9AF, UK.

LANGFORD, Audrey, b. 28 June 1912. Rochdale, Lancs., UK. Musician; Singer. Educ: ARCM., Singing Perfs. m. Andrew Field, 2 d. Debut: at Royal Opera House, Covent Gdn. Career: Prin. Soprano, Royal Opera House, Covent Garden; BBC Radio; major concerts, etc.; currenlty tchng. in London, RNCM, Manchester & USA. Mbr. ISM. Hobbies: Gardening. Address: 55 Hayes Rd., Bromley, Kent BR2 9AE, UK. 3.

LANGHAM, Jennifer, b. 9 Feb. 1948. Macon, Ga., USA. Cellist. Educ: B Mus, Peabody Conserv. Music, 1969; M Mus, Univ. Tex., 1971; Navarra Master Class, 1973; Piatigorsky Master Class, 1974 '75; Marlboro Music Festival, 1975. Debut: Purcell Room, London, 1974. Career: Solo perfs. for Am. Educl. TV & Tortelier Master Calss Series, BBC-TV, 1974; Mbr., New String Trio, NY; NY String Sextet; Num. concert apps. UK, Germany, Switzerland & USA; Tchr., cello, Pomona Coll., Claremont, Calif., & Calif. State Univ., Northridge. Recordings: Max Reger String Trios, Op. 77B & Op. 141B, & Frank Martin Piano Trio & String Trio w. New String Trio, NY, for BASF. Mbr., Mu Phi Epsilon. Addres: 948-D 12th St., Santa Monica, CA, USA.

LANGLAIS, Jean Francios Hyacinthe, b. 15 Feb. 1907. La Fontenelle, France. Organist. Educ: Nat. Inst. for Young Blind, Paris; studies w. André Marchal, Marcel Dupré, Paul Dukas: Hon. Dr., Tex. Christian Univ., Ft. Worth, Duquesne Univ. Pitts. m. Jeanne Sartre, 1 s., 1 d. Career: Organ Tchr., Nat. Inst. Young Blind, 1930-68; Schola Cantorum, 1961-76; Organist, St. Clotilde Basilcia, Paris, 1945-. Comps: Passion (commd. by Fr. Radio); Missa Salve Regina (Prix Madame Rene Coty); 3 concertos for organ & orch.; approx. 250 organ works; vioce & organ works; piano & harpsichord works. Mbrships: Hon. Mbr., Am., Brit. Guild of Organists. Hons. incl: Decorated Officer Legion of Honor, Palmes Academiques; Kt. Order St. Gregory Ct.; Bronze medal, Paris; Vermeil medal arts, scis. & letters; Grand prix Friends of Organ, Paris; Prix Rossini; named hon. citizen New Orleans. Address: 26 rue Duroc, 75007 Paris, France.

LANGLEY, James, b. 22 Sept. 1927. Birmingham, UK. Music Producer. Educ: Assoc., Birmingham Schl. of Music; FTCL. m. Beryl Skidmore, 2s. Career: Music Producer, BBC, Manchester. Comps: Overture & Beginners; Coloured Counties; Sinfonia for 10 wind instruments; Overture for a Restoration Comedy; Te Deum Laudamus; Suite for Trombones; var. brass instrumental works; music for brass band. Mbrships: ISM; CGGB. Address: 43 Ennerdale Dr., Sale, Cheshire, UK.

LANGLEY, Kenneth John, b. 26 Sept. 1948. Bayonne, NJ, USA. Violinist; Teacher. Educ: B Mus, Manhattan Schl. of Music, NY, 1970. Career: Co-concermaster, Ruffino Opera Co. of NY, 1968-70; Violin Tchr., Performing Arts Schl. of NJ, 1972-74; Violinist, NJ, Symph. Orch., 1970-73, Berlin String Quartet, NJ; Berlin Chmbr. Orch., Mbr. & soloist, 1970-74; Violin Tchr., Wittenberg Univ., Ohio, 1974-; Mbr., Springfield Symph. Orch., 1974-; Recitalist on Radio WNYC, NY. Hobbies: Record & tape collection. Address: 18 Hillside Rd., Old Bridge, NJ 08857, USA.

LANGLEY, Robin Patrick, b. 17 Feb. 1944. London, UK. Writer; Musicologist; Pianist. Educ: ARCM; London Univ., B Mus, King's Coll. Career: currently Music Ed., Oxford Univ. Press. Publs: English 18th century chamber & keyboard music, 1975-76; Weber in London, 1976; John Field's Piano Sonatas, 1976. Contbr. to: Grove's Dict.; Music & Letters; Musical Times; Early Music. Mbrships: Life, Royal Musical Assn. Address: 44 Conduit St., London W1R ODE, UK.

LANGRIDGE, Philip Gordon, b. 16 Dec. 1939. Hawkhurst, Kent, UK. Concert & Operatic Tenor. Educ: LRAM; GRSM. m. Margaret Hilary Davidson, 1 s., 2 d. Career incls: apps. at major fests, Britain & Europe; opera apps. incl: L'Incoronazione di Pappea (Monteverdi), 1971, 73, 74, Idomeneo (Mozart), 1976, Il Barbier di Siviglia (Rossini), 1976, Dorian Gray (Hans Kox), 1977, All Netherlands Opera; Eritrea (Cavalli), 1975; Wexford Fest. Opera; Justified Sinner (Thomas Wilson), 1976, Scottish Opera. Has recorded for many labels. Hobby: Collecting Edwardian & Victorian postcards. Mgmt: Ibbs & Tillett, London. Address: 9 Marsworth Ave., Pinner, Middx., UK.

LANKESTER, Michael John, b. 12 Nov. 1944. London, UK. Conductor; Musical Director; Professor of Conducting. Educ: ARCM; GRSM. m. Hannah Mary Francis. Career: Musical Dir., Nat. Theatre of GB, 1969-; Comp., Cond., music for num. Prods., ibid.; Cond., Surrey Phil. Orch., 1972-; Engl. Chmbr. Orch.; Fndr., Contrapuncti, Radio, TV Broadcasts, BBC; Collaborator w. Young Vic. Theatre Co. var. Prods.; Cond., Cheltenham Fest.; Sadler's Wells, & at opening of Royal Northern Coll. of Music, 1973 Musical Dir., Nat. Theatre, 1969-75. Recordings: Gordon Crosse, Purgatory, Ariadne. Mbr. Noise Abatement Soc. Recip. WatneySargent Conducting Scholarship, 1967. Hobbies: Reading; Walking; Cricket. Mgmt: Ibbs & Tillett, 124 Wigmore St. London, W1, UK. Address: 21 Birchington Rd., London N8, UK.

LANKSTON, John, b. 29 May 1939. Lawrenceville, Ill., USA. Tenor; Actor; Dancer. Educ: BMus, Cinn. Coll. Conserv. of Music. Debut: Pedrillo (Seraglio) NYC Opera, 1966. Career: apps. w. NYC Opera, Houston Grand Opera, Wash. Opera, Phila. Opera, Milwaukee Opera, Chatanooga Opera, Harford Opera, Wolf Trap & Caramoor fests.; title roles in US Premiers of Ashmedai (Josef Tal) & Prodigal Son (Britten); TV apps.; rolses incl: Tamino, Werther, Tom Rakewell, Florestan, Don José, Hoffman, Bacchus (Ariadne auf Naxos), Duke (Rigoletto), Peter Quint (Turn of the Screw), Lohengrin, Canio, Peter Grimes, etc. Hobbies: Painting; Antique Collecting; Weight Lifting; Ballet. Address: 155 W 81st St. 4E, NYC, NY 10024, USA.

LÄNNERHOLM, Torleif, E T., b. 22 Jan. 1923. Waxholm, Sweden. Oboist. Educ: Acad. of Music, Stockholm, m. Brittan Lannerholm 1 c. Debut: Stockholm, Career: Mbr. of the Orch. Royal in Stockholm, 1943-46; Solo Oboist in Sweden Radio Symph. Orch. in Stockholm, 1946-; Sev. solo perfs. on Swedish radio & TV & on major stages; Many chamber music apps. Recordings: Lille Bror Soderlundh Oboe Concertino; var. chamber music. Hons: Jetton, Acad. of Music, Stockholm, 1943; Swedish Royal Acad. of Music; Swedish State Scholarship for Art, 1968. Hobby: Boating. Address: Mastvågen 1, 18143 Lindingö, Sweden.

LANZA, Andrea, b. 30 June 1947. Turin, Italy. Musicologist. Educ: Grad. in Classics, Fac. of Letters & Philos., Univ. of Turin; Lic. in Hist. of Music, Conserv. of Alessandria; Pvte. tutor in Pianoforte, Harmony & Comp. Career: Dir., Lib. of Conserv. of Alessandria 1975-78; Dir., Biblioteca Civica Musicale, A Della Corte, Turin, 1979-; Mbr., Directorate Committee of Rivista Italiana di Musicologia', 1973-78. Mbrships: Italian Musicol. Soc. Contbr. to: Rivista Italiana di Musicologia; Nuova Rivista Musicale Italiana; Parole & Metodi; Grove's Dict.; La Musica Ency. Address: Via Umberto I 79, Pecetto Torinese, 10020, Italy.

LANZKY-OTTO, Ib, b. 8 July 1940. Gentoste, Denmark. Horn player. Educ: Royal Acad. of Stockholm, 1957-62. Career: Horn player, w. Stockholm Royal Opera Orch., 1958-61; Assoc. 1st horn, Stockholm Phil. Orch., 1961-67; Solo horn, ibid., 1967-; Tchr., Int. Horn Workshop, 1970-62; Tchr., Inst. de Hautes Etudes Musicales, Montreaux, Switzerland, 1973-; Soloist in var. countries in Europe & USA. Recordings: Horn sonata (Hindemith); Horn Concertino (Lars Erik Larsson); Alarme per Corno (Ake Hermansson); Tranist II (Bengt Hambreus). Mbrships: Int. Horn Soc.; Marlboro Music Festival; Mazers Music Soc. Address: Selmedalsvagen 2, 5 tr., S-126 55 Hagersten, Sweden.

LANZKY-OTTO, Wilhelm, b. 30 Jan. 1909. Copenhagen, Denmark. Pianist; Organist; French Horn Player. Educ: Grad., 1927; MA, 1928, Univ. of Copenhagen; Dips., piano, 1930, organ, 1931, Conserv. of Copenhagen. m. Anna Margrete Foss, 3 s. Debut: as pianist, 1932; as French horn player, 1936; Solo Horn, Danish Radioorch., 1936-44, Royal Opera, Copehagen, 1944-45, Iceland Symph. Orch., Reykjavik, 1946-51, Gothenburg Symph., 1951-56, Stockholm Phil., 1956-74; Former tchr. of French horn, Piano & Chmbr. music. Has made recordings. Hon. Mbr., Int. Horn Soc. Hobbies: Mushrooms; Bicycling. Address: Gimmerstavägen 6, 12536 Älvsjö, Sweden.

LAPIN, Geoffrey Scott, b. 14 Oct. 1949. Balt., Md., USA. Cellist; Pianist. Educ: Dip., Peabody Conserv. of Music; BS, Ind. Ctrl. Univ. Indpls.; MM, Butler Univ., Indpls., Ind. Career: Cellist, Indpls. Symph. Orch.; Prin. Cellist, Indpls. Civic Orch., 1970-72; Cellist, Esch Piano Trio. Mbrships: Am. Fedn. of Musicians; Phi Mu Alpha Sinfonia. Author of prog. notes for Indpls. Symph. Orch. Young People's Concerts. Recip., Rauh Music Perf. Schlrships., 1969. Hobbies: Botany; Landscaping; Refinishing antiques. Address: 618 E 46th St., Indpls., IN 46295, USA.

LAPP, Arthur Edward, b. 25 Sept. 1952. Markham, Ont., Can. Professional Tuba Player. Educ: B Mus Ed, McMaster Univ., Hamilton, Ont. Debut: w. McMaster Symph. Career: Freelance Tuba player, Toronto; Tuba Soloist w. Ont. Youth Concert Band, European tours, 1973, 75; Pres. & Asst. Cond., McMaster Univ. Concert Band, 1972-75; Guest Cond., McMaster Univ. Symph.; Mbr., Hamilton Brass Quintet; Perfs. w. Bach-Elgar Singers, TV & Radio, Hamilton; Player w. Thunder Bay Symph. Orch., 1975-76 season; Tchr. of Instrumental Music, night schls., var. Northern Ont. communities. Recordings w. Ont. Youth Concert Band, Switzerland, 1973. Hobbies: Photography; Ahtletics. Address: 530 Harold St., Thunder Bay ''P'', Ontario P7B 2E1, Can.

LARDE, Christian Pierre, b. 3 Feb. 1930. Paris, France. Flautist; Professor. Educ: Conserv. Nat. Supérieur de Musique, Paris, m. Marie-Claire Jamet, 2 s. Debut: Flute solo, Radio Eirann, Dublin, 1949. Career: Int. Flute soloist, w. apps. in Paris, London, Berlin, NY, Montreal, Tokyo, Johannesburg, Rome, Istanbul, San Fran., New Delhi, Copenhagen, etc.; Prof., Conserv. Nat. Supérieur de Musique de Paris. Num. recordings. Hons: Chevalier des Arts et des lettres; Num. prizes, l'academie du disque & l'academie Charles Cross. Mgmt: Werner, Paris, Address: 25 Allee du Rendez-Vous, 93320 Pavillon s/bois, France.

LARDROT, André, b. 5 Mar. 1932. Nevers, France. Oboist. Educ: Paris Conserv. m. Brigitte Chatelanat, 3 children. Debut: Mozarteum Orch., Salzburg, 1954. Career: 1st Solo Oboe, Mozarteum Orch., Salzburg, 1954-57, Radio Zurich Orch., 1957-71, Radio Symph. Orch., Berlin, 1961-62, Radio Symph.

Orch., Basle, 19623-; Prof., Mozarteum Acad., Salzburg, 1962-65, Volkwang Hochschule, Essen, 1965-67, Basle Music Conserv., 1975. Num. recordings incl: Albinoni; Bach.; Bellini; Donizetti; Handel; Haydn; Mozart; Telemann; Vivaldi. Mbr. IDRS, USA. Recip. 1st Prize, Int. Music; Perf. Competition, Geneva, 1956. Mgmt: Kunstlersekretariat Bahr, 7164 Obersontheim German Fed. Repub. Address: Hinterzweienstrasse 87, 4132 Muttenz, Switzerland.

LAREDO, Jaime, b. 7 June 1941. Cochabamba, Bolivia. Violinist. Educ: Curtis Inst. of Music, Phila., USA. m. Sharon Robinson, Id. Debut: Carnegie Hall, NY, 1959. Career: has app. w. major orchs. in Europe & Am., incl. London Symph., Boston Symph., Chicago Symph., NY Phil., Phila. Orch., etc. under Barenboim, Mehta, Ormandy, Davis, Ozawa, Leinsdorf, Szell & Krips. Recordings incl: Complete Bach Sonatas, w. Glenn Gould; Schubert Trout Quintet w. Rudolf Serkin; Mendelssohn, Bruch, Mozart & Bach concertos w. Boston Symph. Hons. incl: 1st Prize, Queen Elisabeth of Belgium Int. Music Competition, 1959; stamps w. his picture issued by Bolivian Govt.; Handel Medal, NYC, 1960. Mgmt: Harold Holt Ltd., 124 Wigmore St., London, UK. Address: 22 Riverside Dr., NY, NY 10023, USA.

LARNER, Gerald, b. 9 Mar. 1936. Leeds, UK. Music Critic. Educ: New Coll., Oxford; BA (Oxon.). m. Celia Ruth Mary White, 2 d. Career: Asst. Lectr., Manchester Univ., 1960-62; Mbr. Guardian Staff, 1962-; Northern Music Critic of Guardian, 1965-. Comps: Libretto of The Lion, the Witch and the Wardrobe (Novello), 1971. Regular contbr. to Musical Times; The Listner. Mbr. Critics Circle. Hobbies: Wine Drinking; Art Glass Collecting Address: 11 Higher Downs, Altrincham, Cheshire WA 14 2QL, UK. 3.

LARNER, Justina Helen, b. 7 Mar. 1950. Leicester, UK. Private Music Teacher. Educ: Cambridge Coll. of Arts & Technol.; Grad., Trinity Coll. of Music, London; Lic., Pianoforte Teaching, ibid. m. Adrian Larner, 1 child. Career: Tchr., Notting Hill Ealing HS, GPDST; Pvte. teaching; Mbr., CUMS Choir & London Bach Choir. Mbr., Incorp. Soc. of Musicians (Treas., Conventry Ctr.). Hobbies: Sewing; Gardening; Art Appreciation. Address: 7 Adelaide Rd., Leamington Spa, Warwicks. CV31 3PN, UK.

LARO, Johannes Petrus, b. 19 Mar. 1927. Breda, Netherlands. Lieutenant-Colonel; Inspector of Military Music in the Netherlands. Educ: Dips. for clarinet, tchng. & conducting, Royal Conserv. the Hague. m. M S M Hofland, 1 s. Career: Cond., Johan Willem Friso Army Band, 1953-64; Dir. of Music, Cond., Marine Band of Royal Netherlands Navy, 1964-75; Major Dir. of Music, Insp. of Mil. Music in Netherlands, 1975-; Lt.-Col.; sev. TV & radio progs. throughout world. Comps. incl: March of the Dutch Marines; Qua Patet Orbis; Inspectionmarch; March of the 1st Army Corps; Hollands Glorie March; etc. Mbrships: Netherlands Conds. & Offs. Socs. Recip. Prize of Culture, 1963. Address: Schiedamsedijk 11 E, Rotterdam, Netherlands.

LARSEN, Bjarne, b. 28 Mar. 1922. Oslo, Norway. Violinist. Educ: studied violin since age 6. m. Ruth Steger Larsen, 1s. Debut: Aulaen, Oslo, 1937. Career: solo apps. in Norway & Scandinavia & on Norwegian radio & TV; Leader, Orch. of Oslo Nat. Theatre, 1947-57; Leader, Oslo Phil. Assn., 1958-. Recordings: Grieg sonatas. Hons: Critics' Prize for perf. of Nielsen's violin concerto, 1967; Oslo Town culture prize, 1967. Hobby: Cars. Address: Waldemar Thranesgt. 62c III, Oslo 1, Norway.

LARSEN, Hans Juhl, b. 29 July 1943. Bjernede, Soro, Denmark. Music Librarian. Educ: Libn., Danish Library Schl., 1969; Music Libn., ibid., 1972. Career: Ed., Musiknyt fra Slagelse Centralbibliothek, 1970-. Mbrships: Danish Br., Int. Music Lib. Assn.; Lib. Rsch. Grp. for Music Libns. Address: 12 Sostjernevej, Bildso Strand, DK-4200 Slagelse, Denmark.

LARSEN, Jens Peter, b. 14 June 1902. Copenhagen, Denmark. Professor of Musicology. Educ: MA, Univ. of Copenhagen, 1928; PhD, ibid., 1939. m Ruth L Wöldike, 1 s., 1d. Career incls: Asst. Prof., Univ. of Copenhagen, 1928; Lectr., 1939; Prof., Musicol., 1945-70; Organist, Vangede, 1930-45; Musicologist-in-Res., John F Kennedy Ctr., Wash. DC, USA, 1975. Publs. incl: Handel Studies, 1972; Die Haydn Uberlieferung, 1939; Drei Haydn Kataloge, 1941; Handel's Messiah, 1957; 1972; Den Danske Koralbog (w. M Wöldike), 1954, 2nd ed. 1973. Contbr. to var. profl. jrnls. Mbrships. incl: Royal Danish Acad. of Sci. & Letters; Hon. Mbr., Hungarian Acad. of Sciences; VP, G F Handel Soc., Halle (Saale), Joseph Haydn Inst., Cologne. Hons. incl: Kt. 1st Calss, Danebrog Order; Grand Golden Cross of Hon., Austria. Hobby: Gardening. Address: Bernstorffsvej 244, 2920 Charlottenlund, Denmark. 3.

LARSEN, Naomi Ruth, b. 25 Oct. 1909. Chgo., Ill., USA. Pianist; Contralto Soloist; Professor; Choral Conductor. Educ: B Mus, Olivet Nazarene Coll., 1933; Mus M, Am. Conservatory, 1941; Mus M, ibid, 1947; Postgrad. work, Univ. of Ill. & RAM, London, UK; Special cert. in piano pedagogy. m. Walter B Larsen Special cert. in piano pedagogy. m. Walter B Larsen (dec.), 1 s. (dec.). Career: Tchr., Olivet Nazarene Coll., Kankakee. Ill., 1935-75, Cond.; Orpheus Choir, 15 yrs.; Currently Cond., Oratiorio Chorus, 1957-; Min. of Music, Coll. Ch., Bourbonnais, Ill., 20 yrs.; Acting Chmn., Div. of Fine Arts, Olivet Nazarene Coll., 1957-60; Tchr., European Nazarene Bible Coll., Büsingen, German Fed. Repu. (sabbatical leave), 1969. Co-Author w. husband, Fundamentals of Voice Building (text book for class or pvte. voice), 1944. Mbrships. incl: Nat. Assn. of Tchrs. of Singing; Am. Choral Dirs. Assn.; MENC; Upsilon Chapt., Delta Kappa Gamma; Charter mbr., Louise Robyn Fndn.; Corres. Sec., Kaukakee Community Hons: Alumni "O" Award, 1960, Quadrennial Merit Award & special citation, 1972; Choral Award w. special citation, 1972. Hobbies: Travel; Sewing; Reading. Address: 302 E Olivet St., Bourbonnais, IL 60914, USA. 5.

LARSEN, Peter Harry, b. 20 Mar. 1927. Melbourne, Aust. Music Educator; Head of Music Section. Educ: Cert., Melbourne Tchrs. Coll.; B Mus, Dip. Music (Violin & Piano), BA, B Ed., Melbourne Univ.; M Ed studies, La Trobe Univ. m. Lillian Patricia Mary McMahon, 3 s. Career incls: Music Master, Melbourne High Schl., 1951-56; Music Dept. Staff, Huddersfield Tech. Coll., UK, 1957-58; i.c. Music, Geelong Tchrs. Coll., 1960-67; Hd., Music Dept., State Coll. of Vic. at Coburg, 1968-; Cond., Geelong Madrigal Choir, 1960 62, Geelong Symph. Orch., 1960-63; State Coll. Vic. Madrigal Choir, 1968-; Box Hill Choral Soc., 1971-76; Jubilate Singers, Melbourne, 1976-; Choral broadcasts for Aust. Broadcasting Commission, 1973-77. Mbr., Aust. Soc. Music Educ. (Pres., Vic. chapt., 1974-76); Assn. of Music Educ. Lectrs. Hobbies incl: Bushwalking & Mountaineering; Cultivation of Native Plants. Address: 3 Waterdale Rd., Ivanhoe, Vic. 3079, Aust.

LARSEN, Robert L, b. 28 Nov. 1934. Walnut, Iowa, USA. College Professor; Opera Conductor; Pianist; Teacher. Educ: BM, Simpson Coll., 1956; MM, Univ. of Mich., 1958; Mus D, Ind. Univ., 1971; Study of piano w. Sven Lekberg, Joseph Brinkman, Rudolph Ganz, Walther Bricht; Conducting w. Wolfgang Vacano, Tibor Kozma; Opera stage direction w. Boris Goldovsky, Tanglewood. Career: Prof., Chmn., Div. of Fine Arts, Simpson Coll.; Artist Dir., Des Moines Metro Opera Co.; Concert pianist & accompanist; Cond., The Madrigal Singers. Mbrships: Phi Mu Alpha; Pi Kappa Lambda; Alpha Psi Omega. Hons: Gov.'s Award for Contribution to the Arts in Iowa, 1974. Address: 713 W Ashland, Indianola, IA 50125, USA.

LARSEN, Wayne Erik, b. 7 Oct. 1946. Mpls., Minn., USA. Musician (Conductor, Trombone, Euphonium, Piano). Educ: BA, Columbia Univ., 1968; pvte. study of Harmony, Theory & Piano; studied Brass w. Roger Smith, & w. Ralph N Wige of Sousa's Band. Career: Dir., Int. Arts Olympics; Asst. Mgr., Goldman Band, NYC. Recording: The Unknown Sousa, 1976. Publs: Ed., Complete Works of J P Sousa, to be published over next 10 yrs. Conbtr. to jrnls. & newspapers. Mbrships. incl: Int. Sousa Soc. (Pres.); NY Soc. of Chmbr. Winds (Pres. & Music Dir., 1974-75). Hons. incl: Interlochen Scholarship, 1963; Detroit Concert Baton, 1974, 75. Hobbies incl: 18th & 19th Century European Literature; Late 19th Century American Piantings. Address: 333 W 56th St. Apt. 4-G, NY, NY 10019, USA.

LARSON, David Dynes, b. 25 Nov. 1926. Evanston, Ill., USA. Conductor; Music Eductor. Educ: B Mus, M Mus, Univ. of Mich.; Dr. of Sacred Music, Union Theol. Sem., NY; pvte. choral study w. Julius Herford & Margaret Hillis. m. Margaret Montogmery, 1 s., 2 d. Career: Asst. Prof. & Chmn., Music Dept., Wilmington Coll., Ohio, 1950-54; Prof. of Music & Chmn., Music Dept., Kobe Coll., Nishinomiva, Japan, 1954-66; Guest Cond., Tokyo Phil. Chorus, Osaka NHK Radio Orch. & Chorus; Osaka Phil. Orch., etc.; Lectr. at var. Japanese Univs. & Colls.; Prof. of Choral Music, Chgo. Musical Coll. of Roosevelt Univ., 1966-; Min. of Music Highland Pk. Presby. Ch., Ill., 1968-; Cond., N Shore Choral Soc., Evanston, 1973-. Publs: Hymns of the Church, 1963. Contbr. to: Am. Choral Review; NATS Bulletin; Reihai to Ongaku (Worship & Music). Mbrships: Am. Choral Dirs. Assn.; Am. Choral Fndn.; Music Lib. Assn.; Pres., Kobe Col. Corpn. Recip: Roosevelt Univ. Rsch. Fellowship, 1974. Hobbies: Hiking; Travel. Address: 2743 Broadway, Evanston, IL 60201, USA.

LARSSON, Lars-Erik, b. 15 May 1908. Akarp, Sweden. Composer; Conductor. Educ: Stockholm, Leipzig & Vienna. m. Brita Holm, 1936. 1 s. Career: W. Royal Swedish Opera, 1930-31; Music Critic. 1933-37; Cond., Swedish

Broadcasting Co., 1937-54; Prof., Royal Music HS, 1947-59; Dir. of Music, Uppsala, 1961-65. Compositions: 3 Concert overtures; Sinfonietta for String Orch.; Serenade for Strings; Divertimento; Pastoral Suite; Music for The Orch.; Orchl. Variations; 3 Orchl. Pieces; Lyric Fantasy; Due Auguri; Saxophone Concerto; Violin Concerto; 12 Concertinos; Incidental music for the Writer's Tale; The Sundial & The Urn (solo, choir & orch.); Missa Brevis & Three Quotations (unacc. choir); var. chmbr. music pieces, songs & piano works. Mbrships: Coun., Swedish Assn. of Composers. Address: Inäster Ernstgatan 6A, 25233 Helsingborg, Sweden.

LASEROMS, Wim, b. 27 DeC. 1944. Oudenbosch, Netherlands. Music Teacher, Composer; Conductor. Educ: Study of condng. & composition w. Henk van Lynschooten, Rotterdam. m. P de Ryk, 1 s. Career: Music tchr., 1970-; Cond., 1966-; composer, 1973, specialising in works for brass bands, frequently performed on Dutch Radio, etc. Compositions incl: Marches-Festivo, Immer Fest; So Long; Dumbo; moder Fantasy-In Festive Mood; Paso Dobel-Paso Bravo; Trumpet & cornet Trios-Holiday for Trumpets; Three Jolly Trumpets; Trombone Trio-Trombonella-Mozaiek. Publ: Book of Music Lectures Contbr. to var. mags. Mbrships: Dutch Musical Soc.; Jurist, music exam. body of Holland. Hobby: Football. Mgmt: Fa. Tieroloff, Roosendaal. Address: Marykestraat 10A, Bosschenhoofd, Netherlands.

LASH, André Duane, b. 18 May 1947. Coffeyville, Kan., USA. Organ Recitalist; Teacher of Organ & Piano; Church Musician. Educ: B Mus Ed, Kan. State Coll., 1969; M Mus, Southwestern Bapt. Theol. Sem., 1974; Eastman Schl. of Music; pvte. study w. Arthur Poister. Career: Organist, Southern Bapt. Ch. Music Conf., 1975; Organist, chs. of var. denominations, 1963-; Instr. of Keyboard Instruments, Brewton-Perker Coll., Mt. Vernon, Ga. Mbrships: AAGO; Am. Music Scholarship Assn.; Southern Bapt. Ch. Music Conf.; Ga. Bapt. Ch. Music Conf.; Am. Musicol. Soc.; Phi Mu Alpha Sinfonia. Hons. incl: Student Soloist, Coll. Symph. Hobbies incl: Swimming; Camping; Watching baseball games. Address: 4081/2 McIntosch, Vidalia, GA 30474, USA.

LASHOF, Sheryl Beth, b. 24 Oct. 1955. Silver Spring, Md ., USA. Violinist. Educ: Jacksonville Univ.; Maryland Teaching Cert. Career: Violinist, Montgomery Co. Youth Orch. m, Md., 1968-73. & Jacksonville Symph. Orch., Fla., 1973-77; Tchr., Fallston High Schl., Maryland; Concertmastress, Harford Community Orch. Recordings: w. Montgomery Co. Youth Orch. (inclng. 2 for TV). Hons: Schlrships., Wolf Trap Am. Univ. orch. summer 1973. 0 Jacksonville Univ., 1973 & 74. Address: 10125 Ashburton Lane, Bethesda, MD USA.

LASKIEWICZ, Eugene, b. 1 Mar. 1950. Toronto, Ont. Can. Accordionist; Teacher (free-bass accordian, music history, theory). Educ: BEd, Univ. of Toronto, 1977; Royal Conserv. of Music, Univ. of Toronto, 1969-75; BMus, Queen's Univ., Kingston, 1974; MMus, Univ. of Toronto, 1976. m. Gloria Alexandra Hlynka. Career: 1st accordionist candidate for B Mus degree, Queen's Univ.; recitals in Can., France, Sweden, Denmark & Netherlands; represented Can. in Int. Accordion Competitionsi in Vichy, France & Stockholm, Sweden; Can. contemporary music perfs. on CBC radio; chmbr. music apps. w. Chamber Players of Toronto, Stratford Ensemble & mbrs. of Nat. Arts Ctr. Orch.; perfs. w. orchs.; tchr., Royal Conserv. of Music, Toronto, & Mohawk Coll., Hamilton, Ont. VP, Classical Accordian Soc. of Can., Inc., 1979-. recip., Royal Conserv. of Music Scholarship, 1972, '73, '74. Hobbies: Readings; Travel. Address: 445 Arnhem Drive, Oshawa, Ont. L1G 2J2, Can.

LAST, Gert, b. 4 June 1921. Vienna, Austria. Composer; Musician (flute, bass, guitar, piano). Musical Educ: Studied flute & theory of music, film & opera comp. Music Acad., Vienna; Grad., ibid. m. 1 s. Career: Theatre, Ingolstadt & mil. music, 1943-44; Own dance orch., 1946-; Bar musician, 1953-. Compositions: dance & light music; Arrangerments for radio & records inclng. Bilder aus Wien (Suite). Italienische Rhapsodie, Ländiche Miniaturen, Erwachende Grosstadt, Barock Waltz, Musik zum Träumen, Als du gingst, Wann 1 amal ausgeh; zeit in Musik; In Paris; Happy Sunday. Mbrships: Bd. of Dirs., Österreichischer Komponistenbund; Bd. of Dirs., Musicians' Sect., Osterreichischer Gewerkschaftsbund. Address: Hahngasse 12/16, 1090 Vienna, Austria.

LAST, Joan, b. 12 Jan. 1908. Littlehampton, Sussex, UK. Professor of Piano; Examiner; Adjudicator; Lecturer. Educ: pvte. study w. Mathilde Verne & York Bowen; LRAM (Tchrs.) ARCM (perfs.) Debut: Aeolian Hall, London, 1926. Career: Has travelled extensively in UK, USA, S Am. & Scandinavia lecturing on art & tchng. & perf. & making radio & TV broadcasts; Prof., RAM. Has Publd., over 100 educl. albums for Piano. Publs: The Young Pianist, 1954; Interpretation in Piano

Study, 1961. Contbr. to: The Music Tchr., UK; Keys, USA. Mbrships: RAM Club; Comps. Guild; ISM. Recip. Hon. ARAM, 1966, & Hon. RAM, 1976. Hobbies: Golf; Photography; Recoroding. Address: 11 St. Mary's Close, Littlehampton, Sussex, BN17 5PZ UK. 3.

LATARCHE, Pauline Winifred, b. 1 Apr. 1937. Twickenham, UK. Teacher. Educ: studied w. Hilda M Ross & Eileen F Rowe; W London Inst. fo Higher Educ. - dip. course; LLCM (TD); ALCM. m. Kenneth Charles Latarche, 1 s., 1 d. Career: Pianist; pvte. music tchrs. (piano & theory); tchr., Eileen Rowe Pianoforte Schl. Mbrships: hon. treas., Ealing & Dist. Music Tchrs. Soc.; EPTA; ISM; committee, piano section, Ealing Music Fest. Hobbies: Dressmaking; Knitting; Driving. Address: 25 Sidmouth Ave., Isleworth, Middx. TW7 4DW, UK.

LATCHEM, Malcolm, b. 28 Jan. 1931. Salisbury, UK. Violinist. Educ: RCM (w. Albert Sammons); ARCM. m. Gill Latchem, 3d., 1 s. Career: fndr. mbr., Acad. of St. Martin-in-the-Field; mbr., Dartington Str. Quartet. Recordings: Boyce, Trio Sonata; num. solo recordings w. Acad. of St. Martin-in-the-Fiedl. Hon: MMus. Hobby: Gardening. Address: Station House, Staverton, Totnes, Devon., UK.

LATEINER, Isidor, b. 8 Jan. 1930. Havana, Cuba. Concert Violinist. Educ: studies w. Diego Bonilla, Cuba; grad., violin & chmbr. music, Curtis Inst. of Music, Phila. m. Edith Grosz. Debut: Havana, aged 5; Carnegie Hall, NY, 1957. Career: Soloist w. Berlin Phil., Concertgebouw & many other orchs. in Europe & USA; perfs. of 20th century classics; concerts & recitals in Mexico, S Africa, Turkey, Iran, India & Afghanistan; commissioned to play premiers of concerti by Milton Babbitt & Hans Kox; apps. at num. fests; tchr., violin & chmbr. music, Royal Conserv. of Music, The Hague; plays on 1696 Guarnerius. var. recordings. Hobbies incl: Chess; Bridge. Address: Tweede Constantijn Huygensstraat 83, Amsterdam.

LATHAM, Christopher Paul, b. 16 Apr. 1935. Worcester, UK. Schoolmaster. Educ: RAM; GRSM; LRAM; ARCM. m. Jennifer Mary Nevard. Career: Mbr., Full-time Music Staff, Bedales, 1958-62, Frensham Heights, 1962-70 (Dir. of Music, 1965-70); Dir. of Music, Sidcot Schl., 1970-78; Dir. of Musig., Scotch Coll., Melbourne, Aust., 1978-. Mbr., ISM. Hobbies: Photography; Bridge. Address: 13 Larkspur Ave., Doncaster, Vic. 3108, USA.

LATHAM, Lorran, b. 14 July 1916. Nelson, UK. Violinist. Educ: Dip. in Machine Design, Rochester Inst. Technol., USA, 1945; Hochstein Mem. Music Schl., Rochester, 1930-35; B Mus, Eastman Schl. Music, Univ. of Rochester, 1939. m. Esther Elizabeth Payne, 1 s., 1 d. Career: Mbr., Hochstein Schl. Str. Quartet; Instructor in Violin, Rochester Publ. Schls.; Instructor, Ga., State Tchrs. Coll.; Univ. Interchange Concerts, Valdosta, Milledgville, Athens, Statesboro, Savannah, Ga. & num. community functions; Mbr., Concertmaster, Asst. Dir. Rochester Music Guild Orch., 1943-50; Mbr., JYMA Symph., Rochester, 1951-54; Charter Mbr., All-Univ. Symph. Orch., Univ. of Rochester, 1955-; Concertmaster, ibid, 1957-65. Compositions incl: Legende; Ballade; Pensance; Verse; Redolence. Recording: Berlioz; Requeim, 1965 (w. All Univ. Symph. Orch., Glee Clubs, Orpheus Chorale & Cecelian Chorale, Univ. of Rochester). Mbrships: incl: VP, Rochester Poetry Soc., 1968-70; Fndr. Contbr., Acad. Am. Poets. Hobbies incl: Poetry; Photography. Address: 1923 Baird Rd., Penfield, NY, NY USA.

LATHAM, Richard Oskatel, b. 2 May 1906. London, UK. Organist. Educ: St. George's Choir Schl., Windsor Castle; FRCM; FRCO. m. Sylvia Stubbs, 1s, 1d. Career: Prof. of Organ, Theory & Choir Trng., RCM; Organist, St. Paul's Ch., Knightsbridge, London, & Fndr. & Cond., St. Paul's Fest. Choir; Dir., of Music, The Madrigal Soc. Comps: Choral & instrumental music. mbr., coun. RCO. Hobby: Book Collecting. Address: 29 Emperor's Gate, London SW7, UK. 1.

LATHAM, William Peters, b. 4 Jan. 1917. Shreveport, La., USA. Composer; University Professor. Educ. BS in Mus Ed., Univ. of Cinn., Ohio. 1938; B Mus in comp., Coll. of Music Cinn., 1941; M Mus, ibid, 1942; PhD in comp. Eastman Schl. of Music, Univ. of Rochester, 1951; studied comp. w. Eugene Goossens, Howard Hanson & Herbert Elwell; instrumental Cert. in Trumpet. Cinn. Conserv. of Music -1938. m. Joan Seyler, 1 s. 2 d. Career: Fac., Mbr., N Tex. State Univ., Denton, Tex., 1938-39; Eastern Ill. State Tchrs. Coll., Charleston, 1946; Univ. of N Iowa, Cedar Falls, 1946-65; Prof., ibid. 1959-65; Prof. & Co-ord. of Comp., N Tex. State Univ. Schl. of Music, Denton, Tex., 1965-; Dir. of Grad. Studies in Music, ibid., 1969-; (appointed Disting. Prof., 1978-). Compositions incl: Choral works; Chamber Works; works for Band Orch.; Solo works w. Orch.; Solo works w. Wind Ensemble, Mbr., Profl.

orgs. Hons. incl: Annual Awards, ASCAP, 1962-; 1st prize, Alumni Div., Phi Mu Alpha Comp. Contest. Address: 1815 Southridge Dr., Denton, TX 76201, USA 2, 15, 125, 128, 139, 140.

LATOSZEWSKI, Zygmunt, b. 26 Apr. 1902. Poznań, Poland. Conductor. Educ: DMus, Univ. of Poznań. m. Czestana (Karczewska) Latoszewska, 1 s., 1 d. Debut: 1929. Career: Artistic Dir., & 1st Cond., Polish Operas, 1933-72; guest cond., opera houses & orchs. in Poland & other countries; Prof. of Music, Poznań Conserv., 1961-; Prof., Warsaw Conserv. Recordings for Polish radio. Hons: award from Min. of Culture. Address: ul Bracka 20a m 39, 00028 Warsaw, Poland.

LAUBSCHER, Philippe, b. 25 Dec. 1936. Porrentry, Switz. Organist. Educ: Tech. Schl. Neuchâtel; Conserv. La Chaux-de-Fonts; Conserv. Geneva. m. Eliane Kälin, 1c. Debut: 1964. Career: Concerts throughout Europe; Radio prod. in Switz., France, Czechoslovakia; TV prod. in Switz. Recordings: C Franck. Mbrships: Assn. of Romand Organists, vie-pres.; mbr. Organ exam committee Benoise Ch.; occasional mbr. exam Committee Conserv. Hons: 1st Prize Organ virtuosity, Geneva. Hobbies: Railway models. Address: Ch-3052 Zollikofen, Landgarbstr. 53, Switz.

LAUDERDALE, John Frederick, b. 9 May 1935. Houghton-le-Spring, Co. Durham, UK. Tutor of Brass Instruments; Professional Trumpet Player. Educ: Trumpet studies w. Ernest Hall, George Eskdale, RAM, London. div., 2 d. Career: Prin. Cornet, RAF Bands, Royal Liverpool Phil. Orch.; Freelance player, LSO, etc.; Prin,. Trumpet, NZ Symph. Orch.; Asst. Cond. & Prin. Trumpet, Dunedin Civic Orch. NZ; Brass Tutor, Otago Univ. & Educ. Dept., Otago, NZ; Freelance Trumpet Player; Fndr., Dir., Southern Youth Brass Ensemble; Num. Broadcasts. Recordings: Lilburn 2nd Symph., Farquar 1st Symph., Mahler Symphs., NZ Symph. Orch.; NZ Jazz Orch. Mbr., NZ Musicians Club. Hons: Radio NZ Study Bursary, 1969-70. Hobbies: Trout fishing; Swimming; Interior decoration. Address: 9 Heriot Row, Dunedin, NZ.

LAUFER, Wolfgang, b. 18 Dec. 1946. Timisoara, Romania. Cellist; Cello Teacher. Educ: Music Conserv., Romania; Acad. of Music, Tel-Aviv, Israel. m. Mariana-Eva Laufer, 1 d., 1 s. Debut: Tel-Aviv, 1962. Career: solo apps. in Europe, N & S Am., 1962-; mbr. Fine Arts Quartet, Univ. of Wis., USA, 1979-. Recordings for Swedish & Hamburg radio. Hons: Israel awards, 1962-65; 1st prize, Cultural Contest, Sweden, 1972. Hobby: Photography. Address: Zellerstr. 13, Hamburg 73, German Fed. Repub.

LAURENCE, Anya. Toronto, Can. Concert Pianist; Author. Educ: Bachelor's degee, Skidmore Coll., Saratoga Springs, NY; piano studies w. G Sigrid Helgason & Maria Vegara, Toronto, Rudolf Firkusny, NY, & Denise Restout, Lakeville, Conn. 1s., 1d. Debut: Carnegie Hall, NY, 1968. Career: apps. on radio & TV, Can. & US; adjudicator, fests. & competitions; tchr. of piano; soloist w. orchs.; many concert apps. Publs: Women of Notes. Contbr. of num. articles on music to newspapers & jrnls. Mbrships: Fndr., Kinderhook Musical Soc.; American Liszt Soc.; Am. Women Comps. Inc. Hons: Amicus Poloniae Decoration (Poland), 1974; St. Cecilia Medal, 1961. Hobbies: Reading; Histroical Research. Address: RD 1, Kinderhook, NY 12106, USA.

LAURICELLA, Remo, b. 22 May 1918. London, UK. Violinist; Composer. Educ: ARCM; RAM; Dip., Accademia Chigiana, Siena, Italy; Dip., Musica en Compostela, Spain, Career: Soloist w. num. orchs.; Radio Perfs. in UK, Italy, Spain, France, Denmark, Switz., Belgium, S Africa, Aust.; Ldr., Anglo-Polish Ballet Orch.; Mbr. LPO, LSO. Comps. incl: (publd.) 2 symphs.; Petit Suite; Fleet St. Overture; Preludio Africa; Strolling Minstrel; Sinfonietta ad Archi; Sinfonia Breve; Sinfonietta No. 3, for chmbr. orch.; Overture Moirae; Overture From the Ukranian Highlands, (recorded) Boliviana; Londinium; Violin & Piano Sonatina; African Interlude; Danza Siciliana; Tango Sicilliano; Echos From Santiago. Recordings: Own violin works; Nardini, Concerto in E Minor. Mbrships: CGGB; Performing Rights Soc.; Mechanical Rights Soc.; GEMA. Hons: Katherin Howard Prize, 1932; Societa del Quartetto, Vercelli, Italy, 1955. Address: Trinacria, 10 Brondesbury Rd., London NW6, 6AS, UK.

LAURIE, Alison Margaret, b. 5 Jan. 1935. Glossop, Derbyshire, UK. Music Librarian. Educ: Glasgow Univ.,1952-57; MA, BMus; Cambridge Univ., 1957-60; PhD: ARCM. Career: Sr. Asst., Glasgow Univ. Lib., 1961-63; Music Librarian, Reading Univ. Lib., 1963-. Publs: Eds. of Purcell -Dioclesian, 1960, Dido & Aeneas, 1961, King Arthur, 1971 & King Arthur (vocal score), 1972. Contbr. to: Bent & Tilmourht, South materials & the interpretation of Music; I Spink (Ed.),

English Music in the 17th Century; Musical Times & other jrnls. Mbrships: Purcell Soc.; Royal Musical Assn.; Int. Assn. of Music Librarians; Lib. Assn. Hobbies: Hill Walking; Gardening. Address: 123 Nightingale Rd., Woodley, Reading RG5 3LZ, UK.

LAURIE, Cynthia, b. 12 Apr. 1924. London, UK. Concert Singer (Soprano); Teacher. Educ: FTCL (Singing); ATCL (Ptve. Teaching); Studied w. Elena Gerhardt, 1950. m. Trevor Hill, 1 d. Career: Recitals & Broadcasts in England & Scotland, 1949-64; 1st recital of Mabler & Berg songs on Norwegian radio, 1957; Tutor, Univ. of Ghana & broadcasts on Ghana radio, 1964-65; Series of recital seminars on German & French romantic songs at Simon Fraser Univ., Can., 1969; Tutor in Singing, Craigie Coll. of Educ., Ayr currently tchng. in Khartoum, Sudan. Mbrships: ISM; Former mbr., Edinburgh Soc. of Musicians Women's Sect. (convener 1959-61). Hobbies: Pastel Drawing; Reading. Address: Dundas & Wilson, C S, 25-28 Charlotte Square, Edinburgh EH2 3EZ, Scotland, UK. 3.

LAURISTON, Michael Owen, b. 9 Nov. 1951. Kingston, Ont., Can. French Horn Player; Conductor. Educ: B Mus Ed, Dalhousie Univ., Halifax, NS, 1972; M Mus, Univ. of Wis.-Madison, 1975. Career: Atlantic Symph.; Madison Symph., Wis. Ballet, Wis. Chmbr. Orch.; Ottawa Symph., Nat. Arts Ctr. Orch., Ottawa, Ont. Recordings: CBC. Mbrships: Am. Fedn. of Musicians; Int. Horn Soc. Hobbies: Yoga; Philately; Physical Fitness. Addres: 323 Catherine St., No. 3, Ottawa, Ont., Canada K 1R 5T4.

LAUSCHMANN, Richard Otto, b. 12 June 1889, Altenburg Thür, German Dem. Repub. Professor; Oboe Player. Educ: Conserv. of Music, Leipzig, m. Lisbet Felgenträger, 1 d. Career: Solo Oboist, Orchs. in Münich, Bern & Kiel; tours, Germany & abroad; Tchr. of Oboe & Chmbr. Music, Music Acads. in Kiel, Lübeck & Mannheim; Prof., State Acad. of Music, Berlin, 1942-45; Hd., Collegium Musicum Univ., Mannheim, 1954-. Publs. incl: Eds. & Arrs. of oboe sonatas, concertos, chmbr. music, esp. B Marcello, G Schwencke, Ph. Em. Bach, P Prowo, Sammartini, G Fr. Händel, E Förster, Graupner, G Ph. Telemann, Stölzel, etc. Mbr., musical assns. Hobbies: Lit.; Wandering. Address: Ilvesheimerstr. 58, 68 Mannheim 51, German Fed. Repub. 30.

LAVIOLA, Marisa Anne, b. 3 Feb. 1954. Phila., Pa., USA. Pianist; Teacher; Accompanist. Educ: B Mus, (piano perf. & music hist.), Bowling Green State Univ., Ohio; MMus (piao perf.), ibid. Career: college instructor in piano, pedagogy, music hist. & piano lit.; now on fac., Asbury Coll., Wilmore, Ky., 1978-, pursuing doctoral studies, Cinn. Coll-Conserv. of Music. Mbrships: incl. Pi Kappa Lambda; Phi Kappa Phi; VP, Gamma Omicron Chapt., Sigma Alpha Iota; MTNA; Am. Musicol. Soc.; MENC; Coll. Music Soc.; Hons: Sigma Alpha Iota leadership award for Mich. & N W Ohio, 1976-77. Hobbies: Horticulture; Gosepl Pianist; Ch. Bible Tchr. Address: 300 W. Coll. St., Wilmore, Ky., USA.

LAVOTHA, Elemer Odon, b. 18 Apr. 1952. Budapest, Hungary. Cellist. Educ: Sibelius Acad., Helsinki; Solo Dip. & Jeton, Music Conserv., Stockholm; Studied w. Pierre Tournier, Zurich & Geneva; Gregor Piatigorsky, Los Angeles. Debut: Stockholm, 1970. Career: Solo-Cellist, Stockholm Phil. Orch.; Apps. on Swedish & German Radio & Swedish TV. w. Stockholm Phil. Orch. Address: Tvistevagen 16, 162 24 Vallingby, Sweden.

LAW, Daniel Ping-Leung, b. 3 May 1946. Hong Kong. Composer; Conductor; Theorist. Educ: BA, Chinese Univ. of Hong Kong; MMus, Northwestern Univ., Ill., USA; PhD, ibid. m. Irene Wong, 1 d. Career: lectr. in music, Chinese Univ. of Hong Kong; cond.; num. choirs in mainly a cappella works; cond., num. orchs.; formerly asst. music ed.; Summy Birchard Publications Ltd.; examiner, Hong Kong Univ. extra-mural studies. Comps. incl: Medieal Suite, 1977; Trio, for oboe, bass clarinet & piano, 1978; Alleluia, for a cappella choir, 1979; Variations on a Chin Theme, for violin, piano, flute & tape, 1977. Publs: Perspectives on Church Music, 1978. Mbr. num. profl. socs. Hon: Pi Kappa Lambda. Address: D-32, Staff Residence, Chinese Univ. of Hong Kong, Station, NT, Hong Kong.

LAW, Nellie Winifred, b. 23 Mar. 1901. Devonport, UK. Pianist; Lecturer; Broadcaster; Adjudicator; Examiner; Conductor. Educ: RCM, London; ARCM; MRST; further pvte. study w. Herbert Fryer (piano) & Louise Trenton (singing). Career: Sr. Music Mistress. N Grammar Schl., Portsmouth, Hon. Cond., Tangmere Choirs, Solo Artist, Pianist & Singer., 1932-39; Sr. Music Mistress, Westonbirt Schl., Hon. Cond., Fndr., Westonbrit & Dist. Music Club, 1940-53; Schl. broadcasts, 1943-63; O'seas (E & S Africa, Rhodeisa, Cairo, Malta, Cyprus, Singapore, Borneo, Hong Kong, NZ). Examiner,

Lectr., Recitalist, Broadcaster. 1964-68; Adjudicator at Fest., GB & O'seas & Examiner, 1962-. Mbrships: ISM; Warden of Schl. Music Sect., ibid., 1958. Hobbies: Walking; Knitting; Reading. Address: Brabourne, Old Bristol Rd., E. Brent, Highbridge, Somerset TA9 4HU, UK. 3.

LAWLEY, John William Graham, b. 11 July, 1944. Stafford, UK. Musician (Oboe & Cor Anglais). Educ: RAM; LRAM; ARCM; GRSM; studies w. Leonard Brain, 1963-67. Career: Prin. oboe, Eng. Nat. Opera, 1967-77; oboist, Londn Symph. Orch., 1978-. Hobbies: Squash; Tennis; Walking. Address: 9 Dukes Ave., London N3, UK.

LAWLOR, Thomas, b. 17 June, 1938. Dublin, Ireland. Bass-Baritone. Educ: BA, Univ. Coll. Dublin; Performer's Course, GSM, 3 yrs. m. Pauline Wales, 1 d. Career: Prin. Roles, D'oyly Carte Opera Co.; ENO; Phoenix Opera; 'Glyndebourne Fest. Opera; Wexford Opera Fest.; Kent Opera; Engl. Music Theatre Co.; Glyndebourne Touring Opera; Royal Opera House, Covent Gdn.; Netherlands Opera, 1977. Recordings: HMS Pinafore & Yeoman of the Guard (Decca); Cox & Box (Pye). Hobbies: Reading; Theatre; Cinema; DIY. Mgmt: Music Int., 13 Ardilaun Rd., Highbury, London N5. Address: 51 Fitzjohns Rd., Lewes, Sussex, UK.

LAWRENCE, Anne Dorothy, b. 11 Mar, 1922. Glasgow, Scotland. Music Administrator-Teacher. Educ: RSAM, 4 yrs. Dip., in Musical Educ: LRAM. (Ptte.t); Tchr. Trng. Qual., Jordanhill Coll. of Educ. Career: Music Tchr. Trng. Scotland, London, Wilts.; Nat. Music Advsr., YWCA of GB, 1949-52; Asst. & Co. Music Advsr., Glas. LEA, 1954-58; Co. Music Advsr., W Sussex Co. Coun., 1960-69; Sr. Lectr., Bognor Coll. of Educ.; Fndr. Hd., Dept. of Music, Chichester Coll. of Cond., Chichester Singers, 1960-; Guest Cond.; Adjudicator, E Eussex, Wilts., Northants., Yeovil & Malta. Mbrships: ISM. Hons: Bronze Medal, RSAM; Medals for Piano, Harmony & Counterpoint; Students Soc. Prize; Macfarlane & Schlrship for Singing. Hobbies: Singing; Cond.; Reading; Gardening. Address: 11 Belgrave Crescent Chichester PO19 2RY, Sussex, UK.

LAWRENCE, Arthur Peter, b. 15 July 1937. Durham, NC, USA. Associate Professor of Music; Organist; Harpsichordist; Teacher; Conductor. Educ: AB., Davidson Coll.; AMLS., Univ. of Mich.; M Mus., Schl. of Music, Fla. State Univ.; DMA., Stanford Univ.; ChM., AAGO., AGO; Presiding Bishop's Cert., Protestant Episc. Ch. of Am. Career: Dir. of Music, All Souls Parish, Berkeley, Calif., 1963-66; Asst. Univ. organist, Stanford Univ., 1966-68; Acting Univ. Organist, ibid., 1968; Instr., Music, Centre Coll. of Ky., 1968-69; Assoc. Prof., Music, & Acting Chmn., St. Mary's Coll., Ind., 1969-; Ed., The Diapason, 1976-; Organ, Harpsichord Recitals, num. churches, cathedrals & univs., USA, UK, France, Germany, Austria. Publs: Co-ed., Harpsichord Music in Print, 1974. Contbr. to profl. jrnls. Mbrships: Dean, St. Joseph Valley Chapt., Treas., San Fran. Chapt., AGO; Am. Musicol. Soc.; Coll. Music Soc. Music Lib. Assn.; AAUP. Hons: Theodore Presser Fndn. Schlrship., 1958; Selected Student Cond., Aspen Choral Fndn., 1970. Hobbies: Organ building; Gardening. Address: Dept. of Music, St. Mary's Coll., Notre Dame, IN 46556, USA.

LAWRENCE, David John, b. 12 Sept. 1955. London, UK. Piano Accompanist; Solo Painist; Conductor; Piano Teacher. Educ: B Mus, Univ. London, 1974-77; Lic., Royal Acad. Music, London, 1974-78; Assoc., Royal Coll. Music. Debut: Leighton House, 1979. Recordings: Harmonium player in Shostakovich Ballet, Age of Gold w. London Phil./Haitink; Austrian Radio recording of Sonatina by Walter Kainz, Radio Graz, 1979. Mbrships: Incorp. Soc. of Musicians; The Musicians' Union. Recip. Pianoforte Professors' Mem. Prize, Royal Acad. Music, 1975. Hobbies: Touring; Travel; Films. Address: 2 Malborough Ave., Edgware, Middx., HA8 8UH, UK.

LAWRENCE, Douglas Howard, b. 26 Sept. 1942. Los Angeles, Calif., USA. Baritone; Voice Teacher. Educ: B Mus, Univ. of Southern Calif., M Mus., ibid. m. Darlene Brudi Lawrence, 1 s. 1 d. Career: has sung with most major US symph. orchs. & opera cos.; num. perfs. in Germany. Recordings: w. S German Radio; Britten's War Requiem (Klavier Records). Mbr., Nat. Asn. of Tchrs. of Singing. Hons: Nat. Opera Inst. Grant, 1972; Sullivan Fndn. Grant, 1972. Hobby: Tennis. Mgmt: Hurok Concerts Inc. Addess: 23142 Dolorosa St., Woodland Hills, CA 91364, USA.

LAWRENCE, Lucile. New Orleans, USA. Harpist; Teacher. Educ: Studied w. Salzedo & Edgard Varesé. Career: 123 Concerts, Aust. & NZ, 1925; Fac. Mbr., Curtis Inst., 1927; Toured as soloist w. Salzedo Harp Ensemble, 1927; Organized & toured w. Lawrence Harp Quintette; Guest Tchr., Denver Coll. of Music, 1928; num. solo apps., USA; Organized harp

Dept. at Pa. Musical Acad., 1932-33; w. Radio City Music Hall, 1932-39; Freelance perf., radio, concerts, ballet, TV, chmbr. music; Concerts for Young Audiences, w. Claude Monteux, Balt. & NY, 1955; Brattleboro Music Center, 1964; Panelist, 19th Biennial Conference of the E MENC in Buffalo, 1964; Recitalist, Lectr., Harp Week, van Beinam Fndn., Netherlands, 1966; Harp clinic, Houston, 1966; Tchr., 1967-; currently Tchr., Boston Univ., The Manhattan Schl., Mannes Coll. num. recordings. Ed., num. works by CPE Bach, GF Handel, etc. Publs. incl: The ABC of Harp Playing; Method for the Harp (w. Carlos Salzedo). Mbrships: 1st Pres., Am. Harp Soc. Address: 7 Roosevelt Ave., Larchmont, NY 10533, USA.

LAWRENCE, Martin, b. 26 Sept. 1909. London, UK. Opera Singer. Educ: Pvte. study of Voice w. Mark Raphael, Spencer Clay, George Cunelli & others; Musical studies w. Georg Knepler & Alberto Erede. m. Lily Altman, 1 s. 1 d. Debut: w. Carl Rosa Opera Co., Hull, 1944. Career: Concerts, Musical Comedy, Pantomime, Oratorio; Opera at Covent Garden, Sadlers Wells, New London Opera at Cambridge Theatre perfs. in Wales, Repub. of Ireland, Aust., etc.; Film, radio & TV apps.; Dir., of Music, New London Synagogue, St. Johns Wood, London, 1965-. Recordings: Duet from Donizetti, Don Pasquale, w. M Stabile; Showboat; Chu Chin Chow; Negro Spirituals. Contbr. to musical & other jrnls. Mbr., profl. assns. Hobbies: Reading; Listening to & Performing Music. Address: 46 W Heath Drive, London NW11 7QH, UK.

LAWRENCE, Robert, b. 18 Mar. 1912. NYC, USA. Conductor; Author; Critic; Lecturer. Educ: BA, CCNY; MA, Columbia Univ.; Dip. in Cond., Juilliard Grad. Schl. Career: Artistic Dir. & Cond., Friends of French Opera; Assoc. Prof. Music, Temple, Univ.; Cond., Phoenix, Ariz. Symph., 1949-52, & Presidential Symph. of Turkey, 1957-59. cond. symph. orchs. in USA, Europe & S Am. Recording: (as Cond.) Mozart Arias, Eleanor Steber & Symph. of Air. Publs: Victor Book of Ballet, 1949; The World of Opera, 1956; A Rage for Opera, 1971; The Great French Operas & the Famous (in preparation). Contbr. to: High Fidelity; Musical Am. Mbr., The Bohemians Club. Hobbies: Travel; Languages. Addess: 140 E 28th St., NY, NY 16016, USA. 2.

LAWRENCE, Sheila, b. 12 Dec. 1945. Ootakamund, India. Concert Organist. Educ: RAM; LARM; GRSM. m. Peter Mitton, 1 s. Debut: Purcell Room, Dec. 1973. Career: Dir. Music, Servite Priory, London; Radio 3 broadcasts; Recitals, major ch. network; Special interest, Organ reform & has had built portable chmbr. organ; Specialises in early mid Baroque music, esp. N German & Italian schls.; Recitals, Germany, Denmark, Netherlands & Italy; Fndr. Mbr. BOA & NEOS. Mbrships: RCO; ISM; ISOB; Organ Club. Hobbies: Gardening; Walking; Cooking; Arch.; Stained glass windows. Mgmt: Terry Stasberg Agency. Address: 22 Liverpool Rd., Kingston-upon-Thames, Surrey, KT2 7SZ, UK.

LAWRENCE, Sidney Jason, b. 28 Oct. 1909. New Rochelle, NY, USA. Author; Composer; Inventor; Adminstrator; Teacher; Lecturer. Educ: Metropolitan Music Schl., NYC; CCNY; studied Comp. & Piano w. var. tchrs. m. Yvette Geller, 1 s., 2 d. Career: Pres., Neighbourhood Music Schl., 1940-53; Problem Cons., Hd. of Rsch. Div., ibid., Harbour Conserv. & Metropolitan Music Schl., NYC; Fndr., Harbor Conserv. for Musical Growth, Hewlett, NY, 1951-; Assoc. Ed., Musician Mag. Comps: Over 40 piano & instrumental, incl. Driftwood (flute); Tandem (clarinet duet). Publs: incl: Remedial Sightreading for Piano Student, 1964; This Business of Music Practising, 1967; Behavioral Profile of Piano Student, 1978. Contbr. to music jrnls. Mbrships: incl: ASCAP; MENC. Hobby: Bicycling. Address: 229 Oakford St., W Hempstead, NY 11552, USA.

LAWRENCE-ARCHER, E A, b. 6 Apr. 1943. Preston, UK. Timpanist; Percussion; Orchestral Adminstrator. Educ: RAM; LRAM; ARAM. Career: Free-lance work w. most ldng. orchs., London & UK, major ballet & opera cos.; Musician, mgr., Engl. Music Theatre Co. (formerly Engl. Opera Grp.), 1976-; Admnstr., Philomusica of London; Mng. Dir., Conchord Mgmt. Ltd. Hobbies: Riding; Spanish; Guitar; Reading; Painting. Address: 8 Deepdene, 58 Luttrell Ave., London, SW15, UK.

LAWRY, Eleanor McChesney, b. 17 June 1908. Pitcairn, Pa., USA. Musicologist; Piansit; Teacher. Educ: Pitts. Musical Inst., Pa., 1925-28; studied piano w. Wynne Pyle, NYC, 1929-41; AB., Washinghton Sq. Col., NY Univ.; attended Harold Bauer's Master Classes, 1931-32; MA, Grad. Schl. of Arts & Sci., NY Univ., 1947; PhD (musicol.), ibid., 1954. Career: Recitals & Lectures; Illustrated Radio lecture for Charles Maubiel, 1943. Publs: Historical Chart of Composers, 1937; Co-Author, Chapt. on 16th Century Italian Instrumental Music, Reese, Music in the Renaissance, 1954; The Psalm Motets of Claude Goudimel, 1954; Claude Goudimel, Oeuvres Complétes, vols. II, IV, VI,

VIII, 1967-73. Contbr. to: Ency. Americana; Diapason. Mbrships: Int. Musicol. Soc.; Am. Musicol. Soc.; Renaissance Soc.; Music Lib. Assn.; AAUW; Music Tchrs. Nat. Assn.; NY State Music Tchrs. Assn.; NY Fedn. of Music Clubs; Nat. Guild Piano Tchrs. (Fac. Mbr.). Hon: Fellowship for Study in French Libs., AAUW, 1955-56. Hobby: Playing Cello in Ensemble. Address: 186 Pinehurst Ave., NY, NY 10033, USA. 6, 11.

LAWSON, Peter, b. 11 Apr. 1950. Manchester, UK. Concert Pianist; Piano Tutor. Educ: Royal Manchester Coll. of Music; Royal Northern Coll. of Music; GRSM; ARMCM. m. Ariane Lawson. Career: Concert Pianist; apps. throuthout UK, Europe & USA; Broadcasts for BBC, French, Dutch & Belgian radio; apps. w. Royal Liverpool Phil. Orch. Mbrships: Musicians Union; ISM. Address: Slimtop Cottage, Cross St., Broadbottom, Hyde, Cheshire, UK.

LAWTON, Sidney Maurice, b. 28 Oct. 1924. Stechford, UK. Director of Music. Educ: Mus B., ARCO; ARMCM; Manchester Univ. & RMCM, 1942-43, 1945-47. Career: Dir. of Music, Queen's Coll., Taunton, UK., 1947-. Compositions & Arrangements (OUP): The Young Clarinettist, 3 vols.; A Book of Clarinet Duets; The Young Flautist, 3 vols.; The Clarinettist's Book of Carols; The Young Trumpet Player, 3 vols.; The Brass Quartet, 2 vols.; The Young Oboist, 3 vols.; Handel, Overture in C, Ed., 3 clarinets; A Book of Clarinet Trios; The Young Trombonist, 3 vols.; The Young Horn Player, 3 vols.; Telemann, Musique Heroique; The Windband Book; Old Engl. Trumpet Tunes; Windscore Series, Nos. 1-10 (Novello); Fugue On A Nursey Theme (New Wind Music Co.). Author, The Wind Orchestra (OUP) Contbr. to A Handbook For Music Teachers, 1968 (London Univ. Inst. of Educ. & Novello). Mbrships: RCO; ISMMusic Masters Assn.; Brit. Soc. of Dowsers. Hobbies: Dowsing; Healing Techniques. Address: Dir. of Music, Queen's Col., Tauton, Somerset, UK. 3, 28, 30.

LAY, Kenneth John, b. 14 Aug. 1953. Broken Hill, NSW, Aust. Music Educator; Pianist; Organist; Violist; Teacher. Educ: Newcastle Conserv., dip., music educ., 1975; accredited pvte. music tchr., keyboards. Debut: as pianist, Broken Hill, 1976. Career: tchr., secondary schls., NSW; lectr., Univ. of NSW, Robinson Coll.; prin. violist, Broken Hill Civic Orch. Mbrships: incl: chmn. & asst. cond., Broken Hill Civic Orchestra; fndr. & cond., Broken Hill Baroque Ensemble & Vocal Consort; sec., Broken Hill Branch, Arts Coun. of SA; Aust. Soc. for Music Educ.; local organising sec., Music Examinations Advsry. Bd. Address: 299 Iodide St., Broken Hill, NSW 2880, Aust.

LAYCOCK, Geoffrey Newton Stephen, b. 27 Jan. 1927. York, UK. Lecturer in Music, Organist; Pianist; Harpsichordist; Conductor. Educ: RCM; GRSM; ARCM; LRAM; LTCL; ARCO. m. Audrey Jamson, 2 d. Career: Prin. Lectr. in Music, Keswick Hall Coll. of Educ., Norwich Publs: New Catholic Hymnal, 1971. Contbr. to num. profl. jrnls. Mbr., num. profl. orgs. Hobby: Daydreaming. Address: 37 Brettingham Ave., Cringleford, Norwich, Norfolk, NR 4 6XJ, UK. 3.

LAYCOCK, Jolyon, b. 31 July 1946. Bath, UK. Composer; Teacher; Artist Working in Audio-Visual Media. Educ: BMus, Nottingham Univ., 1968; Master of Philos., 1970; ARCM (pianoforte tchrs.), 1965. m. Katherine Anna Price, 1s. Career: Birmingham Arts Laboratory, Dir. of Sound Workshop, 1970-74; Freelance touring Artist, 1973-77; Dir. of Sound Studio, Spectro Arts Workshop, Newcastle, 1976-78; Music & Dance Co-ordinator, Arnolfini, Bristol, 1979-; Lectr. for Extra-mural, Univ. & Coll. Depts.; Num. one-man shows of Audio Visual & Electronic installations at major provincial British Galleries. Publs: Tyrannos- 12 Audio-Visual Cycles. Contbr. to: Contact. Mbrships: Nottingham Midland Group of Artists; British Electro-Acoustic Music Assn.; British Section Panel, ISCM. Hobbies: Gardening; Wine-making; Cooking. Address: 18 Monmouth Rd., Bishoptown, Bristol 7, UK.

LAYTON, Billy Jim, b. 14 Nov. 1924. Corsicana, Tex., USA. Composer. Educ: B Mus, New England Conserv. of Music, 1948; M Mus, Yale Univ. Schl. of Music, 1950; PhD., Harvard Univ., 1960. m. Evro Zeniou, 1 s., 1 d. Compositions: 3 Dylan Thomas Poems for Mixed Chorus & Brass Sextet; Divertimento for Violin, Clarinet, Bassoon, Cello, Trombone, Harpsichord & Percussion. Recordings of own work: 5 Studies for Violin & Piano, Opus 1; String Quartet in 2 Movements, Opus 4; 3 Studies for Piano, Opus 5. Contbr., past mbr., Ed. Bd., Perspectives of New Music, Mbrships. Trustee, Am. Acad., Rome; Mbr. of Bd., Am. Music Ctr.; ASCAP; Am. Soc. of Univ. Composers: Am. Musicol. Soc. Address: 4 Johns Rd., Setauket, NY 11733, USA. 2, 6.

LAYTON, Robert, b. 2 May 1930. London, UK. Music Talks Producer, BBC. Educ: Worcester Coll., Oxford; MA (Oxon.); Univs. of Uppsala & Stockholm; studied comps. w. Edmund

Rubbra, hist. of music w. Egon Wellesz; further studies w. Prof. Carl-Allan Mobert. m. Ingrid Nina Thompson. Career: Swedish Film Industry, 1954-55; tchr. in Londn, 1956-59; BBC Music Division, 1959- (music presentation, 1959, music talks, 1960) Gen. Ed., BBC Music Guides, 1973-. Publs. incl: Franz Berwald, 1959; Jean Sibelius, 1965; Sibelius & his World, 1970; Dvorak Symphonies & Concertos, 1977; Sibelius, 1981. Contbr. incl: The Symphony (ed. R Simpson), 1966; The Gramophone; The Listener; The Times, etc.; profl. jrnls. in UK & Sweden. var. mbrships. Address: 112 Goldhurst Terr., London NW6 3HR, UK. 14.

LAZAR, Joel, b. 19 Mar. 1941. NYC, USA. Conductor. Educ: AB magna cum laude Harvard Univ., 1961; AM, ibid., 1963; Cond's Course, Aspen Music Fest., 1959-61 & '64 & at Berks. Music Ctr., 1962-63; Student of Richard Burgin, 1959-65; Asst. to Jascha Horenstein, 1971-73. m. Susan Gaber. Debut: Cambridge, Mass., 1959. Career: Tchr. & Cond., Harvard Univ., 1959-71; NY Univ., 1966-69, Univ. of Va., 1969-71; USA & Local premieres of maj. works of Honegger, Mahler, Nielsen, Piston, Holst; Fndr. & Cond., Cantabrigia Orch., Cambridge, Mass., 1965-71; European debut w. BBC Northern Symph. Orch., 1973- Apps. w. Danish Radio Symph. Orch. & Tivoli Concert Orch., Copenhagen, 1973-74; Scottish Baroque Ensemble, 1975. Contbr. to: Notes, High Fidelity. Mbrships: Phi Beta Kappa, 1960; Hon. Mbr., Bruckner Soc. of Am., 1969. Hons: Scholarships & Fellowships from Harvard Univ., Wesley Weyman Fund, Frank Huntington Beebe Fund, Koussevitsky Fellowship, 1963. Hobby: Cats; Chinese food. Mgmt: Robert Angles, Ltd., London. Address: 37a Newington Green, London N 16 9PR, UK.

LEACH, Andrew James Barnett, b. Dec. 1937. Willerby, nr. Hull, UK. Church Organist; Harpsichord Player; Private Teacher; School Music Master. Educ: Royal Manchester Coll. of Music, 1957-60; ARMCM in organ tchng. & schl. music. Debut: (Europe) organ recital Nicolaikerk, Appingedam, N Holland, 1976. Career incls: Asst. Organist, Beverly Minster, 1960-67, 74-78; Master of Music, Howden Minster, 1967-72; Organist & Choirmaster, Elloughton Parish Ch., N Humberside, 1972-77; Organist & Choirmaster, Welton Parish Ch., N Humberside, 1977-; pvte. tchng., organ, piano, theory; var. schl. appts., Hd. of Music, Howden Schl., 1967-; Organ & Harpsichord Continuo, E Riding Co. Choir, 1968-; Organ Recitalist, inclng. local & nat. BBC broadcasts; broadcast ch. servs., Radio Hilversum, BBC radio & TV, ITV. Mbrships: RCO; ISM; Inc. Assn. of Organists; Pres., Hull & Dist. Organists Assn., 1975-76; Brit. Inst. of Organ Studies; Die Gesellschaft der Orgelfreunde. Hons: FRSA. Address: 4 The Octagon, Willerby, Hull, HU10 6BL, UK. 3, 28, 29.

LEACH, John, b. 29 July 1931. London, UK. Composer; Cimbalom Player. Educ: TCL, State Acad., Vienna, Austria. m. Joanna Leach, 1 s. 1 d. Career: Freelance Cimbalom Player w. major Symph. Orchs. of Europe; Freelance Comp. of documentaryu films, plays for BBC, etc. Comps: Variations for Cimbalom; Dithyrambs for Harp & Cimbalom; Suite for Unaccompanied Double Bass; Sinfonia Orientalis. Recordings: Kodály, Háry János Suite, w. Vienna Phil., LSO, Phil. Hungarica, & Berlin Radio Symph. Orch.; Stravinsky, Renard w. Suisse Romande. Contbr. to: Music & Letters; Consort; Composer. Mbrships incl: Gov. & Hon. Archivist, Royal Soc. Musicians; Fellow, Royal Asiatic Soc. Recip., Arts Coun. Award, 1955. Hobby: Walking. Address: 7 Felden St., London SW6 5AE, UK.

LEA-COX, Peter, b. 21 June 1945. Bournemouth, UK. Organist; Harpsichordist; Conductor; Administrator. Educ: RAM; BMus; FRCO; ARAM; GRSM; FTCL; ARCM. Career: Asst. Course Off., RAM, 1973-; Master of Music, St. Jude-on-the-Hill, NWII, 1973-; Organist, St. Mary-at-Hill, EC3, 1976-; Cond., People's Palace Choral Soc., 1975-, North London Opera, 1976-, Music in Central Sq., 1976-; Harpsichordist, London Baroque Ensemble & Regent Sinfonia. Mbrships: Sec., N London Soc. of Organists; Deanery rep. (W. Barnet), Royal Schl. of Ch. Music. Recip., Stewart Macpherson Prize, RAM, 1966. Hobbies: Gardening; Meteorology; Astronomy. Address: St. Jude-on-the-Hill, Central Sq., London NW11, UK.

LEADER, Harry, b. London, UK. Music Director; Musician; Clarinet, Saxophone, Flute, Novelty Instruments. Educ: Grammar schl.; Pvte. study w. father, Trumpet, m. Rona. Career: Band Ldr., Hammersmith Palais, 4 yrs., Astoria Danse Salon, 15 yrs., Regent Ballroom, Brighton, 4 yrs.; Toured UK. w. stage shows, one night stands; Own TV show, 1948; BBC radio apps. compositions: Over 350, inclng. Tonight's the Night, Dragon Fly, South Paw Special, Dance Dance Dance, Back to Those Old Kentucky Days, Lead the Way. Recordings on all maj. labels. Mbrships: Chmn., Music Conds. Assn., Performing Rights Soc.; Mechanical Copyright Protection Soc.; BBC Club; Song-writers Guild of GB; Barker, Variety Club of GB. Hons: Winner, All-England Brass Band Contest, for march comps. & arrs. Brit. Brass

Band Conds. Assn., 1970; Gold Badge of Merit (services to British music), Songwriters Guild of GB. Hobbies: Judo; Snooker. Address: Prestone, 114 Preston Dr., Brighton, Sussex, UK.

LEAH, Philip John, b. 23 Oct. 1948. Dulwich, London, UK. Teacher of Flute. Educ: GNSM, Northern School of Music, Manchester; Post grad. Cert. in Educ., Padgate Coll. of Educ., Warrington. m. Joyce Woolridge. Comps: Fanfare for a Golden Jubilee, 1970; Conversation for Flute & Piano, 1971: Acme, a suite for chmbr. orch.; Sinfonia for Chmbr. Orch.; Prelude and Scherzo for String Quartet; Wind Quintet. Mbrships: ISM; Musicians Union. Hobbies: Football; Social Scis. Address: 18 Compton Rd., Halesowen, W Midlands B62 9TD, UK. 3, 28.

LEAR, Evelyn. Soprano. Educ: NY Univ.; Hunter Coll.; Juilliard Opera Workshop; Fulbright Schlrship. to Germany, 1955. M. Thomas Stewart. Debut: Ariadne auf Naxos, Berlin Opera, 1957. Career: Four Last Songs w. LSO, UK, 1957; Mourning Becomes Electra, Met. Opera, NYC, 1967; Wozzeck, La Scala Milan, 1971; regular apps. w. opera cos. & orchs., Europe & USA; Guest apps., Berlin Opera, Vienna State Opera; many recitals. Roles incl: Marie, Wozzeck; Marschallin, Der Rosenkavalier, Countess, Marriage of Figaro; Fiordiligi, Cosi fan Tutti; Desdemona, Othello; Dido, The Trojans; Donna Elvira, Don Giovanni; Tatiana, Eugene Onegin; Lavinia, Mourning Becomes Electra; Lulu. Recip. Concert Artists Guild Award, 1955, 16.

LEASK, Margaret Louise (Cameron), b. 9 Julyu 1929. Cornwall, Ont. Canada. Violinist; Teacher. Educ: Qualified Infant Mistress, Scotland; Var. music tutors inclng. J Peebles Conn. m. John Jamieson Leask, 1s., 1 d. Debut: Carnegie Hall, Dunfermline. Career: Ldr., Barry, Ostlere & Shepherd Orch., Kirkcaldy, 1953-57; Dpty. Ldr., Dunfermline Orchl. Soc., 1955-57; Fndr. & Cond., Tankerton String Players, 1964-; Fndr. & Cond., Whitstable Jr. Orch., 1971-; Tchr., violin, Kent Music Schl., Jr. King's Schl. & King's Schl., Canterbury. Mbrships: ISM; E Kent Dist. Comm., Kent Music Schl. Hons: Dux Music, Dunfermline HS, 1945-46; Highest Award, Fife Music Fest., 1947. Hobbies: Painting; Drawing. Address: 3 Foxgrove Rd., Tankerton, Whitstable, Kent, UK.

LEAVINS, Arthur, b. 14 July 1917. Leicester, UK. Violinist. Educ: LRAM (Perf. Tchrs.); ARAM. m. Mary Baddeley, 2 s. Debut: New Zealand, 1925. Career: W Catterall Quartet; Ldr., RPO; Sub-Ldr., BBC Symph. Orch.; Ldr., BBC Concert Orch. Recordings: Orchl.; Histoire du Soldat. Mbr. Royal Soc. of Musicians. Recip. of Jonathan North Medal. Hobbies: Readings; Gardening; Golf. Address: 17 Highfield Dr., Bromley, Kent, UK.

LEAVITT, Donald Lee, b. 2 Sept. 1929. Annapolis, Md., USA. Librarian. Educ: BA, Am. Univ.; Ind. Univ. (musicol.). m. Nadine Slater Leavitt, 1d., 1 s. Career: Chief, Music Div., Lib. of Congress, Wash., DC. Contbr. to: Notes; Fontes Artis Musicae; Library Trends; Phonographic Bulletin. Mbrships: Pres., Record Libs. Commission, Int. Assn. of Music Libs.; Pres., Int. Assn. of Sound Archives; Music Lib. Assn.; Am. Musicol. Soc., etc. Address: 12602 Crimson Ct., Bowie, MD 20715, USA.

LEAVITT, Joseph. Chelsea, Mass., USA. Musician; Arts Administrator; Producer; Author; Teacher. Educ: AB, Am. Univ., Wash. DC; New Engl. Conserv. of Music; Boston Univ.; Manhattan Schl. of Music. m. Sally Elissa, 1s., 1 d. Career: Percussionist & tympanist w. var. orchs. on radio, TV & film soundtracks, 1949-69; Gen. Mgr., NJ Symph., 1969-71, Balt. Symph. Orch., 1973-; Exec. Prof., Wolf Trap Fndn. for Performing Arts, Vienna, Va., 1970-73; former fac., mbr., Peabody Conserv. & Cath. HS, Balt.; Prin. Instr., Arts Mgmt. Intern Prog., Univ. of Md., 1974-. Publs: Reading by Recognitions, 1960; The Rhythms of Contemporary Music, 1962. Contbr. to jrnls. Sev. recordings. Mbrships. incl: Bd. of Dirs., Int. Soc. Performing Arts Admnstrs. Recip. var. hons. Address: Hampton Garth, Towson, MD 21204, USA. 2, 3.

LEBERMANN, Walter K H, b. 23 Feb. 1910. Karlsuhe, Germany. Violinist; Violist; Musicologist; Lexicographer. Educ: Music Coll., Karlshue; Dr. Hoch's Conserv., Frankfurt. m. Erla T Diekmann, 2 s., 1 d. Career: w. Radio Symph. Orch., Frankfurt, 1937-64; worked w. many publrs. inclng. Barenreiter, Breitkopf & Härtel, Eulenburg, Peters, Polsky Wydawnictwo Muzyczne, Silorski, Simrock, etc. Comps: incl: Kadenzen zu Instrumentalkonzerten. Has edited works by many comps. Contbr. to publs. in field. Mbrships: Arbeitsgemeinschaft für mittelrheinische Musikgesichte; Int. Viola Rsch. Soc. Address: Stift Tepl Str. 6, D-638 Bad Homburg, German Fed. Repub.

LEBIČ, Lojze, b. 23 Aug. 1934. Prevalje, Korosko, Yugoslavia. Composer; Conductor. Educ: MA, Archaeol.; M Mus, Comp. & Conducting. m. Ukmar Jelena-Lebic, 1 child. Career: incls: Cond., Chmbr. Choir, Ljubljana Radio-TV, 1962-72; Concerts throughout Europe; TV & Radio apps; Prof. of Pedagogical Acad. Comps. incl: Burnt Grass (cantata); Korant (for Orch.); Sentence (orch. & 2 pianos); Glasovi (strings); Kons A, B (chmbr. ensemble); Tangram (chmbr. orch.); Atelier II (electronic music); Vocal & Choral Music; Music for Stage, etc. Recordings icnl: Anthology of Croation Music; Motets & Madrigals: I Fiamminghi in Europa. Mbr. var. orgs. Hons. incl: Winer, class trophy (contemporary music), Let the People, Sing, BBC, 1972; Preseren Fond Prize, 1966, '70; 9 awards at Yugoslav Radio Music Fests. Hobby: Archaeol. Mgmt: Musikverlage Hans Gerig Colgne Drususgasse 7-11. Address: Celovska 127, 61000 Ljubljana, Yugoslavia.

LEDBETTER, David John, b. 19 Aug. 1943. Dublin, Ireland. Lecturer; Harpsichordist. Educ: MusB (Dublin); MA (Dublin, Oxon.); ARCM; Dip. of Staatliche Hochschule für Musik, Freiburg. Career: Lectr., Royal Northern Coll. of Music; Concerts & broadcasts, England, Ireland, Germany. Contbr. to: MGG. Mbrships: Royal Musical Assn.; The Lute Soc. Address: Royal Northern Coll. of Music, 124 Oxford Rd., Manchester M13 9RD, UK.

LEDERER, Franz Joseph, b. 16 June 1936. Moosburg, Germany. Director of Studies. Educ: Civic Acad. of Music, Munich; musicol. studies, Regensburg; PhD. Career: production of Bavarian Radio broadcast, Deutsche Messe zu Ehren des H1. Gregorius, for 4 voices a capella; Deutsche Messe Nr. 2, Requiem in memoriam patris. Comps. incl: 3 masses; 4 Advent songs; 4 Communion songs; 2 funeral songs; Num jauchzt den Herren, motet; Ehre sei Gott in der Höhe, canonic motet for 3-voice female choir; Credo song; Offertorium. Publs: monograph on the Catholic Werke eines süddeutschen Klosterkomponisten. Mbrships: Soc. for Music Rsch., Cassel; Assn. of Bavarian Music Masters. Hobbies: Musicology; Literature; Philosophy. Address: Ganzemllerstr. 19, 8050 freising, German Fed. Repub.

LEDERMAN, Sidney. London, UK. Violinist; Teacher. Educ: ARCM, FLCM (perf.); studied w. Max Rostal & Campoli. m. Joan Teresa Field. Career: solo perfs. throughout UK; mbr., Israel Symph. Orch., 1955-66; mbr., Eng. Nat. Opera, 1967-. Hobbies: Composing music; Writing Poetry; Painting & Repairing Porcelain. Address: London, UK.

LEDGER, Philip Stevens, b. 12 Dec. 1937. Bexhill-on-Sea, UK. Conductor; Organist; Harpsichordist; Pianist. Educ: MA, Mus B, King's Coll., Cambridge; FRCO; LRAM; ARCM. m. Mary Erryl Wells, 1 s., 1 d. Career: Master of the Music, Chelmsford Cathedral, 1962-65; Dir. of Music, Univ. of E. Anglia, 1965-73; Dean, Schl. of Fine Arts & Music, ibid., 1968-71; Artistic Dir., Aldeburgh Fest. of Music & the Arts, 1968-; Cond., Cambridge Univ. Musical Soc., 1973-; Dir. of Music & Organist, King's Coll., Cambridge, 1974-. Recordings: As Cond. (since 1974 at King's Coll.); as Harpsichordist w. Benjamin Britten & Pinchas Zukerman; as Pianist w. Robert Tear. Publs. incl: Ed., Anthems for Choirs 2 & 3, 1973; Six Carols with Descants, 1975. Contbr. to: Musical Times. Mbr., ISM; Athenaeum. Hons. incl: Silver Medal, Worshipful Co. of Musicians, 1961. Hobbies: Swimming; Theatre. Address: 15 Dane Dr., Cambridge CB3 9LP, UK. 1, 3.

LEDLOVA-KOPECKY, Dagmar, b. 22 Sept. 1935. Bystrice Pod, Hostynem, Czechoslovakia. Concert Organist; Lecturer; Teacher. Educ: State Conserv. of Music, Brno, Czechoslovakia, 1951-56; Franz Liszt Acad. of Music, Weimar, Germany, 1956-57; Acad. of Music Arts, Prague, Czech., 1957-61. m. Ernest John Kopecky, 1 s. Debut: Solo Concerts in Czech., 1956; Germany, 1957; Russian, 1959; Concerts w. Orch., Prague, Czech., 1958; NY, USA, 1971, etc. Career: Concerts given in all maj. cities in Czech., Russian; Int. Organ Fest. at EXPO '67, Montreal; Nat. Conven., AGO, Buffalo, NY.; NY Phil., Lincoln Ctr., NY; Toronto, Hamilton, etc. Recordings: Supraphon Records; Canadian Broadcasting Corp's 'Organists in Recital' (mainly Czech & Canadian Organ muisc). Mbrships: RCCO, Toronto; Czech. Soc. of Arts & Scis., USA; Am. Fed. of Musicians; Fac. Assn., Royal Conserv. of Music, Univ. of Toronto. Hons: Hon. recognition, Int. Organ Comp., Prague, Czech., 1958; Winner, Prague Academy's Organ Comp., 1961. Hobbies: Reading; Travel; Visiting Art Galleries. Address: 52 Holmesdale Cresc., Toronton, Ont. M6E 1Y, Can. 27, 29.

LEDUC, Claude Alphonse, b. 22 July 1910. Lieusaint, France. Music Publisher. m. Blanche Lerouc, 3 s., 1 d. Career: Music Publr., 1928-; Successor to father, 1951; Jt. Mgr. & Co-Proprietor (w. brother, Gilbert Leduc.), Editions Alphonse Leduc. Publs. eds. of num. composers, inclng. Alain, Albeniz, Bitsch, Bozza, Casteréde, Jaques Charpentier, Ibert, Jolivet, Messiaen, Mihalovici, Pierné, Rivier, Sauguet, Romasi, & W Weber. Mbrships: VP, 1965, Pres., 1971, Union Chmbr. of French Music; Publrs.; VP, Nat. Committee on Music, 1970-; VP, SACEM (Soc. of Authors, Composers & Publrs. of Music);

Edec., Committee for the Protection of Music, 1965-; Fndr., Mbr., Hunt Soc.; Cercle Foch; Interallied Union. Hobbies: Stag Hunting; Fencing. Address: 175 rue St.-Honore, Paris, 75040, France.

LEDWARD, James Henry, b. Sept. 1954. Liverpool, UK. Director; General Editor; Oboe Professor. Educ: London Coll. of Music Perfs. Course; 2 yrs. advanced course, RAM; FLCM. m. Teresa Ledward. Career: Dir. & Gen. Ed., Nova Music; Oboe Prof., London Coll. of Music. Publs: var. eds. for oboe & piano. Hobby: Sport. Address: 48 Franciscan Rd., London SW17, UK.

LEE, Byong Won, b. 20 Dec. 1941. Yongp'yong, Korea. Professor of Ethnomusicology (Korean music & dance). Educ: BMus, Korean Music, Seoul Nat. Univ., Korea, 1964; MA, Ethnomuculogy, Univ. of Wash., 1971; PhD, Ethnomusicology, ibid., 1974. m. Jin Young Chung. Career: Asst. Prof. of Ethnomusicology, Univ. of Hawaii, Honolulu, 1974-. Contbr. to: Grove's Dict., 6th Ed.; Essays on Asian Music and Theater; The World of Music No. 2; Korean Studies I; Asian Music; The World of Music. Mbrships: Soc. for Ethnomusicology; Int. Folk Music Coun.; Coll. Music Soc.; Korean Musicological Soc. Hons: Fulbright-Hays Fellow, 1972-73; SSRC-ACLS Fellow, 1977. Hobbies: Mountain Climbing; Travel. Address: Music Dept., Univ. of Hawaii, 2411 Dole St., Honolulu, HI 96822, USA.

LEE, Chung, b. 28 April 1942. Tokyo, Japan. Professor of Piano. Educ: Hochschule f. Musik in Wien (Acad.); Dip., piano & chmbr. music (hons.). m. Yoshiko, 2 d. Debut: Vienna, 1967. Career: Concerts, TV & radio apps., Austria, Germany, France, Switz., UK, Poland, USA, Korea, Japan, etc. Sev. recordings. Mbr., Internationale Chopin Gesellschaft in Wien. Hons: Hong Ran Pa Hon., Korea, 1975; First prizes, competitions in Japan & Austria. Hobbies: Photography; Skiing. Mgmt: CH. et. C Kiesgen, Paris; Kajimoto, Tokyo. Address: Steingasse 33/18, A-1030 Vienna, Austria.

LEE, Dennis Ean Hool, b. 2 Dec. 1946. Penang, Malaysia. Pianist. Educ: B Mus, London Univ., 1967; M Mus, RCM, 1968; LRSM; ARCM (Piano Perf.); ARCM (Violin Tchng.); Concert Pianist's Dip., Acad. for Music, Vienna, Austria. Debut: Purcell Room, London, 1969. Career: has app. at Wigmore Hall & Royal Fest. Hall, London; perf. w. BBC Welsh & Northern Orchs., Royal Liverpool Phil.; Radiotelevision Italian (Milan). & Slovak Chmbr. Orch. (Bratislava); has made live & recorded broadcasts for BBC-Radio 3; app. at Cheltenham Int. Fest.; has toured Far E. & Europe. & has recorded Ravel duets w. Phillippe Entremont (CBS) & for radio & for TV in Bremen, Bavaria, Bavaria, Italy, Malaysia, Singapore, Taiwan, Czechoslakia & Cannes; opps. in the Philippines & Adelaide Fest., Aust. Mbr: ISM. Recip. of many awards inclng: 1st Prize, Royal Overseas League Fest., 1968, & Stepanow Competition, Vienna, 1969. Hobbies: Reading; Theatre; Travel. Mgmt: Ingpen & Williams Ltd., 14 Kensington Ct., London W8, UK. Address: 36 Burleigh Road, Sutton, Surrey SM3 9NE.

LEE, Douglas Allen, b. 3 Nov. 1932. Carmel, Ind., USA. Professor of Musicology & Piano. Educ: B Mus, De Pauw Univ., M Mus, PhD, Univ. of Mich.; Studied piano & Musicol. w. var. tchrs. m. Beverly Haskell. Publs: The Works of Christoph Nichelmann, 1971; Christoph Nichelmann Clavier Concertos in E & A (Ed.), 197; Six Embellished Sonatas of Franz Benda (Ed.), in press; A Thematic Index of the Works of Franz Benda (in prep.) Contbr. to: Musical Quarterly; Grove's Dict., 6th ed. Kan. Music Review. Mbrships: Am. Musicol. Soc.; Nat. MTA (Chmn., histl. instruments, 1970-72); Am. Soc. for 18th Century Studies; Phi Kappa Phi; Pi Kappa Lambda. Hobby: Photography. Address: Coll. of Fine Arts, Wichita State UKniv., Wichita, KS 67208, USA. 8. 28.

LEE, Gary Thomas, b. 4 Feb. 1946. Provo, Ky., USA. Classical Guitarist; Guitar Instructor. Educ: BA, Univ. of Louisville, Ky., 1972. m. Jane F Lee (div.), 1d. Debut: 1969. Career: Classical Guitarist & Instr., 1965-; Guitar Instr., St. Robert Bellarmine Col., Louisville, Ky.; WAVE TV, 1972; Guitarist w. profl. Shakespearean troupe, summer 1975; Var. concerts. solo & ensemble, Bellarmine Coll., 1972-. Comps: Jota Aragonese, 1975; Classical Variation, Music of the Masters of the 19th Century. Mbrships: Am. String Tchrs. Assn.; Louisville Soc. of the Classical Guitar; Pres., ibid., 1968-71. Guitar Ed. & Contbng. Rschr.-Writer, Int. Guitar & Violin Makers Jrnl., 1968-70. Hobbies incl: Wood instrument repair & rebuilding. Address: 170 Gillette Ave., Louisville, KY 40214, USA.

LEE, Hye-ku, b. 10 Jan. 1909. Seoul, Korea. Radio Executive; Professor. Educ: PhD, Seoul Univ.; pvte. study of violin & 2 Korean instruments. m. (1) Kui-nam Song (dec.); (2) Ki-yong Chong; 3 s., 3 d. Career: Chief of radio stn.; Prof., Dean, Prof. Emeritus, Coll. of Music, Seoul Nat. Univ. Publs: Studies in Korean Music, 1957; Musical Instruments of Korea, 1962; Topics in

Korean Musical Instruments of Korea, 1962; Topics in Korean Music, 1967; Music in the Annals of King Sejong, 1973; Essays on Korean Music, 1976. Contbr. to jrnls. Mbrships: Nat. Acad. of Arts; Pres., Korean Musicol. Soc.; Advsr., Korean Music Coun.; Soc. for Ethnomusicol. Hons: incl: Prize of ARt, 1973. Address: 2-206 Wang-gung Apt. Ichon-dong, Yongsan-ku, Seoul, Korea.

LEE, Robert Charles, b. 22 Mar. 1927. Youngstown, Ohio, USA. Musicologist; Pianist; Composer; Professor. Educ: AB, 1951, MusB, 1956, MusM, 1957, Wichita State Univ., Kan.; Univ. of Warsaw, Inst. of Musicol., 1968-69; PhD, 1970, Univ. of Wash.; pvte. tchr. of piano, theory & comp., Seattle, Wash., 1960-; Educator, Seattel Pub. Schls., 1973-; Sr. Rsch. Fellow (Exchange prof.), Am. Coun. of Learned Socs., Budapest, Hungary, 1970-72; num. solo recitals, chamber & concerto perfs. Comps. incl: Elegy, 1956; Tribute to Domenico Scarlatti, 1963; Cantus Chromatica, 1966; 13 Sketches for Children, 1963, etc. Publs: num. articles for profl. jrnls. esp. on Liszt & Am. Jazz. num. critical eds. & arrs. Mbrships: Fndr., 1964, Pres., 1964-72, & mbr., Bd. of Dirs. (1967-), Am. Liszt Soc.; ASCAP; MTNA & other profl. Assns. num. fellowships, grants & hons. Hobbies incl: Sculpture; Jewellery design; Jogging; Raising Weimaraner hounds. Address: 2557 Queen Anne Ave. N, Seattle, WA 98109, USA. 23, 28, 29.

LEE, Sung-Sook. Korea. Singer (soprano). Educ: BA (Music), Sook Myuug Women's Univ.; Juilliard Schl. of Music, NYC, USA. m. Jimmy Hu. Career incl: leading role, world premiere of Gian Carlo Menotti's 'Tamu Tamu', Chgo., 1973; leading operatic roles at Spoleto Festival, 1974; San Fran. Opera, 1974; La Scala, Milan, 1975; Covent Gdn., 1975; Frankfurt Opera, 1976-77; Seattle Opera 1978-; Miami Opera, 1978. concert appearances w. Buffalo Phil., Seattle Symph., Dallas Symph. & Pitts. Symph.; NYC Opera, 1975-76. Recording: Rossini's Stabat Mater (Vox). Mbr: Am. Guild of Musical Artists. Hons: incl: Silver Medal, Int. Madam Butterfly Competition, Japan, 1973. Mgmt: Columbia Artists Mgmt. Hobbies: Sports; Photography. Address: NYC, USA.

LEECH, Alan Bruce, b. 19 Oct. 1944. Lima, Ohio, USA. Bassoonist; Saxophonist; Conductor. Educ: B Mus, M Mus, Coll.-Conserv. of Music, Univ. of Cinn. m. Karen Davidson Leech, 1 d. Career: Soloist & Prin. Bassoon, Pierre Monteux Domaine Orch.; Prin., Knoxville Symph. Orch., Tenn., Am. Wind Symph. Orch., Pitts., Bozeman Symph., Mont., & Lexington Phil., Ky.; Assoc. Cond. & Prin. Bassoon, Cinn. Pro Musica Chmbr. Orch.; Bassoon, & Saxophone, Montana Mix, Gallatin Woodwind Quintet, Mont. State Univ., & var. other grps.; chmbr. & music & solo perfs.; Tchr., var. Univs.; now Prof. & Dir., of Bassoon & Saxophone, Co-Dir., Annual fest. for contemp. music, Mont. State Univ., Bozeman. Contbr. to: Klimko, Bassoon Performance Practices & Teaching in the US & Canada. Mbr., profl. assns. Hobbies: Hiking; Camping; Winemaking. Address: 12 No. Western Drive, Bozeman, MT 59715, USA. 9.

LEECH, Karen Davidson, b. 17 Dec. 1945. Cleveland, Ohio, USA. Flautist. Educ: BA, Smith Coll., Mass., MM, Coll. Conserv. of Music, Univ. Cinn.; Marcel Moyse Flute Seminar. m. Alan B Leech. Career: Perfs. incl: Prin., Monteux Domaine, Orch.; Am. Wind Symph. Orch., Pitts; Knoxville Symph. Orch., Tenn.; Prin., Bozeman Symph., Mont.; Prin., Cinn. Pro Musica Chmbr. Orch.; Smith Coll. Woodwind Quintet, Gallatin Woodwind Quintet, Mont. State Univ.; Tchr: Univ. Tenn.; Nat. Flute Assn.; Fac. Advsr., Music Educators Nat. Conf.; Coll. Music Soc.; Am. Fedn. of Musicians. Recip. Grad. Fellowship at Cinn. Conserv., 1967. Hobbies; Hiking; Camping; Cooking. Address: 522 S Third Ave., Bozeman, MT 59715, USA.

LEFANU, Nicola Frances, b. 28 Apr. 1947. UK. Composer. Educ: MA (Oxon). Career: Broadcasts & perfs., GB, Europe & USA. Comps: Over 20 vocal, choral, solo, chmbr., orchl. theatre, ballet, etc. inclng: Variations for oboe quartet, 'The Sam Day Dawns' for soprano & choral ensemble; 'Columbia Falls' for orch.; 'But Stars Remaining' for soprano; Dawnpath (chmbr. opera). Mbr., Coun., Soc. for Promotion New Music. Hons: Cobbett Chmbr. Music Prize, 1968; 1st prizc, BBC comps. competition, 1971; Mendelssohn Schlrship., 1972: Gulbenkian dance award, 1972; Harkness Fellowship, 1973. Address: 53 Barkston Gdns., London SW5, UK.

LEFEBVRE, Gilles, b. 30 June 1922. Montréal, PQ, Canada. Musical Director & Administrator. Educ: Ottawa Univ.; studied violin & hist. of music, Montreal, Ottawa & Paris, 1946-50. Career: Fndr., Les Jeunesses Musicales, Can., 1949, & The Art Ctr., Oxford, 1951; Organised World Congressses for the Int. Fedn. of Jeunesses Musicales, 1955 & 67; Organised 1st Nat. Music Competition JMC, 1961; Assoc. Artistic Dir., EXPO, Montreal, 1964-67; Dir., Canadian Cultural Ctr., Paris, 1972-;

Prof. Violinist, 1942-; & esp. between 1949-52. Mbrships. incl: Pres., Int. Fedn. for Jeunesses Musicales, 1955-57, 1967, 1970-74; Pres., Can. Arts Conf., 1970-72; Pres., Commn., Peoples Orch., Youth Music, June, 1974; Rep., Int. Music Coun. & UNESCO, for the Int. Fedn. of Jeunesses Musicales, June, 1974. Address: Centre Cultural Canadien, 5, Rue de Constantine, 75007 Paris, France.

LEFEBVRE, Philippe André, b. 2 Jan. 1949. Roubaix, France Organist; Composer; Conservatory Director. Educ: 5 1st Prizes, Conserv. of Lille; 4 1st Prizes, Conserv. of Paris; studied w. Pierre Cochereau, Maurice Durufle, Rolande Falcinelli. m. Dominique Woets. Debut: Notre-Dame Cathedral, Paris, 1968. Career: Titular Organist, Cathedral of Arras, 1968-; many recitals in France; concert tours, Spain, Germany, Belgium, Italy, Netherlands; Organ Tchr., Conserv. of Arras.; Dir. Conserv. in Marq-en-Baroeul. Comps. incl: Mass for organ; Hommage â Ravel (chmbr. orch.); songs, hymns, motets. Recordings incl: Le chemin de la corix, Marcel Dupre; L'oeuvre d'orgue de Robert Schumann. Contbr. to jrnls. Mbr. profl. orgs. Recip. many hons. Address: Domaine des Cascades, 327 rue Verte, 59170 Croix, France.

LEFELD, Jerzy Albert, b.17 Jan. 1898. Warsaw, Poland. Composer. Educ: Dips. in Piano & Comp., Warsaw Conserv., 1917. M. Stefania Siwecka, 1 s., 1 d. Debut: 1917. Career: 1st comp. performed by Warsaw Phil., Jan. 1919; Symph. no. 2 performed Warsaw Phil., 1925; other comps. recorded & broadcast, Polish Radio. Comps. incl: 2 Symph.; Str. Sextet; Songs for Voice & Piano; 4 Piano Preludes; Variations on Folk Theme for Piano; 4 Piano Preludes; Variations on Folk Theme for Piano; Nocturno (piano); Mazurkas (piano) (recorded) Symph. no. 1; Internezzo for Orch. Recordings: num. as accomp. & chmbr. pianist. Mbrships incl: Union of Polish Comps.; Assn. Polish Musicians. Hons. incl: Golden Cross of Merit; Off.'s Cross, Polonia Restituta; State Prize of Poland. Hobbies: Astronomy; Climbing; Photography. Address: 05-500 Siedliska 43, poczta Piaseczno, Poland. 14.

LE FLEMING, Christopher Kaye, b. 25 Feb. 1908. Wimborne, Dorset, UK. Musician; Composer; Lecturer. Educ: Brighton Schl. of Music; RSCM. m. Phyllis Tanner, 3 s. Career: Var. positions connected w. music in educ. Var. comps. Contbr. of articles to music jrnls. Mbrships: Chmn., Composers' Guild of GB, 1971; Chmn., Kent Co. Music Comm., 1964-71; Chmn., of Govs., Kent Music Schl., 1972-. Hobbies: Railways; Walking. Address: 1B Yardley Park Rd., Tonbridge, Kent TN9 1NE, UK.

LE FLEMING, Naomi, b. 4 May 1944. Nelson, Lancs., UK. Cellist; Teacher. Educ: LRAM (Perfs.); Paris Conserv.; GSM. m. (1) Dr. Hugh Macdonald (2) Antony Le Fleming, 5 c. Debut: London Recital Club, Wigmore Hall. Career: Freelance player for var. London Chmbr. Orchs. incl. English Chmbr. Orch., Monteverdi Orch. & Richard Hickox Orch.; Cello Tchr., Cambridge, 1965-70; Mbr., De Frevillo Trio, 1967-70; Tchr.; Mbr. Tchng. Staff, Birmingham Schl. of Music, 1975-; Recitals, concerts. Mbrships: ESTA Midlands Rep.; West Midlands Arts Panel. Hons: 4 prizes, RAM. Hobbies: Painting; Drawing; Medicine; French food; Tennis; Playing Double Bass & Flute, etc. Address: 34 Mayfield Rd., Moseley, Birmingham 13, UK.

LEFRANCOIS, André, b. 9 Mar. 1906. Domont, France. Professor. Educ: Licencié es Sciences, Paris. m. Mme. Ginsiano. Career: Prof., lycée Fresnel, Paris; Prof., Jeunesse Musicales de France. Publs: Analyses musicales d'operas de Wagner: L'Or du Rhin, 1975; La Walkyrie, 1975; Tristan et Isolde, 1976; Les Maîtres-Chanteurs, 1977; Siegfried, 1978; le Crépuscule des Dieux, 1979. Contbr. to: Bulletin du Cercle Wagner. mbr., Cercle Richard Wagner. Address: 3 rue Lecourbe, 75015 Paris, France.

LEGETI, György, b. 28 May 1923. Diciosanmartin, Rumania. Composer. Educ: Conserv. of Klausenburg; Dip. of Comp., Acad. of Music, Budapest. m. Vera Ligeti, 1 s. Career: Asst. Prof., harmony & counterpoint, Acad. of Music, Budapest, 1950-56; staff mbr., Studio for Electronic Music, WDR, Cologne, 1957-59; Lectr., Darmstadt Courses for New Music, 1959-; Vis. Prof., Stockholm Music Acad., 1961-70; Comp-in-Res. & Vis. Prof., Stanford Univ., USA, 1972; Lectr., Tanglewood Music Courses, 1973; Prof. of Comps., Hamburg Music Acad., 1973-. Comps. incl: orchl. works; solo instrument w. orch.; chorus, soloists & orch.; Chmbr. music; instrumental music; vocal music w. chmbr. ensemble; works for a cappella choir; opera; electronic music. Author of 2 harmony texts, 1954, 56. Contbr. to jrnls. Mbr. profl. orgs. Recip. var. hons. Address: Movenstr. 3, 2000 Hamburg 60, German Fed. Repub. 19.

LEGGATE, Robin, b. 18 Apr. 1946. W Kirby, UK. Singer (tenor). Educ: BA (oxon), (Engrng. & Econ.); MBA Cranfield

(Business Admin.); RNCM. Career: Prin. tenor, Royal Opera House, Convent Garden. Recordings: Fanciulla del West (puccini); Armida (Haydn). Recip. Richard Tauber Memorial Prize, 1975. Mgmt: Harrison/Parrott, Ltd., London. Address: 26 Baronsmere Rd., London N2 9QE, UK.

LEGGE, Harry, b. 24 Apr. 1914. Liverpool, UK. Conductor; Violist. Educ: BA, Oxford Univ.; RCM. Career: Cond.; Rehearsal Orch., Brit. Youth Wind Orch., & Brent Symph. Orch. Dir., RPO, 1963-73. Compositions: Boccherini's Roundabout for String Orch. Recordings: w. Brit. Youth Wind Orch. Address: Garden Flat, 62 Messina Ave., London NW6, UK.

LEGRADY, Thomas Theodore, artist name THOMAS, Ted. formerly TASSY, Tamás, b. 22 Mar. 1920. Budapest, Hungary. Composer; Conductor; Arranger. Educ: PhD, Erzsébet Univ., Pécs, 1946; Masters degree, Comp., Bartok Conserv., Budapest, 1953. m. Katherine Varady, 3 s. Debut: Budapest, 1942. Career incls: Staff Arr., Radio Budapest, 1949-56; Staff Arr., CBC TV, Montreal, Can., 1956-59; Instrucotr of Theory, McGill Univ., 1966-67, Loyola Coll., Montreal, 1967-72, N York Bd. of Educ., 1972-. Comps. incl: Diverimento & Suite (brass quintet), 1963; Three Dates, 1973; Music for Winds; French-Can. Folksongs for Band; The Mailman; (some works recorded). Publs: V'Lá L'bon vent, Beginners Band Textbooks, 1979; Musical textbooks. Mbr., profl. assns. Hons: 1st Prize, Can. Comp. Competition, 1963. Hobbies incl: Oil Painting; Sailing. Address: 58 Van Horne Ave., Willowdale, Ont., Canada M2J 2S9.

LEGRAND-SCHWAKOPF, Krystyna, b. 25 June 1925. Warszawa, Poland. Pianist. Educ: Matriculation, Lyceum in Warsaw; Dip., Warsaw Conservatoire Acad. of Music. m. Jerzy Jan Schwakopf, 1 s. 1 d. Career: Apps. as soloist & in chmbr. music in Poland, Austria, Bulgaria, Czechoslavia, Albania, Belgium & Hungary; Radio apps. in Poland & Belgium. Mbr. Soc. of Polish Musicians Artists SPAM in Warsaw. Hobby: Antiquity. Address: ul. Tucholska 11 m 28, Warsaw 01 618, Poland.

LEHANE, Maureen. London, UK. Concert & Opera Singer. Educ: Guildhall Schl. of Music & Drama. London. m. Peter Wishart. Career: Soloist w. all major choral socs.; Regular broadcasts inclng. Promenade Concerts; Tours of USA, Australia, Far & Middle East; Soloist at Glyndebouren, Sadlers Wells, TV, etc. Num. recordings inclng: Handel's Belshazzer, cond. N. Harnoncourt. Recip. of many hons. Hobbies: Cooking; Gardening. Mgmt: Artists Int. Mgmt., 3 & 4 Albert Tce., London. NW1, UK. Address: 26 Pleydell Ave., London W6, UK. 1.

LEHEL, György, b. 10 Feb. 1926. Budapest, Hungary. Chief Conductor & Music Director of the Budapest Symphony Orchestra. Educ: Acad. of Music, Budapest. m. Dr. Zsuzsanna Markovits. Debut: Budapest, 1946. Career: Regular concerts in USA, Japan, USSR, England, Germany, Italy, France, Switz. Yugoslavia, etc. Many recordings w. Westminster, Deutsche Gramophon Gesellschaft, Suprahon, Huangaroton, etc. Hons: Franz Liszt Prize, 1955, '62; Merited Artist, 1967; Lossuth Prize, 1973; Hon. D Mus, Chicago Conserv. Coll. Mgmt: Interkonzert, 1051 Budapest, Vörösmarty Ter. 1. Address: 1121 Budapest, Normafa ut 17/a. Hungary. 4, 30.

LEHMAN, Paul Robert, b. 20 April 1931. Athens, OH, USA. Professor of Music; Associate Dean. Educ: BS Ed., Ohio Univ., Athens; M Mus, PhD, Univ. of Mich., Ann Arbor. m. V Ruth Wickline, 1 s., 1 d. Career incls: Instr., Asst. Prof., Univ. of Colo., Boulder, 1962-65; Assoc. Prof., Prof., Univ. of Ky. Lexington, 1965-70; Music Specialist, US Off. of Educ., Wash. DC, 1967-68; Prof., Eastman Schl. of Music, Univ. of Rochester, NY, 1970-75, Univ. of Mich., Ann Arbor, 1975-; Assoc. Dean, ibid., 1977-. Publs: incl: Tests & Measurements in Music, 1968; The School Music Program; Description & Standards (w. others), 1974; The Harmonic Structure of the Tone of the Bassoon, 1965. Contbr. to profl. publs. Mbrships. incl: Chmn., Nat. Committee on Instrn., MENC, 1975-78; Chmn., Music Educ. Rsch. Coun., MENC, 1964-70; Am. Musicol. Soc. Addresss: Schl. of Music, Univ. Mich., Ann Arbor, MI 48109, USA.

LEHMANN, Arnold O., b. 12 Apr. 1914. Surprise, Neb., USA. Music Educator; Conductor; Musician (clarinet & piano); Singer (tenor). Educ: BA (Langs.), Northwestern Coll.; B Mus, MA (Music), Univ. of Wis.; PhD (Musicol.), Western Reserve Univ. m. Esther J Burhop, 3s. Compositions: Large no. of works & arrangements for male voice chorus. Recordings: 17 records of male voice choirs. Publs: A Concise Dictionary of Liturgical Terms, 1978; The Church Musician's Enchiridion, 1978; The Liturgical Church Year, 1979. Contbr. to: The Lutheran Chorale. Mbrships: Am. Musicol. Soc.; Life, Phi Mu Alpha Sinfonia; Coll. Band Dirs. Nat. Assn. Recip: Fac. Fellowship for further music study, 1965-66. Hobbies: Water skiing, Woodworking; Boating. Address: Rte. 4, Watertown, WI 53094, USA. 8, 130.

LEHMANN, Hans Ulrich, b. 4 May 1037. Biel, Switz. Professor; Composer. BA, 1956; Univs. Berne, Zurich & Basle, 1956-67; Dip., violoncello, 1960; Dip. music theory, 1962; Master Calss, comp., 1960-63. m. Janine Lehmann, 1 s., 1 d. Career incls: Prof., theory & Comp., Musikhochschule, Zürich, 1972-; Dept. Dir., ibid., 1974-. Dir., All Zürich Music Insts., 1976-; Lectr., Zürich Univ., 1969-. Comps. incl: Quanti I, 1962; Regions, 1963; Episoden, 1963-64; Mosaik, 1964; Tractus, 1971; ... zu streichen, 1974; zu blasen, 1975-76; Mondog, 1976; Tantris, 1976-77; Air, 1977; Motetus Paraburi, 1977-78. Contbr. to profl. publs. Mbr. profl. orgs. Hons. incl: Prize, Conrad Ferdinand Meyer Fndn., 1973. Address: In der Looren 38, CH-8053, Zürich, Switz.

LEHMANN, Markus Hugo, b. 31 Mar. 1919. Ceská Lipa, Czech. Composer; Conductor; Teacher; Pianist; Organist. Educ: Univ. of Salzburg, Austria; North-Western Music Acad., Detmold; Darmstadt Kranichstein. m. Aretje van de Graaf. Career: Organist & Choir Cond., Salzburg, 1948-50; Cond., sev. opera houses, Germany, 1953-62; Rdr., B Schott's Söhne, Mainz, 1962-63; Musical Dir., Opera Grp., Staatliche Hochschule für Musik, Freiburg, 1963-. Comps. incl: (operas) (Der Präsident, 1970) (ballets) L'enfer sur terre, 1962 (vocal works); Lied der Kentauren, 1953; works for orch.; concerts for solo instruments, etc. Mbrships: Die Künstlergilde. Hons: Cultural Award for Music, 1976 (Sudenten German Culture Prize). Address: Urach Str. 39, D-7800 Freiburg, German Fed. Repub. 19, 23, 29, 30.

LEHNER, Franz Xaver, b. 29 Nov. 1904. Regensburg, Germany. Composer; Organist. Educ: Munich Coll. of Music; Master class for comp. m. Anne Marie Kroen, 1 s. Career: Choir Dir., Landshutlsar, 1938; Tchr. at ch. music schl., Regensburg, 1938; Prof., Würzburg Coll. of Music, 1948; Prof. of comps., München Coll. of Music, 1958. Comps. incl: Die schlaue Susanne; Die Erbschaft; Die Vielsetigen; Die Stationen des ehrenwertigen Don Geronimo order Der Schafstall; Alle Tage ist (k)ein Aschermittwoch; Die kleine Stadt; Gamaliel; Faust dritter Teil. Recordings: Chmbr. music; concertos for clarinet, cello, organ, (Bavarian radio). Hons: Musikpreis, Munich, 1966; Kilturpreis, E Bavaria, 1971. Address: 8031 Olching, Ludwig-Thomasstr. 1, German Fed. Repub.

LEHNERTS, Frances, b. Mpls., Minn., USA. Concert Singer; Voice Teacher. Educ: BS, Univ. Minn.; MA, Tchrs. Coll., Columbia Univ., NYC; Artists Dip., Juilliard Schl. Music. Debut: Town Hall, NYC. Career incls: Concert & opera apps. throughout USA; Soloist & Recitalist, TV & tours, USA & Europe; Tchr., singing, Bronx House Music Schl., 1955-; Tchrs. Coll., Columbia, 1960-; NY Univ., 1968-. Mbr., Mu Phi Epsilon. Recip: 5 yr. Fellowship, Juilliard Schl. Music, 1939-45; Tanglewood Schlrship., 1945. Hobby: Gardening. Address: 440 Riverside Dr., NY, NY 10027, USA.

LEHRER, Thomas Andrew, b. 9 April 1928. NY, USA. Songwriter; Teacher; Performer. Educ: BA., Harvard Univ., 1946; MA, ibid., 1947; Grad. study, 1947-53, 1960-65. Career: Night club appearances, USA; Concert appearances, USA, Canada, UK, Australia, NZ., Denmark., Norway; Major TV appearances, UK, Australia, Canada, German Fed. Repub., Norway; Minor TV appearances, USA. Comps. recorded: Songs by Tom Lehrer, 1953; More of Tom Lehrer, 1959; Tom Lehrer Revisited, 1960; That Was the Year that Was, 1965; An Evening Wasted with Tom Lehrer, 1959. Publs: The Tome Lehrer Song Book, 1954; Tom Lehrer's Second Song Book., 1968. Mbrships: ASCAP; MCPS; Comps. & Lyricists Guild of Am. Address: 11 Sparks St., Cambridge, MA 02138, USA. 1, 2.

LEHRFIELD, Robert, b. 9 Aug. 1925. Newark, NJ., USA. Oboist. Educ: BA., Eastman Schl. of Music. m. Florence Seakwood, 2 d. Career: NY. Phil.; Little Orch. Soc. of NY.-; Indianapolis Symph.; New Orleans Symph. Address: 13 Pal Dr., Wayside, NJ 07712, USA.

Le HURAY, Peter Geoffrey, b. 18 June 1930. London, UK. University Lecturer; Organist. Educ: BA, St. Catharine's Coll., Cambridge Univ., 1951; Mus B., ibid., 1952; PhD., 1958. m. Bridget K A Payne, 1 s., 1 d. Career: Lectr. in Music, Cambridge & Fellow of St. Catharine's Coll., 1959; BBC recitalist, Promenade Concerts, 1962; Barclay Acheson Prof. of Int. Studies, Macalester Coll., St. Paul, Minn., USA, 1969-70. Recordings: Sonata on Ps.94 (Julius Reubke); Variations on Wienen, klagen, sorgen, sagen (Liszt); Lizst; Bach; Ad nos Fantasias. Publs: Music & the Reformantion in England, 1549-1660, 1967; Treasury of English Ch. Music, vol II,

1965; The Sources of English Ch. Music, 1549-1660 (w. R T Daniel), 1972; Music & Aesthetics in the 18th-early 19th centuries, Cambridge Source Readings in the History of Music, etc. Ed. Tudor Ch. Music series. Contbr. to: Musica Britannica; The Diapason, etc. Mbrships incl: Coun. Mbr., 1963-& Ed. of the RMA Proceedings, 1963-66, Royal Musical Assn.; Pres., Inc. Assn. of Organists, 1970-72; Editl. Bd., Early Engl. Ch. Music, 1970-. Address: St. Catharine's Coll., Cambridge, UK. 3.

LEICHTLING, Alan Robert, b. 16 Apr. 1947. Bklyn., NY, USA. Composer; Teacher; Conductor. Educ; B Mus Juilliard Schl. Music, 1968; MS, ibid., 1969; DMA, 1971. m. Anita Sue. Career incls: Musical Dir. & Cond., var. chmbr. ensembles, 1963-; Prod., Dir. & Commentator, 'Music in the 20th Century', KDICFM, Grinnell, Iowa, 1975-; Asst. Prof. Music, Grinnell Coll., 1975-; Res. Comp., ibid., 1975-; Dir., Electronic Music Studio, 1975-. Comps. incl: Fantasy Piece II (cello & piano), 1976; Sonata (cello & piano) Opus 68, 1976. Mbrships: ASCAP; Am. Music Ctr. Hons. incl: ASCAP Standard Award, annually 1971-76; Pulitzer Prize nominee, 1970, '71; num. grants & awards. Mgmt: Seesaw Music Corp., 177 E. 87th St., NY., NY 10028. Address: 538 10th Ave., Grinnell, IA 50112, USA.

LEIGHTON, Kenneth, b. 2 Oct. 1929. Composer; Professor of Music. Educ: Queen's Coll., Oxford; DMus; MA; LRAM; studies w. G Petrassi, Rome. m. Lydia Vignapiano, 1 s., 1 d. Career: Prof. of theory, RNCM, 1952-53; Gregory Fellow in Music, Leeds Univ., 1953-56; lectr. in comp., Edinburgh Univ., 1956-58; lectr in music & Fellow of Worcester Coll., Oxford, 1968-70; Reid Prof. of Music, Univ. of Edinburgh, 1970-. Comps. incl: 2 Symphs.; 3 piano concertos; concertos for violin, cello, viola & 2 piano; Symph. for str. orch.; 2 str. quartets; piano quintet; 2 sonatas for violin & piano; 3 piano sonatas; Partita for cello & piano; Burlesque, Passacaglia, Chorale & Fugue; Fantasia Contrappuntistica, for piano; organ & piano music; Ch. music; music for radio & TV. Address: Faculty of Music, Univ. of Edinburgh, Alison Mouse, Nicolson Sq., Edinburgh, EH8 9BH, UK.

LEININGER, Robert, b. 11 May 1916. Richmond Hill, NY, USA. Orchestral Bassist. m. Mildred Lieninger, 2 d. Career: Bassist, Les Brown Dance Orch., 1941-46; Mbr., 1948-, currently Asst. Prin. Bassist, Pitts. Symph. Orch., Pa.; Fac. Music Schl., Duquesne Univ., Pitts., Pa. Hobbies: Golf; High Fidelity. Address: 2418 Collins Rd., Pittsburgh, PA 15235, USa.

LEINSDORF, Erich, b. 4 Feb. 1912. Vienna, Austria. Conductor. Educ: State Acad. of Music, Vienna; Mozarteum, Salzburg. m. Vera Graf, 3 s. 2 d. from previous marriage. Debuts: Vienna, 1933; NYC (Metrop. Opera), 1938. Career incls: Cond. & for Music Dir., NY Metrop. Opera, Cleveland Orch., Rochester Phil., Boston Symph.; Guest Cond. w. most ranking symph. orchs. inclng. Boston, Chgo., Cleveland, NY Phil., Los Angeles, Berlin, Vienna, London, Amsterdam, Paris. Recordings: over 100 LP's inclng: 19 full length operas; all Mozart symphs.; all Beethoven; all Brahms. Publs: Cadenza (autobiog.); var. musical essays & articles. Recip., var. hon. docts. & awards for recordings. Hobbies: Reading; especially History; Puzzles; Walking; Writing. Address: 146 Saconesset Rd., Falmouth, MA 02574, USA.

LEITE, Clarisse, b. 11 Jan. 1917. Sao Paulo, Brazil. Professor of Piano; Composer; Inspector of Arts. Educ: Dip., Sao Paulo Conserv. on Music & Drama, 1930. m. Cesar Dias Baptista, 3 s. Career incls: contracted to Sao Paulo Educl. Radio, 1932-37; tours for State Dept. of Culture, Sao Paulo, var. concerto apps., 1937-59; perfs. in Vienna, 1959; var. TV apps.; Prof. of Piano, Carlos de Campos-Tatui Conserv. Comps: var. keyboard concerto & instrumental works; songs. Mbrships: Soc. of Brazilian Comps. of Serious Music; Soc. Pro Arte; State Commn. of Music, Sao Paulo, 1962. Recip., num. hons. & competition prizes. Address: Avendia Angélica 1106, Apto. 97, 01-227 Sao Paulo SP, Brazil.

LEITERMEYER, Fritz, b. 4 Apr. 1925. Vienna, Austria. Violinist; Composer. Educ: Tchrs. Coll.; Acad. of Music, Vienna. m. Ingeborg Kieseberg. Debut: State Opera, Vienna, Career: Mbr., Vienna State Opera Orch., Vienna Phil. Orch., Vienna Court Music Orch. Comps. publd. incl: Epigramme; 72 Dialoge; 24 Bicinen; Konzert, contrabass & strings; Prolog; 12 Baskontraste; Posaunissimo; Adventgespräch für oboe und streicher op. 68; 6 Duos für Flöte und Fagott op. 69; Trompetissimo für trompete solo op. 70; Monolog für flöte solo op. 71; (recorded) 12 Episodes. Mbr.; profl. orgs. Hons: Förderungspreis, City of Vienna, 1963; State Prize, 1963; Prize of the Vienna Art Fndn., 1973; Hon. Circle, Vienna Phil., 1971; Prof., 1967; Österreichische Ehrenkreuz für

Wissenschaft und Kunst, 1978;Würdigungspreis der Stadt Wien, 1978. Hobbies: Hiking; Mountaineering; Sauna. Address: 2/18 Landskrongasse, A-1010 Vienna, Austria.

LEITNER, Ferdinand, b. 4 Mar. 1912. Berlin, Germany. Conducotr. Educ: State Acad. of Music, Berlin. m. Gisela Büsing, 1 s. Career: Music Dir., State Opera, Hamburg, 1945; Opera Dir., State Opera, Munich, 1946; Opera Dir., Symph. Dir., State Opera, Stuttgart, 1947; Gen. Music Dir., ibi, 1950; Prof., ibid, 1961; Cheif Musical Dir., Zürich Opera, 1969-; Guest Cond., maj. cities of N & S. Am., Europe, Australia, Asia. Recordings: over 100, inclng. Busoni, Doktor Faust; Carl Orff, Prometheus, Carmina Burana, Catulli Carmine, Trionfi Di Afrodite. Mgmt: Interartist, The Hague, Holland. Address: Opera House, Zurich, Switz.

LEIVISKÄ, Helvi, b. 25 May 1902. Helsinki, Finland. Composer. Educ: Dip. In Comp., Sibelius-Acad., Helsinki, 1927; study w. Prof. A Willner, Vienna, 1928-29. Début: Comp. concert, 1935. Career: Piano pedagogue, 1922-38; Libn., Sibelius Acad., 1933-68. Comps. incl: 3 Symphs.; Sinfonia Brevis, 1962; Folk Dance Suite; Piano Concerto; Triple Fugue; Cantata for choir & orch.; Piano quartet; Violin Sonata; Motion-Picture music, etc. Publs: Music critic for evening paper Ilta-Sanomat, 1957-61; Musical essays. Mbrship: Zonta Int. Hons: Recip., Pro Finlandia Medal, Kalevala Medal. Address: Kirkkokatu 1 a C, 00170 Helsinki 17, Finland.

LEJET, Edith, b. 19 July 1941. Paris, France. Composer; Professor. Educ: Conserv. Nat. Supérieur de Musique de Paris. Career: Prof., Solfége, Conserv. Nat. Supérieur de Paris, 1972-; Comps. incl: Music for trumpet & brass quintet, 1968; Monodrame, for violin & orch., 1969; Journal d'Anne Frank, for girls' choir & instrumental ensemble, 1968-70; Saxophone Quartet, 1974; Espaces Nocturnes, for 2 flutes, clarinet, bass clarinet, percussion, harp & double bass, 1976; Harmnie du Soir, for 13 strgns., 1975-77; Concert for cello & instrumental ensemble, 1978; Triptuque, for organ, 1979; Gémeaux for guitar, 1978; concerto for flute, 1979. Hons. incl: num. 1st prizes at Conserv.; Premier 2nd Grand Prix de Rome, 1968; Prix Florence Gould, 1970; Prix Hervé Dugardin, 1974; Gránd Prix de La Musique de Chambre, SACEM, 1979. Address: 49 rue Laugier, 75017 Paris, France.

LEKFELDT, Jørgen, b. 27 Mar. 1948. Copenhagen, Denmark. Composer; Musicologist; Pianist; Grammar School Teacher. Educ: MA (Musicol.), Univ. of Copenhagen; piano studies w. Elisabeth Klein. m. Lene Duus, 1 s. Debut: (as comp.) public concert, 1976. Career: radio broadcasts on new music; fndr., Group for Intuitive Music (GIM), 1974; sev. concerts w. GIM, 1974-. Comps. incl: Mantra-Spiral, 1975; Quintet, 1976; Madison Music, 1976; Organum, 1977; Natus Sum, 1977: Arua, 1977; Prelude for organ, 1978; Fable for orch., 1978-79; Piano Concerto, 1978-79; DIM, 1979, for horn, synthesiser, cello. Contbr. to: Dansk Musiktidsskrift (DMT); Bladet. Mbrships: Danish Comps. Soc.; Det Unge Tonekunstnerselskab (DUT); Group for Intuitive Music. Hobbies: Zoology; Philsophy. Address: Sostrup Elle 12, Sostrup, 4300 Holbaek, Denmark.

LELAND, James Miner, b. 31 March 1940. Mpls., Minn., USA. College Organist & Choirmaster; Professor of Music. Educ: Akademie Mozarteum, Salzburg, 1960-61; B Mus, Oberlin Coll. Conserv. of Music, 1962; M Mus., Northwestern Univ. Schl. of Music, 1963; Mus D., ibid., 1972; Acad. of Music, Berlin, 1963-64. Career: Harpsichord Soloist w. Robert Shaw Chorale; Organ Soloist, Detroit Symph. Orch., Atlanta Symph. Orch.; num. solo recitals in Am. colls. & univs.; currenlty Coll. Organist & Choirmaster & Prof. of Music, Hollins Coll., Roanoke, Va. Contbr. to: The Diapason; Roanoke World News. Mbrships: Coll. Music Soc.; AGO. Recip. of Fulbright Fellowship for European Study, 1963-64. Address: Dept. of Music, Hollins Coll., Roanoke, VA 24020, USA.

LEMARE, Iris Margaret Elsie. London, UK. Musician. Educ: Cert., Inst. Jacques Dalcroze, Geneva, Switzerland, 1921-24; ARCM in Music. ARCM in Elocution. Royal Coll. of Music. London, 1925-29. Appts. incl: Co-Fndnr., Macnaghton-Lemare Concerts, 1931-33; Fndr., Lemare Concerts, 1934-37; Conductor, Polland Opera Co., 1935-39, Oxford Chmbr. Orch., 1939-40, Carlyle Singers, 1930-39, BBC Orch., 1936-37 (1st woman to do so), Durham Co. Opera, 1965-66, Opera Nova, Teeside, 1970-; Conductor & Artistic Dir., Lemare Orch. 1945-; Examiner to Assoc. Bd. of Royal Schls. of Music, 1930-. Mbrships. incl: Coun. Mbr., Inc. Soc. of Musicians, 1967-70; British Fedn. of Music of Festivals; Musicians Union; Nat. Trust; English Speaking Union. Recip., Dove Prize, Royal Coll. of Music 1917. Hobbies: Bell-ringing; Climbing; Skiing; Bird-Watching. Address: 10 St. Hilda's Craft, Askham Bryan, York, UK.

LEMKES, Bouwe, b. 27 June 1924. Alphen ad Rijn, Holland. Violinist. Educ: Soloist Cert., Conserv. Amsterdam, 1951; Study w. Oscar Back. m. Jeanne Elisabeth Vos. Debut: Amsterdam. Career: Concertmaster, Amsterdam Phil.; Perfs. w. Netherlands Chmbr. Orch.; Ldr., 1st Violin Sect., Utrecht Symph.; Tours, as duo-violinist w. wife, of European, UK, Israel & USA. Tchr., Violin, The Hague & Amsterdam Conservs. Recordings:: Music for 2 violins by Henk Badings, Hans Kox, Alan Ridout. Contbr. to Mens & Melodie. Address: van Hogendorpstraat 9, 3581 KB, Netherlands.

LEMMON, Alfred E, b. 8 Dec. 1949. Lafayette, La., USA. Musicologist; Organist. Educ: BM, Loyola Univ., 1971; MA, Tulane Univ., 1974; PhD, ibi. (in progress). Publ: ed., Sonate e Variacoens, by Marcos Antonio Portugal, 1976. Contbr. to: Liturgrical Arts; Nat. Studies; Heterofonia, Archivum Historicium Societatis Iesu; The Americas; Music; The Am. Organists; The Soundboard; Revista Musical Chilena; Tlalocan; Current Musicol.; The World of Music; Sydney Organ Jrnl.; Readings in Belizean Hist.; Jrnl. of San Diego History. Mbrships: Am. Musicol. Soc.; Int. Musicol. Soc.; Am. Guild of Organists; Am. Acad. of Franciscan Hist.; New Orleans Friends of Music (Bd. of dirs.). Address: 806 Johnston St., Lafayette, LA 70501, USA. 29.

LEMPFERT, Majorie O E, b. 2 Dec. 1921. South Kensington, London, UK. Viola Player & Teacher. Educ: ARAM; LRAM; ARCM. Career: Chmbr. Music Viola Player, Engl. String Quartet, 1954-73; Freelance Chmbr. Orchl. work w. Engl. Chmbr., Jacques, Geraint Jones & other orchs. Recordings w. above-named orchs. Mbr. ISM. Hobbies: Country Walking; Riding. Address: 53 Sterne St., London W12, UK.

LENCSES, Lajos, b. 18 Jan. 1943. Dorog, Hungary. Oboist. Educ: Music Coll., Budapest; Dip., Bartok Conserv., 1961; Dip., Music Acad., Budapest, 1966; Dip., Conserv. de Paris, France, 1967; m. Veronika Janssen. Debut: Budapest, 1966. Career: Solo Oboist, Radio Symph. Orch., Stuttgart, German Fed. Repub.; Concerts as Soloist, Budapest, Paris, Geneva, Lisbon, Athens, Berlin, Hamburg, Stuttgart; TV apps., Budapest, Paris, Stuttgart; Radio broadcasts, Germany, France, Austria. Recordings: Haydn-Dittersdort, Oboe Concertos; Wolf-Ferrari, Oboe & English Horn. Concertos. Hons: Laureate, Int. Competition in Musical Execution, Geneva, 1968. Hobbies: Travel; Photography. Mgmt: Konzertdirektion Erwin Russ, Stuttgart. Address: 7 Stuttgart 1, Reinsburgstrasse 140, German Fed. Repub.

LENDVAY, Kamillo, b. 28 Dec. 1928. Budapest, Hungary. Composer. Educ: Dip., Franz Liszt Acad. of Music, Budapest, 1959. m. 1 child. Debut: as Cond., Opera Co., Szeged Nat. Theatre, 1956-57. Career: Prof. Franz Liszt Acad. of Music, Budapest, 1973-. Comps. incl: stage works; vocal, orchl., chmbr. & instrumental music; Concertino for piano, winds, percussion & harp (recorded), 1959; Orogenesis, musicians, 1969; The Magic Chair, light TV opera, 1972; Expressions for strings, 1974; Pezzo Concertato, violin & orch., 1975; Dispositions for cimbalom, 1975; Pro Libertate, cantata, 1975. Mbr., Hungarian Fedn. of Musical Arts. Hons: Erkel Comp. Prize, 1962 & 64; SZOT Comp. Prize, 1966; 2nd Prize, Trieste City Prize, 1975. Hobby: Gardening. Address: Kacsoh P ut. 141d, H 1142 Budapest, Hungary.

LENNEBERG, Hans H., b. 16 May 1924. Olpe, Germany. Music Librarian; Associate Professor of Music. Educ: AB, Bklyn. Coll.; AM, musicol., NY Univ.; MLS, Pratt Inst. m. Johanna Sonnenfeld, 1 s., 2 step-s. Publs: Co-ed., Aspects of Medieval & Renaissance Music, 1964; Ed., reprint Henry Fothergill Chorley's Modern German Music, 1973; History of Musical Biography (in prep.). Contbr. to num. profl. publs. Mbrships: Am. Musicol. Soc.; Int. Assn. Music Libs.; Music Lib. Assn.; Soc. 18th Century Studies; Soc. Ethnomusicol. Address: Joseph Regenstein Lib., Univ. Chgo., Chicago, IL 60637, USA. 8, 11.

LENNOX, David, b. 4 Apr. 1928. London, UK. Singer; Lecturer. Educ: BA (Hons.), Univ. of London; Postgrad. Cert. in Educ., ibid.; LRAM (Singing, Perfs.); Studied w. Charles Kennedy Scott & Alexander Young. m. Mary Hill. Career: Opera, Glyndebourne; BBC studio operas; Resident/Guest, Royal Opera House, Covent Garden, 1967-76; Perfs. in Berlin & Paris; Lectr., Schl. of Music, Huddersfield Polytechnic, 1972-. Recordings: Mozart, Marriage of Figaro; Berlioz, The Trojans; Strauss, Salome. Hobby: Walking. Address: Nethercroft, Huddersfield Rd., Penistone, Sheffield, S30 6BU, UK. 3.

LENOIR, Yves Roger Désiré, b. 10 Aug. 1950. Etterbeek, Brussels, Belgium. Musicologist. Educ: Univ Louvain, Budapest, dip. Hungarian Language and Lit.; Music Acad.

Woluwe St. Lambert; B Mus; MA Mus, Louvain. Career: Prof. Musical Hist., Music Acad. Woluwe Saint-Pierre; Prof. Musical Educ., Lycée Descartes de Rabat (Maroc), 1976-78. Mbrships: Assn. of Graduates in Art Hist. and Archeol., Cath. Univ. Louvain. Publs: Life and Works of Béla Bartok in the USA, 1940-1945, 1976. Contbr. to: Documentation on Central Europer, 1972, 1973; Blend of Musicol., Louvain, 1974; Keys for Music, 1974. Hobbies: Linguistics; Sports; Travel. Address: 19 Rue Château Kieffert, 1200 Brussels, Belgium.

LENOT, Jaques, b. 29 Aug. 1945. St. Jean d'Angely, Charente Maritime, France. Composer. Educ; Autodidact. Debut: Festival Royan, 1967. Career: Concerts, conferences, Royan, Paris, Aix en Provence, La Rochelle, Berlin, Rome, Milan, Warsaw, Trie ste, Zagreb, Amsterdam, Donaueschingen, Persepolis. Comps: De Elegia Prima; Amarlied; Oper'Avvent; Exile Allegories; Piano concerto; Concert melody; Symph.; Quartet. Hons: Vocation Fndn., Paris, 1974; SACEM, 1976. Address: 45 Boulevard A Briand, 17200 Royan, France.

LENTZ, Donald Anthony, b. 24 Jan. 1908. Brookings, SD, USA. Ethnomusicologist; Conductor; Composer; Flutist; Teacher. Educ: BS, SD State Univ., 1930; MFA, Univ. of SD, 1935; pvte. study w. Georges Barrere, flute; Albert Stoessel, cond.; Vladimir Bakaleinikoff, cond. & orch.; Virgil Thomson, comp. & orch.; study of tradl. music systems & instruments of India, Java, Bali, Taiwan & Iran w. tchrs. in those areas. m. Velma Gildemeister. Career: Prof. of Ethnomusicol., author & lects.; Dir. of Bands, Univ. of Neb., 1937-73; Dir., Univ. Orchs. , Univ. of Nebraska, 1937-41; Originator of Band Day in USA; Former flutist w. NY Symph., Sousa Band, Barrere Little Symph., etc.; Vis. Prof. in summer sessions at Univs. of Idaho & Wyo., at. Nat. Music Camp at vankton Coll.; Cond. of Music Fests. throughout USA; Rsch. work in Sumatra & Burma, 1975. Comps. incl: The Gamelan Music of Java & Bali, 1965. A Few Thoughts on Synthesis, 1968; Eastern & Western Wind Instrument Intonations, 1972, etc. Num. recordings as Cond. w. Univ. of Neb. bands. Mbr. of many profl. orgs. Hons. incl: Chinese Classical Music Medal for Sino-Am. Interchange & Understanding, Taipeh, 1975. Address: Route 3, Lincoln, NE 68505, USA.

LEONARD, Lawrence, b. 22 Aug. 1923. London, UK. Conductor. Educ: RAM, London, LRAM; L'Ecole Normale de Musique; studied pvtly. w. Ansermet & Kleiber. m. (1) Josephine Duffey, 1 s., 1 d. (2) Katharina Wolpe. Career: Asst. Cond., BBC Northern Orch., 1 yr.; Asst. Cond., Halle Orch., 5 yrs.; Music Dir., Edmonton Symph. Orch., Canada, 5 yrs.; World wide freelance concerts. Comps: 4 Pieces for Orch.; Group Questions for Orch.; Var. arrangments. Recordings: Francesca Da Rimini; Sleeping Beauty Suite; Complete Harpsichord Concerti (Bach); Telemann Flute Suite. Mbrships: Comps. Guild (Chmn., 1977); Musicians Union. Hons: FRAM; FGSM. Hobbies: Chess, Mountain Walking. Mgmt: Basil Douglas. Address: Wellside, Well Walk, London NW3, UK. 2, 3.

LEONARD, Nels, Jr., b. 16 Feb. 1931. Ashland, Ky., USA. Music Educator; Oboist; Classical Guitarist. Educ: AB, Marshall Univ.; MM Univ. of SD; PhD, W. Va. Univ.; Cinn. Coll. Conserv. of Music; Hart Coll. of Music; TCL, UK; Winona Coll. m. Barbara Jean Bias, 1 s., 1 d. Career: Public Schl. Music Tchr., Ky., Ind., 1952-55; Asst. Dir. of Music, NC State Univ., 1957-59; Woodwind Instructor, Asst. Dir. of Bands, Univ. of SD, 1955-57; Dir., Music Educ., Prof. of Music, W. Liberty State Coll., W Va., 1959-; Acting Chmn., Dept. of Music, ibid, 1971; Oboe Instructor, W. Va. Univ., 1962 63; Teaching Asst., ibid., 1964-65; Dir., Wheeling Symph. Trng. Orch., 1960-61; num. Classical Guitar Perfs.; num. Apps. as Oboe Soloist w. var. orchs.; num. Radio Apps., WWVA; Ed., Notes as Tempo, 1961-67; Cons., Reviewer, Parker Publishing Co. Recordings: Century Records. Contbr. to: Instrumentalist; Woodwind; World; Notes a Tempo. Mbr., Off., num. Profl. Orgs. Recip. var. Hons. Hobby: Skiing. Address: 15 Crestview Dr., Wheeling, WV 26003, USA. 6, 28.

LEONARD, Stanley Sprenger, b. 26 Sept. 1931. Phila. Pa., USA. Tympanist; Percussionist; Composer; Teacher. Educ: BM & Performer's Cert. in Percussion, Eastman Schl. of Music, Univ. of Rochester, 1954. m. Margaret Holman Leonard, 2 s. Career incls: Prin. Tympanist, Pitts. Symph. Orch., 1956-, apps. in major cities throughout world; Timpani & Percussion Soloist, ibid., 1958, 64, 66 & 73; Sr. Lectr. in Percussion, Carnegie-Mellon Univ., 1958-. Comps. icnl: Fanfare & Allegro for timpani & trumpet; Bachiana; Circus; Prelude; Solo Dialogue. Recordings: 35 w. orchs. for Mercury, Capitol, Everest, Columbia & Command Records. Contbr. to Percussive Notes, PAS. Mbrships. incl: Am. Fedn. of Musicians; Bd. of Dirs., Percussive Arts Soc.; ASCAP. Hobbies: Fishing; Church Activities. Address: 551 Sandree Dr., Pittsburgh, PA 15243, USA.

LEONE, Mae Grace. Baldwin, NY, USA. Musician; Conductor; Composer; Musicologist. Educ: BA; MEd; PhD, NY Coll., NYC D Mus Ed; Applied Music, Ch. Music Cond., Music Educ., Music Lit., Music Merchandising, Music Therapy, Studio Music, Jazz, Theory, Comp. Certs. Debut: Town Hall, NYC; CBS TV; WEAT-TV; WPTV. Career: Dir., Music Radio Broadcast, Freeport, NY; Dir., Prod., Radio, TV Religious Prof.; Organist; Music Dir., Our Lady of Fla. Monastery, N. Palm Beach, Fla. Comps. incl: Marching Band Music; Chmbr. Music; Choir works; Collegium Musicum works; Guitar Ensemble Music. Reocordins: 9 Albums. Publs: The Modern Approach To Musicology, 1965; The Spirit of Music, 1968. Contbr. to: Musical Arts; Ethnomusicol. Mbr. Nat. Guild of Musicians; Nat. Assn. of Organ Tchrs.; Int. Piano Tchrs. Assn. Hons: Community Ldr. of Am. Awards 1970-74; Personalities Of The South Awards, 1970-74; Bicentennial Award in Hlth. & Music. Hobbies: Golf; Tennis; Swimming. Address: 417 Ebb Tide Dr., N Palm Beach, FL 33408, USA.

LEONE, Raphael, b. 20 Aug. 1948. Basel, Switz. Flute Teacher & Player; Piccolo Player; Alto Flute Player. Educ: Dip. Flute Tchng.; Diplomprüfung, d. Career: Flute Player, Collegium Musicum Basel, Filharmonisk Selskap, Oslo, Norway, & Wiener Symphoniker, Vienna, Austria; Recitals in Basel, Oslo, Paris, & Vienna, Austria; Recitals in Basel, Oslo, Paris, & Vienna; Recordings on Radio Oslo & Rdio Vienna. Mbr., Osterreichischer Gewerkschaftsbung. Recip. Förderungspreis, Migros Competition, 1972 & 74. Hobby: Philosophic writers; Hist. of architecture; Painting. Address: A-1120 Vienna, Schlöglgasse 7, Austria.

LEONHARDT, Gustav, b. 30 May 1928. Graveland, Holland. Musician (harpsichord & organ). Educ: Basle Schola Cantorum. m. 3 c. Debut: Vienna, 1950. Career: Concert appearances throughout the world; Prin. role (as J S Bach) in Jean-Marie Straub's film "Chronik der Amma Magdalen Bach", 1967. Recordings of var. workds in Telefunken, Harmonia Mundi & Philips labels. Publs: The Art of Fugue, 1952 Sweelinck, Opera Omnia, Vol. 1 1968; Het Huis Bartolotti, 1976. Address: Herengracht 170, Amsterdam. Holland.

LEONTIS, Christos, b. 11 May 1940. Herakleion Crete, Greece. Composer; Performer (Piano, Lute). Educ: Studied Harmony, Fugue, Counterpoint, Conserv. of Athens, & Conserv. Nat. de Musique, Paris. div., 1 d. Career: Comp. for theatre & films. Compositions: 35 works for theatre perfs., inclng. 6 pieces for tradedies; 15 pieces of film music. Recordings: 7 LPs. Mbr., Union of Greek Comps. & Lyricists (VP). Hons: 1st Prize for film music, 6th Salonica Cinema Fest., 1966. Hobbies: Theatre; Movies. Address: 537 Messoghion Ave., Athens, Greece.

LEPAGE, Jane Weiner, b. 7 May 1931. Montague, Mass., USA. Music Educator. Educ: BMus, Boston Univ.; MSc, Univ. of Mass.; trombone & music education. m. William E. LePage, 5c. Career: chairperson, Music Dept., North Adams State Coll., N Adams, Mass. Publs: Women Composers, Conductors & Musicians of the Twentieth Century, 1980. Contbr. to: Nat. Music Educators Jrnl., Mass. Music News. Mbrships: Pres., Am. Assn. of Univ. Women (Berkshire Co.); Nat. Music Educators Assn.; Mass. Music Educators; Int. League of Women Comps. (affiliate mbr.); Advsry. Bd., Berkshire Community Coll., 1970-75. recip., grant from Mass. Music Educators for Reach Out & Create Proposal, 1975; Fellowship, Learned Socs. of Am.-Contemporary Music, 1960. Hobbies: Golf; Reading; Skiing. Address: 46 Saulnier Dr., Williamstown, MA 01267, USA.

LEPAK, Elizabeth R., b. 20 Jan. 1943. Detroit, Mich., USA. Violist; Teacher. Educ: BA, W. Mich. Univ., MA, Mich. State Univ.; Study w. Robert Schneiber, Joseph Work, Nathan Gordon. m. David E Lepak, 1 d. Career: Voilist, Battle Creek (Mich.) Symph., Kalamazoo (Mich.) Symph., Dearborn (Mich.) Symph., Twin Cities (St. Joseph-Benton Harbor, Mich.) Symph. Mbr., Kalamazoo Symph., String Quartette, 1973-74; Pvte. Tchr., Violin & Viola. Mbrships: AFM; Sigma Alpha Iota; Kalamazoo Symph. Women's Assn. Hobbies: Gardening; Bowling; Water Skiing; Sewing; Travel. Address: 5832 Belard, Portage, MI 49081, USA.

LEPPARD, Raymond John, b. 11 Aug. 1927. London, UK. Conductor. Educ: MA, Cambridge Univ. Career: associated w. Engl. Chmbr. Orch. since its inception; Prin. Cond., BBC Northern Symph. Orch., 1973-; opera, Glyndebourne, Covent Gdn., Coliseum, Santa Fé, San Fran., Aldeburgh, Drottingholm, Oslo; opera realisations, Monteverdi; Ballo della Ingrate, L'Orfoeo, L'Incoronasione di Poppea, Il Ritorno d'Ulysse, & Cavalli, L'Ormindo, La Calisto, L'Egisto, L'Orione, Messa Concertata, etc.; film scores, Laughter in the Dark, Lord of the Flies, Alfred the Great; Brit. Acad. Lectr., 1970; RSA Lectr.,

1973. Has recorded over 100 discs. Realisations publd. by Faber Music. Hons. incl: D Litt. Bath, & Commendatore della Repub. Italiana, 1974. Mgmt: Ibbs & Tillet, London. Address: 16 Hamilton Terr., London NW8, UK. 1.

LEPSØE, Albert, b. 20 June ¢926. Bergen, Norway. Amateur Pianist & Recorder player. Educ: HS of Comm. of Norway, Bergen; Piano lessons from age 6. Mbrships: Hd. of Admin., Bergen Chmbr. Music Soc., 1957-; Comm. of 'Harmonien', Bergen Symph. Orch.; Coun., Festival of Bergen; Ed., Ch. Mag., Cathedral of Bergen; num. cultural clubs & Socs. Publ: 25-year report, Bergen Chmbr. Music Soc., 1935-60; Ed., weekly prog. Harmonien, 1971-73; author of progs. & notes of Chmbr. Music Soc. Hobbies: Music; Ch.; Theatre; Walking; Nature; Political work. Address: Storhaugen 23, 5000 Bergen, Norway.

LEQUIEN, Colette, b. 19 Dec. 1920. Versailles, France. Viola Player; Teacher. Educ: Conservatoire Nat. Supérieur de Musique de Paris. m. Pierre Potet. Career: Viola soloist in num. French orchs. & chmbr. ensembles incl. Orch. Pasdeloup, Orch. de l'ORTF, Sonia Levis & Feminin de Paris str. quartets; currently mbr., Quintette M. Claire Jamet, Trio de Versailles; soloist on French & foreign radios; apps. at Fests. in Aix-en-Provence, Menton, Bordeaux, Avignon, Strasbourg, Stuttgart, etc.; num. tours, France & abroad; Prof. of viola, Conserv. Nat. Supérieur de Paris. Recordings: works by Mozart, Milhaud, Schönberg, Hindemith etc. Hons: num. 1st prizes at Conserv. Nat. Supérieur de Paris; Grand Prix du disque, 1961, '70. Address: 7 rue Jean Bologne, 75016 Paris, France.

LERCH, Richard, b. 24 Oct. 1913. Gleiwitz, Germany (now Poland). Professor; Conductor; Performer (Violin & Piano). Educ: Univ.; Dips. for Violin, Piano, Cond. & Theory, Music Acad., Vienna, Austria. m. Herma Lerch. Debut: Gleiwitz. Career: Violinist, & late Cond.; Prof., Univ. of Posen; Dir. of Studies, Univ. of Mainz, German Fed. Repub.; Cond. & Tchr., Mainze. Compositions: 2 Symphs.; Missa Festiva; Der Gnom (The Gnome), opera, num. chmbr. music & choral works. Recordings of many of his concerts. Hons: Hon. Cond., Wiesbaden Orch. Hobby: Electronic Music. Address: 62 Wiesbaden-Bierstadt, Karl; Salzbach-Str. 10, German Fed. Repub.

LE ROUX, Jean-Louis, b. 15 Apr. 1927. Le Mans, France. Oboist; Conductor. Educ: Dip., Ecole Superieure de Commerce de Paris; Conserv. Nat. de Musique de Paris. m. Marta Bracchi, 2 s., 1 d. Career: Prin. Oboe, San Fran. Symph. Orch.; Assoc. Cond., San Fran. Ballet; Music Dir., San Fran. Contemporary Music Players. Recordings: Three West Coast Composers; Educl. recording. Pres., Bring Your Own Pillow Inc. Addres: 2874 Wash., St., San Fran., CA 94115, USA.

LE SAGE, Sally. b. Farnborough, Kent, UK. Singer. Educ: RCM; ARCM. Career: concert, opera & oratorio perfs. Winner, singing competition, s'Hertogenbosch, Netherlands, 1967. Hobbies: Painting; Reading. Mgmt: Ingpen & Williams. Address: 26 Haven Lane, Ealing, London W5, UK.

LESINSKY, Adam Peter, b. 16 Dec. 1893. Old Forge, Pa., USA. Music Educator; Conductor; Cornettist; Composer. Educ: AB, B Mus, Valparaiso Univ.; M Mus, Am. Conserv. of Music; D Mus, St. Joseph's Coll. m. May Coleman, Dec. 2 d. Career incls: Mbr., Sousa's Gt. Lakes Band, 1918-19; Assoc. Prof. of Music, St. Joseph's Coll., Ind., 1957-66, Guest Tchr. num. univs. in USA; Toured Eastern USA & 10 Countries in Europe as Cond., Father Lach's Boys Symphonic Band; Judged dist., state & nat. contests Comps. incl: Fife, Jug & Bottle Band Novelty, 2 vols., 1951 Belwin. Publs. incl: The Rhythm Master Method for Violin, Viola, Cello & bass, 3 vols. 1937. Contbr. to profl. mags. Mbrships: incl: Phi Mu Alpha. Hons. icnl: St. Cecilia Award, Notre Dame Univ., 1967. Hobbies: Flower Gardening; Viewing Sports. Address: 528 Fleming Blvd., Rensselaer, IN 47978, USA. 2.

LESJAK, Borut, b. 25 May 1931. Ljubljana, Yugoslavia. Composer; Pianist; Percussionist. Educ: Acad. for Music, Ljubljana, 1954. m. Mica Lesjak, 2 d. Debut: as comp., film music; Don't Wait on May, 1957. Career: Free-Lance Comp.; Ldr. & Cond., The Jolly Tobbaggan, Children's radio & TV broadcasts. Comps. incl: num. works for orch.; music for theatre & radio plays; pop songs; film scores (short & long films, documentaries); num. songs, suites, instrumental pieces, musical stories, arrs., etc. for children. Mbr., Soc. of Slovenian Composers, Ljubljana. Hobbies: Mountaineering; Skiing. Address: Rozna dolina c 114, 6 1000 Ljubljana, Yugoslavia.

LESKE, Clemens Theodor, b. 24 Sept. 1923. Aust. Pianist; Director of Conservatorium. Educ: BMus, Melbourne Univ., 1947; Dip., Paris Conserv., 1949; Master course w. Edwin

Fischer, Lucerne. m. Beryl Kimber, 4 s., 1 d. Debut: w. Melbourne Symph. Orch., 1947. Career: soloist w. Melbourne & Sydney Symph. Orchs.; concert tours in USSR, UK, USA, Denmark, German Fed. Repub., Italy, Switz., Netherlands, Malta; Assoc. pianist for Kimber, Ricci, Zukerman, Fried on Aust. tours; Dir., Elder Conservatorium, Univ. of Adelaide, 1977-. Mbrships: Chmn., Univ. Music Soc. & SA Music Examinations Bd.; Patron, Aust. Soc. for Keyboard Music & Adelaide Eisteddfod Soc. Recip., Nat. Critic's Award, 1977. Address: Univ. of Adelaide, Adelaide, SA, Aust.

LESNIAK, Lech Janusz, b. 28 Apr. 1941. Krakow, Poland. Piansit. Educ: MA, High Schl. of Music, Warsaw; Dip., Acad. of Music; Warsaw. m. Magdalena Lesniak, 2 s. Debut: On radio, Krakow, 1955. Career incls: Apps. w. Nat. Phil.; TV & radio; Conservatoire n Moscow; Conservatoire of Geneva; Acad. of Music in Munich; Mbr., Phil. Classic Piano Trio; Tchr., HS, of Music, & Acad. of Music. Recordings of Schubert, Schumann, Saint-Saens. Pederewski & Mozart. Mbr., Polish Soc. of Musicians. Hons: Disting. Award, Int. Competition, E Germany, 1970; Competition as accomp., Poznan, 1974. Hobbies: Skiing; Swimming; Sailing. Address: 02-611 Warszawa, ul. Krasickiego 25, Poland.

LESSER, Laurence, b. 28 Oct. 1938. LA, Calif., USA. Cellist. Educ: BA Harvard Univ., 1961; studied w. Gregor Piatigorsky, m. Masuko Ushioda Lesser. 1 d. Career: Num. concert perfs., USA, Europe, Japan & S Am. apps. w. Boston Symph., Los Angeles Phil., London Phil. & other major orchs.; Asst. to Piatigorsky, teaching at Univ. of Southern Calif., Los Angeles Tchr., Peabody Inst., Balt., Md.; currently teaching at New England Conserv., Boston, Mass. Recordings: Schoenberg Monn Concerto; Lazarof Concerto; Chmbr. Music in Heifetz-Piatigorsky Series Mbr., Phi Beta Kappa. Hons: Cassado Prize, Siena, Italy, 1952. 4th Prize, Tchaikosky Competition, Moscow, USSR. 1966. Mgmt: (Europ), Interartists, The Hague, Netherlands; (Japan), Kajimoto Concert Mgmt; Tokyo, Japan. Address: 65 Bellevue St., Newton, MA 02158, USA.

LESTER, Daphne F, b. 7 Feb. 1931. Wednesbury, Staffs., UK. Head of School Music Department. Educ: Royal Acad. Music, 1949-52; GRSM; LRAM; ARCM. Career: Hd., Music Dept., Ancaster House, Bexhill, Sussex, 1957-60; Kendal HS, Cumbria, 1960-80; Kirkbie Kendal Schl., 1980-; Conductor, Kendal Choral Soc., 1967-. Mbr., Incorp. Soc. Musicians. Hobby: Gardening. Address: Freten Cottage, 1 Ch. View, Natland, Kendal, Cumbria, UK.

LESTER, Eugene, b. 6 Mar. 1921. RI., USA. Musician (Piano, Organ, Harpsichord); Conductor; Composer. Educ: BA, Brown Univ., 1942; B Mus., Yale Univ., 1947. Career: Cond. & Rehearsal Pianist, Martha Graham Dance Co., 1948-; Cond., Jose Limon Dance Co., 1965, '66, & '72; Asst. Cond., Harkness Ballet, 1965; Cond., Batsheva Dance Co., NYC, 1962. Commissions for moder dance choreographers incl: Cortege of Eagles, 1967, The Plain of Prayer, 1968; The Archaic Hours, 1969, all for Martha Graham; Psalm, 1967 for Jose Limon; The Pass, 1960, Eclipse. 1961, Ceremony of Serpents, 1963, for Robert Cohan; Excursions, 1966, Footnotes, 1970, Sight Seeing, 1971, for Paul Sanardo. Hobbies: Coins; Chess; British rock music. Address: 75 Bank St., NY, NY 10014, USA.

LETHCO, Amanda Vick Robbins, b. 29 Oct. 1921. Vicksburg, Miss., USA. Pianist; Harpsichordist; Composer; Teacher; Writer. Educ: B Mus Ed, M Mus, Northwestern Univ.; postgrad. study, Juilliard Schl. of Music, & Columbia Univ.; pvte. study w. Rudolph Ganz, Chgo., James Friskin, Juilliard Ruth Burr, Houston. m. William C. Lethco (dec.), 2 s. 3d. Career: Has given lectures, master classes & workshops, throughout USA & in Japan. Publs: Creating Music at the Piano (18 book series of piano instruction books, w. Dr. W.A. Palmer), 1971-76, Japanese transls., 1976. Mbrships: Pi Kappa Lambda; Sigma Alpha Iota; Nat. MTA. Hon. Doct. Humanities, Whitworth Coll. Hobbies: Art; History. Address: 12467 Queensbury Lane, Houston, TX 77024, USA.

LEUBA, (Julian) Christopher, b. 28 Sept. 1929. Pitts., PA., USA. Professor of Music; Conductor; French Horn Player. Educ: B Mus, Roosevelt Univ., Chgo., 1951: Carnegie Inst. of Technol.; pvte. study, cond., Pierre Monteux, Dr. Richard Lert. div. Career: Prin. Horn, Chgo. Symph., Mpls. Symph., Philharmonia Hungarica; Chmbr. Music Perfs.; apps. in Chgo. & Las Vegas; Guest apps. as Cond.; Cons., Mirafone Corp. & Produtitiv Genossenschaft Waldkraiburg; Prof., Univ. of Wash. Recordings incl: Horn Omnibus (Everest); Mozart Beethoven (Audiophile). Ed. musical pubs. Contbr. to profl. jrnls. Mbrships: Galpin Soc.; AAUP. Hobbies: Hiking; Cycling; Linguistics. Address: 4800 N E 70th St., Seattle, WA 98115, USA.

LEUCHTMANN, Horst, b. 16 Apr. 1927. Braunschweig, Germany. Musicologist. Educ: State Music Schl., Braunschweig; pvte. teaching; PhD, Univ. of Munich, 1957. m. Brita-Angela von Wentzel, 1 s., 2 d. Publs. incl: Ed., Musik in Bayern; Ed., 2nd ed., Complete Works of Orlando di Lasso; Orlando di Lasso; I Sein Leben, 1976, II, Seine Briefe, 1977; Terminorum musicae index septem linguis redactus (polyglot dict. of musical terms, English, French, German, Italian, Spanish, Hungarian, Russian, 1978-1980 ed.-in-chief; transl. of books from English & French into German, authors J Guiart, E Stein, E Ansermet, C M Bowra, R Kirkpatrick etc. Contbr. to num. profl. jrnls. Address: Markgrafenstr. 50, 8000 Munich 82, German Fed. Repub.

LEUKAUF, Robert, b. Apr. 1902. Vienna, Austria. Conductor; Composer. Educ: Vienna Univ., Vienna Acad. of Music; Vienna Coll. of Music. m. Helene Elsner. Debut: as Cond., at the Municipal Theatre, Meissen, Germany. Career: apps. at Municipal Theatres in Hanau, Ingolstadt, & at Geman Theatres, Olmütz & Budweis; has broadcast over ORF Vienna & TV stns. in Munich & Vienna. Compositions incl: Vier Heitere Claudius-Lieder; Hesse-Lieder; Vier Galgenlieder for mixed choir; Varterunser-Psalm for baritone, mixed choir & orch.; Fungensonate 1 for Piano; Indianische Suite for orch.; Altspanische Suite for flute & guitar; Quintet for flute, oboe & str. trio; Bläserquintett; Sinn der Kunst for men's & mixed choirs; "Wenn jeder" for mixed choir. Recordings: Divertissement für Kammerorchester Nr. 1 & Nr. 2; Vieer Orchesterstcke zu einer ungarischen Komödie. Publs: Der Terror Der Lüge oder Musik Als Denksport, 1974. Contbr. to musical jrnls. Mbrships: Austrian Composers' Guild; Austrian Soc. for Contemp. Music; Vienna Mozart Assn. Hons. incl: appointed Prof., 1957; Theodor Körner Prize, 1960. Address: Meyrinkgasse 13, A-1238 Vienna, Austria. 3.

LEUPOLD, Wayne Harvey, b. 13 June 1943. Joliet, Ill., SUA. Organist; Musicologist; Editor. Educ: BM, BA, Valpáraiso Univ.; MM, Syracuse Univ., NY. Career: Ed., Romantic Organ Lit. Series; Ed., The Organists' Companion; Co-fndr., Int. Romantic Organ Music Symposium, Cornell Univ., Ithaca, NY. Contbr. to: AGO Music; The Diapason. Mbrships: AGO; Organ Historical Soc.; Am. Musicol. Soc.; Ctrl. NY Assn. of Music Tchrs. Hobby: Collecting Oriental & Victorian Art. Address: 7 Evergreen Ln., Cazenovia, NY 13035, USA.

LEUZINGER, Rudolf, b. 2 Mar. 1911. Zürich, Switz. Musician m. Helen Schlatter, 3 c. Career: Prin. Bassoon Player, Radio Orchester Lugano, Teatro Municipal Rio de Janerio, Tonhalle-Orchester Zürich; Music Tchr., Musikhoschule Zürich; Mbr. of Jury. Int. Music Competitions of Geneva & Prague; Soloist in concert w. var. orchs. Contbr. to: The World of Music; Schweizerisches Musikerblatt. Mbrships: Hon. Mbr., Swiss Musicians' Union; Gen. Sec., Int. Fedn. of Musicians. Pres., Swiss Perfs. Soc. Recip., 2nd Prize, Int. Music Competition of Geneva, 1939. Hobby: Yachting. Address: Waserstrasse 83, CH 8053 Zürich, Switzerland. 19.

LEVARIE, Siegmund, b. 24 July 1914. Austria. Professor; Author; Conductor. Educ: PhD, Univ. Vienna, 1938; Cond. Dip., Vienna Conserv., 1935. m. Norma Levarie, 1 d. Career: Fndr. & Cond., Collegium Musicum Univ. Chgo., in many 1st perfs. of old music, 1938-52. Publs. incl: Le Nozze di Figaro, 1952; Fundamentals of Harmony, 1954; Guillaume de Marchant, 1954; Musical Italy Revisited, 1963; Tone, 1968, (w. Ernst Levy); The Nature of Opera, 1974; (ed.) Lucu Van-Jung Page (1892-1972); Contbr. of articles & reviews to profl. jrnls. Address: 624 Third St., Brooklyn, NY 11215, USA.

LEVARY, Tibor (Formerly Farkas Tiberiu), b. 5 Sept. 1914. Sibiu, Romania. Composer; Pianist; Choir Conductor. Educ: Musical Conserv., Brasev, 1931; MA, Bucharest Univ.,1935; Profl. qualification, Assn. Comps., Bucharest, 1949. div., 1 s. Debut: Bucharest, 1949. Career: Fest. apps.; radio broadcasts, Romania; in Israel, 1969-. Comps: Zold erdönek lombjai közt; Szureti dal; Arany-völgy (musical) Nu voi uita niciodata; Numai tu esti visul meu; Cintecul Plutasilor 52 children's songs & lullabys; relig. songs & hymns. Mbrships: Assn. of Romanian Comps. (1946-58); ACUM, Israel. Hobbies: Trips; Poetry. Address: PO Box 854, 16 Shamai St., Jersulem, Israel.

LEVETT, James Alfred, b. 7 Mar. 1909. Rochester, Kent., UK. Organist. Educ: ARCO; CHM. m. Dorothy Joan Sowerby; Career: Num. Ch. Appts., inclng. Asst. Organist, Rochester Cathedral. Accomp. & Organist, Rochester Choral Soc.; Radio & TV Appearances. var. Cathedrals & Chs. Mbrships: Cond., Rochester Jr. Choral Soc.; Chmn., Rochester Music Club. Hobbies: Reading; Walking; Gardening. Address: St. Mary's House, 30 St. Margaret's St., Rochester, Kent ME 1 1TU, UK. 1.

LEVIN, Gregory John, b. 8 Mar. 1943. Wash., DC, USA. Composer; Conductor; Pianist. Educ: BA, Harvard Coll., 1967; MFA. Brandeis Univ., 1969, PhD, ibid., 1975; studied comp. w. Arthur Berger, Luciano Berio, Pierre Boulex, Leon Kirchner, Billy Jim Layton & Seymour Chaloff. m. Susan A. Harpel. 2 s. Debut: Nat. Gall. of Art. Career: Asst. Cond., Brandeis Choral Union, 1968-70; Liner notes for Acoustics Rsch. Inc. & Deutsche Grammonphon Gesellschaft, 1969; Musical Dir. & Cond., Syracuse New Music Ensemble, 1970-72; Cond., Syracuse Univ. Orch. & Symph. Orch., 1971; Asst. Prof. of Music Theory & Comp., Syracuse Univ. Schl. of Music, 1970-72; Musical Dir. & Cond., The Levin Ensemble, 1972-; Middle & HS Tchng. Specialist, RI Coun., on the Arts, 1972-; Vis. Asst. Prof. of Music Theory & Comp., Univ. of RI, 1972-73; Comp.-in-Res., Ind. Univ., South Bend. 1972; Asst. Prof. of Music Theory & Comp., Univ. of Calgary, Canad, 1973—; Dir., Calgary Chmbr. Players, 1974-. Compositions incl: Dee's Toast, 1972; Spring Tide, 1973; The Temple of Love (forthcoming). Recordings: The White Goddess (film & score), etc. Contbr. to Musical Quarterly. Pres., Raga-Mala Music Soc. Recip., sev. grants, commissions, prizes, awards & scholarships. Address: 2852, 24 St. NW, Calgary, Alta. T2N 1N4, Canada.

LEVIN, Philip Arthur, b. 9 Sept. 1945. Phila., Pa., USA. Musician, Recorder. Modern & Baroque Bassoon, Historical instruments; Maker of Historical instruments. Educ: B Mus., Manhattan Schl. of Music. Career: Perf. w. Music for A While, Touring Grp. based at Sarah Lawrence Coll., Bronxville, NY; Freelance Musician, Perfs. in Carnegie Hall, Carnegie Recital Hall, Tully Hall, NYC; Dir., Participant, Early Music Workshops throughout USA; Designer, Maker, Repair Specialist of Historical Woodwind, Instruments. Recordings: Mercury, 1750 Arch.; Vanguard. Hobbies: Hi Fidelity Sound Systems; Flying; Skindiving; Collecting Woodwind Instruments; Cooking. Mgmt: Sheldon Soffer Mgmt., Inc., 130 W. 56th St., NY, NY 10019, USA. Address: 112 1st Ave., NY, NY 10009, USA.

LEVIN, Rami Yona, b. 27 Feb. 1954. Brooklyn, NY, USA. Composer; Oboist; Teacher. Educ: BA, Yale Univ.,1975; MA, Univ. of Calif., San Diego, 1978; Aspen Music Schl., 1977; comp. study w. Kenneth Gaburo, Yehudi Wyner, Robert Morris, Bernard Rands, Miriam Gideon & others. Career: Oboist, Yale Repertory Theatre, 1972-73, Bar Harbor Music Fest., 1976, & Sonor (Contemporary Music Ensemble), 1976-77; perf. at var. comps. recitals; pvte. tchr. of oboe, recorder & piano. Comps: Now We Are Six (song cycle), 1975; Str. Quartet, 1978; Doubletake for 2 pianos, 1976; Ambages for Guitar, 1976; Connections, for oboe solo, 1976; other works for wind instruments & piano. Mbr., League of Women Comps. recip., 1st prize, Aspen Music Fest. Comps. Competition, 1977. Hobbies: Work with Children; Writing Children's Books; Cycling. Address: c/o Bresler, 12 Lindberg Ln., New City, NY 10956, USA.

LEVIN, Robert Jacob, b. 7 June 1912. Oslo, Norway. Pianist. Educ: piano w. Prof. Arpad Lehner & Nils Larsen; comp. w. Gustav Lange & Fartein Valen. m. Solveig Bernstein, 2 children. Debut: Oslo, 1932. Career: Concert Pianist, Soloist w. all orchs. in Norway; num. broadcasts on radio & TV, Norway & Scandinavian Broadcasting; Accomp. for many noted artists in Norwayh & abroad; Prof., Rector, Norwegian Acad. of Music. Has recorded w. many artists. Mbrships: TONO (comps. assn., Norway); Bd., Oslo Phil. & Norwegian Soc. of Art of Music. Hons: Royal Order of St. Olav, Kt. 1; HM the King's Gold Medal of Merit. Address: Gebelsgate 46 b, Oslo 2, Norway.

LEVINE, Amy Miller, b. 11 Mar. 1939. Brooklyn, NY, USA. Composer; Teacher; Conductor. Educ: BA, Bennington Coll.; comp. fellowship, Brandeis Univ. m. Joel Robert Levine 2c. Comps: 5 duets for 2 violins; Largo for solo violin. Contbr. of reviews to Independent Jrnl. Newspaper; San Rafael Pointer Newspaper. Mbrships: ASCAP; League of Women Comps. Hons: Commissions from Inverness Music Fest. & Marin Symph. Assn. Hobbies: Music; Art; Theatre. Address: 22 Bradcliff Ct., San Rafael, CA 94901, USA.

LEVINE, Jeffrey Leon, b. 19 Sept. 1942. Brooklyn., NY, USA. Composer; Performer on Double-Bass. Educ: AB, Brown Univ., Providence, RI; M Mus, Yale Univ.; Dip. d'Onore, Accademia Chigiana, Siena, Italy. 1s. Career: Specialist in contemporary music as perf. on double-bass. Comps. Parentheses (string); From (2 pianos); Cadenza (solo piano); Harpsichord quartet (w. flute, clarinet & viola); Divertimento (10 solo strings); Trigonon (2 violin & viola). var. recordings of contemporary music & chmbr. music. Mbr., ASCAP. Hons: Tanglewood Commission, 1967; Fulbright Scholar, 1968-69; Oakland Ballet Commission (for Crystals), 1975. Address: 4133 Webster ST., Oakland, CA 94609, USA.

LEVITAN, Fanny, b. 5 JuNe 1928. Etterbeek, Brussels, Belgium. Pianist; Accompanist; Mezzo-soprano. Educ: Académie de Musique d'Anderlecht, Brussels; Charles Scharrés Superior Schl. of Piano; grad. (singing), Académie de Musique, Brussels. m. Samuel Levitan. Career: num. solo apps. in recitals, oratorios, concerts, in Can.; accomp. for disting. artists & for opera prod. in Waterloo, Ont.; apps. on CBC; vocal coach, tchr. of piano, Royal Conserv. of Music, Toronto, Ont. Mbrships: Toronto Musicians' Assn.; Musicians Guild of Montreal; Friends of the Metropolitan Opera, NY; Nat. Travel Club, USA. Hons: num. prizes at colls.; dip. of excellence as piano accomp., Int. Jury of Musical Studies in Brussels; semifinalist, Int. Vocal Competition, Brussels, 1962. Hobbies: Books on History; Biographies; Music; Travel. Address: 563 Castlefield Ave., Toronto, Ont. M5N 1L7, Can.

LEVY, Frank, b. 15 Oct. 1930. Paris, France. Cellist; Composer. Educ: BS, Juilliard Schl. of Music; MA, Univ. of Chgo.; pvte. study, comps. w. Hugo Kauder, Cello w. Leonard Rose & Janos Starker. m. Barbara Levy. Career: many Solo & Chmbr. Music apss.; Prin. Cello, Radio City Music Hall Orch. Has publd. 36 comps. inclng: Go Down Death, for narrator, trumpet, harp & solo dancer; Seven Bapetelles for oboe, cello & piano; Symph. No. 3; Sonata for Violin & Piano. Recordings: Boar's Head Festival; Duo for Violins; Clarinets Sonata; Introduction & Rondo for 3 Clarinets; Suite for Horn & Piano; Brass Quintet. Contet. to The Nation. Mbrships: ASCAP; Am. Music Ctr.; Nat. Soc. of Lit. & the Arts. Hons. incl: Am. Music Ctr. Comp. Assistance Grant, 1973, 78. Hobbies: Photography; Gardening; Hiking. Address: 19 Virginia St., Tenafly, NJ 07670, USA.

LEVY, Gerardo, b. 23 Oct. 1924. Berlin, Germany. Flutist; Conductor; Teacher. Educ: Grad., Coll. Musicum, Buenos Aires, Argentina; B Mus, Boston Univ., USA. Debut: Buenos Aires, aged 18. Career: (past) Soloist, var. chmbr. ensembles, USA, Europe & S Am.; Prin. Flutist, Orquesta Filarmónica, Radio Nacional Orquesta Sinfónica & Amigos de la Música, Buenos Aires; (present) Tchr., Sarah Lawrence Coll. & NY Univ.; Prin. Flutist, Music for Westchester Orch., Clarion Orch., Co-Prin. Flautist, NYC Opera; Fac., Sessions Senese per la Musica l'arte, Siena, Italy & Mich.-Sarah Lawrence Summer Sess., Florence; Dir. & Cond., Caecilian Chmbr. Ensemble, NY; Soloist, var. chmbr. ensembles, Europe & S Am. Recordings: CRI, Vox, Vanguard, Ricordi & Serenus Labels. Mbr., Bd. Dirs., NY Flute Club. Hobby: Philately. Address: 151 W 93rd St., Apt. 3-S, NY, 10025, USA.

LEVY, Michael Sigmund, b. 21 Oct. 1945. Johannesburg, S Africa. Musicologist; Teacher of Piano, Organ & Theory of Music; Organist. Educ: BA, 1968, BAHons. 1969, MA, 1974, Univ. of Witwatersand, ATCL (Tchrs.), 1970. Career: Asst. to Concert Mgr. of Nat. Symph. Orch., Admnstv. Off. of SABC Jr. Orch. & Sec. of SABC Choir, South African Broadcasting Corp.; currently Musicol., Southern African Music Rights Org. (SAMRO), Johannesburg, Choirmaster & Organist, Music Tchr. for both individual & Class tuition, piano, organ, percussion band, Orff instruments. Publ: Catalogue of serious Music, Orginial Works, Arrangements & Orchestrations, Published & in Manuscript, SAMRO, 1979. Hobbies incl: Art; Theatre, Colour photography. Address: 71 Delft, 50 Olivia Rd., Berea, Johannesburg 2198, S Africa.

LEVY, Morten, b. 28 Jan. 1939. Copenhagen, Denmark. Musicologist; Ethnomusicologist; Scholar of Musical Semiotics. Educ: Musical theory & musical hist. at Conserv. of Copenhagen, 1964. m. 2s. Career: Music Stage Mgr., Royal Theatre of Copehagen, 1964-67; Advsr. on Folk Music to the Danish Broadcasting, 1966-70; Archivst, Danish Folklore Archives, 1967-73; Scholarship, Inst. of Musicol., Univ. of Copehagen, 1973-79. Publs: Den Staerke Slatt, 1974 (on Magic Music of Medieval Scandinavia & its survival by Fiddle Players of Norway). Address: Dag Hammarskjölds Allee 3, 2100 Copehagen 0, Denmark.

LEWANDO, Ralph, b. 28 April 1898. Boston, Mass., USA. Specialist in vioce production; Violinist Violist; Music critic; Music editor. Educ: Univ. of Vienna, Austria; Dip., Vienna Acad. of Music & Dramatic Art; Studied w. Leopold Auer & Ottoker Sevcik, ibid.; Studied cond. w. Franz Schalk, voice w. Rosa Papier-Paumgartner. m. Olga Wolf Lewando. Debut: Violin soloist, Vienna Phil., Vienna. Career: Former ed. music publr., Music & Artists Mag., assoc. ed., Music Jrnl., music critic, Scripps-Howard Pittsburgh Press (28 yrs.); Currently chief ed., Musical Living Mag.; Music fac., Chatham Coll. & Duquesne Univ.; Ensemble instr., Vienna Acad. of Music. Mbrships. incl: Music Critics Assn.; Metropol. Opera Nat. Coun.; Am. Fedn. of Musicians; MENC; Music Tchrs. Nat. Assn.; Am. Symph. Orch. League; Int. Soc. of Performing Arts Admnstrs.; Assn. of Coll., Univ. & Community Arts Admnstrs. Hobbies: Playing chmbr.

music; Editing music mags. Address: 303 W 66th St., NY, NY 10023, USA.

LEWENTHAL, Raymond, b. 1926. San Antonio, USA. Pianist; Editor; Musicologist; Writer. Educ: Juilliard Schl. of Msuic; Chigiana Acad., Siena; studied w. Lydia Cherkassy, Olga Samaroff-Stowkowski, Alfred Cortot & Guido Agosti. Career: has made concert tours thru'out USA, Europe & S Am.; perf. Liszt cycle, 1965, 66 & 67; specializes in music of 19th century. Publs: Ed., Piano Music of Alkan; Ed. Piano Music for One Hand; Ed., Alkan, Funeral March for Pappagallo, Hons: Kt. of Arts, & Letters, 1970; Gainesborough Award; Winner, Young Artists Contest, UCLA; Harriet Cohen Award. Address: 51 E 78th St., NYC, NY, USA. 3.

LEWIN, Frank, b. 27 March 1925. Breslau, Germany. Composer; Teacher; Musical Director; Associate Professor. Educ: Cert., Baldwin (LI) Conserv. of Music; B Mus, Yale Univ. Schl. of Music m. Elsbeth Gaertner Lewin, 3d. Career: Assoc. Prof. of Comp., Yale Univ. Schl. of Music, New Haven, Conn., USA; Assoc. Prof., Columbia Univ. Schl. of the Arts, NYC. Comps. incl: Theater music; operas; concert music (concertos, song cycles, historical outdoor plays); TV (series & specials); films. Recordings incl: Requiem for Robert F Kennedy. Publs incl: Expo 67; Man and His Sound, 1968. Contbr. of articles on music, sound to num. periodicals. Mbrships: Soc. of Motion Picture & TV periodicals. Mbrships: Soc. of Motion Picture & TV Engrs.; Nat. Acad. of TV Arts & Scis. Mgmt: Polygon Artists, New Haven, Conn. Address: 113 Magnolia Lane, Princeton, NJ 08540, USA.

LEWIN-RICHTER, Andrés, b. 22 Mar. 1937. Miranda, Spain. Composer. Educ: Dr. of Indl. Engrng., Barcelona Univ.; MSEE, Columbia Univ., NYC. m. Cristina Vidal-Quadras, 1 s., 1 d. Career: Exec. Dir., Conjunt Catalá de Música Contemporánia, Barcelona, & Phonos Electronic Music Lab., Barcelona. Comps. publd. incl: Study No. 1; Study No. 2; Densities; Sequenza No. 1 for percussion & tape; Sequenza per Anna for vioce & tape; film & stage music. Comps. recorded: Study No. 1 Electronic Music. Mbr., Acoustical Soc. of Am.; Sec., Catalan Comps. Assn. Contbr. to Spanish musical & musicol. publs: Address: Reina Cristina 1, Barcelona 3, Spain.

LEWIS, (Sir) Anthony Carey, b. 2 Mar. 1915. Bermuda, Conductor; Editor; Composer. Educ: Mus B., MA., Cantab. m. Lesley Lisle Lewis. Career: BBC Music Dept., 1935-46; Peyton-Barber Prof. of Music Birmingham Univ., 1967-68; Prin., RAM, 1968-. Compositions: Trumpet Concerto; Horn Concerto; A Tribute of Praise for unaccomp. chorus. Recordings: Monteverdi; Vespers; Handel; Semele, Sosarme; Blow; Venus & Adonis; Rameau; Hippolyte et Aricie Purcell; Come ye sons of art, Fairy Queen, King Arthur, Publs: Fndr. & Gen. Ed., Musica Britannica; Ed., Handel, Apollo & Daphne, Semele (co-ed.), Athalia, Purcell, Fairy Queen, Sacred Music (co-ed.), Contbr. to musical jrnls. Pres., Royal Musical Assn., 1963-69. Hons: Kt., 1972; CBE., 1967; Hon. Mus D., Birmingham; Hon. RAM; FRCM; FTCL; GSM. Hobby: Gardening. Address: RAM, Marylebone Rd., London NW1, UK. 1.

LEWIS, Anthony David Stanley, b. 9 Nov. 19049. Leeds, UK. Cellist. Educ: LRAM. m. Ann Wells. Debut: w. Medici String Quartet, Wigmore Hall, London, 1973. Career: Mbr., Medici String Quartet (res., York Univ., 1974-77), 1971-; BBC Radio broadcasts; Yorks; ITV prog., 1976. Recordings: w. Medici String Quartet, EMI. Hobbies: Golf; Real Ale. Address: B 26 Langwith Coll., Univ. of York, Heslington, York, UK.

LEWIS, Arthur, b. 30 Oct. 1935. Philadelphia, Pa., USA. Violist; Educator. Educ: BA, BM, Mus. Ed., Coll. of Pacific; New England Conserv. of Music; DM, Ind. Univ.; Tanglewood, 1958. m. Nancy Glorian Thomas, 2 s., 1 d. Career: Solo apps. & Prin. Viola, Balt. Symph.; Violist w. Phila. Orch.; Chmbr., Symph. of Phila.; Buffalo Phil.; First desk, Apsen Festival Orch.; Solo & Chmbr., Nat. Educl. TV; Fac. Int. Congress of Strings; Peabody Conserv.; Assoc. Prof., Ill. State Univ.; Ed., Aspen Festival Prog. Notes. Publs: Ed., Notes on Music, Idea & History by Kurt Oppens. Mbrships: Phi Kappa Phi; Pi Kappa Lambda; Phi Mu Alpha. Recip. num. awards & scholarships. Hobbies: Backpacking; Bicycling; Chess. Address: Rte. 1, Bloomington, IL 61701, USA. 3.

LEWIS, Eric Michael, b. 27 Feb. 1946. Bronx, NY, USA. Violinist. Educ: BM., MMus, Manhattan Schl. of Music; Postgrad. study in quartet perf., SUNY Binghampton. m. Judith Glyde. Career: Perfs. w. LSO, Am. Symph. Orch., Pro Arte Chmbr. Orch., Springfield (Mass.) Symph., NY Community Symph., New World Symph.; Fndr., N. Bergen Chmbr. Orch. & Soc.; Concertmaster, Manhattan Orch.; First Violin, Manhattan String Quartet, 1970-; Quartet in Res., Corfu Music Fest., Greece; Fac. Mbr., Quartet in Res., Cornell Univ. Fac. Mbr.,

Quartet in Res., Grinnell Coll., 1972-; Patriot for Me (play), Love Story (film), num. educl. TV progs. Mbrships: Coll. Music Soc.; AAUP; Pub. Events Comm., Grinnell Coll.; Local 802, Am. Fedn. of Musicians. Hons: Full schlrships., Manhattan Schl. of Music; Tchng. Fellowship, SUNY; Iowa Arts Coun. Grant for Quartet Perf.; NY State Arts Coun. Grant; Masterworks Fndn. Young Artists Award, 1968; Finalist, Naumberg Chmbr. Music Award, 1974. Hobbies: Reading; History; Philosophy; Golf; Ping-pong. Mgmt: Thea Dispeker, NYC. Address: 1589 Sylvan Rd., Mohegan Lake, NY 10547, USA.

LEWIS, Henry, b. 16 Oct. 1932. LA, Calif., USA. Conductor; Clarinettist; Double Bassist. Educ: Univ. of Southern Calif. m. Marilyn Horne, 1 d. Career: Double Bassist, LA Phil. Orch.; Mbr., 7th Army Symph. Orch., 1955-57; Cond., ibid., making many radio broadcasts w. orch.; Fndr. & Dir., String Soc. of LA (later LA Chmbr. Orch.) touring Europe in 1960's; Cond., LA Phil., 1961-65, Am. Symph. Orch., Carnegie Hall, 1967, NJ Symph. Orch., 1968-, & Met. Opera, 1972; Guest Cond., num. orchs. inclng. LSO, RPO, & La Scala Opera Orch.; Music Dir., LA Opera Co., 1965. Address: NJ Symph. Orch., 1020 Broad St., Newark, NJ 07102, USA.

LEWIS, Jeffrey, b. 28 Nov. 1942. Neath, S Wales, UK. University Lecturer; Composer; Organist; Pianist; Conductor. Educ: B Mus, M Mus, Univ. Coll., Cardiff; ARCM (Organ, perfs.) Studied w. Stockhausen & Ligeti, Darmstadt, w. Boguslaw Schaffer, Krakow, w. Don Banks, London; PhD, Univ. of Wales. Career: Pianist, Paris Chmbr. Ensemble, 1967-68; Lectr. in 20th Century Comp. Techniques & Expmtl. Music, City of Leeds Coll. of Music, 1969-72; Lectr., Dept. of Music, Univ. Coll. of N Wales, Bangor, 1973-. Mutations I (orch.); Mutations II (organ); Antiphony for 4 Grps. of Instruments; Memoria; Chmbr. Concerto (orch.); Esultante (organ). Mbrships. incl: Performing Right Soc.; CGGB. Hons. incl: Welsh Arts Coun. Bursary, 1967-68; 2nd Prize, Int. Organist-Comp. Compeition, Zwolle Netherlands, 1972; 2nd Prize, Stroud Fest. Int. Comps. Competition, 1972. Address: Ael-Y-Bryn, Sling, Tregarth, Bangor, N Wales, UK. 3. 4.

LEWIS, Lorna Jane, b. 24 July 1937. Worcester, UK. Recitalist (Flute, Recorders & Early Woodwind); Teacher (Flute); Director. Educ: BA, Univ. Coll., London, 1960; ALCM; pvte. study, Flute, Baroque Flute & Recorders, Var. tchrs. m. J V V Twycross-Lewis, 2 d., 1 s. Debut: Southbank, London, 1971. Career: Tchr. of Flute, Stratford-upon-Avon Grammar Schl. for Girls, 1970-73, 1976- & S Warwicks. Coll. of Further Educ. & S Warwicks. Music Ctr., 1971-73; Flute Tchr., Univ. of Warwick & Wroxall Abbey, 1975-76; Pvte. tchr.; Fndr., Age of Gold Ensemble, 1973, for Flute & Early Woodwind Music, perfs. throughout UK & on Nationwide TV; Lecturer-recitals to schls., 1974-. Contbr. to: Recorder & Music Mag. Mbrships: ISM; Musicians Union; Galpin Soc. Hobbies incl: Thinking; Reading. Address: 30 Grove Rd., Stratford upon Avon, Warwicks., CV37 6PB, UK. 23, 27, 29, 30.

LEWIS, L Rhodes, b. 27 Nov. 1919. Emporia, Kans., USA. Orchestral Conductor; Music Educator. Educ: B Mus, Baker Univ.; MS., Kans. State Univ.; PhD, Univ. of Iowa; Dip., US Navy Schl. of Navy Schl. of Music; studied cond. w. Robert Sedore, Eugene Ormandy, James Dixon Alfred Wallenstein. m. Roberto Palmquist Lewis, 3 s., 1d. Career: Cond. & Musical Dir., Am. Community Symph. Orch., 1961-; European Concert Tours to Denmark, Norway, Sweden, Finland, Soviet Union, Poland, Czech., Austria, Germany, France, England, Yugoslavia, Italy, Switz., Luxembourg, The Netherlands, Belgiu.; Prof., Dept. Chmn., Univ. of Wis., Eau Claire, 1963-73. Publs: A Study of the Am. Community Symph. Orch. in the USA, 1956. Mbrships. incl: Am. Soc. of Comps. & Conds.; Bd. Dirs., Am. Symph. Orch. League, 1956-59; Pres., Wis. Symph. Orch. Assn., 1966-68. Hons: Outstanding Alumni, Kans. State Univ.; Croix du Commandeur, French Legion of Hon., Paris, 1961. Hobby: Travel. Address: Box 101, Eau Claire, WI 54701, USA. 2, 12.

LEWIS, Marcia Ann, b. 27 Feb. 1941. Dodgeville, Wis., USA. Singer; Professor of Voice and Opera. Educ: B Mus, Univ. of Wis., Madison; Mus M, ibid.; Doctoral work, Northwestern Univ., Evanston, Ill. Career: Vocal solo recitals at Northwestern Univ., Blossom Music Festival, Aspen Music Schl., Augustana Coll., Northeastern Ill. Univ., Carleton Coll. & Univ. of Wis.; Alto soloist w. Trinity Coll. Mens' Glee Club, Augustana Concert Band, Keuka Pk. String Quartet, Chgo. Early Music Ensemble, Northwest Lyric Opera Guild, N. Shore Chmbr. Choir, Chgo. Symph. Chorus, Rockefeller Chapel Choir, Anshe Emet Synagogue & sev. ch. & coll. choirs. Mbrships: Bd., Chgo. Chapt., Nat. Assn. Tchrs. of Singing; Phi Kappa Phi; Musicians Club of Women of Chgo.; Am. Choral Dirs. Asns.; Metropolitan Opera Guild; Sigma Alpha Iota; Am. Guild of Musical Artists;

MENC; Music Tchrs. Nat. Assn.; AAUW; Sigma Epsilon Sigma; Pi Lambda Theta. Hons: Sev. awards, Sigma Alpha Iota, 1962-63; 1st. place, Composition Contest, Univ. of Wis., 1965; Fac. Growth Award, Am. Luth. Ch. & Augustana Coll., 1967; Upper Midwest Metropolitan Opera Contest Winner, 1968. Hobbies: Golf; Reading; Sewing. Address: 9630 Higgins Rd., Rosemont, IL 60018, USA.

LEWIS, Raymond, b. 28 Jan. 1947. London, UK. Pianist; Organist; Conductor. Educ: FTCL, GTCL, ARCO; Rucky van Mill, Denys Darlow, TCL. 1s. Debut: Harrogate Fest.; Purcell Room, S Bank. Career: Num. recitals as solo pianist & in chmbr. music; Dir. of Music, Ch. St. Stephen, Westminster & Scottish Nat. Ch., Covent Gdn.; Vis. Lectr., Music Dept., Winchester Schl. of Art; formerly Dir. Marcello Ensemble & pianist, Vitali Trio. Hons: Ricordi Cond. Prize. Hobbies: Classic Sports Cars. Mgmt: Terry Slasberg Agency. Address: Melbury Grange, Mavelstone Rd., Bickley, Kent BR1 2SZ, UK.

LEWIS, Richard. Concert & Operatic Singer (tenor). Educ: RMCM (w. Norman Allin); RAM; FRAM; FRMCM; LRAM. Career: apps. in num. operatic incl. premieres of Rape of Lucretia (Britten); Troilus & Cressida (Walton), Midsummer Marriage (Tippett), Moses & Aaron (1st. Brit. perf.); regular apps. at Glyndbourne; guest artist, opera houses at San Francisco, Chgo., Vienna, Berlin, Buenos Aires, etc.; num. oratorio & recital apps. in UK, USA, Aust., NZ, etc.; apps. on TV & radio. num. recordings. recip., CBE, 1963. Addresss: White Acre, Highgate Road, Forest Row, W Sussex, UK.

LEWIS, Victor Joseph, b. 29 July 1919. Golders Green, London, UK. Impresario; Conductor; Composer. Chairman & Managing Director. Educ: Ravensfield Coll., Mill Hill, London. m. Jill Anstey, 1 d. Career: Appeared as Actor in films, "Goodbye Mr. Chips" & "Date With a Dream", (also composed film score for the latter); Fndr., Coll. Band at age of 12, & became Prof. Musician, 1937; Played w. Ted. Heath & Stephane Grappelly, 1945-; Launched Jazzmen w. Jack Parnell, (on record), 1944, and later made personal apps; Launched 20 pieces Inovations Concert Orch., 1950; Cond., USA, S Africa, Can., Venezuela & most European countries. Comps. incl: Romance for Violin; Beyond the Hill; My Special Friends; Serenade for Strings; Red (tribute to Shostakovich); Expressions; Have I Changed; Lapis Lazuli, etc. Recordings incl: Mine & Theirs, (w. RPO); Big Band Bash; My Life My Way; My Friends the Stars; My Friends The Bandleaders; Academy Award Winners, etc. Mbr., num. profl. orgs. Hobbies: Cricket; Golf; Tennis; Philately; Photography; Record Collectng Address: 36 Pine Grove, Totteridge, London N20, UK.

LEWISTON, David, b. 11 May 1929. London, UK. Musician; Writer; Photography. Educ: Lic., 1952; Grad., 1953, TCL. Career: Mag. Writer & Ed., 1956-72; Staff Ed., Forbes & Banking Mag.; Photojrnlst., specialising in musical, dance & Far Eastern subjects; musical field work, Far E, 1966-67, Ctrl. & S Am., 1967-68 & 75-76, Himalayas, 1972-. Recordings: ethnomusical anthols. for Nonesuch Explorer Series & BBC Sound Archives. Address: co Nonesuch Records, 1855, Broadway, NY., NY, USA.

LEYTENS, Luc M E L., b. 14 Nov. 1936. Antwerp, Belgium. Secretary-General of "Jeugd en Muziek-Jeunesses Musicals" (Youth & Music), Belgium. Educ: J D & Can. mus., Univ. of Louvain. m. Mimi Boereboom, 3 children. Career: Barrister, Antwerp 1960-63; Fndr. (1963) & Sec., Antwerp Cathedral Concerts; Asst. Sec.-Gen., Youth & Music, Belgium, 1963-69; Sec.-Gen., ibid., 1969-; Prof. of Musical Hist., Schl. for Journalists, Brussels, 1971-; Mbr. Perm. Juridical Commission, Int. Fedn. "Jeunesses Musicales", 1964-74; Lectr., Royal Flemish Conserv. of Music, Antwerp, 1966-. Publs: Peter Benoit, 1972. Jef Van Hoof, 1974 (w. Paul de Raedt). Contbr. to jrnls., encyclopediae, etc. Mbr. ed. bd., 'Gamma'. Mbrships. incl: Flemish Soc. for Musical Hist.; Assn. of ARt Histns., Louvain. Hobbies: Reading; Collecting Books & Records. Address: Cogels Osylei 72, B-2600 Berchem-Antwerp, Belgium.

LHOTKA-KALINSKI, Ivo, b. 30 July 1913. Zagreb, Yugoslavia. Composer; Voice Teacher. Educ: Degree in Law; 2 Dips., Zagreb Music Acad.; studied w. Lldebrando Pizzetti, Rome. m. Bosiljka Zec, 1 s. Career: Voice Tchr., 1940-. Comps. (all operatic, except as noted) incl: Pomet the Matchmaker, 1944; Croatian Chronicle (cantata), 1952; The Llliterate, 1954; The Legend (ballet), 1955; The Journey, 1956; The Button, 1957; Power Politics, 1958; The Rogue's Song (cantata), 1959; The Shining City, 1967. Recordings: Radio Zagreb. Publs: The Art of Singing, Book 1, 1953, Book II, 1975. Mbr., Croation Assn. of Comps. Mgmt: Aklor-Ed. (Barenreiter-Verlag) Kassel; Peters Musikverlag, Frankfurt. Address: Primorska 14, Zagreb, Yugoslavia.

LI, Judith Anderson, b. 27 July 1938. Bedford, Ind., USA. Violinist; Mezzo-Soprano; Professor of Music History. Educ: PhD, Musicol. & MM, Cath. Univ. of Am.; BM Violin & BME, Ind. Univ. m. Karl G Li, 1 s., 2d. Career: Prof. of Music Hist., Univ. of DC, Wash. DC; Vis. Assoc. Prof., Univ. Md., Catonsville; Assoc. Prof. of Music Hist. & Voice, Bowie State Coll., Md.; Violinist w. fac. trio, Univ. of DC performing in Wash. DC area; Apps. as Mezzo-Soprano & Alto Soloist locally; Visiting Prof., China Culture Coll., Taipei, Taiwan; Lecture & seminar East, 1977, '78. Publs: English Comic Opera: The Works of Stephen Storace, 1978; Stephen Storace: His Life & Works, 1979. Mbrships: Am. Musicol. Soc.; Am. String Tchrs. Assn. Hons: Award for Outstanding Contributions to Music in Taiwan, Hong's Fndn. for Educ. & Culture, Taipei, Taiwan, 1977. Address: 49 Stonegate Dr., Silver Spring, MD 20904, USA. 29.

LIANG, Ming-Yüeh, b. 11 Oct. 1941. Peking, China. Ethnomusicologist; Composer; Performer of Chinese Instruments. Educ: Cert., Taiwan Art Acad.; B Mus, Univ. of HI; MA & PhD, UCLA. m. Naomi Kami, 2 children. Debut: City Hall, Hong Kong, 1964. Career incls: Chmn., World Music Dept., San Fran. Conserv. of Music; Free Univ., Berlin; Guest Soloist, broadcasts in USA, Germany, France; solo recitals & lectures at major Am. & Asian univs., etc.; currently Assoc. Prof., Univ. of BC. Comps. incl: Yü Lo Ch'un Hsiao for ming-cheng; T'ai Shan Hsing for sheng; Shen-Yu for orch. & ch'in solo; Floating Clouds for small orch.; Liang Hsiao for string orch. Recordings: Lyrichord; EMI-Royal; CBS-Sony; Four Seas. Musik für Ch'in. Publs: The Chinese Ch'in, Its History & Music, 1972. Contbr. to: Grove's Dict.; Chinese Culture; World of Music; Essays on Asian Music & Theatre. Mbrships: Soc. for Ethnomusicol; Int. Folk Music Coun.; Advsr., Chinese Nat. Music Assn. Recip., Artwater Kent Comp. Awards 1967 & 69; Canada Coun. Research Grants, 1974; '75; Deutscher Akademischer Austauschdienst. Address: Dept. of Music, Univ. of BC, Vancouver BC Can.

LIARDET, Jean-Paul,b. 5 Oct. 1939. Lausanne, Switz. Conductor; Composer; Harpsichordist; Pianist. Educ: Degree in Bus. Econs., Lausanne Univ.; Geneva Music Conserv. m. Sylvie Liardet, 2 .d Debut: Madrid. Career: Piano concerto performed in Bern; Cond., Detmold Operhaus; Radio & pub. perfs., TV perfs., etc., w. Collegium Academicum de Geneva, Studio de Musique Contemporaine, & Orch. de Chambre de Lausanne, etc. Comps. incl: Piano Concerto; Piano Sonatas; Macbeth (stage music); Ballads; Pieces for Harpsichord; Film & TV music. Recordings incl: William Byrd; Claude Daquin; Francois Couperin; J S Bach. Mbr., Assn. des Musiciens Suisses. Prod. of 4 musical educ. films. Recip., var. hons. Hobbies incl: Yachting. Address: 65 Grand-Rue, CH-1170 Aubonne, Switz.

LIBAEK, Sven Erik, b. 20 Sept. 1938. Oslo, Norway. Composer; Conductor; Arranger. Educ: Juilliard Schl. of Music, NY, USA; studied w. Joseph Raieff. m. Lolita Libaek, 2d. Career: Pianist, film Windjammer; Cond., Sound 71-74 Concert Orch., Aust; own TV Show, Aust.; Comp., num. TV, Film, Theatre Scores. Compositions incl: (publd.) 6 Moods for 2 Flutes; 6 Lyrical Bagatelles, piano; 6 Musical Pictures, guitar; num. works for piano, piano & voice; (Recorded) Australian Suite orch.; My Thing; musical Grass; Symph. No. 1, The Fifth Continent; var. Film, TV Series Scores. Recordings: own works, & Classical Piano Favourites. Contbr. to The Aust. Comp. Mbrships: VP, Fellowship of Aust. Comps.; Dir., Asian Composers League; Dir., Australasian Performing Rights Assn. Recip. Aust. Record Award, Best Instrumental, 1968. Hobbies: Bridge; Tennis. Address: 35 Kendall St., W Pymble, NSW 2073, Australia.

LIBBACH, Roland Anton Bruno Friedrich (Pseud. Rolf van Lingen), b. 7 Feb. 1914. Dresden, Germany Music Teacherl; Librettist. Composer. Educ: Coll.; Dresden Conserv.; Akademie Mozarteum, Salsburg; studies w. Prof. Leo Ertl, Salzburg. m. Hermine Kralik, 4 c. Carerr: Apps. w. own ensemble in German Fed. Repub., Switzerland, Austria over 25 yrs.; radio broadcasts in German Fed. Repub., Switzerland, Austria, France & Belgium. Comps: Choir music; religious songs; folk songs; dance music; light music. Publs: Mozart Anno Übermorgen, 1972. Mbrships. incl: Austrian Comps. Union; Verband Österreichischer Textautoren. Hons: Silver Award of the OGB Sect., Kunst, 1973. Hobbies: Films. Address: Bocksbergerstr. 16, A.-5033 Salzburg, Austria.

LIBBERT, Jürgen, b. 18 May 1941. Posen (now Poland). German citizen Teacher of Classical Guitar. Educ: State Exam., Vienna Acad. of Music, Austria, 1966; Concert Dip., Vienna Conserv., 1968. Career: Tchr. in Vienna & in Flensburg, Germany; Tchr., Fachakademie für Kath. Kirchenmusik & Musikerziehung, Regensburg, & Regensburg Univ. 1971-; Studies in musicol., ibid., 1972-; Tchr., Fachakademie Leopold-

Mozart -Konservatorium, Augsburg, 1974-. Publs. incl: de Visée Suite in E major for Guitar (w. R Brojer); articles in Gloria DeoPax Hominibus (Festschrift), 1974; Ed., Guitar works of F Sor, 1976 & Guitar works & arrs. of Erwin Schaller, 1976-. Contbr. to profl. jrnls. Mbrships: Gesellschaft für Musikforschung; Guitar Fndn. of Am. Address: Werftstr. 21, D 8400 Regensburg, German Fed. Repub.

LIBBY, Patrick Charles, b. 15 Mar. 1942. Bournemouth, Hants., UK. Stage Director. Educ: Kingston Schl. of Art. Career: varied experience in most branches of theatre; dance, opera & films; Staff Prod., Sadlers Wells Opera Co., 1965-68; Asst.Prod.-Assoc. Prod., Glyndebourne Fest. Opera, 1969-74; Dir. of Prod., Batignano Fest., Italy, 1974-; Dir., of Productions, Engl. Nat. Opera N (1978-). has directed for Royal Opera Covent Gnd., Met. Opera, San Fran. Opera, Wexford Fest., Camden Fest., Glynebourne Fest. Opera. Hobby: Pottering. Mgmt: M Epstein, Columbia Artists Mgmt., NY 10019, USA. Address: 30 Hamilton Terr., London NW8, UK. 3, 30.

LICHTENSTEIN, Alfred, b. 30 Mar. 1901. Koenigsberg, Germany. Flautist. Educ: Flute & comp. studies w. var. tchrs., Germany, Switzerland & France. m. Georgette Wegh. Debut: Berlin, 1920. Career incls: Formerly Tchr., Conservs. in Europe & Egypt; Freelance Solo Flautist, num. concert tours, esp. in Europe, 1920s, & Eastern USA, 1953-; Film & TV perfs.; radio apps., USA & abroad; Berlin Fests., 1975. Comps: Var. works for Flute & Piano. Recordings for major record cos. Contbr. to profl. & popular publs. Mbr., profl. assns. Hons: Recip., Gold Jewelled Flute, King of Greece, 1921; Rumanian Cross of Kts., 1922; Dip. Merit, Pres. of Argentina, 1941; D Mus, Ariz. Univ., USA, 1971. Hobbies incl: Photography; Film Making. Mgmt: Int. Alfred Lichtenstein Fan Club Inc. Address: PO Boxz 138, Wall St. Station, NY, NY 10005, USA.

LICHTMANN, Margaret Stevens, b. 7 Aug. 1945. Gilmer, Texas, USA. Professional Musician; Teacher (flute, piccolo, music theory); Assistance Professor of Music. Educ: BMusEd, Univ. of Texas at Austin, 1967; MMus, Flute perf., Univ. of Denver, 1972; DMA, Flute perf., in progress at Boston Univ. m. Theodor D Lichtmann. Career: formerly Prin. Flautist, Boston Fest. Orch.; Solo recital tour, W Europe, 1976; Substitute, Denver Symph. Orch., 1971-74; Played w. Denver Lyric Opera Co., Central City Opera; Free-lance, Denver-Boulder, Colo. area, 1971-74; Org. & Co-Fndr., The Denver Philo-musica, chmbr. music ensemble; Flute Instructor, Rivier Coll., Univ. of Iowa, Arapahoe Coll.; currenlty Asst. Prof. of Music, Univ. of Miss. Mbrships: Nat. Flute Assn.; Am. Musicol. Soc.; Denver Musicians Local 20-623; VP, Univ. of Texas Chapt., 1964, Pres., Boston Univ. Chapt., 1976, Mu Phi Epsilon. Hons: Finalist, Int. Sterling Staff Competition. Hobbies: Reading; Flying; Tennis; Skiing. Address: Box 2886, University, MS 38677, USA.

LICHTMANN, Theodor David, b. 25 Dec. 1938. Bern, Switzerland. Pianist (Soloist & Chamber Music); University Professor. Educ: Tchrs. Dip., Univ. of Zurich; Akademie für Musik, Vienna, Austria; Hochschule für Musik, Munich, Germany; M Mus., Univ. of Tex., USA; Piano Studies w. Irma Schaichet, Zürich, Leonard Shure, NYC. m. Margaret Lichtmann, (Flautist). Debut: Bern, 1954. Recitals in Zürich, Berlin, Vienna, Hamburg, London & smaller cities in Switzerland; Broadcasts on Swiss Radio & TV; Recitals in Phila., Denver, Austin, Roswell, USA; Broadcasts on Radio & TV, Denver, Colo.; Prof., Schl. of Music & Chmn., Piano Dept., Univ. of Denver. Recordings: Var. records for Decca, London, UK. Contbr. to ARBA; Libraries Unlimited. Mbrships: AAUP; Coll. Music Soc. Hobbies: Literature; Photography; Mountaineering. Address: 1015 Monaco Parkway, Denver, CO 80220, USA. 139.

LIDDELL, Nona Patricia, b. 9 June 1927. London, UK. Musician (Violinist). Educ: RAM, London; LRAM; ARAM. m. Ivor McMahon, dec., 1 d. Debut: Promenade Concerts, 1947. Career: Ldr., Engl. String Quartet, 1957-73; Ldr., London Sinfonietta & Monteverdi Orch.; Mbr., Richards Piano Quartet (1964-79) & Schiller Trio; Broadcaster as Soloist and w. all mentioned ensembles. Recordings: Martinu & Chausson Piano Quartets, w. Richards Piano Quartet; Complete Chmbr. Works of Schönberg, w. London Sinfonietta; Gemini, Leo & Libra, of Roberto Gerhard, w. London Sinfonietta; Piano Quartet, Fantasy String Quartet & Rhapsodic Clarinet Quintet (by Herbert Howells) w. Richards Piano Quartet & Richards Ensemble, Violin Concerto by Kurt Weill w. Londn Sinfonietta -Grand Prix du Disque. Mbr., ISM. Addres: 40 Ridge Rd., London N8 9LH, UK.

LIDELL, Alvar, b. 11 Sept. 1908. London, UK. Singer; Speaker; Broadcaster (Announcer/New Reader). Educ: BA,

Exeter Coll., Oxford; pvte. study, singing, piano, cello & piccolo. m. Nancy Corfield, 1 s., 2 d. Debut: As singer, Nat. Gallery, London, 1943. Career: Announcer & Newsreader, BBC, 1932-69; Free-lance Singer & Speaker in musical works. Recordings: 2 discs of ballads for HMV, 1941; Over 215 Talking Books for RNIB, 1937-. Contbr. to: Radio Times; Listener; Spectator. Recip. of MBE, 1964. Hobbies: Gardening; Golf; Travel. Mgmt: Basil Douglas Ltd. Address: 6 Davenham Ave., Northwood, Middx. HA6 3HN, UK. 3.

LIDHOLM, Ingvar, b. 24 Feb. 1921. Jönköping, Sweden. Composer; Conductor; Viola Player. Educ: High Schl. of Music, Stockholm & w. Hilding Rosenberg, Stockholm & Matyas Seiber, London. m. Ulla Lidholm, 1 s. Career: viola player, Royal Opera Orch., Stockholm; Cond.; Ötebro Symph. Orch.; Prof. of Comp., Stockholm; Hd. of Artistic Planning, Swedish Broadcasting Corp. Comps: works for stage (opera, ballet, TV music drama), orch., a capella & accomp. choir, solo vocal music, chmbr. instrumental music. num. recordings of own works. Mbr., Royal Acad. of Music, Stockholm. Hons: Christ Johnson Music Prize, 1958; ISCM, 1959; Koussevitsky Int. Recording Award, 1965; Salzburg Opera Prize, 1968. Address: Uttringe Hages V. 33, 15024 Rönninge, Sweden.

LIDKA, Maria. Berlin, Germnay. Violinist. Educ: studied w. Max Rostal; Hon. RCM. m. Walter May (dec.), 2 s. Career: Prof., RCM; Soloist & chmbr. music perfs., UK & Europe. Recip., Freeman of City of London; Hon. RCM. Address: 68 Lowther Dr., London SW13, UK.

LIDL, Vaclav, b. 5 Nov. 1922. Brno, Czechoslovakia. Composer. Educ: Grad., Bus. Acad.; Brno Conserv. m. Eva Hronadkova, 1 s. Career incl: writer of many musical scores for films & TV. Compositions incl: Diverimento for flute, clarinet & bassoon; Third String Quartet; Dandelions, for flute, soprano & harp; Symph. for Grand Orch.; Cantus Variabilis for violin, clarinet & piano; Hic Homo Sum, Cantata for mixed choir, tenor, piano & percussion; Our Little Drummer, Cantata for child's voice & Grand Orch. 2nd Symphony for chamber orchestra. Mbrships: Union of Czechoslovak Composers. Hobby: Skiing. Mgmt: Music Information Ctr., Besedni 3, 118 00 Praha 1. Address: Soukenicka 14, 110 00 Praha 1, Czechoslovakia.

LIDRAL, Frank Wayne, b. 11 Apr. 1920. Algoma, Wis., USA. Professor of Music; Conductor; Woodwinds (Clarinet). Educ: BS, Univ. Wis., 1941; M Mus, Northwestern Univ., 1947; PhD, Eastman Schl. of Music, Univ. Rochester, 1956. m. Martha Elise Kasten. 1 s., 2 d. Career: Assoc. Prof. of Music, Ctrl. Mo. State Univ., 1947-56; Prof. of Music, Ind. State KUniv., 1956-60; Prof. of Music, Univ. Vt., 1960-; Chmn., Music Dept., ibid., 1960-73; Compositions incl: Prelude for Orch. Var. choral & orchl. recordings. Publs. incl: Syllabus for American Indian Music, 1975. Contbr. to profl. jrnls. Active mbr. num. profl. orgs Hons: Pi Kappa Lambda; Pi Lambda Phi Hobbies: Bridge; Chess; Golf; Swimming. Address: 10 Country Club Dr., RD 1, S Burlington, VT 05401, USA. 2, 6.

LIEBERMAN, Fredric, b. 1 Mar. 1940. NY, NY USA. Ethnomusicologist; Composer. Educ: BMus, Eastman Schl. of Quartets; Leaves of Brass; Sonatina for Piano; Suite for Piano; Psalm 147. Publs: Chinese Music: an annotated bibliography, 1979. Contbr. to: Ethnomusicology; Asian Music; other profl. jrnls. Mbrships: Soc. for Ethnomusicol. (Ed., Ethnomusicol.); Coll. Music Soc. (Exec. Bd. mbr. for Ethnomusicol.), 1973-77. Recip., 1st prize, Atwater-Kent Award in Musicol., 1967. Address: Schl. of Music, Univ. of Wash., Seattle, WA 98195, USA.

LIEBERMANN, Rolf, b. 14 Sept. 1910. Zurich, Switz. Opera Manager; Composeer. Educ: studied law, Univ. of Zürich Conserv. of Music. m. Gioconda Schmit, 1 s. Career: w. Music Dept., Swiss Radio Corp., 1945-50; Hd. of Orch., Swiss Radio Beromünster, 1950-57; Music Dir., N. German Broadcasting System, Hamburg, 1957-59; Gen. Mgr., Hamburg State Opera, 1957-73; Mgr., Paris Opera, 1973-. Compositions incl: Polyphonic Studies for chmbr. orch.; Une des Fins du Monde; volkslieder Suite; Furioso; Symphony No. 1; Concerto for jazz band & orch.; Symphonie des Echanges; Leonore 4045 (opera); Penelope (opera) School for Wives (opera). Hons. incl: Art Prize, City of Zürich; Commandeur de la Légion d'Honneur, 1974; Doctorate, Univ. of Berne, 1975. Address: Theatre National de l'Opera, Place de l'Opera, 75009, Paris, France.

LIEBERSON, Peter Goddard, b. 25 Oct. 1946. NYC, NY, USA. Composer; Conductor. Educ: Bachelor's Degree, NY Univ.; Master's Degree in Comp., Columbia Univ. m. Ellen Kearney. Career: Comps. perf. & commissioned by Boulez & the NY Phil., Tashi (w. Peter Serkin), Berkshire Music Ctr., Tanglewood, Speculem Musicae & Group for Contemporary Music. Comps: Concerto for Groups of Instruments (recorded); Cello Concerto;

Piano Fantasy (recorded); Accordance; Tashi Quartet. Hons: Charles Ives Award, 1974; Martha Baird Rockefeller Recording Grant, 1975; Nat. Endowment for the Arts Grant for comp. Address: 2 Soldiers Field Pk., Boston, MA 02163, USA.

LIESE, Johannes, b. 28 May 1908. Landsberg, Germany. Composer. m. Ursula Reisshuus. Comps: Opera 5 symphs.; Orchl. works; keyboard works; 60 songs. Hobbies: Collecting Bells. Address: M Lutherstr. 124, Berlin 62, German Fed. Repub.

LIESS, Andreas Karl Friedrich, b. 16 June 1903. Klein-Kniegnitz am Zobten, Prussian Silesia. Emeritus Professor; Musicologist; Pianist. Educ: Musicol. Inst., Vienna; State Acad. of Music, Vienna; PhD, New Vienna Conserv., 1928. Career incls: Music Critic, Musicologist; Lectured in num. Univs. & elsewhere in Paris, Rome, Barcelona, Berlin, Holland, Bulgaria; Instructor, Music History, Conserv. of the City of Vienna, 1952, Music & Cultural History, Acad. of Music & Performing Arts, Vienna; Sr. Lectr., ibid, 1964; Assoc. Prof., ibid, 1973-. Publs. incl: Claude Debussy, das Werk im Zeitbild, 2 vols., 1936, 1978; Carl Orff, Idee & Werk, 1955, '77 (Engl. edn., 1965); Protuberanzen Bd. I, Zur Theorie der Musikgeschichte, 1970; Claude Debussy und der Art Nouveau, Studi musicali, Rome, 1976; 15 other titles. Contbr. to very num. profl. jrnls. Mbr., profl. orgs. Hons. incl: Cross of Hon. for Science & Art, 1968; Theodor Korner Prize, 1958, 61; Ehrenmitglied der Oesterr. Gesellschaft fur Müsikwissenschaft, 1978; num. other Hons. Address: 41/11 Semperstr., Vienna 1180, Austria. 30.

LIFCHITZ, Max, b. 11 Nov. 1948. Mexico City, Mexico. Pianist; Conductor; Composer; Teacher. Educ: BMus, MS, Juilliard Schl., 1971; MMus, Harvard Univ., 1973. m. Merle Sonia. Debut: (as pianist) Mexico City, 1955. Career: Pianist, Juilliard Ensemble, 1968-74; num. concerts & recordings; Asst. prof. of comp., Columbia Univ. NYC; num. perfs. of own works in USA; num. apps. at fests. in USA & Europe. Comps. incl: (chmbr. orch.) Tiempos, 1969; Globes, 1971; Roberta, 1972; Intervencion, 1976; (band) Mosaico Mexicano, 1979; (chmbr. ensemble) Fibers, 1967; Rebellions, 1976; Music for Percussion, 1977; Episodes, 1978; Rhythmic Soundscape, 1978; Winter Counterpoint, 1979; (piano) Elegia, 1971; Adelante, 1974; Implications, 1979; (stage) Bluebells, 1973; (tape) Pearls for Merlie Perlie, 1974; (vocal) Kaddish, 1973. Mbrships: Am. Music Ctr.; AFM; Jr. Fellow, Univ. of Mich. Soc. of Fellows. num. hons., awards & prizes incl. 1st prize, Gaudeamus Competition for perfs. of Contemporary Music, Rotterdam, 1976. Hobbies: Lit.; Photogrpahy; Sports. Address: 862 W End Ave., NY, NY 10025, USA.

LIGHTOLLER, Elisabeth Susan, b. 16 Jan. 1945. Hertford, UK. Freelance Harpsichordist & Pianist. Educ: ARCM (Tchrs.). 2 s. (adopted). Career: Num. apps. in GB as soloist & mbr. of var. ensembles; W Baroque Chmbr. Grp. (Fndr. Mbr.); Piano duo w. Peter Jacobs. Mbr. ISM. Hobbies: Reading; Walking. Address: 24 Eversley Cress., Spring Grove, Isleworth, Middx., UK.

LIGOTTI, Albert F., b. 26 Feb. 1927. NYC, USA. Symphonic, Trumpeter; University Professor. Educ: BA., Quenn's Coll., NYC; MA., Columbia Univ., NYC; pvte. trumpet study w. Wm Vacchiano & Jack Borodkin, NYC; cond. pupil of Michael Fevievsky. m. Arlene Ligotti. Career: Bell Telephone TV Orch.; Broadway Co. of The Man of La Manche; Trumpeter, NY Phil., Met. Opera, & freelance; Univ. Prof., tchng. & cond. (opera & wind ensemble). Recordings: 1st trumpet w. Modern Brass Ensemble; Extra Trumpet w. NY Phil. recording, 1960-68. Publs: Arr. for Brass Quintet, Tritsch-Tratsch Polka (J Strauss), 1966; Arr. for Brass Quintet, Trumpet Voluntary, John Stanley, 1967. Mbrships: MENC; CMS; NACWPI; Int. Trumpet Guild; Nat. Wind Ensemble Mbr.; GMEA. Hobbies: Golf; Tennis; Old clocks. Address 220 Greencrest Dr., Athens, GA 30605, USA.

LILBURN, Douglas Gordon, b. 2 Nov. 1915. Wanganiu, NZ. Professor of Music. Educ: Canterbury Univ. Coll.; RCM. Career: Composer; Prof., Music, Vic. Univ., Wellington; Dir., Electronic Music Studios, ibid. Comps. incl: (publd.) Symphony no. 3; Allegro for strings; Two sonatinas for piano; 'Sings Harry' song cycle; Elegy song cycle; Thre songs for baritone & viola; (recorded) Symphony no. 3; Allegro for strings; 'Sings Harry' Overture 'Aotearoa'; Landfall in Unknown Seas; Festival overture; Dance Sequence for Expo '70; Symph. No. 2 Mbrships: Composers' Assn. NZ; Brit. Guild Composers. Hons. incl: Cobbett Prize, RCM, 1939; 3 NZ Centennial Awards, 1940; APRA Award, 1945; Hon. D Mus, Univ. Otago, 1969. Hobbies: Gardening; Walking. Address: 22 Ascot Terr., Wellington 1, NZ.

LILL, John Richard, b. 17 Mar. 1944. London, UK. Concert Pianist. Educ: RCM. Debut: Royal Fest. Hall London, 1963.

Career: Concert Apps. in most major cities throughout Europe, USA, USSR, Far E., Aust. etc.; Apps. as Soloist w. leading orchs.; worldwide radio & TV apps. Recordings: complete Beethoven Concertos & Sonatas; complete Brahms concertos. Hons: 1st Prize, Int. Tchaikowsky Competition, Moscow, 1970; OBE, 1978; Hon. DSCc., Univ. of Aston, Birmingham, 1978. Hobbies: Walking; Chess; Psychic Rsch. Mgmt: Harold Holt Ltd. Address: c/o Harold Holt Ltd., Wigmore St., London W1H ODJ, UK. 1. 3, 122.

LILLEY, John Mark, b. 24 Mar. 1939. Converse, La., USA. Conductor; Professor of Music & Assistant Dean. Educ: BMus Ed., Baylor Univ., 1961; BMus., ibid, 1962; MMus, ibid, 1964; DMus A, Univ. of Southern Calif., 1971. m. Betty Durham, 1 s., 1 d. Career: Gave 1st perf. of Kubik's Scholastica, & 1st W Coast perf. of Ives' The Celestial Country; Prof. of Music & Asst. Dean, Coll. of Arts & Scis., Kansas State Univ. Recordings: Gail Kubik, Scholastica-A Medieval Set. Contbr. to: The Journal of Nontraditional Studies. Mbrships: Omicron Delta Kappa; Pi Kappa Lambda; Phi Mu Alpha Sinfonia; Am. Choral Dirs. Assn.; Coll. Music Soc. Hobbies: Golf; Bridge. Address: 1806 Laramie, Manhattan, KS 66502, USA. 9.

LIM, Kek-Tjiang, b. 21 Mar. 1928. Bandjermasin, Borneo, Indonesia. Conductor; Violinist. Educ: Grad., Amsterdam Conserv. of Music; Dips., Conserv. Nat. de Musique, Paris, Conserv. Int. de Musique; L'Ecole de Jacques Thibaud. m. San-Fang Tijiok, 2 s. Career: Music Dir., Jakarta Radio Orch.; Music Dir. & Prin. Cond., Peking Ctr. Radio Symph. Orch.; Prof. of Violin Peking Ctrl. Conserv. of Music; Music Dir. & Prin. Cond., Hong Kong Phil. Orch.; has given violin recitals in Europe & Asia. Recordings: Fung Hang Recording Co. & Music City Record Co., Hong Kong. Hons. incl: among 3 finalists, Concorso Int. Arrigo Serator-Serato, Rome, 1954. Hobbies: Chinese Boxing; Meditation; Yoga. Address: 33 Ventris Rd., Apt. 1B, Happy Valley, Hong Kong.

LIMA, Arthur Moreira, b. 16 July 1940. Rio de Janeiro, Brazil. Concert Pianist. Educ: Baac. in Maths & Physics, Rio de Janeiro Mil. Schl.; studied French Lang. & Lit. at the Lycee Francais, Rio & Alliance Francaise, Paris; studied piano pvtly. w. Lucia Branco, Rio de Janeiro; harmony & comp. w. Renzo Massarani; pupil of Marguerite Long & Jean Doyen, Academie Marquerite Long, Paris; Tschaikowsky Conserv., Moscow, 1963-69; post grad. pupil of Rudolf Kehrer. m. Eliana Cardoso Moreira, 2 d. Debut: Brazilian Symph. Orch., Rio de Janeiro, 1950. Career: Concert tours to UK, USSR, USA, Canada, Spain, Poland, Switz., Yugoslavia, The Netherlands, Czech., France, Germany, Austria, Latin Am.; Has played w. Moscow Phil. Orch., Moscow Chamber Orch., USSR Radio Orch., ORTF, Paris, Warsaw Phil., Suisse Romande, BBC Northern, Northern Sinfonia, Royal Liverpool Phil. Orch., under the batons of well-known conds. Recordings incl: Sev. for Melodiya, USSR, inclng. solo works by Liszt, Chopin, Rachmaninov, etc.; Orchl. works by Mozart; Recording for BBC, etc. Hons. incl: 2nd Prize, Chopin Competition, Warsaw, 1965; Special prize, Best interpretation of a Chopin Sonata, Warsaw, 1965; 3rd Prize, Leeds Competition, Moscow, 1970. Mgmt: Harold Holt Ltd., London. Address: Hagenberggasse 8, Vienna 1130, Austria.

LIMA, Candido de Oliveira, b. 22 Aug. 1939. Viana do Castelo, Portugal. Pianist; Composer; Professor. Educ: Studied Philos., Cath. Univ.; Conservs. of Oporto & Lisbon. m. Maria José Lima, 1d. Debut: Brage & Lisbon. Career: Concerts in public on Radio & TV. Comps. published in Oporto in Milan, Italy & France. Publs: Short treatises on Aesthetics, Music & Sociology, Harmony, etc. Mbr., Soc. of Portuguese Authors. Hobbies: Sports. Address: Travessa das Antas 220, Oporto, Portugal.

LIMA, Luis, b. 12 Sept. 1948. Cordoba, Argentina. Tenor. Educ: studied voice w. Carlos Guichandut, Buenos Aires & Gina Cigna, Italy. Debut: as Pinkerton, Madama Butterfly, Lisbon. Career: Has sung at major opera houses incl. Munich, Vienna, Milan, Paris, Zürich, Strasbourg, Barcelonoa & Liége; US debut, concert perf. of Gemma di Vergy, Carnegie Hall, 1976; debut, La Scala (Faust), 1977; Alfredo, La Traviata, Metropolitan Opera, 1978-79; NYC Opera, La Boheme & Rigoletto, 1979; repertoire incls. leading tenor roles in Don Giovanni, Werther, Roméo et Juliette, Faust, Tosca, Macbeth, Lucia di Lammermoor, Manon. Mgmt: Columbia Artists Mgmt. Inc., 165 W 57th St., NY, NY 10019, USA. Address: c/o Mgmt.

LIMOLI, Michael David, b. 18 June 1948. Cleveland, Ohio, USA. Clarinetist; Pianist; Ballet Dancer. Educ: BMus, MMus. (clarinet); BS Mus. (Ballet); DMus., (clarinet), Ind. Univ. Debut: Carnegie Recital Hall, 1978. Career: Solo concerto apps. w. Orchs. in Salzburg, Austria (Mozart woche Festspiel); Bad Reichenhall, BRD; Bloomington, Ind. Recordings: Michael Limoli in Concert. Mbr., Pi Kappa Lambda. Hons: Winner, var.

Compeitions; Fellowship, Ind. Univ., 1971-72. Hobbies: Opera; Playing Bagpieces. Mgmt: Norman J. Seaman Concerts, NYC, USA. Address: 124 Thompson St., NY, NY 10012,;USA.

LIN, Cho-Liang. b. 29 Jan. 1960. Shine-Choo, Taiwan. Violinist. Educ: Profl. Children's Schl., NYC High Schl. Dip.; Sydney Conserv. of Music, Aust.; Juilliard Schl., NYC. Debut: aged 7, Taiwan, NY 1979. Career: num. recitals & concerto apps. in S E Asia, Spain, German. Fed. Repub., & USA. Recordings: Franck, Sonata; De Falla, Spanish Suite; De Sarasate, Zapateado. Hons. incl: Taiwan Nat. Youth Violin Competition, 1970; Aust. Broadcasting Commission Concerto Competition, 1975; Queen Sofia Int. Competition, Madrid, 1977; Juilliard Schl. Violin Competition, 1978; Aspen Music Fest. Violin Competition, 1978. Hobbies: Baseball; Reading. Mgmt: Harrison/Parrott Ltd., 22 Hillgate St., London W8 7SR, UK. Address: c/o mgmt.

LIND, William Reinhold, b. 3 Nov. 1911. Boras, Sweden. Conductor; Arranger; Pianist. Educ: Royal Swedish Acad. of Music. m. Ulla-Britt, 3 c. Debut: pianist w. Boras Symph. Orch., 1925. Career: Pianist in Swedish radio, 1938-43; Cond., ibid., 1943-59; cond., Swedish radio & TV, 1959-76; guest cond. in Scandinavia & most European countries. Comps: music for radio, TV & films; light music; num. arrs. Recordings: about 200, incl. Yuletid (gold & diamond award). Mbrships: STIM; SKAP; Wilhelm Peterson-Bergerstiftelsen; Lions. Hons: Royal Swedish Acad. of Music, 1936. Hobbies: Music; Chess. Addess: Hjortstigen 8, Gävle, Sweden.

LINDBERG, Nils, b. 11 June 1933. Uppsala, Sweden. Composer; Arranger; Organist; Piansit. Educ: Univ. of Uppsala; Royal Acad. of Music, Stockholm. m. Annemarie, 3 s. Career: Perfs. on Swedish Radio & TV; Accomp. to Judy Garland during her Northern Tour; apps. on Norddeutscher Rundfunk, Hanover, Hamburg, & Madrid TV; tours of Brazil & USA. Comps. incl: 7 Dalecarlian Paintings; Trisection; Blues for Bill; Reflections; Petra; Zodiac; Brand New; Ars Gratia Artis; Trumpet Song; In Memoriam Rolf Billberg; Polska with a Trumpet; Lapponian Suite; Noahs Ark; Curbits; Storm Warning; Concert Grosso. Recordings: Music with a Jazz Flavour (Alice Babs); Jan Allan With Music by Nils Lindberg.; own comps. Hons: Grammis (important Swedish record prize), for Jan Allan's record of his music, 1970. Hobby: Music. Address: Adellorgsvägen 10, 78041, Gagnef, Sweden.

LINDE, Hans-Martin, b. 24 May 1930. Werne, German Fed. Repub. Educator; Performer on Flute & Recorder. Educ: State HS for Music, Freiburg, Germany. m. Gundrun Olshausen, 1 s., 2 d. Career: concert tours, Europe, USA, S Am., Middle & Far E, 1955 ; Tchr., baroque flute, recorder, ensemble, 1957-; Cond., vocal ensemble, 1965-; & chmbr. orch., 1970-, Schola Cantorum Basiliensis, Basle, Switz.; 1st Flute, Cappella Coloniensis of Western Germany, Radio Cologne, 1957-; Co-Ed., Zeitschrift für Spielmusik, 1966-. Comps: Chmbr. music for flute or recorder, Recordings for EMI Electrola; DGG; Harmonia; Mundi & RCA. Publs: Ornamentation in Ancient Music; Handbook for recorder players; methods for recorder & ensemble playing. Hons: Grand Prix du Disque; Edison Preis; Deutscher Schall. Plattenpreis. Address: Kuntmattring 5, CH-4107, Ettingen, Switz. 2.

LINDEMAN, Lucas, P M, b. 30 Apr. 1926. Hertogenbosch, Netherlands. Institute Director. Educ: Lic., Pontifical Inst. of Sacred Music, Rome; Degree in Music Educ. & Choir Direction, Conserv. of Tilburg, Netherlands. Career: Tchr. of Music in HSs, 11 yrs.; Dir., Lennards-Inst. of Music Educ., Roemond, 1965-. Mbrships: Int. Soc. for Music Educ.; Dutch Assn. of Music Educators Vereniging Lereren Schoolmuziek; Govtl. Commission for Renewal of Music Educ. of Schls. Chief Redactor, & Ex Ore Infantium (music pedagogical reviews). Hobby: Travelling. Address: Lennards-Instr., Steegstraat 16, Roermond, Netherlands.

LINDEMAN, Osmo, b. 1929. Pianist; Composer. Educ: studied w. Eino Linnala (theory) & Nils-Erik Fougstedt (comp.), Sibelius Acad.; Dip. in Comp.; studied w. Carl Orff in Munich (on UNESCO grant). Career: Tchr. of Harmony, Counterpoint, Electronic & Computer Music, Sibelius Acad.; His works have been perf. by Helsinki City Symph Orch., etc. Comps. incl: (orchl. works) Symph. 2, 1964; Variable, 1967; (solo works w. orch.) Piano Concerto 1, piano & orchs, 1963; Piano Concerto 2, piano & orch., 1965; (chamber works) Str. Quartet, 1966; Music for Chamber Orch., 1966; Concerto for Chamber Orch., 1966; Partita for Percussion, 1962; Two Expressions, vibraphone & marimba, 1965; (electronic music) Kinetic Forms, 1969; Mechanical Music for Stereophonic Tape, 1969; Tropicana, 1970; Midas, 1970; Ritual, 1972; Spectacle, 1974; var. music for films; radio plays, etc. Recordings: Ritual. Publs: Introduction of Music Theory, 1976; Technology of

Electronic Music, 1974. Recip. 1st prize for comp. 'Ritual in the VI Int. Comp. Contest, the Electronic & Computer Music Category, arr. by the Italian Soc. for Contemp. Music. Address: Vaahtorinne 3A3, 01600 Vantaa 60, Finland. 30.

LINDEMANN, Thomas, b. 10 Feb. 1940. NYC, USA. Music Educator (Tuba). Educ: BSMusEd., SUNY, Fredonia; MSMusEd., Ithaca Coll., NY; Eastman Schl. Music, Rochester, ibid. m. Genevieve Gilbert Lindemann, 2 s. Career: Public Schl. (Dept. Hd.) instrumental music tchr. Mbrships: AFM; MENC; NYSSMA; NYSUT. Hobbies: Gardening; Fishing; Reading; Photography; Swimming; Sailing; Travel. Address: Arizona Way, Marcellus, NY 13108, USA.

LINDER, Albert, b. 15 Oct. 1937. Copehagen, Denmark. Musician, Horn. Educ: studied w: Knud Sorensen, Gottfried Frieberg, Franz Gerzendorfer. m. Karen Linder, 2 d. 2 s. Debut: Copenhagen 1954. Career: Horn Soloist, Mozarteum Orch., Salzburg, Austria, 1954-57, Stuttgart Radio Orch., Germany, 1957-60, Gothenburg Symph. Orch., Sweden, 1960-; Horn Soloist, 35 different Orchs. in Europe, Africa, Can., USA. Japan; Ldr., Gothenburg Woodwind Quintet. Recordings: Mozart Horn Concertos 1-4, w. Vienna State Opera Orch.; Musik Fur Waldhorn; Chmbr. Music Of The Late 18th Century; Music For Hunting Horn & Strings. num. recordings inclng: Beethoven sonata; Shuman Adagio and Allegro. Recip. 1st Prize, Int. Competition, Geneva, Switzerland, 1956. Hobby: Photographing Wild Animals. Address: 1 Hallstamsvagen, 43600 Askim, Sweden.

LINDER, Hans, b. 17 Jan. 1917. Wuppertal, Germany. Teacher; Pianist. Educ: Music Acad. Munich. m. Ursula Munzner-Linder, 1, 1d. Debut: Bremerhaven, 1939. Career: Cond., City Theatre Bremerhaven, 1939-52; In the army, 1940-45; Tchr., var. schls., 1952-; Chmbr. music, 1946-; Cond., Music Soc. Bremerhaven, 1952-. Comps. incl: Chmbr. music; String Trio; Violin Sonatino; Piano Trio; Serenade for String Orch., etc. Recordings w. Radio Bremen. Publs. incl: How Our Musical Life Used To Be (a Music History of Bremerhaven), 1959. Contbr. to: Var. mags. & newspapers. Mbrships: Bd. of Dirs., Assn. German Amateur Orch.; Dis. Pres. Bremen Contest, Youth and Music; Soc. of German Music Pegagogues and Concert Musicians. Hobbies: Music; Stamps. Address: Gaustr. 68, 2850 Bremerhaven-Lehe, German Fed. Repub.

LINDER, Judith Anna Ingegerd, b. 14 Jan. 1930. Torpa, Sweden. Conductor; Musical Director (Piano, Organ, Violoncello, Song). Educ: Superior Organ Examination; Superior Precentor Examination; M Mus; Pvte. study in Stockholm, Berlin, Hiversum & Lucerne. m. Alf Linder, 1 d. Career: Precentor, S Maria Magdalena Ch., Stockholm; Tchr., Liturgical Song, Theological Fac., Univ. of Uppsala & Theological Inst. in Stockholm; Radio & TV apps. in Sweden & Finland; Concert tours in W Germany, Holland, Belgium 2 France. Recording of French Meditative Sacred Music. Hobbies: Drawing; Painting; Psychology. Address: Fredrikshovsgatan 3A, 115 22 Stockholm, Sweden.

LINDER, Ursula, b. 25 July 1922. Bremerhaven, Germany. Violinist. Educ: State Music Acad. Berlin. m. Hans Linder, 1 s., 1 d. Debut: Bremerhaven, 1946. Career: Chmbr. concerts, Bremerhaven, 1946-; Chmbr. Orch. Fritz Stein, Berlin, 1941-44; First Violinist, Music Soc. Bremerhaven, 1952-; Concerts, UK, France, Netherlands, Denmark. Recordings w. Radio Bremen, 1947-. Hobbies: Gardening; Needlework. Address: Gaustr. 68, 2850 Bremerhaven-Lehe, German Fed. Repub.

LINDGREN, Floice Rhodes, b. 1 July 1938. Atlanta, Ga., USA. Flautist; Music Educator & Researcher. Educ: B Mus, Univ. of Tenn.; M Mus, Northwestern Univ. Ill.; Summer Cert., Kodaly Musical Trng. Inst.; pvte. studies, Hungary & USA. div. 1 s., 1 d. Career incls: Flute Soloist, Knoxville Symph. Orch., & Shreveport, La., Symph. Orch.; Soprano & Flute Soloist, Caribbean Chorale, St. Thomas, Virgin Islands; Fndr., St. Thomas Chmbr. Singers, ibid.; Dir., Materials Resource Ctr., Kodaly Musical Trng. Inst.; Wellesley, Mass.; Soloist, summer concerts, ibid.; TV apps. Recordings: Flute Soloist on album of New Herrnhut Moravian Choir. Mbr., profl. assns. Hons incl: Prize for Comp., Kodaly Musical Trng. Inst., 1975. Hobby: Photography. Address: 73 Summer St., Natick, MA 01760. USA.

LINDGREN, Kurt, b. 10 June 1937. Stockholm, Sweden. Composer; Headmaster of Seminary. Educ: Studied Doublebass, Univ. of Music, Stockholm; pvte. study of comp. m. Kerstein, 2 s. Career: Tours in Europe as Bass Player, inclng. Jazz Fests. & Broadcasts; perfs. of chmbr. & symphonic music, Sweden; Musical Ldr., Stockholm Town Theatre, 1965-68;

Leading part, Swedish film, Djavulens Instrument. Comps. incl: A Herdsman's Song (chorus & orch.); Striden om en ton (Drama for chorus & rhythm sect.); stage music; TV ballet music. Recordings: Karin Krog, 1964; Lars Gullin, Portrait of my Pals, 1964. Mbr., Swedish Govt. scholarships. Mgmt: Univ. of Music, Stockholm Electronic Music Studio, ibid. Address: Orrspelsvgen 58, 161 40 Bromma, Sweden.

LINDHOLM, Berit Maria, b. 18 Oct. 1934. Stockholm, Sweden. Oper Singer (soprano). Educ: Stockholm Opera Schl. m. Hans Lidholm 2d. Debut: Countess in Le Nozze di Figaro, Stockholm, 1963. Career: Perfs. all over the world incl. Metropolitan, NY, Carnegie Hall, San Francisco, Chicago, London, Paris, Hamburg, Berlin, Munich, Bayreuth, Moscow, Napeles, Madrid, Geneva, Zürich, Vienna, Prague, Budapest, Barcelona, Marseilles, etc.; repertoire incl. Brunnhilde, Isolde, Kukndry, Tosca, Turan dot, Salome, Elektra. Recordings: Walkure (Wagner); Les Troyens (Berlioz); songs by Swedish comps. Hon: Opera Singer by appointment of the King of Sweden. Mgmt: Artistsekretariat Ulf Törnqvist, Norrtullsgatan 26, 11345 Stockholm, Sweden. Address: c/o mgmt.

LINDHOLM, Teppo Untamo, b. 16 Sept. 1920. Conductor. Educ: Degree in Conducting, Sibelius Acad., 1957; Dip. in conducting, ibid., 1957; Degree from Conservatoire, 1957. m. Ester Sofia Loukiainen. Debut: Conductor, Sibelius Acad. Public concert, 1957. Career: appeared num. times on Finnish Radio; Conductor of orch. in Savonlinna, 1957-61. Comps. incl: Concert Waltz "Unten Mailla"; Num. arrangements for symph. orchs.; composer of var. minor wks. Recorded var. pieces of light music. Publs. incl: helsingin yliopiston kirjaston Sävellyskäsikir joitusluetto. Contbr. to num. mags. Address: Yllinkulma B 12, 62 100 Lapua, Finland.

LINDLEY, Simon Geoffrey, b. 10 Oct. 1948. Barnhurst, Kent, UK. Cathedral Organist; Chorus Master. Educ: RCM, London; FRCA (CHM); GRSM; FTCL; ARCM; LRAM. m. Carel Louise McMiram 2s. Career incls: Dpty-Organsit, Westminster Cathedral, 1970-75; Dir. of Music, Leeds Parish Ch., 1975-; Chorus Master, Leeds Phil. Soc., Halifax Choral Soc., 1975-; RSCM Special Commissioner, 1975-; Leeds City Organist, 1976-; Music Tutor, Leeds Polytechnic, 1976-; Comps. Come sing and dance (carol). Recordings incl: Solo Recital of Romantic Organ Music. Contbr. to profl. publs. Mbrships incl: RCO; (coun.) ISM; RSCM; Cathedral Organists' Assn. Recip., Geoffrey Tankard Organ Prize, RCM, 1968. Hobbies: Cooking; Driving; Churches & Cathedrals. Mgmt: Ibbs & Tillett. Address: Stoneleigh, 48 W Pk. Grove, Roundhay, Leeds LS8 2DY, UK.

LINDROOS, Paul Bertel, b. 19 Sept. 1910. Karis, Finland. Precentor (organ & piano). Educ: Sibelius Acad., Church Music Inst.; Comp. studies w. Prof. Eino Linnala & Prof. Selim Palmgren. m. Hjordis Linnea Maria Westerholm, (2) Estrid Anna-Lisa Nylund, 3 s. (1 dec.), 1 d. Career: Cond., male & mixed choirs, Finnish broadcaxsting; Fndr., Cond, "Hembygdens Sangare i Pojo r.f.", 1943; Cond., mixed choir, "Fiskars Sangarbroder", 1036-65; Cond. of ch. congregation choirs, Pojo, 1935-65; Concert tours in Stockholm, Sweden & Helsinki, Finland; Cond., choir fest., S Finland. Comps: Agnus Dei, for soli, choir & organ; Music for the 600th anniversary of the Pojo (Pohja) community, 1959. Contbr. to local newspapers, music critic. Mbrships: Soc. of Swedish Musicians; Ch. Commissioners in Pojo (Pohja) Congregation. Hons: Directus Cantus, 1943. Hobbies: Hunting; Fishing; Growing flowers. Address: 10420 Skuru, Tunavik 213, Finland.

LINDSAY, Sylvia, b. 29 May 1925. near Rye, Sussex, UK. Pianist; Directing Secretary, Council for Music in Hospitals. Educ: RCM, RAM; LRAM; ARCM. m. David F M Lindsay, 2s., 1 d. Career: Concerts in hosps., cathedrals, chs., clubs, etc.; 1st perfs. of Exequy, & Omar Khayaam by Ivor Walsworth; TV & radio apps. for Coun. for Music in Hosps., 19/6. Conbtr. to: Soc. Servs. Quarterly; Int. Poetry Mag. Mbrships: Royal Overseas League; Dolmetsch Fndn.; Brit. Soc. for Music Therapy. Hobbies: Early Music & Old Instruments; Poetry; Comparative Religion. Address: Elmhurst, Lower Rd., Little Bookham, Surrey KT23 4EF, UK. 3.

LINDSAY-DOUGLAS, Carole, b. 21 Dec. 1946. E Ruston, Norfolk, UK. Soprano; Director of Lindsay Music Publisher. Educ: Bretton Hall Coll. of Educ.; Cert. of Educ. (Leeds); Pvte. studies w. Audrey Langford. m. Douglas Coombes. Career: Mbr. of Chorale, WNO, 2 yrs.; Apps. as Soloist; Royal Festival Hall; Queen Elizabeth Hall; Fairfield Hall; Huddersfield Town Hall; Free Trade Hall; Oratorio perfs. in provinces; Apps. on radio & TV; Voice & harp duo w. John Marson; one woman show in USA, 1976, 79. Recordings: A Frog He Would a Wooing-Go; Guitar Schl. Publs. incl: Cat Duet (Rossini), 1974; Lindsay Carol Book I, 1978. Contbr. to the Tchr. Mbrships: Brit.

Actors Equity; ACE Int. Hobbies: Dressmaking; Philately; Sketching; Driving. Mgmt: Lindsay Music Entertainments, Brook House, 24 Royston St., Potton, Sandy, Beds., UK. Address: Brook House, 24 Royston St., Potton, Sandy, Beds. SG19 2LP, UK.

LINDSAY, Mort, b. 21 March 1923. Newark, NJ, USA. Conductor; Composer; Orchestrator; Pianist. Educ: BA, Columbia Coll., NYC, 1944; MA., Columbia Univ., NYC, 1948; EdD., Tchrs. Coll., ibid. 1974; pvte. study in comp. w. Wallingford Riegger, Paul Creston, Tibor Serly; cond. w. Tibor Serly. m. Betty Jane Lindsay, 3 c. Career: Staff Pianist, NBC Network, 1948-50; Staff Cond., CBS, 1954-56, Staff Cond., ABC 1957-59; Musical Dir., for Judy Garland, 1960-65; Musical Dir., Merv Griffin TV Show, 1965-; Orchestrator, Broadway Theatre 'Bajour', 1965-;Musical Dir., on TV for Barbra Steisand, Carol Channing, Andy Williams. Comp. of motion picture scores incl: 40 Pounds of Trouble, Universal, I Could Go On Singing, UA. Stolen Hours, UA (11 recordings of title song,); The Best Man, UA.; The 7 Ages of Man, ballet; Real-Life, 1978. Recordings: Hip Grimm Fairy Tales, Roulette, 1960; Great Sounds of Mort Lindsey, Dot, 1959; Great Band; Great Songs; Great Sounds, etc. Mbrships: ASCAP; CLGA; AGAC; Phi Mu Alpha. Hons: Grammy Award (Nat. Acad. of Recordings Arts & Scis.) - Musical Dir. (Album of the Yr.), Judy Garland at Carnegie Hall, 1962; Emmy Award (Nat. Acad. of TV Arts & Scis.) - Outstanding Individual Achievement in Music, for musical direction of A'Happening in Ctrl. Pk'. Address: 6970 Fernhill Dr., Malibu, CA 90265, USA.

LINDSTRÖM, Anders, b. 25 Nov. 1947. Lund, Sweden. Composer; Actor; Vocalist; Instrumentalist. Educ: Musicdramatical course, Theatre Schl. of Malmö. Debut: (as actor) Royal Opera, Stockholm; (as Comp.) for Musikteatergruppen. Career: Comp., music for over 40 musical theatre plays; Radio & TV perfs.; Tchr., vocal presentation, Theatre Schl., Malmö. Comps. incl: Rallare Rej, 1971; Det finns aldrig avslutad sang, 1972; Modern (Brecht, Eisler), 1973 (recorded); Familjen Larsson, 1974; Aina B. dansar inte pa rosor (opera), 1975; Palestina - mitt blod, min väg, mitt land (recorded), 1976; Varför ta det lilla lugna, 1977; Resenarerna, 1978; Dubbla Bottnar, 1979. Mbr., Teatercentrum. Hobbies: Work; Political Activities; Nature. Address: Hagested 43, S270 20 Löderup, Sweden.

LINGE, Morrell Kennedy, b. 18 Apr. 1918. McKeesport, Pa., USA. Violinist. Educ: Duquesne Univ.; Grad. Schl. of Carnegie-Mellon Univ.; studies w. Oscar del Bianco & Roland Leich (comp.), Paul Sladek, Andre Benoist (violin). m. Nora Harris Linge, 1 s., 1 d. Debut: Duquesne Univ., 1940. Career: Tchr., pub. & pvte. for 40 yrs.; mbr.; Pittsburgh Symph. Orch., 40 yrs.; num. TV & radio apps.; mbr., Civic Light Opera, Pittsburgh Opera & Ballet. Mbrships: Pittsburgh Musical Soc.; Local 60, Union rep. to the Pittsburgh Symph. Orch. Hobbies: Painting (acrylics); Writing & Arranging. Address: 615 Bower Hill Rd., Mt. Lebanon, PA 15243, USA.

LINGE, Ruth, b. 13 Oct. 1927. Porsgrunn, Norway. Opera Singer; Lyrical Soprano. Educ: pvte., Oslo, Stockholm, Vienna. m. Tormod Linge. Debut: as Norina in Don Pasquale, Oslo, 1951. Career: Norsk Operaselskap, 1951-58; Mbr., Den Norske Opera, 1958-; main roles incl: Zerlina, Donna Elvira, Donna Anna, Cherubino, Papagena, Adina, Gidla Rosina, Musette, Olmpia; apps. in TV opera prods., radio concerts, etc. Mbrships: Sec., Bd., Soc. of Norwegian Opera Singers; Soc. of Norwegian Musica Artists. Address: Ths. Heftyesgt 64A, Oslo 2, Norway.

LINK, Joachim-Dietrich, b. 18 Oct. 1925. Magdeburg, Germany. Conductor; Composer; Pianist; Publisher. Educ: Music Acad., Leipzig. m. Karin Rohn, 1 s., 1 d. Debut: Leipzig, 1941. Career: Musical Dir. & Comp., Municipal Theatre, Leipzig; Musical Dir., Weimar & var. theatres; Orch. Ldr., Comic Opera, Berlin; Cond. & Musical Dir., Acad. for Music Hanns Eisler; Cond., Robert Schumann Conserv., Zwickau. Comps. incl: violin Concerto; 3 Piano Concertos; Sonatas for all instruments; vocal & piano works; 2 Operas; 3 Musical Comedies; 5 Children's Operas; num. Film Music. Recordings: Bela Bartok; Village Scenes. Publs. incl: Gen. revisions of piano ed., var. operas classical & mod. Contbr. to profl. jrnls. & newspapers. Mbr., Janácek Soc., Brno, CSSR. Hons. incl: Hon. Medal, DDR, 1959; Art Prize, 1966. Hobby: Gardening. Mgmt: Artists Agency, DDR Berlin. Address: Hecht Str. 52, 1166 Berlin, German Dem. Repub.

LINKE, Norbert, b. 5 March 1933. Steinau-Oder, Schlesien, DDR. Composer; Teacher. Educ: DPh, Hamburg Univ. m. Marianne Conrad, 3 d. Career: Music Tchr., Hamburg, 1960-72; Prof., Lubeck, Darmstadt, 1972-. Comps. incl: Works for orch.; chmbr. music; vocal works. Recordings: D66;

Colosseum; Camerata; Hohner; Orion. Publs: Muski zwischen Konsum und Kult, 1972; New Roads in Contemporary Music, 1975; Philosophy of Musical Education, 1976. Contbr. to Nationalzeitung Basel; New Music Jrnl., Regensburg. Hons: Stuttgart, 1962; Hamburg, 1968; Hof, 1969; Hamburg (2), 1970; Stuttgart, 1977. Hobbies: Reading; Hiking. Address: Torfstuce 23, D-2000 Hamburg 62, Germany.

LINKER, Robert White, b. 22 Oct. 1905. Salisbury, NC, USA. Musicologist. Educ: AB, 1925, Am, 1928, PhD, 1933, Univ. of NC. m. Dorothy Lavinia Insley, 1 s., 1 d. Publs: French Secular Music of the Late 14th Century (w. W Apel), 1950; Music of the Minnesinger & Early Meistersinger, 1962; Egerton 3307 (w. G S McPeek), 1963; The Unica in the Chansonnier Cordiforme (w. E L Kottick), 1967. Contbr. to: Jrnl. Am. Musicol. Soc.; Boletin de la Real Academia Española. Mbrships: Medieval Acad. of Am.; Am. Musicol. Soc.; S. Atlantic Mod. Lang. Assn. (Pres., 1972). Hons: Chevalier, 1975, Off., 1973, Ordre des Palmes Académiques; Lt.-Col., Aide-de-Camp to Gov. of Ga., 1972, 76; Medieval Studies in Honour of R W Linker, 1973. Address: 480 W Lake Drive, Athens, GA 30601, USA. 2, 11, 28.

LINNARTZ, Hans, b. 7 Nov. 1936. The Hague, Netherlands. Music Educator; Recorder Player. Educ: Univ. of Amsterdam; Muzieklyceum Conserv., Amsterdam. m. Marijke Best, 2 children. Debut: NCRV Radio, Hilversum. Career: num. broadcasts in Netherlands; Asst., TV prods. & also concerts in Netherlands, Belgium, Austria, France, & UK; Hd., Pedagogical Dept., Royal Conserv. for Music, The Hague; Tchr., Gen. Music Educ., Baarnsch Lyceum, Baarn. Recordings: 4th Brandenburg concerto. Contbr. to: Tijd-Maasbode; Sonorum Speculum. Mbrships: KNTV; Vereinging Voor Nederlandse Muziekgeschiedenis. Hobby: Reading. Address: Prof. Drionlaan 21, Baarn, Netherlands.

LINSCOME, Sanford Abel, b. 2 Jan., 1931. Houston, Tex., USA. Music Educator; Singer. Educ: BME., McNeese State Coll., Lake Charles La., 1954; MM., Univ. of Ill., 1959; DMA., Univ. of Tex., Austin 1970. m. Aileen Read, 2 d. Career: Singer, Robert Shaw Chorale, 1954-55; Recital, Oratorio Apps., midwestern, southern USA, 1955-65; Tchr. of Singing, Choral Dir., Univ. of Ala., 1958-60; Res. Tenor, Prof. of Music, Tchr. of Singing, Music Hist., Bibliog., & Coord. of Grad. Studies, Schl. of Music, Univ. of N Colo., 1965-; Cons., William C Brown & Co., Publrs. Author, A History of Musical Development In Denver, Colorado-1858-11908, 1970. Contbr. to: Colo. Mag.; Grove's Dictionary of Music & Musicians. Recip. 1st Place, Southern USA Young Artist Contest, 1953. Hobbies: Hunting; Gardening. Address: 2659 16th Ave., Greeley, CO 80631, USA.

LINTHICUM, David H, b. 7 May 1941. Balt., Md., USA. Freelance Composer; Author; Lecturer. Educ: Western Md. Coll., Westminster; B Mus, Peabody Conserv., Bald., 1964; M Mus, Cath. Univ. Am., Wash, DC, 1969; DMA, Univ. Ill., 1972. Career: Formerly, Coll. Prof. Music, hist., theory, comp. & ethnomusicol.; Currently, Freelance comp., author & lectr. Comps: Pour la fluste seule, 1969; Music for Cello, 1975. Contbr. to: The Composer; Music Review. Mbrships: Am. Musicol. Soc.; Soc. Ethnomusicol. Inc.; Am. Soc. Univ. Comps. Hon s: Marie K. Thatcher Award, Peabody Conserv., 1964; Univ. Ill. Fellowship, Music, 1970-71, '71-72. Hobbies: Lib. vol. work; antiques; Raising Old Engl. sheepdogs; Gourmet cooking. Address: 224 Warren Ave., Baltimore, MD 21230, USA.

LIPKIN, Malcolm Leyland, b. 2 May 1932. Liverpool, UK. Composer; Pianist; Lecturer. Educ: pvte. studies, piano, Gordon Green, 1944-59, comp., Matyas Seiber, 1954-57; RCM, 1949-53; D Mus London; ARCM; LRAM. m. Judith Frankel, 1 s. Debut: Gaudeamus Fndn. Music Week, Netherlands, 1951. Career: Lectr., Depts. of External Studies, Univ. of Oxford, 1965-75, Univ. of Kent Canterbury, 1975-. Comps. incl: Metamorphosis for Harpsichord, 1974; Interplay for Treble Recorder, Percussion, Harpsichord & Viola da Gamba, 1975; The Pursuit symph., 1975-76; Four Departures for Voice & Violin, 1972; Psalms 92, 117 & 121 for a cappella choir, 1969-73. Contbr. to Comp. mag. Recip. var. hons. Hobbies: Long country walks; Reading. Address: Penlan, Crowborough Hill, Crowborough, Sussex TN6 2EA, UK. 3.

LIPPMANN, Friedrich, b. 25 July 1932. Dessau, Germany. Musicologist. Educ: PhD, 1962. m. Gudrun Schuppa. 1 child. Career: Mbr., Joseph Haydn Inst., Cologne, 1962-64; Dir., Music Hist. Dept., German Histl. Inst., Rome, 1964-. Publs: Ed.: J Haydn Harmoniemesse, 1966; Vincenzo Bellini und die Italienische Opera seria seiner Zeit, 1969. Contbr. to profl. jrnls. Mbrhips: Int. Musicol. Soc.; German Soc. for Music Rsch.; Italian Musicol. Soc. Hobbies: Lit.; Art. Address: 391 via Aurelia antica, I-00165 Rome, Italy.

LIPPOLD, Klaus Eberhard, b. 26 Feb. 1938. Plauen Vogtland, Germany. Musicologist. Educ: PhD. m. Monika Lippold, 2 c. Publs: Die Licht'schen Chöre-ein Beitrag zur Geschichte der deutschen Arbeitersängerbewegung, 1966: Zur Frage der Asthetischen Inhalt-Form-Relationen in der Musik, 1971. Contbr. to var. anthologies. Mbrships: Int. Soc. for Musicol.; Soc. of Comps. & Musicologists of the German Democratic Repu. Recip. Hon. Prin. E. German Soc. of Comps. & Musicologists. Address: 77 Philipp Reis Str., DDR 7033 Leipzig, E Germany.

LIPSCOMB, William Nunn, Jr., b. 9 Dec. 1919. Cleveland, Ohio, USA. Professor; Clarinetist. Educ: BS., Univ., of Ky., 1941; PhD., Calif. Inst. of Technol., 1946; MA (Hon.), Harvard Univ., 1959; DSc (Hon.), Univ. of Ky., 1963. m. Mary Sargent Lipscomb, 1 s., 1 d. Career: Abbott & James Lawrence Prof. of Chem., Harvard Univ.; w. Pasadena Civic Orch., Calif., 1944-46; Mnpls. Civic Orch., 1954-59; TV perfs. of Chamber Music, Mnpls., Minn., 1958-59; Chmbr. Music Concerts, Mnpls., Minn., 1958-59; Chmbr. Music Concerts, Mnpls., Boston, Cambridge (Mass), Cambridge, UK, 1953-74; Chamber Orch., New England Chmbr. Opera Grp., 1973; Orch. & Chamber Music Concerts in Weston, Vt., 1962 0 '65-73. Mbrships: Bd. Mbr., New Friends of Chamber Music, Mnpls. 1958-59. Hobby: Tennis. Address: 26 Woodfall Rd., Belmont, MA, USA. 1, 2.

LISCHKA, Rainer, b. 25 April 1942. Zittau, Germany. Composer. Educ: Dip. music, Dresden, 1966; rsch. asst. 1966-69; hd. rsch. asst. 1974. Career: comp. for Staatskapelle, Dresden; State Opera, Dresden; Berlin radio; State Theatre, Dresden; Comps: "Die heilige Elisabeth", "Der grosse Held Tartarin", "Die Frauen von Montecano", chmbr. music; choral music. Recordings: "Traum in den Morgen", "Kontakte für Altflöte, Kontrabass & Vibraphon", "Die Stimmen der Tiere"; music for children, theatre & cabaret. Hons: Mendelssohn Scholarship, 1969 & 70; 1st prize, World competition, Budapest, 1974. Hobbies: reading; travel. Address: DDR-808 Dresden, Zur neuen Brücke 10, German Dem. Repub.

LISSA, Zofia, b. 19 Oct. 1908. Lwow, Poland. Professor of Musicology. Educ: PhD; Dr. Hist.; Golden Dip. of Conserv. (piano & organ). Debut: 1st scientific works from 1930. Career: Prof. of Conserv., 1930-39; Dir., Inst. of Musicol., Warsaw Univ., 1947-75; Docent of Musicol., ibid., 1947-51; Asst. Prof., ibid., 1951-57; Full PRof., ibid., 1957-. Publs. incl: 18 books translated in 14 langs. inclng. Japanese & Chinese; 495 scientific articles; Books incl: Zur Musikaestetik (essays), 1969; Studia nad tworczoscia Fryderyka Chopina, 1970. Leipzig; Acad. of Art, Berlin; Acad. of Sci., Meinzz. Hons. incl: State Prize, 1953; Prizes of Min. of Culture & Min. of Sci. Address: Miazynska 37, Warsaw 02-637 ul, Poland.

LISTER, Craig L. George. b. 7 Nov. 1950. St. Louis, Mo., USA. Professor of Music; Historian; Organist; Harpsichordist. Educ: AB, Wash. Univ., 1968; MMus, ibid, 1972 (Organ & Harpsichord); PhD, Univ. of NC at Chapel Hill (Musicol.), 1979. m. Margaret Mary Lister. Career: Num. organ & harpsichord recitals, incl. J S Bach's Die Kunst die Fuge (complete), histl. programs, 15th-20th Centuries, 1972-. Publs: Theoretical Traditions of Keyboard Performance from 1650-1750, 1979. Mbrships: AAUP; Am. Musicol. Soc.; Coll. Music Soc.; Music Lib. Assn. Hobby: Instrument Construction with emphasis in early keyboard instruments. Address: Univ. of Texas of the Permian Basin, Odessa, TX 79762, USA.

LISZCZ, Kazimierz, b. 24 March 1937. Stykow, Rzeszow, Poland. Musician; Lecturer. Educ: Music Hs, Cracow; MA. m. Lucja Lesniak, 2 c. Debut: w. Phil. Orch., Rzeszow, 1960. Career: Mbr., Lublin Phil. Orch.; St. Lectr. in Music, Lublin, Univ.; Lyricist; Perfs., clubs & cultural homes; num. radio apps.; Lectr., Universal Scientific Soc., Labour Univ., Musicians Co. Lublin. Comps: Arrs. of Folk Songs & Folk Music. Publs: Collections of popular regional music for Mus. of Rzeszow & Lublin. Mbrships: Polish Musicians Assn.; Polish Ethnol. Soc.; Polish Trade Union of Culture & the Arts; Polish Touring Soc. Hobbies: Folk Songs; Music; Poetry. Address: ul. Pana Balcera 1/115, 20-631 Lublin, Poland.

LITTLE, Florence Elizabeth, b. 7 July 1911. Streator, Ill., USA. Teacher (retired). Educ: BA, Mich. State Univ., 1932; Western State Coll., Gunnison, Colo., 1959: MSE; Drake Univ., 1962; Denver Univ., 1962. m. Alfred Lamond Little (dec.), 1 s., 1 d. Career: Accomp., Mich. State Univ., 1933-36; tchr., var. schls. in USA incl. Des Moines, Iowa, 1953-73; pvte. tchr., piano & voice, 1932-56. Mbrships: Mu Phi Epsilon; Kappa Kappa Iota; Am. Bus. Women's Assn.; NEA; Iowa State Educ. Assn.; Des Moines Educ. Assn.; Izaak Walton League; Mid-Iowa Orchid Soc.; Int. C B Operator Assn. Hobbies:

Genealogy; Crafts; Crocheting; Needlework; Weaving; Orchids. Address: 1020 69th St., Des Moines, IA 50311, USA.

LITTLE, Francis E (Frank) b. 22 Apr. 1936. Greeneville, Tenn., USA. Operatic Tenor. Educ: BS, E Tenn. State Univ.; M Mus, Univ. of Cinn.; D Mus, Northwestern Univ. m. Carolyn Jo Sauter, 2 d., 2 s. Debut: Chgo. Lyric Opera, 1970. Career incls: Leading tenor roles, Chgo. Lyric Opera, 1970-76; Wash. Opera, 1973-74; Phila. Lyric Opera, 1973-75. Apps. w. Chgo. Symph. Orch., Cinn. Symph. Orch., Milwaukee Symph. Orch. & in major Am. summer fests.; Broad career as concert artist & recitalist, specialising in songs of Franz Liszt & Charles Ives. Mbr., Pi Kappa Lambda. Contbr. to Music Jrnl. Recip., var. hons. Hobbies incl: Fishing. Address: 150 Thackeray Lane, Northfield, IL 60093, USA. Mgmt: Colbert Artist's Mgmt., 111 W 57th St., NY, NY 10019, USA.

LITTLE, Pauline Mary, b. 1942. Beds., UK. Concert Pianist. Educ: LRAM; Pvte. Studies w. Claude Pollard & Peter Katin. Debut: Wigmore Hall, 1965. Career: Recitals & concerts in GB & abroad; Broadcasts for BBC. Mbr. ISM. Recip. Royal Amateur Orch., Bronze Medal, 1966. Hobbies: Tennis; Antiques; Walking. Address: Sunfields, 7 Lyndhurst Dr., Harpenden, Herts., UK.

LITTLE, Wm. A., b. 28 July 1929. Boston, Mass., USA. Musicologist; Organist; Educator. Educ: BA, Tufts Coll., Mass., 1951; MA, Harvard Univ., 1953; LTCL, 1952; PhD, Univ. of Mich., 1961. Career: Asst. Prof. of German Organist & Choirmaster of the Coll., Williams Coll., Williamstown, Mass., 1957-63, Assoc. Prof. & Chmn., Geman, Tufts Univ., Medford, Mass., 1963-66; Prof. & Chmn., German Dept., Univ. of Va., Chorlottesville & Organist/Choirmaster, St. Paul's Ch., Ivy, Va., 1966-; Mbr., Editorial Bd. for new Historischkritische Gesamtausgabe Felix Mendelssohn Bartholdy. Publs. incl: Gottfried August Burger, 1974; FMB. Kompositionen für Orgel, Vol. 1, 1978. Contbr. to: Diapason; Am. Organist; Ed.; German Quarterly, 1970-. Mbrships. incl: Am. Musicol. Soc.; AGO; Bach Gesellschaft. Hobbies: Tennis; Antiques; Gastronomy. Address: Kirklea, Ivy, VA 22945, USA. 2, 4, 11, 29.

LITTLEJOHN, Joan Anne, b. 20 Apr. 1937. London, UK. Composer; Musicologist; Writer. Educ: RCM; GRSM; LRAM; postgrad. study w. Herbert Howells, Lennox Berkeley, Racine Fricker, Nadia Boulanger & others. Career: sev. 1st perfs. of comps. at Purcell Room & other concert halls; many perfs., Londn & elsewhere; Adminstv. staff, RCM, 1960-; piano tchr., Harrow Schl., 1972-73; Deputy Keeper, Parry Room, Lib. RCM, 1972-; pvte. teaching & coaching. Comps. incl: over 150 songs, incl. sev. song-cycles; The Bonny Earl of Murray (commissioned for Avalon Singers, 1975); St. Juliot, Cornwall, other settings of Rachel Pearse; Vier Lieder of Friederike Schnabel. Recording With my Father A-Ploughing (song & poetry recital, 1972). Contbr. to: Composer Magazine; Envoi Poetry Magazine, etc. Mbrships: PRS; Songwriters' Guild of GB; Mozartgemeinde, Vienna; Society of Genealogists; Heraldry Soc.; Life mbr., Brit. Fed. of Music Fests. & Brontë Soc. Hons: Ralph Vaughan Williams Trust Award. Hobbies incl: Writing Poetry. Address: c/o Royal Coll. of Music, Prince Consort Rd., London, SW7, UK. 27.

LITTON, James H, b. 31 Dec. 1934. Charleston, W Va, USA. College Professor; Organist; Choral Conductor. Educ: B Mus, M Mus, Westminster Choir Coll., Princeton, NJ; Post Grad. study, Canterbury Cathedral. m. Lou Ann Hall, 3 s., 1 d. Career: Protestant Hour Radio Recordings: ABC TV, Winter Star. Recordings: Hamilton: Epitaph for This World and Time; Var. radio recordings; series of Liturgical tchng. cassettes. Contbr. to num. profl. mags. inclng: Music, AGO mag. Mbrships: AGO (Dean, Indpls., 1966-68, Dean, Central, NJ, 1977-79); Nat. Pres., Asns. of Anglican Musicians, 1966-68; Standing Commission on Ch. Music, 1972- (Vice Chmn., Treas., Service Music Chmn.); Assn. of Choral Conds.; RCO. Hobbies: Record collecting; Travel; Organ Hist. Address: 8 Carnation Pl., Lawrenceville, NJ 08648, USA.

LIVINGSTON, Jay, b. 28 Mar. 1915. McDonald, Pa., USA. Composer; Songwriter; Pianist. Educ: BA, Univ. of Pa.; UCLA. m. Lynee Livingston, 2c. Career: Freelance, NYC, up to 1947 & since 1957; contracted to Paramount Picture Pictures, during which wrote songs for over 100 films, 1947-57. Comps. incl: 2 Broadway musicals (Oh Captain, 1958; Let It Ride, 1961); 206 publd. songs, 1976; TV themes for Bonanza & Mr. Ed. num. recordings of his songs. Mbrships: icnl: Exec. Bd., Acad. of Motion Picture Arts & Scis. & Comps. & Lyricists Guild; Fndr., Nat. Acad. of Recording Ars & Scis.; ASCAP. Hon. incl: Motion Picture Acad. Awards, 1948, 50 & 56; elected to Songwriters Hall of Fame, 1972. Hobby: Travel. Mgmt: Alvin Bart, Bart-Levy Agcy. Address: ASCAP, ASCAP Bldg., One Lincoln Plaza, NY, NY 10023, USA. 2.

LIVINGSTONE, Ernest Felix, b. 9 Sept. 1915. Berlin, Germany. Professor of Musicology & Cultural History. Educ: Univ. of Berlin; Ed.M, Univ. of Rochester, USA: BMus, MA, PhD, Musicol. m. Teresa Marotta, 1 d. Career: Prof., Musicol. & Cultural Hist., Rensselaer Polytechnic Inst. & Eastman Schl. of Music, Rochester Univ.; Chmn., Dept. of Fine Arts & Chmn., For, Land. Exam. Comm., Rensselaer; Guest Lectr., Univs. of Copenhagen & Gottingen. Contbr. to profl. jrnls., Papers read at Int. Musicol. Congresses, Bonn, 1970, Berlin, 1974. Mbrships: Am. Musicol. Soc.; Past Chapt. Pres., Am. Assn. of Tchrs. of German; AAUP. Hons: Disting. Fac. Award, Rensselaer; Citation, NY Bd. of Regents, 1968. Hobby: International travel. Address: 50 Grange Rd., Troy, NY 12180, USA. 11, 12, 13.

LIVINGSTONE, Laureen, b. 3 Feb. 1946. Dumbarton, Scotland, UK. Educ: Singing studies w. Ena Mitchell, 3 yrs.; Piano & violin study at RSAM; Jordanhill Coll. of Educ.; London Opera Centre; pvte. studies w. Vera Rozsa (singing); Dip. Mus Ed., RSAM; Tchrs. Cert. m. Philip Mayer, 2 c. Career: Num. concerts throughout UK; Perfs. w. Glynebourne, Engl. Nat. Opera & Scottish Opera; BBC Promenade Concerts at Royal Albert Hall; Concerta Opera perfs., Germany, Switz., Poland, Holland, Belgium, Portugal, Naples; Concerts w. Northern Sinfonia; LSO & SNO; Broadcasts for BBC radio & TV. Recordings: Sev. recital progs. for BBC. Hons: Winner, Peter Stuyvesant Scholarship, 1969. Mgmt: Music International. Address: 12 Pymmes Brook Dr., New Barnet, Herts., UK.

LJUNGDAHL, Olle, b. 11 MAy 1911. Karlstad, Sweden. Cathedral Organist. Educ: Higher Organist Examination, Higher Ch. Choir Examination, Higher Music Tchr., Examination, Acad. of Music, Stockholm; Pvte. studies in Choir Conducting & Vocal Polyphony (Palestuna Style). m. Annie Olsson, 1 child. Career: Organ recitals on Swedish & Norwegian radio; Radio progs. & tours w. Karlstad Motet Co. in Scandinavian Countries. Recordings: LP w. Karlstad Motet Co. Hons: Varmland Co. Coun's. Froding Award, 1967; Karlstad Municipality Culture Award, 1971. Hobby: Lit. Address: O. Kyrkogatan 6, 652 24 Karlstad. Sweden.

LLEWELLYN, William Benjamin James, b. 6 May 1925. Farnworth, Widnes, UK. Director of Music. Educ: Emmanuel Coll., Cambridge; RAM; B Mus (London); FRAM; ARCO; LRAM. m. Mildred Stott, 2 s., 1 d. Career: Asst. music master, Charterhouse Schl., 1950-65. Fndr. & Cond., Linden Singers, 1950-59; Dir. of Music, Charterhouse, 1965-; Cond., The Llewellyn Singers. Comps: hymns in Anglican Hymn Book; 100 Hymns & Songs; Hymns for Celebration: New Church Praise. Recordings: w. Linden Singers. Mbrships: RAM; Pres., ISM, 1977; Chmn. Godalming Music Fest., Musical Dir., Music for Youth. Hobbies: Photography; Railways; Sound Reproduction. Address: Westron Wynde, Mark Way, Godalming, Surrey GU7 2BW, UK.

LLORENS, José-Maria, b. 8 Nov. 1923. Guissona, Lérida, Spain. Educ: Seminario Diocesano, Barcelona, Spain, 1949: Master, Sacred Music, Instituto Ponticicio de Música Sagrade, Rome, T Italy, 1945; Doct. Musicol., ibid., 1968. Career: Sci. Rschr., Higher Coun. of Musicol. Sci. Rschs. Num. publs. in musicol. field. Contbr. to: Die Musik in Geschichte und Gegenwart; Enciclopedia Italiana; Enciclopedia Salvat de la Música (Barcelona); Gran Enciclopedia Catalana (Barcelona); Grove's Dictionary of Music. Mbrships: Royal Acad. of Fine Art, San Fernando; Int. Musicol. Soc.; Catalan Musicol. Soc.; Catalan Liturgical Studies Soc. Hons: Gold Medal from Pope Paul VI for presenting his doctoral theses. Address: Plaza de los Angeles 4, Barcelona, Spain.

LLOYD, Albert Lancaster, b. 29 Feb. 1908. London, UK. Arthur; Ethnomusicologist; University Lecturer. Educ: MA (Hon. Open Univ.) m. Charlotte Maria Adam, 1 s., 1 d. Career: has done much ethnomusicol. field work, esp. in Balkan countries; has made between 30 & 40 LPs of Engl., Aust. & Balkan folk music, most issued by Topic Records in the UK & by Columbia Records in the USA. Publs: Come Ye Bold Miners- Songs & Ballads of the Coalfields, 1952; Penguin Book of English Folk Songs (w. R Vaughan Williams), 1959: Folk Song in England, 1967. Contbr. to jrnls. & profl. inclng. Encyclopedia Britannica & Grove's Dictionary of Music & Musicians. Mbrships: Ed. Bd., Engl. Folk Song & Dance Soc.; Int. Folk Music Coun. Address: 16 Crooms Hill, London SE 10, UK.

LLOYD, David Bellamy, b. 22 Nov. 1937. Stockport, UK. Piano Accompanist. Educ: ARMCM (Perf. & Tchr.). Debut: recital w. Heddle Nash, Wigmore Hall, 1956. Career: Accomp. to Jan Peerce, Fest. Hall, London & tour of France, Germany, Switz., Austria & Netherlands; TV apps. w. Jack Brymer, Adele Leigh; regular accomp. to Jack Brymer, Leon Goossens & Elizabeth Harwood in recitals & broadcasts, Singapore, Hong Kong, India, NZ & Spain. Recordings: Brahms Clarinet Sonata op. 120/1 concertante: The Art of Leon Goossens. Mbr., ISM. Recip., Hilary Haworth Prize, RMCM, 1958. Hobbies: Opera; Travel; Railways; Photography; Motor Cars. Mgmt: Ibbs & Tillett; Terry Slasberg. Address: 5 Thornhill Rd., Heaton Mersey, Stockport, Ches. SK£ 3HJ, UK.

LLOYD, Gabriel Frederic Garnons, b. 1 July 19198. Oxford, UK. Musicologist; Opera General Manager; Lecturer; Author. Educ: Hon. FRAM. m. Valerie Fraser, 2 s. Career incls: Regional Dir., Arts Council of Gt. Britain, 1943-50; Chmn., Notts. Co. Music Comm., 1947-49; Festival of Britain Dir. of Oxford, 1951; Chmn., Theatre Mgrs. Assn. Prodng. Mgrs. Comm., 1958-67; Pres., Theatre Mgrs. Assn., 1967-70; Gen. Mgr. & Sec., D'Oyly Carte Opera Trust; Gen. Mgr., Savoy Theatre; Chmn., Savoy Orpheans Ltd.; Dir. of Entertainments, Savoy Hotel Grp. Contbr. of articles on Elgar, Beethoven, Gilbert & Sullivan to music publs.; author of progs. notes, record sleeves etc. Mbrships: Gov., RAM; Dir. Royal Gen. Theatrical Fund; Gov., Royal Choral Soc.; Advsry. Coun., The Rehearsal Orch.; Life Gov., Royal Phil. Orch.; Advsry. Coun., Philomusical Ltd.; Past Chmn., Appeal Comm., Malcolm Sargent Cancer Fund for Children; Worshipful Co. of Musicians. Hons: OBE; JP; Hon. FRAM. Hobbies: Fishing. Address: 18 Clifton Hill, St. John's Wood, London, NW8 0QG, UK.

LLOYD, George Walter Selwyn, b. 28 June 1913. St. Ives, Cornwall, UK. Composer; Violinist. Educ: studied violin w. Albert Sammons, comp. w. Harry Farjeon & counterpoint w. Dr. Kitson. m. Nancy Juvet. Debut: conducting 1st symph. w. Bournemouth Symph. Orch., 1933. Comps. incl: 3 operas inclng. lernin, The Serf, John Socman; 9 symphs; 4 piano concertos; 1 violin concerto; miscellaneous pieces for orch., piano, violin. Comps. recorded: An African Shrine. Address: 199 Clarence Gate Gnds., Glentworth St., London NW1 6AU, UK.

LLOYD, Robert Andrew, b. 2 Mar. 1940. Southend-on-Sea, UK. Bass. Educ: Grad., Keble Coll. Oxford, 1962; London Opera Ctr. m. Sandra Watkins, 1 s., 3 d. Debut: as Fernando in Fidelio, London Univ. Opera. Career: Schoolmaster, 1962-63; Instrucotr Lt., Royal Navy, 1963-66; Lectr. in Int. Affairs, Bramshill Police Coll., 1966-68; Prin. Bass, Sadlers Wells, London Coliseum, 1969-72, Royal Opera House, Covent Gdn., 1972-. Recordings: EMI; Decca. Hobby: Sailing. Mgmt: HarrisonParrot Ltd. Address: 41 Birley Rd., Whetstone, London N20, UK.

LLOYD-JONES, David Mathias, b. 19 Nov. 1934. London, UK. Conductor. Educ: Westminster Schl.; BA, Magdelen Coll., Oxford. m. Anne Carolyn Whitehead, 2 s., 1 d. Career: Apps. w. opera at Covent Gd., ENO at Coliseum; Wexford, Bath & Camden Festivals; Scottish Opera, Welsh Nat. Opera; Radio in Amsterdam & Paris; Cond. most maj. orchs. in GB; Many BBC TV operas; Music Dir., ENO N, 1978. Recordings: Music of Russian Nationalists w. LPO. Publs: incl: Boris Godunow (ed. full score). 1976. Contbr. to profl. jrnls. Hobbies: Theatre; French Cuisine; Travel. Address: 3 Harley Gdns., London SW10 UK.

LLOYD WEBBER, Julian, b. 14 Apr. 1951. London, UK. Solo Cellist. Educ: RCM; RAM; ARCM, 1967. studied under Pierre Fournier, Geneva, 1973. m. Celia M Ballantyne. Debut: Wigmore Hall, London, 1971. Career: perfs. w. ldng. Brit. orchs. & at major UK concert halls, inclng. Royal Fest. Hall, Queen Elizabeth Hall, (London), Usher Hall (Edinburgh), Ulster Hall (Belfast); London premiere of Bliss Concerto, Queen Elizabeth Hall, 1972; Royal Fest. Hall debut w. Elgar Concerto, 1974; Perfs. in Finland, Germany, Holland, Luxembourg. Recordings: incl: Mod. Brit. Cello Music; Delius cello sonata Bridge, Oration; Ireland, Piano Trio. Contbr. to: Sunday Times; Strad; The Composer. Mbrships: ISM; Orient F C Sportsmans Club. Hons. incl: Seymour Whinyates Award, 1971; Percy Buck Award, 1972. Hobbies: Keeping turtles; Soccer; Countryside. Mgmt: Ibbs & Tillett, 24 Wigmore St., London, UK. Address: c/o mgmt.

LLOYD WEBBER, Willam Southcombe, b. 11 Mar. 1914. London, UK. Professor; Musical Director. Educ: Organ Scholar, RCM, London, 1931-37; FRCM; FRCO; FLCM; Hon. RAM; DMus. (London). m. Jean Hermoine Johnstone, 2 s. Debut: First organ broadcast at age 13 yrs. Career: Organist & Choirmaster, Christ Ch., Newgate St., London, 1929-32, St. Cyprian's, Clarence Gate, 1933-39, All Saints, Margaret St., 1939-48; Prof. & Examiner in Theory & Comp., RCM, 1945-; Examiner to the Associated Bd. of the Royal Schls. of Music, 1945-64; Dir., London Coll. of Music; Musical Dir., Central Hall, Westminster, Comps. incl. many instrumental & choral works, both sacred & secular. Contbr. to Musical Times & Musical Opinion. Mbrships: Past Pres. of Hon. Mbr., London Assn. of Organists; Coun. Mbr., RCO, 1946- & Hon. Treas.,

1953-64; Master of The Worshipful Company of Musicians, 1973-74; VP, Inc. Assn. of Organists, etc. Hons: CBE; var. organ & theory prizes at RCM & RCO. Hobbies: Bridge; Chess. Address: 13A Sussex Mansions, Old Brompton Rd., London SW7 3J2, UK. 1, 3.

LOBAUGH, Harold Bruce, b. 19 Feb. 1930. Toledo, Ohio, USA. Professor; Clarinettist. Educ: BSc, Muskingum Coll., New Concord, Ohio, 1952; M Mus, Eastman Schl. of Music, Univ. of Rochester, NY, 1960; PhD, ibid., 1968. m. Charlotte R, 2 s. Career: Instructor in Music, schls. in Kansas City & Cleveland; Asst. Prof., Hartwick Coll., Oneonta, NY, 1960-64; Assoc. Prof., Univ. Regina, Sask., Can., 1966-. Publs: Ten Rennaisance Dances (arr. for recorders), 1969. Contbr. to: Grove's Dictionary of Music & Musicians, 6th ed.; Jrnl. of Lute Soc. of Am.; Lute Soc. Jrnl., UK. Mbrships: Am. Musicol Soc.; Can. Assn. of Univ. Schls. of Music; Am. Lute Soc.; Can. Music Educators Assn. Hobby: Electronics. Address: 36 Cardinal Crescent, Regina, Sask., Canada.

LÖBERG, Per, b. 28 March, 1942. Oslo, Norway. Musician (Double Bass, El. Bass). Educ: Pvte. studies w. Knut Guettler, Bjorn Holmvik, Gary Karr. m. Mona, 1 s., 1 d. Debut: Oslo, 1961. Career: Oslo Phil.; The Norwegian Radio Orch.; Opera Orch., 3 yrs.; Sev. Jazz Orchs.; Jazz Fests., Europe; Studio Musician (TV, radio & record studios). Comps. incl: Opus 1, Bossa Mona; Bossa Nostra; En Sang For Atte Ore (recorded); Jeg Sa Et Skip Som Seilte (recorded). Mbrships: Oslo Musikerforening; Norsk Jazzforbund. Hons: 2nd Prize, Amateur Jazz, 1963. Address: Ammerudhellinga 35, Oslo 9, Norway.

LOCK, William Rowland, b. 27 Feb. 1932. Toronto, Ont., Canada. Vocalist (Baritone); Conductor; Teacher. Educ: ARCT, Royal Conserv. of Music, Toronto; B Mus, MacPhail Coll. of Music, Mpls., USA; M Mus, ibid.; DMA, univ. of Southern Calif.; grad. study in Austria & UK. m. Margaret Annie MacLean, 1 s., 1 d. Career: Prof. of Voice, Conducting & Ch. Music, Biola Coll., La Mirada, Calif. Fndr.-Dir., William Lock Singers. Min. of Music, Mpls., Minn.; Whittier, Calif.; Long Beach Calif.; Solo appearances in recital, on Radio & TV in Canada & USA; Fndr., William Lock Chorale & Orch. Compositions: Var. vocal & choral works & arrs. Contbr. to: Ency. of Music in Canada; Jrnl. of Ch. Music; Choral Review Ed., Worship & Arts, 1971-; Ed., The Sounding Board, 1967-72. Mbrships: Pres., LA Choral Conds. Guild, 1972-74; Am. Choral Dirs. Assn.; The Hymn Soc.; Choristers Guild; RSCM; Nat. Ch. Music Fellowship. Recip. Gold Medal, Royal Conserv. of Music, Toronto, 1954. Address: 13967 Whiterock Dr., La Mirada, CA 90638, USA.

LOCKE, Ralph, b. 9 Mar. 1949. Boston, Mass., USA. Musicologist; Teacher. Educ: BA, Harvard Coll.; MA, PhD, Univ. of Chgo. Comps: music to Brecht's Mother Courage. Contbr. to: Grove's Dict., 6th ed.; Nineteenth Century Music; JAMS; Revue de Musicologie; Fontis artis musicae; Berlioz Soc. mag.; var. Boston newspapers, etc. Mbrships: Am. Musicol Soc.; Société française de musicologie; Association Nationale Hector Berlioz. Hons: DAAD, German Govt. Award, 1970; French Govt. Exchange Fellowship, 1974, & Bourse d'Eté, 1976; Outstanding Young Men of the Year, 1978. Address: 26 Gibbs St., Rochester, NY 14604, USA.

LOCKETT, David Robert, b. 13 Jan. 1951. Stirling, SA, Aust. Pianist (Performer & Teacher); Lecturer. Educ: Elder Conserv., Adelaide, 1963-67; B Mus, Univ. of Adelaide, 1972; RCM, UK, 1972-73; L Mus A; ARCM. m. Alison June Sandow, 1 d. 1s. Career: Pvte. Tchr. Performer, to 1973; Teaching Fellow, Univ. of New England, Armidale, NSW, 1974; Lectr. in Music (Keyboard). Murray, Pk. Coll. of Advanced Educ., 1975-; Concerto perfs. w. leading Aust. orchs.; regular radio apps. for Aust. Broadcasting Commission, & on commercial TV. Mbr., profl. assns., Aust. Hons. incl: Eva Lines Memorial Prize, 1964; SA Winner, Aust. Broadcasting 'Commission Competitions, 1968, 69; Athol Lykke postgrad Award; var. grants & scholarships. Hobbies: Reading; Gardening; Walking. Address: 12 Lawrence Ave., Rostrevor, SA 5073, Aust.

LOCKHART, James Lawrence, b. 16 Oct. 1930. Edinburgh, UK. Conductor; Musician (keyboard). Educ: B Mus, Edinburgh Univ.; Royal Coll. of Music; FRCO; ARCM. m. Sheila Grogan, 2 s., 1d. Career: Asst. Organist & Chorus Master, St. Giles Cathedral, Edinburgh, 1946-51; St. Mary's Episc. Ch., ibid., 1950-51; Organist & Choir Master, St. John the Divine, Kennington, London, 1951-53; All Souls, Langham Pl., ibid., 1953-54; Apprentice Cond., Yorks. Symph. Orch., 1954-55; Repititeur & Asst. Cond., Munster City Opera, Germany, 1955-56; Bavarian state Opera, 1956-57; Glyndebourne, Festival Opera, 1957-59; Repetiteur, ibid., 1962-68; Prof., Royal Coll. of Music, 1962-72; Music Dir., Welsh Nat. Opera, 1972-. Hobbies: Travel; Hill walking; Driving. Address: 105 Woodcock Hill, Harrow, Middx. HA3 0JJ, UK.

LOCKLAIR, Dan S(teven), b. 7 Aug. 1949. Charlotte, NC, USA. Church Musician; Composer; Instructor of Organ & Piano. Educ: B Mus, Mars Hill Coll., NC, 1971; MSM, Schl. Sacred Music, Union Theol. Sem., NCY, 1973; Postgrad. study, comp., SUNY, 1975-. m. Suzanne Aycock Locklair. Career: Organist, Choirmaster, Ch., Musician, since aged 14; Instructed music, coll. level; Organ Recitalist, NYC inclng. Cath. Ch. St. John the Divine, St. Thomas Ch. & St. Patrick's Cathedral Instructor of Music, Hartwick Coll., Oneonta, NY. Comps. incl: In Praise of Easter, 1975; Triptych for Manuals, 1976; O God of Earth & Altar. Mbrships. incl: ASCAP, Past Dean, Coll. Chapt., AGOÇ; MENC. Hons. incl: Crisp Medal, Most Outstanding Music Student, Mars Hill Coll., 1971; 1st prize, Nat. Comp. Contest, DC Chapt. AGO, 1972; Copyist Assistance Grant, Martha Baird Rockefeller Fndn. & NY State Coun. on the Arts, 1978. Hobbies incl: Collecting pipes. Address: 139 Matthews St., Binghamton, NY 13905, USA.

LOCKWOOD, Normand, b. 1906. NY., USA. Composer; Teacher. Educ: Univ. of Mich. Schl. of Music; studied w. Nadia Boulanger, Paris. Career: Tchr. in many colls. & univs. inclng. Oberlin Coll., Columbia Univ., Westminster Choir Coll.; Composer-in-Res., Assoc. Prof. of Music & Theatre, Univ. of Denver. Compositions incl: var. orchestral works; oratorios & choral works; music for keyboard; chmbr. music, 5 operas; integrated & incidental music for plays. Mbrships. incl: AGO; Fellow, Am. Acad. in Rome; Am. Composers' Alliance. Hons. incl: Publn. Award, Soc. for Publn. of Am. Music; Award in Music, Nat. Inst. of Arts & Letters; Swift Prize. Address: c/o Am. Comps. Alliance, 170 W 71st St., NY, NY 10023, USA.

LOCKWOOD, Ralph Gregory, b. 21 Feb. 1942. Cleveland, OH, USA. Horn Player; Pianist; Harpsichord Player; Organist; Conductor. Educ. incls: B Mus, Baldwin-Wallace Coll. Conserv. of Music; M Mus, New Engl. Conserv. of Music, Boston;·D Mus A Cand., Univ. of Cinn. Coll. -Conserv. Career: Music in Me. Chmbr. Orch., 10 yrs.; Horn Player & chmbr. music perf., Eastern Music Fest., Greensboro, NC; num. TV apps. as Recitalist & chmbr. musician; Tchr., Univ. of NC; currently Asst. Prof., Ariz. State Univ., on leave to play Asst. Prin. Horn, Clevelnad Orch., 1975-76. Num. publd. transcription of classical works for Brass Quintet & Brass Choir. Mbrships: NACWPI; Galpin Soc.; Int. Horn Soc.; Phi Mu Alpha Sinfonia. Hobbies incl: Yoga; Jogging; Swimming. Address: 17713 Grovewood Ave., Cleveland, OH 44119, USA.

LODÉON, André Maria Marcel, b. 25 Mar. 1928. Fort-de-France, Martinique. Conservatory Director; Conductor. Educ: Nat. Higher Conserv. m. Renée-Paul Symphor-Monplaise, 4 s., 2 d. Career: Dir., Nat. Conserv., Grenoble Region; Dir. of Concerts in France, Romania, Poland; TV interviews on Grenoble Conserv. Comps: (publs.) var. instrumental pieces. Contbr. to: Music & Educ.; Music & Myth; etc. Mbrships. incl: European Assn. of Conserv. Dirs.; Assoc. Sec., French Assn. of Conserv. Dirs. Hons. incl: Kt., Nat. Order of Merit, 1973; Kt., Order of Arts & Letters. Hobbies: Reading; Swimming; Sailing. Address: 6 Chemin de Gordes, 38100 Grenoble, France.

LOEB, Arthur L, b. 13 July 1923. Amsterdam, Netherlands. Musician (recorder, voice, viola da gamba, harpsichord). Educ: BS Chem, UKniv. Pa., 1943; AM, Harvard, 1945; PhD, ibid, 1949; New England Conserv. of Music; Musiek Lyceum, Amsterdam; Longy Schl. of Music; Cambridge, Mass. m. Charlotte I Aarts. Career: King's Chapel & Old North (Boston) Choir; Boston Renaissance Ensemble; Cambridge Ct. Dancers; Collegium Iosquinum; Sr. Lectr. on Visual Environmental Studies & mbr. Early Music Ensemble, Harvard Univ. Recordings for Cambridge Records. Contbr. book reviews in Leonardo. Mbrships: Life Fellow, Royal Soc. of Arts; Life Fellow, Am. Inst. of Chemists; Soc. for Hist. of Music in Netherlands; Viola da Gamba Soc. of Am.; Signet Soc., Harvard. Address: 29 Shepard St., Cambridge, MA 02138, USA.

LOEVENDIE, Theo, b. 17 Sept. 1930. Amsterdam, Netherlands. Composer; Saxophonist. Educ: Amsterdam Conserv. m. J Dedeoglu, 2 d. Career: apps. as comp., performer & ldr. of his own grps. at all major jazz fests. in Europe, since 1968, also comp. of "serious" music; Sr. Tchr. of Comp., Rotterdam Conserv., 1970-. Comps. incl: Incantations for bass clarinet & orch., 1975; Orbit for 5 french horns & orch.; Timbo, for 6 percussions, 1974; Strides, for piano, 1976; Six Turkish Peoms, for female voice & 7 instruments, 1977; Scaramuccia, for clarinet & orch., 1969. (all recorded). Contbr. to num. profl. jrnls. Hons: Edison Award, 1969. Address: Adm. de Ruyterweg 400 HS, 1055ND Amsterdam, Netherlands.

LOFT, Abram, b. 7 Jan. 1922. NYC, NY., USA. Violinist; Professor of Music. Educ: BMA., Columbia Coll., 1942; MA., Columbia Univ., 1944; PhD, ibid, 1950. m. Mildred S. Loft,

2s., 1 d. Career: Freelance Violinist-Violist, NYC, 1944-46; Asst. Prof. of Music, Columbia Coll. (Columbia Univ.), 1946-54; Mbr., Fine Arts Quartet, 1954-; Assoc. Prof., Univ. of Wis., Milwaukee, 1963-67; Prof. of Music, ibid., 1967-. Recordings (w. Fine Arts Quartet): Beethoven, Bartok, Haydn, & Brahms Quartet Cycles; Mozart Viola Quintets; other quartet & mixed ensemble works from Bach to Wuorinen & Babbitt, etc. Publs: Violin & Keyboard -The Duo Repertoire (Vol. 1: From the 17th Century to Mozart. Vol. 11: From Beethoven to the Present), 1973. Contbr. to: Musical Quarterly; Jrnl. of the Am. Musicol. Soc.; Notes. Mbrships: Review Ed., Jrnl., Am. Musicol. Soc., 1949-53; AAUP. Hobbies: Woodworking; Photography. Address: 4067 N. Lake Dr., Milwaukee, WI 53211, USA. 2.

LOGOTHETIS, Anestis, b. 27 Oct. 1921. Burgas, Bulgaria. Austrian Citizen. Composer. Educ: Dip., Acad. of Music, Vienna. m. Maria, 1 d. Career: Radio plays; Instrumental music. Compositions publd. by Universal edit., Vienna, Edit. modern, Munich, Ricordi Verlag, Munish, Gerig Verlag, Cologne, Edit. Ariadne, Vienna. Recordings for Wergo, Columbia, Thorophon. Contbr. to: Melos; Neues Forum; Wort & Wahrheit; Osterrichische Musikzeitschrift; Erhad Karkoschka, Das Schriftbild der Neuen Musik; John Cage, Notations; Otto Breicha, Aufforderung zum Misstrauen. Mbrships: Int. Soc. of Moder Music; Grazer Autorenversammlung. Hons: Fellowship to Rome; 1st Prize, Athens Comp. for Moder Music, Athens, 1962; Theodor Koerner Prize, Vienna, 1960. Address: Hegergasse 4/9, 1030 Vienna, Austria.

LOGUE, Joan Anne, b. 15 Aug. 1936. Grand Rapids, Minn., USA. Singer. Educ: BA, Univ. of Minn.; MA, Univ. of Wash.; studied voice w. Re Koster; Dip., Aspen Schl. of Music; Opera coaching w. Luigi Ricci; Italy; Chmbr. music w. Piero Guarino & Giorgio Favaretto. Debut: Venice, S Bussotti, Lorenzaccio. Career: Laborintus II (soprano soloist), Venice, Teatro Massimo (Palermo), Maggio Musicale (Florence); Per Massimiliano Robespierre (Terza Donna), Teatro Comunale (Bologna) & tour; Rara Requiem (mezzo-soprano solista), Biennale of Venice, Milan Radio Orch.; La Pazzia Senile (soprano soloist), Teatro dell'Opera Rome; Tirsi e Clori (soprano soloist), Piccola Scala, Milan; Num. concerts, tours & recitals; Fest. apps.; Radio pers. Recordings: Reportage da Isola di Utopia (w. Giorgio Gaslini); Contemporary Music; Music for Voice, Horn & Piano (w. D Ceccarossi). Mbr., Phi Beta Kappa. Hons: 2nd prize, 1st Int. Contest for interpretation of moder music, ISCM, 1973; Fulbright Scholarship to Italy, 1965. Hobbies: Swimming; Golf; Tennis. Address: Via Pietro Tacchini 6, Rome, Italy.

LOHMANN, Heinz Friedhelm, b. 8 Nov. 1934. Gevelsberg, Germany. Organist; Harpsichordist; Precentor. m. Erdmute Goetze, 1 s., 2 d. Debut: Gevelsbert, 1949. Career: Organist, Wolfsburg, 1958-60, in Paris, 1960-61, Düsseldorf, 1961-71, Kirche Zum Heilsbronnen, W Berlin, 1971-; Tchr. of Organ Art, Berlin Ch. Music Schl., 1974-; concerts throughout Europe, Israel Lebanon, America & USSR. Comps: unpubld., principally organ & choral works. Num. recordings of organ works on Da Camera, RBM & Pelca labels. Publs. incl: keyboards and orchl. works ed. for Breitkopf & Härtel, Wiesbaden; Ed., G Rietschel's Die Aufgabe der Orgel im Gottesdienste bis in das 18. Jahrhundert, 1971; Handbuch der Orgelliteratur, 2 vols., 1975. Contbr. to: German musical jrnls. Mbrships: New Bach Soc.; Soc. of Friends of the Organ; Int. Heinrich Schütz Soc.; Soc. for Music Rsch. Hobbies: Wandering; Reading; The Table. Address: Rheinstr. 6/7, 1 Berlin 41, German Fed. Repub.

LOHSE, Fred, b. 9 Apr. 1908. Leipzig, DDR. Comps., Tchr. Educ: Dph 1959, Lectr. 1967. m. Elli Lohse-Claus. Career: 1928-1952 Music pedagogue; 1952-1968 Tchr.; 1973 Prof. Karl Marx UKniv. Leipzig. Comp. incl: Orch. works; Chmbr. music; Piano music; Choir music. Recordings: Divertimento for str. orch.; Our Moder Music, nr 22. Mbrships: Assn. of Comp. and Musicologists DDR. Hons: Art Prize Leipzig, 1970; Kunstpreis der DDR, 1978. Address: Kreuzstr. 4, Leipzig 701, German Dem Repub.

LOMBARD, Alain, b. 4 Oct. 1940. Paris, France. Conductor. Educ: studied w. Mme. Talleul, Suzanne Demarquez Gaston Poulet. Debut: salle Gaveau, age 11; Am. Opera Soc., NYC, 1963. Career: Cond., Lyon Opera Orch., France, 1961-; Asst. Musical Dir., l'Opera d'Aran Opening, Paris; Asst. Cond., NY. Phil. & Summer Fest., Salzburg, 1966; Musical Dir., Miami Orch., Fla., 1967, Strasbourg, 1972-; Guest Cond., Miami, Fla., Met. Opera, NY, Phil., USA, Scheveningen Fest., Holland, Berlin Phil., Hamburg Opera Orch., W. German, l'Orchestre de Paris, France, Salzburg Fest. Recip. Gold Medal, Dimitri Mitropoulos Competition, NY., USA. 1966. Address: co SA. Gorlinsky Ltd., 35 Dover St., London W1X 4NJ, UK.

LOMBARDI, Nilson, b. 3 Jan. 1926. Sao Paulo, Brazil. Composer; University Profesor. Educ: Dip. of Piano & Musical Educ., 1954; Musical Comp., w. Camargo Guarnieri, 1954-69. Career: Prof. of Piano, Official State Conserv. Dr. Carlos de Campos, Tatui, Sao Paulo, Prof. of Musical Educ. in var. Colls. & Insts. of Educ., State of Sao Paulo; Prof. of Structure of Musical Lang., Fac. of Music, Official State Conserv., Maestro Juliao, Sao Bernardo de Campo. Comps: (recorded by Attilio Mostro Giovanni); Ciclo Miniature; 10 Ponteios for piano; Cantilena for piano. Mbrships: Affiliated to the Order of Sao Paulo Brazilian Musicians. Hons: 1st Prize, State Music Commission, 1962; 3rd Prize, Municipal Commission of Culture, Sao Paulo, 1966. Address: Rua das Palmeiras 225 apto 3 12, Sao Paulo, Brazil.

LOMBARDO, Robert Michael, b. 5 Mar. 1932. Hartford, Conn., USA. Composer; Professor. Educ: B Mus, M Mus, Hartt Coll. of Music, Univ. of Hartford, Conn.; PhD, Univ. of IA. m. Kathleen Lombardo, 2 d. Career: Prof. of Theory & Comp., Comp.-in-Res., Chgo. Musical Coll., Roosevelt Univ. Comps. incl: 2 chmbr. operas, Sorrows of a Supersoul & the Dodo, to libretti by Kathleen Lombardo; Orchl. Fantasy; Orchl. Aphorisms; 2 string quartets; Watergate Music; a bitter suite for clarinet & piano; Nocturne for double bass alone (recorded); multimedia works; Largo for string quartet (recorded). 12 Contemp. Piano Pieces for Children, 1965; In My Craft or Sullen Art, 1967. Mbrships: Sec., Chicago Soc. of Comps.; Am. Comps. Alliance; BMI; Am. Soc. of Univ. Comps. Recip., num. comp. prizes & commissions. Hobbies: Film-making; Writing Poetry. Address: 1040 W Wellington St., Chicago, IL 60657, USA.

LONDEIX, Jean-Marie, b. 20 Sept. 1932. Libourne, Gironde, France. Professor; International Concert Artist. Educ: Conserv. Paris. m. Janine Coudreau, 2 children. Debut: 1953. Career: Num. concerts & recitals, Europe, USA, Canada, USSR, Japan; TV & recitals, Europe, USA, Canada, USSR, Japan; TV & Radio apps. Comps. incl: Playing the Saxophone, 1965; Le Detache, 1968; Planche des doigtes compares pour les Harmoniques, 1971. Recordings incl: Scaramouche (w. orch.), 1960; Rhapsody (Debussy), 1972; Duos w. P. Brodies, 1975. Publs. incl: 125 years of Music for Saxophones, 1971. Contbr. to jrnls. Pres., Assn. French Saxophonists. Hons: 1st prize & Hon. prize, Conserv. Paris, 1953; Officer Arts & des Lettres, 1971. Address: 9 rue de Mulhouse, 33000 Bordeaux, France.

LOMON, Ruth, b. 8 Nov. 1930. Montreal, Can. Composer; Pianist; Teacher. Educ: Conserv. de Que., McGill Univ.; New Engl. Conserv. m. Earle Lomon, 3 c. Debut: w. Montreal Symph. Orch. Career: perfs. as 2 piano team w. Iris Graffman Wenglin; lecturing & perfng. on women comps., contemporary music & standard repertoire; apps. on radio & TV. Comps: Soundings, for piano duet; Dust Devils, for harp solo; 5 songs after poems by William Blake, for mezzo-soprano & viola; Triptych, for 2 pianos; The furies, for oboe, d'amore & Engl. horn; Requiem, for soprano, chorus, brass & woodwind; Recordings: Celebration, Nimbus & the Sun God, for 2 harps. Mbrships: Am. Music Ctr.; Broadcast Music Inc., Am. Women Comps.; Int. League fo Women Comps.; Nat. Music Tchrs. Assn. Hons: Yaddo Fellow, 1977; Helene Wurlitzer Fndn. grant, 1978; fellow at Ossabaw Island Project, 1978; Am. Women Comps. Recording Contest for Celebrations for 2 harps. 1979. Hobbies: Travel; Hiking. Address: 18 Stratham Rd., Lexington, MA 02173, USA.

LONDON, Edwin Wolf, b. 16 Mar. 1929. Phila., Pa., USA. Composer; Conductor; Educator; French Horn Player; Post Horn Player. Educ: Mus. B., Oberlin Coll., Conserv., Ohio, 1952; PhD., Univ. of Iowa, 1961; Pvte. Comp. Study w. Philip Greeley Clapp, Philip Bezanson, Luigi Dallapiccola & Darius Milhaud. m. Janet MacLeod London, 2 s. Career: Prof., Music, Univ. of Ill. Chmn.-elect, Comp., Theory Div., Univ. of Ill. Schl. of Music, Compositions (publs.); Trio, 1956; Woodwind Quintet, 1958; Overture to the Imaginary Invalid, 1958; Song & Dance, 1959: The Bear's Song, 1960; 3 Settings of Psalm XXIII, 1961; The Third day, 1961; Five Haiku, 1961; Sonatina Viola & Piano, 1962; Wash. Miscellany, 1963; Osanna, 1965; Brass Quintet, 1965; Portraits of Three Ladies, 1967; Four Proverbs, 1967; Christmas Music, 1969; Dream Thing, 1970; Day of Desolution, 1971; Enter Madmen, 1971; Polonius Platitudes, 1971; Genesis 21:6, 1972; Geistliche Musik, 1972; Roll, 1973; Sacred Hair, 1973; Better Is, 1974: (recorded) Viola Sonatina; Portraits of Three Ladies. Trio. Contbr. to: MLA Notes; Smith Quarterly; Iowa Review. Mbrships: ASCAP; Chmn., Mid-West Region, Am. Soc. of Univ. Comps.; Coll. Music Soc.; Am. Fedn. of Musicians; Hons: Fellow, MacDowell Colony, 1965, '66, '71, '74. Guggenheim Fellowship, 1969. Address: 910 W. Hill St., Champaign, IL 61820, USA.

LONDON, George, b. 30 May 1920. Montreal, Can. Operatic Bass-Baritone; Music Administrator; Operatic Stage Director. Educ: LA City Coll., USA. Debuts: Hollywood Bowl, 1941, San Fran. Opera, 1944, Vienna State Opera, 1949, Metrop. Opera, 1951; La Scala, Milan, 1952. Career: Metrop. Opera, 1951-66; Regular apps., Bayreuth Fest., 1951-64; Salzburg Fest., 1952; Edinburgh Fest., 1950 Guest apps., Buenos Aires, Venice, Zagreb, Belgrade; 1st Am. to sing title role in Boris Goudonov at Bolshoi Theatre, Moscow, 1960; Debut as Stage Dir., Seattle Opera, 1973. Num. recordings incl: Title role in Boris Goudonov, Don Giovanni, The Flying Dutchman, Wotan in Die Walkurie & Das Rheingold; Num. solo recordings. Contbr. to jrnls. & mags. Hons: Title of Kammersänger, Austria, 1954; Mozart Medal, Vienna, 1971. Hobby: Antique cars; Mgmt: Columbia Artists Mgmt., Inc., NYC. Address: 8000 Glengalen Lane, Chevy Chase, MD 20015, USA.

LONDON, S J, b. 15 Oct. 1917. NY, NY, USA. Physician; Medical Musicologist. Educ: BA, Univ. Louisville, 1937; MD, ibid., 1941. m. Estele Steinfeld, 1 s., 1 d. Career: Prac. internal med., 1949-58; Med. Rsch., clin. pharmacol., med. musicol., 1958-. Contbr. to: Jrnl. Am. Med. Assn.; New England Jrnl. Med.; Archives Internal Med.; MD; NY State Jrnl. Med.; High Fidelity. Mbr., Am. Musicol. Soc. Hobbies: Writing; Archeology. Address: 85-28 215 St., Hollis Hills, NY 11427, USA. 6.

LONEY, June Ellen, b. 22 Apr. 1930. Sydney, Aust. Harpist. Educ: FCTL; LMus (Aust. Music Bd.). Career: Prin. harpist, Sydney Symph. Orch., 1962-; num. apps. as soloist on radio & TV; Tchr. of harp, Sydney Conserv. of Music. Recordings: Debussy, Danse Sacrée et Danse Profane; Ravel, Introduction & Allegro. Contbr. to Sydney Harp News, 1969-70. Mbrships: Fndr. & Pres., Sydney Harp Assn. Recip. MBE, 1978. Hobby: Photography. Address: 2 Cogan Pl., Lane Cove, Sydney, NSW, Aust.

LONG, Carole Wilson, b. 30 May 1937. Ft. Morgan, Colo., USA. Musicologist; Educator; Conductor; Organist; Harpsichorist; Composer; Arranger. Educ: B Mus, Colo. State Univ. MA, Eastman Schl. of Music, Univ. of Rochester; PhD Cand., Univ. of Mich. m. Page Long. Career incls: Solo organ recitals & Accomp. & Choir Dir., for var. chs. & for concerts in Colo., Ariz., & Mich.; Violinist & Violist, orchs. in Colo. & Ariz.; Recorder Player & Harpsichordist, var. grps. in Mich.; Asst. Prof. of Music, Univ. of Ariz., 1960-63; Instr., Saginaw Valley Coll., 1973; Vis. Asst. Prof. of Music, Alma Coll., 1974-; Cond. of combined ch. choirs & college choirs, 1973-; Organ Instructor, 1st Congl. Ch., St. Pauls Sem., Saginaw Valley State Coll., 1965-; Asst. Dir. of Music, 1st Congregational Ch., 1965-; Cond., Camerata Campanella, 1978-; Cond., Saginaw Valley Choristers Guild fest., 1979; Mbr., Camerata Consort. Mbr., var. profl. assn. inclng. Am. Musicol. Soc. Recip., var. hons. Hobbies incl: Swimming; Films; Reading. Address: 4608 Colonial Dr., Saginaw, MI 48603, USA.

LONG, Jack Edward, b. 21 Jan. 1911. Bournemouth, Hants. Solo voiloncellist. Educ: Schl., London Violoncello Schl. m. Alexandra Margaret Smith, 2 children. Debut: Wigmore Hall. Career: Solo Cellist, SA. Broadcastin Corp., 1928-31; Prin. Cellist, LPO, 1951-58; Sub-Prin. Cello, LSO, 1959-; Soloist, BBC; Tchr., Chamber Music. Hobbies: Motoring; Gardening, (Rose-Growing). Address: 28 Cissbury Ring South, Woodside Park, London N12, UK 3.

LONG, Newell Hillis, b. 12 Feb. 1905. Markle, Ind., USA. Professor of Music Education. Educ: Ed.D, Ind. Univ., 1965; MA, ibid, 1939; MS, Northwestern Univ., 1934. m. Eleanor S Rice, 1 s. Career: Secondary Schl. tchr. for 9 yrs.; Dir., Band & Orch., Ctrl. Mich. Univ., 1929-31; Prof. of Music, specializing in trombone & arrs.; 1935-75; Rsch. speciality, tests of music discrimination. Comps. incl: Art Show (recorded); Concertino for woodwind quintet & band (recorded); Journey toward Freedom (recorded); Lincoln Lyric Overture; American Rhapsody. Recordings: Indiana-Oregon Music Discrimination Testo. Publs: Rubank Elementary Method of Trombone, 1934; Collegiate Trombonist, 1951; Newell Long Brass Sextet Album, 1951; Devotional Solos (for wind instruments), 1944. Contbr. to num. profl. jrnls. Mbrships: num. profl. socs. Hons: Fellowship in comp., Huntington Hartford Fndn., 1961, '65; Hall of Fame Award, Phi Beta Mu, 1977. Hobbies: Railroads. Address: 1304 E Univ. Ave., Bloomington, IN 47401, USA. 8.

LONG, Page Carroll, b. 7 Apr. 1933. Lima, Ohio. USA. Organist; Conductor; Composer; Pianist; Harpsichordist; Recorder player. Educ: Grad., Western Reserve Acad., Hudson, Ohio; B Mus., Oberlin Conserv., 1955; MA., Univ. of Iowa, 1956 FAGO cert., 1962; DMA., Univ. of Ariz., 1963. m. Carole Wilson. Career: Instr., Univ. of RI, 1956-57; Instr. Western Reserve Acad., 1957-61; Organist-Choirmaster, 1st Recorder, Organ, etc., 1969-. Compositions: Seven

Benediction Responses, 1969; The Toybox Suite (recorded trio), 1972; Lenten Elegy (organ), 1972. Contbr. to: Diapason; Jrnl. of Ch. Music; AGO Mag. Mbrships: Fellow, AGO; Am. Recorder Soc.; Pres., Saginaw Valley Chapt., Choristers Guild; Int. Soc. of Harpsichord Bldrs. Hons: Compositions prizes, 1963, 1971. Hobbies: Harpsichord bldg.; Photography. Addess: 1st Cong. Ch., 412 Hayden St., Saginaw, MI 48607, USA.

LONGHURST, John Thomas, b. 23 June 1940. Sacramento, Calif., USA. Associate Professor of Music; Organ Recitalist. Educ: B Mus., Univ. of Utah, 1964; M Mus., ibid., 1966; DMA., Eastman Schl. of Music, Univ. of Rochester, 1970; FAGO. m. Nancy May Meldrim, 2 s. Career: Assoc. Prof., tchng. organ & music theory Univ.; Carillonneur Mbr. of Grad. Music Fac. & Chmn., Music Scholarship. Comm., Brigham Young Univ.; Fac. Recitalist, ibid.; toured w. Brigham Young Univ. Fac. Artists' Bur.; Guest Organist, Salt Lake Mormon Tabernacle; gave world premier perf. of Robert Cundick's Organ Concerto; Adjudicator, Gtr. Spokane Music & Allied Arts Fest., 1974; Chmn. of Organ Music & Ch. of Jesus Christ of Latter-day Saints Gen. Music Committee. Mbrships: State Chmn. for Utah, AGO; Phi Beta Kappa Phi. Address: 85 S. 350 E., Orem, 84057, USA.

LONGYEAR, Rey Morgan, b. 10 Dec. 1930. Boston, Mass., USA. Musicologist; Educator; Timpanist. Educ: AB, Los Angeles State Coll., 1951; AM, Univ. NC, 1954; PhD, Cornell Univ., ADCM; 1957; Peabody Conserv.; Tanglewood (Berks. Music Ctr.). m. Katherine Marie Eide. Career: Tchr., Univ. Southern Miss., Univ. Tenn.; Currenlty, Prof., music, Hd., musicol., div., Univ. Ky.; Orchl. apps. w. NC Symph.; Balt Symph.; Gettysburg Symph.; Knoxville Symph., etc. Publs. incl: 19th Century Romanitcism in Music, 1969, 2nd enlarged ed., 1973. Contbr. to profl. jrnls. Mbrships. incl: Int. Musicol. Soc.; Am. Musicol. Soc.; Austrian, German, Italian Musicol. Soc. Hon: Guggenheim Fellowship, 1971. Hobbies incl: Hiking; Reading. Address: 405 Dudley Rd., Lexington, KY 40502, USA. 7,11.

LÖNN, Anders, b. 5 Mar. 1943. Stockholm, Sweden. Musicologist. Educ: Stockholm Univ.; Uppsala Univ. Career: Staff Mbr., Swedish Music History Archive, Stockholm, 1965-; occasional Lectr., Göteborg, Uppsala Univs.; Chief Ed., Swedish Jrnl. of Musicol., 1972-. Contbr. to: Acta Musicologica; Sohlmans Musiklexikon, 2nd. ed., Musicol. Ed.; MGG; Grove's Dictionary of Music & Musicians, 6th Ed.; Svenskt Biografiskt Lexikon; Swedish Jrnl. of Musicol. Mbrships: Chmn., Sub-Commission, Répertoire International Thesaurus de Littérature Musicale, 1971-; Sec., SwedishNat. Committee, ibid, 1968-; Bd., Swedish Soc. for Musicol., 1972-; Gen. Sec., Assn. Internationale des Bibliotheques Musicales, 1974-; Bd., Swedish Sect., ibid: 1974. Swedish Committee, 1973-. Address: co Svenskt Musikhistoriskt Arkiv, 82 Strandvägen, 115 27 Stockholm, Sweden.

LOOMIS, James Phillip, b. 28 Dec. 1929. Bowling Green, Ohio, USA. Professor of Music; Band Director. Educ: BSE., Bowling Green State Univ.; MM., DMA., Univ. of Mich. m. Jacquilyn Van Wienen. Career: Chmbr. music concerts at maj. US univs.; Clarinetist, Toledo Symph. Orch.; TV, radio apps. w. USAF Band & Univ. of Mich Symph. Band; Adjudicator, Mid-West state-level music competitions, MENC; Prof., Music, Bowling Green State Univ., Valparaiso Univ.; Wheaton Coll., Ft. Wayne Bible Coll. Recordings: Univ. of Mich. Band on Parade. Publs: Co-compiler, A Bibliography of Ensembles & Solo Repertoire for Wind Instruments. Mbrships: Past Mbr., State Planning Comm. on Higher Educ. for Ind., (IMEA Conf.) Coll. Band Dirs. Nat. Assn.; NACWPI; Past Chmn., Wood Co., Ohio, MENC; NEA; Kappa Kappa Psi. Hobbies: Golf; Chess. Address: 7327 Kern Valley Dr., Fort Wayne, IN 46815, USA.

LOOSLI, Arthur, b. 23 Feb. 1926. La Chaux d'Abel, Berner Jura, Switz. Concert Singer. Educ: Conserv. of Berne w. Felix Loeffel; studies w. Mariano Stabile, Venice, & Arne Sunnegard, Stockholm. m. Theresia Röthlisberger, 1 s. Debut: Berne, 1958. Career: Perfs. in Switz., Belgium, Sweden, Netherlands, Germany & Italy; guest artist at Stadttheater, Berne. Recordings: Elegie, Nachhall, Lieder (Othmar Schoeck); Winterreise (Schubert). Mbrships: Othmar Schoek Assn.; Swiss Music Tchs. Assn. Recip. 1st prize, Int. Singers' Comp. (bass-baritone), 'sHertogenbosch, Netherlands, 1959. Further profi. activities: Painting & Graphics; Drawing Master at Gymnasium, Thun, Switz. Address: Steigerweg 21, 3006 Berne, Switz.

LOOTS, Joyce Mary Ann, b. 30 Sept. 1907. Durban, Natal, S. Africa. Composer; Pianist. Educ: LTCL: Dip., Cape Town Coll. of Music; studied comps. w. Prof. Bell, & piano w. Colin Taylor. m. Dr. J H Loots, 1 s., 1 d. Comps. incl: Four South African Lyric Pieces for Orch.; Walt Whitman's Death Carol for mezzo-soprano & full orch.; Pathfinders for mixed voices; Three Pieces for Orch.; The Crescent Moon (4 songs); The Golden Threshold (3 songs); Aspects of Time; miscellaneous songs. Var. works recorded for S. African Broadcasting Transcription Lib. Contbr. to profl. mags. Mbrships: Wanderer's Club, Johannesburg. Address: 203 Murrayfield, Corlett Drive, Illovo 2196, Johannesburg, S. Africa. 3, 27.

LOPES-GRACA, Fernando, b. 17 Dec. 1906. Tomar, Portugal. Composer; Writer. Educ: Hist. & Philos., Lisbon & Coimbra Univs.; Musicol., Sorbonne, Paris, France; Piano, Comp. & Theory, Conserv. Nacional, Lisbon, Portugal. Comps. incl: For a Child about to be Born; Three Portuguese Dances; Sinfonia for Orchestra; Gabriela, Cravo & Canela; Five Funeral Steeles; Poem of December; Suite Rústica no. 1; Canto de Amor e de Morte; Four Sketches (all recorded). Publs. incl: A Música Portuguesa e os seus Problemas, III, 1973; Um Artista Intervém e Cartas com Alguma Moral, 1974. Contbr. to profl. publs. Mbr.; Soc. Française de Musicol. Hons: Comp. prize, Círculo de Cultura Musical, 1940, '43, '44, '52; Comp. prize, Prince Rainer II of Monaco, 1965. Address: El mio Paraiso 2, Av. da República, Parede, Portugal. 4.

LOPEZ, Raymond V, b. 20 Sept. 1921. Los Angeles, Calif., USA. Organist; Pianist; College Teacher. Educ: organ study w. var. tchrs.; B Mus, 1947, MScEd, 1969, Univ. of Southern Calif.; Life Tchng. Credentials, music & gen. second. educ., Calif.; 10 yrs. rsch. on music of Mexico. Career: Tchr., Coord., Cons., Los Angeles City School, 1947-; specialist on music of Mexico; Instr., Music of Mexico course, E Los Angeles Community Coll.; recitals at Int. Fest. of Organsits, Morelia, Mexico; Organist & Accomp., Gtr. Los Angeles area. Contbr. to Heterofonia, Mexico City. Mbrships: AGO; Phi Kappa Phi. Mexican hons. Hobbies: Exploring Deserts; Mountaineering. Address: 1521 Oneonta Knoll, S Pasadena, CA 91030, USA.

LOPEZ-CALO, José, b. 4 Feb. 1922. Nebra, Spain. Professor. of Musicology; Roman Catholic Priest. Educ: Lic., Philos., Univ. of Comillas, 1949; Lic., Theol., Theol. Fac. of Granada, 1956; Master of Relig. Music, 1959, Doctor in Mesicol., Pontifical Inst. of Sacred Music, Rome, 1963. Career: Musical Advsr., Vatican Radio, 1962-70; Asst. Prof., Musicol., Pontifical Inst. for Sacred Music, Rome, 1964-65; Prof., ibid., 1965-70; VP, ibid., 1967-70; Prof., Univ. of Santiago de Compestela, Spain, 1973-. Composition: Musica Granadina del Siglo XVI; Missa de Angelis; Ganti Sacri per la Santa Messa. Publs. incl: La Musica de la Catedral de Granade en el Siglo XVI, 2 vols., 1963; Presente y Futuro de la Música Sagrada, 1967, Italian Ed., 1968; Catálogo Musical del Archivo de la Santa Iglesia Caterdral de Santiago, 1972. Contbr. to num. jrnls., Grove's Dictionary. Mbrships. incl: Int. Musicol. Soc.; French, Italian & Am. Musicol. Socs.; Reales Academias de Bellas Artes de San Fernando, Madrid & Granada; Dolmetsch Fndn.; Int. Soc. for Sacred Music. Address: Primo de Rivera 31, Santiago de Compostela, Spain, 14, 19.

LOPEZ COBOS, Jesus, b. 25 Feb. 1940. Toro, Zamora, Spain. Conductor. Educ: PhD, Univ. of Madrid; studied comp. & conducting. m. Gloria Ruiz Ramos, 1 s. Debut: as orchl. cond., Prague, 1968; as operatic cond., Venice, 1969. Career: Res. Cond., Venice Oera, German Opera, Berlin; Guest Cond., operas in Paris, London, Munich, Hamburg, Cologne, Milan, Vienna, San Fran. Chgo.; Cond. num. orchs inclng. LSO, RPO, New Philharmonia; Concertbouw Orch., Munich Phil., Stuttgart & Munich Radio Orchs., Nat. Orch., Spain, Recordings of works by Arriaga & Mozart w. Engl. Chmbr. Orch. Lucia di Lammermoor; Otello. Hons: 1st Prizes, Mitropoulos Competition, 1968, Besancon Competition, 1969. Hobby: Philosphy Mgmt: Harrison/Parrott, 22 Hillgate St., London W8, UK. Address: c/o mgmt.

LOPEZ-SOBA, Elias, b. 17 April 1927. Ponce, Puerto Rico. Pianist; Musicologist Music Professor. Educ: Sr. & Soloist Dips., Longy Schl. of Music, Cambridge, Mass.; MA, 1953, Bennington Coll., Vermont; Reifeprufung, 1956, Akademie für Musik, Vienna, Austria. m. Carmen Irene Marxuach de la Cúetara. Debut: Vienna, Austria, 1956. Career: Concert tours, Austria, Italy, Spain, Central Am. & the Caribbean; Concert presentations, UK & USA; Soloist w. num. Am. Orchs.; Chmbr. music concerts; Austrian Radio Network, Radio Televisión de España, RAI in Italy, Canadian Broadcasting Corp., Radio & TV in Puerto Rico; Concert Lectures; Fest. apps.; Univ. of Puerto Rico, Assoc. Prof., 1961-65; Hd. Dept. of Music, 1963-64, Dir., Dept. of Cultural Acitivities, 1964-65, 1967-71, Fac. 1978; Fest. Casals, Inc., Exec. Dir., 1973-74, Exec. VP, 1974-75; Pres., 1975-77. Mbrships: Bd. of Dirs., Inst. of Puerto Rican Culture, 1968-72; Am. Musicol. Soc. Hons. incl: Fulbright Scholar, 1953, '54, '55; Gold Medal, Concours Int. d'Interpretation Musicale Geneve, Switz. Address: Calle del Parque 352, Penthouse, San Juan, Puerto Rico 00912.

LORAINE, Keith Edward, b. 26 Sept. 1942. St. Louis, Mos., USA. Bassonist; Player of Early Wind Instruments (also Hurdy Gurdy). Lecturer; Instructor. Educ: BA., Brigham Young Univ. m. Barbara Elizabeth Ballantine. 1 d. Career: Perf. & Assoc. Dir., Brigham Young Univ. Ancient Instrument Ensemble; Musical Dir., Utah Renaissance Faire; Perf. for NET-TV, Utah Shakespearean Fest. & Music Perf. Trust Funds; Bus. Mgr., Utah Civic Oratorio Soc.; Bandsman (Bassoonist) Salt Lake Civic Symph. Orch., Payson Community Theatre Orch. & Auditioner, US Army Band, Brigham Young Univ. Symph. Orch. & Symphonic Band, Utah Valley Symph. & Westminster Community Symph. Orch. Mbrships: Am. Fedn. of Musicians; Galpin Soc.; Dolmetsch Fndn.; Am. Recorder Soc.; Musica Sacra & Profana. Hobbies: Photography; Gardening; Mechanical Tinkering; Hand Ball; Paddle Ball. Address: 859 Sunshine Lane, Grapevine, TX 76051, USA.

LORAND, István, b. 14 June 1933. Budapest, Hungary. Composer. Educ: Dip., Univ. Fac. of Arts; Comp. degree. Acad. of Music; Studied comp. at the Acad. of Music, Budapest as a pupil of Ferenc Szabo & later of Ferenc Farkas. m. Olga B Szarka. Debut: 1953. Career: Music Tchr., then Dir. of music schl. from 1957-60; worked w. Editio Mcsica, Budapest; currently Tchr. at a sec. schl. Comps. (cantatas) May Ode; For the First Time Shone the Star; American Worker's Song; Children's Cantatas; Hey, You Danube; Mourning Movement; (choral works) They Died for You; To the Last; Mourning Chorus for Male Choir; Twilight Madrigal; Corn-husking; In Your Two Arms; Camping at Lake Baaton, etc.; (orchl. works) Symph. for Str. Orch.; Song Feast Overture for Wind Orch.; (Chmbr. music) Str. Quartet; Sonata for violin & piano; Sonata per flauto; (instrumntl. pieces) Rondo for piano; Small pieces for piano, for violoncello & for violin; choral works, children's choirs, etc. Mbrships: Assn. of Hungarian Musicians; Art Fndn. of the Hungarian People's Rep.; Nat. Coun. of Choirs; Dpty. Dir. of the Art Comm., Budapest Coun. of Choirs. Hons: Art Prize of the Hungarian Trades Union Coun., 1960 & '74. Address: Szakasits Arpad ut 52b, 1115 Budapest XI, Hungary.

LORAND, Thomas, b. 31 Mar. 1923. Budapest, Hungary. Violist; Teacher. Educ: Liszt-Ferenc Music Acad., Budapest; studied w. Waldbauer, Zathurecky, Lukacs, Weiner. m. Susan Ohlbaum, 2 d. Career: State Symph., Budapest; Prin. Viola, Rotterdam Phil.; Arco-Str. Quartet; Radnai Str. Quartet; Rotterdam Harp Quintet; Rotterdam Str. Quartet; Tchr., Viola Str. Quartet, Rotterdam Conserv. Recordings: Schubert, Trout Quintet, w. Trio Hongrois; w. Rotterdam Phil. Address: 7 Burgemeester Le Fevre De Montigny Plein, Rotterdam 3013, Holland.

LORCINI, Marie Iösch, b. 1 Jan. 1930. Montreal, Canada. Musician; Harpist; Teacher. Educ: Conservatoire de Musique dd Quebec; Premier Prix de Harpe, ibid, 1951. M. Gino Lorcini, 2 s., 2 d. Career: 1st Harpist, Montreal Symph. Orch., 1946-69; 1st Harpist, London Symph. Orch. & Hamilton Phil. Orch., 1969-; Soloist, CBC Radio & TV; Stratford Fest., Ont.; Nat. Film Bd. of Canada. Str., Univ. of W. Ont. London, Ont. Hobbies: Weaving; Gardening. Address: 282 Ramsay Rd., London, Ont. N6G 1N6, Canada.

LORD, David Malcolm, b. 3 Oct. 1944. Oxford, UK. Composer; Conductor; Lecturer. Educ: Pupil of Richard Rodney Bennett, RAM; LRAM; GRSM. Career: Currently Vis. Lectr. in Music, Univ. of Bath, & Newton Pk. Coll., Bath Co-Dir., Recording Co. Comps: Newton Pk. Coll., Bath. Co-Dir., Recording Co. Comps: The Ferryman; How the Stars Were Made; The Sea Journey; The Magic Fruit; The Worldmakers; History of the Flood; The Wife of Winter; Nonsongs; Soliloquy forGuitar; Incantage for Orch.; Harpsichord Concerto; Music for radio, TV, theatre & films; Ch. & choral music; music for dance. Recordings: Pantalone's Pantomime; Gelineau Psalms (arrs.). Hobby: Recording. Address: 6 Camden Cres., Bath BA1 5HY, Avon, UK.

LORD, John Malcolm Shaw, b. 23 Jan. 1932. Manchester, UK. Singer (Bass-baritone); Teacher of Singing (Private). Educ: Dulwich Coll; Northern Schl. of Music, Ellis Keeler; LRAM; Pvte. studies w. M Brown; Lucie Manen, Bruce Boyce, Nina Davis-Reynolds. m. Hilary Wilson, 1 s. Debut: Wigmore Hall. Career: Salder's Wells Opera Co., 1961-63; BBC Chorus, 1963-65; Glynebourne Festival Opera, 1965; Opera for All, 1965-66. Mbr. ISM. Hobbies: Hillwalking; Climbing; Swimming. Mgmt: Music INt. Address: Hillcrest, Sheffield Rd., Hathersage, Sheffield S30 1DA, UK.

LORD-WOOD, June, b. 20 June 1922. Glenolden; Pa., USA. Librarian. Educ: BA, MA, Columbia Univ.; Peabody Conserv., Balt., Md. Appts: Bibliog. Asst., Rare Book & MS Lib., Columbia Univ.; Choir Mbr., 2nd Presby. Ch. of Phila., Brown Mem. Ch. of Balt. & Riverside Ch., NYC; pvte. recitals. Contbr. to:

International Folk Music Council Yearbook, 1975. Mbrships: Am. & Int. Musicol. Soc.; Music Lib. Assn.; Am. Inst. for Verdi Studies. Address: Apt. 131, 410 Riverside Dr., NY, NY 10025, USA. 4.

LORENC, Antoni, b. 23 Sept. 1909. Skopje, Yugoslavia. Radio & TV Music Editor. Educ: Philos. Fac., Skopje. m. Filomena Lorenc, 7 children. Career: Music Ed., Radio TV Pristina. Comps. incl: Lovely Bride (instrumental); Albanian Chorus (vocal); Three Songs from Opoja; Dances & Wedding Songs (vocal-instrumental); 2 Collections of chorus songs for children; Sparrows Musical Folklore (7 volumes). Contbr. to profl. mags. Mbrships: Soc. of Comps. of Kosovo; Soc. of Folklore of Servia. Soc. of Comps. of Kosovo; Soc. of Folklore of Servia. Hons. incl: Vuk's Prize of Cultural & Educ. Union of Serbia, 1972. Hobbies: Philately; Numismatics. Mgmt: Radiotelevision Pristina, Yugoslavia. Address: 6/11, Pristina, Yugoslavia.

LORENGAR, Pilar. Zaragoza, Spain. Operatic Soprano. m. Jürgen Schaff. Career: apps. at La Scala, Covent Gnd., Berlin Opera, Salzburg Fest., made 1st app. w. San Fran. Opera, 1964, & w. Met. Opera, 1966; recitals. Address: Franken Allee 12, Berlin 19, German Fed. Repub. 2.

LORENTZEN, Bent, b. 11 Feb. 1935. Stenad, Denmark. Composer. Educ: Dip. exam. from the Royal Danish Music Conserv.; Docent, 1964. m. Edith Lorentzen, 4 c. Debut: w. the opera, Haughty Little Mette, 1963. Career: Studies for Two, Nordic Music Days, Helsinki, 1970; The Bottomless Pit. commissioned for the Nordic Music Days, Oslo, 1972; Euridice perf. at the Arhus Opera, 1973; Die Musik kommt mir ausserst bekannt vor! Kiel Opera, Germany, 1974. Comps. Euridice (opera); Shiftings (orch.); Quadrata (str. quartet); Syncretism (cl., trbn., vlc., pno); Umbra (guitar solo); New Choral Dramatics, choral songs to texts of Mao; Thus Morning (choir); Song of my Country (choir); Intersection (organ); Puncta (organ); 5 simple piano pieces; Friisholm (music theatre for film); The Sound of Your Echo (film opera). Recordings: Water, electronic music for children. Pubs: Ej sikkelej, 1967; New Choral Dramatics, 1971; Recorder System, 1962-64; Musikens ABC, 1969; Mer om musiken, 1972; An introduction to Electronic Music, 1969. Contbr. to profl. jrnls. Mbr., Danish Comps. Soc. Hons: Prix Italia for Euridice, 1970; 1st Prize, Nylon Film Fest. for the Sound of Your Echo, 1973 & at the Stockholm Organ Fest. Puncta. Mgmt: Wilhelm Hansen, Copenhagen. Address: Sotoften 37, 2820 Gentofte, Denmark.

LORENZ, Andrew Bela, b. 17 Oct. 1951. Melbourne, Aust. Violinist; University Lecturer. Educ: DSCM, Perfs. Dip. & Tchrs. Dip., Sydney Conserv. of Music, 1970. m. Wendy Joy Lorenz. Career incls: Recitals, concerto, radio & TV perfs.; Dpty. Ldr., Melbourne Elizabethan Trust Orch., 1972-; Led for D'Oyly Carte Opera Co., Sadlers Wells, UK, 1973-74; Ldr., New England Ensemble, res. piano quartet, Univ. of New England, Armidale, NSW, Aust., & Lectr., Music Dept., 1975—; Fndn. Mbr. & Ldr., New England Sinfonia; World tour w. New Engalnd Ensemble. Recordings: Works by Beethoven, Turina & Margaret Sutherland. Hons. incl: Victorian ABC Concerto Competition Winner, 1972. Hobbies: Sport; Reading. Mgmt: Musica Viva Aust., Sydney, Aust.; Terry Slasberg, London, UK. Address: 6 Gordon St., Armidale, NSW 2350, Aust. 4.

LORENZ, Ellen Jane, b. 3 May 1907. Dayton, Ohio, USA. Music Editor; Arranger; Composer; Choral Conductor. Educ: BA, Wellesley Coll.; MSM., Wittenberg Univ.; Study w. Nadia Boulanger. m. James B. Porter, 1d. Career: Ed., Lorenz Publng. Co., 1932-68; lectr., folk hymnudy, handbell methods; cond., choirs, etc. Publd. Comps: Num. anthems, cantatas, organ pieces, handbell pieces. Publs incl: Handbell Music in Church, 1963; The Learning Choir, 1968. Contbr. to profl. jrnls. Mbrhsips. incl: ASCAP; Mu Phi Epsilon; Pres., Dayton, Chmbr. Music Soc.; Dayton Chormasters Club; Bd. Mbr., Dayton Music Club. Num. hon. incl: Prize for Profl. Women, Paris, 1932; 4 Prize, for anthems, Chapel Choir Guild, 1938-45; Prize for string quartet, Mu Phi Epsilon, 1972; Mus D, Lebanon Valley Coll. Hobies: Travel; Cooking; Gardening. Addess: 324 Oak Forest Dr., Dayton, OH 45419, USA. 3, 5, 8.

LORENZ, Wendy Joy, b. 25 Oct. 1950. Sydney, Australia. Pianist; Teacher. Educ: Perfs. & Tchrs. Dips., Sydney Conserv., 1970; L Mus A, 1968; studied w. Maria Curcio, London, 1973-74. m. Andrew Bela Lorenz. Career incls: recital, broadcast & concerto-soloist apps., Aust., Europe, Am. & Asia; Pianist, Young Sydney Piano Trio, 1968-71; Piano Tchr., NSW Conserv., 1971; currently Pianist, New England Ensemble & lect., in music, Univ. of New England, Armidale, NSW, Aust. Hons. incl: Beethoven Bicentenary Medallion, German Fed. Repub., 1970. Hobbies incl: Reading; Nature; Walking. Address: 6 Gordon St., Armidale, NSW, Australia 2350.

LORIMER, Michael, b. 13 Jan. 1946. Chgo., Ill., USA. Classical & Baroque Guitar Player. Educ: studied w. Andres Segovia. Debut: Los Angeles, 1960. Career: World-wide perfs.; 1st Am. guitarist to tour USSR, 1975, '77, works by Ohana, Previn, Moreno-Torroba, Bolcom, etc., written for & dedicated to him. Pubs: num. eds. of guitar music inc. works by Albeniz, Bach, L Couperin, Dowland, Froberger & Weiss. Contbr. to Guitar Player. Mgmt: Harold Shaw, 1995 Broadway, NY, NY 10023, USA. Address: c/o Robert Levin, 180 West End, NY, NY 10023, USA.

LORIOD, Yvonne, b. 20 Jan. 1924. Houilles, Seineet-Oise, France. Pianist. Educ: Nat. Conserv. of Music, Paris. m. Oliver Messiaen. Career: Solo recitals in most European countries, N & S Am., & Japan, w. leading orchs.; 1st Performances in Paris of Concerti by Bartok & Schonberg & many works by Jolivet & Messaien; Prof. of Piano, Paris Conserv.; Master Classes at summer schls., Darmstadt & Bayreuth. Recordings of num. works issued. Hons: 1st Prize for Piano, etc., Paris Conserv.; Chevalier, Legion of Hon.; Grand Prix du Disque. Address: 230 rue Marcadet, 75018 Paris, France.

LORTAT-JACOB, Bernard, b. 1 Jan. 1941. Paris, France. Ethnomusicologist. Educ: Schola Cantorum (harmony, counterpoint); Music Hist., Institut de Musicologie; Bachelor's degree in Sociology; Doct. in Linguistics (Paris). m. Anita Lortat-Jacob, 2d. Career: Researcher, French Nat. Centre of Scientific Rsch. Publs: La Saison des Fetes dans une Vallée du Haut-Atlas (Co-Authur), 1978; Musique et Fetes au Haut-Atlas (co-Ed.). Contbr. to: Musique en Jeu (Ethnomusicol. Sect.); Author, Revue de Musicologie. Hobbies: Tennis; Wine. Address: 3 Rue Collardeau, Etiolles, 91450 Soisy-sur-Seine, France.

LOSONCZY, Andor, b. 2 June 1932. Budapest, Hungary. Pianist; Composer. Educ: Dip., Piano & Comp., F. Liszt Zenemüveszeti Föiakola, Budapest, 1955-59. m. Klara Kupor, 1 s., 1 d. Debut: w. Maderna, Darmstadt, 1955. Career: Concerts & pers. throughout Europe; TV & radio apps; USA tour, 1978. Comps. incl: Ensemblemusik, 1959-61; Descort, 1971; Untitled, 1976; Sätze, 1966; Phonophobie, 1975; Growth Structures, 1978; Black Box Choir Ensemble, 1970; Dues for var. Instruments, 1963; Sketch-book, Trio, 1975; 4 Piano Pieces, 1959; Panorama for 2 Pianos, 1972; for strings 1, 1967, 2, 1973; Changes, for chmbr. ensemble, 1977. Mbrships. incl: Austrian Ensemble for New Music; Austrian Comps. Union; Coop. for Computer Music. Hons: Int. Piano Competition, Warsaw, 1955; Liszt-Prize, Budapest, 1956; Kranichsteiner Music Prize, Darmstadt, 1960; Comp. Prize, Graz, 1974. Address: Etrichstr. 5, 5020 Salzburg, Austria.

LOTZENHISER, George William, b. 16 May 1923. Spokane, Wash., USA. Conductor, Composer; Educator; Musician (trombone). Educ: B of Ed., Eastern Wash. State Coll., Cheney, 1946; BA, ibid, 1947; M Mus., Univ. of Mich., 1948; EdD, Univ. of Ore., 1956. m. B. Kathryn, 2s. Career incl: 1st trombone w. var. orchs. incl. Spokane Symph., 1960-62, Tucson Symph., 1948-60; Assoc. Cond., ibid., 1957-60; Asst. Prof. of Music, Univ. of Ariz., 1949-56; Assoc. Prof., ibid, 1956-60; Prof. of Msuic, Eastern Wash. State Coll., 1960-69; Hd., Div. of Music, ibid, 1960-61; Dir., Div. of Creative Arts, 1961-69; Dean, Schl. of Fine Arts, 1972-. Compositions incl. num. small pieces for brass ensembles; brass, woodwind & percussion solos; Minuet C., for String Orch. & Piano. Publ: Music 200 (Programmed Music Theory Text). Mbrships. incl: MENC (var. offs.); Pres., Eastern Wash. Music Educators, 1965-67; Phi Kappa Phi; Phi Kappa Lambda; Phi Mu Alpha Sinfonia; Kappa Delta Pi; Phi Delta Kappa; Kappa Kappa Psi; Tau Beta Sigma; Delta Chi. Address: Route 2, Box 146, Cheney, WA 99004, USA.

LOUDOVA, Ivana, b. 8 Mar. 1941. Chulmec, Czech. Composer. Educ: Prague Conserv.; Prague Acad. of Arts & Music; Study of comps. w. M. Kabelác, Emil Hlobil; Grant for 6 months study w. Oliver Messian & André Jolivet, Paris, 1971. Recordings: Meetinf with Love; Air-duo for bass clarinet & piano; Kuroshio; Chorale. Spleen, (homage to Baudelaire); Corale per orch. Hymns, 1975; Concerto, 1976. Hons: 1st Prize, Vocal Fest., Jihlava, for Meeting with Love, 1966. 1st Prize, Composition Contest, Jirkov, for Mummy, children's a capella chorus, 1967. Hobbies: Tennis; Skiing. Address: Pod Stráni 2166, 100 00 Prague 10, Czech. 27.

LOUGHRAN, James, b. 30 June 1931. Glasgow, UK. Coductor. Educ: studied in Bonn, Amsterdam & Milan. m. Nancy Coggon, 2 s. Debut: Royal Fest. Hall. London 30 Mar. 1961. Career: Assoc., Bournemouth Symph. Orch., 1962-65; Prin. Cond. BBC Scottish Symph. Orch., 1965-71; Prin. Cond. & Musical Advsr., Halle Orch., 1971-. Has recorded w. Halle Orch. & Leicestershire schls. Recip. of 1st Prize, Philharmonia Orch. Conds. Competition, 1961. Mgmt: Harold Holt Ltd.,

London. Address: Halle Concerts Soc., 30 Cross St., Manchester, UK.

LOUIS, Leslie Bertram, b. 13 Aug. 1948. Singapore. Pianist; Organist; Cellist; Accordionist. Educ: RCM; ARCM (piano perf.); TCL for cond. Debut: Franck's Symphonic Variations at Hayes, 1972. Career: Co. pianist & Asst. Music Dir. for Northern Ballet Co., 1974-75, with whom num. perfs. throughout Engl. & Wales; freelance pianist, 1975-; app. as pianist & cellist w. Hayes Orch.; 2nd Bass, London Phil. Choir. Mbrships: ISM; Musicians' Union; Int. Songwriters Assn.; Anglo-Austrian Music Soc. recip., 1st prize in Alec Rowley Piano competition, TCL, 1974. Hobbies: Stamps; Tennis; Badminton; Table Tennis; Swimming. Address: Four Seasons, 31 Broadwater Close, Burwood Pk., Walton-on-Thames, Surrey KT12 5DE, UK.

LOUTTIT, Mark Edgar, b. 6 June 1948. Canton, Ohio. Music Teacher; Performer (French Horn). Educ: BA, Univ. of Ariz.; BMus, Schl. of Music, ibid; Studies w. John Woldt, Edward W Murphy, Keith Johnson. Career: USAT Bands, 1968-72; Tucson Ballet Orch., 1973-74; Tucson Symph. Orch., 1974-75; Manachetta Horn Quartet, 1973-74; Asst., Univ. of Ariz. Band, 1977-; Dir. of Instrumental Music, Casa Grande Union High Schl., Ariz. Recordings as mbr. of var. Univ. of Ariz. Ensembles. Mbrships: Phi Mu Alpha Sinfonia; MENC; Ariz. Band & Orch. Dirs. Assn.; Kappa Kappa Psi; Nat. Educ. Assn.; Phi Alpha Theta; Final County Five Arts Coun. Hons. incl: Scholarships; Outstanding mbr., Univ. of Ariz. Band, 1976. Hobbies: Travelling; Reading. Address: 2175 N Tuebell D-3, Casa Grande, AZ 85222, USA.

LOUVIER, Alain, b. 13 Sept. 1945. Paris, France. Composer; Conductor. Educ: Paris Conserv. m. Marie-Cecile Milan, 1 child. Career: Boarder, Acad. of France, Rome, 1969-72; Concert, Royan Fest., 1972; Perf. in France of Trans. by Stockhausen; Dir., Nat. Music Schl., Boulogne-Billancourt, 1972-. Comps. incl: (publs.) Etudes pour Agresseurs for claviars, 1964-72; 3 Atmosphéres, for clarinet & orch., 1974; (recordings) Shima & Candrakala, for 6 percussion instruments, 1970. Hons. incl: 1st Prize, Paris Conserv.; Prize, Vocation Fndn., 1966; 1st Grand Prize, Rome, 1968; Arthur Honegger Prize, 1975. Hobbies: Botany; Entomol. Address: 45 rue Escudier, 92100 Boulogne, France.

LOUWENAAR, Karyl June, b. 11 Jan. 1940. Grand Rapids, Mich., USA. Pianist; Harpsichordist. Educ: BM, Wheaton Coll., Ill., 1962; MM, Univ. of Ill., 1964; DMA, Piano. Eastman Schl. of Music, Univ. of Rochester, 1974; Cert. in Harpsichord, Staatliche Hochschule für Musik, Cologne, 1972. Debut: Orchestra Hall, Chgo., 1967. Career: Concerts, USA & sev. W. German cities, inclng: Cologne & Bonn; Perfs., Cologne, Hannover radio; Carnegie Recital Hall, NYC, 1974; Instr., Piano Wheaton Coll., 1963-68; Asst. Prof., Piano & Harpsichord, Schl. of Music, Fla. State Univ., Tallahassee. Recording: Wm. Penn, Fantasy for harpsichord. Mbrships: Pi Kappa Lambda; Wheaton Coll. Scholastic Hon. Soc. MTNA; New Bach Soc. Hons: NDEA Title IV Fellowship, Eastman Schl. of Music, 1969-70; Grant, Deutscher Akademischer Austauschdienst, 1970-72. Hobbies: Photography; Travel; Cooking. Address: 517 Westwood Dr. N. Tallahassee, FL 32304. USA. 5, 29.

LOVEC, Vladimir, b. 6 Apr. 1922. Maribor, Yugoslavia. Professor of Piano, Harmony, Counterpoint, & History of Music. Educ: Bachelor's Degree, Coll. Dip., Univ. of Ljubljana; Dip. in comp., 1950, conducting, 1951, Acad. of Music, Ljubljana. m. Zdenka Bartol, 2 d. Career incls: Dir., Schl. of Music, Prof., ibid.; Koper, 1953-66; Radio broadcasts; Stage perfs.; TV apps. Comps. incl: Concert for Piano & Orchestra, 1959; Dramatic Overture, 1972; Concertino for Flute & Orchestra, 1975; Trio 76, 1976; Koper Symph., 1977; Sonatina for recorder, 1978. Recordings: Dramatic Overture, 1972; Partita for Wind Instruments Quintet, 1976. Mbr., Assn. of Slovene Comps., Ljubljana. Contbr. to Newspapers & reviews. Hons. incl: Reward of town of Koper, 1972. Address: JLA 5, 66000 Koper, Yugoslavia.

LOVEJOY, Michael Saunders, b. 11 July 1941. Farnham, Surrey, UK. Violinist; Composer. Educ: RCM, 1959-63; ARCM; studied comp. w. Herbert Howells. Career: violin solos in Children's Hour for BBC, 1957; mbr. Nat. Youth Orch. of GB, 1955h58; toured Austria as Rustic Fiddler w. Clifton Coll. Morris Dancers, 1958; mbr., Eng. Nat. Opera Orch., 1963-. Recordings: in Eng. Nat. Opera perfs. on Wagner's Ring. Mbrships: Elgar Soc. Hons: var. scholarships & awards inclng. Gold Medal, Grade VII, Associated Board Examinations. Hobbies: Italian Language; Recording scenes from Shakespeare w. friends. Address: 23 Wakefield Ave., Bournemouth BH10 6DS, UK.

LOVELAND, Kenneth, b. 12 Oct. 1915. Sheerness, Kent, UK. Music Critic. m. Anne Edwards. Career: Music critic, var. profl. publs., own music mag., Radio Wales; music progs. for Radio Telefis Eireann, Dublin; BBC Kaleidoscoper, etc. Contbr. to: The Times; South Wales Argus; Opera; Musical Times; Country Life. Mbrships: Critics Circle; Press Club; Pres., Guild of British Newspaper Eds., 1962; Pres., Nat. Training Coun., 1968. Hons: Golden Statue of Vienna, 1970; Cavaliere Iralian Govt., 1970. Hobbies: Watching cricket & soccer; Travel; Walking; Food & Wine. Address: 20 Monmouth House, Cwmbran, Gwent, NP44 1QT, UK.

LOVELL, Patricia Mary, b. 16 Apr. 1923. Reigate, Surrey, UK. Musician; Violinist. Educ: ARCM; GRSM. Career: BBC Symph. Orch.; Royal Opera House, Covent Gdn.; BBC London Studio Players; Tchr., Balls Pk. Coll. of Educ., Watford Schl. of Music, RAM. Mbrships: Royal Musical Assn.; Londno Orchl. Assn. Hobbies: Dressmaking; Gardening. Address: 65 Meadway, Southgate, London N14 6NJ, UK.

LOVELL, Percy Albert, b. 13 Apr. 1919. Warmley, Bristol, UK. Lecturer & Tutor in Music. Educ: MA, King's Coll., Cambridge Univ.; Mus B, ibid.; LRAM. m. Mary Priestman Clark, 4 s. Career: Formerly Dir. of Music, Bootham Schl., York; Sr. Lectr. in Music, Northumberland Coll.; currently Snr. Lectr. in Music, Univ. of Newcastle upon Tyne; Cond., Newcastle Bach Choir; Dir., Opera Summer Schl., Nat. Operatic & Dramatic Assn.; Cond., Tyneside Chmbr. Orch.; Dir., Camerata Singers. Publs: Quaker Inheritance, 1871-1961, 1970; Ed., Roger Clark, Somerset Anthology, 1975. Contbr. to: Music & Letters; Grove's Dictionary of Music & Musicians (new ed.). Mbrships: Royal Musical Assn.; ISM; Viola da Gamba Soc. Hobbies: Walking; Photography. Address: West Lea, Wylam Wood Rd., Wylan, Northumberland. NE41 8HZ, UK.

LOVETT, Terence George, b. 2 July 1922. London, UK. Conductor (Pianoforte, Timpani & Percussion, Viola, Horn, Trumpet, Organ). Educ: FRAM; LRAM. m. Selina Dorothy Clark, 3s. Debut: London, 1941. Career incls: Organist & Choirmaster num. Chs.; Cond. & Artist Dir., Hull Phil. Soc.; Cond: London Jr. & Sr. Orchs.; ERMA Choir; Nordiska Ungdomsmusikveckor in UMEA, Sweden; Freelance Cond. w. BBC Orch. & maj. orchs. in GB, Europe, Scandinavia, Middle & Far EAst. Mbrships: Royal Phil. Soc.; ISM; RCM Club; Le Petit Club Francais. Recip. RAM Club Prize, 1942. Hobbies: Fencing; Reading; Cooking. Mgmt: Ibbs & Tillett Ltd., London UK. Address: 15 Beauchamp Rd., E Molesey, Surrey KT8 OPA, UK. 3.

LOWDELL, John b. 12 Mar. 1935. London, UK. Cellist. Educ: RAM; LRAM. m. Janet Harvey, 3 c. Career: City of Birmingham Symph. Orch., 1958; Royal Philharmonic Orch., 1960-73 (chmn., 1968-73); London Philharmonic Orch., 1973-. Hon. Life mbr., Royal Phil. Orch. Hobbies: Farming; Tennis. Address: Chequers Farm, Five Ashes, Mayfield, Sussex, UK.

LOWE, John Stanley, b. 31 Oct. 1906. Grantham, Lincs., UK. Pianist. Educ: MA., Mus B., Sewlyn Coll., Cambridge Univ.; RCM, ARCM., ARCO. m. Barbara Gibbon, 2 s. (1dec.), 2 d. Career: Tchr., Chigwell & Eastbourne Coll.; WWII Serv., Anglo-Am., Liaison, E Anglia; Cond., Cambridge Phil. Soc., 1935-47; In charge of music, BBC 3rd Prog., 1947-50; Cond. BBC Midland Singers, 1947-62; Hd. of Music. Midland Region, BBC, 1950-62; Artistic Dir., Coventry Cathedral Festival, 1962; Dir., Malvern Festival, 1962-64; Dir., Commonwealth Arts Festival, Liverpool, 1965. Mbrships: ISM; Sec., Nat. Commission for Cath. Ch. Music. Hobbies: Oboe & trumpet in amateur music. Address: 9 The Cobbles, Wingate Way, Cambridge CB2 2HD, UK. 28.

LOWE, Timothy Malcolm, b. 20 Jan. 1953. Tonbridge, Kent, UK. Concert Pianist; Teacher. Educ: Yehudi Menuhin Schl., RCM; Studied w. Vlado Perlemuter, Paris, France; ARCM Dip. Debut: Soloist w. Brit. Youth Symph. Orch., Royal Festival Hall, Londn, 1970. Career: Apps. on radio as Soloist w. Brit. Youth Symph. Orch. in Youth Orchs. of the World; Apps: Aldeburgh Festival; Plymouth Mayflower Celebrations; Wigmore Hall, 1970; Chopin Soc. Recitals. Mbr. ISM. Hons: 2nd Prize, S London Heat Sr. Sect., Nat. Jr. Piano Playing Competition; Chopin Prize, RCM. Hobbies: Films (Cinema); Walking; Yoga. Address: co The Oast House, Sandy Lane, Ightham Common, Near Sevenoaks, Kent, UK.

LOWENS, Irving, b. 19 Aug. 1916. NYC, NY, USA. Educator; Administrator; Writer; Lecturer; Musicologist; Music Critic. Educ: BS (Music), Columbia Univ., NY, 1939; MA, Univ. of Md., 1957 m. Margery Morgan Lowens. Career: now Dean & Assoc. Dir., Peabody Inst. of the John Hopkins Univ.; chief music critic & Ed., The Washington (DC) Star, 1961-78. Publs: Music & Musicians in Early America, 1964; A Bibliography of

American Songstars Published before 1821, 1976; Ananias Davisson's Kentuck Harmony (1816), 1976; Music in America & American Music, 1978; Haydn in America, 1980 A Bibliography of American Tune Books Published before 1811 (co-author), 1981. Contbr. to encys., Grove's Dict., 6th ed., scholarly jrnls., etc. mbr. num. profl. socs. num. hons. Address: 5511 N Charles St., Balt., Md., USA. 2.

LOWRY, Elizabeth Alaire Howard, b. 4 June 1943. Phila., Pa., USA. College Teacher; Choral Conductor; Harpist. Educ: BA, Southern Meth. Univ., 1965; M Mus, 1969; D Mus A, 1972, Univ. of Tex., Austin. m. Thomas Wells Lowry, 2 s. Career: Harpist, Dallas Symph. Orch., Dallas Summer Musicals, 1959-67, Austin Symph. Orch., 1967-; of fac., St. Mary's Cath. Schl., Austin, 1965-66, Ursuline Acad., Dallas, 1966-67, Southwestern Univ., 1972-74, Univ. of Tex. at Austin, 1974-; Fest.Cond.; Clinician; Adjudicator. Author: Semele, Music Drama by George Frideric Handel-Contemporary Performance Practice Considerations, 1972. Contbr. to Choral Jrnl; Record Review. Mbrships. incl: Pres., Coro d'Amici of Austin; Tex. Choral Dirs. Assn. Recip. acad. hons. Hobbies: Reading; Camping; For. Travel. Address: 1802 Rogge Ln., Austin, TX 78723, USA.

LOWRY, Karen Lynnette, b. 4 May 1955. Louisville, Ky., USa. Performer & Teacher of Violin. Educ: BMusEd., Univ. of Louisville, 1977; MMus, Univ. of Texas at Austin, 1979; Doct. Cand., ibid. Career: Louisville Orch., 1975-77; Kentucky Opera Assn., 1976-77; Louisville Bach Soc. Orch., 1976; Aspen Fest. Orch., summer, 1977; Austin Symph. 1977; Suzuki trained tchr., Univ. of Texas String Project; tchr., Aschaffenburg, GfR, 1979. Mbrships: Local 11-637 Am. Fedn. of Musicians (Louisville, Ky.); Local 433, Austin Texas. Hons: Francis T Roberts Music Scholarship, Univ. of Louisville, 1976-77. Hobbies: Backgammon; Tennis. Address: 3303 Kirby Ave., Louisville, KY 40211, USA. 2.

LOYONNET, Paul Louis, b. 13 May 1889. Paris, France. Concert Pianist. Educ; Conservatoire National, Paris. m. Edith Tourn, 1 d., 1 s. Debut: Paris, 1906. Career: Played chmbr. music w. Marsick, Capet, Szigeti Pierre Founier, R. Le Roy & many others; Appearances w. orchs. in France, Germany, Netherlands, Belgium, Sweden, Norway & Denmark; Film, Nocturno de Amor, Mexico, 1951; TV Recital, ibid., 1952; Appearance on radio in Stockholm, Hamburg, Cologne, Berlin, Paris, Lyon, Montreal, Montevideao, Mexico, Geneva, Lausanne, Milan, Athens; Appearance on radio-TV Francaise prog., Music For You, 1961. Recordings: Beethoven sonatas; Music by Gabriel Faure, Jacques Ibert, Schumann, Couperin. Author of Beethoven le mal connu & Les 32 sonates, journal initime de Beethoven, 1976. Contbr. to: Courrier Musical; Revue Musicale. Mbrships. incl: Assn. of Univ. Tchrs.; Assn. des Professeurs de Quebec. Hobbies: Collect. of paintings; Philosophical studies; Yoga. Address: 4584 Hingston Ave., Montreal, H4A 2K1, Canada.

LUBIN, Ernest Viviani, b. 2 May 1916. NYC, USA. Composer; Pianist; Writer. Educ: BS., MS., Tchrs. Coll., Columbia Univ.; studied comp. w. Ernest Bloch & Darius Milhaud. m. Eleanore Casseen, 2 s., 1 d. Debut: w. Mr. Jay Gottliev, as a piano duet team, Carnegie Recital Hall, 1972. Career: appearance of Lubin-Gottlieb duet on 'The Listening Room', Stn. WQXR, NYC, 1972, & at Alice Tully Hall, NY., 1974. Compositions: Songs of Innocence; Suite in the Olden Style for String Orch.; A Purcell Suite for Orch.; Pavane for Flute & Strings; Variations for Piano Orch.; Publs: The Piano Duet, 1970; The Pianist Chord Manual, 1971; Beethoven & His Circle, 1975; Chopin & His Circle, 1975; Teacher & Pupil, 1976. Contbr. to var. jrnls. Music Critic for NY Times, 1945, '49-50. Mbrships: ASCAP; MacDowell Colony. Recip., Bearns Prize, Musical Comp., 1938. Hobbies: Chess. Address: 336 Ft. Washington Ave., NY, NY USA.

LUBIN, Steven, b. 22 Feb. 1942. NYC, USA. Pianist; Musicologist. Educ: AB, Harvard Coll.; MS, Juilliard Schl. of Music; PhD, NY Univ. m. Wendy Lubin, 1 s. Career: Solo piano recitals in many cities in E USA; Lectr. num. campuses; In charge of grad. studies in theory, Cornell Univ., 1971-75; Tchr., SUNY, Purchase, NY; Works of Mozart played on authentic replica of 18 century piano built by self; Fndr. Mbr., The Mozartean Players, chmbr. group perf. on authentic classical instruments. Recordings incl: Brahmsp-Paganini Variations for Jose Limón Dance Co. Publs: Techniques of Development in Middle-Period Beethoven, 1974. Contbr. to: The Music Jnrl. Mbr. in Am. Musicol. Soc. Hons: Winner, WQXR Young Instrumentalists Competition, 1955. Hobbies: Drawing; Painist; Cabinet-making. Mgmt: Charles Hamlen Mgmt, NY, USA. Address: 500 Kappock St., Bronx, NY 10463, USA.

LUBOTSKY, Mark, b. 18 May 1931. Leningrad, USSR. Violinist; Soloist; Professor. Educ: w. Prof. A Jampolsky,

Moscow Conserv., 1953; w. Prof D Oistrakh, Pris d'excellence, 1958. m. Mirsky Nathalie, 1 s. Debut: Bolshoi Hall of Moscow Conserv., 1950. Career: Concerts w. major orchs. of USSR, UK, Netherlands, Germany, Sweden, Finland, Czech., Denmark, etc.; Many radio & TV apps. Recordings: B Britten, Violin Concerto; Torelli, Glück, Violin Concertos; Mozart Violin Concerto Schubert, Rondo; A. Schnittke Violin Concerto; Bach, 6 Sonatatas; Brahms, 3 Sonatas, etc. HOns: Mozart Int. Competition, Salzburg, 1956; Chaikovsky Int. Competition, Moscow, 1958. Hobby: Dogs. Mgmt: Dr. De Koos & Co. Address: Manilladreef 16, Utrecht, Netherlands.

LUCAS, David John, b. 19 Jan. 1942. Southampton, UK. Music Teacher; Pianist; Composer. Educ: RAM, 1961-64; GRSM; LRAM (Piano Tchr.); Music Tchrs. Cert., Inst. Educ., Univ. London. m. June Marjorie Dunnings. Career: Asst. Organist, St. Marylebone Parish Ch., 1962-65; Music Master, Pk. Schl., Swindon. 1965-69; Hd., Music Dept., Devizes Schl., 1964-; Music Dir., Devizes Light Operatic Soc., Comps. incl: Magnificat & Nunc Dimittis for boys voices, 1967; 3 musical plays for children 'Travel of Odysseus', 1973; 'Prince Haetic', 1974, & 'Thats Another Story', 1975; var. pieces for piano; Sinfonietta, 1978. Mbrships: ISM; Asst. Masters Assn. Hobbies incl: Cricket; Golf; Reading. Address: 1 Lynchet Close, Market Lavington, Devizes, Wilts., UK.

LUCAS, William Roy, b. 2 May 1932. Alexandria, La., USA. Opera Singer; Academician. Educ: BMus, La. State Univ.; M Mus., ibid; grad. study for DMA. m. Peggy Joan Dawson, Career: Leading Baritone in over 700 perfs., of over 40 roles in Germany, Austria, France, Luxembourg, Belgium, Switz. & USA; Stage Direction w. Franco Zeffirelli & Walter Felsenstein; Prof. ov Voice & Dir. of Choral Activities, N. Assn. of Tchrs. of Singing; Phi Mu Alpha. Hons: Rockefeller Grants, 1962-1963; Nat. Finalist for Am. Fedn. of Music Clubs, 1956. Hobbies: Basketball; Tennis. Address: 1509 Chickess St., Johnson City, TN 37601, USA.

LUCCHESI, Margaret (Peggy) Ann Cunningham, b. 12 June 1928. Oakland, Calif., USA. Symphony Percussionist & Teacher. Educ: AB, Univ. of Calif., Berkeley, 1949; Calif. State Tchrs. Credential & MA, San Fran. State Coll., 1957; Cond. Course, RAM, London, UK; LRAM in orchl. cond., 1952. m. Dino V Luccesi, 3 c. Career: Mbr., Percussion Sect., San Fran. Symph., 1955-; Mbr., San Fran. Opera Orch., 1961, 1964-; Mbr., San Fran. Percussion Ensemble, 1960-72; On Fac. of San Fran. Conserv. of Music & the Univ. of Calif., Berkeley, Applied Music Prof.; Perf. throughout San Fran. Bay area; Perf. 13 yrs. at the Carmel Bach. Fest.; Lectr. on percussion "sounds & techniques" for schls. & adult audiences. Var. recordings as a mbr. of the San Fran. Symph. Orch. Mbrships. incl: Phi Beta Kappa; Pi Lambda Theta; San Fran. Women's Musicians Club. Hons. incl: Farejon Prize (harmony), RAM, London, 1952; Mann Prize, Ernest Read Prize in Orchl. Cond., 1954. Var. hobbies. Address: 31 Yorshire Dr., Oakland, CA 94618, USA.

LUCIE, Lawrence (Larry), b. 18 Dec. 1914. Emporia, Va., USA. Guitar, Banjo, Mandolin & Clarinet Player. Educ: Studied Music by Correspondence, Chgo. Acad. of Music, 1923; Bklyn. Conserv. of Music, NY; Paramount Profl. Music Schl., NYC, 4 yrs. Career incl: Played in family band; Played w. Duke Ellington, Cotton Club, 1934; w. Louis Armstrong Band, 1940-45; Ldr., own combo, 1946-; guitar tchr., Jazzmobile Workshop, NYC. Comps. incl: Down at Rubina; Psycho; Crazy Winnie; After the Sun Goes Down; A Swingin' Cause. Recordings incl: Sophisticated Lady/After Sundown; Jazz & Blues Series - This Is It. Publs: Special Guitar Lessons, Book 1, 1971, Book 2, 1972, First Beginners Book, 1975. Mbrships. incl: Hon. Mbr., Local 802 A F of M; NYC; Assoc. Mbr., NY Jazz Repertory Co. of NY. Address: 400 W 43rd St., Suite 19H, NY, NY10036, USA.

LUCIUK, Juliusz Mieczyslaw, b. 1 Jan. 1927. Brzeznica, Poland. Composer. Educ: Magister Phil. Musicol., Jagiellonian Univ., 1952; Dip., Theory, 1955, Composition, 1956, State Higher Schl. of Music, Cracow, Study w. Nadia Boulanger, Max Deutsch, Paris, 1958-59. m. Domicela Dabrowska, 2d. Debut: Three Songs, perf. 1954. Num. compositions, sev. recorded by Polish Radio, BBC, Sender Freies Berlin, ORTF, Italian Radio Palermo, Netherlands Radio, incl: songs, works for piano, (Lirica di timbri; Pacem in terris, etc.) piano & violin, (Capriccio), woodwinds, ballets, (Niobe), opera-ballet, works for solo vioce & chmbr. ensembles, (Floral Dream; Le souffle); du vent; Pour un Ensemble; solo voice & orchestra, (Tool of the Light; Poeme de Loire), orch. works. Recordings: Maraton; Lirica di timbi; Pacem in terris. Mbrships: Union of Polish Composers; Soc. of Polish Authors. Num. Polish, int. composition awards, inclng: Silver Medal, Int. Competition for Composers, Vercelli, 1960; Netherlands Radio AVRO Prize, Int. Competition, Bilthoven, 1962; Honourable Mentions, Prince Pierre Competition,

Monaco, 1971 & 1973; 1st Prize, Prince Pierre Competition, Monaco, 1974. Golden Cross of Merit, Poland, 1975. Address: Os. Kolorowe 6m10, 31-938 Krakow-Nowa Huta, Poland.

LUCKETT, Richard, b. 1 July 1945. Lymington, Hants., UK. University Lecturer; Journalist. Educ: St. Catharine's Coll., Cambridge; BA, 1967; PhD, 1972. Career: Prods. for Cambridge Univ. Opera Soc. incl: Orfeo ed Euridice, 1965 & Ariadne auf Naxos, 1966. Publs: Ed., H Purcell, Sonata's of III parts, 1975. Contbr. to Music & Letters; The Spectator. Mbr. Royal Musical Assn. Address: Magdalene Coll., Cambridge, UK.

LUCKY, Stepan, b. 20 Jan. 1919. Zilina, Czechoslovakia. Composer. Educ: Composition Dept., Master Schl., Prague Conserv., 1947; Music Dept. of Philos. Fac., Prague Conserv., 1947; Music Dept. of Philos. Fac., Prague Univ., 1948. 2 d. Carer: Music Critic, var. newspapers & weeklies, 1945-49; Hd., Music Dept., Prague TV, 1954-58. Comps. incl: Concertos for piano, 'cello, violin & Double Concerto for violin & piano; Midnight Surprise (one-act opera); var. works for 2 instrments or small ensembles; sev. works for string orch.; sev. song cycles; choral pieces, most for children; music for about 100 films. Many of works have been recorded. Publd. (w. Vladimir Bor) Trojan, monograph about his music for films & the operatic scene, 1957. Mbr: Ctrl. Committee. Assn. of Czech. Composers. Hons: State Order for Outstanding Accomplishments, 1969; Artist of Merit, 1972. Hobbies: Touring; Swimming; Chess. Address: Praha 6, Lomena 24, Czech.

LUDEWIG-VERDEHR, Elsa, . 14 April 1936. Charlottesville, Va., USA. Clarinettist. Educ: B Mus & B Mus Ed., Oberlin Conserv. of Music, Ohio; M Mus., D Mus. A & Perf s. Cert., Eastman Schl. of Music, Rochester, NY. m. Walter Verdehr (Verderber). Debut: Carnegie Recital Hall, NYC, 1959. Career incls: Clarinettist, Verdehr Trio (concerts in USA & Europe), Richards Wind Quintet (concert in USA & Can.); Marlboro Music Fests. (Music from Marlboro tours), apps. on NET-TV & Int. Clarinet Symposium; Recitalist, Boston NYC, Denver, Wash. DC., & var. univ. campuses; Orchestral Soloist, Houston & Lansing Symph.; Prin. Clarinet, Brevard Fest. Orch., Grant Teton Orch., Lansing Symph., Eastman Wind Ensemble & Eastman Philharmonia' Prof. of Music, Mich. State Univ., East Lansing. num. recordings. Int. Clarinet Soc.; NACWPI. recip., Disting. fac. awards, Mich. State Univ. 1979. Mgmt: PAA, 265 Parklake Ave., Ann Arbor, MI 48103, USA. Address: 1635 Roseland, East Lansing, MI 48823, USA. 5, 8.

LUDGIN, Chester Hall, b. 20 May 1925. New York City, USA. Operatic Baritone. Educ. incl: Am. Theatre Wing Profl. Trng. Prog.; Vocal study w. Wm. S Brady, etc. Debut: Scarpia (Tosca) Expmtl. Opera Theatre of Am., New Orleans, 1956. Career incl: leading operatic roles w. major cos. in Can., USA & Mexico. Repertoire incl. Escamillo in Carmen, Mephistopheles in Faust (Gounod), Figaro in Barber of Seville. Appeared in sev. World Premieres inclng. opera by Ward, Ellstein, LaMontaine, etc. Hobbies: Portrait, Painting; Photography. Mgmt: Thea Dispeaker Artists' Rep., 59 E 54th St., NY., NY 10022. Address: 205 W End Ave., NY., NY 100023, USA.

LUDWIG, Christa. b. Berlin, Germany. Singer. m. Paul-Emile Deiber, 1s. from former marriage. Debut: as Orlovsky in Die Fledermaus, Städtische Bühnen, Frankfurt. Career incls: Frankfurt; Darmstadt; Hanover; Mbr., Vienna State Opera; guest apps. in opera, concerts & recitals, NYC, San Fran., Los Angeles, Chgo., Buenos Aires, Tokyo, Paris, Milan. Rome, London, Berlin, Munich, Moscow, Washington, Montreal, Toronto, Hamburg, etc.; apps. a prin. fests. of Europe & Am. Recordings incl: Fidelio; Carmen; Cosi Flute; Die Fledermaus; Rosenkavalier; Walküre; Götterdämmerung; Tristan & Isolde; Tannhäuser; Parsifal; num. concert & recital discs. Hons. incl: Kammersaengerin, Austrian Govt., 1962; 1st Class Cross of Hon. for Sci. & Art, Mozart Medal, 1969; Priz des Affaires Culturelles, 1972. Hobbies incl: Listening to Music; Theatre; Philosophy; Cooking. Mgmt: Music & Arts SA, Tobelhofstr. 2, CH-8044 Zurich. Address: Vidolin Hoferstr. 17, CH-6045 Meggen, Switzerland, 2, 19, 27.

LUENING, Otto, b. 15 June 1900. Milwaukee, Wis., USA. Composer; Conductor; Flautist; Educator; Pioneer in Electronic Music. Educ: State Acad. of Music, Munich; Municipal Conserv. of Music, Zurich; Univ. of Zurich; Privately w. Ferruccio Busoni. m (1) Ethel Codd (div.); (2) Catherine Brunson. Debuts: as flautist, Munich, 1915; as cond. & comp., Zurich, 1917. Career: Prof., Eastman Schl., Univ. of Ariz., Bennington Coll., Columbia Univ. & Juilliard Schl., 1925-75. Comps. incl: Elegy; Entrance & Exit Music; Fanfare for a Festival Occasion; Gargoyles for Violin & Tape; Lyric quartets; Evangeline (opera). Num. comps. recorded by CRI, Desto, Louisville, Golden Crest & Columbia. Contbr. of num. writings to profl. publs. Mbrships.

incl: Co-Pres., CRI; Bd., Int. Soc. of Contemp. Music; Nat. Inst. of Arts & Letters; Am. Acad. in Rome. Hons. incl: D Mus, Wesleyan Univ.; DFA, Univ. of Wis., 1977: DMus, Wis. Conserv. of Music, 1979; 3 Guggenheim Fellowship; Nat. Endowment for the Arts Award. Hobbies: Swimming; Yoga; Psychology; Medicing; History. Address: 460 Riverside Dr., NY, NY 10027, USA. 2.

LUISI, Francesco, b. 27 April 1943. Bari, Italy. Musicologist. Educ: Dip., Musical Paleography & Philol., Univ. of Pavai; Dip. in Composition & choral Music, Conserv. of Bari. Mbrships: Artistic Exec. Comm., G P da Palestrina Fndn.; Exec. Comm., Italian Soc. of the Flauto Dolce; Exec. Comm., Pro Musica Studium, Rome. Publs. incl: Il secondo libro di frottole di A. Antico. cirtical ed., 2 vols., 1975-76 (The 2nd book of Frottle of A Antico); Atti del Convegno di Studi Palestriniani, 1975 (Study forum on Palestrina); Del cantar a libro... o sulla viola, 1977. Contbr. to var. music jrnls. inlclng. New Italian Musical Review, etc. Address: Via del Masherino 75, 00913, Rome, Italy.

LUKASZCZYK, Jacek, b. 11 Mar. 1934. Warsaw, Poland. Pianist. Educ: Dip., Acad. of Music, WArsaw, 1957; Dip., Acad. of Music, Vienna, 1964. Career: concerts, radio & TV broadcasts & recordings, Poland, USSR, Austria, German Fed. Repub., Italy, France, Netherlands, Soloist & Mbr. of piano duo w. brother Mociej Lukasczyk. Recordings: Muza. Mbrships: Dpty. Gen. Sec., Chopin Soc., Vienna; Presidium, Chopin Soc., German Fed. Repub. Hobbies: Mountaineering; Swimming; Roulette. Address: Herbeck Str. 46/17, 1180 Vienna, Austria.

LUKE, Ray E., b. 30 May 1928. Ft. Worth, Tex., USA. Conductor; Composer; Professor. Educ: B Mus, Tex. Christian Univ., 1949; M Mus, ibid., 1950; PhD, Eastman Schl. Music, Univ. Rochester, 1960. m. V Faye Smith, 1 s., 1 d. Career incls: Assoc. Cond., Okla. City Symph. Orch., 1968-73; Music Dir. & Cond., ibid., 1973-74; Prof., instrumental music & comp., sev. univs., 1950-; Currently, Okla. City Univ. Comps. incl: Dialogues for Organ & Percussion; Prelude & March; Rondo; Sonics & Metrics for Concert Band. Mbrships: ASCAP; Am. Music Ctr. Hons. incl: Grand Prix Gold Medal, Queen Elisabeth of Belgium, Int. Competition in Comp. for 'Concerto for Piano', 1970; ASCAP Award, contbns. to serious music, 12 consecutive yrs. Hobby: Travel. Address: 6017 Glencove Pl., Oklahoma City, OK 73132, USA.

LUKOWICZ, Jerzy, b. 1 April 1936. Krakow, Poland. Pianist. Educ: Dip., Panstwowa Wyzszy Szkola Muzyczna w. Krakowie; MA, Acad. of Music; Accademia Chigiana, Siena. m. Elzbieta Stefanska Lukowicz. Career: Concerts in num. countries inclng: Poland, Czechoslovakia; E & W Germany; Hungary, Italy, France, Norway, Yugoslavia, Belgium, USSR, USA; Int. Festivals; Prof., Acad. of Music, Krakow; Pianist in Cracow Trio, 1963-. Recordings for Polish radio & TV; Disc recordings for Polskie Negrania, MUZA. Hons. incl: Premio Antonio Vivaldi w. Cracow Trio in Accademia Chigiana, Siena, 1965; Prize of Krakow City, 1975. Mgmt: PAGART, Polish Artists Agcy., Warszana, pl. Zwyciestwa 9. Address: ul. Garncarska 3, 31-115 Krakow, Poland.

LUMB, Harold, b. 25 July 1919. Slaithwaite, Huddersfield, Yorks., UK. Professional Singer. Educ: RAM, London; LRAM, singing tchrs., ARCM, singing perfs. Debut: Engl. Opera Grp., 1950. Career: Westminster Abbey, 1951-52; BBC Singers, 1952-; Solo broadcasts. Recordings: w. BBC Singers. Mbrships: ISM; Equity. Recip. HP Lunn's Music, Prize, 1934. Hobbies: Chess; Swimming; Rambling; Tennis. Address: 10 St. Georges Ave., Kingsbury, London NW9 0JU, UK. 3.

LUMBY, Herbert Horace, b. 8 Oct. 1906. Birmingham, Warwicks., UK. Composer; Instrumentalist & Teacher (violin, viola & piano). Educ: Birmingham Schl. of Music; ABSM (violin & viola). m. Muriel Normansell. Career: Solo & Orchl. (CBSO). Comps. for Full Orch. incl: Symph. in A minor op. 27; Lyric Suite op. 20; Ankerdine Suite op. 21; Summer Pastorale op. 26; Festive March op. 53. Comps. for string orch. incl: The Lovely Rosalind op. 11; Spring Pastorale op. 16; Idyll op. 29; Carol for the Nativity op. 38; Aubade op. 47; Variations, op. 50; Scherzo Ostinato op. 51; Sonatas for violin & piano, viola & piano; str. & piano trios; str. quartet, pieces for piano, piano duet & 2 pianos, harp, violin, viola, clarinet, cello, guitar; many songs. Publs: Violin Class Tutor Books 1 & 2, 1958; The Cuckoo for Piano No. 5. Mbrships: ISM; Musicians Union. Hobbies: Fishing; Gardening. Address: 71 Cole Valley Rd., Hall Green, Birmingham B28 0DE, UK. 1. 14.

LUMSDAINE, David Newton, b. 31 Oct. 1931. Sydney, Aust. Composer; Lecturer. Educ: Sydney Conserv., Sydney Univ., RAM; pvte. study w. Matyas Seiber. m. Nicola Lefanu, 2d. Career: Lectr., Sr., Lectr. in Music (comp.), Univ. of Durham,

1970-. Comps: about 25 comps. incl. major works for orchl, chmbr. & vocal mediums; electronic music. Address: The Music Schl., Palace Green, Durham City, UK.

LUMSDEN, David James, b. 19 Mar. 1928. Newcastle-on-Tyne, UK. Organist; Choral Conductor; Harpsichordist; University Lecturer. Educ: MA, D Phil, Mus B, Selwyn Coll., Cambridge Univ. m. Sheila Daniels, 2 s., 2 d. Career: Organist; Southwell Minster; Fellow & Organist, New Col., Oxford; Fndr., Cnd., Nottingham Bach Soc.; Solo appearance at Proms, RFH, QEH; Mbr., London Virtuosi; Vis. Prof., Yale Univ., USA. Prin., Royal Scottish Acad. of Music & Drama, 1976-. Many recordings incl: The Organ in the Sheldonian; In Quires & Places, No. 7; Christmas Music from new College; Evensong at New College, Oxford; Choral Masterpieces by S S Wesley; Boyce Trio Sonatas; Gerald English Sings Baroque Music; Bach -David Lumsden; recitals. Ed., An Anthol. of English Lute Music 1953; Ed., Thomas Robinson's Schl. of Music 1603, 1971; Music for the Lute (Gen. Ed.) 6 vols., 1966-. etc.Mbrships: ISM; Past Pres., Inc. Assn. of Organists. Recip., Barclay Squire Prize, 1951; Hon. FRCO, 1976. Hobbies: Mountain walking; Bird watching; Reading. Address: RSAMD, 58 St. George's Pl., Glasgow, Scotland, UK. 1, 5.

LUMSDEN, Norman, b. 16 Sept. 1906. London, UK. Bass Singer. m. Irene Palmer, 1 s. Career: Engl. Oprea Grp., 1947-72; Singer w. most leading choral socs. in GB & in BBC Symph. & Promenade Concerts, etc.; Chosen by BBC to sing bass solos in 200th anniversary of 1st perf. of Messiah, later repeated in Westminster Abbey where comp., buried; Apps. at Covent Gdn., Glyndebourne, Sadler's Wells & In concerts & opera perfs. in Germany, France, Can., USA, Holland, Belgium, Czechoslavakia, Switzerland, Norway & Denmark; Original prin. in many of Britten's operas & in Walton's The Bear. Num. recordings & TV operas. Hobby: Golf. Address: 70 Cawdor Cres., London W7 2DD, UK.

LUMSDEN, Ronald, b. 28 May 1938. Dundes, UK. Pianist. Educ: Harris Acad., Dundee; RCM, London; ARCM; LRAM. m. Annon Lee Silver, dec., 1 s. m. Alison Paice Hill, 1975. Career: Pianist in Res., Univ. of Southamptom, 1965-68; Sir Henry Wood Promenade Concerts 1973 & '74; Soloist in Arts Coun. Contemporary Music Network, 1974-76. Vis. Piano Tchr., N.E. Essex Tech. Coll. & Schl. of Art, 1971-; Frequent broadcasts & recitals in UK, Netherlands, Sweden, Yugoslavia. Recordings: Messiaen's Canteyodjava for Gaudeamus Foundation Camilleri's Mantra (Vista VPS 1007). Mbr., Exec. comm., Soc. for Promotion of New Music, 1975-; ISM. Hons: First prize-winner, Int. Competition for Interpreters of Contemporary Music, Utrecht, 1968. Hobby: Gardening. Address: 50 Grosvenor Rd., Caversham, Reading, Berks. RG4 OEN, UK.

LUND, Lilleba, b. 21 Apr. 1940. Nord-Reisa, Troms, Norway. Opera Singer. Educ: studied w. Prof. Erna Berger, Hamburg, 1962-63, w. Prof. Erik Werba, Vienna, 1972-74. m. Johan Kuandal, 1 d. Deubt: opera, Augsburg, 1963; Soloist, Oslo Phil., Oslo, 1969. Career: Soloist, NRK Girls Choir, Norwegian Broadcasting, many radio & TV concerts, 1952-57; Opera Singer, Augsburg, 1963-65, Wurzburg, 1965-67; Dortmund, 1967-70. Recordings: Children's Songs by David Monrad Johansen, Philips. Mbrships: Norwegian Broadcasting Competition, 1955: 3rd Prize, 15th Int. Music Competition, Munich, 1965. Hobbies: Music; Wandering; Literature; European History. Address: Box 122, 1312 Slependen, Norway.

LUNDBERG, Kjell, b. 6 June 1922. Gothenberg, Sweden. Composer; Musician (organ, bassoon). Educ: Music Schl. of Gothenberg, 1939-41; Royal Music HS, Stockholm, 1945-49; Summer course in Engl. Ch. Music, w. David Willcocks, Cambridge, UK, 1973. Comps: Coena Domini (mass); Canticum Sacrum (mass); Gratia Dei (mass); 3 cantatas for organ; Oculi (toccata), Ludium Gaudium; Concerto for oboe & orch.; 4 Suites for orch.; 5 woodwind quintetti; vocal pieces; choral songs. Recordings: 4 choirsongs (Freton); Marsch (Telefunken); Fuo (Fuoep). Publs: Music Critic, Boras Tidning newspaper, 1964-; Contbr. of articles on Swedish comps. to Boras Tidning. Mbrships: Cond., Confedn. Choir. Hobby: Travel. Address: Vastergardsgatan 4, 502 49 Boras, Sweden.

LUND CHRISTIANSEN, Anne, b. 11 Sept. 1928. Copenhagen, Denmark. Opera Singer (Soprano). Educ: Royal Opera Schl., Copenhagen, 1954-57; Studied in Vienna, Rome, Seina; Music Tchrs. Degree, Royal Danish Conserv. Music, Copenhagen, 1970. Debut: Aarhus, Donna Anna, 1957. Career: Staff, Royal Opera, Stockholm, 1958; Royal Theatre, Copenhagen, 1961; Tchr., Royal Danish Conserv. Music, Copenhagen, 1970-. Address: Snaregade 8, 1205 Copenhagen K, Denmark.

LUNDE, Ivar Jr., b. 15 Jan. 1944. Tonsberg, Norway. Composer; Oboist. Educ: AA, Tonsberg Hoyere Almenskole, 1964; Conserv. of Music, Oslo; Akademie Mozarteum, Salzburg. m. Nanette Gomory Lunde. Debut: (oboist) Tönsberg, 1964; (comp.) Lund, Sweden, 1965. Career: Asst. Prof. of Oboe & Theory, Univ. of Wis., USA; Oboist, Den Norska Opera, 1964-66, Nat. Gall. Orch., Wash., DC, USA, 1966-68. Comp. of over 70 works inclng. sev. works for large wind ensemble & symph. orch., choir, & chmbr. music. Mbrships. incl: Soc. of Norwegian Comps. Contbr. to The Wis. Schl. Musician, etc. Hons. incl: 1st Prize, Oslo Concert Hall Comp. Contest, 1976; 1st Prize, Univ. of Maryland/Kendor Music Clarinet Choir Comp. Contest. Hobbies incl: Camping. Address: 3432 Cummings St., Eau Claire, WI 54701, USA.

LUNDE, Nanette Gomory, b. 3 Feb. 1943. Darby, Pa., USA. Instructor of Harpsichord & Piano. Educ: B Mus, Oberlin Conserv., Ohio, 1965; 2 Certs. for Harpsichord, Akademie Mozarteum, Salzburg, Austria, 1965; M Mus, Northwestern Univ., Ill., 1966. m. Ivar Lunde Jr. Debut: Wash. DC, 1965. Career: Instr. of Harpsichord & Piano, Univ. of Wis., Eau Claire, 1969-; Coulee Region Harpsichord Worshops, La Crosse, Wis., 1969, 71, pvte. studio Tchr.; Recitalist, USA & Europe. Contbr. to The Harpsichord; Clavier Magazine. Mbrships. incl: Pi Kappa Lambda; Sigma Alpha Iota; Schubert Club, St. Paul, Minn. Recip., var. scholarships. Hobbies: Harpsichord Building; Winter Sports; Fishing. Address: 3417 Riley St., Eau Claire, WI 54701, USA.

LUNDGREN, Olav, b. 14 May 1941. Höyanger, Norway. Clarinettist. Educ: Philos. Degree, Oslo Univ.; Perfs. Dip (Reifeprufung), Musikakademie, Vienna (w. Prof. Rudolf Fette1). 1 c. Career: Solo clarinettist, Wiener Volksoper, 1972; Solo clarinettist, Norwegian Opera, Oslo, 1974; Solo clarinettist, Norwegian Opera, Oslo, 1974; Solo clarinettist, NRK Radio Orch., Oslo, 1977; Apps. as soloist, Norway & abroad. Address: Nedre Skogvei 4C, Oslo 2, Norway.

LUNDQUIST, Torbjörn Iwan, b. 30 Sept. 1920. Stockholm, Sweden. Composer; Symphonist. Educ: Studied w. var. tchrs. m. (1) Maud Elisabeth Lagergren (dec.), 2 s., 1 d., (2) Marianne Elisabeth Lagergren. Debut: Cond., Stockholm, 1949. Career: Cond., Drottningholm Theatre, 1949-56, Torbjörn Lundquist Chmbr. Orch., 1949-56; Apps. as Cond., Stockholm Phil. Orch., State Orch. etc., 1970-. Compositions incl: Concerto Grooso (violin, cello & strings), 1974; Trio Fiorente (piano, violin & cello), 1975; Symph. No. 3 (Sinfonia Dolorosa), 1971-76; Violin Concerto (Fantasia Pragenese), 1976-78; Symph. No. 1 (Chmbr. Symph.), 1956; Symph. No. 2, (...for freedom), 1956-70, etc. Recordings incl: Bewegungen; Duel; Teamwork. Mbr. var. profl. orgs. Hobby: Mountaineering. Hons: Ture Rangström Scholarship, 1975; Swedish State Award for Comp., 1976; Artist Reward, Swedish Govt., 1978-. Address: Freyvgen 5 B, 133 00 Saltsjöbaden, Sweden. 4.

LUNDQVIST, Alf-Roger, b. 15 Sept. 1957. Stockholm, Sweden. Student. Educ: Statens Normalskola Music Dept. (chmbr. music, cond., comp., violin, music hist.); Pvte. Conserv. of Stockholm w. E Nordwall & Jacob Moskowitz (piano); studied choir comp., comp., counterpoint etc. w. Prof. Waldemar Söderhalm. Debut: reykjavik, 1977. mbr., Am. Musicol. Soc. recip., UNM prize for young Scandinavian comps., 1977. Hobbies: Long walks in the country. Address: Klensmedsvägen 19 n.b.t.v., 12637 Hägersten, Stockholm, Sweden.

LUNDSTEN, Ralph, b. 7 Oct. 1936. Ersnäs, Lulea, Sweden. Composer; Electronic Musician; Film Maker. Career: Comp. of Ballet Music, Music for Theatre, Films, TV Radio & Exhibitions; Owner of Sweden's only pvte. electronic music studio, Andromeda; Subject of Swedish Radio portraits, 1971, 1972, Swedish TV portrait, 1973. Compositions incl: The Water Sprite; Carvings; Upbeat; Stretch; Universe Callings; Gunnar of Lidarände; Icelandic Dancing Pictures; Johannes & The Lady of the Woods; Paternoster; Nightmare; Erik XIV & Gustav III (2 Ballets about Swedish Kings); Num. recordings for HMV & Swedish Radio. Mbr., Assn. for Swedish Comps. Hons: Grand Prix Biennale, Paris, France, 1967; about 40 other awards for music & film-making. Hobbies: His profession excludes all others. Address: Frankenburgs Väg 1, 13200 Saltsjö-Boo, Sweden.

LUNN, Roger Francis, b. 22 Nov. 1938. Surbinton, UK. Musician; Cello Treble & Bass viol Player. Educ; ARCM (Cello, Perf.); Lic., GSM, London (Cello Tchr.). m. Sara Anne, 1 s., 1 d. Appts: Bournemouth Symph. Orch., 1960-62; Freelance w. London orchs., 1962-72; LPO, 1972-; Elizabethan Consort of Viols, 1967-; Tchr. of Cello, Borough of Romford, London

Borough of Havering, Kingston upon Thames Corp., Surrey Co. Coun. & others, 1961-71; Pvte. Tchr. of Cello, 1962-. Many recordings w. all the London orchs. & Elizabethan Consort of Viols. Mbrships: Musicians Union; ISM. Recip. Andrew Carnegie Scholarship to GSM, Worshipful Co. of Musicians, 1958. Hobbies incl: Steam railways; Model railways. Address: 57 Brown's Rd., Surbinton, Surrey, KT5 8SP, UK. 4.

LUPER, Albert T(homas), b. 10 Jan. 1914. Jacksonville, Tex., USA. Musicologist. Educ: BMus, Tex. Christian Univ., 1934; MMus, Eastman Schl. of Music, 1938; post-grad. study, ibid., 1946-48, '51; Cert., Conservatório Nacional de Música, Lisbon, Portugal. m. Elisabeth Mayhew Luper, 1d., 1s. Career: Instructor, violin & music theory, John Tarleton Coll., Stephenville, Tex., 1935-38; Instructor & asst., Prof., Univ. of Tex., 1938-48; Asst. prof., assoc. prof., then full prof., Schl. of Music, Univ. of Iowa, 1948-; Publs. incl: Music of Argentina, 1941; Music of Brazil, 1941: Bibliography of the writings of J A Westrup, 1957. Contbr. to: Grove's Dict., 6th ed.; Musical Quarterly; Jrnl. of the Am. Musicol. Soc.; Music Library Assn. Notes, & other jrnls. Mbrships: Am. Musicol. Soc.; Int. Musicol. Soc.; Coll. Music Soc.; Music Lib. Assn.; Int. Musicol. Soc.; Coll. Music Soc.; Music Lib. Assn.; Int. Assn. of Music Libs.; Medieval Acad. of Am.; Am. Assn. of Univ. Profs. Address: 213 McLean St., Iowa City, IA 52240, USA. 2, 11.

LUPTON-SMITH, Lilian Ruth Gladys, b. 7 Nov. 1896, E London, S Africa. Teacher of Piano & Theory. Educ: pvte.; S African Licentiate (piano). m. Arthur Walter Lupton-Smith (dec.), 3s. Career: Prin., secondary Govt. Schls.; pvte. tchr.; lead singer in num. amateur prods. Comps: Waltz, The Brook; num. songs. Contbr. to: The S African Music Tchr.; Modern Keyboard Review; NCW News. Mbrships: S A Soc. of Music Tchrs. (var. offices); Nat. Coun. of Women (life mbr.); Durban Soroptomist Club; D'Urban Women's Club; past mbr., English Speaking Union, London. Hobbies: Reading; Bridge, Crosswood Puzzles. Address: 54 Nicolson Rd., Durban 4001, S Africa.

LUPU, Radu, b. 1945. Romania. Pianist. Educ: Moscow Conserv. Career incl: appearances w. leadin UK, European & US Orch.; Toured E. Europe w. LSO; USA tour, 1972. num. recordings incl. all Beethoven concertos. Hons: 1st Prize, Van Cliburn Competition, 1966: 1st Prize, Leeds Int. Competition, 1969. Mgmt: Harrison Parrott Ltd., 22 Hillgate St., London, W8, UK. Addess: c/o mgmt.

LÜTGE, Elizabeth Marie (nee Sivertson), b. 31 Oct. 1928. Durban, S. Africa. Music Teacher. Educ: LRSM (Tchrs.); LTCL (Tchrs.); Gold Medal, Natal Soc. for Advancement of Music; B Mus; M Mus. m. Ronald Frederick Lütge, 1 s., 3 d. Career: sev. broadcasts for S. African Broadcasting Corp.; Soloist w. Durban Civic Orch. & E. London Phil. Soc.; Matriculation music, Berea Girls HS. Comps: Grazing Sheep, A Gallop; The Lost Lamb (short piano pieces for children). Mbrships: Past Pres., mbr., S. African Soc. of Music Tchrs.; Convocation of Natal Univ.; Natal Tchrs. Soc. Recip. many awards inclng. Gold Medal, Eisteddfodau (Natal Soc. for Advancement of Music), 1939-45. Hobbies: Swimming; Reading; Theatre. Address: 10 Cradock Pl., Fynnland, 4052, S. Africa.

LÜTOLF, Max, b. 1 Dec. 1934. Altishofen, Switz. University Teacher. Educ: MA; PhD; D Musicol. m. Sylvai Hunkeler; 3 d. Career: Prof., Univ. of Zürich, 1977. Recording: Harpsichordist, Archive Prod. 198 196. Publs: Die mehrstimmigen Ordinarium missae-Sätze vom ausgehenden 11. bis zur Wende des 13, zum 14. Jahrhundert, 2 Vols., 1970; Ed., Andre Campra, Les Festes Venitiennes, 1972. Contbr. to var. profl. jrnls. Mbrships: Int. Musicol. Soc.; Swiss Music Rsch. Soc; Italian Musicol. Soc. Recip. Edward J Dent Medal, 1973. Address: 8 Arosastrasse, CH-8008 Zürich, Switz.

LUTOSLAWSKI, Witold, b. 25 Jan. 1913. Warsaw, Poland. Composer. Educ: Warsaw Univ.; Piano degree, 1936, Composition degree, 1937. Warsaw State Conserv. of Music; m. Maria-Danuta Dygat. Debut: 1st Pub. Perf. of Orchestral Work, Warsaw Phil., 1933. Career: Played daily in Warsaw cafes under German occupation, 1939-45; 1st perf. of orchestral work, Paris, 1946; 1st perf., Symph. No. 1st 1948: Series of works based on Polish folklore, 1945-55; Tchr., Composition, Berkshire Music Ctr., Tanglewood, USA, 1963, '64, Dartington Summer Schl. of Music, UK, 1968, Conserv., Aarhus, Denmark; Cond. of own works, in Europe & in recordings, 1963-. Num. compositions incl: Symphonic Variations, 1938; Symph. No. 1, 1947; Musique Funebre (string orch.), 1958; Jeux Venitiens, 1961: Symph. No. 2, 1967; Concerto for cello & orch., 1970; Preludes & Fugue for 13 solo strings, 1972. Most. prin. works have been recorded. Mbrships. incl: Polish Composers Union; Hon. Mbr., Int. Soc. for Contemp. Music; Hon. Mbr., Swedish Royal Acad. of Music; freie Akademie der Kunste, Hamburg; Bayerische Akademie der

Schönen Kunste. Akademie der Knste, W. Berlin;Extraord. Mbr., Deutsche Akademie der Künste, E. Berlin; Mbr., Prof. Commission, Warsaw Autumn Fest.; Chmn., Prof. Coun., Polish Music Publs.; Int. Music Coun. Num. hons. incl: City of Warsaw Prize, 1948; Koussevitsky Int. Recording Award, 1964: State Music Prize, 1952, 1955 & 1964; Léone Sonning Music Prize, 1967; Sibelius de Wilhuri Prize, Helsinki, 1973; Maurince Ravel Prize, Paris, 1971. Hobbies: Other arts; Sailing. Address: Smiala 39, 01-523 Warsaw, Poland, 2, 3, 4.

LUTSCHG, Andrej, b. 2 Sept. 1926. Mollis GL, Switzerland. Violinist. Educ: Zürich Acad. Music; Prof. Moravec, Vienna. m. Evelyne Dubourg, 1 s., 1 d. Career incls: Soloist w. num. orchs. inclng. Berlin Radio Orch., Brussels Radio Orch., Orch. Maggio Musicale Fliorentino, N German Radio Orch. Hamburg; Dir., Master class, Zürich Acad. Music, 1964-. Recordings incl: J S Bach's Complete Sonatas & Partitas for Solo Violin; Wladimir Vogel's Concerto for Violin & Orchestra. Mbrships incl: Schweizerischer Tonkunstlerverein; Schweizerischer Musikpadagogischer Verband. Mgmt: Knozergesellschaft Zürich GmbH, Steinwiesstrasse 2, 8032 Zürich. Address: Klusdorfli 6, 8032 Zürich, Swizerland.

LUTYENS, Elisabeth, b. 9 July 1906. London, UK. Composer; Educ: RCM; Ecole Normale, Paris, France. m. (1) Ian Glennie, (2) Edward Clark, 2 s., twin d. Comps: about 200 publd. works; 80 film scores; 100 radio scores; works recorded by Argo, Decca & EMI. Publs: Author of one book, sev. articles. Hon: CBE; Hon Univ. (York). Mgmt: Universal Edition (music); David Higham (films). Address: 13 King Henry's Rd., London NW3 3QP, UK. 4, 14.

LUTZEN, B(ernhard) Ludolf, b. 23 Apr. 1939. Leipzig, Germany. College Professor. Educ: studied theory of music, Germanics, psychol., pedagogy & sociol., Univs. of Frankfurt & Cologne; State exams in Germanics; studied at Coll. of Music, Frankfurt; State exams in Schl. Music; Assessor exams; promoted to Musicol. m. Renate Lützen-Blume, 1 s. Career: specialist in Renaissance & early Baroque wind instruments, 1964-; early music prog. for TV & radio; Dir., Odhecaton Ealy music ensemble, Cologne. Recordings: Chrisnach voor 400 Jahren; Von Tod und Leben-Motxetten zur Passion; Musikalishe Feste in fürstlichen Gärten. Contbr. to publs. in field. Mbrships. incl: Committee, Int. Arbeiskreis für Musik. Address: Friedrichstr. 10, 5000 Cologne (Porz), German Fed. Repub.

LUXON, Benjamin, b. 1937. Camborne, UK. Baritone Singer. Educ: Westminster Trng. Coll.; GSM. m. Sheila Amit, 1 d. 2 s. Career: Phys. Educ. Tchr. until turning profl. as singer, 1963 w. lieder, folk musicoratorio & operatic repertoire; apps., Aldenburgh, Covent Gdn., BBC TV, Glyndebourne, Engl. Nat. Opera. Recordings incl: Hugo Wolf's Mörike Lieder, 1974. Hons. incl: Gold Medal GSM, 1963: FGSM, 1970, appointed Bard of Cornish Gorseld, 1974. Hobbies: Collecting English Drawing & Watercolours; Swimming; Tennis. Adress: 4 Prospect Rd., New Barnet, Herts., UK. 1.

LUXTON, Lesley Vivienne, b. 9 Apr. 1955. Newton Abbot, Devon, UK. Concert Cellist; Cello Teacher. Educ: BA (mus), Univ. of Southampton; 3 yrs. grad. study, RNCM. m. M H Ismail. Career: 2 yrs. w. Nat. Youth Orch. of GB; Piano Trio tour of Yugoslavia incl. perf. at Jeunesses Musicales conference, Rovins, 1976; solo concerts & broadcasts in Bahrain; duo recital tours of UK. recip., Merguerison Clay & Helen Porterhouse Scholarship form Herman Bantock Fund. Hobbies: Painting; Drawing; Tennis. Address: 12 Courtenay Pk., Newton Abbot, Devon TQ12 2HD, UK.

LUYPAERTS, Guy Philippe, b. 3 May 1931. Wilrijk, Belgium. Pianist; Composer; Conductor. Educ: Superior Dip., piano, Royal Music Acad., Brussels; Solfeggio, Harmony, Counterpoint & Fugue, ibid. m. Paulette Heusch, 4c. Career: Prof. of Piano & Solfeggio, Music Acads. of Watermael Boitsfort & Anderlecht, 1957-66; Dir. of Music Acad. of Verviers; Soloist, Symph. Orch. of Liége, 1961-69; Prof. of Practical Harmony, Royal Acad. of Liége, 1963-; Cond., Chmbr. Orch. of Verviers, 1966-; Toured France, Holland, Portugal, Austria, Germany & Zaire as pianist & lectr.; Apps., Belgian radio & TV. Comps. incl: (for piano) Rhythmic Triptich; Art Childhood; Caprice Rapsodie; Suite for Bassoon & Piano; Syncopation in Liberty for trumpet & piano; Prologue & Rhythms for oboe & piano. Author of solfeggio for musical tuition establishments. Mbr., num. profl. orgs. Hons: Laureate, Prize of Comp. Emile Doehaerd, 1975. Address: 4, rue Chapuis, 4800 Verviers, France.

LYALL, Max Dail, b. 14 Feb. 1939. Mazie, Okla., USA. Pianist; Tenor; Teacher. Educ: AA, Northern Okla. Jr. Coll. Tonkawa, Okla.; B Mus, Okla. Bapt. Univ., Shawnee; M Mus, Univ. of Okla., Norman; Geo. Peabody Coll. for Tchrs.,

Nashville, Tenn.; student of Leon Fleisher & Julio Esteban, Peabody Conserv. of Music, Balt., Md. Career: Music Ed. (3 yrs.) w. Ch. Music Dept., Bapt. Sunday Schl. Bd., Nashville, Tenn.; Assoc. Prof. of Music (8 yrs.) Belmont Coll., Nashville; Elected to the fac., Golden Gate Bapt. Theol. Sem., Mill Valley, Calif., 1974; Piano & Harpsichord Soloist w. Nashville Symph. Orch., Nashville Chamber Orch. & Tenor Soloist w. the Nashville Chamber Singers, Nashville Pro Musica, Louisville Sem. Oratorio Chorus, Golden Gate Bapt. Theol. Sem. Oratorio Chorus; Calif. Bapt. Coll. Chapel Choir. Compositions; many choral, organ & piano arrangements publd. by Broadman Press, Nashville. Recordings: Max Lyall at the Piano, by So. Bapt. Radio & TV Commn., Ft. Worth, Tex. Publs: Hymn-Tune Preludes for the Piano; Favorite Hymns for the Piano; Music from Way Back When. Mbr. var. profl. orgs. Hobby: Writing. Address: Golden Gate Bapt. Theol. Sem., Strawberry Point, Mill Valley, CA 94941, USA.

LYDDON, Paul W, b. 6 Oct. 1931. Fairport, NY, USA. Professor of Music (Piano). Educ: Dip., Phillips Acad., Andover, Mas., 1950; B Mus, Eastman Schl. of Music, NY, 1954; M Mus, Univ. Ill., Urbana, 1955. m. Vicki Federer, 1 s., 3 d. Career: Prof. of Music (piano), Univ. of Wyo., Laramie; Recitals, apps. as soloist w. many orchs.; Mbr. several chmbr. music ensembles; Profl. accomp.; Over 700 concerts in USA, UK, Germany & Austria. Mbrships: Pi Kappa Lambda; Phi Mu Alpha Sinfonia. Address: 157 Custer St., Laramie, WY 82070, USA.

LYDIATE, Frederick. Salford, UK. Pianist; Composer; Teacher. Educ: studied w. Dr. F H Wood; LRAM. m. Audrey Petttinger, 2 s., 1 d. Career: Concert Pianist/Accomp.; Theatre Conducting; Tchr. at schls. & pvtly; Perfs., BBC, Wigmore Hall etc. Comps. incl: 2 Str. Quartets; Chamber Concertino (piano & 9 Instruments); Clarinet Quintet; Quartet for Oboe, violin, viola, harp; wind Quintet; Four Pieces for Wind Quartet; Poem for Flute & Harp; Piano Sonata; Midinetts; Blarney Stone; 'Crisis' (words by Hassall for tenor voice, clarinet, horn & str. quartet) Piano Quintet 1975; Sonata for violin & piano, 1975; Dialogues for flute & harpsichord/piano, 1974. Recordings incl: Touch & Go; Thunder God (orchl.); Piano Sonata No. 1, Mbr., CGGB. Hobbies: Art; Philosophy. Address: 274 Binley Rd., Conventry CV3 1HT, UK.

LYDZINSKI, Kazimierz Alexander, b. 10 Aug. 1917. Nieder-Stradam, Germany. Cellist; Composer. Educ: Grad., Coll., Torun & Poland; Grad., Conserv., Torun, 1939; London Violoncello Schl. of Prof. Herbert Walen, 1946-47; studied cello w. Dr. Ruth Waddel, Edinburgh, bagpipe w. Wm. Ross, Edinburgh & comp. w. Karol Szymanowski. Career: solo, chmbr. & symph. activities throughout N & S Am.; Former mbr., Havana Philharmonic, Havana, Cuba; currently Cellist, Okla. Symph. Comps: Concerto for bagpipe & orch.; Souvenir of Scotland for bagpipe & orch.; Symphonic Ldyll for bagpipe, harp & orchl Antiphonia Rexis Poloniae (adagio for cello & organ); Concerto for Flute & Orch.; Symph. No. 1 in C major. var. orchl. transcriptions of chmbr. & solo works for cello. Hobbies: Gardening; Numismatics. Address: 434 N W 20th St., Oklahoma City, OK 73103, USA.

LYKKEBO, Finn, b. 1 Jan. 1937. Sollerod, Holte, Denmark. Professor. Educ: Studied Organ, Theory, Music Hist., Comp., Royal Danish Conserv., 7 yrs. m. Kristen Lykkebo, 4 children (1 from former marriage). Debut: Nordic Youth Music Fest., 1962. Career: Sev. perfs. of works on radio; Music Drama on TV. Comps: Gravure 1 (Cello); Gravure 11 (Bassoon); Gravure III (Flute); Gravure IV (piano); Ikoner (Organ); 3 Songs, sonnets by Keats soprano, cello, clarinet & harp. Contbr. to Dansk Musiktidsskrift. Mbrships: Danish Asns. Comps; Young Musicians Union. Hons: Grants, State Cultural Fund, 1973. 75. Address: Sondersig PR68955, Outrop, Denmark.

LYMPANY, Moura, b. 18 Aug. 1916. Saltash, UK. Pianist. Educ: FRAM; Studied w. Ambrose Coviello, RAM; W. Paul Weingarten, Vienna; Mathilde Verne, Tobias Matthay & Edward Steverman. Debut: Harrogate, UK, aged 12 yrs. Career: Apps. worldwide & w. maj. orchs. Recordings on HMV; Decca 1.

LYNCASTER, Rhodes, b. 27 Aug. 1927. Burnaby, BC, Can. Singer; Pianist; Composer; Actress. Educ: studied piano voice & comp. w. pvte. tchrs., Vancouver, BC; 3 yr. voice scholarship, Nan-Goodwin Studios, Vancouver, 1945-48. Debut: Theatre Under the Stars, Vancouver, 1948. Career: Singer, Your Guest show, CBC radio-Vancouver, 1950; Singer-Actress, Roadshow series, CBC radio-Montreal, 1951-52; TV apps., Singer-Dancer, Los Angeles, 1950, ABC & CBS. Comps: The Christmas Bells; By My Lovin' Baby. Recordings: It's Christmas in Hawaii, 1960. Mbrships: incl. PRO Can.; Am. Fedn. of Musicians, Local 145. Hobbies: Gardening; Astrol.; Astronomy. Mgmt: Amalgamated Artists (Alex McCallum), 1227 Richards St., Room 1, Vancouver, BC, Can. Address: No. 109-2233 W. 3rd Ave., Vancouver, BC, Can. VK, 1L5.

LYNE, Peter Howard, b. 21 July 1946. Northampton, UK. Composer; Music Teacher. Educ: Worcester Coll., Oxford; BA (Music); BMus (Oxon); MA (Oxon). m. Annika Ingeborg Eriksson, 1 d. Career: Hd. of Music, Kursverksamheten vid Stockholms Universitet, 1973-; Music Advsr., Studieforbundet Folkuniversitet, 1977-. Comps: Grisens röst (The Voice of the Pig), for soprano, & 12 instruments, 1972; Contracts for Orch., 1974-75; Conflict (text, Matthew Arnold) for baritone & 4 Str. Quartets, 1976-77; Fern Hill (Text, Dylan Thomas), for soprano, 6 instruments & percussion, 1977. Recording: 3 Epigrams for recorder quartet, 1974. Publs: Hilding Rosenberg - a catalogue of works, 1977; Hilding Rosenberg, 197; co-author, Musiklyssning, 1979. mbr. Swedish Comps. Assn. Hon: Hadow Music Scholar, Worcester Coll., Oxford, 1965-68. Hobby: Chess. Address: Väntorsvägen 221, 12532 Älvsjö, Sweden.

LYNEX, Penelope Norah, b. 30 Aug. 1936. London, UK. Cellist. Educ: RAM, ARAM, 1965. m. John Hugh Hamon Massey Stewart, 1 s., 1 d. Debut: Wigmore Hall, London. Career: recitals & concerto perfs., UK; broadcasts, Netherlands & UK; apps. on TV & BBC TV; Tchr., Exhibitioners, RAM. Mbr., ISM. Hobbies: Reading; Gardening; Nature Study. Address: 32D Abbey Rd., London NW8 9AX, UK.

LYON, David Norman, b. 29 Dec. 1938. Walsall, Staff., UK. Composer; also as Leo Norman; Pianist. Educ: RAM. m. Kate, 1 s. Compositions: Divertimento for Small Orchestra; Dance Prelude; Little Suite for Brass Trio; Trio for Violin; Horn & Piano. (as Leo Norman), Short Suite for Strings; Overture 'Joie de Vivré; Piano Concerto; God's Grandeur (song cycle); Horn Trio; String Quartet; The Reckoning (children's opera); var. works for light orch. inclng: Divertimento; Short Suite for Strings; Fantasia on a Nursery Song; Dance Prelude. Hons: RAOS Young Composer Award, 1963, Eric Coates Prize, 1964; Royal Phil. Soc. Prize, 1964. Hobbies: Cinema; Home Brewing. Address: Coombe Terr. House, Coombe, Rd., Wotton-under-Edge, Glos., G212 7NA, UK. 3, 28.

LYON, James, . 26 July 1954. Lausanne, Switz. Cellist; Cello teacher. Educ: Lauréat de Conserv. de Lausanne, Bordeaux; pupil of Jacques Neilz, Paris, & Willy Hauer, Lausanne. Debut: Orch. de Chambre de Bordeaux, 1973. Career: mbr. var. orchs. incl: Orch. Nat. de France, Orch. des Concert Lamoureux Paris), Orch. Paseloup (Paris), Ensemble Instrmental Andrée Colson; solo recitals & concerts in France, Belgium, Switz., Italy, Egypt, India, Thailand, Hong Kong, Korea, Bulgaria; mbr., Duo w. pianist H Surmelian; Prof. of Cello, l'École Nat. de Musique, Troyes, France. Recordings: sonatas for cello & piano by Alberic Magnard & Yvon Bourrel. mbr., Société des Concerts Pasdeloup. recip., Médaille d'Honneur ville de Bordeaux Musique de Chambre, 1974. Address: 29, Chemin de Chandieu, 1006 Lausanne, Switz.

LYON, John Thomas, Jr., b. 21 Sept. 1930. Rochester, Vt., USA. College Music Educator; Choral Director; Singer (Tenor); Specialist in Music Education. Educ: BS, Univ. of NH; MA, Music & Music Educ., Columbia Univ.; PhD Music Educ., Ind. Univ.; studied voice w. Karl Bratton, Margaret Harshaw. m. Joyce Glascock, 3 s., 1 d. Career: Has taught at W Va. Inst. of Technol., Tarkio Coll. & James Madison Univ., Va.; Tchr., Vocal & Instrumental Music Pub. Schls., Va.; Tenor Soloist, Oratorios, Opera, TV; Cond., Civic, indl., fraternal & fest. choruses; Clinician; Adjudicator; currently co-ord. of Music Educ., James Madison Univ. Contbr. to: W Va. & Va. Music Educ. Asns. Jrnls. Mbrships. incl: State Rsch. Chmn., State Student Chmn., MENC; Coll. Sect. Pres., Va. Music Educ. Assn. Hobbies: Gardening; Carpentry. Address: 620 Circle Dr., Harrisonburg, VA 22801, USA. 29.

LYON, Raymond Michel (pseud. Michel Lorin), b. 27 Oct. 1908. Neuilly-Seine, France. Music Critic; Musicologist. Educ: Bach. és Sciences, Faculté des Sciences de Paris; musically self-taught. m. Isabelle Legros, 3 s., 1 d. Career: music critic, 1928-; musicologist, 1945-; radio progs., 1932-35; radio prod., 1949, 1961-63, 1976-78; designer & producer musical prods. sev. recordings. Publs: Jacques Offenbach, 1946; Guide de l'Amateur de Microsillon, 1955; Apercus sur la Musique, 1959. Contbr. to: Dictionnaire Bordas, Ency. Clartés; Ed., Le Courrier Musical de France; Ed., late Guide du Concert et du Disque; articles in var. mags. mbr., num. profl. socs., incl. SACEM, Société Francaise de Musicologie. Hons: Chevalier de la Legion d'Honneur (France); Officier du Merite Cultural (Monaco). Hobby: Photography. Address: 7 Residence Beausoleil, 92210 Saint Cloud, France.

LYONS, James, b. 3 Sept. 1954. Balt., Md., USA. Pianist; Musicologist; Teacher. Educ: BA, Frostburg State Coll.; studied musicol., Univ. of Md. studied piano w. Shoko Gesell & James Pierce; studied comp. w. Jon Bauman. m. Loretta Lyon. Career:

Specialist in vocal music, Carroll Co., Md., Public Schls., 1979; Dir. of Music, Trinity United Methodist Ch., Cumberland, Md., 1974-76; special interests in musicol. studies in conjunction w. other humanistic disciplines, Stravinsky, condng. & accompng., comp. Mbrships: Am. Musicol. Soc.; Phi Mu Alpha Sinfonia. Hobbies: Lt.; Cooking; Gardening; Hiking. Address: 50 Main St., PO Box 37, New Market, MD 21774, USA.

LYONS, (Lorna) Jean Elderkin. b. Vancouver, BC, Can. Musician. Educ: ATCM Dip., Royal Conserv. of Music, Toronto, Can.; Cornish Schl. of Music, Seattle, USA: LRSM; piano studies w. Alberto Gurreto, Arthur Benjamin, Max Pirani, Stephen Balogh, comp. w. Healey Willan, & orchestration w. Ettore Mazzoleni. Career: Piano Tchr., Conserv. of Music, Vancouver; estbld. Jean Lyons Schl. of Music; Dir., Pacific Publrs., Publs: Grade One Theory (revised 1975); Grade Two Theory (revised 1977); Harmony (2 vols.); A History of Music (2 vols.); Form in Music. Mbrships: Dir., Can. Music Competition; ARCT Assn.; Jeunesses Musicales. Address: Suite 38-777 Burrard St., Vancouver, BC, Canada V6Z 1X7. 27, 29.

LYONS, Vicky. b. London, UK. Music Teacher. Educ: Studied clarinet w. Prof. O'Keefe, Trinity Coll., London & privately; London Coll. Music Dip., ALCM (CLT PFG). Career: Clarinet Tchr., Winchester Coll., Coll. Quiristers & Pilgrims Cathedral Schl., 1968; Sr. Clarinet Tchr., Winchester Coll., 1971; Sr. Clarinet Tch., Bedales Schl., Petersfield, 1972; Pvte. Tchr., Clarinet, Piano, Musicianship & Theory. Mbrships: Incorp. Soc. of Musicians; ISM Profl. Register of Pvte. Tchrs. of Music; ISM Southampton Dist. Ctr. Committee. Hobbies: Politics; Current Affairs; Reading. Address: 15 Woodgreen Rd., Winchester, Hants., UK.

LYSY, Alberto. b. 11 Feb. 1935. Buenos Aires, Argentina. Violinist; Teacher. Educ: studied w. Ljerko Spiller, Argentina, div. 4 c. Career: solo recitals & perfs. w. orchs. in Italy, France, Belgium, Switz., Netherlands, Germany, UK, Spain, Greece, Israel, Japan, India, USA, USSR, S Am.; Dir., Camerata Lysy Gstaad; Dir., Int. Menuhin Acad., Gstaad. Hons. incl: Prizewinner, Queen Elisabeth of Belgium Int. Competition, Brussels, 1955. Hobbies: Cross Country Skiing; Chess; Football. Address: Chalet Angela, Gstaad, Switz.

M

MA, Hiao-Tsiun, b. 11 July 1912l, Ningpo, China. Professor; Music Director; Conductor. Educ: BA, Nat. Ctrl. Univ., Nanking; Ecole Cesar Franck, Paris, France; Conserv. Nat. Musique Paris; PhD, Univ. Paris. m. Marina Loo, 1 s., 1 d. Career: Music Dir. & Cond., Children's Orch. NY, USA, 1962-; Dir., Ecole Cesar Franck, Paris, 1976. Comps. incl: Etudes for string orch.; Hommage a Bach for string orch.; Suzy (comic opera). Publs: La Musique Chinoise de Style European, 1941; Man-t'an yin-yue ti hiue-si yu kiao-hiue, (Causerie sur les etudes et l'enseignement de la musique), 1976. Contbr. to var. profl. publs. Mbrships: Soc. Authors, Comps. & Music Eds., Paris; Soc. Dramatic Authors; Int. Soc. Musicol. Hobby: Painting. Address: Ecole Cesar Franck, 8 Rue Git-le-Coeur, 75006 Paris, France.

MA, Si-Hon, b. 3 Apr. 1925, Canton, China. Violinist. Educ: Master's Degree, 1950, Artist's Dip., 1952, New England Conserv. of Music. m. Kwong-Kwong Tung. Debut: NYC, 1956. Career: 2 world tours, 1960, 1964; Concerts in USA & Can., 1963-; Recorded extensively for European radios, 1957-. Recordings: Beethoven, Sonata Op. 47, A Maj. for Violin & Piano; Mozart, Sonata in C, K 296 for Piano & Violin. Mbrships: Fndr. & Pres., Si-Yo Music Soc. Fndn., Inc., NYC; Music Dir., Pace Univ. Chmbr. Music Series. Inventor of Roth-Sihon mutes for violin, viola, cello & doublebass. Hons. incl: Am. Heritage Award, JFK Lib. for Minorities, 1972. Mgmt: Columbia Artists Mgmt. Address: 1553 Stratford Dr., Kent, OH 44240, USA.

MAAG, Peter, b. 10 May 1919, St. Gallen, Switz. Conductor; Pianist. Educ: Univs. of Zürich & Geneva; studied under Ernest Ansermet, Wilhelm Furtwängler, Alfred Cortôt. m. Marika Franchi, 1 d. Career: Chief Cond., Bonn Opera, 1954-59; Freelance until 1964; Chief Cond., Vienna Volksoper, 1964-67; Art Dir., Parma Opera, 1971-77; Artistic Dir., Turin Opera, 1977-; Freelance Cond. w. concerts throughout the world. Recordings: Decca; DGG; Vox; Japan Columbia. Hons: Toscanini Medal, Parma, 1971; Toscanini Baton, ibid., 1975. Hobbies: Skiing; Sailing; Swimming. Mgmt: ICM (USA) Hilbert, Paris (World). Address: Crastota, Pontresina, Switz.

MAASSEN, Jacques Johannes Josephus Maria, b. 4 Dec. 1947, Breda, Netherlands. Musicologist; Music Teacher; Carillonneur. Educ: State Univ., Utrecht; Dutch Carillon Schl., Amersfoort. m. Jentje Baker. Debut: Breda, 1966. Career: Sev. broadcasts, Dutch Broadcasting Org.; carillon recitals in Netherlands, UK, German Fed. Repub., France, USA, Can.; Ed., Klok en Klepel mag. Comps: Praeludium, Variatio en Fugato, 1968; Passacaglia, 1970; Reflexies, 1974; Inscripties; 4 Etudes (all for carillon). Publs: Klokkenspellen te Breda, 1501-1742, 1972. Contbr. to: Klok en Klepel; Mens en Melodie; Muziek en Onderwys. Mbrships: Exec. Committee, Dutch Carillon Guild (VP); Exec. Committee, World Carillon Fedn.; Dutch Musicol. Soc.; Dutch Guild of Music Tchrs. Recip., num. prizes as carillonneur, also 1st Prize, Toon van Balkom comp. competition, 's Hertogenbosch, 1974. Address: Generaal van der Plaatstraat 14, Breda, Netherlands.

MAASZ, Gerhard, b. 9 Feb. 1906, Hamburg, W. Germany. Comp: Cond. Educ: Autodidact. m. Beatrice Ballmer, 2 s. Debut: Arosa, 1922. Career: 1922-1925 European tours w. Hass-Berkow-Spielen; Cond. City Theater Osnabruck, Regional Theater Braunschweig; 1929-1936 Cond., program advsr. Radio Hamburg; 1939-1944 Cond. Würtemberg Regional orch., Stuttgart; since 1951 Mus. dir. TV operas; freelance comp. & cond., 1966-; Visiting cond.; Lectrs. Comp. incl: Orch. works; Chmbr. music; Schl. music; Dance music; Piano works; Choir works; Music for folkloric instruments; Opera; Theater, film music. Recordings: var. of own works. Mbrships: Brahms Soc., Hamburg (hon. mbr.). recip. Brahms Medal, Hamburg. Hobbies: Brahms Archives. Address: Ronco 5, Ascona, Capella Gruppaldo, CH 6622, Switz.

MAAZEL, Lorin, b. 6 Mar. 1930, Neuilly, France. Conductor. Educ: Univ. of Pitts., Pa., USA, 1951; studied baroque music, Italy, 1951; Berkshire Music Ctr., Tanglewood, Mass., summers 1951, 1952; studied Cond. & Violin w. Vladimir Bakaleinikoff, Pitts. m. Israela Margalit, 1 s., 2 d. Career: Cond., Bayreuth Fest., 1960, 1968, 1969; Cond., Met. Opera, NYC, 1962; Artistic Dir., W Berlin Opera, 1965-71; Music Dir., Berlin Radio Symph. Orch., 1965-; Cond., La Scala, Milan, 1966 & 1967, & Vienna Opera, 1966; Assoc. Prin. Cond., New Philharmonia of London, 1970-72; Music Dir., The

Cleveland Orch., Ohio, USA. 1972-. Recordings: num. recordings, w. above orchs., & other major orchs. thru'out Europe, inclng. works of Bach, Beethoven, Mozart, Strauss, Tchaikovsky, Prokofiev & Stravinsky. Mbrships: Int. Platform Assn.; Pitts. Musical Soc. Hons: Fulbright Fellowship, 1951; D Mus., Pitts., Univ., 1968; HHD., Beaver Coll. Address: The Cleveland Orchestra, Severance Hall, Cleveland, OH 44106, USA. 2, 4.

MACAL, Zdenek, b. 8 Jan. 1936, Brno, Czech. Conductor. Educ: Conserv. of Music; High Schl. of Music, Janacek Acad. Career: Cond. of leading orchs. throughout Europe & Am.; Czech Phil. Orch., 1966-68; Gen. Music Dir., Cologne Radio Symph. Orch., 1970-74; currently Music Dir., Hannover Radio Orch. num. recordings esp. w. Czech Phil. Hons. incl: Int. Conds. Competition, Besancon, 1965; Mitropoulos Competition, NY, 1966. Address: Postfach 117, 6000 Lucerne 14, Switz.

MCALLISTER, Forrest Lee, b. 8 July 1912, Joliet, Ill., USA. Editor & Publisher; Composer; Author; Lecturer; Conductor; Adjudicator. Educ: De Paul Univ.; VanderCook Coll. of Music. m. Lois June Cooley, 3 d. Career: Hd. of Music Dept.; Schl. for Special Servs., Wash. & Lee Univ., Lexington, Va., 2 yrs. during WWII; Dir. of Recreation for the five Northwest States of the VA, following WWII; Dir. of Rsch. & Educ. of the Am. Music Conf., 1948; Has judged band, orch. & choral contests in almost every state, which includes, State, Regl. & Nat. categoreis; Acts as Guest Cond., clinic dir., curriculum cons., adjudicator & lectr.; Has adjudicated at Canadian-Am. Music Fests. held at Moose Jaw, Sask., Abbotsford, BC & London, Ont.; Has been Guest Cond. in Nice, France & Tokyo, Japan; has been an annual adjudicator & guest cond. of the combined hon. band, orch. & chorus at the Tri-State Music Fest., Enid, Okla., over 20 yrs.; Ed. & Publsr. of the Schl. Musician Director & Tchr. Mag., 1951-; Cons. to Am. Schl. Band Dirs. Assn., Phi Beta Mu, Nat. Cath. Bandmasters Assn., over 10 yrs.; Bd. Dirs., John Philip Sousa Meml., Inc. & the ABA Rsch. Ctr.; Took active part in the formation of the N. Am. Band Dirs. Coordinating Coun. & is the perm. Exec. Sec.-Treas.; Bd. Dirs. Compositions: Karen Overture; Pastore D'asiago - Carl Fischer, etc. Fine Arts Fndn. of Phillips Univ., Enid, Okla. Recip. many hons. Address: 516 Middletree Rd., Sugar Creek, Joliet, IL 60433, USA.

MCALLISTER, Maureen, b. 1 Sept. 1941, London, UK. Organist; Recorder Player; Teacher. Educ. incls: FRCO; LRAM; ARCM; A Mus TCL; LTCL; 2 Dip. de Merito, 1 Dip. Effetivo, Acad. Musicale Chigiana, Siena. m. Robin Jackson, 1 s. Career incls: num. recitals in cathedrals, town halls, at fests., etc.; Prof., London Coll. of Music; Vis. Organ Lectr., Hendon Polytechnic; Recorder Tchr., Inner London Educ. Auth.; adjudicator, UK fests. Has recorded for BBC. Contbr. to: Recorder & Music Mag. Mbrships: RCO; LCM Soc.; Soc. or Recorder Players. Recip. Italian Govt. scholarships, 1966, 67. Hobbies: Reading; Theatre; Cooking; Gardening. Mgmt: Helen Jennings Concert Agcy.; Terry Slasberg Agcy. Address: Lamorna, The Forsters, Langley Heath, Maidstone, Kent, UK.

MACATSORIS, Christofer, b. 25 Dec. 1936, Phila., Pa., USA. Conductor; Pianist. Educ: Univ. of Pa.; Tempe Univ.; Grad. in Comp., Phila. Conserv. of Music; studied comp., Milan, Italy. Debut: w. Phila. Lyric Opera Co., 1964. Career: Cond., Phila. Lyric Opera Co., Wilmington Opera, Pa. Opera Co.; Cond., Ambler Fest.; Accomp. for sev. Met. Opera singers; Musical Dir., Weekly TV opera prog., NBC, Phila., 1963-65; currently Fac. mbr., Curtis Inst. of Music, Phila. Mbr., Nat. Inst. Lit. & Sci. Hobbies: Art History; Oenology. Address: 1142 Snyder Ave., Phila., PA 19148, USA.

McBAY, Alexander Douglas, b. 24 Mar. 1943, Aberdeen, Scotland, UK. Teacher of Music (organ, piano, voice); Conductor. Educ: Dip. Mus. Ed., RSAM, 1964; ARCO, London, 1971. m. Lesley Elizabeth McLeod Martin, 1 s., 1 d. Career: Music Tchr., Renfrew Educ. Comm., 1965-67, Aberdeenshire, 1967-72, Dumfriesshire, 1972-74, Borders Reg. Coun., 1975-76, Dumfries & Galloway, 1976-; Organist & Choirmaster, Langholm Parish Ch.; Musical Dir., Langholm Town Brass Band. Recordings: The Bard. Mbrships: ISM; RCO. Hons. incl: Dunbartonshire Prize, RSAM, 1964. Hobbies incl: Walking. Address: 1 Esk Pl., Langholm, Dumfries & Galloway, DG13 OBD, UK.

MCCABE, John, b. 21 Apr. 1939, Huyton, Lancs., UK. Composer; Pianist. Educ: MusB, Manchester Univ.; Royal Manchester Coll. of Music; Munich Music Acad. m. Monica Christine Smith. Career: Concert & recital pianist & chmbr. music performances in var. countries; Radio & TV appearances in UK & USA. Compositions incl: Symphs. & Concerti; Notturni ed Alba for soprano & orch.; The Chagall Windows for orch.; Hartmann Variations for orch.; opera - The Play of Mother Courage, & The Lion, The Witch, & The Wardrobe; ballets - Mary Queen of Scots, & The Teachings of Don Juan; var.

orchl. works; chmbr. music; organ, piano & choral music. Recordings: complete piano music of Haydn, Nielsen, etc. Publs: Rachmaninov, 1974; Bartok's Orchestral Music, 1974. Mbrships: Exec. Comm. & Coun., Soc. for Promotion of New Music; Inc. Soc. of Musicians. Hobbies incl: Books; Films; Cricket. Address: 49 Burns Ave., Southall, Middx., UK.

McCABE, Robin, b. 7 Nov. 1949, Puyallup, Wash., USA. Pianist. Educ: BMus, Univ. of Wash., 1971; MMus, 1973, DMus A, 1978, Juilliard Schl. Debut: Carnegie Recital Hall, NYC, 1975. Career incls: concerts throughout USA, Can. & Europe; US State Dept. recital tours in S. Am., 1975-76; Artist-Tchr., Fac. of Shawnigan Summer Arts Fest., Victoria, BC, Can., 1975-79; Nat. TV recitals; Duo recital w. violinist Ruggiero Ricci, Carnegie Hall, NYC, 1976; fac., Juilliard Schl. Recordings: Solo and as duo w. Ruggiero Ricci. Contbr. to: NW arts Mag. Mbrships: Nat. Mortar Bd. Soc.; Alpha Lambda Delta; Mu Phi Epsilon. Hons. incl: Winner, Nat. Music Tchrs. of Am. Competition, 1971 Concert Artist's Guild Int. Competition, 1971 Concert Artist's Guild Int. Competition, 1975; Recip., Matha Baird Rockefeller Grant, 1978. Hobbies: Jazz; Literature; Skiing; Tennis; Swimming; Mushroom Hunting. Mgmt: Herbert Barrett, 1860 Broadway, NYC 10023, USA. Address: 160 W 73rd St., NYC, NY 10023, USA.

McCAIN, Barry Reid, b. 27 Oct. 1951, Jackson, Miss., USA. Performer on Bagpipes & Guitar. Educ: Jackson State Univ. div., 1 d. Career: plays Scots Highland Bagpipes; Folk Guitarist; apps. at local functions. Mbr., Clan Donald Soc., USA. Hobbies: Reading; Backpacking; Ancient & Medieval Gaelic Culture. Address: 1879 Smallwood, Jackson, MS 39212, USA.

McCALDIN, Denis, b. 28 May 1933, Nottingham, UK. Conductor. Educ: BSc., PhD, Nottingham Univ.; BMus., B'ham Univ. m. Margaret Smith, 1 s., 1 d. Career: Cond., Dir., Lancaster Univ. Concerts; Guest appearances cond. Royal Liverpool Phil. Orch., London Mozart Players, Royal Phil. Orch., Cumbria Concertante, etc., 1970-; BBC Radio 3, etc. Publs: Stravinsky, 1972; Contbr. to Beethoven Companion, 1972; Ed., Berlioz Te Deum, 1973. Contbr. to: Music Review; Musical Times; Music & Musicians; Music in Education; Times Higher Educ. Supplement; Soundings, etc. Mbrships: ISM; RMA. Hobbies: Good food & music. Address: co the Music Rooms, Lancaster Univ., Lancaster, UK. 3.

McCANN, John R, b. 23 Nov. 1933, San Mateo, Calif., USA. Cornett Maker. Educ: BA, San Jose State Univ., 1955; MA, Univ. of Southern Calif., 1974. m. Monica Hammond McCann. Career: began making instruments as hobby, turning professional in 1975. Mbrships: AMIS; Am. Recorder Soc. Hobbies: Outdoor activities. Address: 5918 Merritt Pl., Falls Church, VA 22041, USA.

McCARROLL, Jesse Cornelius, b. 12 July 1933, Dayton, Ala., USA. College Professor; Pianist. Educ: B Mus (Piano), Cleveland Inst. of Music, Ohio; MA, Profl. Dip., EdD, Tchrs. Coll., Columbia Univ.; Mannheim Schl. of Music, Germany; NY State Cert., Music Supvsr., Secondary Schls. Career: Asst. Prof., NYC Community Coll., CUNY; Lectr., workshops & confs.; Concert apps., W Africa, & USA. Mbrships: MENC; NY State MTA; NY State Music Theory Soc.; Doct. Assn. NY Educators; AAUP; Phi Mu Alphs Sinfonia (Pres., Beta Gamma Chapt., Tchrs. Coll., Columbia, 3 yrs.); Phi Delta Kappa; Kappa Delta Pi; Profl. Staff Congress, CUNY. Hons. Scholarship Student, Karamu House, Cleveland, 1959-60. Hobbies: Bike Riding; Reading; Travelling. Address: 645 Water St., NY, NY 10002, USA.

McCARTHY, Eileen, b. London, UK. Violoncellist. Educ: RAM; ARAM; LRAM. m. Herbert Arthur Lawrence, 1 s., 1 d. Debut: Wigmore Hall, London. Career: Mbr., Boyd Neel Orch. & the Philomusica; apps. w. Menuhin Fest. Orch.; Mbr., Carter String Trio; BBC radio & TV broadcasts; has toured 15 countries. Recordings: w. Boyd Neel Orch. & Philomusica; horn quintets. Mbr., ISM. Hons: Sir Edward Cooper Prize; Herbert Withers Prize; Alessandro Pezzo Prize. Address: Flat 5, 93 Elm Park Gdns., London SW3, UK.

McCARTHY, Margaret Patricia, b. 27 Sept. 1928, Melbourne, Aust. Music Librarian; Teacher. Educ: Dip. (piano, singing), Melbourne Univ., 1948; BMus, ibid., 1950; Dip.Ed., ibid., 1970; Dip., Librarianship, Melbourne State Coll., 1977; Assoc., Lib. Assn. of Aust., 1978. m. Neville J McCarthy, 3 s., 2 d. Publs: A Report on Victorian Educational String Music, 1976; Report on Music Libraries Visited (1975-76) in UK, 1976; A Descriptive Inventory of Music Manuscripts & Research Materials Held on Microfilm in Australian Libraries, 1978. Contbr. to: Aust. Jrnl. of Music Educ.; Continuo. Mbrships: Int. Assn. of Music Libs.; Int. Soc. for Music Educ.; Liub. Assn. of Aust.; Aust. Soc. for Music Educ.; Aust. Strg. Tchrs. Assn. Hobbies: Youth Music Activities; Viola Playing;

Horticulture; Reading. Address: 891 Glenferrie Rd., Kew, Melbourne, Vic. 3101, Aust.

McCARTY, Frank L, b. 10 Nov. 1941, Pomona, Calif., USA. Composer; Clarinettist; Assistant Professor of Music; Performer on Electronic Instruments, Percussion, Clarinet & Saxophone. Educ: BA San Diego State Univ., 1963; MMus, Univ. of Southern Calif., 1965; PhD Univ. of Calif., San Diego, 1975. div., 1 s., 2 d. Career: Asst. Prof. of Music, Cal-State, Fullerton, 1966-71, & Univ. of Pitts., 1971-; Percussionist, San Diego Symph. Orch., 1967-71; Mbr., BIOME - Live Electronic Music Ensemble, 1970-. Compositions: Clocks (percussion ensemble); Color Etudes (solo tuba); Five Situations for Four Saxophones; Tam-Tammany I-II (concrete tape & lights); Suite - The Bacchae (electronic tape); Exitus for Band; Introduction to Percussion, arrangement so haydn Musical Clock Pieces for Mallet-Percussion Duos & Trios. Contbr. to jrnls. in field. Mbrships: Percussive Arts Soc.; Nat. Fedn. of Music Clubs; Phi Mu Alpha; LA Electronic Music Club; Musical Engrng. Soc. Hobbies: Designing Electronic Music Systems; Cooking. Address: 6819 1/2 Thomas Blvd., Pittsburgh, PA 15208, USA.

McCATHREN, Donald E, b. 6 July 1924, Gary, Ind., USA. Conductor; Clarinettist; Music Professor. Educ: BS in Musical Educ., Ind. State Univ.; Grad. Cert., USN Schl. of Music; MM, Ind. Univ. m. Millicent F McCathren, 1 s., 3 d. Career incls: USN Musician & Off.; Tchr., Chgo. Musical Coll., Ind. Univ. & Duquesne Univ.; Dir. of Educl. Servs. for the G Leblanc Corp.; Musical Dir., Am. Youth Symph. & Chorus & S Hills Symph. of Pitts., Pa.; num. fest. & other apps. as Cond. or Solo Clarinettist. Recordings: w. Am. Youth Symph. & Chorus, Duquesne Univ. Symphonic Band & Duquesne Univ. Symph. of Winds. Publs. incl: Saxophone Notebook; Clarinet Notebook; Bassoon Notebook; Oboe Notebook & Flute Notebook; Clarinet & Saxophone Fingering Charts. Contbr. to musical & educl. jrnls. Mbrships: incl: ASCAP; Conds. Div., Am. Symph. Orch. League; Pres. & Fndr., Am. Youth Symph. & Chorus; MENC. Recip., num. hons., inclng; D Mus, Huron Coll., 1969; Hon. Citizen of Interlaken, Switz., 1970. Address: 3651 Ashland Dr., Bethel Pk., PA 15102, USA.

McCAULEY, John J, b. 16 Nov. 1937, Des Moines, Iowa, USA. Pianist; Conductor; Teacher. Educ: BS, B Mus, Univ. of Ill.; MS, Juilliard Schl. of Music. Debut: Carnegie Recital Hall, NYC, 1975. Career: Num. concerts, also & chmbr. music, US East Coast & Midwest, & in Europe; frequent radio & TV apps. Mbrships: Int. Soc. for Contemporary Music; Am. Music Ctr. Hons: Tanglewood Fellowship, 1960; Juilliard Fellowship, 1964; Aspen Schl. Fellowship, 1964. Hobbies: Languages; Travel; Mountain Climbing; Literature. Address: Riverdale Country School, 253rd St. & Post Rd., Bronx, NY 10471, USA.

McCAW, John, b. 3 Nov. 1918, Kaitangata, NZ. Performer on Clarinet & Basset Horn. Educ: Studied privately w. father. John McCaw Sr., NZ.; LTCL, ARCM, RCM, London, UK. m. Ann Broomhead; 2 d. Debut: NZ. Broadcasting Serv. at age of 18 yrs. Career: Prin. Clarinet, NZ. Nat. Orch., London Phil. Orch., New Phil. Orch.; Solo appearances w. these orchs. & others; Concertos & chmbr. music for BBC radio, inclng. recitals w. pianist wife Ann Broomhead; Prof. of Clarinet, RCM. Recordings: Mozart & Nielsen Clarinet Concertos w. New Phil. Orch.; Josef Holbrooke Clarinet Quintet w. Delme Quartet. Mbr., ISM. Mgmt: B Graham, 35 Northwick Pk Rd., Harrow, Middx. Hobbies: Rsch. into acoustics & mechanics of clarinet; Gardening; Drawing; Cabinet making. Address: 15 Leinster Ave., London, SW147JW, UK. 3.

McCHESNEY, James, b. 2 Apr. 1941, Airdrie, Scotland, UK. Pianist. Educ: Perfs. Course, RSAM; Master Classes w. Paul Badura-Skoda, Alfred Brendel & Jörg Demus; Pvte. study w. P Badura-Skoda & Prof. Viola Thern. Debut: Troon. Career: Apps. in UK, Austria, Germany & Greece; apps. on Austrian & BBC radio; TV apps. in Scotland, Greece, Austria; Master-Class Asst. to Paul Badura-Skoda at the Folkwang Musikhochschule, Essen (Ruhr), Germany; Teaching Appt., Vienna Conserv.; Mbr., New Vienna Piano Trio. Recordings: Frank Sonata & Constantinidis Dances for Violin & Piano; Schumann "Scenes from Childhood" (w. Takis Ktenaveas). Mbr., ISM & Austrian Union for the Arts & Freelance Professions. Hobby: Trout & Salmon Fishing; Aviation. Mgmt: Choveaux Mgmt.; Mancroft Towers, Oulton Broad, Lowestoft, Suffolk, Uk. Address: 1160 Vienna, Thaliastrasse 96/21, Austria. 3, 28, 29, 30.

McCLARTY, Jack, b. 11 July 1938, Kalispell, MOnt., USA. Bands Director; Educator; Adjudicator; Professor of Music. Educ: B Mus. Ed., Univ. of Mont., 1960; M Mus Ed., Andrews Univ., 1964; Ed D., Univ. of Mont., 1968. m. 1 d. Career: Dir. of Bands, S. Missionary Coll., Tenn.; Band perfs., Houston Astrodome, 1970, Disney World, 1973, '76, '79; Judge, World Competition of Drum Crops, Notre Dame Univ., 1974; band Clinician. 1 band recording. Contbr. to profl. jrnls. Mbrships: Coll. Band Dirs. Nat. Assn.; Fellowship of Christian

Musicians; Nat. Security Coun.; Pi Kappa Lambda; Sigma Phi Epsilon; Deta Tau Kappa; Phi Mu Alpha. Hobbies: Musical judging; Water skiing; Tennis. Address: PO Box 544, Collegedale, TN, USA.

McCLEERY, Janet Mary, b. 10 May 1943, London, UK. Pianoforte & Organ Accompanist. Educ: RAM; FRCO; CRSM; LRAM (Pianoforte); LRAM (Singing). m. John H Box. Career: 3 concerts, Royal Fest. Hall; Many concerts, London, Home Cos., & Yorks; Sound track (w. Valerie Pardon) for film documentary on the piano ind. Recordings: 3 pvte. recordings for the Cathedral & Abbey Ch. of St. Albans, Herts., for St. Albans Schl. Mbrships: ISM; RAM Club. Hons: Henry Eyres Prize, RAM, 1964; May Turtle Gift, RAM, 1964. Hobbies: Reading; Cooking; Swimming. Address: 20 Gillian Ave., St. Albans, Herts, AL 12QH, UK.

McCLELLAN, William Monson, b. 7 Jan. 1934. Groton, Mass., USA. Music Librarian. Educ: BA (Music). Colo. Coll., Colo. Springs, 1956; AMLS. (Lib. Sci.), Univ. of Mich., Ann Arbor, 1959; MA (Musicol.), Colo. Coll., Colo. Springs, 1961. m. Jane Muir McClellan, 4 d. Career: Choral Music Instructor, Alamosa High Schl., Colo., 1956-58; Music Libn. & Instructor in Music, Univ. of Colo., Boulder, 1959-65; Music Libn. & Prof. of Lib. Admin., Univ. of Ill. at Urbana-Champaign, 1965-. Contbr. to panels & sessions at meetins of Music Lib. Assn.; Abstractor for Notes (jrnl. of Music Lib. Assn.), 1967-71, Editor of Notes, 1977-. Mbrships: Music Lib. Assn. (Pres. 1971-73); Assn. for Recorded Sound Collections: Int. Assn. Music Libs.; Am. Musicol. Soc. Hobbies: Gardening; Conjurer & Amateur Magician; Carpentry. Address: 1020 W Hill St., Champaign, IL 61820, USA.

McCLINTOCK, Robert Bayles, b. 3 Apr. 1946, Reno, Nev., USA. Conductor; Railwayman. Educ: BA, Calif. State Univ., Sacramento. Debut: as Cond., 1970. Career: Cond., Southern Pacific Railroad & AMTRAK; sev. apps. on local TV; Own radio show, Symphony Preview; Music Reviewer, Suttertown News. Comps. incl: num. chmbr. works, for instruments and/or voices; Hiawatha (ballet); Song Cycle; August Requiem. Hobby: Study of Japanese music, culture, language & lit. Address: 3016 Garfield Ave., Carmichael, CA 95608, USA.

McCOLL, William Duncan, b. 18 May 1933, Port Huron, Mich. USA. Clarinettist. Educ: Oberlin, 2 yrs.; Manhattan Schl. of Music, 1 yr.; Grad. w. Reifezeugnis, State Acad. of Music & Representational Arts, Vienna. m. Sue McColl. 1 s. Career: Solo Clarinettist, US Seventh Army Symph. Orch., 1957-58 & Philharmonia Hungarica, Vienna, 1959; Clarinettist. Festival Casals: Solo Clarinettist, Puerto Rico Symph. Orch. & Clarinet Instructor, Puerto Rico Conserv., 1960-68; Clarinettist. Soni Ventorum Wind Quintet, 1963-; Assoc. Prof., Univ. of Wash., 1968-; Bass clarinettist, Orquesta Filarmonica de las Americas (Mexico City), summers 1976-78. Recordings incl: Villa-Lobos Quintette en Forme de Choros; Villa - Lobos, Chorus No. 2; Villa-Lobos, Trio for bassoon, clarinet & oboe, quarter ditto w. flute; Reicha Quintet in G maj; Haydn Clock Organ pieces (arr. for Wind Quintet) Beethoven, Clock Organ pieces (arr. for Wind Quintet). Reicha-Quintet in E Minor; Danzi-Quintet in F major Poulene, Duo for clarinet & bassoon: Villa-Lobos, Trio for Clarinet, bassoon & piano. Address: c/o Dept. of Music, Univ. of Wash., Seattle, WA 98105, USA.

McCOLLOM, Thomas Oscar, b. 29 Jan. 1934, Stillwater, Okla., USA. Music Educator. Educ: B Mus, Okla. State Univ., 1956; B Mus, Yale Univ., 1957; M Mus, ibid., 1958; Cand. for D Mus Ed., Okla. Univ., 1976. m. Joyce Marie Megee, 2 d. Career: Soloist in performances of Mozart & Beethoven concerti w. Lawton Phil. Orch., Okla. & Okla. State Univ. Orch.; Tchr., Nat. Baldwin Keyboard Achievement Awards Winner, 1967; Asst. Prof. of Piano. Mbrships: incl: MTNA; Okla. MTA; Past Pres., Lawton MTA; Phi Mu Alpha Sinfonia, Nat. Guild Piano Tchrs.; Phi Kappa Phi; Phi Eta Sigma. Sev. hons. & awards. Hobbies: Camping; Motor Cycling. Address: 14 NW 60th, Lawton, Okla., USA.

McCORKLE, Donald M(acomber), b. 20 Feb. 1929, Cleveland, Ohio, USA. Musicologist; University Professor. Educ: B Mus, Bradley Univ., Peoria, Ill., 1951; MA, Ind. Univ., 1953; PhD, ibid., 1958; Post-doct. rsch., European music archives, 1967, 69, '71, '75 m. Margit Lundstrom McCorkle. Career incls: Dir. & Ed.-in-Chief, Moravian Music Fndn. Inc., Winston-Salem, NC, 1956-64; Prof., Musicol., Univ. Md., Coll. Pk., 1964-72; Univ. BC, 1972-; Hd., Dept. Music, ibid., 1972-75; Ed., num. eds. 18th-century music, Am., Engl. & German Moravians. Publs. incl: Moravian Music in Salem: A German-American Heritage, 1959; Compiler, A Descriptive Catalogue of the Autographs of Johannes Brahms, 1976. Contbr. to Jrnls. Mbr. profl. orgs. Hons. incl: Moramus Award, disting. serv. to Am. music, 1964. Hobbies incl: 18th Century antique furniture. Address: 1819 Acadia Rd., Vancouver, Canada V6T 1R2.

McCOY, Marvin M, b. 27 Dec. 1933, Clemons, Iowa, USA. Musician (French Horn); Freelance Artist; Horn Instructor. Educ: Univ. Iowa, 3 yrs.; w. Philip Farkas, Chgo., 1954-55; Froydis Ree Wekre, Oslo, Norway, 1975. m. Karen Mae Landsness, 4 children. Career: w. Dick Schory Percussion Pops Orch.; Henry Mancini & Andy Williams Tours; Chgo. Little Symph. Tours, Chgo. Chmbr. Orch. Tours; Solo Horn, St. Paul Opera Orch., 7 yrs.; Horn Instructor, var. colls., Minn., 1960-. Recordings: Dick Schory on Tour (w. Percussion Pops Orch.), 1964. Contbr. to Woodwind World, 1960-63. Mbrships: Int. Horn Soc.; Galpin Soc. Hobbies: Magic esp. sleight-on-hand & close-up work. Address: 3204 W 44th St., Minneapolis, MN 55410, USA.

McCREDIE, Andrew Dalgarno, b. 3 Sept. 1930, Sydney, NSW, Australia. Musicologist. Educ: BA, Univ. of Sydney, 1951; MA, ibid., 1958; Post-grad. Dips., Univ. of Copenhagen, 1956, Univ. of Stockholm, 1957; Dr. Phil., Univ. of Hamburg, 1963; NSW, State Conserv. of Music, 1949-52; RAM, London, 1953-55. m. Gertrud Rosner, 1 d. Career: Tutor, Lararehogskolan, Stockholm, 1957-59; Lectr. in Music for British Coun., Germcny, Austria; Italy & Yugoslavia, 1961-63; Guest Lectr., Univs. of Amsterdam & Utrecht, 1964; Sr. Rsch. Fellow in Musicol., Univ. of Adelaide, 1955-69; Sr. Lectr. in Music, ibid., 1970-73; Rdr. in Music, 1974-77; Prof., ibid., 1978-. Publ: Instrumentarium & Instrumentation in the North German Baroque Opera, 1964 Fndr. & Ed., Miscellanea Musicologica, 1966-. Ed. & contbr to var. music publs. inclng: Music & Letters, Music & letters. Mbrships. incl: Int., Am., French & German Musicological Socs.; Chmn., SA, Div., Int. Assn. of Music Libs.; Pres., Musicol. Assn. of SA; Chmn., Aust. Musicol. Cttee, Recip var. awards incl: rsch. fellowship & grant; Edward J Dent Medal, Fellow, Aust. Acad. of the Humanities, 1975. Hobbies: Travel; Collecting art books; Walking. Address: c/o Schl. of Music, Univ. of Adelaide, Adelaide, SA, Australia 5001.

McCRORY, Martha, b. 15 Aug. 1920, Quincy, Ill., USA. Educator; Cellist. Educ: B Mus, Univ. of Mich., 1941; M Mus, Eastman Schl. of Music; Artist's Dip. in Violoncello, ibid.; Postgrad. study, Univ. of London, UK. Career: All Am. Youth Orch.; Rochester Phil.; San Antonio Orch.; Nashville Symph.; Soloist, Chattanooga Symph., Huntsville Symph. etc.; Mgr., Chattanooga Symph; Assoc. Prof. of Music, Univ. of the S; Dir., Sewanee Summer Music Ctr. Mbrships: Nat. Fedn. of Music Clubs; Music Educators Nat. Assn.; AAUP; Past Pres., Tenn. Unit, Am. String Tchrs. Assn.; Musicians Union; Naras. Hobbies: Golf; Travel. Address: Univ. of the South, Sewanne, TN 37375, USA. 5, 7, 27.

McCUAIG, Ewen, b. 27 May 1931, Rosecrown, Sask., Canada. Organist & Pianist. Educ: ARCT, (piano); B Mus., Comp., Univ. of Toronto; Post grad. studies at the Hochschule für Musik, Frankfurt, Germany. m. Jane Martin. Career: Num. CBC radio recitals as soloist & as accompanist; Sev. CBC-TV & CTV-TV appearances as duo-pianist & accompanist; Num. public recitals; Complete organ works of Franck in two recitals in Ottawa, 1973; Soloist in concert of organ & brass at the Nat. Arts Ctr., Ottawa, Sponsored by NAC - CBC, 1974; Organist, Anglican Ch. of St. John the Evangelist, Ottawa. Recordings: Songs of Shakespeare for Folkways of NY w. tenor Tom Kines. Mbr., CCO. Address: 134 McLeod St., Ottawa, KP2-OZ7, Canada.

McCULLOH, Byron, b. 1 Mar. 1927, Okla. City, USA. Bass Trombonist; Lecturer. Educ: BMus, MMus, Perf. Cert. in Trombone, Eastman Schl. of Music, Rochester, NY. m. Natalie Martin McCulloh, 1 s., 1 d. Career: Bass-trombonist, Okla. City Symph., 1951-52; St. Louis Symph., 1952-56; Pittsburgh Symph., 1956-; Chautauqua Symph., summers, 1959-69; Artist-Lectr., Carnegie-Mellon Univ., 1969-; Assoc. Prof., Eastman Schl. of Music, 1977-78. Comps. incl: 1 symph. 2 str. quartets, instrumental music, esp. for trombones & other brass. Mbrships: ASCAP; Am. Music Ctr.; Fndr. mbr., Pittsburgh Alliance of Comps.; Coll. Music Soc.; Int. Congress of Symph. & Opera Musicians. Hobbies: Sailing; Cooking. Address: 1306 Penn Ave., Pittsburgh, PA 15221, USA.

McCULLOUGH, Charles Harold, b. 29 Mar. 1938, Dallas, Tex., USA. Pianist; Teacher. Educ: B Mus, Southern Meth. Univ., Dallas, Tes.; M Mus, Univ. Ind., Bloomington. m. Juliette Anne Norman, 1 d. Debut: w. Paul Kletski & Dallas Symph. Orch., Dallas. Career incls: Apps. in USA, Europe & Mexico; Instr., piano, Ithaca Coll., NY, 1973-75; currently, Asst. Prof., piano, N Tex. State Univ., Denton. Mbrships: Pi Kappa Lambda; Phi Mu Alpha. Hons. incl: Winner, GB Dealey Piano Competition, 1960; Special Citation 'Outstanding Virtuoso', Alfredo Casella Int. Piano Competition, 1964; Fulbright-Hays Schlrship., Germany,

1966-67. Hobbies: Making wine & beer. Address: co Music Schl., N Tex. State Univ., Denton, TX 76203, USA.

McCULLOUGH, Oscar James, b. 17 Aug. 1922, Cleveland, Ohio, USA. Opera & Concert Singer (Baritone); Educator. Educ: B Mus, Baldwin Wallace Coll., 1948; M Mus & Perfs. Cert., Eastman Schl. of Music, Univ. of Rochester, NY, 1952; Summer Sessions, Mozarteum, 1961 & Meadow Brook Schl. of Music, 1967 & '68. m. Marion H Schuster, 1 s., 1 d. Debut: NYC, 1963. Career: Recitals & Guest Soloist w. Orchs. in Opera Oratorio & Chmbr. Orchs., USA. Can., Dublin, Repub. of Ireland, Paris, France, Stuttgart, Freiburg & Bonn, Germany; Guest Soloist, Colonial Williamsburg, Gov's. Palace Candlelight Concerts, 10 yrs.; Perfs. w. Robert Shaw, Roger Wagner & Howard Hanson, Assoc. Prof., Music, Hollins Coll., Va., USA. Recordings: Handel's Italian Cantata - Cuopre tal volta il cielo; Hermann Reutter Lieder. Mbrships: Phi Mu Alpha Sinfonia; Nat. Assn. of Tchrs. of Singing. Hobby: Gardening. Address: Hollins Coll., VA 24020, USA.

McDERMOTT, Vincent, b. 5 Sept. 1933, Atlantic City, NJ, USA. Composer; Ethnomusicologist; Educator. Educ: BFA, Univ. of Pa.; MA, Univ. of Calif., Berkeley; PhD (Music), Univ. of Pa.; Electronic music study, Univ. of Toronto; Ethnomusicol. study, Inst. of Ethnomusicol., Univ. of Amsterdam, Holland; Study of Javanese Music, Acad. Seni Karawitan, Indonesia; Study of tabla, w. Aakir Hussain, Calif. A Charlene, (div.) 2 s., 1 d. Career: Fac. Mbr. & Adminstr., Wis. Concerv.; Performer on tabla in concerts of N Indian music throughout USA, 1970-; Co-dir., Pro Musica Wis. Nova (profl. new music perf. grp.). Compositions performed throughout US: Swift Wind, Cantata No. 2 for voice & contrabass; Orpheus for tape & videotape; Siftings upon Siftings, Symph. No. 1; Time Let me Play & be Golden in the Mercy of his Means (sonata for guitar & harpsichord). Mbrship: Soc. for Asian Music. Address: 2804 E Linnwood Ave., Milwaukke, WI 53211, USA.

MacDONAGH, J A Terence, b. 3 Feb. 1908, Woolwich, London, UK. Oboist (& Cor Anglais); Professor of Music. Educ: Piano w. Arthur de Greef, Brussels Conserv.; Oboe studies w. Mystil Morel, Paris; RAM. m. Mary Corrick, 2 d. Career: Prin. oboe, British Nat. Oper Co., 1928-29; BBC Scottish Orch., 1929-30; BBC Symph. Orch. (Cor Anglais), 1930-33; Prin. oboe w. same orch., 1936-47, 1962-73; Prin. oboe, RPO under Sir Thomas Beecham, 1947-62; Bd. of Profs., RCM. Recordings: num. w. BBC Symph. Orch., RPO, London Wind Soloists (Complete Mozart & Beethoven Wind Music, etc.). Hons: BEM (for service in NFS); FRAM, 1951; FRCM, 1963. Hobbies: Sailing; Tennis; Walking; Foreign Travel. Address: 6 Normanhurst Drive, E Twickenham, Middx., UK.

McDONALD, Gerald, b. 12 Aug. 1913, Wallasey, UK. Musical Administrator. Educ: Mt. St. Mary's Coll. & Dresden; singing w. J G Veaco, Liverpool & Frank Titterton; violin w. J Matthews; gen musicianship w. Imogen Holst. m. Jeanette Pearson, 2 s., 1 d. Career: Reg. Dir., Arts Coun. of GB (Southern, Eastern & N Regs.), 1948-56; Gen. Mgr., Royal Liverpool Phil. Orch., 1956-64; BBC Hd. of Music, N, 1964-69; Gen. Mgr., New Philharmonia Orch., 1969-74; Admnstr., Musicians Benevolent Fund, 1974-78; Vis. Tutor, Arts Admin. Course, City Univ.; Admnstr., Nat. Opera Studio, 1978-; Chmn., Central Music Advisory Committee, BBC. Contbr. to: BBC talks progs; specialist jrnls. Mbrships: Arts Coun. Music Panel. Royal Phil. Soc. Committee; RVW Trust Committee; ISM; Brit. Fedn. of Music Fests. Hons: MA, Liverpool; FRSA. Hobbies: Singing Lieder & English Songs; All Games & Outdoor Activities. Address: 40 Onslow Gdns., London N 103JU, UK.

MACDONALD, Hugh John, b. 1940, Newbury, UK. University Lecturer. Educ: Pembroke Coll., Cambridge. m. Naomi Butterworth, 1 s., 3 d. Career: Gen. Ed., New Berlioz Ed., 1965-; Asst. Lectr. Cambridge, 1966-68; Lectr., 1968-71; Fellow, Pembroke Coll., 1963-71; Cond., Cambridge Phil. Soc., 1969-71; Cond., Cambridge Players, 1969-71; Lectr. in Music, Oxford, 1971-; Cond., Oxford Univ. Orch., 1977-. Publs: New Berlioz Edition, Vol. 19 (Grande Symphonie Funèbre et Triomphale), Bärenreiter, 1967; Vol. 3 (Les Troyens), Bärenreiter, 1969-70; Berlio Orchestral Music, 1969; Skryabin, 1978. Hobby: Typewriters. Address: Fac. of Music, 32 Holywell, Oxford, UK. 3.

McDONALD, Ian Donald, b. 1 Apr. 1937, Wellington, NZ. Composer. Educ: B Mus, M Mus, Victoria Univ. of Wellington; Tchrs. Cert. m. Mary Margaret McDonald, 1 s., 1 d. Career incls: apps. in NZ Broadcasting Corp. Music Progs. documentary Notes On a Film Track (TV). Comps. incl: Miniatures for piano, 1964; 3 Easy Pieces (piano), 1967; Piano Duo, 1967; Nynke's Composition, 9 orchl. instruments, 1968; Easter Fragments (piano, violin & tenor), 1971; M (string quartet), 1971; High Country Clusters (brass band); The Taniwha (opera), 1973; Te Papaeioa (histl. pageant), 1973; Cantata for Joanna, 1975; Sounds of Dunedin, 1978. num. works

recorded. Contbr. to: Comment; NZ Listener. Mbrships: Comps. Assn. of NZ; NA Musicians Union. Recip., Wellington City Coun. Music Prize, 1967. Hobbies: Yoga; Gardening; Walking. Address: 928 Cumberland St., Dunedin, NZ.

MACDONALD, James V, b. 31 Jan. 1945, Portage la Prarie, Man., Can. French Horn Player. Educ: BA, Queen's Univ., Kingston, Ont.; MMus, Univ. of W Ont., London, Can.; Janacek Acad., Czech.; studies in London, UK, & Stockholm. m. Susan, 2 s. Career: perfs. w. Toronto Symph., Nat. Arts Ctr. Orch. & many major Canadian orchs.; Fndr., Yorkwinds Wind Quintet; extensive tours, special tchng., broadcasts, etc. Recordings: some classical, many commercial & pop. Contbr. to profl. jrnls. Mgmt: Sound Prism, 100 Lyall Avenue, Toronto. Address: 100 Lyall Ave., Toronto, Ont. M4E 1W5, Can.

MacDONALD, John Alexander, b. 1 Jan. 1929, Durant, Okla., USA. Choral Conductor; Musicologist & Professor of Music; Choral Clinician. Educ: B Mus Ed., Oberlin Coll., 1951; MA, 1957, PhD, Musicol., 1964, Univ. of Mich. m. Linda McMillan, 2 s., 1 d.; 1 d, 3 s., (1 dec.), by previous marriage. Debut: Akron, 1962. Career: Instr., Grand Rapids, (Mich.), pub. schls., 1955-58; Choral Cond., Akron Symph., 1962-; Asst. Choral Dir., Blossom Fest. Chorus, 1968-74; Min. of Music, High St. Christian Ch., Akron, 1964-; Fac. Mbr., 1957, Head, Dept. of Music, 1967-77, Prof. of Music, Univ. of Akron. Contbr., Notes of Music Lib. Assn., 1973. Mbrships: Pi Kappa Lambda; Past Sec., State Admnstrs. of Music Schls. of Ohio; Am. Musicol. Soc.; Coll. Music Soc.; Local 24, Am. Fedn. of Musicians. Hobbies: Photography; Ornithology; Hiking; Boating; Woodwork. Address: 1721 Deepwood Dr., Akron, OH 44313, USA. 8.

MACDONALD, John Roy, b. 13 July 1948, Gimli, Man., Can. French Horn Player. Educ: BMus, Univ. of Toronto, 1971; studied horn w. Eugene Rittich, Toronto & Barry Tuckwell, London & Frantisek Solc, Brno. m. Katalina Maria Bogyo, 1 s., 1 d. Career: solo tours, N Am. & Europe; 1st horn, Bamberg Symph. Orch., 1972-75; prin. solo horn, Radio Symph. Orch., Frankfurt. Recordings for W German radio & in Can. Hons: num. fest. awards since age 12; silver medal, Int. Competition, Geneva, 1971; 1st prize, Int. Competition of Prague Spring Fest., 1974; 1st prize, CBC competition, 1977; Top prize, Int. Competition of German Radio Networks, Munich, 1978. Hobbies: Sailing; Skiing. Mgmt: Annie Alber, Munich. Address: Egerländerstr. 9, 6390 Usingen, German Fed. Repub.

MACDONALD, Malcolm, b. 26 Oct. 1916, Bedford, UK. Composer; Critic; Teacher; Jazz Pianist. Educ: MA, MusB, Cantab; RCM. m. Margaret Kerslake. Career: Bandmaster RAF Command Bands, 1942-45; Sr. Lectr., Cape Town Univ., 1948; Prof., RAM, 1954-; Lectr., Royal Acad. Dancing, 1962-67; Examiner, Associated Bd., 1964-; Dir., Jazz Course, RAM, 1975-. Comps. incl: Harpsichord Concerto; Cuban Rondo. Contbr. to Gramophone, 1952-. Hons: RAM; Arts Coun. Award, Sinfonietta, 1951; Royal Phil. Soc. Prize, Symph. II, 1952. Address: 43 Crown St., Harrow, Middlesex, UK.

MacDONALD, Malcolm (Calum), b. 26 Feb. 1948, Nairn, Scotland, UK. Musical Writer & Journalist. Educ: Downing Coll., Cambridge. Career: Freelance Writer; Musical Jrnls.; Music Copyist; Ed.; Mng. Ed., Tempo Mag.; Compiler, Gramophone Classical Catalogue. Comps: Surface Measure & Before Urbino (2 songs w. orch.); At the Firth of Lorne & other songs w. piano; piano pieces; arrangements of var. contemp. works. Publs: incl Havergal Brian: Perspective on the Music, 1972; John Foulds: His Life in Music, 1975; Schoenberg, 1976. Contbr. to: The Listener; Musical Times; Tempo; Musical Events; Records & Recordings; Adam; etc. Address: 95 King Henry's Rd., Swiss Cottage, London NW3, UK.

MacDONALD, Robert James, b. 25 Aug. 1927, Boardman, (Ohio), USA. Educator; Librarian; Lecturer; Performer (Tenor). Educ: BSc, Youngstown Coll.; MA, Lib. Sci., Univ. Mich.; PhD, ibid.; MMus., Mich. State Univ.; Cleveland Inst. Music; Conserv. Royal Musique, Brussels; Voice w. Bernardo de Muro & Beniamino Gigli; Piano Beryl Rubinstein & Arthur Loesser. m. Sarah Campbell Ramsay (dec.), 1 s. Debut: Piano solo, Youngstown Symph., 1947; Operatic debut, Palermo, 1951. Career: Frequent oratorio perfs. Publs. incl: Problems in the Authentication & Dating of Later 18th Century Imprints of French Instrumental Music, 1974; Personnel Lists of Public Orchestras in Paris 1751-1793, 1976. Mbr. profl. orgs. Hons. incl: Fulbright Schl., 1964-66. Hobbies incl: Tennis. Address: 10033 Groh Rd. No. 36, Grosse Ile. MI 48138, USA.

McDONALD, Susann Hackett, b. 26 May 1935, Rock Island, Ill., USA. Concert Harpist; Teacher. Educ: École Normale Superieur de Musique, Paris; grad., Paris Conserv., 1955; studied w. Julius Hayford, NY. Debut: Carnegie Hall, NY. Career:

Concert Harpist touring Europe, USA, S Am. & the Orient, 1960-76; Concert Harpist, Columbia Artists, Inc., 1976-79. Publs: (ed.) Rosetti Sonatas (complete). Recordings: Dussek sonatas; Rosetti sonatas; Spohr, Sonata for violin & harp; 20th century harp music; Mediterranean Reflections; The Romantic Harp; The Virtuoso Harp; Masters of Flute & Harp, 2 vols. Mbrships: Sigma Alpha Iota (nat. hon. mbr.); Delta Kappa Gamma. Recip., Premier Prix, Paris Conser., 1955. Mgmt: Columbia Artists, Inc. Address: 504 S Catalina, Pasadena, Calif., USA. 27.

McDONNELL, Thomas Anthony, b. 27 April 1940, Melbourne, Aust. Singer (Baritone). Educ: Law Degree, Melbourne Univ.; Arts Degree, ibid.; Melba Conserv., Melbourne, w. Lennox Brewer; Pvte. study w. Maestro Ricco, Rome, 1969-70. m. Mary Jennifer Smith, 1 s., 1 d. Debut: Belcore, L'Elisir d'amore, Brisbane, Aust., 1965. Career: World Premieres, Ice-Break, We Come To the River, Vasco, Royal Hunt of the Sun, Dawnpath; British Stage Premieres, War & Peace, Bassarids, Saul & David; War & Peace, Tannhauser, Operning Sydney Opera House, 1973. Recordings: Israel in Egypt; La Fanciulla Del West; Tancredi; Donizetti Rarities; Darwin - Song for a city. Hons: Showcase Aust., 1965; Joan Sutherland/Women's Day Vocal Quest, 1965; Lever hulme Youth & Music Scholarship to Rome. Hobbies: Shakespeare; Chmbr. Music; Poetry; Architecture; Jogging; Tennis. Mgmt: Music Interational. Address: 25 Talbot Rd., London, N6, UK.

MacDOUGALL, Robert Bruce, b. 2 May 1931, Brooklyn, NY, USA. Musician (oboe, cor anglais, oboe d'amore); Educator. Educ: Rutgers Univ., NH, 1949-50; US Army Band Schls., NJ & Germany; B Mus, Juilliard Schl. of Music, NYC, 1957; MA, Columbia Univ., 1958. m. Céline Janelle, 3 s., 1 d. Career: Secondary Schl. Music Tchr. & Mbr., Symph. Orch., Regina, Sask., Canada, 1958-59; Fndr., Band Orch., instrn. in Engl. Schl. System, Quebec City, 1960-63; Tchr. & Mbr., local symph. orch., Ithaca, NY, 1963-65; Co-dir., Instrumental music instrn., City Schl. Dist. Plattsburgh, NY, 1965-; Oboist & cor anglais w. Vt. State Symph., 1965-; Oboe d'amore w. Montreal Symph., 1970, Concl. Schl. Band, EXPO '67; Charter Mbr., US 7th Army Symph. Orch., 1952-53. Compositions: Mass of Hope (Chorus & Orch.); Reverie du Printemps (piano); The Dead of Paoli (Chorus & Cor Anglais). Hons: US Army in Europe Hon. Bandsman, 1952; Merit Schlrship., Juilliard Schl., 1956. Hobbies: Gardening; Hiking; Camping; Philately; Numismatics. Address: 51-B Prospect Ave., Plattsburgh, NY 12901, USA.

MACEDA, Corazon S, b. 10 May 1911, Biñan, Laguna, Philippines. Educator. Educ: BSE, Univ. of the Philippines, 1931, Conserv. of Music, ibid., 1939; MA, Eastman Schl. of Music, Univ. of Rochester, 1948. Career incls: currently Assoc. Dean, Coll. of Music & Fine Arts, Philippine Women's Univ. Comps: Pangarap; Ave Maria; Araw na Dakila (Christmas song). Recordings: Araw na Dakila. Publs: incl: Pointers for Music Teachers, 1957; Philippine Choruses for all Occasions; A Series of workbooks in Music. Ed., Mod. Tchr. Mag. Contbr. to: profl. jrnls. Mbrships. incl: Pres., Philippine Soc. for Music Educ.; Treas., Music Promotion Foundation of the Philippines; Nat. Music Coun. of the Philippines. Hons: City of Manila Award in Music, 1978. Hobbies: Handicraft; Painting; Attending Concerts. Address: '841 F Agoncillo St., Malate, Manila 2801, Philippines. 23, 27.

MACEDA, José, b. 31 Jan. 1917, Manila, Philippines. Ethnomusicologist; Composer. Educ: Acad. of Music, Manila; Ecole Normale de Musique, Paris; E Robert Schmitz Schl., San Fran., AB, Queen's Coll., NYC; PhD, UCLA. m. Madelyn Clifford, 4 d. Career: piano recitals in Philippines & USA, 1937-57. Comps: Ugma-Ugma; Agungan; Kubing; Pagsamba; Cassettes 100; Ugnayan; Udlot-Udolot; Ading. Contbr. to: Ethnomusicol.; World of Music; Sarawak Mus. Jrnl.; Ency. Britannica; Grove's Dict. of Music. Mbrships: Soc. of Ethnomusicol.; Current Anthropol. Recip., Repub. Heritage Award, Philippines. Address: Univ. of the Philippines, Coll. of Music, Quezon City, Philippines.

MACÉDO, Nelson de, b. 6 Mar. 1931, Barbosa, Brazil. Composer; Conductor; Violinist; Violist; Guitarist. Educ: Medal for Sculpture, Fine Arts Univ., Salvador; Dip., Musical Inst. of Bahia, 1952; Dips., Music Schl., Fed. Univ., Rio de Janeiro; studies w. Serge Collot, Etienne Ginot & Jacques Ripoche, Paris. m. Lucia Franco de Macédo, 1 s., 1 d. Career incls: 1st Viola, Soloist, Municipal Theatre Symph. Orch., Rio de Janiero; Viola Tchr., Villa-Lobos Inst.; Guest Cond., Orquestra Sinfonica Brasileira & Municipal Theatre Symph. Orch. of Rio de Janeiro; Fndr. & Cond., The Camerists & Artis Canticum Choir; Guitarist & Fndr., Duo Paganini. Comps: Fantasia Concerto for tenor trombone & orch.; Invocacao (choral); Fantasia Capricho, for sax.-Alto & String. Mbrships: Order of Brazilian Musicians; Dir., Revista do Musico. Hons: incl: 2nd Prize, 1st Nat. Ballet Comp. Contest, Rio de Janeiro, 1976. Address: Apt. 304, R.

Commendador Martinelli 96, Grajau, 20.000 Rio de Janeiro, Brazil.

McELFRESH, Clair Thomas, b. 20 Oct. 1931, Pitts., Pa., USA. Conductor; Composer; Professor. Educ: BS, Ind. Univ. of Pa., 1953; MA, Case-Western Reserve Univ., 1959; m. Emily Shelton McElfresh, 2 s., 4 d. Career: Prof., Coll. of Arts & Scis., Dir., Fac. Scholars, & Dir., Choral Activities, Fla. Int. Univ., Miami; Guest Cond., Cleveland Orch., N Miami Beach Symph. Orch., Cleveland Women's Orch., All-State Choruses in Fla., Va., SC, NC, Tenn. & Pa. Comps: Alleluia; O Ye People; A Very Merry Christmas; Mistletoe; Life Has a Tender Meaning; Please, Don't Leave Me, Brother; Images of Love; Lost Tomorrow; We Believe; Robin O Robin; O Precious Lord; Still Only You. Recordings: The Church Militant; Hope for the Future. Mbr., profl. assns. Hons: Mus D, Combs Coll. of Music, Phila., 1969. Hobbies: Boating; Fishing. Address: 7625 SW 167th St., Miami, FL 33157, USA.

McELHERAN, N Brock, b. 6 Jan. 1918, Winnipeg, Canada. Conductor; Musical Director. Educ: BA, Univ. Toronto, 1939; MusB, ibid., 1947; studied conducting at Tanglewood & w. Pierre Monteux; voice w. Ernest Vinci, Banff Summer Schl. Fine Arts. m. Jane Gooding Munro, 1942. Debut: Univ. Toronto Symph. Orch., 1938. Career: Crane Schl. Music, State Univ. Coll., Potsdam, NY, USA, 1947-; Coord., Choral Activities, ibid.; Dir., Saratoga-Potsdam Choral Inst.; Cond., Saratoga; Potsdam Chorus (res. chorus for Phila. Orch., Saratoga Festo); Musical Dir., Montreal Elgar Choir. Comps: sev. short choral works. Recording: Handel's Saul, 1952. Publ: Conducting Technique, 1966. Contbr. to profl. jrnls. Hobbies: Travel; Photography; Sport. Address: State Univ. Coll., Potsdam, NY 13676, USA.

MACENAUER, Bedrich, b. 8 Apr. 1929, Prague, Czechoslovakia. Conductor; Chorus master. Educ: State Conserv., Prague; Dip. (Cond.), Acad. of Music, Prague, 1956. m. Nadezda Vanickova, 2 s. Debut: Cond., FOK Orch. & Opera Grp. of Acad. of Music, Prague. Career: Chorus master & Cond., Opera Ceske, Budejovice & Opera House, Pilsen, 1957-; regular concerts w. Female Chmbr. Choir, Children's Choir & Chmbr. Orch. of Pilsen, 1962-. Compositions: works for children, broadcast on Radio Pilsen. Mbrship: Czech Music Soc. Hobbies: Travel; Nature walks; Tape recording; Record collecting. Address: Zelenohorska 6, 31704 Pizen 17, Czech.

MACER, Aubrey William John, b. 9 mar. 1924, Ashbourne, Derbyshire, UK. Músic Teacher; Organist. Educ: piano & organ studies w. pvte. tchrs.; trng. as Specialist Tchr., schl. music, Coll. of St. Mark & St. John, Chelsea; LRAM; ARCO; Cert. in Educ.; London Univ. Inst. of Educ. Career: Organist & Choirmaster, sev. parish chs.; Music Tchr., sev. schls.; Pvte. Tchr., piano orgsn & singing; Coach for GCE & ISM exams. Comps: Two Quintet Pieces (organ); Postlude in A flat (organ); Choral Improvisation on the tune "Mannheim" (organ). Mbr., ISM. Hobby: Philos. & math. reasoning. Address: c/o "Old Chapel", Burrow Hill, Chobham, Woking, Surrey, UK.

MACEROLLO, Joseph, b. 1 Oct. 1944, Guelph, Ont., Can. Accordionist & Educator. Educ. incls: MusB, 1965, MA, 1969, Univ. of Toronto; studied accordion w. Nicholas Antonelli & Charles Camilleri. m. Frances Slingerland, 1 d. Debut: Toronto. Career incls: has made num. apps. & broadcasts as Soloist, w. orchs., jazz grps., etc.; has premiered many contemp. works for accordion inclng. world Premiere of Gerhard Wuensch's Music without Pretensions (accordion & str. quartet); Tchr., accordion, hist. of music, analyist & contemp. music, Royal Conserv. of Music, Toronto; Studio Inst., Queen's & York Univs., Fac. of Music Univ. of Toronto. Has recorded for CBC Int. Transcription Serv. Contbr. to jrnls. Mbrships. incl: Pres., Contemp. Music Showcase Assn.; Dir., Can. Music Competitions. Recip. many hons. inclng: Can. Accordion Champion, 1963, 64. Hobby: Film. Address: 3296 Cindy Cres., Mississauga, Ont. L4Y 3J6, Canada.

McFARLAND, J Patrick, b. 13 Feb. 1939, Rio de Janeiro, Brazil. Symphony Musician (English Horn, Oboe d'Amour, Oboe); Businessman. Educ: BA, San Jose State Coll., San Jose, Calif., USA. m. Anne A McFarland, 2 d. Career: Prin. English Horn, Atlanta Symph. Orch., Ga.; Owner, McFarland Oboe Shop (business dealing w. oboe sales, serv. & accessories). Address: co Atlanta Symph. Orch., Atlanta, GA 30329, USA.

McFERRIN, Sara Elizabeth Copper, b. 10 Sept. 1924, Wash., DC, USA. Singer. Educ: Howard Univ., Wash., DC; Univ. of Calif., Los Angeles; Calif. State Univ., ibid.; Univ. of Southern Calif., Los Angeles; Teaching credential, Calif. Community Colls. div., 1 s., 1 d. Career: Hollywood Greek Theatre Opera Chorus; NY City Ctr. Opera Chorus; Broadway prod., Lost in the Stars; in films Porgy & Bess, & Elmer Gantry. Symph. soloist, solo recitalist & oratorio soloist throughout USA. Christmas

Specials, TV-CBS; currently Chmn., Voice Dept., Fullerton Coll., Calif. Mbrships. incl: Exec. Bd. & prog. chmn., Los Angeles Chapt., Nat. Assn. Tchrs. of Singing; Music Tchrs. Nat. Assn.; Calif. Assn. Profl. Music Tchrs. Hobbies: Golf; Plants. Address: The Water Gardens, 2925 Barrington CT, Fullerton, CA 92631, USA.

McGEE, Robin, b. 28 Dec. 1934, High Wycombe, Bucks., UK. Cello, Piano, Double Bass Player; Director; Professor. Educ: LRAM (tchrs. pianoforte); ARAM. m. Elizabeth Rosemary Cooper, 2 s. Career: RPO; Co-Principal, LSO; Fndr. Mbr. & Principal, London Sinfonietta; now Dir.; Prof., RAM; Concerts at home & abroad inclng. 16 visits to USA; 2 extensive world tours w. LSO; Played w. all maj. symph. orchs. & chamber orchs. Recordings: Most of the symphonic repertoire w. LSO; Contemporary music w. London Sinfonietta. Mbrships: MRSM; ISM; Coun., London Sinfonietta. Hons: Thalberg Scholarship, RAM, 1952; Sir James Caird Award, 1955. Hobbies incl: Reading; Swimming; Gardening. Address: Glebe Cottage, Ashmead Lane, Denham, Bucks, UK.

McGEGAN, (James) Nicholas, b. 14 Jan. 1950, Sawbridgeworth, Herts., UK. Baroque Flautist; Harpsichordist; Operatic Conductor; Teacher. Educ: LTCL, 1968; BA, 1972, MA, 1976, Corpus Christi Coll., Cambridge. Career: Prof., RCM; Supvsr., King's Coll., Cambridge. Recordings: 6 Sonatas, JC Bach, w. Christopher Hogwood, L'Oiseau-Lyre; num. recordings w. Acad. of Ancient Music, The Music Party & The Engl. Concert. Publs: Tom Jones by Philidor, 1976. Hobbies: Archaeology; Food. Address: 26 Barchard St., London SW18, UK.

McGILL, Gwendolen Mary Finlayson, b. 29 Apr. 1910, Ayr, Scotland, UK. Cellist; Pianist; Clarsach (Celtic Harp) player. Educ: studied in Ayr, Edinburgh, Vienna (w. Buxbaum), Paris (w. Bazelaire), Salzburg (w. Mainardi), & Prades (w. Casals). Debut: as solo cello recitalist, Vienna. Career: Solo Cello Recitals, London, Vienna, Paris, Amsterdam, BBC-Radio Scotland; Concertos w. Vienna Concert & Scottish Orchs.; Mbr., London Chmbr. Orch.; Tchr., pvtely. Comps. (unpubld.) for cello, piano & clarsach. Mbrships. incl: ISM; Fndr., Ayr Music Club; Life Mbr., Clarsach Soc., An Commun Gaidhealach & Saltire Soc. Hons. incl: Major Trophy for clarsach & singing in Gaelic, Scottish Nat. Mod., 1960. Hobby: Tapestry. Address: 17 Walker St., Edinburgh EH3 7NE, UK.

McGLAUGHLIN, William, b. 3 Oct. 1943, Phila., Pa., USA. Conductor; Trombonist. Educ: BMus, 1967, MMus, 1969, Temple Univ., Phila.; pvte. studies in Cond. & Trombone, m. Katherine Pancoast Palmer, 1 s., 1 d. Career: Assoc. Cond., St. Paul Chmbr. Orch.; Asst. Cond., Pitts. Symph. Chmbr. Orch.; Assoc. Prin. Trombone, Pitts. Symph.; Asst. Prin. Trombone, Phila. Orch. Hons: Sponsorship as Exxon Arts Endowment Cond., 1975-77. Mgmt: Affiliate Artists Inc., 155 W 68th St., NY, NY 10023. Address: 1973 Lincoln Ave., St. Paul, MN 55105, USA.

McGOUGH, Neil Vincent, b. 18 Mar. 1939, Pukekohe, NZ. Trombonist; Conductor. Educ: Pvte. study, trombone, orchestration & theory. m. Pamela Clouston, 1 s., 2 d. Career: Prin. Trombone, Symphonia of Auckland; Freelance recordings for Radio, TV; Musical Dir. for Theatrical prods., 1963-; Arranger, Orchestrator for TV & theatre. Mbrships: Sec., NZ Musicians Union; Life Mbr. & Past Nat. Sec., Actor's Equity of NZ; Mbr., NZ Queen Elizabeth II Arts Coun.; Chmn., Northern Regional Arts Coun.; Past Chmn., Auckland Operatic Soc.; Past Chmn., Symphonia Opera Co. Hobbies: Painting; Reading. Address: 59 Martin Ave., Mt. Albert, Auckland, NZ.

McGREGOR, Bruce Howard, b. 22 July 1952, Toronto, Ont., Can. Conductor; Trumpeter; Pianist; Educator; Adjudicator. Educ: BEd, Queen's Univ., Kingston, Ont.; BMus, Univ. of Toronto; MMus, ibid. m. Carolyn Mary Martin. Debut: cond., Peterborough Symph. Orch., 1975. Career: Cond., Peterborough Symph. Orch., 1975; gave premiere of Lothar Klein's Voices of Earth; fndr., cond., Peterborough Symph. Chorus; tchr., Univ. of Toronto (cond. & trumpet); musician-in-residence, Trent Univ.; tchr., Sir Sandford Fleming Coll.; musical dir., Belleville Theatre Guild & Trenton Musical Assn., 1979-; musical dir., E Ontario Concert Orch.; music educator, Dr. F J Donevan Collegiate Inst., Oshawa. Mbrships: Am. Symph. Orch. League; AFM; Ont. Music Educators Assn.; Ont. Secondary Schl. Tchrs. Fed. Hons: num. prizes & awards incl. 1st prize, Heinz Unger Cond. Competition, 1975. Hobbies: Badminton; Tennis; Swimming; Travel; Audiophile. Address: 50 Centennial Dir., Port Hope, Ont. L1A 3X2, Can.

McGREW, Esther Gertrude (Harris), b. 5 Jan. 1907, Wash., DC, USA. Teacher of Piano & Organ. Educ: BA, Univ. of W Fla.; studied w. Prof. William Beal, Mrs. Pearl Hauer, James P Hussong, William Bates. m. Clinton Jackson McGrew, Sr., dec., 1 s., 2 d.

Career: Piano & Organ Tchr., 8 yrs. Hons: Nat. Piano Playing Auditions Nat. Honour Roll of Guild Tchrs., 1977, '78. Mbrships: NGPT; Music Tchrs. Nat. Assn.; Fla. State Music Tchrs.; The MTA of Pensacola; Music Study Club, Pensacola; AGO (Sec., Pensacola Chapt.). Hobbies: Horticulture; Swimming. Address: 8255 Fordham Dr., Pensacola, FL 32504, USA. 4, 5.

McGUIRE, Barbara, b. 10 Oct. 1940, Manchester, UK. Singer (Mezzo-soprano); Professor of Singing. Educ: ABSM, Birmingham Schl. of Music. m. Robert Lawton Pettifer, 2 s. Debut: Wigmore Hall, London, 1975. Career: Num. perfs., UK; Recitals, Vienna & Dijon; Broadcasts incl. perf. w. NPO, Cond. Sir Adrian Boult; Elgar's Sea Pictures, CBSO Proms; Prof. of Singing, Birmingham Schl. of Music. Hons: Vaughan Williams Scholarship, 1971. Hobbies: Reading; Walking; Children. Address: 8 The Grange, Cubbington, Leamington Spa, Warwicks., UK.

McGUIRE, Colin John, b. 17 June 1947, London, UK. Teacher & Musician (clarinet). Educ: Royal Acad. of Music. Debut: w. Mayfair Ensemble, Purcell Room, 1973. Career: Freelance clarinet player, London; Mbr., Kent Opera Orch.; Admnstr., Mayfair Ensemble. Mbrships: Royal Soc. of Musicians; Inc. Soc. of Musicians; Assoc., Royal Phil. Soc.; RAM Club. Hobby: Squash. Address: 34 Woolmer Rd., London N18 2JT, UK. 147.

McGUIRE, Edward, b. 15 Feb. 1948, Glasgow, Scotland, UK. Composer; Folk Music Performer; Flute Teacher. Educ: RSAM, 1965; Studied Comp. & Flute, RAM, 1966-70; studied Comp. w. Ingvar Lidholm, Sweden, 1971; ARCM, Flute. Career: Mbr., Whistlebinkies (folk grp.), perfs. on Scottish radio & TV, & at Int. Folkmusic Fests., Brittany & German Dem. Repub.; radio talks on music. Comps. incl: (broadcast) 5 Pieces for Saxes; Music for Low Flutes; Solo for Clarinet(s); Martyr (Viola); (commissions) Rebirth-Interregnum-Liberation (trilogy for ensembles); 1974-75; Symph., 1976. Mbr., profl. assns. Hons. incl: E Hecht. Comp. Prize, RAM, 1968; Winner, Nat. Young Comps. Competition, 1969; var. scholarships. Hobbies: Trade Union & Political Activity. Address: 18 Highburgh Rd., Glasgow G12 9YD, UK.

McGURK, Molly, b. 23 Aug. 1929, Armadale, W Aust. Pianist; Singer; Teacher. Educ: LMus (piano). m. John David Browne, 2 s., 1 d. Debut: (as pianist) 1948; (as singer), 1953. Career: num. perfs. as pianist in standard concerto repertoire; perfs. as singer in oratorio, operatic arias & lieder; apps. on radio & TV; guest soloist w. all Aust. orchs. & w. NZ Choral Soc.; Tchr. of singing, 1968-. Recordings: songs by Samuel Barber, Duparc, Rachmaninoff, Fauré & Debussy etc. mbr., WA Music Tchrs. Assn. Hons: Churchill Fellowship, 1967; num. exhibitions for piano. Hobbies: Cryptic crosswords; Cooking; Knitting. Address: 41 Doney St., Alfred Cove, WA 6154, Aust.

MACHADO SANTOS, Maria de Graca, b. 15 Aug. 1933, Sao Luis-Maranhao, Brazil. Assistant Teacher of Theory & Preception, Federal University, Bahia; Teacher of Musical Education, School of Dance & Integrated Arts, Salvador, Bahia. Educ: Music Grad., State Univ., Bahia; Conserv., Bahia. Comps. incl: Collection of songs for jr. schls. Contbr. to APEMBA, Bahia, Brazil. Mbr. of Assn. Tchrs. of Musical Educ. of Bahia. Hons: Finalist competition comp. & choral arr. on themes of Brazilian folklore. Address: Rua 8 de Dezembro, 85 ap. 303, 40.000 Salvador, Bahia, Brazil.

McHAFFIE, Iain, b. 30 June 1944, Eaglesham, Scotland, UK. Guitarist; Arranger; Composer. Educ: Pvte. studies. w. K Muir, R Moore, Lee Konitz, J Watson. m. Iris McHaffie, 1 s. 1 d. Career: Freelance, Recordings Studios, BBC radio & TV, STV; Guitarist, BBC Scottish Radio Orch. Comps: Beautiful Lady; Klink (w. Irish McHaffie); Straight Home; Night Caperas; Original music for films, Glasgow, 1980, Raindrops; num. other comps. & arrs. for documentaries; signature tunes. Recordings: Mood Chevalier (w. Peggy O'Keefe Quartet). Mbrships: PRS; MCPS; Songwriters Guild; Glasgow Soc. of Musicians. Hobbies: Snooker; Films. Address: 135 Albert Rd., Glasgow G42 8UE, UK.

MACHATIUS, Franz-Jochen, b. 18 Apr. 1910, Rawitsch, Poland. Musicologist; Conductor. Educ: Conserv. Leipzig 1930-1933; Univ. Leipzig 1930-33; Univ. Heidelberg 1933-35; Free Univ. Berlin West 1949-52, DPh 1952. Career: City Theatre Cottbus 1939-41; German Nat. Theater Osnabrück 1941-45; State Theater Oldeburg 1946-47; Comic Opera Berlin, 1947-49; Tchr. Berlin Music Schl., 1955-57; since 1965 Dist. Dir., GEMA, Berlin. Comp. incl: Theater music; Songs. Mbrships: Soc. for Music Rsch. Publs: incl: The Tempo in Music Round 1600, Berlin, 1952; Eroica The Transcendental Ego, Kassel, 1962; Lit. essays, lyrics. Contbr. to: Music in Past and Present; Music Rsch.; Congress bulletins, Cologne, Kassel. Address: Dickhardstr. 3, L 000 Berlin 41, Germany.

MACHAVARIANI, Alexei Davidovich, b. 1913, Gori, Georgia, Russia. Composer. Educ: Tbilisi Conserv. m. Pachkoria Ekaterina, 1946, 1 s. Comps. incl: Mumli Mukhasa (symphonic suite), 1939; Mother & Son (opera), 1941; The Bridge (symphonic suite), 1942; Concerto for piano & orch., 1944; 1st Symph., 1947; Concerto for Violin & Orch., 1950; Ten Uacc. Choral Pieces, 1952; My Country's Day (oratorio), 1953; Othello (ballet), 1957; 3 Suites (Symph. Orch.), 1958; Hamlet (opera), 1967; 2nd Symph., 1976 (recorded); Children's Album, 1976; Georgian Frescoes, 1977; Musical Youth, 1977; Bug, musical comedy. Recordings: Concerto for Symph. Orch. & Violin; 5 Vocal Monologues w. orch. Mbrships: Exec., USSR Comps. Union; Exec., Georgian SSR Comps. Union. Recip. var. hons. incl: Order of Lenin, 1966; Gold Medal, Centro Culturale, Braidense, Italy, 1973. Hobbies: Sports; Motoring. Address: Composers Union of Georgia, Tbilisi, USSR.

MACHL, Tadeusz, b. 22 Oct. 1922, Lwow, Poland. Composer; Organist; Lecturer. Educ: Music Lyceum, Lwow; State Coll. of Music, Krakow. m. Irena Paszkiewicz-Machl, 2 c. Debut: Cantata-The Day of Work, Poznan, 1948. Career: works played thru'out Poland & recorded in Poland & abroad; music for 11 short films, 8 plays & 1 TV show; Lectr., State Coll. of Music, Krakow; Dean of Fac. of Composition, Theory & Conduction, ibid., 1967-69; Pro-rector, 1969-72; Dir. of Chair of Composition, 1966-72; Pres. of Disciplinary Commn. of Pedagogical Staff, 1972-. Comps. (publd.) incl: Organ Concerto No. 1; Harpsichord Concerto; Two Pieces for Great Organ; Organ Etude No. 5; An Organ Piece in Five Parts; Organ Mini-Suite. Compositions (recorded) incl: 5 symnphs.; 16 instrumental concertos; 2 concertante cantatas; 4 str. quartets. Recordings: 2 organ etudes; many tapes for archives of Polish Radio. Mbrships: Union of Polish Composers, Warsaw; Pres., Local Circle, Union of Polish Composers, Krakow; Sec., Revision Commission of Coun., Union of Polish Composers, Warsaw. Hons. incl: Gold Cross of Merit for work as Tchr. & Composer, 1965; Award as Active Man of Culture & Art, Warsaw, 1971. Hobbies: Aviation; Motoring. Address: ul. Bol. Chrobrego 29/27, 31428 Cracow, Poland.

MACIEJEWSKI, Tadeusz, b. 22 June 1936, Warsaw, Poland. Musicologist; Medievalist. Educ: Magister, Musicol., Univ. of Warsaw; Dr., Musicol., Ctr. d'Etudes Supérieures de Civilisation Médiévale à l'Université de Poitiers, Franced. m. Elzbieta Maria Tchorzewska, 1 d. Publs. incL: The Pelpin Tablature Choral Compositions; Transcriptions of the Works of M Vulpius in Antiquitates Musicae in Polonia, Warsawa - Graz, 1970; Gradual z Chelmna. Dokument do dziej&w monodii diecezjalnej w Polsce w XII w. Bydgoszcz 1971; Zaqsób utworów z ksiag Archikonfraternii Literackiej w Warszawie 1668-1829, Warszawa, 1972; The Chelmno Gradual in Musica Medii Aevi, t. IV, 1973; Notatki z przeszlos musycznej Lozicza, in Muzyka, 1973. Gradual Karmelitanski z 1644 roku o. Stanislawa ze Stolca, 1976; Kyriale w reisach polskich do XVII w., 1976; Z przestości muzycznej towicza, towicz, 1978. Mbrships: Assn. of Polish Comps; Treas. & VP, Publicity Commn., Contemp. Polish Music Foreign Ed., "Current Musicology", Columbia Univ., NY, USA. Address: ul. Braci Zaluskich 3 m. 73, 01-773 Warsaw, Poland.

McINDOE, Sanna, b. 23 Dec. 1930, Richmond, Yorks., UK. Singer; Teacher. Educ: MA (Edinburgy); (singing tchr.); LTCL (singing perf.); T cert. (SED); Chapter VI (music specialist) tchng. dip., Moray House Coll. of Educ.; study w. Winifred Busfield, Hans Oppenheim (Scotland), Joyce Warrack, Miette Dernbach & Peter Gellhorn (London). m. 1) J W M Smart, 1 d., 1 s.; 2) W I McIndoe, 2 s., 1 d. Career: Concert perfs., recitals, lecture-recitals in Scotland & Hull; apps. at Edinburgh Fest.; operatic roles w. Beaufort & Carlos Opera Groups; app. on TV; repertoire incl. lieder, 16th & 17th century songs, Bach, Handel, Mozart etc; mbr., Living Music. Mbrships: ISM; Edinburgh Univ. Staff Club. Hobbies: Reading; Cooking; Embroidery. Address: 35 Fitzgerald Ave., London SW14 8SZ, UK.

McINNES, Donald, b. 7 Mar. 1939, San Fran., Calif., USA. Concert Violist; University Professor. Educ: AB, Univ. of Calif., Santa Barbara, 1963; MMus, Univ. of Southern Calif., 1966; Dips., Music acad. of West. m. Christine R McInnes, 2 s., 1 d. Career incls: Assoc. Prof. Viola & Chmbr. Music, Univ. of Wash., 1966; Solo apps. in recitals throughout USA & Can., & w. major orchs. inclng. NY Phil. & Boston Symph.; Pgh. Symph.; Masterclass, Int. Viola Congress, Ypsilanti, Mich., 1975; perfs. at var. Fests. Recordings for var. labels. Mbr., profl. assns. Hons. incl: Winner, Ford Fndn. Prog. for Young Concert Artists, 1971. Hobbies: Tennis; Swimming; Gardening. Mgmt: Ibbs & Tillett Ltd., London, UK. Address: School of Music, Univ. of Washington, Seattle, WA 98195, USA.

McINTOSH, Thomas, b. 3 Dec. 1948, Washington, DC, USA. Pianist; Conductor. Educ: George Washington, Columbia &

NY Univs.; BSc, MSc, Juilliard Schl. of Music, NY. Debuts: aged 12 in Mozart concerto w. Nat. Symph. Orch.; aged 16, NY Town Hall recital. Career: perfs. as pianist or cond. in over 55 countries; active in producting & conducting opera incl. world premiere of S Dodgson's Margaret Catchpole; Dodgson's Piano Concerto & Percussion Concertante written for him; cond., City of London Chmbr. Orch.; Artistic Dir., Brett Valley Soc. for the Arts. Recordings: works by Liszt. Publs: mbr., editorial panel, Garland Series. mbr., ISM. Hons: 1st prize, Int. Kranichsteiner Piano competition; prizewinner, Bolzano Busoni Piano competition. Hobbies: Gardinging; Painting. Mgmt: Minstrel Productions Ltd. Address: The Old School, 5 Bridge St., Hadleigh, Suffolk IP7 6BY, UK.

McINTYRE, Donald, b. 22 Oct. 1934, Auckland, NZ. Opera Singer (Baritone). Educ: Tchrs. Cert., Auckland Tchrs. Trng. Coll.; Guildhall Schl. of Music, London. m. Jill Redington, 3 d. Debut: as Zaccarria in Nabucco, w. Welsh Nat. Opera, Cardiff, 1959. Career incl: concert & oratorio singer incing. broadcasting on NZ Radio; Mbr., Sadlers Wells Opera, 1960-67, w. leading roles in Cosi fan Tutte, Marriage of Figaro, Gounod's Faust, etc.; Mbr., Royal Opera House, Covent Gdn., 1967-; annual appearances at Bayreuth Festival; guest performances w. Metropol. Opera, NYC; Vienna State Opera; Hamburg State Opera; La Scala, Milan, etc. Recordings of num. operatic works. recip., OBE, 1977. Hobbies: Sport; Gardening; Painting. Mgmt: Ingpen & Williams Ltd., 14 Kensington Ct., London W8. Address: 2 Roseneath Close, Orpington, Kent, UK.

McINTYRE, Richard Rawlings, b. 22 Nov. 1914, Good Pine, LaSalle Parish, La., USA. Instrumental Music Teacher; Violoncellist. Educ: BMus, La. State Univ.; MMusEd., ibid.; MMus, cello, Tulsa Univ.; Inst. Musical Art, NYC. m. Ruth Blossom McIntyre, 3 s. Career: Mbr., cello sect., New Orleans Symph., La., Houston Symph., Tex. & currently, Tulsa Phil., Okla.; Instrumental Music Tchr., Tulsa Pub. Schls.; Pvte. cello instructor. Mbrships: Sec., Pres., Beta Omega Chapt., Phi Mu Alpha; MENC; OMEA; NSOA; ASTA; NEA; OEA; TTCA. Hobbies: Philately; Photography; Gardening. Address: 3802 S Knoxville, Tulsa, OK 74135, USA.

McINTYRE, (Robert) John, b. 23 June 1938, Sarnia, Canada. Concert Pianist; Professor of Music. Educ: ARCT., Royal Conserv. of Music, Toronto, 1955; Artist Dip., Univ. of Toronto, 1959; Study, Paris Conserv., 1960-61; MM, Boston Univ., 1968. Career: Num. solo chambr. music & concerto perfs., Can., USA & Europe; CBC Radio & TV perfs.; Adjudicator, music fests., Can. & USA; Pianist in Res., Concordia Coll., Minn., 1965-69; Assoc. Prof., Music, W. Wash. State Coll., 1969-75; Assoc. Prof. of Music, Univ. of Miss., 1975-. Recordings: Solo perfs. of works by Schumann, Ravel & Prokofieff, on Artist label. Mbrships: Am. Fedn. of Musicians; MTNA. Hons: Schlrship., Univ. of Toronto, 1957-60; Winner, Ravel Medal, for perf. of French music, French Consulate, 1960; Eaton Schlrship., Univ., of Toronto, 1960; Can. Coun. Grant for study in Europe, 1960-61; Study Grant, Concordia Coll., 1967. Mgmt: Off. of Cultural Events, UMKC-5100 Rockhill Rd., Kansas City, MO 64110, USA. Address: 4335 Oak Ap 10, Kansas City, MO 64111, USA.

McKAY, Neil, b. 16 June 1924, Ashcroft, BC., Canada. Composer; Teacher. Educ: BA, Gen. Arts & Dip. in Comp., Univ. of Western Ont., 1953; MA, Comp., Eastman Schl. of Music, 1955; PhD, Comp., ibid., 1956. m. Marion Dyer, 1 s., 1 d. Career: Canadian Navy Band, 1944-46; Freelance arr. in Canadian radio, 1946-53; Prof. of Music, Univ. of Wis. at Superior, 1957-65; Prof. of Music, Univ. of Hawaii, 1965-. Compositions incl: E F Kalmus - Symph. No. 1, Str. Quartet No. 1, Dance Overture; Shawnee Press - Gamelan Gong, Evocations, Fantasy on a Quiet Theme; Media Press - Triologue; Music 70 - A Dream Within a Dream; Comps., Authograph Publs. - Ring Around Harlequin; Rochester Music Publsrs. - Prelude & Fugue for Band. Mbrships: ASCAP; Fellow, MacDowell Colony. Hons: First Prize for Canadian Comps., Ottawa Phil., Canada, 1955; Edward Benjamin Prize for Quiet Music, 1956; ASCAP Awards, 1965-74. Hobbies: Golf; Fishing; Swimming. Address: 3310 Keahi St., Honolulu, HI, USA.

MACKAY, Penelope, b. Bradford, UK. Soprano. Educ: AGSM. Debut: Glyndebourne, 1970. Career: operatic roles w. Glyndebourne touring & fest. Cos.; Engl. Opera Grp., New Opera Co., Engl. Nat. Opera & Engl. Music Theatre; app. in premieres of Britten, Lutyens & Henze; concerts & oratorio apps. throughout UK; apps. in Brussels, Venice, Copenhagen, Schwetzingen, Florence, The Maltings, Snape & Royal Opera House, Covent Gdn. Recordings: minor roles in Britten's Death in Venice, 1974. Mbrships: ISM; Equity. Hobbies: Cooking; Reading; Needlework. Mgmt: Lies Askonas; Fraser & Dunlop. Address: 25 Bark Pl., London W2 4AT, UK.

McKEE, Richard, b. 29 Dec. 1941, Hagerstown, Md., USA. Concert, Recital & Operatic Bass-Baritone. Educ: BA, Yale Univ., 1964; MMus, Peabody Conserv., Univ. of Ill., 1969. m. Francine Fenn McKee, 2 d. Debut: Goldovsky Opera, 1971. Career: Wexford Fest., Ireland, 1973, '74; Théatre National Lyrique, Paris, 1975; NYC Opera, 1974-; Major Symphs. & Regional Opera Cos. in USA. Mbrships: Bd. of Dirs., AGMA. Hobbies: Tennis; Golf; NYC Opera Softball Team. Mgmt: Tornay Met Inc., NYC. Address: 182 Daniel Rd., Hamden, CT 06517, USA.

McKELLAR, Hugh Christopher, b. 11 April 1948, Salt Lake City, Utah, USA. Violist. Educ: BMus, Univ. of Utah; studied Viola w. Sally Peck. m. Marsha Nelson, 2 s. Career: Mbr., Utah Symph., 1966-70, & 1971-, & Prin. Violist, 1975-; Prin. Violinist Spokane Symph., 1970-71; Mbr., Meridian Str. Quartet, 1970-; Instructor of Viola, Utah Univ., 1973-; Mbr., Utah Str. Quartet, 1973-. Recordings: Var. records w. Utah Symph. Hobbies: Wilderness Backpacking; Amateur Radio; Cooking; Gardening; Reading; Art History; Archery. Address: 1185 Hudson Ave., Salt Lake City, UT 84106, USA.

McKELLAR, Kenneth, b. 23 June 1927, Paisley, Scotland. Singer, Tenor. Educ: BSc., Aberdeen Univ., 1947; RCM, London. m. Hedy Christine Matisse, 1 s., 1 d. Debut: BBC Scottish Symph., 1947. Career: Prin. Tenor, Carl Rosa Opera Co., 1953-54; Regular TV, Radio Series, A Song for Everyone, 1954-70; Concert & Oratorio, Engl. Opera Group, Aldeburgh & Paris. Compositions: The Tartan; The Twa Corbies; Royal Mile; Island Love; The Long Ships; The Tartan Ribbon; Prayer to the Guardian Angel, var. arrs. Recordings: over 39 LP's, inclng. Messiah (Boult), Folk, Oratorio, Opera, Lieder. Author, The Romantic Scotland of Kenneth McKellar. Contbr. to The Scotsman; Scottish Daily Express. Mbrships: Dir., Radio Clyde Ltd., Glasgow; Fellow, Royal Soc. of Arts; Burns & Pushkin Club, Moscow; Saints & Sinners Club, Scotland. Recip. Henry Leslie Prize, RCM, 1952. Hobbies: Cooking; Reading. Address: 39 Victoria Rd., Lenzie, Glasgow, G66 5AR, UK. 3.

MacKENZIE, Melissa Taylor, b. 23 Sept. 1925, Brownsville, Tenn., USA. Teacher of Music Education, Piano, Voice, Organ; Soprano Soloist & Pianist. Educ: BA, Peabody Coll., Nashville, 1946; Postgrad. work, ibid., 1946; studied piano & voice w. var. tchrs., Memphis, 1946-48; voice study w. Hans J Heinz, speech w. late Julia Duncan, French diction w. Simone France, NY, 1948-50; Postgrad. work, Memphis State Univ., (Summers), 1969-70, UT at Martin, (Summer), 1978, 1980. Div. 1 d. Career: Soprano, Memphis Open Air Theatre, 1948; Soprano, Episcopal Actor's Guild of NY, 1949-51; Am. Theatre Wing, NY, 1949-51; Concert Singer, 1948; Pvte. tchr., piano, voice, organ, 1953-; Tchr., Music Educ., Haywood Co. Bd. of Educ., Brownsville, 1953-; Soprano Soloist & Dir. of Music, Gay Valley Camp, Brevard, NC, 1959-62. Mbrships: Grace Moore Opera Schlrships. Comm., 1966; Nat. Fedn. of Music Clubs; VP, & Parliamentarian, Tenn. Fedn. Music Clubs; Nat. Guild of Piano Tchrs., (Fac. accredited music tchr.) Am. Coll. of Musicians; VP, W Tenn., Prog. Chmn., Tenn. Music Tchrs. Assn; Regent, David Craig Chapt., DAR, 1979-; Rehearsal Club Alumnae Assn., NY; Alpha Delta Kappa; Haywood Co. Histl. Soc.; United Daughters of the Confederacy. Hons. incl: Am. Coll. of Musicians, Hall of Fame, 1969; var. awards & piano schlrships. Hobbies: Antiques; Histl. orgs. Address: 647 W Main St., Brownsville, TN 38012, USA.

MACKEPRANG, Grete, b. 1 Sept. 1937, Copenhagen, Denmark. Pianist. Educ: Dip., Royal Danish Conserv.; Summer Course, Acad. Chigiana, Siena, Italy; Study in Rome w. Guido Agosti. Debut: Copenhagen, 1963. Career incl: concert appearances in Copenhagen & var. Danish cities, etc. Mbr: Danish Musicol. Soc. Hon: 1st Prize, Berlingske Tidende Competition, 1950. Address: Ostervoldgade 4B, Copenhagen K, DK-1350 Denmark.

MACKERNESS, Eric David, b. 21 June 1920, Old Stratford, Northants., UK. Reader in English Literature. Educ: MA, Pembroke Coll., Cambridge; PhD, Manchester Univ. m. Margaret Shaw. Career: currently Rdr. in Engl. Lit., Sheffield Univ. Publs: A Social History of English Music, 1964; Somewhere Further North: A History of Music in Sheffield, 1975. Contbr. to: Musical Times; Music & Letters; Music Review; Can. Music Jrnl.; Monthly Musical Record; Musical Opinion; Grove 6. Hobbies: Industrial Archaeology; Discography; Art History. Address: 3 Peel Terrace, Wilkinson St., Sheffield, UK.

MACKERRAS, Alan Charles (Sir), b. 1 Nov. 1925, Schenectady, USA. Orchestral Conductor. Educ: NSW Conserv. of Music; Acad. of Music, Prague. m. Helena Judith Wilkins, 2 d. Career: Prin. Oboist Sydney Symph. Orch., 1943-46; Cond., Sadler's Wells Opera, 1948-53; Prin. Cond., BBC Concert Orch., 1954-56; First Cond., Hamburg State Opera,

1966-70; Musical Dir., Engl. Nat. Opera, 1970-77; Chief Guest Cond., BBC Symph. Orch., 1976-; Guest Cond., Deutsche Oper, W Berlin, 1978-; Guest Cond. w. most Brit. & European Orchs., Australian Orchs. & w. many Am. Orchs. Compositions: (ballet arrangements) Pineapple Poll; The Lady & the Fool. Recordings: Handel: Messiah; Saul; Israel in Egypt; Fireworks Music; Janacek, Sonfonietta; Wagner, Gotterdammerung excerpts; Donizetti, Roberto Devereux; Dvorak, Symph. No. 8; Purcell, Dido & Aeneas. Contbr. to: Opera Mag.; Music & Musicians. Mbr., ISM. Hons: CBE, 1974. Hobbies: Sailing. Address: 10 Hamilton Terr., London NW8 9UG, UK. 1, 3, 15.

MACKERRAS, Joan C, b. 28 Jan. 1934, Sydney, NSW, Aust. Violinist; Teacher of Violin. Educ: MA, Sydney Univ.; RAM, London; LRAM; ARCM. m. Graeme E Hall, 4 s. Career: Rsch. in Hist. of Violin Playing; Mbr. of Orpheus Ensemble. Contbr. to Musicology (Sydney). Mbr., ISM. Hobbies: Antiques; Architecture; Gardening. Address: Hazedell, Elton Pk., Hadleigh Rd., Ipswich, Suffolk, UK.

MACKEY, (Sister) Mary Lourdes, b. 8 Jan. 1905, Chgo., Ill., USA. College Professor; Pianist; Violinist; Organist; Vocalist. Educ: BS, BA, St. Mary-of-the-Woods Coll., Ind.; M Mus, Northwestern Univ., Evanston, Ill.; PhD, Cath. Univ. of Am., Wash., DC. Career: Coll. Prof., Music Educ., Music Hist., Music Theory, Liturgical Music; Chmn., Coll. Music Dept., 16 yrs.; Supvsr. of Music & Music Educ. for Sisters of Providence; Elem. Tchr., Chgo. Pub. Schls.; Ch. Organist; Parish Musical Dir.; Mbr. sev. civic symph. orchs. (violin). Mbr., sev. musical assns. Publs: Ed. in Chief, To God Through Music Series, 1942-59; Making Music Your Own, Book 7, 1968, Book 8, 1971; Doct. dissertation, The Leading Tone in Western European Music to C. 1600 AD. Address: St. Mary-of-the-Woods, IN 47876, USA.

MACKIE, David, b. 25 Nov. 1943, Greenock, Scotland, UK. Chorus Master; Conductor; Pianist; Accompanist. Educ: Greenock Acad.; RSAMD; Univs. of Glasgow & Birmingham; MA; BMus; DipMusEd.; RSAM; ARCM. Career: Schlmaster, 1965-69; extra-mural lectr., 1968-75; chorus master & assoc. cond., D'Oyly Carte Opera Co., 1975-; tours of Am., Can., Aust., NZ; num. radio & TV apps. as accomp. Comps: unpubld. comps. & arrs. Publ: The Songs of Arthur Sullivan, A Catalogue & Commentary (thesis). Recordings: in Gilbert & Sullivan operas as chorus master; advsr., recording of Sullivan's lesser known works. Mbrships: ISM; Brit. Music Soc.; Sullivan Soc. Hobbies: Travel; Reading; Cartology; Collecting Second-hand Books & Victorian Music; Playing Piano Duets; Sullivan Rsch. Address: c/o Bridget D'Oyly Carte Ltd., 2 Savoy Ct., London WC2R OHE, UK.

MACKIE, Neil, b. 11 Dec. 1946, Aberdeen, Scotland, UK. Tenor. Educ: Dip Mus Ed., RSAMD; Dip., ibid.; ARCM. m. Kathleen Mary Livingstone. Career: BBC Radio & TV; recital & concert apps. throughout Brit., Europe & USA. Recordings: Decca. Mbrships: Serving Brother, Most Venerable Order of St. John; Fellow, Soc. of Antiquaries, Scotland. Hobbies: Reading; Walking. Mgmt: Ibbs & Tillet Ltd., London, UK. Address: 127 Headstone Lane, Harrow, Middx. HA2 6JS, UK.

MACKIE, Shirley M, b. 25 oct. 1929, Rockdale, Tex., USA. Composer; Clarinetist; Conductor. Educ: BM, 1949, MM, 1950, LS Univ.; Aspen Inst., Colo.; Conserv. de Musique, France; studied w. Darius Milhaud, Nadia Boulanger, Reginald Kell & Marcel Jean. Career: Dir. of instrumental music, Riesel High Schl.; Fndr./Cond., Chmbr. Orch. of Waco, Tex.; Clarinetist; Clinician; Adjudicator. Comps. incl: Mister Man (opera); Symph. for the Bicentennia; Comments 1976; Gemini's Journey (ballet); 3 Movements for Solo Clarinet; etc. Contbr. to profl. jrnls. Mbr., num. Musical & educl. assns. Hons. incl: Awards for Comp. from Univ. of NC, Tex. MS Soc., Friends of Harvey Gaul, & others; num. perf. awards & commissions, 1950-. Hobbies incl: Photography; Crafts; Motorhoming. Address: Rt. 1, 100 Wilderness Rd., Waco, TX 76710, USA. 4, 5, 7, 27, 29.

McKIE, (Sir), William Neil, b. 22 May 1901, Melbourne, Vic., Australia. Organist. Educ: RCM, London; MA, DMus., Worcester Coll., Oxford Univ. m. Phyllis Birks, 1956. Career: Dir. of Music, Clifton Coll., Bristol, 1926-30; City Organist, Melbourne, 1931-38; Organist, Magdalene Coll., Oxford, 1938-41; Organist & Master of the Choristers, Westminster Abbey, 1941-63; WW II Serv. w. RAF, 1941-45; Dir. of Music, Coronation of Queen Elizabeth II, 1953. Mbrships: Hon. Sec., RCO, 1963-67. Hons: MVO; Hon. Fellow, Worcester Coll., 1954; DMus., Univ. of Melbourne; Cmdr. w. Star, Order of St. Olav. Address: 10 Driveway, Apt. 1401, Ottawa, Ont., Canada K2P 1C7.

McKINLEY, Sharon, b. 11 Dec. 1941, Penticton, BC, Can. Cellist; Teacher. Educ: Univ. of BC; GSM, UK, 5 yrs. Career: Chmbr. music player; Recitals & concertos; BBC radio & TV apps.; Tchr. of Cello, & Prof. of Cello, GSM; Res. Cellist, Southampton

Univ., 1968-72; Cellist, Orion Piano Trio, Recordings: Goehr, Piano Trio; Camilleri, Piano Trio. Mbr., Musicians Union. Hons: 1st Prize, Royal Overseas League C'wlth. Competition, 1964; Gold Medal, GSM, 1964; 1st Prize, BBC Beethoven Competition, 1969. Hobby: Outdoors. Mgmt: Ingpen & Williams (HHH). Address: 7 Eaton Rise, Ealing, London W5, UK.

McKINNEY, Elizabeth Richmond, b. 8 Dec. 1927, Oakdale, La., USA. Piano Teacher. Educ: B Mus., La. State Univ., 1949; MMus., ibid., 1950. m. Dr. James C McKinney, 3 s. Career: Fac., Glorieta Bapt. Assembly; Res. Tchr. of Piano, Southwestern Bapt. Theol. Sem.; Adjudicator, NGPT & var. contests; Frequent Apps., Recitals, Concerts w. Husband; Accomp. Met. Opera Soprano Irene Jordan, tour of Nigeria, 1973. Mbrships: Phi Kappa Phi; Delta Omicron; Past Pres., La.State Univ. Chapt., ibid; NGPT; Euterpean Club; Sem. Women's Club. Named Outstanding First-Year Music Student. La State Univ. Hobbies: Cooking; Travel. Address: 5604 Wedgmont Circle N., Ft. Worth, TX 76133, USA.

McKINNEY, James Carroll, b. 11 Jan. 1921, Minden, La., USA. Administrator. Educ: La Polytechnic Inst., 1938-40; Stanford Univ., 1943-44; BMus, La. State Univ., 1949; MMus., ibid., 1950; MusD Arts, Univ. of Southern Calif., 1969. m. Elizabeth Richmond McKinney, 3 s. Career: Num. Vocal Perfs., Oratorio Recital & opera, S, SW & Calif.; Baritone's Soloist, First Presby. Ch., Hollywood, Calif., 1957-69; Perfs. w. Beaumont Civic Opera, F. Worth Opera, Shreveport Symph. Tex. Choral Clinics, Ala. Address: 5604 Wedgmont Circle, Ft. Worth, TX 76133. 2, 7.

McLAREN, Lorna J R, b. 17 May 1953, Dundee, UK. Violinist. Educ: Pvte. study of violin, piano & clarinet to 1970; Studied piano w. Miles Coverdale, Violin w. Roger Raphael, RSAM, 1970-73; Tchrs. & Perfs. Dip., ibid. Debut: City Hall, Perth, 1973. Career: w. BBC Scottish Symph. Orch., 3 yrs., giving regular radio & TV perfs.; BBC Club. Hons: R. Highgate Scholarship for Violin, 1971; Prize for Sightreading, 1971; Subject Prize for Violin, 1973; J D Miles & Hilda Bailey Prizes for Violin, 1973. (all RSAM). Hobbies: Cycling; Swimming; Anything mentally or physically stimulating. Address: 17 N Gardner St., Glasgow G11 7BU, UK.

McLEAN, Barton, b. 4 Aug. 1938, Poughkeepsie, NY, USA. Composer. Educ: MA, music theory, Eastman Schl. Music, 1965; MusD, composition, Ind. Univ., 1972. m. Priscilla McLean. Career incls: Hd., composition-theory, & Dir., electronic music ctr., contemporary chmbr. ensemble, Ind. Univ. S Bend, 1969-; Num. apps. w. wife, electronic music duo 'McLean Mix', throughout USA. Compositions incl: Spirals; Dimensions II; The Sorcerer Revisited; Genesis (all recorded). Mbrships: incl: Exec. Comm., Am. Soc. Univ. Composers. Recip., num. grants. Hobbies: Mtn. climbing; Canoeing. Address: 58412 Locust Rd., S Bend, IN 46614, USA.

McLEAN, Priscilla Anne Taylor, b. 27 May 1942, Fitchburg, Mass., USA. Composer; Teacher; Performer. Educ: BME, Mass. State Coll., Lowell, 1965; MMus, Ind. Univ., 1969. m. Barton Keith McLean. Career: Assoc., Ind. Univ., Kokomo, 1971-73; Assoc., St. Mary's Coll., Notre Damr, Ind., 1973-; Composer-in-Res., Ind. Univ. S Bend; Mbr., McLean Mix, composing-performing duo. Comps. incl: Variations & Mozaics on a Theme of Stravinsky (orch.), 1967-69, rev. 1974; Ah-Syn (all-harp & synthesizer), 1974. Recordings: Dance of Dawn; Interplanes. Mbrships incl: Exec. Comm., Am. Soc. Univ. Composers; Co Dir., Nat. Radio Contemporary Music Series, ibid., 1974-. Hon: Martha Baird Rockefeller Grant, orchl. work, 1975. Hobbies incl: Skiing; Mountain climbing. Address: 58414 Locust Rd., S Bend, IN 46614, USA.

McLELLAN, Irene Mary, b. 1 Feb. 1928, Toronto, Ont., Can. Performer & Teacher of Piano & Voice; Adjudicator; Examiner; Lecturer. Educ: Grad., ARCT, Royal Conser., Toronto; Piano studies w. E R Schmitz & Karl Ulrich Schnabel; Voice studies w. Eilene Law, Ernesto Vinci & George Lamber; Dance studies w. Sabina Nordoff, NYC. m. H C Kretz (div.). Career: Recitalist, NBC & CBC radio; recital tours in major cities in USA & Can., & in Bermuda; Hd. of Music, Rudolf Steiner Schl., NYC, 1957-63; Cond., Scarborough Light Opera Co., 1964-67; Mbr., Bd. of Examiners, RCM; on edl. bd., RCM Grade Books. Comps: num. works for Sabina Nordoff dance group; Studies for Human Voice (w. Halim el Dabh); 1 electronic comp. Contbr. to Rudolf Steiner Schools, 1962; Toronto Life Mag., 1978. Mbr., sev. profl. socs. Hons: Royal Conserv. Scholarships, 1944, '45, '46; Mirror Drama Awards, Best Dir., Musical Comedy, 1965-66. Hobbies: Painting; Needlework; Fishing; Hiking. Address: 2365 Kennedy Rd., Apt. 401, Toronto, Ont. M1T 3S6, Can.

McLELLAN, Michael J, b. 29 Apr. 1941, Auckland, NZ. Violinist; Conductor; Teacher. Educ: RCM, London, 1961-63;

LTCL; LRSM; FTCL. m. Anne S McLellan, 1 s., 2 d. Debut: as violinist w. Royal Liverpool Phil. Orch. under Boult, 1964. Career: Tchr., Auckland Educ. Dept.; regular broadcasts on Radio NZ; perfs. w. Symphonia of Auckland & Nat. Youth Orch. of NZ; Fndr. Cond., Auckland Jr. Trng. Orch., 1967; appointed Cond., Auckland Jr. Symph. Orch., 1974. Hobbies: Swimming; Carpentry; Reading. Address: 4 Kitirawa Rd., Remuera, Auckland 5, NZ.

MACLEOD, Bobby, b. 8 May 1925, Tobermory, Isle of Mull, Scotland, UK. Musician (Accordeon). Educ: RAF Wartime Educ. Course, Aberdeen Univ. pvte. study of Bagpipe music, Gaelic & traditional Folk. m. Jean MacCulloch, 3 s., 1 d. Career: Touring Dance Circuit, UK, Ireland, France, Moscow, USSR; Broadcasts from 1948 inclng. TV White Heather; apps. at major theatres in UK; US venues incl. Solo apps. at Carnegie Hall, NYC. Compositions: Num. Scottish airs. Recordings for Decca, EMI, Phillips, RCA, Pye, BBC archives. Publ: Bobby MacLeod Arrangements & Compositions. Contbr. to: Accordeon Times. Mbr., Glasgow Soc. of Musicians. Hobbies: Sailing; Rowing; Music; Drinking; Fishing. Address: Royal Building, Tobermory, Isle-of-Mull, Scotland, UK.

McLEOD, Jennifer Helen, b. 12 Nov. 1941, Wellington, NZ. Composer; Pianist. Educ: B Mus, Victoria Univ. of Wellington; studied w. Oliver Messiaen at Paris Conserv. & w. K-H Stockhausen at Cologne Course for New Music. m. Bruce Henry Greenfield. Appts: Lectr., 1967-70, Prof. of Music, 1971-76, Victoria Univ., Wellington; Nat. Progs. Supvsr., Divine Light Mission, Auckland, 1976-. Comps. publd: Piano Piece, 1965; For Seven; Earth & Sky. Comps. recorded: Cambridge Suite, Kiwi; Piano Piece, 1965, Kiwi; Earth & Sky, Philips; Under the Sun, Philips. Mbrships: Australasian Performing Rights Assn.; Hobby: Meditation. Address: c/o Divine Light Mission, Not. Office, PO Box 68471, Auckland, NZ.

McLEOD, John, b. 8 Mar. 1934, Aberdeen, Scotland, UK. Composer; Conductor; Director of Music. Educ: ARAM; LRAM; ARCM; FTCL. m. Margaret Murray, 2 c. Career: Cond., Perth Choral & Orch. Socs., 1965-73; Cond., Glasgow Orchl. Soc., 1971-75; Guest Cond., Scottish Nat. Orch., BBC Scottish Symph. Orch.; Cond., Edinburgh Royal Choral Union, 1977-; Dir. of Music, Merchiston Castle Schl., Edinburgh. Comps: Orchl. Works: Chmbr. & Instrumental Music & Vocal Music. Contbr. to Comp. Mag. Mbrships: Scottish Br., Comps. Guild of GB; BBC Scottish Music Advsry. Comm.; ISM. Hons. incl: Arthur Hinton Prize for Comp., RAM, 1961; Guinness Prize, 1979. Hobbies: Lit.; Art; Var. indoor & outdoor hobbies. Address: The Fairway, Merchiston Castle Schl., Edinburgh EH13OPT, UK.

McMASTER, Gloria, b. Montreal, Wis., USA. Singer; Teacher. Educ: Univ. of Minn.; Columbia Univ.; Univ. of Detroit; SUNY, Brockport, BS, Juilliard Schl. of Music, 1951; MMus, Eastman Schl. of Music, 1955. m. Martin Juhn II, 3 s., 2 d. Debut: Juilliard Schl. Opera Theatre, 1950. Career: TV apps; soloist, Nat. GOP Convention, 1968; radio broadcasts in Mich., Minn., & NY; solo apps. w. Mpls. Symph., Buffalo Phil. & Rochester, NY, Phil.; concerts in recitals & oratorios in Rochester, Mpsl., NYC, NJ, Buffalo & in Frankfurt & Munich, W Germany. num. recordings. Publ: Survey of Singers' Diction in American Music Colleges, 1974. Mbrships: Nat. Assn. of Tchrs. of Singing; NY State MTA; Nat. Opera Guild; Fndr. & Dir., Dansville Music Theater; Assoc. Prof., Houghton Coll., 1971-75; SUNY, Genesio, 1968-71. Hons: Perf. Cert., Eastman Schl., 1957; Nat. Cert., MTNA. Address: 26 Bromley Rd., Pittsford, NY 14534, USA.

McMEEKIN, Colleen, b. 2 Aug. 1917, Sydney, NSW, Aust. Cellist. Educ: studied w. Gladstone Bell, NSW Conservatorium of Music, Sydney, 1936-41; studied w. Maurice Eisenburg, London, UK, 1948-49; studied viol da gamba. m. Ivan McMeedin, 2 d. Career: w. Sydney Symph. Orch., 1941-47; Soloist & freelance musician, London & provinces, UK, 3 yrs.; joined staff of NSW State Conservatorium (tchng. chmbr. music & cello), 1962; currently tchng. at Sydney Conserv., Sydney Grammar Schl.; Examiner, Aust. Music Examination Bd.; Cello Tutor, Sydney Youth Orch.; var. sonata & chmbr. music perfs. Address: 61 Prices Circuit, Woronora River, NSW, 2232, Australia.

MacMILLAN, Mary Lynn Prough, b. 17 Jan. 1944, Mishawaka, Ind., USA. Percussion Teacher; Percussionist. Educ: B Mus., Western Mich. Univ., Kalamazoo, Mich.; studied w. Bob Tiles & Bobby Christian, Chgo. m. Duncan MacMillan Jr., 1 s., 1 d. Career: has played w. Kalamazoo Concert Band, Kalamazoo Symph. Orch., Lansing (Mich.) Symph. Orch., S Bend (Ind.) Symph. Orch., Elkhart (Ind.) Symph. Orch., Ind. Univ. (S Bend) Chmbr. Orch., Mich. Symphonette, & Twin Cities Concert Band, S Bend, & in Musical Theatre, S Bend; currently Timpanist, S Bend Symph. Percussion Instr., St. Mary's Coll., Notre Dame, Ind.

Publs: Notes; Get a Set; Snare Drum Music. Contbr. to: The Percussionist. Mbrships: Percussive Arts Soc.; AAUW. Address: 1702 Winston Dr., South Bend, IN 46635, USA.

MACNAGHTEN, Anne Catherine, b. 9 Aug. 1908, Whitwick, UK. Violinist. Educ: Leipzig Conserv. of Music. m. Arnold Richardson Ashby, 1 s., 1 d. Debut: Dublin, 1931. Career: FndrLdr., Macnaghten String Quartet; Co-Fndr., Macnaghten Concerts (now New Macnaghten concerts). Mbrships: ISM; Musicians Union; European String Tchrs. Assn. Recip., Gold Medal for servs. to chmbr. music, Worshipful Co. of Musicians. Address: 23 Wymondley Rd., Hitchin, Herts., UK. 14.

McNAUGHT, Anthony Jonathan, b. 8 Apr. 1956, Carlisle, UK. Teacher of Violin, Organ & Piano. Educ: Royal Coll. of Music; GRSM; ARCM, Organ Teaching; LRAM, Violin Teaching; Music Tchrs.' Cert., London Univ. Inst. of Educ. Career: Peripatetic Violin Tchr., London Borough of Hillingdon; Asst. Dir. of Music, Bishop's Stortford Coll. Mbrships: Incorp. Soc. of Musicians; Royal Coll. Organists. Hobbies: Cricket; Walking; Swimming. Address: 63 Homewood Rd., Northenden, Manchester, M22 4DG, UK.

MacNEIL, Cornell Hill, b. 24 Sept. 1922, Mpls., Minn., USA. Operatic Baritone. Educ: Julius Hartt Schl. of Music, Univ. of Hartford; var. pvte. tchrs. m. Tania Rudensky, 5 c. by previous marriage. Debut: in Menotti's The Consul, Broadway, NYC, 1950. Career incls: Broadway Actor, Sweethearts, 1947 & Where's Charley, 1949; Menotti's The Consul, 1950; debut w. NYC opera as Germont in La Traviata, 1953; debut as La Scala as Charles V in Ernani, 1959 & at Metrop. Opera as Rigoletto, 1959; has sung in ldng. opera houses of Europe & the Ams. Recordings incl: Rigoletto; La Fanciulla Del West; Aida; Ballo in Maschera. Mbrships: Pres., Am. Guild of Musical Artists, 1971-77. Recip., Alumnus of the yr., Hartt Schl. of Music, 1976. Hobbies: Cooking; Gardening; Woodworking. Mgmt: Ronald Wilford, Columbia Artists Mgmt. Inc., 165 W 57th St., NY, NY 10019, USA. Address: c/o Mgmt.

McNEILL, Marguerite Grace, b. 1 Dec. 1935, Sydney, NSW, Aust. Amateur Singer. Educ: Pvte. studies; Convent Schsl., NSW State Conserv. of Music. Career incls: TV apps. (Philatelic World Music & Theatre); Eisteddfods, opera & oratorio apps.; Collector & Annotator of over 1,000 pages associated w. the perf. arts, Philatelic World of Music & Theatre in Miniature; num. pvte. exhibitions of collection; Pub. Festivals, Sutherland Civic Ctr., 1978; Festival of Sydney, 1979. Press Book of Joan of Sutherland CBE & Richard Bonynge CBE. Contbr. to: Theatre Aust. Mbrships: Friends of the Aust. Opera; Ladies Committee, Archives of Theatrical Memorabilia (Opera & Ballet); Libn., Joan Sutherland Soc. of Sydney. Hobbies: Stamp collecting; Reading; Copper plaques of scenes of opera & singers; Records. Address: c/o 26 Colebourne Ave., Mortdale, NSW 2223, Aust.

MACONCHY, Elizabeth, b. 19 Mar. 1907. Composer. Educ: Pvte.; RCM, London; studied w. Vaughan-Williams, ibid. m. William Richard Le Fanu, 2 d. Debut: 1st public perf., Piano Concerto, w. Prague Phil. Orch., 1930. Career: Has had many of her num. comps. perfd. at Fests. etc., inclng. "The Land", perfd. Henry Wood Promenade Concerts, 1930; var. works, 3 Fests. of Int. Soc. for Contemporary Music, Prague, 1935, Paris, 1937, Copenhagen, 1947; Also broadcasts, UK & abroad. Num. comps. incl: Reflections, for Oboe, Clarinet, Viola & Harp, (Gedok Int. Prize, 1961); Ariadne (C Day Lewis), for Soprano & Orch., King's Lynn Fest., 1971; 3 One Act Operas, The Sofa, The Three Strangers, The Departure; The Leaden Echo & the Golden Echo (G M Hopkins), 1978; Heloise & Abelard, dramatic Cantata for 3 soloists, chorus & orch., 1978; num. other works. Mbrships: Chmn., Composers' Guild of GB, (1st Woman Chmn.), 1960; Chmn., SPNM (Pres., 1977). Recip., Medal, Worshipful Co. of Musicians for services to Chamber Music, 1970; CBE, 1977; Hon. Fellow, St. Hilda's Coll., Oxford, 1978. Address: Shottesbrook, Boreham, Chelmsford, Essex, UK. 1, 3, 27.

McPHEE, George, b. 10 Nov. 1937, Glasgow, Scotland, UK. Lecturer; Organist & Choirmaster. Educ: Dip. Mus Ed., RSAM; BMus, Edinburgh Univ.; FRCO. m. Margaret Ann Scotland, 1 s., 2 d. Career: Lectr., RSAM; Organist & Master of the Choirsters, Paisley Abbey. Recordings: (solo organ) Mangificat; Modern French Organ Music; (choral) Schutz & Monteverdi; Sacred Songs & Hosanna w. Kenneth McKellar & the Choir of Paisley Abbey; O Sing a New Song; Glory to God; The Choir of Paisley Abbey; Hymns for Everyone; The Organ of Paisley Abbey. Mbr., ISM; Royal Troon Golf Club. Hons: Silver Medal, Worshipful Co. of Musicians, 1962; Limpus Prize, FRCO exam., 1962; Sir D F Tovey Prize, Edinburgh Univ., 1963. Hobbies: Golf; Swimming. Address: 17 Main Rd., Castlehead, Paisley PA2 6AJ, UK. 3.

MACPHERSON, Gordon Clarke, b. 14 Nov. 1924, Moose Jaw. Sask., Canada. Professor of Piano; Conductor; Acting Director. Educ: MMus, Ind. Univ.; Artist Dip., Univ. of Toronto; Lic. Dip. (LRCT), Royal Conserv. of Music, Toronto. m. Billie MacPherson, 1 s., 1 d. Career: Concerts & broadcasts as Soloist & Chamber Music player; Cond. for radio & TV; Music Adviser to CBC (Maritimes) & Acting dir., Maritime Conserv.; currently Prof. of Piano, Conductor & Acting Dir., Brandon Univ.; Mbr., Brandon Univ. Trio. Recordings: RCA ccCCS - 1023; CBC Radio Canada Broadcasts Recording SM-245 Stereo, w. Brandon Univ. Trio; other recordings for CBC Int. Serv. Mbrships: Pi Kappa Lambda; Canada Music Council; CAUSM; MRMTA. Recip., Canada Coun. Fellowships, 1962, '74. Hobbies: Reading; Hi-Fi. Address: 3032 Park Ave., Brandon, Manitoba R7B 2K3, Canada.

McQUATTIE, Sheila, b. 23 Mar. 1943, Edinburgh, Scotland, UK. Singer; Pianist; Composer; Lecturer. Educ: ATCL (piano tchng.), 1959; ATCL (singing), 1960; LTCL (piano), 1961; LTCL (singing); 1961; LTCL (class tchrs.), 1962; GTCL, 1963; BMus, 1964. m. John Tudhope, 2 c. Career: recital & oratorio work; 1st broadcast concert perf. of Turina's Canto à Sevilla; Mbr., Florian Ensemble; comps. frequently perf. in concerts. Comps. incl: 2 children's cantatas, Christmas Music for Children & Bambleford Minor. Mbrships: Chmn., Concert Committee of W London Inst. Hons: Winner, BBC comp. competition, 1958; David Taylor prize, 1960; State Scholarship, 1961; Piano Scholarship to TCL, 1961; Alec Rowley Prize, 1963. Hobby: Painting. Address: Tiled Lodge, Iver Heath, Bucks., UK.

MACUDZINSKA, Sylvia, b. 11 Nov. 1906, Mojmirovce, Czechoslovakia. Pianist. Educ: Music Acad., Bratislava; State Music Conserv., Brno; Dip., State Music Conserv., Prague. m. Prof. Rudolf Macudzinski, 1 s. Debut: Brno, 1926. Career: Concert pianist w. Czech. Phil. in Tchaikovsky & Dvorak Concerto; Piano duo w. husband, 1925-; performances in most European music ctrs. Recordings incl: works by Busoni. Saint-Saens, etc. Mbr: Zvaz slovenskych skladatelov. Hon: Frico Kafenda Prize, 1967. Hobby: Cooking. Mgmt: Slovkoncert, Bratislava. Address: Uprkova 39, 809 00 Bratislava, Czechoslovakia.

MACUDZINSKI, Rudolf, b. 29 Apr. 1907, Opatija, Yugoslavia. Concert Pianist; Professor of Music. Educ: German Univ., Prague, Czech.; State Conserv., Brno.; Dip., State Conserv., Prague. m. Sylvia, 1 s. Debut: Brno, 1925. Career: Accompanist to Henri Marteau, 1926-31; Pianist & broadcaster, Czech. radio, 1931-45; w. Nat. Theatre Opera, Bratislava, 1946-53; Prof. of Piano & Pro Dekan, Music Fac., Bratislava Acad. of Music, 1953-74. Compositions incl: Monte Cristo (4-act opera); Le Reve de Coubertin (Ballet on the Olympic Games 1896-1976); Die Warnung von El-Amarna (2-act opera). Mbrships: Slovak Composers Union; Slovak Authors Union. Hons. incl: Kafenda Prize, 1967. Hobbies: Philately; Filming; Travel. Mgmt: Agcy. Slovkoncert, Bratislava. Address: Uprkova 39, 809 00 Bratislava, Czechoslovakia.

MACURDY, John, b. 18 mar. 1929, Detroit, Mich., USA. Bass singer. Educ: Wayne State Univ., Detroit; vocal study w. Avery Crew, Detroit. m. Justine May Votypka, 1 s., 1 d. Debut: New Orleans Opera, 1952. Career: NYC Center Opera, 1959-62; Metropolitan Opera, 1962-; Apps. w. San Francisco Opera, Paris Opera, La Scala, Salzburg Fest., Orange Fest., Aix-en-Provence Fest., Chicago, Hollywood Bowl, Miami Opera, Scottish Opera etc.; apps. w. leading symph. orchs. Commendatore in film of Don Giovanni, 1979. num. recordings. Mbrships: Bohemian Club, NY. Hons: City of Detroit medal, 1969; Rockefeller Foundation Grant, 1959. Hobbies: Antiques; Gardening; Tennis; Golf. Mgmt: AIM, 3 & 4 Albert Terr., London NW1 7SU. Address: Tall Oaks Court, Stamford, CT 06903, USA. 2.

McVEAGH, Diana M, b. 6 Sept. 1926, Ipoh, Malaya. Freelance Music Writer. Educ: ARCM.; GRSM. m. C W Morley. Career: Tutor Extramural Dept., London Univ., UK, 1952-65; Ed., RCM Mag., 1959-65; Asst. Ed., Musical Times, 1964-67; Exec. Comm. Mbr., Grove's Dictionary, (6th Ed.). Publs: Edward Elgar, 1955. Contbr. to: The Times; The Musical Times; The Listener, etc. Mbrships: Royal Musical Assn. Coun., 1961-75, VP ibid., 1975. Address: Ladygrove, The Lee, Great Missenden, Bucks, HP16 9NA, UK.

McVICAR, George Christie, b. 17 Mar. 1919, Dumbarton, UK. Music Adviser. Educ: Dumbarton Acad.; Dip. Mus Ed., Royal Scottish Acad. Music. Publs: Opera Airs for Boys' Classes; In the Minor Mode; A First Minor Reader; The Oxford Scottish Song Book. Mbrships: Vice Chmn., Scottish Amateur Music Assn.; ISM; Hon. Fellow, Tonic Solfa Coll. of Music. Address: 22 Queen St., Stirling, UK. 3.

McWILLIAM, Clement Charles, b. 19 Jan. 1934, Blackheath, London, UK. Organist; Teacher; Harpsichord

Continuo. Educ: RCM, London; BMus., Trinity Coll., Dublin (externally); ARCM. m. Deborah Jane Stokes, 1 s., 1 d. Career: Sub-Organist, St. George's Chapel, Windsor, 1959-65; Sub-Organist, Winchester Cathedral, 1967-75; Dir. of Music, Pilgrims' Schl., Winchester, 1969-. Compositions: Hymn tune, Dulwich (Anglican Hymn Book); Carol arr., 'Unto Us Is Born a Son' (recorded). Three recordings as Organist of Winchester Cathedral Choir. Mbrships: RCM Union; RCO. Hons: Worshipful Co. of Musicians Silver Medal (FRCO) & Limpus Prize, 1958. Hobbies: Railways; Gardening; Crosswords; Mathematics. Address: 62 Middle Brook St., Winchester, Hants. SO23 8DQ, UK.

MADDOX, Robert Lee, b. 22 Jan. 1935, Ranger, Tex., USA. Music Educator; Conductor; Trumpeter. Educ: BA, N Tex. State Univ., 1956; MMus Ed., ibid., 1957; PhD, NY Univ., 1973; Condng. study w. Pierre Derveaux, Int. Summer Acad., Nice, France. m. Irene Newcomb, 2 d. Career: Trumpet, Charlotte Symph., 1963-; Assoc. Cond., Charlotte Symph. Youth Orch., 1963-72; Music Dir., Youth Symph. of the Carolinas, 1973-; Dir. of Instrumental Music, Garinger HS, Charlotte, NC, 1963-; Cond., Charlotte Summer Pops Orch. Contbr. to: The Instrumentalist; NC Music Educator mag. Mbrships: Pi Kappa Lambda; Phi Mu Alpha; State Orch. Chmn., NC Music Educators Coun., 1970-72. Hobbies: Travel; Reading. Address: 4508 Carriage Dr., Charlotte, NC 28205, USA.

MADDOX, Walter Allen, b. 17 Jan. 1935, Portland, Ore., USA. Violinist. Educ: Violin Dip., Juilliard Schl. of Music, w. Joseph Fuchs; Post Grad., Juilliard Schl. of Music, w. Oscar Shumsky. m. Myrna Lynn Maddox. Career: Pitts. Symph. Orch., 1960-62; Juilliard Orch. European Tour, 1958; Detroit Symph. Orch., 1964-. Recordings: w. Pitts. Symph. & Detroit Symph. Hobbies: Bicycling; Body Building. Address: 1931 Fleetwood, Grosse Pointe Woods, MI 48236, USA.

MADEY, Boguslaw, b. 31 May 1932, Sosnowiec, Poland. Conductor; Composer; Pianist. Educ: Dip., Comp., Acad. of Music, Poznan; Dip., Piano, ibid.; Dip., Cond., ibid.; GSM, UK. m. Anna Malewicz-Madey, 1 s. Debut: Cond., Poznan, 1958. Career: Asst. Cond., Poznan Phil., Piano Tchr., Acad. of Music, Poznan, 1958-59; Cond., Grand Theatre of Opera & Ballet, Warsaw, 1960-72; Tchr., Cond. & Opera Ensemble, Acad. of Music, Warsaw, 1960-67; Prof. of Cond., Acad. of Music, Warsaw, 1967-; Hd., Cond. Dept., ibid., 1969-71; Artistic Dir. & Prin. Cond., Grand Theatre of Opera & Ballet, Lodz, 1972-77; Dean, Fac. of Comp., Cond. & Theory of Music, Acad. of Music, Warsaw, 1975-78; Rector, ibid., 1978-; Guest Cond., num. opera cos.; Concerts in Europe, USA & S Am.; var. Radio, TV & Film perfs. Comps. incl: Allegro, Viariations, Sonatina, Preludes, piano; Concerto, piano & orch.; Suite, Dancing Impressions, Ballet Scene, Dramatic Overture, Scherzo Vantastico, orch.; Concereto, flute & orch.; Transfigurations, voice & instruments. Mbr. var. profl. orgs. Hons: Medal of 30 yrs. of Poland & Gold Cross of Merit; Prize of Ministry of Culture & Art, Warsaw, 1976; Medal of Assn. of Authors & Comps. ZAIKS, Warsaw, 1978. Hobbies: Painting; Swimming. Address: 27/33 m. 36 ul. Slowackiego, 01-592 Warsaw, Poland.

MADSEN, Clifford K, b. 3 May 1937, Price, Utah, USA. Professor. Educ: Eastman Schl. of Music, 1956; AS, Coll. of Eastern Utah, 1957; BA, Brigham Young Univ., 1959; MA, ibid., 1960; PhD, Fla. State Univ., 1963. m. Mary Marakis, 3 c. Publs: Experimental Research in Music (w. C H Madsen, Jr.), 1970; Research in Music Behavior; Modigying Music Behavior in the Classroom (Ed. w. R D Greer & C H Madsen Jr.), 1975. Contbr. to: Music Educators Jrnl.; Jrnl. of Rsch. in Music Educ.; Music Therapy Jrnl.; Jrnl. of Rsch. in Music Educ.; Music Therapy Jrnl.; Jrnl. of Acoustical Soc. of Am.; Jrnl. of Applied Behavioral Analysis; Instrumentalist, etc. Mbrships: AAAS; MENC; MAMT; AAUP; Phi Mu Alpha; Kappa Kappa Psi; Phi Delta Kappa; Phi Kappa Phi; Pi Kappa Lambda; Edit. Bd., Jrnl. of Rsch. in Music Educ. & Jrnl. of Music Cherapy. Recip: Keeler Award, Most Outstanding Musician, Brigham Young Univ., 1960. Addrss: 1929 Belle Vue Way, Tallahassee, FL 32304, USA. 7, 28.

MADSEN, Cornelia May Bates, b. 15 May 1939, LA, Calif., USA. Trumpeter; Choir Director; Pianist; Conductor. Educ: BS, Brigham Young Univ.; MA, ibid.; PhD, Univ. of Utah. m. Gary Madsen, 2 s., 1 d. Career: Perfs. in Dance Bands on Las Vegas TV; 1st Trumpet, Utah Valley Symph. Brass Choir. var. bands & orchs.; Choir Dir., Ch. of Jesus Christ of Latter Day Saints; Cond., Special Mormon Youth Choirs; Tchr., Cond., Junior High & Elementary Schl. Orch.; Tchr. Gen. Music; Pvte. Tchr. Piano, Trumpet; Mbr. Utah State Music Textbook & Curriculum Committee. Contbr. to: Instrumentalist Mag.; Utah Music Educator. Mbrships: Sec., Local 272, Am. Fedn. of Musicians; Sec., Utah Valley Symph. Bd.; Life, MENC; Life, NEA; Utah Valley Fine Arts Coun.; Music Ldrship, Alpine Schl. Dist.; Nat. Hons.

Soc. Recip. num. Hons. Hobbies: Homemaking; Literature; Art; Sewing; Cooking; Travel; Gardening. Address: 2857 N. Iroquois Dr., Provo, UT84601, USA. 76.

MADSEN, Norma Lee, b. 2 Dec. 1927, Tremonton, Utah, USA. Symphony Violinist; Violin Teacher; University Adjunct Professor of Music; Assistant Concertmaster. Educ: Brigham Young Univ., 1947; BS, Univ. of Utah, 1951. Career incls: Apps. w. ASTA Festival String Quartet & Utah String Quartet; Frequent Contest Adjudicator; w. Utah Symph. on tours of Europe, Ctrl. & S Am. & UK; Dir., ASTA Nat. String Conf., 1970-. Recordings: As violin soloist w. LDS Tabernacle Choir (CBS); sev. as mbr. of Utah Symph. Publs: Mu Phi Epsilon Composers & Their Works, 1956, 3rd Edn. w. supplements, 1958. Contbr. to num. profl. mags., etc. Mbrships: Mu Phi Epsilon; 1st VP, Utah Fedn. of Music Clubs; Music Tchrs. Nat. Assn.; Utah Music Tchrs. Assn. Recip. of var. awards inclng: 30-yr. Silver Bowl, Utah Symph., 1974; Tchr. Recognition Award, MTNA, 1970-72. Hobbies: Fishing; Golf; Tennis; Scrapbooks; Travel. Address: 2809 Connor St., Salt Lake City, UT 84109, USA. 9, 29.

MADSEN, Trygve, b. 15 Feb. 1940, Fredikstad, Norway. Composer. Educ: Studies in comp. w. Egil Hovland, & in piano w. Ivar Johnsen, 1957-62; studied at Acad. for Music & Fine Arts, Vienna, Austria, 1969-71. m. Brigitte Barbara Hambrusch, 1 d. Career: Music for TV Musical, The Blue People, 1975, & TV satire, Well, Well, Well, 1975 & other TV progs. & films; broadcasts of song cycles in Scandinavia & Belgium. Compositions incl: Suite for Flute & Piano, 1968; 3 Gags for Wind Quintet, 1972; Piano Sonata No. 1, 1972; 5 Launen des Herrn Mephisto Foss (wind quartet), 1973; Concert overture for Symph. Orch., 1975; 40 Lieder; (recorded) 2 Songs for Children, 1973; The Blue People, 1975. Mbr., profl. assns., Norway. Hobbies: Literature; Philosophy; Cooking. Address: Sorlistien 12, 1473 Skarer, Norway.

MADUREIRA António José, b. 24 Nov. 1949, Macau, Brazil. Violist; Orchestral Director. Educ: Art Schl., Univ. Fed., Pernam buco Brazil; Guitar studies w. Prof. José Carrion. m. Sevy de Barros Madureira Ferreira, 1 d., 1 s. Career: Comp. music for the theatre, inclng. Benjamin Santos play, Barca d'Ajuda; Dir., Orch. Romançal Brasileira, Recife; Apps. in all Brzilian capitals & Player of viola nordestina w. Quinteto Armorial in Georgia, USA. Comps: Revoada; Toré; Repente; Toada e Dobrado de Cavalhada; Excelencia; Romances da Bela Infata e de Minervina. Recordings: Quinteto Armorial. Mbrships: Brazilian Soc. of Contemporary Music; Cultural Committee, Recife. Hons: Quinteto Armorial, considered best Brazilian instrumental group of 1974 by Sao Paulo Art Critics Assn.; Quinteto Armorial's record was voted to be in the top 10 of 1974. Mgmt: Discos Marcus Pereira, Rua Novo Horizonte 266, Sao Paulo. Address: Rua Souza Bandeira 87, Cordeiro, Recife-PE, Brazil.

MAEDEL, Rolf, b. 17 Mar. 1917, Berlin, Germany. Pianist; Composer; Conductor; Professor of Music-Theory. Educ: Music Acads., Berlin & Salzburg; Dip., piano; Dip., tchng. m. Caterina Deringer, 5 c. Career: Tours as comp. pianist & cond. (operas), throughout Europe; Radio broadcasts, Germany, France, Spain, Switzerland, Portugal, Austria, Italy, etc.; Tchr., Music, Theory. Mozarteum, Salzburg. Comp: Chmbr. music; Songs; Lieder; Piano pieces, etc. Recordings: Cembalo-Concert (OEKB). Publ: Das Transzendentale Tonsystem, 1975. Mbr. profl. orgs. Recip: Forderungspreis, Austrian Govt., 1956. Address: Konst. Weberg. 12, 1-5020 Salzburg, Austria.

MAEGAARD, Jan Carl Christian, b. 14 April 1926, Copenhagen, Denmark. Professor; Composer. Educ: Dip., Conserv. of Music; Mag-art., 1957, Dr. Phil., 1972, Univ. of Copenhagen; Post Grad. studies, UCLA, Los Angeles, 1958-59. m. Kirsten Offer Maegaard, 2 d. Career: Lectr., 1959, Prof., 1971, Univ. of Copenhagen; Prof., UCLA, Los Angeles, 1978. Comps. incl: Trio for oboe, clarinet & bassoon; Elegy of Equinox for soprano, cello & organ; Chamber Concerto No. 2; Octomeri for violin & piano; 5 preludes for violin solo; Serenade for violin, cello, piano; Musica riservata no. 1 for string quartet; Musica riservata no. 2 for reed quartet; Due tempi for orch.; Pastorale for 2 clarinets; Sic enim amavit for soprano and/or choir, trumpet & organ. Publs: Musikalsk Modernisme, 1964, '71; Studein zur Entwicklung des doderkaphonen Satzes bei Arnold Schönberg, 1972; Praludier til musik af Schönberg, 1976. Contbr. to: Die Musikforschung; Melos; Zeitschrift für Musiktheorie; Dansk Musiktidsskrift. Mbrships: Int. Musicol. Soc.; Int. Soc. for Contemporary Music (Pres., Danish Sect., 1956-58). Address: UCLA Dept. of Music, 405 Hilgard Ave., LA, CA 90024, USA.

MAES, Ernest Paul, b. 13 July 1939, Dendermonde, Belgium. Horn Player; Professor of Horn, Conservatorium, Brussels; Director-Conductor of Flemish Chamber-Opera, Antwerp. Educ: Conservatorium, Brussels. m. Josee de Mulder, 3 children. Career: Horn Soloist, Phil., Antwerp, 18 yrs.; Prof. of Horn, Conservatorium, Brussels & Lemmens Inst., Leuven. Num. recordings as horn soloist; Mozart Concerto w. Orch. de Liege; concerto Telemann-Corelli-Franco, Chmbr. Orch. of Antwerp. Hons: Laureaat, Stravinsky Concours for Orch. Cond., Brussels. Hobbies: Lectures; Sports. Address: Pieter Van Den, Bemdenlaan 1, Belgium.

MAGALOFF, Nikita, b. 8 Feb. 1912, St. Petersburg, Russia. Pianist. Educ: began studies w. Serge Prokofieff; studied w. Isidore Philipp, Paris Conserv.; 1st Grand Prix when aged 17. m. Irene Szigeti, 1 d. Debut: as soloist, 1937. Career: collaborated w. Joseph Szigeti; Soloist w. major symph. orchs. throughout world; apps. at most important European fests.; noted as interpreter of Chopin. Comps: Sonatina for Violin & Piano; songs. Num. recordings for DECCA, Philips & Concert Hall. Recip. Cmdr. de l'ordre de Leopold II, Belgium. Hobby: Chess. Mgmt: Interartists, Det Haag. Address: Le Crépon, 1815 Baugy/Clarens, Vaud, Switz.

MAGDIC, Josip, b. 19 Mar. 1937, Ogulin, Yugoslavia. Composer; Teacher at Academy of Music. Educ: Tchrs. Trng. Coll.; Acad. of Music; Postdip. degree comp. m. Danica Magdic, 3 d. Debut: Cond. & Comp., Concerto for flute & orch., 1963. Career: Tchr., Acad. of Music, Sarajevo. Comps. incl: Rhythmic Expressions (piano); Small Zoo (piano); Five Satyric Anecdotes (viola & piano); Images (violin, clarinet & percussion); Phantasm (orch.); Constellation (orch.); Music for children, choral music, stage music. etc. Mbrships: Comps. Soc. of Bosnia & Herzegovina; Union of Organisations of Comps. of Yugoslavia. Hons: The Presern Prize, 1964; Skoj Award, 1969; UK BiH Award, 1972; BiH Assn. Award, 1974. Hobbies: Sports; Camping; Cooking. Address: Zagrebacka 67, 71000 Sarajevo, Yugoslavia.

MAGEE, Bryan, b. 12 Apr. 1930, London, UK. Member of Parliament. Educ: BA, 1952, MA, 1956, Oxford Univ. studied w. Anthony Milner. m. Ingrid Söderlund (dissolved), 1 d. Career: Music Critic & broadcaster, 1959-; MP w. special interest in music & the arts, 1974-. Publs: Aspects of Wagner, 1968. Contbr. to: BBC; Musical Times; Opera; Music & Musicians; nat. newspapers in UK. Mbrships. incl: Coun., Critics' Circle; Soc. of Authors: Committee, Garrick Club. Hobbies: Travel; Theatre. Address: House of Commons, London SW1, UK. 1, 3.

MAGG, Fritz, b. 18 Apr. 1914, Vienna, Austria. Cellist; Professor of Cello & Chamber Music; Department Chairman. Educ: Hochschule fur Musik, Cologne, 1932-33; Berlin, 1933-34; Ecole Normale de Musique, Paris, 1936. m. Natasha Kugel, 1 child. Debut: Dvorak Concerto w. Vienna Symph. Orch., 1935. Career: 1st cellist, Vienna Symph. Orch., 1934; New Friends Music Orch., NYC, USA, 1938; Metrop. Opera Orch., 1947; Cellist, Gordon & Berks., String Quartets & Trio Concertante; Tours, USA & abroad; Prof., cello & chambr. music, & Chmn., string dept., Schl. Music, Ind. Univ., Bloomington, Ind., 1948-. Recordings incl: Dvorak, Chmbr. Music. Publ: Cello Exercises, 1963. Address: 1320 E Univ. St., Bloomington, IN 47401, USA.

MAGRAW, Donald Keith, b. 3 Apr. 1935, Wigan, UK. Organist; Educator. Educ: BA, Durham Univ., 1957; MusB, ibid., 1957; Cert. Educ., Reading Univ., 1958; MA, Liverpool Univ., 1964; LTCL (Piano Perf.), 1952; FRCO, 1957. Career incls: Organist & Choirmaster, St. Thomas's Ch., Wigan, 1958-70; Accomp., Wigan Masonic Choir, 1970-75; Hd. Music Dept., Cowley High Schl., St. Helens, Merseyside, 1968-. Mbrships. incl: Royal Schl. Ch. Music; Liverpool Phil. Club; Merseyside Music Tchrs. Assn.; ISM. Hons: Rotary Club, Wigan Prize, 'to boy who put serv. before self', 1954; Hewlett Music Prize, 4 yrs., 1954↑-54 Hobbies: Walking; Travel. Address: 519 Ormskirk Rd., Pemberton, Wigan, Lancs., WN5 9LQ, UK.

MAGUB, Roshan, b. 2 July 1941, Bombay, India. Concert Pianist & Teacher. Educ: 3 yrs., RCM; 2 yrs., Vienna Acad. of Music; LRSM; ARCM. m. George Magub, Violinist, Ldr., St. Paul's Chamber Orch. Debut: recital in Vienna, 1965. Career: Recitals & broadcasts in India, Austria & UK; now teaching. Mbrships: ISM. Hons: Sir Adrian Boutl Cup, 1959; Austrian Govt. Scholarship, 1963, '64. Hobbies: Languages; Literature. Address: 83 Erskine Hill, London NW11 6HJ, UK.

MAGUIRE, Hugh, b. 2 Aug. 1927, Dublin, Ireland. Violinist; Conductor. Educ: Belvedere Coll. S J, Dublin. m. Suzanne Lewis, 5 c. Career: Dir. of Strings, Britten-Pears Schl. for Advanced Music Studies; Ldr., Melos Ensemble; Prof., RAM. Mbrships: Irish Arts Coun. Hons: Hon. MMus (Hull); FRAM. MgMt: Ibbs & Tillett, London. Address: 1 Alverstone Rd., London NW2, UK. 1.

MAGYAR, Gabriel, b. 5 Dec. 1914, Budapest, Hungary. (US Citizen). Cellist. Educ: Nat. Schl. Music, Budapest, 1932;

Master's degree, Franz Liszt Conserv., ibid., 1936. m. Julie Dora. Career: Concert Cellist, Europe, 1932-41, S Am., 1947-49, USA, 1949-; Tchr. & Solo Cellist, 1949-56; w. Hungarian Str. Quartet, 1956-72; Prof. Cello & Chmbr. music, Univ. of Okla., 1951-56, Univ. of Ill., Urbana, 1973-; Prof. Chmbr. music, var. summer schls. Recordings for Deutsche Grammophon, Pathe, Marconi & Vox records. Mbrships incl: Sinfonia Fraternity of Am.; Pi Kappa Lambda. Hons: Grand Prix du Disque (for Beethoven quartets), Paris; Prix de Discophile, ibid. Hobby: Photo graphy. Address: 708 Dover Pl., Champaign, IL 61820, USA. 2.

MAGYAR, Thomas (Tamás Aurél), b. 16 Feb. 1913, Budapest, Hungary. Violinist. Educ: Master Degree, Ferenc Liszt Acad. of Music. m. Henriette François. Career: Concert & solo apps. throughout world; has given premieres in var. European countries of violin concertos of comps. inclng: Khachaturian, Walton, Wellesz, Harmann, Martinu & Panufnik; Prof., Conserv. Rotterdam, 1950-55; Ldr.; Netherlands Chmbr. Orch., 1955-78. Recordings: Philips. Mbrships: Royal Dutch Musicians Soc. Hons: Reményi Prize, Budapest, 1932, Warsaw, 1935, Vienna, 1937; Kt., Order of Orange-Nassau, 1969; 1st honour-medal of the City The Hague, 1978. Hobbies: Filming; Photography. Address: Hanenburglaan 160, 2565 GZ The Hague, Netherlands.

MAHAN, Jack Harold, b. 10 Aug. 1911, Ft. Worth, Tex., USA. Educator. Educ: BS Mus, Tex. Wesleyan Coll.; MMus Ed, Southern Meth. Univ.; Chgo. Conserv. Music. m. Florence Elizabeth Pender. Career: Chmn., Music Dept. & Dir. of Bands, Univ. of Tex., Arlington (ret'd.) Author, Quick Steps to Marching, 1955. Contbr. to: The Schl. Musican; Music Jrnl.; La. Music Educator Mag.; past Ed. & Bus. Mgr., Tex. Music Educators Mag. Mbrships: Past Pres., Past Bd. Chmn., & current Sec./Treas., Am. Bandmasters Assn.; Hon. Life Exec. Sec., Phi Beta Mu; Past Chmn., N. Am. Band Dirs. Coord. Coun.; Past Pres., Tes. Music Educators Assn.; Tex. Bandmasters Assn.; Rotary Int.; Mason; Shriner; Hon. Mbr., Japanese Band Dirs. Assn., Phi Mu Alpha Sinfonia, Kappa Kappa Psi, Tau Beta Sigma. Hobbies: Swimming; Photography; Cabinet Making; Cooking. Address: 2019 Bradford Dr., Arlington, TX 76010, USA.

MAHAN, Katherine Hines, b. 16 June 1928, Pontotoe, Miss., USA. Professor of Musicology & American Music; Mezzo-Soprano Singer. Educ: BMus, Okla. Univ., 1950; MMus, Peabody Coll., 1956; Eds (psychol.), Auburn Univ., 1963; PhD, Fla. State Univ., 1967; Fulbright Scholar, Osmania Univ., Hyderbad, India, 1974; Cert. in Humanities, Brown Univ., 1975. m. Joseph B Mahan Jr. Career incls: Choral Dir., toured w. choruses, Mid-W, 10 yrs.; TV broadcasts; Prof., Columbus Coll., Ga., 17 yrs. Comps: Alma Mater; Six Songs for Children; A Childs Prayer (song). Publs: Show Boats to Soft Shoes - 100 Years of Music, 1968; A History of Education in Columbus, Ga., 1976. Contbr. to jrnls. Active mbr., profl. orgs. Recip. var. hons. Address: 2339 Burton St., Columbus, GA 31904, USA. 7.

MAHDI, Salah, b. 9 Feb. 1925, Tunis, Tunisia. Music & Arts Director. Educ: Fac. of Letters, Ex Zaitouna Univ.; Certs. in law & Arabic. m. Rafia Osman, 3 children. Career incls: Former Orch. Cond. & Prod., Radio & TV; Dir., Music & Popular Arts, Min. of Culture, 1961-. Comp. of 400 comps. inclng. The Tunisian Nat. Anthem. Recordings incl: Tunisian symphs.; Sev. Arab Sons. Publs. incl: Arabian Music; The Tunisian Musical Inheritance, 8 vols.; 14 Arabian Songs. Contbr. to var. profl. publs. Mbrships. incl: Fndr., Royalty Soc.; Pres., 1968-75; Pres., Interarabian Acad. of Music. Off., Order of the Tunisian Repub. Hobbies: Reading; Backgammon. Address: 22 rue du Brésil, Tunis, Tunisia.

MAHLE, Ernst, b. 3 Jan. 1929, Stuttgart, Germany. Music Teacher; Conductor; Composer. Educ: Comp. & Conducting, Conserv. Dramático e Musical, Sao Paulo, Brazil, 1958. m. Maria Aparecida Romera Pinto, 3 s., 2 d. Career: Artistic Dir., Escola de Música de Piracicaba, 1953-. Comps. incl: Sonatina for piano, 1956; Sonatina Modal; Toccata (piano 4 hands); Sonatina for oboe, 1970. Recordings: Sonata (viola), 1968; Some pieces for Voices. VP, Brazilian Soc. Contemporary Music. Hons: 1st prize, Univ. Bahia, 1961; 3rd prize, Inst. Goethe (Concurso Nacional), 1974. Address: Rua Sao Francisco de Assis 983, 13400 Piraciaba, Brazil.

MAHLER, David Charles, b. 13 Aug. 1944, Plainfield, NJ, USA. Composer & Performer of New Music. Educ: BA Educ., Concordia Tchrs. Coll., Ill.; Vandercook Coll. of Music, Ill.; Univ. of Portland, Ore.; MFA Comp., Calif. Inst. of Art, Valencia. m. Irene Mervine, 1 child. Comps. incl: In Soundings, 1972 & 74; Very Much It Sleeps; Still Life; Whitman Sampler; Children in the Grasses; Ear Mag, 1975 & 76; I am From; Visitor from the Islands; Piece in Lieu of War; Pieces, 1975; Wind Hymn; Illinois Sleep; Early Winters; Pieces II, 1976; Winter Man; Seven Songs;

Soundfields & Crystalbells; Compline; Wind Circle. Hobbies: Printmaking; Food; Drink; Baseball. Address: 705 Summit E, Seattle, WA 98102, USA.

MAHLER, Fritz, b. 1901, Vienna, Austria. Conductor; Musical Director. Educ: Vienna Coll. for Music; Univ. of Vienna. m. Pauline Koner. Career: Cond., Broadcasting Co., Copenhagen, 1930-36, also at Mannheim, Berlin & w. Copenhagen State Orch.; Guest Cond. w. major orchs. thru'out world; specializes in interpreting the symphinic works of Gustav Mahler. Recordings: sev. fro Vanguard & Decca labels. Publs: Musical Analysis of Wizzeck. Contbr. of articles to jrnls. Address: 340 West 72nd St., NYC, NY 10023, USA. 3.

MAHRENHOLZ, Christhard, b. 11 Aug. 1900, Adelebsen, Germany. Musicologist; Theologian. Educ: Gard., Theol., Univ. of Gottingen, Univ. of Leipzig, 1922; PhD, Univ. of Gottingen, 1923. m. Ursula Von Jouanne, 3 s.; 1 d. Career: Organist; Choir Dir., 1917-24; Minister, 1925-30; Lectr., Ch. Music Univ. of Gottingen, 1930-; Prof., ibid., 1946-; Mbr. Land Ch. Office, hannover, 1931-; VP, ibid; Abbot, Amelungsborn, 1960-; Ed., Musik & Kirche, 1929-. Publs: Samuel Scheidt, Leben & Werk, 1924; Die Orgelregister, ihre Geschichte & ihr Bau 1930-44; Generalbasschorale, 1938; Eds. of works of Samuel Scheidt, 1932-; Glockenkunde, 1948; Choralbuch zum Ev. Kirchengesangbuch, 1950-60. Contbr. to num. profl. jrnls. Mbrships: Pres., New Bach Soc.; Pres., German Protestant Ch. Choir Soc.; German Music Coun.; Int. Musicol. Soc.; Soc. of Dutch Musicians; Soc. for Music Rsch.; Eds. Coll., New Bach Ed. Recip. Hon. D Theol., Univ. of Gottingen, 1948. Address: 28 Kerstingstr., 3 Hannover, German Fed. Repub.

MAHRER, Walte, b. 16 Feb. 1912, Mohlin, Switzerland. Viola Player. Educ: Conserv. Basel; Tchrs. Dip. m. Lucie Kuhn, 3 children. Solo concerts & w. Neves Zurcher trio, 1936-37; Radio Sextet, Basel, 1937-42; Radio Orch., Zürich, 1942-76; Viola, Tonhalle Orch., Zürich; num. concerts, classical & mod. works. Contbr. to profl. publs. Mbrs. profl. orgs. Hobbies: Lit.; Hist. Address: Huttenstrasse 53, CH-8006 Zürich, Switzerland.

MAI, Peter Bernhard, b. 10 Apr. 1935, Chemnitz, Germany. Composer; Music pedagogue. Educ: 1953-58 Music Acad. Leipzig, State exam. m. Rudolfa Mai-Schröder. Career: Tchr. var. Music Schls.; Since 1972 Conserlv. Halle: Since 1974 Lectr. Music Acad. Leipzig. Comps. incl: Sonatine for violin and piano, 1971; Suite for recorder quartet, 1972 Sonatine for soprano recorder and piano, 1972; Miniatures for horn and piano, 1974. Mbrships: VKM, Assn. for Comp. and Musicologists, GCR. Hons: 3rd Prize Comp. for Folk instruments, 1961, VKM contest. Address: Leninstr. 5, 44 Bitterfeld, German Dem. Repub.

MAIBORODA, Georgi Illarionovich, b. 1 Dec. 1913, Pelikhovshchina, Ukraine. Composer. Educ: Kiev Conserv. m. Davidenko Tamara Petrovna, 2 s. Comps. incl: Symphs., 1940, 1952; Gutsuli Rhapsody, Rhapsody, 1951; Friendship of the Peoples (cantata); Zaporozhtsy, 1954; Milana (opera), 1956; The Arsenal (opera), 1960; King Lear (suite for symph. orch.), 1959; Taras Shevchenko (opera), 1967; num. songs etc. Mbrships: Chmn., Ukrainian Composers Union; Bd., USSR Comps. Union. Hons: Honoured Worker of the Arts, Ukrainian SSR, 1957; People's Artist of USSR, 1960; Order of Red Banner of Labour, 1963. Address: Composers Union of Ukrainian SSR, Pushkinskaya St. 32, USSR.

MAILLARD, Jean Henri O, b. 19 Apr. 1926, Paris, France. Teacher. Educ: Docteures-Léttres, Univ. of Paris; State Secondary Schl. Tchr., Musical Educ. m. Francine Cabos, 1 s., 3 d. Career: Tchr., Lydée, Fontainebleau. Recordings: Chansons de Troubadours & Cantigas d'Alfonse le Sage; Les Trouveurs du Moyen-Age, Musique de Tous les Temps; Trovères & Ménestrels. Publs. incl: Lais & Chansons de Ernoul de Gastinois, 1964; Livre d'Or du Centenaire de Guy Ropartz, 1966; Anthologie de Chants de Trouvéres, 1967; Anthologie de Chants de Troubadours, 1967 2nd ed. 1973; Co-author, Présence des Troubadours, 1970; Les Symphonies d'Arthur Honegger, 1974; Parsifal de Richard Wagner (w. Jacques Chailley) in prep. Contbr. to: Revue Belge de Musicol.; Musica Disciplina; Musica; Grands Muciens; Musik in Geschichte & Gegenwart; & other profl. jrnls. Pres., Friends of the organ Assn. Mbrships: Soc. Française de Musicol.; Soc. Int. Arthurienne; Inst. d'Etudes Occitanes. hons: Croix de Guerre, 1939-45; Chevalier des Palmes Académiques, 1971. Hobbies: Popular Traditions & Poetry; Fine Arts. Address: 14 Boulevard Thiers, Fontainebleau F. 77300, France.

MAILLARD-BACK, Andrée, b. 4 Jan. 1945, Lowestoft, Suffolk, UK. Professional Soprano Singer. Educ: RCM; Studied singing w. Hervey Alan, Margaret Bissett & Boriska Gereb. m.

Nicholas Choveaux, 2 d. Debut: Wigmore Hall, London, 1970. Career: Specialist in Oratorio, Lieder & French Song; major perfs. throughout W Europe w. leading choirs & orchs. inclng. Antwerp Phil., Bavarian Radio, Berlin Symph., Brussels Phil., Frankfurt Radio, Lamoureux Paris, Munich Phil., N German Radio, English Chmbr., Philharmonia, Royal Phil., etc.; Radio & TV apps. throughout W Europe & UK. Mbr., ISM; RCM Union. Hons: Maggie Teyte Prize, 1970. Hobbies: Photography; Cookery; Reading; Children; Travelling. Mgmt: Choveaux Mgmt. Address: Mancroft Towers, Oulton Broad, Lowestoft, Suffolk NR32 3PS, UK. 27.

MAILMAN, Martin, b. 30 June 1932, NYC, USA. Composer. Educ: BMus, Eastman Schl. of Music, 1954; MMus., ibid., 1955; PhD, 1960. m. Mary Nan Hudgins, 1 s., 1 d. Career: Has served as Guest Composer & Cond. at over 30 colls. & univs. in USA.; Currently Prof. of Music, N. Tex. State Univ. Num. Compositions inclng: Theme Music for Concepts (TV), 1965; The Rise & Fall: A Choral Fable (R BM), 1968; Associations No. 1, for Band (R BM), 1968-69; Symphony No. 1, for Orch. (R BM), 1969; Generations 2, for 3 Str. Orchs. & Percussion (R BM), 1969; Two Fanfares, for Brass (SM), 1970; In Memoriam Frankie Newton, for Lab Band (SM), 1970; Requiem, Requiem (R BM), 1972; Shouts, Hymns, & Praises for Band, 1972. Mbrships. incl: ASCAP; Phi Mu Alpha; Pi Kappa Lamba. Hons: 1st prize, Edward Benjamin Award for Quiet Music, 1955 & B'ham, Ala. Arts Fest., 1966. Address: Schl. of Music, N. Tex. State Univ., Denton, TX 76203, USA.

MAIORCA, Alfonse Anthony, b. 16 June 1927, Brooklyn, NY, USA. Professional Trumpeter. Educ: Manhattan Schl. of Music. m. Sandra Stone, 1 s., 3 d. Career: Has played w. Ballet Russe de Monte Carlo, Radio City Music Hall, Sauter Finnegan Band, Staff NBC Orch., Bell Telephone Hour, Sound of Music, George M Westbury Music Fair Orch., Westchester Symph., Brooklyn Philharmonia Benny Goodman Orch., City Ctr. Ballet Orch. Recordings w. Radio City Music Hall Quintet for RCA, United Artists, Decca, etc. Mbr., Int. Trumpet Guild. Hobbies: Reading; Gardening. Address: 151 Academy Pl., W Hempstead, NY 11552, USA.

MAIORESCU, Dorella Teodora, b. 6 Jan. 1948, Bucharest, Romania. Harpist. Educ: BMus., Bucharest Acad. of Music, 1968; MS, Juilliard Schl. of Music, NY, USA. 1972; studied w. Liana Pasquali, Marcel Grandjany. Debut: Bucharest, Romania, 1968. Career: Solo Harp Recitals, Romanian Broadcasting Co., 1967-69, Romanian Athenaeum, Bucharest, 1969, Alice Tully Hall, NY, USA, 1972; Harpist, Am. Symph. Orch., 1970-72, NY. Harp Ensemble, Artists-in-Res.; Univ. of Bridgeport, Conn.: Tours of USA, Europe, S Am. Recordings: w. NY Harp Ensemble. Mbrships: Am. Harp Soc.; Am. Fedn. of Musicians. Recip. Bronze Medal, 1st Int. Harp Competition, Hartford, Conn., 1969. Hobbies: Reading; Painting; Swimming; Hiking; Gardening. Mgmt. M Bichurin Concerts Corp.; Albert Kay Assocs Inc. Concert Artists Mgmt, NY, NY, USA Address: Apt. 10 E, 165 W. 66th St., NY, NY 10023, USA.

MAIRANTS, Ivor, b. 1908, London, UK. Musician (Guitar). m. Lily, 1 d., 1 s. Career incl: Guitarist w. Mantovani Orch.; Solo Guitar w. Manuel & His Music of the Mountains; num. apps. as freelance in Films, Tv & Radio; Fndr.-Prin., Ctrl. Schl. of Dance Music, 1950-60. Comps. incl: Little Bo Bleep; Russian Salad; Spring Fever; Pepper & Salt; Summer Madness; 6 solos for Classic Guitar; Flamenco Album No. 1; Meditation & Moto Perpetuo for 2 guitars, etc. Publs. incl: Bundle of Blues; Spirit of New Orleans; Arranging for the Guitar; Composers Guide to the Guitar; Music of the Modern Masters (12 short pieces); Perfect Pick Technique; Finger Style Guitar; num. instrnl. books on guitar. Mbrships: Fndr./dir., Ivor Mairants Musicentre Ltd.; Musicians Union; Music Trades Assn. Hon: Fellow, Int. Assn. of Arts & Letters. Hobbies: Hist.; World Travel; Swimming. Address: 4 Hollies End, Mill Hill Village, London NW7, UK.

MAISKY, Mischa (Michael), b. 10 Jan. 1948, Riga, USSR. Concert Cellist. Educ: Moscow Conserv.; studied w. Mstislav Rostropovich; master class w. Gregor Piatigorsky. Debut: w. Leningrad Phil. Orch., 1965. Career: apps. at Carnegie Hall, Royal Fest. Hall, Berlin Phil. Hall, etc.; recitals w. Martha Argerich, Radu Lupu, Malcolm Frager, etc.; TV & radio apps. in UK, Germany, Netherlands, France, Spain, Mexico, USA, Israel & USSR. Hons: All-Russian Cellists Competition, 1965; Tchaikovsky Int. Competition, Moscow, 1966; Gaspar Cassado Int. Competition, Florence, 1973. Hobby: Music. Mgmt: Harrison/Parrott Ltd., 22 Hillgate St., London W8 7SR, UK. Address: c/o Mgmt.

MAJOR, Blyth, b. Daventry, UK. Director of Music; Teacher of Violin & Vila. Educ: LRAM. m. Myriam Davis, 1 d. Career incls: Cond., Coventry Symph. Orch., 1934-39; Ldr. & Dpty. Cond., Leicester Symph. Orch., 1945-47; Dpty. Ldr., City of

Birmingham Symph. Orch., 1947-51; Dpty. Dir. of Music & Cond., City of Durban Orch., 1951-53; Gen. Mgr. & Sec., City of Birmingham Symph. Orch., 1953-59; Concerts Mgr., London Mozart Players, 1960-63; Fndr. & Musical Dir., Midland Youth Orch., 1956-; Co-Fndr. & Fest. Dir., Int. Fest. of Youth Orchs., 1967-. Mbrships: ISM: Royal Soc. of Tchrs. Address: 20 Redcliff Sq., London SW10 9JZ, UK.

MAJOR, Margaret, b. Coventry, UK. Violist. Educ: ARCM, RCM, London. Debut: Wigmore Hall Recital w. Gerald Moore, London, 1955. Career: Prin. Viola, Netherlands Chmbr. Orch., 1956-59; Prin. Viola, Philomusica of London, 1960-65, Viola, Aeolian String Quartet, 1965-; Prof. of Viola, RCM, London, 1969-. Recordings: Currently engaged in recording complete String Quartets of Haydn. Hons: Lionel Tertis Prize, 1951; Int. Music Assn. Concert Award, 1955; MA, Univ. of Newcastle-on-Tyne, 1970. Hobby: Good food. Address: 13 Upper Park Rd., Kingston Hill, Kingston-upon-Thames, Surrey, UK. 3, 27.

MÄKINEN, Timo Juhani, b. 6 June 1919, Sortavala, USSR. University Professor of Musicology; Pianist. Educ: mA, 1947; Phil. Dr., 1964; studied Piano, Sibelius Acad., 1938-47; studied w. O Wibergh Stockholm, 1946, & C Marek, Zürich, 1948-52. m. Miette Yvonne Forel, 2 s., 1 d. Career: Mbr., Violin & Piano Duo, w. Paavo Rautio, 1955-63; TV & radio perfs., Chmbr., Lieder & Piano concerts; Prof. of Musicol., Univ. of Jyväskylä, Finland. Publs. incl: Musica Fennica (w. Seppo Nummi), 1965, Engl. & other transls., 1967; Robert Schumann as Music Critic, 1967; Piae Cantiones: Source Investigations, 1968; Mozart-The Magic Flute, 1978; Talks with Joonas Kokkonen. Mbrships. incli: Finnish Acad.; Finnish Musicol. Soc.; Kalevala Soc.; Jyväskylä Arts Fest.; Savonlinna Opera Fest. Address: Dept. of Musicol., Univ. of Jyväsklylä, 40100 Jyväskylä 10, Finland.

MAKLAKIEWICZ, Tadeusz Wojciech, b. 20 Oct. 1922, Mszczonow, Poland. Composer. Educ: MA, Law Dept., Jagiellonian Univ., Krakow; Grad., State HS of Music, Warsaw. m. Maria Pawlúskiewicz, 3 d. Debut: Fest. of Polish Music, Warsaw, 1951. Career: Dean, Music Educ. Fac., State HS of Music, Warsaw, 1968-69; Dpty. Rector, ibid., 1969-72; Hd., Music Educ. Dept., 1973; Rector, 1975-78. Comps. incl: Cantata, Peace, Friendship, Work; Epitaphium for symph. orch.; Rondo for clarinet & piano or orch.; Vienna vocalisation for soprano & orch.; Polonaise of the Tank Corps; The Clocks are Ringing; Songs for Children for voice & piano, 1977; Mazovian Dance, for piano, 1977; Hands Friendly with Hands, for mixed choir & organ, 1977; Above Clouds, for mixed choir a capella, 1978. Mbrships: Pres. of Bd., Authors Agcy. Ltd., Warsaw; VP, Bd. of Soc. of Authors ZAIKS, Warsaw; Union of Polish Comps. Recip. num. hons. incl: Golden Cross of Merit, 1971; Cross of Chivalry, 1977. Address: ul. Smolna 8/90, 00-375 Warsaw, Poland.

MAKOWER, Mary, b. London, UK. Professor of Singing. Educ: Guildhall Schl. of Music; Vienna Acad. Career incl: Broadcaster on Vienna Radio; Mbr., Bach Soc., Vienna; Concert & oratorio singer in UK & Europe; Prof. of Singing, Royal Acad. of Music; Pvte. music tchr. Recordings: Hebridean Songs (EMI). Mbr: Inc. Soc. of Musicians. Recip: Hon. ARAM. Address: 50 Belsize Pk. Gdns., London NW3, UK.

MAKRIS, Andreas, b. 7 Mar. 1930, Salonika, Greece. Violinist; Composer. Publisher. Educ: Grad., Nat. Conserv. Salonika, 1950; Grad., Mannes Coll. of Music, NY, 1956; studied comp. w. Nadia Boulanger, Fontainebleau, France; Aspen Music Fest. m. Margaret Lubbe, 2 s. Career: at invitation of tchr., Totenberg, joined his nine-mbr. Instrumental Ensenble, with which he made concert tours throughout USA & Canada; Past Prin. Violinist, Dallas Symph., Past 1st Violinist, St. Louis Symph.; Mbr. of the Nat. Symphs. first violin sect., 1961. Compositions: Concertino for Strings (premiered by the Nat. Symph. Orch.), 1967; Aegean Fest. Overture (premiered by Nat. Symph. Orch.), 1968; Anamnesis (Nat. Symph. Orch., cond., Antal Dorati) 1971; Viola Concerto (commissioned & premiered by the St. Paul Chamber Orch.), 1970; Efthymia; Concertino for Trombone; Str. Quartet, & other chamber works; Fanfare, Fantasy & Dance; Mediterranean Holiday; Quintet for Vioice & String Quartet. Recordings: Aegean Fest. Overture. Hons: Nat. Endowment for the Arts Grant; Martha Baird Rockefeller Fndn. Award; Damrosch Grand 1st Contemporary composer to be performed at the Kennedy Ctr. Concert Hall, cond., Antal Dorati. Address: 11204 Oakleaf Dr., Silver Spring, MD 20901, USA.

MALAN, Jacob Daniel, b. 15 July 1919, Darling, S Africa. Music Lecturer; Organist & Choirmaster. Educ: BMus, Univ. of Cape Town; M Mus, Univ. of Stellenbosch; UPLM (organ), UTLM (piano), Univ. of S Africa. m. Alice Ida Rouillard, 3 s., 1 d.

Career: Organ recitalist, broadcasting regularly, 1945-, toured Cape Prov. (arr. by CAPAB), gave series of weekly recitals, Die Groote Kerk, Cape Town; recitals in UK, Germany; Choral Cond. w. orch. & organ, Die Groote Kerk; Organist & Chirmaster, Die Groote Kerk; Music Tchr., leading Cape Town Schl., 1943-60; Inspector of Music, 1960-68; currently Sr. Lectr., Barkly House Trng. Coll. Publs: Koraalboek (jt. author), 19056; Harmonie by die Klavier, 1967. Contbr. to Die Kerkbode. Mbrships: Past Pres., S African Soc. of Music Tchrs., Cape Guild of Organists. Address: 10 Muswell Hill Rd., Mowbray, Cape Town, S Africa.

MALAS, Spiro, b. 28 Jan. 1935, Baltimore, MD, USA. Singer (bass). Educ: BS, Towson State Coll. m. Marlena Kleinman, 2 s. Debut: Balt., 1960. Career: Opera performances w. Covent Gdn., San Fran. Opera, Chgo. Opera, Vienna State Opera, NY Opera; Festival appearances at Edinburgh & Salzburg; Concert & Opera tours of Australia w. Joan Sutherland; TV appearances in Who's Afraid of Opera; Abduction from the Seraglio; Daughter of the Regiment; Boris Goudonov (PBS-TV). Recordings incl: L'Elisir d'Amore; Dille du Regiment; Semiramide; Griselda; Julius Caesar. Hobby: Model airplanes & trains. Mgmt: Columbia Artists Mgmt.; Matthew Epstein. Address: 245 W 104th St., NY, NY 10025, USA.

MALCOLM, George (John), b. 28 Feb. 1917, London, UK. Harpsichordist; Conductor. Educ: MA, BMus., Balliol Coll., Oxford Univ., RCM. Career: Master of Music, Westminster Cathedral, 1947-59; Trainer of Boys Choir for which Britten's Missa Brevis was written; Frequent tours of Europe as harpsichordist & cond.; Artistic Dir., Philomusica of London, 1962-66; Frequent performer as soloist & in jt. recitals w. Menuhin, Bream & other leading instrumentalists as festivals incl. Aldeburgh, Bath & Edinburgh; Co-cond., w. composer, of original perfs. of Britten's A Midsummer Night's Dream. Hons: CBE., 1965; Cobbett Gold Medal, Worshipful Co. of Musicians, 1960; Papal Kt., Order of St. Gregory the Gt., 1970; Hon. RAM.; Hon. Fellow, Balliol Coll.; Fellow RCM; Hon. MusD, Univ. of Sheffield. Address: 38 Cheyne Walk, London SW3, UK.

MALCOLMSON, Kenneth Forbes, b. 29 Apr. 1911, London, UK. Cathedral Organist; School Director of Music. Educ: MA, BMus, Exeter Coll., Oxford; RCM; Schl. of Engl. Ch. Music; FRCO. m. Belle Dunhill. Career: Commissioner, FRSM, 1935-36; Temporary Organist, St. Albans Cathedral, 1936-37; Organist, Halifax Parish Ch., 1937-38; Organist & Master of the Music, Newcastle Cathedral, 1938-55; Fndr. & Cond., Newcastle Cathedral Choral Soc., 1946-55; Precentor & Dir. of Music, Eton Coll., 1956-71; Cond., Windsor & Eton Choral Soc., 1956-71. Mbrships: ISM; Pres., Music Masters' Assn., 1966-67. Hobbies: Gardening; Walking; Reading. Address: Llanvapley Ct., Abergavenny, Gwent, UK.

MALCUZYNSKI, Witold, b. 10 Aug. 1914, Warsaw, Poland. Pianist. Educ: Warsaw Conserv.; Warsaw Univ. m. Colette Gaveau, 2 d. Debut: Paris, 1940; Carnegie Hall, 1942. Career: since 1949 has toured in Europe, USSR, N & S Ams., NZ, Aust., Near & Far E; Juror in int. contests. Recip. Off.'s Cross, Order of Polonia Restituta, 1970. 16.

MALDYBAYEV, Abdylas, b. 7 July 1906, Karabulak, Kirghiz, Russia. Composer. Educ: Frunze Tchrs. Trng. Inst.; Moscow Conserv. Compositions incl: the first Kirchiz operas - Aichurek, 1939; On the Banks of the Issyk Kul, 1950; Manas (opera), 1944; Choral Symphs. - The Party - Our Happiness, 1954; Glory to the Party; Toktogul (opera); Jt. composer of music of Kirghiz SSR Anthem, w. Vlasov & Fere; Over 300 songs & choral pieces, etc. Hons: People's Artist of USSR; Order of Lenin; 3 Orders of Red Banner of Labour; Bade of Hon.; Medal for Disting. Labour; WWII Medal. Address: Union of Composers, Frunze, USSR.

MALEADY, Antoinette Kirkpatrick, b. 9 Dec. 1918, Powell, Wyo., USA. Librarian. Educ: BS, Business Admin.; BA, Spanish; MLS, Libnship. m. Thomas J Maleady, 1 d. Career: Hd., Acquisitions Dept., Lib., Sonoma State Coll., Rohnert Park, Calif., USA. Publs: Record & Tape Reviews Index, 1971-75; Analysis of the music in Don Quixote (in preparation); Amalia, Jose Marmol, Engl. Ed., (in preparation); Repertoire International de Litterature Musicale, abstracts of Record & Tape Reviews index. Mbrships: Music Lib. Assn.; San Francisco Opera Guild; Assn. of Recorded Sound Collections; Am. Recorder Soc.; Am. Choral Soc.; Pvte. Libs. Assn.; World Affairs Coun.; Am. For. Serv. Assn.; Diplomatic & Consular Officers; Sierra Club. Hobbies: Rsch. & Study; Painting; Golf; Travel. Address: 1040 Butterfield Rd., San Anselmo, CA 94960, USA.

MALESKI, Alice V K, b. 5 May 1951, Edison, NJ, USA. Organist; Pianist; Musical Director. Educ: BA, Douglass Coll., Rutgers Univ., 1973; MMus, Manhattan Schl. of Music, 1976; studied organ w. Frederick Swann, piano w. Vittorio Verse, Robert

Dix Lincoln & Robert Goldsand. Debut: piano recital, Carnegie Recital Hall, 1962. Career: Music Dir., Diocese of Paterson, NJ; organ concerts throughout NY Met. area, Riverside Ch.; Sacred Heart Cathedral, etc. Comps: Chrism Mass Responsorial Psalm, The Heart of the Just Man; Eucharist Prayer No. 1, for children. Publs: Gen. Ed., Assn. of Ch. Musicians Newsletter, 1978-. Mbrships: Rutgers Preparatory Schl. Bd. of Trustees; AGO; Am. Musicol. Soc.; Nat. Pastoral Musicians. Hons: hons. study w. Dr. Carleton Sprague Smith (musicol.), 1972-73; Meta Thorne Waters Award, 1960-73. Hobbies: Horse Riding; Gardening. Address: Laura Lane, Bedminster, NJ 07921, USA.

MALET, Kathleen Mary, b. 4 Feb. 1934, Rangoon, Burma. Violinist; Baroque Violinist. Educ: Studied w. Sascha Lasserson, London, UK; LRAM; ARCM. m. Peter Hamburger. Career: Recitals & Radio & TV Broadcasts, esp. w. Baroque Stringed Instruments; Ldr., Allemande Baroque Ensemble; Arco Dolce Duo (Baroque Violin & Harpsichord) w. John Engleheart; tours throughout Europe & USA; TV apps.; Tchr. of violin, Cheltenham Music Ctr. sev. recordings. Mbr., ISM. Hobbies: music of Fritz Kreisler; Constructing Gardens; Snorkelling. Address: The Mill, Woodmancote, Cheltenham, Glos., UK.

MALFITANO, Joseph John, b. 25 July 1920, Newark, NJ, USA. Concert Violinist; Teacher of Voice & Violin & vocal teacher & coach to Catherine Malfitano. Educ: Studied violin w. Raphael Bronstein, Valentin Blumberg & Louis Parsinger. m. Maria Maslova Flynn, 1 s., 2 d. Debut: Carnegie Hall, 1957. Career incls: var: World Premieres; The 1st pas de trois choreograhed for dancer, singer & violinist to Suite for Voice & Violin By H Villa Lobos, Alice Tully Hall, 1975; Malfitano Duo tours of USA & Can. performing repertoire for voice & violin solo & w. piano. Num. recordings. Mbr. The Bohemians (NY Musicians Club). Hobbies: Astronomy; Sci. Fiction. Mgmt: Columbia Artists Mgmt. Inc. Address: Malfitano Assocs. & Prods., 251 W. 92nd St., 7B, New York, NY 10025, USA.

MALGOIRE, Jean Claude, b. 25 Nov. 1940, Avignon, France. Conductor. Educ: Paris Conserv., oboe prize, 1960, Chmbr. music prize, 1960. 1 s., 1 d. Carer: Operas of 17th & 18th Centuries; Rinaldo, Fest. Hall; Hippolyte et Aricie (Rameau) Covent Gdn.; Tiencrede (Campra) Copenhagen Royal Opera; Coronation of Poppea, Stockhnolm Royal Opera; Les Indes Galantes (Rameau) Versailles Opera Royal; sev. apps., English Bach Fest.; Permanent Cond., La Grande Einric et la Chambre du Roy. Recordings: Rinaldo (complete); Xerxes (complete); Hippolyte et Aricie, etc. Hons: Prix Int. de Geneva, oboe, 1968. Address: 63 Boulevard Lefebvre, 75015 Paris, France.

MALIGE, Alfred, b. 11 Jan. 1895, Oels, Schlesien, Germany. Composer; Instrumentalist; Conductor. Educ: Music Acad.; Autodidact; Conserv. Leipzig. m. Katherina Malige. Career: Orch. mbr.; Cond.; Music Tchr. Comp.; 2 Symph.; Prelude and Fugue in FDGB; 4 Overtures; var. concertos for var. instruments; 6 str. Quartets; Srt. Trio; 4 Wind Quintets; 2 Horn Quartets; Leinin Cantata for Solo, Choir & orch.; Songs, Folk music, Studies. Mbrships: Assn. of Comp. and Musicologists, German Dem. Repub.; German Music Paper, Berlin; Music Mag.; Leipzig; Music and Soc., Berlin; Daily newspapers. Hons: Medal for excellent perf. 1951, 1952, 1963, 1966; Art Prize, Leipzig, 1967; Patriotic Merit Order, German Dem. Repub., 1965 bronze, 1975 silver. Address: Landsbnergstr. 84, Leipzig 7022, German Dem. Repub.

MALININ, Dorothy Rearick, b. 28 July 1935, Danville, Ill., USA. Violinist. Educ: BA, Agnes Scott Coll., 1957, MS, Univ. of Va., 1960; studied under Joel Belov. Univ. of Miami, Fla.; studied w. John Adam. Prin. Violist of the Atlanta Symph. m. Dr. Theodore Malinin, 2 s., 2 d. Career: currently perf. as a Mbr. of the Biscayne Piano Quartet. Mbrships: Phi Beta Kappa; Chi Beta Phi; Sigma Xi; Mortar Bd.; Miami Fed. of Musicians. Hons: Fla. State Soloist at Fla. State Univ. String Clinic w. Albert Spalding & Ernst von Dohany, 1953. Address: 360 Atlantic Rd., Key Biscayne, FL 33149, USA. 7.

MALINOWSKI, Jan Tadeusz, b. 7 June 1915, Honoratówka, Poland. Oboist; Conductor; Educator. Educ: BMus, State Acad. of Music, Gdansk, 1953. m. Krystyna Malik, 2 d. Debut: as Cond., State Phil. Orch., Gdansk, 1953. Career: Cond. & Artistic Dir., Opole Forlkloristica, Radio Opole; Dir., I & II Degree State Schls. of Music, Opole. Contbr. to bar jrnls. Mbrships: Chmn., Opole Chapt., Polish Muscial Assn.; Gen. Bd., Polish Soc. of Choirs & Orchs.; Artistic Dir., Opole Chapt., ibid. Recip., State hons. Hobbies: Mountain Walking; Numismatics; Philately. Address: ul. Krakowska 39 m 1, 45-075 Opole, Poland.

MALLAH, Hossein-Ali, b. 1921, Tehran, Iran. Musician; Violin & Sytar. Educ: Grad., BA, Conserv. of Nat. Music. m. Badry Vaziri. Career: Prof. of Hist. of Music; Perfs. on Radio Tehran;

Musical Dir., Radio Tehran. Publs: Damghani & Music, 1960; Few Words about History of Iranian Music, 1970; Hafez & Music, 1972; History of Military Music in Iran, 1976; Glorious Period in History of Iranian Music, 1976. Mbr., Int. Comm. of Music. Hobbies: Transl. of books; Lit.; Poetry. Address: 30 Jourabchi Alley, Farvardin Ave., Darous, Tehran, Iran.

MALLANDAINE, Jean Patricia, b. Worthing, Sussex, UK. Accompanist; Repetiteur (piano & harpsichord); Music Administrator. Educ: Royal Acad. of Music; LRAM (Tchrs.); ARCM (Performers). Career: Broadcast recitals as soloist pianist & accompanist, BBC Radio; Music Staff, Chief Coach & Continuo Player, Glyndebourne; Recitals at Wexford Fest. & Europalia Fest., Brussels, w. Anne Howells & Ryland Davies; Accompanist to Kirk Te Kanawa, recitals, NYC, USA, 1974, '75; Hd., music staff & chief coach, Houston Grand Opera; Dir. of Musical Studies, Houston Music Studio, Houston Univ., Tex. Mbrships: Inc. Soc. of Musicians. Hobby: Horse Riding. Address: Merryfields, Windsor Lane, Little Kingshill, Gt. Missenden, Bucks., UK.

MALLARD, Donna Suzanne Staton, b. 9 Nov. 1948, Jacksonville, Fla., USA. Teacher; Solo & Ensemble Director of Adult Special Music (vocal). Educ: BMusEd (cum laude), Stetson Univ., Deland, Fla., 1970; MMusEd, Fla. State Univ., Tallahassee, Fla., 1971; Certified in music grades K-12, Elementary Educ. & Reading. m. Larry E Mallard. Career: Public Schl. Music Instr., Middle & High Schl. Choral Dir., Charlton Co. Schl. System, Ga., 1971-74; Pvte. Music Instr. (piano, vocal & instrumental music), 1968-76; Tchr., Folkston Elem., 1974-76; Tchr., Southside Elem., Ark., 1976-80; Solo & Ensemble Dir. of Adult Special Music (vocal), First Baptist Ch., De Witt, Ark. Mbrships: Ark. Educs. Assn. & Nat. Educ. Assn.; Phi Beta; Kappa Delta Pi; Tau Beta Sigma. Sev. Acad. hons. Hobbies: Collector Items; Antiques; Needlepoint; Decorating. Address: 503 S Circle Dr., De Witt, AR 72042, USA.

MALLETT, Lawrence Roger, b. 27 Aug. 1947, Centerville, Iowa, USA. Recitalist on Clarinet; Instructor, Clarinet & Woodwinds; Director of Wind & Jazz Ensembles; Conductor. Educ: B Mus. & B Mus. Ed., Univ. of Iowa, 1969; MMus., Ohio State Univ., 1971. m. Mary Jean Mikels. Career: Clarinetist, Columbus (Ohio) Symph. Orch., 1969-71; Solo & Prin. Clarinetist w. Univ. symphs., Tchng. Asst. & Asst. to Dir. of Bands, Ohio State Univ., 1970-71; Instr. of Music, Luther Coll., Decorah, Iowa, Instr., Clarinet & Woodwinds & Educ. courses, Dir. of Varsity Band & Jazz Ensemble, 1971-73; Instr. & Asst. Dir., Purdue Univ., Dir. Wind Ensemble, Collegiate, Varsity & Ceremonial Bands, & jazz Ensemble, Woodwind instr., Clinician & Adjudicator on Clarinet, Woodwinds & Bands, 1973-; Dir. of Bands, Asst. Prof. of Woodwinds, Bemidji (Minn.) State Univ. Has made sev. recordings both as Recitalist & as Ensemble Dir. Mbrships. icnl: Pi Kappa Lambda; VP, Beta Xi Chapt., Phi Mu Alpha Sinfonia; Kappa Kappa Psi; Nat. Band Assn. Nat. Assn. Coll. Wind & Percussion Instrs.; Pres. Ohio State Univ. Grad. Music Students Assn. Hobbies: Reading; Farming. Address: 703 Lake Blvd., Bennidji, MN 56601, USA.

MALM, William Paul, b. 6 Mar. 1928, LaGrange, Ill., USA. Musicologist; Ethnomusicologist; Lecturer. Educ: BMus, Northwestern Univ., 1949; MMus, ibid., 1950; PhD, UCLA, 1959. m. Joyce Rutherford Malm, 3 d. Career: Pianist-composer, mod. dance, NY, Am. Dance Fest., Jacob's Pillow, Perry-Mansfield Schl. of Theatre; Tchr., Univ. Ill., US Naval Schl. Music; Prof., Univ. Mich. Publs: incl: Music Cultures of the Pacific, the Near East, and Asia, 1967 (2nd edn., 1977); Japanese Music & Musical Instruments, 1959. Contbr. to profl. jrnls. Mbrships: incl; Pres., Soc. Ethnomusicol.; Am. Musicol. Soc. Hons. incl: Henry Russel Award, outstanding tchng., 1966. Address: Schl. Music, Univ. Michigan, Ann Arbor, MI 48109, USA. 11.

MALMLÖF-FORSSLING, Carin G, b. 6 Mar. 1916, Gävle, Sweden. Composer. Educ: Organist, Cantor dip., Uppsala, 1938; MMus, Royal Acad. of Music, Stockholm, 1942; studied w. H M Melchers (counterpoint & comp.), ibid., 1938-43; studied comp. w. Nadia Boulanger, Paris, 1957. m. Stig Forssling, 1 s. Comps. incl: works for organ, solo cello, solo flute, str. orch.; songs, choral music, electronic music. Recording: Release, for str. orch. Mbrships: Soc. of Swedish Comps.; STIM (Int. Office of Music for Swedish Comps.). Hons: Prize of Culture, City of Falun, 1973; Swedish State Comps. Grant, 1976, '79. Hobbies: Religious Philos.; Country Activities. Address: Varlidsvägen 23, 79100 Falun, Sweden.

MALMSTE'N, Georg, b. 27 June 1902, Helsinki, Finland. Conductor; Singer; Composer; Cornet; Piano. Educ: Helsinki Musikkiopisto, 9 yrs. m. Ragnhild Ceciloa, 2 c. Debut: Concert (singing), 1929. Career: ldng. parts, Händel's Julius Casear; Madetoja's Pohjalaisia; Films; Meidän Poikamme Merellä & Sano se Suomeksi; num. radio & TV apps. Compositions incl: (operettas)

Vetoketju; Lennokki; (children's play) Pikku Annin Seikkailut; over 1000 for orch., TV, radio, theatre, film, brass bands, etc. Recordings: 841. Publ: Geog Malmste'n Duurissa ja Mollissa (autobiography), 1964. Mbr. profl. orgs. Hons. incl: Prize Hon., Svenska Kulturfonden, 1974; num. music awards. Hobby: Farming. Address: Lutherinkatu 2B 15, 00100 Helsinki 10, Finland.

MALONE, Carol, b. 16 July, Grayson, Ky., USA. Opera Singer (Soprano). Educ: BMus. Ed., Ind. Univ.; Hamburg Music Acad.; Cologne Music Acad. m. Dr. John E Parker. Debut: Cologne Opera. Career: Performances in opera houses of La Scala, Milan; La Fenice, Venice; Deutsche Oper, Berlin, Bavarian State Opera, Munich; Hanburg State Opera; San Francisco Opera; Metropolitan Opera. Edinburgh Festival; Aix-en-Provence Festival; Salzburg Festival; TV appearances in Magic Flute w. Hamburg State Opera, & in Preussisches Märchen, w. Deutsche Oper, Berlin; Pemanent Mbr., Deutsche Oper, Berlin, 1971-. Hons: Fulbright Schlrship., 1964-65; German Govt. Grant, 1965-66. Hobby: Plants. Addres: Lützelsteiner Weg, Berlin, German Fed. Repub.

MALONE, (Mary) Eileen, b. Victor, NY, USA. Harpist. Educ: BM & Perf. Cert., Eastman Schl. of Music, 1931; Studied w. Marcel Tournier of Paris Conserv., France & w. Marcel Grandjary, NYC. Career: Prof. of Harp, Eastman Schl. of Music, 1936; Featured Soloist. NBC Radio & TV, 1936-60; Harp Advsr., Nat. Fedn. Music Clubs, 1973-74; Solo Apps. w. num. Symphs. inclng. Rochester, Buffalo, & Okla. & w. NYC Phil.; num. Recitals & Chmbr. Music Concerts; Mbr. var. juries. Recordings: Orchl. records w. Rochester Phil. for Victor, Columbia & Mercury. Cont;br. to Mini Course in Music for Schools. Mbrships: Mu Phi Epsilon, NY State Music Assn.; AAUP; Am. Harp Soc. (Original mbr., Int. Fndg. Committee, & present, Nat. Bd.). Hons. incl: Citizen for a Day, Rochester, NY., 1936; Mbr. of Jury, first Int. Harp Competition, Israel, 1959, 1970, 1973; Chmn., 6th Nat. Conf., Am. Harp Soc., 1969; Musician of Year, Mu Phi Epsilon, 1970. Address: Eastman Schl. of Music, 26 Gibbs St., Rochester, NY, USA. 5.

MALTA, Alexander, b. 28 Sept. 1942, Visp, Switz. Opera Singer; Concert Singer. Educ: Music High Schls., Frankfurt & Milan; Accademia Chigiana Siena; Studies w. Desider, Kovàcs, Barra-Carracciolo, Enzo Mascherini. m. Janet Perry, 1 d. Debut: State Opera, Stuttgart. Career: State apps., Munich, Berlin, Hamburg, Frankfurt, Strasbourg, Paris, Madrid, Venice, Zürich, Geneva, Amsterdam, Vienna, San Fran., etc.; Num. radio apps., Europe & USA; TV films, Damnation de Faust, Merry Wives, Zaubergeige, La Bohème, Emperor of Atlantis (Prix d'Italia RAI Award, 1978). Recordings: Samson & Delilah; Orfeo, Monteverdi; Merry Wives of Windsor; Lady Macbeth of Mtsensk. Hobbies: Writing; Stage Directing. Mgmt: Harrison/Parrott, London; Boettger, Berlin. Address: Hiltenspertgerstr. 28, 8 Munich 40, German Fed. Repub.

MALTHER, Lars, b. 8 Apr. 1943, Copenhagen, Denmark. Musician; Double Bass. Educ: Grad., Royal Danish Music Acad., 1968, m. Charlotte Vilmann, 1 s., 1 d. Career: Jazz Bassist, Jazzhouse Montmartre, Copenhagen, 1960-65; Classical Bass Player, Alborg Symph. Orch., 1968-70; Soloist, Tivoli Concert Hall Orch., 1970-72; Royal Danish Orch., 1972-. Recording: Lucanus (Carl-Petter). Address: 17 Ravnsnaesvej, 3460 Bikerod, Denmark. 30.

MALYCKE, Steven, b. 14 July 1920, Cleveland, Ohio, USA. Professor of Music; Professional Musician; Piano Technician. Educ: BS Educ., Ohio Univ.; MMus, Cinn. Conserv. of Music; Cert. Piano Technol., ibid. m. Lois C Naff, 1 s., 3 d. Career incls: Apps. w. num. orchs. inclng: Cleveland Symph.; Charleston Symph.; Soloist w. Warren Symph.; Parme Symph. etc.; Over 800 perfs. of Broadway musicals (30 different shows); Instr. of Piano Technol., Nat. Music Camp. Interlochen, Mich.; Tchr., Public Schls., Ohio, 7 yrs. Prof. num. univs. in USA. Mbrships. incl: Music Educators Nat. Conf.; Am. Fedn. of Musicians. Hobbies: Fishing; Wine making; Bowling; Restoring Player Pianos; Study of French, Spanish, German & Ukrainian Langs. Address: 2616 Ridgewood, Alliance, OH 44601, USA.

MAMES, León, b. 2 Apr. 1933, Leipzig, Germany. Musician (oboe, Cor Anglais, Oboe d'Amore, Heckelphone). Pvte. music educ. w. Grman Ehrenhaus, Edmond Gaspart & Pedro Pablo Cocchiararo; Dr. of Chem., Nat. Univ. of Buenos Aires. m. Beatriz Chinski, 3 s. Career: Mbr. of Orchs. incl: Youth Orch. of LRA Radio Nat.; Symph., Orch. of LRA Radio Nat.; Phil. of Buenos Aires; Nat. Symph.; Cor anglais, permanent orch. of Colon Theatre, 1958-; Chmbr. music performer w. Trio Argentino de Cañas; Trio Am. de instrumentos de Viento; Trio de Oboes de Buenos Aires; Camerata Instrumental de Buenos Aires; Mbr., Trio Barroco de Buenos Aires, 1977-. Recordings: Beethoven-Trio Op. 87 for 2 oboes & cor anglais; Claudio Guidi Drei-Tres Liricas; Gerardo Gandini-Concertino III; Werner Wagner-10 miniatures

for Cor Anglais & Piano. Publs: Translactions into Spanish of var. books on musical subjs. Mbrships: Argentine Musicians Syndicate; Assn. of Profl. orchs.; Argentine Assn. of Interpreters. Recip: 2nd prize, Collegium Musicum de Buenos Aires, 1953. Hobby: Philately. Mgmt: Org. de conciertos Gerard, Corrientes 127, of. 407, Buenos Aires. Address: Marcelo T de Alvear 1239, 11C Buenos Aires, Argentina.

MAMLOK, Ursula, b. 1 Feb. 1928, Berlin, Germany. Composer; Pianist; Professor of Music. Educ: BMus., MMus., Manhattan Schl. of Music, NY; Mannes Coll. & studied w. George Szell, Roger Sessions, Stefan Wolpe, Ralph Shapey. m. Dwight G. Mamlok. Career: Composers Forum. WNYC; many perfs. in USA & South German Rundfunk; Prof. of Music. CUNY; Nat. Endowment for the Arts, etc. Compositions Fac. Manhattan Schl. of Music, 1970-73. Comps. incl: 5 Capriccios for oboes piano; Variations & Interludes for 4 percussionists; Festive Sound for Woodwind Quintet. Variations for Solo Flute; Straybirds for Soprano, Flute, V. Cello. Contbr. to Contemporary Music Newsletter Vol. III, no. 1-2, 1969. Mbrships: Am. Composers Alliance; Am. Soc. for Univ. Comps.; Am. Music Ctr. Recip. var. Hons. Address: 315 E 86th St., NY, NY 10028, USA. 27.

MANA-ZUCCA, b. 25 Dec. 1894, New York, NY, USA. Composer; Pianist. Educ: D Mus, Univ. Miami; Studied NYC & Berlin, Germany. m. Irwin M Cassel, 1 s. Debut: At age of 4 yrs. Career incls: Concert w. NY Phil., Carnegie Hall; Appeared in Rudolf Friml's High Jinks operetta, dancing w. Clifton Webb, playing daughter to Will Rogers in Town Topics on Broadway; Toured w. Comedy Team Gallagher & Sheen. Comps: Over 1100 published works inclng: Big Brown Bear; Nichevo (Nothing Matters); Valse Brilliante (piano); Love's Dart; It Was No Dream; Sonata No. 3 (piano). Num. recordings. Mbrships: Sigma Alpha Iota; SAI; Hon. Mbr., Pen Women League. Hobby: Little Piano Collection (over 200). Address: 4301 Adams Ave., Miami Beach, FL, USA.

MANCINI, Henry Nicole, b. 16 Apr. 1924, Cleveland, Ohio, USA. Composer; Conductor. Educ: Juilliard Schl. of Music, 1942-43. m. Virginia O'Connor Mancini, 1 s., 2 d. Career incls: Concerts, USA, Can., Israel, Japan, Brazil, UK, Aust., NZ, Germany; Royal Family Command Perf., London Palladium, UK, 1966; Guest Cond., Leading Symph. orchs., USA & around the world; Own TV music series. Num. comps. incl: complete dramatic musical scores & recordings for num. films; Author, Sounds & Scores, 1962. Mbrships. incl: Former Bd. of Dirs., ASCAP. Num. hons. incl: 13 Acad. Award nominations; 3 golden Oscars; 20 Grammy Awards; 6 Gold Album Awards; hon. DMus, Duquesne Univ. Hobbies incl: Photography; Skiing. Mgmt: Regency Artists Ltd., 9200 Sunset Blvd., Los Angeles, CA 90069, USA. Address: 9229 Sunset Blvd., Suite 304, Los Angeles, CA 90069, USA.

MANDAC, Evelyn, b. 16 Aug. 1945, Bukidnon, The Philippines. Lyric Soprano. Educ: BA, Univ. of the Philippines; MA, Juilliard Schl. of Music, USA. m. Sanjoy Bhattacharya. Debut: Salzburg, Austria, 1973. Career: Perfs. in Opera in USA, Can., France, Italy, Switzerland & UK; apps. w. num. major US orchs. inclng. Los Angeles, Dallas, Chgo., Phila. & Cleveland. Roles incl: Leading parts in operas of Bizet, Donizetti, Handel, Mozart, Puccini, Strauss, Verdi & num. others. Recordings: Camina Burana W. Boston Symph.; Mahler 2nd Symph. w. Phila. Orch. Mbr., Am. Guild Musicians & Actors. Hons. incl: Met. Opera Audition Prize, 1965; Brussels Competition Prize, 1966. Hobbies: Cooking; Reading. Mgmt: c/o mathew Epstein, Columnbia Artists Mgmt. Address: 165 W 57th St., NY, NY 10019, USA.

MANDEL, Alan Roger, b. 17 July 1935, NY, NY, USA. Concert Pianist; Professor of Music; Recording Artist; Composer. Educ: BS Mus, Juilliard Schl. music, 1956; MS Mus, ibid., 1957; Dip., Acad. Mozarteum, Salzburg, Austria, 1962; Dip., Conserv. Monteverdi, Bolzano, Italy, 1963; 16 grad. courses. Univ. Pa., 1966-69. m. Nancy Siegmeister. Debut: Town Hall, NYC, 1948. Career incls: Num. concerts, maj. cities USA, 1965-; Num. apps. & concert tours, Europe, Mid. East, N Africa, etc.; TV & radio perfs.; Chmn., piano dept., Am. Univ., Wash., DC. num. perfs. & tours w. wife as violin & piano duo. Recordings incl: Elie Siegmeister: A Musical Profile. Contbr. to Profl. publs. Mbr. var. orgs. Hons. incl: Brundage Award, Pa. Univ., 1966. Hobbies incl: Gourmet Cooking; Mtn. Climbing. Mgmt: Aust. Concert Direction; Promotion et Action Musicale, Paris; Sedgley Claire Mgmt., Wash., DC. Address: 3113 Northampton St. NW, Washington, DC 20015, USA.

MANDEL, Nancy Anne Siegmeister, b. 20 Feb. 1943, NYC, USA. Concert Violinist; Musicologist. Educ: BA, Sarah Lawrence Coll.; Grad. Studies in Musicol., Univ. of Pa. & NY univ.; pvte. musical studies w. father (comp. Elie Siegmeister) & other tchrs. m. Alan R. Mandel. Debut: Carnegie Recital Hall, NYC. Career: Concert apps. as solo violinist in over 35 countries throughout world; star of num. radio & TV shows, Europe, Near East & USA. recording: New Music of Elie Siegmeister, Violin Sonata, no. 4 (w. pianist A Mandel). Publ: Ed., Karl Loewe, Grand Duo for Violin & Piano (w. A Mandel), 1976-77. Contbr. to: the New Music Lover's Handbook, 1973; Clavier. Mbr., Prof. assns. Hobbies incl: Art & Art History; Archaeoogy. Mgmt: Aust. Concert Direction, 129 Canterbury Rd., Canterbury, Vic. 3126, Aust. Address: 3113 Northampton St., NW, Wash., DC 20015, USA.

MANDELKERN, Rivka Iventosch, b. 3 May 1916, Hartford, Conn., USA. Violinist; Pianist. Educ: 2 yrs. of Univ. of Calif. at Berkeley; Grad., Juilliard Schl. of Music. m. Bernard Mandelkern, 1 s., 1 d. Debut: Town Hall, NY. Career: Many appearances as soloist w. orchs.; Countless solo recitals & chamber music perfs. Tchr. of violin Rosary Hill Coll.; Mbr., Buffalo Phil. Orch. Mbrships: Chromatic Club; Wednesday Morning Musical; Zonta. Hons: San Francisco Music Week 1st Prize, 1931. Hobbies: Needlework; Gardening. Address: 380 Woodbridge Ave., Buffalo, NY 14214, USA. 5.

MANDER, Noel Percy, b. 19 May 1912, Crouch, Kent, UK. Maker of Pipe Organs. m. Enid Watson, 3 s., 2 d. Career: Army Serv., 5 yrs.; Organ Builder; Appointed Organ Builder to St. Paul's Cathedral, London, 1971; Appointed organ builder to Canterbury Cathedral, 1978; Builder of Winston Churchill Memorial Organ, Fulton, Mo. Author, var. pamphlets on historic organs. Contbr. to: Organs; Musical Opinion. Mbrships: Savage Club; Fellow, Soc. of Antiquaries; Liveryman, City of London (Musicians Co.); Past Master, Worshipful Co. of Parish Clerks. Hobbies: Country Life; Reading; Hist.; Old Clocks; Travel. Address: Earl Soham, near Framingham, Suffolk, UK. 3.

MANDUELL, John, b. 2 Mar. 1928, Johannesburg, S Africa. Composer; Principal. Educ: Jesus Coll., Cambridge; RAM; FRAM, FRNCM, hon. FTCL. m. Renna Kellaway, 1 d., 3 s. Career: BBC, 1956-68 (Prod., 1956-61, Hd. of Music, Midlands & E Anglia, 1961-64, Chief Planner, The Music Prog., 1964-68); Dir. of Music, Univ. of Lancaster, 1968-71; Prin. RNCM, 1971-; Prog. Dir., Cheltenham Fest., 1969-; sev. admin. appointments in Arts Coun. of GB, Univ. of Lancaster, etc. Comps: Symphony; Viola Concerto; Overture, Sunderland Point; Diversions for chmbr. orch.; Str. Quartet; Cameos for Clarinet, other chmbr. music, songs, etc. Publs: Training Musicians, 1978. Contbr. to: The Symphony (ed. R Simpson), 1966; Radio Times; The Listener, etc. Mbrships: Comps. Guild; ISM; Royal Soc. of Musicians, Chopin Soc., Warsaw. Hons: PRS Scholarship, 1954; Theodore Holland, 1956. Hobbies: Cricket; Travel; French Life, lang. & lit. Address: RNCM, 124 Oxford Rd., Manchester M13 9RD, UK. 1, 14.

MANES, Stephen G, b. 11 Apr. 1940, Bennington, Vt., USA. Concert Pianist; Professor of Music. Educ: BS, MS, Juilliard Schl. of Music; Vienna Acad., Austria. m. Frieda Green, 1 s., 1 d. Debut: NYC, 1963. Career: Soloist, major US orchs.; Recitalist & Chmbr. Music Specialist; Perf. w. Cleveland, Rowe & Tokyo Str. Quartets; participant, Marlboro Music Fest; radio broadcasts incl. BBC, 1975, WQXR-NY, 1976. Recordings: Tchaikovsky, Sonata in G major, op. 37; Busoni, Indianisches Tagebuch. Mbrships: NY State Music Tchrs. Assn.; Coll. Music Soc.; AAUP. Hons. incl: Harriet Cohen Int. Beethoven Prize, 1964. Hobbies: Jogging; Bridge; Chess; Spectator sports. Mgmt: Hamlen Mgmt., NY; Interarists, The Hague, Netherlands. Address: 384 Voorhees Ave., Buffalo, NY 14216, USA.

MANFORD, Barbara Ann, b. 13 Nov. 1929, St. Augustine, Fla., USA. Contralto; Teacher of Applied Voice. Educ: BMus, 1955, MMus, 1970, Fla. State Univ. Career: Artist in Res., Ball State Univ., Munice, Ind.; Asst. Prof. of Applied Voice in Musical Perf. & Italian Diction, ibid.; Res. in Europe, performing major mezzo-soprano roles in 12 major Italian opera houses, & concerts & recitals throughout Italy & Paris, France, 1951-68; Num. apps. in USA. Recordings: Songs of Spohr and Brahms. Mbrships: Sigma Alpha Iota; Pi Kappa Lambda; Nat. Assn. of Tchrs. of Singing. Hons: Semi Finalist, Parma Vocal Contest. Address: Colonial Crest Apts., 104, Muncie, IN 47304, USA. 5.

MANGAHAS, Ruby Kelley, b. 27 May 1916, Manila, Philippines. Music Educator; Researcher; Administrator. Educ: AB, Psychology, Univ. of the Philippines; MA, Lib. Sci., Univ. of Mich.; Grad. in piano, Acad. of Music of Manila; PhD, Indian Music, Univ. of London. m. Federico Mangahas, 3 s. Career: Music Fac. Mbr., Univ. of the Philippines, 1947-; Coll. Sec., ibid., 1947-53; Music Libn., ibid., 1955-61; Dir., Inst. of Lib. Sci. ibid., 1966-69; Music Dean, ibid, 1969-78; Fndr., Philippine Youth Orch., 1974. Publ: The Development of Ragalaksana, with Reference to Other Modal Systems. Contbr. to profl. publs. Mbrships. incl: Nat. Music Coun. of the Philippines, Pres., 1976-78, Sec.-Gen., 1974-76; Chapter Sec., Phi Kappa

Phi, 1960-61; Fndr., Philippine Recorder Soc. Recip., fellowship grants. Address: P-5 Area 14, U.P., Quezon City 3004, Philippines.

MANGESHKAR, Hridaynath, b. 26 Oct. 1937, Sangli, Maharashtra State, India. Composer; Singer for Television, Films, Radio & Stage. Educ: Studied w. Ustad Amirkhan, Shri Husnalal, & Shri Ramprasad. m. Bharati Malwankar, 2 s. Debut: At age 7. Career: Participated in nearly all maj. confs. of India; Sang in prof. organized by Maharashtra Mandal, London, UK. Comps. incl: Meerabai; Mirza Galib; Geeta & Gyaneshwari; Chala Wahi Desh; num. comps. based on classical folk, natya sangit, light, Wester & semi-classical music. Mbrships. incl: Dir., Mangesh Melodies Pvt. Ltd. Publs: Muktak; Majhe Gani. Contbr. to: Dainik Maratha; Sandarbha. Hons. incl: Swami Haridas Award, 1970. Hobbies incl: Painting. Address: 101 Prabhu-Kunj, Peddar Rd., Bombay 400026, India.

MANGOLD, Arland Alza, b. 21 Sept. 1937, Ogallah, Kan., USA. Supervisor of Music; Music Educator; Adjudicator in Band, Brass; Instructor of French Horn; Guest Conductor; Clinician; Composer. Educ: Ft. Hays Kan. State Coll.; BMus, Emporia State Tchrs. Coll.; Master in Perf., French Horn, Kan. City Conser. m. Rosemary Stephens, 1 c. Career: Prin. French Horn, Kan. City Phil. Orch., St. Louis Symph. & Denver Symph. Comps: Concertino for Band; Quartl Piece; Chinook for Woodwind Quintet. Mbrships: Nat. Band Assn.; Can. Band Dir. Assn.; Phi Mu Alpha. Hons: Winner, Nat. Young Artists Auditions, USA, 2 consecutive yrs. Hobbies: Record Collecting; Camping. Address: Box 1964, Taber, Alta., Can. TOK 2G0.

MANIATES, Maria Rika, b. 30 Mar. 1937, Totonto, Can. Musicologist. Educ: Assoc., Royal Conserv. of Toronto, (Solo piano), 1958; BA (Music), Univ. of Toronto, 1960; MA (Musicol.) Columbia Univ., USA, 1962; PhD (Musicol), ibid., 1965. Career: Prof. of Musicol. & Chmn., Dept. of Hist. & Lit. of Music (1973-78), Fac. of Music, Fellow of Vic. Coll., Univ. of Totonto; Specialist, Renaissance period & Philos. of music; Dir. & perf., Renaissance Music Grp.. CBC TV show Ars Nova Musica, 1969; Vis. Prof. of Music, Columbia Univ., 1976. Publ: Combinative Techniques in Franco-Flemish Polyphony, 1965; Mannerism in Italian Music & Culture, 1530-1630, 1979. Contb;r. to var. profl. jrnls. Mbrships. incl: Int. Musicol. Soc. (Can. Rep., Bd. of Govs., 1973-82); Am. Musicol. Soc. (Coun. 1972-74, 1976-78, Einstein Award Committee, 1976-79). Hons. incl: Can. Coun. Predoctoral Fellow, 1962-64; President's Fellow, Columbia Univ., 1962-63; Rockefeller Grant in Musicol., 1964-65; Humanities & Soc. Sci. Grant, Can. Coun., 1970-73. Address: Fac. of Music, Univ. of Toronto, Toronto, Ont., Can. M5S 1A1. 11, 14.

MANICKE, Dietrich, b. 29 Oct. 1923, Wurzen, Germany. Composer; Musicologist; Professor. Educ: Grad., Acad. for Music & Theatre, Dresden, 1947; Univ. of Berlin; Univ. of Münster Westfalen; PhD, Free Univ., Berlin, 1955. m. Annelies Western, 1 s., 1 d. Career: Lectr., Music Theory, State Acad. of Music, Dresden, 1948-50, German High Schl. for Music, Berlin, 1950-53, Berlin Ch. Music Schl., 1957-60; Music Program Manager, Amerika Haus Berlin, 1956-66; Northwest German Music Acad., Detmold, 1960-; Prof., ibid., 1967-. Comps. incl: var. orchl. works; Trio, violin, cello, piano; Wind Sextet; var. Chmbr. Music; Songs; piano, organ Sonatas; organ Partita; Sinfonia brevis for orch.; quattro pezzi concertati for violin & piano; sonatine for brass sextet; num. vocal & choral works. Publs: Die Sprache als musikalischer Gestaltträger in Mozarts Zauberflöte, 1955; Der polyphone Satz, Teil 1, 1965, Teil 11, 1979; Ed., Balladen von G A Bürger, 1970. Contbr. to var. profl. jrnls. Mbr. num. profl. orgs. Recip. Carl Maria v. Weber Prize, City of Dresden, 1949; Prof., 1967. Hobby: Walking. Address: 18 Friedrich Pieper Str., D4930 Detmold 14, German Fed. Repub.

MANIKHAO, Narong, b. 30 Mar. 1930, Ayudhaya, Thailand. Music Teacher; Lecturer; Consultant (Violin, Viola, Guitar, Organ, Piano). Educ: PhD; MusD; LTCL; ATCL; A Mus LCM. m. Viyada Manikhao, 5 s., 1 d. Career: Music Tchr., Lectr. & Cons.; Owner, Prin. & Dir., Bangkok Metropolis Music Schl. (licensed by Min. of Educ., Bangkok). Publs: Form of Music, 1975. Hobbies: Photography; Reading. Address: GPO Box 990, Bangkok, Thailand. 29, 30.

MANITAS DE PLATA, (Baliardo Ricardo), b. 1 Aug. 1921, Sete, France. Guitarist. m. Jeanne Maille, 9 children. Debut: Carnegie Hall, NYC, 1965. Career: Leading perf. of flamenco gypsy guitar music; apps. on Ed Sullivan Show, Tom Jones Show, Grand Echiquier. Comps. publd. in Paris & NYC. Recordings for Barclay, Vanguard, Connoisseur Soc., CBS & Philips. Publ: Musique aux Doigts (memoirs), 1976. Contbr. of interviews to num. major mags., worldwide. Mbrships: Variety Club, Paris; SACEM-SDRM, ibid. Hons: Grand Prix du Disque; Disque d'Or;

Royal Command Perf., London, UK; Gala, UNICEF, Paris, 1967. Hobbies: Cars; Women. Mgmt: André Bernard, 17 Rue Coysevox, 75018 Paris. Address: c/o Clergue, 17 Rue A, Briaud, 13632, Arles, France.

MANLY, Ann (Susan), b. 6 Aug. 1949, London, UK. Soprano Singer; Writer. Educ: BA in Music, Oxford Univ. m. Guy Protheroe, 1 d. Career: freelance concert mgmt. & promotion based in London, 1971-77; singing career incl. solo apps. at Queen Elizabeth Hall, St. John's Smith Sq., etc. in London & elsewhere in UK; mbr., leading chmbr. choirs; now co-dir., Spectrum Contemporary music ensemble. Contbr. of programme notes & as programme designer to BBC & ldng. concert promoters. Hobbies: Fashion; Food & Drink; Swimming; Tennis; Cricket. Address: 55 Leconfield Rd., London N5 2RZ, UK.

MANN, Alan, b. 24 July 1914, Sydney, NSW, Aust. Orchestral Player (French Horn); Teacher. Educ: Dip. Educ., Sydney Tchrs. Coll.; Dip. of Music, Sydney Conserv., 1936; studied w. Prof. Wili Kruger of Leipzig; Dip. Radiography, London, UK. m. Ruth Mann, 1 s., 1 d. Debut: Sydney Conserv., 1936. Career: Prin. Hornist, Sydney Symph. Orch., 1954-62; Tchr. of Horn, Sydney Conserv., 1945-; Tchr. Harmony & Theory, ibid.; High Schl. Tchr., NSW Dept. of Educ.; currently Prin. Hornist, Sydney Opera House. Recordings: Num. orchl. works w. major conds. Mbr., var. univ. & academic socs. Hobbies: Science; Horticulture; Literature. Address: 142 Wallumatta Rd., Newport 2106 NSW, Australia.

MANN, Laurence, b. 1 July 1931, Skelmanthorpe, Huddersfield, UK. Mineworker; Bass Trombonist. Educ: Trained w. Brass Band & RAF. m. Brenda Mann, 1 s., 1 d. Career: w. all standards brass bands since 11 yrs. old; Currently, Mbr. & Sec., Carlton Main Frickley Collery Band. Recordings: w. Carlton Main Frickley Colliery Band. Hons: Approx. 80 prizes, Open Solo Competitions. Hobby: Music. Address: 39 Manor Rise, Skelmanthorpe, Huddersfield, Yorks, UK.

MANN, William Somervell, b. 14 Feb. 1924. Critic & Broadcaster. Educ: BA, MusB, Magdalene Coll., Cambridge. m. Erika Charlotte Emilie Sohler, 4 d. Career: Music Critic, Cambridge Review, 1946-48; Radio Broadcaster on Music, 1949-; Asst. Music Critic, 1960-, The Times, London; Assoc. Ed., Opera mag., 1954-. Publs. incl: Introduction to the Music of J S Bach, 1950; Let's Fake an Opera (w. F Reizenstein), 1958; Richard Strauss's Opera, 1964; Wagner's Tristan, Introduction & Translation, 1968; Mozart's Operas, 1977. Contbr. to: Musical Times; Opera; Gramophone. Mbrships: Critics' Circle; CAMRA; Royal Musical Assn. Hobbies incl: Winemaking; Darts; Camping; Foreign Languages; Interior Decoration. Address: 135 Cottenham Park Rd., London SW20 ODW, UK. 1.

MANNEKE, Daniël, b. 7 Nov. 1939, Kruiningen, Netherlands. Organist; Conductor; Composer. Educ: studied comp.; Dip. in organ. m. Gisina Manneke, 1 s., 1 d. Career: Organ recitals; concert for Belgian TV; made a recording on the monumental Del Haye organ (built 1770) in Bergen op Zoom. Comps: Diaphony; Three Times (for choir & 13 instruments); Motet for Renaissance Instruments; Sinfonia for Strings; Diapora for Organ; Plein Jeu for Brass; Jeux for flute solo. Author of essays on educ. & musical improvisation. Mbrshipos: Geneco; KNTV; Toonkust. Recip. Prize of Zeeland, 1967. Address: Breda 4304, Baronielaan 306, Netherlands.

MANNING, Jane Marian, b. 20 Sept. 1938, Norwich, UK. Singer (Soprano). Educ: LRAM, 1958; GRSM, 1960, ARCM, 1961; Scuolad di Canto, Cureglia, Switz. m. Anthony Payne. Debut: Pk. Lane Grp., 1964. Career: Regular apps. in leading concert halls in London, Europe, N America, Aust.; Apps. maj. fests.; Specialist in contemporary music; Frequent broadcasts for BBC; Occasional lecture recitals. Num. recordings in UK, Spain & USA. Contbr. to Composer. Mbrships. incl: Music Panel, Gtr. London Arts Assn.; ISM. Hons: ARAM, 1972; Special Award, CGGB, 1973. Hobbies: Cinema; Cooking; Ornithol. Mgmt: Clarion Concert Agcy., 64 Whitehall Pk., London N19. Addrss: 2 Wilton Square, London N1, UK. 27.

MANNING, Peter David, b. 2 July 1948, Hampstead, London, UK. Senior Experimental Officer in Music. Educ: Choral Schl., Dept. Music, Durham Univ., 1967-69; BA, ibid., 1970; Doct. rsch., 1970-73. m. Elizabeth Locke. Career: Co-reviser, aural tests grades I-VIII, Assoc. Bd., Royal Schls. Music, 1971-72; Snr. Experimental Off., Dirham Univ. Electronic Music Studios, 1973-. Comps: The Night Visitors (ballet for electronic tape w. Peter Wiegold), 1975. Contbr. to: Contract: GSM Review. Mbrships: Coun.; Soc. Promotion New Music, 1973-; Exec. Comm., ibid., 1975-76; Royal Musical Assn. Hobbies: Cooking; Meterol.; Gardening. Address: 19 Rowantree Ave., Gilesgate Moor, Durham City, DH1 1DX, UK.

MANNONI, Raymond, b. 11 July 1921, Pitts., Kan., USA. Professor of Music. Educ: BS, Kan. State Pitts., 1944; MMus Ed, Univ. of Mich., 1947; MMUs, Northwestern Univ., 1949; EdD, Chgo. Musical Coll., Roosevelt Univ., 1955. m. Karen W Mannoni, 1 d. Career: Served w. USA, World War II; Dir. of Bands, Univ. of Southern Miss., 1952-60; Mbr., LeBlanc Music Educators Nat. Adv. Bd., 1958-68; Prof. of Music & Dean, Coll. of Fine Arts, ibid., 1960-. Publs: Music Theory for Beginners, 1956 (co-author). Mbrships. incl: Phi Delta Kappa; Kappa Kappa Psi; Phi Mu Alpha Sinfonia; Pi kappa Lambda; Altha Psi Omega; Phi Kappa Phi; Omicron Delta Kappa. Hobbies: Golf; Swimming; Fishing. Address: Rte. 10, Country Club Estates, Hattiesburg, MS 39401, USA. 2, 12.

MANNS, Angela M, b. 5 Nov. 1942, Gerrards Cross, UK. Performer & Teacher of Flute & Piano. Educ: Royal Acad. Music; LRAM; ARCM; GRSM. m. Phillip D Manns, 1 s., 1 d. Mbr., Incorp. Soc. of Musicians. Hobbies: Writing; Walking; Sailing. Address: Post Cottage, Wood Lane, Kidmore End, Nr. Reading, Berks., UK.

MANSER, Philip Simon Andrew, b. 18 April, 1951, London, UK. Lay Vicar; Music Master; Director. Educ: Dip. Ed., St. Paul's Coll., Cheltenham Spa; GGSM. Career: Lay Vicar, Southwark (1969-72), Gloucester (1972-73), Windsor (1973-77), Lincoln Minster; Hd. of Music, St. Piran's Schl., Maidenhead, 1973-76; Music Master, Ermine Middle Schl., Lincoln; Dir., Minster Consort of Voices. Recordings: Music From St. Georges, Windsor; Five Centuries at St. George's, Vaughan Williams Choral Music. Mbrships: ISM; AMA; Prayer Book Soc.; Lincoln Soc. Address: 'St. Anne', 50 Westgate, Lincoln, Lincs., UK.

MANSHARDT, Thomas, b. 23 Mar. 1927, Wai, India. Concert Pianist. Educ: Conserv. of Lausanne; Ecole Normale, Paris; Academia Chigiana, Siena; studied w. Alfred Cortot. Debut: Vienna, 1954; Bonn, 1954; London, 1956; LA, USA, 1964; NYC, 1965. Career: Concert Tours in Germany, India, Pakistan, USA; num. Apps. as Soloist w. Orch.; num. Radio & TV Apps.; Assoc. Prof. of Music, Univ. of Sask., Can., 1966-. Mgmt: Albert Kay Assocs. Inc., Concert Artists Mgmt., 58 W 58 St., NY, NY 10019, USA. Address: 1004-1830 Coll. Ave., Regina, Sask. S4P 1C2, Can.

MANSO, Carlos, b. 10 Sept. 1928, Buenos Aires, Argentina. Pianist. Educ: Piano Prof. & MMus, Nat. Educ. Coun., Buenos Aires; pvte. studies, Argentina, Brazil, USA, Spain & Portugal. Debut: Cervantes Nat. Theatre, 1955. Career: Concerts, recitals, radio & TV broadcasts in Argentina, Brazil, Uruguay, Portugal, USA, Philippines, India, Japan, Formosa, Spain, UK, Hong Kong & Gibraltar; Hispanic music concert lectures at var. colls., hosps., etc. Contbr. to music jrnls. in Argentina, Brazil & Spain. Mbrships: Gen. Sec. & Music Advsr., Coll. Mayor Hispano-Am. Ntra. Sra. de Guadalupe, Madrid, 1962-66. Hobby: Painting. Address: French 2278 (planta baja-dto. 1), Buenos Aires 1125, Argentina.

MANSON, Eddy Lawrence, b. 9 May 1919, NYC, USA. Harmonica Virtuoso; Composer. Educ: CCNY; NYU; UCLA; grad. Juilliard Schl. Music, 1942. m. Paula Meriam Douse, 1 s. Debut: Brooklyn Acad. Music, 1947. Career incls: Comp.; Arranger; Cond.; Producer; Harmonica Virtuoso; Pres., Margery Music Inc., Eddy Manson Prods. Inc.; Soloist, Town Hall, Carnegie Hall, Royce Hall UCLA, Alice Tully Hall, Lincoln Ctr., NY; USSR, 1959. Comps. incl: Little Fugitive (film score); Day of the Painter (film score); The River Nile (TV document); Symph. No. 1; Fugue for Woodwinds; Chorale Fantasy for Orch.; Bachiana Americans; Trilogy for Woodwinds; Str. Quartet. Recordings incl: Harmonica Impressions; harmonicas Wild; Suite from Little Fugitive (folkways), & num. others. Author, Little Songs That Teach, 1960. Contbr. to var. profl. jrnls. Mbrships. incl: past Pres., Am. Soc. Music Arrangers; Past Gov., Nat. Acad. TV Arts & Sci.; ASCAP. Hons. incl: Elizabeth Sprague Coolidge Award in Comp., 1942; Acad. Award for "Day of the Painter", 1961; 2 TV Emmy Nominations; 5 Venice Festival Awards; 11 ASCAP Standard Panel Awards; 16 clios. Hobbies incl: Gold; Graphology. Address: 2616 N Beachwood Dr., Hollywood, CA 90068, USA. 3.

MANTEL, Gerhard Friedrich, b. 31 Dec. 1930, Karlsruhe, Germany. Cellist. Educ: Music Acads. in Mannheim & Paris; Studied w. August Eichhorn & Pierre Fournier; Musikhochschule, Saarbrucken. m. Renate Mantel, 1 s. Career: Solo Cellist; Belgen Symph., Norway; WDR Radio Symph., Cologne; Soloist toured worldwide, mainly w. Erika Friesar, Pianist; Prof., Frankfurt Musikhochschule, 1973-; Asst. Dir., ibid., 1975-. Recordings w. Erika Frieser incl: Mendelssohn, Strauss, Grieg. Publs: Cello Technik, 1973, Gerig Verlag Koln; Transl. Cello Technique, 1975. Ind. Univ. Press, USA. Mbr. European string Tchrs. Assn. (Rep. for Hessen). Recip. Kulturpreis der Stadt Karlsruhe,

1955. Hobbies: Reading; Family. Address: 6236 Eschborn 2, Feldbergstr. 44, German Fed. Repub.

MANTHEY-KOTZUR, Sonia, b. 7 May 1922, Poznan, Poland. Opera Singer (Coloratura Soprano). Educ: Dip., Acad. of Music. m. Witold Kotzur, 2 d. Debut: as Musette in La Boheme, Poznan. Career: apps. at Poznan opera, Polish Theatre & w. Phil. Orchs. in Poznan, Szczecin, Cracow & Bydgoszcz; TV & radio recitals. mbr., SPAM. Hons: Dip., w. gold medl, 1953; medal for suervices to culture, 1972. Hobbies: Cinema; Swimming. Mgmt: Poznan Phil. Orch. Address: Engla 12 m 5, Poznan, Poland.

MANTIA, Aldo, b. 20 Jan. 1903, Rome, Italy. Music Master; Pianist; Composer; Professor of Piano. Educ: Piano Dips., State Conserv. S. Pietro a Majella, Naples, & Accademia di Santa Cecilia, Rome; Study w. Ida Boissio, Wladimir De Pachmann. m. Del Bianco Lucrezia Romana, 1 d. Career: Concerts, Italy, Europe, Africa, Far East; Prof., Prin. Pianoforte, State Conserv. of Music Santa Cecilia, Rome, 1939-; Prof., Piano, Nat. Inst. of Music, Rome; Artistic Dir., Concerts of Artists Int. Assn., Rome, 15 yrs. Num. compositions incl: Il giardino del Ricordo; Sancto Francesco; Istorie dai Bagdad; Children's Songs; Vieux Clavecin; Una vita solitaria; Num. arrs. Num. recordings. Contbr. to profl. jrnls. Mbrship: Mbr., accademia Tiberina, Rome. Hons. incl: Kt. of Order of Crown of Italy, 1938; Gold Medal & Benemerit Mbr., Artist Int. Assn., Rome, 1946; Gold Medal, Fondazione Sgambati, Rome, 1964; Bronze Medal, Govt. of India, 1961. Address: Via Monte Santo 25, 00195 Rome, Italy. 3, 19, 28.

MANTOVANI, Annunzio Paolo, b. 15 Nov. 1905, Venice, Italy. Conductor (now retired). Educ: TCM. m. Winifred Kathleen Moss, 1 s., 1 d. Career: formed orch. at Midland Hotel, Birmingham, 1923; has given recitals in Wigmore Hall, Queens Hall, etc.; Cond., Orch. of Hotel Metropole, London; has broadcast for BBC, 1927-; formed Timicia Orch., 1932; Theatre Cond., 1940; Musical Dir. for Noel Coward, 1945; formed present orch., 1950; had own TV series during 1960s; Musical Dir. for many shows inclng. Ace of Clubs, Pacific 1860, And So To Bed, & Bob's Your Uncle. sev. comps. Recordings incl: Charmaine; Dancing with Tears in My Eyes; It Happened in Monterey; Mixicali Rose; Greensleeves; La Cumparsita. Hons. incl: Gold Disc for Charmaine; many gold discs for LPs; Novello Award, 1956; Silver Zither Award, Paris, 1975. Hobbies: Motoring; Photography; Bridge. Address: Chestnuts, 61 Sandown Pk., Tonbridge Wells, Kent TN2 4RT, UK. 2.

MANUEL, Handel, b. 27 Apr. 1918, Madras, India. Radio Producer; Pianist; Organist; Conductor; Music Critic. Educ: BA, Univ. of Madras; Practical ATCL. m. Alice Manuel, 1 child. Debut: as pianist, aged 6. Career: piano & organ recitals; num. radio broadcasts; Cond., orchl. & choral concerts; Dir., stage prodns. of Gilbert & Sullivan; app. as soloist w. Mahalia Jackson; accomp. to sev. int. artists inclng. Isobel Baillie & Alberto Lysy; Prod., Western Music, Univ. of Madras. Recip., dedication of Alan Hovhaness 'Arjuna' symph., 1960. Hobby: Tennis. Address: 43/c Ranganathan Ave., Madras 10, India.

MANZ, André, b. 15 Dec. 1942, Chur, Switzerland. Musician (Organ, Piano, Harpsichord); Teacher. Educ: Music Acad., Zurich; Conserv., Winterthur; Hochschule für Musik, Cologne, German Fed. Repub.; Masters degree, Organ & Piano; Concert Dip., Organ. m. Irene Pomey. Debut: 1964. Career: Recitals, Switzerland & German Fed. Repub.; now Ldr., Swiss Baroque Soloists, Amriwwill; var. radio series. Compositions: Play b-a-c-h (6 organists & assts.), 1971. Recordings incl: Swiss Baroque Soloists (music by John Stanley, etc.); Late-romantic organ music (Liszt, Karg-Elert, Mulet etc.); organ music by Armin Schibler. Publs: Max Regeras organ composer. Contbr. to musical jrnls. Mbr., profl. assns. Recip., musical prizes & scholarships. Hobbies: Collecting records of great pianists; Long-distance running. Address: Brunnenfeld strasse 11, 8580 Amriswil, Switzerland.

MARBE, Myriam Lucia, b. 9 Apr. 1931, Bucharest, Romania. Composer. Educ: Grad., music fac., Bucharest (piano & comp), 1944-54; summer courses, Darmstadt, 1968, '69, '72. Career: Musical ed., Bucharest Film Studio, 1953-54; Tutor, Music fac. of Bucharest, 1954; asst., ibid., 1960; Lectr., ibid., 1966; Assoc. Prof., ibid., 1972-; concerts; conferences; radio apps. Comps. incl: Ritual for the Thirst of the Earth (recorded), 1968; Concerto for viola & orch., 1977; Sonata for clarinet solo (recorded), 1964; Le Temps Inevitable, for piano, 1968-71; 7 F G Lorca lieder, 1961; Jocus Secundus (recorded), 1969. Publs: Co-author, George Enescu, 1972; Georges Enescu, monte contemporain, 1975. Contbr. to: Revista Muzica, Contemporanul & other profl. jrnls. Mbr., Composers' Union. Hons: 2nd prize, Int. Competition GEDOK, Mannheim; Comps. Union Prize; Prix Bernier de L'Academie des Beaux-Arts,

Paris, 1972; 1st prize, GEDOK, 1976. Hobbies: Driving; Mountain trips. Address: Str. Grigore Alexandrescu 32, 71129 Bucharest, Romania.

MARCELLE, Pauline, b. 16 Oct. 1911, Ixelles, Belgium. Concert Pianist; Professor of Piano. Educ: Royal Conserv. of Brussels; studied w. Emile Bosquet. Debut: Concert Guller, 1932. Career: Recitals in Belgium, Holland, Italy, Spain, Germany, USA; Nat. Orch., Belgium; Liege, Ghent, Mons Conserv. Orchs.; Radio Orch. of Luxembourg; Orch. of Barcelona; Chmbr. Music w. Alfonse Onnou, Albert Einstein; Piano Duo Perfs. in Russia, Argentina, Israel, Germany, France; Prof. of Piano, Royal Conserv. of Liege; Prof. Extraordinaire, Queen Elisabeth Chapelle; Vis. Prof., Ball State Univ., Muncie, Ind., USA. Recordings: Musique de Schmit, w. Nat. Orch. of Belgium; Psautier, de Schmit, w. Chant Trio a Anches; Movements Concertants, for pianos & str. orch.; de Jacwueling Fontyn; Belgian works for 2 pianos by Marcel Quintet, Fontyn, W Woronoff, J Absil & Joseph Joneen; Schumann-Brahms, for 2 pianos; Debussy-Bizet. Contbr. to Polyphonie. Mbr. var. profl. orgs. Hons. incl: Order of Leopold, 1960. Hobbies: Chess; Travel; Literature. Mgmt: A Carton. Address: 12 Parklaan, B-1980 Tevueren, Belgium.

MARCELLUS, John Robert, III, b. 17 Sept. 1939, Overton, Tex., USA. Professional Musicians; Teacher of Trombone; Principal Trombone; Lecturer in Music. Educ: BS, Univ. of Md., 1964; MMus, Cath. Univ. of Am.; DMA, ibid., 1973. 2 s. Career: Profl. Musician; Tchr. of Trombone; Prin. Trombone, NSO, 1964-; Lectr. in Music, Cath. Univ. of Am. Soloists w. NSO, Norfolk Chmbr. Orch., Chmbr. Music, Recitals, Wash., DC. Recordings: w. NSO, 1970-75; 19th Century Ballroom Music. Contbr. to: Instrumentalist; Nat. Assn. of Coll. Wind & Percussion Instructors Bulletin; Int. Trombone Assn. Newsletter & Jrnl. Mbrships. incl: Bd. of Dirs., Coord. Resource Lib., Int. Trombone Assn. Hobbies: Boating; Fishing; Camping; Tennis. Address: 2407 Seminary Rd., Silver Spring, MD 20910, USA.

MARCH, John Quarles, b. 22 July 1949, Utrecht, Netherlands. Public Schl., Director of Music; Organist; Choir Director. Educ: BA, Durham Univ.; postgrad. cert. in Educ., Cambridge Univ.; FRCO; FTCL. Career: Asst. Dir. of Music, Brighton Coll., 1972-79; Dir. of Music, Workshop Coll., 1979-; Dir. of Music, St. Paul's Ch., Brighton, 1972-75; Fndr. & dir., St. Paul's Singers, Brighton, 1973-75; Dir., Brighton Monteverdi Choir & Orch., 1975-79. Mbrships: ISM; Music Masters' Assn. Hon: Organ Scholar, St. Chad's Coll., Durham, 1970-71. Address: Worksop Coll., Worksop, Notts. S80 3AP, UK. 29, 30.

MARCHAL, André, b. 6 Feb. 1894, Paris, France. Organist. Educ: Prix d'Orgue & Improvisation, Conserv. Nat. de Musique, Paris, 1913; Prix d'Excellence (for counterpoint), Nat. Conserv. of Music, Paris, 1917. m. Suzanne Greuet, dec., 1 d. Debut: 4 histl. recitals Paris Conserv., 1923. Career: Organist, St. Germain des Près, 1914-45, St. Eustache, 1945-63; Soloist, ORTF. Recordings: entire works of César Frank; Bach; num. concert tours in Europe, N Africa, Middle East, USA, Canada, Australia. Mbrships: Hon. Pres., Soc. of Friends of the Organ; Commn. for the Histl. Monuments; Jury, Conserv. de Paris. Hons: Off., Legion of Hon.; Off. des Arts & Lettres. Hobby: Collector of Clocks & Watches. Address: 22 rue Duroc, 75007 Paris, France.

MARCHWINSKI, Jerzy, b. 6 Jan. 1935, Truskolasy, Poland. Pianist. Educ: piano, Maria Wilkomirska, accomp., Kiejstut Bacewicz, Warsaw Music Acad.; further study w. Carlo Zecchi. 1 d. Career: solo apps. & chmbr. perfs., major cities in Europe & Am.; Accomp. for many instrumentalists & singers, esp. violinist Konstanty Kulka; Mbr., Polish Radio Piano Quartet; apps. at many fests. inclng. Perth, Aust.; gave series of lectures, Orford Arts Ctr., Can.; Prof., Warsaw Music Acad. Has recorded for radio & TV stns. in Europe & N Am. Sev. records for MUZA label. Author: An Accompanist. An attempt to define him in light of contemporary requirements, 1976. Contbr. to: Ruch Muzyczny. Mbrships: VP, Assn. des Artistes Musiciens Polonais; F Chopin Soc. Hons: 1st Award of Polish Radio, 1978. Hobbies: Mountain climbing; Cars. Address: PAGART, Plac Zwyciestwa 9, 00-078 Warsaw, Poland. 28.

MARCHWINSKI, Wladyslaw, b. 28 Mar. 1945, Lodz, Poland. Violinist. Educ: MA, Grad. Lodz Conserv., 1968. m. Alena Kulberg. Debut: w. Lodz Phil. Orch., 1963. Career: Concert Soloist; Mbr.; Danish Radio Symph. Orch. Recordings of broadcasts. Hons: 3rd Prize, All-Polish Music High Schls. Students Competition of Baroque Music, 1964. 1st Prize, All-Polish Students Competition of Classical Music, 1968. Hobbies: History of Fine Arts; Theatre; Cinema; Sightseeing. Address: 2100 Copenhagen O, Halsskovgade 4 Dor 1, Denmark.

MARCIL, Monique, b. 28 April 1934, Montreal, Can. Pianist. Educ: Studied Piano, Conserv. de Montréal; pvte. lessons, Vienna, Austria & NYC, USA. Career: Concerts & Recitals; Broadcasts & TV perfs. in Can.; Tchr., Conserv. de Montréal, 1963-69; Fndng. Mbr., Int. Music Inst. of Can., 1963; Dir.-Gen., Montreal Int. Competition, 1965-. Recip., 1st Prize, Conserv. de Montréal, aged 16. Address: 106 Dulwich Ave., St. Lambert, PQ, Can.

MARCINIAK, Stanislaw, b. 24 May 1939, Warszawa, Poland. Conductor; Composer. Educ: Grad., Warsaw Conserv. of Music; Panstwowa Wyzeza Szkola Muzyczba. div. 1 child. Career: Cond. & Musical Dir., Musical Theatre Komedia. Warwaw & var. Army Bands & ensembles; Chief, Festival Sect., Polish Radio, Warsaw, 1973-; Freelance Cond. of recording sessions. Comps. incl: Works for symphonic orchs., army bands, pop songs, theatre music, children's songs. Polish Radio & TV recordings for lib. Mbr. num. profl. orgs. Hons. incl: Prizes in light music field, festival competitions at Opole, Kolobrzeg, Army Song Competition, Scouts Song Competition & num. other awards. Hobbies: Fishing; Hunting; Bridge. Mgmt: Pagart, Warszawa, Plac Zwyciestwa 9. Address: Warszawa, ul. Broniewskiego 26 m 151, Poland.

MARCINIAK-GOWARZEWSKA, Stanislawa, b. 1 Jan. 1937, Tarnopol, Poland. Dramatic Soprano. Educ: Grad., Acad. of Music, Katowice, 1960. m. Wawrzyniec Gowarzewski, 1 d. Debut: Silesian Opera, Chanosan, 1960. Career: Turandot, in Puccini's Turandot; Cho-Cho-San in Puccini's Madame Butterfly; Aida in Vedi's Aida; Elizabeth in Verdi's Don Carlos; Verdi's La Forza Del Destino; Lady Billars in Briten's Albert Herring; Marschalin in Strauss' Rosen die Cawalieren; Senta in Wagner's Der Fliegende Hollander; Soloist, Bytom Opera Co.; prof., Acad. of Music, Katowice. Recordings: The Bybrok Coal Areal Phil. Orch. & Its Soloists. mbr., Soc. of Polish Musicians. Hons. incl: Grand Prix, Liege, 1961. Hobbies: Gardening. Address: Katowice, ul. Armil Czerwoney 7819, Poland.

MARCO, Guy Anthony, b. 4 Oct. 1927, NYC, USA. Musicologist; Librarian; University Dean. Educ: BMus, Am. Conserv. of Music, Chgo., 1951; MA Musicol., 1952, MA Lib. Sci., 1955, PhD, Musicol., 1956, Univ. of Chgo. m. Karen Csontos, 1 s. Career: Formerly Tchr., Music Hist. & Theory, Chgo. Musical Coll. & Chgo. City Coll.; Dean, & Tchr. of Music Bibliography, Schl. of Lib. Sci., Kent State Univ., Ohio; currently, Chief, Gen. Reference & Bibliography, US Lib. of Congress. Publs. incl: The Earliest Music Printers of Continental Europe, 1962; The Art of Counterpoint (w. Claude Palisca), 1968; Information on Music, I, 1975, II, 1977, III, 1979, VI, 1975; Area Ed., Abstracts, Repertoire Int. de la Litterature Musicale. Contbr. to num. profl. jrnls. Mbr., Am. & int. profl. assns. Hobby: Ttavel. Address: 349 O St., SW Wash., DC, 20024, USA. 2, 30.

MARCOVICI, Silvia, b. 30 Jan. 1952, Bacau, Rumania. Concert Violinist. Educ: High Schl. of Music, Bucharest. m. Dr. Aldea Turai. Debut: The Hague, Netherlands, 1968. Career: London debut w. LSO & Stokowski, 1972; NY debut, 1977; Berlin debut, 1980; apps. w. major orchs incl. NY Phil., LA Phil., all London Orchs., Amsterdam Phil., Stockholm Phil., etc.; TV apps., UK & France. Recordings: Beethoven Sonatas w. U Gheorghiu; Glazunov Concerto. Hons: 1st Prize, George Enescu, Bucharest, 1970. Hobbies: Fashion; Interior decorating; Animals. Mgmt: Harrison/Parrott Ltd., 22 Hillgate St., London W8, UK. Address: c/o Mgmt.

MARCUS, Adabelle Gross, b. 8 July 1928, Chgo., Ill., USA. Composer; Pianist. Educ: DePaul Univ. Music Schl., Chgo., 1939-44; studied Comp., Am. Conserv. of Music, 1954, Roosevelt Univ., Chgo., 1959, & w. var. masters. m. Isadore Marcus, 2 d. Career: Concerts, mid-West, 1947-; Soloist w. major symphs.; Perfs. of own comps. in Chgo. & on TV, 1954-74; fac., Chgo. Conserv. Coll. Comps. incl: Snow (chmbr. opera) Shakespearean Dup; Song for Flute, 1970; Symphony of the Spheres; Zen; Outward Bound; num. piano pieces & songs. Mbrships incl: ASCAP; Am. Music Ctr. Inc.; Int. Soc. for Contemporary Music; Kodaly Acad. & Inst. (Hon. VP). Hons. incl: Prize for Song Cycle (R Fost text), Int. Soc. Contemporary Musicians, 1963. Mgmt: Rhapsodia Concert Mgmt. Address: 9374 Landings Lane Apt. 502, Des Plaines, IL 60016, USA. 5, 27.

MARCZYK, Stefan, b. 1 Jan. 1924, Rzeszów, Poland. Concuctor. Educ: MA, Cracow High Schl. of Music; Higher Nat. Dip. in Music (condng. & playing violin). m. Iskra Marczyk, 1 s. Debuit: w. Warsaw Phil., 1951. Career: Concerts in Berlin, Leningrad, San Francisco, Budapest, Rome, Mexico City, Salzburg, Ljubljana, Dubrovnik and many other fests.; TV & radio apps. in Poland, Yugoslavia, Mexico & Cuba. Mbr. of Coun., Polish Musical Artists Soc. Recip. Polish nat. awards for musical activity. Hobbies: Photography; Dogs. Mgmt: State Phil., Szczecin. Address: Mickiewicza 27/30, 01562 Warsaw, Poland.

MARCZYNSKI, Zdzislaw, b. 2 Sept. 1916, Wybranowo, Poland. Double Bass Player; Professor of Double Bass. Educ: Conserv. of Music, Poznan, 1931-39; Acad. of Music, Poznan, 1946-50, Dip. (w. distinction); MA. m. Janina Ciesielska, 1 s. Debut: Cracow Symph. Orch., 1941. Career: 1st solo double bass of the opera & symph. orch., Poznan, 1945-55; 1st solo double bass, Wardsaw Nat. Orch. (1955-57) & Warsaw Nat. Opera (1957-69); Prof. of double bass, Conserv., Poznan (1951-56), & Acad. of Music, Poznan (1956-69); Prof. of double bass, Conserv. de Musique, Quebec & Trois-Rivieres, Can.; Recordings for radio & TV. Publ: Receuil des orchestres pour la contrebasse, 1965. mbr. Assn. des Artistes Musiciens Polonais (SPAM). Recip., 1st prize, with distinction, Conserv. of Music, Pozanan. Hobbies: Do it Yourself; Fishing; Gardening. Address: 7120 Hurteau, Montreal, Que. H4E 2Z1, Can.

MAREK, Czeslaw Józef, b. 16 Sept. 1891, Przemyśl, Poland. Teacher of Piano & Composition. Educ: Univ. of Lwów; Conserv. of Lwów; Acad. of Music, Vienna, Austria. m. Claire Marek-Hofer. Career: Prof., Lwów Conserv., 1914; Dir., Poznán Nat. Conserv., 1929-30; Tchr. of Piano & Comp. Zürich, Switzerland. Comps. (publs.) incl: Suite for orch.; Serenade, for violin & orch.; Prelude, Air & Ballad, for piano, 1975. Publs: What is 'Musical?', 1961; Teaching Pianists, 1972. Contbr. to Swiss Music Review. Mbrships: Swiss Musicians Assn.; Swiss Music Tchrs. Assn. Hons. incl: Hans Georg Naegeli Gold Medal, Zürich, 1971; Prize, Pro-Arte Fndn., Fed. Palace, Berne, 1973. Hobby: Mtn. excursions. Address: Möhrlistrasse 71, 8006 Zürich, Switzerland.

MAREK, Jaroslav, b. 19 Jan. 1939, Prague, Czechoslovakia. Singer. Educ: Degree, Fac. of Geol., Karl's Univ., Prague; Musical Acad., Prague. m. Alena Markova, 2 s. Debut: As tenor solo, Silesian Theatre, OpavaSou-Chong, 1970. Career: Moravian Double-Songs by Dvorak, radio, 1964; Songs of Macha, Nezval & Pushkin by Jaroslav Jezek, TV, 1965; Silesian Theatre, Opava, 1970-73; Salda's Theatre, Liverec, 1973-; 6 concerts of Czech. songs, German Fed. Repub., 1975; Mbr., Canzona Sempre Viva, w. J Picek. Author of Umelecky zpev (The Art of Singing), 1965; text of children's cantata, A Little Safari by J Picek. Mbr., Esperanto Club, Liberec. Hobbies: Stamp collecting; Cycle touring. Astronomy; Philosophy; Psychology; Study of for. langs. Address: Trojanova 1, 120 00 Prague 2, Czechoslovakia.

MARGARITIS, Harry, b. 1 May 1947, Athens, Greece. Musicologist; Pianist; Teacher. Educ: Proficiency, Cambridge, 1968; MLitt. (Classics), Univ. of Athens, 1972; Conserv., Athens; Conserv. Nat. Superieur de Musique de Paris; Dr. (Ethnomusicol.), Sorbonne, Univ. of Paris IV, 1975; Agregation de Musique et de Chant Choral, 1979; studied piano w. Jacques Fevrier. m. Régine Lachaussée. Career: piano recitals in Greece; perfs. in Italy & France; preparing thesis (w. Jacques Chailley) on Popular Music of the Peloponnese. Contbr. to: Ency. Laurosse; Mélanges offerts à S Baud-Bovy. mbr., Société Francaise de Musicologie. Hons: Piano prize, Athens Conserv., 1968; 1st prize in hist. of music, Conserv. Nat. de Paris, 1972. Hobbies: Reading (French, Engl., German & Greek Lit.); Swimming. Address: 8 rue Marsouland, 75012 Paris, France.

MARGGRAF, Wolfgang, b. 2 Dec. 1935, Leipzig, Germany. Musicologist. Educ: Studied at Univs. of Leipzig & Jena, 1952-57; PhD, Leipzig, 1964. m. Annemarie Lorz. Publs: Franz Schubert, 1967, 2nd ed., 1978; Giacomo Puccini, 1977; Giuseppe Verdi. Contbr. to profl. jrnls. Mbrships: Bach Soc.; Union of Comps. & Musicologists of the German Dem. Repub. Address: Goethestr. 24a, DDR-59 Eisenach, German Dem. Repub.

MARGONI, Alain, b. 13 Oct. 1934, Neuilly-Plaisance, France. Composer; Professor of Analysis. Educ: Conserv. Nat. Supèrieur de Musique, Paris. m. Kondo Fusako. Career: Dir. of Music, La Comédie Française, 1966-71; Prof. of Analysis, Conserv. Nat. Superieur de Paris, 1973. Comps: Over 100 scores of stage music for Nat. Theatre & Radio France; Le Roi Lépreux (opera); Break-Broke-Broken, Ballet for brass instruments; Pedagogic music. Hons. incl: 1st Grand Prize of Rome, 1959. Address: 20 rue du Commandant Mouchotte, 75014 Paris, France.

MARIĆ, Ljubica, b. 18 March 1909, Kragujevac, Yugoslavia. Composer; Professor. Educ: Dip. in comp., Schl. of Music, Belgrade; Cert., Postgrad. Dept. of Quarter-tone Music, Alois Haba; Dip. of Master Schl. of Comp. (Josef Suk), Cert. in conducting, Prague Conserv.; Cert., Nicolay Malko's conducting course; Cert., Die Musikalische Arbeitstagung, Strasbourg. Career: comps. recorded for TV & radio broadcasts; Prof., Acad. of Music, Belgrade. Comps. incl: Sonata for violin & piano; Songs of Space (cantata for choir & orch.); Passacaglia for symph. orch.); Wind

Quintet; Music of Ochtechos cycle. Author, The Tractate on Monothematic & Monolithic Form of the Fugue, 1964. Mbr. profl. orgs. Recip. many hons. & awards. Hobby: Painting. Address: Dzordza Vasingtona 36, Belgrade, Yugoslavia.

MARIETAN, Pierre, b. 23 Sept. 1935, Monthey, Switzerland. French Horn Player; Music School Director. Educ: Geneva Conserv., 1955-60. 1 s. Career: Simultaneous Broadcast, radio & TV, French Switzerland, 1969; Deutschlandfunk; 12 Progs., Workshop on Radiophonic Creation, ORTF. Comps. (publs.) incl: Interfaces; Images of Time, 1964-74; Medium & Environment; Initiatives; Music-Antimusic. Recordings: initiative No. 1; Systems. Publs. incl: Medium & Environment: Music in Life, 1968. Contbr. to: Swiss Musical Review; Fine Arts Review, Paris; Opus Int. Mbr. Music Study & Perf. Grp. Hons: Gaudeamus, Netherlands. Comp. Prize, Boswil, Switzerland, 1972. Address: 119 Rue Damremont.

MARIGO, Francisco, b. 2 Jan. 1916, Padua, Italy. Pianist; Conductor; Composer; Professor. Educ: Cert. for piano, studied organ & orchl. conducting, Acad. Chigiana; studies w. Alfredo Casella & Arturo Benedetti Michelangeli. m. Lidia Perez, 4 children. Debut: Padua. Career: concerts in major cities of Italy, France, Spain, Uruguay, Argentina, etc.; Radio & TV broadcasts. Comps: orchl. works; chmbr. music for many instrumental combinations inclng. trumpet, harp & clarinet, duos, oboe & harp, clarinet & harp, recorder & guitar, violin & guitar, etc. Mbr., Soc. of Comps. Hons. incl: premio Guitarristico Argentino, 1960. Hobbies: Painting; Swimming. Address: Lamadrid 370 Lomas de Zamora-Pcia. Bs. As., Argentina.

MARINELLI, Carlo, b. 13 Dec. 1926, Rome, Italy. Musicologist. Educ: Laureate in letters, Univ. of Rome. Apps. incl: Prof. Hist. of Music, Fac. of Arts, Univ. of Aquila & Conserv. of Aquila. Publs: La musica strumentale da camera di Goffredo Petrassi (Instrumental Chmbr. Music of Petrassi); Lettura di Messiaen; Cronache di musica contemporanea; Le Cantate Profane di J S Bach. Contbr. to var. music dictionaries & jrnls. inclng. Italian Review of Musicol.; broadcaster on Italian Radio-TV 3rd prog. Mbrships: Int. Am., & Italian Musicol. Socs. Address: Via dei Monti Parioli 61, 00197 Rome, Italy.

MARK, Peter, b. 31 Oct. 1940, NYC, USA. Opera Conductor; Concert Violist. Educ: BA, Columbia Univ., 1961; MS, Juilliard Schl. of Music, 1963. m. Thea Musgrave. Career: Boy Soprano, NYC Opera, 1953-54, Met. Opera, 1955-57; Prin.Violist, Juilliard Orch., 1960-63, Lyric Opera of Chgo., 1964-66; Asst., Prin. Viola, Los Angeles Phil. Orch., 1968-69; Solo Violist, USA, S Am. & European recital tours, Concerto apps. in UK & USA, in film Lady Caroline Lamb; has periered works by noted contemp. comps.; Assoc. Prof., Univ. of Calif., Santa Barbara; Artistic Dir. & Cond., Va. Opera Assn., 1975-79. Has recorded for EMI, London, Avant, Custom Fidelity & Angel labels. Mbrships. incl: Musicians Union, London, NY & Los Angeles. Recip. var. hons. Mgmt: Ingpen & Williams, Ltd. Address: c/o Va. Opera Assn., 300 Boush St., Room 501 Norfolk, VA 23510, USA.

MARKEVITCH, Igor, b. 27 July 1912, Kiev, Russia. Composer; Conductor. Educ: Coll. de Vevey, Switz.; Ecole Normale de Musique, Paris. m. (1) Kyra Nijinsky, 1936, 1 s., (2) Topazia Caetani, 1947, 4 children. Career: Ldr. of Orch. of Florence & Maggio Fiorentino, Italy, 1944-46; Perm. Cond., Stockholm Phil. Orch., 1952-55, Montreal Symph. Orch., Canada, 1955-60, Havana Phil. Orch., 1957-58, Lamoureux Orch., Paris, 1956-61; Fndr. & Perm. Cond., Radio & TV Orch. of Spain, 1965-; Perm. Cond., Orch. of Santa Cecilia Acad., Rome, 1973-, Monte Carlo Opera, Monaco, 1967-72; Created & taught at Cond. courses, Mozarteum, Salzburg, Austria, Mexico, Moscow Conserv., Madrid, Monte Carlo & Weimar. Comps. incl: Rebus, 1931; Icare, 1932; Psalm, 1933; Paradise Lost, 1935; Le Nouvel Age, 1938; Lorenzo il Magnifico (cantata), 1940; Variations & Fugue, for piano, 1942. Recordings: Over 240 works w. num. symph. orchs. Publs: Made in Italy, 1946; Point d'Orgue, 1961; Introduction to Music; The Encyclopaedic Edition of Beethoven Symphonies. Hons: Off., Legion d'Honneur; Cmdr. des Arts & Letters; Cmdr. of the Order of Merit (Italy); num. record awards. Address: 2 Place du Marché, Vevey, Switz.

MARKHAM, Richard, b. 23 June 1952, Grimsby, UK. Pianist. Educ: pvtely. w. Max Pirani; RAM; LRAM; ARCM; RAM Recital Dip. Debut: Queen Elizabeth Hall, 1974. Career: recitals & concerto perfs. throughout UK & abroad; sev. London recitals at Wigmore Hall & Purcell Room; apps. at fests. in Aldeburgh, Camden, Harrogate, City of London & York; regular broadcasts of recitals & concertos for BBC & Swiss radio. Recordings: Kabalevsky, Stravinsky & Rachmaninov w. Raphael Wallfisch (cello). Mbrships: ISM; RAM Club. Hons: Chappell Medal; 3rd prize, Geneva Int. competition, 1972; Countess of Munster Musical Trust

Scholarships, 1973-74; Frederick Shinn Fellowship, 1975; Gulbenkian Foundation Fellowship, 1976. Hobbies: Cycling; Playing Cards. Address: 27a Ashburton Rd., Croydon CRO 6AP, UK.

MARKIEWICZ, Leon, b. 23 Sept. 1928, Vilnius, USSR. Music Critic; Musicologist. Educ: MA, Pedagogy of Music, Theory of Music, Higher Schl. of Music, Katowice; Doctor of Musicol., Inst. of Musicol., Warsaw Univ. m. Danuto Markiewicz, 2 d. Career: Prorector, Higher Schl. of Music, Katowice. Publs: Over 300 articles, reviews, in Polish prof. & popular press, radio & TV. Mbrships: VP, Assn. des Artistes Musiciens Polonaise & Pres., Critis Sect.; Mbr., Musicol. Sect., Union of Polish Composers; Assn. of Friends of Int. Youth Fest. Meeting, Bayreuth. Hons: Mdsic Critic's Prize, Warsaw, 1964; Musical Prize, Assn. des Artistes Msiciens Polonaise, 1971. Hobbies: Motoring; Touring. Address: 27 styczina 23/13, 40-026 Katowice, Poland.

MÄRKI, Josef, b. 16 Jan. 1928, Wilshofen, Germany. Professor, violin & chmbr. music. Educ: Staatl. Hochschule für Musik, Munich. m. Brigitte Märk-Jaenisch, 3 children. Debut: Radio Stuttgart, 1947. Career: Violinist, Radio Symph. Orchs., Munich, Stuttgart, SWF-BAden Baden; Concertmaster, Düsseldorf Symph.; Prof., violin & chmbr. music, Rheinische Musikschule, Cologne; Mbr., Andrea Wendling Quartet & Stross Quartet; Primarius, Märkl Quartet. Mbr., European String Tchrs. Assn. Hons: 1st Wettbewerb für junge Künstler (Radio Stuttgart), 1947. Hobby: Tchng. chmbr. music to amateurs. Address: 4047 Dormangen 5, Lukasstrasse 2, German Fed. Repub.

MARKOPOULOS, Yannis, b. 18 Mar. 1939, Ierapetra, Crete, Greece. Composer. Educ: Dip., Athens Conserv.; pvte. study of comp. w. Yannis Papaioannou & Yannis Christou; studied Eastern Music, London, UK, 1967-70. Debut: Ierapetra, 1954. Career: Music for stage prods., UK, 1963-, inclng. Aristophanes Lysistrata, Aldwych, 1968, & The Tempest, Chichester, 1968; num. apps. on TV, Greece, BBC, German FEd. Repub. & USA. Comps. incl: Pycchichii, 1, 2, 3, 1966; Oracles, 1968; (LP) Theseus, Estrtangement, Chronicle, etc.; Music for 20 films inclng. Young Aphrodites, 1962, & Death of Alexander, 1966. Contbr. to newspapers & jrnls. Hons: Prizes, Cinema Fest. of Salonica, 1963, 64; Critics' Prize, ibid., 1966; Gold Medal, Charles Cross Acad., for LP, Rizitika, 1976. Hobbies incl: Cinema; Writing Poems. Address: Kerkyras 30, Kypseli, Athens, Greece.

MARKS, Alan, b. 14 May 1949, Chgo., Ill., USA. Pianist. Educ: studied w. Shirley Parnas Adams, 1963-67, Irwin Freundlich, 1967-71, Leon Fleisher, 1972-73; BMus, Juilliard Schl., 1971. Debut: Carnegie Recital Hall, NY, 1971. Carer incls: apps. w. noted US Orchs.; Affiliate Artist, Los Angeles Music Ctr. 3 yrs.; has broadcast on many US radio & TV stations, also BBC radio; played w. violinst Ani Kavafian for 6 yrs., var. chmbr. music apps. w. Contemporary Chmbr. Fnsemble, Harvard Chmbr. Players, Orchl. apps. w. num. Am. Symphs. inclng. Buffalo, St. Louis & Am. Symphs.; Solo recitals in US, Japan, London & Amsterdam. Recordings: Works of Boulez, Chávez, Sessions. Recip. many awards & grants inclng: winner, Univ. of Md. Piano Competition, 1973; winner, Nat. Chopin Contest, 1975. Mgmt: Sheldon Soffer Mgmt, Inc. Address: 465 W End Ave., Apt. 5C, NY, NY 10024, USA.

MARKS, Paul Frederick, b. 24 Mar. 1933, Chgo., Ill., USA. Musicologist; Assistant Professor. Educ: BA, UCLA, 1956; MMus, Univ. of Tulsa, Okla., 1959; PhD, in Musicol., Univ. of Wash., Seattle, projected, 1975; studied viola & violin pvtly. w. Sanford Schonbach, Philip Goldberg, Tosca B Kramer; chamber music w. Feri Roth (Roth Str. Quartet); w. Peter Meremblum Youth Orch. m. Isabel Jane Marks, 1 s., 1 d. Career: Asst. Prof. of Musicol., McGill Univ., Montreal, Canada; Frrelance Violist. Publs: Bibliography of Literature Concerning Yemenite-Jewish Music, 1973. Contbr. to: Int. Review of the Aesthetics & Sociol. of Music;o The Music Review; Eighteenth Century Culture; Jrnl. of the McMaster Assn. for Eighteenth Century Studies. Mbrships: Am. Musicol. Soc.; Int. Musicol. Soc.; Soc. for Ethnomusicol.; Am. Soc. for Aesthetics; Int. Soc. for Aesthetics; Am. Soc. for Eighteenth Century Studies. etc. Hobbies: Wine tasting; Gourmet food. Address: 5579 Queen Mary Rd., Hampstead, Quebec, Can. H3X 1W6.

MARKS, Virginia Pancoast, b. 9 Feb. 1940, Phila., Pa., USA. Music Educator. Educ: Settlement Music Schl., Phila.; BS, Temple Univ., 1961; MA (music) Am. Univ., Wash., DC. m. Edward J Marks, 1 s., 1 d. Debut: Town Hall, NYC, 1967. Career incls: Solo, Chmbr. Music Recitals, throughout USA; Soloist w. num. orchs., quintets, etc. in US. Guest Artist, Spoleto, Italy, Fst.; Opera Coach, ibid & Temple Univ. Music Fest., Goldovsky Opera Workshops; TV & radio apps., NY, Wash. etc. Tchr., Cornell Univ., 1966-67, Ithaca Coll., 1966-67, Temple

Univ., 1968-69. Temple Univ. Music Fest., 1968-70; Asst. Prof. of Perf. Studies, Piano Dir., Preparatory Div., Creative Arts Prog., Bowling Green State Univ., 1970-77; Assoc. Prof. of Performance Studies, 1978-. Recordings: Portuguese Music. Contbr. to Piano Quarterly. Mbrships: Mu Phi Epsilon; Ohio MTA; Friday Morning Music Club, Wash., DC Recip. num. Hons. Hobby: Gardening. Address: 1313 Bourgogne Ave., Bowling Green, OH 43402.

MARKSON, Richard Charles, b. 16 May 1949, Glasgow, UK. Cellist. Educ: Paris Conserv. w. Paul Tortelier & Pierre Fournier. m. Mayumi Fujikawa. Debut: Wigmore Hall, London, 1970. Career: major tours of E & W Europe, Latin Am. & Far East. Hobbies: Eating; Cooking; Sleeping; Reading. Mgmt: Ibbs & Tillett. Address: 18 Oakwood Ct., London W14, UK.

MARKWARD, Edward, b. 8 Sept. 1944, Dubuque, Iowa, USA. Professional Singer (Baritone); Conductor; Teacher. Educ: BME, Drake Univ., 1966; MMus, ibid., 1968; DMA, Univ. Mich., 1974. Debut: Profl. singing, Young Artist Competition winner, Des Moines Symph., 1967. m. Cheri Dee Markward, 1 s., 1 d. Career: Recitals, oratorio & opera apps., eastern US; Apps., Marlboro, RI Civ. Chorale, Des Moines Symph.; Ldng. Baritone, Univ. Mich. Opera Theatre; Guest artist, num. coll. campuses; Cond., Ann Arbor Cantata Singers & Chmbr. Orch., Ann Arbor Civ. Theatre; Guest Cond., Providence Singers, RI, & All-State Chorus Choral Workshops, New England; Asst. Prof. Music, RI Coll. Mbr. profl. orgs. Hons. incl: Pi Kappa Lambda Outstanding Musician, 1968. Hobbies incl: Outdoor Sports. Address: 24 W View, N Providence, RI 02911, USA.

MARLOW, Richard Kenneth, b. 26 July 1939, Banstead, Surrey, UK. University Lecturer. Educ: Chorister, Southwark Cath.; FRCO, 1958; Selwyn Coll., Cambridge (organ Scholar) BA, 1961; MusB, 1962; MA, 1965; PhD, 1966. m. Annette Bateman, 2 s. Career: Rsch. Fellow, Selwyn Coll., Cambride, 1963-65; Lectr. in Music, Southampton Univ., 1965-68; Lectr. in Music, Cambridge Univ. & Fellow, Organist, Dir. of Music & Lectr., Trinity Coll., 1968-. Compositions: Male-Voice Preces & Responses, Oxford, 1972; Anthem: O Lord God, SATB (Novello), 1972. Recordings: Organ Music from Cambridge No. 3 (Grosvenor Records, GRS 1007). Publs: Giles & Richard Farnaby; Keyboard Music (musica Britannica XXIV) London, 1965. Contbr. to: Music & Letters; Musical Times; Proceedings of the Royal Musical Assn. Mbrships: Dir., Cambridge Univ. Chamber Choir; Hon. Gen. Ed., Ch. Music Soc. Hons: Harding Prize, RCO, 1958; John Stewart of Rannoch Scholar, Sacred Music, Cambridge, 1960. Hobbies: Sport; Walking; Architecture. Address: Trinity Coll., Cambridge, UK. 3.

MARLOWE, Sylvia, b. 26 Sept. 1908, NY, USA. Harpsichordist. Educ: Ecol. Normale de Musique, Paris; w. Nadia Boulanger. m. Leonid Berman (dec.). Debut: NY, Complete Well Tempered Clavier, CBS Network. Career: Concerts; Recordings: Teaching; Fac. Mbr., Mannes Coll. Music. Recordings: Num. of Bach, Handel, Haydn, etc. & many contemporary composers. Publ: Selected Harpsichord Music of Francois Coupein. Music Dir., Harpsichord Music Soc. Inc., NY. Hon: Named Chevalier des Arts et des Lettres by French Govt.; Handel medallion, NYC. Hobbies: Reading; Writing; Tennis; Swimming. Address: 108 E 60 St., NY, NY 10022, USA.

MAROS, Miklós, b. 14 Nov. 1943, Pecs, Hungary. Composer; Teacher; Chamber Orchestra Leader. Educ: Comp. & Theory, Acad. of Music, Budapest; Comp., State Coll. of Music, Stockholm. m. Ilona Maros. Career: Tchr. of Electronic Music, State Coll. of Music, Stockholm; Ldr., Maros Ensemble; Comps. frequently perfd. in Europe & USA. Comps. incl: Turba (choir); Denique (soprano & orch.); Symph. Nos. 1-2; Oolit (chmbr. orch.); Divertimento (chmbr. orch.); Chmbr. music, electronic music, etc. Recordings: Descort (soprano, flute, double bass); Manipulation No. 1 (bassoon & live electronic); Divertimento (chmbr. orch.); Oolit. Mbrships: Sec., Soc. of Swedish Comps.; Soc. for Contemporary Music (ISCM Swedish Sect.); Soc. for Experimental Music & Arts. Address: Krukmakargatan 18, S-116 51, Stockholm, Sweden. 4, 29.

MARÓTHY, János, b. 23 Dec. 1925, Budapest, Hungary. Musicologist. Educ: comp., Budapest Acad. of Music, 1951; musicol. w. B Szabolcsi, ibid., 1954; PhD, Aesthetics w. G Lukács, Budapest Univ., 1948; Cand. in Musicol. Studies, 1959; Acad. Dr. of Musicol., 1966. m. Mária Bereznyei, 3 c. Career: Ed. of Music Jrnls. Eneklô Nép, 1949-50 & UJ Zenei Szemle, 1950-51; Asst. Lectr., then Rsch. Wkr., The Budapest Acad. of Music, 1954-61; Rsch. Wkr., Inst. for Musicol., Hungarian Acad. of Sci., 1961-. Publs: Az európia népal születése (The Birth of European Folksong), 1960; Zene és polgár, zene és proletár, 1966 (& in Engl. Music & the Bourgeois - Music & the Proletarian, 1974); Szabó Ferenc indulása (Ferenc Szabó's Early Development), 1970; Music,

Revolution, Socialism, 1975; Assoc. Ed., From Peasant Song to Worker Song, 1968. Contbr. to profl. jrnls. Mbrships: Assn. of Hungarian Musicians; Musicol. Comm., Hungarian Acad. of Scis.; Edit. Bd. Mbr., Magyar Zene, Hungarian Music & Studia Musicologica. Hons: Erkel Ferenc Prize, 1961; Arts Prize of the Hungarian Trade Unions Coun., 1969. Address: H 1116 Latinka S. u. 80, 11.28, Budapest XI, Hungary. 14, 30.

MAROUFI, Javad, b. 5 May 1912, Tehran, Itan. Pianist. Educ: Dip. of Iranian Music, Conserv. of Iranian Music. m. Shams Zaman, 4 c. Debut: 1932. Career: radio perfs.; music for film score. Recordings: Mahur; Isfahan Rhapsody; Chargah; Prelude. Contbr. to: Music Mag.; Viewer (Tamasha). Mbr., Music Coun. of Radio. Recip. Homayoun Medal from HIM the Shah. Hobbies: Reading; Writing. Address: No. 4, Kuche Baharestan 3, Saltanatabad, Tehran.

MARRINER, Neville, b. 14 Apr. 1924, Lincoln, UK. Conductor. Educ: ARCM. m. Elizabeth Marriner, 1 s., 1 d. Career incls: Music Dir., Minn. Orch.; Artistic Dir., Meadowbrook Fest.; Dir., Acad. of St. Martin-in-the-Fields. Recordings: 120 recordings. Mbr., Garrick Club. Hons: Hon. LRAM; Mozart Gemeinde Prize (3 times); Deutsche Schalplaten (twice); Edison Award (5 times); Grand Prix du Disque. Address: c/o Harold Holt, 134 Wigmore St., London, UK.

MARROCCO, William Thomas, b. 5 Dec. 1909, W NY, NJ, USA. Musicologist; Violinist; Professor of Music. Educ: Royal Conserv. of Music, Naples, 1930; BMus, Eastman Schl. of Music, Univ. of Rochester, 1934; MA, Univ. of Rochester, 1940; PhD, Uriv. of Calif., 1952. m. Audrey Jeannette Grein, 1 s., 1 d. Career: 1st Violin, Rochester Phil. Orch., 12 yrs.; Mbr., Roth String Quartet, 14 yrs.; Prof. of Music, UCLA. Recordings (w. Roth String Quartet) incl: String Quartets, Op. 74 & 95, Beethoven, 1967. Publs. incl: Polyphonic Music of the Fourteenth Century, Italian Secular Music, Vol. VI, 1967, Vol. VII, 1970, Vol. VIII, 1972, Vol. IX, 1975, Vol. X, 1977, Vol. XI, 1978; Music in America - An Anthology (w. Harold Gleason), 1964; The Oxford Anthology of Medieval Music (w. Nicholas Sandon), 1977. Contbr. to var. profl. jrnls. Recip. var. hons. Address: 1950 Mandeville Cyn Rd., Los Angeles, CA 90049, USA.

MARSDEN, Joan, b. 6 May 1933, London, UK. Teacher of Piano, History & Theory of Music; Composer. Educ: ATCL, Piano Teaching Dip. widowed, 2 c. Career: Fndr., Staines Festival of Music, now in its 5th yr. to be publd., General Musicianship for Children. Hobbies: Writing novels; Composing; Recorder Consort Playing. Address: 21 Green Lane, Addlestone, Weybridge, Surrey, UK.

MARSEE, Susanne, b. 26 Nov. 1941, San Diego, Calif., USA. Opera Singer (Lyric Mezzosoprano). Educ: BA, Hist., Univ. of Calif.; Elementary Tchng. Dip., Calif.; Opera Workshop, UCLA; Juilliard Schl. of Music; 1 yr., Am. Opera Center. m. Brett B Hamilton. Debut: Roberto Devereux (Donizetti), NYC Opera, 1970. Career: TV apps. incl: Roberto Devereux, from Wolftrap, Rachel, La Cubana (Henze), Turk in Italy (Rossini); perfs. w. opera cos. incl. San Fran. Opera, NYC Opera, Boston Opera, Houston Grand Opera, San Diego Opera, Memphis Opera, Phila. Lyric Opera, New England Opera, etc.; Int. perfs. incl: Spoleto Fest., Aix en Provence Fest., Canary Islands Fest., Bellas Artes (Mexico City), Teatro Municipal Caracas (Venezuela), Cervantes Fest. (Mexico). Recordings: Tales of Hoffmann (w. Beverly Sills). Hons: Recip., grants; 1st Place, Liederkranz Contest, NY, 1970; 2nd Place, Metropolitan Opera Regional Finals, 1968; 2nd Place, San Fran. Opera Regional Finals, 1968. Hobbies: Tennis; Bridge. Mgmt: Shaw Concerts, 1995 Broadway, NY, NY 10024, USA. Address: c/o Mgmt. 2.

MARSH, Gwendolen, b. 17 Mar. 1908, Chetopa, Kan., USA. Concert Pianist & Teacher. Educ: Kan. City Conserv., 1921-27; Advanced study, Piano, Voice & Opera Scores, NYC, 1927-32; pvte. study w. Allen Hinckley (opera scores) & Carl Friedberg (piano). Career: Piano Recitals; Master Classes; Adjudicator, NGPT, throughout USA. Comps: Songs, trios for Women's voices & elementary piano pieces. Contbr. to: Musical Leader (Kan. City critic, 1965-67). Mbrships: Am. Coll. of Musicians; Pederated Music Tchrs. of Kan. City; Clef Music Club; Kan. City; Christian Ch. Hons: Outstanding Comp. Award, No. Fedn. of Music Clubs, 1974. Hobbies: Sewing; Designing; Taking Snapshots of Cats. Mgmt: Community Conserts. Address: 1120 E. 44 St., Kansas City, MO 64110, USA. 2, 5, 8, 27.

MARSH, Milton Rudolph William, b. 29 Sept. 1945, Hamilton, Bermuda. Composer; Arranger; Saxophonist; Flautist. Educ: Gen. Certs. in Educ., Univ. of London; BMus, Berklee Coll. of Music, Boston; MMus, New England Conserv. of Music, Boston. m. Doreen Marsh, 1 d. Career: Num. concert apps. incl. A Fest. of

New England Comps., Jordan Hall, Boston, 1971; A Weekend of Contemporary Jazz, SUNY/AB Buffalo, NY, 1975. Comps. incl: Ode to Nzinga; Poems for Saxophone Quartet; Metamorphosis; Behaviour Control; Music for woodwind quintet. Recordings: Monism. Contbr. to profl. publs. Mbrships: Coll. Music Soc.; Am. Assn. of Univ. Profs. Hons: Noteworthy Americans & Community Leaders Award, 1978. Address: PO Box 635, Astor Station, Boston, MA 02123, USA. 4.

MARSHALL, Adelaide, b. 17 May 1906, Reading, Pa., USA. Singer; Organist; Pianist. Educ: New England Conserv.; studied w. William King, Marian Anderson, Ellen J McDowell. m. Orlof Olson. Debut: New England Conserv. Career: Organist. Mt. Hebron Bapt. Ch., Phila., Pa.; Tchr., Brooklyn Acad., NY.; Piano, Voice Tchr., Harlem Art Schl., NY; Soloist, Accomp., Carnegie Hall; num. perfs. as Vocalist, Organist, Pianist, var. Supper Clubs, Operas, Concerts, Ch.'s Phila., Pa. & NYC; Specialist in Opera, Swing, Gospel. Mbrships: Hon. mbr., Coun., Am. Fedn. of Musicians. Local 802, NYC; Serin Musicians Assn. Local 802 AFLCIOI., 1972-; YWCA; Legion of Mary, Rosary Soc., St. Catherine of Seanna Cath. Ch. Address: 116-34 Newburg St., St. Albans, LI., NY 11412, USA.

MARSHALL, Elizabeth, b. 31 Mar. 1937, Phila., Pa., USA. Concert Pianist. Educ: Degree in Perf., Vienna Acad. of Music, 1958; BMus, MMus, Manhattan Schl. of Music, NY. Debut: Town Hall, NY, 1963. Career: about 300 solo recitals, NY, Boston, Wash., Newark; 5 tours of Am. colls. & univs.; 3 tours in Europe, inclng. Athens, Greece, & Teheran; Guest Artist, Manhattan Percussion Ensemble, for US Govt. sponsored tour of Europe & Middle E. Recordings: complete piano works of Nicolas Flagello (3 albnums); Vittorio Rieti, Sonata for Piano, Leonardo Balada, Musica in Quatro Tiempos. Ed. piano scores for Gen. Muisic Publng. Co., NY. Hons. incl: Martha Baird Rockefeller Award, 1962. Hobbies: Reading; Travel. Mgmt: Elwood Emerick Mgmt., Barbara Hilborn. Address: 311 Prospect St., S Orange, NJ 07079, USA.

MARSHALL, Ingram Douglass, b. 10 May 1942, Mt. Vernon, NY, USA. Composer; Pedagogue. Educ: BA, Lake Forest Coll., 1964; grad. facs., musicol., Columbia Univ., 1964-66; MFA, Calif. Inst. of Arts, 1971. Career: Comp. Fac. (electronic music), Calif. Inst. of Arts, 1971-74; Comp. Fac., San Fran. Conserv. of Music, 1976; num. solo concerts of live electronics, USA, Germany, Netherlands, Denmark, Sweden, Norway, Iceland. Comps. incl: Non Confundar (string sextet, al. flute, clarinet, electronics); Matter (tape comp.); Waterwalk (sound sculpture for 24 speakers & outdoor environment); Text-soundelectronic: The East is Red; Weather Report; The Emperor's Birthday. live electronic: Gambuh; Ikon (Syiasma); Landscape Parts. Contbr. to: Soundings; Numus West; Nutida Musik. Recip. Fulbright Scholarship, Sweden, 1975; Grant from NEA, 1978. Hobbies: Ski touring; Fly fishing; Enol. Address: 504 Cole St., San Francisco, CA 94117, USA.

MARSHALL, J Richard, h 28 July 1929, Schenectady, NY, USA. Opera Conductor; Producer; General Manager. Educ: BA, Univ. of Rochester; MMus., D Mus., Ind. Univ. m. Jean Deresienski. Career: Hd., Opera & Choral Depts., Univ. of Buffalo; Hd., Opera, Boston Conserv.; Dir., Buffalo Opera Singers; Pres. & Gen. Mgr., New England Regl. Opera, 1967-. Publs: Musical-Dramatic Analysis of 'The Turn of the Screw' of Benjamin Britten, 1963. Mbrships: Nat. Opera Assn.; Ctrl. Opera Serv.; AGO; Mass. Tchrs. Assn. Hons: Award for Contbns. to Opera in New England, Assn. for Perf. Arts, Boston, 1973, etc. Hobbies: Photography; Travel. Address: 25 Grayfield Ave., W Roxbury, MA 02132, USA.

MARSHALL, James, b. 12 Oct. 1941, Seattle, Wash., USA. Composer; Bassoonist; Teacher. Educ: BA in Music, Whitman Coll.; MA in Comp., Univ. of Wash.; DMA in Comp., Coll.-Conserv. of Music, Cinn. m. Karen R Pape. Career: Instr. in Theory & Bassoon, Drake Univ., 1966-68; Montclair State Coll., 1968-712; Asst. Prof. of Theory & Comp., Cleveland State Univ., 1974-; several bassoon recitals; Asst. Dir., Contemporary Music Ensemble, Univ. of Cinn., 1972. Comps. incl: String Quartet, 1966; Symph. No. 1; Sonace 1; Sonace 111; Suite in Five Movements; Rondellus; Later, Perhaps (film); Elevation of Imagery; Incidental music for var. plays. Mbr., profl. orgs. Hons: Perf. Asst., Univ. of Wash., 1965-66; Presser Fndn. Scholarships, 1959-63; Fac. Award, Montclair State Coll., 1970; Grad. Assistantships, Univ. of Cinn., 1971-74. Hobbies: Performing; Reading. Address: 7N710 Lucerne Dr., Apt. R34, Cleveland, OH 44130, USA.

MARSHALL, Lois, b. 1924, Toronto, Can. Concert & Opera Soprano. Educ: grad., Royal Conserv., Toronto. Career: recitals from age 15; apps. w. leadin Can. orchs.; Town Hall, NY, 1952; Soloist for Missa Solemnis under Arturo Toscanini; perfs. of Handel & Mozart w. Sir Thomas Beecham; made debut in

opera w. Boston Opera Co., 1959 (La Boheme); apps. incl. Royal Fest. Hall London, Amsterdam Concertgebouw, Edinburgh Fest., etc. Hons: Eaton Award, Toronto Conserv.; Naumburg Award, 1952-2.

MARSHALL, Nicholas, b. 2 June 1942, Plymouth, UK. Composer. Educ: MA, Cambridge Univ.; RCM. Career: In addition to work as comp., plays the horn professionally. Comps. (publd.) incl: Inscriptions for a peal of Eight Bells, for SATB; Sonatina for solo flute; Arion and the Dolphins; Two Minuets, arr. cello & piano; Nine Recorder Trios (arr.); Nine Recorder Quartets (arr.); An album for the horn (arr.); Suite for guitar, flute, clarinet, violin & cello; Partita, for guitar; Trio (for recorders). Recordings: Music from Dartington. Mbr., CGGB. Hobby: Keeping fit. Address: 2 The Mount, Totnes, Devon TQ9 5ES, UK.

MARSHALL, Robert Lewis, b. 12 Oct. 1939, NYC, USA. Musicologist. Educ: AB, Columbia Univ., 1960; MFA, 1962, PhD, 1968, Princeton Univ. m. Traute Maass, 2 children. Career: Assoc. Prof. & Chmn.; Dept. of Music, Univ. of Chgo., 1972-. Author: The Compositional Process of J S Bach, 1972. Ed: Studies in Renaissance & Baroque Music in Honor of Arthur Mendel, 1974; Johann Sebastian Bach: Harpsichord Fantasy in C minor, BWV 906 - a facsimile edition, 1976. Contbr. to jrnls. Mbrships: Am. Musicol. Soc.; Chmn., Am. Chapt., New Bach Soc., 1974-77. Recip. Otto Kindeldey Prize, 1974. Hobbies: Travel; Hiking. Address: Dept. of Music, Univ. of Chgo., 5835 S University Ave., Chicago, IL 60637, USA.

MARSH-EDWARDS, Michael Richard, b. 7 Apr. 1928, Westgate-on-Sea, UK. Composer. Educ: LTCL Dip.; pvte. studies w. Spencer Dyke; Trinity Coll., London. m. (1) Stella K Parrott, 1 d; (2) Ann Wardleworth. Career: Cond., Lucton Bach Orch., 1949-63; Luton Symph. Orch., 1952-63; Dir. of Music, Luton Industrial Mission & Luton Community Centre, 1952-62. Comps. inc: (Orchl.) Toccata for Percussion & Orch.; Dance Overture; Music 1/2/3/4; marcia Burlesca; Revolutionary Overture; Chester Overture; Fantasy of the Waltz of Diabelli; (Instrumental) Variations (8 percussionists); Abstractions (clarinet & viola); Aphorisms (piano); Mobile (oboe); Labyrinth (alto flute); Concerto for 11 Instruments; 3 Studies (12 percussionists); Experiments (8 var. orch. ensembles); Oppositions (2 orchs.); Metastasis (12); (Electronic) Electron 1/2/3; Transition 1/2/3; Mu; num. vocal & instrumental pieces for children. Author, radio scripst & concert notes. Mbrships: ISM; Royal Phil. Soc. (Assoc.). Hobbies: Reading; Walking; Travel. Address: Rose Acre, Station rd., Rossett, Wrexham, Clwyd LL12 OHE, UK. 3, 23, 28, 29, 30.

MARTEL, Fernand, b. 11 Aug. 1919, Quebec City, PQ, Can. Singer; Organist. Educ: Laval Univ.; La Sorbonne; Dip., Juilliard Schl. of Music, 1948. Debut: as Pelleas in Pelleas & Melisande, opposite Maggie Teyte, NYC Opera Co., 1948. Career incls: radio broadcasts, Montreal CBC, TV work, Montreal & Toronto, 1950-60; began playing organ, 1960; currently Organist Singur in rootauranto. Comps. recorded incl: M'aimes tu?; En te disant que je t'aime; Toi et moi; Viens m'ebrasser; Pour toi je chante; Marman; Les Chauffeurs de taxi; Je suis si bien; Do You Need Me. Recordings: Presenting Fernand Martel at the Rogers Theatre Organ, 1973. Concert Records. Mbrships: ATOS Organ Club, Hollywood; Los Angeles, Long Beach & Orange Co. Organist Clubs, all in Calif. Hobbies: Physical Culture; Swimming. Address: 439 W 9th St., Long Beach, CA 90813, USA.

MARTELLI, Henri Ernest, b. 25 Feb. 1895, Bastia, Corsica, France. Composer. Educ: Bachelor, Latin scis. & philos., Acad., Aix en Provence; Lic., Acad., Paris; studied comp., w. Charles Marie Widor, nat. Music Conserv., Paris. m. Marie Ricaud. Compositions incl: Bas-Reliefs Assyriens (w. Sere Koussevitzky & The Boston Symph., Mar., 1930); Ouverture pour un Conte de Boccace; La Chanson de Roland; Opera, Le major Cravachon; Chrestomathie for 3 voices; Sur des Vers de la Pleiade, songs; Epigrammes de Clement Marot; 3 symphs., 3 symph. suites, Sinfonietta, variations for str. orch., 3 quintets, 2 str. quartets, 1 quartt for clarinet, 5 trios, 4 piano suites, 11 sonatas, 20 pieces for piano, 10 concetos. Recordings: Sonate fulute et piano; Scherzetto berceuse et final. Mbrships: Pres., French section, Int. Soc. for contemporary music, (SIMC), 1953-73; Sec. Gen. Nat. Music Soc., 1948-. Hons: Hector Lefuel prize for chamber music, 1957; Florent Schmitt prize, Inst. of France, 1971. Address: 14 Rue de l'Etoile, Paris, France.

MARTENOT, Ginette, b. 27 Jan. 1902, Paris, France. Piano Soloist. Educ: Conservatoire Nat. Seperieur de Musique, Faculte des Lettres, Paris. m. Didier Lazard. Debut: Concert at age 5 yrs. Career: Piano Soloist, 1928-; Soloist of Ondes Martenot Instrument in Orchs. inclng: Opera de Paris; orch. Nat.; LSO; Berliner Phil.; NY Phil.; Concerts & recitals of contemporary music worldwide; Fndr., Martenot Art Schl., France & abroad. Comps: Music for num. films & TV. Num. recordings. Publs: incl: La

Musique, l'Interpretataion et l'Art du Geste, 2 vols.; L'Étude vivante du piano (technique liè á l'interprétation), 3 vols.; Cours supérieur d'interprotation, e Bach à Messiaen, 1 vol. Hons. incl: Grand Priz de l'Exposition Internationale, Paris, 1937. Address: 8 rue Delabordère, 92200 Neuilly, France. 3, 19, 27.

MARTIN, Carolann Frances, b. 20 Nov. 1935, Woodward, Okla., USA. Cellist; Conductor; Music Educator. Educ: BMusEd, Okla. City Univ., 1957; MA, Ohio State Univ., 1964. Career incls: Prin. Cellist, Sioux City Symph.; Cond., Siouxland Youth Symph.; Dir., Morningside Coll. Opera Theatre; Tchr., Cello, Conducting & Music Lit., Morningside Coll.; Mbr., Peninsula Fest. Orch., Fish Creek, Wis., 1968-; Has given num. recitals. Mbrships. incl: Pres., Sioux City Symph. Players Assn.; VP, NW Iowa Reg. Am. String Tchrs. Assn.; Am. String Tchrs. Assn. Hobbies: Tennis; Reading. Address: 1628 S Alice St., Sioux City, LA 51106, USA. 5.

MARTIN, Charlotte, b. 8 Feb. 1923, Mexico City, Mexico. Concert Pianist; Teacher. Educ: AA, Santa Barbara Jr. Coll.; Mex. Nat. Conserv. of Music; Tchrs. Dip., & Study w. Alfred Cortot & Nadia Boulanger, Ecole Normale de Musique, Paris, France, 1937-39; Soloist Dip., Piano, & study w. Nadia Boulanger & Boris Goldovsky, Longy Schl. of Music, Cambridge, Mass., USA, 1940-42. Debut: NYC, 1947. Career: Num. Concerts, Recitals, Lectures & Orchl. perfs., 1942-69; Concert Tours in USA & Europe; 5 Latin-Am. tours inclng. 17 Concerts, Dominican Repub., as Goodwill Ambassador from Mexico; num. Radio Broadcasts in NY, Can. & Europe, 1945-49; Coach & Accomp., Acad. of the West, Santa Barbara, Calif., w. Lotte Lehmann, 1954-64; Titular Prof., 3 Chairs, Schl. of Music, Univ. of Mexico, 1966-; Artist-in-Res., Okla. Bapt. Univ., Shawnee. Recordings: Num. records as Soloist & Accomp., & Master Class records, 1958-, Educo Records, Calif. Mbrships: Okla. & Calif. Music Tchrs. Assns.; Sigma Alpha Iota. Recip., Hon. Doct., Nat. Univ. of Mexico. Hobbies: Interior Decorating; Petit Point. Mgmt: Van Wyck, London, UK. Address: 2126 N. Beard St., Shawnee, OK 74801, USA.

MARTÍN, Edgardo, b. 6 Oct. 1915, Cienfuegos, Cuba. Composer; Pianist. Educ: Bach., EdD, Univ. of Havana; Havana Conserv. m. Aida Rodríguez, 2 d. Career incls: Comp. of juvenila (22 works), 1928-39; Profl. Comps., 1940-; Prof., Music Hist. & Aesthetics, 1942, Musical Comps., 1949, Havana Conserv. Comps. incl: Fugues for Strings, 1947; 6 Preludes for piano, 1949; Variations for guitar; String Quartet No. 1, 1968, No. 2, 1969; vocal, choral & instrumental works. Publs: Panorama Histórico de la Musica en Cuba, 1971; over 2800 articles in musical mags., etc. Mbrships: Nat. Cuban Union of Writers & Artists; Nat. Comm., Music, UNESCO; Interam. Assn. of Music, Caracas. Recip., Nat. Music Prize, 1951 & 52. Hobbies incl: Gymnastics; History; Shortwave Radio. Address: Calle 41 No. 951, apto. 7, Nuevo Vedado, Havana 6, Cuba.

MARTIN, John Horwood, b. Rugby, UK. Teacher; Administrator; Critic. Educ: BMus, Manchester; ARMCM. m. Sylvia Margaret Holmes, 2 s. Career: Dir. of Music, Workshop Coll., Notts.; S Wiltshire Grammar Schl., Salisbury, UK; Sr. Lectr., Dir. of Jr. Dept., Royal Scottish Acad. of Music, 1975-. Contbr. to: Guardian (Music Critic, 1975-). Hobbies: Theatre; Reading; Travel. Address: 5 Beverly Rd., Newlands, Glasgow G43 2RT, UK.

MARTIN, Peter, b. 23 Feb. 1939, NYC, USA. Conductor. Educ: BS, State Univ. Coll., Potsdam, NY; MS, Juilliard Schl. of Music, studying w. Jean Morel; other studies w. Elliott Carter, Renée Longy, Roger Sessions, Luciano Berio, Jacob Druckman. Career: Cond. w. The Garden State Opera Co.; Music Dir., ibid., 1969-; Cond., Merrick Symph., 1976-77; Cond., SOHO Chmbr. Ensemble of NY, 1976-. Address: 645 Water St., NY, NY 10002, USA.

MARTIN, Thomas M, b. 22 July 1940, Cinn., Ohio, USA. Double Bass Player & Teacher. Educ: Eastman Schl. of Music w. Oscar Zimmerman; Curtis Inst. of Music w. Roger Scott. Career: asst. prin., Buffalo Phil.; co-prin., Israel Phil.; prin., Montreal Symph.; prin., London Symph. Orch.; solo bass, Acad. of St. Martin-in-the-Field. Recordings: Schubert, Trout Quintet & Octet. Hobby: Violin making. Address: 22 Eastbury Ave., Northwood, Middx ., UK.

MARTIN, Vivian, b. 9 May 1942, Detroit, Mich., USA. Soprano. Educ: BS, Wayne State Univ.; Detroit Conserv. of Music. m. Clement A McDowell. Career incls: Soloist w. Munich Phil. & Nuremberg Symph. Orch. & Phil. Chorus, 1970; debut as Lenora in La Forza del Destino, 1971; Rezia in Weber's Oberon, Wexford Opera Fest., Ireland, 1972; Royal Opera of Ghent, Stadt Opera Essen, Badische Opera Karlsruhe, Stadt Opera Bonn,

Mainz Opera, Royal Opera Lisbon, Stadtheater Bremen, etc.; TV boradcasts, BBC & BRT Belgium, Romania, Czech.; radio broadcasts, Bavarian Radio, WDR Cologne. Recordings: RCA; Command Records. Mbrships: Am. Fedn. of TV & Radio Artists. Recip., Premier Peix de Chant, Fontainbleau, France. Hobbies incl: horticulture Reading; Fashion Designing. Mgmt: Music Int., London; Artivis Artists, Holland & Belgium; Austrian Concert Mgmt., Europe & Asia. Address: Apt. A-6, Leifstr. 18, 8000 Munich 90, German Fed. Repub. 4, 30.

MARTIN, Walter Callahan, Jr., b. 29 May 1930, Artesia, NM, USA. Professor of Voice; Opera & Concert Singer (Baritone). Educ: BMus., Univ. of Ore., 1952; MMus, ibid., 1964; studied at State Acad. of Music, Stuttgart, Germany, 1954-56; DMusA, Univ. of Southern Calif., 1976. m. Katarzyna Wanda Chalupka. Debut: State Opera, Stuttgart, 1954. Career: has app. w. State Opera, Stuttgart, Nat. Theatre, Mannheim, & Heidelberg & Koblenz Municipal Operas; has made concert apps. thru'out Western Germany, USA, Can. & Ireland; has made radio broadcasts in Germany & USA. Mbrshipos: Assoc. Ed. ic of music review, NATS Bulletin, Nat. Assn. Tchrs. of Singing; Pi Kappa Lamt.da; Phi Mu Alpha Sinfonia; Delta Pi Alpha. Address: 429 Lotus Court, Redlands, CA 92373, USA.

MARTINEZ, Odaline de la, b. 31 Oct. 1949, Matanzas, Cuba. Composer; Conductor; Pianist. Educ: BFA, Tulane Univ., 1968-72; RAM, 1972-76; GRSM (comp. & piano); MMus (comp.), Univ. of Surrey, 1975-77. Career: comps. broadcast by BBC, Radio Istanbul, Radio Cork, Radio Belgrade, Romanian Radio, KPFA San Francisco; pianist, BBC, Radio Belgrade, Romanian Radio. Comps: After Sylvia (song cycle); Phasing, for chmbr. orch.; A Moment's Madness, for flute & piano; Improvisations for solo violin; 2 American Madrigals, for mixed chorus. Contbr. to Contact Mag. Mbrships: League of Women Comps.; SPNM, New MacNaghten Concerts. Hons: Danforth Fellowship; Marshall Scholar; Watson Fellow; Nat. Ebdowments for the Arts (USA); Joyce Dixie Prize; Manson Scholarship. Hobbies: Travel; Eating Out; Films. Mgmt: Magenta Music. Address: 356 Camden Rd., London N7 OLG, UK.

MARTINO, Donald, b. 16 Mar 1931, Plainfield, NJ, USA. Composer. Educ: BM, Syracuse Univ., 1952; MFA, Princeton Univ., 1954. m. Lora Harvey, 1d., 1 s. Career incls: Assoc. Prof. of Theory of Music, Yale Univ., 1959-69; Chmn., Comp. Dept., New England Conserv. of Music, 1969-. Comps. incl: (recorded) Cinque Frammenti; A Set for Clarinet; B,a,b,b,it,t; Notturno; Paradiso Choruses; Impromptu for Roger, 1977; Triple Concert for clarinet, bass & contrabass clarinets & chmbr. orch., 1977. Mbrships: Am. Soc. of Univ. Comps.; Am. Music Ctr.; Broadcast Music Inc. Contbr. to profl. jrnls. Hons. incl: Pulitzer Prize, 1974; Nat. Endowment for the Arts Commission, 1976. Hobby: Tennis. Address: 11 Pembroke St., Newton, MA 02158, USA. 2, 6.

MARTINO, Thomas James, b. 10 Oct. 1948, Bronx, NY, USA. Musician, Bassoon, Clarinet, Saxophone; Musicologist. Educ: BA, Yankton Coll.; BMus, ibid.; MMus., Brooklyn Coll. m. Jeanette H Martino, 1 d. Debut: Town Hall, NYC, 1971. Career: Studio Musician, TV & Movie Sound Tracks, Broadway Musicals; Co-Fndr., Musica Ars Nova; Specialist Ed., 18th Century Neapolitan compositions, Ed. Jommelli's Te Deum, 1970, Requiem, 1972. Recordings: Reconstruction & Ed. of Jommelli's Te deum. Mbrships: Music Dir., Westchester Jazz Ensemble; Co-Fndr., Music Dir., Musica Ars Nova. Hobbies: Skiing; Hiking. Address: Coach n' Four Manor, Jefferson Valley, NY 10535, USA.

MARTINS, Roberto, b. 1 Nov. 1943, Sao Paulo, Brazil. Teacher; Conductor & Choir Director. Educ: Grad. as primary, & lang. & lit. Tchr.; studied Choir Cond. w. Klaus Dietter Wolff, 1967-74, studied contemporary music w. Giberto Mendes, 1968-70. Debut: 1971, as Comp. Career: Dir., & Cond., Madrigal Ars Viva de Santos (choir ensemble); CoñDir., Fest. Música Nova de Santos; TV apps.; comp. commissioned for Fest. de Quro Preto, 1975. Compositons incl: (Vocal) Rosa Tumultuada; Alfa Mysthicum Omega; Salmos; Suplice. Publ: Book on Artistic Educ. to appear 1977. Contbr. to Editora do Autor. Mbrships. incl: Brazilian Soc. Contemporary Music. Hons: Prize for Best Experimental Comp., Sao Paulo Critics, 1973. Address: Caixa Postal 394, 11100 Santos, SP, Brazil.

MARVIN, Frederick, b. 11 June 1923, Los Angeles, Calif., USA. Concert Pianist; Professor of Piano. Educ: Los Angeles City Coll.; Curtis Inst. Music, Phila., Penn.; Southern Calif., 1939; Carnegie Hall, NY, 1949. Career: Concert Pianist, USA, Europe & India; TV apps., USA & Europe; Radio broadcasts, USA, Rueope & India; Prof., Piano, Artist-in-Res., Syracuse Univ., NY. Publs. incl: Padre Antonio Soler, 6 vols. Piano Sonatas; Fandango for Piano Choral Works; 4 Villancicos; Salve; Lamentation;

Stabat Mater. Recordings incl: All Liszt Program; Sonatas by I Moscheles & L Berger. Contbr. to profl. jrnls. Mbr. var. profl. orgs. Hons. incl: Kt. Cmdr., Orden del Mérito Civil, Spain, 1969; La Medaille de Vermeil, Soc. Acad. Arts-Scis.-Lettres, France, 1974. Hobbies incl: Opera. Mgmt: Ernst Schuh, 246 Houston Ave., Syracuse, NY 13224; Address: 246 Houston Ave., Syracuse, NY 13224, USA.

MARYNOWSKI, Jan, b. 13 Feb. 1924, Wloclawek, Poland. Musician; Conductor; Pianist-Accompanist; Teacher of High School Music. Educ: Dip., Cond., High Schl. of Music, Wroclaw; MA, ibid. m. Wanda Marynowska, 3 children. Debut: State Opera House, Wroclaw, Poland: St. Moniuszko, Halka. Career: Cond., State Opera House, Wroclaw (50 operas & ballets); Vis. Cond: German Democratic Repub.; Czechoslovakia; USSR; Tchr. of High Schl. of Music, Wroclaw. Publs: Operatic Pianist-Tutor's Work, Musical Books, 1975. Mbr. Assn. of Polish Musicians. Hobby: Foreign Travel. Address: Pl. Nowy Targ 25-4, 50-144 Wroclaw, Poland.

MARX, Karl Julius, b. 12 Nov. 1897, Munich, Germany. Composer; Professor. Educ: Acad. of Music, Munich; Studied w. Carl Orff. m. Novema Fellman, dec. 1974, 3 s. Career: Lectr., Music High Schl., Munich, 1924-39, State Musical Trng. High Schl., Graz, 1939-45, State Music High Schl., Stuttgart, 1946-66. Comps. incl: Und endet doch alles mit Frieden, (Hölderlin) op. 52; Cantata for solo, choir & Orch.; Fantasia sinfonica for orch. op. 67; All types of Opera. Recordings: Karl Marx, Kammermusik Calig; Karl Marx, Mädchen tanze, sing und springe; Es war einmal ein Segelschiffchen, FidualFON. Publs: ANalyse der Klaviersonate B-dur von WA Mozart, KV 333, 1966; Zur Einheit der zyklischen Form bei Mozart, 1971. Mbrships: German Music Coun.; 1st Chmn., Nat. Assn. of German Musicians & Music Tchrs., Baden-Wurttemberg. Hons: Munich Music Prize, 1932; DSC, 1st Class, German Fed. Repub., 1966; Hon. Senator, Music High Schl. Stuttgart, 1966. Hobby: Mountaineering. Address: 69 Gänsheidestr., D-7000 Stuttgart 1, German Fed. Repub.

MASANETZ, Guido Bruno, b. 17 May 1914, Friedek, Czech. Composer; Conductor; Pianist. Educ: w. Dr. Hans Jelen, Friedek, & Prof. Gustav Götz, Sumperk (piano); Prof. Josef Bartovsky, Plzen (theory & comp.). m. Angelika Rohde, 2 c. Career: before WW II, concert pianist, Radio Brno; after WW II, cond., Municipal Theatre, Zittau; Mus.dir., Stage Song & Dance, Ensemble, Berlin; freelance comp. & cond., Berlin, 1955-. Comps: sev. operas incl. The Miraculous Bird, Explosive for Santa Ines & Vasantasena; Musical, Who Needs Money; num. songs & film scores. Mbr. Union of Comps. & Musicologists of German Dem. Repub. Recip., Art prize of the German Dem. Repub., 1960. Addrss: Buchholzerstr. 70, 1108 Berlin, German Dem. Repub.

MASARIE, Jack F., b. 25 Nov. 1942, San Fran., Calif., USA. Horn Instructor; Performer. Educ: BMus, Juilliard Schl. Music, 1966; MMus, Bowling Green State Univ., 1973. m. Gayle Anderson Masarie, 1 d. Career: Asst. Prin. Horn, Detroit Symph. Orch., 1966-68; Co-Prin. Horn, Toledo Symph., Toledo Opera, 1968-72; Brass Instructor, Mary Manse Coll., Toledo, 1968-72; Hornist, Bowling Green Woodwind Quintet, 1970-71; Horn Instructor, Univ. NC; Prin. Horn, Greensboro Symph.; Hornist, E Wind Quintet & Brass Art Quintet. Mbrships. incl: Int. Horn Soc. Hobbies incl: Veteran Cars; Historic Instruments. Address: 2600 Duck Club Rd., Greensboro, NC 27210, USA.

MASHOKO, Simon, b. 3 Nov. 1918, Ft. Vic., Rhodesia. Catechist. m. Teresa, 4 s., 4 d. Career: Catechist, using the mbira as an aid in religious teachings; Main character, vocational film on R C priesthood. Comps. (recordings): Mbiri Viri; Magonde; Relig. songs from New Testament e.g. the Prodigal Son, the Birth of Jesus & others. Recordings incl: Bhiza Rashe; Psalm 145; The Story of the Resurrection; Tambarara ndiikutumbure munzwa; Bhutsu Mutandarikwa. Chmn., Legion of Mary. Recip. Trophy for traditional dances, 1952; Best Mbira Player in Rhodesia Award. Hobbies: Playing mbira; Reading. Mgmt: Mambo Press, Gwelo. Address: Gareria RC Ch., co Makuvaza, P Bag Glen Clova, Ft. Victoria, Rhodesia.

MASIN, Ronald, b. 9 Aug. 1937, Rotterdam, Netherlands. Violinist. Educ: Dipl., Royal Brussles Conserv. m. Maria Keleman, 1 s. Debut: w. Orch., aged 14, Johannesberg, S Africa. Career: solo & chmbr. perfs., Netherlands, Belgium, France, Switz., Hungary, USSR, Italy, Denmark & S Africa; num. solo apps. w. Concertgebouw of Amsterdam; Ldr., Amsterdam Phil. Orch. & Amsterdam Kern Ensemble. Recordings: EMI. Hobbies: Photography; Cycling. Address: Maartenplein 7, 2585 Vreeland, Netherlands.

MASON, Anne C, b. 18 Jan. 1936, Hattiesburg, Miss., USA. Music Teacher; Musician (violin, viola). Educ: Univ. of Ala.; Miss.

Coll.; BMus., MMusEd. m. George W Mason, 4 children. Debut: Tchaikowsky Viuolin Concerto, 1960. Career: Prin. Viola, Jackson Symph. Orch., incl. Concert & TV appearances; Recording artist w. strings, Malaco & NARC Recording Studios, for jazz, rock & commercials; 1st violin, Tupelo Symph. & Greenville Symph.; Prin. Viola, Opera S; Viola & Violin w. Jackson Opera Guild. Mbrships: Sec.-Treas., Orch. Div., Miss. Music Educators Assn.; Delta Omicron. Hobbies: Swimming; Sailing; Painting. Address: 1131 Annalisa Ln., Jackson, MS 39204, USA.

MASON, David Frederick, b. 2 Apr. 1926, London, UK. Orchestral Musician (Trumpet). Educ: RCM; ARCM. m. Rachael Godlee, 1 s., 1 d. Career: Prin. Trumpet, Covent Gdn.; RPO; NPO; Prof., RCM, London. Mbrships: ISM; RSM. Hobbies: Golf; Theatre. D1Y. Deepfield, orley Farm Rd., Harrow, Middx., UK.

MASON, Eric Morris, b. 21 Dec. 1925, London, UK. Musical Publicist & Critic. m. Doreen Mary Singleton, 1 s., 2 d. Career: London Music Critic, Westminster Press, Provincial Newspapers, 1949-64; Asst. Critic, Daily Mail, London, 1955-64, Music Critic, 1964-71; Publicity & PR Mgr., London Phil. Orch., 1971-75. Publs. & Advertising Mgr., 1975-. Contbr. to Var. publs. Hobby: Canal & River Cruising. Address: 121 Sussex Way, Cockfosters, Herts., UK. 3.

MASON, Frances Gillian, b. 1939, Farnborough, Hants., UK. Concert Violinist. Educ: ARCM (Violin Perf.) m. Alan Foster, 1 d. Career: Soloist, Prom. Concerts & broadcasts, also chmbr. music broadcasts; Prof., RCM, 1970-. Hons: 1st Violin Prize, RCM, 2nd Prize. Flesh Int. Violin Competition & BBC Violin Competition; 1st Prize, Nat. Fed. Music Soc. Award. Hobby: Gardening. Address: 16 Stonehill rd., London SW14, UK. 3.

MASON, (Lt. Col.) James Robert, b. 14 March 1930, Castle Eden, UK. Principal Director of Music. Educ: RAM; LRAM; ARCM; LGSM; Royal Marinos Schl. of Music. m. Alice Chamberlain, 1 d., 1 s. Career: Jr. Musician, Bandmaster, 2nd Lt. (Dir. of Music), Lt. Col. (Prin. Dir. of Music), Royal Marines Band Service; Service in H.M. Ships Bands; Dir. of Music, H.M. Yacht Britannia, 1970-78. Recordings: Colonel Bogey on Parade; Colonel Bogey Series II; H.M. Royal Marines; By Land Sea and Air; Rule Britannia; The Best of the Royal Marines; Famous Concert Marches. Mbrships: Royal Commonwealth Soc.; Naval Club. Hons: M.V.O., 1977. Address: Royal Marines Schl. of Music, Deal, Kent, UK.

MASON, Ralph (John Francis), b. 3 Sept. 1938, Brighton, Sussex, UK. Operatic Tenor; Television Actor. m. Anne Sessions, 1 d. Debut: w. D'Oyly Carte Opera, Stratford Mem. Theatre, 1960. Career incl: Prin. Understudy, 1960-63, Prin. Tenor, 1965-73, D'Oyly Carte Opera; Prin. Understudy & Prin., My Fair Lady Co., 1963-65; Guest Artist, D'Oyly Carte Opera Co., 1975; Prin., English Opera For All Co., 1975-77; Full time mbr., Welsh Nat. Opera Co., 1977-; num. minor parts & prin. roles on Brit. TV. Recordings: Decca. Mbr., Brit. Equity. Hobbies. History, Swimming. Address: 11 Rhododendron Cl., Greenways, Cyncoed, Cardiff CF2 7HS, UK.

MASON, Timothy George Stewart, b. 29 Apr. 1948, Thurcaston, Leics., UK. Musician (cello & baroque cello). Educ: BA, MusB, King's Coll., Cambridge Univ.; Study in Paris w. Maurice Gendron; study of composition w. Hugh Wood; ARCM. Career: Mbr., Capricorn Chmbr. Ensemble, 1973-; Mbr., BBC Symph. Orch., Apollo's Banquet, Wren Consort; Freelance Cellist, London. Hobbies: Reading; Composing; Walking. Address: 1 Malvern Rd., Landon E8 3LT, UK.

MASON, Vito Edward, b. 6 Jan. 1928, Elizabeth, NJ, USA. Choral Conductor. Educ: BS, NY Univ.; MS, Ithaca Coll. m. Rosina E Mogensen, 3 d. Career: Dir., Univ. Choirs, The Am. Univ., Wash., DC; Guest Cond., over 100 Choral Festivals, throughout USA. Compositions: Burst of Applause, 1972; Choral series: Vito Mason Choral Selections; Ed., The American Univ. Choral Series. Contbr. to: Jrnl. of Rsch. in Music Educ. Mbrships: Chmn., Wash., DC, area. Am. Choral Dirs. Assn., 1968-70; MENC. Recip; Porter W Averill Award, for outstanding work in Music Educ. & Choral Conducting, 1965. Address: 306 Coleshill Manor Dr., Silver Spring, MD 20904, USA. 7.

MASSENKEIL, Günther, b. 11 Mar. 1928, Wiesbaden, Germany. Music Educator; Concert Singer (Baritone). Educ: Studied Musicol., Univ. of Mainz & Sorbonne, Paris, France; DPhil., Mainz, 1952; Grad. study in Music Educ. & Hist., ibid. m. Ursula Gross, 4 children. Career: Asst. Music Instr., Mainz, 1954-; Prof. & Dir., Musicol. Seminars, Univ. of Bonn, 1966-; Chmn., Curatoria of Max Reger Inst., Bonn, 1972-; Dir., Beethoven Archives, ibid., 1972-74; num. appearances as concert singer, 1954-. Publs. incl: Untersuchungen zum Problem der Symmetrie in der Instrumentalmusik W.A. Mozarts, 1962; Das Oratorium, 1970; Mehrstimmigmentationen aus der ersten Hälfte des 16. Jahrhunderts, 1965. Contbr. to: Riemann Musiklexikon; Grove's Dict.; Dict. de la Musique, Ency. della Musica Ricordi, etc. Address: D.-534 Bad Honnef, Böckingstr. 3, German Fed. Repub.

MASSERA, Giuseppe, b. 24 Mar. 1912, Bologna, Italy. Musicologist; University Lecturer. Educ: Laurea in law & political science; Dip., Musical Paleography. m. Maria Ladini. Publs: num. books, monographs & articles on many aspects of Italian music. Mbrships: Accademia Filharmonica di Bologna; Accademia Tiberina di Roma. Address: Via Ildebrando Bocchi 36, 43100 Parma, Italy.

MASSÉUS, Jan, b. 28 Jan. 1913, Rotterdam, Netherlands. Composer; Pianist; Educator. Educ: Conserv., Rotterdam. m. Hermana Noordemeer, 1 s. Debut: The Hague, 1950. Career: Radio & Concert Appearances as Pianist, esp. Interpreting own comps.; Tchr., Muziekpedagogische Akademie, Leeuwarden. Compositions: Ballet Music; Chamber Music; Orchl. Music; Music for choir & film. Mbrships: Genootschap van Nederlandse Componisten, Amsterdam; Koninklijke Nederlandse Toonkunstenaars Vereniging, ibid. Hons: Visser-neerlandia Prize, 1956; 2nd Prize, 30 yr. jubilee, AVRO Radio, 1953; Silver Medal. Soc. des Arts, Scis. Lettres, Paris, 1973. Hobbies: Painting; Lit. Address: Woelwijk 29, Tietjerk (Fr.), Netherlands.

MASSEY, Andrew John, b. 1 May 1946, Nottingham, UK. Conductor. Educ: BA (Oxon), Merton Coll., Oxford, 1968; MA in analysis of contemporary comp. technique, Nottingham Univ., 1969. Debut: Elgar prog. w. Cleveland Orch., USA, 1978. Career: Asst. Cond., Cleveland Orch., 1978-; fndr., cond., Apollo Symph. Orch. Comps: Theatre music. Mbrships: ISM; Musicians' Union. Hobbies: Computing; Trees. Address: c/o The Cleveland Orch., Severance Hall, Cleveland, OH 44106, USA.

MASSEY, Pamela Grace, b. 14 Nov. 1948, Los Angeles, Calif., USA. Music Librarian. Educ: BMusEd., MMus, Northwestern Univ.; AM Lib. Sci., Univ. of Mich. Career: Music Cataloguer, SUNY at Fredonia, NY. Mbrships: Music Lib. Assn.; Am. Musicol. Soc.; Soc. for Ethnomusicol. Hobby: Trombonist. Address: 350 Central Ave., Apt. A-2, Fredonia, NY 14063, USA.

MASSEY, Roy Cyril, b. 9 May 1934, Organist; Conductor. Educ: BMus, Univ. of Birmingham; pvte. study w. David Willcocks; FRCO (CHM); ADCM; ARCM. m. Ruth Carol Craddock Grove. Career incl: Organist, St. Augustine's, Edgbaston, 1960-65; Croydon Parish Ch., 1965-68; Warden, RSCM, 1965-68; cond., Croydon Bach Soc., 1966-68; Organist to City of Birmingham Choir, 1954; Organist & Master of the Choristers, Birmingham Cathedral, 1968-74; Dir. of Music, King Edward's Schl., Birmingham, 1968-74; Organist & Master of the Choristers, Hereford Cathedral, 1974-; cond., Three Choirs Fest. Hon: FRSCM for dist. services to Ch. Music, 1972. Address: 14 College Cloisters, Hereford HR1 2NG, UK.

MASSIP, Catherine, b. 12 May 1946, Paris, France. Librarian. Educ: Licenciée ès lettres (archiviste-paléographe); Conserv. Nat. de Musique de Paris. Career: Curator, Bibliothèque nationale, Paris. Publ: La Vie des musiciens de Paris au temps de Mazarin, 1976. Contbr. to: Rsch. on French Classical Music; Fontes artis musicae; Bulletin de la Bibliothèque nationale, etc. Mbrships: AIBM; SFM. Hons: 1st Prize in hist. of music & in musicol., Conserv. Nat. de Musique de Paris. Address: 7 rue de l'Aigle, 92250 La Garenne-Colombes, France.

MASSOUDIEH, Mohammad Taghi, b. 12 June 1927, Meshed, Iran. Professor of Musicology. Educ: LLM, Teheran Univ.; M Harmony, Ecole Normale de Musique de Paris; M Comp., Musikhochschule Leipzig; D Musicol., Univ. of Cologne. Career: Prof. of Musicol., Teheran Univ. Comps: Two Movements for Str. Orch., 1978. Mbrships: Gesellschaft für Musikforschung; Int. Musicol. Soc. Publs: incl: Musik in Busehr, Süd-Iran (w. Josef Kuckertz), 1976; Awaz-e-Sur, Zur Melodiebildung in der persischen Kunstmusik, 1968; Hochzeitsleider aus Balucestan. in: Jahrbuch Für musikalsche Volks-upVölkerkunde, Berlin, 1973. Contbr. to profl. jrnls. Address: Dept. of Music, Fac. of Fine Arts, Univ. of Teheran, Teheran, Iran.

MASTERS, Dennis Joseph, b. 25 Mar. 1923, Oldbury, UK. Teacher; Conductor; Adjudicator; Cornet & Trumpet Player. Educ: L Mus TCL; studied w. Dr. Christopher Edmunds. m. Jean Masters. Career: Cond., The Langley Band, 1946-; Prin. Cornet, Worcestershir Regiment Band, 5 yrs.; Cond., Ransome & Marles Works Band, 10 yrs.; num. TV & radio broadcasts. Comps: Num. published & recorded works. Recording: Sev. records. Recip., var. prizes as player, & winner of num. contests as cond. Hobbies: Reading; Walking. Address: 12 Church Walk, Areley Kings, Stouport-on-Severn, Worcs., UK.

MASTERSON, Robbie Gowan, b. 27 Oct. 1918, Bemis, Tenn., USA. Musician (piano & harpsichord); Educator. Educ: BA, Lambuth Coll., Jackson, Tenn.; Music Educ. Cert., ibid.; Piano study w. pvte. tutors. m. John Thornton Masterson, 1 s., 1 d. Debut: Times Hall, NYC, 1949. Career incl: Concert performances at Town Hall & Carnegie Hall, NYC; Broadcasts from Stn. WYNC; Recitals, NYC Mus. Mbrships: Leschetizky Assn.; Pres., Music Tchrs. Coun. of Westchester, 1975-77; Nat. Guild Piano Tchrs.; Bd. of Adjudicators, ibid., 1975-. Hobbies: Travel; Philosophy; Poetry. Address: 53 Byron Ln., Larchmont, NY 10538, USA.

MASTERSON, Valerie, b. Birkenhead, UK. Opera Singer. Educ: Matthay Schl. of Music, Liverpool; Royal Coll. of Music. Career incl: Performances in Falstaff, Il Turco in Italia & Der Schauspieldirektor, Landes Theatre, Salzburg; Mbr., D'Oyly Carte Opera Co. inclng. appearances in film version of The Mikado; Mbr., Engl. Nat. Opera, 1972-, inclng. leading roles in Orpheus in the Underworld; The Marriage of Figaro; The Rhinegold; Siegfried; La Traviata; Carmen, etc.; debut at Covent Gdn. in The Rhinegold, 1974; Guest appearances w. Glyndebourne Touring Opera, Handel Opera Soc. & Keynote Opera; Broadcasts in the Mikado, 1973 & the Yeomen of the Guard, 1974 (BBC-TV); appearances in Toulouse & Aix-en-Provence Festival, 1975. Recordings incl. sev. complete Gilbert & Sullivan operas. Address: co Engl. Nat. Opera, London Coliseum, St. Martin's Ln., London WC2N 4ES, UK.

MASTROGIOVANNI, Attilio, b. 24 April 1939, Rio de Janeiro, Brazil. Pianist; Professor. Educ: Superior courses, piano, chmbr. music, harmony, musical analysis, music hist.; Extension courses of Piano High Interpretation, Rome & Moscow. m. Luiza Maria de Saboia Mastrogiovanni. Career: Recitals & Concerts, Theatre, Radio & TV in Brazil, USA, USSR, Italy & Switz.; Mbr. of Jury, num. Nat. & Int. Piano Contests; Mbr., Swiss Chmbr. Players; Prof., Alcantara Machado Fac., Sao Paulo. Recordings: Attilio Mastrogiovanni interpreta Nilson Lombardi; Album of Brazilian Comps. Mbrships: Musical Commission of the State of Sao Paulo; Tech. & Pedagogical Coun. of Tatui Conserv., Sao Paulo; Ordem dos Musicos do Brasil. Hons: 1st Prize, Liszt Piano Contest, Rio de Janeiro, 1961; 1st Prize, Moscow Conserv. Soviet Music Piano Contest, 1966; Record Prods. Assn. Award, Rio de Janeiro, 1976. Hobbies: Gymnastics; Cinema. Address: Rua Sud Mennucci, 320 Villa Mariana, Sao Paulo, 04017, Brazil.

MATA, Eduardo, b. 5 Sept. 1942, Mexico City, Mexico. Conductor. Educ: Nat. Conserv. of Music, Mexico; Berkshire Music Ctr., USA. m. Carmen Ginici-Ventallo. Career: Conducted 1st Mexican performances of avant-garde music of the 1960s (Boulex, Stockhausen, etc.); Musical Dir., Mexican Ballet Co., 1963-64; Musical Dir., Guadaljara Symph. Orch., 1965-66; Musical Dir., Orch. Phil. UNAM, Mexico City, 1966-; Prin. Cond. & Musical Advsr., Phoenix Symph. Orch., Ariz., USA, 1972-; Artistic Dir., Puebla Int. Musical Festival, 1974-; musical dir., Dallas Symph., 1977-78; guest cond., ldng. US Symph. Orchs. Compositions: Symph. works; chmbr. music; vocal pieces; Multimedia. Recordings: Var. works on sev. commercial labels, 1967-. Mbrships: Mexican Soc. of Composers. Hons: Golden Lyre, Mexican Union of Musicians, 1973; Prize, Mexican Assn. of Music Critics, 1967. Mgmt: Hurok Concerts (USA); Harold Holt (Europe). Address: PO Box 26207, Dallas, TX 75226, USA. 2, 9.

MATÉ, Janos, b. 16 Apr. 1944, Budapest, Hungary. Violinist. Educ: Dip., virtuosity & pedagogy, Budapest, 1965; Dip., supérieur, Brussels, 1976; studied w. Kadar, Galamian, Ida Haendel & André Gertler. m. Annik Lenepveu, 2 d. Career: 1st concert master, Antwerp Phil., 1977; 1st concert master, Brussels Ch. Orch., 1978; 1st concertmaster, Munich Opera, 1975; concerts & recitals throughout Europe, USA & Can. Recordings: 3 Schubert Sonatinas. Hons: winner, Prix Vieuxtemps, 1974; 2nd prize, Int. Curci Competition, Naples, 1974. Hobbies: Photography; Squash; Mountaineering. Addrss: 61 Blvd. de Dixmude, 1000 Brussels, Belgium.

MATEER, David Gordon, b. 16 Apr. 1946, Belfast, N Ireland. University Lecturer in Music. Educ: BMus, PhD, Queen's Univ., Belfast; MMus, King's Coll., London; Music Tchrs. Cert., London Univ. m. Delise Leadbitter. Career: Lectr. in Music, Herts. Coll. of Higher Educ., 1976-77; Lectr. in Music, Univ. Coll. of Wales, Aberystwyth, 1977-. Contbr. to: Grove's Dict., 6th Ed.; Musical Times; Music & Letters. Mbr., Royal Musical Assn. Hobbies: Book collecting; Playing squash; Learning langs. Address: 52 Bryncastell, Bow Street, nr. Aberystwyth, Dyfed, Wales, UK.

MATESKY, Ralph, b. 4 Jan. 1913, NYC, USA. Conductor; Composer; Violinist; Violist; Educator. Educ: BS Music Educ., Columbia Univ.; MMus, Univ. of Southern Calif.; Dip. & Tchrs. Dip. in Violin, Juilliard Schl. of Music; studied violin & comp., var.

masters. m. Betty Blumberg, 1 s., 1 d. Career incls: Fndr.-Musical Dir., Compton Civic Symph. & Compton Youth Symph., Calif., 1948-63; Cond., Stockton Symph., 1963-67; Fndr.-Cond., San Joaquin Youth Symph., 1964-67; Cond., Tour Orchs., Europe & Mexico; Dir., String Educ., Utah State Univ., 1967-. Comps. incl: num. works for full orch., educl. works, radio film & theatre music, etc. Publs. incl: Group Piano Manual (w. B Matesky), 1975. Contbr. to profl. jrnls. Mbr., profl. assns. Recip. num. awards & citations. Hobbies incl: Gardening; Reading. Address: 2015 NE Country Estates, N Logan, UT 84321, USA. 4, 9.

MATHER, Betty Bang, b. 7 Aug. 1927, Emporia, Kan., USA. University Music Professor (Flute). Educ: Hunter Coll.; BMus, Oberlin Conserv.; MA, Tchrs. Coll., Columbia Univ.; studied at Paris Conserv., France, Freiburg Musikhochschule, Germany, Juilliard Schl., NYC, Tanglewood. m. Roger Mather. Career: Music Prof., Univ. of Iowa. Recordings incl: Jenni, Musique Printaniere (flute & piano); Cucumber Music (Flute, Viola, Celeste, Percussion); Hervig, Chamber Music for Six Players (Flute, Clarinet, Piano, Percussion, Violin, Bass). Publs. incl: Interpretation of French Music for Woodwind & Other Performers; Additonal Comments on German & Italian Music, 1973; 30 Virtuoso selections for Unaccompanied Flute, 1975; Free Ornamentation in Woodwind Music 1700-1775 (w. D Lasocki), 1976; 3 Opera Duets arranged by Berbiguier for 2 Flutes, 1976; 60 Favourite Airs in the Gallant Style for Unaccompanied Flute, 1978; The Classical Woodwind Cadenza: A Workbook (w. D Lasocki), 1978. Contbr. to profl. jrnls. Mbr., profl. orgs. inclng. Nat. Flute Assn. (Dir., 1975-76); Am. Recorder Soc., Ed. Bd., 1979-. Address: 308 4th Ave., Iowa City, IA 52240, USA. 4, 5.

MATHER, Christine Kyle, b. 29 May 1929, York, UK. Musicologist; Former Bassoonist; Player of Early Wind Instruments. Educ: ARCM; PhD, Univ. of Mich., USA. Career: Freelance Bassoonist, London, UK, 1952-56; Bassoon Instructor, RSAM, & Bassoonist, var. Scottish orchs., 1956-62; Fndr. & Dir., Man. Consort, Can., apps. thru'out Can. & in Brit., Germany & Switzerland, 1963-70; Musicologist, Univ. of Man., 1964-70; Musicologist, Univ. of Victoria, BC, 1971-75; Dean, Fac. of Music, Wilfrid Laurier Univ., Waterloo, Ont., 1975-. Recordings: Num. transcriptions recordings for CBC, & for BBC, Radio Suisse Romande & Hessische Rundfunk. Contbr. to: Jrnl. of Can. Assn. of Univ. Schls. of Music; Early Music. Mbrships: Am. Musicol. Soc.; Int. Musicol. Soc. Hons: Can. Coun. Doct. Fellowships, 1968, 1969, 1970. Hobby: Gardening. Address: Fac. of Music, Wilfrid Laurier Univ., Waterloo, Ont. N2L 2C5, Can.

MATHER, Roger Frederick, b. 27 May 1917, Loneon, UK. Flute Teacher. Educ: MA, Univ. of Cambridge; MSc., MIT, USA. m. Betty Bang Mather, 1 s., 1 d. Career: Tech., Managerial positions in steel, automotive Inds., Nat. Aeronautics & Space Admin., USA; Adjunct Prof., Univ. of Iowa; Flute Clinician; Pvte. tchr., Flute. Contbr. to: Woodwind World; Instrumentalist. Mbrships. NACWPI, Galpin Soc., Am. Recorder Soc.; Am. Musical Instrument Soc.; Nat. Flute Assn. Address: 308 4th Ave., Iowa City, IA 52240, USA.

MATHESON-BRUCE, Graeme, b. 19 July 1945, Dundee, Scotland, UK. Singer (Tenor). Educ: RSAM, 1965-69; Dip., RSAM, 1968; Royal Manchester Coll. of Music, 1969-70; London Opera Ctr., 1973-74. m. Elizabeth Anne-Marie Ives, 1 s. Debut: English Nat. Opera, 1973. Career: Apps. w. English Nat. Opera as Gaston in La Traviata, 1973, English Opera Grp. as Prunier in La Rondine, 1974, Glyndebourne Fest. Opera as the Gnat in Cunning Little Vixen, 1975, & Glyndebourne Touring Opera as Sellem in Rake's Progress, 1975. Hobbies: Walking; Gardening. Mgmt: Music Int. Address: 45 Hyacinth Ct., Nursery Rd., Pinner, Middx. HA5 2AP, UK.

MATHEW, Gladys Hagee, b. 3 Mar. 1896, Denver, Colo., USA. Singer; Writer; Teacher of Singing. Educ: BA, Univ. of Colo., 1918; MA, Tchrs. Coll., 1940, Dip. of Specialization in Opera, 1941, Columbia Univ.; Dana Schl. of Music. m. Steere de Montfort Mathew. Career incls: Opera Singer in USA; tours of USA, Austria Czech.; roles incl: Violetta, Gilda, Lucia, Rosina, Mimi Maguerite. Comps: num. songs inclng. song cycles Tell Me, Love & Wild Flowers. Recordings: collect. of songs, NY Municipal Radio. Publs: Singer Know Your Voice: The Balances Breath, The Neglected Tongue, The Perfect Vocal Tone, 1967; The Opera Singer On Stage & Off, 1971. Contbr. to musical jrnls. Mbrships. incl: nat. & NY Fedns. of Music Clubs; Bd. of Dirs., Ctrl. Opera Serv. Committee, Metrop. Opera Co.; Fndr. & Pres., Community Opera Inc., 1953-79. Recip., Citation for Serv. to NYC Cultural Environment, from Mayor of NYC, 1969. Address: 160 W 73rd St., Apt. 3-1, NY, NY 10023, USA.

MATHEWS, John Fenton, b. 27 Mar. 1926, Pontiac, Michigan, USA. Musician, (double bass). Educ: Wayne State Univ.; Detroit Inst. of Musical Art; Double bass study w. Gaston Brohan; Peabody Conserv. Debut: Detroit Inst. of Art, 1956. Career: Prin. double bass, Balt. Symph. Orch., 1959-; Tchr. of double bass, Peabody Conserv., John Hopkins Univ. & Cath. Univ., Wash., DC; Artist in res. (summer), Kniesel Hall, Blue Hill, Maine. Hobbies: Sailing; Cycling. Mgmt: Festivals Inc., Baltimore. Address: 1410 Bolton St., Balt., MD 21217, USA.

MATHEWS, Justus Frederick, b. 13 Jan. 1945, Peoria, Ill., USA. Teacher; Composer. Educ: BA (Music), Calif. State Univ., Northridge, 1967; MA, ibid., PhD (Music Composition), SUNY, Buffalo, 1973. m. Barbara Lynne Sugarman, 1 s. Compositions incl: num. works for var. instrumental & vocal media, electronic & computer music, & music for the theatre. Mbrships: Coll. Music Soc.; AAUP; United Profs. of Calif.; Nat. Assn. of Composers USA; Int. Soc. for Contemporary Music, Electronic Music Soc., Los Angeles. Hons. incl: 1st prize, chmbr. ensemble competition, 1967. Hobby: Swimming. Address: 245 Harvard Ln., Seal Beach, CA 90740, USA.

MATHEY, Paul André, b. 14 Apr. 1909, Chaux-de-Fonds, Switzerland. Organist; Pianist; Violinist. Educ: Zurich Conser. m. Paule-Amélie Pettavel, 2 d. Debut: Radio Lausanne. Career incls: Tchr. of Music, Chaux-de-Fonds Secondary Schl.; Organist, Locle, then Grand Temple, Chaux-de-Fonds; Organ concerts given in Paris, Rotterdam, Rome, Cairo, Switzerland, Germany, Lebanon. Comps. (publs) incl: Preludes for Piano; Children's Pieces for Piano. Contbr. to var. jrnls. Mbrships: Dir., Union Male Voice Choir, Colombier; Liederkranz Male Voice Choir, Locle. Hons. incl: 1st Prize, Chaux-de-Fonds Cantonal Song Fest., 1969. Hobbies: Climbing; Chess. Address: Montbrillant 11, 2300 Chaux-de-Fonds, Switzerland.

MATHEZ, Jean-Pierre, b. 3 Mar. 1938, Bienne, Switzerland. Trumpet Player; Teacher; Editor. Educ: Music Dip. (trumpet), Geneva Conserv. m. Gabi Wunderlin, 1 s., 1 d. Career: Theatre Orch., Bienne; Berne Symph. Orch.; Solo trumpet, Niedersachsisches Symph. Orch., Hannover; Solo trumpet, Lausanne Chmbr. Radio Orch.; Edward H Tarr Brass Ensemble; Dir., Bur. d'Info. Musicales; Ed., Brass Bulletin. Recordings: w. I Musici (Philips); Edward H Tarr Brass Ensemble (CBS,m harmonia Mundi & EMI); Michel Corboz & Lausanne String Ensemble (ERATO). Publ: New Concept of Trumpet Teaching, 3 vols. Mbr. profl. orgs. Hobbies: Thinking; Sport. Address: BIM c.p. 12, CH 1510 Moudon, Switz.

MATHIAS, William (James), b. 1 Nov. 1934, Whitland, Dyfed, UK. Composer; University Professor. Educ: BMus, Univ. Coll. of Wales, 1956; Lyell-Taylor Schol., RAM, 1956-58; LRAM; FRAM. 1965; DMus (Wales), 1966. m. Margaret Yvonne Collins, 1 d. 1959-68; Sr. Lectr., Univ. of Edinburgh, 1968; Prof. & Hd., Dept. of Music, Univ. of Coll. of N Wales, 1970-; Artistic Dir., N Wales Music Fest., 1972-; Cond.; Pianist; Broadcaster on musical affairs. Num. comps. incl. orchestral, choral, chmbr., instrumental, organ & ch. music. Recordings of own work incl: Ave Rex; Clarinet Concerto; Sinfonietta; Vivat Regina, for Brass Band; Wind Quintet; 2 Piano Sonatas; Divertimento for flute, oboe & piano; Concertino; Partita, Chorale (for organ); Wassail Carol; Elegy for a Prince, for baritone & orch.; Cantata, This Worlde's Joie; Magnificat and Nunc Dimittis; Lift Up Your Heads; Missa Brevis; Communion Service in C; Psalm 150; Fantasy for Organ; Capriccio for flute & piano; Opera, The Servants (w. Iris Murdoch), etc. Mbrships. incl: Welsh Arts Coun.; Music Advsry. Comm. to Brit. Coun.; ISM; CGGB; ISCM (Brit.); Welsh Advsry. Comm. to Brit. Coun. Hons: Bax Soc. Prize for Comp., 1968. Address: Y Graigwen, Cadnant Rd., Menai Bridge, Anglesey, Gwynedd LL59 5NG, UK. 1, 3, 29.

MATHIESEN, Aksel Helge, b. 16 Aug. 1931, Fredericia, Denmark. Conductor; Soloist (organ, harpsichord); Organist & Cantor; Scientist; Teacher of Music. Educ: Royal Danish Music Conserv., Univ. Copenhagen; Organist & Kantor, Royal Danish Music Conserv. m. Irmgard Knopf Mathiesen, 2 children. Debut: Organ soloist, 1958; Orch. Ldr., Copenhagen, 1961. Career: Radio prods. & concerts as organ soloist in Denmark, Sweden, Netherlands & Germany; Ldr., The Concentus Musicus of Denmark w. concerts in Europe, USA & Can.; Radio prods. for Danish Broadcasting Corp. Comps: Ch. Music. Num. recordings. publs: Concentus Musicus (w. Wife). Recip. New Yr. Prize, Danish Broadcasting Corp., 1974. Hobbies: Electronic Equipment; Author, Scientific Articles. Address: Hulvejen 2, Stokkebjerg mark, 4450, Jyderup, Denmark.

MATHIS, Edith, b. 11 Feb. 1938, Lucerne, Switz. Opera & Concert Singer. Educ: Concert dip., Conserv., Lucerne. m. Bernhard Klee, 1 s., 1 d. Debut: Stadttheater, Lucerne, 1956. Career incls: apps. at major opera houses & fests. in Europe, UK & USA; tours in Far E & Aust.; TV apps. in Figaro, Freischütz, Zauberflöte, Arabella. Recordings incl: Beethoven's Fidelio; Mozart's Masses & Requiem; Bach Cantatas; Brahms Requiem;

Lieder records of Mozart (complete), Wolf, Brahms, etc. Mbmt: H U Schmid, Hannover, Germany. Address: Thurbergstr. 11, 8570 Weinfelden, Switz.

MATHIS, George Russell, b. 22 July 1926, USA. Choral Conductor; Music Administrator. Educ: BM, Ill. Wesleyan Univ.; MMusEd., EdD, Univ. of Ill. m. Barbara Beth Browns, 2 s. Career: Tchr., pub. schl.; AUS; Assoc. Dir., Choral Activities, Univ. of Ill.; Prof. of Music, Univ. of Okla.; Cond., Schl. & univ. choirs throughout US, Can., Europe; Workshops in schl. vocal music & ch. music. Contbr. to Music Educators Source Book III, 1966, & profl. jrnls. Mbrships: Nat. VP, Am. Choral Dirs. Assn.; Past Nat. Choral Chmn., Music Tchrs. Nat. Assn.; Bd., Interamerican Choral Dirs. Assn.; Bd., SW Jeunesse Musicale, Carnegie Hall; AAUP; Past Province Gov., Phi Mu Alpha Sinfonia; Pi Kappa Lambda. Hons: Guest of Ambassadors of Friendship, Romania, 1973, Poland, 1974; Choirs chosen for var. nat. musical meetings & at Vienna, 1969, '72. Address: Univ. House, Univ. of Okla., Norman, OK 73069, USA.

MATIC-MAROVIC, Darinka, b. 6 Feb. 1937, Herceg-Novi, Yugoslavia. Musician; Conductor; Docent Faculty of Music Art (pianoforte). Educ: Piano & Theory, Acad. of Music, Belgrade; Cond. Orch. & Choir & Docent of Fac. of Music Art, Belgrade. m. Debut: Public Concerts, Belgrade. Career: Apps. w. Academic Chmbr. Choir Collegium Musicum, Belgrade, symph. & chmbr. orch. & var. choirs at concerts, music festivals, on radio & TV in Yugoslavia, Italy, France, UK, Belgium, W & E Germany, Russia, Norway, Czechoslovakia, Poland & Mexico; Worldwide soloist, singer & folk dancer. Comps. incl: arrs. of Yugoslav nat. music performed in Yugoslavia & abroad. Mbr. num. profl. orgs. Recip. var. hons., prizes & dips. Hobbies: Swimming; Rowing; Travel; Folk Dancing. Address: Fac. of Music Art, Marshall Tito Str. 50, 11000 Belgrade, Yugoslavia.

MATOUŠEK, Lukáš, b. 29 May 1943, Prague, Czech. Composer; Clarinettist; Performer on Mediaeval Instruments. Educ: Prague Conserv. of Music; studied comp. w. Miloslav Kavelác, 1969-. m. Zuzana Matousková, 1 d. Debut: cond. Smetana's Ma Vlast, Prague Symph. Orch. Career: Artistic Ldr., Ars Cameralis; num. apps. as perf., ibid. & w. Prague Madrigalists, both live & broadcast on radio & TV, throughout Europe. Comps. incl: orchl. works, inclng. Stories for orchestra; Concerto for percussion & winds; chmbr. music inclng. Orpheus Overwhelmed (flute, viola & harp or piano); vocal works inclng. Cnatata (Vulgata) & Klarka's Rhymes (children's choir); electronic & theatre music. Recordings: Panton label, Czech. Contbr. to Opus Musicum, Bron. Mbrships: Youth Grp., Union of Czech. Comps. & Artists; Umelecká Beseda. Recip., sev. comp. awards. Hobbies: Mediaeval Notation; Constructing Mediaeval Instruments; Mountaineering; Skiing; Canoeing. Mgmt: Music Info. Ctr., HIS, Besedni 3, 118 00 Prague. Address: Vápencová 10, 147 00 Prague, Czech.

MATSON, Sigfred Christian, b. 17 Feb. 1917, Chgo., Ill., USA. Music Teacher; Pianist. Educ: BA, Ohio Wesleyan Univ., 1943; BMus, Am. Conserv. of Music, 1937; MMus, piano, ibid., 1938; MMus, comp., 1939; PhD, comp., Eastman Schl. of Music, 1947. m. Mildred Zimmer Matson, 2 s., 4d. Career: Fac. Mbr., Sioux Falls Coll., Sioux Falls, SD, 1939-41; Ohio Wesleyan Univ., Delaware, Ohio, 1941-44; Monmouth Coll., Ill., 1947-490; Miss. Univ. for Women (Hd. of Music Dept.), 1949-; Mbrships. incl: Chmn., Region VII, Nat. Assn. of Schls. of Music, 1962-64; Exec. Bd., Music Tchrs. Nat. Assn., 1971-74; 1976-80; Exec. Bd., Southern Div. of Music Tchrs. Nat. Assn., 1971-73; 1976-80; VP, Prog., ibid., 1974-76; Pres., ibid., 1976-78; Pres., Miss. Music Tchrs. Assn., 1966-69; Pres., Miss Music Educators Assn., 1961-62. Recip. many comp. grants from Miss. Univ. for Women. Musician of Yr., Miss. Fedn. of Music Clubs, 1973. Hobbies: Gardening; Raising registered Polled Hereford Cattle. Address: Star Rte., Box 220-2 Columbus, MS 39701, USA. 2, 7, 12, 23.

MATSUDAIRA, Yori-Aki, b. 27 Mar. 1931, Tokyo, Japan. Composer. Educ: Grad., Biol., Fac. of Sci., Tokyo Metrop. Univ., 1953; DSc, ibid., 1965. m. Yoko Tanabe, 1 d. Compositions incl: Orbits for Flute, Clarinet & Piano; Co-Action for Violoncello & Piano; Distributions for String Quartet & Ring Modulator; What's Next? for Soprano & 2 Noise Makers; coherency for Flute, Clarinet, Percussion, Harp & Electric Piano; Brilliancy for Flute & Piano. Recordings: Rhymes; Co-Action; Allotropy. Contbr. to jrnls. Mbrships: Exec. Sec., Japanese Sect., ISCM; Mbr., TranSonic composers grp. Hons: Selected, ISCM Fests., 1958, '67, '69, '72, '75; Award for Contempl. Music, Nippon Roche Co., Tokyo, 1967. Hobby: Collecting butterflies. Address: 31-9, 3 chome Kasugacho. Nerima-ku, Tokyo, Japan.

MATSUMAE, Norio, b. 11 Feb. 1931, Tokyo, Japan. Musicologist. Educ: Grad., Tokyo Univ. of Arts; studied Musicol. w. Kazuyuki Tohyama, Comp. w. Tomoziro Ikenouchi; studied in

France. m. Sumiko Ikeda, 2 children. Career: Prof., Grad. Schl., Tohkai Univ.; Dir., Rsch. Inst. of Arts, ibid; Dean, Faculty of Humanities & Culture, ibid. Publs. incl: (as transl.) W P Malm, Music Cultures of the Pacific, the Near East & Asia, 1967; Bruno Nettle, Folk & Traditional Music of the Western Continents, 1973. Contbr. to: Proceedings Jrnl., Fac. of Letters, Tohkai Univ., 1967; Jrnl. Japanese Musicol. Soc., 1973. Mbrships: Int. Musicol. Soc.; Japanese Musicol. Soc. Address: 12-11, 2 Nishi-Kamakura, Kamakura, Japan.

MATSUMOTO, Shigemi, b. Denver, Colo., USA. Soprano. Educ: BM, Calif. State Coll. at Northridge. m. Martin J Stark. Debut: San Fran. Opera Fall Int. Season, 1968. Career incls: San Fran., Portland, Tucson, Augusta, Lake George, Toledo-Dayton & Ark. Operas; Spring Opera Theatre; San Fran., Pittsburgh St. Louis, Houston & Wichita Symphs.; Minnesota Orch.; Antwerp Phil.; over 150 recitals throughout USA & Can., inclng. San Fran., Los Angeles, Vancouver, Houston, San Antonio & Kansas City. Hons. incl: Reg. Winner, Metrop. Opera Auditions, 1967; 1st Prize, San Fran. Opera Nat. Auditions, 1968; Award Winner, Geneva Int. Competition, 1971; Japanese Woman of the Yr., for S. Calif. Hobbies: Camping; Antiques; Pets. Mgmt: Columbia Artists Mgmt., 165 W 57th St., NYC, NY 10019, USA. Address: 60 Riverside Dr., Apt. 1D, NYC, NY 10024, USA.

MATSUMURA, Vera Yoshi, b. Oakland, Calif., USA. Concert Pianist; Music Educator. Educ: Collegiate Degree, Coll. of Holy Names, Oakland, Calif., 1938; studied w. F Moss, M Shapiro, L Kreutzer, P Jarrett. m. Jiro Matsumura, 1 s. Career: num. concerts in Japan, Thailand, Far East; num. Radio perfs., USA & Japan; var. Teaching Appts., presently Dir., Int. Music Coun. Mbrships: Alpha Phi Mu; Music Tchrs. Nat. Assn.; MTA of Calif.; Int. Platform Assn. Names to Hall of Fame, Piano Guild, 1968. Address: 2 Claremont Cres., Berkeley, CA 94705, USA. 27.

MATTHEN, Lida Etta Rice, b. 15 May 1936, Knoxville, Tenn., USA. Professor of Music; Organist-Choirmaster. Educ: BA, Univ. of Richmond, Va., 1957; MMus, 1958, DMus, 1973, Ind. Univ.; grad. studies, Schl. of Sacred Music, Union Theol. Sem., NYC, Schl. of Music, Northwestern Univ., Evanston, Ill.;o pvte. study, piano w. Hilton Ruffy; Organ w. Oswald G Ragatz; Harpsichord w. Gustav Leonhardt. m. Paul Seymout Matthen, 1 d. Career incls: organ recitals; Adj. Prof. of Music, Ind. State Univ., Terre Haute, 1964-; Asst. Organist Choirmaster, 1965-72, Organist-Choirmaster, 1973-, 1st Presby Ch., Bloomington, Ind. Mbrships: Phi Beta Kappa; Pi Kappa Lambda; AGO; Mortar Bd.; Kappa Delta Pi. Hobbies: Art Hist.; Sewing; Tennis. Address: 1333 E. Davis St., Bloomington, IN 47401, USA.

MATTHEN, Paul Seymour, b. 5 May 1914, Pawling, NY, USA. Bass Baritone; Professor of Music. Educ: BA, Bard-St. Stephen's Coll., Columbia Univ., 1937; grad. work, Columbia, 1937-39; pvte. study in voice & organ. m. Lida Etta Rice, 1 d. Career incls: Soloist, Radio City Music Hall, 1940-43; apps. w. major symph. orchs., recitals, concert tours, USA, Can., Europe; Leading Baritone, Stuttgart State Opera, Germany, 1955-57; Dir., Am. Bach. Soc., NY, 1949-51; Fac. appts. at var. colls., univs., etc. 1945-, Prof., Schl. of Music & Grad. Schl., Ind. Univ., 1958-. Has made num. recordings. Contbr. to Notes. Mbrships. incl: Am. & Int. Musicol. Soc.; Music Lib. Assn. Recip. hons. Mgmt: Albert Kaye Assocs., 58 W 58th St., NYC. Address: Schl. of Music, Ind. Univ., Bloomington, IN 47401, USA. 3.

MATTHEW, Jean Foster, b. 17 June 1945, Ft. Myers, Fla., USA. Associate Professor. Educ: BA, MA, PhD, Fla. State Univ. m. Charles Fredrick Matthew II, 1 s., 1 d. Career: Assoc. Prof., Music & Interdisciplinary Studies also trombone, Norfolk State Coll., Va., Engl., Geo. Wash. Univ., Wash., DC; Lectr. on musical subjects. Contbr. to: Pan Pipes (former assoc. ed.); Fla. Libs. Mbrships. incl: Nat. Bd., Tau Beta Sigma; Sigma Alpha Iota; Am. Musicol. Soc.; AGO; Int. Trombone Assn.; MENC. Hons. icnl; Sword of Hon., Tallahassee Sigma Alpha Iota, 1975. Hobbies: Sailing; Skiing; Tennis. Address: 5666 Heathwood Ct., Virginia Beach, VA 23462, USA. 23, 29.

MATTHEWS, Bruce R, b. 12 Apr. 1949, Madison, Wis., USA. Musician (horn). Educ: BMus, Univ. of Wis.; MMus, Univ. of Idaho. m. Susan Hoeft, 2 d. Debut: Performance of Mozart's 3rd Horn Concerto, age 17. Career: currently mbr., Spokane Symph. Orch., & Northwest Wind Quartet; Instr. of Horn, Univ. of Idaho; broadcast in 6-pt. TV series w. Northwest Wind Quatet, PBS-TV. Mbrships: Int. Horn Soc. Hon: Full Schlrship. to Univ. of Wis., 1967. Hobbies: Basketball; Softball; Gardening. Address: E. 11120 26th Ave., Spokane, WA 99206, USA.

MATTHEWS, Clifford, b. 31 Oct. 1937, Holywell, N Wales, UK. Music Advisor. Educ: BA, Open Univ.; RMCM;

ARMCM; LRAM; ARCM. m. Betty Matthews. Career: Hd., Music Dept., Trinity Fields Secondary Schl., Stafford; Hd., Music Dept., Leek Boys Grammar Schl., Staffs.; Lectr. in music, St. Paul's Coll., Rugby; Music Advisor, Wakefield Metropolitan Dist. Coun. Mbr., Music Advisors' Nat. Assn. Hobbies: Mountaineering; Reading; Music. Address: 25 Hill Top Rd., Grenoside, Sheffield, Yorks., UK.

MATTHEWS, David Henry, b. 12 Apr. 1949, Leicester, UK. Violinist. Educ: LRAM. m. Sheila Gibbard. Debut: w. Medici String Quartet, Wigmore Hall, London, 1973. Career: Mbr., Medici String Quartet (res., York Univ., 1974-77); var. BBC broadcasts; Yorks. TV, 1976. Recordings: EMI. Hobby: Real Ale. Address: Music Dept., Univ. of York, York YO1 5DD, UK.

MATTHEWS, Denis, b. 27 Feb. 1919, Coventry, Warks., UK. Pianist; Professor of Muslc. Educ: RAM. m. (1) Mira Howe, 1941, 1 s., 3 d. (2) Brenda McDermott, 1963, 1 s., 1 d. Debut: London, 1939. Career: Num. recitals & tours in UK, USA, Can.; World Tour, 1964; Tours of Latin Am., 1968, 1970; Tchr. & Lectr.; Prof. of Music, Univ. of Newcastle upon Tyne, 1971-. Publs: In Pursuit of Music, 1966; Beethoven's Piano Sonatas, 1967. Mbrships: Arts Coun. of Gt. Britain, 1972-. Hons: CBE; MA (Newcastle); Hon. DMus, (St. Andrews); Hon. DMus, (Hull); FRAM; Hon. FTCL. Hobbies: Astronomy; 18th Century Engl. Furniture; Reading. Address: Dept. of Music, Univ. of Newcastle upon Tyne, UK.

MATTHEWS, Enid Noel, b. 25 DEc. 1905, Hawthorn, Vic., Aust. Organ Historian; Writer. Educ: grad., Assoc. in Theology. m. Charles Ivor Matthews, 2 c. (dec.). Career: 14 yrs. rsch. into hist. of early chs. & organs in Aust. Publs: Colonial Organs & Organbuilders, 1969; The Sound of Strings, 1975; I'll Be Better Tomorrow, 1979. Contbr. of 8 articles on early chs. & organs to The Age, 1964-65; sev. other articles for Organ Histl. Trust of Aust. News & Vic. Organ Jrnl. Mbrships: Vic. Soc. of Organists (hon. life mbr.); Organ Histl. Trust of Aust.; Vic. Fellowship of Aust. Writers. Hobbies: Handicrafts; Teaching Children; Writing; Music. Address: 11 Cambridge Rd., Mooroolbark, Vic. 3138, Aust.

MATTHEWS, Justus Frederick, b. 13 Jan. 1945, Peoria, Ill., USA. Composer; Clarinettist; University Professor. Educ: BA, Calif. State Univ., Northridge; MA, ibid.; PhD, SUNY, Buffalo. m. Barbara Lynne Sugarman, 1 s., 1 d. Career: Perfs. of original comps. in USA & abroad; Univ. Prof.; Clarinettist. Comps: Bionic Music, for 4 channel tape; comps. incl. num. works for var. instrumental & vocal media, electronic & computer music, & music for the theatre. Mbrships: Int. Soc. for Contemporary Music; Writer affiliate of SESAC, NY. Hons: Dean's List, Calif. State Univ., 1963-64; 1st Prize in Comp., ibid., 1964-65; 1st Prize in chmbr. ensemble competition, ibid., 1967. Hobby: Swimming. Address: 245 Harvard Lane, Seal Beach, CA 90740, USA.

MATTHEWS, Michael Gough, b. 12 July 1932, Wanstead, Essex, UK. Pianist; Music Administrator. Educ: Studied w. Sir Percy Buck, Frank Merrick, RCM; ARCM Dips. in Piano, Organ Schl. Music; ARCO; Dip., Corso di Perfezionamento, S Cecilia Acad., Rome; pvte. studies w. Harold Craxton, Carlo Zecchi, Rome, & Dziewiecki, Warsaw. Career: Supvsr., Jr. Studies & Sr. Lectr., RSAM; Dir., Jr. Dept. & Prof., RCM; Registrar, ibid., 1976-; Recitals, Concertos, most European countries & BBC. Publs: Musical Entertainments Based on Aesop Fables (co-author); Nine Lessons & Carols. Mbr., ISM. Hons: Hopkinson Gold Medal, RCM, 1953; Nagrocki PRize, Chopin Int. Piano Competition, 1955; FRCM, 1972. Address: Royal Coll. of Music, Prince Consort Rd., London SW7 2BS, UK.

MATTHUS, Siegfried, b. 13 April 1934, Mallenuppen, Ostpreussen, (now) USSR. Comp. Educ: German Music Acad. Berlin, State exam; German Art Acad. m. Helga Matthus-Spitzer, 1 s. Career: since 1958 permanent musician TV, Radio, Film; Perf. symph. works, ballet, opera in all European countries. Japan, USA, South Am., Aust. Comp. incl: Concert for violoncello and orch., 1975; Operas; Ballets; Chmbr. music. Recordings: many of own works. Mgmt: Artists Agency DDR, Krausenstr. 8-10, 102 Berlin. Mbrships: var. profl. orgs. Hons: 1961 Bronze Medal Song Contest, Vienna World Festival; 1963 Ernst Zinna Prize, Berlin; 1969 Hans Eisler Prize; 1970 Art Prize DDR; 1972 Nat. Prize DDR. Hobbies: Travelling. Address: Elisabethweg 10, 110 Berlin, German Dem. Repub.

MATTHYS, Abel, b. 29 Dec. 1921, Lovendegem, Belgium. Piano Teacher; Conservatory Director. Educ: Dips. in piano & harmony, 1940, chmbr. music, 1941, piano (higher dip.) & fugue, 1943, Royal Conserv. of Ghent. m. Denise van Wanseele, 5 children. Career: piano recitals & concerts w. orchs. in Belgium, France, UK & Netherlands; radio perfs. in Belgium & UK & Netherlands; radio perfs. in Belgium & Netherlands; TV perfs. in

Belgium; Dir., Conserv. of Kortrijk; Piano Tchr., Royal Conserv. of Ghent: Prof. of Piano, Royal Conserv., Brussels, 1978-. Hons. incl: Laureate, Nat. Music Competition, Brussels, 1945. Address: Abdisstraat 10, 9000 Ghent, Belgium.

MATTILA, Edward Charles, b. 30 Nov. 1927, Duluth, Minn., USA. Professor of Music Theory & Composition. Educ: BA; MMus; PhD. m. Nancy Norton, 1 s., 1 d. Career: has taught in sev. colls. & univs., currently Prof., & Dir. of Electronic Music Studio, Univ. of Kan. Compositions: has done works for chmbr., choral & orchestral ensembles & for electronic media, inclng. Paritions for String Orchestra, Six Arrays for Piano, Thirteen Ways of Looking at a Blackbird for reciter, chorus & chmbr. ensemble. Contbr. reviews to newspapers. Mbrships: Am. Soc. of Univ. Composers; Am. Music Ctr.; Coll. Music Soc.; Kan. Composers Forum; Pi Kappa Lambda. Recip. of sev. univ. rsch. grants for composition, 1968-. Hobbies: Painting; Photog.; Astron. Address: Schl. of Fine Arts, Univ. of Kan., Lawrence, KS 66044, USA.

MATTINGLY, Richard Egart, b. 20 Feb. 1950, Louisville, Ky., USA. Percussionist. Educ: BMus Ed., Univ. of Louisville, 1972; MMus, ibid., 1975. Career: Percussionist, Louisville Orch., Kentucky Opera Assn., Kurt Siegert Orch. Recordings: var. works w. Louisville Orch. (1st Edition Records). Contbr. to: Modern Drummer Mag. Mbrships: Percussive Arts Soc.; Am. Fedn. of M usicians, local 11637. Address: 18000 Woodbourne Ave., Louisville, KY 40205, USA.

MATTMANN, Erwin, b. 21 March 1942, Trimbach, Switz. Organist Choir leader. Educ: Basle conserv.; Freiburg Univ., Switz. Debut: Bach organ recital, Bern. Career: Num. concerts all over Europe; fndr. of "Orgelmusik nach Feierabend" (organ music after work), Bern. Comps: Deutsche Messe, op. 1, 1975; Psalm 84 op. 2, 1975; Passion nach Johannes op. 3, 1976. Contbr. to: Katholische Kirchenmusik; Schweizerische Musikzeitung. Mbrships: Schweizerische Musik-pädagogischer Verband (Swiss Soc. of music tchng.). Hobbies: Lit.; politics; swimming; hiking. Address: Sprünglistr. 15, 3006 Bern, Switz.

MATTSON, Sally Jeanne, b. 26 Mar. 1948, Augusta, Maine, USA. Music Educator; Performer, Viola da Gamba (Flute, Clarinet & Alto Saxophone). Educ: BMus, Northern Conserv. Music, 1969; Grad. studies, Kent State, Cleveland State & Cornell Univs.; Viola da Gamba, Baldwin Wallace Conserv., Renaissance Consort & Cornell Univs., Barea, Ohio. m. James Robert Mattson. Career incls: Music Dir., Bratenahl HS, Ohio; Perfs. w. Hal Butler's Orch., Baldwin Wallace Collegium Musicum; Cleveland State Univ. Collegium; currently w. Ganassi Early Music Ensemble & The Gtr. Perfect System Early Music Ensemble. Mbr. profl. orgs. Hobbies: Snow Skiing; Tropical Plant Growing; Trng. & showing Airedale terriers. Address: 10207 Foster Ave., Bratenahl, OH 44108, USA.

MATUSZCZAK, Bernadetta, b. 10 Mar. 1937, Thorn, Poland. Composer. Educ: Dip. (comp.), Music Acad., Warsaw, 1964; Dip. (Piano, theory), Music High Schl., Poznań, 1958. Comps: Septem Tubae, for choir, organ & orch.; Juliet & Romeo, Chmbr. opera; Humanae Voces, oratorio; Rilke's songs for baritone & orch.; Salmi, for quintet; The Mystery of Heloise, opera; Diary of a Fool, chmbr. opera. Recordings: Salmi; Elegy of a Polish Boy, for soprano & orch.; chmbr. drama, Apocalypsis. Mbr. Polish Comps. Assn. Hons: Young Comps. award, 1965; Grzegorz Fitelberg Comps. prize, 1966; Jeunesses Musicales award, 1967. Address: J S Bacha 34 m. 407, 02743 Warsaw, Poland.

MATZ, Rudolf, b. 19 Sept. 1901, Zagreb, Croatia, Yugoslavia. Cellist; Conductor; Composer; Teacher; Music Writer; Music Therapist; Poet. Educ: Dip., Zagreb Music Acad., Zagreb Univ., 1926. m. Margita Matz. Career: HS Tchr., 1930-50; Music Acad., 1950-72; E O Prof., ibid., 1952-62; O Prof., ibid., 1962-72; Ret'd., 1972. Comp. of var. works for piano, string & wind instruments, chmbr. music, orch., choir, solo voice w. accomp., pieces for the theatre. Mbrships. incl: Hon. Mbr., Assn. of Music Tchrs. in Croatia; Pres.; Soc. for Promotion of Music Therapy, Zagreb. Publs: The First Years of Violoncello (32 vols.). Contbr. to profl. jrnls. Recip., var. hons. Address: Zagreb 41000, Mesnicka 15, Yugoslavia.

MAUCERI, John Francis Peter, b. 12 Sept. 1945, NYC, USA. Conductor; Educator. Educ: BA, Yale Univ., 1967; MPhil, ibid., 1971; Conducting Fellow, Berkshire Music Fest., 1971. m. Betty Weiss Mauceri. Career incls: Cond., Metropol. Opera; Los Angeles Phil.; San Fran. Symph.; Nat. Symph.; L'Orch. Nat. de France, Eurpean premiere, Bernstein 'Mass', Vienna, 1973; European premiere, Menotti 'Tamu-Tamu', Spoleto, 1974; W Coast premiere Britten 'Death in Venice', San Fran., 1975; Santa Fe Opera; New Orleans Opera; Israel Phil.; Phila. Orch.; Scottish Opera; NYC Opera; Welsh Nat. Opera; PBS/BBC/EuroVision TV broadcast; Cond. NSO for Leonard Bernstein's 60th Birthday

Concert. Recordings incl: Bernstein 'Candide'. Contbr. to Yale Alumni Mag. Mbr., Elizabethan Club. Hobbies incl: Tennis; Yoga. Mgmt: Columbia Artists. Address: c/o Columbia Artists (Conductors' Division), 165 W 57th St., NY, NY 10019, USA.

MAUD, Arthur, b. 1932, Bradford, UK. Composer; Head of Music Department, Metropolitan Community College, Minneapolis, Minn., USA; Soloist; Organist. Educ: BA, MA & Ed. Cert., Univ. Utah; Hochschule fur Musik, Munich, Germany; PhD, Univ. Minn. Career incls: Dir., Concentus Musicus, 12 yrs.; Ch. Organist & Choir dir. num. chs. inclng. Christ Episc. Ch., St. Paul; Dir., Univ. of Minn., Men's Glee Club; Teaching Asst., Humanities Dept., Univ. Minn., 2 yrs.; Music Cons., Minnemath, 2 yrs.; Dir., Met. Chorale & Renaissance Ensemble, 5 yrs.; Dir. of Music, Breck Schl., 1 yr.; Chmn., State Jr. Coll. Fine Arts Assn., 1 1/2 yrs.; Dir., Project TV, Experimental Music Schl., 4 yrs.; Chmn., Music Dept., Metropolitan Community Coll. Address: 116 Warwick SE, Minneapolis, MN 55414, USA.

MAUERHOFER, Alois, b. 12 June 1946, Fürstenfeld, Austria. Ethnomusicologist. Educ: studied guitar, HS for Music; Dr phil., musicol., also studied hist. & philos. Author: Leonhard von Call, Musik des Mittelstandes zur Zeit der Wiener Klassik, 1974. Contbr. to var. musical publs. inclng: Grove's Dictionary of Music & Musicians 6; Österreichische Musikzeitschrift; Die Musikforschung. Hobby: Classical & flamenco guitar. Address: 8265 Gschmaier 41, Austria.

MAULTSBY, Portia, b. 11 June 1947, Orlando, Fla., USA. Assistant Professor of Ethnomusicology; Ensemble Director. Educ: BMus, Benedictine Coll., Atchison, Kan., 1968; Univ. Salzburg, Austria, 1966; MMus, Univ. Wis., 1969; PhD, ibid., 1974. Career: Asst. Prof., Ethnomusicol., Afro-Am. Studies Dept., Ind. Univ., Bloomington; Dir., Ind. Univ. Soul Revue (performing ensemble, instrumentalists, vocalist, dancers, poets, masters of ceremonies & tech. staff). Comps: Tell Me 'Bout It (Instrumental); Wait Until Morning (Vocal); You Bringin' me Good Vibes (Vocal). Contbr. to var. publs. inclng: Freeing the Spirit, Vol. X, 1976; The Black Perspective in Music, 1976. Mbr. profl. orgs. Hons. incl: 1st prize, comps. Guest Ed., Jrnl. of the Soc. for Ethnomusicol., 1975. Hobbies incl: Tennis. Address: 537 Plymouth Rd., Bloomington, IN 47401, USA.

MAUNDER, Peter Anthony, b. 16 Jan. 1936, Bradford, UK. Clarinettist. Educ: RCM; ARCM. m. Elizabeth Griffiths, 1 s., 1 d. Career: London Phil. orch., 1966-; London Bach Orch. Mbr. Royal Soc. of Musicians. Hobbies: Sailing; Cooking. Address: 86 Lakenheath, Southgate, London N14, UK.

MAURICE-AMOUR, Lila Elisabeth, b. 16 Feb. 1906, Paris, France. Musicologist; Music Critic; Professor. Educ: Lic. ès Lettres, Univ. of Lille; musical studies w. Maurince Amour. m. Maurice Amour (dec.), 1 s., 1 d. Career: Broadcasts on French radio on "Les Poetes et leur Musiciens" & musical hist.; tchr., Univ., Paris-Sorbonne, 1955-; tchr. Univ. Sorbonne Nouvelle, 1960-; Prof., hist. of music, Univ. of Paris (Paris III & IV). Contbr. to num. profl. publs. Mbrships: French Musicol. Assn.; Int. Assn. of French Studies; Friends of Mozart Soc.; Claudel Soc.; Paul Valéry Soc.; Jean Giraudoux Soc.; sec.-gen., Chateaubriand Soc. Hons: Chevalier de la Légion d'Honneur, 1951; Off. des Arts et Lettres, 1955; Off. de l'Ordre Nat. du Mérite, 1972. Address: 122 Boulevard de Courcelles, 75017 Paris, France.

MAUST, Ezma M. (Cobb), b. 29 Jan. 1914, Palco, Kan., USA. Piano & Organ Teacher. Educ: AA (Music); Dip., Sherwood Music Schl., Chgo.; Tchrs. Trng. Cert. m. Paul C Maust, 1 s., 3 d., 1 step-d. Career: Tchr. of piano, harmony & theory, & spinet organ, 22 yrs. Mbr: Nat. Guild of Piano Tchrs. Recip: Cert., Nat. Hon. Roll of Guild Tchrs., 1973. Hobbies: Reading; Cooking; Sewing; Crochet; Camping; Music. Address: 5714 Academy Dr., Paradise, CA 95969, USA.

MAW, Nicholas, b. 5 Nov. 1935, Grantham, Lincs., UK. Composer. Educ: RAM, 1955-58; study w. Nadia Boulanger & Max Deutsch, Paris, 1958-59; FRAM., 1973. Compositions:O One-Man Show, 1964, The Rising of the Moon, 1970 (operas); Scenes & Arias, 1962, Sinfonia, 1966, Sonata for Strings & 2 Horns, 1967, Concert Music for Orchestra, 1972, Serenade for Small Orchestra, 1973, Life Studies for 15 Solo strings, 1974. Odyssey for Orchestra, 1974-79, (concert works); Chamber Music, 1962, String Quartet, 1965 (chamber works). Recip., Lili Boulanger Prize, 1959. Address: c/o Boosey & Hawkes Ltd., 295 Regent St., London W1A 1BR, UK. 1, 3, 14.

MAWBY, Colin, b. 9 May 1936, Portsmouth, UK. Conductor; Composer; Broadcaster; Writer; Lecturer; Organist; Percussionist. Educ: Westminster Cathedral Choir Schl.; RCM. Career: Master of Music at Westminster Cathedral, 1961-78;

Fndr., Westminster Cathedral Str. Orch. & New Westminster Chorus; apps. on British & Italian TV & Eurovision; broadcasts on BBC, French, Canadian, German, Dutch, Belgian & Am. radio; Prof., TCL; has given sev. 1st perfs.; apps. at Promenade Concerts & at fests. at Flanders, Windsor, City of London, Westminster & Merton; has cond. BBC Singers, London Mozart Players, Pro Cantione Antiqua. Comps: 6 masses, many motets & psalms. num. recordings. Contbr. to: The Times; Listener; Tablet. Mbrships: Musicians' Unin; VP, Engl. Pueri Cantotes. Hons: Off. of Merit, Knights of Malta. Hobby: Wine drinking. Address: 16 Stafford Mansions, Stafford Pl., London SW1, UK. 1, 28.

MAXIMOFF, Richard Michael, b. 26 May 1943, Evansville, Ind., USA. Concert Viola Soloist. Educ: BMus, MMus, Juilliard Schl. of Music; pvte. studies w. Emanuel Vardi. m. Ingeborg Maria Groner, 2 d. Debut: Town Hall, NYC, 1963. Career: participant in world première chmbr. concerts w. num. major contemporary musicians; TV apps.; J F Kennedy Memorial Recital, Wilmington, Del., 1963; radio recitals; Owner, 16th century viola, "The Ex-Furmansky". Comps: Mrs. H H A Beach Quintett; Sir Arthur Foote Quintett (both piano & strings); Andrew Imbrie Octet; Ives Fest. (chmbr. orch.). Recordings as soloist w. US Army Studio Orch., 1966-69, Newport Romantic Music Fest., 1971, etc. Hons. incl: Jan & Bertha Werther Prize, Juilliard Schl. of Music; Efrem Kurtz Scholarship, NY Univ.; Chancellor's Award, Univ. of Kansas.

MAXTED, George Alfred, b. 1911, London, UK. Professor of Trinity College of Music, London. Educ: TCM. m. Beryl Victorine Cousens. Career: Covent Garden Opera Co., 1932; Prin. Trombone, Scottish Orch., 1933-36; Glyndebourne Orch., 1936-; Prin. Trombone, BBC Theatre Orch., 1936-39; LPO, 1944-55, Sadler's Wells Opera Orch., 1963-70; Prof., TCM, 1937-48, & 1970-. Publs: 20 Studies for Tenor Trombone, 1953; Talking about the Trombone, 1970. Hobby: Horticulture. Address: Berylands, Horley Lodge Lane, Salfords, Surrey RH1 5EA, UK. 3.

MAXWELL, Barbara, b. 1941, Greeley, Colo., USA. Librarian. Educ: BA, Pomona Coll., 1962; MA, 1965, MLS, 1967, Univ. of Calif., Berkeley; studied organ w. Lee Suitor. m. Douglas L Maxwell. Career: Ref. Libn., Univ. of Calif., Berkeley, 1966-69; Ref. Libn.-Music Libn., SUNY Binghampton, 1969-73; Music Cataloger, Lib. of Congress, 1973-75; Chief Ref. Libn., Geo. Wash. Univ., 1975-. Contbr. to Antiphony. Mbrships: Music Lib. Assn.; Am. Musicol. Soc. Mediaeval Acad. of Am. Recip. Phi Beta Kappa, 1962. Address: 4410 Davenport St., NW, Wash., DC 20016, USA.

MAXWELL, Melinda Sara, b. 23 Oct. 1953, London, UK. Oboist; Performer on Baroque Oboe & Cor Anglais. Educ: BA, Univ. of York; ARCM; LTCL. Debut: tour w. Fitzwilliam Quartet. Career: Freelance, Recording. w. Deutsche Bach Solisten. Hobby: Painting in Water Colour. Address: Nettles, Stanton St. Bernard, Marlborough, Wilts., UK.

MAXWELL, Michael, b. 6 Jan. 1936, Westport, NZ. Symphony Orchestra Manager. Educ: Auckland Univ. Career: Prog. Off., NZ Broadcasting Corp., 1955-59; Orch. Mgr., Phil. Orch., London, 1960-63; Tour Mgr., Royal Phil. Orch., 1963; Mgr., Princeton Chmbr. Orch., 1964-65; Promotion Dir., NY Phil., 1965-66; Asst. Mgr., Cleveland Orch., 1966-76; Gen. Mgr., ibid., 1976-; Man. Dir., Opera Co. of Boston, 1976-. Contbr. to Am. Record Guide, 1965-66. Mbrships: incl: Advsry. Comm.; Jr. Commn., Engl. Spkng. Union, Cleveland; Bd. Dirs., Cleveland Ballet Guild. Hobbies: Photography; Golf. Address: 1 Bratenahl Pl., Bratenahl, OH 44108, USA.

MAXWELL, Michael Somerset Cullen, b. 30 Mar. 1921, London, UK. Composer; Teacher of Wind Instruments. Educ: MMus, Dunelm; LRAM (pfte. tchng.). m. Hilary Trevor Clarke, 2 d. Composer, Duets for Treble & Tenor Recorders. Mbrships: CGGB; ISM. Hobbies: Walking; Swimming. Address: 40 St. Mary's Grove, London W4 3LN, UK. 3.

MAXWELL-TIMMINS, Donald, b. 25 June 1927, Newcastle on Tyne, UK. Senior Adviser in Music. Educ: Bede Coll., Durham; RAm & RCM; LRAM; ARCM. m. Margaret Tinsdeall. Career: Music Master at Glaisdale Schl., Nottingham & Newark Magnus Grammar Schl., 1952-62; Lectr. for WEA, Univ. of Nottingham Extra Mural Dept.; Music Adviser, Halifax, 1962-74; Cond., Brit. Youth Choir; Examiner to the Associated Bd. of the RSM; Sr. Advsr. in Music, Calderdale Metro. Borough Educ. Dept. Comps: Three Nonsense Songs (words by Spike Milligan) for voices & percussion. Publ: Hymn Book for Secondary Schls., 1968; Music is Fun, a 5 Book series for Jr. Schls., 1969; Morning has Broken, Jr. hymn book, 1974; Forty Plus Ten (Jr. Song Book), 1978. Contbr. to: BBC Radio Sports. Mbr., ISM. Hobbies: Watching football; Reading. Address: 8 Kelvin Ave., Trimmingham, Halifax, Yorks. HX2 7LU, UK. 4.

MAY, Ernest Dewey, b. 8 May 1942, Jersey City, NJ, USA. Assistant Professor of Organ & Musicology. Educ: AB, Harvard Coll., 1964; MFA, Princeton Univ., 1968; PhD, ibid., 1975; music tchrs. incl. Nadia Boulanger (theory), 1964-66, & André Marchal (organ), 1964-66. m. Eileen Mayhew, 2 s., 5 d. Career incls: Organist & Choirmaster, St. James' Ch., Greenfield Mass.; Asst., St. George's Engl. Ch., Paris, 1965-66; Asst. Organist to Carl Weinrich, Princeton Univ. Chapel, 1967-68; Instructor in Music, Amherst Coll., 1969; Asst. Prof. of Music, ibid., 1971-; Dir., Amherst Coll. Glee Club, 1970-71; Fndr. & Dr., Early Music Consort of Amherst, 1972-; Asst. Prof. of Organ & Musicol., Univ. of Mass., Amherst; Concerts, USA & Europe. Recordings: Music for Trumpet & Organ. Publs: incl: Breitkopf's Role in the Transmission of J S Bach's Organ Chorales, 1974. Contbr. to profl. publs. Mbrships: Am. Musicol. Soc.; AGO; New Bach. Soc., etc. Recip., Rockefeller Fellowship, 1971-72. Address: RD2, Amherst, MA 01002, USA.

MAYER, Abby S, b. 6 July 1928, Bklyn., NY, USA. Solo French Hornist. Educ: BM, New England Conserv. of Music, 1950; Dip., US Naval Schl. of Music, 1965; MA, Columbia Univ., 1968; Profl. Dip., ibid., 1971. m. Marianne Mayer. 2 s. Career: Soloist & Sect. Ldr.; Educ. NCO; Race Rels. & Equal Opportunity NCO; Master Sgt., US Army; Fac., Eastern Ky. Univ., Richmond, Ky.; Cond., Orange Co. Commun. Coll. Band; Prominent Horn Tchr., 1959-; Solo French Hornist, ISMA Band, US Military Acad., West Point. Recordings incl: o R Strauss Concert No. 1 for Horn. Publs: Schmetzig (Humorous Series). Contbr: IMS Mag.; Ky. Tchrs. jrnl. Hobbies: Skiing; Canoeing; Sailing; Philately. Address: 6 Cedar Lane, Box 388, Cornwall, NY 12518, USA.

MAYER, Alfred, b. 11 Nov. 1921, Newark, NJ, USa. Composer; Accordionist; Organist; Conductor; Teacher; Instrument Designer. Educ: Newark Schl. of Fine & Industrial Art; BS. comp., Juilliard Schl. of Music. m. Annette Siegeler, 2 s., 2 d. Career: Army films; Radio NBC; Appearances nationally on var. TV stns., Concertizing as soloist & W Mayer Accordion Ensemble (4 accordions w. full orch.); Soc. band in met. NY, area; Pres., Lonic Inds. Inc.; Pres., Doric Organ Co. Compositions: A Coquette's Chatter; That Old Black magic; Accordion Carnival; Perform Now; Sudatory in Sudan; Lover; Singing Accordion, Electronic Music; Alfred Mayer's Class Method; Great Moments in Music, etc. Recordings: A Holiday in Paris (Pierre & his Left Band Musicians). Contbr. to: World Book Ency.; Perform Now; Electronic Music for the 70's; NY mag.; Life Mag., etc. Mbrships. incl: Am. Fedn. of Musicians (NY, Newark, Morristown); Audio Engrng. Soc. Hobbies: Concertizing; Broadway shows; Reading. Address: 128 James St., Morristown, NJ 07960, USA.

MAYER, George Louis, b. 17 Sept. 1929, Somerville, NJ, USa. Music Librarian. Educ: BA, NY Univ.; MSLS, Columbia Univ.; grad. study under Fulbright grant; Univ. of Cologne, Germany, 1960-61. Career: Music Libn., Music Libn., NY, Pub. Lib., 1955-65, Supvsng. Music Libn., Lib. & Mus. of Performing Arts, Lincoln Ctr., 1965-73; Prin. Music Libn. & Coord., ibid., 1978-. Contbr. to: Hi-Fi Music at Home; Am. Record Guide; Saturday Review; Previews; Am. Reference Books Annual; Lib. Jrnl.; Opera Review; NATS Bulletin Music Bibliographies for Funk & Wagnalls New Ency. Mbrships: Music Lib. Assn.; Chmn., NY Chapt., Music Lib. Assn. Address: 150 W End Ave., NYC, NY 10023, USA. 6, 42.

MAYER, Günther, b. 6 Nov. 1930, Berlin, Germany. Musicologist; Philosopher. Educ: Univ., dip. musicol., phil., 1958-59; Lectr., 1972. m. Irene Mayer-Dölling, 1 d., 1 s. Career: Radio talks, Music and Document, Radio GDRII, 1969; Hans Eiler and Tradition, Radio GDR II, 1968; Hans Eisler on Intelligence in Music, Radio GDR II, 1969; Hegel and Music, Radio GDR II, 1970. Mbrships: Assn. for Comp. and Musicologists GDR, mbr. bd. of dir. since 1972; Cultural Soc. GDR, mbr. bd. of dirs., pres. Central Commission for Music since 1972. Publs: incl: Hans Eisler, Music and Politics, 19245, 1948, Leipzig, München, 1973. Contbr. to: var. profl. jrnls. Address: Bintstr. 49, 110 Berlin, German Dem. Repub.

MAYER, John, b. 28 Oct. 1930, Calcutta, India. Composer; Violinist. Educ: Calcutta Schl. of Music; RAM; studied w. Matyas Seiber. m. Gillian Hepton, 2 s. Comps: Concerto for Orch.; Flute Concerto; Violin Concerto; Clarinet Concerto; Shivanataraj (symph. dances); Sri Krishna, for flute, piano & Tampura. Recordings: Indo-Jazz Fusions 1, 2 & 3; Indo-Jazz Études; Dhammapada; Raga Music for Clarinet; Shanta Quintet for sitar & strgs. Publs: Plain Man's Guide to Indian Music, 1979. Contbr. to: The Composer. Mbr. PRS. Recip., Bombay Madrigal Scholarship. Hobbies: Boxing; Reading Philosophy. Address: 1 Lanark Mansions, Lanark Rd., London W9, UK.

MAYER, (Sir) Robert, b. 1879, Mannheim, Germany. Philanthropist. Educ: Conserv. of Mannheim. m. Dorothy Moulton

Piper, 2 s., 1 d. Career: Co-Fndr., Robert Mayer Concerts for Children; Fndr., Youth & Music, Chmn., Colin Smythe Ltd.; Assoc., LSD, Engl. Chmbr. Orch., Polyphonia, Musicians Benevolent Fund, Anglo-Israel Assoc. of Christians & Jews, Morley Coll., & Saffron Walden Music Clubs. Publs: Young People in Trouble. Hons: MusD, Cleveland Univ., Ohio; Hon. LLF, Leeds; DSc., City Univ.; LOM, Germany; Order of the Crown, Belgium; FRCM; FTCL; Hon. GSM. Address: 11 Bloomfield St., London, EC2, UK. 3.

MAYER-LISMANN, Else Mitia, b. 17 Apr. 1914, Frankfurt, Germany. Musician; Lecturer; Artistic Director. Educ: State Dip., Piano, Dr. Hochs Conserv., Frankfurt. Career: Lectr. on Opera; Artistic Dir., Mayer-Lismann Opera Workshop. Recip. Hon. Degree, RCM. Hobbies: Cooking; Sleeping; Conversation; Bridge; Chess. Address: 61 King's Ct., N, King's Rd., London SW3 5EQ, UK.

MAYER-MARTIN, Donna Jean, b. 26 Feb. 1947, Billings, Mont., USA. Musicologist; Theorist; Teacher of College-level Music. Educ: BMus, St. Mary Coll., Leavenworth, Kane., 1969; MMus, 1972, PhD cand., Coll.-Conserv. of Music, Cinn., OH. m. Donald W Martin. Mbrships: Am. Musicol. Soc.; Coll. Music Soc.; Medieval Acad. of Am. Address: Music Dept., Wake Forest Univ., Winston-Salem, NC 27109, USA.

MAYFIELD, Lida Louise Kendrick, b. 13 Mar. 1948, Tuscaloosa, Ala., USA. Flute Instructor. Educ: BMus, Cinn. Conserv. of Music, Ohio. m. James Robert Mayfield, 2 s. Career: 1st Flautist, Columbus Symph. Orch., Gs., 1964-66; Solo Flautist, w. performing grp. "From Then to Now", 1972; Solo Flautist, Auburn Baroque Ensemble, 1974-76; Flute Instructor, Auburn Univ., 1970-. Publs: Flute Brochure for Ala. All-State Students "Fundemental Flute Tips". Mbrships: Nat. Assn. of Coll. Percussion & Woodwind Instructors; MENC; Nat. Flute Assn. Hons. incl; Cinn. 3 Arts Grant, 1968-70. Address: 1105 Cumberland Dr., Auburn, AL 36830, USA.

MAYGER, Graham, b. 4 Dec. 1942, Middx., UK. Flautist; Piccolo Player. Educ: ARCM; Paris Conserv. m. Jennifer Jane Lesser, 1 s. Debut: Little Symph. Orch. of London, Royal Overseas League, 1967. Career: Prin. Piccolo, BBC Symph. Orch., 1967; Freelance Perf., 1968; played w. LPO, RPO, Halle Orch., Liverpool Phil., London Mozart Players; Bournemouth Sinfonietta & Northern Sinfonia; Proms. solo debut, 1972, w. Northern Sinfonia; BBC recital, 1978; mbr., Charis Trio; Prof., RCM, 1967-. Recordings: Brandenburg 4, w. Northern Sinfonia Orch. Recip., var. musical Prizes & schlrships. UK & France. Hobbies: Reading; Sport; Aircraft Recognition; DIY; Walking. Address: Hillside Cottage, Gt. Horwood, Bucks., UK. 4.

MAYR, Rupert Erich, b. 1 Apr. 1926, LinzDonau, Austria. Professor of Music & Musicology; Pianist; Organist; Conductor. Educ: studied w. Prof. G Pasztory-Göllerich (piano), Prof. H Schmeidel (conducting) at Mozarteum; Bruckner conserv., Linz; LRSM; PhD, Univ. of Innsbruck. m. Erna Mayr, 3 s. Career incls: Tchr. of Piano & Organ, Bruckner Conserv., Linz; successively Lectr., St. Lectr., Rdr. & Prof. & Dept. Hd., Rhodes Univ., Grahamstown, S Africa, 1955-; Co-Ed., Contributions to the development of the piano sonata (series), 2 vols. publd., 1968-70. Contbr. to S African Broadcasting Corp. Hobbies: Photography; Tennis. Address: 22 Southey St., Grahamstown, S Africa.

MAYS, Sally Ann, b. 22 Apr. 1930, Melbourne, Aust. Musician; Pianist. Educ: Univ. Conserv. of Music, Melbourne; RCM; FTCL; ARCM; LRSM; AMusA. m. John Elsom, 2 s. Debut: Melbourne, 1950. Career: Recitals in UK, Europe, Aust., S Africa and Far East, broadcasts in all these countries; apps. w. chmbr. music ensembles. Recordings: Ives, Harris & Rheinberger Trios; Barry Anderson, Piano Pieces I, II & III. Mbrships: ISM; Musicians' Union. Hons: Clarke Scholarship, 1950; Chappell Gold Medal, 1953. Hobbies: Bicycling; Swimming. Mgmt: Choveaux Mgmt., Lowestoft, Suffolk, UK. Address: 39 Elsham Rd., London W14 8HB, UK. 27.

MAZER, Henry. Conductor; Pianist. Educ: Carnegie-Mellon Univ.; Duquesne Univ.; studied w. Georges Enesco, Paris. m. Kathryn F Mazer, 1 s., 1 d. Career: Pianist w. Pitts. Symph., before WWII, returning as Pianist, Personnel Mgr. & 1st Apprentice Cond. under Fritz Reiner; Cond., Wheeling Symph. Orch., W Va., 1948-c.58, & Fla. Symph. Orch., until 1966; Assoc. Cond. under Wm. Steinberg, Pitts. Symph., 1966-70; Music Dir., Mendelssohn Choir; Assoc. Cond., Chgo. Symph., 1970-; Music Dir., Congress of Strings, Cinn., Ohio, 1971 & 72. Address: The Sovereign, 1040 Cananiele Ave., Chgo., IL 60660, USA.

MAZUR, Krzyaztof Antoni, b. 15 Sept. 1929, Warsaw, Poland. Musicologist; Composer; Teacher. Educ: Cert., Theory,

State Coll. of Music, Lodz, 1956; Cert., Comp., State Coll. of Music, Warsaw, 1958; Dr. of Philol., Warsaw Univ., 1968. m. Iwona Mazur, 1 s. Career: Chief Libn., State Coll. of Music, Warsaw, 1959-69; Asst. Prof., ibid., 1969-. Composer, Solemn March. Publs: Pierwodruki Stanislawa Moniuszki, 1970; Polskie edytorstwo muzyczne miedzy powstaniem IIstopadowym a styczniowym, 1971; Ed., Stanislaw Moniuszko: Chamber Music, 1972. Contbr. to: Muzyka; Ruch Muzyczny. Mbrships: Assn. of Authors; Assn. of Polish Comps.; Warsaw Musical Soc. Recip: Prize, Polish Army Comps. Competition, 1964. Hobby: Angling. Address: 15m 37 un. Nowolipki, 00-151 Warsaw, Poland.

MAZZA, Lynne S, b. 6 Apr. 1949, NYC, USA. Musicologist; Writer; Pianist; Teacher; Conductor. Educ: BA, Hunter Coll., NYC, 1971; MA (Musicol.), Queens Coll., NYC, 1975; Dip., Piano/Cond., G B Martini Conserv. of Music, Bologna, Italy, 1972. Publs: Bibliography of the Periodical Articles on Ferrucio Busoni, 1980. Contbr. to: US Trade Jrnls.; Italian Jrnls./Newspapers. Mbrships: Alton Jones Assocs.; Am. Musicol. Soc.; Busoni Soc.; Int. Piano Archives; Wagner Soc. Recip., Scholarship. Hobbies: Photography; Carpentry; Long Walks. Address: 400 W 23rd St., NYC, NY 10011, USA.

MAZZEO, Rosario, b. 5 Apr. 1911, Musician; Executive; Educator; Author; Inventor; Photographer; Ornithologist. m. 2 c. Career: Mbr., Boston Symph. Orch., 1933-66; Bass Clarinetist, ibid., 1939-66; Perf. num. chamber music & solo pieces throughout career; Cond. many works for larger chamber music ensembles at Tanglewood; Many comps. (Hindemith, Piston, Schuman, Harris, etc.) have written solo parts especially for him; currently Mbr., Crown Chamber Players; Personnel Mgr., Boston Symph. orch:, 1942-66; Treas. & Dir., ibid Pension Instn., -1966; Fac., Berkshire Music Ctr., Tanglewood, Lennox, Mass., 1940-66; Chmn., Woodwind Dept.; Instr. of Clarinet, Chamber Music Coach; New England Conserv., Boston, -1966; currently on Fac., Univ. of Calif., Santa Cruz (Fellow of Crown Coll.); Coord. of Pub. Progs., ibid.; Has lectured at var. univs.; Cons., Lectr. & Clinician, H & A Selmer, Inc.; Inventor of the Mazzeo Clarinet which is used extensively by the maj. orchs. & schl. systems. Publs. A Brief Survey of Chamber Music; Manual for the Mazzeo Clarinet; Musings for Mazzeo; The Clarinet Master Class; Ed. of solo pieces for the clarinet. Mbr. of var. music & ornithol. orgs. Address: Rte. 1, Box 213, Carmel, CA 93923, USA.

MBANDE, Venancio Notico, b. 4 Oct. 1928, Chisiko, Nr. Zavala, Mozambique. Timbila Xylophone Composer & Performer. m. Alzira, 3 c. Career: ldng. musician, Chopi people, in composition, perf. & constrn. zylophone; Ldr., Chopi xylophone orch. Witwatersrand gold mines; Demonstrator & Lectr., Chopi music, Univ. Pa., USA, 1973. Compositions: Many 'Mgodo' xylophone orchl. suites over 25 yrs. Recordings: sev. suites on tape, Int. Lib. African Music. Hon: Winner, African Arts music competition, USa, for 'mgodo' xylophone orchl. suite. Address: Wildebeestfontein Mine, Room No H7, PO Witgould, S Africa.

MEALE, Richard Graham, b. 24 Aug. 1932, Sydney, Aust. Composer; Reader in Music. Educ: NSW Conserv. of Music. Career: Comps. presented at ISCM World Music Days, Warsaw Autumn Fest.; Rdr. in Music, The Univ. of Adelaide. Comps incl: Las Alboradas (recorded); Images (Naguata); Very High Kings (recorded); Clouds now and then (recorded); Soon it will die; Incredible Floridas; Nocturnes (recorded); Interiors/Exteriors; Coruscations (recorded); Evocations; String Quartet; Viridian; Homage to Garcia Lorca (recorded). Mbrships: ISCM (Aust. Sect. Pres.); Coun. Mbr., Music Bd. of Aust.; Adelaide Fest. Centre Trust; Comps. Guild of Aust. Hons: MBE for services to music in Aust., 1971. Hobby: Contemporary English Lit. Address: Music Dept., The Univ. of Adelaide, SA 5000, Aust.

MECH, Raymond Andrew, b. 25 Dec. 1923, Alden, NY, USA. Professor of Voice; Bass-Baritone Singer Choral Conductor. Educ: BS, Fredonia State Univ. grad. studies, Alfred Univ., & Westminster Choir Coll., MMus, Eastman Schl. of Music, Univ. of Rochester; TEC. Opera Course. m. Dorothy Jane Stuart, 3 s., 1 d. Debut: on Star of Tormorrow prog., WBEN-Radio, Buffalo, 1946. Career: gave weekly radio recital WWHG Presents Ray Mech., Hornell, NY, 1947-49; gave voice recitals, Kilbourn Hall, Rochester, 1957, Seaford, NY, 1960; Bass Soloist, oratorios & masses; Voice Tchr.; Dir., ISU Concert Choir; compiled Syllabus of Vocal Study (Grades K-12) for Seaford Pub. Schls., 1966. Compositions: solo setting for 84th Pslam; Road to Avrille (words by Edna St. Vincent Millay) for soloist; Lord's Prayer for mixed choir. Recordings: solo recital of sacred & secular songs on Crest Records. Mbr., profl. orgs. Hobbies: Travel; Camping. Address: 7140 Williamsburg Lane, Terre Haute, IN 47802, USA.

MECKERT, Ruth Louise, b. 21 Aug. 1927, Evansville, Ind., USA. Flautist. Educ: BA, Univ. of Evansville; Master classes w.

Pellerite & Rampal. m. Kermit F Meckert, 1 s., 1 d. Career: Flautist, Evansville Phil. Orch., Tri State Band; Recitalist; Soloist for ch. & civic functions; Adjudicator; Pvte. Flute Instructor. Mbrships: Sigma Alpha Iota; Am. Heritage Music Chmn., DAR, Guide, Reitz House Aux.; nat. Flute Assn. Hons. incl: Youth Soloist, Evansville Phil. Orch., 1945; Soloist, Tri State Band, 1972. Hobbies incl: Hist. homes; Dress designing; Collecting old popular music & folk music. Address: 1507 Cass Ave., Evansville, IN 47714, USA.

MECKNA, Robert Michael, b. 13 Feb. 1945, Long Beach, Calif., USA. Musicologist; Horn Player; Guitarist. Educ: BA, Calif. State Univ., Long Beach; grad. study, Boston Univ. & Univ. of Calif., Santa Barbara; horn study w. Fred Fox; guitar study w. Gilmagno de Jesús. m. Eva Elizabeth Kartinen. Career: Long Beach Symph., 1965-66; host for radio concert prog., Santa Barbara; music critic, Santa Barbara News-Press; prog. annotator, Santa Barbara Symph. Publs: Folkguitar, 1977; co-ed., The Melk Circle; Albrechtsberger, Paradeiser & Schneider, 1980. Contbr. to: The Musical Times; Österreichische Musikzeitschrift; Santa Barbara News-Press. Mbrships: Am. Musicol. Soc.; Music Critics Assn.; Int. Horn Soc.; MENC. Hons: Long Beach Symph. Young Artist Award, 1965; Phi Kappa Phi, 1977; Pi Kappa Lambda, 1979. Hobbies: Gardening; Hiking. Address: c/o Music Dept., Univ. of Calif., Santa Barbara, CA 93106, USA.

MEDEK, Tilo, b. 22 Jan. 1904, Jena DDR. Composer. Educ: Humboldt Univ. Berlin, 1959-64, dip. musicol., 1964; German Music Acad., Berlin, 1959-64; German Art Acad. Berlin, 1964-67. m. Dorothea Siewert, 3 d. Debut: Holland, 1967. m. Dorothea Siewert, 3 d. Debut: Holland, 1967. Career: Radio broadcasts of his own works; since 1962 independent. Comp. incl: Theater works; Ballet; Orch. works; Concertos; Chmbr. music; Electronic music; Songs; Music for Radio, TV, Film. Mbrships: Assn. of Comp. and Musicologists DDR (VKM), mbr. bd. of dir. dist. Berlin. Publs. incl: Re-ed. Correspondence between Caspar Nehev and R Wagner-Regency, Berlin, 1968. Hons. since 1967 var. distinctions at Int. Comp. Contests; Int. Tribune of Comp., UNESCO Paris, 1975; Int. Folk Prize, Radio Bratislava; 1st Prize Winkler Prins Redaktie, Nederland, 1975. Address: Am Zirkus 2, 104 Berlin, German Dem. Repub.

MEEKS, Quincy D, b. 13 Nov. 1910, Palatka, Fla., USA. Concert Violinist; Teacher. Educ: Nat. Acad. of Music, Wash., DC. m. Leslie Frankfurt, 3 d. Career: Tchr. of Violin, Wash. Conserv. of Music & Expression, & Thrieldkel Studios, DC; Sev. concert tours inclng. St. Francis de Sales HS, Powhatan, Va., 1968. Recordings: Cable TV, Daytona Beach, Fla., 1968-69. Mbrships: Dir., Fr. Village String Orch., DC, 4 yrs.; Am. Musicol. Soc.; Nat. Assn. of Negro Music; Nat. Soc. of Lit. & Art; Pres., Christian Endeavor Soc., 19th St. Bapt. Ch., DC, 1976. Contbr. to The Balt. Area Messenger, 1959; Afro-Am. Newspaper, 1959. Hons. incl: Bowling; Jogging. Address: 3815 SD Ave. NE, Wash., DC 20018, USA. 4.

MEEUWS-TONNAER, Henny, b. 21 Apr. 1944, Roermond, Netherlands. Concert Singer, soprano. Educ: Tchr. Trng. Coll.; Conserv., dip. solo singing w. distinction. m. Hans Meeuws, 2 s. Career: 4 Broadcasts w. Dutch Cath. Radio Company (KRO), song recitals, 1972, 1973; Lieder recitals, 1975-78. Mbrships: Royal Dutch Soc. for Musicians (KNTV); Dutch Assn. for Musicians, DONEMUS. Contbr. to: Key Notes; Harmony; Man and Melody; Music and Educ.; Gaudeamus; Ex Ore Infantum; Pyramid. Hobbies: Reading; Walking; House plants; Correspondence; Collecting family photographs; Playing piano. Mgmt: Koffieconcert (Schubertliederer). Address: Keizer Frederikstr. 13, 6085 CN Horn, Netherlands.

MEHEGAN, John, b. 6 June 1920, Hartford, Conn., USa. Musician; Jazz Musicologist. Educ: Julius Hartt Schl. of Music. m. Gay Griscom Mehegan, 3 s., 2 d. Career: Jazz Instructor, Juilliard Schl. of Music, 1947-64; Columbia Tchr. Coll., 1957-60; Jazz Critic, NY Herald Tribune, 1957-60; Univ. of Bridgeport, 1968-; Lectr. in Jazz, Yale Schl. of Music, 1974-; Var. tours & jazz clinics. Recordings incl: The First Mehegan; Reflections; A Pair of Pianos; The Act of Jazz. Publs. incl: Jazz Improvisation, Vols. 1-4; The Jazz Pianist (3 vols.); Piano Styles (3 vols.); Contemporary Styles (3 vols.). Contbr. to musical jrnls. Address: 1 Weathervane Hill, Westport, CT 06880, USA. 2.

MEHLER, Friedrich Julius, b. 27 Sept. 1896, Frankfurt (Main), Germany. Festival Director; Artistic Director; Stage Manager; Composer; Violinist; Pianist; Conductor; Teacher. Educ: Hannover Conserv. (violin); Berlin Music Acad., Robert Kahn (comp.); Acad. of Arts Hans Pfitzner (comp., Cond.); w. mother (piano). m. Hildegard Ginzel, 1 s., 1 d. Career: Mbr. (violin), Opera Orch., Berlin - Charlottenburg; Tours w. opera singers as accomp., piano soloist, N Germany; Toured Czech. (Chmbr. music, solo violinist); Cond., Visby, 1921-; Guest

Cond., Stockholm Phil. Orch., 1927, 1945; Tchr., Schls. in Visby & pvte.; Radio & TV broadcasts world-wide. Comps. incl: Kassation for string quartet; 2 symphs.; 2 violin concertos; comps. for soli, choir & orch.; chmbr. music; songs; Gotlandic Dances, etc. Recordings: Petrus de Dacia, A Mystic Pageant Opera. Contbr. to profl. publs. Mbrships: Union of Swedish Comps.; STIM; Order of Freemasons. Hons. incl: Vasa Order, 1946; Illis Quorum, 1976; Culture prize, Community of Gotland. Hobby: Rose Gordon. Address: Tranhusgatan 47, S-621 00 Visby, Sweden.

MEHTA, Zubin, b. 1936, Bombay, India. Conductor. Educ: Vienna Acad. of Music. Career: Cond. in Belgium & Yugoslavia; Chief Cond., Montreal Symph. & Los Angeles Phil. Orch.; Cond. at festivals incl. Holland, Prague, Vienna, Salzburg & Spoleto; Cond., La Scala, Milan, 1966; Regular perfs. w. Vienna, Berlin & Israel Phil. Orchs.; Musical Advsr., Israel Phil., 1968-; Music Dir., Maggio Musicale, Florence, 1969. Hon: Winner, Liverpool Int. Conds.' Competition, 1958. Address: 135 N Grand, LA, CA 90012, USA.

MEIER, Bernhard, b. 15 Dec. 1923, Freiburg im Breisgau, Germany. Musicologist; Professor. Educ: Studies in musicol., Univ. of Freiburg i. Br., 1946-52; PhD, 1952; Habilitation, Univ. of Tübingen, 1963. m. Helga Baitz. Career: Prof., Musicol., Univ. of Tübingen. Publs: Die Tonarten der klassischen Vokalpolyphonie, 1974; Ed.; Cirpriani Rore Opera Omnia, 1959-77, & Jacobi Barbireau Opera Omnia; Co-ed., Lucae Marentii Opera Omnia & Adriani Willaert Opera Omnia. Contbr. to num. profl. jrnls. Mbrships: Int. Gesellschaft fur Musikwissenschaft; Vereniging voor Nederlandse Muziekgeschiedenis; Gesellschaft fur Musikforschung. Address: Tulpenweg 5, 7403 Pfäffingen bei Tübingen, German Fed. Repub.

MEIER, Gustav, b. 13 Aug. 1929, Wettingen, Switz. Conductor; Professor of Music. Educ: Dip. Certs., Zürich (Switz.) Conserv., 1948, '53. m. Emalou Greer, 4 c. Career: Fac. Mbr., Schl. of Music, Yale, New Haven, Conn., 1960-, Assoc. Prof., 1964-70, Prof., 1970-73; Prof. of Cond., Eastman Schl. of Music, Rochester, NY, 1973-76; Prof. of Cond., Schl. of Music, Univ. of Michl.; Dir. of Orchs. & Opera; Guest Cond., NYC Opera, Santa Fe Opera, San Fran. Opera, Zürich Opera; Musical Dir., Cond., Greater Bridgeport (Conn.) Symph. Orch., 1972-. Num. recordings. Mbrships: Swiss Hist. Soc.; Coll. Music Soc.; Am., Swiss Fedn. of Musicians. Hons: Fellow, Calhoun Coll., Yale, 1964. Address: 2023 Seneca, Ann Arbor, MI 48104, USA.

MEIJER, Axel, b. 24 Aug. 1940, Ultrecht, Netherlands. Musicologist; Cellist. Educ: Doct. in musicol., Univ. of Utrecht. m. Hubertha Hermina Holleman, 2 d. Career: Libn.-Tchr. of music theory-currently Sub-Dir., Utrechts Conservatorium. Author: Conservatory Libraries. Contbr. to orchl. progs., booklets. Mbrships: Soc. of Dutch Music Hist.; Dutch Soc. of Libns.; Bds. of sev. orgs. in field of music libs., & of Alphons Diepenbrock Fund, Amsterdam. Hobbies: Sailing; Spanish culture. Address: Prins Hendriklaan, 70, 3584 Utrecht, Netherlands.

MEISEL, Maribel, b. 23 June 1936, Fairmont, W Va., USA. Musicologist; Musical Instrument Historian. Educ: AA, Cottey Coll.; BA, Oberlin Coll., 1957; BM, Am. Conserv. of Music, 1960; MM, W Va. Univ., 1971; Study of musicol., Univ. of Copenhagen, Denmark, 1965-70. m. Philip R Belt. 1 d. Career: Guide, Custodian, Claudius Collect. of Musical Instruments, Copenhagen, 1967-70; Rsch. Assoc., Stearns Collect. of Musical Instruments, Univ. of Mich., 1927-73; Lectr., Denmark & USA. Contbr. to jrnls., Grove's Dictionary; Ed., Belt-Stein Fortepiano Kit Manual, 1972. Mbrships: Am. Int. Musicol. Socs.; Music Lib. Assn.; Am. Musical Instrument Soc. Hons: Marshall Fellowship to Denmark, 1968-70. Hobbies: Archaeology; Singing. Address: 26 Stanton St., Pawcatuck, CT 06379, USA.

MEITUS, Juli Sergeyevich, b. 28 Jan. 1903, Kirovograd, Ukraine. Composer. Educ: Musical-dramatic Inst., 1923-31. m. Vasilyeva Alexandre Ivanovna, 1 s. Comps: 14 operas; 5 suites for symph. orch.; 3 cycles of Ukrainian folk songs for voice, chorus & orch.; over 200 romances, ballads, etc. for vocalist & piano; var. choral & instrumental works; theatre & film music, etc. Num. recordings. Publs: 6 Operas. Mbrships: Communist Pty. USSR; Comps. Union. Hons: Hon. Wkr. of Art, Ukr. SSR, 1947, Turkmen SSR, 1944; State Prize, USSR Laureate, 1951; People's Artist, Ukr. SSR, 1973; Order of Labour, Red Banner, 1960, '71. Hobby: Philately. Address: Vladimirskaya ul. 14, kv. 8, Kiev 25, USSR.

MEKEEL, Joyce, b. 6 July 1931, New Haven, Conn., USA. Composer. Educ: Paris Conservatoire; BM, MM, Yale Univ.

Schl. of Music. Career: Pvte. Tchr., piano & theory, Princeton, 1960-64; Theory Fac: New England Conserv., 1964-70; Boston Univ., 1970-; Harpsichordist w. New Haven Symph., New Haven Chorale & Princeton Symph.; Organizer of Concerts on Baroque Music for Berkeley Coll. & Yale Univ.; Comp. for prods. at McCarter Theater, Princeton. Comps. incl: White Silence (SATB); Shape of Silence (solo flute). Recordings: Corridors of Dream; Planh. Publs. incl: book reviews. Contbr. to profl. jrnls. Mbrships: Pi Kappa Lamba. Hons. incl: Fellowships, scholarships & awards. Hobby: Sculpture. Address: 119 Pembroke St., Boston, Mass., USA. 27.

MEKLER, Mani, b. Haifa, Israel. Operatic Soprano. Educ: study w. Tito Gobbi. Career: apps. at Royal Opera, Stockholm, Frottningholm Court Theatre, Welsh Nat. Opera, Wexford, Düsseldorf; roles incl. Leonora (Il Trovatore), Fiordiligi (Cosi fan Tutte), Senta (Dutchman), Mimi (La Boheme), Tosca. Mgmt: Artistsekretariat Ulf Förnqvist, Norrtullsgatan 26, tr. 4, 11345 Stockholm, Sweden. Address: c/o mgmt.

MELAMED, Nissan Cohen, b. 23 Mar. 1906, Shiraz, Persia, (Israeli res., 1908-) Composer; Educator. Educ: Tchrs. Coll.; Conserv., Jerusalem. Esther Shalgui, 2 s., 1 d. Career: Israeli Radio & TV; Lectr., Dept. of Music, Bar-Ilan Univ.; Fac. of Music, Tel-Aviv Univ. & Yelin's Music Tchrs. Coll. Comps: over 200 Israeli songs; 100 liturgical Jewish songs. num. recordings. Publs: Rinati, Vol. I 1942, Vol. II, 1946, Vol. III, 1953; Renamim, 1972. Contbr. to: Bat Kol; Tazlil; Duchan. Mbrships: Sec., Soc. Comm., ACUM; Comps. Assn., Musicols. Assn., Israel. Address: 1 Kiryat Sefer Str., Tel-Aviv, Israel.

MELE, Frank, b. 13 Oct. 1921, Rochester, NY, USA. Violinist; Violist; Author. m. 1 s., 1 d. Career incls: Mbr., var. times, Rochester Phil., Pitts. Symph. & Symph. of the Air; Violist, Mod. Art String Quartet at fests. of Am. Music, Yaddo, Saratoga Springs & Woodstock, NY; Solo Viola apps. w. Northern NY Philharmonia; Lectr., Kan. Univ. Publs: Polpeto, 1973, to be republd. as Cosimo; short stories; articles. Mbrships: Fndr. & Dir., Woodstock Soc. for New Music. Hobby: Fly Fishing. Address: PO Box 35, Woodstock, NY, USA.

MELIK-ASLANIAN, Emanuel, b. 13 Sept. 1915, Tabris, Iran. Composer; Pianist; Professor of Piano; Artistic Adviser. Educ: Dip. in comp., conducting, piano, Aklad. Musikhochschule für Musik, Berlin, Germany. m. Lidia Haroutounian, 1 s., 1 d. Debut: Piano Recital, Berlin, 1940. Career incls: frequent apps. as pianist on radio & TV; Many comps. frequetly performed on radio & TV; Music composed for documentary film depicting tribal life in Iran; Frequent apps. as soloist w. Teheran Symph. Orch. Comps. incl: Dance Variations, for orch., 1952; Poème Symphonique; Burlesque for orch.; Myth of creation, ballet. Contbr. to sev. profl. pubs. Mbr., GEMA, Berlin. Hons. incl: Taj Medal; Homayrun Medal. Hobbies: Philos.; Cinema; Lit. Address: Abasad, Apadana Ave., Farhad St., No. 11, 15 Teheran, Iran.

MELIN, Bengt E, b. 5 Jan. 1928, Stockholm, Sweden. Journalist; Composer. Educ: Self-taught in music. m. Eva Stenström. Career: Jazz Musician (trumpet), 1945-48; Critic & Journalist, 1948-. Comps: Lyrics to Swedish tunes; Transl. lyrics into Swedish; Le Marteur d'Or. Publs: När, var, hur, 1968-78; Tribun, 1956; Sohlmans Music Lexicon, 1976. Contbr. to: Aftonbladet, Stockholm. Mbrships: STIM; Swedish Soc. of Popular Music Comps., Lyricists & Arrs.; Fedn. of Int. Jazz Critics. Hobbies: Racing; Lit. Address: c/o Stenström, Folkungagatan 132 c, 116.30 Stockholm, Sweden.

MELKONIAN, Zaban, b. 20 June 1931, Tehran, Iran. Cellist. Educ: Masters degree (artists license), Tehran Conserv.; Grad. Fellow, New Engl. Conserv., USA. m. Virginia Melkonian, 1 s., 1 d. Debut: Lalo Concerto w. Tehran Symph. Orch., Royal Command Perf. Career: Mbr., 23 yrs., currently Prin. Cellist, Tehran Symph. Orch.; frequent chmbr. music perfs.; Guest Artist, Tehran Opera Orch., NIRTV Chmbr. Orch.; Prof. of Cello, Tehran Conserv. Recip. Artists decoration 2° (recognition of continued serv.), 1951. Hobbies: Stamps; Gems; Antiquities. Address: Abasabad, Mir Emad, kouche 9 No. 4, Iran.

MELKUS, Eduard, b. 1 Sept. 1928, BadenWein, Austria. Violinist. Educ: Musicology, Univ. of Vienna; Dip., Violin, Viola, Acad. of Music, Vienna. m. Marlis Melkus-Selzer, 4 children. Debut: Wien, 1944. Career: Mbr., Ensemble Eduard Melkus, playing mainly on instruments in original measurements of 18th century; Capella Acad., Wien; Prof., Violin & Viola, Hochschule for Musik, Wien; Vis. Prof., Univ. of Ga., USA, 1973-74; Concerts in England, Holland, Belgium, Germany, Switzerland, Sweden, Italy, Yugoslavia, Czechoslovakia, Mexico & USA. Recordings of music by Bach, Handel, Haydn, etc. Contbr. to profl. jrnls. Hons. incl: Kornerpreis, 1967. Hobbies: Sightseeing; Music.; Collecting old Violins. Address: 1020 Wien 2, Obere Donaustrasse 57/14, Austria.

MELL, Gertrud Maria, b. 15 Aug. 1947, Ed, Sweden. Composer; Organist; Music Teacher. Educ: Organ Dip., Conserv. of Music, Lund, 1967; Tchr. of Music Dip., Stockholm, 1968. Debut: Swedish TV, 1972, playing own piano composition. Career: Own radio & TV progs., 1973-; currently studying navigation. Comp: Strakkvartet (string quartet) No. 1, 1969; Fantasie (piano), 1961; Improvisation (piano), 1971; 4 Symphonies. Recording: LP - 'Mell' incl. string quartet no. 1, played by Royal Ct. Orch., Sweden, 1971. Mbrships: KMR (Ch. Musicians Soc.); STIM (Swedish Composers Int. Off. of Music). Hons: Älvsborgs Läns Landstings Kulturstipendium 10,000. Hobbies: Boating (has taken skipper's exam.); Pistol shooting; Driving; Swimming; Animals; Nature. Address: Strömstadsvagen 30, 66001 Ed, Sweden.

MELLERS, Wilfrid Howard, b. 26 Apr. 1914, Leamington Spa, UK. Professor; Composer; Writer. Educ: BA, Cantab., 1936; MA, 1945; DMus, Univ. of Birmingham, 1963; Comp. studies w. Egon Wellesz, Edmund Rubbra. m. Pauline Peggy Lewis, 2 d. Career: Coll. Supvsr. in Engl. & Lectr. in Music, Downing Coll., Cambridge, 1945-48; Staff Tutor in Music, Extra-Mural Dept., Univ. of Birmingham, 1948-59; Andrew Mellon Prof. of Music, Univ. of Pitts., Pa., USA, 1960-63; Prof. of Music, Univ. of York, UK, 1964-; Org., Attingham Park Summer Schl. Music, 13 yrs.; Lectr. in Aust., USA & Can.; work for Radio & TV. Comps. incl: Life Cycle (for 3 choirs & 2 orchs.); A May Magnificat; Sun-flower; Rosae Hermeticae. Recordings incl: Voices & Creatures; Cloud Canticle; Opus Alchymycum. Publs: Francois Couperin, 1950; Man & his Music, 1957; Music in a New Found Land, 1964; Caliban Reborn, 1966; Twilight of the Gods, 1973. Address: Dept. of Music, Univ. of York, York, UK.

MELLES, Carl, b. 15 July 1926, Budapest, Hungary. Conductor. Educ: Acad. of Music, Budapest. m. Gertrud Dertnig, 1963, 1 s., 1 d. Career: Cond. of major European Orchs., incl. Vienna & Berlin Phil.; New Philharmonia, London; Guest Cond., Salzburg & Bayreuth Festivals; Concert tours of Japan. S Africa & Europe. Recip. Franz Liszt Prize, Budapest, 1954. Address: Grunbergstrasse 4, 1130 Vienna, Austria.

MELLNÄS, Arne, b. 30 Aug. 1933, Stockholm, Sweden. Composer. Educ: Acad. of Music, Stockholm; Hochschule für Musik, Berlin. m. Marianne Melinäs 1 s. Comps: (orchl. works) Collage (C F Peters); Aura (Wilhelm Hansen); Transperance (STIM); (chamber music) Guestes Sonores (WH); Tombola (Tonos); Per caso (Tonos); Quasi niente (Peters); Capricorn Flakes (Peters); (choir) Succsim (WH); Dream (WH); Aglepta (WH); (solo works) FixationsOrgan (Peters); DisparitionsOrgan (WH); SchizofopniPiano (WH). Recordings: Succism (DGG); Intensity 6.5 (HMV); Conglomerat (SR Records); Eufoni (Caprice); Aglepta (Col.); Cabrillo (Caprice); Far Out (SR Records); Schizofoni (Fermat); Fragments for Family Flute (EFG). Hons: Stichting Gaudeamus, Holland, Int. Compositions comp., 1st prize, 1963 (Collage for orch.). Address: Näsbydalsvägen 14/15, S-18331 Täby, Sweden.

MELLY, George, b. 17 Aug. 1926, Liverpool, UK. Jazz Singer & Writer. m. D Melly, 1 s., 1 step-son, 1 step-daughter. Debut: Youth Club, Croydon. Career: w. Mick Mulligan's Magnolia Jazz Band, 1948-61; John Chilton's Feet Warmers, 1971-. Comps: Lyrics for 'Smashing Time', 1967. Recordings: The World of George Melly, 1950s; Nuts, 1972; Son of Nuts, 1973; It's George, 1974; Melly is at it Again, 1977; Melly sings Hoagie, 1978. Publ: Revolt Into Style, The Pop Arts in Britain. Contbr. to: Melody Maker; New Musical Express; Jazz Jrnl. Mbrships: Musicians Union; Equity; Nat. Union of Journalists; Mbr., Colongy Room. Hons: Voted top Brit. Jazz Singer, 1955/56, '57, '73; Top Int. Jazz Singer (Jazz, Jrnl. Int.), 1979. Hobbies: Trout Fishing; Collecting early blues & mod. paintings. Mgmt: Jack Higgins, European Int. Artistes. Address: 35 St. Lawrence Terr., London W10 5SR, UK.

MELMUKA, Radomir, b. 23 Sept. 1938, Prague, Czechoslovakia. Professor; Pianist. Educ: Prague Conservatory; Acad. of Music, Prague. m. Helena Melmukova, 2 s. Debut: 1960. Career: Concerts throughout Czechoslovakia & Italy, Yugoslavia, France, Germany & Poland. Mbrships: Soc. of Czech Compositiors & Artists; Frederic Chopin Soc. Hons: 4th Prize, piano competition, Prague, 1963; 1st Prize, piano competition F Chopin, Marianske Lazne, 1963; 6th prize, piano competition of A Cassela, Naples, Italy, 1964. Hobbies: Travel; Cars; Cycling; Chess; Mushrooming in Czech forests. Mgmt: Pragoconsert, Maltezske Namesti 1, Prague 1, Czechoslovakia. Address: Krymska 27, 10100 Prague 10, Czechoslovakia.

MELVILLE, Clarissa Brayton, b. 30 May 1941, Newbury, Berks., UK. Flautist; Orchestral Manager; Teacher of Flute & Piano. Educ: Recital Dip., RAM; LRAM; ARCM; Accademia

Musicale Chigiana, Siena. m. Richard John Holttum, 1 s., 1 d. Career: Bournemouth Symph. Orch., 1965-69; Mgr., Orch. of Sadlers Wells Royal Ballet, 1970-78; Tchr., Pimlico Schl. for Talented Children, 1970-; Freelance flute player; pvte. tchr. Mbrships: ISM; Musicians' Union. Hobbies: Sailing; Home Renovation. Address: 51 Stradella Rd., London SE24, UK.

MELVILLE, Derek. Composer; Pianist. Educ: RCM; RAM. Career: Recitals, Broadcasts, UK & abroad. Comps: 2 17th Century Songs of Sleep; Sweet Jesu, King of Bliss (carol). Publ: Chapt., Beethoven's Pianos, in the Beethoven Companion 1971 (paperback), 1973; Chopin, put Clive Bingley, 1977. Address: Magnolia House, Yoxford, Saxmundham, Suffolk IP17 3EP, UK. 29, 30.

MELVIN, Sophia B, b. 9 Feb. 19126, Chattanooga, Tenn., USA. Associate Professor of Piano, Temple University. Educ: BSc & BMus, Univ. of Chattanooga (now Univ. of Tenn.); MMus, Fla. State Univ.; Dip., Cadek Conserv.; Juilliard summer schl.; studied piano w. Katherine Bacon, Mildred Dassett, Harold Bauer & Edward Kilenyi. m. Mael A Melvin, 2 s. Debut: Town Hall, NYC, 1948. Career: Concerto Soloist, Chattanooga & Tallahassee Symphs.; Featured Soloist, Orcas Island Fest. of Arts, Wash.; apps. in Phillips Gall., Wash. DC; presented piano series on WAPO, Chattanooga, & progs. on WDOD, Chattanooga, & WQXR, NY; has given many concerts in Tenn., N Ga., Fla., NY, Conn. & Calif. Mbrships: Pres., Tallahassee Music Tchr's. Assn.; Comm. on Piano Materials, Fla. Music Tchrs.'s Assn.; Sec., State Convention held in Phila., Pa., Music Tchr's. Nat. Assn., 1969. Hobbies: Swimming; Aikido; Travel. Address: 1524 N 13th St., Philadelphia, PA 19122, USA.

MEMINGER, Minna Shklar, b. 29 Dec. 1930, Toronto, Can. Violist. Educ: Toronto Conserv. of Music; New Schl. of Music, Phila., USA; Tanglewood; Serkin's Camp., Marlboro. m. Donald Meminger, 1 s., 1 d. Career: Toronto Symmer Symph; New Orleans Phil., USA; New Chmbr. Orch. of Phila; Rochester Phil.; Shklar Quartett; Tchr. of Music. Hobbies: Camping; Bicycling. Address: 125 Cloverdale Rd., Rochester, NY 14616, USA.

MENDEL, Arthur, b. 6 June 1905, Boston, Mass., USA. Educator. Educ: BA, Harvard Coll., 1925; Ecole Normale de Musique, Paris, 1925-27. m. Elsa M Wissell. Career: Tchr., Dalcroze Schl. of Music & Diller-Quaille Schl. of Music, NYC, 1938-50; Lit. Ed., G Schirmer Inc., 1930-38; Music Critic, The Nation, 1930-33; Ed., Am. Musicol. Soc., 1941-44; Ed., Assn. Mus. Pub., 1941-47; Prof. of Music, Princeton Univ., NJ, 1952, Emeritus 1973; Chmn., Dept. of Music, ibid., 1952-67; Lectr., Columbia Univ., 1949; Lectr., Univ. of Calif., 1951; Cond., Cantata Singers, small chorus specializing in 17th & 18th century music, NYC, 1936-53. Recordings: Cond., The Christmas Story & Musicalische Exequien by H Schütz; Dir., Little Sacred Concerts by H Schütz. Publs. incl: Translator, Paul Hindmith's Craft of Musical Compositon, Theoretical Part, 1942; Ed., The Bach Reader (w. Hans T David), 1945; Studies in the History of Musical Pitch (w. A J Ellis), 1968; Pitch in Western Music since 1500 - A Re-examination, 1979; Ed., J S Bach, Johannes-Passion, 1973-74 (Neue Bach-Ausgabe, II/4). Contbr. to many profl. jrnls. Mbr., num. profl. orgs. Hons. incl: Guggenheim Fellow, 1949-50; DMus, Rutgers Univ., 1973; Hon. Mbr., Am. Musicol. Soc., 1974-; D Humane Letters, Brandeis Univ., 1976. Address: Woolworth Ctr. of Musical Studies, Princeton, NJ 08540, USA. 2.

MENDELSOHN, Jack, b. 5 May 1946, Galatz, Roumania. Cellist. Educ: Acad. Music, Tel Aviv, Israel; Manhattan Schl. Music, NY, USA. m. Alice L Kennedy. Career: Mbr., Israel Chmbr. Orch., 1966-69; Asst. Prin. Cello, Montreal Symph. Orch., Canada, 1970-75; Mbr., Musica Camerata Montreal & Ensemble Pierre Rolland; Soloist perfs., Montreal Symph. & Canada Symph; Prin. cellist, Vancouver Symph. Orch., 1975-. Recordings: CBC Radio & TV. Hobbies: Chmbr. Music; Photography; Cross Country Skiing; Gourmet Food. Address: 63 Glenmore Dr., W Vancouver, BC V7S 1A5, Canada.

MENDES, Gilberto, b. 13 Oct. 1922, Santos, Brazil. Composer; Professor; Journalist. Educ: Santos Conserv., 1941-48; w. Brazilian comps. Claudio Santoro, 1954, & G Olivier Toni, 1958-60; Darmstadt summer courses, 1962, '68; Comps. w. Pierre Boulex, Henri Pousseur & Karlheinz Stockhausen. m. Eliane Ghigonetto, 3 s. Career incls: Tchr., music hist. & esthetics, Clube de Arte, Santos, 1956; Escola de Jovens, 1966; Colégio Vocacional Stella Maris, 1968-. Comps. incl: Nascemorre; Vai e Vem; Music for 12 Instruments; Beba Coca-Cola; Blirium C-9; Santos Football Music; Piano Music n.1. Hons: Asociação Paulista de Criticos Teatrais Award, 1974. Address: Av. Vicente de Carvalho 27, ap. 23, 11, 1000 Santos, Brazil.

MENDL, Robert W S, b. 28 July 1892, London, UK. Author. Educ: MA, Univ. Coll. Oxford; Pupil of Sir Percy Buck, Harrow Schl. m. Dorothy Williams, 1 s. Career: Army Off., WWI & II; Temporary Civil Servant, WWII; Barrister; Joined Shell Organization & ret'd. 1952; since 1952, author. Publs: From a Music Lover's Armchair, 1926; The Appeal of Jazz, 1927; The Soul of Music, 1950; The Divine Quest in Music, 1957; Adventure in Music, 1964; Reflections of a Music Lover, 1971; Contbr. to: The Musical Quarterly; Musical Opinion; The Chesterian; The Penquin Music Mag.; The Music Tchr.; The Music Lover; Music & Letters; The English Review; The Musical Times; The Radio Times; The Quarterly Review; The Daily Telegraph; The Daily Mirror; The Strad. Mbrships: Union Club, Oxford; Oxford Soc. Hons: 2nd Prize, Bricoe Eyre Prize for Music, Harrow Schl. Address: 53 Manor House, Marylebone Rd., London NW1 5NP, UK. 3.

MENDOZA, Anne Elizabeth, b. 29 May 1914, London, UK. Music Teacher; Lecturer; Writer; Arranger of Folk Music. Educ: ARCM; GRSM; RCM. m. Philip Goldesgeyme, 1 s. Career: Sr. Music Tchr., Barr's Hill Schl., Coventry; Prin. Music Lectr., Froebel Educl. Inst., Roehampton; Freelance Lectr. & Advsr., 1956-78. Comps. incl: Hey Betty Martin; First (& Second) Tunes for Recorders & Voices; Graded Rounds; More Graded Rounds; Three Times Three; Lanky Lucy Listener. Recordings arr. w. Joan Fimmer on Argo label; Songs for Children; Rhyme & Rhythm (4); Oats & Beans. Author of about 50 books incl: Tops & Tails; Sociable Songs. Contbr. to: Music Tchr.; Music in Educ. Mbrships. incl: ISM; Engl. Folk Song & Dance Soc. Address: 41 Fordington Rd., Highgate N6 4TD, UK. 3, 27.

MENGELBERG, Karel Willem Joseph, b. 18 July 1902, Utrecht, Netherlands. Composer; Conductor. Educ: State Acad. of Music, Berlin, Germany; studied comp. w. Willem Pijper. Compositions: Liederen, 1925; Barcelona, 1934; Catalunya, 1934; Strijkkwartet I, 1938; Sonate, 1939; Trio, 1940; Requiem, 1946; Divertimenti, 1948; 3 Liederen, 1949; Concert, 1950; Jan Hinnerik, 1950; Anion, 1950; Klompendans, 1951; Soliloquio, 1951; Ballade, 1952; Serenade, 1952; Recitatief, 1953; Suite, 1954; Roland Holst kantate. 1955; Soneria, 1958; Mbr., Soc. of Dutch Comps. Address: Uiterwaardenstraat 406, Amsterdam, Netherlands.

MENGER, Reinhardt, b. 27 Nov. 1936, Wernigerode/Harz, Germany. Organist; Carillon Player; Educator. Educ: Johann Wolfgang Goethe Univ.; studied under Heinz Wunderlich, Johann Ernst Köhler & Helmut Walcha; Netherlands Schl. of Bell Ringing, Amersfoot. Career: num. broadcasts, radio & TV, Germany & abroad. Recordings: var. prods. w. histl. instruments. Mbrships: Galpin Soc., UK; Soc. for Music Rsch., Kassel; German Soc. of Organ Lovers. Publs: Das Regal, 1973. Contbr. to profl. jrnls. Hobby: Collecting Historic Musical Instruments. Address: Abtei, 6302 Armsburg, Germany.

MENKE, Werner, b. 10 Jan. 1907, Diepholz, Germany. Music School Director. Educ: Dip., Conserv. of Music; PhD, Erlangen, 1940. m . Ingeborg Menke-Heisen. Debut: as Trumpet Soloist, Hanover, 1928. Career: Solo Trumpeter, Hanover, 1928-32; Tenor Soloist, concerts & broacasts (Leipzig, Munich & Stuttgart radio), Guest Soloist in oratorio, cantatas & Nuremberg Opera, concerts w. Choruses from the Leipzig Thomas Ch., Regensberg Domspatzen & Munich Dom Chorus, 1933-; conducted own Opera Schl. in Nuremberg; HS Music Tchr., 1952; Lectr. in Music Schls., 1963; Dir., Taunus Music Schl., 1968-. Publs. incl: The Study of the Vocal Work of Georg Philipp Telemann, 1941; History of the Trumpet of Bach & Handel, 1934. Contbr. to: La Musica Ency., Turin, 1967; musical jrnls. Hobbies: Painting; Architecture. Address: Brüder Grimmstr. 1, 6236 Eschborn/Ts., German Fed. Repub.

MENNIN, Peter Antony, b. 17 May 1923, Erie, Pa., USA. Composer; President of The Juilliard School. Educ: Oberlin Conserv.; BMus, MMus, Eastman Schl. of Music; PhD, Univ. Rochester. m. Georganne Bairnston, 1 s., 1 d. Debut: NY Phil., Leonard Bernstein Conducting the Premiere of Symphonic Allego, Met. Opera House. Career: Pres., The Juilliard Schl., 1963-. Comps. incl: 8 Symphs. for Orch.; o Cantata de Virtute (Tenor & Baritone Soloists), Narrator, Children's Chorus, Double Mixed Chorus & Orch.; Cello Concerto; Piano Concerto; Concerto for Orch. (Moby-Dick). Num. recordings. Mbr. var. profl. orgs. inclng: Past Pres. & Chmn., Nat. Music Coun. Hons. incl: Naumberg Am. Music Recording Award, 1952. Address: Juilliard Schl., Lincoln Ctr., New York, NY 10023, USA. 2, 6.

MENOTTI, Gian-Carlo, b. 7 July 1911, Cadigliano, Italy. Composer; Pianist. Educ: Curtis Inst., USA. Career: began composing at age 6 & wrote 1st opera at age 112; during teens was popular Pianist, Milan; Hd. of Composition Dept., Curtis Inst., USA. Compositions incl: Amelia Goes to the Ball (opera); The Old Maid & the Thief (opera); The Medium (opera); The Telephone (opera); The Consul (musical drama); Amahl & the Night Visitors (opera, frequently on TV); The Saint of Bleecker St. Hons. incl: Schlrship. to Curtis Inst.; Am. Acad. of Arts & Scis. Grant, 1945; Pulitzer Prize for The Saint of Bleecker St., 1954. Address: Caprichorn, Mt. Kisco, NYC, NY, USA.

MENUHIN, Hephzibah, b. 1920, San Francisco, USA. Concert Pianist. Educ: Pvte., esp. w. Marcel Ciampi. m. (1) Lindsay Nicholas (dissolved), 2 s., (2) Richard Hauser. Career: Num. perfs., tours as Soloist & w. brother Yehudi. Num. recordings: Chamber Music & Concertos. Co-author (w. husband), Fraternal Society & other sociological works. Mgmt: Harold Holt Ltd., 122 Wigmore St., London W1, UK. 3.

MENUHIN, Jeremy, b. 2 Nov. 1951, San Francisco, Calif., USA. Pianist; Conductor. Educ: Scuola INglèse, Florence; Chalet Flora, Switz.; Westminster, Eton, UK; studied w. Signor E Nardi, Marcel Gazelle, Marcel Ciampi, Nadia Boulanger, Hans Swarowski (Viennese Acad.). Career: BBC, Swiss TV, German TV, NBC, CBS, France & Holland; Perf. in Brazil, Switz., Germany, Holland, UK, Russia, USA, France, Israel. Recordings: Fauré Quartet; Mozart Concerto (both for EMI). Hobbies: Astronomy. Mgmt: De Koos. Address: 2 The Grove, Highgate, London N6, UK. 3.

MENUHIN, Yaltah, b. 7 Oct. 1921, San Fran., Calif., USA. Concert Pianist. Educ: studied piano w. Marcel Ciampi, Paris, Silverstri, Rome, & Carl Friedberg, Juilliard Schl. of Music, NYC. m. Joel Ryce, 2 s. Career: has appeared worldwide as soloist & w. leading instrumentalist; Duo Pianist w. husband Joel Ryce; has appeared at leading European summer fests.; has made TV broadcasts in Paris, London, NYC & Geneva. Recordings: sev. solo & duo piano works for Everest Recordings. EMI, World REcord Club & DGG, Recip. w. Joel Ryce of Harriet Cohen 1st Prize Int. Music Award, 1962, Mgmt: Ibbs & Tillett, London, UK. 4.

MENUHIN, Yehudi, b. 22 April 1916, NY, USA. Violinist. Educ: Pvte. w. Sigmund Anker, Louis Persinger, Georges Enesco & Adolf Busch. m. (1) Nola Nicholas, 1 s., 1 d. (2) Diana Gould, 2 s. Debut: San Francisco aged 7. Career incls: num. perfs. world-wide, initiated Fest. Gstaad (Switz.), annually 1957-, Bath, 1959-68, & Windsor 1969-72; visited Russia, 1945, India (at invitation of Prime Min.), 1952; has promoted visits of Russian artists to USA & Indian artists to the W; Fndr., Yehudi Menuhin Schl. of Music, Stoke d'Abernon, Surrey, UK, 1963; Pres., Trinity Coll. of Music, 1971; has commissioned num. works from composers inclng. Bartok, Walton, Bloch, etc.; num. TV apps. UK & USA. Num. recordings as Soloist & Cond. of Menuhin Fest. Orch. Publs: The Violin - Six Lessons with Yehudi Menuhin, 1971; Theme & Variations, 1972; Unfinished Journey, autobiography, 1977. Hons. incl: KBE (Hon.), 1965; Legion d'Honneur (France); Order of Leopold (Belgium); Order of Merit (German Fed. Repub.); Ordre de la Couronne (Belgium); Ordre des Arts et des Lettres (France); Order of the Phoenix (Greece); Royal Phil. Gold Mdl.; num. hon. degrees. Mgmt: Harold Holt Ltd., UK; CAMI, NY, USA. Address: c/o Harold Holt Ltd., 134 Wigmore St., London W1H 0DJ, UK.

MERCIER, Philippe, b. 25 March 1940, St. Gilles, Brussels, Belgium. Professor of Musicology. Educ: Royal Conserv. of Music, Brussels; Dr. in Musicol., Univ. of Louvain, 1968. Career: Prof. of Musicol., Univ. of Louvain, 1968-; Prof. of Hist. of Music, Music Acad. of Court-St. Etienne & Ottignies, 1972; VP, Société Liegerised Musicologie, 1974; Dir., St-Remy Choir. Recordings: Works of Belgian Composers A F Gresnick, H Renotte, D Raick, C Franck, Delplanque, Dizi, Leplae, etc. sev. publs. in field. Contbr. to: Revue des Archéologues & Historiens d'Art de Louvain; Grove's Dictionary, etc. Recip: Prize of Royal Belgian Acad., 1968. Address: rue Roberti 7, 1340 Ottignies, Belgium.

MEREDITH, Henry Morgan, b. 10 Oct. 1946, Douglas, Ariz., USA. Trumpeter; Musicologist; Specialist on valveless baroque trumpet & piccolo trumpet; Brass & Jazz Teacher; Ethnomusicologist; Conductor; Clinician; Composer; Arranger. Educ: BMusEd., Ind. Univ., Bloomington, 1968; MMus Ed., Specialist cert. in multiple arts, ibid., 1970; DArts, Univ. of N Colo., Greeley, 1980. m. Victoria Steward Meredith. Career incl: Prin. trumpet, Bloomington & Duluth Symphs.; soloist w. num. bands & orchs., incl. Baroque Fest. Orch. & New Chmbr. Orch.; Prof. of trumpet & Dir. of Historical Brass, Univ. of W Ont., London, Can.; ldr., 1st trumpet, United Brass Ensemble; mbr., Trumpet & voice duo, Clarino e Canto; guest soloist, recitalist & tchr. in USA, Can., UK & Austria. Comps: Quintessence for Brass Quintet, 1974; Scherzo, for Woodwind Trio, 1975. Publs: eds. of music incl. The Instrumental Canzoni of Girolamo Frescobaldi (15 vols.), 1979-. Contbr. to num. jrnls. mbr. num. profl. socs. recipient, num. fellowships &

scholarships. Hobbies incl: Antique Brass Instruments. Mgmt: Cantata Artists Mgmt. Address: 1667 Richmond St. N, London, Ont. N6G 2N3, Can.

MEREDITH, Victoria Steward, b. 27 April 1949, Berkeley, Calif., USA. Soprano; Voice Instructor; Choral Conductor; Adjudicator. Educ: BME Ind. Univ., 1971; MM in Voice Perf., Univ. of N Colo., 1975; Study at GSM, London. m. Henry M Meredith, Jr. Career: Instr., Voice, Univ. of Wis.; Cons., Voice, Northland Coll., Wis.; Instr. of voice & vocal techniques, Univ. of Western Ont. Dir. of Choirs, Pilgrim Luth. Ch.; Dir. of choirs, Hd. of Music Dept., St. Joseph Acad., London, Ont.; Mbr., Trumpet & voice duo, Clarino & Canto; Mbr., Duluth (Minn.) Symph. Chorus, Duluth Opera Chorus, Little Theatre of the Rockies Opera Chorus & Univ. of N. Colo. Opera Guild. Mbrships: Metrop. Opera Guild; MENC; Pi Kappa Lambda; Sigma Alpha Iota; Schubert Club. Hons: Perf. Schlrships., Ind. Univ., 1967-71; & Univ. of N Colo., 1974-75. Address: 1667 Richmond St. N, London, Ont. N6G 2N3, Can.

MERINEAU, André Henri, b. 5 Oct. 1929, Montreal, PQ, Canada. Organist. Educ: 1st Prize, Organ, Conserv. Music PQ, 1950; 1st Prize, Harmony, ibid., 1952; Dips., Organ & Comp., Conserv. Santa Cecilia, Rome, Italy, 1957. m. Madeleine Toupin. Debut: Montreal, 1949. Career: Organ recitalist; Prof., Harmony, Organ & Improvisation. Recordings incl: Canadian Broadcasting Serv. No. 254, Bach, Couperin, Champagne, Piche 1967; Pathe-Marconi VSM (30) CO65-1269, Tournemire, Chorlas-poèmes pour les sept paroles du Christ, op. 67; Mbr., Assn. Profs. Conserv. PQ. Hons: Prix Casavant, Montreal, 1949; Medaille Joseph Bonnet, ibid., 1949; Croix de Latran, Rome, 1957. Hobbies: Gardening; Woodwork. Mgmt: Madeleine Toupin-Merineau, 25 Vincent d'Indy Ave., Montreal, PQ, H2V 2S8, Canada.

MERKER, K Ethel, b. 20 July 1923, Chgo. Hts., Ill., USA. French Horn Player; Professor. Educ: BMusEd, MMus, Northwestern Univ. Career: 1st Horn, NBC Symnph. Orch., 1943-49, Boston Pops tour, 1965, Chgo. Opos Orch., 1970-76; Extra Horn, 1950-69, Asst. 1st Horn, 1969-71, Chgo. Symph. Orch., 3rd Horn, Chgo. Lyric Opera Co., 1956; w. Univ. of Chgo. Chmbr. Players, 1968-69; TV broadcasts w. Artists Show Case, WGN, 1968-72; also radio & TV commercials; has played for sev. ballet cos. Prof. of French Horn, Ind. Univ., 1972-. Recordings: w. Chgo. Symph.; on pop songs; film soundtrack, Super Fly. Contbr. to jrnls. Mbr. profl. orgs. Hobbies: Chmbr. Music; Travel. Address: c/o Schl. of Music, Ind. Univ., Bloomington, IN 47401, USA. 27.

MERKÙ, Pavle, b. 12 July 1927, Trieste, Italy. Teacher; Italian Radio (RAI) employee. Educ: degree in Slavic philos., Univ. of Ljubljana, 1950; degree in Arts, Univ. of Rome, 1960. m. Marta Jeric, 1 s., 1 d. Career: Secondary Schl. Tchr., 1950-65; employed by RAI, 1965-; radio & TV interviews in Italy, Yugoslavia & Switz. Comps. incl: opera, orchl. works, cantatas, chmbr. & instrumental music, choral & vocal music. Publs: Aspetti della critica verdiana presso gli soloveni fino al 1918, 1969; Josko Jakoncic, slovenski skladatelj, 1970; Identiteta in ostrostvo Marija Kogoja, 1976. Contbr. to num. profl. jrnls. Mbrships: Società Italiana di etnomusicologia, Rome; Slovenski raziskovalni institut, Trieste. Hons: Nagrada Presernovega sklada, Ljubljana, 1971 for violin concerto. Hobbies: Wine tasting; Mountaineering; Mushroom gatherings. Address: Via Rossetti 113, 34139 Trieste, Italy.

MERLET, Dominique, b. 18 Feb. 1938, Bordeaux, France. Concert Pianist; Organist; Professor. Educ: Conserv., Bordeaux, 1949-53; Conserv. Nat. Supérieur de Paris, 1953-57. m. Michelle Thibault, 2 s., 1 d. Career: Prof. of piano, Conserv. Nat. Supérieur de Paris; Organist, Notre-Dame des Blancs-Manteaux, Paris; Concert apps. w. major orchs. in France & abroad, incl. Germany, Brazil, Can., USA, UK, Italy, Poland, Portugal, Switz.; fest. apps. at Berlin, Bordeaux, Paris, Hong Kong; perfs. on radio & TV. Recordings: works by Bartok, Schumann, Shostakovich, Brahsm, Weber. Contbr. to: (book) The Piano, 1979; profl. publs. Hons: sev. 1st prizes at Conserv. de Paris; Grand Prix de L'Académie Audisque Francais, 1966; Grand Prix de l'Académie Charles Cros, 1966. Hobbies: Ping Pong; Swimming; Walking; Photography; Wine Tasting. Mgmt: Ch. et C Kiesgen, Paris, France. Address: 14 Avenue des Cottages, 78480 Verneuil-sur-Seine, France.

MERRICK, Frank, b. 30 April 1886, Clifton, Bristol, UK. Pianist; Composer. Educ: w. Leschetisky in Vienna, 1898-1901 & 1905. m. (1) Hope Squire 1910, (2) Sybil Case, 1938, 2 s., 1 d. Debut: Clifton, Bristol, 1895. Career: Piano solos at Clara Bitt concerts, 1902; English Provinces & Australasia, 1907-8; Prof. of Piano, Royal Manchester Coll. of Music, 1900-28; Royal Coll. of Music, 1928-56; Trinity Coll. of Music, 1956-. Comps. incl: Variations on a Somerset Folk

Song; 3 Part Invention; An Ocean Lullaby; 2 Concertos; Sonata for pfte. & cello; 'I Smell a Rat' for female voices. Publs: Practising the Piano, 1958 (revised, 1978). Mbrships: Leschitisky Soc.; RCM Union; ISM; CGGB; Songwriters Guild. Hons: Hon. MMus., Bristol Univ., 1958; Hon. FTCL, 1958; Hon. RCM, 1929; Dip. of Merit for Comp., Int. Rubenstein Comp. in Petersburg, 1910; Prize, Columbia Gramophone Co's Comp., 1928; CBE, 1978, etc. Address: 16 Horbury Cres., London W11 3NF, UK.

MERRILL, Nathaniel Chase, b. 8 Feb. 1927, Newton, Mass., USA. Opera Producer & Stage Director. Educ: BA, Dartmouth Coll., 1949; MA Boston Univ. Grad. Schl. of Music, 1953; special student, New England Conserv. of Music, 1949-53. m. Louise Sherman Merrill, 1 s., 1 d. Career: Leading Stage Dir., Metropolitan Opera Assn., NY. Dir., Tech. Servs. & permanent stage Prod., Opera du Rhin, Strasbourg, France; opera dir., in many other companies. Hobbies: Model Trains. Address: 321 W 78th St., Apt. 2-D, NY, NY 10024, USA.

MERRILL, Robert, b. 4 June 1919, Bklyn., NY, USA. Baritone Singer. m. Marion Machno, 1 s., 1 d. Debut: Met. Opera, NYC, 1945. Career: Num. radio & TV apps., USA; film, Aaron Slick from Punkin Crik; stage, Fiddler on the Roof; operatic perfs. throughout USA, Cuba, Mexico, Buenos Aires, Royal Opera House Covent Gdn., Venice, Tokyo & Paris. Recordings: 15 complete operas; highlights from Fiddler on the Roof & Kismet. Author, Once More From the Beginning, 1965; Between Acts, 1976; The Divas, 1978. Hons: Harriet Cohen Int. Music Award Opera Medal, 1961; Handal Medal, NYC, 1970; DMus, Gustavus Adolphus Coll., 1971. Hobbies: Golf; Collecting art. Mgmt: CAMI, 165 W 57th St., NY, NY 10019, USA. Address: c/o Met. Opera Assn., Lincoln Ctr., NY, NY 10023, USA.

MERRIMAN, Nan, b. 28 April 1920, Pitts., USA. Concert & Opera Mezzo-Soprano. m. Tom Brand. Debut: w. NBC Orch. under Toscanini, NY, 1943. Career: annual concert tours in USA & Can., appearing w. num. orchs.; apps. at major European fests.; concerts in many European cities also Johannesburg, S Arica, & Buenos Aires, Argentina; has appeared w. La Scala Opera, Milan & Glyndebourne Fest. Opera, UK. Has recorded for Angel, RCA Victor, Epic & Philips labels. Mbrships: Sigma Alpha Iota; Dominant Club, Los Angeles. Recip. 1st Prize, Nat. Fedn. of Music Clubs, 1943. Mgmt: Columbia Artists Mgmt., Inc., 165 W 57th St., NY, NY 10019, USA. 2.

MESNEY, Dorothy Taylor, b. 15 Sept. 1916, Bklyn., NY, USA. Singer; Pianist; Teacher of Piano & Voice. Educ: BA, Sarah Lawrence Coll.; Columbia Univ.; Queens Coll.; New Schl. for Soc. Rsch.; Juilliard Schl. of Music; Manhattan Schl. of Music. m. Peter Michael Mesney, 1 s., 2 d. Debut: Carnegie Recital Hall, NYC. Career: Num. perfs. of Am. music of all periods & types, colls., clubs, museums, schls., histl. socs., etc.; in some progs. self-accompanied w. autoharp & dulcimer; Fndr. & Prod., "The Am. Experience" (quintet); Co-Fndr., The Elizabethan Experience & the Elizabethan Encounter, featuring Elizabethan music. Comps. incl: hymns; vocal works; instrumental trios & quartets. Recordings: "Patchwork & Powderhorn-Folkways"; American Daguerrotype. Contbr. to jrnls. Mbrships. incl: Nat. Fedn. of Music Clubs; Metropolitan Opera Guild; NGPT. Hobbies incl: Tennis; Swimming; Writing; Art; Theatre. Mgmt: Lecture Cons. of LI, Mineola, NY, USA. Address: 324 Manor Rd., Douglaston, NY 11363, USA. 4, 5.

MESSENGER, Thomas, b. 15 Oct. 1938, Edinburgh, UK. Lecturer; Conductor. Educ: Organ Scholar, Univ. of Glasgow, 1957-61; BMus, ibid.; Fulbright Scholar & Grad. Asst., Wash. Univ., USA, 1961-62; ARCM, 1956; ARCO, 1960. m. Joan Helen Kelly, 2 s. Career: Grad. Asst., Wash. Univ., 1961-62; Lectr., Royal Scottish Acad. of Music, 1961-68; Cond., New Consort of Voices, 1966-68; Lectr., Dept. of Music, Univ. Coll. of N Wales, 1968-; Examiner, Royal Schls. of Music, 1969-; Cond., Monteverdi Singers, 1970-. Publs: Two Part Counterpoint from the Great Masters, Novello, 1970; Editions: Three Chansons for Three Recorders, Universal, 1971; Five Imitations for Three Recorders, Universal, 1971; Five Imitations for Three Recorders, 1972. Contbr. to var. music jrnls. Mbrships: Assn. of Univ. Tchrs.; Royal Musical Assn.; ISM. Hobbies: Reading; Travelling; Opera. Address: 16 Victoria Pk., Bangor, UK.

MESSERVY, George Thomas, b. Trinity, Jersey. Composer. Educ: TCL; LRAM. Career: "Symbols of Night" for soprano & ensemble perfd. at 1976 Camden Fest.; Comps. performed by Bournemouth Symph. Orch. & Guildford Cathedral Choir; Choral Music broadcast by BBC. Comps: Channel Island Folk Tales Suite for recorder trio; Jersey Folk Song arranged for voice & piano. Mbrships: CGGB; Friend of Soc. for Promotion of New Music. Hobbies: Cycling; Gardening. Address: 71 Rouge Bouillon, St. Helier, Jersey, Channel Islands.

MESSIAEN, Olivier, b. 10 Dec. 1908, Avignon, France. Music Educator; Composer; Organist. Educ: Paris Conserv. m. (1) Claire Delbos (dec. 1959), 1 s.; (2) Yvonne Loriod, 1961. Career: Organist, Trinité, Paris, 1931; Co-fndr., Jeune France movement, 1936; Prof., Ecole Normale & Schola Cantorum, 1936-39; Prof. of Harmony, Paris Conserv., 1941-47; Prof. of Analysis, Aesthetics & Rhythm, ibid., 1947-; Prof. of Comp., 1966-. Comps. incl: Livre d'Orgue, 1951; Orchl. works - Trios Petites Liturgies de la Presence Divine, 1944; Turangalila Symph., 1946; Couleurs de la Cité Céleste, 1964; Works based on birdsong, incl. Regeil des Oiseaux, 1953; Oiseaux exotiques, 1955; num. vocal & chmbr. music works, incl. Sept Haikai, 1963; La Transfiguration de Notre Seigneur Jesus Christ, 1968; Fauvette des Jardins, 1970. Recip. num. hons. incl: Grand Officier, Legion d'Honneur; Grand Off., Nat. Order of Merit; Erasme & Sibelius Prize, 1971.

MESSITER, Christine Marian, b. 18 Nov. 1948, Burbage, Leics., UK. Flautist. Educ: RCM; GRSM; ARCM (flute). m. Malcolm Messiter, 1 d. Career: Sub-Prin. Flute, Bournemouth Symph. Orch. & BBC Symph. Orch.; Co-Prin. Flute, BBC Symph. Orch. Recordings: 3 poèmes de Mallarme Ravel w. Boulez. Hons: RCM Flute Prize, 1970; Mozart Mem. Prize, 1971. Address: 67 Crescent W, Hadley Wood, Herts. EN4 OEQ, UK. 2.

MESSITER, Malcolm Cassan, b. 1 April 1949, Kingston, UK. Oboist. Educ: Paris Conserv., 1967; RCM; ARCM. m. Christine Messiter, 1 d. Debut: Purcell Rm., London, 1971. Career: Prin. Oboe, BBC Concert Orch., 1972-77. Hons: Royal Amateur Orchl. Soc. Bronze Medal, 1969; RCM Oboe Prize, 1970. Hobbies: Model Aircraft; Winemaking. Mgmt: Norman McCann Ltd., 16 Irving St., London WC2 7AU. Address: 67 Crescent W, Hadley Wood, Herts. EN4 OEQ, UK. 2.

MESTRES-QUADRENY, Josep M, b. 4 March 1929, Manresa, Barcelona, Spain. Composer. Educ: BSc Student of Cristofor Taltavull. Debut: 1957. Comps. incl: Suite Bufa, 1966; Perludi, 1968; Poemma, 1969; Micos i Pappollones, 1970; Essential Variations, 1970; Homage to Joan Prats, 1972. Recordings: Chmbr. Music No. 1; Music for Anna; Quartet by Catroc; Invention Mobile No. 2; Three Canons in Hon. of Galileo; Micos i Papallones; Divertimento La Ricarda; Double Concerto. Mbrships: Music Laboratory Phonos Catalan Assn. of Comps.; Catalan Ensemble of Contemporary Music; Fundació Joan Miró. Address: Av. Coll. del Portell, 41, 6e, 2a, Barceloa 12, Spain.

METIANU, Lucian, b. 3 June 1937, Cluj, Romania. Composer. Educ: Bucharest Conserv., 1957-63; Hochschule für Musik, Cologne, 1969-71. m. Georgeta Duhalm, 1 d. Comps. incl: 2 symphs., 2 str. quartets, Concerto for strgs., Evolutio '74, Sonata for cello, Duo for cello & bass, Pythagoreis (electronic), music for art films, documentaries & cartoons. Recordings of own works. Contbr. to Revue Roumaine d'histoire de l'art, Vol. 22, 1975 - an organised system of musical structure. Mbr., Romanian Union of Comps. Hons: Romanian Comps. Union prize, 1969. Hobby: Tennis. Address: Intrarea Nicolae Iorga 3, Apt. 3, Bucharest, sect. 1, Romania.

METSÄLÄ, Juha Einari, b. 23 May 1925, Raisala, Finland. Conductor. Educ: BA Helsinki Univ., 1953; Politices Magister, 1957; Sibelius Acad., Helsinki. m. Vappu Linnea Kuusiluoto. Debut: Helsinki, 1951. Career: Cond., orchs. in Kemi & Veitsiluoto, 1951-52, Jyvaskyla, 1955-56, Kerava, 1959-. Jarvenpaa, 1965-; Vis. Cond., Finland, Sweden. Comps. incl: works for voice & piano, solo instruments, chmbr. ensemble, choir, Ed., Pelimannisavelmia III, 1973. Mbr. Finnish orch. Conds. Recip. var. Comp. Prizes in academic competitions, 1951, 1953. Hobbies: Chess; Travel. Address: 17 Sepontie, 04200 Kerava, Finland.

METZ, Donald Edward, b. 8 April 1935, Cleveland, Ohio, USA. Associate Professor of Music Education; Organist. Educ: BA, Wooster Coll., 1957; MA Music Educ., Western Reserve Univ., 1963; PhD, ibid., 1968. Compositions: Sev. works for schl. use. Contbr. to Coun. for Rsch. in Music Educ., & The Choral Jrnl.; Ed., The Gen. Music Jrnl., Vol. 1 No. 1; Junior High General Music, (Ed.,), 1980. Ed. Comm., Jrnl. of Rsch. in Music Educ. Mbrships: Nat. Assn. for Humanities Educ.; Coun. for Rsch. in Music Educ.; MENC; Ohio Music Educators Assn. Address: 10597 Gloria Ave., Cincinnati, OH 45231, USA.

METZLER, Richard (Appleton), b. 12 Nov. 1948, Chicago, Ill., USA. Pianist. Educ: Harvard Univ.; Pvte. studies of piano w. Roberto Szidon, Luise Vosgerchian, David Del Tredici & Leon Kirchner. Career: Perfs. in Argentina, Belgium, Brazil, France, Germany, Italy, Netherlands, Switz. & USA; Soloist w. var. orchs. inclng. Philharmonia Hungarica; Apps. at Int. music fests. of Campos do Jordao, Geneva Sao Paulo & Siegborg; Actor & interpreter in Second German TV film "Brahms, der

unromantische Romantiker". Recordings incl: Works by Ives, Lekeu & Villa-Lobos. Recip. of Wister Memorial Award, Harvard Univ., 1970. Hobbies: Painting; Sports; Philately; Gastronomy; Airplane Watching; Photography. Mgmt: Concertos Maria Abreu, Praia do Flamengo 300, apart. 503, BR-22210, Rio de Janeiro RJ, Brazil. Address: Buchenweg 15, D-8019 Abersdorf, Post Steinhöring, German Fed. Repub. 28, 29.

MEWS, Eric Douglas Kelson, b. 22 Sept. 1918, St. John's, Nfld., Can. Composer; Organist. Educ: United Ch. Coll. & Mem. Univ., St. 'John's Nfld. TCL; BMus (London), 1939, FRCO, 1938, FTCL, 1956; DMus (London), 1961. m. Constantia (Nancy) Radius, 2 s., 1 d. Career: Prof. & Examiner, TCL, UK, 1946-63; Lectr., Colchester Tech. Coll., 1963-68; Sr. Lectr., then Assoc. Prof., Univ. of Auckland, Conservatorium of Music, NZ; Dir. of Music, St. Patrick's Cathedral, Auckland. Comps. incl: Ghosts, Fire, Water (choral); Gigue de Pan (organ & small drums); Joshua (trombone concerto). Recordings incl: Organ of St. Thomas, Tamaki, Auckland. Recip. Missa Brevis Competition Prize, Ont., Can., 1975. Hobbies: Music; Meccano modelling. Address: 10 Patey St., Remuera, Auckland 5, NZ.

MEXIS, Konstantin Filotas, b. 14 June 1913, Trieste, Italy. Pianist; Professor of Music. Educ: Musikakademie, Vienna. m. Elsemarie Muller, 2 s. Debut: Vienna, 1959. Career: Concerts in Vienna, London, Paris, Zürich, Lucerne, Salzburg, Athens, Salonika, Munich; Radio & TV apps. in Vienna, Salzburg & Paris. Comms: Var. Comps. for Piano. Sev. recordings. Mbr. Schlaraffia. Hons. incl: Musikpreis, Vienna, 1957; Silbermes Ehrenzeichen Niederosterreich, 1974; Silbemes Ehenzeichen Repub. Osterreich, 1974; Golden Ehrenplakette, Wien-Perchtoldsdorf, 1975. Hobbies: Medicine; Hist. Address: 2380 Wien-Perchtoldsdorf, Lohnsteinstrasse 37, Austria.

MEYER, Brigitte, b. 1 Oct. 1944, Bienne, Switz. Pianist. Educ: Conservs., Bienne & Lausanne; Acad. of Music, Vienna, 1 s. Career: 1st concert w. orch. aged 11; recital, chmbr. & concerto perfs. in most European countries, notably w. Vienna Symph. Orch., N German Radio Orch. of Hamburg, Orch. of the Suisse Romande; apps. w. Symph. Orch. of the Suisse Romande; apps. w. Symph. Orch. of Montreal; Fest. of Montreaux-Vevey 1974; Fest. of Vienna, 1975. Recordings: Gallo. Mbr., Assn. of Swiss Musicians. Hons: Bösendorfer Prize, 1971; Clara Haskil Prizes - 3rd, 1973, 2nd, 1975. Hobbies: Napping; Japanese Cooking; Cinema. Mgmt: Euphonia, Case postale 214, 1000 Lausanne 9, Switz. Address: Av. Davel 4, CH-1004 Lausanne, Switzerland.

MEYER, Ernst Hermann, b. 8 Dec. 1905, Berlin, Germany. Composer; Musicologist; Professor. Educ: Univ. of Berlin; Univ. of Heidelberg. PhD. m. Marjorie Stokes, 3 d. Career: num. apps. on film, TV & radio. Comps: oratorios, cantatas, songs, film music, opera (Reiter der Nacht); Orchl. & chmbr. music. num. recordings in GDR, USSR, Bulgaria, France, UK. Publs: English Chamber Music, 1946, '56, '74; Die mehrstimmige Spielmusik, 1933, Musik im Zeitgeschehen, 1956; Aufsätze uber Musik, 1977. Contbr. to profl. jrnls. in English, German, Russian, French, Dutch, Bulgarian & Czech. Mbrships: Int. Soc. for Musical Rsch.; Komponisten und Musikwissenschaftler der DDR; Handel Soc.; Acad. of Arts, Berlin & Milan. Recip. hon. doct., Univ. of Halle-Wittenberg, 1972. Hobbies: Working; Picking Mushrooms. Address: Bogenstr. 12, 1167 Berlin-Hessenwinkel, German Dem. Repub.

MEYER, Eve Rose, b. 29 Oct. 1927, Phila., Pa., USA. Musicologist; Professor of Music History. Educ: BS, 1949, EdM, 1956, Temple Univ.; PhD, Univ. of Pa., 1963. m. Saul Meyer. Career: on fac., Temple Univ., 1956-; TV series, Music appreciation, Univ. of the Air. Ed: An Introduction to Music by David Boyden, 1970; Ed., Divertimenti a Tre and a Quattro of Florian Leopold Gassmann; Benj. Carr's Musical Miscellany. Contbr. to: 18th Century Studies; Music Review; Music Educators Jrnl. Mbrships: Coun., Am. Musicol. Soc.; Music Lib. Assn.; Coll. Music Soc.; Sonneck Soc.; Soc. for 18th Century Studies. Recip. acad. hons. Address: Coll. of Music, Temple Univ., Philadelphia, PA 19122, USA.

MEYER, Kerstin, b. 3 Apr. 1928, Stockholm, Sweden. Operatic & Concert Mezzo-Soprano. Educ: RAM, 1948-50; Opera Schl., 1950-52; Mozarteum, Salzburg; study in Italy. Debut: Azucena, Il Trovatore, Royal Opera, Stockholm, 1952. Career: has appeared w. Vienna State Opera, Hamburg Opera, Met. Opera, San Fran. Opera, Paris Opera, at Covent Gdn. London, Teatro Colon, Buenos Aires, etc.; apps. at leading European fests. inclng. Bayreuth Fest., 1962-; concert tours incl. NZ & Orient, 1963. Aust., 1967. Mbr: Royal Musical Acad., Stockholm, Hamburg Opera; Berlin State Opera; Stockholm Opera. Address: Banergatan 71, Stockholm, Sweden. 2.

MEYER, Krzysztof, b. 11 Aug. 1943, Cracow, Poland. Composer; Music Theorist; Pianist. Educ: HS of Music, Cracow; Am. Conserv. Fontainebleau. m. Zofia Golab-Meyer, 1 s., 1 d. Debut: Warsaw Autumn, 1965. Career: num. radio, TV & film apps.; Prof., HS of Music, Cracow. Comps: Opera Cyberiada; 4 symphs.; violin, flute, cello, oboe & trumpet concertos; Polish Chants, soprano & orch.; 5 str. quartets; 5 piano sonatas; Harpsichord sonata; violin sonata; Hommage á Nadia BNoulanger, flute, alto & harp; Quartettino, soprano, flute, cello & piano; 24 preludes for piano; Lyric Triptich, Tenor & Orch.; Fire-Balls for Orch. Publs: Dmitri Shostakovich, 1973. Contbr. to jrnls. Mbr., Union of Polish Composers. Hons. incl: Brazilian Govt. Medal, 1975. Address: 5 Biala Droga, Cracow, Poland.

MEYEROWITZ, Michael, b. 7 Nov. 1926, Capetown, S Africa. Clarinettist. Educ: Dartington Hall Schl., 1936-41; Capetown Coll. of Music, 1941-45; RAM, 1947-51. m. Rosalie Louise Meyerowitz, 2 s., 1 d. Career: Capetown Municipal Orch., 1943-46; Prin. Clarinet, BBC Midland Light Orch., UK, 1953-58 & Clarinet, BBC Midland Light Orch., UK, 1953-58 & BBC Concert Orch., 1958-; Num. broadcasts as a clarinet soloist. Hons: John Solomon Wind Prize, RAM, 1951. Serious Interest in the Further Development of Clarinet Mouthpieces. Hobbies: Photography; Jewellery Making. Address: 36 Cambridge Rd., Teddington, Middx. TW11 8DN, UK. 3.

MEYERS, Emerson, b. 27 Oct. 1910, Wash., DC, USA. Pianist; Professor of Piano. Educ: Artist Dip., Peabody Conserv. of Music, Balt., Md. m. Emma Catherine Holt. Debut: Wash., DC, 1922. Career: Soloist w. Nat. Symph. Orch., Wash., DC; Nat. Gall. Orch., ibid & Liege Symph., Belgium; Solo recitals, Wash., DC, NY, Cleveland, Brussels & Liege; Lectr. on electronic music, Berlin, Florence, Brussels, Lisbon, Vienna, Wash., DC, NY & Phila.; Dir., Profl. Music, Nat. Capitol Sesquicentennial Commn., US Govt., 1950; Prof. of Music Emeritus, The Cath. Univ. of Am., Wash., DC, 1976-; Dir., Electronsonic Music Studio, itid. Recorded Comps. incl: Intervals 1; In Memoriam; Chez Dentiste; Rhythmus; Moonflight Space Music; Rhapsodie Frantastique; Marches Militaires; Metaphoriquement. Contbr. to: Notes; Am. Music Tchr. Mbrships: Cosmos Club; Am. Soc. of Comps., Authors & Publrs.; Am. Music Ctr.; Music Tchrs. Nat. Assn. Hons: Award for Disting. Contribution to Music in Wash., 1950; Plaque, Outstanding Serv. as Pres., Eastern Div., Music Tchrs. Nat. Assn., 1966; Peabody Conserv. Disting. Alumni Award, 1968. Address: 3006 29th Ave., Hyattsville, MD 20782, USA. 2.

MEYLAN, Jean, b. 22 Dec. 1915, Geneva, Switz. Conductor. Educ: Lic. in Law, Univ. of Geneva; Conservs. of Geneva & Lausanne; pvte. studies (also in Paris); studied w. Felix Weingartner, Carl Schuricht, Paul Klecki & Eugène Bigot. m. Elisabeth Buscarlet, 1 s., 1 d. Debut: w. Collegium Musicum, Geneva, 1941. Career: Guest apps., Paris (Lamoureux), Florence & Cologne (Gürzenich-Orch.); Chief Cond., Radio Orch., Cologne, 1949-; Main Guest Cond., St.-Gall, 1953-56; Cond., Geneva Chmbr. Orch. & Radio Orch. Beromunster, 1954-56; Choir Master & Cond., Opera House (Soc. romande de spectacle), Geneva, 1958; Musical Ldr., ibid., 1960; Permanent Guest Cond., Grand-Théâtre de Genève, 1962-; Guest Cond., num. orchs.; w. Suisse Romande Orch., Geneva. Recordings: Beethoven, Schubert, Falla & Prokofiev, on Supraphon. Contbr. articles to anthols. & jrnls. Mbrships: Chmn., Geneva Competition for Young Performers, 1969-; AMS; Rotary Club; Assoc. Mbr., Acad. fu Chablais, France. Hons: Arnold Bax Mem. Medal, 1958; Dvorak Medal, 1974. Hobbies: Walking; Reading; Mountaineering. Address: 6 route de Drize, CH-1227 Carouge, Switzerland.

MEYN, Richard, b. 7 July 1949, Terre Haute, Ind., USA. Instructor of Performing Arts; Double-Bass Player. Educ: Degree in Applied Arts, Lane Community Coll., Eugene, Ore.; Univ. of Ore. Career: Prin. Double-Bass, All-Northwest Youth Orch., 1966; Prin. Double-Bass, Univ. of Ore. Symph., 1968-69; Instructor of Performing Arts, Lane Community Coll., Eugene, 1975-; Prin. Double-Bass, Eugene Symph. Orch., 1976-; Asst. Mgr., Viscount Records Inc. Hons: 1st Place, Ore. State Solo Contest, 1967; John Philip Sousa Band Award, 1967. Hobbies: US & Brit. Numismatics & Philately; Long Distance Swimming & Bicycling; Study of Brit. & US Social History. Address: 243 St. Apt. 11, Springfield, OR 97447, USA.

MICEK, Isabelle Helen, b. 28 July 1922, Shelby, Neb., USA. Piano & Voice Instructor. Educ: BMus, St. Louis Inst. of Music, 1943; MMus, ibid., 1972; Peabody Conserv., 1971. Career incls: Pvte. piano, voice & theory, Columbus, Neb., 1946-; Choir Dir., Organist, Profl. Accomp., 1946-51. Author, History of Keyboard Music to JS Bach, 1972. Mbrships: Music Tchrs.

Nat. Assn.; Pres., NE Dist., Neb. MTA; Nat. Guild Piano Teaching. Hons: Medallion of Merit Award, Art Publ. Soc., 1957; Pres., Community Conserts Assn., Columbus, Neb., 1965-67; Scholarships for Seminars in Music, Mexico, Europe & S Am. Hobbies: Camera Club; Cath. Daughters of Am. Address: 2408 1/2 13th St., Columbus, NE 68601, USA. 5.

MICHAELS, Timothy Croak, b. 1 Oct. 1951, Lock Haven, Pa., USA. Tenor. Educ: BMus, Eastman Schl. of Music, Rochester, NY, 1971; Opera Theatre, Ind. Univ. Schl. of Music, Bloomington, Ind., 1972-73. Debut: Chautauqua Fest., NY, 1970; Stockholm Konserthuset, Sweden, 1975. Career: Chmbr. music concerts; Solo recitals in Scandinavia, Italy, Austria, Spain, USA; Radio & TV apps. in Norway & Sweden; European premier of Am. comp. Frank Ahrold & Ernst Bacon; Swedish premier of music by William Walton & Peter Lyne; Official emissary for Promoting Enduring Peace Inc., People to People Int. & USA Chapt. of UNESCO w. concert tours. num. recordings. Mbrships: Official Emissary, Promoting Enduring Peace; Nat. Fedn. of Music Clubs; UNESCO; People to People; Int.; Svensk-Amerikansk Sallskap; Int. Soc. for Contemporary Music. Hons: Grant for young artsts, Pa. Assn of Music Clubs, 1969; Award for outstanding recitals, Nat. Fedn. of Music Clubs, 1970, 1972; Oberlin Opera Awards, 1972. Hobbies: Writing; Reading; Cycling. Address: Tellusborgsvägen 110 11, Hägersten 12637, Stockholm, Sweden.

MICHALAK, Thomas, b. Krakow, Poland. Music Director; Violinist. Educ: Violin studies w. Irene Dubiska. m., 2 d. Career: Violinist, Warsaw Phil., Phila. Orch.; Cond., Ballet Russe of Monte Carlo, 1964; Asst. Cond.; Chmbr. Soc. of Phila., 1964; Marlborough Music Fest., 1965/66; Fac. Mbr., Hd. of Orch., Ithaca Coll., 1967; Music Dir., Phil. Soc. of Northeastern Pa., 1973; Exxon Affiliate Cond., Pitts. Symph. Orch., 1974; Music Dir., Canton, Ohio Symph. Orch. & Cond., Pitts. Youth Symph., 1976; Music Dir., NJ Symph. Orch., 1977-. Recordings: w. Marlboro musicians under Pablo Casals. Hons: Silver Medal, Moscow Int. Competition (violin); Koussevitzky Prize in Cond., Tanglewood, 1972. Address: c/o New Jersey Symph. Orch., 213 Washington St., Newark, NJ 07101, USA.

MICHALEK, Allen S, b. 11 Sept. 1940, Berea, Ohio, USA. Educator; Jazz Musician. Educ: MA (Music), Univ. of SC; Univ. of Nevada; Berklee Coll. of Music (Dip.). m. Karen Ann Michalek. Career: profl. reed player in Boston, Las Vegas, Toronto & Reno for all major media; tchr. of jazz, Humber Coll., Berkeley Coll, Boston & Univ. of Nevada; chmn., Bd. of Govs., Reno Int. Jazz Fest.; cond., Humber Coll. Jazz Ensemble, which toured Europe & perf. at Montreaux Jazz Fest., Switz. num. comps. recorded & published. Recordings incl: Vioces; 1st Take; On the Way to Montreaux; Fusions 1. Publs: Modern Harmonic Progression, 1977; Composition, 1980. Hons: Winner, Can. Stage Band Fest. w. Humber Coll. Band, 1976; Juno Nomination, 1979; featured artist, num. concert & fests. Address: RR No. 4, Tottenham, Ont. LOG 1WO, Can.

MICHALOWSKI Kornel, b. 23 Feb. 1923, Poznán, Poland. Music Librarian; Music Bibliographer; Musicologist. Educ: studied w. Aldolf Chybiński, Poznán Univ., 1947-51. m. Helena Mindak, 2 s., 1 d. Career: w. Poznań Univ. Lib., 1945-; Hd., Music Div., ibid., 1950-. Publs. incl: Opery polskie (Polish Operas), 1954; Bibliografia polskiego piśmennictwa muzycznego (Bibliog. of Polish music lit.), 1955, Supplement, 1964; Karol Szymanowski. Katalog tematyczny dzieł i bibliografia (Thematic catalogue of works & bilbiog.), 1967; Bilbiografia chopinowska 1849-1969, (Chopin Bibliog.), 1970. Contbr. to jrnls. Mbrships: Bd., Musicols.' Sect., Polsih Composers Union; Vice-Chmn., Music Libs. Sect. & Nat. Grp. of AIBM, Polish Libs. Assn.; Rsch. Couns., Chopin Soc., Warsaw; Poznań Musical Soc. Hons: Golden Cross of Merit, 1972; Cultural Award, City of Poznań, 1971. Address: Orzeszkowej 9/11, 60-778 Poznań, Poland.

MICHAUD, Armand Herve, b. 13 Aug. 1910, Warwick, RI, USA. Violinist; Teacher. Educ: BA Philos.; New England Conserv.; Providence Coll.; Rhode Island Coll. m. Eveline Truchon, 8 c. Career: Schl. Music Tchr., grades through coll.; Apps. on TV & regular progs. on radio; Apps. w. Providence Symph. Orch.; RI Phil. Orch.; Boston People's Symph. Orch.; Pro-Art Quartet; Tours, Europe & S Am. Comps. incl: Fantasie for orch. & string orch.; Several short pieces for orch.; Mass in A minor; 3 songs commemorating the Am. Centennial, 1976. Contbr. of articles to newspapers. Mbrships: Musicians Union; Chopin Club; Providence Symph. Soc. Recip. Tanglewood Scholarship. Hobby: Hist. Address: New London Turnpike, Wyoming, RI 02898, USA.

MICHEL, Madelon, b. 6 Aug. 1939, Amsterdam, Netherlands. Singer. Educ: Tchrs. Schl. Music. m. Ronald Kok, 3 c. Debut: 1956. Career: Solo concerts & perfs. w. choirs; Oratorium concerts throughout Holland, 1973-; Mbr., Polish Baroque Ensemble 'Alla Polacca', vocal quartet 'De Lorme Quartet', & NOS radio chmbr. choir. Mbrships: KNTV; NTB. Hobbies: Piano playing; Collecting flutes; Animals; Camping. Address: Valkenhoflaan 2, Hilversum, Netherlands.

MICHEL, Paul, b. 8 Oct. 1918, Greiz, Germany. Musicologist; Music Educator. Educ: Univ. of Jena; PhD, Humboldt-Univ. of Berlin, 1957. m. Brigitte Michel, 1 c. Career: Lectr., Music Psychol., Educ., Franz Liszt Acad. of Music, Weimar, 1951-; Vice-Chancellor, ibid., 1951-; Dir., Inst. of Educ. & Methodol., ibid., 1960-; Prof., ibid., 1953; Sr. Prof., 1959-. Publs: Musikalische Fähigkeiten & Fertigkeiten, 1961, 1963, 1966, 1971; Musik & Hörer in unserer Zeit, 1967; Psychologische Grundlagen der Muzikerziehung, 1968. Contbr. to: Musik in der Schule; Musick & Gesellschaft; Beiträge zur Musikwissenschaft; Yr. Books of Int. Soc. for Music Educ.; Num. reports of ISME Rsch. Sems., etc. Mbrships: Bd. of Dir., Int. Soc. for Music Educ.; Pres., Nat. Ctr. of Music Educ., GDR; Psychol. Soc., GDR; Int. Soc. for Musicol Managing Committee, Union of Comps. & Musicologists; Nat. Music Coun. of GDR; Fellow of Scientific Coun. of Acad. of Pedagogical Sciences in GDR; Rsch. Commission of Int. Soc. for Music Educ. Address: 15 Gutenbergstr., Weimar, German Dem. Repub.

MICHEL, Paul-Baudouin, b. 7 Sept. 1930, Haine-St-Pierre, Hainaut, Belgium. Composer; Professor of Music History & Harmony; Professor of Music Composition. Educ: Royal Conservs., Mons & Brussels; Grad. in Comp., Queen Elisabeth Chapel of Music, m. Francoise Wel, 2 c. Career incls: Dir., Woluwe-St-Lambert Acad. of Music; Prof. of Music Hist. & Harmony; Prof. of Music Comp., Royal Conserv. of Mon; Lectr., radio. Comps. incl: Symphonic Variations, for orch., 1960; Concaténation, for chmbr. orch., 1967; Musicoïde, for 2 pianos, 1971; Libration; Paysage Polyphonique, 1978; Toreutique I-VI. Recordings: T Inframorphoses, for strings; Prismes for clarinet quartet; Musique Contemporaine for piano. Contbr. to var. profl. jrnls. Mbrships. incl: CeBeDeM; Belgian Lects. Assn.; Jeunesses Musicales. Hons. incl: Gold Medal & Cup, Lutèce Acad., 1974; Paul Gilson Prize, 1977. Hobbies: Chess; Sci. fiction. Address: Rue du Zéphyr 30, 1200 Brussels, Belgium.

MICHELANGELI, Arturo Benedetti, b. 5 Jan. 1920, Italy. Concert pianist. Educ: Conserv. G Verdi, Milan & w. pvte. tutors, incl. Paolo Chiuieri, Brescia & Giovanni Anfassi, Milan. Career incl: concert perfs. throughout the world. Hons: Winner, Grand Prix of Geneva, 1939; Gold Medal of Italian Repub. Address & Mgmt: Harold Holt Ltd., 122 Wigmore St., London W.1, UK.

MICHELET, Michel, b. 27 June 1899, Kiev, USSR. Composer; Cellist; Pianist; Conductor. Educ: Grad., Leipzig Conserv., Germany where he studied comp. w. Max Reger, cello w. Julius Klengel & piano w. Robert Teichmuller; Grad., St. Petersburg Conserv.; Studied Comp. w. Reinhold Gliere, Kieff Conserv. m. Edith Michelet. Career: Prof., Cello, Neues Wiener Conserv., Vienna, Austria; Musical Dir., Russian Romantic Theatre, Berlin, Germany; Cellist in num. concerts w. Boris Kroyt Quartet; Scorer of 108 films. Compositions (publd.) incl: (concert comps.) String Quartet; Alexandria-Songs; Romantic Trio; Chinoiserie; Elegy; Homage to Bach, 4-part suite for symph. orch.; Hanelle, opera after Gerhart Hauptman; Cathedral Windows, oratorio (text by John Rufus Sharpe III); 3 Violin Sonatas; A Cello Sonata; 10 Cello Preludes; Sanctuary; A Sonata for Balalaika & Piano; Harmonie du Soir; (film scores) Le Rosier de Madame Husson (w. Fernande); Les Yeux Noires (w. Harry Bauer, Simone Simone & Jean Pierre Aumont); Diary of a Chambermaid, dir. by Jean Renoir; The Journey; M; The Chase; Last Film Score, 1974, Challenge; Hannele (opera), 1973. Recordings: Many popular songs from films inclng. Concert Songs & Arias (Orion Records), 1973. Mbrships: SACEM (French Comps. Soc.), Paris, France. Hons: 2 nominations for Oscar Awards, Acad. of Motion Pictures. Hobbies: Photography. Address: 1624 N Courtney Ave., Hollywood, CA 90046, USA.

MICHELOW, Sybil, b. Johannesburg, S Africa. Contralto Singer; Pianist. Educ: Music Dip., Univ. of Witwatersrand. m. Derek Goldfoot. Debut: London, 1968. Career: concert perfs. w. leading orchs. & conds., UK & abroad; frequent radio & TV broadcasts; perf. Rule Britannia, las night of Proms, 1968; ic singing classes & musical prods. RADA. Comps. incl: incidental music for RADA prods. of 2 Brecht plays & children's stories w. music for S African Broadcasting Corp. Recordings: Bach Cantatas 78 & 106; Bliss Pastoral; Madrigals; Dallapiccolo Sicut Umbra. Mbr., ISM. Large scale orchl. works w. voice specially written for her by Wilfred Josephs. Hobbies: Playing piano in chmbr. grps.; Gardening. Address: 50 Chatsworth Rd., London NW2 4DD, UK. 3, 27.

MICHELUCCI, Roberto, b. 29 Oct. 1922, Livorno, Italy. Violinist. Educ: Violin Dip., Florence Conserv. m. Adriana Bruni (div.), 2 c. Debut: Aged 9, Milan. Career: Soloist, Musici di Roma; recitals w. important pianists; Soloist w. European Orchs.; TV & radio apps. Recordings incl: works by Tommaso Albinoni, Francesco Bonporti, J S Bach, Pietro Antonio Locatelli, Felix Mendelssohn, W A Mozart, A Vivaldi & Guiseppe Tartini. Mbr., Academia Nazionale di Lettere ed Arti Luigi Cherubini, Florence. Hons: Primo premio assoluto of Rassegna Concertisti, Rome, 1950; Disco d'oro Tokio, 1970; Grand Prix du Disque, Parigi, 1963. Hobby: Sports cars. Mgmt: Konzertagentur Pio Chesini, Basel CH. Address: Via di Catigliano 164, 50066 Vaggio-Reggello (Firenze), Italy.

MICHII, Makoto, b. 10 Nov. 1935, Hokkaido, Japan. String Bassist; Piano Technician; Craftsman. Educ: BMus, BA, Musashino Acad. Musicae, Tokyo; Tchrs. Cert. String Bass instruction; Reg. Piano Technician Craftsman, Piano Technician's Guild, USA. m. Takako Michii, 2 s. Debut: Tokyo, 1960. Career: String Bassist, Japanese Phil. Orch., Tokyp, 1960-62; Prin. String Bassist, Yomiuri Nippon Symph. Orch., ibid., 1962-66; Ctr. for Creative & Perf. Arts, SUNY at Buffalo, USA, 1966-68; String Bassist, Buffalo Phil. Orch. Soc. Inc., 1967-; Solo recital, Buffalo, 1967. Recordings: Various, USA. Publ: Harmonics of String Bass, 1963. Mbr., profl. assns. Hons. incl: Henry B Cabot Award, 1967; Kouusevitzky Fellowship, 1967; Fulbright Fellow from Japan to USA, 1966-68. Hobbies: Skiing; Swimming; Travelling. Mgmt: Buffalo Phil. Orch. Soc. Inc. Address: 116 Getzville Rd., Buffalo, NY 14226, USA.

MICKIEWICZ, Halina, b. 7 Nov. 1923, Stolpce, Poland. Singer. Educ: Dips. & special qualification in singing, HS of Music. Widow, 1 d. Debut: Warsaw, 1943. Career: Soloist w. Warsaw State Opera, 1946-59; broadcast appearances on Polish Radio, 1945-, & TV, 1974-75. Recordings: var. operatic arias etc. from works of Verdi, Donizetti, Bellini, Stauss, Gounod, etc. Mbrships: Soc. of Polish Musicians; Soc. of Polish Theatres & Films; Soc. of Friends of Music, Gdansk. Recip. var. Polish State Hons. inclnd. Gold Medals of Cultural Workers, 1972 & '74. Hobby: Record Collection. Address: ul. Abrahama 84-15, Gdynia 81-387, Poland.

MIDDAUGH, Benjamin, b. 23 Feb. 1934, Aquila, Tex., USA. Singer (baritone); Opera Director; Conductor; Teacher. Educ: BMus, N Tex. State Univ., 1956; MMus, Mich. State Univ., 1962; MusD, Fla. State Univ., 1968; vocal study w. pvte. tutors. m. Pamela Arkin, 1 s., 2 d. Debut: Carnegie Recital Hall, NYC, 1965. Career: Solo appearances w. Operas Cos. of Miami, Birmingham (Ala.); & in concert w. Birmingham Symph., Mobile Symph. & Brevard Music Ctr. Orch.; Fndr.-Dir., The Southern Regional Opera Co., Birmingham, Ala.; oratorio & recital apps. in S & E US; Musical Dir., Cond., Center Playere, Birmingham, Ala., 1969 73. Contbr. to: NATS Bulletin. Mbrships. incl; Ala. State Gov., Nat. Assn. Tchrs. of Singing; Nat. Bd. Dirs., Nat. Fedn. of Music Clubs, 4 vrs.; MTNA; Pi Kappa Lambda; Phi Kappa Phi; Am. Fedn. of Musicians. Recip. var. music hons. Hobbies: Stamp Collecting. Address: PO Box 66, Ontevallo, LA 35115, USA. 7.

MIDDENWAY, Ralph, b. 9 Sept. 1932, Sydney, Aust. Production Director; Theatre Consultant; University Administrator; Music Critic. Educ: Arts degree, Univ. Sydney; Bassoon, Music, NSW Conserv.; Singing, Univ. Adelaide. m. Gillian Kennedy, 3 d. Career: University Administrator; Prof. Dir., var. operas, mainly Univ. Adelaide Dept. Music; Theatre Cons., Univ. Adelaide. Comps: Missa Omnibus Sanctis (capella choir); Mosaics, 1, 2, 3 (brass percussion); Child of Heaven (choir, brass, percussion). Contbr: Opera & Music Critic, Adelaide Advertiser, 1971-76; Adelaide Opera & Music Critic; The Australian, 1976-. Fellowship, Aust. comps.; SA Rep., ibid. Hobbies: Canoeing, Kayaking; Rafting; Bushwalking; Cycling. Address: 13 Grandview Grove, Toorak Gdns., SA 5065, Austalia.

MIDDLETON, Jaynne Claire, b. 14 Nov. 1947, Memphis, Tenn., USA. Lyric Soprano. Educ: BMus, Fla. State Univ., 1969; MMus, ibid., 1972. Career: Soloist, Robert Shaw Chorale, The Atlanta Symph., Messiah, 1973; sev. ldng. operatic roles; soloist, Black, Magnificat, 1978. Mbrships: Nat. Assn. of Tchrs. of Singing; Pi Kappa Lambda; Sigma Alpha Iota. Recip. Award, Theodore Presser Fndn., 1965-66. Address: Schl. of Music, Hardin-Simmons Univ., Abilene, TX 79603, USA.

MIDNEY, Barbara Joan, b. 15 Jan. 1954, Bridgeport, Conn., USA. Musician (oboe & English Horn). Educ: BMus, Boston Conserv. of Music, 1976; Music history studies, Harvard Univ., summer, 1977. Career: Prin. oboe, Boston Conserv. Orch., 1974-76; Prin. oboe, Harvard Cantabrigia Orch., 1976;

Newport (RI) Fest. Orch., Mozart-at-Newport Orch., 1976; Des Moines Metro Opera Orch., 1977; Richmond, Va., Symph., 1977-78; Richmond Civic Opera Orch., 1977-78; Fac., Va. Commonwealth Univ. Community Music Schl.; Concert Ballet of Va. Orch., 1977-78; Solo recitals, Boston, Va., & Conn. Recordings: commercials. Mbrships: Am. Symph. Orch. League; Int. Double Reed Soc. Hobbies: Cooking; Jogging. Address: 97 Douglas Drive, S Meriden, CT 06450, USA.

MIEG, Peter, b. 5 Sept. 1906, Lenzburg, Switz. Composer. Educ: Univs. of Zürich, Basle, Paris; PhD; Studied piano w. Hans Münich (Basle), Emil Frey (Zürich); theory w. C A Richter (Lenzburg), further studies w. Frank Martin. Career: Freelance comp.; music critic for Swiss & foreign jrnls. Comps. incl: Sinfonie, Rondeau Symphonique, Concerto da Camera, Concerto Veneziano, Toccata, Combray, Concertos for piano, flute, 2 flutes, cello, cembalo; songs for tenor & orch. Recordings: Toccata, Concerto for 2 flutes, Piano Concerto No. 2, Kammermusik, tenor songs. Publs: Erinnerungen an Bartok, 1958; ed., Frank Martin texts. Contbr. to profl. jrnls. Mbr. Schweizerischer Tonkünstlerverein. Hons: Ehrensenator der Kulturstiftung Pro Argovia; Kulturpreis der Stadt Lenzburg. Address: Schlossgasse 50, 5600 Lenzburg, Switz.

MIEHLER, Otto, b. 24 Aug. 1903, Passau, Niederbayern, Germany. Music Director; Composer; Pianist. Educ: qualified at Tchr. Trng. Coll.; studied piano & dir. w. Prof. Hermann Zilcher, Bayerisches Staats Konservatorium Würzburg; qualified in comp.; studied musicol., Würzburg Univ. m. Elisabeth Müller-Brunn, 1 d. Career incls: Music Dir., Städische Bühnen (staged) Flensburg, & Dir. of choir & Phil. Concert, 1938-50; Freelance Comp., Guest Cond., Piano Accomp., 1951-61; Lectr., State Coll. for mixed choir & organ or orch.; hymns. on text by Friedr. Wilh. Weber; Marienkantate for soprano, female choir & orch.; Arie, Serenade und Elegie on text by Fleming & Mörike; chmbr. music. Recordings incl; Musik zur Bewegung (4 records). Mbr. profl. orgs. Address: Maerkircherstr. 12, D-8000 Munich 80, German Fed. Repub.

MIERZECKA, Elzbieta, b. 4 Aug. 1943, Warsaw, Poland. Singer (Soprano). Educ: MA; Chopin's Schl. of Music, Warsaw; State Higher Schl. of Music, Warsaw; Postgrad. Pedagogical Musical Studies. m. Zdzislaw Mierzecki, 1 d. Debut: Opera debut in Verbum Nobile, The Great Theatre, Warsaw, 1969. Career: Soloist, Warsaw Autumn Festival; Soloist w. The Polish Army Artistic Ensemble in apps. in Greece, Czechoslovakia, German Democratic Repub., Bulgaria, Hungary, Can. & USA. Num. recordings of Nat. Polish songs for Polish radio. Mbrships: Polish Assn. of Artists-Musicians; Trade Union of Arts & Culture Employees. Hobbies: Antiques; Sewing. Address: ul. Walbrzyska 15 m. 517, 02-739 Warszawa, Poland.

MIERZEJEWSKI, Mieczystaw, b. 10 Nov. 1905, Poznan, Poland. Orchestra Conductor; Pianist. Educ: Dip. State Debut: Poznan. Career: Orch. Cond., Polish Radio; Warsaw State Opera & Phil.; Rep., Polish State Ballet w. apps. in Paris, Toulouse, London, Berlin, num. other European countries, USA. Recordings incl: King Roger; Opera in 3 acts by K Szymanowski. Hons: Dip. d'honneur, Paris, 1937; Polish Commodore Polouia Restituta, 1956; Warsaw Capital Prize, 1958; Order of Banner of Labour, 1959; Merited Worker of Culture, 1969. Address All Armii WP 11 m. 29, Warsaw 00-580, Poland.

MIES, Paul, b. 22 Oct. 1889, Cologne, Germany. Musicologist. Educ: PhD, Univ. of Bonn, 1912. m. Louise Jackels, 2 d. Career: Asst. Schl. Master, 1918-45; War Service, 1914-18, 1939-45; Dir., Inst. for Schl. Music, & Prof., Music Acad., Cologne, 1946-54. Author, Die Bedeutung der Skizzen Beethovens zur Erkenntnis seines Stiles, 1925, 1928, 1932, 1969. Contbr. to: Rheinische Musiker, Vol. 1, Vol. 8; Music in Geschichte & Gegenwart; Beethovenjahrbuch; Die Musikforschung; Musikhaneld; Musica Sacra. Mbrships: New Bach Soc.; Int. Bach Soc.; Soc. for Music Rshc.; Inst. Soc. for Music Rsch. Hons: Hon. Mbr., Beethoven House Soc.; Bonn; Hon. Mbr., Heimatvereins Alt-Köln, Cologne. Address: 23 I Grafenwerthstr., 5 Cologne 41, German Fed. Repub.

MIETELSKI, Marek Stefan, b. 27 Feb. 1933, Krakow, Poland. Pianist. Educ: Dip. Piano, Acad. of Music, Krakow; MA piano; Artist Musician. m. Krystyna Ungeheuer. Debut: Piano recital in Krzystofory Gall., Krakow at Cracow Spring of Young Musicians Fest., 1963. Career: Apps. as soloist & mbr. of MW 2 Ensemble on stage, film, TV & radio in Poland & num. other countries; Istanbul Fest., Fest. of Arts Shiraz-Persepolis, 1976; Warsaw Autumn Fest., 1978; Sec., MW 2 Ensemble, 1962-; Film apps. in Paris, Geneva & London; Lectr., Acad. of Music & Lyceum of Music, Krakow. Recordings w. MW 2 Ensemble. Mbr. Polish Artists & Musicians Assn. Num. awards. Hobbies: Sightseeing; Camping; Photography; Walking. Mgmt: Polska

Agencja Artystuczna "Pagart" Biuro Muxyki, pl. Zwycietwa 9, 00-078 Warszawa, Poland. Address: ul. Na Blonie 3/121, 30 147 Kraków, Poland.

MIGNONE, Francisco, b. 3 Sept. 1897, Sao Paulo, Brazil. Composer; Pianist; Conductor. Educ: Sao Paulo Conserv. Career incls: Prof. of Harmony & Piano, Sao Paulo Conserv.; toured USA, 1942. Compositions incl: Sinfonia de Trabalho; Momus Caramaril for orch.; Congada for orch.; Contratador de Diamantes (opera); Four Churches for Orch.; El Jayon (opera); Batucage (ballet); Babaloxa (ballet); Maracutu de Chico-Rei (ballet); O espantalho (ballet); Yara (ballet). Recip. of Govt. Grant, 1920.

MIHALJINEC, Stjepan, b. 1 Dec. 1935, Zagreb, Yugoslavia. Composer; Conductor; Pianist. Educ: Music Theory, Music Acad., Zagreb. m. Elvira Voća, 1 c. Career: Music Redactor, Radio Zagreb; Comp. of musicals, popular songs, instrumental music, music for children; Pianist, light music; Ldr., own ensemble Stjepan Milhaljinec, 20 yrs.; Radio & TV prod.; Music for films. Comps: Approx. 200 popular songs; musical, I and my other I; Musicals for children, Cinderella, The Clever Rooster; Phantasy for Piano & Symph. orch.; Tears at Daybreak (Proplakat če zora); The Last Cab (Zadnji fijaker). Recordings: approx. 100 single, 20 LP, Tape Recordings. Mbrships: Pres., Croatian Musicians Assn.; Dir., Fest. of Popular Songs, Krapina. Hons: 1st Prize, Int. Fest., Split, 1971; Sev. 2nd & 3rd prizes, in light music fests. Hobby: Postage stamps. Address: Turinina 2/5, 41000 Zagreb, Yugoslavia.

MIHÁLKA, György, b. 22 April 1924, Kělcse, Hungary. Professor; Choral Director. Educ: Dips., Music High Schl. & Univ.; DMus. m. Maria Sirotka, 2 c. Debut: Debrecen, 1970. Career: Num. prizes for female choir, Hungary, Yugoslavia, France & UK; Concert tours, Yugoslavia, 1973, '74, '75, Bulgaria, 1973, German Fed. Repub. & Czech., 1975; Tchr. of Choir Dir.; Ldr. & Dir. of Female Choir; Dir., Secondary Music Schls. Choir, Szeged, 2 Workers' Choirs, Szeged; Tchr. at Tchrs. Coll., Szeged. Publs: Folk-music instruments in Szeged, 1961; Development of music-life in Szeged, 1971; History of Hungarian Choruses - Problems in Chorus Directing, 1979. Mbrships: Hungarian Music Artists' Soc.; Fndn. mbr., Hungarian Musicians Soc. (Kodály). Hons. incl: Main music Prize, Szeged, 1976; Juhasz Gyula Prize for Culture, 1978. Hobbies: Family; Travelling. Address: Madách u. 17, 6721 Szeged, Hungary.

MIHALY, Andras, b. 6 Nov. 1917, Budapest, Hungary. Composer; Professor of Chamber Music. Educ: F Liszt Conserv. of Music Budapest. m. Klara Pfeifer, 1951, 2 s. Career: Solo Cellist, Budapest Opera House Orch., 1946-47; Gen. Sec., Budapest Opera, 1948-49; Prof. of Chmbr. Music, F Liszt Conserv., 1950-; Rdr. of Contemporary Music, Hungarian Broadcasting Corp., 1959-. Compositions incl: Concerto for Cello & Orch., 1953; Concerto for Piano & Orch., 1954; Fantasy for Wind Quintet & String Orch., 1955; Songs on the Poems of James Joyce, 1958; Concerto for Violin & Orch., 1959; String Quartet, 1960; Symph., 1962; Together & Alone (2-act opera), 1965. Hons: Kossuth Prize, 1955; Erkel Prize, 1950, 1965; Labour Order of Merit, Golden degree, 1970. Hobby: Reading. Address: Verhalom ter 9b, Budapest 2, Hungary.

MIHULE, Jaroslav, b. 1 Dec. 1930, Prague, Czechoslovakia. University Professor; Musicologist; Composer. Educ: Charles Univ., Prague, 1949-53; Music Conserv., Prague, 1952-55; PhD, 1972; Candidatus Scienciae, 1973. Career: Asst. Prof., FTVS, Charles Univ., Prague. Publs: Bohuslav Martinu's Symphonies, 1959; Martinu in Images, 1964; Bohuslav Martinu, 1966 (transls. in German, Engl., French & Russian); Bohuslav Martinu, 1972, 2nd ed., 1975. in German, French, Engl., Spanish, Swedish, Italian & Russian; Bohuslav Martinu, His Life & Work, 1974. Contbr. to profl. jrnls. Address: Raisova 7, 160 00 Prague 6, Czechoslovakia.

MIKELSONS, Rudolfs Oskars, b. 11 Aug. 1905, Riga, Latvia. Violinist; Professor of Violin. Educ: studied w. Leopold Auer, Lucien Capet. m. Mirdza Alksnis, 1 s. Debut: Age 5. Career: Concerts, Recitals in Latvia, Russia, Germany, France, Australia; Violinist, St. Louis, Symph., USA; Violin Tchr., Latvia, Germany, Australia, USA, 1927-; Concertmaster, Cond., num. orchs. Address: 1400 Orchard Lakes, St. Louis, MO 63141, USA.

MIKKELBORG, Palle, b. 6 Mar. 1941, Copenhagen, Denmark. Trumpeter; Arranger; Composer. Educ: Royal Acad. of Music, Copenhagen. Career incls: Club Vingaarden, 1961-64; Mbr., 1964-67, Ldr., 1967-70, Danish Radio Jazz Grp.; Mbr., 1965-71, Ldr., 1975-, Danish Radio Orch.; participant in radio & TV broadcasts; fest. apps. throughout Europe. Comps. incl: works for jazz & symph. orchs. separately in combination. 12 LP records. Mbr., Theosophical Soc. Hons. incl: Jazz Musician of the Yr., Denmark, 1968; Lange-Müller Prize, 1976; Danish Conds. Union Prize of Honour, 1977. Hobbies: Painting; Sculpture. Address: Ellegaardsvaenge 5B, 2820 Gentofte, Copenhagen, Denmark.

MIKÓ, Andràs, b. 30 June 1922, Budapest, Hungary. Producer. m. Eva Rehák. Debut: Opera Studio Budapest, Cosi Fan Tutte, 1948. Career: Chief Prod. of Opera Budapest, Covent Garden, Bolschos, Copenhagen, Turino, Rome, Brussels, Cologne, Helsinki, Berlin State Opera, etc.; currently Prod., State Opera Budapest; Prof., Acad. of Music, Budapest. Hons: Kosuth Prize. Address: Uri-Utca 44-46, 1014 Budapest 1, Hungary.

MIKOWSKY, Solomon Gadles, b. 10 Mar. 1936, Havana, Cuba. Pianist; Teacher. Educ: Attended Univ. of Havana, 1954-55 & CUNY, USA, 1958-60; BS Juilliard Schl. of Music; MS ibid., 1961; EdD, Columbia Univ., 1973. Debut: Havana, 1956. Career: Concert Perfs., Cuba & USA; Piano Fac. Mbr., Juilliard Schl. of Music, Manhattan Schl. of Music, NY. Univ. & Phila. Musical Acad. Publs: The Nineteenth-Century Cuban Danza and its Composers, with Particular Attention to Ignacio Cervantes (1847-1905), 1973. Contbr. to: OAS Americas. Mbrships: AAUP; Music Tchrs. Nat. Assn. Hons: Cuban Govt. Scholarship for Piano Studies Abroad, 1955-60; Piano Scholarship, Juilliard Schl. of Music, 1957-63; Cintas Fellowship, Inst. of Int. Educ., 1965-66. Address: 390 Riverside Drive, NY, NY 10025, USA. 29.

MILA, Massimo, b. 14 Aug. 1910, Turin, Italy. Music Critic; Journalist. Educ: pvte. piano studies; doct., Fac. of Letters, 1931. m. Francesca Rovedotti. Debut: 1929. Career: former Prof., Conserv. Giuseppe Verdi, Turin, & Turin Univ.; Contbr. to RAI, Radio Svizzera Italiana & ORTF (radio & TV); Music Critic, La Stampa, Torino; Co-Ed., Nuova Rivista Musicale Italiana. Publs: Il melodrama di Verdi, 1922; Cent'anni di musica moderna, 1944; Saggi mozartiani, 1945; Breve Storia della musica, 1946; L'esperienza musicale e l'estetica, 1950; Giuseppe Verdi, 1958; La giovinezza di Verdi, 1974; Bruno Maderna musicista europeo, 1976; Lettura della Nona Sinfonia, 1977. Contbr. to many reviews. Address: Corso Mediterraneo 130, 10129 Torino, Italy.

MILANOV, Zinka, b. Zagreb, Yugoslavia. Operatic Soprano. Educ: Dip., Zagreb Acad. of Music; studied w. Marie Kostrencic, Milka Ternina, Profs. Carpi, Stueckgold & Bozidar Kunc. Debut: Leonora, Il Trovatore, Yugoslavia. Career: leading roles w. Met. Opera, Chgo. Civic Opera, San Fran. Opera, Cinn. Summer Opera; apps. in Buenos Aires, Rio de Janeiro, Sao Paulo, Vienna, La Scala Milan, Covent Gdn. London, etc.; participant in Salzburg, Lucerne & other fests; concert tours in USA, Can., Mexico, Ctrl. Am., S Am., Europe; TV & radio broadcasts. Recorder w. RCA Victor. Address: c/o Norman McCann Ltd., 19 Charing Cross Rd., London WC2, UK. 2.

MILANOVA, Stoika, b. 5 Aug. 1945, Plovdiv, Bulgaria. Violinist. Educ: studied w. father, Trendafil Milanov & w. David Oistrakh at Moscow Conserv. 1 d. Career: has given duo recitals w. Radu Lupu & Malcolm Frager; apps. w. prin. UK orchs., 1970-, num. London apps.; apps. in most European countries; recitals & apps. w. Yamiuri Nippon Symph. orch., Japan, 1976; apps. w. Halle Orch., Hong Kong Fest., 1976; tour for Aust. Broadcasting Commission, 1976. Recordings: Balkanton (Bulgaria), some of which released by Harmonai Mundi; w. Malcolm Frager, BASF; w. Stuttgart Chmbr. Orch. under Karl Munchinger, Decca. Hons. incl: 2nd Prize, Queen Elisabeth Competition, Brussels, 1967; 1st prize (alo Carl Flesch Prize), City of London Int. Competition, 1970; Grand Prix du Disque, 1972. Mgmt: Harrison/Parrott Ltd., 22 Hillgate St., London W8 7SR, UK.

MILANOVA, Vanya Josifova, b. 12 Jan. 1954, Razgrad, Bulgaria. Solo concert violinist. Educ: Lower & Middle Music Schl., Sofia; Grad., Conserv. of Sofia, 1976. m. Paul de Keyser. Debut: Solo recital, age 9. Career: Concerts & recitals; Bulgarian Radio Broadcasts; Tours, Czech., DDR, Hungary, Poland, Italy, Sweden, Malta, Egypt & USSR. Hons. incl: Queen Elizabeth Int. Competition, Belgium, 1971; Paganini Competition, Genoa, 1973; Tchaikovsky Competition, Moscow, 1974; City of Leeds Prize, 1977. Hobbies: Cooking; Theatre; Cinema; Restaurants; Concerts; Opera. Address: 7 Hazelmere Rd., London NW6, UK.

MILCHEVA-NONOV, Alexandrina, b. 27 Nov. 1939, Sofia, Bulgaria. Opera Singer. Educ: High Schl. of Music, Sofia, w. Prof. G. Z1.-Cherkin; Sofia Conserv. m. Christo Nonov, 1 d. Debut: as Dorabella (Cosi fan Tutte), Varna Nat. Opera. Career: Apps. in Vienna, Moscow, San Francisco, Paris, Palermo, Budapest, Warsaw, W Berlin, Hamburg, Munich, London, Glydebourne, Copenhagen, Brussels, Geneva, Bucharest, Prague,

Madrid, Barcelona, The Hague, Salzburg, Monte Carlo, Athens, Ann Arbor, Belgrade, etc. Recordings: Aida (Amneris), Carmen, Khovantschina (Marfa), Boris Godounov (Marina), Verdi's Requiem; operatic arias; song recitals. Mbrships: Coun. of Bulgarian Musicians. Hons: People's Artist of Bulgaria; Order of Kyril & Methody, 1st class; Premier Grand Prix, Int. Singing Competition, Toulouse, 1966. Hobby: Gobelins. Mgmt: Dr. Raab, Vienna; Mariedi Anders, San Francisco. Address: Flotowgasse 18/3, 1190 Vienna XIX, Austria.

MILES, Colin Lewis, b. 22 Feb. 1944, Regina, Sask., Can. Regional Director, British Columbia Branch of Canadian Music Centre. Educ: BA, Univ. of Alta.; BMus, Univ. of Calgary; MMus, Univ. of Vic.; pvte. studies in viola, viola da gamba & keyboard. Publs: (co-author) A Survey of Community Noise Legislation in Canada, 1972; The Vancouver Soundscape (recordings & booklet), 1973. Contbr. to: Ed., Can. Music Ctr., BC Newsletter; BC Music Educator. Hobbies: Chamber Music; Folkdancing; Hiking. Address: 3550 W 17th Ave., Vancouver, BC, Can. V6S 1A1.

MILES, James, b. 17 Dec. 1949, London, UK. Music/Arts Administrator. Educ: BA in Hist., Exeter Univ.; Diup. in the Admin.of the Arts, Polytechnic of Ctrl. London. Career: Box Office Mgr./Publicity Officer, Cockpit Theatre, London; Arts Officer, London Borough of Greenwich; Artistic Dir., Greenwich Fest.; currently Sr. Arts Officer, London Borough of Camden & Fest. Admnstr., Camden Fest. Hobbies: Photography; Architectural Hist.; Squash; Parachuting. Address: 9 Melville Rd., Walthamstow, London E17 6QS, UK.

MILETIĆ, Miroslav, b. 22 Aug. 1925, Sisak, Yugoslavia. Composer; Violist. Educ: Zagreb Music Acad.; studied viola w. L Cerny & comp. w. P Borkovec. m. Branka Miletić, 1 d. Debut: w. Zagreb Phil. Career: Soloist, Radio Symph., Bratislava, Slovenska Phil., Ljubljana; Fndr., Ldr., Pro Arte Zagreb Str. quartet, touring to most major cities in Europe & to USA & USSR. Comps. incl: Les enfants dansent (piano); Croatische Suite für Gitarre; Songs & Dances (recorders); Symphonic Suite w. toys. Records for Yugoton. Contbr. to: Muzika; Zvuk. Mbr. of staff, Int. violin competition V Huml, Zagreb. Recip. many awards. Hobbies: Music ethnog.; Mountaineering; Ping-Pong. Mgmt: Concert Mgmt. Zagreb Music Info. Ctr., YU 41000 Zagreb, Trnjanska b.b. Address: Mikulićeva 22, 41000 Zagreb, Yugoslavia.

MILKINA, Nina, b. 27 Jan. 1919, Moscow, USSR. Concert Pianist. Educ: Paris Conserv.; studied w. Marguerite Long, Harold Craxton, Tobias Matthay & M Conus (former Prof. of Moscow Conserv.). m. ARM. Sedgwick, 2 c. Debut: w. Lamoreux Orch., Paris. Career: 1st broadcast, 1930; Mozart Specialist; Perf. all Mozart Sonatas & Haydn Trios, BBC; Mozart Bicentenary Recitalist, Edinburgh Int. Fest. Comp: publd. at age 11, Mozart Concertos. UK. Recordings: CPE Bach Sonatas; Scarlatti Sonatas; Haydn; Mozart: JS Bach; Prokofiev; Rachmaninov; complete Chopin Mazurkas; (for Westminster & Pye) Mbr: ISM. Hobbies: Reading; Chess. Mgmt: Non-Exclusive, London. Address: 20 Paradise Walk, London SW3 4JL, UK. 1.

MILLAR, Keith Hamilton Park, b. 20 July 1946, Edinburgh, UK. Symphonic Percussionist. Educ: Geo. Watson's Coll., Edinburgh. Career: Prin. Percussionist w. SNO, 1963-68, RPO, 1968-72 & LPO, 1972-. Recorded w. RPO & LPO during before-mentioned periods. Hobbies: Record Collecting; Driving. Address: 6 bKnollcourt Farquhar Rd., London SE19 15P, UK.

MILLER, Carol M. b. 18 Feb. 1931, Chgo., Ill., USA. Instrumental Director of Music; Flautist; Educator. Educ: BMusEd., Northwestern Univ., Evanston, Ill., 1953; MMus, ibid., 1954. m. Robert B Miller. Career: Dir. of Instrumental Music, Schls. in Ill. & Chgo., 1954-60, Lake Forest Country Day Schl., Ill., 1960-61; 1st Flautist, W Suburban Symph. Orch., Cook Co., Ill.; Asst. 1st Flautist, Evanston Symph. Orch., & Flute & Fiddle Club (Chmbr. Orch.), Highland Park; Dir. & VP, Sealanes Int. Inc., Chgo., 1959-68 & Trade Routes Inc., NY & Conn., 1968-. Contbr. to: Baton. Mbrships: Phi Beta (Nat. Pres., 1974-80, Nat. 1st VP, 1959-62; num. other offices); Alpha Chi Omega. Recip., var. scholarships & awards. Hobbies incl: Sailing; Antique Packard Cars. Address: Shorefront Pk., S Norwalk, CT 06854, USA. 5, 6, 23, 27, 29.

MILLER, Clement A, b. 29 Jan. 1915, Cleveland, Ohio, USA. Musicologist. Educ: BM (piano), Cleveland Inst. of Music, 1936; MM (Music theory), ibid., 1937; MA, Western Reserve Univ., 1942; PhD (Musicol.), Univ. of Mich., 1951. m. Jean M Miller, 2 s., 1 d. Career: Instructor, Hd. of Music Hist. Dept., Dean of Fac., 1937-65, The Cleveland Inst. of Music; Prof. of Music, Fine Arts Dept., John Carroll Univ., 1967-. Publs: Heinrich Glarean; Dodecachordon, 1965; Franchinus Gaffurius: Musica Practica, 1968; hannes Cochleaus: Tetrachordum Musices, 1970; Sebald Heyden: De Arte Canendi,

1972; Hieronymus Cardanus (1501-1576); Writings on Music, 1973. Contbr. to: The Musical Quarterly; Jrnl. Am. Musicol. Soc.; Musica Disciplina; The Am. Recorder; Die Musik in Geschichte & Gegenwart; Grove's Dictionary of Music & Musicians, 6th ed. Mbrships: Am. Musicol. Soc.; Renaissance Soc. of Am.; Medieval Acad. of Am.; Dolmetsch Soc.; Lute Soc. of Am.; Recorder Soc. Hon: Guggenheim Fellowship, 1974-75; Outstanding Educator of Am. Award, 1975. Hobbies: Swimming; Lute Playing. Address: 18975 Van Aken Blvbd., Apt. 411, Shaker Heights, Cleveland, OH 44122, USA. 8, 12.

MILLER, Clyde Elmer, b. 29 Sept. 1917, Downers Grove, Ill., USA. French Hornist; Teacher. Educ: BMusEd., Northwestern Univ., Evanston, Ill.; MA, Tchrs. Coill., Columbia Univ., NYC; pvte. study w. Louis Dufrasne, Josef Franzl; clinics w. Barry Tuckwell, Philip Farkas, Wm. Robinson, John Barrows, Froydis Hauge, Charles Kavaloski, James Winter. m. Patricia Swiercinsky, 2 d. by previous marriage. Career: Solo Prin. Horn, Dallas Symph., 16 yrs.; On tour w. Met. Opera Orch., NY Ballet Soc. Orch., Chgo. Gran Pk. Summer Orch., Dallas Civic Opera Orch., etc.; Played w. NY Phil. Orch., Chgo. NBC Orch., etc.; Pvte. tchng. since 1934; currently Horn, Ft. Worth Symph. & Ballet Orch., 15 yrs.; Mbr. of N Tex. Univ. Andraud Woodwind Quintet; on Tchng. Fac., N Tex. State Univ., Denton; TV & radio commercials; Adjudicator for var. area concerts. Var. recordings. Mbr., profl. orgs. Address: 2907 Wilsonwood Dr., Denton, TX 76201, USA.

MILLER, Ernest Arthur, b. 29 May 1925, Burlington, IA, USA. Salvation Army Officer; Baritone; Conductor of Brass Band. Educ: BMus, Northwestern Univ. Schl. of Music, 1949; Salvation Army Schl. for Offs. Trng., Chgo., 1950; Int. Coll. for Offs., London, UK, 1966. m. Mary June Klass. Career incls: Host & Vocal Soloist, The Living Word, TV series, 300 stns.; USA & Can., 1957-70; Music Dir., Salvation Army Schl. for Offs. Trng., Chgo., 1961-63; Music Sec., Salvation Army Ctrol. Territory, USA, 1963-70; Dir., Ctrl. Music Inst., Camp Lake, Wis., 1964-69; Bandmaster, Chgo. Staff Band, 1966-74; apps. as Vocal Soloist, Massey Hall, Toronto, Avery Fisher Hall, NYC, Royal Fest. Hall, London, Orch. Hall, Chgo., etc. Comps: sev. hymns. Recordings: Zondervan; Pilgrim; Fidelity. Publs: Ed., Salvationist Songs of a Century, 1964. Contbr. to musical & relig. jrnls. Mbrships: incl: Nat. Ch. Music Fellowship; Hymn Soc. of Av.; Nat. Band Assn. Hobbies: Hiking; Photography. Address: 1001-14th St. NW, Washington, DC 20005, USA. 7.

MILLER, Glenn David, b. 12 July 1940, Hummelstown, Pa., USA. Director of Bands; Clarinetist. Educ: BMusEd., Baldwin-Wallace Coll., Berea, Ohio, 1962; MMus, Univ. of Mich., Ann Arbor, 1963. m. Nancy Celesta Meares Miller, 2 d. Mbrships: MENC; Contest Chmn., 4 yrs., Regl. Orch. Chmn., 2 yrs. on Bd. of Dist. 1 of Ohio Music Educ. Assn., ibid.; Nat. Band Assn.; Nat. Schl. Orch. Assn.; Am., String Tchrs. Assn.; NEA; Ohio Educ. Assn.; Northwestern Ohio Educ. Assn.; Bryan Educ. Assn.; Guild of Carillonneurs in N Am.; Lions Club; Bryan; Am. Guild of Engl. Handbell Ringers, etc. Hobbies: Promotion of bells & carillons; Model Railroading; Golf & Baseball. Address: Rte. No. 2, Bryan, OH, USA.

MILLER, Janet, b. 10 Jan. 1916, Spokane, Wash., USA. Musicologist; Music Librarian; Piano Teacher. Educ: BA (major in Music); MA (Libnship); MMus (Musicol.). Career: High Schl. Music Tchr. (Choral Dir., Piano Tchr.), 1940-47; Asst. Prof. Music, Walla Walla Coll., 1947-54; Fine Arts Libn. (inclng. music), 1954-. Mbrships: Pi Kappa Lambda; Am. Musicol. Soc.; Int. Assn. Music Libs.; Music Lib. Assn.; Pacific Northwest Lib. Assn.; Spokane Allied Arts Coun. (Sec.); Zonta Club, Spokane (Sec.). Hobbies: Photography; Travel. Address: 523 W Mansfield, Spokane, WA 99205, USA. 5, 27.

MILLER, John Robert, b. 11 May 1947, Mpls., Minn., USA. Opera & Concert Singer (Lyric Mass). Educ: Chapman Coll., Orange, Calif.; Merola Opera Trng. Prog., San Fran. Opera. m. Gwendolyn Jones. Debut: San Fran. Opera, 1973. Career: Res. Basso, San Fran. Opera, 1973, '74; Perf. Mahler 8th w. Oakland Symph.; St. Matthew Passion, San Fran. Symph.; w. Los Angeles Civic Light Opera, 1975; Appt. w. Affiliate Artists Inc. NY w. Quad Cities Iowa/Ill. Arts Coun., 1975. Mbrships: Nat. Hon. Soc. Second. Schls.; Bohemian Club, San Fran. Hons: San Fran. Opera Auditions Finalist, 1971; Metro. Opera Auditions Dist. Sponsors' Award, 1976. Hobbies: Trout fishing; Cooking. Address: 1459 Green St., San Francisco, CA 94109, USA.

MILLER, Niven, b. 24 June 1929, St. Monans, Fife, UK. Baritone. Educ: Strathclyde Univ., Glasgow; pvte. study w. noted tchrs. m. Margaret Morris, 1 d. Debut: in Marriage of Figaro, Edinburh, 1950. Career incls: Recitals in Royal Albert & Royal Fest. Halls, London; many tours, NZ, Aust., S Africa,

USA, Can., USSR, Netherland, Belgium; has made 2 Royal Command Perfs.; radio series in over 40 countries; own TV series in Can. & USA, 8 yrs. (still running) & in Aust. Has made 17 LP recordings. Contbr. to One World. Mbrships: ISM; Concert Artists Assn. Hobbies: Gardening; Reading; Writing poetry; Music. Mgmt: Elwood Emerick Mgmt., 596 Crystal Lake Rd., Akron, OH 44313, USA. Address: 56 Oakhill Rd., Ashtead, Surrey, KT21 2JF, UK. 3.

MILLER, Ralph Dale, b. 17 Mar. 1909, Whitehall, Ill., USA. Educator; Composer. Educ: BEd, Ill. State Univ., 1936; MA, Univ. Iowa, 1939; MFA, ibid., 1941; PhD, 1942. m. (1) Lucille Rynell, 1932 (div.), 1 s.; (2) Charlene Peura, 1947, 1 s., 1 d. Career incls: Assoc. Prof. & Chmn., Div. Fine Arts, Univ. Minn., Duluth, 1947-50; Prof. & Chmn., Div. Humanities, ibid., 1950-70; Prof. & Dir., Electronic Music Ctr., 1970-. Comps. incl: 3 American Dances for Quintet & Piano, 1948; Arabesque for Flute, 1963. Recordings incl: Symphony for Band, 1974. Mbr., AAUP. Recip: Rsch. study grants & leave in Europe, 1960, '63. Address: Schl. Fine Arts, Univ. Minn., Duluth, MN 55812, USA. 2, 11.

MILLER, Richard, b. 9 Apr. 1926, Canton, Ohio, USA. Lyric Tenor; Professor of Singing. Educ: BM, MM, Univ. of Mich.; Dip. di Canto, L'Accademia de Santa Cecilia, Rome. m. Mary Norman Dagger, 3 s., 2 d. Debut: Stadttheater, Zürich, 1952. Career: Ldng. Lyric Tenor, ibid. & San Fran. Opera; Perfs. w. var. civic opera cos., USA, & Soloist w. maj. orchs. inclng. Cleveland Orch. & St. Louis Symph.; Town Hall recital, NYC, 1967. Tchng. Career: Dir., Univ. Choir & Lectr. in Voice, S Ill. Univ., 1957; Assoc. Prof., Voice, Univ. of Mich., 1957-62, Baldwin-Wallace Conserv., 1962-64; Prof., Singing, Oberlin Conserv. of Music, 1964-; Fac. Mbr., Nat. Music Camp. Interlochen, 1957-62, Blossom Music Fest, 1968-71, Mozarteum, Salzburg, 1972, 78; Vocal Consultant, Am. Music Tchr. jrnl., 1960-72. Publs: English, French, German & Italian Techniques of Singing, 1977. Contbr. to assn. bulletings. Mbrships: Nat. Assn. of Tchrs. of Singing; MTNA; Pi Kappa Lambda; Pi Kappa Phi. Hons: Fulbright Award, Rome, 1951; Silver Medalist, Geneva Int. Contests, 1952. Hobbies: Gardening; Oil painting; Stamp collecting. Address: 221 Forest St., Oberlin, OH 44074, USA.

MILLER, Robert, b. 5 Dec. 1930, NYC, USA. Concert Pianist; Attorney. Educ: BA (Music), Princeton Univ., 1952; LLB, Columbia Law Schl., 1957; studied Piano privately from age 4. m. Victoria Pearson Miller, 3 s. Career incls: Solo apps. throughout the USA, Europe & Latin Am.; Fac., Berkshire Music Ctr., 1970, 71; Manhattan Schl. of Music, 1976, Univ. of Cal. Davis, 1977; num. comps. written for him by Mario Davidovsky, Milton Babbitt, Stefan Wolpe & other leading comps. Recordings incl: Crumb, Makrokosmos vo. II; Wuorinen, Piano Sonata; Wolpe, Form, Form IV, G Perle, Toccata. num. others. Mbr. &/or Dir., Advsr. Committees, var. contemporary music assns. Mgmt: Ruth Uebel, 205 E 63rd St., NY, NY 10021. Address: 47 Valley Rd., Bronxville, NY 10708, USA.

MILLER, Terry Ellis, b. 19 Feb. 1945, Dover, Ohio, USA. Musicologist; Ethnomusicologist. Educ: BMus, Coll. of Wooster, 1967; MMus, Ind. Univ., 1971; PhD, ibid., 1977. m. Betty L, 2 d. Career: Asst. Prof., Musicol. & Ethnomusicol., Kent State Univ., Ohio; organist & choirmaster, var. chs., for 10 yrs.; guest lectr., Oberlin Coll., Ohio Univ., Univ. of Zurich, Switz. Publs: The Covered Bridges of Tuscarawas County, Ohio, 1975. Contbr. num. articles to profl. jrnls. and to Grove's Dict., 6th ed. Mbrships: Am. Musicol. Soc.; Siam Soc.; Soc. for Ethnomusicol. Hobby: Covered Bridges. Address: 717 Avondale, Kent, OH 44240, USA.

MILLER, Thomas W., b. 2 July 1930, Pottstown, Pa., USA. Dean, Northwestern University School of Music. Educ: BS, W Chester State Coll., Pa., 1952; MA, Music, E Carolina Univ., 1957; Mus A D, Boston Univ., 1964. m. Edythe Edwards, 4 c. Career: US 2nd Army Band, 1952-55; Dir., Instrmtnl. Music, Susquenita HS, Pa., 1955-56; Trumpet instr. & Dir., Varsity Band, E Carolina Univ., 1957-61; Doctoral Fellow & Asst. Dir., Univ. Bands, Boston Univ., 1961-62; Asst. Dean, E Carolina Univ., 1962-69; Dean, Schl. of Music, ibid., 1969-71; Dean, Schl. of Music, Northwestern Univ. Contbr. articles, reviews to profl. jrnls. Mbrships: Life Mbr., MENC; MTNA; Nat. Pres., Pi Kappa Lambda; Hon. Chapt. Mbr., Zeta Psi Chapt., Phi Mu Alpha Sinfonia; NASM Grad. Commission, 1974-. Address: Northwestern Univ., Schl. of Music, Evanston, IL 60201, USA. 7.

MILLER, (William) Douglas, b. 10 Dec. 1888, Liverpool, England. Pianist; Composer; Teacher. Educ: studied 4 yrs. w. Leopold Godoswsky, Berlin & Vienna. m. Dorothy Bateman, 1 s., dec., 1 d. Debut: St. George's Hall, Liverpool. Career: num. apps. as Piano Soloist on radio; gave radio talk on Godowsky Centenary, 1971; 2 piano concertos of own composition broadcast.

Compositions: Three Pieces for Piano (publd.); Recollections (9 pieces for piano - publd.); Air & Fling (publd.); Two Noctures (publd.); Soliloquy for piano & cello (publd.); 3 piano concertos; 3 ballets for small orch. Contbr. to: Musical Opinion. Recip. MA (hc), Liverpool Univ., 1978. Address: 42 Catharine St., Liverpool L8 7NL, UK. 3.

MILLIGAN, Thomas Braden, Jr., b. 31 May 1947, Kingsport, Tenn., USA. Musicologist; Pianist. Educ: BA, BMus, Carson-Newman Coll.; MA, 1974, PhD, 1978, Eastman Schl. of Music, Univ. of Rochester; Piano study w. Frank Glazer. Career: Fac. mbr., Carson-Newman Coll., 1978-. Publs: The Concerto in London, 1790-1800 (1978). Mbrships: Am. Musicol. Soc.; Phi Beta Kappa; Alpha Chi; Pi Kappa Lambda; Phi Mu Alpha Sinfonia. Hons: Fulbright Scholar to Austria, 1971-72. Address: Route 2, Talbott, TN 37877, USA.

MILLINGTON, Andrew, b. 2 May 1952, Willenhall, UK. Organist; Choirmaster; Conductor. Educ: pupil of Christopher Robinson & Harry Bramma, Worcester Cathedral; studied piano w. Phyllis Palmer, Cambridge; studied organ w. Ralph Downes, London; FRCO, 1972; Downing Coll., Cambridge, 1971-74; BA (Cantab.), 1974; MA, ibid., 1978. Career: Accomp. to City of Birmingham Choir, 1969-71; Cond. of the Aldwyn Consort of Voices, Midlands, 1969-; Music Master, Malvern Coll., 1974; Organ Scholar, Downing Coll., Cambridge, 1971-74; Cond. of Opera Primavera, London, 19734-; Cond. St. Cecilia Singers, Glos., 1975-; Asst. Organist, Gloucester Cathedral, 1975-. Recording: Quires and Places. Address: 10 Pitt St., Gloucester, Glos., GL1 2BH, UK.

MILLIOT, Sylvette, b. 6 June 1927, Paris, France. Violoncellist; Musicologist. Educ: Doct., Musicol.; studied violoncello, Nat. Conserv. Music, Paris (1st prize), Helene Victor Lyon prize, solo artist's guild prize. Career: Rsch. Asst., Nat. Ctr., Sci. rsch. (musicol.); Asst., Instr. Music, Nat. Conserv. of Music, Paris; Soloist, ORTF; var. concert tours. Publs: Documents inedits dur les luthiers parisiens de 18 siécle, Paris, 1970. Contbr. to: Revue Francaise de Musicol.; Recherches sur la Musique francaise classique, etc. Mbrships: French Musicol. Soc.; French Soc. of 18 century studies. Hobbies: History of Art; Psychology. Address: 6 Villa de la Reunion, 75016 Paris, France.

MILLS, Betty, b. Shanghai, China. Flautist; Pianist; Woodwind teacher. Educ: RAM; ARAM; GRSM; tutors incl. Gerald Jackson, Gareth Morris & Harold Craxton. Career: Prof. of Flute, RAM; Prin. Flute, Sadlers Wells Opera, Royal Ballet Covent Gdn. & for many foreign opera & ballet orchs.; Flautist; Oriana Trio; Oriel Trio & New Engl. Ensemble; Recitals as Flautist & solo pianist for BBC. Schls., Music Clubs, & Univs. throughout UK.; appearances w. Halle Orch.; BBC Symph.; & other London orchs. Pt-time tchr., Winchester Coll., Sherborne Schl. & Haileybury Coll. Mbrships: ISM; RAM. Hobbies: Travel; Countryside. Address: Ferndene, Bracken Close, Storrington, Sussex, UK. 3, 27, 29, 30.

MILLS, Bronwen Elizabeth, b. 15 Oct. 1951, Birmingham, UK. Soprano Singer. Educ: BMus, Univ. of London; LRAM; Cert. of advanced studies, GSM. Career: apps. w. Kent Opera, Monteverdi Choir, BBC Singers, Hickox Singers, London Sinfonietta; extensive oratorio work in London & provinces. Recordings: Schütz & Monteverdi duets. Mbr., ISM. Hons: Allcard Trust (Worshipful Co. of Musicians) Scholarship, 1976-78; Chown Scholarship, 1974-78. Hobbies: Knitting; Gardening; Swimming. Mgmt: London Int. Mgmt., 47 Randolph Ave., London W9. Address: 88 Lower Queens Rd., Buckhurst Hill, Essex, UK.

MILLS, David, b. 29 Jan. 1929, Moose Jaw, Can. Singer (bass); Writer; Poet. Educ: BA (music); ARCT (vocal perf.). m. Marjorie Mutter. Debut: CBC radio. Career: recitals of art & classical songs; apps. in oratorio & opera in N Am., UK & Europe; radio, TV & film apps. Recordings: David Mills Sings Pop Concert Favourites; David Mills Sings Canadian Art Songs; Cry of the Prophet. Mbrships: ACTRA; AGVA; AEA; CAPAC. Hobbies: Histl. Rsch.; Tennis; Swimming. Address: 445 Oriole Pkwy., Toronto, Ont. M5P 2H7, Can.

MILLS, Donn Laurence, b. 7 Dec. 1932, Indpls., Ind., USA. Conductor; Composer; Author; Music Educator. Educ: MMus, Eastman Schl. of Music, Univ. of Rochester; BMus, Northwestern Univ., Evanston, Ill.; Cond. study w. Max Rudolf, Leopold Stokowski, Sixten Ehrling, Pierre Monteux. m. Joan Geilfuss Mills (div.). Career: Music Dir./Cond. of sev. symph. orchs. in the USA as well as Ballet Cos. & Opera; Am. Educ. Dir., Yamaha Music Fndn., 1973-; Fndr./Owner of Sienna Publs. Inc. Comps: Orchl. & vocal publs.; Educl. work in all media. Recordings: Warsaw Phil., Works by Ginastera & Khachaturian; pieces by contemporary Am. Comps. Publs: Composition for Teachers, 1974; Craft of the Conductor, 1980. Contbr. to: The Instrumentalist as Orch. Ed.;

all Am. music mags. & newspapers. Mbrships: ASCAP; Pres., Nat. Schl. Orch. Assn.; Am. Symph. Orch. League, etc. Mgmt: Eric Semon Assocs., NY. Address: 3205 Los Feliz B1. 11-105, Los Angeles, CA 90039, USA.

MILLS, Isabelle Margaret, b. 3 Sept. 1923, Fleming, Sask., Canada. Associate Professor of Music. Educ: BA, Univ. of Man.; Assoc., Royal Conserv. of Muisic, Torotno; MA, Columbia Univ., NYC; Profl. Dip., Music & Music Educ., Tchrs. Coll., ibid.; EdD in Music (choral, vocal), ibid. Career: Tchr., Piano, Dept. of Prof., Music Educ., Fac. of Educ., ibid., 1959-67; Assoc. Prof., Music, Univ. of Sask., 1967-; Dir., ch. choirs & Educ. Chorus, Brandon Coll.; Regular radio, TV perfs. w. latter; Choral clinician; Workshops ldr.; Maj. speaker on Can. music. Recordings: Come Let Us Sing. Contbr. to profl. jrnls. Mbrships: Can. Fedn. of Registered Music Tchrs.; Can. Music Educators Assn.; MENC; Can. Fedn. of Univ. Women; Sask. Registered Music Tchrs. Assn.; Can. Folk Music Soc.; Sigma Alpha Iota. Hons: Frank Ross Chambers Schlrship. Fellowship, Tchrs. Coll., Columbia Univ., 1970-71; Prin.'s Rsch. Award, 1972, Dean of Art's Rsch. Award, 1972-73, 1973-74, Univ. of Sask. Hobbies: Reading; Handcrafts; Horticulture; Entertaining; Christian Education work in United Church. Address: 320 5th Ave. N, Apt. 177, Saskatoon, Sask., Canada S7K 2P5.

MILLS, John, b. 13 Sept. 1947, Kingston-upon-Thames, UK. Classical Guitarist. Educ: ARCM, 1968. Debut: Wigmore Hall, 1971. Career: UK apps. incl. recitals at Newcastle & Tilford Fests.; twice featured, BBC series The Classical Guitar, Radio 3; frequent apps. on local TV & radio stns. throughout UK; extensive tours, Can., USa, Aust., Sweden. Recordings: Five Centuries of the Classical Guitar; Music from the Student Repertoire, Series 1 & 2. Publs: Music from the Student Repertoire, series 1, 1974, & 2, 1975. Mbr., ISM. Hobbies incl: Golf; Astronomy. Mgmt: Helen Jennings Concert Agcy., 60 Paddington St., London W1M 3RR, UK. Address: 31 Fleece Rd., Long Ditton, Surrey KT6 5JP, UK.

MILNE, Hamish, b. 1 Apr. 1939, Salisbury, UK. Pianist. Educ: w. Harold Craxton, RAM; w. Guido Agosti (Rome). m. Margot Gray, 1 s., 2 d. Debut: London, 1962. Career: Soloist in GB & Europe; Prof., RAM. Recordings: works by Reubke, Liszt-Busoni, Medtner, Mozart, Haydn, Liszt & Chopin. Contbr. to BBC radio music talks. Hons: Collard Fellow of Worshipful Co. of Musicians, 1977; FRAM (1978). Address: 111 Dora Rd., London SW19 7JT, UK.

MILNER, Anthony Francis Dominic, b. 13 May 1925, Bristol, UK. Composer; Music Educator. Educ: BMus, DMus, London Univ.; RCM; ARCM; FRCM. Career: Tutor in Music Theory & Hist., Morley Coll., London, 1962; Ext. Lectr. in Music, Univ. of London, -1965; Lectr., Course for Dip. in Hist. of Music, ibid., 1958-62; Staff, RCM, 1961-; Lectr. in Music, King's Coll., London, 1969-71; Sr. Lectr. in Music, Goldsmith's Coll., Univ. of London, 1971-74. Prin. Lectr. in Music, ibid., 1974-; Lecture tours, USA & Canada 1964, '66, '69, 1973-78; Composer-in-Res., Summr Schl. of Liturgical Music, Loyola Univ., New Orleans, 1965-66; Dir. & Harpsichordist, London Cantat Ensemble, 1954-65. Compositions incl: Variations for Orch., 1958; Divertimento for String Orch., 1961; Symph. No. 1, 1972; Symph. No. 2, 1978; Oratorio, The Water & the Fire; Cantatas, The City of Desolation; Salutario Angelica; Roman Spring; num. works for Chorus, Organ & Instruments; Music for var. Radio & TV films, etc. Publs: incl: Harmony for Class Teaching, 2 vols., 1950. Address: 19 Wricklemarsh Rd., Blackheath, London, SE3 ONF, UK. 3.

MILNES, Sherrill, b. 10 Jan. 1935, Hinsdale, Ill., USA. Opera Singer. Educ: Drake Univ.; Northwestern Univ.; BMus; studied w. Boris Goldovsky, Rosa Ponselle, Andrew White & Hermanes Baer. m. Nancy Stokes, 2 s., 1 d. Career: Goldovsky Opera Coi., 1960-65; NYC Opera Co., 1964-67; Leading Baritone, Met. Opera, 1965-; apps. w. most US city opera cos., 1962-72; apps., San Fran. Opera, Hamburg Opera, Covent Gdn., London, Teatro Colon, Buenos Aires, Vienna State Opera, Paris Opera, Chgo. Lyric Opera, 1973-75. Has recorded for RCA Victor, London Decca, EMI Angel, Philips, RCA. Mbrs., Chmn. of Bd., Affiliater Artists Inc. Recip. 2 hon. degrees. Hobbies: Table tennis; Swimming; Horseback riding. 16.

MILNES, William Harold, b. 7 Aug. 1903, Shipley, Yorks., UK. Organist; Teacher of Piano, Singing, Organ & Paper Work. Educ: RCM, 4 1/2 yrs.; ARCO; FRCO; LRAM; ARCM. m. Sheila May Stewart. Career: Asst. Music Master, 34 yrs., Dir. of Music, 3 yrs., Caterham Schl., Surrey; Organist & Choirmaster, St. Luke's Old St., London EC, 1926-27, Foundling Hosp., 1927-34, Guards Chapel, Caterham, 1934-55, St. Paul's Presby. Ch., Croydon, 1955-73, St. Mary's Ch., Caterham, 1973-; Examiner, LCM, 1964-. Mbrships: Pres., Caterham Community Choir; ISM. Hon. FLCM. Hobby: Cricket.

Address: 232 Croydon Rd., Caterham, Surrey CR3 6QG, UK. 3.

MILOSAVLJEVIĆ, Radojica, b. 7 Oct. 1926, Aleksinac, Serbia, Yugoslavia. Conductor; Music Teacher. Educ: Secondary Music Schl.; Acad. of Music; Tchrs. Trng. Schl. m. Ljubica Milosavljević. Debut: Yugoslav Choral Festival, Nis, 1958. Career: Art Mgr. & Cond., Dr. Vojislav Vucković youth choir, Nis; Tchr. of music, Nis.; profl. collaborator of Acad. of Music, Belgrade. Recordings for radio in Yugoslavia & Belgium. Mbrships: Sec., Nis Dept., Assn. of Music Artists of Serbia; Music Committee, Amateur Assn. of Servia; VP & Mbr., artistic commission, Organisation of the Yugoslav Choral Fest. num. prizes & awards incl: Winner, BBC Let the People Sing choral competiion, schl. class, 1976; Winner, Yugoslav Youth Choral Fest., 1973; Golden Token of Cultural & Educational Community of Serbia, 1976; Winner, Europees Musikfest., Belgium, 1972; 1st Prize, Fest. of Amateur Choirs, 1978. Address: Ulica Carnojevica 12/71, 1800 Nis, Yugoslavia.

MILOSEVIC, Predrag, b. 4 Feb. 1904, Knyazevatz, Yugoslavia. Conductor; Composer. Educ: Conserv. of Music, Prague; Masterclass for comp. w. Josef Suk. Div. Career: Cond., Opera House Belgrade; Prof. of Comp. & Conducting, Fac. of Music Art, Belgrade. Comps: Little Suite for Piano; Sonatina for Piano; String Quartet; Simfonietta for Orch.; Songs w. Piano; Film Music. Recordings: Sonatina; Sinfonietta. Contbr. to profl. mags. Mbr. Assn. of Comps. Yugoslavia. Recip. 1st Prize in Competition for String Quartet, 1930. Address: Nikolaja Gogolja 3811, Belgrade, Yugoslavia.

MILSTEIN, Nathan, b. 31 Dec. 1904, Odessa, Russia, (Citizen of USA). Violinist. Educ: St. Petersburgh Conserv.; Study w, Stoliarsky & Leopold Auer; & w. Eugene Ysaye, Belgium. Career: Tours of USSR as soloist & in jt. recitals w. Vladimir Horowitz; Annual tours of European capitsls, 1925-39; Tours of S & Ctrl. Am.; USA debut 1929; Extensive world tours, 1945-. Mbrship: Acad. of St. Cecilia, Rome. Hons: Legion d'Honneur, France; Cross of Hon., Austria. Mgmt: Hurok Concerts Inc., 730 5th Ave., NY, USa. Address: 26 Cours Albert 1er., Paris 8e, France.

MILVEDEN, J Ingmar G, b. 15 Feb. 1920, Göteborg, Sweden. Composer; Assistant Professor. Educ: Lic. of Philos., 1951, PhD, 1972; Musical Theory, counterpoint, comp. w. Dr. S E Svensson, Uppsala; Musicol. w. Prof. C A Moberg; Schola Cantorum Basiliensis, Basel, m. Ulla Milveden, 1 s., 1 d. Debut: Serenade for Strings. The Phil. Orch. of Göteborg, cond. Issay Dobrowen, 1942. Career: Asst. Prof. of Musicol. w. Prof. C A Moberg; Schola Cantorum for the Cath. of Uppsala, 1969; Pezzo Concertante for Orch. & Soloists, 1971; Clarinet Concerto, 1972; 'Nu' (Now), a cantata to Linnean texts for choir & orch.; Gaudeat Uppsala, a cantata for the 500th anniversary of the Univ. of Uppsala. Publs: Zu den liturgischen Reimoffizien in Schweden. Liturgi-und choralges-chictliche Untersuchungen, 1972-. Mbr. Royal Swedish Acad. of Music; Royal Acad. of Arts & Scis. of Uppsala; Chmn. Musikaliska Konstföreningen. Hons: Upplands landstings kulturpris, 1969; Scholarship of the Swedish Musical Acad., 1972 & '73. Hobbies: Swedish ch. life. Address: Torkelsgatan 16B, 2-753. 29 Uppsala, Sweden.

MIMAROGLU, Ilhan, b. 11 Mar. 1926, Istanbul, Turkey. Composer. Educ: Dip. (BA), Law Schl., Ankara Univ.; MA, Tchrs. Coll., Columbia Univ., NYC, USA. m. Gunger Bozkurt, 1 stepson. Comps. incl: 3 str. Quartets; September Moon (orch.); Piano Sonata; Cristal de Boheme (percussion ensemble); Idols of Perversity (strs.); Monologues (solo instruments); (recorded) Pieces Sentimentales (piano); La Ruche; Tract; To Kill a Sunrise; Session, etc. Publs: sounds of America, 1956; The Art of Jazz, 1958; A History of Western Music, 1961. Contbr. to prof. pubs., Turkey, Italy & USA. Hons: Rockefeller Fellowship, 1955; Guggenheim Fellowship, 1971. Hobby: Cinema. Address: 435 W 119 St., NY, NY 10027, USA. 2.

MIMURA, Tsutomu, b. 11 Mar. 1924, Chan-Chu-Rin, Manchuria. Harpist; Conductor; Educator. Educ: BComm., Univ. of Takushuku, Tokyo, 1945; harp, keyboards, conducting, theory, all self-taught. m. Nobuyo Mimura. Debut: Tokyo. Career: Apps. at concert halls in Tokyo & other halls in Japan, Tel Aviv, Israel, Amstrdam, Netherlands, etc.; broadcasts on NHK, Fuji, TBS and many other radio & TV progs. Comps: much music arr. for harp ensemble, inclng. works by Handel, Boieldieu, Mozart, Albrechtsberger & Miyagi. Recordings: Music of the World by Harps, Nos. 1 & 2. Publs: Harp Method, Vols. 1-5, 1966-72. Mbrships: Pres., Nippon Harp Ongakuin; Chmn., Nippon Harp Promotion Soc.; Cond., Mimura Harp Ensemble; Chmn., Tokyo Youth Symph. Orch. Hons: Judge of Hon., Int. Harp Contest in Israel, 1962, '65; Judge at Int. Harp Contest, USA, 1969. Hobbies: Langs; Photography. Mgmt: Mimura Harp Ensemble; Int. Concerts Exchange, Los Angeles, USA. Address: 5-10-16 Higashi-Nakano, Nakano-ku, Tokyo, 164 Japan. 30.

MINAGAWA, Tatsuo, b. 25 Apr. 1927, Tokyo, Japan. Musicologist. Educ: Tokyo Univ.; Fulbright Exchange Schlr., NY, & Columbia Univs., USA; Basel Univ. m. Reiko Ishizuk, 1 s., 1 d. Career: Prof. of Musicol., St. Paul's (Rikkyo) Univ., Tokyo. Publs: History of Musical Notation; Chief Ed., Music vol., Encyclopedia Genre Japonica. Contbr. to: History of Mediaeval Music (on-gaku-Geijutsu). Mbrships: Int. Musicol. Soc.; Dir., Japanese Musicol., Soc. & Toyama Music Lib. Hobbies: Wine; Skiing. Address: Roppongi 6-4-24, Minato-ku, Tokyo, Japan.

MINDE, Stefan, b. 12 Apr. 1936, Leipzig, Germany. General Director, Portland Opera Association. Educ: w. Thomaner Chorus under Prof. Ramin, Leipzig, 1947-54; studied w. Prof. Raumgartner, Mozarteum, Salzburg, 1954-58. m. Edith Minde, 2 s. Debut: Wiesbaden State Theatre, 1961. Career: Repetitor, FrankfurtMain; Solo Repetitor & Cond., Wiesbaden; 1st Cond. of Opera. TrierMosel; at Tanglewood & Berkshire Music Fests., USA, 1970; w. San Fran. Opera, 1968-70; Gen. Dir., Portland Opera Assn., Inc., Oregon, 1970; guest apps. USA & Can. Mbrships: Am. Symph. Orch. League; Opera Am.; Opera W Recip. of CD Jackson Prize for cond., Tanglewood, Mass. Hobbies: Swimming; Jogging; Reading. Mgmt: Thea Dispeker, NY. Address: PO Box 8598, Portland, OR 97207, USA. 9.

MINES, Anatole, b. 21 July 1915, Cambridge, UK. Violist; Chamber Music Player. Educ: RCM. Debut: w. Carter Str. Trio, London, 1940. Career: w. Carter Str. Trio (formed 1940), app. 20 times at Nat. Gall. Concerts, apps. at Int. Music Fest., Prague, also in Brno, Pilsen & Bratislava (progs. incld. oboe quartets w. Léon Goossens), 1946 (sent by Brit. Coun.), in Edinburgh Fest., 1947, 48, 54, toured Germany for For. Off., 1949, & made num. live, radio & TV apps. in UK; has also played w. Marjorie Hayward Str. Quartet & MacGibbon Str. Quartet. Mbrships: Assoc., Royal Phil. Soc.; ISM. Recip. Alfred Gibson Prize for viola, RCM, 1938. Address: 11 Bulstrode St., London W1, UK. 14.

MINKOFSKI-GARRIGUES, Horst, b. 23 July 1925, Dresden, Germany. Concert Pianist; Composer; Professor. Educ: Music Acad. & Conserv. of Dresden: Studies w. Prof. Herbert Wuesthoff, Romana Lowenstein, Karl Knochenhauer, Hermann Werner Finke, Schneider-Marfels. m. Edeltraude Peschke, 2 d., 1 s. Debut: W. Stte Orch. of Dresden, Dresden. Career: Num. apps. in concert & radio broadcasts throughout the world. Comps: Variations on a Theme by Tchaikowsky op. 3; Tagebuch op. 5; 5 Sketches op. 6; Variations on a Lullaby op. 9; 2 Impromptus op. 11; 2 Preludes op. 12; Sonatina op. 13, Bilder eines Kindes op. 16; Aprés la pluie vient le beau temps op. 18; Tel qui rit vendredi, pleurera dimanche op. 19; Canadian Landscapes op. 21; Sonata No. 1 op. 23; Neuf Miniatures op. 26; Klaviermusik op. 15; Piano Concerto No. 1; 5 Miniatures for 4 hands op. 27; Expo '67 for 2 pianos; Aquarium for 2 pianos op. 32. Recordings: (w. orch.) Haydn Concerto; Bach Concerto for 2 pianos (w. Lothar Kilian); Klaviermusik by Minkofski-Garrigues; Num. solo recordings; Complete works or Schubert, Mozart & Beethoven for 4 hands w. Lothar Kilan. Hons: Frankfurt, 1955. Hobbies: Antiques; Paintings; Stamps; Gardening. Mgmt: Bureau Artistique d'Athenes, Georges P Kouakos, 30 Univ. Avenue, 33-35 Pesmatzoglou Blvd., Athens, Greece. Address: 205 Edison Ave., St. Lambert/Montreal, Quebec, Canada. 28.

MINOR, Alan James, b. 9 Oct. 1947, St. Helens, Ore., USA. Instructor of Percussion; Performer. Educ: BSc, Univ. of Ore., 1970. Career: Pvte. Instr. of Percussion, Eugene, Ore., & Lane Community Coll.; Eugene; Mbr., Eugene Symph. & Eugene Wind Ensemble. Mbr., Percussive Arts Soc. Hobbies: Backpacking; Tennis; Studying Am. hist. & native Am. culture; Photography. Address: PO Box 5243, Eugene, OR 97405, USA.

MINOR, Andrew C, b. 17 Aug. 1918, Atlanta, Ga., USA. Musicologist. Educ: BA, Emory Univ., 1940; MMus, Univ. of Mich., 1947; PhD, ibid., 1950. m. Catherine Hogan Minor, 2 d. Recordings: as cond. of Collegium Musicum of the Univ. of Missouri-Columbia, 2 Masses by J Michael Haydn, Handel's Joshua & Gossec's Messe des Morts. Publs: Gen. Ed. for Am. Inst. of Musicol. of Jean Mouton's Opera Omnia, Vols. I (1967), II (1969), III (1969), IV (1974). Assoc. Ed., Accademic Musicale - 17th century vocal & instrumental music, 10 vols., 1970. Contbr. to: Grove's Dict., 6th ed. Mbrships: Am. Musicol. Soc.; MTNA; Missouri MTA; Assoc. Ed., American Choral Review. Address: 919 Timberhill Rd., Columbia, MO 65201, USA. 8, 4.

MINTON, Yvonne, b. Sydney, Australia. Mezzo Soprano. Educ: Sydney Conserv. of Music. m. W Barclay, 1 s., 1 d. Career: joined Royal Opera House, Covent Gdn., 1965; Guest Artist, Cologne Opera, 1969; roles incl: Octavian (Der Rosenkavalier). Dorabella (Cosi Fan Tutte), Marina (Boris Godunov), Orpheo, Sextus (Titus). Recordings: Rosenkavalier; Cosi Fan Tutte; Figaro; var. concert recordings. Recip., Hon. RAM. Hobbies: Gardening;

Family. Mgmt: Ingpen & Williams, Kensington Ct., London W1. Address: 57 Park View Rd., London W5, UK. 1.

MINTZ, Shlomo, b. 30 Oct. 1957, Moscow, Russia. Artist; Violinist. Educ: Juilliard Dip. Debut: Carnegie Hall. Career: apps. w. major symph. orch. in 4 continents; Recitals; TV apps. Sev. recordings. Hons: Leventrit scholarship, Juilliard. Hobbies: Swimming; Chess; Reading. Mgmt: I C M Artist, 40 W 57 St., NY, NY, USA. Address: c/o Mgmt.

MIRANTE, Thomas, b. 11 Oct. 1931, Utica, NY, USA. Composer; Music Educator. Educ: BS in Music, SUNY at Potsdam; MS in Music, Ithaca Coll., NY; postgrad. work, Colgate Univ., NY; pvte. study of Comp. w. Earl George & David Diamond. m. Lucy Fiore, 2 d. Comps: 8 recital Encores (piano); 8 Recital Solos (piano); A Musical Journey (piano); Prelude & March (sax); Andante & Allegro (trumpet); The House on the Hill; I Am; Silent Snow (all choral); The War Poems of Walt Whitman (large chorus & orch.) Symph. no. 1; Piano Sonata; Str. Quartet; Concerto for Viola & Orch.; Portrait for Strings. Contbr. to Oneida Daily Dispatch (reviews); NY State Schl. Music News. Mbr., profl. assns. Recip., var. grants. Hobbies: Reading; Travelling. Address: 208 N Main St., Canastota, NY 13032, USA. 6, 21, 28.

MIRCHEV, Zahari, b. 5 Aug. 1941, Plovdiv, Bulgaria. Violinist. Educ: Dip., Bulgarian Musical Acad., Sofia, 1966. Career: Soloist, Stockholm Phil. Orch. & other Swedish orchs.; Chmbr. Concerts, Bulgaria, Ireland, Sweden; Radio apps. Bulgaria, Ireland, Sweden; TV apps., Sweden; Concertmaster, Sofia Radio Orch., 1965-68, Stockholm Phil. Orch., 1970-74, Stockholm Royal Opera, 1975. Recip., Prize, Nat. Music competition, Sofia, Bulgaria, 1959. Hobbies: Skiing; Fishing. Address: Grondalsvagen 118 111 tr., S 117 46 Stockholm, Sweden.

MIROLYBOV, Peter, b. 8 Feb. 1918, Terijoki, Finland. Choir & Orchestra Conductor; Composer. Educ: Grad., Russian Coll., Terijoki; Coll. of Music, Viborg. m. Irana Gretschaninoff, 1 s., 1 d. Career: Cond., Ch. Choir of Terijoki (orthodox), 1935, Helsinki, 1949, Uspenski-Cathedral Choirs, Helsinki, The Balalaika Orch. of Helsinki (as Pekka Mirola), 1956, sev. radio & TV perfs. Comp. of orthodox music, vesper, liturgy & sev. hymns to the St. Virgin orch. music, balalaika music, choir music & vocal music. Recordings: 3 recordings of orthodox music as cond.; 3 recordings of Russian folk music as arr. & cond. Mbr., Soc. of Finnish Musicians. Hons: Dir. Cantus, 1973. Hobby: Lit. Address: Tuulimyllyntie 2 A 8, 00920 Helsinki 92, Finland.

MISCHAKOFF, Anne, b. 12 May 1942, NY, USA. Violist; Teacher. Educ: BA, Smith Coll.; MA, Univ. Iowa; DMA, Univ. Ill.; Chautauqua Schl. Music; Cummington Schl. Arts; Berkshire Music Ctr., Tanglewood; Kneisel Hall, Blue Hill, Maine. Career: Prin. Violist, Evansville Phil. & String Quartet, 1965-66; Violist, Contemporary Chmbr. Players, & Lexington String Quartet (Chgo.), 1966-68; Detroit Symph. & Mischakoff String Quartet, 1968-72; Sierra String Quartet, 1975-; Asst. Prof., viola & music hist., Univ. Pacific, 1975-. Recordings: CRI; Motown. Mbr. profl. orgs. Hons. incl: Rsch. & Fellowship Grants. Hobbies incl: Swimming; Art; Gardening. Address: 843 W Alpine, Stockton, CA 95204, USA.

MISHORI, Ya'acov, b. 16 June 1937, Ramat Gan, Israel. Horn Player; Teacher; Journalist. Educ: BA (Pol. scis.), Hebrew Univ., Jerusalem, 1961; studied violin; studied horn w. Horst Salmon; profl. dias., studying w. Jan Bos, Amsterdam. m. Edna Mishori, 1 s., 2 d. Career: 1st Horn, Mil. Symph. Band, Radio Orch., Jerusalem; Guest Horn w. Concertgebouw, Amsterdam; Solo Horn, Israel Phil. Orch., 1965-, also w. Radio Symph.; chmbr. ensemble & recital perfs. on TV & radio; Lectr. on music & music educ.; Ed., Musical Progs., Israel Broadcasting Serv. Has made sev. recordings. Contbr. to var. jrnls. Mbr., Int. Horn Club. Address: 102 Bnei-Dan Str., Tel-Aviv, Israel.

MISRA, Lalmani, b. 11 Aug. 1924, Kanpur, India. Teacher; Musicians; Vichitra-Veena. Educ: MA in Hindi, Sahitya Ratna; PhD, Art & Architecture; Masters Degree, Vocal music; Doct. in Instrumental Music (Vichitra Veena Perf.). m. Srimati Padmavati, 1 s., 1 d. Debut: As vocalist, 1933. Career: Child Actor; All India Radio Artist, 1945-; Music Dir., Late Udai Shankar's troupe, 1952-54; Dean, Fac. of Perf. Arts & Hd., Dept. of Instrumental Music, Fac., BHUY, Varanesi, India. Comps: Opera, Meera; 50 Indian Orchl. comps. Publs: Bharatiya Sangit Vadya; Sangit Sarita; Tabla Vigyan. Contbr. to: Sagit Kala Vihar, Bombay; Sangit, Hathras; Nadrup, Varanasi. Mbrships: Exec. Committee, Sangit Natak Akademi, 1972-77; Grants Committee, ibid.; Res. Sc. Committee, ibid.; Gen. Coun., U.P. ibid.; Fndr. Mbr., Bharatiya Sangit parishad, Kanpur; Fndr. Mbr., Gandi Sangit Mahavidyalaya, Kanpur; Fndr. Mbr., Orchl. Soc., Kanpur. Hons. incl: Sev. gold & silver medals as child; Gold Medal, All India Music Conference Trust, 1957; Prize, Best Vichitra Veena Playing of Sangit Natak Acad., 1971. Hobbies:

Badminton; Reading. Address: Qrs No. Old E/7, Banarus Hindu Univ., Varanasi, India.

MISRAKI, Paul, b. 28 Jan. 1908, Constantinople (Istanbul), Tukey. (French Nationality). Composer. m. Cécile Seuzaret, 3 c. Debut: as Composer-Arranger w. Ray Ventura & ses Collégiens (stage orch.), 1931. Career: musical scores for 140 films; popular songs, 1931-; 1st audition of symphonic work, Rhapsodia Brasiliera, by Concerts Colone, Paris, 1966. Compositions incl: Tout va très bien, Madame la Marquise; Chez Moi; Sur Deux Notes; Insensiblement; Sans Vous; Dans Mon Coeur; Chiens Perdus; Maria from Bahia; La tete à l'Ombre; Les Volets Clos; num. other songs; scores for films inclng. And God Created Woman, Mr. Arkadine, Alhaville, Montparnasse 19, Nous Irons à Paris, La Minute de Vérité, Heartbeat, La Main à couper, Les Cousins & Le Doulos. Mbrships: SACEM; SACD. Recip. of Grand Prix de la Chanson Francaise, 1964. Hobbies: Parapsychology; Comparative Religion. Address: 35 ave. Bugeaud, 75116 Paris, France.

MISSIN, Russell Arthur, b. 15 July 1922, Wisbech, Cambs., UK. Organist & Choirmaster; Church Musician; Teacher. Educ: Ely Cathedral; FRCO (CHM); ADCM; LTCL. m. Muriel Quinn, 2 s. Career: Asst. Organist, Ely Cathedral; Organist & Master of the Choristers, St. Mary's Nottingham & Nottingham Univ., 1957-67; Master of the Music, Newcastle Cathedral, 1967-. Publs: Adaptations of standard sacred works for the modern liturgy. Contbr. to: "Promoting Church Music". Special Commissioner, etc., RSCM. Hobbies: Travel; Motoring; Swimming. Address: 71 Bridge Pk., Newcastle upon Tyne NE3 2DX, UK.

MITANI, Yoko, b. 6 Mar. 1935, Tokyo, Japan. Musicologist (Music History, Ethnomusicology). Educ: BA, Ochanomizu Women's Univ., Japan; MA, Columbia Univ., USA; MA, PhD, Tokyo Univ. Career: Professor, Sagami Women's Univ., 1976-; Vis. Fellow, Clare Hall, Cambridge, 1975-76. Publs: Higashi-Ajia Kin So no Kenkyu (A Study of the Long Zithers & their Music in the Far East), 1976. Contbr. to Jrnl. of Japanese Musicol. Soc.; Jrnl. of Soc. for Sch. in Asiatic Music. Mbrships: The Soc. for Rsch. in Asiatic Music; The Japanese Musicol. Soc.; The Soc. of Ethnomusiol., USA; Int. Folk Music Coun. Hobbies: Reading; Listening to music. Address: 4-13, 2-chome, Fujigaoka, Fujisawa-shi, Kanagawa-ken 251, Japan.

MITCHELL, Alasdair, b. 16 May 1947, Glasgow, UK. Orchestra Conductor; Cellist. Educ: BMus, Edinburgh Univ., 1970; Post-grad. studies, RAM; Conducting w. Igor Markevitch & Monte-Carlo Nat. Orch., 1968-72; Conserv. St. Cecilia, Rome & Musical Acad., Chigiana, Siena, 1971-723. m. Fiona Macdonald, 1 s. Debut: w. BBC Scottish Symph. Orch., 1972. Career: 1st undergrad. musical dir., Univ. Music Soc. Orch., Edinburgh, 1969; Apps. w. Ulster Orch., Belfast, Reid Orch., Edinburgh; Scottish Nat. Orch.; Cond., 1st perf. in Brit., Benjamin Frankel's 5th Symph., 1973; App., Danish Radio, 1974; Fndr. & Musical Dir., Edinburgh Camerata, 1975; Norrköping Symph. Orch. (Swedish Radio), 1976. Hons. incl: 2nd prize & Special Merit Prize, Best Knowledge Scores Nicolai Malko Int. Conducting Competition, 1974. Hobbies incl: Food. Address: 26 Mertoun Pl., Edinburgh EH11 1JY, UK.

MITCHELL, Donald Charles Peter, b. 1925, London, England. Music Critic; Publisher. m. Kathleen Burbridge. Career: Fndr. & Co-Ed., Music Surv., 1947-52; London Music Critic, Musical Times, 1953-57; Ed.; Tempo, 1958-62; Hd., Music Dept., Faber & Faber Ltd., 1958; Music Critic, Daily Telegraph, 1959-64; Advsr., Boosey & Hawkes Ltd., 1963-64; Music Critic, The Listener, 1964; Mng. Dir., Faber Music Ltd., 1965; Vis. Fellow, Univ. of Sussex, 1970. Publs. incl: The Mozart Companion (co-ed. w. H C Robbins Landon), 1956; Gustav Mahler, the Early Years, 1958; The Language of Modern Music, 1963, rev. ed., 1966. Contbr. to: Times; Times Lit. Supplement; Encyclopaedia Britannica; Music Review; Opera; Music & Letters; etc. Mbrships: BBC Ctrl. Music Advsry. Comm., 1967; Reform Club; Gen. Coun., Performing Rights Soc. Address: Lawn Cottage, Barcombe Mills, nr. Lewes, Sussex, UK.

MITCHELL, Geoffrey Roger, b. 6 June 1936, Upminster, Essex, UK. Counter-Tenor; Conductor; Choral Manager. Educ: studied w. Alfred Eller & Lucy Menen. Career: Counter-tenor Lay-clerk, Ely Cathedral, 1957-60; Westminster Cathedral, 1960-61; Vicar-choral, St. Paul's Cathedral, 1961-66; Fndr.-Cond., Surrey Univ. Choir, 1966; Mgr., John Alldis Choir, 1966-, Cantores in Ecclesia, 1967-77, BBC Choral Manager, 1977-; Cond., New London Singers, 1970-, Geoffrey Mitchell Choir, 1976-; Prof., RAM, 1974-; Singing Tchr., King's Coll. & St. John's Coll., Cambridge, 1975-. Recordings: w. John Alldis Choir, Cantores in Ecclesia & Pro Cantione Antiqua. Mbrships: BBC Club. Hobbies: Collecting Antique Prints; Swimming; Food. Address: 51 Glengarry Rd., E Dulwich, London SE22, UK. 3.

MITCHELL, Gifford Jerome, b. 29 April 1913, Cobden, Ont., Can. Pianist; Organist. Educ: BA, McGill Univ.; BMus, Toronto Univ. m. Phyllis Rogers, 2 d., 2 s. Comps: Choral Suite (Lonesome Valley) Frederick Harris. Recordings: McGill Choral Soc.; Elgar Choir of Montreal. Publs: Hymns for Schools (5 vols.), 1957-58; Choral Texts for Intermediate Grades, 1965-66. Contbr. to: CMEA Nat. Mag.; Celebration Periodical United Ch. of Can., etc. Mbrships: Past Pres., Exec. Dir., Can. Music Educs. Assn.; Exec. Mbr., Nat. Committee for Worship, etc. Hons: Outstanding Graduate Award for Service to McGill Univ., 1965. Address: 802 Parkland Ave., Mississauga, Ont. L5H 3G8, Can.

MITCHELL, Max Allen, b. 17 Dec. 1914, Frederick, Okla., USA. Music Educator. Educ: BSc, Okla. State Univ., 1936; MMus, Univ. of Mich., 1937; Prof. Dip. in Music Educ., 1950, EdD, 1950, Tchrs. Coll., Columbia Univ. m. Susan Jane Barber, 2 s., 1 d. Contbr. to Southwestern musician. Mbrships: Nat. Pres., Kappa Kappa Psi; Province Gov., Phi Mu Alpha; State Pres., Okla. Music Tchrs. Assn.; Sec.-Treas., Okla. Music Educators Assn.; Reg. Chmn., Nat. Assn. of Schls. of Music. Hobby: Travel. Address: 1512 Wildwood Ct., Stillwater, OK 74074, USA. 4.

MITCHINSON, John. Concert Tenor. Educ: grad., Manchester Coll. of Music, 1955. Career incls: apps. w. Leading orchs. & choral socs., UK & abroad; apps. at major fests. inclng. La Coruna, Santander, Taormina, Flanders, Granada, Aldeburgh, Israel, etc. Repertoire incls: Mahler, 8th Symph., Das Lied von der Erde; Verdi Requiem; Beethoven, 9th Symph., Missa Solemnis; Britten, War Requiem; title role, Stravinsky's Oepidus Rex; Berlioz, Beatrice & Benedict, Lelio, Romeo & Juliet; Damnation of Faust; Bach, Mass in B minor; Handel Judas Maccabeus; Rachmaninov, The Bells; Wagner, Tristan; etc. Recordings inclk: Mahler's 8th Symph.; Berlioz Lelio. Mgmt: Ibbs & Tillet, London, UK.

MITT, Tiina, b. 4 July 1956, Toronto, Ont., Can. Pianist. Educ: ARCT, Royal Conserv. of Music; BMus (perf.), Univ. of Toronto. Debut: Estonian Cultural Org., NY, 1971. Career: St. Lawrence Centre for Perf. Arts., 2 perfs., 1976; Eaton's Auditorium - Concert Hall, 1975, '76; Soloist, Int. Music Schls. final perf. concerts, Mozarteum, Salzburg, Austria. 1975, '76, '78; Concerts, Helsingborg & Lund, Sweden, 1979; Soloist for E York Symph. Orch., Toronto, 1976; Perf. w. André Gagnon, Massey Hall, Toronto, 1979; 3 recitals, The Univ. of Toronto; Soloist for Estonian Male Choir, ibid. Hons: Aga Wagstaff Harris Ltd., 1975; 3 Kiwanis Music Fest., 1970, '73, '79; Salzburg Fest., 1975, '76, '78. Address: 75 Emmett Ave., Apt. 203, Toronto, Ont. M6M 5A7, Can.

MIXTER, Keith Eugene, b. 22 May 1922, Lansing, Mich., USa. Musicologist. Educ: BMus, Mich. State Univ., 1947; Univ. of Basel, Switzerland, 1947-49, 1952-53; MA, Univ. of Chgo., 1951; PhD, Univ. of NC, 1961. m. Beatrice Mary Ruf, 3 s., 1 d. Career: Music Libn., Univ. of NC, 1953-61; Asst. Prof.-Assoc. Prof., 1961-74, Prof., 1974-, Chmn. of Grad. Studies in Music, 1977-, Ohio State Univ. Publs: Johannes Brassart, 6 Motetten, 1960; General Bibliography for Music Research, 1962, 2nd ed., 1975; An Introduction to Library Resources for Music Research, 1963; J Brassart, Opera Omnia, 1965-71. Contbr. to musical jrnls., encys. etc. Mbr., profl. assns. Hons: Fellow, Chgo. Univ., 1951; Jt.-recip., Harriet Cohen Prize for Musicol., 1962. Hobbies: Chess; Sailing. Address: 4455 Shields Pl., Columbus, OH 43214, USA. 11.

MIZERIT, Klaro, b. 12 Aug. 1914, Monfalcone, Italy. Conductor; Music Director; Composer. Educ: studied violin, comp. & conducting; Dips., conducting & comp., Music Acads., Ljubljana, Yugoslavia & Veinna, Austria. m. Magda Soukal, 3 children. Career: Tchr., violin, piano, theory, counterpoint, var. music schls.; Music Dir., Fest. Orch., Dubrovnik, Yugoslavia, 1951-58, Rhenish Phil. Koblenz, W Germany, 1958-68, Atlantic Symph. Orch., Halifax, Can., 1968-; Co-Dir., Monteux Schl. for Condus. & Orchl. Trng., Hancock, USA, 1968-; Guest Cond. throughout world. Recorded w. Rhenish Phil. & Atlantic Svmph. Mbrships: Can. Assn. or Comps.; Am. Fedn. of Musicians; Am. Symph. Orch. League. Recip. comp. prize Glasbena Matica, Yugoslavia, 1943. Hobby: Poetry. Address: 8 Fleming Dr., Halifax, NS, Canada.

MNGOMA, Khabi, b. 18 Nov. 1922, Johannesburg, S Africa. Musicologist; Singer; Choral Conductor; Accompanist. Educ: UTLM (SA); UPLM (SA); LRSM (tchng. & perf.). m. Grace N Mondlhana, 1s., 1 d. Debut: Johannesburg, 1953. Career: fndr. & cond., The Ionian Choir, Soweto; 1st perfs. in S Africa of Judas Maccabeus, Samson, Israel in Egypt (all by Handel), Mendelssohn's Hymn of Praise & Brahms Rhapsody; Fndr., Dept. of Music, Univ. of Zululand. Recordings: Zulu folk songs w. Ionian & Univ. of Zululand choirs; Handel's Samson for S African Broadcasting Corporation. Contbr. to var. jrnls. fndr. mbr., Bureau for Zulu Language & Culture. Hobby: Writing Fiction. Address: Music Dept., Univ. of Zululand, P/B KwaDlangezwa 3886, via Empangeni, S Africa.

MOATS, Brenda Gail, b. 9 April 1952, Moose Jaw, Sask., Can. Musician (flute & piccolo). Educ: BMus, Univ. of Regina, 1975; currently studying for Masters degree in flute perf., Univ. of Ariz. Debut: Soloist w. Regina Symph. under guest cond. Arthur Fiedler. Career: Flautist, Regina Symph. Orch., 1970-78; Flautist, Ariz. Opera Orch., 1978-79. Mbrships: Am. Fedn. of Musicians; Nat. Flute Assn.; Tucson Flute Club. Hons: Winner, Provincial Woodwind Fest., 1971-73; Winner, Can. Nat. Competitive Fest. of Music, Toronto, 1974; Moose Jaw Medal of Merit, 1974. Hobbies: Reading; Swimming. Address: c/o Rural Route No. 1, Regina, Sask., Can. S4P 2Z1.

MOBBS, Kenneth William, b. 4 Aug. 1925, Higham Ferres, UK. Pianist; Harpsichord Player; Organist; Conductor; Educator. Educ: pvte. study w. Rev. Greville Cooke & Dr. M P Conway; LRAM (piano perf.), 1941; FRCO, 1949; BA, 1946, MusB, 1949, Clare Coll., Cambridge; RCM, 1949-50. 3 d. Career: on staff, 1950-, Sr. Lectr. in Music, 1965-, Univ. of Bristol Music Dept.; Musical Dir. of Bristol Opera Schl. (now Co.), 1954-64; violin & piano duo w. William Reid, 1962-65; Harpsichord Player, Pianist & Organist, Bristol Sinfonia, 1964-. Comp. w. George Rowell, Engaged!, comic opera adapted & arr. from Gilbert & Sullivan, 1963. Contbr. to ISM Music Jrnl. Mbrships: ISM; Royal Musical Assn.; Musicians Union; Assn. of Univ. Tchrs. Recip. var. hons. Hobbies: Photography; Hill Walking; Early Pianos. Address: 16 All Saints Rd., Bristol BS8 2JJ, UK. 3.

MÖDL, Martha. Opera Singer. Educ: Munich & Nuremberg Conservs. Career: num. apps. at opera houses in Germany & abroad; participant in Bayrouth Fest., 1951 ; Mbr., Staatsoper Stuttgart, 1953-. 16.

MODUGNO, Anne Depardo, b. Providence, RI, USA. Music Educator; Author; Lecturer. Educ: BMus & MusEd, New England Conserv. of Music; MA & Profl. Dip., Tchrs. Coll., Columbia Univ. m. Victor D Modugno. Career: Music Tchr. of Theory, Electronic Music, Harmony & Counterpoint, Greenwich HS; Staff, Grad. Course in Electronic Music, Univ. of Bridgeport; sev. demonstration & summer workshops & on TV in electronic music. Mbrships. incl: NEA; Kappa Delta Pi; Int. Soc. of Music Educators; MENC; Chapt. Pres., State Music Chmn., Delta Kappa Gamma. Contbr. to profl. jrnls. Hobbies incl: Golf; Tennis. Address: 126 Hunting Ridge Rd., Stamford, CT 06903, USA.

MOECK, Hermann, b. 16 Sept. 1922, Lüneburg, Germany. Publisher; Instrument Maker. Educ: Univs. of Göttingen & Münster; Dr.phil., 1951. m. Elfriede Goldkühler, 4 d. Career: Owner, Moeck Verlag & Musikinstrumentenwerk. Contbnr. to profl. jrnls. Hobbies: Collecting Musical Instruments; Boating. Address: Postfach 143, D 31 Celle, German Fed. Repub. 14.

MOERDŸK, Marie-Cécile, b. 24 May 1929, Zuiddorpe, Netherlands. Singer. Educ: Music Conserv. m. Jan Daundey, 1 d. Debut: Caracas, Venezuela. Career: Docent, Maastricht Conserv.; Concerts in 50 countries; 160 TV progs. weekly 3/4 hour radio prog., 8 yrs.; Ethno-Musicol. expeditions, S. Am., Africa, etc.; Dir., Netherland Folk Music Soc. Comps. Songs (words & music). Recordings: 20 records of Folksongs, classical songs, operetta & oratorio. Publs: Var. songbooks. Contbr. of over 300 articles on folk music to weeklies & musical jrnls. Recip., var. musical hons. Hobbies: Teaching; Writing; Singing; Gardening; Expeditions to 48 countries. Address: De Strype, Leende, N.Br., Netherlands.

MOERK, Alice Anne, b. 1 Mar. 1936, Phila., Pa., USA. Musicologist; Teacher; Pianist; Choral Director. Educ: BMus, Carthage Coll.; MFA, Ohio Univ.; PhD, WVa. Univ.; Eastman Schl. Music; Northwestern Univ.; Dips., piano & pipe organ. Career: Hd., Music Dept., Marion Coll., Va.; Prof. Music, Vardell Hall, NC; Dir. Music, Lees Coll., Ky.; Prof. Music, Fairmont State Coll., WVa. Publs: Patterns of Sound, 1972; Perspectives: A Guide to Comprehensive Music, 1973; A Short History of Popular Music, 1975. Contbr. to: Choral Jrnl. Mbr. profl. orgs. Hon: Rose Hon., Sigma Alpha Iota. Hobbies: Beachcombing; Hiking; Cycling. Address: 1101 Fleming Ave., Fairmont, WV 26554, USA.

MOESCHINGER, Albert Jean, b. 10 Jan. 1897, Basle, Switz. Pianist; Professor of Theory & Pianoforte. Educ: Berne, Leipzig, Munich; Grosser Kunstpreis, Basle, 1954. Career: Prof. of Theory, Conserv. of Berne, 1937-43. Comps. incl: Lieder; Quartet 'Images'; 5 symphs.; Amor & Psyche, ballet; 5 piano concertos; violin concerto; Ballade Symphonique; Saxophone concerto; Pianoforte pieces; trumpet concerto; Fantasie for strings; Sonatina for oboe & strings; var. chmbr. works. Mbr., Swiss Musicians Soc. Hons. incl: Swiss Comps. Prize. Address: Bel Tramonto, 6612 Ascona (Ticino), Switzerland.

MOEVS, Robert Walter, b. 2 Dec. 1920, La Crosse, Wis., USa. Composer. Educ: Ba, Harvard Coll., 1942; Nat. Conserv. of Music, Paris, study w. Nadia Boulanger, 1947-52; AM, Harvard Univ., 1952. m. Maria Teresa Marabini, 1 s., 1 d. Career: Fac., Harvard Univ., 1955-64; Rutgers Univ., 1964-; Chmn., New Brunswick Dept. of Music, 1974-. Comps. incl: Heptachronon for Cello; The Aulos Player for 2 choruses & 2 organs; Games of the Past for 2 pianos; Phoenix & Collana Musicale for piano. Recordings: Sonata for pianoforte; Variazioni sopra und Melodia, viola & cello; Musica da Camera I; Brief Mass. Contbr. to profl. jrnls. Mbr., profl. orgs. Hons: Rome Prize Fellow, Am. Acad. in Rome, 1952-55; Nat. Inst. of Arts & Scis. Award, 1956; Guggenheim Fellow, 1963-64; ASCAP Awards, 1967; Stockhausen Int. Prize, Italy, 1978. Address: The Brookie, Blackwell's Mills, Belle Mead, NJ 08502, USA. 2, 6, 14.

MOFFAT, Alan Lyndon, b. 10 Nov. 1949, Sydney, Aust. Organist; Music Librarian. Educ: FTCL; LMus, Aust. Music Examinations Bd. Career: Federal Music Librarian, Aust. Broadcasting Commission, 1975-; Deputy Organist, St. Andrew's Cathedral, Sydney, 1968-. Recordings: works by Franck, Messiaen, Vierne & Dupré for ABC. Contbr. to: Royal Schl. of Ch. Music (NSW branch) Jrnl.; Sydney Organ Jrnl. Mbrships: L'Association des Amis de l'Art de Marcel Dupré; Royal Schl. of Ch. Music. Hon: 2nd prize, Ernest Truman memorial organ contest, Sydney, 1973. Hobbies: Reading; French Organ Music since 1850. Address: 59 Bardwell Rd., Bardwell Pk., NSW 2207, Aust.

MOFFO, Anna, b. Wayne, Pa., USA. Opera Singer. Educ: Music study w. Mme. Euphemia Giannini-Gregory; Fulbright Schlrship. for study in Italy. m. Robert Sarnoff. Debut: in Madam Butterfly (Italian TV Prod.). Career: leading roles w. Metropol. Opera, NY, & opera cos. of San Fran., Chgo.; La Scala, Milan; Vienna State Opera; Budapest; Stockholm; Berlin & Munich; TV appearances incl. The Anna Moffo Show (35 shows per year on Italian TV shown throught S Europe); Frequent appearances on US TV incl.. Johnny Carson Show, Dean Martin Show, etc. Recordings incl: num. operatic works on RCA Victor & Angel labels; Canteloube's Songs of the Aubergne (RCA Victor), for which Grand Prix du Disque was awarded. Other hons. incl: Cmdr., Order of Merit, Repub. of Italy. Mgmt: Columbia Artists Mgmt., NYC. Address: co Edgar Vincent Assoc., 145 E 52nd St., NY, NY 10022, USA.

MOHR, Wilhelm, b. 18 Feb. 1904, Hamburg, Germany. Composer; Pianist; Organist; Harpsichordist; Musicologist. Educ: Dr. jur., Hamburg; Brahms Conserv., Hamburg; studied w. Anton Penkert. m. Eva Kopff, 9 c. Career: Music Critic, Hamburger Fremdenblatt; Cond., Wandsbeker Friends of Music Soc.; Pres., Hans Pfitzner Soc.; Organist, Martin Luther Ch., Falkenstein Taunus. Compositions: dance suite Merry Old England, large orch., arr. for plucked orch.; Brautwalzer, plucked orch.; Variationen uber das Lied vom Heuschreck, str. quartet; Kleine Suite, flute & piano; Suite, alto recorder & Harpsichord; Romanze, violin & piano. Author, Cesar Franck Biographie, 1st ed., 1942, 2nd ed., 1969. Contbr. to num. profl. jrnls. Mbrships: New Bach Soc.; Handel Soc.; Brahms Soc., Hamburg; Int. Soc. for Music Rsch.; Soc. of Friends of Music, Bad Soden am Taunus; German Mozart Soc. Hobby: Collecting Music Medals & Music Stamps. Address: 16 Am Wiesenhang, 624 K&onigstein 2, German Fed. Repub.

MÖHRINGER, Karel Johannes Frederik, b. 26 July 1937, Zwolle, Netherlands. Cellist. Educ: High Schl., Conserv., Univ. & Music Acad. Debut: Antwerp, 1951. Career: solo cellist, Rheinisches Kammerorchester, Cologne; now solo cellist & gamba player, Rotterdam Phil. Orch.; perfs. all over the world & on film, TV and radio. num. recordings. Contbr. to num. mags. Mbrships: Alpine Club; Rotary Club. Hons: Kammermusikert der Stadt Köln; 2nd prize, Str. Quartet competition, Liège. Hobbies incl: Painting; Film; Photography. Address: J Braakensiekstr. 119, 3119 NN Schiedam, Netherlands.

MOHRMANN, Margaret Nabors, b. 2 Jan. 1944, Little Rock, Ark., USA. Woodwind Teacher; Co-owner of Musical Research Company; Theoretician. Educ: BMusEd., Univ. of Central Ark.; MMus, Northeast La. Univ.; PhD, Univ. of S Miss. m. Harry William Mohrmann. Career: Supvsr., of Music, Dir. of Bands, Monticello, Ark., HS, 1966-69; Instructor of Music, Univ. of S Miss., 1972-73; Instructor of Woodwinds, Univ. of Ctrl. Ark., 1973-74; Co-owner, Dir., of Musical Rsch., Computer Products Unlimited, Little Rock, Ark. Publs: A Method

for Harmonic Symbolization of Twentieth-Century Music Written in Convenvional Notation, 1976. Mbrships: Soc. for Rsch. in Psychol. of Music & Music Educ.; Musical Engrng. Grp.; Nat. Assn. for Coll. Wind & Percussion Instructors; Am. Mensa; S Calif. Computer Soc.; Tau Beta Sigma. Hons: Homer A Brown Award for Musicianship, Leadership & Service, 1966. Hobbies: Reading; Musical Analysis & Rsch. using computers; Experminentation w. synthesized music; Arranging &/or transcribing works for symph. wind band. Address: 2412 Broadway, Little Rock, AR 72206, USA.

MOKSNESS, Ingrid Blakstad, b. 18 Aug. 1929, Oslo, Norway. Pianist; Organist; Accompanist. Educ: Organ Dip. (Ch. Music); Oslo Music Conserv. (tchr., pre-schl. children); studied music therapy. m. Gunnar Moksness, 3 c. Debut: Oslo Concert Hall. Career: Pianist, Oslo & London; Repetitör, Norwegian Opera; Ch. Concerts, Oslo; Cond., Concerto for Choir & Organ; Accomp., var. soloists; Organist, Saner Ch. Mbrships: Oslo Music Soc.; Norway's Organist Soc. Hobbies: Writing; Religious Activities; Gardening; Politics. Address: Ullevalsalléen 14, Oslo 8, Norway.

MOLBERG, Karl-Theo, b. 18 July 1951, Bonn, German Fed. Repub. Horn Player. Educ: studied w. father, Theo Molberg, 1965-69; study w. Prof. E Penzel, 1971-76, Musikal Reifeprüfung (1 mit Auszeichnung), 1975, State HS for Music, Cologne. Career: Solo Horn Player, Youth Orch. of Germany, 1969-74; played w. Int. Youth Orchs., meetings of youth orchs. in Berlin, 1970, Vienna, Aberdeen, London, 1973; w. Syrinx Quintet, 1971-. giving concerts & making many TV & radio apps. in Belgium & Germany; currently Horn Player, Düsseldorfer Symphoniker (Deutsche Oper am Rhein). Recip. Many prizes w. Syrinx Quintet. Address: Am Bungert 12, D-5300 Bonn-Beuel, German Fed. Repub.

MOLCHANOV, Kirill Vladimirovich, b. 7 Sept. 1922, Moscow, USSR. Composer. Educ: Moscow Conserv. Compositions incl: Concerto No. 1 for Piano & Orch., 1945; Concerto No. 2 for Piano & Orch., 1947; Concerto No. 3 for piano & Orch., 1953; Operas, Stone Flower, 1950; Dawn, 1956; Del Carno Street, 1960; Romeo, Juliet & Gloom, 1962; Incidenal music for films - It Happened in Penkovo, 1950; Vast is My Land, 1958; Stars of May, 1959; To the Seven Winds, 1962; Shore Leave, 1962; Music for plays - Girboyedov, 1951; Mary Stuart, 1956; Three Fat Men, 1956; Last Stop, 1957; Attacking the Storm, 1965; Music for Radio & TV. Hon: Honoured worker of the Arts of RSFSR, 1963. Address: Composers Union of the RSFSR, 8-10 Ulitsa Nezhdanovoi, Moscow, USSR.

MOLL, Marques Juan, b. 8 Mar. 1936, Palma de Mallorca. Pianist. Educ: Bachillerato Superior; Titulo de Professor, Piano, Palma & Valencia; Higher Conserv., Barcelona. m. Bienvenida Thomás Andreu, 2 s., 1 d. Debut: Ciutadella, Menorca, 1952. Career: Concert w. orch., Festival of Aarhus, Denmark, 1967, Barcelona, Valencia & Palma, Spain, Bochum, Hagen, Monchengladbach & Krefeld, W Germany; 2 Recitals for radio stn. Westdeutscher Rundfunk, Cologne. Recording: The Works composed by Chopin at Mallorca. Mbrships: VP, Young Musicians Assn., Palma; Prof. de Virtuosismo del Piano, Auditorium, Palma de Mallorca. Hons: Premio Nacional Alonso, Valencia; 1st Prize, Claude Debussy Int. Competition, Munich, W Germany, 1962; 1st Prize, Int. Piano Competition, Aarhus, Denmark, 1967. Hobby: Fishing. Address: Plaza de Espana, 86, 30, 2a, Palma De Mallorca, Spain.

MOLL, Phillip, b. 16 Sept. 1943, Chicago, Ill., USA. Pianist; Accompanist; Harpsichordist. Educ: BA, Harvard Univ., 1966; MMus, Univ. of Texas, 1968. Career: Repetiteur w. Deutsche Oper Berlin, 1970-78; widespread activity as Accomp. for recitals, radio & TV broadcasts throughout Europe, UK, USA, Africa & Japan; Arrangements for flute & piano of James Galway favourites. Num. recordings. Hobbies: Cycling; Writing Limericks; Swimming. Address: Magdeburgerplatz 2, 1000 Berlin 30, German Fed. Repub.

MOLLENHAUER, Bernhard, b. 27 Feb. 1944, Fulda, Germany. Register master woodwind manufacturer (flute, recorder). Educ: Master dip.; study of flute, Conserv., Vienna. m. Elisabeth Mollenhauer-Klüber, 2 c. Career: Managing Dir. & Co-Partner, Conrad Mollenhauer GmbH; Manufacturer of Woodwind instruments. Address: Weichselstr. 27, D-6400 Fulda, German Fed. Repub.

MØLLER, Peter, b. 4 Mar. 1947, Copenhagen, Denmark. Organist; Pianist; Composer. Educ: Royal Danish Music Conserv., Copenhagen, piano & organ, 1964-73; master class, ibid.; Int. Summer Acad., Haarlem w. Hans Haselböck & Anton Heiller. m. Kirsten Martinsen. Debut: Ch. of Our Saviour, Copenhagen, 1973. Career: Concert apps. in Germany, UK & Finland; perfs.

on TV & radio. Comps: Organ symph., Transfiguration (recorded); Passacaglia (recorded); 42 Chorale Preludes; 12 Danish songs. Publs: Application in the Keyboard Works of J S Bach, 1976. Mbrships: Soc. of Danish Organists & Choir Conds.; Soc. of Carillon Players in Denmark; Soc. of Campanologists; Int. Gustav Mahler Gesellschaft. Hobby: Genealogy. Address: Borgergade l (III TV), 6700 Esbjerg, Denmark.

MOLLOVA, Millena, b. 19 Feb. 1940, Razgard, Bulgaria. Pianist; Teacher. Educ: Dip. in piano perf., Bulgarian Music Acad.; studied w. Emil Gillels, Moscow Conserv. m. Ivan Minneff, 3 c. Debut: aged 6. Career: Recitals & concertos in Bulgaria, USSR, Japan, Poland, Hungary, Germany, Belgium, Czech., Cuba, Romania & Yugoslavia; Prof., Bulgarian Acad. of Music. Recordings: works by Tchaikovsky, Beethoven, Mozart, Liszt, Vladigeroff & D Christov. Comps: Piano album for children (composed at age 6/7). Contbr. to Balgarska Muzika. Mbrships: Union of Bulgarian Comps.; Union of Bulgarian Musicians. Hons: Special prize, 1st Bulgarian competition, 1949; 1st prize, 6th world fest., Moscow, 1957; 5th Prize, Tchaikovsky competition, Moscow, 1958; 3rd prize, Long-Thibaud, Paris, 1959; 3rd prize, Int. Competition, Munich, 1962; 4th prize, Int. Beethoven competition, Vienna, 1969. Hobby: Reading. Mgmt: Sofia Concert. Address: Blvd. 9th Sept. 41, Block 24/5, Sofia 1612, Bulgaria.

MOLNAR, Anthony, b. 7 Jan. 1890, Budapest, Hungary. Composer; Author; Viola Player. Educ: High Schl. of Music, Budapest (theory, hist.), 1919-59; Mbr. of Quartett Dohnányi-Hubay-Kerpely-Molnár (viola), 1916-18; Many radio lectures about music. Many comps. publd. or in MS for orch., chamber music, for singing, for choir. Recordings: Choir of Children, 1926. Publs: incl; Aesthetics of Music, 1936; Practical Aesthetics of Music, 1970; a novel about Boëthius, 1972; Memoirs, 1974. Contbr. to: Musica Enciclopedia, Torino. Mbr. of all music socs. in Hungary. Hons: Kossuth Prize, 1957; 'Prominent Artist', 1971. Hobbies: Travel; Engl. lit. Address: Karinthy-ut 14, 1111 Budapest, Hungary.

MOLNAR, Ferenc, b. 15 Nov. 1896, Budapest, Hungary. Viola Soloist; Chamber Music Authority; Educator in Music & Engineering; Founder-Director of Festivals & in the Chamber Music Center at San Francisco State Univ. Educ: Grad., Royal Hungarian F. Liszt Acad. of Music, Budapest; Grad., Royal Jozsef Univ. of Technol., Budapest, m. Maria Rosthy, (author), 1 d., Ava Molnar Heinrichsdorf (author). Career: Capt. in Austro-Hungarian Army & Prisoner in Servia, WWI; Fndr.-Violist, Roth Str. Quartet in Paris, 1926-39; Violist, San Francisco Str. Quartet, 1939-54; Prin. Violist, San Francisco Symph. orch. under Pierre Monteux, 1944-63; solo concert tours in USA, Canada, Europe, Mex., 1944-71; Prof. of Mechanical Engrng., Stanford Univ. 1939-44; Chamber Music Ctr., San Francisco State Univ., 1952-70; Fndr.-Dir., Music at the Vineyards, Saratoga, Calif. 1956-63. 23 maj. Comps. written for & ded. to FM. Recordings & TV: Solo & Chamber music recordings w. Columbia, Victor, Argo (London); KPIX Westinghouse TV Network presented 3 series, called Molnar on Music, to demonstrate the Molnar Chamber Music Method, 1966-67; Three progs. dedicated to Ferenc Molnar's Life, Westinghouse TV network, 1967. Recip. many hons. & awards. Address: 1133 Skycrest Dr. No. 6, Walnut Creek, CA 94595, USA.

MOLNAR, John William, b. 31 May 1909, Toledo, Ohio, USA. Music Educator; Violist; Choral & Orchestral Conductor. Educ: pre-med. studies, Univ. of Toledo; BSc., Md., & DrEd., Univ. of Cinn.; BMus & Dip. in Vila, Cinn. Conserv. of Music. m. Bonnie Hannaford, 1 s., 1 d. Career: Tchr., Maysville, Ky., 1933-34; Newport, Ky., 1934-40; Cinn. Pub. Schls., Univ. of Cinn. & Conserv., 1940-49; Prof. Emeritus, Music Dept., Longwood Coll., Farmville, Va., 1940-; Guest Prof., Fla. State Univ.; arr. Schubert's Omnipotence for band, 1960. Publs: Songs from the Williamsburg Theatre, 1972. Contbr. to num. publs. in field. Mbrships: MENC; Music Lib. Assn. Hobbies: Model Railroading; Model Ship Building. Address: 900 High St., Farmville, VA 23901, USA.

MOLNAR, Josef, b. 7 Sept. 1929, Gänserndorf, Austria. Harpist; Vocalist. Educ: Acad. of Music & Dramatic Art, Vienna. Debut: as orchl. harpist w. Vienna Symph. & Vienna Phil. Career incls: 1st Haprist, NHK Symph. Orch., ABC Symph. Orch. & Yomiuri Symph. Orch., Tokyo; Prof., Geno Gakua Music Coll., Toho Gakuen Music Coill. & Kunitachi Music Coll.; TV broadcasts, Japan, France, Switz., Yogoslavia, USSR; concerts in Japan, Philippines, USA, Netherlands, Germany, Switz., USSR & Yguoslavia; Dir., Karuizawa Music Summer Schl., Japan. Comps: Phantasie for flute & harp; works for solo harp. Num. recordings. Publs: Harp Method in 2 vols. Contbr. to: Nippon Harp News; Ongaku no Tomo. Pres., Japanese Harp Assn. Hons. incl; Cross of Hon., Sci. & Culture, Austria, 1968. Hobbies: Cooking; Skiing. Address: Meguro-ku, Mita 2-18-10, Tokyo 153, Japan.

MOLYNEUX, Christopher John, b. 31 Aug. 1941, Exeter, UK. Senior Administrative Officer; Director of Cemeteries. Educ: MBA, BComm; Assoc., S African Inst. of Mgmt.; MABM; LRSM (Tchr., Organ); LTCL (Perf., Organ); FTCL (Perf., Organ.). m. Jennifer Mary Thomas, 1 s., 1 d. Mbrships: Musical Dir., Cape Town Male Voice Choir; Past Treas., Cape Town Br., Royal Schl. of Ch. Music; Past Pres., Cape Organ Guild; Past Chmn. & Asst. Cond., Philharmonia Choir of Cape Town; Organist & Choirmaster, St. Peter's Ch., Mowbray, St. Andrew's Ch., Newlands; S African Soc. of Music Tchrs.; RCO. Contbr. to: S African Music Tchr. Hobbies: Squash; Photography; Philately; Records. Address: 7 Shaw Rd., Rondebosch, S Africa.

MONCRIEFF, Margaret, b. Edinburgh, Scotland, UK. Cello Soloist & Chamber Music Player. Educ: Edinburgh, London & Paris (w. Pierre Fournier); ARCM. m. Alexander Kelly, 2 d. Career: Concerts throughout UK, Europe (incl. Romania & Bulgaria) & Far East; fnd.mbr., London Cello Ensemble; Cellist of Lyric Trio & Mazzanti Piano Quartet; mbr., Piano Trio w. Jean Harvey & Alexander Kelly. 2 recordings. mbr., ISM. Hons: Bucher & Andrew Fraser scholarships awarded by Edinburgh Univ., 1946; Caird Travelling scholarship, 1948. Address: 32 Gerard Rd., Barnes, London SW13 9RG, UK.

MONELLE, Raymond, b. 19 Aug. 1937, Bristol, UK. Lecturer; Pianist. Educ: MA, Univ. of Oxford; RCM, 1964-66; ARCM; BMus. m. Hannelore E M Monelle, 2 d. Career: Lectr. in music, Univ. of Edinburgh; ldr., Raymond Monelle Trio (jazz). Comps: num. choral pieces. Contbr. to: Music Review; Music & Letters; Brit. Jrnl. of Aesthetics. Mbrships: Royal Musical Assn.; Brit. Soc. of Aesthetics. Hobbies: Poetry; Philosophy; Sailing. Address: Salisbury Gn., Pollock Halls of Residence, 69 Dalkeith Rd., Edinburgh, Scotland, UK.

MONEY, David, b. 4 Jan. 1912, London, UK. Piano Accompanist & Teacher; Coach for Opera, Songs & Chamber Music; Music Critic. Educ: RCM; studied w. Louis Kentner, Kathleen Long & George Reeves. m. Diana Stone, 4 c. Debut: Wigmore Hall, 1935. Career: num. apps. as accomp. throughout UK, Eurpe & Middle E; broadcasts on BBC Radio & TV, ITV & STV as accomp. & reviewer of records; Asst. Music Critic, Daily Telegraph. Recordings: Parlophone; Waverley; Scots Discs. Contbr. to; Concise Ency. of Music & Musicians. Mbrships: Critics Circle; ISM; Musicians Union. Hobby: Gardening. Mgmt: Raymond Gubbay, 125 Tottenham Ct. Rd. W1P 9HN. Address: 16 Devon Rise, London N2 OAA, UK. 3.

MONGOR, Ernest, b. 7 Mar. 1926, London, UK. Music Educator. Educ: ARCM. m. Dorothy Dines, 1 s., 1 d. Career: Asst. Reg. Dir., Yorks. Reg., Arts Coun. of GB, 1951-52; Music Master, Allerton Grange Schl., Leeds, 1954-56; Hd., Music Dept., Foxwood Schl., Leeds, 1956-60; Music Advsr., Borough of Wallasey, 1961-66; Cond., Surrey Co. Youth Orch. & o. Music Insp., Surrey, 1967-. Mbrships: Chmn., Music Advsrs. Nat. Assn., 1975-76. Address: Educ. Dept., County Hall, Kingston-upon-Thames KT1 2DJ, UK.

MONK, Karin, b. 19 July 1903, Copenhagen, Denmark. Coloratura Soprano. Educ: studied w. Emil & Katharina Holm, Copenhagen; Berlin. Debut: Stockholm, Sweden (broadcast), 1928. Career: 1st engagement, Wuppertal, 1931-33; oratorio & ch. music, Denmark; Danish Broadcasting Corp.; apps. in London & Wales; presently w. Royal Danish Opera. Recordings: HMV. Hons: musical prizes, 1949, 50, 66 & 78. Hobby: Vocal Instruction. Address: Kastelsvej 9, 2100 Copenhagen, Denmark.

MÖNKEMEYER, Helmut, b. 26 Sept. 1905, Göttingen, Germany. Educator. Educ: Civic Music Acad. in Berlin, Charlottenburg. m. Else Bormann, 3 s. Career: Solo Hornist, Rhine-Westphalia Symph. Orch.; Schl. Music Tchr., Oberhausen; Dir., Music Schl., City of Krefeld, 1959-. Publs: incl: Krefelder Liederbuch, 1936; Antiqua-Chorbuch, 10 parts, 1951; num. pedagogical works, esp. methods for histl. instruments. Contbr. to: Hausmusik; Handbuch des Musikunterrichts; var. festschriften & yearbooks. Mbr., Soc. for Music Rsch., Cassel. Adddress: Friedrich-Ebert-Str. 287, 415 Krefeld, German Fed. Repub.

MONNARD, Jean-Francois, b. 4 Nov. 1941, Lausanne, Switzerland. Conductor. Educ: LLM, Univ. Lausanne; Music Acad. Lausanne; Orch. Conducting Dip., 1968; Folkwang Hochschule, Essen, German Fed. Repub.; Int. conds. course w. maestro Jean Fournet, Hilversum, Holland. Debut: Cond. operas, Kaiserslautern, German Fed. Repub. & Graz, Austria. Career: Cond., important orchs., Switzerland, currently at Stadttheater, Trier; Radio apps., Basel, Geneva, Lausanne, Lugano & Zurich. Contbr. to newspapers. Mbr., Assn. Musiciens Suisses. Address: Chemin de l'Eglise, 1066 Epalinges, Switzerland.

MONNIKENDAM, Marius, b. 28 May 1896, Haarlen, Holland. Composer. Educ: Conserv., Amsterdam. m. AMA. Van

Gendt, 7 c. Career: Tchr., Conserv., Rotterdam, Music Lyceum, Amsterdam; Music Ed., De Maasbode (newspaper); Amalgamation of De Maasbode & De Tijd, 1960; Perm. Staff, ibid, 1960-. Compositions incl: Labour, Variations symphoniques, Sinfonia Mouvement symphonique (orchl. works); Rondena, Concerto, Toccata, Terma con Variazoni, Sonata da chiesa, 12 Inventions, Serie I & II, Toccata II, 2 themes w. variations, Toccata-Batalla, Prelude The Bells (organ music); Te Deum, Noe, Magnificat, Madrigalesca (works for mixed choir & orch.); Ballade des Pendus, Sinfonia Sacra, Veni Sancte Spiritus, Veni Creator (works for mixed choir & orch.); Ballade des Pendus, Sinfonia Sacra, Veni Sancte Spiritus, Veni Creator (works for male choir & orch.); Missa Festival, Via Sacra (Ch. music). Publs. incl: Biography of Stravinsky; Biography of César Franck. Hons. incl: Chevalier de l'Ordere St. Gregoire-le-Grand; Chevalier de l'Ordre d'Orange-Nassau; Off., d'Acad.; Gold & other Medals, Arts, Sciences et Lettres, Paris. Address: Neuhuvskade 61, The Hague, Netherlands.

MONN-IVERSEN, Egil, b. 14 April 1928, Oslo, Norway. Conductor. Educ: Pvte. tchrs.; Music Conserv., Oslo. m. Sölvi Wang, 1 s., 1 d. Career: Hd. of Music, Cond., The Norwegian Theatre, Oslo; Music Cons., Norwegian TV & The Norwegian Culture Fndn./Coun.; Film Prod. Comps: Music for over 50 Norwegian, Danish, German & Am. Films; Theatre music incl. 5 musicals; music for num. Scandinavian TV series. Recordings: Approx. 800 recordings; Prod. of series w. classical Norwegian music. Mbrships: Musicians Union of Norway; ISCM Norway. Hobbies: Art collecting; Skiing; Fishing. Address: Gjökbakken 9, Oslo 3, Norway.

MONOD, Jacques-Louis, b. 25 Feb. 1927, Asnieres-Paris, France. Composer; Conductor; Former Pianist. Educ: DMA, Columbia Univ., NYC, USA. m. Margrit Auhagen, 1 d. Debut: (pianist) Paris, France, 1949. Career incls: Pianist, -1956; Voice & Piano Duo w. Bethany Beardslee, USA, 1950-55; Chmbr. Ensemble Concert Series, Aust. & Italian Insts., London, UK, 1962-66; Cond., maj. orchs. & chmbr. ensembles, BBC 3rd Prog., London, 1960-; Orchl. concerts & broadcasts in Europe, Scandinavia, N & Ctrl. Am., 1956-; Dir. of Publs., Boelke-BomartMobart, Inc., Hillsdale, NY. Comps. incl: Chamber Aria; Cantus contra Cantum I, II & III. Num. recordings as pianist & cond. Mbrships. incl: Pres., Assn. Rene Leibowitz, Paris, Comps.' Guild for Perf., NY. Author of 3 eds. Recip., sev. hons. Address: 395 Riverside Dr., Apt. 10-B, NY, NY 10025, USA.

MONOSOFF, Sonya b. 11 June 1927, Cleveland, Ohio, USA. Concert Violinist; Professor of Music. Educ: Artist's Dip., Juilliard Schl. of Music. m. Carl Eugene Pancaldo, 4 d. Career: Concerts, USA & Europe; Radio apps., Germany, Denmark, Norway, USA; TV Perfs.; Prof. of Music, Cornell Univ. Recordings: Music of Biber, Bach & Corelli. Contbr. of reviews to Notes, Notes for Corelli recording. Mbrships: Fellow, Radcliffe Inst.; Am. Musicol. Soc.; Am. Musical Instrument Soc. Hons. Best Record of Year Award, Stereo Review, 1970. Hobby: Chamber Music. Mgmt: Ruth Uebel. Address: Cornell Univ., Dept. of Music, Ithaca, NY 14850, USA.

MONTAGU, Jeremy Peter Samuel, b. 27 Dec. 1927, London, UK. Timpanist & Percussion Player; Lecturer, History of Instruments; Conductor; Teacher; Ethnomusicologist. Educ: Trinity Coll., Cambridge; GSM. m. Gwen Ellen Ingledew, 1 s., 2 d. Debut: as cond., Montague Str. Orch., Hampstead, 1952. Career incls: reconstructs mediaeval percussion instruments; Lectr., UK & abroad, regularly at London Univ. Records w. Musica Reservata & other early music ensembles. Publs. incl; Early Percussion Instruments (co-author), 1976; Making Early Percussion Instruments, 1976; The World of Medieval & Renaissance Musical Instruments, 1976; The World of Baroque & Classical Musical Instruments, 1979. Contbr. to jrnls. Mbr. profl. orgs., inclng. Hon. Sec., Fellowship of Makers & Restores of Historical Instruments. Hobbies: Collecting musical instruments; Camping. Mgmt: Terry Slasberg Agcy., 3 The Lodge, Richmond Way, London W12 8LW, UK. Address: 7 Pickwick Rd., Dulwich Village, London SE21 7JN, UK.

MONTGOMERY, Kenneth Mervyn, b. 28 Oct. 1943, Belfast, UK. Conductor. Educ: Royal Belfast Academical Instn.; RCM, London. Deubt: Glyndebourne, 1967. Career: Staff Cond., Sadlers Wells, 1967-70; Asst. Cond., Bournemouth Symph. Orch., Bournemouth Sinfonietta; Dir., Bournemouth Sinfonietta, 1973-75; Musical Dir., Glyndebourne Touring Co., 1974-76; Prin. Cond., Omroep Orkest (Dutch Radio), 1976-; Guest Cond., Netherlands Opera, Glyndebourne Fest. Opera, Welsh Nat. Opera, BBC, Royal Opera House Covent Gdn., Canadian Opera, etc. sev. recordings. Hons: Silver Medal, Worshipful Co. of Musicians, 1963; Tagore Gold Medal, RCM, 1964. Hobbies: Cooking. Mgmt: Artists Int. Mgmt. Address: 24a Crescent Grove, London SW4 7AF, UK. 2, 4, 30.

MONTGOMERY, Lee Boyd, Jr., b. 28 Mar. 1936, Slaton, Tex., USA. Conductor of Bands; Supervisor of Music. Educ: BMus, Tex. Tch. Univ., Lubbock, Tex., 1958; MA in Music Educ., W Tex. State Univ., Canyon, Tex., 1964; working on DMA, Univ. of Tex. at Austin. m. Gwendolyn Elaine Nix, 2 c. Career: Band Cond. in the pub. schls. Mbrships: Phi Beta Mu; Kappa Kappa Psi; Tex. Music Educators Assn.; Tex. Bandmasters Assn.; MENC; Nat. Educators Assn.; Tex. State Tchrs. Assn.; Nat. Jazz Educators Assn.; 2nd VP, Nat. Bands Assn.; Am. Schl. Band Dirs. Assn. Hobbies: Gold; Fishing; Music. Address: 4905 Timberline, Austin, TX 78746, USA.

MONTGOMERY, William L, b. 28 Mar. 1934, Waco, Tex., USA. Flautist; Professor of Music. Educ: BMusEd., Cornell Coll., Iowa, 1953; MMus, Cath. Univ. of Am.; PhD, ibid., 1975; Marlboro Schl. of Music; Curtis Inst. of Music. m. Kathleen Lewis, 3 c. Debut: Carnegie Hall, NYC, 1960. Career: Prin. Flute, US Marine Band & Orch., 1954-63, Nat. Gallery of Art Orch., 1965; Theatre Chmbr. Players, 1968-; Prof. of Music, Cath. Univ. oif Am., 1959-64, Geo. Wash. Univ., 1963-65; Prof. of Music, Univ. of Md., 1964-. Contbr. to: Grove's Dictionary; Flute Ed. Mbrships: VP, nat. Flute Assn., 1975-76; Pres., ibid., 1976-77; Pres., Wash. Flute Soc., 1978-80. Address: 13400 Forest Dr., Bowie, MD 20716, USA.

MONY, Walter Alexander, b. 14 Apr. 1930, Winnipeg, Can. Violinist; Violist; Conductor; Lecturer. Educ: Dip. Educ.; RCM; LRAM; LRSM; ARCM. m. Anneliese Hoenigsberg, 3 s. Career: (as violinist), apps. on TV & radio; concert tours; (as cond.) Lausanne Int. Fests.; tours, S Am. & S Africa; Dir., Nederburg Trio (harp); concerts in London, Amsterdam, Paris, BBC etc.; fndr. & cond., SABC JO Training Orch.; Sr. Lectr., Univ. of Witwatersrand, 1970-; Strg. Dept., Univ. of Pretoria, 1961-. Recordings: solo violin recital; w. Nederburg Trio; author, aural training series, Let us Hear. Mbrships: Pres., S African Harp Soc. Recip. RCM prizes, 1948. Mgmt: W. van Wyck. Address: PO Box 52-210, Saxonwold 2132, S Africa.

MOOMEY, Katherine Walling, b. 25 Apr. 1917, Champlain, NY, USA. Music Educator; Pianist; Organist. Educ: Pvte. studyt of Piano; Woman's Coll., Univ. of NC., 1934-35; 10-yr. Cert., 1939, BS Music Educ., 1941, MS Educ., 1969, Crane Schl. of Music, Tchrs. Coll., SUNY at Potsdam; grad. studies; Westminster Choir Coll., St. Lawrence Univ. m. Raymond Everett Moomey, 1 s., 3 d. Career: Solo pianist & Tchr.; Fest. Choral Dir. & Accomp.; Schl. Music educator, esp. in choral field, Adjudicator NY & Ill., 22 yrs. (Orff-Kodaly oriented); Mbr., Rackham Symph. Choir (w. Detroit Symph.) & Flint Community Choir, Mich. & St. Lawrence Univ. & N Country Community Coll. Choruses, NY. Mbrships: Julia E Crane Alumni Assn. (Bd. of Dirs.); MENC; Phi Sigma Mu. Hobbies: Photography; Swimming; Oil Painting; Hiking; Sewing. Address: Lake Ozonia, St. Regis Falls, NY 12980, USA.

MOON, Harry Edward, b. 8 July 1937, Potsville, Iowa, USa. Tenor; Conductor; Educator; Clinician; Composer & Arranger. Educ: BMus, Coe Coll.; BA (Music Educ. & Voice), ibid.; MMus, Univ. Mich.; currently studying at Univ. of Iowa for DMusArts in Choral Cond. m. Marlene Hudson Moon, 1 s., 1 d. Career: Chmn., Music Dept., Athens Coll.; Artist-in-Res., Oglethorpe Coll.; Asst. Prof. of Sacred Music, Emory Univ. Comps. incl: Let This Mind Be In You, Op. 7; O Come Emmanuel, Op. 9 No. 1; O Come, All Ye Faithful, Op. 9 No. 3. Recordings: The Chandler Choraliers; Carols From the Earth, Vol. I; Hymns For All Seasons. Mbrships: Fellowship of United Meth. Musicians; Am. Guild of Organists; Assn. of Choral Conds. Hobbies: Hist.; Art; Riding; Tennis; Hiking; Reading. Address: 593 Hawkeye Ct., Iowa City, IA 52240, USA.

MOONEN, Janet Elisabeth, b. 31 July 1937, Coventry, UK. Viola Player. Educ: ARMCM; Akademie für Musik & darstellende Kunst, Vienna, 4 yrs. m. Johannes Hubertus Moonen, 2 s. Career: Viola Player, The Brabant Orch., Netherlands. Hobbies: Photography; Wine-making. Address: Antilope 18, Huizen, Netherlands.

MOONEY, Gerard Antony, b. 11 Nov. 1953, Thundersley, Essex, UK. Administrator; Professor; Examiner; Music Publisher; Organist. Educ: LCM, 1972-75; GLCM, 1975; FLCM, 1976; LLCM TD, 1975. m. Carmel O'Donnell. Career: Asst. Registrar, Professor of Music & Examiner, LCM; Asst. Organist, St. Joseph, Upminster, 1971-74; Organist & Choirmaster, St. Augustine, Barkingside, 1974-; Musical Dir., Chigwell Row Opera. Address: 10 Westminster Close, Barkingside, Ilford, Essex IG6 1PQ, UK.

MOORE, Barbara Hill, b. 28 Dec. 1942, St. Louis, Mo., USA. Mezzo Soprano; Associate Professor of Voice. Educ: BS, Lincoln Univ.; MS, Univ. of Ilkl. m. Leandrew Moore. Career: solo apps. incl. St. Louis Symph., 1965, St. Louis Municipal Opera,

1966, Springfield (Ill.) Symph., 1973 & 74, Dallas Civic Symph., 1974, San Antonio Symph., Pensacola (Fla.) Symph., 1975, Dallas Symph. Orch., 1976; num. recitals, oratorios & opera apps.; Assoc. Prof. of Voice, Southern Meth. Univ., Dallas, Tex., Mbrships: Pi Kappa Lambda; local Treas., Nat. Assn. Tchrs. of Singing; MENC. Hons. incl: St. Louis Friends of Music Award, 1961; Ill. Artist Award, 1973-74. Hobbies: Fashion Modelling; Cookery; Tennis; Reading. Address: 2616 Dalgreen Ct., Plano, TX 75075, USA.

MOORE, Carole Torrence, b. 14 Mar. 1938, Va., USA. Flute & Piano Teacher. Educ: Bachelor's degree, Cinn. Coll.-Conserv. of Music & Univ. of Cinn. Tchrs. Coll.; Studied flute w. Robert Cavally & Mark Thomas; Studied piano w. Margaret Belser; Studied organ w. Virginia Banfield & Raymond Herbek. Career: appeared on educl. TV in Cinn. as Flutist & in woodwind ensembles; Appeared w. Roanoke (Va.) Symph. Orch. while in coll., playing flute & piccolo; taught choral music. Petersburg City & Chesterfield Co. Pub. Schl. & at Bollingbrock (pvte. schl.); currently Tchng. Flute & Piano, Va. C'wealth Univ. Community Schl. of Music, Ricmond; Woodwind Instr., Student Orch., Va. Music Camps, (3 yrs.); Flute Tchr., Longwood Coll., Va., 1978-79; Organist & Choir Dir., St. John's Episcopal Ch., Chester, Va. Mbrships. incl: MENC; Past Mbr. & Rep. of the Choral Dirs. Dist. Ill, Bd. of Control for Va. Choral Dirs. Assn.; Am. Choral Dires. Assn.; Richmond, Va. & Nat. MTAs; NGPT. Address: 203 Biltmore Dr., Colonial Heights, VA 23834, USA. 5.

MOORE, Dale (Kimberly), b. 22 May 1932, Olathe, Kan., USA. Baritone Singer; Teacher. Educ: BMus, Univ. of Kan., 1954; Fulbright Scholar to Salzburg Mozarteum, 1954-55; MMus, Univ. of Kan., 1956. m. Rosanne Greenwood, 1 s., 2 d. Debut: Town Hall, NYC, 1960. Career: 9 Recitals in NYC; Solo appearance w. Cleveland Orch. & St. Louis Symph.; Minn. Orch.; Columbus Symph., etc.; Leading Baritone, Lake Erie Opera Theatre; Soloist, Baldwin-Wallace Bach Festival & Bethany Coll. Messiah Week Festival; Recital at the White House; Over 300 concerts & recitals in var. cities of USA; Prof. of Music & Chmn., Voice Fac., Southern Ill. Univ.; Voice Fac., St. Louis Conserv.; Artist-in-Res. & Prof. of Music, Wash. Univ., St. Louis, 1975-. Recording: On the Road to Mandalay & Other Favorite American Concert Songs (Cambridge), 1973. Mbrships: Ctrl. Region Gov., Nat. Assn. of Tchrs. of Singing, 1972-74; Int. Hugo Wolf Soc.; Pi Kappa Lambda; Phi Mu Alpha Sinfonia; Omicron Delta Kappa; Delta Phi Alpha; Nat. MTA. Hons. incl; MusD, Lincoln Mem. Univ., 1964. Address: 5257 Westminster Pl., St. Louis, MOI 63108, USA.

MOORE, Gerald, b. 30 July 1899, Watford, Herts., UK. Pianist. Educ: Univ. of Toronto, Can.; study w. Prof. Michael Hambourg, Toronto. m. Enid Richard, 1936. Career: Returned to UK, 1920, became accompanist & chmbr. music player associated w. world's leading vocalist & instrumentalists; Perfs. at all European Fests.; Lectr. & broadcaster on Music & art of accompaniment in USA annually for many yrs.; Master classes in song interpretation in var. countries, 1949-67; Ret'd., 1967. 50 yrs. of recording. Publs: The Unashamed Accompanist, 1943; Singer & Accompanist, 1953; Am. I Too Loud? (Memoirs), 1962; Schubert Song Cycles, 1975; Farewell Recital (Further Memoirs), 1978. Mbrships: Pres., ISM, 12962. Hons. incl: Gold Medal, Worshipful Co. of Musicians, 1951; Grand Prix du Disque from var. countries; DMus (h.c.) Cambridge Univ.; Hon. DLitt, Univ. of Sussex; Hon. RAM; CBE. Hobbies: Reading; Gardening; Bridge; Walking. Address: Beechwood Cottage, Penn Bottom, Penn, Bucks., UK.

MOORE, James, III, b. 27 Sept. 1940, Richmond, Va., USA. Classic Guitarist; Lutenist; Violinst; Vocalist. Educ: studied w. Frederick Neumann, Frank Wendt, Helen Travis Crawford, Philip Lewis & John Runge. Debut: Richmond, Va. Career: Instructor of Guitar & Lute, Univ. of Richmond & Va. C'wlth. Univ.; provided soundtrack music for State Dept. of Educ. film The Visiting Tchr., 1964; Org. & Dir., James Moore Broken Consort, Moore-Raff Guitar & Lute Duo & Baroque Consort; has app. on Richmond TV channels & radio stns., at museuims, colls., chs. & hist. homes; asst. John Runge in ed. 3 vols., Lute Songs & Folk Songs, 1965-71. Mbrships: Lute Soc. of London, UK; Co-Fndr., Soc. of Classic Guitar, Richmond. Hobbies: Fencing; Boating; Antique Collecting. Mgmt: Elihu Woodson. Address: 1709 Grove Ave., Richmond, VA 23220, USA.

MOORE, Philip Douglas, b. 20 May 1918, Ilford, Essex, UK. Musician (French Horn & Piano). Educ: London Acad. of Music; RAM; ALAM, 1933; FRCM, 1965. Career: w. BBC Symph. Orch., 1937-68; Prin. Horn, ibid., 1948-68. Hobby: Motoring. Address: Moorcroft, Burnt Common, Send, Surrey, UK.

MOORE, Philip John, b. 30 Sept. 1943, London, UK. Organist. Educ: BMus; RCM; FRCO; GRSM; ARCM. m. Camille

Sara Louise Margaret Marquand, 2 d., 1 s. Career: Organist, Choirmaster, St. Gabriel's Ch., Cricklewood, London, 1962-65; Asst. Music master, Eton Coll., 1966-68; Asst. Organist, Canterbury Cathedral, 1968-74; Organist, Master of the Choristers, Guildford Cathedral, 1974-. Compositions: Anthems, organ pieces. Recordings: 4, w. Choir of Canterbury Cathedral; 1 w. choir of Guildford Cathedral; 1 solo organ (Vierne Symphonie I). Hons: RCM Organ Playing Prize, 1965; Limpus Prize, Read Prize, RCO, 1963; Turpin Prize, RCO, 1965. Hobbies: Motoring; Reading. Address: 3 Cathedral Close, Guildford GU2 5TL, UK. 30.

MOORE, Ronald Gresham, b. 15 Dec. 1926, Shrewsbury, Salop., UK. Clarinettist; Special in Eb Clarinet Playing. Educ: ARCM (Perfs.). m. Mary Bernadette Evett, 1 d. (by previous marriage). Career: 1st Clarinet, Fest. Ballet, 1950; Sub. Prin. Clarinet, Sadlers Wells, 1950-51; Sub. Prin. Clarinet & Eb Clarinet, LSO, 1951-; Dir., LSO Ltd., 1953-61, 1964-75; Sec., LSO Sickness & Benevolent Assn., 1969-. Recordings: 2nd Clarinet w. London Wind Soloists in recordings; 2nd Clarinet w. London Wind Soloists in recordings of J C Bach Wind Sinfonias, & wind arrs. of Beethoven's Fidelo & Mozart's ll Seraglio; Eb Clarinet or 2nd Clarinet, majority of LSO recordings, 1951-; Prin. Clarinet, some LSO recordings, 1951-61. Mbr. Delius Soc. Hobbies: Gardening; Home brewing; Exploring the Cotswolds. Address: Kingsclere, 9 Fitzgerald Ave., London, SW14 8SZ, UK.

MOORE, Timothy, b. 19 Feb. 1922, Cambridge, UK. Composer; Educator. Educ: MA, MusB, Cantab.; RCM. Compositions: Suite for 3 Recorders; Andante for Cor Anglais & Piano; 3 2-Part Inventions for Piano; The Scrapyard; Reciprocal Rumbas; Night Song; Sing Lullaby. Mbrships: CGGB; PRS. Hons: Madrigal Soc. prize, 1947; Farrar Prize, 1947; Royal Phil. Soc. Prize, 1948. Hobby: Reading. Address: Dartington Hall Schl., Totnes, Devon TQ6 6EB, UK. 3, 28.

MOORLAND, Carol, b. 28 Aug. 1907, Pass Christian, Miss., USA. Pianist. Educ: w. Lucie Caffaret, Paris, France; Sternsches Konserv., Riga, Latvia; under Simon Barere, Stockholm, Sweden. m. Edwin M Marshall, 3 s., 1 d. Debut: Stockhom, Sweden. Career: Concert & Radio apps., throughout Europe & USA, 1933-42; Mbr., Piano Fac., North's Schl. Music, Greenwich Conn.; Pvte. tchr.; Artist (under Carol Moorland-Marshall), over 400 commd. portraits, esp. children, 1957-68-; Sculptor, porcelain & ceramic show dogs, 1968-; Works in collects., Palais de Monaco, UK, Aust., Hawaii, NZ, France, Canada & USA. Publ: 4 Octaves in 5 Lessons, 1959. Contbr. to: NY Herald Tribune.Mbr., var. orgs. Hobby: Breeding & Showing Show Borzois. Address: 30371 Morning View Dr., Malibu, CA 90265, USA.

MORA, Vera (SESAN, Karolina Vera), b. 3 May 1908, St. Petersburg, USSR. Concert & Opera Singer; Musicologist; Writer. Educ: Cernauti Conserv., Romania, 1925-31; Prague Conserv., Czechoslovakia, 1931-35. Career: Vis. Mbr., Opera Houses, Cluj & Bucharest, 1933-38; roles in Tosca, Aida, Madam Butterfly, etc.; Prof., Prague Conserv., 1939-56; Jt. Organiser, Karel Capek Exhib., Bucharest, 1970; Prof. of Ch. Music, John Huss Theol. Fac., 1976. Publs. incl: (play) Fairytales of an Evening, 1934; Romanian Song (in Czech), 1937; Romanian Puppet Shows, 1931; var. transls. inclng. Czech Nat. Anthem in Romanian. Mbr., Dvorák & Smetna Socs., Prague. Address: Vysehradská ul. 27, 128 00 Prague 2-Vysehrad, Czechoslovakia.

MORALES, Abram, b. 30 Nov. 1939, Corpus Christi, Texas, USA. Opera Singer (Lyric tenor). Educ: BME, MMus, Southern Methodist Univ. Career: Apps. incl: Almaviva (The Barber of Seville), Alfredo (La Traviata) w. Can. Opera Co.; Tonio (The Daughter of the Regiment), Houston Grand Opera, Opera Theatre of Hawaii; Astrologer, (Le Coq d'Or) w. NYC Opera, NY & Kennedy Center, Wash., DC; Rodolfo (La Boheme) Kentucky Opera; Apps. w. Metropolitan Opera, Opera Co. of Boston, etc. Mgmt: Harold Shaw. Address: 165 West End Ave., Apt. 19A, NY, NY 10023, USA.

MORAN, Gerald, b. 25 May 1926, Eston, Sask., Can. Music Editor. Educ: Mt. Angel Abbey, Ore., USA. Career: Organist, St. Paul's Cathedral, Saskatoon, Sask., Can., 1950-57; Ed., Music Publs., Province of Alta.; Ed., Music Calendar, monthly, 1970-, Music in Alberta, quarterly, 1972-74. Hobby: Photography. Address: 31 Chatham Dr. NW, Calgary, Alta. T2L 0Z4, Can.

MORAWSKI, Jerzy, b. 9 Sept. 1932, Warsaw, Poland. Musicologist. Educ: Theory, Warsaw Conserv., 1957; Piano, ibid., 1961; MA, Inst. Musicol., Warsaw Univ., 1958; PhD, Inst. Arts, Polish Acad. Scis., 1970. m. Katarzyna Morawska. Career: Asst., Dept. Theory & Hist. Music, Inst. Arts, Polish Acad.

Scis., 1956-70; Doct., Hd. Hist. Music Sect., ibid., 1970-; Lectr., Warsaw Univ., 1968-70; Acad. Cath. Theol., Warsaw, 1970-73; Jagiellonian Univ., Cracow, 1971-. Publs. incl: The Problems of the Tropes' Technique. Contbr. to profl. publs. Mbrships. incl: Past V-Sec. & Pres., Polish Composers' Union, Musicol. Sect.; Int. Musicol. Soc. Address: ul. Dluga 24 m. 43,00-238 Warsaw, Poland.

MOREAU, Félix, b. 8 Sept. 1922, AigrefeuilleMaine, Loire-Atlantique, France. Composer; Organist. Educ: studied music w. Maurice Duruflé & Marcel Dupré; Disciple of Messiaën. Debut: when aged 12. Career: Organiste Titulaire du Grand Orgue, Cathedral of Nantes; Int. Concert Perf., UK, Switz., Can., etc.; Soloist on French radio. Comps. incl: 3 Motets (organ & chorus); Ave Maria (organ & chorus); pastorale de Printemps (2 recorders & piano); Suite Modale (organ). Recordings: les 3 corals pour Orgue, Cesar Franck; le Grand Orgue de la Cathédrale de Nantes; Musique Francaise a l'Orgue de la Cathédrale de Luçon. Author: le Grand Orgue de la Chatédrale de Nantes, 1971. Contbr. to jrnls. Mbrships. incl: Prof., Ctr. of Sacred Music of the W. Recip. comp. prize for sacred music, 1956. Address: 5 Quail André Rhùys, 44 200 Nantes, France.

MOREIRA DA ROCHA, Persio, b. 7 Mar. 1934, São Paulo, Brazil. Music Teacher; Composer; Pianist. Educ: Grad., Dramatic & Musical Conserv. of São Paulo, 1953; Grad., Choir Conserv. of São Paulo. m. Celina Anna Botana M Rocha, 1 d., 2 s. Career: Pub. Tchr., -1972; Musical Tchr., Ind. Social Serv., 1955-; Educl. Asst. & Musical Supvsr., ibid., 1961-; Mgr.-Owner w. wife, O Mundo da Criança (elem. educ. schl.). Comps. incl: (orch.); Suite 25th January; Suite Piratini; (piano); Children's Suite Nos. 1 & 2; Baião (Brazilian dance); Chmbr.); String Quartet, 1974; Quartet for Flute, Clarinet, Bassoon & Piano, 1965; var. songs; Piano Waltz (recorded); Suite Infantil No. 1. Mbr., Soc. Brasileira de Música Contemporánea. Recip. sev. musical prizes. Address: Rua Guararapes 202, Lapa, São Paulo, CEP 05077, Brazil.

MORELLE, Maureen, b. 16 Aug. 1934, Aldershot, Hants., UK. Singer (mezzo soprano). Educ: ARCM. 1 s. Debut: Rosina in Barber of Seville, Welsh Nat. Opera. Career incl: guest appearances w. Glyndebourne Opera, Royal Opera House, Covent Gdn., Engl. Nat. Opera; Recitals & other broadcasts for BBC; Madrid Festival Opera; Engl. Opera Grp.; appeared in world premiere of Punch & Judy (Birtwhistle). Recordings: var. Greek songs (Jupiter records). Hons. incl: Dame Clara Butt Award, RCM, 1960; Queen's Prize for Women Singers, 1963. Hobbies: Sewing; Gardening; Cooking. Mgmt: Music & Musicians. Address: Flat 4, 8 Westbury Rd., London W5, UK.

MORENO, Sara, b. 23 Mar. 1928, Buenos Aires, Argentina. Pianist. Educ: Superior Tchr. of Music, Nat. Conserv. of Music & Scenic Arts, Buenos Aires; Collegium Musicum of Buenos Aires. m. Miguel Muller, 1 d. Debut: LRA, Radio Nacional of Buenos Aires. Career: Apps. incl: LS1 Radio Municipal; House of Theater; Municipality of Campana; Lomas de Zamora; Quilmes; Cultural Dept. of Educ.; Min. of La Plata: 4 concerts of old music playe£d on historic pianoforte at Hist. & Art Mus.; Concert at Colegio Mayor Argentino in Madrid sponsored by Argentine Embassy, 1974. Mbrships. incl: Promociones Musicales. Hobbies: Reading; Writing Poetry & Stories; Study of Percussion Instruments; Composing Children's Songs. Address: Independencia 831, 1653 Villa Ballester, Prov Buenos Aires, Argentina.

MORES, Renaat, b. 12 Dec. 1909, Ronse, Flanders, Belgium. Organist; Professor of Music. Educ: Royal Conservs., Ghent & Brussels. m. Alma de la Fortrie, 1 d. Career: Organist, St. Mary Ch., Dendermonde, Flanders; Prof., Acad. of Music, ibid; Organist, Collegial Ch. of St. Martin, Aalst; comps. performed in Flanders, Germany, Luxembourg, Austria & Italy. Comps. incl: 6 masses (incl. Mass for 5 voices & organ); Cantat for the Hallowing of Clocks; works for organ, (inclng. Variations, Fugue & Hymn), choir & solo voice. Recip., Gold Medal for servs. to ch., schls. & colls., from local Bishop. Address: Acaciastraat 21, 9300 Aalst, Flanders, Belgium.

MORET, Norbert Eloi, b. 20 Nov. 1921, Ménières, Switz. Composer. Educ: studied under Olivier Messiaen, René Leibowitz, Arthur Honegger & Paul Kletzky. m. Germaine Fivaz, 3 d. Debut: Philharmony, Vienna, 1950-51. Career: Prof. of Music, Norman Schl., Fribourg, 1952-. Comps. incl: Hipster for orch., 1967; Concerto for strings, trumpet & piano, 1972; Germes Concerto for strings, trumpet & piano, 1972; Germes en Eveil for soprano solo, chorus, flute & percussion, 1973; Toi for soprano & piano, 1974, version for soprano & chmbr. orch., 1975; Gastlosen for organ, 1975; Rituels for harpsichord, 1975; Hymnes de silence for strings, organ, trombones & percussion, 1976. Mbrships: Swiss Musicians Assn. Recip., Music Prize, City of Fribourg, 1974. Hobby: Mountaineering. Address: Jolimont 13, CH 1700 Fribourg, Switz.

MORETTO, Nelly, b. 20 Sept. 1925, Santa Fe, Rosario, Argentina. Composer; Pianist. Educ: Musical Professorship Schl. of Rosario; Nat. Conserv. of Music, Argentina; Univ. of Ill. Music Schl., USA; electronic music courses, Di Tella Inst. of High Musical Studies, Buenos Aires. m. Oreste Moretto, 1 s., 1 d. Career: gives Lectures & musical progs. on Municipal Radio of Buenos Aires. Compositions incl: Trio for violin, 'cello & oboe; Composition No. 7 for flute, viola, bass clarinet & guitar; Composition No. 10 for str. quartet & magnetic tape. Composition No. 11, for Symph. Orch.; Composition No. 12, String Quartet; Composition No. 13, for trumpet & stereo magnetic tape; Composition No. 14, for piano, voice, trumpet & magnetic tape. Mbrships: VP, Argentine New Music Assn., Bd., Villa Gessel Musical Camp. Address: Segurola 1448 Vincente Lopez, Buenos Aires, Argentina.

MORGAN, Carole Montgomery, b. 6 Dec. 1939, Hobart, Okla., USA. Flautist. Educ: BMus, Univ. Houston, Tex. m. Robert P Morgan. Career: Mbr., Houston Symph., 1965-67; Fac., Temple Univ., 1967-; Ambler Inst., 1969-70; Fac., Glassboro State Coll., 1975-76; Mbr., Penn Contemporary Players; Pro Arts Woodwind Quintet; Glassboro Fac. Quintet. Recordings incl: George Crumb's Vox Balanae, Columbia Records. Hobbies: Skiing; Cooking. Address: 2203 1/2 St. James, Philadelphia, PA 19103, USA.

MORGAN, David Sydney, b. 18 May 1932, Ewell, Surrey, UK. Composer; Conductor. Educ: NSW Conserv. of Music, Sydney, Australia. Study of Composition w. Matyas Seiber; Study of Conducting w. Walter Goehr & Norman Del Mar; BMus, Durham Univ.; ARCM. m. Crisetta Mary MacLeod, 1 s., 2 d. Career: Cor Anglais w. Sydney Symph. Orch., 1958-59; Tutor in Theoretical Music Subjs., Elder Conserv., Univ. of Adelaide, 1959-61; Music Libn., British Coun., London, 1964-68; Staff, Music Room, British Mus., 1968-71; Tchr. of woodwind & cond. of orchs. & wind bands, 1971-75; Comp. & Arranger, Educ. Authority, S Aust., 1975-. Compositions: 5 symphs.; Chmbr., instrumental & choral works; Music for Wind & Brass Band; Orchl. pieces; Part-songs. Hons: Sydney Gordon Vicars Composition Schlrship., 1950-52; Martin Musical Fellowship, 1966. Address: c/o Music Branch, 22/ Sturt St., Adelaide, 5000, S Aust. 3.

MORGAN, Genie Boinest, b. 29 Apr. 1897, Florence, SC, USa. Piano Teacher. Educ: BM, Elizabeth Coll., Salem, Va.; Tchrs. Cert., Peabody Conserv., Balt., Md.; Studied w. George F Boyle, Ernest Hutcherson, Guy Maier. m. Charles Kemper Morgan, dec. Contbr. to: The Clavier; The Piano Tchr.; The Piano Quarterly; The Piano Guild Notes. Mbrships: Life, Nat. Fedn. of Music Clubs; Union Music Club; Delta Kappa Gamma Soic.; SC Music Tchrs. Assn.; Nat. & State Tchrs. Assn.; Nat. Guild of Piano Tchrs. Hons:O Hall of Fame, Piano Guild, 1968; Award for Contemporary Achievement, 1975. Hobbies: Travel; Bridge. Address: 112 Douglass Heights, Union, SC 29379, USA. 5, 30.

MORGAN, Geoffrey David, b. 1 June 1945, Hayes, Middx., UK. Organist & Choirmaster; Teacher. Educ: TCL; Newton Pk. Coll., Bath; FRCO (CHM); FTCL (Organ); GTCL; LRAM (Organ tchng.); ARCM (Organ perf.); LTCL (Piano perf.); Cert. Educ.; BA. Career: Dir. of Music, Papplewick Schl., Ascot, 1970-76; Organ Scholar, Magdalen Coll., Oxford, 1976-78; Organist, Alexandra Choir; Solo organ work, Royal Albert Hall & Queen Elizabeth Hall; num. organ recitals throughout UK; Sev. BBC broadcast organ recitals; 2nd Asst. Organist, Westminster Abbey, 1979-. Recording: The Story of Jesus; Thomas Timkins. Contbr. to Musical Opinion. Mbrship: RCO. Hons: Lady Maud Warrender Prize for Piano Playing, 1966; 1st Prize, London Organ Week Competition, 1975. Hobbies: Cars; Hi-Fi; Wine-making; Photography. Address: 5 Albemarle Rd., Bournemouth, Dorset, UK.

MORGAN, Paula, b. 11 Aug. 1935, Modesto, Calif., USA. Music Librarian. Educ: AB, Mills Coll., Oakland, 1957; MA (Musicol.), Columbia Univ., 1959; Grad. study, musicol., Univ. of Calif., Berkeley, 1959-63; MLS, ibid., 1964. Career: Music Libn., Princeton Univ. Lib., Princeton, NJ, 1964-. Contbr. to: Grove's Dict., 6th Ed. Mbrships: Music Lib. Assn.; San Fran. Single Reed Soc. Hobbies: Playing the clarinet; Cooking. Address: Firestone Lib., Princeton Univ., Princeton, NJ 08544, USA.

MORGAN, Richard Paul, b. 18 May 1945, Wellingborough, UK. Organit & Director of Music. Educ: RCM, London, 1963-65; Organ Scholar & Asst. Cathedral Organist, Christ Ch., Oxford Univ., 1965-68; MA, Oxford; BMus, London; FRCO(CHM); ADCM; LRAM (Clarinet tchr.); ARCM (piano perf.). m. Heather M Neal. Career: Music master, Beachborough Schl., Northants., 1968-69; Sub-organist, Exeter Cathedral, Pt.-time Lectr. in Music, Exeter Univ., & Dir. of Music, Exeter Cathedral Schl., 1969; Deputy Cond., Exeter Musical

Soc., 1969-. Organ recitals for BBC. Recordings: Organ Music from Christ Church, Oxford. Mbrships: ISM; RCO; Exeter Musical Soc. (Dpty. Cond.). Hons: A. Bull Memorial Prize, RCM, 1963; Turpin Prize, RCO, 1965. Address: 4 Cloister Garth, Cathedral Close, Exeter, UK.

MORGAN, Robert P, b. 28 July 1934, Nashville, Tenn., USA. Professor of Music. Educ: AB, Princeton Univ.; MA, Univ. of Calif., Berkeley, 1958; MFA, Princeton Univ., 1960; PhD, ibid., 1969; Acad. of Music, Munich, Germany, 1960-62. m. Carole Montgomery. Career: Prof. of Theory & Composition, Temple Univ.; Composer; Reviewer, High Fidelity mag.; Advsry. Ed., Musical Newsletter. Compositions incl: Music for chmbr. ensemble, voice & orch. Contbr. to var. music jrnls. & mags. Mbrships: Am. Soc. of Univ. Composers; Am. Musicol. Soc.; AAUP. Hons. incl: Woodrow Wilson Fellowship. Address: 2203 1/2 St. James, Phila., PA 19103, USA.

MORGENSTERN, Dan Michael, b. 24 Oct. 1929, Munich, Germany. Jazz Critic & Historian; Editor; Lecturer; Producer. Educ: Brandeis Univ. m. Ellie Schocket, 1 s. Career: Ed.-in-Chief, Metronome Mag., 1960-61; Prod., Jazz in the Gdn., Mus. of Mod. Art, NYC, 1961, 1963-66; Ed. & Co-Fndr., Jazz Mag., 1962-63; Assoc. Ed., 1964-67, Ed.-in-Chief, 1967-73, Down Beat Mag.; Co-Prod., TV series Just Jazz, Pub. Broadcasting Serv., 1970-71; Prod., Hall of Fame Concert, Newport Jazz Fest., 1975, Dir. Inst. of Jazz Studies, Rutgers Univ., 1976-, other concerts. Publs: Jazz People (w. Photographer Ole Brask), 1976. Contbr. to Am., UK & Japanese musical & audio jrnls. Mbrships: incl: Music Critics Assn.; NY Chapt. Gov., 1971-76, Nat. Trustee, 1972-74, 1975-, Nat. Acad. of Recording Arts & Scis.; Cons. to Music Progs., Nat. Endowment for the Arts, 1974-. Hons: Grammy Awards for Best Album Notes, Nat. Acad. of Recording Arts & Scis., 1973, 74. Hobbies: Collecting Records & Books; Walking. Address: 365 West End Ave., NY, NY 10024, USA. 6.

MORGENSTERN, Frank, b. 17 July 1928, Kleinhartmannsdorf, Germany. Conductor. Educ: Dip., Acad. of Music, Leipzig. m. Erika Reinwald, 2 s., 1 d. Career: Cond., theatres, Stralsund & Cottbus; Chief Cond. & Music Dir., Cottbus, 1963-; Cond., concerts, Czech., Poland, Hungary, Bulgaria, Romania. Mbrships: Soc. of Comps. & Musicols., German Dem. Repub.; Verband der Theaterschaffenden, ibid. Hons: Carl Blechen Prize; Badge of Merit, Comps. Union. Hobby: Angling. Address: Körnerstr. 5, 75 Cottbus, German Dem. Repub.

MØRK, John Frithjof, b. 16 May 1927, Oslo, Norway. Cellist. Educ: Cello study in Oslo & Copenhagen w. Karl Andersen, Rolf Storseth & Erling Blondal Bengtson; studied theory in Oslo w. Karl Andersen. m. Turid-lill Otterbech, 4 c. Debut: Oslo, 1948. Career: 2nd solo cello, Bergen Symph. Orch., 1958-66; 1st solo cello, Norwegian Opera, Oslo, 1966-75; solo cello, Symph. & Radio Orch., Stavanger, 1977-; soloist w. orch. in Bergen & Oslo, Bergen Int. Fest., & Fest. at Harstad; Recitals & chamber music; broadcasts on radio & TV; Tchr. in conserv. & coll. Mbrships: Norwegian Music Fedn., Contemporary Music Soc. Address: Polluxgate 21, 4000 Stavanger, Norway.

MÖRNER, (Carl-Gabriel) Stellan, b. 10 July 1915, Ystad, Sweden. Musicologist. Educ: PhD, Uppsala Univ., 1952. m. Inga-Lisa Blanck, 1 d. Career: Ldr., Record Dept., Swedish Radio, 1953-67; num. individual progs. & series, Swedish Radio, 1947-; Guest Instr., Univs. of Stockholm & Gothenburg, & Librarians Acad., 1953-74; Asst. Prog. Dir., Music, Swedish Radio, Stockholm. Publs. incl: Haydn, 1945; Mozart, 2nd ed., 1965; Lp-boken, 1960; Katalogoch klassifikationsregler för grammonfonskivor och band, 1962, 1970; eds. of works of Haydn, Mozart. Contbr. to musical & musicol. jrnls. Mbrships: incl: haydn Inst., Cologne; Neue Mozart-Ausgabe, 1958-; Sec., Bellmanssällskapet; Bd., Jenny Lind Sällskapet. Address: Birger Jalsgatan 69, 113-56 Stockholm, Sweden.

MORONEY, Davitt, b. 23 Dec. 1950, Leicester, UK. Harpsichordist; Musicologist. Educ: BMus, 1971, MMus, 1972, King's Coll., Univ. of London; PhD studies, Univ. of Calif., Berkeley, 1975-; organ studies w. Susi Jeans; harpsichord studies w. Kenneth Gilbert; ARCM (harpsichord perf.); LRAM (harpsichord tchng.). Career: Harpsichord tchr., San Francisco Conserv. of Music. Recordings: The Harpsichord Music of Louis Couperin; Chamber Music of François Couperin. Publs: Ed., Maurice Greene, A Collection of Lessons for the Harpsichord (1750), 1977; John Farmer, Madrigals to Four Voices (1599), 1978; John Bennet, Madrigals to Four Voices (1599), 1979; Thomas Chilcot, Six Harpsichord Suites (1734), 1980. Contbr. to: Grove's Dict., 6th ed. & profl. jrnls. Mbrships: RCO; Am. Musicol. Soc.; San Francisco Early Music Soc. Hons: Harkness Fellowship, Commonwealth Fund of NY, 1975-77; Hertz Fellowship, 1978-79; Eisner Prize, Univ. of

Calif., 1977. Hobbies: Calligraphy; Jacuzzis; Bread Baking. Mgmt: Lynn Glaser & Assocs., Berkeley, Calif., USA. Address: Dept. of Music, Univ. of Calif., Berkeley, CA 94720, USA.

MORONEY, Edward Francis Pius, b. 5 Jan. 1949, Toronto, Ont., Can. Organist-Choirmaster; Pianist-Accompanist; Conductor. Educ: ARCT, 1965; ARCO, 1970; ARCO (CHM), 1970; MusB, 19723, BEd, 1973, Univ. of Toronto; ARCCO (CHM); RCCO Cert. of Proficiency in Service Playing; FIBA. Career incls: Organist, Royal Can. Inst., Toronto, 1966-76, 1978-; Accomp. & Asst. Cond., Univ. of Toronto Concert Choir & Chorus, 1968-72; Organist & Choirmaster, Willowdale United Ch., Toronto, 1971-76; Asst. Cond. & Accomp., Toronto Youth Choir, 1972-73; Music Master, St. Joseph's Convent Schl., Toronto, 1973-75; Cond., York Univ. Chorus, 1975-76; Cond., Durham Univ. Chmbr. Choir, 1977-78; Dir. of Music, St. John's & St. Margaret's Schls., Elora, Ont., 1978-. Mbr., profl. assns. Hons. incl: Silver Medal for Organ, Royal Conserv., Toronto, 1961; F. Silvester Organ Scholarship, ibid., 1967; L Bell Choral Cond. Scholarship, 1973. Hobbies: Genealogy; Heraldry; Antique Silver. Address: 1 Elliotwood Ct., Willowdale, Ont., Can., M2L 2P8. 23, 28, 29.

MORONEY, Mary Emmeline (Sister), b. 16 Apr. 1942, Melbourne, Aust. Carmelite Nun; Organist. Educ: BMus, Melbourne Univ., 1947; MMus, ibid., 1976. Career: Carmelite Nun of the Monastery of Kew, Vic.; Chief Organist, ibid. Comps: var. liturgical works incl. masses & a setting of complete 4 week cycle of the Liturgical Hours. Publs: The Song of Songs & the Medieval Love Lyric, 1976; sev. research papers incl. Music in Medieval England, 1975. Hons: Commonwealth scholarships, 1960, '71; postgrad. rsch. award, Melbourne Univ., 1974-75. Hobbies: piano & Choral music; Reading; Hist.; Art. Address: Carmelite Monastery, 94 Stevenson St., Kew, Vic. 3101, Aust.

MORREAU, Annette Scawen, b. 4 Feb. 1946, Altrincham, UK. Music Administrator. Educ: BA, Durham Univ.; Univ. of Ind. at Bloomington, USA. Career: Fndr., The Contemporary Music Network, UK; Music Admnstr., Arts Coun. of GB. Contbr. to: Tempo; Contact. Mbrships: Sec., British Sect., ISCM. Hons: 1st Woman to win Durham/Bloomington scholarship exchange. Hobbies: Cooking; Swimming; Sailing; Cello. Address: Flat 2, 3 The Park, London N6, UK.

MORRIS, Christopher John, b. 13 May 1922, Clevedon, UK. Organist; Music Publisher. Educ: ARCO. m. Ruth Early, 2 c. Career: Asst. Organist, Hereford Cathedral; Organist & Choirmaster, St. George's Ch., Hanover Square, London; Hd. of Music Publishing, Oxford Univ. Press. Compositions incl: var. Organ & Choral Works. Co-Author. Editing Early Music, 1963. Mbrships: RCO; ISM. Address: 3 Vicarage Gate, London W8 4HH, UK. 3.

MORRIS, Paul, b. 26 Jan. 1938, Buryport, Wales, UK. Music & Drama Adviser; Pianist; Viola Player. Educ: Univ. Coll. of S Wales & Mon., Cardiff. m. Claire M Morris, 2 c. Career: Tchr., 1960-70; Educ. Advsr., music & drama, Metropolitan Borough of Knowsley, Merseyside, 1970-; apps. on local radio & TV. var. comps. Record reviews. mbr., Nat. Assn. of Inspectors & Advsrs. Hobbies: Rugby; Car Racing; Reading; Working w. Young People. Address: 23 Standhouse Ln., Aughton, Ormskirk, L39 5AR, UK.

MORRIS, Robert Daniel, b. 19 Oct. 1943, Cheltenham, UK. Composer; Pianist; Electronic Music Synthesizer; Professor of Music. Educ: BMus, Eastman Schl. of Music, USA. 1965; MMus, 1966, D Musical Arts, 1969, Univ. of Mich. Career incls: Instructor, Univ. of Hawaii, Honolulu, 1968-69; Asst. Prof.-Assoc. Prof. of Comp., Yale Univ., 1969-; Dir., Yale Electronic Music Studio, 1972-; Chmn., Comp. Dept., Yale Schl. of Music, 1973-. Comps: Reservoir; Phases (2 pianos); Continue for Orch.; Thunders of Spring over Distant Mountains (electronic); In Different Voices (wind ensemble). Contbr. to profl. jrnls. Mbrships: AAUP; Am. Soc. Univ. Comps. Recip., num. Fellowships & Awards. Hobbies: Mathematics; Go; Camping. Address: School of Music, Yale Univ., New Haven, CT 06520, USA.

MORRIS, Wyn, b. 14 Feb. 1929. Conductor. Educ: RAM; Mozarteum, Salzburg. m. Ruth Marie McDowell, 1 s., 1 d. Career incls: Fndr.-Cond., Welsh Symph. Orch., 1954-57; Observer, at invitation of G Szell, Cleveland Symph. Orch., 1957-60; Cond., OH Bell Chorus, Cleveland Chmbr. Orch. & Cleveland Orpheus Choir, OH, 1958-60; Choir, Royal Nat. Eisteddford of Wales, 1960-62; Cond., Royal Choral Soc., 1968-70, Huddersfield Choral Soc., 1969-74. Bruckner-Mahler Choir, 1970-. Hons. inclk: Mahler Mem. Medal, Bruckner & Mahler Soc. of Am., 1968; FRAM, 1964. Hobbies:

Rugby; Chess; Climbing. Address: Orchard Gate, North Dr., Virginia Water, Surrey, UK. 1.

MORRISON, Jeannine Romer, b. 26 Mar. 1930, Atlanta, Ga., USA. Concert Pianist; Teacher. Educ: BMus, Rollins Coll., Fla.; MA, Columbia Univ. m. Don T Morrison, 2 s., 1 d. Debut: Town Hall, NYC, 1958. Career: Piano recitals throughout Eastern USA, & in Bermuda & Toronto, Canada; Frequent broadcasts on Radio & TV, 1950-60. Soloist w. Ctrl. Fla. Symph.; Winter Pk. Community Orch.; Atlanta Symph.; Atlanta Community Orch.; Emory Univ. Orch.; Tchr. of Keyboard Instruments, Clayton Jr. Coll., Ga. Contbr. to: The Music Educators Jrnl.; Staff Notes. Mbrships: Nat. MTA; Ga. MTA; Decatur MTA, 1st VP, 1970-74; NGPT; Am. Coll. of Musicians; Lescheitzsky Assn. of Assn. of Am. Phi Beta, Pi Kappa Lambda. Hobbies:O Cycling; Sightseeing w. children. Address: 609 E Ponce de Leon Ave., Decatur, GA 30330, USA.

MORRISON, Ray, b. 19 Oct. 1946, Asheville, NC, USA. Bass Singer. Educ: AA, Ind. Univ. Schl. of Music; BA, ibid.; MusM; Coll. Conserv. of Music, Univ. of Cinn., Ohio; Mars Hill Coll. Debut: Santa Fe Opera. Career: Perfs. w. Santa Fe Opera, Cinn. Opera, Ind. Univ. Opera Theater, NY Lyric Opera, Bel Canto Opera, Mannes Opera, Bronx Opera & Metropolitan Opera Studio; Sang Am. or world premier of Koenig Hirsch (Henze), Boulevard Soltitude (Henze), The Duel (Al Carmines), The System (Jan Bach) & The Nose (Shostokovitch). Mbrships: Am. Guild of Musical Artists; Nat. Assn. of Tchrs. of Singing. Address: 55 W 76, No. 4-B NYC, NY 10023, USA.

MORRISON, Ronald Alexander, b. 29 June 1934, Rothesay, Scotland, UK. Baritone; Classics Teacher. Educ: MA, Glasgow Univ., 1956 (Choral Scholar, 1954-56); Studies w. Marjorie Blakeston, Glasgow, Ettore Campogalliani, Mantova. Debut: Prince Yamadori in Madame Butterfly, Scottish Opera, 1965. Career: 200 perfs. w. Scottish Opera in roles inclng. Sharpless, Marcello & Rev. Gedge, also Edinburgh fest., tours of Italy, Germany & Iceland; Lieder recitals for BBC; Oratorio & concerts in Scotland; "Opera for All" (ACGB); "Opera for Schools" (Scottish Opera): Phoenix Opera at York, Chichester & Chester Fests. Recordings: Music of Baroque Scotland (BBC): Scotland in the Festival (Saltire Music Grp.). Mbrships: ISM: Brit. Actor's Equity Assn.; Scottish Secondary Tchrs. Assn.; Glasgow Univ. Grads. Assn.; Victory Ex-Services Club. Hons: Silver Medal in Practical Subjects of AB of RSc. Music, 1956. Gervase Elwes Trophy & Ailie Cullen Memorial Prize, Glasgow Fest., 1957. Hobbies: Cricket; Reading; Model Railways. Address: 56 Kethers St., Motherwell, ML1 3HJ, Scotland, UK.

MORRISON, (Stuart) Angus, b. 28 May 1902, Maidenhead, Berks., UK. Pianist. Educ: Open Scholarship, RCM, 1918; studied w. Harold Samuel (piano) & Thomas Dunhill & Ralph Vaughan Williams (comp.). m. Kathleen Dillon, 2 d. Debut: Wigmore Hall, 1923. Career: Concert appearances in Englany & many countries abroad, Gave recitals & broadcasts in Malaya, Hong Kong & different parts of India, 1954; Prof. of Piano, RCM, 1926-; currently Sr. Prof. of Piano, RCM, 1926-; currently Sr. Prof., ibid; Constant Lambert dedicated to him his most popular work, The Rio Grande, Mbr., ISM. Hons: FRCM, 1954; Hon. RAM, 1976. Mgmt: Basil Douglas Ltd., Address: 132 Holland Park Ave., London W11 4UE, UK. 14.

MORRONGIELLO, Lydia Anne, b. 16 Dec. 1942, Salem, Mass., USA. Music Educator. Educ: BS Music Educ., Crane Schl. of Music, SUNY at Potsdam, NY, 1964; MA Music Educ., 1966, Profl. Dip., 1967, EdD Music Educ., 1975, Tchrs. Coll., Columbia Univ. m. Charles T Morrongiello. Career incls: Tchr., Vocal Music, Theory, Humanities, Garden City Sr. High Schl., NY, 1967-; Musical Dir., Celestones (girls' choir), 1967-; Instructor Keyboard Studies, Juilliard Schl. of Music, 1970-72. Publs: Music Symbolism in Selected Cantatas & Chorale Preludes of J S Bach, 1975. Contbr. to Music Educators Jrnl. Mbr., var. profl. assns., inclng. Bd. of Dirs., WNCN radio station, NY. Recip., musical awards & scholarships. Hobbies: Travel; Garment Design & Construction; Collector of Rolls Royces & Bentleys. Address: 18 School Lane, Lloyd Harbor, NY 11743, USA. 27.

MORROW, Grace Elizabeth Kline, b. 9 Apr. 1909, Mt. Gilead, Ohio, USA. Teacher of Voice, Diction, Piano & Music Education; Performer. Educ: BA, Oberlin Coll., Ohio, 1931; Cinn. Conserv. of Music, Ohio, 1936-38; MA, George Peabody Coll. for Tchrs., Nashville, Tenn., 1956. m. Garland Augustus Morrow, 2 d. Career incls: Asst. Prof. of Music, Hardin-Simmons Univ., Abilene, Tex., 1959-66; Assoc. Prof. of Music, ibid., 1966-76; now ret'd. Author, Sharing & Serving Through Music, The Story of the Abilene Alumnae Chapter of Sigma Alpha Iota, 1961-1976, 1975. Ed., profl. jrnls. Mbr. num. profl. orgs. Recip. var. hons. Hobbies incl: Horticulture; Travel; Photography. Address: 1525 Minter Lane, Abilene, TX 79603, USA. 5, 7, 27.

MORROW, Ruth Elizabeth, b. 7 May 1945, Nashville, Davidson Co., Tenn., USA. Violist; University Professor. Educ: BMusSci., Juilliard Schl., 1967; MMus, ibid., 1969; Dip. of Hon., Chmbr. Music Perf., Accademia Musicale Chigiana, Siena, Italy, 1970; Study at Nordwestdeutsche Musikakdemie, Detmold, Germany, 1969-70, 1970-71, 1971-72. Debut: Solo app. w. Abilene Phil., Abilene, Tex., 1959. Career incls: Solo apps., White House Concerts for Young People, Wash., USA, 1960: Viola concertos perfd. w. Nashville Youth Orch., Abilene Phil. & German orchs.; Recitals in USA & Germany, 1959-76; Prin. Violist, Abiline Phil., 1959-63; Juilliard Concert Orch., 1968-69; Brevard Music Ctr. Fest. Orch., 1958-59; Tibor Varga Kemmerorchester, 1969-70; Kurpfalzisches Kammerorochester, 1970-73; Extensive concert tours of Europe; Radio & TV apps. in USA; Pvte. studio tchng., Abilene, NYC, W Caldwell, NJ, Boulder, Colo., USA & Mannheim, Germany; Tchr., W Caldwell Pub. Schls., 1967-69; Asst. Prof., Viola & Chmbr. Music, Univ. of Colo., Coll. of Music, 1973-. Num. recordings. Mbrships: MENC; MTNA; Am. Str. Tchrs. Assn. Hons: Young Artists of Nashville Award, 1959; 2nd Prize, Perini Award, 1965; Elsie & Walter Naumberg Scholarship, 1963-64, 1965-66. Hobbies: Leatherwork; Watercolour Painting; Riding; Swimming; Rsch. on viola lit. of 17th, 18th & 19th centuries. Address: 830 20th St., 205 Boulder, CO 80302, USA.

MORS, Rudolf Ernst Theodor, b. 16 July 1920, Munich, Germany. Composer; Conductor. Educ: Master Dip., Music High Schl., Munich, 1950; studied w. Richard Mors, Joseph Haas & Karl Höller. m. Agnes Knapp, 2 c. Career: Cond., Theatre Comp., City Theatre, Ingolstadt, 1950-51, City Stage, UlmDonau, 1951-63, City Stage, Bielefeld, 1963-74. Compositions incl: opera, Vincta; Symphonic Cantata; Symph. No. 2, fantasia, Die Flamme; Konzert für Klavier und Orch., 1976; Str. Quartet; Violin Sonata; Sonatina, violin & piano; Piano Sonata, 4 hands; Lyrische Suite, flute & piano, Bagatellen, wind quartet; Quintet, horn & str. quartet; 4 Lieder collections; var. Musicals; over 100 comps. for dramas & airy tales. Mbrships: Munich Musicians Soc., VDMK; GEMA; German Comps. Grp. Recip. 1st Richard Strauss Scholarship, City of Munich, 19590. Hobbies: Horseback Riding; Swimming; Mountaineering. Address: Goldschmiedenweg 8, 48 Bielefeld 12, German Fed. Repub.

MORTENSEN, Otto Jacob Hübertz, b. 18 Aug. 1907, Copenhagen, Denmark. University Lecturer. Educ: Organ & Piano, Royal Coll. Music, Copenhagen, 1929; MA, Univ. of Copenhagen, 1956. m. Inger K J Bentzon, 3 s., 2 d. Debut: 1930 (as pianist). Career: Soloist & chmbr. music perf., 1930-37; Musical staff, Theatre Royal, Copenhagen, 1937-55; Tchr.-Sr. Lectr., Royal Coll. Music, 1943-66; Hd. master, Opera Acad., 1959-66; Tchr., Univ. of Aarhus, 1966-74. Comps. incl: Str. Quartet; Piano Quartet; Oboe Sonata; (recorded) Danish & English Songs; Danish Folksongs. Publs. incl: Harmonisk Analyse efter Grundbas-Metoden, 1955. Contbr. to musical publs. Mbr., Int. Musicol. Soc. Recip., var. awardss. Address: Iammerisvej 20, 8240 Hiisskov, Denmark.

MORTENSEN, Tage, b. 9 Oct. 1932, Aarhus, Denmark. Conductor; Composer; Lecturer. Educ: BA, 1959, MA, 1961, Aarhus Univ.; Paedigogicum, Hjorring Gymnasium, 1965; studied Piano, Organ & Cond., Aarhus; Cond. course, Mozarteum, Salzburg, Austria, 1965. Career incls: Prod., Danish radio, 1959-; Ldr., Nordjysk Pigekor, 1961-; 1st Cond., Danish RadioTV Girls' choir, & Ldr., Chorus Schl., 1965-; apps. as Cond., abroad; Guest Cond., RadioTV Youth Symph. Orch.; Tchr., Gymnasium, Frederikshavn, 1965-71. Comps. incl: Crucify Him (TV oratorio), 1971; Passacaglia for orch.; about 100 children's songs, 1957-; cantatas. Recordings of Danish hymns, 1968, 75. Contbr. to Dansk sang. Mbr., profl. coord. organisation. Hobbies: Literary studies; Fishing. Address: Vinkelvej 4, 9900 Frederikshavn, Denmark.

MORTON, Richard Edward, b. 30 May 1952, Barnsley, UK. Singer (tenor). Educ: Choral scholarship, King's Coll., Cambridge; BA, MA, 1977; 1 yr. Post Grad. study, RCM; Pvte. study w. Tito Gobbi & Helga Mott. m. Brenda Valerie Morton, 1 s. Career: Regular radio apps., BBC radio. Recordings incl: Coronation Ode (Elgar), w. LPO, for Silvr Jubilee of Queen Elizabeth II; Canticum Sacrum (Stravinsky); Rejoice in the Lamb (Britten); Music to the Tempest (Locke). Mbrships: FRSA. Hons: Countess of Munster Musical Trust Award, 1975; Runner-up, kathleen Ferrier Competition, 1976; Travel Scholarship, Royal Soc. of Arts, 1978. Hobbies: Sports; Bird watching. Address: 24 Great Close Rd., Yarnton, Oxford, UK.

MORTON, William, b. 9 Jan. 1937, Sheffield, UK. Flautist. Educ: Pvte. study w. David Snademan, Geoffrey Gilbert, William Bennett, Alexander Murray; ARCM (flute & picolo). m. 1 s., 2 d. Career: Flautist, Ctrl. Band of RAF, 1955-60; Royal Opera

House Orch., Covent Garden, 1960-; Co-prin. Flautist, 1962-; Qualified Tchr. of F Mathias Alexander Technique. Mbrships: Royal Soc. of Musicians of GB; Soc. of Tchrs. of Alexander Technique. Hobbies: Walking; Modern languages; Astronomy; Natural history. Address: 90 Cleveland Rd., Ealing, London W13 OEJ, UK. 3.

MOSBACHER, Carl E, b. 26 Sept. 1920, Frankfurt/Main, Germany. Pianist. Educ: Grad., Royal Conserv. of Music, The Hague, Netherlands. Debut: Pianist w. Aedian Trio, Town Hall, NYC, USA, 1951. Career: Ext. perfs. as chmbr. music player & recitalist throughout USA; Former Mbr., Palestine Phil. Orch., Israel; Large student following; Fac., Mannes Coll. of Music, NY Univ., NYC. Address: 605 Water St., NY, NY 10002, USA.

MOSER, (Sir) Claus, b. 24 Nov. 1922, Berlin, Germany. Chairman, Royal Opera House. Educ: KCB; CBE; BSc (Econ.): FRAM; FBA; Pvte. lessons. m. Mary Moser, 1 s., 2 d. Mbr., Govng. Body, RAM; Dpty. Chmn., BBC Music Advsry. Committee. Hobby: Music Advsry. Committee. Hobby: Music. Address: 3 Regents Pk., Terrace, London NW1 7EE, UK. 1.

MOSER, Edda Elisabeth, b. 27 Oct. 1942, Berlin, Germany. Opera & Concert Singer. Educ: Berlin Conserv. m. Peter Csobadi. Debut: Constance in Mozart's II Seraglio. Munster. Career: appearances at Easter Festival, Salzburg, 1968; Vienna Festival; Salzburg Festival, 1970-72; w. opera cos. inclng. Metropol. Opera NYC, Vienna State, Hamburg, Berlin, Munich & Paris; num. concerts under conds. of int. reputation. Recordings incl: Lieder of Richard Strauss, Hans Pfitzner & Robt. Schumann (EMI); var. operatic works inclng. Magic Flute, Idomeneo, etc. (EMI); Hons: Grand Prix du Disque for Mozart Arias LP; Cross of Merit, German Fed. Repub. Mgmt: Columbia Artists Mgmt., NYC. Hobby: Cooking. Address: Elsenborner Str. 19, D5 Cologne 41, German Fed. Repub. 5.

MOSHINSKY, Elijah, b. 8 Jan. 1946, Shanghai, China. Theatre & Opera Director. Educ: BA, Melbourne Univ., Australia; DPhil, Oxford Univ., UK. m. Ruth Dyttman. Career: Dir., w. Royal Opera House, 1973-75; Assoc. Prof., ibid., 1975-; Dir. of Plays w. Nat. Theatre; Freelance dir., inclng. prod. of Wozzeck for Aust. Opera at Adelaide Festival, 1975, & of Salome for Dallas Civic at Houston Grand Opera, USA; Lohengrin for Royal Opera House, Covent Garden. Hobbies: Painting; Moutain climbing. Mgmt: Harrison-Parrott Ltd. Address: 5 Camden Row, London SE3, UK.

MOSKOVITZ, Harry H, b. 1 July 1904, Lithuania. Flautist; Clinician; Teacher. Educ: New England Conserv., Boston; Juilliard Grad. Schl., NY. m. Florence Kramer, 1 d. Career: Played formerly w. NBC Symph., CBS Symph., St. Louis Symph., NYC Ctr. Symph. & Opera Orchs., the Voice of Firestone Orch., NY Phil. Stadium Concerts; Solo Flute of the Goldman Band & Bell Telephone Hour; Asst. Prof. Music Dept., Queen's Coll., NY. var. solo & lecture recitals. Recordings: The Flute Family, Mark Educl. Records; The Armstrong Quartet, The Classic Guitar Trio, Flute Sessions, Golden Crest Records. Publs: 24 Progressive Duets by Devienne, 1973. Contbr. to: Instrumentalist; Woodwind World; Music Jrnl. Mbrships: Pres., NY Flute Club, 6 terms; currently VP ibid.; Bd. Dirs., Nat. Flute Assn.; Am. Musical Instrument Soc. Hobbies: Horology; Hist. of antique musical instruments. Address: 6769 Groton St., Forest Hills, NY 11375, USA.

MOSONYI, Pierre, b. 17 Dec. 1918, Szombathely, Hungary. Pianist; Conductor; Musicologist; Lectuer. Educ: Dip., Franz Liszt Music Acad., Budapest, 1965; pvte. study w. Agi Jambor; Paris Conserv., Pupil of Lazare-Lévy, 1953; Accademia Chigiana, Siena. m. Myriam Mason, 1 d. Debut: Budapest, 1942; Budapest Radio, 1946. Career: broadcast recitals, Paris, Hiversum, Lisbon, NYC; solo & chmbr. recitals, Europe, USA & UK; London debut, Purcell Rm., 1967; attached to London Univ. Extra-Mural Dept. Recordings: Selmer-Ducretet-Thomson, Paris; Peter Bartok Records, NYC. Hons: 2nd Prizes, Int. Liszt Comp., Paris, 1947, Int. Chopin Comp., ibid., 1949. Address: 6A Fairbourne Rd., London N17 6PT, UK.

MOSS, Lawrence Kenneth, b. 18 Nov. 1927, Los Angeles, Calif., USA. Composer; Professor of Composition. Educ: MA in Comp., Eastman Schl. of Music, 1950; PhD in Comp., Univ. of Southern Calif., 1957. m. Graydon Hinsley Moss, 1 s., 3 d. Career: Prof. of Comp., Univ. of Md. Comps. incl: (operas) The Queen & the Rebels; The Brute; Ariel (Soprano & Orch.); Fantasy for Piano; Omaggio (piano); Remembrances (8 instruments); Evocation & Song (saxophone & tape); (recorded) Elegy; Timepiece; Auditions (woodwind quintet & tape); Violin Sonata; 4 Scenes for Piano. Contbr. to profl. jrnls. Mbr., ASUC. Hons. incl: Guggenheim Fellowships, 1958, 68; Nat. Endowment for Arts Grant, 1974. Address: 220 Mowbray Rd., Silver Spring, MD 20904, USA.

MOSS, Randolph Marshall, b. 23 June 1908, Woodbine, NJ, USA. Violinist. Educ: Peabody Conserv.; Juilliard Schl. of Music. m. Saimi Marie Fassett, 1 s. Debut: Town Hall, NYC, 1935. Career incls: Apps. on Radio; Inventor of Electrofonic Vilin, 1930; Tech. Advsr. var. films inclng: Counterpoint; Recitals & Soloist w. num. orch.; Fndr. & 1st Violin, Am. String Quartet; Fac. Mbr., NY Coll. of Music; Int. Coll.; Henry St. Settlement Schl., NY; Concertmaster & Asst. Cond., Wash., DC Nat. Symph. Orch. Num. recordings. Contbr. to Jrnl. of Am. Musicol. Soc. Mbrships. incl: Int. Musicol. Soc.; Renaissance Soc.; Am. Fedn. of Musicians. Hons. incl: Walter W Naumburg Fndn. Award, 1935. Address: 1740 N Arteique Rd., Topanga, CA 90290, USA. 4.

MOSS, William, b. 21 Dec. 1942, Castleford, UK. Composer; Pianist; Teacher. Educ: Leeds Coll. of Art (NDD); RAM (w. James Iliff & Vivian Langrish); pvte. study w. Nadia Boulanger; GRSM; LRAM. Comps: major works incl. Concert, for 11 pianists, 1966 (recorded); Grande Étude, solo for prepared piano, 1970 (recorded); recent works for mixed chmbr. ensembles. Address: High Street, Fulbeck, Nr. Grantham, Lincs., UK.

MOSTAD, Jon, b. 21 Apr. 1942, Oslo, Norway. Composer. Educ: MDivinity; Intermediate grade of music, Univ. of Oslo, 1969; Dip., comp., Music Acad. of Oslo, 1974. m. Ase S Folleras Mostad, 2 c. Comps. incl: children's choral works, orchestral, instrumental, piano, organ and chmbr. music. Contbr. to Ballade. Mbrships: Norwegian Comps. Assn.; Chmn., Fredrikstad sect. & mbr. Nat. Committee of Ny Musikk (Norwegian branch of LSCM). Hons: Norwegian Broadcasting competition prize for comps. for children's & youth choirs, 1972. Hobbies: Forest & Mountain Walking; Skiing; Gardening. Address: Skovbolev 3, 1600 Fredrikstad, Norway.

MOSTARD, John, b. 5 Mar. 1942, Susteren, Netherlands. Bassoonist. Educ: studied w. Nico van Wieringen; Conservatorium at Tilburg. Career: Solo Bassoonist, Radio Phil. Orch., Hilversum, 1965. The Hague Phil. Orch., 1971, Rotterdam Phil. Orch. under Edo de Waart, 1973; Bassoon Tchr., Royal Conservatorium The Hague, Conservatorium Amsterdam, Conservatorium Rotterdam. Address: De Wulp 20, Ouderkerk AD Yssel, Netherlands.

MOSZUMANSKA-NAZAR, Krystyna, b. 5 Sept. 1924, Lwów, Poland (now USSR). Composer; Professor. Educ: Studied Comp. w. S Wiechowicz & Piano w. J Hoffman, State Coll. of Music, Cracow, 1 s. Career: Hd., Comp. Dept., State Coll. of Music, Cracow; music performed in num. Cracow, 1 s. Career: Hd., Comp. Dept., State Coll. of Music, Cracow; music performed in num. countries thru'out world, & at Fests. of contemporary music inclng. Warsaw Int. 1963, 1965, 1968, 1971, 1973, & Jean Villar Avignon, France, 1973. Compositions incl: (publd.) 5 Duets for Dlute & Clarinet, 1959; Exodus (symph. orch. & tape), 1964; Variazioni per flauto e orchestra da camera (1965-1966); Intonations (2 choruses & symph. orch.), 1968; Implications (2 pianos & percussion), 1969; Bagatelles for Piano, 1971; Bel canto for Soprano, Celeste and Percussion (1972); Str. Quartet, 1973-74. (recorded) Music for Strings, 1963; Hexaedre (symph. orch.), 1965; Interpretations for Flute, Tape & Percussion (1968); Pur Orchestre, 1969; Constellations for Piano, 1972. Madonny polskie, 1974, for chorus & orch. Mbrships: union of Polish Comps. (Pres., Cracow Sect. 1967-71); Presidium, ibid. Hons. incl: Gold Medal, Int. Competition of Comps., Buenos Aires, Argentina, 1962; Prize, Szywanoshi Comps. Competition, 1974, Warsaw. Prize, Polish Min. of Cutlure, 1971. Address: Swierczewskiego 2/3, 31-116 Cracow, Poland.

MOULDER, Earline, b. Buffalo, Mo., USA. College Professor; Organist. Educ: BA (French & biol.), MusB (piano, organ & thory), Drury Coll.; MMus, Ind. Univ.; post-grad., Amsterdam Conserv. Career: Concert Organist, concentrating on Middle Eastern music; apps. in 11 countries of Europe, 1964, inclng. perfs. on organ Schubert played at Heiligen-Kreuz, & in chapel of St. Peter's, Rome; Organist, St. Paul Meth. Ch., Springfield; Prof., Hd. of Organ Dept., Drury Coll., Springfield. Comps: Crucifixion (organ); Psalm 150--dedicated to USAF Acad., 1970. Mbrships: Mortar Bd.; Sigma Alpha Iota. Writer on music & culture of contemp. Mid-E & organ constrn. Address: Box 522, Buffalo, MO 65622, USA. 5.

MOULE-EVANS, David. Professor of Harmony, Counterpoint & Compositions; Composer; Conductor. Educ: RCM; DMus, Oxon., 1930. m. Monica Warden Richardson Evans. Career: Prof., Harmony, Counterpoint & Composition, RCM, 1945-74; comps. have been perf. at num. pub. concerts & broadcast on radio; sometimes conducts own works. Comps. incl: Spirit of London; Vienna Rhapsody; The Haunted Place for string orch.; Old Tupper's Dance; chmbr. works; instrumental pieces; songs. Hons: Carnegie Publn. Award for Concerto for string orch., 1928;

1000 Prize of Govt. of Aust. for Symph. in G major, 1952. Hobbies: Reading; Walking. Address: Merry Down, Harrow Rd. W., Dorking, Surrey RH4 3BA, UK. 1.

MOUNTAIN, Peter, b. 3 Oct. 1923, Shipley, Yorks, UK. Musician (Violin). Educ: RAM; Violin pvtely. w. Sascha Lasserson. m. Angela Dale, 1 s., 2 d. Debut: Wigmore Hall, London, 1950. Career: Regular BBC broadcasts w. Angela Dale; Wide experience chmbr. music; Formed Peter Mountain String Quartet; Mbr., Boyd Neel String Orch.; Phil. Orch. (played in 2 Brahms concerts, cond. Toscanini at his last London app.); Ldr., Royal Liverpool Phil. Orch., 1955-66; Concertmaster, BBC Trng. Orch. (later Acad. BBC), 1968-75; Coach, num. Youth orchs., incl. Nat. Youth Orch. & Scottish Nat. Youth Orch., 1979. Currently, Hd., String Dept., Royal Scottish Acad. Music & Drama, Glasgow. num. recordings w. orchs. & ensembles. Mbr. profl. orgs. Hon: FRAM, 1963. Hobbies incl: Photography; Gliding; Camping; Reading. Address: 23 Kingsborough Gdns., Glasgow G12 9NH, UK.

MOURÃO, Isabel, b. 25 Jan. 1936, Sao Paulo, Brazil. Concert Pianist; Piano Teacher. Educ: studied w. noted tchrs. in Brazil, USA & France. div., 1 adopted d. Debut: Sao Paulo, Brazil. Career: num. concerts in major cities in Europe, UK, USA, S Am.; Radio rectials, UK, France, Portugal, etc.; var. radio & TV broadcast in S Am.; Piano Tchr., Brasilia's Univ., Teresopolis Summer Course, Pro Arte Seminarios de Musica, etc.; Jury Mbr., num. piano competitions in Brazil. Recordings incl: Works by O Lacerda, 1 LP; Grieg Piano Music (2 albums, 6 discs); Piano Festival (2 discs of famous waltzes); Chantecler (LP of works by Dinora de Carvalho); Ricordi & 50 Ponteins (2 LPs of works by Camargo Guarnieri). Recip. var. hons. Hobbies incl: Greek lit. & hist. Mgmt: Joseph Stuhl, 2437 Brown St., Phila., USA. Address: R Martins Fontes 248, apt. 91, São Paulo, Brazil.

MOUTSOPOULOS, Evanghelos A, b. 25 Jan. 1930, Athens, Greece. University Professor. Educ: MA, Univ. of Athens; State PhD, Univ. of Paris; comp., Athens & paris. m. Michèle Montigne. Comps: Suites for orch.; Chamber music; Lieder. Publs: approx. 20 books & over 150 articles, inclng: La musique dans l'oeuvre de Platon, paris, 1959; Aesthetic Categories. An Introduction to the Axiology of the Aesthetic Object, Athens, 1970; Rhythms & Dances of Greeks & Bulgarians, Laographia, 197, 1959, pp. 505-548; La Philosophie de la musique dans la dramaturgie antique; Formation et structure, Athens, 1975; Platon, Dictionnaire de la Musique, vol. II, Paris, Bordas, 1970. Contbr. to: Revue Philosophique; Diotima; Les Etudes Philosophiques, etc. Mbr., Société Francaise de Musicologie. Address: 40 Hypsilantou St., Athens 140, Greece. 2, 19.

MOYER, Birgitte Plesner, b. 13 Aug. 1938, Hellerup, Denmark. Musicologist; Violinist; Singer; Associate Professor of Music. Educ. incls: BA, 1960, MA, 1961, PhD, 1969, Stanford Univ , USA. m. Carl Bailey Moyer, 1 s., 1 d. Career incls: Pvte. Tchr., violin, 1965-; former Concert Mistress, Stanford Chmbr. & Symph. Orchs.; Master Sinfonia (first violin), 1975-; Cond., Ladera Children's Orch., 1975-; frequent perfs. (violin & singing), local ch. & chmbr. music; Music Judge, Brazil, Can. & Am.; Recitals annually in N & S Am., Italy, Portugal, Switz., Can. & Brazil; Assoc. Prof. of Music, Hartt Coll. of Music, Univ. of Hartt, Conn. Recordings: Music of Portugal; Liszt/Villa - Lobos Solo Recital; Bartok's Sonata for 2 pianos & percussion. Publs: A Bibliography of Theoretical Works on Music Published 1700-1750, 1750-1800, 2 vols., 1962. Contbr. to: Clavier Mag. Mbrships. incl: Am. & Danish Musicol. Socs. Hobbies incl: Gardening; Tennis. Mgmt: Sula Jaffe, Rio de Janeiro; Jean Michel Hubert, Portugal. Address: 160 Erica Way, Menlo Park, CA 94025, USA. 3.

MOYER, J Harold, b. 6 May 1927, Newton, Kan., USA. Professor of Music. Educ: AB, Bethel Coll., Kan., 1949; MA, Geo. Peabody Coll., Tenn., 1951; PhD, Univ. of Iowa, 1958; Additional study, Univ. of Ill., 1966-67. m. Rosemary Linscheid Moyer, 2 d. Career: Prof. of Music, Chmn., Dept. of Music & Div. of Fine Arts, Bethel Coll., N. Newton, Kan.; Num. perfs. of comps. Compositions incl: Psalm 95; Thou Grace Divine; Organ Preludes; Hymns & harmonizations for Mennonite Hymnal, 1969; Symphony No. 1; Job, Cantat for Mixed Voices & Orch.; Triology for Choirs & Orch. Recording: Praise the Lord (Male Chorus comps.). Contbr. to: Mennonite Life; Mennonite Weekly Review; Kan. Music Jrnl. Mbrships: Music Tchrs. Nat. Assn.; Past VP & Prog. Chmn., Kan. Music Tchrs. Assn.; Past Auditions Chmn., Wichita Piano Tchrs. League; Kiwanis Int. Recip., Kan. Comp. of the Yr. Award, 1971. Hobbies: Jogging; Spectator sports; Music. Address: Bethel Coll., N. Newton, KS 67117, USA. 8.

MOYLE, Richard Michael, b. 23 Aug. 1944, Paeroa, NZ. Ethnomusicologist. Educ: LTCL, 1965; MA, Univ. of Auckland, 1967; PhD, ibid., 1971. m. Linden Averil Evelyn Duncan.

Career: Vis. Lectr. in Anthropolgy, Ind. Univ., 1971-72; Asst. Prof. of Music, Univ. of Hawaii, 1972-73; Rsch. Fellow in Ethnomusicology, Aust. Inst. of Aboriginal Studies, 1974-77; Rsch. Grant, ibid., 1977-80. Recordings: The Music of Samoa; Traditional Music of Tonga; Tonga Today (compiler). Publs: Songs of the Pintupi, 1979; Fagogo: Fables from Samoa, 1979. Contbr. to num. profl. jrnls. Mbrships. incl: Aust. Inst. of Aboriginal Studies; Polynesian Soc.; Int. Musicol. Soc.; Int. Folk Music Coun., etc. Recip., Annual Prize in Music, Univ. of Auckland, 1967. Hobby: Photography. Address: Australian Inst. of Aboriginal Studies, PO Box 553, Canberra, ACT 2601, Aust. 30.

MOYZES, Alexander, b. 4 Sept. 1906, Klastor poa Znievom, Czechoslovakia. Composer; Music Educator. Educ: State Conserv., Prague. Career: Prof. of Theory of Music & Composition, Acad. of Music & Dramatic Arts, Bratislava, 1928-48; Chief of Music Sect., Czech. Radio, ibid., 1937-48; Prof., Coll. of Music & Dramatic Arts, 1949-; Rector, ibid., 1967, 1969. Compositions incl: Sonata in E Minor, 1925; String Quartet, 1939; Wind Quartet, 1933; Vocal works--Colours on the Palette, 1928; 12 Folk Songs from Saris, 1929; They are Singing in the Mountains, 1933; They Are Singing, Playing, Dancing, 1938; Whose Organ are Playing?, 1947; Ballad Cantata, 1960; In the Autumn, 1961; Orchl. works--7 symphs.; Concerto for violin & orch., 1958; Concerto for flute & orch., 1967; The Brave King (opera), 1962. Mbrships. incl: Chmn., Union of Slovak Composers, 1969-70. Recip. var. awards & prizes. Address: Coll. of Music & Dramatic Arts, Bratislava, Sturova 7, Czechoslovakia.

MRACEK, Jaroslav John Stephen, b. 5 June 1928, Montreal, Can. Musicologist. Educ: Assoc. Dip., Royal Conserv. of Music, Toronto, 1948; BMus, Univ of Toronto, 1951; MA, Ind. Univ., USA, 1962; PhD, ibid., 1966. m. Virginia Chambers, 2 s. Career: Prof. of Music, San Diego State Univ.; has presented num. papers at meetings & congresses. Publs: Seventeenth-Century Instrumental Dance Music, Stockholm, 1976. Contbr. to: The New Grove Dictionary of Music & Musicians; sev. learned jrnls. Mbrships: Chmn., Southern Calif. Chapt., Am. Musicol. Soc., 1972-74; Int. Musicol. Soc.; Czech. Soc. of Arts & Scis. in Am.; Am. Music Lib. Assn. Recip. of num. grants. Hobbies: Stamp & Book Collecting; Hiking; Swimming. Address: 5307 W Falls View Dr., San Diego, CA 92115, USA.

MRAVINSKY, Yevgeni Alexsandrovich, b. 4 June 1903, St. Petersburg, Russia. Conductor. Educ: Leningrad Conserv. Career: cond., Kirov State Acad. Opera & Ballet Theatr, Leningrad, 1932-38; Cond., Leningrad State Phil. Orch., 1938-; Concert tours of UK, Austria, Germany, Finland, Czechoslovakia, Switzerland, USA, etc. Hons: Winner, All Union Conds.' Competition, 1938; People's Artist of USSR, 1954; Badge of Hons., State Prize & Lenin Prize, 1961. Address: Leningrad State Phil. Orch., 1 Ploshchad Iskusstv, Leningrad, USSR.

MROWIEC, Karol, b. 24 Oct. 1919, Ruda Sl., Poland. Organist; Musicologist; Composer. Educ: Acad. of Music, Cracow; ThD, Cath. Univ. of Lublin. Career: Organ Concerts, Radio, Ch.'s Mgr., Ch. Musicol. Inst., Cath. Univ. of Lublin, 1969-. Compositions incl; Woz, 4 voices; var. Masses. Publs: Polska piesn koscietna worpracowaniu kompozytorow XIX wiekn, 1964; Plankty polskie I, 1968; Pasje Wielogtosowe e Przesztosc; Ruch Biblijny, Liturgiczny, Muzyka. Mbr. Musicol. Sect., Soc. of Polish Comps. Hons: Meritorious Worker of Culture, 1972; 1st Prize for Choir Comp., Poznan, 1958. Address: Katolicki Uniwerstytet Lubelski, 7 ul. Nowotki, 20-039 Lublin, Poland.

MRYGOŃ, Adam Wieslaw, b. 23 Nov. 1935, Pyzdry, Poland. Musicologist; Conductor. Educ: Musicol. Inst., Warsaw Univ.; State HS of Music, Warsaw. m. Ewa Maria Szemetyllo. Career: Chief, Dept. of Music Collect., Univ. Lib., Warsaw; Choir Asst., State HS of Music, ibid., 1962-71; Dir., Choir, Inst. of Ch. Musicol. Cath. Univ., Lublin, 1963-72, Dept. Ch. Musicol., Acad. Theol., Warsaw, 1971-; Radio broadcasts w. ensemble Scholares Lublinenses pro Musica Sacra, 1966, '68. Recordings: Laudemus Nomen Domini, w. Students' Choir of Musical Acad. Theol., Warsaw, 1977. Publs: Emil W Smietanski, Polish pianist, composer & educator, 1968; co-author, Bibliography of Polish Musicological literature from 1945, 1966, '72; co-ed., Karol Szymanowski--King Roger, score, 1973; Polish Code for cataloging of Music, 1974. Mbrships: Union Polish Comps.; Assn. Polish Libns. (2nd sec., music sect.). Address: Graniczna 4m. 1212, Warsaw 00 130, Poland.

MUDE, Hakurotwi, B. 6 Aug. 1938, Hartley, Rhodesia. Upholsterer & Mbira Player. Educ: as upholsterer & Mbira player & musician. m. w. 8 c. Debut: 1968. Career: Mbira player & musician for 12 yrs. Comps: 60 recorded. Hobbies: Mbira playing & singing; Upholstery. Address: 5534 New Canaan, Highfield, Salisbury, Rhodesia.

MUEGEL, Trudy Drummond, b. 28 Mar. 1936, Chgo., Ill., USA. Performer on Percussion & Euphonium; Percussion Instructor. Educ: Cert., Am. Conserv., Fontainebleau, France; BMus, Coll.-Conserv. of Music, Cinn., Ohio; BSc, Univ. of Cinn.; MSc., Juilliard Schl. m. Glenn A Mugel, 3 d. Career: Freelance Perf., percussion & euphonium; Percussionist, Cinn. Symph. Orch., 1958-62, & Cinn. Summer Opera, 1960-62 & 68-; Tympanist, Minot (ND) Coll.-Community Symph., 1962-65; Lectr. on Percussion Instr., Northern Ky. State Coll. Recordings: Asst. Soloist on New Music for Double Bass, Piper Records. Mbrships: Cinn. Alumnae, Sigma Alpha Iota; Pi Kappa Lamda; Perussive Arts Soc.; Kappa Delta Pi. Hobbies: Designing & Making Own Clothes; Camping. Address: 4027 Thimbleglen Dr., Cincinnati, OH 45239, USA.

MUELLER, Frederick A, b. 3 Mar. 1921, Berlin, Germany. Composer; Musicologist; Bassoonist. Educ: BM, Univ. Houston, USA, 1957; Eastman Schl. of Music, 1959; BMus, Fla. State Univ., 1961; NY Pro Musica Inst.; Oakland Univ.; Meadowbrook Schl. of Music; Fortran Seminar, MSU. m. Mary-Fay Moore. Career incls: Perfs. w. Kan. State Phil.; Houston Symph. Orch.; Chmbr. & Symphonic Ensembles; Dir. of Music & Assoc. Prof., Spring Hill Coll., Ala., 1960-67; Prof., Morehead State Univ., Ky., 1976; Dir., Collegium Musicum, MSU. Comps: Var. commissions, all media plus bassoon pedagogy. Num. recordings. Contbr. to profl. jrnls., etc. Mbrships: incl: Phi Kappa Phi; Phi Mu Alpha; Pi Kappa Lambda. Hobby: Learning among children ages 2-10. Address: Music Dept., MSU, Morehead, KY 40351, USA. 11.

MUELLER, Harold, b. 28 Jan. 1920, Austin, Tex., USA. Conductor; Flautist; Educator. Educ: BMus, Univ. of Mich., 1941; MMus, ibid., 1946; PhD, Univ. of Rochester, 1956; Juilliard Schl. of Music, 1947; perfs. cert. (flute) Eastman Schl. of Music, 1955. m. Beatrice Baldinger, 2 s. Career incl: flautist w. var. orchs.; asst. prof., Univ. of Minn., 1956-57; Assoc. prof., prof., dept. chmn., Austin Coll., 1958-67; Prof., Dept. Hd./Chmn., (1967-75), Marietta Coll., 1967-; Musical Dir., Parkersburg (WV) Choral Soc., 1977-; Cond., Marietta Coll. Civic Symphonette & Oratorio Soc., 1967-; music commentator, WMRT/FM, 1976-. Publs: Ed., 10 cantatas by Andreas Hammerschmidt; other eds. & arrs. Contbr. to num. profl. jrnls. Mbr. var. profl. socs. Hons: Senior hons., Univ. of Mich., 1941; Award of Merit, Nat. Fedn. of Music Clubs, 1973, '75. Hobbies: Sailing; Photography; Genealogy; Antiques. Address: 518 4th St., Marietta, OH 45750, USA. 2, 7, 8, 29.

MUELLER, Otto-Werner, b. 23 July 1926, Bensheim, Germany. Symphony Conductor; Teacher. Educ: Musisches Gymnasium, Frankfurt. m. Margarethe Mueller, 3 s. Career incls: Dir., Chmbr. Music Dept. Radio Stuttgart at age 19; Fndr., Cond. Radio Stuttgart Kammerchor; Cond. of Opera, Operetta, Ballet & Symphonic concerts, Comp. & Arr., CBC 1951; Tchr. & Cond., Conserv. de Musique & d'Art Dramatique, Montreal, 1958; Fndr. & Dean, Vic., BC Schl. of Music, 1963; Prof. of Music, Univ. of Wis., 1967; Prof. of Conducting, Yale Univ. Schl. of Music, 1973-; Guest Cond., Moscow, Leningrad, Montreal, Vancouver, Quebec & Nashville Symph. Orchs., USSR, 1968-73. Hons. incl: Int. Emmy Award, US Acad. of TV Arts & Scis., 1965. Hobby: Langs. Mgmt: Polygon Artists Assn., 8 Prospect Pl., New Haven, CT 06511, USA. Address: 185 Mansfield St., New Haven, CT 06511, USA.

MULFINGER, David Robert, b. 4 July 1937, Syracuse, NY, USa. Concert Pianist; Professor of Piano. Educ: BMus, Oberlin Conserv., 1959; MMus, Ind. Univ., 1962. Debut: Town Hall, NYC. Career: Radio progs. aired over CBC network, & NYC radio WNBC; Over 100 solo recitals in US & Can.; Performed complete cycle of 24 Preludes & Fugues, Vol. II, from Well-Tempered Clavier of JS Bach in coll. & univ. music schls., USA; Accompanying seminars presented on keyboard works of Bach. Mbrships: Pi Kappa Lambda; Coll. Music Soc. Hons. incl: State Winner, Nat. Fedn. of Music Clubs contest, 12965. Hobbies incl: Athletics. Address: 213 Hurlburt Rd., Syracuse, NY 13224, USA.

MULFINGER, Joan Elizabeth Wade, b. 20 July 1933, New Milford, Pa., USA. Violinist; Violist; Prof. of Strings, Bob Jones Univ. Educ: BM, Eastman Schl. of Music, Rochester Univ.; Grad. study, Syracuse Univ.; Study of violin w. Ralph Wade; Violin & viola, Francis Tursi; Chmbr. music, John Celantano; Violin & chmbr. music, Louis Krasner. m. George Leonidas Mulfinger, Jr., 2 s., 9 d. Career: Violist, Krasner String Quartet, 1958, 1960-61; String Quartet Series, NY State Educl. TV; Soloist, Bob Jones Symph. Orch.; Chmn., String Dept., 1968-75, Bob Jones Univ.; Violinist, Blvd. Bapt. Ch. Recordings: Tapes of

original hymn arrs., WMUU radio. Mbrships: Am. String Tchrs. Assn.; MTNA; Sigma Alpha Iota. Hons: Hardy Meritorious Award, 1970. Hobby: Gardening; Piano. Address: 25 Springdale Dr., Greenville, SC 29609, USA.

MULGAN, Philip Anthony, b. 5 Apr. 1927, London, UK. Joint Head, Music Dept., Oxford Univ. Press. Educ: MA, BLitt (Oxon). m. Anne Catherine Gough, 3 c. Mbrships: Royal Musical Assn.; Int. Musicol. Soc.; Int. Soc. Music Educ.; Am. Musicol. Soc. Address: Ely House, 37 Dover St., London, W1, UK.

MULHOLLAND, Raymond, b. 26 Apr. 1928, Manchester, UK. Youth Music Adviser. Educ: Royal Marines Schl. of Music; Liverpool Matthay Schl. of Music; TCL.; Assoc., Inst. of Municipal Entertainment (AIM Ent.); Assoc. Mbr., Brit. Inst. of Mgmt. (AMBIM). m. Louise Lily Elliott, 1 s. Career: Enlisted as a band boy, Royal Marines, 1942-58; Active serv. in Malaya & Korea; Musical Dir., Liverpool Corp., 1960-67; Youth Music Committee, 1967-; Interview, ''Music in Cities'', BBC World Serv., nat. BBC. Contbr. to: Isme Paper; Music Teacher; Times Educl. Supplement; Youth Scene (Publd. by DES). Hobbies: Landscape Painting; Fishing; Cricket; Reading. Address: 69 Manor Rd., Woolton, Liverpool 25, UK.

MULLER, Günther, b. 28 Aug. 1933, Dresden, Germany. Accordionist; Pianist; Organist; Composer. Educ: Music High Schl., Dresden; State Accordion Lectr. Dip., 1954. m. Edith Müller-Achermann. Career: Ldr., Musette-Grp., Instrumental Grp., Radio Dresden, 1950-53; Staff Mbr., Josef Preissner Music Publrs., Munich, 1954; Accordionist, Elektronium Soloist, Hohner Accordion Symph., 1955-58; Rdr., Edition Melodie Publrs., Zürich, 1958-59; perfs. in Europe, 1960-65; Fndr., arOnda Records, 1965; Fndr. Guensther Mueller Music Publrs., 1967; Fndr., Hohner Musikstudio. Compositions: suite, Auf einem Volksfest, Ein Ferientag, Freunde fur Immer, Hyme, Kleine Konzert-Suite, Pastorale & Scherzo, Kleine Suite, accordion orch.; Studie in Blue, piano solo, Konzertion in d-moll, accordion w. orch.; album Moderne Akkordeonsoli, Solisten-parade, vols. 3 & 4, Kleine Suite, Toccata, accordion solo. Mbr. German Comps. Grp. Address: 6380 Bad Homburg v.d.H., Frankfurter Landstrasse 7, Gerrman Fed. Repub.

MÜLLER, Karl Franz, b. 1 May 1922, Vienna, Austria. Composer; Pianist; Organist; Harpsichordist. Educ: State Acad. for Music, Vienna; pvte. studies w. Hans Pfitzner. m. Marie Müller, 1 s. Debut: Vienna, 1940. Career: Symphs. & concerts for Austrian Broadcasting Corp. & Musikverien, Vienna. Comps: 9 Symphs.; 4 concerts; var. other comps. for orch.; songs. Publs: Johann Sebastian Bach, 1950; Richard Strauss-zum Gedächtris, 1950; In Memorian Hans Pfitzner, 1950; Köchel-Verzeichnis (reorganization), 1951. Contbr. to: Oesterr. Musikzeitschrift. Mbrships: Austrian Soc. for Mod. Music; Aust. Comps. Union. Hons. incl: Oesterr, Ehrenkreuz für wissenschaft und Kunst, 1972. Address: Strassberg. 43/6/8, Vienna 1190, Austria.

MULLER, Mette Vibeke, b. 11 Jan. 1930, Odense, Denmark. Curator at the Music History Museum, Copenhagen. Educ: Cand.mag., Univ. of Copenhagen. m., 1 s. Publs: Classical Indian Musical Instruments, 1969-70; Traek & Tryk & Pust & Sug, 1971; From Bone Pipe & Cattle Horn to Fiddle & Psaltery, 1972. Contbr. to: Kulturhistorisk Leksikon for Nordisk Middelalter; Dansk Musiktidsskrift; Solhmans Musiklexikon; Die Musikforschung; Dansk Arborg for Musikforskning; Studia instrumentorum Musicae popularis. Mbrships: ICOM; ISM; Dansk Selskab for Musikforskning. Address: Musikhistorisk Museum, 1124 Copenhagn, Mus., Abrena 34, Denmark.

MULLER, Paul (also Muller-Zurich), b. 19 June 1898, Zurich, Switz. Composer. Educ: Conserv. Music, Zürich. m. Elisabeth Sigg. Career: Tchr., theory, comp., conducting, Conserv. & Univ. Zürich; Cond., choir & orch. Comps. incl: Choraltoccata uber 'Ein feste Burg', 1953; 'Christ ist erstanden', 1957. Recordings incl: Sinfonia I fur Streinchorch, op. 40; Sinfonia II fur Streichorch und Flote, op. 53; Sonata fur Streichorch op. 72. Mbr. profl. orgs. Hons: Musikpreis der Stadt Zürich, 1953; Komponistenpreis des Schweiz.; Tonkunstler-vereins, 1958. Hobbies incl: Reading; Travel. Address: CH 8253 Dissenhofen, Zum Goldener Leuen, Schmiedgasse 9, Switz.

MULLER, Per E, b. 4 Sept. 1932, Hamburg, W Germany. Singer (bass, baritone). Educ: Studied singing w. Helge Birkeland, Norway. 2 c. Debut: As Kezal in Bartered Bride, Norwegian Opera Co., 1963; Concert singer (lieder & opera), 1975. Career: Profl. singer, 1960-; Radio & TV apps.; Apps. at Nord Ring Festival, 1974 & Inverness, 1976, together w. 6 other countries, BBC host. Num. recordings. Recip. 1st Prize, Nord Ring Radio Festival, Groningen, Holland, 1974. Hobbies: Music of all kings, especially Light Music; Classic Operas. Address: Eltonveien 6, Oslo 5, Norway.

MULLER, Sylvia Ruth Barbush, b. 1 Mar. 1935, E. Chgo., Ind., USA. Pianist; Organist; Piano & Organ Teacher; Clinician; Critic; Adjudicator. Educ: BMus, Sherwood Music Schl., Chgo., Ill., 1957; MMus, ibid., 1961; courses at Ind. Univ., N. - W.; studied w. Leo Podolsky, Ralph Sunden, Harold Berlinger & Florence Grandland Galajukian. m. Paul William Muller Sr., 2 s. Career: Perf. Shostakovich's Piano Concerto No. 2 w. Sherwood Symph., Orchestra Hall, at commencement, 1961; Adjudicator, NGPT & Int. Assn. of Organ Tchrs. Recordings: Guest organist w. Lake Central Concert Choir, Christmas Albums, 1974, '77. Contbr. to: The Organ Tchr. Mbrships: Pres., 1975-76, 1978-79, Ind. Music Tchrs. Assn.; Fndr., N W Chapt., ibid.; Music Tchrs. Nat. Assn.; St. Michael-Alter & Rosary; former Mbr., Schererville J-Shees; Am. Guild of Organists; former Pres., Student Coun., Coll.; Nat. Hon. Soc., HS. sev. hons. Hobbies incl: Boating; Sewing; Swimming w. Retarded & Handicapped Children; Tchng. Music as Special Education; Writing; Reading. Address: 108 North Rd., Schererville, IN 46375, USA.

MUNCASTER, Clive, b. 24 Jan. 1936, Hove, Sussex, UK. Composer; Conductor. Educ: LRAM, RAM, MMus & RMT, Fla. State Univ. m. Ursula Brotherton-Ratcliffe, 5 s. Debut: First perf. of original comp. 'The Happy Hypocrite' w. Oxford Chamber Ensemble under composer's direction at The Queen Elizabeth Hall, London. Career: num. broadcasts of comps.; 'The Enthusiasts', a prog. concerning his life & activities, BBC TV (Southern), Nov. 1970; Fndr. & Musical Dir., Churchill Meml. concerts, Blenheim Palace, 1966-; Fndr., Gov., The Music Therapy Charity, 1969-. Compositions: Romance for Violin & Orch.; Fantasy for Oboe & Orch.; Pastorella for String Orch.; 'Cows' for voices w. instrumental accomp.; Num. other short pieces; maj. unpub. works incl. The Hidden Years, The Musical Giant, Society Symphony. Mbrships: Royal Musical Assn.; Composers Guild; Brit. Soc. for Music Therapy; Nat. Assn. for Music Therapy, Inc. Hobbies: Sailing. Address: The Manor Stables, Gt. Haseley, Oxford, UK. 3.

MUNDIGL, Josef Otto, b. 8 Oct. 1942, Langquaid, Germany. Composer, teacher. Educ: tchr. trng., Regensburg; degree in music, Regensburg, 1976-77; study of electronic music. m. Ilonka Blechinger, 1 d. Career: Adult educ. tchr. at Acad. for advanced tchr. trng., Dillingen, Hessisches Inst. & adult educ. ctr., Regensburg. Comps. incl: Ringspiel Nr. 1, 1973; Kristalle, 1974; Reflexe, 1975; Ringspiel Nr. 2, 1975; Baal Sebub's Tanz, 1975; Sequenzedrstudien 1-5 1974-75; Orchesterkonzert Nr. 1, 1975; Ringspiel Nr. 3, 1976; Ringspiel Nr. 4, 1978. Publs: Musik aus Strom (Music from electricity), 1975; Handbuch zur Acht Okta Filter-Bank (Eight octave filter bank handbook). Contbr. to: "Die Musikforschung". Mbr. var. profl. orgs. Address: 8424 Saal/Donau, Abensbergerstr. 31, German Fed. Repub.

MUNGER, Dorothy M, b. 16 Apr. 1915, Fostoria, Ohio, USA. Pianist; Harpsichordist. Educ: BMus (piano), 1940; piano studies w. Karin Dayas, Harold Triggs, Guy Maier, Rosina & Josef Lhevinne. m. Charles R Munger, 1 d. Career: Concert apps. w. orchs. & chmbr. music ensembles; accomp.; solo recitals; tchr. Arthur Jordan Conserv. of Music, Indpls., piano & theory, 1937-51; soloist & pianist, Indpls. Symph. Orch., 1938-44; Ind. Ctr. Univ. (piano, theory & appreciation), 1960-72; pianist, harpsichordist & celeste player, Indpls. Symph. Orch., 1960-; Artist Assoc. in piano, Butler Univ., Jordan Coll. of Fine Arts, Indpls., 1977-. Recordings w. Indpls. Symph. Orch. mbr. num. profl. socs. & orgs. Hons: Steinway Artist, 1952; Dorothy Munger Piano Chair, Indpls. Symph. Orch., 1979. Hobbies incl: Music; Music Pedagogy; Grandchildren; Travel. Address: 5753 N Coll. Ave., Indpls., IN 46220, USA. 5, 30.

MUNKACHY, Louis, b. 23 Nov. 1928, Kassa, Czech. University Professor of Music; Choral Conductor. Educ: Chorus Cond. Dip., Music Educ. Dip., Liszt Acad. of Music, Budapest; MM, Comp., Duquesne Univ., USA; PhD, Musicol., Univ. of Pitts. m. Emily Botos, 1 s., 1 d. Career: Choral Cond., profl. & amateur ensembles, Hungary, 1951-56, USA, 1960-; Prof. of Music Theory, Duquesne Univ. Contbr. to Grove's Dictionary. Mbrships: NEA; MENC; Assn. of Cath. Musicians. Hons: Hungarian Cultural Medal, 1956. Address: 1362 Craigview Dr., Pittsburgh, PA 15243, USA.

MUNN, Alexandra Marguerite, b. 16 Sept. 1934, Calgary, Alta., Canad. Music Educator; Pianist; Chorus Director. Educ: LRSM; AMus, LMus (Western Bd. of Music); Dip., Juilliard Schl. of Music; piano study w. pvte. tutors in Canada, USA & Italy. Debut: Soloist, Calgary Women's Musical Club, 1956. Career: Perfs. w. orchs. of Edmonton, Winnipeg, Vancouver CBC; Accompanist & Dir., Da Camora Singers on CBC Nat. Radio & TV networks; Opera Coach, Banff Schl. of Fine Arts, & Musical Dir., Musical Theatre Div., summers, 1952-67; Adjudicator at Music fests. throughout Canada; Cond., Richard Eaton Singers, 1967-73, incl. concert tour of UK, 1970; Prof. of Music, Univ.

of Alta.; Chorus Dir., Edmonton Opera Assn. Apps. w. Calgary Phil. Orch. Mbrships: CAUSM; ARMTA; Beta Sigma Phi; Royal Commonwealth Soc. Hons. incl: Gold Medal, Db. of Govs., Univ. of Alta., 1953. Hobbies: Golf; Bridge. Address: Dept. of Music, Univ. of Alta., Edmonton, Alta., Canada T6G, 2C9.

MUNN, Katrina Jeanette, b. 24 Dec. 1911, Bradford, Vt., USA. Teacher of Piano & Organ; Accompanist; Organist & Choir Director. Educ: BS, Univ. of Vt., Burlington, Vt.; Dip. in Piano, Inst. of Musical Art, Juilliard Schl. of Music; pvte. study of both piano & organ. Career: Tchr. of Piano & Organ, Bradford, Vt.; Organist & Choir Dir., United Ch. of Christ, Bradford; Accomp. for N Country Chorus. Mbrships: Sec., Vt., Chapt., 3 yrs.,m Dean, 2 yrs., Registrar, 3 yrs., AGO; Adjudicator, Accredited Tchr., Chmn., Bradford Ctr., NGPT; Accredited Tchr., 1st VP of Vt. Assn., 1 yr., Music Tchrs. Nat. Assn.; Scholarship Auditions Comm., Vt. Fed. of Women's Clubs. Hobbies: Playing Chamber Music; Vegetable Gardening, etc. Address: Box 244, Bradford, VT 05033, USA.

MUNNS, Robert Ellis, b. Purley, Surrey, UK. Concert Organist; Harpsichord Player; Conductor; Examiner; Adjudicator. Educ: RAM. m. Sally Johnson. Career: Dir. of Music, Holy Trinity Brompton, London, & Cond., Brompton Choral Soc., 1959-73; Prin., Blackheath Conservatorie, Cond., Blackheath Str. Orch., Dir. of Music, Woodford Parish Ch.; BBC Recitalist & Accomp.; frequent tours abroad & overseas; broadcast, Netherlands, Germany, USA, Can., Eire. Recordings made in var. chs. & cathedrals. Publs: Organ Scores of Creation & Elijah, Peters ed. Contbr. to mags. Mbr., ISM. Recip. var. hons. inclng. works written for him by var. contemp. comps. Hobby: Boating. Mgmt: Ibbs & Tillett Trio Mgmt. Address: 25 Tandridge Drive, Orpington, Kent, UK.

MUNRO, William Henderson, b. 13 Feb. 1936, Bangor, N. Wales, UK. Educator. Educ: Corby Coll. Further Educ.; ALCM; RMSM. Career: Tchr. of pianoforte, brass & woodwing. Mbr., Inc. Guild Ch. Musicians. Hobbies: Oboist; Angling. Address: 34, Stour Rd., Corby, Northants. NN17 24X, UK.

MURA, Péter, b. 21 June 1924, Budapest, Hungary. Conductor. Educ: HS of Music, Budapest. m. Rose Tóth, 1 d. Debut: Hungarian State Opera House, 1948. Career: Solo repetitor, Hungarian State Opera House, 1945-; Cond. of the Stàgione of the Hungarian State Opera House, 1950-53; Dir. & Chief Cond., Miskolc Nat. Theatre Opera Co., 1953-57; State Opera Cond., Warsaw, Poland, 1957-58; Cond., Silesian Opera, Bytom, Poland, 1958-61; Dir. & Chief Cond., Miskolc Symph. Orch., Hungary, 1961-. Recordings: (Mozart) IdomeneoOverture & ballet; Symph. in AK.134, Hungaroton, 1974. Mbrships: Union of Hungarian Musicians; Mbr. of Presidum, ibid. Hons: Liszt Ferenc Prize, 1966; Merited Artist of the Hungarian People's Rep., 1972. Mgmt: Interkoncert, Budapest, Hungary. Address: Rudas L.u.63, H-1064 Budapest VI, Hungary.

MURADIAN, Vazgen, b. 17 Oct. 1921, Ashtarak, Armenia. Composer; Viola d'Amore Player. Educ: Grad., Benedetto Marcello State Conserv. of Music, Venice, 1948. m. Arpi Kirkyasharian, 2 s. Debut: NY. Lincoln Ctr., Alice Tully Hall. Career: Taught violin, solfeggio & theory of Music, Collegio Armeno, Venice, Italy, 1945-50; Played as Violist in a number or Orchs. on arrival in USA inclng. New Orleans Phil. & Wagner Opera Co.; Has appeared as Viola d'Amore soloist in USa & abroad; Extensive perfs. of his work in Europe & Am. by var. artists. Compositions incl: Concerto, op. 52 for violin & orch.; concerto op. 23 for Viola d'amore & orch.; Adagio & Fondo op. 11 for violin & orch.; 6 sonatas for solo violin; 3 sonatas for violin & piano; op. 21, 22, 24; 2 sonatas for piano, op. 16, 18; Sonata for viola d'amore, p. 38; Var. songs; Sinfonia, Op 56; Concerto for bassoon & orch., Op. 53; Concerto for ud (or guitar) & orch., Op. 57. Contbr. of articles about the forms of music & viola d'amore in var. reviews. Mbr., ASCAP. Hons: Tekeyan Prize, 1962. Hobbies: Chess Playing. Address: 269 W 72nd St., NY, NY 10023, USA.

MURAIL, Tristan, b. 11 Mar. 1947, Le Havre, France. Composer; Electronic Keyboard Player (Ondes Martenot, Organ, Synthesizers). Educ: Lic., Economics; Political studies, Inst. d'Etudes Politiques; Conserv. de Paris, Comp. w. Olivier Messiaen. Career: Manager, L'Itinéraire (Ensemble for New Music, Paris). Comps. incl: Couleur de Mer; Altitude 8000; Au-Delà du Mur du Son; Sables; Mémoire/Erosion; Territoires de l'oubli; Tellur; Ethers; Treize Couleurs du Soileil Couchant; Les Courants de l'espace. Recordings: Mémoire/Erosion & Ethers (Ensemble l'Itinéraire). Hons: Prix de Rome, 1971. Hobby: Science fiction. Mgmt: Maité Barrois, 40 rue de Bretagne, 75003 Paris, France; Editions Musicales Transatlantiques, 50 rue Joseph de Maistre, 75018 Paris, France. Address: 40 rue de Bretagne, 75003 Paris, France.

MURCHIE, Leslie Graham, b. 23 Aug. 1918, Middlesborough, Yorks, UK. Pianist; Professor; Examiner; Accompanist; Adjudicator. Educ: GSMD, London; FGSM; LRAM; AGSM. m. Elizabeth Brameld, 2 s., 1 d. Career: Professor, Guildhall Schl. of Music & Drama; One-time opera coach, Royal Opera House, Glyndebourne, Nat. Welsh Opera; Adjudicator, Brit. Music Fest. Mbrships: ISM; Music Advsr., Savage Club & London Press Club; Worshipful Co. of Musicians. Hobbies: Gardening; Golf; Walking. Address: 33 Fitzwarren Gdns., London N. 19, UK.

MURDOCH, Dennis, b. 9 Jan. 1914, Nuneaton, UK. Pianist. Educ: Studied w. Sauer & Steurmann, Vienna; RAM; FRAM, 1960; ARCO. m. Sue Pawsey, 1 s., 2 d. Debut: Wigmore Hall, 1946. Career: solo recital & concerto perfs., inclng. Royal Fest. & Royal Albert Halls; num. solo broadcasts from London & all the UK regions; 1960-, mainly Tchr., RAM, adjudication & examining. Mbr., RAM Club. Hons. incl: Macfarren Gold Medal, 1939. Hobbies: Golf; Motoring. Address: Orchard Lea, Harefield Rd., Rickmansworth, Herts., UK.

MURDOCH, James Arthur, b. 25 Jan. 1930, Sydney, Aust. National Director, Australian Music Centre. Educ: Sydney Conserv. of Music; Conservatorio Real de Madrid. Career: Staff mbr., Aust. Broadcasting Commission, 1948-51; Asst. Dir., Museum of Modern Art, Melbourne, 1956-58; Musical Dir., Lusillo & his Spanish Dance Theatre, 1958-62; Asst. Music Dir., Aust. Ballet Co., 1962; Mgr., Universal Record Club Pty. Ltd., 1963-64; Exec. Mbr., World Record Club Pty. Ltd., 1964-68; James Murdoch Mgmt. Pty. Ltd., Concert & Artists Mgmt., 1968-71; Music Cons., Music Bd., Aust. Coun., 1972-74; Nat. Dir., Aust. Music Centre, 1974-. Comps: La Espera, ballet, 1960. Publs: Australia's Contemporary Composers, 1972. Contbr. to profl. publs. Mbrships. incl: Chmn., Int. Assn. of Music Libs. Aust. & NZ (NSW); Committee Mbr., ibid (Fed.); Dir., Music Rostrum Aust.; Pres., Chiron Coll. Ltd.; Advisory Panel, Sydney Int. Piano Competition; Music Planning Committee, Sydney Coll. for the Arts. Hobbies: Photography; Theatre; Ballet. Address: PO Box N9, Grosvenor St., Sydney, NSW 2000, Aust.

MURDOCH, Mary Hersey, b. 16 Apr. 1931, Chessington, UK. Musician (oboe, oboe d'amore, cor anglais). Educ: Downe House, Newbury; RAM; LRAM (perf.). m. George Miskin, 1 s., 2 d. Career: Prin. oboe, Royal Liverpool Phil. orch.; prin. oboe, Sydney Symph. Orch.; mbr., Portia Wind Ensemble & Tilford Ensemble; num. solo & chmbr. music perfs. for BBC. Recordings: Bach, Art of Fugue & Musical Offering; Handel, Trios & Oboe Concertos; Warlock, The Curlew. Mbr., ISM. Hons: Ross Scholar, 1950; N London Orchl. Soc., 1951; John Solomon Wind prize, 1951. Hobbies: Tennis; Swimming; Gardening. Address: Hankley Edge, Tilford, Farnham, Surrey GU10 2DD, UK.

MURGIER, Jacques, b. 30 Sept. 1912, Grenoble, France. Violinist; Composer; Conductor. Educ: Paris Coinserv. m. Simone Peyrot, 1 s. Career: Asst. Lectr., Fac. of Letters, Grenoble, 1934-39; Cond., French Radio-Diffusion; Fndr., Paris String Trio. Comps: Quartet in D flat; Concerto for oboe & orch.; 3 Flute Pieces; 3 Odes; String Trio; Symph. for Strings; Spiral (ballet) The Book of Hours; 2nd Str. Quartet; Concerto for Saxophone; Concerto for tuba or double bass & piano. Recordings: Haydn's Trios; Lyre Bird. VP, Nat. Music Committee. Recip. 1st Prize for Violin, Paris Conserv. Address: 14 rue Carnot, 5110 Reims, France.

MURO, Don, b. 29 July 1951, Freeport, NY, USA. Composer; Performer; Educator. Educ: BS, music educ., Hofstra Univ., 1973. Career: Lectr., Performer, Clinician, schls., colls. confs., esp. electronic music. Comps: A Little Space Music; Current Events; I Will Lift Up Mine Eyes; O Be Joyful in the Lord; Badlands Overture; A New Season. Publ: An Introduction to Electronic Music Synthesizers (filmstrip), 1975. Contbr. 'Jazz & the Electronic Medium', Nat. Assn. Jazz Educators 'Educator', 1976. Mbr. prof. orgs. Recip. ASCAP Award, 1978. Hobby: Tennis. Address: 91 Whaley St., Freeport, NY 11520, USA.

MURPHY, Dennis, b. 19 Jan. 1934, Plainfield, NJ, USa. College Music Teacher. Educ: BMus, MMus, Univ. of Wish., Madison; PhD (ethnomusicol.), Wesleyan Univ., Middletown, Conn. m. Patricia LaBreche Murphy, 2 d. Career: Tchr., Goddard Coll., Plainfield, Vt., for 10 yrs; Performer, Bassoon, tenor voice, & renaissance instruments; interested in design & constrn. of musical instruments w. special emphasis of Javanese gamelans (classical orchs). having build two & encouraged building of sev. others. Comps. incl: A New Psalm (SATB chorus). Author: The Autochtonous American Gamelan, 1975. Contbr. to: Jrnl. of Music Acad. Madras; African Music. Mbrships: Soc. for Ethnomusicol.; Coll. Music Soc.; Phi Mu Alpha. Hobbies incl: Playing chmbr. music; Painting; Photography. Address: Box 47, Plainfield, VT 05667, USA.

MURPHY, Kathleen G, b. 12 Nov. 1952, Auburn, NY, USA. Cellist. Educ: BMus, MMus (Perf.), Eastman Schl. of Music. Career incls: Solo recitals, Eastman Schl.; Rochester Phil., 1974-; Aspen Fest. Orch., 1975, '76; Aspen Chmbr. Orch., 1977; Tchng. Asst., Chmbr. Music Asst., Eastman Schl., 1975-78. Mbr., NY Cello Soc. Hons: Winner, Eastman Concerto Competition, 1974; Winner, Music Acad. Concerto Competition, 1974; Finalist, Hudson Valley String Competition, 1975. Hobbies: Sewing/Needlepoint; Cross-country skiing; Skating; Cooking; Reading. Address: 2135-D East Ave., Rochester, NY 14610, USA.

MURPHY, Kevin Edgar, b. 23 Mar. 1928, Sydney, Aust. Orchestral Clarinetist & Saxophone Player. Educ: studied w. Edward Simson, NSW State Conservatorium, 3 yrs.; w. Jack Brymer, UK, 1964. m. Beryl Barber, 2 s., 2 d. Career: began playing w. dance bands; w. Aust. Broadcasting Commission Nat. Mil. Band; played in theatres (musical comedy, opera, ballet etc.), 2 yrs.; Mbr. & soloist on both instruments, SA Symph. Orch., Adelaide, 15 yrs.; Assoc. Prin. Clarinet, also soloist & mbr. of sextet ("Sydney Wind Soloists"), Sydney Symph. Orch., 1967; Radio Recitals, Aust. Broadcasting Commission; Tchr., NSW Conservatorium for sev. yrs. Recorded Wm. Lovelock's Concerto for saxophone & orch. Hobbies incl: Gardening; Bible study. Address: 6 Maxwell Pde., French's Forest, NSW, Australia 2086.

MURRAY, Bain, b. 26 Dec. 1926, Evanston, Ill., USA. Composer; Professor; Music Critic. Educ: AB, Oberlin Coll., 1951; AM, Harvard Univ., 1952; studied musicol. w. Suzanne Clercx, Univ. of Liège; additonal study w. Walter Piston, Harvard Univ. & Nadia Boulanger, Paris, France. m. Laurie W Murray, 1 d. Career: Prof. of Music, Cleveland State Univ.; joined Univ., 1966; Lectr., Fenn Coll., 1963-65; Assoc. hd., Theory Dept., Cleveland Music Schl. Settlement, 1958-69; Instructor, Oberlin Conserv. of Music, 1955-57; Tchng. Fellow, Harvard Univ., 1954-55; Music Critic, Cleveland Plain Dealer, 1957-58, Sun Newspapers, 1959. Comps. incl: (recorded) On The Divide (chorus & wind quartet); Safe in their Alabaster Chambers (chorus, cor anglais & cello); Three Songs; other vocal works. Publs: Music Ed., Our Musical Heritage, 1964. Contbr. to num. profl. jrnls. Mbrships: ASCAP; Am. Soc. for Univ. Comps.; Cleveland Comps. Guild (Pres. for 4 yrs.). Hons: Fulbright Grant; ASCAP Awards; Medal of Distinction, Polish Comps. Union, etc. Hobbies: Mountain Hiking; Renovating log cabin; Travel. Address: 1331 Cleveland Heights Blvd., Cleveland Heights, OH 44121, USA.

MURRAY, Margaret, b. 11Mar. 1921, Lille, France. Lecturer on Orff-Schulwerk; Accompanist; Cellist; Recorder Player. Educ: RCM; ARCM (accomp., piano perf., cello tchng.); LRAM (piano tchng.). Career: some public concerts; music mistress, Marlborough Coll., 1942-43, & Wycombe Abbey, 1946-52; sec., Orff-Schulwerk Soc., 1964-. Publs: 5 vols., Engl. ed., Orff-Schulwerk, 1958-66; 8 English Nursery Songs, 1963; Wee Willie Winkie, 1965; 9 carols, 1973; transl., Gunild Keetman's Elementaria, 1974, Barbara Haselbach's Sance Education, 1971, Carl Orff's The Schulwerk, 1976, & Gertrud Orff's Orff Music Therapy, 1980. Recordings: Music for Children (Orff-Schulwerk). Mbrships: ISM; Royal Musical Assn.; Soc. for Rsch. in Psychol. of Music & Musicol. Educ. Hobbies: Films; Reading. Address: 31 Roedean Cresc., London SW15 5JX, UK.

MURRAY, Niall, b. 22 Apr. 1948, Dublin, Ireland. Opera Singer (Baritone). Educ: Royal Irish Acad. of Music, Dublin. m. Dr. Barbara F M Murray, 1 d. Debut: Boy Soprano, Pantomime, Dublin, 1952; Baritone, Curly in Oklahoma, Dublin, 1970; Opera Debut, Bomorzo, Coliseum, London, 1976. Career: Baritone lead, 52 musicals; currently, Prin. Baritone roles, Engl. Nat. Opera, London; TV & radio apps., England & Ireland. Recordings: Niall Murray Sings (Shaw Songs); Niall Murray Sings (Irish Songs); Danilo, The Merry Widow; Robert, The Drum Major's Daughter. Mgmt: Music Int., 13 Ardulaun Rd., Highbury, London N5 2QR, UK. Address: c/o Mgmt.

MURRAY, Paul (Burns), b. 21 Mar. 1927, Saint John, NB, Can. Organist; Choral Conductor; Adjudicator; Teacher; Consultant; Freelance Broadcaster & Writer. Educ: BMus, Univ. of Toronto; RCM; ARCM; ARCO; FRCO; ARCT; ACCO; FCCO. m. Helen Mary, 1 s., 1d. Career: Organist & Choirmaster, London (UK); Metropolitan United Ch., Toronto; Music Chmn., Jr. High Schl., N York, Ont.; Cons., Dept. of Educ. for NS; local music critic for CBC; Host of Organists in Recital (CBC); fndr., cond., Halifax Chmbr. Choir. Comps: 4 Short Introits. Contbr. to: The Can. Music Educator; Oepra Canada. Mbrships: past-pres., Can. Music Educators' Assn.; VP, Can. Music Coun.; VP, RCCO RCO. recip., Turpin Prize, RCO, 1954. Hobbies: Fishing; Walking; Flying; Broadcasting; Badminton. Address: 15 Alderwood Dr., Armdale, NS, B3N 1S6, Can.

MURRAY, Robert P, b. 24 Oct. 1936, South Bend, Ind., USA. Violin player & teacher. Educ: BMus, Am. Conserv. of Music, Chgo., 1959; MMus, ibid., 1960; DMus, Ind. Univ., Bloomington, 1976. m. Janet Slapikes, 1 s. Debut: Orch. Hall, Chgo., 1957; Town Hall, NY. Career: Concertmaster & Soloist, Chgo. Chamber Orch., Amici della Musica Chamber Orch., Bach Festival Orch. (Calif.) & num. Metropolitan orchs; Artist-in-Residence, Univ. of Santa Clara, Calif.; Assoc. Prof. of Music, UNC, Greeley, Colo., 1972-76; ibid., Baylor Univ., WACO, Tex., 1976-78; ibid., Va. Commonwealth Univ., Richmond, 1978-. Recordings: Complete violin sonatas by A Rubinstein; violin sonatas by C Saint-Saens. Mbrships: Pi Kappa Lambda; Phi Mu Alpha Sinfonia; Am. String Tchrs. Assn. Hons: 1st prize, Am. Conservb., 1957; Premiere, L Sowerby 3rd sonata for violin & piano, 1964; Hobby: Audio Engineering. Mgmt: Critics Choice Artists Mgmt. Address: Dept. of Music, Va. Commonwealth Univ., Richmond, VA 23284, USA.

MURRAY, Sterling Ellis, b. 19 May 1944, Balt., Md., USA. Teacher; Musicologist. Educ: BMus, Univ. of Md.; MA, Univ. of Mich.; PhD, ibid. m. Constance Wright Murray, 2 d. Career: Assoc. Prof. of Music Hist. & Lit., W Chester State Coll. Publs: Antonio Rosetti (1750-1792) & His Symphonies, 1973; Manual for Joseph Kerman's Listen, 1975. Contbr. to: Musical Qarterly; Current Musicol.; Music & Letters; Groves' Dict., 6 ed.; Am. Choral Review. Mbrships: Regional Off., Am. Musicol. Soc.; Int. Musicol. Soc.; Soc. for 18th Century Studies; Phi Mu Alpha; Music Lib. Assn. Recip. Grant, Am. Philos. Soc., Phila., Pa. Address: 344 W Union St., W Chester, PA 19380, USA.

MURRAY, Thomas, b. 6 Oct. 1943, Los Angeles, Calif., USA. Organist & Choirmaster. Educ: BA, Occidental Coll., Calif., 1965; studied Organ w. Clarence Mader. Career: Organist & Choirmaster, Cathedral Ch. of St. Paul, Boston, Mass.; Recitals, Denver, NYC, Boston, Atlanta & other major US cities; European tour, 1970, inclng. perfs. in Vienna, Copenhagen & Amiens, & broadcast recitals, Vatican Radio. Recordings: Complete works of Mendelssohn & Cesar Franck on historic New England organs. Contbr. to: Organ Club (UK) Jubilee Book; Oschse, History of the Organ in the US, (photographs); profl. jrnls. Mbrships incl: AGO; Am. Musical Instrument Soc. Hons. incl; 1st Place, AGO Nat. Competition, 1966. Hobbies incl; Photography; Antique Furniture. Address: 1 Oak St., Newbury, MA 91950, USA.

MURRAY, Thomas Wilson, b. 24 July 1925, Omaha, Neb., USA. Hornist; Teacher. Educ: BMus. Educ., Northwestern Univ., 1950. m. Frances Peterman Murray, 1 d. Career: Past Prin. Horn, US Army Band, Wash., DC; Horn Tchr., Coll. prep. level; Natural Hornist & alto saxhornist, Smithsonian Inst., Wash., DC; Freelance hornist, horn soloist (valve & natural horns); Fac., Geo. Mason Univ. & Northern Va. Community Coll. Recordings: 19th Century American Ballroom Music (Nonesuch); Music from the Age of Jefferson (Smithsonian Instn.); Our Musical Past (US Lib. Congress). Mbr. profl. orgs. Hobbies Incl; Books. Address: 3814 N Vernon St., Arlington, VA 22207, USA.

MURRAY, William Bruce, b. 13 Mar. 1935, Schenectady, NY, USA. Opera Singer. Educ: BA (Music Educ.), Adelphi Univ., NY; Fulbright Schlrship., Rome, 1956. m. Nancy Lee Adams, 2 s., 1 d. Debut: Spoleto, Italy in Susanna's Secret, 1956. Career: Leading Baritone, Munich State Opera & German Opera, Berlin; appearances at major opera houses in Europe, Japan & USA. Recordings: var. operatic works for Bavarian Radio, inclng: Simone; Sim Tjong; Antingonae, etc. Address: Hilssteig 27, 1 Berlin 37, Germany.

MURRELLS, Joseph, b. 1 Nov. 1904, Highbury, London, UK. Musicologist; Pianist; Composer; Lyricist; Author. Educ: Studied w. Lilian Bayliss; Bronze & Silver Medallist, Victoria Coll. of Music; Cert. in Theory (Schls. Examination), RAM; ARCM. m. Edith Jane Cuthbert, 1 s. Debut: in Notions Revue, 1924. Career: Pianist, Tom Priddy's Tango Band, 1926, broadcasting from Nottingham Palais de Danse; Pvte. Society engagements, 1927-35; Orchl. Lib., BBC, 1936; Variety Libn., BBC, WWII; Prof. Mgr., Ascherberg, Hopwood & Crew, Music Publsrs., 1944-58. Comps. incl: (publd. & recorded) Count your Blessings (under pseudonym Edith Temple); Those Were the Days; Mia Mantilla; The Engagement Waltz; It's a Grand Life in the Army; (publd.) Heavenly Bread; Pearls; Hope & Pray; Publs: Books of Golden Discs, 1966 revised ed. 1974; British Hits 1907-1966. Cont;br. to Press. Mbrships: PRS; Songwriters Guild of Gt. Brit. (former Councillor). Hon: Winner (w. J Prenctice), News of the World 1000 Prize, (1953); Gold Bade of Merit, Songwriters Guild, 1977. Hobbies: Music Research (Popular Music); Motoring; Gardening. Address: 35 Beechfield Rd., OLondon N4 1PD, UK. 3, 30.

MUSGRAVE, Thea, b. Edinburgh, Scotland, UK. Composer. Educ: Edinburgh Univ.; Studied w. Nadia Boulanger, Paris. m. Peter Mark. Career: Tchr., Extra Mural Dept., London Univ.; Vis.

Prof., Univ. Calif., Santa Barbara, USA; Mbr., Ctrl. Music Advsry. Panel for BBC; Lectr. num. univs. in UK & USA; Cond. of own music inclng: Beauty & the Beast (ballet); The Voice of Ariadene; Orchl. works w. BBC Symph., BBC Scottish Symph., London Symph. & Engl. Chmbr. Orchs. Comps. incl: The Five Ages of Man (chorus & orch), 1963; The Decision (opera), 1964-65; Mary, Queen of Scots (opera), 1975-77; A Christmas Carol (Opera), 1979; num. chmbr. 2 orchl. works inclng: Chmbr. Concerto No. 3, 1966; Night Music, 1969; Memento Vitae, 1969-70; Space Play, 1974; Songs incl: Primavera (soprano & flute), 1971. Hons: Koussevitzky Award, 1973; Guggenheim Fellowship, 1974-75. Address: c/o J & W Chester, Eagle Ct., London EC1 5QD, UK.

MUSKAT, Thomas, b. 16 Mar. 1943, Pécs, Hungary. Keyboard Performer (piano, organ, synthesizer). Educ: Conserv. m. Anita Rödseth, 1 s. Debut: First album, 1971. Career: 5th place, Topteen, Norway, 1977. Recordings: 7 solo LP's. Mgmt: CBS, Norway. Address: Bölerlia 45, Oslo 6, Norway.

MUSKETT, Michael, b. 23 June 1928, Blackpool, UK. Musician (Recorder, Clarinet; Early & Traditional Instruments). Educ: ARCM. m. Doreen Taylor, 2 d. Career: Clarinet Soloist, Chmbr. & Symph. orchs., London & S Africa; Recorder Soloist, Chmbr. concerts & recitals; Lecture Recitals w. wife inclng. Flutes, reeds & whistles, & Drums, Drones & Dulcimers; Series of recitals, Michael Muskett's Museum of Music, Purcell Room, London, 2 yrs.; concerts for children; var. TV & radio apps. Exhibs. mounted in France & UK. Contbr. to mags. & jrnls. Mbrships: Galpin Soc.; ISM; Musicians Union; Soc. of Recorder Players; Northumbrian Pipers Soc. Hobbies: Making Instruments; Field Research in Folk Music. Mgmt: Helen Acton, Amadeus House, Church St., Framlingham, Woodbridge, Suffolk IP 13 9BE. Address: Piper's Croft, Chipperfield Rd., Bovingdon, Herts., HP3 OJW, UK.

MUSSER, Willard I, b. 2 Feb. 1913, Mohnton, Pa., USA. Professor of Music; Conductor/Clinician. Educ: BME, MME, Ithaca Coll., NY. m. Gloria Hvizdos, 1 s., 1 d. Career: Dir., Instrumental Music, secondary schls., NY & Pa.; Assoc. Prof., Music, Dir. of Bands, Hartwick Coll.; Prof. Music, SUNY, Potsdam, 1956; Fndr., Crane Wind Ensemble; Brass Ed., Brass & Percussion mag. Comps: Arabesque for Band; March Globil for Concert Band, 1977; Num. transcriptions. Publs: Author, Co-Author, workbooks, manuals, studies; Ed., var. trumpet works; Ed., The Band Director's Guide to Instrument Repair, 1973. Contbr. to profl. jrnls. Mbrships: Pres. Elect, Am. Concert Band Assn.; Past Pres., Exec. Field Cons., NY State Music Assn.; Past Mbr., Planning Comm., Pres.; E Div., MENC; Am. Bandmaster's Assn.; Am. Fedn. of Musicians. Hons: Life Mbrships., Ringold Band, Reading, Pa., & Local 135, Am. Fedn. of Musicians; Alumni Award, Kappa Gamma Psi. Hobby: Fishing. Address: POB 71, Greentown, PA 18426, USA.

MUSSULMAN, Joseph Agee, b. 20 Nov. 1928, E. St. Louis, Ill., USA. Professor of Music. Educ: BMus, 1950, MMus, 1951, Northwestern Univ., PhD, Syracuse Univ., 1966. m. Emma Jo-Anne Stafford, 2 d. Career incls: Instr. in Voice, Northwestern Univ., 1952-54; Asst. to Dean, & Asst. Dir., Choral Orgs., Ripon Coll., Wis., 1954-57; Asst. Prof. Music, Univ. of Mont., Missoula, 1957-. Publs: Music in the Cultured Generation, 1972; The Uses of Music, 1974; Dear People... Robert Shaw, 1979. Contbr. to profl. jrnls. Mbr., Popular Culture Assn. Hons: Danforth Tchr. Study Grants, 1961-62, 64-65; Rsch. Grant, Nat. Endowment for Humanities, 1967-68. Hobbies: Conservation Work; Hiking & Backpacking; Ski Touring. Address: Dept. of Music, Univ. of Montana, Missoula, MT 59812, USA. 11.

MUSTONEN, Aimo Mainio, b. 15 Jan. 1909, Tampere, Finland. Editor; Composer. m. Annikki Mustonen, 4 c. Comps: Num. marching songs & pieces of light music; 230 songs for children. Publs: March Songs, 1939-44; 6 books of Songs for Children, 1970-78. Mbr., ELVIS (Soc. of Film & Light Music Comps.). Hons: Dir. musices, 1974. Hobbies:O Sports; Chess. Address: 01860 Perttula, Finland.

MUTI, Riccardo, b. 28 July 1941. Conductor. Educ: Dip. (piano), Conserv. of Naples; Dip. (comp. & cond.), Milan. m. Christina Mazzavillani, 2 s., 1 d. Career: Prin. cond., New Philharmonia/Philharmonia Orch., 1975-; concert tours in USA w. Boston, Cleveland, Chgo., Phila. & NY orchs.; apps. at Fests in Edinburgh, Salzburgh, etc.; apps. as operatic cond., Covent Garden, Florence, Vienna, etc. num. recordings. Address: via Corti Alle Mura 25, Ravenna, Italy.

MYCIELSKI, Zygmunt, b. 17 Aug. 1907, Przeworsk, Poland. Composer; Music critic. Educ: Cracow & Paris. Career: Ed., Ruch muzyczny (bi-monthly musical jrnl.). Compositions: Orchl. works incl: Polish Symph.; Piano Concerto; Nowy lirnik Mazowiecki (Cantata); Overture Silesienne; 2nd & 3rd Symphs.; String Trio;

5 Preludes for Piano; Ballet - Narcyz; Zabawa w. Lipnach; choral works, etc. Mbrships: Pres., Union of Polish Composers, 1949-50. Hons: State Prize, 1952 (for Polish Symph.); Union of Polish Composers Prize, 1955; num. decorations. Publs: Ucieczki z Pieciolinii (musical essays); Notatki o muzyce, 1961. Address: Ul. Rutkowskiego 10-31, Warsaw, Poland.

MYERS, Herbert W, b. 17 March 1943, Bell, Calif., USA. Performer & Teacher of Renaissance & Baroque Woodwinds & Strings; Maker of Renaissance Woodwinds & Strings. Educ: BA, Stanford Univ., Calif., 1964; MA, in Music, ibid., 1966; cand. for Dr. of Musical Arts in Perf. Practices of Early Music. m. Margaret Anne Urling, 1 s. Career: Perf. for three yrs. w. the NY Pro Musica Antiqua Inc., Concert Ensemble in extensive tours of the US & S Am., Perf. in Pro Musica on Recorder, Shawm, Dulcian, Crumhorn, Renaissance Flute, Rackett & Vielle; currently Lectr. in Early Music, Stanford Univ. & Dir. of the Stanford Renaissance Wind Band. Recordings: Recorder II of the 4th Brandenburg on Columbia - Bach - The Six Brandenburg Concertos - Anthony Newman & Friends, 1972. Publs: Tunes for the Recorder, edited & transcrivbed from Restoration recorder tutorts, Instrumenta Antiqua Publs., 1976. Contbr. to: The Am. Recorder; Renaissance Qtly. Mbrships: Galpin Soc.; Am. Musical Instrument Soc. Address: 2180 Monterey Ave., Menlo Pk., CA 94025, USA.

MYERS, Philip Frederick, b. 25 June 1949, Elkhart, Ind., USA. French Horn Player. Educ: BFA, Music, BFA, Music Educ., Carnegie-Mellon Univ., Pitts., Pa. Career: 1st Horn, Pitts. Symph., Pitts., Pa., 1974-. Recordings: Atlantic Brass Ensemble. Hobbies: Tennis; Table Tennis; Running; Bicycling. Address: 1242 Wisconsin Ave., Pittsburgh, PA 15216, USA.

MYERS, Rita Koors, b. 29 Sept. 1942, Paterson, NJ, USA. Pianist, Harpsichordist, Music Educator. Educ: Eastman Schl. of Music; BSc, 1964, MSc, 1965, Juilliard Schl. of Music. m. William Ira Myers. Debut: Carnegie Recital Hall, 1972. Career: has concertized as Soloist & w. chmbr. ensembles at many halls, univs. & other instns. on E Coast of USA; apps. on CBS TV network & var. NY radio stns.; Prof. of Music, Dept. of Fine Arts, Bergen Community Coll., Paramus, NJ. Recordings: Sonatas for the Harpsichord, Pianoforte & Flute of Johann Christian Bach, complete 4 vol. collect., Musical Heritage Soc. label. Mbrships. incl: Alton Jones Assocs.; Am. & Nat. Recorder Socs; Music Tchrs. Nat. Assn.; NEA. Recip. Acad. hons. Hobbies incl: Playing recorders & medieval harp; Reading; Hiking. Address: 73 Oak Dr., Upper Saddle River, NJ 07458, USA. 4.

MYERS, Stanley, b. 6 Oct. 1933, Birmingham, UK. Composer. Educ: MA, Balliol Coll., Oxford Univ.; w. Band of the Royal Berkshire Regt. m. (1) Eleanor Fazen, (2) Yvonne Stammose, 1 s. Career: Thirty feature films, inclng: 'Ulysses', 'Janice', 'Zee & Co', 'Percy', 'No Way to Treat a Lady', 'Otley', 'Raging Moon', 'Kaleidoscope', 'The Wilby Conspiracy', 'The Apprenticeship of Duddy Kravitz & num. others; Num. plays, series & documentaries for TV inclng: 'Divorce His & Hers', 'Up the Junction', 'Robin Hood', 'Diary of a Young Man', 'Shoulder to Shoulder'. Many TV commercials. Recordings: Loguerythms (soloist, Annie Ross); Changes (soloist, John Williams); sev. sound track albums. Recip. Ivor Novello Award, 1978. Mgmt: First Composers Ltd. Address: 44 Redcliffe Rd., London SW10, UK.

MYERSCOUGH, Clarence Percy, b. 27 Oct. 1930, London, UK. Violinist; Professor of Violin. Educ: FRAM., Paris Conserv.; studied w. F Grinke & Rene Benedetti, Pierre Pasquier & Marcel Devaux. m. Marie-Louise Scherer, 1 s., 1 d. Career: apps. & broadcast as Soloist in major European capitals & for ATV & BBC Open Univ.; Ldr., Fidelio Quartet, 1965-72; Prof. of Violin, RAM. Recordings: Tippett quartets 1-3, Britten quartets 1 & 2, Delius & Arriaga quartets 1 & 2 w. Fidelio Quartet; Alun Hoddinott Sonata for Violin & Piano. Mbr., ISM. Hons: 2nd Prize, Carl Flesch Int. Comp., 1952. Hobby: Microscopy. Address: 17 Salterton Rd., London N7, UK. 3.

MYHREN, Helge, b. 17 Apr. 1951, Arendal, Norway. Pianist. Educ: Piano studies w. Erling Westher, Oslo, & Maria Curcio Diamand, London; Comp. studies w. Conrad Baden, Oslo. Debut: As soloist, Oslo, age 19. Career: Soloist, Oslo Phil. Orch., Bergen Phil. Orch., Radio Orch., Oslo; Pianist, Oslo Phil. Orch.; Chmbr. music concerts w. Norwegian Woodwind Quintet; Radio & TV apps., Oslo; Concerts, Bergen & Harstad Fests., Norway; Radio recordings, Sweden. Contbr. to: Norwegian Music Soc. Mag. Mbrships: Norwegian Music Soc.; Contemporary Music Soc. Hons: Aust-Agder fylkes kultur pris, 1972. Hobby: Model Building. Mgmt: Norsk Konsertdireksjon/Leon Farner, Oslo 1, Norway. Address: Brentedalen I, 4800 Arendal, Norway.

MYKLEGÅRD, Åge, b. 18 Aug. 1904, Oslo, Norway. Cathedral Organist. Educ: Exam Artium. m. Ingeborg Christensen, 4 c. Career: Organist & Choirmaster, Tonsberg, 1928; Cathedral Organist, Tonsberg, 1948-73; Annual perfs. of Oratorios etc.; Servs & Concerts on TV & Radio. Comps: Supplement: 6 Orgel Koraler, 1975. Address: Bulls gt. 16, 3100 Tonsberg, Norway.

MYRVIK, Donald Arthur, b. 13 June 1936, Minnesota, Minn., USA. Musicologist; College Administrator; Choral Conductor. Educ: BA, Augsburg Coll., 1958; Augsburg Theol. Sem., Mpls., 1958-60; MA, 1963, PhD, 1975, Univ. of Minn., Mpsl. m. Rhoda C Dahl, 2 s. Career: Choral Cond., 1958-68; Admnstr., Luth. Soc. for Worship, Music & Arts, 1961-69; Admnstr., coll. servs., Coll. of Liberal Arts, Univ. of Minn., 1969-. Publs. incl: Musical & Social Interaction for Composers & Performers: Difference between Source Music & the 1950 Avant Garde, 1975. Contbr. to Ch. Music. Mbrships: Am. Musicol. Soc.; Coll. Music Soc.; Soc. for Ethnomusicol.; Luth. Soc. for Worship, Music & the Arts. Hobbies: Racquetball; Automobiles. Address: 6012 Tenth Ave. S, Minneapolis, MN 55417, USA.

MYSLIK, Antonin, b. 3 Sept. 1933, Humpolec, Bohemia. Musician (Clarinet); Music Researcher; Recording Director. Educ: Prague Conservatorium. m. Vlasta Bimova-Myslikova, 1 c. Debut: Chmbr. Music w. Collegium Musicum Pragense, 1963. Career: Orch. of E F Burian Theatre, Prague, 1961-69; Freelance Musician; W. Collegium Musicum Pragense Festivals in Vienna, Salzburg, Prague; Broadcasting in Vienna, Salzburg, Graz, Stockholm, W Berlin & Prague. Comps. incl: Musica Viva Historica; Reconstruction & Ed.; Antonin Vranicky: Marsche fur Harmonie, 1970. Num. recordings. Publs. incl: Haydns Jahrbuch, 1976. Contbr. to Gramorevue, Prague. Hons. incl: supraphon, Prix de la Dramaturgie. Mgmt: Pragokoncert, Maltezske nam. 1, 118 13, Praha 1. Address: Namesti Kubanske revoluce 1321/18, 100 00 Praha 10, Czechoslovakia.

N

NABARRO, Margaret Constance Dalziel Nunes, b. 16 Oct. 1923, Darwen, UK. Musicologist; Violinist; Violist; Pianist; Organist; Harpsichord Player. Educ: MMus, Univ. of Witwatersrand; DMus, Ethnomusicol., S Africa; GBSM, Dip. Ed., Univ. of Birmingham. m. Prof. F R N Nabarro, 5 c. Career: Lectr. in Musicol., Ethnomusicol. & musical appreciation; Music Critic, The Star, Johannesburg. Publs: num. rsch. papers on music of Western Sephardic Jews & Portuguese Mananos. Contbr. to: Ars Nova; S African Jewish Affairs; Estudos Gerais do Universidade de Moçcambique. Mbrships: S African Soc. of Music Tchrs.; Royal Commonwealth Soc., London. Hobbies: Cooking; Reading; Chmbr. Music. Address: 32 Cookham Rd., Auckland Pk., Johannesburg, S Africa.

NAESTEBY, Kai J Angel, b. 26 June 1920, Oslo, Norway. Violinist. Educ: studied w. Henrik Due, Odd Gruner-Hegge. m. Rigmore Karin Naesteby, 1 d. Debut: Oslo, 1947. Career: Violinist, Oslo Phil., 1944-; Soloist, ibid; Mbr. Oslo Str. Quartet, 15 yrs.; Cond., Sarpsborg Musikkforening, 1956-; Guest Cond., num. orchs. inclng. Oslo Broadcasting Orchestra. Recordings: w. num. Ensembles, inclng. own, Old-Fashioned Dance Music, Devotional Music. Hons: Mbr. Borg Symfoniorchester, 1971; Kt. of the Golden G Key, Norwegian Musicians Union, Oslo Dept., 1970; Culture Prize, Scarpsborg Town, 1973; Oslo Phil. Orch. Honour, 1977. Hobby: Fresh Air; Gardening, at Summer Cottages. Address: 11 b Edvard Griegs Alle, Oslo 4, Norway.

NAGAN, Zvi Herbert, b. 27 Oct. 1912, Gelsenkirchen-Buer, Germany. Music Teacher. Educ: BA, MA Cand., Tel-Aviv Univ.; Comp. w. Ben Haim, Tal & Berkeley. Soc. m. Rita Katz, 1 s. Career: Music Tchr., primary schl. Comps: sev. works for recorder ensemble; 7 pieces for 4 hands; music for 2 recorders, harpsichord & small orch. Mbr., Israel Comps. League; Israel Musicol. Soc. Hobbies: Playing Chamber Music; Reading. Address: 12 Frankfurt St., Tel-Aviv, Israel.

NAGEL, Robert Earl, Jr., b. 29 Sept. 1924, Freeland, Pa., USA. Musician (Trumpeter, comps., cond.) Educ: Cinn. Conserv., summers of 1938 & '41; Dip. in Trumpet, Juilliard Grad. Schl., 1942-43; BS in Comp., Juilliard Schl. of Music, 1948; MS in Comp., ibid, 1905. m. Bernice Jensen, 1 s, 3 d. Career: Freelance trumpet artist in concerts, recordings, television & film recording in NYC, 1947-68; Fndr. & Dir., NY Brass Quintet, 1954; Soloist & Chamber Music Artist in tours throughout the USA & Europe. Face. Mbr., New England Conserv. of Music, Boston, Mass., 1st Trumpet, Chautauqua Symph. Orch., Dir. of Music, Candlewood Bapt. Ch., CT., Compositions incl: Brass Trios Nos. 1 & 2; Rhythmic Studies; Trumpets on Parade; Concerto for Trumpet & Strings; Speed Studies; Studied in Contemporary Music; Hymns for Brass. Recordings incl: Concerto for Trumpet by Vagn Holmboe; Brandenburg Concerto No. 1; The Sound of Trumpets, 1977. Publs: Baroque Music for Trumpet, 1969; The Regal Trumpet, 1971. Mbrships: Co-Fndr., Int. Trumpet Guild, 1975. Contbr. to music jrnls. Mbr., var. profl. orgs. Mgmt: Columbia Artists Mgmt. Address: Broadview Dr., Brookfield, CT 06804, USA.

NAGLE, (Sister) Mary Ellen, b. 25 April 1928, Toledo, Ohio, USA. Musicologist; Pianist. Educ: B Mus, Mary Manse Coll., Toledo, 1950; M Mus (piano), 1964, PhD (musicol.), 1972, Univ. of Mich.; Dip. of Gregorian Studies, Gregorian Inst. of Paris, France. Career: Musicol. tchng. music hist., seminars in medieval & renaissance music. Mbrships: Am. Musicol. Soc.; Pi Kappa Lambda; Music Tchrs. Nat. Assn. Ohio Unit; Mu Phi Epsilon, Nat. Music Sorority. Hons: Pi Kappa Lambda, 1964; Winner, Mu Phi Epsilon Nat. Musicol. Rsch. Contest, 1972. Hobbies: Sports; Travel. Address: 415 Erie St., SE, Apt. 201, Minneapolis, MN 55414, USA.

NAGY, Robert D., b. 3 March, 1929, Lorain, Ohio, USA. Opera Singer (tenor). Educ: Cleveland Inst. of Music, 3 yrs. m. Vincenza Ianni Nagy, 1 s., 2 d. Debut: Metropolitan Opera, 1957. Career: Apps., opera houses throughout world; w. Metropolitan Opera Co., 22 yrs. Hons: Chicagoland Music Fest., 1956; 1st Male Winner of 1st Metropolitan Opera Guild (Auditions of the Air), 1957. Hobbies: Boating; Fishing. Mgmt: Mr. Peter Lustig. Address: 536 7th Ave., New Hyde Pk., Ny, Ny, USA.

NAHATZKI, Richard C, b. 15 Jan. 1949, Balt., Md., USA. Tubist. Educ: B Mus, Peabody Conserv.; Special Student, New England Conserv. Career: Brass Art Quintet, 1969-71; New England Scholarship Brass Quintet, 1971-72; Tubist, Kassel Staatstheater, German Fed. Repub., 1972-74; Solo Tuba, Saarländischer Rundfunk, 1974-; Fndr., 20th Century Brass Quintet (ensemble dedicated to perf. of modern brass comps.), 1976. Recordings: Hindemith, Tuba Sonata; Vaughan William Tuba Concerto; Gunther Schuller, Brass Quintet; Eugene Bozza, Sonatino; M Kagel, Mirum for Tuba. Hons: Full Scholarship, Peabody Conserv., 1967; Scholarship Brass Quintet New England Conserv., 1971. Hobbies: Sports Cars; Sailing; Skiing. Address: Leharstr. 22, 66, Saarbrücken 2, German Fed. Repub.

von der NAHMER, Wolfgang, b. 14 Apr. 1906, Remscheid, Germany. Professor of Music; Conductor. Educ: Dr. Hoch Conserv., Frankfurt; Prof., 1955. m. Irmingard Scheidemantel. Career: Asst., Dresden State Opera, 1932; Orchl. Dir., State Theatre, Schwerxin, 1934; Prin. Cond., Düsseldorf Opera, 1937-44; Municipal Music Dir., Saarbrücken, 1944; Prin. Cond., Cologne Opera; Hd., Schl. for Opera, State ACad. of Music, Cologne; guest apps. in concert halls & opera theatres in Spain, the Netherlands, Luxembourg, Switz.; broadcasts on German radio; Cond.; num. premieres; promoter of mod. music. Address: 52 Euskirchner Strasse, 5 Cologne-Sülz, German Fed. Repub.

NAIDITCH-COOPER, Eva, b. 28 Oct. 1907, Winnipeg, Man., Can. Pianist; Teacher. Educ: studied w. Wanda Landowska (France); Isador Philipp, Lazare-Levy, Alfred Cortot (Paris), Percy Grainger & Josef Lhevienne (Chgo.). Musical Coll. (scholarship). m. Ben Cooper, 2d. Career: perfs. w. George de Lausnay Orch., Paris, 1933, Winnipeg Symph. Orch., 1934; num. recitals in Chgo., Winnipeg, Brandon (Can.) & Los Angeles, Calif.; pvte. tchr., coach, master classes, 1942-; mbr. Applied Music Fac., Mt. St. Mary's Coll., Los Angeles. Hons: 1st prize, Concours Int. de l'Union des Femmes Artistes Musiciennes, 1932. Hobby: Music. Address: 730 N Alfred St., Los Angeles, CA 90069, USA.

NAISH, Bronwen, b. 19 Nov. 1939, Burley, Hants., UK. Solo Double-Bassist; Teacher of Cello & Bass. Educ: ARMCM; study w. Gary Karr in USA. m. Roger Best, 2 s, 3 d. Debut: King's Hall, Newcastle upon Tyne; Purcell Room, London, 1976. Career: Features on Look North, South Today, Wales Today; Interviews for BBC Radio 2; Only exponent of Gary Karr virtuoso bass technique in UK, & restricts apps. to solo perfs.; Teaches this technique & aims to project bass as total musical voice in it own right. Mbrships: European Str. Tchrs. Assn.; Int. Soc. Bassists; ISM. Hobbies: Gardening; Home Improvements. Address: Moelfre, Cwm Pennant, Garndolbenmaen, Gwynedd, UK.

NAKARAI, Charles F T, b. 25 Apr. 1936, Indpls., Ind., USA. Music Educator; Musicologist; Organist; Pianist. Educ: BA, Butler Univ., Ind., 1958; MM, ibid, 1967; PhD work, Univ. of NC at Chapel Hill, 19657-70. Career incls: Organist & Dir. of Choirs, Northwood Christian Ch., Indpls., 1954-57; Min. of Music, Broad Ripple Christian Ch., Indpls., 1957-58; Asst. Prof. of Music, Milligan Coll., Tenn., 1970-72; Pvte. Tchr. of Organ & Piano, 1972-. Comps: Three Movements for Chorus, 1971. Mbrshps. incl: Am. Musicol. Soc.; Coll. Music Soc.; Am. Guild of Organists; Music Tchrs. Nat. Assn. Contbr. to profl. publs. Recip., var. schlrships. Hobbies incl: Art. Address: 3520 Mayfair St., Bldg. 3, Apt. 205, Durham, NC 27707, USA.

NAKAS, Vytas, b. 4 Dec. 1947, Salzburg, Austria. Singer; Musicologist; College Faculty Member. Educ: BA, Roosevelt Univ., MM, Ind. Univ. Debut: Ind. Univ. Opera Theatre. Career: chosen by Xenakis for role of Coryphor in Am. premiere of Oresteia; created role of Burdovsky in TV opera Myshkin by J Eaton; Soloist, Indpls. Symph. Orch., Lithuanian Opera of Chgo., Ind. Univ. Opera Theatre; recitals in USA, Can., France & Austria. Contbr. to the Lithuanian quarterly Lithuanus. Hobby: Swimming. Address: Kaulbachstr. 68, 8 Munich 22, German Fed. Repub.

NALLINMAA, Eero Veikko, b. 14 Feb. 1917, Vanaja, Finland. Conservatory Director. Educ: Phil. D. m. Sole Raevuori, 2 d. Career: Dir., Conserv., Tampere, Finland. Comps: Opera Jaakko Ilkka; Songs; Comps. for Symph. Orch., piano, etc. Recording: Amores. Publs: Musiikillisen hahmotuksen ongelmia (Problems of the Musical Gestaltung), 1964; Erik Ulrik Spoofin nuottikirja (the Musical Manuscript of Erik Ulrik Spoof), 1969; Barokkimenuetista masurkkaan (From the Baroque Menuet to the Mazurka), 1979. Mbrships: Musicol. Soc. of Finland. Hobby: Geneal. Address: Hämeenpuisto 43-45 A 20, 33200 Tampere 20, Finland.

NANAVATY, Daulat, b. 27 Nov. 1917, Bombay, India. Musicians; Pianist; Music Critic. Educ: TCL; ram; Tobias Matthay Schl., London; LRAM; LTCL; FTCL; Licentiate, Tchrs. Training Dip. Debut: Wigmore Hall, London. Career: Prod. of

Western Music, All-India Radio, Delhi, 1958-71; Chief Prod. of Western Music, All-India Radio, Bombay, 1972-76; recitals in India, UK, France, Poland & Czech.; Tchr., Bombay Sch. of Music, 1972-; piano recitals on TV, Tehran, Shirazand, & Isfahan, 1976; radio career from 1937-76; (Vis. fellow, W Music, North-Eastern-Hill Univ., Shillong, 1977-79). Recordings: num. for radio. Contbr. to: Gramophone; da Scala; Span. Mbrships: Bombay Chmbr. Music Soc.; Time & Talents Club; Delhi Symph. Orch. Soc. Hons: FTCL gold medal; LTCL gold medal; David Nesbit prize, TCL, 1944. Hobbies: Reading; Nature; Walking; Sports; Record Collecting. Address: New India Ctr., Flat 4A, 4th Floor, 17 Cooperage, Bombay 400039, India.

NANCEKIEVILL, Paul David, b. 28 Sept. 1952, London, UK. Church Musician; Organ Recitalist. Educ: Kent Univ., 1971-73; ARCM, 1971; Musikhochschule, Cologne, 1973-76. Career: Ch. Musician Organ Recitalist, Porz, Cologne, Germany; Dir. of Music, Markuskirche, Cologne-Porz. Hobbies: Study & perf. of Renaissance music, esp. choral music; Sport Reading hist. books. Address: 31 Greenacres Ave., Ickenham, Middlesex, UK.

NANIA, Salvatore, b. 25 Nov. 1915, Catania, Sicily, Italy. Conductor; Violinist; Violist. Educ: Degree in Mod. Philol.; Dips., Violin & Viola. m. Wanda Flore, 4 c. Career: 1st Violin & 1st Viola, Concert perfs. Comps. Four Sonatas for Viola & Piano; Concert for Viola & Orch. Contbr. to Midwest Folklore (ind. Univ., USA). Mbrships: Acad. Musicale, Naples; Viola Forschungsgesellschaft, Schone Aussicht, Kassel, Germany. Hon: Deutsches Musikinstitut für Ausländer, Salzburg, 1940. Hobby: Fishing. Address: Naples, Piazza Pu, Umberto, 4-CP. 80142, Italy.

NANUT, Anton, b. 13 Sept. 1932, Kanal, Yugoslavia. Conductor; University Professor. Educ: Univ. Music Acad. m. Milojka, 2 s. Debut: w. Slovene Phil. Orch., 1954. Career: has given concerts w. major orchs. in Yugoslavia; Permanent Cond., Dubrovnik Fest.; Music Dir., Slovene Phil. Orch., Ljubljana; has given concerts in Italy, Belgiu, Austria, Czech. , Romania, Poland, Switz., Hungary, London, Germany, etc., & for broadcasting corps. in many of these countires. Mbrships: Soc. of Univ. profs.; Yugoslav. Music Artists Union. Hons. incl: Slobodna Dalmacija, 1970. Hobbies: Water sports. Mgmt: Yugokoncert, Belgrade; Concertna Direkcija, Zagreb; Caecilia, Geneva. Address: Koseze Blok B 1, 61000 Ljubljana, Yugoslavia.

NAPIER, Marita, b. Johannesburg, S Africa. Soprano singer. Educ: TCL; Norwestdeutsche Musikakademie, Detmold. m. Wolfram Assmann. Debut: Bielefeld, 1970. Career: apps. at opera houses & fests., La Scala, Rome, Florence, Covent Garden, Vienna State Opera, Lisbon, Madrid, Barcelona, Bayreuth, Hamburg, Berlin, Frankfurt, Stuttgart, Munich, Amsterdam, Cologne, Orange, Paris, Toulouse, Strasbourg, Marseilles, Geneva, Zürich, San Francisco, Minneapolis, St. Puals, Los Angeles, Miami, Toronto. num. recordings. Contbr. to: Capital; Interior; Vogue, etc. Hobbies: Reading; Archeology; Interior Decorating. Mgmt: Germinal Hilbert, Paris. Address: Bergkoppelweg 7, 2 Hamburg 63, German Fed. Repub.

NAPOLI, Jacopo, b. 26 Aug. 1911, Italy. Composer; Music Educator. Educ: S Pietro a Majella Conserv. of Music, Naples: Dips. in Compositions, Organ & Piano, Career: Prof. of Counterpoint & fugue, Cagliari Conserv. & Naples Conserv.; Dir., S Pietro a Majella Conserv., 1955-62; Dir., G Verdi Conserv., Milan; Dir., Scarlatti Arts Soc., 1955-. Compositions: Operas - Il Malato Immaginario, 1939; Miseria e Nobilita, 1946; Un curloso accidente, 1950; aNasaniello, 1953, I Pescatori, 1954; Il Tesoro, 1958; Oratorio - The Passion of Christ, Il Rosario, 1962;; Il Povero Diavolo, 1963; Piccola Cantata del Venerdi Santo, 1964; Orchl. works -Overture to Love's Labours Lost, 1935; Preludio di Caccia, 1935; La Festa di Anacapri, 1940. Address: 55 Via Andrea da Isernia, Naples, Italy.

NARCINI, Deborah Antoinette, b. 20 Apr. 1953, Trenton, NJ, USA. Mediaevalist. Educ: BA (summa cum laude), Trenton State Coll., 1975; Dip., Brooklyn Coll. Latin Inst., 1975. MTS, Harvard Univ., Cambridge, Mass., 1977; MA, MPhil, Yale Univ., 1979. Pvte. study of piano, harpsichord & voice. Career: Sev. apps. (both solo & ensemble) in local perfs., mainly of opera & early music; Organist & choir dir., St. Jame's Ch., Trenton; Currently investigating manifestations of philos. & theol. trends in mediaeval music, Harvard Univ.; Has written prog. notes & transls. Mbrships: Mediaeval Acad. of Am.; Am. Musicol. Soc.; Int. Musicol. Soc.; Delta Omicron Int. Music Fraternity; Historian of Local Chapt., 1971-74. Hons: Kate D Stout Scholarship for Grad. Study, 1975. Roothbert Fellow, 1975. Hobbies; History of the silent cinema; Painting; Sewing.

Address: 57 Main Blvd., Trenton, NJ, USA. 27, 29.

NARCISSE-MAIR, Denise Lorraine, b. 19 Jan. 1940. Kingston, Jamaica. University Professor of Music; Pianist; Harpsichordist; Choral Conductor. Educ: RCM, Assoc. Bd., Royal Scholar, 1958-61; ARCM (Pianoforte Tchng.) Hons., 1969; LRAM (Pianoforte Perf.) Hons., 1960; GRSM, 1961; Postgrad. Studies, RCM, 1961-63; B Mus. (Musicol.) Hons., Goldsmiths Coll., London Univ., 1971: PhD (Ethnomusicol.) London Univ., in progress. div. 1 d. Career incls: Tchng. piano, RCM, 1960-61; Lectr., Inst. of Educ., London Univ., 1969-70; Snr. Lectr., ibid., 1970-71; Snr. Lectr., Coord. of postgrad music courses, 1970-72; Asst. Prof., Dept. of Music, Queen's Univ., Kingston, Canada, 1972-; Assoc. Prof., ibid; 1976-; num. lectures in UK, USA & Can; Adjudicator; Cond., num. fests. & concerts worldwide. Comps: Incidental music for plays; Space Song for Infants, 1971; Tableau Vivant (musical Song for Infants, 1971; Tableau Vivant (musical drama); Arr. of 2 W Indian Spirituals for SATB, 1974. Mbr., num. profl. orgs. Address: Music Dept., Queen's Univ., Kingston, Ont. Canada.

NASH, Harold John, b. 26 Aug. 1931, Treorchy, S Wales, UK. Orchestral Musician; Teacher of Trombone & Bass Trumpet. Educ: LRAM & ARCM, 1950; ARAM, 1972. m. Elizabeth Shelley, 2 s. Career: Trombonist, RPO, 1947; Prin. Trombonist, Sadlers Wells Opera Co., 1952, & Royal Opera House, Covent Gdn., 1956-; Prof. of Trombone & Brass Tutor, RAM; Ed., Sounding Brass. Recordings: Passacajlia by Buxton Orr; 4 Pieces for 4 Trombones by Gareth Wood. Contbr. to: The Composer; Int. Trombone Fend. Mag. Mbr: Royal Soc. of Musicians of GB. Hobbies: Gardening; Preservation of Real English Ale. Address: 9 Boileau Rd., Ealing, London W5 3AL, UK. 3, 28.

NASH, Mary Frances Heddle, b. 20 Nov. 1928, Wellington, NZ. Accompanist; Repetiteur. Educ: LRAM; ARCM; ARAM. Div., 3 d. Career: worked w. BBC Radio & TV; Philips; Royal Opera House, Covent Gdn.; Engl. Nat. Opera; Engl. Opera Grp.; Engl. Music Theatre; Scottish Opera; Welsh Nat. Opera; New Opera Co.; Kent Opera; Harold Holt Pk. Lane Grp.; Chelsea Opera Grp.; London Opera Ctr.; RAM; LSO; Arts coun. GB. Mbrships: RAM Club; Musicians Union; LSM. Hobbies: Gardening; Crossword Puzzles; Sci. Fiction. Address: 38 King Henry's Rd., London NW3 3RP, UK.

NASH, Norman Graham, b. 28 July 1940, Toronto, Ont., Can. Pipe Band Side Drummer; Dance Band Drummer. Educ: Group 2 cert., Can. Army (Militia). m. Marilynne Dianne Stone, 3 d., 1 s. Career: apps. on Ed Sullivan Show, Observer TV prods.; sev. perfs. in Massey Hall, Toronto; Scottish World Fest., 1972-78. Recording: Here Comes the Famous 48th; Scottish Heritage; Octoberfest in Can. Contrbr. to Piper & Dancer Bulletin. Mbrships: Toronto Musicians Assn.; Pipers & Pipe Band Soc. of Ont. (as drummer & adjudicator). recip. num. solo drumming awards, 1955-. Hobbies: Teaching Young People Music & Drumming. Address: 26 Amberdale Dr., Scarborough, Ont. M1P 4C1, Can.

NATANSON, Tadeusz, b. 26 Jan. 1927, Warsaw, Poland. Composer. Dip., Music Educ., High Schl. of Music, Wroclaw, 1952; Dip., Comp., ibid. 1956. m. Maria Czurczak, 1 s. Career: Pvte. Lectr., High Schl. of Music, Wroclaw; Dean Instrumental Fac., ibid., 1965-; Dean, Fac. of Comp. & Music Theory, ibid.; Cathedral Dir., Comp., Music Theory; Dir., Inst. for Music Therapy, & Dept. of Musicotherapeutics. Prorector, 1975. Compositions incl: 5 Symphs.; 3 Concerti; 2 Trios; cantata Opamietajcie Sie; ballet Quo Vadis; opera Tamango; num. orchl., chmbr. works; var. music for choir & orch., choir, vocal soloists & orch. Publs: Contemporary Composers Techniques, Vol. 1, 1970, Vol. 11, 1972. Contbr. to Wiadomosci Mbrships: VP, Wroclaw Sect., Polish Comps. Union; Committee Mbr., Int. Fest. of Modern Music, Warsaw Autumn; Committee for Doctorate-Affairs, High Schl. of Music, Warsaw; Hon. Mbr., Silesian Music Soc. Recip. num. Hons. Hobbies: Car. Travel. Address: 48 ul. Wyścigowa, 53 012 Wroclaw, Poland.

NATHAN, Hans, b. 5 Aug. 1910, Berlin, Germany (US Citizen). Musicologist. Educ: Dph., Friedrich Wilhelm Univ., Berlin, 1934; postgrad. study, Harvard Univ., USA, 1936-38; pvte. study w. var. masters. m. Jael Nathan. Career: Fac. mbr., Mich. State Univ., 1946-. Prof., ibid, 1964-; Vis. Prof., Tufts Univ., 1945, Univ. of Rome, Italy, 1952-53, Tulane Univ., 1966, Inst. for Advanced Study Princeton, 1957-58. Publs. incl: Ed., The Continental Harmony (1794) of William Billings, 1961; Dan Emmett & the Rise of Early Negro Minstrelsy, 1962; William Billings: Date & Documents, 1976. Contbr. to musical jrnls. & encys. Mbr., profl. assns. Recip., num. grants, Fellowships, awards. Hobby: Horseback Riding. Address: Dept. of Music, Michigan State Univ., E Lansing. MI 48824, USA. 11, 14, 28.

NATRA, Sergiu, b. 12 Apr. 1924, Burcarest, Romania. Composer. Educ: MA, Nat. Music Acad., Bucarest, Romania, 1952; Studied Comp. w. Leo Klepper. m. Sonia Natra, 2 s., Career: Commissions of symph. works, chmbr. music, stage & film music in Romania; Maj. commissions in Israel by the Israel Fest., the Israel Phil. Orch., the Israel Radio, Israel Comps. Fund: Prof. of Comp.; Examiner for the higher musical educ., Israel Min. of Educ. & Culture, 1964-71; Commission for Testimonium, 1968. Comps. (publd.) 3 Corteges in the Street, 1945; Suite for Orch., 1948; Sinfonia for Strings, Music for Violina & Harp, Music for Harpsichord & 6 Instruments, 1964; Music for Oboe & Strings, 1965; Sonatina for Harp. 1965; Song of Deborah, 1967; Variations for Piano & Orch., 1966; Prayer for Harp. 1972; Sonatina for Trumpet. 1973; Sonatina for Trombone Solo, 1973; Sacred Service, 1976; From the Diary of a Composer. Recordings: Suite for Orch. (Electrecord-Bucarest), 1948; Music for Harpsichord & 6 Instruments (CBS, Israel); Song of Deborah (CBS, Israel); Sonatina for Harp (ARS Nova, USA). Mbrships: Romania Comps. Union, 1945-58. Committee Mbr., 1948-58. Israel Comps. League, 1961-. HOns: Georges Enesco Prize, 1945; Rumanian State Prize, 1951; Milo Prize, Writers & Artists Club. Tel Aviv, 1966; Engel Prize, Tel Aviv Municipality, 1969. Address: 10 Barth St., Tel Aviv 69104, Israel.

NATSCHINSKI, Gerd, b. 23 Aug. 1928, Chemnitz, Germany. Composer; Conductor. Educ: Coll. of Music, Dresden; Acad. of ARts, E Berlin. m. Ingeburg Raschke, 1 s., 1 d. Debut: as cond., RAdio Broadcasting Orch., Studio Leipzig, 1949. Career incls: Chief Cond., Gt. Radio Orch., E Berlin; Cond. of own comp., Messeschlager Gisela, Metropol Theatre, E Berlin, Comps: music for 65 films; 400 popular songs; orchl. works. Comp. of musicals: Messeschlager Gisela, 1960; Servus Peter, 1961; Mein Freund Bunbury, 1964; Terzett, 1974; ABC der liebe (Decamerone), 1975; Casanova, 1976. Recordings: as cond., 12 LPs & 200 singles. Contbr. to: Musik & Gesellschaft; Theater der Zeit; daily press. Mbrships: Volkskammer (Parliament) of the German Dem. Repub.; Nat. coun., ibid.; Soc. of Comps. & Musicols.; CIAM, UNESCO. Hons. incl: Nat. Prize, German Dem. Repub., 1961 & 74. Address: Ostendorfstr. 10, 117 Berlin, German Dem. Repub.

NAVARRA, André, b. 13 Oct. 1911, Biarriz, France. Violoncellist. Educ: Toulouse Conserv.; pvte. studies. Career: Tours throughout Europe and Am., solo recitalist; soloist w. all leading orch.; App. at Cheltenham Fest. in Elgar's Concerto. Address: 14 Rue de Moscou, Paris, France.

NAVARRO, Paul Louis, b. 15 Aug. 1943, Oakland, Calif., USA. Musician (French Horn). Educ: BM Horn, Ind. Univ., 1967; MMus, Horn, Western Mich. Univ., 1969. Carer: Horn Instr: Western Mich. Univ., 1967-69; Chgo. Conserv. Coll., 1970-; W. Chgo. Lyric Opera Co., 1970-; Grant Pk. Symph. Orch., 1790-; Currently w. Chgo. Chmbr. Consort, Studio, TV & film recordings in Chgo. Mbrships: Pi Kappa Lambda; Int. Horn Soc. Address: 810 Michigan Ave., Evanston, IL 60202, USA.

NAVON, Shmuel, b. 16 Aug. 1904, Dunaevzi. Russia. Musician; Supervisor of Education. Educ: Univ. educ. in psychol., educ. & philos. m. Ruth Navon, 2 s. Comps: folk songs publd. in 3 books & recorded in hundreds of records issued throughout the world, inclng. famous folk song 'Artza Alinu'. Publs: Alinu, 1936; Alinu, 1948; Artza Alinu, 1963. Mbrships: Israeli Comps. Assn.; Int. Comps. Assn.; Israeli Supvsrs. Assn.; Int. Rdng. Assn. Address: 16 Gottlieb St., Tel-Aviv, Israel.

NAYLOR, Judy Anne, b. 10 Dec. 1956, Sydney, NSW, Aust. Teacher; Librarian. Educ: B Ed, Canberra Coll. of Advanced Educ. Publs: A Reader's Guide to Music, 1977; A Union List of Music Serials held in the ACT, 1977; Union List of Music Books held in High Schl. Libraries in the ACT, 1977-78; Union List of Music Books held in Secondary College Libraries in the ACT, 1978; Secondary College Libraries & Music Curricula, 1978; A Basic Collection of Music for Secondary College Libraries, 1978-79. Mbrships: Lib. Assn. of Aust.; Northern Territory Tchrs. Fed.; NSW Tchrs. Fed.; Aust. Fellowships of Evangelical Students. Hobbies: Hockey; Playing & Teaching Guitar, Mandoline & Banjo Mandoline. Address: 36 Ocean View Dr., Terrigal 2260, Aust.

NAYLOR, Peter Russell, b.5 Oct. 1933, London, UK. Composer. Educ: MA, Cambridge Univ., 1957; B Mus, London, 1961; FRCO, 1961; ARCM, 1962. Career: Lectr., City Lit. Inst., London, 1963-65; Organist, Ashwell Fest., Herts., 1964-69; Lectr., Harmony, Couterpoint, etc., RSAMD, 1965-71; Music Assoc., Scottish Opera for Youth, 1975-. Comps. incl: Movement (organ); Eastern Monarchs; Air & Variations (2 pianos); Beowulf, symph. poem for wind band.

Clarinet Quintet; Violin Sonata; Bird Songs; Tides & Islands (orch.); The Mountain People (children's opera); Pied Piper (1-act opera). Mbr., CGGB. Hons: London Univ. Convocation Trust Prize, 1959; Ascherberg Comp. Prize, 1959. Hobbies: English Literature; Walking. Address: 216 Anniesland Rd., Glasgow G13 1XF, UK. 3, 4.

NAYO, Nicholas Zinzendorf Kofi, b. 4 Apr. 1922, Kaika-Buem, Ghana. Musician; Composer; Conductor (Piano, Brass). Educ: Tchrs. Cert. A; M Mus, Boston Univ., USA; LRSM (London); Dip. African Music (Legon); CTVCM (London). m. Comfort Addae, 6 children. Debut: 1st orchl. work played by GBC Orch., Accra, 1972. Career: 1st Dir., Nat. Acad. of Music, Winneba, 1973-75; TV apps. as cond. of 2 new works for chorus & orch. w. Nat. Acad. of Music Chorus & Orch., Accra, Ghana, 1975. Recordings incl: New Era w. GBC Symph. Orch.; 2 Choruses w. Acad. Orch. Contbr. to The Black Perspective in Music; Radio & TV Times, Ghana; African Music. Hobbies: Photography; Volley Ball. Address: Schl. of Music & Drama, Univ. of Ghana, Legon, Ghana. 25.

NAZZARO, Lou, b. 12 Feb. 1939, Dover, NJ., USA. Percussionist. Educ: BS Juilliard Schl. of Music; MA Instrumental Music, Columbia Tchrs. Coll.; Profl. Dip., Instrumental Specialist, ibid; finished course work for Ed D in Coll. Tchng. of Music, div., 2 s. Debut: Ballet Theatre, NYC. Career: pers. w. many orchs., bands, inclng: Am. Symph. Orch.; Am. Opera Soc., Carnegie Hall; Symph. of the Air; Am. Ballet; US Army Band; Juilliard Symph. Orch. & Opera Orch. Broadway musicals incl: Fiddler on trhe Roof; Funny Girl; Man From La Mancha; Charlie Brown. Var. TV spectaculars & Can. musicals, inclng: Johnny Belinda & Hamlet; Asst. Cond. & Percussionist, Holiday on Ice Show. Num. recordings inclng. ballet, symphonic musicals, musical sound tracks; Publs: Developing Afro-Jazz Rhythmic Concerts, 1979. Mbr., Musicians Union. Var. hobbies: Address: 42 McDavit Pl., Dover, NJ 07801, USA.

NEAL, Gordon, b. 6 July 1929, Wombwell, UK. Double Bassist. Educ: Royal Manchester Coll. of Music, ARMCM. Career: W the Halle Orch., 1950-52; Mbr., City of Birmingham Symph. Orch.; LSO, 1957-. Hons: Assoc., Royal Manchester Coll. of Music, 1950. Hobbies: Radio Control Model Aircraft; DIY. Address: 674 High Rd., Buckhurst Hill, Essex, IG9 5HN, UK.

NEAL, Harold, b. 31 Aug. 1916, London, Ont., Can. Church Musician; Choral & Orchestral Conductor; Violinist & Violist. Educ: BA, Univ. of Toronot, 1949; M Mus, Univ. of Ind., 1959; doctl. studies, Univ. of Mo., Kansas City. m. Margaret Imogene Hewitt, 2 s. Career: Cond., ch. choirs, community orchs., bands; Can. Army Bandmaster; Violin & Viola, Toronto Phil. Orch., 1936-53; FAc., Hd. of Music & ARts Dept., Graceland Coll., Lamoni, Iowa, 1953-66; Dir. of Music, World HQ, Reorganized Ch. of Jesus Christ of Latter Day Saints, Independence, Mo., 1969-; Dir., Independence Messiah Choir & Auditorium Chorus; Cond., Auditorium Symph. Orch.; Violinist, Auditorium Str. Quartet. Contbr. to jrnls. Mbrships. incl: ASTA; Am. Symph. Orch. League; Am. Choral Dirs. Assn. Recip. acad. hons. Hobbies incl: Horseback riding. Address: Box 178 B, Rt. I, Blue Spring, MO 64015, USA.

NEAL, Lenora Ford, b. 6 Jan. 1947, Ogden, Utah, USA. Pianist; Educator. Educ: Bm, Univ. of Utah. Carer: Fac. Mbr., Music Dept., Univ. of Utah; completed 5 month USO tour of Alaska & the Far E; has perd. w. Utah Symph. & Chmbr. Orchs.; Soloist, Utah Symph. & Ballet W. 1975; Guest Pianist, Snowbird Music Fest., 1975; Guest Perf. w. Muhlfeld Trio on tour; gives pvte. instruction. Mbrships: Music Tchrs. Nat. Assn.; Mu Phi Epsilon; Nat. Fedn. of Music. Hons. incl: Utah Concert Coun. Competition; 1st Pl., Utah State Fair Adv. Piano Competition; state & reg. piano competitions. Music Tchrs. Nat. Assn.; Best Pianist w. hon. mention, Sterling Staff Int. Competition, 1974. Address: 362 W 3300 S, Countiful, UT 84010, USA.

NEAL-SMITH, Denys John, b. 7 Aug. 1915, Richmond, Surrey, UK. Organist; Choir Trainer. Educ: Univ. of London; pvtly. w. Alec Rowley, Edgar Moy, AG Iggulden, GT Pattman AJ Pritchard; RSCM; FRCO (CHM). m. Joan Doris Wilcock, 2 s., 2 d. Career: Dpty. Organist to the Parish of Richmond, 1933-40; Dir. of Music, ibid, 1965-; Organist & Master of Choristers, St. Matthias, Richmond, 1940-; Cond., Engl. Ch. Music Singers, 1951-65; Cond. of Sunday Half-Hour (BBC) Richmond, 1963; Organist, ibid, Ham, 1973; Chmn., Richmond Upon Thames Music Fest., 1960-73; Music Dir., TV serv., Richmond, 1971; Cond., Songs of Praise, Richmond, 1978; Sev. broadcasts, Richmond Carol Fests. Contbr. to num. articles to The Organ. Mbrships: Chmn., E. Surrey Assn. of Organists, 1960-70; Chmn., W. London Soc. of Organists,

1963-69; Pres., London Assn. of Organists, 1970-72. Hobbies: Bell-ringing; Photography (of churches & organs). Address: 95 Cole Pk. Rd., Twickenham TW1 1HZ, UK. 3.

NEAMAN, Yfrah, b. 13 Feb. 1923, Sidon, Lebanon. Violinist. Educ: Primier Prize, Conservatoire National de Musique, Paris. m. Gillian Shaw, 1 s, 1 d. Debut: Salle Gaveau, Paris, 1939. Career: Recitals & concerts w. the major orchs. in most European countries, N Am., Africa & Asia; radio & TV apps. worldwide; Hd. of the Dept. of Solo Studies, GSM, London. Recrodings: Concerto by Roberto Gerhard; Concertos by Racine Fricker & Don Banks; Trios & Sonatas, by John Ireland. Publs: Ed., William Primrose, Technique is Memory; Ed., sev. works by var. comps. Mbrships: Dir., Carl Flesch Int. Violin Comp., Lond; Artistic Cons., Portsmouth Int. String Quartet; Musical Advsr., The Nat. Assn. for Gifted Children. Hons: FGSM; Freeman, Worshipful Co. of Musicians. Mgmt: Ibbs & Tillett, London, UK. Address: 11 Chadwell St., London EC1R 1XD, UK, 3, 30.

NEARY, Martin Gerard James, b. 1940, London, England. Organist; Harpsichordist; Conductor. Educ: MA., Gonville & Caius Coll., Cambridge; FRCO. m. Penelope Jane Warren, 1 d. Career: ASst. Organist - Organist & Master of Music, St. Margarets, Westminster, 1963-71; Prof. of Organ, TCL., 1963-; Organist & Master of Music, Winchester Cathedral, 1972-; num. recitals & for tours in Europe, USA & Can. Recordings: as choral cond., organist & harpsichordist (EMI Oryx & Abbey labels). Publs: incl: arr. of choral music; eds. of organ works. Mbrships. incl: Cond., Twickenham Musical Soc., 1966-72, Hons. incl: Dip., 3rd Int. J S Bach Competition, Leipzig, 1968; Hon. FTCL.; Hon. Citizen of Tex.; Prize, Int. Organ Fest., St. Albans, 1963. Hobby: Cricket. Address: The Close, Winchester, Hampshire, UK.

NEBE, Michael, b. 28 July 1947, Nordenbeck/Waldecik, German Fed. Repub. Cellist. Educ: Dip. & Tchng. qualifications, Dortmund Conserv.; MMus, King's Coll., Univ. of London; LRAM, Post Grad. studies, RAM, London. Debut: Wigmore Hall, London, 1977. Career: Mbr., Place Duo (w. Robert Bouffler), Place Consort (w. Valerie Morgan & Robert Bouffler), Chmbr. music, London; Mbr., Percy-Pryma-Nebe Trio, perfs. Britain, tours, German Fed. Repub., Holland, USA & Can.; Tchr.; Freelance musician; Translator. Publs: Translation into German of Eta Cohen's Violin Tutor, 1979. Mbrships: Solo Perfs. Sect., ISM; Musician's Union. Hons: German Music Assn. (Deutscher Musikrat) Scholarship, 1968; City of Dortmund Scholarship, 1969, '70; Peter Stuyvesant & Reemstsma Fndn. Scholarships, 1971, 73. Hobbies: REading; Comp.; Tehatre. Mgmt: Choveaux Mgmt. Address: Flat 6, 44 Nightingale Lane, London SW12, UK.

NEDBAL, Manfred Josef Maria, b. 20 Oct. 1902, Vienna, Austria. Composer; Violoncellist. Educ: MD.; Study of counterpoint, composition. m. Gertrude Knapp. Career: Violoncellist, concerts & radio perfs.; Critic; Composer. Compositions: 50 songs, 35 chmbr. music works, choral music, symphs. Recordings: Sonatine for Strings; Preludio & Fugue for Orchestra; Variations & fugue for Orchestra; Rondino for Orchestra. Contbr. to newspapers. Mbrships: IGNM; Osterr. Komponistenbund; osterr. Gesell. fur Zeitgenossische Musik; VP & Chmn., Culture Sect., Austro-Czech Soc. Hons: Chmbr. Music Prize, IGNM, 1949; Choir Prize, City of Vienna, 1952; Title of Prof., Austrian Govt., 1965; Silver Medal, City of Vienna, 1973. Smetana Medal 1975. Hobbies: Riding; Bridge; Stamps. Address: A-2500 Baden, Peterhofg 8, Austria.

NEDYALKOV, Hristo, b. 1 Sept. 1932, Dryanovo, Bulgaria. Choral Conductor. Educ: Bulgarian State Conserv. m. Dobrina Nedyalkova, 1 s. Career: Cond.; Children's Choir of Bulgarian Radio & TV; num. apps., stage, film, TV & radio. Comps: num. childrens songs. Num. recordings. Editor, Musical Collections. Mbrships: Union of Bulgarian Comsp.; Union of Bulgarian Musicians. Hons: Honoured Artist of Bulgaria, 1972-. Hobby: Fishing. Address: 5 Malusha Str., Sofia 1164, Bulgaria.

NEEDHAM, Hilary Margaret, b. 31 Dec. 1934, Manchester, UK. Piano Teacher; Pianist. Educ: scholarship to RCM; ARCM (perfs.); LRAM (tchng.); LGSM (perfs.). m. Godon C Waddingham, 2 s. Debut: Manchester. Career: radio broadcasts while aged 8-15 yrs.; before marriage performed in Mancheaster, Stockport, Blackpool, Salford & Lond; currently gives concerts for charities; Tchr., Manchester, London, E Grinstead. Mbrships: ISM; Soc. of Women Musicians; Ctrl. Bd., Vice-Chmn., London & Home Cos. Area Coun., Brit. Fedn. of Music Fests. (inc. Music Tchrs. Assn.); Chmn. & Piano Sec., E Grinstead Music & Arts Fest.; Royal Stuart Soc.; RCM Union; Elgar Fndn. Recip. exhib., RCM, 1954; European Piano Tchrs. Assn. Hobbies: Scottish dancing & hist.; Travel; Geology; Walking; Gardening. Address: 'Donary' 45 Fairlawn Dr., E Grinstead, Sussex, UK.

NEEDHAM, Louise (Chapman), b. 24 Feb. 1938, Brandon, Can. Professor of Music; Pianist. Educ: BA, Brandon Univ.; Assoc. Mus, Piano Perf. Univ. of Man.; Grad. Dip. Music, Brandon Univ.; M Mus, Ind. Univ., USA. m. Lucien Needham. Career: Solo recitals; Chmbr. music recitals Concerto perfs. w. orch. Adjudicator & Examiner. Mbrships: Can. Assn. Univ. Schls. of Music; Can. Assn. Univ. Tchrs.; Can. Fedn. of Music Tchrs. Assn.; Alta. Registered Music Tchrs. Assn.; Am. Fend. Musicians. Recip., Orchard Memorial Scholarship in Music, 1957. Hobbies: Travel; Reading; Gardening; Cooking. Address: 20 Ave. S, 1533 Lethbridge, Alta., Can.

NEEDHAM, Lucien, b. 5 Apr. 1929, Hull, Yorks., UK. Professor of Music; Conductor; Pianist. Educ: Guildhall Schl. of Music, London; AGSM; ARCM; GGSM. m. M Louise Chapman. Debut: London. Career incl: Frequent concert, radio & TV appearances as cond. & pianist in Western Can. & on CBC; Examiner, Western Bd. of Music; Festival Adjudicator, Can. & USA; Lecture-recitals, etc.; Prof. of Music, Univ. of Lethbridge. Compositions: Christmas Gradual; The Fields Abroad (both SATB a capella). Contbr. to var. music jrnls. Mbrships. incl: past Pres., Man. & NW Ont. Area Coun. of Music Festivals; Past Pres., Man. Registered Music Tchrs. Assn. Hons. incl: Fellow, Guildhall Schl. of Music, 1965; Grants & fellowships from Can. Coun. Nuffield Fndn. & Brit. Coun. Address: Univ. of Lethbridge, Canada, 9, 129, 130, 139.

NEEL, Louis Boyd, b. 19 July 1905, K. Conductor. Medical Practitioner; University Professor. Educ: MA., Gonville & Caius Coll., Cambridge Univ.; MRCS; LRCP. St. George's Hosp., Career: Qualified & parctised as Dr. of Med.; Fndr. & Cond., Boyd Neel Orch., 1933-; Appearances at Salzburg Festival, 1937; Tour of Portugal, 1939; Returned to med. work during WWII; Tours w. orch. of Europe, Australia & NZ., N. Am., 1947-52; Guest cond., Glyndebourne festival 1934, Sadler's Wells Opera, 1945, D'Oyly Carte London Seasons, 1948-49, Edinburgh Festival 1948, 1951, Mayer Children's Concert, London; Dean, Royal Conserv. of Music, Toronto, Canada, 1953-71; Formed Hart House Orch., 1954, w. perfs. at Brussels World Fair, 1958, tours of Canada & Europe, EXPO 67, Montreal. Recordings of num. works. Hons: CBE., Hon. RAM Order of Canada. Publ: The Story of an Orchestra, 1950. Address: c/o York Club, 135 St. George St., Toronto, Ont., Can.

NEES, Vic, b. Mar. 1936, Mechelen, Belgium. Composer; Conductor. Educ: Conservatoire of Antwerp. m. Lea de Keersmaecker, 2 d. Career: Regular Radio Apps. as Cond., BRT Chorus. Compositions: (publd.). European Stabat Mater; Rachel Mammon; Vigilia; Birds & Flowers For Flor's & William's Birthday; (recorded) Five Motets; Gezelle-Songs. Contbr. to Vlaams Muziektydschrift; Adem; Gamma. Mbrships: SABAM; CVKV. Hons: Albert De Vleeshouwer Prize, 1960; Eugene Baie Prize, 1973. Hobby: Literature. Address: 7 Max Havelaarlaan, 1850 Grimbergen, Belgium.

NEGRI, Vittorio, b. 16 Oct. 1923, Milan, Italy. Conductor. Educ: studied comp.; cond., & violin, Milan. m. w. 3 c. Career: Asst. cond., Salzburg Mozarteum, 1952; guest cond., ldng. orchs. in Europe; apps. at fests. in Flanders, Salzburg, Montreux, Versailles, Orange, Sagra Musicale Umbra, etc. num. recordings inclng. music by Mozart, Vivaldi & comps. of Venetian Baroque. Mbrships: fndr. mbr., Italian Soc. of Musicol. num. awards for recordings. Mgmt: Anne Armes, 19 New End, London NW3, UK. Address: Chemin des Cuarroz 8, 1807 Blonay, Switz.

NEIDLINGER, Gustav, b. 21 Mar. 1912, Baritone Singer. Educ: Opernschule, FrankfurtMain. Career: apps., Stadttheater Mainz, Stadttheater Plauen, Staatsoper Hamburg, Staatsoper Stuttgart, Bayreuth Fest., Deutsch Oper Berlin, La Scala Milan, Covent Gdn., London, Grand Opera St. Carlo Naples; currently mbr. of Staatsoper Stuttgart. 16.

NEILL, William, b. 17 March, McAllen, Tex., USA. Opera & Concert Singer (Tenor). Educ: Bmus, MMus, Univ. of Texas at Austin, 1966 & 68; pvte. vocal study w. Joseph Frank Poùhe. m. Dixie Ross Neill, 1 s. Debut: Steuermann in Fliegende Hollander, Essen, German FEd. Repub., 1968; Tamino in Magic Flute, Portland, Oire., USA, 1970. Career: World premiere of Bruno Madern's Satyricon (Trimalchoi), Amsterdam, 1973 (filmed for Amsterdam TV); Lohengrin in San Francisco, 1978; Title role, Can. premiere of Peter Grimes, Toronto, 1980; Perf. over 30 leading roles w. major cos. in Europe, USA, Can. & S Am.; Leading roles in over 10 world or Am. premieres, etc. Hons: San Fran. Opera Auditions, 1967; Metropolitan Opera Auditions, 1965; Martha Baird Rockefeller Grant, 1968, 69. Hobbies: Family; Travel. Mgmt: Shaw Concerts, Inc., NY, USA. Address: 780 Riverside Dr., 5-F, NY, NY 10032, USA.

NEILSON-FRANSEN, Janis, b. 13 Apr. 1943, Toronto, Ont., Can. Pianist. Educ: Univ. of Toronto; ARCT, Royal Conserv. of Music, Toronto; Aspen Summer Schl.; Siena w. Guido Agosti & Alfred Cortot; fac. of music, Toronto, w. Harvey Olnick & John Beckwith. m. Delbert Fransen. Career: pianist for Nat Ballet of Can., 1967-74; pianist for Sol Hurok Concerts Inct., 1974-75 (Royal Swedish Ballet, Stuttgart Ballet); pianist for Joffrey Ballet, 1976-78; prin. pianist, Nat. Ballet Schl., 1979-. Publs: arr. rehearsal scores etc., for ballet cos. Mbr. AFM. Hons: pianist for num. dancers dirs. incl: Nureyev, Erik Bruhn, John Cranko, Roland Petit, Elio Field, Robert Joffrey. Hobbies: Knitting; Cooking. Address: 8 Laurier Ave., Toronto, Ont. Can.

NELSON, Douglas Raymond, b. 17 Jan. 1934, Boyd, Wis., USA. College Professor. Educ: B Mus., Univ. of Colo., Boulder; MA, Stanford Univ., Calif.; PhD., Univ. of NC., Chapel Hill; Postgrad. study, Univ. of Oslo, Norway, Univ. of Vienna, Austria & Univ. of Mich., Ann Arbor. Career: Perfs. in opera theatre, musical comedy; Ch. soloist; Prof. of Music & Chmn., Div. of Fine Arts, Limestone Coll., Gaffney, SC Contbr. to Grove's Dictionary of Music & Musicians. Mbrships: Am. Musicol. Soc.; AAUP; MENC; Music Tchrs. Nat. Assn.; Phi Mu Alpha Sinfonia. Recip., schlrships., Univs. of Colo., Stanford, NC & Oslo. Hobbies: Writing; Drama; Tennis; Table Tennis; Classic Mystery Writing. Address: 100 Victoria Lane, Gaffney, SC 29340, USA.

NELSON, Havelock, b. 25 May 1917, Cork, Ireland. Conductor; Accompanist (piano); Organist; Composer; Adjudicator; Broadcaster; Writer; Examiner. Educ: MA., MSc., PhD., Trinity Coll., Dublin Univ.; Pvte. tuition & Royal Irish Acad. of Music, Dublin; D Mus.; LRAM. m. Hazel Guthrie Lutton, 2 s., 1 d. Career: Served in RAF, 1943; Joined the BBC (Northern Ireland), 1947; Cond., Studio Symph. Orch.; Dir., Ulster Singers; Artistic Dir., Studio Opera Grp.; I V - 'Songs of Praise' (as cond.). 'The Nelson Touch', 'Portrait of a Mu ician', 'Sounding Voices', 'Music for Pleasure', all series. Comps. incl: orchl. works, ballet, choral suite, song cycles, choral works, works for piano, radio plays, TV plays, films. Recordings: Celtic Songs (w. Veronica Dunne); Highlights of Irish Opera (cond.); Irish Rhythms (cond.); She Moved through the fair (pianist); Irish Songs of Praise (cond.). Mbrships: Pres., Brit. Music Soc.; Bd. Mbr., Fend. of Music Fests.; ISM. Hons: OBE; Fest. of Britain, 1951; Radio Eireann Carolan Composition Prize, 1950; MusD, Queen's Univ., Belfast, 1977. Hobbies: Theatre; Cine-photography; Swimming; Travel. Address: 30 Rosetta Pk., Belfast 6, UK.

NELSON, Jon, b. 24 Aug. 1936, Okmulgee, Okla., USA. Professor. Educ: B Mus., M Mus., Univ. of Tulsa, Okla.; grad. work Hochschule fur Musik, Stuttgart & Munich, Germany, Univs. of Wis., Okla., Calif., Wash. Career: Recitalist & Symph. Soloist, var. orch. inclng. 7th. Army Symph. Orch.; Apps. w. New Rochelle Symph., Okla. City Symph., Enid-Phillips Symph., Tri-State Symph., etc.; Recitals, Kan. City, Tulsa, Seattle, Calif., NY., Germany, etc.; currently Prof., musicol. & piano, Phillips Univ., Enid, Okla. Recordings incl: Rachmaninoff 2nd. Piano Concerto in C minor, Op. 18; Shostakovich Piano Concerto No. 2; Poulenc Piano Concerto; Franck Symphonic Variations. Mbrships: Phi Mu Alpha; Kappa Delta Pi; Okla. MTA; Nat. MTA; Am. Musicol. Soc. (specialty: 19th & 20th Century Music); Okla. Music Educators Assn.; Okla. Educ. Assn. Hons: Theodore Presser Fndn. Schlrship., 1952; Chandler Schlrship., 1954. Hobbies: Herpetol. & Zool.; Engl. Hist.; Philos.; Poetry; Swimming; Writing. Address: P O Box 2162 Univ., STn., Enid, OK 73701, USA.

NELSON, Louise, b. 10 Mar. 1902, London, UK. Singer. Educ: TCL, London, FTCL.; ATCL. Debut: Queens Hall, London. Career: Soprano; Operatic & Lieder Singer; Radio broadcasts, UK, Germany & S. Africa; Soloist, Chamber Music & Orchl. Soc.; Num. Recitals; Soloist, Metropolitan Opera Co. Mbr., Soc. Women Musicians, London Adjudicator for solo & choral singing, British Fedn. of Music Fest. Recip., Grosvenor Gooch Prize, 1926. Hobby: Tennis. Address: 7 Grove Ave., Tunbridge Wells, Kent TN1 1UP, UK.

NELSON, Peter, b. 27 May 1932, Ripon, UK. Secondary uchool Music Teacher. Educ: MA/Queen's Coll., Cambridge, 1955; Cert. Ed., Univ. of Leeds, 1956; LGSM, Tchng. of Singing, Orchl. Conducting, 1969; LRAM; ARCM; LTCM. m. Margaret Whitaker, 2 s. Career: Music Master, Ossett Grammar Schl., Yorks, 1956-59; Leeds Modern Schl., 1969-63; Lectr.-Prin. Lectr. in Music, Trent Pk. Coll. of Educ., Barnet, Herts., 1963-74; Hd. of Music Dept., Townsend C o E Comprehensive Schl., St. Albans, Herts., 1974-; Cond; Enfield Choral Soc., 1971-. Mbrships: Schl. Music Sect., ISM. Recip., W Riding of Yorks. Co. Music Schlrship., 1950. Hobbies: Semi-profl. solo singing as baritonetenor; Woodwork, inclng. musical instrument making; Painting & Sketching. Address: 95 Byng

Dr., Potters Bar. Herts EN6 1UJ, UK.

NELSON, Philip Francis, b. 17 Feb. 1928, Waseca, Minn., USA. Music School Dean. Educ: AB, Grinnel Coll., 1950; Am, Univ. of NC., 1956; PhD, ibid. 1958; Dip., Univ. de Paris, France, 1957; Conserv. Nat. de Paris, 1956-57. m. Georgia Ann Nelson, 1 s., 1 d. Career incls: Asst. Prof.-Assoc. Prof., Dept. of Music, Ariz. State Univ., Temple, 1958-63; Music Critic, Phoenix Gazette, Ariz., 1958-61; Dir. of Music, Ascension Luth. Ch., Scottsdale, Ariz., 1959-63; Prof. of Music & Dept. Chmn., Harpur Coll., SUNY at Ginghamton, 1963; Dean, Schl. of Music, Yale Univ. Publs. incl: Nicolas Bernier, a Resume of his Work, 1960; Principes de Composition de M Bernier, Paris 1961-62, transl. NYC 1964; Gen. Ed., Symposium (Coll. Music Soc. Jrnl.), 1966-69. Contbr. to var. profl. jrnls. & publs. Mbrships incl: AAUP; Am. Musicol. Soc.; Coll. Music Soc. (Nat. Coun. 1965-71); Int. Musicol. Soc.; Soc. Françcaise de Musicol. Hons: Fulbright Scholarship, Paris, 1956-57; Recip., var. rsch. grants, Ariz. State Univ. & SUNY at Binghamton. Hobbies: Model Building; Swimming; Golf; Sailing. Address: 870 Prospect St., Hamden, CT 06511, USA. 2, 11.

NELSOVA, Zara, b. Winnipeg, Man., Can. Cellist. Educ: studied in London. Debut: w. Malcolm Sargent at age 13. Career: num. apps. in Italy, Spain, Portugal, Switz., Holland, UK, USA & Scandinavian countries. Address: 300 Ctrl. Pk. W. New York, 24, NY, USA.

NEMENYI, Lili, b. 28 Nov. 1908, Iglo, Hungary, Vocalist; Dramatic Artist (Soprano). Educ: Hungarian Acad. of Music. Debut: Sluj, Romania, 1922. Career: Teatrul Magiar, Cluj, 1922-28; Magyar Szinhaz, Favorosi Operetts-zinhaz, Budapest, 1928-32; Csckonai Szinhaz, Debrecen, Hungary, 1936-40; Hungarian Opera House, 1945-68; Britten, Albert Herring (Lady Billows); Guest apps.; Belgium, France, UK, DDR, USA, China, Romania, Poland, Yugoslavia, Czechsolovakia, Mongolia, Austria; Radio, TV perfs., Hungary, Romania, Shanghai. Recordings: Opera, operetta, Bartok & Kodaly songs. Mbrships: Soc. of Music Artists of Hungary; Hungarian Theatrical Assn. Hons: Golden Order of Labour, 1956, '70; Merited Artist of Hungarian Peoples Repub., 1957; Honoured Artist, ibid, 1967. Hobbies: Singing chanson; Sculpting. Address: Tanacs korut 13-15, 1075 Budapest, Hungary VII.

NEMES, Katalin, b. 5 Oct. 1915, Debrecen, Hungary. Pianist. Educ: Piano Tchrs. Dip., Music Acad., Budapest (as student of Béla Bartòk). m. György Nemes, 1 s., 1 d. Debut: Hungary, 1937. Career: Radio apps. & concerts, Hungary, France, Italy, USSR, mostly 1945-; Repertoire includes works by romantic comps., Beethoven. & contemporary Hungarian & foreign comps.; Prof., Piano Dept., Music Acad., Budapest, 1951-. Recordings: Works by Chop, Schubert, Schumann, E Dohnányi & M Mosonyi (19th century Hungarian comp.). Publ: Ed., Piano Pieces from Mid-European Music. Mbrships: Fndn. mbr., Liszt Ferenc Soc.; Hungarian Assn. of Musicians. Hons: Liszt Ferenc Prize, 1962. Hobbies: Cooking; Gardening. Address: Budapest II, Palánta u. 1a, Hungary.

NEMESCU, Octavian, b. 29 Mar. 1940, Pascani, Romania. Composer; Lecturer, University of Brasov. Educ: Comp. Dip., Conserv. of Bucharest; DMusicol., 1978. m. Erica Nemescu. Comps. incl: Sonata for Clarinet & piano, 1962; Triangle for big orch., 1964; Ego (multi-media perf.), 1970; The Play of Senses. A music for a pair of ears, of eyes, of hands, a nose & a mouth, 1973-76; Cromosom. imaginary music, 1974; Natural!! music in space, 1974; Calendar, permanent music for the environment of a room, 1976; Semantica, metamusic for lovers of music, 1978. Recording: Polyrithmies; Concentric. Mbr., Comps. Union of Romania. Contbr. to jrnls. Recip. Aaron Copland comp. prize, 1970. Address: Bu. Dinicu Golescu 23-25, BL B, Scara 3, Ap 65, Sector VII, Codul 77112, Bucharest, Romania. 4.

NEMET, Mary Ann, b. 10 June 1936, Budapest, Hungary. Violinist. Educ: A Mus A, Univ. Conservatorium, Melbourne, Studied w. Stella Nemet, Max Rostal & Arthus Grumiaux, div. 3 children. Debut: Beethoven Violin Concerto w. Sydney Symph. Orch., 1955. Career: Concert tours, radio & TV apps. in Aust. & Far East; Toured most European countires w. pianist Roxanne Wruble (Duo Landolfi); Appointed to Sydney Conservatorijm, 1970; Soloist, E Germany, 1972; Ldr. of Nemet String Trio & Piano Quartet, London; Chmbr. music & solo work throughout Aust.; Lectr. in Strings, Victorian Coll. of the Arts. Num. recordings. Address: c/o Victorian Coll. of the Arts, 234 St. Kilda Rd., Melbourne 3004, Vic., Aust.

NEMETH, Gyula, b. 17 July 1930, Budapest, Hungary. Conductor. Educ: Acad. of Music, Leningrad. m. Anina Bitzerhadi, 2 c. Debut: w. Leningrad Phil. Orch., 1957. Career: Ast. cond., Leningrad Phil. Orch.; cond., Santiago Symph.

Orch., Chile; cond., orchs. in Germany, Bulgaria, Poland, Czech., Chile, Yugoslavia, Portugal, UK, Venezuela, Peru, Cuba & Turkey. Recordings: about 24 LPs. incl. Golden Disc of Liszt pieces. Hon: Hungarian Liszt prize. Hobbies: Swimming; Fishing; Skin Diving; Gliding. Mgmt: Interkoncert, Budapest. Address: Budapest, 1146 Abonyi utca 8, Hungary.

NENDICK, Josephine Anne, b. 2 Feb. 1931, Sevenoaks, UK. Singer. Educ: RCM. Debut: Aldeburgh Fest., 1957. Career: concerts & broadcasts throughout Europe; num. fest. apps.; has given premieres of works by Boulex, Berio, Bussotti, Barraque & others; num. works written especially for her. Recordings: Muza; EMI; Argo (Decca); Valois. Mbr., ISM. Hobbies: Walking; Travel; Cooking; Interio Decoration. Mgmt. Ltd. Address: Flat 3, 9 Ennismore Gdns., London SW7 1NL, UK.

NERBE, (Nils Hugo) Lennart, b. 20 Feb. 1917, Tysteberga, Sweden. Conductor; Musician (Piano, Clarinet, Violin). Educ: RAM. m. May Hallen, 4 children. Debut: w. Stockholm Radio Orch., 1948. Career incls: Perfs., Stockholm Orchl. Soc., Swedish Radio Orch., Gothenburg Orchl. Soc., Co. Gavleborg's Orchl. Soc., Norrkoping Orchl. Soc. & Stockholm Promenade Concerts. Recordings: Tapes for Swedish Radio. Hons: Stockholms Kulturnamnd, 1958, '74; Konstnarsstipendienamnden, Stockholm, 1964, '71, '75. Hobbies: Swimming; Tennis. Mgmt: Svensk Konsertdirection, Henrik F Lodding, Junigatan 27, 415 15 Goteborg. Address: Atterbomsvagen 32, 112 58 Stockholm, Sweden.

NESBITT, Dennis, b. 23 Feb. 1919, Monkseaton, Whitely Bay, UK. Cellist; Performer on Viola da Gamba & Tremble Viol. Educ: RCM. m. Nancy B Neild. Debut: Phil. Soc., Newcastle-on-Tyne. Career: lectures & recitals on TV, USA, Switz., Finland, Portugal, France, Germany, Netherlands, Aust. & England; Prof. RAM, London. Comps: arrs. recorded on HMV & Columbia. Recordings: HMV; Columbia; Philips; Decca; Argo; Vogue; Westminster; Pye; Arco. Publs: The Viol Family; Makers of English String Instruments. Mbrships. incl: Dir., Elizabethan Consort of Viols, Fidelio Quartet, Music & Dance & Pro Arte Orch. Recip., Hon. ARAM; MSSA, Switz. Hobbies: Farming; Antiques; Donkey Breeding. Address: 5 Cranmore Way, London N10, UK. 4.

NESCHLING, John Luciano, b. 13 May 1947, Rio de Janeiro, Brazil. Conductor; Pianist. Educ: Seminários de Musica Pro-Arte, Rio de Janeiro; studied Choral & Orchl. Cond. w. Prof. Hans Swarosky, Acad. for Music & Performing Arts, Vienna, Austria, studied w. Leonard Bernstein, Berkshire Music Ctr., Tanglewood, USA. Debut: w. Nat. Symph., Rio de Janeiro, 1968. Career: Concerts w. Major European Symph. Orchs., in Berlin, Vienna, Lisbon, Bratislava & Florence, & w. all Brazilian Orchs.; Concerts w. Berkshire Music Ctr., Orch., USA; Cond.; operatic perfs. in Tanglewood & Lisbon; TV perfs. in Rio de Janeiro, & Radio broadcasts in Brazil & Europe. Comps: music for Penna, Desgraçcas de Uma Criançca, 1973; music for Dumas, Dama das Camélias, 1974; Film Music for Os Condenados, 1973. Hons: Assoc. Cond., Symph. Orch. of Porto-Alegre, Brazil; Critics' Award for Best Cond., Brazil, 1969; Prize Winer, Int. Competition, Florence, Italy, 1969; Prize Winner, Int. Competition of London Symph., UK, 1973. Mgmt: Spectrum, Nüremberg, Germany; Project Int. Music, London, UK. Address: Rua Alm. Saddock de Sá 133C-02, ZC-37, 20.000 Rio de Janeiro, Brazil.

NESERITIS, Andreas, b. 30 Nov. 1897, Patras, Greece. Composer. Educ: STudied w. Denis Lavrangas, Conserv. of Athens, Greece. m. Rena Skoufou. Compositions incl: 3 Symphs.; (operas) King Aniliagos, Hero & Leander; Symphonic Music; Instrumental Music; Vocal Music. Mbrships: Pres., League of Greek Comps. Hons: Award, Acad. of Athens, 1952; Gold Cross, 1965 Silver Medal, Acad. of Athens, 1971; 1st Prize Fine Arts Acad. of Athens, 1975. Hobby: Gardening. Address: Eptanissou 54, Athens 807, Greece, 19.

NESS, Arthur J., b. 27 Jan. 1936, Chgo., Ill., USA. Musicologist; Clarinettist; Composer. Educ: Bm, Univ. of Southern Calif., 1958; AM, Harvard Univ., 1961; PhD cand., NY Univ. Career: Prof. of Music, Univ. of Southern Calif., 1963-75; Prog. Annotator, LA Concert Assn.; Chmn., Dept. of Music, Daemen Coll., 1976-. Publs: The Lute Works of Francesco da Milano, 1971. Contbr. to: Groves Dictionary. Mbrships incl: Sec.-Treas., Southern Calif., Chapt. Am. Musicol. Soc.; Int. Musicol. Soc.; Music Lib. Assn.; Coll. Music Soc.; Lute Soc. of Am.; Lute Soc. Recip. of Fulbright Fellowship (Germany), 1965-68. Hobby: Horticulture. Address: 184 Campus Dr., Amherst, NY 14226, USA.

NESTAAS, Eirik, b. 9 Feb. 1948, Bergen, Norway, Cellist; Ciochemical Engineer. Educ: M Sc. Schl. of Chemistry, Univ. of Trondheim, 1974; Cello student, Nordwestdeutsche Musikakademie, Detmold, German Fed. Repub., for 3 yrs. from 1970. m. Anna Maria Busse Nestaas, 1 d. Debut: Trondheim, 1974. Career: Num. concerts, mainly of chmbr. music, Germany & Norway, 1970-; Radio & TV apps.; Mbr., Trondheim String Trio & Trondheim Str. Quartet. Recreations: Family Life; Travelling. Address: Romulslia 58, 7000 Trondheim, Norway.

NETHSINGHA, Lucian Alaric, b. 3 May 1936, Colombo, Ceylon. Cathedral Organist; Conductor. Educ: RCM; FRCO; ARCM; LRAM; MA, King's Coll., Cambridge. m. Jane Symons, 1 s., 1 d. Career: Organist & Dir. of Music, St. Michael's Coll., Tenbury, Worcs., 1959-72; Organist & Master of the Choristers, Exeter Cathedral & Cond., Exeter Musicol. Soc., 1973-; num. radio & TV broadcasts as organ recitalist & choral cond. Recordings: w. choirs of St. Micheal's Coll. & Exeter Cathedral. Mbrships: Coun., RCO; Royal Musical Assn. Hons: Gold Medals for piano, TCL, 1952 & Assoc. Bd., 1953. Mgmt: Mrs. J Goldsbrough, Lower Haresbrook, Tenbury Wells, Worcs. Address: 11 The Close, Exeter, UK.

NETOLICKA, Karel, b. 23 Nov. 1929, Vilimovec, Czechoslovakia. Assistant Principal Bass, Milwaukee Symphony Orchestra. Educ: studied violin & clarinet as a child; studied bass w. Rudolf Tulácek, State Conserv. of Music, Brno, Czechoslovakia, for 5 yrs.; at Janácek Acad. of Music, Brno, for 4 yrs. m. Libuse, 1 s., 1 d. Debut: Brno, 1950. Career: gave many recitals during student yrs.; Prin. Bass, Symph. Orch. SOKB, Brno, 1951-52 & Army Opera, Prague, 1953-55; w. Radio Symph. Orch., Prague, 1955-68; Symph. Orch., Munich, German Fed. Repub., 1968-69; Milwaukee Symph. Orch., 1969-70; Oslo Phil., Norway, 1970-71; Asst. prin. Bass, NC. Symph., USA, 1971-72; & Milwaukee Symph. Orch., Wis., 1972-; did some teaching while in Czechoslovakia; tchr. of bass, Wis. Univ., 1977-; played wld premiere of bass concerto by Jiri Mindle, dedicated to Netolika, 1976. Hobby: Walking in the country; especially mountains. Address: 176 N. 67th St., Milwaukee, WI 53213, USA.

NETTL, Bruno, b. 14 Mar. 1930, Prague, Czechoslovakia. Musicologist. Educ: AB, Ind. Univ., Bloomington, 1950; MA, ibid, 1951; PhD, 1953; MALS, Univ. of Mich., Ann Arbor, 1960. m. Wanda White, 2 d. Career: Instr. in Music, Wayne State Univ., Detroit, Mich., 1953-54; Asst. Prof. of Music, ibid, 1954-56, '59-64; Assoc. Prof. of Music, Univ. of Ill., Urbana, 1965-67; Prof. of Music, & Anthropol., ibid., 1967-. Publs. incl: Music in Primitive Culture, 1956; An Introduction to Folk Music in the US., 1960; Cheremis Musical Styles, 1961; Theory & Method in Ethnomusicology, 1964; Folk & Traditional Music of the Western Continents, 1965, 2nd edn., 1972; Daramad of Chahargah, a study in the perf. practice of Persian music, 1972; Contemporary Music & Music Cultures w. C Hamm & R Byrnside, 1975; Eight Urban Musical Cultures, 1978. Contbr. to var. prof. publs. Mbrships: Pres., Soc. for Ethnomusicol., 1969-71; Ed., Yearbook of the Int. Folk Music Coun., 1974-77.Ed., ibid, 1960-64; Am. Musicol. Soc.; Int. Folk Music Coun.; Int. Musicol. Soc. Hons: Fulbright Fellowships, Germany, 1956-58 & Iran, 1968-69. Address: 1423 Cambridge Dr., Champaign, IL 61820, USA. 2.

NEUBAUER, Vlastimil, b. 7 Mar. 1923, Berehovo, Czechoslaovakia. Tympanist. Educ: studied law, Charles Univ., Prague; Gard., Prague Conserv. div. Career: Prin. Tympanist, Icelandic symph., opera & radio orchs., & Prof. at Conserv., Czechoslovakia; Tympanist, Icelandic State Symph. Orch., Reykjavik, 1969-. Mbrships: Icelandic Musician's Union; Am. Symph. Orch. League; Percussive Arts Soc. Icelandic Symph. Orch. Mbrs.' Club; Brit. Soc. for Music, Therapy. Hobby: Nature. Address: Sunnuvegur, 23, Reykjavik, Iceland.

NEUBERT, (Ernst) Günter, b. 11 Mar. 1936, Crimmitschau, German Dem. Repub. Compser; Soudn Control Technician. Educ: pvte. study of violin, piano & organ; Conserv. of Leipzig, 1954-55, Conserv. Hanns Eisler, Berlin, 1955-60; Dip. as Sound Control Techn., 1960; Extgramural student in comp. w. Prof. Wagner-Regeny, 1960-65; qualified in tchng. of theoretical subjects in music, Conserv. of Berlin, 1965-67; master classes w. Profs. Wagner-Regeny & Paul Dessau, Acad. of Arts in GDR, 1968-71. m. Emmi Bauer, 3 d. Career: Sound Control Techn., Rundfunk, Leipzig, 1960-. Has had 14 works publd. or recorded; Prin. Works: Chmbr. music, choral works, vocal symphonic; music for radio & TV. Mbrships: Soc. of Comps. & Musicols. in GDR; Kommission für Kammermusik und Sinfonik in Berlin. Address: 2 Arthur-Hausmann-Str., 7021 Leipzig, German Dem. Repub.

NEUBURGER, Hans, b. 3 Feb. 1934, Amsterdam, Netherlands. Musician; Viola. Educ: Amsterdam Conserv. m. Carla van Dantzich, 2 s. Debut: Amsterdam, 1953. Career incls: Prin. Vila, Radio Filharmonisch Orkest, Hilversum, 1960-;

Mbr., Gaudeamus Str. Quartet; Solo apps., GB, Can., Germany, Finland, Netherlands; Radio apps., BBC, CBC, RAdio Helsinki, Radio Hilversum, N German Radio, Hamburg, W. German Radio, Cologne; Tchr., Conserv. of Arnhem, Netherlands. Recording: Gaudeamus Str. Quartet, works by George Crumb, Enrique Raxach & Ton de leeuw. Mbrships: ESTA, Netherlands; Register of Netherlands Musicians. Hobby: Collecting mod. graphic art. Mgmt: Fndn. Gaudeamus, Postbox 30, Bilthoven, Netherlands. Address: Speenkruidstraat 11, Soest, Netherlands.

NEUGEBAUER, Hans, b. 17 Nov. 1923, Karlsruhe, Germany. Regisseur; Producer; Stage-Designer. Educ: Studied piano & voice. m. Martina Neugebauer, 2 children. Debut: Hd. of Prod., City Opera, Heidelberg. Career: Hd. of Prod: Kassels, 1962-64; Cologne Opera House, 1964-; Guest Prof: 5 Festivals at Glyndebourne, Wiesbaden, Shwetzinger; Opera Prods: Chgo.; Berlin; Trieste; Geneva; Copenhagen; Tokyo; Frankfurt on Main, etc.; Regisseur of World Premier, Die Soldaten by B A Zimmermann, Cologne, 1965. Publs: Transls. of operas for Ricordi (Macbetto, Barbiere). Schott Sons (Faust's Damnation) in German. Hobbies: Conducting; Tennis. Address: Voigtelstrasse 23, 5 Koeln 41 (Cologne), Germany. 3.

NEUHAUS, Max, b. 9 Aug. 1939, Beaumont, Tex., USA. Composer; Percussionist. Educ: B Mus., Manhattan Schl. of Music, 1961; M Mus., ibid, 1962. Carer: US Tour w. Contemp. Chmbr. Ensemble cond. by Pierre Boulez, 1962-63; Percussion Soloist touring USA & Can. w. Karlheinz Stockhausen, 1963-64; Solo Recital, Carnegie Recital Hall, NYC, 1964 & 65; Artistin-Res., Univ. of Chgo., 1964-65; 15 Solo Recitals in major European cities & Spoleto Fest., Italy, 1965-66; Rev. Fisitor, Bell Telephone Labs., Murray Hill, NJ, 1968-69; 25 realizations of WAter Whistle & other works, USA & Can., 1970-74; Prem. installation of Walkthrough, Metropolitan Transporation Bldg., NYC, 1973. Comps: Listen (1-5), 1966-69; Public Supply (1-5), 1966-73; Fan Music, 1967; Bi-Product (1, 2), 1966-67; American Can (1, 2), 1966-67; Drive-in-Music, 1967-68; Telephone Access, 1968; Water Whistle (1-17), 1971-74; Walkthrough, 1973. Recordings: Electronics & Percussion, 5 Realizations by Max Neuhaus (BCS); Fontana Mix-Feed; K, Stockhausen's Zuklus for Solo Percussionist (Wergo). Contbr. to num. jrnls. Hons. incl: Fndn. for Contemp. Performing Arts, 1965; Creative Artists Pub. Serv. Prog., 1974. Address: 210 Fifth Ave., New York, NY, 10010, USA.

NEULS-BATES, Carol, b. 1 Dec. 1939, NY, NY, USA. Musicologist. Educ: BA, Wellesley Coll., 1961; PhD, Yale Univ., 1970. m. William Boulton Bates, Jr., 1 d. Career: Instructor, Univ. of Conn., 1966-68; Asst. Prof., Hunter Coll., CUNY, 1973-75; Adjunct Asst. Prof., Brooklyn Coll., CUNY, 1978-; var. admin. & cons. appointments. Publs. incl: co-author, Women in American Music: a bibliography of music & literature, 1979; var. articles on women musicians in USA. Contbr. to: Notes (Jrnl. of the Music Lib. Assn.); Ms. mag. Mbrships: Coll. Music Soc.; Am. Musicol. Soc.; Music Lib. Assn.; Sonneck Soc. Hons: Junior Sterling Fellow, 1963-64; Wellesley Scholar, 1961; var. rsch. grants & fellowships. Address: 145 E 16th St., New York, NY 10003, USA. 5.

NEUMANN, Friedrich, b. 30 Oct. 1915, Salzburg, Austria. Composer; Musical Theorist; Teacher for Composition. Educ: Univ. of Vienna; Mozarteum, Salzburg; studied comp. w. J N. David, Leipzig; cond. class w. Clemens Krauss, Abendroth; musicol. studies, Univ. of Graz; Doctorate (Federhofer), 1958. m. Gerda Keller, 3 c. Career: Theory Tchr., Mozarteum, 1947; Comp. class at Acad. of Music in Vienna, 1966; Extraordinary Prof., 1968; Ordinary Prof., 1972; Chief of Dept. for Comp., Music Theory & Cond., Hochschule fur Musik und Darstellende Kunst, 1972-. Compositions incl: Sinfonia in Sol for Orch.; Concert for Str. Orch.; Launische Empfindung & Melancholie for mixed chorus; 4 str. Quartets; 5 Sonatas for Piano; Quintet for Wind Instruemnts. Recordings: Concert for Str. Orch., Preiser Records. Publs: Synthetische Harmonielehre, 1951; Tonalität und Atonalität, Versuch einer Klärung, Landsberg am Lech, 1955; Die Zeitgestalt, eine Lehre vom musikalischen Rhythmus, 1959; Die Tonverwandtschaften, Phänomen und Problem 1973, etc. Mbr. var. profl. orgs. Address: Lambrechtgasse 10/12, 1040 Vienna, Austria. 14.

NEUMANN, Karl, b. 12 Aug.1903, Prostejov, Czech. Professor Emeritus of Music; Cellist; Violist da Gamba. Educ: LLD, Univ. of Prague; MFA, Carnegie Inst. of Technol., Pitts., Pa. m. Editha S Schlanstedt. Career: Co-Fndr., Antique Players, Pitts., Pa. & Chief Gambist, ibid.; num. apps. throughout USA, in London, Paris & at Brussels World Fair; Prof. Emeritus, Univ. of Southern Miss. Recordings: w. Antique Players, Classic Eds. Contbr. to: Miss. Recordings: w. Antique Players. Classic Eds. Contbr. to: Music Revue; Jrnls. of Am. Musicol. Soc. & Viola dea Gamba Soc. of Am.; Southern Quarterly. Mbrships: Pres.,

Am. Viola da Gamba Soc., 1964-69; Am. Musicol. Soc.; Hon., Engl. Viola da Gamba Soc. Hobbies: Reading; Writing. Address: 315 Beverly Lane, Hattiesburg, MS 39401, USA.

NEUMANN, Klaus L, b. 19 Aug. 1933, Innsbruck, Austria. Musicologist; Radio Producer. Educ: studied musicol. at Hamburg & Kiel. m. Ingeborg Rindfleisch, 1 s., 1 d. Career: Music Off., Deutsches Rundfunkarchiv Frankfurt/Main, 1964-71; Hd., Sound Archives, WDR Cologne, 1971-76; Hd., Early Music Dept., ibid., 1976-. Recordings: num. as prod. Publs: Oktavmelodik bei Naturvölkern und in alter Volksmusik, 1963. Contbr. to Fonoforum. Address: Westdeutscher Rundfunk, Alte Musik, Postfach 101950, 5000 Cologne 1, German Fed. Repub.

NEUMANN, Vaclav, b. 29 Sept. 1920, Prague, Czechoslovakia. Conductor. Educ: Prague Conserv. Career: Viola player w. Smetana Quartet; Czech Phil. Orch.; Dpty. cond. for Rafel Kubelik, 1948; Cond., orchs. in Karlovy Vary & Brno; Cond., Prague Symph. Orch., 1956-63, Prague Phil., 1963-64; Chief Cond., Komische Opera, Berlin, 1957-60; Cond., Leipzig Gewandhaus Orch. & Gen. Music Dir., Leipzig Opera House, 1964-67; Cond., Czech Phil. Orch., 1967-68; Chief Cond., ibid, 1968-; Tours of Europe & UK., 1964, USA & Japan. Hons: Nat. Prize of German Democratic Repub., 1966; Honoured Artist, 1967. Address: Prague 1, -Stare Mesto, Siroka 10, Czechoslovakia.

NEUMANN, Věroslav, b. 27 May 1931, Citoliby, Czechoslovakia. Composer. Educ: Grad., Acad. of Musical Arts, Prague, 1954. m. Jana Hoskova, 2 d. Career: Cond. & Artistic Dir., sev. youth ensembles, Prague, 1947-; Sec., Gen. Sec. & Pres., Union of Czechoslovak Composer, 1962-69; Prof., Popular Conserv., Prague, 1969. Comps: The Chimney Opera, 1965 (also made into TV Film, Czech TV, Prague); Panorama of Prague (3 symph. pictures for baritone & orch.), 1962; Ode for Symph. Orch., 1965; The Solitary Woman (4 songs for soprano & piano), 1964; Invitation to a Cocktail (orch.), 1967; 5 Pieces for 2 violins, 1968; String Quartet, 1969; Green Years (Children's 2 partsongs 2. 2 violins & piano, 1961; The Lament of Ariadne Abandoned, according to Monteverdi (female choir), 1970; In Memoriam to Pablo Neruda (Mixed Choir), 1975; num. children's songs & choral pieces. Hons: Winner, var. competitions for comp. of songs & choral pieces. Address: Smeralova STr. 9, 170 00 Prague 7, Czechoslovakia.

NEUMEYER, Fritz, b. 2 July 1900, Germany. Professor Music; Harpsichordist; Composer. Educ: Univs. of Cologne & Berlin; Study w. F. Bosche, A von Fielitz, J Kwast & W Klatte. Career: Cond., Saarbrucken Municipal Theatre, 1924-27; Ldr., Saarbrucken Assn. for Early Music & Harpsichordist, 1927; Mbr., Chmbr. Trio for Early Music (w. Scheck & Wenziger), 1935-62; Lectr., HS. for Music, Berlin, 1933-44; Prof. of Histl. Keyboard Instruments, HS for Music, Freiburg/Breisgau, 1946-69; Concert harpsichordist w. Capella Coloniensis & Wiener Solisten & duo on histl. keyboard instruments w. Rolf Junghanns, 1968-. Compositions incl: Ballads, songs, choral works, 4 Meditations for String Trio. Recip: Johann; Stamitz Prize; Bundesverdienstkreuz. Hobby: Collection of old keyboard instruments. Address: 78 Freiburg/Breisgau, Silberbachstrasse 21, German Fed. Repub.

NEUPERT, Hanns, b. 22 Feb. 1902, Bamberg, Germany. Piano & Harpsichord Manufacturer. Educ: Univ. Studies: Physics, Music & Piano-bldg. m. Emma Hartmann, 1 d., 2 s. Career: Harpsichord Maker, J C Neupert, Bamberg, Nuremburg, in workshops for histl. keyboard instruments. Publs: Vom Musikstab zum modernen Klavier, 1924, 4th ed. 1956; The Clavichord, 1965. Contbr. to Ency., Musik in Geschichte und Gegenwart. Hon. Mbr., Soc. Music Rsch., 1953-. Address: 86 Bamberg, Am Knöcklein 9-13, German Fed. Repub. 14.

NEVEL, Eva Mary, b. 13 Aug. 1924, Binghamton, NY, USA. Teacher. Educ: B Ed., Cortland State Coll. for Tchrs., 1945; Additional courses, Syracuse Univ., Oneonta State Coll. for Tchrs., Cornell Univ.-towards Ny State Certification in Admin. & Spvsr. of Elem. Educ.; Univ. of Scranton; var. Courses, Broome Commun. Coll., Baptist Bible Sem. & Practical Bible Trng. Schl.; B Mus Ed., Syracuse Univ., 1951; MM (Mus Ed), ibid, 1960; Num. additional adv. credits & study, ibid: NY State Cert. to teach any area of music, vocal & instrumental. Career: Tchr., Jr. high, vocal music, ibid, 1967-70; Tchr., vocal music grades 4-6, 1970-; Min. of music & ch. musician, (clarinet & trombone); vocal soloist & sometime mbr., Ginghamton Choral Soc.-perf. in the World Premier of John Peterson's Christmas Contata, 'The King of Kings', 1973, & in the 1st choir & orch. presentation of 'The Last Week', 1974. Compositions: Chorus, 'Glorify God Together'; Song, 'Love is Kind', Publs: 'An Intermediate Grade Chronology' (hist. & cultural chart for classroom use). Mbrships: Charter mbr., Cortland Chapt.,

Kappa Delta Pi, 1945; Beta Iota Chapt. Pi State, Delta Kappa Gamma, 1969; Life mbr., Nat. Educ. Assn.; MENC & NY Schl. Music Assn.; ZPres., Sec. & var. cttees., Binghamton Tchrs. Assn.; Pres., Intermediate Assn. of Childhood Educ. in Binghamton, 1956. Hobbies: Experimenting with new musical instruments; Travel; Photography; Outdoor life. Address: Box 1, Pennsylvania Ave. RD2, Binghamton, NY 13903, USA. 23, 27, 29.

NEVILLE, David James, b. 3 Sept. 1949, Cardiff, Wales, UK. Composer; Conductor. Educ: BSc; MA (Cantab). m. Diana Rosemary Neville, 1 s. Career: BBC Broadcast, 1978; Elgar Festival, Hereford, 1980. Compositions: The Canle Indoors (Chorus & Orch.); The Wreck of the Deutschland (Solo, Chorus & Orch.). Contbr. to: Catholic Herald. Address: 28 St. Agnes Rd., Heath, Cardiff, Wales, CF4 4AD, UK.

NEVILLE, Diana Rosemary, b. 23 Dec. 1949, Manchester, UK. Soprano. Educ: BA, Special Hons., Music, Bristol Univ.; Royal Northern Coll. of Music, Manchester. m. David James Neville, 1 s. Career: BBC TV Soloist, Bach Christmas Oratorio, Dec. 1977; Former BBC Northern Singers soloist, NW Engl. Mbr., Incorp. Soc. of Musicians. Address: 28 St. Agnes Rd., Heth, Cardiff, Wales, CF4 4AP, UK.

NEVILLE, Margaret, b. 3 Apr. 1939, Southampton, UK. Opera Singer (Lyric Soprano). Educ: ARAM. m. John Neville Mould. Debut: Royal Opera House, Covent Gdn. Career: Sadlers Wells Opera, 7 yrs.; Cologne Opera; Guest apps: Covent Gdn.; Glyndebourne; Scottish Opea; WNO; Barcelona; Aixen-Provence; Dusseldort; Berlin; Hamburg; Roles incl: Pamin, Zerlina, Susanna, Despina, Gilda, Norina, Gretel; Num. recitals for BBC Music Prog.; Several TV apps. Recordings: Gretel in Hansel & Gretel (HMV). Recip. Mozart Memorial Prize, 1962. Hobby: Walking w. Basset called Henry. Mgmt: Lies Asconas, London; Robert Schulz, Munich. Address: 15 The Ave., Bedford Pk., Chiswick, London W4, UK.

NEW, Leon John, b. 8 June 1933, London, UK. Music Educator. Educ: BA (music), Christ's Coll., Cambridge; music tchrs. cert., London Univ. Inst. of Educ. Career: wide experience of schl. music tchng. in UK inclng. Hd., Music Dept., Bramcote Hills Grammar Schl., Notts., 1964-67; Educ. Off., Zambia, 1967-70; Dir. of music., Nairobi Schl., Kenya, 1970-72; Sr. lectr. in Music, Univ. of Nigeria, 1973; acting Hd. of Dept., ibid., 1975-; rsch. worker into W African cert. examinations in music; recording & transcribing Igbo music. Contbr. to: Music Tchr.; Aust. Jrnl. of Music Educ.; papers at confs. of Int. Soc. of Music Educators. Mbrships. incl: Soc. of Authors; Royal Soc. of Musicians; London Buddhist Soc.; Royal Overseas League (life mbr.). Hobbies: Tennis; Chess; Travel. Address: 16 N Park, Eltham, London SE9, UK. 23, 28.

NEWANDER, Mary Clarice, b. 17 Sept. 1935, St. Louis, Mo., USA. Music Educator; Coloratura Soprano; Piaist. Educ: AB, 1967, MA Educ (Music Educ), 1963, Ed.D. Music Educ., 1976, Wash. Univ., St. Louis, Mo. Career: Grad. Asst., Wash. Univ., St. Louis, 1963-64, 1964-65; Univ. Fellowship, ibid. 1965-66. Contbr. to: Opera Kit for the Elementary Schl: Hansel & Gretel. Mbrships: Mu Phi Epsilon; MENC; Mo. Music Educators Assn.; Am. Musicol. Soc.; NEA; Int. Folklore Fedn. of St. Louis Inc.; Soc. for Ethnomusicol.; Swedish Coun. of Am.; Swedish Pioneer Histl. Soc.; Slavic & E European Friends. Hons: Mbr., Mo. State Coun. on the Arts, 1971. Hobby: Operatic Singing. Address: 587 Westborough Pl., Webster Groves, MO 63119, USA. 29.

NEWBERRY, Andrew, b. 17 Nov. 1949, Chesterfield, Derbyshire, UK. Organist; Conductor. Educ: Chorister, Kings Coll., Cambridge Univ.; Organ Scholar, Selwyn Coll., Cambridge Univ., 1968-71; MA; RCO, 1967-68; FRCO (CHM); ADCM, 1975. Career: Asst. Master of the Music, Peterborough Cathedral, 1971-; BBC broadcast servs. & Continental tours, 1975, 76, as organist w. cathedral choir; BBC broadcast recital, 1975; Organ recitals throughout UK, inclng. Scottish tours, 1975, 76; Asst. Cond., Peterborough Phil. Soc. Chmn.; local organists' assn.; Cond. St. Peter's Singers; Pt.-time Tchr., Oundle Schl. & adult educ. Recordings: 2 LPs w. Cathedral Choir. Mbrships incl: RCO; RSCM; ISM; Hobbies: Travel; Current Affairs. Address: The Vineyard, Minster Precincts, Peterborough PE1 1XU, UK.

NEWMAN, William S, b. 6 Apr. 1912, Cleveland, Ohio, USA. Musicologist; Author; Pianist; Composer. Educ: BS, 1933, MA, 1935, PhD, 1939, Western Reserve Univ., Cleveland, Ohio. m. Claire Louise Murray, 1 s. Debut: Cleveland, 1928. Career incl: fac., University of NC, Chapel Hill, 1945; Prof., ibid., 1955; Alumni Disting. Prof., 1962; retired 1977. Publs. incl: The Sonata in the Baroque Era, 1959; The Sonata in the Classic Era, 1963; The Sonata since Beethoven, 1969; Ed., var. critical

eds. of Baroque & Classical Sonatas. Contbr. to Grove's Dict., 6th ed.; Ebciclopedia della musica; Musical Quarterly; Notes; Jrnl. of Am. Musicol. Soc.; Music Review; Music & Letters, etc. Mbr. num. profl. socs. Hobbies: Automobile Mechanics; Chess; Literature. Address: Univ. of N Carolina, Chapel Hill, NC 27514, USA.

NEWMAN, Yvonne, b. 2 Mar. 1924, Buxton, Derbyshire, UK. Singer; Pianist. Educ: LRAM; ARCM; LGSM. m. (1) T R Dean, (2) B Walker-Smith, 2 s. Debut: Royal Fest. Hall, London. Career: D'Oyly Carte Opera Co.; Merrie England, Princes Theatre; Glyndebourne Opera; BBC Singers; Contgralto Soloist, BBC Panel, var. Broadcast, Promenade Concerts. Recordings: Decca; RCA. Mbrships: ISM; Adjudicator, Brit. Fedn. of Music Fests. Recip. Silver Medal, GSM, 1946. Address: 709 Clive Ct., Maida Vale, London 39, UK.

NEWMARK, John, b. 12 June 1904, Bremen, Germany. Accompanist. Educ: Hond. D Mus, McGill Univ., Can.; Studied w. Anny Eisele, Leipzig. Recordings on Decca, Club du Disque, Pathe-Marconi, RCA Victor, Folkways, Westminster, Radio-Can. Transcriptions. Hons: Off. of Order of Can.; Grand Prix du Disque (w. Kathleen Ferrier), 1952. Hobby: Painting. Address: 3261 Forest Hill Ave., Apt. 47, Montreal, Canada H3V 1C4.

NEWSON, Roosevelt Jr., b. 30 Aug. 1946, Rayville, La., USA. Concert Pianist; Teacher. Educ: BMus, Southern Univ., 1968; M Mus, Peabody Conserv. of Music, 1971; DmusA, ibid, 1977. m. Ethel Rae Whitaker Newson, 2 c. Career: Perfs. throughout USA; Toured Europe, 1978; many radio & TV perfs. inclng. cablevision lecture-perfs. Publs: A Stylistic Analysis of the Solo Piano Music of George T Walker (b. 1922). Hons. incl: Ford Fndn. Fellow, Peabody Conserv.; Winner of sev. local piano competitions; Winner, Triad Presentations, Inc., Annual Auditions, 1978; Belin Arts Award, 1978. Hobbies: Carpentry; Reading. Mgmt: Affiliate Artists Inc., NYC. Address: 12 S Broadway, Balt., MD 21231, USA.

NEWTON, Betty, b. 12 May 1922, Stockport, UK. School Teacher. Educ: Teaching Dip., Emergency Trng. Coll., Risley; extra-mural studies, Piano & Aural Trng., Northern Schl. of Music, Manchester; studied Recorder w. D A Bamforth; Perfs. Lic., TCL; Recorder courses, USA. Career: Hd. of Music, Gt. Moor Jr. Schl., 1955; Dpty. Hd., ibid., 1970; Fndr. Mbr., 1969, & now Vice-Prin., Stockport Recorder Coll.; Asst. Tutor, NW Recorder Workshop, Univ. of Wash., USA, 1974; Jt. Organiser, recorder mettings for jr. schl. children. Contbr. to Northern Recorder Mag. Mbr., Soc. of Recorder Players. Hobbies: Travel; Books. Address: & Holly Rd., High Lane, Nr. Stockport, Cheshire SK6 8HW, UK.

NEWTON, George, b. 18 Jan. 1908, Kankakee, Ill., USA. Teacher of Singing; Choral Director; Singer (Bass-baritone). Educ: AB., Princeton Univ.; Juilliard Grad. Schl., NYC m. Melba Nesbit, 1944, 1 d. Debut: Recital, NY, 1933. Career: Am. Vocal Quartet, 1930-33; Soloist, Chautaugua Inst., 1930, '33; Soloist w. Indpl. Symph. Orch., many times; Soloist, num. choral orgs. in E. & Midwest US; Song recitalist; Ch. Choir Dir.; Pvte. Voice Studio, Indpls., 1933-; Artist-tchr., Chmn., Voice Dept., Ball State Univ., 1936-74; Lect. & Recitals at vocal workshos, etc., throughout US. Contbr. to num. music publs. Mbrships: Regional Gov., Nat. Assn. of Tchrs. of Singing, 1956-60; Bd. of Dirs., ibid, 1967-74; Organizer, Ind. Chapt.; Nat. MTA; Ind. MTA; Am. Musicological Soc. Hobbies: Tennis; Squash; Bridge; Bowling; Reading. Address: 747 N. Graham Ave., Indpls., IN 46219, USA.

NEWTON, Harold R, b. 10 Oct. 1906, Chicago, Ill., USA. Violist; Violinist; Teacher; Conductor. Educ: BM (violin). m. Naomi Hendricsk, 4 s. Career: Violist, Soloist, w. sev. orchs. inclng. Chgo. Symph.; Chmbr. music w. Northwestern Univ. Fac. Quartet; Tchr., Northwestern Univ. Schl. of music, DePaul Univ., Wheaton Coll., Univ. of Tampa, Fla.; Cond., Little Symph. or Chgo. & others. Num. recordings w. var. orchs. Mbrships: Am. String Tchrs. Assn.; Am. Fedn. of Musicians. Hobbies: Woodcarving; Fishing. Adddress: 3935 Harrisburg St., NE, St. Petersburg, FL 33703, USA.

NEWTON, Ivor, b. 15 Dec. 1892, London, England. Pianist-Accompanist. Career: concert tours of all 5 continents w. artists from Dame Nellie Melba & Maria Callas, & from Ysaÿe to Yehudi Menuhin & Casals. Recordings: HMV; Decca. Publs: At the Piano - Ivor Newton, 1966. Recip. of CBE.; FRCM. Hobby: Idling. Address: Kirsten House, Kinnerton St., London SW1, UK. 1.

NEWTON, Raymond Nicholson, b. 4 June 1944, Sunderland, UK. Instrumentalist (Double Bass, Violone & Bass Guitar). Educ: RMCM & RNCM; ARNCM; Int. Schl. of Virtuoso Bassists. BBC Symph. Orch.; apps. on TV & radio. Contbr. to Jrnl. of Int. Soc.

of Bassits. mbr., Int. Soc. of Bassists. Hobby: Walking. Address: 1 Kings Ave., Bromley, Kent BR1 4HN, UK.

NEWTON, Rodney Stephen, b. 31 July 1945, Birmingham, UK. Composer; Conductor; Timpanist & Percussionist. Educ: Studied Timpani & Comp., Birmingham Schl. of Music, 1962-67. m. Jennifer K. Williams. Career: BBC Trng. Orch., Bristol 1967-68; Freeland w. RPO, BBC Symph. Orch. & other major orchs., 1970-73; Sub-Prin. Percussionist, English Nat. Opera Orch., 1973-79; Co-Prin., ibid., 1979-; Percussion tutor to var. Educ. Committees; has cond. chamber concerts incl. own comps. Comps. incl: 9 Symphs.; Operas, The Shadowbride, Legend of King Kenelm & Titus Groad; Ballet, The Story of Jacob; Meditation for Brass; Wind Quintet. Recordings w. var. orchs. incl. Locke Brass Ensemble. Contbr. to: Music & Musicians; Newsleter of Havergal Brian Soc. Mbrships: Havergal Brian Soc.; Performing Right Soc.; CGGB; Elim Pentecostal Ch. Hons: Wangford Fest. Comp. Prize, 1977. Hobbies: Astronomy; Horse Riding. Address: 13 Chetwynd Ave., E. Barnet, Herts EN4 8NG, UK. 29, 30.

NEZERITIS, Andreas, b. 30 Nov. 1897, Patras, Greece. Composer. Educ: Conserv. of Athens. m. Irena Skoufou. Career: Apps. as comp., Nat. Lyric Scene, Nat. Orch., radio. Comps. incl: 2 opera, The King Aniliagos & Hero & Leander; 3 symphs.; concertos for str. orch., wioln & orch., piano & orch.; ballet music for str. orch.; Two Greek Rhapsodies (full orch.); Greek Dance Suite on Cyprian themes; Five Psalms of David (4 soloists, mixed chorus, orch.); vocal music; piano music; etc. Mbr., Union of Greek Comps. Hons: Gold Cross, Order of King George 1st, 1965; Silver Medal & Prize, 1971, 1st Prize in Fine Arts, 1975, Acad. of Athens. Hobby: Gardening. Address: Eptanissou 54, Athens (807), Greece. 19.

NIBLOCK, James F, b. 1 Nov. 1917, Scappoose, Ore., USA. Composer; Violinist; Teacher; Administrator. Educ: BA & BEd, Wash. State Univ.; MA, Colo. Coll.; PhD, Univ. of Iowa. m. Ruth Helen Beall, 1 s., 1 d. Career: Mbr., Beaumont String Quartet, 1948-63; Concertmaster, Lansing Symph., 1962-64; Prof., Mich. State Univ., 1948-; Chmn., Music Dept., ibid., 1962-. Comps. of over 70 maj. works, w. 24 publis. Mbrships: ASCAP; Phi Kappa Phi; Pi Kappa Lambda; Phi Mu Alpha; Phi Delta Kappa. Publs: Music for the High School Chorus, 1967. Hobbies: Flying; Sports. Address: 215 Elizabeth St., E Lansing, MI 48823, USA. 2, 8.

NICA, Grigore, b. 14 Oct. 1936, Ploiesti, Romania. Composer; Editor. Educ: Ciprian Porumbescu Conserv., Bucharest; grad., Bucharest Conserv. m. Anca Rodica, 1 d., 1 s. Debut: (as comp.) Symph. for large Orch., 1969. Career: Musical ed., Romanian Radiotelevision; author, num. radio & TV progs. Comps incl: The Good Soldier Svejk, for oboe, clarinet, harp, soprano & percussion, 1973; 4 songs for voice & piano (1975); (recorded comps); 3 Sketches for orch.; concerto for violin & orch.; Suite for orch.; Piano sonata; Cello sonata; 2 str. quartets. Contbr. to Muzica Review. mbr. Comps. Union of Romania. recip. 2nd prize, Ion Vidu contest; 2nd prize, choir comp. contests. Hobbies: Swimming; Cycling. Address: Calea Calarasi Rd. 109, Sect. 3, 74101, Bucharest, Romania.

NIC⁻, Carter, b. 5 Apr. 1940, Jacksonville, Fla., USA. Conductor; Violinst. Educ: B Mus., Eastman Schl. of Music, 1962; M Mus., Manhattan Schl. of Music, 1964. m. Elizabeth Nice, 2 c. Debut: NY Carnegie, 1965. Career: currently Asst. Cond. & Concertmaster, New Orleans Symph.; Prof., Loyola Univ. Recordings w. New Orleans Symph. Hobbies: Sailing; Golf; Tennis. Address: PO Box 15465, New Orleans, LA 70175, USA.

NICHIFOR, Serban, b. 25 Aug. 1954, Bucharest, Romania. Composer. Educ: Bucharest Acad. of Music; comp. w. Aurel Stroe & Doru Popovici; cello w. Serafim Antropov & Radu Aldulescu. Comps. incl: Source for solo voices, choir & orch., 1978; Gloria, for choir & orch., 1978-79; Constellation, for orch., 1977; Shadows, for orch., 1979; Anamorphosis, for str. quartet (1976); Trois Nouvelles Impressions, for flute, cello & harp, 1979. Contbr. to: Muzica. Mbrships: Romanian Comps. Union; GEMA, W Berlin. Hons: 1st prize, Gaudeamus Int. Comps. Competition, Netherlands, 1977; prize winner, Comps. Competition, Int. Choral Congress, Tours, France, 1977; ISCM Prize, Athens, 1979. Hobby: Skiing. Address: Blvd. Dr. Petru Groza 41, Ap. 1, 76241 Bucharest, Romania.

NICHOLAS, John Kenneth, b. 16 April 1923, Penrith, Cumberland, UK. Director of Music; Organist; Pianist. Educ: Royal Manchester Coll. of Music; ARMCM; GRSM. m. Betty Jean Lawton, 1 s., 1 d. Career: Dir. of Music, St. Phillips Grammar Schl., Birmingham; Cond., St. Philips Singers; BBC TV & ITV Appearances, 1971, 72 & 75. BBC Radio Broadcasts, 1972, 73 74, 75, & 76; Tour of France, April 1974. Tour of

Ital, 1975. Compositions: Jacobs Ladder)for soloist, chorus & orch.); Anglican Responses in Tudor Style; Introits; Settings of Anglican Communion Serv. Recordings: recordings of St. Philips Singers, 1959, '72; Carols from St. Philips, 1972; Palestrina Mass, Missa Aeterna Christi Muneri w. Motets, 1974; Music of Engl. Renaissance to 20th Century. Hons: 1st Anglican to conduct in St. Peters Basilica, Rome; Presented Gold Medal by Pope Paul VI, 1975. Hobbies: Car Maintenance; Woodwork; Cine Photography. Address: 31 Weymoor Rd., Harborne, Birmingham, UK.

NICHOLAS, Louis Thurston, b. 2 Oct. 1910, Trimble, Tenn., USA. Professor of Music, George Peabody College for Teachers; Tenor; Pianist; Conductor. Educ: AB., Southwestern at memphis, 1934; M Mus., Univ. of Mich., 1939; Dip., Specialists in Music Educ., Tchrs. Coll., Columbia Univ., 1952. m. Sarah Elizabeth Lacey, 3 s. Career: Recitalist, 36 progrs. without repetitions incl. a series of. 8 histl. lecture-recitals covering 7 centuries & 10 countries & 3 on important song cycles; has made num. apps. as oratorio & orch. soloist. Contbr. to many profl publs. inclng: Chapt. in CHoral Director's Guide (Neidig & Jennings, eds.), 1967; Cricit, Music Editor, The (Nashville) Tennessean, 1951-75. Mbrships. incl: Fellow, Am. Inst. of Vocal pedagogy, holder of many offs., inclng. Pres., 1962-63; Nat. Assns. Tchrs. of Singing; Am. Acad. Tchrs. of Singing; phi Mu Alpha, Sinfonia; Music Tchrs. Nat. Assn.; MENC. Hobby: Collecting Recordings; music & books. Address: 207 Craighead Ave., Nashville, TN 37205, USA. 2, 11, 12.

NICHOLAS, Michael Bernard, b. 31 Aug. 1938, Isleworth, Middx., UK. Cathedral Organist. Educ: MA., Jesus Coll., Oxford Univ.; FRCO. (CHM); studied privately w. John Webster & C H Trevor. m. Heath G. Rowdon, 2 s. Career: Organist & Choirmaster, Louth Parish Ch., Lincs., 1960-64; Organist & Choirmaster, St. Matthew's Ch., Northampton & Cond., Northampton Bach Choir, 1965-71; Organist & Master of the Choristers, Norwich Cathedral, 1971-. Pt.-time Lectr. in Music, Univ. of E Anglia, 1971. Recordings: In Quires & Places Where They Sing. No. 4, St. Matthews, Northampton & No. 9, Norwich Cathedral; Christmas Music from Norwich Cathedral, 1974; Organ Favorites; Six Pieces by H. Howells; Favorite Hymns & Anthems. Publs: Sightsinging, 1966; Muse at St. Mathew's, 1968. Contbr. to Organists' Review. Mbrships: RCO; Norfolk Guild of Organists; Cathedral Organists Assn. Hobbies: Sailing; Bridge; Politics; Drinking real ale. Address: 53a The Close, Norwich NR1 4EG, UK.

NICHOLAS, Robert Michael, b. 8 Oct. 1945, Frome, UK. Instrumentalist (Trumpet & Related Instruments). Educ: LRAM; ARCM. m. Marian Elizabeth Clark, 1 s., 1 d. Debut: Crosby Civic Hall, 1976 (recorded by BBC). Career: 2 TV apps. w. Atarah's Band; Trumpet Player, Royal Liverpool Phil. Orch. (also Flugel Horn, Cornet, Post Horn & Piccolo B-flat Trumpet). Recordings: w. Atarah's Band & Liverpool Brass Ensemble Recip., Cousin's Mem Medal, 1964. Hobbies: Squash; Riding; Judo; Swimming; Reading. Address: Haven, 5 Birkey Lane, Formby, Lancs., UK.

NICHOLLS, John Whitburn, b, 16 Oct. 1916, Bendigo, Vic., Australia. Organist. Educ: Chorister, St. Paul's Cathedral, Melbourne; FRCO; ARCM. m. Jean Howarth Harris. Career: City Organist, Hobart Tas.; Organist & Master of Choristers, St. David's Cathedral, Hobart; Examiner, Schls. Bd. of Tas. & Australian Music Examinations Bd.; Adjudicator; Lectr.; Broadcaster; Cond. Address: 23 Kunama Dr., Kingston, Tas., Aust. 3, 15.

NICHOLLS, Leslie John, b. 30 Sept. 1948, Welwyn Gdn. City, Herts., UK. Classical Guitarist; Private Teacher. Educ: Guildhall Schl. of Music & Drama, London; Lic., ibid.; Pvte. studies. Career: Tchr. of classical guitar to pvte. pupils. Mbr., Incorp. Soc. of Musicians. Hobbies: Reading; Theatre; Cinema. Address: 52 Grant Ct., Waltham Abbey, Essex, EN9 3DY, UK.

NICHOLSON, David, b. 28 Nov. 1919, Regina, Sask., Can. Benedictine Monk & Priest; Choirmastr. Educ: BA, Christ the King Sem., BC, Can., 1945; M Mus, Northwestern Univ., 1968; Doct. Cand., Univ. of Edinburgh. Career: Choirmaster, Mt. Angel Abbey, Ore. Recordings: sev. recordings of Gregorian Chant, Gregorian Inst. of Am.; other recordings for RCA Victor. Publs: Singing in God's Ear, 1956; Musical & Vernacular in the Mission, 1964; Dictionary of Plainsong, forthcoming. Mbrships: Am. Musicol. Soc.; Schola Gregoriana, Cambridge. Recip., 'Gramy' for Best Choral Recording, 1960. Hobbies: Swimming; Weightlifting. Address: Mt. Angel Abbey, St. Benedict, OR 97373, USA.

NICHOLSON, David Michael Prudhoe, b. Newcastle on Tyne, UK. Flautist. Educ: Lic., GSM (Perfs.); Lic., GSM (Tchrs.). m.

Josephone Nicholson, 2 children. Career: Fndr., Bernicea Ensemble; Mbr., Amphion Wind Quintet; Fndr. Mbr., New Music Grp. of Scotland, app. 1st time at Edinburgh Int. Fest., 1974; Prin. Flute, Scottish Chmbr. Orch.; Dir., Scottish Phil. Soc.; Prof. of Flute, RSAM, Glasgow; Soloist; Frequent broadcasts; Concerts Mgr., Edinburgh Univ. Fac. of Music. Recording: RAmeau Piéces de Clavecin en Concerts. Mbr. Solo Perf. Sect., ISM. Recip. Silver Medal for Highest Dip. Marks, GMS, 1963. Hobbies: Climbing; Walking; Photography. Address: 37 Charterhall Rd., Edinburgh, EH9 3HS, UK.

NICHOLSON, Elizabeth Ann, b. 13 June 1932, Murree, India (now Pakistan). Singer. Educ: Ctrl. Schl. Speech & Drama; pvte. voice study w. Joseph Hislop, London; BA's, music hist. & musid educ., Southern Meth. Univ., Dallas, Tex.; MA cand. (musicol.), Univ. of Ky. m. David P Nicholson, 1 s., 1 d. Mbrships: Pi Kappa Lambda; Mu Phi Epsilon. Recip. Mu Phi Epsilon Prize, 1972. Hobbies: Reading; Cooking; Collecting antiques; Travel. Address: 117 Colonial Ct., Little Rock, AR 72205, USA.

NICHOLSON, Ralph Ward, b. 15 June 1907, London, UK. Composer; Conductor; Violinist; Teacher; Adjudicator. Educ: ARCM. m. Gillian Ringland, 2 s., 2 d. Career: Violinist, LSO, 1937-62; Cond., Croydon Youth Orch., 1945-78; Cond., Bookham Choral Soc., 1954, Guildford Symph. Orch., 1960, Redhill Soc. of Instrumentalists, 1962-73; Brighton & Hove Harmonic Soc., 1973; Prof., RCM, 1963-77; Pt.-time music adviser, Co. of Surrey, 1960-72. Comps. incl: Concerto for oboe & strings; Bassoon Concerto; Rhapsody for clarinet & orch.; Impromptu for contra-bassoon & orch.; March for brass quaretet; Intermezzo for woodwind; var. songs, wedding marches & fanfares; 2 carols, A Winter Birth & Herrick's Carol. Mbrships: Performing Right Soc. Hons: Tagore Gold Medal. Hobbies: Golf; Tennis; Cricket. Address: Capel House, Capel, Surrey, UK.

NICKEL, Heinz, b. 28 July 1935, Seulberg/Ts., Germany. Musicologist; Music Teacher; Guitar Teacher. Educ: studied musicol., hist. of arts, hist. of Spanish lit.; pvte. study of guitar w. Curd Gudian; Doct. in musicol. (hist. of guitar). m. Ute Görlich, 3 s. Career: Gymnasium Tchr. of Music. Publs: Beitrag zur Entwicklung der Gitarre in Europa in Biblioteca de la Guitarra, 1972. Contbr. to: Instrumentenbaumusik international. Mbrships: Gesellschaft für Musikforschung; Verband deutscher Schulmusiker. Hobbies: Painting; Diving. Address: 5488 Adenau, Näsbach 9, German Fed. Repub.

NICKSON, Noel John, b. 5 Jan. 1919, Melbourne, Aust. Professor of Music, B Mus., Univ. of Melbourne, 1938; ARCM., RCM, London, UK, 1939-40, 46-47; Mus B, Univ. of Dublin, 1948; Must D., ibid, 1949. m. Margaret G Wortley, 1 s., 1 d. Career incl: Fndn. Prof. & Hd., Dept. of Music, Univ. of Old.; 1st Dean, Fac. of Music, ibid., 1967-69, 1971-74. Compositions: Sonata for Violin & Viola, 1964; Sonatina for Pianoforte, 1966; var. other comps. & tchng. materials. Contbr. to: Miscellanea Musicologia; The RCM Mag.; Aust. Jrnl. of Music Educ.; Vestes; Studies in Music. Mbrships: VP Aust. Soc. for Music Educ., 1969-71; Pres., ibid 1971-74; Hon. Life Mbr., 1974-; VP, Dalcroze Soc. of Aust.; Patron, Music Tchrs. Assn. of Qld.; Int. Soc. for Music Educ.; Soc. for Ethnomusicol.; Am. Soc. for Eastern Arts; RCM Union; Patron, Kodaly Educ. Inst. of Aust. Hons: FRCM, 1977. Address: Dept. of Music, Univ. of Qld., St. Lucia, Qld. 4067 Aust. 3, 15, 28.

NICODEMO, Oswaldo, b. 17 Nov. 1915, Sao Paulo, Brazil. Professor of Music, ¿Violin, Viola, Paino). Educ: Dips: Prof. of Violin, Concertist, Chorus Maestro; Prof. of Harmony, Dramatic & Musical Schl. of Sao Paulo. m. Luzia Siciliano Nicodemo, 2 s. Debut: Playing Violin at Municipal Theatre of Sao Paulo, 1938. Career: Prof. of Viola, Municapl Symphonic Orch. of Sao Paulo & State Phil. Orch., Sao Pualo; Violinist, Viotti Quartet, Sao Paulo. Comps. incl: Marcha Fantastica (violin & piano); Melody (violin & paino); Romance (violin & piano); Valse Triste (violin & paino); Var. pieces for Chant & Paino. Recordings incl: Tapes for Voice of Am. Hons: Hon. in Campana D'Oro, Salerno, Italy, 1955. Address: Rua Sergipe 627, Sao Paulo - SP, Brazil.

NICOLET, Aurèle, b. 22 Jan. 1926, Neuchatel, Switz. Instrumentalist; Professor of Music. Educ: Conserv. of Paris, France. m. Christiane Gerhard. Career: Mbr., Winterthur Orch., 1948-58, Berlin Philharmonic Orch., 1950-59: Prof., Music Schl., Berlin, 1950-; concert apps. throughout Europe, num. recordings: 1965-. Hons. incl: 1st Prize, Conserv. of Paris; 1st Prize, Int. Competition, Geneva, 1948; Music Critics' Prize, Berlin, 1963. Address: 4102 Binningen, Neubadrain 14, Switz.

NICULESCU, Mariana, b. Brasov, Romania. Soprano singer. Educ: grad. Barsov Conserv. (violin); studied singing at Cluj Conserv., & Conserv. di S Cecilia, Rome, w. Jolanda Magnoni.

m. Franco di Santis. DY debut as Violetta, 1977. Career: apps. at NY City Opera, Metropolitan Opera, Los Angeles, Cincinnati, Toronto, Frankfurt, Stuttgart, Rome, Trieste, Venice, Turin, Florence, Treviso, Spoleto, etc.; num. concert apps; roles incl. Violetta, Mimi, Marguerite, Gilda. Hons: winner, Rossini Competition, Italy, 1972. Mgmt: Columbia Artists Mgmt. Inc., 165 W 57th St., NY, NY 10019, USA. Address: c/o mgmt.

NICULESCU, Stefan, b. 31 July 1927, Moreni, Romania. Composer; Musicologist; Pianist. Educ: Bucharest Polytechnic Inst.; MA, Bucharest Conserv.; Studio Siemens for Electronic Music, Munich. m. Colette Demetrescu. Career: Prof. of Comp. & Music Analysis, Bucharest Conserv.; Guest, Deutscher Akademischer Austauschienst, W Berlin, 1971-72. Comps. incl: Symph., 1956; 3 Cantatas, 1959, 60 & 64; Hétéromorphie, 1967; Aphorismes d'Heraclite, choral, 1969; Ison for 14 soloists, 1971; Le Livre avec Apolodor, opera, 1974; Concerto for winds & percussion, 1975. Recordings: Electrecord (Bucharest); Erato (Paris). Publs: George Enescu (co-author), 1971. Contbr. to: Muzica & Revue Roumaine d'histoire de l'art (both Bucharest). Mbr., Exec. Bd., Romanian Comps., Union. Hons. incl: George Enescu Prize for comp., Romanian Acad., 1962. Hobby: Reading. Address: Intrarea Sublocotenent Staniloiu 4, Sector III, 73228 Bucharest 31, Romania.

NIEDERDORFER, Otto Josef, b. 18 April 1953, Eisenkappal, Austria. Pianist. Educ: Dip., Hochschule fur Musik, Graz, Austria. Debut: Graz, 1971. Career: Concerts in Graz, Salzburg, Vienna, Paris, Warsaw, Klagenfurt, Bergamo Rotinj, Yugoslavia; Apps. w. orchs.; 1st TV app. at Rovinj, Yugoslavia; Radio apps. in Austria & several foreign countries. Recip. var. prizes & hons. Hobbies: Book; Records; Sports; Philately. Address: A-9135 Eisenkappel 16, Austria.

NIEDERHOFFER, Milton Lester, b. 28 April 1943, Violinist. EDuc: CCNY; pvte. violin study w. H Silverman, Lewis Kaplan, Vaclay Benkovic, Steven Staryk & Gwen Thompson. m. Margaret Ann Johnson, 1 s. Career: Mbr., Cosmopolitan Young People's Symph., 3 seasons; 2nd violin sect., Vancouver Symph. Orch., 1970-. Hobby: Tennis. Address: 4171 W. 14th Ave., Vancourver, BC V6R 2X6, Can.

NIELSEN, Bjarne, b. 3 Jan. 1954, Roskilde, Denmark. Double Bassist. Educ: Pvte. studies. w. Preben Fanhoe, Denmark; Master classes & workshops. Career: Soloist, Royal Danish Orch., Dittordsorf & Koussevitzky, etc.; Recordings w. Orchs. for Radio & TV. Mbrships: Int. Soc. of Bassists. Hons: Jacob Gade's Legat, 1973. Address: Bakkedraget 3, 4130 Viby SJ, Denmark.

NIELSEN, Finn, b. 9 Aug. 1919, Bergen, Norway. Pianist. Educ: Conserv. of Music, Bergen; Pvte. studies w. Gottfrid Boon, Stockholm; Georg Varsarhelyi, Copenhagen; Ilona Kabos, London; Conrad Hansen, Hamburg. m. Anne-Marie Gjerland, 3 c. Debut: Oslo & Bergen, 1947. Career: Concert tours: Norway, Sweden, Denmark, England, Scotland, Ireland, Holland, USA, etc.; Concerts: Norwegian Radio & other countires; Played Grieg Comps. in Norwegian Cultural Film; Grieg Recital for Eurovision, 1963 in Grieg's Home, Troldhaugen; Soloist & accomp., Bergen Festivals, 1953-. Recordings of Norwegian Comps. Mbrships. incl: Norwegian Musicians Assn.; Norwegian Music Tchrs. Soc. Address: Erleveien 9F, N-5030 Landaas, Norway. 24.

NIELSEN, Finn Fausing, b. 31 May 1950, Copenhagen, Denmark. Bass Guitarist. Educ: Pvte. studies. m. Bente, 2 s. Debut: Cirkus Benneweiz, Copenhagen, 1968. Career: Svend Nicolaisens Orch., 1969-. Recordings: Approx. 100 LP records as studio musician. Mbr., Danish Musician & Orch. Union. Address: Jyllingevej 264, 2610 Rodovre, Denmark.

NIELSEN, Niels Henrik, b. 21 July 1935, Copenhagen, Denmark. Organist. Educ: Organist exam. (Master's degree), Royal Danish Conserv. Music, 1954; Organ w. Anton Heiller & French horn w. Gottfried Freiberg, Vienna, Austria, 1957; Organ w. Gaston Litaize & Conducting w. Robert Blot, Paris, France, 1959-60. m. Randi Habersaat, 1 s. Debut: Copenhagen, 1955. Career incls: Organ tchr., Conserv. Music, Aalborg, 1966-75; Cathedral Organist, Copenhagen, 1972-; Frequent concert tours & solo perfs. Europe & Danish TV. Recordings incl: Messiaen; La Nativité du Seigneur & L'ascension. Hons. incl: Danish Music Critic's Prize, 1969; Prof. Ove Christensen Prize. Hons., 1971. Address: Boeslundevej 13, 2700 Brenshoj, Denmark.

NIELSEN, Svend, b. 20 Apr. 1937, Copenhagen, Denmark. Composer. Educ: Studied Music, Univ. of Copenhagen; STudied Theory, Royal Danish Acad. of Music. Compositions;

Duets for Soprano & Contralto & Chamber Ensemble, 1964; Metamorphoses for 23 Solo Strings, 1967; Nauges for Orch., 1972; Romances, 1970-74; Chmbr. Cantata, 1975; Sonnets of Time, 1978. Recordings: Romances; Chambercantata. Address: H C Andersensvej 10, 8230 Aabyhoj, Denmark.

NIELSEN, Tage, b. 16 Jan. 1929, Frederiksberg, Denmark. Composer; Director. Educ: MA, Univ. of Copenhagen, 1955. M. Aase Grue-Sörensen, 3 c. Career: Dpty. Hd., Music Dept., Danish Radio, 1957-63; Dir., Prof., Royal Acad. of Music, Aarhus, 1963-. Comps. publd: 2 Nocturnes for piano (also recorded); Il Giardino Magico for orch.; Marker og Enge, divertimento for organ; 3 Characteristic Pieces & an Epilogue for piano. Comps. recorded: Attic Summer for soprano, guitar & percussion; Recitativ & Elegy for guitar solo. Contbr. to: Dansk Musiktidsskrift. Mbrships: Ghmn., Music Comm., Danish State ARt Fndn., 1971-74; Prog. Comm., Danish Radio, 1967-71; Bd., Aarhus Symph. Orch., 1974-. Recip., Anker Prize, 1975. Address: Bredkaer Tvaervej 37, DK 8250 Egaa, Denmark.

NIEMAN, Alfred (Abbe), b. 25 Jan. 1913, London, UK. Composer; Pianist. Educ: RAM; FRAM; ARAM; FGSM. m. Aileen Steeper, 2 s. Career: Concert apps. in 2 piano team; perfs. w. BBC 5 yrs; Prof. of Comp. & Piano, Lectr., GSM. Comps. (recorded): 2nd Piano Sonata; 9 Israeli Folksongs; Chromotempera for cello & paino; Paradise Regained, for cello, piano & Chinese cymbals; Tongs & Bones, for trombone solo. Other comps. incl: 2nd Symphony; Arie Fantasie for organ; Variations & Finale for piano; 2 Serenades for piano; Adam (cantata) for tenor, 4 trombones, 5 percussion & piano; var. songs. Publs: Schumann (Symposium); Tension in Music (Symposium). Mbrships: CGGB; Brit. Assn. of Music Therapy; Consultatn, Nat. Assn. for Gifted Children. Hons. incl: McFarren Gold Medal. Hobby: Cricket. Address: 21 Well Walk, London NW3, UK. 29.

NIEMCZYK, Waclaw, b. 2 July 1907, Warsaw, Poland. Violinist. Educ: Warsaw Conserv., Inst. Moderne de Violin (Paris); Study w. Bronislaw Hubermann. m. Jean Morrell, 1 child. Debut: w. Warsaw Phil., 1920. Career: Prof., Conserv. at Danzig, 1938; Ldr., Cracow Phil., 1946. Comps. incl. num. works for violin & paino & solo violin, cadenzas for concerti by Mozart, Beethoven, Paganini, others; Transcriptions for violin & piano inclng. & Caprices by Paganini. Recordings w. Radio Free Europe, Radio & TV Françcaise, Polish RAdio, BBC London & Manchester. Hons: Winner, Int. Competitions for Violin, Vienna, 1932, Warsaw, 1935. Hobbies: Theatre; Literature; Dogs; Gardening. Address: 23 Goldsmith Rd., London W3 6PX, UK. 3.

NIEMOTKO-BRZEZICKA, Krystyna, b. 33 May 1938, Szczebrzeszyn, Poland. Pianist; Teacher. Educ: Acad. of Music, Warsaw, 1955-61; MA, 1961; studies in Venice, 1964, Budapest, 1967, NY & Boston, 1974-75 m Waldemar Niemotko, 2 s., 1 d. Debut: Wroclaw, 1954. Career: apps. as soloist & w. orchs. in all major Polish cities, in Bulgaria, Czech., UK, W & E Germany, Hungary, Italy & USA; mbr. jury, Int. competition for pianists & lyric singers, Enna, Sicily, 1974, 79; Prof., master course for pianists, Northampton, UK, 1977; mbr., Educ. Committee, New Nat. Chopin Ed., 1961-67. num. recordings for radio in Polan, Czech., UK, Italy & USA. mbr. Soc. of Polish Artists & Musicians, Hobbies: Architecture; Sculpture; Painting; Travel. Mgmt: Pagart, Warsaw, Address: Plac Konstytucji 6/31, 00550 Warsaw, Poland.

NIESSING, Paul, b. 5 May 1917, Rotterdam, Netherland. Concert Pianist; Musicologist. Educ: studied w. Willem Andriessen. m. Marianne Niessing-Polak Daniels, 1 s. Debut: aged 18. Career includes: aps. w. ldng. Dutch orchs. inclng. Amsterdam Concertgebouw, Hague Residentie, Radio Phil.; recitals in Holland, Belgium, France, Germany & Switz.; Accomp.; Pedagogue; Musicol. Contbr. to num. Dutch music jrnls. & cyclopedias. Mbrships: Bd. of Examiners, Govt. Exams. in piano & musicol.; Pres., Johan-Wagenaarstichting & Hans-Schouwmanstichting. Recip., Arts-Scis.-Lettres, France. Hobby: Literature. Address: Backershagenlaan 28, Wassenaar, Netherlands. 19.

NIEVA, Ignacio Morales, b. 18 Dec. 1928, Valdepeñas, Spain. Conductor; Organist. Educ: Profl. Dip., pianoforte, harmony, Real Conservatorio de Música de Mardrid; Cond. & modern music, Manhattan Schl. of Ny. m. Maria de las Mercedes Vizoso Arandes. Career: Musical & Zarzuela (Spanish Comic Opera) Cond., Chmbr. Music Cond.; Choir Cond. & Organist; Music (Form & Analysis) and Humanities, Conserv. of Puerto Rico. Comps: Sinfonia I (Hebráica); Sinfonia II (De la América Hispana); Concerto Grosso; Preludio y Fuga; Chmgr. Music No. 2; Quinteto con Piano; String Trio, etc. Contbr. to: El Mundo; Vocero. Mbrships: Ateneo Puertorriqueño, Hato Rey, Puerto Rico 00918, USA.

NIKOLOV, Ventseslav, b. 20 Apr. 1943, Rousse, Bulgaria. Cellist. Educ: studied w. Janor Starker & on master course at Moscow Conserv, w. M Rostropovitch & N Shakhovskaia. m. Anda Nikolova, 3 d. Debut: 1st Bulgarian perf. of Shostakovitch's 1st concerto, 1966. Career: apps. w. all major orchs. in Bulgaria; num. guest apps. in many countires inclng. USSR, Czech., Hungary, GDR, Begium, Switz., Austria, Cuba, Romania. Recordings: works by Shostakovitch, Pipkov, Josiffov, Hindemith, Beethoven & contemporary Bulgarian comps. Contbr. to Union of Bulgarian Musicians Bulletin. Hons: 4th prize, Nat. Bulgarian competition, 1964; 4th prize, Int. Tchaikovsky competition, 1970. Mbr. Union of Bulgarian Musicians. Hobbies: Books; Cooking; Tourism. Address: 17 Dimiter Polyanov Str., 1504 Sofia, Bulgaria.

NIKOLOVSKI, Vlastimir, b. 20 Dec. 1925, Prilep, Yugoslavia. Composer; Professor of Composition. Educ: Grad., Acad. of Music, Belgrade, 1955. m. Vera Talevska-Nikolovska, 1 d. Career: Prof., Comp., Acad. of Music, Skpije; Dean, ibid., 1966-71; Dir., Skopie Opera, 1956-57. Publd. comps: 41 works, inclng: Parodii, op. 10, 1954; Picanterii, op. 19, 1966; Satyr No. 1, op. 22, 1967; Sonata, op. 28, 1970; Jugendalbum, op. 17 no. 1, 1971; Suita, op. 1 no. 3, 1971; Makendonka, op. 23, 1975. 31 works recorded on disc andor tape. Contbr. to: Macedonian Musical Folklore; Razgledi; Svuk; Sovyetskaya muzika; Nova Makedonija. Mbrships. incl: Pres., Union of Yugoslavian Comps., 1961-65, Union of Macedonian Comps., presently. Recip., num. Yugoslavian musical hons. Hobbies: Drawing Caricatures; Writing. Address: ul. Dame Gruev 78, 91000 Skopje, Yugoslavia.

NILES, John Jacob, b. 28 Apr. 1892, Louisville, Ky., USA. Dolklorist; Folksinger & Composer; Dulcimer. Educ: Univ. of Lyon, France; Cinn. Conserv.; Schola Cantorum, Paris. m. Rena Lipetz, 2 s. Career: Concerts of Am. folk music, USA, UK O Europe. Num. compositions; Recordings of songs inclng. I Wonder as I Wander, Black Is the Color of My True Love's Hair, num. others. Publs: The Ballad Book of John Jacob Niles, 1961; Christmas Carols for Young Actors, Folk Ballads for Young Actors, 1962. Mbrships: ASCAP; Am. Folklore Soc.; Am. Dialect Soc. Hons: HOn. degrees from Cinn. Conserv., Univ. of Ky., Univ. of Louisville, Transylvania Univ., Episc. Theol. Sem. of Ky. Hobbies: Gardening; Woodcarving; Painting. Address: Boot Hill Farm, RFD 10, Lexington, KY 40511, USA. 2.

NILSEN, Grethe, b. 15 Dec. 1952, Oslo, Norway. Violinist. Educ: Studied w. Prof. Herbert Bergene. Career: Norwegian Radio Corp. Orch. Mbr., Norwegian Musicans Union. Address: Helgesensgt. 83, Oslo 5, Norway.

NILSSON, Birgit, b. 17 May 1918, Sweden, Opera Singer (soprano). Educ: Stockholm Royal Acad. of Music. m. Bertil Niklasson. Career: w. Stockholm Opera, 1947-51; Appearances at Glyndebourne, 1951; Bayreuth, 1954; Munich, 1955; Hollywood Bowl, Buenos Aires & Florence, 1956; Bayreuth & Covent Gdn., London, 1957; La Scala, Milan, Naples, Vienna, Chgo. & San Fran., 1958; Metropol. Opera, NY., 1959; Bayreuth, 1960; Covent Gdn., 1962-63; Leading roles in Turandot, Paris, 1968; Josen, NY., 1968; Elektra, London, 1969; noted for Wagnerian repertoire. Num. recordings especially of Wagner. Hons: Royal Ct. Singer, 1954; Austrian Kammersangerin & Hon. Mbr., Vienna State Opera, 1968; Cmndr., Order of Vasa, 1968; Medal Litteris & Aribus, 1960; Medal for Promotion of Art of Music, Royal Acad. of Music, Stockholm, 1968. Address: Waldheimstr. 6, Zürich, Switz.

NILSSON, Bo, b. 1 May 1937. Composer. EDuc: studied counterpoint w. Micha Pedersen & Karl-Birger Blomdahl. m. Monica Nilsson, 3 d. Debut: as Comp. w. Zwei Stücke for chmbr. orch., Cologne, 1956. Comps: Frequences; Quantitäten; Stunde eines Blocks; Zwanzig Gruppen; Reaktionen; Brief an Gösta Oswald; Déj u; Déjà connu; Versuchungen; Entrée Séance; Revue; Vier Prologen; Flöten aus der Einsamkeit; Lisa; La Bran; Carillon de Madeleine; Tua Fatumeh; Chanson de Monique; Fragments; Audiogramme; Swedenborg dreaming; Szene I - III; Rendez-vous; music for films, theatre & TV. Publs: Spaderboken (The Mad Book), 1966. Hons: 1st Prize, Ein Irrender Sohn, Rome, 1958; Christ Johnson Prize, Brief an Gösta Oswald, 1974. Mgmt: Universal Ed., Vienna; Edition Tonos, Darmstadt; Wilhelm Hansen, Copenhagen. Address: Stockholmsvägen 60C, S?18142 Lidingo, Sweden.

NILSSON, Erling Marten, b. 4 Oct. 1947, Nederkalix, Sweden. Communal Music Director; Pianist. Educ: Music tchrs. exam., People's HS Framnas, 1971. Career: Communal music tchr., Alvsbyn's commune, 1972-73; Ragunda commune, 1973-75; Communal music dir., Ragunda communal music schl., 1976-. Hobby: Reading. Address: 6a, Skalgrand, 840 70 Hammarstrand, Sweden.

NILSSON, L, b. 20 Feb. 1939, Malmö, Sweden. Composer. Educ: Music Coll., Stockholm; Studies of composition, Paris. m. Sissi, 1 s. Career: Worked on Fylkingen & the Swedish Electronic Music Studio, EMS. Compositions: Over 40 works; multi-media works; music for film & TV. Recordings: Swedish Radio; Rikskunserter Sweden; HMV; CCRC. Publs: Sohlman; Nutida Musik; Tonfallet. Mbr., FST, Swedish Composers' Union. Recip. Swedish State Music Grant. Address: Ljungbyholmsv. 52, 26091 Förslöv, Sweden.

NILSSON, Raymond, b. 6 May 1920, Sydney, Australia. Singer; Professor of Voice and Opera. Educ: Univ. of London, UK; BA., Sydney Univ., Australia; LRSM., Sydney Conservatorium of Music. m. Mildred Hartle Stockslager, 1 s., 2 d. Debut: Royal Opera House Covent Garden, London, 1953; San Fran. Opera Co., Calif., 1961. Career: Int. opera & concert singer, 1956-; Opera & concert tours. Am., Europe, S. Africa & Australia, 9145-68; apps. at opera houses in Germany, Holland, Belgium, USA, Spain, Aust., S. Africa; Prin Tenor, Royal Opera House Covent Garden, 1953-61; Prin. Tenor, San Fran. Opera Co., 1961-; Prin. Tenor roles in 10 full-length operas for BBC, 1953-62; Broadcasts of recitals, operas & major choral works for BBC, 1951-; Promenade Concerts, Royal Albert Hall, London, 1953-63; TV broadcasts, Holland & Belgium; Creator, major tenor roles of Quint in 'Turn of the Screw' (B Britten), Bramble in 'Our Man In Havana' (M Williamson) & Beau Brummel in 'The English Eccentrics' (M Williamson); Prof. of Voice & Dir., of Opera, San Jose State Univ., Calif. Recordings: 'Peter Hungaricus' by B Britten; 'Psalmus Hungaricus' by Kodaly. Hobbies: Golf; Refereeing Rugby. Address: 1285 Middle Ave., Menlo Pk., CA 94025, USA. 4, 15, 28, 19.

NIN-CULMELL, Joaquin, b. 5 Sept. 1908, Berlin, Germany. Composer; Pianist; Conductor. Educ: Dip. de fin d'Etudes, Schola Cantorum, Paris, 1930; Premier accessit de comp. Musicale, Paris Conserv., 1934. Career: Prof. of Music: Williams Coll., Mass., 1940-50; Univ. of Calif., Berkeley, 1950-; Prof. Emeritus, ibid. Comps. incl: Piano Concerto; Cello Concerto; El burlador de Seville (ballet); Dedication Mass (mixed chorus & organ); La Celestine (opera); Le Rêve de Cyrano (ballet); Piano Quintet; Aano Sonata; Songs; Cantata by José Pradas for voice, string orch. & harpsichord. Mbrships: Corres. Mbr., Royal Acad. of Fine Arts of San Fernando, Madrid; Fellow, Inst. of Creative Arts, Univ. Calif., Berkeley. Address: 165 Hillcrest Rd., Berkeley, CA 94705, USA. 2, 9, 19.

NISKA (Mullen), Maralin, b. 16 Nov., San Pedro, Calif., USA. Singer (soprano). Educ: BA, UCLA; pvte. studies, piano, violin, voice, coaching in opera. m. William P Mullen, 2 stepchildren. Debut: Metropolitan Opera Nat. Co., 1965. Career: NYC Opera, 10 1/2 hrs., 25 roles; Metropolitan Opera, 6 yrs., 6 roles; Metropolitan Opera Nat. Co., 2 yrs., 8 roles; Radio interview show host, NY; Many TV interview apps.; Major Orchs. of USA, BBC Symph. w. Boulez, Israel Phil.; Most opera cos. of the US; Netherlands Opera; Caracas Opera, Puerto Rico, Mexico City; Recitals, USA, Can., Mexico. Recordings: Music from Spain. mbrships: Equity; Screen Actors Guild; Am. Guild of Musical Artists (Bd. of Govs.). Hobbies: Sewing; Keeping house; Knitting; Reading; Cooking. Mgmt: Tony Hartmann, 250 W 57 St., Suite 1128A, NY, N7 10019, USA. Address: 32 Cibola Circle, Rt. 3, 109 NM Santa Fe, NM 87501, USA.

NITSCHKE, Manfred, b. 5 Jan. 1926, Leipzig, Germany. Composer; Pianist. Educ: pvte. study in Leipzig w. Felix Petyrek & Joseph Achtelik; Hochschule für Musik, Berlin. Career: Editor & Prod., radio & TV. Comps. incl: Overtures, Suites, Instrumental & orchl. works, songs, stage & film music. Recordings: sev. of own works. Mbr., Verbandes der komponisten und Musikwissenschaftler der DDR. Address: Müggelseedamm 250, 1162 Berlin-Friedrichshagen, German Dem. Repub.

NIVERD, Raymond, b. 5 Oct. 1922, Paris, France. Music School Director. Educ: Nat. Conserv., Paris. m. Eliane Niverd Papazian, 3 c. Career: currently Dir., Nat. Schl. of Music, Troyes. Comps: Suite Provençcale; Concerto for piccolo; Trio; Quartet; etc. Publs: pedagogical works, inclng. Méthode de Hautbois, Kt., Legion of HOn. Address: 1 rue Diderot, 10000 Troyes, France.

NJIRIĆ, Nikša, b. 13 Apr. 1927, Dubrovnik, Yugoslavia. Composer; Music Teacher. Educ: Grad., Zagreb Acad. of Music, 1951. m. Zdenka Jardas, 1 s. Debut: 1948. Career: Music Tchr., HS, Zagreb. Comps. incl: Symphony; Symphonietta; Concertino for Piano, Strings & Percussion; Variations for Oboe & Strings; 3 stringquartets; Windquintet; Dialogues for Clarinet

& Piano; Solo songs; Metamorphoses (ballet); Variations on an Ancient Croatian Choral Song (organ music); music for children. Recordings incl: Songs for Children. Mbrships: Soc. of Croatian Comps.; Soc. of Music Pedagogues of Croatia. Contrbr. to 2 textbooks & profl. jrnls. Recip., var. music hons. Hobby: Photography. Mgmt: Union of Orgs. of Yugoslav Comps., Beograd. Address: Ruzmarinka 3/IV, 41000 Zagreb, Yugoslavia.

NKETIA, Joseph Hanson Kwabena, b. 22 June 1921, Mampong-Ashanti, Ghana. Ethnomusicologist; Composer; Writer; Educationist. Educ: BA, Univ. of London; TCL; Juilliard Schl. of Music, NY, USA; Columbia Univ.; Schl. of Music, Northwestern Univ., Ill. m. Lily Agyeman-Dua, 4 c. Career: Prof. of Music, & Dir., Inst. of African Studies, Univ. of Ghana, Legon; Prof. of Music, UCLA, USA. Comps: 4 Flute Pieces; Canzona for Flute, Oboe & Piano; 4 Akan Songs; Monkamfo No (SATB). Publs. incl: African Music in Ghana, 1962; The Music of Africa, 1974. Contbr. to var. jrnls. Mbr., num. profl. orgs. Hons. incl: Cowell Award, African Music Soc., 1958; ASCAP Deems-Taylor Award, 1975. Address: Inst. of African Studies, Univ. of Ghana, Legon, Ghana.

NOACK, Fritz, b. 25 Sept. 1935, Greifswald, Germany. Pipe Organ Builder. Educ: some study of violin & organ; apprentice in organ building w. Rudolph V Becherath, Hamburg. German Fed. Repub. 1954-58. m. Marjorie A Noack (nee Korman). Career: worked w. two Am. builders before fndng. The Noack Organ Co. Inc., 1960; has bult about 80 tracker orans for schls. & chs. in USA; Tchr., bi-yrly. courses for organ majors on organ design, New Engl. Conserv., Boston Conbr. to: The Diapason; Jrnl. of Ch. Music; ISO-Info.; Music Mag. Mbrships: Assoc. Pipe Organ Builders of Am., Int. Soc. Organ Builders; AGO. Hobbies incl: Rsch. on hist. organs. Address: 38 W Main St., Georgetown, MA 01833, USA.

NOBLE, Ann, b. 24 Sept. 1955, Oakland, Calif., USA. Composer; Flautist, Copyist. Educ: Bmus (comp. & flute), Univ. of Redlands; MA (comp.), Mills Coll. Career: mbr., Improviser's Orch., 1974-79; now working w. Independent Comper's Assn., Los Angeles, presenting New Music Concert Series, also prod. classical music concerts & pub. rels. Hunger Project Concert Comm., Los Angeles. Comp: ...saved in prisms of honey... Recordings: w. Improviser's Orch. Mbrships: League of Women Comps.; Am. Women Comps., Inc. recip., Sigma Alpha Iota Comps. Award, 1979. Hobbies: Backpacking; Hiking. Address: 1953 1/2 Argyle Ave., Los Angeles, CA 90068, USA.

NOBLE, Jeremy, b. 27 Mar. 1930, London, UK. Musicologist; Critic; Broadcaster. Educ: Worcester Coll., Oxford, 1949-53; pvte. music studies; Rsch. Fellow, Barber Inst., Birmingham, 1964-65; Fellow, Harvard Inst. for Renaissance Studies, Florence, 1967-68; Leaverhulme Rsch. Fellow, 1975-76. Career incls: Music Critic The Times, 1960-63; The Sunday Telegraph 1972-76; Assoc. Profl., SUNY, at Buffalo, 1966-70 & 1976-. Contbr. to many profl. jrnls.; many broadcasts for BBC radio 3. Address: Dept. of Music, SUNY, Buffalo, NY 14214, USA.

NOBLE, John, b. Southampton, UK. Baritone Singer. Educ: MA, Univ. of Cambridge. Career: Regular broadcasts, concerts, opera, recitals, Fest., UK & Europe; toured USA, Italy & USSR in opera & oratorio. Recordings: Delius, Sea-Drift; Vaughan Williams, Pilgrims Progress; Orff, Carmina Burana; Britten, Albert Herring. Mbrships: Lords Taverners; Brit. Actors Equity (Councillor). Address: c/o 8 Harley St., London W1, UK.

NOBLE, Noël Alfred, b. 31 Dec. 1923, Melbourne, Vic., Aust. Operatic & Concert Singer; True Bass Baritone. Educ: Melbourne Univ.; Conservatorium of Music, ibid.; Grad., Perfect Voice Inst., Ill., USA. m. Joyce Frances Noble. Debut: Melbourne, aged 8. Career: Contracted Singer, Aust. Braodcasting Commission; Bass Soloist, St. Paul's Cathedral, Melbourne; Guest Prin., Sadler's Wells Opera, Welsh Nat. Opera, Glyndebourne, & orchs., choral socs., opera cos. throughout the world; Regular per. at Albert Hall, Royal Fest. Hall, Queen Elizabeth Hall & concert halls, throughout UK & abroad; Qualified speech therapist; num. radio & TV apps. as perf. & adjudicator. Mbr., musical assns. Contbr. to musical publs. & athletic mags. Recip., num. awards. Hobbies incl: Reading biog. Address: 47 Greenend Rd., Bedford Pk., Chiswick, London W 1AH, UK.

NOBLE, Richard Desmond Clunliffe, b. 2 Apr. 1930, Hindhead, Surrey, UK. Music Critic & Journalist; Gramophone Record Retailer. Educ: Eton Coll.; BA, Keble Coll., Oxford. Career: Asst., BBC Gramophone Lib., 1958-61; Dir., William Lennard Concerts Ltd., 1962-; Ed., The Consort, 1960-72; Dolmetsch Histl. Dance Soc. Jrnl., 1973-; Reviewer, Records &

Recordings, 1978-. Contbr. of many articles, reviews, etc., esp. to The Consort; Recorder & Music Mag; Records & Recording. Mbrships: Royal Musical Assn.; Music Lib. Assn.; Dolmetsch Fndn. (Gov.); Dolmetsch Histl. Dance Soc.; Brit. Music Soc. Hobbies: Cartophily; Gardening. Address: Fonthill, Hurtmore, Godalming, Surrey GU7 2RE, UK.

NOBLE, Weston, Conductor; Clinician. Educ: Arts. D. Augustana Coll., SD. Career: Dir. of Music Activities, Luther Coll., Decorah; Iowa; Guest Dir., Music Festivals in USA & Can.; Four concert tours in Europe; Guest fac. mbr. num. colls. & univs.; App. w. Luther Nordic Choir at Kennedy Ctr., Wash., DC & Lincoln Ctr., NY. Apps. w. Luther Coll. Concert Band at Lincoln Ctr., NY; Adjudicator at Int. Festival of Three Cities (Vienna, Budapest & Prague); Mbrships: Am. Choirmaster Assn.; Am. Bandmasters Assn. Address: Luther Coll., Decorah, Iowa, USA. 3, 12, 28.

NOBLEMAN, Maurice, b. 29 Nov. 1927, NYC, USA. Orchestra Conductor. Educ: Gen. Arts Music Major, CCNY; Music student of Fimitri Metropoulos, Zoltan Kodaly & Victor de Sabata. m. Robert Dolby Nobleman, 2 d. 1 s. Debut: Brooklyn Museum Concerts, NY, 1952. Career: Guest Speaker; Lectr. for radio broadcasting; Directed num. concerts in the NY area. Recordings: Complete radio broadcast transcriptions. Contbr. to: Musical America; Musical Courier. Mbrships: Assoc. Musicians. of Gtr. NY; Am. Fed. of Musicians - AFL. Hobbies: Collecing out of print recordings & tapes. Mgmt: Al Michelson (Mgr.), NY. Address: 110 Beacon St., Dumont, NJ, USA.

NOBRE, Marlos, b. 18 Feb. 1939, Pernambuco, Recife, Brazil. Composer; Pianist; Conductor. Educ: Recife Fed. Univ.; Dip., Piano, Theory, etc., Univ. of Recife; Dips. in Comp., var. instns.; Postgrad. Dip. Comp., Inst. Torcuato di Tella, Buenos Aires. m. Leonora Nobre. Debut: Rio de Janeiro. Career: Musical Dir., Brazilian Nat. Symph. Orch., & Brazilian Nat. Broadcasting (Radio MEC); Participant num. fests. contemporary music; Broadcasts on Radios Suisse Romande, ORTF, Berlin, etc. Comps: incl: Concerto Breve; Ukrinmakrinkrin; Mosaico; Rhythmetron (many recorded). Contbr. to books on music & Brazil. Mbr., num. profl. assns. Recip., num. musical hons. Mgmt: Argentina. Address: Rua Paissandu 93 Apt. 601, ZC-01, Rio de Janeiro (20.000), Brazil.

NOEL, Barbara Hughes McMurtry, b. 27 Feb. 1929, Mt. Vernon, Wash., USA. Dean of Humanities & Fine Arts. Educ: Oberlin Conserv. of Music; BMus, 1951, MMus, 1952, Univ. of Ky.; Univ. of Wash.; PhD, Univ. of Ill., 1972. m. Hugh R Noel, Jr., 2 d. Career incl: Asst. Prof. of Music & Music Libn., Univ. of Richmond, 1972-75; chmn., music dept., ibid., 1973-76; Assoc. Prof. of Music, ibid., 1975-76; chmn., music dept., Prof. of Music, Mankato State Univ., 1976-78; acting chmn., music dept., Prof. of Music, Texas Woman's Univ., 1978-79; Dean, Coll. of Humanities & Fine Arts, ibid., 1978-. Publs: Louis Ferdinand, in Grove's Dict., 6th ed. Mbrships: Am. Musicol. Soc.; Coll. Music Soc.; Nat. Assn. of Schls. of Music; MENC; Coll. Art Assn.; Modern Lang. Assn.; Am. Theatre Assn.; Am. Assn. for the Advancement of the Humanities; Am. Assn. for Higher Educ. Hons: Pi Kappa Lambda; scholarships & awards. Hobbies: Reading; Travel. Address: 1825 Westridge, Denton, IX 76201, USA.

NOEL, Jacques, b. 25 Feb. 1930, Sherbrooke, PQ, Can. Pianist; Arranger; Singer; Teacher. Educ: BSc, Ecole Supérieure de Sherbrooke. Career incls: Pianist for Chrysler Show, La Place des Arts, Montreal, 1965; Pianist Accomp., La Boite a Chansons, Expo 67; Band Ldr., L'Antre du Diable, Expo 67; Pianist, Arranger, CBC TV; Apps. nightly, Atlific & C'wlth Holiday Inns, 1968-; Commissioned by Kazumi Ujiharallo Tominaga (Japan) to translate & adapt the Yamaha Music Course. Mbrships: ISM; Musician's Guild of Montreal; Mbr. at Large, Lions' Club. Recip. Laureatus, Tchr.'s Concert Symposium, Univ. of Long Beach, Calif., USA, 1970. Hobbies incl: Sci. reading. Address: 215 Montée des Trente, Mont St. Hilaire, PQ, Can., J3H 2R5.

NOJIMA, Minoru, b. Japan. Pianist. Educ: studied w. Aiko Iguchi; Toho Music Schl.; studied w. Lev Oborin, Moscow. Debut: Carnegie Hall, 1970. Career: has perfd. throughout the world, inclng. over 60 apps. w. NHK Orch. in Tokyo. HOns: 1st Gradn Prize, Music Concours, Japan; 2nd Prize, Van Cliburn Competition, 1969; Schlrship., USSR (for studies w. Lev Oborin), 1966. Address: Nat. Orchl. Assn., 111 W 7th St., Room 1500, New York, NY 10019, USA.

NOLEN, Timothy, b. 9 July 1941, Rotan, Tex., USA. Lyric Baritone - Opera. Educ: BA, Trenton State Coll.; MA, Manhattan Schl. of Music. m. Paulette Haupt-Noeln, 1 d. by previous marriage. Debut: San Fran. Opera. Career: Opera houses, San Fran., Chgo., Portland, Seattle, Boston; San Diego, Phila.,

Houston, Cologne, Amsterdam, Rouen, Bordeaux, Aix-en-Provence, Toulouse, Angers, Nancy, Zürich; TV, L'Eisir D'Amore - Don Pasquale; Die Fledermaus; Concerts, Boston Symph., LA Phil., Paris Nat., Paris Radio Orch. Hobbies: Painting; Writing; Musical Comp.; Fencing; Tennis; Golf. Mgmt: CAMI - Matthew Epstein, USA; Claude Stricker, Europe. Address: 210 Riverside Dr. 8E, NYC, NY 10025, USA. 4.

NOLL, Ernst-Diether, b. 22 Sept. 1934, MerzigSaar German Dem. Repub. Conductor. Educ: Music Acad. Weimar, State exam, 1957; Franz Liszt Music Acad. m. Karin Noll-Möbius, 2 s., 1 d. Debut: Erfurt. Career: Cond. Erfurt, 1958-1963; Leipzig, 1962-65; Karl-Marx-Stadt, 1965-69; since 1969 Musical Dir. Eisenach. Comps: 7 Oratoria; 1 Opera, King Drosselbart; Cantatas; Chmbr. music; Songs; Music for Children; Theater music. Mbrships: Assn. for Comp. and Musicologists (VDK); Theater Soc. (TV); Soc. for German-Sovjet Friendship (DSF). Hobbies: Riding. Address: Heinrich Strasse 39a, 59 Eisenach, German Dem. Repub.

NOLTE, Ewald Valentin, b. 21 Sept. 1909, Utica, Neb., USA. Musicologist. Educ: Cert., Concordia Tchrs. Coll., Seward, Neb., 1929; B Mus, 1944, M Mus, 1945, PhD, 1954, Northwestern Univ.; Grad. studies, Yale Univ., 1950-51. m. Irene Schmidt, 1 s., 1 d. Career: Organist & Choir Dir., Luth. Chs., Ohio & Ill., 1929-44; Asst. Prof. Music, Northwestern Univ., 1944-64; Exec. Dir. & Bulletin Ed., Moravian Music Fndn., Winston-Salen, NC, 1964-72; Prof. Music, Salem Coll., ibid., 1964-; vis. lectur., var. Univs. Comps: Ed., about 50 18th & 19th century works from Am. Moravian Archives. Publ: Creative-Analytical Theory of Music (co-author), 1948; Ed., Four Sinfonias by J. C. F. Bach, 1978. Jrnl. of the Am. Musicol. Soc.; Notes; Church Music. Mbr. profl. assns. Hons. incl: Moramus Award, 1972. Address: 1016 Willowlake Rd., Winston-Salem, NC 27106, USA. 7, 29.

NOMURA, Yosio Francesco, b. 8 Oct. 1908, Tokyo, Japan. Professor Musicology & Aesthetics. Educ: Fac. of Letters (Bunqakusi), Tokyo Univ.; studied Theory & paino w. Dr. Klyoske Kanetune, Oriental Music w. Prof. Hisao Tanabe, Enharmonium w. Dr. Shôhei Tanaka. m. Yosiko Agnes Miyajima, 1 d. Career: Prof. at Keio Univ. & Sophia Univ.; Lectr., Tokyo Univ., 20 yrs., & at Kyoto, Tôhoku & Kyûsyû Univs.; Prof. of Musicol. & Dir. of the ARt Mus., Tokyo Univ. of Arts, until 1976; currently Prof. of Musicology at Uenogakuen Univ. & Elisabeth Univ. of Music. Publs: incl: (in Japanese) Musical Aesthetics, 1953, revised ed. 1978. History of Music as History of Spirit, 1956, 13th ed., 1977. World History of Religious Music, 1967, 2nd ed., 1973; Music in World History, 1971; 3rd ed., 1978. Contbr. to: Rythmes du Monde, 1956; Dokumente & Berichte, 1962; Acta Musicologica, 1963; Festschrift für K. G. Fellerer, 1973. Mbrships: Japanese Musicol. Soc. Int. Musicol. Soc.; Intergu: Consociatio Internationalis Musicae Sacrae: ICOM. Hobby: Swimming. Address: 4-16-37 Sekimatı-kıta, Nerima-ku, Tokyo, Japan. 14.

NONO, Luigi, b. 29 Jan. 1924, Italy. Composer; Teacher. Educ: study w. Bruno Maderna & Hermann Scherchen. Career: Tchr., New Music Summer Schl., Kranichsteiner Music Inst., Darmstadt, 1957-; Dartington Hall Music Summer Schl., Devon UK. 1959-60. Compositions: Variezioni canoniche sulla serie dell op. 41 di A. Schoenberg, 1950; Polifonica-Monodia-Ritmica, 1951; Composzione per Orch. No. 1, 1952; Epitafio per F. Garcia-Lorca, I, II, & III, 1952-53; Liebeslied; Der Rote Mantel (ballet; 1954; Omaggio a Emilio Verdova (electronic music), 1960; Sul Ponte di Hiroshima, 1962; Dal Diario Italiano, 1964; La Fabrica illuminata, 1966; Recorda Cosa tia Hanno Fatto in Auschwitz, 1966; Per bastiana taiyangcheng, 1967. Address: Giudecca 882, Venice, Italy.

NOON, David, b. 23 July 1946, Johnstown, Pa., USA. Composer. Educ: BA, Pomona Col., 1968; MA, NY Univ., 1970; MMA, Yale Univ., 1972; DMA, ibid., 1977. Comps: Inflections (piano, prepared piano, harp, harpsichord, vibraphone); Labyrinth (chmbr. orch.); Introduction, Dirge & Frolic (flute, clarinet, bassoon, trumpet, brombone); Duo (2 violas); Ai, Ai (orch.); Sonata (clarinet, prepared piano, vibraphone); Song & Toccata (trombone); Fantasy (violin, piano duet); Cadenzas (violin); Berceuse Seche (orch.); Motets & Monodies (oboe, english horn, bassoon). Mbrships: ASCAP; Am. Musicol. Soc.; MLA; Pi Kappa Lambda. Recip. num. prizes, awards, grants & fellowships. Address: 1563 Elmcroft Ave., Pomona, CA 91767, USA.

NOONE, Lana M, b. 30 Dec. 1946, NYC, USA. Musician (flute, piccolo). Educ: CCNY; SUNY; Mannes Coll. of Music. m. Byron M Noone, 1 d. Career: Soloist w. Am. Concert Band, Orch. of Am.; Recitalist, Edinburgh Fest. Fringe Soc., Scotland, UK; Flutist; Huntington Symph., Orch., New Chmbr. Orch., Am. Concert Band, L'Amore di Musica; radio & TV apps., NYC.

Mbrships: Local 802, Am. Fedn. Musicians; Nat. MTA; Nassau Music Educ. Assn. Hons: Awards, LENA, NYC Competition, 1965; Int. Youth Orch., Berlin, 1965. Hobby: Swimming. Address: 232 Kilburn Rd. S, Garden City, NY 11530, USA.

NORAS, Arto Erkki, b. 12 May 1942, Turku, Finland. Cellist. Educ: 1st Prize, Conserv. Nat. Superieur de paris, France (studied w. Paul Tortelier). m. Marja Kantola, 2 children. Career: Regular concert apps. all over the world; Prof.'s Chair, Sibelius Acad., Helsinki. Hons: 2nd Prize, Tchaikovsky Competition, Moscow, USSR, 1966. Mgmt: Musik Fazer, Helsinki. Address: Mesaanikuja 7, Helsinki, Finland.

NORBY, Erik, b. 9 Jan. 1936, Copenhagen, Denmark. Composer. Educ: Dip., Royal Danish Conserv. of Music, Copenhagen & Aarhus. m. Solveig Lumholt, 2 d. Debut: Stockholm, 1966. Career: Tutor in Music Theory & Solfege, Music Conserv., Aalborg, 1966-. Comps. incl: 2 Songs, 1963; Music for 8 sextets, 1966; Sinfonia da Requiem, 1968; Chromatikon (recorded), 1971; 3 Songs for soprano & 11 instruments, 1973; Cortege for orch., 1974; Schubert-variations for 4 flutes (recorded), 1974; The Rainbow-Snake, symphonic poem, 1975. Mbr., Danish Comps. Soc. Recip., commns. & awards. Address: Parkbo 6, 2500 Valby, Copenhagen, Denmark.

NORDENFELT, Dagmar, b. 31 Jan. 1908, Bofors. Karlskoga, Sweden. Concert Pianist; Teacher; Composer. Educ: Studied Piano w. Gottfrid Boon, Stockholm, Henrik Knudsen, Copenhagen, & Paul Weingarten, Vienna; studied Comp. w. var. tchrs. m. Nils Kindahl (1946-56). Debut: Stockholm, 1932. Career: Concert tours in Sweden, & in Norway, Finland, Denmark, Paris, Vienna, Ankara & Istanbul; Soloist w. symph. orchs.; chmbr. music; num. broadcats; Comeback Concert, after being crippled by arthritis, 1975. Comps: Sev. songs & piano pieces (broadcasts). Contbr. to Sydsvenska Dagbladet (Music Critic, 1965-67). Mbr., Swedish Piano Tchrs. Assn., Recip., Swedish State Artists Scholarship, 1976. Hobbies: Reading (esp. Art & History). Address: Viskg. 10A, Helsingborg S-25247, Sweden.

NORDGREN, Pehr Henrik, b. 19 Jan. 1944. Saltvik, Finland. Composer. Educ: Musicol. study (lic. es lettres), Helsinki Univ.; study of composition w. Prof. Jonas Kokkonen, Helsinki; Study of composition & trad. Japanese music, Tokyo Univ. of Arts & Music, 1970-73. m. Shinobu Suzuki, 1 c. Compositions incl: Orch. works - Euphony No. 1, 1967; Epiphrase, 1967; Euphony No. 2, 1967; The Turning Point, 1972; Concerto for violin & orch., 1969; Concerto for viola & orch., 1970; Concerto for Clarinet, Folk Instruments & Orch., 1970; Symph., 1974; Choral works w. orch. - Angus Dei, 1970; 4 Pictures of Death (chmbr. music), 1968; 3 Enticements for wind quintet, 1970; Hoichi the Earless (piano), 1972; Autumnal Concerto for Trad. Japanese Instruments & Symph. Orch., 1974; Piano Concerto, 1974; Quartet for Trad. Japanese Instruments, 1974; Wind Quintet, 1975; Euphony No. 3, 1975; Oshidon (piano), 1976. Mbrships: Bd., Finnish Composers Assn.; Bd., Musikki (music mag.); Bd., Kaustinen Folk Music Festival. Recip: 1 st Prize, Finnish Broadcasting Co. Composers Comp., 1969. Address: Eknävägen 31, 132 00 Saltsjö-Boo, Sweden.

NORDQUIST, Charles Paul, b. 4 Mar. 1947, Denver, Colo., USA. Trumpeter; Educator; Conductor. Educ: BME, Univ. of Denver, 1969; MA in Trumpet, 1972. Career incls: Trumpet, inclng. prin., Brico Symph. Orch.; Denver, Colo., 1964-72; Prin. Trumpet, Anchorage Symph. Orch., 1973-75 (personal leave of absence, 1975-76); Prin. Trumpet, AK Fest. of Music, Anchorage, 1973 & 74; Lectr. in Trumpet, Anchorage Community Coll., Univ. of AK, 1973-; num. symph., band, ensemble & solo apps. Mbrships. incl: Am. Musicol. Soc.; Int. Trumpet Guild; Soc. for Rsch. & Promotion of Brass & Wind Music. Hobbies: Flying; Skiing; Photography; Drawing. Address: 8636 Boundary Ave., Anchorage, AK 99504, USA.

NORDSTROM, Tor Wilhelm, b. 22 Mar. 1944, Ekenas, Finland. Church Musician. Educ: Higher Ch. Musical Educ., 1971; Musical Dir.'s Degree, 1972; Singing Dip., Sibelius Acad., 1974. m. Anneli Sommar. Career: Soloist & Accomp., ch. concerts; Local radio perfs. (singing); Tchr., Ekenas Music Schl., piano & recorder. Contbr. of reviews to newspaper, Vastra Nyland. Mbrships: Raseborg Choral Singing Dist., V Chmn.; Ekenas Music Bd., Sec. Hobbies: Travel; The Finnish Archipelago. Address: Hoijersvagen 6, 10600 Ekenas, Finland. 29.

NØRGARD, Per, b. 13 July 1932, Gentofte, Denmark. Composer; Teacher. Educ: BA; MA in Music, Royal Danish Music Conserv., 1955; studied w. Nadia Boulanger, Paris, 1956-57. Career: Tchr., Jutland Music Conserv. Compositions

incl: Metamorphosis; Sonate; 3 orchl. symphs.; Triptychon; Fragment IV; ARcana; Sub Rosa; Nova Genitura; (recorded); Voyage into the Golden Screen; Constallations; Piano Works 53-68. Contbr. to: Numus West; other music mags. Mbrships incl: Int. soc. for Contemporary Music; Danish Comps. Assn. Hons. incl: Lily Boulanger Prize, 1957; Danish Ballet & Music Prize, 1964; Harriet Dohen Medal for Ballet Music, 1967; Music Prize, Nordic Coun., 1974. Hobby: Astrology. Mgmt: Ed. Hansen, Gothersgade 9-11, 1123 Copenhagen K. Address: Norrebrogade 90, 2200 Copenhagen N. Denmark.

NORHEIM, Thoralf Andreas, b. 24 May 1912, Notodden, Norway. Dominican Father; Pianist; Organist. Educ: piano, organ & theory at Oslo Conserv. of Music & w. pvte. tchrs., 1930-45; philosophy, theorly & music, Paris, France, 1945-52; ordination, Oslo, 1950. Debut: as piannist, Oslo, 1939. Career: Apps. in concerts & broadcasting, 1939-; concert tours in Scandinavia, France, UK, USA, Can., 1952-73; piano recitals, soloist w. orchs., chamber musicion. Comps: Catholic liturgical music. Recordings: sev. made in Calif., 1959-65. Contbr. to: magazine, St. Olav; newspaper, Aftenposten, Oslo. Mbrships: Norwegian Union of Musicians; Norwegian Performing Artists League; Norwegian Organists Alliance. Hobbies incl: Reading. Address: Ovre Lunden 5, Oslo 5, Norway.

NORMAN, Jessye, b. Augusta, Ga., USA. Operatic & Concert Soprano. Educ: Howard Univ., Wash., DC; Peabody Conserv., Baltimore, Md.; Univ. of Mich., Ann Arbor, Mich.; Debut: (operatic) Deutsche Opera, Berlin, 1969. Career: apps. in leading roles in opera houses all over the world; num. int. concert apps. Recordings: Il Corsaro & Un Giorno di Regno (Verdi); The Marriage of Figaro & La Finta Giardiniera (Mozart); La Vera Costanza (Haydn); Armida (Haydn); works by Tippett, Wagner, Schumann, Mahler, Schubert, Berlioz & French comps. Hons: Winner, Int. Musikwettbewerb, Bavarian Radio, Munich. Mgmt: Harry Beall Mgmt. Inc., 119 W 57th St., NY, NY 10019, USA. Address: c/o mgmt.

NORMAN, Philip Thomas, b. 16 Oct. 1953, Christchurch, NZ. PhD student in musicology. University of Canterbury. Educ: BA (Engl. Lit.), MA (Music), Univ. of Canterbury, NZ, 1972-76; Dip., Tchng., Christchurch Tchrs. Coll., 1977. Career: var. comps., inclng. comic operetta, incidental music for theatre, chmbr. music; arrs. for radio, TV etc.; cond., jazz pianist, bass player, chorister. Comps: Interface 640. mbr. (Sec.), Comps. Assn. of NZ, 1978. Hobbies: Sports. Address: 46a Matai St., Christchurch 1, NZ.

NORRINGTON, Roger Arthur Carver, b. 16 Mar. 1934, Oxford, UK. Orchestral, Operatic & Choral Conductor. Educ: BA, Cambridge Univ.; RCM. m. Susan Elizabeth McClean (May) 1 s., 1 d. Debut: London, 1962. Career: Musical Dir., Kent Opera; Musical Dir., Schütz Choir of London; Musical Dir., London String Players & London Baroque Ensemble; worldwide guest apps. num. recordings. Contbr. to: Musical Times; Music & Musicians; BBC radio. Hobbies: Reading; Sailing; Walking. Address: 52 King Henry's Rd., London NW3, UK. 1.

NORRIS, Geoffrey, b. 19 Sept. 1947, London, UK. Musicologist. Educ: ARCM, 1967; BA, Univ. of Durham, 1969; Univ. of Liverpool, 1969-70; 1972-73; Inst. of Theatre, Music & Cinematog., Leningrad, 1971. Career: Ed., Grove's Dict. of Music & Musicians, 6th ed., 1973-; Lectr. in Music Hist., RNCM, 1975-77; Ed. (scholarly & reference music books), Oxford Univ. Press, 1977-. Publs: Rakhmaninov, 1976; (with others) Encyclopedia of Opera, 1976. Contbr. to: Grove's Dict.; Everyman Ency.; Musical Times; Musical Quarterly; Tempo; Music & Letters; BBC broadcasts. Mbr. Royal Musical Assn. Address: Flat D44, Du Cane Ct., London SW17 7JH, UK.

NORRIS, Michael John, b. 28 Mar. 1934, Hayes, Middx., UK. Bassoon Player. Educ: TCL; RAM; LRAM. m. Pauline Chase, 1 s., 1 d. Career: Prin. bassoon, Coldstream Guards Band, 1954-57, Scottish Variety Orch., 1962-66, BBC Scottish Symph. Orch., 1970-, (contra-bassoon 1966-70); broadcasts of concertos by Mozart, Hummel, Stamitz. Comp: Diversions, for brass band. Hobbies: Swimming; Chess; HOme DIY. Address: 31 Hawthorn Ave., Bearsden, Glasgow, Scotland, UK.

NORRIS, Richard, b. 25 May 1927, LA, Calif., USA. Concert Pianist. Educ: BA, Pomona Coll.; 12 yrs. study w. Egon Petri; 15 yrs. study w. Alexander Libermann. Debut: NY, 1961. Career: Concert tours of W Europe, 1961, 62, 69; Recitals, Can., USA, Hawaii. Recordings: Richard Norris Plays Liszt; Richard Norris Plays Chopin; Richard Norris Plays Liszt - Années de Pèlerinage - Italie. Address: PO Box 10485, Honolulu, NI 96816; PO Box 169, Gualala, Mendocino County, CA 95445, USA.

NORTH, Nigel John, b. 5 June 1954, London, UK. Lutenist; Specialist in 16th-18th century music. Educ: RCM; ARCM; GSM. Debut: Mgmore Hall, London, 1978. Career: Mbr., New London Consort, Acad. of Ancient Music, Hagen Trio, Early Music Consort, London Consort Players; Prof. of Lute, GSM. Recordings: as consort & continuo player, BBC, EM. Saga, DGG; Decca, Harmonia Mundi & Erato. Publs: William Byrd, 1976, Alfonso Ferrabogio, 1976. Mbr., ISM. Address: 8 Garden Lodge Ct., Church Lane, London N2, UK.

NORTH, Roger Dudley, b. 1 Aug. 1926, Warblington, Hants., UK. Composer; Lecturer; Broadcaster. Educ: Univ. Coll., Oxford Univ., 1944-45; RAM, 1943-44 & 48/51; LRAM. m. Rosamund Shreeves, 2 d. Career: Approx. 100 broadcast talks, BBC, 1960-; Has taught at Morley Coll., 1965-; Var. tchng. posts, lecture series, etc. Compositions: Clarinet Sonata, 1953; 3 Pieces for Orch., 1970; num. unpubld. works. Recordings: Talks 'Harmony for the Listener', BBC Transcription Serv.; 'Mood Music' for Boosey & Hawkes; own electronic comps.; var. arrangements, 1977. Book I of New Musical Companion. Mbrships: CGGB; Light Music Soc.; Soc. for the Promotion of New Music. Hons: William Wallace Exhbn., RAM, 1949; Battison Haynes Prize, RAM, 1949; Oliviera Prestcott Gift, RAM, 1950. Hobbies: Sailing. Address: 24 Strand-on-the-Green, Chiswick, London W4 3PH, UK. 3.

NORTHCOTT, Bayan Peter b. 24 Apr. 1940, Harrow-on-the-Hill, Middx., UK. Music Critic. Educ: BA, Dip. Ed., Univ. Coll., Oxford; B Mus, Southampton Univ. Career: Music Critic, New Statesman, 1973-76; Snday Telegraph, 1976-. Contbr. to: Grove's Dict., 6th ed.; Music & Musicians; Listener; Musical Times; Musical Newsletter (NYC); Daily Telegraph; Guardian; Tempo; Dansk Musiktidsskrift; New Statesman (music critic, 1973-76). Mbr., Music Sect., Critics Circle, 1974-. Address: 52 Upper Mall, London W6, UK.

NORTHCOTT, Brian Richard, b. 17 June 1944, Bath, Somerset, UK. Counter-tenor; Music Teacher. Educ: RCM; GRSM; ARCM; studied w. Alfred Deller & Gerald English. m. Ann Valerie Northcott, 1 s., 1 step-d. Career: Alto Lay Clerk, Tenbury Wells, 1965-67, St. George's, Windsor, 1967-70, Guildford Cathedral, 1970-73; Hd. of Music, Haymill Schl., Slough, 1967-70; Dir. of Music, Frensham Heights, 1970-73; Bembridge Schl., Isle of Wight, 1973-75. Carisbrooke HS, 1975-; Musical Dir., Ryde Phil. Soc., 1973-; Cond., Isle of Wight Youth Choir, 1974-. Recordings: w. Martindale Sidwell Singers, Guildford Cathedral & St. Bartholomew Singers. Address: 53 Newport Rd., Cowes, Isle of Wight, UK.

NORUP, Bent, b. 7 Dec. 1936, Hobro, Denmark. Opera Singer. Educ: Studied w. Kristian Riis (Copenhagen), Karl Schmitt-Walter (Munich) & Herta Sperber (NY); Opernschule am Königlichen Teater, Copenhagen; Copenhagen Opernchor am Königlichen Teater, Debut: Kurwenal, Tristan und Isolde, Royal Opera, Copenhagen, 1970. Career incls: Apps., Europe & USA; Staatstheater Graunschweig, 1973/78; Stadtische Buhnen, Nürnberg, 1978; Opera Soloist, Koniglichen Teater, Copenhagen, 1968; Radio apps. Hons: Dänische Kritikerpreis, 1971. Address: Schultheissallee 75, 8500 Nürnberg, German Fed. Repub.

NOSS, Luther, . 21 July 1907, Leland, Ill., USA. Educator; Organist. Educ: St. Olaf Coll., Northfield, Minn., 1924-27; B Mus., Northwestern Univ., Evanston, Ill., 1930; B Mus., Yale Univ., 1931; M Mus., ibid, 1932; Pvte. Comp. study w. Alban Berg, Vienna, Austria, 1932-33; Organ STudy w. Marcel Dupre, Paris, France, 1934. m. Osea Calciolari. Career: Univ. Organist, Cornell Univ., USA, 1935-39; Univ. Organist, Yale Univ., 1939-54; Univ. Choirmaster, 1939-61, Master of Silliman Coll., 1953-62, Dean, Schl. of Music, 1954-70, Prof. of Music, 1949-76. Curator, Paul Hindemith Collection. Compositions (publd.); Psalms & Humns of Early Am., 1956. Recordings: 3 recordings of Baroque Organ Music (Overtone Records). Publs: Assoc. Ed., Hymnal Colleges & Schools, 1956; Ed., Christian Humns, 1963; Ed., Vol. III, 8, Paul Hindemith Collected works, 1977. Contbr. to: Notes. Mbr.; num. profl. orgs. Hons: Bach Medal for Organ Playing Harriet Cohen Int. Fndn.; LHD., Colgate Univ., 1963; D Mus., St. Olaf Coll., 1967. Hobbies: Travel; Photography. Address: Sch. of Music, Yale Univ., New Haven, CT 06520, USA. 2, 3, 11.

NOTT-BOWER, Jill, b. Colyford, UK. Mezzo-Soprano. Educ: GSM; ARCM. m. Robert Spencer, 2 s. Career: over 1000 recitals & broadcasts since 1958 in duo w. husband (specialising in lute & guitar accomp. songs). Recip. of Silver Medal, Worshipful Co. of Musicians. Hobbies: Dressmaking; Winemaking; Horseback Riding. Address: c/o Ibbs & Tillett, 124 Wigmore St., London W1H 0AX, UK.

NOVÁK, Géza, b. 22 June 1921, Budapest, Hungary.

Flautist; Director of Chamber Wind Ensemble. Educ: Music Acad., Budapest. m. Jana Novák, 1 d. Debut: Prin. flautist, State Orch. of Budapest. Career: Prin. flautist, Broadcasting Orch., Budapest; Opera, Budapest; Broadcasting Orch., Bratislava, Czech.; Prin. flautist, Czech Phil. Orch. Recordings: All Czech Phil. & Wind Quintet; solo records of Bach, Mozart, Debussy; mbr. num. int. juries in different countires. Hons: Laureate mbr., Czech Phil. Hobbies: Books; Nature. Mgmt: Hudlební fond, Prague. Address: Mostecka 17, Prague 1, Czech.

NOVAK, Jiri, b. 5 Sept. 1924, Horni Jeleni, Czechoslovakia. Violinist. Educ: Conserv. of Prague; Acad. of Music, Prague. m. Dagmar Novakova, 1 d. Career: Ldr. of V Talich's Czech Chmbr. Orch., 1945-48; 1st Violinist, Smetana Quartet. Recordings: Paganini Concerto No. 1 w. Prague Symph. Orch.; Mozart Concerto No. 4 w. Czech Phil.; Orch.; °. Smetana Quartet. Recip. Czechoslovak Artist Award of Merit, 1966. Hobbies: Drawing; Painting. Address: Praha 5, Na Smukyrce 14, Czechoslovakia.

NOVICK, Melvyn J, b. 7 Aug. 1946, Brooklyn, NY, USA. Singer (Tenor). Educ: Bmus, 1968, MMus, 1970, Manhattan Schl. of Music. Career: apps. w. NY City Opera, Syracuse Symph., Dayton-Toledo Opera Assns., Opera Classics of NJ, State Opera of Conn., Alvin Ailey Dance Co. and at Spoleto, Artpark & Aspen music fests.; fac. mbr., Wagner Coll.; Artistic Dir., Warminster Symph. Opera. Mbrships: Donizetti Soc.; Phi Mu Alpha Sinfonia. Mgmt: Helena Blue, Artist Rep. Address: 459 Hillside Ave., Palisades Pk., NJ 07650, USA.

NOVOTNY, Bretislav, b. 10 Jan. 1924, Vsetin, Czechoslovakia. Violinist. Educ: Fac. of Philos., Charles Univ., 1945-47; Grad., Conserv. of Music, Prague, 1950. m. Estela Roldan, 3 c. Debut: Soloist w. Prague Symph. Orch., 1949. Career incl: Mbr., Old Prague Quartet, 1951-55; Concert Master, Prague Symph., 1954-61; 1st Violin & Ldr., Prague STring Quartet, 1955-; Instr., Prague Music Acad., 1970-; Concert tours of Switzerland, 1947; Poland, 1948; E. Germany; 1958; Mexico, 1965; New Zeland, 1966; Austria, 1971; USSR, 1972; num. tours world-wide w. Prague String Quartet. Recordings: Sonatas & Partitas for solo violin (J S Bach, in his own arr. (realisation) - Supraphon-Artia label); Hexentank (N Paganini), Supraphon; Num. recordings w. Prague Str. Quartet, (Dvorak). Contbr. to: Hudebni rozhledy, Prague. HOns: Prize of City of Prague (presented to Prague String Quartet for thei prominent work for City & State), 1967; Prize for Recording of Bach works, Supraphon, 1973; Artist of Merit Award from Czech Govt., 1974. Mgmt: Pragokoncert, Prague. Address: Na Lysinach 15, 14700 Praha 4, Czechoslovakia.

NOVOTNY, Jan, b. 15 Dec. 1935, Prague, Czechoslovakia. Pianist. Educ: Prague Conserv.; Dip., Acad. of Musical ARts, Prague. Debut: Prague, 1954. Career: concert pianist in most European countires, & in Brazil, India & Burma, Thailand, Malaysia, Hong Kong, Philippines, etc.; Frequent performances on TV & Radio; Rectals, Prague Sp-ring Festivals, 1972, 74, 75. Recordings incl: Sonatas by Beethoven, Brahms, Hindemith, etc.; num. works of Smetana & other Czech Composers (Pragkoncert label). Hon: 2nd Prize, Int. Piano Competition, Prague Spring Festival, 1957. Hobbies: Chmbr. Music; Cooking. Address: Rosickych 6, 150 00 Prague 5, Czechoslovakia.

NOVY, Donald Andrew, b. 23 Apr. 1932, Oak Park, Ill., USA. Compsoer; Conductor; Trumpeter; Teacher. Educ: B Mus., Northwestern Univ., 1954; M Mus., ibid, 1955; Univ. of Colo.; Denver Univ. m. Joyce J. Novy, 3 c. Career: Soloist, Northwestern Univ. Band, Univ. of Colo. Band, Denver Municipal Band, Brico Symph. Trumpet, var. Symphs.; Perfs. w. Tex Beneke, Ted Weems, Nat Cole, Henry Mancini, Jerry Lewis, Red Buttons, Billy May, Paul Whiteman, Vikki Carr, Helen O Connell, var. others. Tchr. Instrumental Music, Denvre Public Schls. Pvte. Tchr., Trumpet Music Dir., Denver Winter Sports Show, 1965-66, Alpine Musicamp, Inc., Aspen, Colo, 1968-71; Pres., Alpine Music Studio Inc.; currently w. Art Gow Orch., Denver. Composer, Sonatina for Brass. Recordings: The Denver Affair. Publ: Brass Wind Instrument.Mbrships: Local 20, Am. Fedn. of Musicians; MEND; CMEA; NAJE; NEA; DCTA; DEA; Pi Kappa Lambda. Hons: Winner, Young Man With a Horn Contest, Chgo., Ill., 1950, 3rd Place Award, Comp., Thor Johnson Brass Comp. Contest, Cinn. Conserv., 1954. Hobbies incl: Skiing; Tennis. Address: 1234 S Quince Way, Denver, CO 80231, USA.

NOWAKOWSKI, Mieczyslaw, b. 13 Oct. 1934, Wlodzimierz, USSR. Director of Orchestra. Educ: Dip. of Cond., State High Schl. of Music. m. Helena Kasprowicz-Nowakowska, 1 s. Debut: Nat. Phil., Warsaw, 1959. Career: Cond., Theatre of

Music, Gdynia, 1959-61; Cond., Great Theatre, Warsaw, 1961-69; Dir. of Orch., Hd. & Artistic Dir., State Opera, Poznań, 1969-71; Hd., Musical Polish TV Theatre, Warsaw, 1972-73; Cond., Great Theatre, Warsaw, 1974-77; Musical Mgr., ibid, 1978-. Num. recordings; special recordings for Polish Radio & TV. Hons: Golden Prague for Morning, by Tadeusz Baird, Prague, 1974. Address: 8 Moliera St., Ap. 44, 00-076, Warsaw, Poland.

NOWAK-ROMANOWICZ, Alina, b. 14 Jan. 1907, Warsaw, Poland. Musicologist. Educ: Warsaw Univ.; Dip., Conserv. of Music, Warsaw, 1932; M Musicol., Jagiellonian Univ., Cracow, 1936; D Musicol., ibid, 19651. m. Edward Romanowicz. Career: Lectr., State HS Music, Katowice, 1947-52; 57-59; Ed., Polish Music Publr., PWM. Cracow, 1956-61; Lectr., Jagiellonian Univ., 1960-78. Publs: incl: Józef Elsner, 1957; Polish Music in the Age of Enlightenment and the Early Romanticism, 1966; Somes problems of Polish opera 1796-1830, 1967; Elsner's Music Style, 1969; J Elsner & Chopin, 1973. Contbr. to Polish Acad. Scis. Inst. Lit. Rsch.; Muzyka. Mbr., Union Polish Comps. Hobby: Travel. Address: 40 524, Katowice, ul. Kościuszki 164, Poland.

NUNN, June Aubretta Linda, b. 9 June 1929, Slough, UK. Specialist in School Music; Pianist (solo & accomp.). Educ: RCM; GRSM; ARCM; AMusTCL. Career: Music Specialist, Bradenham House Schl., High Wycombe, 1950-54; Music Specialist, Bucks CC, 1956-67; Hd., Music Dept., Herschel High Schl., Slough, 1968-. Mbrships: ISM; Schls. Music Assn. (hon. mbrships. sec.). Hons: Gold Medallist (piano), Assoc. Bd. Finals. Hobbies: Reading; Walking; Motoring; Handcrafts. Address: Jack's Park, Upper Gordon Rd., Camberley, Surrey GU15 2HN, UK.

NUTTING, Geoffrey Howard, b. 14 Oct. 1936, Wolverhampton, UK. Assistant Librarian; Lecturer in Music. Educ: BA (Durham), 1958; MA (Durham), 1961; Dip. in Theology (Oxon), 1960; Associateship, Lib. Assn. of Aust., 1977. m. Julis Lesley Wakefield Nutting, 1 d, 1 s. Career: Lectr. in Music, Univ. of Nigeria, Nsukka, 1961-66; Lectr. in Music, Monash Univ., Aust., 1966-; Snr. Lectr., ibid, 1976-; Asst. Libn., ibid, 1977-. Contbr. to: The Music Review; Tape Recorder; The Musical Quarterly; Una Sancta; Int. Review of Music Aesthetics & Sociology; Miscellanea Musicologica; Interchange; Parergon; Tyndale Paper. Mbrships: Lib. Assn. of Aust.; Musicol. Soc. of Aust.; Tyndale Fellowship of Aust.; Vic. Rep., RISM (Aust.). Hons: The Music Prize, Wolverhampton Grammar Schl., 1955. Hobbies: Music Recording and Reproduction; Theology. Address: 52 Peel St., Berwick, Vic. 3806, Aust.

NYBERG, Gary B, b. 9 Feb. 1945, Lewiston, ID, USA. Director of Bands; Teacher of Low Brass. Educ: BA, Univ. of ID; MMus, Univ. of Wis.; PhD, Brigham Young Univ.; conducting, trombone & comp. studies w. var. tchrs. m. M Karen Nyberg, 3 c. Career: Dir. of Bands & Music Theory, Lower Columbia Coll.; trombone soloist, Univ. of Idaho, Greenville, Miss. Symps. Comps: Beta Lyrae, for chmbr. orch.; Manifesto: Summer, 1968, for trombone & tape; 6 Arabesques, for solo tuba. Publs: Introduction to Schenker Analysis, 1978. Mbrships: Am. Musicol. Soc.; Int. Trombone Assn.; MENC; Phi Mu Alpha Sinfonia; Pi Kappa Lambda; Sigma Alpha Epsilon (pres.); AFM. recip. Robert Bollinger Award, 1963. Hobbies: Stamp Collecting; Canoeing; Gardening. Address: Lower Columbia Coll., Longview, WA 98632, USA.

NYGAARD, Eline, b. 5 July 1913, Sandefjord, Norway. Pianist; Piano Teacher. Educ: studied w. Dagmar Walle-Hansen, Nils Larsen & Simon Barer. m. Kjell Riisnaes, 2 s., 1 d. Debut: Oslo, 1939. Career: piano recitals, Norway, concert tours, Am., 1949; recitals, Norway from S to N, 1956; Soloist w. orchs., Oslo, Bergen, & other cities; sev. radio broadcasts; Piano Tchr., 1967-. Asst. Prof., 1971-. Univ. of Oslo. Mbrships: Music Tchrs. Assn. of Oslo; Norwegian Musician Artists Assn. Address: Niels Juels gate 1, Oslo 2, Norway.

NYGHT, Kim Alvin, b. 11 July 1953, Des Moines, Iowa, USA. Percussionist; Band Director. Educ: B Mus Ed., Drake Univ. Career: Timpanist & percussionist, Des Moines Metro Opera Pit Orch., 1973-75; num. large scale Orchl. Ch. Progs.; Percussionist & Prin. Timpanist, Des Moines Symph., 3 yrs. Publ: co-author, Roger Maxwell's 14 Weeks to a Better Band, 1973. Mbrships: Percussive Arts Soc.; Des Moines Musicians Assn.; NEA; Iowa State Educ.; Perry Educ. Assn. Hobbies: Tennis; Cycling; Bowling; Billiards; Golf. Address: 2811 Warford Apt. 3, Perry, IA 50220, USA.

NYHLEN, (Lars) Lennart (Elias), b. 11 Apr. 1936, Stockholm, Sweden. Musician (Guitar, Banjo, Mandolin). Educ: pvte. studies of guitar, comp., harmony etc. m. Regnhild Gunilla, 3 d. Career: studio work; a ccomp. num. Int. stars; num. TV & film apps.; tours of Sweden & Europe w. different groups; composer & arr., 1970-; cond. & comp., children's progs. Recordings: 3 LPs, 1 single, num. radio & TV recordings. Hons: mbr. of trio winning Swedish newspaper AT contest for amateur jazz groups, 1954; mbr. of Dixieland band winning Swedish TV contest for amateur jazz groups, 1956. Hobbies: Photography; Film. Address: Selmedalsvägen 64/VII, 12655 Hägersten, Sweden.

NYSTEDT, Knut, b. 3 Sept. 1915, Oslo, Norway. Composer; Organist; Choral Director. Educ: (organ) w. Arild Sandvold, Oslo, & Ernest White, NY; (comp.) w. Bjarne Brustad, Oslo, & Aaron Copland, USA. m. Birgit Nystedt, 3 c. Debut: as organist, 1938. Career: Organist, Torshov Ch., Oslo, 1946-; Dir., Norwegian Soloist's Choir; TV & radio apps. w. Norwegian Soloists' Choir in Norway, Sweden, Denmark, USA, France, Japan & Korea. Comps. incl: Orchl., choral, organ & chmbr. music. num. recordings of own works. Mbrships: Soc. of Norwegian Comps.; Chmn., Oslo Organists Soc., 1956-65. Hons: Kt. of St. Olaf, 1966; Disting. Service Citation, Augsburg Coll., Minneapolis, 1975. Address: Vestbrynet 25, Oslo 11, Norway. 29, 30.

NYSTROEM, Margot, b. 8 June 1935, Soderhamn, Sweden. Pianist. Educ: Degree in Piano, Borgarskola, Stockholm. m. Nils G. Nystroem, 1 s., 2 d. Debut: Stockholm. Career: Concert apps. in W. Germany & Austria, 1972; London, 1973; USA, France, Rome & Iceland, 1974. Tour in USSR, 1975. Mbrships: Treas., Gottfrid Boon Soc., Stockholm. Recip: Royal Schlrship. for Artists, Swedish Govt.; Stockholm Scholarship for Artists, 1973, 1975. Mgmt: Edward Rye, Birger Jarlogatan 123, Stockholm. Hobbies: Gardening; Cooking; Skiing. Address: Tantogatan 43, S-117 42 Stockholm, Sweden.

NYTTENEGGER, Esther E., b. 20 July 1941, Zürich, Switzerland. Cellist. Educ: Winterthur Conserv.; Zürich Conserv. m. Ernst Kern. Career: Solo cellist & parmanent soloist, Lucerne Fest. Strings, 1962-67; Num. concert tours, Western Europe, Middle E, S Africa, Canada, Mexico & USA. Recordings incl: Joseph Haydn's Cello Concert Nr. 1, C-Major; Henrich Suter Meister, 2 concerts for violoncello & orch. Mbr., Schweizerischer Tonkuenstlerverin, Lausanne. Hons: 2nd prize, 3rd Pablo Casals Int. Violoncello Competition, Israel, 1961; Solistenpreis des Schweizerischen Tonkuenstlervereins, 1962. Hobbies: Archaeol. Travel. Address: Im Straler 30, CH-8047 Zürich, Switzerland.

NZEWI, Meki Emeka, b. 21 Oct. 1938, Ninewi, Anambra State, Nigeria. Academic; Traditional Drummer; Playwright; Specialist in African Music; Composer. Educ: BA. m. Philomena Nnennaya Nzewi, 4 c. Career: musical comps. perfd. on Nigerian radio & TV; Writer & Dir. of musical playes staged and broadcast throughout Nigeria; Sr. Rsch. Fellow in Ethnomusicol. & Drama, Inst. of African Studies, Univ. of Nigeria, Nsukka. Contbr. to: Ibadan Jrnl.; Conch; The Black Perspective in Music. Mbrships: Int. Folk Music Coun.; Soc. to Ethnomusicol. Hobby: Travel. Address: Inst. of African Studies, Univ. of Nigeria, Nsukka, Nigeria.

O

OAKES, Rodney Harland, b. 15 April 1937, Rome, NY, USA. Composer & Teacher of Electronic Music. Educ: BA, 1960, MA, 1966, San Diego State Univ.; DMA, Univ. of S Calif., 1973. m. Jeannette L Oakes, 2 d. Career: Perf. throughout USA; TV, LA, PBS-Chant Chance, CBS-Steps to Learning; num. radio interviews. Comps. incl: The Primrose; Song for Two Voices; Dialogue for Flute & Tape Recorder; Six by Six; Introspecturm in Six Refractions: Variations on an 1th Century Hymn Tune. Mbr., MENC; Am. Soc. of Univ. Comps.; Audio Engrng. Soc.; Phi Delta Kappa. Contbr. to: The Comp.; Synapse. Hons: Celia Buck Grant-In-Aid Award, 1966; Delius Fndn. Hons. Mention, 1970; Nat. Endowment of the Arts Commn., Synergy (ballet), 1975. Hobbies incl: Reading. Address: 5000 Prospect Blvd. Pasadena, CA 91103, USA.

OBADIA, Heskel H (known professionally as **Hakki Obadia**), b. 15 Jan. 1924, Baghdad, Iraq. Violinist; Oudist. Educ: studied at Fine Art Inst., Baghdad, 1941-46; San Fran., Conserv. of Music, USA, 1948-50; studied violin w. Sidney Griller; studied under French, Italian, English, Rumanian, Russian, Lebanese & Am. Music Tchrs.; AA & BA in Music (& post grad work in comp.), Univ. of Calif., Berkeley. m. Rebecca Musaffi, 2 s., 1 d. Career: Soloist, Carnegie Hall, NYC; Cond. of Middle E. Music Grp. & Solo Violinist, Phil. Hall, Lincoln Ctr., 1963 & '64; Appeared at World Fair in NY, 1963-64; Var. TV commercials, NYC (arr. & comp.); Ldr. of own Grp. & NY, Radio Progs. Comps. incl: over 20 albums of Middle E. Music & over 250 comps. & arrs. Recordings: on MGM; Decca; Audio Fedility; Scepter; Oriental Record Co., etc. Publs: The Hakki Obadia OUD Method Book; Middle East Mood for Orchestra, 1976. Contbr. to var. jrnls. Recip. medals for musical achievement. Hobbies: Taping & collecting old recordings. Address: 54 Clay Pitts Rd., Greenlawn, NY 11740, USA.

OBELKEVICH, Mary Helen Rowen, b. 29 Mar. 1945, NYC, NY, USA. Musicologist; violinist; violist. Educ: PhD, Columbia Univ. Schl. of Grad Studies, 1973; violin studies w. Louis Persinger, William Kroll; Theory studies w. Adele T Katz; comp. studies w. Darius Milhaud, Irving Fine, Otto Luening, Vladimir Vssachevsky. m. David Obelkevich. Career: specialist in hist. of music philosophy & its application to practice. Comps: elementary piano comps. in Instant Piano. Publs: Philosophy & Art in the Music of Seventeenth Century France, 1973; (co-author) Instant Piano, 1979. Contbr. to: Current Musicol.; Musical Quarterly. Mbrships: Am. Musicol. Soc.; CMS; MLS: MOG; Friend of the Columbia Univ. Libraries; Friend of the NYPL; Bd. of Dirs., Community Opera Inc. recip. Young Artist Award, Nat. Arts Club (violin), 1965. Hobbies: Travel; Sweater Designing. Address: 115 Clr. Pk. W, NY, NY 10023, USA.

OBER, Carol Jean, b. 28 Nov. 1940, Muskegon, Mich., USA. Clarinettist; Clinician; Teacher. Educ: BMus, Univ. of Mich., 1963; MMus, ibid., 1965; Mich. Permanent Tchng. Cert., 1968. Debut: Ann Arbor, Mich., 1964. Career: 1st Clarinet, NC Symph., 1965-66; 1st clarinet, Can. Opera Co., 1968-73; clarinettist & ldr., Toronto Woodwind Quintet, 1970-77; clarinet & bass clarinet, Mich. Opera Theatre, Detroit, 1978-; Asst. prin. clarinet, Detroit Concert Band, 1966-; num. recitals in Toronto, Mich. & elsewhere; num. clinics; sev. tchng. posts in Mich. & Can.; pvte. instructor & lectr. sev. recordings. Publs: Clarinet Mouthpiece Designs & Acoustics (article), 1965. Mbrships: Tau Beta Sigma (former sec.); AFM. recip., Arion Award, 1958. Hobbies: Travel; Tennis: Dog Training; Work on Clarinet Mouthpieces. Address: 1418 Morton Street, Ann Arbor, MI 48104, USA.

OBERLIN, Russell, b. 11 Oct. 1928, Akron, Ohio, USA. Countertenor. Educ: Dip. in voice, Julliard Schl. of Music, 1951. Career: num. apps. in concerts, opera, at chs., univs. museums, etc. USA, Can. & UK; Leading Soloist, NY Por Musica Antiqua, 1953-59; Soloist, Play of Daniel (Christmas prod.), 1957-; sang incidental music for the Lark, 1955, Am. Shakespeare Fest. Theatre prods., 1957-58; participant in fest.; many TV apps. Has recorded for Decca, Columbia, Esoteric, Expériences Anonymes Records. Co-Ed: Purcell songs, 1959. Mgmt: Colbert Artist Mgmt., 850 7th Ave., NY, NY 10019, USA. 2.

OBETZ, John Wesley, b., 29 June 1933, Locust Dale, Pa.., USA. Organ Recitalist; Professor of Music (Organ). Educ: B Mus Ed, 1954, M Mus, 1955, Northwestern Univ., Evanston, Ill.; D Sac Mus, Union Theol. Sem., NYC, 1962; Int. Summer Acad. for Organist, Haarlem, Netherlands, 1966. m. Grace Spencer Obetz, 1 s. Career: Prof., Albion Coll., Mich., 1962-67, Conserv. of Music, Univ. of Mo-Kansas City, 1970-; weekly broadcasts, The Auditorium Organ, sponsored by Reorganized Ch. of Jesus Christ of Latter Day Ss., 1967-. Has made 6 redcordings for Célèbre Records. Contbr. to Music Ministry. Mbrships. incl: Reg. Chmn. (10 states), AGO. Hobbies: Sailing; Tennis. Mgmt: Célèbre Mgmt., PO Box 1959, Independence, MO 64051, USA. Address: 8841 Fairway, Leawood, KS 66206, USA.

OBRADOVIĆ, Aleksandar, b. 22 Aug. 1927, Bled, Yugloslavia. Composer; Professor of Composition. Educ: Grad., Belgrade Acad. of Music, 1952. m. Biljana, 1 s. Career incls: Asst. Prof.-Assoc. Prof.-Prof., Belgrade Acad. of Music (now Fac. of Music Art), 1954-; comps. perf. in 14 countries. Comps. incl: 5 symphs.; many other orchl. works, many vocalinstrumental works; ballet, A Springtime Picnic at Dawn; chmbr. works; film music; music for radio dramas; electronic music. Publs: Orchestration, I & II, 1976, III in preparation; Electronic Music & Electronic Instruments, 1978. Contbr. to var. publs. Mbr., Soc. of Comps. of Sebia. Recip. 17 prizes & sev. grants to study abroad. Address: Branka Djonovića 8, Belgrade 11000, Yugoslavia.

O'BRIEN, Donna Bray, b. Baker, Mont., USA. Harpist; Soprano; Musicologist. Educ: incls: BS, Univ. of Ore.; studied w. var. Bunratty Castle Harpists, Shannon, Ireland. Am. Debut: Ore. Soc. of Artists Hall, Portland, European Debut: Dromoland Castle, Co. Clare, Ireland, Career: num. recitals, coll. concerts, radio & TV broadcasts; concert-lectures, Irish Heritage in Song, KOAP-TV Portland & KOAC-TV, Corvallis, Ore., Cable TV, Portland, Comps: Rosie, The Elephant (children's song); Thanksgiving Song. Contb. (Irish Harp Ed.), Folk Harp Jrnl. Mbrships: incl: VP, Portland Chapt., Am. Harp. Soc.; Bd. of Dirs., AAUW; Irish-Am. Cultural Inst.; Am.-Irish Bicentennial Committee. Hobbies incl: Winter Sports: Swimming; Dancing; Tennis. Address: 2402 N. Webster St., Portland, OR 97217, USA.

O'BRIEN, Peter Adrian, b. 7 Apr. 1936, Poole, Dorset, UK. Snoir Lecturer in Music; Organist; Pianist. Educ: MA, Mus B, Cantab; FRCO (CHM); Cert. Educ. m. Hazel Enid Stringer, 1 s., 1 d. Debut: Accomp. to Janet Howd, Wigmore Hall, 1973. Career: Music Master, Skinners Schl. Tunbridge Wells, 959-61; Asst. Dir. of Music, St. Luke's Coll., Exeter, 1964-; Accomp., BBC, Bristol, 1974; Mbr., Duo Gagliano; Music Dir., South West Opera; Cond., Minehead Fest. Orch. Recordings: W. Herbert Downes on BBC Radio 3. Mbrships: RMA, RCO; ISM. Hobbies: Chess; Orinthol.; Gardening. Address: 'Lyndewode,' 29 Argyll Rd., Exeter, Devon, UK.

O'BRIEN, Robert Felix, b. 24 June 1921, Bresse, Ill., USA. Band Director; Associate Professor of Music. Educ: Navy Schl. of Music, Wash. DC, 1942-43, B3c, Southern Ill., Univ., 1947, MA, State Univ. of Iowa, 1949; further studies, Univ. of Colo., 1951-52. m. Catherine Casey, 3 s. Career: USN fleet band, Pacific area, 1942-46; Tchr., pub. schls., Iowa, 1947-51, & St. John's Univ., Collegeville, Minn., 1954-55; Assoc. Prof. (applied brass, instrumental techniques, band arr. & music educ.), & Dir. of Bands, Univ. of Notre Dame, Ind., 1952-54, 55-; Acting Chmn., Music Dept., ibid, summers 1970 & 71; has made local, regional & nat. TV & radios apps. as univ. band dir.; has made sev. recordings w. Univ. of Notre Dame Band. Compositions: Damsha Bua (Victor Clog). Contbr. to jrnls. Mtr., num. profl. orgs. Recip. of many awards. Hobbies: Reading; Record & Tape Collecting; Fishing; Camping. Address: 1452 Glenlake Dr., S. Bend. IN 46614, USA. 7.

O'CONNELL, Raymond, b. 1922, Melbourne, Aust. Teacher of Piano. Educ: Licentiate, Assoc. Bd., Royal Schls. of Music; LRSM (Aust.); ARCM. m. Cecilia J Airey, 2 s., 2 d. Career: On Staff, RCM, 1947-49 & 1954-55; Examiner, Assoc. Bd., Royal Schls. of Music, 1954-; Prin. Tchr. of Piano, Elder Conservatorium, Adelaide Univ., 1949-53, & RSAM, 1955-64; Sr. Lectr. & Supvsr. of Adult Pt.-Time Studies, ibid, 1964-; Hd. of Piano Dept., ibid, 1978-. Hons: Hopkinson & Chappell Gold Medals; Dannreuther, Corbett & Queens Prizes; Worshipful Co. of Musicians Medal, 1942. Address: 19 Cricket Field Lane, Houston, Renfrewshire, PA6 7JD, UK. 3.

ODEI, Matthew Asare, b. 11 Julyu 1927, Akim Swedru, Ghana. Teacher of School Music, Piano, Voice, African Drumming, Music & Culture. Educ: Wesley Tchr. Trng. Coll., Kumasi; Music Specialist Course, Kumasi Coll. of Technol; Schl. Music Course, Winneba Specialist Trng. Coll.; Gen. Dip. in Music, Univ. of Ghana, Legon. 5c. Debut: Swedru Methodist Ch., 1947. Career: Schl. Music Tchr., Organist, Singer; Conductor & Accomp. for TV & Radio; Senior (tutor) Superintendant; Hd of Music & Culture Dept., Berekum Trng.

Coll. Conserv.; Brong Ahafor Reg; Arts Council of Ghana Rep., music section. Comps: Songs, Preludes, Anthems etc., for voice &/or orch.; African music w. drum accomp. Recordings: Choral songs. Publs: African Music. Contbr. to local jrnls. Mbrships: Chmn., Berekum Annual Musical Fest.; Dir., Wesley Singers; Chmn. & dir., Dramatic Soc. Hons: sev. prizes, awards & scholarships. Hobbies: Farming; Games & Athletics; Reading. Address: Berekum Trng. Coll., PO Box 74, Berekum B/A, Ghana.

O'DETTE, Paul, b. 2 Feb. 1954, Pittsburgh, Pa., USA. Lutenist. Educ: Schola Cantorum Basiliensis, Switz.; studied w. Eugen Dombois & Thomas Binkley. Career: Concerts in NY, Wash., Pittsburgh, Toronto, Detroit, Houston, Atlanta, London, Amsterdam, Hamburg, Vinna, Zürich, etc.; app. on CBS TV, The Heyday of the Lute; Dir. of Early Music, Eastman Schl. of Music. Recordings: works by Byrd, Dowland; Duetti Italiani; Estampie; L'Agonie du Langue d'Oc; Musik der Spielleute. Contbr. to Lute Soc. of Am. Newsletter. Mbrships: Lute Soc. of Am.; Lute Soc. (UK). Hons: Columbus (Ohio) Symph. Young Musicians Auditions, 1971. Hobbies: Cooking; Camping. Address: 13 S Goodman St., Rochester, NY 14607, USA.

O'DONNELL, John David, b. 6 Oct. 1948, Sydney, Aust. Organist; Harpsichordist; Lecturer; Musicologist. Educ: Perfs. & Tchrs. Dips., NSW State Conserv. of Music; BMus, Univ. of Durham; Fellowship & Choirmaster's Dips., RCO; Archbishop of Canterbury's Dip. in Ch. Music. m. Gail Jenne DeVoss, 2 s., 1 d. Career: Lectr., NSW State Conserv. of Music, 1941-74; Organist, St. Mary's Cathedral, Sydney, 1971-74; Snr. Lectr., The Vic. Coll. of the Arts, 1974-; Organist, St. Peter's, Eastern Hill, Melbourne, 1974-; Perfd. complete organ works of Bach in Melbourne, 1974; Frequent recital tours in N Am., 1977-. Contbr. to: Musicology; The Diapason; Early Music, etc. Hons: Student of the Year, NSW State Conserv. of Music, 1966; Limpus Prize, RCO, 1969; Winner, Nat. Organ Playing Competition, Southport, UK, 1969. Hobbies: Reading. Mgmt: Hart/Murdock Artists Mgmt., Toronto. Address: 729 Malvern Rd., Toorak, Vic., Australia.

O'DONOVAN, Una Margaret, b. 6 Dec. 1943, Dublin, Repub. of Ireland. Harpist. Educ: Mus B, Pt. I, Sr. Tchng. Cert., Univ. Coll. Dublin; Pvte. harp tuition, Maria Korchinska, London, & Phia Berghout, Amsterdam. Career: Prin. Harpist, City of Birmingham Symph. Orch., Royal Opera House Covent Gdn., RPO (currently); chmbr. music w. London Sinfonietta & Nash Ensemble; Apps. on Ulster TV, Irish Radio & TV, BBC Radio, Dutch Radio & TV; Recorded Henze Doppio Concerto for Hilversum Radio, etc. Hobbies: Reading; Walking. Mgmt: Dr. G de Koos & Co., London Br. Address: 17 Castelnau, Barnes, London SW 13 UK.

O'DUINN, Proinnsias, b. 18 Oct. 1941, Dublin, Eire. Orchestral Conductor. Educ: mainly pvte. m. Patricia Higgins, 1s., 1d. Debut: Dublin. Career: Prin. Cond., Iceland Symph. Orch.; Prin. Cond., Orquesta Sinfonica Nacional del Ecuador; Prin. Cond., RTE (Irish radio & TV) Singers; now Permanent Prin. Cond. of RTE Concert Orch. Hons: Fellowship from Irish Arts Coun.; Radio & TV Critics Award. Hobbies: DIY; Gardening. Address: Tankardrath Cottage, Tankardrath, Towland of Gibbstown, Co. Meath, Eire.

OFSDAL, Steinar, b. 4 Oct. 1948, Oslo, Norway. Musician (Recorders, Hardangerfiddle, Cello, Double Bass). Educ: Dip., Orff Inst., Slazburg, Austria. m. Nina Frostrup. Career: Played in symph. orchs., jazz bands & chamber music, 1962-74; apps. at Salzburg Fest., 1970-71; concert tours, radio & TV shows in Scandinavia, Germany, Austria, Switz., France & Iceland, w. traditional folk music & folk singing. Comps: commission from Ny Musikk (Norweigian Sect., ISCM), 1974; Incidental music for Peer Gynt, 1978. Recordings: contributed to about 40 LPs; solo album, Floytesprell. Publs: Veslefrikk - en musikkpantomime, 1976. Mbrships: Union of Norwegian Musicians: Hammerfest Icebear club. Hobbies: Norwegian traditional folk music; Photography. Address: Jens Bjelkes Gate 4, Oslo 5, Norway.

OGBE, George Korjosey, b. 2 June 1932, Lolobi, Volta Reg., Ghana. Teacher of Violin, Viola, Piano & Drums; Specialist in Orchestration. Educ: Cert., Schl. of Music, Kumasi Coll. of Techonol.; 1st Ghanaian to qualify as violin tchr., through LRSM; Dip. in music Educ., Bela Bartok Conserv. of Music, Budapest, 1967. m. Peace Ama Osena, 4 children. Debut: as soloist w. Orch. of Kumasi Coll. of Technol., 1958. Career incls: radio broadcasts, Ghana & Hungary, 1962-63; TV appa., Ghana, 1967-. Comps. incl: At the Lagoon (violin & piano); At the Volta Fest. (orch. & percussion); short pieces for strings. Recordings: Ghana Broadcasting Corp. Publs: Notes on Education & Research in Africa Music, 1975. Mbrships. incl:

Nat. Sec., Ghana Music Tchrs. Assn., 1973-; Ghana Nat. Planning Committee, World's Fest. of Black Arts & Culture. Recip., 1611 Amati Bros. & 1713 Stradivari violins through well-wishers. Hobbies incl: Gardening; Literature; Photography. Address: Nat. Acad. of Music, PO Box 25, Winneba, Ghana.

OGDON, John Andrew Howard, b. 27 Jan. 1937, UK. Concert pianist. Educ: Royal Manchester Coll. of Music. m. Brenda Lucas. Career: Concert perfs. throughout the world, incl. London, Edinburgh, Spoleto, Moscow, Milan, Antwerp; 2-piano recitals w. wife; Jt. Dir., Cardiff Festival of 20th Century Music. Recordings incl: concertos by Michael Tippett & Busoni. Compositions: var. works for piano. Hons: 2nd Prize, Liverpool Int. Piano Competition, 1959; Tchaikwsky Award, Moscow, 1962, Liszt Prize, 1961; Harriet Cohen Int. Award. Address: 13 Chester Terr., Regent's Pk., London NW1, UK.

OGSTON, Bruce Robin, b. 18 May 1944, Chester, UK. Singer (Baritone). Educ. incls: FTCL (Singing perf.); FTCL Pianoforte (perf.); Conserv. di Benedetto Marcello, Venice; Vienna Acad. Debut: New Opera Co., Sadlers Wells Theatre, 1973; Wigmore Hall, 1976. Career incls: Phoenix Opera; New Opera Co.; Opera Rara; BBC Singers, 1974-76; apps. w. Engl. Nat. Opera & Royal Opera House, Covent Garden, 1979; BBC Radio 2 "Among Your Souvenirs"; "An Evening of Nostalgia & Laughter". Recordings: The Thief of Bagdad, Film Music of Dimitri Tiomkin w. RPO; Recital of Songs by C W Orr. Mbrships: ISM; Equity. Hons. incl: Elizabeth Schumann Leider Prize & John Halford Pianoforte Prize, 1969; Countess of Munster Musical Trust Award, 1972. Hobbies: Cooking; Cycling; Beer. Mgmt: HHH Ltd. Concert Agency, 5 Draycott Pl., London SW3 2SF; Int. Celebrities Mgmt. Ltd., 12 Drumlin Dr., Milngavie, G62 6LN. Address: 79 Delaware Mansions, Delaware Rd., London W9, UK.

OGTEROP, Bep Alberta Bernarda, b. 5 May 1909, Amsterdam, The Netherlands, Singing Teacher; Pianist; Conductor of Choirs; Member of Juries. Educ: studied music for govt. examination. m. R J J Knaven. Debut: as Piano Accompanist of choir & soloist, 1920; As Singer (altomezzo soprano), 1929; as Cond. of Choirs, 1946. Career: Stage Perfs. of opera & oratorio in Holland; Radio perfs. in Holland (especially AVRO) & Belgium (singing & cond.); TV perfs. in Holland (jury & cond.). Mbrships: Koninklijke Nederlandse Toonkunstenaars-Vereniging; Register of the Nederlandse Toonkunstenaars - Raad. Recip.: Gold Award for Music Achievement, City of Amsterdam, 1975. Hobbies: Animals; Football. Address: Bilderdijkkade 18 Huis, Amsterdam (Oud-West), The Netherlands.

OHANA, Maurice, b. 12 June 1914, Gilbraltar. Composer. Educ: Philos. degree; Study of piano, composing; Schola Cantorum, Paris; Santa Cecilia Conserv., Rome. Num. comps. incl: Sibylle (voice & percussion), 1968; Auto da Fé (opera), 1972; 24 Preludes (piano), 1973; Office des Oracles (3 choral & orchl. grps.), 1974; T'Haran-Ngo (orch.), 1975; Anneau Tamarit (cello & orch.), 1975; Mass, 1977; Trios Contes de l'Honorable Fleur, (chmbr. opera), 1978. Recordings of most of the above & var. other works. Mbrships: SACEM; Musique Sacrée. Hons. incl: Prix de la Rai, 1961; Prix Italia, 1969; Grand Prix du Disque, 1970, '70; Nat. Grand Prix of Music, 1975; Officier des Arts & Lettres. Hobby; Tennis. Mgmt: Edition Jobert, 79 rue Quincampoix, Paris 3. Address: 31 rue du General Delestraint, Paris XVI, France.

O'HARA, Nolene (Thomson), b. 11 Dec. 1935, Sydney, Aust. Pianist; Organist; Music Teacher. Educ: Perfs. & Tchrs. Dip., Sydney Conserv. of Music; A Mus A; Grad. studies Ch. music, New Orleans Bapt. Theol. Sem., USA 2 yrs. m. John O'Hara, 3 s. Debut: Sydney, 1948. Career: Prof., Newcastle Conserv. of Music, 1956; Stage Accomp., & accomp. soloist, TV & radio broadcasts; Arr. & Perf., Ch. music events inclng Billy Graham Crusades; Ch. music seminars & clinics; Music examiner. Recordings: Sing, Make a Joyful Sound (accomp.), USA, 1967; Bapt. Centenary Yr. Fest. of Music, 1968; Baptist Jubilee, Caringbah, Sydney, 1979. Contbr. to profl. publs. Hons: Finalist, Aust. Broadcasting Commission Concerto Competition, 1953; var. scholarships & awards. Hobbies: incls: Reading; Cooking. Address: 47 Langer Ave., Caringbah, NSW 2 229, Australia.

OHLSSON, Garrick, b. 3 Apr. 1948, White Plains, NY, USA. Pianist. Educ: studied w. Thomas Lishman at Westchester Conserv. of Music; w. Sascha Gorondnitski & Rosina Lhevinne at the Juilliard Schl. of Music; pupil of Olga Barabini. Career: Maj. perfs. in 1969 incld. appearances in Boston, Montreal; Invited by Eugene Ormandy to debut w. the Phila. Orch. in

Philharmonic Hall, NY & in Phila. Acad. of Music, 1970; Recital Metropolitan Mus. of Art, 1970; Concert tours to London, Berlin, Vienna, Rome, Milan, Dusseldorf & Baden-Baden; Concerts in NY, Wash., Boston, Chgo. & invitation to play at the White House for P M Edward Heath, 1970-71: Appeared w. many symph. orchs. in USA & Canada inclng. San Fran., Mnpls., Buffalo, Houston, Toronto, Winnipeg & Chicago, & perf. for approx. 12 coll. concert series & univs., 1971-72; Debut perfs. at all the Saratoga Fest. of the Performing Arts, Hollywood Bowl, Grant Park, Tanglewood, & the Caramoor Fest., Katonah, NY, summer 1971; Var. TV appearances. Sev. recordings of Chopin & Liszt for EMI. Hons. incl: 1st prize, Warsaw Int. Chopin Competition (first Am. prize winner), 1970. Address: 1 Hubbard Drive, White Plains, NY, USA.

OHMIYA, Makoto, b. 1 July 1924, Tokyo, Japan. Professor of Musicology; Conductor. Educ: Grad. Laws & Politics, Kyoto State Univ., 1974; Grad., 1951, Finished Master Course, 1953, Tokyo State Univ. (Aesthetics of Music); studied comp. w. Prof. Koji Taku; studies cond. w. Prof. Noboru Kaneko. m. Lina Sugawara, 2 d. Debuts: as Cond., 1950. Career: as Cond., num. concerts w. local orchs. & chmbr. ensembls, 1950-; Musical Dir. & Cond. of Haydn Ensemble, Tokyo, 1971-; apps. in Belgian & French music fests. w. Haydn Ensemble, 1975, '77; as Commentator, num. apps. on NHK Radio & TV prog. series, 1951-; Prof. of Musicology, Ochanomizu State Univ., Tokyo. Many comps. for 2 pianos, chmbr. ensembles & orchs. Recordings: Joseph Haydn; Notturni, 1971; 6 Scherzandi, 1975; 4 Divertimenti a Nove, 1977. Publs: Joseph Haydn, 1962; Guide to 200 Famous Orchl. Works, 2 Vols., 1965; Joseph Haydn's Comps. for Lira (in English), 1973; Joseph Haydn Werke, VI Concerti mit Radleiern, 1976; var. musical texts, ect. Mbrships: Joseph Haydn Inst., Cologne; Int. Musicol. Soc., etc. Address: Ogigaya 4-19-17, Kamakura, Japan.

O'HOGAN, Roger Matthew, b. 6 Sept. 1917, Durban, Natal, S. Africa. Supervisor of Music, Musical Script Writer & Programme Announcer, South African Broadcasting Corporation; Organist, St. Martin's Church, Rosebank, Johannesburg, 1967-78. Educ: Lic. in Music for Organ (Tchr.); Univ. of S. Africa; LTCL. m. Jennifer Mary Schonland, 1 s. Career: has had own radio prog. 'O Come, Let Us Sing', Engl. Serv., SABC, 1949-, now also on SABC Overseas Serv. & Rhodesia Broadcasting. Compositions: Joseph & the Angel for boys' voices & organ (recorded only). Has recorded organ works for SABC. Contbr. to SABC mag. "Radio & TV". Mbr: Special Commnr., RSCM. Hobby: Swimming. Address: 3 Water Lane, Gardens, Johannesburg, 2192 S. Africa. 3.

OHYAMA, Heiichiro, b. 31 July 1947, Kyoto, Japan, Assistant Professor of Music; Performer (Violin, Viola). Educ: Toho-Gakuen Music High Schl. & Music Coll.; AGSM; Ind. Univ., USA. m. Gail Jean Allen, 1 s. Debut: NYC. Career: Appts. at Ind. Univ. & NC Schl. of the Arts; currently Asst. Prof. Music, Univ. of ALIF., Santa Cruz; player w. Chmbr. Music Northwest, Bradenburg Ensemble, Music from Marlboro, & Crown Chmbr. Music; Perfs. at Fests., etc. Recordings for Columbia Records. Mbrships: Musicians Union. UK; Am. Fedn. Musicians; AAUP. Hons. incl: Winner, num. competitions, Japan, USA & UK, 1966-; Regents Fac. Fellowship, Univ. of Calif., 1975. Hobbies incl: Sailing; Carpentry; Cooking. Mgmt: Young Concert Artists, NYC. Address: 204 Coronado Drive, Aptos, CA 95003, USA.

ÖIEN, Ingegärd, b. 1 May 1940, Falkenburg, Sweden. Musician (horn). Educ: Royal Acad. of Music, Stockholm; studies in Brno, Czechoslovakia & Chgo., USA. m. Per Öien, 1 s, 1 d. Career incl: Solo horn, Norwegian Opera, Oslo. Mbr. Norwegian Musicians Union. Hobby: Gardening. Address: Konvallveien 24, N-1473 Skarer, Norway.

ÖIEN, Per (Olav), b. 31 Oct. 1937, Bergen, Norway. Flutist; Educator. Educ: Bergen Conserv. Music. m. Ingegärd Öien, 1 s., 1 d. Debut: Bergen, 1956. Career: Solo Fluist, Norwegian Radio Orch., Bergen Symph. Orch., Oslo Phil. Orch.; Soloist & Chamber Music Perfs., Norway & abroad; Radio & TV Appearances; Mbr., Norwegian Wind Quintet; Tchr., Musikkhögskolen, Oslo. Num. recordings. Mbr., Norwegian Musicians Union. Hons: Princess Astrid's Music Prize, 1965; Alf Andersen Prize, 1966. Hobbies: Sailing; Skiing. Mgmt.: Norsk Koinsertdireksjon AS Klingenberggt. 4, Oslo. Address: Konvallveien 24, N-1473 Skarer, Norway.

OIESEN, Mabel Lucile, b. 13 Jan. 1904, Franklin Pa., USA. Voice Teacher; Choral Director; University Administrator. Educ: B Mus., Coll. of Wooster, Ohio 1928; M.s., Cincinnati Conserv. of Music, 1942; Columbia Univ., summer 1946; Ithaca Coll., summer 1964. m. (1) Eugene Morgan Hawkins, dec., (2) Remo Rebecchi. div. Career: Dir., John Brown Univ.

Cathedras Choir Annual Christmas Progs., Mutual Broadcastings System, 1946-65; toured USA & Can. as Dir. of same choir; Chmn., Music Dept., John Brown Univ. Siloan Springs, Ark., 1944-73. Recordings: collect. of anthems & Brahms Requiem, w. Cathedral Choir; soprano solo recitals, 1973; & 73. Publs: A Guide to Beautiful Singing, 1978. Mbrships: Pi Kappa Lambda, 1942; Ark. Music Tchrs. Assn.; Nat. Assn. of Music Tchrs.; Nat. Assn. of Tchrs. of Singing. Hons: Chalmers Clifton Prize, 1942; Hon. D Mus, Theol. Sem. of LA. 1949; Elected Outstanding Educ. of Am., 1972. Address: 124 N Dogwood, Siloam Springs, AR 72761, USA. 3, 5, 7, 27, 29.

OISTRAKH, Igor Davidovich, b. 27 April 1931, Odssa, USSR. Violinist. Educ: Music Schl. & State Conserv., Moscow. Career: many concerts w. father David Oistrakh; many for. tours. Num. recordings. Hons. 1st Prize, violin competition, Budapest, 1952, & Wieniawski competition, Poznan; Honoured Artist of RSFSR. 16.

OKAMOTO, Kelly G, b. 1 Oct. 1950, Chgo., Ill., USA. Tubaist. Educ: BS in Music Educ., Ind. State Univ. Career: Prin. Tubaist, Norad Command Band, Colo. Springs Symph. Mbrships: Tubaist Universal Brotherhood Assn.; Phi Mu Alpha Sinfonia. Hobby: Archery. Address: 2329 Robin Dr., Colo. Springs, CO 80909, USA.

OKAMURA, Takao, b. 25 Oct. 1931, Tokyo, Japan. Operatic & Concert Bass. Educ: Dip., St. Cecilia Conserv., Rome; Music Acad., Vienna; Grad., Waseda Univ., Tokyo. m. Kazuko Okamura, 1 child. Debut: w. Italian Opera Troupe, Tokyo, 1959. Career: BerlinDeutsche Oper; Munich Staatsoper; Cologne; Düsseldorf; Verona Arena; Rome Teatro del Opera; Tokyo Fujiwara & Nikikai; roles incl: Filippo II, Sarastro, Boris Godunov, King Mark, Rocco, Mephistopheles (Faust), Don Basilio, Grand Inquisitor, Recordings: Fratelli: Westminster; Japan. Publs: Eds. of collections of songs by Italian comps. Mbrships: incl: Tokyo Nikikai. Hons: 1st Prize, Int. Singing Competition, Toulouse, 1960. Mgmt: Rudolph Raab, Austria; Robert Schulz, German Fed. Repub. (Lothringestr. 23, 5000 Cologne 1); Million Concert, (exclusively Japan; Japan Arts (elsewhere). Address: 2 chrome, 16-4-1004 Komazawa, Setagaya-ku, Tokyo, Japan.

O'KEEFE, Bradshaw Dennis, b. 12 Jan. 1946, Balt., Md., USA. Librarian; Researcher. Educ: BMus (Hon), Peabody Conserv. of Music, 1969. Career: asst. music libn.,Peabody Inst., 1976-79; rschr. in the fine arts. Publ: The 1643 Theatrum Biblicum of Nicolaes Visscher & its Musical Iconology, 1970. Contbr. to: rsch. for TV prog., Ralph Kirkpatrick Plays Bach, 1978; prog. notes for Peabody Conserv., 1978-79. Mbrships: Int. Assn. of Music Libs.; Music Lib. Assn.; Am. Musicol. Soc. Hobbies: Rare Book Collecting; Fine Bookbinding; Conservation of Library Materials & Works of Art on Paper. Address: 7109 Greenbank Rd., Balt., MD 21220, USA.

OKON, Krzysztof, b. 23 Jan. 1939, Warszawa, Poland. Musician; Cellist. Educ: Conservatoire of Music, Cracow; Accademia di Santa Cecilia, Rome. 1 s. Debut: 1957. Career: Soloist & w. Cracow Trip, 1957-; apps. in all maj. cities of Poland; Germany; Brussels, Belgium; Antwerp, Holland; Zagreb & Ljubljana, Yugoslavia; Detroit, USA; Alger, Algeria; Taskent & Karaganda, USSR. Recordings incl: 2 long-playing records by Cracow Trio of Polskie Nagrania. Mbr. Assn. of Polish Musicians & Artists. Hons. incl: 1st Prize & Gold Medal as soloist w. Chmbr. Orch. Hobby: Painting. Address: Lobzowska 24 A3, 31-139 Krakow, Poland.

OLÁH, Tiberiu, b. 2 Jan. 1928, Arpasl, Transylvania, Romania. Composer; Professor. Educ: Conserv., Cluj, 1946-49; Dip., Tchaikovsky Conserv.; PhD. m. Yvonne Olah. Career: Comps. perfd. world-wide; Prof., Bucharest Conserv. Comps. incl: Evenimente - 1907; Armonii II, II, III, 1975, '76, '78; Sonata for solo flute, 1978; The Time of Memory, (to the memory of N & S Koussevitsky), for 9 soloists, 973; Timpul Cerbilor, choral symph., 1973; Music for film, The Last Crusade; num. vocal-symph., symph., chmbr. music, choral music, music for stage & film. Recordings: Sonata for Clarinet Solo; Sonata for flute solo; Columna Infinita; Translations for 16 Strings; Perspectives, for 15 instruments; Invocations; Espace et Rythme; The Time of Memory. Publs: Weberns vorseriells Tonsystem, 1969; The Symbol Sound in Bartok's Sonatina for Piano, 1976. Mbrships: Union o Roumanian Comps. Hons: G Enescu Comp. Prize of Romanian Acad., 1965; The Int. Koussevitsky Recording Prize, 1967; Koussevitsky Fndn. Commission Work for Chmbr. Music Soc. of Lincoln Center, 1971. Address: Dionisie Lupu 65, Bucharest, Sector 1, Roumania.

OLÁH, Tibor, b. 11 May 1937, Sopron, Hungary. Violinist; Conductor; Teacher. Educ: Instrumental Specialist; BA (music); Tçhr.-Cond.; Tchrs. dip., Lszt Acad. of Music, 1956. 1 d.,1 s. Debut: cond., symph. orch., Sopron, 1954. Career: radio concerts in Can. as violinist; 1st violin, N York Symph. Comps: Overtures, Fantazia of Schubert's Unfinished, Songs. Recordings: trios & quartets. Publ: First Finger Plus Three I-II-III (violin class method book). Contbr. to: Recorder; How to select a violin tchr. Mbrships: Toronto Musicians Assn.; AFM. Hobbies: Gardening; Painting. Address: 14 Clematis Rd., City of N York, Will, Ont. M2J 4X2, Canada.

O'LEARY, Jane Strong, b. 13 Oct. 1946, Hartford, Conn., USA. Composer; Teacher of Piano & Harmony; Pianist. Educ: BA, Vassar Coll.; MFA, PhD, Princeton Univ. m. Patrick M O'Leary, 1 s. Career: Lectr., Swarthmore Coll., Pa., 1971-72; Tchr. of Piano & Harmony, Coll. of Music, Dublin, 1974-77; Radio perfs., RTE; num. perfs., Ireland; Fndr., Dir. & Pianist, "Concorde" (contemporary music group). Comps: Trio (flute, cello, piano); Begin (mixed choir & flute); Piano Piece, 1973; Trio, for flute, clarinet & piano, 1977; Movements for 10 Instruments, 1970; Quartet for clarinet, bass clarinet, violin & violoncello, 19569; Three Voices - Lightning, Peace, Grass, 1977; Poem from a 3-Yr. Old; I Sing the Wind Around; The Prisoner. Mbrships: Assn. of Irish Comps.; PRS; Dublin Fest. of 20th Century Music; Music Assn. of Ireland; MCPS: Sev. prizes & fellowships. Address: 1 Avondale Rd., Highfield Pk., Galway, Eire.

OLEVSKY, Estela Kersenbaum, b. 13 Aug. 1943, Buenos Aires, Argentina. Concert Pianist. Educ: Prof. Superior de Musical, Nat. Conserv., Buenos Aires; Vocal & Instrumental Conducting, Teatro Colon Art Inst., Buenos Aires. m. Julian Olevsky, 1 d. Debut: Buenos Aires, 1953. Career: Concert tours, S Am., Ctr., & N Am., Far E. NZ, Israel; Am. debut w. Mozart Orch., NY, 1967; Tchr., piano, Univ. Mass., 1968-. Recordings: w. Julian Olevsky, all violin & piano works by Mozart. Mgmt: Conciertos Gerard, Buenos Aires, Argentina. Address: 68 Blue Hills Rd., Amherst, MA 01002, USA.

OLEVSKY, Julian, b. 7 May 1926, Berlin, Germany. Concert Violinist. Educ: Violin w. Russian Master, Alexander Petschnikoff. m. Estela Kersnbaum, 1 s., 2 d. Debut: at age 10. Career: Concertizing since 10 yrs. old; 2 World-wide tours inclng. Europe, Far E, NZ, Israel, USA & Latin Am. Recordings incl: All Bach Sonatas & Partitas for Solo Violin; 12 Vivaldi Concerti; 15 Handel Sonatas; All violin & piano works by Mozart w. Estella Olevsky; A Violin Recital. Hobby: Fishing. Address: 68 Blue Hills Rd., Amherst, MA 01002, USA.

OLGINA-MACKIEWICZ, Olga, b. 24 June 1904, Jaroslawl, Russia. Former Opera Singer; Professor of Singing. Educ: pvte. singing lessons; Dip. as pianist, Conser., Leningrad. m. Zygmunt Mackiewicz. Debut: in Verdi's Traviata, Vilno, Poland, 1922. Career: leading coloratura soprano roles for Warsaw Opera & other Polish theatres; Guest apps. throughout Europe; recitals & radio broadcasts throughout Europe inclng. UK; currently Porf., Music Acad., Poland. Recordings operatic arias w. orchl. accomp.; duos w. Frank Titterton (tenor) w. orchl. accomp.; songs, accomp;. by Ivor Newton (piano). Contbr. to musical mags. Mbr.; Soc. of Polish Musicians. Recip. many awards tchng. Hobbies: travel. Address: 90-132 Lodz, Narutowicza 67-6, Poland.

OLIAS, Lotar, b. Königsberg, Germany. Composer. Educ: Klindworth-Scharwenka Koinserv., Berlin. m. Reiny, 1s. Career: Comp. light music, songs, satirical songs, film music, musicals, popular music; Owner, Edition Esplanady GambH, Hamburg. Num. recordings, inclng. You, You, You; Junge, komm bald wieder; So ein Tag, so wunderschön wie heute; Lotar's Theme; Blue Mirage; Tango of the Drums; Die Gitarre und das Meer; Unter fremden Sternen; Tipsy Piano; Oh Ellie-Lou; Tango in the Rain; Hallelujah 2000; Concert Music, Sahara; Alasca. Over 1000 titles published. Num. Hons. incl: Citation of Achievement. Broadcast Music Inc., USA, 1953; 78; Golden Records for songs & productions; winner, sev. song contests. Address: CH 6612 Ascona, Switzerland.

OLIPHANT, Naomi Joyce, b. 24 Jan. 1953, Toronto, Ont., Can. Pianist; Lecturer; Singer. Educ: MMus (perf. & lit.), Univ. of Toronto, 1975-76; BMus (perf.), ibid., 1971-75; ARCT (piano), Royal Consrv. of Music, Toronto, 1967; ARCT (voice), ibid., 1973. Debut: (piano) w. Toronto Symph. Orch., 1965. Career: Recitals throughout Ont. & on radio; perfs. w. sev. orchs., incl. Toronto Symph. & Hamilton Phil.; recital accomp. in Can. & USA on radio; official accomp. var. orgs.; opera coach & accomp., Toronto Opera Repertoire; solo recitals as singer; soprano soloist w. orchs. & choirs; Lectr., Brock Univ., 1976-; Univ. of Toronto, - 1978; fac., Banff Schl. of Fine Arts, 1979-.

mbr. Univ. Women's Club of Toronto. Hons: winner of num. scholarships, 1960-; 1st prize, United Appeal Competition, Toronto, 1967; winner, Hamilton Phil. Young Artist Competition, 1974. Hobbies: Reading; Swimming; Needlework. Address: 43 Stratheden Rd., Toronto, Ont. M4N 1E5, Canada.

OLIVEIRA, Elmar, b. 28 June, 1950, Waterbury, Conn., USA. Violinist. Educ: Hartt Coll. of Music, Hartford, Conn.; Manhattan Schl. of Music, NYC. Debut: Town Hall, NYC. Career: Apps. w. orchs. inclng. NY Phil., Cleveland, Balt., Chgo., Phila., Dallas, NJ, Minn., Montreal, Moscow Phil., etc. Recordings incl: Husa Sonata; Layman Melodia. Contbr. to: Music Jrnl.; Fugue Mag. Hons: 1st prize, G B Dealey Dallas News Award; 1st Prize, Naumburg Competition; Gold Medal, Tchaikovsky Int. Competition, Moscow, 1978. Hobbies: Antiques; Art; String Instrument Collection; Pool; Billiards. Mgmt: Shaw Concerts, Inc. Address: c/o Robert Levin Assocs., 250 W 57th St., Suite 1332, NY, NY 10019, USA.

OLIVEIRA, Jocy de, b. 11 April 1936, Curtiba, Paraná, Brazil. Pianist; Composer. Educ: MA, Wash. Univ. St. Louis, Mo., USA, 1968; studied Piano w. Marguerite Long, Paris. M. Elezar de Carvalho (div.), 2 s. Debut: Sao Paulo, 1944. Career: Recitalist, & Soloist w. num. major orchs., S. Am., USA & Europe, inclng. Brazilian Symph. Orch., Belgian Nat. Orch. & St. Louis Symph.; broadcasts, Brazil & Europe; Environmental & mixed media concerts; Assoc. Prof., Univ. of S. Fla., Tampa, 1972-73. Compositioins incl: Probabilistic Theater I-II, 1967-68; Polyinteractions I, 1970. Recordings incl: Messaie, Catalogue des Oiseaux. Publs incl: Apague meu Spotlight (1-act play), 1961. Recip. num. musicals hons. Mgmt: Edition Wilhelm Hansen, Gothersgade 9-11, 1123 Copenhagen, Denmark. Address: 18 W. 70 St., NY, NY 10023, USA.

OLIVEIRA, Willy Corrêa de, b. 11 Feb. 1938, Recife, Pernambuco, Brazil. Composer; Conductor. Educ: Studied comp. w. G. Olivier Toni & Henri Pousseur. m. Marta Ferreira de Salles, 1 s., 1 d. Career incls: Music Critic for A Tribuna, 1963; Tchr. of Information Theory & Poetics, Escola Superior de Propaganda, 1963; Dir. Music & Film, J W Thompson Co., 1964-68; Dir. Film & TV, Mauro Salles Publicidade, 1968-72; now Prof. of Comp., Univ. of São Paulo. Compositions incl: Kitschs (piano); Um Movimento (choir, also recorded); Impromptu para Marta; 2 Intermezzos; 2 Preludes; Phantasiestück III. Publ: Composicäco: Reflexoës, 1976. Contb. to jrnls. Mbr.; profl. assns. Hobbies incl: Loving; Reading; Writing., Address: ECA USP (Departmento de Musica), Caixa Postal 8191, São Paulo, Brazil, 14.

OLIVIER, Gerrit Cornelius, b. 6 Nov. 1945, Villiers, S. Afirca. Musicologist; Accompanist; Choral Conductor; Organist. Educ: BMus, 1967, Dip. in Ch. Music, 1967, M Mus (Comps.), 1976. Pretoria Univ.; Transvaal Higher Educ. Dip., 1968. Debuta: (as Accomp.) 1972. Career: Lectr., Conserv. of Music, Pretoria, 1979: Music Master, Pretoria Boys High Schl., 1971-75; Lectr., Dept. of Musicol., Univ. of S. Africa; Ch. Organist, since age 14. Comps: Incidental theatre music; 2 song cycle; organ sowks. Contbr. to newspapers. Mbr.; profl. assns. Hons: incl: 1st Prizes, Conc., Organ & Improvisation, Nat. Univs. Arts Fest., 1965; Brit. Coun. Scholarship, 1976; SABC commission to comp. song-cycle, 1976. Hobbies incl: Ethnomusicol. Writing short stories. Address: Dept. of Musicology, Univ. of S. Africa, PO Box 392, Pretoria 0001, S. Africa.

OLKUSNIK, Joachim, b. 27 March 1927, Kostrzyna, Poland. Composer; Music Editor. Educ: Dip., State Acad. of Music, Warsaw, 1960. m. Malgorzata Kociolek, 2 s., 1 d. Debut: 1957. Career: Ed., Dept. of Serious Music, Polish Radio, 1964-70; currently Ed.-in-Chief, Authors Awcy. Music Publs. Comps. incl: Piano Sonata, 1957; Retrospections for 2 string orchs., woodwinds, brass & percussion, 1961 & 2, 1968; Spectrophonographics for female choir, 52 instruments, 2 harps, 2 pianos & percussion, 1964; Sequences No. 2 for violin & piano, 1969, No. 2 for flute & harpsichord, 1973. Recordings; Polish Radio. Contbr. to: Polish musical jrnls. Mbrships: Bd., Union of Polish Comps.; Sect. of Music Works, Soc. of Authors (ZAIKS). Recip., prize for Spectrophonographics, G Fitelberg Competition, 1964. Hobby: Motoring. Address: Maltanska 5/53, 02-761 Warsaw, Poland.

OLLESON, (Donald) Edward, b. 11 Apr. 1937, South Shields, UK. University Lecturer. Educ: BA, Hertford Coll., Oxford Univ., 1959; MA, ibid., 1963: D Phil, 1967. m. Eileen Gotto, 1965, 2 s., 1 d. Career: Asst. Lectr., Hull Univ., 1962-63; Rsch. Lectr., Christ Ch., Oxford, 1963-66; Fac. Lectr., Oxford Univ., 1966-72; Univ. Lectr. in Music, ibid., 1972-; Fellow, Merton Coll., 1970-; Publs: Ed., Proceedings of the Royal Musical Assn., vols. 94-100. Essays on Opera & English Music in

Honour of Sir Jack Westrup (w. N Fortune & F W Sternfeld), 1975; Music & Letters, (w. Denis Arnold), 1976-; contbr. to var. music publs. Hobbies: Condng., gardening, cooking. Address: Fac. of Music, 32 Holywell, Oxford, UK.

OLMSTEAD, Gary J, b. 4 Feb. 1941, Portland, Mich., USA. Assoicate Professor of Percussion Instruments. Educ: BM Univ. of Mich.; MFA Ohio Univ.; DMA Cleveland Inst. of Music. m. Barbara S Burkholder, 1 s, 1 d. Career: Assoc. Prof., Percussion Instruments Ind. Univ. of Pa. Publs: The Snare Drum Roll, 1979. Contbr. to the Percussionist jrnl. Mbrships: Pres., Bd. of Dirs., Percussive Arts Soc.; Pi Kappa Lambda. Address: 1245 Oak St., Indiana, PA 15701, USA. 8.

OLSEN, (Carl Gustav) Sparre, b. 25 April 1903, Stavanger, Norway, Composer. Educ: Akademische Hochschule, Berlin; Violin . H van der Vegt. m. (1) Edith Davidsen (2) Astri Almestrand. Career: Violinist w. orchs. in Oslo, 1923-33; Bergen, 1935-36; Tchr., Conserv. of Bergen, 1934-40; Cond. of choral socs., Bergen 1935-39; Music Critic, Bergens Tidende, 1935-40. Comps: Orchl. works incl: Canticum for Orch., 1974; Chmbr. music incls: String Quartet, 1972; Contemporary music from Norway. Publs: Memories of Tor Jonsson, 1968. Contbr. to Norsk Musikktiddsskrift. Mbrships: Soc. of Norwegian Comps.; Prog. Coun., Norwegian Broadcasting. 1950-59. Hons. incl: Kt. of St. Olav, 1968. Address: Olav Aukrustsvei 9, 2600 Lillehammer, Norway.

OLSEN, Poul Rovsing, b. 4 Nov. 1922, Copenhagen, Denmark. Composer; Ethonomusicologist. Educ: Univ. of Arhus, 1940-40; Univ. of Copenhagen, 1942-48; Cand. jur., 1948; Royal Danish Conserv. Music, 1943-46; Dip. in piano, harmony & counterpoint, 1946; Studies w. Nadia Boulanger, Paris, 1948-49. m. Solange A M Petit-Dutaillis, 1 s., 2 d. Debut: Arhus, 942. Career: Music Critic, Morgenbladet, 1945-46; Information, 1949-53; Berlingske Tidende, 1954-74; Hd. Ethnomusicol. Sect. Danis Archives of Folklore, 1960-; Lectr., Univ. of Lund, Sweden, 1967-69, Univ. of Copenhagen, 1969-. Comps. incl: Belisa (opera), 1964; The Marriage, 1966, The Stranger, 1969 (ballets); Sinfonia II, 1966, Au Fond de la Nuit, 1968 (orchl. works). Publs: Musiketnologi, 1974; Music & Musical Instruments in the World of Islam, (w. Jean Jenkins), 1976. Contbr. to var. profl. jrnls. Mbrships: incl: Fndn. Danish Comps., 1971; Pres., Int. Folk Music Coun., 1977-. Recip., hons. Address: Tuborgvej 99, 2900 Hellerup, Denmark.

OLSON, Howard Stanley, b. 18 July 1922, St. Paul, Minn., USA. Assist Editor, Africa Theological Journal. Educ: BA, 1943; MDiv, 1946; PhD, 1965; LLD, 1970. m. A Louise Anderson, 2 s., 2 d. Career: Linguist, Anthropol. & Pastor, Tanzania, 1946 ; Mbr. of Fac., Luth. Theol. Coll., Makumira, 1964-; has made tape recordings of music of many ethnic groups in E Africa. Ed. & field worker, Tumshangilie Mungu (Let us Praise God, in Swahili), 1968, 5th enlarged ed., 1979; Compiled "Lead Us Lord", 1977; ed., Spoken Rimi. Contbr. to: African Initiatives in Religion, 1971; African Music, 1978; Hons: Disting. Alumnus Award, Lutheran Schl. of Theol., Chgo., 1978. Hobbies: Athletics; Mountain climbint; Gardening; Singing. Address: Box 55, Usa River, Tanzania. 4.

OLSSON, Mats Fredrik, b. 3 Nov. 1929, Stockholm Sweden. Record Company Director; Arranger; Composer; Conductor. Educ: BA, Univ. of Stockholm, 1953; Cantor's Exam, Uppsala Cathedral, 1948; Dip., RAM, Stockholm 1959; Pvte. studies counterpoint, instrumentations, arrang. & cond., 1950-55 1950-57. m. Maj-Britt Elisabeth Olsson, 2 s., 2 d. Debut: 1949. Career: Musician, 1949-54; Arr., 1954-57; Record Prod., 1957-59; Dir., A & R, CBS Records Sweden, 1970-; Comp. of film music & music for TV & radio. Comps: Suite for Orch.; Riksväg 13; Tennelbenepolka; Ballet Music; Pop songs; Adaptions of Swedish folk songs. Arranger of recordings by Swedish vocal artists. Mbrships: STIM; SKAP. Recip., 2 schlrships. Hobbies incl: Tennis. Address: Gryningsvaḡan 28, 163 53 Spanga, Sweden.

OLSSON, Rolf Nils Sture, b. 3 Sept. 1919, Upsala, Sweden. Timpanist. Educ: Orch. Schl.; Studio of Electronic Music, Stockholm; Univ. of Gothenburg. m. Solveig Sawra Elsy Olsson, 1 d., 1 s. Career: Jazz & Restaurant Musician, Orch. Ldr., 1941; Tchr., Acad. of Music, Gothenburg; Timpanist, Opera Gothenburg, 1956-. Comps: Film & theatre music; Orch. works; About 4000 arrs. Mbr., STIM. Publs: Schl. songbook; Drum Tutor Parts I & II; Tutor in Latinamerican Drumming; Kroumata (drum ency. Recip., Govt. Cultural Schlrship., 1973. Hobbies: Music; Philately. Address: Lökullavägen 8, 433 00 Partille, Sweden.

OMATA, Sumio, b. 26 July 1947, Yamanashi, Japan. Research Director; Editor. Educ: BA, Int. Christian Univ.; MA, Queen's Coll., CUNY; PhD, Inst. of Philological Studies. 1d. Career: Rsch. Dir., RISM project, Japan; Ed. Bd., Gendai Guitar. Puls: Kyrie prosulae in the Madrid ms. 19421, 1979; Guitar Music Guide, (Ed.), 1977; Ed., Master Works of Guitars, 1978. Contbr. to: Gendai Guitar. Mbrships: Am. Musicol. Soc.; Am. Musical Instrument Soc.; French Lang. Soc.; Japan Musicol. Soc. Hobbies: Driving; Hiking; Tennis. Address: 450 Nagufusa, Hachioji, Tokyo, Japan.

OMMER, Andrea, b. 4 Dec. 1945, Glasgow Scotland, UK. Orchestral Player; Teacher of Violin. Educ: Ommer Schl. of Music; RSAM; Dr. SAM (Tchr. & Perf.); LRAM (Tchr.); Brussels Conservatoire. m. Vincent Brogan, 1 s, 2 d. Career: Perfs. w. SNO. Redcordings w. SNO. Hons: Ailie Cullen Memorial Prize, 1960; Chmbr. Music Prize of RSAM, 1964, 66; Robert Highgate Scholarship, 1965; Hilda Bailey Prize, 2966. Hobbies: Family; Music. Address: 29 Kessington Dr., Bearsden, Galsgow G61 2HG, UK.

ONDERDENWYNGAARD, Toos A J, b. 27 Aug. 1926, The Hague, Netherlands. Classical Pianist. Educ: Amsterdam Conserv. Career: Plays regularly w. major orchs. & conds., in recitals for radio & TV in Holland, Germany, Austria, Belgium, France, & Czechoslovakia; Also concert tours to Middle E, India, Rumania, Turkey, S Am., Cuba, & Mexico. Hons: Elisabeth Everts Prize for most promising young musician in Holland, Amsterdam, 1949; Laurel Wreath, Circle of Friends of the Concertgebouw Orch. Hobbies incl: Detailed music studied of Haydn, Schumann, Liszt, & unknown Czechoslovakian comps. Address: Papeweg 4, Wassenaar, Netherlands.

O'NEAL, Christopher, b. 22 Mar. 1953, Surbiton, UK. Oboe Player. Educ: RCM w. Terence MacDonagh & Edwin Roxburg, 1971-75; ARCM; Staatliche Hochschule für Musik, Freiburg, W. Heinz Holliger, 1975-76. Debut: 1976: BBC Recital 1978. Career: Concert mgr., mbr., Elysian Wind Quintet; plays w. Park Lane Players, Capricorn & Osten Muse; gave world premiere of David Sutton's oboe concerto; dedicatee & 1st perf. of David Sutton's Tenebrae for solo oboe; recitals & solo apps. at Purcell Room & Queen Elizabeth Hall. mbr., ISM. Hons: semi-finalist, Leeds Nat. Music Platform, 1974, '77; semi-finalist, Prague Spring Fest. Competition, 1974. Hobbies: Squash; Tennis: Good Food; Photography; Chess. Address: Flat B, 16 Castelnau, Barnes, London SW13, UK.

ONISHI, Aiko, b. 26 Nov. 1930, Tokyo, Japan. Pianist; Professor of Music. Educ: B Mus, Eastman Schl. of Music, Rochester, NY, USA; Performer's Cert. & Artist's Dip., ibid. Debut: Tokyo, 1957. Career incl: Num. concerts in USA & Japan; Radio & TV broadcasts; Prof. of Music, San Jose State Univ., Calif. Mbrships: Am. Matthay Assn.; Calif. Assn. of Profl. Music Tchrs.; Piano Guild; Calif. MTA. Hons: Hon. Citizen of San Jose; Mu Phi Epsilon Artist; President Annual Scholar, 1977. Hobbies: Reading; Sewing. Address: 321 Brookwood Ave., San Jose, CA 95116, USA. 5. 9.

OOST, Gert, b. 13 Sept. 1942, Raamsdonksver, Netherlands. Musicologist; Organist. Educ: Dr. (musicol.), Univ. of Utreht; Conserv. of Amsterdam (prix d'excellence for organ). m. Maria Hermien Blomberg, 2d. Career: num. concerts & recitals annually. nu. recordings. Publs: The Organmakers Bätz, 1975; Nederlandse Klaviermuziek, 1975. Mbrships: Ned. Toonkunstennaars Verenigjng; Verenigjng van Nederlandse Musikgeschiedenis. Address: Zr. Spinhovenlaan 16, Bunnik, Netherlands.

OPPENS, Ursula, b. 2 Feb. 1944, New York, NY, USA. Pianist. Educ: BA, Radcliffe Coll., 1965; MS, Juilliard Schl., 1967. Debut: NY 1969. Career: Perfs. throughout USA & Europe as soloist & mbr. of Speculum Musicae, 1976; Apps. w. NY Phil & other orchs.; Recitals at Tully Hall, Kennedy Ctr. Num. recordings. Mbrships: Dir., Am. Music Ctr.; Mbr-Dir., Speculum Musicae. Hons: 1st Prize, Busoni Int. Piano Competition, 1969; Avery Fisher Prize, 1976. Mgmt: Shelton Soffer, Inc., USA. Address: 777 West End Ave., New York, NY 10025, USA.

OPPER, Jacob, b. 4 Nov. 1935, Lódz, Poland. College Professor. Educ: CCNY, USA, 1953-55; Univ. of Miami, 1955-58; Fla. State Univ., 1958-60, 1961-70, B Mus 1960, M Mus 1965, PhD, 1970; NY Univ., 1960-61. Publ: Science & the Arts: A Study in Relationships from 1600 to 1900. Mbrships: Am. Musicol. Soc.; Am. Soc. for 18th Century Studies; Pi Kappa Lambda. Address: 126 Center St.,Frostburg, MD 21532, USA.

ORAM, Daphne B, b. 31 Dec. 1925, Devizes, Wilts., UK. Composer; Inventor; Lecturer. Career: BBC Music Balancer,

1943; Dir. & Co-Fndr., Radiophonic Workshop, 1958; Dir., Oramics Studio, 1959-; Inventor, Oramics Graphic Sound; Concert/Lecture, Edinburgh Fest., 1962; num. TV, radio & film apps. Compositions incl: Four Aspects; Episode Metallic: Pulse Persephone; Bird of Parallax (ballet); Sacdonica (piano & Oramic tape, w. I Walsworth). Recordings: Electronic Sound Patterns; music for films inclng. The Innocents. Publs: An Individual Note of Music, Sound & Electronics, 1972. Mbrships: CGGB; Inst. Patentees & Inventors. Recip., 2 Gulbenkian Fndn. Awards. Hobbies: Reading; Archaeology; Animals. Address: Tower Folly, Fairseat, Wrotham, Kent TN15 7JR, UK. 27.

ORELLY, Sally, b. 23 Oct. 1940, Dallas, Tex., USA. Violinist; Pianist. Educ: BS., Tex. Women's Univ.; MM., Ind. Univ.; Royal Conserv. of Music, Brussels; N. Tex. State Univ.; studied w. Marjorie Fulton, Dr. Jack Roberts, Ivan Galamian, Josef Gingold, Carlo Van Neste. m. Dennis Dalton, 2 d. Debut: Soloist Dallas Symph., Tex., 1957. Career: Concertmaster, Solo Violinist, Int. String Congress, Puerto Rico; Orchl. Soloist, Recitalist, USA, Europe, Can.; Fac. Mbr., Manhattan Schl. of Music, NYC; Violinist, NY Piano Trio mbr. Caecilian Trio, Recordings: works by Ravel, Lalo, Fauré etc. Mbrships: Sigma Alpha Iota; Pi Kappa Lambda. Hons: Ind. Univ. Perf's Cert.; Van Katwijk Conducting Award, Dallas Symph., 1958; Perf. w. Dallas Symph., Hendl Award, 1957; Dealey Award, Merriweather Post; Nat. Fedn. of Music Clubs Young Artist; Fulbright-Hayes Scholarship; Belgium Ministry of Culture Speical Grant. Hobby: Creative Writing. Mgmt: Raymond Weiss Mgmt., NYC. Address: 240 Ctrl. Pk. S., NY, NY 10019, USA.

ORFF, Carl, b. 10 July 1895, Munich, Germany. Composer. Musical Educ: Akademie der Tonkunst, Munich, until 1914; Studied w. Heinrich Kaminski, 1921. m. Liselotte Orff, 1 d. Career: Cond., Münchner Kammerspiele, 1915-17; Cond. Nationaltheater, Manheim, & Landestheater, Darmstadt, 1918-19; Fndr. (w. Dorothee Günther), Güntherschule, 1924; Cond., Münchner Bachverein; Dir., master class for comp. Staatliche Hochschule für Musik, Munich, 1950-60; Dir., Orff Inst. Akademie "Mozarteum", Salzburg, 1961-. Compostions incl: Carmina Burana, 1935-36; Die Bernauerin, 1944-45; Astutuli, 1945-52; Antigonae, 1947-48; Comoedia de Christi Ressurectione, 1955; Ludus de Nato Infante Mirifucus, 1960; Ein Sommernachtstraum, 1962; Prometheus, 1963-67; De Temporum Fine Comoedia, 1969-71; Rota, for choir & instruments, 1972. Num. recordings of works by var. orchs. Mbrships: Hon. Pres., Deutsche Stiftung Musikleben, Bayerische Akademie der Schönen Künste. Hons: incl: Doct., Univ. of Munich, 1972; Ramano Guardini Prize, Catholic Acad., Bavaria, 1974. Address: D-8918 Diessen am Ammersee, German Fed. Republic.

ORKISZ, Andrezj, b. 21 Dec. 1937, Lwów, Poland. Cellist. Educ: State Conserv. of Music, Cracow; Dip., ibid; studies w. Joseph Mikulski & Paul Tortelier. m. Anna Orkisz, 2s. Debut: Cracow, 1959. Career: Apps. as soloist all over Europe, USSR, Japan, Aust., India, Egypt, Iran, Hong Kong; Polish radio & TV; Nippon TV; mbr. Warsaw Piano Quintet; tours w. Warsaw Piano Quintet in USA, Can., UK, Mexico, Switz., France, Germany, Austria, Eire, S Am., etc; Prof., Warsaw Acad. of Music. Recordings: (as soloist) works by Saint-Saens, Tadeusz Baird, M De Falla; (w. Warsaw Piano Quintet) works by Brahms, Dvorak & Grazyna Bacewicz. Mbrships: Assn. of Polish Musicians. Recip., 3rd prize, Polish Min. of Culture, 1974. Hobbies incl: Painting; Sport; Tourism; Family; Education. Mgmt: Pagart, Poland; Mariedi Anders, USA; Hans Fehr, German Fed. Repub.; Marcel de Valmalete, France. Address: 10 Ludna St., 00414 Warsaw, Poland.

ORLAND, Henry, b. 23 Apr. 1918, Saabrucken, Germany. Composer; Conductor; Educator. Educ: Cert. d'Etudes, Univ. of Strasbourg, France; BM., MM., PhD., Northwestern Univ., Ill., USA. Career: Cond., SW German Broadcasting System Orch.; Cond., Goodman Theatre, Chgo. & other US, European orchs. Comps. incl: Symphs. concertos, choral-orchl. works, solo & chmbr. music. art songs, theatre music. Recordings of choral comps. for Vox, Desto. Contbr. to Music & Man. (mag.); Music, Lit. Critic, St. Louis Post-Dispatch, St. Louis. Globe-Democrat. Hons: Delius Prize for Comps., 1972; Fromm Fndn. Award, 1958; Chgo. Music Critics Award, 1952. Hobbies: Tennis; Swimming; Hiking; Chess; Reading. Address: 21 Bon Pric Terr., St. Louis-Olivette, MO 63132, USA. 8, 12, 21, 23, 28.

ORLEDGE, Robert Francis Nicholas, b. 5 Jan. 1948, Bath, UK. University Lecturer in Music. Educ: Clare Coll., Cambridge Univ., 1965-71; BA, 1968; MA (Cantab.), 1972; PhD (Cantab.), 1973; ARCO, 1964. Career: Univ. Lectr. in Music, Liverpool. Publs: L'Oeuvre de Charles Koechlin (Catalogue), w. Madeleine Li-Koechlin, 1975; Gabriel Fauré, 1979. Contbr. to: Musical Times; Music & Letters; The Music Review; Current Musicol.; Musical Quarterly, etc. Mbrships: Royal Musical

Assn.; Centre de Documentation Claude Debussy. Hobbies: Swimming; Playing jazz piano. Address: 13A Westmoreland Rd., Wallasey, Merseyside L45 1HU, UK.

ORLOFF, Vladimir, b. 26 May 1928, Odessa, Russia. Cellist. Educ: Bucharest Conserv. m. Marietta Demian, 1 d. Debut: Bucharest, 1947. Career: Concerts in Austria, UK, France, W. Germany, Switzerland, Czechoslovakia, Eire, Turkey, Can., Austria; Film Apps., Romania, Czechoslovakia; Prof. Extraordinaire, Vienna Acad. of Music, Austria, 1967; Prof. of Univ. of Toronto, Can., 1971-. Compositions: Cadenza for Haydn C Major Concerto; Arr. Ed., var. Cello Music. Num. recordings, Prague Bucharest, USA & German Fed. Repub. Mbr. Toronto Musicians Assn. Hons: 1st Prize, Bucharest Int. Competition, 1947; 1st Prize, Warsaw Int. Competition, 1955; 2nd Prize, no 1st awarded, Geneva Int. Competition, 1957. Hobby: Autos. Mgmt: Ibermusika, Madrid, Spain; Ann Summers Int., Toronto, Can.; R Slotover, London, UK; Mariedi Amders, San Francisco, USA; Casetti-Giovani, Geneva, Switzerlnd; Lodding, Goteborg, Sweden. Address: Apt. 2314, 85 Throncliffe Park Dr., Toronto, Ont. M4H 1L6, Can. 1.

ORMANDY, Eugene, b. 18 Nov. 1899, Hungary (US Citizen) Conductor. Educ: Royal State Acad. of Music; Univ. of Budapest. Careet: Hd. of Master Classes, State Conserv. of Music, Budapest, 1919; Dpty. Cond. to Toscanini w. Phila. Orch., USA.; Cnd., Mpls. Symph. Orch., 1931-36; Music Dir. & Cond., Phila. Orch., 1936-. Hons: Cmndr., Legion d'Honneur, France; Order of Dannebrog, Denbark; Kt., Order of White Rose, Finland; Order of Merit, Juan Pablo Duarte, Dominican Repub.; Cmdr., Order of Lion, Finland; Hon. Cross for Arts & Scis., Austria; Sibelius Medal; Presidential Medal of Freedom, 1979; Hon. KBE; Hon. doctorates from num. acads. & univs. in USA. Address: c/o Ronald Wilford Assocs., 165 W. 57th St., NY, NYU 10019, USA.

ORNADEL, Cyril, b. 2 Dec. 1924, London, UK. Composer; Conductor. Educ: RCM. m. Shoshana, 2 s., 1 d. Career: Musical Dir., theatre prods., Call me Madam, Kiss me Kate, Kismet, Pal Joey, My Fair Lady, London Palladium, 1957-59; TV Musical Dir., Sunday Night at the London Palladium, 1957-61. The Strauss Family, 1973, Edward the Seventh, 1975; Apps in own series, The Piano Can Be Fun, ATV; Films, Subterfuge, Some may Live; Christina; Man of Violence; Brief Encounter; Cool it Carol; Dir. of recording & musical supvsn. for The Living Bible w. Sir Lawrence Olivier; Cond., Starlight Symph. Orch., 1960-68; Fndr. & Dir., RCA. Stereoaction Orch. series, 1970. Compositions: (Theatre) Pickwick; Ann Veronica; Starmaker; Treasure Island; Pied Piper; Great Expectations; Music for Beatrix Potter stories, HMV.; Children's recordings inclng. Ali Baba, Johah & the Whale & Thumbelina. Author of the Piano Can be Fun (w. Harry Junkin), 1973. Hon. mbr., Johann Strauss Soc. of Gt. Britain. Hons: Ivor Novello Award for Portrait of my Love, 1961, If I Ruled the World, 1963; BMI Award for Portrait of My Love; Gold Record LP for The Strauss Family, w. LSO; Ivor Novello Award; Best British Musical, Treasure Island, 1975. Hobby: Photography. Mgmt: Richard Stone, 18/20 York Bldgs., London, WC2N 6JU, UK. 3.

OROZCO, Rafael, b. 1946, Cordoba, Spain. Concert Pianist. Educ: Conserv. of Music, Cordoba & Madrid; Acad. Chigiana, Siena, Italy, Hons: 1st prizes at Int. Piano Competitions in Jaen, 1963, Bilbao, 1963, Vercelli, 1964, & Leeds, 1966; Extraordinary Prizes, Cordoba & Madric Conservs.; Hon. Mbr., Acad. of Beaux Arts of Cordoba; Dip. de Honore, Acad. Chigiana, Siena, Mgmt: Harrison/Parrott Ltd., 22 Hillgate St., London W8 7SR, UK.

ORR, Buxton Daeblitz, b. 18 Apr. 1924, Glasgow, UK. Composer; Conductor. Educ: Med. educ., Middx. Hosp., London; MBBS, BSc. (Physiol.); Music Educ., LGSM. (Cond.); FGSM. m. Jean Grant Latimer. Career: Prof. of Comp. & Gen. Musicianship, GSM. Cond., London Jazz Comps. Orch., 1970-; Talks for BBC Radio 3 Comps: Theatre & film music, Chmbr. music & songs; Orchl., brass & woodwind music; Opera 'The Wager'. Recordings: (on Apollo label) Bagatelles for Piano; Ballad of Mr & Mrs. Discobbolos; Cycle of solos & duets on poems of E E Cummings. Contbr. to: Record News; The Listener; Grove; Mbr.,Bd. of Examiners, Univ. of London. Address: 11 Gledhow Gdns., London SW5 OAY UK. 3.

ORR, Robin, b. 2 June 1909, Brechin, UK. Composer; Emeritus Professor of Music. Educ: RCM, London; Organ Scholar, Pembroke Coll., Cambridge Univ.; MA, Mus D; studied pvtly. w. Casella & Boulanger. m. Margaret E Mace, 1 s, 2 d. Career: Asst. Lectr. in Music, Univ. of Leeds, 1936-38; Organist, Dir. of Studies in Music, St. John's Coll., 1938-51 & Fellow, 1948-56; Univ. Lectr. Cambridge, 1947-56; Prof., RCM, 1950-56; Prof. of Music, Glasgow Univ., 1956-65; Fellow, St. John's Coll., Cambridge & Prof. of music, 1965;

Chmn, Scottish Opera, 1962-. Comps. incl: 3 symphs.; 2 operas Oedipus at Colonus (Greek play); Spring Canata: chmbr. music, 3 song cycles w. str. orch., etc. Recordings: Symph. in One Movement, 1963; some church & organ music. Mbrships: Musician's Co., London; Royal Musical Assn.; CGGB; ISM. Hons: FRCM, 1965; Hons. RAM, 1966; CBE, 1972; D Mus (Glasgow), 1972; LLD (Dundee), 1976. Address: c/o St. John's Coll., Cambridge, UK. 1, 3, 14, 28.

ORR, Wendell Eugene, b. 23 July 1930, Gilman, Ill., USA. Bass Singer; Choral Conductor; University Professor. Educ: BS, Lawrence Coll., 1952; BMus, Conserv. ibid, 1955; MMus, Univ. of Mich., 1957; pvte. study in Rome, London & Edinburgh. m. Nancy Brannan, 1 s., 1 d. Career incl: Opera, oratorio, concert, TV & radio apps. as singer & cond., in Midwest & Eastern States of USA & New England; 4 apps. on Boston Pops prog.; Bass singer, Lyric Opera Quartet; Dir., Youngstown State Univ. Men's Chorus; Past Dir., Opera Workshop, Univ. of NH. Mbrships: Nat. Assn. of Tchrs. of Singing; Am. Choral Dirs. Assn.; Int. Platform Assn.; Ctrl. Opera Serv.; Ohio Educ. Assn. Hobbies: Sports; Reading; Record collecting. Address: 7197 Elmland Dr., Poland, OH 44514, USA. 8, 12, 28, 29.

ORREGO-SALAS, Juan A, b. 18 Jan. 1919, Santiago, Chile. Composer; Musicologist. Educ: BA, State Univ. of Chile, 1938; Dip. in Archt., Cath. Univ. of Santiago, 1943; Nat. Conserv. of Music, State Univ. of Chile, 1936-43; MA, ibid, 1942; Columbia & Princeton Univs. & Tanglewood Summer Schl., USA, 1944-46; PhD., State Univ. of Chile, 1953. m. Carmen Benavente, 5 children. Career: Cond., Cath. Univ. Chorus, Santiago, 1937-44; Prof. of Musicol., State Univ. of Chile, 1942-47; Prof. of Comp., ibid., 1947-61; Chmn., Music Dept., Cath Univ. of Chile, 1959-61; Dir., Latin-Am. Music Ctr. & Prof.of Compositions, Schl. of music, Ind. Univ., Bloomington, USA, 1961-; Chmn., Comp. Dept., Ind. Univ. Schl. of Music. Comps: Over 70 comps. inclng. String Quartet, Sonata a Quattro, Madrigals, Missa in Tempore discordiae, Variaciones Serenas, The Days of God (oratorio); Dead End Street (opera in 3 acts). Num. recordings. Contbr. to many profl. jrnls. Mbrships. incl: Chilean Acad. of Fine Arts; Chilean Nat. Assn. of Comps.; Inter-Am. Music Coun.; Am. Soc. Univ. Comps.; Am. Musicol. Soc.; Pi Kappa Lambda. Num. Hons. Hobbies: Gardening; Skiing. Address: RR12, Box 225, Bloomington, IN 47401, USA. 14.

ORREY, Leslie Gilbert, b. 11 Sept. 1909, Hawnby, Yorks., UK. Pianist; Organist; Conductor; Writer. Educ: RCM; ARCM; FRCO; Mus B, Durham Univ. m. Elsa Todd. Career: Tchr., Westminster Schl., & Morley Coll., London; RAF, 1939-45; Music Lectr.-Hd., Music Dept., Goldsmiths' Coll., Univ. of London, 1945-71. Publs: Koechlin, Gabriel Fauré (transl.), 1946; Saint-Foix, The Symphonies of Mozart (transl.), 1947; Foundations of Harmony & Compositions, 1948; Music at the Keyboard, 1965; Bellini, 1969; A Concise History of Opera, 1972; Programme Music, 1975; Gluck, 1976. Contbr. to: The Beethoven Companion, 1971; Musical Times; Musical Opinion; Music & Letters: Listener. Address: 176 Kew Rd., Richmond, Surrey, UK.

ORSELLI, Cesare, b. 17 May 1941, Piombino, Italy. Professor of History of Music. Educ: BA, Univ. of Florence, 1964; 2 yr. musicol. course, Accad.Musicale Chigiana, Sina; pvte. music studies. m. Fausta Cianti. Career incls: interiews on Puccini & his opera, opera ''Verista'', Italian theatres, Berlioz etc., Rai (Italian Broadcast); Pof. of Italian Lit., Univ. of Siena, Italy. Num. publs. inclng: Problemi di critica pucciniana, 1966; Arrigo Boito; un riesame, 1968; Butterfly & C., 1968; Boheme, o la Scapigliatura borghese, 19 72; Don Pasquale, 1973; Andrea Chenier, 1974; Petrarca e la musica, 1974; Il castro Carmen; verismo e verita storica, 1974; Turandot, 1976; M Cartelnuovo Tedesco, 1978; Schubert Piano music, 1978; L'Angelodi Fuoco di Prokovier, 1978. Contbr. to concert progs., jrnls., etc. Mbrships: Soc. Italiana di Musicol. Address: Piazza P Leopoldo 5, Florence, Italy.

ORTA NADAL, Enrique, b. 31 Aug. 1918, Rosario, Argentina. Concert Pianist; Accompanist. Educ: engrng. studies to degree of Land Surveyor, var. instns.; capatability dip. in French; Superior Prof., Piano, Gold Medal Conserv. Schenone, Rosario; Nat. Conserv. Buenos Aires; studies w. Jorge de Lalewicz, Oreste Castronuovo, Ruwin Erlich. m. Sere Beatriz Klien, 1 d. Debut: Buenos Aires, 1940 Career: num. recitals, Rosario, Buenos Aires, Argentine Brazil, & Japan; radio & TV broadcasts. Mbr., Fndr., Conciertos Arte. Recip. Fellowship, Comision de Culture de la Provincia de Santa Fe, 1942. Address: Entre Rios 521, Buenos Aires, Argentina.

ORTHEL, Leon, b. 1905, Roosendaal, Composer; Pianist; Music Master. Educ: Royal Conserv. of Music, The Hague;

Berlin Acad. for Music. m. Sara Gerarda Joosting, 2 s. Career: Sr. Master of Piano, Royal Conserv. of Music, The Hague, 1941-71; St. Master of Comp., Amsterdam Conserv., 1949-71. Comps. incl: 6 Symphs.; sev. smaller works for orch.; chmbr. music; var. works for piano; Sonata per Organo; Comps. for harp; Une Martyre, for soprano & orch., to works by C Baudelaire; Tre Movimenti Ostinati per Orch.; Trumpet Concerto. Mbr., Dr. Johan Wagenaar Stitching (Chm. of Committee). Hons: Kt., Order of Orange Nassau; Silver Medal of Soc. of Arts, Scis., & Letters, Paris; Silver Medal of The Hague. Hobbies: Philos; Theatre; Film; Chess. Address: Aarbeistraat 10, The Hague, Netherlands.

ORTIZ, Cristina, b. 17 Apr. 1950, Bahia, Brazil. Concert Pianist. Educ: studied w. Magda Tagliaferro, Paris & Rudolph Serkin, Phila.; Degree Dip., Brazilian Music Conserv., Rio de Janeiro, Brazil; Special Dip., Curtis Inst. of Music, Phila., Pa. Recital Debut: Carnegie Hall, 1971, (w. Frühbeck de Burgos & Detroit Symph.), Carnegie Hall, 1973, Royal Festival Hall (w. Andre Previn & LSO), 1973. Career: Concerts all over the USA, Brazil, Japan, N. Zealand & most countries all over Europe & Scandinavia. num. recordings. Hons: First Prize, VI Nt. Piano Competition, Rio de Janeiro, 1965; First Prize, VIII Inst. M. Tagliaferro Piano Competition, Paris, 1966; Prize Winner, IV George Enesco Int. Piano Competition, Bucarest; First Prize Winner, III Int. Van Cliburn Contest, Ft. Worth, Tex., 1969. Hobbies: Reading; Sports; Painting; Dancing. Mgmt: Harrison/-Parrott Ltd., 22 Hillgate St., London W8 7SR. Address: 50 Dale St., London W4, UK.

ORTLEPP, Christa, b. 21 Apr. 1933, Hamburg, Germany. Concert Singer. Educ: 3 yrs. voice trng. w. Prof. Karl Oskar Dittmer, 1953-56; 7 yrs. music instrn. w. Russell Green, 1965-72. m. Reinhold Ortlepp, 2 d. Debut: Opening concert at Victoria Coll. Summer Schl. Concerts Series, 1957. Career: Sang w. select grp. of a Hamburg Radio Choir for the arrival of PM Nehru & Indira Gandhi (songs in Bengali), Hamburg; Quartet work for NWDR, & background music for movies, Hamburg; Recital for Vic. Coll. Summer Session Concert Series, Messiah soprano solo w. Vic Choral Soc., Guest Soloist (opera arias) for the German-Canadian Soc. Choir Concert, Sang for CHEK TV, Vic., Concert at Oak Bay Beech Hotel w. Richard Proudman & Malcolm Hamilton, Vic., 1956-59; Guest Soloist w. Univ. Str. Quartet, Sask.; 8 recitals of songs at the Mendel Art Gall., 1969-72; 3 half-hour recitals for CFNS; Interview & one song for CFQC, TV; Recitals of songs & arias sponsored by the Order of the Eastern Star; 4 recitals sponsored by the Royal Canadian Coll. of Organists. Recordings: one rec. of Russell Green's latest works, 1971; appeared as soloist w. a Hamburg Radio Choir, for Philips Records, 1955. Mbrships: RCCO (Prog. Comm., Sask. Ctr.); Musical Art Club, Saskatoon. Address: 2603 Cascade St., Saskatoon, Sask., Canada.

ORTMANS, Kay (Kathleen) Muriel, b. 18 Sept. 1907, London, UK. Composer; Teacher. Educ: RAM; Tchrs. Cert., Dalcroze Schl. of Eurythmics, London; Ann Driver Schl. of Music & Movement, ibid. m. Kenneth F B Pawley, 1 s. Career: Tchr. of movement to music; Broadcaster, BBC radio, 1941-43; Own weekly prog., CBC, Canada, 1947-50; TV appearances, Canada & USA; Lecture performances, Univs. in BC & USA; Fndr.-Dir., Well-Springs Fndn., Ben Lomond, Calif., for tchrng. prog. for personal growth through the arts. Compositions: Garibaldi Mountain Suie for orch. & solo; Let's Play Suite for children; num. short pieces for movement. Recordings made of these works & musical sketches. Publ: Reminder from Well-Springs, 1967. Contbr. of Chapt. to Sir Herbert Read's New Educ. Curric., 1943. Recip. Canadian Radio Award for outstanding prog., 1949. Hobby: Gardening. Address: Well-Springs, 11667 Alba Rd., Ben Lomond, CA 95005, USA.

OSAFO, Felix Onwona, b. 24 Oct. 1923, Obomeng-Kwahu, Ghana. Senoir Superintendent of Music (Piano, Clarinet, Singing, Composition). Educ: Tchrs. Cect. A; LRSM; FVCM; CTVCM; Dip. M Ed, Univ. Adelaide, Aust. m. Alice Asiedua Osafo, 8 children. Career: Cond. in charge, Presby. Trng. Coll. Choir, Akropong-Akwapim, Ghana; TV & Radio apps. w. Choir. Comps: Over 100 Ghanaian comps; 50 songs. Recordings of 30 songs by Ghana Broadcasting Corp. Contbr. to: African Music; Ghana Tchrs. Jrnl. Mbrships: incl: Ghana Music Tchrs. Assn.; Int. Folk Music Coun; African Music Soc. Hons: Music Prize, Univ. of Adelaide. Hobbies: Lawn Tennis; Photography. Address: Presby. Trng. Coll., PO Box 27, Akropong-Akwapim, Ghana.

OSBORNE, Charles, b. 24 Nov. 1927, Brisbane, Aust. Critic; Author. Educ: Studied piano w. Archie Day & Irene Fletcher & voice w. Vido Luppi & Browning Mummery. div. Career: Asst. Ed., London Mag., UK, 1957-66; Asst. Lit. Dir., Arts Coun, of Gt. Brit., 1966-71, Lit. Dir., 1971-. Publs: Opera 66, 1966;

The Complete Operas of Verdi, 1969; Ed., Letters of Giuseppe Verdi, 1971; The Concert Song Companion, 1974. Contbr. to: Opera; London Mag.; Spectator; Times Literary Supplement; Encounter: New Statesman; Observer; Sunday Times. Hobby: Travel. Mgmt: Richard Scott Simon Ltd., London. Address: Richard Scott Simon Ltd., 36 Wellington St., London WC2, UK. 3, 14, 15, 28.

OSBORNE, Chester Gorham, b. 18 Sept. 1915, Portsmouth, NH, USA. Composer; Author. Educ: Dip., orchl. course in trumpet, 1936, B Mus, 1937, New Engl. Conserv. of Music; M Mus, Northwestern Univ., 1950. m. Mary E Rooney, 2 s., 3 d. Career incls: former Trumpeter, Boston Symph. & other orchs.; 355 ASF Band; Tchr. of Music, Ctr. Moriches, NY, 1938-41, 1946-70. Comps: Treasure Island Overture (band); British Eighth March (band); Christmas Cards (brass sextet); Two Irish Folk Songs (SSAA chorus); Diversions for Drummers, (collection); Aisling (horn); Lowlands (tuba). Recordings of own comps: Connemara Sketches; The Silver Anchor. Contbr. to profl. publs. Mbrships: MENC; NY State Schl. Music Assn. (adjudicator); Pi Kappa Lambda. Recip. acad. hons. Hobbies: Fishing; Do-it-yourself home maintenance. Address: PO Box 517, Center Moriches, NY 11934, USA. 6, 29.

OSBORNE, Gwendolen M S, b. 7 Jan. 1912, Norton Lindsey, Warwick, UK. Music Teacher, Piano, Organ & Singing. Educ: RAM; GRSM, London; LRAM (piano tchr.). Career: Sr. Music Mistress, Gardenhurst, Burnham-on-Sea, 1938-41, St. George's Schl., Ascot, 1941-45; Hd. Singing Dept., Howell's Schl., Denbigh, 1945-72; Ret'd but still tchng. pvtely. Mbrships: Vice-chmn., Denbigh Music Soc.; St. Asaph Choral Soc. Hobbies: Motoring; Dressmaking; Cooking; Gardening. Address: 29 Nant-y-Patrick, St. Asaph, Clwyd, N Wales, UK. 1.

OSBORNE, José, b. 3 Mar. 1934, Hucknall, Nottinghamshire, UK. Private Teacher of Piano & Singing. Educ: FLCM, Singing; ATCL, Piano Perf. m. D G Osborne, 3 children. Mbr., Incorp. Soc. of Musicians. Hobbies: Oil Painting; Walking. Address: Highfields, 15 Derby Rd., Risley, Draycott, Derbyshire, UK.

OSBORNE, Neville, b. 14 Sept. 1928. South Shields, UK. Conductor; Examiner; Adjudicator; Lecturer. Educ: London Univ.; TCL; RAM & pvte. studies w. Harold Darke; FRCO; GRSM; LRAM: ARCM. m. Eveline Marion Page, 2d. Career: Hd. of Music Dept., Dartford Grammar Schl., 1957-62, Lichfield Friary Schl., 1963-64, & Sidney Webb Coll. of Educ., 1967-71; Music Advsr., Newcastle-upon-Tyne Educ. Committe, 1965-67; prin. lectr. in music, Chelmer Inst. of Higher Educ., Essex, 1971-78; Examiner, Assoc. Bd., 1974-. Comps: Sing to the Lord; From Glory to Glory; part-songs for chours. Contbr. to music jrnls. Hon: FRSA. Hobbies: Gardening; Travel; Fly-fishing. Address: 6 Abbot's Close, Crofton Ln., Orpington, Kent BR5 1HW, UK.

OSBORNE, Tony Roy Stuart, b. 10 Nov. 1947, Slough, UK. Double Bass Player; Teacher; Composer; Arranger; Bass Guitarist. Educ: RAM, London, 1966-69, w. John Walton (double bass) & Richard Stoker (comp.); LRAM., 1969. m. Jocelyn S. Levy 1971, 1 s. Career: Freelance Bassist, Symph. Orch. inclng. BBC Proms, etc., etc., Opera, Ligh Music, Jazz, Dance band; Seasons at Convent Garden, Royal Ballet, Theatre Royal Windsor; short spells, D'Oyly Carte; Bass Guitar, Dance work, recordings; Vis. Instrument Instructor for Bucks (now Berks.) Co. Coun. & at the Haberdasher's Aske's Schl., Elstree; Profl. Asst., RAM Orchs. (when required). Compositions commissioned; Piano Trio, Fantasia for Cello & Piano for Little Missenden Fest.; also Essay for Orch., 3 pieces for Orch., Elegy for Chorus & Orch.; Sonatina for Oboe & Bassoon; var. other small works. Sev. recordings as bass player, arranger & musical dir. Mbrships: CGGB; RAM Club. Hobbies: Studying Music; Walking; Gardening, etc. Address: 42 Parkland Ave., Slough, Berks. SL3 7LQ, UK. 30.

OSGOOD, Donald, b. 23 Jan. 1921, Wellington, Somerset, UK. Professor of Brass and Scoring; Lecturer; Adjudicator. Educ: Toynbee Hall, London; Pvte. studies; LTCL. m. Madge McEwen, 2 s, 1 d. Career: Prof. of Brass Band Scoring, GSM; St. Lectr., Southall Coll. of Technol., Middx.; Adjudicator, Nat. Brass Band Championships of GB; Dir., Nat. Summer Schl. of Music for Salvation Army; Trombonist w. var. brass bands & RAF Ctrl. Band, 1941-46; Num. broadcasts. Comps: Var. comps. for Brass Band & Choir (recorded). Publs: Ed., num. publs. inclng: The Creation, 1961. Contbr. to Sounding Brass. Recip. 1st Prize, BBC Int. Competition for Brass Band Comps., 1958. Hobbies: Reading; Watching Cricket; Church Activities. Address: 18 Speart Lane, Heston, Hounslow, Middx., UK.

OSIANDER, Irene, b. 9 Dec. 1903, Tiflis, Russia. Composer; Pianist. Educ: Stern Konservatorium, Berlin; Music Prof. State Authorize, Copenhagen. m. Dietrich Vogel. Debut: Berlin,

1932; Copenhagen, 1945. Career: Compositions in Concert Halls & on Radio in Denmark, German Fed. Repub. & German Dem. Repub. Compositions: Quartet for Strings; Ballet Suite 'Tamara' for Orch.; The Danish Spring; 'Fatima' Symph.; Pictures from Kaukasus, symph.; childrens songs; piano pieces, etc. Mbrships: Danish Composer Soc. Hobby: Music. Address: Landskronagade 41, Copenhagen 2100, Denmark.

OSINCHUK, Juliana Lidia, b. 17 May, 1953, NYC, USA. Pianist. Educ: B Mus, M Mus, Juilliard Schl. of Music, 1975; Doct. cand., ibid; pvte. study of piano w. var. tchrs. from age 5; Ećole d'Art Americaine, Fontainebleau, France, 1964, '65, '66, '68 (w. Nadia Boulanger). Career: Num. solo recitals, 1965-; Chmbr. music recitals, 1971-; TV app., NYC, 1960; Radio perfs., NYC, 1965, '73, '75, '76; European tour, 1978; Radio broadcasts, NCRV Holland; Recitals in Brussels, Athens, Greece & Koper, Yugoslavia. Hons. incl: 1st Medal, Conserv. Nat. Superieur de Musique, Paris, France, 1966; Walter Damrosch Scholarship, 1968; NY State Regents Award, 1971; Juilliard Schl. Scholarship, 1972-74; Josef Lhevinne Scholarship, 1973; Mason & Hamlin Prize, 1974; Morris Leob Memorial Prize, 1975; Nat. Arts Club Prize, NYC, 1977; Piano Tchrs. Congress Int. Competition Winner, 1976, NYC. Hobbies incl: Stamp Collecting; Photography. Mgmt: Int. Concert Administratie, Amsterdam, Netherlands. Address: 35 E 7 St., NY, NY 10003, USA.

OSKAMP, Gerard Hubertus Marinus, b. 21 Dec. 1950, Bussum, Netherlands. Conductor. Educ: Solo Dip., Cello, Utrecht, 1975; Cond. studies w. Edo de Waart, Prof. Hans Swarowski, Ferdinand Leitner. m. Maria Louise Kool, 1 c. Career: Cellist, Rotterdam Phil. Orch., 1973-76; Staff Cond., Bournemouth Symph. Orch., 1976-78; Regular Guest,UK, Scandinavia, Netherlands & Germany, 1976-. Hons. Hans Haaring prize of radio Salzburg, 1974; Cond., final concert Vinna Mastercourse, 1975; Winner, John Player competition, for young conds., London, 1976. Hobby: Photography. Mgmt: Harrison Parrott Ltd., 22 Hillgate St., London W8 7SR, UK. Address: c/o Mgmt.

OSTADI, Nader Mortezapour, b. 6 Sept. 1951, Tehran, Iran. Double Bass Player. Educ: Dep., Tehran Music Conserv.; Dip., Tehran Univ.; BM, Univ. of Mo.; Aspen Music Fest.; Tanglewood Music Fest. Career: Houston Civic Symph.; Sandiego Symph.; Prin. Bass., Tehran Symph. Comps: Naghmeh, for 12 Double Basses; Serenade, for 2 Double Basses. Contbr. to Inst. Musician Paper; Symphony News. Mbrships: Int. Soc. of Bassists; Am. Fed. of Musicians. Hobbies: Running; Writing music; Practising. Address: Ave. Mihan, 27 Farmanieh, Shemiran-Tehran, Iran.

ØSTBYE, Rolf, b. 16 Dec. 1918, Oslo, Norway. Pianist; Organist; Choir master. Educ: Piano studies w. Nils Larslen, Erling Westher, Oslo; Organ studies w. Arild Sandvold, Oslo; Lang., Hist. of Art, Musicol. studies, Univ. of Fribours, Switz. Debut: as accomp., Oslo, 1940. Career: Cond., Choir of St. Olav's Catholic Cathedral, Oslo, 1940-; Cathedral Organist, ibid, 1947-; Repetitor, Music Conserv. Oslo, 1945; Repetitor for soloist & choir, Norwegian Opera, 1958-70; Repetiteur, Norwegian Opera, 1970-; Sev. concerts, TV & radio apps., Scandinavia, UK, Switz., Italy, Yugoslavia & Russia. Mbr., Soc. of Norwegian Artists. Recip. of scholarships. Address: Seilduksgaten 4, Oslo 5, Norway.

ØSTERENG, Thorleif, b. 28 March 1912, Oslo, Norway. Editor. Educ: Studies in Oslo, Copenhagen & NY. m. Kari Ostereng, 5 d. Debut: Oslo. Career: Editor, Music Dept., Norwegian Broadcasting Corporation; Radio apps., own Jazz Big Band. Recordings: Over 100. Publs: Translations of musical books from English & Spanish to Norwegian. Recip., scholarship from NRK. Hobby: Studying langs. Address: Lindebergveien 34, 1342 7AR, Norway.

OSTHOFF, Helmuth, 13 Aug. 1896, Bielefeld, W. Germany. Prof. musicol. Educ: Univ. Berlin, PDh 1922, Prof. 1938; Univ. Frankfurt 1938. m. Heidi Osthoff, 1 s. 1 d. Career: Pianist; Cond.; Musical Dir. Univ. Frankfurt 1938; Prof., musicol., Univ. of Frankfurt, 1938-66. Mbrships: Int. Soc. for Musicol.; Soc. for Music Rsch. Publs. incl: The Lute player Santino Garsi da Parma, 1926, 1973; Adam Krieger, 1929, 1970; The Dutch and the German Song, 1938, 1967. Contbr. to: Music Rsch.; Archive for Musicol.; Swiss Music Mag. Address: Lange Bögen 18, 8700 Würzburg, German Fed. Repub.

OSTHOFF, Wolfgang, b. 17 Mar. 1927, HalleSaale, Germany. Musicologist. Educ: Frankfurt Conserv. w. Kurt Hessenberg & others; Univs. of Frankfurt & Heidelberg w. H Ostoff, T Georgiads & others. m. Rente Goetz, 3 s. Career: Asst.-Docent, Munich Univ., 1957-68; Prof., Würzburg Univ., 1968-. Publs. incl: Das dramatische Spätwerk Claudio

Monteverdis, 1960; Beethoven Klavier Konzert c-moll, 1965; Theatergesang & darstellende Musik in der italienischen Renaissance, 2 vols., 1969; Heinrich Schütz, 1974. Contbr. to musicol. jrnls. Mbrships incl: Int. Musicol. Soc. Hubby: Musicology. Address: Institut für Musikwissenschaft, University of Würzburg, Residenzplatz 2, D 87 Würzburg, German Fed. Repub.

OSTOVA, Greta, b. 22 Aug. 1916, Bilsko (Bieltz), Poland. Cellist. Educ: Akademie für Musik & darstellende Kinst, Vienna, Austria; Perfs. Dip. w. hons. (cello); Masterclass Cassado. m. Frederick Ost. Career: Prof., Masaryk Schl. of Music; Solo recitals w. var. pianist, Radio Ostrava; Chmbr. music, Macak Quartet, Prof. K Holub Trio; Radio Bratislava solo recitals & chmbr. music w. Macuzinski Trio; Troppau recitals w. Josy Tesarik, Dr. S Kral; Charity Concerts, solo recitals & chmbr. music, UK & NZ; Radio & TV apps., NZ; Prin. cellist, Chmbr. Ensemble touring NZ w. Bolshoi Ballet, 1959; Chmbr. Music Classes, Univ. A.E., NZ; Concerts w. NZ String Trio, ABC Concert Orch.; Prin Cellist, Jesus Superstar, Sydney, Aust., 1972-73; Tchr., advanced students; Prin. Cellist, Symphonia Auckland. Comps: Sev. arrs. Hons: Cellist in quartet participating at NZ Investiture of Queen Elizabeth II, Wellington, NZ, 1954. Hobbies: Chmbr. music; Gardening; Art Collecting. Address: 32 Williamson Ave., Belmont, Auckland, 9, NZ.

OSTROVE, Geraldine E, b. 22 July 1938, Astoria, NY, USA. Music Librarian. Educ: AB, Goucher Coll.; MLA, Univ. of Md. Schl. of Lib & Info. Servs.; M Mus, Peabody Conserv. Contbr. to: Notes; Fontes Artis Musicae; Musical Am. Mbrships: Recording Sec., Music Lib. Assn., 1972-78; Int. Assn. of Music Libs.; Coun., Am. Musicol. Soc., 1975-77; Beta Phi Mu Int. Lib. Sci. Hon. Soc. Address: Peabody Conserv. Lib., 21 E Mt. Vernon Pl., Baltimore, MD 21202, USA.

OSTROWSKY, Avi, b. 1939, Israel. Conductor: Musical Director. Educ: Tel Aviv Robin Music Acad.; Acad. of Music & Representative Arts, Vienna. Career: Musical Dir. & Perm. Cond., Haifa Symph., Orch., 1969-, also Israel Phil. Orch. Israel Chmbr. Ensemble, etc.; broadcasts on Israel Broadcasting; has app. in Scandinavia, UK, Netherlands, Romania & Austria. Recip. of Am.-Israel Culture Fndn. Schlrship. Address: Rachel St. No. 3, Haifa, Israel.

OSTRYNIEC, James Paul, b. 27 Sept. 1943, Erie, Pa., USA. Oboist; Teacher; Composer. Educ: B Mus, Univ. of Louisville, 1965; MFA, Univ. of Hawaii, 1967; DMA, Univ. of Mich., 1972. m. Jane Wealthy Elkinton, 1 d. Debut: Phillips Collect., Wash. DC, 1975. Career: Oboist, Balt. Symph., 1970-; Fac., Peabody Inst. of Balt., 1971; Artist-in res., Towson State Coll., 1972-; One of foremost exponents of contemporary oboe techniques in US; num. recitals & concert apps. Comps: Movements for Orchestra, 1967. Mbrships. incl: Phi Kappa Phi. Contbr. to Dissertation Abstracts, 1972. Recip., var. hons. Hobbies incl: Antiques. Mgmt: Emily Sattell Artists Mgmt. Inc., 3408 Tulsa Rd., Balt., MD, USA. Address. 721 31. Johns Rd., Balt., MD 21210, USA.

OSTWALD, David Frank, b. 20 Jan. 1943, Stage Director. Educ: BA, Reed Coll., Portland, Ore.; MFA, Carnegie Inst. of Technol., Pitts., Pa.; PhD, Carnegie-Mellon Univ., Pitts., Pa. Career: Opera Dir., Western Opera Theater, San Fran. Opera Merola Prog.; Kan. City Lyric Theater Valley Opera Assn., Schl. of Orpheus, San Fran. Community Music Ctr., Carnegie Tech. Opera Workshop, Inverness Music Fest. Compositions: Dance-Dramas, Xoregos Performing Co.; Plays, Drama Dept., Univ. of Calif. Lunchbox Theatre. Hobbies: Skiing; Chmbr. Music. Address: 484 W 43rd St. Apt. 28K, NY, NY 10036, USA.

OTEY, Orlando, b. 1 Feb. 1925, Mexico City, Mexico. Music Executive; Educator; Theorist; Pianist. Educ: DMus, Imov. of Mexico, 1945; Curtis Inst. of Music, Phila., Pa., 1945-48; studied under sev. masters. m. 2), 1d., 1s.; 2) Diane McAnney, 1s. Career incl: pianist, Mexico, USA; recitals & w. orchs., 1929-; 1 of 3 Am. pianists, Chopin Centennial Fest., Warsaw, Poland, 1949; Musical Dir., Jewish Community Ctr. Orch. 1974-78; Dir., Otey Music Schl., 1970-; organist & choirmaster, Mt. Salem Meth. Ch., Wilmington, Del., 1973-. Num. comps. incl: Arbesque, 1950; Sinfonia Breve, 1956; Suite for Strings, 1957; Tzintzuntzan for strings, 1958; Poetica for solo trumpet & orch., 1970. Publs: Otey Music Teaching Method, 1973; Discoverer, Natural, Exotic & Non-septonic musical keys, 1978. mbr. num. profl. orgs. Address: 2391 Limestone Rd., Wilmington, DE 19808, USA.

O'TOOLE, Catherine Mary, b. Newton, Mass., USA. SupervisorActing Director, Department of Music Education, Boston Public Schools; Educ: SFA, Boston Univ., 1930; AB, Boston Coll., 1936; New Engl. Conserv. of Music; pvte. study, piano, organ, recorder. Career: Supvsr., Music Educ.,

1934-71; Acting Dir., 1969-71; OrganizerSupvsr., music prog. under Title I, sev. schls., 1965-66; OrganizerAdmnstr., prog. combining music, painting, dance & drama, summer 1966; OrganistChoir Dir., St. John's Ch., Wellesley Hills, Mass., 1972-; Portraits in Music & Art based upon the Liturgical Year. Contbr. to Music Educators Jrnl. Mbrships. incl: Fndr.Dir., Canterbury Ensemble of Cape Ann, Mass. (perf. of early music), 1971-; MENC; AGO; Am. Recorder Soc. Hobby: Hiking. Address: 5 Allen Ave., Rockport, MA 01966, USA.

OTTEN, Daniel, b. 20 Nov. 1938, Rotterdam, Holland. Violinist. Educ: Soloist Dip., Tchng. Dip., Muzieklyceum, Amsterdam. m. Marijke Delmonte, 2 c. Career: Ldr., sev. orchs., -1976; currently Soloist & Tchr. Var. Recordings. Mgmt: Nederlands Impresariaat, Int. Concertadministratie, Address: Paulinelaan 1, Muiderberg, Holland.

OTTEN, Kees, b. 28 Nov. 1924, Amsterdam, Netherlands. Leader of the ensemble Syntagma Musicum, Amsterdam. Educ: Muzieklyceum, Amsterdam. Debut: Amsterdam, 1945. Career: perfs. in UK, USA, Mexico, Aust., NZ, Indonesia; Japan & all over the continent. num. recordings. Contbr. to num. Netherland publs. Hons: Edison Prize, 1967 & 1969; Grand Priz du Disque, 1969; Japanese Critics) Prize, 1970. Mgmt: Nederlands Impresariaat, van Breestraat 77 Amsterdam. Address: Grote Oost 75, Hoorn, Netherlands.

OTTER, Hens, b. 22 May 1945, Amsterdam, Netherlands. Musician (Clarinet; Bass Clarinet; Saxophone). Educ: Conserv., Amsterdam. m. Iréne Baylé 2 d. Career: Mbr., Netherlands wind Ensemble, 1963-; Netherlands Ballet Orch.; var. jazz grps., occasionally. Recordings: w. Netherlands Wind Ensemble, works by Beethoven; Stravinsky; Mozart; Richard Strauss. Hons: Sev. Edison & Flotenuhrpreis, Wiener Mozart Gemeinde (w. Netherlands Wind Ensemble). Hobbies: Improvisation; Electronics; Dogs; Cactus plants. Address: Woonboot Tholonioue, Yobaonpad Stoiger 3, Amsterdam, Netherlands.

OTTERBACH, Friedemann Gotthard, b. 31 Mar. 1942, Stuttgart, Germany. Musicologist; Music Writer. Educ: PhD (Musicol.), Univ. of Freiburg; study of Flute, Trossingen Music Acad. Debut: radio prog. on Musik & Sprache, Sudwestfunk. Career incl: Author of sev. radio progs. on music. Publs: Kadenzierund & Tonalität im Kantilenensatz Dufays. Ein Beitrag zur Harmonik des späten Mittelaters, 1974; Schöne Musikinstrumente, 1975. Mbrships: Soc. of Music Rsch. Hobbies: Philos.; Literary criticism. Address: Goethestr. 43, 78 Freilburg, German Fed. Repub.

OTTO, Irmgard, b.15 July 1912, Berlin, Germany. Musicologist. Educ: Univ. of Berlin. Career: Asst., Friedrich Wilhelms Univ., Berlin (Musicol.), 1938-; Staff Mbr., Musikinstrumenten-Mus. Berlin, 1950-74, retiring as Musicol. Conservator. Publs: incl: num. mus. catalogues & related works. Contbr. to profl. jrnls. Mbrships: incl: Soc. for Music Rsch., Kiel; Int Soc. for Musicol. Basle; German Soc. for Eastern Music, Berlin; Int. Assn. of Musical Instrument Collects. Hobbies: Chamber Music; Painting; Collecting Musical Instruments Made as Toys. Address: Lefevrestr. 28, D 1000 Berlin 41, German Fed. Repub.

OTTO, Lisa, b. Dresden, Germany. Concert & Opera Singer. Educ: Bus. Schl.; Music Acad., Dresden. m. Albert Blind. Career: w. State Theatre, BeuthenOS House, Opera of Nürnberg, Germany; w. Staatsopher Dresden, 1946-50; German Opera, Berlin, 1950-. Roles incl: Zerlina, Don Giovanni; Blondchen, Abduction from the Seraglio; Papagena, Magic Flute; Despina, Cosi Fan Tutti; Susanna, Marriage of Figaro; Sophie, Der Rosenkavalier; Marcelline, Fidelio; Ighino, Palestine. Address: 20 Weinmeisterhöle, Wedenweg, 14, 1 Berlin, Germany. 2.

OTTOSEN, Kirsten, b. 2 Jan. 1938, Arhus, Denmark. Solfége Teacher; Pianist. Educ: Conserv. Dip. in Solfége & Piano. m. Knud Ottosen, 3 c. Career: Lectr., Inst. of Musicol., Univ. of Aarhus, 1958-74; Lectr., Royal Acad. of Music Arhus, 1974; Perfs., Danish TV & radio; Harpsichord player, The Chmbr. Orch. of Aarhus. Publs: Music reading/writing program for th Suzuki system. Contbr. to: Dansk Musiktidsskrift. Mbrships: Danish Soc. of Music Educ. Hobbies: Chmbr. Music; Accompaniment (piano & harpsichord); Gastronomy. Address: Tousvej 20, DK 8230 Abyhoj, Denmark.

OUBRADOUS, Fernand Robert, b. 1903, Paris, France, Professor; Conductor. Educ: Nat. Conserv., Paris. m. Gilberte Pimbert, 2 d. Career: Fndr. Trio d'Anches, 1927; Prof. at Salzburg Summer Acad., Aust.; Prof. of Chmbr. Music, Paris Conserv., 1941; Pres.-Dir., Int. Music Acad., Nice, 1959; Cond. at num. fests. inclng. Aix-en Provence, Salzburg; & Munich; Juryman, Int. Concoureses; Geneva & Munich,

Compositions incl: trios, quintets & other chmbr. works; reconstructions of French histl. musical works by such composers as Rameau, Couperin, Leduc, Corrette, Pleyel, etc. Publs: The Technique of the Bassoon; French Historical Works. Mbrships: Pres., chmbr. Concerts. Music, 1960-. Hons: Off., Legion of Hon. Hobby: Fishing. Address: 89 bis, Ave. Sainte-Marie, Sainte-Mande, Seine, France.

OVENS, Raymond John, b. 14 Oct. 1932. Bristol, UK. Violinist. Educ: RAM; ARAM. m. Shelia Margaret Vaughan Williams, 1 s.,1 d. Debut: Wigmore Hall, London, 1970. Career: 1st Violin, LSO, 1951; Prin. 2nd Violin, RPO, 1956, Asst. Ldr., ibid., 1972; Concertmaster, Vic. Symph., 1967; Ldr., BBC Scottish Symph. Concerts & recitals for BBC; Ldr., Lyra Str. Quartet; ldr., Ceol Rosh Chmbr. Group. Hons: FRAM. Hobbies: Painting; Golf. Mgmt: R Ingles, co RSAM, Glasgow, UK. Address: 18A Westbourne Gdns., Glasgow G12 9XD, UK.

OVERBY, Karl Edvard, b. 30 July 1938, Northfield, Minn., USA. Horn Player; Instructor; Private Teacher. Educ: BA St. Olaf Coll., Northfield, Minn., 1960; MA, Univ., of Iowa, 1964; MFA, ibid; 1965; pvte. study (French Horn) under Christopher Leuba. m. 2c. Career: Instr. in Brass, Dir., of the Thiel Coll. Wind Ensemble & Assoc. Cond. of the Thiel Chamber Orch., Thiel Coll., Greenville, Pa. 1965-68; Asst. Conc., Greenville Orch., 1966-68; Third Horn in the Phoenix Symph.; Ldr. of Phoenix Brass Quintet; Fndr. & Chmn., Music Dept., Gerard HS; Private Tchr. of French Horn. Recordings: Phoenix Boys' Choir Sings Noel w. The Phoenix Brass Quintet. Mbr., Am. Fed. of Musicians, local 586. Recip., Ford Fndn. Stipend to participate in workshop, researcing & designing educl. progs. for small ensembles to present in schls., 1972. Hobbies: Camping; Conservation. Address: 1732 E Pickrell Dr., Phoenix, AZ 85040, USA.

OVEREND, Susan Elizabeth, b.6 Mar. 1955, Bristol, UK. Music Teacher; Conductor. Educ: Royal Acad. Music, 1973-76; Grad., Royal Schl. Music, 1st Class hons.; Lic., Royal Acad. Music; Assoc., Royal Coll. Music; Royal Acad. Music Profl. Cert. m. Roger Philip Overend, 1 d. Career: Hd. of Music, N Foreland Lodge, 1976-79; Pvte. Tchr., Piano, Woodwind & Theory, 1979-; Co-Fndr., Artistic Dir., Edgeborough Ensemble. Mbrships: Incorp. Soc. of Musicians; Royal Acad. of Music Club. Recip. City Livery Club Prize, 1976. Hobbies: Reading; Writing; Riding; Swimming.

OVERGARD, Graham T, b. 9 Oct. 1903, Humboldt, Kan., USA. Teacher; Composer; Conductor; Professor of Music Education. Educ: D Mus.; LL D. m. Estelle S Sutherland, 1 s., 2 d. Career: Apps. NBC Radio, 15 Yrs.; CBS TV Prog. for Nat. F B League, 10 yrs.; Judge & Guest Cond., State & Nat. Music Festivals; Adjudicator & Guest Cond: World's Fair, 1938, 64; Disney Land, Calif., etc. Comps. incl: Ballade Bravara; The Force of Freedom; Fanfare & Fable; Gridiron Heroes; Forever Fathful; Motor City Parade; The Peace Corps Song, etc. Num. recordings. Mbrships: ASCAP; Phi Delta Kappa; Rotary Int.; Phi Mu Alpha. Hons. incl: Diamond Medal of Artistics Serv., Am. Fedn. of Musicians. Address: 723 Waterway, Venice, FL 33595, USA.

OVERHOLDT, Elaine Rosalie, b. 21 May 1952, Woodstock, Can. Singer; Pianist; Teacher; Actress. Educ: BMus (voice perf.), Univ. of W Ont., London, Can.; ARCT, Royal Conserv., Toronto; Banff Schl. of Fine Arts. Career: num. apps. on radio & TV commercials; piano concert tour of Barbados; singing tour of Engl.; guest apps. on TV shows on CBC, CTV etc. comps: songs perf. & recorded. Mbrships: Assn. of Can. TV & Radio Artists; Toronto Musicians' Assn.; CAPAC; Pres., E Overholt Enterprises Ltd. & E Overholt Publishing. Hons: num. awards at children's fests.; 2nd prize, Int. Youth for Christ talent comp. as pianist. Hobbies: Reading; Jogging; Dancing; Cinema. Mgmt: Richk Sands Assocs., Toronto. Address c/o 5431A Yonge St., Willowdale, Ont. M2N 5R6, Can.

OWEN, Angela Maria b. Cert. in Cond., Boston Conserv. of Music, 1953; PhD in Musicol., Boston Univ., 1957. M. Sidney Owen, 2 c. Career incls: Instrumental Music Supvsr., Pub. Schls., Weymouth, Mass., 1956-59; Instr. in Music Appreciation, Theory, Recorder. Palo Alto Community Adult Schl., Palo Alto, Calif., 1962-; Instr. in Music Appreciation, Recorder, Sequoia Adult Schl., Menlo Pk., Calif., 1979-; Instr. in Recorder & Violin, Community Schl. of Music & Arts, Mountain View, Calif., 1968-74; Dir., Mid-Peninsula Recorder Orch., 1967-; Instr., Music Lit & Hist., Foothill Jr. Coll., 1974-75; Music reviewer, Peninsula Times Tribune, 1977-. Comps: Theme & Var. for 3 Recorders; Conversations for 4 Recorders; Villancicos for 2 Recorders (arr. & ed.), 1976; Favourite German Folksongs for 2 Recorders, 1976. Publs: Prelude to Musicianship, 1979. Contbr. to music jrnls. Mbr., profl. orgs. Hons. Pi Kappa Lambda, 1957; 1st pl. Recorder

Comp. Contest, ARS Miami Chapt., 1972 & San Francisco ARS Bay area, 1979. Hobbies: Tennis; Hiking, etc. Address: 246 Walter Hays Dr., Palo Alto, CA 94303, USA. 5.

OWEN, Barbara, b. 25 Jan. 1933. Utica, NY, USA. Organist; Teacher. Educ: Mus B, Westminister Choir Coll., 1955; M Mus, Boston Univ., 1962; N German Acad., 1975, '77. Career: Organist, chs., Wash., DC, Portland, Conn., & Fall River, Mass., 1956-60; Assoc. w. CB Fisk Inc. organ bldrs., 1961-; Organist & Choir Dir., 1st Religious Soc., Newburyport, Mass., 1963-; Lectr. & Recitalist. Publs: The Organs & Music of King's Chapel, 1965; The Organ in New England before 1900, 1976; Compiler & ed., 3 Early American Carols, 1973; A Century of American Organ Music 1776-1876, 1975; 10 American Hymn Preluded from the 19th Century, 1976; The Victorian Collection, 1978; 4 Centuries of English Organ Music, 1979. Contbr. to profl. publs. Mbr. profl. orgs. Recip: Nat. Endwoment for Humanties Rsch. Fellowship, 1974-75. Hobbies: Gardening; Antiques; Cats. Address: 46A Curtis St., Pigeon Cove, MA 01966, USA.

OWEN, Beti Mary, b. Llannon, Llanelli, Wales, UK. Lieder & Concert Singer. Educ: Cartrefle Coll., Wrexham; Carmarthen Trinity Coll.; Vienna Acad., Austria. Debut: Lieder Recital, Wigmore Hall, London, 1973. Career: Liedr recital, Purcell Room; Recitals, Wigmore Hall; Broadcasts on BBC & Independent radio & TV; Engagements in Sweden; Num. recitals & oratorio perfs. throughout UK. Recordings: Lieder; Sacred Songs in Welsh, "Iesu biau'r gân"; Engl. & Welsh hymns, "Good Tidings"; Welsh Folk Songs; Welsh Art Songs, "Songs We Love". Mbr. ISM; Equity, Hons. Scholarship to study w. Prof. Ferdinand Grossman & Lajos Szamosi, Austria; Austrian State Scholarship to study Leider & oratorio at Vienna Acad. Hobbies: Reading; Vegetarian cuisine; Organic Gardening; Walking. Address: 30 Atney Rd., Putney, London SW15 2PS, UK. 29.

OWEN, Blythe, b. 26 Dec. 1898, Bruce, Minn., USA. Pianist; Cellist; Composer. Educ: B Mus, Chgo. Musical Coll., 1941; M Mus, Northwestern Univ., 1942; PhD, Eastman Schl. of Music, 1953; Ecole des Americaines, Fontainebleau, France. div. Debut: Young Artist Series, Chgo., 1927. Career: made many apps. as Soloist, in clubs, onradio, w. orchs., in chmbr. ensembles, etc. Comps. incl: Trio for Oboe, Clarinet & Bassoon; Two Inventions; Saraband & Gigue for 4 Tubas; Toccata for piano; Variations on Am. Folk Songs; Fanfare & Professioinal, organ & brass quartet; Peace Hymn of the Republic (choral); Remember When (5 pieces for piano). Recordings of own works: Festival Te Deum. Mbrships: The Fontainebleau Assn.; The Art Inst. of Chgo.; NGPT; Music Tchrs. Nat. Assn.; Am. Music Ctr., Inc.: ASCAP; Am. Assn. of Univ. Comps.; Int. Inst. of Art & Letters, Switz, Recip. of num. awards. Address: 115 Kephart Lane, Berrien Springs, MI 49103, USA. 2, 4, 29.

OWENS, Jerry Hubert, b. 29 Apr. 1944, St. Louis, Mo., USA. University Professor of Vocal Music, Educ: B Mus Ed, M Mus, Kan. State Coll. of Pitts.; grad. study, Univ. of Kan. 1 s. Career: Fndr. & Dir., The Designed Xpression choral & dance ensemble (800 perfs. inclng. TV specials & oversear tours to Europe, Caribbean, Orient, USSR, Romania, 1970-); Jt. Fndr., Fine Arts Dept., Univ. of Mo. at Farmington. Author: A Transcription & Analysis of Ten Anthems & Verse Anthems, 1968. Mbrships: Am. Choral Dirs. Assn.; Phi Mu Alpha Sinfonia; Kappa Delta Pi. Hobbies: Tennis. Address: 23 Middle St., Farmington, ME 04938, USA.

OXLEY, Harrison, b. 3 Apr. 1933, Sheffield, UK. Organist; Choirmaster; Conductor; Piano Accompanist; Examiner & Adjudicator. Educ: BMus, MA, Univ. of Oxford; ARCM; ARCO; FRCO; studied w. Willis Grant. m. Dorothy Mary Tanton, 2s., 1 d. Career: Organist & Master of the Chorister, St. Edmundsbury Cathedral; Cond., St. Edmundsbury Bach Choir & orch., 1958-; recitals in England, Germany & Switz., 4 tours of USA & Can. Comps: Anthems, Organ music, Carol arrs. Recordings: Great English Organ Music; Hymns of Praise; Organ music from St. Edmundsbury. Contbr. to Musical Times & Musical Opinion. Mbr., ISM. Hons: Read Prize, Sawyer Prize, Turpin Prize (all from RCO). Hobby: Stroking the Cats. Address: 1 Conyers Way, Gt. Barton, Bury S t. Edmunds, Suffolk, UK.

OXLEY, John Ernest Barrington, b. 19 Nov. 1922, Bristol, UK. Teacher of Singing. Educ: Royal Coll. of Music, 1947-50. m. Mary Ellen Evans, 2 s., 1 d. Career: singer, BBC Radio, 1950-, W End Stage, London, 1951-55; var. TV & concert apps.; Tchr., Music & Class Singing, Bristol & Bath Schls.; Chorus Master, Bristol Opera Schl.; Pvte. Tchr., 1961-75; Singing Tchr., Bristol Old Vic Theatre Schl.; Guest Prof., Theatre Dept., York Univ., Toronto, Can., 1972, '74; Assoc. Prof., ibid, 1975-78; Guest Prof., Drama Dept., Univ. of

Toronto, 1976-78. Recip: Silver Medal, Grade VIII Exam., Assoc. Bd. Royal Schls. of Music, 1942. Hobbies: Gardening; Badminton; Sports. Address: 75 Weston Rd., Lond Ashton, Bristol, UK. 28, 29, 30.

OZAWA, Seiji, b. 1 Sept. 1935, Hoten, Manchuria. Symphony Orchestra Conductor. Educ: Grad., Topho Schl. of Music, Tokyo, Japan. m. Vera Ilyin, 2 children. Debut: Tokyo, Japan, w. NHK Orch. Career: Music Dir., Toronto Symph. Orch. 1965-69, San Fran. Symph., 1970-76, Boston Symph. Orch., 1974-; Music Dir., Ravinia Fest., 1964-68; Guest Cond., LSO, New Philharmonia & other major orchs. Recordings for Philips, DG, EMI, RCA, CBS. Hons: 1st Prize, Int. Competition, Besancon, France; 1st prize, Koussevitzky Scholarship, Tanglewood, Mass; USA. Hobbies: Tennis; Skiing. Mgmt: RA Wilford, Columbia Artists Mgmt Inc., 195 W 57th St., NY, NY 10019, USA. Address: c/o Mgmt.

OZGA, Kazimierz, b. 23 Oct. 1931, Tarnow, Poland. Pianist; Composer. Educ: piano studies w. Z Siekierska & K. Abratowski, Tarnow, Prof. Milinowska, Wroclaw, & at piano school of Sacré Coeur convent, Zblitowska Gora; comp. w. Profs. Jamka & Bukowski, Wroclaw. 1s. 1d. Debut: Wroclaw. Career: Apps. on stages & concerts halls in Poland (Warsaw, Wroclaw, Tarnow, Sopot, Opole), Yugoslavia (Belgrade, Dubrovnik, Sarajevo, Mostar) & Norway (Oslo, Kristiansand, Drammen, Skien, Tonsberg); TV & radio broadcasts in Poland & Norway; now pianist at Norwegian Opera in Oslo. Comps: 5 songs (recorded); 2 ballets. Mbrships: Norsk Komponistforeninge Int. Muikkbyra TONO. Hons. incl. 1st prize, jazz fest., Wroclaw, 1962; TV Grand Prix, song fest., Opole, 1964. Hobbies: Drawing; Painting. Address: Den Norske Opera, Storgt. 23, Oslo 1 Norway.

OZIM, Igor, b. 9 May 1931, Ljubljana, Yugoslavia. Violinist. Educ: Music Acad., Ljubljana; Dip., RCM, London; Pvte. study w. Prof. Max Rostal, London. m. Dr. Breda Volovsek, 1 s., 1 d. Debut: Ljubljana, 1947. Career: Tours of Europe, USA, S. Am., Australia, NZ & Japan; Broadcasts, all European countries. Num. recordings. Publs: Ed., num. contemporary violin works. Ed., Pro Musica Nova, 1974. Hons: Carl Flesch Medal, Int. Competition, London, 1951; 1st Prize, German Broadcasting Stns. Ind. Competition, Munich, 1953. Hobbies: Photography; Table tennis. Mgmt: Ibbs & Tillett, London. Address: Breibergstr. 6 5000 Cologne 41.

OZOLINS, Arthur Marcelo, b. 7 Feb. 1946, Lubeck, Germany. Concert Pianist. Educ: fac. of music, Univ. of Toronto, 1962-63; BSc (music), Mannes Coll. of Music, NY, 1964-67; piano studies w. Pablo Casals, Jacques Abram, Nadia Boulanger, Nadia Reisenberg & Vlado Perlemuter. Career: apps. in NY, Wash., London, Paris, Montreal, Stockholm, Sydney, Sao Paulo, Hamburg, Leningrad, Los Angeles, etc.; soloist w. Toronto Symph., Stockholm Phiul., Hallé Orch.; recital tour of USSR; perfs. on TV & radio for CBC, BBC, Swedish radio, Polish radio, etc. Recordings incl: works by Provoviev, Rachmaninov, Chopin, Bartok, Bach, Franck, Kenins, J Medins, etc. Mbrships: AFM; Engl. Speaking Union, Can. Hons: 7 Can. Coun. Awards; 1st prizes, Edmonton Nat. Competition, 1968 & CBC Talent Fest., 1968; Van Cliburn Int. Competition Special Prize, 1973. Hobbies: Swimming; Reading Books on Philos. & Phychol. Mgmt: Richard von Handschuh, Toronto. Address: 159 Colin Ave., Toronto, Ont. M5P 2C5, Canada.

OZOLINS, Egils, b. 20 May 1945, Peisenberg, Germany. Musicologist; Pianist. Educ: BA (music), Univ. of Calif., Los Angeles, 1967; MA (music), ibid., 1969; studied musicol. w. Edwin Hanley, Frnk D'Accone, Walter H Rubsamen; studied piano w. Alice Ehlers, Aube Tzerko, Johana Harris. Debut: (Piano) Chgo. Orchestra Hall, 1962. Career: as musicologist specializes in baroque music; formerly tchng. assoc., music dept., Univ. of Calif. at Los Angeles; now conducts pvte. piano studio in Los Angeles; Rare Books & Microfilm Bibliographer, Music Lib., Univ. of Calif., Los Angeles. Mbrships: Am. Musicol. Soc.; Nat Honors Soc. Hobbies: Non-contact Sports. Address: 1636 S Beverly Glen Blvd., Los Angeles, CA 90024, USA.

OZOLINS, Janis Alfreds, b. 29 Sept. 1919, Riga, Latvia. Violoncellist; Concert Singer (Bass): Orchestral Conductor. Educ: Dip., Solo Violoncello, Conserv. of Latvia, Riga, 1944; studied w. Prof. E. Mainardi, Rome, Italy, 1947-49; studied Comp., Riga, & Royal Acad. of Music, Stockholm, Sweden; Singing Tchrs. Examination, Stockholm, 1958; studies for Fil.Kand. in Musicol., Univ. of Uppsala, 1962. m. Adine Uggla, 2 s., 1 d. Debut: (Violoncello) Riga, 1943. Career: Concert, Radio Recitals, & Solo perfs. w. orch., Latvia, Sweden, Denmark, UK, Italy & Switz.; Music-master, 1956-; Cond., Landskrona Symph. Orch., 1957; Bass Soloist; Beethoven's Ninth Symph., w. H Blomstedt, Norrköping, 1961; Dir., Växjö Municipal Schl. of Music & Municipal Music Dor., Vöxjö, 1964-; Cond. of Opera, Martha, ibid, 1970. Mbrships: Municipal Bd. of Culture, Växjö, Bd. of Symph. Orch., ibid; Mazerska Soc. of Chmbr. Music, Stockholm. Address: Eddervägen 26, S 352 41 Växjö, Sweden.

P

PACE, Carmelo, b. 17 Aug. 1906, Valleta, Malta. Music Teacher; Composer. Educ: FLCM; LRSM. Career: Fndr. & Condr., Malta Cultural Inst. Concerts, 1948-; Viola player in own chmbr. music ensemble; Lectr. of hist. & theory of music. Comps. incl: Works for Pianoforte Solo & var. other instruments; orch., choral, vocal solos & chmbr. music; operas incl. Caterina Desguanez, I Martiri, Angelica & Ipogeana. Mbrships: Organizer, Malta Cultural Inst. Concerts, 1948-; Performing Rights Soc., London. Hons. incl: 1st Prize for comp., Rediffusion Chmbr. Music competition, 1955-58; 1st Prize, Performing Right Soc., London, 1962, 72, 73; Kt. of the Order of St. John: Gold Medal of the Soc. of Arts, Manufactures & Commerce: Malta Gold Medal of Merit. Hobbies incl: Reading. Address:14 St. Dominic St., Sliema, Malta, 30.

PACINI, Renato, b. 4 Dec. 1909, Utica, NY, USA. Violinist; Conductor. Educ: Acad. of S. Cecilia, Rome, Italy; grad., New Engl. Conserv. of Music, Boston, Mass., 1932. m. Stella (dec.), 1 s., 1 d. Career: ldr., New Engl. Conserv. Orch., State Symph. Orch., Boston; deputy ldr., People's Symph. Orch.; mbr., Indpls. Symph. Orch., 1938-; deputy ldr., ibid., 1938-77; Asst. Cond., ibid., 1950-55: Assoc. Cond., 1955-68; Fndr., Cond., Indpls. Pops Orch.; Dir. & cond., Lafayette (Ind.) Symph. Orch., 1957-; dir., Schola Cantorum of St. Peter & St. Paul Cathedral & St. Vincent Schl. of Nursing Girls' Choir; fac., Jordan Coll. of Music, 1940-45; pvte. tchr., 1945-; soloist NBC network, Mendelssohn violin concerto, 1932. Mbrships: Ind. Chapt., Nat. Soc. of Arts & Letters. Hons: Doct., Marian Coll., Indpls.; Sagamore of the Wabash, 1978. Hobbies: Golf; Fishing. Address: 7815 Somerset Bay, Apt. A, Indpls., IN 46240.

PACIORKIEWICZ, Tadeusz, b. 17 Oct. 1916. Sierpe, Poland. Composer; Organist; Teacher; Educ: Episcopal Organist Schl., Plock., 1932-36; studied Organ w. Prof. B Rutowski & Comp. w. Proif K Sikorski, Warsaw Conserv., 1936-43. m. Zofia Wiaczkis, 2 s., 1d. Career: Prof. of Harmony, Counterpoint, Instrumentation & Comp., State Musical Acad., Warsaw. Comps. incl: 2 Pianoi Concertos, 1952 & 1954; Wind Quintet, 1953; Concerto for Violin & Orch., 19055; 2nd Symph., 1957; String Concerto, Adagio & Allegro, 1960; Ushiko, radio opera, 1962; Liegea, radio opera, 1964; Trio for Flute, Viola & Harp. , 1965; Concerto for Organs & Orch., 1967; Concerto for Trombone & Orch., 1971; Six Miniatures for 4 Trombones, 1972; Oratorium de Revolutionibus, 1972. Mbrships: Polish Comps. Assn.; Frederick Chopin Assn.; ZAIKS, Assn. of Comps. & Publrs.; Warsaw Musical Assn. Hons. incl: Award for Choral Comp., Chopin Centenary Competition 1949; 3rd Prize, Min. of Nat. Defence, 1968; 3rd Prize, Min. of Nat Defence, 1968; 3rd Prize for an opera, & 1st Prize for Outstanding Servs., Min. of Culture & Arts, 1969. Address:01-863 Warsaw, ul. M Jasnorzewkiej 9m.25, Poland.

PACKER, Dorothy, S, b. 2 April 1923, Boston, Mass., USA. Musicologist. Educ: BMus, MA, PhD, Boston Univ. m. Leo S. Packer, 1 d., 2 s. Career: Lectr., Hist of Music & Counterpoint, Boston Univ., 1944-48; Lectr., Am. Music, Am. Studies Program, SUNY at Buffalo, 1956-60; Lectr., Hist. of Music, Nazareth Coll. of Rochester, 1964-66. Contbr. to: Revue de Musicologie; The Musical Quarterly; Jrnl. of the Am. Musicol. Soc.; record notes, etc. Mbrships: Am., Int. & French Musicol. Soc. Hons: Grant, Am. Coun. of Learned Socs., 1973. Address: 2933 Garfield St., NW, Wash. DC 20008, USA.

PACLT, Jaromir, b. 24 Feb. 1927, Hradec Kralove, Bohemia. Musicologist; Violinist. Educ: PhD., Univ. of Prague, 1953; CSc., ibid, 1966. div. Career: Ed., Kniznice Hudebnich rozhledu, 1955-60; Dir., Exposition Hall, Theatre of Music, Prague, 1961-63; Czech. Acad. of Scis., 1963-. Publs: Ed., Tri Kapitoly o Z Nejedlem, 1957; Ed., Strawinsky u nas, 1957; Ed., Tvurci moderni hubdy, 1965; Ed., Kresba a avuk., 1969; Ed., Hubda v ceskem divadle a cinohre, 1972; Ed., Slovnik svetovych skladetelu, 1971. Contbr. to: Hudebni rozhledy; Slovenska hubda; Kvety; Tvorba; Mlada fronta; Svobodne slovo; Literni noviny; Sesity; Ruch Muczyczny, Poland; Musica. Hi-Fi Stereophonie, W. Germany. Hons: 1st Prize, Czech Radio, 1967; 2nd Prize, Int. Music Competition, Radioi Brno, 1970. Hobbies: Painting; Motoring. Address: 2672 Nad Palatou, 150 00 Prague, 5, Czechoslovakia.

PADBERG, Helen Swan, b. Shawnee, Okla., USA. Performer of & Teacher of Violin; Pianist; Harpist. Educ: AA, Stephens Coll.; BFA, Univ. of Okla.; M Mus., Northwestern Univ.; pvte.

study of violin w. Jacques Gordon, Bertha Eisen & Scott Willitts, & harp w. Ruth Cobb. m. Frank Padberg, 1 s., 1 d. Career: solo recitals from age 12; Recitalist and soloist w. orchs. of Stephens Coll., Univ. of Okla., Northwestern Univ.; soloist & 1st violin, USO Orch. during WWII; Mbr., Chgo. Women's Symph., Okla. Symph., Chgo. Civic Orch., Am Youth Orch. (NY), & Nat. Orchestral Assn. (NY); Asst. Concertmaster, Chgo. W Suburban Symph.; Concertmaster, Little Rock (Ark.); violinist, Ark. String Trio; num. solo appss. on radio & TV; many solo recitals. Mbrships: Pi Kappa Lambda; Am. Harp Soc.; Mu Phi Epsilon; Am. Fed. of Musicians; Co-fndr., Little Rock Chamber Music Soc. Recip. num. hons. Hobbies: Cooking; Water Skiing; Tennis; Travel; Community Service. Address: 175 E Delalware Pl., Chgo., IL 60611, USA.

PADDOCK, Ralph Austin, b. 21 Nov. 1921, Chelsea, London, UK. Oganist; Teacher. Educ: Tchr. Trng. Coll.; Piano Studies, Trinity Coll. of Music; Pvte. Organ Studies; Lic., Royal Acad. Music. m. Frances Barbara Kitson, 1 s. Career: Organist, Choirmaster Holycross Priory Church, 1948-. Contbr. to: Musical Opinion. Mbrships: Incorp. Soc. of Musicians; Leicestershir Organists' Assn.; Nat. Union of Tchrs. Recip. Papal Medal Beni Morente, 1975. Hobbies: Fishing; Imbibing. Address: 28 Meadhurst Rd., Leicester, UK.

PADE, Else Marie, b. 2 Dec. 1924, Aarhus, Denmark. Composer; Producer. Educ: RAM, Copenhagen; Pvte. Studies w. Vagn Holmboe (comp.) & Jan Meagaard; Electro-acoustic; MSc. Holger Lauridsen; Ferienkurse fur neu Musik, Darmstadt; Experimental Sect. of French Radio. Career: Prod. & Advs. for Contemporary Music, Denmarks Radio, 1964-73; Collaborator on rsch. project for handicapped children, Univ. Clinic, Copenhagen, 1973-. Comps. incl: The Blade of Grass (ballet), 1964; Immortella (ballet), 1969; Maria (Essay of magnetic tape, coloratura soprano, speaking voice, mixed choir), 1975R. Hons. incl: Rsch. scholarships & awards. Hobbies: Reading: Nature. Address: Soondre Fasanvej 95, 2500 Valby Denmmark.

PADGETT-CHANDLER, David E, b. 18 Jan. 1945, Weston Super Mare, UK. Organist; Education Officer. Educ: Cert. of Educ: (Music & Engl. Lit.), King Alfreds Coll., Winchester; Bristol Cathedral Schl.; studied w. Clifford Harker, Bristol Cathedral & Alwyn Suplice, Winchester Cathedral. Career: Asst. Organist, Bishipston Parish Ch., Bristol, 1960-64; Organ Scholar, Bristol Cathedral Schl., 1962 & King Alfreds Coll., Winchester, 1964-67; Organist & Choirmaster, All Saints PC., Winchester, 1968-70 & Richmond Parish Ch., Surrey, 1970-. Publs: Music at Hyde (Winchester), 1970; The Organs & Music at St. Thomas Church, Winchester, 1969. Mbrships: Hon. Sec. Richmond Arts Fest. Assn.; RCO. Contbr. to: The Richmond & Twinckenham Times; The Musical Times; Musical Opinion. Hobbies: Reading; Do it Yourself; Graphic Design. Address: 49 The Grove, St. Margarets, Twickenham TW1 3EW, UK.

PADILLA, Antoine, b. 11 June 1944, Oran, Alegria. Composer; Conductor; Pianist; Professor. Educ: MMus (comp.), Laval Univ., Que.; studied comp. & cond., Acad. of Music, Munich, German Fed. Repub. m. Liliane M. Blanc. Career: regularly composing & conducting for CBC/TV, Montreal; composing for theatre & TV plays. Comps: Drama scores for TV, Montreal; Chmbr. Symph.; Fresque québécoise, for 8 recorders, cello & harpsichord (recorded). Mbrships: Can. Music Coun.; Can. League of Comps. Hons: Outstanding young man of the year, 1978; Anik Pize, 1978 (CBC/TV for best frama score in Can.). Hobbies: Reading; Swimming; Exercising; Trips. Address: 3355 Queen Mary Rd., Apt. 109, Montreal, Que. H3V 1A5, Canada.

PADMORE, Andrew Paul, b. 15 May 1951, Birmingham, UK. Cathedral Organist; Conductor; Adjudicator; Examiner. Educ: MA; BMus; FTCL; FLCM; LRAM; ARCM; ARCO. m. Eileen Mary Godfrey. Career: Organist & Master of the Choiristers, Cork Cathedral; fndr., cond., E Cork Choral Soc. (250 voices); Dir., Cork N Monastery Boys' Choir. Comps: Anthems; Communion Setting in F; sev. arrs. for choirs. Recordings: The Organ of Cork Cathedral; The Cork N Monastery Boys' Choir. Mbrships: FRSA; RCO. Hobbies: Motoring in Morgan Cars; Swimming. Address: Organist's House, 8 Dean St., Cork, Erie.

PADWA, Vladimir, b. Krivyakino, Russia. Composer; Pianist; Educator. Educ: Imperial Conserv., Petrograd.; State Conserv., Berlin, Germany; Leipzig Conserv.; Pupil, Ferruccio Busoni, Michael Zadora, Paul Juon. m. Natalie J Lozier, 1947, 1 s., 1 d. Career incls: Directed & perfd. 1st broadcast all-electronic music, Berlin, Germany, 1932; Assoc. Prof., Music Educ., NY Univ., 1968-; Num. concerts throughout USA, Europe, Far E, S Am. S Africa; Adjudicator. Quebec Music Fests., Canada, 1961-; NB Competitive Music Fests., 1965-. Compositions incl: Ballet Suite 'Tom Sawyer'; Concerto for 2 pianos & strings; Symphony in D Contbr. to profl. jrnls. Mbr. var. orgs.

Hons. incl: Nat. Fedn. Music Clubs Award Merit, 1973. Address: 736 Riverside Dr., NY., NY 10031, USA. 6.

PAESKY, Efrain, b. 29 Oct. 1931, Gancedo, Chaco, Argentina. Pianist; Piano Professor. Educ: Grad. in piano & chmbr. music, Nat. Univ. of Rosario. m. Emma Alcira Garmendia. Debut: Soloist w. Nat. Symph. Orch. of Buenos Aires, 1949. Career incl: Recitalist in num. countries of N & S Am. & W Europe; Pianist, Trio Estable of Rosario Univ. Currently Hd., Tech. Unit on Music of org. of Am. States & Sec.-Gen. of Inter-Am. Music Coun. Recordings: Musica Americana para ninos; works of Beethoven & Mozart, etc. Mbrships. incl: Inter-Am. Music Festival, Wash. DC; Piano MTA; Inter-Am. Music Coun.; Interam. Music Ctr., Rosario. Hons: 1st Prize, Chopin Contest, Rosario, 1949; Outstanding Personality award, Rosario Jr. Chmbr., 1968. Hobbies: Chess; Films. Address: 5340 28th St. NW, Wash., DC 10015, USA.

PAETZOLDP-HRDLIČKOVA, Nadja, b. Sophia, Bulgaria. Harpist. Educ: State Conserv. Prague, Study w. Prof. Marie Zunová-Skalská; div., 1 d. Career: apps. w. State Symph. Orch., Poznan. Poland; Radio & Film; Symph. Orch., Prague, Czech.; Konzertverein, St. Gallen, Switz.; Stadttheather Biel, Allgemeine Music Gesellschaft, Lucerne; solo recordings for radio, Katowic, Munich, Zürich & Bern. Mbrships: Janáček Soc., Zürich; Schweizerischer Musikerband. Hobbies incl: Adapting works of old unknown comps.; Ballet. Address: Zähringestr. 1, 6003 Lucerne, Switzerland.

PÄFFGEN, Peter K, b. 18 Nov. 1950, Düsseldord, Germany. Musicologist; Editor & Publisher of Music. Educ: Univ. of Cologne. Publs: Hans. Newsidler: Ein Newgeordent Künstlich Laurtenbuch (ed.), 1974; Ed., JB Besardus: Instrucktionen für Laute, 1974; Der Lautenist Hans Newsidler. Studien zu Lute und Lautenmusik in der ersten Hälfte des 16. Jahrhunderts, forthcoming. Contbr. to Die Musikforschung. Address: GbR Junghänel, Päffgen, Schäfer, Postfach 309, 4040 Neuss/Rhein, German Fed. Repub.

PAGANUZZI, Enrico, b. 18 Jan. 1921, Asmara, Ethiopia. Professor of Literature. Educ: musical studies w. David Begalli & Arrigo Pedrollo; Dip., Musical Paleography, Cremona; Grad. in Humanities. Contbr. to: Revista Musicale Italiana; Convivium; Cultura neolatina; Vita Veronese; Enzyclopädie Die Musik in Geschichte und Gegenwart; Enciclopedia della Musica (Rizzo-Richordi); Grove's Dictionary of Music & Musicians, 6th ed.; La Muisica a Verona. Mbrships: Libn., Philharmonic Acad., Verona; Italian Soc., of Musicol.; Corres. Mbr., Veronese Acad. of Agric., Sci. & Letters. Address: Lungadige Matteotti 9, 37126 Verona, Italy, 30.

PAGE, Kenneth, b. 8 Dec. 1927, Birmingham, UK. Violinist; Violist; Conductor. Educ: Birmingham Schl. of Music (ABSM); LRAM. m. Brenda Gane, 1 s., 1 d. Career: Violinist, Archduke Trio (Res., Leciester Univ.); Ldr., Found., Musical Dir., Orch. da Camera; Cond. Birmingham Phil. Orch.; concerts, UK & abroad. Recordings; Delius, Brigg Fair, w. Birmingham Phil. Orch.; Josephs, Piano Concerto No. 2 (world premiere), w. Orch. da Camera. Recip: Hon. M. Mus, Leicester Univ., 1975. Hobbies: Model Railways (OO Gauge); Photography. Address: 41 Fishponds Rd., Kenilworth, Warwicks, CV8 1EY, UK. 2.

PAGELS, Jurgen Heinrich, b. 16 April 1925, Lubeck, Germany. Ballet Master; Educator; Educ: Opera House Ballet Schl., Lubeck; Legat Schl. of Russian Ballet, Tunbridge Wells, UK; Adv. Tchrs. Degree of Russian Ballet (MARB); Adv. & Soloist Degree of Assoc. of Russian Ballet (MRBS). m. Angela M. Granados Aburto. Debut: Lubeck Opera House. Career: Ballet Soloist, Lubeck, & Dortmund Opera; Ballet Theatre Co., Europe; Yugoslav Nat. Ballet; Ballet Étoile, Paris; Ballet Legat; Guest Soloist in major European Cities in USA; Ballet Master & Assoc. Prof., Ind. Univ. Schl. of Music, USA; Choreographer for sev. opera & ballet prods; Guest Mestro & Guest Artistic Dir., Ballet Guatemala. Mbrships: Nat. Soc. of Arts & Letters; Russian Ballet Soc., UK; Assn. of Russian Ballet, UK, Goethe Soc., Dallas, Tex. Contbr. to: Dance News; Dance Mag. Recip of Award of Community Leaders & Noteworthy Americans. Hobbies: Sculpture; Mosaic; Steel Welding. Address: Ballet Dept., Schl. of Music, Ind. Univ., Bloomington, IN 47401.

PAIGE, Norman, b. NYC, USA. Singer (Tenor). Educ: NY Univ.; Juilliard Schl. of Music; Am. Theater Wing/Profl. Trng. Prog. m. Inci Bashar, 1 d. Debut: Matteo, Strauss Arabella, Linz, Landestheater, Austria, 1958. Career: Linz, Landestheater, 1958-61; Civic Opera, Cologne Opera, 1961-65; Met. Opera Nat. Co., 1956-67; NYC Opera, 1967-68; Europe, Chgo., 1969-77; guest apps. in Europe & USA; over 80 lyric & character roles; Dir., Division of Voice, Schl. of Fine Arts, Univ. of Kans. Recordings: First officer -Zimmerman's Die Soldaten. Mbrships: Pi Kappa Lambda;

AAUP. Recip. grants. Hobbies: Engl. entymol. Mgmt: Jim Scovotti Assocs., 185 W End Ave., NYC. Address: Schl. of Fine Arts, Univ. of Kan., Lawrence, KS 66045, USA.

PAIKOV, Shaike (Yeshayahu), b. 5 July 1937, Tel Aviv, Israel. Composer; Arranger; Conductor. Educ: Univ. Entrance; Music Tchr., Musicol. Career: Apps. at Israeli Fests.: Childrens Int. Fest., Malta; Chassidic Fest., Israel; Int. Fest., Chile, 1976, '78; Perf. of Music of Israeli Films & Plays. Comps: More than 400 Israeli Songs. Recordings: Lovely Israel (3 records): Songs from Ilan & Ilanit: En-Den-Dino, Folklore Israel; Music from Movies (2 records); Songs of the Fests. (2 records); Records from var. singers. Mbrs. Accum, Israel. Num. hons. inclng: 1st Prize Oriental Fest., 1971; 1st Prize Chassidic Fest., 1975; 2nd Prize, ibid, 1976. Hobbies: Growing Flowers; Music. Address: Kibbutz Mishmar Hasharon, Israel.

PAILLARD, Jean-Francois, b.12 Apr. 1928, Vitryle-Francois, France. Conductor; Musicologist. Educ: 1st prize Music Hist., Conserv. Nat. Sup., Paris; studied cond. w. Igor Markevitch, Salzburg, Austria; Lic., scis., maths., Sorbonne, Paris. m. Anne-Mrien Beckensteiner, 3 s. Debut: Fndn., J F Paillard Chamb. Orch., 1953. Career: About 120 annual world-wide concerts, inclng. tours of Japan (4), Korea, N. & S. Am.; Org. & Tchr. Cond. Courses, Spring & Summer, France. Recordings; Approx. 200 w. Erato. Publs: La Musique Francaise Clasique, PUF, 1960, 3rd. Ed., 1973; Achives de la Musique Instrumentale, Archives de la Musique Religieuse. Mbrships: French Musicol. Soc.; French Soc., 18th century. Hons: 10 Grands Prix du Disque (Acad. Charles Cros. Disque Francais, Disque Lyrique), Prix Edison, Holland, German Record Prize, Gold Record, Japan. Hobbies: Piloting Aircraft; Sailing. Mountaineering. Address: 23 rue de Marly, 7860 Etang la Ville, France.

PAÏTA, Carlos, b. 10 March 1932, Buenos Aires, Argentina. Conductor. Educ: Piano w. Juan Neuchoff; Harmony, counterpoint, fugue, comp. & instrumentation w. Jacobo Fischer. m. Elisabeth de Quartrebarbes, 7 c. Debut: Theatro Colon, Buenos Aires. Career: Apps. in London, Paris, Edinburgh, etc. Recordings: Festival Wagner; Grands Overtures; Requiem de Verdi; 3éme de Beethoven; Overtures Rossini; lère de Mahler; Symph. Fantastique de Berlioz. Hons: Off. Govt. invitation to visit USA, 1965; Grand Prix Académie Charles Cros, Paris, 1969; Grand Prix de L'Académie Francaise, 1978. Mgmt: Martin Taubman, Impresariat, Bohlstrasse 23, 6300 Zug, Switz. Address: 15, Chemin du Champ D'Anier, 1209 Geneva, Switzerland.

PAJARO, Eliseo M, b. 21 Mar. 1915, Badoc, Illocos Norte, Phillippines. Composer; Conductor; University Professor. Educ: Grad. Music Dip., Univ. of Philippines, 1947; M Mus, 1951; PhD, 1953, Eastman Schl. of Music. m. Joaquina Tobias, 2 s.,3 d. Career: Prof. of Comp., Coll. of Music, & Special Asst. to Pres. on Cultural Affairs, Univ. of Philippines. Comps. incl: 4 concertos, 3 symphs., 3 choral cycles & 5 song cycles; Binhi Ng Kalayaan (opera); Mirinisa (ballet); 2 str. quartets. Publ: Himing Pilipino I-II, 1972, 74. Contbr. to var. jrnls. Mbrships incl: Pres., Regional Music Commission, S.E. Asia. Hons. incl: Repub. Cultural Heritage Award, 1964, 70; Pres. Award of Merit, 2966; Outstanding: 2 Marilag St., U.P. Village, Diliman, Quezon City, Philippines.

PALADI, Radu, b. 16 Jan.1927,Storojinezh, Romania. Composer; Pianist; Conductor; Professor. EducZ: MA, Ciprian Porumbescu Conserv., Bucharest. m. Marta Paladi, 1 s., 1 d. Debut: as pianist, 1943; as cond., 1967. Carree: periodical piano concerts; Cond., Botosani Phil Orch., Romania, 1968-72; duo concerts (viola & piano), 1975-76; Prof., Theatre & Film Acad., Bucharest. Comps. incl: Eliberarea (oratorio); Fluierasul fermecat (symph. suite); Ciulini Baroganului (symph. suite); str. quartet in minor; wind quintet; piano music; choral music. Mbr., Comps. Union, Bucharest. Hons. incl: Comps. Union of Romania Prize, 1969, 72. Address: Lucaci St. 55, 7000 Bucharest IV, Romania.

PALAY, Elliot J, b. 18 Dec. 1948, Milwaukee, Wis., USA. Opera Singer (Helden Tenor). Educ: B Mus, Ind. Univ. m. Susan W. Palay. Career: Appd. in Opera Houses, NYC, USA; Deutsche Oper Am Rhine, Frankfurt, Munich Staatsopher, Stuttgart, Dortmund, Frieburg, Lubeck, Kiel, Darmstadt, & Wuppertal, Germany; Roles incl: Berg, Tambourmajor (Wozzeck); Janacek, Boris (Katja Kabanova); Wagner, Walter (Meistersinger) & Tristan (Tristan); Strauss, Kaiser (Frau Ohne Schatten) & Matteo (Arabella); Verdi, Radames (Aida) & Ismaele (Nabucco). Hobbies: Golf; Tennis. Mgmt: Stoll Agcy., Germany. Address: Deutsche oper am Rhein, 4 Düsseldorf, German Fed. Repub.

PALECZNY, Piotr Tadeusz, b. 10 May 1946, Rybnik, Poland. Pianist. Educ: MA, Dip. w. distinction, 1970, HS of Music, Warsaw. m. Barbara Paleczny. Debut: Moscow, 1967. Career:

concert rours, most European countries, USA, Cuba, Japan, Aust. Recordings incl: Mussorgski's Pictures at an Exhibition; Chopin Studies op. 25. Mbr., Soc. of Polish Musicians. Hons. incl: 1st Prize, Best Perf. of Russian & Soviet Music, Katowice, 1961, 1963, 1964; Gold Medals, Int. Piano Competitions, Sofia, 1968; 3rd Prize, Int. Piano Competition, Munich, 1969; Chopin Competion, Pleven, 1972; Bordeaux, 1972 (also) Grand prix); Gold Medal of Merit, 1974. Hobbies: Theatre; Old paintings; Cars; Animals. Mgmt: Pollish Artist Mgmt: PAGART & Polish Radio & TV Impresario. Address:Mickiewicza 30/39, 01-616 Warsaw, Poland.

PALING, Edwin John, b. 29 Dec. 1948, Nottingham, UK. Orchestra Leader. Educ: RAM; Studied w. Sidney Griller. m. Elizabeth Pitts. Career: Ldr., Scottish Nat. Orch.; Violinist w. Bournemouth Symph. Orch.; City of Birmingham Symph. Orch.; BBC Midland Light Orch. Hobby: Golf. Address: 19 Craigmarloch Ave., Torrance, Glasgow, G64 4AY, UK.

PALISCA, Claude Victor, b. 24 Nov. 1921, Fiume (now Rijeka, Yugolsavia) Professor of History of Music. Educ: BA., Queens Coll., Flushing, NY, 1943; MA., Harvard Univ., 1948; PhD., ibid, 1954; MA (Hon.), Yale Univ., 1964. m. Jane Pyne 1 s., 1 d. Career: Instr. in Music, Univ. of Ill., 1953-54; Asst. Prof., ibid., 1954-59; Assoc. Prof. of the Hist. of Music, Yale Univ., 1959-64; Prof. of Hist, ibid., 19643-; Dir. of Grad. Studies in Music, 1957-70; Chmn., Dept. of Music, Yale Univ., 1967-, etc. Publs: (books) Giralomo Mel: Letters on Ancient & Modern Music to Vincenzo Galilei & Giovanni Bardi, 1960; Seventeenth Century Science & the Arts (w. 3 others), 1961; Musicology (w. others), 1963; Baroque Music, 1968; Trans. w. Guy Marco, Zarlino, The Art of Counterpoint, Le istutioni harmoniche, 1558, Part III, 1968; Contbr. to var. profl. publs. Mbrships incl: First VP., AM. Musicol. Soc., 1965-67; Pres. Nat. Coun. of the Arts in Educ., 1967-69; VP., New Haven Symph., Inc., 1969-; VP, Arts Coun. of Gtr. New Haven, 1975.; Pres. Am. Musicol. Soc., 1970171., Recip. sev. fellowships. Address: 68 Spring Rock Rd., Pine Orchard, Branford, CT 06405, USA. 2, 11.

PALLER, Ingrid, b. 24 Dec. 1928, BruckMur, Austria. Opera and concert singer; Music pedagogue, Educ: Music Acad. Mozarteum, Salzburg; Music Acad. Vienna. Debut: Klagenfurt. Career: Lyrical coloratura soprano, City Theater, Basel Heidelberg; German Opera Düsseldorf; Concert tours through Europe and South America; app. TV, opera. Recordings; Rigoletto; Don Giovanni, Hobbies: Traveling; Sport. Address: Kempstenestr. 58, 8 München 71, German Fed. Repub.

PALM, Richard Dennis, b. 26 Feb. 1945, Seattle, Wash., USA. Instrument Maker (records, baroque bassoons & dulcians). Educ: BS. in Elec. Engrng., Univ. of Wash., 1967; MS. in Elec. Engrng., ibid, 1970; studied bassoon w. Arthur Grossman, 1969-71; worked for Friedrich von Huene (recorder maker), 1972-74; Set up own shop in Cambridge, 1975-. Contbr. to Jrnl. of the Assn. for the Adv. of Med. Instrumentation (A Solid State Fiberoptics Oximeter), w. others, 1971. Mbrships: Am Recorder Soc.; Gaplin Soc.; Tau Beta Pi; Am Civil Liberties Union. Address: 33 Lee St., Apt. 7, Cambridge, MA 02139, USA.

PALM, Siegfried, b. 25 Apr. 1927, Barmen, Germany. Cellist: Professor of Music. Educ: pvte. studies m. Brigitte Heinemann. Career: Solo Cellist, Municipal Orch., Lübeck, 1945-47, NW. German Radio Symph. Orch., 1947-62, Mbr., Hamann Quartet, 1951-62; Dir. of Music, Cello Class, Nat. Coll. of Music, Cologne, 1962-; Mbr., Rostal-Palm chröter Trio; Lectr., Darmstadt Vacation Courses in Mod. Music, Cologne, 1962-; Vis. Lectr., Dartmouth Coll., USA & Swedish Radio, Stockholm; solo guest apps. & concert tours throughout the world; apps. incl. Holland Fest., Warsaw Autumn Fest., Prague Spring Fest., Venice Munich Fest., Barcelona Fest. & Marlboro (USA) Fest. Recordings: num., avant-grade works a speciality (e.g. Zimmermann, Penderecki) Hons. incl: German Record Prize (Deutsche Schallpolattenpreis), 1969. Address:26 Gartenstr., 5038 Rodenkirchen, Nr. Cologne, German Fed. Repub.

PALMER, Cedric King, b. 13 Feb. 1913, Eastbourne Sussex, UK. Composer, Conductor, Author, Lecturer. Educ: RAM; ARAM; LRAM; FRSA. m. Winifred Henry (dec.), 1 s., 1 d. Career: Conc. & Lectr., City Literary inst., 1939-; Cond., The King Palmer Light Orch. (BBC), 1939-; Cond., Euphonic Symph. Orch., N. London Orch., Sevenoaks Musical Soc., W. End Theatrical Prods., Film Orchs., etc. Compositions: Film scores for Dark Eyes of London; Cockney Kids Adventure; Secrets of the Stars; Rythm of the Road; Holiday Time; Signs of the Times, etc.; Operettas -Gay Romance; The Snow Queen; The Film Opens (11th hour melody); 3 Atonal Studies, etc. Publs: Teach Yourself: Music, 1946; Teach Yourself: to Play The Piano, 1957; Teach Yourself: to Compose Music, 1947; Teach

Yourself: Orchestration, 1968; The Musical Production, 1953; ABC of Church Music, 1971; Your Music & You, 1938; Granville Bantock, 1939. Mbrs. of num. music orgs. Hons. incl: JP., 1968; Freeman, City of London, 1963. Address: Clovelly Lodge, 2 Popes Grove, Twickenham TW2 5TA, Middx., UK.

PALMER, Elizabeth Ann, B. Bristol, UK. Bassoonist; Teacher of Orchstral Wind Instruments. Educ: Scholar, RCM; ARCM Bassoono Tchr. Perf.; studied w. Archie Camden & Ernest Hall. Career: During 17 yrs. in London, played in orchl. concerts & symphonic & chmbr. music recitals in all main concert halls. Mbrships: ISM; (Coun. Mbr., 1977-); Music Masters Assn. (Committee, 3 yrs.; Elected Mbr. of Coun., 1976); MRSM., Life, Nat. Trust. Hobby: Reading. Address: The Oak, Knoll Hill, Bristol BS9 1QU, UK. 3.

PALMER, Felicity Joan, b. 6 Apr. 1944. Soprano. Educ: GSM; AGSM. Career incls: concerts in UK, Belgium, France, Italy, German, Spain, USA; Europe tour w. BBC Symph. Orch., 1973; opera debut in Marriage of Figaro, Houston, Tex., 197 3. Recordings incl: Poullenc Song Recital w. John Constable: Poems pour Mi w. Boulez; Holst Choral Symph. w. Sir Adrian Boult. Recip., Kathleen Ferrier Mem. Prize, 1970. Address: 22 Greville Rd., London NW6 5JA, UK. 1.

PALMER, Larry Garland, b. 13 Nov. 1938, Warren, Ohio, USA. Harpsichordist; Organist; Educator; Author. Educ: BMus., Oberlin Conservatory of Music, 1960; M Mus., Eastman Schl. of Music, Univ. of Rochester, NY, 1961; Dr. of Musical Arts, ibid, 1963; Assoc. & Choirmaster Dips., Am. Guild of Organists (AAGO.; Ch M.). Career incls: Prof. of Music & Dir., Choral Acitvities, Norfolk State Coll., Va., 1965-70; Prof., Harpsichord & Organ, Meadows Schl. of the Arts, Southern Meth. Univ., Dallas, Tex., 1970-; Organist & Choirmaster, St. Luke's Episcopal Ch., Dallas, 1971-; Organ & harpsichord recitals, USA, France, Germany & Austria; Featured harpsichord artist, Am. Guild of Organists Nat. Convention, Dallas, 1972; Int. Congress of Organists, Phila., 1977; Int. Organ Weks, Nürnberg, 1978. Comps. (Anthems); 'Twas in the Year That King Uzziah Died; Matin Responsory for Advent. Recordings: The Harpsichord Now & Then: a solo recital of early 20th Century music; The Organ Works of Hugo Distler. Author of Hugo Distler & His Ch. Music, 1967. Ed. & Contbr., var. books & jrnls. Mbrships: AGO, (Chapt. Dean, 1968-70, 1977-79); Pi Kappa Lambda; Hymn Soc. of Am. Address: 10125 Cromwell Dr., Dallas, TX 75229, USA. 7.

PALMER, Peggy, b. 18 Apr. 1912, Hyde Park, Adelaide, SA, Aust. Pianist; Piano & Theory Teacher. Educ: Elder Conservatorium, Adelaide; studied w. Prof. Max Pauer, Leipzig (now Mendelssohn) Conservatorium, Germany, 4 yrs. Career: sev. piano recitals in Adelaide Town Hall before going to Germany; since return to Aust., about 100 piano recitals for Aust. Broadcasting Commission Radio, Adelaide & Sydney, also Concerto Soloist w. SA Symph. Orch., Town Hall & Radio Studio. Mbrships: Advsry. Bd. Mbr. for Music, Univ. of Adelaide; Examiner Coun. Mbr., SA Music Tchrs. Assoc. Inc. Hons: Elder Scholarship, 1925-27; Adeliade Karl Grimm Scholarship, Leipzig, 1930-32. Hobby: Collecting china. Address: 19 Alexandria Ave., Rose Park, Adelaide, SA, Austria.

PALMER, Willard Aldrich, b. 31 Jan. 1917, McComb, Miss., USA. Music Editor; Composer; Musicologist; Lecturer; Harpsichord 1st; Pianist. Educ: BS, Millsaps Coll.; Post-Grad. studies at Univ. of Houston, 2 yr. scholarship, Leipzig Conserv. m. Ruby Lenoire Touchstone, 2s., 1d. Career: 34 yrs. experience as ed., choral dir., concert artist; Dir., Memorial Lutheran Ch. Choir, 1959-77; Mbr., Music Fac., Univ. of Houston, 1946-64; Lectures & workshop tours in USA & Can., 1968-; now Keyboard Ed.-in-Chief for Alfred Publishing Co. Comps: num. works, arrs. & eds. for choir; Baroque Folk (piano), 1972; Contemporary Album for the Young (piano), 1977. Publs: 300 books written or edited; num. keyboard works, classical & modern written or edited; (w. Amanda Vick Lethco) 16 vols., Creating Music at the Piano, 1970-76; (authors ed. w. Margery Halford) An Introduction to the Baroque Era, 1976; An Introduction to the Classical Era, 1977; An Introduction to the Romantic Era, 1978. Mbrships. incl: Houston Harpsichord Soc.; ASCAP. Hon. D.Humanities, 1971. Address: 9602 Winsome Ln., Houston, TX 77063, USA.

PALMITER, Lloyd Frank, b. 9 June 1954, Detroit, Mich., USA. Cellist; Teacher. Educ: BMus (chmbr. music & strg. tchng.), Univ. of Evansville, Ind.; grad. studies at Univ. of Evansville, Ind. Univ., S Bend & W Ky. Univ., Bowling Gn. Career: cellist w. Owensboro Symph., Owensboro, Ky; grad. asst. Dept. of Music, W Ky. Univ.; pvte. cello tchng. Recip., Pres.'s Award for outstanding achievement in music, Univ. of Evansville, 1977. Address: 17346 Willshire Dr., S Bend, IN 46635, USA.

PALOLA, Juhani Antero, b. 25 Nov. 1952, Helsinki, Finland. Violinist; Teacher. Educ: w. Prof. T. Poqezeva, Oula Conserv. of Music, 1967-69; w. Prof. A Ignatius, Sibelius Acad., Helsinki, 1974-76; Summer Courses w. Prof. Igor Bezrodnigi, Eli Goren, Takaya Urakowa. m. Liisa-Maria. Career: Perfs. as soloist w. Finnish Symph. Orchs. inclng. Finnish Radio Orch.; Chmbr. music perfs., Sweden, Norway, Austria, Hungary, Czech., USA, 1976; 2nd Concertmaster, Oula Symph. Orch.; Tchr., Oula Conserv. of Music. Hobby: Squash. Address: 90850 Martinniemi, Finland.

PALOMBO, Paul Martin, b. 10 Sept. 1937, Pitts., Pa., USA. Composer; Educator; Administrator. Educ: BS, Ind. Univ. of Pa.; PhD, Eastman Schl. of Music. m. Joyce Fletcher Palombo. Debut: Balt. Symph. Orch., Md., 1965. Career: recip., 25 commns.; Assoc. Dean for Acad. Affairs, Prof. of Comp., Dir. of Electronic Music Studio, Coll. -Conserv. of Music, Univ. of Cincinnati, OH. Comps: Proteus for orch.; Sonos I for harpsichord & electronic tape; Ritratti Anticamente for viola & piano; Et. Cetera, electronic ballet; Montage for violin & piano; Sonos IV for string trio & electronic tape; Miniatures for organ & electronic tape; Morphosis: electronic music for dance (recorded); Methatheses for flutes, oboes, harpsichord & double bass (recorded); Sonos III for double bass & electronic tape (recorded). Publs. incl: The Graphic Language of New Music, forthcoming. Mbrships. incl: Am. Soc. Univ. Comps.; Coll. Music Soc.; Audio Engrng. Soc. Recip., prizes in comp. Address: 234 Glenmary Ave., Cincinnati, OH 45221, USA. 3.

PALOTAY, Irene Banyay, b. 18 Oct. 1902, Kaposvar, Hungary. Pianist; Organist. Educ: Franz Liszt Acad., Budapest; M Mus, Univ. of Southern Calif.; studied under Bela Bartok & Zoltan Kodaly. m. Julius Palota, 1 s. Career: radio & TV perfs. in Europe & USA. Contbr. to num. publs. Mbrships. incl: Nat. Assn. of Am. Comps. & Conds.; Nat. Guild of Piano Tchrs.; Pres., Int. Club, Los Angeles; Am. Musicol. Assn. Hobbies: Sport; Reading. Address: 3000 Leeward Ave., Apt. 713, Los Angeles, CA 90005, USA.

PÁLSSON, Páll Pampichler, b. 9 May 1928, Graz, Austria. Conductor; Composer. Educ: Studied Trumpet & Cond. Acad. of Music, Graz, & Hochschule für Musik, Hamburg, Germany. m. Astrídur Eyjólfsdóttir Pálsson, 2 s, 1 d. Career: Mbr., Graz Phil. Orch., 1945-49; Mbr.,1949-59, Cond., 1960-, Iceland State Symph. Orch.; Cond., Reykjavlk City Band, 1949-74; Cond., Icelandic Singers (male choir), 1964-. Compositions: Orchl., Chmbr. & choral works, inclng. Requiem for Mixed Chorus (recorded). Hobby: Swimming. Address: Grettisgate 94, Reykjavlk, Iceland.

PANDI, Marianne, b. 30 Aug. 1924, Budapest, Hungary. Musicologist. Educ: Dip., Franz Liszt Acad. Music, Budapest, 1956. M. Endre Schwimmer, dec., 1 s. Career: Ed. in Chief, Guide de Concerts, sponsored by Nat. Phil, Budapest, 1958-, Hungarian Music News, 1969-, Music Critic, Hungarian daily newspaper Magyar Namzet; Lectr., Hungarian Radio. Publs: History of the Italian Music, 2 vols., 1960; Monteverdi, 1961; Gyorgy Kosa, 1966; Musical Criticism of Hunderd Years in Hungary, 1967; Concert Guide I, Orchestral Works, 1972; Concet Guide II, Concetos, 1973; Concert Guide III, Chamber Music, 1975. Contbr. to profl. jrnls. Mbrships: Hungarian Musicians Corp.; Liszt Soc. Hobbies: Cooking; Swimming; Car Driving. Address: 1071 Budapest, Damjanich u.42, Hungary.

PANUDLA, Dusan, b. 19 July 1923, Kosice, Czechoslovakia. Violinist; Conductor; Educator; Composer; Music Critic. Educ: Brno & Prague Conservs.; Pvte. studies. m. Renata Hlaváckóvá, 1 s. Debut: Cond., Brno, 1943-45. Career: Concert Master, Prague Nt. Theatre's Opera; Nearly 1600 concerts worldwide; Fndr. Cond., Prague Chmbr. Orch., 1950; 30 quartet world premieres; Radio perfs. & recordings in Germany, Engl., France, Scandinavia & Switzerland; 28 world premieres as soloist. Publs. incls: 18 scores by Haba, Martinu, etc; More than 50 string quartets recorded. Fndr., Pandula quartet, 1969. Publs: Essays on contemporary comps. Mbr. Comps. Union, Prague. Hobbies: Colleclting Mod. Paintings & Sculpture; Motoring. Address: 7 Stuttgart 50, Obere Waiblingerstr. 150 B, German Fed. Repub.

PANGBORN, Robert C, b. 31 Dec. 1934, Painesville, OH, USA. Percussionist. Educ: Eastman Schl. of Music; Westers Reserve Univ.; Juilliard Schl. of Music; Oakland Univ. 2 children. Debut: Cleveland Orch., 1958. Career incls: Mallet Percussionist, Cleveland Orch., 1957-63; Prin. Percussionist, Detroit Symph., 1964-; Hd., Percussion Dept., Cleveland Inst. of Music, 1958-63, Detriot Community Music Schl., Geo. Szell & Detroit Symph. under Sixten Ehrling. Recordings. Cleveland Orch., Epic Records; Symphonic Metamorphosis, London Records; Detroit Symph., Columbia Records. Mbr., Percussive Arts Soc. Hobbies: Gardening; Art Collecting; Antique Percussioin Instruments. Address: 301 S Pleaslant St., Apt. 2, Royal Oak, MI, USA.

PANHOFER, Walter, b. 3 Jan. 1910, Vienna, Austria. Pianist. Educ: HS of Music & Dramatic Art, Vienna. m. Getraut Schmied. Career: Concert tours throughout Europe & overseas; Prof. of Music, Univ. of Vienna, 1971-. Recordings: var. works w. Vienna Octet (Decca label). Recip: Austrian Cross of Hons. for Sci. & Art. Hobbies: Books; Skiing; Mountains. Address: Erdbergerstr. 35, 1030 Vienna, Austria.

PANNELLA, Liliana, b. 13 Apr. 1932, Teramo, Italy. Musicologist. Educ: BA., Univ. of Rome; Dip., Piano, Conser. of St. Cecilia, Rome; Dips., Polyophonic Vocal Compositions & Ch. Music Hist., Univ. of Parma. Career: Asst. in Spanish Lit., Fac. of Letters, Univ. of Rome, 1956-58; Instructor, Music Hist. & Libn., Morlacchi Conserv. of Music, Perugia, until 1970; Instructor, Hist. & Aethetics of Music, St. Celilia Conserv. of Music, Rome, 1970-. Publs incl: Spunti di poesie popolari nelle comiposizioni musicali de codici cortonesi 95-96, 1960; Il canto della 'Ramacina' nelle tradizione letteraria e musicale, 1961; Jouly mariner, un' antica 'chanson' alcuni momenti della sua storia e sopravvivenza nella tradizione ne popolare odierna, 1965; Le composizioini profane di una raccolta fiorentina del Cinquyecento, 1968; Valentino Bucchi, un musicista contemporaneo italiano, 1974; Valentino Bucchi. Anticonformismo e politica musicale italiana, 1975. Contbr. to: Dizionario biografico degli Italiani; Istituto Enciclopedia Italiana; Lares; Rivista Italiana di musicologia. Mbrships: Fndr. Mbr., Italian Soc. of Musicol.; Etruscan Acad., Cortona; VP Associaziene Musicale Valentine Bacchi. Address: via Ubaldino Peruzzi 20,00139 Rome, Italy.

PANTALEONI, Hewitt, b. 22 Mar. 1929, NYC, USA. Choral Conductor; Scholar. Educ: incls: AB, Harvard Coll., 1953; AMT, 1953, AM, 1956, Harvard Univ.; PhD, Wesleyan Univ., Conn., 1972. m. Patricia Curtis Hamilton, 4 d., 1 s. Career incls: Instr.-Full Prof., SUNY Oneonta, 1960-; Dir. of var. choirs, glee clubs, etc.; African drumming concerts, 1968-. Recordings: African dances & games, S & R Records, 1968. Ed: var. music publs.; Ballad book of John Jacob Niles, 1959; Songs & stories from Uganda by Wm Moses Serwadda, 1974. Publs: The 5:02 to Boston, 1966, The Rhythm of Atsia dance drumming among the Anlo (Eve) of Anyako, 1972. Contbr. to jrnls. Mbrships. incl: Bd., African Music Soc. Address: 81 Elm St., Oneonta, NY 13820, USA.

PANTILLON, Francois, b. 15 Jan. 1928, La Chaux-de-Fonds, Neuchatel, Switz. Orchestral Conductor; Composer. Educ: Dip., Violinist, Swiss Soc. of Musical Padagogies; Royal Conserv., Brussels. m. (1) Antoinette Van Stokkum, 1 s, 1 d. (2) Rose-Marie Tschanz, 1 s. Debut: Violinst & Choral Cond. w. Pantillon Trio. Career: Chief Cond., Thun Symph. Orch.; Guest Cond. w. num. Swiss & foreign Orchs. Comps. incl: Works for Orchs.; Visiones, 1968; Psaume 75, 1975; Joel's Hymne, (choir, soloist & orch.); 1976. Mbr. num. profl. orgs. Hons: Van Hal. Prize for Violin, 1952; Prize for Comp., La Societe Federale Suisse de Chant, 1960. Hobbies: Skiing; Canoeing. Mgmt: Konzertgesellschaft Zürich; Choveaz Mgmt., London; G Juhar, Roma. Address: Haupstrasse 32, CH 3280 Montiler, Switzerland.

PANUFNIK, Andrzej, b. 24 Sept. 1914. Composer. Educ: Dip. w. Distinction, Warsaw State Conservatoire (theory & comp. of music); State Acad. of Music, Vienna (cond. w. Prof. Felix Weingartner). m. Camilla Jessel, 2 c. Career: Cond., Cracow Phil. Orch.; Music Dir., Polish State Fil Productions; Dir., Warsaw Phil. Orch.; Has cond. leading European orchs.; Musical Dir. & Cond., City of B'ham Symph. Ordh., UK. Compositions incl.: 5 Symphonies, Piano and Violins Concertos, vocal and chamber works; Sinfonia di Spere, 1974-79: Dreamscape, 1976; Str. Quartet, 1976; Sinfonia Mistica, 1977; Metasinfonia, 1978. Recordings incl: Sinfonia Sacra; Sinfonia Rustica; Nocturne; Autumn Music; Tragic Heroic Overture; Universal Player. Violin Concerto; Sinfonia Concertante. Mbrships: Composers Guild of GB; PRS; Pres., Richmond Concert Soc., UK. Hons. incl: var. Polish decorations; 1st prize, Prince Rainer Competition, Monaco, 1963; The Sibelius Centenary Medal for Comp., London, 1965. Hobbies: Traveling; All Arts. Address: Riverside House, Twickenham, Middx, TW1 3DJ, UK. 1, 21, 18.

PANULA, Forma Fuhani, b. 10 Aug. 1930, Kanhajoki, Finland. Conductor; Composer. Educ: Ch. Music & Sibelius Acad. m. Helena Haanisto, 4 children. Debut: Helsinki, 1954. Career: Nat. Opera; Helsinki Phil.; Chef Aarchus; tours in Europe, USSR, USA; Prof. of conducting. Comps. Musicals; TV & Radio plays; chmbr. music; light music. Has recorded w. Helsinki Phil. Mbr. many profl. orgs. Hobby: Light music. Address: Espoo 61 Finland.

PAOLONE, Ernesto, b. 30 Oct. 1904, Mafalda (Molise) Italy. Director; Professor. Educ: Dip., comp., w. Amilcare Zanella & Antonio Cicognani; piano w. A Zanella; musicol. w. Prof. Giulio Fara. m. Anna Zedda, 3d. Career: Dep. Dir., Biblioteca Oliveriana, Pesaro, 1936-40; Lectr. in hist. & aesthetics of music, Lib., Conserv. di Musica G Pierluigi da Palestrina, Cagliari, 1940-75. Contbr. to Rivista Musicale Italiana; Grove's Dict., 6th ed.; Rassegna Dorica; Musica d'Oggi; Ricordiana; Rivista Italiana di Musicologia, etc; aricles on Beethoven's Hammerklavier Sonata, Op.106. Mbrships: Società Italiana di Musicologia; Associazione Int. Biblioteche Musicali (gruppo Italiano); Academmia Tiburtina. Hobbies: Gardening; Research. Address: via Bresciani 17, 09100 Cagliari, Italy.

PAPACH, Gary, b. 22 Oct. 1944, S Bend, Indiana, USA. Composer; Businessman; Principal desk bassoon. Educ: BMus Perf., Cinn. Conserv. of Music, 1966; Bach. Business Sci (Accounting), Ind. Univ., 1979. m. Eiko Ito Papach, 2d. Debut: Cinn., 1965. Career: Cinn. Symph.; State Dept. World Orchl. Tour; USA Navy Band; Lake George, NY Opera Fest.; Bolshoi Ballet, NYC; Prin. desk bassoonist w. S Bend Symph.; Music Advsr., Montessori Schl. of S Bend, Ind. Comps: Beethoven Symph. No. 10, The Lost (adapted from Quintet op. 29). Recordings: as mbr. of Cinn. Symph., 1960's. Address: 374 Pin Oak E. Mishawaka, IN 46544, USA.

PAPAELIAS, John, b. 5 Apr. 1949, Salisbury, Rhodesia. Singer; Pianist; Guitar Player. Educ: High Schl. Tchng. Dip., Univ. of London; Assoc. Bd., Grades II & III (piano). m. Lois Maureen. Career: 5 yrs. profl. solo entertainer in London (UK), W Europe, W Indies, S Africa, Rhodesia, Can. & USA. Comps: several songs (recorded). mbr., AFM. Hons: Quarterfinalist in Am. Song Fest., 1979. Hobbies: Travel; Photography. Address: 70 Cambridge Ave., Toronto, Ont. M4K 2L5, Canada.

PAPAI, Ray Andrew, b. 15 Dec. 1932, South Bend, Ind., USA. Woodwind Artist; Composer; Arranger; Record Producer; Music Director; Conductor. Educ: BM, Ind. Univ.; MA, Northwestern Univ. m. Carolyn Lee Klein Papai, 2 d. Debut: Soloist w. Chgo. Symph. Orch. Career incls: Soloist w. Chgo Symph. & Chgo Chmbr. Orchs.; Num. TV apps.; Musical Dir. var. theatres; Musical Dir., Contemporary Arts Quintet; Pres, Ultra Nova Records & Publrs. Comps: incl: New Child; Once Upon a Spring; Our Happiness in Love. Recordings: Handel's Water Music w. Chgo. Chmbr. Orch. Mbr. num. profl. orgs. inclng; Nat. Acad. of Recording Arts & Scis. Hobbies: Golf; Tennis; Photography; Para-Psychol. Address: 501 E Providence Rd., Palatine, IL 60067, USA.

PAPAS, Sophocles Thomas, b. 18 Dec. 1894, Epirus, Greece, Professor of Guitar; President of Columbia Music Company. Educ: Studied langs., Cairo, Egypt; Guitar self-taught. m. 1) Evaline Monico, 1 d., 2) Mercia Lorentz, 2 s. Career: Tchr. of Guitar & Publr. of Guitar Music, Wash. DC, for over 55 yrs.; One of earliest artists to appear on radio stns. in Wash. DC; Perf. & Lectr. on hist. of guitar in num. schls. & to guitar soc. in USA; Mbr.; Jury at Int. Competition of Guitarists in Orense, Spain, 1961; Fac. Mbr., Am. Univ., Wash. DC, 1962-64. Publs: The Most Comprehensive & Complete Method for the Clasical Guitar. Contbr. to profl. jrnls. etc. Mbrships. incl: NY Soc. of Classic Guitar; ASCAP; ASTA. Hobbies: Reading; Etymol. of Words. Address: Music Co. 13446 Connecticut Ave., NY, Washington, DC, 20036 USA.

PAPASTEFAN, John James, b. 28 July 1942, Milwaukee, Wis. USA. Assistant Professor of Music. Educ: BEd. in music, Univ. of Wis., Whitewater, 1966; MA in Music, Appalachian State Univ., Boone, NC, 1967; DA courses in progress, Univ. of Miss.; PhD, Walden Univ.; Adv. percussion study w. Jay Collins & Gordon Peters. m. Linda J. Morgan. Career: Timpanist & Prin. Percussionist, Mobile Symph. Orch. (now defunct); Grad. Asst., Percussion Instr., Fndr. & Dir. of the Percussion Ensemble, Appalachian State Univ., 1966-67; Instr. in Music, Univ. of S. Ala., 1967-; Fndr. & Dir. of the Univ. of S. Ala. Percussion Ensemble, which perf. at the 1971 MENC So. Div. Meeting at Daytona Beach, Fla. Contbr. to: The Percussionist; The Intrumentalist: NACWPI. Jrnl. 0 WWBP Journal (reviewer). Mbrships incl: Precussive Arts. Soc.; MENC; Life Mbr., Phi Mu Alpha; AFM, local 407. Hons. John Philip Sousa Band Award, 1961. Grad. Assistantship, Appalachian State Univ., 1966. Hobbies: Lawn & Gardening; Old Instruments. Address: 209 Vanderbilt Dr., Mobile, AL 36608, USA.

PAPAVASILION, Ernest John, b. 1 May 1937, Lancaster, Pa., USA. Violinist; Concertmaster; Conductor. Educ: B Mus., Eastman Schl. of Music; Colo. Coll.; Univ. of Mich.; Millersville State Coll.; violin studies w. Joseph Knitzer, Raphael Bronstein, Ivan Galamian, Mischa Mischakoff, Oscar Schumsky; cond. studies w. Jonel Perled, Hugh Ross. Debut: Bruch Violin

Concerto, w. Eastman-Rochester Symph. Career: Concertmaster on Broadway for musicals; Soloist w. Eastman-Rochester Symph., Lancaster Symph., Columbia Symph. Vivaldi Chamber Orch.; Recitalists; Musical Dir. & Cond. of St. Paul's Choral of Hempstead, NY & N Shore Chorus of LI., NY.; Violinist w. Am. Symph. Orch. under Leopold Stokowski, 4 yrs.; Rochester Phil., 7th Army Symph. Orch.; Touring w. Royal Ballet of London, Leingrad-Kirov Ballet, NY City Ballet, etc.; currently Violinist, Met. Opera Orch.; Concertmaster, Lancaster Symph. Orch.; Tchr.-Violin. Specialist, Hempstead Pub. Schls., LI., NY. Pres., Musical Arts Soc. (Nat. Fed. of Music Clubs). Hobbies: Swimming; Running; Bicycling. Address: 242 W. 76th St., NY., NY 10023, USA.

PAPE, Naomi, b. 8 Jan. 1907, Kingwilliamstown, Cape Prov., S Africa. Lecturer; Music Examiner. Educ: Stellenbosch Univ. Conserv. Music: RAM, 3 1/2 yrs.; FRAM; ARAM; GRSM; LRAM; ARCM; (UTLM & UPLM S Africa). Career: Lieder singer, 46 Radio recitals, all stns. S Africa; Lectr., singing & piano, Univ. Potchefstroom, 1951-53; Stellenbosch Univ., 1954-64; Cape Town Coll. Music, Univ. Cape Town, 1971; Lectr., singing & piano & Music Examiner, Univ. S Africa, Pretoria, 28 yrs. Pres., SASMT, 1950. Recip: Cert. Merit, singing, RAM, 1931. Hobbies: Motoring; Walking. Address: 6 Kilarney Ct., Inverleith Terr., E London, S Africa. 3.

PAPINEAU-COUTURE, Jean, b. 12 Nov. 1916, Montreal, Canada. Composer; Professor of Music. Educ: studied piano w. Francoise d'Armour, Montreal, 1927-39, w. Leo-Pol Morin, ibid, 1939-40; studied writing of music w. Gabriel Cusson, ibid, 1837-47; Bacc., Music, (comp., cond., piano), New England Conserv. of Music, Boston, 1941; studied w. Nadio Boulanger, 1941-43, 1954-45. m. Isabelle Baudouin, 1 s., 2 d. Career: Tchr. theory, Music Conserv., Montreal, 1946; Sec., Music Acad., Quebec, 1947-54; Tchr., theory, Music Fac., Univ. of Montreal, 1951; Sec., ibid, 1952; Prof. ibid. 1963; Sub Dean, ibid. for orch., Aria, 1949, Poème, 1952; for grps. of instruments, Canons, 1964, Dialogues, 1967; Paysage, 1968; Chanson de Rahit, 1972; Obesession, 1973; for solo instruments, Suite, (piano), 1942-43; Aria, (violin), 1946; Dyarchie (harpsichord), 1971; Slano (string trio), 1976; Le Debat du Coeur et Du Corps Devillon (narrator, cello & percussion), 1977. num. other works for choir, voices & accomp., theatre, etc. Recordings incl: Concert Grosso, 1943, rev., 1955; Etude en si bemol, 19456; Psaume CL, 1954; Quatuor No. 1, 1953, No 2, 1967, etc. etc. Contbr. of articles, reviews, to var. profl. jrns. Num. Mbrships. Recip., num. hons. Address: 657 Rockland Ave, Outremont, Montreal, H2V 2Z5, Canada.

PAQUETTE, Daniel, b. 7 Apr. 1930, Morteau, France. Musicologist; Composer; Cellist; Pianist. Educ: BA, 1961; Cert. in Musicol., Sorbonne, 1961; Doct., 1968; 1er. Prix: Cello, Nat. Conserv. of Music, St. Etienne; 1er Prix Composition Musicale (1st Prize Musical Comp.), Nat. Conserv., Dijon. m. Madeleine Moungel, 3 children. Career: num. radio & TV broadcasts for ORTF Paris, Tele-Enseignement of the E. of France TV Ext., in Mainz & Milan; Lectr. in Musicol., Univ. of Strasbourg; Asst. Lectr. in Music Hist., Univ. of Dijon -St. Etienne; currently Proif. of Musicol., Univ. of Lyons II. Compostitions incl: Les Dames des Entreportes (symph. poem); Str. Quartet; Str. Trio; Choral Works: Les Fantomes du Val au Faon (children's operetta). Contbr. to Dictionnaire de Musique, Bordas Responsable Iconographie; Musik in Geschichte und Gegenwart; Musica; La Revue Musicale Suisse; etc. Mbrships: SACEM, Paris; Past Pres., " Voix Amies", Dijon; Past Pres., "Assn. of Students of Music His.", Strasbourg; Pres., "Collegium Musicum", Lyons. Recip. of Medal, Bi-Millenaire, City of Mainz. Hobbies: Electronics; Graphology. Address: LLes Furtins, Berzé la Ville, 71960 Pierreclos, France.

PARATORE, Ettore, b. 23 Aug. 1907, Chieti, Italy. Professor ofLatin Literature. Educ: Dip., Fac. of Ancient Letters, Univ., 1927. m. Augusta Buonaiuti, 2 d. Career: Prof. of Latin Lit., Univ. of Rome; TV & radio apps., Italy & France. Publs: works on classical & mod. lit.; transls. from Latin & Greek; Contbr. to book "Moderni e Comtemporanei", 1975. Contbr. to: profl. jrnls., newspapers, etc. Mbrships incl: Pres., Roman Assn. of Friends of Music; Arcadia; Accademia dei Lincei; Dir., latinitas; Pres., Romanisti Assn.; Pres., Abuzzo Studies; Dir., Classical & Mideaval Culture mag. Hons. incl: Laureate, Univ. of Poitiers, 1964, Univ. Paris-Sorbonne, 1978; Gold Medal; Rome Cultural Prize, 1976. Hobbies: Concerts; Opera; Philosophy; Philology; Sports. Address: Via Giacinto Carini 2, 00152, Rome, Italy. 2.

PARDEE, Margaret, b. 10 May 1920, Valdosta, Ga., USA. Violinist; Violist. Educ: Dip., Inst. of Musical Art of the Juilliard Schl. of Music, 1940; Postgrad. Dip., ibid., 1942; Dip., Juilliard Grad. Schl., 1945. m. Daniel R. Butterly. Debut: Town Hall, NYC, 1952. Career: Played solo & in chmbr. music grps. in tours throughout USA; Played w. symph. orchs. in NYC, Wash. DC., NJ., Miss. etc.; Concert Master of Great Neck Symph., NY.; Fac. Mbr., Juilliard Schl. & Meadowmount Schl. of Music; Has held String Seminars in univs. in USA; Has taught students from USSR, S Africa, Iran, Israel, S. Korea, Canada, Aust., USA. etc. Assoc. Music Tchrs. League, NYC; MTNA; NY State Music Tchrs. Assn.; Viola Rsch. Soc. (Int.). Mbrships: Bd. Dirs., Soc. for Strings, NYC; Recip. var. hons. & awards. Hobbies: Gardening. Address: c/o The Juilliard Schl., Lincoln Center Plaza, NYC, NY 10023, USA. 3, 27, 29.

PARES, Philippe, b. Paris, France. Composer; Conductor. m. Geneviéve Pillet, 1 d. Career: Artistic Dir., Columbia Records, Pris, 1927-31; writes incidental music for radio, films, & TV. Compositions incls: Lulu (operetta); L'eau á la bouche (operetta); La Petite Dame du train bleu (operetta); Le Moulin sans souci (operetta); film scores for Le Million, Un soir de Rafle, Toboggan, Une jeune file savait; sev. songs. inclng. Si l'on ne s'était pas connu & Tout est au Duc; Hyme de la Légion d'honneur. Mbrships: Pres., SDRM (Paris), 1950-60, & Authors' Composers' & Publrs. 'Mechanical Rights Soc., Paris. Hons: Kt., Legion of Hon. Address: 86 Rue de Varenne, Paris 7e, France.

PARIK, Ivan, b. Aug. 1936, Bratislava, Czech. Composer. Educ: Conserv., Bratislava; Acad. of Music, Bratislava. m. Magdalene Barancok, 2 children. Career: Music Dramaturg, Bratislava TV, 1959-68; Lectr., Music Theory & Lit., Acad. of Music, Bratislava, 1962-. Comps. incl: Sonata for Solo Flute (recorded); Songs About Falling Leaves (4 piano pieces -recorded); Music for an Opening (flute & tape - recorded); Music for Three (flute, oboe clarinet - recorded); Music for a Ballet (full orch. - recorded); Fragments, (ballet), Tower Music for 12 Brass Instruments, 2 MG Tapes & Bells; electronic works; In Memoriam Ockeghem; Cantica feralia (electronic music); In the Mountains (ballad), Epitaph for Flute & Guitar; num. works for film, radio, TV & the theatre. Publs: Notes on Composer's Education, 1974. Mbr: Slovak Composers Guild, Bratislava. Hobby: Modern Graphics. Address: Legionarska 15, 801000 Bratislava, Czechoslovakia.

PARIKIAN, Manoug, b. 14 Sept. 1920, Mersin, Turkey. Violinist. Educ: TCL; FTCL. m. Diana Margaret Carbutt, 2 s. Career incls: Ldr., Liverpool Phil. Orch., 1947-48, Philharmonia Orch., London, 1949-57; Prof. of Violin, RAM, 1959-; solo apps. in all European countries & ldng. fests.; has given 1st pub. perfs. on works by Goehr, Rawsthorne Thea Musgrave, Iain Hamilton, Hugh Wood, Gordon Crosso & Elizabeth Maconchy; tours of USSR, 1961 & 65, S Am. 1974; Sir Robert Mayer Vis. Lectr., Leeds Univ., 1974-75. Mbrships: incl: Hon. RAM, 1963, Jury, Tchaikovsky Violin Competition, Moscow, 1970. Hobbies: Backgammon; Collecting Early Armenian Printed Books. Address: The Old Rectory, Waterstock, Oxford, UK. 1

PARIS, Alain, b. 22 Nov. 1947, Paris, France. Conductor. Eudc: Lic., Law, 1969; Studied piano, solfége, hist of music, w. Bernadette Alexandre-Gorges, 1951-65; Studied harmony w. Georges Dandelot, cond., w. Pierre Dervaux, l'Ecole Normale de Musique, Paris, 1965-68; Studied cond. w. Louis Fourestier, (1968), Int. Summer Chls., Nice, Paul Paray, (1972-74) m. Marie-Stella Abdul Ahad. Debut: 1968; Career: Cond., num. Orchs. l'Ilé de France, 1975, Orch. de la Suisse Romande, 1975, Orch. Symphonique de Radio-Luxembourg, 1975, Orch. Philharmonique de Radio-France, 1975, Orch. du Capitole de Toulouse, 1976, Orch. de Lyon, 1976, New Chamber Orch., ORTF, Chamber Orch., Paris, 1972, Orch. Lyrique de l'ORTF, 1973, Orch de Nice - Cote d'Azur de l'ORTF, Nice, 1973, Symph. Orch. of N. Greece, Thessalonica, 1973, Iraqi Nat. Symph. Orch., Bagdad, 1974, Orch. Lyrique et Choeurs de l'ORTF, 1974; Orch. de Paris, 1974; Orch. de Nice, Cote d'Azur de l'ORTF, 1974; Prod., Musical Broadcasts, ORTF. Contbr. toi: Scherzo; Ency. Universalis. Recip., 1st prize, Int. Competition, Besancon, France, 1968. Hobbies: Tennis; Bridge. Mgmt: Opéra & Concert, Paris. Address: 87 Rue de Monceau, 75008 Paris, France.

PARKER, Andrew Lindsay, b. 8 June 1950, Hanover, German Fed. Repub. Music Bibliographer & Palaeographer. Educ: BA, 1971, Mus B, 1972, MA, 1975, King's Coll., Cambrdige. Mbrships: Royal Musical Assn.; Bibliographical Soc. of London. Publs: Ed., var. items of 16th Century polyphony, Oxford Univ. Press, 1970-; Ed. of anthems by Handell & Prucell, Argo & EMI Record Cos.; Sub-Ed., Oxford Book of Madrigals, 1978. Hons: Choral Schlrship. King's Coll., Cambridge, 1968; William Barclay Squire Prize for Mus B, 1972; William Barclay SquireEssay Prize, Cambridge Univ., 1972. Hobbies: Electronics; Commercial tape-recording. Address: King's Coll., Cambridge, UK.

PARKER, Craig Burwell, b. 11 Feb. 1951, Leavenworth, Kan., USA. Trumpeter. Educ: BMus (trumpet), Univ. of Ga., 1973; MA (histl. musicol.) Univ. of Calif., Los Angeles, 1976; trumpet study w. Robert DiVall, Albert Ligotti, Robert Grocock, Clyde Noble & Olin Parker; piano & comp. studies. m. Susanna Hays Parker, 1'd. Career: Trumpeter w. American Wind Symph. Orch., 1970, Spoleto Fest. Orch., 1975, Long Beach Symph. Orch., 1976- Composers Brass Quintet, 1977-; solo recitals in Calif., Ga. & Utah; num. freelance recordings in Los Angeles area. Comps: Fugue in A minor, for piano, 1970: The Grass Menageria (song cycle), 1971; Suite for 2 trumpets, 1972; Nocturne, for trumpet & piano, 1972; Sonata for bassoon & piano, 1973; 3 Miniatures, for clarinet & piano, 1975. Contbr. to: Brass Bulletin; Int. Trumpet Guild Jrnl.; Composer (USA); MACWPI Jrnl. Mbrships: Am. Musicol. Soc.; Coll. Music Soc.; Int. Trumpet Guild; Nat. Assn. of Coll. Wind & Percussion Instructors. Hons. incl: Atwater Kent Musicol. Competition, 1974, '79; var. fellowships. Hobby: Record Collecting. Address: 6702 Santa Barbara Ave., Gdn. Grove, CA 92645, USA.

PARKER, Hilary Anita, b. 12 Aug. 1953, Lincoln, UK. Private Piano Teacher; Local Performer. Educ: Royal Manchester Coll. of Music; Royal Acad. of Music; Grad., Royal Schl. of Music; Hochschule für Musik, Munich, Fed. German Repub. Debut: Lincoln, UK. Mbr., Incorp. Soc. of Musicians. Hons: Gold Medal for Highest Distinction Marks in GB & Ireland in Grade VIII Assoc. Be. Exams., 1967; German Acad. Exchange Serv. Schlrship., 1975. Hobbies: Cookery; Dancing; Reading. Address: 242 Hykeham Rd., Lincoln, LN6 8BE, UK.

PARKER, Vaninne Darynth, b. 27 Sept. 1949, Bromley, Kent, UK. Singer. Educ: RAM, 1969-75; LRAM, 1972; master classes w. Dame Janet Baker & Pierre Bernac. Debut: Wigmore Hall, London, 1977. Career: apps. w. Engl. Music Theatre incl. Death in Venice, Covent Garden & Adelburgh Fest.; apps. at Schwetzingen, Edinburgh & Florence Fests.; radio apps. BBC & in Germany; perfs. w. Scottish opera; now w. Kent Opera; oratorio & recitals in London & home counties. Mbrships: ISM; RAM Club. recip., English song Prize, RAM, 1974. Hobbies: Reading; Walking; Archaeology; Ch. Architecture. Address: 60 Fordmill Rd., London SE3 3JN, UK.

PARKES, Joanna, b. 29 July 1944, Sydney, Aust. Music Librarian; Performer (viola da gamba, recorder, flute, Renaissance winds); Teacher (viola da gamba, recorder); Lecturer. Educ: BA (Sydney); Dip. Lib. (Univ. of NSW); NSW Conserv. of Music (flute); Schola Cantorum Basiliensis. Career: Renaissance Players, Sydney, 1962-71, 1974-75; Musica Antiqua, Adelaide, 1974-; ldr., Univ. of Adelaide Viol Consort; freelance work radio, TV, film, concerts on flute, recorder & viol; tours of Aust., S E Asia, NZ; music broadcaster, Adelaide; music libn., Univ. of Sydney, Schola Cantorum BAsiliensis, Univ. of Adelaide. Mbrships: Musicol. Soc. of Aust.; Int. Assn. of Music Libs. (VP, Aust./NZ branch); Int. Assn. of Sound Archives; Viola da Gamba Soc.; Lute Soc.; Early Music Soc. of SA. Hobbies: Collecting Musical Instruments; Chinese Language & Cultural; Travel. Address: Dept. of Music, Univ. of Adelaide, Adelaide, SA 5001, Australia.

PARKHOUSE, David, b. 1 Dec. 1930, Tegnmouth, UK. Concert Pianist. Educ: RCM; ARCM. m. Eileen Croxford, 2 s. Debut: Wigmore Hall, Festival Hall. Career: Solo & Chamber Music recitals, & concertos Brahms-Handel Variations; Gershwin-Varitions (piano & orch.); Rauel-Trio; Debussy-Sonatas; Beethoven-Archduke Trio; Beethoven-Kreutzer Sonata; Beethoven-Ghost Trio; Mendelssohn-Piano Trio; Rachmaninoff-Sonata, cello & piano; Barber-Sonata, cello & piano; Kodaly-Sonata, cello & piano; Schubert-Trout Quintet; Vaughan Williams-Sonata, violin & piano; Vaughan Williams-Hymns; Elgar-Sonata, violin & piano; Bush-Trio. Mbr. ISM. Hons. Chappell Gold Medal, 1948; Queens Pize, 1953; Boise Fndn. Award, 1952; FRCM. Hobbies: Flying; History. Address: 63 Madrid Rd., London SW13, UK.

PARKIN, Eric, b. 24 Mar.1924, Stevenage, UK. Concert Pianist; Music Educator. Educ: B Mus, FTCL, Trinity Coll. of Music. Debut: Wigmore Hall, 1948. Career: Regular broadcaster on radio & TV; many apps. w. leading orchs.; Henry Wood Proms. Recordings incl: John Ireland's Concerto & Legend; Phantasy Sonata; CelloPiano Sonata; 2 VionlinPiano Sonatas; Piano Music (3 vols.); Baines & Moeran Piano Music; Rozzo Film Music. Mbr., ISM. Contbr. to Music Tchr. Hons: Silver Medal, Worshipful Co. of Musicians, 1947. Hobbies: Listening; Reading. Mgmt: Ibbs & Tillett. Address: 23 Matlock Rd., Caversham, Reading, RG4 7BP, UK.

PARKIN, Simon, b. 3 Nov. 1956, Manchester, UK. Composer; Pianist; Teacher. Educ: Yehudi Menuhin Schl., 1967-74; MusB, Univ. of Manchester, 1977; GRNCM, 1978;

ARCM, 1973. Career: perfs. in St. John's, Smith Sq., London, Wigmore Hall & Queen Elizabeth Hall, London; apps. at Gstaad & Windsor fests. Comps. incl: Ted Spiggot & the Killer Beans (opera); Ensemble pieces: Jingle Bells; Polygamy etc. mbr., Musicians Union. recip. univ. & coll. prizes. Hobbies: Reading; Writing; Sport; Science Fiction. Address: 8 Crescent Rd., Southport, Merseyside PR8 4SR, UK.

PARKINSON, John Alfred, b. 2 Feb. 1920, Croydon, UK. Music Librarian. Educ: Jesus Coll., Cambrdige, 1939-40, '46-49; Ma (Cantab); RAM, 1945-46; ARCM. m. Marie Hupka, 3 s. Career: Dir. Music, Trinity Schl., Croydon, 1949-64; Rsch. Asst., Brit. mus. (now Brit. Lib.), 1964-. Publs: (ed.) Oxford Book of Carlos, 1964; Renaissance Song Book, 1971; Index to the Vocal Works of the TA Arne & Michael Arne, 1972, Many eds. renaissance & baroque vocal & instrumental music. Contbr. to: Musical Times; Music & Letters; Monthly Musical Record. Mbr., ISM. Hobby: Victorian Music Covers. Address: 130 Farley Rd., Selsdon, S Croydon, CR2 7NF, UK.

PARKINSON, Ruth-Christine, b. 7 July 1956, Manchester, UK. Concert Pianist. Educ: Chetham's Hospital Schl. of Music; RNCM; ARCM; GRNCM; pvte. study w. Sir William Glock. Career: solo recital at music clubs, concerts w. var. orchs.; took part in Granada TV, A Gift for Music, 1972; Recording; radio recording of Manchester Midday Recital, 1978. mbr., ISM. Hons: ABRSM Gold Medal, 1971; Sheila Mossman Award, 1971. Hobby: Going to Cricket Matches. Address: 66 Heaton Rd., Heton Moor, Stockport, Cheshire, UK.

PARKS, James Hays, b. 25 Aug. 1943, Topeka, Kan., USA. Singer (Baritone, Countertenor). Educ: B Mus, Washburn Univ., Topeka; MS Music, Kan. State Coll., Pittsburg, Kan.; Helen Jordan Schl. of Musicianship, NYC; Inc. Schl. of Music; studies at Zürich Opera, Switzerland. Debut: Harvard Univ. & St. Paul Opera Assn., Boston. Career: Artist; Tchr.; Min. of Music, St. James Luth. Ch.; Baritone Lead, US Premier Egk Opera, St. Paul Opera, Educl. TV Opera. Recordings at Dist. Fests. & Area Band Fests. Cntbr. to US Govt. sponsored Model Cities Project. Mbrships: MENC; Omega Psi Phi; Phi Mu Alpha Sinfonia; Kappa Kappa Psi. Hons. incl: 4 yr. Scholarship, Topeka Civic Symph. Hobbies: Photography; Hunting Small Game. Address: 3620, 43rd St. 306, Moline, IL 61265, USA. 8.

PARMELEE, Paul Frederick, b. 3 May 1925, Chgo., Ill., USA. Professor of Music; Concert Pianist. Educ: Am. Conserv. of Music, Chgo.; B Mus, Perfs. Cert., Piano, Eastman Schl. of Music, 1947; Juilliard Schl. of Music; M Mus, Univ. of Colo., 1949; D Mus, Fla. State Univ., 1960. Div. 2 d. Debut: Town Hall, NYC, 1963. Career: Solo recitals, USA, inclng. NYC, Detroit, Milwaukee, Ore. & Calif.; Pianist; Pablo Casals Trio, num. concerts in USA; Soloist w. major orchs.; Prof. of Music, Univ. of Colo. Recordings: George Crumb, Night Music I; Brahms Trio Op. 87, Ives Trio. Mbr., musical assns. Hons: Trio awarded name of Pablo Casals Trio by Casals himself, 1972. Hobbies incl: Reading; Jogging. Mgmt. Dahlgren Arts Assoc., Denver (for trio). Address: 2000 Walnut Apt. 2, Boulder, CO 80302, USA.

PARMER, Edgar Alan, b. 14 Sept. 1928, NYC, USA. Physician; Musician. Educ: AA, in Music, UCLA, 1950; AB; MA; MD. m. Judith Parmer, 1 s, 1 d. Career: Soloist, NYC Symph. Orch., 1940; Orch. only - Burbank, Glendale, MGM Symph., Westchester Symph. Orch. Recordings w. before mentioned symph. orchs. Mbrships: Pres., Doctor's Symph. Orch., 1970-72; Westchester Symph. Orch.; Amateur Chamber Music Soc. Address: Premium Point Pk., 7 Shore Dr., New Rochelle, NY 10801, USA.

PARNAS, Leslie, b. 22 Nov. 1932, St. Louis, Mo., USA. Concert 'Cellist; Professor of Music, Boston University. Educ: Grad., Curtis Inst. of Music. m. Ingeburge Parnas, 2 s. Debut: Town Hall Recital, NYC, 1959. Career: Solo Cellist, annual world-wide concert tours. Has recorded for Pathe-Marconi & Columbia Records. Mbrships: Chmbr. Music Soc. of Lincoln Ctr., NYC; Dir., "Kneisal Hall" Summer Music Schl., Blue Hill, Me. Hons: Pablo Casals Prize, Paris, 1957; Primavera Trophy, Rome, Italy, 1959; Prize Int. Tschaikovsky Competition, Moscow, 1962. Hobbies: Langs; Photography; Tennis. Mgmt: Columbia Artists Mgmt. Address: 6 Brentwood Ave., Newton Ctr., MA, USA.

PARNELL, David Andrew, b. 17 Feb. 1954, Stockport, UK. Organist; Teacher. Educ: BA, MA, Cantab.; FRCO; Organ Study w. Kenneth Beard, Nicolas Kynaston. m. Sally. Debut: Southwell Minister, for Nottingham Soc. of Organist. Career: Num. organ recitals; Asst. Master of the Music, St. Albans Cathedral & Dir. of Music, St. Albans Schl. Recordings: The Questioning Cross. Mbrships: ISM. Hons: Limpus & Frederick Shinn Prizes, for FRCO, Jan. 1974. Hobbies: People; TV. Address: 175 Camp Rd., St. Albans, Herts, UK.

PAROLARI, Egon, b. 21 Sept. 1924, Brugg/Aargau, Switz. Oboist; professor. Educ: Orch. dip. Zürich conserv., M Saillet 1943: Study under Ra Lamorlette & P Bajeux, Paris, 1948-50. m. Gertrud Ott, 1 s, 1 d. DEbut: Geneva, 1943, 1943. Career: Oboe solo, musikkollegium orch., Winterthur, from 1944; Swiss Festpielorch., Lucerne, trom 1944; Zürich chmbr. orch.; Colleghium musicum, Zürich; Munich Bach Orch. Recordings: Oboe concertos D min.F Maj., Vivaldi; Concerto da Camera, Honegger; Concerto for violionoboe, Bach; Six Metamorphoses after Ovid, Britten; Concerto, Peter Mieg; Concerto in Eb. maj., Handel; Concerto in C maj., Stamitz. Publs: "Medizinische Untersuchungen an Bläsern') Swiss music jrnl. 19636. Mbr. var. profl. orgs. Hons: 2nd prize, Int. Music Competition, Geneva, 1952. Address: St. Georgenstr. 68, 8400 Winththur, Switzerland.

PARRIS, Robert, b. 21 May 1924, Phila., Pa., USA. Composer; Pianist; Harpsichordist; Teacher. Educ: BS MS, Univ. of Pa.; BS, Juilliard Schl. of Music; Berks. Music Ctr.; Columbia Univ.; Ecole Normale de Musique, Paris. m. Anna Rosalind elkes Parris. Comps. (publs.): Fantasy & Fugue for solo cello; Concerto for Five Kettle Drums & Orch.; Lamentations & Praises for Brass & Percussion; Sonata for unaccompanied Violin. Recordings: Concerto for Trombone & Orch.; The Book of Imaginary Begins. Contbr. to Wash. (DC) Evening Star; Kenyon Review; Juilliard Review. Hons: Fulbright Grant, 1952-53; Grants, Nat. Endwoment for the Arts, 1974, NY State Coun. on the Arts, 1974. Address: 3307 Cummings Lane, Chevy Chase, MD 20015, USA. 2.

PARRISH, Lillian Alberta, b. 14 Dec. 1917, Boston, Mass., USA. Concert Pianist; Piano Teacher. Educ: Soloist Dip., New England Conserv. Music, Boston; Fellowship, Juilliard Grad. Schl.; Master Classes, Cornell Univ.; BS, music educ., Columbia Tchrs. Coll. m. William Parrish, 2 s. Debut: Boston, Mass., 1940. Career: Fac., Westchester Conserv. Music, NY; Dir., N Stamford Piano Studios, Conn.; Soloist, Boston Pops, 1939; Num. apps., clubs, museums, radio stns., univs.; Currently, Dir., Alamaden Piano Studios, Calif. Mbr., profl. & hon. socs. Hons: Winner, Mason & Hamlin Grand Piano Competition, 1939; NY Cosmopolitan Club Recital Award, 1955; NY Debut Recital Awrd, Madrigal Soc., 1956. Hobbies: Gardening; Hiking. Address: 6661 Leyland Pk. Dr., San Jose, CA 95120, USA. 5.

PARROTT, Andrew Haden, b. 10 Mar. 1947, Welsall, UK. Conductor. Educ: BA, Merton Coll., Oxford. m. Emma Kirkby. Career: Dir. of Music, Merton Coll., Oxford, 1969-71; Cond.; Schola Cantorum, Oxford, 1968-71, Musica Reservata, 1973-76, Taverner Choir & Players, 1973-. Recordings: w. Musica Reservata: As Asst. Cond. to Stokowski, w. LSO,; S Chorus-Master, Acad. of St. Martin's; w. Taverner Choir; w. London Cornett & Sackbut Ensemble, Contbr. to: Early Music. Hobbies: Food; words. Address: 24 Avondale Pk. Gdns., London W11 4PR, UK.

PARROTT, Ian, b. 5 Mar. 1916, London, UK. University Professor Music. Educ: RCM, 1932-34; New Coll. Oxford, 1934-37; ARCO, 1936; D Mus (Oxon), 1940; MA (Oxon), 1941. m., Elizabeth Olga Cox, 2 s. Comps. incl: The Black Ram (opera), 1957; sev. orchl. works; Chmbr. music & songs; Ceredigron of Harp, 1962; Flamingoes (song); Soliloquy & Dance (harp); Welsh Folk Song Mass, 1973-74. Recordings incl: Contemporary Welsh Choral Music, 1969; Contemporary Music for Harp & Flute, 1967-70. Mbrships. incl: VP, Elgar Soc. Publs incl: Elgar, 1971; The Music of Rosemary Brown, 1978. Contbr. to profl. jrnls. Hons. incl: Harriet Cohen Int. Musicoll. Medal, 1966. Hobbies incl: Wine making. Address: Henblas, Abrmad, 'Nr. Aberystwyth, Dyfed SY23 4ES, UK. 3.

PARROTT, Michael Ian Edwin, b. 16 Sept. 1942, Colwyn Bay, UK. Orchestral Musician (Cellist). Educ: Imperial Coll., London; LGSM. Career: Mbr., Royal Liverpool Phil. Orch.; Ebrle Ensemble piano quintet. Mbrships. Musicians Union; ISM. Hon: Cello Prize, GSM, 1964. Hobby: Railways. Address: 9 Salisbury RD., New Brighton, Merseyside, UK.

PARRY, Wilfrid, b. 17 Feb. 1909, Birmingham, UK. Pianist. Educ: TCL; FTCL. m. Eileen Grainger. Debut: Trinity Coll. Concert, Queen's Hall, London. Career: regular broadcasts as Soloist, Chmbr. Musician & Accomp., 1928 ; BBC Staff Accomp., 1961. Recordings: num. chmbr. works w. var. ensembles; records w. Evelyn Rothwell, Anthony Pini, Owen Brannigan, Dennis Brain, Florence Hooton, et al. Mbr., ISMI. Hons: Chappell Gold Medal, c. 1926; Hon. RAM, c. 1970. Hobbies: Photography; Motoring. Address: 18 Foxfield Close, Northwood, Middx, HA6 3NU, UK. 3.

PARSONEAULT, Catherine Jean, b. 16 June 1950, Freeport, Ill., USA. Musicologist. Educ: BMus (piano), Univ. of Wyoming,

1973; MMus, Southern Methodist Univ., Dallas, 1977; study for PhD, NM Tex. State Univ. m. Thomas Parsoneault. Career: var. tchng. & lib. posts; pvte. piano tchng.; organist, Emanuel Lutheran Ch., Dallas, Tex., 1977-. Publ: Opera at North Texas, in Current Musicology, 1978. Corres. Ed., Current Musicol., 1977-. Mbrships: Am. Musicol. Soc.; RIDIM/RCMI; AAUP; AAUW; Coll. Music Soc.; MTNA; Pi Kappa Lambda; Delta Omicron; MENSA. Hons: Mu Phi Epsilon; Outstanding Grad. Student in Music, Southern Meth. Univ., 1976-77. Hobbies: Reading; Photography; Gardening. Address: 2016 Custer Pkwy., Richardson, TX 75080, USA.

PARSONS, Geoffrey Penwill, b. 15 June 1929, Sydney Aust. Pinoforte Accompanist. Educ: NSW State Conservatorium of Music. Career: Toured Aust. w. Essie Auckland, 1948, Aust. & NZ w. Peter Dawson, 1949; Came to UK as Accomp. to Peter Dawson, 1950; Assoc. w. world's leading singers & instrumentalist inclng. Elisabeth Schwarzkopf Victoria de los Angeles, Janet Baker, Nicolai Gedda, Hans Hotter, Gerhard Hüsch, & Nathan Milstein; Concerts in 40 countries & all 6 continents, inclng. 15 return tours of Aust.; Appts. at num. fests.; Artists in Res., NSW State Conservatorium of Music, 1975; Many recordings. Hons. incl: Harriet Cohen Int. Award, 1968; Hon. RAM, 1975; OBE, 1977. Hobbies incl: Tennis. Address: 176 Iverson Rd., London NW6 2HL, UK.

PARSONS, John Anthony, b. 5 Oct. 1938, Leicester, UK. Musician; Trombonist. Educ: RAM; ARAM, 1973. m. Sarah Joyce Jones, 2 d. Career: Former Mbr., Sadlers Wells Opera Orch., & Halle Orch.; Co-Prin., Trombone, BBC Symph. Orch.; Prof. of Trombone, LCM. Hons: Hon. FLCM, 1974. Hobbies: Learning for. langs.; Wine-making; Sailing; Gardening; Writing doggerel verse. Address: Delft Cottage, Burnt House Lane, Kirton, Nr. Ipswich, Suffolk, UK.

PARTOS, Oedoen, b. 1907, Budapest, Hungary. (Israeli citizen). Composer; Musician (viola); Educator. Educ: Study in Budapest of violin w. Hubay & composition w. Kodaly. Career: Ldr. of Viola Sect., Israel Phil. Orch., 1938-56; Dir., Israel Acad. of Music, Tel-Aviv, 1951; Prof., Tel-Aviv Univ., 1961-. Compositions incl: Concerto (violin & orch.); Sinfonia Concertante (viola & orch.); Yiskor (strings); Visions (flute, piano & strings); Makamat (flute & string quartet); Ein Gev (symphonic fantasy); Images (orch.); Symphonic Movements; 5 Israeli Songs; Tehilim (string quartet); Agada (viola, piano & percussion); Nebulae (woodwind quartet); Litur (12 harps); Pino pieces, etc. Mbrships: Fndr. Mbr., Int. Soc. for Contemporary Music, Hons: UNESCO Prize, 1952 & Israel State. Prize, 1954, FOR 'Ein Gev'. Address: 25 Tsimchei Hayehudim St., Ramat Aviv, Tel-Aviv, Israel.

PARTRIDGE, Ian, b. 12 June 1938, Wimbledon, London, UK. Concert Singer (Tenor). Educ: LGSM. m. Ann Glover, 2 s. Debut: w. Bexhill Choral Soc. under Harold Partridge, 1958 Career: hundreds of broadcasts for BBC Radio; num. live apps., Royal Fest. Hall, Royal Albert Hall. Concertgebouw Amsterdam, etc. Recordings: Schubert, Die Schöne Müllerin; Schumann, Dichterlieb, Liederkreis op. 39; Chanson d'Amour, songs of Faure & Duparc; Vaughan Williams, on Wenlock Edge; Warlock, The Curlew. Mbr., ISM. Recip. var. awards. Hobbies: Cricket; Horse racing; Bridge. Mgmt: Ibbs & Tillet, London, UK. Address: 127 Pepys Rd., Wimbledon, London SW20 8NP, UK.

PARTRIDGE, Jennifer, b. 17 June, 1942, New Malden, UK. Accompanist. Educ: AGSM Piano Perfs. & Singing Perfs.; LRAM. m. David Smith. Career: Recitals, Concerts, TV & Radio apps. w. singers & instrumentalists; Famous duo w. brother, Ian Partridge. Recordings incl: Music All Powerful (w. Purcell Consort); Vaughan Williams Songs; Die Schöne Müllerin & Dichterliebe, Schubert Lieder, An Album of English Songs (w. Ian Partridge); French Songs (w. Ian Partridge); Part Songs (English), Schubert Part Songs w. Baccholian Singers. Mbrships: ISM; Musician's Union. Recip., Eric Rice Mem. Prize for Accomps., Overseas League, 1964. Hobbies: Dogs; Sport. Address: 50 Howberry Rd., Thornton Heath, Surrey, CR4 8HY, UK.

PARTRIDGE, John Albert, b. Nov. 1941, Reginaw, Sask., Can. Music Educator; Organist; Choir Director. Educ: BEd., Univ. of Sask., Regina; Assoc. in Music, ibid. Career: Piano, Harpsichord Concert Perfs., Solo & w. Orch.; Profl. Accomp. esp. Vocalists: Piano Adjudicator, Sask. Music Fest. Assn.; Jr.High Schl. Music Specialists; Ch. Organist & Choirmaster; Canadian Broadcasts. Publs: Division III Music Programme (w. David Escott). Mbrships: Sec.-Ttreas., Sask. Music Educators Assn.; Local Chmn., RCCO. Hons: C M Willoughby Piano Scholarship, 1959; C N Drake Piano Scholarship, 1960. Hobby: Harpsichord Building. Address: 2737 McCallum Ave., Regina, Sask. S4T 1L5, Canada.

PASCAL, Claude, b. 19 Feb. 1921, Paris, France. Composer; Critic; Director of Studies. Educ: Conserv. Nat. Supérieur de Musique, Paris. m. Gwendolen Rooke, 1 d. Career: Dir. of Studies at Conserv. Nat. Supérieur de Musique, Paris. Comps: Concertos for cello & orch., piano & chmbr. orch., harp & orch.; Octet for wind; 2 sonatas & a sonatina for violin & piano; Suite for piano; Saxophone quartet; var. chmbr. works. Recordings: 2nd Sonata for violin & piano; Trios Légendes for clarinet & piano; Saxophone quartet; (w. Marcel Bitsch) orchestration of Bach's Art of Fugue (Grand Prix de l'Academie du Disque Francais, 1967). Contbr. to Le Figaro, Pris. mbr. SACEM. Hons: Officier de l'ordre des Arts et Lettres; Chevalier de l'ordre national du Mérite; Premier Grand Priz de Rome, 1945. Hobby: Tennis. Address: 10, rue Darcet, 75017 Paris, France.

PASCHKE, Donald Vernon, b. 22 Oct. 1929, Menominee, Mich., USA. Professor Music; Singer; Teacher of Singing. Educ: BS, B Mus, 1957, M Mus, 1958, Univ. of Ill.; D Musical Arts, Univ. of Colo., 1972; pvte. voice study & lit. coaching. m. Helen Inez Burton, 1 s, 1 d. Career: Recitalist, German Lieder & French Melodie; Oratorio Soloist; app. w. Lexington Symph. in Memotti, Amahl & the Night Visitors; Instr. in Music, Berea Coll.,Ky., 1958-62; Prof. of Music; Coach in Lieder & Melodie, Eastern N M Univ., Portales. Publs: Transl., Ed. & Collator, A Complete Treatise on the art of Singing, Part II (1847 & 1872 eds.), 1975; Part I (1841, 1872 eds.) in progress. Mbr., profl. assns. & hon. socs. Recip., var. awards. Hobbies: Photography; DIY. Address:228 Kansas Dr., Portales, NM 88130, USA. 29.

PASCU, George, b. 14 Jan. 1912, Iasi, Romania. Professor of Music. Educ: Dip., Music Acad., Iassy 1934. M. Elisabeta Catalina. Career: Cond., Episc. Choir of Roman, 1934-38, Metropol. Choir, Cracova, 1943, & Phil. Choir, Iasi, 1953-59; Cond., Nat. Theatre Orch., Iasi, 1946-53; Phil. Orch., ibid., 1944-56; Music Tchr., 1934-44; Prof., Iasi Conserv. 1944-77; Dan, Fac. of Instrunemtal & Vocal Music, ibid. 1964-69; Chmn., Musicol. Dept., 1964-76. Author of var monographs & musicol. studies. Contbr. to var. jrnls. inclng. Muzica; Cronica, etc. Mbrships: Union of Roumanian Composers; Corresp., Acad. of Soc. & Pol. Scis. Hon: 2nd Prize, Roumanian Min. of Educ., for musicol. writing. 1964. Address: str. N. Gane 12 et 1 ap 3,R- 6600 Iasi, Romania.

PASHLEY, Anne, b. 5 June 1937, Skegness, UK. Singer (Soprano). Educ: GSM, London. m. Jack Irons, 1 s, 1 d. Debut: In Semele, Handel Opera Soc., London. Career: Regular apps. in operas at Convent Gdn., Welsh Nat., Scottish Nat., Adelburgh Festival, Sadlers Wells, Glyndebourne, Wexford, etc.; Concerts in France, Germany, Portugal, Spain, Belgium, Italy, Israel, Sweden, Holland, etc.; Leading roles in 8 BBC TV operas & num. radio apps. Recordings incl: La Morte de Cleopatra, Berlioz; Magnificat, Bach; Peter Grimes, Britten, etc. Mbr. Brit. Actors Equity. Contbr. to the Listener. Hobbies: Gardening; Winemaking; Table Tennis; Tennis; Art Collecting; Interior Design. Address: 289 Goldhawk Rd., London W 12, UK.

PASRICHA, Aruna, b. 12 Dec. 1942, Lahore, Pakistan. Music School Principal; Concert Pianist; Classical Guitarist; Player of Recorder & Clarinet. Educ: ARCM; studied piano & clarinet, RCM, London, 1959-61. M. Surindar Lal Pasricha. Career: Concert Pianist, also appos. as soloist, in duets & accomp. to leading violinists; Regular perfs. on All-India Radio; Mbr., Auditioning Panel, All-India Radio; Prin., Calcutta Schl. of Music; Hd. of Music, Harry Gosling Schl. London, 1964-67 Mbr. profl. orgs. Hobbies incl: French cookery; Breeding dogs. Address: 217 Cromwell Mansions, Cromwell Rd., London SW5 OSD, UK.

PASTORE, Giuseppe Alfredo, b. 13 March 1915, Naples, Italy. Musicologist; Teacher; Conservatory Director. Educ: Dip.in Composition & Piano. m. Doria Michela Pastore, 3 children. Career: Asst. in Music Hist., Univ. of Lecce; Music Critic, La Gazzetta del Mezzogiona daily, Barl; currently Dir., Tito Schipa Conserv. of Music, Lecce; Instr. in Music Hist. ,ibid. Compositions: Vocal Chmbr. Music. Publs: Leonardo Leo, 1945; '77; Ed., Paiano Galatina, 7 instrumental w orks of Leonardo Leo (stage overtures & sinfonias & chmbr. concerto); Toccata for harpsichord by Nocola Fago, Ed., Zanibon Padova; Tammaso Traetta - 'La Pace di Mercurio', Bari 1975. Contbr. to: num. musicol. jrnls., inclng. Studi Salentini, Il Sagittaro, Nosto tempo, Brudisii res. Address: 2 via Redipuglia, 73100, Leece, Italy.

PATACHICH, Iván, b. 3 June 1922, Budapest, Hungary. Composer. Educ: Dip. in Comp. & Cond., Franz Liszt Acad. of Music, Budapest, 1948; studIed comp. w. A. Siklós & F. Szabo, cond. w. J. Ferencsik. m. Ibolya Markovics,1 d. Debut: Opera Budapest, 1946. Career: Musical Dir., Hungarian Film Studios, Budapest. Compositions (publd.): Concerto per Arpa, 1956; Tre Pzzi, 1961; petite Suite, 1961: Theomachia (1 act opera), 1962; Symphonietta Savariaensis, 1965; Contorni per Arpa, 1968; Concerto per Violino & Pinaforte, 1956: Puente Ovejuna (3 act opera), 1971: Concerto per Organo, 19734: Spetti (electronic music), 1974. (also recorded); Ritmi Dispari, 1966; Music of the Bible (cantata), 1968; Quartetino per Sassonfoni, 1972 (USA). Publ: On Film Music, 1972. Mbrships: Hungarian Assn. of Musical Artists; Artisjus, Budapest. Hons: World Youth Fest. Prize, Moscow, 1954; Niveau Prize, Hungarian TV, 1972. Address: Budapest 1016. Naphegy tér. 9, Hungary.

PATEKAR, Bhalchandra Vaman, b. 23 March. 1928. Maharashtra, Dhulia, India. Professor of Music (Vocal). Educ: incls: BA (econs.) & ILB, Univ. of Bombay; D Mus, AB Gandharva Mahavidyalaya Mandal; PhD Cand., Baneres Hindu Univ. m. Sumitra B Patekar, 1s., 2d. Career: Tchr., grad. & post-grad. level for over 12 yrs., w. Women's Coll. Banares Hindu Univ., 1961-; Cultural rep. & tchr., Fiji, 1975-78: SINGS Khrupad, Dahmar, Khayal, Tappa, Thumri, Bhajan, Drama songs, etc., & plays tabla & harmonium, & have given over 500 perfs. on stage, radio & TV in India, Australia & Europe; Actor & Dir. in many dramas. Comp. dramas, dances, ballets, orchs. etc. (unpubld.) Has recorded sev. LPs. Mbr. many profl. orgs. Recip. num. hons. & awards. Address: Women's Coll., Banares Hindu Univ., Varanasi-5 (UP), India.

PATENAUDE, Joan, b. 12 Sept. 1944. Ottawa, Can. Opera Singer (soprano). Educ: BMus, Univ. of Montreal. m. Bruce Yarnell (dec.) Debut: NYC Opera. Career: Opera, NYC Opera, San Fran. Opera, Can. Opera; Concerts, Warsaw, Poland 1978. Orient 1979, Aust. 1980. Recordings: Songs of the Great Opera Composers, vols. 1, 2 & 3; Medea in Corintha. Contbr. to: Opera Can. Hons: Can., Coun. Award (4); Metropolitan Opera Auditions. Hobby: Writing. Mgmt: Ludwig Lustig & Florian, 111 W 57th St., NY, NY 10019 USA. Address: c/o Mgmt.

PATES, Gennilla Atkins, b. 29 May 1908, Vladez, Alaska, USA. Piano Teacher. Educ: Averett Coll., Danville, Va.; B Mus., Shenandoah Conservatory of Music, Winchester, Va.; BS., Mus. Ed., Mary Wash. Coll. Univ. of Va. m. James Scott Pates, 1 d., 1 s. Career: Tchr., Pineland Coll., Salemburg, NC., 3 yrs.; Tchr., Oneida Coll., Oneida, Ky. (now extinct), 1 yr.; Pvte. piano tchr. Mbrhsips: Chmn., Nat. Guild of Piano Tchrs., 12 yrs.; 3rd VP., Va. Fedn. of Music Clubs: Va. State Chmn. (Sr.); Int. Platform Assn; Alpha Psi Omega. Hons: Hallof Fame, NGPT, 1972. Hobbies incl: Ceramics; Gourmet cooking; Oil Painting. Address: 1500 Augustine Ave., Fredericksburg, VA 22401, USA. 4, 5, 27.

PATEY, Bent, b. 12 June 1952, Oslo, Norway. Composer. 1 s. Career: Sev. radio & TV progs., Norway & Sweden. Comps: Bazar's 2nd albumn, recorded 1974: Lotus' 1st album, recorded 1978. Recordings: Approx. 10 w. sev. bands. Mbrships: Norwegian Musicians Union. Hobby:Being with son, Thomas. Address: Jacob Aallsgt, 15, Oslo 3, Norway.

PATEY, Edward Raymond, b. 23 June 1940, Jersey City, NJ, USA. Violinist. Educ: BM, 1963, MM, 1965, Manhattan Schl. of Music. m. Kathleen Gail Ptey, 1 s., 1 d. Career: Violinist w. Balt. Symph. Orch. Mbrships: Balt Astron. Soc., Md. Acad. of Scis.; Smithsonian Assocs.; Ars Viva String Quartet, Balt., Md. Hobbies: Collecting Works on Philosophy; Astronomy; Tennis: Jogging. Address: 4012 Deepwood Rd., Baltimore, MD 21218, USA.

PATIST, Johan, b. 17 Dec. 1912, Utrecht, The Netherlands. Pianist. Educ: Leaving Cert., Soloist Dip. (cum laude) Utrecht Conserv.; Dips. Govt. Exams; Finishing studied w. Willem van Otterloo (comp., cond.), Paul Frenkel, Jaap Spaanderman, Paul Baumgartner Bale, Jan Smeeterlin (piano), London, m. Hendrica Hirdes, 2d. Debut: Recital, Utrecht, 1930, w. Symph. Orch., 1937, w. Radio Symph. Orch., 1938. Career: Approx. 450 radio & TV apps., recitals, broadcasts & solo apps. (w. orch.) in Holland, Belgium, France, Germany, Austria, Switz., the Dutch Antilles, Venezuela & Surinam; Apps. w. orch. cond. by Willem van Otterloo,Bernard Haitink a. o.; more than 4000 Schl. concerts in Netherlands; Appeared w. prominent singers & instrumentalists (Dutch, Am., German, Belgian, French); Tchr. for sev. yrs. at the conserv. of Amsterdam & Utrecht; VP., Municipal Music Lib. of Utrecht. Hons: Kt. of the Order of Orange - Nassau, 1978. Hobbies: Billiards; Caravanning; Travelling, etc. Address: Frans Halsstraat 53, Utrecht., The Netherlands. 1, 30.

PATON, John Glenn, b. 21 Feb. 1934, New Castle Pa., USA. Singer; Teacher of Singing. Educ: BS., Cinn. Conserv. of Music, student of Sonia Essin, 1955, MM & Perfs. Certs. in Voice & Opera, Eastman Schl. of Music, student of Julius Huehn, 1959: Studied Lieder w. Prof. Hermann Reutter, Stuttgart, Germany,

1960-61. m. Marion Wilma Anderson, 1 s. Career: Recitals in collaboration w. Prof. Hermann Reutter, accompanist, Stuttgart, Germany, & NYC, San Francisco, Baton Rouge & num. other cities, USA; Tchr. of Singing, Univ. of Wis., 1961-68; Assoc. Prof. Voice, Univ. of Colo., 1968-. Recordings; Supporting role in Lohengrin, w. Boston Symph.; recorded Broadcasts for radio studios in Basel, Frankfurt, Baden-Baden, & Helsinki, Publ: Ed., Nicola Vaccai, Practical Method of Italian Singing, 1974. Address: Coll. of Music. Univ. of Colorado, Boulder, CO 80309, USA.

PATRICK, David Michael, b. 8 Dec. 1947, Exeter, Devon, UK. Director of Music; Concert Organist. Educ: Royal Coll. of Music, 1966-70; ARCM (Organ performer). Career: many recitals in Parish Chs. Abbeys & Cathedrals in GB, inclng. Westminister Abbey & Westminister Cathedral; regular broadcaster, BBC-Radio 3; Dir. of Music, St. Michael's Schl., Tawstock, Barnstaple, Devon. Recordings: French Organ Music at Buckfast Abbey, Devon. Mbrships: Solo performers sect., Inc. Soc. of Musicians; Past Pres., Exeter & Dist. Organists Assn. Hons: Stuart Prize, RCM, 1967; Walford Davies Prize for Organ, ibid., 1968. Hobby: Sailing. Address: 12 Matford Ave., Exeter, Devon, EX2 4PW, UK.

PATRICK, Philip Howard, b. 12 Aug. 1946, Bridgend, UK. Computer Musician. Educ: B Mus, Univ. Wales, 1968; MFA, Princeton Univ., USA, 1971; PhD, ibid., 1973. m. Rosalind Elizabeth Davies. Comps. incl: Gwald; Suspensions; & Reflections (countersynthesised sound); Movement for String Quartet: Threesome (flute, oboe & clarinet); 7 Variations for (flute, viola & harp); Gwald (soprano & alto chorus & harp); Love songs (soprano, alto, baritone, 2 flutes, 2 clarinets & harp). Contbr. to profl. jrnls. Mbrships: Am. Soc. Univ. Composers; Coun. Exceptional Children. Hons. incl: Hon. mention, New Music for Young Ensembles Competition, 1975. Address: Apt. 609 Sussex House, 4970 Battery Lane, Bethesda, MD 20014, USA.

PATTEN, James, bv. 30 July 1936, Sheffield, UK. Composer. Educ: TCL; FTCL; GTCL; LTCL; Houchschule für Musik, Berlin. m. Philippa Willis, 3 c. Carrer: Tchr. (comp.) TCL; music for BBC radio & TV; progs. for BBC schls. radio; Tutor, Open Univ.; Peripatetic music tchr.; comps. played at Bath, Cheltenham & Stroud fests. Comps: Piano Sonata I; Ofan; Multiple; A Lef Falls; Taiko; Sunrise Song; Music for 2 guitars & tape; Trochee; Night Music; Other Sounds; Str. Quartet, etc. Contbr. to BBC Music Club. Mbrships: CGGB; Assoc., PRS; ISM. Hons: Royal Phil. Soc. comp. prize, 1963; German Academic Exchange Scholarship, 1963; Arts Councilo of GB bursary, 1973; London Saxophone Quartet prize, 1973. Address: Butchery Farm Cottages, Hornigsham, Warminster, Wilts., UK.

PATTERSON, Andy James, b. 20 Feb. 1929, Gordon, Tex., USA. Professor of Music; Chairman of Grad. Studies in Music; Head of Theory & Compositions Department. Educ: BA, MMus, Tex. Christian Univ.; DMus. Comp., Fla. State Univ. m. Jane Shaw, 3 s. Career: Prof. of Music, Hd., Music Theory-Comp. Dept., Chmn., Grad. Music Studies, Hardin-Simmons Univ., Abilene, Tex. Comps. incl: Symphony No. 1 for Orch.; Collection of Songs, Solo Sonatas for Brass, Woodwind Instruments & Piano; Works for Organ; Works for Band. Publs: Musical Form, 1960; Musical Composition, 1969; Harmony, 1970; History of the Bassoon, 1957; Contbr. to: newspapers; Tex. Choirmaster Mag. Mbrships. incl: Am. Music Ctr. Inc.; Am. Soc. Univ. Comps.; Southeastern Comps. League; Tex. Comps. Guild; Nat. Assn. of Comps., USA. Recip., 1st Prize, Orchl. Comp., Tex. Comps. Guild, Nat. Fedn. Music Clubs, 1969. Hobby: Photography. Address: 1642 Swenson, Abilene, TX 79603, USA. 2, 7, 12.

PATTERSON, James Hardy, b.,12 Oct. 1935, Kingston, Ga., USA. Professional Musician (Woodwinds, Flute, Clarinet, Saxophone, Oboe & Bassoon); Conductor; Woodwind Instructor. Educ: AB Music, Clark Coll.; M Mus, Univ. Mich. m. Lois G. Patterson, 2 d. Debut: Cond., Freda Payne Show, Venetian Room, Fairmont Hotel, Atlanta, Career: Apps. on TV w. Jack Jones TV Speical, etc.; Mbr. Duke Pearson's Big Band; The Mowtown Band; Atlanta Symph. Orch.; Atlanta Pops Orch.; 7th Army Band, Stuttgart; Staff Orch. accompanying Ice Shows, Circuses, ect. Comps. incl: Arrs. for Billy Taylor Trio & Band. Num. recordings. Contbr. to profl. jrnls. Mbr. num. orgs. Hobbies: Tennis; Arranging. Address: 413 Fielding Lane SW, Atlanta, GA 30311, USA.

PATTERSON, Jeremy David Kyle, b. 15 June 1934, Solihull, Warks, UK. Senoir Lecturer. Educ: Accoc., Birmingham Schl. Music (ViolinViola Tchr.); Grad., ibid. Career: (past) Jr. & Second. Schl. Tchr.; Choirmaster, St. Mark's Smothwiok; Cond., Birmingham Anglo-Orthodox Choir; Cond., Bromsgrove String Orch.; Cond., Clent Hills Choral Soc.; currently Cond.,

Birmingham Fest. Choral Soc.; Spkr. & Cond., BBC radio; Adjudicator; St. Lectr., Faculty of Educ. City of Birmingham. Polytech. Mbr., ISM. Hobbies: Laughter; Friends. Address: 6 Pine Close Flats, Redlake Rd., Pedmore, Stourbridge, W Midlands, DY9 OSA, UK.

PATTERSON, Paul, b. 15 June 1947, Chesterfield, UK. Composer. Educ: ARAM; 1973 Privately w. Richard Rodney Bennett. Career: Manson Fellow, RAM, 1970-; Dir. of Contemporary Music, Warwick Univ., 1974-; Apps. on radio & TV; Music for TV seriels; Vis. Lectr., var. univs. Comps: Time Piece; Requiem; 3 concertos for clarinet, trumpet, horn; many orchl. works; electronic music; TV signature tunes; brass band music; chmbr. music; organ music. Recordings incl: Florescense (Author Wills); Visions (Author Wills); Jubilate (Christopoher Gower); Time Piece (Kings Singers); Kyrie (London Chorus). Mbrships. incl: Exec. Committee, SPNM. Hons. incl: Theadne Holland Scholar, 1968. Hobbies incl: Sailing. Address: 2 Jadesa Ct., 43 Somerset Rd., Barnet, Herts., UK.

PATTERSON, Russell, b. 31 Aug. 1928, Greenville, Miss., USA. Conductor; Artistic Director. Educ: BA.; B Mus., M Mus.; La. State Univ.; New England Conserv. of Music; State HS. for music, Munich, Germany; Univ. of Mo., etc. m. Sharon Hayden, 2 s. Career incl: Cond. of var. orchs. incl. New Orleans Opera Assn.; Bayrische Staatsoper; Guest cond. w. var. orchs. in USA., Netherland Radio Orch., etc.; Gen Dir., Kan. City Lyric Theater; Artistic Dir., Point Lookout Festival; Lectr. in Music, Univ. of Mo., Kan. City. Recordings: Operas - The Sweet Bye & Bye, by Beeson (Desto); Taming of the Shrew, by Giannini (CRI); excerpts from Rigoletto, by Verdi & Barber of Seville, by Rossini (Damon). Capt. Jinks of the Horse Marines. Mbrships: Phi Mu Alpha Sinfonia; Phi Kappa Lambda; Ctrl. Opera Serv.; Bd. of Dirs., OPERA, Am. Nat. Opera Assn.; Dir., Co-Opera. Hons. incl: Fulbright Scholar; Sinfonia Music Man of the Yr., 1969. Hobbies: Tennis; Golf; Chess. Address: 4928 Wornall Rd., Kansas City, MO 64106, USA.

PATTERSON, T Richard, b. 28 Apr. 1917, South Bend, Ind., USA. Professor of Piano, Educ: B Mus & M Mus., Oberlin Conserv. of Music, Oberlin Coll., Oberlin, Ohio. m. Mary Graham Patterson, 1 s, 2 d. Career: Professor of Music (Piano), State Univ. Coll., Fredonia, NY, 1947-. Recordings: Sonata for viola & piano, Op. 11, No. 4, by Paul Hindemith, Fantasy -Theme w. variations -Finale, Mary Patterson, viola, T Richardson Patterson, piano, recorded on Fredonia Music Series 1957, Crest Records. Mbrships incl: VP., Eastern Div., 1964-67, NY State Schl. Music Tchrs. Assn., 1971; Mbr. 1st US Music Tchrs. nt. Assn. Ldrs. People-to-People Travel Delegn. to Western & Eastern Europe, May-June 1974. Hobbies: Swmming; Antiques; Architecture. Address:404 Lake Shore Dr. W. Dunkirk, NY 14048, USA.

PATTISON, Bruce, b. 13 Nov. 1908, Felling-on-Tyne, UK. Professor of Education. Educ: MA (Dunelm); PhD (Cantab). m. Dorothy Graham. Career: Emeritus Prof. of Educ., Univ. of London. Publ: Music & Poetry of the English Renaissance, 1948, 2nd ed. 1970. Mbr., Royal Musical Assn. Recip: William Barclay Squire Prize, Musical Palaeography, Cambridge, 1931. Hobbies: Music; Chess. Address: Coombe Bank, 6 Church Rd., Kenley, Surrey, CR2 5DU, UK.

PAUER, Fritz, b. 14 Oct. 1943, Vienna, Austria. Pianist; Composer; Arranger. Educ: Vienna Conserv. m. Christl Pauer, 1 step-d. Debut: Adebar Jazz Club, Vienna. Career incls: Piano Tchr., Jazz Inst., Vienna Conserv., 1969-; Mbr., Austrian Radio Big Band, 1970-; Mbr., Erich Kleinschuster Sextet; TV & fest. apps. Comps: Modal Forcs (Parts I & II), 1971; Meditations for Piano Solo, 1979: 23 Poems for Piano Solo, 1972; num. jazz pieces & popular tunes. Mbrships: AKM; AGAC; Austrian Comps. Union. Recip. 1st Prize, Jazz Piano, Int. Competitions for Mod. Jazz, Vienna, 1966. Hobbies: Painting; Yoga Address: Einsiedlerpl. 127, A-1050 Vienna, Austria.

PAUK, György, b. 26 Oct. 1936, Budapest,Hungary. International Concert Violinist. Educ: pupil of Profs. Zathureczki Weiner & Kodaly, Franz Liszt Acad. oif Music, Budapest. Debut: (British) Recital & Fest. Hall, 1961. m. Susan Mautner, 1 s, 1 d. Career: Has played w. most maj. orchs. in Europe, toured Aust. Extensively (3 times), visited NZ (twice), Israel, Middle & Far East & the Carribbean, S Africaw (6 tours); workd w. many ldng. conds. incl. Barbirolli, Boulez, Davis, Maazel, Giulini, Dorati, Solti; played w. Chgo. Symph. at Solti's invitation, 1970; playd w. Chgo. Symph. at Solti's invitatioin, 1970; plays w.ldng. Am.Orchs. twice yearly tours; has played w. all orchs. in GB & toured Europe w. RPO, Bournemouth Symph. & London Mozart Players; soloist w. Royal Danish Orch. on UK toured; Has played at Edinburgh, Bath, Lucerne, Chelthenham & other fests; regular perf. at Promenade concerts; 3 visits to

native Hungary. Num. recordings. Recip. num. hons. Mgmt: Ingpen & Williams Ldt., 14 Kensington Ct., London, W8, UK.

PAUL, Ernst Julius, b. 18 Nov. 1907, Vienna, Austria. French Horn Soloist; Musicologist; Composer. Educ: qualified in theory of music, 1930, Dr. Phil., 1934, Vienna Univ.; studied horn w. Prof. K Stiegler, Acad. for Music & Interpretive Arts, Vienna; pvte. study of comp. w. var. tchrs. m. Wilhelmine P. Monn, 2 s., 2 d. Career incls: Solo Horn, Vienna Broadcasting Orch., 1944-53; Mgr. of Archives, 1954-60; Musicol. Cons., Austrian Broadcasting Serv., 1960-72; Tchr., pvte. students & Vienna Coll. of Music, 1962-75; now retired. Comps: over 200 works for symph. orch., chmbr. orch., ensembles, solo instruments, choirs, etc. Recordings: Klassische Österreich.Volksmusik und Jagdmusik. Publs. incl: Die Jagd in Oestereich, 1963: Johann Georg Albrechtsberger, 1975. Contbr. to jrnls. Mbr. profl. orgs. Recip. many hons. Addrss: Weidling bei Klosterneuburg NÖ, Weidlingbachgasse 1 c, A-3400 Austria. 19.

PAUL, James, Conductor. Educ: Oberlin Coll. Conserv. of Music; Mozarteum, Salzburg, Austria; pvte. studies of piano, organ, oboe, clarinet & voice. Career: Guest Cond. Boston Ballet Co., 1965-68; Cond., Red Fox Music Camp, New Marlboro, Mass., 1966, 68 0 69: Choral Dir., Winterfest, Boston, 1957; Music Dir. & Prin. Cond., Cambridge OperaCambridge Opera Workshop, Mass., 1969-70; Music Dir., Bach Soc. of St. Louis; Cond., Kinder Konzert Series, St Louis Symph.; Guest Cond., Boston Philharmonic; Prin. Cond., ibid, 1974-75; Music Dir., Civic Symph., Webster Groves; Assoc. Cond., Kan. City Philharmonic 1972-; Music Dir., Kan City Balley, 1974-. Hons: Leonard Bernstein Cond. Fellow, Tanglewood, 1967; Eleanor R Crane Mem. Prize, ibid, 1967; Serge Koussevitsky Mem. Cond. Prize, ibid., 1967; Cond. Fellow, St. Louis Symph. Orch., 1970-71. Address: 700 E 8th St., Kansas City, MO 64106, USA.

PAUL, Ouida Fay, b. 18 Jan. 1911, Deatsville, Ala., USA. Music Educator; Conductor; Contralto; Voice Teacher. Educ: BA., Huntington Coll., Montgomery, Ala., 1930; BS., ibid, 1933; MA., Tchrs. Coll., Columbia Univ., 1943; EdD., ibid, 1957. Career incls: Schl. Music Tchr., 1930-45; Asst. Prof. of Music Educ., Greensboro Coll., NC., 1945-49, Univ. of Fla., Gainesvilles, 1949-61, Univ. of Hawaii, Manoa, 1961-69; Instructor of Voice of Musicol., Leeward Community Coll., Univ. of Hawaii, 1968-77; Ch. Soloist, 1946-49; Ch. Choir Dir., 1950-; num. Solo Recitals, Concerts; pvte. voice tchr., 1977-. Contbr. to Choral Jrnl. Mbrships: MENC; Committee on Music for the Handicapped, ibid; State Sponsor, Student Chapts., ibid; Adjudicator, ibid; num. other Offs., ibid; Hawaii Music Educators Assn.; 1st VP, ibid; Chmn., State Coven., ibid; Am. Choral Dirs. Assn.; Hawaii State Chmn., ibid, 1963-66: Mbr., Off., num. othjer Profl. Orgs. Recip. num. Hons. Hobbies: Painting; Sewing; Cooking; Swimming; Gardening. Address: 5740 Haleola St., Honolulu, HI 96821, USA. 27, 183.

PAUL, Steven Everett, b. 6 Dec. 1937, Atlanta, Ga., USA. Record Producer; Editor; Musicologist; Flautist. Educ: BA, Columbia Univ.; MA, Yale Univ.; PhD, Can., King's Coll., Cambridge; Juilliard Schl. of Music. Career: Perfs. in amateur & profl. ensembles & orchs., in NY, Boston, London, Cambrdige & Aldeburgh. Ed. & Prod., CBS Records, 1966-72; Broadcasts on BBC Radio 3 & WNCN, NYC; Currently, Engl. Ed., Deutsche Grammophon (Polydor), Hamburg. Mbrships: Royal Musical Assn.; Am. Fedn. of Musicians. Author of sleeve notes for CBS, DDG & RCA recordings. Contbr. to profl. publs. Hons: Kinne Award in the Humanities, Columbia Univ., 1955; Phi Beta Kappa, 1958; Woodrow Wilson Fellow, Yale Univ., 1959; Fulbright Schlr., Univ. of London, 1965; Grant, Vaughan-Williams Trust, 1975. Address: Harvestehuder Weg 1, D-2000 Hamburg 13, German Fed. Repub.

PAULI, Hansjörg, b. 14 Mar. 1931, Winterthur, Switzerland. Writer on Music; Filmmaker; Teacher. Educ: Winterthur Conserv.; Pvte study w. Hans. Keller, London. m. Friederike Staub, 1 s. 1 d. Career: Critic var. Swiss newspapers, 1956-60; Prod., Zürich Radio broadcasts on mod. music, 1960-65; Hd., Music Dept., Hamburg TV, 1965-68; Free-lance, 1968-; Broadcasts, Swiss & German radio; Films, German 3rd Channels; Lectr., Switzerland, Germany, Austria. Contbr. to Swiss, German, Austrian, English, Swedish music jrnls. Dutton's Dictionary & Solomann's Musiklexikon. Mgmt: Schweizer Tonkunstlerverein. Address: "Cá Rossa", Via Patocchi, 6644 Orselina, Switzerland.

PAULS, Cherry-Willow, b. 22 May 1946, Reigate, UK. Organist; Harpsichordist. Educ: GRSM; ARCM (Piano & Organ Perf.); LTCL (Organ); w. Anton Heiller, Peter Hurford & Luigi Ferdinando Tagliavini. Career: Organ/Harpsichord Tchr., St. Paul's Schl., London; Solo & concerto perfs. in UK & Europe;

Organist, Ealing Abbey, London, 1977-. Recordings: Royal Albert Hall, June 1974. Publ: 17/18th Century Organ Music, 1979. Mbrships: Royal Musical Assn. Hobbies: Reading; Swimming; Cookery. Address: 10 Kestrel Ave., Moormede Pk., Staines, Middlesex, TW18 4RU, UK. 3.

PAULSON, Leone, b. 17 July 1920, Utica, NY, USA. Harpist. Educ: Grad., Juilliard Schl. of Music, NYC; studied w. Carlos Salzedo. m. Milton Paulson, 1 d. Career: Soloist, Symph. Orchs. in USA. Europe; Dir., Paulson Harp Ensemble, 7 Harps; Harp Tchr., Nat. Music Camp. Interlochen Mich., The Schl. of Creative Arts, Martha's Vineyard, Mass., Ukrainian Music Inst. of Am.; num. Radio, TV Perfs., USA & Eire. Compositions: Arrs. for 7 harps. Recordings: w. Paulson Harp Ensemble. Contbr. to Am. Harp Jrnl. Mbrships: Am. Fedn. of Musicians, Local 16; Harp Chmn., Nat. Fedn. of Music Clubs; Am. Harp Soc.; Past Pres., NJ Chapt., ibid. Mgmt: Int. Artists Alliance. Address: 74 Ralston Ave., S Orange, NJ 07079, USA.

PAULUS, Stephen Harrison, b. 24 Aug. 1949, Summit, NJ, USA. Composer. Educ: BA, 1971, MA, 1974, PhD, 1978, Univ. of Minn., Mpls. m. Patricia Stutzman Paulus. Comps: num. works publd. by AMSI of Mpls., Hinshaw Music Inc. of NC & Charl Fischer, NYC. Co-Dir./Fndr., Minn. Comps. Forum. Mbr., Pi Kappa Lambda. Recip. Minn. State Arts Bd. Grant & Nat. Endowment for the Arts Fellowship. Hobbies: Tennis; Golf; Reading. Address: 1710 Jefferson Ave., St. Paul, MN 55105, USA.

PAULY, Reinhard G, b., 9 Aug. 1920, Breslau, Germany. Music Historian; Violinist; Viola Player. Educ: AB, AM, Columbia Univ.; MMus, PhD, Yale Univ. m. Constance Hare, 2d., 1s. Publs. incl: Music in the Classic Period, 1965, '73; Music & the Theater, 1970; La Musica en el periodo clasico, 1975; eds. of works by Michael Haydn, Ernst Eberlin, Antonio Caldara; 18th Century Choral Music, etc. Contbr. of articles to Grove's Dict., 6th ed. & profl. jirnls. Mbrships: Pres., NW Chapt., Am Musicol. Soc.; Coll. Music Soc. Address: Lewis & Clark Coll., Portland, OR 97219, USA. 14.

PAUTZA, Sabin, b. 8 Feb. 1943, Calnic-Resita, Romania. Composer; Conductor; Professor. Educ: Music Acad. Ciprian Porumbescu, Bucharest, 1960-65; Post Grad. Specialization in Comp. w. Franco Donatoni, Accademia Musicale Chigiana, Siena, Italy, 1970. m. Corina Popan Pautza, 2 c. Debut: As Cond., Music Acad. Choir, Bucharest, 1965. Career: Cond., Int. Jugend Festspieltreffen, 1974, '77, '78, Int. Music Holidays, Romania, 1974-78, Fest. of Romanian Music, Iassy, 1974-78; Fndr., Gen. Dir. & Cond., Animosi Choir, & Chmbr. String Orch. of George Enescu Music Acad., Issay, Romania; TV apps. as comp., cond. & tchr., Romanian TV; Radio apps., Bucharest & Iassy. Comps. incl: Musica per Due; Seykylos Hymn; Lauds; Homadg to the Children of the World; Five Pieces for Large Orch.; Columbus (Cantata); Jocuri II, for string orch.; String Quartet No. 3; Another Love Story, opera for children. Contbr. to: Musical Writings; Musica Review. Mbr., Comps. Union of Romania. Hons: George Enescu Prize for Comp., Romanian Acad., 1974. Address: Bul. Alexlandru eel bun, 40, BL. D 3, SC. D, AP, 39, 6600 Iassy, Romania.

PAVIOUR, Paul, b. 14 Apr. 1931, Birmingham, UK. Comopser; Educator. Educ: BA, B Mus, London Univ.; M Mus RCM; FRCO; ARCM; FLCM; FTCL; LGSM; LRAM. m. Janet Margaret, 3 s. Career incls: Dir., Music, All Sts. Coll., Bathurst, NMSW, Aust. & Organist & Choirmaster, All Sts. Cathedral, Bathurst, 1969-75; Lectr., Compositions, Goulburn Coll. Adv. Educ., 1975-. Compositions incl: (orchl. works) Symph. No. 4; Sir Arthur Lives; September Romance; (vocal) Crazy Jane; (chmbr. music) Frank Gardiner is Caught; (choral) So I Walk On; Psalmus Anglicanus; Christ for The World We Sing; (keybd.) Missa Australis, Make a Note of This, 2 vols.; Lydaldia. Contbr. to var. jrnls. Mbrships incl: FRSA; Pres., Aust. Soc. Music Educ: Hons. incl: Harding Prize, 1960. Hobbies incl: Reading; History. Address: 4 Beppo St., Goulburn, NSW 2580, Australia.

PAWLOWSKI, Walerian Henryk, b. 18 Dec. 1920, Kielce, Poland. Conductor; Composer; Music Journalist; Professor of Music. Educ: Dip. State High Schl. of Music, Cracow. m. Isabella Ferenz. Debut: June 1951. Career: Cond: Polish Radio Orch., Bydgoszcz; State Phil., Szczecin; Guest Prof., High Schl. of Music; Pres., Artistic Bd. of Music Soc. Compositions incl: The Man (for big orch.); The Mad Cat (song); Exercises in Vocalization (choral); Music for TV & theatre. Recordings: Symphonic & light music. Contbr. to Polish radio & press. Mbrships: Polish Musicians Assn.; Soc. of Stage Authors & Comps. Hons. incl: Award of the Province, 1975. Hobbies: Photography; Travel; Collecting Records & Tapes. Address: 71 143 Szczecin, ul. Stanislawa Kostki 1 K, Poland.

PAYER, Premysl, b. 16 June 1898, Chrastany, Litomerice, Bohemia. Conductor; Organist. Educ: Inst. of Machinery, Prague; Pvte. study of comp. & harmony w. Prof. Jar Kvapil, Brno. m. Dagmar Laiderova (div.). Debut: Acad. Theater, Brno, 1927. Career: Theatre Music Cond., Prague, 1933-38; Collaboration w. Radio Brno, 1928-32; Cond., AB Filmateliers, Prague, 1939-44; Theatre Cond. & Children's Choir, Karlovy Vary, 1945-61. Comps. Theatre Music for Shakespere's Twelfth Night, 1945; Merry Wives of Windsor, 1949; Romeo & Juliet, 1956: Lope de Vega's Fuente overjuna, 1950; Clever Child, 1961; J B Priestley's They Came to a City, 1946. Recordings: 3 popular music records, 1933-45. Mgmt: Concert Agcy., Plzen. Address: 360 00 Karlovy Vary, Nebozizek 3, Czechoslovkia.

PAYNE, Anthony Edward, b. 2 Aug. 1936, London, UK. Composer; Writer on Musical Subjects. Educ: BA, Mus., Durham Univ. m. Jane Manning. Comps. incl: Sonatas & Ricercars for Wind Quintet; Paean, Piano Solo; Concerto for Orch.; First Sight for Her & After (16 voices): Fire on Whaleness (brass band); The World's Winter (soprano & 8 players); Paraphrases & Cadenzas for clarinet, viola & piano; The Sea of Grass (chorus & Organ); Three Little Cantatas for Choir a capella; String Quartet. Recordings: The Music of Anthony Payne; Phoenix Mass.; The World's Winter. Publs: Schoenberg (Oxford Studies of Composers), 1968; Frank Bridge, 1976. Contbr. to Musical Times, Tempo, Music & Musicians, other mags. & newspapers. Mbrships: Past Chmn., Soc. for Promotion of New Music; Co-Chmn., Macnaghten Concerts, 1967. Hons: Phoenix Mass chosen as Engl. entry for 1974 ISCM Fest.; Radcliffe Finalist, 1975; Concerto for Orch. perf. at ISCM fest., 1976. Hobbies: English countryside; Reading; Cinema. Address: 2 Wilton Square, London N1 3DL, UK.

PAYNE, Stanley Vincent, b. 27 Feb. 19824, Winchester, UK. Teacher; Trumpeter. Educ: BA (music & langs.) Univ. of London, 1949; cert. of Educ., Southampton Univ. Inst., 1950. m. Barbara Joy Sacree. Career: on music staff, Winchester Coll., 1960-; freelance symphony, chmbr. & theatre work in S England since 1950. Mbrships: ISM; Musicians' Union. Hobbies: Steam Railway Operation; Pistol Shooting. Address: Boyne Mead, Nations Hill, Kingsworthy, Winchster, Hants. S023 7QY, UK.

PAYNE, Victor William, b. 14 Aug. 1924, Southampton, UK. Music Lecturer. Educ: LTCL (TTD); ARCM. m. Eileen Payne, 2 d. Career: Music Master, Stratford Green Schl., London E15, 1948-54; Hd., Music Dept., William Morris Schl., London E17, 1954-59; Hd., Music Dept., Edge Hill Coll. of Educ., 1954-74; Hd., Dept. of Music, City of Birmingham Coll. of Educ., 1974-; Examiner, TCL, 1964-. Compositions: Ed. & Contbng. Comp., projected series, Spectrum. Publ: Ed., G. Self, Make a New Sound, 1974-75. Contbr. to: Music in Educ. Mbr., ISM. Hon: FTCL. Hobbies: Music; Cooking. Address: 356 Valentine Rd., Kings Heath, Birmingham, B14 7AN, UK.

PAYNTER, John Frederick, b. 17 July 1931, London, UK. University Teacher; Composer; Writer on Music Education. Educ: TCL; GTCL; Dr. Philos., Univ. of York. m. Elizabeth Paynter. 1 d. Career incls: Dir., Schls. Coun. Project, Music in the Secondary Schl. Curriculum, 1973-80. Comps. incl: Landscapes, 1972; The Windhover, 1972; May Magnificat, 1973; God's Grandeur, 1975; Sacrament's of Summer, 1975; Incarnatus, 1976; Galaxies for Audience & Orch., 1977; The Wild Swans (opera), 1978. The Voyage of St. Brendan (ch. opera), 1979; The Visionary Hermit, 179; num. short choral & instrumental works and music theatre works for children. Publs: Sound & Silence (w. Peter Aston), 1970; Hear & Now, 1972; The Dance and the Drum (w. Elizabeth Paynter), 1974; All Kinds of Music, 1976, '79; Sound Tracks, 1978. Contbr. to num. profl. publs. Address: Westfield House, Newton on Derwent, York, UK. 1, 3.

PAYVAR, Faramarz, b. 10 Feb. 1932, Tehran, Iran, Santour Player (Persian Traditional Instrument). Educ: Master of Persian Traditional Music. 1 d. Career: Perfs. on Stage, Radio, & TV; Prof. of Santour, Nat. Schl. of Persian Music. Comps. incl: 30 pieces of music for Santour; Songs; Orchl. works. Recordings: 15 records, solo & w. groups & singers. Publs: A Method for Santour, 1962; 8 piecers for Santour, 1978. Affiliate, Minn. of Culture & Arts. Hons: Trophy from Iran Am. Soc., 1957;. Prize from Cambridge Univ., 1964; Prize from London Univ., 1964; Hobby: Swimming. Address: Post Box 66/1610, Farid Ave., Agdasieh Rd., Tehran, Iran.

PEAK, Edward Ernest, b. 15 Oct. 1951, Moreton, Chesire, UK. Double Bass Player. Educ: Royal Manchester Coll. of Music. Career: Double Bass Sect., Royal Liverpool Phil. Orch. Hobbies: Photography; Sound recording. Address: 10 Burden Rd., Moreton, Wirral, Cheshire, L46 6BQ, UK.

PEAKE, Luise Eitel, b. 11 Jan. 1925, Konigsberg, Germany. Musicologist. Educ: BA, Univ. of Tenn., Knoxville, USA, 1949; Stern Conserv., Berlin, 1948, MMus (piano), Chgo. Musical Coll., 1951; MMus (musicol.), ibid., 1952; PhD, Columbia Univ., 1968. m., 2 s. Publs: The Song Cycle; A Preliminary Study, 1968; Assoc. Ed., The Piano Quarterly, 1959-67. Contbr. to: Musical Quarterly; Jrnl. of Am. Musicol. Soc.; Grove's Dictionary. Mbrships: Am. Musicol. Soc. (Chmn., SE Chapt., 1971-74); Music Lib. Assn. Address: 516 Santee Ave., Columbia, SC 92205, USA.

PEARCE, Alison Margaret, b. 5 Aug. 1953, Bath, Somerset, UK. Soprano Singer. Educ: Dartington Coll. of Arts, Devon; GSM; AGSM; cert of advanced musical studies. Debut: Wigmore Hall, London. Career: num. recitals, oratirio perfs.; soloist in premiere of Hoddinott's Sinofonia Fidei; apps. on BBC radio; fest. apps. incl. Wigmore Hall Summer Fest., Fishguard, Music Armenia, Cardiff 20th century. Recordings: Songs of the Hebrides; Medieval & early Renaissance music; Renaissance music. Mbrships: ISM; Equity; Royal Overseas League. Hons: Southern Arts Assn. Young Musician, 1976; Brighton Phil. Soc. Herbert Menges Memorial Award, 1977; Susan Longfield Memorial Award, 1977; Arts Coun. of GB Mirian Licette Scholarship, 1977; 2nd prize, Kathleen Ferrier Competition, 1977; Countess of Munster Award, 1978; Greater London Arts Assn. Young Musician, 1978/79; ISM Young Artist, 1979; Henry & Lily Davis Award. Hobbies: Theatre; Travel; Continental Cuisine. Mgmt: Basil Douglas Ltd., London. Address: 232 Goring Rd., Goring-by-Sea. Worthing, Sussex BN12 4PG, UK.

PEARCE, Elaine Julia, b. 1 June 1946, London, UK. Singer (soprano). Educ: Royal Coll. of Music; GRSM; ARCM. Career incl: performances as a schoolgirl in Britten's Let's Make an Opera, Vaudeville Theatre, & in Noyes Fludde, St. Pancras Arts Festival; freelance soloist & mbr. of chmbr. choirs; Pvte. tchr. & turor; Schutzvecka in Sweden & Finland; num. recitals of Lieder & Chanson in London & S England. Hobbies: Walking; Swimming; Reading. Address: 3 Halliwick Rd., Muswell Hill, London N10, UK.

PEARCE, George Geoffrey, b. 19 Sept. 1943, Cottingham, Yorks., UK. Educator; Organist; Choirmaster. Educ: GRSM; FTCL; ARCO; ARCM; ALCM. Debut: Organ Solo, RCM Chamber Concert, 1964. Career incls: Asst. Organist, Beverley Minister, Yorks., 1969; Music Tchr., Kingston upon Hull inclng. Hd. of Music, Hull Grammar Schl.; Currently Instructor of Pinoforte, Harlaw Acad. & Organist & Master of the Choristers, St. Andrews Episcopal Cath.,Aberdeen; Special Commissioner, Royal Schl. of Ch. Music, & cond., Aberdeen Orpheus Choir; Organ Recitalist; Organist, Servs., Radio & TV. Mbrships: ISM; RCO; Inst. Adv. Motorist. Recip., RCO Sawyer Prize, 1965. Hobbies: Scenic Driving; Reading Thrillers; Hill Climbing; Visting Bldgs. of Archl. Interest. Address: c/o Harlaw Acad., Albyn Pl., Aberdeen AB9 1RG, UK.

PEARCE, Max Macauley, b. 24 Mar. 1922, Maitland, S Australia. Bass Singer. Educ: King's Coll., Kensington, SA; Studied Singing at Elder Conservatorium. Widower, 1 s. Career: Bass Prin. in Operas inclng: Don Carlos, Faust, die Entfuhrung aus dem serail, The Heavyweight (Krenck), Gilbert & Sullivan Operettas; Prin. Bass, Aust. Broadcasting Commission's Adelaide Consort. Hobbies: Part-time Grazier on property 16 miles from Adelaide; Wood Carving. Address: Grasby Rd., Balhannah, S Australia 5242.

PEARCE, Melvin Michael, b. 13 July 1943, La Mesa, Tex., USA. Teacher; Conductor; French Horn Player. Eudc: BA Music Educ., Eastern NM Univ., 1965; MA, Univ. of Iowa, 1967; MA, Univ. of Northern Colo., 1976. m. Sharon Ann Roether Pearce, 2 s. Career incls: High Schl. Band Dir., Albuquerque, NM, 4 yrs.; Band-Orch.-Jazz Dir., Lakewood High Schl., Colo., 5 yrs.; Horn Player, Bands & Orchs., Eastern NM & Iowa Univs.; Asst. 1st Horn, Albuquerque Symph., 1967-70; 1st Horn, 1972, Guest Cond. 1973, Jefferson, Colo. Symph. Orch.; Ed., String Vibrations. Comp: (Arr.) Purvis, Poeme Mystique. Recordings: Homage to Capitan (perf.); 2 as Band Cond. Mbr., assns. Recip., num. awards for self & bands. Hobbies incl: Archaeology; Reading. Address: 7633 W Elmhurst Dr., Littleton, CO 80123, USA.

PEARCEY, Leonard Charles, b. 6 June 1938, London, UK. Musician (songs w. guitar); Broadcaster; Writer; Arts Administrator; Producer. Educ: MA, Corpus Christi Coll., Cambridge Univ. Career: Music Dir., GSM, and Sec., Int. Violin Competition, 1966-70; Dir., Merton Fest., 1972-76; Dir., Debut recitals for young musicians at Purcell Room & seminars for young musicians; Admnistr., Radio Tims 50th birthday, inclng. lauching of drama awards, 1973; TV and radio activities incl. all major arts & relig. progs., biographical progs. &

documentaries, adult & children's music progs. & own series; songs w. guitar in major concert halls & cathedrals & at leading fests.; var. tours; lectr., speaker, compere, radio work as chmn., presenter, critic, interviewer, reporter. Comps: Num. songs, some arrs.; several LPs. Publs: The Musician's Survival Kit, 1979. Mbrships: W Highland White Terrier Club; Music Box Soc. Hobbies: Food; Drink; Travel. Address: 53 Queens Road, London SW19, UK.

PEARLMAN, Leonard Alexander, b. 12 Jan. 1928, Winnipeg, Can. Conductor; Professor of Orchestras. Director of Orchestras. Educ: BA, 1949, MD, 1953, Univ. of Man., Can.; MM. SUNY at Buffalo; Dip., Vienna State Acad. of Music, Austria, 1956. Career: Cond.,St. Catharines Symph. Orch., Ont., Can., 1958-64; Vis. Prof., Univ. of Md., 1965; Prof., Peabody Inst., Balt., Md., 1966-73; Chmn., Dept. of Orchl. Activities, Conserv. of Music, Univ. of Mo. at Kan. City., 1973-74; Prof., Peabody Inst., 1974-77; Prof. of Music, Univ. of Arizona Schl. of Music; Dir. of Orch. & Cond. of Univ. Opera, ibid, 1977-. Recordings: Sev. recordings. Mbrships: incl: Bd. of Dirs., Coll., Conserv. & Univ. Div., Am. Symph. Orch. League; Am. Musicol. Soc. Contbr. to: Grove's Dict. of Music & Musicians, 6th ed. Hobby: Chess. Address: 225 E Calle Turquesa, Tucson, AZ 85704, USA.

PEARS, (Sir) Peter Neville Luard, b. 22 June 1910, Farnham, Surrey, UK. Tenor Singer. Educ: Lancing Coll.; Oxford Univ.; RCM. Career: BBC Singers, 1934-37; New Engl. Singers, 1936-a38: Am. & European tours w. Benjamin Britten & w. Julian Brean, 1956-; recitals w. Osian Ellis & w. Murray Perahia; Sadler's Wells Opera, 1943-46; app. as Peter Grimes, 1945, '60: Engl. Opera Group, 1947; Covent Garden Opera, 1948; pres., ISM, 1970; first perf. num. new works by Britten, Tippett, Berkeley, etc.; co-fndr., Aldeburgh Fest., 1948; Crab lectr., Univ. of Glasgow, 1961; co-find., Britten-Pears Schl. for Advanced Musical Studies. num. recordings. Publs: w. B Britten, Purcell Ed., 1948. mbr., Reform Club. num. hons. incl: CBE, 1957; knighted 1978; FRCM; hon. RAM; hon docts. from Univs. of York, Sussex, Cambridge & Edinburgh. Mgmt: Pears-Phipps Mgmt. Address: c/o Phipp, 8 Halliford St., London, N1, UK. 1.

PEARSON, Keith William, b. 7 June 1938, London, UK. Clarinettist. Educ: RAM; LRAM; ARCM. m. Virginia Kate Henson, 1 s., 1 d. Career: Prin. Clarinettist, SNO, 1962-; Mbr. of Staff, Royal Scottish Acad. of Music & Drama. Mbrships: ISM. Hobbies: Photography; Keeping tropical fish. Address: 3 Victoria Circus, Glasgow G12 9LB, UK. 3.

PEARSON, William Dean, b. 28 Sept. 1905, Huddersfield, Yorks., UK. Music Educator. Eudc: BSc., Leeds Univ.; B Mus., Durham Univ.; FRCO; Hon. FLCM; study w. Dr. Gordon Slater & Sir. Edward Bairstow. m. Shelia Colston Rees, 1 s. Career: Co. Music Advsr., Cornwall, 1947-58; Insp. (Music), Manchester Educ: Committee, 1958-70; Lectr. in Music, St. John's Coll. of Further Educ., 1970-. Comps: Part songs; Unison songs; Organ pieces; Woodwind & recorder pieces; Violin & Viola pieces; Edits. & Realisations of music by Handel, Corelli, Valentine, Marcello, etc. Publ: Troubadour Song Books, 2 vols., 1965. Contbr. to: Making Music, etc. Mbrships: ISM; Rural Music Schls. Assn. Hobbies: Travel; Lit.; Maths. Address: 15 Ellesmere Rd. S., Manchester M21 1TE, Lancs., UK. 3.

PEART, Donald Richard, b. 9 Jan. 1909, Fovant, Wilts., UK. Professor; Violinist; Viola & Viola da Gamba Player. Educ: BMus, MA, Univ. of Oxford; RCM; ARCM; FRCM. m. Ellen Lilian Germon, 1d., 1s. Career: Emeritus Prof. & Fndn. Prof., Univ. of Sydney. Publs: Ed., John Jenkins, Consort Music in 6 Parts, Musica Britannica, 1977. Contbr. to: Musicology; Opera Australia; Jrnl. of Viola da Gamba Soc.; Music Now (Ed.). Hons: John Lowell Osgood Prize, Univ. of Oxford, 1932. Hobbies: Walking; Bushwalking; Reading; Cooking; Wine; Music. Address: 14 Windward Ave, Mosam, Australia. 2088. 1, 3, 14, 15, 29.

PEASE, Edward, b. 29 May 1930, Gilman, Ill., UDA. Musicologist; Dance Historian. Educ: PhD, Ind. Univ.; Further study, Univ. Freiburg, Germany, 1 1/2 yrs. m. Betty Kuhlman Pease, 1 d. Career: Prof., Music, Western Ky. Univ., 1967-; Lectr., dance hist. & humanities; French hornist, regional concerts & fac. recitals of chmbr. music. Publs: Music from the Pixérécourt Manuscript, 1960; Encountering Ivan Illich, 1974. Contbr. to profl. jrnls. Mbrships: Am. Musicol. Soc.; Comm. Rsch. in Dance (US). Hons: Fulbright Schlrship., Deutsche Akad. Austauschdienst Dankstipendium; Rsch. Fellow, Am. Coun. Learned Socs. Hobbies: Aviation; Travel. Address: 823 Merideth Dr., Bowling Green, KY 42101, USA.

PEASE, Lois Joyce Elda (Schatz), b. Detroit, Mich., USA. Piano Teacher; Choir Director. Educ: AA., Univ. of Calif., LA,

1948; BA, ibid, 1952; Calif. Pub. Schl. Teaching Credential, 1953. m. Fred Ansel Pease, 1 s., 1 d. Career: Children's & Youth Choir Dir.; TV appearance w. children's grp. Contbr. to The Flammerion. Mbrships: Area Chmn., Nat. Guild of Piano Tchrs., 1974-75; Music Tchrs. Assn. of Calif.; Musical Arts Club. of Orange Co.; Choral Conds. Guild; Orange Co. Chapt., Orff-Schulwerk Assn. Hons: Nat. Honor Roll, Nat. Guild of Piano Tchrs., 1969-74; YMCA Serv. to Youth Award, 1966-67; PTA Serv. Award, 1972; Nat. Certification by Am. Coll. of Musicians, 19709-. Hobbies: Youth Acitivities; ''Pease Pipers'' (singing & instrumental family grp.); Clarinet; Sewing; Bowling; Camping. Address: 14524 Rio Blanco. Rd., La Mirada, CA 90638, USA.

PECKHAM, Margaret (Elizabeth), b. 29 Nov. 1939, Hastings, UK. Mezzo-contralto. Educ: LRAM; ARCM; Concert Dip.; Staatliche Hochschule für Musik, Frankfurt. Career: w. Engl. Nat. Opera, 3 yrs.; Now freelance throughout Europe; Concert & Recital work; toured NZ, 1977. Contbr. to jrnls. Mbrships: ISM; Royal Musical Assn.; Deutscher Künstler Verbund. Hon: Schlrship., German Acad. Exchange Serv., 1969-71. Hobbies: Walking; Reading; var. handcrafts. Address: 102 St. Helens Rd., Hastings. TN34 2EL, Sussex, UK.

PEDERSEN, Gunner Møller, . 5 Feb. 1943, Arhus. Denmark. Composer. Educ: Diplomeksamen, 1968 & Musick Paedagogisk Eksamen, 1969, Det Jyske Musikkonservatorium, Ahrus; supplementary studies w. Cornelius Cardew, London, 1969. Debut: as Comp.in Harderslev, w. a mil. march 'Awake & Faithful', 1963; as perf. artist in Trondheim, Norway w. music theatre piece 'Tumlingen', 1969. Career: Comp. music for num. films & theatre plays, opera & electronic music: Concerts. etc. Compositions incl: Symph., 1967; Clouds, 2 songs, 1968; Sonata in White, piano, 1969; (electronic works) in Terra Pax, 1966; Organism, 1969; Minos Music, 1970; 'Stoned', an electronic symph., 1973; (opera) 'Show Bix', 1969; (TV) August 1969, puppet play, 1972; (concerts) Musikzag; Electronic Music: Here; Phoenix; Da Niente; Matin; Mars Suite 1977; A Sound Year. Mbrships: Dansk Komponistforening; DUT, the Danish Sect. of JSCM. Fndr. Danish Electronic Music Soc., 1976. Address: Dunhammervej 7, DK 2400, Copenhagen NV, Denmark. 30.

PEDERSEN, Paul Richard, b. 28 Aug. 1935, Camrose, Alta., Canada. Professor of Music Composition of Theory. Educ: BA, Univ. of Sask., 1957; M Mus., Univ. of Toronto, 1961; PhD., ibid, 1970. m. Jean Frances Stollery, 4 children. Career: Music Dir., Camrose Luth. Coll., Alta. 1962-64; Assoc. Prof., Fac. of Music, McGill Univ.,Montreal, 1966-74; Chmn., Dept. of Theory, ibid, 1970-73; Dir., Electronic Music Studio, 1969-74; Assoc. Dean, 1974-76; Dean. Fac. of Music, 1976-; Exec. Prod., McGill Univ. Records. Composer of choral works inclng. Psalm 134 & On the Nativity of Christ, 1963, chmbr. music inclng. An Old Song of the Sun & the Moon & The Fear of Loneliness, 1973, orchl. music & electronic music. Recordings: For Margaret, Motherhood & Mendelssohn; An Old Song of the Sun & The Moon & The Fear of Loneliness. Contbr. to: Jrnl. of Acoustical Soc. of Am.; Jrnl. of Music Theory; Can. Psychol. Review. Mbrships: Canadian League of Comps.; Comps., Authors & Publrs. Assn. of Canada. Recip. of hons. Address: 125 Percival, Montreal West, PQ, Canada. 2.

PEDERSEN, Tove, b. 4 June 1938, Oslo, Norway. Cellist. Educ: Cello studies in Oslo, Copenhagen, Paris & Zürich. Career: Cellist, Orch. of Musikeselskabet Harmonien, Bergen, 1967-; Mbr., Harmonien String stage, radio & TV. Address: Heien 21, 5000 Bergen, Norway.

PEEBLES, Anthony Gavin Ian, b. 26 Feb. 19456, Southborough, Kent, UK. Pianist. Educ: Trinity Coll., Cambridge; Mus B (Cantab.); LRAM (Piano Perfs.). Debut: Wigmore Hall, London, 1969. Career: Recitals in over 50 countries; has played at Royal Fest. Hall, Royal Albert Hall, Fairfield Hall, Queen Elizabeth Hall, etc.; Num. broadcasts with BBC; over 20 concertos w. var. orchs. inclng. Royal Phil., Royal Liverpool Phil., & Hallé Orch. Recordings incl: Copland, Fantasy; Bartok Studies; Dallapiccola; Quaderno Musicale di Annelibera; Autumn Music & Nocturne w. LSO Mbr., ISM. Hons: 1st Prize, BBC Piano Competition, 1971; 1st Prize, Debussy Competition, 1972. Hobbies: Cricket; Tennis. Address: 2a Forthbridge Rd., London, SW11 5NY, UK. 28, 29, 30.

PEERCE, Jan, b. NYC, USA. Tenor Singer. Educ: studies violin.m., 1s., 2 d. Career: worked as orchl. Violinist; made debut as singer w. NBC Symph. under Toscanini; Radio City Music Hall broadcasts, also many TV apps. on network Shows; num. concerts, USA. Can., Europe. Mexico. Ctrl. Am., Jamaica, S Am., Israel, UK, etc., tours in USSR, S Africa, Aust.; operatic apps. w. Met. Opera, San Fran. Opera, Vienna State Opera, Munich State Opera, etc.; fests. in Europe & Israel,

1968-; has starred in 4 films. Has recorded for RCA Victor, Westminister, Vanguard & United Aritsts. Mgmt: Maurice Feldman, 745 Fifth Ave., NY., NY 10022, USA. 2.

PEETERS, Flor, b. 4 July 1903, Tilen, Belgium. Organist; Composer; Teacher. Educ: Lemmens Inst., Mechelen. m. Marieke van Gorp, 1 s., 2 d. Career: num. Organ Recitals all over the world, inclng. 10 tours of USA, 2 tours of USSR; Organist, Cathedral Mechelen, 1923-; Organ Prof., Lemmens Inst., 1923-52; Organ Tchr., Royal Conserv., Ghent, 1931-48; Tchr. Organ & Comp., Conserv. Tilburg, Holland, 1935-48; Organ Tchr., Royal Flemish Conserv., Antwerp, 1948-68; Dir., Tchr. Comp., ibid, 1952-68; Ed., De Praestant, 1952-71. Compositions incl: over 500 organ comps; (publd.) incl: over 3000 Chorale Preludes; 3 Concertl; Chmbr., Piano Music; 9 Masses, var. Ch. Music; Lieder; (recorded) Lied Symph.; 3 Preludes & Fugues; Variations & Finale on a Flemish Song; Elegy; Toccata, Fugue & Hymn on Ave Maris Stella; Passacaglia & Fugue; Concerto for Piano & Orch. Recordings: Old Netherland Masters; Old Italian Masters; Old Engl. Masters; Orgelwerke de Romantik & Neuzeit; Bach; Sweelinck, Buxtehude; Organ Music of N Germany & the Netherlands; Organ Music of the Netherlands; Flor Peeters Plays Peeters. Author w. MA Vente & others, The Organ And Its Music in The Netherlands, 1971. Contbr. to var. profl. jrnls. Mbr. Royal Acad. of Sci's. Letters & Fine Arts. Hons: RAM; Dr. Honoris Causa, Cath. Univ., Wash. DC; Dr. Honoris Causa, Cath., Univ. of Louvain, Belgium; made Baron, Belgium, 1971. Address: Adagio, 123 Stuivenbergbaan, 2800 Mechelen, Belgium.

PEETERS, (Jan Willem) Paul, b. 22 June 1953, Weert, Netherland. Student of Musicology & Organ. Educ: pvte. study, piano, 1961-71, organ, .1971-73, Schl. of Music, Weert; Utrecht, 1976, musicol., Univ. of Utrecht, 1972-; student, prin. subject - organ, Conserv. of Utrecht, 1976-78. Career: Organist, Matthias Ch., Weert, 1968-72, Chapel of Nunnery of Ursulien, Weert, 1970-72, St. Willibrordus Ch., Bodegraven, 1975 (3 months); OLV Ch., Werkhoven, Organist & Choral Cond., 1977-79. Pvte. recordings of organ works. Mbrships: Vereniging voor Nederlandse Musiekgeschiendenis; Nederlandse Organisten Vereniging; Gesellschaft der Orgelfreunde. Hobbies incl: Methods of organ bldg.; Philos.; Sports. Address: Rijnesteinhof 12, 3525 EN Utrecht, Netherlands.

PEHARDA, Zdenko Ivan, b. 2 Mar. 1923, Zagreb, Yugoslavia. Conductor; Pianist. Educ: Grad. (as pianist), Conserv. of Zagreb; Grad. (as cond.), Music Acad., Zagreb & Ljubljana, 1946. m. Mirjana Dancuo, 3 children. Debut: 1947. Career: app. as Solo Pianist, Accomp., Cond., Choirmaster, Trombonist or Arr., most operhouses & on radio, Yugoslavia; Cond. orchs: Europe & USA; Tchr., Music Schl. in Rijeka Sarajevo, Yugoslavia; Jazz Orch. Leader, 1938-; Cond., Opera Rijeka, 1946-; Music Dir., ''Komekija'', Zagreb & Theatre Varazdin, 1957-; Ldr. of Operatic Schl. & Opera Cond., Oslo, Norway, 1964-; TV & radio apps., Oslo, Norway; Asst. Music Dir., Norwegian State Opera, Oslo, 1977-. Has had sev. original choral & folk choir works recorded in Yugolsavia. Contbr. occasional articles to newspapers. Mbr: Norwegian Union of Musicians; Hon. Mbr., Kiwani's Club, Lillestrom, Norway. Hobbies: Photography; Mechanics. Address: Nedre Kalbakkvei 2D, Oslo 9, Norway.

PEINEMANN, Edith, b. 3 Mar. 1939, Mainz, Germany. Violinist. Educ: GSM; violin studies w. Robert Peinemann (father), Heinz Stanske & Max Rostal. Debut: Munich, 1956. Career: soloist w. ldng. orchs. in Europe, USA, Aust., Japan, S Am. & S Africa. apps. at fests. in Lucerne, Salzburg, Helsinki, Vienna, Munich, etc; Prof., Acad of Music, Frankfurt. Recordings: Dvorak, Concerto; Ravel, Tzigane; Brahms sonatas w. Jorg Demus. Hons: 1st prize, Int. Competition, German Radio, Munich, 1956; Plaquette Eugene Ysaye, Liège. Hobbies: Cross Country Skiing; Hiking; Reading; Fine Arts. Mgmt: Dr. Goette, Hamburg; Barbara Graham, London; Mariedi Anders, San Francisco. Address: Hegibachstr. 54, 8032 Zürich, Switzerland.

PEIRICK, Elyse Mach, b. 12 Jan. 1941, Cngo., Ill., USA. Author; Concert Pianist; Professor of Music. Educ: B Mus Ed., Valparaiso Univ., Ind., MMus, PhD., Northwestern Univ., Evanston, Ill.; studied Piano w. Clarence Eidam & Louis Crowder; Master Classels w. Vronsky & Babin. m. John Edward Peirick, 1 s. Debut: Gary, Ind. Career: Prof. of Music (Piano), Northeastern Ill. Univ., Chgo.; TV app. as Soloist w. NBC Symph. orch., Chgo., Radio perfs. as Soloist w. Netherlandische Omkoerst Orch. & Nederlandische Symph. Orch., Hilversum, Holland; num. recitals for Dutch radio & for Swiss Broadcasting Co., Zürich. Recording: Elyse Mach & Her Piano. Publ: The Liszt Studies: Essential Selections from the Origal 12 Volume Set of Technical Studies for the Piano...

Selections, Editions & Engl. Trans; 1973; Contemporary Class Piano, 1976. Contbr. to: The Piano Quarterly; Clavier. Mbrships incl: Am. Liszt Soc. (Exec. Sec.); Int. Liszt Ctr., London, UK (US Rep.); Cons., Assn. Francaise Franz Liszt. Hons: Chgo. Achievement Medal, 1959; 1st Place, Farwell Piano Competition, Chgo., 1962. Hobbies incl: Skiing; Horseback Riding. Address: 6551 N Wauesha Ave., Chicago, IL 60646, USA.

PEJMAN, Ahmad, 9 July 1935, Lar, Iran. Composer; Chariman, University Music Department. Educ: BA, Tchrs. Coll.; MA in Comp., Acad. of Music, Vienna, Austria. m. Homa Bahreini, 2 s.,1 d. Career: Chmn., Music Dept., Tehran Univ. Comps.: (published) Sonatine for Viola & Piano; (performed) 2 Ballets; 2 Operas; orchl. & chmbr. music; film music; music for children; music for Persian instruments. Hobbies: Reading; Books; Collecting Music Books. Address: Music Dept., Columbia Univ., NY, NY, USA.

PEJOVIĆ, Roksanda, b. 11 Dec. 1929, Belgrade, Yugolsavia. Writer on Music; Music & Art. Historian. Educ: Hist. of Art, Philos. Fac., Belgrade Univ., 1957; Piano, Josip Slavenski Music Schl., 1959; Hist. of Music, 1955, MA, 1963, Acad. of Music; Doct. degree, Ljubljana Univ. 1975. m. Vojislav Pejović, 1 d. Career: Prof. Stanković Music Schl., 1957-75; Docent, Fac. of Musical Art, 1975-. Publs incl: History of Music, I-II, 1969; Oskar Danon, 1972; 50 Years of the Belgrade Philharmonic Orchestra. Contbr. to: Zvuk; Pro Musica; Arts Musicae; Fontes Artis Musicae; Narodno stvaralastvo; other jrnls; musical congresses. Mbr., Soc. of Comps. & Music Writers. Address: Braće Jerković 71, 11040 Belgrade, Yugolsavia.

PELINSKI, Ramon Adolfo, b. 31 Aug. 1932, Corpus, Misiones, Argentina. Musicologist. Educ: Lic. Filosofia, Univ. Cordoba; Aesthetics, Univ. Cracow, Poland; MA, Univ. Munich, 1966; PhD, ibid., 1969; Piano & comp., Conserv. Music, Cordoba; Music analysis, Conserv. Paris; Musicol., Sorbonne, Paris, 1 s. Career: Orgnsr., music sect., Exhib. 'World Cultures & Mod. Art'; Assoc. Prof.of Coord., Musicol. Div., Dept. Music, Univ. Ottawa, Canada, 1973-. Publs. incl: Die Weltiliche Vokalmusik Spaniens Am Anfang des 17. Jhs., 1971. Contbr. to profl. publs. Mbrships. incl: Gesellschaft fur Musikforschung, German Fed. Repub.; Am. Musicol. Soc. Soc. Francaise Musicol. Hobbies: Skiing; Langs: Address: 173 Daly Ave., Apt. P, Ottawa, Ontario K1N 6E8, Canada.

PELLANT, Jiří, b. 2 Dec. 1950, Prague, Czech. Double Bass Player. Educ: Prague State Conserv. under Frantisek Posta, 6 yrs.; grad., 1972. Debut: Prague, 1972. Career: 1 yr., Orch. of Nat. Theatre, Prague; 3 yrs., ldr., Symph. Orch. of Radio Yugolsavia;1 yr., Symph. Orch. FOK, Prague; now in Symph. Orch. of Czech. Radio, Prague. Recordings: Dvorak, Str. Quintet, Op.77; Dittersdorf, Sinfonia Concertante. Hons: winner of 2 competitions, Symph. Orch., FOK, Prague, & Radio Symph. Orch. Hobbies incl: Music; Sport; Tourism; Car; Books; People. Address: Tylovo námestí 4, Prague 2, Czechoslovakia. 2.

PELLEGRINO, John, b. 23 Mar. 1930, Providence, RI., USA. Teacher; Performer (trumpet); Professor of Music. Educ: B Mus Ed., Boston Conserv. of Music, 1958; M Mus., Univ. of Miami, 1959; Yale Univ.; Boston Univ. m. Alice M. Kays, 1 s., 1 d. Career: TV taping Peloquin Chorale, 1969; Nat. TV Boston, 1972; Mbr. Miami Symph. Orch.; Prin. Trumpet, RI Phil. Orch.; Portland (Me.) Symph., RI Civic Choral & Orch., Peloquin Chorle & Orch., Westerly Community Chorus & Orch.; Ldr., RI Phil. Brass Quintet; Trumpet Recitalist throughtout the New England area; Prof. of Music, RI Coll., 1964-. Recordings: Peloquin Chorale, 1965, '67, '72, '74; The Music of Arthur Custer, 1975. Contbr. to the RI Music Educ. Review. Mbrships: MENC; RI Music Educators Assn.; Int. Trumpet Guild; Nat. Assn. for Humanities Educ.; 1st VP, Warwick Arts Fndn. Recip., var. scholarships & awards. Hobbies: Gardening; Camping. Address: 39 Natwick Ave., Warwick, RI 02886, USA.

PELLERITE, James John, b. 30 Sept. 1926, Clearfield, Pa., USA. Musician (Flute); Professor. Educ: Juilliard Schl. of Music, NYC.; Wayne State Univ., Detroit; Pvte. study of flute w. Wm. Kincaid. m. Helen Mae Kraut, 2 s. Career: Solo flute, w. Indpls. Symph. Orch., Detroit Symph., Radio City Music Hall, NYC., Chautauqua Symph., NY.; Solo flute, Phila. Orch., 1960-; Prof., Schl. of Music, Ind. Univ. Recordings incl. wide solo flute repertoire for Golden Crest Records - Coronet Recording Co.; Orchl. recordings w. Columbia & Mercury. Pres., Zalo Publs & Servs. Mbrships: VP , Nat. MTA. Recip. Disting. Alumni Award, Valley Forge Mil. Acad., 1961. Hobbies: Cycling; Philately. Address: 109 N. Glenwood Ave. W., Bloomington, IN 47401, USA.

PELLETIER, Louis Philippe, b. 7 Aug. 1945, Montreal, Can. Concert Pianist. Educ: Grad., Conserv. of Music, Montreal, studying w. Lubka Kolessa; further studies w. Claude Helffer, Karlheinz Stockhausen, Harold Boje & Aloys Konstarsky. m. Luoise Larose, 1 s. Career: recitals throughout Europe, in N Africa & USA; toured on behalf of Jeunesses Musicales of Can., 1977-78; num. apps. on CBC & recordings for Radio-Can. Int.; noted for perfs. for contemporary music & has given many premieres. Hons: 1st prize (piano) Conserv. of Montreal, 1968; 1st prize, Int., Arnodl Schönberg piano competition, Rotterdam, 1979. Address: 1558 Van Horne, Outremont H2V 1L5, Canada.

PELLETIER, Wilfrid, b. 20 June 1896, Montreal, PQ, Can. Conductor; Pianist. Educ: degrees from Univs. of Montreal & of Banff, Laval Univ., McGill Univ., Univ. of Quebec, Hobart & NYC Colls. m. Rose E Bampton, 2 s. Career: Metrop. Opera, NYC, 1971-50; San Fran. Opera; Cincinnati, Ohio; NY Phil.; Montreal Symph.; Quebec Symph.; Rvinia Opera; Dir. of Music, Min. of Cultural Affairs, PQ. Recordings: RCA Victor; Columbia. Publs: Une Symphonie Inachevee (biog.) Hons. incl: Salle Wilfred Pelletier, Montreal, Chavalier, Legion of Hon., France; GMG, UK; CC, Can.; Prix D'Europe, 1915. Address:322 E 57 St., NY., NY 10022, USA. 2.

PELLINI, Giovanni, b. 14 Oct. 1912, Milan, Italy. Lutenist; Player of the Theorbo, Chitarrone, Recorder, Crumhorn, Psaltry & Gittern. Educ: law degree. m. Enrica Berrini. Career: Fndr., Symposium Musicum di Roma, 1958, Symposium Musicum di Milano, 1962; hundreds of concerts in Italy & abroad; TV & radio broadcasts in Italy & abroad. Recordings: Frottole (songs for voice & luto from the early 16th century), Candide-Vox CE 31017; Il Seicento, La musica per strumenti diversi, vol. 2 of Storia della musica italiana, RCA LM 40001-9. Publs: catalogue of musical intsruments in the Theatrical Mus., La Scala, Milan. Contbr. to: Museo Teatrale del Teatro all Scala di Milano, 1971. Address: Via Cartesio 2, 20124 Milan, Italy.

PELNAR, Ivana, b. 30 Dec. 1946, Czech. Musicologist. Educ: Pargue Conserv.of Music, 1961-64; Western Reserve Univ., USA, 1966-67; B Mus, McGill Univ., Can.,1969; Yale Univ., 1969-70; PhD Cand. Univ. of Munich, German Fed. Repub. Contbr. to: 6th ed. Grove's Dictionary of Music & Musicians; var. record jacket notes, ARIOLA-EURODISC, Munich. Mbr., German Assn. of Univ. Women. Hobbies: Langs.; Lit.; Theatre; Composing songs. Address: 8 Blueberry Lane, Lexington, MA 02173, USA.

PENA, Angel, b. 22 Apr. 1921, Laoag City, Philippines. Composer; Arranger; Bass Player; Music Teacher. Educ: LRSM, London, UK. m. Josefina Lovinaria Peña, 1 d. Debut: Concerto for Double Bass w. Manila Symph. Orch., 1969. Career: Guest soloist, Manila Symph. Orch. (concerto for double bass & orch. composed by soloist himself); TV interviews, Lects. & adjudications, Philippines & Hong Kong; Bass player, Honolulu Symph. Orch.; Prelude & Fugue for String Orch. Recordings: Popular songs recorded in Philippines & Hawaii. Contbr. to Manila Chronicle & Evening News. Mbrships: PRS; Songwriters Guild Gt. Britain; Am. String Tchrs. Assn.; Am. Fedn. of Musicians. Recip. of hons. Hobbies incl: Hiking; Swimming. Address: 802 Prospect St., Apt. 606, Honolulu, HI 96813, USA.

PENALVA, José de Almeida, b. 15 May 1924, Campinas (São Paulo) Brazil. Claretian Priest; Music & Theology Professor; Conductor. Educ: Theol. Lic., Pontifical Cath. Univ., Sao Paulo; ThD, Pontifical Georgian Univ., Rome, Italy; Cert. in Musical Studies, State Schl. of Music & Fine Arts,Paraná; Comp. courses w. Prof. Savino de Bendictis, São Paulo; Grad. course, Acad. S Cecilia, Rome w. Prof. Boris Porena; Courses in Europe. Career: Prof., State Schl. of Music & Fine Arts, Paraná; Prov., Coll.of Music, Blumenau; Cond., Pro-Musica Choir, Curitiba, Madrigal Choir, Coll. of Music, Blumenau; & of the Chorus, City Theatre, Blumenau. Comps: Sacred music Piano pieces; Madrigal Quadruplo. Recordings: Metanoia (cantata); Agape (cantata-mass). Contbr. to many jrnls. Mbrships: Fndr., Int. Soc. of Contemp. Music (Brazilian branch); Pres., Chmbr. of Arts of State Cultural Coun. of Paraná; Fndr. mbr. & Gen. Sec., Pro-Música de Curitiba. Hons: Silver Plaque, State of Paraná Govt. for Metanoia, 1975; Var. rsch. scholarships. Address: Av. Getúlio Vargas 1193, Caixa Postal 153, Curitiba 80.000, Paraná, Brazil.

PENCIK, Jindrich, b. 14 Feb. 1930, Prostejov, Czechoslovakia. Choirmaster. Educ: Cond.'s Dip., Prague Conserv. of Music.m. Jarmila Zidkova, 1 d. Debut: Prague 1958. Career: Choirmaster & Cond., Artistic Ensemble of the Czech. Army, Prague; State Ensemble of Folklore Songs & Dance, Prague; Choirmaster, Prague Men's Choir; Cond., Guest Ctrl. Bohemian Symph. Orch. & Prague Radio Orch. sev. recordings. Hons:

Czech. Musical Fund Prizes for condng., 1971, '72, '75. Hobby: Maths. Address: No. 89/231 Vysocanska St., Prague, 9, 1900 Czech.

PENDERECKI, Krzysztof, b. 23 Nov. 1933, Debica, Poland. Composer. Educ: State Schl. of Music., Krakow; studied w. Franciszek Sklyszewski. m. Elizabeth Penderecki, 1 s. Career: Prof. of Composition, Krakow Stats Schl. of Music, 1958-66, Flolwang Acad. of Music, German Fed. Repub., 1966-67; vis. USA, 1967; Guest Cond., LSO, Peterborough, UK, 1973; Cond., Polish Radio Orch. in recording of own works. Compositions incl: Psalms of David, 1958; Strophes; 1959; Anaklasis, 1960: Threnudy to the Victims of Hiroshima (str. orch.), 1960; Pslams of magnetic tape, 1961; Florescenses (orch.), 1962: Sonata for Cello & Orch., 1964; Passion of Our Lord Jesus Christ According to St. Luke, (oratoria), 1966; The Devils of Loudun (opera), 1969: Kosmogonia (oratoria), 1970: Utrenja (oratorio), 1971; Canticum Canticorum Salomonis (oratorio), 1972; Symph. No. 1, 1973; Magnificat (oratorio),. 1974; Concerto for Violin, 1977; Paradise Lost (opera), 1978. All prin. works have been recorded. Hons. incl: 1st, 2nd & 3rd Prizes, Competition, Polish Comps. Assn., 1959; UNESCO Award, 1961; Fitelburg Prize, 1960; Polish Min. of Culture Prize, 1961. Address: c/o Lyra Mgmt., 1776 Broadway, NYC, NY 10019, USA.

PENDLE, Karin Swanson, b. 1 Oct. 1938, Minneapolis, Minn., USA. Professor, Musicology & Applied Music, (voice). Educ: BA, Univ. of Minn., 1961; M Mus, Univ. of Ill., 1964; PhD, ibid., 1970. m. Frank Pendle, Publs: Eugene Scribe & French Opera of the 19th Century, 1979. Contbr. to: Musical Quarterly; Music Review; Music & Letters. Mbrships: Am. Musicol Soc.; Nat. Assn. Tchrs. of Singing; Coll. Music Soc.; Am. Assn. of Univ. Profs. Hons: Phi Beta Kappa; Pi Kappa Lambda; Phi Kappa Phi. Address: 2308 Moerlein Ave., Cincinnati, OH 45219, USA.

PENHERSKI, Zbigniew, b. 26 Jan. 1935, Warsaw, Poland. Composer. Comp. Dip., Warsaw Conserv. Music, 1959. M. Malgorzata Penherski, 1 s. Comps. incl: Chamber Primer (for instrumental ensemble); 1964; 3 Recitativi (for soprano, piano & percussion), 1968; Children Improvisations (for instrumenta ensembles), 1979; Instrumental Quartet, 1979: Incantationi 1 Sextet for Percussion Instruments, 1972; Radio Symph. for 2, 1975; Street Music (chmbr. ensemble), 1966: Samson Put on Trail (radio opera), 1968; 3M-HI (electronic piece), 1969; The Twilight of Peryn (opera), 1972; Anamnesis (orch.), 1975. Mbrships: Union Polish Comps.; Zaiks. Hons: 2nd Prize, Young Polish Comps. Competition, 1960; 3rd Prize, Fitelberg Competition, 1963. Silver Cross of Merit, 1975. Address: Al. Wojska Polskiego 20, 01-554, Warsaw, Poland.

PENICKA, Miloslav, b. 16 Apr. 1935, Ostrava, Czechoslovakia. Music Teacher; Composer. Educ: Dip. in comp., Conservatorium of Music, Prague, 1958, AMU., Prague, 1964. M. Janet Edith Harvey, 1 d. Debut: Prague, 1958. Career: Worked for ABC music lib., Sydney, Australia, 1964-69; Tchr., comp., Abbotsleigh HS., 1969-. Num. comps. perf. & or publs. in CSSSR incl: Symph. for full orch.,C Concerto for piano & orch., Divertimento for violin, woodwind; brass & bass, Five songs on Negro Poetry, for baritone & orch., etc. Recent Compositions (not performed or publd.): 2nd String Quartet; Quintet for Clarinet & Strings; 2 Serenades for Small Orch.; Concerto for Clarinet & Orch.; Sonatina for Violin & Piano; Piano Quartet; Nameless Overture, for small orch.; (works perf.), Num. pieces for schl. orchs. & var. instrumentaln grps. Mbrships: OSA (for community bloc countries); Assoc. Writer mbr., APRA; Austrian Musicians Union. Hobbies: Aquariums; Fishing. Address: 43 Lady Davidson circuit, Forestville, NSW, 2087, Australia.

PENLAND, Arnold Clifford, Jr., b. 8 Oct. 1933, Asheville, NC., USA. Professor of Music; Conductor; Singer, Tenor. Educ: BS., Western Carolina Univ., Cullowhee, NC., 1956; M Ed., Duke Univ., Durham, NC., 1966; Cert., Plymouth Drama Schl., Mass., 1957; MA., George Peabody Coll., Nashville, Tenn., 1959: Dalcroze Eurythmics Inst., Nat. Music Acad.; Univ. of NC. m. Joan Eudy Penland, 1 d. Career: Public Schl. Music Tc 1956-60; Supvsr. of Music, Raleigh, NC., 1960-67, SC State Dept. of uc., 1969-70; Dir., Cond., Ch. Choirs, Raleigh Oratorio Soc., Leakville Community Chorus; Dir., Raleigh Cultural Ctr.; Fndr., Dir., Raleigh Musical Theatre For Youth, Raleigh Youth Symph.; Prof. of Music, Dir., Continuing Eudc. in Music, Univ. of Fla., Gainesville, 1970-. Publs: You Can Read Music, 1962; A Time For Music: A Guide For Teachers, 2 vols 1963; Ed., Choral Curriculum Guide for Secondary Schools, 1962; Ed., The Arts in Educations; What, For Whom, How?, 1969; A Descriptive Survey of Music Teaching-Learning In the Florida Middle Schools, 1972. Contbr. var. profl. jrnls. Mbr., Off., num. profl. orgs. Recip. num. Hons. Hobbies: Cooking;

Reading. Address: 2809 SW 81 St., Gainesville, FL 32601, USA.

PENNYCOOK, B., b. 5 Oct. 1949, Toronto; Can. Composer; Assistant Professor of Music & Computing Sci. Educ: BMus (Comp.), Toronto, 1972; MMus (Comp.), Toronto, 1973; DMA (Comp.), Stanford 1978. m. Suzanna D. McClennan, 1s., 1d. Career: Radio perfs., Toronto; Asst. Prof. of Music, Queen's Univ., Kingston, Ont. Comps: August Suite (guitar), 1977 (recorded); Concerto for Double Wind Ensemble & Percussion, 1978; gr, RR (Saxophone quartet, piano, bass tape), 1979 (recorded); Studies in Metal, 1976; Film, A Matter of Choice, 1975. Recordings incl: Computer Music from Colgate, Vol. 1. Contbr. to: Computer Music Jrnl.; Queen's Quarterly. Mbrships: Can League of Comps.; Can. Music Centre; Can. Film Comps. Guild Hons: Can. Coun. Doct. Fellowship, 1976-78; Short Term Grant, Can. Coun., 1973-74: Sir Ernest MacMillan Fellowship (CAPAC), 1973; Fairclough-Lowe Scholarship; Ont. Univ. Open Fellowship for Grad. Studies. Address: Dept. of Music, Queen's Univ., Kingston, Ont. K7L 3N6, Canada.

PENROSE, Timothy Nicholas, b. 7 Apr. 1949, Farnham, Surrey, UK. Educ: TCL; LTCL; FTCL. m. Shirley Margaret Bignell. Debut: (opera) Holland Festival, 1974. Career: num. solo concert apps. throughout UK & many European countries; tours w. Pro Cantione Antiqua of London; solo recitals foir BBC & European radio stns.; concerts w. Medieval Ensemble of London & London Music Players. Recordings: w. Pro Cantione Antiqua, Mideaval Ensemble of London, London Music Players & London Early Music Group. Mbrships: Gentleman-in Ordinary, Her Majesty's Chapel Royal, 1972-75; City Glee Club, London. Recip., Greater London Arts Assn. Young Musicians award, 1975. Hobby: Motor-cycling. Address: 35 Poplar Grove, New Malden, Surrey, UK.

PENTLAND, Barbara (Lally), b. 2 Jan. 1912, Winnipeg, Man., Can. Composer. Educ: pvte. study of piano from age 9; studied compositions w. Cécilen Guthiez, (pvte.) Schola Cantorum, Paris, 1929-30; Grad. Juilliard Grad. Schl. of Music, 1939; studied w. Aaron Copland, Berkshire Music Ctr., Mass., summers, 1941 & 42. m. John Huberman. Career: has played own piano works in Can., USA, London & Brussels, on CBC & on BBC; has composed about 100 works. Compositions Recorded: String Quartet No. 1; Symphony for 10 Parts (No. 3); Duo for Viola & Piano; Toccata; String Quartet No. 3. Res Musica, 1975. Disasters of the Sun, 1976. Contbr. to: Northern Review. Mbrships: Assoc. Composer, Can. Music Ctr., Toronto; Can. League of Composers; Can. Music Coun.; Affiliate, BMI, Can. Ltd.; Juilliard Alumni Assn.; MacDowell Colony Fellowy; Am. Fendn. of Musicians. Hons: Centennial Medal, Govt. of Can., 1967; Bronze Medal, XVI Olympiad, London, 1948. Hon. LLD Univ. of Manitoba, 1976; Diplome d'Hanneur, Can. Conf. of Arts, 1977. Hobbies: Maths; Bird-watching. Address: 4765 W. 6th Ave., Vancouver, BC V6T, Canada, 2, 14.

PENZEL, Erich, b. 5 Aug. 1930, Leipzig, Germany. Professor of Music; French Horn Player. Educ: Nat. Coll. of Music, Leipzig. m. Jutta Wegner. Career: Gewandhaus Orch., 1949—61: Solo French Horn, WDR Radio Symph. Orch., 1961; num. guest perfs.; num. recordings. Recordings incl: Rosetti's Horn Concerto in D minor, w. Mainz Chmbr. Orch. (Turnabout TV34078S). Hons. incl: Prague Spring Prize, 1953. Address: 7 Raderthalgürtel, 5 Cologne 51, Germany.

PEPPIN, Geraldine, b. Marston Magna, UK. Concert Pianist. Educ: studied w. Mabel Lander. m. Randall Swingler (dec.), 1 s., 1 d. Debut: when aged 17. Career: num. concert, radio & TV perfs. in piano duo w. sister Mary Peppin; Prod. of Pianoforte, GSM. Mbr., ISM. Recip. FGSM, 1975. Hobby: All things in Nature. Address: Mount Pleasant, Pebmarsh, Halstead, Essex LO9 2L2, UK.

PEPPIN, Mary, b. Marston Magna, UK. Concert Pianist. Educ: studied w. Mabel Lander. m. R E W Fisher, 1 s., 1 d. Debut: at age 17. Career: num. concert, radio & TV apps. in piano due. w. Geraldine Peppin; Prof. of Pinoforte, Guildhall Schl. of Music & Drama. Mbrships: ISM; Musicians' Union. Hons: Fellowship, GSM. 1975. Hobby: Listening. Address: Great Lenghts, Pebmarsh, Halstead, Essex, UK.

PEPPING, Ernst, b. 12 Sept. 1901, Duisburg, Germany. Composer; Educator. Educ: HS. for Music, Berlin. m. Marianne Scheinpflung, 1977. Career: Tchr., Berlin Kirchenmusikschule, 1934; Prof., Berlin Music HS., 1953-. Compositions incl: 3 Symphs.; Piano Concerto; Te Deum; String Quartet; 4 Piano Sonatas; Organ Concertos & Partitas; Passionsbericht des Matthaus; Deutsche Mess; Missa Dona Nobis Pacem; var. liturgical & ch. music. Mbrship: Akad. der Kunste, Berlin &

Munich. Publ: Der Polyphone Satz. Hons: num. prizes incl: Mendelssohn Prize, 1926; Dusseldorf Robert Schumann Prize, 1955; Bremen Phil. Gesellschaft, 1962; Dr. Phil., Berlin Free Univ., Dr. Theol., Berlin Kirchliche HS. Address: Johannestift, Berlin-Spandau, Germany.

PERAHIA, Murray, b. 1947, NY, USA. Pianist; Conductor. Educ: studied piano from age 4; studied conducting for 3 yrs. Career incl: many recitals & concerts, USA, UK, Amsterdam, Germany, etc.; apps. at Marlboro Music Fest., VT., Aldelburgh & other Brit. summer fests., Bergen Fest., etc.; many chmbr. music recitals inclng. sev. w. Peter Pears. Recordings incl: sev. works by Chopin & Schumann; SoloistCond. for series of all Mozart piano concerto (in progress). Mgmt: Harold Holt Ltd., 122 Wigmore St., London W1H ODJ, UK.

PERCIVAL, Allen Dain, b. 23 Apr. 1925, Bradford UK. Executive Chairman, Stainer & Bell, Publisher; Conductor; Keyboard Player. Educ: BMus, Magdalene Coll., Cambridge; pvte. study, piano, harpsichord continuo, conducting. m. Rachel Hay. Debut: cond., Cambridge Opera Group, 1952; keyboard continuo, Royal Fest. Hall, London, 1955. Career: Music off., Brit. Coun., Paris, 1948-50; Music, Homerton Coll., Cambridge, 1951-62; cond., Cambridge Opera Group, 1952-53; Cambridge Univ. Musical Soc., 1954-58; Dir. of Music, GSM, 1962-65; Prin., ibid., 1965-78. Publs: The Orchestra, 1956; The Teach Yourself History of Music, 1961; Music at the Court of Elizabeth I, 1975; Ed., Partners in Praise, 1979, English Love Songs (1600-1960), 1980; Galliard Book of Carolos, 1980; Ed., Music Jrnl., 1978-. Contbr. to most musical mags. Mbrships: ISM; Worshipful Co. of Musicians:; Royal Musical Assn. Hons: CBE, 1975; FRCM; Hon.RAM; Hon. FTCL; FGSM; Hon DMus (City Univ.), 1978. Hobby: Travel. Address:. 7 Park Parade, Cambridge, UK.

PERCY, Richard Arthur, b. 21 July 1944, Warrington, UK. Solo Clarinettist; Teacher. Educ: Huddersfield Schl. of Muic, 1964; study w. Rudolf Jettel, Vienna State Acad., 1967; Brittish Coun. Bursary to study in Stockholm, 1971; Post Grad. studies w. Sidney Fell, RNCM, Manchester, 1973. m. Irena Pryma. Debut: Wigmore Hall, 1977. Career: Staff, Malvert Coll., 1979-. Contbr. to: Music in Educ. Mbr., Solo Perfs. Sect., ISM. Hobbies: Cond.; Arr.; Writing poetry. Mgmt: Choveaux Mgmt., Mancroft Towers, Oulton Broad, Lowestoft, UK. Address: 15 Arosa Dr., Malvern, Worcs., UK.

PERCY, Staffan W, b. 4 Apr. 1946, Stockholm, Sweden. Guitarist. Educ: pvte. & cello classes. m. Bibi Alling, 2 s. Debut: 1974. Career: comp. primarily of poems by Bo Setterlind; singer & guitarist, concerts & recordings: writer of Swedish & English lyrics. Comps. recorded: 5 LP albums - Barnav Kärleken; Il Visor; Hjärtats Ballader; Under Lyktorna; Drommens Skeppl other songs. Publs: Hjärtats Ballander, 1977; Rytterean Fran Södra Rada, 1979. Mbrships: STIM; SKAP; SAMI; Sallskapet club, Stockholm. Hons. incl: Siösala Priset, 1977; grants for isch. & travel. Hobbies: Sailing, Target Shooting; Greek & Roman Archaeology. Address: Jungfrugaton 19, 2tr, 11444 Stockholm, Sweden.

PERDECK, Rudolf, b. 12 Mar. 1925, Almelo, Netherlands. Pianist; Composer. Educ: Studied Comp. w. Hendrik Andriessen, Conserv. of Amsterdam; Cert. for Piano Soloist, Royal Conserv., The Hague; studied Piano w. Theo van der Pas,ibid. m. Ans Boonen. Career: Var. Comps. performed in Concerts & Radio progs., 1959-. Comps. incl: Capriccio for Flute & Piano; Scherzo for Piano & Orch.; Set Rhythm for piano solo; contbr. children's songs to book, Een Mandje Vol Amandelen. Contbr. as Music Critic to De Stem (daily paper), 1969-72. Mbr., Union of Dutch Comps. (Geneco). Address: Geerten Gossaertlaan 1, Groningen, Netherlands. 3.

PEREIRA-ARIAS, Antonio, b. 20 Apr. 1929, Montevideo, Uruguay. Conductor; Guitarist; Double Bass player; Guitar Teacher at Royal Conserv., The Hague, Netherlands. Educ: guitar & double bass studies, Conserv. de Monteviedeo; studies w. A Rapat & A Segovia (guitar), E Pujol (musicol.) & J Hartinon (cond.). m. J G den Ambtman, 5c. Career: cond., 1959-68 w. Radio Symph. Orch., Montevideo; Double Bass Player, Radio Symph. Orch., Montevideo & Rotterdam Phil. Orch. perfs. as guitarist as soloist & with orch. in S Am., USA & Europe. Comps: Sonata for guitar; Trio for viola, cello & guitar; Exodo II for guitar; transcriptions for classical guitar. sev. recordings. Contbr. to: Guitar Review (NY); Guitar (UK); Il Fronimo (Italy). Mbrships. incl: Centro Guitarristico del Uruguay; Centro Guitarristico de Sao Paulo (Brazil); Ven. Guit. Fco., Targa (Netherlands): Academie de Guitarre de Marseille (France); Peña Guit., Barcelona, Spain. Hobbies: with the Family; Reading. Address: Hendrik van Bontsfortstraat 21, 3067 JM Rotterdam, Netherlands.

PERENYI, Miklos, b. 1948, Budapest, Hungary. Cello Soloist. Educ: Dips., St. Cecilia Acad., Rome, 1962, & Liszt Ferenc Acad., Budapest, 1964; studied w. Miklos Zsamboky & Ede Banda, Hungary, Enrico Mainardi, Rome, Salzburg & Lucerne, & Pablo Casals, Zurmatt. Career: has app. at state concerts in Hungary & at concerts in many European countries; played sev. times at Marlboo Fest., Vt., USA. Address: XII Jakobinusok tere 4b, Budapest, Hungary.

PEREZ-GUTIERREZ, Mariano, b. 11 Sept. 1932, Palencia, Spain. Professor; Principal Director; Director of Orchestra & Choirs. Educ: Lic. & Doct. Arts, Univ. Sevilla; Dips., 1st Class Grad. awards, Conserv. of Madrid; Lic. in Chant Gregorian & Musicol. studies, Pris, 1963, '64, etc. m. Mary Cruz Blanco, 1s. Career: Canon, Cathedral of Santiago de Compostela, 1964; Choir Master, ibid, 1964; Dir. of Orch., Choirs, Chapel of the Cathedral; Prof. of Aesthetics & Hist. of Music, Higher Conserv. of Music of Sevilla, 1969; Hd. of Studies, ibid, 1972; Vice Prin., ibid, 1974; Prin. Dir., ibid, 1978. Comps. inc.: Elegia Cromatic; Secuencias ciclicas, etc. Recordings: Misa jubilar. Publs. incl: Oriegn y naturalera del Jubilus Aleluyatica, 1972; Comprende yama la musica, 1979:; El Universo de la Musica, 1980. Contbr. to profl. publs. Hons. incl: Award, Acad. of Fine Arts of Cordoba, 1979 & Higher Coun. of Scientific Investigation. Hobbies: Art; Pvte. collection of ancient & exotic intruments. Address: Conservatorio Superior de Musica, Jesus del Gran Poder, 49-Sevilla, Spain. 19, 23, 28, 29, 30.

PERIČIĆ, Vlastimir, b. 7 Dec. 1927, Vrsac, Yugoslavia. Composer; Musicologist. Educ: w. Stanojilo Rajicić, Musical Acad., Belgrade; w. Alfred Uhl. Akademie für Musick und darstellende Kunst, Vienna. Career: Prof. of Musical Theory & Hist. of Yugolsav Music, Musical Acad. (Fac. of Musical Art), Belgrade. Comps: Piano Sonata, 1949; String Quartet, 1950; Symphonic Movement, 1951; Sonatina for Violin & Piano, 1951; Piano Sonatina, 1952, Sinfonietta for String, 1952; Songs. Recordings on Radio Belgrade. Publs. incl: The Creative Way of Stanojlo Rajicić, 1971. Contbr. to Zvuk; Pro Musica. Mbr. Assn. of Yugoslav Comps. Recip. Prize at Comp. Competition for String Quartet, Vercelli, Italy, 1950. Address: 11000 Belgrade, Lenjinjradska 6, Yugoslavia.

PERKIN, Maimie, b. 22 Apr. 1919, Blackpool, UK. Singer. Educ: FTCL; Dip., Hochschule für Musik, W Berlin; LTCL (tchrs., perf.); LRSM (tchrs., perf.) tchng. & perf. licentiates, Univ. of S Africa. m. Maurice Albert Perkin. Career: leading roles in opera, Gilbert & Sullivan operas, oratorios & song recitals; apps. on radio, S Africa; prod. & acted plays & musical prods. Mbrships: S African Soc. of Music Tchrs. recip. Univ. of S Africa Tchng. Scholarship, 1960. Hobbies: Reading; Bird Watching; Theatre. Address: 7 Rolina Ave., Florida Glen, 1710, S Africa.

PERKINS, Laurence, b. 22 May 1954, Prescot, Lancs., UK., BAssoonist. Educ: Northern Schl. of Music; RNCM (w. Charles Cracknell); GRNCM (perf.). m. Catherine Hemsley. Career: Manchester Midday Concerts recital, 1976; BBC Radio 2 Music Making recital, 1977; Radio 3 Concert Hall recital, 1979; app. on TV, 1979; Wigmore Hall, London, recital, 1979; Chester Summer Music Fest. recital, 1979. Recording: Bassoon Serenade. mbr., ISM. Hons: RNCM Woodwind prize, 1974; Worshipful Co. of Musicians Silver Medal for musicianship, 1975. Hobbies: Record Collecting; Working w. Sound Equipment; Artwork. Mgmt: Shelia Cooper Concert Artist, Ltd. Address: 142 Bleak Hill Rd., Windle, St. Helens, Merseyside WA10 6DN, UK.

PERKINS, Leeman Lloyd, b. 27 Mar. 1932, Salina, Utah, USA. Professor of Music History. Educ: BFA, Univ. of Utah, 1954; PhD, Yale Univ., 1965. Career: Instructor, Asst. Prof., Music Hist., Yale Univ., 1964-71; Assoc. Prof., Music Hist. & Coord. for Musicol., Univ. of Tex., Austin, 1971-75; Prof. of Music Hist., Columbia Univ., NY, 1976-. Publs: Johannis Lheritier Opera Omnia, 2 vols., 1969; The Mellon Chansonnier, 2 vols., 1979. Contbr. to: Musical Quyarterly; Jrnl. Am. Musicol. Soc: Renaissance Quarterly; Moreana; Fontes artis musicae. Mbrships: Am. & Int. Musicol. Soc.; Renaissance Soc. of Am.; Amici Thomae Mori. Hons. grants & fellowships from Martha Baird Rockefeller Fndn., Yale Univ., Am. Coun. Learned Socs., Univ. Rsch. Inst. of Univ. of Tex., Austin; Nat. Endowment for the Humanties, Phi Beta Kappa, Phi Kappa Phi. Hobbies: Violinist; Lit.; Hist. Renaissance. Address: Dept. of Music, Columbia Univ., NYC, NY 10027, USA.

PERKOWSKI, Piotr, b. 17 Mar. 1901, Oweczacze, Ukraine. Composer. Educ: Dip., Warsaw Conserv. of Music, 1925; studied w. Roman Statkowski, Karol Szymanowski & Albert Roussel (Paris). m. Ewa Moser 1d. Career: Prof., Chief of Dept. of Composition, Music Coll., Warsaw, Ret'd., 1973; compstioins are perf. repeatedly, esp. ballets; all works have been recorded by Polish Radio & are publd by Chester in Londonn Eschig in Pris & Polskie-Wydawnictwo-Muzyczene in Poland. Compositions incl: Nocturne for orch. (recorded for grammophone); Torun Sketches, (record); Wedding Suite (cantata on folk lore themes); UTY Japonskie, songs; Cello concerto, 1973; Poems of Aben Azam, for baritone & orch. Song to verses of Pushkin, Mickiewicz & Staff; Songs of Sappho for soprano; film scores. Contbr. to jrnls. Mbrships: incl. on Warsaw City Coun., Ret'd 1974; Cons., Min. Culture; Union of Authors (ZAIKS); Union of Polish Composers. Recip. of num. awards. Hobby: Social Work. Address: Zaulek 28, Warsaw, Poland.

PERLE, George, b. 6 May 1915, Bayonne, NJ, USA. Composer. Educ: PhD, NY Univ.; studies in comp. w. Wesley LaViolette & Ernst Krenek. m. Barbara Phillips (dec.), 1 stepson, 2 d. Career: Prof. of Music, Queens Coll. CUNY. Comps. incl: Songs of Praise & Lamatation, for soloist, choirs & orch., 1974; 3 Movts for orch., 1960; Cello Concerto, 1966; Concetino for piano, winds & timpani, 1979; 2 Serenades for Chmbr. ensemble, 1962, '67; 7 Str. Quartets; 3 Wind Quintets; Sonata quasi una fantasia, for clarinet & piano, 1972. sev. recordings of own works. Publs: Serial Composition & Atonality; An Introduction to the Music of Schoenberg, Berg, & Weberg, 1962 (4 edn., 1977); Twelve-Tone Tonality, 1977; The Operas of Alban Berg, Vol. 1 (Wozzeck), 1989. Contbr. to: Music Review; Musical Quarterly; The Score; Jrnl. of the Am. Musicol. Soc.; Perspectives of New Music, Schwizerische Musikzeitung, etc. Mbrships: ASCP; Co-fndr. w. Stravinsky & Hans Redlich of the Int. Alban Berg Soc. Hons. incl. mbrship, Am. Acad. of Arts & Letters, 1978. Address: 333 Central Pk., W, NY, NY 10025, USA. 2, 14, 30.

PERLEMUTER, Vlado, b. 1904. Concert Pianist; Professor. m. Jacqueline Deleveau. Career: has app. w. orchs. & as Recitalist in all major European cities; toured USA, Can. & Japan; Prof., Nat. Higher Conserv. of Music, Paris. Recordings incl: Integrale de Maurice Ravele; Integrale des Sonates de Mozarte; Chopin Recital; 24 Preludes (Chopin). Publs: Ravel d'Aprfes Ravel (w. Helen Jourdan-Mouhange). Hons: 1st Prize, Paris Conserv.; Prix d'H onneur; Dix Diemer; Grad Prix du Disque for Chopin Recital, 1972. Address: 21 rue Ampre, Paris 17, France.

PERLIS, Vivian, b. 26 Apr. 1928. Brooklyn, NY, USA. Historian; Lecturer; Harpist. Educ: BMus, MMus, Univ. of Mich. m. Dr. Sanford J. Perlis, 3 c. Career: Historian, specializing in Am. music; Lectr. in Am. Studies, Yale Univ.; Snr. Rsch. Assoc., Yale Schl. in Music; Dir. of Oral Hist. Project, Am. Music. Publs: Charles Ives Remembered: An Oral History, 1974; An Ives Celebration, 1977 (Co-Ed.); Two Men for Modern Music, ISAM monograph No. 9, 1978. Contbr. to: Notes; Musical An.; NY Times. Hons. incl: Award, Nat. Inst. of Arts & Letters, 1971; Kinkeldey Book Award, Am. Musicol. Soc., 1975; Conn. Book Publrs. Award. Address: 139 Goodhill Rd., Weston, CT 06883, USA.

PERLMAN, Itzhak, b. 31 Aug. 1945, Tel-Aviv, Israel. Violinist. Educ: Tel-Aviv Acad. of Music; Juilliard Schl., USA; studied w. Ivan Galamian & Dorothy De Lay. Career: radio recitals when aged 10; recital, Carnegie Hall, 1963; apps. w. major Am. orchs., 1964-; regular tours in Europe & apps. w. European orchs., 1966-; 1st app. in UK. w. LSO, 1968; participant in Israel Fest. & S Bank Summer Concerts, London, 1968, 69. 16.

PERNEL, Orrea, b. July 1906, St. Mary's Platt, Kent, UK. Violinist. Educ: studied w. Mme. Adila Fachiri, London; studied w. Edouard Naduad, Paris Conserv., France. Debut: Wigmore Hall, 1928. Career: concert tours, Europe & USA; many solo apps. w. orchs., Europe & USA, 1943-68; Tchr., Smith Coll., Northampton, Mass., & Bennington Coll., Vt., (for 23 yrs.), both USA. Mbr., ISM. Recip. 1st Prize, Paris, Conserv., 1924. Hobby: Gardening. Address: Townsend. 102 West St., Hartland, Bideford, N Devon EX39 6BQ, UK. 5.

PERNES, Thomas, b. 25 Feb. 1956, Vienna, Austria. Composer. Educ: Hochschule für Musik, Vienna (piano w. Bruno Seidlhofer & Alexander Jenner, comp. w. Alfred Uhl); Dip., comp., ibid., 1976; further studies w. Firedrich Chera & Roman Haubenstock- Ramati. Debut: Steirischer Herbst, 1976. Career: Comps. perf. WDR Cologne & Vienna, by H Schiff, 1976; by Ensemble Kontrapunckte, Franz Schubert Quartet & René Staar, 1977-78; perfs. Paris, Vienna, The Hague, Radio Hilversum. Comps: Reflexionen for cello; 2 str. Quartets; Zyklus for violin; Petits Jeux Cristallins for string orch. 7 6 concertant violins; Variations for piano; Partita for cello; Porträt II for chamber ensemble; Choral for baritone & chamber ensemble; Concerto for chamber orch. mbr. prol. socs. Hons. incl: Würdigungspreis des Bundesministeriums für Wissenschaft und Forschung; 1976; Staatsstipendium fur Kompositon, 1977. Hobbies: Music; Cooking; Sports. Address: Laxenburgerstr. 4913/1/, 1100 Vienna, Austria.

PERNYE, András, b. 19 Nov. 1928, Budapest, Hungary. Musicologist. Educ: Musicol. Dip., 1958. m. Andrea Ernst, 1 d. Career: Broadcasting, 1955-; TV apps., 1958-; Music Critic of the daily paper Magyar Nemzet, 1959-76; Asst. Ed., Editio Muica, Budapest, 1960-63; Prof., Acad. of Music, 1965-; Ldr. of A Sem. for the Hist. of Jazz on the Radio, 1962-69. Publs: (books) Puccini, 1959; History of German Music up to 1750, 1964; Textbook to the pantomime Mario & the Magician by Thomas Mann, music by István Láng, world premiere, Budapest, 1964; Jazz, 1964, 2nd end., 1966; Alban Berg, 1967; Seven essays on Music, 1973; Performing Art & Musical Language, 1974; Musica per la tastiera (Ed.); Italian Keyboard Music from the 16th & 17th Centuries, Vol. I, 1977; (studies) approx. 50 essays & mag. articles, e.g. Alban Berg & die Zahlen, Studia Musicalogica, 1967; Ferenc Szabo, 1964. Mbrships; Hungarian Musicians Corp.; Inst. for Philos.; Liszt Soc. Hons: Erkel Prize, 1975. Hobbies: Paleontology. Address: Madách Imre ut 2-6, 1075, Budapest, Hungary.

PERPER, James Douglas, b. 18 Dec. 1943, Ft. Lauderdale, Fla., USA. Low Brass Specialist (Tuba Major); Band & Choral Director. Educ: BSc (Educ.) 1971, MEd., 1974, Memphis State Univ. m. Delynn Carol Frazier, 1s. Career: 3 Educl. TV progs., Brass Instruction, Memphis; Band & Choral Dir., Public Schls., 9 yrs. Contbr. to: School Musician. Mbrships: MENC; NEA; TEA; WTVA; WTSBOA; TBA; NBA; Tri-M. Hons: Modern Music Masters Int. Sec. Hobby: Racquetball. Address: 325 Center St., Apt. 309, Collierville, TN 38017, USA.

PERRET, André, b. 6 Oct. 19 20, Geneva, Switz. Pianist; Piano Teacher. Educ: Geneva Conserv.; Paris Conserv.; pvte study w. Dinu Lipatti. m. Ursula Gutzwiller., Career: Soloist at recitals & w. major orchs. in most European countries; currently Piano Tchr., Geneva Conserv. Hons. incl: Virtuosity Prize, Geneva, 1938; 1st Prize, Paris Conserv. 1940; 1st Prize for Piano, Geneva Music Competitions, 1941; Judge at num. int. piano competitions. Address: 11 rue Gautier, 1201 Geneva, Switz.

PERRET, Claudine, b. 17 July 1935, les Brenets, Switzerland. Singer. Educ: Dip., Swiss Soc. for Music Teaching. 1959; Examination in song, oratorio & opera, Vienna Acad. of Music, 1964. Career: Num. apps. in oratorios & concertos in Europe; Var. operatic roles inclng. Azucena (Il Trovatore-Verdi), Sextus (Julius Caesar - Handel), The Medium (Menotti), Magdelena (Rigoletto -Verdi). Recordings: Magnificat (Bach); Mass in B Minor (Bach); Selva Morale (Monteverdi); De Profundis (De Lalande). Recip. 1st Prize, Swiss Competition for Young Musicians, 1964. Hobbies: Walking w. dog; Mtn. climbing. Address:Ave. du Leman 43, 1005 Lausanne, Switz.

PERRET, Denise, b. 19 Oct. 1942, Neuchatel, Switzerland. Musicologist. Educ: Lic. es Lettres (ethnol. & musicol.); Cert. in Lute, Conserv. of Nauchatel; Cert. in Hist. of Music, Inst.of Musicol., Sorbonne. Career incl: Specialist in lute music of 15th, 16th & 17th Centuries; In charge of Collection of Musical Instruments, Mus. of Ethnography, Neuchatel; Cataloguer, ibid. Contbr. to:Le Broges; Bulletin des Journes de Musique Ancienne; Bulletin of Conserv. of Neuchatel. Early Music; Il Fronimo; Newsletters. Mbrships: Int. & Swiss Musicol. Socs.; Assn. of Int. Musical Libns.; UNESCO agcies. Mgmt: Journees Int. de Musique Ancienne, Neuchatel. Hobbies: Art; Painting; Travel; Music. Address: Rue des Tunnels 1, 2006 Neuchatel, Switzerland.

PERRETTI, Claudine, b. 8 June 1934, Lausanne, Switzerland. Pianist. Educ: Degrees in Musicol. & Aesthetics; Piano Dip., Nat. Conserv. of Music, Paris, France. Career: Concerts in Europe, the E, Latin Am., Aust., N Africa, Can. Recordings: Recital of Marcello, Scarlatti, Chopin, Debussy, Pegase Records. Contbr. to: French Letters; Concert Guide; Paris Wk. Mbr. Assn. of Swiss Musicians. Hons: 1st Prize, Musical Aesthetics, Nat. Conserv., Paris, 1957; Prize, Nat. Competition for Swiss Musicians, 1958; Prize, Int. Piano Competition, Bilbao, Spain, 1961. Hobbies: Lit.; Dancing; Theatre; Cinema. Mgmt: Yves Dandelot - Salle Pleyel, Paris, France. Address: Ave. Mousquines 12, 1005 Lausanne, Switz. 3.

PERRIN, Jean-Charles, b. 17 Sept. 1920, Lausanne, Switz. Pianist; Professor of Music; Composer. Educ: BA., Univ. of Lausanne; Dip. in Piano Virtuosity, Conserv. of Lausanne. Career: Prof., Conserv. of Lausanne & Conserv. of Sion; Music Critic, Gazette de Lausanne. Compositions incl: 2 Symph. Movement; Hecatombre á Diane; Ouverture bréve pour orch.; 5 Sonatas for piano, violin, cello, flute & horn; Wind Quartet; Partita for strs.; Mass for soloist, choir & orch. Hons. incl: Laureat, Councours of Musical Perf., Geneva. Address: 6 Ave. du Leman, Lausanne, Switz.

PERRIN, Robert Henry, b. 17 Aug. 1924, Tacoma, Wash., USA. Administrator in International Business Machines; Amateur Violinist, Violist, Musicologist. Educ: studied violin & viola from age 6; BA (music), 1948, MA (musicol.), 1953, Univ. of Wash.; studied Old French & Old Provencal resulting in thesis on poetry & music of troubadours (MA), m. Lorna Storgaard (dec.), 1 d. Contbr. to: Jrnl. of Am. Musicol. Soc.; Soc. for Ethnomusicol. Hobbies: Chmbr. music; Translations of mediaevel Romance plays, poems, treaties. Address: 295 Clinton Ave., Brooklyn, NY 11205, USA.

PERRIS, Arnold B, b. Cleveland, Ohio, USA. Music Historian; Ethnomusicologist. Educ: BA, MA, Case-Western Reserve Univ.; PhD, Northwestern Univ. m. Norma Hilyard. Career: Music Fac., Ohio Univ., Mich. State Univ.; Case-Western Reserve Univ.; Ed. & Educl. Dir., Summy-Bichard Co., 1952-62; Author & Narrator, radio series on music, Cleveland, St. Louis, 1971-; Vis. Lectr. in Music, Univ. of Singapore & Min. of Educ., Repub. of Singapore, 1975-76. Author; An Introduction to Symphonic Music, 1975. Contbr. to: Jrnl. of Soc. of Ethnuomusicol.;Musical Am. Mbrships. incl: Pres., St. Louis Chmbr. Orch. & Chorus, 1974-; MENC; Am. Musicol. Soc. Address: Fine Arts Dept., Univ. of Mo., St. Louis, MO 63121, USA.

PERRY, Douglas Arthur, b. 20 Apr. 1953, West Bromwich, UK. Musician (tuba). Educ: Royal Acad. of Music; LRAM. m. Susan Elizabeth King. Career: freelance tuba player w. var. Orchs.; Tuba, Bergen Symph. Orch., Norway, 1973-74. Hobbies: Cooking; Driving; Brewing. Address: 55 Birmingham Rd., Kidderminister, Worcs., UK.

PERRY, Janet, b. 27 Dec. 1947, Minneapolis, Minn., USA. Opera Singer. Educ: BA, Curtis Inst. of Music. m. Alexander Malta, 1 c. CareerZ: apps. in Munich, Hamburg, Vienna, Salzburg Fest., Cologne, Zürich. num. opera & operetta films for German TV. Mgmt: Harrison/Parrott Ltd., 22 Hillgate St., London W8 7SR, UK. Address: c/o Mgmt.

PERRY, Margaret Anne, b. 20 Dec. 1954, Croydon, Surrey, UK., Opera Singer; Recitalist. Educ: GSM, 3 yrs.; AGSM; postdip. opera studied under Vilem Tausky, Continued operatic studied, Nat. Opera Studio. Debut: Papagena (Magic Flute), Kent Opera, 1980. Career: apps. w. Kent Opera, Engl. Opera Group etc., & at Cambridge, GSM, Convent Garden, Aldeburgh, Barbican etc.; roles incl. Susanna (Marriga of Figaro), Micaela (Carmen), Monica (The Medium) & Tytania (Midsummer Night's Dream); concerts oratorios, recital throughout UK. Mbrships: ISM; British Equity. Hons: Gregory Hast Silver Cup for Singing, 1976; Worshipful Co. of Musicians Silver Medal, 1977; Lady Mayoress Prize, 1978; Ricordi prize for Opera, 1978, Stanley Thomas Johnson Fndn. Schlrship. Hobbies: Reading; Eating Out; Listening to Music. Address: 50 Lodge Rd., W Croydon, Surrey, CRO 2PE, UK.

PERRY, Marvin Chapman, II, b. 12 Feb. 1948, Birminghma, Ala., USA. Principal Trumpet Player; Trumpet Instructor. Educ: BMus, Eastman Schl. of Music, 1970; Catholic Univ. of Am., 1973; MMus Educ., Univ. of Montevallo, Ala., 1975. M. Anne Katherine Finne, 1 s, 1 d. Career: Soloist, Arlington Symph. of Arlington, Va., Baroque Arts Chmbr. Orch., Wash. DC, the US Army Band (Pershing's Own) Wash., DC; Trumpeter, Birmingham (Ala.) Symph. Orch., Rochester Phil., & chmbr. music for Young Audiences, Inc.; Vis. Lectr. of Music, Ind. Univ., Bloomington, Ind., 1978-79; Prin. Trumpet, Indpls. Symph. Orch., 1975-; Trumpet Instructor, Butler Univ., 1976- Recordings w. Eastman Wind Ensemble & Eastman Brass Ensemble. Mbr., Int. Trumpet Guild. Hobbies: Family; Photography; Canoeing. Address: 3377 E 62nd St., Indpls., IN 46220, USA.

PERRY, Zenobia Powell, b. 3 Oct. 1914, Boley, Okla., USA. Composer; Pianist. Educ: BS, Tuskegee Inst., Ala., 1938; MA, Northern Colo. Univ., Greeley. 1945; MA, Wyo. Univ., 1954; studied piano w. R Nathaniel Dett, Alan Willman & Gunnar Johansen, comp. w. Charles Jones, Alan Willman & Daurius Milhaud. m. James Roger Perry (div.), 1 d. Comps: Four Mynymns for Three Players (str. quartet no. 2); Narrative for Speaker, Flute & Piano; Threnody-a Song Cycle for soprano & piano. Mbrships. incl: Mu Phi Epsilon; OH Tchrs. of Theory & Comp.; Dayton Chmbr. Music Soc. Recip. Cert. of Award (as judge of annual Scholalstic Music Comp. Contest), Akron Jr. Chmbr. of Comm., 1969. Hobbies: Growing roses; Designing gowns. Address: 1267 E urner Pl., Wilberforce, OH 45384, USA.

PERSICHETTI, Vincent, b. 6 June 1915, Phila., Pa., USA. Composer. Educ: BM, Combs Conserv.; Dip. in Conducting, Curtis Inst.; Mus D, Phila. Conserv. m. Dorothea Persichetti, 2 children. Career: Comp. Dept., Juilliard Schl. of Music, NYC,

1947-; Dir. of Publs., Elkan-Vogel Co., 1952-. Comps: 9 symph.; 4 string quartets: 11 piano sonatas; 10 band works; misc. chmbr. & choral works; song cycles. Recordings: over 50. Publs: 20th Century Harmony, 1961. Contbr. to: Mod. Music; Notes; Musical Quarterly; etc. Mbr., VP, Nat. Inst. Arts & Letters. sev. awards & fellowships. Hobby: Sculpture. Address: Hillhouse, Wise Mill Rd., Philadelphia, PA 19128, USA.

PERTHEN, Avis Ann, b. 31 May 1951, Rainham, Essex, UK. Musician (cello). Educ: Guildhall Schl. of Music & Drama; AGSM (Tchr. & Performer). m. Charles Fullbrook. Career: Mbr., Locrian String Quartet, Capicchioni Ensemble, freelance musician. Mbrship: Inc. Soc. of Musicians. Hons: Merchant Taylor's Schlrship. & Gregory Saltzman Schlrship. 1971; Edith Pleeth Mem. Prize, 1972. Hobbies: Squash; Tennis; Bridge; Swimming; Reading; Driving. Address: 5 Maxwelton Close, Mill Hill, London NW7 3NB, UK.

PERTIS, Zsuzsa, b. 21 May 1943, Budapest, Hungary. Pianist; Harpsichordist. Educ: Dip., Music Acad., Budapest, 1966; Dip., Music Acad., Vienna, 1969. m. Pál Kelemen, 1s. Debut: 2nd Prize, Int. Competition for Harpsichord, Brugge, 1968; (1st Prize not awarded). Career: concerts, Budapest, Vienna, Salzburg, Berlin, Rome, Paris, NYC & Vancouver; Harpsichordist, Franz Liszt Chmbr. Orch.; Adj., Music Acad., Budapest. Recordings: 11 Haydn sonatas for harpsichord; harpsichord music of Bull, Farnaby, Froberger, Louis Couperin, played on old instrument; var. recordings inclng. works by Bach w. Franz Liszt Chmbr. Orch. Publs: Ed., var. baroque keyboard works. Mbrships: Assn. of Hungarian Musician; Nat. Committee, CIM, SIMC & SIEM. Mgmt: Interkoncert, Budapest, Hungary. Address: Mandula u. 25, 1025 Budapest, Hungary. 29.

PERZ, Miroslaw, b. 25 Jan. 1933, Zielonagora, Poland. Musicologist; Choir Conductor. Educ: Dr. of Musicol., Univ. of Warsaw; Study w. Adolf Chybinski, Poznan Univ., Kieronim Feicht, Warsaw; Organ Dip., High Schl. of Music, Warsaw, 1959; Study of composition w. Tadeusz Szeligowski; Conducting w. Bohdan Wodiczko. m. Career: Cond., Chmbr. Choir, Nat. Phil., Warsaw, 1957-59; Cond., Warsaw Musical Soc. Choir, 1962-63; Cond., Warsaw Univ. Choir, 1963-68, 1972; Asst.-Docent, Warsaw Univ. Inst. of Musicol., 1957-; Dir., Chair of Hist. of Polish Music Publs. Monographs, contbns to books, & encys., transcriptions. Contbr. to profl. jrnls. Mbrships: IMS; Musicol. Sect., Polish Composers Assn.; Vereiniging voor Nederlandse Muziekgeschiedenis; Antiquage Musical Italicae Studiosi. Address: Grojecka 41 m 17, PL 02 031 Warsaw, Poland, 14.

PESCHEK, James, b. 17 May 1925, Brampton, Cambs., UK. Schoolmaster; Assistant Music Mast. Educ: King's Schl., Canterbury (Music scholar); MA, MusB, King's Coll., Cambridge (Choral); RAM, 1949-51; ARAM; LRAM; ARCO. m. June Elizabeth Anne Bourne, 1 s., 1 d. Career: Asst. Dir. of Music, Uppingham Schl., 1960-69; Dir. of Music, Monkton Combe Schl., 1960-69; Dir. of Music, Uppingham Schl., 1969-78; Assoc. Cond., Fndn. Mbr., Linden Singers; Fndr., Uppingham Choral Soc., 1959; Choirmaster, Bath Cantata Group, 1964-69; Judge, Koestler Awards for Music Perf. in Prisons, 1973-; Examiner, Assoc. Bd., Royal Schls. of Music, 1976-. Mbrships: Coun., ISM, -1981; Pres., Music Masters Assn., 1972-73. Hons: John Steward of Rannoch Scholarship in Sacred Music (Cambridge), 1949. Address: 62 Stockerston Rd., Uppingham, Rutland, Leics., 6E15 9UD, UK.

PESEK, Libor, b. 22 June 1933, Prague, Czechoslovakia. Conductor. Educ: Grad. Acad. of Musical Arts, Prague, 1966. m. Jana Peskova, 1 s. Career: Fndr., Prague Harmony, 1959: Cond., N. Bohemian Symph. Orch. 1963-69; Fndr., The Sebastian Orch., Prague, 1965; Cond., State Chmbr. Orch., Czechoslovakia, & Frysk Orkest, Netherlands, 1969; Conctradt w. Overyssels Phil. Orkest, Netherlands; Guest Cond., Prague, Paris, Naples, Brussels, Berlin, Amsterdam, Vienna, Warsaw, Basel, Lisbon, etc.; Regular Guest on Prague TV & radio. Recordings incl: Works by Mozart; compositions for orch. by Pavel Vejvanovsky; Concerts for trumpet & orch. by Vivaldi, Telemann & Haydn; Works by Stravinsky & Kluszk; Suite for Winds by Pavel Blatny; 4th Symph. by Zedenek Lukas. Mbr., Perf. Artists St. t., Union of Czechoslovak Comps., 1960-69. Recip., Grand Priz du Disque, 1968. Mgmt: Pragokoncert. Address: Mongolska 5, 160 00 Prague 6, Czechoslovakia.

PESKO, Zoltan, b. 15 Feb. 1937, Budapest, Hungary. Composer; Conductor. Educ: Dip., Liszt Ferenc Music Acad., Budapest, 1962; Master Courses, Italy & Switz., 1963-65. Debut: as Comp. & Cond., Hungarian TV, 1960. Career: Work w. Hungarian TV, 1960-63; Cond., Deutsche Oper, W Berlin, 1969-73; Perf. at Teatro alla Scala, 1970; Chief Cond., Teatro

Communale, Bologna, Italy, 1974-76, Teatro La Fenice, Venice, 1976-77; Radiotelevisione Italiana Milan, 1978-. Comps: Tensions (Str. Quartet), 1967; Trasformazioni, 1968: Bildnis einer Heligen (Soprano, Children's Choir & Chmbr. ensemble), 1969; Jelek, 1974. Var. recordings. Contbr. to: Melos. Hons: Prize for Comp.; Acad. di S. Cecilia, Rome, Italy, 1966; Premio Discografica (for recording debut as Cond.) Italian Critics, 1973. Address: Radiotelevisione Milano, Milan, Italy.

PETERS, Dale Hugh, b. 8 Mar. 1931, Ft. Worth, Tex., USA. Professor; Organist; Harpsichordist. Educ: BM, BA, N. Tex. State, Univ. of Ill. & Univ. of Copenhagen, Denmark. m. Juanita Teal Peters, 2 s. Career: Organ & Harpsichord Recitals in US, Germany & Denmark. Mbr., AGO. Recip. 1st Prize, AGO Young Artists Competition, Nat. Biennal, 1954. Address: 2818 Glenwood, Denton, TX 76201, USA.

PETERS, Geroge David, b. 30 Aug. 1942, Evansville, Ind., USA. Music Educator; Composer; Performer on Trombone. Educ: B Mus Ed. Univ. of Evansville, Ind.; MSc, Univ. of Ill.; D Ed, ibid. m. Jean G. Peters, 2 children. Career: currently Dir. of Computer-Assisted Instruction in Music Educ., Univ. of Ill. Comps: Neumes Triebend; Dactylsung; Reflectus No. 4; Sight Reading Method for Snare Drum; Newburgh Interludes (Joseph Boonin, 1976); 14 Etudes for Trombone (Joseph Boonin, 1976); Anapestic Distortions. Recordings. Graduate Trombone Quartet, Vol. 1. Univ. Brass Recordings Series. Contbr. to: The Instrumentalist. Mbrships: MENC; CBDNA; ADCIS: NCCBMI; Aera; Int. Trombone Assn.; Phi Mu Alpha. Recip. of sev. awards. Address: Schl. of Music, Univ. of Illinois, Urbana, IL 61801, USA.

PETERS, Gordon Benes. b. 4 Jan. 1931, Oak Pk., Ill., USA. Conductor; Percussionist. Educ: BME, Master in Music Theory & Conducting. Eastman Schl. of Music; studied conducting w. Pierre Monteux. m. Catherine Kemper Peters, 2 d. Career incl: US Mil. Acad. Band, W Point, 1950-53; Grant Pk. Symph., Chgo., Ill., 1955-58; Rochester Phil. Orch., 1955-59; Chgo. Symph. Orch., 1959-; Cond., Elmhurst Symph., 1963-68, Civic Orch. of Chgo., 1966- (also Admnstr.). Comps. Swords of Moda-Ling. Recordings: w. Marimba Mastgers (Eastman Schl.of Music); w. Chgo. Symph. as percussionist. Publs: The Drummer; Man, A treatise on Percussion; Ed., Percussion Dept., The Instrumentalist, 5 yrs. Mbrships: Am. Symph. Orch. League; Percussive Acts Soc. Hobbies: Antiquing; Driftwood; Reading; Gardening. Address: 1337 Ashland Ave., Wilmette, IL, USA.

PETERS, Johanna McLennan, b. Glasgow, Scotland, UK. Opera Singer; Professor of Singing; Head of Opera Studies. Educ: Nat. Schl. of Opera, London. Debut: Nozze di Figaro, Glyndebourne, 1959. Career: Royal Opera House, Convent Garden, Sadler's Wells Opera, Welsh Nat. Opera, Scottish Opera, Glyndebourne Fest. Opera, English Opera Group, Phoenix Opera, D'Oyly Carte; Prof. of Singing, GSM; Hd. of Opera Studies, ibid,. Recordings: Albert Herring; Christopher Columbus. Hobbies: Travel; Archaeology; Cooking. Mgmt: Music Int. Address: 59 Marlbourgh Place, London, NW8, UK.

PETERS, Juanita Teal, b. 4 Aug. 1929, Dallas, Tex., USA. Concert Singer; Voice Teacher. Educ: BM, N Tex. State Univ.; Grad. study, Univ. of Minn, RAM, London. m. Dale Peters, 2 s. Debut: Dallas Symph., 1954. Career: Soloist, Dallas Symph., 5 times, LPO, Corpus Christi Symph., Ft. Worth Opera Assn., Wichita Falls Symph.; Num. concerts in USA; Mbr., Music Fac., SE Okla. State Univ. Hons: G B Dealey Award, Dallas Symph., 1954; Wallace Award, Wichita Falls Symph., 1959, '59. Address: 2818 Glenwood, Denton, TX 76201, USA.

PETERS, Roberta, b. 4 May 1930, NYC, USA. Operatic Soprano. Educ: Litt D, Elmira Coll., 1967; Mus D, Utica Coll., 1968. m. Bertram Fields, 2 s. Debut: Zerlina, Don Giovanni, Met. Opera, 1950. Career: many radio & TV broadcasts; in film Tonight We Sing; apps. at Royal Opera House, Convent Gdn., summers 1950-60, Cinn. Opera, summers, 1952-53, 58, Vienna State Opera, 1963, Salzburg Fest., 1963, 64, etc.; concert tours, USA, USSR, Scandinavia, Israel. Has recorded sev. opera. Author: Debut at Met. Hons. incl: Woman of Yr., Fedn. of Women's Clubs. Mgmt: S Hurok, 730 Fifth Ave., NY, NY 10022, USA. 2.

PETERS, Ursula M, b. 10 Feb. 1920, Racine, Wis., USA. Teacher (guitar, violin, piano, organ, voice). Educ: Wis. Coll. of Music, Racine (voice), 4 yrs.: Univ. of Wis. Coll. of Music; studied violin w. Mr. Gilam, 2 yrs. & piano w. Miss Gonsky & John E. Barnhart, 10 yrs. m. Allen Jesse Peters, 1 s., 1 d. Debut: Goodrich Concert Hall, Milwaukee, Admiral Hull, Dallas, Tex., etc. Career: apps. on WRJN, Racine, KGNC, Amarillo & WLS, St. Bonaventure; Goodrich Concert Hall, Milwaukee;

Organist, Our Mother of Mercy, Wellington. Recordings: Man, Land & Love, 1976. Contbr. to: Univ. Soc.; Staff Notes. Mbrships: Tex. Fedn. of Music Clubs; Nat. Fedn. of Music Clubs; VP, 2 yrs., Treas., 1 yr., Wellington Federated Music Club; NGPT (reporter, 5 yrs.) Am. Legion. Hobbies: Knitting; Writing fiction; Tennis, etc. Address: Rte. 1, Box 319, Wellington, TX 79095, USA. 1.

PETERSEN, Alf, b. 6 Feb. 1910, Copenhagen, Denmark. Cellist. Educ: Royal Music Conserv., Copenhagen. m. Edel Wamberg, 1 d., 1 s. Debut: 1936. Career: Fndr. & Mbr., The Chmbr. Quartet (Kammerkvartetten), 1934-43; Tchr., Royal Inst. for the Blind, Copenhagen, 1941-; Mbr., Copenhagen Phil. Orch., 1947 -48; Mbr., Denmark Radio Symph. Orch., 1948-; Tchr. of Cello, Royal Music Conserv., 1951- ; Mbr., Poul Birkelund Quartet, 1951-; Has given solo & chmbr. music concerts. Recordings: num. comps. by new Danish comps.; Mozart, Haydn. Kuhlau w. Poul Birkelund Quartet. Mbr., Soloist Soc. of 1921. Recip., Danish Gramophone Prize, 1957 & 1958. Hobby: Collecting art. Address: Bloustrod Alle 2, 3450 Allerod, Denmark.

PETERSEN, Judith Ann Hellenberg, b. 1 Feb. 1935, Mishawaka, Ind., USA. Educ: BS, MS, Juilliard Schl. of Music, NYC. m. James William Petersen, 1 s., 1 d. Career: Piano Tchr., Morningside Coll., Sioux City, Iowa, 1960-62, & Coñorodia Sr. Coll., Ft. Wayne, Ind., 1963-76; Huntington Coll., Ind., 1975-; Concordia Seminary, Ft. Wayne, Ind., 1977-; Soloist & chmbr. music recitals, Radio & TV performances in Midwest states; Dir. of Choirs & Instrumentalists, St. John Luth. Ch., Kendallville Ind. Mbrships: Ind. Fedn. of Mus. Clubs; Music Educators Book Soc.; Ind. MTA. Hobbies: Interior Decorating; Swimming; Golf; Cycling. Address: Meadow Ln., Kendallville, IN 46755, USA.

PETERSEN, Knud, b. 18 Mar. 1931, Copenhagen, Denmark. Musician, (Organ, Piano, Trumpet, Violin, Clarinet, Saxophone). Educ: Grad. Royal Acad. of Music, Copenhagen, 1954; Dips., 1963, 1964, 1965, Royal Acad. of Music, Stockholm, Sweden. Career: Musician, Norway, Netherlands, Denmark, Sweden, 1954-; Apps. in Sweden, 1966-; Finland, 1968, Israel, Iceland, 1973, Poland, 1975, Denmark, 1978. Arranger, var. works for choir. Recordings: Gunnar Thyrestam, Organ Concerto No. 10. Hobbies: Travel; Languages; History; Music. Address: 4 Valbovägen, 80370-Gälve, Sweden.

PETERSEN, Patricia Jeannette, b. 7 Oct. 1940, Bay City, Mich., USA. Musician (viola). Educ: BS (Med. Technol.-ASCP), Univ. of Colo., 1962; studied w. Horace Jones, ibid, 1956-60; & Martin Fischer, Brown Univ., 1967. m. Gary LeMarr Petersen, 1 s., 1 d. Career: RI Phil. Orch. 1971-; New Music Ensemble of Providence, performs contemp. music, 1973-74; Artist Int. Orch., 1977-. Mbrships: Henschel Club (VP, 1977-79); AFM, local 198; Am. Soc. of Psychoprophylaxis in Obstereic; CEA of RI, 1967-78; La Leche League (Regional Admnstr., 1976-, Area Co-Ordinator, 1973-76). Hobbies: Sewing; Gardening; Camping. Address: 610 Tower Hill Rd., N Kingstown, RI 02852, USA.

PETERSON, LeRoy Henry, b. 2 Sept. 1937, Regina, Sask., Can. Universiry Professor & Violinist in Residence. Educ: BA, Columbia Union Coll.; M Mus, Peabody Conserf. of Music; Artist Dip., ibid. m. Carol Mae Butler, 1 s., 1 d. Debut: Singapore, Malaya at age 13. Career incls: Soloist w. Singapore Symph., NSO, Balt. Symph., Peabody Orch., Worcester Symph., Indpls. Symph.; Concertmaster, Worcester Symph. Orch.; Concert tours, Europe, USA, Far E, Bermuda, Can.; Apps. on radio & TV; Tchr., Columbia Union Coll., Atlantic Union Coll., Pioneer Valley Acad., Andrews Univ. Recordings: 4 Strings & a Soul Evening Song. Mbr. MENC. Hon. incl: Melissa Tiller Mem. Prize, Peabody Conserv. of Music, 1964. Hobbies incl: Photography; Swimming. Address: 217 N Maplewood Dr., Berrien Springs, MI 49103, USA.

PETERSON, Oscar Emmanuel, b. 15 Aug. 1925, Montreal, Canada. Pianist. Educ: Studies w. Hungarian-born Classical pianist, Paul de Markey. Debut: Carnegie Hall, NYC, USA, 1950. Career: Annual global concert tours; N Am., British & European TV & radio apps. Comps: Hymn to Freedom; Hallelujah Time; The Canadiana Suite; num. jazz tunes. Publs: Oscar Peterson New Piano Solos, 1965; Jazz Exercises & Pieces, 1965. Contbr. to: Sound Magazine. Hons: Disting. Citizen Award, Comps. Soc. of Canada; LLD, Carlton Univ., Ottawa, Canada; Medal Disting. Servs. to the city of Toronto; Order of Canada. Hobbies: Fishing; Photography. Mgmt: Norman Ganz, 451 N Cannon Drive, Beverly Hills, Calif., USA. Address: 124 Eight St., Toronto, Ont. M8V 3C4, Canada.

PETERSON, Richard Trenholm, b. 30 Mar. 1934, San Francisco, Calif., USA. Associate Professor of Music; Head,

Department of Percussion. Educ: Trinity Coll., San Antonio, Tex.; San Francisco State Univ., Calif. m. Marilyn Ann Peterson, 1 s. Career incls: Concert Tours, Japan, Europe, Australia, Mexico, as Asst. Cond., Calif. Youth Symph.; Regular TV Apps. w. SFSU Percussion Ensemble & Foothill Percussion Ensemble; Lecture/Demonstrations, Perfs. (Timpanist) w. orchs.; Assoc. Prof. of Music, Hd., Dept. of Percussion, San Francisco State Univ. & Foothill Community Coll. Dist., Calif. Comps. incl: Duets I & II for Sn. Dr. & Timpani, 1975; Allegro for Timpani, 1974; Introduction & Movement for Percussion Ensemble; Overture & Incidental Music for the Trojan Women, 1977. Mbr., profl. orgs. Hons. incl: Janacek medal, Czech. Address: 883 Roble Dr., Sunnyvale, CA 94086, USA.

PETERSON, Wayne Turner, b. 3 Sept. 1937, Albert Lea, Minn, USA. Composer; Pianist. Educ: BA, Univ. of Minn., 1951; AM, ibid, 1953; PhD, 1960; Royal Acad. of Music, London, UK. m. Harriet Grace Christiansen, 4 s. Career: Instr., Univ. of Minn. Music Dept. 1955-59; Professor of Music San Fran. State Univ., 1961-. Recorded Compositions; Free Variations for Orchestra; Phantasmasoria. Publd. Compositions; Can Death Be Sleep (chorus); Earth, Sweet Earth; Psalm 56; Spring; Clusters & Fragments (string orch.); Metamorphoses (wind quintet). Hons: Fulbright Scholar, Royal Acad. of Music, 1953-54; Winner, State Centennial Compositions Contest for Free Variations for Orch., 1958; Ford Fndn. Commn.,1959; Paul Masson Inc. Comm. for ''Transformations'' (string quartet), 1974. Hobbies: Backpacking; Fishing; Sailing. Address: 343 Carvera Drive, Mill Valley, CA 94941, USA.

PETHEL, James, b. 24 Dec. 1936, Gainesville, Ga., USA. Professor of Music; Organist. Educ: BS, Carson-Newman Coll.; MA, Geo. Peabody Coll. m. Martha Pethel. 1 s., 1 d. Career: Prof. of music, Carson-Newman Coll, Comps: 59 works for organ, chorus, vocal solo. Mbrships. incl: AGO; Southeastern Comps League; ASCAP. Hobbies: Photography; Gardening. Address: Rte. 2, Jefferson City, TN 37760, USA.

PETIN, Nikola, b. 19 Dec. 1920, Krasnodar, USSR. Composer; Music Writer; Professor of Counterpoint. Educ: Belgrade Univ.; Musical Acad. of Belgrade; Studied w. N Boulanger, Paris, France. m. Magdalena Petin, 1 d. Debut: 1st Piano Comps. at age 13 yrs. Career: Prof. of Counterpoint, Acad. of Fine Arts, Novi Sad. Comps. incl: Over 60 Opus; Sonnet Cyclus for chmbr. orch.; The Contrasts, suite for string orch.; Piano & choir comps. Num. comps. recorded in Yugoslav Broadcasting Stns. Publs. incl: The Basic Techniques in Choir Arrangements, 1974. Contbr. to profl. mags. Mbr. num. profl. orgs. Hons. incl: Prize of Yugoslav Radio TV for Piano Music, 1971. Hobbies: Photography; Travel; Swimming; Rowing. Address: Mileticeva 8, 21000 Novi Sad, Yugosalvia.

PETIT, Francoise, b. 8 July 1925, Paris, France. Pianist Harpsichordist. Educ: 1st Prize of Hon., Conserv. Supérieur Paris; 1st Prize, Hist. of Music. Career: Concerts; Perfs. on ORTF, BBC, Radio Can., others. Recordings: Piano works of Roussel, Durey, Jolivet, Duphly harpsichord music. Ed., scores, music of Guillemain, Corrette, Balicourt, Duphly. Hons: Bablock Prize, 1957; Chevalier de l'Orde National du Mérite, France, 1972; 2 grads prix du disque. Hobby: Gardening. Address: 140 Boulevard Pereire, Paris 76017, France.

PETIT, Pierre, b. 21 Apr. 1922, France, Composer; Musical Director. Educ: Univ. of Paris (Sorbonne); Conserv. of Paris. Career: Hd. of Course, Conserv. of Paris, 1950; Dir. of Light Music, ORTF (French Radio & TV); 1960; Dir. of Light Musical Prods., ibid, 1964-70; Dir. of Chmbr. Music, 1979-64; Dir. of Musical Prods., ibid., 1964-70; Dir. of Chmbr. Music, 1970-; Dir.-Gen.; Ecole Normale de Musicque, Paris, 1963-; Music Critic, Parisien-Libéré. Compositions incl: Suite for 4 cellos, 1945; Zadig (ballet), 1948; Ciné-Bijou (ballet), 1952; Feu Rouge, Feu Vert, 1954; Concerto for piano & orch, 1956; Concerto for organ & orch., 1960; Furia Italiana, 1960; Concerto for 2 guitars & orchs., 1965. Mbrships: Gov. Coun., Conserv. of Paris. Hons: Off. of Arts & Lettres; Off., Ordre du Cédre du Liban; Premier Grand Prix, Rome, 1946. Publs: Verdi, 1957. Address: 2 rue de l'Amiral-Cloune, Paris 16e., France.

PETKOVIC, Dragiša, b. 17 July 1922, Smederevo, Yugoslavia. Composer; Conductor. Educ: BA, Acad. of Music, Belgrade. m. Ljiljana Petkovic, 1 s., 1 d. Debut: Cond., Youth Choir & Orch., Smederevo & Abrasevic Cultural & Arts Soc., Smederevo & Belgrade. Career: Apps. as cond. & comp. at concert halls in Belgrade & on Radio & TV; Cond., Jadinstvo Cultural & Arts Soc., Belgrade; Ed., Music Progs., Radio Belgrade's Foreign Lang. Prog. Comps. incl: Orchl. Symph. in Two Movements; Cantata for solo baritone, choir & orch.; Instrumental & Vocal comps. Num. recordings. Contbr. to Zvuk

Music Review, Saranjevo. Mbr. Assn. of Comps. of Serbia. Recip. num. awards. Hobby: Chess. Address: Palmoticeva 6, 11, 000 Belgrade, Yugoslavia.

PETRA-BASACOPOL, Carmen, b. 5 Sept. 1929, Sibiu, Romania. Composer; Professor of Composition. Educ: BA (Phil.) DMus, Sorbonne, Paris. m. Alexandru Basacopol, 1 s. Career: Prof. of Comp., Music Aca., Buhcarest; radio & TV apps. Comps. incl: Ronde pour piano, op. 2, 1949; Suite for flute & piano, op. 3, 1950; 6 préludes for harp, op. 14, no. 2, 1960; Sonata for flute & harp, op. 16, no. 2, 1960; Hommage á la vie, for baritone & orch., op. 22, 1963. Publs: L'originalité de la musique roumaine á travers les oeuvres d'Enesco, Joro et Constantinesco, 1978. Contbr. to: Musica. Mbrships: Union des Comps. de la R. S. de Roumaine. SACEM. Hons: Dip. d'honneur du Concours Int. de Comp., Mannheim-Ludwig-shafen, 1961; Prize of Comps. Union, 1974. Hobbies: Reading. Address: 70668 Bucharest 6, Strada Antim No. 40, Romania.

PETRASSI, Goffredo, b. 16 July 1904, Zagarolo, Rome, Italy. Composer. Educ: Dips. in Composition & Organ. m. Rosetta Acerbi, 1 d. Career: Prof., St. Cecelia Conserv., Rome, & St. Cecilia Acad., ibid. Compositions incl: Lyric works; Ballets; Symphonic works; Vocal & instrumental chmbr. music; Symphonic-choral music. Recordings: Coro di Morti; Recreation Concertante; 5 Concerti; Noche Oscura; Serenata; var. quartets, trios, caprices, etc. Recip: Hon. Doctorte, Univ. of Bologna. Address: Via Ferdinando di Savola 3, 00196 Rome, Italy.

PETRESCU, Dinu Mircea Cristian, b. 22 Dec. 1939, Bucharest, Romania. Composer; Conductor; Musicologist. Educ: Grad., Cond. Dept., High Schl. of Music Ciprian Porumbescu, 1964; study w. Tiberiu Olah, ibid, 1964; w. Pierre Schaeffer, Groupe de la Recherche, ORTF, Paris, 1969; Grad., Int. Inst. of Music, Darmastadt, German Fed. Repub., 1972-78. w. Henekis, Stockhauser. m. Hrisanta Petrescu. Career: Musical Jrnl. Romanian Radio & TV, 1975; Musical Adviser, George Enescu Phil. Orch., Bucharest, 1978-; Co-Fndr., 1st electronic music studio in Romania at the High Schl. of Music. Comps. recorded & publd. incl: Symphonia Brevis (Orch.); From Heart, oratorio for voices & magnetic tape; Cosmophony I, II & III; Singing Space I-V Hymn, for voices, childrens voices, wind instruments, percussion, electronic modultions, magnetic tape, light organ, synthesis equipment; Space Study I, II (electronic); Impulses, for programmed piano & generators, Continuum I, II, for voices, percussion, electronic modulation, synthesis equipment; Stage & film music. Contbr. to: Comtemporanul; Muzica. Hons: Medal, 25th Anniversary of the Repub. Price of the Romanian Composers' Union, 1979; Scholarshipa. Address: Str. Stefan Mihăleanu nr. 27, sector 3, 73101 Bucharest, Romania.

PETRESCU, Emilia, b. 12 May 1925, Bucarest, Romania. Vocal Concert Soloist. Educ: Conserv. of Music, Bucarest. m. Mircea Ionescu, 2 children Debut: 1947. Career: Apps., USSR, Europe, USA; Permanent Radio-TV collaborator. Recordings: 15 LP's (Romania), 6 LP's (France). Mbrships: Hon. Mbr., Baldwin Wallace Inst., Cleveland, Ohio; Hon. Mbr., ''Heinrich Schutz'' Soc., Kassel, German Fed. Repub. Hons: Merited Artist of Romania; Golden Ducate of Gottingen, 1973; Hon. Citizen of Ruse-Bulgaria. Hobbies: Minerals; Old Folklore Art; Mountain Climbing. Mgmt: ARIA Bucarest; Margit Drissen, Mainz, German Fed. Repub. Address: Str. Cargea Voda 2, ap. 2, Sector 1, 71149 Bucharest, Romania.

PETRI, Michala, b. 7 July 1958, Copenhagen, Denmark. Recorder Player. Educ: Studied w. Prof. Ferdinand Conrad, Staatliche Hochschule für Musik & Theater, Hannover, Germany. Debut: Danish Radio, 1964. Career: App. as Soloist w. Orch., Tivoli Copenhagen, 1969; Over 400 concerts in Denmark, Norway, Sweden, Germany, Switz., Belgium, Finland, Italy, Iceland, UK: Many fests.; TV & Radio perfs. in these countries. Recordings incl: Music by Henning Christiansen, Berio, Handel, Telemann, van Eyck; Sammartini, Concerto; Vivaldi, Concerto. Hons: Jacob Gade prize, 1969 & 75; Critics Prize of Honour, 1976; Nording Radio Prize, 1977. Address: Noddehegnet 30, 34, 80 Fredensborg, Denmark.

PETRIĆ, Ivo, b. 16 June 1931, Ljubljana, Yugoslavia. Composer; Conductor. Educ: Comp. & cond., Acad. of Music, Ljubljana. Career: Ed.-in-chief, Edicije DSS, Ljubljana. Comps. incl: 3 symphonies; concertos for var. instruments & orch.; sonatas for oboe, bassoon, horn w. piano; orchl. music; instrumental music; sonata for solo violin. Mbr. Assn. of Solovene Comps. (sec.). Hons: 1st prize, Wieniawski Int. Comp. competition, for violin solo (1975); Sollvenian State prize for artists, 1971; Ljubljana prize for artists, 1977. Address: Bilecanska 4, 61000 Ljubljana, Yugoslavia.

PETRIC, Joseph, b. 8 Oct. 1952, Guelph, Ont., Can. Concert Free-bass Accordist; Teacher; Musicologist. Educ: BMus, Queen's Univ., Kingston, Ont., 1975; MA (musicol.), 1977; pvte. study in perf. w. Joseph Marcello (Toronto) & Hugo Noth, Hochschule für Musik, Trossingen, German Fed. Repub., 1977. m. Penelope Marguerite Blake. Career: perfs. in Can., USA. & Germany; premieres of many solo & chmbr. works for accordion; recordings & broadcasts for CBC, 1975-78, '80; num commission for perf. written by Daniel Foley, Hans Kore Jacobsen, M. Mozetich, etc.; prog. of studies in accordion, Royal Hamilton Coll. of Music & Western Conserv. of Music, Ont., 1979. Comps: num arr. of works by Sor Mozart, Roncalli, Beethoven, etc. Recordings; works by Scarlatti, BAch, Haydn & Beethoven. Publs incl: 5 Scarlatti Sonatas, arr. for Free-bass Accordion, 1979. Contbr. to Can. Music Eductors Jrnl.; Ency. of Music in Can., 1978-79. recip. var. scholarships. Address: 50 Warfield Dr., Willodale, Ont. M2J 3S3, Can.

PETRILLO, Clement C, b. 27 Sept. 1914, Philadelphia, Pa., USA. Concert Pianist; College Professor. Educ: B Mus., M Mus, Artist Dip., Tchrs. Cert., Phila. Musical Acad. m. Ida Dussich, 1946, 1 d. Career incl: Chapt., US Army, Italy & N Africa, 1942-46; Lt. Col., AUS, ret'd.; Off. in restoration & rebldng. of La Scala Opera, Milan, 1945-46; Fac., Phila. Musical Acad., 1955-; Prof. of Piano, ibid, 1957-; Chmn., Piano Dept., 1967-70; Coordinator, Applied Div., 1979-; Coordinator, Musicianship Div., 1973-; Coord., Musical studies, 1974-; Dean of the Coll., 1975-. Contbr. to: Opera News: Am. Music Tchr. Mbrships: Past Pres., Pa. Music Tchrs. Assn.; Coll. of Music Soc.; AAUP. Hons. incl: Bronze Star Medal, 1945; Kt., Order of the Crown of Italy, 1945; Kt. Order of Saint' Agatha, Repub. of San Marino, 1945; Kt. Order of San Maurizio e Lazzaro, House of Savoy, 1946; Bronze Medallions, La Scala Opera, Milan & Maestro Arturo Toscanini, 1946; Tchr. of the Yr. Award, Pa. Music Tchrs. Assn., 1971; Outstanding Educator of Am., 1973, 75. Hobbies: Reading; Fishing; Golf. Address: 22 Edgewood Dr., Cherry Hill, NJ 08003, USA.

PETROBELLI, Pierluigi, b. 18 Oct. 1932, Padua, Italy. Musicologist. Educ: Laurea in Letttere, Univ. of Rome, 1957; MFA, Princeton Univ., 1961; studied comp. w. Arrigo Pedrollo, 1952-66. Career: Libn.-Archivist, Inst. di Studi Verdiani, Parma, 1964-69; Libn. & Tchr. of Music Hist., Conserv. G Rossini, Peasaro, 1970-73; Prof., Hist. of Music, Fac. of Higher Educ., Univ. of Parama, 1970-72; Lectr. in Music, Univ. of London King's Coll., 1973-76; Reader, ibid., 1977-. Publs. incl: Giuseppe Tartini-Le fonti biografiche, 1968. Contbr. to many profl. publs. Mbrships: incl. Int. Musicol. Soc.; Royal Musical Assn.; Am. Musicol. Soc.; Societa Italiana di Musicologia. Address: 57 Aberdare Gdns., London NW6 3AL, UK. 19.

PETROV, Vadim, b. 24 May 1932, Prague, Czechoslovakia. Composer; Professor of Composition. Educ: Acad. of Arts, Prague. m. Marta Votapkova, 1 s, 1 d. Career: Hd. of Music Dept., Soc. of Music, Prague, 1957-66: Hd. Conserv. of Dance Music & Jazz, 1966-70; Prof. of Comp., Prague Conserv., 1970-; Cond., Vocal Choir of Blind Girls Carmina Lucis. Comps. incl: Music for theatre, stage & films; More than 460 comps.; Music for films inclng: Jane Eyre, This Horse Must be Off. etc.; Concerto for Violin in G; Symphonic Poem for piano & orch.; The Salt of Earth; Vocal Choruses for male & female voices; Scherzo Poetico; Serenta, etc. Recordings on Supraphon & Panton. Address: 1609 00 Praha 6, Karasovska 8333, Czechoslovakia.

PETROVIC, Danica, b. 2 Dec. 1945, Belgrade, Yugoslavia. Musicologist. Educ: Musicol. & ethnomusicol., Fac. Music, Belgrade. m. Milan Petrovic, 1 child, Career: Asst., Inst. Musicol., Belgrade. Publs: A Liturgical Anthology Manuscript with the Russian 'hammer-headed' Notation from A.D. 1974, Musica Antiqua Europae Orientalis III, 1972; Church Elements in Serbian Ritual Songs, Grazer musikwissenschaftliche Arbeiten 1, 1975: One Aspect of the Slavonic Oktoechos in 4 Chilandari Music Manuscripts, Report 11th Congress IMS, II, 1975. Contbr. to: Zvuk; Arti Musices; Die Welt der Slaven. Address: Inst. Musicol., Knez Mihailova 35, Belgrade, Yugoslavia.

PETROVIĆ, Radmila, b. 21 Jan. 1923. Ethnomusicologist. Educ: BA, Belgrade Univ., MA, ethnomusicol., Acad. Music, Belgrade; Ethnomusicol., Wesleyan Univ., Middletown, Conn., USA, 2 terms. div., 1s. Career: Rsch. fellow, Inst. of Musicol., Serbian Acad. of Scis. & Arts, Belgrade. Publs: Monograph Studies of Zlatibor, Jadar, Leposavic, Vladicin Han, & Banat; The Place of Ethnomusicology in Yugoslav Music, 1970. Contbr. to: Jrnl. IFMC; Yrbook. IFMC, 1971; Int. Review Aesthetics & Sociol. Music, 1974; La musiques serbe a travers les siecles, 1973; Mbr. ed. bd., Int. Review Aesthetics & Sociol Music, Zagreb. Mbrships: Soc. Folklorists Serbia; Exec.

Bd., Int. Folk Music Coun. Hobby: Working w. amateurs in villages. Address: Svetozara Markovica 36, 11000 Belgrade, Yugoslavia.

PERTROVIĆ, Radomir, b. 13 May 1923, Belgrade, Yugoslavia. Composer; Conductor; Professor. Educ: Music Acad., Belgrade. m. Mirjana, 1 d. Debut: as comp., 1951; as cond., 1954. Career: Cond., Branko Cvetkovic choir, Belgrade; Prof., Harmony & counterpoint, Fac. of Musical Art, Belgrade; Musical Writer & Critic. Recorded Comps. incl: Moto Sinfonico (also publd.); Symphony; Sonatina for Oboe & Piano (publd.); Str. Quartet; Sonta in F (for piano); Symphonical Epithaf (voices & instruments); Young men on the belfries, (voices & instruments); Has also done theatre & film music, songs for soloist or á cappella choir, etc. contbr. to jrnls., radio & TV. Mbr. profl. orgs. Recip. many awards & decorations. Address: Jevrejska 30, 11000 Belgrade, Yugoslavia.

PETROVICS, Emil, b. 9 Feb. 1930, Nagybecskerek, Yugoslavia, Composer. Educ: Dip., Liszt Ferenc Acad. of Music, 1957. m. Erzsi Galmabos, 1 d. Career: Dir. of Musical Affairs, Petöfi Theatre, Budapest, 1960-64; Premiere of first opera 'C' est la Guerre', 1962; Prof., Acad. of Dramatic Art, 1964-; Prof.; Fac. of Comp., Acad. of Music Liszt Fernc; 1968-; Premiere of second opera 'Crime & Punishment, 1969. Comps: Cassazione for brass instrument, 1953; Flute concert, 1958; Str. Quartet, 1959; Suite for harpsichord, 1958; C'est la Guerre, opera in one act, 1961; Lysistrate, comic opera for concert, 1962; Brass Quintet, 1965; Book of Jonah, oratorio, 1966; Crime & Punishment, opera in 3 acts, 1969; II Cantata, 1972; many comps. for the stage; films & for choirs, All comps. edited by Editio Musica, Budapest & recorded by Hungarian Radio & Hungaroton. Publs: Ravel, biog. of the composer 1959. Mbr., Presidency of the Assn. of Hungarian Comps. Hons: 2nd prize, Liège, Belgium, for Str. Quartet No. 1, 1959; Kossuth Prize, 1966. Hobbies: Skiing; Gardening. Address: Napraforgó utca 9/a. H-1o21, Budapest, Hungary. 2.

PETRUCCI, Mary Jeanne, b. 30 Sept. 1952, Waterbury, Conn., USA. Violinist. Educ: BMus, MMus, Hartt Coll. of Music, Univ. of Hartford; Dip, Chmbr. Music, Accademia Chigiana, Siena. Debut: (solo w. orch.) Waterbury, 1968. Career: Asst. Concertmistress, Waterbury Symph.; mbr., Hartford Symph. & Chmbr. Orchs.; mbr., I Solisti Fiorentini; mbr. Gruppo Concertistico Toscano; solo & chmbr. music recitals in USA & Italy; now 1st violinist, Maggio Musicale Fiorentino Orch. (Teatro Communale, Florence). Hons: Young Artists award, Waterbury, Conn., 1970; Siena Summer Music Session scholarship, 1973-74; Spoleto fest. orch. scholarship, 1976; Perfs. award, Hartt Coll. of Music, 1974; Alumnae Grad. Scholarship, ibid., 1975-76. Address: Three Mile Hill Rd., Middlebury, CT 06762, USA.

PETRUSHKA, Shabtai Arieh, b. 15 Mar. 1903, Leipzig, Germany. Composer; Arranger; Conductor. Educ: Tech. Univ., Berlin-Charlottenburg; Leipzig Conserv. of Music; Stern's Conserv., Berlin. m. Pnina Dogar, 1 s. Career: orch. Ldr., var. theatres in Berlin, 1928-33; Arr., DGG, Berlin-UFA Film Co., 1933-37; Arr. & Cond., Palestine Broadcasting Serv., Jeru-salem, 1938-48; Asst. Dir. of Music, Israel Broadcastir j Service, 1948-58; Hd., Music Div., ibid, 1958-68; Sr. Lectr., Orchestration & Score Reading, Rubin Acad. of Music, Jerusalem, 1969. Comps. incl: (recorded & Publd.) 5 Oriental Dances; 4 Movements for Band; 3 Movements for Orch.; Piccolo Divertimento for Symphonic Band; 3 Jewish Melodies for String Orch.; Hebrew Suite for band; var. chmbr. music for woodwind & brass; var. choral settings of Israeli folk tunes. Contbr. to: Musica; Jewish Review, Copenhagen. Mbr., num. profl. orgs. Recip. of Am.-Israel Soc. Music Awards, Carnegie Hall, NYC, 1957. Hobbies: Photography; Gardening; Carpentry. Address: 13 Abba Hilkia St., 93183 Jerusalem, Israel.

PETRŽELKA, Ivan, b. 3 July 1928, Brno, CSSR. Musicologist; Opera producercritic. Educ: PhD, music, Brno, 19852; Dip. opera prod., Janackova Acad., Brno, 1954. m. Eva Zavrelova, 1 s. Career: Prof., Brno conserv., from 1954. Prods. G. Verdi, La Traviata, 1954; V. Blodek, Im Brunnen, 1956; R. Kerndl. Ehrbare Familie, 1963; Mozart, Marriage of Figaro, 1974; Pergolesi, La serva padrona, 1975; Gluck, Orpheus & Eurydice, 1976; Jan Antos, Ober Bauernfreiheit oder rebellieren, 1975. Publs. incl: Das Konzertbuch, 1959; Ruská a sovetska hudba (Russian & Soviet music), 1975; Musicalische Momente aus Bulgarien, 1975; Das Kleine musicologische Fensterchen, 1976. Contbr. to var. profl. jrnls. Address: 6110 Brno II, Nerudova 14, Czech.

PETTAN, Hubert, b. 23 Oct. 1912, Zagreb, Croatia, Yugoslavia. Professor of Music School. Educ: LLD; Dip., Musical Acad. of Zagreb. m. Jagoda Vedris, 1 s. Career: Prof.of Musical Schl. Vatroslav Lisinski, Zagreb; Accomp. soloists.

comps.incl: Sonatina for piano, 1963; Solo Songs; Sonata for violin & piano, 1970; Three Rondos for piano, 1972; Opera, Arkun (several arias published separately), 1975. Publs. incl: A Rapid Review of the History of Music (3 volumes), 1965-66; Nine Centuries of Polyphonic Choral Music (3 volumes), 1970-73; Musical textbooks.; ed., Croakian solo song, 1979. Contbr. to num. profl. jrnls. Mbrships: Soc. of Crotian Comps.; Assn. of Musical Tchrs. in Croatia. Address: 41000 Zagreb, Kacicéva 4, Yugoslavia.

PETTERSSON, Allan G, b. 1 9 Sept. 1911, Västra Ryd, Sweden. Composer. Educ: Studied Violin, Viola, Counterpoint, Royal Acad. of Music, Stockholm, 1930-39; Studied Comp. w. Karl-Kirger Blomdahl; studied Viola w. Maurice Vieux, Paris, France; studies comp. w. Arthur Honegger & René Leibowitz, 1951-52. m. Gundrun Gustafson. Career: Viola player, Stockholm Phil. Orch., 1940-50. Comps. incl: 24 Barefoot Songs (voice & piano), 1943-45; Concerto for violin & str. quartet, 1949; Three Concertos for string orch., 1950, 1956, 1957; Seven sonatas for two violins, 1951; 15 Symphonies, 1953-78; Symphonic movement, 1973; 6 Songs, 1935; Vox Hurmana, Solo, Choir, orch., 1974. Mbrships: Royal Acad. of Music, 1970; Soc. of Swedish Comps. Hons. incl: Artist Reward, Swedish Govt. (for life); City of Stockholm Hon. Award, 1968; Award for Outstanding Swedish Work on record, 1970; Swedish Gramophone Award, 1977; Litteris et Artibus, 1977. Address: Bastugatan 30, 11725 Stockholm, Sweden.

PETTY, James Carter, b. 9 July 1928, Murfreesboro, Tenn., USA. Music Director; Conductor. Educ: BMus, Cinn. Conserv. of Music, 1950; BSc, Univ., 1957; SUNY, 1968. m. Polly Adams Petty, 1 d. Debut: cond., Cinn. Conserv. Symph. Orch., Recital Hall, Cinn., 1949. Career incls: Cond., Jackson Symph. Orch., 1961-67; Music Dir., ibid., 1967-; Guest apps., Mex., Can., Hawaii, Calif., NY etc. Comp. Fanfare & Melody, 1973. Author, The Evolution of Conducting, 1956. Contbr. to: Flute Forum; Jackson Sun. Mbr. var. profl. orgs. Hons. incl: Etelka Evans Mem. Scholarship Award, 1951. Hobbies incl: Chess; Math. Address: 64 Glen Eden Dr., Jackson TN 38301, USA. 7.

PEYROL, Annie Mary, b. 10 Dec. 1948, Alencon, France. Teacher. Educ: Conserv. of Le Mans (solfeggio, piano, harmony, singing, etc.); Conserv. of Paris (music hist., musicol., analysis). m. Jean-Pierre Peyrol, 1c. Career: music tchr. in a Lycée. Recordings: w. Ensemble Vocal Stéphane Caillat. Mbrships: Association pour le 150e Anniversaire de la Société des Concerts du Conservatoire. Hons: 1st prizes, music hist. & musicol., Conserv. Nat. Supérièur de Musique de Paris. Hobbies: Piano; Singing; Choral Conducting. Address: 9 rue des Jardins,38420 Domène, France.

PEZOLD, Hans, b. 10 Apr. 1901, Mulsen St. Jacob, Germany. University Professor; Musicologist. Educ: Dr. phil., Univ. of Leipzig; Leipzig Conserv. m. Ilse, 1 s. Career: Grad. asst , Univ. of Leipzig, 1926; Instr., ibid., 1927; Sr. Instr., 1946; Sr. Instr., 1946; Rdr., 1952; Prof., 1965-. Prolific contbr. to var. music publs. inclng: Volk & Wissen; publs. of German Ctrl. Inst. for Second. Educ.; Funk & Schule; Musik in der Schule, etc.; author of intruductory notes & record sleeves particularly of works of Tchaikowski. Mbrships: German Union of Composers & Musicols.; Chmn., Leipzig Local Union of Germany. 1969; Order of Merit of the Fatherland, 1971. Address: Rapunzelweg 8, 703 Leipzig, German Dem. Repub.

PFANNER, Adolf, b. 24 May 1897, Westerheim, Bavaria, Germany. Composer. Educ: Tchrs. Training Coll.; Studied comp. w. Prof. Gottfried Rüdinger, Acad. of Musical Art. Munich. Compositions incl: (publd.) Geistliche Gesänge für Alt. Viola & Orgel, Op. 19, 1922; Rotkäppchen, Bühnenspiel, 1929; Die ewige Liebe; Geistliche Gesänge Op. 271 1932; Der Säemann (Claudius). Op. 35 1935; Lieder, Op. 35, 1937; O Mensch. bedenk (Hesse), Op. 46, 1937; (recorded) Lieder der Einsamkeit, Op. 21; Trio for Violin, Viola & Cello, Op. 47; Piano Trio, Op. 13. Mbrships: Tonkünstler Verein, Munich; Bund Deutscher Komponisten; Gema. Hobbies: Painting; Travels for the sake of Art. Address: D 8000 Munich 70, Stifsbogen 74, App. 624, German Fed. Repub. 2.

PFANNKUCH, Wilhelm, b. 12 Nov. 1926, Kiel, Germany. Musicologist; Conductor. Educ: State Pvte. Exam., 1950; PhD, Univ. of Kiel, 1954. m. Carla Meyer, 1 s, 2 d. Career: Asst. Sci., 1955 (w. Lectrng. duties, 1960), Assoc. Sci., 1964, Sci., 1969, Sci. Dir., 1972, Musicol. Inst., Univ. of Kiel; Cond. Fndr., Kiel Chmbr. Orch., 1952-; Cond., Collegium Musicum, Univ. of Kiel, 1960- Recordings: Telemann's Water Music (TELDEC). Publs: Das Opernschaffen Ermanno Wolf-Ferraris, 1975; Ed., Georg Friedrich Händel, Concerti grossi, 1959-; Ed., Joseph Haydn, Armida, 1975; Co-Ed., Bericht Über den 7. Internationalen Musikwissenschaftlichen Kongress Köln 1958,

1960; Festschrift Friedrich Blume zum. 70. Geburtstag, 1963. Contbr. to: num. profl. jrnls & mags. Mbr., num. profl. orgs. Address: Wilhelmshavener Strasse 4, 2300 Kiel 1, German Fed. Repub.

PFAUTSCH, Lloyd Alvin, b. 14 Sept. 1921, Washington, Mo., USA. Professor of Music; Choral Conductor; Singer. Educ: BA, Elmhurst Coll., Ill.; M Theol, M Sac Mus, Union Theol. Sem., NYC; Hon. LL.D., Ill. Wesleyan Univ. m. Edith Herseth, 3 s., 1 d. Career: Mbr., Robert Shaw Chorale, NBC & CBS Choruses; Prof., Southern Meth. Univ., Dallas, Tex. Over 200 publd. comps. & arrs. Publs: Mental Warm-Ups for the Choral Conductor, 1969; English Diction for the Singer, 1971, Choral Conducting: A Symposium, 1973; Solos for the Church Year, 1957; Solos for the Church Soloist, 1960. Contbr. to var. periodicals. Mbrships: ASCAP; Phi Kappa Phi; Phi Mu Alpha; ACDA; FUMM; Pi Kappa Lambda. Recip. Hon. D Mus, Elmhurst Coll. Address: 3710 Euclid Ave., Dallas, TX 75205, USA. 7.

PFIFFNER, Ernst, b. 6 Dec. 1922, Mosnang, St. Gallen, Switzerland. Choir Leader; Organist; Music Academy Director. Educ: Univ. of Fryburg; Ch. Music Schl., Regensburg; Pontificio Istituto de musica sacra, Rome, Organ Dip., Basel Conserv.; studied w. Oswald Jaeggi, Willy Burkhard, Nadia Boulanger. m. Mar'ese Taschner, 1 d., 2 s. Career: Choir Dir., St. Michael, Basel; Editor; Music Tchr.; Dir., Acad. of Schl. & Ch. Music, Lucerne. (Publd.) Compositions incl: Autosprüche, Geleit-sprüche am Fahrweg. Messe auf die heilige Dreifaltigkeit, Mette, Proprien, Psalms, Motets, Sängerspiegel, choir; var. vocal solo & instrumental works; Brautgesänge; Polyhymnia; Toccates I & II, organ; (recorded) 7 Geistliche Gesänge, soprano, flute, viola, cello; Messe auf die heilige Dreifaltigkeit; Ein Kind ist uns geboren heut; Toccata, organ. Contbr. to: Katholische Kirchenmusik; Gottesdienst; Schwierische Kirchen-zeitung; Musica sacra. Mbrships: Musicians Soc.; Swiss MTA; Ch. Musicians Assn. Hons: 2nd Prize, Organ Competition, Magadino, 1964; 1st Prize, Chmbr. Music, Basel, 1952. Address: 125 St. Johannsring, CH 4056 Basel, Switzerland.

PFOHL, James Christian, b. 17 Sept. 1912, Winston-Salem, NC, USA. Conductor; Music Educator (Organ, String Bass, Trumpet). Educ: Mus B, Univ. Mich. 1933; Mus M, 1939; Mus D, Cinn. Conserv. of Music, m. Carolyn Day Pfohl, 2 s, 1 d. Career incls: Fndr. Dir., Reston Chorale & Reston Chmbr. Orch., 1966-; Cond., N Va. Youth Orch., 1967-; Dir., Choral Music, Robert E Lee High Schl., Fairfax Co., Va.; Cond. num. Symph. Orchs. inclng: Charlotte, Jacksonville & York, Pa.; Organist & Choir Dir., Wash. Plaza Ch., Reston, 1969; Stage, Film, TV & Radio apps. Comps: Series of 26 arrs. of Moravian Music. Contbr. to Mogas Schl. Musician; Instrumentalist. Mbr. num. profl. orgs. Hobbies: Fishing; All Sports. Address: Brokie Green B4, 1000 Country Club Rd., York, PA 17403, USA.

PHELPS, Christopher, b. 21 May, 1943, Cheltenham, UK. Conductor; Organist. Educ: RCM; FRCO (ChM); GRSM; LRAM; ARCM; Akademie für Musik, Vienna. m. Dorothy Ryan, 1 s., 2 d. Career incl: Cond., Colchester Inst. Symph. Orch., Ipswich Orch. Soc., Essex Symph. Orch.; toured Romania w. 2nd Essex Youth Orch. & W Germany w. Colchester Inst. Symph. Orch.; sometime organist, Armagh Cathedral, N Ireland; organ recitalist. Hons: Turpin prize for FRCO, 1964; joint 2nd prize, Walford Davies Competition, RCM, 1964; Deuxieme Mention Concours Int. de jeune chefs d'orchestre, Besancon, 1970; Conds. prize, Radio Salzburg, 1970. Hobbies: Squash; Badminton. Address: 1 Bristol Rd., Colchester, Essex, UK.

PHILIBA, Nicole, b. 30 Aug. 1937, Paris, France. Composer; Professor. Educ: w. Olivier Messiaen, Conserv. Nat. Superieur de Musique de Paris; l'Institut de France; l'Institut Academie des Beaux Arts. Career: num. apps., Radio Television France; Belgian Radio; Radio Can., USA, Italy; Prof., Conserv. Nat. Superieur de Musique, Paris. Comps. incl: Concerto for saxo-phone & orch., 1967; Sonata for flute, 1979; Six Pieces for Piano, 1975; Etudes Rythmiques, 1979; Mosaiques (trumpet), 1977; Inventions, for guitar, 1977; Evocations for piano, 1976; Saxophone Sonata, 1969. Sev. recordings for Radio Television France. Var. acad. hons. Address: 15 rue des Carrières, 92150 Suresnes, France.

PHILIP, Robert Marshall, b. 22 July 1945, Witney, UK. Music Critic. Educ: ARCM, 1964; BA, MA, Peterhouse, Cambridge, 1964-68; PhD, Wolfson Coll., Cambridge, 1975. m. Dr. Maria Lukianowicz. Career: Broadcasts on Radio 3 incl: Changing Orchl. Style; Changing Quartet Style; many contbns. to Record Review, inclng. surveys of all Beethoven's symphs.; 13-part series The Long-Playing Era; Tchr.; Cambridge Music Tripos. Mbrships: Royal Musical Assn. Contbr. to Grove's Dict. of Music & Musicians Assn. Contbr. to Grove's Dict. of Music & Musicians, 6th ed. Hons. incl: Jr. Rsch. Fellowship, Wolfson Coll., Cambridge, 1971-73; Brit. Acad. Award, 1974. Address: Wolfson Coll., Cambridge, UK.

PHILIPS, John Douglass, b. 20 Dec. 1932, Stanton, Tenn., USA. Pianist; Professor of Music. Educ: B Mus, Rollins Coll., 1954; Lic de Concert, Ecole Normale de Musique, Paris, 1956; DMA piano, Peabody Conserv., 1977. Debut: Salle Cortot, Paris, 1959. Career: Recitals, Chmbr. Music, radio & TV apps. Europe & USA; Gulbenkian Fest., 1964; Prof., piano, Acad. Marquerite Long, Paris, 1964-69; Assoc. Prof., Fontbonne Coll., St. Louis, Mo., 1971-; Chmn., Music Dept., ibid., 1975-76; Music Critic, W End Word, St. Louis; Music Dir., BHAM (US Bi-centennial celebration, St. Louis), 1976. Recordings: Milhaud's Suite for ondes martenot & piano. Contrbr. to: Piano Quarterly; Clavier. Mbr. profl. orgs., Recip. schlrships. Hobby: Gourmet cooking. Address: 7556 Parkdale Ave., Clayton, MO 63106, USA.

PHILLIMORE, Cynthia Frances Mary, b. 11 June 1934, London, UK. Teacher of Piano & Oboe. Educ: LRAM; ARCM; ARAM. Career: Prof., Oboe. RAM, piano & oboe, Jr. Exhibnrs., RAM; Piano & Oboe Tchr., Roehampton Inst. of Higher Educ., King's Schl. Canterbury; Piano & Oboe Tchr., Accomp. for choir, Wadsworth Schl. Mbr., ISM. Hobbies: Travel; Fell walking; Church crawling & arch. Address: Flat 4, 207 Stanley Rd., Twickenham TW2 5NW, UK.

PHILLIPS, Burrill, b. 9 Nov. 1907, Omaha, Neb., USA. Composer. Educ: Mus B 1932, MM 1933, Eastman Schl. of Music. m. Alberta Mayfield, 1 s., 1 d. Compositions: (publd. & recorded) Selections from McGuffey's Reader; Concert-piece for Bassoon & Strings; Canzona III (7 instruments & poet); (publd.) Scena (small orch.); Symphony Concertante (small orch.); Serenade (piano, 4 hands); Conversations & Colloquies (violin & viola); Piece for 6 Trombones; Preludes for Brass; That Time May Cease (men's chorus); Trio for Trumpets; Toccata (piano); 4 Latin Motets (SATB); The Return of Odysseus (baritone, speaker, SATB chorus & orch.); (recorded) Sonata for Cello & Piano, Sonata in 2 Movements (violin & harpsichord); Sonata for Organ Solo; Sonatas 1 & 2 for Piano Solo. Commission from var. instns. inclng. League of Comps. 1944, Formm Fndn. 1956. E S Collidge Fndn. 1958. Subject of monograph, Saluting the American Composer Burrill Phillips. Music Clubs Mag., winter 1970-71. Mbr., ASCAP. Hons: Guggenheim Fndn. Grants, 1942, 1961; Fulbright Lectr., Univ. of Barcelona, Spain, 1960. Nat. Endowment for the Arts grant, 1977. Hobby: Life on Farm w. 50 Acres of Woodland, Gardens & Fish Pond. Address: Branchport, NY 11418, USA. 2, 3, 14, 28.

PHILLIPS, Harvey, b. 2 Dec. 1929, Aurora, Mo., USA. Musician (tuba); Music Euducator. Educ: Juilliard Schl. of Music; Manhattan Schl. of Music; Hon. D Mus, New England Conserv. of Music; Manhattan Schl. of Music; Hon. D Mus. New England Conserv. of Music, 1971. m. Carol Ann Dorvel, 3 s. Career incl: Disting. Prof., Indiana Univ.; Pres., Harvey Phillips Fndn., Inc. solo apps. world-wide inclng. Aust., Europe, Japan, etc.; Fndr. & co-Fndr. of num. orgs.; Recitals, Carnegie Hall. num. solo recordings. Contbr. to: num. profl. publs. Mbrships: Tubists Universal Brotherhood Assn. (Bd. of Advisors); Bloomington Chmbr. of Commerce; var. Tchr. & Perf. Unions. Hons: 1st Tubist-Circus Hall of Fame Band; Bi-Centenary Celebrations, 1976; "Harvey Phillips Day" Celebrations, New England Conserv. of Music, 1971; "Harvey Phillips Day", Marionville, Mo., 1976; Kappa Kappa Psi; Dist. Service to Music Award, 1978. Address: Tubaranch, 4769 S Harrell Rd., Bloomington, IN 47401, USA. 6.

PHILLIPS, Jean, b. 24 May 1942, Highbury, London, UK. Concert Pianist & Harpsichordist; Teacher. Educ: Royal Coll. of Music; ARCM (Tchrs.). Div., 2 d. Debut: Wigmore Hall, 1965. Career: Introduced a regular series of concerts for children & parents combining piano & harpsichord music w. stories & poems narrated by Gerard Benson, at Purcell Room & var. provincial halls; Solo recitals at Wigmore Hall, Queen Elizabeth Hall & Purcell Room; Pt.-time lectr., piano & harpsichord, Trent Park-Middx. Polytechnic. Mbr: Inc. Soc. of Musicians. Hons: Margot Hamilton Prize, 1962; Percy Carter Buck Award, 1963. Hobbies: Flower Arranging; Gardening; Toy Making. Mgmt: Warren Redman. Address: 69 Kingsgate Ave., Kingsgate, Broadstairs, Kent, UK. 30.

PHILLIPS, Karen, b. 29 Oct. 1942, Dallas, Tex., USA. Violinist. Educ: BM, Eastman Schl. of Music, Rochester, NYC, 1964; Post-Grad. Dip., Juilliard Schl. of Music, NYC, 1967. Debut: Grace Rainey Rodgers Auditorium. Career: over 300 apps. in solo recitals, Lincoln Ctr., Metropolitan Mus. of Art, Carnegie Hall, Rockefeller Inst., NYC, Los Angeles Music Ctr., Queen Elizabeth Hall, Purcell Hall, London, UK, Mus. of Modern Arts, Paris. Stärasbourg Conserv., etc.; Regular apps. in radio & TV progs. Comps. incl: 1 symph; 2 works for viola & orch.; 2 works for viola & small ensemble; about 40 songs; 1 organ work. Recordings. incl: Music of Berio. Contbr. to profl. jrnls.

Recip., sev. awards. Mgmt: Ibbs & Tillett, London, UK. Address: 258 W 71st St., NY, NY 10023, USA.

PHILLIPS, Lena Margaret, b. 8 Feb. 1944, Pwllygwlaw, S Wales, UK. Solo Singer (Mezzo-Contralto). Educ: LRAM; ALCM; Ancren Eleve, Paris, France; pvte. study w. Constance Shacklock. m. Albert Pratt (dec.). Debut: Recital, Wigmore Hall, London, 1973. Career: Concert & Recital work; Oratorio & Opera; Pvte. teaching & lecturing; fndr. Lena Phillips Opera Workshops for Children, 1978. Mbrships: ISM; Equity. Hons: Vaughan Williams Centenary Prize, 1972; Grover Esdale Recitalist Award, 1972; Dyfrig Owen Prize, 1973; Del Mar Journeaux Prize, Paris, 1975. Hobbies: Record & Mug Collecting; Tapestry; Talking with Friends. Mgmt: Helen Jenning Concert Agcy. Address: 15 Berriedale Drive, Sompting, Lancing. Sussex BN15 OLE, UK.

PHILLIPS, Linda, b. Melbourne, Vic., Aust. Composer; Pianist; Teacher; Adjudicator; Music Critic. Educ: Univ. Conserv., Melbourne; Melba Conserv.; studied Comp. w. Fritz Hart Harmony w. Dr. J A Steele & Piano w. Edward I Goll. m. A M Kauffmann (dec.). 1 d. Career: Num. Broadcasts inclng. own Comps. for Melbourne, Sydney & Brisbane Aust. Broadcasting Commission; Pub. recitals & recitals w. other artists of own chmbr. music works & songs; formerly Melbourne reviewer, Aust. Musical News; Music Critic, Melbourne Sun News-Pictorial, Comps. (publd.): Four Bush Lyrics; Orchard Zephyr; Songs of the Outback, Cradle Song; Plum Tree; Noon (piano); Butterflies (piano), (recorded) Australian Light Classics (chmbr. music & songs), w. Comops. as pianist. Publ: Book of Verse from a City (profl. women). Hons: var. Scholarships; OBE, 1975. Hobbies: Reading; Study of Italian; Gardening. Address: 19 Hughenden Rd. E, St. Kilda, Melbourne, Vic. 3182, Aust. 3, 15.

PHILLIPS, Lois, b. 19 Jan. 1926, London, UK. Pianist; Teacher; Composer; Lecturer. Educ: RAM; FRAM. Career: Recitals & broadcasts in UK, Germany, Switz., solo & w. Oriole Ensemble. Comps: var. educational works. Publ: Lieder Line by Line, 1979. mbr. ISM. Hons: Elizabeth Stokes Open Scholarship, Harold Samuel Bach Prize, Janet Duff Greer Prize, Sterndale Bennett Prize, Am. Women's Club Prize, Walter Macfarren Gold Medal (all at RAM, 1934-49). Hobbies: Languages (German, French, Engl.); Literature; Natural History. Address: 11 Chalcot Sq., London NW1, UK.

PHILLIPS, (Maglona Patricia) Bryony, b. 10 March 1948, Manchester, UK. Composer; Writer. Educ: BA, New Hall, Cambridge Univ., 1971; Studied Comp. & Far Eastern Music, Boston, USA, 1971-72; Postgrad. study of comp. & paleography, New Hall, Cambridge, 1972-73. m. Dr. Richard Phillips, 1 d. Career: Mbr., London Schls. Symph. Orch. & var. orchs. & chmbr. music groups, UK & USA; Sang in choirs, UK, USA & NZ; Recorder soloist, UK & NZ; Radio apps. NZ; Dir., recorder soloist & comp. of Brids of Enlightenment & Relese From Hell, written for 3rd NZ Asian Studies Conference. Comps. incl: Mele Sapphoa, 1968; Autumn Floods, for soprano solo, choir & orch., 1973; Requiem Brevis, 1973; Birds of Enlightenment, Theatre Cantata, 1978; Release from Hell, operetta, 1978; Chitra, Lyric Opera, 1979; First Love, song cycle for soprano & piano, 1979. Num. Radio & TV recordings. Contbr. to: Comps. Assn. of NZ Newsletter; Outrigger (poetry mag.). Mbrships: Sec., 1978-79, Comps. Assn. of NZ. Hons: Prize, Dorian Choir's competition for choral work combining Maori & European elements (Te Waiata 88). Hobbies: Asian studies; Lit.; Playing & listening to music. Address: 14 Carmen Ave., Balmoral, Auckland 4, NZ.

PIAGGI, Anthony Francis, b. 19 July 1952, N Adams, Mass., USA. Director of Music; Organist. Educ: BA, Westfield State Coll., Mass.; MA (music hist.), Smith Coll.; studied piano w. Gilda Glazer, organ w. Yella Pessl, choral cond. w. Iva Dee Hiatt. Career: Dir. of Choral Music, Coll. of Our Lady of the Elms, Chicopee, Mass.; Organist & Choir Dir., Annuciation Ch., Northampton, Mass. Comp: Mass for the Annuciation; hymn tunes. Mbrships: Am. Musicol. Soc.; AGO. Hobbies: Theatre; Medieval Ch. Hist. Address: 15 Ballard St., Apt. Q, Easthampton, MA 01027, USA.

PIAMENTA, Abraham (Albert), b. 6 July 1938, Jerusalem, Israel. Educ: Music Acad., Tel-Aviv. m. Ruchama (Korin) Piamenta. Career: well-known Israeli Comp., Arranger & Band Ldr., fields of jazz & Middle E folk music; num. TV & radio broadcasts, Israel Comps: Mezare Israel (jazz album-recorded); Nimrod (ballet for ethnic gp., Inbal); film scores; var. original rock & roll tunes. Publs: Islamic-African folk & dance music, featuring the music of Sudan, 1975. Mbrships: ASCAP; Israeli Musicians Union Local 802, NYC. Address: 43-23 42nd St., LIC, NY 111104, USA.

PICARDI, Rudolph (John James Falcione), b. 25 May 1927, San. Fran., Calif., USA. Conductor; Pianist; Coach; Stage

Director. Educ: San Fran. Conserv. of Music; piano pedagogy, Univ. of Calif. Ext.; Luigi Cherubini Conserv. of Music, Florence, Italy (comp. w. Vito Frazzi, piano w. Eriberto Scarlino); cond. w. Paul van Kempen, Alceo Galliera, Franco Ferrara, Accademia Chigiana, Siena; cond. w. G L Lessing, Kurt Eichorn, Muzick Hochschule, Munich; cond. w. Hans. Swarowsky, piano w. Doris Leischner, Viola Thern, Vienna State Acad. of Music; Kapellmeister degree, State Acad. of Music, Vienna. Div. Career: Dir., Univ. of Tex. Opera Dept., 1962-64; Asst. Cond.Coach, San Fran. Opera's Merola Prog., 1962-70; Dir. of Univ. of Redlands Opera Workshop, 1969-71; Musical Dir., Cond., San Bernandino Symph. Orch.; Pro Tem Musical Dir., Cond., Redlands Univ., Community Symph.; Artistic Dir., San Fran. Talent Bank; Music Dir./Stage Dir., West Bay Opera Assn., Ross Valley Players. Mbrships: Mu Phi Epsilon; Nat. Opera Assn.; Societa Leonardo da Vinci. Recip., Ford Fndn. Grant, 1969. Mgmt: Rudolph Picardi, 715 De Haro St., San Fran., CA, USA. Address: 715 De Haro St., San Francisco, CA 94107, USA.

PICCHI, Silvano, b. 15 Jan. 1922, Pisa, Italy. Composer; Music Critic. Educ: Grad., Nat. Conserv. of Music & Theatrical Arts. Argentina, 1947. m. Maria Concepción Patrón (Guitarist), 2 s., 1 d. Career: Composer, 1948-; Lectr. in Sol-fa & Harmony, Manuel de Falla Municipal Conserv., Buenos Arires, 1964 & 65; Music Critic, La Presna daily, 1962-; Organiser, Jury, Argentine-Italioan Cultural Fest., 1974. Compositions publd: 3 Little Fugues for flute, clarinet, viola & bassoon, 1952; 3 Microdances for piano, 1948; Argentine Suite for piano, 1967; 5 Pieces for Organ, 1963 (recorded by Qualiton); Prelude & Fugue for organ, 1948. Contbr. to: La Presna, Buenos Aires. Mbr: Argentine Soc. for Authors & Composers, (SADAIC). Hons: Prize, Nat. Arts Fndn., 1966 & 68; Prize, Wagnerian Assn. of Buenos Aires, (for his Trio), 1968. Nat. Arts. Fndn. Prize for Sonata per Violino Solo, 1975. Hobbies: Pencil & Ink Drawing. Address: Aranguren 4682, Dto. 1, Capital Federal, Argentina.

PICHT-AXENFELD, Edith Maria, b. 1 Jan. 1914, Freiburg, Germany. Pianist; Organist; Harpsichordist; Educator. Educ: Studied Piano w. Paula Roth-Kastner, 1920-32; Abitur, Freiburg, 1931; Pvte. Music Tchng. Examination, 1932; Studied Piano w. Anna Hirzel-Langenhan, 1932-34 & w. Rudolph Serkin, 1934-34; Studied Organ w. Wolfgang Auler, Berlin, 1936 & w. Albert Schweitzer. m. Dr. Georg Picht, 3 s., 1 d. Debut: Freiburg, 1927. Career: Piano & Harpsichord Concerts throughout Europe, UK., S. Am. S. Africa & Asia, 1935-; Participant, Int. Fests. inclng. Engl. Bach Fest.; Chmbr. Music Partnership w. Aurele Nicolet & Heinz Hollinger; Piano Trio w. Nicolas Chumachenco & Alelxandre Stein; Prof., Staatliche Hochuschule fur Musik, Frieburg, 1947-. Recordings incl: Bach: Golbert Variations (Erato); Les Clavicistes Allemands (Erato); Six Paritas (Victor); Barok sonaten Oboe & Basso Continuo (Phillips). Hons: Chopin Prize, Warsaw, Poland, 1937. Mgmt: Concert Direction Robert Kollitsch, Berlin. Address: D 7824 Hinterzarten, Altbirklehof, German Fed. Repub.

PICK, Karl Heinz, b. 18 Aug. 1929, RothenburgOberlausitz, DDR. Concert pianist; Comp.; Piano pedagogue. Educ: Music Acad. Leipzig 19481952, State exam; Lectr. 1955. m. Elisabeth Buckisch, 2 d. Debut: DDR, 1950. Career: Concerts DDR, USSR, Poland, Finalnd, Rumania, Hungary, Czechoslovakia, Bulgaria, W. Germany, Korean Democratic Repub., Egypt, Syria; Radio, TV prod.; Prof. Music Acad. Felix Mendelssohn Bartholdy, Leipzig. Comp. incl: Ergänzung; 3 piano concertos; Fairy Tale Suite for piano; Violin concerto; Symphonic overture; Song cycles; Cantata. Recordings incl: Song cyle, The Black Earth; Liederkreis. Mbrships: Var. profl. orgs. Hons: Merit Medal DDR, 1970; Art Prize Leipzig, 1962; Pestalozzi Medal, 1968; Arthur Becker Medal, 1974. Hobbies: Wandering; Animal, Nature lover. Address: Heinrich Büchnerstr. 2,7024 Leipzig, German Dem. Repub.

PICK, Richard Samuel Burns, b. 20 Oct. 1915, St. Paul, Minn., USA. Professor of Guitar. Educ: Univ. of Ill.; Univ. of Chgo.; De Paul Univ.; BS. m. Evelyn Virginia Tomanek, 1 d. Career incl: Guest artist on Radio & TV w. WGN Symph. Orch., St. Louis Symph. Orch.; Premier of Le Chevalier Errand (Jacques Ibert) w. Chgo. Symph.; Premier of own transcription of Vivaldi Concerto for guitar & orch., w. Mich. City Symph.; Mbr., Contemporary Chmbr. Players of Univ. of Chgo.; Prof. of Guitar; Dir., Chgo. Guitar Soc.; recitals in many US cities. Comps. Richard Pick 1st Repertoire for Classic Guitar (22 original pieces), 158; arrs. for solo guitar of num. works by Bach, Handel, etc. Recordings incl: LP albums - Richard Pick -Guitar; Americana; Guitarra Espanola; Above & Beyond. Publs. incl: 5 graded guitar method books, Introduction to Guitar, Introduction to effective accompaniment, First Lesson for Classic Guitar, Lessons for Classic Guitar Book 2, Fundamental Fingerboard Harmony Master Works for 2 Guitars, Vol 1, 1975;

8 Variations on a Carcassi Etude for 2 Guitars. Mbrships: Am. Fedn. of Musicians; Pres., Chgo. Classic Guitar Soc.; Chmn., Chgo. Guitar Soc. Hons: Order of Kentucky Colonels. Address: 9136 Sheridan Ave., Brookfield, IL 60513, USA. 28.

PICKARD, Alan Henry, b. 22 Aug. 1942, Douglas, Isle of Man, UK. Music Adviser; Violinist; Singer. Educ: RMCM; GRSM; FTCL; LTCL; ARMCM. m. Rosemary Curry, 1s., 1d. Career: mbr., Nat. Youth Orch.; sev. tchng. posts incl. Hd. of Music, Castle Rushen High Schl., 1971-77; Music Advsr., Isle of Man Bd. of Educ., 1978-; Dir., Isle of Man Int. Fest. of Music & Dancing, 1972-79. Recordings: 3 w. Manx Girls Choir. Publs: Music in Isle of Man Schools- a Guide, 1978; Music Making in the Isle of Man Schools - a Directory, 1979. Contbr. to: Czechoslovak Life. Mbrships: incl: Music Advsrs. Nat. Assn.; Friends of RNCM; Brit. Diabetics Assn. Hons: Rothschild Open Scholarship to RMCM. Hobbies: Books; Walking; Food; Wine. Address: Bridge House, Shore Rd., Port Erin, Isle of Man, UK.

PIECHLER, Arthur, b. 31 Mar. 1896, Magdeburg, Germany. Conductor; Organist; Composer. Educ: Acad. of Music, Munich. m. Rosl. Kellnberger. Career: Cathedral Organist, Augsburg; Conserv. Instructor, 1925; Orchl. Cond., Ulrichs-münster-Augsburg; Cond., Augsburg Oratorio Soc., 1932; Concert organist, Germany & abroad; Conserv. Dir., 1945-56. Comps incl: 2 operas, 2 large choral works w. orch., num. organ & orchl. works. Mbrships: Hon. Mbr., Admin. Coun. for Music, Cultural Soc. of German Fedn. of Inds.; Rotary Club; Ritter vom HI.Grab. Hons: Joseph-Rheinberger-Preis, 1921; Bundesverdienstrkreuz, 1st class, 1956; Bayerischer Verdienstorden,1959; Bayerishcen Roetenthaler, 1973. Address: c/o Rosl Piechler, Hauptstr.20, 8380 Landau/Isar, German Fed. Repub.

PIECHOWSKA, Alina, b. 29 Aug. 1937, Wilno, Poland. Comoposer; Pianist. m. Claude Pascal, 2 c. Educ: Studied piano & cond. w. Leokadio Urbanowis, Concrad Kaveckas; Studied comp. w. Witold Rudzinski, Warsaw, dip. 1970, Nadio Boulanger, Paris, dip. 1971. Debut: 1965. Career: Films, Theatre, TV & Radio (Poland). Comps: Songs of Bilitis; Ambitus Sonore (recorded); Songs for chorus Zwierzaki; 3 Studies for Voice. Recordings: Anagrams for string quartet; Ballet Music; Imaginaire. Mbrships: ZKP; SACEM. Hobbies: Painting; Theatre. Address: 68 rue Joseph de Maistre, Paris, 75018, France.

PIEKARZ, Ladislaus, b. 11 Apr. 1930, Vienna, Austria. Pianist; Composer. Educ: Lic. Phil.; Philosophical F; Dips., Piano, Conducting, Music Theory, Acad. of Music. Debut: Soloist, 1st Perf. of Casella-Partita for Piano & Orch., Salzburg, 1951. Career: Concerts in Austria & Germany; Austrian Radio, 1951; Radio Switzerland, 1961; Tchr., Harmony, Counterpoint & Piano, Mozarteum; Prof., 1971; Extraordinary Prof., 1976. Comps. incl: String Quarter, 1954; Romanze in E Minor for Little Orch., 1957; Num. Piano Comps., Songs & Spiritual Works. Publs: Contbr. to Der Menschals Personenlichkeit und Problem, Pustet Munchen, 196 3. Hobby: Reading Histl. Books, Hiking. Address: A-5020 Salzburg. Henri-Dunantstr.42, Austria. 29.

PIEL, Walter Karl, b. 6 Sept. 1939, Bochum, German. Senoir Academic Counsellor. Educ: Univ. of Cologne; State Coll. of Music, Cologne; Marburg Univ.; PhD, 1967. m. Anneliese Plume, 3 children. Career: Musicol. Asst., Musicol. Inst., Marburg Univ., 1965-70; Acad. Counsellor, Seminar for Music Educ. tchng. of tchrs. of handicapped children. Rhineland Tchrs. Coll., Cologne, 1971-; Sr. Acad. Counsellor, ibid., 1973-. Publs: Studien zum Leben und Schaffen Hubert Waelrauts unter besonderer Berücksichtigung seiner Waelrauts unter Besonderer Berücsichtigung seiner motetten, 1967. Mbr., Soc. for Music Rsch., Cassel. Address: Longericher Str., 226 D5000 Cologne, German Fed. Repub.

PIERCE, Elnora Retledge Cooper, b. Shreveport, La., USA. Pianist; Organist. Educ: BA, Bishop Coll., Marshall, Tex.; San Fran. Conserv. Music; Sherman Clay Schl. Organ, Oakland, Calif.; MA, Univ. of Tex. Div., 1 s. Career: Tchr., music in Christian Educ., 1952-69, Elem. Pub. Schl. Music, Collins Gdn., 1969-; Radio broadcasts. Mbrships: Nat. Educ. Assn.; Music Educators Assn.; Texas State Tchrs. Assn.; San Antonio Tchrs. Assn. Hobbies: Sewing; Sports. Address: 4822 Creekmoor Dr., San Antonio, TX 78220, USA.

PIERCE, Jane Gail Illingworth, b. 22 Mar. 1948, Hanover, NH, USA. Musicologist; Piano Teacher. Educ: AM, Sweet Briar Coll; PhD, Univ. of NC. m. Richard Norwin Pierce. Career: Pvte. Piano Tchr., 1968-; Instr., RI Coll., 1974. Contbr. to: Jrnl. of Lute Soc. of Am.; Grove's Dictionary, 6th ed. Mbrships: Am. Musicol. Soc.; Lute Soc. of Am. Hons: Phi Beta Kappa, 1968;

NDEA title IV PhD Fellowship, 1969-73; Theodore Presser Music Scholarship, 1967, 68. Hobby: Collecting antiques. Address: 95 Florence Rd., Apt. 1-C Branford, CT 06405, USA.

PIERCE, Jerry Dale, b. 4 Aug. 1937, Muncie, Ind., USA. College Music Teacher; Clarinettist. Educ: BS in Symphonic Instruments, Ball State Univ., Muncie, Ind., 1973; M Mus, ibid, 1977; studied clarinet w. Daniel Bonade for 5 yrs.; studied sòlo clarinet w. Robert McGinnis & Bernard Portnoy. Career incls: Prin. Clarinettist, Va. Symph., 1958-59, Halifax Symph., NS, 1959-61, Birmingham Symph., Ala., 1961-64, Ars. Nova Orch., NYC, 1964-66, Anderson Symph., Ind., 1967-; Player solo clarinet w. the NH Summer Music Fest. Orch., Dean Ryan cond., 1958, the CBC Symph., Halifax, Sir Ernest McMillan cond., 1959-61, & the Augusta Music Fest. Orch., Ga., 1963; Radio premiers of th John Beckwith Fall Scene & Fair Dance for solo violin, clarinet & orch.; US premier of Concerto for Clarinet & Orch. (Jean Francaix). Contbr. to: The Clarinet. Mbrships. incl: Phi Kappa Lambda; Nat. Assn. of Coll. Wind & Percussing Instrs.; Int. Clarinet Soc; Clarinet & Saxophone Soc. of GB. Hobbies: Sports cars; Auto racing. Address: 4611 Mounds Rd., Anderson, IN 46103, USA. 4.

PIERNAY, Rudolf, b. 8 Dec. 1943, Gustrow, Germany. Singer (Bass). Educ: Abitur, Berlin; Stadt Konservatorium Berlin; Staatliche Hochschule fur Musik und darstellende Kunst, Berlin; Dip. Piano, Chmbr. Music & Vocal Accomp.); State Dip. for Piano & Voice Tchng., RAM, London; GSMD. London. Career: Musical Dir., Weald Music Soc., Crawley, Sussex, UK, 1970-; Vocal Coach, Opera Berga Summer Schl., 1973-74; Prof. of Singing, GSM, London, 1974-; Apps. on BBC & several maj. radio stns. in Germany. Hons: Piano Prize, Stadt Conservatorium, Berlin, 1963; Elena Geshards Prize, RAM, 1964; Mirsky Memorial Prize, GSM, 1971. Address: 127 Queens Rd., London SW19, UK.

PIERROT, Noelie Marie Antoinette, b. 1899, Paris, France. Organist. Educ: Schola Cantorum; Nat. Conserv. of Music, Paris. Career: Prof., Schola Cantorum, 1925-31, & Gregorian Inst.; 1943-46; Organist, St. Pierre du Gros-Caillou Ch., Paris, 1929-; Soloist, ORTF, 1935-; has given recitals in many European cities. Compositions incl: Choral for Organ on theme by Gabriel Faure; motets; Melodies for soprano & piano. Publs. incl: eds. of Padovano's works after MSS.; eds. of organ works of 16th, 17th & 18th centuries; New Method for the Keyboard (4 books); Organ Method (w. Jean Bonfils). Recordings: num. organ works by Bach & French composers. Hons. incl: 1st Prizes in Organ & Counterpoint & Fuge, Nat. Conserv.; Alexlandre Guilmant Prize. Hobby: Collecting Antique Organchests. Address: 19 rue Mazarine, Paris 6, France.

PIERSON, Edward, b. 4 Jan. 1931, Chicago, Ill., USA. Opera Singer (Bass-Baritone). Educ: BA Educ., Roosevelt Univ., Ill. m. Myrtle Pierson, 1 s, 1d. Debut: Chgo. Lyric Opera in Don Carlo; 1964; NYC Opera in Don Rodrigo, 1966. Career: W. NYC Opera, 10 yrs.; Engaged by maj. orchs. in USA; Vast Oratorio Repertory; World TV premiere of Fachel, La Cubana (Henze); Specializing in such roles as Flying Dutchman, Scarpia, The Wotans, etc. Recordings: Carrie Nation; Moore (Desto Records); Treemonisha; Joplin (Deutsche Gramaphon). Bd. Mbr., AGMA. Hobbies: Tennis; Bicycling. Mgmt: Thea Dispecker ASC. Address: 72 Summit Rd., Elizabeth, NJ 07208, USA.

PIERSON, Herbert, b. 9 May 1914, Trenton, NJ, USA. Symphonic French Horn. Educ: BA, Curits Inst. of Music; Studied French Horn w. Anton Horner; Studied Violin w. Herbert Fletcher. m. Elizabeth Wayda, 1 s,1 d. Debut: St. Paul's Ch., 1928. Career: 5 yrs. w. Trenton Symph.; 1 yr. w. Kans. City Phil.; 36 yrs. w. Phila. Orch.; Tchr., French Horn, Temple Univ.; Tchr., French Horn, Phila. Musical Acad. Recordings w. Phila Orch., 1938-. Mbrships: Musicians Unions, Local 77 & Local 62 AFM. Hobbies: Gardening; Painting; Swimming; Horse Racing. Address: 28 Endicott Rd., Trenton, NJ, 06690, USA. 2.

PIERSON, Thomas Claude, b. 13 May 1922, Houston, Tex., USA. Professor of Music; Musicologist; Violinist. Educ: B Mus. in Educ., Univ., of Neb.; M Mus., Northwestern Univ.; PhD., Eastman Schl. of Music, Univ. of Rochester. m. Laurel Beth Polhemus, 2 s, 1 d. Career: Prof. of Music, Univ. of Houston; Mt. St. Mary's Coll., I.A., Calif.; Tex. A & I Univ. Publs: The Life & Music of John Alden Carpenter, microfilm Univ. of Rochester, 1953; Lecture (Fac. series) 'In Quest of Personal Freedom', 1969. Contbr. to: Tex. Music Tchr.; Clavier; Tex. Music Tchr. Mbrships: AAUP; Coll. Music Soc. Hobbies: Physical Fitness; Parapsycol. Address: 5909 Fenway Dr., Corpus Christi, TX 78413, USA.

PIGEAUD, Francois André Jean Robert, b. 22 Jan. 1943, Niort, France. Music Administrator; Producer. Educ: Studies of Lettres Classiques, Musicologie, organ. Career: Délégué

Général des Jeunesses Musicales de France, 1969-74; Classical Marketing Mgr., Pathe-Marconi EMI, 1974-76; Délégué Artistique, Ensemble Intercontemporain, 1976-78; Dir. of Music, Marais Fest., 1972, '73, '74; now Sec-Gen., Groupe Vocal de France, Chargé de Mission au Ministère de la Culture et de la Communication (Direction de la Musique), Prod., Radio-France. Publs: Guide des orgues de Paris, 1979; Mendelssohn, 1980. Contbr. to: Harmonie; Panorama de la Musique. Mbrships: Comité Directeur du Concours Int. d'Orgue de Chartres; Sec.-Gen., Association Francaise pour la Sauvegarde de l'Orgue Ancien; Société des Gens de Létteres de France. Hon: VP, la Federation Int. des Jeunesses Musicales, 1974-75. Hobby: The Organ. Address: 26 rue de Meaux, 75019, Paris, France.

PIGGOTT, Audrey Margaret, b. London, UK. Cellist; Pianist; Composer. Educ: RCM, London, (ARCM., perfs.); Ecole Normale de Musique, Paris. Career: num. concert apps. in London & throughout UK; num. broadcasts on BBC inclng. solo perfs. w. BBC Orch.; concert apps. in Vancouver & Victoria,BC &n in Alta., Canada. Compositions: 6 Elizabethan Songs for Female Voice; 2 Two-part Songs -On Westminster Bridge & A Boy's Song; sev. original & adapted plays performed on CBC Radio & TV. Mbrships: Fac., Community Music Schl. of Gtr. Vancouver. Hons. incl: Hoplison Silver Medal, RCM, 1929; 1st presentation, Leonard Borwick Mem. Prize, ibid. Hobby: Reading. Address: 2125 Eddington Dr., Vancouver, BC., V6L 3A9. Canada. 4, 21.

PIGNEGUY, John Joseph, b. 8 July 1945, Shoreham-by-Sea, Sussex, UK. Freelance Horn Player, also plays Descant Horn & Wagner Tuba. Educ: RAM, 1963-66; studied w. James Brown. m. Ruth Smith. Career: 1st Horn, London Mozart Players, 1968-70, also 1st Horn, Royal Opera House Covent Gd., 1972-74; Mbr., Merlot Trio & Nash Ensemble, making radio & TV broadcasts & "Proms" apps.; Musical Dir., Sound of Horns & London Horn Ensemble; Invited by Yehudi Menuhin to Gstaad Fest., Switz., 1978, w. Merlot Trio. Recordins incl: Dumbarton Oaks & Hummel Septet, Nash Ensemble; Baroque double horn concerti w. Gordon Carr & New Cantata Orch. under James Stobard; Sound of Horns-Dreamsville. Recip. Aubrey Brain Mem. Prize, RAM, 1965. Hobbies incl: Squash; Walking holidays. Address: 46 Northumberland Rd., N Harrow, Midx HA2 7RE, UK.

PIGOTT, Raymond, b. 13 Feb. 1935, Nottinghma, UK. Violinist; Music Educator. Educ: Royal Acad. of Music; LRAM (violin tchng.); ARCM (violin performing). m. Shelia M. Filmer, 2 s. Career: Music Master, Watlington Second. Schl. (Icknield Schl.), 1957-59; Violin Tchr., London Co. Coun., 1959-62; Ldr., W Riding String Quartet, 1962-68; String Advsr., Sheffield Educ. Comm., 1968-70; Sr. Lectr. in Music, Bretton Hall Coll., of Educ., 1970; Freelance violinist. Mbrships: Inc. Soc. of Musicians; European Strings Assn., etc. Hobbies: Reading; Travel. Address: 7 Park Grove, Horbury, Wakefield, Yorks., UK.

PIGUET, Michel, b. 30 Apr. 1932, Geneva, Switzerland. Oboist; Recorder Player. Educ: Conserv. of Geneva (Dip.); studied w. Olivier Messiaen, Marcel Delannoy & Roland Lamorlette, Paris. m. Terese Ponghis, 1 s., 1 d. Career: Oboist, 1956-64, Prin. Oboe, 1962-64, Tonhalle Orch., Zürich; Fndr., Ricercare Ensemble, 1963-; apps. as soloist & w. ensemble, Switz., France, Germany, Spain, Sweden, UK & USA; Tchr., Schola Cantorum Basiliensis, 1964-. Recordings: DGG; Eraot; Série Réflexe (EMI). Address: 22 Frankengasse, 8001 Zürich, Switzerland.

PIISPANEN, Sylvi Elisabet, b. Savonlinna, Finland. Concert Singer. Educ: Sibelius Acad., Helsinki; Dip., solo singing, Royal Danish Music Conserv., Copenhagen. Debut: Concert, Helsinki, 1959. Career: Concerts, Finland & Denmark, & sev. radio apps., Finland, Sweden, Norway & Denmark, mainly mod. Scandinavian songs & German Ch. cantatas etc. inclng. works by Hugo Distler, Wolfgang Hufschmidt, Hans Friedrich Micheelsen,Bach, Vivaldi, Hindemith, etc. & 'Geistliche Konzerte'. Publ: A small vocalise-variation for children's voices, 1975. Mbr., Freemasons. Hobbies: Travel; Needlework. Address: Adilsvej 121 st. tv., DK-22000 Copenhagen F., Denmark.

PIKE, Lionel John, b. 7 Nov. 1939, Bristol, UK. University Lecturer; Organist. Educ: BMus, MA, DPhil., Univ. of Oxford; FRCO; ARCM. m. Jennifer Marguerite Parkes, 2c. Career: Lectr., Royal Holloway Coll., Univ. of London. Publs: Eds. of Palestrina & Peter Philips, 1975, '76; Beethoven, Sibelius & The Profound Logic, 1978. Contbr. to Music & Letters; Soundings; The Consort; Musical Times. Mbrships: Pembroke Coll. Soc.; Royal Musical Assn.; RCO. Hons: Organ scholar, Pembroke Coll., Oxford, 1959-62; FRCO Limpus Prize, 1963.

Hobbies: Cricket; Medieval Architecture; Steam Railways. Address: 31B Armstrong Rd., Englefield Gn., Surrey TW20 ORW, UK.

PIKLER, Charles Robert, b. 5 Sept. 1951, Monrovia, Calif., USA. Violinist. Educ: B Math., Univ. of Minn.; studied w. Bronislaw Gimpel, Univ. of Conn.; Roman Totenberg, Berkshire Music Ctr., Tanglewood; Ben Ornstein, Norwich, Conn. Career: Violinist, Mnpls. Symph., Stanislaw Skrowaczewski cond.; Violinist, Cleveland Orch., Lorin Maazel cond.; Violinist, Rotterdam Phil. Orch., Edode Waart, cond., 1976-78; currently violinist, Chgo. Symph. Orch., Sir Georg Solti, cond. Mbr., Pi Mu Epsilon. Hons: Winner of Aetna Life Ins. Competition. Hobbies: Mathematics; Chess; Language Study. Address: c/o 1101 S Hunt Club Dr., Apt. 106, Mt. Prospect, IL 60056, USA.

PILAND, Jeanne Smith, b. 3 Dec. 1945, Raleigh, NC, USA. Singer (mezzo-soprano). Educ: B Mus, M Mus, E Carolina Univ., Greenville, NC. Debut: w. Balt. Opera Co., 1972. Career: Opera singer w. NYC Opera Co., Opera Cos. of Cinn., Louisville, Omaha, Balt., Chautauqua, Nev., Colo. Springs; Columbus Symph., Caramoor & Brevard Festivals. Mbrships: Pi Kappa Lambda;Sigma Alpha Iota. Hons: Prize Winner, Balt. Opera Auditions, 1972-73; Grants from Sullivan Fndn., 1973, Minna Kaufmann Ruud, 1973, Martha Baird Rockefeller, 1975 & Nat. Opera Inst., 1976. Hobby: Needle Mgmt. Jim Scovotti. Address: 515 W 59th St., NY, NY 10019, USA.

PILGRIM, Jack Alfred, b. 4 Jan. 1929, Keighley, UK. Lecturer in Education. Educ: BA, 1950, Cert Ed, 1952, B Mus, 1953, Univ. of Sheffield; 1st Prize, counterpoint & fugue, Conserv. of Lyon, France, 1951. M. Sylvi Peker, 2 s, 3 d. Career: Asst. Master, 1953-64; Lectr., music & music method in tchr. trng., 1964-73, educ., 1973-; Music Advsr., Nuffield Mod. Lang. Proj., 1964-70; Chief Examiner & Chmn. of Music Panel, JMB, 1969-. Publs. incl: Nuffield French Song Book, 1968; about 20 performing eds. of vocal music. Contbr. to musical books & jrnls. inclng: Grove's Dictionary, 6th ed.; Musik in Geschichte und Gegenwart, Mbr., Soc. for Rsch. in Psychol. of Music & Music Educ. Hobbies: Choral conducting. Wine making. Address: 54 St. Margaret's Rd., Horsforth, Leeds LS18 5BG, UK.

PILKINGTON, Charles Vere, b. 11 Jan. 1905, London, UK. Harpsichordist; Clavichordist; Organist. Educ: MA, Christ Church, Oxford. m. Hon. Honor Chedworth Philipps (dec.), 1 s. Career: Former Chmn., Sotheby & Co.; concerts in London, Oxford, Cambridge, Lisbon, & constant use as accomp. Mbrships: Committee, Royal Music Assn.; Contemporary Music Cos.; Musica Britannica. Contbr. of Musical criticisms to the London Mercury, & reviews for the Times Literary Supplement. Hons: Eton Organ Prize, 1922. Hobbies: Playing; Reading; Travelling. Address: Casal da Nora, Colares, Portugal

PILKINGTON, Michael Charles, b. 30 Sept. 1928, Pretoria, S Africa. Singing Coach; Conductor. Educ: MA, St. Catherine's Coll., Cambridge, 1949-52; GSM, 1952-53; LRAM Piano Accomp; LGSM Piano Tchng. m. Carol Ann, 2 d. Career: Fndr. Mbr. of Park Lane Group & Repetiteur for Handel Opera Co., New Opera Co., Opera Schl., 1953-61; Musical Dir., Waltr Gore's London Ballet, 1961-63; Prof., tchng. Harmony & Counterpoint, Keyboard Skills, General Musicianship & Interpretation of Song, GSM, 1964-; Examining Bd., ibid, 1968-; Pianist to LSO Chorus, Royal Phil. Orch. & Fest. Ballet, 1966-71; Cond., East Surrey Choral Soc. Publs: Early Georgian Song, Vols. 1/2; Songs of John Eccles; Songs of Thomas Arne, 1/2; Songs of James Hook; Songs of William Boyce; Stephen Storace, John Blow, The Linleys. Contbr. to: Musical Opinion. Mbrships: Treas., Assn. of English Singers & Speakers. Hons: FGSM, 1972. Hobbies: Reading; Poetry; Watching Plays. Address: 6 Woodstock Rd., Croydon, Surrey, UK.

PILLNEY, Karl Hermann, b. 8 Apr. 1896, Graz, Austria. Pianist; Composer. Educ: Konzertexamen, Hochschule für Musik, Cologne, 1922. m. Elisabeth Feldmann, 2d. Career: Concert tours in Europe; Prof. & ldr., master classes for piano, Hochschule für Musik, Cologne, 1930-61. Comps. incl: completion of Bach's Art of Fugue. Recordings: Parodistische Variationen für Orch. Hons: Sonderpreis des Sozialistischen Kulturbundes Berlin, 1929. Address: Bensberg, Kardinal-Schulte-str. 10, 5060 Bergisch Gladbach, German Fed. Repub.

PILSS, Karl, b. 7 Apr. 1902, Vienna, Austria. Pianist; Harpsichordist. Educ: Music Acad. Vienna, 1927; Vienna Univ., 1927-1930. m. Hertha Pilss. Career: 1932-1966, Assistant choir dir. Vienna State Opera; since 1939 solo choir tutor; 1926-1936, Tchr. Vienna Conserv.; 1960-1967, Tchr. Music Acad. Vienna. Comp. incl: Sonata in S, for trumpet and piano; Introduction Chorale and Hymn, for orch.; Vienna is

Dancing; waltzes for orch.; Baroque Suite, for Str. Orch.; Piano Concerto; Horn Concerto. Hons: Prof. title, 1953; Franz Schmidt Medal, silver, 1958; Hon. Cross for Sci. and Art, 1966; Jubilee ring, Vienna State Opera, 1968. Hobbies: Painting, watercolour, oil. Address: Laufberggasse 12, A1010 Vienna, Austria.

PINDER, Arthur Thomas, b. 31 July 917, Halifax, Yorks., UK. Educator; Choir Conductor & Director. Educ: Holy Trinity Schl., Halifax, Yorks; Fellow, Inst. of Legal Execs.; Fellow, Inc. Guild of Ch. Musicians. m. Edith Pamela Inston, 1 s., 1 d. Career: Treble & Tenor Soloist, Halifax Parish Ch., Yorks.; Past Cond., Datchet Womens Inst. Choir & Slough Male Voice Choir; Choral Lectr., E. Berkshire Coll. of Educ., until 1969; Registrar, Archbishop of Canterbury's Cert. in Ch. Music; Tenor Lay-Clerk, St. Geroge's Chapel, Windsor Castle, Berks., Gentlemen, HM Pvte. Chapel, Cond. & Dir., The Cloister Singers. Publs: History of Halifax Parish Ch. Choir. Contbr. to: The Reader; The Ch. Musician. Hobbies: Snooker; Bowls; Walking. Address: 16 The Cloisters, Windsor Castle, Berks., UK.

PINNELL, Janice Smith, b. 27 Apr. 1929, Tampa, Fla., USA. Teacher of Piano, Music Theory & Pedagogy. Educ: Piano Tchrs. Cert., 1949; BM, Southern Methodist Univ., Dallas, Tex., 1970; Cert., Music Tchrs. Nat. Assn. & Am. Coll. of Musicians. m. Whitney Leroy Pinnell, 1 s., 2 d. Career: studios in Temple Terrace & Tampa, Fla., 1950-55, Bay St. Louis, Miss., 1957-59, Mesquite, Tex., 1962-; Prep. Piano Tchr., Southern Methodist Univ., 1968-70, Dallas Independent Schl. Dist., 1971- 72; Ch. Musician, 18 yrs. Contbr. to: Clavier; Piano Guild Notes; Tex. Music Tchr.; Mesquite Daily News. Mbrships: Student Affiliate Bd. Mbr., Tex. MTA; num. offs., Mesquite, Dallas & Tampa Music Tchrs. Assns.; Organiser of Mesquite Chapts., Music Tchrs. Assn. & Nat. Guild of Piano Tchrs.; Altrusa Int. Hons: Scholarships & Assistantships. Hobbies: Raising Dogs; Writing; Floral Design; Collecting Books & Records. Address: 4329 Chestnut Dr., Mesquite, TX 75150, USA. 4.

PINNELL, Richard Tilden, b. 9 Jan. 1942, Whittier, Calif., USA. Musicologist; Guitarist. Educ: BA, 1967, MA, 1969, Brigham Young Univ.; CPhil, 1973, PhD, 1976, UCLA; guitar studies in Los Angeles & S Am. (Uruguay & Argentine). m. Maria Piedad Yarza of Melo, 3d. Career: former tchr., UCLA, Brigham Young Univ., Santa Monica Coll., Los Angeles City Coll., Los Angeles Valley Coll., Mt. San Antonio Coll.; now asst. prof., Univ. of Wis., Stevens Point. Publs: The Role of Francesco Corbetta in the History of Music for the Baroque Guitar, 1976. Contbr. to: Jrnl. of the Lute Soc.; Soundboard; Early Music; Am. Str. Tchr.; Guitar Player. Mbrships: Guitar Fndn. of Am.; Am. Musicol. Soc.; Coll. Music Soc.; Lute Soc. of Am.; Am. Fed. of Musicians. var. grants & awards. Address: 712 Leonard St., Stevens Point, WI 54481, USA.

PINNELL, Ruth, b. 30 Aug. 1917, Kans., Ill., USA. Singer (soprano); Teacher. Educ: B Mus, La. State Univ., Baton Rouge; M Mus, Univ. of Ill., Urbana; pvte. study w. Bruce Foote, Urbana, Ill.; Frank LaForge NYC; Ettore Verna, NYC; Maggie Teyte, London, UK. Career: Recitals & oratorio apperances in: St. Louis, Mo.; New Orleans, La.; Columbia, Mo.; Lexington, Ky.; Sioux Falls, SD.; Albany, NY.; Syracuse, NY.; Yankton, SD.; Amsterdam, NY.; Monroe, La.; Prof. of Voice, Schl. of Music, Syracuse Univ., NY Contbr. to book review 'Basic Techniques of Voice Production - Heizler' for the Am. Music Tchr., 1974. Mbrships: Nat. Pres., Assn. of Tchrs. of Singing; AAUP; Pi Kappa Lambda; Sigma Alpha Iota; MENC, etc. Hons: Sword of Hon. & Rose of Hon., Sigma Alpha Iota. Hobbies: Gardening; Cooking; Riding. Address: 311 Arnold Ave., Syracuse, NY 13210, USA. 5.

PINNOCK, Trevor David, b. 16 Dec. 1946, Canterbury, UK. Solo Harpsichordist; Educ: RCM, 1964-67; ARCM (piano & organ). Debut: as soloist, Purcell Room, London, 1971. Career: w. Galliard Harpsichord Trio, 1966-72; w. The Engl. Concert (Baroque instruments), 1973-; apps. frequently on radio & at major fests. inclng. City of London, Brighton, Engl. Bach, & Edinburgh; frequent apps. abroad. Recordings: Trevor Pinnock at the Victoria & Albert Museum (Engl. keyboard music); CPE Bach (harpsichord concertos); Rameau (solo keyboard); works by J S. Bach, Vivaldi & others. Contbr. to: Early Music, Mbr. ISM. Recip. of Raymond Russelll Harpsichord Prize, 1967. Mgmt: Basil Douglas. Address: 3 Cannon Lane, London NW3, UK.

PINSCHOF, Thomas, b. 14 Feb. 1948, Vienna, Austria. Flautist. Educ: Artist & Tchr. Dip., Vienna Conserv.; Acad. of Music, Freiburg. Debut: Wiener Musikverein, Brahms-Saal, 1965. Career incls: Mbr., Vienna Symph. Orch., 1971-72; Fndr., Ensemble Melkus Ensemble, 1973-; Artist in Res. w. Ensemble I, Victorial Coll. of Arts, Melbourne, Aust., 1976.

Recordings: Philips; DGG; Adel-Cord. Contbr. to musical publs. & prog. notes. Pres., Soc. of Friends of Ensemble I. Recip., var. musical hons. Hobbies: Cooking; Tennis; Reading; Skiing; Diving. Address: Dennebergpl. 910, A-1030 Vienna, Austria.

PINTO, Alejandro, b. 30 Aug. 1922, Nieswiez, Poland. (Argentine citizen 1954-). Manufacturer; Composer. Educ: Studied Piano, Harmony & Counterpoint w. William Gräetzer. m. Rebeca Efendovich. Debut: (as Comp.) 1948. Compositions incl: (publd.) Five Small Jewish Songs; (recorded) Five Small Chinese Songs; num. other vocal & orchl. pieces, some performed at Colon Theatre; Requiem for Alexandra, 1975. Mbrships: Argentine Soc. of Authors & Comps. of Music (SADAIC); Union of Comps. of Argentina; Young Comps. of Argentina Assn. Hons: Mention, Buenos Aires Musical Competition, 1970, for Alexandra's Time (perf. 1968); Prize, Nat. Fund. for the Arts, 1973, for Requiem for Alexandra (perf. 1973). Address: Serrano 439 1 A., Buenos Aires, Argentina.

PINTO, Carlo D, b. 13 Dec. 1925, Turbe, Yugoslavia. Associate Professor of Muisic. Educ: B Marcello Conserv., Venice; MMus, Composition, Eastman Schl. of Music, Rochester Univ., USA. m. Caterina Colla. Career: Cond.; Pianist, Europe & USA; Piano recordings for Swiss, Can. radio networks; Num. chmbr. music recitals; Master of Coll., SUNY Buffalo, NY, USA. Compositions performed incl: Interference '69; Symposium Overture; Three War Poems (voice & piano). One educl. recording of flute & piano music. Mbrship: AAUP. Address: 8111 Sheridan Dr., Buffalo, NY 14221, USA.

PINZARRONE, Nina Vacketta, b. 16 Apr. 1947, Danville, Ill., USA. Pianist; Accompanist; Arranger; Lecturer. Educ: BMus, Univ. of Ill.; MMus, ibid. m. Joseph Pinzarrone (div.), 1d. Debut: Univ. of Ill., 1971. Career: Accomp.-perf., Nat. Ballet Schl., Toronto, 1974-; TV app. Evening of Ballet perf. demonstrations; perf., contemporary music concerts incl: Mills Coll., Oakland, Calif., 1972, Delaware Belmont Symposium for New Music, 1975, & Int. Symposium for New Music, Tampa, Fla., 1976. Mbrships: Am. Fed. of Musicians; Mu Phi Epsilon. Hons: Can. Coun. grant for rsch. in Europe, 1979; Pi Kappa Lambda, 1969; Phi Kappa Phi, 1969. Hobbies incl: Reading; Needlepoint; Travel; Photography. Address: 68 Gilgorm Rd., Toronto, Ont. M5N 2M5, Canada.

PIRENNE, Maurice Maria, b. 29 Nov. 1928, Tilburg, Holland. Organist; Choirmaster; Music Educator. Educ: Philos. & Theol. study, 1946-52; Brabant Conserv., 1948-50; Pontifical Inst. of Sacred Music, Rome, 1953-59; M Mus (organ), 1956: M Mus (composition). 1957. Career incl: Organ recitalist in Holland, Italy, Germany & Belgium, Organist & Choirmaster; Prof. of Organ, Brabant Conserv.; Prof., Dutch Inst. of Roman Cath. Ch. Music, Utrecht & Municipal Conserv., Arnhem; Choirmaster, St. John's Cathedral, Hertogenbosch. Recordings incl. var. sacred choral works (KRO-Klassiek). Mbrships: Dutch Gregorian Assn.; Dutch Musicol. Assn.; Roman Cath. Organ Coun. Recip: Pascal-Schmeitz Prize for young ch. music composers, 1960. Address: Eikenlaan 1, Rosmalen, Holland.

PIRIE, Peter John, b. 24 Apr. 1916, Wood Green, London, UK Musicologist. Educ: Guildhall Schl. of Music & Drama. m. Mildred May Holmes, 2 s. Publ: Frank Bridge, 1971. Contbr. to: Musical Times; Musical Opinion; Music Review; Music & Musicians; Records & Recording; Haydn Yr. Book; Grove's Dictionary. Mbrships: Critic's Cir. Address: 2A Adur Ave., Shoreham-by-Sea, Sussex BN4 5NN, UK. 3.

PIRNER, Gitti, b. 26 June 1943, Immenstadt, Germany. Pianist. Educ: studied w. Erik Then-Bergh, Conserv. of Munich; advanced studies w. Louis Hiltbrand. Conserv. of Genf; master course w. Wilhelm Kempff. m. Wolfgang Noelle. Debut: at age 7, Augsburg, Germany. Career: has given recitals & orch. concerts in all capitals of Germany, Vienna, Milan, Rome, Genf, Basel, Lisbon, Athens, Bucharest, Warsaw, Brussel, Salzburg, Bayreuth, & Lucerne; has made TV & radio broadcasts in Germany, Switz., Austria & Poland. Compositions: Cadenzas for Mozart's piano concertos. Has recorded for all German broadcasting stns. & france musique. Hons: Gold Medal, Busoni Int. Competition, 1965; 1st Prize, Int. Music Competition, Genf, 1970. Hobbies: Art; Theatre; Skiing; Mountaineering. Mgmt: Erika Esslinger, Grimmstrasse 34, D-7 Stuttgart, German Fed. Repub. Address: Postfach 205, D-8132 Tutzing, German Fed. Repub.

PISCAER, Anny Petronella Henrica Maria, b. 8 Aug. 1902, Oud-en Nieuw Gastel, Netherlands. Musicologist; Pianist. Educ: Final Examination, Tilburg Conserv., 1927; studied Musicol. w. Prof. A Smijers, ibid, 1927-29; Univ. of Brussels, Belgium, 1929-31; Univ. of Utrecht, Netherlands, 1933-36; Courses of study of var. Methods, inclng., Tilburg Conserv., 1927-57, (Sucessor of Prof. Albert Smijers); Tchr., Municipal Schls. at

Breda, 1942-57, & Bergen op Zoom, 1950-68, & Tilburg & Breda Girls High Schl., 1948-68; var. Broadcasts lectures on medieval music, & old Dutch Songs, pre-1939; Lectrs., Old Netherlands Songs w. Laken Choir, Brussels Palais des Beaux Arts, 1946. Publs: Catechism on the History of Music, 1930; Var. articles on Jacob Obrecht. Contbr. to: Musica; Musik im Unterricht; Hausmusik; Gregorius; Ouverture; Preludium; Mens & Melodie; Opera; Acta Musicologica; Cecilia en de Muziek; Mixturen; Sinte Geertruydsbronne; Monumenta Musicae Belgicae; other profl. publs. Mbrships: Assn. of the Hist. of Dutch Soc. Dutch Musicians; Belgian Musical Soc.; Art; Ex Libris; Travelling; Trees & Flowers; Needlework; Book Collecting; Music. Address: Bredase straat 22, Bergen op Zoom, Netherlands.

PISCHNER, Hans, b. 20 Feb. 1914, Breslau, Germany. Teacher; Cembalist; Musicologist; Intendant. Educ: Musicol. studies at Inst. of Univ. of Breslau; keyboard studies w. Bronislaw von Pozniak & Gertrud Wertheim; Prof., 1949; PhD, 1961. Career incl: Hd., Radio music dept., 1950-54; Hd., Music dept., Min. of Culture, 1956-56; Representative, Min. of Culture, 1956-62; Intendant, Deutsche Staatsoper, Berlin, 1963-; num. apps. as soloist & accomp., Europe, Am. & Japan. Recordings: num. works of Bach, both as soloist & continuo player. Publs: Music in China, 1955; Die Harmonielehre Jean-Philippe Rameaus, 1967. sev. articles for profl. jrnls. Mbrships: Pres., Kulturbundes der DDR; Chmn., Neuen Bach-Gesellschaft, Leipzig; Akademie der Künste, Berlin; Exec. Committee, IMC. Hons. incl: Handel prize, Halle, 1961; Nat. prize, 3rd class, 1961; Johannes R Becher medal, 1962; Nat. prize, 1st class, 1976. Mgmt: Künsltler-Agentur, Berlin, German Dem. Repub. Address: Deutsche Staatsopera Berlin, 108 Berlin, Unter den Linden 7, German Dem. Repub.

PISK, Paul Amadeus, b. 16 May 1893, Vienna, Austria. Comopser; Teacher; Musicologist. Educ: PhD., Univ. of Vienna; Dip., Vienna Conserv. m. Irene Hanna Pisk, 1 c. Career: Num. Apps. as Pianist & Cond., Europe & USA; Prof., Vienna Municipal Univ. & Austro-Am. Conserv.; Prof., Univ. of Redlands, USA, 1937-50, Univ. of Tex., ibid, 1950-63, Wash. Univ., St. Louis, 1963-72; num. summer appts.; currently Prof., Calif. State Univ., North Ridge. Comps: 40 works. Co-author, History of Music & Musical Style. Contbr. to: Music Quarterly; Am. Music Tchr.; Notes, Lib. Assn.; Tex. Quarterly. Mbrships: Am. Comps. Alliance; Am. Music. Hons: Grand Prize, City of Vienna, 1925; Tex. Comps. Prize, 1944, '47; Hon. degree, Univ. of Vienna, 1969. Address: 2724 Westshire Dr., Los Angeles, CA 90068, USA. 3, 14.

PISTONE, Danièle, b. 1 Dec. 1946, Belfort, France. Musicologist. Educ: Licence de Lettres Modernes; Licence d'Italien; Maîtrise de Lettros Modernes - Doctorat d'Etat; Conserv. de Besancon; Schola Cantorum de Paris. m. Silvio Pistone, 1c. Career: Musicologist, Université Paris-Sorbonne; Prod., Television Francaise; Prod., Radio-France. Publs. incl: Le Piano dans la litterature francaise des origines jusqu'en 1900, 1975; La Symphonie dans l'Europe du XIXe siècle, 1977; La Musique à Paris de la Revolution à 1914, (in preparation); co-author, sev. books. Contbr. to profl. jrnls. Mbrships: Société Francaise de musicologie; Société internationale de musicologie; Société internationale de musique francaise. Address: 48bis rue Bobillot, 75013 Paris, France.

PITCATHLEY, John, b. 18 Feb. 1955, Motherwell, Scotland, UK. Organist; Teacher (Organ, Piano, Flute & Brass Instruments). Educ: Music Student & Organ Scholar, Glasgow Univ.; BMus, ibid, 1977. Debut: Local Organ recitals. Career: Apps. on BBC Songs of Praise Broadcasts & World Serv. Radio Broadcasts: Asst. Musical Dir., Local Operatic Soc.; Organist, Motherwell Cathedral; Mbr., Glasgow Univ. Chapel Choir. Contbr. to Music Assn., Lanarkshire Sec. of Organists. Hobbies: Cathedral Choir; Harmony; Singing; Playing Piano. Address: 57 St. Vincent Pl., Motherwell, Scotland, UK.

PITCHFORD, Joan, b. 12 May 1918, Melbourne, Aust. Teacher of Piano, Theory & Harmony. Educ: Sydney Conservatorium of Music, 1947, 48, 49, 50; AMSV, 1937; A Mus A, 1947; L Mus A (perf.), 1949; L Mus A (Tchr.), 1950. m. R K Pitchford (dec.). Career: Aust. Broadcasting Commission Broadcasts as soloist & Accomp., 1952-60; Tchr., NEGS, Armidale, NSW, 1952-60, MLC & pvtly. in Adelaide, SA. Mbrships: Pres., 1975-79, Coun. Mbr., 1963-, Music Tchrs. Assn. of SA; Aust. Soc. for Keyboard Music; Assoc. of Musical Soc. of Victoria., Aust. Music Exams. Bd., (Examiner, 1975-). Address: 17 Wahroonga Ave., Wattle Park, SA, 5066 Australia.

PITFIELD, Thomas Baron, b. 5 Apr. 1903, Bolton, Lancs., UK. Composer. Educ: Royal Manchester Coll. of Music; Hon. FRMCM. m. Alice Maud Astbury. Career: Prof. of Comp., Royal

Manchester Coll. of Music (later Royal Northern Coll. of Music), to 1973; var. broadcasts talks, perfs. & incidental music; solo recitals of works, North & Midlands. Comps. incl: Choral Suites; num. Songs, Part-Songs, Orchl. & Instrumental pieces; Piano Solos; Guitar Music; Carols, Ch. Music & Ch. Plays; over 20publrs. incl. USA; (recorded) Prelude, Minuet & Reel; Ballet in Education; Scherzetto from Sonata for Piano Accordion. Publs: Musicianship for Guitarists, 1959; var. non-musical publs. Contbr. to jrnls. Mbr., CGGB. Hons: Oxford Univ. Press Choral Competition, 1943; Welsh Nat. Eisteddfod Chmbr. Music Competition; Centenario della Filarmonica Competition, 1963; FRMCM. Address: Lesser Thorns, 21 E Downs Rd., Bowdon, Altrincham, Cheshire, UK. 3, 14, 16, 19.

PITTMAN, C Earl, b. St. Louis, Mo., USA. Educator; Jazz Historian; Clarinetist; Saxophonist; Bass Violinist. Educ: BME, Univ. Denver; M Mus, Ctrl. State Univ., Edmond Okla. m. Juanita Burnett, 4 children. Career: Profl. musician; Instrumental music classroom tchr., band & orch.; Orgnsr. & Ldr., Earl Pittman Jazz Orch.; Mbr., USN Band, 1942-45; Currently, Gt. Lakes Experience Band to record Documental Music for Veterans, Navy Bands, WWII. Mbrships. incl: Orgnsr. & Past Pres., Okla. Unit, Nat. Assn. Jazz Educators; Bd. Trustee, Local 37t AF of M, 2 terms; Phi Mu Alpha Sinfonia; OBA of Okla.; OMEA. Hobbies: Baseball; Tennis. Address: 838 NE 7th St., Okla. City, OK 73104, USA.

PITTMAN, Richard, b. 3 June 1935, Balt., Md., USA. Conductor. Educ: B Mus, Peabody Conserv.; Conducting w. Sergiu Celibidache, Accad. Chigiana, Siena, Italy; Fulbright Award, conducting, Hochschule fur Musik, Hamburg, Germany; Conducting w. Laszlo Halasz, NY, USA; Pierre Boulez, Basel, Switz. m. Lore Buchtemann, 1 s. Career incls: Cond. & Tchr., orchl. conducting, New England Conserv. Repertory Orch., 1968-; Cond., Concord Orch., Mass., 1969-; Music Dir., Boston Musica Viva, 1969-; Guest Cond., NSO, (Wash.), BBC Welsh Symph. Orch., Hessian Radio Symph. Orch., (Frankfurt) Hamburger Symph. (Hamburg), etc. Recordings: w. Boston Musica Viva & New England Conserv. Repertory Orch. Mgmt: Ingpen & Williams, 14 Kensington Court, London W8, UK. Address: 41 Bothfeld Rd., Newton Ctr., MA 02159, USA.

PITTS, Ruth Eleanor Landes, b. 11 Sept. 1939, Ft. Worth, Tex., USA. Music Teacher. Educ: BME, Baylor Univ., Waco, Tex., 1960; MA, George Peabody Coll. for Tchrs., Nashville, Tenn., 1960; PhD., ibid, 1968. m. William Lee Pitts, Jr. 2 s. Career: Instructor, Free Will Bapt. Bible Coll., Nashville, 1962-66; Min. of Music, 1st Bapt. Ch., Centerville, Ga. 1966-69; Vis. Lectr., Houston Bapt. Coll., Tex., 1969-70. Dallas Bapt. Coll., Tex., 1970-71; Music Tchr., Richardson Independent Schl. Dist., 1972-74; Pvte. Tchr., Piano, Voice, 1962-; Judge. Dallas Symphonic Fest., 1972-75; NGPT, 1974. 1975 & 1976; Muisc History Lctr., Baylor Univ., 1977; Music Instructor, McLennan Community Coll., 1977 . Author, Don Juan Hidalgo, 17th Century Spanish Composer, 1968. Mbrships: Am. Musicol. Soc.; MENC; NGPT; Tex. Music Educators Assn.; Music Tchrs. Nat. Assn.; Tex. Music Tchrs. Assn. Richardson Music Tchrs. Recip. num. Hons. Address: 717 Ivyan Dr., Waco, TX 76710, USA.

PIZARRO, David (Alfred), b. 15 May 1931, Mount Vernon, NY, USA. Organist. Educ: MusB, Yale Univ., 1952; MusM, ibid., 1953; Nordwestdeutsche Musikakademie, 1953-55; ARCO; FTCL; Assoc., AGO. Debut: NY, 1946. Career: 16 European concert tours; recitals in most European countries; num. recordings for radio; titular Organist & Master of the Choristers, Cathedral Ch. of St. John the Divine, NY, 1974-. Recordings: Music of Holy Russia; 75 yrs. of Cathedral Music; French organ music; Christmas at the Cathedral, etc. Contbr. to: The Anglican; The Harvard Alumni mag.; Eds. of old masters. Mbrships. incl: Ch. Club of NY; NY Chapt. of AGO; Royal Schl. of Ch. Music; Alcuin Club. Hons: Sherman Organ prize, Yale Univ., 1953; Flubright grant to Germany, 1953. Hobbies: Philately; Bicycle riding. Address: 29 Pearl St., Mt. Vernon, NY 10550, USA.

PLACEK, Robert Walter, b. 25 Aug. 1932, Chgo. Ill., USA. Associate Professor of Music. Educ: BME, De Paul Univ.; MS, in Mus. Educ.; EdD, in Music Educ., Univ. of Ill. m. Joyce Wolters, 2 d. Career: Pub. Schl. Music Tchr., 11 yrs.; Instr., Univ. of Ill., 2 yrs.; Asst. Prof., 6 yrs., now Assoc. Prof., Univ. of Ga. Publs: (co-author) computer-Assisted Instruction Package, EMUS, 1976. Contbr. to Jrnl. of Rsch. in Music Educ. Mbrships: MENC; Ga. Composers; Pi Kappa Lambda; VP, Nat. Consortium for Computer-Based Musical Instn. Hobbies: Composing; Jazz piano playing. Address: 375 Greencrest Dr., Athens, GA 30601, USA.

PLAISTOW, Stephen, b. 24 Jan. 1937, Welwyn Gdn. City, UK. Critic; Administrator; Pianist. Educ: ARCM; MA, Clare Coll.,

Cambridge. Career: Free-lance Jrnlst., 1961; BBC Music Prod., 1962-74; Chmn., Brit. Sect. of ISCM & Music Sect. of ICA, 1967-71; Mbr., Music Panel, Arts Coun. of GB, 1972-; Chief Asst. to Controller of Music, BBC, 1974-; Chmn., Brit Sect. of ISCM & Arts Coun. Contemp. Music Network, 1976-. Contbr. to: Gramophone Musical Times; Tempo. Mbr., Critics' Circle. Hobby: Travel in France. Address: Flat 5, 33 Gloucester Ave., London NW1 7TJ, UK.

PLANCK, Gerd (Lillemor), b. 26 Sept. 1915, Oslo, Norway. Family Assistant; Composer. Educ: Pvte. studies, piano. m. Henrik Planck, 2 d. Debut: State Artist, Lilla teatern, Helsingfors, Finland, 1955. Career: Stage artist, Helsingfors, Compenhagen & Oslo; Radio apps., Norway. Comps. incl: (recorded) Ett Flickenbarn; Sang med positiv; Nidvisa Till manniskan; Sa kul; Sju dikter om Kärlek; Knäppupp; Roslagen (for chorus). Mbr., children's songs for Swedish TV, 1964; SKAP stipendiary for children's songs, 1967. Hobbies: Music; Lyrics. Address: Olaus Petrigatan 2 nb, S-115 34 Stockholm, Sweden.

PLANTINGA, Leon Brooks, b. 25 Mar. 1935, Ann Arbor, Mich., USA. Music Historian; Pianist. Educ: BA, Clavin Coll., 1957; M Mus, Mich. State Univ., 1959; PhD, Yale Univ., 1964. m. Carol J. Cevaal, 2 s. 1 d. Career: Prof., Music Hist., chmn., music dept., Yale Univ.; Lectures, lecture-recitals, univs., USA, Canada, GB, Germany. Publs: Schumann as Critic, 1967; Muzio Clementi: his Life & Music, 1977. Contbr. to profl. jrnls. Mbrships. incl: Bd. Dirs., Am. Musicol. Soc., 1972-74; Int. Musicol. Soc. Hons: Fellowships, Am. Coun. Learned Socs., Am. Philosophical Soc., Alexander von Humboldt Stiftung, & John Simon Gugggenheim Fndn.; Nat. Endowment for the Humanities Rsch. Fellowship, 1979-80. Hobbies incl: Mountaineering. Address: Music Dept., Yale Univ., Newhaven,CT 06520, USA. 14.

PLANYAVSKY, Peter Felix, b. 9 May 1947, Vienna, Austria. Cathedral Organist; Lecturer. Educ: Music Acad., Vienna, 1959-67; Master's degrees in organ, 1966, ch. music, 1967. m. Maria Planyavsky, 1 d., 1 s. Career: Cathedral Organist, St. Stephens Cathedral, Vienna; Lectr., Musikhochschule, ibid.; Recitals & broadcasts, Europe, Aust., Japan, S Africa & USA. Comps. (publs.) incl: (organ) Sonata II pro organo; Toccata alla Rumba; Veni, quaeso, veni Sancte Spiritus; (organ & voice) Zwei geistliche Gesange; (choir & organ) Deutsches Ordinarium; (choir, organ & other instruments) Zwei Stücke zur Passion. Recordings incl: Franz Liszt Orgelwerke; Austrian Organ Music. Hons. incl: Förderungspreis für Musik der Stadt Wien, 1975. Address: Singerstrasse 22/6, 1010 Vienna, Austria. 19.

PLATEN, Emil, b. 16 Sept. 1925, Düsseldorf, Germany. Conductor; Musicologist. Educ: Univs. of Cologne, Münster & Bonn, PhD, 1957; NW German Music Acad., Detmold; Dip. of Choir-Cond., 1950. m. Helga Bingel, 3 s. Career: Chmbr. Musician & Cond., Düsseldorf, Cologne & Bonn, 1951-; Fndr. & Dir., Collegium Musicum, Bonn Univ. (num. concert tours, Europe & overseas), 1953-; Acad. Contbr., Beethoven Archives, Bonn, 1957-64; St. Lectr., 1959, Acad. Music Dir., 1964, Hon. Prof. of Musicol., 1971, Univ. of Bonn. Contbr. to: Bach-Jahrbuch; Neue Bach-Ausgabe; complete ed. of Beethovens Werke; Die Musikforschung. Address: Im Erlengrund 22, D 5300 Bonn 2, German Fed. Repub.

PLATH, Wolfgang, b. 27 Dec. 1930, Riga (formerly Letland. Music Researcher. Educ: Free Univ. Berlin, musicol., phil.; Tübingen, 1958, DPh. m. Margit Mende, 3 d. Career: since 1960, mbr., Bd. of Dir., New Mozart ed. Publs. incl: Piano book for W Fr. Bach; var. vols New Mozart Ed.; Joseph Schuster, Sei Divertimenti da Camera; Giuseppe Sarti, violin sonate in B op. III/3. Mbrships: Soc. for Music Rsch.; Zentralinst. für Mozartforschung, Salzburg. Contbr. to: Grove's Dict., 6th ed.; Mozart Annual; var. profl. jrnls. Hons: Austrian Cross of Honour 'Litteris et Artibus' 1st Class, 1977. Hobbies: Piano, 4 handed; Mycology; Cooking. Address: Karwendelstr. 19, D-8900, Augsburg, German Fed. Repub.

PLATTHY, Jeno, b.13 Aug. 1920, Dunapataj, Hungary. Composer; Poet. Educ: P. Pazmany Univ., 1942; Tchrs. Dip.; Ferencz J Univ., 1944; MS, PhD, Catholic Univ. of Am., 1965, MS; Ferenc Liszt Conserv., 1943. m. Carol L Abell. Debut: String Quartet, Opus 5, Bruxelles, 1939. Career: Bamboo, Bicentennial Opera of the US 1976, Wash., DC; Exec. Dir., Fed. of Int. Poetry Assns. Comps. Bamboo, Opera in 3 acts, op.78, 1965; Concertum Lyrae, op.11, 1943; Christmas String Quartet, op.80, 1979. Publs: Tavasz; 1948; Summer Flowers, 1960; Autumn Dances, 1963; Winter Tunes, 1975; Springtide, 1976; Bela Bartok, 1980. Contbr. to: Nouvelle Europe. Mbrships: ASCAP; PEN; Int. Soc. of Lit., etc. Hons: D Letters (hon.) Accademica Sinica, 1975; PhD (hon.),

Yangmingshan Univ., 1975; D Lit. (hon.), Univ. Libre Asie, 1977. Address: PO Box 39072, Wash. DC 20016, USA. 6, 10, 28, 29.

PLATTS, Kenneth Michael, b. 22 Apr. 1946, Calcutta, India. Composer. Educ: LCM. Comps: num. songs & carols for children; Cantatas; The Borders of Sleep, The Highwayman; Orchestral Works; Music for the Maltings, Elizabethan Dances, Brighton Fest. Overture; Brass Band; Little Suites No. 1 & 2, Concerto for Brass Band, Overture, Street Party; Incidental music for TV, radio & stage. Recordings: Strand-on-the-Green (own comp). Contbr. to: Making Music; Music Tchr.; Music in Educ. Mbrships: PRS. Hobbies: Swimming; Keep-fit. Address: 69 Portland Rd., Kingston-upon-Thames, Surrey, UK.

PLAVEC, Joseph, b. 1905, Hermanuv Mestec, Bohemia. Professor; Composer. Educ: PhD., Fac. of Arts, Charles Univ., Prague; Stage Conserv. of Music; Sorbonne, Paris, France. m. Anne Cinkova, 1 s, 2 d. Career: Second. Schlmaster. of philol. of music, 1930-48; Tchr., State Conserv. of Music, Prague, 1948; Prof., Pedagogic Fac., Prague, 1948-53, & Pedagogic Dept., Charles Univ., 1954-59; Hd., Chair for Music Educ., 1959-; External Prof., Acad. of Muical Arts, Prague; Cond., sev. choral socs. inclng. Bohemian Mixed Choir. Comps incl: We the Czechoslovak Nation (cantata); Conception (words by Rabhindrath Tagore); many songs, part-songs, song cycles, choir arrs. of folk songs, etc.; Fantasia for violin & piano; Variations on Christmas Carol for piano; Scherzo-Polka for harp; many other instrumental works; sev. orchestral works. Publs: sev. monographs. Contbr. to jrnls. Mbr: Union of Czech Composers. Recip. of many hons. & awards. Address: 53803 Hermaniv Mestec 197, Czech.

PLEETH, Anthony Michael, b. 11 May 1948, London, UK. Musician (Cellist); Professor of Music. Educ: AGSM. Debut: London, 1965. Career: Recitals at Music Clubs, 1965-; Radio perfs., 1966-; Prof., GSM, 1966. Hobbies: Cooking; Carpentry. Address: 8 Garden Lodge Ct., Church Lane, London, N2, UK.

PLEETH, William, b.12 Jan. 1916, London, UK. Cellist; Professor. Educ: London Acad.; London Cello Schl.; Leipzig Conserv. m. Margaret Good, 1 s, 1 d. Debut: Leipzig, 1931; London, 1933. Career: Perfs., BBC TV & Radio; Concerts, London, UK, Netherlands, Germany, France, Italy, Australia & NZ; apps., BBC radio & TV; Prof., Guildhall Schl. of Music & Drama. Recordings: Var. cello & piano sonatas by Brahms & Mendelssohn; Schubert Quintet & Messiaen Quartet, Brahms Sextets. Mbrships: ISM; ESTA. Hon. Fellowship, Guildhall Schl. of Music & Drama. Hobbies: Gardening; Collecting Early English Furniture. Address: 19 Holly Pk., London N3 3JB, UK. 3.

PLESHAKOV, Vladimir, b. 4 Oct. 1934, Shanghai, China. Concert Pianist; Recording Artist; Associate Professor of Music; Musicologist. Educ: Dip., New S. Wales Conserv. of Music, Sydney, Aust., 1953; AB., Univ. of Calif., Berkeley, 1958; B Mus. Arts. Stanford Univ., 1972. m. Svetlana Kossobudsky, 2 s. Debut: Sydney, Aust., 1950. Career: Concerts in Aust., Can., USA, Japan; Discoverer, Perf. of neglected piano music; Assoc. Prof. of Music, Hd., Piano Dept., Univ. of Evansville; Fac. Mbr., Nueva Learning Ctr., Hillsborough, Calif., 1968-. Fndr; Pleshakov-Kaneko Music Inst. Recordings: 10 L P's Piano Solos, Orion; piano works by Joseph Woelfl, Friedrich Wilhelm Rust, Bonifacio Asioli, Paul Dukas, Vincetn d'Indy, Dmitri Shostakovich, Medtner, Chausson, Grieg, Prokfiev, Dussek, Szymanowski, Balakirev. Mbrships: Advsry. Bd., Pacific Musical Soc.; Former Dir., ibid; VP, Global Intercultural Soc. Winner, Aust. Broadcasting Commission Concerto Competition, 1950. Mgmt: Artists Int., Suite 409, 1050 N Point, San Francisco, CA 94019, USA. Address: 470 Romana, Palo Alto, CA 94301, USA.

PLETTNER, Arthur Rudolph, b. 15 Nov. 1904, NYC, USA. Composer; Conductor. Educ: Royal Bavarian Conserv., Wuerzburg, Germany; Juilliard Grad. Schl. of Music, USA, 3 yrs.; B Mus, Univ. of Toronto, Can. m. Isa McIlwraith. Career incls: Assoc. Cond. & Choirmaster, German Light Opera Co., 1924-27, & Floranz Ziegfeld Prods., 1927-30, NYC; Mbr., NY Oratorio Soc. Orch., 1933-42; Chautaqua, NY Symph. Orch., Worcester, Mass., Fest. Orch., Cond., Symph. Orch. Chattanooga, Tenn., 1937-49; Juilliard Prof. of Music, 1937-73, & Chmn., Music Dept., 1966-69, Univ. of Tenn. ibid. Comps. incl: Communion Service in D; Barn Dance (str. orch.); Symph. in G; Appalachia (str. quartet). Publs: Studies in Conducting; articles & reviews. Mbr., Am. Musicol. Soc. Recip., Commissions, prizes & grants. Hobby: Model Railroading. Address: 105 Druid Drive, Signal Mtn., TN 37377, USA. 7.

PLINKIEWISCH, Helen Edwina, b. 22 Apr. 1908, Portland, Ore., USA. Music Educator. Educ: BS in Music Educ., NY Univ., 1931; MA in Music Educ., Columbia Univ., 1934; EdD in Music Educ., ibid, 1955; Dip. in piano & theory, Conserv. of Music, Ore. State Univ., 1929; music study in Rome & Vienna, 1929-30; Piano studies w. Lillian Jeffreys Petrie, Alton Jones & Kiriena Siloti. Debut: Piano recital, Corvallis, Ore., 1929; Concerto w. orch., Corvallis, 1929. Career: Pioneer in use of creative methods to introduce grand opera to the young; 13 Demonstrations of Opera Educ. for the Young, NYC, 1958-71 & in Phil. Hall, NYC, 1973; TV apps. NYC, 1958, '60, '68; Supvsr. of Music, Odessa, NY, 1931-33; Music in Garden City, Pub. Schls., NY, 1935-74; Lectr. in Music Educ., New Paltz State Univ., Farmingdale, NY, 1953 & Hofstr Univ., 1953-70; Tchr., Workshop, Opera in the Classroom, Cultural Arts Center, Syosset, NY, 1977. Cons. in Opera for the Tchrs. Edn. of Music in Our Life & Music in Our Times. Advsr. & Contbr., They Shall Have Opera, 1959, Co-author, A Merry Go Round of Songs. mbr. num. profl. socs. Recip. num. hons. Hobbies: Travel; Poetry; Genealogy. Address: 56 Kingsbury Rd., Garden City, NY 11530, USA. 12.

PLODER, Katherin Norine Olivia, b. Calcutta, India. Violinist. Educ: in London & studied w. Carl Flesch for 3 yrs. from age 12; studied w. Ginette Neveu, Paris, France; Master Classes w. Henri Temianka in USA. div., 2 d. Career: Mbr., Boyd Neel Str. Orch.; Mbr., Edward Silverman Str. Quartet; Solo recitals & broadcasts in UK, Israel & Middle East; Tchr., & coach in chmbr. music; as Sculptor, has exhibited in major London exhibs. Mbrships: ISM; Lake Artists Soc. Hobbies: Sculpture; Old Cottages; Knitting in Mohair; Address: Cherry Tree, Troutbeck, Windermere, Columbria, UK. 3.

PLOTT, Stefan Julius Johannes, b. 25 Dec. 1939, Vienna, Austria. Violinist. Educ: Studied Violin w. mother, 1946-; studied w. Prof. Karl Barylli, Vienna State Conserv., 1950-54; studied at Acad. for Music & Performing Arts, Vienna w. Prof. Vasa Prihoda, 1954-57, & Prof. Franz Samohyl, 1957-60. m. Edda-Solvejg Mallin. Career: Played Violin w. children's orch. in film, Du Bist die Welt für Mich, 1949; Mbr.; Mozart Youth Orch., 1950-54; Concert tour to Switzerland as mbr. of Str. Quartet w. the Sängerknaben vom Wienerwald, 1954; substitute player w. Vienna Phil. Orch. at Var. concert tours in Europe as Guest mbr., Philharmonia Hungarica, 1956-57; 1st Violinist, Vienna Symph. Orch., 1961-; permanent mbr. & 3rd Ldr., ibid, 1969; extensive world wide concert tours; Mbr.; Concentus Musicus, 1966-69. Recordings: Num. recordings w. Vienna Symph. Orch., 1961-, & w. Concentus Musicus. Hons: Bronze Medal, Mozart Orch.; 1st Prize, Vienna State Conserv. Competition. Hobbies: Trout Fishing; Skiing; Tennis; Music; Theatre. Address: A-1210 Vienna, Mayerweckstrasse 28, Austria.

PLOWRIGHT, Rosalind Anne, b. 21 May 1949, Workshop, UK. Opera Singer. Educ: Royal Manchester Coll. of Music; London Opera Ctr.; Perfs. Dip. Debut: Rossweisse in Valkyrie, Engl. Nat. Opera, 1975. Career: Glyndebourne Festival Opera; Maj. roles: Glyndebourne Touring Opera; Engl. Nat. Opera; Kent Opera; Debut Recital: Purcell Room, London, 1976; Apps. in Operas filmed at Glyndebourne for TV; Broadcasts w. Kent Opera for Radio 3. Hons: League of Opera Prize (Awarded at Coll.), 1972; Peter Stuyvesant Scholarship, 1973. Hobbies: Painting; Reading; Cooking; Climbing; Walking. Mgmt: Ibbs & Tillet. Address: 211 Maybank Rd., S Woodford, London E18 1EP, UK.

POAKWA, Daniel Anim, b. 28 April 1936, Konongo, Ashanti-Akim, Ghana. Music Teacher; Composer; Acting Headmaster. Educ: Tchr. Trng. Coll. Cert. A; Gen. Cert. of Educ. O Level; Theory Grade VIII, ABRSM; Gen. Dip. in Music, Univ. of Ghana, Legon. m. Rose Afua Serwaa, 4 c. Career: Acting Headmaster, Akomadan Sec. Schl. Akomadan-Ashanti. Comps: Engl. songs. Problems; The Sportman's World; Sympathetic Teasing; How Did Moses Cross The Red Sea?; Child on Platain Leaves; spiritual; Ibi Nfifirsam Ne Anigyee; Handwork; Twisongs; Enne Yeate De Nne; Ma Me Man Nsore; Yehye Wo Nsam; Nyame Ne Yen Nam. Recordings for Ghana Broadcasting Corp. Mbrships: Ghana Music Tchrs. Assn.; Planning Committee for Ghana Sec. Schls. Syllabus; Soc. for Rsch. in African Music. Hobbies: Listening to classical music; Oware playing. Address: Qsei Kyeretwie Second. Schl., PO Box 3789, Kumasi, Ghana. 28.

PODOLSKI, Michel, b. 9 Apr. 1928, Brussels, Belgium. Lutenist; Musicologist. Debut: Pro Musica Antiqua, 1948. Career: Pro Muica Antiqua, 1948-56; Duo w. Mezzo Christiane Van Acker, 1956-; Cond., Soloist, Renaissance & Early Baroque Recitals & Chmbr., Music; Seminars. Eastman Schl. of Music, Folger Shakespeare Lib., Univs.; Radio, TV Perfs., ORTF, RTB, EMS, CBC. Recordings: 20 Anthologies of Lute Music; HMV; EMS; BAM; Contrepoint. Publs: Ed., Monteverdi, Orfeo, 1966; Ed. several 100's of works for lute, lute & voice, consorts, Early Baroque Operas, Contbr. to: Ctr. Int. de la

Recherche Scientifique Francais; Belgian Musical. Soc. Review; Cles pour la Musique, Brussels. Mbr. Belgian Musicol. Soc. Hobbies: Archaeology; Sociology; Botany. Address: 28 Kelleveld, 1990 Hoeilaart, Belgium.

POELL, Alfred, b. Linz, Austria. Opera Singer (Baritone). Educ: MD, Specialist in Oto-rhino-laryngol., Univ. of Vienna. m. Helene Sigmund. Career incl: Prin. Baritone, Dusseldorf opera, 1928-39; Prin. Baritone Vienna State Opera, 1939. Num. recordings issued. Mbr., Union Yacht Club. Address: Frankenberggasse 3, Vienna, Austria.

POHJOLA, Erkki, b. 4 Jan. 1931, Ylistaro, Finland. Music Institute Director. Educ: Grad., Music Educ., Sibelius Acad., Helsinki. m. Aino Leppihalme,3 s. Career: Cond., Tapiola Children's Choir & Chmbr. Orch., tours in Finland, Sweden, Norway, France, Estonia, Russia, Yugoslavia, UK. Poland, USA & Switz. & TV & radio perfs., UK. German Fed. Repub., Scandinavia & USA. Recordings: Blue & White, 1967; Tapiola Sings, 1969; Sounds of Tapiola, 1972; Christmas in Tapiola, 1974; The Tapiola Children's Choir, 1976. Publs: Pedagogic Book Serial for Schools; Musica I, 1965, 2nd ed., 1975, II, 1967, 2nd ed., 1976, III, 1969, IV, 1974. Mbr., Int. Soc. for Music Educ. Hons. incl: Finnish State Prize for Info. Publng., 1974. Hobby: Sports. Address: Iltaruskontie 4 A 1, 02120 Espoo 12, Finland.

POHJOLA, Maija-Liisa, b. 9 July 1936, Seinäjoki, Finland. Pianist; Piano Teacher. Educ: musical studies in Finland, Vienna, Salzburg, Paris, GFR & Italy. 2c. Debut: Helsinki, 1955. Career: apps. as soloist, recitalists & chmbr. Musician in Finland, Scandinavia, German, UK, Czech., etc.; Prof. of piano & chmbr. music; Sibelios Acad., Helsinki. Recordings: works by Liszt, Bartok, Heininen, Bergman, Meriläinen, Salmenhaara & Ligeti. Hons. Folkwang prize, Essen, 1960; Finnish Comps. prize for advocacy of Finnish comps., 1975. Mgmt: Fazer Concert Agency, Helsinki; Anglo-Finnish Concert Soc., London. Address: Tontunmäntie 17, As.1, 02200 Espoo 20, Finland.

POHJOLA, Paavo, b. 22 Feb. 1934, Seinajoki, Finland. Violinist. Educ: Music Acad., Vienna, Austria. m. Eeva Kontiola, 5 children. Debut: Helsinki, 1955. Career: Violin soloist, Scandinavia, German, France, Hungary etc.; 1st ldr., stockholm Phil. Orch., 1965-73; 1st ldr., Radio Symph. Orch., Helsinki. Recordings: sev. as soloist & mbr. chmbr. grps. Mbr., Finnish ISCM Sect. Address: Metsapirtintie, 02880 Veikklo, Finland.

POHL, William Francis, b. 16 Sept. 1937, Clinton, Iowa, USA. Cantor (Gregorian Chant) & Choir Director. Educ: SB, 1957, SM, 1958, Univ. of Chgo.; PhD, Univ. of Calif. at Berkeley, 1961; pvte. study of muic. Career: Cantor & Choir Dir., De Sales House, Chgo., 1958-59, Newman Hall, Berkeley, 1959-61, MIT Chapel, Cambridge, Mass., 1961-62, St. Ann Chapel, Palo Alto, Calif., 1962-64; Fndr. & Dir., Concentus Musicus, Minn., 1966-73; Cantor. Master of th Chant & Asst. Choir Dir., Ch. of St. Agnes, St. Paul, Minn., 1972-78; Cantor, Twin Cities Schola Cantorum, 1978-. Recordings: Music from the Field of the Cloth of Gold, Concentus Musicis, 197 3. Contbr. to Sacred Music (Assoc. Ed.). Mbrships. incl: Consociatio Internationalis Musicae Sacrae. Address: Dept. of Mathematics, Univ. of Minnesota, Mpls., MN 55455, USA. 8.

POHLREICH, Ferdinand, b. 10 June 1917, Budapest, Hungary. Pianist. Educ: LLD Charles Univ., Prague, Czech., 1945; Dip., Musical Acad. Prague, 1950. m. Marie Rychlikova, 1 s. Debut: Prague, 1950. Career: Concert activity, esp. as pianist of Herman's trio, 1950-70; Radio & TV recordings of chmbr. Orch., mbrs. of Viach's quartet & other instrumentalits & singers; Musical Prod., Radio Prague, 1957-. Comps. incl. most frequent played incl. Beethoven, Schubert, Schumann, Debussy, Dvorak, Smetana. Mbrships: Assn. of Czech Comps. & Instrumentalists. Dvorak Soc. Address: Rimskyu 37, Prague 2, Czech.

POINTON, Barbara, b. 13 Aug. 1939, Stoke-on-Trent, Staffs, UK. Senoir Lecturer in Music. Educ: 1st Class Hons. Birmingham Univ., 1960. m. Malcolm John Pointon, 2 s. Career: Sr. Lectr. in Music, Homerton Coll., Cambridge; Rsch. into the Restoration verse anthem; Second. & Primary tchng.; Occasional schl. broadcasts; Recorder playing; Children's Saturday music club. Comps. incl: Songs for the Pictogram System for Remedial Readers; Triptych for String Quartet, 1968; Hymn to St. Thomas of Canterbury, 1969. Mbrships: Musical Dir., Cambridge Br., Soc. of Recorder Players; Royal Muaical Assn. Hons. incl: Barber Schlrship., 1959 & 60. Hobbies incl: Gardening. Address: Opus One, Lower St., Thriplow, Royston, Herts., UK.

POKORNÝ, Petr, b. 16 Nov. 1932, Prague, Czechoslovakia. Composer; Research Worker. Educ: Charles Univ.; Prague

Conserv.; Pvte. study w. Prof. Pavel Borkovec, Recorded Compositions; Sonatina for clarinet & piano; Duo for flute & clarinet. Publd. Comps.: Solo compositions for clarinet, flute & viol.; Chmbr. music; songs. Hobbies: Travel; Cookery; Writing Short Prose Poems. Address: Na Petrinách 392, 16200 Prague 6, Czech. 2.

POLEWSKA, Ludmilla (nee Timoschenko), b. 8 Sept. 1898, Krakow, Poland. Professor of Music; Concert Cellist. Educ: Kharkow Conserv., Ukraine; Moscow Conserv. m. Prof. Dr. Nicholas Polewsky, 1 d. Debut: Moscow, 1916. Career: Fndr., Ukrainian State Trio; Quartet Leontowich; Prof. of Cello, Moscow, Kharkow & Vienna Conservs.; Soloist w. symph. orch.; own cello recitals; chmbr. music concerts, Europe, USA, Can. Ed. of works of contemporary comps. Mbrships. incl: Assoc. Musicians of Ctr. NY; Am. Fedn. of Musicians. Contbr. to profl. jrnls. Recip., Gold Medal, Moscow Conserv. Hobby: Poetry. Mgmt: Ukrainian Music Inst. of Am. Inc., NYC, USA. Address: 34-40 78 St., Apt. 3H, Jackson Heights, NY 11372, USA.

POLEWSKA, Zoia, b. 31 May 1929, Krakow, Poland. Concert Cellist. Educ: Vienna Acad. of Music. m. Anatole Darow. Debut: Vienna Concert House. Career: num. concerts & recitals, Europe, USA, Can.; Soloist w. symph. orchs. inclng. Vienna Phil., La Scala, Venice Theatre, Radio Italiano; Radio concerts in Europe, Can., USA, inclng. Carnegie Hall & Town Hall, NYC. Comps: Ukrainian Song; many transcriptions for cello. Mbrships. incl: Assoc. Musicians of Ctr. NY; Am. Fedn. of Musicians. Contbr. to profl. jrnls. Hons: Dama d'Onore di Merito del Ordine della Concordia, Rome, 1946. Hobbies: Singing; Dramatic art. Mgmt: M Bichurin Concerts Corp., Carnegie Hall, NY 10019, USA. Address: 34-40 St. Apt. 3H, Jackson Heights, NY 11372, USA.

POLGAR, Tibor, b. 11 Mar. 1907, Budapeast, Hungary. Composer; Conductor; Pianist; Professor of Music. Educ: Univ. of degree in Philos.; Dip. in Composition, Royal Acad. of Music, Budapest, 1925. m. Ilona Nagykovacsi. Debut: Concerts &` radio broadcasts, Budapest, 1925. Career: Cond., Composer in residence, Hungarian Broadcasting Corp., 1925-48; Artistic Dir., Hungarian Radio, 1948-50; Assoc. Cond., Philharmonica Hungarica, Marl-Westpahlen, Germany, 1962-64; Tchng. Staff. Opera Dept., Univ. of Toronto, Canada, 1966-75; York Univ., Toronto, 1976-77. Composition incl: A European Lover (muisical satire in 1 act); The Glove (1 act opera); The Troublemaker (comic opera); The Suitors (opera); The Last Words of Louis Riel (Cantata from Canadian Hist.); Notes on Hungary, (Suite f. Conc. Band), Ilona's Four Faces, (f. Sax.), Lest we Forget the Last Charter of Genesis; Pentatonia, 1975. 200 feature & documentary film scores; Music for CBC radio & TV plays, etc. Mbrships: Past VP., Hungarian Composers & Authors Assn., 1946-51; Toronto Musicians Assn.; CAPAC; Can. Music Ctr. Recip. Ferenc Erkel Prize for Composers, 1953-54; Canada Coun Sr Arts Fellowship, 1966. Address: 21 Vaughan Rd., Toronto M6G 2N2, Ont. Can. 3, 29.

POLGLASE, Joseph, b. 2 Dec. 1940, Dover, UK. Schoolmaster; Cellist; Pianist; Singer. Educ: MA, Oxford Univ. m. Rosemary St. John Sillick, 1 s., 1 d. Career: Mbr., Nat. Youth Orch. of GB, 1956-58; Fndr. Mbr., Clerkes of Oxenford, num. TV & radio broadcasts; Asst. Dir. of Music, Leys Schl., Cambridge, 1963-66; Dir. of Music, Dean Close Schl., Chettenham, 1967-74; Dir. of Music, 1974-, Housemaster, 1976-, Cranleigh Schl., Surrey. Made sev. recordings w. Clerkes of Oxenford. Mbrships: Musicians Union; ISM; Committee Music Masters Assn. Hobbies: Bridge; Gardening; Walking; Reading. Address: Cubitt House, Cranleigh Schl., Cranleigh, Surrey, UK.

POLIN, Claire, b. 1 Jan. 1926, Philadelphia, Pa., USA. Composer; Flautist; Musicologist. Educ: B Mus., M Mus., D Mus., Phila. Conserv. of Music; Study at Juilliard Schl. of Music, Berkshire Music Ctr., Temple Univ., Dropsie Univ.; Pvte. study of flute w. William Kincaid; Comps. w. Vincent Persichetti, Roger Sessions, Lukas Foss, Peter Mennin. m. Merle S Schaff (dec.), 2 s. Career: Prof., Music, Rutgers Univ.; Frelance Flautist; Mbr., Pan-Orphic Duo; Lectr. Comps. incl: Ma'alot for viola & percussion: Paraselene for soprano, flute & piano; Amphion for Symph. Orch.; Windsongs for soprano & guitar; Procris for flute & tuba; Orchl. & choral works. Recordings of own works incl: Summer Settings, for solo harp; synalia for flute, clarinet & piano; for solo viola; Gilgamesh for string orch. & flute. Publs. incl: Art & Practice of Modern Flute (w. W Kincaid), 3 vols., 1967-; Advanced Flautist (w. W Kincaid), 2 vols., 1974; The AP HUM MS, 1979. Contbr. to US, for jrnls. Mbr., profl. orgs. Hons: Leverhulme Fellowship to Univ. Coll., Wales, 1968-69; Fellow, MacDowell Colony; Cedok (Germany), 1977; var. prizes, commissions. Address: Dragon Hill, Baird & Health Rds., Merion, PA 19066, USA. 5, 11.

POLITOSKE, Daniel T., b. 30 Dec. 1935, Indiana, Pa., USA. Musicologist; Organist. Educ: BS Music Educ., Ind. State Coll., Indaian, Pa.; M Mus., Univ. of Mich., Ann Arbor; Cert., Univ. of Louvain, Belgium; Royal Flemish Conserv. of Music, Antwerp; PhD., Musicol., Univ. of Mich., Ann Arbor. Career: Fac. positions at Scotland Schl. of Veterans Children, Pa., Hillsdale Coll., Mich., Univ. of Mich., Ann Arbor, Nat. Music Camp, Interlochen, Univ. of Ga., Athens. Assoc. Prof., Univ. of Kan., 1975- Publs: The Choral Motets of Balduin Hoyoul, 1975; Music, an Introduction to Mbrships: Am. Musicol Soc.; Int. Musicol. Soc.; Coll. Music Soc.; Music Lib. Assn. Hons: Rotary Fndn. Fellowship for int. Understanding; Rackham Fellowship. Univ. of Mich. Hobbies: Tennis; Swimming. Address: 915 W 29th St., Lawrence, KS 66044, USA.

POLL, Melvyn, b. 15 July 1941, Seattle, Wash., USA. Operatic Tenor. Educ: BA, JD, Univ. of Wash., Seattle. m. Rosalind Benaroya Poll, 1 s., 1 d. Debut: Pfalztheater, Kaiserslauten, German Fed. Repub., 1971. Career: Israel Nat. Opera, Tel-Aviv; NYC Opera. Hobbies: Family; Wines; Tennis. Mgmt: Ludwig Lustig & Florian Ltd., NYC. Address: 16 N Chatsworth Ave., Larchmont, NY 10538, USA.

POLLAK, Anna, b. 1 May 1912, Manchester, UK. Opera Singer. Debut: Dorabella, Sadler's Wells, London, 1945. Career: Prin. mezzo-soprano, Sadler's Wells Opera, 1945-62; roles incl. Carmen; guest apps., fests., home & abroad, Covent Garden, Glyndebourne, Aldeburgh, etc.; apps. at concerts & on radio & TV; retired 1970. Recip., OBE, 1962. Hobbies: Gardening; Swimming; Driving; Literature. Address: Hawthorn House, Stanford, Ashford, Kent, UK.

POLLAK, Helen Charlotte Schiller, b. 21 Oct. 1932. Mannheim, Germany. Pianist; Teacher. Educ: BA, Douglass Coll., Rutgers Univ., 1954; MA, Univ. of Chgo., 1957. m. Barth Pollak, 1 s., 1 d. Career: Pianist, Harpsichordist & Celeste Player w. S Bend Symph. & former lectr. in Music. St. Mary's Coll., Notre Dame, Ind.; pvte piano studio; Music Tchr., S Bend (Ind.) Community Schl. Corp.; formerly Tchr., Univ. of Chgo. Lab. Schl. & Charter Mbr., Chgo. Symph. Orch. Chorus. Contbr. to Elem. Schl. Jrnl., 1957-65. Mbr., S Bend Assn. of Piano Tchrs. Address: 239 S Hawthorne Dr., S Bend, IN 46617, USA.

POLLARD, Anthony Cecil, b. May 1929, London, UK. Publisher. Educ: John Lyon Schl. Harrow. m. Margaret Cleveland, 1 s., 1 d. Career: Brit. Army. 1946-49; Joined 'Gramophone', 1949; London Ed., ibid, 1959: Ed., 1961; Publsr. & Mng. Ed., 1972. Hobbies: Music; Literature; Gardening; Golf. Address: The Spinney, Pynnacles Close, Stanmore, Middx, HA7 4 AF, UK.

POLLARD, Brian Joseph, b. 5 April 1930, Padiham, Burnley, UK. Bassoonist. Educ: Bus. Trng. Coll.; ARCM. m. Marion Pollard-Lincklaen-Arriëns, 1 s., 1 d. Career: w. Ballet Joos Orch., 1945; RPO, 1946-47; 3rd Regional RAF Band, Germany, 1948-50; Royal Opera House, Convent Gdn., 1951-53; Solo Bassoonist, Concertgebouworkest, 1953-; mbr. of Danzi Wind Quintet, 1956-. Has recorded chmbr. music for Philips, Zeon, Teldec & Donemus. Address: Michelangelo Straat 60, Amsterdam, The Netherlands.

POLLINI, Maurizio, b. 1942, Milan, Italy. Pianist. Career: apps. w. leading orchs. in Europe & USA inclng. Berlin & Vienna Phil. Orchs., Bayerischer Rundfunk Orch., LSO, Boston, NY, Phila., Los Angeles & San Fran. Orchs.; participant in Salzburg, Vienna, Berlin & Prague Fests. Records for Polydor Int. Recip. 1st Prize, Int. Chopin Competition, Warsaw, 1960. 16.

POLLOCK, Robert Emil, b. 8 July 1946, NYC, USA. Composer; Pianist. Educ: BA, Swarthmore Coll.; MFA, Princeton Univ. m. Klazine van der Vlies-Pollock, 1 d. Debut: Comp. 's Forum, Donnell Lib., NYC, 1974. Career incls: WOXR broadcast of works. Artist in Concert Series, May, 1976. Comps. publd: Movement & Variations for str. quartet (also recorded); Bridgeforms (also recorded); Violament; Theatre Piece; Woodwind Quintet; Revolution; Progessional; Metaphor (I & II). Mbrships: Am. Music Ctr. Inc.; Guild of Comps. Inc. Hons. incl: var. fellowships & commissions. Address: 254 W 20th St., Ship Bottom, NJ 08008, USA.

POLOGE, Steven, b. 10 Jan. 1952, NYC, USA. Musician (Cellist). Educ: B Mus, Eastman Schl. of Music, 1974; MMus, Juilliard Schl. of Music, 1978; studied Cello w. Ronald Leonard & Lorne Munroe; Meadowmount Schl. of Music, summers 1972-72. Career: Player w. Rochester Phil., 1973-74, 1974-75; Mbr., Buffalo Phil., 1975-76; Player uncer contract, Aspen Music Fest., Colo., 1974, 75; Mbr., Am. Ballet Theater Orch., 1978; solo apps., NYC, 1978. Hallies: Political Sci.; Long Distance Running. Address: 750 Mildred St., Teaneck, NJ 07666, USA.

POLUNIN, Tanya, b. 30 Mar. 19 17, Reading, UK. Professional Musician. Administrator; Educator. Educ: maj. studies w. Mabel Landedr, (Asst. to Prof. Leschetizky); RCM; Tchrs. Trng. Course, RAM; LRAM. m. Maj. ADA Wright (dec.), 1 s., 1 d. Career: Chmbr. Music Recitals in Schls. & Coll., 19 48-54; Prin. Tanya Polunin Schl. of Pianoforte Playing. Mbrships: ISM, 1963-, Warden, Pvte. Tchrs. Sect., Committee Mbr. for 10 yrs.; ISM (Mbr. of Coun.). Hobbies: Gardening; Walking; Illuminated Manuscripts. Address: ''Casita'', Landsdowne Rd., Holland Park, London W11 3LS, UK.

POLYZOIDES, Christos, b. 30 Jan. 1931, Drama, Greece. Violinist. Educ: Dip. for Violin, 1951, Dip. for Harmony, 1952, State Conserv., Thessaloniki; Dip. w. distinction, Acad. of Music & Dramatic Art, Vienna, Austria, 1957. m. Katherina Sourvali, 1 s., 1 d. Career: 1st Solo Violinist, Graz Phil. Orch., Austria, 1957-69; Tchr., Graz Conserv. (later Acad. of Music, then Music Univ.) Univ. Prof., 1969-; Soloist & Chmbr. musician, concerts in Austria, Germany, Italy, Hungary, Yugoslavia, & Greece; Radio, TV & Fest. perfs.; Summer courses; Duo w. Katherina Polyzoides. Mbr., ESTA. Address: A-8010 Graz, Morellenfeldz. 20, Austria.

POLYZOIDES, Katherina (née Sourvali), b. Tessaloniki, Greece. Pianist. Educ: Tchng. Dip., 1952, Piano Soloist Dip., 1953, State Conserv., Tessaloniki; Acad. of Music & Dramatic Art, Vienna, Austria, 1959; m. Christos Polyzoides, 1 s., 1 d. Career: Piano Class, Acad. of Music, Graz, 1963-69; Solo Choir direction, ibid., 1972-; Perfs, as Soloist & Chmbr. muisc player, at concerts in Austria, Hungary, Greece, Yugoslavia, & on radio & TV; Summer courses; Duo w. Christos Polyzoides. Address: A-8010 Graz, Morellenfeldz. 20/7, Austria.

POMMER, Max Conrad Wolfgang, b. 9 Feb. 1936, Leipzig, Germany. Conductor. Educ: PhD, Karl-Marx Univ. Leipzig; Dip. cond. & piano, ''Felix-Mendelssohn-Bartholdy'' coll. of music, Leipzig. m. Gisela Grabner, 2 d. Career: ldr. opera orch., Kleist Theatre, FrankfurtOder; Radio prods. Schoenberg, Eisler, Bach & Milhaud w. radio symph. orch., Leipzig & Berlin; TV & film apps. Recordings: Eisler-5 orch. pieces; Chmbr. symph.; The Long March; Cantatas; all w. Gewandhaus orch., Leipzig. Publs: Ed. orch. works, C Debussy (Peters ed.). Mbrships: Comps. & musicians union of German Dem. Repub. Address: 701 Leipzig, Hillerstr. 9, German Dem. Repub.

POMMIER, Jean-Bernard, b. 17 Aug. 1944, Beziers, France. Concert Pianist. Educ: Conservatoire National de Musique de Paris, 1961. M. Chantal Hermite, Career: A worldwide Soloist career inclng. appearance w. Moscow, Tokyo, London Symph. Orchs., Chgo Symph. Orch., the Concert Pinebow in Australia, Orchs. of Dresden & Leipzig, etc.; Many Radio Orchs.; Casals Fests., Puerto Rich; Conds. w. whom he plays incl: Daniel Darenboim, M Von Karajzu, P Boulez, Zubin Melitz, L Foster, etc; Chamber music w. many eniment artists. Var. recordings edited by EMI, inclng. Mozart, Schumann, Debussy, Tchaikovsky, Bach, Beethoven. Hons: Chevalier dans l'Ordre National du Merite, France, 1971; Premier Priz au Concours International des Jeunesses Musicales, 1960; Prix de la Guilde des Artistes Francais; Premier Diplome d'honneur de Concours Tchaikovsky, 1962. Hobby: Reading. Address: 10 rue Lincoln, 75008, Paris, France.

POMYKALO, Igor, b. 30 Dec. 1946, Rijeka, Croatia, Yugoslavia. Musician (Viola, Recorder, Crumhorn, Shawm, Viola de Gamba). Educ: Music Acad., Zagreb. m. Maja Karlovic. Debut: Groznjan, Istria, Yugoslavia, 29 Aug. 1979. Career incls: Concerts w. ensembles Univ. Studiorum Zagrabiensis, Zagreb, & Fridrik Grisogono, Zader; var. ensembles, Belgium, Netherlands & Denmark; Viola player, Zagreb Symph Orch., Radio & TV, Zagreb, 1966-. Recordings: Renaissance Fests, 1974, & Anno Domini 1973, 1975 (w. Univ. Studiorum Zagrabiensi). Contbr. to var. jrnls. Mbr. profl. orgs. Hobbies incl: folk instruments. Mgmt: Koncertna Direkcija Zagreb, Trnjanska bb. 41000 Zagreb. Address: Medvedgradska 40, 41000 Zagreb, Yugoslavia.

PONG, Grace, b. 26 Oct. 1955, Hong Kong. Pianist. Educ: BMus, Manhattan Schl. of Music, NY, 1977. Debut: NYC. Career: perfs. at RTV (Hond Kong), 1972, NJ Theatre, 1974; solo recitals, Manhattan Schl. of music, 1976, chmbr. music perf., ibid., 1977; piano tchr., Toronto Public Schls. Mbrships: Ont. Music Tchrs. Assn.; Can. Bureau for the Advancement of Music. Hons: Awards from the Hong Kong Schl. of Music Fests., 1971-72. Hobbies: Arts; Music; Opera; Drama; Reading; Swimming. Address: 417-250 Cassandra Blvd., Don Mills, Ont. M3A 1V1, Canada.

PONSELLE, Rosa Melba, b. Meriden, Conn., USA. Dramatic Soprano. Edcu: pvte. tutors, NYC. m. Carie A Jackson. Career: joined Met. Opera Co., 1918; played in leading roles w. Caruso;

Tchr., Coach, Artistic Dir., Balt. Civic Opera Co. Address: Villa Pl., Stevenson, MD 21153, USA.

PONT, Kenneth Graham, b. 8 Apr. 1937, Newcastle, NSW, Aust. Philosophy Lecturer. Educ: BA, Univ. of Sydney, 1958; PhD, Aust. Nat. Univ., 1965. Career: Lectr. in Philos., Dept. of Gen. Studies, Univ. of NSW, 1966-; Vis. Assoc. Prof. of Musicol., Grad., Ctr., CUNY, USA, 1973-74. Contbr. to: Nation Review (music & opera critic); Scholarly jrnls. Mbrships: Musicol. Soc. of Aust. (Pres. 1975-77). Hobbies: Environmental Studies; Cookery; Landscape Gardening. Address: Dept. of General Studies, Univ. of New South Wales, PO Box 1, Kensington, NSW 2033, Australia.

POOL, Jeannie Gayle, b. 6 Nov. 1951, Paris, Ill., USA. Musicologist; Music Critic; Lecturer; Expert on History of Women in Classical Music. Educ: BA (music), Hunter Coll., CUNY; grad. work, Columbia Univ., Publs: Women in Music History; A research Guide, 1977; Women Composers of Classical Music, 1980. Contbr. to: Music Educators Jrnl. & other jrnls. Mbrships: Am. Musicol. Soc.; CMS; Nat. Coordinator, 1st Nat. Congress on Women in Music to be held in NYC, 1981. Hon: citation from Nat. Fed. of Music Clubs from promotion of Am. Music, 1979. Address: 752 West End Ave., Apr. 12 E, New York, NY 10025, USA.

POOL, Robert David, b. 21 July 1954, Ickenham, Middx., UK. Violinist. Educ: RCM (Jr. Exhibitioner & full time student); ARCM (perf.). Career: mbr., BBC Symph. Orch.; recitals & concertos in London & home countries; ldr., Prometheus Quartet; perfs. in Hans Werner Henze's workshop in Italy; former mbr., ISM. Hons: Angela Bull Memorial prize; 3 yr. exhibition to RCM; Dove violin prize; Sir James Caird Travelling Scholarship; ARCM; Countess of Munster award. Hobbies: Photography; Cinema. Address: 26B Kingsend, Ruislip, Middx. HA4 7DA, UK.

POOLE, Geoffrey Richard, b. 9 Feb. 1949, Ipswich, Suffolk. Composer; Lecturer. Educ: BA, Univ. of E Anglia; BMus, Univ. of Southampton; LRAM. m. Beth Wiseman, 1s., 1 d. Career: Lect., Manchester Univ. Comps: Wymondham Chants, 1970; Algol of Perseus, 1973; Visions, 1975; Polterzeits, 1975; Crow Tyrannosaurus, 1975; Harmonice Mundi, 1978; Chamber Concerto, 1979 (all broadcasts). Contbr. to: Musical Times; Tempo. Mbrshipos: CGGB; PRS; Chmn., N W Arts New Music sub-committee. Hons: Alfred Clements Memorial prize, 1975; Radcliffe (2nd) Prize, 1977. Hobbies: Cycling; Cooking; Philos.; Psychol.; Astrol. Address: 6 Bamford Grove, Didsbury, Manchester 20, UK.

POOLE, John Charles, b. 5 Feb. 1934, Birmingham, UK. Conductor. Educ: MA, Balliol Coll., Oxford Univ.; FRCO m. Anne Mary Toler, 3 s. Career: Dir., BBC Singers, 1972-. Mgmt: Ibbs & Tillet. Address: Buckettsland Farm, Well End, Boreham Wood, Herts, UK.

POPE, H Lefevre, b. 16 Oct. 1911, Wembley, UK. Director of Music. Educ: FRCO, 1948; Mus B, Trinity Coll., Dublin, 1959. m. Joan Crawford, Career: Ch. Organ Appts., London & Scotland; Organ Recitals from St. George's Hawick. St. Cuthbert's Melrose, BBC; Dir. of Music, Harrogate Coll., 1966-77. Comps: Organ arrs.; Two Christmas Pieces (organ). Recordings: Holly & the Ivy, from Two Christman Pieces. Mbrships: RCP; Fndr.Pres. Melrose Music Soc. Recip. Prout Mem. Prize, Trinity Coll., Dublin, 1959. Hobbies: For. travel; Art. Address: 44 Duchy Rd., Harrogate, N Yorks., HG1 2ER, UK.

POPE, Michael Douglas, b. 25 Feb. 1927, London, UK. BBC Producer. Educ: GSM. m. (1) Margaret Jean Blakeney, 1 s., (2) Gillian Victoria Peck, 1 s., 1 d. Career: Joined BBC, 1954; Musical Dir., London Motet & Madrigal Club, 1954-; Guest cond., RTE; Prod., BBC Music Div., 1966-. Mbrships: Royal Phil. Soc.; Royal Musical Assn.; Savile Club; Past Pres., London Athletic Club; Chmn., Elgar Soc. Author of var. essays & radio scripts on Parry, Elgar & their contemporaries. Hobbies: Reading; Theatre; Travel. Athletcis (Brit. Olympic Team 1948). Address: c/o BBC, Broadcasting House, London W1A 1AA, UK.

POPE, Peter Searson, b. 25 Mar. 1917, London, UK. Composer; Pianist; Teacher of Pianoforte, Educ: ARCM. m. Noreen Iris Abbott, 1 s., 2 d. Debut: 1935. Career: Piano Quartet; on BBC & at Wigmore Hall; Saxophone Quartet: on BBC & at St. John's, Smith Sq. Comps. incl: Sonatina for Recorder (treble) & Piano (Schott); Chmbr. music: The Sea is All About Us (piano); Songs w. piano accomp.; Poems of James Reeves for tenor & harp; Concerto for clarinet & small orch. Mbr. ISM. Hons: Foli Scholarship (Comp.) at RCM, 1935-39; Octavia Travelling Scholarship, 1939; Ellen Shaw Williams Prize (Piano), 1938. Hobbies: Painting; Countryside (Walking,

etc.). Address: 20 St. Augustines Ave., South Croydon, Surrey CR2 6JG, UK.

POPESCU, Paul, b. 29 Apr. 1929, Brasov, Romania. Conductor. educ: Dip. in Art, Music Conserv., Ciprian Porumbescu, Bucharest; Music Acad., Vienna. m. Viorica Firca-Popescu, 1 d. Debut: Phil. Orch., Timisdara, 1954. Career: Cond. of var. symph. concerts & operas in Romania & 15 other countries, inc. ORTF, Paris, Pas de Loup, Paris, Gewandhaus, Leipzig, Komische Oper, Berlin, MAV Orch., Budapest, Phil. Orch., Bordeaux, etc.; Cond., Symph. Orch. of Radio Televisione, Bucharest; Cond. of Romanian film music. var. recordings w. symph. orchs., chmbr. orchs., operas, etc. Contbr. to var. profl. jrnls. Hons: Maritul Cultural, the highest order for artists in Romania. Hobbies: Sports; Reading; Recreation with family. Address: Blu. Magheru 7, Scara I, Ap. 22, Bucharest, Romania.

POPLE, Peter Ravenhill, b. 21 May 1943, Ilford, Essex, UK. Violinist. Educ: GSM, London; LGSM (VT). m. Teresa Cullis, 2 d. Career: Joined Alberni Str. Quartet as 2nd Violin, 1970; Tours of Europe, Aust., NZ & Far East w. quartet; var. periods as Artist-in-Res., Univ. of W. Aust., Perth; perfs. of complete cycle of Beethoven Quartets, Aust, 1973, Wexford Fest., Repub. of Iceland, 1975. Recordings incl: Works by Schubert, Mendelssohn & Schumann (w. Alberni Quartet); currently recording Schumann's complete chmbr. music for CRD. Hobby: Chess. Address: 215 Moorfield, Harlow, Essex, UK.

POPLE, Ross, b. 11 May 1945, Auckland, NZ. Cellist (also Viol da Gamba). Educ: RAM (recital dip.); LRSM; Conserv. Nat. Superieur de Musique de Paris. m. Anne Margaret Stoors, 1 d., 2 s. Debut: London, 1965. Career: Prin. cello, Manuhin Fest. orch., 1969-75; Prin. cello, BBC Symph. Orch., 976-; recitals both contemporary & traditional in UK & abroad. sev. recordings. Hon. RAM. Hobbies: Tennis; Squash; House Building. Address: 61 Ellesmere Rd., Weybridge, Surrey KT13 OHW, UK.

POPOVIC, Berislav, b. 12 June 1931, Zajecar, Yugoslavia. Compsoer. Educ: Fac. of Musical Art. m. Gordana Stefanovic, 1 d, 1 s. Debut: Zagred, 1958. Career: Tchr. of theoretical subjects, Musical Schl. Slavenski, 1960-61; Docent, Fac. of Musical Art, Beograd, 1967-; Vice-Dean, ibid., 1973-75; Vice-Rector, Univ. of Arts of Beograd, 1975-. Comps. incl: Medium Tempus (large orch.), 1973; Diffractions (concerto for orch.), 1967. Mbrships. incl: Soc. of Serbian Comps.; Int. Info. Ctr., Zagreb. Publs: Types of Forms in Contemporary Music, 1967. Contbr. to newspapers & mags. Recip., Octabar Prize of the Univ., 1963. Hobbies incl: Paintings. Address: Aleske Nenadovica 28, YU-11000 Beograd, Yugoslavia.

POPP, Lucia, b. 1939, Bratislava, Czech. Concert & Opera Soprano. Educ: Dip., Bratislava Music Acad. m. Georg Fischer. Career incls: Mbr., Cologne & Hamburg Operas; Leading Singer, Vienna State Opera; apps. w. many other cos.; participant in fests.; num. concerts, TV broadcasts, etc. Roles incl: Romilda, Handel's Serse; Queen of the Night, Magic Flute; Despina, Cosi Fan Tutti; Blondchen & Constanze, Abduction from the Seraglio; Zerlina, Don Giovanni; Marzelline, Fidelio; Rosina, Barber of Seville. Recordings incl: Serse; Cosi Fan Tutte; Rosenkavalier; Magic Flute. Address: c/o Lydia Storle, 8 München 90 Spitzingplatzz, German Fed. Repub. 2, 3.

POPPER, Felix, b. 12 Dec. 1908, Vienna, Austria. Conductor; Pianist. Educ: PhD (Law), Univ. of Vienna; Staatsakademie of music, Vienna; pvte. study w. Hugo Reichenberger. m. Doris Jung, 1 s. Debut: W.Egk, Inspector General, NY City Opera. Career: Cond. & Music Adminstr., NY City Opera, NBC-TV Opera; affiliated w. opera dept., Mannes Coll.; Curtis Inst., Acad. of Vocal Arts, Phila., Pa. Address: 40 W 84th St., NY, NY 10024, USA.

POPPLEWELL, Kenneth Arthur, b. 15 May 1914, London, UK. Violinist. Educ: began apprenticeship as printer when aged 14; mainly self-taught musician, but studied w. Albert Sammons; ARCM (tchrs. Dip.), 1962. Career: RPO under Sir Thomas Beecham, 1946-49; BBC Symph. Orch., 1949-62; currently Co-Ldr., Capriol Orch. of London. Has taken part in many orchl. recordings. Contbr. to var. mags inclng: Symph.; 600 Mag. Mbrships: Musician's Union; ISM. Hobby: Lutherie (violins much sought after by profl. players). Address: 0 Bedford Rd., Bedford Pk., London W4, UK.

POPPLEWELL, Richard John, b. 18 Oct. 1935, Halifax, UK. Organist; Choirmaster; Recitalist; Composer; Accompanist; Teacher. Educ: Chorister & Organ Scholar, Kings Coll., Cambridge; Clifton Coll., Bristol; RCM, London; FRCO; ARCM. m. Margaret Conway, 1 s. Career: Regular broadcaster; Soloist, Henry Wood Promenade Concert, 1965; Recitalist, GB;

tours, Can., Netherlands, France, Portugal; Asst. Organist, St. Paul's Cathedral, 1958-66; Dir. of Music,St. Michael's Cornhill, 1966-79; Prof. of Organ, RCM, 1962-; Accomp. Bach Choir, 1966-79; Organist. Choirmaster & Comp., H.M.'s Chapels Royal, St. James' Palace, 1979-. Comps: (for organ) Suite; Puck's Shadow; Trio Sonata; Chorale Preludes; Easter Hymn & Down Ampney; Elergy; Aria, The Time of the Singing; Variations on a New Year's Carol (SSAATTBB Carol, There is no Rose). Recordings: His Music (own comps.); Carols With Bach Choir; Organ Music from St. Michaels, Cornhill. Mbrships: RCO; ISM; Musicians Union; NATFHE. Hons: ARCO Sawyer Prize, aged 14; RCM Prizes, 1955, '56. Hobbies: Reading; Swimming; Walking. Mgmt: Ibbs & Tillet. Address: 23 Stanmore Gardens, Richmond, Surrey TW9 2HN, UK. 4.

PORFETYE, Andreaa, b. 6 July 1927, Zadareni, Arad, Romania. Composer; Conductor; Teacher; Musical Director. Educ: Sibiu Trng. Coll. for Tchrs.; Fac. of Comp.; Cond.; Dip. Comp., Ciprian Porumbescu Acad. of Music, Bucharest. m. Lotte Hedwig, 3 children. Debut: W. Symph. Sibiu, 1957. Career: Apps. on Radio & TV; Int. Festivals & Symposia; Prof. of Harmony & Counterpoint, Acad. of Music, Bucharest; Musical Dir., St. Joseph's Cathedral, Bucharest. Comps. incl: Concerto for organ & orch.; 1st Sonata for violin & piano. Contbr. to Muzica Review, Bucharest. Mbr. Comps. of Romania. Hons. incl: Prize of Union of Comps. of Romania, 1974. Hobbies: Lit.; Arts; Football. Address: Calea Rahovei 104, Bucharest, Romania. 1.

PORTER, Andrew, b. 26 Aug. 1928, Cape Town, S. Africa. Writer on Music. Educ: MA, Oxon. Career: w. Manchester Guardian, 1949; Music Critic, Financial Times, 1953-74; of the New Yorker, 1972-; Ed., The Musical Times, 1960-67; Vis. Fellow, All Souls Coll., Oxford, 1973-74. Opera Transl. perfs: Verdi, Don Carlos, Rigoletto, Othello, Falstaff; Wagner, The Ring; Handel, Ottone; Haydn, Deceit Outwitted, The Unexpected Meeting; Mozart, Lucio Silla. Recordings: The Ring (Engl. transl.). Publs: A Musical Season (collected essays), 1974; Music of Three Seasons, 1978. Contbr. of articles & papers to: Music & Letters; Musical Qtly.; Musical Times; Proceedings of the Royal Musical Assn.; Atti del Congresso Internazionale di Studi Verdiani, etc. VP, Donizetti Soc; ASCAP, Deems Taylor Award, 1975. Address: c/o The New Yorker, 25 W 43rd St., NY, NY 10036, USA. 10, 23, 28.

PORTER, Evelyn, b. Easton-in-Gordano, Somerset, UK. Teacher & Lecturer on Music; Pianist. Educ: pvte. study w. Claude Pollard & Harry Farjeon; Tchrs. Trng. Course, RAM, 1922-23; Dip. LRAM; qualified for MRST. Debut: Harrow, Middx. Career: Tchng. posts, var. schls. inclng. Wembley Grammar Schl., London; contbr. of series to schls. radio prof., BBC, 1938; w. Educl. Dept., ENSA, 1943-45; Extra-mural Lectr., Univ. of London, 1946-56; pvte. lectr. & writer on musical subjects; chief work as pvte. teacher of piano & musicianship, currently w. own pvte. Schl. of Music. Publs: Music Through the Dance, 1937; Music, a short History, 1940 (publd. in USA as The Story of Music, 1951); Concert-Goer's Guide, 1950. Contbr. to Music Tchr.; Pianoforte Tchr.; Musical Times; Music in Educ.; Child Educ.; The Choir; The Lady. Mbrships: MTA (Chmn. NW Middx. Br. 1943-61); ISM; Royal Music Assn., Hobbies: Gardening; Travel; Photography. Address: Gayton, 38 Ashcombe Gdns., Weston-super-Mare, Avon BS23 2XD, UK. 3, 27.

PORTER, Quincy, b. 7 Feb. 1897, New Haven, Conn., USA. Compsoer; Educator. Educ: Yale Schl. of Music; studied in Europe. Career: Tchr., Cleveland Inst. of Music; Hd., Theory Dept., ibid; Prof. of music, Vassar Coll., 6 yrs.; Dean of Fac., New England Conserv. of Music; Dir., ibid; Prof. of Music, Yale Univ. Compositions incl: Str. Quartets 1-3; Str. Quartet No. 4, 1931; Str. Quartet No. 5 & 6; St. Quartet No. 7, 1943; Hons. incl: Osborne Prize in Composition, Yale Schl. of Music; Steinert Prize in Composition, ibid; Guggenheim Fellowship, 1928; Coolidge Medal for Chmbr. Music, 1943; Pultizer Prize for Concerto for 2 pianos, 1954.

PORTER, Ronald Fowler, b. 21 Mar. 1928, Belfast, N Ireland, UK. Singer; Schoolteacher; Lecturer; Choral Conductor. Educ: BA; FTCL; FLCM; LRSM; MTD; Ulster Coll. & City of Belfast Schl. of Music. m. Mary Tipping Ferguson, 1s., 1d. Debut: aged 17, Belfast. Career: Profl. Bass., Belfast Cathedral Choir; Profl. Ch. Soloist, Melbourne, Aust.; broadcaster, Melbourne, Dublin & N Ireland as singer & cond.; apps. on BBC radio & TV; fndr., Abbey Singers & Consort; fndr., cond., Cantoris. Mbrships: ISM; Ulster Soc. of Organist & Choirmaster. Recip., num. prizes incl. UK Rep., BBC Let the People Sing Competition (large choir sect.). Hobbies incl: Local Hist.; Rsch. in Irish Ethnomusicology. Address: 306 Merville Garden Village, Whitehouse, NewtownAbbey, Co. Antrim, N Ireland, UK.

PORTER, Rosalind, b. 22 Oct. 1950, London, UK. Cellist. Educ: Studied cello w. var. tchrs.; ARCM (Dip.); License de Concert, École Normale de Musique, Paris, France; Reifeprüfung (Dip.), NWD. Musikakademie, Detmold, German Fed. Repub. m. Peter Rosenberg. Debut: Paris & London, 1973. Career: Solo Cellist, Göttingen Symph. Orch., 1974-75; Solo Cellist, NW Deutsche Philharmonic Orch., 1976- perfs. mainly in Germany of concertos of Haydn, Elgar, Dvorak, Boccherini, Beethoven, ect. Hons. incl: Angela Bull Prize, RCM; Suggia Award, 1966; Assoc. Bd. Scholarship, 1969; 2nd Prize, Int. Beethoven Competition, Spain, 1970; Tagore Gold Medal, RCM, 1971; var. scholarships. Hobby: Painting. Address: AM Kalten Born, 35, 34 Göttingen-Geismar, German Fed. Repub.

PORTER, Steven Clark, b. 22 June 1943, NYC, USA. Composer; Conductor; Educator; Pianist; Percussionist. Educ: BS, The Mannes Coll. of Music, 1967; MA, Queens Coll., CUNY, 1969; PhD, CUNY Grad. Ctr., currently. m. Rita Hallinan Porter. Career: Apps. on Voice Am. on Radio; Var. conducting apps. throughout US; guest clinician; var. tchng. posts. Comps. incl: The Creation, 1969; Three Rock Motets, 1972; Behold A King, 1975; 6 arrs. for chorus; The Children of the Lord; Christmas Variations; The Ten Commandments. Recordings incl. Psalm For The New World, 1974. Mbrships: incl. Nat. Music Educators Assn.; Music Educators Nat. Conf. Publs: New Choral Dramatics (Ed.), 1973; Songs for the Jesus Generation (Ed. & Arr.), 1973. Address: 705 E 10th Ave., E Northport, NY 11731, USA.

PORTUGHEIS, Alberto, b. La Plata, Argentina. Pianist; Teacher; Conductor. Educ: BA; Piano, Violin, Conducting, Compositions Dips., Conserv. Scaramuzza, Buenos Aires, Argentina & Conserv. de Geneve, Switzerland. Debut: Wigmore Hall, London, 1968. Career: Soloist, w. orchs. & in chmbr. music, Europe, N. Am., Central Am., S. Am. & Israel. Compositions; Prelude; Air; Gavotte. Sev. Recordings. Recip., 1st prize, Virtuosity Competition, Geneva, 1964. Hobbies: Reading; Theatre; Sports; Cooking. Mgmt: R.W.G. Raybould, 8 Pelham Place, London SW7, UK.

POSPISIL, Frantisek, b. 13 Nov. 1933, Hanusovice, Czechoslovakia. Violinist; Professor. Educ: Dip., Acad. of Music, Prague; Special Master Course of Chmbr. Music, ibid. m. Vlastimila Pipalova, 1 d. Debut: Dvorak Hall, House of Artist, Prague, 958. Career: Fndr., Foerster Trio; Mbr., Dvorak Piano Trio & Collegium Tripartitum, 1970-; Concert tours in Europe, S. Am. & Canada; Prof., Conserv. of Music, Prague. Sev. recordings. Hobbies: Driving; Fishing. Mgmt: Pragokoncert, Prague. Address: Pujmanove 885/19, 14000 Prague 4, Czechoslovakia.

POSPISIL, Ladislav, b. 20 Nov. 1935, Uhrice, Czechoslovakia. Violoncellist. Educ: 9 degrees in gen. educ.; Conserv. of Brno; Dip., Acad. of Music, Prague. m. Vera Stofava, 1 s., 2 d. Career: Mbr., Violoncello Grp., Czech Phil. Orch.; Solo Cellist, Basler Symph. Orch., 1969-71. Hons: 2nd Prize, Moscow Youth Fest. Competition, 1957; 3rd Prize, Prague Spring Fest., 1961. Mgmt: Pragonkoncert, Prague. Address: Novodvorska 34, 142 00 Prague 4, Czechoslovakia.

POSPISIL, Vilém, b. 19 July 1911, Prague, Czechoslovakia. Musicologist; Musician; Critic. Educ: Dr. in Law & Philos. (Musicol.). m. Helena Hosková, 4 children. Career: Music Critic, Svobodné Slovo & Hudebni Rozheledy, 1946; Sec.-Gen., Prague Spring Fest.; Ed.-in-Chief, Hudebni rozhledy (musical monthly); Permanent Mbr. of Jury, Concours des Jeunes Chefs d'Orch., Besancon, France; Mbr., Commission of Juridiction, Int. Music Coun. of UNESCO; Radio Commentator. Publs: Monograph on Václav Talich; Famouns Conductors of the Prague Spring Festivals; Famous Soloists of the Prague Spring Festivals; Monograph on Marie Podvalová; (all publd. 1962-66). Contbr. to: Hudebni rozhledy; Svobodné slovo. Mbrships: Guild Comps.; Bur. of European Assn. of Music Fests., Geneva; Fedn. of Int. Music Competitions, ibid. Hons: Critics' Prize, 1964; Smetana Medal, 1974. Hobbies: Tennis; Swimming; Linguistics. Address: Praha 4 Sporilov, Roztylské sady 21, Czechoslovakia.

POST, Nora, b. 18 Dec. 1949, Bayshore, NY, USA. Oboist. Educ: BA, Univ. of Calif., San Diego; Staatliche Hochschule für Musik, Freiburg, Germany; Perf. Dip., NC Schl. of Arts, Winston-Salem; PhD, NY Univ.; MA, ibid. Debut: Town Hall, NY, 1974. Career: plays both baroque & mod. oboe; Creative Assoc., Ctr., of Creative & Performing Arts, Buffalo, NY; apps. at ORTF, Paris, Musee de l'Art Moderne, Paris, 19th Int. Warsaw Autumn, Carnegie Recital Hall, Alice Tully Hall, Harrogate & Dartington Fests. & BBC London. Recorded for CRI, EMI (ERATO) & Orion. Mbr., Am. Musical Instrument Soc.; Coll. Music Soc. Recip. Walter Anderson Fellowship, NY Univ.,

1973-75; Fellow, De Pauwhof, Wassernaar, Netherlands. Address: 44 Davison Ln. E, W Islip, NY 11795, USA.

POSTLEWATE, Charles Willard, b. 8 Jan. 1941, San Antonio, Tex., USA. Guitar Teacher; Performer. Educ: B Mechanical Engrng., Gen. Motors Inst., Flint, Mich., 1964; B Mus, Wayne State Univ., Detroit, Mich., 1969; M Mus, ibid., 1973. m. Diane Jean Kieffer, 2 s., 1 d. Debut: Detroit Inst. of Arts, 1968. Career incls: Electric (Jazz) Guitarist for Bob Hope, Gordon McRae, Marilyn Maye, 1964-71; Num. solo recitals, N USA; Var. orchl. apps.; Mbr., Perf. Fac., Wayne State Univ., E & W Mich. Univs., Univ. of Mich., Flint; Asst. Prof., Univ. of Tex., Arlington. Contbr. to var. profl. jrnls. Mbrships. incl: Guitar Curriculum Chmn.; Am. String Tchrs. Assn. Recip. var. hons. Hobbies incl: Baseball; Camping. Address: Univ. of Tex. of Arlington, Music Dept., Box 19 105, UTA Stn., Arlington, TX 76019, USA.

POSTOLKA, Milan, b. 29 Sept. 1932, Prague, Czech. Musicologist. Educ: Grad. (Hist.), Charles Univ., Prague, 1956; CSc, ibid, 1966; PhD., 1967; music study w. pvte. tutors, m. Bela, 2 d. Career: Rsch. work, Nat. Mus., Music Div., Prague, 1958-; Lectr. in Histl. Musicol., Charles Univ., 1966-; Rsch. Grp. Ldr., Czech Acad. of Scis., 1972-. Publs: Joseph Haydn a nase hubda 18. stoleti (Haydn & Czech Music of th 18th Century), 1961; Leopold Kozeluh; Life & Work (w. thematic catalogue), 1964; Joseph Haydn (monograph, in press); Critical edits. of: L Kozeluh, 5 Piano Sonatas (w. D Setková-Zahn), 1959; Anthol. of 18th Century Czech. Song, 2 vols. (w. O Pulkert), 1961-62; L Kozeluh Tre Sinfonie, 1969. Contbr. to num. music jrnls. encys., etc. Mbrships: Int. & Am. Musicological Socs.; Int. Asst. of Music Libs.; Fesellschaft für Musikforschung. Hobby: Travel. Address: Vysehradská 15, 128 00 Praha 2, Czech. 14.

POTMESILOVA, Jaroslava, b. 1 Sept. 1936, Prague, Czechoslovakia. Professor of Organ. Educ: Study of Piani, High Schl.of Music; Organ, Prague Conserv.; Dip., Organ, & Pedagogical Qualification, Acad. of Music. Debut: Prague, 1966; Career: Organ concerts, Austria, Switzerland, Turkey; Czechoslovakia, E., W. Germany, Belgium, Poland; 6 films, Organ Music of 7 Centuries, Czech. TV. Recordings: German Baroque Music; Czech Baroque Organ Fugues; Prague Baroque Organ; Eugon Suchon's Symphonic Fantasy upon Bach for Organ & Orchestra, w. Czech. Phil. Orch. Hons: Dip. & Medal of Hon., Bach Competition, Prague Spring Fest., 1966. Hobby: Literature. Address: Pohorelec 24, 11800 Prague-Hradcany, Czechoslovakia.

POTTEBAUM, William G, b. 30 Dec. 1930, Teutopolis, Ill., USA. Associate Professor. Educ: BS in Mus Ed., Quincy Coll., Ill., 1953; M Mus in comp. theory, Eastman Schl. of Music, Univ. of Rochester, NY,1960; PhD, in music comp. ibid, 1974; studied comp. w. Prof. Hermann Reutter, Stuttgart Musika Hochschule, 1954-55; Electronic Music Seminar, Univ. of Toronto, Canada, w. Prof. Myron Schaeffer. Career: 4 yrs. tchng. Grade & HS Instrumental & Vocal & Gen. Music, Pvte. & Class Piano Instrn., 1955-57, '60-62; Assoc. Prof., State Univ. Coll., Brockport, NY, 1963-; Assoc. Chmn., Dept. of Music, ibid, 1969-70. Compositions incl: works for large orch., for chamber orch., for large orch. & chorus, songs, electronic music, piano tchng. pieces, etc. Publs: incl: co-author, Listening in Depth, 1965; Music in Europe, wall map & study manual, 1965; Music in Assisted Instruction Tchr. & Student Manuals, 1967. Contbr. to var. jrnls. Mbrships: MENC; Coll. Music Soc.; NEA, etc. Hons: 1st prize in Am. Music in the Univ. for Concerto for Orch., 1963. etc. Address: Dept. of Music, State Univ. Coll. at Brockport, NY 14420, USA.

POTTENGER, Harold Paul, b. 21 Nov. 1932, Aurora, Mo., USA. Conductor; Composer; Educator. Educ: BS, Univ. of Mo. 1954; MME, Univ. of Wichita, 1958; DME, Ind. Univ., 1969. m. Patsy Lou House, 2 d. Career: Music Tchr., pub. schls., 6 yrs.; Coll. Tchr., SW Bapt. Coll., US Int. Univ., Calif.; Dir. of Bands & Assoc. Prof., Music, Bradley Univ., Ill., 1970-. Compositions; Suite for Band, 1965; Num. short choral works & arrangements, band transcriptions. Publs: Instrumental Handbook, 1971. Mbrships: MENC; Ill. Music Educators Assn.; Coll. Band Dirs. Nat. Assn. Hobbies: Golf; Tennis. Address: 2611 W Barker, Peoria, IL 61604, USA.

POTTER, Archibald James, b. 22 Sept. 1918, Belfast, Ireland, Composer; Singer; Flautist; Conductor. Educ: Clifton Coll., Bristol; RCM; Midland Schl. of Music, Birmingham. m. Dorothy Edith Elizabeth Whiteside (dec'd). Career: Singer, BBC, 1930's-50's; Panelist, Round Brit. Quiz; Bass Soloist, num. Oratorios; Chmn. Concert Hall, Search For A Song. Author, Speaker, The Young Students' Guide To Music, Listening To Music, The Consumer's Guide To Music series, Radio Eireann. Compositions incl: Sinfonia de Profundis, Concerto Da Chiesa,

piano & orch.; ballets Careless Love, Gamble No Gamble, Caitlin Bocht, Full Moon For the Bride; opera Patrick; var. orchl. works. songs, part-songs. Recordings: Variations On A Popular Tune; The Men of The West; White Green & Gold; The Best Of Irish Music; Gems From The Irish Airwaves; The Band of the Irish Army; Ceol Potter, Contbr. to the Comp.; Hibernia; The Irish Times; The Sunday Independent; The Irish Press. Mbr., Off., num. Profl. Orgs. Recip. num. Hons. Hobbies: Travel; Languages; Rambling. Address: Tobar Ceoltora, Greystones, Co. Wicklow, Eire. 3, 14.

POTTER, David Kinsman, b. 7 Jan. 1932, Malden, Mass., USA. Performer of the Contra-Bass; Orchestra Member. Educ: B Mus, Boston Univ. m. Margaret Eileen Hummel, 1 d. Career: Tchr. of String Bass, Colo. State Univ.; Tf. Collins; The Secret Life of an Orch., short documentary for Pub. TV; Mbr., Denver Symph. Orch. Recordings: Milena, Cantata for Soprano & Orch. by Alberto Ginastera, w. Denver Symph. Orch., 1973. Mbr. Kappa Gamma Psi. Hobby: Camping. Address: 1627 S Jasmine St., Denver, Co 80224, USA.

POTTER, Malcolm Frederick, b. 23 June 1933, Adelaide, S Australia. Professional Singer; Teacher. Educ: Dip., Perf. & Tchr. of Music; Assoc., Univ. of Adelaide. m. Nancy Margaret Honey, 1 s. Career: Tenor Soloist in num. operas, musical comedies, Gilbert & Sullivan, oratorios; Recitalist on Radio & in Concert Halls; Mbr., Adelaide Singers; Adelaide Consort of Voices. Recordings: Malcolm Potter Sings; Soloist, Aust. Festival of Music Vol. 1; Tenor Excerpts from Messiah by Handel; Var. ABC Discs. Hobbies: Music; Oil & Watercolour Painting; Sculpture. Address: 63 Pratt Ave., Pooraka, S Australia 5095.

POTTS, June E, b. 12 Oct. 1935, Chgo., Ill., USA. Horn Instructor; Musician (horn); Music Director; Managing Director. Educ: Northwestern Univ.; Univ. of Dubuque, Iowa; Tex. Christian Univ., Ft. Worth. Career: Mbr., Youth Orch. of Gtr. Chgo. & Selbert Opera Guild, Chgo.; Prin. Horn, Dubuque Univ. Orch., Iowa, Wright Coll. Orch., NW Symph. Orch., Women's Symph. Orch., Chgo. Scholarship Orch. & Westside Symph. Orch., all of Chgo.; currently Prin. Horn & Libn., Irving Symph. Orch., Tex.; Music Dir., Ft. Worth Civic Orch.; Mng. Dir., Ridglea Acad. of Music, Ft. Worth, Tex. Mbrships: Musical Dir. & Fndr., Horn Soc. of N Ctrl. Tex.; Dir. & Fndr., Tex. Assn. of Orch. Libns.; Int. Horn Soc.; Am. Fedn. of Musicians. Recip., musical awards & schlrship. Hobbies: Swimming; Horticulture; Classic Sports Cars. Address: 4530 El Campo Ave., Ft. Worth, TX 76116, USA.

POULTON, Diana, b. 18 April 1903, Storrington, Sussex, UK. Lutenist; Historian of the Lute & its Music. Educ: Slade Schl. of Fine Art, Univ. of London; studied Lute w. Arnold Dolmetsch. m. Thomas Leycester Poulton (dec.), 3 d. Career: Num. Broadcasts & TV apps., UK & Europe, 1926-; Concerts & lectures thru'out England; perfs. at Stratford upon Avon, Old Vic Theatre & other London theatres; Musical Dir., Shakespearian prods. at Open Air Theatre, Regent's Park, London, many yrs.; Prof. for the Lute, RCM, 1969-. Recordings: English Lute Songs, w. John Goss, 1927; The History of Music of Shakespeare's Time, Vol. 1. Publs: An Introduction to Lute Playing; John Dowland, 1972; Co-Ed., Collected Lute Music of John Dowland. Contbr. to: Musical Times; Lute Soc. Jrnl.; Consort; Monthly Musical Record; Le Luth & sa sique. Mbrships: Lute Soc. (Pres.); Galpin Soc.; Viola da Gamba Soc.; Soc. for Renaissance Studies. Hon: RCM, 1970. Hobbies: Reading; Theatre. Address: 5 Wilton Sq., Islington, London N1 3DL, UK. 3, 14.

POUMAY, Juliette, b. 12 Sept. 1934, Verviers, Belgium. Pianist; Professor of Piano. Educ: Conserv. Royal de Liège, 1949-53; Diplome Supérieur (piano) w. high distinction & Silver-gilt Medal awarded by the Belgian Govt.; Study in Paris w. Lazare Levy, 1954; Grad., Chapelle Musicale Reine Elisabeth, 1956-59. Career: International soloist, num. recitals in Belgium, Paris, London, Berlin, Hanover, Cologne, Geneva, Lausanne, Vienna, Oslo; sev. radio broadcasts. Recordings: Sonatas for piano & violin (Caésar Franck & Guillaume Lekeu); Concerto for 2 pianos & orch. (René Defossez), w. Suzette Gobert & Orch. Nat. de Belgique; Sonata for piano & violin (Louis Lavoye) w. Charles Jongen. Mbrships: Soroptimst Club of Verviers. Hons: Junior Prize, Union Artistique et Littéraire, 1946; Marie Prize, 1953; Virtuoso Prize awarded by the Belgian Govt., 1955; Dresse de Lebioles Prize, 1956; Chosen by her govt. as rep. of L'École Belge du Piano in Norway for the Tournée de Concerts et Recitals, 1961; Mbr., Conseil de Perfectionnement de l'enseignement de la Musique, 1973; VP, Union of Tchrs. of Conserv. Royal de Liège. Hobbies: Reading; Swimming. Address: 5 Place Henry Vieuxtemps, 4800 Verviers, Belgium.

POUPET, Michel, b. 4 July 1926, Rheims (Marne) France. Specialist in Musical Education, National Centre for Educational

Documentation, Ministry of Education, Paris; Baritone; Musicologist; Music Critic. Educ: univ. degree in law; studied singing w. Charles-Paul of Paris Opera, later w. Marguerite Canal. m. Mazedier Madeleine, 1 s., 1 d. Debut, 1956. Career: Recitalist, specializing in French song, esp. of the 19th & 20th centuries; has worked w. var. opera grps. inclng. Xavier de Courville's Micropera, 1970; Rschr. & interpreter of Georges Bizet, working in collaboration w. Winton Dean, is also working on correspondence of George Sand; Music Critic & London Corresp. (during 1963-64, when was w. French Embassy), L'Entr'acte opera mag., 1962-71. Contbr. many articles to music publs. Mbrships: French Soc. of Musicol.; Assoc. Mbr. Union of Women Profs. & Composers of Music; Music and Tradition. Recip. of 2nd Prize (ex-aequo), Union of Women Musical Artistes (UFAM) Honour Competition, 1970. Hobby: Skiing. Address: 15, rue Cassette, 75006 Paris, France.

POUSSE, Marcel, b. 23 June 1920, Lille, France. Music Teacher; Catholic Priest. Edud: Advanced Studies in Theol. & Philos.; Lille Cathedral Choir Schl.; Insts. of Sacred Music, Lille & Paris; Dips., Gregorian Ward & Orff Methods, IML., Paris. Career: Music Tchr., Primary & Secondary Levels. Comps: Music for TV film, The Gt. Bird; Restorations of 16th & 18th Century Music by musicians from the Oise area. Translator, The Little Singer's Voice. Contbr. to: Ed., Liaison, Assn. of Cath. Music Tchrs.; Liaison Bulletin, Pueri Cantores of France. Mbrships. incl: Pres., Assn. of Cath. Music Tchrs. Address: Instn. St. Joseph du Moncel, BP 53, 60700 Point Sainte Maxence, France.

POWELL, Arlene Karr, b. Chgo., Ill., USA. Pianist; College Professor. Educ: Dip., Juilliard Schl. of Music; B Mus, M Mus, Chgo. Musical Coll., Roosevelt Univ.; Cert., Conserv. Am. de Musique, France; Studies w. Rudolf Ganz, Mme. Rosina Llevinne, Mlle. Nadia Boulanger. Career: Concerts throughout Midwestern & Eastern US as recitalist & soloist w. orch. Comp. of original music for TV, & hundreds of tchng. pieces for piano. Recordings: Bach Suites. w. Stan Kenton's Jazz Workshop, Orange Coast Coll. Mbrships: Pres., Calif. Piano Assn.; Bd. of Dirs., Compton Civic Symph. Assn.; Affiliate, Calif. Music Educators Assn., Music Educators Nat. Assn.; Music Assn. of Calif. Community Colls.; Musicians Union. Recip., Helene Curtis Prize, 1949. Address: 9255 Caladium Ave., Fountain Valley, CA 92708, USA.

POWELL, Morgan E, b. 7 Jan. 1938, Graham, Tex., USA. Composer; Professor; Trombonist. Educ: B Mus, N Tex. Univ.; M Mus, ibid.; Doct. work in comp., Univ. Ill. m. Lucinda Lawrence-Powell, 2 c. Career: Toured w. Univ. of Ill. Jazz Band as Trombonist & Asst. Cond. to Eastern Europe, Ireland & Scandinavia; toured W & E Coasts (incl. Carnegie Hall) w. Contemporary Chmbr. Players, 1975. Comps. incl: Darkness II (brass quintet); Alone; Brass Quintet No. II; Faces; Windows, Commission from Spoleto fest., 1977. Recordings incl: Jazz comps.; Music for Brass; Transitions. Mbr., ASCAP. Hons. incl: ASCAP Awards, 1970-79; Grant, Ctr. for Advanced Study, Univ. Ill., 1972-73; Grant, Nat. Endowment for the Arts, 1974, 1976-77; many commissions. Hobby: Farming. Address: Music Dept., Univ. Ill., Urbana, IL 61801, USA.

POWELL, (Norman) James, b. 7 March 1930, Woonona, NSW. Aust. Pianist; Teacher; Musicologist. Educ: Sydney Conserv. Music, 1948-54; Dip., ibid., 1959. m. Merrill Lorraine Stutchbury, 1s., 1 d. Career: incls: Duo-pianist w. sister, Nola Powell, inclng apps., w. Aust. Broadcasting Commission, 1952-53; Rschr. w. Alan Roberts, into tchng. music by coulour; Cond., Wollogong Symph. Orch., 1974-76. Recordings: 2 gospel recordings. Publ: Pianoforte General Knowledge & Annotations (w. Daphne E Arnold), 1973. Mbr., num. profl. orgs. Recip. Lever Award, $1,000, w. sister, 1952. Hobbies incl: Water Skiing; Fishing. Address: Corner Robson Rd., & Powell Ave. Corrimal 2518, NSW, Australia.

POWERS, Adrian Peter, b. 28 Jan 1945, Hickley, Leics., UK. Organist; Director of Music. Educ: Grad. & Assoc., Birmingham Schl. of Music; Cert. in Educ., City of Birmingham Coll. of Educ.; ARCO. Career: apps. & broadcasts on Radio 2, BBC-TV & BBC Radio Birmingham; Hd. of Acad. Music, Moseley Schl., Birmingham. Mbrships: ISM; Inc. Guild of Ch. Musicians; Birmingham Br., Inc. Assn. of Organists. Hobbies: Reading; Theatre; Ecclesiastical Architecture; Study of Christian Liturgy. Address: Flat 4, 106 Church Rd., Moseley, Birmingham B13 9AB, UK.

POWNING, Graham Francis, b. 20 Nov. 1949, Sydney, Aust. Oboist. Educ: DSCM, FTCL, NSW Conserv. of Music. m. Rosemary Eizabeth Byron, 2 s. Career: Prin. oboe, Sydney Elizabethan Orch.; tchr., NSW Conserv. of Music; progs. for ABC radio on Aust. oboe music. Comps: 5 trios for 2 oboes & cor anglais; var. wind quintets; works for strgs. & brass. Recording; Aust. oboe music. Contbr. to Int. Double Reed mag.

VP, Aust. Double Reed Soc. Recip. Queen Elizabeth Jubilee medal. Hobbies: Conposing; Arranging. Address: 20 Reserve St., Denistone, 2114 Australia.

POWROZŃIAK, Józef, b. 4 Dec. 1902, Staniatki, Poland. Professor of Violin & History of Music 1951-63, 1972-75; Rector of Music Coll., Katowice. Educ: Jagiellonian Univ.; Music Inst. m. Janina Bossowska, 1 d. Publs: Paganini, 1958; The Guitar from A to Z, 1966; Lipinski, 1970; 2 Tutors for the Guitar; 125 anthols. for violin, guitar, accordion & other instruments. Contbr. to var. periodicals. Mbrships: Soc. of Polish Musicians; Pres., Folk Inst. of Music. Hons: Music Prize, town of Katowice; Hon. & Prize, Min. of Art & Culture. Hobby: Sports. Address: Katowice, ul. Paderewskiego 42/10, Poland.

POY, Nardo, b. 28 Apr. 1948, Bronx, NY, USA. Violinist. Educ: BS, Mannes Coll. of Music, NYC. m. Julia di Gaetani. Debut: gave Phila. permiere of Hovhannes' Talin for viola & string orch., 1973. Career: Mbr., Empire Sinfonietta, NYC & Brattleboro Fest. Orch.; currently Prin. Violinist, Opera Co. of Phila., Orch. of the City of NY, Lake George Opera Fest., Mbr., Mostovoy Soloist of Phila. & Philharmonia Orch. of Phila., Artist-in-Res., SUNY at Postdam. Mbrships: Phila. Musical Soc.; Assoc. Musicians of Gtr. NY. Hons. incl: Hans Neumann Award for Excellence in Chmbr. Music, 1970. Hobbies incl: Gardening; Reading; Handicrafts. Address: 345 S 13th St., Phila., PA 19107, USA.

POZAJIC, Mladen, b. 6 Mar. 1905, Zupanja, Yugoslavia. Conductor; Pedagogue; Concert Accompanist; Music Theoretician; Composer. Educ: Dept. of Conducting, Music Acad., Zagreb. m. Zdenka Bukac, 1 d. Debut: 1926. Career: Music Master, 1930-37, Prof., 1937-45, Music Acad. Zagreb; Opera Cond., 1947-65; Prof., Music Acad., Sarajevo, 1965-. Comps: Symph. & chmbr. music; piano comps.; solo songs accompanied by piano & by orch.; choruses. Mbrships: Assn. of Comps.; Assn. of Music Artists of Yugoslavia. Contbr. to a music ency. & lectr. on Radio Sarajevo. Hons. incl: 27th July Prize, Repub. of Bosnia & Herzegovina, 1968. Hobby: Music. Address: 71000 Sarajevo, JNA 35, Yugoslavia.

POZDRO, John Walter, b. 14 Aug. 1923, Chgo., Ill., USa. Composer; Educator. Educ: Am. Conserv. of Music, 1941-42; B Mus, Northwestern Univ., 1948; M Mus, ibid, 1949; PhD, Eastman Schl. of Music, 1958. m. Shirley Winans, 1 s., 1 d. Career: Instructor, Univ. of Iowa, Cedar Falls; Tchng. Fellow, Eastman Schl. of Music; Vis. Prof., Northwestern Univ.; Prof., Music Theory & Compositions, Univ. of Kan., Lawrence, 1950-; Chmn., Dept. of Music Theory, ibid, 1961-; Hd.; univ's annual Symposium of Contemp. Am. Music, 1958-69; works have been heard on nat. radio & perf. by well-known orchs. thru'out USA. Compositions incl: All Pleasant Things; The Creation; They That Go Down to the Sea; The Light; Landscape II; Ostinato; Waterlow Park. Compositions Recorded: Third Symphony; Piano Sonatas Nos. 2 & 3. Contbr. to jrnls. Mbrships: ASCAP; Pi Kappa Lambda; Kan. Music Tchrs. Assn.; Nat. Patron, Delta Omicron Int. Recip. of many awards inclng. Delius Fndn. Award for Preludes for Piano, 1974, Nat. Endowment for the Arts Grant, 1976; ASCAP Award, 1978-79. Hobbies: Fishing; Photography. Address: Dept. of Music, Murphy Hall, Univ. of Kan., Lawrence, KS 660945, USA.

POZNIAK, Piotr, b. 26 Aug. 1939, Cracow, Poland. Musicologist. Educ: Magister degree in Musicol., Jagiellonian Univ. Career: Musicologist. Chiefly music of Renaissance & Baroque Era, especially music for lute & probelms of editing early music. Publs: Works of Dlugoraj, 1964, Diomendes Cato, 2 vols. 1970 & 73. F Maffon, 1970 (each w. biographical & analytical preface); in collective publs. - works on Bakfark & anonymous pieces for lute, 1964, a vocal piece of Gorczycki, 1966, a medieval anonymous composition, 1972; Nedza Uszczesliwiona, Opera, 1978; Var. articles on lute music in periodicals. Mbrships: Int. Musicol. Soc.; Polish Comps. Union, Sect. of Musicol. (Bd. Mbr.). Address: ul. Jaworowa 25, Cracow 30-327, Poland.

PRATT, George, b. 11 Feb. 1935, W Kirby, UK. Senoir Lecturer in Music. Educ: Organ Scholar, St. Peter's Coll., Oxford, 1956-59; B Mus., 1960; MA, 1965; ARCO, 1963. m. Mary Margaret Stewart, 2 s. Career: Dir. of Music, Abingdon Schl., Berks., 1960-64; Dir. of Music, Univ. of Keele, 1964-74; Sr. Lectr. in Music, ibid, 1974-. Comps: Church Anthems (RSCM Press). Recordings: The Organ of Keele University, 1965; Come Living God, 1974. Publs: John Stanley, Op. 1 (edn.), 19712; John Stanley, op. 4 (edn.), 1974; William Babel, Two Sonatas; Thomas Vincent, Two Sonatas; Bach Cello Suites. Contbr. to profl. mags. & jrnls. Mbr., profl. orgs.; chmn., W Midland Arts, 1976-. Hons: Coll. Prize, Oxford, 1959; Read Prize, RCO, 1963. Hobbies: Perf.

wind chamber music; Sailing. Address: Univ. of Keele, Keele, Staffs. ST5 5BG, UK. 3.

PRAUSNITZ, Frederik W, b. 26 Aug. 1920, Cologne, Germany. Conductor. Educ: Juilliard Grad. Schl., 1945. m. Margaret Britten Grenfell, 1 s., 1 d. Debut: Cond., Detroit Symph., 1944. Career: Guest Cond., BBC, LSO, New Philharmonia, LPO, RPO, Engl. Chmbr. Orch., & many orchs. on the Continent, 1957-; Assoc. Dir., Pub. Activities, Juilliard Schl. of Music, 1947-49; Asst. Dean, ibid, 1949-61; Dir., Choral Music & Assoc. Cond., Juilliard Orch., 1956-61; Cond., New Engl. Conserv. Symph. Orch., Boston, 1961-69; Music Cond., Syracuse Symph Orch., 1971-. ch. cond., Peabody Inst., Balt., Md., 1976-. Has recorded for Columbia, EMI, Epic, Angel, Phillips & Argo. Contbr. to sev. jrnls. Mbrships: Dir., Int. Soc. Contemp. Music, 1960-62; Am. Symph. Orch. League; Savage Club, London. Hons. incl: Rockefeller Fndn. Lectr. on Music, Harvard Univ., 1966; Hon. Fellow, Univ. of Sussex, UK, 1970; Special Asst. to Provost, Oakland Univ., Mich. 1976. Address: c/o Syracuse Symphony Orch., 113 E Onondaga St., Syracuse, NY 13202, USA. 6, 14

PREBILIC, Elizabeth J (Sister Susanne), b. 3 July 1918, Eveleth, Minn., USA. Educator; Performer; Conductor; Writer. Educ: BA, Coll. of St. Scholastica, Duluth, Minn.; MM, Northwestern Univ., Evanston, Ill., 1959; Univ. of Minn., Duluth, 1954-61; N Tex. State Univ., Denton, 1967-70; Case-Western Reserve Univ., Cleveland, Ohio, 1970-71. Debut: Piano recital, aged 5; Organ & Violin, aged 7; Clarinet, aged 10. Career: Cond. of schl. orchs., 25 yrs.; Num. concerts & perfs.; Perf. & tchr. of violin, viola, piano, organ, string quartet, ensembles; Accomp. of soloists & choirs; Tchr., Asst. Cond. & Concertmaster, Coll. of St. Scholastica; 1st Violin, Duluth Symph.; pvte. studio, St. Scholastica Priory. Mbr., var. musical socs. Recip., sev. hons. Hobby: Travel. Address: St. Scholastica Priory, Duluth, MN 55811, USA.

PREININGER, John A, b. 5 May 1947, Graz, Austria. Librarian; Jazz Drummer. Educ: Phiol. & Archeol., Univ. of Graz, 1965-; PhD, ibid, 1973; Drums & timpani, Conserv., Graz; Jazz & Jazz drumming, Hochschule für Musik, Graz. Debut: Radio-recording, Studio St. Peter, Graz, 1969. Career: Radio, TV, concerts, Austria, Yugoslavia, Hungary, Germany, Denmark, Spain, USA, FRG, Sweden, Poland; Mbr., Neighbours Jazz Group, Graz. Comps. incl: Knautschlack, A-Skelett, Il bimbo, Floating, Meditation, Graz 345, We Come On First. Recordings incl: Acoustic Space, 1970; Tone Jansa Jazz Kvartet, 1977; Neighbours - Accents, 1978; Neighbours - Live, 1977. Contbr. to Jazz Rsch. Mbr., Int. Soc. Jazz Rsch., Graz. Hobbies incl: Sport; Travel; Astrol.; Humanities. Address: Froehlichgasse 8, A-8010 Graz, Austria.

PREJZNER, Tadeusz, b. 17 Mar. 1925, Radzyn-Podlaski, Poland. Composer; Radio & TV Producer. Educ: MA equivalent; Dip. in Composition, Warsaw Music HS, 1962. m. Elzbieta Kakowicz, 1972, 2 d. Debut: Phil., Cracow. Career incl: Prod., Polish Radio & TV, Music Sect., 1972-. Compositions: Four Preludes for Chamber Orchestra, 1963; Concertino for Piano & Orch., 1961; Trio for Bass, 1966; Quintet for Brass, 1966; 1st Symph., 1969; 2nd Symph., 1972; Music for theatre - Midsummer Night's Dream, 1963. Recordings: Songs to Galczynski's Words, 1962; Trio for Brass, 1971; 4 preludes. Contbr. to: Jazz Forum; var. Jazz mags. & reviews. Mbrship: Assn. of Polish Composers. Hon: 2nd Prize, Young Composers Competition, Poland, 1971; Polish comps. competition prizes, 1972. Hobby: Gardening. Address: Wloscianska 2 m. 63, 01-710 Warsaw, Poland.

PREK, Stanko, b. 12 Mar. 1915, Solkan, Nova Gorica, Yugoslavia. Professor of Classic Guitar; Concert Guitarist; Composer. Educ: Grad., Tchr. Schl., Ljubljana Staatliche Akademie der Tonkunst-Muenchen, 1941, Acad. of Music, Ljubljana, 1944. m. Antonija Orlich. Debut: Ljubljana, 1938. Career: Solo apps. in major towns of Yugoslavia, Germany & Switz.; Apps. on Yugoslavian radio; Prof., Acad. of Music, Zagreb, Acad. of Pedagogics, Maribor. Comps. incl: Symph. in C sharp minor; choral works; Guitar solos; string quartets. Publs. incl: Classic Guitar Tutor 1-6, 1966-70; Methodics of the Classic Guitar I, 1977 (w. Mirko Orlich). Contbr. to profl. jrnls. Mbrships incl: Union of Yugoslav Comps.; Soc. of Music Artists of Slovenia. Recip., Lajovic Prize for Comp., Glasbena Matica, Ljubljana, 1942. Hobbies incl: Collecting folklore materials. Address: 6100 Ljubljana, Streliska 1, Yugoslavia.

PREMRU, Raymond Eugene, b. 6 June 1934, Elmira, NY, USA. Composer; Conductor; Trombonist. Educ: B Mus, Eastman Schl. of Music, USA, 1956; ARCM, UK, 1957; studied comp. w. Gladys Levnton, Bernard Rogers & Peter Racine Fricker, trombone w. Emory Remington. m. Susan Talbot, 2 d. Career: Mbr., Philharmonia & New Philharmonia

Orch., London, 1958-, Philip Jones Brass Ensemble; recip. commns. from fests., orchs., ensembles, socs., etc. Comps; Music From Harter Fell; Quartet for Two Trumpets, Horn & Trombone; Concertane for Strgs; Cavases; Triptych for voices & brass. Concertino for Trombone & Four Woodwind; Tissington Variations. recording; Live At Ronnie Scott's (Bobby Lamb Ray Premru Orch.). Hobbies: Tennis; Walking; Reading. Address: 33 Springfield Gdns., London NW9 ORY, UK.

PREPREK, Stanislav, b. 21 Apr. 1900, Sid, Yugoslavia. Composer. Educ: Tchrs. Trng. Schl. Career: Tchr., organist & cond. of choral socs. & children's choirs; Num. perfs. on radio. Comps. incl: Spring Suite I & IV (piano); Little Theme with 25 Variations (piano); Spring Waters (voice & piano); Death in Ears (voice & piano); Sonata for Flute & Piano; Capriccio for String Quartet; The Waves (piano suite)., String Quartet IV; The Elegiac Poem (voice & piano). Mbr., Comps. Soc. of Yugoslavia, Novi Sad. Hobby: Lyric writing. Address: Preadoviceva 14, 21131 Petrovaradin, Yugolsavina.

PRESCOTT, Thomas Mayhew, b. 11 May 1951, Beckly, W Va., USA. Maker of Historical Woodwinds. Educ: BA, Lake Forest Coll., Ill., 1973; apprenticed to Friedrich von Huene, 1973-75. Produced 1st instrument, 1975. Instruments: baroque flutes, recorders, clarinets, etc., owned by many noted perfs. of early music; 2 instruments accepted for Contemporary Musical Instrument Makers exhibit, Wash. DC. Mbr., Am. Musical Instrument Soc. Hobbies: Playing early instruments; Skiing; Flying. Address: 99 Washington St., Melrose, MA 02176, USA.

PRESS, Seymour Red, b. 26 Feb. 1924, Bronx, NY., USA. Saxophone; Clarinet; Flute. m. Nona Press, 1 s., 1 d. Career: Played musical score of film "Those Were the Days"; Played w. Bobby Sherwood, Tony Pastor, Ralph Flanagan (Chesterfield Radio Show), Tommy Dorsey (TV "Stage Show"), Benny Goodman, Am. Symph. Orch., NYC Ballet Orch. Compositions: Slow Drive; Far Eastern Weekend. Recordings: Park Ave. Patter (w. Don Redman Orch.); Drumorama (Louie Bellson Orch.); Last Moments of Greatness (Tommy & Jimmy Dorsey Orch.); original Broadway cast albums of Gypsy, Jennie, Mame, Applause, Pippin, Cyrano, etc.; recorded w. Charles Mingus, Andre Kostelanetz, Bobby Sherwood, Tony Pastor, Ralph Flanagan. Mbr., ASCP. Hobbies: Swimming; Golf. Address: 77-35 113th St., Forest Hills, NY 11365, USA.

PRESSER, André, b. 12 Sept. 1933, Amsterdam, Netherlands. Conductor. Educ: Studied Cond., & Piano-Soloist, -Tchr. & -Accomp., Royal Conserv., The Hague. widower, 2 children. Debut: Piano, 1942; Cond., 1960. Career: Repétiteur, Nat. Ballet of Holland; Musical Dir., Dutch Nat. Ballet, 1961-. Hond: Awards as Ballet Cond., Paris, 1962, 1970. Hobbies: Horse Riding; Cooking. Address: Bentinckstraat 8, Abcoude 1165, Netherlands.

PRESSLER, Menahem, b. Magdeburg, Germany. Pianist; Professor of Music. Educated in Palestine. m. Sara Scherchen, 1 s., 1 d. Debut: W. Israel Philharmonic; In USA, w. Phila. Orch. under Ormandy. Career: Annual world-wide tours as mbr., & co-fndr., Beaux Arts trio; Solo perfs. Num. recordings as mbr., Beaux Arts Trio, inclng. complete Mozart, Beethoven, Brahms, Schubert & Ravel; Solo recordings. Publs: Ed., 1st publication of Prokoffiev's 9 Sonata. Hons: Grand Prix du Disque, 1964; Deutscher Schallplatten Prize, for complete recordings of Dvorak, 1971; Nominated for Grammy Award, for same album. Address: c/o Schl. of Music, Ind., Univ., Bloomington, IN, USA

PRESTON, George Hamish Hew, b. 26 Nov. 1929, Wellington, UK. Inspector of Music. Educ: ARCM; MA, Kings Coll., Cambridge. m. Janet Elizabeth Preston, 2 children. Career: Cond., Birmingham Choral Soc., 1959-64, Walsall Choral Soc., 1961-70; Hd. of Music, Perry Common Comprehensive Schl., Birmingham, 1963-70; Insp. of Music, Inner London Educ. Auth., 1970-76; Gen. Advsr. w. special responsibility for music, Royal Country of Berkshire, 1976-. Address: Farthings, Whitchurch Hill, nr. Reading, UK.

PRESTON, Jean, b. 3 Sept. 1925, Montpelier, Idaho, USA. Singer; Professor of Voice. Educ: Pvte. instruction in voice, piano & solfegge; Voice study, Vocal & operatic coaching, var. tchrs. m. Donald A Preston, 2 s. Debut: Salk Lake City, Utah. Career: Num. apps. w. Utah Symph. in concert & in leading operatic roles; perfs. w. Houston Symph., Houston Grand Opera, Corpus Christi Symph.; Soloist w. Barbirolli, Previn & other major conds.; Tour w. Utah Symph., 1968; perfs. w. Houston Chmbr. Orch. & Bach Soc.; TV apps. Recordings: Scarlatti, Mass of St. Cecilia; Honegger, King David; Handel, Samson; Robertson, Book of Mormon Oratorio. Mbr., profl. orgs. Recip., num. awards in competitions, etc. Hobby: Travel. Address: 4223 Dumfries, Houston, TX 77035, USA.

PRESTON, Robert, b. 26 Jan. 1942, Bronxville, NY, USA. Concert Pianist. Educ: Dip., in Piano, B Mus, & M Sc. Juilliard Schl. of Music, m. Joanne Polk. Debut: Carnegie Hall, 1965. Career: Perfs. in every maj. city in US in solo recitals & apps. w. maj. symph. orchs.; 5 int. tours w. perfs. in England, France, Italy, Germany, Australia, Netherlands, & Brazil; num. radio & TV perfs.; Subject of a nationally televised documentary film; Assoc. Prof. of music, & Chmn., Piano Dept., Univ. of Bridgeport, Conn., currently. Recordings: Rubenstein Piano Concerto No. 3 & Kabalevsky Piano Concerto No. 3, 1974., Recip., num. awards inclng. Gold Medal, Int. Busoni Competition, Italy. Hobbies incl: Photography. Address: 228 E Columbus Ave., White Plains, NY 10604, USA.

PRESTON, Simon John, b. 4 Aug. 1938. Organist; Conductor; Lecturer. Educ: King's Coll., Cambridge; BA; MusB; MA; ARCM; FRAM. Career: Sub-organist, Westminister Abbey, 1962-67; Acting organist, St. Alban's Abbey, 1967-68; cond., Oxford Bach Choir, 1971-74; Organist, lectr. in music, Christ Ch., Oxford, 1970-. num. recordings. Hons: Dr. Mann Organ Student, King's Coll.; hon.FRCO; Edison Award, 1971. Address: Christ Church, Oxford, UK.

PRESTON, Stephen John, b. 24 May 1945, Skipton, Yorks., UK. Flautist. Educ: AGSM. m. Patricia Anderton, 1 s., 1 d. Debut: w. Galliard Harpsichord Trio, Purcell Room, London, 1968. Solo perf. Purcell Room, 1972. Career: w. Galliard Harpsichord Trio, 1967-71; Prof., baroque flute, GSM; Perf., baroque flute, w. Engl. Concert ensemble; Radio & TV broadcasts; Recitals, Queen Elizabeth Hall, Purcell Room, Wigmore Hall; Festivals, Bath, Brighton, City of London, Cambridge, Leeds, York. & Eng. Bach Festival; Recordings of early flutes from mus. for BBC Sound Archives. Contbr. to Early Music Mag.; Music Teacher Mbr., ISM. Hons: Fernley Flute Schlrship., 1963-66; Dame Myra Hess Award, 1972; Brit. Arts Coun. Award, 1972-73. Hobbies: Cycling; Gardening. Mgmt: Basil Douglas Ltd., 9 St. George's Terr., London, NW1. Address: 64 Lawrie Park Rd., Sydenham, London SE26, UK.

PRETRE, Georges, b. 14 Aug. 1924, France. Conductor. Educ: Conserv. de Douai; Conserv. Nat. Superieure de Musique de Paris; Ecole des Chefs d'orchestre. Career: Dir. of Music, Opera Houses of Marseilles, Lille & Toulouse, 1946-55; Dir. of Music, Operacomique, Paris, 1955-59, l'Opera, ibid,1959-; Dir. Gen. of Music, ibid, 1970-71; Cond. of the Symph. Assns. of Paris; Guest Cond. at Prin. music festivals of the world, & at La Scala, Milan; 1965-66; Metropol. Opera House, NY, 1964-65; Salzburg, 1966. Address: 19 rue de Montbuisson, 78 Louveciennes, France.

PRETTY, Sharman Ellen, b. 12 June 1951, Launceston, Aust. Lecturer in Oboe. Educ: B Mus, Univ. Adelaide; Prufung den Kunstlerischen Reife, Staatliche Hochschule fur Musik, Freiburg, German Fed. Rebup. Career: Formerly Prin. Oboe, Elizabethan Theatre Trust Orch., Melbourne; Solo & Chmbr. Music performances. Aust. Broadcasting Commission; Lectr., Oboe, Canberra Schl. Music, ACT. Mbr: Profl. Musicians' Union Aust. Hon: Winner, SA Final, Aust. Broadcasting Commission Concerto Competition, 1970. Hobbies: Theol. Studies; Swimming. Address: c/o Canberrra Sch. Music, NSW Cresc., Manuka, ACT 2603, Aust.

PREUSSNER, Carltheodor, b. 24 May 1895, Marxguün, Germany. Cellist. Educ: Dortmund Conserv.; Munich Acad. of Music; Leipzig Inst. of Music. m. Emma Schumann. Career: Cello Virtuoso; Soloist & Music Tchr., 1925; Cellist, Dortmund., Leipzig & Munich; Ed., Fränkischer Kulturspiegel; Ed., Deutscher Kulturspiegel, 1948-49. Contbr. to: var. jrnls. Mbrships: Co-Fndr. & Mbr., Exec. Bd., State Assn. of Bavarian Musicians; Fndr. & Press., Assn. of Musicians, Hof & Vicinity; Ch. Coun., Naila-Marxgrün. Address: Landhaus Preussner, 8671 Marxgrün, German Fed. Repub.

PREVIN, André George, b. 6 Apr. 1930, Berlin, Germany. Conductor; Composer; Pianist. Educ: Univ. of Calif., USA; Berlin & Paris Conservatories. m., 3 s., 1 d. Career: Music Dir., Houston Symph., 1967-69; Prin. Cond. & Music Dir., LSO,1968-; BBC TV series annually since 1971. Compositions: Cello Concerto, 1967; Guitar Concerto, 1971; Serenades for Violin, 1972; Symph. for Strings, 1965; Overture to a Comedy, 1967; Wind Quintet, 1974; Brass Quintet, 1974; The Invisible Drummer (Six Piano Preludes), 1974; (stage musicals) Coco, 1969 & The Good Companions, 1974. num. recordings Publs: Music Face to Face (w. A Hopkins), 1971; Andre Previn, by Edward Greenfield, 1973. Contbr. to many mags., jrnls., etc. Mbrships: CGGB; Dramatists Guild; Acad. of Motion Pictures, Arts & Scis., etc. Hons: Motion Picture Acad. Awards, 1958, '59, '62, '63. Hon. degree, GSM, 1972. Hobbies: Collecting folk art; Drawing; Sport (Fencing). Mgmt: Harrison Parrott, London, Address: c/o London Symph. Orch., 1 Montague St., London WC1, UK. 2, 14, 16.

PREY, Hermann, b. 11 July 1929, Berlin, Germany, Baritone. Educ: State Music Acad., Berlin. m. Barbara Pniok, 1 s., 2 d. Career incls: State Opera, Wiesbaden, 1952; Munich, Hamburg, Vienna, Berlin; apps. at Bayreuth, Edinburgh, Vienna, Salzburg, Aix-en-Provence, Tokyo, Perugia & other fests.; Guest Artists, La Scala, Milan, Teatro Colon, Buenos Aires, Metrop. Opera, NYC San Fran. Opera; currently w. Munich State Opera. Hobbies: Cinema; Riding. Address: Fichtenstr. 14, D-8033 Krailling vor München, German Fed. Repub. 16.

PRIANO, Aldo, b. 23 Dec. 1895, La Spezia, Italy. Violinist; Orchestral Conductor. Educ: Dip. of Violin; Comp. w. Renzo Bossi & Gaetano Luporini. m. Elvira Petrilli, 2 d. Debut: Violin concerts, S Am., 1918. Career: As cond., apps. on Italian, Austrian & Yugoslavian radio; as violinist, apps. on Italian radio. Comps: Reverie for violin or cello & piano; Carovana and Danza Delle Bambole for piano; Arr. of a Romance by Mendelssohn, 2 Sonatas by Castrucci. Recordings of violin for Max Glucksmann Soc. Mbrships: Regia Accademia Filharmonica of Bologna; Accademia Nazionale of Florence; Artistic Dir., Musici Luceneses. Address: Via Burlamacchi No. 11, Lucca, Italy.

PRICE, Janet, b. Pontypool, Gwent, S Wales, UK. Soprano Singer. Educ: B Mus, M Mus, Univ. Coll., Cardiff; LRAM (Singing perf. & Piano accompanist); ARCM (Piano perf.). Debut: BBC TV (Wales), 1964. m. Adrian Beaumont. Career: Has sung in all parts of Brit. Isles in USA & Most W Europe countries; Specialists in recreation of neglected heroines in 19th century Italian Bel Canto Opera; Prin. operatic roles w. Glyndebourne Fest. Opera, Welsh Nat. Opera Co., Handel Opera Soc.; Gave Belgian Premiere of Tippett's 3rd Symph. w. Belgian Radio Orch., Fest. of Flanders, 1975. Recordings: EMI; Argo; Composers' Recordings Inc., USA; Unique Opera Recordings; USA. Hons: Winner, Young Welsh Singers' Award, Arts Coun., 1964. Hobbies incl: Fell walking. Mgmt: Ibbs & Tillett, London, UK. 27.

PRICE, John Elwood, b. 21 June 1935, Tulsa, Okla., USA. Composer; Professor; Pianist. Educ: B Mus, Lincoln Univ., Mo., 1957; MMus, Univ. of Tulsa, 1963. Career: Staff Comp.-Pianist, Karamu Theatre, 1957-59; Chmn., Music & Fine Arts, Fla. Mem. Coll., Miami, 1964-74; Fac., Dept. of Music, Eastern Ill. Univ., summer 1970-71, fall 1974. Comp. of 310 works inclng: Invention for Piano I, 1969; Two Typed Lines (voice & piano), 1966. Recordings: Scherzo I for Clarinet & Orch., 1970. Mbrships: incl: ASCAP; Soc. of Black Comps.; Am. Soc. of Univ. Comps. Publs: incl: The Black Musician As Artist & Entrepreneur, 1974. Hons: incl: Comp.-in-Res., Fla. Mem. Coll., 1969-74. Hobbies incl: Painting; Poetry. Address: Music Dept., Eastern Ill. Univ., Charleston, IL 61920, USA.

PRICE, Leontyne, b. 10 Feb. 1927, USA. Opera Singer (soprano). Educ: Ctrl. State Coll., Wilberforce, Ohio; Juilliard Schl., NY. Debut: In Poulenc's Les Carmelites, San Fran., 1952. Career: Leading role of Bess in Porgy & Bess, in Vienna, Berlin, Paris, London & NY, 1952-54; Recitals & soloist, 1954-; Soloist, Hollywood Bowl, 1955-59; Perfs. in Opera, NBC-TV, 1955-58; San Fran. Opera Co., 1957-59, 1960-61; Vienna Staatsoper, 1958-61; Opera appearances at Covent Gdn., London, 1958-59, Chgo., 1959-60, Milkan, 1960-61, Metropol. Opera, NY, 1961-62, '66, '69; noted for role of Aida, Paris Opera, 1968. Recordings of num. works made on RCA-Victor label. Address: 1133 Braodway, Suite 603, NY, NY 10010, USA.

PRICE, Margaret Berenice, b. 13 Apr. 1941, Blackwood, Wales, UK. Operatic Soprano. Educ: TCM. Debut: as Cherubino in Marriage of Figaro, Welsh Nat. Opera, 1962; in same role, Royal Opera House, Convent Gdn., 1963. Career: apps. in 5 major Mozart roles, world's ldng. opera houses, Convent Gdn., Paris, La Scals, Vienna, Salzburg, San Fran., Munich, Cologne, Chgo., Glyndebourne. Recordings; works by Beethoven, Elgar, Handel, Mahler, Puccini, Vaughan Williams; sev. recital, lieder albumns. Hobbies: Coking; Motoring; Reading. Address: 24 Marylebone High St., London W1, UK. 1.

PRICOPE, Eugen, b. 16 Apr. 1927, Oituz-Bacau, Romania. Conductor; Musicologist. Educ: Conserv. of Music, Bucharest; Int. Cond. course, Trier, W German, 1978. m. Eugenia Pricope, 2 s. Debut: 1956. Career: Cond., all symph. orchs. in Bucharest & Romania; num. recordings w. Romanian Symph. Orchs.; apps. on TV & radio; Dir., Museum of Romanian Music, Bucharest, 1979. Publs: Beethoven, 1958; Symphony before Beethoven, 1963; Conductors & Orchestras, 1972; Silvestri, 1975; Contbr. to dicts., encys. & profl. jrnls. Mbrships: Romanian Comps. Union; Assn. of Theatre & Music Workers; mgng. bd., Bucharest Cultural & Scientific Univ. Hons: Czech. Express Gratitude award, 1964; Comps. Union prize, 1976; Beethoven Bicentennial medal, 1970. Hobbies: Camping; Chess. Address: .str. Liviu Rebreanu 20, Bloc A G, Sc.1, Et.1, Ap. 4, La6 Bucharest 57, Romania.

PRIESTMAN, Brian, b. 10 Feb. 1927, Birmingham, UK. Conductor; Musical Director. Educ: B Mus, Univ. of Birmingham, 1950; MA, ibid, 1952; Superior Dip., Cond., Royal Conserv. of Brussels, Belgium, 1952. m. Mary-Ford Stockton Priestman, 1 d. Career: Music Dir., Royal Shakespeare Theatre, 1960-63, Edmonton, Ca., Symph., 1964-68, Denver, USA, Symph., 1970-78; Music Dir., Florida Phil., 1977-; Res. Cond., Balt., USA, Symph., 1968-69; Prin. Cond., New Zealand Broadcasting Corp., 1973-75. Recordings: num. Contbr. to Grove's Dictionary of Music & Musicians; Musik in Geschichte & Gegenwart; Ency. Britannica. Hons: Golden Lyre Award, USA, 1973; Dr. of Fine Arts, Regis Coll., 1972; Dr. of Humane Letters, Univ. of Colo., 1977. Mgmt: Shaw Concerts, NY; Harold Holt, London. Address: c/o Florida Phil., 150 S E 2nd Ave., Miami, FL 33131, USA.

PRIMUS, Constance Merrill, b. 26 Aug. 1931, Denver, Colo., USA. Teacher of Recorder & Flute. Educ: Bucknell Univ.; Univ. Colo. (BMus, 1978); Univ. Denver; Western State Coll.; Studied Piano, Blanche D Matthews Schl. of Music; Tchrs. Cert., Am. Recorder Soc. m. Robert J. Primus, 2 s. Career: Pvte. Tchr. of Recorder & Flute; Schl. Demonstrations on Recorders & Workshops for Classroom Tchrs.; Progs. on hist. of flutes w. musical examples from Collection of antiqua & folk flutes; Former Mbr., The Camerata & var. Chmbr. Music Enselbles. Contbr. to: The Am. Recorder. Mbrships: Am. Recorder Soc. (Nat. Bd. of Dirs., 1978-); Former Music Dir., Denver Chapt., Sigma Alpha Iota & Tau Beta Sigma. Hobby: Travelling; Jeeping. Address: 13607 W Mississippi Ct., Lakewood, Colo., USA. 5, 27.

PRINSEN, Jaap Anton, b. 1 Sept. 1942, Apeldoorn, Netherlands. Horn Instructor. Educ: Horn soloist cert., Amsterdam Conserv. Career: 3rd horn, Concertgebouw Orch.; soloist, ibid., 1970; Chmbr. music recitals, var. provincial Dutch towns; broadcasts w. Radio Phil. Orch., Amsterdam Chmbr. Orch. & Radio Chmbr. Orch.; Horn Instr., Conservs. of Groningen & Friends of the Concertgebouw, Amsterdam, 1967; Prix d'Excellence, Amsterdam Conserv., 1969. Hobbies: Gardening; Fishing. Mgmt: Nederlands Impressariatt. Address: Wustelaan 35, Santpoort, Netherlands.

PRINZ, Alfred, b. 4 June 1930, Wien, Austria. Clarinettist; Composer; Pianist. Educ: Akademie für Musik, Wien. Career: 1st Clarinettist, Vienna State Opera, 1945; Solo Clarinettist, Vienna Phil., 1955-. Comps.; 5 symphs.; Musik für Orchestra, 1959; Klarinettenkonzert, 1971; Violinkonzert, 1973; Kammermusik. Hons: Prof., Hochschule für Musik, Wien, 1972; Wien State Prize for Comp., 1971. Address: 1190 Wien, Paul Ehrlich-Gasse 12, Austria.

PRIOR, Susan Jane, b. 29 Jan. 1946, Ottaws, Can. Performer & Teacher (recorder & Baroque flute). Educ: 2 yrs. maths & physics. Univ. of Toronto; studied recorder w. Hugh Orr, Toronto, & Hans-Martin Linde, Switz.; studied flute w. Robert Aitken, Toronto; studied Baroque flute w. H-M. Linde & Barthold Kuijken. m. William Prior, 1d. Career: perfs. in num. Baroque chmbr. concerts in and around Toronto; recordings for CBC radio & TV; concerts in Vancouver & Victoria, Can.; played for background music for radio, TV & film prods.; regular solo apps. in early music concert series in Toronto & univs. nearby. Contbr. to Continuo mag. Mbrships: Toronto Musicians Assn.; Am. Recorder Soc.; Coll. Music Soc.; Can. Assn. of Univ. Schls. of Music; Royal Conserv. of Toronto Alumni Assn. Hobby: Photography. Mgmt: Matthew James Redsell, Toronto. Address: 70 Jackman Ave., Toronto, Ont. M4K 2X6, Canada.

PRISTER, Bruno, b. 21 Jan. 1909, Zagreb, Yugolsavia. Professor of Music; Composer. Educ: Dip, Hist. of Music, Acad. of Music. m. Ilonka Rac, 2 s. Debut: To the Dead Russian Soldier on Radio Zagreb, 1939. Career: Prof. of Music at var. schls. Comps. incl: Prelude for Piano; 2 Symphonic Scherzos; Songs of Sorrow & Sadness (for tenor & piano); Bar-Kochba in 4 movements (symph. poem); Song of a Lame Devil (baritone & orch.); Two Songs for Soprano; Four Jewish Songs; Song over songs (opera cantata for 3 voices & chorus) Recordings of num. children's choral songs. Mbrships: Assn. of Croatian Comps.; Musical Pedagogues; Croatian Musical Inst. Nums. hons. inclng: Jewish Music Award by Croatian Repub: Fund for Promotion of Culture, 1974. Hobbies: Swimming; Sailing. Address: 41000 Zagreb, Mlinarske cesta 37, Yugoslavia.

PRITCHARD, Arthur J, b. 12 Feb. 1908, Gloucester, UK. Organist; Professor of Harmony & Composition. Educ: D Mus (Dunelm); FRCO; ARCM; Hon. RAM; Hon. FTCL. m. Nell Waters, 1 s. Career: currently Prof. of Harmony & Comp., RAM, Master of Music, St. John's Wood Ch., London. Comps: ch. & organ music; schl. music. Mbrships: Coun., Examiner, RCO; Special Commnr., RSCM. Address: 22 Corringham Rd., London NW11 7BT, UK.

PRITCHARD, Brian William, b. 5 Jan. 1943, Ashburton, NZ. University Lecturer; Conductor. Educ: MA, Univ. of Canterbury; PhD, Univ. of Birmingham. m. Gerda Schoenmann-Roesle, 2 children. Career: currently Lectr. in Musicol., Univ. of Canterbury. Publs: eds. of works by Mendelssohn & Antonio Caldara. Contbr. to: Musical Quarterly; Jrnl. of the Galphin Soc.; RMA Rsch. Chronicle; Grove's Dict., 6th ed. Mbrships: Vice-Chmn., NZ Br., Int. Assn. of Music Libs.; Royal Musical Assn.; Music Lib. Assn., USA; Int. Musicol. Soc.; Australasian Victorian Studies Assn. Address: Schl. of Music, Pvte. Bag, Univ. of Canterbury, Christchurch, NZ.

PRITCHARD, John Michael, b. 1921, London, UK. Conductor. Career: Cond. & Musical Dir., Royal Liverpool Phil. Orch., 1957-63; Prin. Cond., LPO, 1962-66, & Glyndebourne Fest. Opera, 1952-77; Music Dir., ibid, 1969-77; Guest Cond., Royal Opera House, 1952-; Chief Cond., Cologne Opera, 1978-; has made guest apps. at many fests. both in UK & abroad, & w. mnay leading orchs. throughout world, toured Far E. w. LPO, 1969; went to Tokyo & Osaka w. NPO, 1970; toured USA, 1971. Mbr., Spanish Club. Recip. of CBE. Address: c/o AIM, 3/4 Albert Tce., London, NW1, UK.

PROCHAZKA, Zdenek Horymir, b. 25 Aug. 1915, Slany, Czechoslovakia. Composer. Educ: State Conserv. of Music, Prague; Study w. Prof. Rudolph Karel, Prof. Dr. Karel Janlecek, Prof. Metod Dolezil. Career: Tchr., Music, Prague high schls., 1945-53; Lectr., Gymnastic Music, Charles Univ., 19651-53; Prof., Gymnastic Music, Fac. of Phys. Educ. & Sports, 1953-58; Freelance composer, 1958-; Collaborator, Nat. Theater, 1945-47, & other Prague theatres; External Prof., State Conserv., 1970-71; Pianist for gymnastics broadcasts, Czech Radio. Comp. incl: 30 compositions for mass exercises, 12 for stage exercises; Beskydy Suite for Orch.; Choral music, songs for young people. var. exercise compositions, above, are recorded. Publs: Music in Modern Gymnastics (textbook), 1973. Contbr. to Gymnastika, ZTV. Mbrships: Czech Trade Union of Authors; Chmn., Music Sect., Czech Union of Mod. Gymnastics. Hons. incl: Prize, Czech Acad. of Sci. & Art, 1944; Commemoration Medal, for advancement of Socialist Phys. Culture, 1973; Spartakiad Merit Badges, 1955, '60, '65; Award, Min. of Educ., 1970. Hobbies: Literature; Fine Arts. Address: Norska 9, Prague 10 Czech. 28.

PROCTER, Leland, b. 24 Mar. 1914, Newton Mass., USA. Composer; Mechanical Designer & Draftsman. Educ: B Mus., Eastman Schl. of Music, Univ. of Rochester; M Mus., Univ. of Okla.; grad. work, Harvard Univ., 1 yr. Compositions incl: Variations for Orch.; Str. Quartet No. 1; Procantico (orch.); Str. Quartet No. 2; Symph. No. 1; Sonata for Piano; Quintet for piano & strings; Three songs of service; Sonatas for clarinet & piano; Prelude 3 (organ); Fantasy for flute & piano; Tone-Image for cello & piano; Three Choral Preludes for organ & oboe. Recordings: Symphony No. 1, 1967. Publs: Five Easy Piano Pieces, 1952; Kites (in 'Panorama' anthol.); 1953; Tonal Counterpoint (text), 1957; Vikings, 1965. Mbr., Am. Composers Alliance. Hons: 2nd pl. Nation-wide Chamber Music Contest sponsored by Nat. Fedn. of Music Clubs for Str. Quartet No. 1, 1943, etc. Hobbies: Gardening; Reading; Photography. Address: 1 South Rd., Hampden, MA, USA.

PROCTER, (Mary) Norma, b. 15 Feb. 1928, Clethorpes, UK. Concert Singer (Contralto). Educ: vocal studies w. Roy Henderson, musicianship w. Alec Redshaw, lieder w. Hans Oppenheim & Paul Hamburger. Debut: Southwark Cath., London. Career: specialist in concert works & oratorio; has sung in Germany, France, Spain, Portugal, Norway, Holland, Belguim, Sweden, Denmark, Austria, Israel, Luxembourg, S Am; apps. w. all major orchs. & in all major fests. in UK; Convent Gdn. debut in Gluck's Orpheo, 1960. Recordings: Messiah; Elijah; Mahler's 2nd, 3rd 8th symphs. & Das Klagende Lied; Hartman, Symph. No. 1; Julius Caesar Jones; Nicholas Maw's Scenes & Arias; Hermann Suter, Le Laudi. Recip. Hon. RAM, 1974. Address: 194 Clee Rd., Grimsby DN37 8ET, UK. 27.

PROCTER-GREGG, Humphrey, b. 31 July 1895, Kirby Lonsdale, Westmoreland, UK. University Professor of Music; Director of Opera; Composer; Writer. Educ: History & Organ Scholar, Peterhouse, Cambridge; Opera & Comp. Scholar, RCM, London; Mus. B.; MA; FRCM, 1962. Career: Fndn. of Music Dept. at the Univ. of Manchester, 1936, later Rdr., and Prof. of Music, 1954; Dir. for Royal Carl Rosa Opera, 1957. The Arts Coun. (Touring Opera), 1958, The London Opera Ctr., 1960-62. Publs: Sir Thomas Beecham, 1971; Beecham Remembered, 1973; Transl; (opera, etc.). The Int. Music Co., NY, for the BBC & Ricordi, Faber & Faber; Songs & violin sonata. Mbrships: ISM; Royal Musical Assn.; CGGB; Peterhouse Soc.; Nat. Trust. Hons: Emeritus Prof., Univ. of Manchester, 1962; CBE, 1971. Hobby: Painting. Address: 3 Oakland, Windermere, Cumbria, UK.

PROCTOR, Charles, b. 5 Apr. 1906, London, UK. Conductor; Composer; Musician (piano & organ). Educ: Royal Acad. of Music; FRAM; FRCO; FTCL; ARCM; studies in Dresden & Vienna. m. Rosemary Rennie. Career: Fndr. & cond., Alexandra Choir. Compositions incl: Concerto for pinaforte & orch.; Sonatas for Violin & piano; Cello & piano; Organ; Canzona, choral & passacaglia for organ; Chaconne for organ; Missa Brevis; Film music & arrangements; orchl. & choral works. Educl. music, etc. Publs: Harmonization at the Keyboard; The Class Music Teacher (Reason Why series); To be a Professional Musician. Mbrships: ISM; PRS; CGGB; RAM Club; RSA. Hobby: Landscape Painting in oils. Address: Bay Tree House, Winchelsea, Sussex, UK.

PROCTOR, George Alfred, b. 13 May 1931, Toronto, Can. Music Historian; Violinist. Educ: Royal Conserv. of Music, Toronto (Assoc. Dip., 1950); Eastman Schl. of Music, Univ. of Rochester (MM, 1956, PhD, 1960). m. Nancy M Wells, 1s., 1d. Career: Violinist, var. orchs., 1953-68, Univ. of W Ont., 1977-; Dir. of Music, McMaster Univ., 1954-57; Musicologist, Nat. Mus. of Can., 1959-61; Asst.Prof., Univ. of BC, 1961-64; Assoc. Prof., Univ. of W Ont., 1964-65; Assoc. Prof., Eastman Schl. of Music, 1965-67; Pickard-Bell Prof. & Hd. of Music, Mount Allison Univ., 1967-74; Prof. of Music History, Univ. of W Ont., 1974-; Asst.Dean, Grad.Studies, ibid., 1974-78. Publs: The Works of Nicola Matteis, 1965; Sources in Canadian Music, 1975; (in progress) Canadian Music of the Twentieth Century. Contbr. to Grove's Dict., 6th Ed., & num. encys. & profl. jrnls. Hons. Fellowships from Eastman Schl. of Music & Canada Coun. Hobbies: Sailing; Cross-country skiing. Address: 38 Indian Rd., London, Ont., Can., N6H 4A5.

PROFETA, Laurentiu, b. 14 Jan. 1925, Bucharest, Romania. Composer; Pianist. Educ: Philosophical Univ., Bucharest; Piano & Comp., Bucharest & Moscow Conservs. m. Nicola Profete. Debut: Puppet Suite, awarded Enescu's Prize, 1946. Comps. incl: Songs for Children & Youth, 1968; Prince & Pauper (ballet), 1970; Gypsy Songs, 1971; Adventure in the Garden (oratorio for children's choir & symph. orch.), 1973; 6 Humorous Pieces (children's choir & small orch.), 1974; Music for Artistic Pictures. Num. recordings. Contbr. to profl. jrnls. Mbrships: Sec., Union of Comps. of Romania; Nat. Committee, Int. Music Coun. Hons. incl: Order of Cultural Merit, 1969, 72, Union of comps. Prize, 1976; 1st prize, fest. Cantarea Romaniei, 1977. Hobbies: Light Music; Jazz; Slides. Mgmt: Union of Comps., Calea Victorie 141, Bucharest. Address: Street Beloiannis B, Bucharest, Romania.

PROHASKA, Felix, b. 1912. Conductor. Educ: studied w. Wuchner & Steurmann, Vienna, Austria; Univ. of Vienna. Career: Cond., Graz, Duisburg, Strasbours, Salzburg Fest.; Regular Cond., Vienna State Opera, 10 yrs.; 1st Cond., Frankfurt Opera, 1955; Guest apps., Europe & S Am. 2.

PROSEV, Toma, b. 10 Nov. 1931, Skopje, Yugoslavia. Composer; Conductor. Educ: Acad. of Music; Dip. Theory & Folklore, Zagreb, 1956; Dip. Comp., Ljubljana, 1961. m. Nada Prosev, 2 children. Debut: Skopje, 1951. Career: Apps. on stage, radio & TV; Music for film Birds, 1953. Comps. incl: 14 Oratoriums; 3 Operas; 2 Ballets; 13 Concerts; Chmbr. Music; Music for TV, film; 4 Symphs.; etc. Recordings: The Sun of the Ancient Country; Chmbr. Music No. 2 "Integrali" for piano & chmbr. orch.; Music for children. Publs: Zvuk; Razgledi; Sovremenost. Mbrships: SAKOJ, Yugoslavia; DKM, Skopje. Hons. incl: Oct., Nov. Nat. Prize for Comp., 1969. Hobbies: Mountaineering; Gardening. Address: Skopje, ul Pitu Guli 39a, Yugoslavia.

PROSZYNSKI, Stanislaw, b. 31 Jan. 1926, Warsaw, Poland. Composer; Musical Writer; Teacher. Educ: MA, Fac. of Comp., State Acad. of Music, Warsaw, 1953; postgrad. studies in Comp., ibid, 1958. Debut: (theatre music) Lódz45. Career: Tchr., Music Schls., 1954-60; Fac. Mbr., Warsaw Acad. of Music, 1960-; Chmn., Dept. of Problems in Music Educ., ibid, 1968-71; Docent, 1970-. Compositions incl: Little Symph., 1947; Olympic Pictures (baritone, choir & symph. orch.), 1952; The Red Lion (4 act opera), 1953-61; Lyrical Constructions (female choir & chmbr. orch.), 1962; 7 Girls Under Arms (2 act musical), 1968-69; Str. Quartet II (music in 2 pitches), 1969-73; music for ballet, theatre, TV & films. (publd.) East Piano Works, 1955, 1957; Threnody VIII 1963; St. Quartet I, 1974; To Blackthorn (choir), 1974. (recorded) The Lighthouse Keeper. Publs: Tosca, by G Puccini, 1956; Aida, by G Verdi, 1958; Cyganeria (La Boheme), by G Puccini, 1961. Contbr. to profl. jrnls. Hons. incl: 2nd Prize, Polish Students' Assn., Warsaw, 1961; Individual Prize, 2nd degree, Min. of Culture & Art. 1969. Hobby: UL. Lowicka 58 M 5A, 02-531 Warsaw, Poland. 29, 30.

PROTHEROE, Guy, b. 3 Oct. 1947, Worcester, UK. Conductor; Writer. Educ: Magdalen Coll., Oxford (Demyship), 1966-70; GSM, 1970-71; BA (Oxon). m. Ann Manly, 1d., 1s. Career: Cond., Spectrum Contemporary Music Ensemble, Engl. Chmbr. Choir, Vesta Consort, Voices, Guy Protheroe Singers; cond., arr., pop musical incl. The Who, Rich Wakeman, Demis Roussos, Black Sabbath, Steve Harley; guest cond. w. many groups; concerts from Royal Albert Hall & Empire Pool, Wembley, to Brit. tours for Arts Coun. & European tours for Brit. Coun.; apps. on TV & radio; num. recordings. Freelance writer on music; BBC Music Presentation Ed. Contbr. to: British Music Now, 1975. Address: 55 Leconfield Rd., London N5 2RZ, UK.

PROTT, Egon Max, b. 31 Dec. 1932, Bremerhaven, Germany. Violinist. Educ: pvte study of Violin, 1947-53; studies w. Paul Richartz, Conserv. of Bremen, 1953-60. Career: Mbr., 1st Violin Grp., Noordelijk Filharmonisch Orkest, Groningen, Netherlands, 1960-. Hobby: All Kings of Theatre. Address: Westersingel 27, Aduard (Gr.), Netherlands.

PRUETT, Lilian Pibernik, b. 15 Oct. 1930, Zagreb, Yugoslavia. Professor of Music; Pianist. Educ: AB, Vassar Coll., 1952; MA, 1957, PhD, 1960, Univ. of NC, Chapel Hill; Conserv., Zagreb, Yugoslavia, 1936-44; Musikadademie "Mozarteum", Salzburg, Austria 1946-50. m. James Worrell Pruett, 1 s., 1 d. Career: Perfs. in solo recitals; Soloist w. orchs.; w. NC Piano Trio, 1967-; Prof. of Music, NC Ctrl. Univ., Durham. Mbrships: Chmn., 1957-59, Sec.-Treas., 1955-57 & 1976-77, SE Chapt., Am. Musicol. Soc.; Int. Musicol. Soc.; Am. Assn. for the Advancement of Slavic Studies. Contbns. incl: Essays in Musicology, 1967 Die Musik in Geschichte und Gegenwart, 1949; Grove's Dictionary of Music & Musicians, 6th ed., 1976. Address: 343 Wesley Dr., Chapel Hill, NC 27514, USA.

PRUSLIN, Stephen Lawrence, b. 16 Apr. 1940, NY, NY, USA. Pianist. Educ: BA, Brandeis Univ.; MFA, Princeton Univ.; piano studies w. Luise Vosgerchian & Eduard Steuermann. Debut: London, 1970. Career: Concerts, radio, TV worldwide as soloist & w. Fires of London (fndr.mbr.), London Sinfonietta & other groups; num. 1st perfs. of works by Maxwell Davies, Carter, Xenakis, Webern, etc.; films incl. Ken Russell's The Devils & The Boy Friend. num. recordings as soloist and w. Fires of London. Publs: Ed., Peter Maxwell Davies - Studies from Two Decades, 1979; libretto, Punch & Judy, 1968. Contbr. to: Tempo; Music & Musicians; Music in Education. Address: 39a Dansbury St., London N1, UK.

PRYCE, John Maxwell, b. 22 Oct. 1936, Cardiff, Wales, UK. Music Adviser. Educ: BA, Univ. Coll. Cardiff, Wales; Coll. of St. Mark & St. John Chelsea; Postgrad. Cert. in Educ., in London Univ.; Welsh Nat. Coll. of Music & Drama, Cardiff; ARCM (Singing & Perf.). m. Eira Elizabeth, 1 s., 1 d. Career: Hd. of Music, Merrywood Grammar Schl., Bristol, 1958-67; Dir. of Music, Withywood Schl., Bristol, 1967-69; Cond., Bristol Concert Orch., 1965-69; Music Adviser, Warley, W Midlands, 1970-72; Fndr./Cond., Warley Concert Orch., 1971-72; Tenor, BBC West of England Chorus, 1965-69. Mbrships: incl: Asst. Masters & Mistresses Assn.; Nat. Assn. of Inspectors & Educ. Advisers; Exec. Committee, The Schls. Music Assn.; exec. committee, Music Advisers Nat. Assn; Advsry. Coun., Nat. Schl. Brass Band Assn.; Exec. Committee, Standing Conf. for Amateur Music; ISM. Hobbies: Solo Singing; Cond.; Adjudicating; Foreign Travel. Address: 74 Park Rd., New Barnet, Herts. EN4 9Q7, UK. 3, 4.

PRYOR, Gwenneth Ruth, b. 7 Apr. 1941, Sydney, Aust. Concert Pianist. Educ: ARCM.; Dip., NSW State Conservatorium of Music; L Mus. m. Roger Stone. Debut: Wigmore Hall, 1965. Career: Concert Apps., UK, Europe, Aust., N & S Am.; has broadcast frequently for BBC, ABC & Continental radio stns.; has app. on Aust. TV; has made chmbr. music apps.; Tchr., Morley Coll. Recordings: Beethovey-Spring & Kreutzer Sonatas, w. Carlos Villa, Violin); St. Saens-Wedding Cake Caprice Waltz; Moussorgsky-Pictures at an Exhibition; Williamson-2nd Piano Concerto; & Concerto for 2 pianos w. composer; Schumann-Carnaval & Papillons. Mbrships: ISM.; Subscriber, Brit. Int. of Recorded Sound. Hons. incl: 1st Prize, Aust. Musical Assn., 1963; Hopkinson Gold Medal, RCM, 1963. Hobbies: Reading; Cooking; Swimming. Address: 132 London N Rd., London, NW8 OND, UK. 3.

PRZYLUBSKI, Kazimierz, b. 5 Mar. 1945, Sierpc, Plock, Poland. Opera Singer. Educ: Acad. of Music, Warsaw; Conserv., Geneva; Academia Chigiana Siena. Debut: Nat. Touring Opera, Warsaw, 1970. Career: Nat. Ensemble 'Mazowsze', 1963-70; Warsaw Chmbr. Opera, 1970-72; Opera Bytom & Bydgoszcz, 1972-74; Opera Poznan, 1975-; radio & TV recitals, Poland, Italy, Romania, German Dem.

Repub., Czech. Mbr., Polish Musical Artists Assn. Hons. Prize of the Min. of Art & Culture, Polish Vocal Competition, Wroclaw, 1969; Silver Medal, Int. Music Competition, Geneva. Hobbies: Literature; Travel; Theatre. Address: Generala Zajaczka 19/27, O1-505 Warsaw, Poland.

PRZYSTAS, Czeslaw, b. 6 Aug. 1907, Frysztak, Poland. Violist; Lecturer. Educ: State Conserv., Katowice. m. Janina Lewinska. Career: 1st violist, Polish Radio & TV Gt. Symph. Orch., 1945-58; Mbr., Radio String Quartet; Lectr., State Music Acad. Num. recordings w. quartets, Radio Katowice. Publs: Elementary Rhythm and Sightsinging, 1947; Intonation in the Violin (Transl. 1958). Mbr., Polish Musical Artists. Hons: State Music Prizes, 1972, 73. Hobbies: Maths.; Crosswords; Poetry. Address: ul. Mikolowska 40/3, 40-066 Katowice, Poland.

PSACHAROPOULOS, Nikos, b. 18 Jan. 1928, Athens, Greece. Stage Director. Educ: BA, Oberlin Coll., USA; MFA, Yale Univ.; DHL, Williams Coll. Debut: Stage Dir. of Mummers, Oberlin Coll., Ohio. Career: Artistic Dir., Williamstown Theatre Festival, 1955; Assoc. Prof., Yale Univ., 1956-; Dir., NY Pro Musica, 1957-74 (Play of Daniel, Play of Herod); Stage Dir., NYC Opera (Besson's Lizzie Borden, Rorem's Miss Julie); Dir., Am. Shakespeare Festival), Stratford, Conn., 1969 (Androcles & the Lion); Broadway Dir., 1968 (Langston Hughes' Tambourine to Glory). Publs: Play of Daniel, Play of Herod, Oxford Univ. Press. Contbr. to var. profl. jrnls, etc. Mbrships: AEA; AFTRA; AGMA; SSDC. Address: Box 517, Williamstown, MA 01267, USA. 2, 13, 19.

PTACNIK, Jiri, b. 8 Apr. 1921, Kolin (Bohemia), Czechoslovakia. Violinist; Member of Prague Chamber Orchestra. Educ: Music Schl., Kolin; Master class, Conservatorium, Praha. m. Jitka Ptacnikova, 1 s. Debut: Violin Concerto in G maj. by Siegfried Wagner performed at Conservatorium, Praha, 1943. Career incls: Ldr. of Violin Grp., Konzertmeister, in operatic orchs. in Brno & Praha, 1943-46; Dpty. Ldr., Radio Symph. Orch., Praha, 1947-64; Mbr. Prague Chmbr. Orch., 1951-; Ldr. of Violin Grp. & Artistic Dir., Prague Chmbr. Orch., 1958-70. Comps. tv & recording. Num. recordings. Hobby: Photography. Address: u Vesny 1866, 100 00 Praha 10, Czechoslovakia.

PTASZYNSKA, Marta, b. 29 July 1943, Warsaw, Poland. Composer; Percussionist. Educ: B Mus., Music Lyceum, Warsaw, 1962; M Mus., Warsaw Conserv. of Music, 1967; Artist Dip., Cleveland Inst. of Music, USA, 1974; studied w. T Paciorkiewicz, J Zjodzinski, Nadio Boulanger, C Duff, R Weiner. Career: Concert, Fest Apps., Poland, France, Netherlands, USA; Mbr. Percussion de Srastbourg, Percussion Ensemble of Poznan, Cleveland Inst. of Music Contemporary Ensemble; Percussion Tchr., Warsaw Conserv., 1970; Percussionist, Warsaw Nat. Phil.; Tchr., Comp., Bennington Coll., USA, 1974-; Comps. incl: Improvisations, orch.; Preludes & Scherzo, vibraphone, xylophone, piano; Suite Variee, percussion ensemble & piano; Little Mosaic, percussion ensemble; Variations, flute solo; Little Fantasy Mexican, percussion & piano; Jeu-Parti, harp & percussion. Contbr. to var. profl. jrnls. Mbrships: Union of Polish Comps.; Pres., Circle of Young Comps., 1965-70; Percussion Arts Soc., USA. Hons. 1st Prize, Comps. Competition, Warsaw, 1967; Young Comps. Competition, Poland, 1971; TV Opera Competition, Poland, 1972; Percussive Arts Soc., Comp. Contest, 1974. Hobbies: Painting; Theatre. Address: 1621 Vallejo St., apt. 6, San Francisco, CA 94123, USA.

PUCEK, Anna, b. 4 Oct. 1943, Krakow, Poland. Music Teacher; Pianist. Educ: Acad. of Music; Magister Art. m. Sylwester A Pucek, 1 c. Debut: Wroclaw, Poland, 1962. Career: Ldr. & owner of Billund Musikskole; Apps., Polish & Danish Radio. Mbr., Danish Soc. of Music Tchrs. Hobbies: Gardening; Flowers; Reading; Travelling in Europe. Address: Molleparken 126, DK 7190 Billund, Denmark.

PUDDY, Keith A, b. 27 Feb. 1935, Wedmore, Somerset, UK. Clarinetist. Educ: RAM. m. Marilyn Johnston, 1 s. Career: Prof. of Clarinet, TCM; Mbr., Gabreili Ensemble, New London Wind Ensemble. Recordings incl: Mozart, Brahms Quintets; Mozart Concerto; Beethoven Septet; Prokofiev Sextet; Brahms Trio. Selected & edited Orchestral Extracts for clarinet, 1974. Recip. Hon. FTCL, 1975; ARAM. Hobbies: Early works of art; Early furniture. Address: 20 Courtnell St., London W2 5BX, UK.

PUGH, Donald Wagner, b. 25 June 1931, Houston, Tex., USA. Music Educator; Conductor; Music Administrator. Educ: B Mus., 1955, M Mus Ed., 1957, N Tex State Univ.; DMA, Univ. of Tex., Austin, 1967; Vocal Study w. Allan Guy, Frank

McKinley, Mary McCormick; Cond., w. Frank McKinley; Music educ., w. C Edward Brookhart, m. Delores Earlene Taylor, 2 s., 1 d. Career: Ch. & Schl. Choral Cond.; Guest Cond., San Antonio Concert Orch., N Tex. State Univ., Symph. Ctrl. Tex. State Symph.; Musical Dir., Semi-profl. theater; Adjudicator; Choral Clinician. Contbr. to jrnls. Mbrships: Am. Choral Dirs. Assn; Tex. Choral Dirs. Assn.; MENC; Tex. Music Educators Assn.; Tex. Jr. Coll. Tchrs. Assn.; Tex. State Tchrs. Assn.; Pi Kappa Lambda; Phi Mu Alpha Sinfonia; Phi Delta Kappa; Blue Key. Hobbies: Camping; Rebuilding pianos; Fishing; Travel. Address: 113 Meadowbrook, Lake Jackson, TX 77566, USA. 7.

PUGH, Leonard, b. 1 Nov. 1929, Denbigh, N Wales, Music Adviser; Teacher. Educ: B Mus., Dunelm; FRCO, (CHM); LRAM; Liverpool Matthay Schl. m. Ruth Elizabeth Jones. Career: Prin., City of Belfast Schl. of Music; Snr. Music Advsr., Belfast Schl. of Music; Snr. Music Advsr., Belfast Educ. & Lib. Bd.; Lectr., St. Katherine's Coll., Scarisbrick Hall, 1952-60; Organist & Choirmaster, Childwall PCh., 1955-57, St. Andrew's Southport, 1957-60; Llanelli Parish Ch., 1961-64. Cond. & Concert Organiser, Broughton & Dist. Choral Soc., 1952-60; Hd., Music Dept., Llanelly Boys' Grammar Schl., 1960-64; Hobbies: Making Music of all kinds; Reading. Address: Belfast Educ. & Library Be., 40 Academy St., Belfast BT1 2NQ, N Ireland.

PULLIAM, Lucille E, b. 28 Feb. 1909, Seattle, Wash., USA. Musician (piano, small harps). Educ: BA (Educ.); Tchng. Cert., Sherwood Music Schl., Chgo. m. (1) Ben J Altman (dec.), 1 s., 2 d., (2) Arthur Lynn Pulliam (dec.). Career: since 1955 has been a specialist tchr. & demonstrator of small or minstrel harps, aiming at an advance in the type of music which can be played on these instruments; her work has led to the publ. of the Folk Harp Jrnl. & the introduction of annual Festivals, of which the 1976 Festival showed 15 styles of small (non-pedal) harp. Mbrships: Organiser & 1st pres., Minstrel Harpers of Ore. Hobbies: Langs.; Study of Folk Music. Address: 926 SE Marion, Portland, OR 97202, USA.

PULLIN, Audrey, b. 18 Apr. 1929, Brentwood, Essex, UK. Music Teacher; Cello, Violin, Double Bass, Piano. Educ: LRAM; Schl. Music Dip. m. Stanley Limbrey. Career: Westminister Schl., 1951-; St. Benedict's Schl., 1953-. Publs: Co-Ed., Choose Your Instrument, 1979. Contbr. to the Strad. Mbrships: ISM. Hobbies: Gardening; Violin-making; Do-it-yourself; Writing. Address: 3 W Common Rd., Uxbridge, Middx. UB8 1NZ, UK. 3.

PULS, Gerd, b. 24 Jan. 1927, Neukloster, Germany. Musical Director. Educ: State Music Acad., State exam. m. Ruth Seidel-Publs, 1 s. Debut: City Theater Rostock. Caroor: 1949, Solo repetitor; 1951, 1st Cond.; 1956, Artistic Dir.; 1962, General Musical Dir. Recordings: Gunter Kochan, Music to "Störtobeker", Günter Kochan, 3rd Symph. w. solo soprano. Mgmt: People's Theater Rostock. Mbrships: Assn. of Comp. and Musicologist GDR; Soc. of Theatrical Artists, GDR. Hons. State Prize, 1959; Patriotic Merit Order, 1970. Address: Langestr. 9, 25 Rostock, 1 DDR, German Dem. Repub.

PURCELL, Patricia (Elizabeth Harley), b. 7 Sept. 1925, Egham, Surrey, UK. Pianist; Teacher. Educ: RCM, 1944-47; ARCM, 1945; pupil of Frank Merrick. Debut: Royal Albert Hall, London, 1958. Career: Var. recital/concerto apps., incl. Wigmore Hall, London, 1969; Polish Tour, Frederic Chopin Soc., 1972. inclng. Chopin's Birthplace & 27th Chopinowski Int. Fest., Duszniki, & apps. on Polish radio & TV; Pvte. tchr. Mbr., ISM. Recip., 1st Prize, Piano Concerto Class, London Musical Competition Fest., 1956. Hobbies: Dressmaking; Psychol.; Nature. Address: c/o Barclays Bank Ltd., 85 Aldwick Rd., W Bognor Regis, W Sussex, PO21 2NU, UK. 27.

PURSER, John Whitley, b. 10 Feb. 1942, Glasgow, Scotland, UK. Composer; Poet; Lecturer. Educ: Fettes Coll.; DRSAM, Comp.; DRSAM, Cello; DRSAM, Singing; RAM; studied w. Dr. Hans Gal, Sir. Michael Tippett. m. Wilma Paterson, 1 s., 1 d. Career: Freelance Comp., Poet & Lectr. Comps. incl: Epitaph 1916; Viola Concerto; Cello Concerto; Opus 7; Comedy Overture; Clydefair Overture; Stone of Destiny; Intrada for Strings; Radio opera The Bell; TV opera The Undertaker; Bannockburn, exhibition music; St. Quartet; Love in Season; song cycle Five Landscapes; Clavier Sonata; Circus Suite (4 hands); etc. Contbr. to: Scottish Int.; The Scotsman; Times Educl. Supplement; Prospice, etc. Hons: Caird Scholarship,1963-67; Royal Phil. Soc. Award, 1962; Scottish Arts Coun. Award, 1969; RTE Carolan Prize, 19634; Eire Govt. Prize, 1966; Glasgow Educl. Trust Award, 1974. Hobby: Chess. Address: 27 Hamilton Dr., Glasgov G12 8DN, UK. 30.

PUTNAM, Ashley, b. 10 Aug. 1952, NY, NY, USA. Opra Singer (soprano). Educ: BMus, MMus, Univ. of Mich. Schl. of

Music. Debut: Lucia di Lammermoor, Va. Opera Assn., 1976. Career: apps. w. NY City Opera (debut, 1978), Glyndebourne Fest. Opera, Santa Fe Opera, Houston Grand Opera, Seattle Opera, Wash. Grand Opera, Wolf Trap Fest.; perfs. w. NY Phil. Orch. Bayerische, Rundfunk, Munich, & Opera Orch. of NY; Recitals. Recordings: LaBoheme; Mother of Us All (Angel More). Hons: 1st prize, Met. Opera Nat. Auditions, 1976; Nat. Opera Inst. Grant, 1976, '77; Martha Baird Rockefeller Study Grant, 1979. Mgmt: Colbert Artists Mgt. Inc., 111 W 57th St., NY, NY 10019, USA. Address: c/o mgmt.

PUTNIK, Edwin Vincent, b. 11 July 1924, Chicago, Ill., USA. Educator; Musician. Educ: B Mus, N Western Univ., Evanston, Ill., 1948; M Mus, ibid, 1949. Debut: Chgo. Career: Mbr., Chgo., Denver & Phoenix Symphs.; Extensive solo & clinic work; Instr. of Music, Univ. of Ill.; Prof. of Music, Ariz. State Univ.; Mbr., Gammage Woodwind Quintet. Comps.: Murillo for flute & band. Publs: Flute Pedagogy & Performance, 1952; Music Theory in Outline Form, 1962, rev. edit., 1965; The Art of Flute Playing, 1971, 2nd edit., 1973. Mbr., profl. orgs. Hons: Pi Kappa Lambda, 1948; Chicago Music Clubs Award,

1940. Hobbies: Golf; Tennis; Swimming. Address: 2929 N 55th Pl., Phoenix, AZ 85018, USA. 9, 28, 29.

PUYANA, Rafael, b. 4 Oct. 1931, Bogota, Colombia, Harpsichordist. Educ: studies w. Wanda Landowska. Career: based on Paris, giving concerts, recitals, etc. throughout world. Recordings: CBS; Philips. Hobby: Collecting Old Keyboard Instruments. Mgmt: Basil Douglas Ltd., 8 St. George's Terrace, London NW1 8XJ, UK. 16.

PYLKKÄNEN, Tauno Kullervo, b. 22 Mar. 1918, Helsinki, Finland. Composer. Educ: Dip. in Comp., Sibelius Acad.; BA, Univ. of Helsinki, 1941. Career: Artistic Dir., Finnish Nat. Opera, 1960-70; Critic for daily newspaper; Prof., Sibelius Acad. Opera Studio. Comps. incl: 8 operas inclng: Mare ja Hänen Poikansa, 1945, Opri & Oleksi, 1957, The Unknown Soldier, 1967; Kaarina Maununtytär ballet fantasy, 1960 Concerto for cello & orch.; about 70 songs; sev. song cycles; 4 cantatas. Publs: Oopperavaeltaja, 1953. Contbr. to: Pieni Musiikilehti. Mbrships: Finnish Soc. of Comps.; The Riders, Helsinki., Hons incl: Prix Italia III, 1950. Hobby: Riding. Address: Apollonkatu 13 A 50, Helsinki 10 Finland.

Q

QUEEN, Dorothea Mitchell, b. 1 Nov. 1913, NYC; USA. Teacher; Director of Church Music; Pianist. Educ: BA, Millsaps Coll., Jackson, Miss.; B Mus, Chgo. Musical Coll., Ill.; B Mus Ed, ibid; M Sac Mus, Schl. of Sacred Music, Union Theol. Sem., NYC; postgrad. work at var. univs. m. Dr. Merritt B Queen, 2 s, 1 d. Career: Dir. of Ch. Choirs in Ill., NY, Miss & Tenn.; Piano Tchr.; Gen. Music Tchr. in Pub. Schls. in Ill., Tenn. & NY,currently at Cantiague Schl., Jericho, Li. Publs: O Praise Him! Alleluia! 1963; Ed. of Orff Beat, 1972-74. Contbr. to var. music jrnls. Mbrships: Past Pres., Ll. Chapt., Am. Orff-Schulwerk Assn.: MENC; NY State Music Assn.; Nassau Music Educators Assn.: Am Recorder Soc.; Nat. Fellowship of Meth. Musicians; Hymn Soc. of Am., formerly Exec. Comm.; Sigma Alpha Iota. Hobbies: Early Am. Needlecrafts; Houseplants. Address: 28 Norfolk Dr., Eatons Neck, Northport, NY 11768 USA.

QUEFFÉLEC, Anne, b. 17 Jan. 1948, Paris, France. Pianist. Educ: Paris Conserv. of Music; studied w. Mmes. Bascourret, Lelia Gousseau, w. Jean Hubeau & in Vienna w. Paul Badura-Skoda, Jorg Demus & Alfred Brendel. Career: Recitals & concerts in France, UK, Spain. Italy, Germany, Switz., Netherlands, Austria, etc., USA, Japan, S Africa, Far East; chmbr. music concerts (duos, trios, piano duets); many orchl. concerts; Recordings: works by Scarlatti, Schubert, Chopin, Liszt, Ravel, Bach, etc. Hons: first prizes from Paris Conserv.; 1st prize, Munich Int. piano competition, 1968; 5th prize, Leeds piano Int. competition, 1969. Hobbies: Reading; Philos.; Cooking; Friends; Cycling; Jogging. Mgmt: Bureau de Valmalète, Paris; Gubbay, London. Address: 6 rue de Belzunce, 75010 Paris, France.

QUELLMALZ, Alfred, b. 25 Oct. 1899, Öberdigisheim, Württemberg, Germany. Music Researcher. Educ: studied comp., violin, viola, & piano, Music Coll.; Music Tchr. m. Leonie Blum, 4 children. Career: Music Tchr.; Asst. Musicol.; Music Rschr., German Folksong Archive, Freiburg; Hd., Dept. 2 Folkmusic, State Inst. for Music Rsch., Berlin (disbanded in 1945); Freelance work for Radio Vararlberg, S-W Radio Network & Southern German radio Network; currently pvte. scholar. Publs. incl: Bruder Singer (song book); Südtiroler Volkslieder (sci. documentation), vol. 1, 1968, vol. 2, 1972. vol. 3, 1976, vol. 4, in press. Contbr. to profl. jrnls. Mbrships: Soc. for Folklore; Co-op. for Folkmusic Rsch. Recip. Mozart Prize, 1969. Address: Senefelderstr. 114, D-7000 Stuttgart 1, German Fed. Repub.

QUINE, Hector, b. 30 Dec. 1926, London, UK. Music Teacher; Classic Guitar. Educ: Pvte. study. m. Penelope Engleheart, 1 s., 1 d. Career: Prof., Guitar, TCL, 1958, RAM, 1959, GSM, 1966; Advsr. on Guitar Music, Oxford Univ. Press, 1972. Publs: Studies for Guitar, 1965; Guitar Duet Arrangements, 1969; Modern Guitar Albums, 1961,'74; Tutor for Guitar, 1971; Num. other works transcribed & edited. Mbrships: Royal Phil. Soc.; ISM; Chelsea Arts Club. Hons: Hon. ARAM., 1965; Hon. FTCL, 1969; Hon. RAM, 1972. Hobbies: Cricket; Carpentry; Photography. Address: 22 Limeston St., London, SW10 OHH, UK. 3, 28.

QUINET, Marcel, b. 6 July 1915, Binche, Belgium. Composer. Educ: Conservatore Royal de Bruxelles. m. Jacqueline Rongy, 1 s. Career: Dir., Musical Acad. of St. Josse-Ten-Noodle-Schaerbeek; Prof., Conservatoire Royal de Bruxelles; Prof., Chapelle Musicale 'Reine Elisabeth de Belgique. Compositions incl: (orchl. works) 3 pieces for orch.; Sinfonietta; Variations; Serenade pour cordes; Divertimento; Symphony; Overture pour un festival; Musique pour cordes et timbales, etc.; (chamber music) Trio a clavier; Suite pour 4 clarinettes; Sonatine pour violon et piano; Sonate pour Flute et piano, etc.; var. instrumental music; vocal music; (theatre) les deux Bavards (opera de chambre); La Nef des Fous (ballet). Recordings incl: Variations pour Orchestre; Quintette a vent; Hult petites pieces pour quintette a vent; Ballatella pour Trompette; Sonate pour 2 violons et piano. Mbrships: Commissions du Ministere de la Culture; Commission des Beaux-Arts de la Province de Brabant; Commission des Beaux-Arts de la commune de St. Josse-ten-noddle; Citoyen d'honneur de la ville de Binche. Hons: Chevalier de l'ordre de la couronne & de Leopold; Prix Gevaert; Prix Agniez, etc. Address: Katangabinnenhof 5, 1980 Tervuren, Belgium.

QUINEY, Enid Joyce, b. 23 Nov. 1928, Forest Hill, London, UK. Harpist; Pianist; Teacher. Educ: RAM; LRAM, 1948; ARCM, 1949. Career: Freelance harpist & pianist; Lecture recitals; Accompanist; Engagements w. London & Provincial Orchs.; Fndr. Mbr., Lydian Harp Trio; Peripatetic Tchr. of Harp. Piano & Strings, London & Kent. Mbrship: Musicians' Union. Hons: Julia Leney Prize for Harp Playing, 1948; ARAM, 1962. Hobbies: Reading; Gardening. Address: 83 Birchwood Ave., Beckenham, Kent BR3 3PY, UK. 3, 27.

QUINT, Michael, b. 19 Apr. 1950, St. Louis, Mo., USA. Musician (French Horn). Educ: AA, Jefferson Coll. 1970; B Mus, Univ. Mo., 1972; M Mus, Southern Ill. Univ., 1976. Career: Extra Horn, St Louis Symph.; Mbr., Gateway Brass Quintet & Corian Woodwind Quintet; Fac., Blackburn Coll., Carlinville, Ill. Recordings: 2 w. St. Louis Symph. Mbr., Int. Horn Soc. Recip: Jefferson Coll. Musical Instrument Award, 1970. Hobbies: Football; Model Building. Address: 9545 Montbrook Dr., St. Louis, MO 63123, USA.

R

RAAD, Virginia, b. Salem, WV, USA. Pianist; Musicologist. Educ: BA, Wellesley Coll.; New England Conserv.; Dip., Piano, Music Hist., Ecole Normale de Musique; Paris; Docteur de l'Univ. de Paris. Career: Concerts, lectures, master classes, Univs., colls., galls. throughout USA; Resident Artist, Salem Coll., WV, 1959-70, Musician-in-Residence, NC Arts Coun. & Community Colls., 1971-72. Contbr. to Debussy et l'evolution de la musique au XXe siecle, 1965 & New Catholic Encyclopedia; Articles in profl. jrnls. Mbrships. incl: Am. Soc. Aesthetics; Music Tchrs. Nat. Assn.; Am., Int., French Musicol. Socs.; AAUP. Hons. incl: ACLS Travel Grant (for representing USA at Debrussy Centennial), 1962; Grants, French Govt., Outstanding Woman Educator in W Va.; Delta Kappa Gamma, 1965. Address: 60 Terrace Ave., Salem, WV 26426, USA. 2, 3, 5, 6.

RABÉ, Christiaan, b. 15 Oct. 1915, Amsterdam, Netherlands. Lecturer in Schoolmusic; Teacher of Piano; Expert in Speech & Voice Training. Educ: Staatsdip. Piano A & B; Dip. Logopaedie & Phoniatrie; Schlmusic. B. Career incls: Prin., Tchrs. Trng. Coll., Amsterdam, 1947-66; Co-Dir., ibid, 1966-76; Cond., Schl. Choir, Gem. Lyceum v. Meisjes, 1957-63; Courses Schl. Radio Hilversum, 1957-63. Comps: Hyppolytos (schl. orch. & female choir); Var. pieces for piano; Songs for children. Recording of Zingen van allerlei dingen (songs for children aged 6-12). Publs. incl: 4 vols. w. songs for primary schl. & method Spelend zingen, Zingend spelen (w. R Smith) 1968-72. Mbr. num. profl. orgs. Hobbies: Travel; Gardening. Address: Het Karveel 48, 1398 BX Muiden, The Netherlands.

RABE, Folke (Alvar Harald Reinhold), b. 28 Oct. 1935, Stockholm, Sweden. Programme Director; Composer; Trombonist. Educ: Music Tchrs. Exam, Community Music Schl. Ldrs. Exam, & study of Trombone & Comp., Royal Coll. of Music, Stockholm. m. Ursula Rabe, 1 s., 1 d. Career: Jazz Musician, 1950-; Comp., 1957-; Writer on musical subjects, 1959-; Mbr., Culture Quartet, 1963-; Mbr. staff, Inst. for Nat. Concerts (INC), 1968-; Program Director, ibid, 1977-. Comps. incl: Polonaise (trombone quartet w. Jane Bark), 1965; Eh?? (Electronic music), 1967; No Hambones on the Moon (film w. Culture Quartet), 1971; I'll Remember Karlheinz (Drainpipe extended tubas & washing machine), 1972. Recordings: Rondes; Pièce; Joe's Harp; Eh?? Publ: Sound Workshop (w. Jan Bark), 1974. Contbr. to num. jrnls. & several radio progs. Mbrships: Hon. Mbr., Escuela de Andinismo, Los Condores, Puno, Peru; var. Nat. Bds. in field of music. Hon: Simborgarmärket, 1970. Hobbies: Finnish Sauna Baths. Address: Birkagatan 1, S-113 36 Stockholm, Sweden.

RABES, Lennart, b. 6 Sept. 1938, Eskilstuna, Sweden. Pianist; Harpsichordist; Organist; Lecturer; Editor; Conductor; Musical Director. Educ: studied piano w. S Sundell, Stockholm, E Cavallo, Milan, B Siki, Zürich, M Tagliaferro, Paris, J v. Karolyi, Munich; studied cond. w. C v Garaguly, Stockholm, P v Kempen, Siena, W v Otterloo, Hilversu, Sir Adrian Boult, London; at the Music Acad., Zürich, & at the Acad. Chigiana, Siena; ARCM. Debut: Pianist & Cond., Stockholm Phil., 1951. Career: has played in major cities of Europe & made many recordings for Swedish, Austrian, Swiss & German broadcasting stns.; Ed., Liszt Saeculum, jrnls. of Int. Liszt Ctr. Ltd.; Musical Dir., ibid.; Organist, Swiss Ch. London, 1966-78; Lectr. for rsch. assns. & conservs. Recordings: Piano works by Henning Mankell, 1977. Mbrships: ISM; Musicians Union; VDMK, German Fed. Repub.; Tonkünstlerverband, Munich; Int. Assn. of Music Libs. Recip. of Royal Swedish Scholarship, 1963. Hobbies: Cooking; Walking. Mgmt: Ibbs & Tillett. Address: Tre Kronor, 35 Stanhope Rd., Deal, Kent CT14 6AD, UK. 4, 28, 29.

RABIE, Ilva Katherine, b. 21 Jan. 1927, Bulawayo, Rhodesia. Piano Teacher; Violinist. Educ: perfs. licentiate UPLM, Univ. of S Africa; tchrs. licentiate, UTLM, ibid. m. Dr Noel Rabie (dec.), 2 s., 1 d. Debut: Grahamstown, S Africa, 1946. Career: Violinist; Salisbury Municipal Orch., 1947-50; violinist, Bulawayo Municipal Orch., 1951-58; apps. w. Townsend Girls High Schl. Choir, Bulawayo Eisteddford concert, 9155, 56; apps. w. Emma Hoogenhout Primary Schl. Choir, Windhoek Eisteddfod, 1970, 72; apps. Muizenberg Jr. Schl., Cape Town Eisteddfod, 1973-79; organist, All Saints' Ch., Plumstead. Mbrships: S African Soc. of Music Tchrs. (hon. sec., treas., Salisbury, 1947-50, hon. sec., Bulawayo, 1951-54); Cape Organ Guild; Inst. of Advanced Motorists. Hons: Beit Grant,

1943-46. Hobbies: Music; Gardening; Art Needlework. Address: Benley House, 20 Yarmouth Rd., Muizenberg 7945, S Africa.

RABINOWITZ, Harry, b. 26 Mar. 1916, Johannesburg, S Africa. Musical Director; Conductor; Composer. Educ: Witwatersrand Univ.; GSM, London. m. Lorna Thurlow Anderson, 1 s., 2 d. Debut: BBC Radio as Pianist. Career: West End Theatre, 1948-53; BBC Radio, 1953-60; BBC Tv, 1960-68; ITV, 1968-77 (London Weekend TV); now Freelance; Apps. w. LSO, LPO, RPO, Philharmonia Orch., Royal Liverpool Orch. & freelance orchs. Has comps. var. Film, TV & Radio scores incl: Love for Lydia; Thomas & Sarah. Recordings: Polydor; EMI; Decca, etc. Mbrships: Musicians Union. Hons: MBE, 1977. Hobbies: Wine; Edible fungi; Others making music. Address: Hope End, Holmbury St. Mary, Dorking RH5 6PE, Surrey, UK.

RACE, Steve, b. 1 Apr. 1921, Lincoln, UK. Musician; Broadcaster. Educ: RAM. m. Leonie Mather, 1 d. Career: Many TV & Radio Series, incl: My Music; Many a Slip; Any Questions?; Major Minor. Compositions: Nicola; Cyrano de Bergerac (for Radio 3); The Day of the Donkey; Songs; Mood Music, etc. Recordings for Nat. Gallery, Glasgow Art Gallery. Publs: Autogiography - Musician at Large, 1979. Contbr. to var. publs. Hons: Ivor Novello Award; ARAM, 1968; FRSA, 1975; FRAM, 1977. Address: Martins End Lane, Gt. Missenden, Bucks., UK. 1, 3.

RACEK, Jan, b. 1 June 1905, Bucovice, Moravia, Czech. Musicologist. Educ: PhD, 1929, DSc, 1957, Masaryk Univ., Brno, Czech. m. Pavla Rackov-Kuncova, 2 d. Career: Admnstr., Moravian Musical Archives, 1930-48; Lectr., 1939-48, Prof. of Musicol., 1948-70, Masaryk Univ., Brno; Admnstr., Instructor in Ethnography & Musical Folklore, Czech. Acad. of Scis., Brno; Ed., Monumenta Musicae Bohemicae, I vo. & Musica Antiqua Bohemica, 90 vols. to 1975. Publs: 45 books on musicol. subjects. Contbr. to int. musicol. jrnls. Mbrships. incl: Austrian Acad. of Scis., Vienna; Int. Musicol. Soc.; German Soc. for Music Rsch.; Int. Soc. for Jazz Rsch. Recip., num. hons. inclng: Order of Labour; Gottfried von Herder Prize. Hobbies: Philosophy; History; Art History; Touring. Address: 21 Pod Kastany, 116 00 Brno, Czechoslovakia.

RACETTE, Vicki, b. 4 Apr. 1956, Pk. Falls, Wis., USA. High Soprano; Trumpet Player. Educ: Univ. of Wis., Superior. m. Nicholaus Elliot Racette. Career: 3rd Trumpet, Duluth Superior Symph.; Duluth Arena Auditorium, 1974-75. Recip. Univ. Scholarship, 1974. Hobbies: Soft ball; Hockey; All forms of art; Singing; For. lang. Address: PO Box 34, Winter, WI 54896, USA.

RACHOEN, Stefan, b. 4 Jan. 1906, Ostrów Lubelski, Poland. Violinist; Orchestral Conductor. Educ: High Schl. of Music, Warsaw. m. Debut: Lublin, Poland. Career: Concerts in Poland & abroad; Film, radio & TV work. Recordings for gramophon, radio & TV. Mbr., Soc. Polish Artists of Music. Hons: Work with Cameras. Address: Warsaw 00-040, ul. Warecka 8 m 90, Poland.

RADAUER, Irmfried, b. 7 Jan. 1928, Salzburg, Austria. Composer. Educ: Hochschule f. Musik, Leipzig; Akademi f. Musik 'Mozarteum', Salzburg; Dips. in conducting, music theory &'music educ. m. Agathe Hemetsberger. Career: Music Critic; Contbr. to Salzburg Fest.; Prof., Electronic Music, & Dir., Electroacoustique Dept., Mozarteum; Researcher & Lectr., Computer Music, Stanford Univ., USA, sev. Austria computer ctrs. & Mozarteum; Freelance composer. Comps. incl: Siau-Tschu; Perspectiven auf b-a-c-h; Euphorie; Tetraeder; Akoasmen; Stringquartet; Sinfonia. Contbr. to: Konfigurationen; Melos, Mbr., Int. Soc. of Contemporary Music. Hons. incl: Theordor Körner Prize, 1967; Osterreichischer Staatspreis, 1970. Hobbies incl: Sport; Travel. Address: Daxjuden 2, 5521 Lochen OO, Austria.

RADCLIFFE, Philip Fitzhugh, b. 27 Apr. 1905, Godalming, Surrey, UK. Educator. Educ: Mus B, King's Coll., Cambridge Univ., 1929. Career incl: Univ. Lectr. in Music, Cambridge Univ.; Fellow, King's Coll., ibid. Compositions incl: 4 Songs: sev. short choral works; prelude for double bass & piano; String Quartet; Music for Greek plays. Recording: 'Mary Walked Through a Wood of Thorn' (performed by King's Coll. Choir). Contbr. to: The Criterion; Music & Letters; Music Review; Musical Times. Mbr: Cambridge Univ. Musical Club. Address: King's Coll., Cambridge, UK.

RADDATZ, Otto Wilhelm Richard, b. 31 Dec. 1917, Stettin, Germany. Organist; Composer; Choir Director. Educ: Dr. Jur., Jena Univ. & Munich Univ., 1940; Kuenzelsau Tchrs. Training Coll., 1945-47. m. Erika Raddatz, 2 s. Career: Tchrs., Choir

Dir. & Organist in Southern Germany; appearances on Stuttgart Radio Broadcasting Copr., 1953-55, 1964-65, 1972; Organist, Post Chapel, McKee Barracks, Crailsheim. Compositions incl: Sunny Time, schl. opera; Hohenlohe Cantata; We Love Our Home, dialect songs; Christopherus; Song of Praise in the Mountains; The Eternal is Beautiful; The Christmas Star; I Wonder why I am sorrowful, Motet. Recordings: My Hohenlohe Long-Playing Record. Contbr. to: Lied und Chor. Schwaebesche Saengerzeitung; Haller Tagblatt; Hohenloher Tagblatt. Mbr. German Comp's. Assn., 1960-. Hons: Silver Badge, Swabian Singers' Assn., 1954; Composers' Award, Carl Engls Music, MuelheimRuhr, 1958; Order of Merit (USA), 1974. Hobbies: Swimming; Cycling; Skating; Photography. Address: 718 Crailsheim, 47 Breslauer Strasse, German Fed. Repub.

RADFORD, Winifred, b. 2 Oct. 1901, London, UK. Singer; Teacher of Singer. Educ: RAM. m. Douglas Illingworth (dec. 1949). Debut: Germany, 1931. Operatic debut: Glyndebourne, 1934. Career: Song recitals, Germany, GB & for BBC; Solo roles, Glyndebourne Fests., 1934-38, Brussels Théâtre de la Monnaie, 1939; Toured USA, Can., GB as Prin. Soprano in Intimate Opera, small chmbr. operas; Joined GSM as Tchr. of Singing, 1955. Translator of French lyrics in Interpretation of French Song, by Pierre Bernac. Author, notes on music & transls. of song lyrics for EMI. Mbrships: Pres., Assn. of Brit. Singers & Speakers; ISM. Hon: FGSM, 1960. Address: 38a Hollycroft Ave., London, NW3 7QN, UK. 3, 27.

RADICA, Ruben, b. 19 May 1931, Split, Yugoslavia. Composer. Educ: Grad. Comp. & Cond., Music Acad., Zagreb, 1958; Chigiana Music Acad., Siena, Italy; studied w. Rene Leibowitz, Paris, 1960-61. m. Nada Staudacher 1 s. Debut: (as Comp.) Int. Soc. Contemporary Music Fest., London, 1962. Career: Prof. of Music Theory, Zagreb Acad. of Music, 1963-. Comps. incl: Lyrical Variations (strings), 1961; Prostration (organ & orch.), 1967; 19 & 10 Interferences (speaker, chorus & orch.), 1965; Extension (orch. & piano), 1973; Per Se II (wind quintet & tape), 1975 (recorded); Ka (2 instrumental groups & synthesizer), 1977. Mbr.; profl. assns. Hons: VI. Nazor Prize, 1974. Hobby: Birds. Address: Mestrovićes trg, 9/XI, 41020 Zagreb, Yugoslavia.

RADICE, Anthea Mulso, b. 11 Feb. 1917, Forest Row, Sussex, UK. Piano Teacher. Educ: ARCM (piano); studied w. Marcel Gazelle & Harold Craxton (piano); studied w. Arthur Cranmer & Eric Greene (singing). m. Rev. A A H Radice, 1 s, 1 d. Career: Solo singing in oratorio; piano tchr., Christ Ch. Cathedral Schl., Oxford, 1944-51; vis. tchr., Eastbourne Coll., 1951-54, Roedean Schl., Brighton, Hengrave Hall, Bury St. Edmunds, 1957-60, Riddlesworth hall, Diss, 1964-77 & Newton Ct., Bury St. Edmunds, 1960-; Dir. of Music, Woodbridge Schl., 1954-56; piano tchrs., St. Edmundsbury Cathedral Choir, 1965-. mbr., ISM. Hobbies: Reading Theology; Watching Tennis. Address: The Rectory, Hepworth, Diss, Norfol, IP22 2PS, UK.

RADO, Agi (Agnes), b. 26 Aug. 1931, Budapest, Hungary. Concert Pianist; Professor of Music. Educ: Professorial Dip., 1947. Performing Artist's Dip., 1951, studies w. Zoltan Kodaly & Leo Weiner, Franz Liszt Acad. of Music, Budapest. Debut: soloist w. Hungarian State Phil., 1949. Carer: Performing Artist, Hungarian State Mgmt., 1951-56; since emigrating to USA has made many recital & orchl. apps. there & sev. concert tours in Europe; specializes in Liszt, Bartok & Am. comps. & has commissioned new comps.; Prof. Goucher Coll., Balt., Md. Has made many broadcast recordings. Mbrships. incl: Am. Liszt Soc. Hons. incl: Harriet Coehn Prize, 1962. Hobbies: Collecting art prints & books; Bicycling; Swimming. Address: 4000 N. Charles St., Baltimore, MD 21218, USA.

RAE, Allan McLean, b. 3 July 1942, Blairmore, Alta., Can. Composer. Educ: 3 yrs. in Army Band; grad., Berklee Coll. of Music, Boston, USA; study at Royal Conserv. of Music, Toronto. m. Darlene E, 1 d., 1 s. Career: Comp. of musicals, electronic scores, background sound effects for Nat Arts Centre, Ottawa, Stratford Fest., Theatre Calgary, Theatre Passe Muraille, Toronto & Cameo Prods., Calgary; jazz progs., dramatic music for CBC radio & TV; num. commissions incl. from CBC, Can. Coun. & Contemporary Music Showcase, Toronto; perfs. of own works incl. solo harp work premiered at Carnegie Hall, NY. Recordings: Harp Concerto in D flat; Poems for Trio; Piano Trio; Bass Concerto; On the Wind, for piano trio. Mbrships: Can. League of Comps.; Alta. Comps. Assn.; Can. Music Ctr. Address: 6316-34 Ave. N W, Calgary, Alta., T3B 1M7, Can.

RAEBECK, Lois Rupp, b. 2 Oct. 1921, W Chgo., Ill., USA. Singer; Teacher; Author. Educ: BS, Tchrs. Coll., Columbia Univ., 1946; AM, ibid, 1948. m. Alfred Smallens. Career:

Singer-Guitarist, num. Concerts East Coast, Mid-West USA; Mbr. NY Pro Musica; Workshops for Tchrs.; Music Cons., Vocal Music Tchr., N Merrick, NY, Elementary Schls. Composer num. Children's Songs. Recordings incl: English Medieval Christmas Songs; Elizabethan Songbag For Young People; Festino: 4-5 titles w. NY Pro Musica; Comp., Perf., about 30 albums for children. Publs: Orff & Kodaly Adapted For The Elementary School, 1972, 2nd ed., 1977; New Approaches To Music In The Elementary School, 1964, 2nd ed. 1968, 4th ed., 1980; Who Am I? Activity Songs for Young Children, 1970; An Elizabethan Songbag, 1974. Contbr. to Educators Jrnl. Mbr., profl. orgs. Hobbies: Hiking; Tennis; People. Address: 31 Joralemon St., Brooklyn Heights, NY 11201, USA.

RAGOSSNIG, Konrad, b. 6 May 1932, Klagenfurt, Austria. Guitarist; Lutenist; Professor. Educ: Acad. of Music & Performing Arts, Vienna. m. Wiebke Steiskal, 2 s. Career: Concert tours & TV apps. in Europe, USA, Can., Japan, Africa Middle & Far East. Apps. at Festivals at Salzburg, Ansbach, Strasbourg, Berlin etc. Prof., Acad. of Music and Performing Arts, Vienna, 1960-64; currently Prof., Music Acad., Basle. num. recordings. Publs: Handbook of Guitar & Lute; Ed., Guitar & Lute Music for Schott, Ricordi, Bote & Bock, Eschig. Hons: Grand Prix du Disque; Edison Prize. Mgmt: Rainer Haas, German Fed. Repub.; G de Koos, Netherlands; Musart, Italy; Musica, Inc., Japan; Esther Brown, NY. Address: c/o Sec., Pro Musicis, St. Johanns-Vorstadt 5, 4056 Basle, Switz.

RAGSDALE, John David, b. 30 Aug. 1932, Stockton-on-Tees, Durham, UK. Music Adviser, Rotherham Metropolitan Borough. Educ: RAM; Westminster Coll., London Univ.; AB; Dip. Ed; FTCL; LRAM; ARCM. m. Jessie Elizabeth, 2 s, 1 d. Career: Royal Marines, 1952-54; Tchng., 1956-69; LEA Advsrt., 1969-. Has dones gen. arrs. (vocalinstrumental) for schls. Mbr., Nat. Assn. of of Educl. Advsrs. & Insps. Hobbies: Chmbr. music; Railway hist. & prac.; Swimming; Outdoor Pursuits. Address: 242 E Bawtry Rd., Rotherham S60 3LS, S Yorks, UK.

RAHBARI, Ali, b. 26 May 1948, Varamin, Iran. Conductor; Composer; Violinist; Pianist. Educ: Dip. (violin), Conserv. Tehran; Dip. (cond.), Conserv. Vienna; Dip. (cond. & comp.), Acad. of Music, Vienna. m. Laleh Djavadipour. Debut: as Violinist (playing own comp.), Tehran TV & Radio, 1962; as cond. (own comp.), Conserv. Choir, Tehran 1963. Career: Cond. & Comp. Tehran Opera House & Vienna Radio Symph. Orch.; Cond., Tehran TV, Istanbul Symph. Orch., Tehran Symph. Orch.; Chief Cond., Jeunesses Musicals Iran, & Dir., Iran Nat. Conserv., Tehran. Comp. incl: International Hymn of Human Rights. Hons. incl: Gold Medal of Her Imperial Highness Princess Ashrat & 1st Prize for Human Rights, 1974. Address: Farah Jonuby-Ki. Farahnaz No. 43, Iran.

RAHN, John, b. 26 Feb. 1944, New York, NY, USA. Composer; Theorist. Educ: BA, Pomona Coll., Calif.; Schl. of Music. m. Suzanne Rahn. Career: Lectr., Music Theory, Schl. of Music, Univ. Mich., 1973-75; Asst. Prof. of Theory & Comp., Scshl. of Music, Univ. Wash., 1975-. Comps: Deloumenon (concert band); Trio (clarinet, cello & piano); Num. other comps. Publs: Lines (Of & About Music), PhD dissertation, 1974. Contbr. to profl. jrnls; Contgributing Ed., Perspectives of New Music. Mbrships: Am. Soc. of Univ. Comps.; Am. Musicol. Soc. Recip. num. fellowships & awards. Address: 8052 Meridian N, Seattle, WA 98103, USA.

RAICS, István, b. 25 May 1912, Music Critic; Composer; Pianist. Educ: Budapest Univ.; Pvt. Music Studies. m. Eva Toth. Debut: Accompanist, 1938. Career: Radio Appearances, Hungary, 1939-; TV Commentator, ibid, 1961-; Solo Concerts as Pianist. Compositions: vocal & stage music. Publs: Orosz népdalok (Russian folksongs), 1947; Madrigalok Könyve (Book of Madrigals), 1947; Ed., Magyar Zene (Hungarian Music), 1961, Kóta (chorus periodical), 1971. Contbr. to poetry anthols., Muzsika, Kóta, etc. Mbrships: Assn. Hungarian Musician; Assn. Hungarian Writers; Assn. Hungarian Jrnlsts.; PEN; Hungarian Ference Liszt Soc.; Bd. Art Fndn., Hungarian PR. Hons. incl: Jozsef Attila Prize; Order of Work; Golden Cross. Hobbies: Tourism & Motoring; Photography. Address: 1027 Budapest, Martirok utja 50, Hungary.

RAIDER, Nat, b. 3 Aug. 1929, Montreal, PQ, Can. Trumpet & Flugelhorn Player; Conductor; Bandleader; Conservatoire de Musique, Montreal, Can. m. Beatrice Mager Radier, 2 d. Debut: Les concerts symphoniques, 1947. Career: CBC Radio & TV; CTV Variety TV series; Num. recordings; Personnal apps. all over Can. & USA; Musical Dir., Forum. Comps. (recordings); Curly; Doing My Thing; Ouzo; The Girls; Petrouchka Final Act & Caf' Conc' Theme. Recordings incl: Dixeland; Man & His Trumpet. Mbrships. incl: Am. Fedn. of Musicians; ACTRA. Hons: 1st Prize for Trumpet, 1st Medal for Solfeggio, Adelphi

Univ., & Tanglewood; BME Cert. of Hon., 1969. Hobbies incl: Photography; Golf. Mgmt: Nat Radider Prods. Inc., 5799 Eldridge Ave., Montreal, PQ, H4W 2E3, Can.

RAILTON, John, b. 23 Feb. 1929, London, UK. Director of Music. Educ: FRAM; GRSM. m. Elizabeth Rule, Isgi; 3 s (former marriage) Career: Tchr., Bedford Mod. Schl., Ealing Grammar Schl.; Dir. of Music, N Herts. Coll.; Lectr., Cond., Adjudicator, Examiner, Associated Bd. of RSM; Cond., Ealing Youth Orch., N Herts. Guild of Singers, Ernest Read Music Assn.; Summer Schls., Canford, Downe House, Roedean. Comps. incl: Folk Song Arrangements; Magnificat. Recordings: The Four Seasons (Stephenson), Choir of Ealing Grammar Schl.; Youth Sings (P Tate), W London Youth Choir; Moses & Aaron (Schoenberg), Orpheus Youth Choirs. Hobbies: Woodwork; Motoring; Camping. Address: N Herts. Coll., Cambrdige Rd., Hitchin, Herts., UK. 3.

RAILTON, (Dame) Ruth, b. 14 Dec. 1915, Folkestone, UK. Pianist; Conductor. Educ: RAM, LRAM; ARAM; FRAM. m. Cecil King. Debut: London, 1936-7. Career: Dir. of Music, num. schls. & socs.; Cond., num. choirs & orchs., 1939-47; Concert Tours throughout world; Fndr., Musical Dir., Nat. Youth Orch. & Nat. Jr. Music Schl., 1947-65; Hon. Prof., Conserv., Azores, Chopin Conserv., Warsaw; Adjudicator, Federation of Fests., 1946-; Governor, Royal Ballet Schl., 1966-74; now ret'd. Hons: OBE, 1954; DBE, 1966; Hon. RMCM, 1959; Hon. FRCM, 1965; Hon. FTCL, 1969; Hon. LLD, Aberdeen Univ., 1960. Address: The Pavilion, Greenfield Park, Dubline 4, Repub. of Ireland. 3, 27, 30.

RAIMONDI, Ruggero, b. 1941, Bologna, Italy. Opersinger, bass. Educ: 1961-1962, studies w. Teresa Pediconi, Rome, w. Maestro Piervenanzi 1963-65. Debut: Glyndebourne, 1969. Career: Rome Opera; Prin. Opera Houses Italy; 1970, Metropolitan Opera New York; Covent Garden, London; Munich Opera; La Scala, Milan; Lyric Opera, Chicago. Recordings: 2 Verdi Requiems; complete Operas, Attila, I Vespri Siciliani, La Goheme, Aida, Don Carlos, Forza del Destino, Il Pirata, Norma. Hons: Competition Award, Spoleto. Hobbies: Reading; science, philosophy, social problems. Address: c/o S. A. Gorlinsky, Ltd., 35, Dover Str., London W1X 4NJ, UK.

RAINBOW, Bernarr, b. 2 Oct. 1914, London, UK. Lecturer in Music Education. Educ: Trinity Coll. of Music, London; Leicester Univ.; M Ed.; PhD.; FTCL; LRAM; ARCM; LGSM. Publs: Music in the Classroom, 1956, 2nd ed., 1971; The Land without Music, 1967; Handbook for Music Teachers, 1968; The Choral Revival, 1970. Contbr. to: Grove's Dictionary; Dictionary of Liturgy & Worship; Musical Times; Music in Educ.; Jrnl. of Educ.; etc. Mbrships: Bd. of studies in Music, London Univ.; Chmn., Tonic Solfa Assn.; Dir., Curwen Inst. Address: 6 Townshend Terr., Richmond, Surrey, UK.

RAINER, Jeff, b. 23 May 1947, New York, NY, USA. Concert Pianist; Teacher; Music Journalist; Host, Radio Program; Instrumental & Vocal Accompanist. Educ: BA, Columbia Univ., 1969; Postgrad. Dip. in Piano, Mannes Coll. of Music, 1974; Diploma, Fontainebleau, 1966; MA, NY Univ., 1978. m. Iwona Furmanik, 1 d. Career: Num. recitals, colls., libs., & music Soc., NYC area; Perf. on Young Artists & recital, WNYC radio. Mbrships: Arturo Toscanini Soc.; Wilhelm Fürtwangler Soc. Hons: Accepted, Chopin Int. Piano Competition, Warsaw. Hobbies: Tennis; Bicycling; Collecting records & tapes. Address: 100 N Washington Ave., Hartsdale, NY 10530, USA.

RAINES, Jack William, b. 19 June 1929, Melbourne, Aust. French Horn Player. Educ: studied w. Roy White, Melbourne. m. Vilma Inez Mair, 3 d. Career: 3 yrs. opera & operatta w. Theatre Orch.; 28 yrs. w. Melbourne Symph. Orch.; perfs. in chmbr. music & concertos for 2 horns. Recordings w. Melbourne Symph. Orch. Mbrships: Musicians Union of Aust. Contbr. to The Harp. Hobbies: Record Collecting; Gardening. Address: 94 Manning Rd., E Malvern, Vic. 3145, Aust.

RAINEY, Thomas Jr, b. 8 Feb. 1947, New Castle, Pa., USA. Music Instructor & Supervisor; Orchestra Member; Clinician; Soloist. Educ: BS, Music Educ., Duquesne Univ.; M Mus Ed, Youngstown State Univ.; Morehead, Boston, Berklee Schls. of Music. m. JoAnn (Josephine) Audia Rainey, 2 s. Career: Instr. of Flute, Westminster Coll., Slippery Rock Coll.; Inst. of Woodwind Method Courses, Westminster Coll.; Supvsr. of Music, Laurel Schl. Dist.; Mbr., Youngstown Symph., Bob Edgars Orch., Esquires, From Bach to Rock; Clinican; Soloist. Recordings: Life; Folk Music - A Pleasant Sound. Contbr. to: Instrumentalist; Command. Mbrships. incl: MENC; Pa. Music Educators Assn. Hobbies incl: Antique cars. Address: 3221 Elm Dr., New Castle, PA 16105, USA.

RAINIER, Priaux, b. 3 Feb. 1903, Natal, S. Africa. Composer (violin, horn, tympani). Educ: SA Coll. of Music, Cape Town;

ram, London; LRAM; FRAM; w. Nadia Boulanger, Paris. Comps. incl: Phalaphala; Aecora Lunae; Clarinet Suite; Sinfonia da Camera; Viola Sonata; Solo Suite Cello; Trios & Triads; Vision & Prayer; Primordial Canticles; Concerto for Cello & Orch.; The Bee Oracles; Six pieces for 5 Wind; Pastoral Triptych; Quanta; String Trio; Cycle for Declamation; Barbaric Dance Suite; Dance of the Rain, etc. Recordings: Str. Quartet, Amadeus Qtte.; Quanta, String Trio; London Oboe Quartet; Cycle for Declamation; Peter Pears. Contbr. to: Times & Tide; The Listener. Mbr., Composers Guild of GB. Hons: Colland Fellow of Worshipful Co. of Musicians. Hobbies: Walking; Swimming; Travel. Address: 75 Ladbroke Grove, London W11 2PD, UK.

RAINSFORD, Peter, b. 25 Oct. 1952, Liverpool, UK. Pianist; Flautist (performer & teacher); Director; Administrator. Educ: RNCM; GRNCM; ARNCM; LTCL; postgrad. cert. in Educ., Christ's Coll. of Educ. Career: Dir. of Music, Chester Arts Ctr., 1976-77; Dir., Tafelmusik, 1977-; freelance musician; vis. lectr., Hammond Schl. of Dancing, Chester Coll. of Further Educ.; Burton Manor Coll.; Wirral Coll. of Art & Design & Adult Studies; Dir., Tafelmusik Studios, Birkenhead. Mbrships: ISM; Merseyside Music Tchrs. Assn. Hon: Student of the Year, Liverpool, 1974. Hobbies: Photography; Squash; Organising Musical Activities for Children. Address: 54 St. David's Rd., Eastham, Wirral, Merseyside, UK.

RAJAPUR, Gayathri, b. 16 March, 1938, Holenarasipur, Mysore State, India, South Indian Classical Musician. Educ: BA, Karnataka Univ.; MA, Univ. of HI, USA, 1975; Sangeeta Vidwan, Ctrl. Coll. of Karnatic Music, 1955. m. Gene Kassebaum, 1 s. Career: Concert perfs., India, USA, Sweden; Artist, All India Radio; Lectr., S Indian Music, Inst. of Ethnomusicol., UCLA, USA, 1963-65, Univ. of HI, 1969-; Lectr., Gottuvadyam, SV Coll. of Music, Tirupati, India, 1973-74. Recordings: Ragas of S India. Author, Bharatiya Sangita Darshana, 1960. Mbr. Soc. for Ethnomusicol. Address: 513 Iana St., Kailua, HI 96734, USA.

RAJIČIĆ, Stanojlo, b. 16 Dec. 1910, Belgrade, Yugoslavia. Composer; Pianist; University Professor. Educ: Piano & Comp., State Conserv., Prague, Czechoslovaki. m. Milica, 1 d. Debut: Belgrade, 1928. Career: Prof. of Comp., Acad. of Music, Univ. of the Arts, Belgrade; Subject of musical portaits, Belgrade Radio & TV. Comps. incl: (orch.) 5th & 6th Symphs., 1966, 75; Concertos for Violin, Piano, Violoncello & Clarinet; (song cycles) Na Liparu, 1957; piano sonatas; songs; (recorded for Radio) all foregoing; Mbr., Serbian Acad. Scis. & Arts (Sec., Dept. of Arts). Recip. num. prizes inclng. 7th of July Prize for Life's Work, 1968; G. von Herder Int. Prize, Vienna, 1975. Address: Narodnog Fronta 60, 11000 Belgrade, Yugoslavia.

RAJNA, Elizabeth Faith, b. 21 Feb. 1929, London, UK. Teacher of Alexander Technique (violin, voice). Educ: Constructive Tchng. Ctr., London; RCM; ARCM (violin perf.). Debut: Wigmore Hall, London, 1968. Career: mbr., Macnaghten Quartet, 1951-55; violin & piano duo w. Anthony Green; vis. lectr. in Alexander Technique, Basle Music Acad.; started Alexander Technique dept., GSM; co-prin., Schl. of Alexander Studies, London. Contbr. to: Music Jrnl.; The Musician; Medical World. Mbr., Soc. of Tchrs. of the Alexander Technique (chmn., 1978-80). Hobbies: Running; Swimming. Address: 99 Rosebery Road, London N10, UK.

RAJNA, Thomas, b. 1928, Budapest, Hungary. Pianist; Composer; Teacher. Educ: Franz Liszt Acad. of Music; ARCM; studied w. Zoltan Kodaly, Sandor Veress, Bela Nagy, Leo Weiner, Herbert Howells & Angus Morrison. Career: Prof. of Comp. & Piano, GSM, 1963-; Lectr., Keyboard Hist. & Studies, Univ. of Surrey, 1967-; Sr. Lectr. in piano, Fac. of Music, Univ. of Cape Town, 1970-; Snr. Lectr., ibid., 1974; num. concerts, recitals, UK & S Africa; apps. on radio, BBC & SABC & SATV Comps. incl: Badinerie (Bach-Rajna); Music for Violin & Piano; Dialogues for Clarinet & Piano; Piano Concerto; Movements for Strings; Dance for Orch.; Suite for strings; Cantilenas & Interludes; film & ballet scores. Recordings: Complete piano works of Stravinsky & Granados; works by Messiaen, Bartok, Scriabin, Liszt & Schumann. Contbr. to The Composer. mbr. CGGB. Hons: Liszt Prize, Franz Liszt Acad., 1947; Dannreuther Prize, RCM, 1951. Address: S Africa Coll. of Music, Main Rd., Roseban, Cape Town, S Africa, 7700.

RAKIER, René Alphons, b. 29 Aug. 1936, The Hague, Netherland. Pianist; Organist; Soloist; Teacher. Educ: Piano Solo Dip., 1955, Organ Solo Dip., 1958; Choir Conducting Final Dip., 1958, Royal Conserv., The Hague. Debut: Pianist, w. Res. Orch., The Hague, 1957; Organist, recital, St. Jame's Ch., ibid. Career: Piano & Organ soloist; Radio broadcasts, accomps., chmbr. music. Comps. (publs.): 3 Choral Preludes for Organ. Contbr. to Mens en Melodie. Mbr. Soc. for Dutch Music Hist. Hons: Prix d'excellence for organ, ibid., 1962; 1st

Prize, Rhine Countries Organ Competition, Arnhem, 1964; Choral Prize, Nat. Improvisation Competition, Bolsward, 1965. Address: Harstenhoekweg 135, Scheveningen, Netherlands.

RÁKOSI, Géza Rezsö, b. 19 Apr. 1938, Budapest, Hungary. Violinist; Teacher. Educ: Fac. of Educ., Music Acad. of Hungary, Szeged. m. Clara Masa, 1 d. Career: ldr., Szeged Phil. Orch.; ldr., Szeged Chmbr. Orch.; regular apps. as soloist in Hungary & abroad; Prof., Music Coll. of Szeged. Recordings; as mbr. of Szeged Phil. Orch. on radio; works by Mozart & Liszt. Hobbies: Collecting beat & jazz records. Address: Mikszáth Kálmán u. 10, 6722 Szeged, Hungary.

RALEIGH, Stuart W, b. 22 Aug. 1940, Syracuse, NY, USA. Choral Conductor; Pianist. Educ: B Mus, Syracuse Univ.; M Mus, ibid.; Berkshire Music Festival. Career: Asst. Cond., Syracuse Symph., 1968-71; Cond., Syracuse Univ. Chorus & Orch., 1965-72; Dir., Baldwin-Wallace Choral Ensembles, 1973-. Comps. incl: Requiem Mass; Hallel: A Canticle of Praise. Recordings: maledictions for Symphonic Wind Ensemble; monoliths for Symphonic Wind Ensemble. Mbrships: Pi Kappa Lambda; Cleveland Composers' Guild. Hon: Lena Corgin Fausey Prize, piano, 1961. Hobbies: Philately; Cinema. Address: 12 Baker St., Berea, OH 44017, USA.

RALF, Richard K, b. 30 Sept. 1897, Karlsruhe, Germany. Educ: studied w. Sister, Father & Prof. Hugo Kann; Scharrvenka Conserv., Berlin. Career: Cond., var. Film Theatres, Germany; Freelance work, Concert & Radio Stns., USA. Compositions incl: symphonic poem for large orch.; Str. Quartet; Violin Concerto; num. Film Scores; Cantata, Brothers Arise, for chorus, orch., mezzo-soprano, speaker; Num. works for films. Mbr., GEMA. Hobby: Sailing. Address: 649 S. Barrington Ave., Los Angeles, CA 90049, USA.

RALFE, Kenneth Harry, b. 14 Aug. 1935, Brighton, Sussex, UK. Cornet Player. m. Brenda Merryweather, 1 d. Career: Prin. cornet, Brodsworth Colliery TSB Band for 17 yrs.; Assoc. w. Carlton Frickley Colliery & Grimethorpe Colliery bands; broadcasts on BBC w. Brodsworth band. Recip. var. 1st prizes in solo competitions. Hobbies: Playing in brass bands; Adjudicating. Address: 23 Wash. Rd., Woodlands, Doncaster, Yorks., UK.

RAM, Ralla, b. 16 June 1924, Sangrur, Panjab, India. Violinst. m. Smt Satya, 4 c. Career: Mbr., AIR, Delhi; Film, HMV, TV & Radio apps. Mbr. Delhi Symph. Soc. Hobby: Playing violin. Address: 97 UB, Jawahar Nagar, Delhi - 7, India.

RAMAKERS, Christiane Josée, b. 25 Jan. 1914, Leopoldsburg, Limburg, Belgium. Music Academy Director; Pianist; Organist; Composer. Educ: Dip., Piano & Organ & studied harmony & counterpoint, Limburg Organ Schl.; studied fugure & orchestration by correspondence. m. Georges Givneron, 1 s., 1 d. Career: Teacher of music & singing, Kon. Atheneum, Eisden, 1934-69; Founder & Dir., Maasmechelen Music Acad., 1945-; Founder, Jeugd en Muziek Eisden-Maasmechelen, 1956. Comps. incl: Concertino, Op. 5; Duo Rhapsodique, Op. 6; Petit Cortege, Op. 10; Ballade, Op. 13; Alternator, Op. 17; Drie zangen van liefde en dood, Op. 19. Publs: Van kleuterdreun naar notenleer, 1967; Door volkslied tot notenleer, 1968; Notenboekje 1a, 1971; Musiektheorie in beeld en Grafiek, Books 1 & 2, 1964. Contbr. to profl. jrnls. Mbr. SABAM. Recip. Koopal Prize, Nat. Min. of Culture, 1961. Recip., Limburg Aovinciol Music Prize, 1978. Hobbies: Portrait Painting; Literature. Address: Bremstraat 28, Eisden, Maasmechelen 3630, Belgium.

RAMALHO, Elba Braga, b. 20 June 1940, Limoeiro do Norte, Brazil. Musician (piano & recorder). Educ: BA, Glee Club, Villa Lobos Music Inst., Rio de Janeiro, 1960; BA Mus. Educ. & Advanced Piano, Alberto-Nepomuceno Music Conserv., Fortaleza, Brazil; Recorder, Fed. Univ. of Parana; Fed. Univ. of Gahia; Fed. Univ. of Minas Gerais. m. Ary DaSilva Ramalho, 3 children. Debut: Fortaleza, Brazil. Career: Apps. on local educl. TV, 1974; Recitals at Joze de Alencar Theatre; Encetur Theatre; German Ctr., Fortaleza, Brazil. Mbr. Am. Soc. of Recorder. Recip. 1st Prize, Competition for Young Pianists, City of Fortaleza, 1964. Hobbies: Travel; Reading; Listening to Music; Cooking. Address: Rua Barbosa de Freitas, 991 (Aldeota), Fortaleza, Ceara (60,000), Brazil.

RAMEY, Samuel, b. 28 March 1942, Colby, Kan., USA. Singer (bass). Educ: B Mus, Wichita State Univ. m. Carrie. Debut: in Carmen, NYC Opera, 1973. Career: Leading bass, NYC Opera; opera apps. w. Phila. Opera Co., Houston Grand Opera, Opera Co. of Boston, Festival Gran Canarius, Florentine Operan, Glyndebourne Festival Opera. Recordings: I due Foscari (Verdi); Tosca (Puccini); Lucia di Lammermoor (Donizetti) - all on Philips label. Hon: Nat. Finalist. Metropol. Opera Nat. Coun.

Auditions, 1972. Mgmt: Columbia Artists Mgmt., USA, & HarrisonParrott Ltd., UK. Address: 320 Ctrl. Pk. W. Apt. 7H, NY, NY 10025, USA.

RAMIREZ, Luis Antonio, b. 10 Feb. 1923, Santurce, Puerto Rico. Composer; Professor. Educ: Grad. (Comp.), Madrid Conserv. of Music, Spain, 1964. Career: Prof. of Harmony & Comp., Conserv. of Music of Puerto Rico. Compositions: Tres Piezas Breves; Fantasia sobre un Mito Antillano; 10 Improvisations for Piano; Meditación a la Memoria de Segundo Ruiz Belvis (viola & pinao); Fragmentos (3 symphonic movements for orch.). Recordings: Neuve Cuentos Antillanos (soprano & piano); Sonata Eligiaca (cello & piano). Hons: Premio Cultural del Ateneo de Puerto Rico, 1966, & 1968. Hobby: Motorcar models. Address: 560 Verona St., Villa Capri, Rio Piedras, Puerto Rico 00924.

RAMOVŠ, Primož, b. 20 Mar. 1921, Ljubljana, Yugoslavia. Composer; Librarian. Educ: Dip., Conserv., Acad. of Music, 1941; Accademia Musicale Chigiana, Siena; pvte. study w. Alfredo Casella, Rome. m. Stefanija Schubert, 3 c. Debut: Ljubljana, 1938. Career: Libn., Slovene Acad. of Scis. & Arts, 1945-52; Libn.-in-Chief, ibid., 1952-; Prof. at Conserv., 1948-64. Comps: Symphonic music (5 symphs., Profils, Musique Funèbres, Symphonic Portrait); 19 Concertos for var. instruments & orch.; Chamber music, Instrumental music (sonatas for var. instruments); Piano & Organ works. num. recordings publ. in Yugoslavia & USRR. Mbrships: Assn. of Slovene Comps. (Sec., 1953-65, VP, 1967-71); Assn. of Slovene Libns. Hons: Phil. Soc., 1944; Ljubljanski Festival 1958; Presernov sklad, 1962; Yugoslav Radio, 1967, 69, 70; Slovene Acad., 1977. HObbies: Mountaineering. Address: Gorupova 2, 61000 Ljubljana, Yugoslavia. 28.

RAMPAL, Jean-Pierre Louis, b. 7 Jan., 1922, Marseilles, France. Flautist; Music Educator. Educ: Univ. of Marseilles. m. Francoise-Anne Bacqueyrisse, 1947, 1 s., 1 d. Career: World-wide tours, 1945-; Perfs. at major int. festivals incl. Rio de Janciro, Aix, Menton, Salzburg, Edinburgh, Prague, Athens, Zagreb, Granada, Tokyo; Ed. for Ancient & classical Music, int. Music Co., NYC. 1958-; Prof., Nat. Conserv. of Music, paris. Mbrships: French Musicological Soc. HOns: Chevalier, Legion d'Honneur; Chevalier, Order des Arts & Lettres; Grand Prix du Disque (7 awards, 1954-64); Oscar du Premier Virtuose Francais, 1956. Hobbies: Tennis; Deep-sea diving; Film-making. Address: 15 Ave. Mozart, Paris 16 ea., France.

RAMSBOTTOM, Derek, b. 5 April 1933, Halifax, UK. Organist; Pianist; College Teacher. Educ: LCTL; ARCO (ChM); Cert. Educ: BA. m. Anne Veronica Hartley, 3 s. Career: Hd. of Music, Huddersfield Tech. Coll. Comps: short comps. & arrs. Mbrships: RCO; Royal Schl. of Ch. Music; Asst. chorus master, Bradford Fest. Choral Soc. Hobbies: Walking; Water Skiing. Address: 9 Pennine Close, Ambler Thorn, Queensbury, Bradford, W Yorks. BD13 2NG, UK.

RAMSDEN, Lawrence Earl, b. 15 March 1939, Islip, NY, USA. Professional Drummer; Percussionist; Music Educator. Educ: B Mus, Boston Conserv. of Music, Mass, 1961; studied at Berklee Schl. of Music, Boston; grad. studies, NY Univ. Schl. of Educ., 1963-64. m. Virginia Knox Ramsden, 1 s., 1 d. Career: Profl. perfs. in NYC & Boston area, 1951-; TV perfs. on 'Wide, Wide World' & 'Startime Variety' shows; Radio perf. on 'Voice of America'; Newport Jazz Fest. perf., 1957; Percussion Demonstration & Perf. at Conn. Tchrs. Conven. & All-Eastern Band & Instrumental Clinic, 1962; Mbr., US Army-navy Band & Fac. Concert 1962; Mbr., US Army-Navy Band & Fac. Concert Band, Naval Schl. of Music, Wash, DC, 1961-62; Bandsman, US First Army Band, Fort Jay, NY, 1961-65; Bandsman, US First Army Band, Fort Jay, NY, 1961-64; Pvte. Instr., 1957-; Pub. Schl. Music. Instr., John F Kennedy Schl., E islip, NY, 1965-. Mbrships incl: Life Mbr., Phi Mu Alpha; Am. Fedn. Musicians, local 802. Hobbies: Photography. Address: 1618 Spur Dr. S, Islip, LI, NY, USA.

RAMSELL, Hilary Keith, b. 30 Dec. 1933, Sheffield, UK. Violinist; Teacher. Educ: LCM, 1951-54; LLCM; Manchester Univ., 1954-58, MusB, 1959; LRAM. div., 2 s. Debut: Tchaikovsky violin concerto, London, 1963. Career: perfs. on radio & TV; concerto repertoire incl. Elgar & Nielsen; prof. of violin, LCM; tchr., Williams Schl. of Ch. Music, Harpenden; tchr. of young beginners for London Borough of Barnet; pvte. tchng. practice. Contbr. to var. jrnls. Mbrships: ESTA; ISM; Musicians Union; Elgar Soc. etc. Hons: Margaret Ann Knowles scholarship, Manchester Univ., 1954-57; Gambier Holmes scholarship, LCM, 1951-54; State scholarship, 1954-57. Hobby: Practicing Scales. Address: 37 Victoria Road, New Barnet, herts. EN4 9PH, UK.

RAMSELL, Kenneth, b. 24 Feb. 1904, Sheffield, UK. Pianist; Teacher; Composer. Educ: studied piano & harmony w. his father. m. Aileen, 1 s., 2 d. (1 step-d). Career: Dance bands in 1920-s; Silent Cinema Orchs.; Liners; Cabaret Accompanist; Tchr., 1932-; Radio Buenos Aires, 1931; Radio Sheffield (talks). Compositions: Opera (Thrall); Nativity Music; 2 symphs. piano sonata; Trios; Duos; Violin concerto; Cello concerto; Piano concerto; 2 Sax. Quartets for LSQ. Mbr., CGGB. Hobbies: Writing music; Poetry. Address: Barber Nook House, Sheffield S10 1EE, UK.

RAMSEY, Gloria C, b. 6 Jan. 1926, Daytona Beach, Fla., USA. Conductor; Teacher; Player of Clarinet, Recorder, Rackett, Drummhorn, Dulcian & Rauschpfeife; Lecturer on Early Music & Instruments. Educ: MA Univ. of Souther Calif., 1958; Eastman Schl. of Music, Rochester, NY; Dip., Nat. Conserv. of Music, Paris, France, Ecole Normale de Musique; Accademia Musicale Chigiana, Siena, Italy. Career: Cond., Mozart Fest. Chmbr. Orch.; Dir., Ramsey-Kellerman-Raynaud Trio, Amati Chmbr. Players; Tchr., UCLA; Assoc. Prof., Univ. of Southern Calif.; Workshops in Can. & Europe; Aix Fext., 1978. Sev. recordings. Mbrships. incl: Am. Recorder Soc.; AFM Local 47. Contbr. to profl. jrnsl. Hons: Fulbright Scholar, 1950-51. Hobbies incl: Dachshunds. Address: Au Jasmin, 84560 Ménerbes, France. 4, 27, 29, 30.

RAMSIER, Paul, b. 23 Sept. 1937, Louisvell, Ky., USA. Composer; Pianist; Educator. Educ: B Mus., Univ. of Louisville; M Mus., Fla. State Univ. PhD., NY Univ.; Special studies, Juilliard Schl. of Music; Electronic Techniques, Composers workshop, Ny Univ. Career: Prof., Music, Ohio State Univ., NY Univ. Compositions incl: Divertimento Concertante on a Theme of Couperin for Contra-Bass & Orch.; The Man on the Bearskin Rug (1-act opera); Suite from Pied Piper, Ballet: The Moon & the Sun, Eden, Wine (choruses). Publs: My Hamster Crawls, & Other Piano Pieces Composed & Illustrated by Children, 1965. Mbrships: L'Association des Musiciens Suisses; Fndg. Mbr., LI Ballet Guild; ASCAP; Pi Kappa Lambda. Hons: Yaddo Fellow, 1969; Huntington Hartford Fellow, 1960; MacDowell Colony Fellow, 1960; Annual ASCAP Awards, 1966-74; NY Univ. Founders Day Award, 1973. Address: 210 Riverside Dr., New York, NY, USA.

RAN, Schulamit, b. 21 Oct. 1949, Tel Aviv, Israel. Composer; Pianist. Educ: Dip., Mannes Coll. Music; Comp. & Piano w. var. tutors. m. Clifford L. Colnot. Debut: NY, USA, 19 Apr. 1967. Career incls: TV & radio apps., CBS, NET, BBC; Asst. Prof., music, Univ. Chgo., 1973-. Comps. incl: O The Chimneys (recorded); Hatzvi Israel Euology (recorded); Concert Piece for Piano & Orchestra; Structures for Piano; Ensembles for 17; 3 Fantasy Pieces for Cello & Piano. Mbrships: ASCAP; Am. Music Ctr. Recip. num. grants & commns. Mgmt: Sheldon Soffer Mgmt. Address: 1455 N. Sandburg Terr., Apt. 2009, Chicago, IL 60610, USA.

RANDAZZO, Arlene, b. 17 June 1943, Chicago, Ill., USA. Opera Singer. Educ: High Schl. of Perf. Arts, NYC; Henry St. Music Settlement, NYC. m. Salvatore Randazzo, 1 d. Debut: Lucia Di Lammermoor, Tulsa Opera Assn. Career: Spoleto Fest. of Two Worlds; NYC Opera; Phila. Conn. Opera; Toledo & Dayton Operas; Opera Theatre of NJ; Chatanooga Opera; Caracas Venezuela; State opera (Stamford); Rochester Opera Theatre; Art Park Fest.; Duluth Opera; Symph. of Puerto Rico; Syracuse Symph.; Utica Symph.; First Nat. Tour of NYC Opera Theatre; Fla. Opera; Aspen Music Fest. Hons: Lieder Kranz Fndn., 1964; Opera Singer of the Year, 1977. Hobbies: Collecting old recordings & antique fans. Mgmt: Eric Semon Assocs. Address: 221 W 82 St., NYC, NY 10024, USA.

RANDELL, Sheila, b. 21 Feb. 1930, High Wycombe, UK. Concert Pianist; Teacher. Educ: Bucks. Schl. of Music; Conservatorij, Lucerne; LRAM (Perf.). m. Robert Oswald Cooke, 1 s., 1 d. Debut: At Wigmore Hall, aged 17. Career: Regular Broadcasts; Wigmore Hall Recitals; Concerts in UK; W. Philharmonia Orch. at Royal Festival Hall; W. London Symph. Orch. at Royal Albert Hall; TV apps.; Apps. w. all leading orchs. Recordings incl: Fantasy Waltzes & Sonata Alla Toccata by William Alwyn, Lyrita. Mbr. ISM. Hons: Gold Medal for Highest Marks in GB any subject, Assoc. Bd., 1945; Challenge Cup, London Competition, 1946; RAM Scholarship, 1946. Hobbies: Reading; Gardening; Needlework; Mathematics. Address: Glenview, 34 The Ridgeway, River, Dover, Kent, CT27 ONW, UK.

RANDOLPH, David, b. 21 Dec. 1914, New York, NY, USA. Conductor; Author Lecturer; Broadcaster. Educ: BS., CCNY; MA., Tchrs. Coll., Columbia Univ. m. Mildred Greenberg. Career: Cond. The Masterwork chorus & Orch., the St. Cecilia Chorus & Orch., Carnegie Hall & Avery Fisher Hall Kennedy Ctr. Wash. DC. num. choral works inclng. Bach's B Minor Mass & St. Matthew Passion, Brahms' Requiem, Mozart's Requiem, Haydn's Mass in Time of War, Orff's Carmina Burans,

Beethoven's Mass in C; Cond., David Randolph Singers; Radio broadcasts, The David Randolph Concert, WNYC radio, 1946-; Host, Lincoln Ctr. Spotlight, WQXR radio; Lectr., NY Univ., The New Schl.; Prof. of Music, SUNY, Coll. at New Paltz; Fordham Univ.; Montclair State Coll., NJ. Comps: A Song for Humanity. Num. madrigal recordings w. David Randolph Singers; Satie's Mass for the Poor; As Cond., The Masterwork Chorus, works by Monteverdi, Schütz, others, & Handel's Messiah; The Instruments of the Orchestra; Stereo Review's Guide to Understanding Music, Publs: This is Music, 1964; The NY Times Guide to Listening Pleasure (contbr.). Contbr. to music mags. Address: 420 E 86th St., NYC, NY 10028, USA. 2, 29, 30.

RANDOLPH, David Mark, b. 7 May 1945, Chgo., Ill., UK. Tuba Player; Professor. Educ: BMus, W Va. Univ., 1967; MMus, Eastman Schl. of Music, 1972; perfs. Cert., ibid., 1973; DMA, ibid., 1978. m. Peggy Andrews Randolph. Career: Tuba player w. Abbey Brass Guild of W Va. Univ., 1964-67; Am. Wind Symph. Orch., 1966; Rochester Brass Quintet, 1967-68; US Army Band, 1968-71; Univ. of Ga. Brass Quintet, 1973-; Asst. prof., Univ. of Ga., 1973-. Mbrships: tuba (Int. rep., Ga.-Fla. Dist.); MTNA (Ga. Brass chmn.); MENC; NACWPI; Pi Kappa Lambda. Hobbies: Golf; Tennis. Address: 165 Watson Dr., Athens, GA 30605, USA.

RANDOLPH, Dorothy Overn, b. 29 Feb. 1928, St. Paul, Minn., USA. Violinist; Teacher. Educ: BA, Univ. of Minn., Mpls., 1949; MAT, 1969, Ed D, 1974, NM State Univ., Las Cruces; Violin studies w. Robert Anderson, 1948-51; Bruno Mazurat (Heidelberg Conserv., Germany), 1964-65, & Ernst Glaser (Oslo, Norway), 1965-66. m. Paul H Randolph, 3 s., 3 d. Career: Violinist, El Paso Symph. Orch., Tex., 1967-70, Des Moines Symph. Orch., Iowa, 1975-; Instructor, Iowa State Univ., Ames, 1975-. Address: 524 Hayward, Ames, IA, USA. 27.

RANDS, Bernard, b. 2 Mar. 1935, Sheffield, Yorks., YK. Composer; Conductor. Educ: M Mus., Univ. of Wales; Study of composition in Italy w. Dallapiccola & Berio; Study of Conducting in France & Germany w. Boulex & Maderna. Career incl: Lectr., Univ. of Wales; Vis. Fellow, Princeton Univ., USA; Composer in Residence, Univ. of Ill.; Granada Fellow in Creative ARts, Univ. of York, 1969-70; Music Fac., ibid, 1974-; Fellow in Creative ARts, Brasenose Coll., Oxford Univ., 1972-73; Prof., Univ. of Calif.; Compositions performed at leading Int. Festivals incl: Venice; Warsaw; La Rochelle; Darmstadt; Prague; Avignon; Zagreb; Buffalo; Camden; Cheltenham & York; Lectr. & Concert tours of USA & Australia; Works for films produced in var. electronic music studios; Cond. of won & contemporary composers' music. Compositions incl: Wildtrack 1-3; Mesalliance; Ology; Aum (Orchl.); Madrigali for orch., 1977; Canti Lunatici for soprano & ensemble, num. vocal, instrumental & educl. poieces. Recordings of var. works issued in Austria. Mbrships incl: PRS; Am. Soc. of Univ. Comps.; SPNN. Hobbies: Reading; Talking; Cooking. Address: c/o Universal Edition (London Ltd.), 2/3 Fareham St., (Dean St.), London W1V 4DU UK. 2, 28.

RANEY, Carolyn, b. 14 Aug. 1924, Los Angeles, Calif., USA. Musicologist; Teacher; Singer; Writer; Opera Director; Pianist. Educ: BM., Eastman Schl. of Music; MMus, Cleveland Inst. of Music; PhD., NY. Univ.; Univ. of Perugia; Univ. of Florence. m. Saul Schechtman, 3 d. Debut: Pittsburgh Bach Fest., 1938. Career: Created role of Angel More, Mother Of Us All, Virgil Thomson, Gertrude Stein; Am. Premier, Suite from Lulu, Balt. Symph., 1951; 1st Perfs. of songs by Robert Ward, Theordoe Chanler, William Ames, Saul Schechtman, Hall Overton, Yves Baudrier, Darius Milhaud. Author, lyric, Remember Us. Contbr. to: Groves Siz; Dictionary of Contemporary Music, 1974; Memorie Federico Ghisi, 1974; Mozart Verzeichnis, 1970; Music & Letters; NATS Bulletin; Balt. Sunday Sun; Music Mag.; Music Educators Jrnl. Mbrships: Coll. Music Soc.; Chmn., Committee on Status of Women, Ed., jrnl. Symposium, ibid; Am. Musicol. Soc.; ASCAP; Nat. Assn. of Tchrs. of Singing; Nat. Assn., Womens Deans, & cnslrs. Adminstrs. AAUP; MENC. Recip. var. Hons. Hobbies: Gourmet; Travel; Mineral & Shell Collecting; Rare Plants. Address: Dir., Opera Dept., Peabody Conserv. of Music, Balt., MD 21202, USA.

RANGANATHAN, Tanjore, b. 13 Mar. 1925, Madras, India. Musician (mrdangam - S. Indian drum). Edc: Study w. Subramania Phillai. m. Edwina, 2 c. Debut: 1938. Career: Profl. musician & accompanist, 1938-; Tours of USA., Europe & UK., incl. perf. at Edinburgh Festival, 1963; Fac. Mbr., Wesleyan Univ. & Calif. Inst. of the Arts; Lecture - demonstrations w. Viswanathan (flute) at var. Am. Univs., 1967-. Recordings: accompanied Ramnad Krishnan on 2 LPs (Nonesuch Elektra Co.); accompanied T. Viswanatham, 2 LPs (World Pacific & Nonesuch). Address: 264 Court St., Middletown, CT 06457, USA.

RÁNKI, Dezsö, b. 8 Sept. 1951, Budapest, Hungary. Pianist; Teacher. Educ: Dip., Liszt F. Music Acad., 1973. Debut: 1st Prize, Schumann Int. Competition, Zwickau, 1969. Career: Concert tours, Europe, America & Far East, 1970-; Tchr., Liszt Music Acad., Budapest, 1973-. Recordings: approx. 25 records. Hons: Grand Prix du Disque, 1972; Liszt Prize, 1973; Kossuth Prize, 1978. Hobbies: Record collection; Cooking. Mgmt: Interconcert, Budapest. Address: Kertész u. 50, Budapest VII, Hungary, 1073.

RÁNKI, György, b. 30 Oct. 1907, Budapest, Hungary. Composer. Educ: studied comp. w. Zoltan Kodaly, Music HS., Budapest, 1926-30; Bachelor's degree. m. Anna Dekány, 2 c. Career: Comps. perf. w. The New Music Grp., Budapest, 1931; Perfm. opera, Stage, Film, Radio, Concerthall & some TV apps., 1945-. Comps. incl: The Boatman in the Moon (opera), 1978; 1st & 2nd Symph.; Concertino; The Magic Drink, ballet, 1975; The Tragedy of Man, opera, 1970; var. other symph., chmbr. & vocal music, educl. works, childrens operas etc. Recordings of comps. incl: King Pomades Nw Clothes; The Tragedy of Man; Three Historical Tableaux. Mbr., Hungarian Film Club. Hons. incl: Erkel Prize, 1952-57; Kossuth Prize, 1954; Golden Medal of Labour, 1967; Medal of Socialist Hungary, 1977. Hobbies: Yoga; Swimming; Gardening. Mgmt: Artisjus & Editio Musica, Budapest; Sikorsky, Hamburg. Address: 36 Gülbaba utca, 1023, Budapest, Hungary.

RANKIN, John, b. Clydebank, Scotland, Organist; Choirmaster; Adjudicator. Educ: B Mus, Glasgow Univ.; RSAM; LRAM; LTCL. m. Margaret D McDonald. Career: Organist, High Ch., Dumbarton, 1934-36; Wellington Ch., Glasgow, 1936-51, Jordan Hill Ch., 1971-; Cond., Glasgow Phil. Choir, 1935-51 & 56-67; Lectr., RSAMD, 1938-51; Tchr., HS of Glasgow, 1947-51; HM Insp. of Schls., 1951-75. Mbrships: Hon. Local Rep., Glasgow Ctr., ISM; Chmn., Glasgow Music Fest. Assn. Hobbies: Golf; Swimming; Reading. Address: 82 Weymouth Dr., Glasgow G12 OLY, UK.

RANSOME, Antony, b. 29 Sept. 1940, Melbourne, Australia. Singer (Baritone). Educ: BA, Univ. of Melbourne; studies w. Lucie Manen. m. Helen Marchant, 2 s. Career: Has broadcast & appd. in concerts & recitals in Australia, Canada & Europe; Has sung w. Engl. Chmbr. Orch. & w. Schütz Choir of London; perfs. at Aldeburgh, Harrogate, Windsor & Wexford Fests.; Fndr., the Wren Consort, specializing in baroque chmbr. cantatas; Tchr. of singing at Tonbridge & Sevenoaks Schls. Recordings: Italian Cantatas, w. Wren Consort, Mbrships: ISM; Brit. Actors' Equity. Hons: Award from Martin Musical Scholarship Trust Fund, 1971; Winner of the Australian Musical Assns. Competition, 1972. Hobbies: Art & architecture. Mgmt: Basil Douglas Ltd., 8 St. George's Tce., London NW1 8XJ. Address: Evergeen, Main Rd., Knockholt, Sevenoaks, Kent TN14 7JL, UK.

RANTS, Pamela Cohick, b. 2 Nov. 1952, Altadena, Calif., USA. Harpist. Educ: B Mus., Univ. of Redlands, Calif., 1974. m. Jack V Rants, 1 d. Career: Harpist, All Southern Jr. High Schl. Orch., 1966-67, & All Southern High Schl. Honor Orch., 1968-69; Soloist, young profl. concerts, Calif., 1969; App. w. Am. Harp Soc. Workshop & Harp Ensemble, Univ. of Calif., at LA, 1970; Perfs. w. Univ. of Redlands Concert Band, Chmbr. Orch., Choir Concert Choir, & Univ.-Community Symph. Orch. 1970-74; Harp Instructor, Calif. Bapt. Coll., Riverside, 1974-; Harpist, San Bernadino Symph. Orch., 1977-. Recording: Sound track music, The Chambered Nautilus (art film), 1972. Mbrships: Pi Kappa Lambda; Sigma Alpha Iota (Sigma Eta Chapt.); Mortar Board; Riverside Symph. Orch.; Univ.-Community Symph. Orch., Redlands; Inter-Varsity Christian Fellowship; Volley Ball Team, Univ. of Redlands. Hons: Helen Johnston Memorial Perf. Award for Prize Winner, Mu Phi Epsilon Scholarship Competition, Riverside, Calif., 1973; Winner, Redlands Bowl Young Artists' Competition, 1973. Hobbies: Hiking; Volleyball. Address: 2469 Paloma St., Pasadena, CA 91104, USA.

RAPAPORT, Rosemary, b. 29 Mar. 1918, Gerrard's Cross, Bucks., UK. Violinist. Educ: RAM; FRAM. m. Gerard P K Heller. Career: Mbr., Hallé Orch., 1943-43; Solo Violinist; Sonata Ensemble w. Fanny Waterman, 1943-47, & w. Else Cross, 1948-; Co-Fndr., Ctrl. Tutorial Schl. for Young Musicians (now called Purcell Schl.), 1962; Prof. of Violin, RAM, 1947-; has broadcast reciatls & concertos; Chmbr. Music Coach & Lectr., summer schls. Contbr. to var. musical jrnls. Mbrships: Royal Soc. of Musicians: Univ.'s Fedn. for Animal Welfare. Hons: Assoc. Bd. Schl. & Special Talent Exhibnr., RAM, 1937-42; ARAM., 1948; FRAM., 1958. Hobbies: Reading; Gardening. Address: the Latch, Newton Blossomville, Bedford MK43 8AN, UK. 27.

RAPF, Kurt, b. 15 Feb. 1922, Vienna, Austria. Conductor; Pianist; Organist; Harpsichordist; Composer. Educ: Grad.,

piano, organ & cond. schl., Hochschuel für Musik. m. Ellen, 1 d. Debut: Vienna, 1945. Career: Fndr. & Cond., Collegium Wien (Vienna String Symph.), 1945-56; Asst. Cond. to Hans Knappertsbusch, Opera House, Zürich, Switzerland; Prof., State Acad. of Music, Vienna; Accompanist to singers & instrumentalists inclng. Schwarzkopf, Lipp, Mainardi, Odnoposoff; Dir. of Music, Innsbruck, 1953-60; Broadcast & TV activities, num. tours abroad, appearances at festivals 9Vienna, Salzburg, Bregenz), 1960-; Chief, Music Dept., Vienna, 1970. Composer of works for orch., choir, chmbr. orch., organ & piano. 60 Records as cond., harpsichordist, organist, pianist. Mbrships incl: Pres., Austrian Composers' Soc.; Bd. of Dirs., Int. Schönberg Soc.; Osterreichischer Musikrat. Recip., Title of Prof., 1970. Hobby: Swimming. Mgmt: Gerhild Baron, Dornbacher Strasse 41/111, A-1170 Vienna, Austria. Address: Bossigasse 35, A-1130 Vienna, Austria.

RAPHAEL, Mark, b. 7 Apr. 1900, London, UK. Singer; Singing Teacher; Composer. Educ: studies w. Raymond von Zur Müklen (London), Emilio Piccoli (Milan) & Henri Albers (Paris). m. Eva Taglich, 1 s. Career: lieder singer. Comps: mainly songs. sev. recordings. mbr., ISM. Address: 17 St. John's Wood Terr., London NW8 6JJ, UK.

RAPHAEL, Roger Bernard, b. 10 Feb. 1929, London, UK. Violinist. Educ: Studied w. Rostal & Laserson, London; Comp. w. Matyas Seiber; Brussels Conservatoire; Premier Prix for Biolin & Chmbr. Music; Dip. Superieur, Violin. m. Irene Russell, 1 s. Debut: Brussels. Career: Soloist & Ch. Music Player on Radio & at recitals in Europe; Staff of Winterhur Conserv., Switzerland, 1964-68; Currently on Staff of RSAM & St. Mary's Music Schl., Edinburgh. Publs: Collaborated w. Menuhin on Violin: 6 Lessons w. Menuhin, 1971. Contbr. to profl. jrnls. Mbr. European String Tchrs. Ass. Hons. incl: Belgian Govt. Scholarship, 1951. Hobbies: Reading; Play-going; Table Tennis. Mgmt: Pro Arte Musica, Edinburgh. Address: 11 Melville Pl., Edinburgh EH3 7PR, Scotland, UK.

RAPHLING, Sam, b. 19 Mar. 1910, Ft. Worth, Tex., USA. Composer; Pianist. Educ: B Mus, M Mus, Chgo. Musical Coll. Comps. incl: Pres., Lincoln (4-act opera); Liear, Liar! (children's 1-act opera); Overture; Ticker-Tape Parade; 1st & 3rd Piano Concertos; Trumpet Concerto w. Strings; Timpani Concerto; Warble for Lilac Time (flute & strings); 5th & 6th Piano Sonatas; Piano Solo Version of complete ballet of Stravinsky's Rite of Spring; Song Cycle; Shadows in the Sun. Recordings on Serenus; Concerto for Piano & Percussion; Remembered Scene; Sonatina No. 2 for Piano; Movement for Piano & Brass Quintet. Mbr. ASCAP. Hons. inlc: 1st Prize for String Suite, 1947. Hobby: Playing Piano & Writing Own Libretti. Address: 2109 Broadway, New York, NY 10023, USA.

RASCH, Kurt, b. 3 Nov. 1912, Weimar, Germany. Composer. Educ: Univs. Jena & Berlin; HS Music, Weimar & Berlin. m. Eve Maria Wittlinger, 3 c. Comps: Sinfonietta Maurice Ravel in Memoriam op. 28; Toccata for orch. op.27; Ostinato for orch. op.19; Concert for orch. op.25; Concert for piano & orch. op.30; Songs w. orch. op.30; Toccata for orch. op.27 (also recorded); Ballet Der Damon op.36 (perf. Bolschoi Theatre, Moscow, 1953). Mbr., Deutscher Komponistenverband. Hons: Thuringischer Orgelpreis, 1929; Comp. prize, Berli, 1941. Hobbies: Painting; Drawing. Mgmt: Eulenburg, Schott, Breikopt & Hartel, Universal Edn., Vienna; N Simrock, Bote & Bock, Berlin. Address: Hähnelstr. 3, 1000 Berlin 41, German Fed. Repub.

RASCHER, Sigurd Manfred, b. 15 May 1907, Elberfeld, Germany. Saxophonist. Educ: Staatliche Hochschule für Musik, Stuttgart, 1925-27. m. Ann Mari Wigen, 4 c. Debut: Allgemeines Deutsches Musikfest, Hannover, 1932; Berlin Philharmonic Orch., Berlin, 1932. Career: Radio & TV pers. all over world; Soloist w. Royal Philharmonic, BBC Symph., London Symph., Halle, Boston Symph., NY. Philharmonic, Phila., Nat. Symph., Cleveland, Detroit, Berlin Philharmonic, Stockholm Philharm., Czech Philharmonic, Oslo Philharm., Zurich Tonhalle, Amsterdam Concertgebouw, Residentie Orkest, The Hague, Orquesta Pablo Casals, Barcelona, Budapest, Warsaw, Sydney Philharmonic, Honolulu & Melbourne orchs. Compositions: Top Tones for the Saxophone, 1941-61; 158 Saxophone Exercises, 1935-68; 24 Intermezzi, 1958; Scales for the Saxophone, 1965. Recordings: Debussy; Rhapsody Rascher Saxophone Quartet; Rascher Saxophone Ensemble. Saxorhapsody, by Eric Coates; Concerto for Saxophone & Orch., by Lars. Eric Larsson; Concerto for Saxophone & Orch., by Erland von Koch; More than 75 transcriptions of baroque, classical & romantic music for saxophone & piano & saxophone & orch. Contbr. to num. profl. jrnls. Num. mbrships. Hobbies: Gardening; Forestry. 3.

RASKIN, Judith, b. 21 June 1928, NYC, USA. Opera & Concert Soprano. Educ: BA, Smith Coll., 1949. Career incls: TV opera debut, Dialogues of the Carmelites, NBC, 1957; NYC Opera debut, Cosi Fan Tutte, 1959; Met. Opera debut, Marriage of Figaro, 1962; Ford Fndn., recital winner, NYC, 1964; Lieder recital, NY Town Hall, 1965; has appeared w. symph. orchs. in Mpls., Phila., NYC. Opera apps. at Glyndebourne, Metropolitan, NY City Opera, Santa Fe, Chgo. Lyric Opera, NBC-TV Opera, num. recordings. Mbrships: Trustee, Rockefeller Fund for Music. Address: c/o M-Kaplan, Inc., 50 Riverside, NY, NY 10023, USA. 2, 5.

RASMUSSEN, Arne Skjold, b. 19 May 1921, Copenhagen, Denmark. Pianist; Professor at Royal Danish Academy of Music. Educ: Royal Danish Acad. of Music. Debut: Copenhagen, 1943. Career: Soloist & Player of Chmbr. Music in Scandinavia, GB, Italy, France, Switzerland & Austria. Recordings: Carl Nielsen's piano works (Fona); Beethoven Sonatas & Brahms Piano Pieces op. 116-118; Gade & Hartman violin sonatas & piano sonatas. Publs: Carl Nielsen, Centenary Essays & Chmaber Music in 100 Yrs. Committee Mbr., Chmbr. Music Club Copenhagen. Hons. incl: Arnold Bax Medal. Hobby: Gardening (flowers, especially spring flowers). Address: Veras Allé 2, 2720 Vanlöse, Denmark.

RASMUSSEN, Fritz, b. 26 Jan. 1917, Vigorg, Denmark. Pianist. Educ: Grad., Royal Acad. of Music, Copenhagen; Piano studies, Geneva & Rome. m. Birte Hoffmeyer, 2 c. Debut: Copenhagen, 1944. Career: Radio perfs., soloist concerts w. accompanying orchs. in Scandinavia, Holland & Switz., 1946-55; Played own comps., France, Monte Carlo & Denmark. Mbrships: Assn. of Music Tchrs.; Assn. of Soloists of 1921. Hons: Cruz De Honra, for introduction of Brazilian music in Denmark. Hobbies: Psychology; The Far East. Address: Nyvej 18, 5-1851 Copenhagen V, Denmark.

RASMUSSEN, Henning Bro, b. 6 May 1924, Copenhagen, Denmark. Educator; Organist. Educ: State Cert., Tchr. of Singing, 1945; Organist exam., 1949; MA in Musicol., 1953. m. (1) Grete Amtorp Olesen, 1955-73, 3 c.; (2) Bodil Boiehoj, 1974, 2 c. Career: Prof., N Zahle's Tchr. Trng. Coll., 1948-; Organist, Bellhoj Ch., 1963-; Danish State Supvsr. of Music Educ. at Tchr. Trng. Colls., 1973-. Publs: Musikkundskab, 1962; Viser og ballader, 1974, Musik for os, 1976. Contbr. to: Dansk Musiktidsskrift (Danish Music Jrnl.); Int. Music Educator. Mbrships: Sec.-Gen., Int. Soc. for Music Educ., 1968-76; Pres., Nordic Union of Music Educators, 1968-71; Pres., Danish Music Tchrs. Assn., 1960-72; Nat. Danish Music Committee, 1976-79; VP, Int. Soc. for Music Educ., 1976-80. Address: 133 Carinaparken, DK3460 Birkerod, Denmark.

RASMUSSEN, Jane Edith, b. 23 Feb. 1928, Mpls., Minn., USA. Flautist; Choral Director; Teacher. Educ: AB, Coll. of St. Scholastica, Duluth, Minn.; MFA, Univ. of Ga., Athens; Presby. Schl. of Christian Educ., Richmond, Va.; summer sessions in music, Eastman Schl. of Music & Columbia Univ.; chmb r. music ast Summer Acad. Nice, France, St. Prex., Switz.; PhD, Musicology, Univ. of Minn. Career: Choral Dir., 2nd Presby. Ch., Prin. Flautist & Solo Flautist, Roanoke Symph. & Lectr. in Flute, Hollins Coll., 1959-74; Tchng. Asstship., Univ. of Minn., Mpls. Has made some recordings, most non-commercial. Contbr. to RILM. Mbrships: former Sub Dean & Sec., AGO; Humn Soc. of Am.; Sigma Alpha Iota; NACWPT; Student Rep., AMS, Univ. of Minn., 1977-78. Hons: Phi Kappa Lambda, 1976. Hobby: Travel. Address: 4101 Parklawn S, Apt. 210, Edina, MN 55435, USA.

RASMUSSEN, Karl Aage, b. 13 Dec. 1947, Kolding, Denmark. Composer. Educ: Dip., Music Theory & Hist., Conserv., Aarhus: studied comp. w. Per Noergard. m. Charlotte Schietz. Carer: perfs. in all Scandinavian countries; appearances (inclng. Radio & TV) in Germany, Italy, Israel, USA; formerly Reviewer, Demokraton, Aarhus; Currently Tchr., Theory & Orchestration, Aarhus Conserv.; connected w. Danish Radio Compositions: This Moment (3 sopranos, flute, percussion), 1966; Symphony for Young Lovers (orch.), 1967; Crapp's Last Tape (radio opera after Beckett), 1967; Symphonie Classique (chamber orch.), 1968; Recapitulations (orch.), 1968; protocol & Myth (accordion, electric guitar & tape), 1970; Anfang & Ende (orch.), 1970-73; Resonance (piano, prepared piano, mistuned piano, celesta), 1972. A Ballad of Game & Dream, 1975; Antifoni, 1976; Jefta, 1976. Contbr. to: DMT (Danish Music Mag.); Nutida Musik, Sweden. Mgmt: Wilhelm Hansen, Copenhagen. Address: Brokbjerggard, 8752 Oestbirk, Denmark.

RASMUSSEN, Niels Christian, b. 27 Apr. 1950, Froslev, Bov, Denmark. Composer. Educ: theory, hist. & comp., The Royal Danish Music Conserv. (Niels Viggo Bentzon); The Music Conserv. of Arhus (Pelle Gudmundsen Holmgren, Per Norgard);

The Music Conserv. of Alborg (Erik Norby). Comps. incl: Kredse, Fl., Cor., Cel., Piano, 1973; Nocturne, soprano, orch., 1973; Drommen om et Swineherf; The Tinderbox (texts by H C Andersen); Se (choir), 1974; 2 Songs for Choir, 1975; Music-dramaic works for children, 1974-78. Most comps. have been played on Danish Radio. Mbrships: Soc. of Danish Comps. Hons: Schlrship, Danish State, 1975. Address: Hojvang, Lindetvej, Gaerum, 9900 Frederikshavn, Denmark.

RASPE, Paul, b. 18 Mar. 1942, Jette (Brussels), Belgium. Musicologist. Educ: Royal Conserv. of Music, Brussels; studied harmony w. Pierre Moulaert; Licencié en Philosophie et Lettres, Free Univ. of Brussels, 1970; Doctorandus. Career: Violist. 'Queen Elizabeth' Orch. of Young Musicians, 1963; Prof. of Music Hist., Acad. of Music, Ixelles (Brussels), 1964-70 & Higher Inst. of Hist. of Art & Archeol., Brussels, 1972-; Music Critic, 'La Libre Belgique' (jrnl.), 1967-68; Sci. Asst., Brussels Mus. for Musical Instruments, 1971-; Asst. Lectr., Organol., Free Univ. of Burssels, 1973-; Lectr., Hist. of Music (summer courses), ibid, 1974-. Publs: Françcois-Joseph Fétis et les progrés de la facture instrumentale em Belgique 1820-1870, 1970; Françcois-Joseph Fétis et la vie musical de son temps 1784-1871 (jt. author) , 1972. Contbr. to sev. musical publs. Mbrships: Int., Belgian & French Musicol. Soc.; Hainaut Soc. of Scis., Arts & Letters. Hons. incl: Laureate of Belgian Vocation Fndn., 1966; Laureate of Belgian Royal Acad., 1972. Address: Place Masui, 17 B-1000 Brussels, Belgium.

RASTALL, (George) Richard, b. 5 Dec. 1940, Nottingham, UK. University Lecturer; Publisher. Educ: BA, 1963, MA, 1967, Mus B, 1964, Christ's Coll., Cambrdige; PhD, Manchester Univ., 1968. m. Jane Oakshott. Career: Univ. Lectr. in Music, leeds Univ.; Ptnr., Boethius Press. Mbrships: Royal Musical Assn.; Inc. Soc. of Musicians; Assn. of Univ. Tchrs. Publs: (ed.) Benjamin Rogers, Complete Keyboard Works, 1972; Ed., All publs. of Boethius Press, 1973-. Contbr. to var. publs. Hobby: Cond., Leeds Guild of Singers. Address: 5 Albert Grove, Leeds, LS6 4DA, UK. 3.

RATCLIFFE, Desmond Hayward, b. 8 Dec. 1917, Teddington, Middx., UK. Music Editor. Educ: Choir Boy, St. Paul's Cathedral, London; RAM., 6 yrs. (interrupted by service in WWII); LRAM.; FRCO. m. Shirley Ratcliffe. Career: Music Ed., Novello & Co., Ltd. (Music Publrs.). 1947-. Compositions: Choral & Organ Music; Ed. & Arr. num. works. Recordings: Faure Requiem, St. John's Coll., Cambridge, Conducted by George Guest. w. Genjamin Luxon, Baritone (ARGO), 1976. Publs: Fauré Tequiem, arr. for female voices (SSA). w. orchl. accomp., using mezzo-soprano in place of baritone if desired. (Novello & Co. Ltd.) Hon. William Elkin Memorial Prize, RAM, 1946. Hobby: Listening to Gramophone Records & Radio Concerts. Address: Uplands, 16 Linslade Rd., Orpington, Kent, UK.

RATH, John Frédéric, b. 10 June 1946, Manchester, UK. Opera and Concert Singer (Bass-Baritone). Educ: BA, Manchester Univ.; RMCM; Opera Schl., Basle; studied w. Elsa Cavelti, Max Lorenz, Otakar Kraus. Debut: Ramphis in Aida, RNCM. Career: English Music Theatre Co. (Ben Benny in Britten's Paul Bunyan; N Ireland Opera Trust (Sparafucile in Rigoletton); Glyndebourne Opera, 1977-; tours w. Glyndbourne as Masetto in Don Giovanni. Fugliemo in Cosi fan tutte & Melibeo in La Fedelka Premiata; apps. as priest, 2nd armed man in Die Zauberflote & Gurnemanz in Parsifal; apps. in France, 1978-. Mbr. Handel Opera Soc. Hobbies: Home; Great singing before WW II. Mgmt: (Opera & Concerts in UK) Robert Clark; (concerts in UK) Ltd.; Organisation Artistique int. (Michael Rainer, Paris). Address: 733 Wandsworth Rd., London SW8, UK.

RATHBONE, Christopher, Bruce, b. 5 July 1947. Croydon, UK. Organist; Educator. Educ: Ba., Cambridge Univ., 1969; Mus B., ibid. 1972; MA, 1973; FRCO., 1966; GSM., 1964-66. m. Isobel Isherwood, 1 d., 1 s. Career: Asst. Organist, Carlisle Cathedral, 1970-73 num. TV & Radio Broadcasts as Accomp. to Cathedral Choir & Abbey Singers; Recitals in Chs. & Cathedrals; Tours as Organist w. Abbey Singers, Germany, Holland and Sweden; currently Organist & Asst. Dir. of Music, Marlborough Coll., Wilts. Recordings of Liszt, Howells, etc. Mbr., ISM. Hobbies: Fell Walking; Reading. Address: 4 River Park, Marlborough, Wilts., UK.

RATHBONE, Joyce Isabel, b. 1929, NY, USA. Pianist; Harpsichordist; Teacher. Educ: RAM; Lausanne Conserv. Career: specializes in perf. of 18th century works; solo apps. at concerts & on radio; chmbr. music ensembles incl. Dickson-Rathbone Duo. Radio talks for BBC. Mbrships: ISM. Address: 31 Chepstow Place, London W2, UK.

RATIU, Adrian, b. 28 July 1928, Bucharest, Roumania. Compser. Educ: studied comp., Music Conserv., Bucharest. m.

Ileana Ratiu, 3 c. Debut: str. quartet, 1955. Career: Var. Musicol. Broadcasts, Radioffusion, Roumania; Contbr. to Int. Fests. & Symposia. Prof., harmony. Conserv., Bucharest. Compositions incl: 3 symphs.; Concerto pour Hautbois; bassoon & orch. à cordes; Studi per archi; Six Images pour orch.; Concerto pour piano & orch.; Ode à la Paix; Quator à Cordes; Vision nocturne; Partita pour quintette at; Concertino per la Musica Nova; Impressions pour ensemble de chambre; Fragment d'un Arc de triomphe pour Beethoven; Monosanta I & II; Trois Madrigaux, (Shakespear), etc. Recordings: Concertino per la Musica Nova. Publs: Georges Enesco, monograph in 2 vols., w. others, 1971. Contbr. to: Revue Muzica, Bucharest, etc. Mbr., Mgmt. Committee, Roumanian Comps. Union. Hons: 2 prizes, Roumanian Comps., Union, 1969, 72; Gernier prize for monograph. French Inst., 1972. sev. award. Hobbies: Literature; Travel. Address: Rue Ave. Vasila Fuica No. 5. Bucharest, Roumania.

RATJEN, Hans Georg, b. 26 May 1909, Berlin-Charlottenburg, Germany. Music Director. Educ: Cologne Inst. for Music. m. Elisabeth Soyter, 1939. Career: w. Kroll Opera, Berlin, 1932, & State Opera Unter Den Linden, Berlin, 1933; 2nd Cond.; & Choir Dir., Würzburg Civic Theatre, 1935; Musical Dir., ibid, 1936; Dir. of Symph. Concerts, Innsbruk Civic Theatre, 1939; 1st Cond., Munic State Opera, 1945; Gen. Music Dir., Oldenburg State Theatre, 1950, & Wuppertal, 1955. Address: 68-70 Lindenstr., 4 Düsseldorf, Germany.

RATTLE, Simon, b. 1954, Liverpool, UK. Conductor. Educ: RAM. Career: Prin. cond., London Choral Soc.; Asst. Cond., BBC Scottish Symph. Orch.; Assoc. cond., Royal Liverpool Phil. Orch.; cond., City of Birmingham Symph. Och., 1980-; Artistic Dir., S Bank Summer Music, 1981-83. Hon: winner, Bournemouth Int. Cond. Competition, 1973.

RAUCH, Joseph, b. 16 Oct. 1904, Munich, Germany. Composer. Educ: Study of harmony, counterpoint, composition & instrumentation w. Prof. Joseph Haas. m. Astree Ernst. Debut: on Bavarian Radio, 1930. Career incl: performances on US & Geramn Radio. Compositions incl: Fantasy for Organ; Antonius-Gesänge; Heitere Nachtmusik; Binding-Lieder; Symph.; Piano Quintet; Sonata for Clarinet & Piano; Ein deutscher Psalter; Ergänzung: Symphonisches Tedeum; Opera: Don Quijote. Num. works recorded. Mbr.: GEMA (German Composers Union). Address: Dreitorspitzstr. 19. D-8100 Garmisch-Partenkirchen, German Fed. Repub.

RAUHE, Hermann, b. Mar. 1930, Wanna, Germany. Professor. Educ: Hamburg Univ., 1951-55, 55-59; State Exams for Grammar Schl. Tchng., Music & German; Dr. Phil., 1959. m. Annemarie Martin, 1 d. Career: Asst., 1960. Lectr., 1963, Prof. of Musicol., 1965-, Music Coll., Hamburg; Dir. of Dept. of Music Educ., 1968, Full Prof. of Music Educ., 1970-, Univ. of Hamburg; Pres., Acad. of Music & Perfng. Arts, Hamburg, 1978. Sev. recordings. Publs. incl: Musiklehrerausbildung an der Universität, 1974; Hören und Verstehen, 1975; Perspektiven musiksoziologischer und musikpaedogogischer Forschung, 1976. Contbr. to jrnls. Mbr. profl. orgs. Recip. Musikpaedogogischer Wanderpreis, 1973. Address: Gredengrund 18, D-2104 Hamburg 92, German Fed. Repub. 19.

RAUSCH, Carlos, b. 15 Mar. 1924, Buenos Aires, Argentina. Composer; Conductor; Teacher; Pianist. Educ: BA, Buenos Aires; Mannes Coll.; Columbia Univ.; MA, SUNY at Stony Brook; DMA Cand., Manhattan Schl. of Music. m. Anna Williams. Career: Adj. Prof. of Music, Suffolk Co. Community Coll., 1975-; Music Dir., The Royal Winnipeg Ballet, 1965-71; Brit. C'wlth. Arts Fest., 1965; Paris & Nervi Dance Fests., 1968-71; Symph. & Chmbr. Music Concerts. Comps. incl: Para Gerardo, 1973; Momentum 75, 1976; Chaconne for Soprano & Paino, 1976. Mbrships incl: Am. Musicol. Soc.; Am. Comps. Alliance. Recip., sev. schlrships. Hobby: Flying. Address: 5 Thompson Hay Path, Setauket, Ny 11733, USA.

RAUSSI, Paavo, b. 19 March 1901, Virolahti, Finland. Organist; Professor. Educ: Organ Dip., Music Conserv., Helsinki, 1926; studies w. Karl Straube, Music Conserv., Leipzig, 1926-26. m. Ingrid Ingeborg Kullman (dec.), 1 c. Debut: Helsinki, 1924. Career: Organ Tchr., Sibelius Acad., 1926-39; Sr. Tchr., ibid, 1939-57; Prof., ibid, 1957-68; Organist, Paulus Ch., Helsinki, 1931-71; Radio apps., Finnish Broadcasting. Mbrships: Chmn., Cantor-organist Assn. of Helsinki Dist., 1950-61; Chmn., Finlands Cantor-organist Union, 1960-74; Kallio-Berghäll Rotary Club, Helsinki, 1951- (Pres., 1963-64). Hons: Dir. musices 1944; Mbr. of hon. of 3 Cantor-organist orgs. in Finland; 2 Freedom Medals; Commander of Finlands Lion Order, 1965; Helsinki-prize, 1955. Address: Adolf Lindforsintie 7 A 10, 00400 Helsinki 40, Finland. 19.

RAUTAVAARA, Einojuhani, b. 9 Oct. 1928, Helsinki, Finland. Composer; Professor. Educ: MA., Univ. of Helsinki, 1954; Dip. (com.), Sibelius Acad., Helsinki; studied comp. w. Vincent Persichetti, Juilliard Schl. of Music, NYC, USA, Aron Copland & Roger Sessions, Tanglewood, ibid, 1955-56, Wladmir Vogel, Ascona, Switzerland, 1957, Rudolf Petzold, Cologne, Germany, 1958. m. Mariaheidi Rautavaara, 2 s., 1 d. Career: Art Prof., 1971-76; Prof. of Comp., 1976-. Compositions incl: 3 Str. Quartets, 1952, 1958, 1965; Symph. No. 3, 1961; The Temptations (ballet), 1965; Independence Cantata, 1967; A Soldier's Mass (orch.), 1968; Anadyomene (orch.) 1968; Cello Concerto, 1968; Piano Concerto, 1969; Apollon Contra Marsyas (comic opera), 1970; True & Fals Unicorn (choral work), 1971; Cantus Articus (concerto for birds & orch, 1972; Runo XLII (opera), 1974. Marjaita, (opera), 1975; A Dramatic Scene, (opera), 1975-76; . Violin Concerto, 1976; Organ Concerto, 1976. num. other orchl., instrumental & vocal works. Recip., Sibelius Prize, 1965. Royal Swedish Acad., 1975-. Hobbies: Painting; Literature. Mgmt: Finnish Music Info. Ctr., Runeberginkatu 15 A 00100 Helsinki 10. Address: Westendintie 65, 02160 Westend, Finland.

RAUTIO, Erkki Ilmari, b. 5 Oct. 1931, Hensinki, Finland. Professor of Cello. Educ: studies w. Yrjö Selin, Enrico Mainardi & Pierre Fournier. m. Adelheid Mörike, 5 c. Career: concerts in USA, Can., Japan, USSR & in most European countries; Prof. of Violoncello, Sibelius Acad., Helsinki. Recordings: EMI; Camera. Hons: Violoncello Prize, Harriet Cohen Int. Music Awards, London, 1968; Pro Finlandia Medal, 1968. Mgmt: Music Fazer, Helsinki. Hobbies: Lappland-Rambling; Chess. Address: maamiehentie 8, 01630 Vantaa 63, Finland.

RAUTIOAHO, Asko A J, b. 23 Apr. 1936, Vyborg, Finaldn. Organist. Educ: High er Organist Exam., Sibelius Acad., Helsinki, 1961. m. Eila Mäkelä, 1 d. Career: Tchr., Sibelius Acad., Helsinki, 1959-; Organist, Hakavuori Parish, Helsinki, 1961-; Organ Designer of over 70 organs & facades; Lecture series on the organ for Finnish radio. Mbrships: Advsry. Committees, on Finnish Ch. Organs, 1959-; Chmn., Assn. of Organists, Helsinki; Finnish Organ Soc.; Die Gessellschaft der Orgelfreunde. Publs. incl: Accompaniment to Masses, 1970. Contbr. to encys. & profl. jrnls. Hons: Dir. Cantus, 1975; Dir. Musices, 1977. Hobbies: Organ hist.; Geneal. Address: Ohjaajanti 22 A 8, SF 00400 Helsinki 40, Finland.

RAWLINS, Caroline Bessie, b. 6 Sept. 1898, London, UK. Solo Violinist. Educ: TCL. m. F R Winton, 1 d. Debut: w. Hamilton Harty, Wigmore Hall, 1919. Career incls: 1st broadcasts, Cesar Franck, Savoy Hill, 1923; formed duo w. Harriet Cohen for sev. years; num. perfs. South Pl. Concert, 1921-45; Mbr., quartets, etc. Mbr., Solo Perfs. Soc., ISM. Hobbies: Food; Wine; Plants; History. Address: 32 Arkwright Rd., London NW3, UK.

RAWLINS, Joseph Thomas, b. 7 Nov. 1936, Lakeland, Fla., USA. Tenor; University Professor. Educ: AA, Univ. of Fla.; B Mus, La. State Univ.; M Mus, ibid.; D Mus A; studied w. Dallas Draper, Frank McKinley & Peter Paul Fuchs. m. Elizabeth Johnson Rawlins, 2 d. Debut: Jackson Opera Guild, 1959. Career: w. Millsaps Coll., Auburn Univ., Univ. of W Fla.; Grad. Asst., La. State Univ.; Grad. Fellow, N Tex. State Univ.; 11 opera roles performed; 15 recitals, Ala. Educl. TV Network & 13 State Radio Network; Soloist w. Memphis Symph., Columbus (Ga.) Symph., State Symph. of Fla., Univ. of Fla. Symph. & Choral Union, etc.; Assoc. Prof. of Music, Univ. of W Fla., pensacola; Soloist, pensacola Symph., & Oratorio Soc., 1975. Recordings: Handel's Elijah w. Jackson Choral Soc. Publs: The Songs of Charles Wilfred Orr with Special Emphasis on His Housman Settings, 1972. Contbr. to: Nat. Assn. of Tchrs. of Singing Jrnl. Mbrships: Nat. Voice Comm., Music Tchrs. Nat. Assn., 1968-70; Am. Choral Dirs., Assn.; Nat. ASsn. of Tchrs. of Singing; MENC; Pi Kappa Lambda; Phi Mu Alpha Sinfonia. Hons: Voice Schlrship., La. State Univ., 1957-59; Schlrship., New Orleans Opera Guild, 1960, Baton Rouge Music Club, 1959, 1961; Semi-finalist, Auditions of the Air, 1966. Hobbies: Fishing; Oil Painting; Gardening; Sports. Address: Fac. of Music, Univ. of W Fla., Pensacola, FL 32504, USA. 28.

RAWLINSON, Griselda Maxwell, b. 23 Aug. 1930, Heswall, Merseyside, UK. Concert Pianist; Teacher; Accompanist. Educ: studied w. Harold Craxton, 7 yrs.; RAM, 5 yrs.; LRAM. m. J K M Rawlinson, 2 s., 1 d. Debut: Bluecoat recital, 1951. Career: Concerts & radio broadcasts; currently Accomp. & Piano Tchr. Occasional contbr. to jrnls. Mbrships: Comms., Merseyside Music Tchrs. Assn. & Hoylake Chmbr. Concert Soc.; ISM. Recip. Ada Lewis Scholarship, 1948. Hobbies: Painting; Fell walking. Address: Glenburn, Oldfield Rd., Heswall, Merseyside L60 6SE, UK.

RAWSTHORNE, Noel, b. 24 Dec. 1924, Birkenhead, Cheshire, UK. Organist. Educ: FRCO; FRMCM; LRAM. m. Elizabeth Cooper, 3 c. Career: Organist, Liverpool Cathedral; Radio Appearances; Recital tours. Am., Canada, USSR. Recordings: Great Cathedral Organs; Toccate Spectacular. Author, The Organs of Liverpool Cathedral, 1958. Mbr., Coun., RCO. Hobbies: Gardening; Cooking. Address: 12 Ashbourne Ave., Blundellsands, Liverpool L23 8TX, UK.

RAY, Ian Patrick, b. 8 Dec. 1946, Hendon, UK. Lecturer in Music; Freelance work as Pianist, organist, baritone & Choral Conductor. Educ: studied music at N E Essex Tech. Coll. & Schl. of Art, 1965-69; ARCM (Hons.) Pinaforte Tchng.; LRAM, Singing Tchr.; FRCO; studied Pianofrte w. Allan Granville & Virginia MacLean; singing w. Norman Tattersall; organ w. Douglas Mews & Douglas Hawkridge; harmony w. Donald Hughes. Career: Organist & Choirmaster, Lion Walk Ch., Colchester, 1969-; Dir. of Music, Felixstowe HS., 1969-71; Lectr. in Music, Colehester last. of Educ., 1972-; Cond., Colchester Choral Soc., 1976-. Mbrships: ATTI; RCO. Hons: Canon Jack Award in Music, NE Essex Tech. Coll., 1967- 68. Hobbies: Mountain Walking; English Poetry. Address: 6 Old Heath Rd., Colchester, Essex CO1 2ES, UK.

RAY, O.P., Mary Dominic (Sister), b. 5 Sept. 1913, Burlington, USA. Author; Music Consultant; Pianist; Lecturer. Educ: Bmus, Cinn. Conserv. of Music, 1937; studied paino w. George Gruenberg, Berlin, 1937-38; Debut: San Francisco, 1939. Career: Fnd.-Dir., Am. Music Rsch. Ctr., Dominican Coll.; Asst. Prof., ibid; music fac., San Francisco State Univ.; Guest lectr., Univ. of Calif., Los Angeles; consultant, perf., lectr. on the Bicentennial series at M H de Young Memorial Museum, San Francisco, 1976; concert pianist, 1939-47; chmbr. music perfs.; recitals in Oakland, San Francisco, Belmont, 1962-; rsch. in Early Am. music, USA & UK. Publs: Gloria Dei, The Story of California Mission Music, 1975 (co-author); Introduction & Music Analysis of The Gold Diggers Song Book, 1975. Contbr. to profl. jrnls. Mbr. profl. socs. Hons: 1st prize, Nat. Fed. of Music Clubs for rsch. in early Am. music; num. rsch. grants. Hobbies: Art; Sculpture. Address: Dominican Coll., San Rafael, CA 94901, USA. 2, 9.

RAY, Ruth, b. 19 July 1899, Alvin, Ill., USA. Violinist; Teacher. Educ: Univ. of Chgo.; Mus M, Eastman Schl. of Music, Univ. of Rochester; Student of Leopold Auer for over 6 yrs. Debut: Carnegie Hall, NY, 1919. Career: Soloist w. many major orchs. inclng. NY Phil., Chgo. Symph., Balt. Symph., Nat. Symph., Mnpls. Symph.; Recitals throughout USA & Canada & in Germany. France, Holland & Switz; Radio recital series on WMAG & apps. on WOR, & WMBD. Compositions: Short pieces for violin & piano; Currently Tchng. Mbrships: Soc. of Am. Musicians (on Bd.); Mu Phi Epsilon; Pi Kappa Lambda; AAUP. Hobbies: Reading; Knitting; Stamp collecting. Address: 815 Judson Ave., Evanston, IL 60202, USA. 2, 5, 8.

RAYMOND, Edwin Matthew, b. 25 Mar. 1920, Berlin, Germany. Music Adviser. Educ: Studies in Berlin & London leading to B Mus (Dunelm), LRAM (flute perf.)., ARCM (orch. cond.), ARMCM (schl. music). m. Elsie Coldwell, 1 s., 1 d. Career: Hd. of Music, var. schls., UK, 1949-58; Music Organist for Middlesbrough, 1959-68; Music Advsr. for Teesside Educ. Authority, 1968-74; Advsr. w. special responsibility for Music for Cleveland Co., 1974-; Fndr. & Cond., Teesside Symph. Orch.; Hon. Music Dir., Teeside Int. Eistenddfod; Cond. (fndr.), Eisteddfod Choir, ibid; Cond., Eleveland Youth Orch.; Fndr.; Cond., Cleveland Choir & Cleveland Symph. Orch.; Author of some arrangements for recorder ensemble. Mbrships: present & past mbr., var. music comms., nat., regional & local level inclng. Exec., Standing Conf. for Amateur Music, 1961-71; Northern Arts Music Panel, BBC Radio Cleveland Advisory Coun. Hobbies: Listening to records; Cond. Address: 1 Walton Ave., Linthorpe, Middlesbrough, Cleveland, UK. 3, 28.

RAYNER, Clare Grill, b. 19 Aug. 1931, Galt, Ont., Can. Musicologist; Professor of Music. Educ: ARCT., Royal Consev. of Music, Toronto, Can., 1953; BM, Univ. of Toronto, 1954; MMus, Ind. Univ., Bloomington, 1959; PhD, ibid, 1963. Career: Asst. Prof. of Music, Calif. State Polytechnic Univ., San Luis Obispo, 1963-67; Prof. of Music, Calif. State Univ., 1967-; Fis. Prof. of Music, Univ. of Calif. at Santa Barbara, 1973-74. Publs: Ed., Christian Erbach, Collected Keyboard Compositions - Corpus of Early Keyboard Music No. 36, 5 vols., 1971-74; Ed., Giovanni Paolo Cima, Ricercar e Canzoni alla Francese ... 1060 - Corpus of Early Keyboard Music No. 20, 1969; Ed., Christopher Gibbons, Keyboard Compositions - Corpus of Early Keyboard Music No. 18, 1967; Ed., Hieronymous Praetorius, organ Magnificats on the Eight Tones - Corpus of Early Keyboard Music, No. 4, 1963. Contbr. to: Musica Disciplina; Am. Music Tchr.; Galpin Soc. Jrnl.; Harvard Dictionary of Music, 1969; Grove's Dict., 6th ed.; var.

anthols., prof. notes, etc. Mbrships: Chmn., S. Calif. Chapt., Am. Musicol. Soc., 1969; Galpin Soc.; Int. Musicol. Soc. Recip. of var. acad. hons. Hobby: Building Harpsichords, Clavichords & Virginals. Address: 5201 Burnett St., Long Beach, CA, USA. 9.

RAYNOR, Henry Broughton, b. 29 Jan. 1917, Manchester, UK. Schoolmaster; Critic; Lecturer; Broadcaster. Educ: pvte. study of violin. Career: Tchr. in var. schls. of all sorts. Publs: Haydn, 1961; A Social History of Music from the Middle Ages to Beethoven, 1972; Mahler, 1975; Music & Society since 1815, 1976. Contbr. to: The times; Music Review; Musical Times; Monthly Musical Record; Chesterian; Grove's Dict., 6th ed.; Concise Ency. of Music & Musicians, 1958; sev. books on music; Histoire de la Musique (Ency. de la Pleiade), 1960 & 63; Dict. de la Musique (Bordas), forthcoming; The Orchestra, A History, 1978; Mozart, 1978. Elected to Critics' Circle, 1965. Hobbies: Books; Theatre; Conversation. Address: 4 Fairhall, Colley Lane, Reigate, Surrey RH2 9JA, UK.

READ, Donald William, b. 19 Sept. 1914, Saugus, Mass., USA. Voice Teacher; Tenor Soloist; Choral Conductor. Educ: AB, Boston Univ.; AM, ibid., Dip., Voice, Juilliard Schl. of Music; Postgrad. Dip., Voice & Choral Conducting, ibid. m. Saimi L Keto, 1 d. Career: Concert, Oratorio Soloist, US, Canada, Japan; Tchr., French, var. Public Schls. & Juilliard Schl. of Music; Pvte. Studio Tchr., Manhattan, 1950-; Fac. Mbr., Mannes Coll. of Music & Preparatory Div., Manhattan Schl. of Music; Fac. Mbr., Juilliard Schl. of Music, Prep. Div., 1949-69; Cond., UN Singers, 1955-72, Concerts, TV Apps., UK, USA, Can., Scnadinavia. Recording: Folk Songs From Around The World. Publs: Compiler, Arr., United Nations Singers Folksong Series; Songs Of The United Nationsl Singers, 1965. Mbrships: Am. Acad. of Tchrs. of Singing; Publs. Off., ibid; NY Singing Tchrs. Assn.; Pres., ibid, 1972-74; Nat. Assn. of Tchrs. of Singing; Lt. Gov., ibid, NY State, 1970-74; Pres., NY Chapt., ibid, 1969-71; ASCAP. Recip. Medal of Merit, City of Ystad, Sweden. Hobbies: Bowling; Stamp Collecting; Travel. Address: 32-42. 89th St., E Elmhurst, NY 11369, USA.

READ, Gardner, b. 2 Jan. 1913, Evanston, Ill., USA. Composer; University Professor. Educ: B Mus, 1936, M Mus, 1937. Eastman Schl. of Music; studied comp. w. var. masters inclng. Jan Sibelius, Finland, 1939, & Aaron Copland, Tanglewood, Mass., summer 1941; studied piano, organ, cond. & theory w. var. masters. Career: Tchr. of Comp. & Theory var. instns., 1940-; Prof. of Comp. & Music Theory, Schl. of fine & Applied Arts, Boston Univ., Mass., 1948-; guest Cond. major orchs. inclng. Boston Symph. 1943, 1954, & Phila. Orch. 1964; Originator & Host, weekly educl. radio series, Our American Music, 1953-60. Comps: Num. commissioned works inclng. Passacaglia & Fugue, Ravinia Fest., Chgo., 1938, & A Bell Overture, Cleveland Orch. 1946; num. other orchl. works performed by major orchs. in USA & abroad; works for chmbr. or str. orchs., & solo instruments; Toccata Giocosa & Night Flight; choral & vocal music; opera, Villon, 1967; chmbr. music; Organ & piano music. Publs: incl: Music Notation, 1964, 2nd ed. 1969; Contemporary Instrumental Techniques, 1975; Modern Rhythmic Notation, 1978; Style & Orchestration, 1978. Contbr. to profl. jrnls. Recip. num. scholarships, Fellowships, prizes & musical hons. inclng. D Mus, Doane Coll., Neb., 1962. Address: 47, Forster Rd., Manchester, MA 01944, USA. 2, 3, 11, 12, 14, 16, 21.

READ, Helen Frieda (Mrs.), b. 20 Mar. 1902, Hampstead, London, UK. Musical Administrator. Educ: London Schl. of Dalcroze Eurythmics; Hon. aram. Widow of Ernest Read, 2 d. Career: Music Admnstr., 1925-; Dir., Ernest Read Music Assn., 1965-77. Contbr. to profl. jrnls. Mbrships: ISM; NFMS; RAM Club. Recip. OBE, 1973. Hobbies: Reading; Drama. Address: 143 King Henry's Rd., London NW3 3RD, UK.

READ, Thomas Lawrence, b. 3 July 1938, Erie, Pa., USA. Professor of Violin & Music Theory. Educ: BM, Oberlin Conserv.; MM, New England Conserv.; DMA, Peabody Conserv. m. Evelyn R Read, 2 s, 1 d. Career: Prof., Univ. of Vt.; mbr., Univ. strig. quartet, Vermont State orch. & Con Brio chmbr. ensemble. Comps: Sonata for cello & piano; Comibnation for violin & paino; Concatenation for flute & pinao; Quintet 1971 for trombone & strings; Isuchronisms No. 3 for strg. quartet. Mbrships: Am. Soc. Univ. Comps: Am. Music Ctr.; Am. String Tchrs. Assn. Comps: Am. Music Ctr.; Am. String Tchrs. Assn. Address: 32 Cliff St., Burlington, VT 05401, USA.

READE, Paul Geoffrey, b. 10 Jan. 1943, Liverpool, UK. Composer; Pianist. Educ: LRAM; FRSM; London Opera Ctr., 1965-66. m. Mary Clark, 1 s., 1 d. Career: Cond., Opera da Camera, Edinburgh Fest., 1963; Pianist, Opera for All, 1966-67, BBC TV Play Schl. series; Music Staff, Sadler's Wells Opera, 1967-69; Comp., Arr., Musical Dir., num. children's series, BBC TV & radio, inclng. Play Schl., & Crystal Tipps & Alistair, (Cartoon series). Comps. incl: Overture to a City; The Little Match Girl (ballet); David & Goliath (children's opera); The Journey of the Winds (children's cantata); Quintet for Saxophone & Winds (children's cantata); Quintet for Saxophone & Wind. Mbr., Composer's Guild. Address: 12 Clorane Gdns., London NW3.

REAKS, Brian Harold James, b. 21 Oct. 1920, Seer Green, Bucks, UK. Lecturer in Music & Health Education. Educ: Dip., Child Dev., London Univ.; Dip. Schl. Hygiene, Royal Inst. Publ. Hlth. & Hygiene; Dip. Schl. Music, RAM. Career: Music Master, num. Schls. & Colls.; Dr. Lectr., Music & Hlth. Educ., Kingston upon Hull Coll. of Educ.; Int. Lectr. Music Therapy, UNESCO; Lectr., Schls. Music Assn., Brit. Soc. for Music Therapy & Standing Conf. for Amateur Music; Broadcaster, BBC & NZ Broadcasting Co.; Music Critic, Yorks. Post. Comps: Num. songs for children, inclng. Time for Travel; As Fit as a Fiddle & Nursery Songs from Humberside; piano works inclng. Watercolours (suite). Filmstrip, Music Thearpy for Handicapped Children (w. recorded commentary). Contbr. to: Music in Educ.; Recorder & Music Mag.; Special Educ. Mbrships: ISM; Royal Soc. of Hlth.; Royal Inst. Publ. Hlth. & Hygiene; E Riding Branch Sec., The Arthritis & Rheumatism Coun. Hobby: Money Raising for Various Charities. Address: Yellow Sands, 19 Beechfield Dr., Willerby, Hull, N. Humberside, UK. 3, 30.

REALE, Paul, b. 2 Mar. 1943, New Brunswick, NJ, USA. Composer; Pianist. Educ: AB, Columbia Univ., 1963; MA ibid, 1967; PhD., Univ. of Pa. m. Carol A Kirkman. Compositions: Seance for solo cello; Alleluia Sequence for Women's chorus; Piece for Piano, 1967; Terza Prattica for Collegium Musicum; Wit in the Circle of Fifths (solo harpsichord); Miserere (SATB); Growth Myth; Intavolatura I (solo guitar); Clownzona (brass); Vala (solo ch). Mbrships: On Bd., NAACC; ISCM. Hons: Fromm Prize Finalist (Mad Ophelia), 1975. Hobbies; Building & restoring old keyboard instruments. Address: 22125 Gault St., Canoga Park, CA 91303, USA.

REANEY, Gilbert, b. 11 Jan. 1924, Sheffield, UK. Musicologist; Organist; Pianist; Musical Director; Profesor. Educ: BA, 1948, MA 1951; B Mus, 1950., Sheffield Univ.; Sorbonne, 1950-53, BS, Sheffield, 1951; LRAM (Solo Pianist). Career: Dir., London Medieval Grp., on BBC & European tours, 1958; Tchng. career: Rsch. Fellow, Reading Univ., 1953-56; Birmingham Univ., 1956-59; Vis. Prof., Hamburg Univ., 1960; Assoc. Prof., 1960-62, Prof., 1963-, UCLA, USA. Gen. Ed., Corpus Scriptorum de Musica; Asst. Ed., Musica Disciplina (jrnl.), 1956-76. Publs: Early 15th Century Music, 6 vols., 1955-77; Machaut, 1971; Complete catalogue of medieval polyphonic mss. to 1400, 2 vols., 1966, 69; Contbr. to jrnls., encys. Mbrships: Royal Music Assn.; Am. Musicol. Soc.; Int. Musicol. Soc. Hons: 1st Dent Medal, Royal Music Assn., 1961. Hobbies: Walking; Reading; Travel. Address: 1001 3rd St., Santa Monica, CA, USA. 2, 11, 21.

REARICK, Martha Nell, b. 29 Nov. 1938, Danville, Ill., USA. Associate Professor of Music (Flute, Piano). Educ: B Mus, M Mus, Univ. Mich.; Pvte. studies. Career: Assoc. Prof. of Music, Univ. S Fla.; Prin. Flautist, Fla. Gulf Coast Symph.; Flautist, Ars Nova Woodwind Quintet; Accomp. for Julius Baker Flute Master Classes in NY, Atlanta, Calif. & Mont. (summer). Arr. for: Suite in B minor (J S Bach); Andante from Italian Symph. (Mendelssohn); Double Fugue (Berlioz). Recordings: Music Minus One Laureate Series (Piano accomp. w. Julius Baker, flute). Publs: The Fabric of Flute Playing, Studio PR, Lebanon, Ind., 1976. Contbr. to Am. Music Tchr. Mbr. num. profil. orgs. inclng.: Sigma Alpha Iota; Phi Beta Kappa; Sec., Nat. Flute Assn., 1978-79. Hobbies: Fla. Trail Assn.; Swimming; Collecting primitive & antique flutes. Address: C/O Music Dept., Univ. S Fla., Tampa, FL 33620, USA.

REBLING, Eberhard, b. 4 Dec. 1911, Germany. Painist; Musicologist. Educ: Berlin Univ. m. Lin Jaldati, 2 d. Career: Resident in Holland, 1936-51, incl. mbr. of Dutch resistance movement, 1941-45; Music Critic & Pianist, Amsterdam, 1945-51; Chief Ed., Musik, & Gessellschaft periodical, Berlin, 1952-59; Rector, Deutscher HS fur Musik Hanns Eisler, ibid, 1959-71; Prof., ibid, 1959-. Publs: Een neuw Nederlandse Danskunst, 1950; Den Lustelijchen Mey, 1950; Johann Sebastian Bach, 1951; Ballett gestern & heute, 1956; Ballett sein Wesen & Werden, 1964; Ballet von A-Z, 1966; Ballet Heute, 1970; Der Tanz der Volker, 1972. Hons: Nat. Prize, 1954; Peace Medal, 1964. Address: 1251 Ziegenhals, Seestrasse 18 German Dem. Repub.

RECH, Geza, b. 25 June 1910, Vienna, Austria. Professor; General Secretary. Educ: PhD, Univ. Vienna, 1935. m. Erika Graner. Career: Theatre prod. esp. opera, 1935-; Prof. dir., Salzburg Broadcast, 1945-50; Dir., sci. dept., Int. Fndn.

Mozarteum, 1950-; Gen. Sec., Int. ibid, 1968-; Prof., Hochschule Mozarteum, 1950-. Publs. incl: Das Salzburger Mozart-Buch, 1964; Besuch bei Mozart, 1969. Contbr. to profil. jrnls.; Ed., Mozart-Jahrbuch & Mitteilungen der Internationalen Stiftung Mozarteum. Mbrships: Hons., Mozart Socs., Vienna & Graz; Mus. Art, Univ. Kan., USA; Consultative Comm., Early Music, Los Angeles. Hons. incl: Silver Medal, City Salzburg, 1970; Silver Medal, Fed. Govt. Salzburg, 1971; Greal Medal of Republik, 1977. Hobbies incl: Books. Address: Rettenpacherstr. 1, A-5020, Salzburg, Austria.

RECHBERGER, Hermann, b. 14 Feb. 1947, Linz, Austria (Finnish Citizen 1974). Composer; Classical Guitarist. Educ: Graphic Inst., Linz; studied Classical Guitar, Bruckner Conserv., Linz, State Conserv., Brussels, Sibelius Acad., Helsinki, Finland (degree), & w. R Hagen, Zurich; studied comp. w. var. masters, dip., 1976. m. Soile T Jaatinen, 1 s., 1 d. Career: Works commissioned by Finnish Radio; broadcasts on other Scandinavian stations; Mgr., Chmbr. Orch., Why Not. Comps. incl: Loitsut, 1974; Balada de la plazeta, 1974; Studies for children's choir, 1975; Mobile, 1975; Tree-O 1975; Consort Music, 1976; num. other pieces, esp. choral & mixed media works. Publ: Let's Sing Contemporary Music (Finnish), 1975. Mbr., Finnish & int. profil. assns. Hons: 1st Prize (comp.) Finnish Pub. Educ. Soc., 1974. Hobbies incl: Linguistics; Graphic Art.

RECTANUS, Hans, b. 18 Feb. 1935, Worms, Germany. Professor. Educ: Civic Music Acad., Frankfurt am Main; Acad. of Music & Interpretive Art, Vienna; Univ. of Vienna; PhD, Univ. of Frankfurt, 1966. m. Elisabeth Zibauer, 1 s., 1 d. Career: Musicol. Asst., Univ. of Frankfurt, 1963-66; Lectr., Tchrs. Coll., Heidelberg, 1967; Prof. at Heidelberg, 1971-. Publs. incl: Leimotivik & Form in den Musikdramatischen Werken Hans Pfitzners, 1967; Neue Anasätze in Musikunterricht, 1972. Contbr. to: Hans Pfitzner Gesellschaft; Die Musikforschung; Kontakt Materialen zur Lehrerbildung; Lehmittel aktuell; Fiemann-Musiklexikon. Mbrships. incl: Praesidium, Hans Pfitzner Soc., Munich; Soc. for Music Rsch., Cassel. Recip., choir Dir., organist. Address: 6905 Schrieshelm Bergstr., Schlittweg 31, German Fed. Repub.

REDER, Philip, b. 16 Mar. 1924, London, UK. Pianist; Teacher; Lecturer. Educ: Launceston Coll.; Guildhall Schl. of Music; Assoc., ibid.; Assoc., Royal Coll. of Music. Career: Vis. Tchr., Schl. recitalist, Hampshire; Lectr., Class teaching & piano grp.; Tchr., UK & USA. Publs: Music & Rhythm, 1964; Great Piano Virtuosos, 1968; French, American & Prussian Marches, 1965; Pianogroup, 1980. Contbr. to: Piano Journal; Music in Education; Music Teacher; Times Educational Supplement. Mbrships: European Piano Tchrs. Assn. (Committee mbr.; Grp. Piano Tchrs. Sec.); Educ. Sect., Incorp. Soc. of Musicians. Address: The Stuido, 3 Weston Rd., Petersfield, Hants., GU31 4JF, UK.

REDMAN, Joan Dorothea, b. 2 Aug. 1929, Clapham Pk., London, UK. Lecturer in Mathematics; Private Teacher of Piano & Theory. Educ: BA, Birkbeck Coll., London Univ.; Postgrad., Brunel Univ.; FVCM; LLCM. m. Geoffrey William Lewis. Career: pvte. Tchng. of Piano & Theory, 1969-; Open University Tutor-Counsellor, 1978-. Mbrships: Mat. Assn.; Convocation, London Univ. Hobbies: Travel; Gardening; Oil Painting; Yoga; Theatre; Policitcs; Dog breeding; Cat fancying. Address: c/o Mrs. Joan D Lewis, Albamere Kennels & Cattery, Willow Tree Cottage, Lade Bank, Wrangle, Nr. Boston, Lincs., UK. 4.

REDMAN, Roy Alvin, b. 23 Feb. 1938, Wichita Falls, Tex., USA. Organ builder. Educ: BA in Music, N Tex. State Univ., 1960; ThM, S Meth. Univ., 1963; MSM, ibid, 1964. m. Sharon Kay Smith, 1965, 1 s., 1 d. Career: Min. of Music, Meth. Ch., 7 yrs.; Organ builder, 1964-; Estab. Redman Organ Co., 1967. Comps:L Opus 11 completed. Contbr. to The Revival of Tracker Organbuilding in the USA by Uwe Pape. Mbrships: Chmn., Educ. Committee, Am. Inst. of Organbuilders; Organ Histl. Soc. of Am.; Boston Organ Club; AGO; Am. Recorder Soc.; Dolmetsch Soc. Recip. Nita & Jake Aiken Award for outstanding student in Sacred Music, SMU, 1964. Hobby: Photography. Address: 2742 Ave. H, Ft. Worth, TX 76105, USA.

REED, Alfred, b. 25 Jan. 1921, NY, NY, USA. Composer; Conductor; Educator. Educ: B Mus, Baylor Univ., 1955; M Mus., ibid, 1956; Juilliard Schl. of Music; Hon. Mus. D. Int. Conserv. of Music, Lima, Peru, 1968. m. Marjorie Beth Deley, 2 s. Career incls: Staff Comp. & Arr., Asst. Cond., Radio Workshop, NY, 1938-42; Assoc. Cond., Radio Prod. Dir., 529th Army Air Forces Symphonic Band, 150 wkly. broadcasts, & Musical Dir., Army Air Forces Convalescent Trng. Prog., & Radio Script Writer, 1942-46; Musical Dir., Arr. for num. Variety-Theatre Artists, comp., var. Theatre Review Scores, Arr., Var. Recordings. Comp., Arr., Musical Dir., num.

progs., NBN, ABC, Mutual, CBS, NBC-TV Networks, 1948-53; Cond., Baylor Univ. Symph., Musical Dir., WORD Records, Waco, Tex., 1953-55; Exec. Ed., Hansen Publs. incl; NY, Miami, 1955-66; Prof. of Music, Schl. of Music, Univ. of Miami Coral Gables, Fla., Dir., Music Merchandising Prog., ibid, Exec. Ed., Univ. of Miami Music Publs., 1966-; Guest Comp., Cond., Clinician, USA, Can., Mexico. S m., Europe. Comp. incl: Armenian Dances (Parts 9 & II); First suite for Band; Music for Hamlet; Scriabin Nocturne for Band; My Jesus, Oh What Anguish; Testament of An American; over 200 works for Concert Band, Wind Ensemble, Chrous, var. Chmbr. Grps.; num. Film Scores; var. Arrs.; var. study materials. Contbr. to: Schl. Musician; Instrumentalist; Music Educators Jrnl. Mbr. num. profl. orgs. Recip. var. Hons. Hobbies: Photography; Travel; Reading. Address: 1405 Ancona Ave., Coral Gables, FL 33146, USA.

REED, H(erbert) Owen, b. 17 June 1910, Odessa, Mo., USA. Composer; Author; Educator. Educ: Univ. Mo., Columbia, 1929-33; B Mus, La. State Univ., Baton Rouge, 1934; M Mus, ibid, 1936; BA, 1937; PhD, Eastman Schl. Music, Univ. Rochester, NY, 1939. m. Esther Morris Reed, 2 d. Career incls: Chmn. of Theory & Comp., Mich. State Univ., 1939-67; Acting Hd., Music Dept., ibid, 1957-58; Chmn. of Music Comp., ibid, 1967-75; Prof. Emeritus, ibid, 1976-; Guest Prof., Lectr., Guest Cond. at many Univs. Comps. incl: (orchl.) La Fiesta Mexicana, 1964; The Turning Mind, 1968; (band) For the Unfortunate, 1972; (stage) Living Solid Face, 1974; (chmbr.) El Muchacho, 1963; (choral) A Tabernacle for the Sun, 1963; Earth Trapped. Works also recorded, Kinescoped & videotaped. Publs. incl: The Materials of Musical Composition (w. Robert G Sidnell), 3 vols., (in preparation), Vol. 1, Fundamentals, 1978; Scoring for Percussion, 1978. Mbr. profl. orgs. Hons. incl: Guggenheim Fellowship; Neil A Kjos Mem. Award, For the Unfortunate, 1975. Hobbies incl: Fishing. Address: 4690 Ottawa Dr., Ikemos, MI 48864, USA. 3, 4, 8, 11, 21, 23, 28, 29.

REED, William Leonard, b. 1910, London, UK. Composer; Lecturer; Pianist. Educ: GSM; RCM; MA & Mus D. Jesus Coll., Oxford. Career: Music Lectr. for Brit. Coun., Scandinavia, 1937-39; Music Master; Sloane Schl., Chelsea, 1945; Tutor, Adult Educ. classes in music appreciation, Oxford Univ. Delegacy for Extra-Mural Studies & London Educ. Auth., 1962-; Dir. of Music, Westminster Theatre Arts Ctr., 1967-; Compositions incl: Mountain House Suite for Orch.; 6 Facets for orch.; Concert Piece for 2 clarinets & piano; Dr. Johjnson's Suite for str. quartet; num. songs; organ works; arrs. of classical pieces for string orch. Publs. incl; The Treasury & Second Treasury of Christmas Music; The Treasury of Easter Music; The Treasury of English Church Music (gen. ed. w. Dr. Gerald Knight); The Treasury of Vocal Music (jt. ed. w. Dr. Eric Smith). Address: Glenwood, 99 Mycenae Rd., Blackheath, London SE3 7SE, UK.

REES, Ann, b. 31 Dec. 1935, Walsall, UK. Pianist; Teacher. Educ: studied w. Derrick Wyndham, Royal Manchester Coll. of Music; ARMCM (piano tchng. & shcl. music); ARCM (perf.); ARCM & LRAM (tchng.) m. Rev. WDC Rees, 1 d. Career: Piano Specialist, also A Level music (hist. & analysis), Howells Schl., Denbigh; currently Vis. Piano Tutor, Univ. Coll. of N Wales, Bangor, & Penrhos Coll., Colwyn Bay; recitals, N Wales, & concert work as soloist, duo & ensemble player. Recorded recital prog. w. cellist Judith Mitchel, BBC Wales, 1975. Mbr., ISM. Hons: Winner under 18 piano solos, 1953, 2nd, open piano solo, 1953, Royal Nat. Eisteddfod of Wales. Hobbies: Dressmaking; Reading. Address: Anwylfa, fron Pk. Ave., Llanfairfechan, Guynedd, Wales, UK.

REES, Eric Vernon, b. 24 Dec. 1919, Ripon, UK. Minister of Religion; Part-time Baritone Soloist & Teacher of Singing. Educ: St. John's Coll., Durham Univ., 1939-42; MA; Dip. in Theol.; Studies w. Edgar Herbert-Caesari. m. Margaret Thistlethwaite (dec. 1964). Debut: 1946. Career: Concerts w. orchs. in London, oratorio apps. & recitals, 1946-; Gave premiére of Kenneth Pakeman's song-cycle w. orch., Lover's Tenderness, w. Mod. Symph. Orch., London, 1958; Narrator in premiére of Cantata Jericho (Mason Harrison). Engl. Nat. Orch., 1973. Comps. (recordings): Sev. songs; Wedding anthem; Folk-song arrs. Recordings of duets. Author, Libretto of Cantat Jericho, 1975. Contbr. to var. jrnls. Hobbies incl: Record collecting; Writing poetry. Address: 1 Lackmore Rd., Enfield, Middx., EN1 4PB, UK.

REESER, Eduard, b. 23 Mar. 1908, Rotterdam, Netherlands. Musicologist. Educ: Music Schl., Rotterdam; Doct. (Hist. of Art, Musicol.), Univ. of Utrecht. m. Christine Elisabeth van Schaardenburg. Career: Tchr. of Music Hist., Music Schl., Rotterdam, 1930-37; Musical Ed., 'Nieuwe RotterdaMSCHE Courant', 1937-41; Music Advsr., Dept. of Educ., Arts & Sci.,

1945-47; Prof., Musicol., Univ. of Utrecht, 1947-73. Publs: De muzikale handschriften van Alphons Diepenbrock, 1933; De Klaviersonate met vioolbegeleiding, 1939; Muziekgeschiedenis in Vogelvlucht, 1941, transl. into Engl. & German; De Zonen van Bach, 1941, Transl. into Engl. & German; De Geschiedenis van de wals, 1947, transl. into Engl. & German; Een Eeuw Nederl. muziek, 1950; Alph. Diepenbroch - Brieven en Documenten, vol. 1-4, 1962-74, vols. 5-8 in preparation; Stijproeven van Ned. musek, 3 vols., 1962-76. Mbrships: Pres., Int. Musicol. Soc., 1972-; Pres., tot bev. der Toonkunst, 1951-69; Pres., Ver. v. Ned. Muziekgesch., 1957-71; Pres., 'Donemus', 1947-57; Royal Acad. of Sic., Netherlands; For. Mbr., Royal Acad. of Sci., Arts & Lit. of Belgium. Hons: off., Order of Orange-Nassau; Kt. Order of Netherlands Lion. Address: Frans Halslaan 19, Bilthoven, Netherlands.

REESOR, Frederick Alan Edwin, b. 14 June 1936, Markham, Ont., Can. Professor; Department Chairman; Organist. Educ: AMus., Conserv. of Western Ont.; Mus Bac., Univ. of Toronto; MMus., Eastman Schl. of Music, Rochester, NY, USA. m. Barbara Eileen Doucett, 4 d. Career: Secondary Schl. Music Coord., Oshawa, Ont., 1959-70; Organist, Choirmaster, St. George's Anglican Ch., Oshawa, 1959-70; Cond., Oshawa Symph. Chorus. & Oshawa Youth Orch., 1967-70; Prof. & Chmn., Music Dept., Univ. of PEI, 1970-; Cond., PEI Symph., 1970-; Organist & Choirmaster, St. Peter's Anglican Cathedral. Charlottetown, PEI Compositions: (publd.) Preludes on Down Ampney, Puer Nobis Nascitur, Song of the Crib, organ; (recorded) Hymn Tune Marche Document. Mbrships: Can. Music Educators Assn.; Ont. Music Educators Assn.; Conven. Chmn., ibid, 1971; Music Committee, Assn. of Atlantic Univs.; Chmn., ibid, 1971-73; PEI Arts Coun.; Steering Committee, ibid, 1974; PEI Music Fest. Assn.; Pres., ibid, 1974; Dir., Community Concert Assn. 1973-. Hobbies: Cabinetmaking; Photography; History of Organ Building in Canada. Address: 126 Rochford St., Charlottetown, PEI CIA 4P3, Can.

REEVE, Eve Lynne Joan, b. 17 Dec. 1935, Osaka, Japan. Harpsichordist. Educ: B Mus, Beaver Coll.; MA, Univ. Pa.; Artist Dip., Phila. Musical Acad.; Artist Dip. NGPT; AAGO. m. Ronald A V Snyder, Jr. Career: Asst. Prof., Lebanon Valley Coll., 1957-68; Solo concerts in USA; Guest soloist w. num. orchs.; Consultant, Music in the Mountains, 1970-; Mbr., NC Symph., 1971-73; Mbr. Celo Chmbr. Players; Fndr., Music in the Mountains, Chmbr. Fest., NC. Mbrships: Fac. Advsr., Delta Alpha Chapt., Sigma Alpha Iota; NGPT; AGO; Leschetizky Assn. Hons: 5 Gold Medals & 3 Cash Prizes, Int. Recording Competitions, 1961, 63; Citation for Outstanding Achievement, Moravian Sem. for Women. Hobbies: Needlepoint; Cats. Mgmt: Winged Rhythm Assocs. Address: Wingéd Rhythm, Rte. 1, Box 26, Burnsville, NC 28714, USA. 2, 5, 7, 23, 27, 29.

REEVE, Robert Graham, b. 25 July 1947, Chingford, UK. Director of Music. Educ: Magdalen Coll., Oxford; MA (Oxon); PhD Univ. London (Engl. 16th century church music); music tchrs. cert., Univ. of London Inst. of Educ.; LRAM (choral cond.); ARCM (singing). m. Olwen Bushell, 2 s. Career: Dir. of Music, Cambridgeshire Coll. of Arts & Technology; mbr., Clerkes of Oxenford; Lectr., adjudicator, Univ. of Cambridge Extra-Mural Bd., Brit. Fed. of Music Fests., etc.; Course tutor, Int. Music Weeks; GCE Chief Examiner. Contbr. to: Music Tchr.; Grove's Dict., 6th ed. mbr., ISM. Hobbies: Cookery; Engl. Hist. Address: 28 King St., Rampton, Cambridge CB4 4QD, UK.

REEVES, Betty (Joan Elizabeth), b. 16 Nov. 1913, Streatham, London, UK. Teacher; Writer; Pianist. Educ: MA (Occupational Psychol. Dept.), Birbeck Coll., London Univ.; LRAM (piano teaching) Tchr. Trng., Yorke Trotter Musicianship, Inc. London Acad. of Music, 1 yr.; Mus B, Trinity Coll. Dublin (external). m. James Ching (div., dec.), 2 d. Debut: Wigmore Hall, London, 1939. Career: Pub. Perfs., Oxford, 1941-45; Tchr./Lectr., London, & holiday courses in Glasgow, Belfast, Dublin & N Wales; some recitals & pub. perfs. London, 1945-48. Compositions incl: Water Ways; The Pilgrims' Way; Early Days; Later Days; Know Your Notation (mainly teaching albums & annotated classics). Publs: Ourselves & Our Pupils, 1951; Aural Training, 1951; Approach to Piano Teaching, 1955; Teachers' Yearbook for Assoc. Bd. Piano Examinations, annually 1947- (w James Ching 1947-62). Contbr. to: Pianoforte Tchr.; Musical Opinion; Music Tchr. Mbr., ISM. Recip., prize for Comp., Inc. London Acad. of Music. Hobbies: Career Guidance; Teaching Sociology; Walking; Watching Wildlife & humans. Address: 5 Southville Rd., Thames Ditton, Surrey KT7 OUL, UK. 3, 27.

REEVES, Gabor, b. 8 Feb. 1928, Budapest, Hungary. Clarinettist; Lecturer. Educ: Franz Liszt Acad., 1945-48; DSCM (tchr. & perf.), NSW State Conserv. of Music, Sydney, 1950;

MMus, Univ. of Sydney, 1978. m. Anthea Hamilton, 2 s. Career: Prin. Clarinet, Queensland Symph. Orch., 1951-54, Sydney Symph. Orch., 1954-60; freelance work in London, 1960-62; Prin. Clarinet, Melbourne Symph. Orch., 1963-64; Lectr./Sr. Lectr., Univ. of Adelaide, 1964-74; Sr. Lect., Chmn. of Dept. of Woodwind, NSW State Conserv. of Music, tours in S E Asia & for Aust. Broadcasting Commission; regular broadcasts. sev. recordings w. Univ. of Adelaide Wind Quintet. Publs: Playing the Scales for Clarinet; Paganini/Reeves, Moto Perpetuo arr. for clarinet & piano. Address: 249 Darley Rd., Randwick, NSW 2031, Aust.

REGAMEY, Constantin, b. 28 Jan. 1907, Kiev, Russia. Composer; Pianist; Musicographer. Educ: BA, Warsaw, Poland, 1925; MA, Warsaw Univ., 1931; PhD, ibid., 1936; Ecole des Hautes-Etudes, Paris, 1934-35; Habibitation, Warsaw Univ. 1937. m. Anna Kucharska, Career: Music Critic, Warsaw, 1934; Ed.-in-Chief, musical review, Muzyka Polska, Warsaw, 1937-39. Comps. incl: Chansons persanes (baritone & chmbr. orch.) 1942, Quintet (piano, clarinet, bassoon, violin & cello) 1944; String Quartet, 1948; Varizioni e Terna, (orch.), 1948; 4x5 (concerto for 4 quintets) 1964; Etudes pout voix de femme et orchestre, 1956; Mio, mein Mio (opera), 1972. Alpha...(cantata for tenor & large orch.), 1970; Lila (double concerto for violin, violoncello & orch.), 1976. Recordings: Quartet (Decca); Etudes pour voix de femme et orchestre (CT). Publs: Les Musique de 20 siecle, 1966. Tresci 1 Forma w. muzyce, Warsaw, 1973; Witold Malcuzynski, Cracow, 1960; Proba anlizy ewolucji w. sztuce. Cracow, 1973. Contbr. to: num. profl. jrnls. Mbrships: Int. Music Coun., 1971-75; Pres. Coun., Int. Soc. of Contemporary Music, 1969-73; Conseil suisse de musique; Assn. des musiciens suisses. Hons: Officer des Palmes Academiques, 1967; Composer's Prize, Assn. des musiciens suisses, 1971. Hobby: Learning many langs. Address: 14 Chemin de Lucinge, 1006 Lausanne, Switz. 14.

REGUERA, Rogelio, b. 24 Jan. 1926, Madrid, Spain. Guitarist. Educ: Royal Conserv. of Music; studied w. Daniel Fortea (classical guitar), Manuel Serapi & Nino Ricardo (Flamenco guitar). m. Marie Elena Amaro. Debut: as accomp. for Vincente Escudero, when aged 13, Career incls: w. Jose Greco, USA, 1951; num. theatrical & TV perfs., Europe, Africa, NS & Ctrl. Ams., Caribbean, etc.; Soloist w. many well-known perfs.; command Perf., Copenhagen Opera House, for King & Queen of Denmark; formed & toured w. own co. of Flamenco guitariests; films incl: Sombraero. Comps: about 45 classical & flamenco guitar works; film music for sev. French & Spanish prods. Has recorded about 30 records, Europe & USA. Publs: History of Flamenco Music; Complete Flamenco Method; Collection of Flamenco Airs - Ancient & Modern. Hobby: Bullfighting. Address: Hotel Broadmoor, 235 W 102 St., NY, NY 10025, USA.

REHFELDT, Phillip R, b. 21 Sept. 1939, Burlington, Iowa, USA. Professor of Music. Educ: BMEd., Univ. of Ariz., 1961; MM, Mt. St. Mary's Coll., 1962; DMA, Univ. of Mirhc., 1969. m. Sally K. Rehfeldt, 4 s. Debut: Tucson Workshop Ctr. for the Arts. Career: Clarinet Soloist, Concerts of New Music, var. Colls. & Univs.; Prof. of Woodwind Instruments & Musicol., Univ. of Redlands, Calif. Recordings: New Music for Solo Clarinet; New Music for Clarinet, Vol. I, Vol. II; Music By JM Mestres-Quadreny; Music for Clarinet & Tape, 1978; Redlands Music for Clarinet, 1978. Contbr. to: Jrnl. of the Int. Clarinet Soc. & others. Publs: New Directions for Clarinet, 1977; Proceedings of the Am. Soc. of Univ. Comps. Mbrships: Am. Musicol. Soc.; Am. Soc. of Univ. Comps.; Kappa Kappa Lambday. Address: 610 W Cypress, Redlands, CA 92373, USA.

REHFUSS, Heniz J, b. 25 May 1917, Frankfurt-on-Main, Germany. Singer; Professor of Voice & Opera. Educ: Lyceum & Univ. Neuchatel, Switzerland. m. Suze Leal. Career: Apps. w. all maj. opera cos. of Europe, USA, Asia & Africa; Prof. of Music; SUNYAB; Eastman Schl. of Music, Rochester, NY; Conservatoire du Quebec; Montreal; Many summer courses; Tchr., Darmstadt, Dartington, Graz, etc.; Apps. in Films on TV & radio. Num. recordings. Hons: Gold Medal (Naegeli) of Town of Zurich; Many Grand Prix du Disque a.o. Hobbies: Electronics; Photography. Address: 331 Lincoln Parkway, Buffalo, NY 14216, USA.

REHM, Wolfgang, b. 3 Sept. 1929, Munich, Germany. Publisher's Chief Reader; Music Editor. Educ: Univ., FreiburgBreisgau; studied Musicol. w. Willibald Guritt, Hermann Zenck. m. Helga Buck, 3 c. Career: Chief Reader, Barenreiter Publrs., Kassel; Mbr. Ed. Mgmt. Bd., New Mozart Ed. Publs: Co-Ed., Musik & Verlag, Carl Vötterle zum 65. Geburtstag am 12. April 1968; Ed., New Mozart Ed., IX24, Sect. 2 Werke für Klavier zu vier Handen, 1955, Co-Ed., VIII22, Sect. 2, Klaviertrios, 1966. VIII20, Sect. 1, Streichquartette Vol. I,

1966, I1517, Don Giovanni, 1968, Ed., V/; Klavierkonzerte, Vol. 8, 1960; Co-Ed., Wolfgang Amadeus Mozart, Jugendsonaten II: 6 Sonaten für Klavier, Cembalo, Violine, Flöte & Violoncello, KV 10-15, 1969. Contbr. to: Mozart-Jahrbuch; Fontes Artis Musicae; Documenta Musicologica, Series 2, 1958; var. other profl. jrnls., books. commemorative volumes. Mbr., Off., num. profl. orgs. Address: 29/I Heinrich-Schütz-Allee, D-3500 Kassel-Wilhelmshöne, German Fed. Repub.

REIBER, Mina Franke, b. 20 July 1905, Bluegrove, Tex., USA. Pianist; Organist; Teacher. Educ: B Mus, 1928, BA, 1937, Hardin Simmons Univ., Abilene, Tex.; Life Cert. in Piano, Tex. State Dept. of Educ.; Postgrad., SW Bapt. Theol. Sem., Northwestern Univ., Evanston, Ill., & Redlands Univ., Calif. m. Ralph R. Reiber. Mbrships: Pres., & VP, Nevin Music Club; NCAO; Charter Mbr., NGPT; Nat. & State Ret'd. Tchrs. Assns.; Wichita Falls Symph. Soc.; Bapt. Ch. Musician. Hons: 2nd Prize in comps., Fed. of Music Clubs in Tex., 1952. Hobbies: Attending concerts. Addres: 402 S Graham, Henrietta, TX 76365, USA. 4, 5.

REICH, Steve, b. 3 Oct. 1936, NY, NY, USA. Composer; Performer. Educ. incl: studied comp. w. Hall Overton, Darius Milhaud & Luciano Berio; MA, Mills Coll., Calif., 1963; studied African drumming, Balinese Gamelaan Semar Pegulingan & Hebrew cantillation. Career: formed own ensemble (1966) which has perf. throughout USA, Can. & W Europe. Comps. recorded incl: Come Out, 1966; It's Gonna Rain, 1965; Four Organs, 1970; Phase Patterns, 1970; Drumming, 1971; Music for 18 Musicians, 1976. Publs: Writings About Music, 1974. Contbr. to: NY Times; Notations; Source mag.; Aspen mag.; Interfunktionen; VH-101; Artitudes. num. grants & fellowships. Address: c/o The Reich Music Fndn., Inc., 1199 Park Ave., NY, NY 10028, USA.

REICH, Willi, b. 27 May 1898, Vienna, Austria. Music Teacher; Writer. Educ: Dr. phil., Univ. of Vienna; studied w. Alban Berg & Anton Webern. m. Etta Naumann. Career: Music Critic, Vienna, 1920-37, Basle, 1938-47, & Zürich., 1968-; Prof. of Musicol., Fed. Inst. of Technol., Zürich, 1959-. Publs: has written about 30 books on musicians. Address: Gorwiden 8, Zürich II, Switzerland.

REID, Charles Stuart, b. 16 Nov. 1900, Bradford, UK. Writer. m. Louise Clapham, 2 s. (1 dec.). Publs: Thomas Beecham, An Independent Biography, 1961; Malcolm Sargent, A Biography, 1968; John Barbirolli, A Biography, 1971; Fifty Years of Robert Mayer Concerts, 1973; Peter Grimes, an analysis, 1947. Music Critic, Profile Feature Writer, 1946-70, The Observer (as Charles Stuart), News Chronicle, Punch, Spectator, NY Times Mag., High Fidelity Mag. (USA), & other periodicals. Correspondence & working papers (the Charles Reid Collection) acquired for 20th Century Archives of Boston Univ., 1974. Mbr., The Critics Circle, London. Hobbies: Exploring S London by bus. Address: 23 Compayne Gdns., London, NW6 3DE, UK.

REID, Helen Ann, b. 28 Sept. 1959, Eureka, Calif., USA. Student of cello & voice. Educ: Coll. of the Redwoods & Humboldt State Univ.; Sequoia Chmbr. Music Workshop; Calif. Music Ctr. Debut: Golterman Cello Concerto w. Coll. of the Redwoods Community Chmbr. Orch., 1978. Career: cellist in 4 Humboldt Light Opera Prods., Eureka; 6 yrs. w. 1st Presby. Church Choir, Eureka. mbr., Soc. for the Prevention of Cruelty to Animals; Clan Donnachaidh Soc. of Calif. Hons: 1st place, State of Calif., Nat. Parent-Tchrs. Assn. Cultural Arts, Reflection Project, for the Treadle Song, 1976; Cameron Allen Music Scholarship, Coll. of the Redwoods, 1978. Hobbies: Cooking; Art. Address: 3535 Dolbeer St., Eureka, CA 95501, USA.

REID, John Stanley, b. 30 Mar. 1948, Hawick, Roxburghshire, Scotland, UK. Music Teacher. Educ: Dip. in Musical Educ., RSAM. m. Carol Mary Frew. Career: Paisley Abbey Choir, 1966-71; Musical Dir./Arr., Glasgow Scout Gang Show, King's Theatre, Glasgow, 1973-77; Fndr., & Musical Dir., Glasgow Youth Band, 1977; Int. Youth Exchange Concert Tours, Bavaria, 1974, Poland, 1975; Chorus Master, Scottish Ballet prod. of The Nutcracker, Theatre Royal, Glasgow, 1978. Comp. & Music Dir. of rock opera, Paul, prod. on BBC TV & radio, 1974. Mbrships: BBC Club, Glasgow, Glasgow Soc. of Musicians; Life mbr., Glasgow Musical Fest. Hobbies: Camping; Swimming. Address: 17 Merrick Gdns., Glasgow, G51 2TN, Scotland, UK.

REIDEMEISTER, Peter, b. 27 May 1942, Berlin, Germany. Musician, flutist; Musicologist; Head of the Schola Cantorum Basiliensis. Educ: Music Acad. Berlin, Tech. Univ. Berlin, DPh 1972; msuic. Career: Flutist Berlin Phil.; Flutist German Bach Soloist, Asst. Auréle Nicolet. Recordings: Bach: 4th, 5th

Brandenburg Concerto; Bach: Musical offerings. Mbrships: New Bach Soc.; Soc. for Music Rsch. Publs. incl: The Chanson, MS 7, München 1973. Contbr. to: Melos; New Music Mag. Hons: 1st Prize German Acad. Competition, flute, 1964. Hobbies: Wandering; Cycling; Chess. Address: Nonnenweg 31, CH-4055 Basel, Switz.

REILLY, Paul Cameron, b. 1 Feb. 1948, Passaic, NJ, USA. Professor of Guitar; Guitarist; Lutenist. Educ: BM, DePaul Univ., Chgo., Ill.; MM, Ball State Univ.; Perf. Dip. Int. Summer Music Acad., Pollensa Mallorca, Spain, 1973. m. Christy S. Reilly. Debut: Chgo., 1968. Career: TV Perfs., Indpls., Ind.; Recitalist, Purdue, Ball STate Univs., Int. Music Acad., Pollensa, Spain; Prof. of Classical Guitar, Ball State Univ., Muncie, Ind. Mbrship: UP, Ind. Soc. of Classic Guitar. Address: 401 Tyrone Dr., Muncie, IN 47304, USA.

REILLY, Tommy, b. 21 Aug. 1919, Guelph, Ont., Can. Harmonica Soloist; Composer. m. Ena Nabb, 1 s. Career: Professional Harmonica Player, 1936-; Tours of UK & Europe (incl. Poland), S Africa, Aust.; 1st Perf., sev. original works; Guest, num. music fests.; Soloist w. leading Orchs., incl. LSO, RPO, Oslo Symph., Krakow Symph., Bergen Symph., Stuttgart Phil., Philharmonia Orch., London Sinfonietta, num. European Radio Orchs. Comps: Background music, inclng. music for BBC series, The Navy Lark. Recordings incl: The Silver Sounds of the Harmonica; Works for Harmonica & Orch. (w. Academy of St. Martin-in-the-Fields); Harmonica Recital; Harmonica Concertos (w. London Sinfonietta); Music for Two Harmonicas. Publs: Play Like the Stars; Tommy Reilly Harmonica Course (2 LPs w. tutor); Progessive Exercises, 1954; Studies for the Chromatic Harmonica, 1954. Mbrships: Musicians Union; Equity; Performing Rights Soc. Hobbies: Photography; Reading. Mgmt: Sigmund Groven (world); Lilian Wick (UK). Address: Hammonds Wood, Frensham, Farnham, Surrey, UK. 14, 30.

REIMANN, Albert, b. 28 May 1925, Bremen, Germany. Teacher; Bassoon Player. Educ: Hochschule für Musik, Frieburg; PHD, Freiburg Univ., 1957. 4 c. Career: Tchr., Goethe-Institut. Publs: Studien zur Geschichte des Fagotts, 1956. Address: Schubertstr. 5, D-7760 Radolfzell, German Fed. Repub.

REIMANN, Aribert, b. 4 March 1936, Berlin, Germany. Composer; Pianist. Educ: Coll. of Music, Berlin; Univ. of Vienna. Compositions incl: Ein Traumspiel (opera); Melusine (opera); Strottreste (ballet); Die Vogelscheuchen (ballet); Elegy for orch.; Concertos for piano & for 'cello; Ein Totentanz for orch.; Hö Iderlin-Fragmente for orch.; Verrá la Morte for orch.; Inane for orch.; Loqui for orch.; Nenia for orch.; Rones for orch.; Zyklus for orch.; Quasimodo-Kantate for chmbr. orch.; Epitaph for chmbr. orch.; Canzoni & Ricercari for chmbr. orch.; Spektren for chmbr. orch.; Trobers for chmbr. orch.; Reflexionen for chmbr. orch.; Nachstück, Engfuhrung & other songs. Mbr: Acad. of Arts, Berlin. Hons. incl: Berlin Art Prize, 1962; Robert Schuman Prize, Düsseldorf, 1965; Critics' Prize, 1971; sev. schlrships. Address: 91, Hohenzollerndamm, 1 Berlin 33, German Fed. Repub.

REIMANN, Margarete Hildegard, b. 17 Oct. 1907, Schiltigheim bei Strassbourg, German Inst. for Music Rsch., Berlin; Prof. of Musicol., Hochschule of Music, Berlin. Publs: Untersüchungen zur Formgeschichte der französischen Klavier-Suite, 1940; Die Luneburger orgel Tabulatur KN208, 1, 2, 1957, 1968; J Matteson, Der volkommen Kapellmeister, 1954. Contbr. to: Zahlreiche Aufsatze; Mf; AfMW; MGG; Kieler Schriften zur M W Mbrships: GfM; IGfM; VNM; Soroptomist Club. Hobbies: Chess; Travel. Address: 31 Marschner Str., 1 Berlin 45, German Fed. Repub.

REIMERS, K. Lennart, b. 31 March 1928, Algutsboda, Sweden. Music & Book Publisher. Educ: Degree in Musicol., Lit. & Philos., Univ. of Uppsala; Dir. of Music Dips., Royal Coll. of Music, Stockholm. m. Gerd. R Wadelius, 1 s., 1 d. Career: Mng. Dir., Nordiska Musikförl aget, Stockholm, 1961-71; Dir., Universal Edition, Vienna, 1971-75; Fndr. & Propriator, Ed. Reimers, Stockholm, 1975-. Publs: A Swedish St. John Passion, 1957; Mozart och Sverige, 1961; Konst-Och Musik historia (w. Gerd Reimers), 1966; Tio Musikanalyer, 1971; Wienervalsen och Familjen Strauss. (w. Gerd Reimers) 1975. Contbr. to sev. musical jrnls. Mbrships: Swedish Royal Acad. of Music; Pres., Publn. Commission, Int. Soc. for Music Educ.; 1968-; Ed., Int. Music Educator, 1968-72, & Musikkultur, Stockholm, 1959-72. Pres.; Swedish Section, ISCM. Recip. of sev. decorations. Hobbies: Travelling; Vinology. Address: Mardvägen 44-46, S-16137, Bromma-Stockholm, Sweden. 19.

REIMS, Clifford Waldemar, b. 1 May 1923, Brooklyn, NY, USA. Teacher; Voice & Opera; Stage Director; Conductor;

Designer; Translator; Singer. Educ: AB, Bucknell Univ., 1949; MM, Voice Ind. Univ., 1951; DMA., Opera, Univ. of S. Calif., 19781. m. Georgette Howell, 1 s., 2 d. Career: Fac. Mbr., Calif. State Univ., Fullerton, Ohio State Univ., Univ. of S. Miss., Ohio Univ, Auburn Univ., Bucknell Univ.; Prof. & Chmn. Dept. of Voice, Dir.; Opera Theater at Roosevelt Univ., Chgo. Publs: Musical Ed. & Singing Translation of Andre Gretry's L'Amant Jaloux, 1971. Contbr. to Opera Jrnl. Mbrships: Past Pres., other offs., Nat. Opera Assn.; Nat. Assn. of Tchrs. of Singing; Chgo. Singing Thcrs. Guild; Pi Kappa Lambda; Phi Mu Alpha Sinfonia; Omicron Delta Kappa; Phi Eta Sigma; Sigma Sonfonia; Omicron Delta Kappa; Phi Eta Sigma; Sigma Alpha Epsilon; Opera III (VP, 1979, Pres., 1980). Hons: Titcomb Award, best Ala. singer, Metrop. Opera Regional Auditions, New Orleans, 1975; Full Schlrship., Opera Ldrship. Schl., Tanglewood, 1958; Outstanding Grad., Opera Dept., Univ. of S. Calif., 1971. Hobbies: Electric railroads; Swimming; Golf. Address: 1815 S. Highland Ave., Lombard, IL 60148, USA. 2, 9.

REIMUELLER, Ross Carl, b. 16 Nov. 1937, Dayton, Ohio, USA. Conductor. Educ: B Mus, Oberlin Conserv. of Music, 1960; M Mus, New England Conser. of Music, 1962; Mozarteum Akademie, Salzburg, Austria, 1958-59. Debut: La Rondine (Puccini), Denver, Colo., 1963. Career: Cond. (opera) - Madame Butterfly, La Boheme, La Traviata, Carmen, Susannah, The Marriage of Figaro, Met. Opera Nat. Co., 1965-67; Carmen, San Fran. Spring Oera, 1968; La Generentola, Rigoletto, Faust, Lucia de Lammermoor, La Traviata, La Boheme, Susannah, Cosi Fan Futte, NY City Opera, 1970-74, tec.; Cond. (Musical Comedy) - Candide, 1491, My Fair Lady, Rosalinda, Dumas & Son, Gigi, Kismet; LA Civic Light Opera, 1967 - 77. etc.; Musical Dir., LA Civic Light Opera, 1967-77. & Houston Music Theatre, 1968, etc. Recordings: Gigi (Lerner & Loewe), original Broadway cast recording, 1973. Pub. in prep.; The Unwritten Vocal Appoggiatura, Mbr., Pi Kappa Lambda. Address: 38 W 87th St. Apt. 5A, NY, NY 10024, USA.

REINECKE, Hans-Peter, b. 27 June, 1926, Ortelsburg, Ostpreussen, Germany. Institute Director. Educ: Goettingen Univ., 1946-48; Hamburg Univ.; Berlin Conserv. 1 s. Career incls: Dir., State Inst. Musicol., Berlin, 1967; Prof., Musicol., Hamburg Univ., 1967; Hochschule für Musik, Hamburg, 1973; Dir., Music Instrument Mus., State Inst. Musicol., Berlin, 1975-. Publs. incl: Stereo-Akustik, 1966; Musik und Verstehen (ed. w. P Faltin), 1974; Hoeren und Verstehen (w. H. Rauhe & W Ribke), 1975. Contbr. to jrnls. Mbr. profl. orgs. Address: Offenbacherstr. 16, 1 Berlin 33 (Wilmersdorf), Germany Fed. Repub.

REINER, Karel, b. 27 June 1910, Zatec, Czechoslovakia. Composer; Former Pianist. Educ: J D, Fac. of Law, also studies in musicol., Fac. of Philos., Charles Univ., Prague; pvte. studies in composition w. Alois Haba, 1929-31; Dips. in composition (Jesef Suk's master class), & quarter -& sixth-ton systems (w. Alois Haba), Acad. of Music. m. Hana Steiner, 2 d. Debut: 1932. Career: Pianist, 1931-47; Musical Collaborator w. E F Burian on theatre 'D', 1935-38; w. gramophone firm, ESTA, 1937-39; w. Opera House of the 5th of May, 1945-47; w. Union of Czech. Composers, 1947-50; Hd., Music Dept., Ctrl. House of Folk Art, 1951 — 59; composing full-time, 1960-. Compositions incl: Over 100 works for pinao, chmbr. ensemble, orch., vocalists, etc., also songs, film scores, & an opera, The Awful Dragon, The Princess & The Shoemaker. Compositions Recorded incl: Sonatas for pinao & for violine; Trio for Flute, Bass Clarinet & Percussion; Concertante Suite for orch.; Three Percussion; Concertante Suite for orch.; Three Compositions for piano; Sujets for guitar. Publs: Singers Ensemble, 1955. Contbr. to: Rytmus review Singers Ensemble, 19655. Contbr. to: Rytmus review (Ed., 1935-38 & 45-47); Musical Ed.; Kulturni politika, 1945-49, & Svobodne Ceskoslovensko, 1945-47. Mbr. of sev. music socs. Hons. incl: Decoration for Outstanding Work, 1961; Merited Artist, 1967. Hobbies: Swimming; Touring. Address: Hviezdoslavova é, 10 Vinohrady, 10100 Prague, Czechoslovakia. 3.

REINHARD, Karol, b. 19 March 1929, Miawa, Poland. Manager; Artistes' Agent. Educ: studied econs. m. Izabella Reinhard, 1 d. Career: Mgr., Tropicale Tmaitii Granda Banda; Agt., Wojewodzka Agencja Impresz Artystycznycm, ul. Wieczorka 10, Katowice. Mbr.: Polskie Stowarzyszenie Yazzowe, Warsaw. Contbr. to: Pagart, Warsaw. Hobbies: Skiing; Travel; Horseriding. Address: ul. Lentza 6101, Krakow, Poland.

REINHARD, Kurt August Georg, b. 27 Aug. 1914, Giessen, Germany. University Professor (retired). Educ: Studied musicol., ethnol., hist. of art. w. Dr's degree in 1938; Pvte. instrn. in piano playing, 1926-33; studies in comp. & paino playing, 1933-36. m. Ursula Honisch, 2 c. Career: Dir., Berlin

Phonograph Archieves, 1948-68; Var. lectures on TV & radio; Perfs. of comps. on radio. Compositions; Many songs for voice & piano or orch., cantatas, piano works, works for orch. &w orks for chamber msuic. Publs: Die Musik Birmas, 1939; Die Musik exotischer Volker, 1951; Chinesische Musik, 1956; Turkische Musik, 1962; Einfuhrung in die Musikethnologie, 1968; Volkslieder von der ostturkischen Schwarzmeerkuste, 1968; Les Traditions Musicales: Turquire, 1969. Contbr. to sci. series 'Beitrage zur Ethnomusikologie', Mbr. of many sci. socs. Recip., Hon. deed for Turkish Govt. Var. hobbies. Address: Vogelsang 29, 6330 Wetzlar, German. Fed. Repub. 19, 23, 29.

REINHARDT, Walter, b. 3 April 1915, Oels/Schlesien, Germany. Educ: at Breslau. m. Luise Weinsheimer. Career: Cond., State Theatre, Giessen, 1945; German Theatre, Munich, 1947-48; Prod. Mgr., & Prog. Arranger, Bavarian Radio; Cond., Walter Rheinhardt Orch. Compositions incl. num. songs. Address: 16 Hangstrasse, 8035 Gauting, Germany.

REINHART, Carole Dawn, b. 20 Dec. 1941, Roselle, NJ, USA. Trumpeter. Educ: BA, Univ. of Miami, Fla., USA; Juiliard Schl. of Music Preparatory Div.; Vienna Acad. of Music, Reifezeugnis; MS, Juilliard Schl. of Music. m. Manfred Stoppacher. Career: Num. solo concerts throughotu the US, Can., Aust., Orient & Europe; Num. TV apps. in USA (among them 'Tonight' Show, Al Hirt Show, To Tell the Truth, etc.). Hong Kong, Aust., Germany & Austria; Radio recordings in Geramny & Austria; Orchl. experience w. Leopold Stokowski, Fabien Sevitzky & others. Recordings: Deutsche Grammophon -Debut 2555 008; BASF - Haydn Concerto & Hummel Concerto, Leopold Mozart Concerto. Mbrships: Int. Trumpet Guild, Bd. of Dirs. Hobbies: Reading; Swimming; Rug-Hooking. Address: Stormstr. 4. D-1000 Berlin 19, German Fed. Repub.

REINOLD, Helmut, b. 11 May 1926, Leipzig, Germany. Music Author. Educ: pvte. study of piano, violin & theory; Cologne Univ., 1946-50. m. Anne Reinold (nee Blum). Career: Freelance team-mbr., W German Radio Network, Cologne, 1947-; some newspaper writing; Librettist for L'Amfiparnaso, Pantalon and Colombine, Nichts Neues aus Pergugia; Transl. operas; worked in Kommunal Kulturverwaltung (Hd. Cultural Off., city of Bergisch-Gladbach). 1970-73. Contbr. var. articles on Methodologie der Musik wissenschaft, zur Musiksoziologie und Theorie des musikalshen Hörens, to var. profl. jrnls. Mbrships: Sox. for Music Rsch.; Int. Soc. for Musicol. Address: Klosterhof 5, 5531 Niederehe (Eifel), German Fed. Repub.

REIS, Joan Sachs, b. 11 Mar. 1922, Louisville, Ky., USA. Lecturer. Educ: BMus (violin), Univ. of Cinn. Coll.-Conserv. of Music, 1944; MMus (musicol.), ibid., 1945; studied music hist. w. Dr. Gerhard Herz, Univ. of Louisville. m. Robert W Reis (dec.), 2 s. Career: fac. mbr., Uiv. of Cinn. Coll.-Conserv. of Music, 1945-70; now Instructor of Music hist. at N Kentucky Univ. Publ: Signs of the Times in Music, 1971. Contbr. to Cinn. Enquirer mag. mbr., Am. Musicol. Soc. & matinee Musicale Club, Cinn. Hons: Peter Froelich Jr. Prize for a contrapuntal comp., Cinn. Coll.-Conserv., 1944; Wanda & Clifton Chalmers Prize for histl. & critical rsch., 1945. Hobbies: Art; Swimming. Address: 1815 Wm. H Taft Rd., Apt. 703, Cinn., OH 45206, USA.

REISSINGER, Marianne, b. 4 Jan. 1945, Marzell/Baden, Germany. Musicologist. Educ: Dr. Hochschen Conserv., Frankfurt am Main; PhD, Univ. of Frankfurt am Main, 1970. Career: Solo Clarinettis & Chmbr. Musician w. num. pub. concerts; Classics Mgr., TELDEC Records GmbH, Hamburg, 1971-78; Musikredakteur und Musikkritiker der 'Abendzeitung', München. Publs: Ernst Eichners Symphonies, 1970; P Hindemith: Sancta Süsanna; P Hindemith: Wind Chamber Music; P Hindemith: Mörder, Hoffnung der Trauen, 1978. Contbr. to: Musikforschung; Mittelrheinisches Tonkünstler-Lexicon; Hindemith-Jahrbuch; Fono-Forum; Frankfurter Rundschau; Frankfurter Neue Presse. Mbrships: Soc. for Music Rsch., Cassell; German Mozart Soc.; Arbeitsgemeinschaft für Mittelrheinische Musikgeschichte. Hobbies: Art History; Travel; Modern Literature; Sailing. Address: Ludolfusstr. 5, 6 Frankfurt am Main 90, German Fed. Repub.

REITZ, Heiner, b. 14 Sept. 1925, Zürich, Switz. Violinist; Pianist. Educ: Tchrs. Dip. Zürich Acad. of Music, 1945; Dip. Concertist, Lausanne Inst. de Ribaupierre, 1947. m. Marianne Bandi, 2 c. Debut: Violin Ricital, Zürich, 1950. Career: Concert Soloist w. Orch. & Chmbr. Music; Violinist & Pianist w. Lucerne Fest. Strings toured S. Am., Europe, USA, Can. & Mexico; Ldr. of Virtuoso Class at Zürich Acad. of Music, 1964-. Comps. incl: 12 Caprices, Violin Solo, 1972; 12 Caprices, Flute Solo, 1973; 12 Caprices, Violoncello Solo, 1976. Publs: The Technique of Violin Practising, 1967; Let's Learn With the Masters, 1969.

Mbr. num. profl. orgs. Hobbies: Chess; Mountaineering. Address: Etzelstrasse 5, 8624 Grüt, B. Betzikon, Near Zürich, Switz.

REJTO, Gabor, b. 23 Jan. 1916, Budapest, Hungary. Concert Cellist; Professor of Music. Educ: Univ. of Budapest; Artists' Dip., Royal Hungarian Acad. Music. m. Alice C. Rejto, 1 s., 1 d. Debut: Budapest; London. Career: Num. concert tours around world; Mbr., Lener, Gordon, Paganini Quartets & Alma Trio; Prof., Music, Univ. Southern Calif., Los Angeles, Promona Coll., Claremont, Calif., & Music Acad. of the W. Santa Barbara, Calif., USA. Recordings: RCA; CRI; Decca; Orion. Mbrships: Am. String Tchrs. Assn.; Music Tchrs. Assn. Calif. Hon: Artist-Tchr. of Yr. Award, Am. String Tchrs. Assn., 1972. Hobbies: Photography; Chess. Mgmt: Mariedi Anders, San Fran. Address: 6230 Warner Dr., Los Angeles, CA 90048, USA.

REJTO, Peter A, b. 5 Dec. 1948, San Mateo, Calif., USA. Violoncellist. Educ: BS, Univ. of Southern Calif., Los Angeles, 1971; Music Acad. of W. Santa Barbara, Calif., 1966, 68, 70; Aspen Music Schl., Colo., 1967, 71. Debut: Hunter Coll. Recital, NYC, 1973. Career: Pers. throghout US in recital & concerto inclng. Boston, Wash., Phila., Mpls., Chgo., Los Angeles & San Fran.; Wigmore Hall Recital, London, UK, 1974; Tour of Bulgaria; Asst. Prof. of Music, Mich. State Univ., E Lansing; Dallas Symph., 1975; St. Louis Symph., 1979. Recordings incl: Duo Fantasy (Zador). Hons. incl: Debut Award, Young Musicians Fndn., Los Angeles, 1971; Chgo. Civic Orch. 1st Prize, 1974. Hobbies: Flying; Skiing. Mgmt: Young Concert Artists Inc., 75 4 55th St., NY, NY, USA. Address: 9129 Geyser Ave., Northridge, CA 91324, USA.

REMEDIOS, Alberto Telisforo, b. 27 Feb. 1935, Liverpool, UK. Opera & Concert Singer. Educ: RAM. m. Judith Hosken, 2 s., 1 d. Debut: Sadlers Wells Opera, 1955. Career: Sadlers Wells Opera (now Engl. Nat. Opera); Welsh Nat. Opera; Royal Opera House Covent Garden; Metropolitan NY; Frankfurt Opera; S Africa, Angers, Rouen, Spain, Orange, San Fran., San Diego, Seattle, etc.; perfs. w. major British Orch.; Frequent broadcaster on Radio & TV. Recordings incl: Mark in Tippett's The Midsummer Marriage; Ring Cycle. Hons: Queen's Prize, RCM, 1957; 1st Prize, Young Int. Opera Singers' Competition, Bulgaria, 1963. Hobbies: Soccer; Record Collecting. Mgmt: S A Gorlinsky, 35 Dover St., London, W1X 4NJ, UK. Address: c/o Mgmt.

REMNANT, Mary Elizabeth Teresa, b. 13 Jan. 1935, London, UK. Musician; Musicologist; Violin, Piano & Medieval instruments. Educ: RCM, 1952-56; St. Anne's Coll., Oxford Univ., 1962-67; MA.; D Phil.; GRSM.; ARCM. Career: Tchr. of piano, violin & recorder, Colet Court, St. Paul's Jr. Schl., 1956-60; RCM (Jr. Exhibitioners), 1961-62; Violin Tchr. & Lectr., Goldsmiths Coll., Univ. of London, 1967-69; Lectr., RCM, 1970-; Tchrs. of piano & violin, London Oratory Jr. Choir, 1973-; performer & lectr. in Italy; France; Belgium; USA. & Switzerland; Mbr., London Medieval Grp. Recordings: Var. items of medieval music. Publ: Musical Instruments of the West, 1978. Contbr. to: Proceedings of the Royal Musical Assn.; Galpin Soc. Jrnl.; Music & Letters; Early Music; Musical Times. Mbrships: Royal Musical Assn.; ISM; Committee, Galpin Soc.; British Archaeological Assn.; Lute Soc. Hons: Tagore Gold Medal, RCM, 1956; Winston Churchill Travelling Fellowship, 1967. Hobbies: Travel; Photography. Address: 15 Fernshaw Rd., Chelsea, London SW10. 27, 29.

RENDALL, David, b. 11 Oct. 1948, London, UK. Opera & Concert Singer (Tenor). Educ: RAM; Recital dip., Mozarteum, Salzburg. m. Kathryn Anne George. Debut: Glyndebourne Touring Opera (Ferrando in Cosi fan Tutte). Career: apps. worldwide incl. Metropolitan, NY, Covent Garden, Paris Opera, San Francisco Opera, Buenos Aires, Hamburg; film of Bruckner's Te Deum w. von Karajan. Recordings: Cosi fan Tutte; Ariodante (Handel). Hons: Young Musician, Greater London Arts Assn., 1973; Bulbenkian Music Fellowship, 1976. Hobbies: Hunting; Walking. Mgmt: Stafford Law Associates. Address: Sandrock, Cornells Bank, Newock, Sussex, UK.

RENDELL, Don, b. 4 Mar. 1926, Plymouth, Devon, UK. Musician (Saxophone; Flute; Clarinet). m. Joan Ruth, 1 d. Career incls: Mbr. num. bands inclng. Oscar Rabin; Ted Heath; Stan Kenton; John Dankworth; Woody Herman; STephan Grappelli; var. own small grps.; Appeared at 1968 Int. Jazz Festival, Antibes, France & Jazz Expo 68, Royal Festival Hall, Lodon; Num. radio & TV appearances, UK & Europe; Tchr., Saxophone, RAM, 1971-; Woodwind instruments, ILEA, Goldsmith Coll. Compositions incl: Train Ride; Ballad of Wyer Hall; Jane Ruth; Suite for Saxophone Quartet. Recordings incl: Space Walk, 1972; 'Live' at Av-Garde Gallery, (w. Joe Palin Trio), 1975. Publs: Robbins Flute Tutor, Pts. 1 & 2, 1973. Mbrships: PRS; Clarinet Saxophone Soc. (VP). Address: 23 Weir Hall Gdns., London N18 1BH, UK.

RENÉ, Jean (René Daugaard), b. 25 Dec. 1935, Copenhagen, Denmark. Jazz Percussionist. Debut: Blue Note, Copenhagen, 1953. Career: Tours throughout world w. artists incl. Jim Hall, Sonny Stitt, Brew More, Herb Geller, Sahip Shibab, Dexter Gordon & Dizzy Gillespie; TV, film & radio apps; apps. w. Delta Rhythm Boys, Platters, Buddy Cole, etc., Madrid. Recordings: 14 LPs, 25 EPs. Hobbies: Music; Billiards.

RENISON, Herbert J. b. 7 April 1915, Quilmes, Argentina. Concert Pianist; Educator. Educ: Grad., Nat. Conserv. of Buenos Aires, 1938. m. Paula Gerard, 1965. Debut: Buenos Aires, 1938. Career incl: Recitals in Argentina, Uruguay & USA; Mbr., Piano Fac., Sherwood Music Schl., Chgo., 1946-; Bd. Dirs., ibid., 1970-. Mbrships: Past Dir. & Pres., Soc. of Am. Musicians, Chgo., 1961-68; MTNA; Cliff Dwellers Club, Chgo. Hobbies: Reading; Coorespondence; Social Life. Address: Sherwood Music Schl., 1014 S Mich. Ave., Chgo., IL 60605, USA.

RENNERT, Jonathan, b. 17 Mar. 1952, London, UK. Organist; Author. Educ: Fndn. Scholar, RCM; Organ Scholar, St. John's Coll., Cambridge; MA, Cantab; FRCO; ARCM; LRAM. Career incls: num. organ recitals, radio & TV progs., UK, France, Belgium, Netherlands, Germany, Switz., W Indies, USA & Can.; Dir. of Music, Holy Trinity Ch., Barnes, 1969-71, St. Jude's Ch., Courtfield Gdns., London, 1975-76, St. Matthew's Ch., Ottawa, Can., 1976-78; Dir., Am. Community Choirs in London, 1975-76; Musical Dir., Cambrdige Opera, 1972-74; St. Michael's, Cornhill, London, 1979-; occasional Course-Dir., RSCM. Has made sev. recordings as Soloist, accomp. harpsichord continuo player. Author: William Crotch (1775-1847) - composer. artist, teacher, 1975; Dr. George Thalben-Ball, a biography, 1979. Contbr. to musical jrnls. Mbr., num. profl. orgs. Recip. var. hons. Address: 8 Ensor Mews, London SW7 3BT, UK. 28, 30.

RENNIE, Susan Elizabeth, b. SS Jan. 1956, Dumfries, UK. Pianist; Teacher. Educ: Buckinghamshire Schl. of Music; RCM; GRSM. Career: Recitals in Essen, Oberhausen, Offenbourg & Oberkirch, German Fed. Repub., 1977, 79; selected for Yehudi Menuhin's Live Music Now scheme, 1979; specialised interest in British piano music; recitals for Brit. Music Soc.; Prof. of piano & chmbr. music, LCM. Hons: Kathleen Long Memorial prize (RCM), 1976; Allcard award, 1978, & Maisie Lewis Recital award, 1979 (Worshipful Co. of Musicians). Hobbies: Walking; Reading; Meditation; Real Beer. Address: 26 Sumner Pl., London SW7 3NT, UK.

RENOUF, David, b. 21 Apr. 1928, London, UK. Music Educator. Educ: TCL; London Univ., MA; Dip. in Educ.; B Mus; FTCL; FTSC; LRAM; ARCM; ARCP. m. Rosemary Pearce, 2 d. Career incl: Hd. of Music Dept., Nottingham Coll. of Educ: Hd. of Music, Trent Polytech., Clifton, Nottingham. Publs: Oxford Student's Harmony, 2 vols., 1965-66; Approach to Music, 6 vols., 1968-71. Ed., The Music Tchr. Address: Trent Polytech., Clifton, Nottingham NG11 8NS, UK.

RENSCH, Gabrielle, b. 20 Sept. 1944, Toronto, Ont., Can. Teacher of Violin & Viola. Educ: ARCT, Toronto. m. Robert. Career: fac., Royal Conserv., Toronto; Freelance playing, NYC; NJ Symph. mbr., AFM, Toronto & NYC. Hons: 2 yrs. on AFM scholarship prog., Congress of Strings; scholarship & silver medals at Royal Conserv., Toronto. Address: 65 High Pk. Ave., Toronto, Ont. M6P 2R7, Can.

RENSIN, Hymen, b. 10 May 1904, NYC, USA. Musician; Conductor; Educator; Mathematician. Educ: BS, CCNY, 1926; AM, Columbia Univ., NY, 1926; var. perm. licenses & certs. of competency; Supv. Schl. Music Dip., Tchrs. Coll., Columbia Univ., 1927; Conds. Dip., Am. Orch. Soc., NY, 1928; PhD (ABD), Music Educ., Tchrs. Coll., NY, 1937. m. Helen L Udowitz, 1 s. Debut: Chas. D Isaacson Concerts, NYC, 1921. Career: Profl. violinist, violist & cond. w. sev. orchs., chamber music grps. & soloist; Music Dir. of summer camps & dev. 'Musicrafts' activity: Spkr., Lectr., Exhbr. & Clinician at convens., schls. & on radio, etc.; Cond., Ev. Sess. Symph. Orch. & Chorus, CCNY & Instr., Music Dept., 1927-39; Chmn., Music Dept., Bx. HS of Sci., 1939-74; Lectr. & Adj. Asst. prof. in Maths at CCNY, 1947-72. Compositions incl: Three Operettas for Childdren, divers orchl. & chmber music works; Alma Mater (words & music, also rec.). Var. recordings. Publs. incl: Basic Course in Music, 1955, 5th rev. edn. '74. Mbr., profl. socs. Recip. many hons. & awards. Var. hobbies: Address: P.O. Box 578, Lenox, MA 01240, USA.

RENTON, Barbara Hampton, b. 29 July 1937, NY, NY, USA. Musicologist; Musical Iconography; Organist; Choral Director. Educ: MA, CUNY, 1968; MPhil, ibid., 1979; PhD, ibid., 1980, m. Joseph A. Renton, 4 c. Career: Ed., Inst. for Studies in Am. Music Newsletter, 1973-74; Chief ed., RIdIM/RCMI

Newsletter, 1977-. Publs: Women in American Music College Teaching, A Statistical Study, 1979. Contbr. to: Coll. Music Soc. Symphosium; Notes, Jrnl. of MLA; Hudebni Rozhledy (Czech.). Mbrships. incl: Int. Musicol. Soc.; Am. Musicol. Soc.; Coll. Music Soc.; Int. Assn. of Music Libs. Music Libs. Assn.; Janacek Soc. (Switz.); Dvorck Soc. of GB; Smetana Soc. (Czech.). Hons: Phi Beta Kappa, 1957; Smetana award (Czech.) Fellowship of Am. Assn. of Univ. Women, 1977-78. Address: 78 E Lincoln Ave., Valley Stream, NY 11580, USA.

RESNIK, Regina, b. 30 Aug. 1922, Operatic Mezzo-soprano. Educ: Hunter Coll., NYC. m. Arbit Blatas. Debut: Bklyn. Acad. of Music, 1942; as Leonore in Fidelio w. NYC Opera, Mexico City, 1943; as Leonore in Il Trovatore, Metrop. Opera, NYC; as Sieglinde, Bayreuth, 1953; London, 1957. Career incls: apps., Chgo. Opera Theatre, San Fran. Opera, Vienna, Berlin, Stuttgart, Buenos Aires; Prod., Carmen, Hamburg State Opera, 1971; Prod. & Actor, Falstaff, Teatr Wielki, Warsaw, 1975. Address: c/o Metrop. Opera Co., NY, NY 10018, USA. 16.

RESTOUT, Denise, b. 24 Nov. 1915, Paris, France. Musician (Piano, Organ, Harpsichord); Writer. Educ: Conserv. Nat. Musique, Paris. Debut: Paris, 1938. Career incls: Dir., Landowska Ctr., Lakeville, Conn. Recordings: Bach Suites, harpsichord solo, REBI; Bach Concerto, accomp. harpsichord, RCA. Publ: Landowska On Music (w. Robert Hawkins), 1965, Contbr. to jrnls. Mbrships: Am. Musicol. Soc.; ALA; AGO; Local 514, Am. Fedn. Musicans. Hons: Citation, Poland Mag. Hobbies: Reading; Cooking. Address: Landowska Ctr., PO Box 313, Lakeville, CT 06039, USA.

RESZKE, Radomir, b. 26 Oct. 1920, Moscow, USSR. Composer & Conductor. Educ: HS of Music, Wroclaw, pedagog. fac., 1952, cond., 1954. comp., 1967. m. Gabriela Swiderska, 5 c. Debut: Wroclaw, 1954. Career: Cond., Wroclaw Phil., 1954-63; Artistic Dir., 1960-63, Mbr. Fac., 1955-, Lectr., 1967-, Prof., 1978-, Dean Fac., 1968, Hd. Music Educ., Wrocalw Conserv. Comps. incl: (overtures) Academic, 1972; Sport, 1957; Suite of Polish Dances, 1966; 2 Trumpte Concertos; Trombone Concerto; Sinfonia De Profundis; Sonata for Cello; Monodrama Ewa, 1978. Recordings for Polish Radio & TV. Publs: The Theory of Conducting, 1965; Knowledge about Instruments with Acoustics, 1966; Special Knowledge About Instruments for Conductors of Amateur Ensembles, 1966; Special Knowledge about instruments for Band Conds., 1966. Contbr. to var. publs. Mbrships: Soc. of Polish Musical Artists; Assn. of Polish Comps.; Soc. of Authors & Comps.; Lower Silesian Soc. Music. Hons. incl: Rewrad of Min. of Culture & Arts, 1969; Reward of Town of Wroclaw, 1972; Gold & Silver Cross of Merit, Polonia Restituta, 1978, etc. Address: ul. Modlinska 77a, 53-152 Wroclaw, Poland.

RETALLICK, Robert Henry, b. 24 Oct. 1935, Leeton, NSW, Aust. Musician (Violin). Educ: Violin w. Florent Hoogstoel, Sydney, Australia & Oskar Back, Amsterdam, Netherlands. m. Penelope Juliet Einzig, 1 s., 1 d. Career: w. Syndey Symph. Orch. & London Symph. Orch.; Ldr., Netherlands Opera & Sadlers Wells, London; Recitalist; Chmbr. Musician. Hobbies: Chess; Reading; Tennis; Crossword Puzzles. Address: 59 S Park Rd., London SW 19, UK.

RETCHITZKY, Marcel, b. 20 Feb. 1924, Geneva, Switzerland. Composer. Educ: Studied Violin & Dir. of Orch., Conserv. of Music, Geneva; self-taught Comp. m. Fanni Jones, 4 children. Comps. incl: The Grass of Error (chmbr. opera); 2 Symphs.; Le Chant de l'Amour Triomphant (ballet); melodies for voice & piano; (recorded by Radio Geneva) 2 Str. quartets; Concerto for Piano & Orch.; Rhapsody for Mezzo-soprano & Orch.; Humulus le Muet (chmbr. opera). Mbrships: Soc. of Dramatic Authors & Comps., Paris; Soc. of Swiss Comps. Address: 14 Boulevard des Philosophes, CH 1205 Geneva, Switzerland.

RETTICH, Wilhelm (Willem), b. 3 July 1892, Leipzig, Germany. Conductor; Composer; Pianist. Educ: Conserv. Leipzig. m. Elsa Barther, 1 d. Career: Cond.-Asst., Opera Theatre, Leipzig, 1912 & 1921-22; Cond., Operas, Plauen, Königsberg, Bremerhaven, Stettin, 1928; Cond., Broadcasting Leipzig, 1928-31, Berlin, 1931-33. Comps. incl: works for orch., chmbr. & vocal music. Contbr. of recordings to most of the radio stns. in Germany & Netherlands & occasional articles to newspapers & music reviews. Mbrships. incl: Dutch Comps. Soc. Recip., Bundesverdienstkreuz, Germany, 1971. Address: Bismarckstr. 3, Baden-Baden, German Fed. Repub.

RETZEL, Frank, b. 11 Aug. 1948, Detroit Mich., USA. Compser. Educ: B Mus, 1972, M Mus, 1974, Wayne State Univ.; early pvte. studies w. Lode van Dessal, Ruth Shaw Wylie, Harold Laudenslager, James Hartway, Ralph Shapey. m.

Kathleen Ann Buhl. Career: Choir Dir. & Msuical Dir., var. Cath. Chs., Detroit area, 1962-74; Fellowship for doct. studies in Comp., Univ. of Chgo., 1974-76; Mgr., Ralph Shapey's Contemporary Players, ibid.; Co-Dir., Co-Fndr. & Comp., improvisation Ensemble, 1975; works broadcasts. Comps. incl: Cables 87, (for soprano & instruments) 1970; 24 Modules, 1972; mainar Flow, 1973; Dreams of Aesop, 1973; Symbiosis, 1974; Tapestries, 1974; Schism I, 1975; Swamp Music, (for amplified ensemble, lighting & dance) 1976. Mbrships: Am. Musicol. Soc.; Am. Soc. Univ. Comps. Hons: P Paray Comp. Award, 1972; H Laudenslager Comp. Award, 1973. Hobbies: Reading Music. Address: 5482 S Greenwood 301, Chgo., IL 60615, USA.

REUTER, Rudolf, b. 15 Apr. 1920, Muenster, Germany. University Professor; Organist; Harpsichordist. Educ: studied Harpsichord w. Imgard Lechner; State Music Tchrs. Exam. in Piano, Organ & Theory; PhD, 1948; Habilitation (musicol.), 1972. m. Dr. Hannelore Hölzen, 3 c. Debut: 1942. Career: regular radio broadcasts, 1946-74; occasional TV broadcasts, 1965-. Recordings: 10 LPs. Publs. Organos Espanoles, 1963; Orgeln in Westfalen, 1965; Die Orgel in der Denkmalpflege Westfalens, 1971; Bibliographie der Orgal, 1973; Veröffentlichung der Orgelwissenschaftlichen Forschungsstelle, 1965-78. Contbr. to: MGG; Ars Organi; Musikwissensch, Zeitschriften; Zs. Westfalen. Mbrships: Int. Soc. for Musicol.; German Musicol. Soc.; Soc. of Friends of the Organ; French Soc. for the Preservation of Antique Organs; Westphalian Histl. Commn.; German Coll. Assn. Hons: Music Prize, City of Muenster, 1938. Hon. Prof., 1965. Address: Boelestrasse 6, 44 Münster-Angelmodde, German Fed. Repub.

REYMANN, Rita Marie, b. 6 Sept. 1939, Akron, Ohio, USA. Teacher; Pianist; Organist. Educ: BA, Kent State Univ., 1961; Mus M, Ind. Univ., 1966. Career: Instructor in Piano, Univ. of Akron. Publ: Transl., F J Fétis, Traité Complet de la Théorie er de la Pratique de l'Harmonie, I & III, 1966. Mbrships: Nat. MTA; Pres., Summit County Sect., Ohio MTA; NGPT; AGO; Tuesday Musical Club, Akron; Friends of Music; Pi Kappa Lambda; Delta Omicron; Dalcroze Soc. of Am. Hons: Sr. Hon. Prin. Delta Omicraon, 1961; Study Grant, Delta Omicraon Fndn., 1973. Adjudicator, NGPT, 1975. Hobbies: Cooking; Gardening; Reading. Address: 71 Yardley Lane, Akron, OH 44313, USA.

REYNISH, Timothy John, b. 9 Mar. 1938, Axbridge, Somerset, UK. Conductor; Head of School of Wind & Percussion, Royal Northern College of Music. Educ: MA, Caius Coll., Cambridge Univ.; pvte. music study w. Aubrey Brain, Frank Probyn, Sir Adrian Boutl, Dean Dixon; ARCM. m. Hilary Anderson, 3 s., 1 d. Career: Prin. Horn w. Northern Sinfonia, Sadlers Wells Orch., City of Birmingham Symph.; Lectr., Bromsgove Coll. of Further Educ. & Birmingham Extra-Mural Dept., Guest Cond., City of Birmingham Symph., Royal Liverpool Phil., BBC Welsh & Nortghern Orchs., LSO, London Studio Strings, Halle Orch., Amsterdam Sinfonietta, RIAS, Berlin, etc. Mbrships: ISM; Royal Soc. of Musicians. Recip. 3rd Prize, Dimitri Mitropoulos Int. Comp., NY, 1971. Hobbies: Theatre; Squash; Gardening. Mgmt: Ibbs & Tillett. Address: Silver Birches, Bentinck Rd., Altrincham, UK. 3.

REYNOLDS, Anna, b. Canterbury, UK. Opera Singer. Educ: LRAM; FRAM. Debut: Parma, Italy. Career: Apps. at La Scala, Milan & all maj. Italian opera houses; Met. Opera, NY; Lyric Opera, Chgo.; Coven Gdn.; Bayreuth Festival; Salzburg Osterfestpelile; Aix-in-rovence; Edinburgh; Glyndebourne; Berlin & Vienna Festivals; Concerts in all maj. cities. Recordings incl: Messiah (Handel); Orfeo (Monteverdi); Die Meistersinger (Wagner); Beethoven's 9th Symph.; Cantatas (Bach); Mass in B Minor (Bach). Mgmt: Harrison Parrott Ltd., 22 Hillgate St., London W8 7Sr7SR, UK. Address: 37 Chelwood Gdns., Richmond, Surrey, UK. 3, 27.

REYNOLDS, Gordon, b. 30 June 1921, Hull, UK. Organist; Teacher. Educ: RCM; Univ. Coll., Hul; ARCM. m. Lois Mary Rogers, 2 s. Career: has broadcast on radio & TV for 25 yrs.; Organist & Choirmaster, Chapel Royal, Hampton Ct. Palace, 1967-; prof. of Harmony, Royal Mil. Schl. of Music, 1969-. Author of many books on music educ. & ch. music. Consultant Ed.: Music in Education. Mbrships: Athenaeum; RSA. Address: Hampton Ct. Palace, E Molesey, Surrey, UK.

REYNOLDS, Michael John, b. 15 Mar. 1930, London, UK. Music Critic; Editor of 'Music & Musicians'. Mbr. of the Critics' Circle (Music Sect.) Hobbies: Playing the harpsichord. Address: 51A Ifield Rd., London W 14, UK. 3.

REYNOLDS, Stephen Charles, b. 22 Mar. 1947, Southport, UK. Concert Pianist; Composer. Educ: GRSM, ARMCM (Perfs.), ARCM (Tchrs.), Royal Manchester Coll. of Music, 1964-68. Debut: Liverpool, 1961. Career: Many piano recitals

throughout Brit., 1967-76; 3 Chopin recitals, London, 1969; Recital, Vienna Conserv. of Music, 1970; Sev. radio braodcasts & 1 TV app.; Sev. commissions for comps.; Piano Staff, Royal Northern Coll. of Music, Manchester. Comps. of chmbr., piano, choral & orchl. works; The Solitude of the High Mountains, concert piece for organ. Mbr., ISM. Contbr. to Delius Soc. Hons. incl: Silver Medal, Gian Baptista Int. Piano Competiton, Vercelli, Italy, 1972. Hobbies incl: Architecture. Address: 1 Park Rd., Eastham, Wirral, Cheshire L62 8AH, UK.

REZAC, Ivan, b. 5 Nov. 1924, Revnice, Czechoslovakia. Composer. Educ: Grad., Acad. of Music & Dramatic Arts, Prague, 1953; Study of piano w. Frantisek Rauch, composition w. Vaclav Dobias. m. Helena Radischova, 1 d. Career: Asst. Prof., Acad. of Music & Dramatic Arts, Prague, 1966-; Dir., Prague Symph. Orch., 1968-. Compositions (recorded): Piano Trio; Symphonic Overture; The Return, for cello & orch.; Introduction & Allegro for Piano; Piano Concerto No. 2; Duo for Cello & Piano; Sisyphus Sunday, for Piano; Musica da camera. Contbr. to articles & reviews to Czech. jrnls. Mbrships: Union of Czech Composers & Concert Artists; Bd. Mbr., Prague Spring Int. Music Fest. Hons: Special Prize for Overtture to Majakovsky's poem The Right Thing, Artistic Jubilee Competition, 1960. Address: Krakovska 19, 110 00 Prague 1, Czechoslovakia.

REZITS, Joseph, b. 16 June 1925, NY, NY, USA. Concert Pianist; Professor; WRiter; Lecturer; Bibliographer. Educ: Artist Dip., Curtis Inst. of Music; BMus, Univ. of Ill.; MMus, ibid.; Profl. Dip., Columbia Univ.; DMA, Univ. of Colorado. m. Robert Weingart Rezits, 2 s. Debut: w. Phila. Orch., 1950. Career: Tours in USA, Can. & Aust. as soloist, ensemble player, lectr.; adjudicator; reviewer; Fac., Schl. of Music, Ind. Univ. num. recordings. Publs: Source Materials for Piano Techniques, 1965; Teacher's Guide to the New Scribner Music Library, 1973; The Pianist's Resource Guide, 1974 (revised 2nd ed., 1978); Source Materials for Keyboard Skills, 1975. Contbr. to num. profl. jrnls. Mbrships: Pi Kappa Lambda; Coll. Music Soc.; MENC; MTNA. Hons: Winner, Phila. Orch. Youth Auditions, 1949. Hobbies: Photography; Walking. Address: Schl. of Music, Ind. Univ., Bloomington, IN 47401, USA.

RHEA, Claude Hiram, Jr., b. 26 Oct. 1927, Carrollton, Mo., USA. Dean of University Music School. Educ: AB., William Jewell Coll., 1950; B Mus Ed., Fla. State Univ., 1953; M Mus Ed. ibid., 1954; Ed D., 1958. m. Carolyn Turnage, 2 s., 2 d. Career: Concerts, solo vocalist, Europe, Latin Am., SE. Asia, Africa & USA.; Lectures in Brazil, Chile, Japan, Hong Kong, Israel, Jordan, India, Indonesia, Malaysia, Rhodesia, Kenya & Zambia; Dean, Schl. of Music, Samford Univ., Birmingham, Ala.; Prof. of Music Lit. & Voice, ibid. Composer, num. individual children's songs publd. in collection & music periodicals. Recordings: Claude Rhea Sings, 1955; Sacred Masterpieces, 1956; Blessed Assurance, 1957; Majestic Themes, 1960; The Radiance of Christmas, 1965. Publs: A Child's Life In Song, 1965; The Sacred Oratorios of Georg Philip Telemann, 2 volumes, 1958. Contbr. to var. profl. jrnls. Mbrships: Music Educators Nat. Conf.; Pi Kappa Lambda; Phi Mu Alpha Sinfonia. Recip., Birmingham, Ala., Silver Bowl Award, Festival of Arts, 1974. Address: 3701 River Oaks Lane, Birmingham, AL 35223, USA. 7, 12.

RHODES, Burt, b. 17 Apr. 1923, Guiseley, Yorks., UK. Musical Director; Orchestrator; Composer; Pianist; Organist. Educ: self-taught. m. Flora Rhodes, 2 d. Career: dance band pianist; theatre musician; work for BBC incl. Musical Dir., Morecambe & Wise radio shows, & TV shows starring Benny Hill, Beryl Reid, Terry Scott; Musical Dir., Talk of the Town since 1966; Musical Dir., Espresso Bongo. Comps. incl: num. orchestrations incl. Stop the World, I want to Get Off, Dr. No, Mardi Gras, André Previn's Good Companions, BBC-TV pantomimes, 2 Royal Variety Perfs., etc. Recordings: 15 LPs of own comps. Mbrships: ISM; Performing Right Soc.; Musicians' Union; Eccentric Club; MMC; Lord's Taverners; Yorks. Co. Cricket Club. Hobby: Cricket. Address: Roseways, 9 Kingsley Ave., Sutton, Surrey SM1 3RE, UK.

RHODES, Cherry, b. 28 June 1943, Brooklyn, NY, USA. Educator; Concert Organist. Educ: BMus, Curtis Inst. of Music; Phila., Pa., 1964; HS Music, Munich, 1964-67; Pvte. study, Paris, 1967-69; Summer Schls., Harvard & Univ. of Pa., 1961, 62, 63. m. Prof. Ladd Thomas. Debut: Soloist w. Phila. Orch., 2970; London, 1976. Career: Soloist w. Phila. Orch., S German Radio Orch., Chamber Orch. of French Nat. Radio; Recitals at Lincoln Center, NYC, Notre Dame, Paris; num. apps. at nat. & regional conventions of AGO; Perfs. at sev. Bach fests. & at fests. in Bratislava, Nurnberg, Paris St. Albans, Luxembourg & Vienna; Gave opening recital on new organ at John F Kennedy Center in Washington, DC; Brodcast perfs. in US, Canada & Europe. Contbr. to AGO-RCCO mag. Mbrships:

Exec. Comm., NYC Chapt., AGO, 1974-75; AGO dual member (NYC & Pasadena Chapts.) 1976-. Mbr. Corp., Ruth & Clarence Mader Memorial Scholarship Fund. Num. hons. Hobbies: Swimming; Dancing; Travelling; Visiting Museums. Address: School of Music, Univ. of S. Calif., Univ. Pk., Los Angeles, CA 90007, USA.

RHODES, Emma Dora, b. 15 Jan. 1899, Mexborough, Yorks., UK. Teacher of Singing, Piano, Theory & Aural Culture. Educ: Schl. of Art, Sheffield, 1918; Royal Acad. of Music; Lic., ibid., Singing, 1926. Career: Sheffield Radio until 1926; Manchester BBC Singing, 1935; Carl Rosa Opera, 4 yrs.; CHoir mistress, Hillsborough Congl. Ch., 1930; Asst. Adjudicator, Sheffield Music Festival, 1935-38. Mbrships: Sheffield Incorp. Soc. of Musicians; Passed mbr., Nat. Union of Tchrs., Former mbr., Sheffield Musical Union. Hobbies: Bowls; Watching cricket. Address: 235 Middlewood Rd., Sheffield, S6 4HE, UK. 3, 23, 27.

RHODES, Leonard William, b. 4 Nov. 1952, Bournemouth, UK. Pianist; Piano Teacher. Educ: Pvte. studies w. Georgina Zellan-Smith; FRAM; Assoc., London Coll. of Music. m. Karen McFall. Career: 1st. Official Organist Position at 13 yrs.; Music Master, Welling Second. Schl.; Acland Burghley Schl., London; Hd. of Music, Catford Co. Schl., ibid.; Currently engaged mostly in teaching & composition. Mbrships: Incorp. Soc. of Musicians; Musicians' Union. Hobbies: Football; Impressionist Painting. 1323 Guese Road, Houston, TX 77008, USA.

RHODES, Michael, b. 13 Aug. 1923, Brooklyn, NY, USA. Singer: Actor. Educ; Juilliard Schl. of Music; Mannes Schl.; NY Coll. of Music; Actors Studio; Pvte. study for voice & opera. m. Susan Price. Debut: W. NYC Opera, 1947; Concert, Carnegie Hall, 1949. Career: Opera apps. incl: NYC Opera; Berlin State Opera; Berlin Municipal Opera; Paris Opera Nat.; Royal Opera, Amsterdam; Theatre de la Monnai, Brussels; Royal Opera, Copenhagen; Monte Carlo Opera; Broadway apps. incl: Carousel & Most Happy Fella; Radio apps. w. NY Phil.; Telephone Hr.; Firestone Hr., etc.; Opera apps. worldwide. Mbrships: Am Guild of Musical Artists; Deutsche Buhnen Genossenschaft; Brit. Actors Equity Assn.; Lotus Club. Address: Am Roemerquelle 14, 552 Bitburg, German Fed. Repub.

RHODES, Willard, b. 12 May 1901, Deshler, Ohio, USA. Ethnomusicologist; Conductor; Pianist. Educ: BA, B Mus, Heidelberg Coll., Ohio, 1922; MA, Columbia Univ., NY; Ecole Normale de Musique, Paris. m. Lillian Hansen, 1 d. Career incls: Fac. Mbr., Columbia Univ., 1937-69; Prof. Emeritus, 1969-. Recordings: 10 LP records for Lib. of Congress, Wash. DC, of Am. Indian Music; Mormon Folk Songs. Publs. incl: Maria Sabena & her Mazatek Mushroom Velada (w. R Gordon Wasson), 1974. Contbr. to var. profl. jrnls., etc. Mbrships. incl: Fndng. Mbr. & 1st Pres., Soc. for Ethnomusicol.; Am. Musicol. Soc.; Int. Folk Coun. Hons: Fulbright Award, 1958; Award, Am. Inst. of Indian Studies, 1965; Nat. Endowment for the Arts, 1978. Hobbies: Conservation; Gardening. Address: 13615 Redwood Dr., Sun City, AZ 85351, USA. 2.

RHYS-DAVIES, Jennifer, b. 8 May 1953, Risca, Gwent, UK. Soprano Singer. Educ: TCL; LTCL; FTCL; postgrad. music tchrs. cert., Univ. of London Inst. of Educ. m. William John McCreedy. Debut: (opera) 1st Lady (Magic Flute) w. Welsh Nat. Opera, 1979. Career: lieder recitals in London; joined Welsh Nat. Opera Chorale, Aug. 1978; roles include Flora (La Traviata) & Goddess of Fortune (Coronation of Poppea); apps. in Dresden & Leipzig as Miss Jessel in Benjamin Britten's The Turn of the Screw, 1980; recital w. BBC Welsh Symph. Orch. joint runner-up in Triennial Welsh Young Singers competition, broadcast 1979. Hons: Kennedy Scott prize for singing, 1976; 2nd prize, Triennial Welsh Young Singers competition, 1979. Address: 58 Park Pl., Risca, Gwent, NP1 6AS, UK.

RIBÁRY, Antal, b. 8 Jan. 1924, Budapest, Hungary. Composer. Educ: Dip., comp., Acad. of Music, Budapest. 1 s. Debut: 2 Michelangelo songs, 1947. Career: radio interviews; piano recordings for radio. Comps: Pantomime-Suite; Hellas Cantata; Requiem for the Lover; 6 Lines from the Satyricon; Concerto Grosso; 5 quartets; 4 violin & piano sonatas; King Louis Divorces (opera); 2 Michelangelo songs; 5 Shakespeare Sonnets; 5 Villon songs. Recordings: 3 vol. of own comps. Publs: music criticism 1960-70. Mbr., Assn. of Hungarian Musicians. Hons: Liszt prize of the Acad., 1947; Chopin prize, 1949; World Youth Meeting prize, Warsaw, 1955. Hobbies: Pictures; Churches. Address: Felka u. 3, Budapest XIII, Hungary.

RIBBING, Bo Carl Stig, b. 5 Jan. 1904, Jönköping, Sweden. Pianist; Teacher. Educ: pupil of Artur Schnabel & others. m. Maria Magdalena Edenhofer, 2 d. Debut: Stockholm, 1927.

Career: solo & concerto concerts & broadcasts, 1925-; Chmbr. music & ensemble player; piano duos; Prof., High Schl. of Music, Stockholm, num. recordings incl. Scandinavian music & perfs. on old instruments from Stockholm Music Museum. Contbr. to Pro Musica Antiqua, 1977. Mbrships: Music Acad. of Sweden; Swedish Comps. Soc. Address: Östeamalmsgatan 42/III, 11426 Stockholm, Sweden.

RIBER, Anders, b. 20 Sep. 1937, Ribe, Denmark. Organist; Organ Teacher. Educ: Aarhus Conserv., organ exam., 1961, dip., 1964; studies w. Gaston Litaize, Paris, 1964. m. Gunver Rosenkrantz, 4 c. Debut: Copenhagen, 1967. Career: Organist in Skaade, 1963-65, St. Paul's, Aarhus, 1965-73, Aarhus Cathedral, 1973-; concerts in Denmark, France, Germany, UK, Sweden, Iceland & Finland; judge for Int. organ contest, Chartres, 1980; organ tchr., Aarhus Conserv., 1965-. Recordings: music by Reger; Danish romantic music (in prep.). Contbr. of music criticism to Aarhus newspapers, 1959-65. mbr., prog. committee, Aarhus Symph. Orch. Address: Edisonsvej 9, 8260 Viby J, Denmark.

RIBER, Jean-Claude, b. 14 Sept. 1934, Mulhouse, France. Opera Director. Educ: Lic. (sociol.), Univ. of Strasbourg; studied singing, theatre & fine arts, Paris & Munich. m. Liliane Meyer, 1 s., 1 d. Career: Dir., Theatre, Mulhouse, 1969-73, Grand Theatre, Nancy, 1970-73; Dir. Gen., Grand Theatre (Opera), Geneva, Switz., 1973-; Stage Mgr. for prods. in France, Germany, Romania, Switz., Italy, Greece, etc.; has staged almost 49 operas; has adapted num. works for stage; Transl. Address: Residence Jura-Lac, 1296 Coppet, Switzerland; Les Ponsez, 88230 Fraize, France.

RIBLA, Gertrude, b. 14 Sept. 1914, Brooklyn, NY, USA. Dramatic Soprano; Professor of Music. Debut: w. Salmaggi Opera, Brooklyn, NY. Career: Mtrop. Opera Co.; Chgo. Lyric & Civic Operas; NYC Opera, City Ctr.; NBC Symph. concerts under Toscanini; Wozzek w. Phila. Symph.; apps. in Milan & Venice, Italy, Wiesbaden, Germany; Cincinnati Opera; New Orleans Opera; San Carlo Opera; Prof., Univ. of Mo., St. Louis. Recordings: Columbia; HMV; RCA Victor. Mbrships: AAUP; AGMA; Nat. Opera Assn. Hobbies: Cooking; Theatre. Address: 827 S Hanley, St. Louis, MO 63105, USA.

RIBOUILLAULT-BIBRON, Danielle Marie, b. 10 Nov. 1952, Paris, France. Musicologist; Guitarist. Educ: Lic., Mod. Letters; Lic. & Master of Musical Educ., Dir. of Musicol.; Dip., Further Studies of Musicol., Sorbonne-paris. m. Jean-Claude Bibron, 2 c. Career: Writer of musicol. works. Publs: Evolution de la Technique de Guitare en France au XVIIIe siécle, 1976; La Guitare en France entre 1750 et 1850. Contbr. to: La Revue Internationale de Musique françcaise; Colloquia on musicol. w. papers on the dev. of the guitar in France & on 'la datation des sources musicales imprimices en France'. Address: 20 C rue de la République, 94270 Kremlin-Bicétre, France.

RICCI, Robert J., b. 25 Apr. 1938, NYC, USA. University Professor; Author. Educ: BA, Antioch Coll., Yellow Springs, Ohio; M Mus, Yale Univ.; DMA, Univ. Cinn. 2 s., 1 d. Career: Jazz pianist & compser; Assoc. Prof., Music, Western Mich. Univ., 1968-. Comps. incl: Fanfare for two trumpets, 1965; Chacconne for Pianoforte, 1965; Concertato for Wind Ensemble, 1966; Summer Music for Woodwind Quintet, 1967; 2 Songs for Soprano & Piano, 1967; Sonata for Trumpet & Piano. Publ: The Language of Twentieth Century Music (w. Robert Fink), 1975; (co-author) Jazz Improvisation, 1978. Contbr. to profl. publs. Mbr. var. orgs. Hons: John A Hoffman Prize for 2 Songs for Soprano & Piano, 1967. Hobby: Cycling. Address: 928 Wheaton Ave., Kalamazoo, MI 49008, USA.

RICCIARELLI, Katia, b. 18 Jan. 1946, Rovigo, Italy. Lyric Soprano. Educ: Dip., B Marcello Conserv. of Music, Venice. Debut: Community Theatre, Mantua, in La Boheme, 1969. Career: performances at: La Scala, Milan; Municipal Theatre, Florence; Opera Theatre, Rome; La Fenice, Venice; Regio, Turin; Bolshoi Theatre, Moscow; Metropol. Opera, NYC; Covent Garden, London; Vienna State Opera; Berlin; Monaco; Paris Opera; San Fran.; Lyric Opera of Chgo.; Wash., etc. Recordings: complete works of Suor Angelica & Simon Boccanegra (RCA); Due Foscari (Phillips); Due Recitals (RCA). Hons: Winner, AS.LI.CO competition, Milan, 1969; Winner, Parma competition, 1970; Winner; Italian Radio-TV competition, 1971. Mgmt: Columbia Artists, NYC (USA); Ilse Zellermayer (Germany). Address: Via Magellano 2, 20097 Corsico (Milan), Italy.

RICE, Thomas Nelson, b. 6 Feb. 1933, Wash. DC, USA. Composer; Teacher. Educ: B Mus. in Comp., Cath. Univ., Wash. DC; MA, in Musicol., Univ. of NC., Chapel Hill. Career: Num. perfs. of music inclng. Symph. perf., Town Hall, NYC, 1962 & Recital, ibid, 1963. Compositions incl: Six Piano

Pieces; Overture 1970 (orch.); Concerto for Tympani & Orch.; Concerto for 3 violins & Str. Orch.; Str. Quartet No. 2; Brass Quintet; Fully Clothed in Armor...(opera for Soprano, Baritone, Violine, Cello & Cond.); Sonatina for Piccolo & String Bass; Fantasy for Clarinet & Piano; One, Two, Three, Fourth (3 Flutes, 2 Perfs.); La Corona by Donne for tenor, narrator & chmbr. orch.; Genesis, overture for orch. & synthesizer; Sonata for 2 violins & piano; Sonata for recorders; String trio; Music for Brass Ensemble. Mbrships: ASCAP; Southeastern Comps. Soc.; Am. Music Ctr.; MacDowell Colonist; Music Educators Assn.; Va. Music Educators Assn.; Va. Beach Friends of Music. Recip., var. Fellowships & Scholarships, inclng. MacDowell Fellowship. Hobbies: Reading; Recorder Playing; Building Instruments (Clavichord, Dulcimer, Electronic Music Studio for Own Use). Mgmt: Seesaw Music Corp., 177 E. 87th St., NY, NY 10028. Address: 7008 Ocean Front, Virginia Beach, VA 23451, USA.

RICH, Ruthanne, b. 20 Dec. 1941, Salisbury, NC, USA. Performer on & Teacher of Piano. Educ: B Mus, Fla. State Univ., 1963; M Mus, Peabody Conserv., 1964; Piano Tchrs. Dip., Musical Normal Schl., Paris, 1965; Viruosity Dip., Schola Cantorum, Paris & LRAM (piano perf.), UK, both 1966; D Mus A, Eastman Schl. of Music, 1974. m. Raymond Peace. Debut: w. Atlanta Symph. Orch., when aged 14. Career: has given perfs. in UK, France, Portugal, Switz., Germany & throughout USA & the Orient; currently Assoc. Prof. of Piano, Kansas City Conserv. Publs: Selected Piano Recitals in Carnegie Hall - A Record of Changing Musical Tastes, 1974. Contbr. to The Piano Quarterly; The Am. Music Tchr. Mbrships: Pi Kappa Lambda; Phi Kappa Phi; Music Tchrs. Nat. Assn.; Sigma Alpha Iota; Alpha Lambda Delta. Hons. incl: 1st Prizes, Biennial Piano Competition, 1962, & Marie Morrissey Keith Contest, 1962 (both Nat. Fedn. of Music Clubs). Address: Kansas City Conserv. of Music, 4420 Warwick Blvd., Kansas City, MO, USA.

RICHARD, Jean-Charles André Daniel, b. 1 June 1922, Vincennes, France. Concert Pianist; Professor; Conservatory Director. Educ: Nat. Higher Conserv. of Music, paris. m. Marie-Lise Faillot, 4 s., 1 d. Career incls: Prof., Montreuil Conserv., 1966-; Dir., Bobigny Conserv., 1969-; Soloist w. French Symph. Assns. & French & for. radio & TV; Tours in Europe; Participator in var. fests. Recordings incl: Pieces for piano (Franck); Melodies (Ravel); Piano Concerto (Falla); Melodies (Debussy); Liederkreis (Schumann). Mbrships. incl: Competition Juries; CNSM Former Pupils Assn. Hobbies incl: Walking; Reading. Mgmt: Kiesgen Int. Concert Bur. Address: 'La Forlane', 78120 Cady-Raizeux, France.

RICHARD, Lawrence, b. 26 Feb. 1942, London, UK. Opera & Concert Singer (Bass-Baritone). Educ: GSM, 1960-64; studied voice w. Norman Walker, Robert Easton, Antony Benskin & Charlotte Aldenhoff; LGSM, 1962; AGSM, 1963. Career: Blyndesbourne Fest. Chorus, 1964-65; Opera for All, 1964-65; Camden & Bath Fests., 1966; Intimate Opera Co., 1966—67; Phoenix Opera, 1966-; English Bach Fest., 1968; Scottish Opera, 1968-; Gilbert & Sullivan for All, 1969-73; English Nat. Opera, 1970-; Handel Opera Soc., 1971-; Royal Liverpool Phil. Soc., 1974; Hagen City Opera 1976-; guest apps. in opera & concerts throughout W Germany since 1976. Recordings: num. commercial recordings; for BBC since 1968; sev. operetta films for TV. Mbrships: ISM; Equity; Deutscher Bühneangehörigen. Hobbies: Food & Wine; Antique Silver; Theatre. Mgmt: Dido Senger. Address: c/o Dido Senger, The Garden, 103 Randolph Ave., London W9 1DL, UK.

RICHARDS, Antony John, Major, b. 15 Aug. 1930, Rochdale, Lancs., UK. Director of Music. Educ: Royal Military Schl. of Music, Kneller Hall; LRAM; ARCM; LGSM; FTCL. m. Dorothy Richards, 2 d., 1 s. Career: Musician, 13/18th Royal Hussars, 1946-53; Bandmaster, Lancs. Fusiliers, 1956-64; Dir. of Music, Royal Tank Regiment, 1964-70, The Life Guards, 1970-; Dir. of Music, Colchester Searchlight Tattoo; Ed. & Publr. of Music for military & brass band. Comps: March of the Civil Defense; March of the Army Air Corps; num. other marches & fanfares for mounted band & State Trumpeters. Recordings: Sev. LPs w. the Band of the Life Guards; Prod. of records of the Household Division incl. Trooping the Colour, Beating Retreat. Address: 36 Garrick Gdns., W Molesey, Surrey, UK.

RICHARDS, Denby, b. 7 Nov. 1924, London, UK. Music Critic. m. Rhondda Gillespie. Career: Lectures in UK & USA; Writer & Lectr. on music; regular contbr. to Music & Musicians from 1st issue; Music Critic, Hampstead & Highgate Express, 1956-; contbr. to many foreign & UK mags., incl. Philharmonic Times, Records & Recording; Broadcaster, BBC, Radio Eireann, Finnish Radio, etc. Publs: The Music of Finland, 1966; Researcher for Searle's Gilbert & Sullivan 1975. Mbrships:

Brevet Flying Club; Royal Zoological Soc. of London. Hobbies: Puns; Vintage Wines; Flying; Out of the Way Music. Address: Hill House, Hasketon, Suffolk, UK. 3.

RICHARDS, John Kell, b. 21 Mar. 1918, Belgrade, Mont., USA. Musician (Tube); Conductor. Educ: BS., Lewis & Clark Coll.; MMus, Univ. of Southern Calif., D Mus, Phila. Conserv. of Music. m. Dorothy F Richards & children. Career: Prin. tuba, Ore. Symph. Orch. & Portland Opera Assn.; Cond., Portland Symph. Band; mbr. of var. orchs. under conds. incl. Stravinsky, Barborolli, Beecham, Klemperer; Played for var. stage shows incl. South Pacific; The King & I, Hello Dolly; Robert. Compositions: Var. band music pieces & arrs. Publs: Brass Anthology, 1970. Contbr. to: Contemporary Educ.; Nat. Music Educators Jrnl.; Ore. Educ. Jrnl. Mbrships: Chmn., Liaison w. State Bd. of Educ. & AACTE & NCATE; Phi Mu Alpha Sinfonia. Hons: Elected to Honor Soc., NW Band Dirs. Assn.; Elected to All-Am. Select Band; Many prizes & medals in music contests as soloist. Hobbies: Painting; Collecting old musical instruments. Address: 0615 Palatine Hill Rd., Portland, OR 97219, USA.

RICHARDSON, Clive, b. 23 June 1909, -aris, France. Composer; Conductor; Organist; Pianist; Violinist; Clarinettis; Trumpeter; Trombonist; Timpanist. Educ: RAM; LRAM; ARAM. m. 1 d. Career: Asst. Musical Dir., Gaumont Brit. Pictures, 1937-37; made over 500 broadcasts on radio prog. 4 Hands in Harmony, 1945-55; has over 100 compositions in transcriptions recorded for background music, radio, TV & film use; paraphrased & orchestrated 35 Engl. Golksongs for radio prodn., ITMA Compositions; London Fantasia; White Cliffs; Salute to Industry; Beachcomber; Running Off The Rails; Melody on the Move; Shadow Walz. Mbr: Savage Club. Hobbies: Tennis; Snooker. Address: 398 Wimbledon Pk. Rd., London SW19, UK. 3.

RICHARDSON, David Vivian, b. 7 June 1941, London, UK. Orchestra Manager. Educ; Mus B, Univ. of Manchester; GRSM; Assoc., Royal Manchester Coll. of Music; Dip. Ed., Caius Coll., Cambridge. m. Janet Lesley Hilton, 1 s. Career: Profl. Trumpeter, 1963-66; Music Prog. Prod., BBC Manchester, 1966-70; Concerts Mgr., New Philharmonia Orch., 1970-72; Gen. Admnstr., Scottish Nat. Orch., 1972-; Freelance record prod.; cond., brass bands. Recip. Winston Churchill Travelling Fellowships, 1976. Address: Braehead, Blanefield, Glasgow G63 9AP, UK.

RICHARDSON, Dorothy, b. Darras Hall, Northumberland, UK. Professional Singer (Soprano); Professor of Singing. Educ: LRAM; ARCM. Career: Operatic recitals; Concerts; TV recitals; Oratorios; Tchr. of Singing, Homerton Coll., Cambridge; Prof. of Singing, GSM, London. Recordings: Choirchoral recordings. Mbrships: ISM; Soc. of Women Musicians. Hobbies: Sports (Tennis, Squash, Hockey); Sportscars & Rallying. Address: 9 Priory Gdns., Highgate, London N6 5QY, UK.

RICHARDSON, Enid Dorothy, b. 25 Nov. 1905, Tunbridge Wells, Kent, UK. Pianist; Harpsichordist; Educator; Composer; Conductor. Educ: Gen. Cert., London Univ., Studied pinao w. Edward Isaacs, Manchester & Georg Brandt, Germany; ARCM; LRAM. Career: Cond., Censorship Madrigal Choir, Bermuda, 1940-43; Brit. Coun. Music Dept., 1945-47; Music Advsr., Brit. Coun. Eastern Caribbean; Cond., Trinidad Madrigal Choir, 1947-51; Rep., Brit. Coun. Music Dept., Munich & Cond., Englisches Seminaar, Munich Univ., Germany, 1951-56; Music Dir., Manor House, Limpsfield & Cond., Staffhurst Wood Choir, 1957-61; Music Dir., Overstone Sch., 1963-71; Fndr. Cond., Orlando Singers, 1968-; Brodcaster from London, Munich, Cologne, Washington, Trinidad & Guyana. Comps: Choral comps. publd. by Blandfords. Contbr. to: New Life; Music Tchr.; Musical Opinion; Musical Record; ISM Jrnl. Mbrships: Royal Soc. of Choral Cond., European Cantata Fests. Hons: Prizes for piano playing in the Hasting & Buxton Fests. Hobbies: Reading; Travel; Languages. Address: The Croft, Otley, Nr. Ipswich, Suffolk, UK. 3, 27.

RICHARDSON, Marilyn Ann, b. 10 June 1936, Sydney, Australia. Singer. Educ: DSCM (Tchrs.). Syndey Conserv. of Music. m. James Christiansesn, 6 c. Debut: Schoenberg's Pierrot Lunaire, ISCM Concert, Sydney, 1958. Career incls: Num. apps. as Concert Soloist; Radio & TV recitals; Prin. roles in TV operas for ABC; 1st apps. in Aust. of more than 300 songs & vocal works, inclng. works by Messiaen; Num. opera roles for Stadttheater Basel & Aust. opera. Recordings incl: From Within Looking Out; George Dreyfus, Aust. Music Today Vol. 1. Recip. Churchill Fellowship, 1969. Hobbies: Tennis; Squash; Gardening; Reading; Children; Music. Mgmt: Starka, Vienna. Address: 28 Yeltana Ave., Wattle Pk. 5066, South Australia, Aust.

RICHEPIN, Eliane, Pianist. Educ: Nat. Conserv., Paris; studied w. Falkenberg, Marguerite Long, Alfred Cortot & Henri Busser. Career: over 1800 concerts (350 w. orchs. such as Nat. ORTF. Orch., Lamoureux Orch., Phila (Pa.) Philharmonic Orch., LPO, Concertgebouw (Amsterdam) & Israel Philharmonic Orch. throughout Europe, N & S Am. & the Mid. E., 1946-; has played under such Conds. as Jean Martinon, Geo. Solti, Edward van Beinum, Stanislas Wislocki, Carlos Chavez, Sir Alrian Boult & others; worldwide radio & TV perfs. Mbrships: Jruy Mbr., num. int. competitions, inclng. Chopin Competition, Warsaw & Concours Busoni; Fdndr., Int. Music Ctr., Annecy; Fndr.-Pres., City of Montevideo Competition. Hons. incl: Placed, Concours de Rome, 1938; Prix des Beaux-Arts, 1943; Hon. Mbr., Phila. Orch. Chevalier des Arts et Lettres. Address: 151 ave. de Wagram, 75017 Paris, France.

RICHEY, Angela, b. 2 Sept. 1931, Edinburgh, UK. Violinist; Soloist; Chamber Music Player; Orchestral Leader & Player; Teacher. Educ: Waddell Schl. of Music, Edinburgh, 1946-49; LRAM, 1952; Recital Div., 1954. m (1) John Sinfield, d. 1973 (2) Richard Haigh, 1 s., 1 d. Career: Several concerts w. Boyd Neel Orch.; Mbr., City of Birmingham Symph. Orch.; Played in Chmbr. Concerts in Sienna, inclng: w. Otto Uggi; Perfs. w. Delphos Ensemble; Num. broadcasts; Fndr., Richey Quartet; Ldr., Warwicks. Symph. Orch. & St. Edmundsbury Orch.; Tchr., Advanced Violin Students, Coventry Schl. of Music. Mbr. ISM. Hobbies: Gardening; Camping. Address: Harborough Bank, Shelsley Beauchamp. Worcester WR6 6RA, UK.

RICHMOND, Albert, French Horn Player. Educ: BS in French Horn, Juilliard Schl. of Music, 1950; MA in Music Educ., Columbia Univ. Tchr's Coll., 1952. Career incls: Solo Horn, Radio City Music Hall Orch., 1950-60; Staff Mbr., Comp.'s Conf. & Chmbr. Music Ctr., Bennington Coll. & now at Johnson State Coll., Vt., during month of Aug., 19 yrs.; Recorded w. Stravinsky; Played w. Symph. of the Air, City Ctr. Ballet Co., NY City Opera Co., Fest. Winds, NBC Symph. under Toscanini, Met. Opera Co.; Mbr., Pablo Casals Fest. Orch., San Juan, Puerto Rico, 1972-; Newport Chmbr. Music Fest., 1974; Bach Aria Grp., CBS, NBC, ABC; Fac. Mbr., Dwight Schl. Englewood, NJM. Records under var. conds. & arrs. Address: 676 Mildred St., Teaneck, NJ 07666, USA.

RICHMOND, Louis B, b. 16 Sept. 1942, Phila., Pa., USA. Conductor; Cellist. Educ: BM, Eastman Schl. of Music, 1964; MMus, Temple Univ., 1966. m. Betty Ann Richmond, 1 s. Debut: as Cellist, Town Hall, NYC, 1970. Career: Fndr., NW Chmbr. Orch., Seattle, Wash., 60 concerts, 1976-77. Mbrships: Am. String Tchrs. Assn.; Am. Symph. League; Phi MJ Alpha. Hobby: Camping. Address: 1916 E Blaine St., Seattle, WA, USA.

RICHTER, Frederico, b. 6 Feb. 1932, Novo Hamburgo, Brazil. Violinist; Conductor; Composer; Professor. Educ: BA (violin) 1951, & Tchrs. Cert.; D Mus, Univ. of Rio Grande do Sul, 1962; studied music, Europe, 9 yrs. m. Ivone Mendes Richter, 2 s., 1 d. Debut: 1949, Pôrto Alegre RS, Brazil. Career: Mbr. w. brother Nicolau, Duo Richter, (violins), concerts in Europe, Uruguay & Brazil, 1956-; 1st violinist, soloist, Symph. Orch. of Pôrto Alegre, 1950-71; Prof., Univ. of Pelotas RS Brazil, 1960-70; Prof., Univ. of Santa Maria RS Brazil, 1966-; Chief, Music Dept. of Fine Arts Center, ibid, 1971-73; Tchr., Instrumental Schl., Symph. Orch. of Pôrto Alegre, 1975; Cond., Chmbr. Orch., Rio Grande do Sul; Regent & Artists Dir., Chmbr. Group of Santa Maria. Comps. incl: Concertratas, 1-3; Suite for violin solo; Niger Song for Orch., 1974; Lisboa, 1973. Recording: LP w. Univ. os Santa Maria. Publ. incl: Voyage on the Keyboard, 2 vols., 1976-77. Contbr. to profl. publs. Mbr., profl. assns. Hons. incl: Gold Medal of Univ. Merit, 1973; Imembui Prize (Gold Medal & Cert.), 1976. Hobby: Camping. Address: Belvedere House, Apt. 1405, 2175 Blvd. de Maisonneuve Ouest, Montreal, Que. H3H 115, Can.

RICHTER, Hamann Lukas, b. 22 Feb. 1923, Bärenstein, Germany. Wissenschaftlicher Mitarbeiter. Educ: Coll. of music, Leipzig, 1941-2; Humboldt univ. Berlin, 1949-52; doctorate, Berlin, 1957. m. Christa Aügsbürg, 1 s. Publs. incl: Zur Wissenschaftslehre von der Musik bei Platon & Aristoteles, 1961; Der Berliner Gassenhauer, 1969; Musikalische Aspekte der attischen Trag&dienchöre, 1972. Das Musikfragment aus dem Euripiedeischen Orestes, 1973; Schoenbergs Harmonielehre und die freie Atonaltiät, 1968. Contbr. to: Archiv fur Musikwissenschaft; Deutsches Jahrbuch der Musikwissenschart; Beiträge zur Musikwissenschaft; Mbrships: Comps. & Musicians union of German Dem. Repub.; New Bach Soc.; G F Handel Soc. Address: DDR-1199 Berlin, Florian-Geyerstr. 10, German Dem. Repub.

RICHTER, Karl, b. 1926, Plauen, Saxony, Germany. Conductor; Organist; Harpsichordist. Educ: Leipzig Conserv., w. Karl Straube & Gunther Ramin. Career: Organist. Thomaskirche, Leipzig, 1949-51; Fac., Music HS Munich, 1951; Organist, Markuskirche, ibid & Dir., Heinrich Schutz Kreis (now Munich Bach Choir), 1951; Fndr., Munich Bach Orch., 1953; Frequent tours of Europe, N & S Am. w. Bach choir & Orch. Recordings: Many of works of Bach incl: St. Matthew & St. John Passions; Mass in B Minor; Magnificat; num. cantatas & orch. works. Address: co Rubolf Vedder Konzertdirektion 8 Munich 8&. Mauerkirchenstrasse 8, German Fed. Repub.

RICHTER, Marga, b. 21 Oct. 1926, Reedsburg, Wis., USA. Composer; Pianist. Educ: BS, MS, Juilliard Schl. m. Alan Skelly, 1 s., 1 d. Debut: Comps. Forum, NYC, 1951. Career: Num. perfs. of own comps. in solo recital & w. orchs. Comps. incl: (orch.) 2 Piano Concertos; Music for 3 Quintets & Orch.; Blackberry Vines & Winter Fruit; (ballet) Abyss; (string orch.) Lament; (piano solo) Sonata for Piano; Requiem; Remembrances; String Quartet. Recordings incl: Piano Music for Children by Modern Composers; Dances for Four Pianos; lament; Sonata for Piano. Mbr., sev. musical assns. Hons. incl: num. grants, incl. ASCAP Standard Award, 1966-78 & comp. grant from Nat. Endowment for the Arts. Address: 3 Bayview Lane, Huntington, Ny 11743, USA. 27.

RICHTER, Marion Morrey, b. 21 Oct. 1900, Columbia, Ohio, USA. Concert Pianist; Composer; Lecturer; Musicologist; Teacher. Educ: BA, Ohio State Univ.; MA, EdD, Columbia Univ.; Artist Grad., Juilliard Schl., NYC. m. Otto C Richter (dec.), 2 s. Debut: Pianist. Am. premiere, George Antheil's Ballet Mechanique, Carnegie Hall, NYC. Career incls: Pianist w. NYC Symph., preimiere of Ulric Cole's Divertimento; Recitals & radio broadcasts; num. Lecture-Concerts & workshops; tours throughout USA, UK. Mexico, Orient; Around the Wld. w. Am. Music, Oncert tour, 1975. Comps. incl: Sea Chant (chorus for women's voices); This if Our Camp (children's operetta); Timberjack Overture (for band); songs & piano pieces; Distant Drums (opera). Contbr. to musical publs. Mbrships. incl: Pres., NY Fedn. of Music Clubs, 1976-; Coord., NY State Nat. Music Coun. Bicentennial Parade of Am. Music. Recip. many hons. Address: 31 Bradford Rd., Scarsdale, NY 10583, USA. 5.

RICHTER, Svyatoslav Theofilovich, b. 20 Mar. 1915, Zhitomir, Ukraine. Pianist. Educ: Moscow Conserv. Career incl: concert tours throughout the world; Wide repertoire incl. works of Bach (cycle of 48 Preludes & Fugues); Beethoven; Schubert; Rachmaninov; Rubinstein; Myaskovsky; Shostakovich; Scriabin; Prokofiev; Ravel; Debussy; Mozart & Schumann. Hons: 1st Prize, 3rd USSR Competition of Executant Musicians, 1935; State Prize; Lenin Prize; People's Artist of USSR; Order of Lenin. Address: Moscow State Phil. Soc., 31 Ulitsa Gorkogo, Moscow, USSR.

RICHTER-HAASER, Ernst Max Hans, b. 6 Jan. 1912, Dresden, Germany. Pianist; Composer. Educ: Grad., Dresden Music Schl., 1932. m. Elly Sonntag, 3 d. Career: Cond., choirs & orchs., Soloist, Tchr., Dresden, 1930-39; Cond., Detmold Municipal Orch., 1946-47; Tchr., piano, NW German Music Acad., Detmold, 1947-63; concert tours, N & S Ams., Europe, Asia, Aust. Comps. incl: piano concertos; concertos for strings; str. quartet; flute concerto; symph.; chmbr. music; piano music; choral music. Has recorded concertos & sonatas by Beethoven, Brahms, Mozart, Schubert, etc. Hons. incl: Iron Cross 2nd. class; Gold Medal for Merit; Lebanon. Mgmt: Columbia Artists Mgmt. Inc., 1965 W 57th St., NY, NY 10019, USA. Address: 15 Bismarkstr., 48 Bielefeld, German Fed. Repub. 2.

RICHTER-HERF, Franz, b. 17 Dec. 1920, Vienna, Austria. Composer; Conductor. Educ: Dips. in Cond., 1947, & Music Theory, 1948, Mozarteum Acad., Salzburg. m. Maria Richter-Taborsky, 1 s., 1 d. Career: Prof. of Music Theory, Mozarteum Acad., Salzburg; Rector, ibid., 1979-. Comps. incl: (publd.) Konzertstück für Tenorposaune, 1959; Symphonische Szenen für Klavier & Orch., 1960; Konzert für Kontrabass, 1966; Choirs a cappella, 1966; (recorded) Symph., 1960; Musik für Streichorchester, 1961; Music w. microtones (Ekmelische Musik) 1970-; Aus einer Strumnacht (cantata), 1971; Ekmelie nr. 1, 1974; Die Stunde des Pan, 1975; Welle der Nacht, 1977; Odysseus (opera), 1979. Recordings incl: 5 Klavierstucke im labilen Tempo, 1965. Publs: Ekmelische Musik (w. R Maedel), 1972; Die ekmelische Orgel, 1975; Intonationsübungen für ekmelische Musik, 1978. Hons. incl: Michael Haydn Medal, 1972. Hobby: Painting. Address: Fischbachstr. 50, A15020 Salzburb, Austria.

RICKENBACHER, Karl Anton, b. 20 May 1940, Basle, Switz. Conductor. Educ: Tchrs. Trng. Course; Study for Cond., Conserv., W Berlin, 1962-66; Kapellmeister-Reiferprüfung (Opera& Concert) Degree, 1966. m. Gaye Fulton. Debut: RIAS,

Berlin. Career: Asst. Cond., Zürich Opera House, 1966–69; 1st Kapellmeister, Städt Bühnen, Frieburg i Br., Germany, 969-74; Gen. Music Dir., Westphalian Symph. Orch., 1976; Prin. Cond., BBC Scottish Symph. Orch., 1978; Regualr Geust Cond. w. RIAS, Berlin; (Radio Symph. Orch.); Guest Cond. w. Symph. Orch. of Bayerische Rundfunks, Munich; Tonhalle Orch., Zürich; Teatro Massimo, Palermo, etc. Contbr. to var. prog. notes. Hons: Kunstpreis des Kanton Solothurn, Switz., 1971. Hobbies: Lit.; Films; Art; Football. Mgmt: Konzert Direktion, Hans Adler, Berlin; Lies Askonas Concert Agency, London. Address: Dorstenerstr. 16, 4350 Recklinghausen, Germany Fed. Repub.

RIDDELL, Joyce, b. 1921, London, UK. Pianist; Harpsichord Player. Educ: studied w. Franz Osborne, RAM; ARAM. m. BL Wynyard, 1 d. Career: Dir., Youth Music Ctr.; broadcasts frequently; has given many recitals in UK & abroad; has given many 1st perfs. of works by contemp. composers; Chmbr. Music Player. Compositions incl: Many short pices for children's orch. Mbr., ISM. Hobby; Bridge, Crosswords. Address: 5 Springcroft Ave., London N2, UK.

RIDDERSTRÖM, Bo, b. 11 Dec. 1937, Arboga, Sweden. Arranger; Composer. Educ: Dip., Music Instr., Ingesund Music Schl., 1961; Study of Orchestration w. Tor Mann, Counterpoint w. Hans Zetterquist; Study of Oboe, Chmbr. Music & Theory, Music Conserv. of Gothenburg, 1964-67. m. Sara Hallberg. Career: Music Tchr., Stenungsund, 1962-65; Dir., Askim Music Schl., 1965-71; Dir., Falkenberg Music Schl., 1971-. Comps: Betula alba, Swedish folk tunes for pinao; Briza media, Swedish folk tunes for 2 flutes; Side By Side, arrangements for flute duet; Notes 12.78 for 12 instruments. Contbr. to: Hallands Nyheter; Musikkultur. Hobbies: Small boat sailing; Baroque flute playing. Address: Bermansgatan 48, 311 00 Falkenberg, Sweden.

RIDDLE, Pauline Peck, b. 1 Aug. 1932, Memphis, Tenn., USA. Assistant Professor of Music; Church Organist. Educ: BS, SW Mo. State Univ., Springfield; MSM, Schl. of Ch. Music, Southern Bapt. Theol. Sem., Louisville, Ky.; DME, Okla. Univ., Norman. m. Donald R Riddle, 1 d., 1 s. Career: Pub. Schl. Music Supvsr. Asst. Prof. of Music, William Jewell Coll., Liberty, Mo.; Ch. Organist & Coord. of Children's Choirs, Wornall Rd. Bapt. Ch., Kan. City, Mo.; organ recitals & workshops. Mbrshps: Exec. Coun.; AGO; Southern Bapt. Ch. Music Conf.; Sigma Alpha Iota; Delta Kappa Gamma. Publs: Church Organ Method, 1973. Hons. incl: Richie Robertson Music Award, 1949. Address: 508 S Forest, Liberty, MO 64068, USA.

RIDDLE, Peter H, b. 29 Dec. 1939, Long Branch, NJ, USA. Professor; Trombonist; Composer; Arranger. Educ: BS, Lebanon Valley Coll.; Annville, Pa., 1961; MA, Trenton State Coll., NJ., 1972; PhD, Southern Ill. Univ., 1974. m. Gail M Riddle, 1 s., 1 d. Career: Band Dir., N Hunterdon Regional High Schl., Annandale, NJ, 1961-67; Dir. of Music, w. Kings Dist. High Schl., Auburn, HS, Can., 1967-69; Assoc. Prof., Acadia Univ., Wolfville, NS, 1969-. Comps. incl: Arr., 2 Preludes, Shostakovitch; Elegy for Kenneth; In Memoriam; Janis Kalejs; Soliloquy for Tromobne; Psalm XXIII; Song for Euphonium. Contbr. to: Schl. Musicin. Mbr., Profl. assns. Hobbies: Model Railroading; Philately; Camping; Swimming. Addres: 32 Skyway Drive, Wolfville, NS, Canada, BOP 1XO.

RIDGEWAY, Frank, b. 9 Sept. 1931, London, UK. Musician, Trumpet, Flugelhorn, French Horn. m. Dorothy Ann Ridgeway, 2 s., 2 d. Carer: Lead Trumpet, London Palladium Orch., UK, Atlantic Symph., Can.; Pt.-Time CBC Concert Orch., Concert Band, 20 yrs.; CBC Studio Sessions, TV & Radio; CTV; Maritime Command Band, 20 yrs. Fac. of Nova Scotia Summer Music Camp, Brass Clinican. Recordings: Can. Armed Forces Tattoo Record, Centennial Yr., 1967; Can. Brass Record, 1967; Stadacone Band, Maritime Command. Mbrshps: Am. Fedn. of Msuicans; Halifax Musicians Assn.; Atlantic Musicians Assn. Hobbies: Swimming; Walking; Table Tennis; House Building. Address: 80 Hillcrest Ave., Lower Sackville, NS, Can.

RIDLEY, Laurence Howard II (Larry), b. 3 Sept. 1937, Indpls., Ind., USA. Contrabassist; Composer. Educ: Violin Scholar, Ind. Univ., 1955-59; Lenox, Mass., Schl. of Jazz, 1959; BS Music, NY Univ., 1971. Career: Sideman w. num. major jazz perfs., 1960- w. Newport All-Stars, Duke Ellington, Coleman Hawkins, Thelonious Monk, Horace Silver, Sonny Rollins; Ldr., Rutgers/Livingston Jazz Profs.; Prof. of Music & Chmn., Music Dept., Livingston Coll., Rutgers Univ.; Guest Lectr., Cons., Clinician, Norlin Music Inc.; Chmn., Jazz Panel, Nat. Endowment for the Arts, 1976-78. Contbr. to jazz jrnls. Hobbies: Tennis; Anthropology of Educ. Address: 37 Blenheim Rd., Englishtown, NJ 07726, USA.

RIDOUT, Alan John, b. 9 Dec. 1934, Kent, UK. Composer. Educ: GSM; RCM; w. P Racine Fricker, Michale Tippet & Henk

Badings (Netherlands Govt. Schlrships.); ARCM. Career: Tchr., Lectr., Cambridge Univ., 1963-75; Prof., RCM, 1960-. Compositions incl: 8 Operas; Christmas Oratorio for Soli, Chorus & Orch.; Orchestral Music inclng. 5 symphs.; Choral Music; Chmbr. Music; Song Cycles; Organ Music; Piano Music. Recordings: about 20. Publs: Background to Music, 1962; Background to Musical Form, 1964. Contbr. to profl. jrnls. Hons: 3 Royal Phil. Soc. Prizes; Clements Prize; Collard Fellowship. Mgmt: Chappel & Co. Ltd., 50 New Bond St., London W1. Address: 5 Burgate House, Canterbury, Kent, UK.

RIDOUT, Godfrey, b. 6 May 1918, Toronto, Canada. Composer; Music Historian; Professor. Educ: Upper Canada Coll.; Toronto Conserv. of Music; Study of Composition w. Healey Willan; Counterpoint & Organ. Charles Peaker; Conducting, Ettore Mazzoleni; ACTM. m. Freda Antrobus, 1 s., 2 d. Career: Composer; scores for Nat. Film Bd. & CBC; Cond., radio & in concert; Lectr., 1948, now Prof., Hist. & Lit. Dept., Fac. of Music, Univ. of Toronto. Compositions incl: Cantiones Mysticae No. 1 for Soprano & Orch., No. 2 for Soprano, Trumpet & Strings; Folk Songs of Eastern Canada; Pange Lingua, for Choir & Orch.; Fall Fair, Full Orch. (recorded by Toronto Symph.) Publs: Articles & reviews in profl. jrnls.; Papers. Mbrships: CAPAC; Can. League of Composers; Vic. Studies Assn.; Toronto Musicians Assn. Hons: Centennial Medal; LLD, Queen's Univ., Kingston, Ont.; FRCCO, 1975. Hobbies: Railways; both real & model. Address: 71 Rowanwood Ave., Toronto, Canada M4W 1Y8.14.

RIEDEL, Friedrich Wilhelm, b. 24 Oct. 1929, Cuxhaven, Germany. Professor of Musicology. Educ: Christian Albrecht's Univ., Kiel; Dr. Phil, 1957; qualified in musicol., Johannes Gutenberg Univ., Mainz, 1971; trng. as organist & choirmaster, Landesmusikschule, Lübeck; qualified in ch. music. m. Almuth Keller, 4 c. Career incls: Musicol. Asst., Inst. of Musicol., Mainz Univ.; Univ. Lectr., Johannes Gutenberg Univ., Mainz, 1971-; Dir., Capella Moguntina (ensemble for old music), Mainz, 1972-. Recordings incl: Kurmainzer Chamber Music from Rokoko, 1975; Organ & bells der Basilika zum Heiligen Blut in Walldürn, 1976. Ed. sev. musical works. Sev. books in field. Contbr. to profl. jrnls. Mbr. profl. orgs. Address: Im Münchfeld 7, D-6500 Mainz, German Fed. Repub.

RIEFLING, Robert, b. 17 Sept. 1911, Oslo, Norway. Pianist. Educ: studied in Oslo, in Hannover, (w. Karl Leimer), & in Berlin (w. Wilhelm Kempff & Edwin Fischer). m. Borghild Hammerich. Debut: Oslo, 1926. Career: num. concerts in Europe, 4 tours of USA; has given 1st perfs. of works by Fartein Valen, Klaus Egge, Rivertz, & Saeverud; Ldr., Reiffling's Piano Inst., 1941-52; Prof., Royal Danish Music Conserv., Copenhagen, 1967-73, Norwegian Music HS, Oslo, 1973-. Many recordings inclng: Beethoven, 32 sonatas; Haydn, 14 sonatas; Bach, Well Tempered Clavier; Hindemith, Lüdüs tonalis. Hons: Knighted, Order of St. Olav, class 1, King Haakon VII, Noway, & Order of Dannebrog, class 1, Queen Margrethe, Denmark. Address: Lysebu, Voksenkollen, Oslo 3, Norway.

RIEHM, Diethard, b. 5 Jan. 1940, Giessen, Germany Fed. Repub. Lecturer in Musicology; University Music Director; Conductor. Educ: DPh, Univs. of Muenster & Cologne; Acad. of Music, Muenster. m. Ursula Riehm, 2 c. Career: Lectr. in Musicol. & Cond., Collegium Musicum, Univ. of Muenster. Mbr., Gesellschaft für Musikforschung. Address: Grimmstr. 2, D44 Muenster, Germany Fed. Repub. 3.

RIEMERSMA, Coby, b. 16 Dec. 1905, Amsterdam, Netherlands. Singing Teacher. Educ: Studied langs; studied music, esp. singing, Amsterdam & Paris, France; Dip. piano, singing & schl. music. Career: Tchr. of num. famous singers, inclng. Jennie Veeninga, Cristine Deutekom & Marco Bakker; interviews on radio & TV, Netherlands & Belgium, Prof. of Singing, Conserv., Amstgerdam, 1941-75. Contbr. to interviews to num. newspapers & mags. Mbrshps: Fndr., Soc. of Friends of the Lied, 1961 (Bd. of Dirs.); Royal Dutch Union of Tchrs. of Music. Hons: Kt., House of Orange, Netherlands. Hobbies: Photography; Travelling; Cycling; Walking; Debating; Housekeeping. Address: Blekersvaartweg 31, Heemstede, Netherlands. 27.

RIEPE, Russell Casper, b. 23 Feb. 1945, Ill., USA. Composer; Arranger; Pianist; Lecturer. Educ; B Mus. So. Ill. Univ., Carbondale, Ill.; MA in Theory & PhD in Music Comp., Eastman Schl. of Music, Univ. of Rochester, NY. m. Elizabeth Young, 1 s. Debut: Shryock Auditorium, So. Ill. Univ., 1963. Career: Fndr. & Dir. of an electronic studio at Southwest Tex., State Univ., San Marcos, Tex., where he is an Asst. Prof. of Music & serves as Hd. of the Comp.-Theory Prog. & teaches piano; Var. comps. and arrangements perf. at Eastman Schl. of Music, So. Ill. Unv., Southwest Tex. State Univ., Lincoln Ctr., NY; Presented series of recitals at Robers Wesleyan Coll., Syracuse & So. Ill. Univ.; Arrangements aired on radio throughout USA.

Compositions incl: Incidental Music for strings; Compositions incl: Incidental Music for strings; Divertimenti for woodwind quartet; Les Heures (electronic music); Child Dying, a cycle of three songs for soprano & orch.; Three Fantasies, for piano; Symphonic Fantasy for large orchestra. Var. recordings as pianist w. Eastman Wind Ensemble & particiated as pianist in recoridngs of own arranagment of Stars & Stripes Forever, Thunder & Lightening Polka, etc. Mbr., var. profl. orgs. Hons. incl: 3 Presser Awards; Woodrow Wilson Fellow; Howard Hanson Prize in Comp., 1972. Hobbies: Ornithology & Reading. Address: 302 Pecan St., San Marcos, TX 78666, USA.

RIEUNIER, Jean-Paul Michel André Marie, b. 27 Jan. 1933, Bordeaux, France. Composer; Professor. Educ: Bordeaux Conserv.; Paris Conserv. m. Françcoise Guinpel. Career: Prof. of Musical Educ., Paris schls., 1957-67; In charge of public musical activities for Paris Dist., Ministry of Culture, 1967-69; Artistic Advsr., in charge of programs for new Phil. Orch. at French Radio, 1976; Prof. in charge of public activities for contemporary music, Paris Conserv. of Music, 1970-. Comps. incl: Cycle of songs, texts by Paul Valéry & Rainer-Maria Fielke; String Quartet, 1962; Symph. Movement, 1962; Symph. for Strings, 1963; Espace, for percussion & sonorized harpsichord; Lineal, for alto-saxophone & piano, 1972; Volume VII, for 7 wind instruments, 1972; Volume III, for flute, viola & harp, 1972; Silences, for trombone, 1977; Antienne, for flute & clarinet, 1978; Forum, for string orch., 1979. Recordings: Music for Mount St. Michel, for small ensemble. Mbrships: SACEM France. Hons: Honour Dip. (comp.), Academia Chigiana, Siena, Italy, 1966. Address: 36 rue Cortambert, 75016 Paris, France.

RIFKIND, Marilyn A, b. 11 Apr. 1949, Tarrytown, NY, USA. General & Vocal Music Teacher. Educ: B Mus Ed., Jacksonville Univ., Fla.; MSc, Music Educ, Univ. of Bridgeport (Conn.), 1975. Career: Tchr. Gen. & Vocal Music, Pleasantville Middle Schl., NY. Mbrships: Mu Phi Epsilon; Pres., Beta Beta Chapt., ibid, 1969-70; Student MENC; Pres., Jacksonville Univ. Chapt., 1969-70; MENC. Hons: Outstanding Secondary Educator of Am., 1974; Notable American Award, 1976-77, 1978-79; Hobbies: Music Theatre; Collecting Records. Address: 11 Lake St., Apt. 6-T, White Plains, NY 10603, USA. 6.

RIGOR, Laura Frances, b. 13 June 1920, Stockton, Calif., USA. Violinist. Educ: Attended Coll., 3 yrs.; Music Major, Univ. of the Pacific, Stockton, Calif.; pvte. Violin studies from age of 9. m. Karl L Rigor, 2 s., 2 d. Career: First Violinist, w. Stockton Symph. 18 yrs., Oakland Symph. 6 yrs., Santa Cruz Symph. 8 yrs., Stockton Sinfonietta, var. Chmbr. Grps. Hobbies: Oil Painting; Gardening; Reading; Swimming. Address: 223 Farley Dr., Aptos, CA 95003, USA.

RIHTMAN, Cvjetko, b. 4 May 1902, Ethnomusicologist; Organist. Educ: Conserv. of Prague & Liepzig; Schola Cantorum, Paris; studied w. Vincent d'Indy. m. Jefa Palavestra, 4 c. Career: Choir Cond. & Orranist, Paris, 1928-32; Choir Cond. & Prof., Tchrs. Trng. Schl., Sarajevo, 1932; after WWII, i/c org. of Middle Music Schl., Sarajevo Opera, Inst. for Study of Folklore & Music Acad., Sarajevo; Prof., ibid. Comps: num. works for choir, children's choir; 6 Folk Songs, voice & piano; Andantino for violin & piano; Preludium & Fuga for piano. Recordings: Pjesma & Cici, for chor. Publs. incl: Polyphonic Forms in the Folk Music of Bosnia-Herzegovina, 1951; Folk Music Traditions of Zepa, 1964; The Traditional Forms of Singing of Epic Songs in Bosnia and Herzegovina, the Anthology of Vaprosi folklora, 1968. Contbr. to: Grove's Dict.; profl. jrnls. Mbrships. incl: Acads. of Sci. & Arts, Bosnia-Herzegovina; Int. Folk Music Coun.; Int. Musicol. Soc. Address: Fadila Jahića Spanca 41, 71000 Sarajevo, Yugoslavia.

RIJAVEC, Andrej, b. 4 March 1937, Belgrade, Yugoslavia. Musicologist. Educ: MA; PhD in musicol. m. Nevenka Petkovsek, 1 s., 1 d. Career: Prof. of Musicol., Univ. of Ljubljana. Publs: Glasbano delo na Slovenskem v obdobju protestantizma (Music in Slovenia in the Protestant Era), 1967; Kompozicijski stavek komornih instrumentalnih del Slavka Osterca (Compositional Technique in the Instrumental Chamber Works of Slavko Osterc), 1972; 20th Century Slovene Composers, 1975. Contbr. to: Muzikoloski zbornik (musicol. annual); Arti Musices; Int. Review of Aesthetics & Social of Music; Musica; World of Music; Current Musicol.; Zvuk. Mbr., Int. Musicol. Soc. Hobbies: Sprots. Address: Kidriceva 4, 61000 Ljubljana, Yugoslavia.

RILEY, Dennis Daniel, b. 28 May 1943, Los Angeles, Calif., USA. Composer. BMus, Univ. of Colo., 1965; MMus, Univ. of Ill., 1968; PhD; Univ. of Iowa, 1973. Career incl: Asst. Prof. of Music, Columbia Univ. Comps: Viola Concerto; Elegy for String Orch.; Concertante Music IIV; Variations IV for Clarinet;

Cantatas I-III; Pinao Pieces I-III; String Trio; Five Songs; Liebeslied; Theme & Variations for Orch.; Elegy for Sept. 15, 1945; Magnificat; Concertino, Beata Viscera. Recordings: Beta Viscera (CBC); String Trio (CRI). Address: c/o C F Peters Corp., 373 Park Ave., S, Ny, NY 10016, USA.

RILEY, John Arthur, b. 17 Sept. 1920, Altoona, Pa., USA. Composer; Cellist; Teacher. Educ: MusB, Eastman Schl. of Music, 1951; MusM, Yale Univ., 1955; Conserv. Nat. de Musique, paris. m. Dorothy Morrow, 1 s., 2 d. Career: Cellist, San Antonio Symph., Rochester Phil., New Haven & Hartford Symph., Hillingdon & Wells Quartets; Instructor of cello, hist., theory, comp., Hartfort Conserv. of Music & Conn. State Coll. Comps: Quartet No. 2; num. unpublished comps. Mbr., Am. Fed. of Musicians. Hons: Tamiment award, 1954, for Strg. Quartet No. 1. Hobbies: Cinematography; Photography. Address: 107 Golf St., Newington, Conn., USA.

RILEY, (John) Howard, b. 16 Feb. 1943, Huddersfield, Yorks., UK. Pianist; Composer. Educ: BA, 1964, MA in Musfc, 1966, Univ. of Wales; M Mus, Ind. Univ., USA, 1967; M Phil. in Music, York Univ., UK, 1970. Career: Prof., GSM, 1970-; Tutor, Barry Summer Schl., 1971-; num. radio, TV, Fest. apps. w. own grp., UK, France, Germany, USA, Can.; Creative Assoc., Center of the Creative & Perf. Arts, Buffalo, NY, 1976-77. Comps. incl: (str. quartets) Textures; Zeroth; Celsius; Changes for string trio; Convolution (8-12 piece grp.); Blox, for solo slute; Nine, for string ensemble; Solo III for one percussionist. LP Recordings incl: Synopsis, 1973; Singleness, 1974; Intertwine, 1975; Shaped, 1976; The Toronto Concert, 1977; Returning, 1978. Contbr. to profl. jrnls. Hons. incl: Arts Coun. Bursaries for Comp., 1969, 73, 75, 77, 78; UK/USA Bicentennial Fellowship in the Arts, 1976-77. Hobbies: Reading; Walking; Football. Address: 2 Bennett Pk., Blackheath, London SE3 9RB, UK.

RIMMER, Frederick William, b. 21 Feb. 1914, Liverpool, UK. University Professor. Educ: MA., Selwyn Coll., Cambridge; B Mus., Dunelm; FRCO. m. Joan Doreen Graham, 2 s., 1 d. Career: Organ Schl., Selwyn Coll., Cambridge, 1946-48; Sr. Lectr. in Music, Homerton Coll., Cambridge, 1948-51; Cramb Lectr. in Music, Univ. of Glasgow, 1951-56; Sr. Lectr., ibid, 1956-66; Organist to Univ., 1954-66; Gardiner Prof. of Music, 1966-; Dir., Scottish Music Archive, 1968-. Compositions: Five Tempers for 2 Violines; Five Preludes on Scottish Psalm Tunes for organ; Pastorale & Toccata for organ; Sing we merrily; Christus natus est, alleluia; O Lord, we beseech thee; Five carols of the Nativity. Many recordings. Co-author, History of Music in Scotland. Contbr. to: Tempo; The Music Review; Organist Quarterly Review; Brit. Book News. Mbrships: Dir., Scottish Opera, 1966-; Chmn., BBC's Scottish Music Advsry. Comm., 1972-; Gov., Royal Scottish Acad. of Music & Drama; Brit. Coun. Music Comm. Recip., Special Award, Composers Guild of GB., 1974. Hobbies: Travel; Reading; Gradening; Collecting Prints. Address: 62 Oakfield Ave., Glasgow G12 8LS, UK. 1, 3.

RIMMER, John Francis, b. 5 Feb. 1939, Auckland, NZ. Composer; University Teacher; Musical Director; Horn Player. Educ: Grad., Univ. of Auckland, NA & Toronto, Can. m. Helen Rimmer, 3 s. Comps., 60 works inclng: Abstracts as White (str. trio); The Ring of Fire (ensemble); Symphony, 1968. Comps. recorded incl: Compositions 2 (wind quintet & electronic sounds); Composition 3 (harp & electronic sounds); Composition 5 (percussion & electronic sounds); At the Appointed Time (orchl.); The Exotic Circle (recorders & percussion); Homage to Paganini (electronic); White Island (electronic); Where Sea Meets Sky 1 (electronic). Contbr. to: CANZ Newsletter. Mbrships: Pres., Comps. Assn. of NZ, 1975; Vice Chmn., Auckland Soc. for Music, Educ., 1975-. Hons: APRA Prize, 1971, 77; philip Neill Prize, 1971; Univ. of Otago, NZ Brass Bands Assn. Prize, 1971; Hon. Mention, Bourges Int. Electro-acoustic Music Competition, 1976. Address; 67 Marlborough Ave., Glenfield, Auckland 10, NZ.

RIMON, Meir, b. 14 Jan. 1946, Vilna, USSR. French Hornist. Educ: BA, Tel-Aviv Univ.; Tel-Aviv Acad. of Music; Amsterdam Conservatorium. m. Irit Rimon, 1 s., 1 d. Debut: Radio Symph. Orch., Jerusalem, 1967. Career: 1st Horn, Israel Phil. Orch., 1970-; Mbr., Israel Woodwind Quintet, 1970-; Artist, Marlboro Music Fest., 1975, 76; Soloist under num. conds. inclng. Daniel Barenboim, & Zubin Mehta; Fac., Tel-Aviv Univ., 1974-. Recordings: Variations on Hayd's Theme for Horn Orchestra, 1971. Mbr. Int. Horn Soc. Contbr. to profl. jrnls. Hons. incl: Nat. Competition of Wind Players in Israel, Israel-Am. Cultural Fndn., 1969. Hobby: Sport. Address: 14 Hashomer St., Holon 58272, Israel.

RINDELL, Matti A, b. 1 Dec. 1934, Karinainen, Finland. Organist; Music Teacher. Educ: Univ. exams. in musicol. &

pedagogy; studied organ w. Prof. Volker Gwinner, Germany, & Prof. Dr. Ferdinand Klinda, Czech.; Exams., Sibelius Acad., Heisinki, as Cantor organist, 1954, Music tchr., 1957, Organ dip., 1961. m. Kaija-Leena Rindell, 3 c. Debut: Helsinki, 1961. Career: num. concert tours, throughout Scandinavia, W Germany, Switz., France; sev. apps. on Finnish radio & TV, Swedish radio, Bremen radio, Germany; recitals, USA & Can.; Organist, Ev. Lutheran Parishers, Helsinki; Tchr., Tehtaanpuiston Yhteiskoulu (second. schl.). Mbrships: incl: Pres., Scandinavian Coun. of Ch. Music; VP Finish Assn. of Cantor-organists; Chmn., Organum Soc. Recip. Director Musices, 1974. Address: Siltavoudintie 13 A, Helsinki 64, Finland.

RING, Guy Layton, b. 31 July, 1922, Auckland, NZ. Musician (harpsichord, clavichord, recorders, viols & crumhorns). Educ: BA, Univ. of NZ; MA, Nottingham Univ., UK. m. Christine Melville Kellie, 2 s. Career: Music Tutor, Adult Educ., Auckland, 1947-50, 1952-54; Mbr., Dolmetsch Ensemble, Haslemere, 1950-; Harpsichordist, Northern Sinfonia Orch., 1962-68; Freeland musician, 1968-75; Prin. Lectr. in music, N Ireland Polytechnic, 1976-78; Sr. Lectr., Music Coll. of Arts & Technology, Newcastle-upon-Tyne, 1978-. Recordings: var. early music works; Hoffnung Festival recording. Publ: Ed., Early Music Discovered Exp. on W Lawes; Delius. Mbrships: Viola da Gamba Soc.; Recorder Soc.; Royal Musical Assn.; Lute Soc. Hobby: Poetry. Address: Low Warden Farmhouse, Warden, Hexham, Northumberland NE46 4SN, UK.

RINGBOM, Nils-Eric, b. 27 Dec. 1907, Abo, Finland. Composer; Musicologist. Educ: MA., Helsinki Univ.; Abo Acad., 1933; PhD., ibid, 1955, div. Guri Tegengren, m. Elisabeth Söderhjelm, 4 c. Debut: Abo, 1933; Helsinki, 1934. Career: Violinist, Turku Symph., 1927-28, 1930-33; Libn., Asst. Mgr., Helsinki Phil., 1938-42; Managing Dir., ibid, 1942-70; Artistic Dir., Sibelius Fest., Helsinki, 1951-60; Organized, Managed Helsinki Phil. Tours of Europe, 1960, 1965, USA, 1968; Music Critic, var. Newspapers. Compositions incl: (publd.) 5 Symphs.; Str. Quartet; num. Chmbr., Choral, Vocal Works; (recorded) Little Suite for Orch. Publs: Helsingfors Orkesterföretag 1882-1932, 1932, Säveltaide, 1945; Sibelius, 1948; Ueber die Deutbarkeit der Tonkunst, 1955; De tva versionerna av Sibelius' tondikt En Saga, 1956; Musick utan normer, 1972. Contbr. to num. profl. mags. & jrnls. Mbr., Off., num. profl. orgs. Hons: Kt.-Cmdr., Order of the Lion of Finland, 1970; Kt., 1st Class, Order of Vasa, Sweden; Kt. of the Dannebrogen, 1958; recip. var. other Hons. Hobby: Mushrooms. Address: Näsudden, 21720 Korpoström, Finland. 14, 19.

RIPPON, Michael George, b. 10 Dec. 1938, Coventry, UK. Singer. Educ: St. John's Coll., Cambridge; MA (Cantab); ARAM. m. Josephine Helena McKimmie, 2 s. Debut: Opera, Covent Gd., 1969. Career: Apps. in Opera, Oratorio, Recitals, Radio Broadcasts, TV; Engl. Opera Grp.; Covent Gdn.; Glyndebourne; ENO; Welsh Nat. Opera; PACT, Johannesburg; Boston Opera; Handel Opera; All leading music fests. & socs. in UK & abroad. Recordings incl: Classics for Pleasure, Belshazzar's Feast; Bach B Minor, Cantatas; Mozart Requiem; Purcell's Ode to St. Cecilia; Handel's Israel in Egypt; Moses & Aaron. Hons: ARAM. Hobby: Reading. Mgmt: Ibbs & Tillett, 124 Wigmore St., London W1H OAX. Address: 31 College Dr., Ruislip, Midd. HA4 8SD, UK. 3.

RISTIĆ, Milan, b. 31 Aug. 1908, Beograd, Yugoslavia. Composer. Educ: Comp. w. Alois Haba, Prague Conserv. m. Ruzica Ristić, 1 s. Comps incl: 9 symphs.; 2 piano concertos; 7 bagatellas for orch.; music for chmbr. orch.; 4 movements for string orch.; concerto for chmbr. orch.; 5 characters for wind quintet; 10 epigrams for ten instruments; 5 sketches for flute, clarinet, viola & harp; music for horn quartet; 7 short pieces for piano. Mbrships: Union of Yugoslav Comps.; Servian Acad. of Sci. & Arts. Hons: Labour Medal w. Red Flag, Yugoslavia; Oct. Prize, Belgrade, 1961; 7th July Prize, 1974. Hobby: Philately. Address: Bulevar Lenjina 185/39, 11070 Beograd, Yugoslavia.

RITCHIE, Elizabeth, b. Ayr, Scotland, UK. Lecturer; Voice Specialist; Ensemble Singer; Choral Conductor; Music Therapist. Educ: RSAMD; Jordanhill Coll.; Roehampton Inst. of Higher Educ.; Dip. (Mus. Ed.), RSAMD; FTCL (solo singing); Dip. T Mus. (music therapy), Roehampton Inst.; Nordoff/Robbins Dip. in Music Therapy. m. James Ritchie, 2 s. Career: Music tchr., Ayrshire Schls., 1950-54; solo singer, London, 1954-56; BBC Singers A, London, 1956-62; lectr. in music, Luton Coll. of Higher Educ., 1969-79; now voice tutor, City Lit. Inst., London, 1969-; music therapist, Harborough Schl. for Autistic Children, London, & St. Thomas's Hospital, London. Mbrships: ISM; committee, Assn. of Tchrs. of Singing; Assn. of Music Therapist; NATFJE; British Equity. recip., Caird Singing Scholarships, 1954. Hobbies: Walking; Sea Fishing;

Chmbr. Music; Accomp. Address: 231 Kinch Grove, Wembley, Middx. HA9 9TF, UK.

RITCHIE, John Anthony, b. 29 Sept. 1921, Wellington, NZ. Composer; Teacher; Professor of Music; Deputy Vice Chancellor. Educ: TD, Dunedin Tchrs. Coll.; Mus B, Otago Univ.; L Mus TCL, UK; LTCL. m. Anita Proctor, 2 s., 3 d. Career incls: Lectr., Music, Univ. of Canterbury, NZ, 1946-61; Prof., Music, 1962-; Vis. Prof., Music Exeter Univ., UK, 1967-68; Depty Vich Chancellor, 1978-. Comps: Concertino for Clarinet & Strings (publ.), 1958; Songs & choral music; Incidental Music for radio plays. Author, chapt. on 'Music', The Pattern of New Zealand Culture, 1968. Contbr. to: Christchurch Press; Aust. Jrnl. of Music Educ.; Music Educators Jrnl., USA; ISME Yrbook.; Educ., NZ. Mbrships. incl: Sec. Gen. (1976-), Int. Soc. of Music Educ. Hobbies: Golf; Gardening; Sport. Address: Schl. of Music, Univ. of Canterbury, Christchurch, NZ. 17.

RIVERA, Graciela, b. 17 Apr. 1921, Ponce, Puerto Rico, USA. Colorature Soprano; Operatic & Concert Artist. Educ: Grad., Juilliard Schl. Music, NY, 1943. m. Joseph Zumchak, 1 s., 1 d. Debut: Title role, Lucia di Lammermoore, Metropol. Opera, 4 Feb. 1952. Career: 300 ldng. soprano roles, USA, Ital, UK., Portugal, Mexico, etc.; Asst. Prof.; Hostos Community Coll., CUNY. Comps: Borinquen (danza); Padre Juestro (sacred song); Campanitas (Christmas carol). Recordings: Christmas Album; Puerto Rican Danzas. Contbr. to: Travel Mag.; Temas Mag. Mbr. profl. orgs. Hons: Pro Arte Musical Medal, Puerto Rico; Exemplary Citizen Award, Inst. Puerto Rico, NY. Hobbies: Swimming; Sewing. Address: 703 Ackerman Ave., Glen Rock, NJ 07452, USA.

RIVERA, Roberto, b. 1 Sept. 1924, Mexico DF, Mexico. Historian of Music; Player of Transverse Flute & Recorders. Educ: UNAM, Escuela Nacional de Musica, Mexico; LLB, LeSalle Univ., Chgo., USA. m. Irma Yolanda Negrete, 1 s. Career: w. Convivium Musicum, Mexico; Soloist, Nat. Symph. Orch. of Mexico, chmbr. grps. & at concerts; Assoc. Prof., Escuela Nacional de Musica; Tchr., Am. Recorder Soc. Contbr. to Heterofonia. Mbrships: Am. Recorder & Musicol. Socs.; 1st Pres., Flauta Barroca AC; Treas, Acad. Mexicans de Musicol. Hobbies incl: Transcription of ancient music. Address: Martin Mendalde 832, Mexico 12 DF, Mexico.

RIVIER, Jean, b. 21 July 1896, Villemomble, Seine, France. Composer. Educ: Nat. Conserv. of Paris. m. Maire Peyrissac, 1 s. Career incl: Prof. (later Emeritus Prof.) of Composition, Nat. Conserv. of Music of Paris, 1945-. Compositions incl: 7 Symphs.; Venitienne (comic opera); works for soloists, choir & orch. incl: Requiem; Psalm LVI; Christus Rex; var. concerti, chmbr. music, choral works, etc. Mbr: Gloxiani (musicians' club). Hons: Florent-Schmitt Prize, 1967; Musical Grand Prix, Town of Paris, 1970; Chevalier, Legion of Hon.; Cmndr. of Arts & Letters; Croix de Guerre. Address: 18 rue Pierre-et-Marie-Curie, 75005, Paris, France.

RIZZA, George Joseph, b. 5 Nov. 1925, Banffshire, UK. Publishing Company Director. Educ: Royal Margaret Lensky, 1 d. Career: Profl. singer, Westminster Cathedral Chor, etc., 1948-54; w. music publrs., J & W Chester Ltd., 1950-72; Mng. Dir., ibid., 1962-72; Mng. Dir., Novello & Co. Ltd., 1972-. Mbrships: Dir., PRS, Park Lane Grp. & Mercury Music; Music panel, Arts Coun. GB; Trustee, Purcell Soc. Trust; Vp, Elgar Fndn. Ltd. Hobbies: Reading; Theatre; Walking. Address: Novello & Co. Ltd., 1-3 Upper James St., London W1, UK.

ROBBINS, Edward (Ted) John, b. 5 June 1920, Toronto, Ont., Can. Conductor; Clinica; Teacher; Euphonium & Trombone Player. Educ: GSM; LGSM; RAF Schl. of Music. m. Margaret Jean Robertson, 1 d., 1 s. Debut: Euphonium soloist, Toronto, aged 12. Career: RCAF, soloist w. Ctrl. Band, Ottawa, 1940; Dir. of brass, Hamilton Conserv. of Music, 1959; re-enlisted RCAF; perfs. w. London Phil. Orch., Ottawa Phil. Orch.; Dir., Orpheus Operatic Soc.; Director of Music, Air Transport Command, 1960; perfs. on CC radio & TV; tchr. var. schls., 12 yrs.; now w. Scarborough Bd. of Educ. Recording: Handel's Harmonious Blacksmith. Contbr. to: The Instrumentalist; num. band transcriptions. Hons: Bronze medal, GSM. Mbrships: Can. Band Dirs. Assn. (pres., Ont. Chapt.); Phi Beta Mu; Toronto Musicians Assn. Hobbies: Woodwork; Carpentry; Reading. Address: 43 Tulane Cres., Don Mills, Ont. M3A 2B9, Can.

ROBBINS, Gerald Martin, b. 1 Dec. 1945, LA, Calif., USA. Concert Pianist. Educ: Pvte. study of piano, LA; BMus, MMus, Univ. of S Calif., ibid; Asst., Master Classes of Heifetz & Piatigorsky, ibid. Debut: Wigmore Hall, London, UK, 1972. Career incls: TV recital & concert apps., USA & Europe; Promenade Concerts, UK, 1976; Concerts w. LA Phil.; Chmbr. music perfs.; Co-Fndr. & Assoc. Cond., Westside Symph.

Orch.; Lectr., Chambr. Music, Univ. of S Calif.; Num. radio & TV apps. Recordings incl: Concerti by Litolff & Reinecke; Dvorak Piano Works. Hons. incl: Van Cliburn Int. :iano Competition Prize, 1969; Dip., Tchaikovsky Int. Competition, 1970. Hobbies incl; Photography; Classical Lit. Mgmt: Basil Douglas Ltd., London, UK. Address: London Musical Club, 21 Holland Pk., London W11 3TE, UK; 12031 Mound View Place, Studio City, Calif., USA. 4.

ROBERT-BLUNN, John, b. 21 May 1936, Manchester, UK. Music Critic. Career: Music Critic; Manchester City News, 1957-60; Manchester Evening News, 1960-; Freelance Contbr: Daily Mail & Daily Telegraph, 1960-68; Artistic Dir., Forum Concerts, 1972-; Artistic Dir., Stockport Sunday Schl. Subscription Series, 1975-; Artistic Dir. Festival of Creative Arts (FOCAL), Canterbury, 1975-. Publs: Northern Accent: The Life Story of the Northern School of Music, 1972. Contrbr. to var. publs. Mbrships: Chmn.-Forum-Music Soc. Ltd., Manchester, Manchester Literary & Philosophical Soc. Address: 22 Clifton Dr., Gatley, Cheadle, Cheshire SK8 4EQ, UK.

ROBERTON, Kenneth Bantock, b. 23 Oct. 1913, Glasgow, UK. Music Publisher. Educ: studied w. Ailie Cullen & Purcell J Mansfield, Glasgow, & Frederic Bontoft, London; LRAM.; Hon. TSC. m. Margaret Elizabeth Potter, 2 s., 1 d. Career: Music Fest. Adjudicator, UK & Hong Kong; Former Musical Dir., S London Muscal Club; Cond., London Scottish Choir & The Roberton Singers; currently Mgng. Ptnr., Roberton Publs. Publs: Orpheus With His Lute (Ed.), 1963. Mbrships: ISM; Brit. Fedn. of Music Fests.; Ed. Bd., Engl. Folk Dance & Song Soc. Hobbies: Walking; Footpath Maintenance; Reading. Address: The Windmill, Wendover, Aylesbury, Bucks. HP22 6JJ, UK.

ROBERTS, Arthur, b. 6 July 1912, NYC, USA. Composer; Librettist; Translator. Educ: Dip., piano, Manhattan Schl. Music, 1933; PhD (physics), NY Univ., 1936. m. Janice Banner, 1 s., 1 d. Career: Tchr., physics, music, New England Conserv., Univ. Chgo.; Special interest, use of computers for generation of music. Comps: many songs; Transl. into Engl. Offenbach's 'La Belle Helene'; 'Grand Duchess of Gerolstein', & 'L Vie Parisienne'. Contbr. to: Music by Computers (ed. von Foerster, Beauchamp), 1969; Bd. Dirs., Contemporary Concerts Inc., Chgo. Address: 1S176 Rochdale Cir., Lombard, IL 60148, USA.

ROBERTS, Bernard, b. 23 July 1933, Manchester, UK. Concert Pianist; Piano Professor. Educ: ARCM Piano Performing. m. Patricia May Russell, 2 s. Debut: Wigmore Hall, 1957. Career: Concerts, recitals & broadcasts, solo & chmbr. music throughout GB, 1958-; Prof., Pinao, RCM. Hobby: Model Railways. Address: 22 The Avenue, Kew Gdns., Richmond, Surrey, UK.

ROBERTS, Christopher Morrell, b. 28 Jan. 1943, Manchester, UK. Lecturer; Piano Accompanist. Educ: RMCM; ARMCM, 1964; FRSM, 1965; MusB, Manchester Univ., 1965; Dip., Educ., Durham Univ., 1966. Career: Asst. Dir. of Music, Leighton Pk. Schl., Reading, 1966-74; London Opera Centre, 1975; lectr. in music, Mabel Fletcher Coll., Liverpool, 1976; accomp., Colchester Inst. of Higher Educ., 1979-; continue player in num. recitals, London & UK, 1969-. Mbrships: ISM; Penn Club. Hobbies: Antiques; Photography; Walking. Address: Schl. of Music, Colchester Inst., Sheepen Rd., Colchester, Essex, UK.

ROBERTS, Dagmar, b. 11 Sept. 1910, Sydney, Aust. Concert Pianist; Teacher of Piano & Harmony; Accompanist; Coach. Educ: Perfs. & Tchrs. Dips., NSW State Conservatorium of Music, 1927 & 1928; A Mus A, Aust. Music Exam Bd. m. William Hunstead, 4 children. Career: Profl. concert work & recitals; Concert Tour, Qld., 1933; Tour of all States for Aust. Broadcasting Commission, 1937; Regular broadcast on TV; Sr. Examiner, Aust. Music Exam Bd.; Adjudicator at Eisteddfodau & Fests; Chmbr. music w. local & vis. artists. Mbrships: Aust. Soc. for Music Educ.; NSW Musical Assn. Hons. incl: Trinity Coll. Medallist, Piano & Theory, All Grades, 1919-22. Hobbies incl: Surfing. Address: 47 Wairakei Rd., Wamberal, NSW 2260, Australia.

ROBERTS, Donald Lowell, b. 13 Aug. 1938, Dodge City, Kan., USA. Music Librarian; Ethnomusicologist. Educ: BA, Friends Univ., 1961; AMLS, Univ. of Mich., 1963; Studied bassoon at Curtis Inst. of Music. m. Sally M Meador. Career incls: Bassoonist, Albuquerque Symph. Orch., 1963-68; Fine Arts Libn., Univ. of NM, 1963-68; Hd. Music Libn., Northwestern Univ., 1969-. Mbrships: incl: Nat. Endowment for the Arts Music Progs. Jazz/Folk/Ethnic Advsry. Panel, 1974-78; Chmn., New Worl Records Ed. Committee, 1975-78; Pres., Commission on Educ. & Trng., Coun. Mbr., Int. Assn. of Music Libs., Sec./Treas., US Br., Int. Assn. of

Music Libs.; Mbr. of Bd., Music Lib. Assn., 1976-78; Treas., Soc. for Ethnomusicol., 1978. Contbr. to 3 books & var. profl. jrnls. Hons. incl: Coun. on Lib. Resources Fellowship, 1972-73. Hobby: Travel. Address: Music Lib., Northwestern Univ., Evanston, IL 60201, USA.

ROBERTS, Eric, b. 27 May 1905, Wallasey, Cheshire, UK. Violinist, Conductor. Educ: Royal Manchester Coll. of Music. m. Margaret Finlay Dow, 2 children. Debut: Wigmore Hall London. Career: Concert Violinst, giving many recitals & concerto perfs. between the Wars; Mbr., BBC NI Orch., BBC Scottish Orch., Halle Orch., Liverpool Phil. Orch.; has conducted BBC Welsh Orch., Northern Sinfonia Orch., & City of birmingham Orch.-; has made many broadcasts on 3rd Prog. w. own Str. Orch., & in Scandinavia; Fndr. & Dir., Edinburgh's Connoisseur Concerts for 20 yrs. Mbrships: Pres., Edinburgh Soc. of Musicans; Coun., Scottish Arts Club; ISM. Hobbies: All Country pursuits, esp. Trout Fishing. Mgmt: Pro Arte Musica. Address: 5 Lonsdale Terr., Edinburgh 4H3 9HN, UK.

ROBERTS, Gertrud Hermine Kunzel, b. 23 Aug. 1906, Hasting, Min., USA. Concert Harpsichordist; Composer. Educ; BA, Univ. of Minn., 1928; student. Leipzig Conserv., of Music, 1930-31; pvte. study w. Mme. Julia Elbogen, Vienna, Austria, 1932-33. m. Joyce O Roberts, 1 s., 1 d. Career: Annual concert tours in Am., 1960-. Comps. incl: Musica for incl. film 'Pineapple Country Hawaii', harpsichord, 1960; Music for Shakespeare's 'Tempest', harpsichord, 1962; Cycle, voice & piano, 1962; Herma's Lullabye, voice & piano, 1962; Music for stage prodn. of Lorca's Yerma, two harpsichords, 1961; Waltz, two harpsichord, 1962; Elegy, piano or orch. for John F Kennedy, 1965; Twelve Time Gardens, piano, 1967; Das Kleine Buch der Bilder, harpsichord; Double Concerto, for 2 harpsichords & orch., 1976, etc. Publs: Chaconne for Harpsichord; Rondo-Hommage to Couperin. Mbr., many profl. orgs. incing. Pres., Nat. Soc. of Arts & Letters, 1971-74. Hons: Hon. Life Mbr., Honolulu Community Theatre; Most Disting. Citizen in Am. in Music, Alpha Gamma Delta, 1975. Address: 4723 Moa St., Honolulu, HI 96816, USA. 5, 9, 23, 27, 29.

ROBERTS, John Peter Lee, b. 21 Oct. 1930, Sydney, Aust. Music Administrator. m. Christina (van Oordt) Roberts, 1 s., 2 d. Career incl: prof., CBC Radio, Toronto, 1955-; special advsr., music & arts, ibid., 1975; mbr. exec. committee, Int. Music Ctr., Vienna; mbr., exec. committee, Int. Music Coun., Paris, 1973-, (VP, 1975, pres., 1978-79); pres., Can. Music Ctr., 1971-77; dir.-gen., ibid., 1977-; pres., Can. Music Coun., 1968-71, 1975-77; dir., Fest. Singers of Can., 1965-77; dir., Nat. Youth Orch. of Can., 1971-; Chmn., Int. Vocal Competition, Rio de Janeiro, 1979. Publs: major chapts. in Aspects of Music in Canada, 1969; Fifty Years of Music on Radio. Contbr. to; The Canadian Forum; Canada Music Book; Les cahiers canadiens de musique; Music Magazine, etc. Address: Can. Music Ctr., 1263 Bay St., Toronto, Ont. M5R 2C1, Can. 2.

ROBERTS, Paul Anthony, b. 2 June 1949, Beaconsfield, UK. Pianist. Educ: BA, Univ. of York, 1970; Recital Dip., RAM 1973. m. Nicola Hadley. Debut: as Soloist, Wigmore Hall, London, 1975. Career: Mbr., Duke Piano Trio; Wigmore Hall recitals, 1974 & 75, Purcell Room, 1976, BBC Radio 3 braodcast, 1975; Solo recital, Wigmore Hall, 1976, 78; Regular contributor to BBC Radio 3 talks on musical topics. Contbr. to The Times. Recip., var. prizes, RAM, incl. May Hodgson Fellowship, 1978-79. Hobbies: Literature; History. Mgmt: Elizabeth Skinner Concert Mgmt., 19 Cheyne Court, London SW3. Address: 3 St. Mary's Lane, Bootham, York, UK.

ROBERTS, Stephen Pritchard, b. 8 Feb. 1949, Denbigh, Wales, UK. Baritone Singer. Educ: RCM (Assoc. Bd. Scholar), 1967-72; GRSM; ARCM. Career: Mbr., male vocal ensemble Pro Cantione Antiqua; Lay Clerk, Westminster Cathedral, 1972-76; num. apps. in London w. major choral socs. & orchs.; apps. at Promenade Concerts & on BBC radio & TV; apps. at fests. incl. Aldeburgh, City of London, Bath, Three Choirs, Lucerne, Bordeaux, Barcelona, Israel, Flanders & Holland; tours of USA, Italy, Belgium & most of Europe; premieres of works by Holloway, Hoddinot & LeFanu. Recordings incl: Bach's Magnificat & St. Matthew Passion, Charpentier's Te Deum & Handel's Messiah. Mbr. RCM Union. Hobbies: Cooking; Eating; Walking; Collecting; Travelling. Mgmt: Harrison/Parrott Ltd. Address: 144 Gleneagle Rd., Streatham, London SW16 6BA, UK.

ROBERTS, Verna Dean Smith, b. 11 Apr. 1925, Sherman, Tex., USA. Teacher of Piano & Voice; Contralto; Accompanist; Organist; Adjudicator; Choral Director. Educ: Guy Maler master classes, Am. Conserv. of Music, Chgo., 1943; BMusEd, Phillips Univ., Enid, Okla., 1947; MS, Okla. State Univ., 1950; studies at William R Harper Coll., Ill., 1975-. m. James B Roberts, 1 s.,

2 d. Debut: (piano) S E State Coll., Durant, Okla., 1943; (vocal), Phillips Univ., Enid, Okla., 1947. Career: pvte. tchr. of piano, 1940-; pvte. tchr. of voice, 1945-; num. posts as tchr.; currently at Sacred Heart of Mary High Schl., Rolling Meadows, Ill.; adjudications; choral dir., mbr. sev. choirs. mbr., num. profl. socs. Hons. incl: Nat. Piano Guild Hall of Fame, 1973; Nat. Hon. Roll., fac. mbr., NGPT, 13 yrs. Hobbies: Swimming; Bowling; Reading; Riding; Cooking. Address: 623 Sycamore Dr., Elk Grove Village, IL 60007, USA. 27, 29.

ROBERTS, Wilfred Bob, b. 26 Feb. 1921, Detroit, Mich., USA. Trumpet; Brass; Piano; String Bass; Arranger; Composer; Conductor; Teacher. Educ: BMus.Ed., Univ. of Mich., 1947; BMus., Theory Comp., ibid, 1949. m. Lois M Roberts. Career: Studio work w. Recording Cos.; TV Networks; Theatre; Films; Concerts; Solo Recitals; 1st Trumpet. Radio City Music Hall Symph. Orch., 1952-72; Instrumental Tchr. & Coll. Instructor in Music, 10 yrs.; Dir., a univ. concert band & wind ensembles. 4 yrs.; Dir., Music Projects, Christian Science Publishing Co., Boston, 1972-. Publng. Soc. Music Ed., Boston, Mass. Comps. (publd.) incl: Coliseum March; Spirit of Nassau March; Serenade for Trumpet; Duo for 2 Winds; Miniature for 3 Winds; A Day in the Country; Variations on an English Tune; Tango; 3 Headlines Transitions Crosscurrents; Suite for 7 woodwinds. Contbr. to: Var. Music Mags. Mbrships: ASCAP; AFM; Phi Mu Alpha Sinfonia; Phi Beta Lambda; Kappa Kappa Psi; Int. Trumpeters Guild. Address: 780 Boylston St., Boston, MA 02199, USA.

ROBERTS, William Herbert Mervyn, b. 23 Nov. 1906, Abergale, N Wales, UK. Composer; Teacher; pianist. Educ: BA, Trinity Coll., Cambridge, 1928; ARCM; LMus, TCL; ALCM. m. Eileen Margaret Easom, 1 d. Career: Music Staff, Clarendon Schl., Abergale, 1953-56; Christs Hospital, Horsham, 1963-67. Music Staff, Clarendon Schl., Abergale, 1953-56, Christs Hospital, Horsham, 1963-67. Compositions: Sonata, Sonatina, pinao, Variatoiins on an Original Theme, 2 Chorales, 2 pianos; 4 Preludes, 3 Pastoral pieces, The Day Before Yesterday, piano solo; var. Songs. voice & piano; Partsongs; Arrs. of Welsh Folksongs. Contbr. to: Music in Educ.; Jrnl. of the Welsh Folksong Soc.; Anglo-Welsh Review. Mbrships: CGGB; Guild for the Promotion of Welsh Music; Oxford & Cambridge Musical Club. Recip. Edwin Evans Prize ·for Piano Sonata, 1950. Hobby: Reading. Address: 41 Worthing Rd., Horsham, Sussex RH12 1TD, UK. 3, 14.

ROBERTS, Winifred, b. Lismore, NSW, Australia. Violinist. Educ: RCM; Study w. Antionio Brosa, Albert Sammons. m. Geraint Jones. Career: Nat. Gallery Concerts, UK; Promenade Concerts; 3 Choirs Fest.; Lake Dist. Fest.; Salisbury Fest.; Manchester Fest.; Soloist, Festival Hall & Queen Elizabeth Hall; Tours, Italy, Spain, USA.; BBC radio & TV apps. Recordings: EMI History of Music; Biber Sonata; Vivaldi Double Concerto; Harpsichord & Violin Sonatas w. husband. Hons: Tagore Gold Medal, 1st Prize, Violin Playing, RCM. Hobbies: Swimming; Reading; Cooking; Gardening; Walking. Address: The Long House, Arkley Lane, Barnet, Herts, EN5 3JR, UK. 3, 27.

ROBERTSON, Donna Nagey, b. 16 Nov. 1935, Ind., Pa., USA. Organist; Harpsichordist; Composer; Teacher. Educ: BS, Indiana Univ. of Pa.; M Mus., Eastman Schl. of Music; AAGO. m. Joseph Robertson. Career: Comp. perf. at many fests. throughout the Southeast; Perf. as Organ Recitalist throughout Southeast USA. Compositions: Trio for Violin, oboe and harpsichord; Recitation w. Five Reflections for Trombone & piano, Nocturn for trombone & tenor; Psalm for a Festive Procession; Love (motet for treble voices); No Single Thing Abides for d.b. chorus; Psalm for an Academic Procession; 6 Psalms of Ascension for low voice & piano. Ed., Music Now, 1973-. Mbrships: AGO; Delta Omicron; Delta Kappa Gamma; Bd. Dirs., League of Women Compoers; Ed., Newsletter, Southeastern Composers' League; Bd. Dirs., Music in the Mountains; chmber music fest. Recip. / Award, Nat. Fed. of Music Clubs for Str. Quartet No. 1, 1960. Address: Box 223, Mars Hill, NC 28754, USA.

ROBERSTON, Duncan, b. 1 Dec. 1924, Hamilton, UK. Singer (tenor). Educ: FGSM; LRAM; Dip., Scottish Nat. Acad. of Music. m. Mary Dawson, 1 s., 1 d. Career: appearances at most major Brit. Festivals; Opera roles w. Covent Gdn., Scottish Opera, Blyndebourne Opera & Engl. Opera Grp.; staff mbr., RSAM, Glasgow, extensive tours abroad; broadcast apps. on Radio & TV. Hobbies: Reading; Walking; Tavel. Address: 256 Nithsdale Rd., Glasgow G41 5AJ, UK.

ROBERTSON, Ian, b. 7 Oct. 1947, Dundee, UK. Pianist; Harpsichord Player; Conductor. Educ: Dip. in Music Educ., RSAM: B Mus. Univ. of Glasgow. m. Carolyn-Joan Scott Robertson. Career: Recitalist, Soloist w. Orchs., Scotland; Accomp., Wigmore Hall, London, Soloist, New Music Grp. of Scotland, concert, Edinburh Fest., 1975; sev. BBC radio broadcasts. Mbr., ISM. Address: 16 Tannahill Terrace, Dunblane, UK.

ROBERTSON, James, b. 17 June 1912, Liverpool, UK. Conductor. Educ: MA, Winchester Coll., Trinity Coll., Cambrdige Univ.; Conservatorium Leipzig; RCM, London. m. Rachel June Fraser, 2 s. Career: Chorus Master, Carl Rosa Opera, 1938-39; Music Staff, Glyndebourne Opera, 1937-39; cond., CBC, 1939-40; Dir. & Cond., Sadler's Wells Opera, 1946-54; Cond., Nat. Orch. of MZ Broadcasting Serv., 1954-57; Cond., Carl Rosa Opera, 1958; Cond., Touring Opera, 1958; Guest Cond., Sadler's Wells, 1958-63; Advsr. on Opera to Theatre de la Monnaie, Brussels, 1960; Artistic Dir., NZ Opera & Cond., Concert Orch. of NZBC, 1962-63; Dir., London Opera Ctr., 1964-77; Consultant, ibid., 1977-78. Mbrships: ISM; Royal Phil. Soc. Hons: Hon. GSM, 1953; FRCM, 1964; Hon. RAM, 1969; Hon. FTCL, 1969; CBE, 1969. Hobbies: Languages, Wine. Mgmt: Ibbs & Tillet Ltd. Address: Ty Helig, Llwyn Mawr, Llangollen, Clwyd LL20 7BG, UK. 1, 28.

ROBERTSON, John Seymour, b. 20 Sept. 1938, Galashiels, UK. Tenor Singer. Educ: BSc, Edinburgh Univ. m. Marjorie Claire Nicholson, 1 s., 3 d. Debut: Glasgow, 1963. Career: Prin. tenor, Scottish Opera, 1963-; apps. throughout UK, Iceland, Germany, Portugal, Poland, Switz. in about 40 roles; broadcasts on STV & BBC; apps. w. Phoenix Opera & w. Scottish Opera at Edinburgh Fest., 1968, 72, 77, 79, w. LPO, 1969, & w. Edinburgh Fest. Opera, 1975-76; apps. w. Ambrosian Singers, London, 1978. Recordings: Marriage of Figaro. Mbrships: Scottish Comm., British Equity Actors Assn.; ISM. Hobbies: Sports; Reading; Motoring; Watching TV. Mgmt: Basil Douglas Ltd., London. Address: 14 Baronald Dr., Glasgow G12 OHZ, Scotland, UK.

ROBERTSON, Paul Allan Reuben, b. 1 Nov. 1952, London, UK. Violinist; Quartet Leader. Educ: RAM. Debut: Wigmore Hall. Career: Ldr., Medici String Quartet. Recordings: Var. BBC; Haydn opus 64 quartets 1-6. Hons. incl: Associated Bd., Schlrship.; GLAA Young Musicians Prize; Inter Coll. Quartet Prize. Hobby: Appreciating things. Address: Music Dept., Univ. York, York, UK.

ROBIN, Joann Cohan, b. 5 Aug. 1928, Bridgeport, Conn., USA. Pianist; Music Therapist. Educ: Studied w. Muriel Kerr at Juilliard Schl. of Music at age 13; studied w. Zosla Jacynowicz, Conn. Coll.; BA., ibid; Special Educ., New Haven State Tchrs. Coll.; intensive course in Music Therapy Musical Guidance, Boston, Mass.; Clinical Trng., Boston State Hosp; Registered Music Therapist, 1957. m. Richard S Robin, 1 s., 1 d. Career: Pvte. Piano Lessons. New Haven Conn.; FAc. of the Julius Hartt Schl. of Music, 1951; Accomp. for vocal & instrumental students. Tchr. of Piano, Acting Dir. of Chapel Choirs, Mt. Holyoke Coll., 1963; Dir. of Music for the ABC Prog., ibid, 1965, 66; Music Therapy Experience at Yale Psych. Inst. (estab. music prog.). Payne Whitney clinic of the NY Hosp., Cornell Med. Ctr., West Haven VA Hosp., etc.; Var. perfs. of chmbr. music progs., choral & orchl. & solo recitals; Lectrs. on music therapy at var. univs; Dance accomp., Mount Holyoke Coll., 1975; Lect. in Dance, 1977. Has written articles on music therapy. Mbr., sev. profl. orgs. Hons: Phi Beta Kappa. var. Hobbies: Address: 78 Woodbridge St., South Hadley, MA 01075, USA.

ROBINSON, Bernard Wheeler, b. 8 June 1904, Coventry, UK. Physicist (Ret'd.). Educ: Oundle Schl.; Trinity Coll., Cambridge; MA; PhD. Career: Chief Organizer & Cond., The Music Comps. 1927-; Cond., Royal Amateur Orchl. Soc., 1933-36; Fndr. & Cond., Informal Chmbr. Orch., 1936-72. Hobby: Chmbr. Music. Address: Pigotts. North Dean, High Wycombe, Bucks., UK.

ROBINSON, Douglas, b. 5 Sept. 1913, Leeds, Yorks., UK. Chorus Master. Educ: Mus B, Dunelm; FRCO. m. Norah Cannell. Career: Organist & Choirmaster, var. Leeds. chs., Christ Ch., Harrogate, 1946; Chorus Master, Royal Opera House, Covent Gdn., 1946-74, Lyric Opera, Chgo., 1976; Chorus Master & Assoc. Cond., Huddersfield Choral Soc., 1972; Gen. Cond., BBC, etc.; Lectr. & Adjudicator. Recordings: Chorus Master, All Covent Gdn. recordings, 1946-74. Publs: All Beginners Please, 1967; Act Two Beginners Please, 1970 (collects. of operatic choruses). Recip., OBE, 1975. Hobbies: Painting; Cooking. Address: 30 Upper Pk. Rd., London, NW3 2UT, UK.

ROBINSON, Forbes, b. 21 May 1926, Macclesfield, Cheshire, UK. Bass singer. Educ: Dip. in Phys. Educ., Loughborough Coll.; I a Scuola di Canto, Scala Theatre. Milan, m. Marion Stubbs, 2 d. Debut: Monterone in Rigoletto, Covent Gdn., 1954. Career: Concert & opera singer throughout Europe & in N & S Am.; Prin. Bass, Royal Opera Co., Covent Gdn.; 5 opera apps. on TV; Own radio show. Recordings: Anniversary Album of Covent Garden (Decca); Handel Arias (Argo); An Evening with Forbes Robinson (Tower); Christmas with Forbes Robinson (Tower); Among Your Souvenirs (Decca); Ballads, Songs & Snatches (Argo). Mbrships: Savage Club, London. Hons: Mario Lanza Schliship., 1952; Opera Medal; Harriet Cohen Int. Music Awards, 1963. Hobbies: Gardening; Rugby Football. Address: 225 Princes Gdns., London W3, UK. 1.

ROBINSON, Helene Margaret, b. 30 May 1914, Eugene, Ore., USA. Professor of Piano; Soloist; Accompanist; Lecturer; Author; Composer. Educ: BA, Univ. of Ore.; M Mus, Northwestern Univ., Ill.; study toward DMA, Univ. of So. Calif., piano study w. Aurora Underwood, Pauline Manchester, Egon Petri & Lillian Steuber. Career: Perfs. on many TV & radio stns.; Lectr. at Workshops for Music Tchrs. on Univ. & Coll. campuses of many western States; Prof., No. Ariz. Univ., 1942-50; So. Ore. State Coll., 1950-67; Vis. Prof., Calif. State Coll., Fullerton, 19661-62 & at Univ. of Calif., Santa Barbara, 1963-64; currently Prof., Ariz. State Univ., Tempe, 1967- & Coord. of Piano Classes; Adjudicator for piano contests & study progs. sponsored by state orgs. of Music Tchrs. & the NGPT. Speaker, 3 Nat. Convens., Music Tchrs. Nat. Assn., 1974, 1976; Speaker, 12 regional & nat. convens., Music Educators Nat. Conf. Publs: Basic Piano for Adults, 1964; Intermediate Piano for Adults, vols. I & II, 1970; Teaching Piano in Classroom & Studio, 1967. Contbr. to var. jrnls. Mbrships. incl: Pres., Ariz. State Music Tchrs. Assn., 1976-; MENC (on Piano Comm., State Chmn. of Student Chapts. in Ore. & Speaker at 10 regl.-nat. convens.) Recip. var. hons. Address: Music Dept., Ariz. State Univ., Tempe, AZ 85281, USA. 3, 5, 27.

ROBINSON, Lucy, b. 23 Dec. 1949, London, UK. Musicologist; Viola da Gamba Player & Teacher. Educ: Ba, Univ. of York; studied at York & Cambridge Univs., Royal Music Conserv., Brussels. Career: perfs. in UK, Europe & Aust.; mbr. Concordia & The Churchill Players; Tchr., Winchester Coll., Purcell Schl. & Open Univ.; lectr. & supervisor at num. Univs. in UK & abroad. Publs: Francois Couperin, Pièces de Violes, 1973; notes for record sleeves. Contbr. to: Gorve's Dict., 6 Ed.; Early Music. Mbrships: Societé Francaise de Musicologie; Royal Musical Soc.; ISM. Recip., Churchill Travelling Fellowship, 1976. Hobbies: Chmbr. Music; Cooking; Gardening; Walking. Address: 20 Springfield Rd.; Cambridge, UK.

ROBINSON, Michael Finlay, b. 3 March 1933, Gloucester, UK. University Lecturer in Music. Educ: BA, 1956, B Mus, 1957, MA, 1960, DPh, 1963, New Coll., Oxford Univ. m. Ann James, 2 s. Career incls: Lectr. in Music, Univ. of Durham, 1961-65; Asst. Prof. of Music, McGill Univ., Montreal, Can., 1965-67; Assoc. prof. of Music, ibid., 1967-70; Lectr. in Music, Univ. Coll., Cardiff, UK, 1970-75; Sr. Lectr., ibid, Int. Musicol. Soc. Royal Musical Assn.; Am. Musicol. Soc. Publs: Opera Before Mozart, 1966, 2nd ed., 1972; Naples & Neapolitan Opera, 1972. Contbr. to var. profl. publs. Hons. incl: Rsch. Grant, Leverhulme Trust, London, 1975. Hobbies incl: Watercolour painting. Address: Northridge House, Shirenewton, Gwent NP6 6RZ, UK. 14.

ROBINSON, Paul E., b. 21 March 1940, Toronto, Ont., Can. Conductor; Broadcaster; Writer. Educ: MA, Univ. of Toronto; Dip. in Cond., Salzburg Mozarteum. m. Marita, 1 s, 1 d. Career: Music Dir., Vic. Chmbr. Symph., Hong Kong, 1967-69; Music Dir., CJRT-FM Toronto, 1972-; Music Dir. & Cond., CJFT orch., 1972-; Music Dir., Toronto Arts Prodns., 1979-. Publs: Art of the Conductor, Karajan (1975), Stokowski (1977), Solti (1979). Address: CJRT-FM, 297 Victoria St., Toronto, Ont. M5B 1W1, Can.

ROBINSON, Stanford, b. 5 July 1904, Leeds, Yorks. Orchestral & Opera Conductor; Lecturer on Conducting & Musical Themes. Educ: RCM, Lonon, ARCM (Hons); Hon. GSM; studied abroad. m. Lorely Dyer, 1 d. Career: w. BBC, 1924-66; Chorus Master, ibid, until 1932, during which time formed the BBC Choral Activities in London, inclng., the BBC Singers, The Choral Soc., The BBC Chorus, & was Cond., The Wireless orch., wide variety of Progs.; Cond., BBC Theatre Orch.; Opera Dir., Assoc. Cond., BBC Symph. Orch., 1946-49; Cond., Opera Orch., & Opera Org., BBC, 1949-52; Toured Aust., NZ, cond. ABC & NZBC Orchs. in num. Cities, 1966-67; Chief Cond., Queensland Symph. Orch., 1968-69. Comp. incl: Orchl. Music, Brass Band Music, part Songs, Choral Arrangements, Songs, etc. Num. Recordings. Recip., OBE, 1972. Hobbies: Photography; Gardening. Address: 2 Stanley House, 103 Marylebone High St., London W1M 3DB, UK. 1, 3.

ROBINSON, Virginia Morgan, b. 8 Aug. 1910, Providence, RI, USA. Harpist. Educ: Pianist, studied w. Alfred Holy & Lucille Delcourt (harp) & Adamowsky (cello); New England Conserv.; Paris Conserv.; studied in France w. Marcel Tournier, Marcel

Grandjany, Pierre Jamet & Mlle Henriette Renié. m. Welford S. Robinson, 1 s. Debut: Solo harp in paris, 1929; Orchl. soloist, Cannes, 1929; NY, 1930. Career: Played w. sisters (Marguerite, pianist & Frances, violinist), throughout Europe & USA; Played one of the first radio broadcasts from Providence RI, one of the first broadcasts from France to Am. & for sev. yrs. had 3 to 5 radio braodcasts a week; Played for the BBC as well as the num. public & pvte. musicalles; Harpist w. Maitre Pierre Monteux in San Fran. Symph., 15 yrs.; Ballet & Opera Harpist; Tchr. at Morgan Music Studio, Mills Coll., San Fran. Conserv., etc.; Mbr. of num. Harp juries; Has been making a film on the Centennial of Mlle Renie, past Pres., No. Calif. Harpists Assn. & 'Harp News'; UK Harpist Assn.; Amis de la Harpe. Address: 163 Monroe St. N, Denver, CO 80206, USA.

ROBISON, Charles Wright, b. 20 Feb. 1925, Batesville, Miss., USA. professor of Music Education; Choral Director. Educ: B Mus., Univ. of Miss.; M Mus Ed., Univ. of Mich.; D Mus Ed., Univ. of Okla. m. Shirley Walker, 1 s., 1 d. Contbr. to: Schl. Musician; Okla. Schl. Music News; Music Tchrs. Workshop. Chmn., Dept. of Art & Music, Angelo State Univ., San Angelo, Tex. Mbrships: Past State Chmn., Am. Choral Dirs. Assn.; MENC; Nat. Assn. Tchrs. of Singing; Tex. Music Educators Assn.; Tex. Choral Dirs. Assn. Hons. incl: Taylor Medal Award. Hobbies: Tenning; Swimming; Gridge. Address: 2921 Southland Blvd., San Angelo, TX, USA.

ROBISON, Paula, b. 8 June 1941, Nashville, Tenn., USA. Flute Soloist; Teacher. Educ: Univ. of Southern Calif.; BS, Juilliard Schl. of Music; Study w. Julius Baker, Marcel Moyse. m. Scott Nickrenz. Debut: NYC, 1961. Career: Soloist w. NY Phil., L'Orchestre de la Suisse Romande; Recitals, Carnegie Hall, Jordan Hall, Boston, Marlboro & Spoleto Fests.; Tours w. Orpheus Trio; Regular pers., Tully Hall, NYC, Kennedy Ctr., Wash. DC, & Fisher Hall, NYC; Res. Artist, Chmbr. Music Soc. of Lincoln Ctr., NYC; Fac. Mbr., New England Conserv. of Music, Boston. Recordings incl: Schubert's Introduction & Variations, w. Rudolph Serkin; Paula Robison plays flute music of the romantic era. Contbr. to Music Jrnl. Hons: 1st Prize, Geneva Int. Competition, 1966. Hobbies: Reading; Growing plants; Travel. Mgmt: Kazuko Hillyer Int., NYC. Address: 57 Brimmer St., Boston, MA 02108, USA.

ROBLES, Maria Esther (D'Attili, Maria), b. 6 Aug. 1921, Fajardo, Puerto Rico. Singer; Voice Teacher. Educ: Juilliard Schl. Music, 2 yrs.; sev. disting. pvte. tchrs. m. (1) Glauco D'Attili, 1 s.; (2) Juan Luis Marquez, 1 d. Career incls: Premiered, Gian Carlo Menotti's 'The Telephone', Paris, London, USA; Starred & premiered, Sir Charles B Cocchran's 'Tough at the Top'; Radio apps., UK, USA, Spain & Puerto Rico; TV, NY & Puerto Rico; Num. Concerts, operas & operattas; Dir., Opera Work Shop & Voice Tchr., Pablo Casals Conserv. Music, Puerto Rico. Recordings incl: Maria Esther Robles canta Danzas Puertorriquenas; Mi Aguinaldo de Navidad. Mbr. prof. orgs. Hons. incl: Medal Merit & Grand Puerto Rican Prize Music, Aacad. Arts & Sics. Puerto Rico, 1974. Address: Villa Internacional II. Casa 13, Punta Las Marias, Santurce, Puerto Rico 00913.'

ROBLES, Marisa, b. 4 May 1937, Madrid, Spain. Solo Harpist; Chamber Musicians. Educ: degrees in harp, harmony & comp., Royal Conserv. of Music, Madrid. 2 s., 1 d. Debut: Madrid, aged 9. Career: regular apps. at Royal Fest. Hall, Queen Elizabeth Hall, Wigmore Hall, London; broadcasts for BBC TV & radio & ITV; apps. in sev. European capitals, in S Am., Can., Africa, Israel; former prof., Royal Conserv., Madrid; Prof., RCM.; harp tchrs., Nat. Youth Orch. of GB. num. recordings. Mbrships: UK Harpists' Assn.; Am. Harp Soc.; Anglo-Spanish Soc. num. hons., prizes & awards. Hobbies: Living Truly & Honestly; House Plants; Films & Theatre; Photography; Children & Animals needing Care. Mgmt: J van Walsum, London. Address: 38 Luttrell Ave., London SW15, UK.

ROBOTHAM, Barbara, b. 15 Jan. 1936, Blackpool, UK. Mezzo-soprano. Educ; Assoc., Royal Manchester Coll. of Music; Hon. Fellow, ibid. m. Eric Waite, 1 s. Career: profl. perfs. in oratorio, opera, lieder; BBC- broadcasts; regular visits to France, Germany, Switz., Italy, Spain, Portugal, Czech.; Tchr. of singing, Royal Manchester Coll. of Music, 1959-65; Prof. of Voice, Lancaster Coll. of Music, 1959-65; Prof. of Voice, Lancaster Univ., 1976-. Recordings: Stravinsky's Cantata on Old Engl. Texts; Walton's Gloria. Mbrships: NW Arts Music panel; Fylde Arts Exec. Committee & Music Panel; ISM. Hons. incl: Imperial League of OPera Prize & Curtis Gold Medal for Singing, 1958; 1st Prize, Liverpool Int. Singers Competition, 1960; 2nd Prize, Int. Concours, Geneva, 1961. Hobbies: 49 Blackpool Rd., N, St. Annes on Sea, Lancs. FY8 3DF, UK.

ROBSON, Elizabeth, b. 17 Jan. 1939, Dundee, Scotland, UK. Opera Singer. Educ: Royal Scottish Acad. of Music (DRSAM).

m. Neil Howlett, 2 d. Debut: Engl. Nat. Opera Co., London. Career: apps. at Covent ZGdn., La Scala Milan, San Carlo Naples, throughout France & Germany; apps. w. Scottish Opera & Welsh Nat. OPera Co.; Concerts; BBC TV & radio. Recordings for EMI. Mbr., Counfrarie Dis Eschansoun Dou Rei Reinie. Recip. Sir James Caird Travelling Scholarship, 1959. Hobbies: Family; Theatre; Pottery; Collecting Hogarth prints. Mgmt: S A Gorlinsky Ltd. Address: Craven Lodge, 42 Inner Park Rd., London SW19 6DD, UK.

ROBY, Paul Edward, b. 5 June 1935, Akron, Ohio, USA. Violinist; Teacher; Conductor. Educ: BM Violin, Oberlin Conserv.; MM Violin, Cath. Univ. of Am., Wash. DC; D Musical Arts, Univ. of Colo., Boulder; studied w. Andor Toth & William Kroll. m. Linda Grace Lowe, 1 s. Career: Mbr., USAF Orch.; Concertmaster, Shreveport Symph., La.; Soloist w. Wash. Civic Symph., Okla. City Symph. & USAF Orch.; Fac. Mbr., Okla. Univ., Norma; Fac. Mbr., Kan. State Univ., Manhattan; Cond., Kan. State Univ., Orch.; 1st Violin, Resident Quartet, ibid; Orch. Dir., Univ. of Lowell; Cond., NH Phil. Mbrships: Am. String Tchrs. Assn.; MENC; MTA; ASTA; CMS; AFM. Hobby: Tennis. Address: 175 Freeman St., Brookline, MA 02146, USA.

ROCCA, Lodovico, b. 1895, Torino, Italy. Composer; Conservatory Director. Educ: Turin Univ.; studied w. Giacomo Orefice, Milan Conserv. m. Guiseppina Dellapiana, 1 s. Career: Dir., Turin Conserv., 1940-66. Compositions incl: Il dibuk (opera); In terra de leggenda (opera); Antiche Iscrizzioni for soprano, bass, choir & orch.; La Cella Azzurra; Chiaroscuri; Proverb di Salomone for tenor, small choir of women & 12 instruments; Salmodia for baritone, small choir & 11 instruments; Storiella for quintet; Birbu occhi di rana for baritone & str. quartet; Schizzi francescani for tenor & octet; 4 Melopee su epigrammi sepolcrali greci; 2 Songs to Tennyson. Mbr: Rotary Club. Recip. of many prizes & awards inclng: Artists Medal of Hon., Italian Repub.; Kt. Cmdr. of Italian Repub. Address: Via Principe Tommaso 94, 10125 Torino, Italy.

ROCHAT, Andrée, b. 12 Jan. 1900, Geneva, Switzerland. Composer; String Musician. Educ: Music Dip., Music Conserv., Geneva; Comp. Studies w. A Gedalge, paris, France, G Orefice, Milan, Italy & Wladimir Vogel, Ascona. m. Dr. E Aeschlimann. Career: Participant, Working Women's Exhib., Zürich, Switzerland; Radio Perfs., Rome, Italy, Burssels, Belgium, Milan, Italy & Zürich, Switzerland. Compositions (publd) Chmbr. & Strings Music (Carisch Milan). Recordings: w. Musikkollegium Winterhur & Schloss Schwetzingen. Publs: Journal D'Un Amateur De Musique. Contbr. to: Schweizerische Musikzeitung. Hons: Gedock, 1957. Address: Minervastrasse 144, 8032 Zürich, Switzerland.

ROCHBERG, George, b. 5 July 1918, Paterson, NJ, USA. Composer, Educ: B Mus, Curtis Inst. of Music, 1948; MA, Univ. of Pa., 1949. m. Gene Amuer Rosenfeld, 1 s. (dec.), 1 d. Career: works performed by all major orchs. in USA; Violin Concerto perfs., Paris & London, 1977; chmbr. works performed internationally. Comps. publd. byu Theo. Presser & Galaxy Music. Comps. recorded: 2nd Symph., Columbia; 3rd Quartet, Nonesuch; Wnd Quartet, Tableaux, Trio, Vox; Chmbr. Symph., Music for the Magic Theatre, Desto; others. Publs: The Hexachord. Contbr. to: Perspectives of New Music; New Lit. Hist. Mag.; Int. Soc. for the Study of Time; others. Mbrships. incl: ASCAP; Am. Musicol. Soc.; Am. Music Ctr. Hon. incl: Gershwin Prize; Prix de Rome. Hobbies: Cinema; The Seashore. Address: Univ. of Pa., Philadelphia, PA, USA.

ROCHE, Jerome Laurence Alexander, B. 22 May 1942, Cairo, Egypt. University Lecturer in Music. Educ: MA, MusB, PhD, St. John's Coll., Cambridge; ARCO. m. Elizabeth Nicholls. Career: Univ. Lectr., Writer, Ed., Continuo Player. Publs: Palestrina, 1971; The Madrigal, 1972; The Penguin Book of Italian Madrigals, 1974; eds. of Italian motets. Contbr. to: New Oxford Hist. of Music, Vol. V; The Monteverdi Companion, 1968; Music & Letters; Musical Times; Music Review; Early Music; The Consort; Soundings. Mbrships: Comm. Mbr. & Chapt. Rep. to Coun., Nothern Chapt., Royal Musical Assn.; RCO; Int. Musicol. Soc. Hobbies: Railways; Meteorology; Architecture; Political Statistics. Address: The Music Schl., Palace Green, Durham, UK.

ROCHE, Michel Sylvain Nizier, b. 16 May 1936, Saint-Etienne, France. Cellist. Educ: Conservs. of Paris & Amsterdam. m. Hesseltje Belksma, 2 d. Debut: w. Radio Orch. of Lyons, aged 16. Career: Mbr., Radio Orch., Hilversum, Netherlands; currently Solo Cellist, Rotterdam Phil. Orch.; Cellist, Netherlands String Quartet (tours of UK, Germany, France & USA); Tchr., Utrecht & Rotterdam Conservs. Hobby: Film. Address: Tiendweg-Oost 29, Lekkerkerk, Netherlands.

ROCZEK, Paul, b. 9 June 1947, Vienna, Austria. Musician (Violin). Educ; Dip. w. Distinction. Musikhochschule, Vienna, 1966; studies w. Prof. Samohyl, & w. Max Rostal, Berne; studies in comp. w Friedrich Neumann, Vienna. Debut: Vienna, 1966. Career: Mbr., Vienna Opera Orch., 1964; Mbr., Chmbr. Orch. Wiener Solisten, 1965; Ldr., Roczek Quartet, now Austrian Str. Quartet, w. concerts throughout Europe & USA, 1966-; Violin Prof., Mozarteum, Salzburg, 1969-. Recording: sev. records as Solo Violinist, & w. Austrian Quartet, Austria & USA. Hons: Prize Winner, Int. Violin Competition, Vienna, 1966. Mgmt: Trude Kleinheisteskemp, Wileheimerst 28a, Stuttgart, BRD. Address: A 5081 Anif, Neu Anif 89, Austria.

RODAN, Mendi, b. 17 April 1929, Jassy, Roumania. Conductor; Professor & Department Head of Rubin Academy of Music, Jerusalem. Educ: Acad. of Music, Arts Inst., B Mus; MA. m. Judith Calmanovici, 2 c. Career: Perm. Cond., Radio & TV Orch., Bucharest, 1953-58; Fndr. & perfm. Cond., Jerusalem Chmbr. Orch.; Chief Cond. & Musical Dir., Jerusalem Symph. (IBA), 1963-72; Perm. Guest Cond: Israel Phil. Orch.; Israel Chmbr. Ensemble; Concert tours in Europe, USA, Aust., S Africa, S America, Far East w. orchs. inclng: Permanent guest cond., Israel chamber Ensemble; Israel Phil. Oslo Phil., Vienna Symph., Berlin Radio Symph. Orch., NOP, London. Num. recordings. Mbr. of segveral profl. orgs. & Int. Juries. Hons. incl: M Rodan Stipoendium for Conds.; Hebrew Univ., Jerusalem; Hon. Citize of Tucson, Ariz. Address: 6 Shiler St., Jerusalem, Israel. 30.

RODDA, John, b. 17 Sept. 1940, Corryong, Vic., Aust. Piano Teacher. Educ: BSc, Univ. Melbourne; Dip. Mus, ibid.; A Mus A; Lic., Royal Acad. of Music; Lic., Guildhall Schl. of Music; A Mus LCM. 3 c. Mbr., Incorp. Soc. of Musicians. Hobby: Horticulture. Address: 11 Frederico St., Highett, Vic. 3190, Aust.

RODEN, Anthony, b. 19 Mar. 1937, Adelaide, Aust. Opera & Concert Singer (tenor). Educ: Assoc., Aust. Insurance Inst.; Licentiate, Adelaide Conserv. m. Doreen, 4 c. Debut: Glyndebourne. Career: Apps. at London Opera Ctr., Glyndebourne, Netherlands fests., Engl. Nat. Opera, Welsh Nat. Opera, Krefeld Opera; num. concerts for BBC & w. London orchs. Recordings for Aust. Broadcasting Commission. Hons: John Christie award, 1971; Opera prize, Adelaide Conserv. Hobbies: Antiques; Golf. Mgmt: Robert Clarke, Trafalgar Perry. Address: 33 Castlebar Rd., Ealing, London 35 2DJ, UK.

RODERICK JONES, Richard Trevor, b. 14 Nov. 1947, Newport, Gwent, UK. Composer; Lecturer; Pianist; Conductor. Educ: RCM; ARCM; GRSM. Career: Hd. of Music, S Warwicks. Coll., Stratford-upon-Avon. Comps: Me & My Bike (opera commnd. by BBC); The Altar Fire (scenic celebration); piano concerto; 2 chamber concertos; num. choral & chamber works; 2 Sinfoniettas, Symphony (1977-78); scores for theatre & TV plays. Contbr. to Welsh Music. Mbrships: Guild for the Promotion of Welsh Music; CGGB; performing Right Soc.; Royal Coll. of Music Union. Recip. Cobbett Prize for Comp., 1970. Hobbies: Walking; Record Collecting; Reading. Address: Chadley House, Loxley Ln., Wellesbourne, Warwicks., UK. 30.

RODETSKY, Samuel, b. 9 Mar. 1906, Sevastopol, Russia. Concert Pianist; Teacher of Piano. Educ: studied music w. father & w. var. pvte. tchrs. in Siberia, China, Japan & USA, inclng. J G Jacobson, S Rader & E Robert Schmitz; St. Joseph's Coll., Japan; Polytechnic Hi, San Fran., USA. m. Valerie Upright. Debut: San Fran. Career: has app. in num solo concerts & recitals in W & as Soloist w. sev. orchs. inclng. NBC Symph. (on continent-wide broadcasts); has app. repeatedly as Soloist & Speaker, State & Regional conventions of Music Tchrs.' Assn.; Adjudicator, contests throughout Calif. Contbr. to: A. Music Tchr.; Music of the W Mag.; Music Clubs Mag.; The Wouthwestern Musician; Bulletins of the MTA of Calif. mbrships: Life Mbr., State & Local Music Tchrs.' Assns., also Past State Pres. & past Pres., San Fran. Br.; Life Mbr., Alumni Assn. of Calif. Plan; Past Pres., Haskalah Club; Starr King Lodge No. 344, F & AM. Hobbies: Swimming; Walking; Gardening. Address: 165 Stanyan Blvd., San Francisco, CA 94118, USA. 4.

RODIO, Jolanda Caterina Letizia, b. 1 Mar. 1914, Zürich, Switzerland. Concert & Opera Singer; Teacher of Singing; Professor. Educ: Dip. in Singing Educ., Royal Danish Music Conserv., Copenhagen; Concert Dip.; Studies w. Nadja Boulanger & Marya Freund, paris; Academia Chigiana & Benedetto Marcello, Italy. 2 c. Concert debut: Copenhagen Conserv., 1948; Opera debut: Aarhus, 1958. Career incls: Prof., Aalborg Music Conserv., Denmark; Concerts throughout Scandinavia & most of Europe; Formed own chamber music grp., PRISMA, 1963, & vocal quartet, PRISMA. Recordings: Liebeslied-Walzer (Brahms); Die schwarze Spinne (Suter-meister). Mbr. var. profl. orgs. Hons. incl: Order of Danebrog.

Denmark, 1974. Hobby: Work. Address: Kulturmühle Lützelflüh, 3432 Lützelflüh, Switzerland.

RODRIGUES, Luis, b. 6 July 1906, Felgueiras, Portugal. Catholic Priest. Educ: Advanced Course, Cath. Univ.; Musical Conserv., Portugal; course in Paris, France. w. Charles Koechlin, 7 yrs. Career: Works performed in TV concert, & on radio. Comps. incl: Miscelania Musical, 1937; Missa Credo, 1939; Missa Laudate, 1939; Missa Regina Caeli, 1940; Missa Liturgica, 1943; Cantanibus Organist, 1943; Missa Christus Manet, 1944; Quartet of psalms, 1978; works published in Netherlands, Italy, Spain & Portugal; (recorded) var. religious Christmas songs. Mbr., Portuguese Writers' & Comps.' Soc. Hobby: Composing music. Address: Rua Delfim Maia 334, Oporto, Portugal.

ROE, Charles Richard, b. 24 May 1940, Cleveland, Ohio, USA. Singer (lyric baritone). Educ: B Mus, Baldwin-Wallace Coll., 1963; M Mus, Univ. of Ill., 1964; grad. study, Univ. of Mich., 1970-73. Divorced, 2 s. Debut: NYC Opera, 1974. Career incl: Apps. w. Mich. Opera Theatre; Miss. Opera Assn.; Caramoor Music Festival; Meadowbrook Music Festival; Music Theater of Wichita; Detroit, Toledo, Wichita, Grand Rapids & Flint Symph. Orchs.; Instr. of Music, Tex. Tech. Univ., 1964-68; Asst. Prof. of Music, E Mich. Univ., 1968-74. mbrships: Am. Guild of Musical Artists; Actors Equity; Nat. Assn. Tchrs. of Singing. Hobbies: Sports; Theatre. Mgmt: Assoc. Concert Artists. Address; 2633 Whitewood, Ann Arbor, MI 48104, USA.

ROE, (Eileen) Betty, b. 30 July 1930, London, UK. Singer; Composer; Accompanist; Organ & Choir Trainer; Musical Director. Educ: RAM; FTCL; LRAM; ARCM; GRSM. m. John Bishop, 2 d., 1 s. Career: Proprietor, Thames Publishing; music tchr. in grammar schls.; TV commercials; Adjudicator; Dir., musicals & children's operas. Comps. incl. solo songs, ch. & choral music, revue songs, musicals, opera, instrumental pieces & music for children. sev. recordings of own works. Mbrships: Musicians Union; Equity; Brit. Fed. of Music Fests.; ISCM; RAM Club. Hobbies: Cooking; Knitting; Yoga. Address: 14 Barlby Rd., Kensington, London W10 6AR, UK.

ROE, Helen Mary Gabrielle, b. 1 Nov. 1955, Bournemouth, UK. Composer. Educ: Reading for BA, Jesus Coll., Oxford Univ.; studied Violin w. Roger Best, 1969-71, Comp. w. David Lumsdaine, 1973-75. Comps. incl: Ash Wednesday for solo piano (perf. in BBC recital, 1976); Die Blaue Blume (soprano & chmbr. ensemble). Mbr., Oxford Univ. Contemporary Music Grp (Pres.). Hobbies: Reading; Walking. Address: St. Oswald's Wicarage, Church St., Durham City, UK.

ROEDERER, Juan G, b. 2 Sept. 1929, Trieste, Italyl. Professor of Physics. Educ: PhD, Univ. of Buenos Aires, 1952; studied organ w. Hector Zeoli, Buenos Aires, & Hans Jendis, Göttingen, Germany. m. Beatriz Cougnet, 2 s, 2 d. Career: Rsch. Phys., Argentine & German Insts., 1952-59; Prof., Univ. of Buenos Aires, 1959-66, Univ. of Denver, USA, 1967-77, Univ. of Alaska, 1977-; Cons., US Govt., 1967-; Chmn., Int. Workshops on Physical & Neuropsychological Fndns. of Music, Carinthian Summer Fest., Austria, 1973, 77. Publs: Introduction to the Physics & Psychophysics of Music, 1973, 2nd ed., 1975, German transl., 1977, Japanese transl., 1978. Mbrships. incl. Acoustical Soc. of Am.; Assn. Francaise pour le Sauvegarde de l'orgue ancien. Address: 105 Concordia Dr., Fairbanks, AK 99701, USA.

ROEDL, Linda L, b. 13 Dec. 1944, Okla. City, Okla., USA. Pianist; Piano Teacher; Mezzo-soprano. Educ: BMus (perf.), Univ. of Colo., Boulder, 1968; studies piano w. Kenneth G Mills, Toronto, David Burge, Boulder, & Rober R Laughlin, Okla. City. m. James A Roedl. Career: Pianist & singer w. The Star-Scape Singers; Can. debut of this ensemble, Toronto, 1977; USA debut, Carnegie Recital Hall 1979; profl. musician & tchr. Recordings (w. The Star-Scape Singers) On This Rock, 1977; An Evening of Poetry & Song, 1978; Flame on the Heart, 1978; Alive at Ontanaka, 1978; Sing Those Wonderful Words, 1979. Hobbies: Decorating. Mgmt: Sun-Scape Records, Toronto. Address: c/o PO Box 793, Stn. F, Toronot, Ont. M4Y 2N7, Can.

ROELLE, Valdemar Zbigniew, b. 9 Dec. 1935, Gdansk, Poland. Soloist; Music Teacher (piano, clarinet, organ). Educ: Music Schl., 5 yrs.; Acad. of Music, Gdansk, 5 yrs. m. Jessie Hielsen, 1 d. Debut: Acad. of Music, 1960. Career: apps. Danish TV, 1973-75. Sev. recordings. Publs: Orgel Kurses (Organ School). Contbr. to: Danish Newspapers & Mags. Mbrships: Danish Music Union. Hons: 1st Prize, Yamaha Electone Fest., Denmark, 1977; Dip. in European Yamaha Electone Fest., 1973, 77. Hobby: Photography. Address: Hyldegards Tvervej 49, 2920 Charlottenlund, Sjelland, Denmark.

ROESSLER, Ernst Karl, b. 18 Oct. 1909, Pyritz, Pommerania, Germany. Composer; Organist; Musicologist. Educ: MA; Univs. of Leipzig & Freiburg. m. Anneliese Kroll, 2 d. Debut: Königsberg Cathedral, Copenhagen. Career: Radio apps., maj. European stations; Musical perfs. w. organ, choir, orchs. & as soloist. Comps. incl: Weihnachtsmusic, for organ; Klangfunktion und Registrierung; Dreizehntoniehre; Praeludium und Meditation zum 46 Psalm, for organ; Orgelmensuierungen (Freiburg....) Jamunder Cantionale für Singstimme, Orgel bzw. Kammerorchester 1-8. Recordings incl: Passionsmusik für Orgel - Psallite; Ecumenical Mass in memory of Albert Schwertzer; Petsch-Partita (organ); Requiem Mass; Solo sonata for violin. Publs. incl: Farbverfremdungen und die Orgel, 1975. Contbr. to var. publs. Recip., many hons. Hobby: Ornithol. Address: 7744 Königsfeld 3, Bergberg, Glaswaldstr. 38, Germany. 19, 29, 30.

ROETSCHER, Konrad Felix, b. 7 May 1910, Aachen, Germany. Composer; Conductor; Pianist; Teacher. Educ: Final examination in comp., cond., piano, High School for Music, Cologne. m. Erika Legart, 1 d. Debut: as cond., Stadttheater Munster. Career: Cond. at Grand Opera, Kiev; Cond. of own comps. & comps. by others on all German radio stations & in W Berlin w. Philharmonic Orch.; songs & chamber music on radio & in concerts. Comps: works for large orch., chamber music, song cycles, perf. on radio in Germany, Austria & N. Am. Mbr., GEMA. Hons: Prof., High Schl. for Music & Perfng. Arts, Berlin; European VIP Service Establishment Persönlichkeit des Jahres 1974-75. Hobbies: 3rd, 6th & 8th tone music; Birdson. Address: Stubenrauchstr. 50, 1000 Berlin 41, German Fed. Repub.

ROETTGER, Dorye, b. 22 Oct. 1932, Utica, NY, USA. Musicologist; Oboist. Educ: Ithaca Coll.; B Mus, Univ. Ext. Conserv., Chgo.; PhD, Univ. of Eastern Fla. Career: Oboist, concerts, theatre, film, symphs., opera, chmbr. ensembles, recording studios, 1951-; Fndr.-Dir., Fest. Players of Calif., 1957; Prof., annual 'Ch. Music for Children' Fest., Artists in Schls. Conference-Showcase; Artistic Apprenticeship & other projects; monthly concerts w. commentary, Nat. Pacifica Radio, 1971-; Originator, 'Music & People: a survey of world cultures' lecture course; Syndicated columnist; Bridging the Culture Gap. Contbr. to musical publs. Mbrships. incl: Am. Musicol. Soc.; Calif. Music Coun., Nat. Fedn. of Music Club. Recip. num. hons. Hobbies incl: Philosophy; Aniaml car & trng. Address: 3809 Delongpre Ave., Los Angeles, CA 90027, USA. 5, 6, 23, 27.

ROETTGER, Heinz Martin Albert, b. 6 Nov. 1909, Herford, Germany. Conductor; Pianist. Educ: DPhil, Univ. of Munich, 1934; studied theory, comp., piano w. Prof. Luther, Hannover; studied condng., master class, Akademie der Tönkunst, Munich. m. Eva Roettger-Johnn. Career: Cond., Augsburg Theatre, Stralsund Theatre; Gen. Musical Dir., Rostock Theatre; Gen. Musical Dir., Dessau; Guest cond., Staatsoper Berlin & Dresden, Poznan opera; num. concert apps. in Germany & abroad; radio & TV apps. Comps. incl: Symphonies, chmbr. music, opera & songs. Publs: Da Formproblem bei Richard Strauss, 1937. Mbr., Verban Deutsche Komponisten und Musikwissenschäftler. Hons: Prof., 1963; Handelprize, 1961; Merit Medal of Friedensrat, 1962; Wilhelm Müller Art prize, 1975. Hobbies: Nature; Goethe studies. Address: Bauhausplatz 3, 45, Dessau, German Dem. Repub.

ROFFMAN, Frederick S, b. 10 Feb. 1945, Baltimore, Md., USA. Conductor; Composer; Arranger; Writer; Director. Educ: Directing, Boston Univ.; Cond., Peabody Conserv. Career incls: Lctr., Light Opera & Musical Comedy, 92nd St. Y Schl. of Music, NYC, Ambler Music Fest., Temple Univ. & Richland Coll., Dallas, Tex.; Librettist, Musical & State Dir., Babette (1976), Sweethearts (1977), Red Mill (1978), Bel Canto Opera Co., NY; Cond., Librettist, Naughty Marietta, 1978; Arranger, One For The Money, NYC, 1972; Cond., Haddon Hall, 1971, Rose of Persia, 1972, Knickerbocker Holiday, 1973, var. others. Comps. incl: incidental music for Brecht's A Man's A Man, Twelfth Night, The Wountry Wife, Galileo, A Touch of The Post; children's shows Treasure Island, Puss In Boots. Recordings: W S Gilbert & Frederic Clay, Ages Ago, 1971. Contbr. to num. profl. publs. Mbrships: Am. Fedn. of Musicians; Dramatists Guild & Author's League of Am.; BMI Theatre Comps. & Lyricists Workshop. Hons: Village Voice Opera OBIE for Red Mill, 1978. Hobbies: Fancy Cooking; Fancy Eating; Opera & Musical Comedy Memorabilia; Writing Lyrics. Address: 230 Riverside Dr., NY, NY 10025, USA.

ROGÉ, Pascal, b. 6 April 1951, paris, France. Pianist. Educ: Nat. Conserv. of Music, paris. m. Annick Aubergé, 1 d. Debut: Paris, 1969. Career incl: TV & radio broadcasts, France, UK, USA; Regular apps. in major European musical centres; Apps. in major cities incl. NY, Chicago, Wash., LA; Toured NZ, S Africa,

Japan. Recordings incl: Complete Ravel & Debussy Cycles; All Saint-Saens & Bartok Piano Concertos. Hons. incl: Acad. hons.; Ensecu Prizeweinner, 1967; 1st Prize, Marguerite Long -Jacques Thibaud Int. Competition, 1971. Hobbies: Readking; Tennis; Record Collecting. Mgmt: Harrison/Parrott Ltd., 22 Hillgate St., London 28, UK. Address: c/o Mgmt.

ROGELL, Irma, b. Malden, Mass., USA. Concert Harpsichordist; Pianist; Adjunct Professor of Music. Educ: AB, Harvard Coll., var. pvte. tutors inclng. Wanda Landowska. m. Bernard C Roggell (dec.), 2 s, 1 d. Debut: Boston, Mass, & NY, 1960. Career: Concert tours, Europe, S Am.; Coll. tours, USA; Apps. w. maj. orchs. inclng. Boston & Brazil Symphs.; Harpsichordist, Camerata, Boston Mus. Fine Arts; Performer, Fest. Orch., Aegina Arts Ctr., Greece; Radi & TV apps., Lausanne, Boston & NY; Adj. Prof. Music, York Coll., CUNY. Recordings incl: Live from Jordan/Hall; Sounds of Celebration. Sec., Piano Tchrs. Congress. Hobbies: Drawing; Painting; Poetry. Address: 165 W. End Ave., NY, Ny 10023, USA.

ROGERS, Calvin Y, b. 22 Nov. 1922, Pittsburgh, Pa., USA. Professor of Music; Violinist; Conductor; Academic Administrator. Educ: Mus B & Mus M. Oberlin Conserv. of Music; Univ. of Mich.; violin studen to f Jan Wolanek, Charles Rychik, Reber Johnson, Gilbert Ross; master student of Pierre Monteux, Domaine Schl. of Cond.; choral cond. under Robert Shaw, Roger Wagner & Gregg Smith. m. Helen M Noxton, 3 d. Career: Concertmaster, Akron Symph. Orch., 1950-66; Asst. Cond., 1952-60; Assoc. Cond., 1960-66; TV-Voice of Firestone-Final Perf.; 1958-62; Prof. of Music, Ashland Coll.; Concertaster, Lakeside Summer Orch., 1976-. Mbrships: pres., Ohio Music Educ. Assn., 1966-69; 1st VP, ibid, 1968-70; Bd. of Trustees, 1956-; Pi Kappa Lambda; MENC; Pres. Ohio Unit; Am. Choral Dirs. Assn.; Trustee & Pres., Ashland Country Club. Hobbies: Golf; Photography; Recreation; Trave. Address: 1005 Country Club Lane, Ashland, OH 44805, USA.

ROGERS, David Claude, b. 3 April, 1939, Oxford, Mich., USA. Associate Professor of Music; Assistant to the Dean; Hornist. Educ: BMus, Mud Ed., Instrumental, Univ. of Mich. 1961; MMus, ibid, 1963. m. Marie Arlene Massey, 1 s. Career: Solo horn, N Carolina Symph. Orch.; Mbr., Toledo, Ohio Symph. Orch.; currently mbr., Toledo Summer Concert Band; Horn Instr., Inter-Provincial Music Camp, Ont., Can. Recordings: Solo horn, The Univ. of Mich. Band on Tour; Touchdown, USA, Hail Sousa. w. Univ. of Mich. Band. Mbrships: Int. Horn Soc.; Ohio Music Educ. Ass. Hobbies: Running; Swimming. Address: 916 Lambert Dr., Bowling Green, OH 43402, USA.

ROGERS, Delmer Dalzell, b. 7 Sept. 1928, Spokane, Wash., USA. Musicologist. Educ: B Mus, 1952, M Mus, both piano, 1953, Univ. of Southern Calif.; PhD, musicol., Univ. of Mich., 1967. M. W Jean Young, 2 s., 2 d. Career: lecture demonstrations & many papers presented to clubs & profl. socs.; Hd., Theory/Comp. Div., Univ. of Texas at Austin, 1978-. Publs: Guide for the Music History & Literature Contests, 1967; Handbook for the Study of Musical Form, 1972. Contbr. to profl. books & jrnls. inclng: Grove's Dictionary, 6th ed. Mbrships: Sec.-Treas., SW Chapt., Am. Musicol. Soc.; Am. Studies Assn.; Coll. Music Soc.; Soc. for Ethnomusicol.; Sonneck Society. Recip. Summer Rsch. Grant, Univ. of Tex. Rsch. Inst., 1964. Address: Musit Dept., Univ. of Texas at Austin, Austin, TX 78712, USA.

ROGERS, Eric G, b. 25 Sept. 1921, Halifax, UK. Composer; Conductor; Arranger. Educ: Swansea Grammar Schl.; Piano & Organ Lessons, 2 yrs. m. Betty Lucia Haley, 2 s. Career: Served RAF, 5 1/2 yrs.; Comp. of music for film documentary ' a Dawns to Sydney', 1946; Band Ldr., Trocadero Restaurant, London, 1949; Comp. of Music for Films, Radio & BBC TV; Music Dir., London Palladium, 1954-57; Music Dir., Decca Record Co., 1952-64. Compositions incl: Music for some 100 feature films inclng. twenty of the 'Carry On' series; Music for num. documentary & children's films; Music for theme tune 'Sunday Night at the London Palladium' & Sev. TV series. Num. recordings. Mbrships: Lord's Taverners. Hobbies: Rugby; Cricket. Address: 'Kraal'. Woodside Hill, Chalfont St. Peter, Bucks, SL9 9TF, UK.

ROGERS, George, b. 2 Apr. 1911, Trieste, Italy. Professor of Piano. Educ: Maestro in pianoforte, Italy; Conserv. St. Cecilia, Rome; Ecole Normale de Musique de Paris; RCM; ARCM; Delegue pour l'enseignement de la methode Alfred Cortot. 1 s. Career: Music Critic, Il Popolo di Trieste; Music Critic, Le Monde Musical; Adjudicator, Int. Piano Comps.; Lectr. & recitals in Colls. in Cambridge, Dublin, France & on Italian Radio; Prof., GSM; Sr. Prof., Tobias Matthay Schl., Bournemouth; Prof., Inst. Musicale Giuliano, Italy; currently Prof. of Paino, RAM. Contbr. to: British Jrnl. of Aesthetics; The Composer. Mbrships:

ISM. Recip. Hon. ARAM. Hobbies: Motoring; Swimming; Psychol., Relig. Address: 3 Westbury Rd., London W5 2LE, UK. 3.

ROGERS, Herbert, b. 22 June 1929, Wichita Falls, Tex., USA. Pianist; Associate Professor of Music. Educ: Dip., Juilliard Schl. of Music. Debut: Town Hall, NYC, 1958. Career: Lectr., Univ. of Calif., Santa Cruz, 1966-68; Assoc. Prof. Music, Hunter Coll., NYC, 1968-; Perf. in Young Artists Series, Metropolitan Mus., 1963; Chmbr. music & solo Concerts, & Soloist w orchs. in 48 states of US, all provinces of Can., & capitals of W Europe. Recordings: Chopin Favourites; American Composers (2 records, CRI & Dorian). Mbr., Bohemian Club, NYC. Hons: Int. Recording Prize, 1952. Hobbies: Astronomy; Linguistics. Address: 99 Bank St., Apt. 7H NY, NY 10014, USA.

ROGERS, James Douglas, b. 1 Jan. 1947, Hove, Sussex, UK. Teacher & Performer (Guitar). Educ: RAM. Debut: Purcell Room, London, 1974. Career: BBC TV; Nationwide; Fest. Lineup (Edinburgh); Radio perfs., UK; Purcell Room, 1974, 75; Wigmore Hall, 1976; St. Johns Smith Square, 1977; Stage, radio & TV, Hong Kong, 1977, 79; Royal Shakespeare Co., Stratford, 1973. Publs: Arr. of The Entertainer (S Joplin) for guitar, 1975. Mbr., Musicians Union. Hons: Julian Bream Prize, 1967. Hobbies: Model building; Drawing; TV watching. Address: 52 Tennyson St., London SW8, UK.

ROGERS, Nigel David, b. 21 Mar. 1935, Wellington, Shropshire, UK. Singer (Tenor). Educ: BA, 1956, MA, 1960, King's Coll., Cambridge; studied singing at Cambridge & London & at Hochschlule für Musik, Munich. m. 1 d. Career: Fndr., Studio der Frühen Musik (quartet), 1960, touring Europe & Asia; Solo concert apps. in most major European cities; Leading roles in opera, Vienna, Amsterdam & Sadlers Wells, London; Num. broadcasts, BBC & Euope; Tchr., var. seminars & Summer Schls.; Prof. of Singing, Schola Cantorum Basiliensis, Basle, Switzerland; Prof., RCM. Recordings incl: Monteverdi, Vespro della Beata Vergine; Orfeo (Monteverdi), title role; Die Schuone Müllerin (Schubert), Canti Amorosi (Caccini, etc.); Morley, The First Book of Ayres (1600); Bach, The St. Matthew Passion, BWV 244; Monteverdi, Virtuoso Madrigals; Sacred Concertos, Il Ritorno D'Ulisse in Patria. Hons: Var. Prizes for records, inclng. Edison Award, Grand Prix du Disque, Engl. Record Critics' Record of Yr. Mgmt: Clarion Concert Agcy Ltd. 64 Whitehall Pk., London N19, 3TN. Address: 137 Avenell Rd., Highbury, London, N5, UK.

ROGG, Lionel A, b. 21 Apr. 1936, Geneva, Switz. Organist; Harpsichordist. Educ: studied piano w. Nikita Magaloff, organ w. Pierre Segond. m. Claudine Effront, 3 c. Debut: complete Bach organ works, Geneva, 1961. Career: concerts in Switz., France, Italy, Spain, Portugal, Austria, Germany, England, Ireland, Denmark, Netherlands, Scandinavia, Poland, Hungary, Czech., USSR, USA, Can., Australia; currently Prof., Organ & Improvisation, Conserv. of Music, Geneva. Comps: 12 Organ Chorales. Recordings: EMI; Harmonia Mundi; Oryx. Contbr. to: Ency. Britannica; Musical Times; La Tribune de l'orgue, Lausanne. Hobbies: Mountaineering; Chess; Reading. Mgmt: UK; Nicholas Choveaus, Lowestoft, Suffolk. Address: 38 A rte. de Troinex, CH-1227, Carouge, Geneva, Swtiz.

ROGNE, Sture, b. 20 April 1947, Örsta, Norway. Accordionist. Educ: Pedagogical & musical, Tchrs. Trng. Coll., Univ. of Oslo. Studies w. Prof. Finn Mortensen. Career: TV & radio apps., sev. European countries & USA; Represented Norway in the Euro-Light & Nord-Ring radio series; Extensive works, theatre msuic; Prod./Dir., Norwegian Broadcasting Copr. Comps. & arrs. for radio & recordings. Recordings: Det glad Aalesund, 1975; Sture Rogne, 1977. Hons: Spellemannprisen, Norway, 1975. Address: Bygdöy allé 20B, Oslo 2, Norway.

ROHAN, Jindrich, b. 14 May 1919, Brno, Czechoslovakia. Conductor; Professor of Prague Music Academny. Educ: Maturity Examination, Prague Coll.; Cond. Dip., Prague Acad. of Musical Arts. m. Milada Rohanova 2 c. Debut: Chief Cond., Symph. Orch. of Czechoslovak Army. Career: Since 1954 Asst., Cond. & currently Chief Cond., Prague Symph. Orch. Recordings incl: Svatopluk Havelka; Symph., Prague Symph.; Lubomir Zelezny, Violin Concerto, Bruno Belcik, soloist; A Dvorak Piano Concerto, Michael Ponti, piano, Prague Symph.; Jan Tausinger; Music evolutive, Prague Symph. Hobbies: Music; Lit.; Art; Skiing; Motoring. Mgmt: Pagokoncert Maltezske nam. 1, Praha 1, Czechoslovakia. Address: Na baste Sv Ludmily 13, 16000 Praha 6, Czechoslovakia.

ROHARD, Jutta, b. 12 June 1927, Copenhagen, Denmark. Pianist. Educ: studied w. Esther Wagning, Georg Vasarhelyi & Bruno Seidelhofer. m. Arne Ryming, 2 s. Debut: Copenhagen,

1950. Career: Soloist, Danish Radio, 1951-; UN Soloist, Greenland, Faroe Islands, Egypt, Cypress, Congo, Netherlands & Germany, 1960-; Soloist w. orch. at Town Hall, Birmingham & Royal Fest. Hall, London; Prof., Roya Acad. of Music, Copenhagen. Mbrships: Soloist Soc. of 1921; Danish Soloist Soc.; Music Educl. Soc. Hons: Artist's Prize, Musicians' Fndn.; Music Reviewers' Artist Prize. Address: Skd. Markus Plads 10, 1921V Copenhagen, Denmark.

ROHLFS, Eckart, b. 23 Dec. 1929, Tübingen, Württemberg, Germany. Manager; Editor. Educ: PhD, Univ. Munich, 1961. m. Holle Hartmann, 4 c. Career: Lectr. of Dreiklang-Dreimasken-Verlag, Munich, 1957-59; Gen. Sec., Musikalische Jugend Deutschlands/Jeunesses Musicales, 1959-74; Mgr., Nat. Competition, Jugend musiziert, German Music Coun., 1963-; Gen. Sec., Verband Deutscher Musikerzieher und Konzertierender Künslter VDMK, 1964-77; Pres., Gewerkschaft Deutscher Musikerzieher und Konzertierender Künstler in der Gewerkschaft Kunst im DGB, 1975-; VP, Arbeitsgemeinschaft Musikberufe des Deutschen Musikrates, 1977-; Ed., Neue Musikzeitung, 1952-; Prod., Disc Series 'Jugend musiziert', 1964-. Publs: Die deutschsprachigen Musiperiodica 1945-57, 1961. Contbr. to: num. profl. jrnls. & books. Mbr., num. profl. orgs. Hobbies incl: Walking; Gardening; Skiing; Sailing; Playing Chmbr. music. Address: Jahnstr. 31a, D-8032 Gräfelfing-Lochham, Kr. Munich, German Fed. Repub.

ROHLOFF, Ernst, b. 17 Apr. 1899, Graudenz, Germany. Musicologist; Organist. Educ: Leipzig Conserv.; PhD. Univ. of Leipzig, 1926. m. Sigrid Zahn. Career incls: Master. second. schl., 1931; Radio DDR broadcast, 1959. Comps. incl: Sternsinger Kumpanei, choral singspiel for the open stage, 1939; Der fahrend Schler bannt den Teufel. Publ. incl: Studien zum Musiktraktat des Johannes de Grocheo, 1930; Der Musiktraktat des Johannes de Grocheo, 1943; Die Quellenhandschriften zum Musiltraktat des Johannes de Grocheio, 1972. Mbrships: German Soc. for Music Rsch.; German Red. Repub.; Soc. of Comps. & Musicols. of the German Dem. Repub. Address: Am. Kugelberg 8, DDR 485 Weissenfels, German Dem. Repub.

ROHMANN, Imre, b. 25 June 1953, Budapest, Hungary. Pianist. Educ: Final Examination, Béla Bartòk Music Schl., Budapest; Artist-tchr. dip., Ferenc Liszt Acad., Budapest; master classes w. Jörg Demus, Stuttgart. Debut: Budapest, 1973. Career: Recitals in all countires of E Europe, in Finland, Netherlands, France, Italy, W Germany, Austria, USA & Japan; perfs. w. ldng. European orchs at concerts & on TV. Recordings: Schumann Intermezzi, Op. 4 & Fantasiestck, Op. 12; Bach. Concerto for 4 pianos; Schubert, Duets w. András Schiff. Hons: Special prize, Hungarian Radio piano competition, 1973; 3rd prize, Int. Liszt piano competition, Budapest, 1976. Mgmt: Intgerkoncert, Budapest. Address: Márvány u.40, 1126 Budapest, Hungary.

ROHNER, Wilhelmine Georgine, b. 12 Sept. 1908, Muntok, Indonesia. Pianist; Piano Teacher. Educ: Dip., Amsterdam Conserv.; Ecole Marguerite Long, Paris. m. H Volten. Debut: Zeist, Netherlands. Career: Recitals, Radio Nirom, Djakarta, Indonesia; Accomp. to Vocalists, Instrumentalists, throughout Dutch Indies; Piano Tchr. Mbr. Royal Dutch Soc. of Musicians. Hobbies: Literature; Linguistics; Horseback Riding. Address: 22bis Adelaarstraat, Utrecht, Netherlands.

RÖHRL, Manfred, b. 12 Sept. 1935, Augsburg, Germany. Opera Singer. Educ: Leopold Mozart Conserv., Augsburg. m. Helga, 1 d. Debut: Masetto (Don Giovanni), Augsburg, 1958. Career: apps. at opera houses in Brussels, Nancy, Strasbourg, Athens Fest., Berlin, Bonn, Cologne, Hamburg, Kiel, Munich, Augsburg, Lucerne, Karlsruhe etc.; apps. in films, on TV & radio; recitalist; perfs. w. symph. orchs.; Fac., Hochschule für Musik, Berlin. Recordings: Der Junge Lord (Henze); Zauberflöte, Berlin, 1974. Address: Seehofstr. 64F, 1000 Berlin 37, German Fed. Repub.

ROHWER, Jens, b. 6 July 1914, Neumünster, Germany. Composer; Musicologist; Professor. Educ: PhD, Univ. of Kiel, 1958. m. Gabriele Zimmermann, 3 s, 3 d. Career: Instr., Reg. Music Schl., Posen, 1943; State Music Schl., Lübeck, 1946; Schleswig; Holstein Music Acad., Lubeck; Dir., ibid, 1955-72; Instr. & Prof., Musikhochschule Lübeck, 1972-. Comps. incl: orchl., chmbr., instrumental vocal & choral works, inclng: Concerto for violin & orch., 1952; Chmbr. Concerto for violin, viola & string orch., 1967; String Quartet, 1968; Sonata for flute & piano, 1971; Paulusbrief, oratorio, Minitures for female voice & orch. (or piano), 1976. Recording: Christus Triumphaton. Publs. incl: Sinn und Unsinn in der Musik, 1969, Harmonische Grundlagen der Music, 1970. Mbrships incl: Soc. of Musicol.; Amnesty Int. Hons. incl: Schleswig-Holstein Art

Prize, 1952. Address: 16 Lutherstr., 24 Lübeck, German Fed. Repub. 19.

ROIKJER, Kjell Maale, b. 14 June 1901, Malmo, Sweden. Bassoon Player; Composer. Educ: studied w. Johs. Andersen, Hjalmar Bull, N O Rasted, Axel Jorgensen; Karel Kadraba; Knud Lassen. m. Gudrun Henriksen, 3 c. Debut: Hälsingborg, 1924. Career: Bassoon, Hälsingborg Sinfoniorkestra, 1924-26; Copenhagen Philharmonie & Tivoli, 1926-44; Royal Operoorchester, 1938-71; Mbr. Danish Woodwind Quintet, 1932-48; Concerts in Denmark, Sweden, Norway; Perfs. in Denmark, Sweden, Norway & Holland. Comps. incl: Concerto for Xylophone and Orch., Tube & Orch.; Cappricio for Tuba & orch.; Invention for 2 Tubas; Variations & Fugue for 2 trumpets, trombone & tuba; Variations & Fugue for 4 trombones, woodwind quintet; Divertimento for flute & viola; Introd. and Variations for solo viola. Recordings: Scherzo for 2 trumpets, horn, trombone & tuba; Variations & Finale for 2 trumpets, horn trombone & tuba. Address: Amundsensvej 26, 2800 Lyngby, Denmark, 1.

ROLAND, Claude Robert, b. 19 Dec. 1935, Pont-de-Loup, Belgium. Organist; Conductor; Composer; Musicologist. Educ: Royal Atheneum & Acad. of Music, Chatelet; Conservs. in Mons, Liege, Paris, Brussels. m. Anne-Marie Girardot, 1 s. Debut: Mons, 1961. Career: Organist, St.-Christoph's Basilica, Charleroi, 1963-67; Dir., Music Acad., Montingnies-le-Tilleul, 1966-75; Prof., Burssels Conserv., 1972-; Recitals & concerts as organist & cond. Comp. of 56 works inclng. works for orch., piano, organ, guitar, flute, violin, chmbr., vocal & choral music. Recordings incl: Concert au Chateau. Mbrships. incl: Cebedem; Fndn. Pres., Musique Vivante; Sabam. Ed. of works by var. comps. Contbr. to profl. jrnls. Hons. incl: Prix Doehaerd, 1971. Hobbies incl: Grecian arts. Address: 11 rue Bierque, B 6418 Gozee, Belgium.

ROLLAND, Paul, b. 21 Nov. 1911, Budapest, Hungary. Professor of Violin. Educ: BM., Simpson Coll., Indianola, Ind. USA; MM., Liszt Acad. of Music, Budapest, Hungary. m. Clar Székely, 2 s. Debut: Budapest, 1936. Career: 1st Violist, Budapest Symph.; Violist, Pro Ideale & Lener Str. Quartets; Fac. Mbr., Simpson Coll., Indianola, Ind. & Univ. of Iowa; Prof. of Violin, Univ. of Ill., Urbana; Soloist w. Symph. Orchs., Recitalist, Chamber Music player; Organizer & Dir., String Tchrs. Clinics & Workshops, USA., Austria, UK, Can.; Lecture-recital & workshops, NZ, Aust., Sweden; Dir., Int. String Workshop, 1972-. Publs: Basic Principles of Violin Playing; Prelude to String Playing, 1971; Ed., New Tunes for String (w. Stanely Fletcher), 1971-72; Teaching of Action in String Playing. w. Marla Mutschler, (17 Films, Book, Wall-chart), 1971-74; Tunes & Exercises for the String Player (music records), 1974. Contbr. to var. profl. jrnls. Mbrships: Am. String Tchrs. Assn. (Fndg. Mbr., 1st Ed., Past-Pres. Publ. Chmn.); MENC; Nat. Schl. Orch. Assn. Hons: Fellowship, Westminster Choir Coll., Princeton, NJ., 1938-40; Grants from US State Dept. 1961, US Off. of Educ., 1965, 1966-70. Bronze Medal & hon. mbrship. Ysaÿe Fndn., Bruxelles, 1975; Outstanding Tchr., Univ. of Ill. Campus Award, 1976. Hobbies: Swimming; Chess; Ping-pong. Address: 404 E. Oregon St., Urbana, IL 61801, USA.

ROMANIC, Teodor, b. 4 Mar. 1926, Bjelovar, Yugoslavia. Conductor. Educ: Dip., Music Acad., Zagreb. m. Zorica Romanic, 2 c. Debut: Symph. Concert in Karlovac, 1952. Career: Symph. concerts, opera perfs., tape recordings on educ. on radio; Dir. of Opera & Philharmonie. Mbr. of Assn. of Music Union of Yugoslavia; Prof., Music Acad., Sarajevo. Contbr. to Odjek Sarajeva. Hons: Decoration of Work & Decoration of Merit by Pres. of Repub.; Prize of City of Sarajevo, 1963; Prize of Assn. of Musical Artists of Bosnia & Herzegovina, 1965; Prize of Assn. of Comps. of Bosnia & Herzegovina, 1968. Hobby: Travel. Address: VI Proleterske brigade 13, 71000 Sarajevo, Yugoslavia.

ROMANINI, Giorgio, b. 22 Feb. 1935, Turin, Italy. Teacher of Horn, Music Conservatorium, Turin; Professor of Orchestra, RAI Symphony Orchestra, Turin. Educ: Horn Dip., Turin Conservatorium. m. Bonadonna Giovanna, 1 s. Debut: 1953. Career: 1st Horn, Alessandro Scarlatti Orch., Naples, 1953-55; w. RAI (Italian broadcasting system) Symph. Orch., Turin, 1955-. Hobbies: Motorcycle sports; Collecting antique lamps. Address: Via Pesaro 36, 10152, Turin, Italy.

ROMANIUK, Jerzy, b. 26 Mar. 1943, Skierniewice, Poland. Pianist. Educ: MA; Dip., High Schl. for Music, Warsaw. m. Iolanta Latkowska, 1 d., 1 s. Debut: Nat. Phil., Warsaw. Career: Concerts in Poland, USSR, W Germany, Spain, Yugoslavia, Netherlands; apps. on Polish radio & TV, on BBC & Hilversum radio. Hobby: Problems of the Universe. Mgmt: Pagart, Warsaw. Address: ul. Roztogi 4 m.48, Warsaw, Poland.

ROMANOVSKY, Erich Maria, b. 11 July 1929, Vienna, Austria. Professor; Composer; Organist; Musicologist; Music Manager. Educ: Dip. Ch. Music, Acad. of Music & Dramatic Art, Vienna, 1949; Dip. Cond., ibid, 1954; PhD., Univ. of Vienna, 1953. m. Erika Engel, 1 s., 5 d. Career: Choirmaster, Vienna, 1950-56; Sec., 2nd. Int. Congress of Cath. Ch. Music, Vienna, 1954; Prof., Musikhochschule (former Acad.), Vienna, 1955-; Gen. Sec., Int. Music Competition, Vienna, 1958-69. Comps. incl: Sinfonic Fantasy (orch.); Sinfonic Prologue (orch.); Cello concerto; Organ concerto; Serenade (orch.); Concerto for chamber orch.; Sinfonietta; Music for Strings I & II; Dürer Triptychon (strings); Chamber music from trio to nonet; Sonata (organ); Partita (organ); Triptychon super Veni Creator (organ); Preludes & Fugues (organs, piano); Choral Preludes (organ); Toccata (piano); 5 Latin Masses; 4 German Masses; Requiem; Motets; Magrigals; Contata. Publs: Liturgische Orgelimprovisation, 1960; Chaps. in Allgemeine Musikgeschichte, 1972. Contbr. to musical jrnls. & ency. Mbrships: Soc. of Authors, Comps. & Publrs., Vienna; Austrian Soc. for contemporary music; Comps. Union, Vienna. Hons. incl: Austrian State Prize, 1952; Papal Order Pro Ecclesia et Pontifice, 1955; City of Vienna Prize, 1959. Hobby: Collecting Postage Stamps. Address: Goergengasse 9-11-XIV-3, 1190 Vienna, Austria. 3, 19.

ROMAŃSKA-GABRYŚ, Jadwiga, b. 23 Apr. 1928, Sosnowiec, Poland. Soprano Singer. Educ: Dip., solo singing, State Coll. of Music, Katowice. m. Marian Gabryś, 1 s. Debut: as Gilda in Rigoletto, Cracow, 1954. Career: Apps. in ldng. roles in 30 operas in Cracow, Warsaw & other Polish cities, 1954-; guest perfs. in Czech., USSR; concerts & recitals in Poland, Switz., German Fed. & Dem. Repubs., USSR, Czech., Bulgaria, Romania, Hungary, Austria, Denmark, Italy; num. broadcasts. num. recordings on radio & disc; asst. prof., solo singing, State Coll. of Music, Katowice. Mbrshps: Polish Artists Musicians Assn; Trade Union of Cultural Workers. num. hons., incl. 1st prize, Int. Competition for Singers, Munich. Hobby: Flower Gardening. Mgmt: Pagart, Warsaw. Address: ul. Chopina 3 m. 1, 30047 Cracow, Poland.

ROMERO, Celedonio, b. Málaga, Spain. Concert Guitarist. Educ: Grad., Real Conserv. de Madrid & Real Conserv. de Málaga. m. Angela Gallego Monlina, 3 s. Debut: Madrid, 1940. Career: for past 20 yrs. has averaged 100 concerts per yr. in USA & Can. & 50 concerts per yr. in Europe & rest of world. Comps. (recorded) incl: Noche en Malaga; Zapateado; Fantasias Nos. 1 & 2; 3 Romantic Preludes; etc. Has recorded for Phillips & mercury labels. Mbr., ASCAP. Hobbies: Poetry comps.; Philos. essays. Mgmt: Columbia Artists for N & S Am.; Hans Schlote, Salzburg, for Europe, Africa, Asia, etc. Address: 2229 El Amigo Rd., Del Mar, CA 92014, USA.

ROMERO, John J, b. 14 Mar. 1920, Cimarron, New Mexico, USA. Teacher; Director of Bands. Educ: BA, NM Highlands Univ., Las Vegas; MA, ibid. m. Leota Valverde, 5 c. Career: USAF, 1942-45; Dir. of Bands & Music Coordinator, Ojo Caliente Independent Schl. Dist., NM, 1969-70; High Schl. & Elementary Schl. Prin., ibid., 1970-71; High Schl. Prin., ibid, 1971-75; Dir. of Instruction, ibid., 1975-76; Elementary Schl. Prin., Cimarron Municipal Schls., 1976-; var. tchng. posts, 1947-69; pvte. tchr., brass instruments; Adjudicator, trumpeter & violinist; organizer & cond., Boy Scouts Drum & Bugle Coprs & Dance Band, El Rito, NM. Mbrships: Nat. Educ. Assn.; NM Educ. Assn.; Am. Schl. Band Dirs. Assn. Hons: Kappa Sigma Kappa; Kappa Kappa Psi. Address: PO Box 215, Cimarron, NM 87714, USA.

ROMERO, Redentor L., b. 25 Aug. 1929, Manila, Philippines. Symphony Conductor. Educ: Conserv. Music, Univ. Philippines; B Mus, San Fran. Conserv. Music, Calif.; Mills Coll., Music Acad. of the W, Am. Symph. Orhc. League. m. Dolores Garcia, 1 s., 1 d. Debut: As violinist at 15, conductor at 20. Career: Cond. & Music Dir., Nat. Phil. Orch.; 1st & only Filipino Cond. touring world as guest cond., symph. orchs. Comps. incl: var. orchls. works, violin concertos., incl. Moscow Symph., USSR State Orch., Am. Symph. Orch., Mexico State Orch., RPO. Publ. Comps. incl: var. orchls. works, violin concertos, Recordings w. num. orchs. Publ. An American Affair, 1976. Contbr. to var. jrnls. Mbrships. incl: Pres., Philippine Fulbright Schlrs. Assn. Hons. incl: 1 of 24 most outstanding young men of Philippines, 1963. Hobbies incl: Tennis; Photography. Address: PO Box 865, Manila, Philippines. 4. 28, 30.

ROMNEY, Hans Charles, b. 25 Sept. 1911, Frankfurt-on-Main, Germany. Charted Accountant; Retired Bank Manager. Educ: LLB. Edinburgh Univ.; German & Scottish Matriculation Examination; Fellow, Inst. of Chartered Accountants, England & Wales. m. Mary Winifred Peerson, 1 s., 1 d. Career: Ret'd Gen. Mgr., Lloyds Bank Int. Ltd. Mbrshps: Chmn. & Fndr. Comm. Mbr., Royal Tunbridge Wells Green Room Club; Reform Club; Royal Overseas Club, Music Circle. Hobbies: Mountaineering; Swimming; Theatre; Music. Address: Tinkers Farm, Steel Cross, Crowborough, Sussex, TN6 2SS, UK. 28.

RONAYNE, John Edward Joseph, b. 16 Oct. 1931, Dublin, Ireland. Violinist; Orchestra; Leader. Educ: Coll. of Music, Dublin; AGSM., 1952; studied w. Max Rostal. m. Elgin Strub, 2 c. Debut: Dublin, 1947. Career: Mbr., Trio, Gate Theatre, Dublin; Mbr., Light Orch. & subsequently Symph. Orch., Radio Eireann; Mbr., London Philharmonic, London Symph. & Royal Philharmonic Orchs.; Co-Ldr. & Ldr., Royal Philharmonic Orch. under Beecham; Ldr., Radio Telefis Eireann Symph. Orch. & Munich Radio Orch., Bavarian Radio; gave 1st perf. in Ireland of solo violin works of Strauss, Prokofiev, Webern, Shonberg, Henze & Hindemith. Hobbies: Photography; philately. Address: 44 Vineyardhill Rd., London SW19, UK.

RÖNNBLOM, Anders F., b. 9 May 1946, Stockholm, Sweden. Author; Composer; Singer; Musician (guitar, banjo, mandolin). Educ: Self-taught. Career: Stage, radio & TV apps. Comps: Over 335 comps., 103 recorded. Recordings incl: Din Barndom Skall Aldrig Dö; Ramlösa Kvarn; Masarna Lämnar Gotland Och Hela Sverige Tittar Pa; Alternativ Rock 'n Roll Cirkus; Det Hysteriska Draget; Komedia - En Tripp Nerför Tarschan Boulevard; Vem Har Satt Mina ßAnglar I Bur. Hobbies: Listing to music; Playing the guitar; Writing songs. Address: Roslagsgatan 11, 113 55 Stockholm, Sweden.

RÖNNOW, Ola, b. 2 Dec. 1952, Oslo, Norway. Bass Trombone Player. Educ: Oslo Music Conserv., 1969-73; Norwegian Music High Schl. (soloists' class), 1974-75; studied w. Denis Wick, London. Career: Iceland Symph. Orch., 1974-75; Freelance in Oslo, 1975-78; Stockholm Opera, 1978-. Mbr. Int. Trombone Assn. Hobbies: Literature; Collecting Jazz records; Billiards; Astronomy; Politics. Address: Arkadvägen 22, 12147 Johanneshov, Stockholm, Sweden.

RONSON, Raoul R., b. 22 Mar. 1931, Fiume, Italy. Music Publisher; Corporation President. Educ: DBA., (Beaux Arts, Musicol. Jrnlsm.) Rome, 1950; MA, New Schl. for Social Rsch. NY, 1957; Postgrad. studies, Miami, 1968; NY Univ., 1972-. m. Susan Kohn Ronson, 1 s. Career: Publr., Classical & serious Contemporary Music; Fndr. & Pres., Seesaw Music Corp. & Okra Music Corp.; num. radio & TV apps. on panels, discussions, criticism, etc.; Univ. & Conserv. Lectr. on contemporary music & the business of music. Recordings: prod., Classical music records. Contbr. to: Major music jrnls. & mags.; record jackets; prog. notes; etc. Mbrships: ASCAP; BMI; Int. Platform Assn. Hons: Cert. of Recognition, Performing Arts Soc., 1975; Bd. of Dirs., Sibelius Soc., 1978-. Hobby: Philately. Address: Suite 45, 1966 Broadway, NY, NY 10023., USA. 6, 8, 29.

RÖNTGEN, Joachim, b. 27 Oct. 1906, Amsterdam, The Netherlands. Musician; Violinist; Viola Player. Educ: Gymnasium Amsterdam, 4 yrs.; Hochschule Koln, 1924-28; studied w. Prof. C Flesch, 1929-30. m. Anne-marie Tütsch. Debut: Concertgebouw Amsterdam, 1924. Career: Concertmaster, Townorchestra Winterhur, Violin Tchr., Music Schl., Winterhur, Switz. Ldr., Winterhur Str. Quartet, 1928-39; Violin Tchr., Royal Conserv., The Hague, 1939-71; Ldr., Rontgen Str. Quartet, 1940-68. Compositions publd: Scales for violin. Recordings: Elite (Turicaphon-Zurich); String Quartets of Haydn, Mozart, Schubert, Dvorak, Mbrships: Rotary, The Hague. Hobby: Gardening. Address: Bankastraat 132, The Hague, The Netherlands.

ROOCROFT, Stanley James, b. 20 June 1937, Little Lever, Nr. Bolton, UK. Music Adviser; Conductor. Educ: LTCL.; Assoc., Coll. of Preceptors; Bretton Hall Coll. of Educ. for Tchrs. of Music, Art & Drama; Cert. in Educ., Leeds Univ. Inst. of Educ. m. Barbara Hogg, 3 d. Career: Musical Dir., Crucible Theatre, Sheffield, for prodn. of 'Irma La Douce' ; Harpsichordist, Schl. for Scandal, ibid; Music Advsr., Educ. Dept., Sheffield; Musical Dir., Theatre North, Sheffield; Musical Dir. Advsr., Theatre N., Cond. of orchs., brass bands, mil. bands, operatic socs., etc. Adjudicator, Exec. Comm.; Yorks Area, Nat. Fedn. of Music Fests Musical Dir., Charles Vance Prods.; Musical Dir., BBC TV. Mbrships: ISM; Nat. Assn. of Brass Band Conds.; Mbrship Sec., Mil. Band Assn. Address: Clints House, Gayle, Nr. Hawes, N Yorkshire, DL83R, UK.

ROOLEY, Anthony, b. 10 June 1944, Leeds, Yorks., UK. Musician (Lute); Director; Lecturer. Educ: LRAM. m. Carla Rooley, 3 d. Career: Apps. on BBC-TV & Radio; French TV & Radio; German TV & Radio; Int. Fests. (Europe, Scandinavia, Am.); Dir., The Consort of Musicke. Recordings: 30 records inclng. complete works of John Dowland (21 record cycle). Publs: A New Varietie of Lute Lessons, (record & book), 1975; The Penguin Book of Early Music, (record & book), 1979.

Contbr. to Lute Soc. Jrnl.; Early Music Mag.; Guitar Mag. Mbrships: Lute Soc.; Viola da Gamba Soc.; Galpin Soc.; Wine Soc. Hobbies: Renaissance Philos.; Wine. Address: Flat B, 6 Harvist Rd., London NW6, UK.

ROOPE, Jesse William Thomas, b. 30 May 1903, London, UK. Lecturer in Musical Instrument Technology. Educ: Northern Polytechnic, London; pvte. tuition, paino & organ. m. Louise Florence Hudson. Career: Organ building, 1941-59; lectr. in electronics, Northern Polytechnic, 1959-71; lectr. in charge of Musical Instrument Technology, London Coll. of Furniture; Examiner & Vis. Assessor, City of Guilds Inst., 1977-. Publs: Ed., Anatomy of the Piano, 1978. Contbr. to Music Trades Review (later Music Int). Mbrships: Piano committee, Furniture Training Bd.; Brit. Standars Inst. for electronic organs, brass, woodwind, percussion committee; VP, Inst. of Musical Instrument Technology (Hon. Sec., 15 yrs., Pres., 1966-67); Fndr. mbr., Organ Club, 1926. Hobbies: Organist; Choirmaster. Address: 11 Park Ave., Potters Bar, Herts. EN6 5EN, UK.

ROOPER, Jasper, b. 30 June 1898, Penkridge, Staffs., UK. Composer; Music Educator. Educ: Royal Coll. of Music; ARCM (composition). m. Sheila Fraser, 2 c. Career: Dir. of Music, Lancing Coll., 1934-49; Staff music lectr. Extra-mural delegacy, Oxford Univ., 1952-67; Pt.-time lectr., Sussex Univ. Compositions: Christmas Rhapsody for voices & organ; Cantata for All Seasons; 5 Songs Probable & Improbable; Kezia & the Kelveys (schl. opera); Overture 'My Life by the Sea'; Little Orphan Annie (speaking voice & orch.) num. Songs & part songs. Mbr: CGGB; PRS. Address: 77 Greenacres, Shoreham-by-Sea, Sussex, BN4 5WY, UK.

ROOS, Ingemar, b. 22 Dec. 1945, Helsingborg, Sweden. Trombonist. Educ: Higher organist degree w. solist dip., Music Acad., Stockholm; Trombone studies, Malmö Conserv., GSM, Civlc Orch. of Chgo., (Final degrees & soloist dip.). m. Eva Fredriksson, 1 d. Career: Sev. fest. perfs.; Num. apps., Scandinavian Radio & TV as soloist & w. chmbr. groups; Solo trombone, The Norwegian Opera, 1971-; Solo trombone, Gothemburg Symph. Orch., 1978-; Prof. of Trombone, Oslo & Gothemburg Conservs. of Music; Mbr., The Norwegian Brass Quintet. Hobbies: Music; Family life. Address: Blabärsvägen 23, 72155 Va Frölunda, Sweden.

ROOSEGAARDE BISSCHOP, Eugéne, b. 4 Mar. 1916, Overveen (NH), The Netherlands. Concert Pianist; Private Teacher. Educ: LL.B. (Neths.), Univ. of Leiden, 1937; studied w. Annie Kroeze., Theo van der Pas, Ludwig Otten, Willem Andriessen & Johan van den Boogert at Royal Coll. of Music, The Hague. m. Alberdina Vogel. Career: Army Office in Europe & O'seas & in Underground Forces in Holland during WWII, 1937-66; During time in Army gave concerts to the forces & the public; After leaving the army, became fulltime Concertpianist, Ldr. of 'Concertino' & Compositions incl: La Courtine Mars; 5e Divisie Mars; Semper Parate, etc.; radio & TV perfs. Many recordings. Mbrships. incl: Chmn., Royal Netherlands Musicians Soc., Arnhem Sect.; Bd. Mbr., Emergency Fund for Artists; Bd. Mbr., Netherlands Musicians Soc. for Promotion of Music. Recip., Johan Wagenaar Prize, awarded to his Ensemble 'Concertino' for outstanding perfs. of Dutch chamber music, 1971. Var. hobbies. Address: Morletpad 15, 6815 EZ, Arnhem, The Netherlands.

ROPEK, Jiri, b. 1 July 1922, Prague, Czechoslovakia Professor of Organ; Organist. Educ: Philos. & Pedagogical FEc., Charles Univ., Prague, 1950; Prague Conserv., 1946; Prague Acad. of Arts, 1950. m. Jirina Ropková-Kupková, 1 d. Career: Recitals in Czechoslovakia, 1950-, & in other European countries, 1960-; Perfs. regularly in USSR, Holland, UK; First Czech Organist to play in the Royal Festival Hall, London (two recitals), & a recital for the BBC; Radio perfs. in most European countries; Prof. of Organ, Prague Conserv.; Organist, St. Jacob's Ch., Prague. Comps: Organ variatrions on Victimae Paschali Laudes, OUP, 1964 & recorded in 1970 at St. Giles, Cripplegate, Ch. music, masses, etc. in Ms. num. recordings incl. Sussex Univ. organ, Czech organ music. Hobbies: Reading in English; Films, etc. Address: U. Plátenice 1960/2, 15000 Prague 5-Smichov, Czech.

ROREM, Ned, b. 23 Oct. 1923, Richmond, Ind., USA. Composer; Author; Pianist. Educ; Music Schl. of Northwestern Univ., 1940-43; M Sc., Juilliard Schl. of Music, NYC, 1948; Berkshire Music Ctr., 1946 & 47. Career: Music Copyist for var. cos.; Prof. of Composition & Composer-in-Res., SUNY, Buffalo, 1959-61; Composer-in-Rex., Univ. of Utah, 1965-66. Comps. incl: A Childhood Miracle (opera); Cycle of Holy Songs; Six Irish Poems; Design for Orchestra; The Poets' Requiem; Progressions (ballet); Poems of Love Rain; music for plays inclng. Suddenly Last Summer, Motel & The Lady of the Camellias. Publs. incl: The Paris Diary of Ned Rorem, 1966;

Music from Inside Out, 1967. Publs: 8 books. Mbr: ASCAP. Hons. incl: prix de Biarritz for melos (ballet), 1951; Eurydice Choral Award, 1954; Pulitzer Prize, 1976. Address: c/o Boosey & Hawkes, 30 W 57th , NYC, NY, USA.

ROSADO FERNANDES, Cremilde, b. 7 Dec. 1940, Lisbon, Portugal. Harpsichordist. Educ: piano, clavichord, harpsichord & chmbr. music at Nat. Conserv., Lisbon & Conserv., Würzburg. m. Gerhard Doderer. Career: Prof., piano, Nat. Conserv., Lisbon, 1973-75; Prof., Historical keyboard instruments, Hermann-Zilcher Conserv., Würzburg; 1975-; Harpsichord & Clavichord recitals in European & Am. countries & on radio & TV. Recordings: Portuguese harpsichord & clavichord music. Publs: Joao Costa de Lisboa, Tencao, 1963; Antaloga de organistas do sec. XVI, 1969; Joao Rodrigues Esteves, Obras selectas, 1979. Contbr. to Anales Lusitanae Musicae (Portugal). Hobbies: Musicol.; Cinema. Address: Heinrich Zeunerstr. 42, 87 Würzburg, German Fed. Repub.; Alameda D A Henriques 48-5, Lisbon, Portugal.

ROSAND, Aaron, b. 15 Mar. 1927, Hammond, Ind., USA. Concert Violinist. Educ: Dip., Chgo. Musical Coll.; Curtis Inst. of Music; studies under Leon Sammetini, Efrem Zimbalist & Wm. Primrose. m. Maree Macpherson Rosad, 1 d. Debut: as Soloist w. Chgo. Symph. Orch., 1937. Career: num. guest apps., CBS-TV; Soloist w. most symphs. of the world; annual tours of Europe & USA; average 100 concerts a yr. num. recordings. Hons: Merite Cultural et Artistique, France; Ysaÿe Medal, Belgium. Hobbies: Gardening; Golf; Philately; Rare Prints & Books. Mgmt: Yves Dandelot, Europe; Jacques Leiser, USA. ; Gorlinsky, UK. Address: 100 W 57th St., NY., NY, USA; Belica 62, Cogoleto, Italy. 2, 3.

ROSCHER, Wolfgang, b. 29 May 1927, Komotau, Czech. Professor; Composer; Conductor. Educ: Dr. Phil. m. Eva Nagel, 1 d. Career: Prof. of music & auditive communication; concerts of early & modern music & own comps.; improvisatory perfs. in theatre & on film, radio & TV; dir. of courses on polyaesthetics. Comps: for vocal & instrumental ensembles. num. recordings. Publs: Polyästhetische Erziehung, Cologne, 1976; Ästhetische Erziehung/Improvisation/Stage music, 1970. Mbrships: Inst. of Intercultural Rsch., Heidelberg; Sektion Polyästhetische Erziehung der Gesellschaft für Musikpädagogik; Gesellscharft für Musikforschung, etc. Hons: Johann-Wenzel-Stamitz-Förderpreis, 1964. Hobbies: Old Austria; Churches & Convents; Wine. Address: Carlo Mierendorffstr. 53, 3200 Hildesheim, German Fed. Repub.

ROSCOE, Martin, b. 3 Aug. 1952, Halton, Cheshire, UK. Concert Pianist. Educ: studied w. Marjorie Clementi & Gordon Green; master classes w. Alfred Brendel, John Lill, Stephen Bishop-Kovacevich, Vlado Perlemuter & Sir William Block; RMCM; ARMCM (tchrs. & perfs.); GRSM. m. Joan Rosemary Threlfall. Career: sole apps. at Cheltenham Fest., Wigmore Hall & Purcell Room, London; soloist w. Royal Liverpool Phil. Orch. & City of Birmingham Symph. Orch.; num. solo perfs. on BBC. mbr., ISM. Hons: Worshipful Co. of Musicians Silver Medal, 1974; Dayas Gold medal, 1974. Hobbies: Reading; Cooking; Walking. Mgmt: Sheila Cooper Concert Artists. Address: 1 Clayton Grove, Clayton-le-Dale, Blackburn BB1 9HJ, UK.

ROSE, Beatrice Schroeder, b. 15 Nov. 1922, Ridgewood, NJ., USA. Harpist; Educator. Educ: Inst. of Musical Art, NYC, 1940-41; Mannes Coll. of Music (scholarship), 1942-44. m. William H. Rose, 1 s. Debut: Concert & radio debut, NY World's Fair, 1939. Career: Soloist, Damrosch Music Appreciation Hour, Broadcast, 1940, for Duke of Windsor's Save The Children Fund, Govt. House, Nassau, Bahamas, 1941; Assoc. Harpist, Radio City Music Hall Orch., NYC, 1944-51; Concert Artist, Italy, USA, Canada, 1952, 53; Prin. Harpist; Houston Symph., 1953-; Fac., Univ. of Houston, 1953-; Rice Univ., 1977-; Former Mbr., Contemporary Music Soc., soloist 1959, 60, under Stokowski; Fndr., Dir., Houston Harp Ensemble. Recordings w. Houston Symph., under Leopold Stokowski. Publs: Enchanted Harp, album of descriptive pieces; co-auth. of 'Outline of Six-Year Harp Course for Elem., Jr. & Sr. HS.', guide for tchrs.; The Troubadour Harp & its Music. Mbrships incl: Am. Harp Soc.; Phi Beta Music Frat.; Judge, Tex. Music Educators Assn., 1962, 63, 64, 74. Recip. var. hons. Address: 1315 Friarcreek Ln., Houston, TX 77005, USA.

ROSE, Bernard William George, b. 9 May 1916, Little Hallingbury, Herts., UK. University Lecturer; Organist; Choral Director; Composer. Educ: RCM; BA (Cantab.), St. Catharine's Coll.; MusB, MA, ibid. m. Molly Daphne Marshall, 3 s. Career: Organist & Fellow, Magdalen Coll., Oxford, 1957-; Organist & Fellow, Queen's Coll., Oxford, 1939-57; VP, Magdalen Coll., Oxford, 1973-75; Cond., Eglesfield Music Soc., 1939-57, & Oxford Symp. Orch., 1971-73; Pres., RCO, 1974-76; Frequent radio broadcasts as choral dir. & speaker. Comps: var.

ch. music. num. recordings of choral music. Publs: (Ed.) Thomas Tomkins, 1963, 64, 73 (in Early English Ch. Music); Handel's Susanna, 1967. Contbr. to: Musical Times; Music & Letters. Mbrships: ISM; PRS. Hons. incl: Stewart of Rannoch Scholar in Sacred Music (Cambridge), 1935-39; DMus (Oxon.), 1956. Hobbies: Photography; DIY. Address: Appleton Manor, nr. Abingdon, Oxon., UK. 1.

ROSE, Earl Alexander, b. 5 Sept. 1946, NYC, USA. Pianist; Composer; Arranger; Conductor. Educ: BS in Music, Mannes Coll. of Music, 1970; studied music at Vienna Acad. of Music, 1967-68, cond. at Juilliard Schl. of Music, NY. Career: Perfs. in semi-classical & pop concerts & night clubs throughout USA; has written music & served as Asst. Music Coord. of NBC TV's Tonight Show; Music Coord. Asst. for ABC TV's Dick Cavett Show; Prodn. Asst. to peter Nero in latter's tour of Australia, 1973; Past mbr., Lehmann Engels Musical Theater Workshop; Comp., Arr. & Co-Producer of songs for CBS TV's Captain Kangaroo series. Comps. incl: Yes I Know (winner, 1976 Am. Song Fest.); Linnea My Love; Overnight Success. Recordings: Grand Piano; Overnight Success. Recordings: Grand Piano; Overnight Success. Mbrships: ASCAP; NARAS; AGAC. Hobbies: Swimming; Record Collecting; Films. Address: c/o Franklin, Weinrib, Rudel & Vassalle, 950 3rd Avenue, NY NY 10022, USA.

ROSE, John, b. 4 Apr. 1948, Gainesville, Ga., USA. Concert Organist & Director of Music. Educ: BA, Rutgers Univ. Career: Concert Organist & Dir. Organiser of Music, Cathedral of the Sacred Heart, Neward, NJ., 1968-; Org. & Dir. of major concert series at the cathedral; regular perfs. throughout USA & Can., & in UK, France & Netherlands; former mbr. Music Fac., Newark campus, Rutgers Univ.; Artist in Res., Trinity Coll., Hartford, Conn. Recordings: John Rose at the Great Organ of the Methuen Memorial Music Hall; Music from Star Wars, 1978. Contbr. to: Music (NYC); Music Jrnl. (NYC). Mbrships: AGO; Nat. Assn. Cath. Cathedral Organists; Mayor of Newark's Commission for POerforming Arts; Archdiocesan Music Commission. Hons: Young Artist of Yr., Musical Am. mag., 1974. Hobbies: Photography; Travel. Mgmt: Arts Image Ltd. (USA). Address: c/o The Chapel, Trinity College, Hartford, CT 06106, USA.

ROSE, John Luke, b. 19 July 1933, Northwood, UK. Composer; Pianist; Tutor in Music. Educ: B Mus., PhD., TCMUniv. of London; L Mus TCL. Career: Ext. Lectr., Univ. of Oxford, 1959-66, & Workers Educl. Assn.; Prof. & Examiner, TCM, 1960-62; Res. Staff Tutor in Music, Univ. of London, 1966-; Adjudicator and recitals, USA, Can., Fiji, NZ & India. Compositions incl: Piano Concerto; Cantata, The Pleasures of Youth; var. songs; three Symphonies. Publs: Wagner's Music Dramas & the Romantic Movement, 1979. Mbrships: Composers' Guild of GB; Chmn , TCM Guild; Assn. of Univ. Tchrs. Hons: Royal Phil. Soc. Prize for 1st Symph , 1957 & 2ns Symph., 1958; Hon. Fellow, TCM, 1961. Hobbies: Painting; Reading; Writing; Poetry; Photography. Address: Kalon, 113 Farnham Rd., Guildford GU2 5PF, UK. 3, 28.

ROSE, Juanelva Marie, b. 3 July 1937, Tulia, Tex., USA. Professor of Music. Educ: BMusEd, W Tex. State Univ., 1958; MA, Eastman Schl. of Music, 1959; PhD, Univ. of Calif., Santa Barbara, 1970. Appts: Instr. in Music, McNeese State Univ., 1959-63, Organist, 1st Meth. Ch., 1959-65, Lake Charles, La.; Prof. & Chmn., Dept. of Music, Tunghai Univ., Taichung, Taiwan, 1965-; perfs. in USA, Repub. of China, India, Pakistan & Ceylon (piano, organ, clarinet). Publs: Ed., Carl Philipp Emanuel Bach, 6 Sonatas for Clavier, WQ, l. Mbr., AGO. Hobby: Chinese Musical Instruments. Address: Box 947, Tunghai Univ., Taichung, Taiwan.

ROSE, Leonard, b. 27 July 1918, Washington, DC, USA. Concert Cellist; Teacher. Educ: Grad., Curtis Inst. of Music, Phila., 1938. m. Xenia Petschek, 1 s., 1 d. Debut: Orchl. solo, NY Phil., Carnegie Hall, 1944. Career incl: recitalist & soloist w. major orchs. throughout the world; Cello tchr. Juilliard Schl., 1951-; Cello tchr., Curtis Inst., 1951-62; num. film, radio & TV appearances. Compositions: ed., bulk of standard cello lit. for Int. Music Co., NY. Recordings incl. num. cello works (CBS). Hons: Ford Fndn. Grant, 1963; MusD, Hartford Univ., 1965. Hobbies: Golf; Bridge; Dancing; Cooking. Mgmt: Sheldon Gold, ICM. Corp. Address: 19 Overlook Rd., Hastings-on-Hudson, NY 10705, USA.

ROSE, Michael Edward, b. 11 Jan. 1934, London, UK. Music Adviser. Educ: RAM; ARAM; FTCL; GRSM; LRAM; ARCM. m. Ann phillips, 2 c. Career: Music Master, 1956-62; Music Advsr., Middx. Co. Coun., 1962-65; London Boroughs of Harrow & Hillingdon, 1965-68; Asst.-in-Charge, BBC Trng. Orch., 1968-72; Many recordings & live broadcasts for BBC, w. BBC Trng. Orch.,

Northern Orch., Symph. Orch., Welsh Orch., 1967-72. Comps. (publs.): Winter Music (cantata); Summer Music (cantata); Var. ch. anthems; Var. vocal & instrumental pieces for children. Mbrships: ISM; MAIEA. Recip. Clements Mem. Prize, 1957. Hobbies: Reading; Bird watching; Jigsaws. Address: 63 Chaucer Rd., Bedford, UK.

ROSE, Michael Paul, b. 7 Dec. 1945, Brooklyn, NY, USA. Conductor; Company President. Educ: BA, Brooklyn Coll., 1966; MA in Musicol., Univ. of Iowa, 1968; PhD in Musicol., Univ. of Mich., 1971. m. Judith Lynne Hyman. Career: Teaching Fellow, Univ. of Mich., 1969-71; Asst. Prof., Univ. of S. Fla., 1972-75; Established Prometheus Music (Pres.), 1975. Contbr. to Grove's Dictionary, 6th ed. Address: 1902 Ave. L, Brooklyn, NY 11230, USA.

ROSE, William H, b. 8 July 1926, Owensboro, Ky., USA. Musician; Educator. Educ: Parks Air Coll. of Engrng.; US Navy Schl. of Music; Juilliard Schl. of Music. m. Beatrice Schroeder, 1 s. Career: formerly Tubist w. CBS Symph., NY., 1947-48; Goldman Band, NY., 1947-51; UN. Symph., NY., 1948-49; Charter Mbr., NY. Brass Ensemble, 1947-48; currently Tuba Player w. Houston Symph. Orch., 1949-; Houston Grand Opera; Houston Brass Quintet; Fac., Univ. of Houston, 1959-. Recordings w. Houston Symph. Orch. & Houston Brass Ensemble. Contbr. to Instrumentalist Mag. Mbrships: Tubists Universal Brotherhood Assn.; Nat. Assn. of Coll. Wind & Percussion Instrs.; Tex. Music Educators Assn. Hobby: Reading. Address: 1315 Friarcreek Ln., Houston, TX 77055, USA.

ROSEBERRY, Eric Norman, b. 18 July 1930, Sunderland, Co. Durham, UK. Lecturer in Music; Administrator. Educ: BA, BMus., Univ. of Durham, 1948-51. m. 1) Elspeth Campbell, 2) Jill Sharp, 4 d. Career: Dir. of Music, STand Grammar Schl. for Boys, Whitefield, Manchester, 1953-58; Co. Music Organizer, Hunts., 1958-64; Music Asst., BBC, London, 1964-69; Radcliffe Lectr. in Music, Univ. of Sussex, 1969-72; Sr. Lectr. in Music, Bath Coll. of Higher Educ. 1972-; Broadcast talks on music for BBC; Cond.; Bath Symph. Orch., 1978. Comps. incl: Recorder Music. Publs: Beethoven, Mozart (Great Master Series), 1960; The Faber Book of Christmas Carols, 1969; Of German Music (Schoenberg & Hindemith), 1976. Contbr. to: The Listener; Tempo; Music & Musicians. Hobbies: Reading; Cooking; Walking. Address: Corner House, Church St., Croscombe, nr.Wells, Somerset BA5 3QS, UK.

ROSEMAN, Ronald Ariah, b. 15 Mar. 1933, Brooklyn, NY, USA. Oboist; Composer; Teacher. Educ: BA, Queen's Coll., NY; oboe studies w. Lois Wann & Harold Gomberg; comp. studies w. Karol Ratthaus, Elliott Carter & Ben Weber. m. Okkyu Kim Roseman, 1 s., 2 d. Career: num. solo recitals in USA & Can.; solo tour in Far East, 1964; num. solo apps. w. NY orchs.; oboe player in var. orchs. & ensembles incl. NY Woodwind Quintet, 1961- (tours of USA, Europe, Asia, USSR & S Am.); acting co-prin., NY Phil., 1973-74, 1977-78 & on European tours, 1975, 76; fac., Juilliard Schl. of Music, 1976-; Artist in Residents, State Univ. of NY, Stonybrook; fac., Waterloo Summer Fest., 1976-. Comps. incl: 2nd Str. Quartet; Suite for solo cello; Trio for 2 oboes & Cor Anglais; Sonata for 2 oboes & harpsichord; 3 Psalms for soprano, flute, clarinet, viola & cello. Recordings: solo works by Handel, Telemann, Schumann, etc; more than 25 chmbr. music recordings. Publs: Renaissance Suite for Woodwind Quintet. Mbrships: The Boheminas; Intl. Double Reed Soc. sev. scholarships & hons. Hobbies: Reading; Cycling; Swimming. Address: 156 W 86 St., NY, NY 10024, USA.

ROSEN, Carole Margaret, b. 18 March 1934, London, UK. Singer. Educ: MA, Somerville Coll., Oxford Univ.; Reifeprufung, Vienna Acad. for Music & Dramatic Art, Austria; pvte. study w. Helene Isepp, Lucie Manen, Otakar Kraus. m. Peter Marsh, 1 s., 1 d. Debut: St. Pancras Arts Fest., 1962. Career: Leading Mezzo, Flensburg City Opera Co., German Fed. Repub., 1964-65; has worked as guest w. Royal Opera, Covent Garden, Engl. Nat. & Scottish Opera, & in Israel, Italy, Canada, USA, Sweden, Czechoslovakia & Brazil; 2 TV opera apps.; frequent BBC recitals; Recitals, London & extensive concerts, UK & abroad; Jury Mbr., Int. Singing Competition, Brazil, 1975. Contbr. to num. BBC music progs. as musical jrnlst. Hobbies incl: Cooking; Dress marking; Listening to people talking. Address: 136 Park Rd., Chiswick, London, W4, UK.

ROSEN, Charles, b. 5 May 1927, NYC, USA. Pianist. Educ: Juilliard Schl. of Music; Princeton Univ.; piano studies w. Moritz Rosenthal & Hedwig Kanner-Rosenthal. Debut: recital, NYC, 1951. Career incls: recitals & orchl. soloist, Europe & Am.; premiered Elliott Carter's Double Concerto, NYC, 1961; Prof. of Music, SUNY, 1972-; gave Messenger Lectures, Cornell Univ., 1975. Recordings incl: 1st complete recording of

Debussy's Etudes, 1951; Stravinsky's Movements, w. the comp. conducting, 1961; Beethoven's last 6 sonatas, 1972; Boulez; Piano Music, Vol. I. Publs: The Classical Style: Haydn, Mozart, Beethoven, 1971; Schoenberg, 1975. Hons. incl: Nat. Book Award, 1972. Address: 101 W 78th St., NY, NY, 10024, USA. 16.

ROSEN, David B, b. 21 Sept. 1938, San Fran., Calif., USA. Musicoloist. Educ: BA, Reed Coll. Portland Ore.; Grad. work in Hist., Columbia Univ.; MA & PhD in Music, Univ. of Calif. at Berkeley; studied Piano w. James Beail, Daniel Pollack & Frederic Rothchild. m. Carol Bilson Gosen. Career: Teaching posts at Dartmout Coll. Chgo. Musical Coll. (Roosevelt Univ.), Brandeis Univ., & Univ. of Wis. Publs: The Genesis of Verdi's Requiem (diss.); Critical Edition of Verdi's Requiem. Contbr. to: Musical Quarterly; Rivista italians di musicologia; MLA Notes; Opera News; other musical publs. Mbrships: Am. Inst. for Verdi Studies (Advsry. Bd.); Am. Musicol. Soc.; Int. Musicol. Soc.; Coll. Music Soc. Recip., Martha B. Rockefeller Grant-in-Aid, 1968-69; NE4 Fellowship, 1979. Address: Schl. of Music, Univ. of Wis., Madison, WI 53706, USA.

ROSEN, Jerome William, b. 23 July 1921, Boston, Mass., USA. Composer; Clarinetist; Professor of Music. Educ: MA., Univ. of Calif., Berkeley, 1949; Special student in clarinet. Nat. Conserv., Paris. m. Sylvia T Rosen, 1 s., 3 d. Compositions: Sonata for Clarinet & Violoncello, publd. Boosey & Hawkes, 1954, rec. Fantasy Records; Str. Quartet No. 1, publd. Percussion, publd. by Music for Percussion, Inc., 1975; Petite Suite for Four Clarinets, publd. by Leblanc, 1962; Three Songs for Chorus & Piano, publd. by Boosey & Hawkes, 1968, Five Pieces for Violin & Piano, rec. by Orion Records. Contbr. to var. music jrnls. & articles to Grove's Dictionary of Music & Musicians. Mbrships: Am. Composers Alliance; Am. Musicol. Soc.; Music Lib. Assn. Hons: George Ladd Prix de Paris, 1949-51; Fromm Fndn., 1952, 53; Guggenheim Fellowship, 1958. Address: Dept. of Music, Univ. of Calif., Davis, CA, USA. 14.

ROSEN, Mary K, b. 1 June 1918, Chgo., Ill., USA. Violinist; Conductor. Educ: Bogulawski Coll. of Music; Columbia Schl. of Music; Artist's Dip., Chgo. Conserv. of Music. m. David Rosen, 1 s., 1 d. Debut: Auditorium, Chgo., at age 10. Career: Cond., Metrop. Youth Orch.; Guest Cond., 8 European countries; Mbr., City Symph. of Chgo; Cond., DePaul Youth Str. Orch.; Fac. Mbr., DePaul Univ. Schl. of Music. Mbrships: Treas., Am. Str. Tchrs. Assn.; Sec., City Symph. of Chgo. HOns: Soloist by selective competition, Diamond Jubilee of Chgo. Conserv., at age 22; Victory Award for sale of US, Bonds, WWII. Hobbies: Crossword Puzzles; Travel. Address: 7157 Laramie, Skokie, IL 60076, USA. 5, 8, 27.

ROSEN, Myor, b. 28 May 1917, NY, NY, USA. Harpist; Composer. Educ: Grad., Juilliard Schl. of Music. m. Esther Rosen, 1 d., 1 s. Debut: Mexico City, 1941. Career: soloist w. NY Phil., Minneapolis Symph. Orch., CBS Symph., Mexico City Symph.; Recitals. Comps: for NBC series, Arts & the Gods; for CBS Camera 3 prod. of Solomon the King.´ num. recordings. Publs: The Writing Technique for the Harp, 1957. Mbrships: The Bohemians. Hobbies: Building Harpsichords; Chess; Stained Glass. Address: 243 Cherry Lane, Teaneck, NJ 07666, USA.

ROSEN, Nathaniel Kent, b. 9 June 1948, Altadena, Calif., USA. Cellist. Educ: BMus, Univ. of S. Calif., 1972. m. Jennifer Langham. Debut: Carnegie Recital Hall, 1970. Career: apps. on TV in Previn & the Pittsburgh, Today Show & on Mike Douglas show. Recordings: complete cello & piano music by Chopin. Contbr. to Am. Strg. Tchr. Mbrships: Musicians Union, local 47; NY Violoncello Soc. Hons: 1st prize Naumburg Competition, NY, 1977; 1st prize Tchaikovsky Competition, Moscow, 1978. Mgmt: Columbia Artists Mgmt., NY. Address: 175 Riverside Dr., NY, NY 10024, USA.

ROSENBERG, Herbert, b. 13 Oct. 1904, FrankfurtMain, Germany. Musicologist. Educ: Dr. Phil., Univ. of Berlin, 1931. m. (2) Elinor Mortensen, 1 s., 2 d. Career: Tchr., Music Hist., Theory, Pedagogy, Klindworth Scharwenka Conserv., Berlin, 1932-35; Res., Copenhagen, 1935; Tchr., Copenhagen Music Schl., 1937-63 except 1943-46, Music Dir., Stockholms Privata Konservatorium; Recording. Mgr., Danish Br., EMI, 1946-64; Mbr., Music Record Dept., Nationalmuseet, Copenhagen, 1964-73; Lectr., Musicol., Univ. of Lund, Sweden, 1966-. Num. publs. in German & Engl., w. Swedish eds., inclng: The Scandinavian His Master's Voice M-series 1920-33, (co-author), 1966;I Edition Balzer - A History of Music in Sound in Denmark, 1966; Jussi Bjorling (co-author), 1969; Wilhelm Furtwängler (co-author), 1970. Contbr. to encys. Recip. hon. Doct., Univ. of Lund. Hobbies: Gardning; Mountain climbing. Address: Langkaervej 16, DK-2720 Vanloese, Denmark.

ROSENBERG, Hilding Constantin, b. 21 June 1892, Bosjökloster, Sweden. Composer. Educ: Royal Acad. of Music, Stockholm. m. Vera Josephson, 2 d. Comps. incl: 8 symphs.; 2 violin concertos; 2 cello concertos & num. other orchl. works; 6 operas; ballets; choral music; 12 strg. quartets & other chmbr. music; songs; music for pinao & organ, etc. num. recordings of own comps. recip. num. prizes & awards. Address: c/o Swedish Music Information Ctr., Tegnerlunden 3, 11185 Stockholm, Sweden.

ROSENBERG, Kenyon Charles, b. 9 Sept. 1933, Chgo., Ill., USA. Critic. Educ: AA, Latin, LA City Coll.; AB, English/Pre-Librarianship, Univ. of Calif. at LA; MS, Lib. Sci., Univ. of S Calif.; LA City Coll.; UCLA; pvte. study, Chgo. Schl. of Music, var. pvte. tchrs. m. Judith Karen Campbell, 4 d. Career: RAdio progs. on new recordings & understanding music, Ohio. Contbr. to: Lib. Jrnl.; Previews; Akron Beacon Jrnl.; B'nai B'rith Messenger. Mbr., Music Critics Assn. Hobbies: Poetry; Tennis. Address: 2154 White Oak Dr., Stow, OH 44224, USA. 8, 28, 29.

ROSENBLITH, Eric, b. 11 Dec. 1920, Vienna, Austria. Violinist. Educ: Dip. Execution, Ecole Ncrmale Musique, Paris, 1934; Lic. Concert, ibid., 1936. m. Carol Elinor Child, 1970. Debut: Paris, 1936; NY, 1941. Career incls: Concertmaster, San Antonio Symph. Orch., 1952-53; Indpls. Symph. Orch., 1953-66; Recitalist & soloist w. orchs. throughout USA, Canada, Europe, Israel & Far E; Num. radio & TV apps.; Solo violinist w. Phila. Composers' Forum premiering works by Appleton, Crump, Felciano, Hovda, Maiguashca, Thome, Thorne & Wernick; Fac., Butler Univ., 1953-66; Bennington Coll., 1966-68; New England Conserv. Music, 1968-; Chmn., String Dept., ibid., 1970. Recordings incl: Beethoven Sonata (Golden Crest). Mbrships: Bohemians, NY; Pi Kappa Lambda. Mgmt: Ann Van Wyck, 96 Ave Versailles, Paris; Tower Music, London. Address: 1330 Beacon St., Waban, MA 02168. 6.

ROSENBLUM, Myron, b. 12 Oct. 1933, NYC, USA. Violist; Violla d'Amore Player; Teacher. Educ: BA, Queens Coll., NYC, 1956; MA, 1969, PhD, 1976, NY Univ.; musical studies w. Wm. Primrose, Walter Trampler, Karl Stumpf, Lillian Fuchs, Joseph Fuchs & Ralph Hillyer. m. Phyllis Ilene Rosenblum, 1 s., 1 d. Career: Solo reciatls on viola & viola d'amore; chmbr. music concerts; Violist, Greenwich Quartet; Freelance Perf., NY Phil., NYC Opera, Clarion Concerts, Am. Opera Soc., Friends of French Opera, Pro Art Orch., Music in Our Time, etc. Publs: incl: eds. of music for viola d'amore. Contbr. to: Grove's Dict., 6th ed.; musical jrnls. Mbrships: Dir., Viola d'Amore Soc. of Am.; Pres., Am. Viola Soc.; Am. & Coll. Music Socs.; European Viola Rsch. Soc. Address: 39-23 47th St., Sunnyside, NY 11104, USA.

ROSENBLÜTH, Leo, b. 11 Jan. 1904, Fürth, Germany. Composer; Concert Singer; Cantor. Educ. incls: Hoschsches Konservatorium, Univ., FrankfurtMain; studied singing w. N Naumow-Fleischmann. m. Rosa Benkow, 1 d. Debut: 1929. CAreer: Chief-Cantor, Synagog at Stockholm; Soloist, w. Scandinavian, Finnish, & Israeli symph. orchs., also broadcasts in Scandinavia (inclng. Finland), German Fed. Repub. Rome & Jerusalem. Has composed music for Royal Theatre, theatres at Malmö & Helsingborg, Sweden, for Swedish Broadcasting & for Stockholm Synagog. Has recorded. Mbrships: Assn. of Swedish Comps.; STIM. Hons. incl: Kulturstipendium, City of Stockholm, 1974. Address: Kungsholms strand 155, S-122 48 Stockholm, Sweden.

ROSENBOOM, David, b. 9 Sept. 1947, Fairfield, Iowa, USA. Composer; Performer (piano, violin, viola, percussion, trumpet). Educ: Pvte. studies; Univ. Ill.; NY Univ. Career: Assoc. Prof. of Music & Interdisciplinary Studies, York Univ., Toronto, Can.; Dir., Laboratory of Experimental Aesthetics, Aesthetics Rsch. Ctr. of Can.; Fndg. Dir., Artists Rsch. Collective, Berkeley, Calif.; Comps. performed worldwide; Num. TV apps; Guest Lectr., var. Univs., etc.; Mbr. several performing grps. Comps. incl: Patters for London (keyboards & jazz ensemble), 1975. Num. recordings w. famous artists. Publs: Books incl: Biofeedback and the Arts; The Results of Early Experiments, 1974. Contbr. to profl. jrnls. Mbrships. incl: Sigma Alpha Iota. Recip. num. scholarships, grants, etc. Hobby: Gliding. Address: Music Dept., York, Univ., 4700 Keele St., Toronto, Ont., Canada.

ROSENFELD, Gerhard Klaus, b. 10 Feb. 1931, Konigsberg, Germany. Composer. Educ: German Coll. of Music, Berlin, German Dem. Repub. 1952-57; German Acad. of Arts, ibid., 1958-61. Career: Lector in Theory of Harmony. German Coll. of Cinema Art, Postdam-Babelsberg, & Lectr., Int. Lib. of Music, Berlin, 1961-64; Freelance Comp., 1964-. Comps. incl: (publd.) Concerto for Violoncello & Orch.; Concerto for Flute & Orch.; Das Alltägliche Wunder (3-act opera); (also recorded) 2

Concertos for Violin & Orch.; Concerto for Piano & Orch; (operas) Der Mantel nach Gogol; Das Spiel von Liebe und Zufall. Mbr., profl. assn. Hons. incl: Th. Fontane Prize, City of Potsdam, 1968; H Eisler Prize (radio), 1968, 70; Arts Prize, German Dem. Repub., 1973. Hobbies: Literature; Fine Arts. Address: Begas-strasse 1A, DDR 1505 Bergholz-Rehbrucke, German Dem. Repub.

ROSENFELD, Jayn, b. 10 Nov. 1938, Pittsfield, Mass., USA. Flautist. Educ: BA, Radcliffe Coll., Cambridge, Mass., 1960; M Mus, Manhattan Schl. of Music, NYC, 1965. m. Edward F Seigel, 2 d. Debut: as recitalist, Carnegie Recital Hall, NYC, 1970. Career: 1st Flute, Am. Symph. Orch. under Leopold Stokowski, 1963-66. Master Virtuosi of NY under Gene Farrell, 1964-69; concedrts as Soloist & w. chmbr. ensembles inclng. NY Camerata (flute, cello, paino). Perfs. Committee for 20th-Century Music, & Academia Int. di Musica da Camera, Rome; Assoc. Tchr., Princeton Univ. Recordings: Cimarosa, Concerto for 2 flutes; Ned Rorem, Trio for flute, cello & piano. Address: 151 Hartley Ave., Princeton, NJ 08540, USA.

ROSENFELD, Pamela Jean, b. 16 June 1950, Dulwich, London, UK. Violinist; Violist; Teacher. Educ: RCM Grad., Guildhall Schl. of Music & Drama; Debut: recital, Henry Wood Prom Circle. Career: Tchr. of Music, Sydenham HS, 1971-75; var. violin recitals & lectr. recitals on viola d'amore; Fndr. Mbr., Rosenfeld Piano Trioé; Peripatetic Tchr. of Violin & Viola, Cornwall Educ. Comm.; Dir. Cond., St. Austell Area Youth Orch. Mbrships: ISM; European String Tchrs. Assn.; Viola d'Amore Soc. Hobbies: History & Care of Stringed Instruments; Motoring; Swimming. Address: 9, Metna Park, St. Newlyn East, Cornwall, TR8 5LO, UK.

ROSENHART, Kees, b. 8 July 1939, Haarlem, Netherlands. Organist; Harpsichordist. Educ: Studied organ & harpsichord, Amsterdam Conserv.; Dips. for ch. organist, solo organ & harpsichord. m. Annemieke Husslage. Career: Prof. of Harpsichord, Conserv. of Arnhem & Amsterdam; Organist, Walloon Ch., Haarlem; num. organ & harpsichord recitals; radio recitals. Publs: The Amsterdam Harpsichord Tutor I, 1977, & II, 1978. Contbr. to: Het Orgel; Gregoriusblad; Mens en Melodie. Address: Leidsevaart 132, 2013 HD Haarlem, Netherlands.

ROSENSTIEL, Léonie, b. 28 Dec. 1947, NYC, USA. Musicologist; Writer; Lecturer; Violinist. Educ: BA, Barnard Coll.; Cert., Juilliard Schl.; MA, MPh, PhD, Columbia Univ. Carer: Perfs., WKCR-FM, NYC; Concertmaster, All LI String Fest. Orch.; Fndr.; Dir., Columbia Univ. Chmbr. Music Soc.; Perfs., LI Little Orch., Accademia Monteverdiana; Dir., Manhasset Chmbr. Music Ensemble; Perfs., Europe, Latin Am., USA; Speical Projects Ed., Current Musicol.; Conds. Ed.; Da Capo Press Music Series. Mbrships: incl: Int. Musicol. Soc.; Authors Guild of Am. Publs. incl: The Life & Works of Lili Boulanger, 1978; Musica Enchiriadis, 1976; Biography of Nadia Boulanger, 1980. Contbr. to books & mags. Recip., num. hons. Hobbies incl: Yoga. Address: 4 Old Mill Rd., Manhasset, NY 11030, USA.

ROSENSTOCK, Joseph, b. 1895, Cracow, Poland. Conductor. Educ: Vienna Acad. of Music; Vienna Univ. m. Marilou Harrington. Career: Prof., Acad. of Music, Berlin, 1920-21; Cond., Stuttgart, 1921-22; Gen. Music Dir., Darmstadt, 1922-27, Wiesbaden, 1927-29, Met. Opera, NYC, USA, 1929, Mannheim, Germany, 1930-33, & Symph. Orch. of Tokyo, Japan, 1936-41 & 45-46; Cond. & Gen. Dir., NYC Opera, USA. 1948-56; Music Dir., Aspen Fests., Colo., 1949-56; Dir., Opera House, Cologne, 1958-60; Dir., Met. Opera, NYC, 1961-; Hon. Music Dir. & Cond., Japanese Broadcasting Orch., Tokyo. Compositions incl: Piano Sonata; Symphonic Concerto for piano & orch.; Overture for orch.; Variations for orch. Address: 63 E 9th St., NYC, NY 10003, USA.

ROSENTHAL, Albi, b. 5 Oct. 1914, Munich, Bavaria, Germany. Antiquarian Bookseller. Educ: Warburg Inst. (Univ. of London); pvte. studies in musicol., Oxford; studied violin since age 7. m. Maud Levy, 1 s., 2 d. Career: proprietor w. M Rosenthal of A. Rosenthal Ltd., Oxford, & Otto Haas, London, expert in music MSS, early printed music and books on music. Contbr. to: Jrnl. of Warburg Inst.; Burlington Magazine; Annales Musicologiques; Essays presented to Egon Wellesz (ed. J. A. Westrup), 1966; Notes; Fontes; Music & Letters; Das Antiquariat; Grove's Dict., 6th ed. & other Encys. & jrnls. Mbrships. incl: Worcester Coll., Oxford; Pres., Oxford Univ. Orch.; Int. Musicol. Soc.; Aust. Musicol. Soc.; Committee, Oxford Subscription Concerts; Garrick Club, London; Groiler Club, NY; Bibliographical Soc., etc. Hons: MA (hc), Oxford Univ., 1979. Hobby: Chamber Music. Address: Half Acre, Boars Hill, Oxford, UK.

ROSENTHAL, Carl A, b. 16 April 1904, Vienna, Austria. Music Editor; Musicologist. Educ: PhD, Univ. Vienna, 1926; m. Else Rosenthal, 1 s., 1 d. Career: Asst. to Prof. Dr. Guido Adler, 1927-40; Sec., Denkmaler der Tonkunst in Oesterreich, 1927-38; Music Ed., Oxford Univ. Press, NY, USA, 1967-; 7 lectures, Radio Wien, 1933-37; Lectures Mozarteum, Salzburg, 1971, 73. Publs. incl: Practical Guide to Music Notation, MCA, 1967; Over 100 reports on Austrian Music Hist.; Contbr. to Encyclopedia Italiana, etc. Mbrships: Int. Musicol. Assn.; Am. Musicol. Assn.; Soc. for Ethnomusicol. Hobby: Hiking. Address: 564 Park Ave., Yonkers, NY 10703, USA.

ROSENTHAL, Harold David, b. 30 Sept. 1917, London, UK. Editor; Lecturer; Broadcaster. Educ: BA, Univ. Coll., London; Inst. of Educ., London. m. Lillah Phyllis Weiner, 1 s., 1 d. Career incls: Ed., Opera Mag. Publs: Sopranos of Today, 1956; Two Centuries of Opera at Covent Garden, 1958; A Concise Oxford Dictionary of Opera (w. John Warrack), 1964, 1972, 1979; Great Singers of Today, 1966; Mapleson Memoires (Ed. & annotated), 1966; The Opera Bedside Book, 1965; Opera at Covent Garden, 1967; Covent Garden, 1976; Ed., Loewenberg's Annals of Opera 1597-1940, 3rd Ed., 1979. Contbr. to OPera. Mbrships: Committee, Arts Coun. Patrons of Music Fund, 1960-70; Coun., Friends of Covent Garden, 1962-; Chmn., Music Sect., Critics' Circle of GB, 1965-67. Hons: Cavaliere Ufficiale, Order of Merit of the Repub, (Italy), 1977. Hobbies: Travel; Food; Collecting Playbills, prints, programmes, etc. Address: 6 Woodland Rise, London N10 3UH, UK. 1.

ROSENTHAL, Laurence, b. 4 Nov. 1926, Detroit, Mich., USA. Composer; Pianist. Educ: MusB, MusM, Eastman Schl. of Music, Univ. of Rochester; studied w. Nadia Boulanger; Nat. Conserv., Paris, France; Mozarteum, Salzburg, Austria. m. Barbara Stander, 2 d. Career: Comp. for film, theatre, TV; Concert Pianist (mostly chmbr. music). Comps. incl: The Wind in the Mountains (ballet); theatre scores for Rashomon, Becket, A Patriot for Me, etc.; film scores for The Miracle Worker, Requiem for a Heavyweight, Becket, The Comedians, Hotel Paradiso, Return of a Man Called Horse, etc.; Ode for Orch.; Four Orphic Tableaux. Mbrships: ASCAP; Acad. of Motion Pictures Arts & Scis. Hons. incl: Emmy, 1966. Mgmt: Mark Newman Agency. Address: 441 Buena Vista Rd., New City, NY 10956, USA.

ROSENTHAL, Manuel, b. 19 June 1904, Paris, France. Composer; Conductor. Educ: paris Conserv.; studied w. Maurice Ravel. m. Claudine Verneuie, 2 s. Career: Musical Dir. & Cond., Nat. Orch., Paris, 1945-48, Seattle Symph. Orch., Wash., USA, 1949-51, & Royal Orch. of Liege, Belgium, 1964-67; Composer-in-Res., Coll. of Puget Sound, Wash., 1948-49; Guest Cond. w. var. orchs. in USA; Prof.; of Orch. Conducting, Nat. Conserv. of Paris, 1902-. Compositions inol: Sonata for 2 violines & piano; La Fete, du Vin for Orch.; Musique de Table for orch.; Magin Manhattan; Desese Deo Gratias; La Poule Nore; Les Femmes au Tombeau. Hons: Kt., Legion of Hon.; Off. of Arts & Letters. Address: 83 Rue du Moulin des Pres., Paris, 13e, France.

ROSEVEAR, Robert Allan, b. 9 July 1915, E Orange, NJ, USA. Professor Emeritus of Music Education; Conductor. Educ: AB, Cornell Univ.; BM, MM, Eastman Schl. of Music; Indiana Uiv., Bloomington; French Horn w. Arkadia Yegudkin, Cond. w. Karl Van Hoesen & Wolfgang Vacano. m. Clara Helen Rhodes, 1 s. Career: Former Asst. to Dir. of Fac., & Chmn., Music Educ. Dept., Univ. of Toronto, Can.; Former Prof. of Music Educ. (instrumental music, french horn, cond.), ibid; Adjudicator num. music fests., USA & Can.; Guest Cond., Music Camps. Bands & Orchs., USA & Can.; Arr., Bell, Glorious is the Land, 1955. Contbr. to: Harvard Dicct. of Music, 2nd Ed., 1969; Grove's Dict., 6th Ed., 1979; Instrumentalist. Mbrships: Ont. Music Educators Assn. (Pres. 1949-50); Can. Music Educators Assn.; Am. Bandmasters Assn.; Toronto Musicians Assn; MENC; Phi Beta Mu. Hons: DMus (hc), Univ. of W Ont., 1979; Life mbr., Ont. Music Educators Assn.) Hobbies: Photography; Camping; Travel. Address: 2714 Saratoga Rd., N, DeLand, FL 32720, USA.

ROSINSKA-SZKLARZEWICZ, Maria, b. 1 Nov. 1915, Ploskinow, USSR. Singer. Educ: Dip., music, Kielce; studied w. profs. Maria & Sophia Koztowska, conservs. in Warsaw & Lvov; also w. Profs. Ada Sari & Jadwiga Szamatulska; MA (biology), Univ. of Jagellon, Cracow. m. Jerzy Szklarzewicz, 3 s. Debut: Polish Radio, 1950. Career: public concerts, recitals & recordings mainly for Polish radio over 25 yrs.; soloist & ensemble music; old Polish songs & Engl. songs of 19th century. Mbrships: SPAM; Music Soc. of Warsaw; Radio Workers Union. recip. prize for services to culture, 1975.

Hobbies: Music; Languages. Address: Dubois 8 m 64, 00188 Warsaw, Poland.

ROSKELLY, William, b. 4 May 1919, Falmouth, Cornwall, UK. Violoncellist Educ: LRAM; ARCM; Post. grad. study w. Pablo Casals, Prades, France. m. Beryl Boskelly, 3 s. Career: Violoncellist, LSO, 1946-56; Freelance & solo chmbr. work, 1956-59; Royal Opera House, Covent Gdn., 1959-64; Tchr. in charge, Newham Acad. of Music. London. Orchl. recordings on HMV & Decca Records. Mbrships: Musicians Union; ISM. Recip. Open Scholarship RCM, 1938. Hobbies: Motorcars; Sailing. Address: 147 Elgin Cres., Holland Pk., London W11 2JH, UK.

ROSNER, Francis, b. 19 Mar. 1916, Vienna, Austria. Concertmaster; Violinist. Educ: Dip., Vienna State Acad. of Music. m. Margaret Matuschka, 1 s., 2 d. Career: First Concertmaster (Ldr.). Violinist, Symph. Orch., Radio-TV, Luxembourg, Recordings; solo - on all recordings of Le Grand Orch. de Radio-Télé Luxembourg; Ldr., Luxembourg Str. Quartet., Contbr. to: Violins & Violinists, Chgo., USA; Das Orchester, Mainz, Germany. Hons: Honoured with the title of 'Professor' by the Austrian Govt. for servs. rendered to music in sev. countries. Hobbies: Photography; Collecting Violin Bows; Collecting Antiques. Address: 1 Rue des Pins, Senningerberg, Luxembourg.

ROSS, Barry Fred, b. 25 Feb. 1944, Boston, Mass., USA. Concert Violinist; Conductor; Teacher. Educ: BA, Hart Coll. of Music, hartford, Conn., 1966; MMA, Yale Schl. of Music, 1970; DMA, Yale Schl. of Music, 1975. Career: Instr. of Violin, Wesleyan Univ., Middletown, Conn.; New England Conserv. Est. Div., Boston, Mass.; Concertmaster & Solo Violinist w. the following Orchs.: Conn. Chmbr. Orch.; Am. Chmbr. Orch. (tour of Greece); Hartford Festival Orch., North Country Festival, Lake Placid, NY; Kalamazoo Symph. Orch.; Kalamazoo Bach Soc.; Cond., Kalamazoo Coll. Chmbr. Kalamazoo Coll. Music Dir., Kalamazoo Festival Theatre. Hons. incl. var. acad. schlrships: Lucy G Moses Fellowship, Yale, 1969. Hobbies: Glider pilot; Sailing. Address: 415 Eldred St. Kalamazoo, MI 49001, USA.

ROSS, Colin Archibald Campbell, b. 7 Dec. 1911, Brecon, UK. Organist; Conductor; Composer; Accompanist. Educ: Brecon & Hereford Cathedrals; RCM, FRCO, (CHM); ARCM; LRAM; ADCM. m. Leila Joyce Hodges, 1 d. Career: Asst. Organist, Hereford Cathedral, 1935-40; Organist. St. Paul's Cathedral, Melbourne, 1948-51; Master of the Music, St. Nicholas' Cathedral, Newcastle upon Tyne, 1955-66; currently Tchng. at Chichester Coll. of Further Educ., 1973-. Compositions: Ostinato, for organ & Unison Song 'The Invaders' (Cramer); Improvisation on 'Ich ruf zu Dir', for organ (Novello); Lorna's Song (Cramer); The Cherry Hung With Snow (Curwen); Let This Mind Be in You, anthem for SATB & organ (Curwen), The Wind Called; Gently The Breeze Blows. Contbr. to: Musical Opinion. Mbrships: ISM; Hon. Sec., The Cathedral Organists Assn., 1956-66. Hons. Steir Prize for Cond., RCM. 1942; Farrer Prize for Comp., ibid, 1942. Hobbies: Motoring; Walking. Address: 63 Chesswood Rd., Worthing, Sussex, UK. 3.

ROSS, Gilbert, b. 30 Oct. 1903, Lincoln, Neb., USA. Concert Violinist; Music Educator. Educ: Chgo. Musical Coll., Ill.; studied Violin w. Leon Sametini & Leopold Auer; theoratical & hist. studies w. var. masters. m. Gertrude H Tuthill, 1 s., 1 d. Debut: Berlin, Germany, 1922. Career: Extensive concert work in Europe, USA, Can. & S Am.; Soloist, Berlin Phil. Orch., Chgo. Symph., Mpls. Symph. & other orchs.; Fndr. & 1st Violinist, Stanley Quartet, Univ. of Mich.; Asst. Prof., Cornell Univ.; Prof. of Music, Smith Coll., Prof. of Music & Chmn. Str. Dept., Univ. of Mich.; Vis. Prof., Univ. of Wis. & Yale Univ. Compositions. Num. transcriptions & arrs. for violin & viola; Eds. of 18th century Italian instrumental music. Recordings: (w. Stanley Quartet & var. artists); Ross Lee Finney, String Quartet in E. Quintet for Piano & String Quartet; Darius Milhaud, Quintets Nos. 1 & 2; Quincy Porter, String Quartet No. 8. Publs: Articles on music & travel. Contbr. to: Travel Mag., Michigan Quarterly Review. Mbrships. incl: Phi Kappa Phi; The Bohemians; Pi Kappa Lambda; AAUP; Am. Musicol. Soc. Hons: Diamond Medal, Chgo. Musical Coll., 1917; Disting. Fac. Achievement Award, Univ. of Mich., 1957. Hobbies: Travel; Bridge. Address: 3 Highland Ln., Ann Arbor, MI 48104, USA. 2, 3, 28.

ROSS, Jerrold, b. 8 Feb. 1935, NYC, USA. Educator. Educ: BS in Music Educ., PhD in Music, NY Univ.; MS in Music Educ., Queens Coll., CUNY. Career: Tchr., Pub. Schls. of NY State, 1957-61; Fac. mbr., NY Univ., 1961-63; Chmn., Tchr. Educ. Dept., NY Coll. of Music, 1963-65; Pres., NY Coll. of Music, 1965-67; Chmn., Dept. of Music & Music Educ., NY Univ., 1967-; Dir., Town Hall, NYC, 1971-74; Hd., Div. of Arts & Arts Educ., NY Univ., 1974-. Acting Vice Dean, Schl. of Education, NYU, 1978. Publ: Interpreting Music Through

Movement, 1963. Contbr. to profl. jrnls. Mbrships incl: Pres. of Bd., Usden Ctr. for Creative & Performing Arts, 1973-; Am. Assn. for music Therapy (sec. 1971-); Broadway Assn. (Bd. of Dirs.). WNCN Citizens Advsry. Bd. Hon. Dir., Mu Phi Epsilon Scholarship Fund., 1965-; NY State Fedn. of Music Clubs, (Bd. of Dirs.). Address: 2 Washington Square Village, NY, NY 10012, USA. 2, 6.

ROSS, Susanna, b. 28 Oct. 1950, Stockton-on-Tees, UK. Opera Singer. Educ: studied w. Vera Rozs. Royal Manchester Coll. of Music, 5 yrs.; ARMCM (perfs. Singing); London Opera Ctr., 2 yrs. m. Philip Griffiths. Debut: as Barbarina, Marriage of Figaro, Glyndebourne Tour, 1973. Career: Susan, Arden Must Die, New Opera Co., Sadler's Wells, 1974; Barbarina, Glyndebourne Fest., 1974, Covent Gdn., 1976; Anne Truelove, The Rake's Progress, Glyndebourne Tour; apps. w. Scottish Opera & at Aix Fest. Covent Gdn. Scholarship, 1973. Mgmt: Neil Dalrymple. Address: 1 Priory St., Lewes, Sussex, UK.

ROSSEELS, Gustave A, b. 19 Jan. 1911, Mechelen, Belgium. Professor of Music. Educ: Grad., Royal Conserv. of Music, Brussels. m. Jacqueline Crepin, 1 s., 2 d. Career: concertised w. Paganini Str. Quartet, USA, Europe & S Am.; films for Univ. of Souther. Calif. Cinema Dept.; TV & radio apps. in USA; currently Prof. of violin & chmbr. music, Schl. of Music, Univ. of Mich., Ann Arbor Recorded w. Paganini Str. Quartet for RCA, HMV & Decca. Mbrshps. incl: AAUP; ASTA. Recip. Harold Haugh award, 1978. Hobbies: Swimming; Golf; Table tennis; Reading myster novels. Address: 1233 Bending Rd., Ann Arbor, MI 48103, USA. 8, 28.

ROSSELLINI, Renzo, b. 2 Feb. 1908, Italy. Composer; Music Critic. Educ: Conserv. of Music of St. Cecilia, Rome. Career: Dir., GB Pergolesi Musical Inst., Varese, 1933-40; Vice-Dir. & Prof. of Composition, G Rossini Conserv., Pesaro; Music Critic, Il Messagero, Rome. Compositions: Lyric operas - La Guerra, 1956; Il Vortice, 1958; Le Campane, 1959; Uno Squardo dal Ponte, 1961; Il Linguaggio Dei Fiori, 1963; La leggenda del Ritorno, 1966; L'Avventuriero, 1967. Mbrships: Nat. Coun. of UNESCO, 1958-; Mgmt. Committee, Nat. Orch. of Monte Carlo, 1965-; Italian Authors & Writers Soc.; Nat. Acad. of St. Cecilia; Cherubini Acad., Florence; Acad. Filarmonica, Bologna. Publs: Polemica Musicale, 1962; Pagine di un Musicista, 1964. Address: Palais Heracles, Monte Carolo, Monaco, & 12 Via Lisbona, Rome, Italy.

RÖSSEL-MAJDAN, Hildegard, b. 30 Jan. 1921, Moosbierbaum, Austria. Opera Singer (contralto). Educ: HS for Music & Dramatic Art, Vienna. m. Dr. Karl Rössel-Majdan, 1 d. Career: Concert & Oratorio Singer under leading Austria & foregin conds., 1948-51; Mbr., Vienna State Opera, 1951-; prof., HS for Music & Dramatic Art, Vienna; Concerts, opera & oratorio, Europe & Am. Address: Agnesgasse 13, Vienna, Austria. 2, 5.

ROSSI, John L, b. 7 Jan. 1927, Wash. DC, USA. French Hornist. m. Loretta M Rossi, 1 s.; 1 d. Debut: Nat. Theatre, Wash. DC, 1946. Career: Nat. Symph. Orch., Wash. DC; RCA Records & Radio, NYC; NYC Ballet & Opera; Am. Symph. Orch. under Stokowski, NYC; Voice of Firestone & Telephone Hour, TV, NYC; Metrop. Opera Auditions of the Air, NYC; Solo Horn, NBC Opera, Goldmn Band, NYC; Brodway theatres, NYC; also internationally known as Luthier & Dealer in Violins. Mbr.; Bd. of Dir., Violin Soc. of Am. Address: 84 Bobwhite Lane, Hicksville, NY 11801, USA.

ROSSI, Massimo, b. 21 Oct. 1933, Supino, Italy. University Professor; Composer; Arranger. Educ: B Mus., Univ. of Montreal, Canada; Licence degree in Music, ibid. m. Teresa Sugar, 1 S. Career incl: Prof. of Harmony, instrumentation, Orchestration, Organography & Organology, Univ. of Montreal; Organ recitalist. Hobbies: Home building of small pipe organ; Gardening. Address: 9 Linden Cres., Kirkland, PQ, Canada H9H 3K5.

ROSSI, Nick, b. 14 Nov. 1924, San Luis, Obispo, Calif., USA. Professor of Music; Author; Arranger; Conductor. Educ: B Mus, Univ. Southern Calif., Los Angeles, 1948; M Mus, ibid., 1952; Supvsr. Credential, Sacramento State Coll., Calif., 1968; PhD, Sussex Coll. Technol., 1971. Career incls: Prod., num. operas inclng: Worl premiere, Liberty? (Roy Harris); Cond. & prod., Importance of Being Earnest (Castelnuovo-Tedesco) world premiere; Prod., radio, TV shows, operettas, etc. Arr. num. works inclng: We Hasten, O Master, 1968; Wondrous Night, 1968. Recordings incl: (Prod.). Music of Puerto Rico; Music of USSR. Publs. incl: A Musical Pilgrimage, 1971; The Sound of Music, 1976. Contbr. to jrnls. Mbrships. incl: pres. & Fndr., Int. Castelnuovo-Tedesco Soc. Inc. Hobbies incl: Philately. Address: Apt. 5-C, 44 W 63nd St., NY, NY 10023, USA. 28.

ROSSI, Robert Ralph, b. 6 Sept. 1933, Vandergrift, Pa., USA. Music Teacher; Band Director; performer (String Bass, Tuba,

Bariton-Euphonium, Accordion-Piano). Educ: BS, Ind. Univ. Pa.; M Mus, W Va. Univ. m. Gustina Jane Jackman, 1 s. Career incls: Tchr., Carroll Twnships.; Pub. Schl., Monongahela, Pa., 1956-61; Charleroi Area Pub. Schls., Pa., 1961-74; Dir., Monogahela Valley Community Band, 1965-; St. Jerome's Cath. Ch. Choir, 1963-; Instrumentalist w. num. artists inclng: Pearl Bailey, Chubby Checker, Four Aces, Four Freshmen, & Allen & Rossi; Pvte. Tchr. Recordings incl: 'Sounds of the Seans' w. St. Valentine's Ch. Mixed Choir, 1974. Mbr. profl. & community orgs. inclng: NEA; MENC; Phi Beta Mu; Conslr., Boy Scouts Am. Address: Box 321, RD 1, Menongahela, PA 15063, USA.

ROSSI-LEMENI, Nicola, b. 1920, Istanbul, Turkey. Concert & Opera Bass. m. (1) Vittoria Serafin; (2) Virginia Zeani. Debut: in opera, Venice, Italy, 1946. Career: apps. at Major opera houses inclng. La Scala, Milan, Met. Opera, NYC, Covent Gdn., London; concert tours, Spain, USA, S. Am., France, GB, Germany, etc., 1950-; radio & TV broadcasts; reading of poetry & philos. Address: c/o Grolinsky, 35 Dover St., London W1, UK. 2.

ROSTAL, Max, b. 7 Aug. 1905, Teschem, Austria. Concert Violinist; Professor of Music, Educ.; Studied violin w. Prof. Arnold Rose & Prof. Carl Flesch; comp. w. Ernil Bohnke, Staatliche Hochschule für Musik, Berlin, m. Baroness von Hohenblum, 2 d. Debut: at age 6, Teschen. Career: Concertised in many European countries as a prodigy between ages of 6 and 14; started concertising as adult at age 17 & since then has appeared all over the world; Asst. to Prof. Carl Flesch., 1927-30 Prof., State Acad. in Berlni; Prof., GSM. London, 1934-58; Prof. at the State Acad. in Cologne & at the Conservatoire in Berne, 1967-; Var. comps. & arrangements as well as new edns. Published by Novellos in London, Chesters in London & Schott's in Mainz. Recordings: Decca, HMV; Argo;p Concert Hall Soc.; Deutscher Grammophon. Mbrshis: pres., European String Tchrs. Assn., ISM; Musikpädago-gischer Verein, Switz. Hons: Mendelssohn Prize, Berlin, 1925; FGSM, 1945; Siler Medal, State Acad. of Music, Cologne, 1965; Cundesverdienstkreuz First Class of the German Fed. Repub., 1968; Music Prize of the City of Berne, 1972, CPE, 1976. Hobbies: Motoring; Photography; Filming; Reading; Swimming. Address: Chalet Promusica, Ausserschwand, CH-3715, Adelboden, Switz.

ROSTIROLLA, Giancarlo, b. 11 Mar. 1941, Rome, Italy. Musicologist. Educ: Dip., Musical Paleography, Univ. of Pavia. Appts: Ed., Nuova Rivista Musicale Italiana; Dir. & Fndr., Instr. of Musical Bibliography. Mbrshps: Pres., Italian Flute Soc.; Italian Musicol. Soc.; Italian Commn., RILM. Publs: Catalogue of the Works of Alexander Scarlatti, 1972; The Missarum Liber Primus of G Pierluigi da Palestrina, 1975. Contbr. to Nuova Rivista Musicale Italiana. Address: Largo Tenente Bellini 9, 00197 Rome, Italy.

ROSTROPOVICH, Mstislav Leopoldovich, b. 27 Mar. 1927, Baku, USSR. Violoncellist; Conductor. Educ: Moscow Conserv. m. Galina Vishnevskaya. Debut: 1942. Career incls: num. concert tours in USSR & abroad, notably in trio w. Leonid Kogan & Emil Gilels; Prof., Conservs. of Moscow & Leningrad, 1960-; Am. debut: 1974. Hons. incl: 1st Prizes, All-Union Concours of Musicians, 1945, Int. Cellists Competition, Prague; State Prize, 1951; People's Artist of the RSFSR & Lenin Prize, 1964; People's Artist of the USSR; Gold Medal, Royal Phil. Soc., 1970; D Mus, Cambridge Univ., 1975. Mgmt: Victor Hochhauser, 4 Holland Pk. Ave., London W11, UK. 16.

ROTH, Daniel, b. 31 Oct. 1942, Mulhouse, Haut Rhin, France. Organist; Professor of Organ. Educ: Nat. Higher Conserv. of Music, paris. m. Odile Mangin, 2 s., 1 d. Career incls: Dpty. Organist, Sacré Coeur Basilica, Paris, 1963-72; Hd. Organist, ibid., 1972-; Prof. of Organ, Nat. Conserv., Marseille, 1973-; Vis. Tchr., Organ, Cath. Univ. of Am. & Artist in Res., Nat. Shrine of the Immaculate Conception, Wash. DC, USA, 1974-76; Recitals in Europe & USA; Radio apps. Comps. incl: (publs.) 5 Verses on Veni Creator, for organ; Ave Maria, motet for choir. Recordings incl: 19th Century Organ Music; Bach on the Great Organs of Charters. Mbrships: SACEM, Paris; Frieds of the Organ, ibid. Hons. incl: 1st Grand Prix, Chartres, 1971. Mgmt: McFarlane, NYC, USA. Address: 9 rue Engéne Carriére, 75018 Paris, France.

ROTH, David Robert, b. 9 Mar. 1936, Stockton-on-Tees, Co. Durham, UK. Violinist. Educ: Univ. Edinburgh, 1953-54; RAM, 1954-59; LRAM. m. Ruth Elaine West, 2 s. Debut: West Linton, Peebles, 1954. Career: W. Netherlands Chmbr. Orch., Amsterdam, 1960-64; Played Bloch Sonata No. 1 on KOT Israel Radio Tel Aviv, 1961; Dpty. Ldr., Northern Sinfonia Orch., Newcastle-upon-Tyne, 1966-68; 2nd Violin, Allegre String Quartet, 1969-. Recordings: w. Allegri String Quartet,-

1969-. Recordings: w. Allegri String Quartet; Records for Open Univ. Mbrships: ISM; MU. Hons: M Mus, Hull, 1975. Hobbies: Chess; Theatre; Reading. Mgmt: Van Walsum, Richmond, Sussey. Address: 16 Oman Ave. London NW2 6BG, UK.

ROTH, George, b. 7 Sept. 1904, Budapest, Hungary. Cellist. Educ: Franz Liszt Acad. Music, Budapest. m. Catherine Molnar, 1 s. Debut: Wigmore Hall, London, UK, 1920. Career: Num. apps. BBC & most European TV & Radio stns.; Frequent apps. w. Lener Quartet; Fndr. w. brother Nicholas, Budapest Trio, app. in Ravel Fest., Paris, 1932; joined London Phil. Orch., 1932; Civ. Def. & toured with Kathleen Ferrier & appd. at Nat. Gall. concerts during WWII; w. Benjamin Britten's Engl. Opera Grp.; London Soloists' Ensemble, 1960's; Toured w. Royal Phil. Orch., USA, 1963 & still a mbr. Recordings: Solo & w. Budapest Trio & Soloists' Ensemble. Hon: Winner, Popper Competition, Budapest, 1924. Hobbies: incl: Photography. Address: 6 Snowdon Mansions, Condar Gdns., London NW6 1ES, UK. 14.

ROTH, Nicholas, b. 1910, Budapest, Hungary. Violinist. Educ: Artist Dip., Royal Hungarina Conserv. m . Rucky Anny van Mill, 5 d. Career: Radio & TV apps. throughout Europe; hd., Chmbr. Music, Dutch Broadcasting, many yrs.; Dir., London Soloists' Ensemble; Violinist; Budapest Trio; Hd., Strings, Poole Tech. Coll.; Prof., violin & chmbr. music, TCL. Recordings: CBS. Hons: Prix de Excellence, Royal Hungarian Conserv.; Hon. FTCL. Hobbies: Philately; Old Maps. Mgmt: Ibbs & Tillett. Address: Flat 11, Cheyne Ct., 37 Surrey Rd., Bournemouth, UK. 3, 14.

ROTHENBERGER, Anneliese, b. 19 June 1926. Operatic Soprano. Educ: Music Acad., Mannheim. m. Gerd W. Dieberitz. Debut: Coblenz Theatre, 1947. Career: Hamburg Opera House, 1948; Vienna State opera, 1967-; apps. incl. La Scala, Metrop. Opera, Salzburg, Glyndebounne & Edinburgh Fets., etc.,film apps. in Die Fledermaus, 1955, Der Rosenkavalier. Recordings: 150 LP's. Address: Quellenhof, 8268 Salenstein TG, Switz.

RÖTHLISBERGER, Max, b. 27 Sept. 1914, Burgdorf, Switz. Opera Designer. Educ: Univ. Berne (Switz); Reinhardt Seminar, Vienna (Design & Acting). m. Gertrud R, 2 c. Debut: Design & Dir.,'Woyzeck'. Career: Actor, Designer, minor Swiss theatres; Chief Designer, Zurich Opera, 1944; Guest Designer, num. European Operas, incl. La. Scala, Fenice, S Carlo, Vienna, Hamburg, Munich; Prof. of Scenic Design, Ind. Univ. Schl. of Music, 1973. Contbr. to: Schweizer Theater-Jahrbuch. Hons: Reinhard-Ring, 1977 (Switz.) Address: 44 Freiestrasse, Zürich, Switz.

ROTHMULLER, Marko Aron, b. 31 Dec. 1908, Trnjani, Yugoslavia. Concert & Opera Singer; Author; Composer; Educator. Educ: studied composition & conducting. Music Acad., Zagreb, Yugoslavia, & w. Alban Berg, Vienna, Austria, & singing w. Jan. Ourednik, Zagreb, & Franz Steiner, Vienna. m. (1) Ella Reiss, div., (2) Catherine Anne Blanchard, div., 2 s. Debut: Schiller OPera, Hamburg-Altona, Germany, Sept. 1932. Career: app. in opera houses, Germany, Austria, Switz., France, UK, Argentina, & USA; perf. chmbr. music, songs, etc.; Prof. of Music (Voice), Ind. Univ. Schl. of Music, Bloomington. Compositions incl: chmbr. music & songs. Has recorded for HMB (London & Qurich), London Records, Decca & Bartok Records. Publs: The Music of the Jews, revised ed., 1967; Pronunciation of German & German Diction for Singers, 1974. Mbr: AAUP. Address: 1005 E Wylie St., Bloomington, IN 47401, USA. 2, 8.

ROTHMUND, Doris, b. Mannheimm, Germany. Concert Pianist; Lecturer. Educ: Conservs., Heidelberg, Mannheim, Saarbruen (studied w. Martin Steinkrüger & Prof. Richard Laugs); master class, Prof. Walter Gieseking. Career: repertoire concentrates on romantic, impressionist & modern music; concerts, Germny, Spain, Austria, France, England, Ireland, Belgium, Egypt, Ethopia, Tanzania, Algeria, Tunisia, Congo, India, Madagascar, Columbia; Lectr., Staatliche Musikhochschule, Mannheim. Address: T.6.26, 68 Mannheim, German Fed. Repub.

ROTHSCHILD, Myrtle, b. 7 July 1936, Krugersdorp, S Africa. Music Teacher (Piano); Pre-school music educator. Educ: BMus (Wits.); LRSM; UTLM; LTCL. m. Hanns Joseph Rothschild, 1 s., 1 d. Career: Music Tchr.; Pre-schl. music tchr. Mbrships: S African Soc. of Music Tchrs. Address: 112 Albert Dr., Northcliff View, Johannesburg 2195, S Africa.

ROTHSTEIN, Albert Jeffrey, b. 21 Feb. 1947, Brooklyn, NY, USA. Conductor; Composer; Educator. Educ: BA in Music, Hofstra Univ., NY; MS in Educ., SUNY, New Paltz; Perm. Tchng. Cert., State of NY. m. Helene, 1 s., 1 d. Career: Dir. of Music, City of Poughkeepsie Public Schls.; Music Dir. & Fndr.,

Poughkeepsie Performing Arts Orch.; Has directed 90 Miles off Broadway Theatre prods. of Pajama Game, Little Mary Sunshine, Guys & Dolls, South Pacific & Of Thee I Sing; Music Dir. for Mid Hudson Opera Co. prods. of Gianni Schicchi, La Traviata & Gala perfs.; Music Dir., Poughkeepsi Ballet Theatre prod. of Nutcracker. Mbrships: MENC; NYSSMA; Past Treas., Ulster So. Music Educators; NEA; MYSTA; Nat. Hon. Soc., Pershing Rifles; Hofstra Univ. Music Hon. Soc. Hons: Phi Delta Kappa. Hobbies: Water Sports; Piano Tuning & Repair; Clock Repair. Address: 17 Cherry Hill Road, New Paltz, NY, USA.

ROTMAN, Johan, b. 26 Feb. 1923, Utrecht, Netherlands. Institute Director. Educ: State Dips., vocal soloist, mucial educ.; Dip., whoir cond. Career: Advsry. Expert in music in educ., currently Dir., Dr. Gehrels Inst. for music in educ., Amersfoort. Address: Utr. weg 137 Amersfoort, Netherlands.

ROTT, Josef, b. 13 May 1929, Miskolc, Hungary. Violinist; Teacher. Educ: Dip., Byelorussian State Univ., Minsk, USSR. m. Stepanova Svetlana Rott, 2 s. Career: 1st violin, then concertmaster, Tomsk Phil. Symph. Orch., 1953-70; violin tchr., Tomsk Coll. for music study, 1953-70; mbr., N Kaukas Phil. Orch., chmbr. music ensemble, soloist, tchr., 1970-78; Ordzjonikidze City; concertmaster, Oshawa Symph. Orch., Can., 1978-. Recordings: works by Mozart, Bach, Beethoven, Tchaikovsky, Bartok, Grieg, etc. Contbr. of music reviews to Tomsk newspaper, 1965-70. Mbrships: Soviet Artists Profl. Assn., 1951-78; Toronto Musicians Assn., 1978-. Recip., Lenin medal, Ordzjonikidze City, 1970. Address: 2700 Bathurst St., Apt. 703, Toronto, Ont. M6B 2Z7, Can.

ROTUNDO, Emil, b. 17 Sept. 1928, Botosani, Romania. Opera Singer (baritone). Educ: Ciprian Porumbescu Conserv., Bucharest. m. Georgeta Rotundo, 1 d. Debut: Figaro (Barber of Seville), Timisorara. Career: ldng. baritone, Timisoara opera house; guest apps. at Bucharest Opera, other major theatres in Romania, in Poland, Czech., Egypt, Germany, Yugoslavia & Eire; radio & TV perfs.; apps. in operettas & musical (My Fair Lady); recitals of lieder & songs of Russion & Romanian comps. num. recordings. Mbr., Theatre & Music Assn., Romania. Hons. incl: Order of Labour, 1964; Medals & Jubilee Distinctions, 1972-74. Hobbies: Car Driving; Swimming; Football. Address: Bv. Lenin 38, Timisoara, Romania.

ROUGET, Gilbert, b. 9 July 1916, Paris, France, Ethnomusicologist. Educ: Lic. in Letters, Sorbonne, Paris. Career: Dir. of Rsch., Nat. Ctr., of Sci. Rsch., paris; Dir., Ethnomusicol. Dept., Mus. of Man, ibid. Author, Music & Trance. Contbr. to: Musicol. Review; Man, French Anthropol. Review; African Soc. Jrnl.; Jrnl. of African Langs.; Hist. of Music (Pléiade Ency.); Ency. of Music (Fasquelle); Grove's Dictionary of Music & Musicians, 6th ed. Mbrships: Int. & French Musicol. Soc.; Ethnomusicol. Soc. Address: 1 rue des Deux-Ponts, Paris 4, France.

ROULEAU, Joseph Alfred, b. 28 Feb. 1929, Matane, Quebec, Canada. Singer. Educ: BA Coll. Jean de Brebeuf, Montreal; Conservatoire de Musique da la Province de Quebec; Studied in Milan. m. Jill Renée Morreau, 2 d., 1 s. Career: Apps. as Bass Singer in Europe incl. opera houses in Paris, Nice, Monte Carlo, Royal Opera House, Covent Gdn., London; Festival apps. at Edinburgh, Aldeburgh, Bath, Wexford, Holland, Empire State Festival, USA; 3 tours of USSR; 4 month tour of Aust. Num. recordings. Hons. incl: Medal, Bene Merenti di Patria, 1967; Bursary, Provincial Govt. Quebec for studies in Italy; Officer, Order of Can., 1977; Silver Jubilee Medal, 1977. Mgmt: AIM, 5 Regent's Pk. Rd., London, UK. Address: 76 Brookside Ave., Beaconsfield, Quebec, H9W 5C6, Can.

ROUSSAKIS, Nicolas, b. 14 June 1934, Athens, Greece. Educator; Clarinettist; Composer. Educ: BA Columbia Coll., 1956; MA Columbia Univ., 1960; Hochschule für Musik, Hamburg, Germany, 1961-63; Ferienkurse fur Neue Musik, Darmstadt, 1962, 63; DMA, Columbia Univ. Schl. of Arts, 1975. Studied comp. w. Otto Luening, Jack Beeson, Henry Cowell, Ben Weber, Philipp Jarnach, etc. m. Vuka Boyovich. Career: Clarinet Tchr., 1958-61; Dir. of the Woodwind Ensemble, Thierd St. Music Schl., NYC, 1960-61; Clarinettist w. The Living Theatre, 1959-60; Freelance Clarinettist, NY, 1958-61; Mbr. of the Erstes Bläserquintett, Musikhochschule, Hamburg, 1961-62, etc.; On Fac., Columbia Univ., 1968; Asst. prof., Columbia Univ.; Pres., Am. Comps. Alliance, 1975; Exec. Dir., Grp. for Contemporary Music, inc., Manhattan Schl. of Music. Comps. incl: Syrtos for Concert Band, 1975; Ode & Cataclysm for Symph. Orch., 1975; March, Song & Dance, for 5 woodwinds, 1959; Composition for Brass Trio, tpt., hn., tbr., 1961; Sextet, fl., cl., vin., cla., vc., pno., 1964; Concert Trio for Oboe, Piano & Contrabass, 1965; Sonata for Harpsichord, 1966-67; Night Speech (chorus & perc.), 1967-68; Six Short Pieces for Two Flutes, 1969; Concertino for Percussion &

Woodwinds, 1973. Sev. recordings. Mbr. of many profl. orgs. Recip. many hons. scholarships, inclng., Fullbrigh Grant, 1961-63; Award, Am. Inst. of Arts & Letters, 1969, etc. Hobbies: Skiing; Tennis; Travel; Mountain Climbing. Address: 225 West 86 St., Penthouse 2F, NY, NY 10024, USA.

ROUTCH, Robert, b. 12 July 1917, Allentown, Pa., USA. French Hornist. Educ: BA, Oberlin Conserv.; MFA, ibid; Paris Conserv. Career: Solo Horn, New Orleans Symph.; Kan. City Symph.; Chgo. Symph.; NY Phil.; Marlboro Fest. Orch.; Prof., Oberlin Conserv.; Juilliard Schl. Music. Recordings: Brahms Horn Trio; num. chmbr. & orchl. works. Publs: Right-Hand Technique for Horn, 1934; French Horn Mute Technique, 1941; Embourchure Aerobics, 1952; Getting Arond on the Horn, 1953. Contbr. to profl. jrnls. Hons. incl: 1st Prize, paris Conserv., 1933. Hobby: Aenol. Address: Box 5, Marlboro, VT, USA.

ROUTH, Francis John, b. 15 Jan. 1927, Kidderminster, UK. Composer; Painist; Writer. Educ: BA, King's Coll., Cambridge Univ., 1951; MA, ibid, 1954; RAM. London; FRCO; LRAM, etc. m. Virginia Anne Raphael, 2 s., 2 d. Career: Appeared as pianist, occasionally cond., in London concerts, regularly on South Bank & elsewhere; Var. radio broadcasts; Fndr., Redcliffe Conserts of Brit. Music, 1963. Compositions: A Sacred Tetralogy for Organ, 1959-74; Sonatina for organ, 1965; Dialogue for violin & orch., 1968; Double Concerto, 1970; Sonata for solo cello, 1971; Concert Aria Spring Night, 1971; Symphony, 1972; Cello Concreto, 1973; Suite 'Cupid & Death' (Locke), 1973; Piano Concerto, 1976. Misc. small pieces & edns. of early Engl. music; Mosaics for 2 violins, 1976; Oboe Quartet, 1977; Fantasy for Violin & Piano, 1977/78; Scenes for Orch., 1978. Publs: The Organ, 1958; Contemporary Music, 1968; The Patronage & Presentation of Contemporary Music, 1970; Contemporary British Music, 1972, early English Organ Music, 1973; Stravinsky, 1974. Contbr. to Organ Music, 1977; Contbr. to var. jrnls. Mbrships incl: CGGB; PRS. Hons: Jasper Ridley Prize, Cambridge, 1951; Limpus Prize, 1954; OUPBach Choir Prize, 1963; Comps. Guild Award for services to Music, 1974. Address: Arlington Pk. House, Chiswick W4 4HD, UK. 3.

ROVICS, Howard, b. 7 May 1936, NYC, USA. Composer; Pianist; College Teacher. Educ: B Mus, 1959, M Mus, 1961, Manhattan Schl. of Music; pvte. study w. Stefan Wolpe. m. Anne Chamberlain, 1 s., 1 d. Debut: Donnell Lib. Ctr., 1961. Career: num. apps. as Comp. & Pianist, primarily in NYC concert halls. Comps. incl: Events II for 10 Players; Concerto for Trumpet & Percussion; Transactions - A Third Stream Jazz Piece; Cantata; Poems of War Resistance; Cybernetic Studies 1 & 2; Transformations for orch.; Three Studies for piano; 28 seting to children's books inclng. Sendak's Where the Wild Things Are, on Weston Woods label. Contbr. to jrnls. Mbrships incl: Am. Comps. Alliance. Recip. var. awards. Hobbies: study of psychol., Senoi Dreamwork, Silva Mind Control, Transactional Analysis. Address: Old Huckleberry Rd., Wilton, CT 06897, USA.

ROVIN, Felix A(sher), b. 16 July 1912, Vilna, Lithuania. Composer-Lyricist; Percussionist; Tympanist; Conductor. Educ: Stephen Batory Univ., Vilan; Grad., Nat. Conserv., ibid.; pvte. study of Comp. & Percussion. m. Helena Tiereshina (Lala Lenskaya, Choreographer-Ballerina), 1 s. Debut: Vilna Symphonic Orch., 1933. Carer incls: w. Nat. Lithuania Radio Symph. & Jazz Ensemble, Vilna; White Russian & Armenian Phil. Orchs.; Georgian Jazz Ensemble; Soviet Circus; Freelance works, USA; Music Dir. Cond., OldNew Americans StageJazz Band, & Lincoln Square Community Ctr. Concert Jazz Orch., NYC. Comps. incl: Mon Amour; The Sinai Saga; Make Me Happy; Fairyland; Cupd's Old Play. Recordings of own works, Europe, USSR & USA. Mbrships. incl: Am. Fedn. Musicians; Profl. Musicians & Vocalists Assn. of New Immigrants (Fndr.-Chmn.) Hobby: Painting. Address: 180 W End Ave., Suite 16B, NY, NY 10023, USA.

ROWLAND, Christopher, b. 21 Dec. 1946, Barnet, Herts., UK. Violinist; Quartet leader. Educ: BA, MA, Trinity Coll., Cambridge; RAM, 1958-63, 1968-71. m. Jennifer Lucy Shaw. Career: ldr., Fitzwilliam Strg. Quartet; perfs. throughout UK, Europe, N America in recital, on TV & radio; Fitzwilliam Quartet tours of USSR, 1975, 78; currently resident quartet at York Univ. Recordings: num. records (w. sev. awards) inc. quartets of Shostakovitch. Contbr. to: Soviet Music; Berlioz Bulletin; Musical Times. Hons: J A Beare prize, RAM, 1969; RAM Principal's prize, 1970; Garland-Harrison Exhibition, 1971; Hooper Declamation prize, Univ. of Cambrdige, 1966: Gray prize, ibid., 1967. Hobbies: Soccer; Golf. Mgmt: de Koos, London. Address: Fountain House, Low St., Burton-in-Lonsdale, via Camforth, Lancs., UK.

ROWLEY, Gordon Samuel, b. 14 Sept. 1943, Detroit, Mich., USA. Musicologist; Librarian; Educator; Organist. Educ: AB, Stanford Univ., 1965; MA, ibid, 1967; MA, Univ. of Iowa, 1976; PhD Cand., ibid. m. Naomi Jean. Career: Rsch. Asst. (music), Stanford Univ., 1966-67; Instr., Music, Simpson Coll., San Fran., 1967-69; Instr., music, & Res. Advsr., Grinnell Coll., Iowa, 1969-70; Rsch. Asst. Organ Lit., Univ. of Iowa, 1970-71; Tchng. Asst., Musicol., ibid., 1970-74; Lectr., musicol., Univ. of Victoria, BC, 1973-75; Lectr., Early Music Workshop, ibid., 1974-75; Tchng. Asst., Lib. Sci., ibid., 1975-76; Music Libn., Northern Ill. Univ., 1976-; organ recitalist, etc. Publs. incl: A Bibliographical Syllabus of the History of Organ Literature; The 19th Century, 1972. Mbr. of num. profl. assns. Recip. sev. adcad. awards. Hobbies incl: Photography. Address: 320 E First St., Kingston, IL 60145, USA.

ROWLEY, Naomi Jean, b. 6 May 1943, Anomosa, Iowa, USA. Musician (organ, harpsichord); Educator; Church Musician. Educ: BMus, Valparaiso Univ., 1965; MA, Stanford Univ., 1966; DMA, ibid, 1969; Univ. of Iowa, 1970-73. m. Gordon Samuel Rowley. Career incl: Asst. Prof., Music, SD State Univ., Brookings, 1967-68; Instr., music, Grinnell Coll., Iowa, 1969-70; Applied instrn., Coe Coll., Iowa, 1970-71, Victoria Conserv. of Music, BC, 1973, & Univ. of Victoria, 1973-75; Instr. & performer, Early Music Workshop, ibid., 1974-75; Vis. Musician, Wilfrid Laurier Univ., Ont., 1975-76; organ & harpsichord recitalist; ch. organist. Mbrships. incl: AGO; Am. Musicol. Soc.; Int. Harpsichord Soc.; Pi Kappa Lambda. Recip. var. Univ. fellowships, etc. Hobbies incl: Cycling. Address: 320 E First St., Kingston, IL 60145, USA.

ROWLINSON, (Geoffrey) Mark, b. 15 Dec. 1948, Antrobus, UK. Baritone Singer. Educ: Christ Ch., Oxford; MA (Oxon.), 1974; RAM. m. Lavinia Johnston. Debut: Queen Elizabeth Hall, London, 1973. Career: num. recitals in London & UK; fest. apps. at Barcelona, Flanders, Europalia, Windsor & Jersey; perfs. on radio in UK, Germany, Spain, Belgium & Holland; TV apps. in Spain & Toronto; num. operatic roles at RAM & elsewhere; producer, BBC. Recordings: Vaughan William's Sir John in Love; Dvorak's Mass in D; Walton's The Twelve. Mbrships: ISM; Equity. Hobbies: Food & Wine; Cricket; Golf. Mgmt: Ibbs & Tillett, London. Address: 133 Abbey Rd., Macclesfield, Cheshire, UK.

ROWNTREE, John Pickering, b. 13 Feb. 1937, Scarborough, UK. Lecturer in Music. Educ: ARCM; Master, Univ. of Newcastle upon Tyne; Adv. Dip. in Educ., Univ. of Southampton. m. Julia Madeline Lorch, 1 s. Career: Civil Eng. in local govt.; Dir. of Music, St Mary's Coll., Southampton; Lectr., Univ. of Reading, currently Lectr. in Music, King Alfred's Coll. of Higher Educ., Winchester. Publs. incl: The Classical Organ in Britain, 1955-75 (w. John Brennan), 1975. Contbr. to: Ch. Music; Music & Liturgy. Mbrships: Hon. Sec., St. Gregory (Roman Cath.) Organ Advsry. Grp. Hobbies: Sailing; Squash; Walking; Reading. Address: The Cottage, 2 Bury's Bank, Greenham Common N. Newbury, Berks. RG15 88Z, UK.

ROXBURGH, Edwin, b. 6 Oct. 1937, Liverpool, UK. Composer; Conductor; Oboist. Educ: RCM (ARCM, LRAM); BA, St. John's Coll., Cambridge Univ.; Ext. degree, Durham Univ. (Mus B); FRCM. m. Julie Cooper, 1 s., 1 d. Career: Has composed two works for London Weekend TV's Aquarius, commissioned by Menuhin; Perfs. & broadcasts throughout the world; Cond./Dir., The 20th Century Ensemble of London. Num. comps. Publs: The Oboe, 1977. Mbrships: Soc. for the Promotion of New Music; Comps. Guild of GB. Hons: Royal Phil. Soc. Prize, 1960; Tagore Gold Medal, 1960; Lili Boulanger Trust Award, 1962. Address: 2 Norman Ave., Twickenham, Richmond upon Thames TW1 2LY, UK.

ROY, Alphonse, b. 14 Nov. 1906, Les Breuleux, Berne Canton; Switzerland. Composer. Educ: Tchng. Dip.; Neuchâtel, Zürich, Geneva & Paris Conservs. m. Elvezia Roy, 3 s. Comps. incl: (publs). Divertissement, for flute & piano; Prelude, for piano; St. Cécile & the Birds, for 3 female voices; Interlude, for flute & piano; Serenade, for clarinet & piano; Pastoral in the Old Style, for flute & piano; Short Piece, for trumpet & pinao; (recording) Str. Quartet. Mbr. Assn. of Swiss Musicians. Recip. Music Prize, Town of Berne, 1972. Hobbies: Reading; Travel. Address: 11 Bldv. du Pont d'Arve, 1205 Geneva, Switzerland.

ROY, Colin Maitland, b. 14 July 1942, Newton-le-Willows, Lancs., UK. Schoolteacher; Organist. Educ: Northern Schl. of Music, Manchester, 1965-66; ARCM. Organ perf., 1966; LRAM. Organ tchr., 1967; Cert. Educ., Univ. of Birmingham, 1967. m. Margaret Goodband, 2 d. Career: Mbr., Liverpool Phil. Choir, 1959-66; Organist & Choirmaster, St. Catherine's Ch., Higher Tranmere, Birkenhead 1961-62 & St. Anne's Ch. Birkenhead 1963-66; Asst. Music Tchr., Queensbridge Schl.,

Moseley, Birmingham, 1967-68; Asst. Organist, Collegiate Ch. of St. Mary the Virgin Warwick (Radio & TV broadcasts & recital tours to Denmark & USA w. Ch. Choir), 1967-69; Dir. of Music, Bordesley Green Boys Grammar Tech. Schl., Birmingham, 1968-72; Organist, Warwick Fest., 1968; Mbr. & Vice-Chmn., Birmingham Singers, 1969-71; Organist & Choirmaster, St. Faith & St. Lawrence Parish Ch., Harborne, Birmingham, 1970-72; Bass lay Clerk, Cathedral, ibid, 1970; Dir. of Music, Whitefield Fishponds Schl., Bristol, 1972-4; Organist & Choirmaster, Chipping Sodbury Parish Ch., 1973-75; Educ. Rep., S. Wales, SW Eng., Publishers, 1974; Organist, The Family Center of St. Nicholas, Yate, 1978-. Mbrships: RCO. Hobbies: Music; Reading; Squash. Address: 120 Woodchester, Yate, Bristol BS17 4TU, UK.

ROY, Nardo, b. 28 Apr. 1948, Bronx, NY, USA. Violist. Educ: BS, Mannes Coll. of Music, NYC, 1971. m. Julia Di Gaetani. Career incls: formerly Mbr., Empire Sinfonietta, NYC, Brattleboro Fest. Orch., Vt.; currently Mbr., Mostovoy Soloists of Phila. (touring Israel 1976, appearing throughout eastern & midwestern USA); Prin. Viola, Phila. Opera Co., Lake George Opera Fest.; Artist-in-Res. w. Carnegie String Quartet, SUNY at Postdam, 1974-76; currently Mbr., An Die Musik, NYC. Mbr., Locals 77 & 802. Am. Fedn. of Musicians. Hons. incl: Hans Neumann Award for Excellence in Chmbr. Music, 1970. Hobbies: Phogoraphy; Gardening; Reading. Address: 345 S 13th St., Philadelphia, PA 19107, USA.

ROY, Will, b. Schenectady, NY, USA. Bass Opera Singer; Painter; Sculptor. Educ: Curtis Inst. of Music, Phila., Pa., Manhattan Schl. of Music, NY. m. Nancy Honegger Roy, 1 d. Career: Leading bass, NY City Opera; apps. w. Grand Theatre de Geneve, Wash. Opera Soc., Ft. Worth Opera, Phila. Grand Oper, Opera Classics of NJ, etc.; app. on French radio; perfs. w. Pittsburgh Symph. & Phila. Symph. orchs. & the Mostly Mozart Fest., Lincoln Ctr., NY. mbr., Bd. of Dirs., AGMA. Mgmt: Ludwig Lustig & Florian Ltd., NY, USA. Address: c/o mgmt.

ROZHDESTVENSKY, Gennadi Nikolayevich, b. 1931, Moscow, USSR. Conductor. Educ: Moscow State Conserv. Career: Asst. Cond., Bolshoi Theatre, 1951; Cond., 1956-60, Prin. Cond., 1964-70, ibid.; Chief Cond., USSR Radio & TV Symph. Orch., 1961-; Guest Cond., orchs. in Europe, Am. & Asia; prin. cond., BBC Symph. Och., 1978-. Hons. incl: Merited & People's Artist of the RSFSR; Lenin Prize, 1970. Address: c/o BBC Symph. Orch., Yalding House, 156 Gt. Portland St., London, W1N 6AJ, UK.

ROZMARYNOWICZ, Andrzej, b. 11 Dec. 1928, Poznanland. Conductor. Educ: Studied violin, Higher Musical Schl., Poznanudied Cond., Higher Musical Schl., Katowice. m. Dobromila Kokorniak, 1 s., 1 d. Debut: (as Cond.) Katowice, 1961. Career: Guest apps. as Cond., 1961-67; Cond., Opera Ilouse, Dytom, 1960-70; Dir. & Artistic Dir., Opera Ilouse, Cracców, 1970-72; Cond., Wrocla Opera House, 1972—76; Apps. as Cond. w. symph. orchs., & on TV & radio; Perfs. w. orchs. in W. Berlin, Bulgaria, Czechoslovakia & USSR. Recordings: Archive Polish music recordings w. Radio Symph. Orch., W. Berlin, Publs: The Problem of Orchestral Violin Playing, 1976. Mbr. Soc. of Polish Artists & Musicians. Hobby: Stamp Collecting. Address: Opera House, Wroclaw. Address: 60-732 Poznan, Rynek Lazarski 11 m. 12, Poland.

ROZSA, Miklos, b. 18 Apr. 1907, Budapest, Hungary. Composer. Educ: Univ. of Leipzig; Grad. (Composition), Conserv. of Music, Leipzig, 1929. m. Margaret Finlason, 1 s., 1 d. Career: 1st Violin Concerto w. Leipzig Symph. Orch., 1929. Career: works performed by leading conds. inclng. Brun Walter, Monteux, Ormandy, Stokowski, Solti, Mehta & Previn & by such artists as Heifetz, Piatigorsky, & Janos Starker. Compositions: Theme, Variations & Finale (orch.) op. 13; Concerto for Strings op. 18; Tripartita (orch.) op. 33; Violin Concerto; Piano Concerto; Sinfonia Concertante for Violin & Violoncello; Cello Concerto; Two Motets (choral); 23rd Psalm (choral). Recordings: all major works recorded, also film scores inclng. Ben-Hur, El Cid, King of Kings, Quo Vadis, Golden Voyage of Sinbad. Mbrships: Pres., Screen Composers of the USA, 10 yrs.; Pres., Young Musicians Fndn., 2 yrs.; Pres., Am. Composers & Conds. Assn., 3 yrs. Hons: Frans Joseph Prize, Budapest, 1937-38; Acad. Award (Oscar), 1946, 48 & 59. Hobby: Art-collecting. Address: co Wm. Morris Agency, 151 El Camino, Beverly Hills, CA, USA.

ROZSA, Suzanne, b. 14 Sept. 1929, Budapest, Hungary. Violinist; Soloist & Chamber Musician. Educ: Vienna State Acad.; RCM; GSM. m. Martin Lovett, 1 s., 1 d. Career incls: Fndr., Dumka Piano Trio; Barbican Ensemble; Prof., GSM. Recordings: Vox; Decca. Mbrships: ISM; European String Tchrs. Assn. Hons: Gold Medal, GSM; Kreisler Prize, Vienna. Hobbies: Swimming; Table Tennis; Walking; Camping;

Cooking. Mgmt: Ibbs & Tillett; Basil Douglas. Address: 24 Remington Gdns., Hampstead, London NW3, UK.

RUBACH, Keith Edward, b. 4 June 1944, Ripon, Yorks, UK. Bassoonist; Pianist. Educ: RAM, 4 yrs.; Rubach, 2 d by 1st marriage. Debut: Martha Graham Dance Co. Career: Martha Graham Dance Co.; New BBC Symph. Orch.; BBC Scottish RAdio Orch.; currently w. NZ Symph. Orch.; Freelance pers. w. Scottish Opera, Sadlers Wells, Kirov Ballett, etc. Compsition: Rose Cheeked Laura Come (words by Thomas Campion). Mbr., PRS, UK. Hobbies: Chamber Music; Cooking; Antique Collecting. Address: co New Zealand Symphony Orchestra, PO Box 2092 Wellington, New Zealand.

RUBBRA, Edmund E. b. 23 May 1901, Northampton, UK. Composer; Pianist. Educ: Reading Univ.; RCM. m. Colette Yardley. Comps. incl: 11 Symphs.; 3 Concertos; 4 STring Quartets; Sonatas for violin, cello, oboe; num. works for whoic, both unacc. & w. orch. Recordings: Symphs. Nos. 2, 7, 10; Festival Overture; Farnaby Improvisations (orch.); Piano Concerto in G; Improvisation for Violin & Orch.; Two Masses; Soliloquy for cello & small orch.; Brahms-Handel Variations crchestrated; Shining River Variations for Brass Band; String Quartet No. 2. Publs: Counterpoint, a Survey, 1960; Holst, a Monograph; Ed., The Evolution of Music, 1964; Edmund Rubbra, Composer. Contbr. to: The Listener. Hons: DMus, Durham, 1948; LLD, Leicester, 1959; CBE, 1960; Fellow, Worcester Coll., Oxford, 1963; Collard Fellowship of the Worshipful Co. of Musicians, 1938; Cobbett Medal for servs. to chamber msuic, ibid, 1955; DLitt., Reading, 1978. Mgmt: A Lengnick & Co., Ltd., 421a Brighton Rd., S Croydon, Surrey. Address: Lindens, Bull Ln., Gerrards Cross, Bucks., UK. 1, 2.

RUBIN, Marcel, b. 7 July 1905, Vienna, Austria. Composer. Educ: Acad. of Music, Vienna; studies w. Darius Milhaud, Paris; Dr. jur., Univ. of Vienna. m. Hilda Eble. Comps: 7 symphs.; Kleider machen Leute (opera); Sinfonietta & Pastorale for strings; concertos for contrabass, bassoon, trumpet & orch.; chmbr. music; songs. Comps. recorded: 5th Symph.; 1st Symph.; Pastorale for strings; Divertimento for violin, cello & piano; Streichquartett; Streichtrio. Mbrships: Kunstsenat, Austria; Pres., Soc. of Authors, Comps. & Music Publrs. (AKM). Hons: Gt. Austria State Prize, 1970; Grand Prize, City of Vienna, 1969. Address: Graf Starhemberggasse 6, A-1040, Vienna, Austria.

RUBIN, Nathan, b. 2 Nov. 1929, Oakland, Calif., USA. Violinist; Teacher. Educ: Univ. of Calif.; Dip., Juilliard Schl. of Music. 3 d. Debut: Oakland, Calif., 1938. Career: Solo apps. w. orchs. under Mitropolous, Milhaud, Stravinsky, Kirchner, Berio, Samuel, Farberman, etc.; extensive chmbr. music perfs., esp. w. Mills Performing Grp.; Dir., chmbr. music perfs., esp. w. Mills Performing Grp.; Dir., Mills Performing Grp., 1960-70; num. TV apps.; Tchr., Mills Coll. & Calif. State Univ. Hayward. Recordings incl: Kirchner, Trio; W O Smith, Cappricio & Duo; Leland Smith, Trio; Bartok, Rhapsodies & Portrait; Ravel, Sonate; Poulenc. Sonate; Satie, Pieces; Christian Wolff, Lines; pop & film recordings. Hons: San Fran. Critics Award, 1949; Hertz Award, 1953. Address: 7962 Terrace Dr., El Cerrito, CA 94530, USA.

RUBINSTEIN, Artur, b. 28 Jan. 1887, Lodz, Poland. Pianist. Educ: Warsaw Conserv. of Music; w. var. pvte. tchrs., Berlin. m. Aniela Mylnarski, 2 s., 2 d. Debut: Berlin, 1901. Career: has made concert tours throughout world; has given many chariety perfs.; played piano for film soundtracks & app. in films inclng. Carnegie Hall, 1947, & Of Men & Music, 1951; Judge, Music Talent in Our Schls., NY; has made TV apps.; is noted for interpretation of Chopin. Recordings incl: Beethoven's Piano Concerti 1-5; Brahms' Piano Quintet & Piano Concerti 1 & 2; num. works by Chopin; Concerti by Rachmaninov, Saint-Saens & Schumann; many recital records. Recip. of num. hons. inclng. Polonia Restituta, Poland; Bronze Medallion, NYC; Gold Medal, Royal Phil. Soc., London. Mgmt: Hurok Attractions, 730 Fifth Ave., NYC, NY 10019, USA. Address: 22 Square de l'ave. Foch, Paris, 16e, France.

RUBINSTEIN, Lubov, b. 16 March 1910, Vladivostock, Russia. Harpist. Educ: Conserv., Leningrad. separated, 2 c. Career: 1st Harpist - Soloist, State Symph. Or Ukraine, 27 yrs. Hobby: Recorder. Address: Nedertoflen 21 - 1 t.h., 2720 Vanlose, Denmark.

RUCK, Hermann, b. 9 Sept. 1897, Sulzbach a. Kocher, Baden-Württemberg, Germany. Composer; Conductor. Musical Educ: Studied organ, piano, theory, comp. & cond., Staatliche Hochschule für Musik, Stuttgart; Grad., composition & conducting, 1926; Studied philos., psychol. & lit., Tech. Univ. Career: Tchr., Stuttgart Conservatory; 1st music tchr., tchr. trng. colls., Künzelsau, Heilbroon & Swabia; Schl. Coun.,

Fanny-Leicht-Gymnasium for girls, Stuttgart; Dir., Bruckner Choir, Stuttgart, 1954-73. Comps. incl: 4 oratorios, 2 piano concertos, sev. orchl. works, 4 sonatas for violin & piano, 2 sonatas for viola & piano, 1 sonata for cello & 1 for flute & piano; 4 solo sonatas for violin, string quartets; Approx. 800 songs & contos; Approx. 100 piano works; Approx. 90 organ works. Author of musical publs. Mbrships. incl: Deutscher Komponistenverband; Freier Deutscher Autoren-verband; GEMA; Tonkünstlerverband. Hons. incl: Gold conducting medal, Deutscher Sängerbund; Title of Prof., 1973. Hobby: Poetry. Address: Im Himmelsberg 10, 7000 Stuttgart, German Fed. Repub.

RUDEL, Julius, b. Vienna, Austria. Conductor; Music Director. Educ: pvte. studies, Vienna; Mannes Schl. of Music. Career incls= Dir., NYC Opera, 1957-79; Cond., over 100 operas; Choral Cond.; Cond., Vienna, Munich, Stuttgart, Cologne, Geneva, Paris, Hambrug, Venic, Bologna, Trieste, Spoleto, Brussels, Genoa, Israel; Cond., num. Orchs. in USA; created serv. fests., Kennedy Center; Past Music Dir., Kennedy Center in Wash., Cinn. May Music Fest., Wolf Trap in Wash., Caramoor Fest. in NY; currently Music Adviser, Opera Co. of Phila.; Musical Dir., Buffalo Phil., 1979-. Recordings incl: Bellini, I Puritani; Boito, Mefistofele; Charpentier, Louise; Finastera, Bomarzo (Wash. Opera Soc.); Janacek, Concertino for Piano Left Hand & Orch. (Caramoor Fest. Orch.); Lalo, Symphonie Espagnole; Massenet, Cendrillon; Mendelssohn, Violin Concerto; Offenbach, Tales of Hoffman; J Strauss, Waltzes (Vienna State Opera orch.). Hons. incl: Julius Rudel Award for Young Conds. created by NYC Opera Co. Bd. of Dirs.; Hon. DMus, Univ. of Vermond, Pace Coll., Univ. of Mich.; Handel Medallion of City of NY; Hon. Insignia of Austrian Govt.; Hon. Cross of Merit of German Fed. Repub.; Hon. Lieutenant, Army of Israel. Hobbies: Swimming; Skiing on snow & water. Mgmt: Edgar Vincent Assocs., 145 E 52nd St., NY, NY 10022, USA. Address: c/o Mgmt

RUDHYAR, Dane, b. 23 Mar. 1895, Paris, France. Composer; Author; Painter. Educ: B Philos., Paris; var. schls. & independent studies. Career: Writing; lecturing, lecture-recitals, all over USA in early yrs.; Concentrates now on writing books for NY & Calif. publsrs. Compositions: (for piano) 4 Pentagrams; 9 Tetragrams; Symph.; (orch.) Sinfonietta To the Real, 3 movements; The Surge of Fire; Five Stanzas (for str. orch.); Threshold (large orch.). Var. recordings. Publs: approx. 25 books on cosmopsychol.; First publ. of piano works & book on Debussy, 1913, (novels) Rania; Return from No-Return; books of poems, etc. Mbrships: Am. Comps. Alliance, NY; Int. Coop. Coun., Calif. Recip., 1000 dollar prize for symphonic poem by L A Phil. Orch., 1922. Address: 3635 Lupine Ave., Palo Alto, CA 94303, USA.

RUDIAKOV, Michael, b. 9 Aug. 1934, Paris, France. Cellist. Educ: Studies w. father, pianist Eliahu Radiakov, Tel Aviv; B Mus, Manhattan Schl. of Music, NY, USA. m. Judith Carol Peck, 1 s., 1 d. Career: Solo & chmbr. music concerts all over word; Artistic Dir., Chmbr. Music, Sarah Lawrence Coll. num. recordings. Recip. Harold Bauer Award, Gold Medal, Casals Competition, Mexico, 1959. Mgmt: Melvin Kaplan Inc. Address: 5500 Fieldston Rd., Riverdale, NY, NY 100471, USA. 8, 14.

RUDIÉ, Robert, b. 12 Feb. 1919, NY, NY, USA. Violinist; Conductor; Educator. Educ: Grad., Schl., Juilliard Schl. of Music, NYC. m. Mertina Johnson, 1 s., 1 d. Debut: NYC, 1929. Career: Concertmaster, Okla. City Symph., 1944-45, 1st Violin, Casals Festival, 1951-73; Concertmaster, NY City Ballet, NJ Symph., var. freelance orchs., NYC, 1955-72; Concertmaster & Asst. Cond., Aspen Festival Nat. Orchl. Assn., Phil. Symph. of Westchester, 1955-72; num. appearances & tours as solo violinist, 1956-; Cond., Rudié Sinfonietta, 1957-61; 1st Violin, Riverdale Str. Quartet, 1959-; Bronx Arts Ensemble, 1973-; Dir., Riverdale Country Schl. & Riverdale Schl. of Music, 1962-; Cond. of Orch. & Tchr. of Violin, Vassar Coll., 1966-69; Co-Dir., Manhattan Schl. of Music Prep. Div., 1970-71; Dir., Manhattan Schl. of Music String Proj., 1971-; Concertmaster, Am. Symph. Orch., 1973-. Hobbies: Photography; Chess; Sailing. Mgmt: Robert W. Gewald, NYC. Address: Riverdale School of Music, Bronx, NY 10471, USA.

RUDNYTSKY, Roman, b. 1 Nov. 1942, NY, NY, USA. Concert Pianist; Professor of Music. Educ: Phila. Conserv.; BS., MS., Juilliard Schl. of Music; D. Musical Arts, Peabody Conserv., Balt., Md.; var. master classes, USA & Europe. m. Suzanne Rouse, 1 d. 1 s. Career: Concerts, USA & Can.; European tours in 15 countries; tour Far East, 1975; Over 100 apps. as Soloist; w. num. major orchs., USA, Can. & Europe; Asst. Prof. of Piano, Dana Schl. of Music, Youngstown State Univ., Ohio. Recordings: E Gold, Symph. for 5 instruments, w.

Israel Baker Ensemble; Liszt, 12 Transcendental Etudes, & 4 other Etudes. Mbrships. incl: Ohio Educ. Assn.; NEA; Ukrainian-Am. Assn. Univ. Profs. Recip. num. musical Prizes inclng. 1st Prize, Juilliard Concerto Competition, Salzburg, Austria; 2nd Prize, Int. Leventritt Competition. Hobbies: Tennis; Travel; Reading. Cinema. Mgmts: M Bichurin Concerts Corp., Carnegie Hall, NY, NY 10019, USA; (W. Europe) Intern Concert Administratie, van Boshulzenstraat 549, Amsterdam 11. Netherlands; Bureau Artistique d'Athenes, Athens. Address: 2050 South Raccoon Rd., no. 1 Youngstown, OH 44515, USA.

RUDOLF, Max, b. 15 June 1902, Frankfurt am Main, Germany. Symphony & Opera Conductor. Educ: Frankfurt Univ.; Dip. in Comp. & Piano. Conserv. of Music, Frankfurt. m. Liese Eder, 1 s., 1 d. Debut: Freiburg im Breisgau, 1923. Career: Opera in Darmstadt, 1923-29; German Opera, Prague, Czech., 1929-35; Met. Opera, NYC, USA, 1945-58; Artistic Admnstr., ibid., 1950-58; Music Dir., Cinn. Symph. Orch., 1958-70; & Cinn. May Fest., 1963-70; Fac. Mbr., Curtis Inst., Phila., 1970-73; Guest Cond. (57 perfs.), Met. Opera 1973-75. Num. recordings. Publ: The Grammar of Conducting, 1950. Contbr. to musical publs. Hons. incl: Docts., Univ. of Cinn., Temple Univ., Miami Univ., Galdwin-Wallace Coll., Curtis Inst. Mgmt: ICM Artists, Inc., NYC. Address: 220 W. Rittenhouse Square, Phila., PA 19103, USA.

RUDZINSKI, Witold, b. 14 Mar. 1913, Siebiez, Russia. Composer; Music Educator; Musicologist. Educ: Magister of Philos., Univ. of Wilno., 1936: MA, M. Karlowicz Conserv., Wilno, 1937; Institut Gregorien, Paris; studied w. Nadio Boulanger, Charles Koechlin. m. Nina Rewienska, 3 c. Debut: 1934. Career: prof., Conserv., Wilno, 1939-41, Lodz, 1945-47, Warsaw, 1957-; Dir., Music Dept., Min. of Culture & Arts, Warsaw, 1947-48; Dir., Warsaw Phil. & Opera, 1947-49; Ed., Muzyka, Warsaw, 1951-55. Compositions incl: (publd.) 5 Operas; 4 Oratorios & Cantatas; 2 symphonic works; var. instrumental & orchl. music; (recorded) The Dismissal of the Grecian Envoys, opera; Gaude Mater Polonia; The Roof Of The World, orch. & choir; Pictures of The Holy Cross Mountains, orch. Publs: Music for Everybody, 1966; Stanislaw Moniuszko, Studies & Materials, vo. I, 1955, vol. II 1961. The Technique Of Bela Bartok, 1965; Moniuszko, 1972; Intro. to Listening to Music, 1975; Musical Rhythm (in prep.). Contbr. to: Ruch Muzyczny, Muzyka, Warsaw, Sovjetskaya Muzyka, Moscow. Mbr. Assn. of Polish Comps. Recip. num. Hons. for Comps. Hobbies: History; Travel. Address: ul. Narbutta 50 m. 6, 12.541 Warsaw, Poland. 1, 3, 14, 16.

RUDZINSKI, Zbigniew, b. 23 Oct. 1935, Czechowice, Poland. Composer. Educ: Comp. Dip. w. Distinction, State HS of Music, Warsaw. m. Ewa Debska, 1 d. Career: Prof. Comp., State HS of Music, Warsaw. Comps: Sonata for 2 str. quartets, piano & kettledrums, rec. Epigrams for flute, choir & perc.; Contra Fidem, for Symph. orch., rec. Study for C, for ensemble and libitum, rec. String Trio, rec.; Moments Musicaux I, for symph. orch., rec. Moments Musicaux II, for symph. orch., rec.; Moments Musicaux III, for symph. orch.; Symph. for choir of men & orch., rec. Quartet for 2 pianos & perc., rec. Music at Night, for small orch., rec.; Requiem, to the victims of Wars, for oech., choir & speaker, rec. victims of Wars, for orch., choir & speaker, rec. Tutti E Solo, for soprano, flute, horn & piano; Sonata for Piano, 1975; Sonata for Piano rec.; 3 songs for tenor & 2 pianos, (recorded); Campbell for percussion ensemble (recorded). Mbr., Union of Polish Comps. Hons: Prize Winner in the competition org. on the occasion of the 150th anniversary of the Warsaw Conserv. of Music, 1960; Prize in the 5th Competition for Young Comps. of the Polish Comps. Union, 1962. Hobbies: Collecting old & folk instruments & old musical pictures. Address: ul. Poznanska 23 m. 26,00-685 Warsaw, Poland. 1, 2.

RUFF, Herbert A, b. 16 Sept. 1918, Vienna, Austria. Pianist; Composer, Arranger; Conductor. Educ: Martin Luther Real Gymnasium, Berlin; Studied w. Lotte Kleiner, Walter Gieseking, Paul Graner, Stern Conserv., Berlin. Debut: Soloist w. Charlottenburg State Opera Orch., Berlin, 1930. Career: Comp. for UFA Films, Berlin; Lucerna Films, Prague; Films for Quebec Min. of Culture; Radio-Can. etc. Comps. incl: more than 2000 songs for Can. TV children's progs. Recordings w. London-Record, Columbia, Fantel, etc. Mbrships: Assoc. Fedn. of Musicians; BMI; Societe des Auteurs, APLL, ISCM. Hons: 1st Prize, UNDA, Monte Carlo; Trophies for best TV Themes etc. Hobbies: Reading; Skiing; Gardening; Philately. Address: 3512 Ave. Grey, Montreal, Quebec H4A 3NG, Canada.

RUFFER, Magdi, b. 19 Oct. 1924, Berne, Switz. Pianist. Educ: Music Tchrs. Dip., Switz.; Ecole Normale de Musique, Paris. m. Sabahattin Eyuboglu (dec.). Debut: Switz., 1943. Career: recitals & broadcasts, Switz., France, Italy, Austria.

Bulgaria, Hungary, Turkey, Germany, etc. Recordings: Durium ms A 77121 (Italy). Contbr. to: Yeditepe; Yeni Ufuklar. Mbr., Swiss Musician Assn. Hobbies: History; Art; Dogs, Cats & Turtles. Address: Bronzsokak 7 Macka, Istanbul, Turkey.

RUFFO, Edgar, b. 30 Jan. 1925, Buenos Aires, Argentina. Choir Director; Teacher of Singing. Educ: BA, Nat. Univ. Coll., Buenos Aires; Philos. Studies, Dept. of Philos., Univ. of Buenos Aires; Conserv. Thibaud-Piazzini; Studies w. Valdo Sciammarella & Carlos Olivares; Technique & Voice w. Mary Melsa & Pedro Tabanelli. m. Agnes Frances Brass, 2 d., 3 s. Debut: as singer, in 1948; as choir dir., in 1958. Career: Recitals in Argentina, oratorios & chmbr. music, specializing in German repertory; Currently Dir., Palomar Polyphonic Choir; Co.-Dir., Nat. Polyphonic Choir, supported by the Argentine Sec. of Culture. Num. recordings of choral concerts. Contbr. to: Diapason; Buenos Aires Musical. Mbrships: Argentine Fedn. of Choirs (Artistic advsr.); Buenos Aires Interchoral Coordination (Deleg.); Italian Inst. of Culture; Goethe Inst.; Art & Life Cultural Assn. Hobbies: His children; The development of culture. Address: Aviadora Earhart 177, Lomas del Palomar (1684), Argentina.

RUFF-STOEHR, Herta Maria Klara, b. 3 Dec. 1904, HanauMain, Germany. Music Teacher; Composer. Educ: Pvte. Study in Voice, Choral Singing, Piano, Violin; Solo w. Orch., Inst. of Music, Univ. of Tubingen. m. Konrad Ruff, 1 d. Comps. incl: num. pieces for piano, violin & piano, flute & piano, string quartette, etc. inclng: Calmato, piano, 1972; Con Spirito, piano, 1975; Andantino, flute & piano, 1967; Allegramente, flute & piano, ,1967; Finale, string-quartett, 1947; Maestoso, string-quartette, 1966; Klarinetten Quintette, organ. Mbrships: Soc. Music Rsch.; German Union of Composers; Int. Soc. Musicol. Hobby: writing songs & poetry (over 390). Address: 7450 Hechingen, Schillerstr. 17, German Fed. Repub.

RUGGERI, Roger, b. 6 Sept. 1939, Middletown, Pa., USA. Musician (Double Bass); Writer; Lecturer; Composer. Educ: B Mus, Eastman Schl. of Music, Univ. of Rochester, 1961; pewrformer's Cert., ibid. m. Janet Fleming Ruggeri, 1 s., 2 d. Career: Prin. Double Bass, Milwaukee (Wis.) Symph. Orch.; Wis. Coll.-Conserv.; Double Bass Soloist w. Eastman-Rochester Orch., Milwaukee Symph., Grand Teton Music Fest.; Appearances as a synthesizer perf.-lectr.; program Annotator, Milwaukee Symph. & NJ Symph. Orchs. Compositions: orchl. works for children's concerts - Wine Kleine Chopsticks, 1971, Around the Sea, 1971; Other orchl. works - Microcosms, 1972 & Wellsprings, 1972; Electronic music - Incidental music for Knock; var. film scores & commercials. Contbr. to: The Bass Soundpost; The Schl. Musician; Am. String Tchrs. Assn.; Prog. Annotations. Address: 3533 N. Shepard, Milwaukee, WI 53211, USA.

RUGGIERI, Alexander F, b. 10 Jan. 1952, Santa Monica, Calif., USA. Conductor; Pianist, Composer. Educ: Bmus, Univ. of S Calif. (theory), 1976; MMus, ibid. (choral music), 1977. Debut: as pianist, Los Angeles, 1964; as cond., Los Angeles, 1974. Career: Cond., Orthodox Concert Choir of Los Angeles; Fndr. music dir., cond., Musical Arts Soc. of Los Angeles Choir & Orch.; cond., St. Peter & Paul A Cappella Choir, Detroit, Mich; cond., Ravanica Serbian Concert Choir, Detroit, Mich.; app. on TV. Recordings (w. Orthodox Concert Choir of Los Angeles) Rachmaninoff, Vespers; An Evening of Orthodox Sacred Music. Mbrships: Pi Kappa Lambda; Am. Musicol. Soc.; Am. Choral Dirs. Assn.; Choral Conds. Guild (Los Angeles Chapt.). Hobbies: Astronomy; Rare Recordings; Old Films; Basketball; Volleyball. Address: 3872 Gilbert, Detroit, MI 48210, USA.

RUGGIERO, Charles Howard, b. 19 June 1947, Bridgeport, Conn., USA. Composer; College Teacher. Educ: BMus, New England Conserv. of Music, Boston, 1969; MMus, Mich. State Univ., 1974; PhD, ibid., 1979. m. Patricia Ann Muller, 1 s., 1 d. Career: Instructor, music theory & comp., Mich. State Univ., 1973-; Prod. & perf. in sev. WKAR-TV & FM radio progs.; Dir., MSU Improvisation Ensemble, 1973-77. Comps: Songs from Emily Dickinson, 1974; Hocket Variations for 2 pianos, 1978; chmbr. music, choral, band & jazz comps. Mbrships: Am. Musicol. Soc.; Am. Recorder Soc.; Soc. for Asian Music; Soc. for Ethnomusicol.; Music Lib. Assn. Hon: Winner, Mich. Music Tchrs. Assn. Comp. commission Contest, 1978. Hobbies: Recorder playing; Reading; Art (drawing); Table Tennis. Address: 712 N Francis Ave., Lansing, MI 48912, USA.

RUGSTAD, Gunnar, b. 5 Sept. 1921, Gjerpen, Norway. Musicologist; Musician (Trombone). Educ: MA Musicol., Univ. Oslo; PhD (Musicol.), ibid, 1977. Lectrs. Degree: Conserv. of Oslo. m. Ingeleiv Ramberg, 2 c. Career: Trombonist, Nowegian Broadcasting Orch. until 1968; Rsch. work at Univ. of Bergen, 1968-74; Hd. of Music Dept., Norwegian Broadcasting TV,

1974-. Publs: Christian Sinding; Biographic & Stylistic Study, 1856-1941. Contbr. to profl. jrnls. Mbrships: Musicians Union, Norway; Norwegian Br., ISCM; Bd. Mbr., Norwegian Culture Fund; Norwegian Soc. of Artists in Music. Address: Hafrsfjordgt 7, Oslo 2, Norway.

RUMP, Alan George, b. 10 Nov. 1947, Norwich, UK. Lecturer; Warden; Trumpeter; Conductor. Educ: BSc (Econ), London Schl. of Economics; BA (Music), Univ. of Bristol; LGSM. m. Arvil M Rump, 1 d. Career: Lectr. in Music & Warden of Churchill Hall, Univ. of Bristol. Publs: Money for Composers, 1977. Mbrships: Music panel, Music Finance committee & Gen. Sub-Committee, Arts Coun. of GB.; Bd., Western Orchestral Soc. Hobbies: Wine; Sport. Address: Churchill Hall, Stoke Pk. Rd., Bristol BS9 1JG, UK.

RUMSEY, David Edward, b. 30 Mar. 1939, Sydney, Aust. Organist. Educ: Lic. in Music, Aust. Music Examinations Bd.; Perf. & Tchr. Dips., NSW State Conserv. of Music; Reifeprüfung, Vienna Acad. of Music. m. Christa Rumsey, 2 d. Career: Tutor in Music, Univ. of Adelaide, 1966; Lectr., NSW State Conserv. of Music, 1969; Organist to Sydney Symph. Orch.; World recital tour, 1970; Concert tours of NZ, 1973, Germany, 1975; Sr. Lectr., Dept. of Organ & Ch. Music, Sydney Conserv., 1974. Recordings: Festive Organ Music of the Baroque, 1968; Deus ex Machina, 1977. Contbr. to profl. jrnls.; Ed., Ch. Music News Bulletin. Mbrships: Pres., Adelaide Organ Music Soc., 1967-68; Bd. of Dirs., Radio station 2MBS-FM, Sydney, 1975-76. Mbr., Sydney City Coun. Organ Committee, 1977-. Hons: Vasanta Schlrship, 1963. Hobbies incl: Fine Wine. Address: 65 Epping Ave., Eastwood, NSW 2122, Aust. 30.

RUNDANS, Anita, b. 30 Aug. 1943, Daugaupils, Latvia. Organist. Educ: BA, Univ. Toronto, Canada, 1967; MA, ibid., 1969; Assoc., Royal Conserv. Music, Toronto, 1969; Dip. Virtuosite, Schl. Cantorum, Paris, 1972. m. Gunars Rundans, 2 s. Career: Recitals, Toronto, Quebec, NY, Cleveland & Phila., USA, London, UK, Hamburg, Lubeck, Goteburg & Stockholm, Europe; App., Canadian Broadcasting Corp. Progs., 'Organists in Recital', 'Best Seat in the House'; Latvian Song Fests., Toronto, Cleveland, Vancouver, Seattle & Cologne. Mbrships: Exec., Toronto Ctr., Toyal Canadian Coll. Organists; Toronto Musicians Assn. Hon: Gold Medal, ARCT, Toronto, 1969. Address: 185 Neville Pk. Blvd., Toronto, Ontario M4E 3P7, Canada.

RUNNER, David Clark, b. 12 Jan. 1948, Long Beach, Calif., USA. Professor. Educ: BMus., Boise State Univ., Boise, Idaho, 1969; MusM., Eastman Schl. of Music, Rochester, NY., 1970; Performers Cert., Organ, ibid, 1971; DMA, ibid. m. Jerralyn Lee. Career: Asst. Prof. of Music (Organ), Milligan Coll., Tenn.; Var. recitals, USA; Organist, World Conven. Christian Chs., Mexico City, 1974. Recordings: Across the Nation with the Milligan College Concert Choir, 1974. Mbrships: Coll. Music Soc.; Pi Kappa Lambda; Am. Guild of Organists. Hons: Winner, Nat. Organ Competition, Worcester, Mass., 1968; Finalist, Nat. Organ Competition, Am. Guild of Organists, 1968; Runner-up, Nat. Organ Competition, Ft. Wayne, Ind., 1971. Hobbies: Travel; Reading. Address: PO Box 416, Milligan Coll., TN 37682, USA.

RUPNIK, Ivan, b. 29 Aug. 1911, Logatec, Yugoslavia. Composer. Educ: Piano, organ studies, State Conserv. of Music, Ljubljana; Grad., New Conservatorium of Music, Vienna; Masters Degree, Comp. & Cond., ibid. Career: Ed., Musical Prod., Radio TV Belgrade, Yugoslavia. Comps: Ode to Fallen Soldiers, Cantata for choir & orch., 1947; You Know Where The Eagles Slip, Symphonic poem for narrator, wind orch. & choir, 1966; Do Not Anger The Sun, Symphonic poem for 2 narrators & full wind orch., 1971; Youth Suite, for Symph. Orch., 1972; Symphonic Pictures, Wind Orch., 1978; Hymn of Peace, for mixed choir & Symph. Orch., 1975; Choir, chmbr. & solo music for piano & organ; comps. for feature & documentary films. Contbr. to var. mags. Mbrships: Assn. of Yugoslav Comps.; Union of Comps. of Serbia. Hons: Sev. awards for comp.; Gold Wreath Medal; Plaque & Gold Badge of the Art Ensemble of the Yugoslav People's Army; Plaque of the City of Belgrade. Hobby: Gardening. Address: 32 Vlajkoviċeva St., 11000 Belgrade, Yugoslavia.

RUPP, Marjorie J, b. 17 Feb. 1943, Phila., Pa., USA. Viola Player. Educ: BS (Music Educ.), State Univ. of NY, 1966; MMus (Educ.), Univ. of Louisville, Ky., 1968; Dip., Schl. of Fine Arts, Antwerp, Belgium, 1965. Career: violin, Antwerp Phil. Orch., 1964-65; violin, Louisville Orch., 1966-68; viola, Okla. City Symph. Orch., 1970-74; viola,/Indianapolis Symph. Orch., 1974-79. Mbrships: Sigma Alpha Iota; Kappa Delta Pi; Altrusa Int. (Indianapolis Club, Bd. of Dirs.). Hons: Am. Fed. of Musicians scholarship to Strg. Congress, Mich. State Univ.,

1960; Berkshire Music Fest. Scholarship, 1967-69; New Schl. Summer Music Fest., Sarasota, Fla., 1968-69. Hobbies: Reading; Gardening; Oil Painting. Address: 5340 Riverview Dr., Indianapolis, IN 46208, USA.

RUSHBY-SMITH, John, b. 28 Sept. 1936, Redcar, UK. Senior sound-balancer; Composer; Sound projection expert; Free-lance record producer. Career: Sound projectionist for Stockhausen's Mantra and Hymnen, tours in UK, France, Italy; Radio talk, The Cave of Harmony (on sound balance); Expert for discussion on sound technique for Music Weekly, Radio 3; Senior sound-balancer w. BBC Radio. Comps: (orchl.) Concerto Grosso; Valse Seriale; (Chmbr.) Saxophone Quartet; Monologue for oboe; Syzygy for flute & piano; Violin Sonata; (Piano) Sonata; Toccata; Elegy; Aspects of Night (duet); Lifespan, for 2 sopranos and tape delay. Recordings: Prod. records for London Saxophone Quartet, BBC Symph. Och. Contbr. to: Studio Sound. Mbrships: CGGB; EMAS; Assoc., PRS. Hobbies: Piano; Singing; Bread-baking; Motoring; Painting; Getting lost in N Scotland; Crosswords; Chess. Mgmt: Allied Artists; Simrock Edition. Address: 11 Lancaster Ave., Hadley Wood, Herts. EN4 OEP UK.

RUSHTON, Julian Gordon, b. 22 May 1941, Cambrdige, UK. University Lecturer. Educ: BA, B Mus, MA, Trinity Coll., Cambridge; DPh, Magdalen Coll., Oxford. m. Virginia Susan Medlycott Jones, 2 s. Appts: Univ. Lectr., Univ. of E Anglia, 1968-74, Univ. of Cambridge, 1974-; Fellow, King's Coll., Cambridge, 1974-. Mbr., Coun., Royal Musical Assn. Publs: Ed., Berlioz, Huit scenes de Faust, 1971, & La Damnation de Faust, 1979. Contbr. to Grove's Dict. of Music & Musicians, 6th ed., & var. profl. jrnls. Address: Kings Coll., Cambridge, UK.

RUSHWORTH, William James Lyon, b. 31 Dec. 1913, W Kirby, Cheshire, UK. Master Organ Builder; Music Retailer. Educ: Wrekin Coll., Salop. m. Margaret Isobel Crawford, 4 s. Contbr., 'The Music Retailers' in Careers in Music by Robert Elkin. Mbrships: incl: Fellow, Inst. Musical Instrument Technol.; Cnslr., Inc. Soc. Organ Bldrs.; FRSA; VP, Fedn. Master Organ Bldrs.; Advsry. Comm., Music Trades Assn.; VP, Music Coun.; Treas., Liverpool Youth Music Comm. & Merseyside Music Tchrs. Assn.; Jr. Fndr., Merseyside Sr. Citizens' Orch. Hons. incl: Sailing; Golf; Beagleing. Address: c/o Rushworth & Dreaper Ltd., 48 Whitechapel, Liverpool, L1 6EF, UK. 3.

RUSSELL, Armand King, b. 23 June 1932, Seattle. Wash., USA. Composer; Professor of Music. Educ: BA., Univ. of Wash.; MA., ibid; DMusA., Eastman Schl. of Music, Univ. of Rochester. m. Lois Russell, 1 s., 1 d. Career: Tchr., Eastman Schl. of Music, summers 1959-63, 1972, ND State Tchrs. Coll., 1958-61, Univ. of Hawaii, 1961-; Chmn., Music Dept., ibid, 1965-71; Double Bass, Seattle Symph., 1948-55, Rochester Phil., Civic Orch., 1956-58, Boston Pops Tour Orch., 1956. Publd. Compositions: Percussion Suite; Pas de Deux; Sonata for Percussion & Piano; Somber Sonatina; Particles; Theme & Fantasia; Chaconne; Two Archaic Dances; Buffo Set; Aria da Capo; Exploration; 2nd Concerto, for Percussion.

RUSSELL, Eleanor, b. 19 Aug. 1931, Denver, Colo., USA. Musicologist; Pianist. Educ: AA, Stephens Coll.; B Mus Ed., Univ. Colo.; MA, PhD, Univ. Southern Calif.; Studied piano w. John Crown & Alicia Lorrocha; Harpsichord w. Alice Ehlers. m. G Truett Hollis, Career: Prof., Calif. State Univ., Northbridge. Recordings: Transcriptions & notes for Blanco y Negro, Side 1, Clavier Records, Los Angeles. Publs: Articles for Grove's Dictionary Vi; Contbr. to & Assoc. Ed. of Festival Essays for Pauline Alderman, 1976, & other profl. jrnls. Mbrships: Am. Musicol. Soc.; State Bd., Educ. Commission, Calif. Congress of Parents & Tchrs., 1974-75; Hon. collaborator, Spanish Inst. of Musicol., 1975-. Recip. num. fellowships & grants. Address: 130 Kenworthy Dr., Pasadena, Calif., USA.

RUSSELL, George Allen, b. 23 June 1923, Cinn., Ohio, USA. Jazz Musician; Lecturer. Educ: Studied comp. w. Stephan Wolpe. Career incls: George Russell Sextet perf. at Pres. John F Kennedy's Int. Jazz Fest., Wash. DC, 1962, at Phil, Hall, Lincoln Ctr., 1963; Tours Europe 1963; Tour of Sweden for Swedish Concert Bur., 1965; Sev. perfs. for Scandinavian radio networks in Oslo, Stockholm & Copenhagen, 1965-71; Perf. at Carnegie Hall, 1974; Tchr. of the Lydian Chromatic Concept, 1953-71. Recordings incl: The Essence of George Russell, 1971; Living Time, 1972; Listen To The Silence, 1973; Ancient Voices of Childrun; Music for a Summer Evening; Lux Aeterna. Publs: The Lydian Chromatic Concept of Tonal Organization, 1953. Mbr., var. musical assns. Recip. num. hons. Address: 6 W 95th St., NY., NY, USA. 2, 6.

RUSSELL, James Reagan, b. 2 Apr. 1935, Alameda, Calif., USA. Clarinettist; Conductor. Educ: BA, Univ. of Calif.,

Berkeley; MMus, Stae Univ. of NY, Stony Brook; studies w. Jack Brymer & Stephen Trier (London), David Glazer (NY) & Rudolf Jettell (Vienna). Career: Asst. cond., Univ. Symph. Orch., Uiv. of Calif., Berkeley, 1958-65; solo clarinettist, Golden Gate Park Band, San Francisco, 1963-71; lectr. in music (clarinet), Univ. of Calif., Berkeley, 1969-. Recording: Music of Macedonia & Bulgaria. recip. Alfred Hertz Travelling Scholarship in Music, .1965-66, 1966-67. Hobby: Photography. Address: 2310 Ellsworth St., Apt. 6, Berkeley, CA 94704, USA.

RUSSELL, Lois Roberta Langley, b. 21 Feb. 1932, Upland, Calif., USA. Percussionist. Educ: Univ. of Wash., Seattle, 1949-52. m. Armand Russell, 1 s., 1 d. Career: Percussionist, Seattle Symph. Orch., 1948-50; Prin. Percussionist, ibid, 1950-55; Timpanist & Prin. Percussion, NC Symph. Orch., 1956; Tympanist, Fargo Symph. Orch., 1958-61; Prin. Percussion, Honolulu Symph. Orch., 1961-; Recitalist & Chmbr. Music Player, performing works for percussion by mod. comps. of Asian & Western countries. Mbrships: Percussive Arts Soc.; Nat. Assn. of Rudimental Drummers; Sigma Alpha Iota. Hobbies: Lapidary; Marksmanship. Address: 3296 Huelani Dr., Honolulu, HI 96822, USA. 5, 9, 27.

RUSU, Liviu, b. 27 June 1908, Cuciurul Mare, Cernauti, Bucovina, Romania. Composer; Musicologist; Professor. Educ: Conserv. of Bucharest, 1928-32; studies in comp. m. Elisabeta. Career: Prof. of comp., Cernauti Conserv., 1932-40; Prof. of hist. & musical forms, Timisoara Conserv., 1945-50; violist & lectr., Filharmonica de stat, Banatul, 1957; Chief ed., Editura Muzicala, 1958-60. Comp. incl: Sonata for violin & piano, 1951; Sonata for clarinet & piano, 1956; 2 Songs by St. O Iosif, 1957; 5 Love Songs, 1955; Polyphonic choruses, 1956. Publs. incl: Music in Bucovina, 1939; Theoretical Perspectives & Preoccupations in the History of Romanian Music, 1966; var. transls. Mbr., Uniunea Comp. si Muzicologilor, Romania. Address: Str. dr. Toma Ionescu 18, Bucharest VI, Romania.

RUT, Josef, b. 21 Nov. 1926, Kutná Hora, Czechoslovakia. Violinist. Educ: State Conserv. of Music, Prague; Study w. Prof. Bedrich Voldan. m. Milada Rutova, 1 s. Debut: Prague, 1951. Career: Violinist, Radio Prague Symph. Orch.; 1953-; Mbr., Prague Chmbr. Orch., 1955-57. Comps. incl: 10 Ensemble Studies for 3 Violins; Studies for 2 Violins; Var. works, composer's own 12-note tonal theory. Manuscripts: 5 Miniatures for Flute & Piano, 1974; Symphony No. 2, 1975; Strg. Quartet; Wind Quintet. Recording, for Radio Prague, Sonate for Double Bass & Strings. Concerto for violin & orch., Radio Lomuc, 1975 Publs: 12 Note Tonal Theory, 1969; Theory of Relativity & Musical Thinking New Physical Theory of Music, 1976; Jan Dostel - Josef Rut: Manual of Rhythm (in press). Hobbies: Scoring, revising, 18th Century music; Touring. Address: Zborovská 40, 15000 Prague 5, Czechoslovakia.

RUTAN, Harold Duane, b. 19 Nov. 1927, Chgo., Ill., USA. French Horn Player; Ethnomusicologist; Professor. Educ: BSc (Educ.), Ohio State Univ.; MFA, ibid.; MEd, Ed.D, Univ. of Ill. m. Marjorie C Rutan, 1 s. Career: Prof. of French Horn & Ethnomusicol., Univ. of Wisconsin; French Horn player, Birmingham (Ala.) Symph. Orch., 1952-53, Nat. Orch. Assn., 1946-47, New Jersey Symph., 1946-47; Asst. Cond. & French Horn player, Duluth-Superior Symph. Orch., 1960-. Mbrships: Soc. for Ethnomusicol.; Int. Horn Soc.; Soc. for Asian Music; Assn. for Asian Studies. Address: 129 Billings Dr., Superior, WI 54880, USA. 8, 12.

RUTGERS, Franciscus Marinus, b. 28 May 1948, Utrecht, Netherlands. Teacher of Violin & Viola; Conductor. Educ: Enschede Conserv.; Conserv. of Utrecht. m. Leonora Maria Dekker. Career: Tchr., violin & viola, Deventer, Enschede & Germany; Ldr., Niggell String Quintet; Fndr., EYO. Mbrships: European String Tchrs. Assn.; NTB; Nederlandse Toonkunstenaarsraad. Hobbies: Sailing; Painting. Address: Assinklanden 211, Enschede, Netherlands.

RUTLAND, Harold, b. 21 Aug. 1900, London, UK. Pianist. Educ: BA., Mus B, Cantab.; AGSM; FRCO; ARCM. Debut: Wigmore Hall, London, 1926. Career: Staff, BBC, Music Div., 1941-56; Ed., Musical Times, 1957-60; Examiner, TCL, 1959-; Lectr.; Adjudicator; Music Critic; Broadcaster. Published Compositions: Toccata, Rigadoon, Siciliana, 2 Sea Shanties (arrangement), Brent Eleigh (piano piece); To the Moon (song). Author, Trinity College of Music; The First Hundred Years, 1972. Contbr. to: Radio Times; Musical Times; Times; Music Tchrs. Mbrships: ISM; Brit. Fedn. Music Festivals; Pres., John Ireland Soc.; past coun. mbr., Royal Musical Assn., Union Grads. in Music. Hons: Hopkinson Gold Medal, RCM, 1924; Organ Schlr., Queens' Coll., Cambridge; Stewart of

Rannoch Schlr., in Sacred Music, ibid; Hon. FTCL. Hobbies: Reading; Walking; Theatre; Photography. Address: 27 Eccleston Sq., London SW1V 1NZ, UK. 3. 14.

RUTLEDGE, George E, b. 29 Mar. 1928, Neodesha, Kan., USA. Music Educator; Company Manager. Educ: BS Music Educ., Lebanon Valley Coll., 1952; M Mus, Instrumental Music Educ., Univ. of Mich., 1955. m. Betty Miller, 2 d. Career: Clarinettist, Official USAF Band, Wash., DC, 1946-49; sang title role, Mikado, Watergate, Wash., DC, 1949-50; Music Dept. Coordinator, Hanover Public Sshls., 1963-77; Mgr., Vibrator Reed Co., 1964-78. Comps: Constellation Overture; Premiere Parade March; Bicentennial March; Silver Jubilee; Samantha Overture. Mbrships: MENC; Pa. Music Educators Assn.; NEA; Pa. State Educ. Assn. Hanover Educ. Assn; Pi Kappa Lambda, 1956; Nat. Band Assn. Hobbies: Antique Automobiles; Genealogy. Address: 221 George St., Hanover, PA 17331, USA.

RUTTERS, Matthias, b. 24 Aug. 1929, Aachen, Germany. Flautist; Professor. Educ: Abitur, Gymnasium, Aachen; NW German Music Acad., Detmold; Concert Dip. w. degree. m. Kyriaki Gaviotakis, 2 d. Debut: Flute Soloist w. Berlin Chmbr. Orch. in France, Spain & Portugal, 1953. Career: Solo Flute; Nat. Orch. of Athens; Berlin Phil. Orch.; Symph. Orch. of Westdeutsche Runelfunk, Cologne; Prof. of Flute, Staatliche Hochschule fur Musik, Ruhr at Essenn, 1972-; Mbr. Woodwind Quintet of Westdeutsche Runelfunk. Recordings: J S Bach 4 Brandenburg Concerto w. Berlin Phil. & Von Karajan. Hons. incl: Prize, Competition of German Radio Stns., Munich, 1953. Hobbies: Collecting Flutes; Greek Lang. Mgmt: Konzertdirektion Drissen Fehr, 65 Mainz Boppstr. 25. Address: 43 Essen 16, Klemensborn 72, German Fed. Repub.

RUUTH, Gustaf, b. 9 Aug. 1920, Stockholm, Sweden. Director of Music (Organ & Music Teacher). Educ: Royal Coll. of Music, Stockholm, 1941-45; Univ. of Gothenburg, 1971-; Univ. of Lund, 1974-76; Phil. cand., 1978. m. Kerstin Thoregard (dec.), 1 s. Career: Organist, Västanfors, 1951, Tidaholm, 1958, Ovanaker, 1959-62, Ljungarum (Jönköping), 1962-; Music Tchr., Per Brahe gymnasium, ibid., 1962-. Publs: Ed., Choral arrs., 1956; Choral works of W C Briegel, 1956, J Vierdanck, 1973, A Hammerschmidt, 1976, A Hackel & G W Heintze, 1969, C E Graff, Sonatas, 1969; Catalogue of Music Collection of Per Brahe gymnasium, Jönköping, 1971, Musicaliska Sällskapet i Jönköping 1779-1839, 1973, w. 3 supplements; Musik i Jönköping, 1808-1883, 1978. Mbrships: Chmn., Collegium of Ch. Musicians in Jönköping. Recip., Cultural Prize, Municipality of Jönköping, 1971. Address: Inre Ljungarumsvägen 18, 2-552 71 Jönköping, Sweden.

RUZDJAK, Vladimir, b. 21 Sept. 1922, Zagreb, Yugoslavia. Opera & Concert Singer; Professor at Academy of Music. Educ: Academic of Music, Zagreb. Debut: Opera, Zagreb, 1947. Career: OPera Singer, Zagreb, Staatsoper, Hamburg, San Francisco, Covent Gdn., London, Met. Opera, NY; Festivals; Edinburgh, Amsterdam, Vienna, Prague & Dubroynik. Num. recordings inclng: Opera; Songs. w. String Guitar; Operatic Arias. Publs: Stephano N Spadina; 6 Sonatas for Violin & Basso, Inst. of Musicol., Zagreb, 1975. Contbr. to Arti Musices, Zagreb. Hons: 1st Prize, Int. Competition, Geneva, 1949; Kammersanger, Hamburg, 1961; Vladimir Nazor Prize, Zagreb, 1964. Address: Galjerova 38, Zagreb, Yugoslavia.

RYAN, Anthony Wayne, b. 31 July 1951, Timaru, NZ. Composer. Educ: MusB, hons. (comp.), Canterbury Univ., 1971; STudied comp. w. John Cousins & David Sell. m. Ursula Summers. Debut: Song Cycle, From a Garden in the Antipodes, 1974. Career: Regular radio perfs. of works, 1974-. Comps: (Song Cycles) From a Garden in the Antipodes; Omi-Kin-Kan; Six Michael Songs; Mass for St. Michael and All Angels, At the Lighting of the Lamps (Symph.); The Vision of Isaiah (choral). Recordings: Song Cycles. Contbr. to: New Zealand Listener; Newspapers; Comps. Assn. Jrnl. Mbrships: Comps. Assn. of NZ; Australasian Perf. Rights Assn.; Artistic Dir., Upper Hutt Arts Fest., 1979-. Hobbies: Var. Musical & Dramatic activities. Address: 129 Fisher Ave., Christchurch, NZ.

RYAN, Colin A, b. 3 Sep. 1953, Montreal, Can. Cellist. Educ: BMus, McGill Univ., Montreal. Career: 1st cellist, Edmonton Symph. Orch.; mbr., Aurora Str. Quartet; numerous TV & radio apps. in chambr. music & solo recitals; soloist w. Edmonton Symph. Orch.; mbr., tchng. staff, Alta. Coll. Hobbies: Squash; Cooking. Address: 11147-70 Ave., Edmonton, Alta. T6H 2G9, Can.

RYAN, Marthinus Johannes, b. 24 Mar. 1951, Johannesburg, S. Africa. Piano Teacher. Educ: BMus; UEDM; ATCL; LTCL; AMusTCL; LRSM; UTLM. m. Martha Maria Kriel.

Career: piano tchr. mbr., S African Soc. of Music Tchrs. Address: Zeerust High Schl., Zeerust, Transvaal, S Africa.

RYBACH, Ladislaus, b. 1 Apr. 1935, Sopron, Hungary. Conductor. Educ: Doct. (Nat. Scis.), ETH, Zurich, Switz; Musical studies w. P Hindemith, Univ. of Zurich; Cond. classes, Zurich Conserv., & Music Acad., Basel; master courses w. R Kubelik & I Markevitch. m. Ruth Kraehenbeuhl, 1 s. Debut: Besancon Fest., France, 1965. Career: Regular Cond. of Univ. Choir, Zürich, & Orchesterverein, ibid. Mbr., Assn. of Swiss Musicians. Hons: 1st Prize, Int. Competition for Young Conds., Besancon, France, 1964. Address: IM Berghof 4, CH-8700 Kuesnacht, Switz.

RYBAR, Peter, b. 29 Aug. 1913, Vienna, Austria. Violinist; Music Professor. Educ: Conserv. of Prague; studied w. Carl Flesch. m. Marcelle Daeppen. Career: toured Europe as Soloist, 1934-38; Concert Master, Winterhur, 1938-65; Ldr., Winterhur Quartet & Orch. Suisse Romand; Tchr., Conserv. of Winterhur, 1971-; Prof., Conserv. of Geneva; has made many apps. at fests., Salzburg, Montreux, Konstanz, Schaffhouse, Lucerne, etc.; makes recital apps. w. wife (pianist); Lectr., in Switz. & abroad; Judge at int. competitions. Has made num. recordings. Hons. incl: Art Prize, Ernst Fndn.; Hon. Prize, Town of Winterhur. Address: Via Stazione, 6987 Caslano, Switzerland.

RYBICKI, Feliks, b. 24 Jan. 1899, Warsaw, Poland. Composer; Conductor; Teacher. Educ: Warsaw Conserv.; Pvte. studies w. Prof. Emil Mlynarski & L Rozycki. m. Helena Penther, 2 d. Debut: Cond., Warsaw Philharmonic Orch., 1926. Career: Tchr. of Orch., Karlowicz Music Schl., Warsaw, 1931-33, Kolegium Muzyczne, Warsaw, 1933-39; Tchr. of Cond., HS of Music, Sopot, 1951-; Tchr. of Orch., HS of Music, Warsaw, 1957-70. Compositions: Concerto for Flute in F major, 1963; Songs for Solo Voice & Piano; Cantata 'Gody Weselne' for 5 soloists, choir & symphonic orch. (recorded); Symphonic Tale 'Marysia Sierotka i Krasnoludki' (recorded); num. film scores recorded; Piano Manual Series; 3 Books of Etudes for Left Hand; Piano Concerto for Small Hands in F minor. Mbrships: Union of Polish Composers, 1928-; Zaiks, Warsaw. Hons: Cross of Polonia Restituta, 1956; Polish Radio Prize for Songs, 1956; State Prize for Music, 1962; PM's Prize for Compositions for Children, 1951; Min. of Culture Award for Compositions for Children, 1960, 61 & 62. Hobby: Handcrafts. Address: Noakowskiego 2612, 00-668 Warsaw, Poland.

RYCE, Joel Willem, I, b. 11 June 1933, Sterling, Ill., USA. Concert Pianist. Educ: Am. Conserv., Chgo.; Curtis Inst., Phila.; studied w. William Kapell, NYC, Rudolf Serkin & Dame Myra Hess, London; BSc (Psychol.), Univ. of London; Trng. & Psychoanalyst. m. Yaltah Menuhin. Debut: Town Hall, NYC, 1956. Career: duo w. Alan Grishman (Am. Violinist), 1956-60; world tour, 1958; annual tours w. Yaltah Menuhin, Am. & Europe, 1960-; app. leading music fests. & on TV, Paris, Hon Kong, NYC, London, Geneva & Cologne. Recordings: solo & duo w. Yaltah Menuhin, for Everest Recordings & EMI World Music Club. Hons: 1st Prize, Munich Int. Competition, 1956, Harriet Cohen Int. Music Awards, 1962 & Am. Conserv. of Music, 1953. Hobbies: Parapsychol.; Swimming. Mgmt: Ibbs & Tillett, 124 Wigmore St., London W1, UK. Address: 85 Canfield Gdns., London NW6, UK. 2, 24, 30.

RYCHLIK, Josef Henryk, b. 12 May 1946, Krakow, Poland. Composer; Music Theorist. Educ: Dips. in Comp. & Theory of Music, Higher Schl. of Music, Krakow. m. Anna Krowicka, 2 d. Debut: Krakow, 1970. Comps. recorded: Muzyka Symfoniczna, II, 1971; Warsaw Autumn, 1971; Wall Music (electronic) 1977; Musica per Gliss, The Poznan Spring, 1972; Grave-ap, 1975; Musinelle (electronic), 1975; Sous titre - Le Reve d'Eurydice)electronic) 1978. Other comps. incl: Points de Suspension, 1974; Warsaw Autumn, 1976. Publs: sev. articles on problems of contemporary music. Mbrships: Union of Polish Comps. Hons: 2nd prize, Young Polish Comps. competition, 1971; 3rd prize, Int. Competition for Organ Work, Szczecin, 1973. Hobbies: Philosophy; Poetry; Photography; Travel. Address: ul. L Teligi 6 m. 9, 30-835 Krakow, Poland.

RYCROFT, Marjorie Elizabeth, b. 19 Nov. 1946, Arbroath, Scotland, UK. Lecturer; Instrumentalist (cello, viola da gamba, tenor viol). Educ: MA, St. Andrews Univ., 1967; MA, 1969, PhD, 1972, Aberdeen Univ.; LRAM; ARCM. m. David Stuart Rycroft. Career: Asst. Music Tchr., Dollar Acad., 1973-75;

Lectr. in Music, Glasgow Univ., 1975-; mbr., Scottish Early Music Consort, 1976-. Hobbies: Cooking; Gardening. Address: 81 Douglas park Cres., Bearsden, Glasgow G61 3DW, UK.

RYDER, Georgia Atkins, b. 30 Jan. 1924, Newport News, Va., USA. Professor of Music. Educ: BS, Hampton Inst., Va., 1944; MMus, Univ. of Mich., 1946; PhD (Music Educ.), NY Univ., 1970. m. Noah Francis Ryder (dec.), 1 s., 2 d. Career: Music Specialist, Alexandria Pub. Schls., Va., 1945-48; Vocal, piano & music educ. tchr., Norfolk State Coll., Va., 1948-67; Prof. & Hd., Music Dept., ibid., 1970-. Contbr. to: The Black Perspective in Music, 1975; Negro Hist. Bulletin, 1976. Mbrships. incl: MENC; Nat. Assn. Tchrs. of Singing; Coll. Music Soc.; AAUP; Pres., Intercollegiate Music Assn. Hons. incl: Achievement Citation, Norfolk Comm. for Improvement of Educ., 1974. Hobbies: Poetry writing; House plants. Address: 5551 Brookville Rd., Norfolk, VA 23502, USA. 5, 27, 29.

RYDZESKI, Burnhart John, b. 10 Aug. 1937, NYC, USA. Professor. Educ: BS, MA, Hunter Coll., CUNY. m. Mary Preparatory Schl., NY, 1960; Dir. of Bands, Lindenhurst Publ. Schls., 1965, E Islip HS, 1970. Assoc. Cond., NYS Army Band, 42 Div.; Stage Band Dir. & Perf., Clarinet & Saxophone, NY; Dir. Broadway Prods. of musical comedies. Mbrships: Kappa Mu Epsilon; Assocd. Musicians of NY; NYS Schl. Music Assn.; Suffolk Co. Music Educators Assn. Hobbies: Theater; Swimming; Tennis. Address: 1521 Sweetman Ave., Elmont, NY 11003, USA.

RYERSON, Adna Mary, b. 23 Aug. 1907, Karuizawa, Japan. Violinist. Educ: RAM; LRAM, 1926; ARAM, 1928. Career: Took part in perfs. of all Haydn Str. Quartets, RAM, 1927-28; Ryerson Str. Quartet, broadcast 1933; New London Orch.; Jacques & Boyd Neel String Orchs. Tchr. of Violin & Viola, Leatherhead Schl. of Music, Fitznells Schl. of Music, Ewell, & privately. Mbr., RSM, Hons: Leonard Borwick Prize, 1928. Hobbies: Reading; Gardening; Playing Quartets for Fun. Address: 31 St. John's Rd., Leatherhead, Surrey, KT22 8SE, UK.

RYGERT, Torsten, b. 3 Feb. 1904, Frinnaryd, Sweden. Director of Music; Organist. Educ: Primary Tchr's. Cert.; Higher Organist & Cantor's Exams. m. Ruth Rosen, 1 child. Career incl: exhibition of paintings of Gothenburg & other places. Compositions: Ch. Festival Cantata; Freemason Cantata; Missa Brevis (choir & orch.); Orchl. suite, Man's Meeting; var. works for organ, songs & pieces; arrs. for choir & instrumental ensembles. Honours: Culture Prize of Savsjo Comm., 1974. Contbr. to local papers of music reviews. Memberships: Rotary Club, Savsjo. Hobbies: Painting; Gardening. Address: Eksjohovgard, 576 00 Savsjo, Sweden.

RYSANEK, Leonie, b. 14 Nov. 1928, Vienna, Austria. Operatic Soprano. Educ: Vienna Conserv. m. Ernst Ludwig Gausman, 1968. Career: NYC; Munich; Milan; London; Edinburgh; Aix-en-Provence; Hamburg; Budapest; Vienna; Paris; Moscow; San Fran.; Bayreuth; Salzburg. Hons: Chapl. I Gold Medal for Singing, London; Kammersängerin, Austria & Bavaria; Austrian Gold Cross 1st Class for Arts & Sci.; Hon. Mbr., Vienna Staatsoper; Silver Rose, Vienna Phil. Address: 8201 Altenbeuern über Rosenheim, German Fed. Repub.

RZEWSKI, Frederic, b. 13 Apr. 1938, Westfield, Mass., USA. Pianist; Composer. Educ: BA, Harvard Coll., 1958; MFA, Princeton Univ., 1960; studies w. Walter Piston, Roger Sessions, Milton Babbitt & Luigi Dallapiccola. m. Nicole Abbeloos, 3 c. Comps: The Poeple United Will Never Be Defeated, 1975; Coming Together, 1972; Les Moutons de Panurge, 1969. num. recordings. Address: 777 West End Ave., Apt. 5B, NY, NY 10025, USA.

RYDER, Kenneth Stanley, b. 22 May 1940, London, UK. Organist; Master of the Music; Pianist; Harpsicordist; Cellist. Educ: Jr. Exhibnr., RAM, London; GRSM (London); LRAM; ARCO. Career: many radio & TV (both BBC & ITV) appearances in conjunction w. the Choir of St. Peter Mancroft, & as Dir. of Clerkes of Mancroft -an all-male voice grp.; Harpsicordist w. Mancroft Players, an instrumental ensemble specialising in perf. of Baraque Chamber Music; Organist & Master of the Music, St. Peter Mancroft, Norwich. Mbrships: ISM; RAM Club. Hobbies: Oil Painting. Address: 56A Cathedral Close, Norwich NR1 4EH, UK.

S

SAARI, Jouko Erik Sakari, b. 23 Nov. 1944. Stockholm, Sweden. Conductor. Educ: Sibelius Acad., 1962-68; Helsiniki Univ., Music Sci., 1965-67; Ind. Univ., USA, Cond., 1969-70; Praecentor Organist degree, 1966; Schl. Music Div. degree, 1966; Conserv. (trumpet) degree, 1966; Music Dir. degree, 1966; Ch. Music div. degree, 1968; Cond. Dip., 1968. m. Raija Syvänen, 1 s. Career: Musical Dir., Helsinki Opera Soc., 1973-74; Cond., Tampere City Orch., 1973-74; Chorus master, Nat. Opera, Finland, 1974-75; Cond. & coach, ibid, 1976-78; Musical Dir., Lahti City Orch., 1977; Broadcast recordings w. Finnish Radio Symph. Orch., 1971, 73-75 & Swedish Radio Symph. Orch., 1974, 76-77. Hobbies: Sports. Address: Etelätie 1. D, 15610 Lahti 61, Finland.

SAASTAMOINEN, Iipo Erkki Aslak, b. 22 July 1942. Pielavesi, Finland. Conductor. Educ: Candidat of Humanistic Scis., Helsinki Univ., 1970. m. Ritva Klemetti, 1 d. Career: Mbr., Soulset Grp., Karelia Grp.; Fndr., Dopplers Phenomenon Grp.; Concerts at Sofia Youth Fests., 1968, Berlin Youth Fests., 1973, & in Cuba; Cond. of Kajaani Big Band. Recordings: w. Soulset, Karelia, Joutsenen Juju-solo LP 1976. Publs: The Plan of Pop/Jazz Education, 1972; Kitarakirja (guitar book), 1975. Contbr. to var. profl. jrnls., newspapers, radio progs. Mbrships. incl: Music Committee, Finnish State, 1970-76. Recip. var. hons. Hobbies: Fishing; Collection of folk music & instruments. Address: Sammonkatu 2B10, 87100 Kajaani 10, Finland. 30.

SABAT, Antoni, b. 16 May 1935. Barcelona, Spain. Manager. Educ: Philos. & Lit. m. Maria Dolors Millet. Career: Gen. Mgr., Forum Musical & Palau de la Música Catalana. Publs: El Palau de la Música Catalana. Contbr. to: Guia Musical. Hobby: Poetry. Address: Amadeu Vives 1, Barcelona, Spain.

SABBE, Herman L(eon Auguste Bertha), b. 24 Aug. 1937. Bruges, Belgium. Assistant Professor. Educ: Prix d'Excellence & State Medal for Cello, Bruges Conserv. of Music, 1954; 1st Prize for Chamber Music & Harmony; Grad., Salzburg Mozarteum Summer Acad., 1956; Dr.Juris & Lic. Not, Gent Stata Univ., 1960; DMus, ibid., 1975. M. Louise Dheere, 1s. 1 d. Career: Asst. Prof. of Musicol., Gent State Univ.; Music Critic, Kunst van Nu, 1964-67; Music Critic, Kunst-en Cultuuragenda, 1968-; Ed., IPEM Yearbook, 1968-70; Co-Ed., Interface, Jrnl. of New Musical Rsch. Amsterdam, 1972-; Ed. of sev. other musical & cultural revies; Contbr. to BRT 3rd Prog. Publs: Het Muzikale Serialisme als Techniek en als Denkmethode, 1977; De Romantiek, 1977; Ed.; Documenta Musicae Novae V, 1977. Contbr. to musical reviews in Europe. Sev. recordings of contemporary chamber music as cellist. Mbrships. incl: Sec., Belgian Section, ISCM; Chmn., ICCEM; VP, Nat. Music Coun. of Belgium; Sec. Gen., Nat. Fedn. fo Jeunesses Musicales, 1963. Hons: Musicol. Award, 1976, Belgian Acad. of Scis., Letters & Arts. Address: Komvest 34B, 8000 Brugge, Belgium.

SABLE, Barbara Kinsey, b. 6 Oct. 1927. Astoria, NY, USA. Professor of Music. Educ: BA, Coll. of Wooster, 1949; MA, Columbia Univ., Tchrs. Coll., 1950; MusD, Ind. Univ., 1966; studied w. Grace LaMar, Cesari Sturani, Roy Royal, Arthur Paulus, Dorothee Manski, m. Arthur J. Sable. Career: Prof. of Music, Univ. of Colo., Boulder; TV app. WCAX, Burlington, Vt., 1954; Vocal Soloist, Concerts, Opera, NY, Calif., elsewhere in wester USA, Germany. Contbr. to: Nat. Assn. of Tchrs. of Singing Review, & Bulletin; Music Review. Mbrships: Nat. Assn. of Tchrs. of Singing; Assoc. Ed., ibid; Ed. Bd. ibid; Pres. Colo.-Wyo. Chapt. ibid; AAUP; MENC; NOA. Hobby: Poetry. Address: 3430 Ash Ave., Boulder, CO 80303, USA. 5.

SACCAGGIO, Adelina Luisa N, b. 29 Oct. 1918. Tren que Lauquen, Buenos Aires, Argentina. Teacher of piano, recorder, guitar. Educ: Theory, Harmony, Nat. Music Conserv., Buenos Aires; 1942; Comp., ibid., 1949. Career: Attended many Music Confs. inclng. 4th Interamerican Conf. of Musical Educ., Santa Fe, 1970; 1st Nat. Conf. on Music Educ., Uruguary, Piriápolis, 1969; Prof. of Music Didactics, Nat. Music Conserv.; Dir., choir, Coralito de Haedo, Organizer, 1st & 2nd Villancico Fests., Haedo, 1974, 75, 76, 77. Num. dissertations. Comps: Duerme...(song); Calma (song & piano). Mbrships: Int. Soc. for Music Educ.; Argentine Soc. of Musical Educ.; Assn. of Music T Tchrs. Hobbies: Swimming; Cycling; Reading. Address: Junin 775, 1706 M J Haedo, Buenos Aires, Argentina.

SACCENTE, Roberto, b. 20 Feb. 1928. Haedo, Buenos Aires, Argentina. Musician; Professor of Music; Choir Director. Educ: BMus, Nat. Conserv. of Music of Argentina. m. Iris Fabrizi. Career: Fndr., Dir., San Justo Women's Choir & San Justo Polyphonic Choir; Choral Dir., Nat. Pol. Choir & Conserv. & Provincial de Morón; Concert tours in USA, S Am. & Europe. Recordings: Gloria (Vivaldi) w. San Justo Polyphonic Choir; var. Argentine & Am. works w. San Justo Women's Choir; Argentine choral pieces w. Nat. Polyphonic Choir. Contbr. to: Buenos Aires Musical; Diapasón. Mbrships: Music Tchrs. Assn.; Italian Inst. of Culture. Hons. incl: Dip., Argentina Assn. of Chmbr. Music, 1970; Dip., Friends of Music, Florence, Italy, 1972. Hobby: Swimming. Address: Nazca 538 4 piso, Dpto. A, Buenos Aires, Argentina.

SACCHI, Leo Joseph, b. 9 Aug. 1934. Chgo., Ill., USA. Horn Player. Educ: BMus, So. Ill., Univ.; MMus, Univ. of Houston. m. Carolyn Thomason Sacchi. Career: Denver Symph.; Prin. Horn, NC Symph.; Prin. Horn, Fla. Symph.; Prin. Horn, NC Symph.; Prin. Horn, Fla. Symph.; 3rd Horn, Houston Symph. Mbrships: AFM; Int. Horn Soc.; AAUP. Hobbies: History & Literature; Bicycling. Address: 3768 Rice Blvd., Houston, TX 77005, USA.

SACHER, Paul, b. 28 Apr. 1906. Basle, Switzerland. Conductor. Educ: Univ. of Basle; Conserv. of Basle. m. Maja Stehlin. Debut: 1926. Career: Fndr., Cond., Basle Chmbr. Orch., 1926; Fndr., Schola Cantorum Basiliensis, 1933; Cond., Collegium Musicum Zurich, 1941-; Dir., Music Acad. of the City of Basle, 1954-69; regular Concerts in most European countries; participant, Lucerne, Glyndebourne, Edinburgh, Aix-en-Provence, Vienna & var. other Fests. Recordings incl: Albinoni, Sammartani, Scarletti, Vivaldi, DGG; Mozart, Cassationen, Klavierkonzerte; Henze, DGG. Ed., book on Adolf Hamm, organist, Basle Cathedral. Contbr. to var. profl. jrnls. Mbrships: Pres., Int. Soc. for Contemporary Music, Swiss Sect., 1935-46; Pres., Assn. of Swiss Musicians, 1946-55. Hons: Mbr., Int. Soc. for Contemporary Music, 1971; Pres., Assn. of Swiss Musicians, 1955; DrPhil h.c., Univ. of Basle, 1951; Schönberg Medal, 1953; Mozart Medal, Salzburg, 1956; Medal, Litteris et ???tibus, Vienna, 1972; Kunstpries der Stadt Basel. Hobby: Gardening. Address: Schönberg, CH-4133 Prateln BL, Switzerland, 14, 16, 19.

SACHS, Klaus-Jürgen, b. 29 Jan. 1929. Kiel, Germany. University Lectr. Educ: Staatsexamen Kirchenmusik, Hochschule für Musik, Leipzig, 1950; Dr. Phil. (Hauptfach Musikwissenschaft), Univ. Freiburg i. Br., 1967; Dr. Phil. Habil. (Musikwissenschaft), Univ. Erlangen-Nürnberg, 1978. M. Eva-Marie Sachs, 2 d. Career: Univ. Lectr. für Musikwissenschaft, Univ. Erlangen-Nürnberg. Publs: Mensura fistularum. Die Mensurierung der Orgelpfeifen im Mittelalter, 1970; Der Contrapunctus im 14, und 15, Jh., 1974. Contbr. to: Archiv für Musikwissenschaft; Riemann-Musiklexikon; Die Musik in Geschichte und Gegenwart; Handwörterbuch der musikalischen Terminologie. Address: Münchauracher Strasse 18, D-8522 Herzogenaurach, German Fed. Repub.

SACHSENSKJOLD, Henrik, b. 17 Apr. 1918. Roskilde, Denmark. Violinist; Conductor. Educ: Royal Acad. of Music, Copenhagen; Conserv. de Musique, Paris, France, study of Cond., Italy; pvte. study of Comp. m. Amalie Malling, 1d. Debut: 1938. Career: Concerts as Violinist, Scandinavia & Europe, w. major Conds.; Cond., Tivoli Symph. Orch.; Guest apps. w. Radio Symph. & other orchs.; Prof. of Violin, Acad. of Music, Aarhus. Recordings of works by A Vivaldi, G F Handel, N W Gade, J P E Hartmann & Carl Nielsen. Recip., Bursary for study in Italy. Address: Ejby, 4070 Kirke, Hyllinge, Denmark.

SACK, Theodor, b. 14 Oct. 1910. Zürich, Switzerland. Pianist; Organist; Music Teacher. Educ: Piano w. Czeslaw Marek; Dip., piano & organ, Schweiz. Musikpaedagogischer Verband. Career: Concerts & radio apps.; Organist; Music Dir. Comp: Horn-Sonata, Missa brevis, Lieder. Recordings: C Franck's 'Les Djinns'; J S Bach's Concertoes for Piano & Concertoes for Harpsichord (Concert-Hall). Mbr., Musikpadagogischer Verband Tonkünstler-Verein. Hons: 2nd prize for piano, Geneva, 1939. Hobbies: Bot.; Lit. Address: Moehrlisrasse 103, CH 8006, Zürich, Switzerland.

SADIE, Stanley (John), b. 30 Oct. 1930. Wembley, Middx., UK. Writer on music; Editor. Educ: MA, MusB, PhD, Gonville & Cains Coll., Cambridge. m. (1) Adéle Bloom, 2 s., 1 d; (2) Julie Anne McCornack, 1d. Career: Prof. TCL, 1957-65; Music Critic, The Times, 1964-; Ed., The Musical Times, 1967-; Ed., The New Grove Dict. of Music & Musicians, 1970-; Ed., Master Musicians Series, 1977-; freelance writer, editor, broadcaster, etc., 1957-. Publs: Handel, 1962; Pan Book of Opera (w. A Jacobs), 1964; Mozart, 1966; Beethoven, 1967; Handel,

1968; Handel Concertos, 1972. Contbr. to: The Musical Times; Gramophones; Opera; Music & Letters; Musical Quarterly, etc. Mbrships: Royal Musical Assn.; Int. Musicol. Soc.; Am. Musicol. Soc.; Critics' Circle; Nat. Union of Journalists. Address: 1 Carlisle Gardens, Harrow, Middx., HA 3 OJX, UK. 1.

SADOWSKY, Reah, b. 17 Dec. 1918. Winnipeg, Man., Can. Concert Pianist; Teacher; Lecturer; Writer. Educ: BA, Colo. Coll., Colo.; MMus, Univ. of Colo., Boulder, Colo; studied piano w. Josef & Rosina Lhevinne, Alberto Jonas, Harold Samuels, Eric Simon & Milan Blanchet; contemporary piano lit. w. David Burge; chmbr. music studies w. Roth Quartet & Felix Salmond; theory, etc. w. num. tchrs. m. Dr F Rand Morton, 1 s. Debut: San Francisco, aged 8. Career incl: recitals & concerts throughout USA, Can., S Am. London; specialist in early Spanish keyboard music; num. radio perfs.; pvte. tchr.; lectr., num. Am. Colls. & Univs.; now artist in residence & Assoc. Prof., Colo. Coll., Colo. Springs. num. recordings. sev. comps., mainly for piano. Publs: Survey of Spanish Music; A Syllabus, 1975; Modern Music, 1850-1940: A Study Guide, 1973. Contbr. to: Am. Music Tchr. sev. hons. Mbrships: Nat. Assn. of Music Tchrs.; Coll. Music Soc.; Am. Assn. of Univ. Profs. Hobbies: Reading; Cooking. Address: 1111 Wood Ave., Colo. Springs, CO 80903, USA.

SAENZ, Pedro, b. 4 May 1915. Buenos Aires, Argentina. Composer; Harpsichordist; Teacher. Educ: Dip., Comp., Carlos Lopez Buchardo Nat. Conserv., Buenos Aires; Dip., Piano, ibid; studied w. Arthur Honegger, Darius Milhaud, Jean Rivier. Debut: Buenos Aires. Career: Pianist, Concerts in Argentina, S Am., Austria, UK, Italy, France, Spain; Harpsichord Recitalist, ibid, & TV Apps., Buenos Aires; (publd.) Comps. Dir., Municipal Conserv. Manuel de Falla, Buenos Aires, 1955-63; Dean, Fac. of Music, Cath. Univ. ibid, 1963-65; Prof., Nat. Conserv. of Buenos Aires,-1963. Tres Piezas Epigramaticas para piano; Preludio y Fuga a la manera de J S Bach; Juguetes, Danza Idilica, Nortena, Variaciones sobre um tema original, Preludio en fa, Aquel Buenos Aires, Policromias, piano; Sonata, violin & piano; Tres Canciones, voice & piano; (recorded) Juguetes; Cinco Canciones, ibid; Seis Piezas para clave and Dieciochesca. Recordings: Harpsichord Recital; Tartini, Didone Ababndonat. Contbr. to: Ars.; var. other profl. jrnls. Mbr. Argentinian Comps. Assn. Recip. num. Hons. Hobbies: Chess; Esperanto. Address: Glorieta Ruiz de Alda 4, 4 B Madrid, 6, Spain.

SAEVERUD, Harald Sigurd Johan, b. 17 April 1897. Bergen, Norway. Composer. Educ: Bergen Acad. of Music, 1916-20; State High Schl. for Music, Berlin, Germany, 1921-22; studied cond. w. Clemens Krauss, Berlin, 1935. m. Marie Hvoslef, 3c. Comps. incl: 9 Symphs.; Concertos (for piano, oboe, bassoon, violin); 3 String Quartets; Sev. works for orch.; 4 Suites for piano; Orch. Suite for theatre, The Rape of Lucrece; 2 Orch. Suites, theatre, Ibsen's Peer Gynt (recorded). Mbrships. incl: Hon., Royal Swedish Acad. of Music; Hon., Harmonien Music Soc., Bergen; Finnish Comps. League; Slovene Acad. Scis. & Arts. Hons. incl: Kt. of St. Olav, 1st Class, 1957; Order of Yugoslav Flag, 1973; Gold Medal, Harmonien, Bergen, 1975; Commander, St. Olav, 1977. Mgmt: Musikk-Huset A/S Oslo, Karl Johansgate 45, Norway. Address: 5046 Radal, Norway.

SAFFIR, Kurt, b. 17 Aug. 1929. Vienna, Austria. Conductor; Coach. Educ: BS, MS, Juilliard Schl. of Music, USA. Debut: Recital, Town Hall, NYC, 1957; Cond., Susannah (Floyd), NYC Opera, 1959. Career incls: NYC Opera, 1953-63; Musical Dir., Actors' Opera, NYC, 1955-62; Chautauqua, 1962; Stadtische Oper, Dortmund, Germany, 1964-67; Lake George Opera Festival, 1963-66; Musical Dir., Queens Opera, NYC, 1968-; Capital Artists, Albany, 1969-; Coord., Cantata Collegium of Int. Bach Soc., 1972-; Deertrees Summer Opera, Me., 1975; Cond., World Premiere Mary Dyer (Owen) w. Hudson Valley Phil., Suffern, NY, 1976; Cond., Capriccio (Strauss), Colo., 1976. Contbr. to profl. jrnls. Mbrships. incl: Int. Bach Soc. Hobby: Reading Murder Mysteries. Address: 175 W 76th St., New York, NY 10023, USA.

SAHAI, Pandit Sharda, b. 23 Mar. 1935. Varanasi, India. Musician (Tabla). Educ: Music study w. father, Bhagawati Sahai, & Kanthe Maharaj. Debut: Solo performance, age 9. Career: Concert perfs. in local towns 1945-, Italee Music Conf., Calcutta, 1951; Concert artist throughout India, 1951-; Tour w. Sarodist, Amjad Ali Khan, to Europe, USA & Canada, 1970; Artist in Residence, Wesleyan Univ., Conn., USA, 1970-75; Vis. Artist, Brown Univ., RI, 1972-; Artist in Residence, ibid., 1975-76; Res., musician, Varanasi; Music degree examiner for Prayag Sangit (non-profit making Univ. for music & dance), Benaras, 1965-. Address: Ram Sahai Bhawan, C22/79 Kabir Chaura, Varasani (UP), India.

SAIDENBERG, Daniel, b. 12 Oct. 1906. Winnipeg, Can. Cellist; Conductor. Educ: Paris Conserv.; Juilliard Schl. of

Music. m. Eleanore Block, 2 s. Career: Cellist & Guest Cond., Phila. Symph. Orch.; Solo Cellist, Chgo. Symph. Orch.; Guest Cond., Chgo. Symph. Orch.; Prof., Chgo. Musical Coll.; Music Dir., Ballet Theatre, NBC & CBS Orchs.; Asst. Artist, Budapest String Quartet; Cellist, Kroll String Quartet; Cond., Saidenberg Little Symph., Town Hall & YMHA, NY; Dir., Saidenberg Gallery, NY. Sev. recordings. Recip. 1st Prize, Naumberg Competition. Hobbies: Art; Golf. Address: 980 5th Ave., NY, NY 10021, USA. 2.

SALA, Oskar, b. 18 July 1910. Greiz, Thueringen, Germany. Composer; Electronic Music Performer & Instrument Builder. Educ: Univ. of Berlin; Music High Schl., Berlin ; studied w. Paul Hindemith. Debut: Berlin 1930. Career: Comp., Perf., Electronic music Germany, 1930-; Builder, Mixtur-Trautonium, electronic studio. Comps. incl: Konzertante Variationen; Scherzo-Etude; Elektronische Tanzsuite; Musik für elektronisches orch.; num. electronic film scores inclng: A Voyage to the Moon (tele-film picture-NASA) w. Manfred Durniok, 1975. Recordings: Stereo-Musik für elecktronisches orch.; Resonanzen, für elektronisches orch.; Suite für. Mixtur-Trautonium kund elektronisches Schlagwerk; Elektronische Impressionen, 1979. Contbr. to: Frequenz, Berlin; Gravesaner Blätter. Mbrships:GEMA; German Composers Grp. Hons: Music Prize, Industriefilmforum, Berlin, 1962: Der Fächer, BASF; Goldene Palme Cannes, for picture & electronic music A fleur d'eau, 1963. Address: 51/55 Charlottenburger Chausee, 1 Berlin 20 German Fed. Repub.

SALABOVA, Libuše, b. 18 Mar. 1929. Nový Bydzov Czech. Opera & Concert Singer (Contralto); Teacher. Educ: Dip., opera & concert singer, Acad. of Music; Dip., tchng. of music, PhD, Charles Univ. m. Ladislav Stros, 2 s. Career incls: num. concerts, Czech., E & W Germany, Hungary, Bulgaria, India, Poland, France, Italy, Belgium, also many radio & TV broadcasts; Chmbr. Opera, Prague, State Theatre, Ustí n. L, Nat. Theatre Prague, Theatre F X Salda-Liberec; recently has specialized in chmbr. duets w. Solisti da camera di Praga & (1974-) Trio Canto camerale. Recordings incl: songs by R Strauss, Brahms, Schumann, Schubert, Beethoven, Czjkovskj, Fischer, Dvorácek, Felix, Simai, E F Burian, Brecht, D C Vackár. Mbr. profl. orgs. Hobbies incl: Jeunesse musical. Address: Hrusická 2511, 141 00 Prague 4-Sporilov, 2 Czech.

SALAMAN, Esther Sarah. Barley, Herts., UK. Singer; Teacher of voice. Educ: RAM, LRAM; Studied w. Elena Gerhardt, Mme Isepp, Alfred piccaver, Lucie Manen, & others m. Paul Hamburger, (div.) 1 s., 1 d. Career: Recitals w. Eng. Opera Grp., London, UK & overseas, (w. Paul Hamburger); English opera Grp. Recitals, BBC Radio, Aust. Broadcasting Corp., S African Broadcasting Corp., Radio Eirann, TV; Hon. Organiser, Concert for Young Professionals, Jewish Inst., London El; Tchr. of Voice, Dartington Summer Schl. of Music; Singing Advsr., Finchley Childrens' Music Grp.; Tchr. of Speech Projection, ILEA Tchrs.; Prof. Guildhall Schl. of Music & Drama; Pvte. Tchr., Singing & Speec. TV appearance, (Interview about voice projection), Nov. 1972. Contbr. to: The Listener, (Radio 3 Broadcast), 1972; Jrnl. of ISM, 1973, '74. Mbr. ISM. Hobbies: Dressmaking; Gardening. Address: 114 Priory Gdns., Highgate, London N6 5QT, UK.

SALAS, Nancy, b. 28 July 1910. Coolgardie, WA, Aust. Professor of Piano & Harpsichord. Educ: LRAM; LRSM; LTCL. Career: Keyboardist w. Sidney Symph. Orch., 1950-55; Regular broadcaster, Aust. Broadcasting Commission; TV Master Classes; Univ. of the Air; Sydney TV; Pt-time tchr., BMus degree, Univ. Sydney; Prof. piano & harpsichord, State Conservatorium Music, NSW. Recordins Early Music, Elizabethan Players (HMV). Publ: (ed.) Baroque Sects., Aust. Music Examinations Bd. Grade Books, 1971. Contbr. to Aust. Jrnl. Music Educ. Mbrships. incl: Pres. & Fndr., Bartok Soc. Aust., 1955; Co-fndr. & Musical Dir., Music Students Overseas Study Fndn., 1972. Hon: Beethoven Commemorative Medallion, German Govt. for outstanding work in field of music, 1970. 2 Student fellowships. Hobbies incl: Gourmet vegetarian cooking. Address: 5 Milner St., Mosman, NSW 2088, Australia.

SALES, Vicente Mercado, b. 15 Feb. 1918. San Juan, Batangas, Philippines. Violinist; Music Educator; Choral Director. Educ: BComm. Sci., Jose Rizal Coll., 1940; Violin cert., Conserv. of Music, Univ. of Philippines, 1948; Gregorian Inst. of Manila, 1961. m. Conception T Peralta, 8c. Debut: 1958. Career incl: Fndr., musical dir., Pasaknungan Philippines Inc. Youth Talent Dev. Ctr., 1065-; Musical dir. & cond. musical plays on stage & concerts, 1958-; TV & radio host, GTV-4, Philippines Broadcasting System, 1976-. Comps. incl: Philippines Folk Mass. Recordings: 10 violin pieces for beginners; Handel's Hallelujah Chorus. Publs: Synon V - Method for Violin Beginners, Bk.I, 1974; (co-author) Music for Young Filipinos, Books I & II, 1962. Contbr. to profl. jrnls. mbr., off., num. profl. orgs. recip. num. hons. Hobbies: Pełota; Gardening. Address: 21-8 Azucena St., Tahanan Village, Parañaque, Metro Manila, Philippines. 29, 30.

SALESKY, Brian, b. 23 Feb. 1952. NY, NY USA. Conductor. Educ: BA, Ind. Univ., 1973; pvte. conducting studies w. Gianfranco Masini. Debut: NY City Opera, 1978. Career: cond., NY City Opera of Herbert's Naughty Marietta, Rossini's Il Turco in Italia & La Cenerentola, Verdi's Rigoletto & La Traviata; at Kennedy Ctr. Summer Opera, Mozart's Der Schauspieldirektor, Offenbach's Chistopher Columbus & Weber's Abu Hassan; at Spoleto Fest., Verdi's Falstaff; Artistic Dir. & cond., Musique á la Mode (NYC); var. musical & admin. posts w. San Francisco Opera, Lyric Opera of Chgo., Settimane Musicale Senese (Italy) & Lake George Opera Fest. Hons: Julius Rudel Award from NY City Op&era, 1977–1980. Hobbies: Cooking; Travel. Address: 515 W 59th St., 18F, NY, NY 10019, USA.

SALISBURY, James-earl, b. 28 Oct. 1951. Twin Falls, Idaho, USA. Conductor. Educ: Piano Student of Paul Pollei, Robert Smith, Tella Bellini, & Jane Lebovitz; Pvte. Trng. in clarinet, bassoon, violin & proficiency in all other orchl. instruments; Studied conducting w. Joseph Rosenstock, 2 yrs. Debut: aged 17. Career: Musical Dir. & Cond., Cottonwood Symph. Orch., Utah; Guest Cond., community, coll. & youth orchs., past 3 yrs.; Amateur & semi-profl. experience in ballet, ballroom & mod. dance, motion picture acting & live theatre inclng. many maj. roles, esp. in Shakespeare. Mbrships: incl: Cond. Serv., Am. Symph. Orch. League. Contbr. to var. mags. Hobbies incl: Theatre & Dance. Address: 2180 E 9th S, Salt Lake City, UT 84108 USA.

SALISBURY-JONES, Raymond Arthur, b. 31 July 1933. Camberley, UK. Chairman; Managing Director. Educ: MA, Modern Hist., Christ Church, Oxford; Piano studied w. Basil Allchin, ibid.; Organ & Piano Studies w. Dr. Sydney Watson, Eton Coll., Windsor. Career: Export Marketing Manager, Dir., Rolls-Royce Motors Int., Rolls-Royce Ltd., 1956-75; Co-Fndr., Dir., London Telemann Ensemble; Promoter young musicians & New Irish Chmbr. Orch.; Chmn., Courtyard Arts Trust Ltd.; Managing Dir., RSJ Aviation Ltd. Mbrships: Junior Appeals Committee, RCM; English-Speaking Union Music Coun. Hons: Lloyd Organ Prize, 1949; Rowe Piano Competition, 1948. Hobbies: Aviation; Skiing; Hill Walking. Address: 12A, Princes Gate Court, Exhibition Rd., London, SW7 2QJ, UK.

SALKELD, Robert, b. 16 Apr. 1920. Newcastle-upon-Tyne, UK. Teacher; Examiner; Editor. Educ: Newcastle Conserv. of Music; RCM; ARCM. m. 1) Eileen Mander, 2s; 2) Bridget Kirk, 1d. Career: var. tchng. posts in schls., 1949-50; tutor, Morley Coll., London, 1950-69; Prof., London Coll. of Music, 1961-69; examiner, ibid., 1961-; extensive work at fests. (Britisch Fed.), Summer schls. & courses, 1949-. Comps: Cradle Song (unison); Concert Pieces (rooordor & piano); 2nd Book of Concert Pieces; For the Left Hand (recorder & piano). Publs: Play the Recorder (3 Bks.), 1966-70; Piano & Percussion Accompaniments (2 Bks.), 1969-71; Scales without Tears, 1968; num. eds. of recorder music & arrs.; Gen. Ed. & contributor, Chester Recorder Series. Contbr. to: Music in Education; Recorder Music. Mbrships: Royal Musical Assn. recip. hon. FLCM, 1977. Hobbies: Reading; Walking. Address: The High House, 58 Bedwin St., Salisbury, Wilts., UK.

SALLINEN, Aulis Heikki, b. 9 Apr. 1935. Salmi, Finland. Composer; Teacher. Educ: Dip., composition, 1960. m. Pirkko Holvisola, 4 children. Career: Tchr., comp. counterpoint & instrumentation, Sibelius-Acad. Comps: 3 Symphs.; 'The Horseman' (opera); Variations sur Mallarmé (ballet); Mauermusik; Chorali for orch.; 4 string quartets; chmbr. music. Recordings: Decca SXL 6431; HMV 5E063-34330; Scandia SLP-575; Da Camera Magna SM 93710; HMV 53063-34283; Finnlevy SFX 11. Mbrships: incl: Bd., TEOSTO; Bd., Finnish Nat. Opera. Address: 01670 Vanta 67, Finland.

SALMI, Vexi, b. 21 Sept. 1942. Hameenlinna, Finland. Record Producer; Lyricist. m. Marja-Leena, 3 children. Recordings: over 800 lyrics released during past 10 yrs. Mbrships: Composers of Film & Popular Music; TEOSTO. Hons: 2 1st prizes, 2 2nd prizes, 3 3rd prizes, MTV Comp. contest of Yr; Prod., 11 Gold LPs, 2 Gold Singles. Address: Vuorimiehenkatu 12 A 5, 00140 Helsinki 14, Finland.

SALMON, Christopher David Baker, b. 21 Dec. 1940. Lower Hutt, NZ. Cellist. Educ: studied cello Wellington, NZ, & Paris, France; LRSM (Tchr.); LTCL (Perf.). m. Heather Anne Salmon, 1 s., 1 d. Debut: as soloist, 1973. Career: Prin. Cellist, NZ Nat. Youth Orch., 1962-63; Cellist, NZ Symph. Orch., 1964-; many solo & chmbr. perfs., frequently broadcasting on Nat. Network of Radio NZ; specialist in contemp. music, esp. by NZ comps.; premiered Lyell Cresswell Solo Sonata, 1973; has backed stage

shows. Records w. ensembles for film, TV & light music sound tracks. Hobbies: Sailing; Cruising; Bush-hiking. Mgmt: NZ. Symph. Orch. P.O. Box 11-440, Wellington, NZ. Address: 6 Sherwood St., Lower Hutt, NZ.

SALOIO, Carlos H, b. 16 Mar. 1931. Ludlow, Mass., USA. Trumpet Teacher & Performer. Educ: BA degree; Grad., USAF Bandsmen Schl.; Grad., Westfield State Coll., Mass. m. Mary W Graham, 5 children. Career: Trumpet Soloist w. Air Force Bands throughout world Chief Arr., & Asst. Bandleader; currently retired from USAF. Mbrships: Am. Fedn. Musicians, Local 171, Springfield, Mass.; Air Force Soc. Addess: 115 John St., Ludlow, MA 01056, USA.

SALOMAN, Ora Frishberg, b. 14 Nov. 1938. Brooklyn, NY, USA. Historical Musicologist; Violinist. Educ: AB, Barnard Coll.; MA, PhD, Columbia Univ. m. Edward B Saloman. Career: solo violin & chmbr. apps. at Baruch Coll., CUNY; Participant, Haydn Fest., Grad. Ctr., CUNY; radio & TV broadcasts, NYC; apps. at Kaufmann Auditorium of 92nd St. YM & YWHA, Mus. of City of NY, Columbia Univ. & Mannes Coll. of Music. Recordings: Archives of Recorded Sound, Lib. of Congress. Contbr. to: Musical Quarterly; Acta Musicol. Recip., rsch. grants & fellowships. Addredss: 14 Summit St., Englewood, NJ 07632, USA.

SALOME, Helene Berthe Elisabeth, b. 24 March 1924. Epinal (Vosges), France. Pianist. Educ: Conserv. Nat. de Nancy; Piano studies w. Edwin Fischer, Lucerne. Career: Concerts, recordings, Radio & TV apps., France, Belgium, Switz., etc. Num. recordings (W. F. Bach, Mozart, Schubert, Louis Ferdinand de Prusse, G Onslow, R. Strauss, etc.). Contbr. to: Musique de tous les temps (France). Mbrships: Pres., Centre Cultural de Valprivas. Hons: Prix Inter-Clubs du Disque, 1969. Mgmt: Centre Cultural de Valprivas, F 43210 Bas-en-Basset, France. Address: c/o Mgmt.

SALT, Valerie Jean, b. 25 Apr. 1956. Tibshelf, Derbyshire, UK. Private Music Teacher of Piano. Educ: Grad., London Coll. of Music; Lic., London Coll. of Music for Pianoforte. m. David Keith Brown. Mbr., Incorp. Soc. of Musicians. Hobbies: Reading; Tennis; Gardening; Walking. Address: 86a High St., Tibshelf, Derbyshire, UK.

SALTEN, Alfred, b. 23 June 1914. Devau, Germany. Conductor; Lecturer. Educ: Rotterdam Conserv. m. Margarethe H Futterknecht, 1 s. Debut: w. KRO Hilversum, 1934. Career: Cond., operetta, 1933-40, '45-54, opera, 1952-55, symph. orch. (Frysk Orkest), 1955-69; Free-lance & Tchr. at sev. conservs., 1969-. Recordings: Jurrian Andriessen, 3rd Symphony; Alfred Salten, Frylans Rom. Mbrships: KNTV; Rotary Club. Address: van Lenneplaan 226, Groningen, Netherlands.

SALTER, Lionel Paul, b. 8 Sept. 1914. London, UK. Harpsichordist; Pianist; Conductor; Musicologist. Educ: LRAM, 1931; BA, Cantab., 1935; BMus., ibid, 1936. m. Christine Fraser, 3 s. Career: Keyboard Perf. esp. Radio, UK & abroad; TV Pianist & Music Asst.; Guest Cond., Radio France Symph.; Asst. Cond., BBC Theatre Orch., 1945; var. sr. posts, BBC, 1948-; Asst. Controller of Music, BBC, 1967-74; Concerts in num. countries; frequent broadcasts; Film, TV Cond.; Lectr.; Adjudicator, Examiner, Romania, Hungary, Brazil; former mbr., London Baroque Ensemble; num. perfs. w. Eduard Melkus & Capella Acadmica, Vienna; Critic, Gramophone, 1948-; The Music Teacher, 1952-; Prog. Ed. Edinburgh Fest., 1951-55; Ed., BBC Music Guides Series. Composition incl: Radio Incidental Music; piano pieces; songs; num. Arrs. & Transcriptions. Publs: Going To A Concert, 1950; Going To The Opera, 1955; The Musician & His World, 1963; Music & the 20th Century Media, 1972; Contbr. to The Years Of Grace, 1950; The Concerto, 1952; The Music Masters, 1954; Music & Western Man, 1956; Decca Book of Opera, 1956; Decca Book of Ballet, 1958; Essays on Music from the Listener, 1967; Die Welt Der Symphonie, 1972, The Symphony, 1973; Gramophonic Guide to Classical Composers, 1978. Contbr. to var. Ency.'s, Musical Reference Works, profl. jrnls. Address: 674 Finchley Rd., London NWII 7NP, UK. 3, 14.

SALTER, Timothy John,, b. 15 Dec. 1942. Mexborough, Yorks., UK. Composer; Keyboard Player; Accompanist & Chamber Music Performer; Conductor (Choral); Teacher. Educ: St. John's Coll., Cambridge; MA (Cantab); MTC (London); LRAM; Hon. RCM. Career: Pianist, accompanying & in chmbr. music on BBC; Several apps. in perfs. of own works; Park Lane Grp. Player; Recitals & apps. as cond.; Dir., Ionian Singers. Tchr., RCM. Comps. incl: Choral music selection (recorded by Apollo Sound); Chmbr. Music & pieces for small ensemble; Songs; Works incl: Cantus (cello & piano); Clarinet Sonata. Num. recordings. Publs: Thomas Campion, Poet, Composer,

Physician (w. A Young & E Lowbury), 1970. Hobbies: Walking; Photography. Address: 26 Caterham Rd., London SE13 5AR, UK. 3.

SALTZMAN, Herbert Royce, b. 18 Nov. 1928. Abilene, Kan., USA. Choral Conductor. Educ: BA, Goshen Col.; MMus, Northwestern Univ.; DMusA, Univ. of Southern Calif. m. Phyllis E Saltzman, 4 d. Career: on Music Facs., Messiah Coll., 1950-52, Upland Coll., 1955-59, Univ. of Southern Calif. 1959-62, & Occidental Coll., 1963; Prof. of Choral Music, Univ. of Ore., 1964-; Assoc. Dean, Schl. of Music, ibid.; Lectr. on Choral Music, Germany, Mexico, France & Costa Rica. Contbr. to: Choral Jrnl. Mbrships: Pres., elect, Am. Choral Dirs. Assn.; Pi Kappa Lambda. Address: 2065 University St., Eugene, OR 97403, USA.

SALVADOR, Mario, b. 13 Apr. 1917. San Pedro Da Macoris, Dominican Repub. Organist; Choir Director. Educ: Pontifical Schl. of Msuic, Rome, Italy, 1931-33; BA, Am. Conservatory of Music, Chgo., Ill., 1939: BA, Loyala Univ., Chgo., 1940; MMus, Am. Conservatory of Music, Chgo., 1940; DMus, Univ. of Montreal, Canda, 1949. m. Isabelle Ann Branham, 1d., 2 s. Debut: Kimball Hall, Chgo., at age of 10 yrs. Career: Concerts in cities throughout USA, Canada, Columbia & Venezuela; Presented in 2 concerts through courtesy of US Army, Univ. Cmd., Florence, Italy, 1945; 1st organ concert ever televised in Venezuela, 1954; Tchr., organ, Fontbonne Coll. & Webster Coll., Prof., music, Marillac Coll., 1959-72; Organist & Choir Dir., St. Louis Cathedral, Mo. Compositions incl: Scherzo for Organ; Three Religious Meditations for Organ; Wedding Album; Music for a Church Service for Organ. Recordings incl: Gregorian Inst. of Am.; Vol. 1 - Pre-Bach; 2 Albums of the Mario Salvador Concert Series. Author of A Method of Organ Playing. Conbtr. to Hammond Organ Mag. Mbrships: Mo. Music Tchrs. Assn.; Cath. Music Tchrs. Assn.; Am. Guild of Organists. Recip., Benemerenti Medal, Pope John XXIII, 1960. Address: 4448 Maryland, St. Louis, MO 63108, USA. 3, 8.

SALZEDO, Leonard, b. 24 Sept. 1921. London, UK. Composer; Conductor. Educ: RCM, 1940-44. m. Patricia Mary Clover, 2 d. Career: Violinist w. LPO, RPO, London Soloists Ensemble, 1947-66; Musical Dir. of Ballet Rambert, 1966-72; Prin. Cond. for Scottish Theatre Ballet, 1972-74.Compositions publd: 7 Str. Quartets; var. ballets; Divertimentos for Wind; Quintet & Brass Sextet; Concerto for Percussion; Songs; Part Songs; Rendezvous (w. David Lindup) for Jazz Quartet & Symph. Orch.; Concerto for Trumpet; Concerto Fervido; var. chamber music & orchestral works. Recordings: Rendezvous, in collab. w. David Lindup for Jazz Quartet & Symph. Orch.; The Wi:ch Boy, ballet suite; Divertimento for Brass, etc. Mbrships incl: ISM; CGGB; Savage Club. Hons: Cobbett Prize for Comp., RCM, 1942; Howard Prize for Violin Playing, ibid, 1942; Tagore Gold Medal, 1943. FIAL. Var. hobbies. Address: 363 Bideford Green, Leighton Buzzard, Beds. LU7 7TX, UK. 3.

SAMELA, Gustavo Gerardo Andres, b. 15 Jan. 1940. Buenos Aires. Argenita. Musical Educator; Recorder & Cembalo Player. Educ: Piano prof. degree. m. Maria Bisceglia, 4 children. Career: Recorded player w. Pro Arte Recorder Consort & Ancient Music Consort, Collegium Musicum Buenos Aires; Approx. 100 apps., Argentina TV, radio & concert halls. Comps: Blues 73 for recorded consort & guitar. Publs: Musica Folklorica Argentina, 1972; Musica Folklorica Latinoamericana, 1974. Recordings: The Recorder: History & Music; The Recorder in France; The Recorder in England. Address: Monroe 4350/4/14, Buenos Aires, Argentina.

SAMPER, Rico Frances, b. 30 Apr. 1926. Valencia, Spain. Concert Guitarist; Composer; Teacher. Educ: degree, Concserv. of Music, Valencia, 1948-54; Music degree, El Micalet Musical Inst., Valencia; pvte. study in guitar w. Pepita Roca Salvador, harmony & comp. w. Francisco Nacher Tatay, solfege & theory w. Manuel Benlloch. m. Nelson Samper, 1 d., 1 d. Debut: Valencia, 1946. Career incl: recitals in USA, Colombia; TV & radio broadcasts, Bogotá, Columbia; guitar tchr., Conserv. of Music, Valencia, 1947-54; Dir. of Acad. of Music Diego Fallon, Bogotá, Colombia, 1955-59; music & guitar tchr., Los Angeles Unified Schl. Dist., 1968-; music & guitar tchr., Rio Hondon Coll., Whittier, Calif., 1971-. sev. guitar comps., tchng. material. Contbr. to: Children's Folk Songs from Spain, by A & P Mills; Colombian newspapers. Mbrships: Music Tchrs. Assn. of Calif.; Calif. State Tchrs. Assn. sev. hons. & prizes. Hobbies: Oil Painting; Travel; Manual Arts. Address: 19037 S Owen Way, Cerritos, CA 90701, USA.

SAMPSON, Peggie, b. 16 Feb. 1912. Edinburgh, UK. Musician (cello & viola da Gamba); Teacher. Educ: MusB, MusD, Univ. of Edinburgh; Lic. de Concert, Ecole Normale de Musique, Paris. Career: soloist in chmbr. music w. Carter String Trio, String Quartet & Trio (in Can.), Man. Univ. Consort,

Jacques String Orch., Hart House Consort of Viols.; apps., Aldeburgh Fest., UK, St. Lawrence Ctr., Toronto, CBC, BBC. Recordings: CBC & BBC transcription servs. Recip., new works for viola da gamba commnd. by Can. Coun. from Adaskin, Rosenboom & Komorous. Hons: Prof., Emeritus, York Univ. Toronto. 58 Hogarth Ave., Toronto, Ont. M4K 1K1, Can.

SAMSING, Freddy, b. 20 June 1946. Copenhagen, Denmark. Organist; Conductor (Choir & Orchestra). Educ: Organist Eksamen; Kantoreics; Dip. Organ; Music Pedagogisk Eksamen; RAM. m. Birte Samsing, 1 child. Debut: Copenhagen, 1969. Career: Concert recitals in Scandinavia & Belgius; Apps. on Radio Denmark; Cond.: Tivoli Concert Hall, Denmark; RAM, Copenhagen; Mus. of Carlsberg Brewery, Copenhagen; Asst. Organist, Cathedral in Roskilde, Seeland, 1969-; Tchr. in Organ Playing; RAM, Copenhagen, 1973-75; Acad. of Music, Aalborg, 1975-. Mbr., num. profl. orgs. Hobbies: Electronics; Organ Bldg.; Nature Walking. Address: Rendsagervej 81 DK-2620 Albertslund, Denmark.

SAMSON, Valerie Brooks, b. 16 Oct. 1947. St. Loius, Mo., USA. Composer; Musicologist; performer on violin & Chinese violin. Educ: BA (music), Boston Univ., 1970; MA (comp.), Univ. of Calif., Berkeley, 1973; pvte. Chinese music study, 1976-. m. Peter Richard Samson, 1 s. Career: num. Bay Area concerts (U.C. Berkeley, Mills Coll., San Francisco Conserv. of Music, art museums, etc.; radio broadcasts, Berkeley, Calif. & Cambridge, Mass.; lectr. on compos. in N Calif. & on women in music. Comps: Encounter, for chmbr. orch., 1973; Blue Territory I & II, for violin & piano, 1975; Montage, a Journey through Youth, for 3 sopranos, piano, dancer, 1975; Night Visits, for chmbr. orch., 1976. Contbr. to: EAR, 1975-; The Composer, 1977-78. mbr., Comps. Cooperative (sect.), League of Women Comps., Music West (treas.). Hobbies: Ski Touring. Address: 1373 Clay St., Apt. 5, San Francisco, CA 94109, USA.

SAMUEL, Harold E, b. 12 Apr. 1924. Hudson, Wis., USA. Musica Librarian; Musicologist. Educ: BA, Univ. of Minn., 1949; MA, ibid, 1955; studied Musicol. w. A Cherbuliez, Univ. of Zurich, 1950-51, w. Hans Heinrich Eggebrecht at the Univ. of Erlangen, 1955-57, & w. Donald J Grout at Cornell Univ. PhD, Cornell, 1963. m. Hella Deffner Samuel, 2 s., 1 d. Career: Music Libn. & Assoc. Prof. of Music, Cornell Univ., 1967- (at Cornell 1957-71); Chmn. of Dept. of Music, Yale Univ., 1971-; Ed.-in-Chief of Notes, the Qtly. Jrnl. of the Music Lib. Assn., 1965-70. Publs: The Cantata in Nuremberg during the Seventeenth Century, 1963. Contbr. of articles to music encys. & jrnls. Mbrships: Am. Musicol. Soc.; Music Lib. Assn.; Coll. Music Soc.; Int. Assn. of Music Libs. Hons: Served on Coun. of Am. Musicol. Soc. & on Bd. of Dirs. of the Music Lib. Assn., etc. Address: Schl. of Music, Yale Univ., New Haven, CT 06520, USA. 14.

SAMUEL, Harry Cecil, b. 23 Apr. 1927. London, UK. Composer; Conductor. Educ: Guildhall Schl. of Music & Drama, London. m. Margaret K Creer, 1s. Career: Dir., Theatre Music Grp., 1950-52; Dir., Aural & Visual Arts Ltd., 1954-56; Tutor, Morley Coll., 1956-; Dir., Morley Coll. Symph. Orch., 1967-. Comps: Youths' Agony, for small orch.; Sequence, for orch.; Concertino, for flute & strings; Divertimento, for orch.; The Romance of Numbers; Improvisation Tapes 1-4; Praeludium, wind organ & perc.; Suite for solo cello; The Turning Worlds (orch.). Contbr. to var. jrnls. Mbr., CGGB. Hons: Morley Coll. Symph. Orch. Comp. Competition, 1957. Hobbies: Making Poetry. Address: 17 Wellgarth Rd., London, NW11 7HP, UK. 3.

SAMUELS, Patrick Stephen, b. 23 Apr. 1940. Ilford, Essex, UK. Tenor Soloist; Conductor; Composer. Educ: NE Essex Tech. Coll. & Schl. of Art, Colchester; AmusTCL; LTCL; LmusTCL; FTCL; FLCM; studied w. Trevor Andrews. m. Pamela Seager-Ashe, 1 d. Debut: Purcell Room, London, 1972; Radio Jamaica, 1969. Career: Musical Dir., Kingston Coll. Choir, Jamaica, 1967-69, Havering Opera Workshop, London, UK, 1970-72, I Soloist Camerati, 1972; Prof. of Voice & Theory, Jamaica Schl. of Music, 1967-69; Recitals, Edinburgh Fest. Fringe, 1973-74; Cond., Father Cornelius, 1975; Cond. own work, From the Blake Songs of Innocence, 1975. Comps. incl: Motets; Study Materials, clarinet, bassoon; operas Shepherds' Delight, The Ring Of The Sea-King. Mbrships: Solo Perfs. Sect., ISM; hon. treas., CGGB; Ch. Music Assn. Recip. Prize, Stroud Int. Comp.'s Competition, 1973. Hobbies: Sailing; Mountaineering. Mgmt: Pro Arte Musica; Camerati Promotions. Address: 11 The Finches, Gullane, E Lothian EH31 2EA, UK.

SAMUELSEN, Roy, b. 12 June 1933. Moss, Norway. Professor of Voice; Bass-Baritone. Educ: BS, Brigham Young Univ.; MMus; Ind. Univ.; Dips., Music Acad. of the W, & San Fran. Opera Schl. m. Mary Lou, 3 s. Career: Served US Army; About 75 opera & oratorio roles; Recitals throughout USA;

Frequent guest soloist,l Norwegian Singing Soc. of Am. convens; Num. perfs. w. orchs. inclng. Minn. Orch., Utah Symph., Indnpls. Orch., Columbus Orch., Louisville Orch.; Perfs. w. NYC, Norwegian Opera, Chgo. Lyric, Chautauqua, Ky., St. Louis, Memphis, Salt Lake City opera cos.; Perfs. w. Ind. Univ. Opera Theater; Artist in Res. & Prof. of Voice, ibid, currently. Recordings: Oratorio to the Book of Mormon, by Robertson; Samson, by Handel. Mbrships: Nat. Assn. of Tchrs. of Singing; Past Pres., Pi Kappa Lambda. Hons: Winner, Metropol. Opera Audition; Henry Lennin Award; Winner, San Fran. Opera Contest; Lotte Lehmann "outstanding vocalist award"; & num. other awards. Hobbies incl: Raquet Ball; Water Skiing. Mgmt: Eric Semon, Inc., NYC, USA. Address: 2012 Montclair Ave., Bloomington, IN 47401, USA.

SAMUELSON, Kathryn Allen, b. 15 Sept. 1921. Allenwood, NJ, USA. Harpist. Educ: BA, music, King's Coll.; Briarcliff Manor, NY; Grad. studies, Engl. Lit., Univ. Pa.; Ariz. State Univ.; Eastern Bapt. Theol. Sem.; Pvte. harp instruction. m. L Philip Samuelson, 1943, 2 s., 2 d. Career incls: Harpist, var. orchs. inclng. Tri-City (Albany, Troy, Schenectady) Symph., NY; Phoenix Symph.; Ariz. & Tulare Co. Symph.; Harpist, 'Young People's Ch. of the Air', 1938-43; Harp Instructor, W HSA, Phoenix, Ariz.; Hamburg, NY Pub. Schls.; Pvtely., 1951-; Ch. Harpist, 1950-. Hobbies: Young Adult Bible Class Tchng.; Spkng. to var. clubs. Address: 195 Oxford Ave., Lindsay, CA 93247, USA.

SANDBERG, Lars, b. 4 May 1955. Stockholm, Sweden. Composer; Teacher. Educ: Royal Acad. of Music, Stockholm (comp. w. Ingvar Lidholm & others) 1973-76; Univ. of Paris, w. Iannis Xenakis, 1977-78. Comps. incl: Fall, for trombone, cello & piano, 1976; Containing, for winds & percussion, 1977; Gatherings, for clarinet solo, 1978; Nomen, for cello solo, 1979; Pertenecia, for mixed chorus, 1979. Mbrships: Soc. of Swedish Comps: ISCM (Swedish Sect.). recip. var. scholarships. Hobby: Cooking. Address: Vindragarvägen 21 11740 Stockholm, Sweden.

SANDELEWSKI, Wiaroslaw Jozef, b. 29 Nov. 1912. Sosnowiec, Poland. Composer; Teacher. Educ: LLM, Univ. of Poznan; Dips. of Composition & Vocal Polphony, Conserv. G Verdi, Milan, Italy. m. Marcella d'Evant, 1 s. Career: Tchr. of Harmony, Conserv. of Parma, 1958-59; Conserv. of Bologna, 1959-63; Tchr. of Musical Theory, Conserv. of Milan, 1963-71; Tchr. of Harmony, Conserv. of Venice, 1971-. Compositions incl: Flute Concerto, 1970; Violin Sonata, 1972; 2 Polish Dances for piano; 4 Miniatures for young pianist. Publs: Puccini, 1962, 2nd edit., 1973; Rossini, 1967. Mbrships: Italian Soc. of Musicol. Address: Via d'Ovidio 1, 20131 Milan, Italy.

SANDER, Peter, b. 9 Sept. 1933. Budapest, Hungary. Composer; Arranger; Piano Teacher; Pianist. Educ: BA, Budapest Univ.; Music Acad. of Budapest; Coll. of Music, Debrecen; GSM; TCL; LGSM. m. 1) Susan Gorocz (div.), 2s. 2) Jacqueline Diana Binns. Career: Lectr. in Comp., City Lit. Inst., London; Pianist & teacher. Comps: Rhapsody for piano & orch.; Ballet Suite for Orch.; String Quartet; Wind Quartet; Brass Quintets; Wind Trio; Fushions, for large orch.; piano music, chamber msuic, light music, film music, etc. Recordings: num. light & rhythmic instrumental LPs; String Quartet; Wind Quintet, Brass Quintet, Exploration for Guitar, etc. Contbr. to: Melody Maker; Music Maker; Into Jazz. Mbrships: PRS; CGGB; Songwriters Guild. Hons: 1st mention, French Radio & TV Comps. Competition, 1974. Hobby: Photography. Address: 73 The Avenue, London NW6 7NS, UK.

SANDERS, Ernest H, b. 4 Dec. 1918. Hamburg, Germany. Musicologist; Professor of Music. Educ: Abitur, Gelehrenschule des Johanneums, Hamburg, Germany, 1937; MA, Columbia Univ., NYC, USA, 1952; PhD, ibid, 1963; studied piano w. Irwin Freundlich, Juilliard Schl. of Music, 1947-50. m. Marion Hollander, 1 d. 1 s. Career: Lectr. in Music, Columbia Univ., 1954; Instr. in Music, 1958; Asst. Prof. of Music, 1963; Assoc. Prof. of Music, 1967; Prof. of Music, 1972; Chmn., 1978; also Instr. in Musicol. & Music Hist., Sarah Lawrence Coll., Bronxville, NY, 1971-77. Publs: The Medieval Motet, in Gattungen der Musik in Einzeldarstellungen, 1973: Polyphony & Secular Monophony: Ninth Century - c. 1300, & England: From the Beginnings to c. 1540, in Music from the Middle Ages to the Renaissance, 1973; English Polyphony of the 13th & Early 14th Centuries, 1979. Contbr. to many profl. publs. Mbrships: Am. Musicol. Soc.; Int. Musicol. Soc.; Royal Musical Assn. Recip. var. fellowships & scholarships. Addess: 885 West End Ave., NY, NY 10025, USA. 14.

SANDERS, John Derek, b. Nov. 1933. Wanstead, Essex, UK. Cathedral Organist. Educ: RCM; MA, MusB, Gonville & Caius Coll., Cambridge Univ.; FRCO; ARCM. m. Janet Ann Dawson, 1 s., 1d. Career: Dir. of Music, Kings Schl., Gloucester, & Asst. Organist, Gloucester Cathedral, 1958-63; Organist & Master of the Choristers, Chester Cathedral, 1963-67; & Gloucester Cathedral, 1967-; Cond., Gloucester Choral Soc. & Glos. Symph. Orch., 1967-; Dir. of Music, The Ladies Coll., Cheltenham, Glos., 1968-; Chief Cond., Three Choirs Fest., 1968, 1971, 1974. Comp: Festival Te Deum. Mbrships: RCO; ISM; Glos. Organists' Assn. (Pres.). Hobbies: Gastronomy; Travel. Address: 7 Miller's Green, Gloucester GL 1 2BN, UK. 1.

SANDERS, Paul Florus, b. 21 Dec. 1891. Amsterdam, Netherlands. Music Critic & Journalist (Ret'd.). Educ: studied w. Semdresden Amsterdam. m. Hilde Surlemont, dec., 1 s. Career: Music Critic; Jrnlst. Compositions: Lieder (publd.); A Capella Choirs (publd.); 2 ballets; chmbr. music. Publs: Het Strykkwartet, 1924; De Piano, her Instrument en zyn Meesters, 1926; Modern Nederlandse Componisten, 1929; Muziek voor de Volksklasse, 1930. Contbr. to: De Muziek (Fndr. & Chief Ed., 1927-33); num. other jrnls. Mbrships: Pres., Netherlands Composers Assn.; Chmn., BUMA; Netherlands Composers Assn.; Chmn., BUMA; Netherlands Fedn. of Profl. Artists. Hons: Hon. Doct., Hamilton Coll., Clinton, NY, 1956; Off., Order of Orange-Nassau, 1952. Address: 14 Pokahoe Dr., N Tarrytown, NY 10591, USA.

SANDERSON, Ronda Beryl, b. 21 Oct. 1921. Adelaide, SA. Musician (pianist). Educ: Adelaide Univ.; Studies w. Louis Kentner; BMus (Perf. hons.), 1943. m. K V Sanderson (div.), 3 s. Debut: Elder Hall, Adelaide. Career: 20 yrs. broadcasting for Aust. Broadcasting Commission & BBC. Recordings: Liszt, Beethoven & Bartok piano concertos; Ravel's Gaspard de la Nuit. Mbrships: ISM; L S Orch. Club. Hons: LRAM prize, 1937. Hobbies: Reading; Writing; Painting. Address: 45 Burlington Lane, Chiswick, London W4, UK.

SANDIFUR, Ann Elizabeth, b. 14 May 1949. Spokane, Wash., USA. Artist; Composer. Educ: BA, Music Comp., E Wash. State Coll.; MFA, Electronic Music & Recordings Media, Mills Coll.; San Fran. Conserv. of Music; Pvte. study w. Paul Creston & Stan Lunetta; PhD prog. in architecture, Univ. of Calif. at Berkeley. Career: Commission, Metropolitan Mtg. & Securities Co., for multimedia environment, Cosmography, 1978-79; Perf./Exhibit, San Fran. Museum of Modern Art, 1977; Perfs., Berkeley, Mills Coll., Buffalo. Comps: Musical score, I Extol the Nestle and Cuddle, 1977. Recordings: Sound Track, The Last Still Life. Contbr.to: Ear Mag. Mbrships: Regional Co-Ord., 1st Nat. Congress on Women in Music; Am. Women Comps., Inc.; League of Women Comps. Hons: Elizabeth Mills Crothers Award (Comp.), 1974; Tchng. Fellowship Center for Contemporary Music, Mills Coll., 1973-74. Address: W 122 Riverside, No. 706, Spokane, WA 99201, USA.

SANDLIN, Dorothy Southerland Johnson, b. 8 June 1927. Rose Hill, NC, USA. Pianist; Educator (piano, vocal, organ). Educ: BS Mus Ed., E Carolina Univ.; Juilliard Schl. of Music, NYC; St. Louis Inst. of Music; Westminster Choir Coll., NJ; Orff Inst. of the Mozarteum, Salzburg, Austria. m. James Delacy Sandlin, Jr. (dec.), 1 s. Debut: Carnegie Recital Hall, NYC, 1961. Career: Music tchr., num. schls. in NJ; Pvte. Tchr. of Piano & Theory, NJ & NC; Adjudicator, Nat. Piano Guild, Austin, Texas; Church Organsit & Dir. 1st Presby. Ch. Plainsboro, NJ; Interima Organist, Dir., First Presby. Ch. in Trenton, NJ. Recordings: Piano Recital, Carnegie Recital Hall, 1961. Publs: Curriculum Guide for Elementary School, 1971. C ontbr. to newspapers. Mbrships: Am. Assn. of Univ. Women; Correspondence Sec., Princeton, NJ, AAUW; Wilmington, NC Chapter, Sigma Alpha Iota, NJ. Hons: Gold medal Recording for Nat. Piano Guild, 1960. Hobbies: Art; Drama; Skiing; Swimming; Walking. Address: 310 Early Dr., Wilmington, NC 28403, USA. 5, 7, 27.

SANDON, Nicholas John, b. 16 Feb. 1948. Faversham, Kent, UK. Musicologist. Educ: BMus, Birmingham Univ. m. Edith Virginia Edwards, 3c. Publs: John Sheppard's Masses, 1976; Oxford Anthology of Medieval Music, 1977. Contbr. to: Early Music; Musica Disciplina; Proceedings of the Royal Musical Assn. Mbrships: Royal Musical Assn.; UK Committee for RILM. Hobbies: Cricket; Farming. Address: Music Dept., Exeter Univ., Devon, UK.

SANDOR, Anna, b. 8 Aug. 1950. Budapest, Hungary. Violoncellist. Educ: Artist & Prof. Dip., Ferenc Liszt Music Acad. m. Dr. Andras Bano. Debut: Violoncello competition of the Liszt Music Acad. Member of the Franz Liszt Chamber Orch. Sev. recordings w. the Franz Liszt Chamber Orch. - Art of the Fugue by J S Bach, Water Music by Handel, Vivaldi Concertos, Mozat Divertimenti, etc. Recip., Great Prize of the Franz Liszt Music

Acad., 1974. Hobbies: Dogs; Records; Photograhpy; Books. Address: Rajk Laszlo utca 14, 1136 Budapsest, Hungary.

SANDOR, Frigyes, b. 24 Apr. 1905. Budapest, Hungary. Conductor; Professor. Educ: Artist & Prof. dip., Liszt Ferenc Music Acad., Budapest. m. Vera Denes, dec., 1 d. Debut: Budapest, 1930. Career: Cond., Liszt Ferenc Chamber Orch.; Num. Concerts Hungary & abroad; Chamber Music Prof., Music Acad., Budapest. Recordings incl: Art of the Fugue (Bach); Divertimenti (Mozart); Harmonia Caelestis (Prince Eszterhazy); 111 Concert (Szollosy); Water Music (Handel). Publs: Violin-Tutor, 5 vols.; Musical Education in Hungary, 1969; Ed., classic violin works, Tartini, Kreutzer, Kayser. Contbr. to Parlando (music review). Mbr., Lizst Ferenc Soc. Hons: Liszt Ferenc Prize; Merited Artist, Hungarian People's Repub. Hobbies: Photography; Books; Dogs. Address: 1132 Budapest, Kresz Geza utca 17, Hungary.

SANDOR, Gyorgy. Budapest, Hungary. Concert Pianist. Educ: Grad., Liszt Conservatorium, Budapest; Study of Piano w. Bela Bartok, Comp. w. Zoltan Kodaly. 1 s. Debut: Carnegie Hall, NYC, 1939. Career: Annual concert tours, USA, Europe, Ctrl. & S Am., Far East, Aust., NZ. Comps. incl: Concert transcriptions of Dukas' Sorcerer's Apprentice, Bartok's Ciaccona & Fuga, Bach organ works (Toccata & Fugue in D minor, Prelude & Fugue in E Flat Major). Recordings: Complete piano music of Bartok, Kodaly, Prokofieff; Works by Chopin, Schumann, Liszt, Brahms, Bach, Beethoven, Dvorak, etc. Contbr. to mags. & newspapers. Hons: Grand Prix du Disque, 1965. Hobbies: Skiing; Swimming. Address: Univ. of Mich., Ann Arbor, MI 48109, USA. 2, 30.

SÁNDOR, János, b. 7 June 1933. Budapest, Hungary. Conductor. Educ: Dip., Ferenc Liszt Acad. of Music, Budapest, 1959; Accademla Chigiana, Siena, Italy, 1960-61. m. Maria Anda, 1 d., 1 s. Career: Music Dir., Györ Phil. Orch., 1967-; cond., Budapest State Opera, 1975-; guest apps. in Austria, Belgium, Bulgaria, Can., Cuba, Czech., Finland, Germany, UK, Netherlands, Iran, Italy, Luxembourg, Poland, Romania, USSR, Spain, Switz., Yugoslavia; cond., Youth Orch., fests. in Switz., UK & Can. Recordings: over 30, inclng. works in the complete Bartok Edition. mbr., Assn. of Hungarian Musical Artists. Hons: 3rd prize, Int. Competition for Conds., Besançon, France, 1957; Liszt award, 1967; Arthur Honegger Prize of Grand Prix Nat. du Disque (for Bartok recordings), 1970: Merited Artist of Hungarian People's Repub., 1973. Hobby: Boating. Mgmt: Interkoncert, Budapest. Address: Tĭkvész ut. 95-97A, 1025 Budapest, Hungary.

SANDOZ, May-Jacqueline, b. 25 June. Lucerne, Switz. Coloratura soprano. Educ: Music Acad., Basle. Debut: Mozart Festival, Interlaken, Switz., 1963. Career: Salzburger Landestheater, 1964; Staatstheater Braunschweig, Barcelona, 1964-66; Landestheater Detmold, 1966-67; Stadttheater Bremerhaven, 1967-69; Städtische Buhnen Dortmund, 1969-74; guest apps., Cologne, Vienna Staatsoper, Frankfurt, Berlin , Munich, Zürich, Israel, Salzburg, Glyndebourne, Metropolitan, NY, Pretoria & Johannesburg. Radio & TV apps. Recordings for Vogue. Hons: Medal at Concours Int. d'Exécution Musicale, Geneva, 1963. Hobbies: Psychology; Zoology; Cycling; Mountaineering; Swimming. Address: Belvedestr. 60, 5000 Cologne 41, German Fed. Repub. 30.

SANDOZ, Paul, b. 25 June 1906. La Chaux-de-Fonds, Switzerland. Singer (Bass-Baritone). Educ: Tchrs. Dip., Neuchatel Conserv.; Opera Schl., Basel. m. Marthe Wickersheimer, 2 d. Debut: Strasburg Opera, 1932. Career: Strasburg Opera, 1932-34; Lucerne Opera, 1934-41; Basel Opera, 1941-49; Guest Perfs., Zurich, Basel & Berne, 1949-; num. concerts & radio apps.; Tchr., Music Acad., Basel; currently Tchr., Lausanne Conserv. Recordings for HMV. Hobbies: Swimming; Mountains. Address: Steinbühlalle 109, Basel, Switzerland.

SANDQUIST, Kathryn Simpson, b. 29 Apr. 1937. Mpls., Minn., USA. Concert Artist (piano, harpsichord); Private Teacher. Educ: BA, Univ. Minn. m. John Maynard Sandquist, 1 s., 2 d. Debut: w. Mp's. Symph. Orch., 1957. Career: Harpsichordist, Musica Primavera; Concentus Musicus, Mpls.; Instr., Music, Hamline Univ., St. Paul, 1965-66; Augsburg Coll., Mpls., 1972-75; Adjudicator, state & local music orgs.; Solo recitals, Minn., Iowa, Wis., N & SD; Guest Artist w. Minn. & Waterloo Symph., Iowa; Local radio broadcasts. Hons. incl: 1st prize, Chgoland. Music Fest., 1948; '53; Edgar Stillman Kelly Award, Nat. Fedn. Music Clubs, 1951. Mbr. profl. orgs. Hobbies incl: Reading; Sewing. Mgmt: Prog. Prods. Inc. of Mpls. Address: 4532 Columbus Ave., Minneapolis, MN 55407, USA.

SANDQVIST, Olof Ingmar, b. 25 Oct. 1927. Falun, Sweden. Musician, French Horn. Educ: Royal Acad., Stockholm. 4 c. Career: 9 yrs., musician, Mil Band; Headmaster & Cond., Musĭc Schl. Orch., Aligsas; Concerts; W Germany, Netherlands; Norway; Radio, TV Apps. Mbr. Rotary Club, Alingsas. Hobbies: Photography; Sailing; Travel. Address: 42 Skolgatan, 441 00 Alingsas, Sweden.

SANDSTRÖM, Sven-David, b. 30 Oct. 1942. Motala, Sweden. Composer. Educ: Stockholm Univ.; Comp., Music HS of Stockholm, 1968-72. m. Gudrum Sandström, 1 d. Comps. incl: The Way; Under the Surface; Close To (recorded); Five Duets for one piano (recorded); Just a Bit (recorded); Inside; The Lost Song; Through & Through Utmost; Openings; In the Meantime (recorded); Disturbances (recorded); Birgitta - Music (recorded); High Above (recorded); Culminations; Con tutta forza; Effort; Agitato; Introduction/Earth's Answer/Spring; Missa da Requiem. Mbrships: Bd., Soc. of Swedish Comps.; Int. Soc. for Contemporary Music, VP, Swedish Sect., Fylkingen. Recip: Christ Johnson Prize, 1974. Address: Hällebergsvägen 61, 141 41 Huddinge, Sweden.

SANDVOLD, Arild Edvin, b. 2 June 1895, Oslo, Norway. Organist; Teacher; Educ: Oslo Conserv., 1906-14 (organists exam., 1912); studied piano w. Karl Nissen; studied organ, piano O comp. w. var. masters, Leipzig. m. Anne Finsen, 5 children (1 dec.). Debut: (as Organist) 1916. Career: Organist, 1914-66. Organist Oslo Conserv., 1917-70; Cond., Land-skoret (Norwegian Christian Youth Assn.), 1922-57, O St. Caecila Assn. Choir, 1928-57; Concerts as organist in Scandinavia O other European countries. Compositions: Misjonkantaten, 1942; ch. music, organ works O chmbr. music (sev. recorded). Mbr., num. profl. assns. Hons. incl: Cmdr., Order of St. Olav; Kt., other Scandinavian orders. Hobbies: Wood Carving; Fishing. Address: Asliveien 1, Bekkelagshogda, Oslo 11, Norway.

SANGER, David John, b. 17 Apr. 1947. London, UK. Concert Organist & Harpsichord Player; Conductor; Organ Consultant. Educ: RAM, 1963-66; ARAM, 1970, FRCO, 1965; studied w. Susi Jeans & Marie-Claire Alain. Career incls: Solo organ concerts; Organ Soloist, num. concerts throughout UK; perfs. in var. fests.; tours in Norway, Germany & Denmark; broadcasts for Norwegian, Danish & E German radio stns. & BBC; Advsr. on Organs, Diocese of Rochester, Kent; Dir. of Music for BBC TV live 'Sung Parish Communion' & Cond. 'Songs of Praise', BBC TV, 1976. Recordings: organ music of Mendelssohn, Franck, Liszt, Bach, also Bach harpsichord music. Contbr. to: Organists' Quarterly Review. Mbr. ISM. Hons: Int. 1st Prizewinner, St. Albans, 1969; Kiel, Germany, 1972. Hobbies incl: Choir trng.; Ch. music. Mgmt: Ibbs & Tillet, 124 Wigmore St., London. Address: 416 Long Ln., Bexleyheath, Kent DA7 5JN, UK.

SANTIAGO-FELIPE, Vilma R, b. 11 Jan. 1932. Manila, Philippines. Music Educator; Music Critic; School Administrator; Pianist; Accompanist. Educ: BMus, Philippine Women's Univ.; Juilliard Schl. of Music, USA; Pvte. studies. m. Fiedl S Felipe, 7 children. Career incls: Premier perf. of Bartok's Third Piano Concerto w. Manila Concert Orch., 1952-53; Script Writer, music appreciation broadcasts, 1953-56; Music Critic & Columnist, Times Jrnl. & Manila Jrnl. (foreign ed.), 1973-; Assoc. & Asst. Prof. in Music, PWU, 1975-. Comps. incl: Dedication (piano solo). Contbr. to profl. jrnls..Mbrships incl: Alpha Tau Chapt., Mu Phi Epsilon. Recip. var. awards. Hobbies: Reading; Handicrafts; Needlework; Creative Design; Cooking. Address: 13 E Maya Dr., Philamlife Homes, Quezon City 3008, Philippines, 27.

SANTORO, Claudio, b. 23 Nov. 1919. Amazones, Manaus, Brazil. Composer; Conductor; Professor. Educ: Conserv. Rio de Janeiro; Conserv. Paris. m. (1) Gisele Louise Portinho Serzedello Correa, 1939, 1 s., 2 d.; (2) 2 s., 1 d. Debut: Violin solo, 1932; Comp., 1939; Cond., 1948. Career incls: Orgnsr., Orchs. Radio Club & Radio Min. Educ., Rio de Janeiro; Chmbr. Orch., Univ., Brasilia; Prof., Dir. & Orgnsr., Music Dept., Univ. Brasilia; Currently, Prof., Mannheim Music HS, German Fed. Repub. Comps. incl: 8 Symphs.; 7 String Quartets; sev. Sonatas for piano, cello, violin, flute, etc.; 7 RCA Victor. Mbr. profl. orgs. Recip. num. prizes & award. Address: Alexander Mackstrasse 6, 6905 Schriesheim, German Fed. Repub.

SANTORSOLA, Guido Antonio Stanislao, di Bari Bruno, b. 18 Nov. 1904. Canosa, di Bari, Italy. Soloist Viola Player. Educ: Phil., theol., Montevideo, 1932; Conserv., Sao Paulo; TCM. m. Sarah Bourdillon, 2 d. Debut: 1913. Career: Dir., Music Acad., Montevideo; Dir., Symph. Orch., Opera & Ballet, Broadcasting Co. SODRE, Montevideo; European tour as violin player for BBC; RAI, Milan; RTF, France; Radio Madrid. Comps. incl:

Concerto for fout trumpets. Publs. incl: 1st & 2nd Book of Choral Harmony; Contrapuntal Harmony; The Language of Music. Mbrships: SODRE; AGADU; AUDEM; Guitar Ctr. of Uruguay. Hons. incl: Min. of Educ., 1937; SODRE, 1942; Ateneo, Montevideo, 1946. Hobbies: Swimming; Cycling. Address: Calle Francisco A Vidal, 722 Pocitos, Montevideo, Uruguay.

SANTOS, Clovis Pereira, b. 14 May 1932. Pernambuco, Caruaru, Brazil. Composer; Arranger; Conductor; String Bassist; Pianist. Educ: Studies w. Guerra Peizxe, 1951; Fed. Univ. of Rio Grande do Noree, course in Theory & Harmony. m. Cristina Pereira dos Santos, 2d. 2s. Debut: November 1968, conducting 1st Symph. work, Lamento e Dança Brasileira. Career: Pianist & arr., Rádio Jornal do Comércio, 1950; Hd., Msuic Dept., TV, 1960; Tour of USA as Brazilian rep. & cond. of the Univ. of Paraiba Chorus, 4th Int. Choir Fest. sponsored by the Lincoln Ctr. for the Performing Arts; 1974; Tchr., Fed. Univs. of Paraiba & Rio Grande do Noree. Comps. (recorded): Chamada Número Um (Cavalo Marinho); Terno de Pifes; Cantiga; No Reino da Pedra Verde; Aboio; Galope; Velhos Sucessos em Bossa Nova; Bossa Nova; Sucessos com Clovis Pereira (Rosenblit Records). Mbrships: Soc. Brasileira de Música Contemporanea. Hons: 1st Prize, Primeiro Concurso Nacional de Arranjos para Coro Misto, sponsored by the Arts Dept., Univ. Fed. of Paraiba, 1966. Hobbies: Audio & Electronics; Magnetic Tape Recordings; Football. Address: Avenida Conselheiro Aguiar 2286 Apt. 602C, Recife, Brazil 50.000.

SANTOS, Murillo, b. 30 Mar. 1931. Rio de Janeiro, Brazil. Musician (piano); Assistant Professor of Composition. Educ: Brazilian Conserv.; Grad., piano, Nat. Schl. Music, 1947; Post-Gr.; Comp. & conducting, 1965. m. Neila Alves dos Santos, 1 s. Debut: Profl. Accompanist, 1953; Comp., 1970. Career: num. apps. piano soloist, recitals, TV, Brazil & Piano Accompanist, Recitals, TV & Tours throughout Brazil, Ctrl. Am., USA, etc. Comps. incl: 'Love Song'; 'Acalanto'. Recordings: Brazilian Sons w. Maria Lucia Godoy & Lia Salgado. Mbr. profl. orgs. Hons. incl: 1st prize, ibid., Goethe Inst. Munich, 1974. Hobbies incl: Lit.; Films. Address: Rua Soriano de Souza 162/601 (Tijuca), 20,000 Rio de Janeiro, Brazil.

SANTOS, Turibio, b. 7 Mar. 1943. Sao Luis, Maranhao, Brazil. Guitarist. Educ: Pvte. studies. m. Sandra Santos, 1 s., 1 d. Career: Duets, guitar & violin w. Yehudi Menuhin, Switz. & France; toured Janpan & Aust., 1976; Concert w. Rostropovitch & Menuhin, UNESCO, Paris, 1976; Concerts, the Y, NY, 1978; Toured USA & Can., 1978. Recordings: (w. Oscar Caceres) Musique Française pour Guitare; Villa-Lobos; Classiques d'Amérique Latine; Musique Bresilienne, Choros do Brazil. Publs: Max Eschig; Ricordi do Brasil. Mgmt: Yves Dandelot, Paris; Helen Jennings; London. Address: c/o Yves Dandelot, 252 Faubourg St Honoré, Paris 8, France.

SARAI, Tibor, b. 10 May 1919. Hungary. Composer. Educ: Acad. of Music, Budapest. m. Ibolya Schwobbl, 1 c. Career: Hd. of Music Dept., Ministry of Culture, 1949-50; Ldr. of Musical Sect. of the Hungarian Radio, 1950-53; Prof. of the Béla Bartók Conserv., Budapest, 1953-59; Prof., Liszt Ferenc Acad. of Music, Budapest, 1959-. Comps: Serenade for String Orch., 1946; Spring Concerto, 1955; 2 String Quartets, 1958. '71; Symph. No. 1 & 2; Musica per 45 corde, 1971; Quartet for flute, violin, viola & cello; De profundis for tenor solo & wind Quintet; Dramma per fiati, for wind quintet; 2 oratorios; 2 cantatas; instrumental, choral, orchl. & chmbr. music. Recordings: Spring Concerto; Serenade for String Orch.; Symph. No. 1 & 2; Diagnosis 69, for tenor & orch.; String Quartets No. 1 & 2; Musica per 45 corde. Publs: The History of Czech Music, 1959. Mbrships: Exec. Comm., Int. Music Coun., 1972-78 (VP, 1976-78); Sec. Gen., Assn. of Hungarian Musicians. Hons: Erkel Prize, 1959; Kossuth Prize, 1975. Address: Maros u. 36, 1122 Budapest, Hungary.

SARAKATSANNIS, Leonidas Nicholas, b. 30 May 1929. Newport, Ky., USA. Professor of Music; Pianist; Composer. Educ: BMus, Coll. of Music, Cinn., 1951; MMus, Coll.-Conserv. of Music, 1956; DMA, Univ. of Cinn., 1968. m. Frances Nicholas, 2 s., 1 d. Career incl: perfs. w. Cinn. Symph., Fla. Symph., Cinn. Community Orch., Coll.-Conserv. of Music Symph., Univ. of Florida Symph., etc.; num. piano recitals, apps. at fests., lectures & chmbr. music throughout USA & Hawaii; perfs. on radio & TV; num. tchng. post incl. chmn., dept. of music, Fla. Technological Univ., 1968-72 & Dir. of Applied Music, Northern Ky. Univ., 1972-77. Compos: Twelve Excursions for the Young Pianist, 1961; num. unpubl. comps. Publ: The Piano Works of Eric Satie, 1968. Mbrships. incl: Pi Kappa Lambda; Phi Mu Alpha Sinfonia; Coll. Music Soc.; Am. Musicol. Soc.; Ky. Dist. chmn, Am. Music Scholarship Assn. sev. awards for comp. & piano. Hobbies: Swimming; Cycling; Tennis. Address: 34 Pentland Place, PO Box 9, Ft. Thomas, KY

41075, USA.

SARDA, Albert, b. 10 Oct. 1943. Barcelona, Spain. Composer. Compositions: Isorritme, 1971; 5 Pieces for Piano, 1970; Le Serpent, 1972; 8 Orchestral Pieces, 1973; String Quartet, 1975. Recordings: 8 Orchestral Pieces (RCA labe)l); Isorritme (EMI); Le Serpent (EDIGSA); Ophiusa (EMI). Hon: March Fndn. Schlrship. Hobby: Sports. Address: C/Balmes, 167. Barcelona, 8 Spain.

SARGENT, Pamela J. (Walter), b. 24 Feb. 1946. Ft. Collins, Colo., USA. String Bass Player. Educ: Music Schl., Northwestern Univ., 1963-64; Assoc. in Applied Sci., Major in Biol. Technol., SUNY, 1967; BS, Kan. State Univ., 1969. m. Steven W Sargent, 1 s., 1 d. Career: Currently playing w. Brico Symph. Mbr., Entomol. Soc. of Am. Hons: Cert. of Award, NY State Schl. Music Assn., 1963. Hobbies: Karate (Tae Kwon Do); Skiing; Breeding Irish Setters; Insect Collecting; Swimming; Softball; Guitar. Address: Rt. 1 Box 48C, Commerce City, CO 80022, USA.

SARGOUS, Harry Wayne, b. 9 Mar. 1948. Cleveland, Ohio, USA. Oboist. Educ: BA, Yale Univ., New haven, Conn., 1970. m. Margaret Kathleen Elaine Mossop. Debut: Severance Hall, Cleveland, 1966. Career: Radio Recitals, Cleveland Radio Stn. WCLV, 1966-71; Marlboro Music Festival, 1970, '71; Bach Concerto for oboe & violin w. David Oistrach, Toronto, 1972; Solo debut, Carnegie Hall, NY, 1975; Prin. Oboist w. Kan. City Phil. & Toronto Symph., radio & recordings; Radio, Blossom Music Festival of Cleveland; Music Critic, Yale Daily News, 1967-70. Hons: Wrexham Prize in Music, Yale Univ., 1970; Joseph Lentilhon Seldon Mem. Award in Music, ibid, 1968; Fortnightly Musical Club of Cleveland Schlrship. Award for Excellence, 1966-70. Hobbies: Travel; Photography. Mgmt: Amy Gilbert Representative, 34 St Cuthbert's Rd., Toronto, Ont. MYG IVl. Address: 255 Elm Rd., Toronto, Ont. M5M 3T9, Canada.

SÁRKÖZY, István, b. 26 Nov. 1920. Pesterzsebet, Hungary. Composer; Professor of Music Theory. Educ: Studied comp., Acad. of Music, Budapest, w. Zoltan Kodaly & other masters; Dip., 1947. m. Elga Ernst, 2 s. Debut: Radio Budapest, 1947. Career: Prof. of Music Theory, Acad. of Music, Budapest. Comps. incl: To Youth, 1953; Sinfonia Concertante, 1963; Who is Pour (soprano, mixed choir & orch.), 1967; Concerto Grosso, 1969; Quatuor pour instruments de bois, 1970; Concerto Semplice, 1973; Quartetto, 1977; musical plays; film, TV & radio music; (recorded) 4 LPs of works. Mbr., Assn. of Hungarian Musicians. Hons. incl: 1st Prize, Int. Coun. of Music. 1957; Merited Artist, Hungarian People's Repub., 1975. Hobby: Woodwork. Address: 1022 Budapest, Fillér u. 62, Hungary. 14.

SARNA, Mohinder Singh, b. 8 Sept. 1926. Montgomery, Pakistan. Vocalist. Educ: BA. m. Devinder Kaur Chadha, 2 s., 2 d. Career: radio broadcasts; film apps.; Comps. recorded; currently w. CMDA, Mahalaxmi Studio, Haines Rd., Bombay. Recip., nat. award for best music, 1969. Hobby: Sports. Address: Talati Cottage, 7 Bangalow, Versova Rd., Andheri, Bombay 61, India.

SAROSI, Bálint, b. 1 Jan. 1925. Csikrákos, Racu, Rumania. Ethnomusicologist. Educ: Grad., Hungarian & Rumanian Lit. & Linguistics, Univ. of Budapest; Doctor's degree, 1948; Grad. in comp. w. Prof. E Szervánszky, & musicol. w. Prof. Kodály, Acad. of Music, Budapest, 1956; Doctor's degree & Candidature, 1966. m. Jolán Benkö, 2 d. Career: Hd. of Dept. of Ethnomusicol., Inst. of Musicol., Budapest. Publs: Die Volksmusikinstrumente Ungarns, Handbuch der europäischen Volksmusikinstrumente I/1, ed. by Ernst Emsheimer & Erich Stockmann, 1967; Ciganyzene, Gypsy music, 1971. (German ed., 1977, Eng. ed., 1978); Zenei anyanyelvunk, 1973. Contbr. to Yearbook of the IFMC, Studia Instrumentorum Musicae Popularis, etc. Mbr., Int. Folk Music Coun. Address: Inst. Musicol., Országház 9, 1014 Budapest 1, Hungary.

SASLAV, Isidor, b. 18 Mar. 1938. Jerusalem, Palestine. Concertmaster; Concert Violinist; Teacher; Lecturer; Editor. Educ: BA, Wayne State Univ., 1961; MMus, 1963, MusD, 1969, Ind. Univ., Staatliche MMus, 1963, MusD, 1969, Ind. Univ., Staatliche Hochschule fuer Musik, Munich, 1958-59; violin study w. Mischakoff, Gingold & Galamin. m. Ann Heiligman, 1 s., 1d. Career incls: Mbr., var. orchs. inclng. Casals Fest. Orch., San Juan, PR, 1958-73; Concertmaster, var. orchs. inclng. Balt Symph. Orch., 1969-; Solo apps. w. many orchs.; on fac., var. instns. inclng. Eastman Schl. of Music, 1975-; Co-Ed., Joseph Haydn Inst., Cologne, 1971-. Contbr. to var. music publs. inclng. Grove's Dictionary, 6th ed. Mbrships: Am. Fedn. of Musicians; Am. String Tchrs. Assn. Address: c/o Balt. Symph. Orch., 120 W Mt. Royal Ave., Baltimore, MD 21201, USA.

SATHYANARAYANA, R, b. 9 May 1929. Mysore, India. Musicologist; Singer. Educ: MSc, Mysore Univ. m. Smt Gowri, 1 d., 1 s. Career incls: Prof. of Musicol., Sri Varalakshmi Acads. of Fine ARts, Mysore. Comps. incl: Sri Veene Namaste; Bhagam dehi Bhagavati; Shreemataram Ashraye. Mbrships. incl: Fellow, Royal Asiatic Soc., London. Acoustical Soc. of India; Int. Folk Music Coun., Can.; Soc. for Ethnomusicol., USA. Publs. incl: Sangeetharatnakara of Sharangadeva, 1968; Sruti, the Scalic Foundation, 1971; Studiesin Indian Dance, 1970; var. transls. Contbr. to sev. Indian jrnls. & mags. Recip., num. hons. Hobbies incl: Yoga; Mantra; Tantra. Address: Ramavilas, Kashipathi, Agrahara, Chamaraja Double Rd., Mysore 570004, India.

SATUREN, David Haskell, b. 11 Mar. 1939. Phila., Pa., USA. Composer; Arranger; University Professor; Performer. Educ: BA, Univ. Pa., 1960; MA, ibid., 1962; DMA, Temple Univ., 1967; New Schl. Music, Phila. Comps. incl: Largo & Allegro for Violin, Cello, & String Orchestra; Ternaria for Organ & Orchestra; Ghandiji; 5 moods in Miniature; Lydian Environment; Dialogue between Harpsichord & String; The 7 Voyages of Sinbad; Evolution for viola, Harpsichord & String Orch.; Trio for Clarinet, Piano & Mallet Percussion; Variation & Fugue for Jazz Combo & Strings. Recordings: Sonata for Clarinet & Piano; Trio for clarinet, Piano & Mallet Percussion. Contbr. to: Perspectives of New Music VI, 1967. Mbr., sev. profl. orgs. Hons. incl: Num. schlrships., fellowships, etc. Hobbies incl: Electronics; Astron. Address: 5 Leonard Tce. Wayne, NJO 7470, USA.

SAUER, Wolfgang, b. 2 Jan. 1928. Wuppertal, Westdeuschland. Singer; Pianist; Radio Journalist. (Blind from birth). Educ: Studied Engl. & German Langs. & Lit. & Musicology in Hamburg, Marburg, Cologne, 1946-52. m. Gisela Pink, 1 s. Career: Singer for EMI Electrola (Recording Co.) of Bestschers, 1954-; Moderator & Prog. Dir. w. nearly all German Radio Stns., 1963-. Num. recordings. Address: Richard Wagner Str. 29, 5000 Koln 5, Germany.

SAULESCO, Mircea Petre, b. 14 Sept. 1926. Bucharest, Roumania (Swedish subject). Violinist. Educ: Bucharest Conserv.; Dip. Bucharest Musical Acad., 1944; studied Violin w. var. masters inclng. Iosif Dailis, Garbis Avachian, Georges Enesco & Jacques Thibaud. Studied Piano & Comp. w. var. masters. m. 2 Gunilla Sandberg-Saulesco, 3 children of 1st marriage. Debut: Bucharest 1941. Career: Mbr., Bucharest Radio Symph. Orch., 1938-50; Fndr., Saulesco Str. Quartet, 1945; Mbr., Bucharest State Phil. Orch. Georges Enesco, 1950-58; Ldr. ibid, 1957-58; num. Chmbr. Music & Solo concerts. E Europe to 1958; Mbr., & one of Ldrs., Symph. Orch., Swedish Broadcasting Corp., 1958-; Fndr., Swedish Saulesco Quartet, 1962. Co-Fndr., Leygraf (piano) Quartet, 1965; num. TV & Radio apps.; var. foreign concert tours. Recordings incl: Alfvén, Violin Sonata; Mozart, Piano Quartets No. 1 G minor & No. 2 E flat major; Atterberg Str. Quartet op. 11; Verdi, Str. Quartet E minor; MBr., Mazer Soc. for Chmbr. Music Hons. incl: Swedish Record Prize, Grammis, 1970, 1972; Austrian Mozart-Prize, 1974. Hobbies: Art Books; Chess; Model Railway. Mgmt: konaertdirektion Inge Daub, Morathonvej 18, 2300 Copenhagen, Denmark. Address: Pepparkaksgränd 26 S-123 55 Farsta, Sweden.

SAUNDERS, Lawrence Ira, b. 15 July 1943. Chgo., Ill., USA. Ethnomusicologist; Violinist; Pianist. Educ: BA, UCLA, 1973; MA, ibid., 1976; Violin w. Louis Debovsky; Piano w. Marie Emerson; Music theory, Los Angeles Conserv. Music & Arts. m. Elsa Coron Saunders, 1 d. Career: Instructor, Mexican folk music, Sanata Ana Coll., Calif. & Chaffey Coll., Alta Loma, Calif.; Tchng. Asst., music cultures of worlds, UCLA. Contbr: 'The Son Huasteco', Proceedings Pacific Coast Coun. on Latin Am. Studies, vol. 3, 1974. Mbrships: Soc. Ethnomusicol.; Int. Folk Music Coun. Recip: Grant, Assocs. Ethnomusicol. to organize & catalogue recordings Mexican music, Donn Borcherdt collect. for Ethnomusicol. Archive, UCLA. Hobby: Books. Address: 408 Via Huueto, Montebello, CA 90640, USA.

SAUNDERS, Neil, b. 19 May 1918. Hove, Sussex, UK. Composer; Lecturer. Educ: MRCS; LRCP; ARCM; music study w. Gordon Jacob & Franz Reizenstein. Career incl: Lectr. in Hist. of Music. Compositions incl: Choral, piano & chmbr. music; Clarinet Concerto; Chmbr. Opera. Publs: Passacaglia; Missa Brevis; Magnificat; Jubilate; Benedic Anima Mea; Choral Songs, etc. Mbrship: Past Comm., CGGB. Hons: Patron's Fund Award, 1949. Hobbies: Reading; Walking. Address: Lodge Farm Cottage, Rossway, Berkhamsted, Herts., UK.

SAUNDERS, Rosamond Metta, b. 27 Dec. 1909. Market Harborough, UK. Flautist; Oboist; Retired Teacher. Educ: Royal Coll. of Music, London. m. M G Menzies, 2 s. Career: Tchr., schls., colls. & pvte. pupils, Worcestershire, Kent & Hampshire; Special Talent Bd., Royal Coll. of Music; Orchestral playing.

Publd. Compositions: The Flute - a Tutor; Clock Duets for Two Flutes; Easy Pieces For Flute Or Oboe. Mbr., Incorporated Soc. of Musicians. Recip., Edmund Grove Exhibition, Royal Coll. of Music, 1935. Hobbies: Collecting antiques. Address: 9 Lionard House, Queens Ave., Canterbury, Kent, UK.

SAUTER, Ernest, b. 9 July 1928. Munich, Germany. Composer. Educ: Thomas Schule (Coll.), Leipzig, 6 yrs.; Pvte. studies, Felix Petyrek, M Landes-Hindemith (piano), R Hindemith. Career: Musical Dir., Junge Ballet-Compagnie, Bonn, 1960-61; Comp., 1975-. Comps: Blue Jeans (Jazz Ballet), 1960; Variations Classiques, 1960; Saitenspiel, 1961; Trois Danses, 1963; Finale (Ballet), 1965; Concertante, 1973; Remontage, 1977. Mbr., GEMA. Address: Route de Malaucéne, F-84330 Caromb/Vaucluse, France.

SAVA, Helen, b. 8 May 1941. Bristol, UK. Lyric Soprano. Educ: Studied Singing w. Florence Wiese Norberg, Pierre Bernac & Peter Pears. m. Keith Bosley, 1 s. Debut: Wigmore Hall, 1972. Career: Soloist w. Early Music & Mod. Grps.; Num. 1st perfs.; Recitals in most maj. London concert halls & throughout UK; perfs. on radio & TV; Concerned w. Music-poetry recitals, particularly in schls. & colls.; Num. broadcasts; Sings in 12 langs. Mbrships: Equity; ISM. Address: 108 Upton Rd., Upton, Slough SL 1 2AW, UK.

SAVAGE, Richard Temple, b. 30 Sept. 1909. Wimbledon, UK. Clarinettist; Music Librarian. Educ: RCM. m. Valerie Patricia Teall, 3 d. Career: Bass Clarinettist, LPO, 1935-46; Bass Clarinettist, Royal Opera House, Covent Garden; Chief Libn., ibid., 1946-. Comps: 3 volumes Clarinet Studies; var. arrs. for string orchs. Hobbies: Gardening; Conducting own amateur orchestra, The Working Mozart Players. Address: 46 Malthouse Lane, West End, Woking GU24 9JE, UK.

SAVAGE, Stephen, b. 26 Apr. 1942. Hertford, UK. Concert pianist; Teacher; Conductor. Educ: Vienna Akademie; RCM. Debut: 1966. Career: Int. recitalist & broadcaster incl. many apps. on BBC radio & TV; Adjudicator in UK and Canada; Profl. of piano, RCM, 1967-; co-dir. 20th century Ensemble, ibid. Address: c/o Royal Coll. of Music, Prince Consort Rd., London, SW7, UK.

SAVALL, Jordi, b. 1 Aug. 1941. Igualada, Barcelona, Spain. Professor of Viola da Gamba & Ensemble Music. Educ: Dip. Cello, Conservatorio Superior de Musica, Barcelona, 1966; Soloists Dip., Schola Cantorum Basiliensis, Basel, 1970. m. Montserrat Figueras, 1 child. Career: Prof., Viola da Gamba & Ensemble Music, Schola Cantorum Basiliensis, Basel, Switz. Concerts in Europe. Recordins incl: Marin Marais; Pieces de Viole 2e Livre, 1975; Musica Barroca Española (Siglo XVII), 1975; Viol & keyboard Music During the Jacobean & Commmonwealth Periods, 1975; François Couperin: Pieces de Violes 1728, 1976; Music from Christian & Jewish Spain, 1976. Address: Flughafenstr. 35, 4056, Basel, Switz.

SAVARD, Claude, b. 16 Oct. 1941. Montreal, Canada. Pianist. Educ: Coll. des Eudistes, Montreal; 1st Prize, Conserv. of Music, PQ; Studied w. Vlado Perlemuter & Suzanne Roche, Paris, France; w. Irving Heller, Montreal, Debut: NY, USA, 1970; Wigmore Hall, London, UK, 1971. Career: Toured w. Jeunesses Musicales in USA, Can., France, Belgium, Germany, Denmark, Poland, Yugoslavia; 17 recitals (Can. Dept. of External Affairs) in Mexico, Guatemala, Venezuela, Brazil, Argentina, Peru, Ecuador & Columbia. 4 recordings for Int. Serv. of CBC & 1 for Select Record Co. Hons. incl: 1st Prize, Int. Competition, Munich, 1966. Hobby: Collecting Opera Recordings & Tapes. Address: 4660 Saint-Denis, Montreal, PQ, Canada.

SAVATTIER, Gérard, b. 1 Dec. 1932. Chatellerault, France. Ecclesiastic. Educ: Gregorian Inst. & César Franck Schl., Paris. Debut: 1962. Career: Mgr., Ctrs. of Sacred Music for the SW of France. Comps: num. liturgical songs & Christmas carol harmonisations. Recordings: w. 650 singers, Poitiers Cathedral; w. Ctr. of Sacred Music, Nevers; w. monks of Abbey of Liguge. Contbr. to: Église qui chante; Pretres diocésains. Mbrships: Assn. F H Clicquot; Assn. St. Ambroise; Soc. of Writers & Comps. of Music (SACEM). Hobbies: Radio & Gramophone; Choral Directing. Address: 10 Rue de la Trinité, 86034 Poitiers-Cedex, France.

SAVERY, Finn, b. 24 July 1933. Gentofte, Denmark. Composer; Pianist; Vibraphonist; Band Leader. Educ: Royal Danish Conserv. of Music, 1953-60. m. Ellen Savery, 1 s, 2 d. Career: Third Stream radio concert, 1961; Freedom, the Best Gold vaudeville theatre, 1961; TV, 1962; Ball at the Bourgeois Soc. (musical, theatre), 1966; Amager Poetry, music film & poetry comp., Tv, 1972. Comps. recorded incl: Freedom the Best Gold; Teenagerlove; Sonata for Double Bass & Piano;

Section I & II; Dualism; Henry; Song of the Surplus Value; Feast in the Mill; New York Series; From 7 Motives to Play; Mountain Air; Three Sections for Piano. Recordings: Finn Savery Trio; Jazz Strings; Music for Mice & Men; Presenting Finn Savery. Contbr. to Profl. publs. Mbrships: Comm., Danish Comps. Soc.; State Fndn. of Art. Hons: 3 Yr. Schlrship., State Fndn. of Art, 1970; Lang-Mülle Stipendium, 1973; Sandby Grant, 1974; 1st Prize, Nordic Jazz Competition for Comps.; num. scholarships. Hobby: Football. Address: Hulsovang 7, 2960 Rungsted Kyst, Denmark.

SAVERY, Janne, b. 26 Feb. 1938. Copenhagen. Denmark. Pianist. Educ: studies w. Prof. Herm D. Koppel, Royal Danish Conserv.; Prof. Carlo Zecchi, pianist & cond. m. Jens Als-Nielsen, 1 s., 1 d. Debut: Royal Danish Conserv., 1960. Career: perf. w. Tivoli Symph. Orch. & Danish Radio Symph. Orch. 2 apps. on Radio WYNC, NYC. Apps. on Danish radio. Hons: 1st prize, Shell, Taormima, 1964. Hobbies: Horse riding. Address: Fuglebakkevej 57, 2000 Copenhagen F, Denmark.

SAVILL, Patrick Stanley, b. 17 Mar. 1909. Westcliff-on-Sea, Essex, UK. Conductor; Music Teacher. Educ: MA, MusB, Peterhouse, Cambridge Univ.; Royal Coll. of Music; LRAM; ARCO. m. Edith Mary Watson. Career: Precentor, Farnborough Schl., 1933-35; War Serv., RAF, VR, 1940-45; Dir. of Music in the theatre, 1936-39, 1945-51; Guest cond., concerts, broadcasts & recordings, 1947-; Prof. of Musical Composition etc., Royal Acad. of Music, 1951-74; Examiner, Assoc. Ed., Royal Schls. of Mlusic, 1962-74; Bd. Mbr., ibid, 1963-74; Pvte. music coach. Recordings: Cond., var. works by Cimarosa, Dittersdorf & Mozart. Mbrships: Comm. of Mgmt., Royal Phil. Soc., 1968-70; Hon. Treas., ibid., 1970-78; RAM Club. Hons: Hon. RAM, 1960; Hon. ARCM, 1966. Hobbies: Gardening; Reading; Travel. Address: 23 Towers Rd., Hatch End, Pinner, Middx., UK. 139.

SAVILLE, Eugenia Curtis, b. 7 July 1913. Clinton, Pa., USA. Associate Professor of Musicology. Educ: BMus, NJ State Tchrs. Coll., Trento, 1934; MA, musicol., Columbia Univ., NY, 1943. m. Lloyd Blackstone Saville, 1 s., 1 d. Career: Assoc. Prof., musicol., Duke Univ., Durham, NC. Publ: Italian Vocal Duets from the Early Eighteenth Century. Contbr. to: Jrnl. Am. Musicol. Soc.; Musical Quarterly; Fontes Artist Musicae; Die Musik in Geschichte & Gegenwart. Mbrships: Int. Musicol. Soc.; Am. Musicol. Soc.; Southeastern Chapt., ibid.; Music Lib. Assn.; AAUP, Recip: Chapelbrook Rsch. Fndn. Fellowship, 1965-66; Duke Rsch. Coun. Grants for vol. on GCM Clari, 18th Century Musician of Pisa, 1966-79. Address: 1103 Anderson St., Durham, NC 27705, USA. 11.

SAVIO, Isaias, b. 1 Oct. 1900. Concert Guitarist; Composer; Teacher. Educ: studied w. Conrado Koch & Miguel Llobet. m. Youki Dubois de Savio, 1 child. Debut: aged 16. Career: concerts, Uruguay & Argentina; tours, broadcasts, Brazil, from 1931; Fndr., Chair of Guitar, Music Conserv. of Sao Paulo, 1947-. Comps: over 50 works for guitar (num. recordings by ldng. S Am. & European artists). Contbr. to: Guitar Review, NYC; Violao e Mestres, Sao Paulo. Mbrships: Fndr., Brazilian Assn. of the Guitar, 1940. Hons: Gold Medal, Ricordi Brazil, 1958; Tchr. of the Yr., Order of Musicians, Brazil, 1969. Hobbies: Photography; Collector of Old Photographic Equipment, Books & Guitars. Address: Rua Dr. Afrodizio Vidigal 448, Vila Maria Alta, 02133 Sao Paulo, Brazil.

SAVOURET, Alain Louis Camille, b. 24 Jan. 1942. Le Mans, Sarthe. Composer; Conductor. Educ: Conservatoire Nat. Superieur de Musique de Paris; Ecole Normale de Paris. m. Marie-Josephe Potoine, 1 d. Debut: Chef d'orchestre des Gds Ballets Classiques de France, 1966. Career: Comp. of electronic music, concert, theatre & Yugoslav TV; Comps. for fests. incl: SIGMA/Bordeauz, Menton, Avigon, Bouges, Munich, SMIP/Paris, etc.; Asst. de l'Orchestre Phil. de Lille; Radio apps. as cond. w. Nat. Orch. & New Phil. Orch. Comps: Kiosque; Selon; Tango; Soltrite; Valse Molle; Suite for pianos a Rallonges; Sonate Baroque; Au loin l'artifice. Recordins: L'arbre etcaetra. Contbr. to: FAIRE; Fest. du Son. Mbrships: Groupe de Musique Experimentale de Bourges; Circuit Int. de Musique Electroacoustique; Journées d'Etudes Internationales des Musiques Electroacoustiques. Hons: 2 commandes de l'Etat; 3 commandes de l'ORTF; Boursier de l'État. Hobby: Rugby. Address: 32 rue G Clemenceau, 92170 Vanves, France.

SAWALLISCH, Wolfgang, b. 26 Aug. 1923. Germany. Conductor. Educ: Music studies w. Profs. Ruoff, Haas & Sachsse. Career: Mil. Serv., 1942-46; Cond., Augsburg, 1947-53; Musical Dir., Aachen, 1953-58; Wiesbaden, 1958-60; Cologne Opera, 1960-63; Cond., Hamburg Phil. Orch., 1960-72; Prin. Cond., Vienna Symph. Orch., 1960-70; Bayerischer Generalmusikdirektor & Music Dir., Bavarian State Opera House, Munich, 1971-; Cond. at many fests. Hon.

Cond., NHK Symph. Orch., Tokyo; Artistic Dir., Suisse Romande Orch., Geneva, 1970. Recordings of num. works issued in USA & UK. mbr., Acad. of Fine Arts, Munich. Hons: Österreichische Ehrenkreuz für Kunst und Wissenschaft; Brahms-Medaille, Hamburg; Verdienstorden Freistaat Bayern; Grosses Silbernes Ehrenzeichen für Verdienste um das Land Wien; Kritikerpreis, 1978. Address: 8217 Grassau, German Fed. Repub.

SAWYER, Philip John, b. 3 Feb. 1948. Birmingham, UK. Organist; Teacher. Educ: RCM, 1966-68; ARCM(OP); ARCO; BA, 1971; MA, 1975; Peterhouse, Cambridge (organ scholar), organ studies w. Piet Kee, Amsterdam, & René Saorgin, Nice Conserv., France. Career: Organ recitals at King's Coll., Cambridge, Westminster Abbey, Notre Dame, Paris, St. Mary's Cathedral, Edinburgh, Glasgow Cathedral, St. Laurence Ch., Alkmaar, Hillsborough Parish Ch., N. Ireland, Univs. of Edinburgh, Aberdeen & St. Andrew's; Lctr.; Napier Coll., Edinburgh. Mbrships: Royal Musical Assn.; ISM; RCO Hon. Sec., Edinburgh Organ Recitals Committee. Hons: Sawyer Prize, 1967, Read Prize, 1968; RCO; Ord Travel Scholarship & Leaf Studentship, 1970; French Govt. Scholarships. Hobbies: Reading; Walking. Address: 19 S Trinity Rd., Edinburgh EH5 3PN, UK.

SAXTON, Beryl, b. 11 Dec. 1934. Sutton-in-Ashfield, Nottinghamshire, UK. Private Teacher of Music. Educ: Pvte. music studies w. Fred Garnett; Assoc., London Coll. of Music; Lic., ibid.; Fellow, ibid.; Lic., Trinity Coll. of Music, London; Fellow, ibid. for voice perf.; Assoc. ibid. for piano teaching. Mbrships: Incorp. Soc. of Musicians; Trinity Coll. of Music Guild; Dip. Holders' Assn., London Coll. of Music. Hobbies: Gardening; Photography; Woodwork; Do-it-yourself activities. Address: Overstones, 41 Dales Ave., Sutton-in-Ashfield, Nottinghamshire, UK.

SAXTON, S Earl, b. 22 May 1919. Berkeley, Calif., USA. Musician (Teacher & Player of French Horn). Educ: BA, Univ. of Calif., 1947; grad. studies, Juilliard Schl. of Music; MME, San Francisco State Coll., 1960. Horn study w. var. teachers, singing w. Mary Groom Jones. m. Marylee Marsch, 1 s., 1d. Career incl: USAF Bands for 4 yrs. during WWII; mbr. San Francisco Symph. & Opera Orchs., 1950-59; Solo horn, Little Symph. of San Fran., 1954-58; Prin . horn, Oakland Symph., 1959-73; 1st horn, Carmel Bach Fest. Orch.; Fndr.-Dri., Brass Choir of First Unitarian Ch. of Berkeley, 1963-; num. coll., univ. & conserv. tchng. posts; Asst. Prof. of Music, San Fran. State Coll., 1955-62. Recordings w. San Fran. Symph. & Little Symph. of San Fran. Publs: (paper) A Brief Summary of the Elements of Hornsinging, 1975. Contbr. to: The Horn Call; Brass Bulletin. Mbrships: Int. Horn Soc.; Bohemian Club of San Fran.; MENC; Sigma Int. Horn Soc.; Bohemian Club of San Fran.; MENC; Sigma Alpha Eta. Hobbies: Painting & Sketching; Gardening; Camping; Travel; Photography. Address: 1773 Walnut St., El Cerrito, CA 94530, USA.

SAYERS, Vera Winifred, b. 19 Mar. 1912. Ealing, UK. Professional Accompanist; Teacher, Piano, Violin, Singing. Educ: Pvte. study w. Arnold Grier, H H L Middleton; LRAM; ATCL; Gold Medallist, LAMDA. m. William Edward Rodway, 1 s., 1 d. Career: Music Mistress, var. schls. inclng. Drayton Manor Grammar Schl., Wynnstay Schl. for Girls, Manor House Schl., Pitmans Coll. Choir, Harvington HS; Also Ealing Mead & Grange Schls.; Accompanist, Drayton Jr. Schl., Grange Schls.; Ealing Grammar Schl. for Girls, Walpole Grammar Greenford Grammar, Herries Schl. Cookham Dean; Keep Fit Assn., Middx.; String Tchr., London Borough of Ealing, 1930-67. Mbrships: Chmn., Vocal, Comm., Ealing Music Fest.; Hon. Life Mbr., Ealing & Dist. Music Tchrs. Soc. Hobbies: Gardening; Motoring. Address: Cheyney House, Strande View Walk, Cookham, Berks., UK. 3, 27.

SAYLOR, Bruce Stuart, b. 24 Apr. 1946. Phila., Pa., USA. Composer. Educ: BMus, 1968, MS, 1969, Juilliard Schl. of Music; Acd. di S Cecilia, Rome, 1969-70; PhD, CUNY, 1978. m. Constance Beavon. Career: Lctr. in Music, Queens Coll., CUNY, 1970-76; Asst. Prof. of Music, NY Univ., 1976-. Comps: Duo for violin & viola, 1970; Loveplay for mezzo-soprano, flute & violn/cello, 1975; Opera, My Kinsman, Major Molineux, 1976; 4 Psalm settings for voice & flute, 1976-78. Publs: The Writings of Henry Cowell, 1977. Contbr. to: Musical Quarterly; Musical Am.; Contemporary Music Newsletter; Grove's Dict., 6th Ed. Mbrships: VP, Sec., mbr. of Bd., League of Comps., ISCM (1973-78); ASCAP. var. awards, scholarships & fellowships. Address: 318 W 85th St., NY, NY 10024, USA.

SCARABINO, Guillermo, b. 1940. Argentina. Conductor; Music Director. Educ: Grad., Music Inst. of Rosario Univ., 1964; MA, Eastman Schl. of Music, Rochester, NY, USA.

1967; studied conducting w. Washington Castro, László Hálász, Walter Hendl & Igor Markevitch. Career: Choirmaster; Fndr. & Ldr., Juventudes Musicales Chmbr. Orch., 1963-65; Guest Cond. w. many orchs. (symph. & chmbr.) in Argentina; Music Coach, Rosario Chmbr. Opera, Opera Theatre of Rochester & Eastman Schl.'s Opera Dept.; Tchr., Rosario Univ. Music Inst., 1967-; Dir., Rosario Univ. Choir, 1969-71; Guest Lectr. at many Argentine instns.; Organizer, Rosario Municipal Conserv., 1971; Special Cons., San Juan State Univ.; Music Dir., Mar del Plata Municipal Symph. Orch., 1972-. Mbr: Pi Kappa Lambda. Recip. of sev. schlrships. & distinctions.

SCATTOLIN, Pier Paolo, b. 30 June 1949. Bologna, Italy. Lecturer; Choral Director. Educ: Dip., choral music & choral direction, Conserv. of Bologna, 1973. Debut: Bologna, 1976. Career: Lectr., gen. musical culture at Conserv. of Bologna; Dir., chorus Euridice, Bologna. Comps: Meunier tu dors, Chevaliers de la Table Ronde, O bella ciao (popular songs arr. for 4 part mixed chorus). Recordings w. Euridice Chorus. Publs: Il trattato teorico de Jacopo da Bologna e Paolo da Firenze in Antiguae musicae italicae scriptores I/2, 1975. Contbr. to: Rivista Italiana di Musicologia; Coro, rivista dei cori italiani; Grove's Dict., 6th ed. Mbr., Societá italiana di Musicologia. Address: Via Mascarella 24, 40126 Bologna, Italy.

SCEK, Ivan, b. 5 Aug. 1925. dec. 20 Jan. 1972. Vipava, Yugoslavia. Teacher of Music & Composition. Educ: Dip. of Comp., Music Acad., Ljubljana. m. Marica Zorc, 1 d., 1 s. Comps. incl: (orchl. music): Concertino for violin & orch., 1958; 2 symph. poems, 1964, '69; (vocal-instrumental music): 10 songs for children's chorus & Orff instruments, 1959; (piano): Seven Images & Istra, 1965; (chmbr. music): Ciacona & Trio for wind instruments, 1965; '68; (scene music): 2 ballets, 1955, '62; (solo songs): 7 grand masses. Mbr., Slovene & Yugoslav music comps. socs. Address: 66000 Koper, Della Valle 7, Yugoslavia.

SCHAAP, Jan, b. 10 May 1928. Zaandam, Netherlands. Conductor; Musicologist. Educ: Clarinet, Choral, Orch. Conducting Dips., Utrecht Conserv.; studied w. Kees van Baaren, Paul Huppers, Igor Markevitch. m. Agatha Helena Kunst. Debut: 1952. Career: Specialist in conducting Military Bands; Cond., Royal Dutch Airlines Band, Dutch State Police Band; Co-Fndr., & Cond., Zaanstad Opera Co., 1969; Tchr., Conducting Alkmaar Music Schl. Recordings: Donizetti, Il Borgomastro di Saardam; num. others w. Military Bands. Author, reconstructed score of Il Borgomastro di Saardam. Mbrships: Royal Dutch Soc. of Musicians; Netherlands Union of Orch. Conds. Hobbies: Flying; Photography. Address: 37 Frans Halsstraat, Wormerveer, Netherlands.

SCHACHTSCHNEIDER, Herbert, b. 5 Feb. 1919. Allenstein, Germany. Opera, concert singer; Tchr. Educ: State Music Acad. Berlin. m. Ingeborg Schachtschneider-Weber, 2 d., 1 s. Debut: Flensburg. Career: Opera House Cologne; Var. Opera houses throughout Europe, and South Am.; TV, Radio app. in Germany, Italy, Belgium, Denmark. Recordings: Schönberg, Gurrelieder; Schnberg, From Today till Tomorrow; Wagner, Logengrin. Mgmt: Theatrical Agents, R. Schultz, München. Hons: 1975, Prof. Music Acad. Saarland. Hobbies: Astronomy; Chess; Swimming. Address: Krementzstr. 1, 5000 Colgne 41, German Fed. Repub.

SCHAEFER, Patricia, b. 23 Apr. 1930. Ft. Wayne, Ind., USA. Librarian. Educ: BMus, Northwestern Univ., 1951; MMus, Univ. of Ill., 1958; MALS, Univ. of Mich., 1963. Career: Audio-Visual Libn., Muncie Pub. Lib., 1959-. Contbr. of weekly column to Muncie Evening Press & prog. notes for Muncie Symph. Mbrships: incl: Am. Musicol. Soc.; ALA; Ind. Lib. Assn. (Chmn., Awards & Hons. Committee); Am. Recorder Soc.; Mu Phi Epsilon. Hobbies: Amateur Musical Groups; Photography. Address: 405 S Tara Lane, Munice, IN 47304, USA. 5, 27, 29.

SCHAEFER, William Arkwell, b. 28 Feb. 1918. Cleveland, Ohio, USA. Professor of Music; Conductor; Arranger. Educ: BEd, MMus, Miami Univ., Ohio; Conducting, Univ. Mich.; Juilliard Grad. Schl. m. Patricia Dyche, 1 s., 1 d. Career incls: Prof., Music, Cond. Wind Orch., Univ. Southern Calif., 1952-; Chmn., Wind & Percussion Dept., ibid., 1952-75; '48 TV Progs., Discovering Music, CBS. Comps: num. eds. & arr., music for concert wind grps., publd. & recorded. Publs. incl: scores for band, works by Bartok, Bizet, J Clarke, Debussy, etc. Contbr. to profl. jrnls. Mbr. profl. orgs. Hons: Annual Awards, contbns. to serious music lit. for band, ASCAP, 1956-; Outstanding Prof. Music Award, Univ. Southern Calif., 1975. Hobby: Antique Instruments. Address: 5050 Angeles Crest Hwy., La Canada, CA, USA.

SCHAFER, R Murray, b. 18 July 1933. Sarnai, Ont., Can. Composer; Author. Educ: LRSM (piano). m. Jean C Schafer.

Career: Artist-in-Residence, Memorial Univ., Nfld., 1963; Prof., Simon Fraser Univ., 1965. Comps. incl: (stage works) Apocalypsis, 1977; Loving, 1966; (orchl.) Untitled Comps. for orch. Nos. 1 & 2, 1963; East, 1973; In Memoriam Alberto Guerro, 1959; Cortege, 1977; Partita for Str. Orch., 1961: (voices & orch.) Adieu Robert Schuman, 1976; Arcana, 1972; Hymn to Night, 1976; Protest & Incarceration, 1960; (instrumental ensemble) Concerto for harpsichord & 8 wind instruments, 1954; The Crown of Ariadne, 1979; Str. Quartets No. 1, 1970, & 2, 1976; (choral) Epitaph for Moonlight, 1968; Gita, 1967; 4 songs on texts of Tagore, 1958; vocal works w. instruments; Polytonality, for piano, 1952; Okeanos, for electronic tape, 1971. num. recordings of own works. num. publs. on musical educ. & modern comps. Mbrships: Can. League of Comps.; Pro Canada. Address: RR No. 5, Bancroft, Ont. KOL 1CO, Can. 2.

SCHANZER, Wolfgang, b. 8 Nov. 1924. Dortmund, Germany. Conductor; University Administrator. Educ: BMus (Piano), BMus, (Comp.), MMus, Manhattan Schl. of Music. m. Whitfield Lloyd, 1 s. Career incls: 7 tours of USA & Can. as Musical Dir./Cond., Concert Opera Grp., Matinee Opera Grp. & Tanglewood Opera Quartet; Musical Dir. & Cond., Turnau Opera Co., Hudson Valley Symph.; Chmn., Dept. of Music, Marymount Coll., Tarrytown, NY, 1951-77; Cond., Chautauqua Opera Co., 1969-; Musical Dir. & Cond., Chappaqua Orchl. Asns., 1969-; Musical Dir. & Cond., Bergen (NJ) Phil. Orch. Recordings: Boston Records. Mbrships: Coll. Music Soc.; Am. Fedn. of Musicians; AAUP. Hons. incl: 1st Prize, Pitts (Pa.) Concert Soc. & NC Symph. Competition; Harold Bauer Mem. Award. Hobby: Travel. Address: Catherine Pl., RFD 2, Katonah, NY 10536, USA. 6.

SCHAT, Peter, b. 5 June 1935. Utrecht, Netherlands. Composer. Educ: Conserv. of Music, Utrecht; Royal Conserv., The Hague; studied w. Matyas Seiber, London, 1958; 2 yrs. study w. Pierre Boulez, Basel. 1 c. Career: Organized political-demonstrative-experimental concert, w. Louis Andriessen & Misha Mengelberg, Carre Theatre, Amsterdam, 1968; w. STEIM Studio for electro-instrumental music & the Amsterdam Electronic Circus, Amsterdam; Sr. Tchr. of Comp., Royal Conserv., The Hague. Comps. incl: Septet, 1957 (recorded); Entelechie II (Bert Schierbeek), scenes for 11 musicians, 1961 (recorded); Dances from the Labyrinth, 1963; Choruses from the Labyrinth, 1964; On escalation, for 6 solo percussionists & orch., 1968; Reconstruction (w. Louis Andriessen, Reinbert de Leeuw, Misha Mengelberg & Jan van Vlijmen), 1969; Thelma, for amplified oboe & orch., 1970 (recorded); To You, 1972 (recorded); Canto general, for mezzo soprano, violin & piano, 1974 (recorded); Houdini, 2 circus opera, 1976 (recorded); Symph. No. 1, 1978 (recorded). Contbr. to: Key Notes; Musical Life. Recip., num. commissions & comp. awards. Address: O.Z. Voorburgwal 119, Amsterdam, The Netherlands.

SCHAVRAN, Henrietta. Manhattan, NY, USA. Musicologist. Educ: BS, 1958; MA, 1965, Columbia Univ., PhD, NY Univ. m. George Schavran, 2 d. Career: Tchr., Brooklyn Community Coll., CUNY; SUNY; Stony Brook; Schl. Dist. 3, Huntington, NY; Pvte. piano lessons. Contbr. to: The Long Islander; Current Musicology. Mbrships: Am. Musicol. Soc.; Coll. Music Soc.; AAUW; Bd., Huntington Township Concert Assn.; Huntington Yacht Club. Recip. Doct. Dissertation Rsch. Grant, AAUW, 1973-74. Hobbies: Sailing; Golf. Address: 79 Cornehlsen Dr., Huntington, NY 11746, USA.

SCHEDL, Gerhard, b. 5 Aug. 1957. Vienna, Austria. Composer; Conductor. Educ: Studies of Music & Sci. at Univ., 4 yrs.; 7 yrs. study of violin, piano & guitar; indep. studies, 1976-; studies of composition w. Prof. E Urbanner, 1978; Dip. Music Theory, Vienna Acad. Career: 1st concert w. own composition, 1972; 2 concerts, Schubertsaal, Konzerthaus, Vienna; 3 radio prods.; TV appearance, 1980. Compositions: op. 12 Fantasie über einen ostinaten Bass (for guitar), 1977. Mbr., OKB, Austrian Composers' Union. Hons: Theodor Körner Prize, 1979; City of Vienna Award of Achievement, 1979. Hobbies: Walking; Painting. Address: 1060 Vienna, Stumpergasse 20/16, Austria.

SCHEFFEL-STEIN, Renata, b. 23 Aug. 1914. Riga, Latvia. Harpist. Educ: Dip. (Theory & Solfeggio), Nat. Conserv. of Paris. m. Werner Stein. Career: Soloist, Ctrl. Europe, 1935-47; Prin. Harp, Philharmonia & New Philharmonia Orch., 1953-75; Prin. Harp, London Symph. Orch., 1975-; Prof. of Harp, Sr. Classes & Master Classes, Royal Acad. of Music, 1975-; Prof. of Harp, Royal Coll. of Music, Mbrships: var. Harp Assns. in UK, France, W Germany & USA. Hon: 1st Prize of Harp, Paris, 1935; Hon. RCM. Hobbies: Gardening; Musical Stamp Collection. Address: 34 Royal Gdns., Wembley, Middx., HA9 8RZ, UK.

SCHEFFER, Eric Johan George, b. 7 Oct. 1909. Delft, Netherlands. Chief Engineer; Honorary Secretary & Treasurer, Utrecht Conservatorium; Amateur Pianist. Educ: IR Degree, Mechanical Engrng., Delft, 1933; Piano studies w. Miss H Theron Mulder & George van Renesse. m. Carina Christina Roeters van Lennap, 2 d. Debut: w. Delft Student Orch., 1934. Career: Num. poets, Netherlands Railways; Mbr. of Bd., Utrecht Conserv., 1948-; Hon. Sec., Utrecht Music Lib., 1958-. Contbr. to: De Koppeling, Rail Jrnl., Utrecht. Mbrships. incl: Fellow, Inst. of Railway Signal Engrs., London; Koninklÿk Instituut van Ingenieurs, The Hague; Hon. Mbr., Utrecht Sect., Maatschappij tot Bevordering der Toonkunst. Hons: Gouden Erelid of DSMG Apollo, Delft, 1934; Erelid, Toonkunst, Utrecht, 1975. Hobbies incl: Music; Writing for rail periodicals; Model railway. Address: El Rancho, 3723 E W Van der Helstlaan 22, Bilthoven, Netherlands.

SCHEID, Paul, b. 13 Jan. 1938. Plattsburg, NY, USA. Organist; Choral Conductor. Educ: BA, Mich. State Univ., 1960; MEd, Rutgers Univ., 1966: Profl. Dip., Tchrs. Coll., Columbia Univ., 1972; Grad. Studies, Westminster Choir Coll., NJ, & Princeton Univ. m. Winifred Potts, 1 s. Career: Ch. musician; Tchr. elem., middle, secondary schls. & community coll.; Organ recitals, NY & NJ; Cond., choral fests. & ch. music workshop. Co-ed., Music Commission News Letter, Diocese NJ. Mbrships: Music Commission, Diocese NJ; Past Dean, Ctrl. NJ chapt., AGO; Exec. Bd., ibid.; RSCM; MENC; Am. Choral Dirs. Assn.; Coll. Music Soc.; Int. Soc. Music Educators; Assn. Anglican Musicians; Hons: Nat. Endowment for the Humanisties Award, 1978. Hobbies: Photography; Trap Shooting. Address: 10 Pershing Ave., Trenton, NJ 08618, USA.

SCHELLER, Stanley, b. 17 Sept. 1940. NY, NY, USA. Bassoonist; Teacher. Educ: BA, music, City Coll., CUNY; Masters Degree of Perf. (Bassoon), Manhattan Schl. of Music, NYC; studied Bassoon w. Sandford Sharoff, Stephen Maxym of Met. Opera, & Harold Goltzer of NY Phil. m. Claire Jacob Scheller. Career: Tours of USA w. Royal Ballet, UK, & Goldovsky Opera Co.; Ctrl. City Opera Co., Colo.; NC Symph.; Young audience ensemble work, NYC & Denver; Woodwind quintet work & freelancing, ibid; currently Bassoonist, Denver Symph. Orch., Bassoon Instructor & Mbr. of Fac. Woodwind Quintet, Univ. of Denver. Mbr., Phi Beta Kappa. Address: 825 Downing St., Denver, CO 80209, USA.

SCHEMPER, Raul, b. 27 May 1921. Buenos Aires, Argentina. Merchant; Composer. Educ: Studied Harmony, Counterpoint & Comp. w. Jacobo Ficher; Piano w. Oreste Castronuovo; Trumpet w. Salomón Flechter; Comp. w. Eduardo Tejeda; Electronic Music w. Francisco Kröpfl. m. Lidia Charnis, 4 children. Debut: 1957. Comps incl: (publd.) Sonata Movements for Piano, 1974; (recorded) Quarter for Woodwind; (other) Prelude Choral & Fugue (piano); Suite for Chmbr. Orch.; 21 Micropieces in 8 parts. Mbrships: Argentine Soc. of Authors & Comps. of Music (SADAIC); Union of Comps. of Argentina; Young Com ps. of Argentina Assn. Recip., Hon. Mention in Musical Competition of 2nd Fest. of Guanabar, Brazil, & in Music Competition of Municipality of Buenos Aires, 1970. Address: Julián Alvarez 350, Buenos Aires, Argentina.

SCHENKEL, Bernard, b. 27 May 1941. Nyon, Switz. Oboist. Educ: Lausanne Univ.; Geneva Conserv. Career: 1st Solo Oboe w. Orch. de Chmbr. de Lausanne, Tonhalle Orch. Zurich, Wurttembergisches Staatsorch., Stuttgart, Orch. de la Suisse Romande, Geneva; apps. as soloist in European concerts, radios & TV; var. recordings. Hons: 1st Virtuosite Prize, Geneva Conserv.; Medal, Concours Int. d'Execution Musicale, Geneva, 1968. Mgmt: Newe Era Int. Concerts, London, & Musica Viva, Farlifang 22, 8126 Zumikon, Switz. Address: Ave. Curé-Baud 47, 1212 Grand-Lancy, Switz.

SCHENKER, Friedrich, b. 23 Dec. 1942. Zeulenroda, DDR. Composer; Trombonist. Educ: German Acad. of Music Hans Eisler, Berlin; State cert. comp., Music Acad., Leipzig; Grad. Acad. of Arts, DDR. m. Heidrun Schenker, 1 s., 1 d. Comps. incl: Listening to the Oboe, 1971; Electrification for Jazz. Beat Grps. & Large Orch., 1972, '73; Sonata for Wind & Percussion, 1973; Solo, Duet, Trio for Violin, Violoncello & Piano, 1975; Flute Symph., 1976. Recordings: Monologue for Oboe, 1974: Symph. In Memorian M L King, 1976; Sonata for JSB, 1977; Double Bass Concerto, 1978; String Quartet, 1979; Landscapes for large orch., 1979. Hons: Prize Carl Maria von Weber, Dresden, 1971; Prize Hans Eisler, State Broadcasting Committees DDR, 1975. Address: Tschaikowski Strasse 25, 701 Leipzig, German Dem. Repub.

SCHENKMAN, Peter, b. 6 Dec. 1937. NYC, NY, USA. Cellist. Educ: Curtis Inst. of Music, Phila., Pa. m. Melinda Evans, 2s. Career: mbr., Boston Symph. Orch.; 1st cellist, St. Louis (Mo.) & Toronto Symph. Orchs.; 1st cellist & featured soloist, Casals Fest., 1974-78; perfs. at Marlboro Fest., Vt.; 1st Can. perfs. of works for solo cello by Pendercki, Colgnass & Schönberg, also Boulez's Messagesquisse (N Am. premiere); fac. mbr., Univ. of Toronto, Royal Conserv. of Music & Nat. Youth Orch. of Can.; host, CBC radio progs. Recordings: works by Brahms, Chopin, Bloch, Davidoff & Frescobaldi. Address: 131 Maclean Ave., Toronto, Ont. M4E 3A5, Can. 29.

SCHERER, B(arry) L, b. 10 Sept. 1949. Marble Hill, NYC, USA. Tenor; Musicologist; Composer. Educ: pvte. vocal studies, 1968-71; AB, Hunter Coll., CUNY, 1972; MA, NY Univ., 1974. Career: num. apps. as Perf., Prod. & Musical Dir., radio stns. WBAI & WEVD, NYC; Guest Lectr., Hunter Coll., NYC Cultural Ctr. & Mus., etc. Comps. incl: The Prisoner of Zollern, or Righteousness Triumphant (2-act opera); Delizia, or the Gypsy's Malediction (21act opera w. ballet); How Beautiful Upon the Mountain; They that Wait Upon the Lord, & other anthems; many songs. Author, concert & record liner notes. Mbrships. incl: Am. Musicol. Soc.; Bd. of Dirs., Jamaica Symph. Orch. Recip. var. hons. Hobbies. incl: Drawing. Address: Parker Towers, 104-20 Queen's Blbd., Forest Hills, NY 11375, USA.

SCHERMERHORN, Kenneth, b. 20 Nov. 1929. Schenectady, NY, SUA. Conductor. Educ: Dip., New England Conserv. of Music, 1950. m. Carol Neblett, 1 s. Career: Asst. Cond., NY Phil.; Music Dir., Am. Ballet Theatre, NJ Symph. Orhc., Milwaukee Symph. Orch.; Opera Music Dir., San Fran. Recordings: Vox. Mbr., Music Panel, Nat. Endowment for the Arts, Wash. DC. Hons: Doct., Ripon Coll.; Serge Koussevitsky Mem. Award. Hobby: Tennis. Mgmt: S Hurok, Inc. Address: 929 N Water, Milwaukee, WI 53201, USA. 2.

SCHERMERHORN, Maja, b. 13 Nov. 1934. Opera & Concert Siner (soprano). Educ: Tchr., Domestic Econ.; Dips. in Opera, Lieder & Concert Singing, Pedagogue for Singing. m. Ir. J Schermerhorn, 1 s., 1 d. Career: Sev. roles in opera; Many concerts in Holland, W & E European countries w. classical & contemporary music; Radio & TVa broadcasts. also in USA. Has made some recordings w. choirs in the Netherlands & Germany. Contbr. to profl. publs. Mb r., KNTV Recip., Second prize of the Nat. Cum Laude Concours, Groningen, 1970. Hobbies: Travelling; Tennis; Lit. Address: Moorveld 75, 6243 AX Geulle, The Netherlands. 30.

SCHERZER, Manfred, b. 2 June 1933. Dresden, Germany. Violinist. Educ: by father Max Scherzer of Dresden state orch., Debut: Berlin, 1950. Career: state orch. Dresden, 1950-3; 1st solo, Komische Oper, Berlin, from 1953; Soloist & 1st concert apps. in Europe, USA, Japan, S America, China; fndr. of Beethoven Trio, 1963. Recordings incl: Max Reger - Sonata in C minor & Chaconne for solo violin; Schubert - Sonatas for violin & piano; Schubert - Trio in E flat maj. op. 100; Vivaldi - Concerto in A minor. Hons: Kunstpreis der DDR; 1964; Preis der Musikkritik, 1969; National preis der DDR, 1972; Smetena medal, CSSR, 1975. Mgmt: Künstleragentur der DDR. Address: 1017 Berlin, Karl-Marx Allee 20g. German Dem. Repub.

SCHEUERLE, Paul Norman, b. 26 May 1926. Manor Pa., USA. Music Educator & Administrator; Band Conductor; Clarinettist; Saxophonist. Educ: BMus., Eastman Schl. of Music; MEd, Pa. State Univ.; DMA, Boston Univ.; Schl. of Music, Univ. of Colo. m. Mary Ann Slater. Career: World tour of Musical Instns. & Orgs., 1971; Guest Cond., Manila, Philippines, 1971, plus many Midwestern States & Alaska; Clarinettist, Prairie Woods Woodwinds Quintet; Baritone Saxophonist; Dakota Saxophone Quartet. Contbr. to: Pa Music Educator Mag.; SD Bandmasters Jrnl. Mbrships: State Chmn., Coll. Band Dirs. Nat. Assn.; Life Mbr., MENC; Life Mbr. & Past Pres. (Chapt.), Phi Mu Alpha; Pi Kappa Lambda; Phi Beta Mu; Phi Kappa Phi; LeBlanc Music Educators Nat. Advsry. Bd. Recip., George Eastman Scholarship, 1951. Hobbies: Golf. Address: 204 West 4th, Mitchell, SD 57301, USA. 8.

SCHEURWATER, Marinus, b. 27 Oct. 1924. Rotterdam, Netherlands. Organist; Pianist; Choir Director; Composer; Arranger. Educ: Dip. Choir Dir., Royal League of Song & Oratorio, 1947; Dip. State Exam. Organ, 1949; Dip., State Exam. Piano, 1950: Solfége, Harmonieleer, Vormleer & Cultuurgesch, Rotterdam Conserv., 1957. m. C W F Takkebos, 2 s., 2 d. Career: Piano Tchr., 1941; Choir Dir., 1945; Organist Chr. Ref. Ch. Rotterdam, 1945-58; Organist, Dutch Ref. Ch. Berkel (Z-H), 1958-; Choir Dir., Social Service Choir, Rotterdam; Music Therapist in geriatric care. Comps. incl: 13 Choir arrs.: Jubilate omnes et cantemus amici, 1974; Uitroep, 1978; Een Waai-wind, 1978; Voorjaar, 1977: Missa in C, 1976; Gloria Patri, 7 Chorale Trios, 2 Chorale Preludes (for organ); Prelude - Invention e fugue, Suite Gymnopaedie,

Concert-Allegro (for piano). Recordings: Hij, die geen liedje zingen kan; Bleiswijk zingt. Publs: Systteem Toonladder-Voetzetting (organ), 1944; Systeem Voetzetting II (organ), 1950; Zingen en luisteren. 30 muzieklessen voor de lagere school (pupil's edition and teachers manual), 1961. Mbr., profl. orgs. Recip., num. prizes. Address: Fioringras 114, 3068 PH Rotterdam, Netherlands. 4.

SCHIBLER, Armin, b. 20 Nov. 1920. Kreuzlingen, Switz. Composer. Educ: Studies in Zürich & London, 1940-46; Inst. Ferienkurse für Neue Musik in Darmstadt, 1949-53. m. Iatana Berger, 3c. Career: Hauptlehrer für Musik an der Kantonsschule, Zürich, 1944-. Comps: Operas; Symphs.; Orchl. Works; Media in Vita (Oratorio); 5 String Quartets; Concertos for all orchl. instruments w. orch.; Works (Ballet Music) for Dance Stage; Chmbr. Music, Hörwerke, after own writings; film music; schl. music. Recordings: Drei Schweizer Orchester spielen Armin Schibler; The Point of Return; Concert pour le temps présent; Schlagzeugkonzerte; Concerto 1959; Musik zu einem imaginaren Ballet; Greina 1975; Epitaph auf einen Machtingen; Das kleine Mädchen mit den Schwefelholzchen; Concerto breve; Tatjana und Armin Schibler spielen das Konzertante Duo; Vier Schweizer Solisten spielen Armin Schibler. Publs: Texte, 1974: Werkreihe zur Musikerziehng. Address: Wolfbachstr. 33, 8032 Zürich, Switz.

SCHIDLOF, Peter, b. 9 July 1922. Vienna, Austria. Violist. Educ: Studied violin w. Prof. Max Rostal. m. Margit Olivia Ullgren, 1 d. Debut: Solo apps. on violin after 1945. Career: Violist w. Amadeus Quartet, 1948-. Recordings w. Amadeus Quartet. Mbr. ISM. Hons: OBE; Crosses Verdienstkreuz of Fed. Repub. of Germany; Crosse Verdienstkreuz für Kunst und Wissenschaft of Austria; Edison Prizes; Grand Prix du Disque; Golden Grammophon; Mozart Prize, etc. Mgmt: Ibbs & Tillet. Address: 6 Powell Close, Edgware, Middx., UK.

SCHIEBE, Ernst Friedemann, b. 18 July 1942. Budapest, Hungary. Organist; Choirmaster. Educ: German A-Prüfung for ch. musicians, 1967; Swedish exam. in Musicol., 1969; Study of Composition, Hamburg, 1970-73; German Staatsprüfung, music masters at secondary schls., 1973. m. Beate Luise Burkartsmaier. Career: Organist, Stockholm, & Staff Mbr., Lib., Royal Swedish Acad. of Music, 1967-69; Organist, Choirmaster, Aumühle, German Fed. Repub., 1969-. Compositions for organ & choir. Mbrships: Nordbischer Kirchenmusikerverband; Stockholms stifts kykomusikerförening; Gesellschaft der Orgelfreunde. Address: Alte Hege 8c, D-2055 Aumfüle, Bez. Hamburg, German Fed. Repub.

SCHIEBLER, Beverly Beasley, b. 9 May 1937. Schelbyville, Ind., USA. Violinist; Singer. Educ: AA Stephens Coll. for Women; Pvte. study, violin, w. Carl Eugene Koerner, Paul Topper; Study of voice, Valfredo Patacchi; Piano study w. Kenneth Abell. m. 1) Robert Wesley Robbins, 1 s.; 2) Carl Robert Schiebler, 1 s., 1 d. Career: Solo Violinist, quartet perfs., Ind. & Mo.; Concertmaster, Alton Civic Orch., Gate way Orch., Northwest Plaza Pops; Assoc. Prin. 2nd Violinist, St. Louis Symph.; Singer, Chatauqua Opera Co. Mbrships: Stephens Ind.; Sigma Gamma Gamma; Sigma Alpha Iota; Stephens Coll. Alumnae Assn. Hons: Schlrships., Ind. Univ. Music Clin., Egyptian Music Camp, Stephens Coll. for Women. Hobbies: Decorating; Sewing; Designing; Riding; Fencing; Singing. Address: 430 Belleview Ave., Webster Groves, MO 63119, USA.

SCHIEBLER, Carl Robert, b. 3 Dec. 1937. Medford, Mass., USA. Musician; French Horn. Educ: Univ. of Wis., study w. John Barrows; Grad., US Naval Schl. of Music. m. Beverly Anne Beasley, 2 s., 1 d. Career: Horn, 7th Army Symph. Orch., 1958-60, St. Louis Symph., 1963-; Mbr., St. Louis Brass Quintet, 1969-; Horn Instr., Webster Coll., 1965-67, Univ. of Wis. Summer Music Camp, 1968, Wash. Univ., 1972-73, St. Louis Inst. of Music, 1974; Instr., Brass Lab., 1972, '73, '74; Personnel Man., St. Louis Symph. Orch., 1977-. Recordings. w. St. Louis Symph. Contbr. to profl. jrnls. Mbrships: Chmn., St. Louis Symph. Orch. Musicians Comm.; Deleg., St. Louis Symph. Rep., Int. Conf. of Symph. & Opera Musicians, 1971, '72; Charter Mbr., In t. Horn Soc.; Orchl. Personnel Mgmt. Conf., 1978-. Hons: Arion Award, 1955. Hobby: Photography. Address: 430 Belleview Ave., Webster Grove, MO 63119, USA.

SCHIER-TIESSEN, Anneliese, b. 11 Oct. 1923. Gleiwitz, Germany. Pianist. Educ: Studied w. Prof. Richard Roessler, Berlin Hochschule fuer Musik. m. Heinz Tiessen. Debut: Soloist w. Berlin Phil Orch., 1945 (Cond. Celibidache). Career: Concert tours in Europer & Asia; Soloist w. Orchestre de la Suisse Romande (Ansermet); Ankara Phil. ORch., etc.; Broadcasts from Germany, Austria, Switzerland, Netherlands, Israel, India, etc.; Several 1st perfs. Mbrships: GEDOK; Budesfachbeirat.

Address: Argentinische Allee 32a, 1 Berlin 37, German Fed. Repub. 19.

SCHIFF, András, b. 21 Dec. 1953. Budapest, Hungary. Concert Pianist. Educ: F Liszt Acad. of Music, Budapest; Pvte. studies w. George Malcolm, Pal Kadosa & Ferenc Rados. Debut: Budapest, 1972. Career: Concerts in Europe, Am. & Far East; TV & radio apps., Hungary, Europe; radio apps., USA; Full lenght film for Japanese TV; Asst., Chmbr. Music Fac., Acad. of Music, Budapest. Recordings of works by D Scarlatti, J S Bach, Mozart, Brahms, Haydn, Beethoven, Schubert & Schumann. Hons. incl: Tchaikovsky prizewinner, Moscow 1974; Leeds Piano Competition Award, 1975; Liszt Prize, 1977. Hobbies: Art; Langs; Sports (Passive). Mgmt: Harrison-Parrott Ltd., 22 Hillgate St., London W8 7SR, UK. Address: c/o Harrison-Parrott Ltd. (as above). 30.

SCHIFF, Heinrich, b. 18 Nov. 1952. Gmunden, Upper Austria. Cellist. Educ: Dip., Vienna High Schl. for Music; pupil of Prof. Kühne & André Navarra. Debut: Vienna & London, 1972. Career: Concert tours in all countries of the world, inclng. major Fests. at Edinburgh, Salzburg, Vienna, Berlin, Warsaw & London Promenade Concerts. num. recordings. Contbr. to: Österr. Musikzeitschrifts; W Berlin Fest. Musical, 1967; Geneva, 1971; City of Vienna, 1973; Warsaw, 1975; E Berlin, 1977; Artist of the Yr. (Phono-Academy), 1978. Hobbies: Skiing; Literature; Cooking; Travelling without cello. Mgmt: Konzertdirektion Schmid, Schmiedestr. 8, Hannover, German Fed. Repub. Address: Belruptstr. 14, 6900 Bregenz, Austria.

SCHILDER, Marie, b. 26 Apr. 1903. London, UK. Concert Singer (Contralto); Artist; Teacher. Educ: Tchr. Trng. Cert., London; Concert & oratorio trng. at Vienna Acad. & Salzburg Mozarteum. m. Dr. Gustav Schilder, 1 d. Debut: Vienna. Career: Recitalist; Oratorio soloist; Symph. & radio performances in UK & European ctrs.; num. performances w. Sir Donald Tovey & the Bach Soc., Edinburgh, 1936-39; Recitals, concerts, radio & symph. performances, Canada, 1939-; Voice Fac., Dept. of Music, Univ. of BC, 1960 74; Pvte. voice tchr., specialising in Lieder, 1974-. Mbrships: Int. Soc. for Contemporary Music; Friends of Chmbr. Music, Vancouver; Coll. Music Soc. Hons: Dip., 1st Int. Comp. for Voice & Violin, Vienna, 1932; Hon. mbr., IODE, Vancouver, 1940. Hobbies: Gardening; Reading; Art collection. Address: 5612 Chancellor Blvd., Vancouver, BC, Canada V6T 1E3.

SCHILLER, Allan, b. 18 Mar. 1943. Leeds, UK. Pianist. Educ: ARCM (perfs. dip.); Moscow Conserv. m. Judith Ann Cowan, 1 s. Debut: w. Halle Orch. under Sir John Barbirolli, Leeds Town Hall, 1954. Career: Promenade concert debut, 1957; subject of Philpott File TV documentary. Recordings: Chopin & Mozart Recitals for Classics for Pleasure. Mbr., ISM. Recip. Harriet Cohen Medal, 1966. Hobbies: Billiards & Snooker. Address: 130 Etchingham Park Rd., London N3 2EN, UK. 3.

SCHILLING, Charles Walter, b. 19 Apr. 1915. Butternut, Wis., USA. Organist; Harpsichordist; Choral Director. Educ: AB, Carleton Coll., Northfield, Minn., 1936; M Sacred Mus, Union Theol. Sem., NYC, 1938; D Sacred Mus, ibid., 1954; AAGO, 1940; FAGO, 1942; Choirmaster, AGO, 1943; LTCL, 1947; FTCL, 1948. m. Sarah Elizabeth Hillyer, 2 s., 2 d. Career incls: Currently, Organist, Carillonneur, Prof. Music, Conserv. Music, Univ. of the Pacific, Stockton, Calif.; Organist & Choir Dir., 1st Congl. Ch., Stockton; Mbr., Stockton Symph. Orch. Comps: Carol; Easter Flowers. Mbr. profl. orgs. Hobbies incl: Antiques; Tropical Fish. Address: Conserv. Music, Univ. of the Pacific, Stockton, CA 95211, USA.

SCHIMMEL, William Michael, b. 22 Sept. 1946. Phila., Pa., USA. Composer; Performer; Educator; Conductor. Educ: Dip., Neubauer Conserv. of Music, Phila., Pa.; BMus, MS, DMusArts, Juilliard Schl., NYC. Career: Tchng fellowship, Juilliard Schl., theory & aural trng. 1969 & 70; Asst. Prof., Brooklyn Coll., CUNY & comp. instructor, Neubauer Conserv., currently; Perfs. w. Phila. Orch., NY Phil., Pitts. Symph.; Cond. 2 Broadway Shows. Comps: 120 works for var. mediums, incl. a one-act opera, 3 hour mass, 22 music theatre prods. Recordings: New Music for Accordion; Three Penny Opera. Publs: Fables, Accordion Solo, 1974; The Spring Street Ritual. Contbr. to: Accord Mag. (Assoc. Ed.); Accordion Arts Soc. Mag.; Am. Accordion Soc. Musicological Mag. Mbrships: Fndr. Mbr., Accordion Arts Soc.; Fellow, Intercontinental Biographical Soc. Hon: Rodgers & Hammerstein Scholarships in comp., Juilliard Schl., 1969 & '70; Tchng. fellowship, ibid, 1969, '70. Address: 242 E 89 St. Apt. 2--D, NY, NY 10028, USA.

SCHINDLER, Hollis, b. 28 Nov. 1930. Crystal Springs, Kans., USA. Organist; Early Music Concert Performer on recorders, krummhorns & guitar. Educ: BMus, Friends Univ., Wichita, Kans.; Postgrad. study, Univ. of Kans., Lawrence; AGO Cert;

study at ISOMATA, Idyllwild, Calif. Haystack Workshop. Debut: on Organ, Wichita, Kans. Career: Concert & Radio apps. in Los Angeles, Calif. Mbrships: AGO; Am. Recorder Soc.; Hymn Soc. of Am.; Am. Guild of Organists. Hobbies: Languages; Handwriting Analysis; Occult Studies. Address: 1407 N Hobart Blvd., Apt. 5, Hollywood, CA 90027, USA.

SCHINDLER, Walter, b. 21 Jan. 1909. Niederschoena, Germany. Organist; Choir Director. Educ: Ch. Music Inst., Leipzig; studied w. Prof. Hoyer, Prof. Kurt Thomas, Fritz Reuter. m. Hedwig Janssen. Career: Organist, Gartenkirche, Hannover, 1932-39; Armed Forces, Russian prisoner, 1939-45; Organist, Choirmaster Gartenkirche, Hannover, 1945-; Lectr., Ch. Music Schl., ibid. 1966-; Tchr., Acad. of Educ., Hannover, 1966-; Ldr., Heinrich Schutz Grp., & Hannover Chmbr. Orch., 1949-; Organist, Concert Tours in E Germany, Sweden, UK, Holland, Switzerland. Compositions incl: Oratorio; Orch. works; Organ works; vocal solos, choir works; Motets. Mbrhsips: German Comps. Grp.; Artists Guild; Assn. of German Music Educators & Concerts Artists; Luth. Ch. Music Soc. Hobbies: Painting; Wandering. Address: 3 Hannover, Böhmerstr. 7, German Fed. Repub.

SCHIPPERS, Thomas, b. 9 Mar. 1930. Kalamazoo, Mich., USA. Conductor; Pianist. Educ: Curtis Inst. of Music, Phila., 1945-47 (completed 4 yr. course); Yale Univ.; Juilliard Schl. of Music; studied w. Paul Hindemith & Olga Samaroff. m. Elaine Phipps. Career: regular Pianist, local radio stn., age 8; Ch. Organist & Operatic Coach, NYC; Music Supvsr., Gian-Carlo Menotti's Opera Co.; Cond. for film & TV; sometime Cond., Met. Opera Co., NY Phil. & NY City Opera; Guest Cond. w. major orchs. thru'out world; Dir., Cinn. Symph. Orch. Co-Fndr. & Dir., Spolete Fest., 1958-; Disting. Prof. of Music & Mbr. of Coll. Conserv. of Music, Univ. of Cinn., 1972-. Address: c/o Capital Records, 1750 N Vine St., Hollywood, CA 90028, USA.

SCHLECKER, Max(called Schleo), b. 2 Aug. 1930. Olten, Switzerland. Publisher; Editor; Company Executive. Educ: has studied theol., law & journalistics & biol.; studied musicol. w. Profs., Dickenmann, von Fischer & Geering, Univ. of Berne, w. Prof. Fischer, Innsbruck, w. Profs. Conradin & von Fischer, Zürich. & w. Prof Schrade, Basle; studied acrobatics, dance & choreog. w. Max Lüem, Berne; studied classical ballet w. Mrs. H Tabajdy, Berne. m. Madeleine Schelup, 2 s., 1 d. Career: Coll. Tchr., Latin & Biol.; Ed.-Reader, Francke Verlag Berne; Reader & Mng. Asst., Raber Verlag, Lucerne; Chief Ed.-Reader, C J Bucher Verlag, Lucerne; currently Publr. of music & books, Mng. Dir., Hortulus AG Publrs. & Book-& Music-Sellers, Effretikon, & Chief Ed., Schleo Press, Lucerne. Mbrships: Int. Musicol. Soc.; active, Luzerner Singer (cond. by Prof. H R Willisegger); Arbeirskreis für Musik in der Jugend; Int. Arbeitskreis für Musik; Schweiz. Verband der Musikalien-Händler und-Verleger; Arbeitskreis Spiel Musik Tan2. Hobbies: Family; Sun; Water; Dance; Luzerner Singer. Address: Bahnhofstrasse 7, CH-8307 Effretikon, Switz.

SCHLEICHER, Neil Clark, b. 21 June 1931. Kansas City, Mo., USA. Vocalists; Director; Educator; Composer; Arranger. Educ: Columbus Boy Choir Schl.; Capital Univ. Conserv. of Music, BSM; MA, Ohio State Univ. of Music, 1960. m. Mary Lou Sickler, 5c. Debut: Town Hall, NY, 1942. Career: Bass soloist, Fred Waring & the Pennsylvanians, 1960-61; musical & dramatic apps. on radio & TV, 1941-62; The Crucifixion performed, Columbus, Ohio, 1961; soloist &/or guest cond. w. Lyric Theatre, Independent Players Club, Babarleon Choral Soc. Comps: The Crucifixion (told in modern verse). Contbr. to Nat Student Musician mag. Mbrships: Bd. of Dirs., Modern Music Masters Int. Honor Soc.; Phi Mu Alpha Sinfonia; charter mbr., Epsilon Phi Chapt. Hobbies: Coach/Player, Soccer & Basketball; Chess; Contract Bridge. Address: 330 Cuba Hill Rd., Huntington, Long Island, NY, USA.

SCHLEIFER, Eliyahu Arieh, b. 8 June 1939. Jerusalem, Israel. Musicologist; French Horn Player; Cantor. Educ: Jerusalem Conserv. of Music, 1950-57; Cert. Tchr. of Music & BMus, Rubin Acad. of Music, 1960-63; Hebrew Univ., Jerusalem, 1962-64; MA & PhD, Univ. Chgo., USA. m. Aya Laipsker. Career: Cantor; Jerusalem, 1952-57; Chgo., USA, 1970-; French Horn Player; Israeli Army Orch., 1957-60; Jerusalem Symph., 1960-63; Lectr. in Music Hist., Rubin Acad of Music, Jerusalem, 1963-67; Var. radio progs. Israeli Broadcasting Auth., 1963-66. Contbr. to Notes. Mbrships: Am. Musicol. Soc.; Israeli Musicol. Soc.; Cantors Assembly of Am. Num. awards. Hobby: Hebrew & Engl. Lit. Address: 2 E Oak St., Chicago, IL 60611, USA.

SCHLEMM, Gustav Adolf, b. 1902. Giessen, Germany. Director of Music; Conductor; Pianist. Educ: studied w. Prof. Bernhard Sekles, Dr. Hoch's Conserv., Frankfurt-am-Main,

1918-23. m. Godrun Reuter, 1 s., 1 d. Career: w. Konigsberg Opera, 1923, & Mönster Theatre, 1924; Music Dir., Herford, 1929; w. Meiningen Nat. Theatre, 1931; 1st Cond., Radio Hamburg, 1935; Freelance Composer & Cond., Berlin Munich & Wetzler, 1937-. Compositions incl: 3 symphs.; Toccata con Fugue; Bermen Suite; Black Forest Masques (ballet); Joyful Overture for Large Orchestra; Sinfonia Ecclesiastica for strings; Media in Vita (oratorio); Pastorale & Scherzo for oboe & strings; Cantata on the Birth of Christ; Der kaiser, musikal Chronist in 10 Bildern. many works for chmbr. ensembles. Address: Merienstr. 4, 633 Wetzler. German Fed. Repub. 1, 28, 29.

SCHLICHTING, Fred Paul, b. 25 Apr. 1922. Minot, ND, USA. Director of Music Education. Educ: BA, Univ. of Wash., 1943: MA, Wash. State Univ., 1961; Violin & viola study w. pvte. tutors. m. Florence Claire Malmo, 3 s., 1 d. Career: Destroyer Off., USN, WWII, Pacific Theatre, 1943-46; Violist, Seattle Symph. & Tacoma Phil., 1946-47; Dir. of Orchs. & Strings, Olympia Schl. Dist., Wash., 1947-69; Supvsr. of Music, ibid., 1961-69; Dir. of Educ., Clover Pk. Schl. Dist., Wash., 1969-; Past Cond., Olympia Symph. Strings; Olympia Symph.; Olympia HS Orch.; current mbr., Tacoma Symph.; Cond., Lakes HS Orch. contbr. to: Music Educators Jrnl.; Am. String Tchr., etc. Mbrships: Phi Mu Alpha; Phi Delta Kappa; Phi Kappa Phi; Past Pres., Wash. String Tchrs. Assn.; Past Pres., Wash. Music Educators Assn.; Am. String Tchrs. Assn.; MENC; Am. Fedn. of Musicians. Hobbies: Collecting Master Violins & Bows; Hunting; Fishing. Address: 10717 Glenwood Dr. SW, Tacome, WA 98498, USA.

SCHLUMPF, Martin, b. 3 Dec. 1947. Aarau, Switzerland. Comp.; Pianist; Tchr. of theory. Educ: Piano tchr., cert., 1971; Cond.; Theory dip., 1972; Comp., Berlin. m. Agnes Schlumpf-Leuenberger. Comps. incl: 3 songs for soprano and chbr. orch.; Evocations, for 6 brass instruments, piano and percussion; Trio, for flute, viola and harp; 5 pieces for large orch.; Fragment, for solo violin and chmbr. orch.; Str. Quartet, 1975. Mbrships: Swiss Music Art Assn.; Swiss Soc. of Music Pedagogues. Hons: 1st Prize Comp. context for young comp., 1972; 1st Prize Comp. contest Concert Hall Soc., Zürich, 1974. Address: Bergstr. 49, CH 8712 Staefa, Switz.

SCHMÄLZLE, Gerhard, b. 10 Jan. 1930. Calw, Gemany. Composer. Educ: Music coll., Stuttgart; Bern conserv.; coll. of music, Berlin. m. Helga Schuldt, 1 s. Career: free-lance comp./violist in var. orchs.; ldr., "Deutche Oper" lib., Berlin, from 1974. Comps: chmbr. music; orch. works; piano works; songs; film/play music. Publs: Nine pieces for piano, 1952; Sonata for 2 violines, 1975; 4 songs after F G Lorca, 1959; 4 pieces for violin and viola, 1959: Little Suiet (orch.), 1954; Brass quintet. Mbrships: SUISA (Swiss writers' soc.). Hons: SRG prize (Swiss Radio), 1954; prize of musical summer schl., Weikersheim, 1954. Hobbies: chess. Address: D-1000 Berlin 12, Schlüterstr. 53, German Fed. Repub.

SCHMID, Erich, b. 1 Jan. 1907. Balsthal, Switzerland. Conductor. Educ: Dr. Hoch's Conserv. Frankfurt am Main, Germany, 1927-30; Master's Class, Arnold Schoenberg, Arts Acd., Berlin, 1930-31. m. Martha Stiefel, 1 s., 2 d. Career: Music Dir., Glarus, Switz., 1934-49; Cond., Tonhalle Orch., Zürich, 1949-517; Chief Cond., Radio Orch., Beromünster, Zürich, 1957 72; Ldr.; Gemischer Choir, Zürich, 1949-75; Ldr., Dir's. Class, Music Acad., Basle. Recordings: Armin Schibler, Passacaglia op. 24; Conrad Beck, Aeneas Silnus, Symph.; Kalus Huber, Des Engels Anerdüng; Rudolf Kelterborn, Elegie; Hermann Goetz; Klavierkonzert op. 18; Xaver Schnyder von Wartensee, Concerto für 2 Klarinetten und Orch., & var. others. Mbrships: Swiss Artists Guild; Pro Musica Zürich, (IGNM). Hons: Mozart Prize, Frankfurt, 1928; Arts Prize, Canton Solothurn, 1973. Address: Obere Lättenstr. 3, 8954 Geroldswil ZH, Switz.

SCHMID, Gretl, b. 8 Feb. 1910. Vienna, Austria. Musician (violin, viola); Educ: Teaching Dip., Vienna Academie, LRAM; London Acad.; Pvte. Violin Studies w. Wolfgang Schneiderhahn & Prof. Ernst Rosenberg. Career: Tchr. of Violin, Viola, Chmbr. Music, String Orchs. Mbrships: ISM; Nottingham Music Club. Hons: Prize for Most Outstanding Perf. at Music Festival, Nottingham, UK, 1974, '75, '78. Address: 71 Plains Rd., Mapperley, Nottingham NG3 5QT, UK.

SCHMID, Hans, b. 31 May 1920. Munich, Germany. Music Historian. Educ: PhD; music studies w. H W von Walterhausen. m. Hanna Auerbach. Career: Rsch. Asst., Music Hist. Seminar, Univ. of Munich, 1952-57; Asst. Prof., Univ. of Munich, 1953-; Rsch. Co-worker, Music Hist. Seminar, Univ. of Munich, 1952-57; Asst. Prof., Univ. of Munich, 1953-; Rsch. Co-worker, Music Hist. Commn., Bavarian Acad. of Scis., 1960-. Contbr. articles sto jrnls. & anthols. in field. Ed. of var. histl. documents. Mbrships: Int. Soc. for Musicol., Basle; Soc. for

Music Rsch., Kassel; Sec., Soc. for Bavarian Music Love, Munich, 1958-; Ed. of Bavarian Musical Documents, ibid. Address: Haupstr. 23, D-808 Emmering, German Fed. Repub.

SCHMID, Manfred Hermann, b. 10 Aug. 1947. Ottobeuren, Bayern. Musicologist. Educ: Abitur, Augsburg, 1967; Studium der Violine, 1965-68 R Koeckert; Magister Artium, Univ. München, 1972; PhD, ibid., 1975. m. Eva-Maria Neumer. Career: Asst., Inst. für Musikwissenschaft an der Universität München. Publications: Das Musikarchiv der Erzabtei St. Peter in Salzburg, Katalog I; L & W A Mozart, J & M Haydn, 1970; Mathias Greiter. Das Schicksal eines deutschen Musikers zur Reformationszeit, 1976; Mozart und die Salzburger Tradition, 1976. Address: Sonnblick 18, D-80818 Straussdorf, German Fed. Repub.

SCHMID, Oscar, b. 14 June 1936. Aarau, Switz. Pianist. Educ: studied w. Geza Hegyi, Zürich; pedagogical & soloist dips.; master courses w. Geza Anda. m. Hanny Loosli, 2 s. Debut: Berne, 1956. Career: concerts throughout the World; apps. at many music fests; TV & radio broadcasts, Switz. & Italy. Mbrships: Schweizerischer Tonkstlerverein; Schweizerischer Musikpaedagogischer Verband. Recip. medals & dips., Concorso internazionale pianistico Ettore Pozzoli, Seregno (Italy), 1963, '65, 67. Hobbies: Fine arts; Italian opera. Address: Landhaus 252A, CH-3055 Suberg, Switz. 28, 30.

SCHMIDBAUER, Hans-Benno, b. 23 Aug. 1934. Munich, Germany. Pianist. Educ: Musicol., Univ. of Munich, (Georgiades) & Innsbruck, (Zingerle); Piano studies w. Kurt Arnold (Munich), Byrnell Figler (St. Louise USA) & Julian v Karolyi (Munich). m. Dr. Walburga Schmidbauer, 2 d. Debut: Munich. Career: var. concert tours in Europe; Own tone studio specializing in piano & chmbr. music recordings. Recordings incl: Piano Sonata op. 37 (Tschaikowsky); Fledermausparaphrase, Künstlerleben, Wein, Weib und Gesang (Strauss-Godowsky); Hungarian Rhapsody Nr. 12 (Liszt); La Válse (Ravel); Diabelli-Variationen op. 120 (Beethoven); Tarantella di Bravura (Liszt). Mbr., Die Musikforschung. Hobbies: Skiing; Visiting ice hockey games. Address: Goethestr. 11, 8023 Pullach, German Fed. Repub.

SCHMID-GAGNEBIN, Ruth, b. 5 Mar. 1921. Neuchatel, Switz. Pianist. Educ: 1st Dip., SMPV, Zürich; studied w. J Blanchard & Yeves Nat. Paris, France; Gt. Dip., Masterclass of Dinu Lipatti, Geneva Conserv. of Music. m. Pierre Schmid, 2 children. Debut: Rome. Career incls: num. Solo apps. at concerts in Italy, Belgium, France, UK, Switz., etc. also many broadcasts for Radio Suisse Romande, ORTF, Radio Italian, etc. Recordings incl: Liszt, Grand Etudes after Paganini; Debussy, Poissons D'or, La danse de Puck, Clair de lune, Feux d'artifice. Contbr. to musical publs. Mbrships. incl: Assn. of Swiss Musicians; Schweizerischer Musikpädagigischer Verband (SMPV); Assn. Pro Musici. Address: CH-2500 Bienne 23, Marche-Neufe, Switz.

SCHMIDT, Christian Martin, b. 10 Nov. 1942. Dessau, Germany. Musicologist; Chief Administrator for Arnold Schönberg's Complete Works. Educ: Dip., d'execution orgue, Ecole Normale de Musique, Paris; studied theory of music, French & Latin, Hamburg, Tübingen, Göttingen & Berlin; Dr phil, Free Univ. of Berlin, 1970. m. Beate-Gabriela Schmitt. Publs: Verfarhren der motivisch-thematischen Vermittlung in der musik von Johannes Brahms, 1970; A Schönberg Sämtliche Werke A Band: Wake für Orgel, Klavier zu vier Händen, zwei Klaviere zu vier Hämden, 1973, Reihe B Band 5: Werke für Orgel etc., 1973, Reihe A Band 19: Späte Chorwerke, 1975. Contbr. to profl. publs. Address: 1 Berlin 45, Margaretenstr. 18b, Germany.

SCHMIDT, Dale, b. 18 Feb. 1942. Cleveland, Ohio, USA. Bass Player. Educ: BMus Ed, Baldwin-Wallace Coll.; Advanced study, Eastman Schl. of Music. Career: Prin. Bass Player, Atlanta Symph. Orch. Hobby: Spiritual Growth. Address: 1168 St. Louis Pl. NE, Atlanta, GA 30306, USA.

SCHMIDT, Hans, b. 1 Sept. 1930. Bonn, W Germany. Musicologist; Lectr. Educ: Univ. Bonn; Univ. Cologne; Doct. Univ. Bonn, 1954; Lectr. 1974, Univ. Hamburg. m. Gudrun Schmidt Seiwert, 3 d. Career: Beethoven lects. in Europe Canada, USA; Sci. co-operator Beethoven archives, Bonn; Sci. ldr. Beethoven House Bonn; Sci. adivser films and TV serials; Private lectr. Hamburg Univ. Recordings: Many explanatory texts to var. records. Publs. incl: Beethoven rsch.; Gregorian and Byzantyne Music; Catalogue of Beethoven Sketches, Bonn, 1964. Contbr. to: Austrian Music Mag.; Beethoven Annual; Music Rsch.; Bonn Univ. Mags. Adress: Klausenbergweg 6a,54 Koblenz-Ehrenbreitstein, German Fed. Repub.

SCHMIDT, Kenneth Julius, b. 23 Aug. 1923. New Orleans, LA, USA. Flute soloist. Educ: La. State Univ.; BM, Loyola Univ., 1950; Dip. Flute, Juilliard Schl. of Music, 1953. m. Fumi Akimoto, 1 child. Debut: Flute recitals, New Orleans, 1950. Career: Apps. w. orchs. inclng: New Orleans Phil. Symph. Orch.; Broolyn Phil Orch.; New Orleans Opera Co.; NYC Opera Co.; Met. Opera House Orch.; Apps. on ABC TV, NBC, CBS; Many Broadway shows; Improvised music for films & TV commercials. Comps. incl: Symph. for Brass, 1953; Quartet for Soprano Voice, 1953. Recordings w. all maj. cos. in USA. Mbrships: Delta Kappa Psi; Alpha Sigma Nu; US Chess Fedn. Hobbies: Chess; Jogging. Address: 212 W 14th St. New York, NY 10011, USA.

SCHMIDT, Liselotte Martha, b. 18 Mar. 1933. W Reading, Pa., USA. College Professor; Musicologist; Pianist; Harpsichordist;k Organist. Educ: BMus, Converse Coll.; Piano, Univ. Mich. Schl. Music; Piano, Juilliard Schl. Music; MA, musicol., NY Univ. Grad. Schl. Arts & Sci.; PhD work ibid.; MMus, Manhattan Schl. Music; Fulbright Schlr., musicol., Univ. Munich, Germany; EdD, Columbia Univ. Career incls: Prof., Music Hist. & Lit. & Dept. Chmn., Schl. Music, W Chester State Coll.; Piano, harpsichord & organ recitalist. Publs. incl: Musical Works of Jachet Berchem, 10 vols., in preparation. Mbr. num. profl. orgs. Hons. incl: Hyatt Prize, composition, Converse Coll., 1953; Schlrships. & rsch. grants. Hobbies incl: Travel; Knitting. Address: 8 Cedarwood Rd., Wyomissing, PA 19610, USA. 27.

SCHMIDT, Lloyd John, b. 6 Dec. 1924. Appleton, Wis., USA. Music Consultant. Educ: BMusEd, Chgo Musical Coll.; MMus, Northwestern Univ. Schl. Music; PhD, Northwestern Univ. Grad. Schl.; Grad., USN Schl. Music m. Marilyn Jean Schmidt, 3 s. Career incls: Music Cons., Conn. State Dept. Educ.; French Horn concerto soloist w. sev. symph. orchs.; Chmbr. & solo recitalis, French Horn & Recorder, USA & Germany. Publs: Booklets for Conn. State Dept. Educ.; Filmstrips. Contbr. to profl. publs. Mbr. & off var. orgs. Recip: Presidential Coun. 'Projs. to Adv. Creativity' Award, 1969. Hobbies: Boating; Sports. Address: 31 Ball Hill Rd., Storrs, CT 06268, USA.

SCHMIDT, Ole, b. 14 July 1928. Copenhagen, Denmark. Conductor; Composer; Pianist. Educ: Royal Acad. of Music. Copenhagen, 1947-55. m. Lizzie Rode, 2 d. Debut: As Comp. & Cond., 1955. Career: Employed by Royal Opera, Copenhagne, 1958-65, as Cond., then freelancing, 1970-71; Chief Cond., Hamburger Sinfoniker, 1971-73; Copenhagen Radio Orch.; currently Freelance Cond. Comps: Raxallo for Brass Quintet, 1974: Toccatas Nos. 1 & 2 for Accordeon. Recordings: Carl Nielsen, 6 Symphs., w. LSO, 1974; Westergard, Cello Concerto, 1975. Mbrships: Danish Comps. Soc. KODA; GRAMEX. Hons: Carl Nielsen Prize, 1975: Gramex Prize, 1975. Hobbies: Composing; Cooking; Teaching; Family Life. Mgmt: Clarion Agcy Ltd., London, UK; Wilhelm Hansen, Copenhagen. Address: Standgade 36, 1, 1401 Copenhagen K, Denmark.

SCHMIDT, William, 6 Mar. 1926. Chgo., Ill., USA. Composer. Educ: BMus, MMus, Univ. of Southern Calif. m. Sharon Davis, 2 d., 1 s. Comps: 86 works publ. 25 works recorded. Mbrships: ASCAP; Pi Kappa Lambda. Hobbies: Photography; Backpacking. Address: 2859 Holt Ave., Los Angeles, CA 90034, USA.

SCHMIDT, Yves Rudner, b. 9 June 1933. Taubaté, Sao Paulo, Brazil. Professor; Composer; Lawyer. Educ: Law studied; Dramatic & Musical Acd., Sao Paulo; Escola Superior de Musica Santa Marcelina, ibid.; & in Lisbon & Hamburg. div. Debut: Taubaté, 1942. Career: State Tchr. Sao Paulo, & Tchr., Music Fac., Marcelo Tupinambá, ibid.; music for 2 Films; Children's theatre; TV & radio perfs. & concerts, Brazil, Latin Am. & Europe. Compositions: 68 piano pieces edited; 3 choral works; var. pieces for piano, voice & var. instruments. Publ: Brasil, Folclore para Turistas, 1963. Contbr. to num. newspapers, reviews, mags., Brazil & Argentina. Mbr., profl. assns. Hons. incl: Prizes for Music, 1967, & Comp., 1973, Prefecture of Taubaté. Hobbies: Travel; Theology; Folklore. Address: Rua Major Sertório 693 apt. 131, Sao Paulo, Brazil.

SCHMIDT-BOELCKE, Werner, b. 28 July 1903. Berlin, Germany. Conductor. Educ: Sternsch Conserv. m. Claire Carriola, 5 s. Career: Concert pianist, 1920-24; 1923-26, Theatre cond., Berlin; 1929-28, Theater cond., München 1928-30; Chief cond. 50 Emelka Theaters in Berlin; since 1928, concerts w. Berlin Radio; 1929, Vis., cond. New York, study trip USA; 1929-34, cond., comp. 57 sound pictures Berlin, München, Paris, Prag; 1934-44, Chief cond. var. theaters Berlin, Dresden; Vis. cond. Düsseldorf, Hamburg, Leipzig, München, Berlin Radio; 1940: Cond. 1st TV operette live broadcast; 1944-45 Military Service w. State Radio Berlin; 1945-46, Dir. light music Radio Hamburg; 1947. Cond. Radio

München; since 1947 vis. cond., pianist. Hons: Federal Merit Cross, 1974. Address: unterbrunnenstr. 46 1/2, 8035 Gauting, German Fed. Repub.

SCHMIDT-SCHEEPMAKER, Ernestine Augusta, b. 8 Sept. 1895. The Hague, The Netherlands. Concert Singer (Mezzo soprano); Teacher of Singing & Piano. Educ: Tchr. grade singing & piano, Koninklijk Conserv., The Hague, 1919; Solo grade singing, 1921; repertoire study; w. Charles Panzéra, Paris. m. Dr. W J Schmidt. Debut: w. Residente Orchestra, in Beethoven Fantaise, 1919. Career: (opera) Title-role, Carmen, Trovatore -Azucena, Soezoeki in Butterfly, Mother Lucia in Cavalleria; Guest at French Opera, at Paris Walkure, Grand Opera, Paris; w. Opera Gent as Amneris (Aida); Many radio song recitals w. well-known artists; Cond. womens choirs at The Hague & Boskoop; Soloist w. Arnhem Orkest Vereniging (Jaap Spaanderman), etc. Mbr., Koninklijke Nederlandse Toonkunstenaar-svereninging. Hobbies: Reading philos. & musical works; Cycling; Swimming. Address: Zinzendorflaan 11, Zeist, The Netherlands.

SCHMIEDEL, Gottfried, b. 24 Aug. 1920. Schmiedeberg, Dresden, DDR. Musicologist. Educ: Conserv. Dresden, Choirmaster, TD, piano, song, theor. Career: Music tchr. Dresden; Lectr. Dresden; Radio, film work. Mbrships: Assn. of Comp. and Musicologists, DDR; Assn. for Journalists, DDR; Cultural Soc. DDR. Publ. incl: A Portrait for You; Kreuz choir Dresden, Leipzig, 1977; A Portrait for You: Benjamin Britten, Leipzig, 1977; Peter Schreier, A Filmstrip, Berlin 1977. Contbr. to: num. newspapers and profl. jrnls.; Lectures with records and concert introductions. Hobbies: Lit.; Beautiful scenery; Enjoying Cats and Dogs. Address: 1 Box 189-70, Zweiter Steinweg 1, Dresden, 8054, German Dem Repub.

SCHMITT, Beate Gabriela, b. 16 May 1949. Berlin, Germany. Flautist. Educ: Music Acad. Tech. Univ. W Berlin. Music Acad. Hamburg 1968-72; Dip, flute; 1972-74 Music Acad. Hamburg, concert exam; m. Dr. Christian Martin Schmidt. Career: Since 1965 concerts W Germany, Europe; Prod. w. var. German, Polish Broadcasting Companies; BBC; TV Prod. Comp: Dev. new wind techniques; many joint works; improvisation groups; projects w. writers and painters to dev. correlation between Arts. Recordings: Record cycles, Opus Musicum, The New Music and its Historical Predecessors, The New Music and its Latest Dev.; Docuementation record 2 of the German Acad. Villa Massimo Rome. Mgmt: Concert dir. Robert Kullitsch, Geisbergstr. 40, 1000 Berlin 30. Hons: 1st Prize Youth and Music, 1965; Scholarship Study Org. of the German People. Hobbies: Lit.; Psychol.; Sport. Address: Margaretenstr. 18b, 1000 Berlin 45, Germany.

SCHMITT,(Sister) Cecilia, OSF, b. 27 Mar. 1928. Rice, Minn., USA. Music Educator. Educ: BA, St. Catherine's Coll., St. Paul, Minn.; MA, Univ. of Minn.; doctoral studies at Univ. of Ill., Urbana, Ill. Career: Tchr., Rschr., Lectr. & Writer; Cath. Sister & Mbr. of the Franciscan Order. Publ: Rapport & Success in Education, 1976. Contbr. to: Music Eduators Jrnl.; Keyboard Arts; Instrumentalist. Mbrships: Nat. Consortium for Humanizing Educ. (Dir.); NGPT (former Dist. Chmn.); Minn. MTA (former Dist. Chmn.); Organ & Piano Tchrs. Assn. Hobby: Research in the Correlation between Music Education & Psychology. Addresss: St. Francis High School, Little Falls, MN 56345, USA. 5.

SCHMITT, Homer Carl Christian, b. 23 June 1911. Cleveland, Ohio, USA. Violinist; Violist; Pianist; University Professor. Educ: Western Reserve Univ., Cleveland; BMus, Cleveland Inst. Music; studied Violin, Piano, Comp. & Theory w. var. tchrs. Debut: Cleveland, 1933. Career incls: Instr. of Violin, Cleveland Inst. Music, 1933-46; Mbr., Cleveland Symph. Orch., 1936-46; Prof. of Violin, Univ. of Ill., Urbana, 1947-; 1st Violinist, Walden Str. Quartet, num. tours US & Europe, inclng. German Fed. Republic for US State, Dept., 1949; Concertmaster, Champaign-Urbana Symph. Orch., & Springfield, Ill., Symph. Orch. Recordings w. Walden Str. Quartet of works by Bergsma, Ives & num. other contemporary comps. Mbr., profl. assn. Recip. var. scholarships. Hobby: Writing Poetry. Address: 401 W High St, Urbana, IL 61801, USA.

SCHMITT, Meinrad, b. 21 Dec. 1935. Wasserburg am Inn, Germany. Professor for Theory of Music. Educ: Study of Comp. Comps. incl: (Orchl.) Canzonaccia; Ikarus; H-a-d-es; Chmbr. Concerto for oboe, horn,l bassoon & strings; (Opera) Der Spielhansl; (Chmbr. Music) 2 Quintets for wind instruments; Chorideon, for flute, violoncello & piano; Incontro, for soprano, flute, clarinet & percussion; Fantasia piccola, for string quartet; Trio for trumpet, trombone & tuba. Recordings: Am. Ende des Regenbogens. Mbrships: Official, German Comps. Guild. Hons: Richard Strauss Scholarship, Munich, 1963; Comp. Prize, Stuttgart, 1969; Kuhlau Comp. Prize, Ülzen, 1970; Comp.

Prize, Marl, 1971. Address: Bahnhofstr. 46, D8031 Gröbenzell b. München, German Fed. Repub.

SCHMITZ, Claude M, b. 24 Apr. 1919. Denver, Colo. , USA. Singer; Chairman, Department of Voice; Opera Producer, Conductor, Director; Choral Conductor; Teacher; Adjudicator. Educ: BA, MA, Doct. candidate, Univ. of N Colo., Ind. Univ., Colo. Univ. m. Anna N Slevin, 2 d. Debut: Denver Grand Opera Co., 1937; Ctrl. City Opera Co., 1938. Career: Profl. Singer-Actor, opera, pub. perfs. in concert, 1937-49; Mbr. of Teaching Staff, Univ. of Colo., 1949-; Fndr., Dir. & Prod., Opera Theatre, 1954; Fndr., Dir., Choral-Aires, Univ. of N Colo., 1955. Mbrships. incl: Nat. Chapt., Nat. Assn. of Tchrs. of Singing, 1951-; Pres., 2 terms. Hons. incls: Blue Key; Outstanding Fac. Mbr., Univ. of N Colo., 1957-58. Hobbies: Photography; Hiking; Travel. Address: 2022-24th Street Rd., Greeley, CO 80631, USA.

SCHMITZ, Hans-Peter, b. 5 Nov. 1916. Breslau, Germany. Professor; Flautist; Musicologist. Educ: PhD, Univ. of Halle; Grad., Flute, Conserv. of Music, Berlin. m. Gisela Fischer (dec.), 2 c. Career: Solo Flautist, Berlin Phil., 1943-50; Concert, Radio & Recording Perfs. publishing activities; Lectr., Northwest German Music Acad., Detmold, 1953-72; State Conserv. of Music, Berlin, 1971-. Recordings: Eterna. Publs. incl: Flötenlehre, 1955; Prinzipien der Aufführungspraxis Alter Musik, 1950; Querflöte & Querflötenspiel in Deutschland wahrend des Barockzeitalters, 1952; Singen & Spielen, 1958; Über die Wiedergabe der Musik Johann Sebastian Bach, 1951: Verteidigung des Dirigenten, 1957; Ed., J J Quantz, Versuch einer Anweisung ..., 1953. Contbr. to num. profl. jrnls. Mbrships: German Music Coun.; German Academic Cultural Exchange Soc.; German Musical Life Fndn.'s Soc. for Music Rsch.; Int. Musicol. Soc. Recip. Silver Medal, Int. Music Competition, Vienna, 1938. Address: Scabellstrasse 12, D 100 Berlin 39, German Fed. Repub. 19.

SCHMITZ, Hans Wolfgang, b. 20 May 1928. Cologne, Germany. Chorus Master; Conductor; Pianist; Lecturer. Educ: Pvte. study, musical theory; Comp. w. Hermann Unger; Piano w. Karl Delseit; Nat. Acad. of Music, Cologne (Cond. w. Peter Hammers). Debut: Four Seasons (Vivaldi), Opera House Wuppertal, 1953. Career: Co-Tutor, Cond., Opera House Wuppertal, 1953-58; Asst. Chorus Master, Opera House Cologne, 1958-60; Chorus Master, Cond., ibid, 1960; Hd. of Opera Schl. & Opera-Chorus-Schl., Lectr. for Chorus Dir., Nat. Acad. of Music, Cologne, 1958-75. Hobby: Music. Address: Hermann-Löns-Strasse 2, D-5000 Cologne 51, German Fed. Repub.

SCHNABEL, Karl Ulrich, b. 6 Aug. 1909. Berlin, Germany. Concert Pianist; Piano Teacher. Educ: Studied w. Leonid Kreutzer, State Acad. of Music, Berlin, 1922-26; studied Comp. & Conducting, ibid, 1922-28. m. Helen Fogel, 1 d. Debut: Berlin, 1926. Career: Appearances in Germany, Austria, UK; London debut, 1931; Concert tours of European countries inclng. Russia, 1933-39; First USA tour 1937; Fac. Mbr., Dalcroze Schl. of Music, NYC, 1938; Hd. of Instrumental Depts., ibid, 1940; Duo appearances w. Helen Fogel, inclng. Holland Festival 1956 & Edinburgh Festival UK 1972; 1939-. Hd. of electronic lab., Mass., USA WWII; Concert tours, USA & Europe, 1945-; Has given Annual Int. Summer Master Courses, Lake Como, Italy, 1947-; num. other Master Courses, 1948-; First concert appearances in Can. 1948, Brazil 1951, Sweden & Norway 1958, Aust. & NZ 1971; Num. perfs. UK, 1951-; Annual perfs., Am. West Coast, 1955-. Recordings: Works of major Comps. inclng. Bach, Mozart, Schumann, Chopin, Liszt, 1931-. Publs: Moder Technique of the Pedal; eds. of Schubert & Weber. Hobbies: Photography; Rock-climbing. Mgmt: Ibbs & Tillet, London, UK. Address: 305 West End Ave., NY, NY 10023, USA.

SCHNEIDER, Hans, b. 23 Feb. 1921. Eichstatt, Bavaria, W Germany. Music Antiquarian; Music Publisher. Educ: Acad. of Music; Univ. Mbrships. incl: Int. Assn. of Music Sci.; Am. Musicol. Soc.; AIBM; Musical Rsch. Assn.; Music Lib. Assn. Address: Mozartweg 4, D 8132 Tutzing, German Fed. Repub.

SCHNEIDER, Laura, b. 19 Sept. 1947. Sacramento, Calif., USA. French Horn Player. Educ. incls: Cleveland Inst. of Msuic, 1966-67; BA, Calif. State Univ., 1970. Career: Prin. Horn, Charlotte Symph. Orch. & Charlotte Chmbr. Orch., Mbr., Charlotte Symph. Woodwind Quintet, 1971-. Mbrships: Int. Horn. Soc.; Charlotte Musicians Assn., local 342, Am. Fedn. of Musicians; Phi Kappa Phi. Hobbies:Hiking; Embroidery; Reading. Address: 3420 Park Rd., Charlotte, NC 28209, USA.

SCHNEIDER, Melvin Frederick, b. 7 Mar. 1904. Lark, Wis., USA. Teacher. Educ: Lawrence Coll., 1922-26; BMus, 1930, MA, 1948, Univ. of Wis.; studied Violin & Piano w. var. masters. m. Naomi J Manshardt. Career incls: Dir. of

Instrumental Music, Neenah High Schl., Wis., 1925-27, S Beloit High Schl., Ill., 1930-32, & Oregon High Schl., Wis., 1932-34; Wis. Dells High Schl., 1934-37; Prairie Du Sac High Schl., 1937-40; Rsch. in Music Educ., Univ. of Wis., 1940-45, & Univ. of Northern Iowa, 1945-60; Independent Rsch. in Music Educ., 1960-. Publs: Music for Every Child, 1947; Tchrs. Manual & Student boos. Contbr. to musical & other jrnls. Mbrships incl: MENC; MTA. Hobby: Restoring Stringed Instruments. Address: 1615 Merner Ave., Cedar Falls, IA 50613, USa. 3, 12.

SCHNEIDER, Richard Stanley, b. 11 Sept. 1952. Gillette, Wyo., USA. French Horn Player. Educ: BMus Ed., Ctrl. State Univ., Okla., 1974; MMus, Ind. Univ., 1976; Perf. Cert., Nordwest Deursch Musikakademie, 1978; studied horn w. Philip Farkas. Career: Soloist, Ponca City High Schl. Orch., 1970-74; Soloist, Central State Univ. Orch., 1970-74; Extra w. Okla. City Symph. Orch., 1971-73; Studio work, Bensen's Sound Studio, Okla. City, 1974; Ind. Univ. Phil. & Opera Orch., 1975-76; Nordwest Deutsch Musikakademie Orch., 1976-78; Tibor Varga Kammerorchester & Deutsche Bach Solisten 1976-78; Mbr., Hamburg Symph., 1978. Mbrships: Int. Horn Soc.; Phi Mu Alpha (Pres., Kappa Tau Chapt., 1973-74); Alpha Chi; Kappa Delta Pi. Hons: J P Sousa Band Awad, 1970; Nat. Schl. Orch. Assn. Award, 1970. Hobbies incl: Scouting & Camping; Climbing; Sky-Diving; Sailing; Swimming. Address: 2417 N W 112th Terr., Okla. City, OK 73120, USA.

SCHNEIDER, Urs, b. 16 May 1939. St. Gallen, Switz. Conductor. Educ: Violin Dip., Zürich Conserv., 1961; Cond. w. Rafael Kubelik, Igor Markevitch & Otto Klemperer. Debut: Aged 15, w. own orch. Career: Fndr., Cond. & Artistic Dir., Ostschweizer Kammerorchester, 1962-; Guest Cond., USA, 1962-; Musical Dir., Camerata Stuttgart, 1968-; Musical Dir., Camerata Academica Salzburg, 1971-73; concerts, operas, radio & TV, Europe, USA, S Am., Australia Africa & Asia; Guest Cond., num. major orchs. Recordings: 15 records. Mbrships: Swiss Musicians Assn.; Schweiz. Berufsdirigenten-Verband. Hons: Cultural Prize, City of St. Gallen, 1967; Master of Fine Arts Int., NY, 1969. Hobbies: Sports; Keep fit; History; Reading; Langs. Mgmt: Christian Lange, Baraislweg 23, D-8132 Tutzing, German Fed. Repub. Address: Gatterstr. 1b, CH-9010 St. Gallen, Switz.

SCHNEIDER, Urs Peter, b. 14 Feb. 1939. Bern. Switz. Composer; Pianist; Piano Teacher; Ensemble Leader. Educ: Dip., Piano Tchng., 1961, Concert Pianist, 1962, Bern & 1965, Cologne. m. Erika Radermacher, 2 s. Career incl: Ldr., Ensemble Neue Horizonte Bern; Mbr., sev. improvisation gps; Concerts & broadcasts all over Europe. Comps. played & broadcast all over Europe. Comps. incl: Raritäten, 1971; Sechs Partien, 1972; Hohe Lieder, 1975; Senfkorn, 1975; Spazieren mit Robert Walser, 1976; Vier Kleine Mysterien, 1977; Siblerlinge, 1977; Liederbuch für Erika, 1979; (Publs.) Babel; kirchweih cycle; Mundwerk; (recorded) Zwei Lieder Verschleiertes; Sechs Lieder; Zeitraum. Recordings: Duette (from Byrd to Cage), 1975; Intime Musik (by Ensemble Neue Horinzonte), 1978. Mbrships: incl: Artistic Mbr., Neue Horizonte Concert Soc., Bern. Publs: Ein Buch, 1971; Noten, 1974. Contbr. to profl. jrnls. Recip., var. hons. Hobbies incl: Wife & sons. Address: Tessenbergstr. 45, CH 2505 Biel, Switz.

SCHNEIDER-CUVAY, Maria Michaela Olga, b. 8 Sept. 1933. Zagreb, Yugoslavia. Pianist; Musicologist. Educ: Univs. of Vienna & Salzburg; PhD, 1975; Dip. Piano, Stattliche Hochschule, Munchen; Mozarteum, Salzburg. m. Josef Schneider, 1 d. Career: Pianist w. Die Salzburger Mozartspieler; Concert tours in France, Spain, Italy, W & E Germany, Austria, Yugoslavia, Netherlands, Belgium, Denmark, Sweden, Hungary; Asst. Prof., Mozarteum, Salzburg & Salzburg Music Schl. Recordings w. Amadeo. Publs. incl: Salzburger Landeskunde, 1955. Contbr. to num. profl. mags. Recip. Osterreichischer Staatspreis, 1956. Hobbies: Gardening; Swimming. Mgmt: Hans Schlote. Address: 5020 Salzburg, Hans Pfitznerstrasse 17, Austria.

SCHNEIDERHAN, Wolfgang, b. 28 May 1915. Austria. Violinist. Educ: studies w. Julius Winkler & Ottokar Sevcik. m. Irmgard Seefried. Career: Prof., Mozarteum, Salzburg, 1936-56, Music Acad., Vienna, 1939-50, Lucerne Conserv., 1949-; Ldr., master classes. Address: Reckenbuhlstr. 20, Lucerne, Switz. 16.

SCHNEIDERMANN, Dina, b. 28 March 1931. Odessa, USSR. Violinist. Educ: Leningrade State Conserv.; Moscow State Conservatoire. m. Prof. Emil Kamilarov, 1 s. Career: First Prizes at many violin competitions; Mbr. of jury of many competition; State Artist, Bulgarian Chmbr. Orch. Recordings: all Beethoven sonata for Piano & Violin; Brahms & Beethoven concertos; Mozart sonatas, etc. Hons: 1st Prize, III Youth Fest., Berlin,

1951; 1st Prize, Int. Violin Competition, Geneva, 1960; Ysaye Fndn. Prize, 1967; Artist emeritus Bulgaria, 1961; Prix Dimitroff, Ordre Cyrille & Méthode, 1963. Address: ul Petko Enev 47 A, 1126 Sofia, Bulgaria.

SCHNITZLER, Michael, b. 7 Aug. 1944. Berkeley, Calif., USA. Leader of the Vienna Symph. Orch.; Member of the Haydn Trio. Educ: Vienna Acad. of Music. m. Ingeborgh Schnitzler, 1s. Career: Vienna Soloists, 1962-67; violin & chmbr. music classes, Hochschule für Musik, Graz., 1967-73; Schnitzler Quarter (Gesellschaft der Musikfreunde series, Vienna), 1971-76; Mbr., Haydn Trio, 1965-; Ldr., Vienna Symph., 1967-; Solo apps. under Giulini, Sawallisch, Jocum, etc. Recordings: Haydn Trio under contract w. Telefunken-Decca. Hobbies: Mtn. climbing; Photography; Mineral & autograph collects.; French wines; Cooking. Address: Sternwartestr. 58, 1180 Vienna, Austria.

SCHNORR, Klemens, b. 22 May, 1949. Amorbach, German Fed. Repub. Organist; Music Historian; Organ expert. Educ: Music Acad., München, 1968/1976, State exam Cath. Ch. Music, 1973, Organ, 1974; München Univ., MA Musicol. 1974. m. Annarosa Schnorr-Nicca, 1 d. Career: Concerts in Germany, Austria, Italy, Switz., Spain; TV prod. w. ARD; many Radio recordings; Tchr. at Music Acad. Munich, 1978. Hons: 2nd Prize, Int. Organ Competition, Avila, Spain, 1973; 1st Prize, Int. Organ Competition, Bologna, Italy, 1975; 2nd Prize, ARD Competition, München, Germany, 1975; 2nd prize, Arnhem, Netherlands, 1976. Address: Siebenbürgenerstr. 15, D-8000 München 70, German Fed. Repub.

SCHOCK, Rudolf, b. 9 Apr. 1915. Duisburg, Germany. Concert & Opera Tenor. m. Gisela Behrends, 2 d. Career: in Opera Choir, Duisburg, 1933-37; leading parts, State Theatre, Brauschweig, 1937-40, German Opera House, Berlin, 1940-43, Opera House, Hannover, 1945-46, State Opera, Berlin, 1946-48; apps. in opera houses in Vienna, Hamburg, Munich, London; participant in Salzburg & Edinburgh fests.; Aust. tour, 1949; TV & radio broadcasts; appeared in film on own life, You are the World for Me, 1953. Recorded for Opera, Gramaphone Records. Hons: Court Singer, Fed. Ministry, Vienna, 1957; German Sports Badge, Gold, 1961. Address: Almeidaweg 7, Starnberg Oberbayern, German Fed. Repub. 2.

SCHOENSTEDT, Friedrich Wilhelm Arno, b. 12 Sept. 1913. Sondershausen Thuringia. Church Musician; Professor of organ & harpsichord. Educ: Dip. ch. music, Hochschule für Musik, Leipzig, 1937; Studied w. Prof. Gunther Ramin, Prof. Joh. Nep. David, Prof. C A Martienssen, ibid. m. Ursula Muff, 2 s., 1 d. Career: Cantor & Organist, St. Matthaw, Leipzig, 1938; Organist, St. Thomae, Leipzig, 1945; Organist, Münster Cathedral of Herford/Westphalian, 1947; Instr. in Organ, Westphalian Ch. Music Schl., Herford; Ch. Music Dir., ibid, 1948; Prof., 1974; Recordings on radio stns. in Europe, USA, Canada, Japan Australia. Recordings w. var. cos. Author of Alte Westfalische Orgeln. Contbr. to Kirchen musik & var. jrnls. Hons: Dr. h.c. of Mus Arts, Wartburg Coll., Waverly, Iowa, USA. Mbrships: Bach Soc.; Schutz Soc.; Soc. of Organ Friends. Hobbies: Travel; Photography; Philately. Address: Stresemannweg 13, 4900 Herford, German Fed. Repub.

SCHOEP, Arthur Paul, b. 13 Dec. 1920. Orange City, Iowa, USa. Musician. Educ: BFA Summa cum laude, Univ. of SD, 1942; Perf. Cert. in Voice, Eastman Schl. of Music, & MusM, Univ. of Rochester, NY, 1945; Artist's Dip., New England Conserv. of Music, 1948: study in Netherlands, 1950-51; DMus Arts, Univ. of Colo., 1962. m. Donna Swainey Philbrick, 1s. Career: Leading Roles, Goldovsky Opera Theatre, 1946-69; Guest Artist, Theatre de la Monnaie, Brussels, Belgium, 1955; Artistic Dir., Denver Lyric Theatre, Colo., USA, 1961-67; Leading roles, num. civic opera cos., USA; Soloist w. num. symph. orchs. inclng. Boston Symph., Rotterdam Phil., Netherlands; Recitals, Netherlands & Germany; Radio perfs., oratorio perfs., Netherlands; currently Prof. of Music, N Tex. State Univ., Denton. Publs. incl: Word-by-word Translations of Songs & Arias (w. D Harris), Part II, Italian, 1972; Bringing Soprano Arias to Life (w. B Goldovsky), 1973. Contbr. to profl. jrnls. Mbrships incl: Nat. Opera Assn. (Pres. 1972, 1973). Recip., Fulbright Scholarship, 1950-51. Hobbies: Photography; World Travel. Address: 1705 Emery Dr., Denton, TX 76201, USA. 2. 7.

SCHOLLUM, Robert, b. 22 Aug. 1913. Vienna, Austria. Pianist; Organist; Composer; Choirmaster. Educ: studied piano, organ, ch. music, conducting, comp., New Vienna Conserv. & Vienna Acad. of Music. 1 s. Career incls: Cond., Organist, Choral Dir., Lectr. on Musicol., 1933-; Tcrh., Vienna HS for Music, 1959-. Comps. incl: Symphs. 1-5; Kontraste for orch.; Konturen for str. orch; Gespräche for chmbr. orch.; var. works for chmbr. ensembles; Psalmkomentare for chorus, 2 pianos.

percussion; etc. Publs. incl: Musik in der Volksbildung, 1961; Egon Wellesz, 1964: Die Wiener Schule, 1968; Singen als menschliche Kundgebung, 1970; Das kleine Wiener Jazzbuch, 1970. Contbr. to profl. jrnls. Mbr. profl. orgs. Hons. incl: Osterreichischer Staatspreis, 1960 & 1961. Grosser Preis der Stadt Wien, 1970. Address: Marokkanergasse 3/3/31, A-1030 Vienna, Austria.

SCHOLZ, Werner, b. 7 July 1926. Dresden, Germany. Musician; Violin Soloist & Tchr. Educ: Acad. of Music, Dresden. m. Ursula Bornemann, 3 children. Debut: Concert master, Dresdner Phil., 1948-51. Career: 1st concert master, Berlin Symph. Orch., 1956-76. Violn Soloist; concerts w. orch. & recitals, world-wide; Num. premiere perfs.; Apps. on radio & TV; Tchr., Acad. of Music, 1952-; Prof. of Music, 1961; Masterclass, 1974, Contbr. to profl. jrnls. Mbrships: Pres., ESTA, sect. GDR. Hons. incl: Merit Medal, 1974. Hobbies: Chess; Table Tennis. Address: Leipziger Str. 43/1904, 108 Berlin, German Democratic Repub.

SCHONBERG, Harold C, b. 29 Nov. 1915. USA. Music Critic. Educ: Brooklyn Coll.; NY Univ. Career: Assoc. Ed., Am. Music Lover, 1946-48; Music critic, NY Sun, 1946-50; Contbng. Ed. & Record Columnist, Musical Courier, 1948-52; Music & Record Critic, NY Times, 1950-60; Sr. Music Critic, ibid, 1960-; Columnist for the Gramaphone (London), 1948-60; Mil. Serv., US Army, 1942-46. Publs: The Guide to Long-Playing Records: Chamber & Solo Instrument Music, 1955: The Collector's Chopin & Schumann, 1959; The Great Pianists, 1963; The Great Conductors, 1967; Lives of the Great Composers, 1970; Contbng. Ed., Int. Cyclopedia of Music & Musicians. Recip: Pulitzer Prize for Criticism, 1971. Address: NY Times, Times Sq., NY, NY USA.

SCHÖNBERG, Stig Gustav, b. 13 May 1933. Norrköping, Sweden. Organist; Composer. Educ: Royal Acad. of Music, Stockholm; studied w. Lars-Erik Larsson & Karl-Birger Blomdahl. Career: organ recitals in Sweden, Finland, Germany, Holland, France; concerts; radio apps.; currently Organist, St. Göran Ch., Stockholm. Compositions incl: num. organ works; Concitalo per orchestra; Sinfonia aperta; Impromptu Visionario; 3 concertinos for str.; ballet music; chmbr. music, inclng. 6 str. quartets & 2 violin sonatas; keyboard music; vocal & choral works; Es sungen drei Engel (organ works - recorded); Lacrimae Comini (organ works - recorded). Recordings: Impressions for piano; Regina Celi for soprano, choir & orch. Mbr: Soc. of Swedish Composers. Address: Svartgarnsvägen 36, 184 00 Akersberga, Sweden.

SCHONFELDER, Gerd, b. 27 Apr. 1936. Köttewitz, Kreis Pirna, DDR. Music critic; Musicologist; Ethnomusicologist; Comps.; Writer. Educ: Univ. Peking, dip. Mod. Chinese, 1959; Central Chinese Music Acad.; DPh Karl Marx Univ. Leipzig, 1969; DSc Martin Luther Univ., Halle-Wittenberg, 1972. m. Elke Schönfelder-Haupt 1 s., 1 d. Career: Vice-pres. Music Acd. Carl Maria von Weber, Dresden; Ordinarius for musicol., ibid. Mbrships: var. profl. orgs. Publs. incl: Music at the Peking Opera, Leipzig, 1972; Socialist Realism in the Symphonic Work of Fritz Geissler, Berlin, 1973; Apfelstädt (satirical novel), 1976. Contbr. to var. profl. jrnls. Hons: Merit Order DDR; Hon. Medal Asssn. for Comp.; Johannes R Becker Medal, DDR. Hobbies: Writing; Driving; Swimming. Address: Pfotenhauerstr. 18/901, 8019 Dresden, German Dem. Repub.

SCHONHERR, Max, b. 23 Nov. 1903. Marburg/Drau (now Jugoslavia). Conductor; Composer. Educ: Konservatorium, Graz, Austria; Dr phil, Univ. of Vienna, 1973. M. Elisabeth Pernitza, 1 s. (decd.). Career: Conductor, opera house, Graz, Theater an der Wien & Volksoper, Vienna, & Radio Vienna, Osterreichischer Rundfunk, 1931-. Compositions: Bauermusik aus Osterreich, 1937; Ballet, Hotel Sacher, Staatsoper, Vienna, 1957; Operetta, Deutschmeiston Kapelle, Raimundtheater, Vienna, 1958; Bombenwalzer, Bayrischer Rundfunk, Munich, 1967. Recordings for var. cos. Publs: Das Jahrhundert des Walzers, Vol. 1, Johann Strauss Vater, 1954; Fr. Lehár Bibliogrphie zu Leben& Werk, 1970; Kompendium zu Bd. 1-120 der Denkmaler der Tonkunst in Osterreich, 1974; C M Ziehrer. Sein Leben, Sein Werk, Seine Zeit. Dokumentation, Analysen & Kommentare, 1974. Contbr. to Osterreichische Musikzeitschrift & to Grove's Dict. Mbrships. incl: AKM; Genossenschaft dramatischer Schriftsteller & Komponisten; Hon. mbr., Johann Strauss Orch., 1971. Recip. of hons. Address: Schubertstr. 10, 2500 Baden bei Wien, Austria.

SCHONTHAL-SECKEL, Ruth, b. 27 June 1924. Hamburg, Germany. Composer; Pianist. Educ: Conserv. Stern, Berlin; Royal Acad. of Music, Stockholm; BMus, Yale Univ.; Comp. studies w. paul Hindemith. m. Paul B Seckel, 3 s. Career: Carnegie Recital Hall; NYC Alice Tully Hall; McMillin Theatre; Wigmore Hall, London; Bellas Artes, Mexico City; WQXR, WNYC TV etc. Comps: Miniatures Vol. I & II; Miniscules; Near

and Far; Potpourrie; Sonata Breve; Variations in Search of a Theme; Four Epiphanies for unaccompanied viola; By The Roadside (Whitman) for soprano & piano. Mbrships: ASCAP; AMA; Program Chmn., Assoc. Music Tchrs. League of NY, 1976-. etc. Hons: Delta Omecron Int. award for string quartet, 1968; ASCAP Award, 1979. Address: 12 Van Elten Blvd., New Rochelle, NY 10804, USA. 5.

SCHÖNZELER, Hans-Hubert, b. 22 June 1925. Leipzig, Germany. Conductor; Musicologist. Educ: NSW State Conserv., Sydney, Aust.; Cond.'s Dip., Conserv. Nat. de Musique, Paris, 1954. m. Margaret Gillian Wingate, 1 s. Career: Cond., 20th Century Ensemble, London, 1957-61; Acting Res. Cond., WA Symph. Orch., Perth, Aust., 1967; Guest Cond., concert, radio & TV perfs., UK, Belgium, France, Germany, Holland, Aust., Çan. Recordings: Unicorn; RCA; Classics for Pleasure; Vox. Publs. incl: Bruckner, 1970; Ed., of German Music, 1976. Mbrships: Int. Bruckner Soc., Vienna; Hon., Dvorak Soc., Prague. Recip., Medal of Hon., Bruckner Soc. of Am., 1971.; Hon. Professorship, Austrian Govt., 1976; Medal of Int. Bruckner Soc., Vienna, 1978. Hobby: Reading. Mgmt: Ibbs & Tillet. Address: Savage Club, 9 Fitzmaurice Pl., London W1X 6JD, UK.

SCHOOLEY, Anne, b. 16 Jan. 1943. Williamsport, Pa., USA. Soprano; Concert Artist; Instructor of Music. Educ: BS, Mansfield State Coll., 1964; MMus, E Carolina Univ., 1968; Prof. & special studies, Aspen Schl. of Music, Chautauqua Schl. of Music, Yale Summer Music Festival, L'Ecole Hindemith. m. John H Schooley, 1 d. Premiere Perf., From a Very Little Sphinx, Fairmont State Coll., 1976. Career: Instr. of Music, Fairmont State Coll., W Va.; Perfs., Aspen Schl. of Music, Yale Summer Festival, Chautauqua Opera, Pa. Opera, W Va. Opera Co., E Carolina Univ. Summer Theatre; Recitals in Ky., NC, W Va., Pa.; Concerto Artist E Carolina Univ. Symph., 1968, Elliot Lake Opera Theatre, 1976; guest artist, Pa. Concert Soc., 1976. Mbrships: Sigma Alpha Iota; Nat Assn. of Tchrs. of Singing. Hons: Perf. grnats, Aspen Schl., 1968 & '69; Ellen Battell Stoeckel Fellowship, Yale Schl. of Music, 1970; Young Artist Winner, Charleston Symph., 1971; Perf. Award, Pa. Opera, 1973; Nat. Fed. of Music Clubs Young Artist, 1977. Address: 113 Morningstar Lane, Fairmont, WV, 26554, USA. 5.

SCHOOLEY, John Heilman, b. 8 Feb. 1943. Nelson, Pa., USA. Associate Professor of Theory & Low Brass (Tuba). Educ: BS in Music Educ., Manfield State Coll., Pa., 1965; Cert. of Merit in Comp., RAM, London, 1966; MMus, E Carolina Univ., Greenville, NC, 1968; var. studies at orther music schls. m. Anne L Weaver, 1 c. Career: Instr. of Theory & Low Brass, Eastern, Ky. Univ., 1968-70; Asst Prof. of Theory & Low Brass Fairmont State Coll., 1970-. Compositions: Partita for Brass Quartet; Serenate for Tuba & Piano; Three Dances for Woodwind Trio; Songs of Victory in Heaven (chorus). Publs: co-auth. w. Dr. H Richard Hensel, A Prospectus for College Theory, Semester 1, first edn., 1972, Semester IV, first edn., 1973, Semester 1, 2nd edn., 1974. Mbrships: ASCAP; So. Composers League. Recip. var. fellowships & grants. Hobbies: Composing music; Gardening; Hunging; Fishing. Address: 113 Morningstar Lane, Fairmont, WV 26554, USA.

SCHOOP, Hans, b. 12 Apr. 1934. Oberaach, Switz. Viola Player. Educ: Dr. phil. 1, Zürich Univ.; Zürich Conserv. m. Vera von Gonzenbach, 2 children. Career: Viola Player, Tonhalle & Theaterorchester, Zürich; Stage mgr. of 18th Century operas (1st apps. for Switzerland) Publs: Entstehung und Verwendung der Handschrift Oxford, Bodleian Lib., 1971. Hobby: Baroque Instruments. Address: Klosbachstrasse 43, 8032 Zürich, Switz. 14.

SCHOOP, Paul, b. 31 July 1907. Zurich, Switz. Composer; Concert Pianist; Conductor; Eduator. Educ: TD, Zurich Conserv.; Concert Dip., Ecole Normale, Paris; Comps. degree, Hochschule für Musik, Berlin; studied w. Boulanger, Hindemith, Dukas, Volkmar Andrea, Emil Frey, Robert Casadesus, Cortot, Schnabel. Debut: Paris, 1927. Career incls: Musical Supvsr. & Comp., Disney Prods. Num. comps. inclng: Maria del Valle (dance drama); var. works for Trudi Schoop Comic Ballet prods. & Danish Royal Ballet; The Enchanted Trumpet (comic opera); songs; marches; music for film; radio, musicals & animated cartoons. Recordings incl: Fata Morgna (symphonic poem); Dance a Story (5 albums). Publd. incl: Impressions for Piano, 3 books. Contbr. to jrnls. Mbr. profl. orgs. Hons. incl: Gold Medallion, Swiss Govt., Mgmt: Eric Schoop, 5757 Ranchito Ave., Van Nuys, CA 91401, USA.

SCHOTT, Howard (Mansfield), b. 17 June 1923. NYC, USA. Musicologist; Harpsichordist. Educ: BA, Yale Univ., 1943; LLB, JD, ibid; Musical studies, Yale & Mannes Coll., NY, 1953-57; DPhil., Oxford, 1978. Publs: Playing the Harpsichord, 1971; Revised Raymond Russell's The Harpsichord & Clavichord, 1973; Ed., Froberger, complete keyboard works, 1970.

Contbr. to: Notes; The Consort; The Galpin Soc. Jrnl; Musical Times; Early Music. Mbrships: Royal Musical Assn.; Am. Musical Instrumental Soc.; Am. Musicol. Soc.; Gesellschaft für Musikforschung; Galpin Soc. Address: 44 Woodland Park Dr., Tenafly, NJ 07670, USA.

SCHOU, Dagmar, b. 29 Sept. 1906. Copenhagen, Denmark. Contralto. Educ: MMus; studied w. Hermann Weissenborn, E Ulrich, & A. Hoeberg. m. Carl Damkjaer, 2 c. Debut: Copenhagen, 1931. Career: num. Concerts, Denmark & Sweden, 1931-70; num. Radio Apps., Denmark. Recordings: Handel, Te Deum; var. others. Mbrships: Soloists Assn., 1921-; Danish Music Educ. Assn. Address: 59 FPE Hartmanns Alle, 2500 Copenhagen, Denmark.

SCHOUSBOE, Torben, b. 6 Oct. 1937. Copenhagen, Denmark. Musicologist; Organist. Educ: Organist, Royal Music Conserv., Copenhagen, 1960; MA, Univ. of Copenhagen, 1968. M. Inge Margrethe Jacoby. Debut: Cathedral of St. Canute, Odense, Denmark, 18 July 1961. Career: concerts as organist & cond., Copenhagen, 1960-; d., radio series Danish Symphonies Through Two Centuries, 1971; Organist & Choirmaster, Emdrup Ch., Copenhagen; Asst. Prof. of Musicol., Univ. of Copenhagen. Publs: Carl Nielson. Kompositioner (w. Dan Fog), 1965; Carl Nielsen, Dagboger og Korrespondance med Anne Marie Carl-Nielsen (Ed., w. Irmelin Eggert Moller), 1979, 2 vols. Contbr. to: RILM; Dansk Musiktidsskrift; Dansk arbog for musikforskning; Dansk arborg for musikforskning; Dansk Kirkesangs arsskrift; Acta musicoliga. Mbrships: Chmn., Nat. Danish Comm., RILM; Sec., Danish Carl Nielsen Soc.; Exec. Comm., Samfundet Dansk Kirkesang & Selskabet Dansk Tidegaerd. Hobbies: Antiquarian Books & Music Prints; Tape Recordings; Gardening. Address: Tryggevaeldevej 132, DK-2700 Copenhagen Bronshoj, Denmrk. 14.

SCHØYEN, Einar, b. 16 Apr. 1952. Stavanger, Norway. Double Bassist. Educ: BA (Highest Norwegian Instrumental/Pedagogical Educ.). m. Nina Rodsrud, 1d. Career: Solos & Chmbr. music, stage, TV & radio; Oslo Phil. Orch.; Norwegian Chmbr. Orch. Mbrships: Int. Soc. of Bassists. Address: Mosseveien 8, Oslo 1, Norway.

SCHRECKER, Bruno Tom, b. 27 Aug. 1928. Frankfurt am/M, Germany. Cellist. Educ: RCM; French Govt. Scholarship; studied w. Pablo Casals; Dutch Govt. Scholarship. m. Doris Wilkinson, 2 s. Career: Peter Gibbs Quartet; Oromonte Str. & Piano Trios; Allegri Quartet; Open Univ.; TV & frequent radio broadcasts; str. quartet tours in Europe, USA, USSR, Far E & India. num. recordings. Mbr., Hans-Ulrich Schmid Concertagem, Hannover, German Fed. Repub. Recip. Hon. MMus, Hull, 1975. Hobbies: Photography; Walking; Restoring old house in Wales; Old bottles. Mgmt: Ibbs & Tillett, London; Mariedi Anders, San Fran., USA. Address: 138 Dora Rd., London SW19, UK. 3.

SCHREIER, Peter Max, b. 29 July 1935. Meissen, Germany. Concert & Opera Tenor. Educ: Music HS, Dresden, 1956-60. m. Renate Kupch, 2s. Career: apps. w. major opera cos., Dresden, Vienna, Munich, Hamburg, Milan, Rome, Buenos Aires, Budapest, London, NYC; participant in Salzburg & Bayreuth fests; specializes in lieder & Mozartean roles; Orchl. Cond., Germany, 1969-; num. recordings as singer. Mbr., Am. Guild of Musical Artists. Hons: Schumann Award in music, 1969; Nat. music prize, German Dem. Repub.; Handel Prize. Address: 19, 8054 Cabberlastr. Dresden, German Dem. Repub. 2.

SCHREINER, Alexander, b. 31 July 1901. Nuremberg, Germany. Concert Organist. Educ: AB, PhD, Univ. Utah, USA; studied music w. John J McClellan, Salt Lake City, & Louis Vierne, Charles M Widor & Henri Libert, Paris, France. m. Margaret Lyman, 2 s., 2d. Debut: Salt Lake Tabernacle, 1921. Career: Chief Organist, The Tabernacle, Salt Lake City, Utah, 1924-; Organ Broadcasts, nat. network, 1929-; Organist & Lectr. in Music, Univ. of Calif. at LA, 1930-39; Annual concert tours, USA, Can. & Europe, 1943-65. Compositions: Concerto for full Orch. & Organ in B Minor; Organ compositions; var. anthems. Recordings: The Great Organ at the Mormon Tabernacle; Christmas at the Mormon Tabernacle. Publs: Organ Voluntaries, Vol. 1 1937, Vol. 11 1945, Vol. 111 1965. Contbr. to: The Clavier; The American Organist; The Ensign; The Instructor. Mbrships: Fellow, AGO; ASCAP; Phi Kappa Phi; Phi Beta Kappa. Hons: LHD, Univ. of Utah; Doct. Fine Arts, Utah State Univ.; Officer's Cross of Merit, W Germany, 1975. Hobbies: Astromony; Physics; Church Work. Address: 1283 East, S Temple St., Salt Lake City, UT 84102, USA. 2, 3, 19,21.

SCHRODER, Jaap, b. 31 Dec. 1925. Amsterdaml, Holland. Violinist. Educ: Dip., Amsterdam Conserv.; 1st Prize, Ecole Jacques Thibaud, Paris, France, 1948. m. Agnés Jeanne Francoise Lefévre, 3 d. Debut: Holland, 1949. Career: Ldr., Radio Chamber Orch., 1950-63; Mbr., Netherlands String Quartet, 1952-69; Fndr., chamber music ensembles Quadro Amsterdam, 1960-66, Concerto Amsterdam, 1962-, Quartettto Esterhasy, 1971-; Prof. of Violin, Amsterdam, Concerto Amsterdam & Quartetto Esterhasy. Hobby: French lit. Address: Gerard Brandstraat 18, Amsterdam, Holland.

SCHRØDER, Jens, b. 6 Nov. 1909. Bielsko, Poland. Conductor. Educ: Dip., State Conserv. of Prague. m. Estrid Schroder, 1 d., 1 s. Debut: Copenhagen Univ. Orch. 1932. Career incls: Music Dir. & Chief Cond., Aalborg Symph. Orch., 1942-; Cond., Municipal Theatre of Aalborg, 1945-; Guest Cond. w. most Scandinavian var. European orchs.; Tour w. grp. from Royal Ballet of Copenhagen to S Am. Mbrships. incl: Dansk Tonekunsterforening; Danskl Solistforening; Dansk Kapelmesterforening. Publs: The Art's Broadcasts of Denmark Radio 1925-50, 1975. Hons. incl: Kt. of Danneborg, King Fredeik IX of Denmark. Hobbies incl: Books. Address: Danmarksgade 12, 9000 Aalborg, Denmark.

SCHROEDER, Gerald H, b. 24 June 1936. Wonewoc, Wis., USA. Associate Professsor of Music. Educ: BS, Univ. of Wis., 1959; MMus, Ind. Univ., 1965; D Musical Arts, Univ. of Colo., 1971; studies w. Helmet Rilinig & Robert Shaw. m. Connie Koepke-Schroeder. Career: Music Tchr., Marshfield Sr. High Schl., Wis., 1960-69; Assoc. Prof. of Music, Univ. of Wis. Ctr., Marshfield, 1968-; Boise State Univ., Idaho, 1978-. Contbr. to: Ch. Music Mag. Mbrships. incl: Am. Choral Dirs. Assn.; Am. Choral Fndn.; MENC. Hons: Outstanding Young Educator of Yr., Marshfield, 1967; Outstanding Tchr. of Yr., Univ. Ctr., ibid., 1972 Outstanding service to Community Award, 1978. Hobby: Camping. Address: 2017 Harrison Rd., Boise, ID83702, USA.

SCHROEDER, Hermann, b. 26 Mar. 1904. Bernkastel, Germany. Composer; Director; Organist; Educator. Educ: Innsbruck Univ.; Rhine Music Schl., 1930; Cathedral Organist Trier, 1938: Music High Schl., Cologne, 1946, Prof., ibid., 1948; PhD, Univ. Bonn, 1975. Comps. incl: Works for choir, organ, orch., piano; Opera: Hero & Leander. Publs: Hons: Robert Schumann Prize, Dusseldorf, 1952; Arts Prize, Rhineland Pfalt, 1956; Bundes Verdienstkreis I Class, 1975. Address: Berhardstr. 245, D 5000 Cologne 51, German Fed. Repub.

SCHROEDER, Linda Ann, b. 4 Nov. 1954. Port Huron, Mich., USA. Violinist. Educ: BMus Perf., Juilliard Schl., 1977. Career: New Jersey Symph. Orch., 1977-78; currently Mbr., Nat. Symph. Orch. Wash. DC, 1978-. Hons: Tchng. Fellowships, assisting Margaret Pardee, 1976, 1976-77; Francis Goldstein Scholarship, 1975; Top Prize winner, Five Town's Music & Art Fndn., 1973: Scholarships, Juilliard, 2 yrs. Hobbies: Needlecrafts; Sports; Furniture Building. Address: 4201 S 31st St., Apt. 826, Arlington, VA 22206, USA.

SCHROEDER, Raymond Lee, b. 15 Nov. 1936. Cincinnati, Ohio, USA. Clarinettist; College Music Teacher; Symphony Conductor: Music Theory Teacher. Educ: BM, Coll.-Conserv. of Music of Cinn., 1958; MMus, Boston Univ. Schl. of Fine 0 Applied Arts, 1959. m. Clementine Schattel, 1 s., 2 d. Career: Cinn. Symph. Orch., 1959-60; Austin Symph. Orch., 1960-; Chautauqua Symph. Orch., 1964-; Solo perfs. w. Austin & Chautauqua Symphs.; Guest Artist, San Antonio Symph.; Cond., Southwestern Sinfonietta. Recordings: Film Score of The Hustler. Mbrships: Pi Kappa Lambda; Phi Mu Alpha Sinfonia. Hobbies: Tennis; Motorcycling. Address: 1203 Country Club Rd., Georgetown, TX 78626, USA. 2.

SCHROTH, Gerhard Otto, b. 6 Mar. 1937. Frankfurt, German Fed. Repub. Music critic; Music pedgague. Educ: Music Acad. Frankfurt, TD; Univ. Frankfurt, musicol. m. Anne Schroth-Eppel, 1 d. Contbr. to: Frankfurte Allgemeine Zeitung, 1971-, music critic since 1966; co-operator Music and Church. Address: Memeler Str. 29, 6370 Oberursel 5, German Fed. Repub.

SCHROYENS, Raymond Jean Joseph, b . 14 Mar. 1933. Mechelen, Belgium. Musician, Organ, Piano, Harpsichord, Virginal, Clavichord, Hammer Clavier. Educ: Lemmens Inst.; Mechelen; Antwerp Royal Conserv. of Music. m. Alleine Harris Lurton, 1 d., 1 s. Debut: Detroit, Mich., USA. Career: First Prod. of Classical Music, Belgian Radio & TV; Prof. of Classical Music, Belgian Radio & TV; Prof. of Harpsichord, Brussles Royal Conserv., Flemish Sect.; Recitalist, Organ & Harpsichord, UK, France, Spain, German, Holland, Denmark, Finland, Bulgaria. Belgium; Tchr. of harpsichord at hometown conserv. Comps: 2 Organ Preludes; 7 works for choir; 3 Suites, recorder quartet; Piano Sonata; 3 songs w. piano accomp.; var. Arrs.; Battery for

Bells, carillon Aureols for Phil. Brass Ensemble; Three Birthday Presents for Daniel. Recordings: Schubert, Die Schone Müllerin; John Loeillet, Sonatas & Harpsichord Dances; William De Fesch, 6 Sonatas. Contbr. to: De Praestant/Tongerlo; Harop/Antwerp; Vlaams Muziektijdschrift; Gamma; Ed. Staff, Muziek & Woord. Hons: 1st Bulgarian State Prize for Piano Accomp., Sofia, 1967; Prize for Carillon Comp., Mechelen, 1971. Hobbies: Reading; Writing, Parapsychol & histl. rsch. Address: 12 Bgmr. Frans Broersstraat, 2800 Mechelen, Belgium.

SCHUBERT, (Ernst) Manfred (Leopold), b. 27 Apr. 1937. Berlin, Germany. Composer; Teacher; Critic; Conductor. Educ: Staatsexamen, Humbolt Univ., Berlin; Dip, comp., Akademie der Künste der DDR. m. Bärbel Schubert, 2 d. Career: Chief music critic, Berliner Zeitung, 1962-. Comps. incl: Cantilena e Capriccio for violin & orch. (recorded), 1974; Clarinet Concerto (recorded), 1971; Suite for orch., 1966; Tanzstudien for small orch.; Esde Hafis, for piano (recorded); Septett in 2 movements; Sonata for solo flute; 2 Strg. Quartets; Canzoni amorosi for baritone & large orch., 1973 (recorded). Contbr. to jrnls. at home & abroad & to radio of DDR. Mbr., Komponistenverbandes der DDR & Kulturbundes der DDR. sev. awards & prizes. Hobbies: Painting in Water Colours; Sports; Swimming. Address: Dolomitenstr. 15, 110 Berlin-Pankow, German Dem. Repub.

SCHUBERT, Zenon, b. 14 May 1934. Grudziadz, Poland. Music Administrator. Educ: Magister of Arts Dip. in Organ & Comp., Poznan, Poland. m. Sabina Marecka, 1 s., 1 d. Career: Dir., Schl. of Music; Num. TV & Radio Apps., Warsaw & Poznan; Concert Apps., Poznan, Wroclaw & Cracow. Comps. incl: Variations for Piano, 1961; Lyric Cantata for Solo Voice, Choir & Orch., 1962; Metamorphoses for Piano, 1963; Triptych for Organ, 1964; Str. Quartets nr. I, II, III, 1964, '66, '73; Overture Concertante for Symph. Orch., 1965; Concerto for Organ & Orch., 1968; Concertino for Oboe & String Orch., 1970; Concerto for Trumpet & Orch., 1973; Oratorio "Gilgamesz" for Solo Voice, Reciter, Two Chorus, Symph. Orch. & Tape, 1974. Mbrships: Assn. of Polish Compositors, Warsaw; Sec., Regional Assn. of Polish Compositros, Poznzn. Hobbies: Car Driving. Address: Osiedle Wielkiego Pazdziernika 7 Dm 33, 61-633 Poznan, Poland.

SCHUCHTER, Gilbert, b. 12 Sept. 1919. Salzburg, Austria. Professor; Pianist; Conductor. Educ: Mozarteum; Berlin Music Acad.; studied under Clemens Krauss. m. Maria Schwaiger, 6 children. Career: apps. at Salzburg, Vienna, Zurich & Majorca Fests., as well as Teatro Colon Buenos Aires, Frankfurt Opera House, Budapest, Brussels; 1976 apps., Moscow & Rome; currently Full Prof., Mozarteum. Recordings: complete piano works of Schubert, Mozart (in progress) & Pfitzner; selected Beethoven piano works; Schumann's Davidsbündler Tänze. Contbr. to: Die Furche; Hi-Fi Karlsrhue; N Zürcher Zeitung. Mbrships: Hon. Mbr., Austrian/Am. Soc. Recip., Prize, Piano, Int. Music Competition, Geneva, 1947. Hobbies: Hiking; Swimming; Reading. Address: Arenbergstr. 19, A 5020 Salzburg, Austria.

SCHUDEL, Thomas Michael, b. 8 Sept., 1937. Defiance, Ohio, USA. University Professor; Bassoonist; Composer. Educ: BS, MM in Theory Composition, Ohio State Univ.; DMA in Composition, Univ. of Mich. m., 1 s., 1 d. Career: Prin. Bassoonist, Regina (Sask.) Symph. Orch., 1964-67, 1968-74; Bassoonist, Regina Univ. Fac. Woodwind Quintet; Solo & ensemble perfs., CBC Radio & TV; Prof., Dept. of Music, Univ. of Regina, Sask., Can. Comps: String Quartet; Set No. 2 for woodwind & brass; Symph. No. 1, Variations for Chamber orch., & Triptych for winds & percussion (CBC commissioned); Nulf's Dance & People who Became (electronic music). Mbrships: Can. Assn. of Univ. Schls. of Music. Hons: 1st Prize, for Symph. No. 1 (unpubld.), City of Trieste Int. Competition for Symph. Compositions, 1972. Address: 149 Shannon Rd., Regina, Sask., Canada.

SCHUHMACHER, Gerhard, b. 20 May 1939. Essen, Germany. Musicologist. Educ: pvte. study, violin, cello, piano & theory; studies w. Prof. J Müller-Blattau, W Salmen, W Wiora & E Apfel; Dr. phil, Univ.of Saarbrücken, 1966. m. Irmgard Schoppen, 2 children. Career: Bibliographer on schlrship. from Deutsche Forschungsgemeinschaft, Das Deutsche Kirchenlied (RISM B VII/1-2), 1966-74; Lectr., Musical Acad. Kassel, 1970-. Publs. incl: Erträge der Forschung: Musikästhetik, 1973: Zur musikalischen Analyse (ed.), 1974; Einführung in die Musikästhetik, 1975; F Mendelssohn Bartholdy, String Quartets op. 12, 13, & 44 (ed.), 1975/76. Co-Ed., Musik & Kirche. Contbr. to var. jrnls. Mbrships. incl: Int. Musicol. Soc. Hobbies: Cooking; Walking. Address: Mozarstr. 4, 3502 Vellmar 3, German Fed. Repub.

SCHULDT, Agnes Crawford, b. 5 July 1902. Pontiac, Mich., USA. Teacher of Piano & History of Music. Educ: BMus, Syracuse Univ., 1924; MMus, ibid., 1927; Oxford Univ., UK, 1958. m. Lester Lorentz Schuldt (dec. 1939). Career: Instructor in music, Univ. of Idaho, 1927-30, Miami Univ., 1930-32; Asst. Prof. of Music, Randolph-Macon Women's Coll., 1941-42; Asst. Prof. & Prof. of Music, Univ. of Idaho, 1946-67; Vis. Prof. of Music, Univ. of Ill., Chgo. Circle, 1968-72; Now Emeritus Prof., Univ. of Idaho. Contbr. to the Am. Scholar. Mbrships: Am. Musicol. Soc.; Coll. of Music Soc.; Chapt. Pres., AAUP, 1960-61. Recip. Gov.'s Award for Execellence in the Arts, 1974. Hobbies: Flower gardening; Reading. Address: 1304 Deakin St., Moscow, ID 83843, USA. 5.

SCHULÉ, Bernard E., b. 22 July 1909. Zurich, Switz. Composer. Educ: Conserv. & Univ. Zurich. m. Olive E Morgan, 1 s. Career: Organist, Brit. Embassy Ch. & Basilique Ste. Clotilde, Paris, France, 1930's; Freelance comps. Switz., 1961-; Composed music for about 50 films. Comps. incl: 'Serenade' for string orch.; 'Chansons dans le style Populaire'; 'Eluminkures' 6 pieces for organ; 'Suite Valaisanne' for orch.; Spiel mit musikalischen Formen' for flute & piano. Recordings. incl:K Die Schiffsreise; Resonances. Publs. incl: L'Accord majeur et l'Accord mineur, Essai d'une nouvelle explication, 1975. Contbr. to Revue Musicale de Suisse Romande. Mbr. prof. orgs. Hons. incl: 1st prize, Comp. competition, Swiss Soc. Music Tchrs., 1969. Hobby: Chess. Address: 11 Rue Butini, 1202 Geneva, Switz.

SCHULER, Richard Joseph, b. 30 Dec. 1920. Minneapolis, Minn., USA. Roman Catholic Priest; Musicologist. Educ: BA, Col. of St. Thomas, St. Paul, Minn., 1942; Ordained Priest, St. Paul Sem., Minn., 1945; MA, Eastman Schl. ofMusic, Rochester, NY, 1950; PhD, Univ. of Minn., Mpls., 1963. Career: Prof., Nazareth Hall Sem., 1945-54, Assoc. Prof., Coll. of St. Thomas, 1955-69, Pastor, Ch. of St. Agnes, 1969-, all in St. Paul, Minn. Publs: Ed., Fourteen Liturgical Works of Giovanni Maria Nanino, 1969; Ed., Engl. ed., Sacred Music & Liturgy Reform after Vatican II, 1969; Ed., quarterly jrnl. Sacred Music, 1975-. Mbrships: VP, Consociatio Int. Musicae Sacrae, Rome, 1967-; Gen. Sec., Ch. Music Assn. of Am., 1972-. Hons. incl: Hon. Papal Prelate (title of Monsignor), 1970; Gold Lassus Medal, Federated Cecilian Soc. of German-Speaking Countries, 1973. Hobbies: Photog; Travel; Gardening. Address: 548 Lafond Ave., St. Paul, MN 55103, USA.

SCHULLER, Gunther, b. 22 Nov. 1925. NYC, USA. President, New England Conservatory of Music. m. Marjorie Black, 2 s. Career: Guest Cond., Boston, Cinn., Minn., Cleveland, Denver, NY, Chgo., Balt., Rochester, St. Louis, Los Angeles, Wash., San Fransisco, Pittsburgh, Atlanta, Montreal, Vancouver Symph. Orchs.; BBC Symph., Phil. Orch. of London; French Radio Orch.; Symph. Orch. of the Bavarian Radio; Tonhalle Orch. of Zurich; prog. 'Contemporary Music in Evolution', WBAI radio, NYC. Artistic Dir., Berkshire Music Ctr. Comps. incl: Horn Concerto; Symph. for Brass & Percussion; Concerto for Orch.; Spectra; 2 Strg. Quartets; 7 studies on Themes of Paul Klee; Music for Brass Quintet; Concerto da Camera; Capriccio Stravagante. Recording incl: Conversations (perf. by the Modern Jazz Quartet - the Beaux Arts str. Quartet, Atlantic Records recording, Third Stream Music); Concertino for Jazz Quartet & Orch.; Lines & Contrasts. Publs: Horn Techinique, 1962; Early Jazz; Its Roots & Musical Development, 1968. num. prized, awards & acad. hons. 167 Dudley Rd., Newton Ctr., MA, USA.

SCHULMAN, Sylvia, b. 21 May 1925. Bulawayo, Rhodesia. Concert Pianist; Accompanist; Teacher. Educ: S African Coll. of Music, Univ. of Cape Town. m. S Benatar, 1 s., 1 d. Debut: w. Cape Town Municipal Orch., 1945. Career: solo apps. w. major orchs., S Africa & Rhodesia; solo accomp. tours & broadcasts throughout Southern Africa; UK apps. as orchl. & recital Soloist; Accomp. BBC Radio 3. Mbr., ISM. Hobby: Ballroom Dancing. Mgmt: Terry Slasberg. Address: 25 Studley Rd., Luton, UK. 3.

SCHULTZ, Svend S, b. 30 Dec. 1913. Nykobing, Denmark. Composer; Conductor. Educ: Royal Danish Conserv. of Music, Debut: 1938. Career: currently Cond., Danish Radio Choir. Comps: 4 symphs; 10 operas; chmbr. music; choral works; etc. Recorded comps: Serenade for strings; choral works; chmbr. music. Mbr., Danish Comps. Soc. Recip. Kt., Order of Dannebrog. Address: Danmarks Radio; Copenhagen, Denmark.

SCHULTZE, Nobert, b. 26 Jan. 1911. Braunschweig, Germany. Composer. Educ: High Schl. of Music, Cologne. m. Jwa Wanja, 6 c. Comps: Lili Marleen; Schwarzer Peter; Das Kalte Herz; Max und Moritz; Struwwelpeter; Peter der dritte;

Käpt'n Bay-Bay; Regen in Paris, etc. Address: Herthastr. 22, 1000 Berlin 33, German Fed. Repub.

SCHULTZ-HAUSER, Karlheinz, b. 1 Sept. 1907. Greifswald, Pommern, Germany. Music Teacher; Editor; Violinist. Educ: studied w. H v. Dameck, S Eberhard, A Wittenberg (violin) & W Klatte (theory & comp.) m. Eva Hauser, 1 d. Career: concerts w. Rüchel Quartet; Concertmaster, Landestheater-Schneidenmühl, 1935-, Theatre of the Residenzstadt Potsdam, 1938-; concerts w. Melante Trio, 1945-; Music Tchr.; Publr. of old music (Telemann Rsch.). Has edited many works by comps. such as Telemann, Quanz, Giordani, Stamitz, etc. for Schott, Peters, Vieweg, Hug, Leuckart & Müller. Mbrships: Soc. for Music Rsch. Soc. Address: 7500 Karlsruhe-Durlach, Rittnerstrasse 51, German Fed. Repub.

SCHULZE, Werner, b. 10 June 1952. Wr. Neustadt, Austria. Professor. Educ: DPh, Vienna Univ. Career: Mbr., Austrian Woodwind Quintet; Concerts in Europe & S. Am.; Prof., High Schl. for Music & Related Arts, Vienna. Comps: 3 Miniatures for Woodwind Quintet; Serenade for 7 Wind Instruments. Publs: incl. Zahl, Proportion, Analogie, 1978. Mbrships: Austrian Comps. Union, Vienna; Cusanus Gesellschaft, Germany. Hons: Wiener Kunstfonds Prize, 1977; Comps. Prize, Niederösterreichische Landesregierung, 1977; Theodor Körner Prize for Knowledge, 1978. Hobbies: Management for concert tours; Travelling. Address: A-2700 Wr. Neustadt, Mozartgasse 9, Austria.

SCHUMACHER, Stanley E., b. 9 Aug. 1942. Indpls., Ind., USA. Music Theorist; Composer; Professor. Educ: BMus, MMus, Butler Univ.; PhD, Ohio State Univ., 1976. m. Susan Schumacher. Career: Prof., Rhode Island Junior Coll., 1978-. Comps: Symmetries (4 performers), 1972; Beat Me Daddy, Eight to a Bar (trombone, piano string bass); Musography I (3 trombones & 2 clarinets). Contbr. to: The Composer Mag. Mbrships: Am. Soc. of Univ. Comps; Am. Musicol. Soc.; Pi Kappa Lambda; Phi Mu Alpha Sinfonia. Hons: 1st Prize, Phi Mu Alpha Sinfonia Comp. Contest, Ohio State Univ., 1967. Address: 305 Greenwich Ave., Apt. B306, Warwick, RI 02886, USA. 29.

SCHUMACHER, Thomas, b. 8 Dec. 1937. Butte, Mont., USA. Pianist. Educ: BMus, Manhattan Schl. of Music, NYC, 1958; Artist Dip., 1960, MS, 1962, Juilliard Schl. of Music, NYC. Debut: Town Hall, NYC, 1963. Career: recital apps. throughout USA, Can., Europe & Japan; Soloist w. major orchs. inclng. NY Phil., Toronto Symph., Warsaw Phil. & Tokyo Phil; world premiere of David Diamond Piano Concerto w. NY Phil.; Artist, Fac., Univ. of Md. Contbr. to Clavier Mag. Hons: Prize, Int. Busoni Competition, 1962, Jugg Competition, 1963. Hobbies: Animals; Bridge; Outdoor Life. Mgmt: Columbia Artists Mgmt., NYC. Address: 7308 Hopkins Ave., College Park, MD, USA.

SCHUMAN, William Howard, b. 4 Aug. 1910. NYC, USA. Composer; Administrator. Educ: Columbia Univ.; Mozarteum, Salzburg, Austria. m. Frances Prince, 1 s., 1 d. Career: on fac., Sarah Lawrence Coll., 1935-45; Dir. of Publs., G Schirmer Inc., NYC, 1944-45; Special Publs. Cons., ibid, 1944-51; Pres., Juilliard Schl. of Music, 1945-62; Pres., Lincoln Ctr. for the Performing Arts, 1962-. Comps: incl: sev. symphs.; sev. quartets; American Festival Overture for orch.; A Free Song (cantata); Undertow (ballet); Prayer in Time of War; New England Triptych; A Song of Orpheus; Newsreel for band; George Washington Bridge for band; Quartettino for 4 bassoons; Variations for String Trio; The Might Casey (opera); film scores & theatre music. Hons. incl: Pultizer Prize; Music Critics' Circle Award; 2 Guggenheim Fellowships; Town Hall League of Composers Award.

SCHUMANN, Wolfgang, b. 23 April 1927. Mönchengladbach, Germany. Director; Composer. Educ: High Schl. for Music, Cologne (State exam., Cond. & Comp. m. Anna-Luise Licht, 1 s. Debut: Bandmaster, Stadttheater Osnabrck. Carer: Theatre & Concert Cond.; Comp. for Radio, films, etc. Comps: Holzbläserlaunen; Indigo; 12 Ballets; approx. 300 Orchl. works; 17 Cantatas; approx. 50 Chmbr. Music works. Sev. recordings. Mbrships: Verband der Komponisten und Musikwissenschaftler der DDR; Mitglied der Bühnengenossenschaft. Hons. incl: Kunstpreis und viele Staatliche Auszeichnungen, 1970. Address: Platanenstr. 30 a, 1254 Schöneiche, German Dem. Repub.

SCHURECK, Ralph John, b. 12 June 1931. Brisbane, Qld., Aust. University Teacher; Musicologist. Educ: Univ. of Qld., MB, BS, DPM (1962), MRANZCP (1970), MRC Psych., (1971); BA (music), 1961, MA, 1966, Univ. of Cambridge (Selwyn Coll.). Career: Fndr., cond., Univ. of Qld. Orchl. Soc.; Asst. organist, St. John's Cathedral, Brisbane; Dir. of Musicol.,

Organ Inst. of NSW. Publ: A Revised List of Autograph Sources for JS Bach's Cantata 188 & Related Works, in Musicology V. Mbrships: Royal Musical Assn.; Musicol. Soc. of Aust.; Early Music Assn. of NSW; Brit. Assn. for Music Therapy. Hobbies: Baroque Chamber Music; Collecting Early Keyboard Instruments; Travel; Food; Wine. Address: 26 Nalya Rd., Berowra Heights, NSW 2082, Aust.

SCHURMANN, Gerard, b. 19 Jan. 1928. Kertosono, Indonesia. Composer. Educ: Radley Coll.; Study of Composition w. Alan Rawsthorne; Piano, w. Kathleen Long. m. Carolyn Nott, 1 d. Career: Netherlands Cultural Attache, London; Orchestral Cond., Dutch Radio, Hilversum; Guest Cond., maj. European orchs.; Broadcaster; Lectr. Comps. incl: Piano Concerto; Violin Concerto; 6 Studies of Francis Bacon (orch.); Scena for Mary Shelley (mezzo Soprano & orch.); Attack & Celebration (orch.); Contrasts (piano); Chuench'i (Soprano & orch.); Variants (orch.); Leotaurus (piano); The Double Heart for unacc. chorus; Dramatic Cantata, Aers Plowman; Music for ballet, theatre, num. Am. & Brit. films var. recordings. Mbrships: PRS; ASCAP; Composers Guild of GB; Phyllis Court Club. Hobbies: Sport; Cooking. Mgmt: Roger Stone Mgmt., GB; Herbert Barrett, USA. Address: 44 Village Rd., Finchley, London N3 1TJ, UK. 3.

SCHWAEN, Kurt, b. 21 June 1909. Katowice, Germany. Composer. Educ: Music, Univs. Breslau & Berlin m. Hedwig Stumpp (dec.). Career: Music Advisor, Deutsche Volksbühne; Sec., Comps. & Music. Logists Union; Pres., AWA. Comps: Piano music; Chmbr. music; Works for Orch.; Opera & Cantatas especially for children; Pinocchio (opera); Koenig Midas; Die Weltreise im Zimmer. Sev. recordings. Publs: Tonweisen sind Denkweisen, 1950; Instrumentationslehre für Volksmusikinstrumente, 1954; Die Adlibitum-Besetzunz, 1954; Kindermusiktheater, 1979. Mbrships: Akademie der Künste der DDR, Sektionl Musik. Hons: Nationalpreis der DDR. Address: Wocholderheide 31, 115 Berlin/Mahlsdorf, German Dem. Repub.

SCHWAGER, Myron August, b. 16 Mar. 1937. Pittsfield, Mas., USA. Professor; Cellist. Educ: Mass. Inst. of Technology, 1955-56; BMus, Boston Univ., 1958; MMus, New England Conserv. of Music, 1961; MA, PhD, Harvard Univ., 1970. div., 1 d., 1 s. Career: Featured speaker on Symphony Preview, WTIC-FM, 1975-77; former fac., Holy Cross Coll.; Worcester Community Schl. of the Perfng. Arts; Jesuit Artists' Inst., Italy; currently Assoc. Prof. of Music History & Music Lit., Hartt Coll. of Music, Univ. of Hartford, 1974-; former prin. cellist, Springfield Symph. Orch. Apps. w. Cambridge Soc. for Early Music, Boston Chamber Players, Consortium Musicale, Hawthorne Trio & Hartford Chamber Orch. Contbr. to: The Creative World of Beethoven (ed. P H Lang), 1971; Music & Letters; Current Musicol.; Musicol Quarterly; Boston Sunday Herald Traveller (1969-72). Mbrships: Am. Musicol. Soc.; Am. Fedn. of Musicians. Address: 18 Sherman St., Hartford, CT 06105, USA.

SCHWANBECK, Bodo, b. 20 July 1935. Schwerin, Germany. Bass Singer (Opera & Oratorio). Educ: Musikhochschule, Munich. Career: Opernhaus, Frankfurt, Koln, Zürich, Dusseldorf; Staatsoper Munich, Hamburg, Vienna; Fest. Aix-en-Provence, Lisbon, Barcelona, NY. Hobby: Horses. Mgmt: David Schiffmann, 57 W 68th St., MY 10023, USA. Address: Parkstr. 9, D 6464 Waldrobe, Germany.

SCHWANDT, Erich Paul, b. 26 July 1935. Paso Robles, Calif., USA. Harpsichordist; Musicologist; Professor of Musicology. Educ: PhD, Stanford Univ., Calif., 1967; studied Harpsichord w. Putnam Aldrich. Career: Prof. of Musicol., Eastman Schl. of Music, Rochester, NY; Prof. of Musicol., Eastman Schl. of Music, Rochester, NY; Prof. of Musicol., Univ. of Victoria, BC, Can. Perfs. in Concerts w. Alfred Deller & Robert Donington, 1964; Recitals in San Francisco, Chgo. & Rochester, NY. Publ: The Ornamented Clausula Diminuta in the Fitzwilliam Virginal Book, 1967; Music & Dance from the Court of Louis XIV, 1975. Contbr. to: Musical Quarterly; Grove's Dictionary of Music & Musicians. Mbrships: Am. Musicol. Soc.; Music Lib. Assn. Hons: Sigma Alpha Iota Prize (in perf.), 1961; Wilson Fellowship, 1965-66. Address: Univ. of Victoria, Victoria, BC, Can. V8W 2Y2.

SCHWANTNER, Joseph, b. 22 Mar. 1943. Chicago, Ill., USA. Composer. Educ: BMus, Chgo. Conserv. Coll., 1964; MMus, DMus, Northwestern Univ., Evanston, Ill., 1966-68; m. Janet Elaine rossate, 1 s., 1 d. Career: Assoc. Prof. of Comp., Eastman Schl. of Music, Rochester, NY, 1970-. Comps. publd: In Aeternum, 1973; Consortium, 1970; Diaphonia Intervallum, 1965; Entropy, 1966; Chronicon, 1976. Comps. recorded: Diaphonia Intervallum; Consortium; In Aeternum; Modus Caelestis; Autumn Canticles. Mbr., Am. Comps. Alliance. Hons. incl: Bearnes Prize in music, Columbia Univ., 1967;

Comps. Fellowship Grants/Nat. Endowment for Arts, 1974, 75. Address: 21 Overbrook Rd., Rochester, NY 14624, USA. 16.

SCHWARTZ, Charles M. NYC, USA. Composer; Author; College Teacher. Educ: PhD, NY Univ. Grad. Schl. of Arts & Sci., 1969. Studied comp. w. Aaron Copland, Darius Milhaud, Roger Sessions, Charles Jones & Arthur Berger. Career: A universe career as comp., author, impresario & music prof., incl. Dir. of Composers' Showcase & mbr., music fac., Hunter Coll., NY; num. TV & radio apps. Comps. incl: 5 symphs., 2 string quartets, songs, orchl. works, solo pieces & instrumental works. Published works incl: Professor Jive (jazz symph.); Mother--, Mother-- (jazz symph.); Comments, for wind and percussion; Motion, for strings; Passacaglia, for orch. Recordings incl: Professor Jive. Publs: Cole Porter, a Biography, 1977: Gershwin, His Life & Music, 1973: George Gershwin, Selective Bibliography & Discography, 1974. Contbr. to: Dict. of Contemporary Music; Grove's Dict., 6th ed. Mbr., num. profl. socs. Hons.: ASCAP award, 1978; Kt. of Mark Twain, 1977; Founders Day Award (NY Univ.) 1970; Fellow, MacDowell Colony, 1968. Hobbies: Collecting brass instruments, paintings & other arts objects. Address: 463 West St. (G-219), NY, NY10014, USa. 2, 28, 29.

SCHWARTZ, Judith Leah, b. 27 April 1943. Jamaica, NY, USA. Musicologist. Educ: MA, 1968, PhD, 1973, NY Univ.; AB, 1964, Vassar Coll.; studied piano w. Donald Yap & Marta Milinowski, harpsichord w. Donald Pearson, Eugenia Earle & Robert Veyron-LaCroix. m. Theodore C Karp. Career: Tchr. of Musicol., Vassar Coll., 1969-70, Univ. of Calif. at Riverside, 1971-73, Northwestern Univ., 1974-. Publs: An Annotated Bibliography of Research Materials for French Baroque Dance and Dance Music. Contbr. to: Music Library Assn. Notes; Grove's Dict., 6th Ed., etc. Mbrships: Am. Musicol. Soc. (Mbr. of Coun., 1978-); Am. Soc. for 18th Century Studies; Music Lib. Assn.; Coll. Music Soc. Hons: Fulbright Award for study in Austria, 1967-68; Am. Philisophical Soc. Grant, 1973-74. Hobbies: Music; Dancing; Photography. Address: 806 Chilton Lane, Wilmette, IL 60091, USA.

SCHWARTZ, Marvin Robert, b. 4 Feb. 1937. NYC, USA. Composer; Educator. Educ. incls: BA, Queens Coll., Flushing, NY, 1957; MFA, Brandeis Univ., Waltham, Mass., 1959; SMD, Jewish Theol. Som., NYC, 1964: musical studies w. many noted tchrs. m. Sherry Ruth Schwartz, 1 s., 3 d. Career: Prof. of Music, Chmn. of Music Dept., 1969-. Queensborough Community Coll., CUNY; Tchr. Queens Coll. & Manhattan Community Coll., both CUNY. Comps. incl: Ruth, a Biblical narrative; Look & Long (opea from play by Gertrude Stein); Scherzo for violin & piano; Lament for Six Million (orchl.); Scenes & Studies for solo viola d'amore. Contbr. to jrnls. Mbr. profl. orgs. Recip. var. hons. Hobbies: Hist.; Middle Eastern philos. Address: 166-10 75th Ave., Flushing, NY 11366, USA.

SCHWARTZ, Paul, b. 22 July 1907. Vienna, Austria. Composer; Conductor; Pianist; Lecturer. Educ: PhD (musicol.), Univ. of Vienna, Dips. (piano & comp.), Vienna State Acad.; Master dips. (comp. & cond.), ibid. m. Kathryn Carlisle Schwartz, 3 d. Career: Chmn., dept. of music, Bard Coll., Annandale-on-Hudson, NY, 1938-47; chmn., dept. of music, Kenyon Coll., Gambier, Ohio, 1947-72; Comp.-in-Residence, ibid., 1976-78. Comps: Violin Concerto; Concerto Grosso; Con Concert Overtures; Sacred Concerto; Cantata, America Celebrates; Smaller choruses; Str. Quartet; Piano Quintet; Piano Trio; Violin Sonata; smaller chmbr. works; songs. Recording: Concertino for Chamber Orchestra. Publ: Hearing Music With Understanding, 1968. Mbrships: Past pres., Ohio Music Tchrs. Assn. & Ohio Theory-Comp. Tchrs. Hons: Commissions from Columbus Symph. Orch., Great Lakes Colls. Assn. & Ohio Bicentennial Commission; fellowship support grant from Ohio Arts Coun. Hobbies: Tennis; Swimming. Address: 203 Ward St., Gambier, OH 43022, USA.

SCHWARTZ, Wilfred, b. 23 Sept. 1923. New York, NY, USA. Violinist; Educator; Conductor. Educ: BS, MS, Juilliard Schl. of Music; Columbia Univ.; Study of violin w. Edouard Dethier, Hans Letz, Louis Persinger; Study of conducting w. Pierre Monteux, Fritz Mahler, Peter Wilhousky, m., 3 children. Debut: Carnegie Hall, NYC, 1949. Career: Concerts, USA & Europe, Radio, TV apps.; Guest Cond., Belgian Nat. Radio, Denver (USA) Symph. Orch., Mexico City Phil., others; Fndr., Cond., Ft. Collins (Colo.) Symph., 1949-; Cond., Cheyenne (Wyo.) Symph. & Choral Soc., 1955-59; Prof., Violin & Orch., Colo. State Univ., 1949-. Recordings: 2 LPs, rare music, produced on grant from Colo. State Univ. Contbr. to profl. jrnls. Mbrships: Am. String Tchrs. Assn.; Nat. Assn. of Composers & Conds.; MENC; Am. Fedn. of Musicians. Hons: Bronze Star, WW II; Nat. Hon. Patron, Delta Omicron. Hobbies: Tennis; Swimming;

Theater; Reading. Address: 1117 Robertson, Ft. Collins, CO, 80524 USA 3.

SCHWARZ, Boris, b. 13 March 1906. St. Petersburg, USSR. Musicologist; Violinst; Conductor. Educ: Sorbonne, Paris, 1925-26; Univ. of Berlin, 1930-36; PhD, musicol., Columbia Univ., NY, 1950. m. Patricia Yodido, 2 s. Debut: Hanover, Germany, 1921. Career: Concertized in Europe, 1921-36; Perf., USA, 1936-; Prof. of Music, Queens Coll., CUNY, 1941-76. Recordings: Complete Bach Sonatas, violin & harpsichord (w. Alice Ehlers); Four Haydn Sontats, violin & harpsichord. Publs: Music & Musical Life in Soviet Russia, 1917-1970, 1972 (German tranls. 1979, 2nd Ed., 1976); Ed., Transl. of Carl Flesch, Violin Fingering, its theory and practice, 1966. Contbr. to: The Musical Quarterly; The Musical Times; The Listener; Musical Am.; Saturday Review; Columbia Masterworks; Slavic Review; Notes; Grove's Dict., 6th Ed. Mbrships: Am. Musicol. Soc.; Int. Musicol. Soc.; Gesellschaft für Musikforschung. Hons: Ford Fndn. Grant, 1952-53; Guggenheim Fellowship, 1959-60; Exchange Scholar, Moscow Acad. of Sci., 1962; ASCAP Award, 1974. Address: 50-16 Robinson St. Flushing, NY 11355, USA. 14.

SCHWARZ, Rudolf, b. 29 Apr. 1905. Vienna, Austria. Conductor. Educ: Vienna. m. Greta Ohlson, 1 s. Mbr: ISM. Hons: Hon. RAM; Hon. GSM; DMushc, Univ. of Newcastle-upon-Tyne, 1972; CBE, 1973. Address: 24 Wildcroft Manor, London SW15 3TS, UK. 1, 3, 14, 16, 21.

SCHWARZ, Vera, b. 31 Jan. 1929. Hamburg, German Fed. Repub. Pianist; Harpsichordist. Educ: Music Acad. Detmold; Music Acad. Vienna. Career: 1964; Prof. for Harpsichord, Music Acad. Graz; 1967, Fndr. and Dir. Inst. for Methods of Perf., Music Acad. Graz. Recordings: var. w. German record companies. Publs: The Young Haydn, Graz, 1971; The Tonal Aspect in the Restoration of old Keyboard Instruments, Graz, 1973; The Violin, the Instrument and its Music, Vienna, 1975. (ed.) Contbr. to: Austrian Music paper. Hons: 1st Prize, Int. Music Contest. Munich, 1958. Address: Neue Welt-Gasse 19, A-1130 Vienna, Austria.

SCHWARZ DU BRUSLE DE ROUVROY, Jean, b. 20 May 1939. Lille, France. Engineer; Composer. Educ: Electronic Engr.; Dips. in Percussion & Harmony, Conserv. of the 10th Dist., Paris. m. Cella Levenez, 2 s. Debut: 1964. Career: Joined Nat. C'tr. for Sci. Rsch., 1965; Joined Music Rsch. Grp., Nat. Audiovisual Inst., 1969; in charge of Accoustical Lab., Dept. of Ethnomusicol., Mus. of Man, Paris. Comps. incl: Hoiku, for tape, 1970; Erda for tape, 1972; Anticycle, for tape & percussion, 1972; Symph.,. for tape, 1974; Fantasy, for piano, 1975. Don Quichotte, for tape, 1976. Recordings: Anticycle; Concrete Music. Contbr. to: Weber Thematic Ency. Mbrships: Sacem; Sacd. Hobbies: Tennis, Golf. Address: 121 rue de Bellevue, 92100 Boulogne, France.

SCHWARZKOPF-LEGGE, Elisabeth, b. 9 Dec. 1915. Jarotchin, Posen (Poznan), Germany. Concert & Opera Singer. Edu: Hochschule für Musik, Berlin; pvte. studies w. Maria Ivogün. m. Walter Legge. Debut: Städtische Oper, Berlin. Career: Berlin Stadtischoper, 1938-43; Vienna State Opera, 1944-50; Royal Opera Covent Gdn., London; La Scala, 1948-64; apps. in every major opera house in Western world; concerts throughout Western world, Japan, Aust., NZ, S Africa, etc.; num. radio & TV broadcasts. Num. recordings inclng: R Strauss; Der Rosenkavalier, Ariadne auf Naxoa, Capriccio; Mozart, all da Ponte operas & Zauberflöte; Wagner, Die Meistersinger; Verdi Requiem; Falstaff; Beethoven, Missa Solemnis; Bach, B minor Mass, etc. Num. hons. inclng: DMus, Cambridge Univ.; Grosses Verdienstkreuz, Germany. Hobbies: Tennis; Mountaineering. Address: c/o Musical Adviser Establishment, Vaduz, Liechtenstein.

SCHWARZ-SCHILLING, Reinhard, b. 9 May 1904. Hannover, Germany. Professor of Compositions; Organist; Conductor. Educ: studied w. Braunfels, Heinrich Kaminski, Boell, Ehrenberg. m. Dusza v. Hakrid, 1 s. Career: Chmbr. Music, Organ, 1927-; Cond., 1929-; Guest Cond., Germany, USA. Korea; Organ & Piano Radio & Concert Perfs. in Germany, Austria, USA, Can., Japan, Korea; TV Apps., 1971, 73. Comps incl: Concerto, for violin & orch.; Partita, for orch.; Sinfonia Daitonica; Symph. in C; Str. Quartet F minor; Klavier-Sonata; Missa In Terra Pax; The Lord's Prayer; Eichendorff-Lieder Cantata Laetare for choir and strings; Motet, Über die Schwelle; Duo for violin & piano, sev. recordings. Contbr. to: Musica; Philharmonische Blatter. Mbrships: GEMA; Deutscher Komponistenverband. Named Honor-Guest of the BRD-Foreign Dept. in the Villa Massimo, Rome, 1966. Address: 24 A Taubert Str., 1 Berlin 33, German Fed. Repub. 28.

SCHWEIKERT, Norman Carl, b. 8 Oct. 1937. LA, Calif., USA. Horn Player. Educ: BMus, Eastman Schl. of Music, Univ. of Rochester, NY; studied w. Odolindo Perissi, Sinclair Lott, Joseph Eger, Morris Secon & Verne Reynolds; orchestral trng. w. Peter Meremblum Calif. Jr. Symph. Orch., Hollywood. m. Sally H Haizlip, 1 s. Career incls: Horn Player w. many orchs. inclng. Rochester Phil., Eastman-Rochester Symph., US Mil. Acad. Band. W. Pt., Aspen Fest. Orch. & LA. Phil.; Instr. of Horn & Mbr., Interlochen Arts Quintet, Interlochen Arts Acad., Mich., 1966-71; 1st Horn & Soloist, Dr. Thor Johnson's Chgo. Little Symph., tours of 1967 & 68, w. Peninsula Music Fest. Orch., 1968, 69 & 70; Soloist w. var. other orchs.; Asst. 1st Horn, Chgo. Symph., 1971-; Tchng. Asst.; Northwestern Univ., Evanston, 1973-; Asst. 1st Horn, Chgo. Symph. 1971-75; 2nd Horn, ibid., 1975-; Assoc. Prof. pt-time, Northwestern Univ., 1975. Guest Artist, Lectr. & Recitalist thru'out USA. Contbr. to: The Horn Call. Mbrships: Advsry. Coun., 1972-. Int. Horn Soc. Sec. Treas., 1970-72; Advsry. Coun., 1972-76. Phi Mu Alpha Sinfonia; Galpin Soc., London; Am. Musical Instrument Soc. Recip. of sev. awards. Hobbies: Collecting Musical Antiques & US Stamps; Reading; Musical Research. Address: 1340 Golf Ave., Highland Park, IL 60035, USA. 2.

SCHWIEGER, Hans, b. 1910. Cologne, Germany. Conductor; Pianist. Educ: Cologne & Bonn Univs.; Music Acad., Cologne. m. Mary Fitzpatrick Shields. Career: Asst. to Erich Kleiber, State Opera, Berlin, 1930; Gen. Music Dir., Mainz, 1932: Guest Cond., Europe, 1932-36; Music Dir., Free State of Danzig, 1936; Cond., Imperial Orch., Tokyo, 1937; Guest Cond., Asia & USA, 1938-48; Music Dir., Kansas City Phil., 1948-; Music Dir., Aspen Music Fest., Colo., 1955; app. w. San Fran. Opera Co., 1956; gave world premiere of Janacek's Opera Schicksal, State Opera, Stuttgart, 1958; frequent Guest Cond. of opera & symph., major German cities; toured Paris, Madrid & Russia, 1972. Hons: HHD; DMus. Mgmt: Hurok Concerts Inc., 1370 Sixth Ave., NYC, NY 10019, USA.

SCHWEITZER, Anton, b. 31 May 1898. Rotterdam, Netherlands. Composer; Violinist. Educ: comp. w. H Zagwin; violin w. L Zimmermann. m. Helene M Peters, 1 child. Debut: 1914. Career: apps. w. var. light music ensembles, 1914-30; w. Rotterdam Phil. Orch., 1918-63. Comps. incl: Notation (solo violin, piano); Story (piano, violin, cello); Symphonical Sketch De Haven; Suite for str. orch.; One Minute, 3 Am. Satires (orchl.); Chorale w. variations (str. orch.); stage & film music. Mbr., Genootschap van Nederlandse Componisten (Geneco). Recip. 2nd prize, Nat. Comp. Contest, Dutch Broadcasting Union, 1941. Hobbies: Sports; Reading. Address: Calandstraat 34, Rotterdam, 3016, Netherlands.

SCHWERTSIK, Kurt, b. 25 June 1935. Vienna, Austria. Composer; Orchestra Musician (French Horn). Educ: Acad. of Music, Vienna, Reifeprufung. m. Christa, 2 c. Career: Mbr., Nieder Osterreichesches Tonkunstler Orchester, 1955-59 & '62-68; Mbr., Wiener Symphoniker, 1968-; Fndr. w. Friedrich Cerha, The Ensemble for Modern Music 'Die Reihe', 1959. Comps. incl: Sonatine fur Horn & Klavier, 1952-72; Trio fur Violine, Horn & Klavier, 1960; 5 Noctures fur Klavier, 1964: Blattaue Schnecken Ohrenkreiser; Draculas Haus & Hofmusik, eine trassylvanische symphonie fur Streicher, 1968; Musik vom Mutterland MU, fur 11 instruments, 1971; Entwurf fur ein Streichquartett, 1974. Der Lange Weg zur gropen Mauer, 1975. Recordings: Kurt Schwertsik's Lichte Momente, Op. 21, BASF. Mbrships: Internationale Gesellschaft fur Neue Musik. Hobbies: Engl. & Am. sci. fiction books; Arts & Architecture. Address: Hockegasse 9, A-1180 Vienna, Austria. 14.

SCHWILLER, Elisabeth. London. Educ: London & Paris (pupil of Dinh Gilly). m. Isidore Schwiller Conductor & Violinist (dec.). 1 s., 3 d. (1 dec.). Prof: Dramatic Soprano & Teacher. Sang under name of Elise Leoni at Covent Gdn. in Beecham Internat. Season In Tosca, Louise, Butterfly, Salome; Var. Touring Opera Roles; Established Elisabeth Schwiller Schl. of Opera 1945; toured China & Far East. Publ: in prep.; A Manual on the Art of Singing. Teaching a method of singing in Rossini tradition as exemplified by Dinh Gilly, as taught Cotogni. Address: 19A Canfield Gnds., London NW6, UK.

SCHWINGER, Eckart, b. 20 Aug. 1934. Freital, German Dem. Repub. Music critic. Educ: Conserv. Dresden, 1953/1955; Music Acad. W Berlin, 1955/1959. m. Bergitt Schwinger, 2 c. Career: Music critic Dresden; since 1966 permanent critic of the Berlin daily Neue Zeit. Mbrships: Permanent mbr. Radio GDR; mbr. German Records; Berlin (ETERNA). Contbr. to: var. profl. jrnls. Hons: Hon. Medal Assn. of Comps. and Musicologists, German Dem. Repub., 1975. Address: Friedrichstr. 125, 104 Berlin, German Dem. Repub.

SCIONTI, Isabel Laughlin. Premont, Tex., USA. Concert Pianist; Teacher. Educ: BMus, Baylor Univ., Waco., Tex.; MMus, Chgo. Musical Coll. m. (i) Silvio Scionti, dec., (ii) William R Hicks, dec. Debut: Rome, Italy, & Carnegie Hall, NYC. Career: 2 Piano Concerts w. Silvio Scionti, Europe, Mex., USA; 1st All-Bach 2 piano concert, Town Hall, NYC, 1941. Var. recordings. Mbrships: Hon. Mbr., Sigma Alpha Iota; State Chmn., Collegiate Artist Competition, sponsored by Nat. MTA. 1969-; Bd., Tex. MTA, 4 yrs. Recip., DMus, Baylor Univ. Hobby: Travel. Address: 1111 Emerson Lane, Denton, TX 76201, USA. 3, 5, 12.

SCIUTTI, Graziella, b. 17 Apr. 1932. Torino, Italy. Concert & Opera Singer. Educ: Dip., Conserv. St. Cecilia, Rome. Debut: concert, St. Cecilia Acad., Rome; opera, Fest. Aix-en-Provence, France. Career: participant in Glyndebourne, Edinburgh, Salzburg & Holland Fests.; apps. at Paris Opera, La Scala Milan, Royal Opera, San Fran. Opera, etc.; tours in S Am. & S Africa; num. radio & TV broadcasts. Hons: Harriet Cohen Golden Medal; Microfono D'Argento; Euro Premio Prize, 1966. Address: La Chaumiére, 24 Rte. de Carra, 249 Puplinge, Geneva, Switz.

SCOFFIELD, William Eric, b. 11 Jan. 1940; Hamilton, Ont., Canada. Conductor; Teacher; Organist; Choir Director. Educ: BA, McMaster Univ., 1961; studied piano w. Eileen McManamy & organ w. George Veary, Hamilton; ARCT (piano solo perf); Specialist Tchng. Certs. in Vocal & Instrumental Music. m. Christa M Bisanz, 2 d., 3 s. Career: Cond. of amateur instrumental & choral grps.; Tchr. of Piano, Organ, Theory, Singing, Winds & Strings in sec. schl.; also Tchr. of Maths; Organist, var. churches; Choir Dir.; Accompanist; Mbrship. in Choirs of Christ Ch. Cath., Hamilton, cond. by George Veary, & St. Mary Magdalene, under Dr Willian. Mbrships: RCCO; V. Chmn., St. Catharines & Peterborough Ctrs., ibid; Canadian Music Educators Assn.; Royal Candadian Coll. of Organists, Chmn. 1974-76; Fndg. Chmn., Port Hope Friends of Music (Concert Soc.); Ont. Music Educators Assn.; Ont. Choral Fedn. Var. hobbies. Address: Campbellcroft, Ont., Canada.

SCOLARI, Henri Louis, b. 25 Sept. 1923. Geneva, Switz. (French citizen). Composer. Educ: Ecole Artistique de Musique, Geneva; Music Conserv., ibid. m. Maria Rosa Bellandi. Career: Controller of Music, Radio-TV Suisse Romande, 1962-. Comps. incl: Le Christ voile (cantata), 1948; Les Stéréos-Symphonies (3 orch.), 1959; Mutations for 15 Instruments, 1961; L'Apothéose d'Alexandre, 1962; Intégration (orch.), 1967; Concerto (cello & orch.), 1970; Arghoul, 1071; Eoliennes (piano), 1975; Concerto (flute & orch.), 1977; Arghoul 2 (clarinet & piano), 1978. Publ: le Trition dénominateur formel du chromatisme intégral, 1950. Mbr., profl. assns. Hons: 2nd Prize, Radio Lausanne Comp. Contest, 1960; Dip. of Hon., Arts-Sciences-Lettres, Paris, 1975. Hobbies: Moder Art; Painting; Photography; Travel. Address: 63 Chemin de Rovéréaz, 1012 Lausanne, Switz.

SCORDINO-HAYES, Judith Marie, b. 7 June 1952. N Babylon, LI, NY, USA. Music Teacher; Violinist; Orchestra Director. Educ: BMus; Perfs. Cert. in Violin, Crane Schl. of Music, SUNY at Potsdam, 1974; Provisional Tchrs. Cert., NY State Educ. Dept.; currently studying for M Ed., CW Post Coll., LI. Career: Music Tchr., & Dir., Jr. High Schl. Str. Orch.; Mbr., Massapequa Symph. Orch.; perfs. w. Con Amore Orch, Utica Symph. Orch. & played background for a Tony Bennett perf.; 1st Orch. Chairwoman, Suffolk County Music Educs. Assn. 1st Elementary Schl. Music Fest. Mbrships: Kappa Delta Pi; Suffolk Co. Music Educators Assn.; NY State Schl. Music Assn. Recip. var. coll. hons. Hobbies: Teaching Swimming; Golf; Volleyball; Playing for Musicals. Address: 617 11th St., W Babylon, NY, USA.

SCOTT, Alexander Robert Crawford, b. 23 May 1932. Kingskettle, Scotland, UK. Lecturer in Music Education; Music Educationist; Conductor; Musicologist. Educ: BMus, 1953, Hons. 2, 1958, Univ. of Edinburgh; Staatliche Hochschule für Musik, Hamburg; Mozarteum, Salzburg; Tchrs. Cert., Moray House Coll. of Educ., 1959. m. Doreen McLaren Low Harley. Career: Edinburgh Int. Fest., Assembly Hall Prodns., 1953, '59; Cond., var. amateur & youth orchs & choirs; Edinburgh Youth Orch.; Black Dyke Mills Band; Edinburgh Royal Choral Union (Chorus Master for broadcasts w. BBC, SSO). 1973-77; Lectr. in Music Educ., Cond., & part-time Lectr., Dept. of Educl. Studies, Univ. of Edinburgh; Hd. of Music Dept. of Moray House Coll. of Educ.; Part-time Cons., GTC for Scotland. Contbr. to: Music & Letters; Music in Educ.; Music Tchr.; The Scotsman; The Educl. Inst. of Scotland Jrnl. Mbrships: Assn. of Lectrs. in Colls. of Educ., Scotland; Chmn., Music Lectrs. Assn. (Scottish Colls. of Educ.). Recip., var. scholarships. Address: 26 Polwarth Tce., Edinburgh, EH11 1NA, UK.

SCOTT, Anthony Leonard Winstone, b. 18 Sept. 1911. Datchet, Bucks., UK. Composer; Organist; Organ Restorer. Educ: RCM. w. Herbert Howells & Henry G. Ley; Pvte. study of composition w. Gerald Finzi; Apprenticed to Rushworth & Dreaper Ltd. (organ bldrs.). m. Ruth Maude Moorsom, 2 s. Career: Organist Lambourn Parish Ch., Berks., 1953-71; Cond., Local Choral Soc., etc.; Music Master, Scaitcliffe Schl., Englefield Green, 1949-52, Lambourn C & E Schl., 1953-55. Comps: Part Songs; Toccata & Fugue for Organ; Prelude & Fugue for Organ; Four Songs from the Princess; Concertos for Violin & Orch.; Organ & String Orch.; Sinfonia for Piano & Orch.; Forgive the Sleeping Man (Baritone, Chorus & Orch.); 2 One-Act Operas, etc. Mbrships: CGGB; Worship Co. of Musicians. Hobbies: Reading; Walking. Addess: Scarth, Winsley, Bradford-on-Avon, Wilts., UK. 3.

SCOTT, Charles Russell, b. 8 Feb. 1898. London, UK. Schoolmaster. Educ: BA, St. John's Coll., Cambridge, 1920; MA, ibid., 1925. m. Irene Keightley Rankin, 3 s., 1 d. Career: Asst. Educ. Sec., Cambs., 1922-27; Asst. Master, Tonbridge Schl., 1927-29; Hdmaster, Cranbrook Schl., 1929-60; JP for Kent, 1943-. Publs: Gen. Ed., Music & the Community, 1933; Jt. Ed., Music & the Amateur, 1951; Ed., Music Centres & the Training of Specially Talented Children, 1966. Contbr. to: Howard Jrnl.; Music & Letters; Making Music; Jrnl. of Educ.; Times Educl. Supplement; Cambridge Review. Mbrships: Chmn., Standing Conf. of Amateur Music, 1946-63, Kent Co. Music Comm., 1932 65; Vice-Chmn. & Treas., Rural Music Schls. Assn., 1958-; Chmn., Kent Coun. of Soc. Serv., 1958-73; VP, 1974-; Advsry. Comm. of Amateur Opera, 1948-63. Hobbies: Social Service; Gardening, Playing Chamber Music (Violin). Address: The Quarry Wrotham, Kent TN 15 7QD, UK. 1, 3, 23, 28, 29.

SCOTT, Derek Brian, b. 28 Feb. 1950. Birmingham, UK. Lecturer. Educ: BA, MMus, Hull Univ. Career: Lectr., Hull Coll. of Higher Educ., & Open Univ. Comps. incl: Sinfonietta, 1975; Brass Quintet, 1976; Lament for 15 solo instrments, 1977. Mbrships: Assoc., CGGB. Hons: Mrs. Sunderland Comps. Prize, 1973; Yorkshire Arts Prize for Comp., 1974; Northern Arts, 1978. Hobbies: Greek Lit.; Motorcycling. Address: 122 Marlborough Ave., Hull, HU5 3JX, UK.

SCOTT, Douglas Michael, b. 5 May 1938. Stirling, Scotland, UK. Teacher of Piano, Singing, Organ & Theory; Choral Conductor; Organist; Lecturer. Educ: Jordanhill Coll. of Educ., Glasgow; LTCL (CMT); LRAM; ARCM; LGSM; ACP. Career: Tchr. of Music, Dunblane Schl., 1961-67; Organist & Choirmaster, Auchterarder, 1966-68; Prin. Tenor & Dpty. Organists, Dunblane Cathedral, 1968-71; Prin. Tchr. of Music, Auchterarder, Secondary Schl., 1969-73; Prin. Tchr. of Music, Bannochburn High, 1974; Prin. Tchr. of Music Auchterarden High, 1975-; Organist & Choirmaster, Barony Ch., Auchterarder, 1971-76; Extra-mural Lectr., Glasgow Univ., 1975-, Univ. of Stirling, 1976-; Mbr., BBC Scottish Singers, 1977; Cond., Clackmannan Choral Soc., 1978-. Mbrships: (incl) Life Mbr., Soc. of Friends of Dunblane Cathedral, Scotland; ISM; RSCM; RCO; Past Pres., Stirling & Dist. Soc. of Organists; FIBA. Hobbies: Photography; Reading; Travel; Gen. Knowledge. Address: 19 Charles St., Dunblane, Perthshire, Scotland FK15 9BY, UK.

SCOTT, Henry G, b. 5 July 1944. Dorothy, NJ, USA. Double Bassist; Professor of Bass. Educ: Grad., Univ. of Rochester, NY, 1966; Eastman Schl. of Music, ibid.; PhD Cand., Heed Univ., Hollywood, Fla. m. Yumi Ninomiya Scott, 2 s. Career: Rochester Phil., 1963-66; Chmbr. Symph. of Phila., 1966-68; Balt. Symph. Orch., 1968-72; Phila. Lyric & Grand Opera Cos., 1972-74; Phila. Symph. Orch., 1974-; toured NZ, Japan, Aust., USA, Can. & Europe as Mbr., NY Phil.; Prof. of Bass, Phila. Music Acad.; Fac. Mbr., New Schl. of Music, Phila. Recordings: as Mbr. of Phila. Orch. Mbrships: Int. Soc. for Double Bassists; Nat. Accreditation Assn. for Psychoanalysis. Address: c/o Phila. Orch., Broad & Locust St., Philadephia, PA 19102, USA.

SCOTT, James, b. 29 March, b. 29 Mar. 1925. Farnworth, UK. Conductor; Adjudicator; Cornet & Trumpet Player & Teacher. Educ: Pvte. studies. m. Ena Scott, 1 d. Career: 1st Broadcast, aged 12, as cornet soloist; Regular broadcasts as player & cond.; Sev. TV apps. as Cond. Recordings: Cornet solos; As Cond., Sev. LP's w. Brighouse & Rastrick and Fodens Brass Bands, etc. Contbr. to: The British Bandsman. Hons: Silver Medal of the Worshipful Co. of Musicians of the City of London for services to Brass Bands, 1977. Hobbies: Walking; Reading. Address: 53 Dibbines Hey, Bebington, Wirral, Merseyside L63 9JU, UK.

SCOTT, John, b. 1 Nov. 1930. Bristol, UK. Composer. Educ: Royal Artillery Band, Woolwich. Career: ldng. Jazz Saxophonist & Flautist, 1960's, also working w. RPO & New Philharmonia; Musical Dir., EMI; Comp., 1965-; Cond., 1968-; in feature films. Comps: num. works for film & TV inclng: Anthony & Cleopatra, Midweek (BBC), Nationwide (BBC); Orpheus & Euridice (ballet); Concerto for saxophone & orch. Comps. recorded: Anthony & Cleopatra (film music); England Made Me (film music). Mbr., Savile Club. Recip., Emmy Award for 'Wild Dogs of Africa', 1971. Hobbies: Music; Skiing. Address: 2 Queen's Gate Pl. Mews, London SW7 5BQ, UK.

SCOTT, John Gavin, b. 18 June 1956. Wakefield, UK. Organist. Educ: BA, MusB, Univ. of Cambridge; pvte. study w. Dr P G Saunders, Jonathan Bielby, Ralph Downes & Gillian Weir. Debut: Royal Fest., Hall, 1979. Career: Solo organ & harpsichord recitals; many recitals w. choir of St. John's Coll., Cambridge, inclng. apps. at Holland Fest., 1975, Promenade Concert, 1975, & BBC Radio 3 broadcasts; Asst. organist, St. Paul's & Southwark Cathedrals. Recordings: w. St. John's Coll. Choir. Hons: Organ Scholar, St. John's Coll., Cambridge, 1974-78; ARCO Limpus Prize, 1971; FRCO Limpus Prize, 1973, & Dr. F J Read Prize, 1974; John Stewart of Rannoch Scholarship in Sacred Music, Univ. of Cambridge, 1975; 1st prize, Manchester Int. Organ competition, 1978. Hobbies: Ecclesiastical arch.; German romantic poetry & lit.; Cinema; Reading; Travel. Address: All Hallows Vicarage, Copperfield St., London SE1, UK.

SCOTT, Leonard, b. 6 Oct. 1908. West Ham, London, UK. Composer. Educ: studied under Herbert Howells, Michael Tippett, Gordon Jacobs, Leslie Orrey, Morley Coll.; trombone under Tom Gutteridge, late of LSO. m. Olive Freda Scott, 3 d. Career: Music jrnlsm., freelance, & w. EMI London. Comps: Part song, 'The Tailor & The Crow' (Galliard); 3rd & 4th Str. Quartets (pvte. recording), (film music). Publs: Sleeve notes on works by Verdi, Bartok, Moussorgsky, Borodin, Boito, Bellini. Booklet on Mozart, Tchaikovsky, Verdi, etc. issued w. the operas of these comps. Notes & transl. on most for the standard operas by major & some minor comps. Mbrships: CGGB; Friend of the Soc. for the Promotion of New Music. Recip., Edwin Evans Prize for Str. Quartet No. 3, 1953. Address: 90 St. John Wood Terr., London, NW7, UK.

SCOTT, Robert Charles, b. 23 July 1935. Wolf Lake, Ind., USA. Educator. Educ: BMus, Knox Coll., Galesburg, Ill., 1957; MA, Tex. A & I Univ., Kingsville, 1963; DMusA, Univ. of Tex., Austin, 1973; studies w. Jess Walters & Walter Ducloux. m. Patricia Darlene Lond, 2 s. Career: St. Louis Municipal Opera, 1955; Little Rock Symph. Orch. Opera, 1957; Music Critic, Corpus Christi Caller-Times, 1964-70; Judge, Met. Opera Reg. Auditions, 1972, '76; Prof., Dir. of Opera Workshop & Summer Music Theatre, also Mbr. of Grad. Coun., Tex. A & I Univ. Contbr. to jrnls. Mbrships: Ctrl. Opera Serv.; Tex. Assn. of Coll. Tchrs.; Actors Equity. Recip. rsch. grant, 1975. Address: 500 College Pl., Kingsville, TX 78363, USA. 7.

SCOTT, Ronnie, b. 28 Jan. 1927. London, UK. Saxophonist; Club Owner. Educ: Pvtw. studies. Career: Mbr., num. famous bands; Formed own band & toured; w. Pete King, opened own jazz club, 1959. Recordings: Ronnie Scott Quintet, Serious Gold. Mbrships: Hon. VP, London Orchl. Assn. Mgmt: Ronnie Scott Directions, 47 Frith St., London W1, UK. Address: Ronnie Scott's Club, 47 Frith St., London W1, UK.

SCOTT, Rupert Nicolas Boileau, b. 24 Dec. 1945. Evesham, Worcs., UK. Composer; Violinist. Educ: RAM, 1964-68; BMus, London, 1967. m. Susan Dickinson. Comps: Suite for 2 Brass Trios, 1970; Towards The New Damascus, 1972; Suite for 4 Saxes, 1973; Bright Blue & Carnival Time, 1974; The Fire & The Rose, 1976; The Red Fox Burning, 1978. Hobbies: Reading; Conversation; Tennis; Squash; Crosswords. Address: 45 Whinmoor Gardens, Leeds 14, Yorkshire, UK. 4.

SCOTT, Samuel Hurley, b. 8 Jan. 1919. Cairo, Ill., USA. Music Theorist & Professor. Educ: BMus., MMus., Jordan Conserv. of Music; PhD Univ. of Iowa. m. Carmen Phyllis Scott. Career: Clarinettist w. Met. Opera Co., etc.; currently Fac. Mbr, N Tex. State Univ. Schl. of Music. Mbrships: Pi Kappa Lambda; Phi Mu Alpha. Publs: Examples of Gregorian Chant & Other Sacred Music of the 16th Century, 1971; Tonal Counterpoint, 1975. Hobbies: Pure bred Whippets: Theoretical rsch. Address: Rte. 3, Box 13, Denton, TX 76201, USA.

SCOTT, Stuart John, b. 29 Jan. 1949. Stretford, Nr. Manchester, UK. Teacher of Flute & Piano. Educ: studied Scis. at Stretford Tech. Coll.; studied Piano & Flute at Chorley Coll. of Educ.; Tchrs. Cert., Lancaster Univ. studied comp. under Lennox Berkeley. m. Jan Beverley Wood. Career: Tchr. of Music in Schls.; Lectr. in Further Educ. Coll.; Public of lectures on Skryabin; Chmn., Stretford Schls. Arts Fest.; Contbr. to broadcast music mag. progs. - talks on Skryabin & on schl.

music Perfs. & broadcasts incl. 'Variations' for two pianos, 'Sonata' & 'Two Pieces' for Brass Sextet, 'Night Piece' for flute & strings, 'March Royal' for full orch., 'Conversations' for wind trio, & var. piano & instrumental solos. Comps. have been perf. in UK, USA, Germany & Scandinavia. First publd. comp. 'An Egyptian Suite' Op. 33 for solo flute. BBC recorded broadcasts of 'Sonata for Brass Sextet' Op. 42. Mbrships. incl: Fndr., Chmn., Brit. Skryabin Soc.; CGGB; PRS; ISM; Barbirolli Soc. Recip. var. awards. Hobbies: Egyptology; Poetry; Woodcraft. Address: Staverley, 6 Colville Grove, Sale Cheshire 1733 4FW, UK.

SCOVOTTI, Jeanette, b. 5 Dec. 1938. New York, USA. Opera & Concert Singer. Educ: HS of Music & Art; 3rd St. Music Schl.; Juilliard Schl. of Music (Dip. in Voice). m. Klaus Andersen. Debut: NYC Opera, 1959; Netropolitan Opera, 1962. Career: opera singer w. San Fran. Opera; Teatro Colon, Buenos Aires; Chgo. Opera; Munich Opera; Vienna State Opera; Metropol. Opera, NYC; Santa Fe Opera; Cinn. Zoo Opera; Hamburg State Opera; appeared in film Eine Nacht in Venedig (German-Italian TV). Recording incl: Excerpts from Die Fledermaus (RCA); Die Schweigsame Frau, (EMI Electrola). Contbr. to Orpheus mag. Hons. incl: Kammersangerin Award, Hamburg, 1973. Hobbies: Sailing; Painting. Mgmt: Organisation Int. Opera & Concert Germinal Hilbert, Paris, Address: Heilwigstr. 25, Hamburg 20, German Fed. Repub. 2.

SCRAGG, Thomas William, b. 19 Sept. 1940. Wirral, Cheshire, UK. Solicitor; Librarian; Discographer; Historical Researcher; Writer. Educ. incl: BA, Schl. of Slavonic & E European Studies, Univ. of London; BPhil. Univ. of Liverpool; Solicitor of the Supreme Ct.; Dip. Lib., Manchester; ALA. m. Isabel Mary Thomas, 2 s., 2 d. Career: Solicitor, 1968-; Music Advsr. & Historical Rschr. for many fests.; Phonographic Cons. & Cataloguer, late Sir Compton Mackenzie's Jethou Record Collect. (1923-30), 1973-75 & Music Lib. Co. FIBA. Granada TV Ltd., 1975-; preparing comprehensive retrospective discography for Claudio Arrau, 1973-; Libn., Knowsley Lib., 1974-. Author in field. Mbrships. incl: Law Soc.; FSA (Scot.); FRGS; FRSA; Royal Musical Assn. Hobbies: Aesthetics; Travel; Antiqurian books. Addess: The Woodcroft, Barnston, Wirral, Cheshire, UK. 4, 29, 30.

SCRASE, David Bernard, b. 13 March 1932. Southsea, City of Portsmouth, UK. Music Teacher, all brass and woodwind instruments, violin; Adjudicator; Brass Band Instructor. Educ: ARCM, 1962. m. Marion Jean Chick, 1 d., 2 s. Career: Brighton Congress Hall Salvation Army, 1939-49; Solo cornet, Royal Army Ordnance Corp., 1952-53; Freelance trumpet player; Teacher; Adjudicator. Mbrships: Nat. Assn. of Brass Band Conds.; Exec. Committee, NABBC; Chmn., Southern Counties Amateur Band Assn. Hobbies: Musical Dir., Brighton Symph. Wind Band & Brighton Silver Band. Address: 7 Hillyfield, Bell Lane, Lewes, Sussex, UK.

SCRIPPS, Douglas Jerry, b. 25 Aug. 1942. Grand Radips, Mich., USA. Orchestral & Operatic Conductor; College Teacher. Educ: BA, Calvin Coll., MMus, Univ. of Mich.; Eastman Schl. of Music; Vienna Acad. of Music. m. Merilee E Collins, 1 d, 3 s. Career: Dir. of Instrumental Music, Grand Rapids Junior Coll.; Res., Cond., Grand Rapids Symph. Orch.; Fndr. & Musical Dir., Kent Philharmonia Orch.; Guest Cond., Midwest USA, inclng. Chicago Civic Orch., W Mich. Opera Assn.; St. Clair Shores Orch.; Calvin Coll. Orch. & Alumni Players; Grand Rapids Ballet. Contbr. to: Grand Rapids Press. Mbrships: Bd. of Dirs., Mich. Coll. Arts & Humanities Assn.; Nat. Assn. of Schls. of Music; Coll. Music Soc.; Grand Rapids Press Club. Hobbies: Sailing; Bridge; Travel. Mgmt: New World Artists. Address: 2622 Oakwood Dr. SE, Grand Rapids, MI 49506, USA. 8.

SCULTHORPE, Peter Joshua, b. 29 April 1929. Launceston, Tasmania, Aust. Composer; Music Educator. Educ: Univ. of Melbourne; Wadham Coll., Oxford Univ. Career: Lectr. in Music, Univ. of Sydney, 1963-; Sr. Lectr., ibid, 1965-; Reader, ibid, 1968-; Comp. in Res., Yale Univ., 1965-67; Vis. Prof. of Music, Univ. of Sussex, 1971-72. Comps. incl: Sonata for viola & percussion, 1960; Sun Music Ballet, 1968; Love 200 (pop group & orch.), 1970; Rain, 1970; Nine String Quartets; Landscape & other works for piano; Tabuh Tabuhan, for wind quintet & percussion; Irkanda series (I-IV) & other chmbr. works; Sun Music series I-IV, for orch.; Music for Japan, (orchl.); Mangrove, & other works for orch.; Rites of Passage (opera) & other vocal, choral & dramatic works. Hons incl: MBE, 1970; OBE, 1977. Hobbies: Reading; Gardening. Address: 91 Holdsworth St., Woollahra, NSW 2025, Aust.

SEAL, Richard Godfrey, b. 4 Dec. 1935. Banstead, Surrey, UK. Choirmaster & Organist. Educ: MA, Christ's Coll., Cambridge Univ.; RCM; FRCO. m. Dr Sarah Helen Hamilton. Career: Asst. Organist, Chichester Cathedral; Choirmaster &

Organist, Salsibury Cathedral. Address: 5 The Close, Salisbury, Wilts., UK.

SEAMAN, Christopher, b. 7 Mar. 1942. Conductor. Educ: Canterbury Cathedral Choir Schl.; King's Schl., Canterbury; MA (Cantab); ARCM: ARCO. Career: Prin. timpianist, LPO, 1964-68; Asst. cond., BBC Scottish Symph. Orch., 1968-70; Prin cond., ibid., 1971; Prin. cond. & Artistic Dir., Northern Sinfonia, 1974-; freelance cond. in UK, Europe, NZ, etc; apps. w. Nat. Youth Orch. Address: c/o Northern Sinfonia, 41 Jesmond Vale, Newcastle-upon-Tyne NE2 1TG, UK.

SEAMAN, David John, b. 14 Feb. 1943. London, UK. Conductor; Accompanist. Educ: BA, St. Catherine's Coll., Cambridge Univ., 1964; MusB, ibid., 1965; Guildhall Schl. of Music (Conds. Course); London Opera Ctr.; Hamburg Music Acad., W Germany. m. Christine Daltry. Career: Repetiteur, Engl. Opera Grp., 1964; Repetiteur, Deitsche Oper am Rhein, Düsseldorf, 1969-72; Repetiteur & Cond., Nuremburg City Opera House, 1972-; 2nd Cond., ibid., 1976-. Address: Flurstr. 8, 8501 Feucht, German Fed. Repub.

SEAMAN, Gerald Roberts, b. 2 Feb. 1934. Leamington Spa, UK. Musicologist. Educ: MA, DPhil, musicol., Univ. Oxford. m. Lorna Vivien Johnston, 2 d. Career: Lectr., music, Nottingham Trng. Coll., 1962-64; Temporary Lectr., Univ. WA, 1964; Sr. Lectr., musicol., Univ. Auckland, NZ, 1965-70; Assoc. Prof., ibid., 1970-; Apps., BBC, Aust. Broadcasting Commn. & Radio NZ. Publs. incl: History of Russian Music, Vol. I 1968. Contbr. to profl. publs. Mbrships . incl: Int. Musicol. Soc.; Chmn., NZ Div., Int. Assn. Music Libs. Hon: Gold Medal, LAMDA, 1952. Hobbies: Langs; Travel. Address: c/o Conservatorium of Music, Univ. Auckland, New Zealand.

SEARCHFIELD, John W, b. 3 Mar. 1930. Chester, UK. Associate Professor; Organist; Conductor. Educ: MA, Magdalen Coll., Oxford Univ.; Royal Acad. of Music; LRAM; ARCM. m. Marijke van Wijk, 1 s., 1 d. Career incl: Organ recitals in UK, Holland, Switzerland, USA & Can.; Frequent appearances on CBC as Cond., Recitalist, Accompanist, Lectr. & Commentator; Guest Cond., Calgary Phil. & Edmonton Symph. Orchs.; Assoc. Prof., Univ. of Calgary; Organist & Choirmaster, Christ Ch., Calgary (inclng. tour of Engl. Cathedrals, 1974); Cond., CBC Calgary String Orch. & Festival Chorus; Harpsichordist, Baroque Ensemble. Recordings: Grieg-Holberg Suite (CBC). Mbrships: RCCO; Can. Assn. of Univ. Schls. of Music. Contbr. to: Opera; Opera News, Can. Music Book. Hobbies incl: Walking; Chess. Address: 1307 18a St. NW, Calgary, Alta., Can. T2N 2H6. 9.

SEARLE, Humphrey, b. 26 Aug. 1915, Oxford, UK. Composer & Writer on Music. Educ: MA, New Coll., Oxford Univ., 1937; RCM, London; Vienna Conserv.; pvtly. w. Dr Anton Webern. m. Fiona E Nicholson. Career: Prodr., BBC Music Dept., 1938-40 & '46-48; Gen. Sec., ISCM, 1948-49; Mbr., Sadler's Wells Ballet Advsry. Panel, 1951-57; Comp. in Res., Stanford Univ., Calif., 1964-65; Prof. of Comp., RCM, 1965-; Guest Comp., Aspen Music Fest., Colo., 1967; Guest Prof., Staatliche Musikhochschule, Karlsruhe, 1968-72. Comps: 5 Symphonies; 2 piano concertos; Trilogy for Speakers, Chorus & Orch. on texts of Edity Stiwell & James Joyce; 3 operas (Diary of a Madman, Photo of the Colonel, Hamlet); 3 ballets (Noctambules, Great Peacock, Dualities), etc. Var. recordings. Publs: 20th Century Counterpoint, 1954; The Music of Liszt, 1954 & '66; Ballet Music, 1958 0 74; Arnold Schoenberg-Structural Functions of Harmony, 1954; Hector Berlioz Letters, 1966; Ed. var. books. Contbr. to dictionaries, encys., jrnls. Hons: UNESCO Radio Critics' Prize for Diary of a Madman, 1960; Italia Prize for The Founding, 1965; CBE, 1968; FRCM, 1966. Address: 44 Ordnance Hill, London, NW8 6PU, UK. 1, 2, 3, 29.

SEARLE, Victor Clark, b. 19 June 1929. Norman, Okla., USA. Organist; Composer; Operatic Conductur. Educ: BMus, Music Theory, Univ. of Okla., 1953; organ w. Mildred Andrews; Opera w. Jan Popper; Choral Work w. J F Williamson. Debut: Pitts., Pa., 1945. Career: Cond., num. perfs., Fujiwara Opera Inst.; Apps. w. Tokyo Symph., Tokyo Phil.; num. organ recitals, opera perfs., choral & orch. concerts; Chmn., Opera & Organ Depts., Nihon Univ.; organ Instructor, Showa Musical Coll.; Dir., I Commendianti in Musica (opera buffa company). Comps: Requiem, for a cappella Male Chorus; Jubilate Deo, for a cappella Male Chorus. Publs: Psychology of Music Education (Japanese translatioin w. T Tomoda, Ongaku No Tomo-sha), 1965. Contbr. to: Music and Worship; Opera News; The Diapason. Pi Ka, Mbrships: Musical Honorary Fraternity; Am. Guild of Organists. Hons: Citation by US Dept. of State, 1955. Hobbies: Building Fairground Organs; Restoring Musical Antiques. Address: 8-8-21-401 Nishi Gotanda, Tokyo, Japan 141.

SEATON, Douglass, b. 8 June 1950, Balt., Md., USA. Musicologist; Conductor. Educ: BMus, Coll. of Wooster; MA, MPhi, Columbia Univ. m. Gayle Ellen Saunders Seaton. Career: Ed. Asst., 1971-72, Asst. Ed.-Assoc. Ed., Hd., Domestic Reports Dept., 1972-74, Hd., Reports, 1974-, Current Musicol. Contbr. to Current Musicol. (ed. in chief, 1977-78); Grove's Dictionary, 6th ed. Mbrships: Am. Musicol. Soc. (Greater NY chapt.); Pi Kappa Lambda. Address: Schl. of Music, Fla. State Univ., Tallahassee, FL 32306, USA.

SEBELL, Tellervo, b. 6 Nov. 1915, Ashtabula, Ohio, USA. Violinist; Pianist. Educ: Cleveland Inst. of Music. m. Raymond Sebell, dec., 1 d. Career: Violin, Am. Community Symph. Orch. tour of Europe, 1968; num. Solo, Chmbr. Music, Orchl. Perfs. in Ch.'s, Community Orchs. Mbrships: Amateur Chmbr. Music Players; Sec., Finlandia Fndn. Hobbies: Reading; Travel. Address: 1833 W 5th St., Ashtabula, OH 44004, USA. 5.

SEBESTYÉN, János, b. 2 Mar. 1931, Budapest, Hungary. Organist; Harpsichord Player. Educ: Dip., Ferenc Liszt Acad., Budapest. Career: Concerts in Hungary; tours of Europe, USA & Japan w. organ & harpsichord concerts; fndr. & prof., harpsichord fac., Acad. of Music, Budapest; musical feature progs. for Radio Budapest. Recordings: more than 40 records inclng. complete organ works of Liszt. Publs: Musical Conversations with Miklos Rézsa, 1979. Hons: Erkel prize (3rd class), 1967; Liszt prize (2nd class), 1974. Hobbies: Collecting old & private records; Collecting old radio progs. & music mags. Mgmts: Interkoncert, Budapest; Musart, Milan. Address: Fillér u. 48, 1022 Budapest, Hungary.

SEBESTYEN, Katalin, b. 12 Feb. 1943, Budapest, Hungary. Musician (violin); Professor of Music. Educ: Royal Conserv. of Music, Brussels, Belgium; Grad., Queen Elizabeth Music Chapel, ibid. Career: Concerts & recitals in var. countries incl: Belgium, Hungary, Holland, Germany, Austria, Switzerland & France; Prof., Royal Conserv. of Music, Brussels & Brabants Conserv., Netherlands; Mbr., Quatuor Haydn; Mbr., Chmbr. music ensemble, contrasts. Award: Winner, Int. Chmbr. Music Festival 'Friedrich Kuhlon', Uelsen, Germany, 1970. Hobbies: Reading; Cinema. Address: Muggenberglei 154, 2100 Deurne, Antwerp, Belgium.

SEDIVKA, Jan, b. 8 Aug. 1917, Slany, Czech. Violinist; Teacher. Educ: Charles Univ., Prague; Prof. O Sevcik; Prague Conserv. (J Kocian); École Normale, Paris; Prof. Max Rostal, London; Master's Dip., Prague; FTCL, London. m. Beryl Sedivka. Career: Hd., Instrumental Dept., Surrey Coll. of Music; Dir., Chmbr. Music Classes, Goldsmith's Coll. Univ. of London; Prof. TCL; Prin. Violin Lectr., Old. Conserv. of Music Brisbane; currently Dir., Conserv. of Music, Hobart, Tasmania; Res. Musician, Univ. of Tasmania; Deputy Chmn., Aust. Music Examinations Bd.; Hon. Life Mbr., Aust. String Tchrs. Assoc.; Vis. Lectr. on String Playing and Pedagogy to num. Univs. & Conservs.; Solo violinist & recitalist; Ldr., London Czech Trio, London Int. Trio; Soloist w. British & Aust. Coun. Address: 17 Brown;s Rd., Kingston, Tasmania 7150, Aust.

SEEBASS, Tilman, b. 8 Sept. 1939, Basel, Switz. Musicologist. Educ: MA; DrPhil. m. Elisabeth Mischler, 2 c. Career: Asst. Schlr., Inst. of Musicol., Basel, 1971-75; Mbr. of a rsch. team for Indonesian Music, sponsored by Swiss Nat. Fund; Dir., Haus der Bucher AG, Basel, 1975-77; Asst. Prof., Duke Univ., 1977-79; Assoc. Prof.; ibid, 1979-. Publs: Musikdarstellung und Psalterillustration im Früheren Mittelalter, 2 vols., 1973; Kunstpen Muziekhistorische Bijdragen to de Bestudering Van Het Utrects Psalterium (w. J H A Englebregt), 1973; Musikhandschriften in Basel, (Catalogue of an Exhibition of Musical Autographs), 1975; The Music of Lombok, (W. G Pandji, N Rembang & Pocdijono), 1976. Mbrships: Int. Musicol. Soc.; Swiss Musicol. Soc.; Am. Musicol. Soc.; Soc. for Ethnomusicol. Address: Dept. of Music, Duke Univ., 6695 College Station, Durham, NC 27708, USA.

SEEFRIED, Irmgard, Concert & Opera Singer. Educ: Augsburg Conservatoire, Aachen, 1940-43. m. Wolfgang Schneiderhan, 2 d. Career: Vienna State Opera, 1943-; apps. abroad inclng. at La Scala Milan, Convent Gdn. London, Met. Opera NYC; participant in Salzburg, Lucerne & Edinburgh Fests.; num. concert tours. Has made many recordings. Hons: Mozart Ring, 1948; Mozart Medal; Lehmann Medal; Österreichisches Ehrenkreuz für Wissenschaft und Kinst; Off.'s Cross of Royal Danish Dannebrog Order. 16.

SEEGER, Horst, b. 6 Nov. 1926, Erkner, Berlin, Germany. Musicologist; Opera Director. Educ: Humboldt Univ., Berlin; Musikhochschule, Berlin. m. Traute Asmus, 2 children. Career: Music Critic, Berlin, 1956-70; Chief Ed., Music u. Gesellchaft, Berlin, 1959-60; Hd., Drama Komische Oper Berlin, 1960-73; Hd. Dresden State Opera, 1973-. Publs: Mozart, 1956; Haydn,

1961; Musiclexikon, 2 vols., 1966; Yearbook of the Berlin Comic Opera, 1961-73; Musikühne (Annual), 1974-77; Oper heute, 1977-; Opera Lexikon, 1978. Mbrships: Int. Musicol. Soc.; Bach & Handel Socs.; Theatre Assn. of German Democratic Repub. Recip. of Lessing Prize of German Democratic Repub. Address: 8051 Dresden, Hainweg 5, Germany.

SEEGER, Michael, b. 15 Aug. 1933, NYC, USA. Lecturer; Collector of Folk Music; Performer on Fiddle, Banjo, Guitar, Autoharp, Dulcimer, Mandolin, Jewsharp, Quills, French Harp & String Bass. m. Alice Gerrard. Career: concerts, radio & TV broadcasts, USA, an., NZ, Aust., Japan, UK. Ireland, Western Europe; apps. at major Folk Fests. Recordings: 5 as soloist; 15 w. new Lost City Ramblers; 1 w. wife; 6 w. sister Peggy; num. field recordings for traditional musicians. Mbrships: Cons. to major folk fests.; Bd. of Dirs., Southern Folk Cultural Revival Prog., Nashville, Tenn. & Nat. Endowment for Arts. Recip. var. hons. Address: Garrett Park, MD 20766, USA.

SEELEY, Paul David, b. 8 May 1949, Harrogate, UK. Orchestral Manager; Repetiteur; Accompanist. Educ: BA & postgrad. cert. in educ., Univ. Coll. of N Wales, Bangor; BMus, Univ. of Edinburgh; pvte. study w. piano w. Norman Yewdall, Colin Kingsley & Antony Peebles; FLCM. Career: tchr., modern langs. before joining music profession; Repetiteur & music asst., D'Oyly Carte Opera Co., 1976-; now also orchl. mgr., ibid.; accomp., D'Oyly Carte artists for concerts & TV appearances; freelance accomp. arr. & cond. Contbr. to: The Savoyard; Delius Soc. Jrnl. Mbrships: ISM; Brit. Music Soc.; Delius Soc.; Sullivan Soc. Hobbies: Photography; Travel; Theatre; Cinema. Address:137 Wilmer Rd., Heaton, Bradford, W Yorks. BD9 4AG, UK.

SEELKOPF, Martin, b. 18 Dec. 1942, Freising, Germany. Librarian. Educ: PhD; Study of Musicol.; Violin, viola & pinoforte, Conserv. of Würzburg. Publs: Das Geistliche Schaften von Alessandro Grandi, 1973. Contbr. to: Die Musikforschung. Mbrships: Gesellschaft für Müsikforschüng; Gesellschaft für Bayerische Musikgeschichte; Verein Deutscher Bibliothekare. Address: Im Grund 13, 8700 Würzburg-Oberdürrbach, German Fed. Repub.

SEFERIAN, Edward, b. 23 Mar. 1931, Cleveland, OH., USA. Violinist; University Professor. Educ: BS, 1957, MS, 1958, Juilliard Schl. of Music, NYC. m. Jan Barbara, 1 s., 2 d. Career: Participant by invitatioin of Pablo Casals, Casals Fest, Puerto Rico, 10 summers; premiered Concerto for Violin & Orch., William Bergsma (commissioined by Phi Beta); Asst. Concertmaster, Seattle Symph., 1960-66; Prof., Music Dept., Univ. of Puget Sound & Cond. & Dir., Tacoma Symph. (both for 20 yrs.). Mbrships: incl. Hon. Mbr., Phi Beta; AAUP. Hons. incl: Nat. Steinway Award for cultural achievement. Address: 4121 N Madrona Way, Tacoma, WA 98407, USA.

SEGAL, Uriel, b. 7 March 1944, Jerusalem, Israel. Conductor. Educ: studied violin from age 7; Rubin Acad. of Music, Israel; studied cond. w. Mendi Rodan & at GSM, London; Dip. of Merit, Int. Conds. Course, Siena, Italy. m. Illana Finkelstein, 3 c. Debut: w. Seajllands Symph. Orch., Copenhagen, 1969. Career: Asst. Cond., working w. George Szell & Leonard Bernstein, NY Phil. Orch., 1969-70; chief cond., Phil. Hungarica, 1979-; Prin-cond., Bournemouth Symph. Orch., 1980-; Phil., Hamburg Phil., Israel Phil., Chgo. Symph., Spanish Nat. Orch., LPO, French Radio Phil., Montreal Symph., NZ Symph., Stuttgart Radio Symph., RAI Rome, Hallé Orch., Scottish Nat., etc. Recordings incl: Stravinsky's Firebird Suite & Symph. in C, w. Suisse Romande Orch.; Mozart's Piano Concerto/Lupu w. Engl. Chmbr. Orch.; Schumann's Piano Concerto/Ashkenazy, LSO; Beethoven, Piano Concerto/Firkusny, New Philharmonia. Hons: 1st Prize, Mitropoulus Cond. Competition, NY, 1969. Hobby: Reading. Mgmt: Harrison/Parrott Ltd., 22 Hillgate St., London W8 7SR, UK. Address: c/o Mgmt.

SEGERSTAM, Leif Selim, b. 2 March 1944, Visa, Finland. Conductor; Composer. Educ: violin, piano, cond., comp., Sibelius Acad., Helsinki until 1963; Cond. Dip., Juilliard Schl., of Music, NY, USA, 1964; Postgrad Dip., violin & comp., ibid, 1966. m. Hannele Angervo, 2 c. Debut: violin, Helsinki, 1963. Career: Cond., Finnish Nat. Opera, 1965-68; Cond., Royal Opera, Stockholm, 1968-72; Musical Dir., ibid, 1971-72; 1st Cond., Deutsche Oper Berlin, 1972-73; Gen. Mgr., Finnish Nat. Opera, 1973-74; Chefdirigent, ORF, Vienna, 1975-; Chefdirigent, RSO Helsinki, 1977-81; Guest Cond., num. leading orchs., Europe USSR, USA & Aust. Comps. incl: orchl. works, solo works w. orch., choral works w. accompaniment, solo songs, chmbr. works, instrumental solo comps., stage works, A cappella choral works, string quartets, num. works for solo or accomp. violin & cello. Var. recordings. Recip. var.

awards. Address: Takojantie 1K, 02130 Espoo 13, Tapiola, Finland.

SEHLBACH, Erich, b. 18 Nov. 1898, Barmen, Wuppertal, Germany. Composer. Educ: State High Schl. for Music, Leipzig. m. Irma Zucca. Career: Prof., Lectr., State High Schl. for Music, Ruhr (Folkwang Hochschule). Comps. incl: Opera, Orch. works, Chamber works, Piano music. Recordings w. Camerata Moseler. Mbr., German Comps. Grp. Recip., Art prize, Wuppertal, 1952. Address: Wintgenhof 9, D 43, Essen 16, German Fed. Repub.

SEHNAL, Jiř, b. 15 Feb. 1931, Radslavice, Czechoslovakia. Musicologist. Educ: PhD, Palacký's Univ., Olomouc; CSc., Purkyne's Univ., Brno. m. Helena Dudesková. Career: Mgr., Inst. of Music History, Moravian Mus., Brno. Publs incl: about 60 studies of 17th & 18th Century Music, History of the Organ in Moravia, Baroque Czech Hymnology; Old Music Eds. in Musica Antiqua Bohemica; HIF Biber, Instrumentalwerke handschriftlicher Überlieferung, 1976. Kirchenmus. Jahrbuch; Die Musikforschung; Archiv f. Musikwissenschaft; Musical Times; Fontes Artis Musicae; Haydn-Jahrbuch; Beiträge zur Musikwissenschaft; Muzikoloski zbornik; Jrnl. of Band Rsch.; Muzyka. Mbrships: Soc. for Eds. of Monuments of Musical Art in Austria; Soc. for Music Rsch.; Soc. of the Friends of Organ. Address: 3 Filipínskéno, 615 00 Brno, Czech.

SEIBEL, Klauspeter, b. 7 May 1936, Offenbach, Germany. Conductor. Educ: Conserv., Nuremberg; Musikhochschule, Munich. m. Jutta Seibel-Reumann, 3 c. Debut: Gärtnerplatztheater, Munich, 1957. Career: Gärtnerplatztheater, Munich, 1957-63; Freiburg, 1963-65; Lübeck, 1965-67; Kassel, 1967-71; Frankfurt, 1971-75; Frieburg (Gen. Music Dir.), 1975-78;Kapallmeister der Staatsoper, Prof. für Dirigieren an der Musikhochschule, Hamburg, 1978-; Guest Cond., Zürich (Opernhaus), Frankfurter Oper, Staatsoper Wien, Deutsche Oper Berlin, Teatro Regio, Torino. Hons: Richard Strauss Stipendium der Stadt München, 1957; Nikolai Malko Competition, Copenhagen, 1965; Dimitri Mitropoulos Competition, NY, 1969. Address: c/o Hamburg Staatsopher, Hamburg, German Fed. Repub.

SEIFERT, Otto Erich, b. 14 Jan. 1912, Dresden, Germany. Organist; Music Educator. Educ: Grad., State Conserv. for Music, Dresden, Germany; Postgrad. Violin Studies w. prof. Popagrama, State Acad., Vienna, Austria. m. Hildegard Seifert. Career: Dir., Music-Schl. Melk & Supvsr., Dist. Music Schls., Melk, Austria; Fndr. & Cond., Lethbridge Chmbr. Orch., Ont., Can.; TV & Radio Apps.; CBC. Publs: Das froehliche Geingenbuechlein, 1943. Mbrships: Can. Fedn. MTA. Hons. Two Schlrships. & One Award, Capital Dresden, Germany, 1939 & 40. Hobbies: Camping; Hiking; Reading. Address: Box 1803, New Liskeard, Ont. POJ 190 Canada.

SEIFFERT, Elaine, b. 4 Aug. 1941, Buffalo, NY, USA. Horn Player; Teacher. Educ: BFA, SUNY at Buffalo, 1965; Grad., theory & comp., Penn State Univ.; Grad., Music Educ., Univ. of W Ont. m. Stephen L Seiffert (separated), 1s, 1d. Career incls: Sev. leading roles, support roles & chorus mbr., 1963-66; Mbr., Reinagel Singers, 961-66; Arr. & Recording Cond., WKBW Buffalo, 1962-63; Mbr., 5 Buffalo area orchs., & Mbr. & Cond., W NY Horn Ensemble; Mbr., Episcopal Ch. Chancel Choir & Asst. Cond., Community Music Schl. Orch. & Univ. of Buffalo Symph., 1966-68; Mbr., Assoc. Cond., Penn State Horn Club, 1968-70; Mbr., State Coll. Woodwind Quintet & Penn State Symph. Orch., 1969; Pvte. instrumental tchr., 1969-; Pt.-time Fac., Fac. of Music, UWO, 1972-. Contbr. to: The Horn Call. Mbrships: Int. Horn Soc.; Am. Fedn. of Musicians; Past mbr., London City Arts Advisory Committee. Hobbies: Swimming; Hiking; Carpentry; Art; Writing. Address: 456 Rippleton Rd., London, Ont. N6G 1M5, Can.

SEIFFERT, Stephen Lyons, b. 14 May 1938, Detroit, Mich., USA. French Horn Performer & Teacher. Educ. incls: BMus & Perfs. Cert., 1960, DMusA, 1968, Eastman Schl. of Music; MA, Brown Univ., Providence, RI, 1963. Debut: w. Eastman Rochester Orch., 1960. Career: Hornist w. var. orchs. in USA & Can., 1959-; Prin. Horn. London (Ont., Can.) Symph., 1970-76; Asst. Prof. of Music, Penn State Univ., 1968-70, Univ. of Western Ont., 1970-76; Prin. Honr, Kingston Ont. Symph., 1976-; Instructor of Horn & Trumpet, Queens Univ., 1976-. Recordings incl: var. w. Eastman Wind Ensemble, 1957-60; The Hornists' Nest, 1968; Hornists' Nest II & III, 1976. Contbr. to profl. jrnls. Mbr. profl. orgs. Hons. incl: Golden Clef Award, RI Fed. Music Clubs, 1962. Address: 90 Brentwood Crescent, Kingston, Ont. K7M 4WI, Can.

SEILER, Mimy, b. 27 Mar. 1906, Neuchatel, Switz. Singer; Pianist. Educ: Music Acad., Zürich; Soprano courses, Lucerne Fest.; studies w. Elisabeth Grümmer, Berlin. m. Walter Lang.

Debut: Vienna. Career: Singer of light soprano roles in Opera in Berlin, Krefeld, Wilhelmshaven, etc., 3yrs.; Singer of J S Bach, Oratorios, Mozart, Great Mass in C Minor, Handel, Messiah, & Lieder of Schubert, Brahms & Schumann; introduced Debussy, Duparc, Roussel & Ravel to Vienna & Berlin. Mbrships: Swiss Music Tchrs. Union; Swiss Musicians Assn. Hobbies: Cats; Dogs; Long Mountain Walks; Swimming. Address: Nadelberg 17, CH-4051 Basel, Switz.

SEINER, Katinka, b. 7 Nov. 1937, Budapest, Hungary. Opera & Concert Soprano. Educ: Musical Gymnasium, Budapest; Franz Liszt Acad. of Music, Budapest. m. Laszlo Ekstein-Easton, 1s., 2 stepdaughters. Career: Opera, operetta & concert tours, radio & TV apps. in UK. Europe, Israel & USA; fest. apps. incl. Glyndebourne, Bergen & Menton; specialises in 20th century comps.; num. premieres of contemporary Brittish & Hungarian works for BBC & in Europe; sings in 15 langs. Recordings: Bartók & Debussy song-cycles. mbr., ISM. Hobbies incl: Collecting Netzukis & small Objets d'Art of Muical Interests; Cross-County Skiing; Langs.; Reading. Address: Hermitage, 6 Salisbury Ave., London N3, UK.

SEITZ, Gerhard, b. 24 Nov. 1922, Munich, Germany. Leader of the Bavarian Radio Symphony Orchestra (violin). Educ: Musikhochschule, Munich. m. Edeltraud, B Miesgang, 1 c. Mbrships: Tonkunstlerverband, Munich; Deutsche Orcestervereinigung. Recip., 2nd prize, Geneva Int. Music Competition, 1949. Address: Prinzregentenstr. 68, Munich 80, German Fed. Repub.

SEIVEWRIGHT, Robert Andrew, b. 22 Apr. 1926, Plunsar, Leicestershire, UK. Cathedral Organist; Broadcaster. Educ: MA, Cambridge Univ.; ARCO. m. Nora Katherine, 2 s. Career: Organist & Master of the Music, Carlisle Cathedral, 1960-; Cond., Abbey Singers; Writer & presenter, num. IBA network progs.; Extramural lectr., Newcastle & Glasgow Univs. Critic, Cumberland News. Hobbies: Motoring; Ball Games; Professional Sport; Architecture; Arts. Address: 6 The Abbey, Carlisle, Cumberland, UK.

SELCH, Frederick Richard, b. 24 Mar. 1930, Royalton, Vt., USA. Founder & President, Federal Music Society; Music Scholar & Collector. Educ: AM, Hamilton Coll., Clinton, NY; MS, Syracuse Univ., NY; NY Univ. Grad. Schl. of Music. m. Patricia Bakin Selch, 4 c. Debut: w. Fed. Music Soc., NYC, 1978. Career: w. Fed. Music Soc. at Carnegie Recital Hall, Hunter Coll. Playhouse, Town Hall, Alice Tully Hall (all in NYC). Recordings: (w. Fed. Music Soc.) Opera in Federal America; Music of Federal America; Music of the Dance. Contbr. of papers to Am. Musicol. Soc; Jrnl. of Violin Soc. of Am. Mbrships: Am. Musical Instrument Soc.(Pres.); Am. Musicol. Soc.; Galpin Soc. Hobby: VP, Keystone Broadcasting, Inc. Address: 132 E 71st St., New York, NY 10021, USA.

SELDEN, Margery Stomne, b. 5 Sept., Chicago, Ill., USA. Music Professor; Musicologist; Pianist; Organist. Educ: AB, Vassar Coll., MA, Yale Univ.; PhD, ibid. m. Paul Hubert Selden, Jr. (dec.), 3s, 1d. Career: Prof. of Music, Wayne State Univ., Detroit, 1950-64, North Central Coll., Ill., 1964-68, Coll. of St. Elizabeth, 1968-. Publs: The French Operas of Luigi Cherubini, 1951. Contbr. to profl. publs. Mbrships: Am. Guild of Organists; Am. Musicol. Soc.; Coll. Music Soc.; Phi Beta Kappa; Sigma Alpha Iota; Sons of Norway; Soc. for Ethnomusicology; Met. Opera Guild; Fndr. mbr., Soc. for Music Theory; Nat. Music Tchrs. Assn. Hons. incl: Asst. Prof. of the Year Award, 1961; Michigan Choral Comp., 1st Prize, 1960; Patriotic Song Contest Winner, 1975. Hobbies: Swimming; Painting. Address: Quentin Court, Maplewood, NJ 07040, USA. 11.

SELÉN, Paul Ebbe, b. 16 Feb. 1920, Alunda, School Teacher; Cantor. m. Birgit Elin (d. 1960), 2 children. Comps: Adaptions of mss in Düben collection of Uppsala Univ. Lib.: Dumont: Magnificat, Stockholm, 1968; Cantate Domino, Stockholm, 1969; Media Vita inMorte Sumus, Stockholm, 1971; Capricornus: Mein Gott und Herr, Hassel, 1972; Albrici: Fader var (Pater noster), Stockholm, 1976; 450 Adaptions from lib's collections. Contbr. of about 60 articles to Svensk kyrkomusik, Misiklivet, etc. Mbr. Swedish Soc., of Musical Rsch. Recip. of Ther Municipality's & Prov. Assemply's awards for cultural activities. Hobbies: Musical Rsch. Hist. of Culture; Lit.; Chess; Travel. Address: Tuna, 2-740 50 Alunda, Sweden.

SELF, George, b. 16 May 1921, King's Lynn, Norfolk, UK. Composer; Lecturer; Teacher. Educ: RAM; GRSM; LRAM. m. Doris Bodsworth, 1 child. Compositions: Many works for schls., publd. by Universal Edition, OUP & Novello. Publs: New Sounds in Class, 967; Aural Adventure, 1958; Make a New Sound, 1976. Contbr. to Music in Educ. Address: 10 Bassett Close, Southampton, UK. 3.

SELFRIDGE-FIELD, Eleanor Anne, b. 29 June 1940, New Orleans, La., USA. Musicologist. Educ: BA, Drew Univ., 1962; MS, Columbia Univ., 1963; D Phil., Oxford Univ., UK, 1969; piano studies w. Konrad Wolff. m. Dr. R Clive Field, 1 s. Career: Author; Ed. of early music; Univ. Lectr.; Prod. of radio broadcasts carried by Nat. Public Radio, USA. Publs: Venetian Instrumental Music from Gabrieli to Vivaldi, 1975; Dario Castello - Selected Ensemble Sonatas, 1977. Contbr. to: Music & Letters; RMA Chronicle; JAMS; Jrnl. of the Hist. of Ideas; Int. Review of the Aesthetics and Sociology of Music, etc. Mbrships: Royal Musical Assn.; Am. Musicol. Soc. Address: 867 Durshire Way, Sunnyvale, CA 94087, USA. 29.

SELL, David Frank, b. 5 Mar. 1930, Oxford, NZ. University Teacher; Author. Educ: Canterbury Univ. Coll.; MusB (NZ); MMus, Durham; DipEd; LMusTCL; LRSM; pvte. study of comp. w. Richard Arnell. m. Christina Ethel Crawford, 1 s., 2 d. Career: Music Educator, secondary schls.; Music Advsr., NZ Educ. Dept.; Univ. of Canterbury Schl. of Music; regular broadcasts. Publs. incl: Musical Textures, 1974; (w. Ian Dando) Beethoven's Piano Concerto No. 1 in C major & its Background, 1975; Listening Guides for 5th Form Music, 1975; Listening Guides for 6th & 7th Form Music, 1976. Contbr. to profl. jrnls. Mbr., profl. assns. & Committees. Hons: Philip Neil Memorail Prize, Otago Univ., 1951. Hobbies: Boating; Skiing; Badminton; Gardening. Address: Schl. of Music, Univ. Canterbury, Christchurch, NZ.

SELLICK, Phyllis Doreen, b. 16 June 1911, Ilford, Essex, UK. Concert Pianist; Professor. Educ: LRAM. m. Cyril Smith, (dec) 1 s., 1 d. Debut: Harrogate, UK. Career: Tours w. husband, Portugal, Belgium, France, Middle East, India, Germany, Russia, NZ, TV apps., w. husband, This is Your Life, No Turning Back; 3 Royal Concerts. Recordings: Sinfonia Concertante, Walton; 2 Piano works & duets, w. husband. Contbr. to Cyril Smith's Duet for 4 Hands. Mbrships: Hon. Mbr., Soroptimists; ISM. Hons. ARAM, 1942; FRAM, 1950; RCM, 1966; OBE, 1971. Hobbies: Reading Hatha Yoga. Mgmt: Ibbs & Tillett, London. Address: 33 Fife Rd., London SW 14 7EJ, UK. 1,3, 27.

SELUCKY, Rosalie Anne (née Butcher), b. 10 June 1943, Tumby Bay, SA, Aust. Musician. Educ: Assoc., Univ. of Adelaide; Dip., ibid. m. Jaroslav Selucky, 1 d., 1 s. Career: Violinist, 2 yrs., French Horn Player, 9 yrs., Adelaide Symph. Orch., 11 yrs. Contbr. to: Horn Call. Address: 34 Thompson Ct., Werribee, Vic., Aust. 3030

SEMEGEN, Daria, b. 27 June 1946, Bamberg, Germany. Composer; University teacher. Educ: BMus, Eastman Schl. of Music; MMus, Yale Univ.; Mus Doc, Columbia Univ.; studied comp. w. Samuel Adler, Burrill Phillips, Witold Lutoslawski, Vladimir Ussachevsky & Bülent Arel. Career: Staff Technician, Columbia-Princeton Electronic Music Ctr., 1972-74; Lectr. in Electronic Music Comp., SUNY at Stony Brook, 1973-74; Asst. Prof. & Assoc. Dir. of Electronic Music Studios, ibid., 1974-79. Comps. incl: Electronic Composition No. 1; Lieder auf der Flucht (soprano & instruments); Chamber works for violin, cello, piano, trombone, clarinet & flute; Music for Violin solo; Triptych for orch.; Dans la Nuit (baritone & orch.). Recordings: Electronic Composition No. 1; Music for Dancers (electronic), 1977. Publs: Trans. & Ed., Kotonski's Percussion Instruments in the Contemporary Orchestra, 1970. Contbr. to Music Journal. Mbr. num. profl. socs. Hons. incl: Nat. Endowment for the Arts Grant, 1975; Prize, ISCM Int. Electronic Music Competition, 1975. Address: Musiuc Dept., SUNY at Stony Brook, NY 11794, USA. 27.

SEMKOW, Jerzy (Georg), b. 12 Oct. 1928, Radomsko, Poland. Conductor. Educ: Jagiellonian Univ., Cracow; HS of Music, ibid.; Leningrad Conserv.; MA (Mus.). m. Barbara Szczepanska, 1966. Career: Asst. Cond., Leningrad Phil. Orch., 1954-56; Cond., Bolshoi Opera & Ballet Theatre, Moscow, 1956-58; Artistic Dir. & Prin. Cond., Warsaw Nat. Opera, 1959-61; Permanent Cond., Royal Opera, Copenhagen, Denmark, 1966-; Guest cond. of num. leading orchs. incl. LPO; NY Phil.; Chgo. Symph.; Boston Symph., & Orchs. in major European cities. Recip: Grand Order, Commanndoria Poloniae Restitutae. Hobbies: Reading; Yachting. Mgmt: Propaganda Musicale, Boncompagnie 47, Rome; & W Hansen Koncertdirektion, Gothersgade 9-11, Copenhagen. Address: U1. Dynasy 6/1, Warsaw, Poland.

SEMLER, Sonny E, b. 19 July 1947, Hvidovre, Copenhagen, Denmark. Singer (Bass); Musician (Trombone, Flute, Keyboard). Educ: Tivoli Gd.; var. tchrs. from Royal Chapel. m. Dido Zimling, 1 d. Career: 6 Bands in 10 yrs.; Sonny Singers, 5 yrs.; TV apps., Denmark, Spain & Sweden. Num. comps. Recordings: Handy Mann, 1967; num. single records incl: Let Me In On Your Love, 1978. Mbrships: Lion Club. Hobbies: Music; Relaxing. Mgmt: Skellingen ApS Booking, Amosevej 107, 4440 Morkov, Denmark. Address: Amosevej 107, Skellingsted, 4440 Morkov, Denmark.

SEMMLER, Rudolf Heinrich Mathias, b. 31 Oct. 1904, Dortmund, Germany. Composer. Educ: Pvte. studies. m. Ida Hardmeyer. Comps: Oratoria, Diario...di Torquato Tasso, 5 Miniature sacre, Cantata Francscana, etc.; Chmbr. music; Lieder; Piano Music; Operas, Hansel & Gretel (Wilh. Busch), Kein Soldat (R Semmler), etc. Publs: Eigenklang der Reihen-Superskala; Drei Musiknovellen. Mbrships: Schweizerischer Tonkünstlerverein. Hobby: Painting. Address: Bellariastrasse 71, CH-Zürich 8038, Switz.

SEMPER, Jean, b. 10 Mar. 1928, Marle sur Serre, Aisne, France. Alto Viola Soloist. Educ: Paris Nat. Conserv., 1948. 1 s. Career: Alto Viola Soloist, Colonne Concerts, Paris, 1948-57; Soloist in Switzerland, France, Germany; Alto Viola Soloist, Basle Symph. Orch., 1957-; Manoliu Quartet, 1957-60; Sempher Trio; Fauré Ensemble, 1973-. Recordings for radio, Basle, Zürich; Dvorák, w. Ensemble Fauré. Hons: 1st Prize, Paris Conserv., 1948; Kt., French Order of Artistic Educ., 1961. Hobbies: Photography; Reading; Swimming. Address: Nonnenweg 8, 4505 Basel, Switz. 4.

SEMSEY, Maria, b. 18 Dec. 1943, Budapest, Hungary. Pianist. Educ: Béla Bártók Conserv., Budapest, to 1962; Music High Schl., Vienna, Austria, to 1970. Debut: Vienna, 1969. Career: Concerto perfs. in Hungary, Austria & Switzerland; Radio apps., Austria & Switzerland. Hobbies: Art; Literature. Address: A 1080 Vienna, Buchfeldgasse 13, Austria.

SENATOR, Ronald, b. 17 Apr. 1928, London, UK. Composer; Author; Conductor; Professor. Educ: Hertford & Trinity Colls., Oxford, & London Univ., PhD, BMus, FTCL. m. Dita Branizka Senator. Career: perfs. (& apps as cond.) at Queen Elizabeth Hall, London, Liverpool & Westminster Cathedrals, etc. & on radio & TV for BBC, ABC (Aust.), NBC (USA) Suddeutsche Rundfunk; Prof. of Music, Univ. of Europe; vis. Prof., MIT, CUNY, London Univ., Inst. of Educ. var. comps. Publs: Musicolour, 1970; Musigramma, 1979. Contbr. to jrnls. & periodicals. Mbrships: ISME; fndr. mbr.; Int. Comps Assn., Sacred Music; MENC; ASMG; CGGB; PRS. Hobbies: Playing with Children. Address: 16 Cumberland Rd., Kew, Surrey TW9 3HQ, UK.

SENGSTCHMID, Johann, b. ¢6 July 1936, Steinakirchen am Forst, Austria. Music Teacher. Educ: Studied Music under Prof. Uhl, Prof. Othmar Steinbauer, Prof. Hans Swarowsky & Prof. R Schmid, Acad. of Music & the Performing Arts, Vienna, Austria. m. Guntrude Sengstchmid, 2 s., 1 d. Over 40 comps. incl.: Rosette ze zwei Stimmen; Rosette zu drei Stimmen; Quadruplum, für Streichquartett; Missa-Adoramus te; Capriccio für Orgelpedal; Der Engel des Herrn. Comps. recorded on Austrian Radio. Publs. incl: Grundlagen der Klangreihenlehre; Anatomie eines Zwölftonspiels, 1971; Kreatives Spielen mit Tönen, 1975. Contbr. to var. profl. jrnls. Hons: Förderungspreis, Lower Austria, 1964; Theodor-Körner Prize, 1969. Address: Buchbayerstrasse. A-3100 St. Pölten, Austria.

SENIOR, John, b. 2 Aug. 1958, Stamford, Conn., USA. Harpist. Educ: Studied w. Lois Bannerman, Lucille Larence, Barton, Hatheway. Career: tour of Romania, 1973; Soloist w. Bridgeport Symph., 1973, Norwalk Symph., 1975, twice w. NY Phil., 1974; radio broadcasts; sev. recitals, 1975-76. Comps: Ballade of the Sea. Mbr., Am. Harp Soc. Hons. incl: Winner, Conn. Am. Harp Soc. Competition, 1973: Gold Cup, Nat. Fedn. of Music Clubs Fest., 1974: Arthur Holde Award, Southern Conn. Young Artist Competition, 1974; Winner, Young Soloist Audition, Norwalk Symph., 1975; awards from Cazaha competition, France, 1977, & Am. Harp Soc. competition, 1978. Hobbies: Reading; Composing; Sports. Address: 4265 Congress St., Farifield, CT 06430, USA. 28.

SENN, Walter, b. 11 Jan. 1904, Innsbruck, Tirol, Austria. Professor. Educ: Univ. Vienna; Music Acad., ibid; State exam., piano, 1930, organ, 1931, schl. music, 1932; PhD. div., 3 ch. Career: Lectr., theory of music, Innsbruck Univ., 1928-38; Music Prof., HS & Sem for Tchrs., Innsbruck, 1928-38; Lectr., musical sci., Univ. Vienna, 1948-50; Prof. Univ. Innsbruck, 1950-; Music histn.; Dir., musical collect, Tyrolese Govt. Museum Ferdinandeum. Author of num. profl. publs. incl: Musik und Theater am Hof zu Innsbruck, 1954; Geschichte der Messe seti 1600, 1963. Contbr. to profl. publs. Mbrships: acting mbr., Gesellschaft zur Herausgabe von Denkmalern der Tonkunst in Osterreich; Assn. for Music Rsch.; Int. Musicol. Soc. (coun.) ; Zentralinstitut fur Mozartforschung, Salzburg (coun.); Josef Haydn Inst., Cologne. Hons: Mozart medals, Int. Stiftung Mozarteum, Salzburg 1956, '74; Theodor Korner Prize, 1961. Address: A 6080 Igls bei Innsbruck, Bilgeristr. 11 b, Austria. 2, 19, 23.

SEQUI, Sandro, b. 10 ov. 1935, Rome, Italy. Director, Debut: Teatro La Fenice, Venice, 1960; More than 50 opera prods. at

La Scala, Rome Opera, Florence Comunale, London Royal Opera House, NY Met. Opera, Chgo. Lyric Opera, Buenos Aires T Colon, Bruxelles T Royal, etc.; Theatre prods. in Italy, plays by Pirandello, Lope de Vega, Orton, Strindberg, etc.; TV prods. in Italy, plays by Isben, Goldoni, Strindberg, Congreve, Sherwood, Henry James, etc. Contbr. to Il Tempo, Rome; Enciclopedia dello Spettacolo. Address: V Monterone 2, Rome, Italy.

SEREBRIER, José, b. 3 Dec. 1938, Montevideo, Uruguay. Conductor; Composer. Educ: Dio., comp., Curtis Inst. of Music, Phila., USA; MA, Univ. of Minn.; studied conducting w. Pierre Monteaux & Antal Dorati; studied comp. w. Aaron Compland. m. Carole Farley, 1 d. Debut: as cond., Montevideo, 1949. Career: Apprentice Cond. w. Dorati, Mpls. Symph., 2 seasons; Assoc. Cond., Am. Symph. Orch., NY, 4 yrs.; NY conducting debut, 1965: Comp.-in-Res., Cleveland Orch., 1968-69, 69-70; former Cond., Cleveland Phil. now conducts extensively in Europe & Ams.; Began composing at age 15. Comps. incl. works for orch., band, voice, chmbr. ensembles, keyboard. Sev. recordings as cond. Contbr. to Jrnls. Mbr. profl. orgs. Recip. many awards & hons. Mgmt: Shaw Concerts, NY. Address: 270 Riverside Dr., NY, NY 10025, USA.

SERENDERO, David, b. 28 July 1934, Santiago, Chile. Conductor; Composer; Musicologist. Educ: Nat. Conserv. of Music. Univ. of Chile; MComp, ibid, 1964; DMusicol, ibid, 1965; Violin Tchr. State Dip., German Fed. Repub., 1962. m. Maria Quinteros, 1957, Maria Alamos, 1964, Ximena Cabello, 1973, 2 d., 1 s. Career incls: Concertmaster, Heilbronn Symph., W Germany, 1961-62; 1st Violin, Nat. Symph., Chile, Tchr., Nat. Conserv. of Music, Univ. of Chile, 1962-65; Cond., Osorno Phil., Fndr., Dir., Music Schl., Osorno, Chile, 1965-66; Cond., Nat. Symph., Chile, 1967-71; Prof., Dir., Nat. Conserv. of Music, Univ. of Chile, 1967-71; moved to W Germany, 1972; Prin. 2nd Violin, Rheinische Phiulharmonie, Koblenz, Cond., Reinisches Collegium Musicum Orch., Wiesbaden, W Germany, 1973-; Guest cond. in Europe and Latin America. Comps. incl: melodrama El Ensayo; musical Astarte; 3 orch. works; 2 Cantatas, choir & orch.; 6 Chmbr. works; 6 songs, rhapsody Reinhild, piano; Alpha Centauris, bassoon solo. Author, La Tetralogia de Richard Wagner, 1965. Contbr. to var. profl. jrnls. Mbrships: Rep. of Chile, Assn. of Friends of the Int. Youth Fest., Bayreuth, W Germany; Nat. Comps. Assn., Chile. Recip. num. Hons. Hobby: Photography. Address: Henrietta-Sontag-St. 5, 5400 Koblenz, German Fed. Repub. 30.

SERKIN, Rudolph, b. 28 Mar. 1903, Eger, Bohemia (US Citizen). Pianist. m. Irene Busch, 1935, 2 s., 4 d. Debut: w. Vienna Symph. Orch., 1915. Career incl: Perfs. of series of sonatas for violin & piano w. Adolf Busch; Am. Debut, 1933; Played w. Toscanini, 1934; w. Nat. Orchl. Assn., 1937; Annual tours of USA, 1934-; Hd., Piano Dept., then Dir., Curtis Inst. of Music; Mbr., Carnegie Commission Report; Pres. & Artistic Dir., Marlboro Schl. of Music; Williams Coll.; Oberlin Coll.; Univ. of Rochester. Mbrships: Am. Acad. of Arts & Scis.; Nat. Coun. on the Arts. Hons: Presidental Medal of Freedom, 1963; MusD, Curtis Inst; Univ. of Vt; Temple Univ. Address: RFD3, Brattleboro, VT 03301, USA.

SERMILA, Jarmo Kalevi, b. 16 Aug. 1939, Hämeenlinna, Finland. Composer-in-residence in Hämeenlinna since 1977. Educ: MA, Helsinki Univ.; Comps. Dip., Sibelius Acad. m. Ritva Vuorinen. Career: Exec. Sec., Finnish Music Info. Ctr.; Comps. perf. on TV, radio & at public concerts. Comps. incl. chamber music & electronic music. Recordings: Monody (Love Records LRLP 57); Odds Against Intervals (Oden 5E062-34854); The Myth is Weeping Again, Don't Cry My Doll (Scandia); Electro Composition I (Fennica Nova); Kai Sinä pelkäsit (Muntra Musikanter). Publs: Finland's Composers, 1976. Contbr. to sev. Finnish newspapers & mags.; Jazz Forum. Mbrships: Bd., Finnish Comps. Guild; Dir. of the Electronic Music Studio, Finnish Broadcasting Co.; Chmn. of the Finnish Sect. of the Int. Soc. for Contemporary Music. Hons. Winner, Comp. Contest, Lahti Men's Choir, 1972 & Pori Jazz Fest., 1972; Recommendation, Finnish Broadcasting Co. & Nordic Cultural Fund, 1973. Address: Niittykatu 7 A 7, SF-13100 Hameenlinna 10, Finland.

SERNKLEF, Harry Torild Wladimir, b. 13 June 1923, Björekulla, Sweden. Conductor; Clarinettist. Educ: Royal Acad. of Music, Stockholm. m. Elsa Birgit Larsson, 1 s., 1 d. Debut: Nielsen's Concerto for Clarinet & Orch., Swedish Radio. Career incls: 1st Clarinet, Royal Opera House Orch., Stockholm, Malmö Symph. Orch., Swedish Radio Light Orch.; Headmaster, Music Schl., Sundbyberg; Mil. Bandmaster, Solleftea, Örebro & Karlstad; Cond., Gävle, Helsingborgs, Nörrkopings Radio Orchs. Recrodings: Ferrmat Strio FLPS 20. Address: Humblegatan 24 B, 17239 Sundbyberg, Sweden.

SEROCKI, Kazimierz, b. 3 Mar. 1922, Toruń, Poland. Composer. Educ: Dip., State High Schl. of Music, Lodz; studied

w. Kazimierz Sikorski, Nadia Boulanger. Comps. incl: Symph.; Choral Symph.; Concerto, trombone & orch.; Sinfonietta, 2 string orchs.; Song Cycles Heart of the Nights, & Eyes of Air; Musical Concertante, chmbr. orch.; Segmenti, 7 instrumental grps.; Episodes, strings & 3 percussion grps.; Symphonic Frescoes; Continuum, for 123 percussion instruments; Forte e Piano, 2 pianos & orch.; Niobe, 2 reciters, choir, orch.; Dramatic Story, orch.; Fantasia Elegiaca, organ & orch.; Arrangements for 1-4 recorders, 1975; Chmbr., Piano Music; Pianophonie for piano, electronics & orch., 1978. Recordings: Muza; Phillips; Wergo; R.C.A. Mbr. Union of Polish Comps. Hons: Polish Nat. Prize for Music, 1952, 1963, 1972; Off., Commander Cross, Polonia Resituta; num. other Hons. Address: PO Box 63, PL 00-957 Warsaw, Poland.

SERVADEI, Annette Elizabeth, b. 16 Oct. 1945, Durban, S Africa. Educ: BMus (S Africa); FTCL; LTCL; (tchng.); LRSM (perf.); Univ. Perfs. & Tchrs. Lic. of Music, S Africa. m. Achille Servadei, 1 s., 1 d. Debut: London 1972. Career: 2 recital tours, Italy; Concerto Perfs., Italy, Germany; Concerto, recital, radio & TV apps., S Africa; Sr. Piano Tutor, Univ. of the Witwatersrand, 1977-. Hons: Recip., scholarships; Samro Prize, 1974. Hobbies: Reading; Italian Cooking. Mgmt: Helen Jennings Concert Agency, London. Address: 275 Mimosa Rd., Blackheath, Johannesburg, 2195, S Africa.

SESSIONS, Roger Huntington, b. 28 Dec. 1896, USA. Comoposer; Teachedr. Educ: Harvard Coll., Yale Univ. Schl. of Music; Pvte. study w. Ernest Bloch; AB; BMus. Career incl: Instr., Smith Coll., 1917-21; Tchr., Cleveland Inst. of Music, 1921-25; Lectr. & Tchr., NY & Boston, 1934-35; Instr., Asst. Prof. & Assoc. Prof., Princeton Univ., 1935-45; Prof. of Music, univ. of Calif., Berkeley, 1945-53; Wm. Shubael Conant Prof. of Music, Princeton Univ., 1953-65; Fac., Juilliard Schl. of Music, NY, 1965-. Comps; incl: 6 Symphs.; Concerto for Violin & Orch., 1937; String Quartet No. 1 in E Minor, 1938; Duo for Violin & Piano, 1948; String Quartet No. 2; Sonata No. 2 for Pinoforte, 1948; String Quintet, 1958; Divertimento for Orch., 1968; Montezuma (opera), 1963; 6 Pieces for Violin Solo, 1966. Publs: The Intent of the Artist, 1941; The Musical Experience of Composer, Performer & Listener, 1950; Harmonic Practice, 1951. Recip. Hon. MusD, Wesleyan, Rutgers & Harvard Univs. Address: 63 Stanworth Ln., Princeton, NJ, USA.

SESTAK, Tomislav, b. 4 July 1931, Karlovac, Yugoslavia. Musician; Violist. Educ: Dip., Music Acad., Zagreb. Debut: Zagreb, Yugoslavia. Career: Concertmaster w. Zagreb Phil; Zagreb Soloists; Solo-Violist, Vienna Symph; Vienna String Trio. Recordings w. Zagreb Soloists (Amadeus), W. New Vienna String Quartet (Deutsche Gramophon). Recip. Vaclav Huml Prize, Zagreb, 1957. Hobbies: Walking; Records; Reading; Slides. Address: 1030 Vienna, Marxergasse 10/22, Austria.

SESTAK, Zdenek, b. 10 Dec. 1925, Citoliby, Czechoslovakia. Composer. Educ: Conserv. for Music, Prague, 1945-50; fac. of Philos., Charles Univ., ibid, 1945-49. m. Marie Zatecka, 2 children. Career: Profl. Composer, 1957-; worked w. dept. of Symph. of Chmbr. Music, Radio Prague, 1968-69; Permanent expert (reader), OSA (Czech Performing Rights Org.), 1970-. Comps. incl: Symph. No. 1 Epitaph (orchl.), 1961; Symph. No. 2 (orchl.), 1970; Symph. No. 3 (orch.), 1971; Symph. No. 4 (string orch.), 1973; Vocal Symph., 1962; Variations-Symph. Fantasy, 1966; Divertimento Concertante (wind quintet), 1966; Hommage a Apollinaarie (mixed choir), 1972; Concertino for French horn, 1972; var. instrumental pieces, choral works & children's songs. Var. works recorded on Panton & Supraphon labels. Publs: Music of the Citoliby Masters of the 18th Century; Music in Citoliby (albums w. works of Czech composer & LP records). Mbrships: Czech Union of Composers. Recip. num. awards for Compositions. Address: Prague 10, Pracska 2594, Czechoslovakia.

SESTERHENN, Peter Bernhard, b. 5 Oct. 1937, Sigmaringen, German Fed. Repub. Violinist. Educ: Music High Schl., Karlsruhe. m. Jane Atlfield, 1 d. Career: Violinist, Bamberg Symph. Orch., 1964-66; Ldr., Düsseldorf Symph. Orch., 1967-. Hobbies: Chess; Sports; Do-It-Yourself. Address: Kantstr. 20, 402 Mettman 2, German Fed. Repub.

SETTO, Kliza, b. 26 Jan. 1932, Sao Paulo, Brasil. Composer. Educ: Postgrad., Univ. of Sao Paulo Conserv. of Music & Drama, 1953. m. Luiz Antonio de Castro Lima, 2 d. Debut: Municipal Symph. Orch., Sao Paulo, Cond., Camargo Guarnieri, 1959. Comps. incl: Oito Variacoes Para Piano, 1972; Lenda Do Céu (Cantata for choral & percussion), 1962; Suite (for chamber orch.), 1961; Dois Momentos (op. 2, blockflute & piano), 1976. Recordins incl: Dois Corais Mistos (a capela), 1967; Folganca (orch. suite), 1969. Contbr. to Revista

Brasileira de Folclore (Min. of Educ. & Cluture, Brasil). Mbrships. incl: Soc. for Ethnomusicology, USA; Comissao Paulista de Folclore, Brazil; Int. Gesellschaft für Jazzfrschung, Austria. Hons. incl: Fellowship, Fundacao Calouste Gulbenkian, 1970; 1st Prize Nat. Brasilian Song contest, 1961. Mgmt: Ricordi Brasileira, Av. Conselheiro Nebia, 1136, Sao Paulo, Brasil. Address: Rua Ceara, 254, 01243 Consolacao, Sao Paulo, Brasil.

SEVENSTERN, Jan, b. 24 Apr. 1949, Hilversum, Netherlands, Musician (Bass Tuba), Educ: Pvte. study w. father, Prof. Wijnand Sevenstern, & pvte. sutdy of theory, 1960-68. Debut: (as soloist) Amsterdam, 1971. Career: Mbr., Dutch Nat. Ballet Orch., Amsterdam; sev. radio perfs./recordings as soloist, inclng. works by Hindemith, Koper, & Andriessen; Soloist, world premiere of Bruno Maderna's opera Satyricon; also TV perf. at La Scala, Milan, 1974, of this opera. Records: var. pop records as session musician. Mbr., Exec. Committee, NTB (Dutch Musicians Union affiliated to Int. Fedn. Musicians). Hobbies: Music; Swimming; Reading. Mgmt: Dr. de Koos Concertdirectie, Laren. Address: Rading 120, Loosdrecht, Netherlands.

SEVERIN, Peder, b. Finderup, Denmark. Opera & Concert Singer (Tenor). Educ: Dip., Royal Theatre Acad. Opera, 1969; St. Cecilia, Rome, Italy; w. Georges Cunelli, London, UK; Anton Dermota, Vienna, Austria. m. Karen Margrete Severin, 1 d. Debut: Lied, Copenhagen, 1971. Career: w. Den Jyske Opera, Arhus, 1971; Royal Theatre, Copenhagen, 1972; Ldng. tenor parts in vr. operas inclng: Coronation of Poppea, Falstaff, Magic Flute; Oratorio, opera & lied concerts, Denmark, Danish Broadcasting Serv., & Danish & Norwegian TV; Apps. in Norway, Sweden, Italy & Germany inclg. 2 opera concerts w. Das Phil. Staatsorchester, Hamburg, 1975. Hons: Prizes, Royal Theatre, 1969; Queen Ingrid's Roman Fond, 1970; Min. Cultural Affairs, 1972. Mgmt: Gosta Schwarck, Dalgas Blvd. 48, 2000 Copenhagen, F. Address: Runevej 8, Tune 4000 Roskilde, Denmark.

SEYMOUR, Joan Dorothy, b. 8 Feb. 1930, London, UK. Concert Singer (soprano); Teacher of Singing. Educ: Trinity Coll. of Music, London; LTCL (TTD) Dip; Pvte. tuition w. Elena Gerhardt & Reinhold Gerhardt. m. Dr. John Seymour. Recital debut in 1957. Career: Many recital & concert appearances in England & Europe. Mbr., ISM (Solo Perfs. Sect.). Hons: Bronze Medal for Pianoforte, Trinity Coll. of Music; Sev. awards & trophies for singing. Hobbies: Needlework; Dressmaking; Antique dolls; Travel. Address: 18 Selborne Rd., Sidcup, Kent DA14 4QY, UK. 3, 27.

SGOURDA, Antigone, b. 6 Aug. 1938, Athens, Greece, Opera Singer. Educ: Nat. Coll. Music, Calomiris, Athens; Akad. Music & Darstellende Kunst, Vienna, Austria. Debut: Donn State Theatre, German Fed. Repub. Career: 'Talkes of Hoffman' & 'Giulietta', German Fed. Repub. TV: 'Katja Kabanowa', Vienna State Opera; 'Giovanni', 'Donna Anna', Edinburgh Fest. & Colon; 'Magic Flute' & 'Cosi Fan Tutte', Glyndebourne. Recordings incl: Don Giovanni. Address: Leitziweg 6, 8006 Zürich, Switzerland, & Eolou 61, Athens, Greece.

SGRIZZI, Luciano, b. 30 Oct. 1910, Bologna, Italy. Harpsichordist; Pianist; Composer; Transcriber. Educ: Dip. Piano, 1924, Dip. Organ, 1928, Dip. Comp., 1929 (all Bologna). Debut: as Pianist, 1924. Career: Piano Concertist from 1924 in Europe & S Am; Pianist at Swiss Broadcasting Cos. from 1931 & at Swiss-Italian Broadcasting (Lugano) from 1947; Harpsichordist at the major European Broadcasting & TV Ctrs. of Swiss & France; Concerts at the Fests of Salzburg, Spoleto (Fest. of two Worlds), of Paris (Fest. du Marais), of Flanders, of Liege (Nuits de Septembre), & at the Fest. of Geneva & Rome. Comps. (for or with orch.) Suite Belge (1952); Suite Napoletna (1953); Viottiana (1954); English Suite (1956); Capriccio for flute (1957); Sinfonietta Roco (1957), etc. (piano & chamber music) Elegia e Scherzo (1956); Ostinati (1958); Suite-Serenata (1957), etc. Many recordings playing piano, harpsichord, Fortepiano. Mbrships: Juries of the Geneva Int. Contest, of the Conservatories of Paris, Geneva, Lausanne, etc. Hons: Grand Prix du disque Charles Cros, 1964-75. Grand Prix des discophiles ORTF, 1965; Grand Prix de Hollande, 1965; Grand Prix Charles Cros, 1972, 75; Grand Prix des Discophiles, Radiotelevisioin Belge, 1977. Address: 6981 Purasca, Ticino, Switz.

SHACKFORD, Charles Reeve, b. 18 Apr. 1918, New York, NY, USA. Composer; Professor of Composition & Theory. Educ: BA, Yale Coll., 1941; PhD, Harvard Univ., 1954; Dip., Music Theory, Juilliard Schl. of Music. m. Jane Elizabeth Wilson, 4 sons (by previous marriage). Career: Instr., Music, Bennett Jr. Coll., 1944-46; Tchng. Fellow, Harvard Univ., 1949-50; Choir Dir. & Lectr. in Music Wellesley Coll., 1952-53; Assoc. Prof.,

Music, Wilson Coll., 1962-65; Prof., Music, Conn. Coll., 1965-. Comps. incl: Fantasy on Vysehrad for 2 pianos & orch; Quintet for clarinet, French horn, vioélin, viola & violoncello; Overture Concertante for concert band; Instrumental, choral works. Broadcast tapes of all the above. Contbr. to profl. jrnls. Mbrships: Am. Musicol. Soc: Am. Soc. of Univ. Composers; Coll. Music Soc; Music Lib. Assn; AAUP. Hons: Percy Lee Atherton Fellow in Composition, Harvard, 1947-49; Wyman Fund rsch. grant, 1949; Rsch. grant, Am. Acad. of Arts & Scis., 1955; Ford Fndn. Fellowship, 1961-62; Composition grant, Conn. Fndn. for the Arts, 1974. Hobbies: Reading; Walking; Climbing; Sailing. Address: 1611 Conn. Coll., New London, CT 06320, USA. 6, 11.

SHACKLOCK, Constance, b. 16 Apr. 1913, Sherwood, Notts., UK. Operatic & Concert Singer. Educ: RAM; LRAM. m. Eric Mitchell (dec.) Debut: Milton's Comus, London Coliseum, 1945-46. Career: Prin. Mezzo, Royal Opera, Covent Gdn.; State Opera, Berlin; Paris Opera House; Liége Opera House; Teatro Colon, Buenos Aires; Rhodes Centenery; Opera, Bulawayo; Bolslhoi, Moscow; Kirov, Leningrad; Elizabethan Opera, Aust.; Amsterdam & Hague Opera Houses; Sound of Music, London Palace Theatre. Recordings: Tristan & Isolde; The Messiah; Beggar's Opera. Mbrships: Pres., Nottingham Operatic Soc., 1966-79; Pres., Engl. Singers & Speakers, 1978-79; Pres., RAM, 1979-80. Hons: FRAM, 1953; OBE, 1970. Hobbies: Tapestry; Gardening; Reading. Address: E Dorincourt, Kingston Vale, London SW15 3RN, UK. 3, 27.

SHAFFER, Jeanne Ellison, b. 25 May 1925, Knoxville, Tenn., USA. Composer; Teacher; Organist. Educ: AA, Stephens Coll., Columbia, Mo., 1944; BMus, Samford Univ., Birmingham, Ala., 1954; MMus, Birmingham Southern, 1958; PhD, Geo. Peabody Coll., 1970. m. Loran O Shaffer (dec.), 1 s, 4 d. Career incls: Soloist w. Paul Whitemn's Orch., 1937-39; appeared in Girl of the Golden West, w. Jeannette MacDonald; soloist w. Birmingham Symph., 1953, Ala. Pops Orch., 1960, Peoria Symph., 1963 & Nashville Symph., 1967; Organist & choirmaster, var. Bapt. Chs.; Prof., Chmn., Dept. of Visual & Perf. Arts, Huntington Coll., Ala., 1976-78. Comps. incl: Four Advent Anthems, 1977; Two Hymn Tune Preludes, 1977; The Ghost of Susan B Anthony (Chmbr. Opera), 1977; Rainbow Ballet Suite, 1978. Art Critic, Montgomery Advertiser-Jrnl. Mbr., var. profl. orgs. Hons. incl: Awards in Comp., Birmingham Fest. of Arts, 1956-61. Address: 2740 Oxford Dr., Montgomery, AL 36111, USA.

SHAFFER, Sherwood, b. 15 Nov. 1934, Bee Co., Tex., USA. Composer; Teacher. Educ: BM, Curtis Inst. of Music; MM, Manhattan Schl. of Music. Career: Fac., Manhattan Schl. of Music, 1962-65; Chmn., Theory Dept., NC Schl. of the Arts, Winston-Salem, 1965-. Comps. publd: Ave Marie. Works recorded: Sonata for contrabasss & piano, The 20th Century Double Bass, Ubres Records. Mbrships: Am. Music Ctr; Nat. Assn. of Am. Comps. & Publrs; Music Tchrs. Nat. Assn. Address: 515 W Sprague St., Winston-Salem, NC 27107, USA.

SHAKESHAFT, Stephen, b. Birmingham, UK. Violinist. Educ: RAM; ARM. m. Gillian Thomas, 1 s., 1 d. Career: Prin. Viola. Scottish Nat. Orch. Hobbies: Radio; Photography. Address: c/o Scottish Nat. Orch., 150 Hope St., Glasgow, UK.

SHAMROCK, Mary Stringham, b. 7 June 1937, Mpls., Minn., USA. Music Educator. Educ: BA, St. Olaf Coll.; MA, WVa. Univ.; trng. in Suzuki violin method; Tchrs. Cert., Orff-Schulwerk, Univ. of Toronto, Can. m. 1) Scott Stringham (dec); 2) Jerome Shamrock. Career incl: Orchl. experience as violinist, 1952-; Instructor of Suzuki violin & Orff-Schulwerk; Assoc. Prof., WVa. Univ.; Instructor for trng. courses in Orff-Schulwerk, Univ. of Toronto, DePaul Univ., Univ. of S Calif.; currently Asst. Prof. of Music, Calif. State Univ., Northridge. Publs: Piano Technique for Classroom Teachers, 1971; Theme & Variations Teaching Unit, 971; Tr. & Ed., Orff-Schulwerk, Background & Commentary; Bibliography of Materials in English concerning Orff-Schulwerk. Contbr. to profl. jrnls. Mbrships: Pres., Am. Orff-Schulwerk Assn., 1978-79; Soc. for Ethnomusicol.; MENC; Am. String Tchrs. Assn. Recip. of Univ. Senate Rsch. Grant, 1972. Hobbies: Gardening; Sewing. Address: 3267 Midvale Ave., Los Angeles, CA 90034, USA. 5.

SHANE, Rita Frances, b. 15 Aug., NY, NY, USA. Dramatic Coloratura Soprano. Educ: BA, Barnard Coll.; sutdies w. Beverley Peck Johnson (voice) & Bliss Hebert (repertoire). m. Daniel F Tritter, 1s. Debut: as Olympia (Tales of Hoffmann), Chagganooga Opera, 1964. Career: apps. at Metropolitan Opera, NY City Opera, Chgo. Lyric, Balt., Santa Fe, La Scala, Munich, Vienna, Scottish Opera, etc.; concert apps. w. Phila., Cleveland, Cinn., orchs., RAI, Santa Cecilia, Austrian Radio

Orch., etc.; fest. apps. at Munich, Salzburg, Vienna, Sagra Umbra, Glyndbourne, Can., Aspen, Mostly Mozart (NY), Handel (Wash.); title role in premiere of Argento's Miss Havisham's Fire, NY, 1979; Hilde Mack in Am. premiere of Hans Werner Henze's Elegy for Young Lovers, NY, 1965; Cecilia Weisz in Am. premiere of Peter Schat's Houdini, Aspen Fest., 1979. num. recordings. mbr., Am. Guild of Musical Artists. Hons: 2 grants. Hobbies: Needlepoint; Gardening; Dachshunds. Mgmt: Herbert H Breslin, USA; Margherita Stafford, Europe. Address: c/o Herbert H Breslin, Inc., 119 W 57th St., NY, NY 10019, USA. 2, 5, 27.

SHANET, Howard, Stephen, b. 9 Nov. 1918, NYC, USA. Conductor; Music Educator. Educ: incls: AB, Columbia Coll., 1939; Am. Columbia Univ., 1941. m. Bernice Grafstein, 1 s. Career incls: Asst. Cond. to Leonard Bernstein, NYC Symph., 1947-48, to Serge Koussevitzky, int. tour, 1949-50; Cond., Berkshire Music Ctr., Tanglewood, Mass., 1949-52, Huntington Symph. Orch., W Va., 1951-53; Asst. Prof. & Cond. of Univ. Orch., 1953, Assoc. Prof., 1959, Prof., 1969, Chmn., Dept. of Music, 1972-78, Dir. of Music Perf., 1978-, Columbia Univ.; Cond., num. 1st perfs. Comps. incl: Allegro Giocoso for String Quartet (or string orch.); Variations on a Bizarre Theme for orch.; works for military band, piano & var. chmbr. ensembles. Recordings: What's New. Publs: Learn to Read Music, 1956; Philharmonic: A History of New York's Orchestra, 1975. Mbr., profl. orgs. Address: Dept. of Music, Columbia Univ., 703 Dodge, NY, NY 10027, USA. 1, 2, 14, 29.

SHANKAR, Ravi, b. 7 Apr. 1920, Benares, India. Sitar player. Educ: studied w. Ustad Allauddin Kahan. m. Annapurna, 1 s. Career: Musician/Dancer in a troupe touring Indian & USA, at age 10; Dir., Composer & Cond., All-India Radio (Vadya Vrinda), 1940-56; Fndr. & Dir., Kinnara Schl. of Music, Bombay, 1962-, & LA (USA), 1967-; Res. Lectr., UCLA, 1964, & CCNY, 1967; currently on staff, Calif. Inst. of Arts; has given recitals worldwide. Comps. incl: film music for Charly, Chappaqua, Panther Panchali, etc; music for TV prod. of Alice in Wonderland; The Discovery of India (ballet); Concerto for Sitar & Orcestra (commissioned by LSO). Recordings incl: West Meets East (w. Yehudi Menuhin, violin). Publs: My Music, My Life, 1969. Recip. of many hons. inclng. Silver Bear of Berlin; Padma Bhushan Award, 1967. Mgmts: Basil Douglas Ltd., London (Europe); Herbert Barrett, NY (USAeE). Address: c/o Mgmt.

SHANKS, Clare Louise, b. 30 May 1939, Glasgow, UK. Teacher; Instrumentalist (Oboe; Recorder). Educ: Ma, St. Andrews Univ; DipEd, Homerton Coll., Cambridge; ARCM, 1961; Baroque Oboe study, Zürich, Switz. Career: TV apps., Baroque instruments, Open Univ; Radio. 'The Baroque Oboe' & w. The Music Party; Concerts w. Engl. Concert, Purcell Room & Victoria & Albert Museum; Apps., Zürich, London, Harrogate, York, Basel, Bruges, Swansea etc. Fests. Recordings incl: Haydn Nocturnes w. Alan Hacker, Music Party; French Music & Handel w. Michel Piguet. Hon: Sawyer Music Prize, St. Andrews, 1960. Hobbies: Reading; Travel; Walking; Natural Hist. Address: 61 Balcombe St., London NW1, UK.

SHANSKY, Daniel, b. 17 Feb. 1920, NY, NY, USA. Teacher; Therapist; Conductor; Composer; now Retired. Educ: NY Univ., 1939-40; Cert. Orchl. Cond., Juilliard Schl. of Music, 1940; BA, Brooklyn Coll., 1955; MS in Educ. ibid 1958. m. Nora Matesky Shansky, 1 s., 1 d. Debut: Rockhill,NY, 1934. Career: Tchr. Wurlitzer Schl. of Music, 1938-45; Bugler & Regimental Band Cond., US Army, 1942-43; Music Therapist, Inst. for Crippled & Disabled, NYC & House of St. Giles the Cripple, Brooklyn, NY, 1945-55; Hd. of Music Dept., Russell Sage Jr. HS, Queens, NY & Nathan Hale Jr. HS Brooklyn, 1955-69; On Detached Serv., as Educl. & Vocational Guidance Counselor at 1S 293, Brooklyn, 1969-. Comps: Four Operettas for Children; Canterbury Tales, str. quartet. Contrbr. to Downbeat Mag., 1939-45. Mbrships: Local 802, Am. Fedn. Musicians; United Fedn. Tchrs.; Guidance Counselors Assn. Recip. Var. HS Medals & Prizes. Hobby: Oil Painting. Address: 2557 4 19th St., Brooklyn, NY 11235, USA.

SHAPINSKY, Aaron, b. 8 Dec. 1925, NY, USA. Concert Cellist. Educ: Juilliard. m. Norma Ehrlich-Sluszny, 2 s. Debut: Town Hall, NY, 1963. Carer: Solo Cellist, Busch Chmbr. Players, 1945; Leopold Stokowski's youngest 1st cellist City Ctr. Symph. & Am. Symph.; Kohon Quartet; num. recitals w. pianist son, Ian, USA & Europe; Film of Beethoven & Brahms Sonata w. Ian; 20th Century Recital Prog., Tully Hall, NY, 1974; Tchr., pvtely., Nassau Community Coll. & Hofstra Coll. Recordings: num. w. Kohon String Quartet (Vox). Hon: Presidental Citation, NY Fedn. Music Clubs, Promulgation of high standards in musical performance, w. son, Ian, 1974. Hobbies incl: Musical Rsch. Mgmt: Annabelle Evans. Address: 19 Belmont Parkway, Hempstead, NY 11550, USA.

SHAPIRO, Joel, b. 28 Nov. 1934, Cleveland, Ohio, USA. Concert Pianist; Teacher. Educ: BA, Columbia Univ.; Premier Prix, Royal Conserv. of Music, Brussels, Belgium; pvte. study w. Stefan Askenase. Debut: As winner of Young Concert Artists Comp., NYC, 1963. London debut w. RPO. Career incl: extensive annual concert tours, incl. piano recitals & concertos in the world's leading music ctrs.; num. radio & TV broadcasts; Prof. of Piano, Univ. of Ill., 1970-. Hons: 1st Prize, Darche Comp., Brussels, 1962; Harriet Cohen Int. Bach Award, London, 1963; Mgmt: Susan Wadsworth, NYC; Maria Graf's Konzertdirection, Hamburg, Germany. Address: Smith Music Hall, Univ. of Ill., Urbana, IL 61801, USA.

SHAPIRO, Laurence David, b. 29 Sept. 1941, Arlington, Mass., USA. Violinst. Educ: BA, Univ. of Dela.; MA, Univ. of Evansville; adv. studies w. noted tchrs. m. Judith Carol Sobel, 3 d. Career: incls: Concertmaster & Soloist, var. orchs. inclng. Evansville Phil.; Fndr., 1st Violin, Dela. Str. Quartet; 1st Violin, Evansville Str. Quartet; Mbr., Soloist, Concerto Soloists of Phila.; Cond., Music, Dir., Univ. Orch., current occupant of Phi Mu Alpha Sinfonia Chair of Music, Assoc. Prof., Univ. of Evansville. Made TV lecture series on chmbr. music for CBS, Phila., 1972. Mbrships. incl: Phi Kappa Phi. Recip. award, Profl. Musicians Competition of Balt., 1969. Hobbies: Tennis; Writing poetry; Yoga. Address: 1671 Bayard Pk. Dr., Evansville, IN 47714, USA.

SHARMA, Pyarelal Ramprasad, b. 3 Sept. 1940, Bombay, India. Music Director; Violinist. Educ: Studied under sev. gurus, m. Sunila Payarelal Sharma, 1 s., 1 d. Debut: Soloist, Indian Symph. Orch., 1958. Career: Cond. of many successful concerts in Indian; Comp. of musical scores of over 1500 Hindi film songs & over 500 songs for 60 Hindi film assignments in hand, inclng. 45 Silver Jubilees, 9 Golden Jubilees, 2 Diamond Jubilees, & 1 Century film. Mbrships: Cine Musicians' Assn.; Cine Music Dirs.' Assn; Indian Performing Rights Soc. Ltd., Bombay. Recip., num. hons. & musical prizes inclng: Golden Disc, Gramophone Co. of India, 1974. Address: Deep Bela, 3rd Floor, Mt. Mary Rd., Bandra, Bombay 400 050, India.

SHARP, Mary, b. 30 Sept. 1907, Wyke, Bradford, UK. Teacher of Piano & Singing. Educ: pvte, mostly w. father; ALCM; LLCM; LRAM. Career: 7 yrs. w. concert choir as soloist & accomp.; many yrs. w. Bradford Educ. as peripatetic pianist & tchr; pvte. piano teacher for 57 yrs. Publs: Theory of Music for Young Musicians, 1923; 5 books of Humor in Music, 1979-77. Contbr. to: Telegraph & Argus; Weekly News. mbr., ISM. Hons: 2nd place, Harrogate Music Fest. for comp. & piano solo, 1964; 2nd place, hymn comp., Huddersfield, 1974. Hobbies incl: Photography; Knitting; Sewing; Crocheting; Writing. Address: 551 Huddersfield Rd., Wyke, Bradford, W Yorks. BD12 8NA, UK.

SHARP, Ronald William, b. 8 Aug. 1929, Sydney, Aust. Pipe Organ Builder. Educ: self-taught organ builder, currently undertaking self-tuition in lutherie & harpsichord building. div., 1 s., 2 d. Has build about 18 organs inclng: St. Mary's Cathedral, Sydney, Knox Grammar Schl. Wahroonga, Univ. of Sydney, Opera House Concert Hall, Sydney, Town Hall, Wollongong, Concert Hall, Perth, Monash Univ., Melbourne. Restoration of 1863 organ by J W WSalker, St. John's C o E Parramatta. Hobbies incl: Power aircraft flying; Guilding; Sailing; Radio controlled model aircrqaft; Studying piano, organ, violin, vioila & cello. Address: 4 Hearne St., Mortdale, NSW 2223, Aust.

SHARVIT, Uri, b. 24 Oct. 1939, Jerusalem, Israel. Composer; Condutor; Ethnomusicologist. Educ: BA, Hebrew Univ., Jerusalem, 1968; Dip., Rubin Acad. of Music Jerusalem, 1965; MA, 1971, PhD, 1976, Columbia Univ., USA. m. Shulamit Sharvit, 4 children. Career: currently Prof. of Ethnomusicol., Bar-Ilan Univ., Israel, & Rsch. Organizer, Jewish Music Rsch. Ctr., Hebrew Univ., Jerusalem. Comps. Heterophonic Study; Divertissement; Duo for violin & cello; Psalm 30; Passcaglia for orch. Transcribor & Ed., Rinatia (traditional tunes), 1968. Contbr. to: Ethnomusicology. Mbrships: Bd. of Music, Ministry of Educ. & Culture, Israel; Bd. of Dirs., Israeli Chmbr. Orch.; Bd. of Dirs., Israeli Inst. for Sacred Music; League of Comps. in Israel; ACUM Ltd.; Israel Soc. of Musicol. Recip. 1st Prize, ACUM annual Competition, 1971. Address: 6 Mann St., Jerusalem, Isarel.

SHASBY, Anne, b. 13 Dec. 1945, Wickham, Hants., UK. Concert Pianist. Educ: LRAM (Perfs). m. Roger Skinner, 1 d. Debut: London, 1971. Career: apps. both as Soloist & in Piano Duo w. Richard McMahon; has performed extensively throughout UK inclng. regular apps. at Purcell Room, Wigmore Hall, Queen Elizabeth Hall & Royal Fest. Hall; TV broadcasts Tribute to Stravinsky, BBC2, & Diversiions, Scottish TV, 1972; frequent broadcasts on BBC Radio 3. Recorded (w. McMahon)

Rachmaninov, Symphonic Dances, & Debussy/Ravel, Nocturnes. Recip. (w. McMahon) Leslie Regen RAM Prize for duo work, 1979. Hobbies: Gardening; Knitting; Cooking; Crochet. Mgmt: Ibbs & Tillett, 124 Wigmore St., London W1, UK. Address: 66 Dartmouth Park Rd., London NW5 1SN, UK.

SHASHOUA, Salim (Shlomo) Samuel, b. 17 Nov. 1930, Baghdad, Iraq. Lawyer; Religious Litigant; Broadcasting Editor. Educ: LLB, Law Coll., Baghdad; Relig. Litigant, Islamic personal law, Jerusalem; Mbr., Israel Bar; Completed Doctoral progs., Columbia Univ., NY, & Hebrew Univ., Jerusalem; Study of flute, Inst. of Fine Arts, Baghdad; Study of Aude & Kamana (ancient musical instrument), Israel. m. Jakcline (Ruth) Gabai. Debut: Lecture, Baghdad Broadcasting Stn., age 13. Career incl: Chief ed. of Israeli Radio progs. incl. Cooperation between Jews & Arabs through the ages; Throught of the morning; Cases from the Relig. Courts. Compositions incl. many songs, publ. in Garlands of Melodies & other books. Publs: Beolam Haor (in the World of Light); Ahmad Shawqi (biography); The Crown of Narcissus (translated stories); Songs to My Country, 1976. Mbr. of var. cultural orgs. Hobbies: Playing music; Writing poetry; Swimming. Address: Nahom St, no. 20, Ramat Chen, Israel.

SHATZKY, Yevgeny, b. 5 Jan. 1941, Uinsk, USSR, Double Bass Player. Educ: qualified as Solo Artist & Tchr., Leningrad Conserv. m. Alla Shatzky, 2 d. Debut: 1967. Career: Perfs. on Soviet TV, w. Leningrad Phil. Orch. & Israel Radio Orch.; currently Orchl. Performer w. Israeli Phil. under Zubin Mehta. Has recorded w. Israeli Phil. Orch. Hons. Jazz Fest., 1966; Conserv. Concours, 1968. Address: Gilo 43/15, Jerusalem, Israel.

SHAVE, Peter Stanley, b. 28 Mar. 1944, Whitchurch, Glam., S Wales, UK. Adviser on Music Education. Conductor; Examiner. Educ: Studied Cello, Piano, Conducting, Comp., RCM, 1962-66; BMus, London; GRSM; ARCM. m. Gillian Stacey, 2 d, 1 s. Career: Advsr. on String Teaching to Inner London Educ. Auth., 1969-76; Cond., Esterhazy Singers, 1971-; Examiner, Assoc. Bd., Royal Schls. of Music; Tutor, Open Univ., 1975-; Former freelance cellist, cond., tchr. Mbr., Musicians Union. Hons: HC Colles Prize; Cobbett Prize. Hobbies: Theatre; Books; Swimming. Address: 68 Strawberry Lane. Tiptree, Essex, UK.

SHAVITZ, Carl, b. 5 Mar. 1940, NYC, USA. Lutenist. Educ: Ny Univ.; Geo. Wash. Univ.; Manhattan Sch. of Music; Univ. of Wis.; French Horn w. Gunther Schuller; Guitar w. Rey de la Torre; voice w. Amanda Evans. Debut: London, 1968. Career: Fndr. mbr., Fortune's Fire (originally Duo Wynford Evans/Carl Shavitz) now a duo, trio w. viola da gamba or quartet w. soprano; Recitals, radio recordings & workshops in most European countries, E Europe, Australian & Japan. Recordings: To Entertain the Stealth of Love, 1977; Mirror of Love, 1978. Publs: Ed., lute song anthologies, Mirror of Love, 1976, & What is Love?, 1978. Mbrships: Lute.; Cyclists' Touring Club. Hons: Fulbright Scholarship, 1966-68. Hobbies: Playing Red Indians; Cycling. Address: 18B Ferntower Rd., London N5 2JH, UK.

SHAW, Christopher Graham, b. 30 July 1924, London, UK. Composer; Pianist. Educ: New Coll., Oxford Univ. m. Jean Margaret Warrand. Comps: Peter & the Lame Man; A Lesson from Ecclesiates; To the Bandusian Spring; Music, When Soft Voices Die (recorded on Argo label); Garden Songs; Sonata for Clarinet & Piano; No Room at the Inn. Mbrships: CGGB; Performing Rights Soc. Contbr. to Tempo mag. Address:38 Hazlewell Rd., London SW 15, UK.

SHAW, Francis Richard, b. 23 June 1942, Maidenhead, UK. Composer; Conductor; Pianist. Educ: LCM; London Univ.; Accademia Chigi (Sien, Italy); Southampton Univ. m. Anne Rosemary Marriott, 3 c. Career incls: Comp., film scores, Great Expectations, ATV, 1978 & Crime & Punishment, BBC TV, 1979. Comps. incl: The Selfish Giant, Opera for young people; 4 Piano Pieces. Mbrships: PRS; MCPS; Songwriters Guild. Hons: 1st prize, Int. Competition for Children's Opera, Welsh Arts Coun., Caerphilly Fest., 1972. Hobbies: Vintage Cars; Pianos. Address: 39 Crane Grove, London N7 8LD, UK.

SHAW, Geoffrey Edward, b. 31 Jan. 1927, Nottingham, UK. Baritone; Teacher. ARCM (Singing Tchng.). m. Helen Harley. Career: Soloist, oratorio & in recital, worldwide; Fndr. Mbr., Purcell Consort of Voices, & Wilbye Consort; Co-Dir., Early Music Consort of London; Prof., Guildhall Schl. of Music Master Classes, Snape Fmb. Recordings: Over 20, w. above grps. & as soloist w. Wandsworth Boys Choir. Hobbies: Clocks; Photography; Sailing. Mgmt: HHH. Address: 50 Kendall Ave. S, Sanderstead, Surrey CR2 0QQ, UK.

SHAW, (Harold) Watkins, b. 3 April 1911, Bradford, W Yorks., UK. Teacher; Writer; Editor. Educ: MA, 1936, DLitt.,

1967, Wadham Coll., Oxford; RCM, 1932-33; var. dips. m. Elanor Horne. Career: Schoolmaster, 1933-46; Sr. Music Adviser, Herts. County Coun., 1946-49; Prin. Lectr. in Music, Worcester Coll. of Educ., 1949-71; Pt.-time Lectr., Birmingham Schl. of Music, 1951-47; Keeper, Parry Room Lib., RCM, 1971-80; Hon. Gen. Ed., Ch. Music Soc., 1956-70; Hon. Libn., St. Michael's Coll., Tenbury, 1948-. Publs. incl: Ed., Musical Educ., 1946; Eighteenth-Century Cathedral Music, 1953; Textual Companion to Handel's Messiah; Hereford Cathedral Organists & Organs. Contbr. to profl. publs. Mbrships: VP, Royal Musical Assn.; VP, Ch. Music Soc.; Fellow, Soc. of Antiquaries. Hons: Osgood Memorial Prize, Univ. of Oxford, 1936; Fellow, RSCM, 1966; FRCM, 1974. Address: Holly Tree Cottage, Broadheath Common, Worcester,WR2 6RP, UK.

SHAW, Hilda, b. 5 Feb. 1922, Manhattan, NYC, USA. Pianist; Composer; Piano Sytlist. Educ: studied piano, theory & comp. at Third St. Music Schl.; pvte. piano pupil of Maybelle Brandenburg of NY; Columbia Univ. m. Daniel Wolfsie, 1s, 1 d. Debut: Town Hall, NY 1939. Career: Played on NY radio stns. beginning in 1941, orginal comps. & improvisations on given theme; Played at jt. piano recitals at Barbizon-Plaza Concert Hall, NY 1941-47; Debut as Jazz Pianist in nightclubs, hotels, supper clubs, 1941; Toured USA w. USO; Many comps. perf. Mbr., Am. Fed. of Musicians, local 802, NY, 1940-. Hobbies: Art. Address: 63-84 Saunders St., Rego Pk., NY 11374, USA.

SHAW, Jeremy Howard, b. 18 Nov. 1956, Bradford, UK. Musician of Clarinet & Saxophone; Director of Woodwind Plub Promotions; Teacher; Lecture Recitlist. Educ: Lic., Trinity Coll. of Music, London, for clarinet teaching; FVCM; Clarendon Coll., Nottingham. Debut: Nottingham Festical, 1979. Career: Appearances in Nottingham Music Theatre; Nottingham Playhouse; Winter Solstice. Mbrships: Incrop. Soc. of Musicians; Musicians' Union. Hobby: Theatre. Mgmt: Woodwind Plub Promotions, Nottingham. Address: 187 Wallaton St., Nottingham, UK.

SHAW, Kenneth Raymond, b. 30 Mar. 1927, Ilkeston, Derbyshire, UK. French Horn Player. Educ: Royal Manchester Coll. of Music, 1948-49. m. Brenda Margaret Lean, 2 d. Career: Buxton Spa, 2 summers, 1949-50; SNO, 1949-50; Halle, 1950-61; Royal Opera House, Convent Garden, 1961-. Recordings w. above orchs Hobby: Transport Address: 22 Oal Hill Cres., Woodford Green, Essex, UK.

SHAW, Lucretia Faye, b. 11 July 1941, Spiro, Okla., USA. Music Educator; Soprano Soloist. Educ: BA, Northeastern State Coll., Tahlequa, Okla., 1964; MME, N Tex. State Univ., 1967. Career: Ch. Choir Dir. & Soloist, 1964-71; Choral Dir., Valliant Pub. HS & Elem. Schl., Okla., 1964-65; Instr. in Music, Southwestern Assemblies of God Coll., Waxahachie, Tex.,1965-58; Asst. Prof. of Music, NE La. State Coll., 1968, Univ. of Southern Miss., 1968-71, Oral Robert Univ., 1971-; Studying langs., Germany, Italy & France; num. operatic & oratorio perfs. Mbrships. incl: MENC; Nat. Assn. for Tchrs. of Singing; AAUP; Hons: Recip. Award, Nat. Heritage Fndn. Ministry Through Music Fndn. Address: P.O. Box 604, Tulsa, OK 74101, USA.

SHAW, Robert Lawson, b. 30 April 1916, Red Bluff, Calif., USA. Conductor. Educ: AB, Pomona Coll., 1938, DMus, 1953; DMus, Coll. Wooster, 1951, Mich. State Univ., 1960, Cleveland Inst. Music, 1966, Emory Univ., 1967, Fla. State Univ., 1968; DFA, St. Lawrence Univ., 1955, Univ. of Alaska, 1966; LHD, Kenyon Coll., 1963, W Reserve Univ., 1966, Westminister Choir Coll., 1975, Univ. of Akron, 1976; Morehouse Coll., 1977; Oglethorpe Univ., 1977. m. (1) Maxine Farley (div.), 1 d, 2 s; (2) Caroline Sauls Hitz, 1 s. Career incls: Guest Cond., num. Orchs. & Fests.; Dir. Choral Music, Berkshire Music Center, 1946-49; Dir. Choral Activities, Juilliard Schl., 1946-49; Cond., San Diego Symph., 1953-58; Assoc. Cond., Cleveland Symph. Orch., 1956-67; Cond., Atlanta Symph. Orch., 1967-, Alaska Fest. of Music, 1956-73; Fndr., Dir., Robert Shaw Chorale, w. annual tours of USA, 1948-66 & world wide tours; Fest. Music Dir., 2nd Int. Choral Fest. Comps. & Conds. Hons: Outstanding Am. born Cond., 1943; Alice M Kitson Award, 1955; Ga. Govs. Award Arts, 1973; Disting. Service Award, Ga. Coll., 1973, SUNY at Postdam, 1975; Nat. Fedn. Music Clubs Award, 1975; Guggenheim Fellow, 1944. Address: 3707 Randall Mill Rd., NW Atlanta, GA 30327, USA.

SHAWE-TAYLOR, Desmond (Christopher), b. 29 May, 1907, Educ: Oriel Coll., Oxford. Career: Music Critic, New Statesman, 1945-58; Music Critic, Sunday Times, 1958-. Publs: Convent Garden, 1948; The Record Guide, w. Edward Sackville-West, 1951-56. Hobbies: Travel, Croquet; Gramophone. Address: 15 Furlong Rd., London N7 8LS, UK. 1.

SHEAD, Hebert Arthur, b. 15 Dec. 1906, Dartford, Kent, UK. Pianist; Teacher. Educ: LRAM (Piano tchrs.); pvte study of music. m. Joyce Shead, 1 s. Career: Gen. teaching of pinoforte w. associated subjects harmony, counterpoint, theory of music, etc.; Teaching at TCL, & at Kent Music Schl., Maidstone. Specialist Knowledge, the History & Technical Background of Pinoforte Design & Construction. Publs: The History of the Emanuel Moor Double Keyboard Piano; The Anatomy of the Piano. Contbr. to The Musical Teacher, OUP Mbr., ISM. Address: 55 Mayplace Rd. E, Bexleyheath, Kent DA7 6EA, UK.

SHEAN, David Charles, b. 12 Aug, 1934, Poole, Dorset UK. Orchestral Violinist. Educ: Pvte. study of music, UK. & Germany. m. Hether Mary Sands, 1 d. Career: Sub-Prin. 1st Violin, Bournemouth Symph. Orch., 1956-. Mbr., Bournemouth Symph. Orch. Benevolent Fund (Chmn.). Hobbies: Theology; Orchestral Soc. Address: Nithvale, 13 Mansfield Ave., Parkstone, Poole, Dorset, UK.

SHEARING, George Albert, b. 13 Aug. 1919, London, UK. Pianist; Jazz Musician. Career: since 1974 more than 300 concerts in USA & Europe; tour of UK w. Stephane Grappelli, 1978; apps. w. ldng. orchs. in classical concertos; num. apps. on TV. num. recordings. mbr. Bohemian Club, San Francisco. num. hons. & awards. Hobbies: Bridge; Cooking; Reading. Mgmt: Kim S Hartstein, 145 W 55th St., Suite 2B, New York, NY 10019, USA. Address: c/o Mgmt.

SHELDEN, Paul M, b. 8 Mar. 1941, Brooklyn, NY, USA. College Professor; Clarinettist; Conductor; Administrator. Educ: BS Juilliard Schl., 1963; MS, ibid, 1965; DMA, Univ. of Md., 1976. m. Pamela E Shelden. Career incls: Asst. Prof. of Music, Dpty. Chmn., Schl. of Gen. Studies, Dept. of Music, Brooklyn Coll., NYC; Chmbr. music perfs.; Clarinettst as soloist & w. orchs., quintets etc.; Solo, chmbr. music & lecture recitals, 1962-; Clarinettist w. Brooklyn Coll. Fac. Trio; Ldr., Paul Shelden Orch., 1956-. Comps: Score for Anouilh's Thieves Carnival. Recordings incl: Athenian Touch. Mbr. var. profl. orgs. Hons. incl: Guest Cond., All-Co. Band, Geauga Co. Ohio Music Fest., 1971. Hobby: Cat fancier. Address: 620 E 85th St., Brooklyn, NY 11236, USA.

SHELDON, Robin Treeby, b. 25 Mar. 1932, Cheltenham, Freelance Musician (Organ & Piano). Educ: MA, Trinity Coll., Cambridge; RAM, London. m. Rachel Margaret Sheldon, 3 s., 1 d. Career: Organist, All Souls' Ch., Langham Pl., London, 1955-58; Asst. Organist, Eton Coll., Windsor, 1958-65; Dir. of Music, King Edwards's Schl., Witley, 1965-74; Dir. of Music, Lancing Coll., Sussix, 1974-76; Mbr., Music staff, Roedean Schl., 1978-; Musical Ed., Scripture Union, 1977-78. Recordings: Hymns from Anglican Hymn Book; Sing Aloud w. Seaford Coll. Choir. Publs: Musical Ed., Anglican Hymn Book, 1965; Songs of Worship, 1979. Contbr. to Life of Faith; Crusade. Mbrships: ISM; Music Masters Assn. Hobbies: Ch. Work; Sailing; Squash; Gardening. Address: Smithy Cottage, Mill Rd., Lancing, Sussex, UK.

SHELEY, Wayne McDowell, b. 23 Apr. 19840, Ellenville, NY, USA. Music Educator; Trombonist. Educ: BS (Music Educ.) Hartwick Coll.; BMus, MMus, Yale Univ.; D Musical Arts, & Perfs. Cert., Trombone, Eastman Schl. of Music. m. Nancy Strow Sheley, 1 s., 1 d. Career: 1st Trombone, Hartford Symph., Nashville Symph.; 2nd Trombpne, Rochester Phil.; 1st Trombone, Eastman Wind Ensemble; Euphonium, Band of Am.; Hd., Dept. of Music/Music Educ., Univ. of Ala., Tuscaloosa. Recordings: Sev. w. above grps. Contbr. to profl. jrnls. Mbrships incl: Bds. of Dirs., Nat. Assn. Schls. of Music, & Yale Schl. of Music. Hons. incl: Fulbright Scholar, 1965; Outstanding Tchr. Award, Kappa Kappa Psi. Hobbies: Golf; Water Sports. Address: 65 Woodland Hills, Tuscaloosa, AL, USA.

SHELLEY, Howard (Gordon), b. 9 Mar. 1950, London, UK. Concert Pianist. Educ: Fndn. Scholar, RCM, 1967-71; ARCM; ARCO; studied w. Vera Yelverton, Harold Craxton, Kendall Taylor, Lamar Crowson, Ilona Kabos. m. Hilary Macnamra. Debut: Wigmore Hall, London, 1971. Career: First TV app. at age of 10 playing Bach & Chopin; since leaving RCM, constant engagements throughout GB & more recently Europe, inclng. Promenade Concerts & regular apps. in London & with the maj. orchs.; Regular broadcaster w. BBC & Continental stns.; Duo w. Malcolm Messiter (oboe); Duo w. Jane Manning (soprano). Recordings: Schumann & Hummel; Favourite Beethoven Piano Sonatas. Mbrships: ISM; Musicians' Union. Hons: Chappell Gold Medal, Peter Morrison Prize & Dannreuther Concerto Prize, RCM; Boise Scholar 1971-72 & Silver Medal, Worshpful Co. of Musicians. Address: 38 Cholmeley Pk., Highgate, London N6 5ER, UK.

SHELTON, Hugh Norman Arthur, b. 19 July 1925, Littleport, UK. Schoolmaster; Organist; Pianist. Educ: MA, Kings Coll., Cambrdige. Career: Gen. Tchr., Bellhaven Hill, Dunbar; Dir. of Music, Cothill House, Abingdon, Berks., Aysgarth Schl., Bedale, Yorks., Caldicott Schl., Farnham Royal, Bucks., 1959-66, Blue Coat Schl., Birmingham, 1966-; Cond., Blue Coat Schl. Choir, ITV broadcast & var. recordings; Asst. Master & Lay Clerk, St. Michael's Coll., Tenbury Wells, Worcs., 1958. Recordings: Abbey Records. Mbrships. incl: ISM; Royal Schl. of Ch. Music; Birmingham Organists Assn.; Life, Railway Correspondence & Travel Soc. Hobbies: Railways; Photography; Dogs. Address: Blue Coat Schl., Birmingham B17 OHR, UK.

SHEPHARD, Richard James, b. 20 Mar. 1949, Gloucester, UK. Composer; School Director of Music; Lay-Vicar. Educ: Corpus Christi Coll., Cambridge; MA (Cantab). Career: Dir. Music, Godolphin School; Lay-vicar, Salisbury Cathedral. Comps: The Addington Service (publd. & recorded); Operas, Rose Ransome, 1974, & Pilgrim's Progress, 1977; Concert Overture, Mayday; Motets, And didst thou travel light and Jesu Dulcis Memoria. Mbr., ISM. Hobbies: Tennis; Squash; Sailing. Address: 52 The Close, Salisbury, Wilts., UK.

SHEPHERD, Adrian, b. 7 Apr. 1939, Upminster, UK. Cellist. Educ: GSM, London. m. Susan Tyte. Career: Prin. Cello, Scottish Nat. Orch.; Dir., Cantilena; Sev. TV series, radio broadcasts; Edinburgh, Cheltenham, Vienna Fests. Recordings: Corelli; The Seasons; Music in England; Scarlatti. Contbr. to: BBC Radio Clyde. Mbrships: Past Pres., Glasgow Soc. of Musicians. Hobbies: Golf; Swimming. Address: 11 Dundonald Rd., Glasgow, G12, UK.

SHEPHERD, Christine, b. 15 Feb. 1948, Malvern, UK. Concert Pianist. Educ: RCM, London, 1966-71; ARCM; FTCL; LRAM; GRSM; Cert. Advanced Studies in Music, London, 1971. m. The Rev. David Shepherd. Career: Solo recitals in Scotland & London; Concerto engagements in N of England. Mbr. ISM. Hons: Austrian Govt. Scholarship, 1971; Scottish Arts Coun. Bursary, 1975. Hobbies: Canvas Embroidery; Psychol.; Poetry; Cordon Bleu Cookery. Address: 25 Blackness Ave., Dundee DD2 1EW, Tayside, Scotland, UK.

SHEPHERD, Donald Paul, b. Apr. 1917, Wallasey, Cheshire, UK. Violinist. Educ: Royal Manchester Coll. of Music; Study of violin w. H Holst; Viola, w. Sydney Errington, Lionel Tertis. m. 1) Muriel Goodwin (dec.); 2) Audrey Bowden. Career: Violinist, Hallé Orch., 1943-. Num. recordings w. Hallé. Mbrships: Musicians Union. Hons: 20-Yr. Medal, Hallé Orch. Hobbies: Snooker; Billiards; Painting & Sketching; Chess; Collecting Art Books, Records; Languages. Mgmt: Hallé Concerts Soc. Address: 21 Broadoaks Rd., Sale, Cheshire, M33 1SR, UK.

SHEPHERD, Paul (Christopher Paul; C Paul), b. 29 May 1935, Hude, Cheshire, UK. Lecturer; Conductor; Violinist. Educ: GTCL; LTCL (Violin Tchr.); LTCL (Violin Perf.). m. Ann Margaret Hitchman, 3 s. Career: Tchr. & Perf., London, inclng. Dpty. Cond., The Dorian Singers, 1957-62; Music Staff, Bretton Hall, Wakefield, 1962-66; Prin. Lectr. & Hd. of Studies in Music, Trinity & All Saints Colls., Leeds, 1966-; Freelance Violinist, 1966-; Cond: Northern Area Schls. Symph. Orch., 1970-; West Riding Singers, 1973-; Music Prod., BBC local radio. Num. recordings. Contbr. to Ch. Music. Mbr. JSM. Hons: Peckskai Scholar, TCL, 1953-56; Ricordi Conducting Prize, 1956. Address: Highland, 1 Larkfield Dr., Rawdon, Leeds LS19 6EL, UK.

SHEPPARD, Elizabeth Honor, b. Leeds, England, UK. Soprano. Educ: RMCM, FRCM. m. Robert Elliott, 1s., 1d. Career: Recitalist, Oratorio Singer, num. English & European Fests.; 1st Soprano, Deller Consort, extensive tours of Europe, N & S Am., 1961-. num. recordings. Hobby: Gardening. Mgmt:˙Ibbs &˙Tillett, London. Address: The Firs, 27 The Firs, Bowdon, Cheshire WA14 2TF, UK.

SHEPPARD, Honor, b. Yorks., UK. Concert Soprano. Educ: studied piano, classical ballet & Greek dancing; vocal studies w. Elsie Thurston & others, Royal Manchester Coll. of Music. Career: Recitalist; Oratorio Singer; apps. at major UK & European Fests.; noted for interpretation of 17th & 18th century music; Prin. Soprano, Deller Consort, touring in Europe, USA, Can. & S Am.; many broadcasts. Has recorded w. Deller Consort. Recip. Curtis Gold Medal, Royal Manchester Coll. of Music. Mgmt: Ibbs & Tillett, London, UK.

SHER, Rebecca, b. 30 May 1950, Munich, German Fed. Repub. Pianist; Composer; Songwriter. Educ: NY Schl. of Music (piano); BA, City Coll., CUNY; Manhattan Schl. of Music; grd. ctr. of CUNY (PhD studies in music). m. Lawrence Jay Sher. Career: Piano recitals in NY (Carnegie Hall, Town Hall, Judson

Hall). Mbrships; Am. Musicol. Soc.; ASCAP; NY Music Soc. (pres., 1969-71). Hons: Phi Beta Kappa, 1972; Edwin Rensin Memorial Award, 1972; medals for piano competitions, 1964, '67. Address: Harmon Cove, 238 Sunset Key, Secaucus, NJ 07094, USA.

SHERE, Charles, b. 20 Aug. 1935, Berkeley, Calif., USA. Journalist; Publisher & Editor; Professor of Music History. Educ: BA, Univ. of Calif., 1961; Studies w. Robert Erickson, San Francisco Conserv. of Music, & Luciano Berio, Mills Coll. m. Lindsey Remolif, 1 s., 2 d. Career: Music Dir., KPFA Fm. Berkeley, Calif., 1964-67; Art & Music Prod., KQED TV, San Francisco, 1967-74; Instructor, Mills Coll., Oakland, Calif., 1974-; Critic, Oakland Tribune, 1971-. Comps. incl: Small Concerto, piano/orch., 1965; From Calls & Singing, 1967; Handler of Gravity, for organ, 1971; Five Piano Pieces after Handler of Gravity, 1975; The Bride (opera), 1978; Tongues for poet & chmbr. orch., 1978. Hons: NEA Grants for art criticism & comps., 1977-78. Address: 1824 Curtis St., Berkeley, CA 94702, USA. 9.

SHERMAN, Ingrid, b. 25 June 1919, Cologne-on-Rhine, Germany. Composer; Lecturer; Author; Counselor. Educ: Piano, Conserv. of Cologne; 15 Hon. Degrees from var. countries. m. Morris Sherman, 2 s. Comps. incl: I Worship Thee; Pathway to Light; O Lord, I'm Asking You; Wake Up; I Walk the Earth. Recordings incl: Music for Therapy. Publs: Works on natural hlth., poetry, predicitions, etc. Contbr. to mags., jrnls. newspapers world wide. Mbrships. incl: ASCAP; Fndr., Peace of Mind Studio; Co-fndr., Acad. of Am. Poets. Hons. incl: Golden Laurel Wreath, United Poets Laureate Int., 967; Awards from num. countries. Hobbies: Watercolour Painting; Philately; Poetry Writing. Address: 102 Courter Ave., Yonkers, NY 10705, USA.,

SHERMAN, Lena Janice, b. 21 Feb. 1938, Kokstad, S Africa. Piano & Percussion Teacher. Educ: Primary Tchrs. Cert.; LTCL; currently studyinig for BMus. m. Ian Clifford Sherman, 1d, 1s. Mbrships: Ars Nova, Univ. of S Africa; S African MTA. Hobbies: Tennis; Violin playing in orch. Address: 87 Willowvale Rd., Blairgowrie Randburg, Transvaal, S Africa.

SHERMAN, Seymour M, b. 30 Nov. 1929, Bklyn., NY, USA. Music Educator; Choral Conductor; Composer; Specialist in Hebrew Liturgical Music. Educ. incls: BS MusEd, 1954, MA Educl. Admin. & Supvsn., 1955, EdD Cand., NY Univ. m. Fronya S. Gallub Sherman, 3 s. Career incls: Choral Music Dir., Plainedge, NY, Pub. Schls., 1959-; Lectr., Gen. & Music Educ., Adelphi Univ., Garden City, NY, 1961-65; Choral Dir., Choir of Plainview Jewish Ctr., 1968-. Comps. incl: These Are the Roots (cantata, recorded); A Sephardic Cycle; Sonatina for Piano; Episodes for str. quartet. Contbr. to profl. jrnls. Mbrships. incl: Phi Delta Kappa; MENC. Recip. NYSSMA Conds. Plaque, 1958. Hobbies: Numismatics; Linoleum cuts; Swimming; Tennis. Address: 7 John Dr., Old Bethpage, NY 11804, USA.

SHERROD, Ronald J, b. 15 Jan. 1945, Abilene, Tex., USA. Classical Guitarist; College Instructor. Educ: BA, UCLA; MA, Calif. State Univ.; Post Grad., San Francisco Conserv. of Music. m. Martha A Sherrod, 1 s. Career: Concert Artist & Tchr. of Classic Guitar; Fac. Mbr., San Diego City Coll. & San Diego State Univ.; Instr., Grossmont Coll., San Diego, Calif. Publications: Guitar Fingerboard Drills and Sight Reading, 1975. Mbr. US Soc. of Classical Guitar. Address: 6829 Mewall Dr., San Diego, CA 92119, USA.

SHIGEOKA, Keni Kinuko, b. Reno, Nev., USA. Japanese Language Instructor; Piano & Piano Theory Instructor. Educ: Sakuragoka Girls Coll., Japan. m. Haruo Shigeoka, 1 s., 2 d. Career: Japanese Lang. Instructor, Waialae Bapt. Acad., Honolulu, Hawaii, 11 yrs.; Piano & Piano Theory Instructor; Piano & Violin Tchr., Hawaii Schl. for the Deaf & Blind. Mbrships. incl: Nat. Guild of Piano Tchrs.; Treas., S Honolulu Dist., Hawaii MTA; Music Tchrs. Nat. Assn. Scholarship Fndn; Music Tchrs. Nat. Assn.; Charter Mbr., Int. Guild Lib. Assn.; Organ & Piano Tchrs. Assn. Hons: Piano Guild Hall of Fame, 1970; Am. Coll. of Musicians Cert.; Music Tchrs. Nat. Assn. Cert; "Kengyoku," Sogetsu Schl. of Kado. Hobbies incl: Sewing; Cooking. Address: 1520 Ahuawa Loop, Honolulu, HI 96816, USA.

SHIGEOKA, Raymond M, b. 11 Apr. 1948, Hilo, HI, USA. Concert Pianist; Professor of Music. Educ: BMus & Profl. dip., Univ. of HI; MMus, Juilliard Schl.; PhD, NY Univ.; piano studies w. Eugene List, Irwin Freundlich, Ozan Marsh & Zenon Fisbein; chmbr. music & musicol. w. sev. tchrs. Debut: Carnegie Recital Hall, NY, 1976. Career: solo, orchl. & chmbr. music perfs. throughout Hawaii, Japan & continental USA; perf. in concert for 150th birthdate of Louis Moreau Gottschalk, Carnegie Hall,

1979; radio & TV apps. in Japan, HI & NY.; major concerts in Germany & UK, 1980-81; Prof. o Music, Turtle Bay Music Schl. & NY Univ. Mbrships: Am. Musicol. Soc.; Coll. Musicol. Soc.; Musical Heritage Soc.; NY Univ. Club; Juilliard Alumni Assn. Hons. incl: winner, Flagler Competition, NYC, 1974; scholarship from Juilliard Schl. HI Univ. Hobbies: Record Collecting; Swimming; Tennis; Composing Music. Mgmt: Connoisseur Artists Mgmt. (USA); Basil Doublas Ltd (UK). Address: 310 W 56th St., Apt. 12C, NY, NY 10019, USA.

SHILLING, Eric, b. 12 Oct. 1920, London, UK. Opera & Concert Singer. Educ: GSM; RCM; ARCM. m. Erica Johns, 2 children. Debut: Sadler's Wells Opera. Career: apps. w. Sadler's Wells & Engl. Nat. Operas; TV broadcasts; Die Fledermaus; Orpheus in the Underworld; Iolanthe; The Visitatioin; Trial by Jury; Tale of Two Cities; The Telephone; Two Shy People. Has recorded for Argo, Saga, L'Oiseau Lyre, HMV, Pye, Supraphon & Charisma labels. Mbrships: ISM: Coun., Equity. Recip. Opera Prize, RCM. Hobby: Motoring. Mgmt: Music Int. Address: 49 Belgrave Rd., Wanstead, London E11 3QP. UK.

SHILLITTO, Walter William, b. 19 Oct. 1927, London, UK. Director of Music, The Band of HM Royal Marines Commando Forces. Educ: Royal Marines Schl. of Music; RAM. m. Constance Mary Shillitto, 1 d. Compositions: Trumpetino, A Concertino for Trumpet & Strings or Wind Band. Recordings: By Land & Sea; Around the Globe; The Best of British; Edinburgh Military Tattoo. Recip., Ernest Read Prize for Cond., RAM, 1959. Address: Royal Marines Barracks, Stonehouse, Plymouth, UK.

SHINDELMAN, Arkady, b. 8 Feb. 1954, Odessa, USSR. Violinist. Educ: Stolarsky Music Schl. for Gifted Children; Accademia Santa Cecilia, Italy; Juilliard Schl. of Music; master class of Jascha Heiftez, Univ. of S. Calif, Los Angeles; Profl. Designation from UCLA. m. Pamela Kuhn Shindelman. Debut: Carnegie Recital Hall, NY, 1977. Career: concert apps. on TV, radio & num. concert halls. mbr. AFM. Hons. incl: 1st Prize, 4th Int. Alberto Curci Violin competition, Naples, 1974; 1st prize, Nat. Competition Fest., Can., 1975; 1st prize, CBC Talent Fest., Can., 1976; Gold mdeal, Peel Music Fest., Can., 1975; winner, Artists Int. Audition for Young Musicians, NY, 1977; Finalist, Concert Artists Guild Competitions, NY, 1977; Can. Arts Grants, 1974, '75, '76. Hobbies: Fencing; Boating. Address: 528 Chatauqua Blvd., Pacific Palisades, CA 90272, USA.

SHINDLE, William Richard, b. 2 Nov. 1930, Van Orin, Ill., USA. Musicologist. Educ: BM, Ill. Wesleyan Univ.; MMus, PhD, Ind. Univ. Career: Instr., State Univ. of NY, Binghamton, 1964-65; Prof. of Music, Kent State Univ., Ohio, 1966-. Publs: Ercole Pasquini: Collected Keyboard Works, 1966; Girolamo Frescoldi; Girolamo Compositions Preserved in Manuscripts, 3 vol., 1968; Girolamo Convarsi: Three Canzona from Canzoni alla Napolitana, 1975; Contbr. to Grove's Dictionary of Music & Musicians. Mbrships: Am. Musicological Soc.; Pa German Soc. Hons: Dissertation Yr. Fellowship, Ind. Univ., 1956-66. Hobby: Genealogy. Address: Schl. of Music, Kent State Univ., Kent, OH 44242, USA.

SHIPLEY, Donald Walter, b. 16 July 1945, Balt., Md., USA. Musicologist. Educ: BSc, Business Admin.; BMus, Theory & Comp.; MMus, Music Hist.; PhD, Musicol. m. Barbara Jane Sanders. Publs: Edition of A Busnois' Missa O Crux Lignum. Mbr. Am. Musicol. Soc. Address: 132 Pickwick Dr., Bethel Pk., PA 15102, USA.

SHIRINIAN, Hampartzoum, b. 20 June 1948, Yerevan, Armenia, USSR. Violist; Instructor of Viola, Violin & Ensemble. Educ: Grad., R Melikian Schl. of Music; Yerevan State Conserv., 2 yrs.; studied Viola w. Rouben Altounian, Yerevan & Louis Kievman, Los Angeles, USA. m. Arletta A Shirinian. Debut: w Yerevan Phil., aged 19. Career: Toured USSR w. Yerevan Polytechnic Chmbr. Orch.; Player Yerevan Phil.; apps. State TV; Prin. Viola, Westside Symph., Los Angeles, USA; played w. Am. Youth Symph. & var. coll. symphs.; currently Assoc. Prin. Viola, Honolulu Symph., & Music Instructor, Pounahou High Schl. Recordings in USSR. Mbrships: Local 47, Musicians Union: Honoluly Symph. Soc. Hobbies: Swimming; Soccer; Pingpong. Address: c/o 1620 N Kinglsey Drive, Los Angeles, CA 90027, USA.

SHIRLEY, George Irving, b. 18 Apr. 1934, Indpls., Ind., USA. Singer (tenor); Teacher. Educ: BS (Educ.), Wayne State Univ., Detroit, Mich.; HHD, Wilberforce Univ., Ohio; pvte. vocal study. m. Gladys Ishop, 1 s., 1 d. Debut: w. Turnau Opera Players, Woodstock, NY, 1959. Career incl: appearances w. Metropol. Opera, NYC, 1961; Teatro Colon, Buenos Aires, 1964; Glyndebourne Festival, 1966; Royal Opera, Covent Gdn., 1967; Scottish Nat. Opera, 1967; Amsterdam Festival, 1975:

Netherlands Opera, 1976; Monte Carlo Opera, 1976. Recordings of num. opera. Contbr. to: Opera News; Opera. Mbrships: Assoc. Dir., Harlem Schl. of the Arts; Bd. Dirs., Boys Choir of Harlem; Bd. Dirs., New Fed. Theatre. Recip. var. awards in opera, Hobbies: Tennis, Sketching. Mgmt: (UK) AIM, 5 Regent's Pk. Rd., London NW1 7TL; (USA) Judd Concert Bur., 127 W 69th St., NY, NY 10023; (Italy) Ann Summers Dossena, Via Mario dei Fiori 42, 00187 Rome, Italy.

SHIRLEY-QUIRK, John Stanton, b. 28 Apr. 1931, Liverpool, UK. Concert & Opera Singer. Educ: BSc, Dip. in Educ., Liverpool Univ.; studied singing w. Austen Carnegie & Roy Henderson. m. Patricia May Shirley-Quirk, 1 s., 1 d. Career: created roles in all Britten operas since Curlew River, notably Mr. Coyle, Owen Wingrave (TV & Convent Gdn., Met. Opera NY); Perfs. w. Scottish Opera & all major orchs. throughout Europe & Am.; created role of Lev. in The Ice Break by Sir M Tippett. Num. recordings. Mbr., ISM. Hons: Hon. RAM, 1973; CBE, 1975; HMus Doc, Liverpool, 1976. Hobbies: Canals; Clocks; Pottering. Mgmt: Harrison/Parrtt Ltd., 22 Hillgate St., London W8 7SR, UK. Address: White House, 82 Heath End Rd., Flackwell Heath, Bucks HP10 9ES, UK. 1, 3.

SHORE, Andrew, b. 30 Sep. 195 2, Oldham, UK. Concert & Opera Baritone Singer; Opera Porducer. Educ: BA (Theology), Univ. of Bristol; RNCM; Dip., London Opera Ctr. m. Fiona Mary Macdonald. Career: app. w. Kent Opera, Edinburgh Fest., 1979; tours w. Opera for All; fndr. mbr., Bristol Intimate Opera, w. who num. apps.; roles incl. Guglielmo (Cosi), Giacomo (Fra Diavolo), Frosch (Die Fledermaus), Ottone (Coronation of Poppea), Tarquinius (Rape of Lucretia); currently mbr., Kent Opera; num. freelance opera & concert apps. esp. Christus in St. Matthew Passion; prod., La Boheme (Sadler's Wells), Der Freischutz, Nabucco, Poppea, Gianni Schicchi & Dido & Aeneas, mbr., ISM. recip., Tim Brandt award in opera production, 1976. Hobbies: Trains & Model Railways; Reading; Hill-walking. Mgmt: Mageta Music, 33 Cholmeley Rd., London N6. Address: 4 Lindal Rd., Crofton Pk., London SE4 1EJ, UK.

SHORE, Bernard, b. 17 Mar. 1896. Violist. Educ: RCM, London; FRCM; Hon. FTCL; ARCM; Hon. RAM. m. Olive, 2 d. Career incls: Mbr., Catterall & Spencer Dyke Str. Quartets; num. apps. as Soloist at Promenade Concerts, giving 1st perfs. of many works by mod. comps.; Prin. Viola, BBC Symph. Orch., 1930-40; HM Inspector of Schls. & Staff Inspector, Min. of Educ., 1948-59; currently Dir. of Music, Rural Music Schls. Assn; rate Prof. of Viola, RCM; Co-Pres., 1st Int. Conf. for Music in Educ., Brussels. Has recorded for HMV. Publs: The Orchestra Speaks, 1937; Sixteen Symphonies, 1947. Hons: Gold Medal, RCM; CBC, 1955. Hobbies: Sketching; Motoring. Address: Flat 6, 3 Palmeira Square, Hove, Sussex, UK. 1.

SHORE, Mary Catherine, b. 9 Mar. 1943, Edmonto, Alta., Can. Organist; Choirmaster; Pianist; Teacher. Educ: RCM; ARCT; ARCM; LRAM; FTCL; BMus, Dip. Educ. & Tchrs. Cert., Univ. of London. Debut: Organ recital, Vancouver, BC, Can., 1962. Career incls: Sub-Organist, Christ Ch. Cathedral, Victoria, BC, Can.; recital tour of Western Can. & USA, 1963-64; currently Hd., Music Dept., St. Joseph's Acad., Blackheath, London & Organist/Choirmaster, Parish Ch. of St. Margaret, Lee; Vis. Examiner, Assoc. Bd; Assn. Examiner. Univ. of London. Radio Contbr. to: RSM Jrnl. Mbrships: incl: Panel of Arts & Humanities & Music Bd., Coun. of Nat. Acad. Awards; sub-grp. panel, Schls. Coun.; Diocesan Exec. Committee, Royal Schl. of Ch. Music, Southwrk; ISM; RCO. Hons: incl: Winner, Vancouver Int. Fest. in Organ Perf., 1964. Hobbies: Qualified Coach in Swimming & Tennis. Address: 74 Micheldever Rd., Lee, London SE12 8LU, UK.

SHORT, Michael, b. 27 Feb. 1937, Bermuda. Composer; Writer. Educ: BSc, Bristol Univ.,, 1958; Dip. in Hist. of Music, London Univ., 1963. Compositions incl: orchl., choral, chmbr. & instrumental works; jingles, incidental music. Publs: Gustav Holts: a centenary documentation, 1974; Gustav Holst: letters to W G Whittaker, 1974. Contbr. to: Brio; Composer. Mbrships: CGGB; Performing Righst Soc. Recip: Mendelssohn Schlrship., 1966. Address: 1 Hospital Ln., Colchester, Essex, UK.

SHRAGER, Pytha (Marleon Germaine), b. London, UK. Pianist, Educ: Conserv. Nt. Superieur de Musique de Paris; Master classes w. Joseph Benvenuti (piano), Joseph Calvert (Chmbr. Music); pvte. piano study, w. George Chavchavadze. Debut: Debussy-Ravel recital (broadcast, Bavarian Radio & BBC), Bayreuth Festival 1966. Career: Concert appearances, broadcasts and TV appearances in most European countries, & E Africa. Recordings incl. Suite 'El Amor Brujo' (Manuel de Falla, piano transcription by Chavchavadze); Gardens of Andalusia, gypsy dances (Joaquin Turina), Chopin allbum, "Chopin, Mon ami," 1976; Mozart; Concerto in D Minor. Mbrships: Pres., Assn. Franz Liszt of Belgium. Recip: Chopin

Insignia, Chopin Soc., Warsaw, 1970. Hobbies: Reading; Theatre; Cinema; Ballet; Opera; Swimming; Works of Da Vinci & Michelangelo. Address: 29 Rue de College, B-1050 Brussels, Belgium. 3, 23, 27, 29, 30.

SHUMAN, Mark Orrin, b. 8 June 1951, NY, USA. Cellist. Educ: BS, MMus, Juilliard Schl. m. Elisabeth Charlotte Kofler. Career: Formerly MBr., The Aulos Ensemble & The Light Fantastic Players; currently Mbr., Comps. String Quartet. Sev. recordings. Hons: 1st Prize, Augusta (Ga.) Symph. Competitioln, 1975. Hobby: Softball. Address: 675 West End Ave., NY, NY 10025, USA.

SHUMIATCHER, Bella (N.M.I.), Pianist & Pedagogue; Lecturer; Consultant; Teachedr. Educ: Grad., Juilliard Schl. of Music; Dip. in perf.; Maturity Dip.; Tchr. training. m. Hyman D Abbey (dec.), 1 s., 1 d. Career: Concert apps. in Canada & USA; Radio & TV progs.; Fndr.-Dir., Shumiatcher Schl. of Music, Larchmont, NY, 1965-; Artist-in-res., Boiberik, Rhinebeck, NY; Pianist, Trio Con Brio; Fac., Juilliard Schl. of Music, 1933-66; Adjunct Prof., NY Univ.; Affiliate piano fac. & vocal ensemble mbr., SUNY Coll., Purchase, NY. Publs: Co-author, Piano & Ensemble Syllabus, 1970,2nd Ed., 1973. Mbrships: Exec. Bd., Assoc. Music Tchrs. Lealgue; Chairperson, Dist. IV, State Piano Chairperson, NY State Music Tchrs. Assn.; Int. Bach Soc. Address: 69 Vine Rd., Larchmont, NY 10538, USA.

SHUTTLEWORTH, Anna Lee, b. 2 May 1927, Bournemouth, UK. Cellist. Educ: BA, Open Univ.; Tchrs. Trng. Cert., Univ. London; ARCM; Studied w. Hainardi & Casals. m. David Sellen. Career: Former Cellist, London Harpsichord Ensemble, Georgian Quartet, Haydn Trio; Currently Prin. Cello, Engls. Sinfonia, Tilford Bach Fest. Orch.; Cellist, Aulos Ensemble, Leonardo Tio, Glickman Trio; Solo recitals, Purcell Room, London, BBC; Prof., RCM; Examiner, Assoc. Bd. of RSM. Recordings: Cello Continuo w. Deller Consort. Publs: Playing the Cello. Mbrships: ISM; ESTA; MU; NAPTHE. Hons. incl: Boise Scholarship, 1955. Address: 33 Stile Hall Gdns., London W4 3BS, UK.

SIBSON, Arthur Robert, b. 9 Feb. 1906, Stockton-on-Tees, Co Durham, UK. Flautist; Conductor; Director of Music Academy; Retired Chartered Engineer. Educ: num. pvte. tchrs. in piano, organ, flute, harmony & counterpoint; Hon. RCM; Ma, Univ. of Rhodesia, 1977. m. Dorothy Eva Williams, 1 d. Career: Flautist & Dpty. Musical Dir., Bulawayo Municipal Orch., 1937-; Dir., Rhodesian Acad. of Music, 1962-; Fndr., Kwanongoma Coll. of African Music, 1961; Pres., Rhodesian Soc. of Music Tchrs., 1970-71. Compositions: Symphony in A minor; Serenada de Mozambique, for piano & orch.; Music for the film 'Pitaniko', 1947; num. short works. Mbrships: CGGB; S African Soc. of Composers; Rhodesian Soc. of Music Tchrs. Hons: Mbr., Legion of Merit (MLM), 1973; Civic Hons. Book, City of Bulawayo, 1971. Hobbies: Indigenous African music; Public affairs; Walking. Address: PO Box 9074, Hillside, Bulawayo, Rhodesia, 3, 18.

SIDDELLEY, Barbara, b. Dunkinfield, Cheshire, UK. Singer; Adjudicator; Teacher of Singing. Educ: ARMCM; studied w. Frank Mullings, Maria Linker of Berlin State Opera & Roy Henderson. Career: Specialist in Oratoria & Lieder; Num. broadcasts; Arts Coun. of GB Concerts. Mbr. Brit. Fedn. of Music Festivals. Hons: Open Scholarship to RMCM; Winner of Hilary Haworth Prize for Lieder Singing. Hobbies: Golf; Walking in the Country; Yachting. Address: Linden Lea, 8A Old Rd., Mottram-in-Longdendale, Cheshire, UK. 4, 27.

SIDDONS, James (DeWitt), b. 1 Nov. 1948, Narsarssuaq, Greenland. Musicologist. Educ: BMus, 1970, PhD cand., N Tex. State Univ., Denton; MMus, King's Coll., Univ. of London, UK, 1971; Mombusho Rsch. Scholar, Dept. of Musicol., Tokyo Univ. of Arts, Japan,1973-74; m. Joy Garbee Siddons. Career: Ed., Musical Analysis (periodical), 1972-74; Asst. Prof. of Music, Liberty Baptist Coll., Lynchburg, Va., 1976-. Contbr. to: Directory of Music Rsch. Libs.; Grove's Dictionary, 6th ed. Mbrships: Int. & Am. Musicol. Soc.; Music Lib. Assn.; Phi Kappa Lambda. Hobbies: Japanalia; Collecting antiquarian books & music. Address: Dept. of Music, Liberty Baptish Coll., Lynchburg, VA 24502, USA.

SIDER, Ronald Ray, b. 10 May 1933, Harrisburg, Pa., USA. Organist; Professor of Music. Educ: BMus., Eastman Schl. of Music, Univ. of Rochester, NY, 1957; MusM, ibid., 1959; PhD, 1967; AAGO, 1963. m. Beth F Kanode. Career: Prof. of Music, Messiah Coll., Grantham, PA., 1958-; Chmn., Music Dept., ibid, 1964-73; Organist & Choirmaster, Grace Meth. Ch., Harrisburg, Pa; Cond., Grantham Oratoria Soc.., 1965-. Publd. Comps: Child in the Manger; Once in Royal David's City; God of Our Fathers; Take Thou Our Minds; Jesus Lives. Contbr. to Inter-Am. Music Bulletin. Mbrships: Bd. of Dirs., Am. Guild of

Organist, Harrisburg, Pa.; Am. Choral Dirs. Assn. Address: RD 3, Dillsburg, PA 17019, USA. 6.

SIEBERT, Lynn Laitman, b. 15 1946, NYC, USA. Musicologist; Violinist; Soprano Singer; Educator. Educ. incls: AB, Vassar Coll.; MA, Rutgers Univ., NB, 1969; PhD, CUNY, 1975; pvte violin study, 17 yrs., & voice study, 5 yrs., w. noted tchrs. m. Donald R. Siebert, 1 d. Career incls: Acting. Mng. Ed.-Rsch. Asst.-Asst. Ed.-German Transl., RILM Abstracts of Music Lit., 1970-71; fac., Bernard Baruch Coll., 1971-72; Pvte. violin instr., 1975-; Vis. Asst. Prof., Drew Univ., NJ, summer 1976; Violinist, w. var. grps. Mbrships. incl: Am. Musicol. Soc.; w. var. grps. Musicians; Am. Chmbr. Music Players. Recip. num. acad. hons. Hobbies incl: Folk singing; Drawing. Address: 116 Madison Ave., Apt. 2, Madison, NJ 07940, USA.

SIEBERT, Wilhelm Dieter, b. 22 Oct. 1931, Berlin, Germany. Composer. Educ: Dip., HS for Music, Berlin & Freiburg. Career: Jazz Soloist; Free-lance Composer. Comps. incl: Frankenstein multemedia show; Der Untergang der Titanic (grand opera); Berenice, solo violin, orch. & tapes. Contbr. to: Musik von A-Z (ed. Alfred A Goodman), 1971; Melos. Mbr: New Music Grp., Berlin. Hons: Int. Summer Course for New Music, Darmstadt, 1964, 66, 67; Cité des Arts, Paris, 1972. PSI, NY, 1978; Berliner Kunstpreis, 1978. Address: Zähringestr. 39, 1 Berlin 31, German Fed. Repub.

SIEGEL, Wayne Perry, b. 14 Feb. 1953, Los Angeles, Calif., USA. Composer. Educ: BA (comp), Univ. of Calif. at Santa Barbara; Diplomeksamen (comp), Jutland Conserv. of Muic, Aarhus, 1977, studying w. Per Norgaard & Karl Aage Rasmussen. Career: num. perfs. of orchl. & chmbr. works throughout Scandinavia & in Calif., incl. radio perfs. of all major works; 2 radio portraits on Danish Radio & KPFK, Calif. Contbr. to: DMT, Copenhagen; Danish Radio. Mbrships: former chmn., Aarhus Young Musicians Organization; Aarhus County Music Commission. Hons. incl: 3 yr. Str. Quartet selected as Danish contribution to Nordic Music Days, Helsinki, 1980. Hobbies: Philosophy; Literature; Collecting Exotic Instruments. Address: Jernaldervej 235 A, 2.th, 8210 Aarhus V, Denmark.

SIEGFRIED, Francoise, b. 6 Mar. 914, Monthey, Switz. Violinist; Teacher of Violin. Educ: Gymnase Vinet, Lusanne; Institut de Ribaupierre, Lausanne; Conserv. Int., Paris; Meisterklasse, Von Sandor Vegh, Basel. m. Walter Siegfried. Career: Tours w. Pianist Pierre Maillard-Verger incl: France, Switz., Spain, Holland, Belgium & Germany; After his death w. Urs Voegelin of Zürich. First auditions of num. French & Swiss Comps. Mbrships. incl: Schweizerischer Tonkunstlerverein; Pro Musica; Soroptmist Club; Swiss Fedn. of Business & Profl. Women. Hons: Premier Prix & Grand Prix de Virtuosite, Conserv. Int., Paris. Hobbies: Fine Arts: Archeology (Romanesque Art). Address: 35 Spiegelhofstrasse, 8032 Zürich, Switz. 3.

SIEGL, Otto, b. 1896, Graz, Austria. Composer; Professor; Violinist; Pianist. Educ: Graz Conserv. m. Adele Wirtz, 2 s. Career: Music Dir., Paderborn, 1926-31; Choir & Orch. Cond., Bielefeld, Essen, Herford, 1931-33; Prof., Koeln, 1933-48, & Styria, 1949-51; Lectr. Prof., State Acad. of Music, Vienna, 1948-. Compositions incl: 2 symphs.; var. smaller works for orch.; choral works inclng. oratorio, cantata & 4 masses; chmbr. music; piano pieces; Lieder. Mbr. Austrian Art Senate. Address: Kunigundenstr. 56, Munich 23, German Fed. Repub.

SIEGMEISTER, Elie, b. 15 Jan. 1909, NYC, USA. Composer; Conductor. Educ: BA, Columbia Univ.; studied piano w. Emil Friedberger, theory w. Wallingford Riegger & Seth Bingham, comp. w. Nadia Boulanger; Dip., Juilliard Grad. Schl. m. Hannah Mersel, 2 c. Debut: as Cond., Town Hall, NY, 1940. Career: comps. perf. by major orchs. in USA, UK. Germany, USSR, Italy, etc. under the baton of int. renowned conds. Comps. publd. & recorded incl: (orchl.) Symphs. No. 3-5; Ozark Set; Sunday in Brooklyn; Western Suite; Concertos for flute & clarinet (piano) Sonata No. 2; (Chmbr. Music) Sonatas No. 1-5, for violin & piano; Str. Quartets Nos. 2 & 3; American Harp, for solo harp; Fantasy & Soliloquy, for solo cello; On This Ground, for piano; Sextet for Brass & Percussion; D5 Operas; Choral, solo instrumental, band music; Songs. Publs: A Treasury of American Song, 1940; Work & Sing, 1944; Invitation to Music, 1961; Harmony & Melody, 2 vols., 1965-66; The New Music Lovers Handbook,1973. Contbr. to profl. pubs. Mbrships. incl: Bd. of Dirs., ASCAP; Exec. Bd., Kennedy Center Competition & Colloquim for Black Music; Chmn., Coun. of Creative Artists, Libs. & Museums. Hons: 15 ASCAP Awards,1963-79; Guggenheim Fellowship; Award of Am. Inst. & Acad. Address: 56 Fairveiw Ave., Great Neck, NY 11023, USA.

SIEGMUND-SCHULTZE, Walther, 6 July 1916, Schweinitz, Germany. Musicologist; Violinsit; Pianist. Educ: Dip., Musicol.; Dr., Sc. m. Dorothea Siegmund-Schultz, 1 s., 1 d. Career: Chair, (Prof., Musicol.), Univ., Halle; Chief Ed., Halle Handel Ed.; Ed., Handel-Jahrbuch, 1955- Publr., Handelfstschriften, 1952-. Publs: Bachs Musik, 1953; Georg Friedrich Handel, 1954; Mozarts Melodik & Stil, 1957; Zu einigen Grundfragen der Musikasthetik, 1962; Georg Friedrich Handel, 1962; G F Handel, Thema mit 20 Variationen, 1965; Johannes Brahms, 1966, 1974; Ludwig van Beethoven, 1975. Contbr. to: Wissenschaftliche Zeitschift der Univ., Halle; Musik & Geslellschaft; Theatre der Zeit; Kunst & Literatur; Musikforum. Mbrships: VP, Dist. Pres., Assn. of Comps. & Musicologists of the German Democratic Repub.; Rsch. Sec., Georg Friedrich Handel Soc.; Int. Musicol. Soc; Int. Music Educ. Soc. Hons: Nat. Prize, German Dem. Repub., 1969; Fatherland Hon. Order, 1959; Handel Prize, 1959; Tchr. Emeritus, 1964; Banner of Work, 1974. Hobby: Chess. Address: 57 b Dölauer Strasse, 402, Halle German Dem. Repub.

SIEKMANN, Frank Herman, b. 20 June 1925, Staten Island, NY, USA. Teacher; Professor of Music; Performer; Conductor; Arranger; Composer. Educ: BS, Schl. of Educ., NY Univ.; MA, Adv. Schl. of Educ., ibid.; EdD, Tchrs. Coll., Columbia Univ. m. Doris M. Pelletier, 2 s., 1 d. Career: Prof. of Music, Kutztown State Coll., Pa.; Cons. Ed. var. textbook publrs. Comps: Astromarch; Patrol March for Band (Pro Art); Discourse for Brass (Seesaw); Arrs. for brass sextet, orch., woodwind quintet & band. Contbr. to The Instrumentalist; Accordion World; Int. Musician; Conn Cord. Mbrships. incl: Bd. Dirs., Reading Symph. Orch., Pa.; Bd. Dirs., Reading Pops Orch.; Reading Musical Fndn.; Reading Musical Soc. Hobbies: Tennis; Photography. Address RD 3, Kutztown, PA 19530 USA. 6, 28.

SIEPI, Cesare, b. 10 Feb. 1923, Milan, Italy. Opera Singer. Educ: Pvte. study w. Maestro Chiesa. Debut: App. as Sparafudile in Rigoletto at Schi, near Venice, Italy. Career: Apps. at La Scala & in opera houses throughout Italy, Spain, Sweden & Switzerland; Leading Baso, Met. Opera; Apps. as Concert Singer; TV career started w. first perf. at Met.; Star of complete color telecast of Don Giovanni; World's leading Figaro & Giovanni. Mgmt: S A Gorlinsky Ltd., 356, Dover St., London W1, UK. Address: c/o S A Gorlinsky Ltd., 35 Dover St., London W1 UK.

SIEVERS, Gerd, b. 16 Oct. 1915, Hamburg, Germany. Musicologist. Educ: PhD, Univ. of Hamburg, 1949; Piano, Music Theory Dips. m. Lieselotte von Hase, 1 s., 1 d. Publs: Die Grundlagen Hugo Riemanns bei Max Reger, 1967; Co-Ed., Koechel-Verzeichnis, 1964; Co-Author, Co-Ed., Max Reger, Eine Gedenkschrift, 1966; Ed., Co-Author, Ex. Deo Nascimur -Eine Festschrift zum 75. Geburtstag Johann Nepomuk Davids, 1970; Ed., 6 vols., Max-Reger-Gesamtuasgabe, 1954-. Contbr. to num. profl. jrnls. Mbrships: Soc. for Music Rsch., Cassel; Int. Soc. for Musicol., Basel; Max Reger Bd. of Trustees, Bonn-Bad Godesberg. Hobbies: Philosophy; Theology; Recent German History; Classical Languages; Photography. Address: 55 Helmholtzstrasse, D-6200 Wiesbaden, German Fed. Repub.

SIEVERS, Heinrich, b. 20 Aug. 1908, Dorum/Wesermünde, Niedersachsen. Professor of Musicology; Music Critic. Educ; D Phil., Univ. Würzburg & Cologne; Bayerisches Staatskonservatorium Würzburg. m. Else-Charlotte Bredlau, 1 d. Career: Music Critic, Braunschwieg u. Hannover für Musik und Theater, Hannover. Comps: Bearbeitung und Herausgabe von Agostino Steffani-Stabat mater. Publs: Die lateinisch-Linturgischen Osterspiele der Stiftskirche St. Blasien zu Braunschweig, 1936; 250 Jahre Brauschweigisches Staatstheater, 1941. Contbr. to: Die Musik in Hannover; Musica curiosa; Musikgeschichte Hannoverische, 1979. Mbrships: Gesellschaft für Musikforschung; Humboldt-Gesellschaft. Hons: Verdiestrkreuz 1 Klasse des Niedersachsischen Verdienstordens, 1976. Address: Holteistrasse 1, 3000 Hannover 1, German Fed. Repub.

SIGMUND, Oskar, b. 13 Aug. 1919, Karisbad, Czechoslovakia. Pianist; Composer. Educ: PhD, German Univ., Prague, 1942; studied w. Dr. Eduard von Chiari, Prof. Vilem Kurz, Prof. Gustav Becking. Debut: Radio Munich. 1946. Career: Comp., var. works for Organ & Piano, chbr. music, Radio Bavaria, Austria, Yugoslavia, Stuttgart, Berlin; Comps. perfd. in Germany, Belgium, Switz. & Yugoslavia. Compositions incl: (publd.) Missa Christo Canamus Principi; La Folia, for 4 violins; (recorded) 5 pieces for 3 trumpets, 2 trombones, tuba & organ; Toccata super BACH for organ. Hons: Kulturpreis der Oba, 1965; Annerkennungspreis Fur Musik der Sudeten-Deutsch Landsmannschaft. 1965. Hobies: Slavic Languages; Literature; Botany. Mgmt: Docent & Stellvertretender Direktor of Fachakademie fur Kath. Kirchenmusik m. Musikerziehung,

Regensburg. Address: 81 Roter Brachweg, 84 Regensburg, German Fed. Repub.

SIGNORELLI, Michael, b. 29 Oct. 1906, Chgo., Ill., USA. Music Educator; Tenor Singer. Educ: Studied, Columbia Univ.; Tchng. Degree, Chgo. Piano Coll. & Schl. of Fine Arts; Studied Violin w. Prof. Joseph Fitzek, Richard Czerwonky, Wolfgang Bachner; Studies Singing w. Forrest Lamont, Madame Mastinelli, Isaac Van Grove, Mary Garden, Dr. Ernst Knoch & others. m. Jeanne Wagler Siognorelli, 5 d., 1 s. Career: App. in Boris Goudonoff w. Ezio Pinza; Sang throughout the western hemisphere as leading tenor w. leading opera cos.; Concert Soloist; Exec. Dir.; Lyric Opera Co., Long Island, Inc.; App. on num. radio & TV stations; Soloist w. Paulist Choir, Chgo., St. Patrick's Cathedral, NYC & Temple Emmanuel, NYC, Contbr. to var. Chgo. Newspapers & Mags. Mbrships: Nat. Assn. of Tchrs. of Singing; NY Singing Tchrs. Assn.; Nat. Opera Soc.; Music Educators Assn. Hobbies: Collector of Paintings, Porcelains, Coins, Stamps, Books, Fine Violins. Address: 344 Middle Rd., Bayport, Long Island, NY 11705, USA. 3.

SIGURDSSON, Elisabeth Gudrun, b. 23 Mar. 1931, Copenhagen, Denmark. Music Professor; Clarinettist. Educ: Piano Dip., Royal Danish Music Conserv., 1950. m. Peter Naur (div.), 2 s., 1 d. Debut: Piano & Clarinet, Tivoli, 1951. Career: Concerts as Soloist & Chmbr. Musician, Denmark, Sweden, Norway & Iceland; Prof., Det Jydsky Musikkonservatorium, Arhus, Recordings: Mozart & Weber Clarinet Quintets (w. Copenhagen Str. Quartet); NW Gade, Fantasistykker; Finn Hoffding, Dialogue for Oboer & Clarinet; Holmboe, Quaretto Medico, PR Rovsing Olsen, Trio Prolana. Mgmt: Wilhelm Hansen, Copenhagen. Address: Marupvej 9, 8240, Risskov, Denmark.

SIJALOWA-VOGEL, Irena, b. 4 Apr. 1927, Kupiansk, USSR. Pianist. Educ: Lwow Higher Schl. of Music, Poland; Consedrv.; Postgrad. studies, Moscow Conserv., 1957; qualified soloist, tchr., chmbr. grp. pianist. m. Jerzy Vogel, 2 s. Debut: Leningrad,1938. Career: Apps. at Festsl.; TV & num. radio perfs.; Assoc. Prof. Music. Recordings: Schumann, Symphonic Etudes, op. 13; (TV) Prokofiev, Sonatas 2 & 9, 1976; num. radio recordings. Publ: Founders of the Soviet School of Pianists, 1979. Contbr. to Mujsikalnaja Zizn. Mbr., Soc. Polish Muicians. Hons. incl: 2nd & Special Prizes, Int. Schuman Competition, Berlin, 1956; Golden Cross of Merit, 1975. Hobbies: Photography; Mountain Climbing; Riding; Hunting. Mgmt: Pagart. Address: Piwarskiego St. 16 apt. 18, 00-770 Warsaw, Poland.

SIKI, Béla, b. 21 Feb. 1923, Budapest, Hungary. Pianist; Professor of Music. Educ: Univ. of Budapest; Artist Dip., Franz Liszt Acad., ibid. m. Yolande Oltramare, 1 s., 1 d. Debut: Budapest. Career: Worldwide Concert Tours. Recordings: Num. recordings for Columbia, Pye, Nippon Columbia, Musical Masterwork Soc., Vox. Hons: Winner, Franz Liszt Compoetition, 1943; Concours Int. d'Exécution Musicale, Geneva, Switzerland, 1948. UK. Address: Univ. of Washington, Seattle, WA 98195, USA. 3.

SIKORSKI, Tomasz,. b. 19 May 1939, Warsaw, Poland. Composer. Educ: MA, Warsaw Conserv. Comps. incl: Echoes II (2 & 4 pianos,chimes, 4 gongs, 4 tam-tams & magnectic tape, 1963; Antiphons (soprno, horn, piano, chimes, 4 gongs & magnetic tape), 1963; Prologues (choir of female voices, 2 concerting pianos, 4 flutes, 4 horns, 3 percussions), 1964; Diaphony (2 pianos), 1969; Homophony (12 brass instruments, piano & gong), 1970; For Strings (3 violins, 3 violas), 1970; Adventures of Sinbad the Sailor (radio opera), 1972; No Title (piano & 3 optional instruments), 1972; Listening Music (2 pianos), 1973; Music Form Afar (mixed choir & instruments), 1974; Other Voices (24 wind instruments, 4 gongs & chimes), 1975; Solitude of Sounds (for tape), 1975; Sickness unto Death (for reciter and 10 instruments) 1976; Music in Twilight (for piano and orchestra) 1977-78. Num. recordings. Address: Polna 40 M 31,00635 Warsaw, Poland.

SILBERMANN, Alphons, b. 11 Aug. 1909, Cologne Germany. Professor. Educ: Univs. of Freiburg, Grenoble, Cologne; Dr. jur.; Study of piano, Cologne Conserv. Career: Prof., Sociol. of Arts & Sociol. of Mass Communications. Univ. of Cologne. Publs. incl: of Musical Things, 1949; La Musique, la radio et l'auditeur, 1954; Die Prinzipien der Musiksoziologie, 1957. Contbr. to jrnls. worldwide. Mbrships: PEN; Soc. Européene de la Culture; Am. Sociol. Assn.; Deutsche Gessell. für Kommunikationsforschung. Hons: Bundesverdienstkreuze 1st class; Laureat, l'Institut de France. Address: Leyboldstr. 62, 5 Cologne 51, German Fed. Repub.

SILCOCK, Norman, b. 5 Jan. 1915, Morley, Yorks., UK. Organist; Pianist; Choirmaster. Educ: Royal Normal Coll. for Blind Students, London; BMus, Univ. of Durham; FRCO; LRAM; LGSM. m. Hilda Sanderson. Comps: Str. quartet, 1957; Think on These Things (anthem); Songs for Cello & Voice, 1972; Comp. for Oboe & Piano, 1974; works for Piano, Organ & Voice. Mbrships: ISM; (Life); Nat. Union Tchrs.; Conservative Club, Gildersome, Yorks. Hobbies: Reading; Chess; Crossword Puzzles. Address: 64 Kent Rd., Pudsey, Yorks., UK.

SILIPIGNI, Alfredo, b. 9 Apr. 1931, Atlantic City, NJ, USA. Conductor; Artistic Director. Educ: pupil of Alberto Erede, cond., 1953; Juilliard Schl. of Music, NYC, 1953; Westminister Choir Coll., Princeton, NJ, 1948. m. Gloria Rose Dibenedetto. Debut: NBC Symph. at Carnegie Hall, NYC. Career: Artistic Dir. & Cond., Opera Theatre of NJ, 1965-; Cond., NBC Symph.; Boston, Brooklyn & Conn. operas; Newark Symph.; Guest cond. in Caracas, Venezuela; San Remo, Italy; Sirmione, Italy; Milan, Italy; Paris, France; Santo Domingo, Dominican Republic; Tampa Opera (Fla.); Providence (RI); Ont., Man., Alta., Canada; Prin. cond., Mex. Nat. Opera; estab. statewide auditioning prog. for young artists, NJ State Opera. Young Artists Prof., 1969; Guest Lects., Glassboro State Coll., NJ; instituted operalogues, Paper Mill Playhouse, Millburn, NJ. 1968. Recordings: Operas ZAZA by Leoncavallo; Excerpts from Verdi Operas, Centra Records. Hons: Centennial Medallion, St. Peter's Coll., 1972; Hon. Citizen, Trenton, NJ, 1972; Disting. serv. to culture award, San Remo, 1972. Mgmt: Hurok, NYC, USA. 2.

SILKOFF, David Michael, b. 9 Oct. 1949, Stratford, E London, UK. Pianist. Educ: GSM w. Ieuan Roberts; RCM w. Kendall Taylor & Cyril Smith; RAM w. Gordon Green. Debut: Wigmore Hall, London, 1975. Career: Recitals & concerts in London, Leeds, Cambridge, The Maltings (Suffolk) & other parts of UK; introduced music of J M Hauer to UK. Hons: Martin Musical Scholarship, 1974; Lloyd Hartley Prize, RAM, 1977. Hobbies: Walking; Swimming. Address: 41A Eastwood Rd., Goodmayes, Ilford, Essex IG3 8UT, UK.

SILLAMY, Jean-Claude, b. 24 July 1932, Algiers, Algeria. Composer of Sacred Music; Musicologist Educ: Dip., psychol., Univ.; 1st prize, comp. m. Maisie, 2 d. Career: Has worked perfd. on records, radio (Corsica) & in Concert Halls, Corsica & Paris. Comps. incl: Quatuor; Musique contemporaine sur des modes bibliques; Gloire aux Morts d'Auschwitz; 5 Chants d'Israel; Quintette á cordes; Promenade dans le Parc; La Reine Esther á Suse; Le Chant des Hirondelles, Psalmes, etc. Recordings: Quator, (by Quator Elyseén); Pièces pour piano, (by Odile Poisson); Pièces pour piano, (by Danièle Salzer); more than 40 records, in var. countries. Publs: Essay on the reconstruction of the music of the Bible, in 6 parts, 1957; La Musique Sumérienne; Les Instruments de Musique des Hebreux; Les Juifs de Djerba; Migrations des Juifs d'Afrique du Nord, etc. Contbr. to: Les Nouveaux Chaiers (Revue); Kadimah; La Terre Retrouvé; L'Education Musicale. Mbrships: French Mjsicol. Soc.; Int. Musicol. Soc. Hons: 1st prize, solfège, 1944, comp., 1952; 1st medal, violin, 1950. Address: 15 Rue Fesch, Ajaccio, Corsica, France.

SILLS, Beverly, b. 1929, Brooklyn, NY, USA. Opera & Concert Singer (coloratura soprano); Administrator, Gen. Dir., NY City Opera. Educ: voice study w. Estelle Liebling; piano study w. Paolo Gallico. m. Peter Bulkeley Greenough, 1 s., 1 d. Debut: Phila. Civic Opera, 1947. Career incls: role of Helen of Troy in Mefistofele, San Fran. Opera, 1953; Rosalinda in Die Fldermaus, NYC Opera, 1955; Mbr., NYC Opera, 1955-; Queen of the Night in Die Zauberflöte, Vienna State Opera, 1967; Violettain La Traviata, La Scala, Milan, 1970; title role in Lucia de Lammermoor, Covent Gdn., London, 1970; Perfs. at major opera houses of Europe & Latin Am.; Num. recitals w. leading orchs. in USA; TV apps. Publs: Bubbles - A Self-Portrait, 1976. Mbrships incl: Chmn. of Bd., Nat. Opera Inst.; Cons. to Coun., Nat. Endowment for the Arts; Bd., NYC Opera. Hons. incl: Hon DMus, Temple Univ., New England Conserv., Harvard Univ., NY Univ., Cert. of Merit, Stereo Review, 1979. Hobbies: Fishing; Bridge. Mgmt: Edgar Vincent Assocs., 145 E 52nd St., Suite 804, NY, NY 10022, USA. Address: c/o Mgmt.

SILSBEE, Ann Loomis, b. 21 July 1930, Cambridge, Mass., USA. Composer. Educ: AB, Radcliffe Coll.; MMus, Syracuse Univ.; DMA, Cornell Univ. m. Robert H Silsbee, 3 s. Career: Fac., SUNY at Cortland, Cornell Univ.; Tchr., piano & music theory; Pianist, solo recitals & chmbr. Music concerts; Darmstadt Ferienkurs für Neue Musik; Works perfd. in USA, France & Germany. Comps. incl: Seven Rituals (orch.); De Amore et Morte, Scroll (chmbr. music); Doors, for piano; Quest, string quartet; Icarus (chmbr. w. chorus); Spirals (chmbr. music); Raft, for narrator & 5 percussionists; Trialogue, for clarinet, violin & piano; 3 Chants for flute solo; 8 Chants, for 2 voices, clarinet & viola; Only the Cold Bare Moon, for soprano, flute & piano; Phantasy, for oboe & harpsichord; Diffraction (chmbr. music w. chorus); River, for 2 groups of players. Mbrships: Am. Comps. Alliance; Am. Soc. of Univ. Comps.; Am. Music Center; Am. Women Comps.; League of Women Comps.; Coll. Music Soc. Hons: 2 Fellowships, Comps. Conference, 1976, '77; Comp. Fellowship Grant, Nat. Endowment for the Arts, 1978-79; 2nd Prize, Burge-Eastman Competition for piano work, Doors, 1978. Hobbies: Hiking; Reading; Chmbr. music. Address: 915 Coddington Rd., Ithaca, NY 14850, USA.

SILSBURY, Elizabeth Alice, b. 1 Dec. 1931, Adelaide, Aust. Lecturer; Critic; Performer (piano, harpsichord). Educ: BA; BMus. m. James Henry Silsbury, 2 d. Career: Sr. Lectr. in Music & Music Educ., Sturt Coll. of Advanced Educ., SA; Prin. Music Critic, The Advertiser, Adelaide; SA correspondent, Opera Mag., London; accomp. & asst. musical dir., Adelaide Choral Soc. Publs: Tertiary Music Directory, 1977; The Arts in Post-Secondary Education in SA, 1978. Contbr. to: The Advertiser, Adelaide; Opera Mag. Mbrships: Chmn., Arts Grants Advisory Committee, SA; mbr., Bd. of Dirs., Aust. Opera. Hons: Churchill Fellowship, 1967; Life mbr., Adelaide Univ. Theatre Guild, 1965. Hobbies: Gardening; Sewing; Soc. for Protection of Abused Words. Address: 44 Tusmore Ave., Tusmore, SA 5065, Aust.

SILVER, Alfred Lindsey Leigh, b. Birmingham, UK. Organist & Pianist; Physician (Industrial Medicine). Educ: MA, Keble Coll., Oxford Univ.; London Hosp., London E1; LMSSA (London); Dip. of Indl. Hlth. (England); wide musical educ. from father, Dr. A J Silver. m. Hilkda Mary Saffin. Publs: Table of Logarithms to Base Two (w. Newby), 1964; Notes on the Duodecimal Divisiion of the Octave, 1964. Contbr. to: Jrnl. Acoustical Soc. Am.; Math. Gazette; Am. Math. Monthly. Mbrships: Fellow, Inst. Musical Instrument Technol. (Past Pres.); Fellow, Brit. Medical Assn. (Pres. Local Divs.). Hons: Organ Exhibitioner, Keble Coll., Oxford, 1925-29; Fellow, Mercator Music Fndn., Rome, Ga., USA. Hobbies: Mathematics; Keyboard Technique; Truffle Hunting; Bee Keeping. Address: Three Lawns, Court Moor., Fleet, Hants, UK. 4.

SILVER, Phillip Alan, b. 15 Apr. 1946, Brooklyn, NY, USA. Pianist. Educ: BMus, MMus, New England Conserv., Boston, USA. m. Noreen Fitzpatrick. Debut: New England Conserv., 1977. Career: mbr., Fitzpatrick/Silver duo w. wife; recitals & concerts in Boston & Arlington. mbr., Pi Kappa Lambda. Hon: 1st prize, Pi Kappa Lambda competition, Boston, Mass., USA, 1977. Hobbies: Films; Collecting Old Records; Cooking; Mythol.; Politics. Address: 4 May Terr., Glasgow G42 9XF, Scotland, UK.

SILVERI, Paolo, b. Ofena, Italy 1913. e: St. Cecilia Acad., Rome, Mo. Perugim. m. Delia Cirino. 1 s., 1 d. Prof.: Lyric Singer; Bass 1941-44; Baritone 1944-56; Sang as Otello 1959; From 1960 sang again all Baritone, Rome Op. as Germont; since 1949 sung all over world. Prof. of voice & singing, St. Cecilia's Conserv., Rome. num. recordings. Hobby: Sailing. Address: Via Ugo Bassi 3, Rome, Italy.

SILVERMAN, Faye-Ellen, b. 2 Oct. 1947, NYC, USA. Composer; Pianist; Author; Assistant Professor. Educ: Dalcroze Schl. of Music, 1951-63; Manhattan Schl. of Music, 1963-64; Mannes Coll. of Music, 1966-67; BA, Barnard Coll. 1968; MA, Harvard Univ., 1971; D Mus Arts, Columbia Univ., 1974. Career: Asst. Ed., 1 yr., Assoc. Ed., 3 yrs., Current Musicol.; Own radio progs., 1972, '76; Works perfd. in Europe (radio) and Asia, (live) & USA (live, radio & TV); Asst. Prof., Goucher Coll. (theory); Mbr., Grad. Fac., Peabody Inst. of John Hopkins Univ (Music Hist. & Lit.). Comps. incl: Stirrings (chmbr. orch.); Speaking Alone (flute); Dialogue (horn, tuba); For Him; Conversations; String Quartet; Windscape (woodwind quintet); Shadings (chmbr. ensemble); Settings (piano solo). Contbr. to: Goucher Quarterly; Current Musicol. Mbr., profl. assns. Hons. incl: Stokowski Comp. Contest, 1961 (age 13); Coll. & grad. schl. awards. Hobbies incl: Ballet; Reading; Travel; Going to Movies. Address: c/o Seesaw Music Inc., 1966 Broadway, NY, NY 10025, USA.

SILVERTHORNE, Paul Adam, b. 8 Jan. 1951, Altrincham, Cheshire, UK. Viola Player. Educ: LRAM & Recital Dip., RAM. m. Sandra Mackay. Debut: w. Medici Str. Quartet, Wigmore Hall, 1973. Career: Mbr., Medici Str. Quartet, 1971-; Res. Str. Quartet, Univ. of York, 1974-77; Var. BBC radio broadcasts; ITV app., 1976. Recordings: Haydn Op. 64, 1-6, & Op. 76, 3 & 4, 1977. Hobbies: Sailing; Campaign for real ale. Address: Flat 1234, Derwent Coll., Univ. of York, Heslington, York, UO1 5DD, UK.

SILVESTER, Victor, b. 25 Feb. 1900 (dec.) Wembley, Middx., UK. Musical Director, dance orchestra. Educ: LCM; TCM. m. Dorothy Newton, 1 s. Career: Regular broadcaster w. own orch., BBC Radio & TV, over 30 yrs. Compositions; 135 dance tunes recorded; num. other recordings; total record sales exceed 55 million, top seller of any dance orch. in the world. Publs: Victor Silvester's Pianoforte Tutor, 1949; Modern Ballroom Dancing (57 edits.); Dancing is My Life (Autobiog.), 1958; num. books on dancing. Mbrships: Pres., Imperial Soc. of Tchrs. of Dancing; Musicians Unipn; Variety Club; Pres., Lord's Taverners, 1972-73. Hons: OBE; Italian Bronze Medal for Mil. Valour. Hobies: Phys. Culture & Weight Trng. Address: 8 Boydell Ct., St. John's Wood Pk., London NWI 6NP, UK. 1.

SILVESTRE, Lourival, b. 14 Nov. 1949, Belo Horizonte, Brazil. Composer; Guitarist. Educ: Comp. sutides w. Ernest Widmer & Bruno Kiefer; Electroacoustic studies in Paris. m. Silvia Beraldo, Comps. (recorded): Impérios; Boi de Acrílico; Eu vou sortir; Le Temps Circulaire; Derriére la Mer et Fantaise; Patricia - all on album, 'Disjuncta', 1975., Recorded: Fiction Musicale. Hons: 3rd Prize, Comp. Competition, Goethe Inst., 1974. Hobby: Walking in the city with my eyes wide open. Address: 90 Rue João de Freitas, 30.000 Belo Horizonete, Brazil.

SILVESTRI, Renzo, b. 15 Oct. 1899, Modena, Italy. Pianist; Composer. Educ: Studied Piano, Parma Conserv., 1919; studied Comp., Florence, 1920. M. Luisa Bandinelli. Career: Piano Tchr. & Dir., Cagliari Conserv., 1922—24; Staff Mbr., Palermo Conserv., 1924-25; Tchr. of Piano, Santa Cecilia Conserv., Rome, 1926-70; Vice-Dir., ibid, 1951-62; Prof. Emeritus, ibid, 1970-. Comps. (for Piano(Faville; Omaggio a Chopin; Ninna Nanna alla Culla Deserta; 6 Divertimenti for 4 Chords; (transcribed for 2 Pianos) Brahms-Paganini Variatins; C Frank, Prelude-Aria-Finale; arrs. of Scarlatti & other Comps.; educl. Scales System for Piano. Mbrships: Superior Coun. of Arts, Min. of Pub. (Instructioin, Rome, 1948-51; Nat. Acad. Santa Cecilia (VP 1962-65, Pres. 1965-70); Royal Phil. Assn., Bologna; Hon. Mbr., Nat. Acad. Scis., Letters & Arts, Modena; Lions of Rome. Hons: Gold Medal, for achievemant in fields of Educ., Culture & Art, Min. of Publ Instruction, Rome, 1967; Grand Off., Order of Merit of Italian Repub., 1970. Address: Via Alamanno Morelli 10, 00197 Rome, Italy.

SILZER, Giorgio W, b. 27 May 1920, Bielitz, Silesia. Concertmaster; Violinist. Educ: studied w. father Hermann Silzer. m. (1) Waltraud Blankenhorn (dec.); (2) div.; 2 children. Career; Mbr., Bernische Orchesterberein, Switz.; Concertmaster, Deutsche Oper Berlin, 1957 ; many concerts & broadcasts as Soloist & w. chmbr. ensembles inclng. own str. quartet (Silzer Quartet), 1960-. Arr. for Zimmerman-Verlag, Frankfurt. Recordings for EMI & Armida. Mbr., Schweitzer Musikpädagogischer Verband. Hons: 2 Silver Medals & a Dip., Concours de Geneve, 1944-50; elected Kammervirtuose, W Berlin, 1962. Hobbies: Art collections; Books; Sports. Address: Falterweg 23, 1 Berlin 19 (W Berlin), German Fed. Repub.

SIMANDL, Josef, b. 29 Aug. 1903, Pilsen, Czechoslovakia. Cellist. Educ: Grad., Music Schl., Pilsen, 1926; Grad., Musical & Dramatic Acad., Bratislava, 1932: PVTE. STUDY IN Vienna, Austria w. Prof. F Buxbavum; Grad., Master Schl., Prague, 1943. M. Emanuela Cecil, (Opera Singer, Emanuela Simandl). Debut: Pilsen 1923. Career: Mbr., Czech Nonet, & Concertmaster & Soloist, Bratislava Radio Orch., 1929-38; Mbr., Brno & Prague Radio Orchs., 1939-44; Prague Symph. Orch., 1956-72; Mbr., Smetana Klavier Trio, 1939-43; Mbr., Prague Czech Str. Quartet, 1941-51; Mbr. Prague Film Orch., 1945-50. Recordings M Reger, D Minor Suite for Cello Solo; Smartini, Vivaldi, Socar Nedbal, Karel Bendl, Saint-Saens, Glazunov; A Dvorák, Dumky, Piano Trio; V Novák, Balad Trio; Brahms, B Major Quartet; Beethoven, B Major Quartet; Janacek, 2nd Quartet; Soloist Tschaikovsky, G Major Piano Concerto. Contbr. to Czech Musical Magazine. Mbr., Czech Musicians Union. Hons: 2nd Prize Svciks String Instrument Competition, 1943; Title Deserving Artist, 1969. Hobbies: Working at Weekend House; Gardening. Address: 120 00 Prague 2, Jeoná 25, Czechoslovakia.

SIMEANUER, Peter W, b. 11 Dec. 1931, Berlin, Germany. Associate Principal Clarinettist. Educ: St. Louis Coll., Tientsin, China, 1947-49; Music studies, Paris & NY. m. Jacqueline Simenauer. Debut: Israel Phil., age 18. Career: Solo and Chmbr. Music apps. in Europe & USA. Assoc. Prin. Clarinettist, NY Phil., 1960-. Recordings: Mozart Clarinet Quintet w. Pascal Sting Quartet. Hons: 1st Prize, Mozarteum, 1952. Mgmt: Columbia. Address: 22 Greenview Way, Upper Montclair, NJ 07043, USA.

SIMIC, Borivoje, b. Nov. 1920, Beograd, Yugoslavia. Conductor; Composer. Educ: Comp. & conducting, High Musical Acad., Beograd. m. Vladislava Nedeljkovic, 1 d. Career: Symphonic, filim & chorus comp.; Cond., Radio-TV Beograd, 30 yrs. Comps: Movimento Dinamico (symph. poem); Quatuor in E (stings); Story of Two Priests; Num. chorus comps. & solo songs. Num. recordings as cond. Critic, Belgrade newspapers Vecernje novosti (Evening News). Hons. incl: 1st Prize, Llangollen Int. Musical Eisteddfod, 1953; October Award, 1958; Plaque d'or of Beograd, 1974. Hobbies: Germanistics; Do-it-yourself. 25 Stojana Novakovica, 1100 Beograd, Yugoslavia.

SIMIONATO, Giulietta, b. 12 May 1916, Forli, Italy. Mezzo-Soprano Singer. Educ: Teatro alla Scala, Milan; studied w. Guido Palumba. Debut: Lola, Cavalleria Rusticana, Montagnana nr. Padua, Italy. Career: 1st app. at La Scala, 1940; apps. in opera houses of Paris, London, Vienna, Mexico City, Geneva, Switz., Lisbon, Portugal, Chgo., NYC, San Fran., etc. Mbr., Met. Opera; Solo recitals; apps. w. Orch., USA & abroad. Operatic roles incl: Maddelena, Rigoletto; Azucena, Il Trovatore. Recorded complete operas for HMV, Decca, Cetra; Leading Mezzo-Soprano for London Records. Recip. Prize for bel canto singing, Florence, Italy, 1933. Mgmt: Columbia Artists Mgmt. Inc., 113 W 57th St., NY, NY, USA. Address: 29/C Vi di Villa Grazioli, Rome, Italy. 2.

SIMMONDS, Paul Edward, b. 24 Apr. 1949, London, UK. Performing Musician & Teacher of Harpsichord & Organ. Eduv: B Mus, Univ. Witwatersrand, S Africa; Freiburg Conservatory, Fed. German Repub.; Pvte. music studies w. Colin Tilney, London. Debut: Purcell Room, London, 1979. Mbrships: Incorp. Soc. of Musicians (Solo Perf. Sect.). Hobbies: Table Tennis; Old Cars; Philately. Address: 21 South Street, Partridge Green, Sussex, RH13 8EL, UK.

SIMMONS, Calvin, b. 27 Apr. 1950, California, USA. Conductor. Educ: Univ. of Cinn., USA; Piano studies w. John Bigg (Prof., RCM); Curtis Inst. o Music, Phila., Pa.; Conducting student w. Max Rudolf & John Pritchard. Career: Glyndebourne Fest. Opera, England, conducting Marriage of Figaro, 1975-76. Hons: San Francisco Opera Kurt Adler Award, 1972; Exxon Arts Endowment Conductor, 1975. Hobbies: Hiking; Hat-collecting; Bicycling. Mgmt: England (Strafford-Law). Address: 2040 Rodney Drive, Los Angeles, Los Feliz, Calif., USA.

SIMMONS, Donald E, b. June 1929, London, UK. Clarinettist; Alto & Tenor Saxophone Player. Educ: Univ. of London; Gordon Delamont Schl. m. Jean Simmons, 3 c. Career: apps. in UK at Royal Fest. Hall, Picton Hall, Cambridge Univ.; ldr., Alex Zanders Ragtime Band, Don Simmons Quartet & Quintet, Casa Loma Jazz Band. Comp: Last Chance Rag. Recordings: 3 w. Eric Silks's Southern Jazz Band, 1951; 1 w. The Bid Muddies at the Ports of Call, 1962. Hobby: Acoustic Design. Address: 767 Greenfield Cres., Newmarket, Ont. L3Y 3B2, Canada.

SIMON, Abbey, b. 8 Jan. 1922, New York, NY, USA. Concert Pianist. Educ: Grad., Curtis Inst. of Music, Phila., Pa. m. Dian Levinson Simon, 1 s. Debut: Town Hall, NYC. Career: Concert tours of 6 continents inclng: S Africa, S Am., USA, Can., Aust., New Zealand, Europe, Russia, Israel; Recitals w. Conds. inclng: Dimitri Mitropoulos, Sir John Barbirolli, Sir Malcolm Sargent, Joseph Krips, William Steinberg, George Szell, Raefael Kubelik, Walter Susskind & num. others. Num. recordings. Hons. incl: Walter W Naumberg Award, NYC; Fedn. of Music Clubs Award, NYC; Elizabeth Sprague Coolidge Medal, London. Hobbies: Tennis; Chess. Mgmt: Harold Shaw Inc., New York, NY; Tower Music, London, UK. Address: 40 Chemin Moise Duboule, Geneva, Switz. 3.

SIMON, Delbert Richard, b. 7 Aug. 1935. Burwell, Neb., USA. Tenor; University Professor of Voice; Musical Director. Educ: BMus., Simpson Coll., Indianola, Iowa, 1955; MMus., Miami Univ., Oxford, Ohio, 1957; DMA, Univ. of Iowa, Iowa City, 1970. M Betty Jean Atkins, 2 s. Career: Concerts on Coll. Campuses in Mich., Ohio, Ill., Iowa, Minn., Tex., Wash.; Artist-In-Res., Bay View Coll. of Music, 1958-61; Oratorio Soloist, Seattle, Wash., Miami Univ.; num. Opera, TV Apps.; Musical Dir., Opera Workshop; Vocal Tchr. & Coach. Author, The Life & Music of Hippolite Monpou, 1970. Contbr. to Grove's Dictionary of Music & Musicians. Mbrships: Auditions Chmn., Ctrl. Region, Nat. Assn. of Tchrs. of Singing; Nat. Opera Assn.; Music Tchrs. Nat. Assn.; Iota Kappa Lambda. Hons: Teaching Fellowship, Univ. of Iowa, 1965-69; Rsch. Fellowship, ibid, 1968-69. Hobbies: Travel; Family Camping. Address: 302 Chamberlin Dr., Charleton, IL 61920, USA.

SIMON, Emil, b. 24 Sept. 1936, Chisinau, Rumania. Orchestra Conductor; Composer. Educ: Dip. in chorus conduction, HS of Music, Cluj, 1954; Dip. in orch. cond. & comp. 'G Dima' Conserv. of Music, Cluj, 1960; grad. studies, w. Nadia Boulanger & at Nat. Higher Conserv. of Music, Paris, France, 1964; studied w. Sergiu Celibidache, Stockholm, 1968. m. Edith, 2 d. Debut: Cluj, 1958. Career: nominated Permanent Cond., Cluj State Phil. Orch., 1960; has toured in USSR, Poland, Czech., Yugoslavia, Italy, France, German Dem. Repub., Sweden, USA & Can. Comps. (recorded): IInd Cantata; Sonata for Orch. Recordings (all w. Cluj Phil. Orch): Debussy's La Mer & Ravel's Dapnis & Chloe; IIInd Suite; Brahms; 2nd Symph.; sev. operatic overtures by Wagner; sev. records of Rumanian contemp. music. Contbr. to Muzica review. Mbrships: ATM; Union of Rumanian Composers. Hons: 1st Prize, Int. Competition for Orch. Conds., Besancon, France, 1964; Order of Cultural Merit, 1968. Hobbies: Fishing; Mountain Touring. Address: Bolyai St. No. 7, Atp. 8, Cluj, Rumania.

SIMON, Stephen Anthony, b. 3 May 1937, NYC, USA. Conductor. Educ: BMus, Yale Univ. Schl. of Music, 1960; Earlier piano studies w. Joel Rosen; Choral cond. w. Dr. Hugh Ross, Dr. Julius Herford; Orchl. sutdies w. Maestro Josef Krips; Cond. seminars w. the NY Phil. under Maestro William Steinberg, 1965, St. Louis Symph. under Maestro Walter Susskind, 1971. m. Ellen Hallo Friendly, 4 s. Debut: NY, 1963. Career: Music Dir. & Cond. of The County Symph., Westchester, NY, 1963-; Music Dir. & Cond. of the Handel Soc. of NY, 1970-74; Guest Cond. Am. Symph., Rochester Phil., NC Symph. Albuquerque (NM) Symph., Chattanooga (Tenn.) Symph., 1975; Sacramento, Denver, Tucson; European cond. in France, also Israel. Comps: Arr. of Pachelbel Kanon in D in Merion Music Rental Catalogue (Presser). Recordings: Complete Mozart Piano Concerti (Lili Kraus, soloist); Works by Handel - Solomon, RCA: Ariodante, RCA; Orlando RCA; Juda Maccabaeus, RCA; Great Scenes from Finaldo, RCA; Guest Scenes fro Athalia, Arli. Contbr. to profl. jrnls. Hons: Nom. for Grammy Award 'Best Choral Recording 1968' Handel's Solomon, RCA; Awarded 'Patron Extraordinaire' by Iona Coll. Inst. of the Arts, 1974. Hobbies: Sports. Address: 281 Garth Rd., Scarsdale, NY 10583, USA.

SIMONEAU, Leopold, b. 3 May 1919, Quebec, Can. Concert & Opera Singer. Educ: BA, Levis Coll., Laval Univ., 1941. m. Pierrette Alaire, 2 d. Career: w. Paris Opera, 1948-51; apps. at La Scala Milan, Vienna State Opera, Colon Theatre, Buenos Aires, etc.; in French premiere of Stravinsky's Rake's Progress, Paris Opera, 1953; concert tours, Europe & Ams. num. recordings. Mgmt: Columbia Artists Mgmt., 111 W 57th St., NY, NY 10019, USA. Address: 11821 Rue De Tracy, Montreal, PQ, Canada. 2.

SIMONIS, Jean-Marie, b. 22 Nov. 1931, Mol. Belgium. Composer; Teacher. Educ: Studied, Royal Conserv., Brussels; 1st prizes, solfege, harmony, counterpoint & fugue; studied orch. & comp. w. Marcel Quintet, cond. w. M Defossez & piano w. Ms. Pueyo & Steyaert. m. Danièle Cancelier, 1 s. Career: Tchr., harmony, Chapelle Musicale Reine Elisabeth, Brussels; Sound Advsr., Belgium Radio & TV, 1961-70. num. publd. comps. incl: L'Automne, 1968, (recorded); Trios Esquisses Symphoniques, 1967 (recorded); Polyphonies pour orch. á cordes, 1973; Suggestions pour flûte & perc., 1970. (recorded); Evocations pour piano, 1974, (recorded); Notturno pour piano, 1977, (recorded); Canzoni a Cinque pour quintette de cuivres, 1977. Mbrships: CEBEDEM; Conseil Supérieur Artistique. Hons: 2nd Grand Prix, Rome, 1961; Queen Elisabeth comp. priz, 1975 & 78. Hobby: Gardening. Address: 83 Rue de Percke, B 1180 Brussels, Belgium.

SIMONITI, Rado Jacobus, b. 15 May 1914, Fojana, Yugoslavia. Musician. Educ: Dip., Conserv.; Dip., Acad. of Music, Ljubljana. m. Ana Bensa, 3 s., 1 d. Debut: in Verdi's La Traviata, Slovenian Nat. Theatre. Career: Prof., music shcl., Spilt, Acad. of Music, Ljubljana; Choral Cond., Concert Organist, Split; Cond., Srecko Kosovel Chorus, Yugoslav Army, Belgrade; Permanent Cond., Ljubljana. Comps: over 100 choral works; more than 30 solo songs; 2 cantatas; The Partisan Ana (opera). Publs: Ed., Our Choruses; Mbrships: Slovenian Comps. Soc.; Yugoslav Comps. Soc.; Interpretive Artist of Yugoslavia. Hons: Preseren Prize, Slovenian Repub., 1949-56 & 76; Prize of the Slovenian Nation, 1967; Hon. Citizen, Nova Gorica; army & civil orders of Yugoslavia. Hobbies: Poetry; Belles Lettres. Address: Gradisce 12, Ljubljana, Yugoslavia.

SIMONKOVA, Dagmar, b. 17 Nov. 1939, Mlada Boleslav, Czech. Solo Pianist; Teacher. Educ: Conserv., Prague, 3 yrs.; Degree, Acad. Arts, Prague, studied w. Prof. Frank Maxian. m. Ing. Krel Horak, 1 d. Debut: Mlada Boleslav, 1957. Career: Piano tchr., Acad. Arts, Prague; Num. TV & radio perfs. inclng. chopin, 4 Nocturnes, Smetana, Polkas, Czech. dances, etc., Czech., USSR, Cuba & Iran.; Concert apps. incl., Czech., Iceland & USSR. Recordings incl: I Jirko, III. concert G dur for piano & orch. (Panton); V J Tomasek, Tre Ditirambi op. 65 (Panton). Mbrships incl: Assn. of Czech. Comps. & concert Artists. Hons. incl: 1st pl. Women's sect., Moscow-Cajkovskys Competition, 1966. Hobbies: Collecting Pictures; Gardening. Address: J M. Sverdlova 4, 160 00 Prague, 6 Bubenec, Czech.

SIMONOV, Yuri Ivanovich, b. 4 Mar. 1941, Saratov, USSR. Conductor. Educ: Leningrad Conserv. Career: Cond., Kislovodsk Phil. Soc., 1967-69; Cond., State Bolshoi Opera & Ballet Theatre, Moscow, 1969-70; Chief Cond., ibid., 1970-; Perfs. in Bolshoi Theatre incl. The Marriage of Figaro; Aida; Boris Godunov; Prince Igor; Pskovityanka; Tours as guest cond. & with Bolshoi Theatre in France, Italy & E Germany. Hons: Laureate, 2nd USSR Competition of Conds., Moscow, 1966; 1st Prize, 5th Int. Competition of Conds., Acad. of St. Cecilia, Rome, 1968. Address: Bolshoi Theatre, 1 Ploschald Sverdlova, Moscow, USSR.

SIMONS, John, b. 24 July 1911, Birkenhead, UK. Pianist. Educ: MusB (Melbourne); studied piano in London & Paris w. Craxton, Matthay, Landowska, Casadesus. Debut: Wigmore Hall, 1934. Career: Concert Artist in England, Europe, Australia; Mbr. of profl. staff, Panel of Examiners & mbr. of the Corp. of Trinity Coll. of Music, London, Contbr. to The Music Tchr. Mbr., ISM. Hons: Hon. FTCL, 1961. Hobbies: Gardening. Address: 2 Ripplevale Grove, London N1 1HU, UK. 3.

SIMONS, Netty, b. 26 Oct. 1913, NY, NY, USA. Composer. Educ: NY Univ. Schl. of Fine Arts; Juilliard Grad. Schl. of Music; 3rd St. Music Schl. Settlement; studied w. Stefan Wolpe. m. Leon George Simons, 1d., 1s. Career: Comp.; Prod.; Scriptwriter, Radio progs. for Am. Comps. Alliance, NYC, 1966-77; Contemporary Music Series, Univ. of Mich. Radio, 1971-; Music for Dance, WNET-TV, NYC. Comps. incl: Variables, Scripio's Drean, 5 other orchl. works; 2 band works; Time Groups No. 1, 5 other piano works; 8 Graphic Scores; var. theatre music; 2 choral works; opera, Bell Witch of Tennessee; 3 songs; violin solo; Str. Quartets; 2 violin sonatas, num. chmbr. works. Recordings: Music for Young Listeners; Design Groups I & II; Silver Thaw. Contbr. to: Music Jrnl., Gallery of living Comps., Comps. of the Am., Notations, John Cage, Anthology of Am. Violin Music, Jerome Landsman. mbr., off., num. profl. socs. recip., num. hons. Hobby: Gardening. Mgmt: Ruth Uebel, NY, USA. Address: 303 E 57th St. - Apt. 47E, NY, NY 10022, USA. 5, 27.

SIMONSEN, Anker Fjeld, b. 15 May 1944, Farum, Denmark. Pianist; Music Teacher. Educ: Econs., Univ. Compehagen; Dip., piano, RAM, Copenhagen, 1967; Tchrs. Degree, ibid, 1971; Summer couses, comp. & piano, Dartington, UK & Gothenburg, Sweden; Bervfsverbot, 1979. Career incls: Royal Opera, Copenhagen, 1969; Co-Fndr., Grp. for Alternative Music, Copenhagen, 1970; Bd. Dirs., ISCM Danis Sect., 1971-75; Radio & TV apps.; Freelance Accomp., RAM, Copenhagen, 1974-; Schl. Tchr. Comps. incl: Sonata for 2 Chmbr. Groups, 1972; Thunder Shower, 1974; Ich Atm, 1974. Recordings incl: Accompaniment, Anthology of Danish Music, 1974. Contbr. to: Anthology of Danish Choir Music, 1973; (Dansk Kor Antologi), 1978-79; Profl. jrnls. Mbr., profl. orgs. Hobbies: incl: Bicycling. Address: Korsgade 353, 2200 Copenhagen N, Denmark.

SIMPSON, Adrienne Marie, b. 26 Nov. 1943, Wellington, NZ. Musicologist; Music Journalist. Educ: BA, MA (Music Hist.), Victoria Univ. of Wellington; MMus, King's Coll., London. m. Richard Henry Chilton. Career: Tutor, King's Coll., London Univ.; Lectr., Goldsmiths Coll. & North East Essex Technical Coll.; Prof., GSM; Freelance, 1973-. Publs: Ed. (w. P Northway) Wm. Williams, Sonata for a Single Flute, 1970; ED., Easy Lute Music, 1975. Contbr. of articles to num. profl. publs. Mbrships: Royal Musical Assn.; Dvorak Soc. Hons: British Coun. Scholar, 1969/70. Hobbies: Reading; Gardening; Philately; Walking. Address: 1 Oliver Place, The Grove, Witham, Essex, UK.

SIMPSON, Dudley George, b. 4 Oct. 1922, Melbourne, Aust. Composer; Conductor; Pianist. Educ: studied piano w. Vera Porter, Leslie Curnow & Victor Stephenson, Melbourne Univ., orchestration w. Elford Mack, Melbourne & Gordon Jacob, UK, & composition w. John Ingram, Melbourne, & Gordon Jacob, UK; Dip., Melbourne Univ. Conserv. of Music. m. Jill Yvonne Bathurst, 1 s., 2 d. Debut: as Musical Dir., Borovansky Ballet, Aust. Career: Guest Cond., Royal Ballet, Covent Gdn., 1960-62; Prin. Cond., ibid, at GB & European major fests., inclng. Monte Carlo, Nice, Athens & Middle E, 1961-63; Musical Dir. for 2 world tours w. Dame Margot Fonteyn, David Blair, Rudolph Nureyev, etc., 1962-64; Composer & Cond. A Voyage of Discovery (1st major work, words by Michael Noonan) for Queen Elizabeth Hall Concert, 1 Mar. 1974. Comps. incl: many TV themes. Recordings incl: In A Covent Garden (w. orch., & synthesizer). Mbr. BBC Club. Hobbies: Gardening; Home Decorating. Address: 'Lanherne'. Beechwood Ave., Weybridge, Surrey KT12 9TE, UK.

SIMPSON, John Michael, b. 3 Oct. 1933, London, UK. LEA Music Adviser. Educ: GTCL. m. Elizabeth Winfield, 2 s. Career: Music Master, St. George of England Schl., Bootle,

1955-56;Hd., Music Dept., Freyerns Grammar-Tech. Schl., Basildon, 1956-66; Music Advsr., Bournemouth Educ. Auth., 1967-69; Music Organiser, Hastings Educ. Auth., 1969-74; Area Music Advsr., E Sussex Educ. Auth., 1974- Comps. incl: Works for Jr. Ensemble; Var. short choral & instrumental works; Cantata; The Prophet; Clarinet Concerto; 2 Symphs.; A Youth Overture; Flute Conderto; Horn Concerto; Brass Quintet. Contbr. to Music Tchr. Mbr., MANA. Hobbies: Reading; Travel; Walking; Cinema. Address: 61 Collier Rd., Hastings, Sussesx, UK. 3.

SIMPSON, Mary Jean, b. 31 Jan. 1941, Bryan, Tex., USA. Instructor of Music, flautist; Flute Clinician. Educ: AA & Cert. in Music, Del Mar Coll.; BS Music (studied flute w. Julius Baker), MMus., Univ. of Tex., Austin (studied flute w. John Hicks). Career: Freelance Tchr., Tex., 1956-62; w. Del Mar Chamber Orch. & Del Mar Theatre Orch., 1959-62; Corpus Christi Symph., Tex., 1961-62; Flute Instructor, Del Mar Coll., Corpus Christi, 1961-62; w. West Side Symph., NYC, 1964-65; Pvte. Instructor in Flute, NYC, 1965; w. Am. Symph. Orch. 1965. 1966, Orch. Symph. de Quebec 1966-67; Lectr. in Music, Centenary Coll., Sherveport, La., & w. Shreveport Symph. & Woodwind Quintet, 1968-70; Instructor in Music Univ. of Mont., Missoula, 1970-; w. Missoula Civic Symph. & Montana Chamber Players, 1970-; Clinician Armstrong Flutes, 1971-; Flute Soloist. Publs: (ed.); Quantz: Sonata 3 for Flute and Continuo (1977). Contbr. to Instrumntalist, Nat. Assn. Coll. Wind & Percussion Instructors Jrnl. & others. Mbrships incl: Nat. Assn. Coll. Wind & Percussion Instructors; Am. Musicol. Soc.; Pi Kappa Lambda. Nat. Flute Assn. Hobbies incl: Show Dogs; Needlework; Gourmet Cookery. Mgmt: Clinician, Edu-tainment Ltd. Address: 106 Sentinel Ave., Missoula, MT 59801, USA.

SIMPSON, Robert, b. 2 Mar. 1921, Leamington, Warwicks., UK. Composer. Educ: DMus, Denelm. m. Besse Fraser. Career: much radio & TV Broadcasting; Mbr., BBC Music Staff, 1951-. Comps. incl: symphs.; str. quartets; piano concerto; violin concerto; violin concerto; piano music; orchl. works; works for instrumental ensembles; Media in vita sumus (motet for choir, brass & timpani); etc. Publs. incl: Carl Nielsen, Symphonist, 1952; The Essence of Bruckner, 1966; BBC booklets - Sibelius & Nielsen & Beethoven's Symphonies. Ed. The Symphony, 1966. Contbr. to var. publs. inclng: Ency. Britannica. Mbr., ISM. Hons: Carl Nielsen Gold Medal, Denmark, 1956; Bruckner Modal of Hon., USA. Hobby: Astron (FRAS) Address: Cedar Cottage, Chearsley, Aylesbury, Bucks. HP10 ODA, UK. 1.

SIMPSON, W Kenneth, b. Bishop Auckland, UK. Teacher; Lecturer in Music Education. Educ: MusB; FRCO; LRAM ARCM. m. Christina Ruth Crawford, 1s., 1d. Career: Hd., Music Dept., Univ. London Inst. of Educ., 1956-75; Examiner & Advsr. to num. univs. & colls.; Chmn., Music Tchrs. Assn.; Cond., Enfield String Players; Alexandra Choral Soc.; Chorus Master, Leicester Phil. Soc. Comps. incl: Evening Serv. in A minor; Six Songs of Christmastide (Legnick). Publs. incl: Rounds & Canons, 1977. Contbr. to num. profl. jrnls. Mbrships: incl: Royal Musical Assn.; ISM. Hobbies: Armchair Gardening; Bookshops; Avoiding Comms. Address: 54 Plants Green, Warminster, Wilts. BA12 9NW, UK.

SIMS, Ezra, b. 16 Jan. 1928, Birmingham, Ala., USA. Composer. Educ: BA, Birmingham So. Coll.; Birmingham Conserv. of Music; BMus., (comp. w. Quincy Porter), Yale Univ. Schl. of Music; MA. (comp. w. Darius Milhaud), Mills Coll. Comps. incl: works for small chorus; chamber orch.; oboe, celeste, percussion; piano; orch.; str. quartet; musique concrete; tape collage; etc. Commissions: Cantata III, Cathy Berberian; Third Quartet, Endicott Fund; Antimatter, McDowell's Fault, Alec, Lion at the Door; The Duchess of Malfi, Pastorale, Interlope; 5 Toby Minutes, Ground Cover, Toby Armour; Cat's Cradle, Ina Hahn; Museum Piece, Carol Beckwith; Tango Variations, Lois Ginades, etc. Recordings: Chamber Cantata on Chinese Poems, ; Midoriguska, Japan, 1978.; Third Quartet,; Elegie-nach Rilke, Contbr. to var. profl. jrnls. Mbrships: BMI; Am. Composers Alliance. Hons: Raphael Sagalyn Prize, Tanglewood, 1960; Guggenheim Fellowship, 1962. Nat. Endowment for the Arts, Cambridge Arts Council; Martha Baird Rockefeller Recording Grant, 1977. Hobbies: Reading; Cooking; Talking; Swimming. Address: 1168 Mass. Ave., Cambridge, MA 02138, USA.

SIMS, Phillip Weir, b. 16 July 1925, Ft. Smith, Ark., USA. Music Librarian; Educator. Educ: BA, Ouachita Coll., 1950; BSM, Southwestern Bapt. Theol. Sem., 1953; MSM, ibid, 1956; DMA, ibid., 1970; MLS, N Tex State Univ., 1973. m. Muriel Edith Evans, 2 d. Careers: Serv. w. USN, 1943-46; Min. of Music, var. chs. in Ark., Ind., Mont. & Tex., 1950-71; Music Libn. & Assoc. Prof. of Music Bibliography, Southwestern Bapt.

Theol. Sem., Ft. Worth., Tex., 1967-. Mbrships: Music Lib. Assn.; Southern Bapt. Ch. Music Conference; Alpha Lambda Sigma; N Tex State Univ. Lib Fraternity. Address: 7308 Ledoux Dr., Ft. Worth, TX 76134, USA.

SINCLAIR, Jeannette, b. London, UK. Opera & Concert Singer. Educ: Mary Datchelor Schl.; LRAM; vocal trng. w. Helene Isepp. m. L I Charin, 1 s., 1d. Career: Prin. soprano, Royal Opera House, Covent Garden, 1956-65; apps. w. major opera cos.; apps. on TV; many radio broadcasts. var. opera recordings. Mbr., ISM. Address: 6 The Lincolns, London NW7, UK. 27.

SINCLAIR, Monica, b. Contralto Singer. Has recorded works of Beethoven, Delius, Gilbert & Sullivan, Handel, Mozart, Purcell, Johann Strauss, etc. Address: 165 Brockley Rise, London SE23, UK. 2.

SINDE RAMALLAL, Clara, b. 28 Dec. 1935, Buenos Aires, Argentina. Guitarist; Teacher. Educ: Lic. in PR; advanced studies of music, guitar & lyric chmbr. song (as soprano). Debut: Teatro Lassalle, 1945. Career: tours as Soloist, major cities of Argentina, Chile, Ecuador, Peru, Columbia & Venezuela; num. perfs. in concert halls & for musical socs.; recordings & broadcasts in Caracas & major Argentine cities; has premiered works written for her by A Galluzzo, Bianchi Piñero & E Calcagno; tours throughout S Am. as Mbr. of Sinde Ramallal Trio (w. Silvia Molinari & Gloria Boschi, both her students), also radio & TV broadcasts, 1971-. Comps. publs: Preludio No. 1; D Scarlatti's Sonata-Gavota (Longo 58, transcription); Barmi. Recordings: Parlophone Label. Mbrships: Dir., & Advsr., Dept. of Guitar, IDEA Inst., Quilmes; Dir., Dept. of Guitar, Spender Inst., Buenos Aires. Recip. of Hon. Dip., Argentine Assn. for Chmbr. Music, 1953. Hobbies: Philately; Literature; Camping. Address: Luca 1771, 7 piso, Dto. "A'", Buenos Aires, Argentina.

SINGER, Jeanne (Walsh), b. 4 Aug. 1924, NYC, NY, USA. Composer; Concert Pianist; Teacher; Lecturer. Educ: Barnard Coll.; BA, Columbia Univ., 1944; 15 yrs. piano study w. Nadio Reisenberg; Artists Dip., Nat. Guild of Piano Tchrs. m. Richard G Singer (dec. 1972), 1 s. Career: Pianist, solo & w. ensembles for 30 yrs.; Radio & TV apps. inclng. many publ. perfs. of own comps.; Lectr.; Pvte. Tchr. Comps. incl: Summons (Baritone); Suite in Ha rpsichord Style; A Cycle of Love (4 songs w. piano); American Indian Song Suite; Composer's Prayer (SSA w. piano). Recordings: Album of own art songs & chmbr. music, 1978. Contbr. to: CAAA Nat. Mag., Music Ed., 1973-. Mbrships. incl: Phi Beta Kappa; Int. Platform Assn.; ASCAP; Comps., Authors & Artists of Am., Inc., 1st VP, NYC Chapt.; Am. Women Comps., Inc. (Bd. of Dirs.). Hons: Over 20 Nat. Awards for music, 1971-; sev. grants, NY State Coun. on the Arts. Hobbies: Breeding prize-winning Siamese cats. Address: 64 Stuart Place, Manhasset, NY 11030, USA. 5,23, 27, 29.

SINGER, Malcolm John, b. 22 June 1940, Coventry, UK. Baritone. Educ: LRAM; Recital Dip., RAM. m. Joy Singer. Career: Ortorio, UK. & Europe; Recitals & Opera, UK & for BBC Radio 3. Mbrships: ISM; Nat. Trust Hons: Prin's Prize, Geo. Grossmith Medal for Opera, John Booth Prize & Lady Maud Warrender Prize, all RAM; Gtr. London Arts Assn. Young Musicians Award, 1969. Hobbies: Bridge; Reading; Gardening; Ornithol. Mgmt: Ibbs & Tillett; Helen Jennings Concert Agcy. Address: 24 St. Martin's Ave., Luton, Beds. LU2 7LQ, UK.

SINGERLING, Jan Willem, b. 23 Aug. 1920, Amsterdam, Netherlands. Conductor; Composer; Teacher. Educ: Dip. Cond., 1961; Music Tchr. Cert., 1962. m. Fracisca Ebinc, 2 s., 2 d. Debut: Comp., 1945; Cond., 1955. Career: Prin. Cond: Royal Wind Band Excelsior, Wormerveer, 1962; Haarlem Police Band, 1969; Mixed Choir, Daniel de Lange, 1972; Koog A/D Zaan Var.; Radio, TV apps. Comps. incl: 4 Flying Spy March; St. Nicholas Parade March; Colours for Band; Var. other works Publs: Comprehensive Method of Euphonium, Bass Tuba. The Clodomir Method. Re-written & extended. Mbr. Musicians Coun. Hobbies: Painting; Photography. Address: 105 Wibautstraat, Zaandam, Netherlands.

SINGH, Prabhu, b. 11 June 1937, Madras, India, Pianist; Conductor; Lecturer in Music. Educ: BMus; FRCO; LRAM (Tchrs. & Perfs.); ARCM (Organ Perf.); ARAM. m. Eleanor Christine Singh, 3 d. Career: Asst. Dir. of Music, Oundle Schl., UK. 1962-66; Dir. of Music, Daunting Schl., 1966-70; Bryanston Schl., 1970-72; Lectr., Schl. of Music, The Polytechnic, Huddersfield, 1972-; Cond., Halifax Orch.; Piano recitals. Mbr., ISM. Hons: Churchill Fellow, 1968-69. Hobbies: Walking; Winemaking; Roman archaeol. in Brit. Address: Woodtop Cottage, Wood Top, Hebden Bridge, W Yorks. H47 6JQ, UK.

SINGLETARY, Robert Thomas, b. 13 Sept. 1935, Cairo, Ga., USA. Educator; Contrabassist; Conductor. Educ: BA, Alaska Meth. Univ.; MMus, Univ. of Idaho. m. Corrine Singletary, 1 d. Career: Music Educator, Band & Orch. Dir., second. schls. & colls., 15 yrs.; Hd., Music Dept., N Idaho Coll.; Cond. & Fndr., N Idaho Symph. Band; Contrabassist, Spokane, Anchorage, Columbus & Idaho-Wash. Symph., also Alaska Fest. Orch. Mbrships: MENC; ID Music Educators Assn.; Phi Mu Alpha; Nat. Orch. League; Nat. Coll. Band Dirs. Assn. Recip., Disting. Serv. Award, 1965. Hobbies: Collecting Books, Paintings & Art Objects. Address: 2421 A St., Coeur d'Alene, ID 83814, USA.

SINIAVINE, Alec, b. 4 May 1916, Odessa, Russia. Composer; Pianist. Educ: 2 yrs. of study at Law Univ., Sorbonne; Dip., Nat. Musical Acad. of Bucarest, Rumania. m. Ramonde Allain, 1 s. Career: Accomp. to num. perfs.; creator in France of sweet rhythmic style of piano music, making num. broadcasts on radio & TV thru-out world. Comps: incl: Attendis-moj Mon Amour; Paris, tu n'as pas changé; Petit train (TV); Bague á Jules; music for 14 films. Recordings: w. Columbia & Decca. Publs: 6 piano books Mbrships: Admnstr., Soc. of Authors, Composers & Eds. of Music (SACEM); Racing Club of France. Recip. of 1st gt. prize of French songs for Reve, mon reve, 1961. Hobbies: Reading; Tennis; Swimming. Address: 6, avenue de New-York, Paris, 16e, France.

SINKO, George, b. 20 July 1923, Budapest, Hungary. Opera Singer; Professor. Educ: Opera Singing, Musical Acad., Budapest, w. Luigi Renzi. m. Eva Hortobagyi, 3 s. Debut: As Raimondo, Lucia di Lammermoor, Opera House, Budapest, 1952; As Colin, La Boheme, Opera House, Szeged, 1953. Career: Has appeared as Philip, Fiesco, Zacharia (Verdi); Sarastro, Leporello, Osmin (Mozart); Baron Ochs (R Strauss); Don Pasquale & Dulcamara (Donizetti); Blue Beard (Bartok); Roco (Beethoven); Daland, Hermann/Tannhauser/Henry the Flower/Lohengrin (Wagner). Sev. recordings. Mbr., Soc. of Hungarian Musical Artistas. Hons: Liszt-Prize winner, 1966; Artist of Merit, 1976. Hobbies: Amateur Cine; Travelling. Address: 5/b Josika Str., Szeged H 6722, Hungary.

SIROKAY, Zsuzsanna, b. 28 Mar. 1941, Ungvar, Hungary. Pianist. Educ: Franz Liszt Music Acad., Budapest; studied w. Peter Solymos, Gyorgy Kurtag, Brendel, Badura-Skoda, Demus & Anda. m. Miklos Dobozi, 2 s. Debut: w. orch. cond. by Janos Ferencsik, Budapest, 1965. Career: concerts throughout Europe (USSR, Poland, England, Ireland, Germany, Italy, Switz., Sweden); tours w. Bamberger Symphony under Istvan Kertez; gave recital 'In Memoriam Clara Haskil', Lucerne Fest., 1973; num. recordings for radio broadcasts (Budapest, London & Glasgow BBC, Cologne, Stuttgart, Lausanne, Zurich, Innsbruck, Vienna). Recordings: Qualiton, Budapest. Hons: Prizes, Leeds, 1963, Vienna, 1967. Hobby: Reading Mgmt: Ingpen & Williams in UK. Address: Klosbachstr. 33 8032 Zürich, Switz.

SIRONEN, Doretha May E, b. Bklyn., NY, USA. Music Educator; Programme Coordinator; Conductor; Dancer; Choreographer. Educ: BA, Bklyn. Coll., 1957; MA, Columbia Univ., 1962; Profl. Dip. music & music educ., Tchrs. Coll., ibid., 1968; PhD, Walden Univ. Inst. Adv. Studies in Educ., 1975. Career: Music specialist, Jerico Pub. Schls., 19 yrs.; Performer, choreographer & musical dir., 21 concerts, Bklyn. Coll. Performing Arts Ctr., 1955-76; 6 prods., NY Workd's Fair, 1964-65; 1 Dance Arts Prog., Opera House, Bklyn. Acad. Music, 1975; Concert, radio & TV apps. Contbr. to profl. publs. Mbr. profl. orgs. Hons. incl: Winner, Annual Conducting Competitions, Columbia Univ., 1960,'62; Participant, Dimitri Mitropoulous Conducting Competition. Hobbies incl: Tap-o-logy; Travel. Address: 267 Birchwood Pk. Dr., Jericho, Lond Island, NY 11753, USA.

SIRUCEK, Jerry Edward, b. 30 June 1922, Cicero, Ill., USA. University Professor; Performer, oboe & Engl. Horn. Educ: BS, Mathematics. m. Lorraine Ella Teichman, 2 s. 1 d. Career: Houston Symph.; Chicago Symph.; Aspen Fest.; Chautauqua Fest.; Chicago Symph. Woodwind Quintet; Am. Woodwind Quintet; Baroque Chmbr. Players; Prof. of Music (oboe), Indiana Univ. Recordings: Solo & chmbr. music. Hobbies: Farming; Flying. Address: 4839 E Ridgewood Dr., Bloomington, IN 47401, USA.

SITHOLE, Elkin Thamsanqa, b. 14 Apr. 1931, Blaauwbosch, Newcastle, S Africa. Zulu Baritone; Pianist; Mbira Drum & Banjo Player; Zulo Baritone Composer; Teacher; Choir Master; Ethnomusicologist; Anthropolost. Educ. incls: BA, Univ. of Natal, 1962; LRAM (singing tchr.), 1966; BMus, Hartt Coll. of Music, Univ. of Hartford, USA, 1967; MA, Wesleyan Univ., USA, 1968; PHD, Queens Univ., Belfast, UK, 1976. m. Regina Thembi Buthelezi, 1 s., 3 d. Career incls: Cond. many perfs., S

Africa, 1962-63; Prof., Music & Ethnomusicol., Northeastern III, Univ., Chgo., 1968-. Comp. many songs. Contbr. to publs. in field. Mbr. Profl. orgs. Recip. var. awards. Hobby: Soccer. Address: Northeastern III. Univ., 700 E Oakwood Blvd., Chicago, IL 60653, USA.

SITSKY, Larry, b. 10 Sept. 1934, Tientsin, China. Pianist; Composer; Musicologist; Teacher. Educ: Sydney Univ., Aust.; Dip., State Conserv. of Music., NSW, 1955; postgrad. studies at Conserv. w. Winifred Burston (pupil of Egon Petri & Ferruccioi Busoni) & then at the San Francisco Conserv. w. Egon Petri, 1958-61. m. Magda Wiczek, 2 c. Debut: First Solo Recital, 1945; Mendelssohn D Minor Concerto, Tientsin, Chine, 1946. Career: Concerts in China from 1945-51; Many concerts, broadcasts in Australia, -1958; Recitals & broadcasts in San Francisco, inclng. own works, 1958-61; Extensive appearances on TV in Celebrity Orchl. Concerts, Aust. Broadcasting Commission, chamber music, solo, etc., 1961-. Comps. incl: Fall of the House of Usher, opera; Apparitions, orchl. piece; Wind Quartet; Sonata for Solo Flute; Little Suite & Sonatina Formalis; Twelve Mystical Preludes (piano); Sonata for Guitar; The Five Elements; Seven Meditations on Symbolist Art; String Quartet; Five Improvisatins for SATB & Piano. Sev. recordings for Aust. Broadcasting Commission & others. Contbr. to var. music jrnls. Mbrships: Music Bd., Aust. Coun. for the Arts; Aust. Performing Right Assn.; Fellowship of Australian Composers. Recip., sev. hons. & awards inclng: Alfred Hill Award, 1968; Fellowship Aust. Coun. for the Arts, 1974; Composition Fellowship to the USSR, 1977. Address: Canberra Schl. of Music, PO Box 804, Canberra City 2601, Aust. 14.

SIVEC, Joze, b. 19 Jan. 1930, Ljubljana, Yugoslavia. Musicologist. Educ: Music Acad., Ljubljana; Fac. of Philos., Ljubljana; PhD, Ljubljana, 1967. m. Irena, 1 d. Career: Prof. of Musicol., Univ. of Ljubljana. Publs: Opera in Ljubljana, 1791-1861 (Opera v Stanovsken gledaliscu v Ljubljani), 1971; Compositional Technique of Wolfgang Striccius (Kompozicijeski stavek Wolfganga Stricciusa), 1972; Opera thorugh the Ages (Opera skozi stoletja), 1976. Contbr. to num. profl. jrnls. Address: Korytkova 5, 61000 Ljubljana, Yugoslavia.

SIVO, Josef, b. Arad, Rumania. Violinist. Educ: studied w. Enescu & Odnoposff; Grad., Franz Liszt Acad., Budapest. Career: Prof , Vienna Coll. of Music, 1964-; Soloist, fests. in Vienna, Salzburg & Taormina; has app. thru'out world. Hons: Corss of Sci. & Culture, Austria, 1970; prizes at int. competitions in Budapest, Prague, Genoa, Warsaw & Geneva. Hobby: Numismatics. Address: Jagdschlossjasse 41, 1130 Austria.

SIXTA, Jozef, b. 12 May 1940, Jicin, Czechoslovakia. Lecturer; Composer. Educ: Conserv., Bratislava; High Schl. of Music, Bratislava; Studied w. Prof. A Moyzes, O Messiaen, A Jolivet. Debut: Bratislava, 1960. Career: Lectr. of Comp., High Schl. of Music, Bratislava. Comps. incl: Recitativo for Vilin, 1974. Recordings: Asynchronia; Solo for Piano; Octeto: Publs: Noneto (score). Mbr. Union of Slovak Comps.; Hons: Prague Spring Festival, 1966; Tribune UNESCO Paris, 1970. Address: 68 Riazanska, 80100 Bratislava, Czech.

SJÖGREN, Albert Johannes Richard, b. 26 Oct. 1934, Lund, Sweden. Headmaster. Educ: High Organist exam., High Precentor exam., Music Tchr. exam., Royal Music High Schl., Stockholm; Comp. studies w. Lars Erik Larsson, Karl-Birger Blomdahl. m. Anna Björkquist, 3 c. Career: Former cathedral organist: Radio & TV apps. as Cond. & Organist; Headmaster, Geijerskolan (People's High Schl. of Music). Comps: Missa Brevis for choir, Descants; Songs for one voice & organ; other music for choir, organ, flutes, etc. Recordings: The Eternal Song of the Church (Cond.). Contbr. to: Svenskt Gudstjänstliv. Mbrships: Pres., Coun. of Scandinavian Ch. Music; Pres., Swedish Ch. Music, etc. Address: Geijerskolan, Ransäter, 684 00 Munkfors, Sweden.

SJÖSTEDT, Sten Johan Kristian, b. 26 Apr. 1945, Malmö, Sweden. Operatic Tenor. Educ: Acad. of Music, Milamö, Opera Schl., Malmö; Mozarteum, Salzburg, Austria. m. Helen Mary Meyer, 1d. Debut: as Rodolfo (La Bohéme), Trier, German Fed. Repub., 1969. Career: Malmö Stadsteatr, 1969; Royal Opera, Stockholm, 1973-; guest apps. in UK, Ireland, Norway, Denmark; roles incl. Faust, Manrico, Don José, Cavaradossi, Turiddu, Nemorini, Max, Gustavus III; num. apps. on Swedish TV & radio. sev. recordings. Hons: Christine Nilsson Scholarship (twice); 1st place, Jussi Bjorling Memorial Fund. Mgmt: Svensk Konsertdirektion AB, Göteborg, Sweden. Address: Helgoagsgatan 26, 41512 Göteborg, Sweden.

SJÖSTRÖM, Nils Gunnar, b. 4 July 1928, Järvsö, Sweden. Pianist; Director. Educ: MA, Uppsala Univ.; State Coll. Music,

Stockholm. m. Angelika Sjöström, 3 children. Debut: Stockholm, 1952. Career: Regular apps., Sweden, 1952-; Concerts, German Fed. Repub., Austria, France, Scandinavia; Dir., State Coll. Music, Gothenburg. Recordings: Works by Swedish comp., Hilding Hallnas (w. other musicians & as soloist), EMI. Mbr. Royal Swedish Acad. Music, 1970-. Address: Krokslatts Parkgata 64, S43138 Molndal, Sweden.

SKABRADA, Jaroslav, b. 8 Jan. 1919, Horusany-Plzenjih, Czechoslovakia. Trumpet Player; Composer. Educ: Prague Conserv. m. Terezie Skabradova, 3 d. Career: Mbr., Ostrava Theatre Orch., 1942-45; currently Mbr., Nat. Theatre Orch., Prague. Comps. (publd. & recorded) incl: Janicka tanci; Teruska; Polka z Presticka; Zlatá muzika; Stoletá; Pisnicky z krabicky; Horusanská Polka; Prestický pochod; Pozdrav Muzikantum; Randostne Sуledáni. Contbr. to profl. publs. Mbr., Union for the Protection of Authors (OSA). Hons: Title, Vzorný pracovník, 1959; 3 Competition Prizes & 3 Commendtions, 1963. Hobbies: Orchestral Conducting; Travelling. Address: Pstrossova 9, 110 00 Prague 1, Czechoslovakia.

SKAGGS, Hazel, b. 26 Aug. 1924, Boston, Mass., USA. Pianist; Composer; Author; Music Psychologist; Group Piano Specialist; Teacher. Educ: BA, Fairleigh Dickinson Univ.; MA, ibid; Grad., NE Conserv. of Music; Artist Dip., Am. Coll. of Musicians; Univ. of Colo.; Univ. of Wis.; Univ. of Minn.; studied w. Ondricek, Dr. Clarence Adler. m. M Paul Skaggs. Career: Tchr., Boston, Catskills, NJ; toured as Adjudicator, NGPT, in USA; Concert, Radio Perfs. as Comp.-Pianist. Comps. incl: Little Girl From Mars; num. Recital Piano Pieces, Summy-Birchard, Schroeder & Gunther, C Fisher, Witmark, J Fischer, Boston Music Co., Century Music. Author, Thumbs Under, technic book. Contbr. to: Music Jrnl.; Piano Quarterly; The Piano Tchr.; Clavier; Etude; Keyboard Jr. Mbrships: Nat. Chmn.; Nat. Compl. Test, NGPT, 1964-; Pres., Piano Tchrs. Congress, NYC, 1975. NJ Music Tchrs.; State VP, ibid, 1963-65; Comps. Forum. NYC; Chmn., ibid, 1968-73; Nat. Fedn. of Music Clubs; State Chmn. of Comps. ibid, 1963-66; ASCAP. Hobby: Folk Dancing. Address: 29 Wayne Ave., River Edge, NJ 07661, USA. 5, 27.

SKEI, Allen Bennet, b. 5 Nov. 1935, Fargo, ND, USA. Musicologist; Music Critic; Clarinettist. Educ: BA, St. Olaf Coll., 1957; MMus, Univ. of Mich., 1959; PhD, ibid, 1965. Nancy Cousins, 1 d., 1s. Career incl: Assoc. Prof., Prof., Calif. State Univ., Fresno; Instructor, Gustavus Adolphus Coll., Iшstructor, Lewis & Clark Coll.; Asst. Prof., Assoc. Prof., Georgia Coll.; Music Critic, The Fresno Bee. Publs: Ed., Jacob Handl, The Moralia of 1596, 1970; Ed., Stefano Rosetti, Sacrae Cantiones, 1973, First Book of 4 Voice Madrigals, 1976 (both in Recent Researches in the Music of the Renaissance). Contbr. to: Musical Quarterly; Music Review; Notes; Jrnl. of Rsch. in Music Educ. Mbrships: Am. Musicological Soc.; Music Lib. Assn.; Music Critics Assn. Hobbies: Photography; Cycling. Address: 3370 W Oswego, Fresno, CA 93711, USA.

SKERIS, Robert A, b. 11 May 1935, Sheboygan, Wis., USA. Hymnologist; Institute Director. Educ: ordained RC priest, 1961; Dr.theol., Bonn. Career: Dir., Hymnology Sect., Int. Inst. for hymnologica & ethnomusicol. studies, Maria Laach. Publ: Chroma theou, On the Orgins & Theological Interpretation of the Musical Imagery used by the ecclesiastical writers of the first centuries, with special reference to the image of Orpheus, 1976. Contbr. to: Sacred Music; Musicae Sacrae Ministerium; Musices aptatio; Musica Sacro CVO; Homiletic & Pastoral Review, etc. Mbrships: Counsellor, Consociatio Internationalis Musicae Sacrae, Rome; Bd. of Dirs., Ch. Music Assn. of Am.; Pres., Catholic Ch. Music Assn; Am. Musicol. Soc.; Music Libs. Assn., etc. Hobby: Constructing Unreal Conditional Sentences. Address: Haus der Kirchenmusik, 5471 Maria Laach, German Fed. Repub.

SKIBA, John Christopher, ACTL b. 11 Aug. 1949, Hillingdon, Middx., UK. Composer; Pianist. Educ: composition w. Edmund Rubbra, Patric Stanford (at GSM) & Adrian Cruft; piano & theory w. David Paul Martin & Otto Karolyi, Watford Schl. of Music; ATCL (Piano perfs. dip.) Comps. incl: Timeless (a journey through the universe), words & music (piano); Educational peices for piano; Contrasts, 4 pieces for high voices; Sonata No. 1 for piano; Wavelenghts for Light for orch.; Hymns for childrens voices & piano; Songs to texts by E E Cummings, voice & piano. Contbr. to: Comp. Mag. Mbr., Comps. Guild of GB. Recip. 1st Prize, Comp., Brent Music Fest., 1973. Hobbies: Golf; Hi-Fi; Reading. Address: 29 The Ave., Ickenham nr. Uxbridge, Middx. UB10 8NR, UK.

SKIDMORE, William, R b. 7 Jan. 1941, Bay City, Mich., USA. Cellist. Educ: BMus, MMus, Univ. of III. m. Dorothy Louise Hubbard, 2 s. Career: Fac. Mbr., Univ. of Md., 1964-74; apps. w. Md. Univ. Trio, Nat. Gall. of Art, Kennedy Ctr., Phillips

Collect., **Eastern** US; solo apps. Ctrl. & S. Am. tour, Nat. Gall. of Art; concerto w. Nat. Gall. of Art Orch.; Cellist, Balt. Symph. Orch., 1974-77; Assoc. Prof. of Cello, WV Univ.; Cellist, Am. Arts Trio & Str. Quartet; Prin. Cellist, WV Symphonette; TV apps. Recordings: Book of Imaginary Beings - R Paris; Clarinet Quintet -R Evett. Mbrships: Am. String Tchrs. Assn.; Am. Fedn. of Musicians. Hobbies: Golf. Address: 331 Bakers Ridge Rd., Morgantown, WV 26505, USA.

SKINNER, Bill (William Alexander Peter) · see **ARMSTRONG, David**

SKINNER, John York, b. 5 March 1949, York, UK. Countertenor. Educ: BMus, London Univ., 1970; York Minster Choir Schl.; LRAM. m. Janet Budden, 1 d. Debut: Britten's Midsummer Night's Dream, Kassel, W Germany, 1974. Career: Concerts, broadcasting & major European Fests.; Scottish Opera, English Music Theatre, Handel Opera Soc., Royal Opera, Covent Garden, Fest. Ottawa; Prof., RCM. num. recordings. Hobbies: Food; Looking at Mountains; Reading. Mgmt: Music Int. Address: 2 Chadwich Court, London Ell, UK.

SKJAER, Henry, b. 5 July 1899, Copenhagen, Denmark. Opera Singer (baritone). Educ: BA, Univ. of Copenhagen; The Royal Danish Conserv.; The Royal Theâtre Opera Acad.; pvte. studies Copenhagen & Paris. m. Ida Levy, 2 c. Debut: The Royal Theatre and Opera House, 1924. Career: The Royal Theatre, Copenhagen, 1930-73, approx. 100 parts, incl. Rigoletto, Scarpia (Tosca), Escamillo (Carmen), Jago (Othello), Count Almaviva (Le Nozze di Figaro), Marcel (La Boheme), Renato (Un Ballo in Maschera), Ford (Falstaff), Crown (Porgy & Bess); Sev. apps, radio, TV, Danish films. Recordings: Bizet - Les Pecheurs des Perles, Verdi - La forza del destino; Danish Songs. Mbrships: Danish Musicians Assn. (Pres., 1965-78, Hon. Mbr., 1978); Danish Actors Soc.; Students Choral Soc., 1916-. Hons: Cross of Dannebrog, Danish Knight, 1941, (1st grade 1955); Royal Court Singer, 1947; Commander of the Thailand Crown, 1960. Address: Pilealle 23A5, 2000 Copenhagen F, Denmark.

SKOLD, Bengt-Göran, b. 10 May 1936, Götenborg, Sweden. Composer; Organist. Educ: Swedish undergrad, examination, 1957; studies at Royal Conserv. of Music, Stockholm, & Staatliche Hochschule für Musik, Stuttgart, Germany. m. Britt Sköld. Career: Organist, St. Olai Ch., Norrköping; Concerts as Organist, Cembalist & Cond., Sweden & abroad; var. radio apps. Compositions incl: Missa Nova for Choir & Beat Grp., 1967; Mässa II, 1969; Fancies towards C (organ), 1970; Agnus Dei (organ), 1971; The Way Back (orch.), 1971; Passion Music for Choir, Children's Choir, Soloist & Orch., 1972; Suite an Max Reger (commissioined for Max Reger Fest., Bonn), 1973; Diaphony for 2 Organists 1973. Triptyk for soprano orch., 1975; Dig Helge Ande for Organ, 1975; Infro & toccata for organ, 1975; Christmas Oratorio, 1975-78; Choral Goole, Diskanthörrn, 1978; Other works for orch., piano, cembalo & organ. Address: Batmansgatan 34,60365 Norrkiping, Sweden.

SKOLOVSKY, Zadel, b. 17 July 1926, Vancouver, BC, Canada. Concert Pianist. Educ: Grad., Curtis Inst., Phila. in Piano & Cond., studied Piano w. Leopold Godowsky & Isabelle Vengerova, Cond. w. Fritz Reiner & Pierre Monteux. Debut: NY Town Hall (as winner of the Walter W Naumburg Acad). Career: Appeared in Recital & as Soloist w. most maj. orchs. in USA, Canada, UK, France, Holland, Belgium, Scandinavia, Italy, Portugal, Mex., S. Africa & Israel. Recordings: Milhaud Fourth Piano Concerto w. comp. cond. French Nat. Orch. (Concerto dedicted to Zadel Skolovsky); Four Piano Sonata, Berg, Hindemith No. 2, Bartok, Scriahin No. 4, all for Columbia Records. Also recorded for Philips records. Mbr. Lotus Club, NYC. Hons: Walter W Naumberg Award, 1939; Nat. Music League, 1941; Nat. Fed. of Music Clubs, 1942; Robin Hood Dell Young Am. Artists Award. Hobbies: Tennis; Chess; Bridge; Art. Mgmt: Wilfrid Van Wyck, London. Address: 240 E 79th St., NY, NY 10021, USA. 2, 30.

SKOMAL, Margaret (Peggy) Elaine, b. 19 Aug. 1958, San Jose, Calif., USA. Harpist; Pianist; Singer. Educ: Univ. Redlands 4 yrs.; var. pvte. tutors; Dip. Merit, Calif. Music Tchrs. Assn. Debut: Redlands Bowl, Calif., May 1975. Career: Perf. w. harp, Miss Teenage Am. Pageant, 1975; Guest Artist Community Chest, Redlands, 1975; 1st chair harpist, HS Concert Orch. & 2nd chair harpist, World Youth Symph. ·Orch., var. Nat. Music Camp, Interlochen, Mich.; Mbr., Univ. Redlands Orch. & Univ. Redlands Harp Ensemble. Contbr. to: Am. Harp Jrnl. Mbr., Am. Harp Soc. Hons. Redlands Bowl Young Artist Award Winner, 1975; Talent Winner, Calif. Jr. Miss Pageant, 1976. Hobbies incl: Dancing; Drama. Address:1831 Valle Vista Dr., Redlands, CA 92373, USA.

SKORZENY, Fritz, b. 1900, Vienna, Austria. Composer; Critic; Violinist. Educ: Vienna Coll. of Music. m. Maria von Keszthely. Comps. incl: Concerto for oboe & orch.; Drei Stucke for orch.; Double Concerto for violin, piano & orch.; Menagerie for chorus & orch.; Enin Lebensfruhling for soprano & orch.; 3 str. quartets; 2 Suites for violin, viola & bass; Duo for 2 violin & viola; var. other works for small ensembles; Viola Sonata; about 70 Lieder; piano music; Sonatas for violin & piano. Hons: Theodor Korner Prize, 1961; Austrian State Prize, 1955. Hobbies: Painting; Studyinig Nature. Address: Obkirchergasse 31, Vienna 19, Austria.

SKRAM, Knut, b. 18 Dec. 1937. Hjörundford, Sunnmöre, Norway. Opera Singer (Baritone). Educ: BArch., 1963, also vocal & musical studies, Mont. State Univ., Bozeman, USA; studied w. Prof. Paul Lohmann, Wiesbaden, & Maestro Luigi Ricci, Rome, 1963-65, Prof. Kristian Riis, Copenhagen. m. Hanne Skram, 1 s., 1 d. Debut: Oslo, 1964. Career: w. Norwegian Opera, Oslo, 1964-, singing 37 leading roles; Glyndebourne Fest. Opera, 7 seasons, 1969-, inclng. app. as Figaro, Southern TV, 1973; Cosi fantutte, Franch TV, 1977; Aix-en-Provence Fest., 1977, '80, '81; Spoleto Fest., Italy, 1978; concert apps, in many countries; regular broadcasts on radio & TV in Scandinavia. Recordings: Knut Skram synger Norske. Romanser; Songs by Chr. Sinding; Oll Sparre Olsen-7 Krokann songs; Bach cantata 82, Ich habe genug. Mbrships: VP, Norsk Operasangerforbund. Recip. var. prizes. Hobbies incl: Skiing. Mgmt: Dido Senger, The Garden, 103 Randolph Ave., London, W9 1DL, UK. Address: Haakon Tveters vei 29, Oslo 6, Norway.

SKŘEPEK, Roman, b. 9 April 193 1, Bratislava, Czechoslovakia. Professor. Educ: Studied Cond. w. Prof. K Schimpl. Comp. w. Prof. Jurovský, Conserv., Bratislava; studied Musicol., Univ., ibid; studied Cond. w. Prof. L Rajter, Music Acad., ibid. m. Sidonia Kmetová-Skrepková, 1s., 1d. Career: w. State Opera, Kosice, 1957-, as Master of Chorus, Cond. & Dramatic; Cond. Ensemble Sluk, Bratislava; Fndr., Chmbr. Orch. of Kosice, num. Concerts w. this & other Orchs.; recordings for Radio Kosice & TV. Compositions: Scenic Music for TV & Theatre; works for Orch.; Choral comps. Contbr. to num. jrnls. inclng. Hudbeni Rozhledy, Hudobný Zivot, Vecer, Páca, Východoslovenské Noviny, Musica, Bulletins of Theatre. Address: Sokolovska 1/VII, 040 01 Kosice, Czech.

SKRIPTSCHENKO, Clara, b. 21 Oct. 1923, Priluky, Ukraine. Concert Pianist; Teacher; Examiner; Adjudicator. Educ: Akademie der Tonkunst, Munich, W Germany; Reife Zeugnis, 1948; Master Class Dip., 1950. m. Philip Harrison. Career: Re. soloist Int. Symph. Orch., Munich & Bundesbahn Orch.; Many apps. w. Bavarian Broadcasting Corp.; Solo recitals of chmbr. music in Germany & Aust.; Apps. for Aust. Broadcasting Commission eg. Sydney Tonight, Startime, Music for Millions, The Commonwealth Bank Hour of Music, Your Home w. Del Cartwright. Recording: Piano Premier, TV Request Prog.; Brahms Handel Variations; (Festival Records). Mbrships: MTA, NSW Aust., Coun. Mbr. Hobbies: Philosophy; Reading; Fashion. Address: 8 Banksia Park Rd., Katoomba, NSW 2780, Aust.

SKROBELA, Katherine Creelman, b. 18 Jan. 1941, NYC, USA. Music Librarian; Teacher of Recorder. Educ: AB, Vassar Coll.; MSLS, Columbia Univ. Schl. of Lib. Serv.; NY Univ.; Brooklyn Coll.; Tchr.'s Cert., Am. Recorder Soc. m. Paul John Skrobela. Career: Music Cataloger, Brooklyn Coll., NY, 1964-71; Music Libn., Middlebury Coll., Vt., 1971-; Dir., St. Stephen's Motet Choir, Middlebury; Tchr., Am. Recorder Soc. workshops in erly music. Contbr. to: Ed., Music Cataloging Bulletin, 1970-74; Mbrships. incl: Cataloging Coun., Music Lib Assn.; Music Lib.Assn. rep. to Am. Lib. Assn.; Catalog Code Revision Committee; Am. Recorddr Soc. Hobbies: Engl. & Scottish country dancing; Gardening. Address: Hamilton House, Bridport, TV 05734, USA.

SKROWACZEWSKI, Stanislaw, b. 3 Oct. 1923, Lwow, Poland. Composer; Conductor. Career: Music Dir. & Cond., Katowice Phil. Orch. & Warsaw Nat. Orch., 1969-59; Music Dir. of Minn. Orch., 1960-. Recordings on Mercury; Philips; EMI; Angel. Hons: President's Medal for outstanding cultural contributions from the College of St. Benedict, St. Joseph, Minn., 1974; DMus, HS, Macalester Coll., St. Paul, Minn., 1973; DMus HS, Hamline Univ., St. Paul, Minn.; Int. Cond. Competitions, 1956. Address: Minnesota Orch., Orchestra Hall, 1111 Nicollet Mall, Minneapolis, MN 55403, USA.

SKUHROVA, Irma, b. 16 Mar. 1925, Zeliezovce, Czech. Professor of Oran. Educ: Dips., piano, 1947, organ, 1950, Conserv. in Bratislava; Organ Dip., Vysoka skola muzickych umeni Bratislava, 1954. Debut: Bach Recital, Bratislava, 1955. Career: concerts, Czech., German Dem. Repub., USSR; Fest. of Organ Music; recitals for TV Brasilava; Prov., Conserv. in

Bratislava. Mbrships: Union of Slovak Comps.; New Bach Soc. Hons: 1st Prize, Brno, 1951, 2nd Prize, Prague, 1952, Czech. Concours of Organists. Hobbies: Music; Tourism. Mgmt: Slovkoncert, Leningradska 5, 800 00 Bratislava, Czech. Address: Schiffelova 24, 801 00 Bratislava, Czechoslovakia.

SKWARA, Zdziskaw Feliks, b. 30 Apr. 1920, Warsaw, Poland, Singer. Educ: MA; Grad, High Schl. of Music, Warsaw, 1953. m. Halina Zalichowska, 1 d. Debut: 18 May 1941. Career incls: Apps. at Polish Festivals of Classical Music, 1950; Solo Singer, Chmbr. Opera of Nat. Phil., Polish Symph. Orchs., 1955-; Polish radio; Concerts in E Germany & apps. on TV & radio; Mgr. & Organiser of Canor Anticus specializing in Middle Age & Renaissance Music, 1970-; Tchr., Secondary Schl. of Music, Warsaw. Recordings for Polish radio; Film on old music for Polish TV; Record in series Musica Antiqua Polonica. Mbr. Assn. of Polish Musicians. Hobbies: Hist. of Art; Archaeol.; Painting. Address: 01-710 Warsaw, Włościańska 10/21, Poland.

SKWIERAWSKI, Edward R, b. Milwaukee, Wis., USA. Violinist; Teacher; Conductor. Educ: BS, Univ. of Wis., Milwaukee; MMus, Northwestrn Univ., Evanston, Ill.; Doctoral sutdy, Ind. Univ., Bloomington; Studied cond. w. Jerzy Bojanowski, Ernst Hoffman, Pierre Monteux. Career: Perfs. w. TriCity Symph., Milwaukee Symph., Duluth Symph., Duluth Opera; Taught at St. Ambrose Coll., Davenport, Iowa., at St. Leo, Fla., & in Ill., Wis., Minn.; Cond. opera & operetta at St. Leo w. Tampa Opera & Symph. Comps: Symph. in C Major; Symph. in C Minor; 2 Violin Sonatas (1 recorded); 2 Piano Sonatas; Fugue for Strings (recorded); Sev. choir pieces. Mbrships: MENC; Duluth Musicians Assn.; Am. Str. Tchrs. Assn.; Suzuki Assn. of Fine Ams.

SKYLLSTAD, Kjell Müller, b. 30 June 1928, Hammerfest, Norway. Asistant Professor of Music. Educ: BA, Andrew Univ., 1950; MA, Walla Walla Coll., 1952; Cand. philol., Oslo Univ., 1960; MA, Musicol., ibid., 1960; Ferienkurse für Neue Musik, Darmstadt, Germany. Career: Radio presentations of historic & avant garde music inclng. series on Monteverdi; Asst. Prof. of Music, Inst. of Musicol., Oslo Univ. Comps: Mixed media works inclng. Abstraction I for Norwegian TV, 1967. Contbr. to var. profl. publs. inclng: Music Ed., Familieboken, 1972-75; Co-Ed., Greig Gesamtausgabe, 1972-. Mbrships: incl: Chmn., Norweigian Musicol. Assn., 1972-75. Hobby: Historic instruments. Address: Sarbuvollveien 40 b, Hovik, Norway. 24.

SKYTTEGAARD, Jørgen, b. 22 July 1940, Odense, Denmark. Oboist. Educ: Royal Acad. of Music, Copenhagen; Studies in Paris & Rome. m., 2 c. Career incls: Apps., Danish Radio & TV; Mbr., Quintet 74; Solo oboe, Aalborg City Orch. Recordings; Chmbr. music & oboe concertos. Address: Koervangs Alle 9, 9000 Aalborg, Denmark.

SLACK, Roy, b. 1912, Cudworth, UK. Music Adviser; Educationalist; Organist. Educ: B Mus (Dunelm), City of Sheffield Coll. of Educ. m. Mary Lofthouse Staniforth, 1 s., 2 d. Career: Organist & Choirmaster, Christ Ch., Cockfosters, 1948-63; Lectr. in Music, Trent Park Coll. of Educ., 1947-49; Advsr. in Music Co. of Middx., 1947-65; Advsr., London Boroughs of Enfield & Haringey, 1965-74; currently Ed., EMI Music Pub. Ltd. Comps. incl: Anthems; Brass band works; schl. music items. Mbrships: Life VP, Schls. Music Assn.; ISM; Int. Soc. for Music in Educ. Address:12 Norrys Rd., Barnet, Herts, EN4 9JX, UK.

SLADE, Heather Anne, b. 9 Mar. 1947, Claughton, Birkenhead, UK. Harpischordist; Accompanist. Educ: BMus., Univ. of Liverpool; Study of piano w. Gordon Green, Accompaniment w. Clifton Helliwell, RMCM; ARCM (performer); ARMCM (performer accompaniment); ARMCM (teacher); GRSM (Manchester); Study of harpsichord w. Huguette Dreyfus, Paris. m. E Barry Lipkin, 2 s. Debut: Age 12. Career: Num. recitals, UK, France; Concert work incls. concerto & continio; Recital, Purcell Room, London 1974; Radio & TV apps. Mbrships: ISM; Musicians Union; Comm. Mbr., Old Students Assn., Royal Northern Coll. of Music. Hons incl: Nat. Harpsichord Competition, 1974; Arts Council award, 1976. Hobbies: Reading; Travel; Swimming; Bridge. Address: Brackenhoe, 20 Clarendon Rd, Sale, Cheshire, UK.

SLATFORD, Rodney Gerald Yorke, b. 18 July 1944, Cuffley, Herts., UK. Double Bassist; Music Publisher. Educ: Bishops Stortford Coll.; RCM. Debut: Soloist, Purcell Room, London, 1969. Career: presently Co-Prin. Double Bass, English Chmbr. Orch., & Prof., RCM; Prin., English Sinfonia, 1966-74; Mbr. Nash Ensemble, 1966-; Fndr., Managing Dir., Yorke Ed., 1969-; num. Chmbr. Music Perfs., London; num. Lecture-Recitals, UK; Soloist, Perfs. on BBC Radio, TV; World recital

tour, 1975; Fndr. Isle of Man Int. Double Bass Competition & Workshop, 1978. Publs: Eds. of works by Rossni, Elgar, Climadro, Giovannini, Michael Haydn, Dittersforf, Lutyens, Berkeley, Machonchy paper on Dragonetti, 1970. Recordings: Music for Double Bass (HMV); Trout Quintet w. Nash Ensemble. Contbr. to: Grove's Dictionary of Music & Musicians; num. Profl. Mags. Mbrships: Royal Soc. of Musicians; Royal Musical Assn. Hobbies: Cooking; Swimming; Physical Training; Gardening. Address: 31 Thornhill Sq., London N1 1BQ, UK. 3.

SLATIN-LEWIS, Sonia, b. 12 Oct. 1910,NYC, USA. Pianist; Musicologist; Music Theorist; Professor of Music. Educ: Damrosch Inst. of Music; Juilliard Grad. Schl. of Music; BS, MA, PhD, Columbia Univ. m. Joseph Lewis. Career: Solo recitals, broadcasts, USA & Can.; Soloist w. CBC Symph. Orch. broadcasts, Montreal, PQ, Can.; Accomp., concert stage & radio broadcasts; Mbr. of Trio, concerts & broadcasts; on music fac., Columbia Univ., 14 yrs.; currently Prof., Bklyn. Coll., CUNY (5 yrs. to date). Contbr. to: Musical Quarterly; Music & Man; Ency. of Music in Can. Mbrships: Phi Beta Kappa; Am. Musicol. Soc.; NY State Music Theory Assn.; Ethno-Musicol. Soc. Recip. acad. hons. Hobbies incl: Nature study; Horseback riding. Address: 2 Consul Rd., Livingston, NJ 07037, USA.

SLATKIN, Leonard, Conductor, Educator. Educ: sutdied w. father, Felix Slatkin, w. Walter Susskind, Aspen, Colo., & Jean Morel, Juilliard Schl. of Music. Debut: w. Youth Symph. Orch. of NY, Carnegie Hall. Career: formed St. Louis Symph. Youth Orch.; Asst. Cond-Assoc. Cond., St. Louis Symph. Orch., 1968-; Tchr., Wash. Univ.; Cond., weekly radio show. Address: 333 W Broadway, Louisville, KY 40202, USA.

SLATTERY, Thomas Carl, b. 31 July 1935, LaCrosse, Wis., USA. Conductor; Clarinettist; Author; Professor. Educ: BM, Eastman Schl. of Music, Rochester Univ.; MA, PhD, Univ. of Iowa. m. Claire L Durr, 2 s. Career: Clarinettist, Eastman Symphonic Wind Ensemble, 7th Army Symph., SE Iowa Symph., Cedar Rapids Municipal Band & Symph. Orch.; Cond., Cedar Rapids Youth Orch., Coe Coll. Band/Orch.; Prof. of Chmn., Dept. of Music, Coe Coll. Publs: The Wind Music of Percy Grainger, 1967; Percy A Grainger - The Inverterate Innovator, 1974. Contbr. to jrnls. & World Book Ency. Mbrships: Past Pres., Iowa Bandmasters Assn.; MENC; Am. Fedn. of Musicians. Hons: Grant, Nat. Fndn. of the Arts of Humanities, 1968. Hobbies: Chss; Piloting; Tennis. Address: 650 30th St. Dr. SE, Cedar Rapids, IA, USA. 8.

SLAVICKÝ, Klement, b. 22 Sept. 1910, Tovacov, Czechsloualkia. Composer; Teacher. Educ: Prague Conservy., 1927-31; Master Classes, 1931-33. m. Vlasta Voborská. Career: Cond. & Musical Dir., Radio Prague, 1936-51; Comp. & Tchr. of Comp., 1951-. Comps. incl: (orchl.) Symfoniettas 1-3, 1940, 62, 72; Moravian Dance, Phantasies (ballet), 1951; Variations Rhapsodic, 1953; (chmbr. works) Suite for Oboe & Piano, 1960; Trialog, 1966; Striaguartel No 2, 1972; Friendship Sonata, 1974; Musica per Tromba & Pianoforte, 1976; 2 Organ works; num. piano pieces, solo & choral songs; Psalmi per coro misto, Soli et Organo, 1970. Mbr., Czech Composers Soc. Hons: Czechoslovak Critics' Prize, 1966; Guild of Czechoslovak Comps. Prize, 1966; Artist of Merit, 1967; Nat. Prize, 1968. Address: Lucemburská 1, 130 00 Prague 3- Vinohrady, Czech.

SLAWINSKI, Adam, b. 27 Nov. 1935, Szamocin, Poland. Composer. Educ: Univ. of Warsaw. m. Krystyna Kisielewska. Debut: Warsaw, 1963. Career: TV Series Singing Letters, 1963-69; Dpty. Dir., Music Dept., Polish Radio, 1974-75. Comps: jazz opera Of The Deepest Dye; Singing Letters (recorded); Ballade for b percussionists (recorded); var. Film Scores, Stage Music, Musicals. Contbr. to: Jazz; Ruch Muzyczny. Mbrships: Assn. of Polish Comps.; Bd., ZAIKS. Hons: 1st & 2nd Prize, Polish Song Fest., Opole, 1966; 1st Prize, Polish Song Fest., Opole, 1967; 1st Prize, Amber Nightingale, Int. Song Fest., Sopot, 1967. Address: 20 M 1514 Walicow, 00-851 Warsaw, Poland.

SLAYDEN, Anne, b. 9 Apr. 1945, Yonkers, NY, USA. French Horn; Antique Natural Horn. Educ: BA, SUNY, Buffalo. Deubt: Recitals at Hamilton Grange, NYC & Morris Jumal Mansion, NYC, 1975. Career: Prin. Horn, Birmingham Symph., Ala., 1967-70; Currently Freelancing, NYC; Antique Natural Horn w. Fed. Music Soc. on TV Feature, 1975. Recordins: Music of the Federal Era. Contbr. to Horn Call, Jrnl. of Int. Horn Soc. Mbrships: Int. Horn Soc.; Fed. Music Soc. (Natural Instrument Organisation). Hobby: Beer & Ale Making. Address: 19 Warren St., NY, NY 10007, USA.

ŠLECHTA, Milan, b. 18 Oct. 1923, Prague, Czechoslovakia. Organist; Professor of Organ. Educ: Nat. Conserv. of Music, Prague, 1942-47; Acad. of Musical Arts, ibid., 1947-51.

Debut: Prague, 1946. Career: Extensive tours throughout Europe, 1956-; Broadcasts in major European cities; TV apps., Prague, 1959, 75, Florence, 1974; Prof., Acad. Musical Arts, 1964-. Repertoire incls. complete organ works of Bach, Mozart & Franck. Recordings incl: works by Mozart, Handel, Franck & Czech comps. Publs: History of Organ & Organ Music, 1967. Contbr. to jrnls. Mbr., Union of Czech Comps. & Concert Artists. Hons: Gold Medal, Burgo-master of Florence, for 5 recitals, 1974. Hobby: Motor Touring. Mgmt: Pragokoncert, Maltézské nám. 1, Prague 1 111 13. Address: Pod Bastami 5, 160 00 Prague 6, Czechoslovakia.

SLEDZINSKI, Stefan, b. 8 Aug. 1897, Zytomierz, USSR. Conductor; Musicologist. Educ: Dip., State Conserv., Warsaw, Poland, 1927; PhD, Univ. Cracow, 1932. m. Jadwiga Sledzinska, 1 child. Debut: w. Phil. Warsaw, 1925. Career: Prof., HS Music, Warsaw, 1924-. Publs. incl: Muzyka Polska, 1968, translated into Japanese, 1975; Mala Encyklopedia Muzyki (ed.), 1969; Orkiestra deta, 1975. Contbr. to: Ruch Muzyczny; Muzyka. Mbrships: Hon. Mbr., Past Chmn., Polish Composers Assn.; Int. Music Coun., Polish Sect., Chmn., & Mbr., JSME. Hons: Prize, Polish Composers Assn., 1974; Prize, Min. Arts, 1975, '76. Hobbies: Canoeing; Fishing. Address: Maltézska 1, Apt. 75, 02761 Warsaw, Poland.

SLEE, Raymond, b. 4 July 1923, Chingford, Essex, UK. Principal Lectures in Music. Educ: MA, St. Catharine's Coll., Cambridge; ARCM; ARCO. m. Beryl Evington, 1 s., 1 d. Career: Asst. Dir. of Music, Bradfield Coll., Berks., 1950-55; Dir. of Music, King's Schl., Rochester, 1955-58; Dir. of Music, Wycliffe Coll., Stonehouse, Glas., 1958-65; Hd. of Music Dept., Hockreill Coll., Bishop's Stortford, Herts., 1965-78. Publications; J S Bach Three-part Inventions, arranged for organ, 1967. Contbr. of articles on the schl. orch. to Piano Tchr. Mbrships: ISM; ATCDE. Hobbies: Reading Listening to Music; Playing Organ & Piano; Conducting. Address: Elmcott, 32 Apton Rd., Bishops Stratford, Herts. CM23 3SN, UK.

SLENCZYNSKA, Ruth, b. 1925, Sacramento, Calif., USA. Concert Painist; Writer. Educ: Univ. of Calif., Berkeley; studied w. Egon Petri, Artur Schnabel, Alfred Corto, Sergei Rachmaninoff & Nadia Boulanger. Career: Prof. of Music, Coll. of Our Lady of Mercy, Burlingame, Calif., 1948-52, San Fran. Acad. of Music, 1950-52. Compositions: small piano works; Candenzas for Beethoven Piano Concertos 1 & 3, Ed., 1& Scarlatti Sonatas. Publs: Forbidden Childhood; Music at Your Fingertips. Hobbies: Writing; Entertaining; Cooking; Walking. Address: 1270 Fifth Ave., New York., NY, USA. 3.

SLENDZINSKA, Julitta, b. 31 July 1927, Wilna, USSR. Pianist; Harpsichordist; Teacher. Educ: MA, Piano, State Conserv., Warsaw, Poland; Piano Virtuoso Dip., ibid., 1958; studied w. Harry Neuhaus, Moscow Conserv., USSR; Studied Harpsichord w. M Trombini-Kazuro; Dip. of Merit, Harpsichord Mastercourse, Acad. Chigiana, Siena, Italy, 1974. div. Debut: 1945. Career: Piano & Harpsichord recitals; Concert tours w. orch. throughout Europe, & in China, Cuba & Korea; num. TV & radio apps. Compositions: Etudes de Concert recorded for Polish radio. Recordings: Chopin piano works; Harpsichord recordings. Mbr., Union of Polish Musicians. Hons: Distinction, Int. Chopin Competition, Warsaw, 1949. Address: ul. Walowa 8 m. 83, 00-211 Warsaw, Poland.

SLIVKA, Meyer, b. 8 Apr. 1923, Mishawaka, Ind., USA. Timpanist; Percussionist (Jazz Trap Drums). Educ: BA, San Francisco State Coll., 1952; Cello, San Francisco Conserv. of Music; Zein harmony, San Francisco State Coll. m. Enid Miller, 5 children. Career incls: Apps. w. San Francisco Symph. Orch.; San Francisco Opera Co.; Little Orch. of San Francisco; Kqed Public TV; Ballet Russe de Monte Carlo; Casals Festival, Puerto Rico; Seattle Symph. Orch.; Seattle Opera Co.; Documentary TV Music. Recordings incl: Venice, Morton Gould, Seattle Symph. Mbrships: Am. Fedn. of Musicians, locals 6, 802, 76. Hobbies: Classic Guitar Maker, experimenting w. electronic music systems. Address: 2343 33rd Ave. S, Seattle, WA 98144, USA.

SLOAN, David W, b. 16 June 1937, Longview, Tex., USA. Professor of Music; Double Bassist; Conductor. Educ: BMus, Univ. Tex., Austin, 1959; MMusEd, Midwestern Univ., 1975; DMA, Univ. Tex., Austin, 1970. m. Timothy Ann Hardy Sloan, 5 s. Career: Bassist, symph. orchs., Austing, Corpus Christi, San Antonio, Midland-Odessa, Wichita Falls; Jazz bassist, Joe Jones, Edmond Hall, Page Cavanaugh, Dick Goodwin Quintet; Cond., clins. for young musicians & musicals, Globe Theatre, SW; Jazz Tour, S Am, 1975, '77; Concert tour, US-E Coast, 1978. Recordings: Studio commercials. Contbr. to profl. publs. Mbrships. incl: MENC; Tex Music Educators Assn. Hobbies incl: Hunting; Fishing. Ad dress: Box 5351, University, MS 38677, USA.

SLOKAR, Branimir, b. 1946, Maribor, Yugoslavia. Trombone Player; Teacher. Educ: Ljubljana Musical Acad.; Conserv. Nat. Superieur de Musique, Paris. m. Ursula Drabert, 2 s. Career: Solo trombone, RTV Orch., Ljubljana, 1967-69; Solo trombone, Orchestre Concerts Colonne de Paris, 1970-71; Solo trombone, Berne Symph. Orch., 1971-77; Solo trombone, Symph. Orch. of Bavarian Radio, Munich, 1977-79; Tchr., Berne Conserv., 1971, Music High Schl., Cologne, 1978; num. concerts in Switz. & other countries as soloist, as mbr., Berne Wind Quartet & Slokar Trombone Quartet. Recordings: num. inclng. music by Albrechtsberger, L Mozart, Purcell, Vivaldi, Telemann, Handel, Marcello. num. prizes & awards. Hobbies: Mountaineering; Sports; Family. Mgmt: Marguerite Dütschler-Huber, Trüelweg 14, 36000 Thun, Switz.

SLOMAN, Jan Mark, b. 10 Apr. 1949, Charleston, WVa., USA. Violinist. Educ: Univ. Scholar, Princeton Univ.; Accepted Curtis Inst. of Music without audition; Studied w. Galamian, Makanowitzky, Laredo & Silverstein. Career: Asst. Concertmaster, Charlotte Symph., 1973-74; Assoc. Concertmaster, Phoenix Symph., Dir., Violin Div., Eastern Music Festival, Greensboro, NC; Apps. incl: Curtis Hall. Phila.; Toured w. Charlotte Chmbr. Orch.; Solo apps. & recitals throughout Eastern USA & w. Phoenix Symph. Recip. Naumburg Grant, Princeton Univ., 1967-69. Hobbies: Creative Cooking; Tennis. Address: 2321 E Highland (303), Phoenix, AZ 85016, USA.

SLOWAKIEWICZ-WOLANSKA, Alicja Maria, b. 12 June 1942, Biecz, Poland. Soprano. Educ: MA, HS of Music, Katowice. m. Jan Wolanski, 1 d. Debut: As Zdenka, Arabella (Strauss), Silesian Opera House, Bytom, 1968. Career: Soloist. Bytom, 1958-73, Wroclaw, 1973-75, Warsaw Chmbr. Opera, 1975-; apps. at Jugendfestspieltreffen, Bayreuth, 1968, '69, '71; roles incl: Queen of the Night, Magic Flute; Lucia, Rigoletto; Rosina, Barber of Seville; Micaela, Frasquita, Carmen; Lucia, Lucia di Lammermoor; Violetta, La Traviata; Musetta, La Boheme; Adela, Die Fledermaus. Mbr., Assn. of Polish Music Artists. Hobbies: Cooking; Swimming. Address: ul. Koscinski 46/10, Katowice, Poland.

SLOWINSKI, Wladyslaw, b. 14 May 1930, Sadino, Poland. Conductor; Composer. Educ: Studied Musicol., Poznań Univ.; Dips. in Comp. & Cond., High Schl. of Music, Poznań. m. Hanna Górzyńska, 1 s. Debut: Posnań Opera. Career: Cond. of Operas in Poznań & L&dź; Symph. Concerts in Poland, USSR & Yugoslavia. Comps: (publd.) 5 Short Pieces for Piano; Sonatina for Piano; (recorded) Makowiski Tales. Recordings: For Muza Records, & Polish Nat. Radio & TV. Mbr., Polish Comps. Union (Gen. Sec.). Hobbies: Literature, History & Politics of the 20th Century. Mgmt: Polish Comps. Soc. Address: Paryska 37/12, 03-945 Warsaw, Poland.

SLUCHIN, Benny, b. 7 March, 1948, Tel-Aviv, Israel. Trombone Player. Educ: BA, 1972, MSc, 1973, Math. Phil., Tel-Aviv, Univ.; Rubin Acad., Jerusalem, 1973-74; Künstlerichen Abschulussprüfung, 1976, Konzertexamen, 1977, Musikhochschule Köln; trombone studies w. Z Ostrowski & V Globokar. m. Shifra, 2 c. Career: Israel Phil. Orch., 1970-71; Jerusalem Symph. Orch. (Israel Radio Orch.), 1971-75; Ensemble Inter-contemporaine (Paris), 1976-; Guest concerts w. Israel Chmbr. Orch., Israel Nat. Opera; Solo recitals & concerts, Israel, France, Germany, Italy, Netherlands, etc. Address: 6 rue Guillaume-Bertrand, 75011 Paris, France.

SMAILOVC, Avdo, b. 14 Aug. 1917, Visoko, Yugoslavia. Music Teacher; Composer. Educ: Higher Schl. of Tchrs. of Music; BA, MA, Music High Schl., Ljubljana. m. Munira,7 children. Career: Prof., Higher Schl. for Tchrs., 1968-; Prof., Acad. of Music, 1976-. Comps. incl: (orchl.) Ad Hominem; Drvar;Podigman, Lyricism from an Ash-Heap (orch. & voice); (chmbr.) Fantasia for Flute & Piano; Pastorale for Oboe & Piano; Wind Trio; Impressions for Violin & Piano; (choral) Freedom, my Beloved City; Poem of Brotherhood from all Sides; Bell from the Valley; Music for children, theatre, etc. (all works taped for radio). Mbr., Union of Comps. of Yugoslavia (exec. coun.) Hons. incl: Dip., City of Sarajevo, 1970. Hobbies: Family; Literature. Address: Strosmajerova 4, 71000 Sarajevo, Yugoslavia.

SMALES, Kathleen Ann, b. 8 Feb. 1943, Tadcaster, York, UK. Opera Singer. Educ: ARMCM; London Opera Ctr.; Studied w. Vera Rosza. m. Alan Opie, 1 s. Debut: Sadler Wells Theatre. Career: Soloist; Glyndebourne Festival; Engl. Nat. Opera; Engl. Opera Grp.; Kent Opera; Cape Town, S Africa, Opera; Oxford Univ. Grp.; Cambridge Univ. Grp.; BBC Radio. Hons: Frances Furness Scholarship, 1968; Peter Stuyvasant Scholarship, 1970. Hobbies: Sewing; Reading; Keep Fit. Mgmt: Ibbs & Tillet. Address: 23 Hill Ct., Hanger Lane, London W5, UK.

SMALL, Rosemary, b. 2 Nov. 1943, Salt Lake City, Utah, USA. University Instructor; Percussionist; Cellist. Educ: BS, Weber State Coll., 1965; MA, Wash. State Univ., 1970; Currently studying for DMA, Hartt Coll. of Music. Career: Grad. Asst., Wash. State Univ., 1968-70; Instr. of Music, ibid, 1970-71; Percussionist, var. perf. orgs., Utah, Wash., Tex., NH & Conn.; Instr. of Music, Tex. A & I Univ., 1971-77; Instr. of Music, Keen State Coll., 1976-; Percussionist, Corpus Christi Symph., 1971-75. Contbr. to: NACWPI Jrnl. Mbrships. incl: Phi Kappa Phi; Percussive Arts Soc.; Nat. Assn. of Coll. Wind & Percussion Instructors; Hartford Musicians Assn. Hons. incl: Outstanding Musician Award, Weber State Coll., 1965. Hobbies incl: Ethnomusicol.; Photography. Address: 68 Blossom St., Keene, NH 03431, USA. 27.

SMALLBONE, Graham, b. 5 Apr. 1934, London, UK. Director of Music; Schoolmaster; Cellist. Educ: MA, Worcester Coll., Oxford Univ.; ARCM; ARCO. m. Dorothea Ruth Low, 2 s., 2 d. Career: Asst. Music Master, Oundle Schl., 1958-61; Dir. of Music, Dean Close Schl., 1961-66; Dir. of Music, Marlborough Coll., 1967-71; Percentor & Dir. of Music, Eton Coll., 1971-. Mbrships: ISM. Hobbies: Golf; Travel. Address: Ballards, Keate's Lane, Eton, Windsor, Berks., UK. 3.

SMALLEY, Cardo Brooks, b. 13 Mar. 1910, London, UK. Violinist; Violist; Musical Director; Conductor. Educ: Royal Conserv. of Music, Toronto; artist pupil w. var. tchrs.; scholaraships student, Univ. of BC, Vancouver, m. Laetitia Kathleen. Career: Concertmaster & Cond., CBC radio & TV, Vancouver studios; Assoc. Concertmaster, Vancouver Symph., also Tour & Assisting Cond., 1932-67; Cond. & Musical Dir., New Westminster Symph., 1967-73; on Tchng. Staff., Douglas Colt., New Westminster, & (currently) Victoria Conserv. of Music. Recip. of Gold Medal, 1932. Hobbies: Boating; Gardening; Woodworking. Address: 999 Carolwood Dr., Victoria, BC, Canada.

SMALLEY, Denis Arthur, b. 16 May 1946, Nelson, NZ. Composer; University Teacher. Educ: DPhil, York Univ., UK; BMus, Victoria Univ. of Wellington, NZ; MusB, Univ. of Canterbury, NZ; Dip. de Musique Electroacoustique et de Recherche Musicale, Paris Conserv.; Dip. Mus. (organ), Univ. of Canterbury, NZ; LRSM; LTCL. m. Rita Knight (separated), 1 s. Career: Hd. of Music, Wellington Coll., NZ, 1969-71; studies w. Olivier Messiaen, Paris & the Groupe de Recherches Musicales, Paris, 1975-76; Lectr. in Music, ibid, 1976-; Perfs. & broadcasts worldwide. Comps: Cornucopia, Gradual (tape w. solo instrument); Pentes, Ouroboros, Darkness After Time's Colours, The Pulses of Time (electro-aucoustic music on tape); Pneuma, Chanson de Geste (amplified voices & instruments). Recordings: Gradual. Contbr. to: Guardian (music critic, 1972-75). Mbrships: Chmn., British Sect., ISCM, 1979-; Music Advisory Panel, Arts Coun. of GB, 1978-; Committee, Electro-acoustic Music Assn. of GB, 1978-. Recip. of Comp. prizes. Address: Music Centre, Univ. of East Anglic, Norwich N54 6TJ, UK.

SMALLMAN, Frederic Basil Rowley, b. 30 June 921, Croydon, Surrey, UK. Professor. Educ: MA, BMus, Oxon.; ARCO. m. Ann Hesketh-Williams, 2 s., 1 d. Career: Lectr. in Music, Univ. of Nottingham, 1950-64; Prof. of Music, Univ. of Liverpool, 1965-; Dean, Fac. of Arts, ibid, 1968-71; Pub. Orator, 1972-73; Pro-Vice-Chancellor, 1973-. Author, The Background of Passion Music, 1957, '70. Contbr. to: Music & Letters; Musical Times; The Choir; Comp.; Listener. Mbrships: Royal Musical Assn.; ISM; CGB. Hobbies: Reading; Crossword puzzles. Address: 25 Gipsy Lane, Liverpool L18 3HL, UK. 3.

SMART, Clive Frederick, b. 14 Apr. 932, Altrincham, UK. Chartered Accountant; General Manager. Educ: Qualified as Chartered Accountant, 1953. m. Audrey Brown, 4 d., 1 S. Career incls: Secretary, Halle Concerts Soc., 1958; Gen. Mgr., ibid, 1961-; Ed., Halle Mag., Mbrships: Assn. of Brit. Orchs.; Manchester Club; NW Arts Assn.; Inst. of Chartered Accountants (FCA). Hons: Queens Silver Jubilee Medal, 1977; Halle Gold Medal, 1978. Hobbies: Music; Photography; Gardening; Sailing. Address: Halle Concerts Soc., 30 Cross St., Manchester, UK.

SMEDEBY, Sune, b. 3 Apr. 1934, Eskilstuna, Sweden. Composer; Teacher of Music Theory. Educ: BA, Uppsala, 1963; Folkliga Musikskolan, Ingesund, 1954-57; Music Acad., Stockholm, 1958-62; Elektronmusikstudion, ibid, 1974-75. m. Birgitta Smedeby, 2 d. Career: Tchr., Framnäs Folkhögskola, 1963-75; Örebro Musikpedagogiska Inst., 1977-. Comps.incl: Och gott öl kom / O guid ale comes (men's chours), 1963; Improvisations I-III, 1968, '69; Vinter (computer music), 1975; Quartetto tramontano (string quartet), 1975; Choral comps.; chmbr. music; Electronic Music. Publs: Musical transcriptions in Lapska sanger II, 1963; Harmonilära, 1978. Contbr. to:

Musikkultur; Swedish Jrnl. of Musicol. Mbr., Assn. of Swedish Comps. Hobby: Playing Contraqbass Tuba. Address: Lyrikgatan 12B, 703 72 Örebro, Sweden.

SMEDLEY, Peter Francis, b. 4 Dec. 1932, Nottingham, UK. Cathedral Organist; Educator. Educ: ARCM; LRAM; LTCL.. m. Teresa Markowska, 1 s. Career: Hd., Music Dept., Corpus Christi Schl., Nottingham, 1958-; Dir. of Music, Nottingham Cathedral, 1964-. Compositions: Motets, Anthems & Choral Settings of Psalms (all publd.); Organ Music; Gebrauchmusik. Recordings: w. Cathedral Choirboys & Schola of Gregorian Plainsong (Cond.). Contbr. to: Church Music; Liturgy. Mbrships: Past Pres., Nottingham Soc. of Organists. Hobbies: Motoring; Travel. Address: Cathedral House, Derby Road, Nottingham, UK. 3.

SMEETS, Leon Joseph Hubert, b. 23 May 1899, Maastricht, Netherlands. Composer. Educ: Musical Acad. of Maastricht. m. M J P Smeets van den Broek, 8 children. Debut: 1918. Comps. for choir incl: Paschalis mis; Sursum cords: Ferialis. Comps. for Brass band incl. Partita Gerlria; Zuid-Holland Suite; Brabantia Nostra. Mbrships: Netherlands Comps. Soc.; Royal Soc. for Musicians: BUM: Stermra. Hobby: Numismatics. Address: Roelofstraat 116, The Hague, Netherlands.

SMENDZIANKA, Regina, b. 9 Oct. 1924, Torun, Poland. Pianist; Teacher. Educ: Dip. w. High Distinction, MMus, State Coll. of Music, Cracow. Debut: Soloist w. Cracow Phil. Orch., 1947. Career: num. concert tours as Recitalist & Soloist w. orchs., Poland & abroad - 30 countries of 3 continents; num. radio & TV broadcasts; tchng., 1964-; Asst. Prof., 1966-, Rector, 1972, '73, State Coll. of Music, Warsaw; has given courses in piano interpretation, lectures, etc. in Warsaw, Tokyo, Weimar, Mexico City, etc. Recordings incl. works by Chopin, Bach, Mozart, Franck, Paderewski, Schubert. Ed., sev. piano works. Contbr. to musical publs. Mbrships: Polish Musicians Assn.; Frederic Chopin Soc.; Instituto Mexicana de Cultura. Recip. num. hons., Polish & for. Mgmt: Polish Artistic Agcy., PAGART, Warsaw, Pl. Zwyciestwa 9. Address: Warsaw, ul Narbutta 76/10, Poland.

SMETÁČEK, Pavel, b. 4 Jan. 1940, Prague, Czechoslovakia. Musician; Clarinet; Saxophone; Bandleader; Composer; Arranger. Educ: Grad., Prague Conserv.; musicol., Charles Univ. of Prague. m. Marta Vysinová, 1 s. Career: Ldr., Tranditional Jazz Studio band; Tours of Europe, USSR, Canaray Islands, USA, 1961-; Apps., Radio & TV; Perfs., maj. European jass fests.; Films, That Cat, Ten People with the Tradition, Italian variations, & documentaries. Comps: Tail Gate Stomp, SOS March for play The Skin of Our Teeth by Thornton Wilder; September Stomp; The Not Knowing Lover; Budulinek The Wanderer, etc. Num. recordings of own compositions & traditional jazz. Contbr. to musical jrnls. Mbrships: OSA, The Authors Protective Union; The Subcommittee for Jazz of the Czech. Comps. & Concert Artists Union. Hobbies: Cultural, historical & sociological relations. Mgmt: Pragokoncert, Prague. Address: Janovskeho St. 20, 170 00 Prague, 7 Czech. 29, 30.

SMETÁČEK, Václav, b. 30 Sept. 1906, Brno, Czech. Conductor; Oboist. Educ: Prague Conserv.; PhD, Charles Univ., Prague. m. Milka Kcvorova, 2 s., 2 d. Career: Cond., all ldng. musical ctrs. of Europe and on all other continents; num. apps. , Theatro Colon, Buenos Arires & as 1st Cond. Cond., La Scala, Milan. Recordings: over 250 titles. Publs: School for Oboe, 1960, 1976; Etudes for Oboe, 1960, 1972. Mbr., Czech. Comps. Soc. Recip., Nat. Artists Award, 1976. Hobbies: Philately; Country House. Address: Klidna 6, Prague 6, Czechoslovakia.

SMETANA, Frantisek, b. 8 May 1914, Ohnistany, Czech. Cellist. Educ: Grad. Comp., State Conserv. of Music in Prague, 1936; Grad. Cello & Chamber Music, Ecole Normale de Music, Paris, 1938; studied cello w. Pravoslav Sadlo in Prague & Pierre Fournier in Paris, etc. m. Rudolfa Urbánková. Debut: First cello recital at age 10; Debut w. Pizen Symph. Orch. at age 16. Career: Mbr. Czech. Quartet, 1939-46; Sev. tours to many European countries as soloist w. orchs. & also as recitalist or in radio broadcasts, 1946-64; Approx. 400 apps. throughout Czech., 1950-55; Tour of China, Korea & Magnolia, 1956; Mbr., Prague Trio, 1958-63; TV apps. & recitals in Jamaica, 1964-66; Solo recitals at Iowa State Univ. & as Mbr. of Amati Trio, recitals throughout Iowa & other states, 1966; Soloist, RPO, London (in Ames) & w. McGill Chamber Orch., Montreal, 1968; Prin. Cellist, Richmond Symph. & Sinfonia, 1973-75; Tchr., cello & chmbr. music, Prague Conserv., 1946-48, Jamaica Schl. of Music, Kingston, 1964-66, Iowa State Univ., 1966-73, Va. Commonwealth Univ., Richmond, 1973-; Has recorded extensively. Mbrships: Czech. Soc. of Arts & Scis. in Am.; Chapt. Hon. Mbr. Phi Mu Alpha, Pi Kappa Lambda. Address: 50 Skipwith Green Circle, Richmond, VA 23299, USA.

SMID, Miroslav, b. 19 Apr. 1932, Gottwaldov, Czechoslovakia. Conductor; Composer; Opera Director & Conductor. Educ: Acad. of Drama & Music, Bratislava. m. Ada Mozjasova. Debut: W Slovak Phil. Orch., 1953. Career: Cond. of 70 films; Cond. of 1250 perfs. w. Lucnica Ensemble, Bratislava; Opera Dir. & Cond., Banska Bystrica. Comps: Num. works for var. ensembles; Comps. for Czechoslovak Radio & TV. Recordings of 45 works. Contbr. to profl. jrnls. Mbr. Union of S lovak Comps. Hons: Priz of Town Gothwaldou; Laurete World Festivals, Moscow & Sofia; Merited Artist of Slovak Min. of Culture. Hobbies: Lit.; Films. Address: 81600 Bratislava, Gabcikova 2, Czechoslovakia.

SMILEY, Pril, b. 19 Mar. 1943, Monhonk Lake, NY, USA. Composer; Percussionist. Educ: BA, Bennington Coll. Career: Res. Comp., 1963-. Instr., 1965-, Assoc. Dir., 1974-, Columbia-Princeton Electronic Music Ctr., NYC; Electronic Music Cons., Lincoln Ctr. Repertory Theatre, 1968-74. Comps: 24 electronic scores for theatre prods.; 10 electronic scores for films inclng. 2 TV documentaries & a feature-length film; an electronic score for skiing ballet. Has been recorded on Vox Turnabout, CRI & Finnadar-4-track labels. Mbrships: Bds. of Dirs., Am. Comps. Alliance & Comps. Recordings Inc. Recip. var. awards & grants inclng: Guggeinheim Fellowship,1975-76. Hobbies: Skiing; Kayaking. Address: Mohonk Lake, New Paltz, NY 12461, USA.

SMIT, André-Jean, b. 24 Aug. 1926, Ville d'Avray, Hauts de Seine, France. Composer; Professor; Director, Academy of Music; Scientific Worker. Educ: Royal Conservs. of Liège & Brussels, Belgium. m. 1 child. Career incls: Prof., Royal Conserv. of Music, Brussels; Dir., St-Gilles-lez-Bruxelles Acad. of Music; Sci. Worker, Mus. of Instruments, Brussels. Comps. incl: (publs). Trio, for reed instruments, 1968; Prelude & Dance, for trombone & piano, 1974; Little Suite, for piano, 1963; Improvisation for flute & piano, 1978. Mbrships: Union of Belgian Comps.; SABAM. Hons: Geevaert Prize, 1969; Triennal Prize, Royal Acad. of Belgium, 1975. Address: 34 rue Sylvain Denayer, 1070 Brussels, Belgium.

SMIT, Leo, b. 12 Jan. 1921, Philadelphia, Pa., USA. Composer; Pianist; Conductor; Teacher. Educ: Curtis Inst., 1930-32; Study of composition w. N Nabakoff. Debut: Piano, Carnegie Hall, 1939; Conducting, Ojai Fest., Calif., 1962. Career: Pianist w. Am. Ballet, 1936-37; US tour, 1940; Pianist, NYC Symph., 1947-48; Orch. apps. w. maj. conds. inclng. Bernstein, Stokowski, Copland, Munich, Stravinsky, 1947-67; Fac. Mbr., Sarah Lawrence Coll., 1947-49; Artist Dir., Concert Hall. Soc. Records, 1947; European tour, 1953-55; Hd., Piano Dept., UCLA, 1957-63; Slee Prof. in Composition, SUNY Buffalo, 1962; Prof. of Music, ibid, 1963-; State Dept. tour, Latin Am., 1967-68. Comps. incl: Caedmon, Copernicus, (choral works); Concerto for Orchestra & Piano; Symphony No. 1; Symphony No. 2; Fantasy: The Farewell, Variations in G (piano); Virginia Sampler (ballet); The Alchemy of Love (space fable in 3 acts); Camera 3, 1977, Leo Smit remembers Stravinsky & Copland; 4 Kookaburra Marches; In Woods, 1978; Magic Waters, chamber opera, 1978. Sev. recordings of own works. Var. vocal/instrumental works. Contbr. to profl. jrnls.; Concert Lectures. Mbrships: Audubon Soc.; Bd. of Dirs., Monday Evening Concerts, LA, 1959-63; ASCAP. Num. hons. awards. Hobbies: Chess; Table Tennis; Photography; Hiking. Address: SUNY, Buffalo, NY 14214, USA.

SMITH, Alan, b. 3 Dec. 1940, Barnsley, S Yorks., UK. Schoolmaster; Musicologist. Educ: BMus, 1963, PhD, 1967, Univ. of Birmingham; Cert. Educ., 1964. Career: Hd. of Music, Hull Grammar Schl., 1969-71; Dir. of Music, Ranby House Schl., Retford, 1971-; rsch. mainly on Elizabethan Ch. music, also on educ. of child of middle schl. age range. Publs: articles on Elizabethan Ch. music in Music & Letters, Proceedings of the Royal Musical Assn. Contbr. of concert reviews to Yorkshire Post, 1970-71. mbr., Royal Musical Assn. Hobbies: Gardening; Church Architecture; Scrabbble; Drama. Address: 8 Lond Causeway, Monk Bretton, Barnsley, S Yorks, S71 2HJ, UK.

SMITH, Alan Benson, b. 31 July 1930, Sheffield, UK. Organist; Music Teacher; Businessman. Educ: Univ. of Durham; Organ scholar, Bede Coll., Durham; LRAM (organ). m. Violet May Waghorn, 2s., 2 d. Career: managing dir. in engineering till 1974; Gen. mbr., Gough Davy, music people, Hull, 1975—79; partner, My Music, Hull (piano & instrument retailers), 1979-; asst. organist, St. John's Ch., Sheffield, 1949-74. Recordings: responsible for 1st recordings of works by German, Bantock, Holbrooke & Brian; organist in works by Brian. Mbrships: Fellow, Inst. of Works Mgrs.; ISM; Organists' Assn., Sheffield & Hull. Address: Aingarth, 39 St. Johns' Rd., Driffield, Yorks., YP25 7RS, UK.

SMITH, Alison, b. 13 Mar. 1914, Edinburgh, Scotland, UK. Vioélinist; Violist. Educ: Waddell Schl. of Music, Edinburgh; Edith Knocker, London; Carl Flesch, Belgium; ARCM; Hon. FTCL. m. Clive Gordon Smith, 2 s. Debut: Freemason's Hall, Edinburgh. Career: Freelance, BBC & var. Leading chmbr. & string orchs.; Prof., TCL; Vis. Lectr., Middlesex Polytechnic, Trent Pk. Mbrships: ISM; Musicians Union; European String Tchrs. Assn. Hons: Sir James Caird Travelling Schlrship., 1931-34 Hobbies: Reading; Art Hist.; Travel. Address: 27A Grove Terrace, London NW5, UK. 3.

SMITH, Barbara Barnard, b. 10 June 1920, Ventura, Calif., USA. Professor of Music; Ethnomusicologist, Univ. of Hawaii. Educ: BA, Pomona Coll.; MMus, Eastman Schl. of Music, Uhiv. of Rochester; Perfs. Cert., Piano, ibid. Career: Piano Recitalist, Soloist w. Orchs. in USA, Korea; Koto Recitalist, Japan, USA. Field Ed., Music in World Cultures, 1972. Contbr. to MGG; Ency. Britannica Int. Ed.; Grove's Dictionary of Music & Musicians, 6th Ed.; IFMC Jrnl.; Ethnomusicol.; Philos. E & W Ongaku Geijutsu; Western Folklore. Mbrships: Soc. for Ethnomusicol.; past Dir-at-Large, ibid; past VP. Coll. Music Soc.; Int. Folk Music Coun.; Int. Soc. for Music Educ.; MENC. Hons. Rockefeller Fndn. Grants, 1956, 1958; Phi Beta Kappa, 1942; Ho'omau I Ka'lke; Sr. Fellow, East-West Ctr., 1973. Hobby: Travel. Address: 3608 Woodlawn Dr., Honolulu, HI 96822, USA. 5, 9.

SMITH, Barry, b. 13 May 1939, Port Elizabeth, S Africa. Oranist & Choirmaster; University Lecturer. Educ: MA, Rhodes Univ., Grahamstown; Assoc. Dip., RSCM, UK, 1972; FTCL (Organ Perf.) ARCO (CHM); LTSM (Organ Tchr.); Tchrs., Perfs., Ch. Organist Dips., Univ. of S Africa. Career incls: Dir. of Music, Michaelhouse, Natal, 1962-64; Organist & Master of Choristers, St. George's Angilican Cathedral, 1964-; Fndr. & Dir., St. George's Singers; Chorus Master, Cape Town Sumph. Choir; Lectr., Fac. of Music, Cape Town Univ.; Organ Solo & Concerto Recitalist; Continuo Player; Radio apps.; Guest Cond.; Cape Town Symph. Orch. Recordings: Music of St. George's Cathedral, Organ Music from Cape Town Cathedral. Contbr. to encys. Mbr., prof. assns Hobbies: Antiques; Pre-Raphelite Art & Design; Travel; Cinema. Address: 15 Belvedere Ave.,, Oranjezicht, Cape Town 8001, S Africa. 28, 29, 30.

SMITH, Billye-Mullins, b. Tex., USA. Author; Concert Pianist; Music Educator; Arts Devotee. Educ: Student of Jeanette Tillet for piano & Helen Shank Emory for voice, Ft. Worth Conservatory of Music; Tex. Wesleyan Coll.; Fla. S Coll.; Master study under Dr. Edwin Hughes, NYC. Debut: Ft. Worth Symph. Orch. Career: Author-in-res., Polk Commun. Coll., Winter Haven, Fla.; Nat. Adjudicator, Nat. Guild Piano Tchrs. Recordings: Billye-Mullins Smith Series of Wedding Music; Repertoire for Organ & Piano; Billye-Mullins Smith Plays Bach to Strauss. Publs: Piano Repertoire Guide; Opus 1 Music Study Program. Contbr. to: Musical America; Contemporary Keyboard; Florida Music Director. Mbrships. incl: Am. Soc. Composers, Authors & Publrs.; Am. Coll. of Musicians; Music Tchrs. Nat. Assn. Hons. incl: Tex. & Nat. Fedn. Music Clubs Awards. Address: PO Drawer 1999, Winter Haven, FL 33880, USA, 27.

SMITH, Calvin L, b. 27 Mar. 1950, Lockport, NY, USA. Hornist. Educ: BMus (Educ.), SUNY at Fredonia, 1972; Grad. study, Ind. Univ. 1972—73; pvte. study of Horn w. Philip Farkas. m. Paula Maxfield Smith. Career: Prin. Horn, Erie Phil. Orch., Pa., 1972; Assoc. Instr. Horn, Ind. Univ., 1973; Hornist, Annapolis Brass Quintet, 1973-76; Tour of major European cities; Mbr., Westwood Wind Quintet, in-res., Ambassador Coll., Pasadena, Calif., & freelance hornist, Los Angeles, 1976-. Recordings: 2 albums w. Annapolis Brass Quintet; Solo album, 1976. Contbr. to Music Jrnl. Mbrships: Nat. Hon. Soc.; Phi Mu Alpha Sinfonia; Fndr., Annapolis Horn Club. Hobbies incl: Canoeing; Spectator Sports. Mgmt: Thea Dispeker Mgmt., NYC; Arists Alliance, Los Angeles, Calif. Address: 937 Lake Drive, Arnold, MD 21012, USA.

SMITH, Carleton Sprague, b. 8 Aug. 1905, NY, NY, USA. Musicologist; Flautist; Librarian. Educ: AB, Harvard Univ., 1927; MA, ibid., 1928; PhD, Univ. of Vienna, 1930; pvte. study, theory & piano, 1922-23; flute studies w. Louis Fleury & Georges Laurent. m. Elisabeth Cowles Sperry, 1d. Career incl: Chief Music Div., NY Public Lib., 1931-58 (established num. important musical collections); Adjunct Prof. of Music, NY Univ., 1939-58; Prof. of Music Hist., Douglass Coll., Rutgers, State Univ. of NJ, 1967-; vis. lectr., num. univs., esp. in Latin Am.; fndr., Music Lib. Assn., 1931; planned Lib. Museum of the Performing Arts, Lincoln Ctr., NY, where NY Public Lib. music collections now reside; solo flautist w. eminent chmbr. music ensembles. Publs. incl. num. articles on music of Latin Am., musical educ., musical libs., etc. Mbrships. inc. Music Lib. Assn. (pres., 1936-37); Am. Musicol. Soc., 1938-39; Bds. of num. musical orgs. Hon. docts., Univs. of Brazil, Bahia, Hamilton Coll. Hobbies: working on own farm. Address: Waldingfield Farm, Wash., CT 06793, USA. 2, 14.

SMITH, Catherine Parsons, b. 4 Nov. 1933, Rochester, NY, USA. Flautist; Musicology Lecturer. Educ: AB, Smith Coll., 1954; MMus, Northwestern Univ., 1957; DMA, Stanford Univ., 1969; Prep. Dip., Eastman Schl. Music. m. Ross Wilbert Smith, 2 s., 1 d. Career: Asst. Prof., Univ. Nev., Reno; Baroque flute perfs., NC & local community orchs., Springfield, Mass., Boston, Chgo., Denver, Rapid City, SD, & Reno; Orgnsr., Black Hills Chmbr. Music Soc. Publs. incl: Freillon-Poncein, Treatise for Oboe, Record, Flageolet (1700), ed. & tr ans., in press. Contbr. to profl. publs. Mbrships. inccl: MS; CMS. Hons. incl: Danforth Fndn. Grad. Fellowships for Women, 1967-69. Hobbies: Jogging; Backpacking. Address: Music Dept., Univ. Nev., Reno, NV 89507, USA.

SMITH, Craig Edward, b. 4 May 1941, Painesville, Ohio, USA. Director of Music. Educ: AB, Union Coll., Schenectady, NY; MSM, Union Theological Seminary, NY; RSCM, Croydon, UK. m. Faith Crandall Jarvis, 2 s., 1 d. Career: Organist/Choirmaster, Kent Schl., Kent, Conn., 4 yrs.; St. George's by-the-River, Rumson, NJ, 6 yrs.; Music Dir., Groton Schl., Groton, Mass. Recordings: Nine Lessons & Carols, Groton Schl. Choir. Mbrships: Anglican Assn. of Musicians: Am. Guild of Organists; RSCM; Ch. Music Commission of NJ Diocese. Hobbies: Golf; Tennis. Address: Farmers' Row, Groton Schl., Groton, MA 01450, USA.

SMITH, David Charles Morgan, b. 30 Sept. 1929. Toronto, Ont. Canada. Music Educator. Educ: ARCT (Clarinet), Univ. of Toronto, 1954; BMus, ibid, 1955; MMus, 1968. m. Muriel Ann Melville, 1 s., 1 d. Career: Secondary Schl. Music Tchr., N York Bd. of Educ., 1956-68; Asst. Prof., Mt. Allison Univ., NB, 1968-69; Assoc. Prof., Queens Univ., Kingston, Ont., 1969-; Cond., Music. Dir., St. Lawrence Summer Theatre, Kingston, 1970-76; Cond., Queen's Univ. Wind Ensemble, 1969-71, 1975-76; Fndr.-Dir., Interprovincial Music Camp, 1962-67; Creative Arts Committee, Ont. Inst. for Studies in Educ., 1965-68. Contbr. to The Canadian Music Educator; The Recorder. Mbrships: Canadian & Ont. Music Educators Assn.; MENC; Canadian Assn. of Univ. Schls. of Music; Coll. Music Soc.; Nat. Assn. of Coll. Wind & Percussion Instrs., Toronto Musicians Assn.; Kingston Musicians Union. Hobby: Puppetry. Address: 171 Sherman St., Kingston, Ont., Canada K7M 4G9.

SMITH, Douglas, b. 25 Oct. 1939, Cincinnati, Ohio, USA. Associate Professor of Church Music. Educ: BS, Carson-Newman Coll.; MMusEd, N Tex. State Univ.; AMusD, Univ. of Mich. m. Rose Davis, 1 d. Career: Knoxville Symph.; Am. Wind Symph.; Waco Symph.; Fort Worth Symph.; Louisville Orch.; currently Assoc. Prof. of Ch. Music (trumpet & cond.), Southern Bapt. Theol. Sem., Louisville. Comps: Wondrous Love (choir & organ); Do I Not Love Thee? (choir & band); All Glory, Laud, and Honor; Star in the East; 8 Christmas Carols for brass, 1978; 61 Trumpet Hymns & Descants, 1977;61 Trombone Hymns & Counter-Melodies, 1979. Contbr. to: Ch. Musician; Instrumentalist. Mbrships: Coll.Band Dirs. Nat. Assn.; Ch. Music Conference; Int. Trumpet Guild. Address: 2107 Alta Ave., Louisville, KY 40205, USA.

SMITH, Douglas Alton, b. 15 Oct. 1944, Jamestown, NY, USA. Musicologist; Lutenist. Educ: BA, Univ. of Puget Sound; BA, MA, Univ. of Wash.; Univ. of Vienna; MA, PhD, Stanford Univ.; studied lute w. Stanley Buetens. Transl. & Ed: Ernst Gottlieb Baron, Study of the Lute (Untersuchung des Intruments der Lauten, 1727). 1976. Contbr. to musical jrnls. & record jacket notes. Mbrships: Assoc. Ed. of Jrnl., Lute Soc. of Am.; Bd. of Dirs., Lute Soc. of Am. Hons: Fulbright Fellowship, 1969-70; Mrs Giles Whiting Fndn. Fellowship, 1975; Humboldt Fellow, 1977. Address: 7919-26th Ave. NW, Gig Harbor, WA 98335, USA.

SMITH, Edwin William, b. 22 Sept. 1914, Sheffield, UK. Lecturer in Music. Educ: Sheffield City Trng. Coll.; ARCO. m. Alice Hill, 1 s., 2 d. Career: Hd., Music Dept., City of Leeds Trng. Coll., 1946-60; Hd., Music Dept., Nottingham Coll. of Educ., 1960-74. Compositions: Var. songs. Publs: The Oxford Student's Harmony; Approach to Music (w. D Renout). Contbr. to Music Tchr. Hobbies: Gardening; Cycling; Photography. Address: Woodmans Cottage, Kilburn, York YO6 4AH, UK. 3.

SMITH, Freda, b. 27 Apr. 1904, Bury, Lancs., UK. Teacher of Music in Schools. Educ: AB, London; Min. of Educ. Tchr.'s Cert.; Nottingham Univ.; LRAM; Studies w. Dr. A. O. Warburton & Dora Gilson. Career: Tchr. of Music; Lecture-recitals; Choir Cond.; Fest. adjudicator; Broadcaster; p.time tutor in music, Manchester Univ. Mbrships: ISM; Committee Mbr., Keswick Music Soc. Hobbies: Walking; Reading; Making

music; Gardening. Address: North Flat, Lingholm, Keswick, Cumbria, CA12 5UA, UK. 3.

SMITH, Gayle, b. 2 Sept. 1943, Los Angeles, Calif., USA. Cellist. Educ: Special Musical Studies Inst., Univ. of Southern Calif.; BA, Univ. of Calif., Los Angeles; Los Angeles Conserv. of Music; pvte. study w. Pablo Casals & Gregor Piatigorsky; Recital Dip., RAM, London, UK (studied w. Douglas Cameron); pvte. study w. William Pleeth & at GSM, London. Debut: Wigmore Hall, London, 1970 (UK); Lincoln Ctr., NYC, 1971 (USA). Career: Apps. Vienna, Austria, & Moscow, USSR, 1970; Engagements & Tours w. UK Orchs. inclng. Liverpool (1975) & Oxford Chmbr. Orchs., Northern Sinfonia, Engl. Sinfonia, Ulster Orch., & w. Oslo Phil. & Bergen Symph. (Harmonien), Norway; Solo apps. incl: Fests. at Avignon, Bath, Harrogate, Nottingham; Radio & TV Broadcasts, BBC, 1973; Broadcasts, Swedish Radio & TV perfs., Norweigian Rikskringkasting; Mbr., Univ. of Calif. Los Angeles Colloquim on the Fine Arts, USA. Recordings: First record to appear June 1974 ON Genesis Records. Hons: Fulbright Scholar; Cello Prize, RAM, 1967; Croydon Soloist Award, 1967; Finalist & Laureate, Int. Tchaikovsky Competition, USSR, 1970. Hobbies: Films, Opera, & The Out-of-Doors. Mgmt: Ingpen & Williams. Address: 21 Holland Pk., London W11 3TE, UK.

SMITH, Gerald L, b. 21 Mar. 1921, Manchester, Iowa, USA. Baritone; Professor of Voice; Choral Conductor. Educ: BA, Univ. of Dubuque, 1942; BM, 1946, MMUS, 1952, Chgo. Conserv. of Music; Further study, opera, French & German song lit., Univ. of Colo., Aspen Inst. of Music. m. Dorothy Laskey, 3 s. Debut: Town Hall, NYC, 1954. Career: Soloist, ABC radio Hymns of All Churches, WGN Theatre of the Air; Soloist, Grant Park Concert Series & w. Chgo. Symph. orch., St. Louis Municipal Opera, Chgo. Sunday Evening Club; Soloist & concert apps., Midwest US; Concerts, Japan, 1973; Aust., 1975; Assoc. Prof., Voice, Northwestern Univ., Dir. of Music, 1st United Meth. Ch., Evanston. Mbrships: Nat. Assn. of Tchrs. of Singing; Pres.; Chgo. Singing Tchrs. Guild; MENC; Am. Choral Dirs. Asn.; Nat. Hon. Patron, Phi Beta; Past Pres., Alpha Chapt., Pi Kappa Lambda; Bd. Mbr., Nat. Assn. of Meth. Musicians; Dir., Ch. Music Summer Schl., Garett-Evangelical Theol. Sem., summer, 1974, 1975, 1976. Hons. DMus Univ. of Dubuque, 1970. Hobbies: History; Collecting foreigh coins; Water sports. Address: 802 Ingleside Pl., Evanston, IL 60201, USA.

SMITH, Glenn Parkhurst, b. 26 Feb. 1912, Oswgo, Ill., USA. Trombonist; Educator; Clinician; Editor. Educ: BMus, Wheaton Coll., Ill., 1934: MMus, Northwestern Univ., Evanston,Ill., 1949; studied w. Jaroslav Cimera. m. Marie C Allen, 3 d.,1 s. Career: Prof. of Music, Trombone, Univ. of Mich. Schl. of Music, 1950-; Fndr., Cond., Univ. of Mich. Trombone Choir. Publs: Ed., 34 Eds. of brass solo & ensemble works by var. Comps. inclng. Gabrieli, Frescobaldi, Marini. Contbr. to: Instrumentalist; Jrnl. of the Int. Trombone Assn. Mbrships: NACWPI; past State Chmn., ibid; Chmn., Rsch. Committee, Int. Trombone Assn.; MENC; Hons: Winner, Chgoland. Music Fest. Trombone Competition, twice, Hon. Mbr., Univ. of Mich. Band Alumni Assn. Hobbies: Travel; Geanology; Antiques. Address: 312 Doty Ave., Ann Arbor, MI 48103, USA. 1, 18.

SMITH, Gregory James, b. 18 July 1952, Croydon, Surrey, UK. Teacher. Educ: Inst. of Educ., 1973-74; Univ. of London tchrs. cert., 1974; chorister, Temple Ch. Choir, 1963-66; GSM, 1970-73; GGSM, 1973. Career: tchr., piano, organ, double bass & choir training; guitar & recorder at elementary level. Mbrships: National Assn. of Schlmasters/Union of Women Tchrs.; ISM; RCO. Hobbies: Sailing; Walking; Chess; Travel. Address: Flat 2, St. John's Vicarge,18 Larcom St., London SE17 1NQ, UK.

SMITH, Henry Charles, b. 31 Jan. 1931, Phila., Pa., USA. Conductor; Trombpne & Euphonium Player. Educ: BA, Univ. of Pa.; Artist Dip., Curtis Inst. of Music. m. Mary Jane D Smith, 2 d, 1 s. Career: Solo trombone, Phila. Orch., 1955-67; Fac., Ind. Univ., 1968-71; Assoc. Cond., Minn. Orch., 1971-. Comps: Hear Us As We Pray (SATB-Choral). Recordings: Over 200 w. Phila. Orch.; 8 w. Phila. Brass Ensemble; 3 solo records. Publs: New Imperial Method for Trombone, 1958; Soles for the Trombone Player, 1972; 12 Easy Duets for Winds, 1972. Contbr. to Am. String Tchrs. Assn. Jrnl. Mbrships: Bd. of Dirs., Int. Trombone Assn.; Bd. of Advisors, Tubist Universal Brotherhood Assn.; Rotary Int. Address: 5640 Woodale Ave., Edina, MN 55424, USA. 2.

SMITH, John Frank, b. 25 Feb. 950, Market Bosworth, Leics., UK. Orchestral Musician (Tuba). Educ: LRAM. m. Sandra Hambleton. Career: Freelance artist for number of yrs.; Prin. Tuba, Engl. Nat. Opera Co., 1975-; Tuba w. London Cabrieli Brass Ensemble & Locke Brss Consort. Num. recordings w. var.

symph. & Opera orchs.; Chmbr. recordings incl: Contrasts in Brass w. Locke Brass Consort. Mbr. Royal Soc. of Musicians. Recip. Sidney Langston Prize for Brass Playing, 1979. Hobby: Do-it-Yourself Projects. Address; 15 St. Margarets Rd., London SE4 1YL, UK. 14.

SMITH, Julian John Hamling, b. 8 Dec. 1929, Hornsey, Middx., UK. Educator; Singer. Educ: Choristr, King's Coll., Edinburgh Univ.; BMus., LRAM; Studied w. Mona Benson, Arthur Reckless, Elena Gerhardt & Roy Henderson. m. Fiona Williams, 1 s., 1 d. Debut: Edinburgh, 1952. Career: Soloist, Maj. Cities, GB; Apps. on Radio 3 & BBC TV; Musical Dir., St. Endellion Fest., 2973-74. Mbrships: ISM. Hobbies: Cricket; Golf; Walking; Gardening; Fan lights. Mgmt: Ibbs & Tillett. Address: Meadow House Kingsgate Rd., Winchester, Hants., UK. 3.

SMITH, Keith Hamilton, b. 19 May, 1928, Rockhampton, Qld., Aust. Lecturer in Music Educ. Educ. Kelvin Grove Tchrs. Coll: AMusA; studied Orff-Schulwerk in Austria, Germany, UK, USA & Can. m. Constance Marie Tunstall, 2 s. Career incl: Tchr., Primary Schls; Featured Int. Tchr. in Orff-Schulwerk, Ball State Univ., Ind., USA; Lectr. in Music var. colls. inclng Kelvin Grove Coll. of Advanced Educ., Brisbane; Organist & Choirmaster var. chs. in Qld.; Leader in Adult Educ.; Demonstrator in Orff-Schulwerk, ISME Perth, 1974, ASME Canberra, 1977. Publs: Questiona & Answers of Orff-Schulwek, 1972, '74, '76. Contbr. to profl. mags. & newsletters. Mbrships incl: Qld. Chapt., Aust. Soc. for Music Educ.; Sec. & Ed., Orff-Schulwerk Assn. of Qld.; 1st Pres., Aust. Nat. Coun. of Orff-Schulwerk Assns. Hons: Travel grant for study in Orff-Schulwerk for 6 months, 1971. Hobbies: Gardening; Visual Art; Ch. Music; Christian Lit. Address: 11 Mirbelia St., Everton Hilla, Qld. 4053, Aust.

SMITH, Kenneth Leslie, b. 6 Aug. 1946, Wolverhampton, Staffs., UK. Orchestral Musician (flute, piccolo & alto flute). Educ: 3 yrs., Cardiff Coll. of Music & Drama, LCCMD; 1 yr., St. Mark & St. John Training Coll., Cert. of Educ. for trng. music. Career: w. BBC Training Orch., 1970-72; w. Bournemouth Symph. Orch., 1973-; Helped form Chmbr. Ensemble, Canzona, 1974; Sev. BBC Broadcasts; Perfs. in Finland & Hong Kong. Mbr., Poole Badminton Club. Hobbies: Badminton; Chmbr. Music; Collecting Records. Mgmt: Western Orchl. Soc. Address: 48 Collwood Close, Poole, Dorset BH15 3HG, UK.

SMITH, Kevin, b. 26 Apr. 1942, Haralson, UK. Counter-Tenor Singer. Educ: GSM; AGSM. div., 2d. Career: 5 yrs. as actor in profl. theatre, TV & Films; perfs. in concerts, oratorio, recitals & opera; BBC recordings of Renaissance & Baroque music; apps. w. Handel Opera Soc., Engl. Opera Group, Kent Opera, Drottningholm Opera, Opera Colon, Buenos Aires, Hamburg Staatsopher & Paris Opera; apps. at most European fests. incl. Göttingen Handel & Wexford Fests; Prof. of Singing, GSM. Recordings: Monteverdi's Marian Vespers; Cavalli's Historia di Jonah; John Taverner's Canciones Espagnoles; Charpentier's Magnificat. Mbrships: ISM; Equity. Hobbies: Renaissance, Baroque & Contemporary Music; Walking; Wine. Mgmt: Stafford Law Assocs., 26 Firlands Ave., Weybridge KT8 OHR, UK.

SMITH, Laurence Fabian, b. 25 Jan. 1909, London, UK. Singer (Baritone); Singing Teacher. Educ: FGSM. m. Nancie, 2 d. Debut: Wigmore Hall, London. Career: Perfs. in Concerts, Oratorio & Opera; num. TV & Radio apps.; currently Hd., Singing Dept., GSM. Contbr. to musical jrnls. of num. articles on singing-teaching, & reviews. Mbr., Arts Theatre Club, London. Hobbies: Reading. Address: 128 Pampisford Rd., Purley, Surrey CR2 2NH, UK. 3.

SMITH, Linda Lee, b. 12 Oct. 1948, Muscatine, Iowa, USA. Bassoonist; Classical Saxophonist. Educ: BM, Bassoon Perf., Univ. of Iowa, 1970; MMus, Bassoon Perf., Manhattan Schl. of Music, 1971; State Univ. of NY at Stony Brook, 1972. Career: Perf., Tully Hall & Avery Fischer Hall, Lincoln Center, Carnegie Hall, Town Hall, Carnegie Recital Hall, Aspen Music Fest., Tanglewood; Tri-City Symph., Davenport, Iowa; Adar Rapids Symph., Iowa; Springfield Symph., Springfield Mass.; Vermont Symph. Publs: A Method for Bassoon, 1973. Mbrships: Int. Double Reed Soc.; Coll. Music Soc.; World Saxophone Congress; Am. Fedn. of Musicians. Hons: Phi Beta Kappa; Pi Kappa Lambda. Hobbies: Skiing; Hiking; Biking; Running; Swimming; Tennis. Address: 154 Amherst Rd., Belchertown, MA 01007, USA.

SMITH, (Sister) Louise, S.S.M.N., b. 9 Dec. 1928, Rawlins, Wyo., USA. Music Librarian. Educ: BA, Our Lady of Victory Coll., Ft. Worth, Tex.; MLib. Sci., N. Tex. State Univ., Denton; MA in Musicol., Cath. Univ. of Am., Wash. DC. Career: currently Collections Libn. for Music, Univ. of Western Ont.,

London, Can. Mbrships: Music Lib. Assn.; Am. Musicol. Soc.; Can. Music Lib. Assn.; Int. Assn. Music Libs. Hobbies: Reading, Philately; Raising African Violets. Address: c/o Mount St. Joseph, 1486 Richmond St., London, Ont. Can., N6A 4X3.

SMITH, Lowell James, b. 22 Oct. 1936, Bakersfield, Calif., USA. Associate Professor of Music; Carillonneur; Organist. Educ: MMUS, Inc. Univ.; Eind Dip., Stitching Nederlandse Beiaardschool. m. Mary W G Trimmer, 1 d. Career: Assoc. Prof., Univ. of Calif., Riverside; Recitals on carillon, USA & Europe; Twice invited competitor, Carillon Competition, Hilversum, Netherlands, as part of Holland Festival. Publs: Ed., Bulletin of the Guild of Carillonneurs in N Am.; 1st Ed. & Fndr., Randschriften (carillon newsletter). Mbrships: Guild of Carillonneurs in N Am., Am. Guild of Organists; Bd. of Dirs., Riverside Opera Soc., Riverside Symph., Riverside Chorale. Address: Music Dept., Univ. of Calif., Riverside, Calif, CA 92502, USA.

SMITH, Malcolm Wallace, b. 6 Mar. 1944, Haslemere, Surrey, UK. Teacher; Composer; Pianist; Organist. Educ: Christ Ch. Cathedral Schl., Oxford; Denstone Coll.; BA, BMus, Leeds Univ.; MA, Otago Univ., NZ; Teacher's cert. m. Delma Marian Harper. Career: var. tchng. posts UK & NZ; mbr., Correspondence Schl. staff Wellington; Hd. of Broadcasting, Wellington; specialises in educ. tape music & electronic music. Comps. incl: Piano Sonata, 1971; music for film of Commonwealth Games, 1974; theatre music for NZ TV series; music for NZ colonial poetry, Nadoo Balantine-Scott & the Pioneer Poets, 1977 (recorded). Mbrships: Comps. Assn. of NZ; Royal Soc. of NZ; Australasian Performing Righs Assn. recip. Leeds Univ. Music Prize, 1963. Hobbies incl: Electronics; Astronomy. Address: Colchester Cres., Newlands, Wellington 4, NZ.

SMITH, Margaret Lillias, b. 26 Mar. 1930, Edinburgh, Scotland, UK. Concert Organiser. Educ: Edinburgh (Tynescastel); Nottingham (Coll. of Educ., Clifton); wide practical experience as Orchl. violinist, choral singer. m. Frank Ivan Smith. Career: Concert Organiser, Music Administration, Univ. of E Angilia, Norwich. mbr., ISM. Hobbies: Singing Adelburgh Fest. Singers & var. choirs; Playing Piano & Violin; Amateur Dramatics; Bird-watching. Address: 5 Station Cl., Lingwood, Norwidh NR13 4AX, UK.

SMITH, Maureen Felicity, b. Leeds, Yorks., UK. Violinist. Educ: Royal Manchester Coll. of Music; Ind. Univ., USA; violin study w. Szymon Goldberg. m. Geoffrey Rivlin, 1 d. Debut: Royal Festival Hall, 1961. Career: Soloist w. Nat. Youth Orch., 1961-64, incl. tours of Poland, Switz, Israel & Greece; D ebut at London Promenade Concerts, 1965; Soloist w. leading British Orchs. & on Radio & TV; Recital debut, Queen Elizabeth Hall, London., 1974. Recording: Medelssohn Violin Concerto Mbrships: ISM; European String Tchrs. Assn. Hons: 1st Prize, BBC Violin Comp., 1965: Gulbenkian Fndn. & Leverhulme Fellowships, 1967. Mgmt: Ibbs & Tillett Ltd. Address: 29 Hall Dr., Bramhope, York LS16 9JF, UK. 2. 27, 30.

SMITH, Meribel, b. 25 Sept. 1902, White Hall, Pa., USA. Retired Piano Teacher. Educ: Bucknell Univ., 1924; Diploma Piano Tchr., 1920. m. Russell T Smith, 1927, 2 s., 1 d. (dec.). Certified in Pa. Music Tchrs. Assn. & Music Tchrs.; Organ & Piano Tchrs. Assn.; Charter Mbr., Alumni Fund, Bucknell Patron; Intercontinental Biographical Assn., 1972. Recip. of Award of Appreciation 1959-60, Bucknell Bison Club. Address: RD No. 1, Muncy, PA 17756, USA.

SMITH, Michael John, b. 7 June 1937, London, UK. Cathedral Organist; Conductor; Examiner; Recitalist. Educ: BMus, MA, Oxford Univ.; Postgrad. Cert. in Educ., London Univ.; DMus, Edinburgh Univ., 1973; LRAM (piano perf.); LTCL (organ perf.); FRCO (CHM); ADCM. m. Marian Lesley Copper, 1d., 1 s. Career: incl: Asst. Choirmaster & Organist, Salisbury Cathedral & Dpty. Cond., Salisbury Musical Soc., 1967-74; Examiner to Royal Schls. of Music, 1969-; Organist & Master of the Choristers, Llandaff Cathedral, & Cond., Llandaff Cathedral Choral Soc., 1974-; Tutor, Univ. Coll., Cardiff, 1974-77. Recordings: w. Salibury Cathedral Choir, 1974. Publs: Ed., 2 Anthems by Michael Wise. Contbr. to: Musical Times & jrnls. Mbrships: Cathedral Organists' Assn.; ISM; RSCM; RCO. Recip. var. awards. Hobbies: Travel; Camping; Old buildings. Address: 1 St. Mary's, The Cathedral Green, Llandaff, Cardiff, UK. 28, 29, 30.

SMITH, Michael Joseph, b. 13 Aug. 1938, Tiline, Ky., USA. Composer; Pianist. Educ: MD; PhD, Biochem.; Pvte. music studies w. David Baker, Ran Blake; New Engl. Conservatory of Music; Juilliard Schl.; Self-taught. m. Kerstin Alli-Maria Andersson Smith, 2 s., 1 d. Debut: Nashville, Tenn., USA. aged 6 yrs. Career: Ballet S Elvira Madigan, Inferno; Film: The

Seventh Level; No Place to Hide; Num. TV appearances in Europe & USA incl. Swedish Drama Series. Compositions: Over 200 works. Recordings: 110 compositions on var. LPs; 30 LPs in Germany, USA, France, Italy, Poland, Japan. Mbrships: Swedish Composers' Soc.; BMI; ISCM; IJF. Hons: Swedish Culture Prize, 1978; Swedish Cultural Coun. Award for World Perf. of Elivira Madigan, 1978. Hobbies: Golf; Piloting. Mgmt: GLF Prods., NY, USA. Address: Svinaberga Skola, S-27057, Sweden.

SMITH, Nicholas Richard Norman, b. 2 Jan. 1948, Manchester, UK. Conductor. Educ: Birmingham Univ.; Northern Schl. Music; studied w. France ferrara, Siena. m. Sally Burlingham. Debut: London, QEH, 1978. Career: Tutor, music hist., Royal Northern Coll. Music, 1973-75; Prin. cond., Northern Chmbr., Orch., 1971-; Prin. cond., Chmbr., Orch., S Yorks, 1975-; Guest cond. Finland & Hungary; Frequent broadcasts, BBC; Fest. Dir., Macclesfield Fest., 1976. Mbr., ISM. Hobbies: Bridge; Squash. Address: 18 Mauldeth Rd., Withington, Manchester M20 9ND, UK.

SMITH, Norman Edward, b. 26 Aug. 1921, Cape Girardeau, Mo., USA. Professor of Music; Trumpeter. Educ: BA, BME, Univ. of Southwestern La., 1943; MME, La. State Univ., 1950; PhD, Fla. State Univ., 1968. m. Aline Jackson Smith, 2 d. Career: Music Tchr., DeRidder, La., High Schk., 1945-48, Terrebone High Schl., Houma, La., 1948-54; Prof. of Music, McNeese State Univ., Lake Charles, La., 1954-. Publs: Band Music Notes (w. Stoutamire) 1977. Contbr. to: NACWPI Journal Int. Trumpet Guild Journal Mbrships: MENC; past State Chmn., ibid; Coll. Band Dirs. Nat. Assn.; past State Chmn., ibid; Phi Beta Mu; past State Pres., ibid; NACWPI; Phi Mu Alpha Sinfonia; Zeta Chi Chapt. Advsr., ibid. Recip. var. Hons: Hobbies: Flying; Boating; Fishing; Cycling. Address: 909 W Claude St. Lake Charles, LA 70605 USA.

SMITH, Patrick John, b. 11 Dec. 1932, NYC, USA. Critic; Writer; Editor; Publisher. Educ: BA, Princeton Univ. m. Elisabeth Munro, 2 s. Publs: The Tenth Muse (A History of the Libretto), 1970; The Musical Newsletter (Publr. & Ed.), 1971-. Contbr. to: High Fidelity; Musical Am.; Musical Times (UK); Opera (UK); Lyrica (Paris, France); Grove's Dictionary, 6th ed. Address: 1185 Park Ave., NY, NY 10028, USA.

SMITH, Richard Langham, b. 10 Sept. 1947, London, UK. Writer on Music; Harpsichordist; Lecturer. Educ: BA, York Univ.; Amsterdam Conserv. m. Joan Dixon. Career: num. recitals w. baroque chmbr. grps.; currently Lectr. in Music, Univ. of Lancaster. Publs: Ed. & Transl., Debussy on Music, 1976. Contbr. to: Times Lit. Supplement; Times Higher Educ. Supplement; Music & Letters, etc. Hobbies: Wine; Gardening; Travel; Languages. Address: Ruckers Cottae, Far Westhouse, via Carnforth, Lancs., UK.

SMITH, Robert, b. Dec. 1922, Whitchurch, Wales, UK. Educator. Educ: BMus, Univ. Coll., Cardiff, Wales, 1946, MMus, 1947; FTCL, 1948. m. Hilda Brangwynne, 1 s., 2 d. Career: External Examiner, A Level Music, Welsh Jt. Educ. Committee, 1962-71 & 1973-; External Examiner, Oxford Polytech. Lady Spencer Churchill Coll. Vice Chmn., Guild for the Promotion of Welsh Music, 1964-66, VP, 1970-. Lectr. in Music, Univ. Coll. of N Wales, Bangor, 1947-69; Sr. Lectr., ibid, 1969-. Comps: Sweet was the Song; Cyfod f'anwyld; Y Wennol; Cath i'r Eos; Pan Oeddwn Fachgen; Ring out, ye crystal spheres; Anghardd; Arr., Duw gadwo'r Brenin, Glan Meddwdod mwyn & Susan llygat-ddu in The St. Deiniol Carol Book. Publs: Six Catalogues of Contemporary Welsh Music, 1959-65. Contbr. to: Music Review; Wales; Anglo-Welsh Review; Welsh Music. Hons: John Edwards Mem. Prize, 1973. Hobbies: Swimming; Walking. Address: Bodafon Villa, Pk. Cres., Llanfairfechan, Gwynedd LL33 OBE, UK. 3.

SMITH, Robert Edward, b. 26 July 1946, Bayonne, NJ, USA. Harpsichordist; Organist; Associate Music Director; Composer. Educ: BS, Mannes Coll. of Music, NYC, 1968. Debut: Carnegie Recital Hall, NYC, 1970. Career: 1st perf. of comoplete harpsichord music of Francois Couperin, NYC, 1972-76; World tour incl. radio broadcasts in Europe & Aust. Comps: 6 Hymns to Our Lady; To Devm; 3 canonic anthems for Passiontide; ibid., for Advent; Partita for organ; 8 Preludes a trad. Christman awards; other ch. music. Hobbies: Cooking; Gardening. Mgmt: Arts Image, Ltd. Address: 150 Scotland Rd., S Orange, NJ 07079, USA.

SMITH, Roger, b. 6 July 1949, Tunbridge Wells, UK. Cellist. Educ: LRAM. m. Felicity Roy, 1s., 1 d. Career: mbr., Acad. of St. Martin-in-the-Fields, London Str. Quartet & Gasliano Trio. Address: The Old Parsonage, Tidebrook Wadhurst, E Sussex, UK.

SMITH, Ronald, b. 3 Jan. 1922, London, UK. Concert Pianist. Educ: Sir Michael Costa Scholar for comp., RAM; studied pvtly. in Paris; FRAM; B Mus, Dunelm. m. Anne Norman, 1d. Debut: Promenade Concert under Sir Henry Wood, 1942. Career: Recitals & illustration talks for BBC, ORTF etc.; sev. tours of Australia, Can. & Far East; Comps: Symphonic Prelude; Comedy Overture; Violin concert MS-MC by BBC. Recordings incl: works by Liszt, Alkan, Balakirev, Chopin, etc. Publs: Alkan-The Man & his Music, 1975; Alkan- the Enigma, 1976; Alkan in miniature, 1978. Contbr. to: Musical Times; Music & Musicians; The Listener. Hons: Pres., Alkan Soc. Hobbies: Walking; Swimming; Gardening. Mgmt: Helen Anderson, 66 Cromwell Ave., London, 6. Address: Tanners House, School Rd., Saltwood, Hythe, Kent, UK. 30.

SMITH, Ronald Aubrey, b. 3 Sept. 1928. London, UK. Advisor for Music; Examiner; Adjudicator; Festival Conductor. Educ: Maud Mary Gooch Organ Schlr., RAM; FRAM; FTCL. m. Moya Kathleen Roberts, 1 s., 2 d. Career: Dir. of Music, Pub. Schls., 1950-63; Co. Music Advsr., W Suffolk, 1963-68; Insp. of Schls. (Music), Bristol, 1968-74; Sr. Advsr. for Music, Co. of Avon, 1974-. Publs: Splendd Zingen Zingen Spelen (Play Sing Sing Play), Books 1-4 (Co-author w. Chris Rabé), 1973-74. Mbrships: ISME; Chmn., 1976-77, ibid. Int. Bd. of Dirs., 1978-80 Music Advsrs.' Nat. Assn.; Exec. Mbr. until 1974, Chmn. 1966-77; ISM 1976-77; Chmn., SW Arts Music Advsry. Panel Address: 35 Pembroke Rd., Clifton, Bristol BS8 3BE, UK. 3.

SMITH, Wayne C, b. 21 July 1953. Salem, Ohio, USA. Teacher; Conductor; Cellist. Educ: BMus, Dana Schl. of Music; MMus, Univ. of Idaho; studies w. Peter N Synnestvedt, William Wharton, Marijke Verberne & Gordon Epperson. m. Dawn A Morrison-Smith, 1 s. Career: Cond., Spokane Falls Community Symph.; Prof. of cello, Spokane Falls Community Coll., 1976-. Mbrships: Phi Mu Alpha Sinfonia; AFM; Am. Str. Tchrs. Assn. recip. Pro Musica Medallion of Dutch Min. of Educ., 1975. Address: S 3905 Sundown Dr., Spokane, WA 99206, USA.

SMITH, Wilford Davis, b. 4 July 1913. Fulton, Mo. USA. Professor of Music. Educ: BS, Tex. Tech. Univ. 1941; MMus, Univ. Tex., 1948; PhD, Geo. Peabody Coll., 1955. m. Montez Snider Smith, 1 s., 1 d. Career: Prof. Music (hist. & lit.), Northeast La. Univ., Monroe, La. Contbr. to: La. Musician; La. Schls. Mbrships: Am. Musicol. Soc.; Music Tchrs. Nat. Assn.; La. Music Tchrs. Assn.; Phi Mu Alpha; Pres., Psi Chapt., Phi Delta Kappa, 1952-53; Pres., La. Chapt., Fellowship United Meth. Musicians, 1965-66; Alpha Chi; Pi Kappa Lambda. Hon: Named Disting. Tchr., Northeat La. Univ., 1971 & '74. Hobbies: Music; Reading; Fishing; Boating. Address: 429 Bayou Oaks Dr., Monroe, LA 71201, USA. 7.

SMITH, Wilfred, b. 8 Aug. 1911. London, UK. Harp-Maker & Repairer; Flautist. Educ: RAM. m. (2) Daphne Ibbott. Career: has app. w. var. orchs. & ensembles inclng. Prin. Flute, Scottish Orch. & Royal Opera House Covent Gdn., Piccolo Player, LPO & BBC Symph. Orch., currently Flautist, London Mozart Players; Dir., Summer Holiday Courses for Flute & Recorder Players. Comps: Orchestral Studies for Flute, 3 vols.; Music for Clarsach & Harp; First Tutor for Delius' & Clarsach. Recordings: Welsh Songs w. Ann Legend' Contbr. to: The Motor-Cycle; Motor-Cycling; var. music mags. Mbr: ISM. Hons: Brough Prize, RAM, 1930; James Prize, RAM, 1930. Address: 15 Castelnau, Barnes, London SW13 9RP. UK.

SMITHER, Howard E, b. 15 Nov. 1925. Pittsburg, Kan., USA. Musicologist. Educ: BA, Hamline Univ.; MA, Cornell Univ.; PhD, ibid. m. Ann M. Woodward. Career: Instr. Music, 1955-57, Asst. Prof., 1957-60, Oberlin Coll. & Conserv. of Music; Asst. Prof., Univ. of Kan., 1960-63; Assoc. Prof., Tulane Univ., 1963-68; Assoc. Prof., 1968-71, Prof., 1971-, Univ. of NC, Chapel Hill. Publ: The Oratorio in the Baroque Era, 1977. Contbr. to: num. profl. jrnls., encys. Mbrships: Am. Musicol. Soc. & Past Coun. Mbr., Past Chmn., SE Chaps.; Int. Musicol. Soc.; Italian Musicol. Soc.; Coll. Music Soc.; Past Mbr., Bd. of Dirs., Music Lib. Assn. Hons: Sr. Grad. Fellowship, Cornell Univ., Fulbright Grant, for study in Germany, 1953-54; Fulbright Sr. Rsch. Grant, for study in Italy, 1965-66; Sr. Fellowship, for rsch. in Italy, Nat. Endowment for the Humanities, 1972-73; Other smaller grants; The Deems Taylor Award of ASCAP, 1978. Address: Dept. of Music, Univ. of NC, Chapel Hill, NC 27514, USA. 11, 14.

SMOLANOFF, Michael Louis, b. 11 May 1942. NYC, USA. Composer; Educator; Editor. Educ: BMus & MS, Juilliard Schl. of Music; Studied w. Aaron Copland, Tanglewood Comp. w. Vincent Persichetti. Married, 1 s. 1 d. Career: App., Carnegie Recital Hall & NYC Town Hall; BBC & Exelandic Radio Broadcasts; Num. Perfs. throughout world inclng. Argentina, 1971, Australia, 1971-72, Austria, 1971, Belgium, 1971,

Can., 1972, Denmark, 1971, Hungary, 1971, Israel, 1971. Comps (publd.) incl: Preludes for Piano, 1967; Canticle for Band, 1966; Concerto for Trombone & Orch., 1968; Essay for Horn & String Orch., 1968; Caricature for Solo Guitar, 1972; Four Haiku Songs, Soprano & Piano, 1973; Kaleidoscope for Band, 1973; Symph. No. III for Wind Ensemble, 1973; Vercingetorix, an opera in one act, three scenes, 1973. Recrodings: Canticle for and (RCA). Contbr. to: 125 Yrs. of Music for the Saxophone, 20th Century Piano Music by Am. Comps. Mbrships: ASCAP; Comps. Workshop, Juilliard Schl. of Music; Nat. Assn. for Am. Comps. & Conds. Hons. incl: Edward B Benjamin Award, 1965; ASCAP Award, 1965-74. Hobbies: Photography. Addess: J 77 Finisterre Apts., Lindenwold, NJ 08021, USA.

SMOLKA, Jaroslav, b. 8 Apr. 1933. Prague, Czech. Musicologist; Composer; Educator. Educ: studied musicol., 1951-56, PhDr, CSc, 1964, Univ. Carolina, Prague; studied w. Profs. Mirko Ocadik & Antonin Sychra; studied compo. w. Prof. Václav Dobiás, AMU, Prague, 1953-56. m. Jara Smolková, 1 s., 1 d. Debut: as comp., Prague, 1955. Career incls: Lectr., Hist. of Music, AMU, Prague; Musical Dir., Supraphon, Panton & other records, TV musical progs., etc. Comps. incl: Under the Blue Sky (10 songs, children's choir, soloist, flute & piano); The Cock Sits Above a Cloud (for women's choir, settings of poems by Vtezslav Nezval; 2nd String Quartet; Sei Poemi per I Due Boemi for bass clarinet & piano; Sonata for Trumpet solo; Fugue Suita after Czech anonyms of 18th-Century for str. quartet. Publs: Ladislav Vycpálek, 1960; Czech Music of Our Century, 1961; Czech Cantata & Oratorium, 1970. Contbr. to musical publs. & Czech radio. Addess: Nad Bertramkou 4, 15& 00 Prague 5 Smichov, Czech.

SMYTH, Brian Mills, b. 15 Oct. 1928. Weymouth, UK. Lecturer. Educ: BA, Open Univ.; RAM; LRAM; ARCM; LTCL. m. Mary Elizabeth Wallis, 1 s., 1 d. Career: Vis. Music Tchr.; Staffs. Educ. Committee, 1953-58; Dir. of Music, Wednesbury Boys High Schl., 1958-60; Dir. of Music, Bushey Grammar Schl., 1960-66; Lectr. in Music, Wall Hall Coll. of Educ., Aldenham, Herts., 1966-68; Snr. Lectr., ibid, 1968; Prin. Lectr. & Hd. of Dept., ibid, 1974-; Hd. of Music Dept., Herts. Coll. of Higher Educ., 1977-. Comps: Songs; piano pieces; incidental music to plays; arrs. for schls. Mbr., RAM Club. Hobbies inc: Hist.; Poetry; Lit. Antiques; Chess; Travel. Address: Clavinia, 54 Belmont Rd., Bushey, Herts. WD2 2JP, UK. 3, 29.

SNAVELY, Jack, b. 11 Mar. 1929. Harrisburg, Pa., USA. Clarinettist; Professor of Music. Educ: BS, Lebanon Valley Coll., Annville, Pa.; MMus, Univ. of Mich.; Additional grad. work, Northwestern Univ. & Peabody. m. JoEllen Bryan Snavely, 2 s. Career: Prof. of Music, tchr. of Clarinet & saxophone & former dir., Symphonic Band, Univ. of Wis.-Milwaukee; Soloist, cond., clinician, recitalist, adjudicator, clarinettist, Woodwind Arts Quintet; Saxophone, Leblanc Fine Arts Saxophone Quartet; Perfs. w. num. orchs. & other musical orgs.; Num. radio & TV perfs. Compositions incl: Clarinet Method for Beginning Students, 1965; Clarinet Studies on the Intermediate Level, 1967; Solo de Concours, by Messager-Snavely, clarinet solo w. band accompaniment, 1967; Largo, Allegro Molto, by Mozart-Snavely, 1974. Recordings: Clarinet Recital, 1970; Woodwind Arts Quintet, 1973. Publs. incl: Basic Technique for all saxophones, 1969; Basic Technique for oboe, 1969; Fourteen Progressive Duets for Clarinets, 1977. Contbr. to num. jrnls. Mbrships: Phi Kappa Phi; Pi Kappa Lambda. Recip. of hons. Hobbies incl: Photogrpahy; Swimming. Address: Univ. of Wis., Milwaukee, WI 53201, USA.

SNIDER, Ronald Joe, b. 4 Aug. 1947. Rotan, Tex., USA. Percussionist. Educ: N Tex. State Univ.; Mills Colls.; Park Point Coll.; studied w. Henk Badings, Pandit Mahapurush Misra, Pandit Ram Narayan, Kalman Cherry, Anthony Civone. m. Joan Weller. Career: Percussionest, Dallas Symph., Dallas Civic Opera; Soloist, Am. Wind Symph., in USA & toured S Am.; Ann Arbor Film Fest., Stanford Univ., Contemporary Music Fest.; In t. Carnival of Experimental Sound, London; perf. w. Winter Consort; recorded for Radio, TV, Phonograph, Films. Contbr. to Percussive Arts. Mag. Mbrships: Int. Cont. of Symph. & Opera Musicians; Am. Soc. for Eastern Arts; Percussive Arts Soc. Hobbies: Collector of Ethnic Instruments; Aquarist; Motorist. Addres: 2343 Rexlawn, Dallas, TX 75227, USA.

SNIŽKOVÁ-ŠKRHOVÁ, Jitka, b. 14 Sept. 1924. Prague, Czech. Pianist; Composer; Professor. Educ: Final exams, Charles Univ., 1948-49; Final exams, Prague Conserv., 1948; Dip., Master Class, ibid., 1948. m. Frantisek Skrhá, 1 s. Career: Concerts & recitals, lecturers at musical congresses; pianist in Ensemble of Nat. Dance & Song; External worker, Nat. Museum; Tchr. in House of Culture; Prof., Prague Conserv. Comps. incl: Zvon, 1966; Rythmicon for 2 pianos, 1973;

Triptych, for soprano & piano, 1976; Stredoveké reminiscence, for organ, 1977. num. recordins inclng. own works. Publs: Musica Polyphonica Bohemiae, 1958; Czech Vocal Polyphony of 16th-17th centuries, 1969; Carmina Festiva, 1978; Jiří Rychnovský: Missa, 1973. Contbr. to profl. jrnls. Mbrships: VP, Mozart Soc. in CSSR/Prague; Soc. of Nat. Museum in Prague; Gesellschaft für Musikforschung. Hobbies: Travel; Minerology. Address: 15000 Prague 5-Smichov, Nad Santoskou 9/74, Czeh.

SNOW, Ursula Mary, b. 8 Dec. 1927. London, UK. Violinist. Educ: RCM, London; ARCM Violin; ARCM. Piano. m. W A Beamist, 2 s., 1 d. Debut: Wigmore Hall, 1960. Career: Chamber music player & recitalist; Mbr. of Croma Piano Trio. Mbrships: ISM; Park Lane Grp. Hobbies: Reading; Theatre; Walking; Camping. Mgmt: Ibbs & Tillet. Address: 4 Mountfort Cres., London N. 1, UK. 3.

SNOWBALL, (Adrienne) Elizabeth, b. 14 Jan., 1939. Bainton, Stamford, Lincs., UK. Musician (Violin, Piano), Teacher. Educ: Peterborough Tech. Coll.; Stamford Schl. of Music, AGSM Dip., GSM. Career: In West End Shows, London, The King & I & West Side Story; London Sr. Orch. BBC TV Monitor, & Saturday Spectacular; Capriol Orch. of London; London Chanticleer Orch.; Engl. Nat. Orch., London; Ulster Symph. Orch.; Billy Connolly Tour, 1976; John Hanson Tour, 1977-78; Taught at: GSM, Jr. Exhib. Scheme; Kings Coll. Schl., Wimbledon; Wimbledon High Schl. for Girls; On Music Staff of James Allens Girls Schl., Dulwich & Inner London Educ. Authority. Mbrships: Musicians Union; European String Tchrs. Assn. Hobbies: Photography; Theatre; Travel; Reading. Address: School House, Bainton, Stamford, Lincs. PE9 3AF, UK. 29, 30.

SNOWDEN, James Wyn, b. 2 May 1943. Lufkin, Tex., USA. Conductor; Music Educator; Trombonist. Educ: BS, MA in Music, Stephen F Austin State Univ.; PhD, Univ. of Colo.; studied Conducting w. Anshel Brusilow, Richard Burgin. m. Shirley Ann Pace, 2 d., 1 s. Career: Dir., Hudson Band, Tex., 7 yrs.; Dir. & Fndr., Longview HS Orch., Tex., concerts in Holland & Luxembourg; Fndr. & Cond., Longview Symph. Orch; Music Dir., Longview Ballet & Community Theatres. Recordings: History in Sound, Longview Symph. Orch.; Judson Band, 3 volumes. Contbr. to: The Instrumentalist; The School Musicians;, The Music Jrnl. Mbrships: Am. Symph. Orch. League; Tex. Music Educators Assn. (Region Orch. Chmn.); Tex. Prof. Educs. Assn. Hons: Leadership & Achievement Award, Tex. Music Educators, 1971; Winner, Honors Competition in Conducting Seminar, Jacksonville, Fla. Hobbies: Tennis; Golf. Address: 29 Country Pl., Longview, TX 75601, USA.

SNOWMAN, M Nicholas, b. 18 Mar. 1944. London, UK. Music Administrator. Educ: Magdalene Coll., Cambridge UKniv. Career: Fndr. & Admnstr., Cambridge Univ. Opera Soc., 1965-67; Asst. to Hd. of Music Staff, Glyndebourne Fest. Opera, 1967-69; Gen. Mgr., London Sinfonietta, 1968-72; Dir., Dept. Artistique, Inst. de Rsch. & Coord. Accoustique Musique (IRCAM), Paris, France, 1972-; Consciller Astutique, Ensemble Inter-Contemporaire, Paris, 1976-. Publs: Co-ed., A Granta Anthology. Address: IRCAM, Ctr. Georges Pompidou, 35 Blvd. Sebastopol, 75001, Paris, France. 3.

SNYDER, Barry, b. 6 Mar. 1944. Allentown, Pa., USA. Concert Pianist; Teacher. Educ: BMus; MMus; Performer's Cert. in Piano; Artist's Dip. in Piano; Eastman Schl. of Music. Debut: w. Allentown Symph. Orch., age 14. Career: Soloist w. Detroit, Atlanta, Nat. & Rochester Symph. Orchs.; Performer of Chmbr. Music w. Composer's, Curtis & Purcell Quartets; Solo recitals throughout USA, Canada & UK Recordings: Suite for Piano by Alec Wilder; Sonata No. 7 in B Flat Major by Prokofiev; Music for Bass Trombone & Piano (All Golden Crest); Piano Monster Concert (Music for Multiple Pianos - Columbia); Recording: An Album of American Piano Music. Mbrships: Pi Kappa Lambda; Na.t MTA; NGPT. Hons: Worcester Festival Prize, 1965; var. prizes, Van Cliburn Int. Piano Comp., 1966. Address: 144 Penn Ln., Rochester, NY 14625, USA.

SNYDER, Mary Susan Smeltzer (profl. name Susan Smeltzer), b. 13 Sept. 1941. Sapulpa, Okla., USA. Pianist; Composer; Teacher; Adjudicator. Educ: BMus, Okla. City Univ., 1963; MMus, Univ. of S Calif. (w. Lillian Steuber), 1967; Vienna Akademie fur Musik (w. Joseph Dichler), 1969-70; further studies w. Gregor Piatigorsky & Rosina Lhevinne. m. Dr. Philip S Snyder. Debut: aged 9, Sapulpa, Okla. Career: extensive solo & chmbr. music recitals throughout S, Mid-West & W USA; apps. w. num. Am. symph. orchs., perfs. on radio & TV. num. unpub. comps. Recordings: Liszt prog. Contbr. to: Sapulpa Herald; Piano Guild Notes; Pasadena Citizen. Mbrships: Pi Kappa Lambda; Sigma Alpha Iota; NGPT; etc. Hons: winner of over 20 artist competitions. Mgmt: Martha Moore Smith

Enterprises, NYC; Community Concerts Inc., NYC. Hobbies incl: Painting; Poetry; Genealogy; Cycling. Address: 8102 Tavenor, Houston, TX 77075, USA.

SOAMES, Cynthia Elizabeth, b. 6 Oct. 1946. Peru, Ind., USA. Percussionist; Timpanist; Teacher. Educ: BMus, Coll.-Conserv. of Music, Univ. of Cincinnati, 1969; MMus, Schl. of Music, Univ. of Miami, 1973. Career: Mbr., Ft. Lauderdale, Nashville & NC Symph.; perfs. w. Cincinnati Percussion Ensemble, Miami (Fla.) Opera Guild, Fla. Family Opera Orch. & Indpls. Symph. Orch.; Tchr. of Percussion, Butler Univ., Western Ky. Univ., St. Joseph's Coll. of Rensselaer, Ind., Univ. of NC at Chapel Hill & Univ. of Wis.-River Falls; Mbr. of Staff, Smith-Walbridge Band Camp. Contbr. to: Percussionist; Percussive Notes; Woodwind World - Brass & Percussion. Mbrships: Historian, Percussive Arts Soc. Address: 115 N Miami St., Peru, IN 46970, USA. 27.

SOARES NETTO, Calimerio Augusto, b. 26 Dec. 1944. Sao Sebastiao do Paraiso, Minas Gerais, Brazil. Pianist; Professor of Piano, Musical Education, Theory, History of Music, Harmony, Musical Pedagogy, Chorale, Folklore. Educ: Tech. course in Music & Music Educ.; Musical Conserv. of Ribeirao Preto (SP); Piano at Coll. of Arts. Univ. of Uberlandia (MG). Debut: 1st Piano Recital in Sao Sebastiao do Paraiso Conserv. of Ituiutaba (MG), Brazil, 1969-; Creator & Dir. of Musical Grp. Arsantika, 1974-. Hons. incl: Medal, Hon. of Merit, State Conserv. of Music, Ituiutaba (MG), 1971; Title of Madrigalist, Second Nat. Contest of Comps. & Choral Arrs., Renaissance Madrigal, Minas Gerais, Brazil, 1976. Address: Rua 26, no. 507, 38300 Ituiutaba, Minas Gerias, Brazil.

SOBOL, Lawrence Paul, b. 10 July 1946. NYC, USA. Clarinettist. Educ. incls: BMus, MMus, Manhattan Schl. of Music; studies w. noted tchrs. Debut: Carnegie Hall, 1969. Career: Recitalist; Clinician; Recording Artist; num. chmbr. music broadcasts on TV & radio; Dir., LI Chmbr. Ensemble of NY; has premiered many comps.; Cons., Alexander Broude Inc. Has recorded num. works by Am. composers inclng: Karel Husa; Roy Harris; David Diamond; Alan Hovhaness. Publs: Eighteen Contemp Etudes, 1971. Contbr. to: Instrumentalist. Recip. Ford Fndn. Scholarship, 1964-65, to study at Peabody Conserv., Balt. Hobbies: Fine restaurants; Execellent cigars; Row boating. Address: 190 N Linden St., N Massapequa, NY 11758,USA.

SODERHOLM, Valdemar, b. 18 Nov. 1909. Moliden, Angermanland, Sweden. Professor; Conductor. Educ: w. Prof. Hans Lampert, Sundsvall (piano, organ, theory); BMus (organist, precentor & music tchr.) The State Coll. of Music, Stockholm; counterpoint w. Prof. Finn Hoffding, Copenhagen. m. Agnes Maria Görtz, 3 c. Career: Prof. in Music Theory, State Coll. of Music, Stockholm; Cond. of the Choir of Hedvig Eleonora Ch., Stockholm. Compositions for organ, choir, solo voice w. organ. Publs: Arbetsboki elementar harmoni Larz, 1950; Arbetsbok i modulation, 1952; Harmonilära 1957; Spelovningar i modulation, 1969; Arbetsboki elementar kontrapunkt, Palestrinastil, 1969. Mbrships: Fellow, Kungl Musikaliska Academien; Stim. Hobbies: Photography. Address: Storgatan 44 III, 114 55 Stockholm, Sweden.

SÖDERSTEN, Gunno, b. 10 Jan. 1920. Stockholm, Sweden. Composer; Church Musician; Pianist; Organist. Educ: Coll. educ., gen. degree in languages, 1939; Royal Music Acad., music dir., 1942, Dip. in comp., cond., & ch. music. m. Barbro, 2 d., 1 s. Debut: as pianist, Stockholm, 1935. Career: Organist & cond., Immanuel Ch., Stockholm, 1943-; perfs. on radio & TV; ch. services in Sweden & USA. Comps. incl: 9 Sacred Songs; Organ-partita; Organ Symph. No. 1; In the Holy Land; 3 organ preludes; other organ works; choral music; works in MSS. sev. recordings as organist & cond. Contbr. to Sohlmans Musiklexicon. mbr., Swedish Soc. of Comps, 1969-. Hons: Stockholm Cultural prize, 1970. Hobbies: Football; Cycling. Address: Bovägen 5, 18143 Lidingö, Sweden.

SODERSTROM, Elisabeth Anna, b. 7 May 1927. Sweden. Opera Singer (soprano). Educ: Study of singin w. Andrejewa de Skilonz & at Opera Schl., Stockholm. m. Sverker Olow, 1950, 3 s. Career: w. Royal Opera, Stockholm, 1950-; Appearance at Salzburg, 1955; Glyndebourne, 1957-64; Metropol. Opera, NY, 1959-63; USSR tour, 1966; frequent concert & TV appearances in Europe & USA; Repertoire incl. Fioridiligi in Cosi fan Tutte; Countess & Susanna in Marriage of Figaro; Countess in Capriccio; leading roles in Der Rosenkavalier. Mbrships: RAM. Hons: Singer of the Ct., Sweden, 1959; Order of Vasa; Stelle della Solidarieta d'Italia; Prize for Best Acting, Royal Swedish Acad., 1965; Literis & Artibus Award, 1969. Hobbies: Sailing; Lit.; Embroidery. Address: 19 Hersbyvagen, Lidingo 1, Sweden.

SOFRAS, Polychronis George, b. 15 Mar. 1930. Piraeus, Greece. Harpist; Musicologist. Educ: Athens Conserv.; Dip. Harp, Juilliard Schl. of Music, NY, USA; BMus & MSc, Cath. Univ., WAsh. DC; PhD Music Hist. m. Pamela Jean Anderson, 1 d. Career: Harp solo apps. w. orch.; Harp recitals in Athens & Bach Fest., London; 1st Harpist, State Symph. Orch., Athens; Athens Opera; Baton Rouge Symph. Orch., USA; Cath. Univ. Symph. Orch., USA; Mbr. Grp. for Contemporary Music, Athens. Comps: Marsyas & Apollo (ballet); Suite on Greek Dances for Harp. Recordings: Megalos Erotikos by Manos Hadjidakis, Lyra. Publs: Rhythmic Analysis for Dancers, 1976; The Harp, 1968. Contbr. to The Pilgrimage. Mbr. num. profl. orgs. Hons. incl: Greek State Scholarship Award, 1962. Hobbies: Instrumental Making; Stage Designing; Hiking; Swimming. Address: 759 Jennifer Jean Dr., Baton Rouge, LA 70808, USA.

SOH, Tomotada, b. 11 June 1948. Tokyo, Japan. Violinist. Educ: Toho Music Schl., Tokyo; 1st Prize, Paris Conserv.; studied w. Joseph Szigeti. m. Elizabeth Stalker. Career: Soloist, perfs. in USA, Europe, Japan, incl. Menuhin Gstaad Fest. & Montreux; var. Radio & TV apps. throughout the world; Asst. to Joseph Szigeti. Recordings: Brahms, Mendelssohn Concertos, Paganini trios, etc. Hons: Geneva Int. Competition, 1963; Long Thibaud, Paganini, 1964. Hobbies: Swimming; Walking. Mgmt: Barbara Graham, London. Address: 1816 Les Bonnettes, Chailly, Switzerland.

SOKA, Ladislav, b. 7 Nov. 1931. Bratislava, Czechoslovakia. Flautist. Educ: Absolutorium, Nat. Conserv., Bratislava. m. Viere Piatkowska, 1 s., 1 d. Debut: Prague 1953. Career: Num. perfs. as soloist, Czechoslovakia & abroad; apps. & recordings for TV & Radio; Mbr., Slovak Phil. Orch. & Slovak Quintet; Prof., Nat. Conserv., Bratislava. Mbr., Union of Slovak Comps. (Br. Soloist). Hons: Int. Contest, Prague, Spring 1953; 3rd Prize, Brass Sect.. Contest for Antonin Rejcha Prize, 1953. Hobbies: Sports, Tennis; Concerts. Address: Steinerova 82/A, Bratislava 801 00, Czechoslovakia.

SOKOL, Vilem, b. 22 May 1915. Pa., USA. Professor of Music; Orchestra Conductor; Opera Conductor; Musical Director (Violin). Educ: Oberlin Conserv. of Music; Fellowship, Juilliard Schl. of Music; Fellowship, State Conserv. of Music, Prague, Czechoslovakia. m. Agatha, Hoeschele, 10c. Career: Prof. of Music, Univ. of Wash.; Cond. & Musical Dir., Seattle Youth Symph. Orch.; Cond. in 1812 segment of hr-long film entitled Relations, 1974 (Acad. Award Winner). Recordings incl: Cond., Seattle Youth Symph. Publs: The Family of Strings & A Listener's Guide to Musical Analysis (TV series). Recip. num. awards inclng: Citations from Seattle City Coun. Hobbies: Photography; Swimming. Address: 6303 NE 185, Seattle, WA 98155, USA.

SOKOLA, Milos, b. 18 Apr. 1913. Bucovice, Moravia. Composer; Violinst. Educ: Brno Conserv.; Master Schl. of Comp., Prague. m. Milona. Debut: Concert, Conserv. of Brno, 1933. Career: Mgr., Music Schl.; Kromertz; Mbr., Nat. Theatre Orch., Prague. Comps. Variations on a theme by Vitezslava Kapralova; Toccata for organ; Lullabies; Concerto for violin & orch.; Valses; Ciaccona for organ; 9th of May; Preludes; Passacaglia quasi; Toccata on theme of Bach; Sonata for violin & piano. Hons: Neuman's Prize, Brno, 1938; Prize, Prague Artists Club comp., 1947; 1st Prize, Czech radio comp., 1948; Prize on hon., Jubilee comp. of Union of Czech Composers, 1960. Hobbies: Chess; Walking. Address: Male Kysice, ul. Miru 59, 273 51 Unhost, Czechoslovakia, 3, 14, 28.

SOKORSKI, Jerzy, b. 3 May 1916. Yalta, Crimea. Composer; Pianist. m. Bogna Sokorska, 1 d. Debut: 1936. Career: Composer, Concert Pianist, Warsaw, 1945-; Rome, 1950; Radio Opera, Warsaw, 1958; Quintet, Warsaw, 1967; Concert for voice & orch., Fest. Mod. Music, Wroclaw, 1972; Concerts, recitals, w. wife (singer), Europe & USA, 1955; Chmbr. concerts, Nat. Phil., Warsaw, 1952-. Comps. incl: Concerto for piano & orch.; Nights of King (opera). Recordings: Radio Opera, Story of the End of the World. Mbr., Soc. Polish Composers. Hobbies incl: Colour photography. Address: 05-820 Piastow, Bradta 2a, Poland. 3.

ŠOLC, Karel, b. 27 Jan. 1893. Milevsko, Czechoslovakia. Pianist; Editor; Arranger. Educ: 1st Piano & Theory w. Prof. Adolf Mikes & Václav Stepán, Prague. m. Ruzena Kusová. Debut: 1917. Career: Concert & Radio perfs. as Soloist, Chmbr. Music player, Accomp. of singers & instrumentalists, 1917- (left hand disabled 1966); Mbr. Editorial Socs., preparing editions of works by Smetana, A. Dvorak, Z. Fibich, J B Foerster, O Ostrcil M Martinu, 1926-; Arr., piano extracts, mainly from works of contemporary Prague. Former mbr., Soc. of Czech Comps. & Concert Artists. Hons: State Distinction, For Excellent Work, 1968; Awards for Propagation of Czech

Music, Suprafon. Hobby: Travel (until 1966). Address: Nezamyslova ul. no. 5, 118 00 Prague 2, Czech.

SOLER, Josep, b. 25 May 1935. Barcelona, Spain. Composer. Educ: studied w. C Taltabull & René Leibowitz. Comps. publd: Edipo y Yocasta (opera); String Quartet; Passio Jesu-Christi; The Solar Cycle; Sonidos de la Noche; Noche Oscura; Requiem for percussion & Orch.; Concertos for cello, harpsichord & other instruments. Comps. recorded: Passio Jesu-Christi; La Transfiguración; Concerto for Harpsichord. Hobbies: Neplatonic philos, & the work of Dionysius the Areopagite. Address: c/o José Bertrand, 15 ático., Barcelona 6, Spain.

SOLER, Pedro Genard, b. 8 June 1938. Narbonne, France. Guitarist. Educ: Study of flamenco guitar by oral tradition. Widower, 1 child. Debut: 1959. Career: Concert appearances at Salle Gaveau; Paris; Mozarteum, Salzburg; Mozart & Brahms Hall, Vienna; Berlin; Queen Elizabeth Hall, London; Civic Theatre of Johannesburg; Municipal Theatre of Sao Paulo; Oslo, Theatre des Nations, Paris; Radio & TV broadcasts w. BBC; ORTF; Austrian TV. Recordings: var. works on labels of RCA Victor (London & Paris); Voga; Chant du Monde (Paris) inclng: Happy Bird (Flamencos). Recip: Int. Grand Prix of Records, Acad. Charles Cros, Paris. Address: c/o Hans Schlote, Danreiterg 4, A-5020 Salzburg, Austria.

SÓLIN, Vladimír, b. 14 July 1911. Hronov, Czech. Music Critic. Educ: Dr, Charles Univ., Prague. m. Milada Drínková. Career: Critic, writer for var. jrns., 1941-; Lectr. in musical problems in Czech., Germany & for schls. & public concerts; Ed., Svobodné slovo (daily); Ed., Hudební rozhledy (monthly musical jrnl.). Publs: Marta Krásová, biography of a singer, Prague, 1960. Contbr. to var. jrnls. & Czech. radio. Mbrships: Dvorák Soc.; Martinu Soc.; Janácek Soc.; Czech. Music Assn.; Assn. of Czech. Comps. & Music Critics. Hons: Award of Czech. Music Fndn. for criticism; Hon. mention of Czech. Comps. Assn.; Merited Culture Officer. Hobbies: Sport; Lit.; Travel. Address: Ulice Hvezdova 39, 140 00 Prague, Czech.

SOLÍS TAIANA, Elsa Inés, B. 14 Jan. 1938. Godoy, Provincia Santa Fe, Argentina. Librarian. Educ: Librnship., Fac. of Philos., Nat. Univ. of Rosario, Argentina; Perito Mercantil Nacional, Colegio Nacional "Juan B Alberdi", Venado Tuerto, Argentina; Piano studies in private conserv., Papávero. Career: Mbr., Juan Sebastián Bach Choir, Venado Tuerto, 1958-; Dir., ibid., 1966-. Hobbies: Active mbr. of the Esperantist movt. Address: Tucumán 50, 2600 Venado Tuerto, Santa Fé, Argentina.

SOLOMON, b. 9 Aug. 1902. London, UK. Pianist. m. Gwendolyn Byrne. Debut: aged 8, Queen's Hall, 1910. Career incls: Wigmore Hall, 1921; tours in UK, France, Germany, Italy, Netherlands, Am., Aust. & NZ. Hons. incl: LLD, St. Andrews Univ.; MusD, Cambridge Univ.; CBE, 1946. Hobbie: Bridge, Motoring. Address: 16 Blenheim Rd., London NW 8, UK. 1.

SOLOMON, Alan, b. 8 July 1938. Johannesburg, S Africa. Violinist; Teacher; Examiner. Educ: Violin; Chmbr. Music; Comp. Debut: w. Johannesburg Symph., Age 17. Career: Soloist, Concerto Perfs. w. Sir Malcolm Sargent, Efrem Kurz, Hugo Rignold, Leo Quayle, Francesco Mander; Regular Recital, Ensemble Broadcasts, SABC; Tchr., Pretoria Conserv. & Pvte. Mbrships: S African Soc. of Music Tchrs.; S African Comps. Soc. Hons: Prizes for Trio for Harp, Flute & Violin, 1964, Violin Concerto, 1966. Hobbies: Reading; Chess. Address: 4 Unity St., Fellside, Johannesburg, S Africa.

SOLOMON, Larry Joseph, b. 17 Apr. 1940. New Kensington, Pa., USA. College Professor; Composer; Theorist; Pianist. Educ: BA, Allegheny Coll., Meadville, Pa., 1962; MMus, Univ. of Ill., 1964; PhD, W Va. Univ., 1973. m. Nancy DeMott. Career: Tchr., music theory, composition & piano, Cornell Univ., 1971, Wells Coll., 1968-73, currently at Pima Coll. Comps. incl: Evolutions (large chorus); Music of the Spheres (marimba); Andromeda 2 1978 (piano); Recording: A Marimba Recital. Publs. incl: A Dictionary of Theoretical Terms, 1976; A Keyboard Theory Workbook, 1978. Contbr. to var. publs. Mbrhsips: Am. Soc. of Univ. Composers; Am. Music Center. Recip. sev. prizes. Address: 5122 Tortolita Rd., Tucson, AZ 85705, USA.

SOLTI, (Sir) Georg, b. 21 Oct. 1912. Budapest, Hungary. Conductor. Educ: studied w. Béla Bartók, Ernst von Dohányi & Zoltán Kodály. Career: sometime Cond., Budapest Opera & Asst. to Arturo Toscanini, Salzburg Fest.; Concert & Recital Pianist, Switz., during WWII; Musical Dir., Bavarian State Opera, 1946-52; Artistic & Musical Dir., Frankfurt City Opera, 1952-62; Prin. Cond., Lyric Opera of Chgo., 1956 & '57; Dir., Royal Opera House, UK, 1961-71; Artistic Dir., Royal Opera House, UK, 1961-71; Artistic Dir., Paris Orch.; Chief Cond.,

Chgo. Symph. Orch.; Guest Cond., Major orchs. thru-out Europe, UK, & USA. Recordings incl: Wagner's "Ring Cycle"; Mahler's 5th, 6th, 7th & 8th Symphonies. Hons. incl: KBE, 1971; DMus, Univs. of Oxford & Leeds; Prix du Disque of French Acad., 8 times; Commemorative medal, Wagner Soc., 1971. Address: Chalet Haut Pré, Villarswur-Ollons, Vaud, Switzerland.

SOLWAY, Kenneth David, b. 6 Feb. 1954. Toronto, Ont., Can. Oboist; Artistic Director. Educ: BMus (oboe), New Engl. Conserv.; student, Royal Conserv., The Hague, Sweelinck Conserv., Amsterdam. m. Susan Graves. Debut: The Hague. Career: specializes in histl. woodwind instruments incl. baroque oboe & recorder; fndr., artistic dir., Teafelmusik (Can.'s baroque orch. w. oringinal instruments); broadcasts on CBC radio. Publ: J S Bach, Reconstruction of concerto for recorder, oboe, violin, strings & continue from BWV 1064, 1978. Contbr. to: Continuo mag.; Tafelmusik News Hons: Can. Coun. Arts Awards, 1976-77, 1977-78. Mgmt: Tafelmusik, 101 Everden Rd., Toronto. Address: 22 Dewbourne Ave., Toronto, Ont. M5P 1Z4, Can.

SOLYMOS, Peter, b. 14 Dec. 1910. Torokbecse, Hungary. Pianist; Professor. Educ: Studied Piano & Comp. in Budapest, Vienna, Paris; Pianists Artist Dip., Budapest & Vienna. Debut: Concert Pianist, Budapest, 1934. Career: Concerts in Hungary & Europe, inclng. BBC, London, UK; Prof. of Piano, F Liszt High Schl. of Music, Budapest, 1948-; Tchr. of num. winners in Int. Competitions; Jury Mbr. num. Int. Competitions; Vis. Prof., Japan, 1973-77. Recordings of works by Bartók, Debussy, Ravel Publs: Eds. of Works by Bach, Scarlatti, Mozart, Beethoven, Schumann, Liszt, Tchaikovsky & Debussy. Mbr. Assn. of Hungarian Musicians. Hons. incl: Franz Liszt Prize, 1957; Merited Artist of Hungarian People's Republic, 1971. Mgmt: Interkoncert, Budapest. Address. Tusnádí, u. 12, 1125. Budapest, Hungary.

SOLYOM, Janos, b. 26 Oct. 1938. Budapest, Hungary. Pianist; Conductor. Educ: Béla Bartók Conserv.; Franz Liszt Acad., Budapest; studied w. Gisella Beres, Arnold Szekely, Kornel Zempleni, Lajos Hernadi, Ilona Kabos, Nadia Boulanger, Magda Tagliaferro. Debut: Sweden, 1959. Career: moved to Sweden, 1956; Pianist, num. TV, Radio Perfs., Sweden & abroad; regular tours, Europe; Tours in Can., USA, S Am., Israel. Recordings: Stenhammar, Liszt, works for piano & orch.; Stenhammar, Liszt, Schumann, Rachmaninov, solo piano works. Mgmt: Konsertbolaget, Stockholm, Sweden. Address: 11 Wivalliusgatan, 112 60 Stockholm, Sweden. 3.

SOM, Laszio, b. 26 July 1934. Budapest, Hungary. Double Bassist. Educ: Eutuos Lorand Univ., Budapest; Dip., Franz Liszt Music High Schl., Budapest. m. Eva Isery, 1 s. Career: Prin. Double Bass, Budapest Opera, & F Liszt Chmbr. Orch., Budapest. Recordings: num., w. F Liszt Chmbr. Orch., Columbia. Hobbies: Gardening; Travel. Mgmt: Interkoncert, Budapest. Address: 9 Kleh Istvan, 1126 Budapest Hungary.

SOMFAI, László, 15 Aug. 1934. Jászlandány, Hungary. Musicologist. Educ: Dip. of Musicol., Ferenc Liszt Acad. of Music. Budapest. m. Dorrit Révész-Somfai, 1 s, 1 d. Career: Musicol.; Hd. of the Budapest Bartók Archives (Inst. of Musicol. of the Hungarian Acad. of Scis.); Prof. of Musicol., Ferenc Liszt Acad. of Music; Music Libn., Nat. Széchényi Lib., Budapest. Publs: co-auth., Haydn als Opernkapellmeister, 1960; Joseph Haydn: Sein Leben in zeitgenössischen Bildern, 1966, Engl. edn., 1969; Anton Webern, 1968; studies on J Haydn, Liszt, Stravinsky, Webern, Bartók; Urtext-edns. in Mozart Neue Ausgabe, Gluck Neue Ausgabe, Musica Rinata; Ed. of Documenta Bartókiana. Mbrships: Presidium, Internationale Stiftung Mzarteum Salburg; Presidium, Assn. of Hungarian Musicians. Address: Néphadsereg utca 12.V.4, 1055 Budapest, Hungary.

SOMMER, Raphael, b. 21 June 1937. Prague, Czech. Cellist; Conductor. Educ: Grad., Rubin Acad. of Music, Jerusalem, Israel, 1956; Grad., Conserv. Nat. Superieur de Musique, Paris; studied under Paul Tortelier & Joseph Calvet. m. Sylvie Ott, 2 s. Career: has been recording for Num. European radio stns. (BBC, Germany, Austria, France, Rumania, Sweden, Norway & in Israel & S Africa; Public concerts as Soloist w. var. orchs.; cello-piano recitals. Mbr. of jury, Int. Cello Competitions, Munich, 1973, Bristol, 1977, Helsinki, 1978; Prof. of Cello, RNCM. Hons: 1st Prize, Cello (under Paul Tortelier), 1961, 1st Prize, Chmbr. Music (under Joseph Calvet), 1962, Conserv. Nat. Superieur de Musique; 1st Prize, Casals Int Competition, Belgium, 1961; 1st Prize, Piatigrosky, Boston, 1962; 2nd Prize, Munich Competition, 1963; Hon. FRCM, 1977 Hobby: Reading. Mgmt: Ibbs & Tillett. Address: 11 Becsize Park, London NW3, UK.4.

SOMMERFELDT, Oistein, b. 25 Nov. 1919, Oslo, Norway. Composer. Educ: Grad., Oslo Conservatorium of Music, 1947; studies w. Josef Marx & Nadia Boulanger. m. Elisabet, 2 s., 1 d. Debut: Oslo, 1954. Num. comps. incl: (orchl. works): Sinfonia La Betulla, 1967; Hafrsfjord, 1972 (piano): Moods Op. 1 Three simple pieces, 1948, revised 1963; 5 sonatinas, 1956-72; (songs & choral works): 3 Blake songs for mixed choir Op. 18, 1967; 4 Norwegina relig. flk songs for mixed choir Op. 23, 1965; (other works): Divertimento for flute solo Op. 9, 1960, revised 1969; Transformation Op. 19, 1970; sev. commissions from Norwegian TV. Sev. recordings, Norwegian Contemporary Music series. Active Mbr., var. music socs. Publcs. incl: Listen & Learn, 1947. Hobby: Nature Address: Fridtjof Nauseus vei 9, 1324 Lysakej, Norway.

SOMMERFIELD, David Fredric, b. 22 Sep. 1941, Queens, NY, USA. Music Librarian. Educ: BA, Brooklyn Coll., CUNY; MS (lib. service), Columbia Univ.; MA (music), Brooklyn Coll. Career: Music Cataloguer & Asst. Music Libn., State Univ. Coll., Potsdam, NY; Record Libn., Peabody Conserv., Balt., Md.; now Sr. Music Cataloguer, Library of Congress. Publs: Proceedings of the Inst. on Lib. of Congress Music Cataloging Policies & Procedures, 1975. Contbr. to: Current Musicol.; ARSC jrnl.; Notes. Mbrships: Music Lib. Assn.; Am. Musicol. Soc.; Int. Assn. of Music Libs.; Assn. for Recorded Sound Collections; Int. Assn. of Sound Archives; Int. Musicol. Soc. Hobbies: Reading; Record Collecting; Concert & Opera going. Address: 101 G St. S W, Apt. A-611, Wash., DC 20024, USA.

SOMOGI, Judith, b. 13 May 1943, Brooklyn, NY, USA. Conductor. Educ: BS, MS, Juilliard Schl., NYC. Debut: NYC Opera, 1974. Career: 1st Woman Cond. on nat. TV, NYC Opera prod. The Ballad of Baby Doe, Lincoln Ctr. broadcast, 1976; debut w. Naumberg Symph. Orch., 1975; debut w. NY Phil., 1977; Asst. Cond., Am. Symph. Orch. Hobbies: Tennis; Swimming; Riding. Mgmt: Herbert Barret Mgmt., Inc. Address: 150 W 82nd St., NY, NY 10024, USA.

SONEVYTSKY, Ihor, b. 2 Jan. 1926, Hadynkiwci, Ukraine. Composer; Conductor; Musicologist. Educ: Univ. of Vienna, 1944-48; Dip. in Comp. & Cond., Staalich Hochschule für Musik, Munich, 1951; PhD, Musicol., Ukrainian Free Univ., Munich, 1961. m. Natalia Palidwor, 3 c. Career: Musical Dir., Dumka Chorus, NY; Assoc. Prof., Ukrainian Cath. Univ., Rome, 1971. Comps: 3 collections of miniature piano pieces, Autumn, Winter, Spring, 1951-61; 2 Art Song Cycles to words of I Franko & V Symoneko. Var. recordings of Art Songs. Publs. incl: Artem Vedel and His Musical Legacy, 1966; Istoria Ukr. Muzyky (Hist. of Ukrainian Music), 2nd Ed., 1961. Contbr., musical reviews, Voice of Am., Wash., 1970-77. Mbrships: Assn. of Am. Comps.; Am. Musicol. Soc.; Ukrainian Acad. of Arts & Scis., USA; Shevchenko Scientific.Soc.; Ukrainian Music Inst., Inc. Hons: First prize, cantata, Love Ukraine, Dumka Chorus, 1962. Address: 62 E 7th St., NY, NY 10003, USA. 29.

SONGAYLLO, Raymond Thaddeus, b. 23 Aug. 1930. Chicopee, Mass., USA. Pianist; Composer; Harpsichordist; College Teacher. Educ: BM, 1951, MM, 1952, Northwestern Univ. m. Mary Ann Seaman, 1 s., 1 d. Debut: Carnegie Recital Hall, NYC, 1947. Appts: Ithaca Coll., NY; Ctrl. Mich. Univ.; Univ. of Denver; currently Assoc. Prof., Simpson Coll., IA. Comps: 10 Short Piano Pieces. Mbrships: AAUP; Coll. Music Soc. Recip., Prize for Duo Concertante for 2 pianos, Delius Comp. Contest, Jacksonville Univ., Fla., 1976. Address: 802 W Clinton Ave., Indianola, IA 50125, USA.

SONNENFELD, Kurt, b. 24 Feb. 1921, Vienna, Austria. Composer. Educ: Studied Piano & Harmony, Konservatorium of Vienna; Comp. w. Fano in Milan. m. Anna Ferrua. Career: RAI Broadcast of two pieces for Tympan & Piano edited by Suvini-Zerboni, Milan. Comps: Concert for Tympan & Orch. edited by Sonzogno, Milan; 2 pieces for Tympan & Piano edited by Suvini-Zarboni. Mbr. SIAE. Recip. of Concorso Lombardo di Composizione Musicale Prize, 1954 by presenting a String Quartet. Address: Via Neera 15, 20141 Milan, Italy.

SONNINEN, Ahti, b. 11 July 1914, Kuopio Co., Finland. Composer; Director. Educ: Sibelius Acad. m. Hilkka Paula, 3 s, 1 d. Debut: first concert of own comps., 1946. Career: Primary Schl. Tchr. at Kajäani Seminarium; Cond. w. many Finnish Orchs. & Choirs; Perf. on radio & TV, etc. Comps: The Lady of Sea (Haavrunva), Opera in 3 Acts; The Finnish Messiade, Oratorium. Num. songs & choral works; ballet, Pessi & Illusia; Symphonic sketches; chamber music. Recordings: Pessi & Illusia (HMV YDLP 1004); The Seven Brothers (Fennica SS 5); Under Lappland's Sky (Fennica SS 11). El amor pasa, 4 poems for Flute, Soprano & Chmbr. Ensemble, Bis, Stockholm. Publs: var. elem. music colls. for children. Address: Apollonkatu 13 A, SF-00100 Helsinki 10, Finland.

SONNTAG, Stanley, b. 25 Feb. 1921, Bklyn., NY, USA. Vocal Coach; Accompanist; College Teacher. Educ: BA, Bklyn. Coll., 1948; MA, NY Univ., 1949. Debut: Town Hall Recital, NY, 1954. Career: Tchr., Hd. Vocal Dept., Manhattanville Coll., NY; Extensive recital accompanying for ldng. artists. Metrop. & NY Opera; Music arr., new adaptation, 1st Am. Ballad Opera, 'The Disappointment'. Publ: Art of Song Recital. Contbr. to: NY Singing Tchrs. Assn. Jrnl. Mbr.; spkr. & judge, NY Singing Tchrs. Assn. Hobby: Painting. Address: 160 W 73 St., NY, NY 10023, USA.

SONSTEVOLD, Elisabeth, b. 7 Sept. 1942, Stockholm, Sweden. Harpist. Educ: harp & comp., Acad. of·Music, Vienna, Austria; dip. of harp, studies w. Marisa Robles, London, UK. m. Jan-Erik Friis, 1 d. Debut: Oslo, Norway, 1968. Career: Prin. Harpist, Oslo Phil. Orch.; Solo apps., also apps. w. major orchs. on radio & TV; Chmbr. music perfs.; Tchr., Oslo Acad. of Music. Recordings: Norwegian Chmbr. Music, Contemp. Music of Norway series. Mbr., Norwegian Soc. of Musicians. Mgmt: Impresario a/s, Oslo. Address: Framnesveien 12, Oslo 2, Norway.

SONSTEVOLD, Maj, b. 9 Sept. 1917, Soleftea, Sweden. Composer. Educ: Piano w. Sven Brandel & Gotfrid Boohn, Stockholm; Piano & theory w. Billy Mayerl, London, UK; Dip., comps. Akademisches Hauptseminar, Vienna, Austria, 1966. m. Gunnar Sönstevold, 1 s., 1 d. Career: Comp. music for stage, film, TV & radio; Oslo, Univ. Oslo, 1971-. Comps: incl: Suite for Piano, op. 1, 1962; op. 2, 1963; Sonata for piano, op. 3, 1964; Stillhet, 1978; Eleven Polytonal Blues, 1978; Veien Min Vise Vil Vandre, for Keyboard Harmony & Improvisation, 1978. Recordings incl: Tornerose; Snow White. Publs. incl: Jazz ABC Mbr., Bd., Acad. Music, Oslo, Hon: Oslo By. Hobby: Music. Address: Majbo, 1890 Rakkestad, Norway.

SONSTEVOLD, Knut, b. 20 Dec. 1945, Oslo, Norway. Bassoon Player. Educ: Dip., Akademi für Musik und darstellende Kunst, Vienna. 1s. Debut: Oslo, 1968. Career: solo bassoon player, Stockholm Phil. Orch.; mbr., Stockholm's Phil. Wind Quintet. Comps: var. electronic works. Recordings: Lars Erik Larson, Bassoon concerto; bassoon & electronics; works by Tansman, Arnold, Hindemith, etc. Mbrships: Fylkingen; FST (Soc. of Swedish Comps.). Address: Lolnvg. 45, 19156 Sollentuua, Sweden.

SOPRONI, József, b. 4 Oct. 1930, Sopron, Hungary. Composer & Professor. Educ: Dip. of Comp. Liszt Acad. of Music. m. Zsuzsa Mohos, 2 c. Comps: Eclypsis for Orch.; Concerto for V'cello; Concerto for Viola; Ovidii Metamorphosis (2 cantatas); 4 Str. Quartets; Chamber Concerto for 13 instruments; Sonata for Flute & Piano; Songs & Choral Pieces; 7 Piano Pieces; Invenzioni sul Bach for piano; Incrustations for piano; Antigone (3-act opera); 3 Symphs.; 6 Bagatelles for wind quintet; Chmbr. music, etc. Recordings: 2 complete records of comps. Mbr., Soc. of Hungarian Composers. Hons: Casella Prize, Naples, 1964; Erkel Prize, Budapest, 1974. Hobbies: Collecting pieces of fine art; Arts; History. Address: Pajzs utca 22/b 1025 Budapest II, Hungary.

SORAA, Jarle, b. 13 Sept. 1932, Alesund, Norway. Pianist; Music Critic. Educ: Oslo Univ.; piano studies w. E Westher & I Johnsen, Oslo. m. Bodil Erna S&raa. Debut: Oslo 1963. Career: Soloist, accomp. & Chmbr. Musician in radio; Soloist, Oslo Philharmonic Orch., Norwegian Broadcasting Corp. Orch.; Piano recitals, London, Copenhagen & Norwegian towns; Radio talks on musical topics; Music Critic, Verdens Gang, Oslo. Mbrships: Vice Chmn., Norwegian Soc. of Drama and Music Critics; Bd. Mbr., Norwegian Soloist Soc.; Norwegian Branch of ISCM (former Bd. Mbr.). Hobbies: Aesthetics; Psychology of Religion. Address: Gjöavn. 5, 1472 Fjellhamar, Norway.

SOREL, Claudette Marguerite, b. 10 Oct. 1932, Paris, France. Concert Pianist; Author; Professor. Educ: BS, Juilliard Schl. Music, 1947; Artist Dip., Curtis Inst. Music, 1953; BS, Columbia Univ., 1954. Debut: Town Hall, NYC, 1943. Career: over 1500 Recitals, USA, Canada, UK, Switzerland, Sweden, Germany, Holland; Soloist, over 200 orchl. perfs. w. major orchs. inclng. NY Phil., Phila., NBC, Boston, LPO, UK; Festivals inclng. Bershires, Aspen, Chautauqua; Nat. TV & Radio Appearances; Nat. Lectures; Disting. Prof., SUNY, Fredonia. Var. recordings. Publs. incl: Compendium of Piano Technique 1969; The 24 Magic Keys, 1973; Mind Your Musical Manners; Rachmaninoff-3 Nocturnes; Smorgasbord Piano Studies. Mbrships. incl: Bd. Dirs., Nat. Music Coun., Mem. Fndn. of Mu Phi Epsilon, Nat. Fedn. Music Clubs, Musicians Club of NY. Hons. incl: Mu Phi Epsilon Citation of Merit, 1968; Vera Dougan Award, Nat. Fedn. Music Clubs, 1969. Hobbies: Stamp Collecting; Cooking; Painting; Sculpture. Mgmt: Eastman Boomer Mgmt., 157 W 57 St., NYC 10019. Address: 333 W End Ave., NY, NY 10023, USA. 2, 5, 6.

SØRENSEN, Inger, b. 8 June 1944, Copenhagen, Denmark. Research Librarian; Freelance Producer. Educ: Cand. phil. (Music), Copenhagen Univ. Career: Rsch. Libn., The Royal Danish Schl. of Educl. Studies/Inst. for Music, 1971-; Freelance Prod., Music Dept., Danmarks Radio, 1977-; TV app. Publs: De musiske udsendelser i Danmarks Radio 1925-1975 Vol. III; Klassisk Musik-Titelfortegnelse, 1978; Musikkens Hvem-Hvad-Hvor; Politikens Operaforer I-II (transl. & Scandinavian version). Contbr. to: High Fidelity (Denmark). Hobbies: Music; Books; Gardening; Theatre. Address: Hyrdevej 21, DK-3060 Espergoerde, Denmark.

SØRENSEN, Jens, b. 18 May 1895, Houer, Vejle, Denmark. Instrument Maker; Cellist. Educ: studied w. Siegfrid Salomon. m. Ursulina Gianelli. Debut: Tivoli Concertsal. Recordings: Gramex. Mbr. Radio Symph. Orch. Address: Sondergade 52, Aeroskobing 5970, Denmark.

SORENSON, Torsten Napoleon, b. 25 Apr. 1908, Tanum, Bohuslän, Sweden. Organist; Composer. Educ: Royal Conserv of Music, Stockholm; studied Organ, Piano, Theory & Comp. w. Carl Orff, Salzburg. m. Sigrid Norling, 2 s., 1 d. Career: Organist, Oscar Fredriks Ch., Gothenburg, 1946-75; Tchr. of Theori, Music High Schl., Gothenburg. Comps. incl: Sinfonia da Chiesa 1 & 2 (1958, '69); Canticum Annae (soprano & organ), 1968; Flaucepi for flute, cello, piano, 1971; Concerto for flute, str.-orch. & percussion, 1976; (recorded(Per quattro archi; Adorazione per organo. Mbr., Musical Acad., Stockholm, 1975. Recip., var. musical prizes, Gothenburg. Hobbies: Drawing. Address: Linnegatan 30, S-413 Gothenburg, Sweden.

SORM, Pavel, b. 1 May 1935, Znojmo, Czech. Violinist. Educ: conserv. Prague, 1958; Dip., Acad. Arts, Prague, 1962. m. Ch. L Lengkeek, 3 children. Debut: Smetana Hall, Prague, June 1962. Career: Concert master, Radio Chmbr. Orch., Hilversum; Apps., Netherlands, TV & Radio; Tchr., Utrecht Conserv. Recordings (radio) incl. solo perfs. comps. by Vivaldi, Mozart, Mandonville, Dvorak, Suk, Fiser, Halek, Bon, Kox, etc. Mbrships: Stamitz Strijkkwartet; Utrecht Kamermuziekensemble; Silvestr Strijktrio. Hon: Sevcik's Prize, Pisek, 1963. Address: Van Wassenaerlaan 14, Hilversum, Netherlands.

SOTHERN, David Annerley, b. 4 Nov. 1921, Brisbane, Qld., Australia. Violinist; Piano & Violin Teacher. Educ: BMus, Univ. of S Africa; LRSM (Piano Tchr. & Theory). m. Caroline Florence Dowie, 2 c., 2 step-c. Career incl: Violinist, S African Broadcasting Co. Nat. Symph. Orch. Comps: Piano Suite; Rhapsodie Havanaise for full orch.; Prelude, 'In Memoriam', 1963. Hobbies: Reading; Homeopathy. Address: 2 Taplow Rd., Auckland Pk., Johannesburg, S Africa.

SOUCHAY, Marc-André, b. 4 Feb. 1906, Stuttgart, Germany. Composer; Librettist; Teacher. Educ: Ph.D, Univ.; studied comp. w. Herman Keller & Paul Juon, Berlin; studied singing w. Oscar Rees, Berlin. m. Lore Volz, 2c. Career: Dramaturg, Staatstheater Stuttgart, 1941-45; Tchr., Musikhochschule Hannover, 1953-63; Lectr., Univ. of Hannover, 1963-. Comps: (Operas) Der Hutzelmann, Alexander in Olympia, Helena und Faust (texts written or arr. by Dr. Souchay). Publs: Europäische Volkslieder, 1950. Contbr. to Zeitschrift für Musikwissenschaft. recip. Opera Prize of Württ. Staatstheater, 1935. Address: Schwarmstedterstr. 71, 3000 Hannover 61, German Fed. Repub.

SOURLIER, Matthias, b. 17 Apr. 1944, Elsau, Winterthur, Switz. Musician (viola). Educ: Dip. for Tchrs., Trng. Coll.; Dip. for Precentor (Choir & Cond.), Konservatorium Zürich w. Jakob Kobalt, 1967; Dip. for viola, ibid, w. George Kertesz, 1969; studied w. George Janzer, 1970-72. Debut: Sinfonia Concertante of Mozart, Tonhalle Zürich, 1969. Career: Violist in the Tonhalle & Theatre Orch. Zürich, 1969-; Solo Violist (Opera Formation), ibid, 1972-; Chamber music player in var. ensembles. Mbrships: Zürich Sect., Swiss Assn. of Musicians; Swiss Musicpadagogic Soc. Hobbies: Mountaineering; Skiing. Address: Birmensdorf 2H, Kirchgasse 1/CH-8903, Switzerland.

SOUROUJON, Léon, b. 28 Jan. 1913, Novi Pazar, Bulgaria. Concert Violinist; Professor of Violin. Educ: Deutsche Akademi für Musik und Darstellende Kunst, Prague, 1933; Ecole Normale, Paris, 1946; studied w. Georges Enescu. m. Ekaterina Kazandjieva, 1 d. Debut: 1929. Career: Concerts & radio apps. in Czech., Poland, Germany, France, Belgium, USSR, Cuba, Vietnam, Korea, China, Israel & Bulgaria. Comps: 6 violin studies; 4 pieces for violin solo; cadenzas for Mozart concertos & Brahms concerto; Improvisation on Schema Israel. Publs: Reflections on the Original Text of Bach's Chaconne; Scales & Technical Exercises. mbr. Profl. Soc. for Musicians, Bulgaria.

Hons: Absolutorium, Deutsche Academie für Musik und Darstellende Kunst, Prague, 1933; Licence de concert, Ecole Normale, Paris, 1945. Address: Harmoniestraat 47, 2000 Antwerp, Belgium; Samuil St. 7A, Sofia, Bulgaria.

SOUSTER, Tim Andrew James, b. 29 Jan. 1943, Bletchley, Bucks., UK. Composer; Instrumentalist; Writer. Educ: BA, New Coll., Oxford, 1964; BMus, 1965; studied comp;. w. Richard Rodney Bennett, Karlheinz Stockhausen. m. Penelope Frances Hales, 2 d. Career: BBC Prod., 1965-67; Comp. in Res., King's Coll., Cambridge, 1969-71; Fndr., Intermodulation ensemble, 1969, Odb ensemble, 1976; Toured widely in UK & Europe; Tchng. Asst. to Karlheinz Stockhausen, Cologne State Music High Schl., 1971-73; Artist in Res., W Berlin Artists Prog., 1974; Leverhulme Rsch. Fellow in Electronic Music, Keele Univ., 1975-79. Comps. incl: Triple Music II, 1970; Wasteland Music, 1970; World Music, 1971-74; Spectral; Heavy Reductions; Arboreal Antecedents; Sonata for cello, piano, 7 wind instruments & percussion. Recordings: Swit Drimz. Contbr. to var. profl. jrnls. Mbrships: PRS; MCPS; Electro-Acoustic Music Assn. of GB. Hons: Bicentennial Arts Fellow US/UK, 1978-79. Mgmt: First Composers Ltd., London; Original Music, London. Address: c/o Music Dept., Keele Univ., Keele, Staffs., ST5 5BG, UK.

SOUTH, Joan Mary, b. 3 Oct. 1915, Brighton, UK. Pianist. Educ: ARCM (piano perf.). m. Robert South, 2 d. Debut: BBC, 1949. Career: Piano duo w. Robert South, recitals, BBC, Swiss Radio; Duo concertos w. Bournemouth Symph. Orch., BBC Welsh Orch., Vivaldi Chmbr. Orch.; Recitals in schls. & music clubs; Music Mistress, Cranborne Chase Schl., 1959-64, Bruton Schl. for Girls, 1964-. Mbr. ISM. Hon: Assoc. Bd. Exhibitioner, RCM, 1932. Hobbies: Mtn. walking; Travel. Address: 2 Welland Gdns., Welland, Malvern, Worcs. WR 13 6LB, UK.

SOUTH, Robert Henry Slater, b. 24 July 1912, Brighton, Sussex, UK. Pianist. Educ: GRSM; ARCM; ARCO. m. Joan Mary Pickett, 2 d. Debut: BBC, 1949. Career: Musical Dir., Michaelhouse Schl., Bruton, Somerset, 1939-73; BBC duo pianist w. wife; Recitals for Music Clubs & Socs. in UK & Switzerland; Concertos w. Capetown Symph. Orch., Bournemouth Symph. Orch. & BBC Welsh Symph. Orch. Mbr. ISM. Hons: Hopkinson Gold Medal, 1934; Chappell Gold Medal, 1934. Hobbies: Astronomy; Mountain walking. Address: 2 Welland Gdns., Welland, Malvern, Worcs., WR13 6LB, UK.

SOUTHERN, Eileen, b. 19 Feb. 1920, Minneapolis, Minn., USA. University Professor of Music. Educ: BA; MA; PhD; Study of piano. m. Joseph Southern, 1 d, 1 s. Career: Prof. of Music, Harvard Univ. Publs: The Buxheim Organ Book, 1963; The Music of Black Americans, 1971; Ed., Readings in Black American Music, 1971; Fndr./Ed., The Black Perspective in Music, 1973- (Jrnl.). Contbr. to: Jrnl. of the Am. Musicol. Soc.; Grove's Dict., 6th Ed.; Acta Musicologica; Musica Disciplina; Symposium. Mbrships: Int. Musicol. Soc; Am. Musicol. Soc. (Bd. of Dirs., 1974-76); Renaissance Soc. Hons: ASCAP. Hobbies: Travel; Camping. Address: Harvard Univ., Cambridge, Mass., USA. 2,5,6.

SOUVARIRAN, Pierre J A, b. 30 July 1911. Montreux, Switz. Pianist. Educ: Bac.lit., Lausanne; Dip. de virtuosité, Rimbaupierre Inst., Lausanne. Career: perf. on BBC 3rd prog., CBC Toronto, Swiss Broadcasts, NWDR Hamburg, Radio Hilversum, Brussels & Munich. Recordings: VDE Gallo. Has recorded on Decca, Hallmark, CBC Select & Jecklin. Mbrships: Assn. of Swiss Musicians; Toronto Musicians' Assn. Hobbies: Mountaineering; Photography. Mgmt: Concert Bur, Fac. of Music, Edward Johnson Bldg., Univ. of Toronto, Toronto, Ont. M5S 1A1, Canada.

SOUZA, José Alves, b. 4 Jan. 1935. Sergipe, Aracaju, Brazil. Professor of Music. Educ: Seminario Sao José; Instituto Villa Lobos, specializing in sacred choral music. m. Nancy Maria Ferreira da Rocha Alves De Souza, 2d. Career incl: Prof. of Muisc, Seminario Sao José, 1959-68; arr. & prod., sacred music comps. for Renovaçao do Canto Sacro no Brasil; Dir , 1st course of Canto Pastoral in Rio de Janeiro, 1963: and subsequent courses. num. recordings. over 100 publs. of choral music of Brazil. Contbr. to num. profl. jrnls. Mbrships: Concselho Regional de Psicologia; Comissao de Música Sacra do Rio de Janeiro; Comissao Nacional de Música Sacra; Federaçao de Corais do Rio de Janeiro. Hobbies: Football; Swimming; Cinema; Theatre. Address: Rua Copaiba No. 149, Vila Kosmos, Rio de Janeiro, Brazil.

SOUZAY, Gerard (Gerard Marcel Tisserand), b. 8 Dec. 1920. Singer. Debut: 1945. Career: Radio & TV broadcasts; tours & apps., Europe, N & S Am., S Africa, Aust., Japan. Recip. 1er

Prix d'Excellence, Paris, Conservatoire. Mgmt: S A Gorlinsky, London; Sheldon Soffer. NY, 16.

SOVIERO, Diana. Jersey City, NJ, USA. Lyric Soprano. Educ: Juilliard Preparatory Schl.; NY; Juilliard Coll., NY; Hunter Coll. Opera Workshop, NY; Boris Goldovsky Opera Theatre. m. Louis Soviero. Debut: Chauttaqua Opera Assn. Career: NYC Opera; Tulsa Opera; Houston Grand Opera; Ft. Worth Opera; New Orleans Opera; Orlando Opera; San Diego Opera; Saint of Bleeker St., TV, 1978. Mbrships: Central Opera Service; Affiliate Artists Inc. Hons: Nat. Opera Inst. Grant, 2 yrs.; Richard Tucker Award. Hobbies: Cooking; Riding; Antique collecting. Mgmt: Columbia Artists Mgmt., NY. Address: 232-22 S Conduit Ave., Rosedale, NY 11422, USA.

SOWELL, Laven, b. 9 Jan. 1933. Wewoka, Okla., USA. Professor of Voice; Choirmaster; Opera Chorus Master. Educ: Aspen Schl. of Music, Colo., 1951, 1952, 1953; BMus, Univ. of Okla., 1955; Manhattan Schl. of Music, NYC, 1956-57; MA, Columbia Univ., NYC, 1964; Conserv. de Musique, Fontainebleau, France, 1966; studied Voice w. Joseph Benton, Martial Singher, John Brownlee, Samuel Margolis; studied Cond. w. Harry R Wilson, Hugh Ross Nadia Boulanger. Career: Toured USA & Can. w. Charles L. Wagner Opera Co.; Tchr., Choral Music, Edison HS, 1961-70; Choirmaster, First Presby. Ch., Tulsa, Okla., 1969-; Dir., Opera Theatre, Univ. of Tulsa, 1970-74; Dir. Choral Activities, ibid, 1974-; Prof. of Voice, ibid; Chorus Master, Tulsa Opera Inc. Mbrships: MENC; Nat. Assn. Tchrs. of Singing; AGO; Music Tchrs. Nat. Assn.; Taught as quest fac. mbr., Evergreen Cert. on Ch. Music, Evergreen, Col., 1972-74. Hons: Citation of Congratulations, House of Reps., Okla. State Capitol (for nat. recognition in choral music); Award for Disting. Serv. to Schl. & Community, Okla. Congress of Parents & Tchrs., Lt. Gov., State of Okla, 1975. Hobby: Travel. Address: 3540 S Wheeling, Tulsa, OK 74105, USA.

SOYER, David, b. 24 Feb. 1923. Philadelphia, Pa., USA. Cellist. Educ: Studied w. Diran Alecanin, Emanuel Feurmann, Pablo Casals. m. Janet Putnam Soyer, 2 s. Debut: W. Phila. Symph. Orch., 1942. Career: Cellist, Guarneri String Quartet; Prof. of Cello, Curtis Inst. of Music, Phila., Pa. Recordings incl: 3 Bach Sontatas for Cello & Harpsichord; Mendelssohn Cello Sonatas; All Beethoven String Quartets; 10 Mozart Quartets; Dvorak, Smetana, Brahms, Schumann Quintets; Sibelius Piano Quartets; Sibelius Piano Quartet w. Arthur Rubinstein. Hobby: Sailing. Mgmt: Harry Beall, New York, NY. Address: 24 Mezzine Dr., Cresskill, NJ 07626, USA.

SPADAVECCHIA, Antonio Emmanuilovich, b.3 June 1907, Odessa, Russia. Composer. Educ: Moscow Conserv. Comps. incl: Jangar (symphonic suite), 1940; (Operas) The Gadfly, 1959; The Good Soldier Swejk, 1961; (Ballet) The Shore of Happiness, 1948; Cincerella, (Opera), 1946; Mine Hostess (comic opera), 1947; The Ordeal (opera), 1949, '53; The Years of Fire, 1966; Lenin is the Heart of the Earth (symph.-oratorio), 1966; Yukki (The Feast of Lanterns), opera, 1968; The Heart of the Violin, operetta, 1969; The Five Lucky Petals (A Shot in the Dark), operetta, 1970; My Mother, children's opera, 1972; The Letter of an Unknown Woman, monodrama, 1974; Moscow, A Hero City, oratorio for soloists, mixed chorus & symph. orch., 1974; The Captain's Daughter, opera, 1975, '77. Hons: Honoured Worker of the Arts, RSFSR, 1963; Order of Badge of Hon., 1967. Address: Sadovo-Triumphalnaia 14/12, Ap. 82, Moscow 103006, U.S.S.R.

SPAHR, Lani Ray, b. 20 Jan. 1947, Mechanicsburg, Pa., USA. Oboist; College Instructor. Educ: Indiana Univ. of Pa., Duquesne Univ., Pitts., Pa. m. Gail C Fatzinger-Spahr, 2 d. Debut: Colo. Springs, 1975. Career: Prin. Oboist, Colo. Springs Symph.; Prin. Oboe, Col. Opera Fest.; Instr. of Oboe, Colo. Coll., Colo. Springs. Mbr., Phi Mu Alpha Sinfonia. Hons: Award for Most Outstanding Woodwind Student at Duquesne Univ., Pitts. Flute Club, 1968. Hobbies: Electronics; Fishing. Address: 409 E San Miguel St., Colorado Springs, CO 80903, USA.

SPANGE, Svend Aage, b. 20 Feb. 1920, Naestved, Denmark. Organist. Educ: Exam. of organist, Royal Danish Music Conserv., Copenhagen, 1942; Exam. of choirmaster, ibid., 1943. studied w. Gaston Litaize in Paris, m. Annalise Brion, 3 s., 1 d. Debut: in Cathedral of Copenhagen, 1946. Career: Substitute Organist, Frederiks Ch. & Vor Frelsers Ch., Copenhagen, 1943-46; 2nd Organist, Roskile Cathedral, 1946-48; Organist & Choirmaster, Thomas Kingos Ch., Odense, 1948-74; Organist & Choirmaster, St. Peders Ch., Naestved, 1974; Recitals in most European countries inclng. Czechoslovakia; Radio transmissions for BBC (3), Radiodiffusion francaise, Radio Hilversuum, Denmark's radio, etc.; Music Critic, Fyens Stifstidende. Coun. Mbr. of Dansk Musikpedagogisk Forening. Recip. grant from Min. of Educ. for studies in Paris,

1961. Address: Fjordlodden 13, 4736 Karrebaeksminde, Denmark.

SPANNHEIMER, Franz Erasmus, b. 7 Nov. 1946, Dettlebach, Germany. Composer; Conductor; Pianist; Organist. Educ: degree music, Würzburg Acad.; Dip. ch. music, Würzburg; master class under Messiaen, Paris. Career: choir dir. & organist, St. Anna, Munich; fndr. St. Anna concerts; fndr. Munich chmbr. music soc.; sork w. Britten & Khatchaturian; cond. in all Europe; TV, radio & film apps. Comps: Evolution; Lionel; Transfiguration; poem for choir & orch.; Perfora (oratorio); Ludus; solo & chmbr. music. Recordings incl: 3 piano concertos - Tschaikovsky; Orgelporträt F E Spannheimer. Publs. incl: Die Formbegriff der neuen music, 1976. Contbr. to var. profl. jrnls. Mbr. var. profl. orgs. Hons: Comp. prize, Würzburg, 1967; Don Carlos di Venosa prize, USA, 1972; Rome prize, 1973. Address: 8000 Munich 22, Thierschstr. 43, German Fed. Repub.

SPANOGHE, Jean Justin, b. 2 Mar. 1945, Schaarbeek, Brussels, Belgium. Pianist. Educ: Premier prix & dip. superieur de piano au conserv. royal d'Anvers; Grad., Chapelle musicale Reine Elisabeth, Belgium. Career: Num. concerts, Belgium, Netherlands, France, Italy & Germany. Hons: Medaille d'argent, Int. Fest. Young Soloists, Bordeaux, 1972; Laureat du concours, Friedrich Kuhlan, chmbr. music, Germany, 1970. Address: Frits van den Berghlaan 1, 2630 Aartselaar, Belgium.

SPARNAAY, Harry Willem, b. 14 April 1944, Amsterdam, Holland. Bass Clarinettist. Educ: Amsterdam Conserv. m. Roswitha Sparnaay-Mol, 2 c. Debut: Amsterdam, 1969. Career: Perfs. w. many major orchs. incl. BBC Symph. Orch., Rotterdam Phil. Orch., ORTF Symph. Orch., Concertgebouw Orch., BRT Chmbr. Orch. (Brussels), Radio Chmbr. Orch. (Hilversum); Soloist, music fests. of Warsaw, Zagreb, Graz, Madrid, Poitiers, NY, The ISCM World Music Days (Boston, Athens & Bonn), Witten, Como, Paris, Naples, etc.; Concerts, Europe & Am.; Prof. of Bass Clarinet & Contemporary Music, Sweelinck Conserv., Amsterdam Rotterdam Conservs & Royal Conserv., The Hague. Recordings. Bass Clarinet Identity; Harry Sparnnay/Lucien Goethals; Composers' Voice; Music by Ton Tbuynèl; Gaudeamus Competition, 1972; Music by Earle Brown; Bass Clarinet Identity 2, The Garden of Delight. Mbr., Bd. Donemus Fndn., Amsterdam. Hons: First Prize, bass clarinet soloist, Int. Gaudeamus Competition, 1972. Address: Z.Buiten Spaarne. 120, 2012 AD Haarlem, The Netherlands.

SPARROW, Andrew Nigel, b. 12 Aug. 1949, Rochford, UK. Viola Player. Educ: 5 yrs. GSM, grad., 1970; 2 yrs. w. Maz Rostal at Hochschule für Musik, Cologne. m. Heleen Sparrow-De Haas, 1 d. Career: solo viola, Zurich Chmbr. Orch., 1972-75; sub-prin. viola, Netherlands Chmbr. Orch., 1975-77; mbr., Residentie Str. Quartet; sub-prin. viola, Hague Phil. Orch.; broadcasts w. Quartet most European countries. Recordings: var. w. Zürich Chmbr. Orch. & Netherlands Chmbr. Orch. mbr. Stitching Nederlands Toonkunstnaarsraad, Amsterdam. Hon: AGSM (distinction). Hobbies: Reading; Cooking. Mgmt: (Residentie Str. Quartet) Nederlands Impressariat. Address: Dirk Hoogenraad Str. 35, The Hague 2586 TB, Netherlands.

SPEARE, Patricia Follett, b. 26 Jan. 1923, Waterbury, Conn., USA. Cellist. Educ: BA, Wellesley Coll.; MA, Univ. of Chgo.; grad. study w. Remi Gassmann on Hindemith's music & theory; cello lessons w. Lieff Rosanoff, Robert Graham, etc. m. Edward Phelps Speare, 5 c. Career: Cellist, Lansing Symph., Mich.; Prin. Cellist, Battle Creek Symph., Mich., 8 yrs.; Fndr., Olivet Chamber Players. Hons: Annie Louise Barrett Fellowship from Wellesley Coll., 1946. Address: 110 Yale St., Olivet, MI 49067, USA.

SPEARING, Robert Michael, b. 22 May 1950, London, UK. Composer. Educ: RCM; GRSM; ARCM. Career: Asst. Dir. of Music, The Purcell Schl. for young musicians, 1973-; Staff, RCM Junior Dept., 1975-78. Comps. incl: (Orchl.) Symphony, 1969; A Legend, 1971; Burlesque, 1972; Sonata Fantasia for Strings, 1979; (Choral) L'Allegro, 1974; Visions of William Blake, 1976; Youth, Sun and Moon, 1977. Publs: H.H. - A tribute to Herbert Howells, 1972. Contbr. to: RCM Mag. Mbrships: CGGB; Royal Automobile Club. Hobbies: Reading; Mountains. Address: 7 Digby Place, Radcliffe Rd., Croydon, Surrey CRO 5QR, UK.

SPEARS, Jared Tozier, b. 15 Aug. 1936, Chgo., Ill., USA. Composer; Professor of Music; Performer (Percussion). Educ: BS Educ., Northern Ill. Univ., DeKalb, 1958; BM 1959, MM 1960, Cosmopolitan Schl. of Music, Chgo., Ill.; DMus. (Comp.), Northwestern Univ., Evanston, Ill., 1965; studied Comp. & Percussion w. var. masters. m. Carla B Spears, 1 s., 1 d. Career: Percussionist, Chgo. area Dance Bands & Chgo. Youth Symph.

Orch.; Tchr., Instrumental music, Maine Township High Schl., Des Plaines, Ill., 7 yrs.; currently Prof. of Music, Ark. State Univ., Clinician, Adjudicator & Cond. Compositions incl: (publd.) Diptych for Organ, 1968; Quartet 66, 1970; Prologue & Jublio (percussion solo), 1971; Scamper (percussion quintet), 1974; (recorded) Kimberley Overture; Chatham Overture; Prologue & Pageant; Neologue; Third Set for Band. Mbrships. incl: ASCAP; Percussive Arts Soc. (State Pres. Ark. Chapt.). Hons. incl: 2 Grad. Awards, Northwestern Univ., 1965, 1966; Faricy Award, ibid., 1966; 1st Prize, Phi Mu Alpha Concert Saxophone Comp. Contest, 1967. Hobbies: Travel; Fishing; Camping; Prospecting. Address: 2917 Turtle Creek Cove, Jonesboro, AR, USA.

SPECHT, Robert John Jr., b. 17 July 1937, Pitts., Pa., USA. Choral Conductor; College Professor of Music History & Literature. Educ: BMusEd, Westminster Coll., New Wilmington, Pa., 1959; MA, Western Reserve Univ., Cleveland, Ohio, 1962; ChM, Am. Guild Organists, 1964; PhD, Case Western Reserve Univ., 1976. m. Joyce Lynn Woodburn, 3 d. Career incls: Assoc. Prof., Music & Cond., Community Chorus, Queensborough Community Coll., Bayside, NYC, 1970-; Co-fndr., Jacksonville Community Chorus; Cons., Music, Am. Bicentennial. Publs: incl: Bibliography of Early American (Choral) Music in Performing Editions, 1974; Instructor's Manual, Student Workbook for Exploring Music, 3rd Ed., 1979. Mbr. var. profl. orgs. Hons: Commendations, furthering Am. music, NY State Am. Revolution Bicentennial Commn. & NYC Bicentennial Corp. Hobbies incl: Cycling. Address: 40 Lawrence Ave., Lynbrook, NY 11563, USA. 6.

SPECTOR, Irwin, b. 11 Jan. 1916, Galwood, NJ, USA. Musicologist; University Professor; Violinist. Educ: BS, NJ State Coll., 1936; MA, Columbia Univ., 1940; PhD, NY Univ., 1952; Univ. of Geneva, 1964-65; Dip., orchl. conducting, Nat. Conserv., Paris Inst. of Musicol., Univ. of Paris, France; pvte. study of comp., violin & chmbr. music. m. Jane Frances Hoffman, 4 s. Career incls: on fac., Ill. State Univ., 1948-; Prof., Acad. Internationale d'Été, Nice, 1971; Vis. Prof., Univ. of Kan., 1968-69. Comps: Pieces in Three (piano solo). Publs: Robert White. Composer. Between Two Eras, 1956; Robert White: The Instrumental Music, 1972. Contbr. to profl. publs. Mbrships: Int. & Am. Musicol. Socs.; Renaissance Soc.; Dolmetsch Soc. Hobbies: Tennis; Chess; Bridge. Address: 903 W College, Normal, IL 61761, USA. 3, 4, 8, 11, 29.

SPEDDING, Frank Donald, b. 21 Aug. 1929, Liverpool, UK. Educator. Educ: DMus (London); ARCM. Career: Hd. Dept., Harmony, Counterpoint, Comp. & allied subjects, RSAMD. Comps: Music for over 24 films; Incidental music, Theatre, Radio & TV; Cello Concerto, Piano Concerto, 'Taylor's Death'; 8 Paganini Impromptus; Toccata a Tre (violin, cello, piano); Num. arrangements & orchestrations; Var. choral songs. Mbrships: ISM; CGGB. Hons: Royal Phil. Soc. Prizeman for Comp., 1951 & '53; Fellowship, RSAMD, 1977. Hobbies: Engl. Lang. Address: c/o Royal Scottish Acad. Music & Drama, St. George's Pl., Glasgow G2 1BS, UK.

SPEER, Klaus, b. 6 Mar. 1911, Berlin, Germany. Organ; Harpsichord; Piano Accompanist; Vocal Coach. Educ: Dip., Humanistisches Gymnasium, Berlin, 1931; Tchrs. Coll., Hamburg-Altona, 1931-32; Halle/Saale, 1932-33; Dip., Akademie für Kirchen - und Schulmusik, 1937. m. Elisabeth Clark Speer, 1 s. Debut: 1932. Career: organ recitals, Europe & USA, 1932-; Coll. Prof. of organ, voice, piano, music hist., var. colls. & univs., USA; Perf. on organ & harpsichord; Ch. Organist & Choir Dir.; Vocal coach; Music Libn. Sibley Music Lib., Eastman Schl. of Music, Univ. of Rochester, NY, 1965-76. Publs: num. articles on organ music & Iberian music in scholarly jrnls. Contbr. to Grove's Dict., 6th ed. & var. profl. jrnls. Mbr. var. profl. orgs. Address: 157 Weldon St., Rochester, NY 14611, USA.

SPEIGHT, John Anthony, b. 27 Feb. 1945, Plymouth, UK. Singing Teacher; Baritone Singer. Educ: GSM, 1964-68; AGSM (Perfs/Tchrs.); Singing w. John Cameron; Comp. w. Buxton Orr & Richard Rodney Bennet. m. Sveinbjörg Vilhjálmsdòttir, 2 s. Debut: 'Messiah', Beverly Minister, Yorks., 1967. Career: Song recitals, Ireland & Iceland; Radio broadcasts, Iceland, 1969, '71, '74, '75; Sang w. Icelandic Symph. Orch.; Oratorio, England & Iceland. Mbrships: Committee, Icelandic Guild of Solo Singers; Musicians Union of Iceland. Hobby: Trout & salmon fishing. Address: Nökkvavogur 32, Reyjavik, Iceland.

SPEISER, Elisabeth, b. 15 Oct. 1940. Zürich, Switzerland. Soprano Singer. Educ: Acad. of Music, Winterthur. m. Hans Jeciklin, 2 c. Debut: Zürich. Career incls: Concerts; all European countries, N & S Am.; Guest, many fests.; Many concerts w. Karl Richter; Opera debut as Pamina, Zauberflöte; Pamina, Ludwigsburger Schloss-Festspiele, 1972-73; Glyndebourne Fest., 1973; Mélisande, St. Gallen, 1974; Euridice,

Ludwigsburger Schloss-Festspiele, 1975; Many Lied-Recitals w. Irwin Gage; TV & Rdio apps., Germany, Italy, Switzerland. Recordings incl: Weltliche Kantaten & Gestliche Lieder (JS Bach); Caecilien-Tonkunstlerverband. Hobbies: Family; Reading; Cooking; Gardening. Address: Luegete 31, 8053 Zürich, Switzerland.

SPELDA, Antonín, b. 12 Mar. 1904, Svihov u Klatov, Czech. Professor of Physics & Musicology. Educ: MSc. Fac. of Sci., Charles Univ., Prague, 1922-27; PhD, DSc, Fac. of Arts, ibid., 1946-48. m. Emilie Speldová-Grubrová, 1 d. Career: Tchrs. Trng. Coll., Pilsen, 1952-73; Grammar Schl., Plzen, 1927-52. Publs: Introduction to Acoustics for Musicians, 1958; Acoustical Foundations of Orchestration (w. J Burghauwer), 1968; Chapters from Musical Acoustics, 1978; Pizzicato of Strings, 1968; The Masking of Individual Tones in Orchestral Music, 1970; Musical Work of Composer Jindrich Jindrich, 1954, 76; Plzen & Music, 1960; Musical Topography of Klatovy District, 1974, & of Domazlice District, 1976. Mbr. Czech. Soc. of Comps. Recip. var. State distinctions, etc. Address: Bolzanova 23, 320 25 Plzen, Czech.

SPENCER, Helen Walker, b. 13 Aug. 1936, Rochester, NY, USA. Museum Projects Director. Educ: Assoc. of Arts, Santa Rosa Jr. Coll., Calif.; Hons. prog., lit., Univ. of Calif. at Berkeley; undergrad. courses in musicol., ibid. m. Henry Benning Spencer II, 1 d., 2 s. Career: Dir., Dept. of Museum & Public Progs., Folger Shakespeare Lib.; Arts Administrator; Producer; co-fndr., The Folger Consert (resident ensemble in early music). Mbrships: Assn. of Coll., Univ. & Community Arts Administrators; Cultural Alliance of Gtr. Wash.; Chmbr. Music Am.; Lib. for the Arts Committee, Wash., DC; Am. Assn. of Musuems. Hon: Washington Review award. Hobbies: Early music on record & tape; Folger Consort; Contemporary poetry & lit.; Theatre; Opera; Travel; Photography. Address: 112 Hesketh St., Chevy Chase, Md., USA. 5.

SPENCER, Joan, b. 1 Aug. 1921, Manchester, UK. Lecturer in Music. Educ: MusB, Victoria Univ. of Manchester; BMus, Univ. of London; Tchr's. Dip., Manchester; Northern Schl. of Music, Manchester; Studied privately w. Dr. Caleb Jarvis; LRAM (aural trng.); (LRAM) (piano tchng.); ARCM (Schl. music). Career: Music Mistress; Schl. of St. Mary & St. Anne, Abbots Bromley, 1943-48; Sr. Lectr. in Music St. Katherine's Coll., Liverpool, 1948-64, w. Midlands Coll. of Educ., 1964-66; Prin. Lectr. in Music, & Hd., Music Dept., Hereford Coll. of Educ., 1966-78; Cond., Hereford String Orch., 1967-76; Examiner in Music, Northern Univs. Jt. Matriculation Bd., 1974-78 (Chief Examiner 1974-78). Comp. of Frolic for Double Bass & Pianoforte. Recip., Hargreaves Prize, Victoria Univ. of Manchester, 1940 & 41. Hobby: Owning & showing Dalmatians. Address: 3 Sollars Close, Whitecross, Hereford, UK. 3, 27.

SPENCER, Joan Mary, b. 8 Feb. 1922, Keighley, Yorks, UK. Teacher & Musician (violin & viola). Educ: Royal Manchester Coll. of Music; ARMCM (perf. & tchr.). Career: Violinist in concerto progs. w. var. orchs.; num. broadcasts in UK, Israel, Yugoslavia, Greece, Belgium, & France; Sonata recitals; Quartet concerts; Duos w. Noel Skinner (piano); Tchr., Violin & Viola, Guildhall Schl. of Music & Drama, London, 1950-. Mbrships: Inc. Soc. of Musicians; European String Tchrs. Assn. Hon: ARCM. Hobby: Philos. Address: 36 Lansdowne Cres., London W11, 2NT, UK.

SPENCER, Robert, b. 9 May 1932, Ilford, UK. Lutenist; Guitarist; Singer. Educ: GSM; Dartington Schl. of Music; LRAM. m. Jill Nott-Bower, 2 s. Career: Prof. of Lute, RAM; Mbr., Deller Consort, 1974-; Toured USA & Europe as mbr. of Julian Dbram Consort; Duo w. Jill NOtt-Bower. Recordings: Over 50 records on RCA Victor, Philips, EMI & Argo labels. Publs: Elizabethan Duets for Two Guitars, 1973; Introduction for facsmilie Lute manuscripts, 1974. Contbr. to: Grove's Dictionary, 6th ed.; Musical Times; Early Music. Mbrships: ISM; Lute Soc. Address: c/o Ibbs & Tillett, 124 Wigmore St., London W1, UK.

SPENCER, Robert Lamar, b. 5 April 1938, Drew, Miss., USA. Music Educator; Singer (Bass-baritone). Educ: BMus, Miss. Coll., Clinton, 1961; MA, Tchrs. Coll., Columbia Univ., NYC, 1962; EdD, N Tex. State Univ., Denton, 1969. m. Peggy Harrell, 1 d. Career: Choral Dir.; Music Educ.; Singer, oratorio, opera & recitals. Mbrships: Nat. Assn. Tchrs. of Singing; Am. Choral Dirs. Assn.; nat. Assn. of Schls. of Music; Tex. Music Educrs. Assn.; Tex. Choral Dirs. Assn. Hons: Finalist, Southwestern Metropolitan Opera Vocie Auditions, San Antonio, 1969. Hobbies: Birdwatching; Fishing. Address: 403 Albemarle Rd., Marshall, TX 75670, USA.

SPENCER, Williametta, b. 15 Aug. 1932, Marion, Ill., USA. Composer; Organist; Musicologist; Associate Professor of Music. Educ: AB, Whittier Coll.; MM, Univ. of Southern Calif.; PhD, ibid. Career: Assoc. Prof. of Music, Rio Hondo Coll.,

Whittier, Calif. Comps. incl: Miss Brevis, At the Round Earth's Imagined Corners, Death Be Not Proud, Nova, Nova, Ave Fit Ex Eve, There Is No Rose of Such Virtue, Welcome Yule, The Mystic Trumpeter, Angelus ad Virginem, Nowell, Nowell, Out of Your Sleep, 4 Madrigals to peoms of James Joyce, Winds of May, In The Dark Pine Wood, Bright Cap & Streams, choir. Mbrships: AGO; Nat. Assn. of Am. Comps. & Conds.; MTA of Calif.; Mu Phi Epsilon; Pi Kappa Lambda. Hons: Fulbright Scholarship to Paris, France, 1953-54; 1st Prize Nat. Comp. Contest, Mu Phi Epsilon, 1952, 1954, 1966; Winner Nat. Comp. Contest, Southern Calif. Vocal Assn., 1968. Hobby: Languages. Address: 6228 Gregory, Whittier, CA 90601, USA. 5.

SPERATI, Carleton (Angelo), b. 1 Sept. 1918, Fergus Falls, Minn., USA. Conductor; Teacher; Performer (Flute & Piccolo); Industrial Scientist. Educ: AB, Luther Coll., Decorah, Iowa, 1938; MA, Univ. of Ill., Urbana, Ill., 1939; PhD, ibid., 1941; Flute Seminar, Indiana Univ., 1973. m. Eloise Morris, 3 c. Career: Orch., Band., Chamber Music, Fergus Falls, Minn., 1931-34 & Luther Coll., 1934-38 (also chorus); Concert band & opera orch., Univ. of Ill., 1938-41; Dir. of Our Saviour's Ch. Choir, Jersey City, Nutley Symph. Orch. (Prin.), West Hudson Symph. Orch., NJ Symph., 1941-50; Cond.; Dupont Expmtl. Stn. Band; Prin. & Asst. Cond., Dupont Employees Concert Band Delaware Symph. Orch.; Wilmington Opera Soc. Orch., etc., 1950-72. Org. orch. & cond. live perfs. for silent films. Mbrships. incl: Am. Fed. of Musicians locals 311-641 & 259; Am. Flute Assn.; Amateur Chamber Music Players. Hobbies: White-water Canoeing; Skiing, etc. Address: 23 Mustang Acres, Parkersburg, WV 26101, USA.

SPERL, Gary Robert, b. 22 June 1950, Waukesha, Wis., USa. Clarinettist; Educator. Educ: BME, Univ. of Wis., River Falls; currently studying for MMus, Ind. Univ. Career: Duluth Symph. Orch.; Mpls. Civic Orch.; Bloomington Fest. Orch.; Assoc. Instr. in Woodwinds, Ind. Univ. Mbr., Mpls. Musicians Assn. Hobby: Scuba diving. Address: 604 S Grand Ave., Waukesha, WI 53186, USA.

SPEZIALE, Marie, b. 4 Apr. 1942, Brooklyn, NY, USA. Trumpeter; Instructor of Trumpet. Educ: BMus, Coll.-Conserv. of Music, Univ. of Cinn., 1964. Career: Appeared on Dave Garroway's Today Show, NBC, 1958; Johnny Carson's Tonight Show, NBC, 1969; Soloist, Cinn. Symph. Orch., 1962, '71, '72; First woman trumpeter in a major symph. orch.; Asst. Prin. Trumpet, Cinn. Symph. Orch.; Instr. of Trumpet, Miami Univ., Oxford, Ohio; Trumpet, Symph. Jazz Septet. Recordings: participated in all Cinn. Symph. Orch. recordings since 1964; Symphony Jazz Quintet, 1972. Mbrships: Pi Kappa Lambda; Sigma Alpha Iota; Province Pres., ibid., 1964-65; Nat. Dir. of Instrumental Activities, 1965-67; MacDowell Soc., 1978-. Hons: Outstanding Woman of the Yr., Fine Arts, Tampa, Fla., 1962; Sigma Alpha Iota, Nat. Fndn. Award, 1962, '64, etc. Hobbies: Photography; Chess; Swimming, etc. Address: 9838 Dargate Ct., Cincinnati, OH 45231, USA.

SPICER, Paul Cridland, b. 6 June 1952, Bowdon, Cheshire, UK. Music Teacher; Organist. Educ: Chorister, New Coll., Oxford; Post Grad. Cert. in Educ., Durham Univ., 1974; RCM & London Univ., 1970-73; BMus; ARCM (organ teaching). Career: Asst. Dir. of Music, Uppingham Schl., Rutland, 1974-78; Dir. of Music, Ellesmere Coll., Salop, 1978-; Organ recitals inclng. Westminster, Durham Cathedrals, New Coll., Oxford; St. Paul's Cathedral; King's & St. John's Colls., Cambridge, etc. Contbr. to Musical Times. Mbrships: ISM; Music Masters Assn. Recip. Walford Davies Prize, RCM (Organ), 1973. Hobbies: Architecture; Old prints. Address: Ellesmere Coll., Elesmere, Salop, SY12 9AB, UK.

SPIEGEL, Laurie, b. 20 Sept. 1945, Chgo., Ill., USA. Composer; Lutenist. Educ: BA, Shimer Coll., Mt. Carroll, Ill., 1967; studied at Lake Forest Coll., Univ. of Ill., Oxford Univ.; Juilliard Schl., NY, 1969-72; MA, Bklyn. Coll., CUNY, 1975; pvte. study of comp. w. Jacob Druckman & Emmanuel Ghent. Career: perfs. at num. museum, galls., univs., fests., inclng. Mus. of Mod. Art, Aspen Music Fest., also radio & TV broadcasts. Comps: chiefly electronic & computer music for dance, theatre, expmntl. video & film. Mbrships: Exec. Coun., Ctr. for New Music; Lute Soc. of Am.; Soc. for Ethnomusicol.; ASCAP. Recip. sev. grants. Address: 173-175 Duane St., NY, NY 10013, USA. 27, 29.

SPIEGL, Fritz, b. 1926, Austria. Flautist; Conductor. Educ: ARAM. Career: Prin. Flautist, Royal Liverpool Philharmonia Orch., 1948-63; Cond., Liverpool Wind Ensemble & Liverpool Singers, 1949-; Dir. & Cond., Liverpool Music Grp.; var. broadcasts, 1951-; Lectr., Royal Manchester Coll. of Music. Publs. incl: What the Papers Didn't Mean to Say; The Black-on-White Misprint Show; A Small Book of Grave Humour; English as She is Wrotten; var. eds. of old music inclng. 1st eds. of works by

Handel, Haydn, Mozart & Bethoven. Hobbies: Research; Vintage Motoring; Musical Automata; Jokes. Address: 4 Windemere Terrace, Liverpool, Merseyside, UK. 3.

SPIES, Claudio, b. 26 Mar. 1925, Santiago, CHile. Composer; Professor of Music. Educ: AB, 1950, MA, 1954, Harvard Univ. m. Emmi Vera Tobias, 1 s., 4 d. Career: Prof., Music, Princeton Univ., Comps. incl: Tempi, Viopiacem; 7 Enzensberger-Lieder; Three Songs on Poems by may Swenson; Animula Vagula, Blandula; Bagatelle for Piano; Shirim Le Hasthunatham; 5 Sonnet settings (Shakespeare). Recordings of own works incl: Impromptu; Viopiacem. Contbr. to Perspectives on Shoenberg & Stravinsky, 1962, & to profl. jrnls. Mbrships: Fndng. Mbr., Past Sec.-Treas., Alban Berg Soc. Ltd.; Fndng. Mbr., Past Exec. Comm. Mbr., Am. Soc. of Univ. Composers; Past Bd. Mbr., League of Composers-ISCM; Mbr., Ed. Bd., Perspectives of New Music. Hons: Composition Award, Ingram Merrill Fndn., 1966; Brandeis Univ. Creative Arts Award Citation in Music, 1967; Award, Nat. Inst. of Arts & Letters, 1969; Fellowship-Grant, Nat. Endowment for the Arts, 1975. Address: Music Dept., Princeton Univ., Princeton, NJ 08540, USA. 2.

SPIETH, Noelle, b. 10 Oct. 1950, Paris, France. Harpsichordist. Educ: Baccalaureat; Conserv. de Paris; Conserv. de Genève. Career: solo concerts in France, UK, Switz., Belgium, Netherlands (UK; radio perfs. in France, Switz., Belgium. Recordings: w. Roger Bernolin (recorder) & "Ensemble Nuove Musiche". Hons: 1st prizes for harpsichord, chmbr. music & music hist., Conserv. de Paris; 1st prize for virtuosity, Conserv. de Genève; 1st prize, Int. Harpsichord Competition, Paris, 1977. Hobbies: Reading; Entertaining Friends. Address: 4 rue Paul Bert, 75011 Paris, France.

SPILLER, Ljerko, b. 22 July 1908, Crikvenica, Jugoslavia. Professor of Violin, Viola & Chamber Music; Conductor. Educ: Artist Dip., Music Acad., Zagreb, Yugoslovaia; Licence de Concert, Ecole Normale de Musique, Paris, France. m. Carola Stella Gielen, 2 s. Debut: Zagreb. Career incls: Prof. & Fndr. of res. str. quartet (1933), Ecole Normale de Musique, Paris, 1930-35; Concertmaster, Alfred Cortot Chmbr. Orch., 1934-35, Radio el Mundo Symph. orch., 1935-48, Philharmon Orch., 1940-45, & L Spiller Chmbr. Orch., 1947; Fndr., Cond. & Concertmaster, Amigos de la Musica, 1947-66; Cond., Youth Orch. of Nat. Radio Buenos Aires, 1977-; Full Prof. of Chmbr. Music, Univ. of La Plata & Collegium Musicum of Buenos Aires; Soloist w. num. symph. orchs. thru'out world; has given 1st perfs. in Buenos Aires of violin concertos by wll-known contemp. composers. Publs. incl: El Pequeno Violinista, 1943, in 6th ed.; Iniciacion para el estudio del violin en grupos, 3 vols., printed in 4 langs. Contbr. to jrnls. Sev. recordings. Mbr., num. profl. organisations. Recip. of many awards inclng: Extraordinary Emeritus Prof., Univ. of La Plata, 1975. Address: Sanchez de Bustamante 2516, 2 p.C. Buenos Aires 25, Argentina.

SPINK, Ian, b. 29 Mar. 1932, London, UK. University Professor. Educ: BMus, TCL, 1952; MA, Barber Inst. Fine Arts, Birmingham, 1958. m. 7 children. Career: Overseas Examiner for TCL, Can.; NZ & Aust., 1958-60; Lectr.-Sr. Lectr. in Music, Univ. of Sydney, NSW, Aust., 1962-69; Hd., Music Dept., (Sr. Lectr.-Prof.), Royal Holloway Coll., Univ. of London, UK, 1969-; Dean, Fac. of Arts, ibid., 1973-75; Dean, Fac. of Music, Univ. of London, 1974-78; Chmn., Bd. of Studies in Music, ibid., 1978. Mbr. of Senate, ibid., 1975-. Publs: Ed., The English Lute-Songs (Stainer & Bell), vol. 17, 1961, 2nd ed., 1974, vol. 18, 1963, vol. 19, 1966; An Historical Approach to Musical Form, 1967; Ed., English Songs, 1625-1660 (Musica Britannica vol. 33); English Song: Dowland to Purcell, 1974; Ed., Arne, The Judgement of Paris (Musica Britannica Vol. 42), 1979. Address: Royal Holloway Coll., Egham, Surrey, TW20 0EX, UK.

SPINNEY, Bradley, b. 11 Feb. 1915, Kittery, Maine, USA. Drummer; Percussionist; Lecturer. m. Catherine Elizabeth Ham, 1 d. Debut: w. Metrop. Theatre Youth Orch., Boston, 1933. Career incls: w. WOR Staff Orch., Mutual Network, 13 yrs.; Currently, freelance musician w. num. grps., orchs. etc. inclng. Met. Opera Orch.; Film work w. 20th Century Fox, Fox Movietone News, Terrytoon & Popeye cartoons; TV series incl: Winston Churchill's 'The Valiant Years'; Fac., NY Univ. & Queens Coll. Comp: Fall of Paris, 1965. Recordings incl: Stravinsky's L'Histoire du Soldat'. Publs. incl: Encyclopaedia of Percussion Instruments & Drumming, Vol. 1, 1955; 2, 1959. Contbr. to Allego. Recip: Prize w. Metrop. Theatre Youth Orch., 1933. Hobbies incl: Old Instruments. Address: PO Box 8842, Ft. Lauderdale, FL 33310, USA.

SPIREA, Andrei, b. 21 Jan. 1932, Bucharest, Rumania. Composer; Teacher of Chamber Music, Piano & Clarinet. Educ: Music Acad., Bucharest. m. Bat-Sheva Spirea, 2 c. Debut: W.

ARAD Phil. Orch., under S Commissiona, 1953. Comps. incl: Sinfonie Breve; 2nd Symph.; 2 Suites for Orch.; String Quartet; Piano Trio; Divertissemento for Orch.; Oboe Concerto; Viole Concerto; Piano Concerto. Num. recordings of own comps. Mbr., Israel Comps. Assn. Address: 29 Brandeis Str., Tel-Aviv, Israel.

SPITZ, Willy, b. 3 Oct. 1936, Seveln, SG, Switzerland. Music tchr. Educ: Conserv. Winterthur, dip, solo singing; Conserv. Zürich, dip. schl. singing. m. Susan Meier, 1 s., 1 d. Debut: Winterthur, 1969. Career: Church concerts; Oratoria; Song evenings in Switzerland and abroad; Radio recordings, Zürich, Lugano. Mbrships: Swiss Assn. for Musical Art; Swiss Soc. for Music Pedgagoues. Address: Riethaldenweg 29, 8200 Schaffhausen, Switzerland.

SPITZENBERGER, Herbert, b. 5 June 1927, Munich, Germany. Concert Pianist. Educ: Leopold Mozart Conserv., Augsburg, 1946-50; studied Piano w. var. masters, Munich. m. Barbara Spitzenberger, 2 c. Debut: Augsburg, 1950. Career: Num. recitals & solo apps., 1950-; Concert tours in Europe, India, Southeast Asia & Japan; Piano tchr., Regensburger Domspatzen Music Schl., 1958-64; Vis. Prof. Piano, Univ. of Arts, Tokyo, Japan, 1965-67; Prof., Hochschule für Musik, Munich, 1968-; radio & TV apps., Europe & Asia. Hons: Prizewinner, Confedn. of Germany Industry, 1955; Professor, 1975. Hobbies: Skiing; Swimming; Motorboating; Table Tennis; Filming. Address: 8021 Hohenschäftlarn, Flossgatter 14, German Fed. Repub.

SPIVAKOSKY, Tossy, b. 4 Feb. 1907, Odessa, Russia. Violinist. Educ: Berlin Hochscule Für Musik; Study w. Profs. Arrigo Serato & Willy Hess. m. Erika Lipsker, 1 d. Debut: Berlin, aged 10. Career: Concerts in Europe until 1933; Concerts, tchng., Australia; 1933-39; US res., 1940-; Concerts, USA, Canada & Europe; Fac. Mbr., Fairfield Univ. & Juilliard Schl. of Music. Comps: Cadenzas to Beethoven Violin Concerto & Mozart's Violin Concertos. Num. recordings. Publs: The Spivakovsky Way of Bowing, by Gaylord Yost, 1949. Contbr. to The Music Review. Mbrships: Am. Musicol. Soc.; The Bohemians. Hons: DLitt, Fairfield Univ., 1970. DMus, Cleveland Inst. of Music, 1975. Mgmt: Albert Kay Assocs., NYC. Address: Westport, CT 06880, USA. 2, 16.

SPOLJARIC, Vlado, b. 23 Jan. 1926, Zagreb, Yugoslavia. Professor of Music; Composer. Educ: Hist. of Music, Music Acad. of Zagreb. m. Olive Zadobosek-Spoljaric, 2 c. Career: Secondary Schl. Prof., 1952-57; Music Ed., Radio TV Zagreb, 1957-62; Prof., Music Schl. Blagoje Bersa, Zagreb, 1962-. Comps: Diptihon (string orch.); Chaconne (oboe, clarinet & bassoon); Movement for Three (flute, oboe & piano). Num. recordings. Mr. Assn. of Croation Comps., Zagreb. Hobby: Photography. Address: Ozegoviceva 12, 41000 Zagreb, Yugoslavia.

SPONG, Jon Curtis, b. 5 Dec. 1933, Des Moines, IA, USA. Concert Organist; Vocal Coach-Accompanist; Composer-Arranger-Editor; College Music Educator. Educ: BMusEd, 1956, MMus, 1958, Drake Univ. Career: recital apps., in USA & abroad; TV & radio broadcasts in USA, Philippines & Orient; currently Artist Tchr., Cinn. Conserv. of Music, Cinn., OH. Recordings: sev. on RCA Red Seal as accomp. to baritone Sherrill Milnes in perfs. of sacred music. Publs: own comps. & eds. of histl. organ music. Contbr. to: Jrnl. of Ch. Music. Mbrships: AGO; Nat. Assn. Tchrs. of Singing; Bd. of Dirs., Nat. Assn. of Organ Tchrs. Hons. incl: Am. Music Rsch. Grant, Electro-Voice, Inc., 1965-66. Hobby: Reading. Address: Coll.-Conserv. of Music, Univ. of Cinn., Cinn., OH 43452, USA. 23, 28.

SPRAGUE, William Hackman, Jr., b. 29 June 1945, Omaha, Neb., USA. Instrumental Music Teacher; French Horn Player. Educ: BME, Univ. of Neb. at Lincoln, 1967; MMus, Univ. of Neb., Lincoln, 1976; Studied w. Philip Farkas, Aspen, 1962 & Marty Morris, Cleveland, 1965. m. Kathleen Rosenbaum, 2 s. Debut: Horn Soloist w. Omaha Symph. Orch., 1962. Career: Tchr. of Instrumental Music, Bellevue Public Schls., currently at Junior High level; Taught at all levels in public schl. instrumental music; Co-ordinator of Elementary Instrumental Music; Omaha Symph., 18 yrs.; Prin. Horn, Lincoln Symph., 7 yrs., Omaha opera Orch.; Omaha Ballet Orch.; Omaha Pops Orch. Recordings: num. commercial and soundtrackts. Mbrships: Pi Kappa Lambda; Phi Mu Alpha Sinfonia (Pres., Upsilon Chapt., 1966); Gamma Lambda Band Fraternity (VP, 1967); Int. Horn Soc. State co-ordinator). Hobbies: Restoration of Antique Cars. Address: 713 E 7th St., Papillion, NE 68046, USA.

SPRATT, Edward Robert, b. 15 June 1926, Kingston-on-Thames, UK. Teacher of Brass Instruments; Performer on Trumpet. Educ: ARAM. m. Renee Clare, 1 s. Career: Perfs. w. Sadlers Wells Opera, LPO & Philharmonia Orch.; Prof., RAM, Vis. Tchr., City of London, Highgate & Westminster Abbey Choir Schls.; Cond.,

Kensington Concordia; Brass Coach, Enfield Young Symph. Orch. Num. recordings. Mbrships: Freemasons; Freeman of City of Londong; ISM; Musicians Union. Hobbies: Reading Hist.; Caravanning. Address: 37 River Bank, London N21, 2AB, UK.

SPRATT, Geoffrey Kenneth, b. 16 Sept. 1950, London, UK. University Lecturer; Conductor; Flautist; Violist. Educ: BA, PhD, Bristol Univ. m. Frances Vivien Squire, 1 s. Career: Lectr., Music Dept., Univ. Coll., Cork; Cond., Univ. Coll. of Cork Chmbr. Choir, Orch. & Choral Soc. num. recordings for Radio Telefis Éireann as lectr. & cond. Contbr. to: Music Review; Musical Opinion; Brio; Counterpoint. Mbrships: ISM; Music Assn. of Ireland; Coun. mbr., Music Tchrs. Assn. of Ireland. Recip., Napier Miles prize for Music, Bristol Univ., 1972. Address: 20 Briarscourt, Shanakiel, Cork, Eire.

SPRINGUEL, France-Virgine, b. 25 Sept. 1956, Ostend, Belgium. Cellist. Educ: Ostend Conserv.; Brussels Conserv.; studying w. Paul Tortelier & André Navarra. Debut: Fest. of Flanders, ORTF. Career: Concerts in Zagreb, Nice, Italy, Germany, USSR, Sweden, Spain & Belgium; Radio & TV apps. Recordings: Record on Pro Civitae & Melodia labels. Hons: Kenipel/Bulcke Prize, 1970; 1st Prize, Pro Civitate 1972; European Prize, 1972; Van Kerklove Prize, 1973; 1st Prizes for Cello & Chmbr. Music, Brussels Conserv; 4th prize, Tchaikovsky Competition, 1978. Hobbies: Painting; Reading; Sport. Address: 111 rue Stevin, 1040 Brussels, Belgium.

SPRONGL, Norbert, b. 30 Apr. 1892, Obermarkersdorf, Germany. Composer. Educ: Dip. comp., music acad., Vienna, 1933; prof., 1956. m. Rosa Schneider. Comps: 4 symphs.; 5 piano concertos; 2 violin concertos; works for large orch.; chmbr. music; songs & choral works; Passacaglia for piano & orch.; Duo for mandoline & guitar; var. piano works. Mbrships: Austrian soc. for contemporary music; Austrian comps. union; hon. mbr. of Mozart circle, Vienna. Hons: Kulturpreis, Lower Austria, 1962; Golden sign of hon., 1967; Plaque of hon., 1972; Austrian cross of hon. for art & science, 1968; Hon. medal for the town of Vienna, 1970. Hobbies: photography. Address: 2340 Mödling, Pfarrgasse 8, Austria.

SPURRELL, Elizabeth Joyce, b. 4 Apr. 1932, Reigate, Surrey, UK. Teacher; Violinist. Educ: RCM; ARCM (piano tchr.); GRSM. Career: Music Dir., King's Coll. Schl., Cambridge, 1957-65; Music Dir., Melbourne C of E. Girls' Grammar Schl., Aust., 1966-71; freelance violinist (now w. Sadlers' Wells Royal Ballet Orch.), 1973-. Hobbies: Chmbr. Music; Walking; Tennis; Art; Ch. Architecture; Gardening. Address: 16 Berestede Rd., Hammersmith, London W6 9NP, UK.

SQUAIR, Jean, b. 19 Jan. 1925, Vancouver, Can. Director. Educ: BA, Stanford Univ.; Grad. work, Univ. of Calif. m. Stuart Davidson Squair, 2 d. Career: Dir., Arts Admin. grad. prog., Golden Gate Univ., Grad. Schl. Mbrships: Pres., Assn. of Calif. Symph. Orchs.; VP, Women's Coun., Am. Symph. Orch. League; Dir., San Fran. Symph. Bd. of Govs. Hobbies: China Collecting; Travel. Address: 6001 Acacia Ave., Oakland, CA 94618, USA.

SQUIRE, Russel Nelson, b. 21 Sept. 1908, Cleveland, OH, USA. Pianist; Emeritus Professor. Educ: BSM, Oberlin Conserv. of Music, 1929; Am, Western Reserve Univ., 1939; PhD, NY Univ., 1942. m. Doris Winifred Squire, 2 s. Career incls: Prof. of Music, Pepperdine Coll. of Los Angeles, 1937-56, Calif. State Univ., Long Beach, 1956-72 (now Emeritus), & Pacific Christian Coll., Long Beach, 1972-73; Adj. Prof. of Educ., Pepperdine Univ., 1973-. Publs: Introduction to Music Education, 1952; Church Music, 1962; Class Piano for Adult Beginners, 1964, 2nd ed., 1971. Contbr. to num. profl. jrnls. Mbr. profl. orgs. Recip. var. hons. Hobbies: Photography; Music composition. Address: 2748 Lakeridge Lane, Westlake Village, CA 91361, USA. 3, 9.

SQUIRES, Shelagh Marion, b. London, UK. Opera Singer (Mezzo Soprano). Educ: AGSM. Career: Glyndebourne Festival Chorus; Solo parts w. Glyndebourne Opera & Phoenix Opera; Prin. w. Engl. Nat. Opera Co. Recordings: ENO recordings of Wagner ring cycle at Coliseum; Wellgunds in Rhinegold; Grimgarde in The Valkyrie. Hobbies: House Painting & Decoration; Do-it-Yourself. Mgmt: Neil Dalrymple, Music Int. Address: 59 Culverden Pk., Tunbridge Wells, Kent, UK.

SREBOTNJAK, Alonjz, b. 27 June 1931, Postojna, Yugoslavia. Composer; Professor. Educ: Dip. in Comp., Ljubljana Acad. of Music; courses at Accademia Musicale Chigiana, Siena; studies w. B Porrena, Rome, & P Racine Fricker, London. m. Dubravka Tomsic, 1 s. Career: works perf. in Europe & USA; Prof. of Comp., Ljubljana Acad. of Music, 1970-; Hd. of Comp. Dept., ibid., 1974-. Comps. incl: Sinfonietta in two movements; Antiphon; Karst Suite; Harp concerto (rec.); Violin Concerto; Cantatas, Ecstasy of Death, A Village Orpheus; Macedonian

Dances (rec.); Letters; 6 pieces for bassoon & piano; Serenata for flute, clarinet & bassoon; Microsongs for voice & 13 instruments (rec.); Music for Strings; Macedonica, for chamber ensemble; choral works; film music. Mbr. Union of Yugoslav Comps. num. hons. Address: Linhartova 1, 61113 Ljubljana, Yugoslavia.

SRI CHINMOY, b. 27 Aug. 1931, Chittagong, Bengal, India. Spiritual Leader; Author; Artist; Composer; Singer; Performer on Esraj, Cello, Violin & Flute. Career: perfs. at pvte. gatherings & pub. mediatations & lectures, 1964-; perf. (w. own students) of own comps., Carnegie Hall, NYC, 1976. Comps: over 1300 devotional songs in Engl. & Bengali; settings of Sanskrit sacred verses. Recordings: Songs of Immortality; My Pilot Supreme; Songs of Eternity; New Creation; Mother, I Bow to Thee; Flame-Waves; Dream-Boat. Publs. incl: God the Supreme Musician, 1974: song books. Contbr. to: Aum Mag.; Meditation at the UN; The Philosopher; Princeton Sem. Bulletin. Mbrships: Dir., Sri Chinmoy Ctr., 1966-, UN Meditation Grp., UN HQ, NYC, 1970-. Hons. inclk: Bronze Medal, NYC, 1975; Sri Chinmoy Day Proclaimed by City of San Fran., Calif. Hobbies: Sport; Photography. Address: PO Box 32433, Jamaica, NY 11431, USA.

SRNKA, Jiri, b. 18 Aug. 1907, Pisek, Czechoslovakia. Composer. Educ: Prague Conserv. (violin); Master Schl. of Vitezslav Novak (comp.); Studied quarter tone & sixth-tone system w. Alois Haba; Grad., Conserv. m. Emilie Sedlackova. Debut: Violinist; Cond. Career: Prof. of film Music, Acad. of Musical Arts, 1950-53. Comps. incl: Orchl. works, chambr. music, vocal music, film music; String Quartet No. 1 w. orch. (recorded). Recordings incl: Suite for full orch.; Concerto for piano & orch.; Concerto for flute & chmbr. orch.; The Children's Yr. (vocal); Film Music to about 50 pictures. Mbr. Assn. of Czech. Comps. Hons. incl: Nat. prioze; 2 State Prizes. Hobbies: Astronomy; Books; Gardening. Address: Podolska 600/1, Podoli, Prague 4, Czechoslovakia.

SROM, Karel, b. 14 Sept. 1904, Pilsen, Czechoslovakia. Composer; Writer. Educ: Pvte. Music Study w. Jan Ev. Zelinka, Sr. & karel Haba; LLD, Charles Univ., 1928. m. Zdenka Hradecka. Career: Critic & Music Reporter, Rytmus, 1940-44; Hd., Music Dept., Czechoslovakia Radio, 1945-50; Chief Ed., State Music Publishing House Orbis & State Publishing House of Lit., Music & Art, 1951-54; Dir., Czech Music Fund, 1954-61; Comp. & Writer, 1961-. Comps: (Orchl. Works) IInd Symph. for large orch., 1951; The Gnome, scherzo for orch., 1953; Sigh on Skates, symphonic allegretto on the theme of the poem by Chr. Morgenstern, 1957; Concerto for piano & orch., 1961; Hayaya, orchl. suite for adults & children, 1961; Etudes for orch., 1970; Scherzi Notturni, 1972; (Chmbr. Music) Whiles, piano trifles, 1942; Seven Pieces for Piano, 1942; Black Hour, cycle of piano comps., 1965; Str. Quartet No. 3, 1966; Sherzo Trio for violin, viola & collo Concertino for two flutes & string quintet or orch., 1971; A Look Back, 1973; Sun & Shadow, orchl. suite, 1976. Publs: Orchestra & Conductor, 1960; Beyond Music, 1965; Karel Ancerl, 1968. Author of num. articles, analyses & criticisms. Address: Podolska 102, 14700 Prague 4, Czechoslovakia.

STAAR, René, b. 30 May 1951, Graz, Austria. Violin Virtuoso; Composer; Conductor. Educ: Helsinki & Stocklholm Conserv. for Music; Vienna Music Acad.; Studies w. Prof. Franz Samohyl & Nathan Milstein (violin), Prof. Alfred Uhl (comp.) & Prof. Hans Swarowsky (conducting). Debut: Helsinki, 1969. Career: Concerts in Austria, Benelux, UK, Hungary, Yugoslavia, Italy, Turkey, France, Scandinavia, etc.; Tchr., Vienna Hochschule. Comps: Chambermusic (for String Instruments); orchl. music; Pieces for Violin & Piano. Hons: Prizewinner, Int. Bach-Mozart Violin Competition, Lisbon, 1973. Address: Viktorg. 12/11, 1040 Vienna, Austria.

STÄBLEIN, Bruno, b. 5 May 1895, Munich, Germany. Musicologist. Educ: Akademie der Tonkunst, Munich, 1914-18; Munich Univ., 1914-18; Dr phil, 1918. m. Hanna Stäblein-Harder, 2 s., 1 d. Career: Opera & Concert Dir., Innsbruck State Theatre & Landestheater Coburg, 1919-30; Music Educ. Tchr., Altes Gymnasium Regensburg, 1930-46; Dir., Inst. for Music Rsch., 1946-60; Prof., 1956, Emeritus, 1963, Hd. of Microfilm archives for Mediaeval Music MMS, 1962, Univ. of Erlangen. Publs: Monumenta Monodica Medii Aevi 1, 1956, 2, 1970; Schrifbild der einstimmigen Musik des Mittelalters, 1975. Contbr. to jrnls. Mbr. profl. orgs. Address: Kleefeld. 10, D-852 Erlangen-Sieglitzhof, German Fed. Repub.

STACHOWSKI, Marek, b. 21 Mar. 1936, Piekary Slaskie, Poland. Composer; Professor of Composition. Educ: BM, Doct., State Acad. of Music, Cracow; studied w. K Penderecki. m. Maria Jablonska, 2 d. Debut: Rotterdam, 1968. Career: num. apps. in TV music progs.; radio & TV interviews; works performed in num.

European countries & USA; Vis. Lectr., Yale Univ., USA, 1975; currently Vice-Rector, State Acad. of Music, Cracow & Dir., Comp. Dept., ibid. Comps: Musica con una battuta del tam-tam; Musica per quartetto d'archi; Neusis II; Chant de l'espoir; Audition; Irisation; II String Quartet; Extensions; Musique solenelle; Poème sonore; Birgs; Chamber Music, Divertimento, Rondeau. All comps. recorded. Mbr., Union of Polish Comps. Hons. incl: 1st prizes, A Malawski Competition, 1968, Szymanowski Competition, 1974; Music Prize, City of Mönchenglabach, German Fed. Repub., 1976. Hobbies: Coins; Egyptology. Address: 29 a ul. Czyzówka, 30-526 Cracow, Poland. 30.

STACY, Thomas, b. 15 Aug. 1938, Little Rock, Ark., USA. English Horn Soloist. Educ: BMus, Eastman Schl. of Music, Rochester, NY, 1960. m. Marie Mann Stacy, 2 s. Debut: Solo debut w. Mnpls. Symph. Orch. under baton of Bernard Haitink. Career: Solo appearances w. NY Phil. Minn. Orch., New Orleans Phil., Minn. Bach. Soc. & Rochester (NY) Civic Orch.; perf. world & NY premieres of Skrowaczewski English Horn Concerto wchich was written for & dedicated to Thomas Stacy; Engl. Horn. Fac., The Juilliard Schl.; Taught Oboe at Univ. of Minn. & Macalester Coll., St. Paul, Minn. Recordings: Concerto for English Horn, by Stanislaw Skrowaczewski, Desto Records; The Swan of Tuonela, by Sibelius, Columbia Records. Publs: Solos for the English Horn Player, edited by Thomas Stacy, 1974; Ed., Int. Music Co. Contbr. to The World's Oboist. Hons: George Eastman Scholarship, 1957-58. Hobbies: Painting; Interior decoration. Address: 74 Sout Pk. Ave., Old Greenwich, CT 06870, USA. 2.

STADER, Maria, b. Budapest, Hungary. Concert Soprano. Educ: studied w. var. noted tchrs. m. Hans Erismann, 2 s. Debut: Int. Competitions, Geneva, Switz., 1939. Career: Solo apps. throughout Europe; apps. w. orchs. in USA; participant in Salzburg, Prades, Berlin, Milan, Perugia, Lucerne, Edinburgh, Munich & Casals Fests. Has recorded for Decca. Hons: 1st Prize, Int. Competitions, Geneva, 1939; Mozart Medal, Salzburg, 1956; Lilli Lehmann Medal; Golden Medal, Zürich, 1962; Austrian Order of Merit for Arts & Scis., 1964. Mgmt: Thea Dispeker, 59 E 54th St., NY, NY 10022, USA. Address: c/o Mgmt.

STADLEN, Peter, b. 14 July 1910, Vienna, Austria. Concert Pianist; Lecutrer; Music Critic. Educ: Piano, theory, Vienna Hochschule für Musik; Piano, theory, cond., Berlin Hochschule für Musik. m. Hedi Simon, 2 s. Debut: 1934. Career: Concert pianist, specializing in Viennese Classics & Second Viennese Schl., touring Austria, UK, Denmark, Netherlands, Italy, Belgium; Pt.-time Lectr., Reading Univ., 1965-69; Vis. Fellow, All Souls, Oxford, 1967-68; Staff Mbr., Daily Telegraph, 1960; Chief Music Critic, ibid., 1977; Num. first perfs., comps. by Webern, Krenek, Schoenberg. Contbr. to num. profl. publs. Mbrships: Royal Musical Assn.; Royal Phil. Soc.; Gesellschaft für Musikforschung; Schoenberg Gesellschaft; Critics' Circle; ISM. Hons: Schoenberg Medal, Austrian Ministry of Culture, 1952. Address: 49 Downshire Hill, London NW3, UK.

STAEHELIN, Marguerite Martha, b. 31 Dec. 1916, Basel, Switzerland. Director of The Swiss Music Library. Educ: Piano & Voice, Basel Conserv.; Dip., Method Jacques-Dalcroze, Geneva, Inst. Jaques-Dalcroze; Basel & Geneva Univs. Debut: Dance; Grand Opera, Demonstration Jacques-Dalcroze. Career: Dir., Swiss Music Lib., NYC, USA; Official Rep., Assn. of Swiss Musicians, Lausanne, Switzerland; Apps. over Radio WNYC, USA. Contbr. of articles to Swiss Am. Review, NY. Mbrships: Int. Soc. for Contemporary Music (Basel & NY); Met. Opera Guild; Advsry. Bd., Swiss Soc. of NY. Hobbies: Swimming; Mtn. Climbing; Cooking. Address: 1 Lincoln Plaza, Apt. 29K, New York, NY 10023, USA.

STAEHELIN, Martin, b. 25 Sept. 1937, Basel, Switzerland. Musicologist. Educ: PhD, Univ. of Basel, 1967; Dip., Tchr. Querflöte, Music Acad. Basel; 1962; Schl. Music Dip., ibid., 1963. m. Elizabeth Schenker. Career: Tchr., Latin, Greek Schl. Music, Basel, 1963; Tchr., Univ. of Zürich, 1971-; Hd., Beethoven-Archives, Bonn, 1976-; Tchr., Univ. of Bonn, 1976-77; Prof., ibid., 1977-. Publs: H Isaac, Messen, 1970, 1973; Der GrüneCosex der Viadrina, 1971; Die Messen Heinrich Isaacs, 3 vols., 1977. Contbr. to: Archiv fur Musikwissenschaft; Die Musikforschung; Fontes Artis Musicae; Schweizerische Beiträage zur Musikwissenschaft; Tijdschrift van de Vereniging voor Nederlandse Muziekgeschiedenis; Schweizerisches Archiv für Volkskunde. Mbrships: Committee, New Josquin Ed.; Bd. of Dirs., Int. Musicol. Soc.; Ctrl. Bd. of Dir., Swiss Music Rsch. Soc.; Musical. Commission, Acad. of the Sciences, Mainz. Hons: Dent Medal, Royal Musical Assoc., 1975. Address: Baumschulallee 19, D-53, Bonn, German Fed. Repub.

STAEMPFLI, (Hans) Jakob, b. 26 Oct. 1934, Bern, Switz. Concert Singer; Singing Teacher. Educ. incls: Bern Conserv.; State

HS for Music, Frankfurt/M, Germany, m. Susanna Zogg, 1 s., 1 d. Debut: 1955. Career incls: Oratorio Singer; Recitalist, noted for Brahms lieder; apps. in major European cities, regularly at Engl. Bach. Fest., 1962-; Tchr., 1960-, currently at Folkwanghochschule Essen, Germany, & Bern Conserv. of Music. Has made num. recordings. Mbrships. incl: Swiss Music Tchrs. Assn.; Swiss Musicians Union. Recip. title of Prof. 'in Würdigung seiner hervorragenden künstlerischen Verdienste', Saarbrücken, 1965. Hobby: Working as recording prod. or balance engr. Mgmt: Konzertdirektion Klaus Menzel, Zürich/Caecilia Geneva/Vitoria Madrid. Address: Haldenweg 24 C, CH-3526 Hünibach, Switz.

STAERN, Gunner Oscar, b. 23 Jan. 1922, Stockholm, Sweden. Orchestral Conductor. Educ: Stockholm Conserv.; Karajan Course, Lurerne, 1955. m. harriett Cronström, 2 s., 2 d. Debut: on Swedish Radio w. Göteborg Symph. Orch., 1949. Career: Repetiteur & Chorus Master, Stockohlm Opera House, 1950-54; Chief Cond., Gävle Phil. Orch., 1954-62; Wexford Fest. Opera, 1963-65; Freelance, 1965-69; Chief Cond., Göteborg Opera House, 1969-; has app. at major fests. & toured all European countries, Far. E & Aust. Recordings: The Moldau, Les Preludes, Tchaikovsky Concerto No. 1 & Violin Concerto, w. LPO; Bo Nilsson, Stunde-eines Blocks, w. Swedish Radio Symph. Orch., Stockholm. Recip. of Arnold Bax Mem. Medal. Hobbies: Art Collecting; Swimming; Fishing; Languages. Address: Haga Kyrkogata 28 a, Göteborg, Sweden. 3.

STAFF, John Gavin, b. 18 May 1933, Bradford, UK. Music Adviser. Educ: tCL, 1951-54; ATCL (pfte); LTCL (TTD); GTCL; Tchrs. Cert., Trent Park Tchrs. Training Coll. m. Shirley Joan Yaxley. Career: Music Tchr., Alderman Catleugh Schl., King's Lynn, 1957-59; Lakenham Boys' Schl., Norwich, 1960-64; Peripatetic Tchr. of Schl. & Choral Music, Norfolk Educ. Authority, 1964-69; Cond., Watton Choral Soc., 1964-66; Blofield Choral Soc., 1964-69; Loddon Choral Soc., 1965-69, Fakenham Choral Soc., 1966-69; N Walsham Choral Soc., 1967-69; Music Adviser, Bournemouth Educ. Authority, 1970-74; Cond., Bournemouth Tchrs. Choir, 1973-75; Music Adviserr, Dorset Educ. Authority, 1974-. Mbr., Music Advisers Nat. Assn. Hobbies: Gardening; Walking. Address: 126 Upton Way, Broadstone, Dorset, BH18 9NA, UK. 3, 4.

STAFFORD, John Michael, b. 23 Apr. 1928, London, UK. Music Broadcaster; Record Critic. Career: Freelance broadcaster, Aust. Broadcasting Commission, 1955-; Prog. Coordinator, Radio 7CAE-FM, Tasmania, 1976-79; Fndr., Archive of Recorded Sound, Tasmania, 1970. Contbr. of music & record criticism to: Mercury & Saturday Evening Mercury, Hobart, 1960-; Australian Broadcasting Commission, 1959-. Mbr. IASA. Hobby: Photography. Address: 669 Nelson Rd., Mt. Nelson, Tasmania 7007, Aust.

STAFFORD, Judith Wolper, b. 1 July 1950, Portsmouth, NH, USA. Assistant Principal Violist. Educ: BMus, MMus, New England Conserv. of Music; Pvte. studies w. Albert Yves Bernard, Bernard Linden & Burton Fine. Career: Asst. Pring. Violist, Eastern Phil. Orch., 1973-79; Sub. mbr., Baltimore Symph. Orch., 1973; Asst. Prin. Violist, Syracuse Symph. Orch., 1973, Portland, Maine Orch., 1974, '75, Opera Co. of Boston, 1974, '75, Richmond Symph. & Sinfonia, 1976-79; Tchr., Eastern Music Fest. Faculty, N Carolina, 1973-77; Lexington, Mass. Public Schls., 1974-75, Groton, Mass. Music Schl., 1974-75; Richmond, Va., 1976-77; Num. radio, TV & solo apps., Boston, Mass., Va. & N Carolina. Recordings: as back-up musician. Mbrships: Am. Fedn. of Musicians. Hobbies: Modelling; Cosmetic sales; Tarot. Address: 3309 W Grace No. 2, Richmond, VA 23221, USA.

STAHL, David, b. 4 Nov. 1949, NYC, NY, USA. Associate Conductor; Conductor. Educ: MA, Queen's Coll., CUNY, 1974; BA, ibid., 1972; Nat. Orch. Assn., 1970-72; Tanglewood, Berks. Music Center, 1975; studied w. Leonard Bernstein, Joseph Rosenstock, Seiji Ozawa & Leon Barzin. m. Ellen Weiss. Debut: Carnegie Hall, 1973. Career: Assoc. Cond., Cinn. Symph. orch., 1976-; Music Dir. & Cond., St. Louis Phil., Cinn. Youth Symph. Orch., 1976-; Asst. Cond., NY Phil., 1976; Guest Cond., num. Am. orchs., 1977-. Mbrships: Am. Symph. Orch. League. Hons: Queen's Coll. Orch. Soc. Award, 1972; Exxon Arts Endowment Cond., 1976-79. Hobbies incl: Hiking; Sports; Photography; Travel. Mgmt: Columbia Artists Mgmt., Inc., NYC, NY. Address: 3203 Golden Ave., Cinn., OH 45226, USA.

STAHULJAK, Dubravko, b. 21 Feb. 1920, Zagreb, Yugoslavia. Conductor; Composer. Educ: Musical Acad., Zagreb. m. Ksenija Taclik, 1 c. Debut: Osijek, Yugoslavia. Career: Stage & radio perfs. Comps. (solo songs) Lyrics Concertant; Venice; Gogo;

Mother; (piano) Child's Dream; Improvizata; (choir & piano) Sorrow & Gladness of Wood; No Justice Between Flowers. Mbr. Croatian Musical Soc., Zagreb. Hobby: Coins. Address: Karlovac, Tuskanova 4, Yugoslavia.

STAHULJAK, Mladen, b. 15 Mar. 1914, Zadar, Yugoslavia. Cellist; Pianist; Organist; Harpsichord Player; Composer; Choir Conductor; Conductor. Educ: grad., theory tchng., organ, comp., Musical Acad., Zagreb; complete studies in Leipzig. m. Branka Dugan, 1 d. Debut: as Cellist, 1932; as Organist, 1935; as Pianist, 1935; as Cond., 1937; as Comp., 1940; on Harpsichord, 1972. Career: Cellist, Zagreb Phil. Orch.; Choir Cond., Zagreb; Lectr., Zagreb Acad.; Maestro del'coro, Sarajevo Opera; Musical Ed., Radio Sarajevo. Comps. incl: works for piano, organ, solo violin, choirs, etc. Mbrships: Comps. Assn.; Assn. of Reproduction Musical Artists. Recip. sev. awards & hons. Hobby: Nature. Address: 71 000 Sarajevo, Obala 16111, Yugoslavia.

STAICU, Paul, b. 7 June 1937, Bucharest, Rumania. Conductor; Professor; Solo Horn Player. Educ: Schl. of Music, Buahrest; Grad., Prague Acad. of Music, 1961 (Horn); Grad., Vienna Acad. of Music, 1970 (Cond.). m. Irina Staicu, 1 s. Debut: Solo horn, 1954; Cond., Bucharest Phil. Chmbr. Orch., 1963. Career: Solo horn, Bucharest Phil., 1961-69; Prof. of Chmbr. Music, 1966, Prof. of Horn, 1969, Bucharest Music Acad.; Chief Cond. of Chmbr. Orch., 1966, Chief Cond. of Symph. Orch., 1975, Bucharest Music Acad.; TV & radio perfs.; Concerts; Prof., summer classes, Bayreuth, Gourdon, etc.; Chief Cond., Constanta Chmbr. & Symph. Orch., 1978. Recordings incl: Works by Beethoven, Mozart, G Enesco, Haydn, Bach, Corelli & modern music. Publs: Studiu Introductiv si Exercitii Zilnice Pentru Corn, 1978. Mbrships: Int. Biographical Assn.; Int. Horn Soc. Hons. incl: Cultural Medal, I Grade, Rumania, 1968; Medal of the H von Karajan Fndn., 1974 w. Chmbr. Orch.; Num. Prizes & Dips., Int. Competitions. Hobby: Pictures. Mgmt: ARIA, Str. Enachita Vacarescu, Bucharest, Rumania. Address: Bd. Republicii 103, 70311 Bucharest, Rumania. 28, 29.

STALDER, Hans Rudolf, b. 9 July 1930, Zürich, Switz. Clarinettist. Educ: Konservatorium Zürich; Bayerisches Staatskonservatorium, Wurzburg, Germany; pvte. studies w. Louis Cahuzac, Paris. Career: Int. Soloist on Çlarinet & Bassetthorn, also w. Chmber Music Grps. (Stalder-Quintet, Zurich Chamber Ensemble). Plays Mozart-Clarinet-Concerto KV622 in orginal version on Bassett clarinet in A, 1968-. Recordings: Mozart Clarinet-Concerto (original version for Bassett Clarinet); Die Klarinette Meisterhaft Gespielt; Brahms Clarinet Sonatas Op. 120; var. recordings on Disco, Electrola, Musicaphon. Mbr., Schweizerischer Tonkunstlerverein. Address: Wengi 2, CH-8126 Zumikon, Switz.

STALMAN, Roger Claude, b. 30 July 1927, Uxbridge, England, UK. Vocalist. Bass; Singing Teacher; Adjudicator. Educ: London Univ.; studied w. Eric Greene, Frederic Jackson. m. Jean Dorothy Kew, 1 s. Debut: 1952. Career: Concerts, Opera, Recitals, throughout UK & Western Europe, also in Israel & Can.; over 250 perfs. of Handel, Messiah, inclng. TV Perfs.; Berlin Fest., 1967; Papal Concert, & tour of Israel in Stravinsky, Oedipus Rex, 1968. Recordings Messiah, Cond. Walter Sussking; Messiah, Cond. Frederick Jackson; Cathedral Music From Salisbury Purcell Odes; Panufnik, Universal Prayer. Mbr. ISM. Recip. Hon. ABSM, 1970. Hobbies: Gardening; Do-it-Yourself. Address: Came House, Monument Lane, Chalfont St. Peter, Bucks. SL9 0HY, UK.

STALMANN, Joachim, b. 2 July 1931, Göttingen, Germany. Musicologist; Theologian; Church Musician. Educ: Studied theology, Musicol., philosophy & ch. music, Göttingen, Tübingen, Munich, Basel, 1951-56; Ordained as Luth. Minister, 1962; PhD, musicology, Tübingen, 1962. m. Christiane Simonis, 4 c. Career: Priest in Bremke near Göttingen, 1962-72; Arbeitsstelle für Gottesdienst und Kirchenmusik, Hannover. Publs: Johann Walters Cantione Latinae, 1962; Johann Walter, Sämtliche Wrke, vol. VI, 1970; Ed. Leader; Georg rhav, Musikdrucke aus den Jahren 1538-1545. Contbr. to: Die Musikforschung; Lutherische Monatshefte; Der Chorleier. Mbr., profl. orgs. Address: 3 Richard-Schöne-Weg 10, D3002 Wedemark 15-Resse, German Fed. Repub.

STALVEY, Dorrance, b. 21 Aug. 1930, Georgetown, SC, USA. Composer. Educ: BMus, Cinn. Coll. of Music, 1953; MMus, ibid., 1955. m. Marilyn Lonzway, 1 s., 1 d. Career incl: var. Composer-Cond. appearances in USA; Exec. Dir., Monday Evening Concerts, LA; Assoc. Prof. of Music, Immaculate Heart Coll., LA. Comps: 5 Little Pieces, piano, 1957; String Trio, 1960; Movements & Interludes, octet, 1964; Changes, piano, 1966; Celebration-prime, brass, percussion & video, 1967; Points-Lines-Circles, sextet & slides, 1968; Togethers I, guitar & tape, Togethers II, percussion, tape & film, Togethers III, clarinet, tape & slides, 1970; Conflicts, Multi-media, 1970; In Time & Not, theatrical concert, 1970; Celebration-Sequent I, chmbr. orch., 1973; PLC-Extract, clarinet solo, 1968; PLC-Abstrat, double bass solo, 1968-72. Mbrships: ASCAP; Am. Music Ctr.; Am. Fedn. of Musicians. Recip: Chmbr. Music Award, Prix de Composition Musicale Prince Ranier III de Monaco, 1961; Fellowship Grant from Nat. Endowments for the Arts, 1975. Address: 2145 Manning Ave., Los Angeles, CA 90025, USA.

STAM, Edward, b. 21 June 1916, Tilburg, Netherlands. University Lecturer; Church Musician. Educ: Laureatus, Acad. for Roman Cath. Ch. Music, 1942; DMusicol., Utrecht State Univ., 1965. m. Maria Jos. Timmen. Career: Cantor, St. Callixtus, Groenlo, 1943-54, St. Martinus, Arnhem, 1954-59, & St. Willibrordus, ibid., 1956-65; High Schl. Music Tchr., 1954-65; Tchr., Royal Conserv., The Hague, 1965-72; Lectr., Inst. of Musical., Amsterdam Univ., 1972-. Comps. incl; 30 Masses; 150 Motets; Organ works & ch. music. Publs. incl: Van Troubadourslied tot Barok, 1956. Contbr. to profl. jrnls. Mbrships. incl: St. Gregorius Assn. (Comps.). Recip., var. prizes for comp. Hobbies: Poetry; Petrography. Address: Hoogeind 5, Driebruggen (lange Ruige Weide), S Netherlands.

STAM, Henk, b. 26 Sept. 1922, Utrecht, Holland. Composer; Author; Lecturer; Pianist. Educ: Utrecht Conserv.; Utrecht State Univ.; Study of composition & music reviewing in Germany. m. Lenske Sterk, 1 c. (3 by prev. marriage). Career: Music Critic, Nieuw Utrechts Daglad; Tchr., Municipal Schl. of Music; Deventer; Prin., Zealand Schl. of Music, 1954-62; Cond., Soc. for Instrumental Music, Middleburg, -1960; Prin., Rotterdam Schl. of Music, 1962-72, Lectr., AVRO (Dutch Broadcasting Assn.). Comps: 5 sonatinas for piano; Overture de Ruyter (orch.); Hommage à Valery (Accordion band); Chmbr. music incl: sonatas for flute, violin, cello & piano; suite for violin & piano; sonata for unaccomp. violin; serenade for unaccomp. cello; 3 string quartets. etc. Publs: Robert Schumann, a biography, 1948; Introduction to Contemporary Music, 1953; Programmemusic, 1959. Recordings: 3rd String Quartet. Mbrships: KNTV (Royal Dutch Soc. of Musicians); Soc. of Dutch Composers. Recip. de Ruytermedal, 1957. Hobbies: Model trains; Stamps. Address: Noorderend 30, Suawoude (Frl.), Netherlands.

STAM, Joop, b. 13 June 1934, The Hague, Netherlands. Composer; Pianist; Conductor & Chorus Master. Educ: Royal Conserv., The Hague; studied comp., piano & organ. m. Ineke Stam-Lalleman, 1 s., 3 d. Career: Tchr., S Africa, 1961-72; Dir. of Music, Performing Arts Coun. of Orange Free State, 1972-. Comps. incl: The Collector, w. F Staff, & other ballet music, Stage & Film music; Ch. music; Chmbr. music; Vocal & electronic music. Recip. commissions from var. bodies. Recordings: tapes of var. works. Contbr. to: Die Burger; Opus; S African Music Tchr. Mbr., profl. assns., S Africa. Hons: Winner, Gaudeamus Competition for Comp., 1959; Oude Libertas Award, 1974. Hobbies incl: Philosophy; Mathematics; Cybernetics. Address: 11 Milner Rd., Waverley, Bloemfontein, S Africa.

STAMAC, Ivan, b. 31 May 1936, Dubrovnik, Croatia, Yugoslavia. Accoustician; Composer. Educ: Dip. Engrng., Electronics & Tech. Acoustics; Medium Grade Musical Schl. m. Stefica Stamac, 1 s. Debut: w. Comp. Quartetto, 1954. Career: Worked at most Yugoslav song festivals since 1958; Var. works for jazz orch.; musicals & stage music; 2 TV shows; choir music. Comps. incl: The Dark Poem (male voice & piano), 1972; Party (musical), 1973; Three Pusketeers (musical parody), 1975. Publs: Song Series ZM-DHS, 1972-. Contbr. to ZVUK, Yugoslav Music Review. Mbrships. incl: Presidium, Union of Comps. Organizations in Yugoslavia. Hons: Num. prizes at Yugoslav Song Festivals, 1966-. Hobby: Sea Fishing. Address: Maksimirska 110, YU-41000 Zagreb, Yugoslavia.

STAMENOVA, Galina, b. 5 Oct. 1958, Sofia, Bulgaria. Violinist. Educ: Sofia & Antwerp Conservs.; Juilliard Schl. of Music, NY. Debut: Sofia, 1970, London, 1978. Career: Concerts in UK, Belgium, Bulgaria & France; TV apps. in Belgium, Bulgaria & Czech. Hons: 1st prize, Bulgarian Nat. Competition, 1973; 1st prize, Shell London Symph. Strg. Competition, 1978. Hobbies: Theatre; Ballet. Mgmt: Ingpen & Williams, 14 Kensington Court, London W8, UK. Address: c/o Mgmt.

STAN, Radu, b. 12 Sept. 1928, Cluj, Romania. Music Critic; Music Librarian. Educ: Musicol., Bucharest Music Conserv., 1962. m. Irina Grecu, 1 s. Career: Hd., Music Sect., State Ctrl. Lib., 1963-. Contbr. to Romania Literara (music critic); var. jrnls., radio & TV progs. Mbrships: Theatre Artists & Musicians Assn. (Committee, Music Critics Sect., 1974-); Muzica Soc. (Bd., 1972). Hobby: Cycling. Address: str. Bujoreni 49 ap. 77, Bucharst sector 7, Romania.

STANDEN, Richard, b. Bolton, England. Singer. (Bass). Educ: GSM. m. Marian Hughes. Debut: Royal choral socs. at prin. Brit. music fests.; num. BBC Radio & TV broadcasts as recitalist & in choral works, also Prom Concerts; for apps. incl: Contemp. Fest. of Music, Cologne, 1958, Haydn Fest., Madrid, 1959, Handel Fest., Barcelona, 1959; has sung in Austria, Belgium & Netherlands; Prof., GSM. Recordings: HMV; Nixa; Westminster; Pye Mbrships: Assn. of Engl. Singers & Tchrs.; ISM. Recip. FGSM, 1969. Hobbies: Walking; Carpentry. Address: 109 Harestone Valley Rd., Caterham, Surrey, UK. 3.

STANFORD, Patric John, b. 5 Feb. 1939, Barnsley, Yorks., UK. Composer; Conductor; Lecturer; Adjudicator. Educ: FGSM; MMus. m. Sarah Blyth Hilton, 2 s., 1 d. Career Comp.; Prof., GSM Adjudicator, Int. Choral Fests. Comps. (publd.): Nocturne; Notte; Bagatelles for string quartet; Preludes for bassoon;o Peasant songs; Piano Trio; Antitheses for string orchestra; Sonata for solo violin; Stabat Mater; Variations for piano; Suite Francaise for wind quintet; Sonatine for recorder; Opera, Villon;o 2 symphs.; 3 string quartets; concertos for violin, piano & cello; Choral & vocal works; music for films, theatre, ballet & TV. Recording: Autumn Grass. Contbr. to Musical Times. Mbrships: CGGB (exec. committee, 1973-); ISM; PRS; RCA. Hons: Royal Phil. Soc. Prize, 1962; Mendelssohn Schlrship., 1964; Premio Citta di Trieste, 1977; Committee of Solidarity Award, Jugoslavia, 1973; Oscar Espla Award, Spain, 1974. Hobbies: Sunshine; Reading; Countryside; Solitude. Address: c/o Radcliffe Edition, Arlington Park House, London W4 4HD, UK. 14, 23, 30.

STANEK, Alan Edward, b. 3 July 1939, Longmont, Colo., USA. College Professor of Music (Clarinet) & Chmn., Music Dept., Idaho State Univ. Educ: BMusEd, Univ. of Colo., 1961; MMus, Eastman Schl. of Music, 1965; D Musical Arts (Clarinet perf.), Univ. of Mich., 1974. m. Janette Elizabeth Swanson Stanek, 1 s., 1 d. Contbr. to Neb. Music Educator (book reviews). Mbrships: MENC; Idaho Music Educators Assn.; NACWPI; Int. Clarinet Soc. (Sec., 1978-80); Nat. Assn. of Coll. Wind & Percussion Instructors (Idaho State Chmn.). Hons: 2nd Place, Nat. Adult Cond. Competition, 1975. Hobbies: Camping; Skiing; Fishing. Address: 4550 Johnny Creek Rd., Pacatello, ID 83201, USA. 8.

STANFIELD, Doreen, b. London, UK. Concert Pianist; Piano Teacher. Educ: Gold Medal, RCM; Silver Medal, Assoc. Ed., LRAM; Study w. Osborn & Craxton, London. m. Eli Goren, 1 s., 1 d. Career: num. radio performances & recitals, mainly on chmbr. music; Prof., London Coll. of Music, 1962-75. Mbrships: Inc. Soc. of Musicians; Mensa. Hobbies: Lit.; Theatre. Address: 11 Lyndhurst Gdns., Finchley, London N3, UK.

STANFORD, E Thomas, b. 2 Jan. 1929, Albuquerque, NM, USA. Ethnomusicologist; Composer. Educ: AB, Univ. of Calif., Berkeley, 1951; MMus. Univ. of Southern Calif., 1953; anthropol. & linguistics, Escuela Nacional de Antropologia, Mexico, 1956-59; folklore musical, Escuela de Posgraduados, Univ. Nacional Autonoma de Mexico, 1956-58. m. Antonia Hernandez Vazquez, 1 s., 2 d. Career: Series of 13 radio progs. Musica popular mexicana, 1968. Has made 6 recordings on Mexican music; ethnomusicologist, Univ. of Tex., 1971-78 & Univ. of NC, 1979-. Publs. incl: An Introduction to Certain Mexican Music Archives (w. Spiess), 1969; El Villancico y el Corrido Mexicano, 1974. Contbr. to jrnls. Mbr. profl. orgs. Hobbies: Electronics design & constrn.; Mechs.; Gardening. Address: Av. Taxqueña 1818-K16, Mexico 21, DF.

STANHOPE, David Richard, b. 19 Dec. 1952, Sutton Coldfield, UK. Pianist; Horn Player; Arranger; Composer; Conductor. Career: authority on works of Percy Grainger; freelance profl. horn player & pianist for 10 yrs. (to 1980); mbr., Adelaide Brass Quintet. Comps. incl: Corettes (horn quartet). Recording: 2 piano music for Percy Grainger. Contbr. to Aust. Jrnl. of Music Educ. Mbr., Percy Grainger Lib. Soc. Address: Flat 5/73, Buxton St., N Adelaide, SA, Australia 5006. 30.

STANLEY, Donald Arthur, b. 11 Jan. 1937, Mansfield, Ohio, USA. Tubist; Conductor. Educ: BS Music Educ., Ohio State Univ.; MFA, Ohio Univ. Career: Dir. of Music, Milan Pub. Schls., Ohio, 1959-62; Grad. Asst., Ohio Univ. Bands, 1962-64; Instructor of Music, Kearney State Coll., Neb., 1964-66; Assoc. prof. of Music, Mansfield State Coll., Pa., 1966-. Contbr. to: Instrumentalist; NACWPI Bulletin; Pa. Music Educ. Assn. News; Getzen Gazette. Mbrships: Kappa Kappa Psi (Nat. VP); Pa Collegiate Bandmasters Assn. (Pres.); NACWPI (Vacancy Notice Serv. Dir.); Phi Mu Alpha Sinfonia; MENC; Coll. Band Brotherhood Assn. Recip: Citation of Excellence, Nat. Band Assn. 1975. Hobbies: Gardening; Record Collecting. Address: Music Dept., Mansfield State College, Mansfield, PA 16933, USA.

STANLEY, Frances Kniffin, b. 9 Nov., Stryker, Ohio, USA. Concert Pianist; Educator; Lecuter. Educ: Pvte. study w. num.

Masters inclng. Ernest Bloch, Beryl Rubinstein, Roger H Sessions, Quincy Porter & others. Cleveland Inst. of Music, 4 yrs.; Columbia Univ. Piano Dept.; Boston Conserv. of Music. m. George Hamilton Stanley, 1 d. Carmen. Career: Had own Radio Prog.; Perf., num. Radio Stns. inclng., WHK, WADC, WFJC, WBBM, WMAQ; & WBKB, CBS TV Stns.; Adjudicator for var. Socs. & Contests; Resource Person, num. Schl. Confs. & Civic Grps. Owner-dir., tchr., Stanley Music Studios. Mbrships: VP Prog. Chmn., Sec., Bd. Dirs., Pres. (1972-74), Chgo. Artists Assn.; Pres., 1956-58, Music Study Club of Chgo, Inc.; Chmn., Cerebral Palsy Fund Drives, 1959-76; VP, 1963-66, Sec., Treas., Lyric Opera of Chgo. Guild, S Suburban Chapt.; Pres., 1962-64, Bd. Dirs., Chgo. Heights Symph. Orch.; Fac. Mbr., NGPT; Am. Coll. of Musicians; Int. Platform Assn.; Int. Soc. for Contemporary Music; Soc. of Am. Musicians; Chgo. Symph. Soc.; Chgo. Women's Musical Club; Nat. Fedn. Music Clubs; Am. Symph. Orch. League Inc. Hons: incl: Voted Hon. Life Mbr., Music Study Club of Chgo. & presented w. gold & diamond gavel, 1958; Hon. Life Mbr., Chgo. Heightys Symph. Orch. Bd. Dirs. & presented w. Gold & Diamond Gavel, 1964; Life Mbr., Zoltan Kodály Acad. & Inst. Hobbies: Travel; Charity Drives & Projects, (Fd. Dirs., Family Service & Mental Health Ctr.; Jones Memorial Ctr. Women's Bd.). Address: Stanley Apts., 2612 Flossmoor Rd., Floosmoor, IL 60422, USDA. 4, 5, 27, 29.

STANLEY, Helen Camille, b. 6 Apr. 1930, Tampa, Fla., USA. Composer; Pianist; Teacher; Lecturer; Writer. Educ: student of Hans Barth & Ernst von Dohnanyi; BMus, Cinn. Conserv. of Music, 1951; MMus, Fla. State Univ., 1954; BS, Muskingum Coll., 1961; Cert. Piano Judge, Fla. State Music Tchrs. Assn. Career: Former lectr. at Jacksonville Univ. & Jones Coll.; now independently tchng., perf. lectures & touring, presenting master classes to tchrs.; Comps. widely perf. on TV & radio; Apps. on TV channels 7 & 12. Comps. incl: Rhapsody for Electronic Tape & Orch.; Duo-Sonata for Tape Recorder & Piano; var. songs & instrumental solos; Battle Hymn, for 2 choirs, organ, percussion, trumpets & flute; Overture for Brass & Timpani; String Quartet. Recordings: Electronic Prelude; Duo-Sonata for Tape Recorder & Piano; Rhapsody for Electronic Tape & Piano. Contbr. to: Music Dir. Mag.; Beaches Leader. Mbr., sev. profl. orgs. Hons. incl: Louis B Pogner Award (comp.), 1950; C Hugo Grimm Award for Ensemble Comp., 1951; FSMTA-MTNA Comp. Commission, 1972. Address: 1768 Emory Circle S, Jacksonville, FL 32207, USA. 5, 27, 29.

STANO, Janina, b. 26 July 1919, Warsaw, Poland. Opera Singer; Artist. Educ: Dip., Commercial Acad., Cracow; Dip., State Higher Musical Schl., Warsaw. div., 1 s. Debut: as Gilda, in Rigoletto, Opera in Cracow. Career: Apps. in Europe incl. Grand Theater of Opera & Ballet, Warsaw, State Opera, Vienna, Operas in Munich, Stuttgart, Dusseldorf, Amsterdam, Luxemburg, Lyon, Leipzig, Dortmund, Hannover, etc.; num. roles; Vocal Mgr., Soloist of Opera, Warsaw Grand Theater; Tchr., Solo Singing, State Higher Musical Schl., Warsaw; Asst. Prof., Hochschule für Musik, Düsseldorf; Hd., Vocal Studies, Deutsche Oper am Rhein. Mbr., Soc. of Polish Artists-Musicians. Hons: Laureate of Int. Singing Competition, Berlin, 1951; Int. Competition of Opera Singers, Vienna, 1961. Hobbies: Learning foreign Langs.; Travelling. Address: ul. Sulkowskiego 12/14 m.5, 01-610 Warsaw, Poland.

STANTON, Royal Waltz, b. 23 Oct. 1916, Los Angeles, Calif., USA. Choral Director; Teacher. Educ: BE, UCLA, 1939; MA, ibid., 1946. m. Norine Parker, 2 d. Career: Dir. of Choral Orgs., Long Beach City Coll., 1950-61; Foothill Coll., Los Altos Hills, Calif., 1961-67; De Anze Coll., Cupertino, Calif., 1967-; Dir., LA Bach Festival, 1959-60; Music Dir., The Schola Cantorum, De Anza Coll., 1964-. Comps: Cantata - God's Son is Born, 1968; Two Motets for Double Choir, 1971; 90 choral compositions & arrs. (anthems, motets, folksong, etc.), 1950-76. Publs: The Dynamic Choral Conductor, 1971; Steps to Singing for Voice Classes, 2nd ed., 1976. Contbr. to: Jrnls. of MENC & Am. Choral Conds. Assn.; Symposium, Jrnl. of Coll. Music Soc. Mbrships: ASCAP; Am. Choral Dirs. Assn.; MENC; Am. Musicological Soc.; The Choral Fndn.; Choral Conds. Guild. Hons: ASCAP Awards, 1969-71; Outstanding Educator of Am. Award 1971, 1974. Address: 22301 Havenhurst Dr., Los Altos, CA 94022, USA. 9.

STAR, Cheryl M, b. 28 Jan. 1947, Miami, Fla., USA. Music Teacher (Flute & Piccolo). Educ: BA, New Coll., Sarasota, Fla., 1968; MS, Fla. Int. Univ., 1975; studied w. Eugene Johnson, Univ. of Miami, Pat Stenberg, Univ. of Southern Fla. & Julius Baker. m. William Joseph Star, 1 s., 1 d. Debut: Sarasota, Fla., 1966. Career: Flute Instr., Miami Dade Community Coll., 1970-; Tchr. of Flute, Fla. Int. Univ., 1972-; Perfs. w. Miami Phil. Orch., Ft. Lauderdale Symph. & Miami Beach Symph.; num. opera & ballet perfs. Hons: Outstanding Young Artist, Sarasota; Finalist, Young Artist Competition, Miami, 1966. Address: 65006 SW 60 St., S Miami, FL 33143, USA.

STARCK, Claude, b. 24 Oct. 1928, Strasbourg, Bas-Rhin, France. Cellist; Teacher. Educ: Nat. Conserv., Paris; studied w. P Tortelier, P Fournier, P Bazelaire. m. Therese Kämpf, 2 s. Debut: Age 4. Career: Concerts in Europe & Can.; Cello Soloist, Strings Fest., Lucerne, 1957, Orch. Quartet, Zürich, 1960-; Ldr., Concert Class, Musich High Schl., Zürich, 1963-. Recordings: Haydn, Stamitz, Concerti; 3 Bach Sonatas; Vivaldi, Concerto; St. Saens, Concerto, Sonata; num. Chmbr. Works. Hons: 1st Prize, Cello, Nat. Conserv., Paris, 1951; Chmbr. Music Medal, ibid., 1950. Hobbies: Drawing; Painting. Mgmt: Konzergesellschaft, Zürich. Address: 19 Singlistr., 8049 Zürich, Switzerland.

STARER, Robert, b. 8 Jan. 1924, Vienna, Austria. Composer. Educ: State Acad., Vienna; Conserv., Jerusalem; Juilliard Schl., NY. m. Johanna Herz, 1 s. Career: Works perfd. by Mitropoulos, Bernstein, Steinberg, Leinsdorf; Composed for Martha Graham, others. Comps. incl: (Opera) Pantagleize; The Last Lover; Apollonia; Coincerti for piano, viola, violin & cello; 3 Symphs.; Choral, Chmbr. Music, etc. Recordings: Viola Concerto, Ariel, for soloists, chorus, & orch.; Concerto atre, Mutabili, chmbr. & solo works. Publs: Rhythmic Training. Mbr., ASCAP. Hons: Guggenheim Fellow, 1957-63; Fulbright Scholar, 1964; Nat. Endowment, 1972, '77; Am. Acad., 1979.

STARIKOFF, Ireyne, b. Odessa, Russia. Concert Pianist; Artist Teacher. Educ: Grad. First Prize Solfege, First Prize for Piano, Conserv., Marseille; BMus & MMus, Ecole Normale de Musique, Paris, under Isidor Philipp. m. Dr. Raymond Jonnard, 1 s. Debut: Paris, NY. Career: Rouen, Lenormand Fest., Paris, Vincent d'Indy Fest.; Sorbonne Amphitheatre before the Pres. of the French Repub.; Radio, Eiffel Tower, Radio Paris; Brooklyn Concert Series, Paterson Symph., Chopin Recital, Steinway Hall, Carnegie Hall, Nat. & Int. Conventions; Radio WNYC, WABC. Music Critic for Courier Musical & Art Musical, Paris & NY. Mbrships: NGPT, FM Judge, Chmn. of Paterson, NJ, 1960-68; Chopin Soc. of NY (Prog. Chmn., 1960-68); Nat. Opera Club of NY; Piano Tchrs. Congress; Associated Music Tchrs. League. Hons: Gold Medal & Cash Prize at the Int. Piano REcording Fest., 1955-56; Biennial Piano Recording Comp., 1961-63; Gold Medal & Cash Prize, Annual Piano Recording Comp., 1970, '73, '74; Winner in Tchr. Category sponsored by NGPT; Hall of Fame, NGPT, 1969. Address: 465 West End Ave., NY, NY 10024, USA. 23, 29.

STARK, Ethel, b. 25 Aug. 1916, Montreal, Canada. Conductor; Violinist. Educ: Grad., Curtis Inst. Phila., Pa., USA, 1934; McGill Conserv. Music; Acad. Musique Quebec; w. Ernest Bloch, Switzerland. Debut: Windsor Hotel, Montreal, 1928. Career incls: Guest Soloist & cond., num. orchs.; Concert tours, soloist & cond., Canada, USA, Europe & Far E; Fndng. Dir. & Cond., NY Women's Chmbr. Orch., 1938; Montreal Women's Symph. Orch., 1940; Canadian Choir, 1952; Montreal Women's Symphonietta, 1955; Ethel Stark Symphonietta, 1968; Tchr., violin, Conserv. Music & Dramatic Art, Montreal, 1952; Lectr., Cardinal Leger Inst., Montreal, 1964. Mbr. var. orgs. Recip. grants & schlrships. Address: 5501 Adalbert Ave., Apt. 110, Cote St. Luc, Montreal, PQ H4W 2B1, Canada.

STARKER, Janos, b. 5 July 1924, Budapest, Hungary. Cellist; University Professor. Educ: Franz Liszt Acad., Budapest. m. Rae Busch Staker, 2 d. Career: Solo Cellist, Budapest Opera Phil., 1945-46, Dallas Symph., 1948-49, Met. Opera, NYC, 1949-53, Chgo. Symph., 1953-58; Prof., now Disting. Prof., Ind. Univ., 1958-; concert tours on all continents. Inventor of the Starker Bridge. Has recorded over 70 LPs for major cos. Publs: An Organized Method of String Playing; Bach suites, cadenzas, & var. other edited works. Mbr., Am. Fed. of Musicians. Hons: DMus, Chgo. Conserv.; Grand Prix du Disque; Geo. Wash. Award. Mgmt: Colbert Artists, NY; Concerto Winderstein, Munich, Germany. Address: Indiana Univ., Department of Music, Bloomington, IN 47401, USA.

STARR, Susan, b. 29 Apr. 1942, Phila., Pa., USA. Concert Pianist. Educ: Dip., Curtis Inst. of Music, Phila., 1961. m. Robert Arrow, 1 s., 1 d. by 1st marriage. Debut: w. Phila. Orch., aged 6, 1948. Career: Debut w. NY Phil., 1951; youngest instrumentalist to appear in regular series, Robin Hood Dell, Phila., 1959; 1st Soloist w. A Symph. Orch., under L Stokowski, Carnegie Hall, NYC, 1962; Annual tours, USA & Can., apps. w. most major N Am. orchs.; Tours in Europe, USSR, Ctrl. & S Am., Far East; Artist-in-Res., Phila. Musical Acad., 1965-; perfs. at Ravinia Fest., Chgo. 1968, & other major US Fests.; num. TV apps. Recordings: w. Arthur Fiedler & Boston Pops Orch. for RCA. Contbr. to Music Jrnl., 1974. Hon. Mbr., Delta Omicron. Hons: 1st Prize, Nat. Merriweather Post Competition, Wash., DC, 1957; Bronze Medal, 1st Int. Dimitri Mitropoulos Competition, NYC, 1961; 2nd Prize, 2nd Int. Tchaikovsky Competition, NYC, 1961; 2nd Prize, 2nd Int. Tchaikovsky Competition, Moscow, USSR, 1962. Mgmt: Herbert Barrett

Mgmt., 1860 Broadway, NY, NY 10023. Address: 2203 Panama St., Philadelphia, PA 19103, USA. 3, 27.

STARYK, Steven S, b. 28 Apr. 1932, Toronto, Ont., Can. Violinist; Professor of Music. Educ: Royal Conserv. of Music, Toronto; pvte. studies in NY. m. Ida Elizabeth, 1 d. Career: former ldr./concertmaster, Royal Phil., London, Concertgebouw, Amsterdam, Chgo. Symph. & other orchs. by age of 35; Prof. at 9 univs. & conservs. in Europe, USA & Can.; organized Quartet Canada, extensive concert tours; radio & TV apps. in N Am., UK, Netherlands, Germany, Switz. Italy, Japan & Korea. Recordings: 170 comps. on 40 albums. Hons: Can. Coun. Arts Awards, 1967, '75; Queen Elisabeth Centennial Award, 1978; Shevchenko Medal, 1974. Address: 41 Foursome Cres., Willowdale, N York, Ont. M2P 1W1, Can. 2, 29.

STATHAM, Keith, b. 24 May 1934, Gloucester, UK. Composer; Arranger. Educ: BA (Hons.), Magdalene Coll., Cambridge. m. Ruth Lawrence, 2 s. Career incls: Gen. Mgr., Northern Sinfonia Orch., 1966-74; Arranger for var. LP's. Comps: Music for West End revues, 'Share My Lettuce' and 'One to Another'; incidental music for theatre; signature tunes & music for num. TV shows. Recordings: Now and Then; Songs of Alex Glasgow; Northern Drift. Mbr., Savile Club. Address: 16 Sanderson Rd., Newcastle upon Tyne, UK.

STAUFFER, George B, b. 18 Feb. 1947, Hershey, Pa., USA. Musicologist; Organist. Educ: BA, Dartmouth Coll.; MA, Bryn Mawr Coll.; MPhil., PhD, Columbia Univ.; Organ study w. Robert Elmore, John Weaver & Vernon de Tar. m. Beatrice Elinor Terrien. Debut: St. Thomas Ch., NYC, 1973. Career: Asst. Organist & Choir Dir., St. Paul's Chapel, Columbia Univ.; Mbr. Ed. Bd., current Musicol. Contbr. to: Current Musicol.; AGO Jrnl.; Nonesuch Records (jacket notes). Mbrships: Am. Musicol. Soc.; Neue Bach-Gesellschaft. Hons: NDEA Fellow in Musicol., Columbia Univ., 1971-74. Hobby: Harpsichord Building. Address: RD 1 Box 220, Hershey, PA 17033, USA.

STAVELEY, Colin, b. 1942, Dublin, Ireland. Violinist. Educ: Royal Irish Acad. of Music; LRAM; Northern Schl. of Music. m. Susan Harris, 1 d. Career: Mbr., Amici Str. Quartet, 1963-66; Ldr., BBC Welsh Orch., 1966-68; Co-Ldr., RPO, 1968-. Mbr: ISM. Address: 44 Newlands Wood, Bardolph Ave., Addington, Croydon, Surrey, UK.

STEAD, Maurice Oliver, b. 11 Jan. 1939, Ballina, NSW, Aust. Violinist. Educ: AMusA, LMus, Royal Schls. of Music. Career: Fndn. Concertmaster of Elizabethan Sydney Orch.; Concertmaster, Elizabethan Melbourne Orch. Hons: Winner of 1st Lever Aard; Num. Aust. Radio Eisteddfod Awards & Championships. Address: 192 Scotchmer St., Fitzroy Nth, Vic. 3068, Aust.

STEADMAN, Jack William, b. 12 Oct. 1920, London, UK. Violinist; Teacher; Examiner. Educ: FRCM, ARCM (perf.), RCM, London. m. Patricia Steadman, 2 s. Career: Mbr., LSO, 1948-; Chmn., Mng. Bd., ibid., 2 yrs.; Dir., 20 yrs.; Prof. of Violin, RCM, London, 1956-; Examiner for Assocd. Bd., Royal Schls. of Music, 1962-. Mbr., ISM. Address: 67 Craddocks Ave., Ashtead, Surrey, UK.

STEADMAN-ALLEN, Raymond Victor, b. 18 Sept. 1922, London, UK. Salvation Army Officer; Music Editor; Composer; Conductor; Lecturer. Educ: Studied w. James Stevens, Dr. Ben Burrows; BMus, Durham Univ., 1955; FTCL, 1960. m. Joyce Foster, 2 d. Career: Ed. staff, SP & S Ltd., 1946-59; Music Ed., Wright & Round, 1960; Freelance Music Ed. SP & S Ltd., 1967-; Lectr., Europe, Can., USA, Aust., UK. Comps: During career as staff comp. & arr., produced over 300 brass, organ & choral works. Recordings: largely band, solo & choral works. Contbr. of tech. & gen. articles to var. jrnls. Hobbies: Gardening; Art; local History. Address: 8 Warwick Rd., New Barnet, Herts., UK. 3.

STEARNS, Peter Pindar, b. 7 June 1931, Greenwich Village, NYC, USA. Composer; Professor; Organist. Educ: Artist Dip., Mannes Schl. of Music; studied w. Bohuslav Martinu. m. Marcia Bush, 1 s., 2 d. Career: Comp., Ch. Organist, Prof., 1957-; Chmn., Comp. Dept., 1961-73, Mannes Coll. of Music, NYC; Asst. Prof., Yale Univ., 1964-65. Comps. incl: 6 symphs.; num. other orchl. works; 5 string quartets; num. works for diverse combinations; keyboard & vocal works; Quintet for Winds (recorded). Mbrships: Am. Comp. Alliance; Hymn Soc. of Am.; Ch. Music Assn. of Am. Address: c/o American Composers Alliance, 170 W 74th St., NY, NY, USA.

STEBBINGS, Ruth, b.11 Mar. 1956, Redhill, Surrey, UK. Teacher of Violin, Viola & Piano. Educ: Grad., Royal Coll. of Music; Lic., Royal Acad. of Music for violin teaching; Assoc., Royal Coll. of Music for piano teaching; Music Tchrs. Cert.,

London Univ. Inst. Educ., 1977-78. Career: Pt.-time tchr., Violin & Viola, London Univ., Goldsmith's Coll., 1974-78 & Croydon HS, 1976-78; Pt.-time tchr., Piano, Croydon Piano Ctr., 1978; Full-time tchr., Bedales Schl., Petersfield, Hants., 1978-; Played w. Croydon Symph. Orch. & Royal Amateur Orchl. Soc. Mbr., Incorp. Soc. of Musicians. Hons: Pearl Elliot Award for piano playing, Croydon HS; Raymond Ffennell Prize for 1st place in GRSM exam., Royal Coll. of Music. Hobbies: Travel; Walking; Swimming; Camping; Cooking. Address: 58B, Ch. Rd., Steep, Petersfield, Hants., UK.

STEBBINS, Robert A, b. 22 June 1938, Rhinelander, Wis., USA. Professor of Sociology specialising in Sociology of Music. Educ: BA, Macalester Coll., 1961; MA, 1962, PhD, 1964, Univ. of Minn. m. Karin Y Olson, 1 s., 2 d. Career: Asst. to Full Prof. of Sociol., Mem. Univ. of Nfld., 1965-73; Prof. of Sociol., Univ. of Tex. at Arlington, 1973-; Prin. Double Bass, St. John's Symph. Orch., Nfld., 1968-73, Dallas Civic Symph., 1975-76; Univ. of Calgary Orch., 1976-. Contbr. to: sociol jrnls.; Ed., column in Int. Soc. of Bassists Newsletter. Mbrships. incl: Am., Int. & Pacific Sociol. Assns.; Chmn. Amateur Div., Int. Soc. of Bassists; Amateur Chmbr. Music Players. Address: Dept. of Sociol., Univ. of Calgary, Calgary, Alberta T2N 1N4, Can.

STECHER, Melvin, b. 14 Aug. 1931, NY, NY, USA. Concert Pianist. Educ: Academic & Musical Studies, New York. Career: Stecher & Horowitz, Duo Pianists, 1951-; Co-Dir., Stecher & Horowitz Schl. of Music, Cedarhurst, NY, 1960-; Ed. Cons., G Schirmer Inc., NY, 1975-. Comps: Learning to Play, Books 1-4, 1963; Playing To Learn, Books 1-4, 1965; Rock With Jazz, Books I-5, 1969; We Wish You A Merry Christmas, Books 1-2, 1971; In The Spirit of '76, 1973; num. Piano Solos. Recordings: Stecher & Horowitz - Duo Piano Recital. Mbr. Music Tchrs. Nat. Assn. Concerto for Two Piano & Orchestra, Walter Piston, dedicated to Stecher & Horowitz, 1961. Mgmt: Columbia Artists Mgmt., Inc. Address: 74 Maple Ave., Cedarhurst, NY 11516, USA. 3.

STEDMAN, Ursula, b. 20 Oct. 1927, London, UK. Violist. Educ: RAM, 1947-51; LRAM (perfs.); Cert. of Merit. m. Bernard Newland, 2 c. Career: Chmbr. Music w. Grissell Piano Quartet & other ensembles & chmbr. orchs., UK; Concerts, Wigmore Hall, Purcell Room; Freelance violist w. major London Orchs.; Prof., Junior Exhibitioner Dept., RAM. Mbrships: RAM; ISM. Hons: Theodore Holland Prize, viola, 1950; Sir Edward Cooper Prize, ensemble, 1949; ARAM, 1972. Hobbies: Reading; Sailing; Gardening. Address: 35 St. Peter's St., London N1, UK.

ŠTĚDROŇ, Bohumír, b. 30 Oct. 1905, Vyskov, Moravia, Czech. Musicologist; Professor. Educ: DPhil, Masaryk Univ. of Brno, 1934; DSc, Charles Univ., Prague, 1969. m. Lidia Linhartová, 1 s., 2 d. Career: Prof., Univ. of Brno. Publs: Monographs on Czech composers: Zd. Fibich, 1952; J B Foerster, 1947; L Janácek, 1958; Vlt.Novák, 1967; J Suk, 1935; F Vach, 1941; Leos Janácek, Letters & Reminiscences, 1946 (Eng. Transl.), 1955; On the Genesis of the opera Jenufa by L Janácek, 1968 (German); Leos Janácek, Life & Work, 1976; The Work of Leos Janácek, (1959 in English). Address: ul Tábor 50 d, 602 00 Brno, Czech.

STEED, Graham (Percy), b. 1 Mar. 1913, Newcastle-upon-Tyne, UK. Organist & Choral Conductor. Educ: BMus (Dunelm); FRCO. m. 1) Elsie 2 s., 1 d. 2) Rita Gellatly Ritchie. Debut: Newcastle-upon-Tyne City Hall (BBC Recital), 1935. Career: Cathedral & ch. apps. in UK, Canada, USA; Recital tours in UK, Aust., Belgium, France, Germany, Holland, Iceland, India, Italy, NZ & Switz. Comps: Variations on the hymn-tune Durham (Ricordi); Le Tombeau de Dupré (ABC Sydney). Recordings: (ORgan Works of Marcel Dupré) Symphonie-Passion. Op. 23, Deuxième symphonie, Op. 26; Evocation. Op.37, Psaume XVIII, OP. 47; Preludes & Fugues, Op. 7; Variations, Op. 20; Annonciation, OP. 56; Deux Esquiisses, Op. 41 (organ symphs. of Widor) No 5 in F, No. 9 (Gothique); complete organ works of César Franck. Contbr. to: Musical Times; Musical Opinion; Sydney Organ Jrnl.; var. Canadian newspapers. Mbrships: RCO; RSCM; Royal Canadian Coll. of Organists; L'associationd des Amis de l'Art de Marcel Dupré. Hons: Appointed 'Ambassadeur' de l'aSsociation des Amis de l'Art de Marcel Dupré, Paris, 1972; Pres.; Assn. Int. pour un Fndn. Marcel Dupré, Paris, 1975. Hobbies: Photography; travel. Address: 67 King St., Truro, NS Canada.

STEEDMAN, Heather, b. 4 Mar. 1953, Glasgow, Scotland, UK. Professional Musician; Teacher of Timpani & Percussion, RCM jr. dept. Educ: Studies of Piano, Royal Scottish Acad. of Music, 1958-69; Studies of Percussion & Piano, Royal Acad. of Music, London, 1969-73; Lic., ibid. Recordings: Blades on Percussion. Mbr., Incorp. Soc. of Musicians. Hons: Hugh Fitch Percussion

Prize, Royal Acad. of Music, 1973; Vivien Langrish Piano Prize, ibid., 1973; Var. schlrships. incl. MacFarlane schlrships. for study at Royal Scottish Acad. of Music. Hobbies: Running; Languages. Address: 79 Danes Ct., N End Rd., Wembley Pk., Middx., UK.

STEEG, Bruce, b. 18 Mar. 1938, Brooklyn, NY, USA. Conductor; Pianist. Educ: BS, MS, Juilliard Schl. of Music. m. Rosemary Waterworth Steeg. Career incls: played Gershwin throughout USA & at Gershwin Mem. Concert in Carnegie Hall (cond. Paul Whiteman), at very early age; num. apps. on radio, TV & w. ldng. orchs. inclng. Denver, Queens Symphs., Cleveland Orch. & NY Phil.; Solo Pianist & Arr., US Mil. Acad. Band & Glee Club, W Point; featured Pianist w. Guy Lombardo & his Orch.; Assoc. Cond., Pianist w. Nat. Ballet, Wash., DC; Assoc. Cond., Dance Arr., musical prod. 'Odyssey' starring Yul Brynner; Prin. Guest Cond., Miami Ballet. Recip., Dip. Aureum Hon. Causa, 3rd World Congress of Poets, 1976. Address: 6000 34th Ave., Hyattsville, MD 20782, USA.

STEEG, Rosemary, b. 6 Aug. 1937, Denton, Tex., USA. Singer; Opera Director; Music Administrator. Educ: Concert Pianist, scholarship student, N Tex. State Univ., Univ. of Tulsa; Fulbright Scholarship, Rome Opera House. m. Bruce Steeg, 2 d. Debut: Tour, USIA, Italy, 1963. Career: Fndr., Artistic Dir., Prince George's Civic Opera; Guest Artist, Balt. Symph.; Dir., Prince George's County, Dimensions in Music (Nat. Award Program), 1971-; Guest Lectr., Wash. Good Music Station; Dir., Bamboo (World Premiere Opera by Platthy); Dir., Alcaste (US Premiere, Lully). Mbrships: Md. State Music Tchrs. Assn.; Central Opera Service. Hobby: Cooking. Address: 6000 34th Ave., Hyattsville, Md., USA.

STEEL, Christopher Charles, b. 15 Jan. 1939, London, UK. Composer; Director of Music. Educ: RAM, 1957-61; studied Comp. w. John Gardner, ibid.; ARAM, 1970; LRAM; GRSM; studied w. Harald Genzmer, Staatliche Hochschüle für Musik, Munich, Germany, 1961-62. m. Anthea Victoria Wilson, 1 s., 1 d. Career: Music Master, Cheltenham Coll. Jr. Schl., 1963-66; Asst.Dir. of Music, Bradfield Coll., Reading, 1966-68; Dir. of Music, ibid., 1968-. Comps. incl: 4 Symphs.; Mass in 5 Movements for Chorus, Orch. & Soloists; Paradise Lost, Dramatic Cantata for Chorus, Orch. & Soloists; Jerusalem, Cantata for Chorus, Orch. & Soloists; Concerto for Str. Quarrtet & Orch.; Island (overture); Concerto for Organ & Chmbr. Orch.; The Rescue (Chmbr. Opera); Odysseus (3 Act Opera); 6 Turner Paintings for Orch.; Music to the Bacchae & Agamemnon.; var. organ works, anthems, music for schls., Piano & smaller chmbr. works. Mbrships: CGGB; ISM. Recip., num. prizes for Comp., RAM, 1960-61. Hobbies: Walking; Reading; especially History; Theatre. Address: Stratford, Bradfield College, Reading, Berks. RG7 6BB, UK. 3.

STEEL, John, b. 29 June 1936, London, UK. Singer (tenor). Educ: AGSM. m. Helen Margaret Walker, 2 s. Debut: 1st perf. of Our Man in Havana by Malcolm Williamson at Salders Wells Theatre, 1963. Career: Apps. w. Cos. at Glyndebourne & Royal Opera House; Freelance soloist concentrating on concerts, oratorio & recital work; Apps. w. choral socs. throughout GB inclng: Festival Hall & Queen Elizabeth Hall, London; Apps. on BBC; Ferando in Goyescus in original Spanish at Morley Coll., 1965; Appeared in Moses & Aaron at Royal Opera House, 1967; Tenor soloist in Requiem Mass (Bruckner) w. LPO; Artistic Dir. to Tadworth & District Arts Fest. Num. recordings. Mbrships: Savage Club, London; ISM. Hobbies: Sports; Detective Fiction; Collecting Records of Gt. Singers of the Past. Address: 3 Downs View, Tadworth, Surrey, UK.

STEELE, (Hubert) John, b. 13 Apr. 1929, Wellington, NZ. University Professor of Musicology. Educ: BA, Vic. Univ. Coll., 1951; MA, Otago Univ., 1952; PhD, Cantab., 1959. Career: Lectr. in Music, Sydney Univ., 1959-61; Lectr.-Assoc. Prof., Otago Univ., 1962-. Mbrships: Royal Musical Assn.; Lute Soc.; Int. Musicol. Soc. Publs. inclk: Sundry eds. of early Engl. organ music, ch. music of Alessandro Scarlatti, etc. Contbr. of articles to Studies in Music & Reviews to Musical Times & Early Music. Hobbies: Organ & lute playing; Travelling. Address: 35 Leven St., Dunedin, NZ.

STEELE, James Eugene, b. S Norfolk, Va., USA. Flautist; Teacher; Choirmaster; Public School Music Administrator. Educ: BS, Coll. of William & mary, 1961; MEd, Temple Univ., 1972; EdD, Nova Univ., 1976; further study at Mozarteum, Salzburg, Reid Schl. of Music, Edinburgh, & Coll. of Preceptors, London. Career: Piccolo player, Norfolk Symph. Orch., 1951-73; Dir. of choral music, Hampton City Schls., Hampton, Va., 1960-65; Supervisor of Music, ibid., 1965-; Dir., All-City Fest. of Music, 1970; Minister of Music, Calvin Presbyterian Ch., 1963-. Publs: The Perceptual Relationship Between Music & Painting, 1974; Duties & Activities of Music

Supervisory Personnel in Virginia, 1975. Mbrships. incl: Nat., Va. & Hampton Educ. Assns.; Va. Choral Dirs.; Va. Band & Orch. Dirs. Assn.; AFM; Int. Reading Assn.; Hampton Assn. for Arts & Hmanities. Hons: Fndr., Dir., Hampton Fest. of Music. Hobbies incl: Hi Fi Projects; Collecting paintings, antiques, old clocks, rare books. Address: 1001 Gates Ave., Apt. 7B, Norfolk, VA 23507, USA. 23, 28, 29.

STEELE, Philip John, b. 15 Feb. 1936. Bass (Opera & Concert). Educ: BS, MS, Juilliard Schl. of Music. m. Sigrid Jaegersen Steele. Career: NYC Opera; Nat. Symph. Orch., Wash., DC; New Orleans, Boston, San Fran., Kansas City Operas; Va. Opera Assn.; Chattanooga, Lake George, Ctrl. City (Colo.) Operas; Worcester Symph.; Knoxville, Dallas, Austin Symphs.; Metrop. Opera Studio; Men of Song Concert Quartet, Nat. Tour, 1971; Affiliate Artist, 3 yrs. Recordings: Columbia Mbr., Am. Guild of Musical Artists. Hobbies incl: Camping; Hiking; Fishing; Carpentry. Mgmt: Hans Hoffman, 200 W 58th St., NYC, NY 10019. Address: 469 Churchill Rd., Teaneck, NJ 07666, USA.

STEEN, Bernt Anker, b. 6 June 1943, Bergen, Norway. Musician (Trumpet, Flugelhorn). Educ: Degrees in Hist. of Art & Classical Archeology, Univ. of Oslo; studies w. Harry Kvebek & Froydis Ree Werke (Oslo), & w. John Wallace (london). m. Ingrid Furseth. Career: Solo trumpet, Norwegian Radio Big Band; Classical Trumpet Player; Num. radio & TV apps. w. own quintet & as soloist, Norway; Twice soloist, Montreux Jazz Fest.; Soloist, Molde & Konsberg. Recordings: Peacemaker. Hons: Scholarships from the Norwegian State, 1977. Hobbies: Scuba Diving; Photography. Address: Agathe Grondahls gate 14, Oslo 4 Norway.

STEEN-NOEKLEBERG, Einar, b. 25 Apr. 1944, Ostre Toten, Norway. Pianist; Professor of Piano; Harpsichordist; Organist; Clavichordist. Educ: Examan Articum, Musicol., Univ. Oslo; Piano Tchrs., Perf. & Organist Dips., Norway; Piano Perf., Comp. & Harpsichord Perf. Dips., Germany. m. Roshan Rastomjee, 2 c. Debut: Oslo, 1970. Career: Concerts in Scandinavia, Germany, UK, France, Greece, Far East; Master Classes, Sion, Switz.; Prof. of Piano. Musikhochschule, Hannover, Germany. Recordings in France & Norway. Contbr. to Aftenposten, Olso. Mbrships: Norwegian Assn. of Perfs.; German Assn. of Profs. Hons. incl: 1st Prize, Artist of the Yr., Norway, 1975. Hobbies: Lit.; Philos. Mgmt: Impresario o/s, Tollbodgaten 3111, Olso. Address: 3 Hannover, Eichstr. 51, German Fed. Repub.

STEFANOVIĆ, Dimitrije, b. 25 Nov. 1929, Pancevo, Yugoslavia. Musicologist; Choir Conductor. Educ: Grad., Facs. of Philos. & Music, Belgrade Univ.; BLitt, DPh, Lincoln Coll., Oxford Univ., UK. m. Olga Stefanović, 1 s., 1 d. Career: Sr. Rsch. Fellow, Inst. of Musicol., Belgrade; Prod., 3 records of Old Serbian Music, & TV Film, Music in Medieval Serbia. Recording: Old Servian Chant, Belgrade, 1971. Publs: Manuscripts of Byzantine Chant in Oxford Bodleian Library (w. N G Wilson), 1963; Old Serbian Music, Inst. of Musicol., vols. 15, I & II, 1974-75. Contbr. to: Sternfeld Music from the Middle Ages to the Renaissance, 1973; Music & Letters. Corres. Mbr., Serbian Acad. of Scis. & Arts, 1976. Address: Inst. of Musicology, Knex Mihailova 35, Belgrade, Yugoslavia.

STEFANOVIC, Pavle, b. 22 Mar. 1901, Krusevac, Yugoslavia. Musicologist; Writer. Educ: Grad. Philos. w. Aesthetics. m. 1 s., 1 d. Career: Lectr. on radio inclng. 'Along the Way of Symphony' & 'Chmbr. Music'. Mbrships: Hd., Committee of Music & Scene Activity, Beograd, 7th season; Assn. of Comps. & Musical Writers of Serbia; Assn. of Writers of Serbia. Publs: Along the Tone, 1958. Contbr. of articles, studies & essays to var. Yugoslavian periodicals. Permanent Music Critic, Press, & Justice, (daily newspapers of Beograd), & var. tech. mags., lit. mags. & newspapers. Hon. Mbr., Assn. of Comps. & Musical Writers of Serbia, 1971. Address: Beograd, Mlatisumina ul. No. 3, Yugoslavia. 3.

STEFANSKA-LUKOWICZ, Elzbieta, b. 7 Sept. 1943, Krakow, Poland. Harpsichordist. Educ: Dip., Panstwowa Wysza Szkola Muzyczna w Krakowie; MA, Acad. of Music. m. Jerzy Likowicz. Debut: Nat. Phil., aged 11. Career: Num. concerts in Poland, Austria, Bulgaria, Czechoslovakia, France, E & W Germany, Hungary, Iran, Italy, Netherlands, Rumania, Spain, Switz., USA; num. int. fests.; Recordings for Polish Radio & TV & many foreign broadcasting stns.; Prof., Acad. of Music, Krakow. Recordings: Muza (7 discs); EMI Electrola. Mbrships. inclk: European Chmbr. Soloists-Masterplayers Orch. Hons. incl: Prize of Krakow City, 1973. Address: 31-115 Krakow, ul. Garncarska 3, Poland.

STEFFEN, Gerhard, b. 31 Oct. 1924, Buschhütten, District Siegen, Germany. Library Director. Educ: Dr. Phil., Musicol., Univ. of Cologne; PhD; Conserv. of Cologne. m. Ingrid Steffen, 1 d. Career: Bibliothecary of Deutsche Musikphonothek,

Berlin, 1962-64; Deputy Dir., 1965-75, Dir. of public library, Hagen, 1975-. Publs: Johann Hugo von Wilderer (1670-1724) Kapellmeister am kurpfälzischen Hofe zu Düsseldorf und Mannheim, 1960. Contbr. to: Die Musik in Geschichte und Gegenwart; Neue Deutsche Biographie; Bibliotheksdienst. Mbrships: Gesellschaft für Musikforschung; Arbeitsgemeinschaft für rheinische Musikgeschichte. Hobbies: Music; Travel. Address: An der Egge 12, D-5800 Hagen 1, German Fed. Repub.

STEGER, Hanns Hermann, b. 19 June 1940, Würzburg, Germany. Pianist; Musicologist. Educ: Concert Dip., State Acad. of Music, Munich, 1966; PhD, Univ. of Regensburg, 1976. m. Gabriele Steger, 1 s. Debut: Sophiensaal, Munich, 1962. Career: concerts, Munich, Hamburg, Würzburg, Leverkusen, Stuttgart, Boston, NYC, Richmond (Va.), Springfield (Mass.), Bucharest, Ploiesti & Sinaia (Romania), The Hague, Sittard (Netherlands); broadcasts, Bavarian Radio, NW German Radio, WGBH Boston, Amherst (Mass.), WDR Cologne; Univ. of Regensburg & Von Müller Gymnasium, Regensburg. Recordings: 57 Lieder by Robt. Franz; works by Alkan, J Landwehr. Publs. incl: Die fünf Späten Sonaten von A Skrjabin, 1976; Der Weg der Klaviersonate bei A Skrjabin, 1976. Mbr., German Soc. for Music Rsch. Address: Odenwaldstr. 1, 84 Regensburg, German Fed. Repub.

STEGLICH, Hanns Hermann, b. 10 Dec. 1929, Radebeul, Germany. Orch. musician; Comp. Educ: Music Acad. Dresden; Music Acad. Hans Eisler Berlin. m. Maria Steglich-Papsdorf, 2 s. Career: Mbr., var. orch.; 1962-74; Musical advsr., Regional Cabinets for Cultural Affairs; Cond. Symph. orch. Karl-Marx-Stadt; Dist. sec. Assn. for Comp. and Musicologists DDR. Chmbr. Music; Choir works. Recordings: many of own works. Mbrships: Assn. Assn. for Comp. and Musicologists DDR. Hons: 1968, 1973 Cultural Award, dist. Karl-Marx-Stadt; 1974 1st Prize Song Contest Karl-Marx-Stadt. Hobbies: Philately; Records of all kings. Address: Theodor-Lessingstr. 1011, 90 Karl-Marx-Stadt, German Dem. Repub.

STEIJEN, P Håkan H, b. 8 July 1949, Stockholm, Sweden. Musician (troubadour, guitar); Composer; Singer. Educ: Univ. 2 c. Debut: 1970. Career: num. radio & TV apps., Sweden; Apps., stage, schls. & institutions. Recordings: (LP's) Here, you have the ocean...; Inspiration (own comps.). Mbrships: YTF; Profl. troubadour Soc. Hons: Stipendiary for Swedish Songwriting, 1978. Hobbies: Music; Lit.; Art. Address: Hägerstensvägen 151, 12648 Hägersten, Stockholm, Sweden.

STEIN, Arlene C, b. 7 July 1935, Utica, NY, USA. Music Educator; Pianist; Flautist; Singer. Educ: BMus, ESM Schl. Music, Univ. Rochester, NY, 1957; MMus, ibid., 1970. m. Harry Melville Stein, 1959, 2 s., 1 d. Career: Music educator specializing in handicapped children & geriatrics; Cond. & Dir., Sarasota Community Orch. (rehab. music prog., sr. citizens 55-95 yrs. old); Mbr., Stein Family Troupe w. Husband & 3 children; Flautist w. Sarasota Concert Band. Contbr. to: Schl. Music News, 1971. Mbrships. incl: Sigma Alpha Iota; Am. Fedn. Musicians. Hons. incl: Arion Nat. Music Award, 1953; Gertrude Curran Music Schlrship., 1953-57. Hobby: Reading. Address: 1950 S Brink Ave., Sarasota, FL 33579, USA.

STEIN, Gertrude Emilie, b. Ironton, Ohio, USA. Educator; Soprano; Pianist. Educ: Capitol Coll.; BA, Wittenburg univ., 1929; MA, 1931, BS in Educ., 1945, PhD, 1948, Univ. of Mich.; Piano, Voice Schlrship. to Cinn. Coll.-Conserv. of Music. Career: Music Supvsr., Centralized Co. Schls., Williamsburg, Ohio, 1932-37; Dir., Jr. HS Music, 1937-68; Assoc. Prof., Piano & Music Educ. & Hd., Dept. of Music, Tex. Luth. Coll., 1948-49. Contbr. to profl. jrnls. Num. mbrships. incl: Donor, Fndr., Rev. Dr. & Mrs. S A Stein Mem. Funds, 1955-; AAUW; Am. Symph. Orch. League; NEA; Ohio Educ. Assn.; Metrop. Opera Guild; MENC; MTNA; Nat. Assn. of Educl. Broadcasters; NY Writers Guild; Associated Councils of the Arts; Assn. of Tchr. Educators; Amateur Chmbr. Music Players; Phi Kappa Phi (Hon.); Pi Lambda Theata (Hon); Zonta Int. Address: 133 N Lowry Ave., Springfield, OH 45504, USA. 2, 5, 8.

STEIN, Gladys Marie, b. 19 Oct. 1900, Meadville, Pa., USA. Teacher of Piano & Theory. Educ: Grad., New England Conserv. of Music; Pa. Coll. of Music, & Aeolian Hall Schl. for Music Rsch.; studied at Thiel Coll., Pitts. Musical Inst., Univ. of Pitts. & Gannon Coll. Publd. comps. incl: Waltz of the Toys; Red-Feather; Soldiers on Parade; Melodies to Play & Sing; Song of the Young Braves; Happy Little Robin; Scouts on Parade; Dancing Along; Redbird; Dancing Americans; Polish Dance; Springtime Frolic; In Tulip Time; Tuned Time Bell & Rhythm Band Instructor & Keyboard Tunes; num. articles & short stories. Contbr. to: Erie Times; Christian Science Monitor; Kindergarten-Primary Magazine; Music Teachers' Review. Dir., Stein Schl. of Music, 1930-50. Lectr.

on rhythm band for Ludwig & Ludwig. Mbrships: MTNA; Pa. Music Tchrs. (num. offices); Erie Music Tchrs.; National Rifle Assn.; Walnut Creek Rifle Assn., 1973. V. Distinguished Serv. Award, State Grp., 1973. Hobbies: Reading; Gardening; Sewing; Hand Gun Shooting. Address: 427 W 31st St., Erie, PA 16508, USA. 3, 4, 29.

STEIN, Leon, b. 18 Sept. 1910, Chgo., Ill., USA. Professor; Composer. Educ: BMus, DePaul Univ., 1931; MMus, ibid., 1935; PhD, ibid., 1949. m. Anne Helman, 2 s. Career: successively Instructor, Assoc. Prof., Prof., Chmn. of the Dept. of Comp. & Theory, DePaul Univ., 1948-66; Dir., Grad. Div., Schl. of Music, ibid., 1948-66; Dean, Schl. of Music, 1966-. Comps: (publd.) 4 Symphs., 18 other orchl. works, 2 operas, num. Chamber Music, Choral & Solo Works; (recorded), 5 String quartets; Three Hassidic Dances, for orch.; Quintet for saxophone & string quartet; Trio for violin, saxophone & piano; 2 sonatas for violin & piano; Sonata for solo violin. Publs: Musical Forms - The Study of Structure & Style in Music, 1962; Anthology of Musical Forms, 1962; The Racial Thinking of Richard Wagner, 19509; An Analytical Study of Brahms's Variations. On a Theme by Haydn, 1944. Contbr. to: The Jrnl. of Musicol.; Chgo. Jewish Forum; Musarts Mag. Mbr., num. profl. orgs. Hons: Winner, Int. Competition, Elkhart Symph. w. 4th symph. Address: 4050 W Greenwood, Skokie, IL 60076, USA. 2, 8, 14.

STEINBECK, Hans David, b. 25 Mar. 1925, Rupperswil AG, Switzerland. Quintet Leader; Archivist. Educ: Zürich Univ.; Sorbonne, Paris, France; Dip., oboe playing, Zürich Conserv. m.Betty Salter, 3 c. Career: Mbr., Winterthur City Orch., 1953-62; Fndr. & Ldr., Winterthur Baroque Quintet, 1958-; Dir., Swiss Quintet. Publs: Schweizer Komponisten unserer Zeit, 1975. Ed., many baroque & early classical chmbr. music works. Mbrships: VP, Int. Assn. Music Libs.; Schweizerischer Tonkuenstlerverein. Hobbies: Chmbr. Music; Editing old music; Gardening. Mgmt: Concerts Int., CH-8706 Meilen, Switz. Address: Baumschulstrasse 5, CH-8524 Wiesendangen, Switz.

STEINBECK, Wolfram, b. 5 Oct. 1945, Hagen, W Germany. Musicologist; Sci. asst. Inst. for Musicol., Univ. Kiel. Educ: Univ. Freiburg, 1965/1972, DPh, 1972. m. Susanne Steinbeck-Schmidt, 2 children. Publs. incl: The Menuet in the Instrumental Music of Joseph Haydn, München, 1973; ANTOC, A New Method to Register Melodies through the Computer, Berlin, 1974; The Use of the Computer in the Analysis of German Folksongs, 1976. To the Method of Analysis of German Folksongs with the aid of Electronic Computers, Cologne, 1976. Address: Arndtplatz 1, D-23 Kiel, German Fed. Repub.

STEINBERG, Ze'ev Wolfgang, b. 27 Nov. 1918, Dusseldorf, Germany. Violist; Composer; Lecturer. Educ: Studied Violin, Theory & Comp. w. pvte. tchrs., Germany & Israel. m. Chavah Weil, 1 s., 1 d. Career: Violist, 1942-71, Asst. Prin. Viola, 1971-, Israel Phil. Orch.; Viola Soloist w. all Israeli Orchs. & Chmbr. Orchs., 1945-; Mbr., Israel Str. Quartet, 1959-. Comps: 4 Miniatures for 2 Recorders; 6 Miniatures for Cello & Piano; Concerto da Camera no. 1 (viola, solo & str. orch.); 2 String Quartets; Festive Prologue; Little Suite; Concerto da Camera no. 2 (Violin solo & 9 instruments); Arr. of Sonata A minor (Schubert); Kartch Prize, Hebrew Union Coll.; Jersalem (for Rehab & the Spies), 1970. Hobbies: Family Research; Grandchildren. Address: 13 Golomb St., Kirat-Ono 55000, Israel.

STEINER, Frances Josephine, b. 25 Feb. 1937, Portland, Ore., USA. Cellist; Conductor; College Professor; Editor of 18th Century Music. Educ: BS, Temple Univ., 1956; MusB, Curtis Inst. of Music, 1956; MA, Radcliff Coll., Harvard Univ., 1958; DMA, Univ. of Southern Calif., 1969; Fontainebleau Schl. of Music, France, 1957; Marlboro Music Festival, Vt., 1952, '53, '57, '58. m. Melvin Israel Tarlow. Debut: NY Town Hall, 1965. Career incls: Assoc. Prof., Calif. State Coll., Dominguez Hills, Calif., 1967-; Full Prof., ibid., 1975-; Hd., Music Dept., ibid., 1978. Cond., Calif. State Coll., Dominguez Hills Chamber Orch., 1967-74; Prin. Cellist, Calif. Chmbr. Orch. & Asst. Prin. Cellist, LA Chmbr. Orch., 1970-73; Music Dir. & Cond., Baroque Consortium, 1974; Prin. Cellist, Glendale Symph. Orch., 1975; 1st woman to conduct profl. symph. orch. at Pavilion of LA Music Center, 1977. Recordings incl: Trio in D, Op. 36, by Beethoven Sonatas for Cello & Pianoby Paul Hindemith. Publs. incl: Six Minutes for Two Celli, 1967; Musicianship for the Classroom Teacher (w. Max Kaplan), 1966. Mbrships: Coll. Music Soc.; Palos Verdes Alumni Chapt., Mu Phi Epsilon; Am. Symph. Orch. League; Conds. Guild; Calif. Symph. Orch. League. Recip. of hons. Hobbies: Gourmet Cooking; Gardening. Address: 21 La Vista Verde Dr., Rancho Palos Verdes, CA 90274, USA.

STEINER, Frederick (Fred), b. 24 Feb. 1923, NY, USA. Composer; Conductor. Educ: Inst. of Musical Art, NYC; BM, Oberlin Conserv. of Music, OH, 1943; Doctl. Cand., Univ. of Southern Calif., 1971-. m. Shirley Laura Steiner, 2 d. Career: Comp., Cond. & Arr., radio in NYC, 1943; Music Dir., radio prog. This is Your FBI. To Lost Angeles, 1947; num. other radio progs.; 1st TV work, Columbia Broadcasting System, 1950; 1st film work, 1950. Major TV credits incl: Andy Griffith; Danny Thomas; Gunsmoke; Have Gun Will Travel; Hogan's Heroes; Movie of the Week; Rawhide; Star Trek; Twilight Zone; Hawaii Five-O. Major film credits: Della; First to Fight; Hercules; The Man from Del Rio; Run for the Sun; St. Valentine's Day Massacre; Time Limit. Comps: Perry Mason Theme; Navy Log March; var. transcriptions & pieces for TV & film. Recordings: King Kong (cond.), Motion Picture Score by Max Steiner. Contbr. to: Jrnl. of the Arnold Schoenberg Inst.; Filmmusic Notebook; Record album notes. Mbrships. incl: Exec. Bd., Comps. & Lyricists Guild of Am.; ASCAP; Am. Fedn. of Musicians; Acad. of Motion Picture. Arts & Scis.; Am. Musicol. Soc. Hobbies: Viola da Gamba; Philately. Address: 4455 Gable Dr., Encino, CA 91316, USA.

STEINER, Gitta Hana, b. 17 Apr. 1932, Prague, Czech. Composer; Pianist; Poetess. Educ: Dip. in Comp., Juilliard Schl. of Music, 1963; MusB, 1967; MS, 1969. Career incls: Pvte. Tchr. of piano, 1960-; Fac., Bklyn. Conserv. of Music, 1963-65; Co-Dir., Comps. Grp. for Int. Perf., 1968. Comps: instrumental, chamber, orchl., choral & vocal works, inclng: Suite for Orch., 1958; Concerto for violin & orch., 1963; Tetark for string orch., 1965; Two Songs, 1966; Concerto for piano & oirch., 1967; String Quartet, 1968; Trio for 2 percussionists & piano, 1969; 5 Poems for mixed chorus, 1970; Duo for cello & percussion, 1971; Four Choruses, 1972. Hons. incl: num. commns.; Gretchaninoff Mem. Prize, 1966; Standard Annual Award, ASCAP, 1972-76. Address: POB 431, Fresh Meadow, NY 11365, USA.

STEINGRIMSSON, Gudmundur, b. 19 Oct. 1929, Hafnarfjödur, Iceland. Drummer; Teacher. Educ: Studied drums w. Robert Grauso, Fibes Drums Corp.; Henry Adler Schl., NY, USA. m. Unnur Gudmundsdóttir, 2 s., 3 d. Debut: w. K K Sextet, Reykjavik, Iceland. Career: Apps. in Hs. of Norden, Reykjavik w. Bengt Hallberg & others; Leningrad TV; Finland Radio; Denmark Radio; Norway Radio; Iceland TV & Radio; Recordings: w. Icelandic Artists, Haukur Morthens, Ragnar Bjarnason, etc. Mbrships: Oddfellow; Reykjavik Jazz Club; Jazz Vakning Hafnarfjörd. Hobbies: Painting; Jazz music. Address: Fögrukinn 5, Box 131, Hafnarfjördur, Iceland.

STEINHARDT, Milton Jacob, b. 13 Nov. 1909, Miami, Okla., USA. Musicologist. Educ: Univ. of Kan., 1926-28; BMus, 1936, MMus, 1937, Eastman Schl. of Music, Univ. of Rochester; PhD, NY Univ.; violin studies, NY, Munich, Paris & Berlin, 1929-33. m. Ilse Boral, 1 s. Career: Asst. Prof., Ctrl. Wash. Coll. of Educ., 1938-42; Instr., Mich. State Univ., 1948-50; Assoc. Prof., Ohio Univ., 1950-51; Chmn., Dept. of Music Hist. & Lit., 1951-75, now Prof. emeritus, Music Hist., Univ. of Kan. Publs: Jacobus Vaet & his Motets, 1950. Ed: complete works, Jacobus Vaet, 7 vols., 1961-68, Alard du Gauquier, 1971; Philippe de Monte, The Motets Vols. 1 & 2, 1975, Vol. 3, 1978. Contbr. to profl. publs. Mbrships. incl: IMS; Am. Musicol. Soc. Recip. acad. grants & fellowships. Address: 1331 Strong Ave., Lawrence, KS 66044, USA. 2, 11, 14.

STEINITZ, Charles Paul Joseph, b. 25 Aug. 1909, Chichester, UK. Lecturer; Conductor; Writer. Educ: BMus, 1934, DMus, 1940. London; FRCO; LRAM, 1930; FRAM. m. Margaret Johnson, 2 s., 1 d. Career: Lectr., London Univ.; Cond. & Fndr., London Bach Soc. & Steinitz Bach Players; Regular radio apps. - Bach cantatas, contemporary music, Handel oratorios; Sev. TV apps.; Promenade Concert, 1972. Recordings incl: Handel Wedding Anthem/Bach Cantata; Bach Magnificat & Cantata 118. Publs. incl: many eds. of Bach, Schütz, Handel, etc.; Eds. of Baroque Music; Sev. Educl. Books; Bach's Passions, 1978, etc. Contbr. to: Records & Recordings. Mbrships: ISM; RCO; Athenaeum Club. Hons: FRAM; Wallis Budge Prize, 1932. Hobbies incl: Gardening. Address: 137 St. Julian's Farm Rd., London SE27 ORP, UK. 2, 30.

STEINITZ, Richard John, b. 16 Oct. 1938, Ashford, Kent, UK. Music Lecturer; Composer; Conductor; Artistic Director. Educ: MA, King's Coll., Cambridge, UK; Accademia di S. Cecilia, Rome; MMus, Univ. of Ill., USA. m. Freda Mary Gardner, 1 d. Career: Artistic Dir., Huddersfield Contemporary Music Fest.; All comps. perf. in public; sev. broadcasts in UK & Netherlands; Cond., Huddersfield Glee & Madrigal Soc. Comps. incl: Songs from the 1001 Nights, 1968; Visions of Emily Dickinson, 1972; Sonata for Trumpets & Trombones, 1964 (rev. 1967); Concenter, 1975; Tableaux of the Heraldic Animals, 1976;

Hymn to Apollo at Delphi, 1976; Three Nymphs, 1978. Contbr. to: Music & Musicians; Musical Times; Contact. Hons: Italian Govt. Scholarship for Comp., 1975; 2nd Prize, BBC Comps. Competition, 1968. Hobbies incl: Walking; Sailing; Gardening; Travel. Address: Oak House, Riley Lane, Kirkburton, Huddersfield HD8 0SZ, UK.

STEINMANN, Conrad Michael, b. 22 Dec. 1951, Rapperswil, Switz. Recorder Player; Professor. Educ: baccalauréat, Matura, 1970; studies w. Hans-Martin Linde, Schola Cantorum, Basel, Switz., 1970-74 (Concert Dip.). m. Regula, 2 c. Debut: 1968. Career: Concerts, many European countries; Radio recordings: Professor, Musikakademie Zürich. Recordings: Vivaldi Recorder Concertos; w. J Savall & H Smith, Italian/English Chmbr. Music. Contbr. to: The Am. Recorder; Tibia. Hons: Winner, 1st Int. Recorder Competiton, Bruges, Belgium, 1972. Hobbies: Children; Cooking; Travelling. Mgmt: Mrs. Ursula Pfaehler, Obere Wart 55, CH-3600 Thun, Switz. Address: Tössertobelstr. 10, CH-8400 Winterthur, Switz.

STEKEL, Eric Paul, b. 27 June 1898, Vienna, Austria. Conductor; Composer; Musicologist; Orchestra Leader. Educ: Acad. of Music, Vienna, 1914; studied w. F Schalk, F Lowe, R Robert, F Ondricek, C Horn, F Schreker & C Proraska. Career: Chorus Master, Vienna Opera, 1919-20; 1st Cond., Lubeck Opera, 1920-22; Prague Opera, 1922-25; Vienna Volksoper & Concert, 1925-28; Saarbrücken, 1928-30; in France, 1930-; concerts & radio operas in France & Europe; Cond., Algiers Orch., 1945-47; Dir., Saarbrücken HS & Univ. Prof., 1947-51; Cond. Conserv. Superieur & Grenoble Symph. Orch., 1951-70. Comps. incl: 4 Symphs.; Grenoble Overture; Various Pieces for Winds; Concerto for violin & orch.; Concerto for piano; Nuits Blanches (opera in 3 acts); Detresse & Esperance (oratorio); Lieder; Alger (symph. evocatins); var. chmbr. works & transcriptions. Publs: Bruckner & Mahler, 1936; l'Ecole Autrichienne Contemporaine, Nouvelle Litteraires, Cahiers du Theatre & Guide du Concert. Mbrships: French Musicol. Soc.; Hon. Pres., Assn. of Conserv. Dirs. & Artists Union. Hons: Off., Legion of Hon.; Kt. of Acad. Palms; Cross of Emporer Charles (Austria-Hungary); Silver Medal of Culture, Italy; Medal of Mil. Bravery. Hobbies: Mountaineering; Swimming. Address: 26 Ave. Albert ler de Belgique, 3800 Grenoble, France. 3, 19.

STEKL, Konrad, b. 21 July 1901, Ragusa, Dalmatia, Yugoslavia. Professor; Conductor; Choirleader; Music Director; Author. Educ: Conserv. & Music Acad., Graz, Austria & Prague, Czech.; Dip. as Comp. & Cond.; studied w. Prof. Roderich v. Mojsisovics. m. Elisabeth Bendl von Hohenstern, 5 c. Career: Professor (Theory); Music Dir.; Cond., sev. orchs. in Graz, Judenburg, Trifail & Kapfenberg; Discoverer, Grazer Fantasie of Franz Schubert, etc. Comps. incl: Der Rattenfänger; Grauli, Anna Iwanowna; Teje; Maria Magdalena; Blaubart; Ein Fest auf Haderslevhuus; Goldene Tränen (symph.); Franz von Assisi (Requiem); Chmbr. Music; music for brass instruments; over 250 songs & cantatas. Recording: Konrad Stekl, Musikverlag Fritz Shulz. Author, over 150 essays. Ed., Mitteilungsblatt des Steirischen Tonkunstlerbundes & Musik aus der Steiermark. Mbrships. incl; Fndr. & VP, Steirischer Tonkunstlerbund, Graz; Int. Gesellschaft f. Neue Musik, Vienna; Richard Wagner Gesellschaft. Recip., num. prizes. Hobbies: Cycling; Sport. Address: A-8020 Graz, Quergasse 3/8, Austria.

STENBERG, (Helge) Sigvard, b. 24 May 1933, Norrköping, Sweden. Violin Teacher. Educ: Univ. of Gothenburg Conserv. of Stockholm, 1949-53; pvte. study w. Prof. Eridre Wolf & W Andersen, Göteborg, 1953-57; studied w. Prof. Juri Jankelevifj, Tjajkovsky Conserv., Moscow, USSR; Violin Tchrs. exam., Conserv. of Göteborg, 1965-67; Musicol. studies, Univ. of Göteborg, 1971-. Career: recitals, Norkoping, Stockholm, Karlstad; TV broadcasts, Sweden & Moscow; w. orchs. of Norrköping & Göteborg, 1953-58, '62-67; Tchr., Karlstad, 1967-, & Norrköping, 1976-. Mbr. Swedish violin tchrs. assn. Recip. scholarships. Address: Drottninggatan 33:171, 59100 Motala, Sweden.

STENHOLM, Rolf, b. 23 July 1937, Vate, Gotland, Sweden. Organist; Choirmaster. Educ: RMA, Stockholm; Studied Organ w. Alf Linder; Flor Peeters, Antwerp, Belgium. m. Solveig Stenholm, 3 c. Career: Num. Radio apps. in Sweden, Norway & Belgium; Organ recitals in Sweden, Norway, Denmark, Belgium, Austria & UK (Royal Festival Hall, London); Organ recital of Entire Organ Works of Cesar Frack, Strangnas, 1973; Cond., Oratories w. Strangnas Choral Soc. Recording of Cathedral w. Organ including works of Franck, Grigny, Reger, Schlick & Hallnas. Hons: 2nd & Public Prizes at Int. Organ Wk. in Bruges, Belgium, 1964. Hobbies: Hist. of Organ Music; Organ Bldg.; Chess. Address: Domprostgrand 4, S 152 00 Strangnas, Sweden.

STENT, Keith Geoffrey, b. 26 Oct. 1934, Portsmouth, UK. Lecturer; Conductor. Educ: TCL; BMus (London); ARCM; GTCL;

LTCL. m. Myrna Clayton, 1 s., 1 d. Career: currently Prin. Lectr., Polytechnic of S Bank, London; previously on staff or Royal Ballet Schl., TCL, Colls. of Educ., independent & State Schls.; currently Cond., Wandsworth Symph. Orch. & Wandsworth Youth Phil.; currently Dir., Litolff Orch.; Freelance engagements; previously Cond. of Operatic Socs., Concert Band & other orchs.; Examiner, TCL, 1963-. Comps: Two Carols in Modern Vie, for Chorus & Orch.; Two Carlos for the Caribbean; Sullivan at Sea (Brass Band); Novello. Contbr. to: Music in Educ. Mbrships: Hon. Sec., London Centre 1960-65, ISM. Hobbies: Model Railways; Victoriana & Edwardiana. Address: 20 Montana Rd., West Wimbledon, London SW20 8TW, UK.

STENZL, Jürg Thomas, b. 23 Aug. 1942, Basle, Switz. Musicologist; Music Critic. Educ: Univs. of Berne, & Sorbonne, Paris, France; Dr.phil, 1968. m. Therese Fürst, 1 c. Career: Asst. to Prof. L F Tagliavini, Fribourg Univ., 1969-75; Privatdozent & Chief de Travaux ibid., 1974-; Ed., Schweizerische Musikzeitung, 1975-. Publs: Die vierzig Clausulae der Handschrift Paris, 1970; Repertorium der liturg. Musikhandschriften der Diözesen Sitten, Lausanne & Genf, 1972-; Contbng. Ed., L Nono, Texte, Studien zu seiner Musik, 1975j; A Corelli, Triosonaten op. 2 & 4, 1979. Contbr. to profl. publs. Mbr., profl. assns. incl: Sec., Swiss Musicol. Soc. Hobbies: Practical Musical Activities; Literature; Arts. Address: au Tronchet, CH-1751 Neyruz, Switz.

STEPAN, Pavel, b. 28 May 1925, Brno, Czechoslovakia. Pianist. Educ: Philos. Fac., 2 yrs.; Acad. of Musical Arts; studied Piano w. grandfather, Prof. V Kurz. m. Eva Kozlovská, 1 s. Debut: 1941. Career: Played w. Czech Philharmonia under R Kubelik, 1943; frequent recitals of classical & contemporary music; num. chmbr. music perfs., esp. w. Smetana Quartet; tours in many countries of E & W Europe; num. apps. at Prague Spring Fest.; Tchr., Prague Acad. of Music & Fine Arts, & at courses at seminars abroad. Merit Artist, CSSR, 1975-. Recordings incl: Mozart, Piano Concertos in A & B (K 488 & K595), in F & C (K 459, K 503), & Sonata in C minor; Prokofiev, Flüchtige Erscheinungen op. 22; D Kabalewski, III Piano Concerto; Dvorak, Piano Quintet in A (w. Smetana Quartet); V J Tomasek, Eglogues; Beethoven, Sonata in A op. 2 no. 2, & sonata in F minor op. 57, Appassionata; Schulhjoff, 2nd Sonata for Piano; Suk, Complete Piano Works. Contbr. to Rudé Právo; Hudebni Rozhledy. Hons: Awards at Prague Spring Fest. 1951, & at World Youth Fests., Berlin 1951, Bucharest, 1953; Wiener Flötenuhr Prize, Austria, 1971. Hobby: Chess. Mgmt: Pragokoncert. Address: Besedni 3, 118 00 Prague 1, Czechoslovakia.

STEPHAN, Rudolf, b. 3 Apr. 1925, Bochum, Germany. Musicologist. Educ: univ. Heidelberg, 1944-47, Cöttingen, 1947-50; PhD, 1950, Habil., 1963, Göttingen. Career: Ord. Prof., Freie Universität Berlin, 1967. Publs: incl: Musik, 1957; Neue Musik, 1958; Gustav Mahler - 4 symphonie, 1966; Über das Musik leben der Gegenwart, 1968; Über Musik und Politik, 1971; Über Musik und Kritik, 1971; Die Musik der 60er Jahre, 1972; Über Musik and Sprache, 1974; Avantgarde und Volkstümlchkeit, 1975; Schulfach Musik, 1976; Musik fremder Kulturen, 1977; Bericht über den 1. Kongress der Internat. Schönberg-Gesellschaft, 1978; Alexander Zemhlinky, 1978. Mbrships: Int. Musicol. Soc. (Basel); Gesellschaft für Musikforschung; Int. Soc. for Contemporary Music; Int. Gustav Mahler Gesellschaft; Int. Schönberg Gesellschaft, etc. Address: Musikwiss. Institut der Freien Universität Berlin, Hundekehlestr. 26a, D1000 Berlin 33, German Fed. Repub.

STEPHENS, Howard, b. 3 May 1921, Hounslow, Middx., UK. Lecturer; Professional Organist; Examiner in Music. Educ: Scholar & Exhbnr., RCM; FRCO; ARCM; BMus, Oxford Univ.; MA, ibid.; Archbishop of Canterbury's Dip. in Ch. Music (ADCM). m. Marjorie Joan Brown, 1 s., 3 d. Career incls: Sub-Organist, Exeter Cath., 1950-54; Tutor, St. Luke's, Exeter, 1952-54; Cond., Exeter Musical Soc. & Honiton Choral Soc., 1952-54; Dir. of Music, Birkenhead Schl., 1955-59; Cond., Hoylake Choral Soc., 1956-59; Dir. of Music, St. Mary's Osterley, 1959-; Prin. Lectr. & Hd. of Music Dept., Borough Rd. Coll. of Educ., 1959-76; Hd., Dept. of Music, W London Inst. of Higher Educ., 1976-78; Special Commnr., RSCM; Examiner, Oxford Local Examinations Bd.; Mbr., Coun. of Curwen Inst. Comps: A Schumann Suite for Brass Band. Contbr. to music jrnls. Publs: Editl. Bd., Handbook for Music Tchrs. Mbrships: ISM; Nat. Assn. of Tchrs. in Further & Higher Educ. Address: 17 Thornbury Ave., Osterley, Isleworth, Middx., UK. 3.

STEPHENS, John Anthony, b. 20 Apr. 1947, St. Louis, Missouri, USa. Singer. Educ: BMusEd; MMus; DMusA. m. Barbara Ann Stephens. Debut: w. Lake George Opera Fest., 1973. Career: Roles w. Metropolitan Opera, Opera Cos. of Boston, Balt.,

Augusta, New Haven, Lake George Opera Fest. & Asolo Opera; Concert apps., J F Kennedy Center, Nat. Cathedral & Saratoga Perf. Arts Center. Recordings: America Independent; La Fiesta de la Posada. Contbr. to: Grove's Dict., 6th Ed. Hons: Fulbright Fellow, 1973; 1st Place, Nat. Assn. of Tchrs. of Singing Contest, III., 1973. Hobbies: Sports; Reading; Woodworking. Mgmt: Thomas Rowe of NYC. Address: 230 West End Ave., 9c, NY, NY 10023, USA.

STEPHENS, Norris Lynn, b. 14 Dec. 1930, Charleroi, Pa., USa. Music Librarian; University Professor; Organist; Choir Director; Carillonneur. Educ: BFA, Carnegie-Mellon Univ., Pitts., Pa.; MFA, ibid.; SMM, Union Theological Sem., NYC; MLS, Univ. of Pitts.; PhD, ibid. m. Donna Lynne Anderson, 1 s., 1 d. Career: Asst. Organist-Dir., & Carillonneur, E Liberty Presby. Ch., Pitts., Pa., 1963-; Bi-weekly radio broadcasts of carillon recitals, WLOA, Braddock, Pa., 1963-77; Music Libn. & Asst. Prof., Univ. of Pitts., Pa. Comps. Num. arrs. for pipe & electronic organs, handbells; Organ scores to many oratorios, requiems. Contbr. to: Ency. of Lib. & Info. Sci.; Grove's Dictionary of Music & Musicians; Union Catalogue of Music & Books on Music Printed Before 1801 in Pitts. Libs.; Western Pa. Histl. mag. Mbrships: Sec.-Treas., Allegheny Chapt., Am. Musicol. Soc., 1969-74; Nat. Coun., 1975-77; Music Lib. Assn.; Int. Music Lib. Assn.; Am. Guild of Organists; Nat. Choral Comm., ibid., 1960-70. Hobbies: Gardening; Model Railroading; Refinishing Furniture. Address: 106 Candlewyck Drive, Glenshaw, PA 15116, USA.

STEPHENS, Paul Day, Jr., b. 7 May 1946, Trenton, Mo., USA. Pianist; Piano Instructor. Educ: BMus, Univ. of Mo. at Kansas City, 1971; postgrad. study, Cleveland Inst. of Music; MMus, Ball State Univ., Munice, Ind., 1976; studied piano & pedagogy w. var. tchrs. m. Janice T Saffir. Career: Teaching Fellow, Cleveland Inst. of Music; Grad. Asst., Ball State Univ.; former Fac. Mbr., William Jewell Coll., Liberty, Mo., Conserv. of Music, Univ. of Mo. at Kansas City, & NE Mo. State Univ., Kirksville; Organist, Trinity Episcopal Ch., Kirksville, Mo. Mbrships: Nat. Music Tchrs. Assn.; Phi Mu Alpha Sinfonia. Address: 423 Glendale Rd., Liberty, MO 64068, USA.

STEPHENS, Rex, b. 25 Apr. 1913, Launceston, UK. Professor of Pianoforte. Educ: FRAM. m. Honor Tolchard. Career: Accomp., num. celebrated soloists, concerts, radio & TV; Prof. of Pianoforte Accomp., RAM, London. Hobbies: Carpentry; Walking. Address: 278 Earl's Ct. Rd., London SW5 9AS, UK. 3.

STEPHENS, William Raymond, b. 12 Jan. 1916, Caerphilly, S Wales, UK. Music Publisher. Educ: Toronto Conserv. of Music; Qualified Bandmaster; Choirleader & Profl. Instrumentalist. m. Eunice H Davies, 2 s. Career: Tuba, String Bass Player w. Princess Patricias Band for 10 yrs. military serv.; Music Mgr., Boosey & Hawkes, Can., 13 yrs.; Gen. Mgr., Frederick Harris Music Co., Univ. Toronto, Can., last 5 yrs.; Orchl. perf. w. BBC Allied Ex-Forces Network, London, UK, 1944; w. CBC Symph., 1949-50. Contbr. to var. Am. & Can. Music Jrnls.; Music & Drama Columnist until 1970. Mbrships: incl. Past Pres., Can. Music Publrs. Assn. Hobbies: Writing; Bird Watching; Sports. Address: 2145 Rebecca St., Oakville, Ontario, Canada.

STEPHENSON, Donald James, b. 15 Feb. 1947, Leeds, UK. Opera Singer; Teacher. Educ: RMCM; ARCM. div., 1 s., 1 d. Debut: Engl. Nat. Opera, 1972. Career: apps. w. BBC Northern Singers, Sadler's Wells Opera, Engl. Nat. Opera, Engl. Opera Group & Engl. Music Theatre; apps. on radio & TV, UK & Belgium. Recordings: Ch. music from Leeds. Mbrships: ISM; Inst. of Advanced Motorists; MG Owners Club. Hons: ARCM w. hons., 1972; Arts Coun. Scholarship, 1975. Hobbies: Golf; Mountain Walking; Motorcycling; Sports Cars. Mgmt: Fraser & Dunlop, 91 Regent St., London W1. Address: 45 Blenheim Rd., Chiswick, London W4 1ET, UK.

STEPHENSON, Eric William, b. 9 Mar. 1930, Streatham, London, UK. Music Adviser; Pianist. Educ: RAM; LRAM; ARMC; FTCL. m., 2 s., 1 d. Debut: Croydon, 19612. Career: Perfs., Royal Fest. Hall, BBC & BBC TV, London Weekend TV; Music Master, Battersea Grammar Schl.; Kingsdale Schl.; Co. Music Advsr., Warwicks; Music Advsr., London Borough of Hillingdon. Compositions: Singplay; Classroom Orchestra. Mbrships: Music Advisers Nat. Assn. Hobby: Sailing. Address: White Falcons, 48 Hatters Lane, High Wycombe, UK. 3.

STEPHENSON, Kurt, b. 30 Aug. 1899, Hamburg, Germany. Research musician. Educ: Univ. Hamburg, Freiburg, Frankfurt, Halle, musicol.; PhD Halle 1924; Lectr. Freiburg, 1937. m. Erika Piel, 1 d. Career: 1939 Lectr. musicol. Univ. Bonn; 1948 Prof. Mbrships: Soc. for Music Rsch., Kassel; Brahms Soc., Hamburg. Publs. inclk: 100 years Phylharmonic Society in Hamburg, 1928; Johannes Brahms and Fritz Simrock, 1960;

Romanticism in Music, 1961; Clara Schumann, 1969; Description and Sources of the History of the German Unitary Movement, 1963/74. Contbr. to: Music Rsch., Kassel; Music in Past and Present, Kassel. Hons: Brahms Medal, Hamburg, 1973. Hobbies: Travelling; Walking. Address: 2357 Bad Bramstedt/Gayen, German Fed. Repub.

STEPHENSON, Loran Dean, b. 22 Oct. 1925, Riverdale, Idaho, USA. Composer; Author; Director; Teacher. Educ: BA, MA, Brigham Young Univ. m. Joyce Barrett, 5 s., 4 d. Career: Asst. Cond. & Co-Fndr., Dist. of Columbia Youth Symph. Orch.; Fndr. & Dir., Stephenson Family Strings; Pub. Schl. Music Tchr.; Tchr., Phila. Music Acad. Composer of Impressions of Children, Trio for 2 violins & cello or flute, oboe & bassoon. Recordings: Stephenson Strings: Greetings. Author of Reading, Rhythm & Rote: Method for Young String Players, Books 1 & 2, 1960, '61. Mbr., Bd. of Dirs. & Nat. Sect., Nat. Schl. Orch. Assn. Hobbies: Arch.; Bus. Address: 401 South 46th St., Phila., PA 19143, USA.

STEPKA, Karel Vaclav, b. 3/ May 1908, Ces. Budejovice, Czechoslovakia. Music Teacher; Composer; Choir Master; Musician (Piano, organ, violin). Educ: Organ Schl.; Dept. for Comp. Music Conserv.; Prague Acad. of Music. m. Berta Jirkalova. Comps. incl; Symph. Suite (Orch.); Hussite Cantata (soloist, choir, organ & orch.); Meditation (String quartet); Due umore (violin & Meditation (string quartet); Due Umore (violin & piano); Sonata (piano); Suite a l'Antique (2 trombes); Tracing the Hussites: Canto bellicoso (mixed choir), brass & kettle drums); Trocnov: festival march (orch.). Publs: Hymnology, 1952; Doctrine of music instruments (Nauka o hudebnich nastrojich), 1961; Art Fighting (umeni bojujici), 1966; ed., var. music publs. Mbrships: Czech Mozart Soc.; Bohemia Music Co.; Czech Authors Union. Hons: Dr. Ch. Farsky Prize, 1950; Mem. medal, Music comp. Adalb. Jirovec, 1969. Hobbies: Touring; Swimming. Address: 66 Manesova St., 120 00 Prague 2, Vinohrady, Czechoslovakia. 3.

STEPTOE, Roger Guy, b. 25 Jan. 1953, Winchester, UK. Composer; Accompanist; Pianist; Teacher of Composition. Educ: BA (Music), Univ. of Reading, 1974; Postgrad., RAM, 1974-77; LRAM; LLCM. Debut: (as comp.) Purcell Room, 1977. Career: Composer-in-Residence, Charterhouse, Surrey. Suite for solo cello broadcast, 1978. Comps. incl: Music for horn & orch., 1975; Overture for Charterhouse, 1977; String Quartet No. 1, 1976; Suite for solo cello, 1977; From Huperion for oboe & piano, 1977; Gaudeamus for organ, 1978; Study for solo violin, 1978; Praises for choir and orch., 1977; King for Macedon (opera), 1978; Sonata for Piano, 1979. Contbr. to Composers Mag. Mbrships: CGGB; Performing Right Soc.; RAM Club; ISM; mechanical Copyright Soc. Hons. incl: Charterhouse Comp. Award, 1976-79; Frederick Corder Prize for comp. & Leverhulme Comp. Award, RAM, 1975; Charles Lucas prize (RAM), 1976. Hobbies: Theatre; Concerts; Reading; Piano Playing. Address: Rosse-Lyn, Compton, Winchester, Hants., UK. 30.

STERK, Ienske, b. 18 June 1940, Utrecht, Netherlands. Violincellist. Educ: Utrecht Conserv.; Amsterdam State Univ. m. Henk Stam, 1 c. Career: Tchr. of Violoncello, Toonkunst Schl. of Music, Utrecht & Hoorn Regional Schl. of Music; Mbr., Frysk Symph. Orch., 1966-; Mbr., Frisian Str. Quartet. Recordings: perfs. of modern Hungarian, Czech & Dutch str. quartets w. Frisian Str. Quartet recorded by Dutch Broadcasting Corp. Mbr., Anouk (Artists' trade-union). Hobbies: Collecting Exotic Musical Instruments; Animals. Address: Noorderend 30, Suawoude (Frl.), Netherlands.

STERN, Isaac, b. 21 July 1920, Kremenietz, USSR. Concert Violinist. Educ: San Fran. Conserv. of Music. m. Vera Lindenblit Stern, 2 s., 1 d. Debut: Concertmaster of San Fran. Symph. w. Naoum Blinder (Bach's Double Violin Concerto), 1934. Career: LA Symph. w. Otto Klemperer, 1935; San Francisco Symph. w. Pierre Monteux; Chgo. Symph. w. Frederick Stock, 1937; Carnegie Hall Debut, NYC, 1943; NY Phil. w. Dimitri Mitropoulis; major tours in recital & w. Dimitri Mitropoulis; major tours in recital & w. ldng. orchs., throughout USA, Can., Europe, Israel, S Africa, Aust., India, Japan, Iceland, Singapore, Hong Kong, USSr; apps. at all major fests., inclng. Prades Fests. w. Pablo Casals, 1950-52; & Puerto Rico, 1953-67; premiered Hindemith's Sonata (1939) at Carnegie Hall, 1945, Wm. Schuman's Violin Concerto w. Boston Symph., 1950 & Bernstein's Serenade for Violin, Strings & Percussion at Venice Fest., 1954; perf. of Mendelssohn's Violin Concerto filmed on Mt. Scopus, Israel following Six Day War, w. Israel Philharmonic cond. by Leonard Bernstein, 1967; num. TV apps.; num. Recordings. Mbrships: Pres., Carnegie Hall; Bd. Chmn., Am.-Israel Cultural Fndn. Inc.; Dir., Jerusalem Music Ctr.; Former Fndr.-Mbr., Nat. Coun. of the Arts. Hons: Grammys, 1971 & 73; Cmdr., Ordre de la Couronne, 1974; num. hon.

docts. Address: c/o Hurok Concerts, 1370 Ave. of the Americas, New York, NY 10019, USA. 2.

STERNBACH, David Joel, b. 5 May 1934, Long Beach, NY, USA. French Horn Player. Educ: BA, NY Univ., 1957; MMus, Ind. Univ., 1964; pvte. study w. noted tchrs. m. Sally Lynn Miller. Career incls: former Solo Horn w. var. orchs. in Denmark, Berlin, Puerto Rico, USA; apps. at fests.; Soloist & Recitalist, Europe, USA, Caribbean, Ctrl. Am.; currently Tchr. of Horn, W Va. Univ., Hornist, Abbey Brass Guild, WVU Fac. Woodwind Quintet, Solo Horn, W Va. Symphonette, Bach Cantata Soloist, Recitalist, Cond. Recordings: w. Danish State Radio Symph.; Jazz recordings w. Kenny Drew & Pedro Biker & w. NY Rock & Roll Ensemble; TV & radio recordings. Ed. var. musical publs. Contbr. to jrnls. Mbr. profl. orgs. Recip. var. hons. Hobbies: Photography; Birdwatching. Address: 321 Morgantown Ave., Morgantown, WV 26505, USA.

STERNBERG, Jonathan, b. 27 July 1919, NYC, USA. Conductor. Educ: Juilliard Schl. of Music, 1929-31; AB, NY Univ., Wash. Sq. Coll., 1939; NY Univ. Grad. Schl., 1939-40; Harvard Summer Schl., 1940; Manhattan Schl. of Music, 1946; L'Ecole Monteux, 1946, '47. m. Ursula Hertz, 1 s., 2 d. Debut: VSO, 1947. Career: Guest Cond., maj. orchs. & opera in Vienna, Salzburg, Berlin, Munich, Stuttart, Zurich, Geneva, Paris, Monte Carlo, Brussels, London, Warsaw, Prague, Buenos Aires, NY, etc. Musical Dir., Royal Flemish Opera, Antwerp, 1961; Harkness Ballet, NY, 1966; Atlanta Opera & Ballet, 1968; Vis. Prof. of Conducting & Cond., Eastman Philharmonia, Eastman Schl. of Music, Rochester, 1969; Prof. of Music, Temple Univ. Coll. of Music, Phila.; Dir. & Cond., Main Line Symph. & Symph. Club of Phila., 1971. Recordings incl: 50 LP records w. Vienna State Opera Orch., Salzburg Mozarteum Orch., VSO on var. labels. Contbr. to A Bibliography of Periodical Literature in Musicology & Allied Fields. Mbrships: Nat. Assn. of Am. Composers & Conds.; Am. Fed. of Musicians; Musical Fund Soc. Hons: Cit. Award for Disting. Serv. to Am. Music (NAACC), 1972; hon. DMus, Calif. Int. Univ., 1976. Var. hobbies. Mgmt: Bureau de Concerts Liliane Weinstadt, 69 rue Langeveld, 1180 Brussels, Belgium. Address: Temple Univ., Coll. of Music, Phila., PA 19122, USA. 2, 6, 23, 28, 29.

STERNDALE-BENNETT, Barry Monkhouse, b. 9 Mar. 1939, London, UK. Singer, Tenor Soloist. Educ: Grad., La Salle Univ., USA; ALCM; DMS; FRSA; FInstAm. Studied w. Prof. Roy Hickman, GSM, then LCM. m. Jane Fitch, 1 s., 2 d. Career: Apps. at leading fests., UK, Canada & Europe; Keeper, Sterndale Bennett Lib., containing important material on Mendelssohn, the Bach Passions, the RAM & Cambridge 1816-75, as gt. gt. grandson of Sir William Sterndale Bennett. Mbrships: Royal Musical Assn.; New Phil. Chorus; RNVR. Hobbies: Photography; Stamp Collecting; Skiing. Address: 115 E Sheen Ave., London SW14 8AX, UK. 3.

STERNE, Colin C, b. 14 Nov. 19231, Wynberg, S Africa. Professor of Music. Educ: BS, Miami Univ., OH, 1943; MS, Juilliard Schl. of Music, 1948; Dip., Paris Conserv., 1951. m. Roberta Bradshaw, 3 d. Career: Prof. of Music, Univ. of Pitts., Pa., 1948-. Comps: 3 Songs (James Joyce); Sonata for Recorder & Harpsichord; Mass for 2-part chorus & organ; Meadow, Hedge, Cuckoo for solo alto recorder; var. motets & choral pieces. Publs: The Son of Getron, 1962; Music & the Listener, 1965; Music for the Recorder (var. eds.). Contbr. to: Music & Letters; Am. Recorder. Mbrships: VP & Bd. Mbr., Am. Recorder Soc.; Am. Musicol. Soc. Hons. incl: Phi Mu Alpha Sinfonia Comp. Award, 1948. Address: 624 Garden City Dr., Monroeville, PA 15146, USA.

STERNEFELD, Daniel, b. 27 Nov. 1905, Antwerp, Belgium. Conductor; Composer. Educ: Dip., Antwerp Conserv.; studied Comp. w. P Gilson, Brussels; Dip., Orch. Direction, Mozarteum, Salzburg, Austria. m. Suzan De Backer, 1 s. Debut: Antwerp Opera House. Career: 1st Cond., Royal Flemish Opera, Antwerp; 1st Cond., Symph. Orch., Belgian Broadcasting, Brussels. Comps. incl: Mater Dolorosa (opera); Pierlala (ballet); Symph. in C. Recording: Symph., Variations for Brass. Hobbies: Reading; Gardening. Address: Ave. R Gobert 83, Brussels 1180, Belgium.

STERNFELD, Frederick William, b. 25 Sept. 1914, Vienna, Austria. Educator. Educ: Cand. Phil., Vienna Univ., Austria, 1937; PhD, Yale Univ., USA, 1943; MA, Oxford UK, 1956. m. Sophia Jung. Career: Rd., Hist. of Music. Publs: Goethe & Music, 1954; Music in Shakespearean Tragedy, 1963; Ed., English Madrigal Verse (w. Fellowes & Greer), 1967; Ed., New Oxford History of Music, Vol. VII (w. Wellesz), 1973. Contbr. to: Musical Quarterly; Music & Letters; Shakespeare Quarterly; Annales Musicologiques. Mbrships: VP, Royal Musical Assn.; Athenaeum. Hobbies: Swimming; Walking. Address: 'Greenwood', Boars Hill, Oxford OX1 5DJ, UK. 3.

STESZEWSKI, Jan Maria, b. 20 Apr. 1929, Koźmin, Poland. Musicologist; Educ: Master of Philos., Poznań Univ.; Dr of Liberal Arts, Inst. of Arts, Polish Acad. of Scis.; Piano Study, HS of Music, Poznań. m. Barbara Zwolska, 3 c. Career: Collaborator, Inst. of Arts, Warsaw, 1952-75; Hd., Musicol Dept., Poznań Univ., 1975-. Publs: Collections of folk songs & music from different regions; Kurpie, 1955; Lubelskie, 1955; Byelorussia, 1958-69; East Carpathians, 1965; Historical Sources of the 17th Century, 1960, 1970. Contbr. to: Muzyka; Polish Music; Jahrbuch für Volksliedforschung; Studia Musicologica; Rocznik Historii Sztuki; Ruch Muzyczny, etc. Mbrships: Chmn., Polish Musicol. Soc., 1969-73; Pres., Polish Comps. Union, 1973-79; Pres., Polish Music Coun., 1979-; Bd. of Dirs., Int. Musicol. Soc., 1977-. Address: Boguslawskiego 6 m. 143, 01-923 Warsaw, Poland. 30.

STEUART, Richard Carson, b31 Jan. 1956, Weyburn, Sask., Can. Trumpet Player & Teacher. Educ: Univ. of Regina; Curtis Music Inst., Pa. m. Carol Joan Powell, 1 d. Career: Mbr., Nat. Youth Orch. of Can.; Mbr., Regina Symph., 5 yrs. Hons. incl: Award for Nat. Jr. Winds, Can., 1967; var. local fest. awards. Hobby: Physical Fitness. Address: Box 1250, Regina, Sask., Canada.

STEVENS, Bernard, b. 1916, UK. Composer. Educ: Study of composition w. E J Dent & R O Morris. Comps. incl: Symph. of Liberation; Unacc. Mass; Concertos for violin & cello; var. chmbr. music pieces & piano music. Recip: 1st Prize, Daily Express music competition, 1946. Address: The Old Forge, Gt. Maplestead, Halstead, Essex CO9 2RE, UK.

STEVENS, Denis William, b. 2 Mar. 1922, High Wycome, UK. Conductor; Musicologist. Educ: Jesus Coll., Oxford; MA (Oxon); DHL, Fairfield Univ.; RAM; Pvte. studies in London & Paris. m. (1) Sheila Elizabeth Holloway, 2 s., 1 d. (2) Leocadia Kwasny. Career: Prod., BBC Music Div., 1949-54; Vis. Prof., Cornell Univ. & Univ. Calif., Berkeley, USA; Cond., Ambrosian Singers, 1956-60; Prof., Musicology, Columbia Univ., 1964-; Pres., Academia Monteverdiana; Guest Lectr., Europe, Can., India, Burma, USA; Concert apps., Europe, Am. & Can. Eds. of many pre-classical works publd. & recorded incl: Monteverdi Vespers, Orfeo, etc. Publs. incl: Tudor Church Music, 1961, '66; Monteverdi - Sacred, Secular and Occasional Music, 1978. Contbr. to profl. jrnls. Mbrships. incl: Am. Musicol. Soc. Hobbies: Travel; Photography. Address: 25 Clarement Ave., NY, NY 10027, USA. 1, 2, 3, 11, 14, 19.

STEVENS, Halsey, b. 3 Dec. 1908, Scott, NY, USA. Composer; Author; Educator. Educ: BMus, Syracuse Univ., 1931; MMus, ibid., 1937; Univ. of Calif., 1944; pvte. study, 1919-26; studied comp. w. Wm. Berwald, 1928-31, '35-37; Ernest Bloch, 1944; piano w. George Mullfinger, 1928-31. m. Harriett E Merritt, 1 s., 2 d. Career: Assoc. Prof. of Music, Dakota Wesleyan Univ., 1937-41; Prof. & Dir., Coll. of Music, Bradley Univ., 1941-46; Prof., Univ. of Redlands, 1946; Univ. of So. Calif., 1946-79; Vis. Prof., Univ. of Wash., 1958; Yale Univ., 1960-61; Univ. of Cinn., 1968; Williams Coll., 1969; Program annotator, LA Phil. Orch., 1946-51; Coleman Chmbr. Concerts, 1966-. Comps. incl: (for orch.) Triskelion; Symphony No. 1; Sinfonia Breve; Symphonic Danes; Concerto for violoncello & orch.; Concerto for clarinet & string orch.; Double Concerto for violin, violoncello & str. orch.; The Ballad of William Sycamore; A Testament of Life; Te Deum; num. chamber & choral works. Var. recordings. Publs: The Life & Music, of Béla Bartók, 1953, rev. edn., 1964, Japanese transl., 1961; Co-Ed., Festival Essays for Pauline Alderman, 1976. Contbr. to var. jrnls. Hons. incl: LittD, Syracuse Univ., 1966. Address: 9631 Second Ave., Inglewood, CA 90305, USA. 2, 3, 9.

STEVENS, J E, b. 8 Oct. 1921, London, UK. Musical Historian; Professor of Renaissance & Medieval English. Educ: MA, PhD, Magdalene Coll., Cambridge. m. Charlotte E M Somner, 4 c. Career incls: Prof. of Medieval & Renaissance English, Univ. of Cambridge; Musical Historian. Publs: Music & Poetry in the Early Tudor Court, 1961, 1979; Ed., Musica Britannica vols. 4, 18 & 36; Medieval Romance, 1973. Mbrships: Fellow, British Acad.; Fellow, Magdalene Coll., Cambridge. Hobbies: Playing the viol; Sailing; Bricklaying. Address:O 4 & 5 Bell's Court, Cambridge, UK. 1.

STEVENS, James, b. 5 May 1930, London, UK. Composer; Pianist; Writer; Director. Educ: GSM, London; Conserv. Nat. de Musique, Paris, France; Hochschüle für Musik, Berlin, Germany. Debut: ORTF, 1952. Career: Comp. of Film Scores & music for TV progs. & series; Prod., var. shows inclng. Paradise is in Your Mind; apps. on Radio & TV. Comps. incl: 3 Symphs.; 2 Musicals; Ghost Story (opera); Infantes Etheria (organ); Etymon (chmbr. grps. & singers); Lion & Unicorn; In a Nutshell; Music for Films & TV

progs. inclng. Horizon, World of Tonight; Bomp's Travels, The Visit (stage shows); (recorded) Queen High; Exploding Galaxy; Rock cantata, Orpeheus in Space; Amo Ergo Sum. for organ. Under the Southern Cross; Another Life; var. pop records, jazz albums & mood music. Contbr. to: New Statesman; Opera; Tempo. Hons: Royal Phil. Prize, 1952; Mendelssohn Scholarship, 1953; Lili Boulanger Memorial Award, 1954. Hobbies: Cooking; Swimming; Car-camping Trips in France. Address: c/o Composers' Guild of Gt. Brit., 10 Stratford Pl., London W1, UK. 3, 13, 14.

STEVENS, Joan Frances (Née WOLLERMAN), b. 14 Jan. 1921, Palmerston North, NZ. School Music Specialist; Teacher (Piano); Music Therapist. Educ: Wellington Tchrs. Coll.; Registered Music Tchr.; LRSM; LTCL; LGSMT (Music Therapy), 1976. m 1) W H B Easterbrook-Smith (div.); 2) J M S Ross (dec.); 3) R S Stevens, 3 stepchildren. Career incls: Schl. Tchr.; Itinerant Music Advsr., Wellington; Asst. Music Lectr., Wellington Tchrs. Coll.; Sr. Tchr., Corres. Schl.; Improvisation for Dance Grps.; Schl. Broadcasts; Accomp. Comps. incl: (published) Song to A Tui; (also recorded) A Child's Song of the New Zealand Bush; The Penguin & other Movement Songs; Koo the Kiwi & Kip the Kangaroo. Mbr., profl. assns., NZ & UK. Hobbies incl: Gardening; Reading; Dance Movement. Address: 57 Friend St., Karori, Wellington 5, NZ.

STEVENS, William Jervis, b. 6 Jan. 1921, Montreal, Quebec, Can. Pianist. Educ: BMus, Piano, Univ. of McGill; Music Specialist, Dept. Educ., Quebec. Debut: Montreal, 1951; Boston, 1952; NY, 1962. Career: Host & Performing Artist on CBC TV wkly, 13 yrs.; Guest apps. on CBC TV Educl. Children's Progs., 6 yrs.; Adjudicator of Music Fests.; Solo Recitals & Perfs. in Secondary Schls. & Colls. in Can., 25 yrs.; Broadcast premiere perf. of 1st Violet Archer Piano Concerto, CBC Symph., Toronto; Master Piano Tchr., École de Musique, Vincent D'hdy & Univ. of Motnreal. Recordings incl: William Stevens Plays the Romantics. Contbr. to: Adagio; Jeunesses Musicales. Hons. incl: Harriett Cohen Commonwealth Medal, 1960. Mgmt: Snyder Prods., 989 Belmont, Manchester, NH. Address: Parmenter Rd., RR1, Sutton, Quebec, Can., JOE 2KO.

STEVENSON, Barbara Thorne, b. 26 Dec. 1919, Portland, Ore., USA. Singer; Lyric Dramatic Soprano. Educ: Pacific Univ., Forest Grove, Ore.; Curtis Inst. of Music, Phila., Pa. m. (1) Donald S Stevenson, 1 s. (2) George E Stephens, 1 s. Debut: Phila. Opera Co., 1939. Career incls: Leading Soprano, Phila. Opera Co., 3 seasons; Has sung extensively throughout USA & Can. in concert & oratorio; Has app. as soloist w. maj. orchs. inclng. NY Phil. Recordings: Mozart Requiem; Debussy Sirenes. Mbr., Sigma Alpha Iota. Hons: Winner, Atwater Kent Radio Audition, State of Ore., 1930, '31, '32; Winner, nat. Fedn. of Music Clubs Biennial, 1933, '35. Hobbies: Music, Writing. Address: 109 Hemenway Apt. 1, Boston, MA 02115, USA.

STEVENSON, Nora Carroll, b. 18 Nov. 1924, Beaumont, Tex., USA. Musicologist; Historian (American History); Violinist; Violist. Educ: BA, Univ. of Tex., 1944; MS, 1949, MMus, 1972, Univ. of Mich.; PhD Cand., Univ. of Va. m. Charles Leslie Stevenson, 5 s. Career: Prin. Violist, Rockbridge Symph., W Va., 1976-78; Violist, Sage City Symph., Vt., 1978-79; Tchr., violin & viola. Mbr., Am. Histl. Assn. Address: Box 14, Wilmington, VT 05363, USA. 27.

STEVENSON, Phyllis Diane Miles, b. 18 Apr. 1944, Montreal, Quebec, Canada. Musician; School Music Teacher. Educ: BMus; Grad. Dip. Mus. Ed. m. John Stevenson, 1 s., 1 d. Debut: (as comp.), Ottawa Unitarian Ch., 1969. Career: Schl. Tchr., 19612-; Pvte. Piano Tchr.; Poetry Readings on TV; w. Milton Acorn; At Yellow Door Coffee House; Public Relations liason to Brit. & Can. musicians; soprano soloist, Temple Israel Choir. Publs: Sight Reading (poetry). Contbr. to Unitarian Newsletter. Mbrships: Nat. Arts Ctr. Orch. Assn.; Bd., Ottawa Symph. Orch. Hobbies: Poetry; Acting (comedy). Address: 3031 Otterson Drive, Ottawa, Canada K1V 7B5.

STEVENSON, Robert Murrell, b. 3 July 1916, Melrose, NM, USA. Musicologist. Educ: AB, Univ. of Texas; MMus, Tale Univ.; STB, Harvard Univ.; BLitt, Oxford; STM, Princeton Univ.; PhD, Rochester Univ.; grad., Juilliard Grad. Schl. of Music, 1938. Debut: NY, 1942. Career: Univ. of Texas, 1941-43, '46; US Army, 1943-46; Westminster Choir Coll., Princeton, NJ, 1946-49; UCLA, 1949-; Ed., Inter-Am. Music Review. Publs: 26 books inclng. Music in Aztec & Inca Territory, 1976; Vilancicos portugueses, 1976; Spanish Cathedral Music in the Golden Age, 1976; A Guide to Caribbean Music History, 1975; Latin American Colonial Music Anthology, 1975; Christmas Music from Baroque Mexico, 1974; Renaissance & Baroque Musical Sources in the Americas, 1970. Contbr. of articles to profl. jrnls. etc., inclng. The New Grove, sev. comps. Mbrships: Corresponding mbr., Hispanic Soc. of Am. & Acad. Real de San Fernando de Bellas Artes, Madrid. Recip., sev. fellowships & awards. Hobby: piano playing. Address: 405 Hilgard Ave., Los Angeles, CA 90024, USA. 2, 30.

STEVENSON, Ronald, b. 6 Mar. 1928, Blackburn, UK. Composer; Pianist. Educ: Assoc., Fellow, Royal Mannchester Coll. of Music; Conserv. di Santa Cecilia, Rome. m. Marjorie Spedding, 1 s., 2 d. Career: Prom debut in own 2nd piano concertos, 1972; Busoni documentary on BBC TV, 1974; 12 Busoni documentary on BBC TV, 1974; 12 Busoni progs., BBC Radio 3, 1973; 36 Reicha fugues played on Radio 3, 1970. Comps. incl: Passacaglia on DSCH for piano (recorded); Prelude & Fugue for organ; Piano concerto No. 1; Piano concerto No. 2; Peter Grimes Fantasy for piano; Anger dance for guitar; Prelude, Fugue & Fantasy for piano. Publs: Ed., The Young Pianist's Grainger, 1966; Western Music, 1971. Contbr. to: Listener; Music Review; Musical Times; Score; Scottish Int. Mbr., Comps. Guild of GB. Hons. incl: Harriet Cohen Int. Music Award, 1966. Hobbies: Hillwalking; Reading. Mgmt: Basil Douglas, London; Pro Arte Musica, Edinburgh. Address: Townfoot House, W Linton, Peeblesshire, UK. 3.

STEWART, Barbara D, b. 17 Sept. 1941, Rochester, NY, USA. Musician, Classical Kazoo. Educ: BA, Cornell Univ.; MS, Simmons Coll.; Flute Dip., Eastman Preparatory Schl.; studied w. Joseph Mariano. m. James Cobb Stewart, 2 d. Career: TV, Radio Apps., Concert, NY Town Hall w. Peter Schickele's PDQ Bach, local perfs., as 1st Kazoo, Mgr. & Creator, The Kazoophony, comprising the Kaminsky Int. Kazoo Quartet, & The Fie-On Arts Ensemble; many schl. & coll. shows. Mbr., Rochester Chmbr. Orch.; Past Pres., Bd. of Dir., ibid. Hobby: Squash Racquets. Mbmt: Arthur Shafman International Ltd. Address: 3485 Elmwood Ave., Rochester, NY 14610, USA. 27.

STEWART, Frank Graham, b. 12 Dec. 1920, La Junta, Colo., USA. Composer; Theorist. Educ: BMus, Eastman Schl. of Music, 1942; MAT, Colo. State Univ., Ft. Collins, 1968; PhD, Mich. State Univ., 1971; Lifetime Standard Teaching Credential, Calif. m. Johanna Kluge, 1 d. Comps. incl: English As She Is Taught; To Let the Captive Go (opera); Metamorph; Heavyweights; Scene - 1970; The First Joy of Marriage; 12 Etudes for Clarinet & Piano; Suite for Piano; Str. Quartet 1. Contbr. to profl. jrnls. Mbr., num. profl. assns. Hons. incl: Opera Contest Winner, Mannes Coll. of Music, 1974; Orpeus Award, Phi Mu Alpha Sinfonia, 1974; num. scholarships. Hobbies: Fishing; Hiking; Gardening; Swimming. Address: PO Box 5261, Mississippi State, MS 39762, USA.

STEWART, Jean, b. 17 Feb. 1914, Tonbridge, Kent, UK. Viola Player. Educ: ARCM; Hon. ARAM. m. G D Hadley, 3 d. Career: Former Viola Player; Menges Str. Quartet, Macgibbon Str. Quartet; Currently Viola Player, Richards Piano Quartet; Adjudicator. Recordings: Chausson & Martinu Piano Quartets w. Richards Piano Quartet; Piano Quartet by Herbert Howells w. Richard Piano Quartet; Fantasy Str. Quartet by Herbert Howells & Clarinet w. The King, Richards Ensemble. Mbrships: Royal Phil. Soc.; ISM; Brit. Fedn. of Music Fests. Recip. Leverhulme Scholarship to RCM, 1938. Hobbies: Cooking; Cats; Gardening. Address: 59 Gloucester Cres., London, NW1 7EG, UK.

STEWART, John, b. Cleveland, Ohio, USA. Opera Singer. Educ: BA, Yale, Brown; New England Conserv. m. Julia Emoed-Wallace, 1 d. Debut: Pinkerton - Santa Fe Opera. Career: apps. w. Opera Cos. & Orchs. in USA & Europe. Address: Eppsteiner Str. 53, 6 Frankfurt am Main 1, German Fed. Repub.

STEWART, Larry Joe, b. 8 Jan. 1940, Indpls., Ind., USA. Bassoonist; University Professor. Educ: BS Music Educ., Ball State Univ., Ind., 1962; MMus, Northwestern Univ., 1963; DMusical Arts, Univ. of Mich., 1972; Pvte. study of Bassoon, 1958-. m. Susan Kay Olson, 1 s., 1 d. Career incls: Prof. of Bassoon, & Mbr., Fac. Woodwind Quintet, Western Mich. Univ., 1965-69; Asst. 1st Bassoon, Nat. Symph. Orch., Wash., DC, 1963-65; 1st Bassoon, Kalamazoo Symph., 1965-69; Bassoon & Theory Prof., Interlochen Arts Acad., Mich., 1971-73, & Glassboro State Coll., NJ, 1973-; 2nd Bassoon, Phila. Philharmonia, 1975-; Solo Bassoon, Phila. Comps. Forum, 1976; Serv. of Bassoons for Custom Music Co., Mich., 1972-. Mbr., profl. assns. Recip., var. scholarships & univ. hons. Hobbies incl: Fishing; Camping; Canoeing. Address: 402 Yale Rd., Glassboro, NJ 08028, USA.

STEWART, M Dee, b. 8 Oct. 1935, Indpls., Ind., USA. Musician, Trombone, Tenor Tuba, Bass Trumpet; Music Educator. Educ: BS, Ball State Univ., 1957; MM, Northwestern Univ., 1962. m. Rozella Stewart, 1 d., 1 s. Career: Trombone, Tenor Tuba, Bass Trumpet, Phila., Pa., Orch.; Fac., Curtis Inst. of Music. Recordings: w. Trombone-Sect., Phila. Orch.; w. Phila. Brass Ensemble, The Glorius Sound of Brass, A Festival of Carols in

Brass, Joy to the World, God of Our Fathers, The Antiphonai Music of Gabrieli. Hobbies: Family; Nature; Organic Gardening. Address: 429 Beechwood Ave., Haddonfield, NJ 08033, USA. 2, 6.

STEWART, Priscilla Kay, b. 7 Feb. 1948, Hamilton, NZ. Pianist; Singing/Opera Coach; Accompanist. Educ: BMus, Univ. of Auckland, NZ; LRSM Dip., NZ; Grad., London Opera Centre; Post Grad. study, RCM. m. Anthony Mathews, 1 s. Debut: Bath Fest., 1973. Career: Recitals, Lincoln Centre, NY, 1977; Tchr., London Opera Centre, 1974-78; Tchr., GSM, 1979-; Concerts & Recitals throughout UK. Hons: Eric Rice Memorial Prize for accompanists (Royal Overseas League). Hobbies: Sailing; Swimming. Address: 22 Rydal Rd., London SW16, UK.

STEWART, (Richard) Murray, b. 20 Feb. 1954, Barnet, Herts., UK. Organist; Educator. Educ: BA, Univ. of Cambridge, 1975; MA, 1979; FRCO; ARCM; LRAM; studied in Paris w. Daniel Roth. m. Susan Grundy. Career: Sub-Organist, Leeds Parish Ch., 1975-76; Asst. Dir. of Music, Wrekin Coll., 1976-79; Organist & Choirmaster, Solihull Schl., 1979-; Cond., Royal Leamington Spa Bach Choir, 1979-. Recital tours of Netherlands, Denmark, & Germany, Sweden & France. Recordings: works by Bach, Vierne etc.; also for BBC & Danish radio. Mbrships: RCO; ISM. Hons: Organ Scholar, Trinity Hall, Univ. of Cambridge, 1972-75; Finalist, Interpretation Competition, 9th St. Alban's Int. Organ Fest., 1977; Recip. Henry & Lily Davis Fund, 1978. Address: 34 Brook Ln., Olton, Solihull, W Midlands B92 7EJ, UK.

STEWART, Robert, b. 6 Mar. 1918, Buffalo, NY, USA. Composer; Violinist; Educator. Educ: MMus, MusEd, Violin & Comp, Am. Conserv., Chgo. m. Sue Ellen Crumley, 2 s. Career incls: Tchr., Theory & Violin, Am. Conserv. of Music, 1939-53; Freelance profl. violinist, Chgo., 1940-53; Concertmaster, Rosnoke Symph. Orch., 1960-64; Chmn., Dept. of Music, Wash. & Lee Univ., Lexington, Va., 1974-; Num. commissions. Comps. incl: Vocal, chmbr., orchl., concertos, string orchs., woodwinds, brass, duos, piano & organ works. Recordings: Three Pieces for Brass Quintet; Music for Brass No. 4; String Quartet No. 3. Mbr. num. prof. orgs. inclng: Dir., Rockbridge Chorus & Orch. Assn. Hobby: Sailing. Address: 205 White St., Lexington, VA 24450, USA. 2.

STEWART, Thomas, b. San Saba, Tex., USA. Opera Singer. Educ: Baylor Univ.; Juilliard Schl. of Music. m. Evelyn Lear. Career: joined Berlin Opera, 1958; apps. at Met. Opera, San Fran. Opera, Royal Opera House Covent Gdn.; apps. at Bayreuth Fest., 1960-; num. recitals w. Evelyn Lear. Roles incl: Wotan, Das Rheingold; Ford Falstaff; Escamillio; Carmen; Golaud, Pelléas el Mélisande; Amfortas Parisfal; Kurvenal, Tristan & Isolde. 16.

STICH-RANDALL, Teresa, b. W Hartford, Conn., USA. Operatic Soprano. Educ: Hartford Schl. of Music; Columbia Univ.; Univ. of Perugia, Italy. Career: noted for interpretations of Mozart roles; created role of Gertrude Stein in world Premiere of Virgil Thomson's Mother of us All, & title role in Otto Luening's Evangeline; tours in USA; apps. in major cities of Europe, Japan & S Am.; participant in Salzburg, Aix-en-Provence, Besançon, Florence, Perugia & other fests. Recip. title, Kammersängerin, Vienna, Austria. Address: Jonnycake Lane, New Hartford, CT, USA.

STILES, Frank, b. 2 Apr. 1924, Chiswick, London, UK. Composer; Conductor; Violist. Educ: BSc, Imperial Coll.; BMus (Durham); LGSM; AGSM; Paris Conserv. m. Estelle Zitnitzky. Career: BBC & ITV. Comps. publs: String Quartets 1 & 2 (also recorded); Duo for Violin & Viola (also recorded); 2 Symphs.; Sev. works for String Orch.; 2 Concertos for Viola; Concerto for Violin; Concerto for Clarinet; Symphonia Concertante; Dramatic cantata, etc. Recordings: Quintet for wind, strings & harpsichord; Intradoes; Oboe Sonata. Contbr. to: The Musician; The Comp. Mbrships: CGGB; PRS; ISM; Song Writers Guild of GB; Musicians Union. Hons: City of London Prize for Comp., 1954. Mgmt: Priory Concertante of London, c/o John Stratton, Flat 3, 31 Parliament Hill, London NW3 2TA, UK. Address: Flat 11, 19 Hanson St., London W1P 7LN, UK. 3, 28, 30.

STILLFRIED, Eleonore Auersperg de, b. 22 Sept. 1919, Grafenstein, Grottau, Czechoslovakia. Violinist; Teacher. Educ: studied violin, HS for Music, Mozarteum, Salzburg. w. Profs. Georg Steiner & Christa Richter-Steiner, 1945-47; Lic. for Tchng. Music, Seminar fur Musik-erzieher, 1947; studied violin & viola, Viennese Acad. of Music w. Prof. Ernst Morawec, 1947-53. m. Wolfgang Graf von Stillfried. Debut: Soloist, Viennese Chamber Orch. under conds. Franz Litschauer & Heinrich Holreiser, 1948-53; Mbr., Nat. Orch. 'Sinfonica Nacional' of music at Conservatorio Nacional, 1953-58; var. recitals of viola-sonatas in concerts, broadcasting & TV; Mbr., Camarata Academica, Salzburg (viola) under cond. of Bernhard Paumgartner

& Géza Anda, 1958-63; Prof. for Violin & Viola, Volks-Musikschule, Salzburg, 1961-72. Mbr., Amateur Chamber Music Players. Recip., 2nd prize for violin, Eistedfodd in Llonglallen, 1948 & '49. Hobbies: Chamber Music, etc. Address: Correo Aereo, Duitama (Boyacà), Colombia.

STILMAN, Julia, b. 3 Feb. 1937, Buenos Aires, Argentina. Composer. Educ: Pvte. studies in Comp. w. Gilardo Gilaroli, Buenos Aires; MMus, Univ. of Md., USA, 1968; D Musical Arts, ibid., 1973; post-doct. studies, Yale Univ., 1974, 2 c. Career: Theory-Comp. Fac., Harvard Univ., Wash., DC; Artist in Residence, Org. of Am. States, 1978. Comps. incl: Chantatas No. 1-4 for soloists, chorus & orch., 1961, 1963, 1973, 1975; (recorded) Cuadrados y Angulos for Chmbr. ensemble, 1966; Rituals for chorus, soloist & orch. (commissioned by Nat. Endowment for Arts), Intensities (Etudes for Woodwind Quintet); Barcarola: Theodore Presser (filmed for NJ TV with NEA Grant); Etudes for String Quartet. Contbr. of paper on Dufay to Am. Musicol. Soc., 1975. Mbrships. incl: Am. Women Comps., Inc.; Am. Soc. Univ. Comps.; ASCAP; Phi Kappa Phi. Hons. incl; Berkshire Music Ctr., Tanglewood, 1975; Nat. Endowment for Arts Fellowship, 1974, 1976; ASCAP Award, 1978. Hobbies: Interrelationships in the Arts. Address: 301 Congressional Lane, Rockville, MD 20852, USA.

STILWELL, F Raymond, b. 30 Sept. 1932, Harrisburg, Pa., UASA. Violist; Instructor. Educ: BMus, Perf.'s Cert., Eastman Schl. of Music; MMus, doctl. cand., Ind. Univ. m. JoAnn, 1 s., 2 d. Career: Mbr., Rochester Phil., Marine Band Orch., on fac., Interlochen Arts Acad. Prin. Violist, Chgo. Little Symph., Peninsula Music Fest. Orch.; Tchng. Asst., Ind. Univ.; currently Prof.Prin. (1977-78), Violist, Cinn. Symph., of Viola, Cinn. Conserv. of Music. has recorded w. Rochester Phil. Eastman Rochester Symph., Marine Band Str. Ensemble, Cinn. Symph. Orch. Mbr., Viola Rsch. Soc. Hobbies: Chess; Stamps; Gardening. Address: 428 Eight Mile Rd., Cincinnati, OH 45230, USA.

STINGL, Anton, b. 25 Jan. 1908, Konstanz, W Germany. Guitarist; Composer; Professor. Lute player. Educ: Univ. Freiburg, maths., phys., 1933; Autodidact in music. m. Lotte Stingl, 2 d., 2 s. Debut: Freiburg, 1930. Career: Radio since 1931; Viola da gamba player, lute player Freiburg Chmbr. Trio for Ancient Music 1935-1942; Russian war prisoner 1942-1949; since 1970 tchr. Music Acad., Frieburg; 1951-1971; guitarist Orch. South West German Radio. comp. incl: Sonatine from nursery rhymes, op: 15a; Chmbr. music; Choir music. Recordings: Vivaldi, lute and mandolin concerto; Ukrainian, Yiddish & German songs. Mbrships: Jury mbr. Int, Guitar Contest ARD, München, 1976. Hons: Federal German Merit Cross, 1974. Hobbies: Botany; Mycology; Bryology; Ornithology; Wandering. Address: Hammerschmiedstr. 6, 7800, Freiburg Br., German Fed. Repub.

STINNETT, Stephanie Gayle, b. 4 Feb. 1954, Albuquerque, NM, USA. Professional Harpist, Organist & Pianist. Educ: BchM, Univ. of NM, 1976; MusEd Cert., 1977 Univ. of Calif. at Los Angeles; Immaculate Heart Coll., ibid. Career: Solo Harp Recitalist; harpist for dinner hour music; Ch. staff Harpist; special perfs. on TV; harpist w. symphn. orchs. Recording: How Great Thou Art (harp solos of relig. music). Mbrships: Am. Harp Soc.; Am. Assoc. of Univ. Women; AGO; Pi Beta Phi; Sigma Alpha Iota (Chaplain, 1975, Pres., 1976); Nat. Hon. Soc.; Coll. Nat. Hon. Socs. (Pres., Blue Key, 1975-76). Recip., sev. perf. scholarships. Hobbies: Ballroom Dancing; Photography; Ice Skating; Reading; Square Dancing. Address: 8104 Connecticut NE, Albuquerque, NM 87110, USA. 27.

STITH, Marice W, b. 29 June 1926, Johnstown, Ohio, USA. Music Educator; Musician (Trumpet). Educ: Studied Trumpet w. Wilbur Crist, Capital Univ., 1936-50; B Schl. Music, ibid.; MA; Ohio State Univ.; studied Trumpet w. Forest Stohl, ibid & Sidney Mear, Eastman Schl. of Music. m. Shirlee Stith, 2 s., 2 d. Career: Trumpet, Syracuse Symph. & Syracuse Symph. Brass Quintet, NY, 6 yrs.; Prof. of Music & Dir. of Bands, Cornell Univ.; Tchr. of Brass Instruments & Electronic Music Comp., ibid; Fndr. & Cond., Cornell Univ. Wind Ensemble; Min. of Music, St. Paul's United Meth. Ch., Ithaca; num. apps. as Trumpet Soloist, Guest Cond., Music Adjudicator. Comp: Band Transcription, Three Dance Episodes from On the Town (Bernstein). Recordings: 7 records of serious trumpet music; 22 records in Cornell Univ. Wind Ensemble series. Publ. Ed., E Div. Newsletter, Coll. Band Dirs. Nat. Assn. Contbr. to Music Educators Jrnl. etc. Mbr. num. profl. orgs. Hobbies: Water Skiing; Fishing; Travelling. Address: Music Dept., Cornell Univ., Ithaca, NY 14850, USA. 6.

STITT, Irene C, b. 30 Aug. 1925, Ramsgate, UK. Teacher of Piano, Violin & Viola; Author; Music Critic. Educ: RAM, London (dip. LRAM); Nat. Conserv. of Music, Paris, France; Acad. for Music & Performing Arts, Vienna, Austria. m. Carroll E Stitt, 1 s., 1 d. Career: Mng. Dir., Stitt Concert Artist; Concert Mgr.,

Germaine Pinault Int. Music Soic. Ltd.; Adjudicator, MENC & NYSSMA. Mbr., Japan Soc. Inc. Author, Japanese Ceramics of the Last 100 Years, 1974. Contbr. to newspapers as music critic. Hobby: Japanese ceramics. Address: 15 Marshall Ave., Floral Park, NY 11001, USA. 27, 29.

STOBART, James, b. 23 March 1938, Staffs., UK. Conductor. m. Judith Swan. Career: Cond., Artistic Dir., The Locke Brass Consort of London (formed 1963); Apps. w. The Locke Brass Consort of London, TV & concerts in Belgium, major tours of N Am., 1980; num. film, TV & radio apps., UK. Recordings: Contrasts in Brass, Volume 1 & 2; Jubilant Brass; Strauss, Complete Brass Music. Address: 21 Butler Ave., Harrow, Middx., UK.

STOCKER, Markus, b. 2 Apr. 1945, Basel, Switz. Violoncellist. Educ: Acad. of Music, Basel; Tchr.'s & Soloist's Dips. m. Mei-Lee Ong, 1 d. Career: Concerts throughout Europe & USA & Far East incl. Vietnam; French TV, Paris; German Radio, Berlin; Debuts in London, Paris, Vienna, Berlin, Lucerne, Salzburg & Menuhin Fests.; Prof., Conserv. of Wintherthr & Zürich; Has made sev. recordings. Mbr., Assn. of Swiss Musicians. Hons: 1st prize, Bloomington, Ind., USA, 1972; Grand Prix, Int. Maurice Marechal Cello Competition, Paris, 1972; Soloist's Prize, Assn. of Swiss Musicians, 1973. Hobbies: Sports; Reading. Mgmt: Konzertgellschaft, Zürich, Switz. Address: Friedenstrasse 21, 8400 Winterthur, Switz.

STOCKHAUSEN, Karlheinz, b. 22 Aug. 1928, Cologne, German Fed. Repub. Composer; Conductor; Lecturer; Professor. Educ: Cologne Univ. & State Conserv., 1947-51; permanent co-operator at studio for Electronic Music, W German Radio, Cologne, 1953-. Since 1958 annual concert tours throughout the wld.; Vis. Prof., Fndr. & Artistic Dir., Cologne Course for New Music; Dir., interpretation grp. for live electronic music, 1964-; Wld. Exhib. Osaka, 1970, performance of own works; over 60 comps., most recent Zodiac; 12 melodies of the star sings & Sirius, electronic music w. 4 soloists, both 1975. Recordings: Over 80 records of own works. Publs: 3 vols. Texte.

STÖCKIGT, Siegfried, b. 8 Dec. 1929, Legenfeld/Vogtland, Germany. Concert Pianist. Educ: Staatsexamen, Hochschule für Musick, Leipzig. m. Annemarie Forkel, 1 s. Career: Int. Concert Pianist, TV & radio apps.; Prof. of Piano, Hochschule für Musik Hanns Eisler, Berlin. Comps: Chmbr. music; Moderne Rhythmen für Klavier; Concerto ritmico, etc. Recordings: Piano music & Piano concertos. Publs: Modernes rhythmisches Klavierspiel, 1968. Mbrships: Mitglied des Komponisten-Verbandes der DDR; Chopin-Gesellschaft - Kulturbund der DDR. Hons. incl: Kuntspreis der DDR, 1966; Professor, 1968; Nationalpreis der DDR, 1974; Ehrennadel in Silber des Komponistenverbandes der DDR, 1974. Address: Uhlandallee 8/10, 1603 Eichwalde, German Dem. Republic.

STOCKMANN, Erich, b. 10 Mar. 1926, Stendal, Germany. Musicologist; Ethnomusicologist. Educ: studied musicol. & German philol., Univs. of Greifswald & Berlin, 1946-52; Dr phil, Univ. of Berlin, 1953. m. Doris Stockmann. Career: Asst., 1953, Ldr. of rsch. grp., 1958-, Acad. of Scis., Berlin; Lectr. in Ethnomusicol., Univ. of Berlin, 1957-. Author of Ed., many books inclng: Des Knaben Wunderhorn in den Weisen seiner Zeit, 1958; Handbuch der europäischen Volksmusikinstrumente, vol. I & following (co-ed.), 1967-; Studia instrumentorum musicae popularis, vol. I & following (ed.), 1969-; Contbr. to profl. publs. Mbr. profl. orgs. Address: Zellinger Weg 12, DDR-110 Berlin, German Dem. Repub.

STOCKMEIER, Wolfgang, b. 13 Dec. 1931, Essen, Germany. Professor; Composer; Organist. Educ: Dr. Phil., Univ. Cologne, 1957; Musikhochschule Cologne. m. Ingrid St., 3 c. Career: Recitals, 1941-; TV & Radio apps., 1952-. Comps: for organ, piano, choir, chmbr. music, orch. Recordings: Nearly all German radio stations; approx. 30 records. Publs. Musikalische Formprinzipien, 1967; Die Programm-Musik, 1970 (Engl. Ed., 1971). Contbr. to: Musica; Musica Sacra. Hobby: Lit. Address: Obere Heeg 4, 562 Velberg-Langenberg, German Fed. Repub.

STOEPPELMANN, Janet, b. 5 Dec. 1948, St. Louis, Mo., USA. Composer; Musician (Harpsichord, Electronic Keyboards). Educ: BA (major in music); MMus in Comp. & Theory; grad. work in comp. w. Jocy de Oliveira; studied electronic music w. Hilton Jones. Comps: (commissioned(Piece for Contemporary Dance; (publd.) 2 choral pieces; The Great Wall of China (theatre piece); piece for Soprano & Ensemble. Mbrships: Southeastern Comps.' League; Soc. for Ethnomusicol. Address: 920 NW 186th Dr., Miami, FL 33169, USA.

STOIANOV, Konstantin Kolev, b. 16 Aug. 1961, Sofia, Bulgaria. Violinist. Educ: Dip., Royal Conserv. of Antwerp, Belgium, 1974. Career: Concerts w. Royal Symph. Orch.,

Antwerp, Buchout Symph. Orch., Turnout Symph. Orch., & many others; Engagements to play in Germany, Holland, France, Austria. Youngest Mbr. & Protjégé, Fndn. Alex de Vries, Antwerp. Hons: 1st Prize, Royal Conserv. of Antwerp, 1974; Dr Aaron Mostowoy & F Werept-Browvers Award, Antwerp, 1974; Chosen for Master Class, Int. Concours for Young Violinists, Glasgow, UIK, 1975. Hobbies: Football; Swimming; Chess; Reading; Pets; Gardening. Address: Jaak Blockx str. 70, Morstel, Belgium.

STOKER, Richard, b. 8 Nov. 1938, Castleford, Yorks., UK. Composer; Professor of Composition. Educ: Huddersfield Schl. of Music; RAM; studied w. Lennox Berkeley, London & Nadia Boulanger, Paris; Mendelssohn Scholar, 1962; FRAM; ARAM; ARCM. m. Jacqueline Margaret Trelfer. Career: Frist music broadcast at age 15 on BBC Home Serv.; Many broadcasts, BBC & in USA, Canada, Germany, Holland, Italy; Perf. at many music fests. & clubs, concert halls, South Bank, Wigmore Hall, etc.; Prof. of Comp. RAM, 1963-. Comps. incl: (operas) Johnson Preserv'd (chamber 3 acts); Thérèse Raquin (3 acts); Ecce Homo, cantata; Sextet; 2 piano trios; Wind Quintet; Variations Passacaglia & Fugue for Strings; Partita; Three improvisations: A Little Organ Book; Variants; (for organ) Sonatas; Sonatinas; Three song cycles; Three str. quartets; chamber works; choral works, etc. Record: Improvisation for Guitar; String Quartets 1-3; Miniature String Trio. Publs: Words Without Music, poems, 1953-73; Outposts. Contbr. to Composer Mag.; Musical Times; Music in Educ., etc. Mbrships: CGGB; Exec. Comm., ibid., 1969-74, 1976-; PRS; Ed., Composers Mag., 1969-. Hons. incl: Coates Meml. Prize, 1961; Royal Amateur Orch. Soc. Prize, 1962; Dove Prize, RAM, 1962. Hobbies: Squash; Tennis. Address: 14 Palmers Ct., Palmers Rd., London N11, UK. 3.

STOKES, Eric, b. 14 July 1930, Haddon Heights, NJ, USA. Composer. Educ: BM, Lawrence Coll., Wis., 1952; MM, New England Conserv., 1956; PhD, Univ. of Minn., 1965. m. Cynthia Crain, 1 s., 1 d. Comps. incl: Horspfal (opera) 1969; Eldey Island, 1971; The Continental Harp & Band Report, 1974; The Jealous Cellist & Other Acts of Misconduct (opera), 1978; Inland Missing the Sea, 1976. Recordings: The Continental Harp & Band Report, 1977. Mbrships: ASCAP; ASUC; Minn. Comps. Forum. Hons: var. commissions; Nat. Endowment for the Arts grants, 1974, '75; Hon. DFA, Lawrence Univ., 1974. Hobbies incl: Canoeing; Ceramics. Address: 1611 W 32nd St., Minneapolis, MN 55408, USA.

STOKES, William James Nicks, b. 24 June 1940, Burlington, NC, USA. Organist; Choral Conductor; Church Musician; University Teacher of Organ. Educ: AB, St. Andrew's Presby. Coll.; BMus, Eastman Schl. of Music; SMM, Schl. of Sacred Music, Union Theol. Sem; Fellow-in-music, Wash. Cath.; AAGO, ch.M. Recordings: (as organist) The Joy of Christmas. Contbr. to: Richmond News-Ldr.; Performed Liturgy & Music. Hobbies: Swimming; Antiques. Address: 3312 Suffolk Rd., Richmond, VA 23227, USA. 4.

STOLARIK, Ivo, b. 17 Oct. 1923, Ostrava, Czechoslovakia. Dramaturgist. Educ: PhD, Philos. Fac. of the Univ. in Brno, 1952. m. Dagmar Slachtova, 1 s., 1 d. Career: Radio Sound Dir. in Ostrava, 1945-53; Cond. of the Radio Children's Choir, 1948-53; Musicol., Slezsky ustav CSAV Opava (Silesian Inst. of the Czech Acad. of Scis. in Opava), 1954-63; Art Dir. of the Janácek Philharmony Orch. in Ostrava, 1963-73; Lectr. of the Musical Folkloristics of the Dept. of the Musical Hist., Univ. of Brno, 1954-58; Dramaturgist of the Janácek Philharmony Orch., Ostrava, 1973-75; Dramaturgist of Supraphon in Prague, 1975-; Lectr. of Musical Folklore Dept. of Music Hist., Charles Univ., prague, 1974-. Var. recordings cond. the Smoll Orch. of the Radio Ostrava & The Radio Children's Choir, Ostrava. Publs: We Sing With the Radio - 4, 1950; The J B Foerster's Putting the Poems by P Bezruc to music, 1956; Hrcava. Ethnographic Monography of the Silesian Village, 1958; The Correspondence L Janácek - J Loewenbach, 1958; Janácek in the Memories of his Countrymen, 1958; The Silesian Themes in J Kricka's Works, 1961; The List of the Complete Works of the Composer J Cernik, 1961; The Opera 'Nitteti' by J Myslivecek, 1963. Mbr. of profl. socs. Hons. incl: Prize of City of Ostrava, 1959; Prize of Young Artists, Prague, 1964; Hon. Dip. for educl. films, Cannes, 1964; Film & TV Prize, awarded by Govt. of Czech, 1965. Address: nam. Rijnove revoluce 3, 701 00 Ostrava 1, Czech.

STOLL, Dennis Gray, b. 1912, London, England. Conductor; Composer; Writer. Educ: MA, Christ's Coll., Cambridge; studied w. Sir Henry Wood & Sir Eugene Goosens. Career: Cond., Ballets de Monte Carlo, 1936; Deputy for Sir Thomas Beecham, LPO, 1940; Critic, Music Jrnl., NYC, 1963-; Music Dir., Int. Cultural Exchange, 1963-67; Freelance Cond., num. symphs., inclng. RPO, 1965-66 & Cairo

Symph., 1965; Artistic Dir., Ancient Egyptian Dance Grp. & Fndr., Nefer Ensemble, 1969. Comps. incl: Akhnaton & Nefertiti (opera); Piano Concerto, 1965; Persian Suite; Homage to Hafiz; Songs of Karnak (opera); Princess Margaret Suite; 3 Str. Quartets; Piano Quartet; Hans Andersen Suite; The Raising of Nefertiti (ballet, recorded); 2 Russian Dances; film scores; num. ballet suites. Publs: Music Festivals of the World; Music Festivals of Europe. Contbr. to: learned jrnls.; radio talks. Mbrships: Composers Guild; Engl.-speaking Union. Address: Heath Mansions, Putney Heath Lane, London SW15, UK.

STOLLBERG, Oskar, b. 18 Oct. 1903, Berlin, Germany. Cantor, Organist; Church Music Director; Lecturer; Choir Director; Organist; Pianist. Educ: Tchr. Trng. Coll.; Conservs. in Berlin, Würzburg & Nürnberg; Music Coll., Munich; State exams in music, 1931; musicol., Munich & Erlangen Univs.; Dr Phil, 1941. m. Irmgard Herold, 1 s., 2 d. Debut: Munich. Career: w. chs. in Munich, Gunzenhausen & Schwabach; Tchr. at City Educ. Peoples' Coll., Nürnberg, & Erlangen Music Inst.; pub. concerts & lectures in many cities in Germany also Austria & Italy. Comps. incl: works for piano, organ, choir; chmbr. music; cantatas; masses; etc. Publs: J G Herzog in Seinen Briefen an Max Herold (1865-1908); Einführung in den Tonsatz, 1978. Contbr. to books & jrnls. in field. Mbrships. incl: New Bach Soc.; Leipzig Soc. for Music Rsch. Recip. var. hons. Address: D – 8540 Schwabach, Südl. Ringstr. 1, German Fed. Repub.

STOLOW, Benjamin, b. 31 oct. 1929, Montreal, Canada. Violinist; Music Educator. Edduc: Teaching Dip., PQ; Conservatoire de Musique, PQ; Juilliard Schl. of Music, NYC, USA; Alumnus of Nat. Orchl. Assn., NYC. m. Bluma Silversmith, 1 s. Career: Violinist: Montreal Symph. Orch.; McGill Chmbr. Orch.; num. Radio, TV & Solo apps.; Prog. Dir., The South Shore String Assn.; Author of a Violin Teaching Method for Children in Grps. Mbr., Quebec Music Educators Assn. Hons: Sarah Fischer Concert Scholarship, 1952; Bourse de Perfectionnement, PQ, 1962. Hobbies: Tennis; Skiing; Chess. Address: 5907 Clanranald Ave., Montreal, PQ, Canada, H3X 2T2.

STOLOW, Meyer, b. 31 Oct. 1929, Montreal, Can. Musician; Violinist. Educ: Studied Music w. J Berljawsky, Montreal, 1945; RAM, UK, 1953-56. m. Gwyneth Margaret Jones, 1 s., 1 d. Career: Ldr., City of Birmingham Symph. Orch., 1960-63; Ldr., London Mozart Players, 1963-68; Ldr., Ulster Orch., 1968-71; Ldr., Royal Opera House, Covent Gaden, 1972-. Mbrships: Musicians Union; ISM. Hons: Dove Prize, RAM, 1956; FRAM, 1975. Hobby: Chess. Address: 86 Wise Lane, Mill Hill, London NW7, UK.

STOLTE, Siegfried, b. 2 Oct. 1925, Halberstadt, Germany. Conmposer; Music Director. Educ: Dip. Bassoon, Leipzig Coll. of Music, 1947; Comp. dip., 1952. m. Hanna Stolte, 2 s. Career: Asst. Lectr., Leipzig Coll. of Music, 1952-54; Dir., Schl. of Music, Altenburg, 1954-58; Lectr., Leipzig Coll. of Music, 1958-73; Prof., Institute of Fine Arts, Baghdad, Iraq, 1960-61; Dir., Schl. of Music, Waren-Müritz, 1973-. Comps: childern's songs; choir music; cantatas; Music for children, for recorders & str. orch.; Music for bassoon & piano; Neubrandenburger Konzert, for youth orch.; Mecklenbürger Tanzweisen, for wind orch.; Kammermusik für Kinder. Recordings: Sechs kleine Geschichten, for children's choir. Publs: Concertino for soprano recorder and str. orch. Mbrships: Comps. & Musicians' Union of German Dem. Repub. Hons: Kunstpreis, Free German youth, 1966; Kunstpreis, Free German Trade Unions, 1975; int. dip. comp. competition, Berlin, 1973. Hobby: Philately. Address: 206 Waren (Müritz), Kurt-Burger-Platz 20, German Dem. Repub.

STOLTZMAN, Richard Leslie, b. 12 July 1942, Omaha, Neb., USA. Clarinettist. Educ: BMus, Ohio State Univ.; MMus, Yale Univ. Debut: Metrop. Mus, NYC. m. Lucy Chapman Stoltzman, 1 s. Career: Recitals w. David Ensemble, London, UK, 1970-72; Guest Artist, Marlboro Music Fest., 10 yrs.; Tashi Chmbr. Ensemble w. Peter Serkin; Mozart Concert Debut, Carnegie Hall, 1976; Soloist w. Amadeus, Cleveland, & other str. quartets; NY Phil., 1979 w. James Leving; Aldeborough Fest. w. Amadeus, 1978. Comp. (recorded); Ed. of Schuberts Arpeggione Sonate. Recordings: A Gift of Music; Beethoven, Trio op. 11, & Quintet op. 18; Messiaen, Quatours pour le fin du temps (w. Tashi); Saint-Säens, Poulenc, Honegger Sonatas; Mozart & Brahms Clarinet Quintets; Stravinsky L'Historie Suite & 3 pieces. Mbr., Nat. Advsry. Bd., Young Audiences Inc. Hons: Avery Fisher Prize, 1977; Yale Univ. Order of Merit. Hobbies: Pastry Chef; Tennis. Mgmt: Frank Salomon Assocs., 201 W 54th St. 4C, NYC. Address: Calif. Inst. of Arts, 24700 McBean Pkway, Valencia, CA 91355, USA.

STONE, David Clifford, b. 25 Mar. 1936, Bristol, UK. Violinist; Conductor; Music Consultant; Adjudicator; University Lecturer. Educ: MA, King's Coll., Cambridge. Career: Ldr., Trio

Pro Musica; Mbr., Martin Quartet; Prin., Menuhin Fest. Orch.; Cond., Avon Youth Orch. & Hong Kong Youth Symph. Orch.; Music Consultant, Hong Kong Govt. & W Aust. Adjudicating Panel, Royal Overseas League Music Fest. & Boise Fndn. Scholarships. var. recordings esp. by Delius. Publs: Ed., Joseph Gibbs violin sonatas, 1974, '76; Spohr, Violin School, 1976. Mbrships: FRSA: ISME: ISM; Delius Soc. Hobby: Theol. Address: The Old Post Off., Leighterton, Tetbury, Glos., UK.

STONE, John, b. 16 Aug. 1903, Odessa, Russia (British subject). Violinist; Violist; Conductor. Educ: studied w. Leon Bergman, Arthur Willie Kaye. m. Sybil M T Thompson. Career: Mbr. Cinema & Theatre Orchs.; Musical Dir., Theatre Royal, Birmingham, 1941-56; Ldr., D'Oyly Carte Opera Orch., 1957-58; Musical Scriptwriter, Radio Birmingham, 1973, Hessischer Rundfunk, German Fed. Repub., 1972-76. Contbr. to: Hinrichsen's Musical Year-Books, 1945-46, 1947-48; Concise History of Music in Birmingham; Who's Who in Birmingham Music; The Times. Hobbies: Reading; Theatre; Films; Playing chmbr. music. Address: 42 Wheats Ave., Harbone, Birmingham B17 ORJ, UK. 3.

STONE, Kurt, b. 14 Nov. 1911, Hamburg, Germany. Music Editor; Musicologist; Writer; Lecturer. Educ: Univ. of Hamburg; Royal Danish Music Conserv. (Grand Exam.); pvte. post grad. study (chiefly Harpsichord & organ). m. Else Nielsen. Career: Var. tchng. positions inclng. 6 yrs. at the Dalcroze Schl. of Music, NY (theory & comp.); Freelance Music Ed. for var. Am. Music Publrs.; Hd. of Orch. & Band Publ. Dept. at G Schirmer, Inc., NY; Ed. in Chief, Associated Music Publsrs., Inc., NY, 1956-65; Dir. of Publs. at Alexander Broude, Inc., NY, 1965-68; currently Dir. of Publs. at Joseph Boonin, Inc., NJ, Cons. Ed. for Music at Charles Scribner's Sons, NY; Dir. of the Index of New Musical Notation at the Music Lib. at Lincoln Ctr., NY. Has edited a large number of musical publs. & books on musical subjects. Contbr. to profl. jrnls. Mbrships: incl: ASCAP; Am. Musicol. Soc.; Chmn., Comm. on Adv. Notation Music Lib. Assn; Mbr. of Exec. Committee of Am. Soc. of Univ. Comps. Hon: Guggenheim Fellowship, 1975-76; ASCAP Standard Awards, 1976/77/78, Dist. Achievement in Educl. Jrnlsm., 1976. Hobbies: Travel; The Arts; Good Food. Address: 922 Madison Ave., NY, NY 10021, USA.

STONE, Robin Domnic Alexander, b. Hoddesdon, Herts., UK. Pianist; Composer; Conductor. Educ: FLCM; LLCM (TD). Debut: Wigmore Hall, London. Career: Prof. & Examiner, LCM; Concert Tour of Am., 1976. Recordings: Records for Adelina de Lara Recording Trust. Contbr. to var. jrnls. Mbrships: Fellow, Royal Soc. of Arts; ISM. Hobbies: Cine-photography; Flying; Collecting Coins & Old Items of Interest. Address: Athinai, 27 Heath Dr., Gidea Park, Essex, UK. 3, 28.

STONE, William, b. 6 May 1915, Columbus, Ohio, USA. Violinist. Educ: student of Paul Sladek & Georges Enesco. m. Louise Wingold Stone. Debut: Pittsburgh, Pa. Career: Mbr., Pitts. Symph. Orch., 1937-42; CBS Symph. Orch., 1945-; CBS Str. Quartet, 1954-57; Kroll Str. Quartet, 1960-71; Phoenix Quartet, 1972-; Chautauqua Symph. Orch., 1972-; served w. USNR, 1942-45 (Mbr., Navy Band Str. Quartet); Solo recitals, Quartet; Phoenix Quartet - works of Berwald - 3 Quartets. Hobbies: Reading; Walking; Playing Str. Quartets w. friends. Address: 65-19 182 St., Flushing, NY 11365, USA. 2.

STORJOHANN, Helmut, b. 8 Apr. 1920, Hamburg, Germany. Artists & Repertoire Manager & Producer Classic. Educ: Dr Phil (musicol & philos.), Univ. of Hamburg, 1953; studied piano, harpsichord, conducting, comp. m. Gisela Schunk-Storjohann. Debut: as cond., Collegium Musicum, Univ. of Hamburg, 1948. Career: Perm. Cond., Collegium Musicum, Hamburg Univ., 1948-53; A & R Mgr. Pop & Classic & Prod. Classic, Philips, Hamburg, 1955-63; Dir. of Clasical Artist Dept. & Prod., EMI Electrola, Cologne. Recordings: many operas, operetas, oratorios, orchl. works, chmbr. works, lieder, mainly by German comps. Mbrships: Counsellor, German Musicarchive German Lib.; Kuratoium der Deutschen Stifung Musikleben; Bd., Deutsche Phonoakademie. Recip. many recording awards. Hobbies: Football; Travel. Address: Birkenallee 1, 5000 Cologne 40, German Fed. Repub.

STORTI, Mauro, b. 23 Jan. 1937, Modena, Italy. Teacher; Classical Guitar Soloist. Educ: Conserv. Milan. Debut: As soloist, Milan, 1964. Career: Tchr., Scuola Musicale, Milan, 1964; Currently, State Conserv., Piacenza; Num. apps. as soloist & w. chmbr. orchs., France, Austria, Belgium, Yugoslavia, Malta, Lybia, Tunisia, Turkey, Hungary & Czech.; Radio apps., Italy & Switz. Recordings: 2 LPs (Bentler & Podium). Didactic Publs. incl: Il Dominio delle Corde. Contbr. to profl. jrnls. Mbrships: Italian Soc. Authors & Publrs.; Advsr., Italian Guitar Assn.; Juries, var. guitar contests. Address: Via Martiri Triestini 7, 20148, Milan, Italy.

STØRUP, Carl, b. 26 Dec. 1908, Skallerup, Denmark. Conductor; Performer on Violin, Clarinet, Saxophone, Vibraphone, Guitar, Accordian & Trombone. Educ: studied w. organists Andersen & Peter Möller, Hjorring, Denmakr. div., 3 c. Debut: Aalborg, 1949. Career: apps. on Danish TV & radio; TV broadcasts, France & Can.; Cond.,orch. of Vin & Olgood, Copenhagen. Recordings: approx. 30. Mbrships: Danish Assn. of Conds.; Danish Soc. of Musicians; KODA. Recip., Hon. Freeman, Tonsberg, Norway. Address: Lilletoften 59, DK-2740 Skovlunde, Denmark.

STOTT, Kathryn Linda, b. 10 Dec. 1958, Nelson, Lancs., UK. Concert Pianist. Educ: Yehudi Menuhin Schl.; RCM; ARCM. m. Michael Ardron. Debut: Purcell Room, 1978. Career: Perfs., Queen Elizabeth Hall, Wigmore Hall, Windsor & Gstaad Fests.; Piano recital for Thames TV; Recordings for Dutch, German & BBC radio. Hons: Martin Scholarship, 1976; Churchill Scholarship, 1979; Croydon Symph. Award; Chappell Medal; Royal Amateur Orchl. Soc. Silver Medal, 1977. Hobbies: Films; Horse riding. Mgmt: De Koos Concert Mgmt. Address: 15E Fitzjohns Ave., London NW3, UK.

STOUGHTON, Bonita Adele, b. 14 July 1949, Xenia, OH, USA. Violinist. Educ: BM & BME, Univ. of Cincinnati Coll.-Conserv. of Music, 1972. m. Michael Gordon Stoughton. Career: Dayton Jr. Phil., 1964-67; Dayton Phil. Orch., 1972-74; NC Symph., 1974-; var. solo chmbr. recitals at art insts., colls. & chs. Mbrships: Recording Sec. & Warden, Mu Phi Epsilon. Hobbies: Cycling; Hiking; Embroidery. Address: 205 Milton Rd., Durham, NC 27705, USA.

STOUGHTON, Michael Gordon, b. 5 Dec. 1942, Wash., DC, USA. Cellist. Educ: Studied w. David Wells, Manhattan Schl. of Music; Schlrship. Student, Berkshire Music Fest., Tanglewood, Mass. m. Bonita A Partlow. Career: Prin. Cellist, Montgomery Co. Youth Orch., Md. All State Orch. & Berkshire Music Fest., Tanglewood, Mass.; Cellist, USAF Band & Symph. Orch., 4 yrs.; Extensive tours as soloist & mbr. of var. chmbr. grps.; Co-Prin. Cellist, Edmonton Symph. Orch., Alta., Can.; Perf. on num. radio & TV broadcasts, CBC; Tchr., Cello, Auto Mechanics & Basic Electronics, Putney Schl., Vt., USA, 3 yrs.; Mbr., Vt. Symph. & the Marlboro Fest.; Tchr., Cello, Keene State Coll., NH; Prin. Cellist, NC Symph. Orch. & Cellist, Chmbr. Players Str. Quartet. Hobbies: Car Mechanics; Rallaye Driving; Hi-Fi & Audio Enthusiast. Address: 205 Milton Rd., Durham, NC 27705, USA.

STOUT, Donald, b. 7 Dec. 1956, London, UK, Clarinettist. Educ: Artist Dip., Univ. of Toronto. Debut: Solo debut w. CBC Vancouver Orch., aged 18. Career: Hamilton Phil.; Can. Opera Co.; Soloist, Can. Chmbr. Orch.; Vic. Symph.; CBC Vancouver Chmbr. Orch.; currently 2nd Clarinet & E-flat Clarinet w. Vancouver Symph. Recording: film recording w. Elmer Bernstein & Maurice Jarre. Hons: First Prize, Vancouver Symph. Scholarship Competition, 1975. Address: 6976 Arbutus St., Vancouver, BC V6P 5S8, Can.

STOUT, Louis James, b. 11 Mar. 1924, Wellsville, NY, USa. Professional Horn Player; Professor of Horn. Educ: BMusEd, Ithaca Coll., NY; studies w. noted horn tchrs. m. Glennis Metz, 3 s. Career: Solo Horn w. var. orchs. inclng. Chgo., Flint, New Orleans, Ann Arbor & Jackson Symphs., Kansas City Phil., Radio City Music Hall & Sigmund Romberg Orchs.; has made many TV shows; currently Prof., Univ. of Mich. Comps: English Folk Song Suite (recorded & publd.); Beethoven Variations on a Theme from Don Giovanni arr. for 3 horns. Recorded w. Chgo. Symph., 1955-61. Author, Special Fingerings for the French Horn. Contbr. to books & jrnls. Mbrships: Life Mbr., Phi Mu Alpha & Pi Kappa Lambda; Int. Horn Soc. Hobbies: Sailing; Tennis; Leather craft; Woodworking. Address: 1736 Covington Dr., Ann Arbor, MI 48103, USA.

STRAESSER, Joep (Hoseph Willem Frederik), b. 11 Mar. 1934, Amsterdam, Netherlands. Composer; Teacher. Educ: Univ. of Amsterdam; Conserv. of Amsterdam. m. Stanny Verster. Career: Tchr. of comp. & musical theory, Conserv. of Utrecht. Comps. incl: (piano) Intersections 3, 1971; (Piiano & instruments) Alliages, 1971; Intersections V-2, 1975; (Quartets) Str. Quartet, 1971; Intersections V plus V-1, 1974, '76; (organ) Splendid Isolation, 1976-77; (choir & instruments) Missa, 1969; (orch.) Chorai Revisited, 1975. Recordings: Herfst der muziek, for mixed choir, 1964; 22 Pages for 3 male voices & instruments, 1965; Ramasasiri, for soprano & instruments, 1967; Intersections V-2, 1975; Canterbury Concerto for chmbr. orch. & piano, 1978; Intervals II, 1979. Contbr. to Mens en Melodie. Mbr. Bd., Union of Dutch Comps. Hons: Gaudeamus prize for Comp., 1965. Address: Hollandstraat 19, 3634 AS Loenersloot, Netherlands.

STRAHL, Dorothy Elizabeth, b. 3 Oct. 1942, Minot, ND, USA. Violinist; Violist; Teacher. Educ: BMus, 1964, MS, 1966, Juilliard Schl. of Music; Yale Univ.; Accademia Musicale Chigiana, Siena. Studies w. Nathan Milstein, Zürich. Career incls: Fac., New England Conserv. of Boston, Riverdale Schl. of Music, NYC, City & Country Schl., NYC; Asst. Concertmaster, Joffrey Ballet Orch.; Prin. Violist, Alvin Ailey Ballet Orch.; Mbr., NY Phil.; solo perfs. w. NH Music Fest. Orch.; recitals in eastern & midwestern US; radio & TV recitals, NYC; Voice of Am. broadcast. Recip., 1st Prize, Nat. Competition, Nat. Fedn. of Music Clubs, 1963. Address: 225 W 80th St., NY, NY 10024, USA.

STRAIT, Pauline Alice, b. 6 Aug. 1928, Australia, Oboe & English Horn Player. Educ: Assoc. Music, Aust. Music Examinations Bd., piano, 1946. m. Leslie Ivan Strait, 1 d. Career: Orchl. musician, playing 2nd, prin., assoc. prin. & English Horn w. most Aust. Orchs. incl. opera, ballet & chmbr. works; Tchr. of oboe, N.S.W. State Conserv. of Music. Comps: small comps. for oboe, written mainly for elementary exams. for the NSW State Conserv. of Music. Mbrships: Profl. Musicians Union; Fndr., Aust. Double Reed Soc. Hobbies: Painting; Sewing; Gardening. Address: 7 Fitzroy St., Killara, NSW 2071, Aust.

STRANGE, Richard Eugene, b. 14 Sept. 1928, Hutchinson, Kan., USA. Conductor; Woodwind Specialist. Educ: BMusEd, Wichita State Univ., Kan.; MMusEd., Univ.of Colo.; DMusA, Boston Univ. m. Marian L, 2 s. Career: Music Tchr., Clifton HS, Kan.; Asst. Dir. of Bands, Boston Univ.; Woodwind Instr., Tex. Coll. of Arts & Inds., Kingsville; Dir. of Bans, Univ. of W Va., Morgantown, Carnegie-Mellon Univ., Pitts., Pa. & (currently) Ariz. State Univ., Tempe, Ariz.; Orch. Cond., Carnegie Civic Symph. & Butler (Pa.) Co. Symph. Orch. Cond., Tempe Symph. Orch.; Guest Cond., Nat. Music camp., Interlochen, Mich. Recordings: as Cond., Carnegie-Mellon Univ. Symph. Band, music by Leonardo Balada & Joseph Wagner; As Cond. of Ariz. State Univ. Symph. Band, Fight Songs of the West. Contbr. to: Band Music Reviewer, The Schl. Musician Dir. & Tchr. Mag. Mbr., profl. orgs. Hons: Incl. Carnegie Mellon Univ. Music Alumni Award, 1967. Hobbies: Photography; Sailing; Skindiving; Travel. Address: Dir. of Bands, Dept. of Music, Ariz. State Univ., Tempe, AZ 85281, USA. 9, 29.

STRASFOGEL, Ian, b. 5 Apr. 1940, NYC, USA. Opera Producer & Director. Educ: AB, Harvard Coll. m. Judith Norell. Career: Opera Prod: NYC Opera; Salome, Il Ritormo, etc.; Opera Soc. of Wash., DC (Kennedy Ctr.): Mahagonny, etc.; Tanglewood Festival: L'Incoronazione di Poppea, num. music theatre pieces; Netherlands Opera; Satyricon (World Premiere); Chmn., Opera Dept., New England Conserv., Boston, 1968-72; Dir., Opera Soc. of Wash., 1972-75; Artistic Advsr., Phila. Lyric Opera, 1973-74; Dir., Music Theatre Project at Brooklyn Acad. of Music, NYC, 1976-. Publs: Ed. Transl., BA-TA-CLAN by Jacques Offenbach, 1971. Contbr. to Opera News Mag. Mbr. Phi Beta Kappa. Mgmt: Matthew Epstein, Columbia Artists Mgmt. Inc., NYC. Address: 915 West End Ave., New York, NY 10025, USA.

STRAUS, Ivan, b. 13 Feb. 1937, Teplice, Czech. Violinist; Teacher. Educ: State Conserv., Prague, 6 yrs.; Acad. of Music, Prague, 6 yrs.; Moscow Conserv., 2 yrs.; studied w. N Kubat, J Pekelsky & G Barinova. m. Eva Strausova, 1 d. Career: Mbr.; Lantern Magic, Chamber Harmony, Czech Trio & Duo B Martinu; Tchr., Acad. of Music, Prague, State Conserv., Pardubice. Recordings: Berg violin concerto & works by Fiser, Slavicky, Klusak, Matej, Barta. Contbr. to Hudebni rozhledy. Mbrships: Union of Czech Comps. & Concert Artists; Japanese Str. Tchrs. Soc. Hons: Competitions in Paris, 1959, Moscow, 1962, Prague, 1964, Montreal, 1966; Grand Prix Charles Cross, 1965; Critics' Prize, Prague, 1965. Hobbies: Cooking; Architecture; Painting. Mgmt: Pragokoncert, Prague. Address: Zborovská 68, Prague 5, Czech.

STRAUSS, Melvin, b. Newark, NJ, USA. Conductor; Pianist. Educ: BA, Rutgers Univ.; MA, NY Univ. Career incls: Music Dir., Turnau Opera Players & Oratorio Soc. of NJ; Assoc. Cond., Cantata Singers, Inc., NYC; Asst. Cond., NJ Symph. Orch.; Cond., Fromm Players, Berkshire Music Ctr.; Tchr., New Schl. of Music, Phila; Assoc. Prof., Univ. of Pa.; Cond., Profl. Tng. Orch. of Phila, Univ. of Pa. Choral Soc., Univ. Orch. & Penn Contemp. Players; currently Assoc. Cond., Buffalo Phil. Orch. (1967-), Dir. of Buffalo Schola Cantorum & Assoc. Prof. of Music, SUNY, Buffalo; Guest Cond., Phil. Orch. of Bogota, Columbia, 1968, conducting Papal Reception ceremony for Pope Paul VI. Hons. incl: Koussevitzky Conducting Award, Boston Symph., 1964; Antek Conducting Prize, NJ Symph. Address: Buffalo Phil. Orch., Buffalo House, 26 Richmond Ave., Buffalo, NY 14222, USA.

STREATFEILD, Simon, b. 5 Oct. 1929, Windsor, UK. Conductor. Educ: Eton Coll.; RCM, London. m. Elizabeth Winship, 2 d. Career: Prin. Viola, Sadler's Wells Opera,

1953-55; Prin. Viola, LSO, 1956-65; Assoc. Cond., Vancouver Symph. Orch., Canada, 1972-77; Vis. Prof., Faculty of Music, Univ. of W Ontario, 1977-. Recordings: Telemann Viola Concerto (Oiseau Lyre). Mbrships: London; Kent Co. Cricket Club. Hobbies: Squash, Cricket; Ornithology. Address: Hurst-An-Clays East, Ship Street, East Grinstead, Sussex, UK.

STREETER, Thomas Wayne, b. 26 Apr. 1943, Kokomo, Ind., USA. Assistant Professor of Music; Musician (Trombone, Tuba, Baritone). Educ: BMusEd, Ind. Univ.; MMusEd, ibid; D Musical Arts, Cath. Univ. of Am. m. Christine Elizabeth Pfeiffer, 2 s., 1 d. Career: Bass Trombone w. USAF The Airmen of Note; Bass Trombone, Richmond Symph.; Bass Trombone & Personnel Dir., Bloomington-Normal Symph.; W. Touring orchs. of Henry Mancini & Nelson Riddle; has played w. Bands backing Andy Williams, Johnny Mathis, Petula Clark, Bob Hope & other major artists. Recording: Music for Bass Trombone; Thursday Night Dues; Contbr. to: Int. Trombone Assn. Jrnl. Mbrships: Int. Trombone Assn. (Past Treas.); Nat. Assn. Jazz Educators; Phi Mu Alpha (Chapt. Advsr.); Kappa Kappa Psi. Hons: Outstanding Educator of America, 1975. Hobbies: Gardening; Camping. Mgmt: Kendor Music. Address: 1711 Ebel Dr., Normal, IL 61761, USA.

STREETS, John, b. /7 Apr. 1928, Bristol, UK. Pianist, Director of Opera; Professor; Accompanist. Educ: FRAM; LRAM; ARCM; Accademia Chigiana, Siena. Debut: Bath, 1945. Career: Pianist, Gabrieli Ensemble; & Trio; Recitals w. int. artists inclng. Janet Baker, Paul Tortelier, Elizabeth Harwood; Num. TV, radio perfs.; Dir. of Opera, Prof., RAM. Sev. recordings. Contbr. to profl. jrnls. Hobbies: Reading; Travel; Cooking. Mgmt: Ibbs & Tillett. Address: 18 Marlborough Rd., Richmond, Surrey TW10 6JR, UK. 3.

STREICH, Rita, b. 18 Dec. 1926, Barnaul, USSR. (German Citizen). Opera & Concert Singer. Educ: study w. Erna Berger & Maria Ivogun. m. Dieter Berger, 1949, 1 s. Career: w. Berlin State Opera, 1st leading role Olympia in Tales of Hoffman, 1947; w. Stadtische Oper, Berlin, 1950-53, Vienna Staatsoper, 1953-; Perfs. at Festivals incl. Bayreuth, 1952-53; Salzburg, 1954-62, 1965-; Aix-en-Provence, 1955; Glyndebourne, 1958; Guest appearances & concert Evangelical Luth. Ch., Oak Park, Mich., 1971; Organist, 1st United Meth. Ch., Wayne, Mich., 1975-76; Fac. Mbr., NGPT. Comps: Lullaby; hymn arrs. Also Librettist. Mbrships. incl: MENSA; Pres., Beta Chapt., Delta Omicron, 1973-76; Reg. Dir., Intertel, 1974-76. Recip. var. hons. Address: 443 W Evelyn St., Hazel Park, MI 48030, USA.

STRELLING, Frank Denys, b. 9 Oct. 1926, Kingston-upon-Hull, UK. Teacher of Piano & Violin. Educ: AGSM. Career: apps. w. Royal Ballet & Opera & on BBC TV Monitor; on music staff, GSM Junior Exhibition scheme & ILEA. Comps: 2 Str. Quartets. Mbr. ISM. Hobbies: Photography; Theatre; Motoring; Reading. Address: 13 Kemble Drive, Bromley Common, Bromley, Kent, UK.

STREVENS, Patrick Keir, b. 8 June 1928, Swansea, Wales, UK. Hornist; Teacher of Bass instrumentalists; Music School Director. Educ: LRAM. m. Nancy Muriel Sweet, 1 s., 1 d. Career: LPO, 1948-53; Royal Shakespeare Theatre Ensemble, 1953 season; Royal Opera House, Covent Gdn., 1953-60; Philharmonia Orch., 1960-64; Kent Brass Specialist, 1964-71; Area Dir., Kent Music Schl., 1971-75; Dir., ibid., 1975-; Fndr., Kent Brass Quintet & Kent Wind Quintet; Ed., Kent friends of Music Bulletin, 1971-76; Cond., W Kent Youth Orch., 1971-. Contbr. to: Horn Call. Mbrships: Musicians Union; ISM; Int. Horn Soc. Hobbies: Sailing; Walking. Address: Esmond Cottage, Lidwells Lane, Goudhurst, Cranbrook, Kent TN17 1EJ, UK.

STRICKER, Rémy, b. 3 Jan. 1936, Mulhouse, France. Musicologist. Educ: Studied Piano w. Yvonne Lefébure; studied Hist. of Music, Musicol. & Musical Aesthetics, Conserv. de Paris. m. Henriette Canac, 1 s. Career: Author of Musical Progs., ORTF France-Musique, 1962-; Prof. of Musical Aesthetics, Conserv. Nat. Supérieur de Musique, Paris. Publs: La Musique Française du Romantisme à Nos Jours, 1966; Musique du Baroque, 1969; Le Lied et La Mélodie, 1974. Contbr. to Larousse, La Musica & Encyclopedia Universalis encys. Hons: 1st Prizes for Hist. of Music, Musicol. & Musical Aesthetics, Conserv. de Paris. Address: 29 rue La Fontaine, paris 75016, France.

STRIPP, Alan Alfred Martyn, b. 17 Oct. 1924, London, UK. Staff Tutor in Music; Conductor. Educ: Dulwich Coll.; Trinity Coll., Cambridge; MA, m. Mary Wadsworth. Career: Staff Tutor in Music, Cambridge Univ. Bd. of Extra-Mural Studies; Cond., Phoenix Orch. comps: Concerto for Flute & Strings; Concerto for Harmonica & Strings; Serenade for Strings. Hobbies: Countryside; Boats. Address: The Old Green, Linton, Cambs., UK.

STROE, Aurel, b. 5 May 1932, Bucharest, Rumania. Composer. Educ: MBA (comp.), Bucharest Music Conserv., 1956. m. Victoria Miescue, 1 d. Career: Perfs. (& first perfs.) at Fest: Royan, Darmstadt, Warsaw, Zagreb. W. Berlin, Bucharest; other perfs. at Copenhagen. W Berlin, Brno, Kassel, Budapest, Vienna; also var. Radio & TV appearances. Comps: Arcades, 1962; Concert Music for Piano, Percussion & Brass, 1964; Laudes I & II for Orch., 1966, '68; Canto I & II for Orch., 1967, '71; Two operas - 'Ca N'Aurapas le Prix Nobel', 1965-69 & 'Aristophane: La Paix', 1973; Musique Pour Oedipe a Colone, choir, brass & perc., 1963; Concerto for clarinet & orch., 1974-75. Var. electronic music. Recordings: Arcades; Concert Music for piano, perc. & brass; Musique Pour Oedipe a Colone, etc. Contbr. to profl. jrnls. Mbrships: Bd., Composers Union. Bucharest. Hons: Rumanian Acad. Prize for music, 1972, etc. Address: Str. Luigi Cazzavillan 35, Bucharest 12, Rumania.

STROHM, Reinhard, b. 4 Aug. 1942, Munich, Germany. Musicologist. Educ: PhD (Musicol.), Tech. Univ. of Berlin, 1971. Career: Ed., Richard Wagner Gesamtausgabe, Verlag B Schott's Söhne Mainz, Munich, 1970; Lectr., Music Fac., King's Coll., Univ. of London, UK, 1975. Publs: Ed., Richard Wagner, Rienzi, 1974-, & Tannhauser, 1977-; Italienische Opernarien des Fruhen Settecento, 1976. Contbr. to: Musikforschung; Rivista Italiana di Musicologia; Analecta Musicologica. Mbrships: Gesellschaft fur Musikforschung; Soc. Italiana di Musicologia. Address: 25A, Menelik Rd., London NW2, UK.

STRØMBERG, Ole-Jergen, b. 24 Feb. 1946. Oslo, Norway. Clarinettist; Bass Clarinettist. Educ: studied w. Richard Kjelstrup & Heinrich Geuser. m. Anne-May Stromberg, 1 s., 1 d. Career: Soloist w. piano accomp. & w. orch., radio broadcasts; Mbr., Oslo Phil. Orch. & Oslo Wind-Quintet of 1972. Hobbies: Cross-country Skiing; Hiking. Address: Kong Ringsv. 39, 2010 Strommen, Norway.

STROMBERGS, Alfred, b. 19 Feb. 1922, Liepaja, Latvia. Conductor; Opera Coach. Educ: Latvian State Conserv. of Music, Riga; ARCT, Royal Conserv. of Music, Toronto, Canada; ARCCO, Royal Canadian Coll. of Organists; Studied w. L Bernstein & L Foss, Tanglewood, Mass., USA, 1953. m. Hilda, 1 d. Debut: Latvia, 1943. Career: Fndr. & Cond., Halifax Symph. Soc.; NS, Canada, 1951-55; Cond., Shakespearian Theatre, 1957-68; Cond., Canadian Opera Co., Toronto, 1969-71; Opera Coach & Cond., Univ. of Toronto, 1960-71, Univ. of Alta., 1971-. Contbr. to Opera Canada. Mbrships: Canadian Assn. of Univ. Music Schls.; Coll. Music Soc., USA. Recip., Canada Coun. Travel Grant for European Opera Studies, 1966. Address: Dept. of Music, Univ. of Alta., Edmonton, Alta., Canada.

STRONG, Joyce Elizabeth, b. 26 May 1933, Kan. City, Mo., USA. College Music Teacher, Piano. Educ: Univ. of Pittsburgh, Pa.; Eastman Schl. of Music, Univ. of Rochester, NY; BS, Juilliard Schl. of Music, 1957; MS, ibid., 1959. Debut: Pittsburgh, Pa., 1953. Career: Asst. Prof., Huntingdon Coll., 1961-63; Instructor, Univ. of Ala., 1963-67; Asst. Prof., Tex. Women's Univ., 1967-; num. Solo & Chmbr. Music Perfs.; Soloist w. var. Symphs. Mbrships. incl: Coll. Music Soc.; Music Tchrs. Nat. Assn.; Mu Phi Epsilon; Denton MTA; Past Pres., Tex. Women's Univ. Music Assn.; Past Pres., ibid. Hons: Pi Kappa Lambda, 1963; Pittsburgh Concert Soc. Award, 1963; Atlanta Symph. Soc. Award, 1946; Award of Merit, Nat. Fed. of Music Clubs, 1977. Address: 112 D Coronado Dr., Denton, TX 76201, USA.

STRONGHILI, Miranda, b. 7 May, 1929, Evia, Halkis, Greece. Pianist; Musicologist. Educ: BA in French & Philos.; Dip. of Engl. Studies, Am. Coll. (Pierce); Soloist Piano Dip. Nat. Conserv. of Athens, 1953; studied w. Yvonne Lefébure, Paris Conserv. (during 1968-69 under a French Govt. schlrship.). & w. Freddy Golbeck; Piano Dip. of Soloist & Prof., Cesar Franck Schl., Paris; 2nd Medal in Counterpoint, Municipal Superior Schl., Paris. Debut: Athens, Rotterdam. The Hague, Amsterdam, London, Wolverhampton, Lausanne, Cholet & Paris; has broadcast in Athens, Paris, Zurich & hilversum; gave series of lecture concerts, Athens YWCA, 1959; gave series of lectures on musical analysis of modern French composers, 1970-71. & 5 Lectures on musical analysis of Gabriel Fauré's work on occasion of 50th anniversary of his death, 1974, both at French Inst.of Athens Conferences & concerts in Greece, 1978-79. Publs: Little History of Music, 1959. Mbrships: Int. Musicol. Soc.; Greek Assn. of Contemp. Music; Alumnae of Am. Coll. (Pierce); Lyceum Club of Athens. Hobbies: Sports; Dancing; Travelling. Address: 44, Amalias Ave., Athens (119), Greece. 27, 29.

STROW-PICCOLO, Lynne, b. 17 June 1943, Waterbury, Conn., USA. Opera Singer. Educ: Univ. degree in Music Educ.; Voice studies w. Cantor Arthur Koret, Carlo Alfieri, Sara Sforni Corti. m. Tommasco A Piccolo. Debut: Teatro dei Rinnovati, Siena, Italy, 1975. Career: Apps. w. Italian & Am. Radio & TV; Leading roles in operas, major opera houses in Italy, USA, Germany, S Am. Hons: 1st Am. to win 1st Prize, Busserto Verdi Voices Contest, 1974; Absolute winner, Italian TV Opera Contest, 1974. Hobbies: Reading; Knitting; Astrology. Address: Via Sciesa 18, 20135 Milan, Italy.

STRUBLE, Larry J, b. 19 July, 1940, Caldwell, Kan. USA. Violinist; Conductor. Educ: BMusEd., Wichita State Univ., MA, Denver Univ., Colo.; Post Grad. studies, Eastman Schl. of Music & Denver Univ.; Studied Cond. w. Vladimir Golschmann. m. Dorothy Lund Struble, 2 d. Career: Violinist w. Symph. Orchs., Opera, Studios, Ballet, Broadway Musicals & Strolling; Cond., Symph. Orchs.; Studio & Classroom Tchr., inclng. Special Assignment, Cherry Creek Schls.; Adjudicator, Young Artists Contest. Recordings: Miscellaneous Studio Work; San Marco Strings. Author, Interrelated K 12 Music Guide, 1974. Mbrships: Colo. VP & Life Mbr., Am. String Tchrs. Assn.; Chapt. MENC; Kappa Delta Pi. Hons: Sr. Hon. 5, 1962; Nafzger Young Artist Finalist, 1963; Sigma Iota Scholarship, Kan. City, 1963. Hobbies: Folk Music; Photography; Camping & Hiking; Dog Training & Showing; Archery; Golf; Rifle Shooting (Hon. Life mbr., Nat. Assn.). Address: 6076 S Leyden, Englewood, CO 80110, USA.

STRUDWICK, Nancy, b. 13 Dec. 1921, Bromley, Kent, UK 'Cellist; Pianist; Double Bass Player; Singer. Educ: London Violoncello Schl.; RAM; LRAM; ARCM; ARAM. m. Hector B Jacks, MA. Career: Concert 'Cellist & Tchr.; Cond. & Adjudicator; Dir. of Music, Bedales Schl., 1959-63. Mbrships: ISM; London Violoncello Club. Hons: Ada Lewis Schlr., RAM, 1938. Hobbies: Watching Cricket; Gardens; Helping Charities (Mgr., Oxfam Shop). Address: Applegarth-Spotted Cow Lane, Buxted Uckfield, Sussex, UK. 3.

STRUNK, Steven, b. 7 Mar. 1943, Evansville, Ind., USA. Composer; Teacher; Pianist. Educ: Berklee Schl. Music, Boston, Mass., 1961-63; BMus, Boston Conserv. Music, 1965; MS, Juilliard Schl., NY, 1967; DMA, ibid., 1971; studied w. Luciano Berio, Vincent Persichetti & Rouben Gregorian. m. Barbara Burke, 2 c. Career: Assoc. Prof., Schl. Music, Cath. Univ. Am., Wash., DC, 1973-. Comps. incl: Quartet II Transformations: Permutations. Contbr. to Contemporary Music Newsletter. Mbr. profl. orgs. Hons. incl: Gretchaninoff Mem. Prizes, comps. Juilliard, 1966, '67, '70. Hobby: Chess. Address: 5603 Chevy Chase Parkway NW, Washington, DC 20015, USA.

STRYJA, Karol, b. 2 Feb. 1915, Cleszyn, Poland. Conductor. Educ: Dip., Conducting, Music High Schl., Katowice. m. 3 d. Debut: 1951. Career: Chief Cond. & Music Dir., Katowice Phil. Orch., 1953 ; Chief Cond., Odense Symph orch., Denmark, 1968-; Concert tours, Europe, Argentina; Radio, TV perfs. Recordings of music by Francaix, Bizet, Schumann, Verdi, Broodin, Rozyki. Hons: Officer Croix Polonia Restituta, 1970; Music Prize, Polish Ministerium of Culture, 1970; Music Prize, City of Katowice, 1973. Address: Gen. Zajaczka 6, Katowice, Poland.

STUART, James Fortier, b. 22 Dec. 1928, Baton Rouge, La., USa. Singer (Tenor); Professor of Voice. Educ: DMus Arts, Eastman Schl. of Music. Univ. of Rochester; BMus, La. State Univ.; MMus, ibid.; Perfs. Cert., Eastman Schl. of Music. Debut: La Traviata, New Orleans Opera Co., 1954. Career: Over 300 perfs. of leading tenor roles in Gilbert & Sullivan operas w. Martyn Green Co. & Am. Savoyards; Leading tenor w. orchs. in NY, Phila., Chgo., New Orleans & Atlanta; W. Boston Opera Co., New Orleans Opera & Atlanta Opera; TV apps. on Perry Como Show & Andy Williams Show; Prof. of Voice, Kent State Univ. Mbrships: Nat. Assn. of Tchrs. of Singing; Phi Mu Alpha Sinfonia. Hobbies: Duck Hunting; Water Skiing. Address: 1474 Stratford Dr., Kent, OH 44240, USA. 8.

STUCKENSCHMIDT, Hans Heinz, b. 1 Nov. 1901, Strasbourg, France. Music Critic; Composer. Educ: studied w. Arnold Schoenberg. m. Margot Lefèbre. Career incls: Free-lance Comp. until 1927; Music Critic, Bohemia, 1928-29, Prager Tagblatt, 1937-39, Der Neue Tag, 1939-41, Prague; Chief, New Music Dept., RIAS Radio, Berlin, 1946; Music Critic, Neue Zeitung, Berlin, 1947, Frankfurter Allgemeine Zeitung, Berlin, 1957-. Prof. of Music Hist., Tech. Univ., Berlin, 1949. Emeritus, ibid., 1967. Comps: Neue Musik (2 piano pieces), 1921. Publs. incl: Twentieth Century Music (in Engl.), 1969; Schönberg, 1974; num. musicol. works in German. Contbr. to: Music & Letters; Musical Quarterly; ldng. German musical reviews. Mbr., Acad. of Art, W Berlin. Hons. incl: Schönberg Medal, 1952; Salzburger Kritik-Preis, 1975. Address: Winkler Str. 22, W Berlin 33, German Fed. Repub.

STUCKY, Steven, b. 7 Nov. 1949, Hutchinson, Kansas, USA. Composer. Educ: BMus, Baylor Univ., 1971; MFA,

Cornell Univ., 1973; DMusA, Cornell Univ., 1978. m. Melissa Whitehead, 1 d. Career: Asst. Prof. of Music, Conserv. of Music, Lawrence Univ. Comps: Quartet for clarinet, viola, cello & piano; Symph. in Two Movements; Kenningar (Symph. No. 4); Movements; Movements III; Schneemusik (soprano & piano). Publs: Witold Lutoslawski and his Music. Contbr. to: Notes; Mozart-Jahrbuch; Musical Quarterly. Mbrships: Am. Soc. of Univ. Comps.; Am. Musicol. Soc.; Soc. for Music Theory; Am. Music Center; Am. Comps. Alliance. Hons: Victor Herbert-ASCAP Prize, 1974; Am. Soc. of Univ. Comps. Prize, 1975; Nat. Endowment for the Arts Comp. Fellowship-Grant, 1978. Hobby: Chess. Address: 409 S Walnut St., Appleton, WI 54911, USA.

STUDEBAKER, Julia Marlene, b. 11 Sept. 1951, Elmhurst, Ill., USA. Professional Musician (French Horn). Educ: Pvte. studies; Northwestern Univ., Evanston, Ill. 1 d. Debut: 1st horn, Berlin Radio Symph. orch., 1973. Career: 1st horn, Berlin Radio Symph. Orch., recordings of solo chmbr. pieces, Pleyel, Stamitz; 1st horn & soloist, Concertgebouw Orch., Amsterdam, 1974-. Hobby: Piano. Address: N Maesstr. 47, 1071 PP Amsterdam, The Netherlands.

STUDER, Pierre André, b. 27 Nov. 1941, La Chaux-de-Fonds, Switzerland. Orchestra Leader; Sound Engineer; Professor of Harmony & Musical Analysis; Artistic Director. Educ: Dips., Orchl. Dir., Musical Culture, Musical Admin. m. Elisabeth press, 1 d., 1 s. Career: Formed chmbr. orch. for concerts & recordings: Works w. Deller Consort, London; Tours for concerts & recordings, France, UK, Switzerland; Prof. of Harmony & Musical Analysis, Geneva Conserv. of Music. Recordings: About 200 records as sound engr. & producer. Mbrships: Fndn. Coun., Geneva Conserv. of Music; Assn. of Swiss Musicians. Recip. num. prizes for records. Hobbies incl: Collection of musical boxes. Address: 14 ave. Godefroy, 1208 Geneva, Switz.

STURMAN, Paul, b. 14 Oct. 1943, Hitchin, Herts., UK. Professor & Lecturer in Composition; Composer; Professional Organist. Educ: RAM, London; Royal Flemish Conserv., Antwerp, Belgium; GRSM (London); LRAM (Organ Perf.); ARCM. Career: As Comp., has been commissioned to write num. works inclng. 10th Anniversary Contemporay Concert of the LCM Junior Music Schl. Comps: Psalm 93, for chorus & orch.; Organ variations; Num. part-songs, My Song is In Sighing, Christ's Complaint; Song Cycle, The Seasons; Piano Pieces, etc. Publs: Creating Music, 1979. Contbr. to: Univ. Mag.; Composer. Mbrships: RAM Club. Hons: Stonex-hare Memorial Prize, 1962. Hobbies: Theatre; Travel; People. Address: 15 Hillside Rd., Thorpe St. Andrew, Norwich, Norfolk, UK.

STYLES, Dorothy Geneva, b. 13 Dec. 1922, Eldorado, Ark., USA. Teacher of Piano, Organ, Theory; Pianist; Organist; Choir Director; Composer. Educ: Grad., Detroit Inst. of Musical Arts, 1945; BMus, Univ. of Detroit, 1947; BS, Columbia Univ., 1954; MA, Eastern Mich. Univ., Ypsilanti, 1970; MA, Univ. of Mich., Ann Arbor, 1970. Career: perf. on WEXL-Radio at age 10; tchng. since age 12; former Organist/Pianist, Hazel Park Baptist Tabernacle; Choir Dir., St. Timothys Evangelical Luth. Ch., Oak Park, Mich., 1971; Organist, 1st United Meth. Ch., Wayne, Mich., 1975-76; Choir Dir., Bethel United Meth. Ch.; Choir Dir., Organist, Calvary United Meth. Ch.; Fac. Mbr., NGPT. Comps: Lullaby; Mrs Santa Claus Loves Mr. Santa Claus (recorded); Pledge of Allegiance to the Flag (recorded); Mother, Tell Me. Publs: Some Implications of the Harmonic Series, 1978. Mbrships. incl: MENSA; Pres., Beta Chapt., Delta Omicron, 1973-76; ASCAP; AGO; Nat. Assn. of Organ Tchrs.; Nat. Honor Soc. Recip., var. hons. Address: 443 W Evelyn St., Hazel Park, MI 48030, USA. 4, 5, 27.

STYLES, John Ernest Fredric, b. 17 Sept. 1913, Lutterworth, Leics, UK. Clerk in Holy Orders. Educ: BA, Bristol Univ., 1934, Oxford Univ., 1949; MA, Oxford Univ., 1954; PhD, James Martin Coll., Hong Kong, 1969; LRAM; ARCM; FLCM; LTCL; LGSM; FTSC; FNCM; FVCM; FRSA Scot; FASA; MChMus; DMus, Central Schl. of Rel., 1975; FPhS, 1975. Career: Chap. & Sacrist, Christ Ch. Cathedral, Oxford, 1947-54; Cond. & Chorus Master, Glossop Choral Soc., 1957-60; Precentor, St. Mary's Cathedral, Edinburgh, 1960-69; Hdmaster., St. Mary's Cathedral Choir Schl., ibid., 1969-73; Precentor, Holy Trinity Ch., Hull, 1973-78; Prin. Victoria Coll. of Music, 1977-; Examiner, ibid., 1975-; WEA Lectr. on Music, 1976-. Hobbies: Reading; Walking. Address: 45 Ash Grove, Beverly Rd., Hull HU5, ILT, UK. 3.

SUÁREZ COUTO, César-Antonio, b. 2 June 1952, Cienfuegos Las Villas, Cuba. Operatic Bel Canto Tenor & Concert Artist. Educ: Cinn. Conserv. of Music; Temple Univ. Coll. of Music; Brevard Music Centre, NC; pvte. study w. Ms. Gina Maretta; Grad., G Verdi Conserv., Milan, Italy; Juilliard Schl. m. Geraldine Elizabeth Novack Suárez, 3 d. Debut: Hartford, Conn.

in L'Elisir d'Amore. Career: Apps. in num. opera houses in N & S America & in Italy in all the leading Italian lyric roles, also in Der Rosenkavalier & Don Giovanni. Sev. TV & radio broadcasts. Recordings: Rossini's William Tell. Mbrships. incl: Am. Guild of Musical Artists. Hons: num. scholarships, awards & prizes in USA & Italy, incl. Premio G Verdi D'Oro, 1976. Hobbies: Sketching; Drawing; Painting; Gardening; Cooking; Metaphysics. Mgmt: Shaw Concerts Inc., 1995 Broadway, NY, NY 10023, USA. Address: 811 N W 92nd Ave., Pembroke Pines, FL 33024, USA.

SUART, Richard Martin, b. 5 Sept. 1951, Blackpool, UK. Baritone Singer. Educ: St. John's Coll., Cambridge; MA (Cantab.); RAM; Dip., RAM. Debut: Wigmore Hall, London, 1979. Career: apps. w. Engl. Music Theatre & Singers Co. Recordings: Elgar's Caractacus w. Royal Liverpool Phil. Orch.; Pergolesi's Miserere, Magdalen Coll., Oxford. Mbr., ISM. Hobbies: Drinking; Home Brewing; Cookery; Decorating. Mgmt: Ibbs & Tillett, London. Address: 7 Douglas Ctr., Quex Rd., London NW6 4PT, UK.

SUBOTNICK, Morton, b. 14 Apr. 1933, Los Angeles, Calif., USA. Composer. Educ: BA; MA in Comp., Mills Coll. m. Doreen G Nelson, 1 s., 1 d. Career incls: Co-fndr., San Fran. Tape Music Ctr.; Asst. Prof., Mills Coll.; Musical Dir., Lincoln Ctr. Repertory Theatre, NYC (1st season); now Assoc. Dean & Dir. Electronic Music, Calif. Inst. of Arts; annual US lecture & concert tours; contract w. Columbia Records. Compositions incl: Misfortune of the Immortals (chmbr. ensemble); (recorded) Silver Apples of the Moon; Sidewinder; Lamination; (mixed media comp.) 2: Game for 2 Players (& No Audience); orchl., solo & theatre works. Mbr., ASCAP. Hons. incl: Guggenheim Fellow, 1975. Mgmt: Sheldon Soffer Mgmt., 130 W 56 St., NYC. Address: 235 S Westgate Ave., Los Angeles, CA 90049, USA. 2, 9.

SUBRAMANIAM, Lakshminarayana, b. 23 July 1947, Madras, India. Violinist. Educ: MBBS, Madras Univ.; MFA, Calif. Inst. of the Arts. m. S Vijayashree. Debut: Ceylon, 1955. Career: Violin soloist, comp.; musical dir. of Navaratna; mbr., violin trio w. brothers; soloist in The Magic Fingers, educl. documentary film; apps. on TV & radio in SE Asia, Europe & USA; perfs. in Europe, USA, Can. SE Asia & Scandinavia; soloist w. Ravi Shankar & George Harrison tour of Europe, Can. & USA; i/c of S Indian Music Dept., Calif. Inst. of the Arts. Recordings: solos, w. violin trio & w. Ravi Shankar & George Harrison. Contbr. to var. mags. Mbrships: Madras Musical Assn.; Friends of Music, Madras. Hons. incl: Awarded title, Violin Chakravarthi, 1972; named Best Violinist of the yr. by Madras Social & Cultural Acad., 1977-78. Address: 650 S Detroit, No. 204, Los Angeles, CA 90036, USA. 23, 28, 29.

SUCHON, Eugen, b. 25 Sept. 1908, Pezinok, Slovakia. Composer; Teacher. Educ: studied piano & comp. w. Fric Kafenda at Musical Schl. & Acad., Bratislava; studiew w. Vitezslav Novák at Prague Cons. Career: Prof. of comp. & theory, Acad. of Music & Drama, Bratislava, 1941-48; Prof. & hd. of Musical Educ., Univ. of Pedagogy, Bratislava, 1948-60. Comps. include: The Whirlpool & Svätopluk (operas); Piano Quartet; Passacaglia for piano; Fantasy for violin & orch.; Metamorphoses for large orch.; Ad Astra, cycle for soprano & orch.; Symphonic Variations on BACH for organ, strng. orch. & percussion; other choral, orchl. chmbr. & instrumental works. Num. recordings of own comps. Hons: National Artist, 1958; triple award of State Prize. Address: c/o Music Information Ctr., Fucikova 29, 80100 Bratislava, Czech.

SUDBURY, Graham, b. 3 Dec. 1925, Ealing, London, UK. Director of Music; Orchestra Associate Director. Educ: Glasgow Univ.; MA, Magdalene Coll., Cambridge; Coll. St. Nicholas (RSCM); FRCO; Choir Trng. Dip. m. Janet (Nita) Paterson Hall, 2 d. Career: Mil. serv., RA, 1943-47; Dir. Music, St. Marty the Virgin, Primrose Hill, London, 1952-53; Wimborne Minster, Dorset, 1954-59; Fndr.-Cond., Wimborne Choral & Orchl. Soc.; Churston Ferrers Grammar Schl. & St. Mary Parish Church, St. Marychurch, S Devon, Cambridge, & Univ. Ch. Gt. Mary; Assoc. Dir., Cambridge Youth Orch. Recordings w. choir of Gt. St. Mary's Cambridge, & both Univ. & Parish organs, 1978. Mbr., ISM. Hon: John Brook Prize, choir trng., 1951. Address: 82 Greystoke Rd., Cambridge, UK.

SUESS, John G, b. 4 Aug. 1929, Chgo., Ill., USA. Educator. Educ: BS, 1951, MMus, 1957, Northwestern Univ., Evanston; Univ. of Chgo., 1951-52; PhD, Yale Univ., 1963. m. Betsy Davenport Suess, 1 s., 4 d. Career: Lectr.-Asst. Prof., Musicol., Ohio Univ., Athens; Asst. Prof.-Assoc. Prof., Music, Univ. of Wis.-Milwaukee, 1966-67; Prof. of Music & Chmn. of Music Dept., Case Western Reserve Univ., 1968-. Contbr. papers & articles to profl. meetings & publs. Mbrships: Am. & Int. Musicol. Socs.; Reg. Chmn., Eastern OH, Mid-W, Int. Repertory of Musical Iconography; Soc. for Aesthetics

& Art Criticism; Coll. Music Soc.; Soc. for Ethnomusicol. Hobbies: Swimming; Tennis; Back-packing. Address: 2224 Devonshire Rd., Cleveland Hts., OH 44106, USA.

SUGAR, Rezsö, b. 9 Oct. 1919, Budapest, Hungary. Professor of Composition. Educ: Comp., Music HS, Zoltan Kodaly, 1942. Debut: as Comp., Hungarian Radio, 1943. Career: Prof. of Comp. in sev. music schls., 1946-; Prof. of Comp., Music HS, Budapest, 1968-. Comps: Hunyadi, Stauromachia (oratorios); Komives Kelemen (cantata); The Daughter of the Sea (ballad); Divertimento; Suite, Concerto, Sinfonia, Partisa, Epilogues, etc. (orchl. works); 2 Str. Quartets; Frammenti Musicali (sextet); Sonata for violin & piano; Rhapsody for violoncello & piano, etc. Recording: Il Str. Quartet, Hunyadi. Mbr., Soc.· of Hungarian Musicians. Recip., Kossuth Prize, 1954. Address: XII Trenesenyi u 62, Budapest, Hungary.

SUITNER, Otmar, b. 16 May 1922, Innsbruck, Austria. Conductor; Musical Director. Educ: Mozarteum Hochschule für Musik, Salzburg. m. Marita Wilckens. Debut: Landestheater, Innsbruck, 1942. Career: Musical Director, Remscheid, Germany, 1952; Gen. Musical Dir., Palatinate Orch., 1957; Hd. of State Choir & State Opera, Dresden, 1960, Berlin, 1964. Recordings: Var. records on EMI, Teldec, Deutsche Grammaphon & Eterna labels. Hons: Professor, 1968; Hon. Cond., NHK Symph. Orch., Tokyo, Japan, 1973; Cmdr., Gregorian Order, 1973. Mgmt: Svensk Konsertdirektion, Göteborg, Sweden. Address: Seefeld/Tirol, Postfach 12, Austria.

SUITNER, Peter, b. 10 Aug. 1928, Ulm, Germany. Composer; Teacher. Educ: pvte. study, Innsbruck. m. Erika Pintgera. Debut: Cond., chmbr. orch., 1947. Career: Freelance comp.; tchr., Conserv., Innsbruck. Comps. incl: Klavierstücke; Chmbr. music; film music; Comps. for zither; num. other comps. Hons: Förderungspreis Stadt Innsbruck, 1968; Kompositionspreis Friedrich Kuhlau, 1970; Preis, Komp. Wettbewerv Südtiroler Sängerbund, 1978; Wurdigungspries, Land Tirol, 1978; Sonderpreis Sänderbund Telfs, 1979. Hobbies: Painting; Swimming; Walking. Address: Michael-Gaismayrstr. 4, 6020 Innsbruck, Austria.

SUK, Josef, b. 8 Aug. 1929, Prague, Czechoslovakia. Violinist. Educ: Prague Conserv. of Music. m. Marie Polakova. Debut: Prague, 1951. Career: Concerts, TV & Radio appearances all over world; Soloist, Czech Philharmonic Orch.; Mbr., Suk Trio. Many Recordings. Author, Transcriptions for Violin and Piano of Music, 1874-1935, Patron, Dvorak Soc., London, UK. Hons: Grand Prix de Disque, 1960, '66, '68 & '74; State Prize, 1964; Artist of Merit, 1970; Edison Prize, 1972; Wiener Flotenuhr, 1974. Mgmt: Pragokoncert. Address: Karlovo Namesti 5, Prague 2, Czechoslovakia.

SULC, Miroslav, b. 4 June 1927, Rychnov, Czechoslovakia. Musicologist. Educ: Studied music hist., Prague Univ. m., 1 child. Career: Currently at Min. of Culture, Prague. Publs: Oskar Nedbat, 1959; Jacques Offenbach, 1977. Contbr. to: Hudebni roshledy; Hudobny zivot. Address: Sporilov II 2719, Prague 4, Czech.

ŠULCOVA, Brigita, b. 10 Feb. 1937, Krzanowicze, Poland. Concert Singer. Educ: pvte. study w. Jan Tausinger. m. Jiri Sulc, 1 d. Debut: Prague, 1968. Career: w. Nat. Theatre, Prague, Czech.; roles incl: Anne, Rake's Progress (Stravinsky); Elsa, Lohengrin (Wagner); Catherine, Krutnava (Suchon); has made TV & radio broadcasts. Recordings incl: J Tausinger's Ave Maria, Gekritze am Himmel, Constelatione; L Kubik's Warrior's Wife, Lamentation; D Shostakovich's Seven Romances. Mbr., Czech. Composers' & Concert Artists' Union. Hons: Czech Critic's Prize, 1968; Prizes, Authors Contest, Unesco, Paris, 1973, '74. Address: Koulova 2, 160 00 Prague 6, Czechoslovakia.

SULIOTIS, Elena, b. 28 May 1943, Athens, Greece. Opera Singer (soprano). Educ: Buenos Aires & Milan. m. marcello Guerrini, 1970. Debut: in Cavalleria Rusticana, Teatro San Carlo, Naples, 1964. Career incl: Amelia in Un Vallo in Maschera, Trieste, 1965; Abigail in Nabucco, La Scala, Milan, 1966; Helen of Troy in Mefistofele, Chgo., 1966; Lady Macbeth, Covent Gdn., 1969; num. perfs. in N, S & Ctrl. Am. & European Capitals; Repertoire incl: Manon Lescaut; La Giaconda; Macbeth; Norma; Otello; Aida; Il Trovatore. Recordings incl: Norma; Cavalleria Rusticana; Nabucco; Anna Bolena & Macbeth on Decca label. Hons. incl: sev. prizes. Hobbies: Country life; Plants & Animals. Address: Villa il Poderino, Via Incontri 38, Florence, Italy.

SULLIVAN, Bartholomew Thomas, b. 7 Sept. 1902, Wishaw, Lanarks, UK. Music Teacher of Adjudicator; Musician (Euphonium). Educ: study of theory & harmony w. var. tchrs. m. Jean Crawford. Career: Music Tchr.; Brass Band Tchr. &

Adjudicator; Euphonium Soloist; Num. radio appearances, TV shows in UK & on the Continent. Recordings: over 100 recordings as Prin. Euphonium & Band Master w. GUS Footwear Band, inclng. 2 solos. Publs: 2 Solo Euphonium Books. Mbrships: Pres., Northants Brass Band Assn.; Chmn., Midland Conds. Assn.; VP, Nat. Conds. Assn. Hons: w. GUS Footwear Band, 5 times Brass Bands Champions, Albert Hall; World Champions, Kirkgrate, Holland; Insignia of Honour, for conspicuous services to brass bands, London, 1973. Hobbies: Motoring; Music. Address: 5 Reservoir Rd., Kettering, Northants., UK.

SULLIVAN, Betty Somers, b. 24 July 1919, Dublin, Ireland. Cellist; Viola da Gamba Player. Educ: studied cello w. Frank Cheatle, Clyde Twelvetrees (at Royal Irish Acad. of Music), & Anthony Pini (london); chmbr. music class, GSM; Dip., LRIAM. div., 1 d. Career: former Prin. Cellist, Radio Telefis Eireann (RTE) Symph. Orch.; in London worked in chmbr. orchs. & Musica Reservata & played continuo on BBC broadcasts; Prin. Cellist, New Irish Chmbr. Orch.; Mbr., Hesketh Piano Trio & Henry Purcell Consort (on viola da gamba); regular broadcasts for RTE; has taught cello in RIAM & Coll. of Music. Hobbies: Walking & climbing; Reading; Dressmaking; Gardening; Playing str. quartets w. friends. Address: 33 Butterfield Ave., Templeogue, Dublin 14, Ireland.

SULLIVAN, Gwynne, b. 6 Aug. 1937, Sutton, Surrey, UK. Singer (Tenor). Educ: MA, Univ. of Oxford. m. Isolde Dawe. debut: La Traviata, Sadlers Wells Opera, 1969. Career: Sadlers Wells Opera, 1968-74; Royal Opera Covent Garden, 1974-; Oratorio & Light Music Concerts. Recordings: Troilus & Cressida; Peter Grimes. Mbrships: Equity; Concert Aritsts Assn. Hons: Southern Area Winner, Cinzano Schlrship., 1968. Hobbies: Antiques; Horticulture. Mgmt: Basil Douglas. Address: 152 Wood End Lane, Northolt, Middx. UB5, 4JR, UK.

SULLIVAN, John Laurence, b. 22 June 1940, Sydney, NSW, Aust. Educ: Comp. Dip., Qld. Conservatorium of Music. m. Lucy Harrison, 2 s. Career: Music Supervisor (NSW), Aust. Broadcasting Commission. Comps: String Quartet No. 2; Tropic for Solo Flute; The Encircled Landscape. Mbrships: Comps. Guild of GB; Fellowship of Aust. Comps.; Aust. Musicol. Soc. Recip., GSM Comp. Prize, 1967. Hobbies: Bushwalking; Camping; Gardening. Address: 114 Fiddens Wharf Rd., Killara, NSW 2071, Australia.

SULYOK, Imre, b. 30 Mar. 1912, Budapest, Hungary. Composer; Organist; Musicologist. Educ: Grad., Acad of Music, Budapest; studied w. Zoltan Kodaly. m. Marta Bodolay, 4 c. Career: Ed., New Liszt Ed.; Organist, Cond., Luth. Ch., Budapest-Kelenfold. Compositions incl: Chaconne, 5 other orchl. works; Organ Dedication Cantata, 4 other works for choir & orch.; Str. Quartet, var. Chmbr. Music; Concerto, Sonata Preludes, var. other organ works; num. Study Materials, songs, arrs., Film & Stage Music. Publs: Critical Eds. of Liszt, Missa Solemnis, Missa Coronationalis. Missa Quatuor Vocum Ad Inaequales, Spetem Sacramenta, Via Crucis, Dante-Symphony, Mephisto Waltz Nos. 1 & 2; Gregor Werner, Te Deum, Symphonia Da Chiesa; Michael Haydn, Three Marches; Albrechtsberger, Six Fugues For Organ. Mbr. Assn. of Hungarian Musicians; Hungarian Liszt & Kodaly Assns. Recip. num. Hons. for Comps. Hobby: Travel. Address: R Moricz Zsigmond Korter, 1117 Budapest, Hungary.

SULZER, Balduin, b. 15 Mar. 1932m, Grossraming, Austria. Composer; Conductor; Teacher; Choir Trainer. Educ: Philosophical & Theological studies, Univ. Pont. Gregoriana, Rome; MA (hist.), Univ. of Vienna; Brucknerkonservatorium, Linz; Hochschule für Kirchenmusik, Rome; Musikhochschule, Vienna. Career: Prof., Musikgymanasium, Linz; Korrepetitor, Brucknerkonservatorium; Dir., Linzer Kammerorchesters. Comps: 1 symph.; 1 Passion (Passio Crucis); Cantatas; Chmbr. music; 6 instrumental concertos; Piano & organ music; Songs. Recordings: Wind Quintet, Violin Sonata No. 3; Toccata for Piano; Notizen (piano); Miniaturen (piano); Sonatine for Str. Orch.; Rondo for Str. Trio; Laudate Dominum (choir). Contbr. of music criticism to Neue Kronenzeitung. Mbrships: Österrichischen Komponistenbundes; Österreichischen Gesellschaft für zeitgenossische Musik. Hons: Förderungspreis des Landes Oberösterrich, 1970; Kulturpreis des Landes Oberösterreich, 1977. Hobby: Fishing. Address: A-4073 Wilhering 1, Austria.

SUMIKURA, Ichiro, b. 27 Oct. 1932, Tokyo, Japan. Professor & Lecturer of Musicology. Educ: Tokyo Nat. Univ. of Fine Arts & Music. m. Fusako Soh, 2 s., 1 d. Career: Music critic to sev. music mags., 1958-63; Commentator on var. music progs., radio & TV, 1960-; Prof. of Musicol., Tokyo Nat. Univ. of Fine Arts & Music; Lectr. of Musicol., Tokyo Univ.; Toho Gakuen Coll. of Music. Publs: J S Bach - Life & Work, 1963, '73; Translator of var. other books, mainly on Bach, by Lud-André Marcel, Max Weber, Karl Geiringer, Rosalyn Tureck

& Howard Ferguson; Ed., Homages to J S Bach, 1972. Contbr. to var. msuic encys., mags., etc. Mbrships: Sec.-Gen., Japanese Musicological Soc.; Int. Musicological Soc.; Neue Bach-Gesellschaft; Soc. Int. Antonio Vivaldi. Hobby: Mountaineering. Address: Ogikubo 3-14-18, Suginami-ku, Tokyo, Japan.

SUMSION, Herbert Whitton, b. 19 Jan. 1899, Gloucester, UK. Cathedral Organist (retired); Pianist; Composer; Adjudicator; Examiner. Educ: articled pupil to Sir Herbert Brewer, then organist of Glocucester Cathedral; FRCO; ARCM (solo piano); BMus (Dunelm). m. Alice Hartley Garlichs, 3 s. Career: Organist, Christ Ch., Lancaster Gate, London, 1922-26; Dir. of Music, Bishop Stortford Coll., 1924-26; Prof., Curtis Inst. of Music, Phila., USA, 1926-28; Organist, Gloucester Cathedral & Cond., Three Choirs Fest., 1928-67; Dir. of Music, Cheltenham Ladies Coll., 1935-68. Comps: ch. & organ music. sev. organ recordings. Mbrships: ISM; RCM Union. Hons: DMus (Cantuar), 1947; FRCM, 1961; CBE, 1961; FRSCM, 1963. Address: Hartley, Private Rd., Rodborough Common, Stroud, Glos. GL5 5BT, UK. 1.

SUNDBERG, Johan E F, b. 25 Mar. 1936, Stockholm, Sweden. Acoustics Researcher. Educ: Organist & Cantor Exam., Uppsala, 1957; PhD, 1966. m. Agneta Hagerman. Career: Lectr., Inst. of Musicol., Uppsala Univ., Rschr., Dept. of Speech Communication, KTH, Stockholm, in fields of musical instrument acoustics & sound perception. Comps: nursery tunes 'composed' by a generative music theory, Swedish Jrnl. of Musicol., 52, 1970. Publs: Mensurens betydelse i öppna labialpipor (The Significance of the Scaling in Open Flute Organ Pipes), 1966; Musikens ljudlära (Sonology of Music), 1973, 2nd Ed., 1978. Contbr. to: Jrnl. of the Acoustical Soc. of Am.; Folia Phoniatrica; Swedish Jrnl. of Musicol.; Acustica & other profl. jrnls.; proceedings of sci. congresses. Mbrships: Acoustical Socs. of Am. & Sweden (Pres., 1976); Stockholm Bach Choir (pres., 1968-77). Address: Dept. of Speech Communication, KTH, S-10044 Stockholm, Sweden.

SUNDERMAN, F(rederick) William, b. Altoona, Pa., USA. Physician. Educ: BS, ScD, Gettysburg Coll.; MD, MS, PhD, Univ. of Pa. m. Clara Louise Baily (dec.), 1 s. Career: Violin Soloist, Chautauqua Summer Series, Pa. String Tchrs. Assn., Gettysburg, Pa., Am. String Tchrs. Assn., W Chester, Pa., Trenton Tchrs. Coll. Orch., NJ, Int. String Conf., W Chester, Pa.; Ed., Annals of Clinical & Laboratory Science; Dir. of Educ., Assn. of Clinical Scientists; Prof. of Pathology, Hahnemann Medical Coll. & Hospital; Hon. Clinical Prof. of Medicine, Thomas Jefferson Univ. Medical Coll. Contbr. to: Bulletin of the Med. Lib. Assn.; Ann. Med. Hist.; Transactions Coll. of Physns. of Phila.; Am. Strin Tchr.; Gettysburg Coll. Bulletin. Mbrships: Am. String Tchrs. Assn.; Past Pres., Am. Soc. of Clin. Pathols., Assn. of Clin. Scis.; Fndng. Gov., Coll. of Am. Pathols.; Life Trustee, Am. Bd. of Pathol. Hobby: Photography. Address: 1833 Delancey Pl., Philadelphia, PA 19103, USA. 1, 2, 28, 29, 30.

SUNDMAN, Ulf Johan, b. 27 Feb. 1929, Stockholm, Sweden. Organist. Educ: Hogre organistexamen; hogre kantorsexamen; musiklararexamen; Dip. Organ Playing; Int. Acad. for Organ, Haarlem, Holland; Pvte. studies. m. Anna-Greta Sundman, 1 d. Career: Organ concerts in Sweden, Finland, Norway, Germany, Austria, DDR, Netherlands, Switz., Czechoslovakia & USSR; Int. Organ Days in Gottingen, W Germany, 1972; Organ Music Festival in Vilnius, USSR, 1974; Concerts on Radio Sweden; Cond., Diocese choir. Recordings: USSR (Melodia); Sweden (Proprius). Hons: P A Berg Medal, Kungl Musikhogskolan; Culture Prize of Town of Skelleftea, 1972 & Province of Vasterbotten, 1973. Address: Varvsgatan 18, S-93100 Skelleftea, Sweden.

SUNG, Alexander, b. 19 Mar. 1947, Tientsin, China. Musician (Piano & harpsichord). Educ: Piano Dip., Mozarteum, Salzburg, Austria, 1967; Harpsichord Dip., Hochschule für Musik und Darstellende Kunst, Vienna, 1971. m. Polly Lin Sung, 2 c. Debut: Carnegie Hall Recital Hall, NY. Career: Piano & Harpsichord Instructor, Va. C'wlth. Univ. & Richmond Univ., USA. Hons: Prize Winner, Int. Harpsichord Contest, Brugge, Belgium, 1971; Int. J S Bach Competition, Leipzig, Gemany, 1972. Mgmt: M Birchurin Concerts Corp., NYC, USA. Address: 10711 Arsenal Dr., Midlothian, VA 23113, USA.

SUNG-TAI, Kim (pen-name - Naksok), b. 9 Nov. 18907, Korea. Composer; Professor of Music; Conductor. Educ: Grad., Dept. of Music, 1939; studied in USA under auspices of the US State Dept., 1955-56. Career: Instructor, Posung Coll., 1941; Prof. Coll. of Music, Seoul Nat. Univ., 1946-; Dean, ibid. Compositions incl: Str. Quartet in C minor, 1939; Suite for Str. Quartet, 1944; Symph. Phantasie, 1944; art songs inclng. Sanyuhwa, 1946, River Paekma, 1954, Azalea, 1955; Festival March, 1958; In Rain & Wind (symph.), 1966; Lullaby & 4 other songs, 1966; Sajasu & other songs,

1967; Suite for Str. Orch., 1969; Sonata for Flute & Piano. Publs. incl: A Collection of Children's Songs, 1934; A Collection of Korean Art Songs, 1955; On Vocal Harmony, 1960; The Art of String & Wind Music, 1961. Mbrships: Participant, Music Seminar, Osaka Schl. of Music, Japan, 1970; Profs. Qualification Judgment Committee, Educ. Min., 1972. Hons: Best Film Music, Asian Film Fest., 1960; Cultural (Presidential) Order, 1962; Sosong Order w. Red Ribbon, 1963; Nat. Acad. of Arts Contribution Award, 1964; Hon. LittD, Yonsei Univ., 1969. Address: 1-8 Tongsung-dong, Chongno-gu, Seoul, Korea.

SUPPAN, Wolfgang, b. 5 Aug. 1933, Irdning, Styria, Austria. Musicologist; Clarinettist. Educ: Dr phil. Univ. of Graz, 1959; Habil., Univ. of Mainz, 1971. m. Elfriede Vass, 2 s. Career incls: Dir., Musicol. Dept., German Folksong Archives, Freiburg, 1963-74; Prof. of Musicol., Univ. of Mainz, 1971-74; Prof. of Musicol., Univ. of Mainz, 1971-74; Full Prof., Dir. of Inst. of Ethnomusicol., Univ. for Music & Theatre, Grax, & Prof. for Comp. Musicol., Philos. Dept., Univ. of Graz., 1974-. Publs., 7 books inclng; Lexikon des Blasmusikwesens, 1973, 2nd ed., 1976; Deutsches Liedleben zwischen Renaissance und Barock, 1973. Contbr. to jrnls., books, etc. Mbrships. incl; Pres., Soc. for Rsch. & Promotion of Brass & Wind Music, 1974-; Sec. Gen., Styrian Soc. for Comps., 1974-. Address: Institut für Musikethnologie, Musikhochschule Graz, Leonhardstr. 15, A-8010 Graz, Austria.

SUR, Donald, b. 1 Feb. 1935, Honolulu, USA. Composer; Associate Professor of Music. Educ: AB, Univ. Calif.; MFA, Princeton Univ.; PhD, Harvard Univ., Div., 1 s. Career: Assoc. Prof. Music, MIT; 'Composer's Forum', Nat. Pub. Radio; 'Composer's Show', Voice Am.; 'Artist Portraits', WGBH, Boston; 'Asian Exchange', WBUR, Boston; 'Musicultura', Dutch Radio, 1974. Comps: The Sleepwalker's Ballad; Red Dust; Piano Fragments; Book of Catenas; Intonation before Sotoba Komachi. Contbr. to: Harvard Dictionary Music, 2nd ed.; Essays in Ethnomusicology, Seoul, 1969. Mbrships: Advsr., Performing Arts Prog., Asia Doc.; Deleg., Int. Conf. New Music Notation, Ghent, Belgium, 1974. Hons: NY Bohemians Club Prize, 'Piano Fragments', 1969; Percussive Arts Soc. mention, 'Red Dust', 1974. Hobby: Korean Chess. Address: 7 Ashton Pl., Cambridge, MA 02138, USA.

SURDIN, Morris, b. 8 May 1914, Toronto, Can. Composer. Educ: Pupil of Louis Gesenway. m. Hazel, 1 s. Career: Radio, TV & Film; Ballet; Irish Guards Band; over 3000 scores for Yodir drama; stage musicals; music for stage dramas, etc. Comps: Serious, Books I & II; Prairie Boy; On Christmas Day; other songs. Recordings: Remarkable Rocket (Ballet); Concerts for Five Bass Accordion & Strings. Mbrships: CAPAC; Can. League of Comps. Hons: All music in the archives of Univ. of Calgary, Alberta, Can. Hobby: Music. Address: 2 Totteridge Rd., Islington, Ont. M9A 1Z1, Can.

SURGENOR, Ingrid, b. 5 May 1946, Belfast, N Ireland, UK. Piano Accompanist; Harpsichordist; Celeste Player. Educ: RAM; GRSM; LRAM; ARCM. m. Gerald Price, 1 d. Career: Piano Accomp., all major London concert halls; official Accomp. to Kathleen Ferrier Mem. Schlrships., 1971-; Mbr., Music Staff, Glyndebourne Fest. Opera, 1972-; Keyboard Player, BBC Welsh Symph. Orch. Mbr., Musicians Union. Hons. incl: Leonard Borwick Mem. Prize, RAM, 1969. Hobbies: Sewing; Eating Out. Address: 86 Waun Fach, Pentwyn, Cardiff CF2 7BD, UK.

SURIAN, Elvidio, b. 10 Jan. 1940, Lussingrande, Italy. Musicologist. Educ: BS; MA. m. Eugenia Venturi, 1 d. Publs: A Checklist of Writings on 18th-Century French & Italian Opera, 1970. Contbr. to: Jrnl. of the Am. Musicol. Soc.; Nuova Rivista Musicale Italian; Grove's Dict., 6th ed.; La Musica, new ed. Mbrships: Exec. Committee, Italian Musicol. Soc.; Am. Musicol. Soc. Coord., Italian Grp., RISM; Italian Grp., RILM. Hobby: Philately. Address: Via Gallucci 3, 61100 Pesaro, Italy. 30.

SURINACH, Carlos, b. 4 Mar. 1915, Barcelona, Spain. Composer & Conductor. Educ: studied w. Enrique Morera, Municipal Conserv., Barcelona, Spain; piano studies at the 'Oberklasse' of Robert Schumman Conserv. in Dusseldorf; studied cond. w. Eugen Papst at the Hochschule in Cologne; comp. under Max Trapp, Akademie der Kunste, Berlin, 1939-41. Career: Cond., Orquesta Filarmonica, Barcelona & Gran Teatro del Liceo Opera House, 1944; num. apps. as cond. of major European orchs., Paris, 1947-51; many commissions by US symph. orchs.; Vis. Prof. of Music Comp., Carnegie-Mellon Univ., 1966-67. Comps. incl: works for orchs., voice & orch., wind symph., chmbr. music, chorus, voice & piano, piano, ballets, discography; many musical scores. Hons. incl: Alexander von Humboldt fellowship (Berlin), 1940; Arnold Bax Soc's Medal of GB for non-c'wealth composers, 1966; Kt. Cmdr. of the Order of

Isabella I of Castile, 1972. Address: 440 E 59 St., NY, NY 10022, USA.

SUSSKIND, Peter, b. 8 Nov. 1944, London, UK. Conductor. Educ: BA, Cambridge Univ.; RCM; ARCM. Debut: London Mozart Players, Queen Elizabeth Hall, 1976. Career: Freelance Cond., BBC Orchs., etc. Mbrships: ISM. Hons: Clarinet Prize, RCM, 1967. Hobby: Reading. Address: 60 Grafton Tce., London NW5, UK.

SUSSMAN, David Ethan, b. NYC, USA. Player of Classical Guitar, Lute & Mandoline. Educ: BA, SUNY at Buffalo; guitar studies w. Leonid Bolotine; master classes w. Oscar Ghiglia & at Juilliard & Aspen Music Schls. Debut: Carnegie Recital Hall, NYC, 1973. Career: num. solo & chamber perfs., mostly in NE USA; soloist w. orchs., inclng. Buffalo Phil.; perfs. w. Ctr. of the Creative & Performing Arts, Univ. of Buffalo, inclng. tour of Europe, 1974; Perfs. w. Coll.; perfs. w. Berks. Music Ctr., Tanglewood, 1972, 1974-77; Instructor of Guitar, Tufts. Univ., Atlantic Union Coll. & Clark Univ. Mbrships: Phi Beta Kappa. Address: 26 Clifton St., Belmont, MA 02178, USA.

SUTCLIFFE, Sidney Clement, b. 6 Oct. 1918, Edinburgh, UK. Musician; Oboe; Oboe d'amore; Cor Anglais; Cello; Teacher & Coach; Conductor. Educ: George Watson's Coll. & RCM, study w. Leon Goosens, John Snowden. m. Marion Roberts, 3 d. Debut: w. Sadlers Wells Orch., 1938. Career: Mbr., LPO, Philharmonia Orch., BBC Symph.; Prof., RCM; Woodwind coach; Var. conducting engagements. Recordings: w. Philharmonia Orch., 1949-62; Solo, chmbr. music. Hons: Hon. ARCM. Hobbies: Music; Golf; Swimming; Photography. Address: 2 The Court, Cascade Ave., London N10 3PS, UK. 3.

SUTER, Louis-Marc, b. 2 Feb. 1928, Fribourg, Switz. Teacher of History & Music & History of Theory of Music. Educ: Cond. Dip.; Licence en pedagogie et psychologie; Licence en musicologie; Dr. Musicol. m. Monique Torche, 4 s. Career: Tchr. of Hist. of Music & Hist. of Theory of Music, Univ. of Berne & Conserv. of Lausanne. Comps. incl; Esquisse; Concerto for flute & orch.; Passacaille, etc. Contbr. to num. profl. publs. Mbrships: Assn. of Swiss Musicians; Swiss Musicol. Soc. Hobby: Gardening. Address: 1, route du Pré de l'Ile, CH-1752 Willars-sur-Glâne, Switz.

SUTERMEISTER, Heinrich, b. 12 Aug. 1910, Feuerthalen, Switzerland. Composer; Music Educator. Educ: Acad. of Music, Munich; Study of Philol., Paris & Munich. m. Verena-Maria Renker, 1948, 1 d. Career: Prof., HS for Music, Hanover, 1963-. Compositions incl: Operas - L'araignee noire; Romeo & Juliet; The Tempest; Botte Rouge; Niobe; Raskolnikoff, Seraphine, Titus Feuerfuchs (burlesque); Madame Bovary; The Canterville Ghost (TV opera); Other works incl: Missa da Requiem; Te Deum, 1975; 3 Piano Concertos; Cello Concerto; 2 Divertimenti; 8 Cantatas; 2 Concertos for Cello; La Croisade des Enfants & The Bottle Imp (for TV). Mbrship: Pres., Schweizerische Mechanlizenz; Bayerische Akademie der Schönen Kunste. Hons: Salzburg Opera Prize, 1965; Assn. of Swiss Composers Prize, 1967. Hobbies: Breeding Belgian shepherd dogs. Address: Vaux-sur-Morges, Lac de Geneva, Switzerland.

SUTHERLAND, Bruce, b. Fla., USA. Composer. Pianist. Educ: BMus, Univ. of Southern Calif.; MMus, ibid. Studied piano w. Ethel Legionska & Amparo Iturbi; comp. w. Halsey Stevens & Ellis Kohs. Debut: w. KFI Symph. Career: Dir., Bach Festivals for Calif. MTA; Harpsichord Soloist w. Telemann Trio; Ch. Organist; Piano Tchr.; Adjudicator, NGPT, Austin, Tex. Compositions: Allegro Fanfare; Quintet; Notturno; String Trio; piano & vocal music. Contbr. of music articles to Christian Sci. Monitor. Mbrships: Pi Kappa Lambda; Nat. Assn. Am. Comps. & Cond.; Am. Music Ctr., NY; Am. Music Schlrship. Assn., Cinn. Hons: 1 of winners, Int. Competition Louis Moreau Gottschalk, New Orleans, 1970; Stairway of the Stars Award, Santa Monica, 1973. Hobbies: Photography; Art; Theatre; Wilderness; Beaches. Address: 2336 Pier Ave., Santa Monica, CA, USA. 2, 28.

SUTHERLAND, Donald S, b. 27 May 1939, Kearney, NJ, USA. Organist; Conductor; Teacher. Educ: BMus, Syracuse Univ., 19612; MMus, ibid., 1963; studied organ w. Arthur Poister. m. Phyllis Bryn-Julson, 1 s., 1 d. Career: Organ fac., Peabody Conserv. of Music, Balt., Md.; Dir. of Music, Bradley Hills Presby. Ch., Bethesda, Md.; cond. & organ soloist at 5 Kennedy Ctr. Fests.; solo apps. w. sev. orchs.; solo recitals throughout USA; radio broadcasts & recodings for Nat. Public Radio, USA, BBC, London & ORF, Austria; TV apps. on CBS; workshops & recitals for regional conventions of AGO. Mbrships: Pi Kappa Lambda; Dean of DC chapt., AGO. Address: 11413 Georgetowne Dr., Potomac, MD 20854, USA.

SUTHERLAND, Donald S, b. 27 May 1939, Kearney, NJ, USA. Organist; Conductor; Teacher. Educ: BMus, Syracuse Univ.,

1961; MMus, ibid., 1963; studied organ w. Arthur Poister. m. Phyllis Bryn-Julson, 1 s., 1 d. Career: Organ fac., Peabody Conserv. of Music, Balt., Md.; Dir. of Music, Bradley Hills Presby. Ch., Bethesda, Md.; cond. & organ soloist at 5 Kennedy Ctr. Fests.; solo apps. w. sev. orchs.; solo recitals throughout USA; radio broadcasts & recordings for Nat. Public Radio, USA, BBC, London & ORF, Austria; TV apps. on CBS; workshops & recitals for regional conventions of AGO. Mbrships: Pi Kappa Lambda; Dean of DC chapt., AGO. Address: 11413 Georgetowne Dr., Potomac, MD 20854, USA.

SUTHERLAND, (Dame) Joan, b. 7 Nov. 1926, Sydney, NSW, Australia. Opera & Concert Singer (soprano). Educ. in Sydney. m. Richard Bonynge, 1954, 1 s. Debut: Dido in Purcell's Dido & Aeneas, Syeney, 1947. Career: w. Royal Opera Co., Covent Gdn., London, 1952-; Leading roles in opera at Vienna State Opera; La Scala, Milan; Teatro Fenice, Venice; Paris Opera; Glyndebourne; San Fran. & Chgo. Operas; Metropol. Opera, NY, etc.; Noted for leading roles in Handel's Samson & Donizetti's Lucia di Lammermoor; Num. concert & operatic tours w. husband (cond.), 1964-. Recip: CBE. Hobbies: Reading; Needlepoint. Mgmt: Ingpen & Williams, London W8. Address: c/o Royal Opera House, Covent Gdn., London WC2, UK.

SUTHERLAND, Iain, b. 18 May 1936, Glasgow, UK. Conductor. Educ: Perfs. Dip., violin, Royal Scottish Acad. of Music. m. Barbara Sutherland, 3 s. Career: many yrs. as Orchl. Violinist, LPO, Engl. Chmbr. Orch., etc.; Cond., BBC Scottish Radio Orch., 1966 72; now Free-lance Cond., making regular radio & TV broadcasts, fest. apps., regular guest apps. w. major orchs. in UK & Europe. Comp. of many light orchl. works, also songs, arrs. & transcriptions. Cond. or Musical Dir. for var. LPs. Mbrships: PRS; Mech. Copyright Protection Soc.; Coun., Songwriters Guild of GB; ISM; Nat. Music Coun. of GB; Life Mbr., Wig Pen Club; Radio Industries Club. Hobbies: Playing golf; Watching football; Current affairs; Reading hist. Address: c/o Concert Artists Representation Ltd., 17 Red Lion Square, London WC1, UK.

SUTHERLAND, Oriel, b. Norfolk, UK. Contralto/Mezzo Soprano Soloist. Educ: Diss Grammar Schl; studied w. Isobel Baillie & Meriel St. Clair, RCM. m. Dennis Sutherland, 1 d. Continental debut: recitals, Germany & Switz., 1968; London debut: Verdi's Requiem (cond., Barbirolli), Henry Wood Centenary Concert, Royal Albert Hall, London, in presence of The Queen, 1969. Career: recitals & oratorios in UK, Netherlands, Germany, Switz., France, S Am.; broadcasts for BBC & Continental stns. Recip. num. awards & prizes incl: Int. Competitions s'Hertogenbosch, 1968; Munich, 1969; Gulbenkian Fndn. Music Fellowship, 1970-73. Hobbies: Reading; Knitting & Crochet; Writing Poetry. Address: 5 Mornington Ave., London W14 8UJ, UK.

SUTHERLAND, Robert, b. Glasgow, Scotland, UK. Concert Pianist; Accompanist. Educ: Royal Scottish Acad. of Music; RCM; ARCM; Hochschule für Musik, Munich, Germany. Career: chmbr. music pianist; Accomp. to instrumentalists & vocalists; has wworked w. num. famous artists; world tour as Accomp. to maria Callas, 1973. Contbr. to: var. musical mags. Mbr., ISM. Recip., 1st Pl., Broadwood Competition, Glasgow, 1951. Hobbies: Art; Cooking. Mgmt: S A Gorlinsky. Address: 41 Cumberland Terrace, Regents Pk., London NW1, UK.

SUTHERN, Orrin Clayton II, b. 10 Nov. 1912, Renova, Pa., USA. Concert Organist; Conductor; Lecturer Black Music. Educ: BA, Adelbert Coll., Western Reserve Univ.; MA, Tchrs' Coll., Columbia Univ. m. Alice Wilson Suthern, 2 d. Debut: Organist, Trinity Cathedral, Cleveland, Ohio, 1929. Career: 1st Black Organ recitalist, Ohio Am. Guild of Organists; 1st Black Organist, CBS Radio Broadcasts w. Tuskegee Inst. Choir & Maj. Southern Symph., New Orleans, La. Recordings: Christmas at Lincoln, Lincoln Univ. Chorale, 1970. Publs. incl: The Case of the Negro Composer, 1965. Mbr. num. profl. orgs. inclng: Mu Phi Alpha Sinfonia. Hons. incl: Esso Fndn. Grant for Studies in Black Music, 1970. Hobby: Photography. Address: PO Box 145, Lincoln Univ., PA 19352, USA. 7, 11.

SUTT, Grzegorz, b. 17 Nov. 1938, Warsaw, Poland. Conductor. Educ: MA; Dips. in Cond. & special Theory, Higher Schl. of Music, Lodz, 1962. m. Barbara Zurowska-Sutt, 1 s. Debut: Lódź Phil., 1962. Career: Cond. w. Phil. Orchs. of Bydgoszcz, Olsztyn, Koszalin, Katowice, Baltic Phil. of Gdansk, & Grand Orch. of Polish Radio & TV; Int. Cond. Competition, Besançon, France, 1967; Music Teaching Fac., Higher Schl. of Music, Gdansk. Recording of concert w. Grand Orch. of Polish Radio & TV. Contbr. of reviews to daily papers. Mbr., Assn. of Polish Musicians. Hobbies: Photography; Films; Excursions. Address: ul. Dabrowszczaków 32/A m. 15, 80-364 Gdansk, Poland.

SUTTER, Milton Joseph Jr., b. 25 July 1940, Passaic, NJ, USA. Musicologist; Organist; Harpsichordist. Educ: BS, Juilliard Schl. of Music, 1963; MMus, Yale Univ., 1966; DMusA, Stanford Univ., 1969; Akademie Mozarteum, Salzburg; Conserv. di Musica S Cecilia, Rome; Syracuse Univ. Debut: NYC, 1960. Career: organ & harpsichord recitals, apps. w. orchs., USA, Italy, Austria; US participant, int. perf. competitions, German Fed. Repub., Switz., Czech.; Asst. Organist, Stanford Univ., 1968-69; currently Assoc. Prof. of music hist., Chmn., Dept. of Music hist., Temple Univ., Phila., Pa., 1975-78. Publs: Ed., Italian Organ Music of the 18th Century, 1970. Contbr. papers to profl. meetings & articles to var. musical publs. inclng. Grove's Dictionary. Mbrships: Am. & Int. Musicol. Socs.; Music Lib. Assn.; Int. Assn. Music Libs.; Coll. Music Soc.; Musicol. Advsry. Bd., European Liszt Centre, Eisenstadt, Austria. Recip. many scholarships & grants. Address: Coll. of Music, Temple Univ., Philadelphia, PA 19122, USA.

SUTTERER, Karen Jerelle, b. 12 Dec. 1949, Birmingham, Ala., USA. French Horn & 18th century Waldhorn player; Professor of Music. Educ: BMus cum laude, 1971, MMus magna cum laude, 1972, post-grad work, 1973, Fla. State Univ.; ARCM, 1974. m. Davey Spencer Thornton. Career: Freelance horn player, London, UK; full time w. orch. of Royal Ballet; Music tchr., London schls.; Waldhorn perf., Colonial Williamsburg Music Shoppe, Va., USA; Prin. Horn, Jacksonville Symph. Orch.; Prof. of horn, theory & music appreciation, Jacksonville Univ.; mbr., Jacksonville symph. woodwind & brass quintets. Mbrships: Pi Kappa Lambda; Phi Kappa Phi; Fla. Music Tchrs. Assn. Hons: Prizewinner, perf. contest, Fla. State Univ. (soloist w. Atlanta Symph. Orch.), 1973; Fulbright Scholar, 1973-74. Hobby: Long Distance Running. Address: 670 Seabrook Pkway., Jacksonville, FL 32211, USA. 27.

SUTTIE, Alan, b. 25 Feb. 1938, Kirkaldy, UK. Conductor. Educ: w. Nat. Youth Orch. of GB; ARCM; studied operatic conducting w. emphasis on Puccini, Italy. m. Ann Caroljne Dennis, 2 s., 2 d. Career: Orchestral Timpanist; Assoc. Cond., Scottish Nat. Orch., 1968-71; Freelance Cond., 1971-, app. w. Bournemouth Sinfonietta, Nat. Youth Orch. of GB (at Royal Fest. Hall), Welsh Nat. Opera Co., Royal Opera Hs., Covent Garden; Chelsea Opera Grp. & var. BBC Orchs.; formed Sinfonietta of Wales, chmbr. orch. giving concerts in Wales & W of Engl., 1973. Mbr: ISM. Hons: Gulgin Medal, 1956; Gulbenkian Schlship. to study conducting, 1965. Hobbies: Photog.; Squash; Tennis. Mgmt (opera only): Greenan & Brown, 19B Belsize Park, London NW3, UK. Address: 2 Berrington Cottages, Lympne, Hythe, Kent, UK. 3.

SUTTLE, Ernest Frank Arnold, b. 18 Oct. 1914, Reading, Berks., UK. HM Inspector of Schools. Educ: MA; BLitt; DMus, St. Edmund Hall, Oxford Univ.; FRCO; pupil of Dr. E T Cook, Southwark Cathedral. m. Judith Mary Gummer, 2 c. Career: Music Staff, Christ's Hosp., Horsham, 1940; WWII Serv., RAF, 1941-45; Dir. of Music, King's Schl., Canterbury, 1946-51; HM Inst. of Schls., 1951-. Comp. Wedding March. Contbr. to: Oxoniensia. Hons: Sawyer Prize, RCO, 1931; Nat. Competition winner w. Wedding March, 1961. Hobbies: Maths.; Walking. Address: The Barnards, Eldersfield, Gloucester GL 19 4PR, UK. 3.

SUTTON, Julia Sumberg, b. 20 July 1928, Toronto, Can. Musicologist; Dance Historian; Dance reconstructor (choreographer) of Renaissance & Early Baroque Dance. Educ: AB, Cornell Univ., 1949; MA, Colo. Coll., 1953; PhD, Eastman Schl. of Music, Univ. of Rochester, 1962. Career incls: Dance Dir., sev. Am. perfs.; Dir., The Elizabethan Dancers; Guest Lectr., Boston Conserv., Cornell Univ., York Univ., Kansas State Univ., Harvard Univ.; Workshops; Fndr., Court Dance Inst. of the Dance Notation Bureau; Vis. Prof., Colo. Coll. Summer Session & Hart Coll.; Currently Chmn., Music Hist. & Musicol. Dept. of New England Conserv. Publs: (led) Arbeau; Orchesography (1588) 1966; Contbr. to: The Musical Quarterly; Jrnl. of the Am. Musicol. Soc.; Jrnl. of the Lute Soc. of Am., etc. Mbrships: AMS; CMS; Phi Beta Kappa; Phi Kappa Phi. Hobby: Folk Dancing. Address: 22 Glenburnie Rd., Boston, MA 02131, USA.

SUZUKI, Hidetaro, b. 1 June 1937, Tokyo, Japan. Violinist; Conductor. Educ: Toho Schl. of Music, Tokyo; Dip., Curtis Inst. of Music, Phila. m. Zeyda Ruga, 3 c. Debut: Tokyo, 1951. Career: Concert tours as soloist, recitalist w. Ruga-Suzuki in USA, USSR, Cuba, France, Belgium, Can., Japan; Concertmaster, Quebec Symph. orch. (1963-78) & Indpls. Symph. Orch. (1978-); Prof. of violin, Conserv. of PQ (1963-79) & Butler Univ., Ind. (1979-); has conducted Quebec Symph. Orch., Canadian Broadcasting Corp. Orch., Tokyo Symph. Orch. & Sapporo Symph. Orch. Recordings: works by Beethoven, Suzuki, Franck & Ravel. Hons: Grand Prix, Japan Nat. Competition, 1951; 6th prize, Tchaikovsky Int. Competition, 1962; 10th prize, Queen Elisabeth Competition, 1963; Montreal Int. Competition, 2nd prize, 1966; Queen Elisabeth Int. Competition, 5th prize, 1967. Hobbies: Walking; Cycling; Being just lazy. Mgmt: Valmalete (W Europe); Musica-Tokyo (E Europe); Kikuchi (Japan). Address: 430 W 93rd St., Indpls., IN 46260, USA.

SVANBERG, Carsten, b. 6 Dec. 1945, Copenhagen, Denmark. Trombonist. Educ: Music Univ.; Pvte. studies w. P I Moller, Th. Graae Jorgensen (Danish Radio Orch.), Denis Wick (London), Ronald Barron (Boston). m. Lilli, 1 s. Debut: Solo perf., Tivoli Concert Hall, 1966. Career: Mbr., Danish Life Regiment Band, Royal Guards, The Royal Opera in Sweden, Danish Broadcasting Light Orch. & Royal Danish Orch., 1975-; Soloist, Denmark, Scandinavian & USA; Fac., Int. Trombone Assn. Recordings: as Mbr. of Copenhagen Brass Quintet; A Festival Recording, Elsinore. Mbrships: 2nd VP, Europe, Int. Trombone Assn.; Int. Gesellschaft zur erforschung der blassmusik. Hons: 2nd Prize, Scandinavian Competition for Brass, 1970; Amongst 5 Best Trombone Players in World, Int. Competition, Munich, 1974. Hobbies: Working in the house; Gardening; Travel. Address: Harespringet 3, DK-2400 Copenhagen, Denmark.

SVANESØE, Robert, b. 24 Aug. 1921, Copenhagen, Denmark. Trumpet Soloist; Conductor. Educ: Royal Danish Acad. of Music. m. Alice Svanesoe, 1 d. Career: Solo Trumpet & Vice-Cond., mil. brass band, Prinsens Livregiment, 1942-60; Dir. of Music, Den kongelige Livgarde, Copenhagen, 1961-73; TV & radio broadcasts as Trumpet Soloist & Cond.; ret'd., 1973. Comps. incl: Prinsesse Margrethe's Honnomarch (recorded by Den kongelige Livgardes Musikkorps on EMI). Mbr., Committee, Danish Conds. Soc.; Int. Military Music Soc., London. Recip., num. hons., inclng: King Frederik IX mem. Medal; Order of Kthood., Tunisian Repub.; Kt., Order of Merit, Repub. of Italy; Cross of Merit, German Fed. Repub.; Das Goldene Ehrenzeichen für Verdienste um die Republik Österreich. Address: Rosenvangsvej 47, DK 2670 Greve Strand, Denmark.

SVEINSSON, Atli Heimir, b. 21 Sept. 1938, Reykjavik, Iceland. Composer. Educ: Philos. Cand., Univ. of Iceland; Künstlerisce, Reifeprufung, Comp., Theory, Staatliche Hochschule für Musik, Cologne. Comps. incl: (recorded) Flute Concerto. Mbrships: Icelandic Comps. Assn. Hons: Nordic Music Prize, 1976. Address: Vesturberg 95, Reykjavik, Iceland.

SVERRISSON, Hjalmar, b. 29 Dec. 1950, Reykjavik, Iceland. Educ: Singing Schl., Reykjavik, 1 s. Debut: In "Prymskvida" (opera), Nat. Theatre of Iceland, 1974. Career: Choir, Nat. Theatre, 1974-; Singing Schl., Reykjavik, 1974-78; TV, radio & film apps.; Toured Can. & Wales. Recordings: Choir of Singing Schl., 1978; Silfurkorinn, 1978, '79. Hobbies: Films; Theatre; Playing Golf; Opera; Fishing. Address: Álmholt 17, Mosfellssveit, Iceland.

SVETLANOV, Eugeni Pyodorovich, b. 6 Sept. 1928, Moscow, USSR. Composer; Conductor. Educ: Gnesiny Music Educ. Inst.; Moscow Conserv. Career: Cond., Moscow Radio, 1953; Cond., Bolshoi Theatre, Moscow, 1954-62; Chief Cond., ibid., 1962-65; Cond., USSR State Symph. Orch., 1965-. Compositions incl: Symph.; Tone-Poems Festival, 1950; Daugava, 1953; Siberian Fantasy, 1953; Rhapsody, 1954; Home Fields (cantata), 1949; Concerto, 1951; 5 Sonatas; 5 Sonatinas; Preludes; approx. 50 romances & songs. Hon: People's Artist of RSFSR. Address: USSR State Symph. Orch., 31 Ulitsa Gorkogo, Moscow, USSR.

SVOBODA, Tomas, b. 6 Dec. 1939, Paris, France. Composer; Pianist; Percussionist; Conductor; Professor of Music. Educ: Conserv. of Music, Prague, 1954-62; Dips. in Percussion, Composition & Conducting; Acad. of Music, Prague, 1962-64; MMus, Univ. of Southern Calif., USA, 1969. Debut: w. FOK Prague Symph. orch., 1957. Career: Compositions perfd. by Radio Stns., Prague Symph. orch. & var. chmbr. orchs., Prague, -1964; Composer in USA; works performed by var. Orchs. & chmbr. grps., 1965-. Compositions incl. over 70 unpubld. works; Choral & Dance for Brass Quintet, 1967. Bagatelles, In a Forest, for piano, 1976. Mbrships: Nat. Assn. of Am. Conds. & Composers; Am. Music Ctr.; ASCAP; Musicians Mutual Assn. Hons: Helen S Anstead Award in Composition, 1967; 3rd Prize, Santa Barbara Comp., 1969. Hobbies: Chess; Photography; Meteorol. Address: 4320 SE Oak St., Portland, OR 97215, USA.

SVORC, Antonin, b. 12 Feb. 1934, Jaromer, Czech. Singer. Educ: Gymnasium, Prague; Conservatoire, Prague. Debut: Liberec, Theatre of F X Salda, Czechoslovakia. Career: Apps. incl: Nat. Theatre, Prague; State Opera, Berlin, German Democratic Repub. Recordings: Arias from Operas (Wagner, Verdi, etc.). Hons. incl: Grand Prize, Concours de Chant, Toulouse, 1958; Meritorious Artist Award, Prague, 1974. Address: 14700 Prague, 4 Podoli, na Klaudiance 13, Czech.

SWAIN, Freda Mary, b. 31 Oct. 1902, Southsea, UK. Composer; Pianist; Speaker; Teacher; Organiser. Educ: Tobias Matthay Piano Schl. & RCM; FRCM (1962). m. Arthur Alexander (dec.). Debut: Queen's Hall, London. Career: Prof. of piano, RCM, 1924-40; broadcasts in London, S Africa & Australia; works perf. in UK, Europe and the Commonwealth. Comps: orchl., choral & chamber works; Works for piano, strngs., woodwind, brass, organ; over 100 songs; anthems & hymns. Mbrships: PRS; CGGB; ISM. Hons: Author, Sullivan prize for Comp., 1921; Ellen Shaw Williams Prize for piano, 1921; Dir., NEMO concerts & Music Ctr. Hobbies: Reading; The English Countryside. Address: High Woods, Chinnor Hill, Chinnor, Oxon OX9 4BD, UK. 2, 3, 30.

SWAINSON, Anthony Robin, b. 7 Dec. 1947, Amersham, Bucks, UK. Tubaist. Educ: studies tuba w. Stuart Roebuck (Halle), Royal Manchester Coll. of Music; GRSM (Manchester); ARMCM (Perfs.); ARMCM (Tchrs.). m. Kathleen Surtees, 1 d. Debut: w. Halle Orch., Free Trade Hall, Manchester, 1968. Career: Tubaist w. BBC Scottish Symph. Orch., 1971-; Radio perf., BBC; Prof. of Tuba, RSAM. Mbr., BBC Club, Glasgow. Hobbies: Sport. Address: 191 Terregles Ave., Pollokshields, Glasgow G41 4RS, UK.

SWALIN, Benjamin F, b. 30 Mar. 1901, Minneapolis, Minn., USa. Musician (Violin & Viola); Conductor. Educ: BS, MA, Columbia Univ.; PhD, Univ. of Vienna; Dips., Inst. of Musical Art, NYC; Dip., Hochschule fur Musik, Vienna; DFA, Univ. NC. m. Maxine McMahon. Career: Broadcasts for TV w. NC Symph. Orch. in series Orchestras of the Nation; Var. apps. on State radio stns. in connection w. concerts for adults & children. Comps: Several for Symph. Orch., Violin & Piano. Publs: The Violin Concerto: A Study in German Romanticism, 1941. Contbr. to num. profl. jrnls. Mbrships. incl: Am. Symph. Orch. League; Torch Club. Recip. Morrison Award for Achievement in Performing Arts, 1968. NC Award for Achievement in Fine Arts, 1966. Address: Box 448, Carrboro, NC 27510, USA. 2, 7, 28.

SWAN, Judy, b. 22 Oct. 1946, Hampstead, London, UK. Viola Player & Teacher. Educ: Royal Coll. of Music, w. Cecil Aronowitz; ARCM Dips. (viola & piano). m. James Stobart. Career: Freelance violist, 1966-70; Violist, London Phil. orch., 1970-. Address: 21 Butler Ave., Harrow, Middx., UK.

SWANN, Donald Ibrahim, b. 30 Sept. 1923, Llanelli, UK. Composer; Pianist. Educ: MA, Christ Church, Oxford, Univ. m. Janet Oxborrow, 2 d. Career: Accomp. & comp. for intimate revues, 1948-56; wrote music for Henry Reed series of features for Third Programme, BBC, in 1950's; on stage in own show w. author Michael Flanders, At the Drop of A Hat, & its successors, 1957-67; comp. & perf. own works largely in concerts, 1967-; Comps: 3 books of new carols and one narration w. songs, for children & young adults; Round the Piano with Donald Swann (children's song); Fesitval Martins & Requiem for the Living (C Day Lewis); Settings of J R R Tokien; The Story of Boritzye Schweig (narration w. music); Songs w. Michael Flanders; songs to texts by John Betjeman & Arthur Scholey; The Yeast Factory (music drama) w. Alec Davison, 1979. var. recordings. Address: 13 Albert Bridge Rd., London SW11, 4PX, UK.

SWANN, Gloria Sheinberg, b. 5 Feb. 1926, Fort Worth, Tex., USA. Pianist; Teacher; Writer. Educ: BA, MMus, Tex. Christian Univ.; grad. study; piano & English, Univ. of S Calif. w. Benjamin Bruister Swann, 2 s., 2 d. Debut: Ft. Worth, Tex., w. symph. orch., 1943. Career: recitalist in var. cities; pvte. piano tchr.; coll. fac., Northern Ariz. Univ.; TCU; Tarrant Co. Jr. Coll.; music critic; freelance writer. Publs: Gustav Mahler: The Poetics of Sound. Contbr. to: Staff Notes; Ariz. Daily Sun; Chicago Spectator & other mags. & jrnls. Mbrships: Pres., Ft. Worth, Piano Tchrs. Forum, 1978-79; fac. mbr., & adjudicator, NGPT; Ft. Worth Music Tchrs. Assn.; Texas Music Tchrs. Assn.; Nat. Music Tchrs. Assn.; Am. Musicol. Assn. Recip. var. awards for music & poetry. Hobbies incl: Reading; Writing; Cooking; Studying languages & philosophy. Address: 900 Chateau Vallee Circle, Bedford, TX 76201, USA.

SWANSON, Walter Donald, b. 19 June 1903, London, UK. Composer; Arranger; Conductor; Adjudicator. Educ: LRAM; ARAM. m. Marjorie Hill, 1 s. Debut: London, 1915. Career: Asst. Cond., Cape Town Symph. Orch., 1927; Staff Cond. & Comp., S Africa Broadcasting Corp., 1935; cond. num. opera, operetta, ballet orchs. Compositions incl: 2 Symphs.; num. stage & radio Musicals inclng: The Mill of Youth (medieval musical legend); Rough Diamond (musical comedy). Contbr. to: Cape Times; Cape Argus; The Monitor; num. other mags. & jrnls. Mbrships: S Africa Music Rights Assn.; Dramatic & Literay Rights Assn.; former Pres., Cape Musicians Assn.; The Owl Club; former Pres., Cape Guild of Organists; var. other profl. orgs. Hons: 1st Prize, Union DeFense Force Marching Song, 1946; SABC Author Prize; Otto Bach

Musical Comedy Prize, 1971. Hobbies: Rotary; Freemasonry; The Turft; Crossword Puzzles. Address: 19 Rondebosch Lodge, Main Road, Rondebosch, Cape Town, S Africa. 3, 18.

SWANSTON, Roderick Brian, b. 28 Aug. 1948, Gosport, England, UK. Director of Music; Teacher; Organist; Conductor. Educ: MA, MusB, Pembroke Coll., Cambridge; Organ Scholar, ibid.; GRSM; FRCO; LRAM; ARCM. Career: Asst. Organist, HM Chapel Royal, Tower of London; Dir. of Music, Christ Ch., Lancaster Gate, 1972-77; Dir. of Music, St. James, Sussex Gdns., 1977-; Prof. of Theory, RCM; Dir. of Music in London of Ithaca Coll., NY; Panel of Tutors, Extramural Dept., London Univ.; Tchr., Jr. Dept., RCM; Organist; Conductor. Recordings: Organ Recital from Framlingham Parish Ch. contbr. to Times Educl. Supplement. Mbrships: Royal Musical Assn.; ISM; Pres., Hegel Soc. Recip. Sawyer Prize, RCO, 1969. Hobbies: Writing; Dialectics; Philosophy; Theology. Address: Flat 3, II Sinclair Gdns., London, W, 14, UK.

SWANWICK, Keith, b. 2 Feb. 1937, Leicester, UK. Musician (conductor); Music Educator. Educ: MEd, PhD, Leicester Univ.; RAM; GRSM; LRAM; ARCO. m. Maureen Anne Pawley, 1 s., 2 d. Career: Hd. of Music, Rutherford Schl., London, 1960-62, Wyggeston Boys Schl., Leicester, 1962-66; Lectr.-Sr. Lectr. in Music Educ., Univ. of London Inst. of Educ., 1966-; Prof. of Music Educ., London Univ., 1967-. Cond. Comps: Five Songs from America; A Day In A Life. Publs: Popular Music & the Teacher, 1968; Chief Reviewer, Handbook for Music Teachers, 1968; Teachers'/Pupils' notes for Fusion/Song & Story (Thames TV). Contbr. to jrnls. Mbr., AUT. Recip., Sawyer Prize, RCO, 1960. Hobbies: Walking; Reading; Thinking. Address: 18 Park Ave., St. Albans, Herts, UK.

SWARTZ, Jack Paul, b. 25 Feb. 1920, Piatt Co., Ill., USA. Music Educator; Singer; Pianist; Composer; Professor, University School of Music. Educ: BM, Ill. Wesleyan Univ., 1941; MM, George Peabody Coll. for Tchrs., 1949; EdD, Univ. Neb., 1956. m. Claire Ritchie Swartz, 4 s. Career: Prof., (ret'd.), Schl. of Music, Fla. State Univ., Tallahassee, Fla. Coordinator of Music Educ., Univ. of Tex. at Arlington. Publs: The Collegiate Class Piano Course (Prentice-Hall, Inc.), 1971. Contbr. to Jr. Coll. Jrnl.; Music Educators Jrnl. Mbrships: Pres., Phi Delta Kappa; Pi Kappa Lambda; AAUP; Pres., Ariz. State Chmn., Int. Assn. of Torch Clubs; Pres., Tallahassee Torch Club. Hobbies: Folk Dancing; Travel. Address: 731 Buckskin Trail, Arlington, TX 76015, USA.

SWAYNE, Giles Oliver Cairnes, b. 30 June 1946, Stevenage, UK. Composer; Pianist. Educ: Trinity Coll., Cambridge; RAM. m. Camilla Brett, 1 s., 3 stepchildren. Career: Perfs. at Aldeburgh & Bromsgrove Fests.; Purcell Room; SPNM Concerts; at Birmingham, Liverpool, Lancaster, Warwick & York Univs.; BBC Radio 3 broadcasts of most works: Music Staff, Glyndebourne, 1973-74; Teaching Staff, Bryanston Schl., 1974-76. Comps. incl: Three Shakespeare Songs (chorus); Chmbr. Music (strings, harp); Cantos 1 5 (solo pieces for guitar, organ, piano, violin, clarinet); Orlando's Music (orch.), 1976; Synthesis (2 Pianos); Music for schl. orchs. & TV. Recordings: Canto 1 (guitar). Mbrships: PRS; Composers' Guild, MCPS. Address: c/o London Mgmt. 235/241 Regent St., London W1.

SWEENEY, Cecily Pauline, b. 8 Sept. 1932, Detroit, Mich., USA. Musicologist. Educ: BA, Wayne State Univ., 1954; MA, 1957, PhD, 1972, UCLA; BMus, 1952, Detroit Conserv. of Music; Artist's Dip., ibid., 1 s. Debut: Liszt, Piano Concerto No. 1, Detroit Symph. Orch., 1952. Contbr. to: Corpus Scriptorum de Musica, vol. 13, 1971, vol. 26, 1976; Musica Disciplina. Mbrships: Phi Beta Kappa; Pres., Los Angeles Alumnae Chapt., Sigma Alpha Iota; Am. Musicol. Soc. Hobby: Chmbr. music. Address: 1161 Linda Flora Dr., Los Angeles, CA 90049, USA.

SWEENEY, Eric John, b. 15 July 1948, Dublin, Eire. Musician (keyboard); Conductor; Composer. Educ: MusB, Trinity Coll., Dublin; LRAM; LRSM; grad. work, Santa Cecilia, Rome. m. Sally Olivia Johnston, 2 d. Career: Cond.; Culwick Choral Soc. & Culwick Consort; Cond., RTE Singers. Comps: Missa Brevis; Canzona; 5 Italian Songs; Symphony; Incidental Music for Abbey Theatre. sev. recordings. Mbrships: Musical Assn. of Ireland; Trinity Coll., Dublin, Assn. Recip., Prout Award, Trinity Coll., Dublin, 1969. Hobbies: Fishing; Gardening. Address: 20 Ballyroan Pk., Dublin 16, Eire.

SWEET, Lonn Milford, b. 22 Nov. 1940, Scotland, SD, USA. College Administrator; Director of Bands. Educ: BS, 1961, MM, 1964, Univ. of SD. m. Dorothy Marie Sweet, 2 c. Career: Music Instructor, Springfield HS, SD, 1961-66; Dir. of Bands & Asst. Prof. of Music, Univ. of SD/Springfield, 1966-74; Dir. of Bands & Chmn., Music Dept., Northern State Coll., Aberdeen, SD, 1974-. Mbrships. incl: SD Bandmasters

Assn.; Coll. Band Dirs. Nat. Assn.; Nat. Band Assn.; MENC. Address: 1722 S 7th St., Aberdeen, SD 57401, USA.

SWIATEK, Lucie, b. 9 May 1906, London, UK. Amateur Pianist. Educ: in London & Brussels; studied piano w. Maurice Jacobson in London & Sidney Rosenbloom in S Africa. Career: Fndr. & Org. of The Chopin Soc. in England (recitals once monthly). Mbr., ISM. Hobbies: Art; Antiques; Preservation of Environment; Period buildings; Animal Welfare. Address: 42 Beechcroft Gdns., Wembley Pk., Middx.

SWIDA-SZACILOWSKA, Helena Maria, b. 22 Feb. 1928, Warsaw, Poland. Vocal Soloist. Educ: Masters in Romantic Philol., Cath. Univ. of Lublin; vocal studies at Second. Music Schl. m. Edmund Szacilowski (div.), 1 s. Debut: Radio Warsaw, 1953. Career: radio broadcasts; w. Warsaw Opera, 1960-62; Soloist w. Lublin Phil. & other Polish orchs. Mbr. Assn. of Polish Musicians. Recip. Distinction in vocal competition, Warsaw, 1951. Hobbies: Lectures; Touring. Address: 20-029 Lublin, Sklodowskiej 8 m 11, Poland.

SWIETLY, Hermann Karl, b. 25 Mar. 1943, Vienna, Austria. International Civil Servant (Chemical Technician) with IAEA; Violinist. Educ: studied violin, 1951-, at dist. music schl., w. Hilda Preissler at Conserv. of Vienna (recip. of upper degree in violin, 1962), w. Peter Guth & currently Christos Polyzoides. m. Ines Vera Irisgler, 1 s., 1 d. Career: has given num. concerts, 1955-; has app. as Soloist & as Chmbr. Music Violinist in chs., adult colls., concert halls, Austrian castles & palaces; temporary mbr. of Vienesse Ensemble "Musica Antiqua" & Wiener Bachgemeinde; apps. on Belgian, Aerwegian, Swedish & Finnish TV. Mbrships: Int. Amateur Chmbr. Music Players; Verein der Freunde der Kammermusik; Int. MENSA Club; Verein der Beethoven-Gedenkstaette; Verein der Freunde des Musischen Heims. Hobbies: Mountaineering & Hiking; Rock Climbing; Reading. Address: Kreitnergasse, 23/9, A 1160 Vienna, Austria.

SWIFT, Richard, b. 24 Sept. 1927, Middlepoint, Ohio, USA. Composer; Educator. Educ: MA, Univ. of Chgo., Ill., 1956; Fellow, Inst. for Advanced Musical Study, Princeton Univ., 1959-60. m. Dorothy Swift, 3 s. Career: Prof. of Music, Univ. of Calif., Davis, 1956-; Chmn., Dept. of Music, ibid., 1963-71; Vis. Prof., Princeton, Univ., 1977. Compositions: Piano Concerto; Domains III; The Pleasures Of Merely Circulating; Quartet IV; Sonata for solo violon; Planctus. Summer Notes; Great Praises. Contbr. to: Perspectives of New Music; Notes; Jrnl. of Am. Musicol. Soc.; Jrnl. of 20th Century Music. Mbrships: Coll. Music Soc.; Am. Music Ctr.; ASCAP. Hons: Louisville Symph.-Rockefeller Fndr. Award, 1954; Rockefeller Fndn. Award, 1968; Comps: Str. Quartet Award, 1974; Am. Acad. & Inst. of Arts & Letters Award, 1978. Hobbies: Reading Philosophy, European & American Literatures; Gardening. Address: 568 S Campus Way, Davis, CA 95616, USA. 2, 9.

SWINDELL, Warren C, b. 22 Aug. 1934, Kansas City, Mo., USA. Instrumental Music Educator; Applied Clarinettist. Educ: BSc, Music Educ., Lincoln Univ. of Mo.; MMusEd (instrumental), Univ. of Mich.; PhD, MusEd, Univ. of Iowa. m. Monica Streetman Swindell, 2 d. Career: Band Cond.; Music Administrator. Mbrships. incl: Bd. of Dirs., Frankfort Arts Fndn.; Kentucky State Dept. of Educ. Advsry. Committee on K-12 Tchr. Certification in Music; VP, Kentucky Assn. of Coll. Music Depts.; KMEA Minority Concerns Committee. Hobbies: Gardening; Out-of-doors activities. Address: 1303 Lago Dr., Frankfort, KY 40601, USA.

SWING, Peter Gram, b. 15 July 1922, NYC, USA. College Professor. Educ: AB, Harvard Univ., 1948; AM, 1951; postgrad. studies, Univ. of Utrecht, Netherlands, 1951-52; PhD, Univ. of Chgo., 1969. m. E A Sherman, 2 s., 1 d. Career: Instructor, Assoc. Choirmaster, Rollins Coll. 1952-53; Instructor, Univ. of Chgo., 1953-55; Fac. Mbr., Swarthmore Coll., 1955-; Assoc. Prof., 1959-69; Prof., 1969-; Dir. Coll. Chorus, 1955-; Chmn., Dept. of Music, 1958-74; Fac. Mbr., Berkshire Music Ctr., Lenox, Mass., 1962-; Nat. Humanities Fac., 1969-70. Publs: Three Christmas Motets of Jean Mouton, edited w. critical commentary, 1973. Mbrships: Chmn., Phila. Chapt., Am. Musicol. Soc., 1969-70; Coll. Music Soc.; Renaissance Soc.; Vereniging voor Nederlandse Muziekgeschiedenis; AAUP; Phi Beta Kappa. Recip., var. hons. Address: 614 Hillborn Ave., Swarthmore, PA 19081, USA. 2.

SWISHER, Gloria Agnes Wilson, b. 12 Mar. 1935, Seattle, Wash., USA. Teacher, Theory, Composition, Piano; Pianist; Composer. Educ: BA, Univ. of Wash., 1956; MA, Mills Coll., 1958; PhD, Eastman Schl. of Music, 1960. m. Donald Prevost Swisher, 2 s. Career: Instructor, Music, Wash. State Univ.,

1960-61, Pacific Luth. Univ., 1969-70, Shoreline Community Coll., 1969-73, Shoreline Community Coll., 1973-. Comps: God is Gone Up With A Merry Noise; Two Faces of Love; Cancion; Concerto, clarinet & orch.; Thanksgivings 1 & II; Sisters; Processions. Author, Syllabus for Music Theory, 1974, Rev. Ed., 1975, '78. Mbrships: Chmn., Int. Music Fund, Sigma Alpha iota, 1974-; Prov. Pres., ibid., 1970-73; Ladies Musical Club; Phi Beta Kappa. Hons: Woodrow Wilson Fellow, 1956-57; Capitol Choir Contest, 1961. Hobbies: Knitting; Embroidery; Reading. Address: 7228 6th NW, Seattle, WA 98117, USA. 5, 29.

SWOBODA, Henry, b. Prague, Czechoslovakia. Symphony, Opera Conductor. Educ: Music Conserv., Prague; PhD, Prague Univ.; Study w. Vaclav Talich, Zemlinsky, Prague, Richard Robert, Vienna. Debut: Symph., choral concert, German Opera House, Prague. Career: Cond., Prague Opera; Cond., Dusseldorf Opera; Cond., Prog. Org., Prague Broadcasting; Guest Cond., Edinburgh, Berlin, Dresden, Vienna Symph.; Music Dir. & Cond., Concert Hall Soc. & Westminster Recordings, NYC; Lectr. & Symph. orch. Dir., Harvard Univ.; Vis. Prof. & Symph. Orch. & Opera Workshop Dir., Univ. of Tex., Austin; Guest Cond., maj. US, European symph. orchs. Recordings: Num. "firsts" of works by Bartok, Bruckner, Dvorak, Hindemuth, Ibert, Janacek, Kodaly, Martinu, Milhaud, others. Publs: Coord., Forum Lects., Voice of Am., 1967. Hons: Grand Prix du Disque, 1950. Hobbies: Reading; Swimming; Walking. Address: 11855 1st East, Treasure Island, FL 33706, USA.

SYKES, James Andrews, b. Atlantic City, NJ, USA. Professor; Administrator. Educ: AB, Princeton Univ.; Eastman Schl. of Music, Univ. of Rochester, MA; Dalcroze Schl. of Music, NY; Austro-Am. Conserv., Mondsee, Austria. m. Clara Hanington, 1 s. Debut: Town Hall, NY. Career: Dean, Lamont Schl. of Music, 1933-35; Chmn., Dept. of Music, Colo. Coll., 1935-46; Chmn., Dept. of Music Colgage Univ., 1947-53; Prof. of Music, Dartmouth Coll., 1953-73 (Dept. Chmn., 1953-59); Am. Specialist Grants from US Dept. of State, visits to 12 countries of Latin Am., 1960, to 14 countries of Far & Middle East, 19645, to Rumanian, 1972; Cond., Handel Soc. of Dartmouth Coll., 1953-73; Round-the-World tours, United Service Organizations, 1945; Protagonist & Writer of 10 program TV series, Music in Focus, 1958; Vis. Fac. Artist, Assn. of Am. Colls., 1937-44. Recordings: Short Piano Pieces of Charles Ives; Works by Clara Schumann; Sonata No. 1, William Sterndale Bennett. Contbr. to: World Book Encyclopedia; Am. Choral Review; Music Lib. Notes; The Listener. Mbr., num. profl. orgs. Recip., sev. hons. Hobbies: Swimming; Travel. Address: 5 Rip Road, Hanover, NH 03755, USA. 2, 3, 30.

SYKES, Malcolm, b. 14 Apr. 1946, Darlington, Co. Durham, UK. Solo Pianist; Lecturer; Visiting Tutor. Educ; GTCL; FTCL; Vienna Acad. for Music & Dramatic Art. London debut: Purcell Room, 6th Feb. 1976. Career: Lectr., Stockton-Billingham Tech. Coll.; Vis. Tutor, Middleton-St.-George Coll. of Educ. & Leeds Polytechnic; Has given recitals & concert apps. in the provinces; Participated in master Class w. Denis Matthews; Has performed w. Alexander Choir under Charles Proctor in London. Mbr. ISM. Hons: Tillett Trust Post-grad. Scholarship; John Halford Pianoforte Prize, 1968; Alec Rowley Pianoforte Recital Prize, 1969; Maud Seton Prize, 1970; Alec Rowley Mem. Prize, 1971. Hobbies: Concerts; Theatre. Mgmt: Ibbs & Tillett. Address: 58 Kingston St., Darlington, Co. Durham, DL3 6AT, UK.

SÝKORA, Václav Jan, b. 10 Oct. 1918, Prague, Czech. Composer; Musicologist; Pianist; Cembalist; Editor; Critic. Educ: Dip., High Music Schl., 1946; Charles Univ., PhD, 1948; CSc, 1963, Prague. m. Vera Hrábková, 2 c. Debut: as pianist, w. Czech. Phil. Career: Concert Pianist & Cembalist, Germany, Sweden, S Am., Netherlands, Austria, Belgim, Switz., Yugoslavia, Poland, etc.; TV, Prague; Radio, Prague, Paris, Zürich, Vienna, Hilversum, Ljubljana, Stockholm. Comps: Polkas, 1961; 5 Études, 1968; Meditation for Bassoon, 19712, etc. Recordings incl: works of Vorisek, Rejcha, Dussek; Old Portuguese Music for Cembalo; Spanish Music for Harpsichord; Harpsichord in Old and New Music; F X Brixi - Partita for harpsichord., etc. Publs: Jan Herman, national artist, 1956; F X Dusek, monographie of old Czech Comp., 1958; Robert Schumann, 1967; Improvisation Yesterday and Today, 1966; History of Piano Arts, 1973; Music of North Europa, 1975; num. eds. & transcriptions. Contbr. to: Hudebni Rzozhledy Praha; Musikforschung; Hudebni veda, Praha. Mbrships: Int. Music Soc.; Union of Czech. Comps. Address: Karlinske nám 11, Praha 8 - Karlin, Czech.

SYMONDS, Norman Alec, b. 23 Dec. 1920, Nelson, BC, Can. Composer. Educ: Royal Conserv., Toronto; pvte. studies w. Gordon Delamont, Toronto. Career: Commentator & Interviewer, Radio. Comps. incl: (recorded) The Nameless Hour, for string orch.

& improvised solo; Diversion, for Brass Quintet; Impusle, for symph. orch.; Concerto Grooso, for Jazz Quintet & Symph. Orch.; Quintette, for Clarinet & synthesizers; Deep Ground Long Waters, song & choral; Pastel Blue, for String Orch.; Laura and the Lieutenant, music play for children; Big Lonely, for Symph. Orch. Hobbies: Reading; Sailing; Card Playing. Address: 33 Harbour Square, Suite 1430, Toronto, Ont. M5J 2G2, Can.

SYMONDS, Stewart, b. 2 Jan. 1937, Sydney, Aust. Interior Designer. Educ: pvte. Career: stage, film & TV apps.; profl. involvment mainly in stage design. Publ: Catalogue for Exhibition, The Pianoforte Past, 1979. Mbrships: Musicol. Soc. of Aust.; Early Music Assn. of NSW.; exec., Soc. of Interior Designers of Aust.; Friends of Elizabeth Bay House; Friends of Museum of Applied Arts & Scis. Hobbies: Collecting & Restoring Antique Pianos. Address: McDonalds Farm, 15-17 Honor St., Ermington, NSW 2115, Aust.

SYNNESTVEDT, Viggo Redmond, b. 13 Mar. 1918, Copenhagen, Denmark. Pianist; Composer. Educ: RAM, Denmark; Storste eksamen med Udmaerkelse ved The Royal Danish Acad. of Music. Debut: Odd Fellow Palaeet, Copenhagen. Career: Recitals as soloist w. Royal Danish Kapel, Odd Fellow Palaeet; Recitals in England, Switz., Sweden, Norway, & on radio. Comps. (publs. & recordings): many songs. Recordings: Mozart; Greig; Bach; Liszt; Sinding; Rubinstein; V Synnestvedt. Mbrships: Solistforeningen 1921-; KODA (Komponistforeningen). Address: Ahlmannsalle 24, 2900 Hellerup, Denmark.

SZABELSKI, Boleslaw, b. 3 Dec. 1896, Radoryz, Poland. Composer; Organist. Educ: degrees in Music, Warsaw; Dip. in Organ, Warsaw Conserv. m. Irene Marmol, 1 d. Debut: Katowice, 1953. Career: Warsaw Autumn Fest., 1953, 56, 58, 61, 68; Musicki Biennale, Zagreb, Yugoslavia, 1964. Comps. incl: Soldier's March (choir & wind orch.) 1948; 4th Symph., 1957; Verses for Piano & Chmbr. Orch., 1963; 5th Symph., 1968; (also recorded) Concerto Grosso for Orch., 1954; Preludes for Chmbr. Orch., 1963; Concerto for Flute & Orch., 1964. Hon. Mbr., Zwigzen Kompozytorow Polshich. Hons. incl; Silesian Music Prize, 1957; Fest. SIMC Prize, 1962, 66; State Prize, 1953, 62, 66; Gold Medal of Merit, 1962; Recip., Polish orders. Hobby: Growing Flowers. Address: ul. Nad Yareni 9, 40-625 Katowice, Poland.

SZABO, Albert (Burt), b. 28 Dec. 1931, Wellington, Ohio, USA. Professor of Music; Composer. Educ: PhD, Mich. State Univ., E Lansing, 1967. Comps. incl: Divertimentissimo for winds, 1962; She is not Fair, for men's voices, 1963; 2 Pieces for Orchestra, 1963; Rejoice & Be Merry, for mixed voices, 1966; A Forest Hymn, for tenor & orch., 1967; Rain, for mixed voices, 1967; 3 Enigmas, for jazz orch., 1969; Impressions for jazz orch., 1970; Diversions of Aries, for symph. orch., 1973; Two Worlds, for mixed voices, 1973; Forboding, for soprano, clarinet & piano, 1973; Serenade for Oboe & Orch., 1975; Soundscapes, for symph. orch., 1977; Chinese Songs, for soprano, flute & piano, 1978. Publs: Theory of Barbershop Harmony, 1976. Mbrships: MTNA; ASUC; ASCAP; Soc. for the Preservation & Encouragement of Barbershop Quartet Singing in Am., Inc. Hons: Perf. award, Univ. of Redlands, Calif., 1964; Perf. award, Dallas, Tex., Symph. Orch., 1965. Hobbies: Sailing; Swimming; Golf; Collecting musical postage stamps. Address: Music Dept., Univ. of Ctrl. Fla., Orlando, Fla., USA.

SZABO, Antal, b. 21 May 1938, Debrecen, Hungary. Flautist. Educ: Middle Schl. of Music, Miskolc, Hungary, 1951-56; Acad. of Music 'Liszt Ferenc', Budapest, 1956-61 (w. Prof. Hartai). Dips. Artists of Flute & Master of Music; w. Prof. Nicolet at his master class in Freiburg i/B, 1966-67. m. Maria Sailer, 2 d. Career: recitals w. Hungarian Radio & Philharmonia; Prof., Ujpest Music Schl. Hobbies: Tourism; Reading. Address: Majakovszkij u. 102 II.3, 1068 Budapest, Hungary.

SZABÓ, Csaba, b. 19 April 1936, Akosfalva-Acátari, Transylvania, Romania. Composer; Lecturer. Educ: Acad. of Music, Kolozsvar, Cluj. m. Szànthò Klàudia, 2 s. Career: Cond., Székely Ensemlbe, Marosvásáhely-Tg. Mures, 1959-63; Lectr., Szentgyorgyi Istvàn Theatrical Art Inst., 1963-; num. apps., Romanian & Hungarian radio & TV. Comps: Csàng & nepdalok nöi Karra (Csangò tunes for female chorus), 1958; String Quartet for Youth, 1964; Egyszesüènekek, I, II (Clear Songs), 1968, '70; Csingi-lingi reggelek (Choruses for Young Children), 1972; Ötkis Kòrus (5 Little Choruses), 1972; Nenia, for orch., 1976; Öt dal Dsida Jenö verseire (5 songs on Dsida Jenö's verses for soprano & orch.), 1976; Parlando, ginsto e corale, for piano, 1979; Roaming Tune, for prepared piano, 1979. Recordings: Passacaglia on a theme by Joannes Kajoni; Among Glass Splinters, variations for orch. Publs: Hogyar tanitsuk korunk zenejèt (How to Teach Contemporary Music), 1977; Ed., Zenetudomànyi Iràsot, 1977. Contbr. to

profl. publs. Mbr., Union of Romanian Comps. Hons: Order for Cultural Merit, 1968; Prize of Union of Comps., 1975. Hobby: Travel. Address: Aleea Carpati 55/a, apt. 13, 4300 Tg. Mures, Romania.

SZABO, Miklós, b.15 Apr. 1931, Szentgotthárd, Hungary. Professor at the Conservatoire of Györ. Educ: Fac. of Sec. Schl. Music Tchrs. & Choir Conds., Franz Liszt Acad., Budapest; State Exam., 1953. Career: Prof., Conserv. of Györ; Vis. Prof., Univ. of Jyvaskyla, Finland, 1974; Lectr., Sibelius Acad., Helsinki, 1974; Cond. of Women's Choir in Györ, giving annual concerts in Budapest & recordings for Hungarian radio; Concerts in Vienna, 1966, Dijon, 1968, Paris, 1970; Concerts in Italy, Vienna, Poland; Prof., Summer Course fo the Kodaly Musical Trng. Inst., Watertown, Mass., USA. Recordings under his dir. incl. works by Bartok, Palestrina, Liszt, Dufay, Lasso, M. Haydn & Monteverdi; Contemporary Hungarian Women's Choirs. Publs: Music Composition-Choral Culture, 1972; Kodály's & Adorno's Common Thoughts about Music Education, 1972. Contbr. Renaissance Polyphony Then & Now, in Muzsika, 1977. Mbrships: var. profl. socs. num. hons. & awards. Address: 49 Tanácsköztarsaság útja, 9022 Györ, Hungary.

SZALONEK, Witold Josef, b. 2 Mar. 1927, Czechowice, Poland. Composer. Educ: Piano Dip., Music Lyceum, Katowice, 1949; Dip. in Composition, MA, HS of Music, ibid., 1956. m. Beata Maria Zygmunt, 2 s. Debut: Katowice, 1954. Career. Asst., HS of music, Katowice, 1956-61; Adj. Prof., 1961-67; Prof. of Composition, 1967-73; Recotr, 1972-73; Prof. of Composition & Theory, HS of Arts, W Verlin, 1973-. Compositions incl: num. orchl. instrumental & choral works, inclng. Pastorales, oboe & piano,oboe & orch.; Dzwon, double choir, Toccata Polyphonica, string orch.; Symphonic Satire; Les Sons, orch.; O Pleasant Earth, Voice & orch. Publs. incl: Claude Debussy, 1862-1918, 1962; On the Unexploited Sonoric Qualities of the Woodwind Instruments, 1968, 2nd ed., 1973. Mbr. & off. var. profl. orgs. Recip. num. hons. Address: Königen Luise Str. 75a, 1000 Berlin 3, Germany.

SZCZEPANSKI, Zygmunt, b. 7 Apr. 1909, Leczyca, Poland. Music Director; Conductor. Educ: Tchng. & Musician's Dips. widowed, 1 s., 2 d. Debut: Warsaw, 1939. Career: Choral & Orchl. Cond., clandestine concerts, Warsaw, 1939-44; Dir. & Cond., Lublin Phil. Orch., 1944-47; Dir., Cond., Stage Mgr., opera & phil. orchs., 1947-72; perfs. as Cond., France, Austria, Switz. & Monaco, 1966, Germany, 1968, Bulgaria, 1971; currently, Music Dir. & Cond., Music Theatre, Szczecin, Cond., Hejnal chorus, Szczecin, also for phil. orch. & opera. Has made radio & TV recordings. Author, 7 books inclng: Spiew w. Szkole Moze Byĉ Piekny. contbr. to profl. jrnls. Mbr. profl. orga. Hons. incl: Zasluzony Dzialacz Kultury, 1975. Hobbies: Touring; Camping; Mountain climbing. Address: Al. Powstancow 4b m 5, 70-110 Szeczecin, Poland.

SZE, Yi-kwei, b. 6 Jan. 1917, Shanghai, China. Bass Baritone; Professor or Voice. Educ: Grad., Nat. Conserv. Music, Shanghai. m. Nancy Lee, 1 s. Debut: Town Hall, 1947; Opera, San Fran. Opera, 1950. Career incls: Created role, Calchas, NY premiere, Walton's 'Troilus & Cressida', NYC Opera; Performed Sarastro, NBC-TV prod., 'Magic Flute', 200th anniversary Mozart's birth; Extensive concert tours throughout world, 1953-; Solos w. Brlin, London & NY Phil. Orchs., Cleveland & Phila. Orchs., Boston Symph., Concergebouw Orch., Amsterdam & var. music fests.; Dir., Hong Kong Arts Fest., Schl., 1974-; Fac. Mbr., Eastman, 1971-. Hons. incl: 1st Order Fine Arts, China, 1957; Grand Gala du Disque, Amsterdam, 1966. Address: 3465 E Ave., Rochester, NY 14618, USA.

SZEKERES, Ferenc, b. 23 Mar. 1927, Murakeresztur, Hungary. Conductor; Music Master. Educ: MusM, Dip, Cond.; Zoltan Kodaly; Attended Cond. course by Franco Ferrara. m. Magda Kelemen, 2 d. Career: Cond. in major European towns & cities; Radio,TV & Film perfs. Recordings: Madrigaux et Motets; Motets by Angelicum 'Milano' Paisiello; Cantata Comica; Christmas Songs; Vivaldi, Judith Triumphans; J Haydn, Il ritorno di Tobia; Oratorio; Die Erwehlung eines Kappelmeisters; etc. Publs: Mixed voices, I-XX; Euqal Voices, I-X; Series of Old Masters, Pieces for Chorus of Works by Monteverdi, Schulz, Lully. Mbr., Hungarian Musicians Assn. Hons: Grand Prize, French nat. Acad. 1973 & 74; Cavaliere dell Ordine al Mérito della Republica Italiana, 1976. Hobby: Tennis. Address: 103 Villáni Str., Budapest, Hungary 1118.

SZELENYI, Istvan, b. 1904, Zolyom, Hungary. Professor of Music;o Composer; Writer; Musicologist. Educ: Dip. in Composition, F Liszt Acad. of Music, Budapest. m. Barbara Kovacs, 1 s. Career: Prof. of Piano, Gymnasium musicum of Hungary, 1948-51; Dir., ibid., 1948-51; Ed., New

Review of Music, Hungary, 1951-56; Prof. of Compositions, Bela Bartok Conserv., Budapest, 1956-, F Liszt Acad. of Music, Budapest, 1966-. Compositions incl: 1st Symph., 1926; 3 Str. Quartets, 1926-31; 6 Sonatas, 1926-56; Virata Oratorium (text by Stefan Zweig), 1936; Spartacus Oratorio, 1959; Ten Days (oratorio), 1964; Violin Duos, 1959; 24 Little Concert Pieces for violin & piano, 1958; num. chmbr. works, Piano music, cantatas, songs & choruses. Publs: Biography of F Liszt; Bartok's Work, For Children; Harmony of Romanticism; New Methods in Modulation; On Modulation; History of Hungarian Music. Contbr. to musicol. jrnls. Hobbies: Youth Education. Address: Bajza U-2, Budapest, Hungary. 3.

SZELENYI, Laszlo (stage-name FARAGO), b. 3 Oct. 1935, Budapest, Hungary. Pianist. Educ: Bartok & Franz Liszt Acads., Budapest; Acad. of Music, Freiburg/Breisgau, 1957-61. Career incls: Opera Cond., 1961; concert apps. as Soloist, 1968-; concert tour of German Fed. Repub., 1972; solo debut, Budapest, 1974; W Berlin debut, 1975; broadcasts in Germany & Austria; Tchr., Conserv., Innsbruck, 1976-. Comps: var. songs, piano pieces & works for stage accomp. Recordings: Kaskade label, German Fed. Repub. Contbr. to musical jrnls. Mbrships: Int. Liszt Soc.; Soc. for German Music Educators & Concert Artists. Recip., 3 1st Prizes, Budapest Conserv. & Music Acad., 1949, 50 & 54. Hobbies: Reading; Collecting Records; Soccer; Swimming; Hiking' Ping-Pong. Address: Serlesweg 5, A-6161 Natters u. Innsbruck, Austria.

SZERVANSZKY, Endrew, b. 27 Dec. 1911, Kisteteny, Hungary. Composer; Professor of Composition. Educ: Fac. of Comp., Music Acad., Budapest. m. Elisabeth Sipos. 1 s. Career: Prof. of Comp., Nat. Conserv., 1942-48; Prof. of Comp., Liszt Ferenc Music Acad., Budapest, 1948-. Compositions: Petöfi Songs; a Capella Petöfi Choirs; Three Spiritual Songs (Soprano, Flute & Piano); 2 Str. Quartets; 2 Wind Quintets; Violin Duets; Suite for 2 Flutes; Two Duets for Flute; 5 Concert Studies for Solo Flute; Trio (Flute, Violin, Viola); Sonata (Violin, Piano); Sonatina (Flute, Piano); Serenade (Clarinet & Orch.); 6 Orchl. Pieces; Variations in Five Movements (orch.); Gloomy Heaven (Requiem for Orch. & Choir); Clarinet Concerto (Clarinet & Orch.); Serenade for Strings; Flute Concerto; Concerto in Memory of Attila Jozsef (orch.); last three also recorded. Mbr., Assn. Hungarian Comps. Hons: Honoured Artist; 2 Kossuth Prizes; 2 Erkel Prizes. Address: 1026 Budapest, Nyul utca 18, Hungary. 3.

SZERYNG, Henryk, b. 22 Sept. 1918, Zelazowa Wola, Poland. Violinist. Educ: w. Carl Flesch, Berlin, Nadia Boulanger, & Gabriel Bouillon; Nat. Higher Conserv. of Music, Paris. Career: Interpreter for Polish Govt. in Exile, 1939-45, also giving num. concerts to Allied troops; has made num. apps. as Soloist thru'out world; Dir., String Dept., Schl. of Music, nat. Univ. of Mexico; appointed Special Music Advsr., Mexican Permanent Deleg. at UNESCO, Paris, 1970. Recordings incl: Violin Concerto by many composers inclng. Mozart, Paganini, Prokofiev, Sibelius, Vivaldi, Bartok, Beethoven, Berg & Wieniaski. Hons. incl; Grand Prix du Diswwue, 6 times; Kt. Cmdr., Polonia Restitua, 1956; Medal of City of Paris, 1960. Mgmt: Wilfrid Van Wyck, 80 Wigmore St., London W1, UK.

SZIDON, (José) Roberto, b. 21 Sept. 1941, Porto Alegre, Brazil. Pianist. Educ. incls: Inst. of Fine Arts of Rio Grande do Sul, Brazil; Fac. of Fine Arts, Univ. of Santa Maria, Brazil; The Piano Schl., NYC; Dip., Suprior Course in Music, 1964; Prof. of Music Educ:, 1965. Debut: Porto Alegre, 1950. Career incls: num. perfs. throughout the Ams., W Europe & Baltic & E Europe, Japan, Hong Kong, S Africa & Singapore; perfs. w. over 70 orchs., inclng. Suisse Romande, LPO, Cleveland & Vienna Symph.; num. fest. & broadcast perfs. Num. recordings. Contbr. to: Correio do Povo, Porto Alegre. Hons: Prize, Sao Sebastiao, Rio de Janeiro, 1966; Simoes Lopes Neto Medal, Porto Alegre, 1974; German Record Prize, Berlin, 1977. Hobbies: Philately; Numismatics; Painting; Gastronomy. Mgmt: Tower Music, Tottenham Ct. Rd. 125, London W1P 9HN. Address: Buchenweg 15, D-8019 Abersdorf, Post Steinhöring, German Fed. Repub. 28, 29.

SZIRMAY, Marta, b. 9 Oct. 12939, Kaposvar, Hungary. Opera & Oratorio Singer. Educ: Bela Bartok Conserv., Budapest. m. Manfai J Csaba. Debut: Hungarian State Oper House. Career incl: appearances w. opera cos. of Vienna, Basle, Moscow, Cologne & Hamburg; Festival appearances incl: Maggio Musical, Florence; Wiesbaden; Prague; Broadcaster on Hungarian & Italian Radio. Recordings incl: Te Deum of Buda Castle - Missa Brevis (Kodaly); Beethoven's 9th Symph.; 5 Hungarian Popula Songs (Bartok); var. songs by Liszt, Bach, Schumann, Brahms, Kodaly, etc. Hons: Liszt prize. Hobbies: Jazz singing; Improvisation; Fishing; Dogs. Mgmt: Nelly Failoni. Address: Kosciuszko Tade 10, 1012 Budapest, Hungary.

SZIRTES, Andrew Peter, b. 19 March 1952, Budapest, Hungary. Violinist. Educ: RCM; TCL. m. Edith Miranda, 2 s. Debut: Wembley Town Hall, 1961, violin solo. Career: Mbr., City of Birmingham Symph. orch.; TV apps. w. City of Birmingham Symph. orch., 1978, apps. in Royal Fest. Hall and Albert Hall. Recordings: 10 w. City of Birmingham Symph. orch. Hons: Silver Medal, Violin Solo, Wembley Music Fest., 1961; 2nd Prize, Vernon Adcock Talent Contest, 1963. Hobbies: Tennis; Golf; Ornithology; Comps. & Arr. Address: 144 Selsey Rd., Edgbaston, Birmingham B17 8JT, UK.

SZKODZINSKI (Sister), Louise, BVM, b. 11 Aug. 1921, Cicerto, Ill., USA. Teacher, piano, theory, music history & literature. Educ: BMusEd., Mundelein Coll., 1943; MMus, Chgo. Musical Coll., 1947; DMus, Ind. Univ., 1976. Career: 100 Piano recitals in 10 states, also in Lublin, Poland; apps. on Artist's Showcase (WGN-TV), 1967; Assoc. Prof. of music, Mundlein Coll. Publs: Doct. documents, A Comparison of Editorial Markings in Three Beethoven Sonatas, & The Polonaises of Chopin. Mbrships: Ill. State Music Tchrs. Assoc.; Chgo. Area Music Tchrs. Hobby: Photography. Address: Mundelein Coll., 6363 Sheridan Rd., Chgo., IL 60660, USA.

SZMOLYAN, Walter, b. 19 Feb. 1929, Vienna, Austria. Writer & Editor. Educ: Vienna Univ.; Studied Voice & Music Theory, Vienna Conserv.; Composition, Vienna Coll. of Music. Career: Ed., Österreichischen Musikzeitchrist, 1961-; Lectr., Lafite Music Publrs. (responsible for the series; Austrian Composers of the 20th Century), Vienna, 1964-. Mbrships: Bd. Dirs., Austrian Union of Composers, 1970-; Gen. Sec., Int. Schönberg Soc., 1972-. Publs: Josef Matthias Hauer, 1965; 50 Jahre Mödlinger Singakademie 1919-1969, 1969; over 100 articles most of them for the Osterreichistchen Musikzeitschrift; Music Critic, Mödlinger Zeitung. Address: Ferdinand Buchbergergasse II, A-2340 Mödling, Austria. 86.

SZOKOLAY, Sandor, b. 30 Mar. 1931, Kunagota, Hungary. Composer. Educ: Budapest Music Acad. m. Sari Fesztay, 1952, 4 s. Compositions incl; Blood Wedding (opera), 1963; Hamlet (opera), 1968; Aziszonyat balladaja (The Ballad of Horrow); Tetemrehivas (Ordeal of the Bier); Oratorios- A tuz marciusa (March Fire); Istar pokoljarasa (Ishtar's Descent to Hell); Cantatas; Choral works; Songs; Chmbr. Music. Hons. incl: Prize in Warsaw, Moscow & Vienna. Hobbies: Motoring; Mountaineering. Address: H-1119 Budapest, Szabados S.-Utica 90, Hungary.

SZOLLOSY, András, b. 27 Feb. 1921, Szászváros, Translyvania. Composer; Music Historian. Educ: Acad. of Music, Budapest (w. Kodály); Accademia di Santa Cecilia (w. Petrassi); PhD, Univ. of Budapest. m. Eva Keménfy. Comps: Tre pezzi per flauto e pianoforte; Concerto No. 3; Concerto No. 4; Musica per orchestra; Transfigurazion; Musica concertante; Preludio Adagio e Fuga; Sonorita; Concerto for harpsichord & strings, etc. Recordings incl: Trasfigurazioni, Musica per Orchestra, 1975. Publs: Art Kodály, 1943; Honegger, 1957; Critical edition of Bartok's Writings, 1967; Other Editions of Writings by Bartók & Kodály. Contbr. to var. music jrnls. Hons: First Prize, UNESCO's International Rostrum of Comps., Paris, 1970. Address: Somló ut 12, 1118 Budapest, Hungary. 28.

SZOMJAS-SCHIFFERT, György, b. 25 Apr. 1910, Dunakeszi, Hungary. Ethnomusicologist. Educ: Comp. & Singing, Szeged Conserv., 1930-3; LLD, Univ. of Szeged, 1934; Librarian Dip., Budapest, 1940; Candidate, Musical Scis., Budapest, 1969. m. Magda Imrik. Debut: w. songs, Paris radio, 1960. Career: Librarian, Ctrl. Office of Statistics, 1936-40; Musical columnist, Korunk Szava, 1936-42; Rapporteur, finally Ministerial Sec., Min. of Educ., Budapest, 1940-49; Scientific Contbr., then Prin. Contbr., Inst. of Musical Sci., Hungarian Acad. of Scis., 1954-76. Recordings: over 6000 collected folk songs. Publs: A finnugorság ösi zenéje nyomában, 1965; Rajnal vagyon, szép piros, Hnekes várvirrasztók és órakieltók, 1972; A finnugor zene vitája, 2 vols., 1976. num. contbr. to profl. jrnls. Mbr., Int. Folk Music Coun. Hobby: Former chess problem compiler. Address: Solymár-u. 8, 1032 Budapest, Hungary.

SZÓNYI, Erzsébet, b. 25 Apr. 1924, Budapest, Hungary. Composer; Pianist; Conductor; Teacher. Educ: Dip., Franz Liszt Acad. of Music, Budapest, 1947; Prix de composition, Conserv. de Paris, 1948; studied under Janos Viski, Ernö Szegedi, Tony Aubin, Nadja Boulanger & Olivier Messaien. m. Dr. Lajos Gémes. Debut: 1945. Career: Tchr., Second Schls., 1945-48, Franz Liszt Acad., Budapest, 1948-; Dir., Schl. Music Fac., ibid., 1960-; has worked in close coop. w. Zoltán Kodály. Compositions incli: 2nd Divertimento for Orch. (publd.), 1951; A Florentine Tragedy (opera), 1957; Concerto for Organ & Orch. (publd.), 1958; Six pieces for Organ (publd. & recorded), 1957; Due Sonetti di Petrarca for Mixed Voices, harp

& Clarinet (publd.), 1960; Piccola Introduzione (publd. & recorded), 1964; Trio Sonata for Violin, Violincello & Piano (publd.), 1965. Publs. incl: Method of Musical Reading & Writing, 1953, incl: Method of Musical Reading & Writing, 1953, Engl. ed., 1974; La Formation de l'Oreille Musicale, 1966; Principles & Practice of the Kodály Method, 1973. Contbr. to: Musical Education in Hungary, ed. F Sandor, 1966. Mbrships: Chopin Soc., Warsaw; VP, Int. Soc. for Music Educ.; Bd., Assn . of Hungarian Musicians & Music Educators Union. Recip. of Erkel Prize, 1959. Hobbies: Photography; Gardening. Mgmt: Edition Musica, Budapest; Boosey & Hawkes, NYC. Address: Tamasi Aron U.3, 1124 Budapest, Hungary.

SZPILMAN, Wladyslaw, b. 5 Dec. 1911, Sosnowiec, Poland. Pianist; Composer. Educ: Frederick Chopin HS of Mujsic; Music Acad., Berlin. m. Dr. Halina Grzecznarowska, 2 s. Career incl: Ldr., Warsaw Piano Quintet; Concert pianist in Poland, Sweden, Finland, Germany, Hungary & Czechoslovakia; Chmbr. Music performances in num. countries in Europe, N & S Am., Japan, India, etc. Compositions incl: Concertino for Piano & Orch.; Piano Suite - The life of Machines; num. works for piano & violin; some 450 songs. Num. recordings on Muza label & for Polish Radio. Publ: Cities of the Dead, 1946. Mbrships. incl: Soc. of Polish Composers; Soc. of Polish Musicians. Hons. incl: Kt., Order of Polonia Restituta; Gold Cross of Merit. Address: 12 Gimnastycina, 02-632 Warsaw, Poland.

SZPINALSKI, Antoni, b. 20 Jan. 1901, Sokolów Podlaski, Poland. Pianist; Composer. Educ: F Chopin Higher Schl. of Music, Warsaw. m. Henrietta Szpinalska. Comps: Opowieść wieczorna (Evening tale, piano & symph. orch.); Tarantella (flute & symph. orch.); Suita ludowa nr. 1 (Folk suite no. 1, symph. orch.); Warszawaska serenada (Warsaw serenade, symph. orch.); Mazur (symph. orch.); Polka staccato (2 piccolos & symph. orch.); Delia (waltz for symph. orch.) all also recorded. Mbrships: Assn. Polish Musicians; Assn. of Authors & Comps. of Light Music. Hobby: Photography. Address: Dabrowiecka 11, 03-932 Warsaw, Poland.

SZURMA-HASANI, Marianne, b. 21 Feb. 1949, Bradford, UK. Pianist; Accompanist; Teacher; Violinist. Educ: RAM; GMVCM; LRAM; ARCM. m. S A Haleem Hasani, 1 s., 1 d. Debut: Bradford, 1965. Career: solo & concerto perfs.; Accomp.; Tchr. of piano, violin, theory & harmony. Mbr., ISM. Hobbies: Languages; Travel; Flamenco Dancing; Judo. Address: 76 Woodside Ave., Alderton, Wembley, Middx., HA0 1UY, UK. 27.

SZUSTER, Julja Isabel. b. 28 Sept. 1946, Yeovil, Som., UK. Musicologist; Music Educator. Educ: BA (Hons.), musicol., Univ. Adelaide, Aust.; Dip., Secondary Tchng. Career: Advsry. Off. Classroom Music, Educ. Dept., SA. Contbr. to Groves Dictionary of Music & Musicians, articles on G W L Marshall-Hall. Mbrships: Am. Musicol. Soc.; Musicol. Soc. of Aust.; Musicol. Assn. SA; Aust. Soc. Music Educ. Address: 2A Elphyn Rd., Kingswood, SA 5062, Aust. 27, 29.

SZWED, Józef, b. 3 Oct. 1929, Tarnowskie Gory, Poland. Teacher of Music & Piano, Musical Academy, Katowice. Educ: MA, Musical Acad., 2 Dips., m. Dorota Szwed, 1 c. Career: Compositions performed on Polish Radio, 1952; made debut as Cond. w. Silesian Opera, 1963. Compositions: about 56 serious works inclng. symph. music, chmbr. music, songs, a 2 act opera (The King's Lover), Concertos for Trumpet; Concertos for trombone; also about 105 pieces of light music for orch. or brass band & about 200 arrangements of other composers' works. Mbrships: Union of Polish Composers; Assn. of 'ZAIKS' Authors. Hons: 2nd Prize for Young Polish Composers, 1967; Distinction for Polish Composers, 1968; 2 Prizes for songs, 1968 & 71. Hobbies: Gardening; Tramping. Address: ul. Jednósci Robotniczej 37, 42-600 Tarnowskie Góry, Poland.

SZWEYKOWSKI, Zygmunt Marian, b. 12 May 1929, Craców, Poland. Musicologist. Educ: MA, Poznán Univ.,

1951; PhD, Jagiellonian Univ., Crácow, 1964. m. Anna Szweykowska. Career: Asst., Musicol. Dept., Poznán Univ., 1950-53; Asst.-Reader, Jagiellonian Univ., Cracow, 1954-; Chmn. & Reader, Musicol. Dept., ibid., 1971-74. Publs. incl: Gen. Ed., Musicalia Vetera (thematic catalogue of early Polish musical MS), 5 vols., 1969-; Zródla do historii muzyki polskiej (Sources for Hist. of Polish Music), 24 vols., 1960-; other eds, of early Polish Music. Contbr. of num. papers & articles to musicol. jrnls. & encys. Mbrships: Union of Polish Comps. (Musicol. Sect.); Int. Musicol. Soc.; Am. Musicol. Soc. Address: Filarecka 24 m. 14, 30-110 Crácow, Poland.

SZYMAŃSKA, Iwonka Bogumiia, b. 11 July 1943, Warsaw, Poland. Composer; Pianist. Ecu: Piano Superior w. MA, 1965, Comp.'s Superior w. MA, 1972, State Higher Schl. of Music, Warsaw. Debut: as pianist, 1951; as comp., 1965. Career: radio broadcasts as pianist, 1964; & comp., 1970. Comps. incl: 3 symphs.; 4 str. quartets; Sonety: I (symph. orch.), II (2 sopranos, choir & orch.), & III (2 pianos & symph. orch.); Mahoniowy koncert (violin & orch.); Wiosenny koncert (piano & orch.); Mobil (symph. orch.); Trilogy (comprising Patria, Copernicus & Homini) solo works for piano & harp; Creation of new music form, 'Sonnet'. Contbr. reviews to Ruch Muzyczny, 1970-72. Mbr., Polish Comps. Union. Recip. sev. comp. awards. Address: al Świerczewskiego 98 m. 145, 01-016 Warsaw, Poland.

SZYMONOWICZ, Zbigniew, b. 3 Feb. 1922, Lwow, USSR. Pianist; Composer. Educ: Dip., Acad. of Music, Lodz, 1946; MA. m. Bozena Matulewica. Career: has given concerts in Poland, Austria, Bulgaria, Czechoslovakia, France, Finland, Germany, The Netherlands, Norway, Rumania, China & USSR; currently Pvte. Lectr. & Pres., Piano Cathedra, Music Acad., Lodz. Compositions: Piano solo works, Preludes, Mazurkas, Triptich, Variations & Fugue on theme B-A-C-H for 2 pianos, songs, Concerto for Piano & Orch., 1966; Dialogues for Piano, String Orch. & Percussion, 1971; 'Per aspera' for Symph. Orch., 1973. Has done recordings for Polish Radio & TV. Mbrships: ZKP (Union of Polish Composers); SPAM (Polish Musicians Assn.); Sec., TiFC (Frederic Chopin Soc.). Recip. of 8th Prize, IVth Frederic Chopin Int. Piano Competition, Warsaw, 1949. Address: Al. 1 Maja nr 3m. 8, 90-717 Lodz, Poland.

SZYMULSKA, Halina, b. 16 Jan. 1921, Lublin, Poland. Soprano Singer. Educ: studied w. Ada Sari, French Govt. Scholarship to study w. Prof. Pierre Bernac, École Normale, Paris, 2 s. Debut: 1950, Polish Radio, Warsaw. Career: concert career until 1962; num. perfs. on radio, Poland & abroad, 1962-; repertoire incls. songs by Moniuszko, Paderewski, Debussy, Fauré, Roussel, Messiaen. Poulenc, Wolf, Britten, Brahms, Schubert, Schumann, Rachmanioff, etc. Has recorded for radio, also LP of Moniuszko's songs, 1972. Mbr., Assn. of Polish Musicians (SPAM). Recip. Golden Cross of merit for propagation of Polish music abroad. Hobbies: Theatre; Film. Address: 00-229 Rynek Nowomiejski-Warsaw No. 27 m. 2, Poland. 2.

SZYROCKI, Jan, b. 29 Dec. 1931, Laziska Rybnickie, Poland. Conductor; Lecurer. Educ: MScEng., Szczecin Tech. Univ.; Dip., Piano, Music Schl.; Rybnik; Dip., Music Schl., Szczecin; Royal Schl. of Music, The Hague, Vienna Music Coll.; Poznań Music Coll., m. Jolanta Szyrocka, 2 d. Career: Fndr., Szczecin Boys Choir 1960; Fndr., Szczecin Tech. Univ. Choir which won 1st prizes in Polish competitions 1960, 61, 63, 67, 69 & 1973-74; prizes in Netherlands, 1969, & Czech., 1977; Pres., Szczecin Polish Choirs & Orchs. Assn.; Lectr., Poznań Music Coll. num. recordings in France, USA & Poland. Mbrships: Polish Musical Artists Assn.; Polish Choirs & Orchs. Assn.; Music Assn. Henryk Wieniawski Memorial, Szczecin. Hons: 1st degree, Polish Choirs & Orchs. Assn., 1968; Award for cond. at All-Polish Acad. Choirs Competition, 1960, 63, 67, 69, 73; Music Award, Szczecin, 1977. Hobbies: Travel; Swimming; Skiing; Photography. Address: Al. Wyzwolenia 11/5, 70 552 Szczecin, Poland.

T

TABACHNICK, Arthur. Violinist. Educ: BMus, Roosevelt Univ.; MMus, ibid. Career: Concertmaster, Ill. Symph. Orch., Chgo.; Staff Artist, WGN Radio & TV; Fac. Mbr., Nat. Music Camp, Interlochen, Mich., 1965-71; currently Concertmaster, Indpls. Symph. Orch., Mbr., Lyric Trio, & Concertmaster (summers), Grant Pk. Orch., Chgo.; has broadcast on nat. network; extensive concertizing throughout USA & Can. Hons. incl: Nat. HS Contest; Interlochen Music Schlrship.; Winner, Juilliard Competition, 1939.

TABACHNIK, Michel, b. Geneva, Switzerland. Composer; Conductor. Educ: Cips. in Comp. & Cond., Geneva Conserv.; Asst. to Pierre Boulez, 4 yrs. w. Christine, 1 s., 1 d. Debut: Fest. of Royan, France. Career: Regular Guest apps. as Cond. w. Berlin Phil., Concertgebouw, Amsterdam, Nat. Orch of France, Suisse Romande Orch., BBC Symph., etc.; Permanent Cond., Gulbenkian Orch., Lisbon, Portugal, 1973-75, and Regional Orch. of Lorraine, France, 1975-76; Artistic Dr., Ensemble Inter-Contemporain, Paris, 1976-. Comps. incl: Mondes; Fresque; Sillages; Movimenti; Eclipses; 3 Impressions; Perseides. Recordings: Works of a Honegger (w. French Nat. Orch.). Hobby: Alpinism. Mgmt: Samama, Houtweg 11, Laren NH Netherlands. Address: 6 Route de Prize, CH1227 Geneva, Switz.

TACUCHIAN, Ricardo, b. 18 Nov. 1939, Rio de Janeiro, Brazil. Professor; Composer. Educ: BS, Col. Pedro II; Grad., piano, Escola de Música, Univ. Fed. Rio de Janeiro, 1961; Comp. & Cond., ibid, 1965; Post grad., comp. & orchestration, 1967. m. Nilce de Oliveira Tacuchian, 2 s. Debut: Imagem Carioca for orch., 1963. Career incls: Comp., 1st Nat. Meeting of Comps., Brasilia, 1975; 1st Biennial Brazilian Music, 1975; Cond., sev. profl. & amateur choirs & ensembles; Prof., Hist. Music, Fed. Univ. Rio de Janeiro & Prof., Musical Educ., State Coll. Rio de Janeiro. Comps. incl: Concertino for piano & string orch.; Estruturas Sinfonicas (orch.); Cantata dos Mortos; Cantata de Natal; Estruthuras Verdes, for violin, cello & piano (recorded); O Canto de Poeta (recorded). Publs. incl: A Música no Século XIX, 1975. Mbr., profl. orgs. Address: Rua Eurico Cruz, 33 Apt. 204, Jardin Botánico, 22461 Rio de Janeiro, RJ Brazil.

TAGLIAVINI, Ferruccio, b. 14 Aug. 1913, Reggio Emiliao, Italy. Operatic Tenor. Educ: studies in electrical engrng.; Conserv. of Music, Parma; voice study w. Italo Brancucci, Parma & Amedeo Bassi, Florence. m. Pia Tassainari. Debut: Rodolfo, La Boheme, Teatro Communale, Florence, 1939. Career: apps. at major opera houses inclng. La Scala Milan, San Carlo Opera, Naples, Teatro Reale, Rome, Met. Opera, NYC, also in S Am.; concert tours in USA, 1946-; has made films in Italy, inclng. Barber of Seville. Recip. 1st Prize for singng, May Fest. competition, Florence, 1939. Mgmt: S A Gorlinsky Ltd., 35 Dover St., London W1, UK. 2.

TAHOURDIN, Peter Richard, b. 27 Aug. 1928, Brämdean, UK. Composer; Academic. Educ: TCL, 1949-52; LTCL; MMus, Univ. of Toronto. m. Jane Todner, 2 d. Career: Vis. Comp., Univ. of Adelaide, 1965; Snr. Lectr. in Comp., Univ. of Melbourne, 1973-. Comps: Orchl., chmbr., choral, electronic music. Recordings: Symph. No. 1; Symph. No. 2; Sinfonietta No. 2; Clarinet Sonata. Publs: Australian Composition in the 20th Century, 1978. Contbr. to: Comp.; Aust. Jrnl. of Music Educ. Mbrships: Chmn., Comps. Guild of Aust., 1978-79; Fellowship of Aust. Comps. Hobbies: Reading. Address: Faculty of Music, Univ. of Melbourne, Parkville, Vic. 3052, Aust. 3.

TAILLEFERRE, Germaine, b. 19 Apr. 1892, Parc St.-Maur, Seine, France. Composer. Educ: pupil of Ravel, Nat. Conserv. of Music, Paris. Divorced, 1 d. Career incl: Mbr., Les Six (w. Auric, Durey, Honneger, Milhaud & Poulenc); Prof. of Accompaniment, Schola Cantorum, 1970-72. Compositions incl: Concerto for baritone, piano & orch.; Concerto for flute, piano & orch.; Concerto for soprano & orch.; Operas - Il était un petit navire; La Petite Sirène; Le Maître; num. film scores, etc. Hons: Musical Grand Prix, Gen. Coun. of the Seine dist., 1960; Grand Prix of music, Acad. of Fine Arts, 1973; Off., Legion of Hon. Hobbies: Tapestry; Interior decoration. Address: 122 rue d'Assas, 75006 Paris, France.

TAIT, Malcolm James, b. 21 Jan. 1931, Vancouver, Can. Cellist. Educ: pvte. study w. Pierre Fournier. m. Myrna MacNeal, 3s. Career: num. perfs. as soloist w. ldng. Can. orchs.

& as recitalist; mbr., Brandon Univ. Trio; formerly prin. cellist, Vancouver Symph., Stratford Fest. Orch. & Toronto Symph. Orch.; former mbr., de Rimanoczy Quartet; app. at Stratford Fest. of Chmbr. Orch.; Artist-in-Residence, Univ. of New Brunswick; Sr. cello tchr., Univ. of Toronto & Royal Conserv. of Music, Toronto. num. recordings. Hobbies: Skiing; Canoeing. Address: 2506 Lorne Ave., Brandon, Man. R7B 0L2, Can.

TAJO, Italo, b. 25 Apr. 1915, Turin, Italy. Opera Singer; Stage Director; Professor of Voice & Opera. Educ: Study of engrng. & violin; Study of voice w. Nilde Bertozzi. m. Inelda Meroni, 1d. Debut: As Fafner in Das Rheingold, Turin, 1935. Career: Int. opera star w. perfs. in all maj. world opera houses; TV, radio, film, musical comedy & drama perfs.; Prof., Music & Opera, & Basso-in-Res., Coll.-Conserv. of Music, Univ. of Cinn., USA; Dir., Int. Opera Fest., Barga, Italy, 1970-. Recordings for HMV, RCA, Telefunken & Cetra-Soria. Mbrships: Nat. Opera Assn.; Coll. Music Soc. Hobby: Carpentry. Address: 5541 Penway Ct., Cincinnati, OH 45239, USA. 2.

TAJVIDI, Ali, b. 6 Nov. 1927, Tehran, Iran. Composer; Conductor; Violinist; Sitar Player. Educ: studied w. father, w. Abolhassan Saba & w. Mr. Ostovar. m. Shokat Tajvidi, 2 children. Debut: Nat. Iranian Radio, 1946. Career: Comps. for Iranian films; Comp., Cond. & Soloist, Nat. Iranian Radio & TV; Chmn., Higher Coun. of Music, ibid. Comps: 70 vocal works; 20 orchl. pieces; (all works recorded by Nat. Iranian Radio & TV). Contbr. to Iranian lit. jrnls. Mbrships: Fellow, Royal Coun. of Music; Chmn., Comps.-Vocalists-Musicians' Syndicate. Hons: Medal of Arts, 1st Class; Homayoon Hedal. Hobby: Reading. Address: 16 Hafezieh Alley, Shiraz Ave. (Vanak), Tehran, Iran.

TAKACS, Jenö, b. 25 Sept. 1902, Siegendorf, Burgenland, Austria. Composer; Pianist; Collector of Folkmusic; Professor Emeritus of the University of Cincinnati. Educ: Hochschule für Musik, Vienna, Austria. m. Eva Takács. Debut: Sopron, Hungary. Career: Concert tours of Europe, Nr.East, Far East, USA. Num. comps. Recordings by Osterreichische Phonotek Vienna, Composers Portrait, 1972. Cons., European Liszt Ctr., Eisenstadt, Austria. Mbrships: AAUP; Austrian Soc. of Comps.; Austrian Komponistenbund. Hons: Fellow, Grad. Schl., Univ. of Cinn., 1972-; Prof. hc given by State Pres., 1952; Merit Cross of Burgenland, 1962; Hon. Citizen of Siegendorf, 1963. Address: A-7012 Siegendorf, Austria.

TAKAHASHI, Yoriko, b. 27 June 1937, Kanazawa, Japan. Pianist. Educ: BA, Tokyo Univ. of Arts, 1961; UCLA, USA, 1964-65; Dips. in Piano, Toho Conserv. High Schl., 1957, Juilliard Schl. of Music, 1964, Akademie für Musik und Darstellende Kunst, Vienna, 1966; Piano studied w. var. tchrs. m. Gabriel Chodos, 1 s. Career: Concerts throughout Japan, USA & Europe; Official Accomp. for NHK, Tokyo; Apps. w. UCLA & Eugene (Ore.) Symph. Orchs., USA; Solo Recitals, Ore. Educl. TV Network & RIAS (Italy). Recordings: Sonatas No. 2 & 3 (MacDowell). Contbr. to: Fujin-no Tomo (Women's Companion); Asahi Newspaper, Tokyo. Hons. incl: Scholarship, Japan Soc., NY, 1964; Winner, Nat. Competition, Tokyo, 1954; Winner, Casella Int. Pianoforte Competition, Italy, 1966. Mgmt: Leo Berkowitz, 254 Plymouth St., New Bedford, MA 02740, USA. Address: 245 Waban Ave., Waban, MA 02168, USA.

TAKEDA, Y, b. 3 Feb. 1933, Yokohama, Japan. Conductor. Educ: Tokyo Univ. of Arts. m. Mary Ellen Carter, 1 s. Career: Guest Cond., Chgo. Symph. Orch., Cleveland Orch., Detroit Symph. Orch., Tokyo Metrop. Orch.; Tokyo Phil. Orch., Tokyo Symph. Orch. & Mich. Opera Theatre; Music Dir., Cond., NM Symph. Orch., Kalamazoo (Mich.) Symph. Orch. Hobby: Skiing. Mgmt: Harold Shaw Mgmt. Address: 6408 Ponderosa NE, Albuquerque, NM 87110, USA.

TAKEMITSU, Toru, b. 8 Oct. 1930, Tokyo, Japan. Composer. Educ: Study of composition w. Yasuji Kiyose, 2 yrs. Compositions incl: Requiem for String Orch.; Asterism for piano & orch.; November Steps; Green for Orch. (November Steps II); The Dorian Horizon for 17 Strings; Two Lentos for piano; Vocalism Ai; film scores for: Hara-Kiri; Woman of the Dunes; Kwaidan; Face of Another. Var. compositions recorded. Address: A301, 3-15-56 Tamako-cho, Higashi Murayama City, Tokyo 189, Japan.

TAL, Josef, b. 18 Sept. 1910, Pinne, nr. Poznan, Germany. Composer; Pianist. Educ: Dips. in piano, harp & tchng., Staatliche Akademische Hochschule für Musik, Berlin. m. Pola Pfeffer, 1 child. Incumbent, Chair of Musicol., Hebrew Univ., Jerusalem. Composer of var. works, inclng: 3 operas Ashmedai, 1971; Massada, 1973 & Die Versuchung, 1976. Publs: Elementary Theorie of Music, 1944; Introduction to Forms in Music, 1951. Contbr. to: the Wold of Music

(UNESCO); Bat Kol (Hebrew mag.). Mbrships: Akademie der Künste, Berlin; Pres., Israel Ctr. of Int. Music Counc.; Art Coun. mbr., Min. of Culture, Israel. Hons: UNESCO Fellowship for rsch. in electronic music, 1949, '64; Engel Prize, 1952; Tel Aviv Prize, 1971; State Prize, Israel. Address: Debora Hanevia Str. 3, Jerusalem, Israel.

TALARCZYK, Joseph, b. 12 Aug. 1919, Grudziadz, Poland. Composer; Conductor; Pianist. Educ: Dips., comp. & conducting, HS of Music, Lodz. m. Edwarda Niewiardwska, 2 children. Debut: w. Filharmonik Orch., Lodz. Career: Cond.; many musical theatre prods.; work for radio, TV & films. Comps. incl: 8 musicals; much symphonic pop music; Three Episodes; Rapsodie for trumpet & orch.; 2 Sinfoniettas; Cappriccio brillante; Three Polish Dances; Quintetto (flute, oboe, clarinet, bassoon & horn); Westerplatte (cantata); Piano concerto; Intrada; 10 musicals; much symph. pop music. Contbr. to: Teatr; Muzyka. Mbrships: Polish Comps. Assn.; Assn. of Polish Actors & Film; ZAIKS. Hons. incl: Golden Cross of Merit, 1957; var. prizes. Hobbies: Sking; Sailing. Address: Majdanska 24 m 2, 04-110 Warszaw, Poland.

TALBOT, Désirée Ruth, b. 24 Oct. 1926. Singer. Educ: LUCT (piano); LUCT (singing); UPLM (singing). Debut: Lady Allcash in Fra Diavolo, Cape Town. Career: Tchr., piano, singing, aural, theory, schsl. & conserv., 1954-60; Milan, 1960-62; Lectr. in Singing, Univ. of Stellenbosch, 1962-66; Snr. Lectr. in Singing, Univ. of Cape Town, 1966-; Prof., ibid, 1979-; Leading roles, over 500 perfs of 28 operas; Sang Judith in 1st British perf. of Duke Bluebeard's Castle, Bartok, 1957. Recordings: SABC & BBC Overseas Services. Publs: For the Love of Singing, 1978. Contbr. to jrnls. Hons: Award, Italian Govt. Hobby: Dressmaking. Address: 517 Sevenaoks, Main Street Newlands, 7700, Cape, S Africa.

TALBOT, Margaret Aimée Eileen, b. 25 May 1925, Melton Mowbray, Leics., UK. Cellist; Peripatetic Cello Teacher. Educ: RCM, (ARCM, Cello & Singing). m. Thomas Talbot, (dec.), 1 stepson. Debut: As cellist & singer, 1946. Career: Cello Tchr., Wyggeston Girls' Schl., Leicester, 1947-48; Music Mistress, King Edward VII Grammar Schl., Melton Mowbray, 1950-51, Knossington Grange Boys' Schl., 1952; Pt.-time Cello Tchr., Collegiate Girls' Schl., Leicester, 1952, Full time Music Mistress, ibid, 1954-56; Music Dir., Melton Mowbray Am. Operatic Soc., 1953-57, Oakham & Dist. Choral Soc., 1960; Fndr. & Mbr., Hull Symphonia Orch.; Peripatetic cello Tchr., Hull Educ. Authority, 1971-. Mbr., ISM. Hobbies: Writing Poetry & religious prose. Address: Tranquillo, 11 Parkside Close, Park Ave., Hull, HU5 3E2, UK. 3.

TALBOT, Michael Owen, b. 4 Jan. 1943, Luton, UK. University Lecturer in Music. Educ: BA Hons., MusB, PhD, Clare Coll., Cambridge Univ.; ARCM, RCM, London. 1 c. Comps: Many Eds. of Baroque Music. Publs: Vivaldi, 1978. Contbr. to: Music & Letters; The Music review; Musical Times; The Consort; Soundings. Mbrships: Histl. Advisor, The Vivaldi Soc.; RMA. Address: Dept. of Music, The University, PO Box 147, Liverpool L69 3BX, UK.

TALMA, Louise, b. 31 Oct. 1906, Arcachon, France. Composer. Educ: Attended Inst. of Musical Art, NYC, 1922-30; Studied Piano w. Isidore Philipp & Comp., Harmony, Organ w. Nadia Boulanger, Fontainebleau Schl. of Music, France, Summers 1926-39 & 1949, '51 & '61; BMus, NY Univ., 1931; MA, Columbia Univ., 1933. Career: Tchr., Hunter Coll., CUNY, 1928-52, Prof. Music, 1952-. Compositions incl: Four-handed Fun, 1939; Piano Sonata No. 1; Terre de France, 1943-45; Toccata for Orch., 1944; Alleluia in Form of Toccata for Piano, 1945; Let's Touch the Sky, 1952; Str. Quartet, 1954; La Corona, 1954-55; The Alcestiad (Opera), 1955-58; A Time to Remember, 1966-67; Voice of Peace, 1973; Summer Sounds for clarinet & string quartet; Piano Sonata no. 2, 1976. Mbrships: Fellow, AGO, 1944; Bd. of Trustees, Fontainebleau Fine Arts & Music Assn., 1950; Corp. Mbr., Edward MacDowell Assn., 1953-; ASCAP, 1962. Hons. incl: Two Guggenheim Fellowships, 1946 & '47; Sr. Fulbright Rsch. Grant, 1955-56; Marjorie Peabody Waite Award, Nat. Inst. of Arts & Letters, 1960; Sibelius Medal for Comp., Harriet Cohen Int. Awards, 1963; Elected to Nat. Inst. of Arts & Letters, 1974; Sanford Medal, Yale Univ., 1976. Hobbies: Travel; Study of Languages. Address: Hunter Coll., City Univ. of NY, 695 Park Ave., NY, NY 10021, USA. 2, 14.

TALMI, Yoav, b. 28 Apr. 1943, Kibbutz Merhavia, Israel. Conductor; Composer. Educ: Dip., Rubin Acad. of Music, Tel Aviv; Post-grad. Dip., Juilliard Schl. of Music, NY; Summer courses at Aspen, Tanglewood, Salzburg & Netherlands. m. Erella Gottesmann Talmi, 2 c. Career: Assoc. Cond., Louisville Orch., 1968-70; Co-Cond., Israel Chamber Orch., 1970-72; Artistic Dir. & cond., Gelders Symph. Orch., Arnhem,

1974-79; Prin. Guest Cond. & Artistic Advsr., Munich Phil. Orch., 1979-. Comps: Music for Flute & Strings, 1965; Overture on Mexican Themes (recorded), 1969. Recordings: Concertos for clarinet by Weber & Rossini; works by Sibelius; works for horn & orch. Hons: Boskovitch Prize for Comp., Israel, 1965; Koussevitzky Memorial Conducting Prize, Tanglewood, 1969. Hobbies: Chess; Painting. Address: Kapellenberglaan 7, Rozendaal (Gld. 6891, Netherlands.

TALMON (Monsohn), Zvi, b. 9 Dec. 1922, Jerusalem, Israel. Composer; Conductor; General & Music Teacher. Educ: Yeshivat 'Etz Hayim' & 'Mizrahi' Sem. for Tchrs.; studied Jewish music at the Shirat Yisrael Inst. under the late Hazzan Schlomo Zalman Rivlin; studied comp. & cond. at The Jerusalem Music Inst., The Israeli Conserv. & The Israel Acad. of Music. m. Rivka (Ronald), 3 c. Career: General & Music Tchr. at Tachk'moni Schl. & Choirmaster for 32 yrs.; Fndr. of the Hechal Shlomo Chorus & Cond. for many yrs.; Music Tchr., Choirmaster & Cond. of the Wind Instrument Orch. at the General Israel Orphans Home for Gils. Compositions: Jewish Liturgical Music for cantor, choir & organ (or piano); Jewish & Israeli songs for choir; Chasidic songs arranged for choirs. Var. recordings as cond. Publs: Lam'nazeach Mismor, 1945; Z'liley Dror Umoledet, 1951; Tav Ron, 1960; Et Hazamir, 1965; Music for Martyrs' & Heroes Remembrance Day, 1965; Rinat Hahechal, 1965; Ron Lan, 1967; Shir Ly, 1970; Mizmorey Shem V'yefet, 1972; Z'liley Shabat, 1974. Mbr., ACUM. Hobbies: Philology. Address: 22 Ben Maymon St., Jerusalem, Israel.

TALSMA, Willem Retze, b. 3 Jan. 1927, Wognum, Netherlands. Pianist; Harpsichord player; Organist; Conductor. Educ: studied law & Musicol., Univ. of Amsterdam. m. Hélène Beatrix Kemmere, 2 s. Career: Concerts & Lecture-recitals of ancient music on appropriate instruments; Advsr. for restoration of organs, State Commission for Monuments; Coaches soloists. Num. recordings, radio & TV apps. Comps: Church hymns. Publs: (Trilogy) Die Wiedergeburt der Klassiker (Renaissance of the Classics): Book I, Anleitung zur Entmechanisierung der Musik, 1979; Book II, Beethoven, 1980. Contbr. & music critic, num. jrnls. and newspapers. recip. Edison prize, 1967. Hobby: Collecing antique keyboard instruments. Address: Chalet El Mirlo, Artola Baja, Marbella, Málaga, Spain.

TALVELA, Martti Olavi, b. 4 Feb. 1934, Hiitola, Finland. Opera & Concert Singer. m. Anna Kääriäinen, 1 s., 2 d. Career: Tchr., Lahti Music HS, 1958; Royal Opera House, Stockholm, 1961-62; apps., Deutsche Oper Berlin, Staatsoper Hamburg, Vienna, Munich, Royal Opera Covent Gdn., Met. Opera NYC, La Scala Milan, Rome, San Fran., Tokyo, Bayreuth, Salzburg, 1962-; Artistic Dir., Savonlinna Opera Fest., Finland, 1972-; TV broadcasts. Has made many recordings. Hons: Pro Finlandia, 1973; Finnish State Prize, 1973. Hobbies: Music; Books; Fishing. 16.

TAMAS, Janos, b. 24 May 1936, Budapest, Hungary. Pianist; Cond.; Comp.; Prof. Educ: Conserv. Budapest, Zürich, Bern; Music Acad. Franz Liszt, Budapest; MA Zermatt; Theory and piano tchr. dip. m. Maria Leentvaar, 2 s. Debut: Zürich. Career: Cond. var. Swiss orch.; Musical Dir. Aargau Opera; Piano accompanist; Choir concerts; Visiting cond. Comp. incl: Little Hungarian Suite; Str. Quartet; Strausiade; The Infernal Supper oratorium; Capriccio, ballet; Eisblumen (piano). Recordings: Sonata for violin & piano; Mosaique; String Quartet; Improvisationen for piano. Mbrships: Swiss Musical Art Assn.; Swiss Comp. Soc.; Swiss Soc. of Music Pedagogues. Hons: 1st Prize Bach contest, Budapest, 1949; 2nd Prize Bartok contest, Budapest, 1954; Prize Musical Art Assn., 1964. Cultural Award Lion's Club, 1971; Werkjahr des Kantons Aargau, 1972. Hobbies: Wandering. Address: Burgstr. 10, 5012 Schönenwerd, Switz.

TAMASSY, Eva, b. 30 July 1936, Budapest, Hungary. Concert Flautist; Lecturer in Flute. Educ: F Erkel Conserv. of Music, Budapest; Franz Liszt Music Acad., Budapest; UPLM, S Africa. m. J P Cronjé, 2 s. Career: num. radio & TV apps.; annual concert tours throughout the country (concertos, recitals, chmbr. music); Teaching. Hobbies: Reading; Swimming. Address: Conserv., Univ. of Stellenbosch, Stellenbosch 7600, S Africa.

TAMASSY, Zdenko, b. 6 Sept. 1921. Vezseny, Hungary. Composer. Educ: Franz Liszt Acad. Music, Budapest. m. Gabriella Fischer. Compositions: Operettas; Musical comedies; Music for theatre, film, radio & TV. Mbrships: Assn. Hungarian Musicians. Hungarian Music Fund. Recip. Erkel Prize, 1966. Address: Balassi Bu7, 1055 Budapest, Hungary.

TAMBLYN, William, b. 5 Dec. 1941, Birmingham, UK. Editor; Composer; Lecturer; Publisher. Educ: BA (Hons.) Music,

Dunelm. Career: Hd., Schl. of Music, Colchester Inst. m. Anne Patricia, 2 s. Compositions: Over 150 inclng. 26 instrumental or vocal works published by Boosey & Hawkes, Novello, OUP, Chapman, St. Martins (RSCM), Chiswick Music. Recordings: Hosanna in excelsis - Apollo Sound; Chiswick Advent - Chiswick Music. Publs: Sing Up, a guide to singing in church, 1971; Ed., Church Music, 1966-74; sheet music, Articles in Church Music; Music in Educ.; Promoting Ch. Music; Liturgy; Times Educl. Supplement; Universe; Catholic Herald. Hobbies: Gardening; Family. Address: Motts Farm, Motts Ln., Marks Tey, Colchester, Essex, UK. 3.

TAMMARO, Ferruccio, b. 5 June 1947, Turin, Italy. Musicologist; History of Music Teacher. Educ: Fac. of Classical Humanities, Turin Univ.; BA; Hist. of Music Deg.; Comp. course & Electronic Music course, Verdi Conserv. of Turin. Career: Winner of Scholarship for research about Sibelius in Finland; Collaborator, Insts. of Musicol., Turin Univ. Comps: 2 Electronic works. Publs. incl: L'imperativo nella musica di Sibelius (The imperative in the music of Sibelius), 1974; Ambivalenza dell' Otello di Rossini (Ambivalence of the Otello of Rossini), 1977; Sibelius e il silenzio di Tapiola (Sibelius and the silence of Tapiola, 1977). Contbr. to: Nuova Rivista Musicale (Italiana); Rivista Della Società Italiana di Musicologia. Mbrships: Società Italiana di Musicologia. Hobby: Archeology. Address: Via Lamarmora 37, 10128, Torino, Italy.

TAN, Margaret Hee-Leng, b. 12 Dec. 1945, Penang, Malaysia. Concert Pianist. Educ: DMus A, Juilliard Schl., NY, 1971. m. Curtis Nelson Crouch. Career: num. apps. as Soloist, Orient & USA, also radio & TV broadcasts; participant, Aspen & Eastern Music Fests.; Mbr., 20th Century Consort; Carnegie Recital Hall, NYC, 1977. Contbr. to Jrnl. of Brit. Inst. of Recorded Sound. Mbr., Percy Grainger Lib. Soc. Recip. many awards & grants. Mgmt: Artist Int. Mgmt., NY; Donald Moore Prods., Singapore. Address: 489 13th St., Brooklyn, NY 11215, USA.

TAN, Melvyn, b. 13 Oct. 1956, Singapore. Harpsichordist; Pianist. Educ: Yehudi Menuhin Schl., Cobham, UK, 1969-74; RCM; ARCM. Debuts: Singapore, 1960; Wigmore Hall, London, 1977. Career: num. radio perfs.; recitals; perfs. w. Int. orchs. Hons: Prizewinner, Leeds Nat. Musicians' Platform, 1977, Royal Overseas League, 1975, Festival Estival de Paris, 1979; Raymond Russell Harpsichord Prize, 1975. Hobby: Keeping Fit. Mgmt: Stephen Hetherington, Queens Theatre, 51 Shaftesbury Ave., London W1. Address: 35 Somerset Rd., London W4, UK.

TANG, Jordan Cho-Tung, b. 27 Jan. 1948, Hong Kong. Composer; Orchestral & Choral Conductor. Educ: BA, Chung Chi Coll., Chinese Univ. of Hong Kong, 1969; MSM, Wittenberg Univ., Ohio, USA, 1971; MMus, Cleveland Inst. of Music, 1973; PhD cand., Univ. of Utah; studied comp. & conducting w. noted tchrs. Career: commission, Children Dance Theatre (The Buttermilk Tree); Asst. Cond., Univ. of Utah Symph., Univ. Chmbr. Orch., Utah Chmbr. Orch., Salt Lake Civic Symph. Orch.; Assoc. Cond., Utah Youth Orch.; Music Dir., SE Christian Ch., Music Dir., New Music Ensemble; currently Music Dir., S W Missouri State Univ. Symph. Comps. incl: Sinfonia Brevissima; Timpani Concerto; Violin Concertino; Elegy for Cello & Strings; String Quartet; Piece for Violoncello & Harp; A Little Suite for Woodwind Quartet; Psalm of Praise; Passio Brevis; Missa Brevis; Sonatinas for piano solo & duet. Mbrships. incl: ASCAP; Musicians Union; Am. Music Ctr.; Am. Symph. League. Recip. many hons. Hobbies: Music; Films. Address: Music Dept., S W Missouri State Univ., Springfield, MO 65802, USA. 8, 9.

TANGGAARD, Svend Erik, b. 25 Jan. 1942. Pianist; Composer. Educ: piano & comp. w. Helge Bonnen, Copenhagen, 1962-67; studies w. Karl Mansker, Munich. m. Lis Rex Pederson, 2 d. Debut: Danish Acad. of Fine Arts, 1962; Career: perfs. of own works by Danish Radio Symph. Orch. & Moritz Fromberg Quartet. Comps. incl: 3 symphs.; 8 str. quartets; Piano concerto; Violin concerto; Overtures Nos. 1 & 2 for chmbr. orch.; Concertos Nos. 1 & 2 for 14 wind instruments, 2 double basses & percussion; other instrumental works; songs. Publs: music ed., Ny Dansk Myte; articles in Danish Musicpcriodical (DMT). Mbrships: Danish Comps. Soc.; Union of Art, Groningen; Union of Young Comps. recip. State Art Fndn. grant for 3 yrs. Hobbies: European Lit.; Painting; Sculpture; Sponges. Address: Nikolaj Plads 7, 1067 Copenhagen K, Denmark.

TANNER, Jerré E, b. 5 Jan. 1939, Lock Haven, Pa., USA. Composer. Educ: BA, Univ. of Iowa, 1960; MA, San Francisco State Univ., 1970; studied comp. w. Dr Roger Nixon. Career: comps. perf. in Hawaii, Calif., Utah, on radio & TV. Comps: Ka Lei No Kane (opera); The Naupaka Floret (opera); Symphonic Song Cycles; Boy w. Goldfish; A Hawaiian Songbook, Book 1;

Kona; Book 2; The Tradion-Monarch; 6 Songs from a Winter's Pillowbook; Song Cycles (w. piano); From an Albion Songbook; Spring Garlands; Ho'oku'ikahi (symphonic); songs & chmbr. music pieces. Recording: Boy w. Goldfish, London Symph. Orch. Mbrships: ASCAP; Nat. Assn. of Am. Comps. & Conds.; Hawaiian Music Fndn.; Bd. mbr., Hawaii Arts Coun. num. fellowships, grants & awards incl: ASCAP awards, 1977, '78, '79. Mgmt: Malama Arts, Inc., PO Box 1761, Honolulu, HI 96806, USA. Address: PO Box 1478, Kailua-Kona, HI 96740, USA. 9.

TANNER, Paul. O. W., b. 15 Oct. 1917, Skunk Hollow, Ky., USA. Trombonist; Educator; Composer; Author. Educ: MA, UCLA. m. Bunny. Career: w. Glenn Miller Orch., Les Brown, etc.; Am Broadcasting System Staff, 16 yrs.; UCLA, 18 yrs. Currently Prof., ibid. Worked in all maj. film, radio, TV & recording studios & under many fine conds. Comps. incl: Concerto for Two Trombones; Aria for Trombone; Concert Duo for Tenor & Bass Trombone. Recordings: num., 1938-. Publs: A Study of Jazz, 3rd ed., 1976; The Complete Practice Method for Tenor Trombone. Contbr. to num. profl. publs. Mbrships. incl: Exec. Dir., World Jazz Assn.; Dir., Higher Curric., Nat. Assn. Jazz Educators. Recip. var. hons & awards. Address: 10966 Rochester Ave., Suite 4C, Los Angeles, CA 90024, USA.

TANSMAN, Alexandre, b. June 1897, Lodz, Poland. Composer; Pianist; Conductor. Educ: Univ. of Warsaw. Debut: at age 15. Career: tours as Pianist & Cond. throughout world; US tour, 1927; composed film scores. Compositions incl: Triptyque, 1931; 8 symphs.; Ricercari (orch.), 1949; Sabbatai Zevi (opera); Dyptique (orch.); 6 Etudes for orch.; La Nuit Kurde (opera); num. guitar works (sev. recorded by ldng. artists); 4 Movements for orch.; Le Serment (opera) The Prophet Isaiah (oratorio); Piano Concerto; Sextuor (ballet); Concerto for orch.; Toison d'or (opera) Viola Concerto; Hommage a Erasme de Rotterdam (orch.); Resurrection (ballet). Num. recordings. Publs: Igor Stravinsky, 1948. Contbr. to profl. publs. Hons. incl: Grand Prize, Poland, 1920; Elizabeth Sprague Coolidge Medal, USA; Berlioz Medal, France; var. hon. degrees. Hobby: Collecting Statuettes & Old Books. Address: 3 rue Florence, Blumenthal, Paris, 16e, France. 3.

TAPLEY, Rolland Sylvester, b. 12 Mar. 1901, Hudson, Mass., USA. Violinist; Conductor. Educ: Studied violin w. Felix Winternitz (grad. of Vienna Conserv.). m. (1) Roma Keddy, 3 children, (2) Augusta Hallet. Career: In 57th yr. w. Boston Symph. Orch.; Cond: N Shore Phil., 25 seasons; Wellesley Symph., 24 seasons; NH Phil., 14 seasons. Recordings on RCA & DGG. Harvard Musical Assn. Hobbies: Bridge; Camping. Fishing. Address: 111 Lincoln St., Newton Highlands, MA 02161, USA.

TAPSONY, Veronica, b. 12 July 1938, Budapest, Hungary. Concert Pianist; Teacher. Educ: Bela Bartok Musical Gymnasium; Tchrs. Dip., Gyor, Hungary; BM, MMus, Univ. of Mo., USA. m. Andrew Tapsony. Career: Concerts, London, Vienna, San Fran., Kan. City, Amsterdam, The Hague; Tchr., William Jewell Coll. & Univ. of Mo., Kan. City. Mbrships: Franz Liszt Soc., USA; Coll. Music Soc.; Nat. Soc. Lit. & The Arts; Mu Phi Epsilon. Hons: Franz Liszt Prize, Gyor 1959. Hobbies: Reading; Sports; Museums. Mgmt: Choveaux Mgmt., UK. Address: 8410 Sagamore, Leawood, KS 66206, USA.

TARABA, Bohuslav, b. 22 Nov. 1894, Sedicany, Bohemia, Czechoslovakia. Composer; Teacher (Retired). m. Milada Tarabová. Compositions: Melodramas on texts of K. Capek; The Funeral of President T G Masaryk; Settings of Shakespearean Sonnets; Czech Nonnet; The Life of Painter Peter (opera); num. orchl., vocal & chmbr. music pieces. Publs. incl: Lion & Dov; Memories on J B Foerster. Mbr., Czechoslovak Assn. of Comps. Hobbies: Painting; Horse-riding (formerly inclng. Long Distance Rides). Address: Bubenecská 8, Prague, Czechoslovakia.

TARACK, Gerald, b. 27 Feb. 1929, Detroit, Mich., USA. Violinist. Educ: Profl. Children's Schl.; Music Schl., Henry St. Settlement. m. Linda Viana Beckley, 1 s., 1 d. Debut: Town Hall, NY, 1952. Career: Freelance concertmaster & chmbr. musician; Dir., Tarack Chmbr. Ensemble; Music cons., NYC Ctr., Joffrey, Alvin Ailey & Paul Taylor Dance Cos.; Fac., Queens Coll. Recordings: Solo & Chmbr. Music, Vanguard, Monitor, Nonesuch, Atlantic, Composer's Recordings & Lyrichord labels. Mbr., Concert Artist's Guild. Hons: Profl. Children's Schl. Alumni Award, for important contbrn to performing arts, 1975. Address: 133 W 94th St., NY, NY 10025, USA.

TARANTO, Vernon Anthony Jr, b. 16 Nov. 1946, New Orleans, La., USA. Composer. Educ: BMus & MMus, La. State

Univ. m. Joyce Gibson, 3 s. Career: Sinfonia Orionis commissioned & premiered by Georgetown Symph. Orch., Wash. DC, 1974; Fantasie On An American Folk Song, USAF Band; Prof. music theory & comp., Nicholls State Univ., Thibodaux, La. Comps: Study 1 for Brass Trio, Comps. Autograph Publs: Rejoice, choral anthem, Pro Art Music Publrs. Mbr. Beta Omega Chapt., Phi Mu Alpha Sinfonia. Hons: Soliloquy for Strings selected for perf. by New Orleans Phil. in concert of student works, 1966; La. Comps. Award, 1978. Hobby: Gardening. Address: Rte. 2, Box 343, Prairieville, LA 70769, USA.

TARANU, Cornel, b. 20 June 1934, Cluj, Romania. Composer; Conductor. Educ: Conserv. of Music, Cluj, 1951-57; 2 Dips., piano, comp.; studied w. Nadia Boulanger & Olivier Messiaen, Paris, 1966-67; Gyorgy Ligeti & Cristopher Caskel, 1968-69; Dr. in Musicol., Cluj Conserv., 1973. m. Daniela Margineanu, 1 d. Debut: as comp. w. string trio, 1952. Career: Works perf. by all Rumanian orchs. (Cluj, Bucharest); Orch. National ORTF; Cleveland, Lausanne, Brussels, Warsaw, Athens, London, etc. w. Ars Nova of Cluj; Cond., Ars Nova of Cluj, contemporary music ensemble; Prof. of Comp., Conserv. of Cluj. Compositions incl: Sonatas for flute, piano; Contrastes; Incantations; Song to a Bright Century; Horia's Oak & Cortège (Cantatas); Lieder, choral, Incidental & Film Music; Don Giovanni's Secret. (Chamber Opera); Il Symph., Aulodica; Rime di Michelangelo (voice & ensemble); Résonances (guitar solo or w. ensemble). Recordings: Electrecord Bucharest (w. Symetries & Sequences). Publs: Enesch in the Consciousness of the Present, 1969; 8 Madrigals. Contbr. to music jrnls. Mbrships: Rumanian Union of Comps.; SACEM, Paris. Recip., Prize of Rumanian Composers, 1972, '78; Prize of the Rumanian Acad., 1973. DMus, 1973. Hobbies: Jazz; Reading, etc. Address: Jorga 7, Cluj, Rumania.

TARCAN, Haluk, b. 1 Sept. 1931, Izmir, Turkey. Pianist; Ethnomusicologist. Educ: Dip. Piano & Solfeggio Tchr., Acad. of Music, Istanbul; Summer courses; Academia Chigiana, Sienna, Italy & Salzburg Mozarteum; Grad., Nat. Ctr. of Scientific Rsch., Paris; Pvte. studies w. J Fevrier, Paris. m. Therese Tarcan. Debut: Istanbul. Career: Perfs. & recitals, chmbr. music & soloist w. orchs. in Istanbul, Ankara, Salzburg & Paris. Recording of J Brahms Piano Solo. Publs: Comptines at Jeux Enfantins Turcs, published by Kultur B K, Milli Folklor Arastirma 16, Ankara, 1976. Contbr. to CNRS, Paris; Music critic, daily Turkish newspaper Cumhurriyet & Orkestra, Istanbul. Hobbies: Hist.; Archaeology; Underwater Fishing; Photography. Address: 20 rue Chappe, 75018 Paris, France.

TARKAM, Ella, b. 12 Nov. 1938, San Francisco, USA. Violist; Violinist. Educ: AA City Coll. of San Francisco; BA San Francisco State Univ., 1969. Career: has broadcast live on KDFC-FM radio w. Berkeley Promenade Orch.; plays w. Old 1st Ch. Orch., San Fran., & Cath. Archdiocese Soc., San Fran. Recordings: Tchaikovsky's Canzonetta; Mozart's Eine Kleine Nacht Music; Brigadoon; St. Gabriel Sings Again; Albinoni's Op. 7 No. 3 Concerti a Cinque (w. Berkeley Prom.). Mbrships: Local 6, Am. Fedn. of Musicians; Soc. of Western Artists; San Fran. SPCA, Recip. of Suzuki Award Cert., Am. String Tchrs. Assn., 1966. Hobbies incl: Chmbr. Music; Hindu & Belly Dancing; Watercolors & Pen & Ink Drawings; Eastern Philos.; Gardening. Addrss: 329 Elizabeth St., San Francisco, CA 94114, USA.

TARP, Sv. Erik, b. 6 Aug. 1908, Thisted, Jutland, Denmark. Composer. Educ: Royal Conserv., Copenhagen. m. Aase Rising, 2 d. Comps: 7 Symphs., overtures, suites for orch.; Chmbr. music; Piano music; Operas; Ballets; Songs etc.; Music for film, stage & TV. Recordings: Symphony nr. 2 in E flat; Te Deum for mixed choir & orch. Contbr. to sev. newspapers. Mbrships incl: Bd. Dirs., Danish Composers Soc.; Pres., Bd., Gen. Mgr., Soc. Publng. Danish Music, 1966-74; Gen. Mgr., Danish PRS, 1960-74; Bd. Dirs., Danish Copyright Soc., 1960-74; Danish Artists Stoc. Hons. incl: Anckerske legat; Lange-Muller prize; Carl Nielsen prize. Hobby: Driving sports cars. Address: Strandvejen 12, 2100 Copenhagen O, Denmark.

TARR, David Eugene, b. 11 Jan. 1932, Washington, Pa., USA. College Professor; Conductor. Educ: BSM, Nyack Coll., NY; MusM, Hartford Univ.; Regina Conserv. of Music, Saskatchewan, Canada; W. Va. Univ.; PhD, Pacific State Univ., 1977. m. Dorothy Gray, 3 s., 1 d. Career: Writer & Dir., "Singspiration," Canadian TV; Command Performance w. "The Young Americans," King of Thailand, Bangkok; Conductor, num. stage & TV appearances on world tour w. "The Young Americans"; Prof. of Music (Vocal), Alderson-Broaddus Coll., Philippi, W. Va.; Conductor, "A-B Singers" in Coun. of Churches TV Special "RAP"; Fndr./Dir., The West Virginians. Mbrships: VP, Coun. of Cultural Coords., W Va.; MENC; AAUP. Hons: Nat. Teaching Fellowship, 1970-71; Outstanding Educator of Am., 1974-75. Hobbies: Oil Painting. Address: Alderson-Broaddes Coll., Philippi, W. Va., USA.

TARR, Edward Hankins, b. 15 June 1936, Norwich, Conn., USA. Trumpet Soloist; Musicologist. Educ: AB, Oberlin Coll., 1957; MMus, Northwestern Univ., 1959; Grad. Study w. Prof. Leo Schrade, Univ. of Basel, Switzerland, 1959-64. m. Madeleine Fiorese, 1 s., 1 d. Career: Tchr., The Musical Acad. & the Schola Cantorum Basiliensis, Basle. Recordings: Num. recordings inclng. Bach's 2nd Brandenburg Concerto & 3rd & 4th Orchestral Suites, on valveless Baroque Trumpet; Hummel Concerto in E; Baroque Masterpieces for Trumpet & Organ, Vol. 1-3 (w. George Kent). Publs. incl: Johann Ernst Altenburg's Essay on an Introduction to the Heroic & Musical Trumpeters' Art (translation), 1974; Die Trompete, 1977 (2nd Ed., 1978); G F Handel, Suite in D Major for Trumpet, Strings, & Basso Continuo, 1733; Johann Nepomuk Hummel, Concerto a tromba principale, in Edur; Claudio Monteverdi, L'Orfeo. Contbr. to: Kongressbericht Bonn; The Diapason; Brass Bulletin; Grove's Dictionary of Music & Musicians, 6th Ed.; Notes; The Musical Times. Mbrships: Pi Kappa Lambda, 1959. Mgmt: Concerto Winderstein, Germany; Utter Mgmt., USA. Address: Oberer Rheinweg 71, CH-4058 Basel, Switzerland.

TASKER, William Decatur Jr., b. 25 July 1943, Winston-Salem, NC, USA. Composer; Conductor; Teacher & Performer on all Keyboards & Recorders. Educ: BA, San Jose State Coll., 1965; MA, UCLA, 1969; studied w. var. noted tchrs. Career incls: Actor (bit part) in film Down to the Sea. Comps: concert works, inclng. Alaska Sketches (orchl.); A Sacred Symphony (brasses, soprano, chorus, percussion); chmbr. music, inclng: I Am a Child (cantata); Concierto Grande de Mariachi (recorder orch.); Suite for Violin; many film scores & commercials inclng. Quality of Man in the Next 100 Years (US Info. Agcy.); pop record arrs. Contbr. to Recorder News. Mbrships: Am. Fedn. of Musicians Local 47; BMI; Am. Soc. of Music Arrs.; Pres., Southern Calif. Chapt., Am. Recorder Soc. Hobbies incl: Railroads & trams. Address: PO Box 197, Topanga, CA 90290, USA.

TATE, Phyllis (Margaret Duncan), b. 6 Apr. 1911, Gerrards Cross, Bucks., UK. Composer. Educ: RAM, FRAM, 1964. m. Alan Frank, 1 s., 1 d. Num. comps. incl. sev. commissioned for BBC, Festivals etc. & many others inclng: Saxophone Concerto, 1944; Str. Quartet, 1952; Choral Scene fromn the Bachhae, 1953; The Lady of Shalott for tenor & Instruments, 1956; London Fields, 1958; Opera, The Lodger, 1960; TV Opera, Dark Pilgrimage, 1963; Gravestones, for Cleo Laine, 1966; Illustrations for Brass Band, 1969; Variegations for Solo Viola, 1970; Serenade to Christmas, Chorus & Orch., 1972; Explorations around a Troubadour Song, Piano, 1973; Lyric Suite, Piano Duet, 1974; The Rainbow & the Cuckoo, (oboe & string trio), 1975; Songs of Sundrie Kindes for tenor & lute, 1975; St. Martha & the Dragon, for narrator, soloist, chorus & orch., 1976; Scenes from Kipling for baritone & piano, 1976; All the World's a Stage for chorus & orch., 1977; Panorama for Strings, 1977. Num. works for Young People inclng: The Story of Lieutenant Cockatoo, Twice in a Blue Moon, A Pride of Lions, Ring Out, Sing Out. Recordings: Sonata, for Cello & Clarinet; Apparitions, for Tenor & Instruments; Nocturne, for 4 voices; 3 Gaelic Ballads; Street Sounds. Address: 12 Heath Hurst Rd., London NW3 2RX, UK. 1.

TATRAI, Vilmos, b. 7 Oct. 1912, Kispest, Hungary. Violinist; Music Educator. Educ: Nat. Conserv., Budapest. m. Zsuzsa Kreisman, 1938, 1 s., 1 d. Career: Tchr., 1946-53; 1st Violin, Budapest Symph. Orch., 1933; Mbr., Radio Orch., 1938; Leading Violinist, Metropol. State Concert Orch., 1940-; Fndr.-Lrd., Tatrai String Quartet, 1946-; Tours of European countries w. Quartet, 1952-; Fndr.-Ldr., Hungarian Chmbr. Orch., 1957-; Prof. of Music, Budapest Acad. of Music, 1965-. Hons: 1st Prize, Bela Bartok Competition, 1948; Liszt Prize, 1952; Kossuth Prize, 1958; Eminent Artist of Hungarian People's Repub. Hobbies: Walking; Photography. Address: Zenemuveszeti Foiskola, Liszt Ferenc ter. 2, H-1136 Budapest XIII, Hungary.

TATRO, Duane L., b. 18 May 1927, Van Nuys, Calif., USA. Film Composer. Educ: BA, Univ. of Southern Calif., Ecole Normale de Musique, Paris, France. m. Françoise, 2 s., 1 d. Career incl: Composer of Film scores for: Green Apple Road; Paper Man; Man Hunter, etc.; TV scores for FBI; Mannix; Mission Impossible; Streets of San Francisco; MASH; Cades Country; Invaders; Young Lawyers; Barnaby Jones, etc. Recordings: Duane Tatro's Music for Moderns; Music to Listen to Red Norvo By; Smack Up (Art Pepper Quintet) - all Contemporary label. Mbrships: Composers & Lyricists Guild of Am.; Am. Fedn. of Musicians. Hobbies: Tennis; Fishing; Hunting. Address: 15705 Superior St., Sepulveda, CA 91343, USA.

TATTERMUSCHOVA, Helena, b. 28 Jan. 1933, Prague, Czechoslovakia. Singer (Soprano); Opera Member, National

Theatre, Prague. Educ: Acad. of Music, Prague. m. Bota Jaroslav, 1 s. Debut: Opera Ostrava, Czechoslovakia, 1954. Career: Opera Ostrava, 1954-56; Opera Prague, 1956-; Perfs. at Music Festivals in Edinburgh, Barcelona, Wiesbaden, Brussels, Amsterdam, Naples, Feneva, Zürich, Lausanne, Bologna, Moscow, Warsaw, Kiel, Vienna, Sofia & Prague. TV & radio apps. Num. recordings. Hons: 2nd Prize, Int. Competition, Prague, 1954; Dip. of Hon., Int. Competition, Geneva, 1958. Hobbies: Gardening; Flowers; Farming on own farm. Mgmt: Nat. Theatre, Prague. Address: Prague 10, Strasnice, Detska St. No. 210, Postal No. 10000, Czechoslovakia. 3.

TATTERSALL, David William, b. 11 Sept. 1935, Manchester, UK. Lecturer in Music Education; Piano & Organ Recitalist. Educ: RCM; RSCM; Auckland Univ., NZ; LRAM; ARCM; ARCO. m. Beatrice May, 1 s. Career incls: Prin., Auckland Schl. of Music & Organist & Choirmaster, St. Thomas, Auckland, 1967-71; Dir. of Music, Mt. Albert Grammar Schl. for Boys, 1968-71, Prior's Ct., Newbury, Berks, 1971-73 & Dilworth Schl., Auckland, NZ, 1973-75; Lectr.-i/c Tas. Conservatorium of Music, Launceston, 1975-. Comps: 3 piano sonatas; variations for piano; organ rhapsody; set of 30 choral introits; brass fanfare; Albertson Overture for wind instruments. Mbrships: Int. Soc. for Music Educ.; Kodaly Soc. for Music Educ. Hobbies incl: Social & Econ. Hist.; Flying. Address: c/o Tas. Conservatorium of Music, Tas. Coll. of Adv. Educ., PO Box 1214, Launceston, Tas. 7250, Aust. 3.

TATTERSALL, Norman, b. 13 Oct. 1924, Burnley, Lancs., UK. Singer. Educ: RAM; ARAM; LRAM. Career: Profl. Singer, Concert, Opera, Recital, Broadcasting; Lectr.; Adjudicator; Dir. of Opera, Music Dept., Colchester Inst. of Higher Educ. Mbrships: Soc. Sec., Solo Perfs. Sect., ISM. Hons: Num. prizes, RAM, 1947-52; Boise Award, 1953. Hobbies: Motoring; Theatre; Cooking. Mgmt: Ibbs & Tillett Ltd. Address: 2 Amyand Park Gardens, Twickenham, TW1 3HS, Middx., UK.

TAUSKY, Vilem, b. 20 July 1910, Prerov, Czech. Conductor; Composer. Educ: Univ. of Brno; Janácek Conserv., Brno; Meisterschule, Prague. m. Margaret Helen Powell. Career incls: Nat. Opera House, Brno, Czech., 1929-39; Musical Dir., Carl Rosa Opera, 1945-49; Guest Cond., Royal Opera House at Covent Gdn., 1951-; Sadler's Wells Opera, 1953-; BBC Cond., 1950-; Dir. of Opera, GSM, 1966-; Artistic Dir., Phoenix Opera Co., 1967-. Comps. incl: Czechoslovak Christmas Carols, 1942; Oboe Concerto, 1957; Concertino for harmonica & orch., 1963; Divertimento for strings, 1966; Soho: scherzo for orch., 1966; Concert Overture for brass band, 1969; Cakes & Ale: overture for brass band, 1971; From Our Village: orchl. suite, 1972. Hons: Czech. Mil. Cross, 1944; Czech. Order of Merit, 1945. Hobby: Country Life. Address: 44 Haven Green Ct., London W5, UK. 1.

TAUSSIG, Walter, b. 9 Feb. 1908, Vienna, Austria. Conductor; Piano Coach & Accompanist. Educ: degree 'Matura', Humanistic Gymnasium, Vienna; some semesters of Univ. of Vienna; Akademie fur Musik und darstellende Kunst, Vienna & Hochschule fur Musik und darstellende Kunst. m. Lenore Ruth Elkan, 1 d. Career: Scv. provincial German Opera Houses, & theatres in Vienna; Tours throughout Europe, Turkey & Egypt; w. S. Hurok touring USA & Canada; Phil. concerts in Havana, Cuba; Orch. concerts in NY Town Hall & Carnegie Hall; w. the New Opera & two prodns. on Broadway; w. Montreal, Chgo.; San Francisco, Pitts. & Ctrl. City, Colo., Opera Cos.; w. Met. Opera, NY, 1949- (first as Asst. Cond. & since 1968 as Assoc. Cond.); w. the Salzburg Fest., Austria, 1964-; w. Vienna Staatsoper at the Worlds Fair, Montreal, 1967; w. La Scala, Milan, 1974 & 1975. Var. recordings. Hons: Fulbright Exchange Prof. in Tokyo, Japan, 1965-66. Hobbies: Philos.; Swimming, etc. Address: 320 Riverside Dr., No. 14 G. NY, NY 10025, USA. 4.

TAUTENHAHN, Gunther, b. 22 Dec. 1938, Kowno, Lithuania. Composer; Teacher; Author. Educ: studied violin, piano & comp. in NY. Career: Comps. widely performed & broadcast in USA; Inventor of clock face whereby children can learn note and time values. Comps. incl: Brass Quintet; Concerto for double bass & orch.; Double Concerto for french horn, timpani & orch.; Concept Three for orch.; Suite for double bass; Concerto for alto saxophone & orch.; Options for flute & double bass; (employing Fiber Movement principle) Numeric Serenade for piano & orch.; Sinfonietta for 12 instruments; Trio for trumpet, tubular bells & cello. Publs: The Importance of One, 1971; Controlled Expressionism, 1976; Fiber Movements, 1978. Contbr. to musical jrnls. Mbrships: incl: ASCAP; Am. Soc. of Univ. Comps.; AMC; NACUSA; ICA. Recip., Young Am. Comps. Award, 1963. Address: 1534 3rd St., Manhattan Beach, CA 90266, USA. 2, 9, 28, 29.

TAVENER, John Kenneth, b. 28 Jan. 1944, London, UK. Composer. Educ: RAM; Hon. FTCL; Hon. ARAM. m. Victoria

Maragopolou. Career: Works perfd. in UK, Ireland, Scandinavia, Netherlands, Poland, USA, Can., Aust., etc. Comps. publd. incl: Pro Concerto; Celtic Requiem; Coplas; Nomine Jesu; Cain and Abel; Ultimos Ritos; Therese (opera); A Gentle Spirit (opera); Kyklike Kinesis. Comps. Recorded: The Whale; Requiem for Father Malachy; Canciones Espanolas; The Divine Liturgy of St. John Chrysostom. Hons. incl: Int. Sacred Music Prize, Perugia, for Ultimos Ritos; Prince Ranier of Monaco Prize for Comp.; UNECSO Prize. Mgmt: Chester Music, Eagle Court, London, UK. Address: c/o Mgmt. 30.

TAYLOE, Marjorie Zaerr, b. 15 Feb., Los Angeles, Calif., USA. Harpist; Singer; Conductor of English Handbell Choirs. Educ: Artist Dip., Samiloff Opera Acad.; Los Angeles Valley Coll.; Whittier Coll.; Occidental Coll.; Los Angeles Music Schl.; Am. TV Schl., Hollywood. m. Ralph Chester Tayloe, 2 s., 3 d. Debut: Los Angeles, 1950. Career: Apps. as organist & harpist on radio & TV; Var. opera roles; Soloist harpist, Beverly Hills Symph.; Dir., Royal Bonnie Bells, Engl. handbell ringers & Tayloe Family Singers & Handbell Ringers. Comps. incl: Praise the Lord, 1976. Num. recordings. Publs. incl: The Welch Harpers, 1975. Coantbr. to profl. jrnls. & mags. Mbr. profl. orgs. Hobbies: Children; Collecting Bells & Harps. Mgmt: The Tayloe Family Recordings. Address: 4527 Kraft Ave., N Hollywood, CA 91602, USA. 5, 9.

TAYLOR, Alexander Macdonald, b. 9 May, 1932, Edinburgh, Scotland, UK. Musician (Viola). Educ: Trinity Acad., Edinburgh; RAM. m. Ruth Marsh, 2 s., 1 d. Career: Prin. Viola, LSO. Recordings: Brandenburgs & Trout: Music for Pleasure. Hobby: Gardening. Address: 21 Pine Gdns., Surbiton, Surrey, UK.

TAYLOR, Anne, b. Johannesburg, S Africa. Concert Pianist; Accompanist; Singer; Teacher. Educ: Studies w. Leff Pouishnoff. Lic. Tchr. & Performer, RAM, London, UK; TCL; Univ. of S Africa. Career: Concert apps. as soloist & assoc. pianist since childhood w. brother, Prof. David Carl Taylor RAM, London, & leading artists; Num. broadcast recitals inclng. progs. of Schubert, Brahms, Hugo Wolf & Goethe; Lieder recitals; Soloist w. City of Johannesburg & Durban Symph. Orchs., S African Broadcasting Symph. Orchs.; Frequent recitals as pianist & singer for Johannesburg Musical Soc.; Many concerts for charity & cultural organizations. Publs: Critical thesis & enlightened approach to Pianoforte. Hons: Tripel Bursar Medallist, Assoc. Bd., Royal Schls. of Music, London; Dip. of Merit, Cambrian Soc. Eisteddfod & S African Broadcasting Co. Hobbies: The Arts; Country Walks; Language Studies. Address: Suite 98, Guildhall, Esselen & Edith Cavell St., Hospital Hill, Johannesburg, S Africa.

TAYLOR, Bernard U., b. 8 Jan. 1897, Olean, NY, USA. Opera, Concert, Recital & Oratorio Singer. Educ: Tchrs. Coll., Columbia Univ.; Pvte. study in Paris, Rome, London. m. Jean Hayes, 1 d. Career: Mbr., Pa. Opera Co., Phila.; Num. US tours in oratorio, concert, recitals; Teacher. Publs: Compiler, Ed. num. song albums, inclng. Classic Italian Art Songs, 3 Vols.; French, German Art Songs; Contemporary American Songs; Great Art Songs of 3 Centuries; Bach Arias for Soprano. Contbr. to profl. jrnls.; Chmn., Ed. Bd., Bulletin of Nat. Assn. of Tchrs. of Singing. Mbrships: Past Pres., NY Singing Tchrs. Assn.; Co-fndr., Past Pres., Nat. Assn. of Tchrs. of Singing; Am. Acad. of Tchrs. of Singing; Metrop. Opera Club. Hobbies: Opera; Travel to European fests. Address: 464 Riverside Dr., New York, NY 10027, USA. 6.

TAYLOR, Charles, b. Manchester, UK. Violinist. Educ: Royal Manchester Coll. of Music; FRMCM; Hon. RCM. m. Mary Donnelly, 1 s., 2 d. Career: Ldr., Taylor String Quartet, 1934-50, Royal Opera House Orch., 1952-76, Brighton Phil. Orch., 1952-. Recip., OBE, 1972. Hobbies: Golf; Chess. Address: 10 Westside, Hendon, London NW4, UK.

TAYLOR, Christopher Corin, b. 3 March 1929, Ewell, UK. Flautist; Recorder player. Educ: GSM; Hon. ARAM. m. Anthea Cox, 2 s., 2 d. Debut: BBC Third programme, 1952. Career: Prin. Flute, Royal Opera House, 1955-59; Prin. Flute, RPO, 1963-67; Prof., RAM, 1974-. Recordings: Brandenburg Concertos; Vivaldi Recorder Concerto; 7 Bach Flute Sonatas; 4 Vivaldi Flute Concertos. Mbrships: PRS; Aston Martin Owners Club; Walton on Thames Sailing Club. Hobbies: Driving Sports Cars; Sailing. Address: The Little House, Weston Green, Thames Ditton, Surrey KT7 OJZ, UK.

TAYLOR, Clara, b. 24 July 1948, London, UK. Pianist; Accompanist; Professor, RAM. Educ: LRAM, 1968. m. Colin Wainwright. Career: Concerts as soloist & Accomp. throughout UK & Europe; apps. on TV; sev. BBC recordings; Prof., RAM, 1974-. Recordings for Pearl Records. Mbrships: ISM; RAM Club. Mgmt: Young Musicians Liaison. Address: Lintalee, Austenwood Ln., Gerrards Cross, Bucks., UK. 23, 27, 30.

TAYLOR, Clifford Oliver, b. 20 Oct. 1923, Bellevue, Pa., USA. Composer; Professor of Music; Clarinettist. Educ: BFA (comp.) & BFA (perf.-clarinet), Carnegie Mellon Univ., Pitts., Pa.; MA in Music, Harvard Univ., Cambridge, Mass., 1950; studied w. Nicholai Lopatnikoff, Dr. Frederick Dorian, Domenico Caputo, Walter Piston, Paul Hindemith, Randall Thompson, etc.; pvte. study of violin w. Gosta Andreasson; pvte. study of clarinet, Rosario Mazzeo. m. Louise Kemp Taylor, 3 s. Career: Asst. Prof., Dept. of Music, Chatham Coll., Pittsburgh, Pa., 1954-61; Assoc. Prof., ibid, 1961-63; Buhl Assoc. Prof. of Humanities, 1962-63; Asst. Prof. of Music & Comp., Coll. of Music, Temple Univ., Phila., Pa., 1963-64; Assoc. Prof. of Music & Comp., ibid, 1964-69; Prof. of Music, 1969-. Cir., Cond., contemporary players & singers. Perf. w. many well-known orchs. & artists. Compositions incl: works for orch., chamber music, str. quartet, voice, choral, piano, organ, percussion. Contbr. to profl. jrnls. Mbrships: Am. Composers Alliance; Am. Soc. of Univ. Composers; Coll. Music Soc.; Am. Music Ctr. Recip. Awards from NEA, Nat. Symph. Orch., Rheta A Sosland Competition, Friends of Harvey Gaul, Inc. Hobbies: Swimming; Winemaking. Address: 149 Fernbrook Ave., Wyncote, PA 19095, USA.

TAYLOR, Derek Noel, b. 20 Feb. 1929, Oldham, UK. Director of Music, HM Welsh Guards. Educ: ARCM; LTCL. m. Rosaleen Taylor, 1 s., 3 d. Career: Bandmaster, 16th/5th The Queens Royal Lancers; Schl. Bandmaster, Royal Mil. Schl. of Music, Kneller Hall; Dir. of Music, Royal Mil. Acad., Sandhurst. Recordings: Sousa Marches; Lennon & MacCartney; Tunes of Glory; Hands Across the Sea; Selections from the Shows. Mbrships: Lansdowne Club; Hon. Mbr., Lions Int. Hobby: Golf. Address: Welsh Guards Band, Chelsea Barracks, London SW1, UK.

TAYLOR, Eric Robert, b. 8 May 1928, Leamington, UK. University Professor of Music. Educ: MA, DMus, Christ Ch., Oxford; Hon. RAM; ARCO. m. Mary Monica Pratt, 2 s. Career: Organ Scholar, Christ Ch., Oxford, & Sub-Organist, Christ Ch. Cathedral, 1945-49; Prof. of Harmony, TCL, 1952-55; Dir. of Music, Stonyhurst Coll., 1955-59; Sr. Lectr. in Music, Univ. of Reading, 1959-68; Prof. of Harmony, RAM, 1959-66; Prof. of Music, Univ. of Durham, 1968-; Examiner to Assoc. Bd., Royal Schls. of Music, 1957-. Publs: A Method of Aural Training, 3 vols., 1959; Playing from an Orchestral Score, 1967; Introduction to Score Playing, 1969. Address: The Music Schl., Palace Green, Durham, DH1 3RL, UK.

TAYLOR, Gerald, b. 20 Nov. 1935, Upholland, Lancs., UK. Music Educator; Organ Recitalist; Director of Music; Accompanist. Educ: RCM; FRCO; FTCL; ARCM. m. Ruth Margaret Lawson, 2 s. Career: Organist & regular weekly recitalist, St. Thomas's Ch., Regent St., London, 1958-60; Music Master, Westminster Abbey Choir Schl., 2nd Asst. Organist, Westminster Abbey, Organist to Westminster Schl., 1964-68; Dir. of Music, Cottesmore Schl., Crawley, Sussex, 1968-; Organist, Warnham Singers, Horsham, Sussex; Recitalist, Chs. & Cathedrals, UK. Mbrships. incl: ISM; Music Masters Assn.; RCO; Westminster Abbey Old Choristers' Assn. Hobbies: Playing the Piano; Gardening; Country Walks. Address: 14 Oaks Close, Amberley Grange, Horsham, W Sussex RH12 4TZ, UK. 4.

TAYLOR, John, b. 18 July 1945, Charing, Ashford, Kent, UK. Organist; Church Musician. Educ: BMus, Univ. of London; DipEd, Univ. of Reading; RCM; FRCO; LRAM; ARCM. Career: Hammond Scholar for Organ, Queen's Free Chapel of St. George, Windsor Castle, 1966-68; Organist & Dir. of Music, Ch. of St. John the Divine, Kennington, London, 1969-72; Asst. Organist, Scottish Episcopal Cathedral Ch. of St. Mary, Edinburgh, & Asst. Dir. of Music, St. Mary's Music Schl., Edinburgh, 1972-77; Organist & Choirmaster, Loughborough Parish Ch., Leics. & Music Tchr., Garenden High Schl. for Boys, Loughborough, Leics., 1977-. Mbrships: ISM; RCO. Hobbies: Photography; Motoring. Address: 25 Pinfold Gate, Loughborough, Leics. LE11 1BE, UK.

TAYLOR, Kendall, b. Sheffield, Yorks, UK. Concert Pianist; Professor of Music. Educ: RCM w. Herbert Fryer (piano); Gustav Holst (compositions) & Sir Malcolm Sargent (conducting); FRCM. m. Mirjana Nikolic, 2 d. Career: Concert pianist, regular appearances at BBC Promenade Concerts; Concertos at Edinburgh Festival; w. Royal Phil. Soc. & all leading British Orchs. & Conds.; Var. recital tours & radio broadcasts; Tours of W Europe, Canada, Australia & NZ, W Indies, Africa, Far E, etc.; Bd. of Profs., RCM; Assoc. Bd., Royal Schls. of Music. Mbrships: ISM. Hobbies: Mountain walking; Scrambling; Reading. Address: 45 Worple Rd., Wimbledon, London SW19, UK.

TAYLOR, Lily Elizabeth, b. Manchester, UK. Musician, Flute, Recorders, Organ, Piano. Educ: Studied w. Dr. Arthur W Pollitt.

m. Stainton de Boufflers Taylor. Career: Flute, Recorder Tutor, Educ. Dept., Liverpool, 1958-, Wallasey, 1961-; Choirmaster & Org., Ch. of Humanity, Liverpool, 1925-31; Mbr. London Phil. Choir, 1933-39; Music Mistress, Marymount Convent, Wallasey, 1962-66; Mbr. Wallasey Singers, 1941-65; Fndr., Dir., Round House Consort, 1950; Musical Dir., Merseyside Soc. Recorder Players, 1951-69; Vis. Tutor, C F Mott Coll. of Educ., 1969. Mbrships: Galpin Soc.; Dolmetsch Fndn.; Soc. Recorder Players. Hobby: Domestic Arts. Address: The Round House, Magazine Lane, Wallasey, Merseyside L45 1LX, UK. 3.

TAYLOR, Maria del Pico, b. 7 May 1935 Havana, Cuba. Pianist; Assistant Professor of Piano; Head of Piano Class. Educ: Degree, Diplomatic Law, Univ. of Havana; Piano & Theory Dips., Conserv. Peyrellade, Havana; Artist & Lic. Dips., Univ. of Toronto, Can.; MMus, Northwestern Univ., USA. m. Raymond J. Taylor, 1 d. Debut: as mbr. of Momento Musicale Trio, Carnegie Hall, 1975. Career: Concerts as soloist & w. orchs., Cuba, USA & Can.; Frequent concerts at colls. & univs.; Special series of lecture-recitals, Chgo. Bd. of Educ.; Asst. Prof. of Piano & Hd., Piano Class, Temple Univ., 1971-; on roster of Young Audiences Inc., perfs. in num. shcl. concerts. Mbrships: Pi Kappa Lambda; Pa. Music Tchs. Assn.; AAUP. Hons. incl: Silver Medal, 1951, Gold Medal, 1952, Conserv. Peyrellade, Havana; "Notalbe American" Plaque, 1978; var. scholarships. Hobbies incl: Travel; Gourmet cooking. Mgmt: Eric Semon Assocs., 11 W 57th ST., NYC, NY, USA. Address: 7950 Henry Ave. Apt. 12A, Phila., PA 19128, USA. 27.

TAYLOR, Millard Benjamin, b. 9 Aug. 1913, Crete, Neb., USA. Concertmaster; Violinist; Professor of Violin. Educ: BMus, Eastman Schl. of Music, 1935; Perf.'s Cert.; Artist Dip. m. Marie Jeanne Capasso Taylor, 2 d. Career: Concertmaster, NSO, Wash. DC, 1938-44, Rochester Phil. Orch., 1945-67, Chautauqua Symph. Orch., 1965-; Prof. of Violin, Eastman Schl., 1944-; Chmn., String Dept., ibid., 1950-; Violinist, Eastman Quartet, Eastman String Trio; Ldr. & 1st Violin, Chautauqua Str. Quartet. Recordings incl: Brahms Piano Quartets Opus 25, 26, 60 (w. Eastman Quartet). Publs. incl: Ed., Violin Parts, 9 Beethoven Symphonies. Contbr. to Instrumentalist. Hons: DMus, Doane Coll., 1967; DLitt, Neb. Wesleyan Univ., 1975. Hobbies incl: Photography; Boating. Address: 25 Coral Way, Rochester, NY, USA. 2.

TAYLOR, Neilson, b. Huddersfield, UK. Baritone Singer. Educ: BA (Geog.), London; Post-Grad. Cert. in Educ.; Adv. Dip., RAM, 1954-59; studied w. Roy Henderson, Ettore Campogalliani, Eduardo Asquez. Debut: in opera, Glyndebourne, 1963. Career incl: ret'd. from profl. football to join Granadiers TV grp., 1958, & Cliff Adams Singers, making regular TV & radio broadcasts; toured Aust. w. Tommy Steele, 1960; Leading roles, Glydebourne Opera Co., 1962-65; recitals in Italy; opera & concerts, Germany, Netherlands, Austria, Portugal; regular radio & TV broadcasts; Guest Artist, Royal Opera House Covent Gdn.; Prof. of Singing, Royal Scottish Acad. of Music. Recordings incl: Annie Get Your Gun; Théerèse (Massenet); Merry Go Down (Warlock anthol.). Hobbies: Golf; Painting. Address: 30 Kilnford Cres., Dundonald, Ayrshire, UK.

TAYLOR, Patricia Anne, b. 20 Dec. 1944, Bramley, Leeds, UK. Mezzo-soprano Singer. Educ: RMCM; ARMCM (tchr. & perf.); GRSM; Hochschule für Musik und Darstellende Kunst, Vienna. m. Roderick Kennedy. Debut: Wigmore Hall, London, 1970. Career: concerts & recitals throughout UK w. most major orchs.; apps. in Spain, Vienna & Paris; apps. w. Scottish, Phoenix, Kent, Engl. Nat. Opera Cos. & w. Chelsea Opera Group; perfs. on radio & TV; roles incl. Mother (The Consul) & Speranza (Orfeo). Contbr. to: Opera. Mbrships: Equity; ISM. Hons: Countess of Munster Award, 1969, '71; Curtis Gold Medal, 1970; Richard Tauber Memorial Prize, 1970; Imperial League of Opera Prize, 1971. Hobbies: Painting; House Plants; Photography; Designing & Producing Operas for amateurs & students. Mgmt: Music Int., London. Address: 211 Maybank Rd., S Woodford, London E18 1EP, UK.

TAYLOR, Robert George, b. 17 Feb. 1915, Seven Kings, UK. Peripatetic String Teacher. Educ: Borough Rd. Trng. Coll., 1934-36; Assoc., Coll. of Preceptors, 1938; LTCL (choral conducting); FTCL (orchl. conducting). Career: Tchr., Brentwood Co. Secondary Schl., 1936-40; Served in Europe w. Royal Field Artillery, 1940-45; Studied pt.-time, TCL, & Music Tchr., var. shcls., 1945-71; Peripatetic String Tchr., Mid-Essex Div., Essex Educ. Auth., 1971-; Free-lance Viola Player. Mbrships: ISM; Nat. Union of Tchrs.; Hon. Musical Dir., var. amateur orchs. & operatic socs. Hobbies: Reading; Swimming; Motoring; For. travel; Amateur acting. Address: 38 Middleton Rd., Shenfield, Essex, CM15 8DJ, UK.

TAYLOR, Ronald L, b. 22 July 1946, Montreal, Canada. Flautist; Concert Artist; Soloist; Professor of Music. Educ:

Regents Dip. Hons. in Music, SUNY, USA; NY State Dip., Rome Free Acad., NY. m. Janice Taylor. Debut: Solo Recital, Nat. Gall., Ottawa, Can. Career: Over 140 solo & jt. recitals throughout Can. & USA; Jt. TV recital (CBC) w. wife; Solo recitals over CBC; Solo apps. w. Montreal Chmbr. Orch.; Former Prin. Flute w. Can. Symph. Orch.; Prof. of Flute, Orford Arts Ctr. of Jeunesses Musicales du Can.; Prof. of Flute, Royal Conserv. of Music, Univ. of Toronto. Pres., Toronto Flute Soc. Hons. incl: B Sharp Music Club Award, Utica, NY, 1964. Hobbies: Langs.; Cooking. Mgmt: Ont. Arts Coun., 151 Bloot St. W. Suite 500, Toronto, Ont. M5S 1T6. Address: 467 Church St., Toronto, Ont., Canada.

TAYLOR, Rossmé Agnes, b. 15 Nov. 1924, Winnipeg, Man., Can. Teacher of Piano, Organ, Harpsichord, Lute. Educ: BMus, Univ. of Toronto, 1950; MMus, Univ. of Wis., USA, 1955; MSc, Columbia Univ., NY, 1966; Assoc. Dip., Toronto Conserv. of Music, 1944. m. Alan W. Taylor. Career incls: Educl. Radio & TV, Univ. of Wis. & Pa. State Univ.; Pvte. study in fortepiano & harpsichord. Contbr. to Am. Music Tchr. Mbrships. incl: Chmn., Bethesda Chapt., Md. Nat. Guild of Piano Tchrs.; Music Tchrs. Nat. Assoc.; Md. State MTA. Hons: Nat. Hon. Roll, Nat. Guild of Piano Tchrs., 1973, 74, 76; Alice Chandler Egan Scholarship in Music, Ore. Shakespearean Fest., 1960. Hobbies incl: Music collections. Address: 7302 Baylor Ave., College Park, MD 20740, USA. 5.

TAYLOR, Thomas Fuller, b. 7 May 1937, Evanston, Ill., USA. Associate Professor of Music History & Musicology; Director. Educ: BA, Physics, Earlham Coll., Richmond, 1969; MMs, Music Hist., 1962, PhD, Music Hist., 1967, Northwestern Univ., Evanston, Ill.; Harvard Univ. m. Nancy Emmons Taylor, 1 d., 1 s. Career: Tchr. of Music, Math., Science, Oakwood Schl., Poughkeepsie, NY, 1959-61; Instructor of Music, Earlham Coll., Richmond, Ind., 1962-64; Lectr. of Music, Ind. Univ., Bloomington, Ind., 1966-67; Assoc. Prof., Music Hist. & Musicol., Univ. of Mich., 1967-; Dir., Collegium Musicum. Recordings: The Emperor Maximilian and Music. Publs: Catalog of the works of Jeremiah Clarke, 1977. Contbr. to: The Musical Quarterly; Diapason. Mbrships: Am. Musicol. Soc.; Coll. Music Soc. Hons: Grants for the Rackham Schl. to pursue rsch. in Spanish Cathedrals, 1977. Hobbies: Woodworking; Hiking; Cross Country Skiing; Skating. Address: 324 Hilldale Dr., Ann Arbor, MI 48105, USA.

TCHAIKOWSKY, André, b. 1 Nov. 1935, Warsaw, Poland. Composer; Pianist. Educ: Paris Conserv.; Warsaw Conserv.; Pvte. studies w. Stefan Askenase (piano) & Hans Keller (comp.). Debut: Paris, 1948. Comps: Sonata for clarinet & piano, 1958; Inventions for piano, 1960; 2 String Quartets; Piano Concerto, 1971; Trio Notturno, for violin, cello & piano, 1978; 2 Song-Cycles to texts by Shakespeare. Recordings: Mozart Piano Concerto K. 503; Bach-Goldberg Variations; Haydn F Minor Variations & 2 Sonatas; Mozart Sonatas; Mozart Klavierstücke; Schubert Ländler & Waltzes. Mbr., Performing Rights Soc. Hobbies: Reading; Chess; Prose Writing; Solitary Walks. Mgmt: Harrison/Parrott Ltd., 22 Hillgate St., London W8 7SR, UK. Address: c/o Mgmt. 1.

TCHEREPNIN, Alexander, b. 21 Jan. 1899, St. Peterburg, Russia. Composer; Conductor; Pianist. Educ: St. Peterburg Conserv.; Paris Conserv. m. Lee Hsien-Ming, 3 s. Debut: London. Career: Worldwide apps. Compositions: Over 100 published works. Recordings for DGR, EMI, Coloseum, others. Mbrships: Nat. Inst. of Art & Letters, NYC; Bohemians, NYC. Hons: Schott Music Composition Prize, 1924; Chevalier of Arts & Letters, French Govt.; Glinka Prize; Am. Opera Soc. Hobbies: Nature; Icon collecting; Books. Mgmt: Ibbs & Tillett, London. Address: 2 Rue Furstenberg, Paris 6, France. 2.

TCHICAI, John Martin, b. 28 Apr. 1936, Christianshaven, Copenhagen, Denmark. Musician (Alto & Soprano Saxophone); Percussionist; Composer. Educ: Acad. of Music. m. Kirsten Tchicai, 1 child. Career: Films Future One, Denmark, Walking Woman, Can.; Radio, TV perfs. in Holland, Belgium, Germany, Sweden & Denmark; Concerts in all above & Italy, Norway, Finland, USA, UK, France, Switz., Iran, Afghanistan & India. Comps: num. songs, incidental music. Recordings: Wiebelfeser Live; Cadentia Nova Danica; Afrodisiaca; Instant Comps. Pool 002, 005, Holland; NY Art Quartet; Norwegian Concert. Mbrships: Narayananda Universal Yoga Trust; Danish Comps. Union; Rumi Soc., London. Hons: Jazz Musician of the Yr., Denmark, 1969; Danish Cultural Ministry Grant, 1968; Scholarship Grant, Deutscher Akademischer Austauschdienst, Berlin, 1978. Hobbies: Cleansing the Mind; Looking at Unpolluted Nature. Address: Hojskolevej 11, 2960 Rungsted, Denmark.

TEAGUE, William Chandler Sr., b. 8 July 1922, Gainesville, Tex., USA. Organist; Pianist; Church Musician; Conductor;

Lecturer; Teacher. Educ: Southern Meth. Univ.; BMus, Curtis Inst. Music; Int. Zomeracad. voor Organistens, Haarlem, Netherlands. m. Lucille Ridinger Teague, 1 s., 1 d. Debut: Gainesville, Tex. Career: Num. perfs., local, state, regional & nat. convens., AGO; Annual transcontinental concert tours, USA; Extensive concert tours, Europe, Mexico, etc.; Radio & TV apps., USA & UK. Recordings incl: Wicks' Organ Recital Series. Contbr. to jrnls. Mbr. profl. orgs. Hons. incl: Shreveport Jrnl. Award, Musician of Yr., 1971. Hobbies incl: Swimming. Mgmt: Ibbs & Tillett, 124 Wigmore St., London, UK; Pagart Agency, Warsaw, Poland. Address: 547 Broadmoor Blvd., Shreveport, LA 71105, USA. 7, 29.

TEALE, Perry Wendel, b. 28 May 1923, Carleton Pl., Ont., Can. Pianist; Organist; Reviewer; Composer; Arranger; Broadcasting Producer. Educ: Dip., Royal Conserv. of Music, Toronto; LTCL; ARCT (Piano solo perf.). Debut: as Pianist, Montreal, 1947; as Organist, w. Atlantic Symph. Orch., 1976. Career: Solo recitals on piano & organ; piano solos w. orch.; sev. CBC radio recitals; Music Prod., CBC. Contbr. to Grove's Dict., 6th ed.; hundreds of reviews. Mbrships. incl: RCO; Royal Can. Coll. of Organists; Atlantic Fedn. of Musicians. Hobbies: Athletics; Judo. Address: RR 1, Musquodoboit Harbour, Halifax Co., NS, Canada B0J 2L0.

TEAR, Robert, b. 8 Mar. 1939. Concert & Operatic Tenor. m. Hilary Thomas, 2 d. Educ: MA, King's Coll., Cambridge. Debut: Covent Garden, 1970. Career: Mbr. King's Coll. Choir, 1957-60; Engl. Nat. Opera Grp., 1964. Worked w. world's famous conds., Karajan, Bernstein & Solti. Appeared in num. roles in operas & major festivals. Close assoc. w. Michael Tippett, 1970-. Appears regularly w. Royal Opera & Scottish Opera. Has worked w. every major recording co. & made num. recordings. Mbrship: Garrick Club. Recip: FRSA. Hobbies: All sport; Digging; 18 & 19 Century Engl. Water colours. Address: 101D Clarendon Rd., London W11, UK. 2.

TEBALDI, Renata, b. 1 Feb. 1922, Italy. Opera Singer (soprano). Educ: Arrigo Boito Conserv., Parma; Gioacchino Rossini Conserv., Pesaro; Study w. Carmen Melis & Giuseppe Pais k in NY. Debut: Rovigo, 1944. Career incl: chosen by Toscanini to appear in re-opening of La Scala, Milan, 1946; Covent Gdn. Debut in Verdi's Otello & the Requiem, conducted by Victor de Sabato, 1950; Sang leading lyric roles in her early career, notably mimi & Desdemona; later developed dramatic roles incl. Tosca & Aida; Cilea's opera, Adriana Lecouvreur, was revived for her in perfs. in NY & Chgo.; Perfs. incl. wide range of leading soprano operatic roles in theatres of European & USA Music Ctrs. Address: 1 Piazza Guastella, Milan, Italy.

TECK, Katherine (Née Weintz), b. 31 Dec. 1939, Mineola, NY, USA. Promoter of Modern Music; Editor & Journalist. Educ: BA, Vassar Coll., 1960; Mannes Coll. of Music, 1961-62; MA, Columbia Univ., 1964; studied horn w. Harry Berv & Gregory Squires. m. Alan Teck, 1 s., 1 d. Career: Concert Music Dept., Broadcast Music Inc., 1964-66; Pres., Mod. Listeners' Record Club, 1966-67; Ed. Staff, Dover Publs. Inc., 1967-69; Horn Player, Westchester Phil. Symph., Yonkers Civic Phil. Orch., Westchester Co. Band, Performing Arts Soc. (Opera). Comp. var. works for winds (unpubld.) Contbr. to musical publs. inclng: Three Facets of French Horn, 1964. Mbrships: Int. Horn Soc.; NY Brass Conf. for Scholarships. Hobby: Playing harpsichord & piano. Address: 11 Clinton Ave., Hastings-on-Hudson, NY 10706, USA.

TEGGIN, Maggie L, b. 8 Oct. 1946, Cheshire, UK. Private Teacher. Educ: Dip. Educ.; Dip. Stage Mgmt.; Dancing quals. incl: MNATD for tap; ANATD for ballet & ballroom; BA (MUS), Univ. Nottingham; Lic., Trinity Coll. of Music, London. m. David Hipperson. Career: Asst. Stage Mgr., Hair; Stage Mgr., Opera for All; Dir., Stage Mgr., Engl. Opera Grp.; Prod., Norfolk Opera Players; Music Tchr., Thorpe Grammar Schl., Norwich; Tchr., Tanya Polunin Schl.; Vis. Tchr., Keswick Hall Coll. & Notre Dame Schl. Contbr. to: Classical Music; ISM Journal. Mbrships: Incorp. Soc. of Musicians (Warden, Pvte. Tchrs. Sect., 1980-81); Int. Piano Tchrs. Cons.; Hon. Local Sec., Norwich Ctr. of ISM. Recip. Arts Coun. Schlrship., 1969. Hobbies: Operatic Prods.; Choral Singing; Gardening. Address: 211 Unthank Rd., Norwich, Norfolk, NR2 2PH, UK. 23, 27.

TEJON, Jose Ignacio, b. 12 Dec. 1920, Tarragona, Spain. Composer; Techer; University President. Educ: B Phil, Univ. of Comillas; B Theol., Sophia Univ., Tokyo, Japan; BMus, Pius X Inst., NYC, USA; MA, Manhattan Schl. of Music; Dip. Counterpoint, Ecole Normale, Paris, France. Debut: (as Cond.) Hiroshima, Japan, 1964. Career: 50 Concerts as Choral Cond., Japan, 1965-; Concerts, Spanish Radio & TV, 1974; Pres., Elizabeth Univ. of Music, Hiroshima; Cond.; Elizabeth Madrigal Singers. Comps: Choral works, inclng. Missa Japonica, Missa Anniversarii, Shizukeki (carol). Recordings: Mozart, Coronation

Mass; own works. Publs. incl: Counterpoint according to the Style of Palestrina, (Japanese), 1971. Contbr. to Gendai Guitar. Address: Elizabeth Univ. of Music, Noboricho 4-15, Hiroshima, Japan.

TE KANAWA, Kiri, b. Gisborne, NZ. Soprano. m. Desmond Stephen Park. Debut: Countess, Marriage of Figaro, Royal Opera House Covent Gdn., 1971. Career: apps. at major opera houses inclng. Metrop. Opera, NY, San Fran. Opera, Paris Opera, Sydney Opera House. Roles incl: Amelia, Simon Boccenegra; Donna Elvia, Don Giovanni; Desdemona, Otello; Mini, La Bohemine; Michaela, Carmen; Pamina, Magic Flute. Recordings: Don Giovanni; Mozart Vespers & Exultate Jubilate (both under Colin Davis on Philips). Recip. OBE, 1973. Hobbies: Golf; Reading; Squash. Mgmt: Artists Int. Mgmt., London.

TELERMAN, Estela, b. 23 Aug. 1946, Buenos Aires, Argentina. Pianist; Teacher. Educ: AA, Palomar Coll., San Diego, Calif., USA; MA, Univ. of Buenos Aires; Municipal Conserv. of Buenos Aires; Collegium Musicum of Buenos Aires; Piano study w. pvte. tutors. Debut: Solo recital, Buenos Aires, age 15. Career: Soloist in recitals; Orchl. concerts & Chmbr. Music recitals, buenos Aires & other cities of Argentina; Recitals in NYC, Wash., Phila. & var. cities of Calif., USA; Recitals & TV broadcasts in Lima & Arequipa, Peru; Local Radio & TV Braodcasts; Int. Bach Soc. Sessions, Lincoln Ctr., NYC, 1968-69; Tchng. Asst., Hist. of Music, Fac. of Philos. & Letters, Univ. of Buenos Aires. Contbr. of articles to local mags. & jrnls. Mbrship: Grad. Coll., Univ. of Buenos Aires; Music Tchrs. Assn. Hobby: Collecting records. Recip: 1st Prize, Juan Carlos Pax, 1975. Address: Beruti 3676 3-B 1425 Buenos Aires, Argentina.

TELLSTROM, Anders Theodore, b. 8 Aug. 1919, Boston, Mass., USA. Music Educator. Educ: DMA; MMus Educ.; BMus. m. Ann Cauvet Tellstrom. Career: Dir. of Music, Pleasantville, NY, 1946-68; Teaching Fellow, Boston Univ. Schl. of Fine & Applied Arts, 1955-56; Cond., Music Div., Readers Digest, 1960; Chief, Bureau of Music Educ., NYS Educ. Dept., 1968-76; Executive Dir., Music Educators Nat. Conf., 1976-. Publs. Music in American Education Past and Present, 1971. Contbr. to profl. jrnls. Initiated & contributed to 14 guides & syllabuses in music educ., NYS Educ. Dept. Mbr. profl. orgs. inclng: Phi Kappa Lambda; Phi Mu Alpha; Nat. Committee, Alliance for Arts Educ., Arts for the Handicapped & Alliance of Assns. for the Advancement of Educ. Hobbies: Fishing; Gardening; Travel; Reading; Swimming. Address: 1902 Association Dr., Reston, VA 22091, USA. 28.

TELMANYI, Emil, b. 22 June 1892, Arad, Hungary. Concert Violinist; Conductor; Chamber Music Player; Teacher of Violin, Viola & Chamber Music. Educ: studied w. Hubay, Koessler & Popper, Music Acad., Budapest; Dips. as Concert Violinist, Composer & Tchr. m. (1) Anne Marie Carl Nielson, (2) Annette Schiöler, 3 children. Debut: w. Phil. Orch. (for 1st continental perf. of Elgar Concerto), Berlin, 1911. Career: started chmbr. orch. concerts (both playing & conducting), 1929; concertized in Europe, USA & Can.; Cond., concert perfs. in Copenhagen, Oslo, Paris, Gothenburg, London & Warsaw. Cond. Stravinsky concert in Budapest w. Composer as Soloist, 1926; gave opera perfs., Royal Opera House, Budapest; started string quintet w. family, touring Scandinavia, Germany & Hungary, 1958; has done many transcriptions & arrs. of works by Handel (sonatas), Beethoven (romances) & Brahms (waltzes); has recorded violin concertos by Carl Nielsen, Sibelius & Mendelssohn, all Bach solo works w. Vega (arched) bow. Contbr. many articles to musical jrnls. Hons: Ove Christensen Legacy, 1942; Carl Nielsen Medal, 1953; Anna Schytte Legacy, 1964; Gramex Prize, 1969. Hobbies: Bridge; Fishing; Billiards. Address: Malmmosevej 19 B, 2840 Holte, Denmark. 3, 14.

TELMÁNYI, Ilona Dorothea Antoinette, b. 20 July 1937, Copenhagen, Denmark. Violinist; Violist; Viola d'amore Player. Educ: pvte. pupil of Emil Telmanyi; Royal Danish Acad. of Music, Copenhagen; Dip. as Music Pedagogue, Det Jydske Musikkonservatorium, Arhus. Debut: w. Pro. Musica Chamber Orch. cond. by Emil Telmanyi, Copenhagen, 1952. Career: Mbr. of the Telmanyi Quintet, touring in Denmark (Radio, TV), Norway, Sweden, Germany, Hungary; Viola Soloist & w. orchs. in Denmark, Norway (Radio), Hungary, Poland, Germany; played viola d'amore in Denmark, Norway (Radio), England (The Viola d'amore Soc.); Lectured at Acad. of Music & Trng. Coll. for Music Tchr. in Bergen, on viola d'amore, 1974; Played at Grieg Fest., Lofthus, 1973 & '74 & at Grieg's home 'Troldhaugen,' 1975. Revisions & arrangements for viola d'amore; Ariosti, sonatas; A Jiranek; Concerto for flute & viola d'amore; Kopriva, Variations on a Hungarian Theme (solowork); J Kral, Nocturne for viola d'amore and the Norwegian Hardanger fiddle; arr. violin & piano: Bull, Sorrow & Solitude sur la Montagne. Recordings: Quintettes by CArl Nielsen, N W

Gade, F Mendelssohn, etc. Mbr., Danish Soc. of Music Pedagogues. Address: Malmmosevej 19B, 2840 Holte, Denmark.

TEMERSON, Leon, b. 26 Aug. 1904, Paris, France. Violinist. Educ: Conservatoire Nat. Superieur de Musique. m. Nadia Kagan. Debut: Paris, 1927. Career: Assoc. Concert Master, Orch. de Paris, w. Montreux; Soloist: French Nat. Radio; NY Phil. etc; Concert tours in USA & Europe; Prof., Sarah Lawrence Coll., NY, USA; Inst. des Haute Etudes Musicales, Montreux, Switzerland; Chmn., NY Phil. Chmbr. Ensemble, 1952, 62. Publs: La Chausvin Français, 1946. Hons: Chevalier des Arts et Lettres. Address: 1391 Madison Ave., New York, NY 10029, USA.

TEMKIN, Ascher M., b. 9 Feb. 1938, Chicago, Ill., USA. Conductor. Educ: BME, Northwestern Univ., 1960; MM, Composition, Butler Univ.; Study of conducting w. Dr Richard Lert, Lukas Foss, Richard Burgin; Study of viola w. William Primrose, Joseph dePasquale, Rolf Persinger; Violin, w. Samuel Arran, others. m. Penelope Carney, 1 s., 1 d. Debut: Violin Soloist, Orch. Hall, Chgo. Career: Prin. Violist, Kan. City Phil., Buffalo Phil., Indpls. Symph.; Musical Dir., Genesee Symph.; Assoc. Dir., Bogata Phil. (Colombia); Guest Cond., USA & S Am.; Musical Dir., Cond., Brockport (NY) Symph. Orch. Mbrship: Am. Symph. Orch. League. Hobbies: Tennis; Swimming; Cooking. Address: 122 Sherwood Dr., Brockport, NY 14420, USA.

TEMPERLEY, Jean, b. Hillingdon, Middlesex, England. Opera singer. Educ: Guildhall Schl. of Music. Career: 1968, Brighton Fest.; perf. in many Opera Halls throughout England, Scotland, Wales; Oratorios, concerts; TV prod. Gilbert and Sullivan Promenade Concert; Barber Inst., Univ. of Birmingham; Camden Fest., 1969; num. broadcasts; Flanders, Lisbon Fest.; 4 month Am. tour incl. New York, Hollywood; Kent Opera. Recordings: Lambert's Rio Grande; var. others. Hons: Marjorie White Memorial Award; 1968, Finalist Kathleen Ferrier Award. Address: c/o Concert Dir. Int. Lyndhurst, Denton Rd., Ben Rhydding, Ilkley, W Yorkshire LS29 8QR, UK.

TEMPERLEY, Nicholas Mark, b. 7 Aug. 1932, Beaconsfield Bucks., UK. Musicologist; Pianist; Educator. Educ: BA, King's Coll., Cambridge Univ., 1955; MusB, ibid, 1956; MA, 1959; PhD, 1959; ARCM, 1952; ARCO, 1958. m. Mary Sleator, 1 s., 2 d. Career: Asst. Lectr. in Music, Cambridge Univ., 1961-66; Fellow, Clare Coll., ibid, 1962-66; Asst. Prof., Yale Univ., 1966-67; Assoc. Prof., Univ. of Ill., 1967-72; Prof., ibid 1972-; Chmn. Musicol. Div., ibid, 1972-75; Revived Edward Loder's Raymond & Agnes Arts Theatre, Cambridge, 1966, also broadcast BBC 3rd Prof., 1966. Composition: Interlude for Organ, 1962. Mbrships: Coun., Am. Musicological Soc.; Int. Musicological Assn.; Royal Musical Assn.; Coun., Sonneck Soc.; Victorian Soc. Contbr. to num. music jrnls. & publs. incl. Music & Letters; Musical Times; Music Review; Grove's Dictionary; Ency. Britannica. Hons: John Stewart of Rannoch Schlrship. in Sacred Music, Cambridge Univ., 1953; Harriet Cohen Medal, Int. Musicological Assn., 1961. Fellowship, Nat. Endowment for Humanities, 1975-76. Hobbies: Bridge; Maths. Address: 805 Indiana Ave., Urbana, IL 61801, USA. 14.

ten BOKUM, Jan Gerardus Arend, b. 6 Mar. 1942. Music Educator & Administrator. Educ: Dip., Utrecht Conserv., 1965; Doct. in Music, Univ. of Utrecht, 1972. m. J. G. M. ten Bokum-van Raaij, 3 d. Career: Dir., Apeldoorn Music Schl., Netherlands; Tchr., Hist. of Music, Pedagogical Acad. of Music, Leeuwarden, Netherlands. Publs. incl: Johannes Gijsbertus Bastiaans, 1972; var. eds. of works by Dutch comps. Contbr. to: Musik in Geschichte und Gegenwart; Grove's Dict., 6th ed. Mbrships: Assn. of Netherlands Music Tchrs. Address: Schopenhauerstraat 62, Apeldoorn, Netherlands.

TENNEY, James, b. 10 Aug. 1934, Silver City, NM, USA. Composer; Pianist; Conductor. Educ: BA, Bennington Coll., 1958; MMus, Univ. of Ill., 1961. m. Ann Holloway, 1 d. Comps: about 50 inclng. Clang for orch.; Quintext; Five Textures for str. quartet & bass; Spectral Canon for Conlon Nancarrow, for harmonic player piano; Chorales for orch.; Three Pieces for Drum Quartet. Author: META HODOS: A Phenomenology of 20th Century Music & an Approach to the Study of Form, 1964. Mbr., BMI. Hons: Nat. Sci. Fndn. Rsch. Grants, 1964, 66; Comp. Fellowship. Nat. Endowment for Arts, 1975. Address: Music Dept., York Univ., Downsview, Ont., Canada.

TEO, Li-Lin, b. 10 July 1953, Penang, Malaysia. Pianist; Teacher; Lecturer. Educ: TAM (w. Dennis Murdoch); LRAM; ARCM; LRSM; pvte. study w. Louis Kentner & Vlado Perlemuter. Debut: Purcell Room, London, 1977. Career: recitals in Singapore, Jersey & var. parts of UK; some concerto apps.; perfs. in Salzburg & Paris; TV & radio apps. in Singapore; pvte. tchr.; lectr., Coventry Schl. of Music & on ILEA music panel. Mbrships: ISM; Chopin Soc.; Nat. Assn. of Tchrs. in Further & Higher Educ. Hons: Assoc. Bd. Scholarship; sev. prizes, RAM, incl. Walter MacFarren Gold Medal, Albanesi Prize, Harold Samuel Prize, Sterndale Bennett Prize; Tobias Matthay Fellowship; Dominion Fellowship Trust. Hobbies: Reading; Calligraphy; Painting. Address: 14, Corringham Rd., Wembley Park, Middx., UK.

TEPPER, Albert, b. 1 June 1921, New York,NY, USA. Composer; Conductor; Music Teacher. Educ: BMus., 1947, MMus., 1948, New England Conserv. of Music; Cert., Composition, Univ. of Edinburgh, 1951; Cert., Cond., Mozarteum, Salzburg, 1951; Advanced study, Princeton Univ., Workshop in Electronic Composition, Trumansburg, 1965. m. Judith Arker, 2 d. Career: Instr., Theory, New England Conserv., 1947-50; Instr., Asst. Assoc. Prof. Music, Hofstra Univ., 1952-68; Prof., ibid, 1968-; Chmn., Music Dept., 1954-58, 1967-73. Compositions incl: Concertino for Oboe & Strings; Euclid (SSA-piano); Spring, The Sweet Spring (SATB); Suite for Clarinet & Bassoon; 3 Jazz Spirituals (SATB-piano). Publs: Tonal Harmony: Vocabulary & Syntax, 1972. Contbr. to profl. jrnls. Mbrships: Past Pres., E Div., MTNA; Am. Fedn. of Musicians; Am. Musicol. Soc.; Coll. Music Soc.; ASCAP; AAUP; Pi Kappa Lambda; Kappa Gamma Psi; Bohemians. Hobbies: Reading; Conversation; Travel; Theater; Cinema; Dance. Address: 36 Honeysuckle Rd., Levittown, NY 11756, USA. 6, 11.

TEREY-SMITH, Mary, b. Budapest, Hungary. Musicologist; Opera Conductor; Vocal Coach. Educ: BMus (Condng. & Composition), Liszt Acad. of Music; MA (Music Lit.), Univ. of Vt., USA; PhD (Musicol.), Eastmans Schl. of Music, Univ. of Rochester. m. C A C Smith. Debut: Cond. of Tatabanya Symph., Budapest, 1951. Career incl: Vocal coach, then Asst. Cond., Hungarian State Opera, 1950-56; Res. Cond., Tatabanya Symph., 1951-56; Vocal coach, Toronto Royal Conserv. Opera Schl., Can., 1957-58; Dir. & regular cond., Western Wash. Univ., 1967-; Musical dir., all prods., ibid; Dir. & harpsichord accompanist, Collegium Musicum ensemble, ibid., 1969-. Mbrships: Am. & Int. Musicol. Socs.; Nat. Opera Assn. Hons. incl: Radcliffe Fellow, 1976. Hobbies: Theatre; Sailing; Embroidery. Address: 1809 Harris Ave., Bellingham, WA 98225, USA. 5.

TERMINI, Olga (Ascher), b. 19 May 1930, Hamburg, Germany. Associate Professor of Music History. Educ: Hochschule fur Musik, Hamburg; Univ. Southern Calif., Los Angeles, USA; BM, 1954; MM, 1957; PhD, 1970. m. Francesco Termini. Career: Music Tchr: Stevenson Jr. High Schl., 1954-57; Fairfax High Schl., 1957-72; Los Angeles City Coll. (pt.-time), 1957-64; Calif. State Univ., Los Angeles, 1972-. Publs: Five Settings of Goethe's Mailied in Relation to his Concept of the German Lied, Festival Essays for Pauline Alderman, 1976; The Transformation of Madrigalisms in Venetian Opera of the later 17th Century, 1978; Formal & Stylistic Changes in the Arias of C. F. Pollarolo, 1978. Contbr. to Grove's Dict., 6th ed. Mbr. num. profl. orgs. inclng: Am. Musicological Soc. Recip. Fulbright grant to Italy, 1966-67. Address: 4278 Sea View Lane, Los Angeles, CA 90065, USA.

TERRAYOVÁ, Maria Jana, b. 29 Apr. 1922, Pribyslavice, Trebic Dist., Czech. Musicologist. Educ: studied organ w. F. Michálek, State Conserv., Brno & Janácek Univ. Acad. of Musical Arts, Brno; PhD., Fac. of Philos., J. E. Purkyne Univ., Brno. m. Elemir Terray, 1 s. Career: gave organ concerts while at Janácek Univ., 1946-49; Libn., Music Sects., Univ. Libs., Brno., 1948-50, & Bratislava, 1951-54; Sci. Worker, Sect. of Hist. of Music, Slovak Acad. of Scis., Sect. of Musicol., 1954-; has transcribed & arr. num. old Slovak musical mss. of the 16th, 17th & 18th centuries, which have been broadcast & used in TV films; has made 6 records for Supraphon (Artia) & Opus labels. Contbr. to many jrnls. in field. Hobbies: Reading; Cooking; Growing Flowers; Touring. Address: Párickova 19, 801 00 Bratislava, Czech.

TERRONI, Raphael, b. 6 Nov. 1945, London, UK. Pianist. Educ: GSCM; ARCM. 1 s., 1 d. Debut: Wigmore Hall, London, 1974. Career: Apps. incl: Fairfield Halls, Royal Festival Hall, several fests. & recitals throughout UK; Prof. of piano, LCM. Mbrships: ISM; LCM socs. Hons: FLCM; Finalist, Nat. Piano Competition. Hobbies: Sport; Art. Address: Toll Cottage, Dorking Rd., Walton on the Hill, Tadworth, Surrey, UK.

TERRY, Kenton F, b. 4 July 1909, Coatesville, Pa., USA. Flautist. Educ: West Chester State Coll., 2 yrs.; Dip., Curtis Inst. of Music. m. Christine Lewis, 1 d. Career: w. Nat. Symph. Orch., 9 yrs.; w. Phila., Pa. Orch., 31 yrs. Tchr. of Flute, Univ. of Ind., Bloomington, Ind., 1975. Compositions: Co-Author, 60

Rambles for Flute, 1969. Address: H-31 Radwyn Apts., Bryn Mawr, PA, USA. 2.

TERRY, Paul Michael, b. 16 Jan. 1949, Erith, Kent, UK. Director of Music. Educ: BA, Hons. in Music, Univ. E Anglia; Cert. Educ., Trinity Coll., Cambridge; Assoc., Royal Coll. of Music. Career: Mbr., Music Dept., Culford Schl., Bury St. Edmunds, Suffolk & City of London Schl.; Dir. of Music, City of London Freemen's Schl., Ashtead, Surrey; Freelance conductor; Assoc. Dir., London Boy Singers; Examiner, Assoc. Bd., Royal Schls., Music, 1980-. Recordings: Broadcasts & recordings w. London Boy Singers. Mbrships: Music Masters Assn.; Incorp. Soc. of Musicians; Freeman, City of London. Address: 2 Avenue Gdns., London, SW14, UK.

TERSMEDEN, Gerard, b. 21 Aug. 1920, Stockholm, Sweden. Composer. Educ: studied w. Iris Törn & Gösta Theselius. m. Britt-Marianne, Peggy, Sjögron, 2 c. Comps. incl: Solitaire; Prelude; Romantisk Rapsodi; Magnolia; Negresco; Mediterranean Rhapsody; Mini Concerto; Rapsodie des Memises; Reverie; Riara; Till Hermine; Lat violinerna tala, Rhapsodie des Etoiles, etc. Recordings: 93 own comps. on disc, 88 on 8 LPs. Mbrships: SKAP; STIM. Hobbies: Sailing; Golf. Address: Villa la Provencale, 1297 Founex VD, Switz.

TESTRUP, Alice, b. 19 June 1929, Copenhagen, Denmark. Pianist. Educ: w. Chr. Chrisiansen, Royal Danish Conserv., 1947-51; w. Freündlich, Juilliard Schl. of Music, USA, 1953-55; w. Zecchi, Mozarteum, Salzburg, 1955. m. Dr. Erik Christensen, 2 c. Debut: Copenhagen, 1951; Town Hall, NY, 1955. Career: Toured Europe w. Paul Doktor, 1955; Fest. Concert, Tivoli Concert Hall, 1956; Soloist, Radio Symph. Orch.; Radio broadcasts; Solo & Orchl. work & concerts w. regional orchs., 1957-65. Publs: Musikkens Hvem Hvad Hvor, 1961. Mbr., Den Danske Solistforening. Hons: Fulbright Scholarship, 1953. Mgmt: Wilhelm Hansen. Address: Skt. Paulsgade 7, 8000 Aarhus C, Denmark.

TEUBER, Ulrich J., b. 22 May 1920, Berlin, Germany. Organist; Musicologist. Educ: BA, 1937; Organ-builder, cantor & organist dip., Royal Acad. of Music, Copenhagen, 1942; Mag. art, Musicology, Univ. of Copenhagen, 1949. m. Grete Bille Hansen, 3 d. Career: Organist, Enghave Kirke, Copenhagen, 1949-; Lectr., Royal Acad. of Music, Copenhagen, 1960; Docent, ibid, 1966-; Pastoralseminarium, Copenhagen, 1972-. Comps: Var. Ch. music. Publs: Cantorinus, 1970; Diskantbogen, 1973; Jubilate, 1978. Contbr. to Danish & foreign jrnls. Mbrships. incl: Danish Union of Organists (Sec., 1961-); Danish Confederation of Professional Assns.; Int. Arbeitsgemeinschaft für Hymnologie (VP, 1962-); Danish Soc. of Music Educ. (Pres., 1978-). Address: Bagsvaerdvej 147A, DK-2800 Lyngby, Denmark.

TEUTSCH, Walter, b. 11 Oct. 1909, Ausburg, Bavaria. Organist; Conductor; Professor of Music (Ret'd.). Educ: Abitur; Referendar; JVD; Dip., Leopold Mozart Conserv. m. Gertrude Oettinger, 2 d. Career: Prof. of Music, Westminster Coll.; Assoc. Cond., Utah Opera Theatre; Cond., Salt Lake Phil. Choir; Prof. of Music (Dir. of Opera Workshop), US Int. Univ.; Organist and/or choir dir. Mbrships: Nat. Opera Assn. (Dir., Gov., VP); Am. Guild of Organists (Subdean, Dean); Ctrl. Opera Serv.; Am. Musicological Soc. Hons: Ernest Bloch Award, 1946; Utah Centennial Exposition, 1947. Address: 4581 Tivoli St., San Diego, CA 92107, USA. 9, 23, 28.

THALBEN-BALL, George Thomas, b. Sydney, NSW, Aust. Concert Organist. Educ: RCM; DMus; ARCM; FRCM; FRCO; FRSCM; FRSA. m. Evelyn Chapman, 1 s., 1 d. Career incl: Organist, The Temple Ch., London, 1923-; Civic & Univ. Organist, Birmingham, 1949; Curator & Organist, Royal Albert Hall; concerts & recitals in UK, USA, Can., Aust., NZ, etc.; regular apps. at Promenade Concerts; num. broadcasts. num. recordings. mbr., num. musical socs. & organisations. Hons. incl: CBE, 1967; Freeman of the City of London. Address: 3 Paper Buildings, Inner Temple, London EC4, UK.

THALLAUG, Edith, b. Oslo, Norway. Operatic Mezzosoprano. Career: Dramatic actress, Nat. Theatre, Oslo; now Prin. singer, Royal Opera, Stockholm; apps. in Gothenburg, Glyndebourne, London, Moscow, Vienna, Linz, Basle, Bonn, Warsaw, Prague, Oslo, etc. & at fests. in Edinburgh, Bergen & Berlin; roles incl. Carmen, Amneris (Aida), Octavian (Rosenkavalier), Eboli (Don Carlos), Magdalena (Die Meistersinger), etc.; apps. on TV & radio. sev. recordings. Mgmt: Artistsekretariat Ulf Törnqvist, Norrtullsgatan 26, tr. 4, 11345 Stockholm, Sweden. Address: c/o mgmt.

THALMAN, Marilynn Carstens, b. 24 Feb. Detroit, Mich., USA. Music Teacher (Piano). Educ: Univ. Iowa; Univ. Ill.; Northwestern Univ.; San Jose City Coll.; Lic. Nat. Keyboard

Arts & Tchr. & Cons., Princeton, NJ. m. Norman J Thalman, 3 children. Career: Establ Choir Schls. at Christ Lutheran Ch., Clarendon Hills; St. Mark & St. Paul Choirs, Christ the King Luth. Ch., Tucson, Ariz.; Estab. Ixoye Co., Christ the Good Shepherd Luth. Ch., San Jose, Calif.; Tchr. & Cons., Nat. Keyboard Arts Assn., Princeton, NJ; Music Dir., Christ the Good Shepherd Ch. Comps: Score for Triptych; A Tapestry in 3 Parts by Mathew. Publs: Songs of Joy Through the Church Year, 1963; Improvisation Syllabus & Guide, 1979. Contbr. to profl. jrnls. Mbr. num. profl. orgs. Address: 2449 Fairoak Ct., San Jose, CA 95125, USA. 27.

THAUER, Anja, b. 1945 Lubeck, Germany. Cellist. Educ: Nuremberg & Stuttgart Schls. of Music; Nat. Higher Conserv. of Music & Music Normal Schl., Paris. Career: makes regular concert apps., Europe, Near & Far E; makes radio & TV broadcasts. Recordings incl: Schubert's Arpeggione Sonata; Reger's Solo Suite; Francaix's Fantasie. Hons: German Ind. Cultural Prize, 1961; Grand Prix, Paris, 1962; City of Nuremburg Cultural Prize, 1964. Hobbies: Painting; Philos. Address: Sonnenbergerstrasse 17, 62 Wiesbaden, German Fed. Repub.

THEBOM, Blanche, b. 19 Sept. 1919, Monessen, Pa., USA. Concert & Opera Singer. Educ: studied voice, dramatics, dance, langs. w. var. pvte. tutors, NYC, 1939-. m. Richard E Metz (div.). Debut: Brahms Alto Rhapsody, Phila. Orch. under Eugene Ormandy, 1941. Career: num. concerts & recitals; apps. w. opera cos. in Europe & USA; many apps. w. Met. Opera Co. in leading roles inclng. Fricka (Die Walkiere), Baba the Turk (Rake's Progress) & Adelaide (Arabella); fests. incl. Glyndebourne Mozart Fest., UK, 1950; Artistic Dir., Atlantic Opera Co., 1967-. Recorded for Victor records. Fndr. & sole contbr., Blanche Thebom Schlrship. Fndn. Inc., 1948. Hons. incl: Order of Vasa, Sweden. Address: c/o Met. Opera Assn., 1947 W 39th St., NY, NY 10018, USA. 2.

THEIMER, Axel, b. 10 Mar. 1946, St. Johann, Tirol, Austria. Vocal Instructor & Coach; Choral Director. Educ: BA, St. John's Univ., Collegeville, Minn., USA; MFA, Univ. of Minn., Mpls. m. Lois Ann, 1 d. Career: Mbr., Vienna Boys Choir; Dir., Chorus Viennensis; apps. as Vocal Soloist on TV in Austria & USA & in concerts in USA; Choral concerts in USA, Bahamas & Rumania; Clinician & Dir. of choral & vocal workshops, Mid-W USA; Dir. of choral & vocal activities, St. John's Univ. Recordings w. St. John's Univ. Men's Chorus. Mbrships: Am. Choral Dirs. Assn.; Am. Choral Fndn.; Ch. Music Assn. of Am.; Intercollegiate Music Coun.; Nat. Assn. of Tchrs. of Singing; Minn. MTA; MTNA. Hobbies: Sailing; Tennis; Skiing. Address: St. John's Univ., Dept. of Music, Collegeville, MN 56321, USA. 8.

THEMELIS, Dimitris, b. 1 May 1931, Thessaloniki, Greece. Director of Conservatory. Educ: PhD (musicol.) Ludwig Maximilian Univ., Munich, 1964; Dip., violin & harmony, 1952. m. Leda Uzuni, 1 c. Career: Lectr. in musicol., Univ. of Thessaloniki, 1969-71; Dir., State Conserv. of Music, Thessaloniki. Publs. incl: Etude ou Caprice, Die Enstehungsgeschichte der Violinetude, 1967; Violintechnik in Österreich und Italien um die Mitte des 18 Jahrhundert (in Der junge Haydn, 1972). Mbrships: VP, Committtion of Arts State Orch. of Thessaloniki; Gesellschaft für Musikforschung. Address: State Conserv. of Music, Thessaloniki, Olympiou Diamanti 7, Greece. 29.

THEODORAKIS, Mikis, b. 29 July 1925, Chios, Greece. Composer. Educ: Conservs. of Athens & Paris. m. Myrto Altinoglou, 1 s., 1 d. Career: Greek resistance fighter against Germans, 1943-45; Arrested & deported during Greek Civil War, 1947-52; Res. in Paris, 1954-61; Returned to Greece, 1961, becoming Mbr. of Parliament; Imprisoned for Pol. Activities, 1967-70. Comps. incl: Sinfonia (oratorio); Adagio (orch.); Passacaglia on a Theme of Instruments; Orpheus (ballet); 1st Symph.; Carnival (ballet); Sonatina No. 1 (violin & piano); Epitaphios, Suita No. 1, 2, 3 (Concerto for pianoforte); Antigone (ballet); Petite Suite (Piano); Axion Esti (oratorio); Music for num. films incl. Zorba the Greek, The Barefoot Battalion, The Trojan Women; Music for Nat. Theatre of Greece; num. songs. etc. Recip. num. hons. incl: Sibelius Award, London, 1963. Address: 111 No Des Champs, Paris, France.

THERON, Anna Margaretha, b. 11 May 1918, Springs, S Africa. Teacher; Lecturer. Educ: BA (Afr. Netherlands & Hist.); MA (Afr. Netherlands); Higher Educ. Dip.; LTCL. m. Jakc Pieter Theron, 5 c. Career incl: Pvte. music tchr., 30 yrs.; tchr. of music, primary & high schls.; Ed., The South African Music Teacher; lectr. in Afrikaans at Witwatersrand Univ.; radio apps. Contbr. to: Die Burger; The Medium; Sarie Marais; Die Huisvrou. Mbrships. incl: S African Music Assn.; Pres.,

Uniondale Music & Art Soc. Hobbies: Music; Books; Tennis. Address: de Hoop, PO Box 16, Avontuur, 6490, S Africa.

THEVENIN, Francis, b. 1 Oct. 1930, Asheville, NC, USA. Violinist. Educ: Univ. of Ga.; Univ. of Wash.; Am. Conserv. of Music, Chgo., Ill.; BMus.; MMus.; studied w. Scott Willits. m. Tine Blees Thevenin, 2 d. Career: Atlanta Symph. Orch.; Fla. Symph. Orch.; Orquesta Sinfónica de Puerto Rico; Chgo. Lyric Opera Orch.; Chgo. Chamber Orch.; Minneapolis Symph. Orch. Hobbies: Astronomy; Woodworking; Electronics; Tennis; Gardening; Camping. Address: 4013 Natchez Ave. S., Edina, MN 55416, USA.

THÉVET, Lucien André, b. 3 June 1914, Beauvais, France. Horn Player; Teacher. Educ: Premier Prix de Cor. Nat. Conserv. of Music, Paris. m. Suzette Varrot, 1 d. Debut: Casino de Cannes, 1936. Career: 1st Horn, Soloist, Radiodifusion Français. Théâtre Nat. de l'Opéra, Orch. de la Soc. des Concerts du Conserv.; concert apps.; Prof., Nat. Conserv. of Versailles Reg. Author, Complete Method for Horn, 2 vols. Contbr. to Grp. d'Acoustique Musicale, Univ. Pierre et Marie Curie, Paris. Mbr., Int. Horn Soc. Hons: Kt. of Arts & Letters, 1967; Bronze Medal of City of Paris, 1970. Hobby: Astronomy. Address: 36 Ave. Mathurin-Moreau, 75019 Paris, France.

THEW, Warren. b. 10 Apr. 1927, Fairport, NY, USA. Pianist; Harpsichord player & performer on all Historical keyboard Instruments. Educ: BMus & perf. cert., Eastman Schl. of Music, Univ. of Rochester, NY, 1949. m. Lisbet Günzburger. Debut: Washington, DC, 1951. Career: perfs. of over 40 piano concertos, cycles of Beethoven's 32 piano sonatas, progs. of works by Bach, Mozart, Schubert, Schumann, Chopin, Liszt, also of Renaissance, Baroque & contemporary music; apps. in Deutsche Mozartfest, Beethoven-Woche, Stuttgart Int. June Fest., Zürich; tours in Europe & USA incl. apps. on radio & TV; tchr., master classes at Music Acad., Zürich, 1965-72. Recordings incl. works by Rachmaninoff, Beethoven, Haydn, Max Kuhn & Hermann Haller. mbr. Assoc. Musicians of Greater NY. Hobbies: Writing Poetry; Entomology; Herbs; Cooking; Cartooning. Address: Schlimbergstr. 24, " 8802 Kilchberg/ZH, Switz.

THIEL, Joern, b. 12 Oct. 1921, Dresden, Germany. Music Film & TV Director; Author; Music Educator. Educ: Univ. of Kiel; Berlin Acad. of Music; Cologne Acad. of Music; Darmstadt Inst. for New Music. Debut: Cologne Radio, 1951. Career: Prod., Author, Broadcaster, sev. German broadcasting stns., 1951-66; Film & TV Dir. for music presentation & documentation, 1959-; Fndr. & Chief, Audio-Visual Dept., Remscheid Acad., 1958-61; Tchr. of Film & TV Directing, Vienna Music Acad., 1970. Comps. incl: Let's Build a Town, 1961. Recordings incl: Japan & the Musical West, 1965; Owner, Three-A-Productions for 3rd World Music Specialities. Mbr., sev. int. music socs. Publs. incl: Music & Media, 1973. Contbr. to profl. jrnls. Hobbies incl: Writing. Address: 8 Munchen 40, Rheinstr. 3/IV, German Fed. Repub.

THIEL, Wolfgang, b. 23 Sept. 1947, Berlin, Germany. Composer; Musicologist. Educ: Dip. in composition, 1974; Dr. Phil., Humboldt Univ., Berlin, 1975. m. Angelika Kaparnick, 1 s. Career: Musical sub-ed., German TV, 1974-75; freelance composer & musicol., specialising in hist. & theoretical problems of film music, 1975-. Compositions incl: Kontakte, piece for Jazz trio & String Quartet, 1972; Sonate fur Klavier, 1973; Grosstadt-Rhapsodie for Concert Organ & Orch., 1976; Oratorio, Awe of the Life, 1978; var. film & TV scores; songs, etc. Publs: Film Music, 1979. Contbr. to: Musik & Gesellschaft. Mbrship: Union of Composers & Musicols. of E Germany. Hobbies incl: Film-art; Organ playing. Address: Seumestrasse 8, 1035 Berlin, German Dem. Repub.

THIELE, Siegfried, b. 28 March, 1934, Chemnitz, Germany. Composer; Conductor. Educ: state exam, music. m. Uta Thiele, 1 s., 3 d. Career: Perfs. of comps. in Europe, India, USSR, Japan. Comps. incl: Pantomime for Orchestra, 1962; Sinfonia in Fünf Sätzen, 1965; Musik für Orchester, 1968; Lydische Suite für kleines Orchester, 1970; Serenade for flute, violin & cello, 1969; Cantilena & Allegro for flute & piano, 1971; Ubungen im Verstummen, 1972; Jeux pour hautbois et orchestre, 1973; Sonatine für Orchester, 1974; Sinfonietta alla Ciaccona, 1974; Deux etudes pour orgue; Wolkenbilder, 1977; Hommage à Machaut, 1977. Contbr. to Neue Zeitschrift für Musik. Mbr. comps. & musicians union of German Dem. Repub. Address: 705 Leipzig, Konstantinstr. 8, German Dem. Repub.

THIEME, Hermann Ernst Maria, b. 18 Jan. 1924, Dresden, Germany. Composer; Conductor/Pianist. Educ: Acad. of Music, Weimar/Munich; Dip. for Conds., Bavarian State Acad. of Music, 1951. m. Inge Walter, 1 d. Debut: as pianist.

Schaubude lit. cabaret, Munich, 1945. Career: Cond. & Comp., theatres & operas Flensburg, 1951, Bonn, 1952-54, Munich Kammerspiele, 1956-61, German & Swiss radio & TV, 1953-; Bavarian State Theatre, 1957; Free-lance Comp. & Cond., 1961-. Comps. incl: Polonisches Konzert, concerto for piano & orch.; chmbr. music; songs; ballet music; musical fairytales; music for stage, 60 comps., film & TV, 600 prod. musicals. Recordings: Goethe Inst. Mbrships. incl: GEMA; Int. Music Ctr., Vienna; German Assn. of Comps. Hobbies: Swimming; Walking. Mgmt: AGZ-Presseagentur, Hirschstr. 83, D-7500 Karlsruhe 1, German Fed. Repub. Address: Dufourstr. 108, CH-8008 Zürich, Switz.

THIEME, Ulrich, b. 5 Aug. 1950, Hamm, German Fed. Repub. Recorder Teacher; Musicologist. Educ: State Dip., Music Teaching, 1973; Concert Dip., Recorder, 1974; PhD, Musicol. Career: Recorder Tchr., Acad. of Music, Cologne, 1973-78; Recorder Tchr., Acad. of Music, Hannover, 1978-; TV apps; Broadcasts for sev. German stations, 1969-; Concert tours throughout Europe, & in E Asia & S Am. 50 concerts, Germany, w. Recorder/Lute-Guitar duo. Recordings: Jüng Baur, Tre Studi per Quattro; Bach, Brandenburg Concertos. Hons: 1st Prize, German Young Musicians Competition, 1967. Mgmt: New Era Int. Concerts Ltd., London, UK. Address: c/o Staatl. Hochschule für Musik, D-3 Hannover, German Fed. Repub.

THIJSSE, Wilhelmus Hermanus, b. 2 Aug. 1916, Delft, Netherlands. Musicologist; Organist. Educ: State Dip. (organ); Royal Conserv. (Musicol.). m. Gijsberta Johanna Schildt, 4 c. Comps: Sonata for recorder & harpsichord; Small pieces for Small Fingers on the Small Harp; The Bells; sev. choral works; 2 operas. Publs: Zeven eeeuwen Nederlandse Muziek (7 Centuries of Dutch Music), 1947; Haydn biography, 1948; About Melody, 1977; Music From Then Till Now, 1978. Contbr. to: Mens en Melodie. Mbrships: Soc. Dutch Comps.; Hague Artists Soc.; Artists Soc.; Dutch Workers Soc. Hobbies: Filming; Gardening; Model Railways. Address: Hyacintweg 44, 2565 RJ The Hague, Netherlands.

THODAY, Gillian, b. 27 July 1948, Worksop, UK. Cellist. Educ: RAM; LRAM; Recital Dip.; NordwestDeutsche Musikacademie, Detmold, German Fed. Repub., w. André Navarra; Reifeprufung & Koncertexamen. Debut: Wigmore Hall, London, 1975. Career: Solo apps. throughout UK (incl. 3 recitals in Purcell Room) & abroad; apps. on BBC radio & TV; premieres of works by Michael Berkeley & Roger Steptoe; apps. on TV in Making A Name & in Jacqueline Du Pré's master class. Recording: Granville Bantock's Sapphic Poem. Mbrships: Musicians' Union; ISM. Hobbies: Swimming; Cross-country Walking; Reading; Dressmaking; Langs. Address: 72 Agamemnon Rd., London NW6, UK.

THOENE, Walter, b. 26 June 1928, Rheydt, W Germany. Musicologist; Harpsichordist; Clavichordist. Educ: Univ. Cologne, musicol., drama, sociol.; 1949. Tchr. cert.; 1958 DPh. Career: 1958/1962 Asst. Musicol. Inst. Univ. Cologne; since 1962 sci co-operator Mus. Musical Instruments, State Inst. for Music Rsch. W. Berlin; Radio, TV prod. in Germany, France. Recordings: num. Mbrships: Soc. for Music Rsch.; Working Community for Music History of the Rhine dist.; German Soc. for Oriental Music. Publs. incl: Music Past and Present, 1962; Christian Gottlieb Neefe, 12 piano sonatas w. epilogue and criticism, re-ed., 1961; Studies for the Music History of the Rhine dis. II, re-ed., 1962. Address: Bambergerstrasse 41, D1000 Berlin West 30, German Fed. Repub.

THOM, Eitelfriedrich, b. 20 Nov. 1933, Stolp, DDR. Educ: Martin Luther Univ.; State exam, PhD. m., 1 s. Debut: Blankenburg. Career: Concertoes, mainly chmbr. orch.; Conf.; Sci. work; Telemann Rsch. + questions of ways of perf. in the 1st half of the 18th Century. Recordings: Tape recordings w. Radio DDR & Radio Berlin. Mgmt: Assn. of Comp. & musicologists DDR; Handel Soc., Halle; Telemann Work Circle, Magdeburg. Publs. incl: Monography: Telemann-Chamber Orchestras, 1965; Re-ed. of the Cycle: The Little Concert, 1972-1976. Contbr. to: Music Forum DDR, Leipzig. Hons: Art Prize Magdeburg; Prize for Creative Folkloric Art. Hobbies: 8-mm Film; Collection of Art objects & instruments. Address: Karl-Marx Str. 2a, Blankenburg, Harz, DDR 372, German Dem. Repub.

THOMAS, A F Leighton, b. 28 April, 1927, Whitchurch, Glamorgan, Wales, UK. Editor; Writer on Music; Organist. Educ: Ellesmere Coll., Salop; New Coll., Oxford; MA (Oxon). m. Sheila Dumayne, 1 d. Career: Lib., Welsh Nat. Opera Co., 1966-71; Ed., Welsh Music, 1968-73; Lectr. in music, Swansea Univ. Coll. Extra-Mural Dept., 1964-77; Ed., The Music Review, 1974-; Organist & Choirmaster, St. Mary's Ch., Burry Port, 1958-66; Organist & Choirmaster, All Saints' Ch., Llanelli,

1971-. Comps: Welsh Folk Song arrs. Contbr. to: The Times; Oxford Times; Western Mail; Anglo-Welsh Review; Radio Times; Musical Times; Musical Opinion. Mbrships: Royal Musical Assn.; Church Music Soc.; Sec., Guild for the Promotion of Welsh Music, 1964-68; Hon. life mbr., Llanelli Organists' Assn. Hobby: Cricket. Address: Glyneitin, Burry Port, Dyfed, Wales, UK. 28, 29.

THOMAS, Beal, b. 14 Mar. 1940, Longview, Tex., USA. Church Musician. Educ: BMus, Southern Meth. Univ., Dallas, Tex.; MSM, Union Theol. Sem., NYC. Career: Organist & Choirmaster, St. Paul's Ch., Flatbush, Brooklyn, NY, 1962-65; Organist & Master of Choir, Christ Ch. Cathedral, Vancouver, BC, Canada, 1965-70; Dir. of Music, Christ Ch. Cathedral, Vic., ibid, 1970-. Mbrships: Primate's Commission on Ch. Music, Anglican Ch. of Canada; Royal Canadian Coll. Organists; Ch. Music Soc. Address: 912 Vancouver St., Vic., BC, Canada.

THOMAS, Brian L, b. 30 Aug. 1937, London, UK. Sub Principal First Violinist. Educ: ARCM; Akademie für Music, Vienna. m. Mary Thomas, 1 d., 1 s. Career: No. 3-Ldr., Sadlers Wells Opera Orch., London, 4 seasons; Played w. symph. & chmbr. orchs., num. recitals & some concerto engagements; Joined LSO, 1965; Subsequently appointed No. 4 (sub principal) violinist, ibid. Hons: Full time schlrship., RCM; Essex Co. Travelling Schlrship. Hobbies: Do it Yourself; Tennis; Motor Racing; Home brewed wine & beer. Address: 16 Montana Rd., Wimbledon, London SW20, UK.

THOMAS, Charles Columbus, b. 10 Sept. 1940, McAlester, Okla., USA. Assistant Professor; Vocalist; Percussionist; Pianist; Conductor; Dancer. Educ: BA, Langston Univ.,Okla.; San Francisco State Coll.; MFA, Brooklyn Coll., NY; Cand. PhD, CUNY. Debut: W Afro-Am. Folklore Troupe, Town Hall, NYC, 1966. Career: Musical Dir. & Actor, Afro-Am. Folklore Troupe, City Ctr. of Music & Drama, NY; Musician & Dancer w. Egbe Omo Nago Folklore Ensemble, Brooklyn Acad. of Music; Actor, John & Mary (film); Progs. for Educl. TV. Recording of Golden Music of Africa w. Egbe Omo Nago Ensemble. Publs: The Black Brother Goose; Rinds for the Revolution, 1970; Contbr. to: Yardbird Review. Mbr. num. profl. orgs. Recip. var. awards. Hobbies: Travel; Art; Designing own wardrobe; Roller Skating. Address: 1245 Park Ave., New York, NY 10028, USA. 2, 30.

THOMAS, Earl Morgan, b. 5 Feb. 1925, Houston, Tex., USA. Clarinettist; Associate Professor of Music. Educ: Juilliard Schl., 1950; BMus, 1966, MMus, 1969, Univ. of Okla. m. Janice E M Thomas. Career incls: Mbr., NY Wind & Brass Ensemble, 1947-52; Solo Clarinet, Dallas Symph., 1950-52, Okla. City, Symph., 1952-69, Lexington Phil. Symph., 1969-; Clarinet Prof., Okla. City Univ., 1960-63, Univ. of Okla., 1963-69, E Ky. Univ., 1969-; Mbr., var. chmbr. grps.; Prod., TV & radio concerts. Comp. Var. chmbr. works. Recordings: Works by Berg, Webern, Walton & other modern comps. Contbr. to press & profl. jrnls. Mbr., profl. assns. Hons: Dedicatee, var. clarinet works. Hobbies incl: Short-wave listening; Tape recording. Address: RR 10 Lakeshore Drive, Richmond, KY 40475, USA.

THOMAS, Elvera, b. 2 Dec. 1912, Middelburg, Cape Province, Repub. of S Africa. Music Teacher; Music Therapist. Educ: BA; BSc; MSc; Univ. Tchrs. Lic. in Music. m. Rev. Evan Thomas (dec.). Debut: Soloist, Sunday Evening Concert, Pt. Elizabeth, aged 13 yrs. Career incls: Organized & Cond., Int. League of Arts Youth Orch., Pretoria rehearsals, 1963; Initiated S African Music Camp, Dept. of Educ., Arts & Science, Div. of Adult Educ., 1st Orchl. camp at Hartbeespoort Dam, 1964; Formed S African Assn. of Music Therapists, 1973; Music Therapist, Alexandra Institution, Cape Town, 1973-78; S African Assn. of Music Therapists delegate to Wrold Congress of Music Therapy II, Buenos Aires, 1976; Designer, 1st S African course in Music Therapy to be given at Pretoria Technikon, 1978-79; sev. radio apps. Contbr. to profl. publs. Mbr., profl. orgs. Hons: Open Profl. Violin Solo, Bloemfontin Eisteddfod A award, 1953. Hobbies: Helping people through music; Playing the organ in church. Address: 27 De Wet Ave., Moselville Uitenhage 6230, S Africa.

THOMAS, Ernst, b. 21 Feb. 1916, Darmstadt, Germany. Instituto Director. Educ: Land Conserv. of Music, Leipzig; studied w. R Teichmüller, H Abendroth, M Hochkofler, M Ludwig, R Oppel; State Examination, Piano, 1937; Mozarteum, Salzburg. m. Lore Gerlt, 2 s. Career: Music Critic, Darmstädter Echo, 1947-56; Music Ed., Frankfurter Allgemeine Zeitung, 1956-62; Dir., Int. Music Inst. of Darmstadt, Ldr., Int. Holiday Course for New Music, 1962-; Publr., Neue Zeitschrift für Musik, 1958-78; Darmstädter Beiträge zur Neuen Musik, 1962-; Zeitgenössische Musiktheater, 1964, K A Hartmann, Kleine Schriften, 1965; Ed., Musica-viva-Konzerte, Munich, 1964-78; Radio Perfs., Series Der neue Musikbericht, Cologne, 1967. Mbrships: German Music Coun.; German Fed. Repub.

Sect., Int. Music Coun.; German Sect., Int. Soc. for New Music; Int. Music Ctr., Vienna. Address: 190 Nieder-Ramstädter Strasse, D-6100 Darmstadt, German Fed. Repub. 14, 19.

THOMAS, Günter, b. 5 June 1932, Leipzig, Germany. Musicologist. Educ: Univs. of Leipzig & Cologne; PhD, 1962. m. Margarete Jansen, 2 s. Career: Mbr., permanent musicol. staff, Joseph Haydn Inst., Cologne, 1962-. Publs: Friedrich Wilhelm Zachow, 1966; Ed., Complete Haydn ed.; The Nelson Mass & the Theresa Mass, 1965; Ed., the Opera La Fedeltà Premiata, 1968; Ed. w. H Lohmann, the violin concertos, 1969; Essays incl. Griesingers Briefe über Haydn, 1966, Studien zu Haydns Tanzmusik, 1973, Gioco filarmonico - Würfelmusik und Joseph Haydn, 1973. Contbr. to: Die Musik in Geschichte und Gegenwart; Grove's Dict., 6th Ed. Address: Junesrotstrasse 15, D-5020 Frechen 4, Königsdorf, German Fed. Repub.

THOMAS, Jess, b. 4 Aug. 1927, Hot Springs, SD, USA. Opera Singer. Educ: BA, Univ. of Neb.; studies for MA Psychol., Stanford Univ., Calif. m. Violeta Rios, 2 s., 1 d. Debut: San Fran. Career: Perfs. at Met. Opera, NYC, Vienna State Opera, Nat. Theater, Munich, Royal Opera, Covent Garden, Paris Grand Opera, W Berlin Opera, Bolshoi Opera, La Scala Opera, Milan, San Fran. Opera & num. others; also apps. w. most major Am. & European Symphs.; Bayreuth & Salzburg Fests. Recordings incl: Siegfried; Frau ohne Schatten; Ariadne; Beethoven, 9th Symph.; Macht des Schicksals (highlights); Ballo; Jess Thomas sings Wagner; Parsifal; Lohengrin; Gurrelieder; Meistersinger. Hons: Wagner Medal, Bayreuth Fest., 1963; Kammersänger, Bavarian Govt., 1963, Austria, 1976; San Fran. Opera Medallion, 1972. Mgmt: Colbert Artists Mgmt., 111 W 57th St., NYC, NY 10019, USA. Address: PO Box 662, Tiburon, CA 94920, USA. 2.

THOMAS, Judith, b. Rugby, UK. Oboist; Performer on Oboe d'Amore & Cor Anglais. Educ: RAM; LRAM; ARCM. Career: currently Oboist, Cor Anglais Player, Engl. Nat. Opera Orch.; Free-lance Soloist, chmbr. music & orchl. player, BBC broadcasts; Tchr. & Youth Orch. Coach. Mbr., ISM. Recip. F Vivian Dunn Prize for woodwind, RAM, 1960. Address: 53 Station Rd., Teddington, Middx., UK.

THOMAS, Lyndon, b. 26 Nov. 1942, Leamington Spa, UK. Double Bass Player. Educ: TCL; LTCL (Mus. Ed.). m. Susan Elizabeth Chambers, 3 c. Career: Played for Ballet Rambert, 1964-65; Mbr., Bournemouth Symph., 1965-. Hobbies: Crayon Drawing; Relief Sculpture. Address: 9 Foxholes Rd., Southbourne, Bournemouth, UK.

THOMAS, Margaret Ann, b. 12 Mar. 1942, Bristol, UK. Colo Soprano Singer; Voice Teacher. Educ: RAM (Assoc. Bd. scholar), 1961-65; ARCM; FLCM. m. Reginald James Dymond, Artist MBE, 1 stepdaughter. Debut: Colston Hall, Bristol, 1965. Career: oratorio apps. as soloist throughout UK; radio perfs. as soloist w. BBC West of England Singers; TV apps.; staff mbr., Birmingham Schl. of Music; Dir. of Music, Amberley House Schl., Bristol; Examiner; Adjudicator; pvte. tchr. of singing. Mbrships: ISM; RAM Club; LCM Sec.; Bristol Music Club. Hobbies: Theatre; Cordon Bleu Cookery; Driving. Address: Barum House, 20 Kersteman Rd., Bristol BS6 7BX, UK.

THOMAS, Mark Stanton, b. 24 Apr. 1931, Lakeland, Fla., USA. Flautist. Educ: Am. Univ., Wash. DC; Int. Graphoanalysis Soc. Inc., Chgo., Ill.; Peabody Conserv. of Music, Balt., Md. m. Judith C Thomas, 4 s., 1 d. Career: Chmn., Woodwind Dept., Am. Univ.; Instructor of Flute, Geo. Wash. Univ.; VP & Mbr., Bd. of Dirs., W T Armstrong Flute Co., Elkhart, Ind.; Recitalist & Soloist, num. apps. USA & abroad; Perfs. before 4 Presidents of USA; num. Film, Stage, Radio & TV appearances; Flute Clinician & Dir. of Master Classes, USA 0 abroad; Instructor of Flute, Notre Dame Univ., 1975. Recordings: Num. Solo & Ensemble & Orchl. records; Flute Recital, Vol. I; Music for Flutes, Vol. I. Publs: The Story of the Flute, 1967; Care & Maintenance of Your Flute, 1970; The Flute Forum, 1971; Learning the Flute (Beginning Method); Learning the Flute (Intermediate Book I & II), 1975; 18 Exercises for Flute by Berbiguier, 1977; My First Book of Christmas Flute Solos, 1976; My First Book of Sacred Flute Solos, 1977; My First Book of Popular Flute Solos, 1978, etc. Contbr. to Woodwind World Mag.; School Musician Mag.; Music Jrnl. Mag. Mbrships. incl: Nat. Flute Assn. Inc. (Fndr., Pres., 1973-, Bd. of Dirs.); Bd. Dirs., Am. Youth Symph. & Chorus, 1975; Pres., Elkhart Symph. Soc., 1978. Hobbies: Ceramics; Flute Collection; Various Sports. Mgmt: W T Armstrong Co. Inc., Elkhart, IN 46514. Address: c/o Mgmt.

THOMAS, Neville Aubrey, b. 22 May 1921, Sydney, NSW, Aust. Musician; Lecturer. Educ: NSW Conserv. of Music, Sydney, 6 yrs.; studied in USA & England; SPTC, Moore Theol.

Coll. m. Valerie Thomas, 1 s., 3 d. Career incls: doubles on 10 woodwind instruments; has played w. Sydney Symph., Elizabethan Trust Orch. (Opera House), Aust. Broadcasting Commn.; Ldr., Sydney Saxophone Quartet; Lectr. in woodwinds, Conserv. of Music, Sydney; Sr. Examiner for all Woodwinds, Aust. Music Exam. Bd.; active Clinician; Pioneered Woodwind Clinics, "Schl. of the Air," Flying Doctor Network; JP Soloist on var. recordings. Publd. monographon Doubling. Contbr. articles & columns to profl. jrnls. Mbrships. incl: Pres., Musicians Union of Aust.; Aust. Chmn., Int. Clarinet Soc.; Licensed Lay Rdr., Chmn., Wind Standing Committee, Aust. Address: 36 Bishop Ave., Randwick, Sydney, NSW 2031, Aust.

THOMAS, Peter, b. 1 Dec. 1925, Breslau, Germany. Composer; Conductor. Educ: Music Highschool. m. Cordula Thomas, 2 c. Career incls: Cond., Peter Thomas Orch. Comps: 550 Comps. for cinema & TV. Num. recordings. Publs: Classic with 1 Finger; High School for Modern Instrumentation. Hons: Twice recip. of Bundesfilmpreisträger. Address: Strada Regina 8, CH-6900 Lugano, Switz.

THOMAS, Richard Vaughan, b. 28 Nov. 1949, Bangor, N Wales, UK. Horn Player. Educ: Royal Manchester Coll. of Music, w. Sidney Coulston, 1967-70. m. Jean Frances Thomas, 1 s. Career: Prin. Horn, Scottish Baroque Ensemble, Chmbr. Orch. & Philharmonia, 1970-74; Freelance work w. all major orchs., & extensive solo & chmbr. work throughout Scotland; currently Prin. Horn & Soloist, Bournemouth Symph. Orch. Recordings: w. Amphion Wind Quintet for BBc; w. Bournemouth Symph., 1974-. Mbr., Musicians Union. Hobbies: Sports; Motoring; Crosswords. Mgmt: Western Orchl. Soc. Address: 11 Scarf Rd., Canford Heath, Poole, Dorset, UK.

THOMAS, Wyndham Harwood, b. 23 Sept. 1938, Bridgend, S Wales, UK. Composer; University Lecturer; Organist; Director, Bristol Early Music Consort. Educ: BA, MA, Dip.Ed., Univ. of Durham; ARCO. m. Kathleen Stubbs, 2 s. Career: Dir. of Music, Woodbridge Schl., Suffolk, 1961-63; Lectr. in Music, Nonington Coll., Kent, 1963-66; Lectr. in Music, Bristol Univ., 1966-. Comps. broadcast: Violin sonata; Song Cycle (3 melodramas & Eulogy); Introduction & Passacaglia for organ; Anthems; radio & TV talks on early instruments. Contbr. to: Comps. Magazine; Musical Times; ISM jrnl. Mbrships: Comps. Guilf of GB; RCO; Performing Right Soc. Hons: Organ Scholar, Univ. of Durham, 1957-60; shared Welsh Arts Council Award for Young Comps., 1966. Hobbies: Gardening; Drinking; Gentle Sports. Address: 15 Cotham Pk., Cotham, Bristol BS6 6BZ, UK. 30.

THOME, Diane, b. 25 Jan. 1942, NY, USA. Composer; Theorist; Pianist; College Professor. Educ: Performers Cert., piano, Eastman Schl. Music; BMus, ibid.; MA, Univ. Pa.; MFA, Princeton; PhD, composition, ibid (1st woman to receive music degree from Princeton). Career incls: Tchr., piano, Princeton Univ., 1970-74; theory, harmony, Rutgers Univ., Camden, 1973-74; theory, 20th century music, SUNY, Binghamton, 1974-; num. apps., fests. & radio. Compositions incl: January Variations; Polyvalence; Los Nombres (recorded). Publ: Music for Percussion. Mbr. profl. orgs. Hons. incl: SUNY Rsch. Grant, 1975; Commn., Int. Women's Arts Fest.; Nat. Endowment of the Arts Comps. Grant, 1977. Address: Schl. of Music, Univ. of Wash., Seattle, WA 98195, USA.

THOMMESSEN, Reidar, b. 7 June 1889, Stavern, Norway. Composer; Professional Piano Player. Educ: Coll., UK, 1 yr.; studied Piano w. Karl Nissen & Mary Barrat Due; stsudied Theolry w. Iver Holter. m. Gudrun Dagny Lindseth, 4 children (2 dec.). Debut: Brighton, UK, 1921. Career: Has worked as Piano Player in major Norwegian restaurants inclng. Kaba & Skansen; currently working daily at Teaterkafeen, Oslo. Comps. incl: Over 150 comps. (many published in NYC); Score of film Laila. Mbr., Assn. of Norwegian Comps. Recordings: 1 LP. Hons: King's Gold Medal for Merit, 1962; Munken Award, Larvik. Hobbies: All active sports. Address: Fredriksborgvn. 21, Oslo 2, Norway.

THOMPSON, Alastair M, b. 28 Dec. 1944, Sherborne, UK. Singer (tenor). Educ: Westminster Abbey Choir Schl.; Lancing Coll.; MA, King's Coll. Cambridge; Dip. Ed., New Coll. Oxford. Career: w. The King's Singers, 1968-78; currently recital, oratorio & opera singer. Recordings: w. The King's Singers. Hobbies: Travel; Reading; Walking. Mgmt: Ibbs & Tillett. Address: 73 Parliament Hill, London NW3, UK.

THOMPSON, Barbara Gatwood, b. 24 Nov. 1923, Nashville, Tenn.,USA. Cellist. Educ: BA, Geo. Peabody Coll.; Cello studies w. Oscar Eiler. m. Vance Maynard Thompson Jr., 2 s., 1 d. Career: Cellist, Charter Mbr., Nashville Symph. Orch.; Cellist, Memphis Symph. Orch. (also charter mbr.), Memphis Opera

Theater, Memphis Concert Orch.; Mbr. Memphis Symph. Strings (on staff of local recording studio). Played under Pablo Casals in perf. of his El Pessebre, Memphis, 1968. Mbr., Past Pres., Renaissance Music Circle. Hobbies incl: Needlepoint; Photography; Singing in choir of 2nd Presby. Ch. Address: 320 E Cherry Circle, Memphis, TN 38117, USA.

THOMPSON, Brian Raymond, b. 9 Apr. 1939, Belfast, N Ireland, UK. Teacher of Piano, Organ & Harmony; Composer. Educ: RAM, 1957-60; Keble Coll., Oxford, 1960-61; Univ. of London Inst. of Educ., 1961-62; MA, Queen's Univ., Belfast, 1968-69; LRAM; GRSM; MTC. Career: Tchr., London, Drogheda, 1962-66; Tchr., Portora Royal Schl., Enniskillen, 1966-68; Tchr., Loreto Convent, Coleraine, 1969-70; Pt.-time lectr., educ. (music), New Univ. of Ulster, Coleraine, 1969-74; Piano tchr., 1963-; Accomp., Coleraine & Portstewart Music Fests., 1976-. Comps: Organ Sonata No. I, E Flat minor, 1959; Piano Sonata, F minor, 1960; Piano Preludes, 1961-63; Deep Ce, for piano, 1965-73; Study in D minor (''Storm on Lough Erne'') for piano, 1967; Harmony Exercise for piano, 1967-68; String Quartet in 2 flats, 1968-69; Symphony No I (''The Long Hot Summer''), 1968-69; Symphony No 2 in G, 1969-71; 3rd & 4th Symphonies in preparation. Mbrships: ISM; RCO, Fellow & Life Mbr.; Ulster Orch. Assn., Life Mbr.; Oxford Union Soc.; Queen's Univ. Assn.; RAC, Life Assoc. Mbr.; Nat. Trust. Hons: Harry Farjeon Prize (for Harmony), RAM, 1958; Henry R Eyers Prize (for Aural Trng.), RAM, 1960. Hobbies: Driving; Weather Statistics; Newspaper Cuttings; Writing about music; Playing symphonies on the piano. Address: 7 Hillside, Portstewart, Co. Derry, BT55 7AZ, N Ireland, UK.

THOMPSON, Carl G., b. 3 July 1931, Friona, Tex.,USA. Educator; Choral Music Conductor. Educ: AA, Frank Phillips Coll.; BMusEd, MMusEd, N Tex. State Univ.; post-grad. study, Colo. Univ. m. Carol Joy Kittinger, 3 s., 2 d. Career incls: Soloist & Choral Cond., Abilene Tex. Symph. Orch. (Amahl & The Night Visitors, opera), 1958; Soloist, Ark. Tech. & Russellville Messiah Prod., 1964; Choral Adjudicator, Ark., 1966-67; Cond., Hon. Chorus, Ark. State Choral Fest., Hot Springs, 1967; Soloist & Chorister, Rochester, NY, Oratorical Soc. & Bach Fest. Chorus, 1969-71; Cond., All-Am. Hon. Musicians Chorus to Greece, 1973; Solo Ensemble, Dirs. Chorus, Am. Choral Dirs. 1st Nat. Conven., 1971; Cond., All-Co. Madrigal Chamber Grp., Whitehall, Upstate NY, Queensbury Ch. of Christ, Glens Falls, NY, & Dir. of Music, Ch. of Christ, Queensberg, NY, 1974; Pub: Schl. Music Tchr., 14 yrs. Mbrships: Life mbr., Am. Choral Dirs. Assn. (state chmn., western area, NY, 2 terms); MENC; Phi Mu Alpha; Nat. Assn. Tchrs. of Singing. Recip., Rockefeller & Cordett Fndn. Grants. Hobbies: Tennis Coach; Photography. Address: RD1 Whitehall, NY 12887, USA.

THOMPSON, David William, b. 8 June 1925, Birmingham, UK. Lecturer; Violist. Educ: Assoc., Birmingham Schl. of Music. m. Susan Rosemary Jervis, 1 d. Career: Violist, BBC Northern Orch., 1950-56; Freelance Violist, London, on music staff, Wellington Coll., Berks., 1956-64; Prin. Viola, SNO, 1964-69; Sr. Lectr., Orange Free State Provincial Admin., & Soloist, broadcasting for S African Broadcasting Corp. Nat. Serv., 1969-. Mbr., ISM. Hobbies: Gardening; Viola practice. Address: PO Box 3514, Bloemfontein 9300, S Africa.

THOMPSON, Edward Ian, b. 25 Feb. 1931, Dunoon, Argyll, UK. Musician; Potter. Educ: MA, BMus, Univ. of Glasgow; ARCO. Career: Libn. & Sr. Libn., Royal Scottish Acad. of Music & Drama; Lectr. in Hist. of Music, ibid; Lectr. in Music, Univ. of Glasgow, Dept. of Extra-Mural Educ.; Libn. & Lectr., 1956-74; Potter, 1974-. Publs: Early English Church Music, Vol. 7 - Rober Ramsey English Church Music, 1965, Vols. 19 & 20 - Robert Ramsey Latin Church Music & Robert Ravenscroft Anthems, in preparation. Contbr. articles & prog. notes to musical publs. Mbrships: Royal Musical Assn.; ISM; Int. Assn. of Music Libs.; Royal Music Assn. Hobbies: Mountaineering & Canoeing; Cooking; Ceramics. Address: The Gatehouse Rodel, Isle of Harris PA83 3TW, UK. 3, 28.

THOMPSON, Elizabeth Zinn, b. 22 Sept. 1941, Detroit, Mich., USA. Professor of Music; Saxophonist; Flautist; Studio Musician; Clinician. Educ: BMus, Univ. Mich., 1965; MMus, Ariz. State Univ., 1967. 1 d. Career incls: Clinician, Mich., NY State, Ariz.; Fac., Cath. Univ., Wash. DC, 1971-72; Univ. Ariz., 1973-; Played w. Phoenix & Tucson Symphs.; Soloist w. Ariz. State Univ. Band, Reston Fest. Orch., Univ. Ariz. BAnd, Ariz. Chmbr. Orch., Gammage Woodwind Quintet, Ithaca Fac. Quintet, Ariz. Woodwind Quintet, USAF Band, Wash. DC; Num. recitals, var. states. Contbr. to jrnls. Mbr. profl. orgs. Recip: Fulbright Grant, Paris, France, 1967. Hobbies incl: Ornithol.; Sailing. Mgmt: Claire Jackson Mgt. Inc., Tucson. Address: c/o Schl. Music, Univ. Ariz., Tucson, AZ 85721, USA.

THOMPSON, Marcus Aurelius, b. 4 May 1946, Bronx, NY, USA. Performer on Viola & Viola d'Amore; Professor of Music, MIT, Cambridge, Mass.; Director. Educ: BMus, 1967, MSc, 1968, DMA, 1970, The Juilliard Schl. Debut: Carnegie Recital Hall, 1968. Career: Soloist w. Nat. Symph. Orch. (Wash. DC), St. Louis Symph., Boston Pops, Symp. of the New World, Cypriot Radio Orch. C.B.C. (Nicosia), The Chmbr. Orch. of San Salvador (El Salvador); Chmbr. Music apps., Marlboro, Sante Fe, Spoleto, Newport, Aspen Music Fests.; w. Chmbr. Music Soc. of Lincoln Center, The Concord String Quartet, The Harvard Summer Schl. Chmbr. Players, The Rhode Island Fest. String Quartet; Num. recitals. Recordings: Sonata da Chiesa (Martin); Der Schwanendreher (Hindemith); Suite Hebraique (Bloch); Youth in a Merciful House (Moore); Kreuz und Quer (Edwards); Corridors of Dream (Mekeel); Consortium I (Schwantner); Viola Quintet (Street). Mbrships: The Viola Rsch. Soc.; The Viola d'Amore Soc. Hons: Winner, Young Concert Artists Inst. Auditions, 1967; 1st Prize, Hudson Valley Phil. Competition, 1967; Recording of Special Merit Award, Stereo Review, 1978. Hobby: Hiking. Address: 19 Florence St., Cambridge, MA 02139, USA.

THOMPSON, Randall, b. 21 Apr. 1899, NYC, USA. Conductor; Composer; Professor of Music. Educ: studied w. Ernest Bloch. Career: Cond., Desoff Choirs; Prof. of Music, Wellesley Coll., Harvard Univ., Princeton Univ., & Univs. of Calif. & Va.; Dir., Curtis Inst. Compositions incl: Symph. No. 1; Symph. No. 2, 1931; The Peaceable Kingdom (chorus), 1936; Alleluia (chorus), 1940; The Testament of Freedom (chorus), 1942; Symph. No. 3, 1948. Hons. incl: Fellowship, Am. Acad. at Rome, Italy, 1922.

THOMPSON, Robert Ian, b. 5 Apr. 1943, Bradford,UK. Tenor Singer; Harpsichordist. Educ: Queen's Coll., Cambridge; MA (Cantab.); RCM; ARCM; ARCO; pvte. study in Italy w. Maestro Campogalliani. m. Judith Welch. Career: BBC Chorus, 1966-67; Vicar-Choral, St. Paul's Cathedral, 1968-77; freelance opera & concert singer; prin. tenor, Berne StadtTheater, Switz., 1978-80; mbr., var. vocal ensembles; broadcasts in UK, Germany, Switz. & Austria. Recordings: w. Pro Cantiones Antiqua, Early Music Consort; as soloist w. Schütz Choir, London; Capella Clementina. Mbrships: ISM; RCO. Hobbies: Mountaineering; Gardening; Cooking; Brewing; Francophilia. Address: 12 Holly Terr., Windermere LA23, 1EJ, UK.

THOMS, Paul Edward, b. 16 Apr. 1936, Lousiville, Ky., USA. Educator; Baritone; Choral Conductor. Educ: BMus, Univ. of Ky.; MMus, Miami Univ., Ohio. m. Marion Cox, 2 d. Career: Rural music supvsr., Brown Co. Schls., Ohio, 2 yrs.; currently Dist. Music Coord., Fairfield Schls.,ibid.; Solo appearances w. Hamilton Symph. Orch. & Hamilton Choral Soc.; past Baritone Soloist, Temple Bene Israel & 1st Ch. of Christ Sci., Hamilton; Cond., Fairfield Choruses, inclng. appearances w. Hamilton Symph. Orch. & local radio & TV broadcasts; Fndr. & Dir., Fairfield Choraliers. Contbr. to var. jrnls. Mbrships: incl: VP, Modern Music Masters; Phi Mu Alpha; Kappa Delta Pi; Alpha Psi Omega; Am. Choral Dirs. Assn.; Treas., Exec. Bd., Hamilton-Fairfield Arts Coun.; Bd. Dirs., Hamilton Fine Arts Coun.; Hamilton Symph. Orch., Hamilton Civic Music Assn. Hobbies: Opera; Theatre. Address: 128 S ''D'' St., Hamilton, OH 45013, USA.

THOMSEN, Niels, b. 24 Apr. 1945, Copenhagen, Denmark. Solo Clarinet Player. m. Jytte Lund. Career: Royal Kings Guard Band, 1963-67; Solo clarinettist, South Danish Symph., 1967-68; Solo clarinettist, Tivoli Symph. (Copenhagen Symph.), 1968-76; 1st Solo clarinettist, Denmark Radio Symph., 1976-. Recordings as soloist w. every Danish orch. inclng. Nielsen Concerto. Hon: Jacob Gade Music Prize, 1969. Address: Arnevangen 16, 2840 Holte, Denmark.

THOMSON, Bryden, b. Ayr, Scotland. Orchestral Conductor. Educ: Dip. MusEd. (Hons), RSAMD; BMus (Dunelm); FRSAMD; LRAM; ARCM. Career incls: Asst. Cond., BBC Scottish Symph. Orch.; Assoc. Cond., Scottish Nat. Orch.; Cond., Den Norske Opera, The Royal Opera, Stockholm; Prin. Cond. BBC Northern Symph. Orch.; currently Prin. Cond., BBC Welsh Symph. Orch.; Artistic Dir. & Prin. Cond., Ulster Orch. Hobby: Golf. Mgmt: Music Int., 13 Ardilaun Rd., Highbury, London, N5 2QR, UK. Address: c/o Mgmt.

THOMSON, Harold, b. 1 Aug. 1906, Rutherglen, Scotland, UK. Pianist; Accompanist; Continuo player; Lecturer; Examiner; Adjudicator. Educ: Dip. SNAM, Scottish Nat. Acad. of Music, Glasgow; BMus, Edinburgh Univ.; Pvt. studies w. Sir Donald Tovey. Career: Asst. in Music, Glasgow Univ., 1934-39; Lectr., W of Scotland Joint Committee for Adult Educ., 1934-39; Vice-Prin., Royal Scottish Acad. of Music, 1939-52;

Music Critic, Glasgow Herald, 1948-52; Hd. of Music (Scotland) BBC, 1952-64; Examiner to Assoc. Bd. of Royal Schls. of Music, 1947-76. Recordings: BBC recordings of talks, piano recitals & chmbr. music recitals. Publs: Academus Text Books on Rudiments of Music (Joint Author), 1933. Contbr. to: Glasgow Herald. Mbr., ISM, 1930-. Hons: Prizes & Scholarships, Scottish Nat. Acad. of Music; Fellow, Royal Scottish Acad. of Music, 1973. Hobbies: Reading; Travel. Address: 22 Overtoun Dr., Rutherglen, Glasgow G73 2QD, UK. 3, 29.

THOMSON, James Cutting, b. 12 June 1909, Chgo., Ill., USA. College Teacher of Musicology; Musician (Violin, Harpsichord, Gamba). Educ: AB, Middlebury Coll., 1929; Staatlich Geprüft, Hochschule Für Musik, Berlin, Germany, 1934; MA, Baylor Univ., USA, 1940; MA, Yale Univ., 1948; PhD, NY Univ., 1959. m. Selma Wertime Thomson, 1 s., 3 d. Career incls. Tchr., Coll. of Ozasks, 1934-35, Baylor Univ., 1935-42, Wilson Coll., 1952-63, Univ. of Kansas, 1963-68; W Chester State Coll., Chmn., Music history & lit., 1968-75; num. radio apps. & solo recitals. Comps: Aria for Violin & Piano (also arr. for str. orch.), 1941. Publs: The Works of Caron, a Study in 15th Century Style, 1960; An Introduction to Philippe Caron, 1964, Music Through the Renaissance, 1968; The Performance of Music Transcribed with Irregularly Placed Barlines, 1970; The Complete Works of Philippe Caron, 1971-74. Contbr. to: Southwestern Musician; Am. Choral Review. Mbrships: Am. Musicol. Soc.; Pi Kappa Lambda; Pa. Assn. for Higher Educ.; Pa. Music Educators Assn.; Masons. Hons: Scholarship, Am. Coun. Learned Socs., 1942; Fellowship, Yale Univ., 1942; Kellogg Fugue Prize, Yale Music Schl., 1949; Fulbright Lecture Award, Iran, 1962. Hobbies: Photography; Model Railroading. Address: 1638 Green Ln., RD 3, West Chester, PA, USA. 6, 8. 11.

THOMSON, Joan Lewis, b. 13 May 1940, Boston, Mass., USA. Musicologist; Music Critic; Pianist. Educ: Smith Coll., 1958-60; BA, Barnard Coll., 1962; MA, Columbia Univ., 1964, PhD, 1972. div., 2 s. Career: Lectr., Met. Opera Guild, NY, Purchase Campus, SUNY, Opera Action, Fairfield-Westchester; Musicologist, Yale Univ., Schl. of Music, Asst. Dir., Oral Hist., Am. Music, 1976-79; Music Critic, Greenwich Time, 1971-78, Patent Trader, 1971-72; Exec. dir., Our Bach Midnight Concerts, Lincoln Ctr., 1974. Contbr. to: Musical Newsletter; NY Times; Opera News; Opera. Mbrships. incl: Music Committee, Greenwich Lib; Am. Musicol. Soc.; Music Critics Assn. Hons. incl: Clarence Barket Fellow in Musicol., Columbia Univ., 1963-65. Hobbies: Swimming; Hiking; Reading. Address: 46 Cherry Valley Rd., Greenwich, CT 06830, USA.

THOMSON, Virgil, b. 25 Nov. 1896, Kansas City, Mo., USA. Composer; Music Critic. Educ: BA, Harvard Univ., 1922; studied w. Nadia Boulanger, Paris; DFA, Syracuse Univ., 1949; DLitt, Rutgers Univ., 1956. Career: Choirmaster & Organist, King's Chapel, Boston; Writer on music for mags. inclng. Vanity Fair, Boston Transcript, Mod. Music; Music Critic, NY Herald Tribune, 1940-54. Compositions incl: Sonata da Chiesa (chmbr.); 3 Str. Quartets; The Plough that Broke the Plains (film music); The Mother of Us All & Lord Byron (operas); Filling Station (ballet); Louisiana Story (film music); Symph. on a Hymn Tune; Missa pro Defunctis; Cantata on poems of Edward Lear; A Solemn Music & a Joyful Fugue. Publs: The State of Music, 1939; The Musical Scene, 1945; The Art of Judging Music, 1948; Music Right & Left, 1951; Virgil Thomson by Virgil Thomson, 1966; Music Reviewed, 1940-54, 1967; American Music Since 1910, 1971. Mbr: Am. Acad. of Arts & Letters. Hons. incl: Off., Legion of Hon., France; Gold Medal, Nat. Inst. of Arts & Leters; Creative Art Award Gold Medal, Brandeis Univ., 1968; Fellow, Am. Acad. of Arts & Scis. Address: 222 W 23rd St., New York, NY, USA.

THOMSON, Warren Milton, b 2 Aug. 1935, Parramatta, Aust. Educator. Educ: BMus, Univ. of Melbourne; Dip. Ed., Melbourne; MACE. Career: Dir. of Music, Trinity Grammar Schl., Kew, 1960-72; Dir. of Studies, Aust. Music Examinations Bd., 1973-74; Hd., Schl. of Ext. Studies, Sydney Conservatorium, 1974-; Num. piano broadcasts for Aust. Broadcasting Commission; FM Radio & Moscow Radio; Fed. Examiner, Aust. Music Examinations Bd., 1972, 73, 74. Recordings: AMEB Pianoforte Course Preliminary Grade (w. Larry Sitsky). Mbrships. incl: Pres. Fedn. of Aust. Music Tchrs. Assns. Publs. incl: Piano Course - A Tutor for Australian Children (w. Miriam Hyde), 1975; Piano Course 2, 3 (w. Miriam Hyde), 1976. Contbr. to profl. jrnls. Hobbies incl: Swimming. Address: 1 Woodward Pl., St. Ives, NSW, 2075, Australia.

THORARINSSON, Leifur, b. 13 Aug. 1934, Reykjavik, Iceland. Composer. Educ: Reykjavik Music Schl.; Vienna Music Acad.; w. Gunther Schuller, NYC. m. Inga Huld Hakonardottir,

3 children. Comps: Two Symphonies (1963, 1976); Violin Concerto; String Quartet; Trio Violin, Violincello, Piano; Violin Sonata; Trio, Flute, Violincello, Piano; Piano Sonatas 1 & 2; Woodwind Quintet, Flute Sonata. Mbr., Comps. Soc. of Iceland. Address: Rosenvaengets Alle 14, 2100 Copenhagen O, Denmark.

THORDAL, Vagn, b. 7 Feb. 1918, Grindersley, Denmark. Singer; Teacher. Educ: Tchrs. Dip., 1940; Speech Tchr., 1945; Music Tchr., 1964; studied w. Gerda Schroder, Ragnar Blennow, Roy Henderson, Iwor Newton, Erik Werba. m. Mimi Jacobsen, 2 c. Debut: Copenhagen, 1950. Career: Recitals in Denmark, Norway; num. Ch. Concerts; frequent apps., Danish Radio; Radio apps., UK, France, Austria; Prof. of Singing, Vestjysk Music Conserv., Royal Theatre Opera Schl., Copenhagen & Copenhagen Univ. Mbrships: MTA; Danish Soloists Assn.; Ctrl. Academic Org. Address: 5 Hoeghs Alle, 2820 Gentofte, Denmark.

THORNE, Francis, b. 23 June 1922, Bayshore, NY, USA. Composer; Pianist-Conductor. Educ: BA, Yale Univ. m. Ann Cobb, 3 d. Debut: 1st major comp. performed by Phila. Orch., 1964. Comps: 51 major comps. in catalogue, 11 published; 12 comps. recorded on 7 LP records. Mbrships: Broadcast Music Inc.; Am. Music Ctr.; Exec. Dir., Am. Comps. Alliance; VP, Contemporary Music Soc. Hons: Nat. Inst. of Arts & Letters Prize, 1968; Nat. Endowment for the Arts Fellowship, 1973; NY State Coun. of the Arts Fellowhip, 1974. Hobbies: Swimming; Rowing; Reading; Jazz piano. Address: 116 E 66th St., NY, NY, USA.

THORNE, Phillip Martin, b. 1 Nov. 1951, Pitlochry, Perthshire, UK. Teacher of Guitar; Principal Teacher of Music. Educ: FTCL (Recital Dip.); LTCL (Perfs. Dip.); LRAM (Tchng. Dip.); Cert. in Secondary Music Educ. m. Shelagh Robertson, 1 d., 1 s. Career: Regular broadcasts, BBC Radio; Extensive recitals in Scotland as soloist, & in var. ensembles; has been active in expanding the contemporary guitar repertoire; Tchr. of Guitar, RSAMD, Glasgow; Prin. Tchr. of Music, St. David's High Schl., Midlothian. Publs: Fugue in D minor & other works by S L Weiss. Address: 26 Rullion Rd., Penicuik, Midlothian, Scotland,UK.

THÖRNER, Helmut, b. 1903, Chemnitz, Germany. Composer; Organist; Pianist; Lecturer. Educ: Leipzig Conserv. m. Marianne Thörner. Career: Organist, Stadtkirche, Chemnitz, 1944-; Prof., Burgstadt Music Schl., 1948; Prof., Piano & Comp. Schumann Conserv., Zwickau, 1955; num. broadcasts, German Radio, 1942-; Solo performances w. Dresden Kreuzchor & Thomaner Chor, Leipzig; Reviewer, Saechsische Neueste Nachrichten, Die Union, etc. Comps. incl: Concert variations on 'Annchen von Tharau' (piano); Toccata & Fugue in E Minor (organ); Sonata in C (violin & piano). Contbr. to Aufgaben der neuen Kirchenmusik, 1967. Mbr., AWA, Berlin. Address: Otto Nuschke Str. 42, Karl-Marx Stadt, 90 German Dem. Repub. 3.

THORNHILL, Margaret Louise, b. 26 Nov. 1950, Palo Alto, Calif., USA. Clarinettist; Teacher. Educ: BA, Univ. of Calif.; MA, DMA, Stanford Univ. Career: Pvte. Studios, Palo Alto & Santa Cruz, Calif.; num. chmbr. music & solo perfs. Lectr. in Music, Univ. of Calif., Santa Cruz; Woodwind Chmbr. Music Coach, Stanford Univ.; Asst. Prof. of Music, Occidental Coll., LA, Calif. Mbr., Int. Clarinet Soc.; Am. Fedn. of Musicians; NACWPI. Address: 250 E Del Mar Blvd., Pasadena, CA 91101, USA. 4,

THORPE, Marion, b. Vienna, Austria. Pianist; Writer; Musical Administrator. Educ: Pvte. study w. Franz Osborn. m. Jeremy Thorpe, 3 s., 1 stepson. Career: BBC talks & interviews; prog. notes. Publs: Ed., Form & Performance by Erwin Stein, 1962; Classical Songs for Children, 1964; 5 vols. of Piano Lessons & Young Pianist's Repertoire w. Fanny Waterman. Contbr. to var. music mags. Mbrships. incl: Pres., Friends of Covent Gdn.; Music Advsry. Comm., Brit. Coun.; Aldeburgh Festival & Snape Maltings Fndn.; Jt. Chmn., Leeds Int. Pianoforte Competition; Gov., Yehudi Menuhin Schl.; Dir., Engl. Music Theatre; Pres., SW Arts Assn.; Corp. of TCL; Music Panel, Gtr. London Arts Assn.; Hobbies: Sightseeing; Swimming; Sunbathing. Address: 2 Orme Square, London, W2, UK.

THORSTEINSDOTTIR-STROSS, Ásdis, b. 26 Nov. 1939, Reykjavik, Iceland. Violinist. Educ: Dip., Reykjavik Conserv., 1959; Staatliche Hochschule für Musik, Munich, German Fed. Repub., 1959-62; Int. Summer Acad., Nice, France, 1973, 74. m. Wolfgang Stross, 3 d. Career: Mbr., Reykjavik Symph. Orch., 1962-; Rekjavikur Ensemble. Mbrships: Icelandic Musicians Union; Soc. of Musicians in Icelandic Symph. Orch. Hobbies: Sewing; Travelling; Reading. Mgmt: Sekretariat Brandi-Stross, 8183 Rottach-Egern, German Fed. Repub. Address: Öldugata 28, Reykjavik, Iceland.

THURM, Joachim, b. 23 Feb. 1927, Ruppersdorf bei Lobenstein, Thüringen, Germany. Composer; Teacher. Educ: Staatsexamina (Comp., theory, piano, ch. music), Musikhochschule Franz Liszt, Weimar. Comps. incl: Sinfonia Piccola; Moments musicaux for electronic sounds & musical instruments; 5 Impromptus for orch.; Trumpet concerto; Partita for 16 brass & kettledrums; lieder; choral music; piano & chmbr. music; music for film & TV. num. recordings of own works. Mbr., Verband der komponisten und Musikwissenschaftler der DDR. Hobbies: Playing old keyboard instruments; Record collecting. Address: Weststrasse 6, 5302, Bad Berka bei Weimar, German Dem. Repub.

THURSTON, Ethel Holbrooke, b. 30 Oct. 1911, Mpls., Minn., USA. Musicologist. Educ: AB, Vassar Coll., 1933; Attended Pontifical Inst. of Medieval Studies, Toronto, Ont., Can.; Dips., Organ & Solfege, Am. Schl. of Music, Fontainebleau, France; 4 Yr. Dip., Gregorian Chant, Pius X Schl. of Liturgical Music, NY, USA; PhD, NY Univ. Career: Tchr., Music Hist & Theory, var. colls., 1942-; Chmn., Dept. of Music Hist., Manhattan Schl. of Music, NYC, 1965-; Vis. Prof., Musicol., NY Univ. Grad. Schl., 1973-74. Publs: The Music in the St. Victor Manuscript, 1959; The Works of Perotin (Transcription w. Commentary), 1970; The Conductus Collections in Manuscript Wolfenbüttel, 1099, 1976. Contbr. to: Catholic Art Quarterly. Mbrships: Am. Musicol. Soc.; Int. Musicol. Soc.; Mu Phi Epsilon, 1946; Mu Sigma, 1951; Phi Beta Kappa, 1933; Music Lib. Assn. Hobbies: Travel; Wildlife conservation. Address: 175 W 12th ST., NY, NY 10011, USA.

THYM, Jurgen, b. 2 July 1943, Bremervörde, Germany. Musicologist; Plays Piano. Educ: State Exam, Freie Univ., Berlin, 1969, Hochschule für Musik Berlin, 1967; PhD, Case Western Reserve Univ., Cleveland, OH, USA, 1974. Career: Tchng. Asst., Case Western Reserve Univ., 1969; Instr., Oberlin Coll. Conserv., 1973, Instr.-Asst. Prof., Eastman Schl. of Music, Rochester, 1973-. Publs: The Solo Song Settings of Eichendorff's Poems by Schumann & Wolf, 1974. Contbr. to profl. jrnls. Mbrships. incl: Am. & Int. Musicol. Socs. Recip. acad. hons. Hobbies: Chess; Hiking. Address: 1450 E Ave., Rochester, NY 14610, USA.

TIELLA, Marco, b. 6 May 1930, Rovereto, Italy. Teacher. Educ: Dip. in Arch. m. Lia Petrolli, 1 s., 1 d. Debut: 30th Fest. of Contemporary Music, Venice, 1967. Career: Concerts w. Complesso Veneziana Strumenti Antichi, la Fontegara, Studio di Musica Antica, Insieme Polifonico Jannequin; soloist on Archicembalo; Prin., Corso per il restauro degli antichi strumenti, Civica Scuola di Musica di Milano. Publs: Intavolatura d'Organo della Scuola dell' Hofhaimer, 1975; A. Scarlatti's Cantata inhumana in regolato cromatico, Andate o miei sospiri. Contbr. to: Engl. Harpsichord mag.; Galpin Soc. Jrnl.; Bollettino dei Musei Civici Veneziani; Musica Viva. Mbrships: Galpin Soc.; Int. Coun. of Mus. Hobby: Making & restoring renaissance musical instruments. Address: Via Rialto 30, 38068 Rovereto, Italy.

TIENSUU, Jukka, b. 30 Aug. 1948, Helsinki, Finland. Composer; Musician (piano & harpsichord); Conductor. Educ: Dips. in Piano & Comp., Sibelius Acad., Helsinki, 1972; Juilliard Schl., NYC, USA, 1972-73; Dips. in Harpsichord & Baroque chmbr. music, State Music HS, Freiburg, W Germany, 1976. Career: Solo piano, solo harpsichord & chmbr. music concerts in Europe, USA; Soloist w. var. Finnish Symph. Orchs.; Tchr., computer music, IRCAM, Paris; Tchr., comp. a.o.t., Sibelius Acad., Helsinki. Comps. incl. orchl., instrumental, vocal & electronic music inclng. commns. from Finnish State Radio & Nordic Comps. Coun. Contbr. to: Melos/NZ; Music & Musicians; Numus-W; Finnish music publs. Hons: Koussevitzky Award, 1973; Leonie Sonning Award, 1978. Address: Fleminginkatu 20 A 5, SF-00510 Helsinki 51, Finland.

TIKKA, Kari, b. 13 Apr. 1946, Siilinjarvi, Finland. Conductor. Educ: Dip., Oboe Perf., 1968, Conducting, 1969, Sibelius Acad., Helsinki; Pvte. study, conducting, w. Arvid Jansons, Luigi Ricci. m. Pirkkoliisa Tikka. Debut: Helsinki, 1968. Career: Cond., Tampere Theatre, 1969-70; Cond., Nat. Opera, Helsinki, 1970-72; Finnish Radio Symph. Orch., 1972-; Swedish Royal Opera House, 1975-; Guest Cond., Scandinavia, USSR, Germany, Poland. Comps: Two Aphorisms; Due Pezzi. Recordings: Triplet, New Finnish Mod. Music; Oopperan Lastenkabaree. Hons: Finnish State Schlrship., 1974-76. Hobby: Spectator sports. Mgmt: Konsertbolaget, Stockholm. Address: Mottitie 30, 00370 Helsinki 30, Finland.

TILBURY, Dorothy Elizabeth, b. 6 June 1946, London, UK. Music Teacher. Educ: Pvte. studies w. Mabel F Lloyd; Jr. Exhibitioner, Guildhall Schl. of Music & Drama, 1958-64; Trinity Coll. of Music, 1964-67; Grad., ibid.; Lic., ibid.; MusEd.

Career: Tchr. of Gen. Music in Schls. & of Piano, Guitar & Clarinet. Mbrships: Incorp. Soc. of Musicians; Exec. Mbr., London Borough of Haringey's Schls. Music Assn. Hons: Winner, many local festivals for piano playing; Winner, The Lily Messenger Silver Salver, London Music Festival, 1963, 1964, 1965. Hobbies: Photography; Travel; Handicrafts. Address: 143 Poynton Rd., Tottenham, London, N17 9SJ, UK.

TILBURY, John, b. 1 Feb. 1936, London, UK. Concert Pianist. Educ: RCM; ARCM; James Gibb; Warsaw Conserv. m. (2) Janice Dykes, 2 d. Recordings: John Cage's Sonatas & Interludes, Decca. Contbr. to: Musical Times; Am., Canadian, English; Polish & Italian musical periodicals. Mbrships: ISM; Musicians Union. Hons: Prizewinner, Gaudeamus Int. Competition for Contemporary Music, 1964. Hobby: Watching Soccer. Address: c/o Allied Artists, 36 Beauchamp Pl., London, SW3, UK.

TILLIS, Frederick Charles, b. 5 Jan. 1930, Galveston, Tex., USA. Composer; Professor of Music. Educ: BA, Wiley Coll., Marshall, Tex.; MA, PhD, Univ. of Iowa. m. E Louise Tillis, 2 d. Career incls: Prof. of Music (Theory, Improvisation & Comp.); currently Special Asst. to the Provost for the Arts & Dir. of Afro-Am. Music & Jazz Prog., Univ. of Mass., Amherst, 1970-. Comps. incl: Music for violin, cello & piano; Freedom for chorus; Niger Symph.; Five Spirituals for chorus & brass choir. Recordings: Music for Alto Flute, Cello & Piano; Freedom for Chorus; Brass Quintet; Niger Symph.; Two Spirituals for Symph. Orch. Mbrships: Am. Comps. Alliance; MENC; Nat. Assn. of Jazz Educs. Recip. var. hons. inclng: Danforth Assoc., 1969-; Rockefellow Grant, 1978. Hobbies: Reading; Poetry; Table tennis. Address: 55 Grantwood Dr., Amherst, MA 01002, USA.

TILMOUTH, Michael, b. 30 Nov. 1930, Grimsby, UK. University Teacher. Educ: Christ's Coll., Cambridge; BA, 1954; MA, 1958; PhD, 1960. m. Mary Jelliman, 2 s., 1 d. Career: Lectr. in Music, Prof. of Music, Dean of Fac. univs. inclng: Glasgow & Edinburgh; Dir., Scottish Opera, 1975-; Mbr. BBC Archives Committee, 1976-. Publs: incl: A Calendar of References to Music in Newspapers published in London and the Provinces, 1660-1719 (Royal Musical Assn. Rsch. Chronicle No. 1, 1961 & No. 2, 1962), 1968; Ed. num. edns. of mainly instrumental chmbr. music of 17th & 18th centuries; Mbr., Ed. Committee, Musica Britannica & Purcell Soc. Contbr. to profl. jrnls. Mbrships. incl: Coun., Royal Musical Assn., 1970-76. Hobbies: Skiing; Squash; Hill Walking. Address: 62 Northumberland St., Edinburgh EH3 6JE, UK. 1.

TILSON THOMAS, Michael, b. 1944, Hollywood, Calif., USA. Conductor. Educ: BMus, Univ. of Southern Calif.; MMus, ibid; studied w. Ingolf Dahl & John Crown; Cond. Fellow, Berkshire Music Ctr., 1968 & 69. Career: Mbr., Berkshire Music Ctr. Fac., 1970; Asst. Cond., Boston Symph. Orch., 1969-70; Assoc. Cond., ibid, 1970-71; Music Dir., Buffalo Philharmonic, 1971-; Vis. Adjunct Prof., Music Dept., SUNY, Buffalo; Cond., NY Philharmonic Orch. Young People's Concerts; Prin. Guest Cond. & Music Dir. of Spectrum Series, Boston Symph. Orch. Recordings incl: Debussy's Images, Tchaikovsky's 1st Symph., Ruggles' Sun-treader, Schuman's Violin Concerto, Ive's Three Places in New England & Piston's 2nd Symph. (all w. Boston Symph. Orch. for DGG). Hons. incl: Musician of the Month, Musical Am. Mag., June, 1970; Young Artists Award, ibid, 1969; Hon. DFA, Hamilton Coll., Clinton, NY, 1971; Koussevitzky Cond. Prize, Berkshire Music Ctr., 1968. Hobbies: Crystallography; Minerology. Address: Buffalo Philharmonic, Philharmonic House, 26 Richmond Ave., Buffalo, NY 14222, USA. 3.

TIMM, Jeanne Margaret, b. Sioux City, Iowa, USA. Flautist; Teacher. Educ: BMus, Morningside Coll. Conserv. Music, 1940; Grad. work, Eastman Schl. Music, 1942-43; La. State Univ., 1955, '66. m. Everett L. Timm, 2 s. Career incls: Flautist w. New Orleans Symph., New Orleans Civ. Opera, Sioux City Symph., Monohan Post Band, Timm Woodwind Quintet res. at La. State Univ.; La. State Univ. Baroque Ensemble, & Prin. Flautist w. Baton Rouge Symph.; Staff flautist, radio stns., KSCJ & WNAX, Sioux City; Tchr., La. State Univ. Mbr. profl. orgs. Recip. Grant, La. Coun. Music & Performing Arts to perform in pub. schls., 6 yrs. Hobby: Cooking gourmet food. Address: 465 Magnolia Woods Dr., Baton Rouge, LA 70808, USA.

TIMM, Kenneth N, b. 2 Nov. 1934, San Fran., Calif., USA. Educator; Instrumentalist (Saxophone, Clarinet, Flute); Arranger; Copyist; Conductor. Educ: BA, Calif. State Univ., Hayward; MA, Mills Coll., Calif.; Doct. Cand., Ind. Univ., Bloomington. m. Virginia, 1 s., 1 d. Career: Freelance perf., arr., comp., 1955-; Asst. Prof., music comp & theory, Cleveland State Univ. Comps. incl: Sonata (Other Streams) (4 celli);

Trichotomy (orch.). Recording: The Joiner & the Die-hard (Crystal), 1976. Publ: A Graphic Representation of Anton Webern's Symphonie, Op. 21, II, 1975. Mbr. Profl. orgs. Recip. prizes for comps. Address: 3385 Kildare Rd., Cleveland Hts., OH 44118, USA.

TIMMERMANS, Ferdinandus, b. 7 Sept. 1891, Rotterdam, Netherlands. Musician (organ, piano, carillon); Singer. Educ: Piano dip., Maatschappijtot bevordering der Toonkunst, 1914; Organ dip., Nederlandse Toonkunstenaars Vereniging, 1912; Carillon dip., Beiaardschl. Mechelen, 1925; Singing dip., 1930. m. Jannetje Smits, 2 children. Debut: Dordrecht, 1907. Career incls: Organist, Remonstrant Ch., Rotterdam, 1924-64; City Carillonneur, Rotterdam, 1924-56; Schiedam, 1926-56; Carillon Tchr., Rotterdam Schl. Music, 1927. Compositions incl: Fantasie en fuga over 'Hoe groot o Heer'; Impromptu. Publ: Luidklokken en Beiaarden in Nederland, 2nd ed., 1950. Contbr. to jrnls. Mbr. profl. orgs. Hons. incl: 1st prizes, carillon competitions, Dutch Carillon Guild, 1927. Hobbies incl: Organ-bldg.

TINSLEY, Pauline Cecilia, b. Wigan, UK. Lyric Dramatic Soprano. Educ: Northern Schl. of Music, Manchester; Opera Schl., St. John's Wood; LRAM. m. G M Neighbor, 1 s., 1 d. Debut: as Desdemona, Rossini's Otello, London, 1961. Career: has made extensive apps. in concerts, oratorios, recitals & broadcasts, UK & abroad, but best known as Opera Singer, Royal Opera Covent Gdn., Engl., Welsh & Scottish Nat. Opera cos., & w. cos. in Europe & N Am.; Leading interpreter of Verdian roles (Abigaille, Lady Macbeth, Aida,etc.), but repertoire also incls. Handel, Mozart, Beethoven, Rossini, etc. Recordings incl: Elettra, (Mozart's Idomeneo). Hobbies: Knitting; Gardening. Mgmt: AIM. Address: Springfield House, Altham Rd., Hatch End, Pinner HA5 4RQ, UK. 3, 27.

TIPPETT, (Sir) Michael Kemp, b. 2 Jan. 1905, London, UK. Composer. Educ: RCM. Career: w. Ran Choral & Orchestral Soc., Oxted, Surrey, & Tchr. of French, Hazelwood Schl., until 1931; Dir. of Music, Morley Coll., 1940-51; Dir. of Bath Fest., 1970-74. Has composed num. works; those recorded incl: The Midsummer Marriage (opera); The Knot Garden (opera); Boyhood's End; Suite for the Birthday of Prince Charles; Magnificat & Nunc Dimittis; The Weeping Babe; The Heart's Assurance; Preludio Al Vespro di Monteverdi; Little Music for Strings; Concerto for Orchestra; Songs for Ariel; Fantasia Concertante on a theme of Corelli; Concerto for Double String Orchestra; Concerto for piano & orchestra; Sonata for 4 horns; Songs for Dov; Fantasia on a theme of Handel; The Vision of St. Augustine; Symphonies No. 1, 2 & 3; 3 str. quartets; 3 piano sonatas. Publs: Moving into Aquarius, 1959, paperback ed., 1974. Recip. of num. prizes & awards for work. Address: Schott & Co. Ltd., 48 Gt. Marlborough St., London WIV 2BN, UK. 3.

TIPPLE, Colin John, b. 24 June 1942, Welwyn Garden City, UK. Organist; Choir Trainer; Schoolmaster. Educ: BMus, London Univ. (RAM); FRCO; GRSM; LRAM; ARCM. Career: Dpty. Organ Prof., RAM, 1964-65; Asst. Dir. of Music, Fettes Coll., Edinburgh, 1965-; Assoc. Cond. & Organist, Scottish Chmbr. Choir, 1970-75; Cond., Scottish Chmbr. Choir, 1975-. Recordings: Monteverdi, Missa in illo tempore, w. Scottish Chmbr. Choir, 1974. Mbrships: ISM; RCO; RAM Club; RSCM; Edinburgh Soc. of Organists. Hons: Henry Richards Prize, 1961; Hubert Kiver Prize, 1963; F A Keene Prize, 1963; Ridley Prentice Meml. Prize, 1964; Margaret & Sydney Lovett Prize, 1964. Hobbies: Reading; Travel. Address: 96 Inverleith Pl., Edinburgh EH3 5PA, UK.

TIRIMO, b. 19 Dec. 1942, Larnaca, Cyprus. Concert Pianist. Educ: RAM, London; FRAM; State Acad. of Music, Vienna. m. Mione Jane Tirimo, 1 s., 1 d. Debut: London, 1965. Career: Int. soloist w. leading orchs., also on TV & radio; 1st public perf. of complete (20) Schubert Piano Sonatas w. own completions of unfinished movements, London. Recordings: Chopin, cassette, 1975; Schubert sonatas, 1978; Brahms' 2nd Piano Concerto, w. Yoel Levi & LPO, 1978. Publs: Urtext Ed. of the Complete Schubert Piano Sonatas. Mbrships: ISM; Eng. Speaking Union. Hons. incl: Winner, Geneva Int. Piano Competition, 1972; Jt. winner, Munich Int. Piano Competition, 1971. Hobbies: Chess, Reading; Football; Travel. Address: 2 Combemartin Rd., London SW18 5PR, UK. 2, 29.

TIRRO, Frank Pascale, b. 20 Sept. 1935, Omaha, Neb., USA. Professor of Music; Author; Composer. Educ: BME, Univ. of Neb.; MMus, Northwestern Univ.; PhD, Univ. of Chicago. m. Charlene Rae Whitney Tirro, 1 s., 1 d. Career incls: Prof. of Music, Duke Univ., Durham, NC. Comps: American Jazz Mass; American Jazz Te Deum; Church Sonata for organ; Melismas for Carillon; Sing A New Song. Publs: Jazz: A History, 1977. Contbr. to: The Musical Quarterly; Jrnl. of the Am. Musicol.

Soc.; Music Lib. Assn.; Notes; Dict. of Contemporary Music; Grove's Dict., 6th Ed. Mbrships: Int. Musicol. Soc.; Int. Soc. for Jazz Rsch.; Am. Musicol. Soc.; Renaissance Soc. of Am.; Mediaeval Acad. of Am.; Music Lib. Assn. Hons: Fellow of Villa I Tatti; ASCAP Standard Comps. Award; Nat. Fedn. of Music Clubs Award. Hobbies: Travel; Motorcycling; Bread Baking. Address: Dept. of Music; Duke Univ., 6695 College Station, Durham, NC, USA. 11, 29.

TISCHHAUSER, Franz, b. 28 March 1921, Bern, Switz. Radio Director; Composer. Educ: Dips., theory & piano. Career incls: Radio Dir., Radio Zürich. Comps: Das Nasobem; Omaggi a Mèlzel; Punctus contra punctum; Seldwyliana; Kontertänze; Eve's Meditation of Love; The Beggar's Concerto; Dr. Bircher und Rossini; Oktett; Kassation; Sonatine. Recordings: Ex Libris. Mbrships: Schweizerischer Tonkünstlerverein. Hons: Conrad Ferdinand Meyer Prize, 1951. Address: In der Stelzen, CH-8428, Teufen, Switz.

TISCHLER, Hans, b. 18 Jan. 1915, Vienna, Austria. Musicologist (Pianist). Educ: Piano Tchrs. Dip. (BMus), Vienna State Acad., 1933; MMus, ibid., 1935, 36; PhD Musicol., Vienna Univ., 1937, Yale Univ., 1942. m. (1) Louise Hochdorf (dec.), 1 s., 1 d., (2) Alice Bock, 1 s., 1 d. Career incls: Assoc. prof., Chgo. Musical Coll. of Roosevelt Univ., 1947-65; Prof., Ind. Univ. Schl. of Music, 1965-. Publs. incl: The Perceptive Music Listener, 1955; Practical Harmony, 1965; A Structural Analysis of Mozart's Piano Concertos, 1966; A Medieval Motet Book, 1973; The Montpellier MS; A New Transcription, 1978; Complete Edition of the Earliest Motets, 1979. Contbr. to num. books & jrnls. Mbr., profl. assns. Hons. incl: Guggenheim Fellow, 1964; NEH Fellow, 1975. Address: 711 E 1st St., Bloomington, IN 47401, USA. 8, 11, 12, 14, 28.

TITCOMB, Caldwell, b. 16 Aug. 1926, Augusta, Maine, USA. Music Professor; University Organist. Educ: AB, Harvard Univ., 1947; MA, ibid., 1949; PhD, 1952; Studied piano, organ, percussion, comp. theory & musicol., w. var. tutors. Career incls: Music fac., Brandeis Univ., 1953; Dir., undergrad. studies in music, 1956-; Music & Drama critic, Harvard Summer News & Harvard Crimson, 1953-. Comps: 13 incidental music scores for stage & film prodns. Publs. incl: Choral Music (co-author), 1963, '66. Contbr. to profl. jrnls. Mbr. profl. orgs. Hons incl: Schurz Prize, 1944; Detur Award, 1944. Hobbies: Reading; Swimming. Address: Slosberg Ctr., Brandeis Univ., Waltham, MA 02154, USA. 6, 11.

TITON, Jeff Todd, b. 8 Dec. 1943, Jersey City, NJ, USA. Ethnomusicologist; Guitarist. Educ: BA, Amherst Coll., 1965; MA, Univ.of Minn., 1967; MA, ibid., 1970, PhD, ibid., 1971. m. Paula Winslow Protze, 1 d. Career: Lazy Bill Lucas Blues Band, 1969-71; Asst. Prof., Tufts Univ., 1971-77; Assoc. Prof., ibid, 1977-. Recordings: Lazy Bill & His Friends; Lazy Bill Lucas. Publs: From Blues to Pop: The Autobiography of Leonard (Baby Doo) Caston, 1974; Early Downhome Blues - a Musical & Cultural Analysis, 1977. Contbr. to num. profl. jrnls. Mbrships: Soc. for Ethnomusicol.; Am. Folklore Soc. Hons: Deems Taylor Prize, ASCAP, 1977. Hobbies: Photography. Address: Dept. of Music, Tufts Univ., Medford, MA 02155, USA.

TITT, Michael George, b. 13 July 1939, Salisbury, UK. Flautist; Performer on Piccolo, Alto Flute, Piano & Organ. Educ: Royal Mil Schl. of Music, Kneller Hall; Berlin Music Conserv.; TCL; LTCL, 1964; FTCL, 1965. m. Rigmor Davidsen Titt. Career: Free-lance Musician; Performed w. most ldng. symphs. in UK; perfs. at Bath, Llandaff, Edinburgh, Berlin, Vienna, Chichester & Bergen Fests.; currently flautist, Bergen Symph. Orch. & Prof., Bergen Music Conserv.& Bergen Laereskole, Norway. Recordings: num. w. Bergen Symph. Orch., NRK & BBc. Mbrships: ISM; KRRC Assn. Recip., 1st Prize, Royal Military Schl. of Music, Kneller Hall, 1957. Hobbies: Travel, Motoring; Cooking. Address: Torgny Segerstedsvei 180, Fyllingsdalen 5033 Bergen, Norway.

TITUS, Graham, b. 15 Dec. 1949, Newark, Notts., UK. Concert & Opera Singer. Educ: MA, Clare Coll., Cambridge Univ. (Organ Scholar); FRCO; Music High Schl., Cologne, German Fed. Repub. Debut: Purcell Room, London, 1974. Career: Glyndebourne Fest. Opera, 1973, '74; apps. w. New Opea Co., Handel Opera, Engl. Nat. Opera; Radio recitals, 1974-76; apps. on Dutch TV & radio; concert tour of S America; Recital & Oratorio work throughout UK; inclng. Aldeburgh Fest., 1975. Hons: Winner, Young Musicians '74 Series, 1974; Winner, Leeds Nat. Musicians Platform, 1974; Winner, '5-Hertogenbosch Singing Competition, 1977. Hobbies: Gardening; Psychic Phenomena. Mgmt: Ibbs & Tillett. Address: 114 Oldfield Rd., London N16, UK.

TIVEY, Roger James, b. 9 Jan. 1942, Wellingborough, Northants., UK. Music Teacher; Organist; Festival Director.

Educ. incl: Organ Schlr., St. Paul's Coll., Cheltenham, 1960-63; Hons. Degree, Music & Educ., Leicester, 1977; Master Music Educ., Univ. London, 1980; Assoc., Lic., Fellow, London Coll., 1963; Lic., Trinity Coll., 1976; Lic., Royal Acad., 1977; Assoc., Royal Coll., 1977. Career incl: Asst. Admnstr., W Theatre Ballet, 1969; Prog. Controller, Wellingborough TV Stn., 1974; Hd., Music & Drama, Wellingborough Breezehill Girls Schl.; Dir. of Music, United Reformed Ch., ibid.; Artistic Dir., Music for All Concert Series. Compositions: Hiroshima, a Requiem for this Age of Fear, 1968; Fire & Ice, 1966. Recordings: w. Tornadoes Grp., 1963-65. Publs: Historical Organs in North Northamptonshire, 1972; Papal Letters of the Early Fifttenth Century, 1974. Mbrships: Int. Soc. Musicians; Royal Coll. Organists. Address: 2 Buckwell End, Wellingborough, Northants., UK.

TOBIN, Ashleigh Hambridge, b. 28 Nov. 1939, Adelaide, Aust. Lecturer; Organist; Conductor. Educ: MMus, Univ. of Adelaide; FRCO; FTCL; LMus. m. Denise Ahern. Career: Sr. Lectr. in Music, Adelaide Coll. of Further Educ.; Adelaide City Organist; Organist & Dir. of Music, Ch. of the Epiphany, Crafers; cond., Crafers Boys' Choir; num. recitals for Aust. Broadcasting Commission, Univ. of Adelaide, Melbourne Fest. of organ & harpsichord. Mbrships: ISM; RCO; Royal Schl. of Ch. Music. Hons: Nat. Finalist, ABC Instrumental & Vocal Competitions, 1957, '60, '62. Hobbies: Walkng; Camping. Mgmt: Crafers Concerts. Address: 509 Kensington Rd., Wattle Pk., S Aust. 5066, Aust.

TOBIN, Candida, b. 5 Jan. 1926, Chingford, UK. Education Specialist; Originator of Tobin Music System. Educ: Hon. FTCL; LTCL. m. John Tobin. Career: formerly music specialist for Herts. Co. Coun.; Tobin Music System featured on sev. radio & TV progs.; lectr., ISME, ISM, ECIS & MENC (USA) conferences. Comps: Didactic material for recorder & guitar; musical plays for schls. Recordings: Audio-Visual material on Diatonic Comp. Publs: Classroom Teacher's Manual - First Steps to Music Literacy, 1979; Manuals on var. aspects of theory; Colour Piping 1 & 2, 1969; Wizard's Way, 1976; Recorder Books; Guitar Instruction Kit & Manual, 1977; Colour & Play Books, Workbooks, etc. Contbr. to: The Guardian; Times Educ. Supplement; Tchrs. World; Music Tchr.; Music in Educ.; She; etc. Mbrships: ISM; ISME; MEUT. Hobbies: Developing Music Teaching System; Composing; Sport. Address: The Old Malthouse, Knight St., Sawbridgeworth, Herts. CM21 9AX, UK.

TOBIN, Caroline, b. 14 May 1941, Chgo., Ill.,USA. Clarinettist. Educ: BA, Music, Univ. of Calif. at Los Angeles, 1962; MA, Clarinet Perf., Calif. State Univ., 1973. m. R D Tobin, 1 d. Career: Participant in chmbr. music concerts, & perfs. w. symphs., Los Angeles & Ventura; currently Fac. Mbr., Ventura Coll. Community Conserv. & Calif. Lutheran Coll. Mbrships: Int. Clarinet Soc.; NACWPI; Southern Calif. Schl. Band & Orchl. Assn. Hobbies: Swimming; Skiing; Horseback Riding. Address: 1273 Knollwood Drive, Newbury Pk., CA 91320, USA.

TOCH, Ernst, b. 7 Dec. 1887, Vienna, Austria. Composer. Educ: Univ. of Vienna (Medicine); Hoch Conserv., Frankfurt-am-Main, Germany. Career: Tchr. for num. yrs.; Tchr. of Composition, Univ. of Southern Calif. Compositions incl: Concerto No. 1; Concerto No. 2 for piano & orch., 1933; Big Ben (orchl.), 1934; Pinocchio, a Merry Overture (orchl.), 1947; Symph. No. 3, 1956. Hons. incl: Pulitzer Prize in Music for 3rd Symph., 1956.

TODA, Kunio, b. 11 Aug. 1915, Tokyo, Japan. Composer; Music Educator. Educ: Grad., Tokyo Univ., 1938; Studied w. Prof. Poppen, Heidelberg Univ., Germany, 1938; Studied Comp. w. Prof. Saburo Moroi, Tokyo, Japan, 1941-43. m. Masako Okada. Career: Prof., Comp., Harmony, Counterpoint, Toho Gakuen Schl. of Music, Tokyo; Dir. Senzoku Gokuen Schl. of Music. Comps: (publd.) Sonatina per pianoforte; Quattro pezzi deformati per pianoforte; Fantaisie sur les sons de koto; Concerto grosso per sei strumenti ed orch.; Sette canti dall'antologia Mannyosyu; Santo Paulo, Oratorio-misterio nella forma di no; (recorded) Sonatas for Violn & Piano & other instruments; Akemi; Kyara Monogatari; Mlranda; Fantaisie symphonique "Légende" for orch.; Sinfonia in Sol. Publs: Prokofiev, 1957. Contbr. to: Sogen Ongaku Koza; Record Ongaku Koza; Cahiers Renaud-Barrault, 1963; Num. Japanese music mags. & daily papers. Mbrships: Sec. Gen., Japanese Nat. Committee of the Int. Music Coun.; Committee Mbr., Japanese Soc. for Contemporary Music. Hons: Japan Victor Prize, 1943; NHK, Jiji Press, Music Contest Prize, 1944, '48, '49. Address: 4-16-13 Seijo, Setagaya-ku, Tokyo PC 157, Japan. 14.

TODD, Diana R, b. 10 Jan. 1943, Adelaide, SA, Aust. Classical Guitarist; Journalist; Entrepreneur. Educ: BA (Music),

DePaul Univ.,Chgo., Ill., USA; master classes w. Manuel Lopez Ramos & Michael Lorimer. Career: TV apps., Adelaide, Aust., TV prog., Ind., USA. Contbr. to Mid-America Guitar Soc. publs. Mbrships: Nat. Entertainment Conf.; Am. String Tchrs. Assoc.; Am. Fedn. Musicans; Guitar Fndn. of Am.; Mid-Am. Guitar Soc.; Galpin Soc.; Aust-Am. Wine Assn. (Pres.). Hobbies: Racquetball; Wine Connoisseur. Address: 155 N Humphrey, Oak Pk., IL 60302, USA.

TODD, Lawrence Edwin Jerome, b. 14 June 1919, Syracuse, NY, USA. Performer (Trombone, Euphonium, Bass Trombone, Bass Trumpet, Valve Trombone); Instr. of Tuba, French Horn, Trumpet, etc. Educ: studied trombone w. James T Harris, Walter Beeler, Ernest Clarke, Davis Shuman, Charles Gusikoff; Music Educ., Ithaca Coll., 2 yrs.; BS in Music, Juilliard Schl. of Music; MA in MusEd., Columbia Univ. Tchrs. Coll. m. Lida Todd, 1 d. Debut: Montclair State Coll. Fac. Recital Series, 1968. Career: Prin. Trombone w. New Orleans Symph., Buffalo Phil., Nat. Symph., Wash. DC, Am. Ballet Theatre Orch., Goldman Band, NYC, NJ Symph., Madison Sq. Gdn. Staff Orch., etc.; Var. perfs. in radio, TV & commercial recording grps.; Supplementary player in perfs. of NY Phil., Met. Opera Orch., Radio City Music Hall Orch.; Var. broadway shows; Instr. of Brass Instruments at Jersey City State Coll., Montclair State Coll., Wm. Patterson State Coll., Upsala Coll.; Brass Cons. for many NJ HS's. Recordings as Prin. Trombonist w. var. orchs. Mbrships: Phi Mu Alpha; Am. Fed. of Musicians. Var. hobbies. Address: 22 Longview Rd., Cedar Grove, NJ 07009, USA.

TODD, Lida Elizabeth Roberts, b. 3 Nov. 1918, Norwalk, Ohio, USA. Performer (Violin, Piano); Instructor. Educ: BA in Music, Oberlin Coll. Conserv.; MA in MusEd, Montclair State Coll. m. Lawrence Edwin Jerome Todd, 1 d. Career: 1st Violinist w. Buffalo Phil., Pitts. Symph., Am. Ballet Theatre Orch., Nat. Symph. Orch., Opera Theatre of NJ; Prin. violinist, Papermill Playhouse Staff Orch., NJ; Asst. Concertmaster, Schubert Theatre Orch., NY for 3 yrs. Broadway run of 'Promises Promises'; Var. perfs. in radio, TV & commercial recording grps, inclng. original cast album of 'Promises Promises'; Asst. Concertmaster, Colonial Symph.; Violinist, Montclair State Str. Quartet in res.; Fellowship tchng. at Montclair State Coll., NJ. Recordings as mbr. of Nat. Symph. Orch., RCA., Pitts. Symph. Orch. & Am. Ballet Theatre Orch., Capitol Records. Mbr., Am. Fed. of Musicians (Locals in NY, NJ, Phila. & Newark, NJ). Hobbies: Ping-pong; Photography; Swimming. Address: 22 Longview Rd., Cedar Grove, NJ 07009, USA.

TODDS, Walter Henry, b. 28 June 1920, London, UK. Television Producer. Educ: MA, Gonville & Caius Coll., Cambridge Unaiv., 1938-41; Dip. Educ., London Univ. Debut: Singer w. Ballet Rambert, 1941. Career: Prod., BBC Radio, 1951-58; Prod., BBC-TV, 1959-65; Sr. Prod., Music Progs., BBC-TV, 1965-. Prods. incl: Int. Concert Hall, Beethoven Symphs. w. Klemperer; num. eds. of musical quiz 'Face the Music'. Mbrships: Arts Coun. Music Panel, 1976; Inc. Soc. of Musicians; Assn. of Broadcasting Staff. Publ: Patrick Hadley, a memoir, 1974. Hobbies: Reading; Astronomy. Address: 17 Prince of Wales Terr., London W8, UK.

TOEBOSCH, Louis Christiaan, b. 18 Mar. 1916, Maastricht, Netherlands. Composer; Conductor; Educator; Organist. Educ: Studied at the Conserv. in Maastricht, Netherlands & Conserv. Royal de Musique, Liege, Belgium, 1934-39. m. Maria Rubens. Debut: Maastricht. Career: Dir. & Organist, Holy Sacrament Ch., Breda, Netherlands, 1940-65; Cond., Municipal Orch., Tilburg, 1946-50; Dir., Brabants Conservatorium, Tilburg, 1965 74. Comps: (Organ) Praeludium et fuga i Fantasie et fuga; Allegro for organ & Orch.; Changements for organ & orch.; Two Postludia; Tryptique; Toccana; Orgelspiegel; (Orch.) Sinfonietta No. 2; Concertante Ouverture; Festival Overture; Adagio e Allegro; Agena; (String Quartet) The King's Quartet; (Piano) Sonate No. 1; (Chmbr. Music) Mayetmâr for recorder, flute & harpsichord; (Brass Band) Variations on a popular song; Eufonie; (Choir) Philippica moderata; Bome; Sinfonietta No. 1. Recordings: Philippica Moderata; moderata; Tryptique. Contbr. to: St. Gregoriusblad. Mbrships: Advsr., Raad Van de Kunst; Int. Jury Organ-Comp. Zwolle. Hons. incl: Order of the Kthood. of St. Gregorius, 1965; Order of the Kthood of Oranje-Nassau, 1969. Hobbies: Travel; Histl. Bldgs. Exhibs. Address: Burgemeester van Meursstraat 13, Tilburg, The Netherlands.

TOFT, Lars Esben, b. 2 March 1928, Hover, W Jutland, Denmark. Trombonist; Pianist. Educ: pupil, Conserv., Aarhus, 1945-49; pedagogical educ., Conserv., Odense, 1966-68; studied w. Palmer Traulsen & Denis Wick. m. Grethe Hess, 1 s., 1 d. Career: Mbr. of Odense Symph. Orch., 1950- (1st trombone); Trombone Tchr., Conserv. of Music, Odense, 1950-; Soloist w. orch.; Radio apps.; Celeste & Harpsichord

Player, Odense Symph. Orch. Hobbies: Crosswords; Lit. Address: Tingvallavej 11, 5210 Odense NV, Denmark.

TOFTE-HANSEN, Paul, b. 27 Aug. 1914, Copenhagen, Denmark. Oboist; Solo-Cor anglais, Danish Radio Symphony Orchestra. Educ: Grad., oboe & Piano, Royal Danish Acad. of Music, 1937. m. Else, 3 children. Debut: 1942. Career: Mbr., Tivoli Symph. Orch. of Collegium Musicum & Emil Telmanyic Chmbr. Orch.; app. as Soloist, Denmark & Sweden; Solo-Cor anglais, Danish Radio Symph., 1946-. Compositions: A Christmas Cantata; Trio (oboe, clarinet & bass); Quartet (flute & strings); Piece for oboe & piano; Suite for piano; Songs & Suite for woodwind quiantet. Recordings: Carl Nielsen's Romance & Humoresce for oboe & piano, op. 2, w. Eyvin Muller; Niels V Bentzon's Sonata for cor-anglais & piano, op. 71, w. the composer. Recip. of Danish Gramophone Prize for Bentzon Sonata, 1956. Address: Finsensvej 122, 2000 Copenhagen F, Denmark.

TOGSTAD, John Olav, b. 28 Oct. 1947, Orkanger, Norway. Flautist. Educ: 2 yrs., Royal Norwegian Military Band, Div. Trondheim; Studies w. Sverre Skagen, J Tonsjo, T Bye, Jean Pierre Rampal, Maxence Larrieu, Paris. m. Jorunn Kolltveit, 1 d. Career: Sev. apps., radio & TV; Soloist, Norwegian Radio Orch. Mbr., Norwegian Music Union. Hobby: Nature. Address: Trondheimsv. 47, Oslo, 5, Norway.

TOIVOLA, Antti Olavi, b. 20 Feb. 1935, Riihimäki, Finland. Headmaster. Educ: BA, 1958, MA, 1960, Univ. of Helsinki; Final Cert., theory of music & comp., Conserv. Dept. of Sibelius-Acad., Helsinki, 1960; Cert. for Music Tchng., Normal Schl. of Helsinki, 1960; further studies, Hamburg, German Fed. Repub., 1966-67. Debut: Helsinki, 1958. Career: Sec. of founding committee, 1960, & Acting Headmaster, 1961, Music Schl., Riihimäki; Headmaster, Music Schl., Savonlinna, 1962-65, & Music Schl. of Ylivieska Dist., 1968-. Comps. incl: 2 symphs. for student orch.; symphonic poem; An die ewigen Sterne for organ; Cantus for trumpet & organ; sonatina for violin & piano, etc. Contbr. to var. newspapers. Mbrships. incl: Assn. for Music Sci. in Finland. Recip. 2nd prize in comp., Nelimarkka Fndn., Helsinki, 1958. Address: Telkkätie 17, 84100 Ylivieska 10, Finland.

TOLANSKY, Jonathan Paul, b. 27 July 1948, London, UK. Orchestral Player; Percussion Player; Lecturer on Music. Educ: Perf. Dip., Piano & Percussion, TCL; BBC Trng. Orch., Bristol; FRSA. Career: Mbr. Engl. Nat. Opera Orch., 1974-; Extensive work w. maj. Brit. Orchs. inclng: RPO; New Philharmonia; Bournemouth Symph.; BBC; Halle; Birmingham, etc; Co-Prin. Percussion, Royal Opera House Orch., 1977-; Guest Lectr., London Univ.; Some Teaching. Num. recordings. Publs: Currently writing book on interpretation of music in opera, symph. & ballet. Mbr. Brit. Inst. of Recorded Sound; Fellow, Royal Soc. of Musicians. Recip. Gertrude Norman Prize, TCL, 1970. Hobbies: Walking; Travel; Collecting Sound Recordings. Address: 16 Sheen Common Dr., Richmond, Surrey, UK. 30.

TOLLEFSON, Arthur Ralph, b. 3 May, 1942, San Fran., USA. Pianist. Educ: AB, Stanford Univ., 1963; MA, ibid, 1964; DMA, 1968; Pvte. studies w. var. tutors. m. Brenda McNasser. Debut: San Fran., 1954, Wash. DC, 1973, NY, 1974. Career: Chmn., Piano Dept., Schl. Music, Northwestern Univ.; num. solo recitals, maj. Am. cities; Soloist w. San Fran., Oakland & Atlanta Symph. Orchs.; Guest artist, sev. Am. music fests.; num. TV & radio apps. Contbr. to profl. jrnls. Mbr. profl. orgs. Hons. incl: Kimber Award, instrumental music, 1958; Nat. Endowment for Humanities Summer Fellowship, 1975. Hobbies incl: Swimming; Ping-pong; Billiards. Mgmt: Albert Kay Assocs., NYC. Address: 1100 Forest Ave., Wilmette, IL 60091, USA.

TOLO, Leland Stanford, b. 9 Jan. 1943, McVille, ND, USA. Professor of Double Bass, Viola da Gamba, Ensemble & Sight-Singing. Educ: Luther Coll., Decorah, Iowa, 1960-62; BA Musicol., Univ. of Minn., 1964; MM Musicol., Univ. of Louisville, Ky., 1966; Höchschule für Musik, Munich, Germany, 1967-68. m. Marian Kay Herrington, 1 s., 1 d. Career: Prof. of Double Bass, Ensemble, Sight-singing & Viola da Gamba, Hartt Coll. of Music, Univ. of Hartford, Conn.; 1st Stand Double Bass, Hartford Symph.; Double Bassist & Gambist, Hartford Baroque Chmbr. Orch. Contbr. frequent articles to Bass Sound Post. Mbrships: Inst. for String Bass; Viola da Gamba Soc. of Am.; Am. Musicol. Soc. Hobbies: Jogging; Swimming; Cycling; Camping; Building & Repairing Own Musical Instruments. Address: 57 Pocahontas Dr., W Hartford, CT 06117, USA.

TOLONEN, Jouko Paavo Kalervo, b. 2 Nov. 1912, Porvoo, Finland. Professor of Musicology; Composer. Pianist. Educ: MA, Helsinki Univ., 1939; PhLic, 1964; PhD, 1969. m. (1)

Lidia Soldarev, m. (2) Alila Kunnas, 6 c. Career: Assoc. Hd., Music Dept., Finnish Broadcasting Co., 1941-46; Hd., Music Dept., ibid, 1946-55; Gen. Dir., Finnish Nat. Opera, 1956-60; Tchr., Choir Technics, Klemetti Inst., 1955-66; Tchr., Theory & Comp., Sibelius Acad. of Music, 1960-66; Cond., Lappeenranta Orch. & Chmbr. Choir, 1960-66; Instructor, Musicol., Univ. of Turku, 1966-; Hd., Music Sect., ibid, 1970; Prof. of Musicol., ibid, 1972; Apps. as Chmbr. Musician, Accomp., Piano Soloist, Choir & Orch. Dir., Finland & Abroad; num. Radio Apps. Compositions incl: Symph.; 3 Arabesques; Andante & Rondo alla burla; Suites, orch.; 2 Cantatas; choir, solo instrumental works; songs. Publs: Problem of Minor Triad & Unitarian Theory of Intervals & Harmonies, 1969; Fugure Themes of Bach & Protestant Choral Melodies, 1971. Contbr. to var. profl. jrnls. Mbr., Off., num. profl. orgs. Hons: Comm. of Finnish Lion; Comm., StdS, Italy. Hobbies: Cultural History; Family. Address: 2.a.4 Tuhkimontie, Helsinki 82, Finland. 14, 19.

TOMASEK, Andrija, b. 4 Oct. 1919, Calinec, Croatia, Yugoslavia. Professor; Musicologist; Writer on Music; Musical Critic. Educ: Dip., Acad. of Music, Zagreb; Fac. of Music, Univ. of Oxford. div., 1 d. Career: Dir., Schl. of Music Pavao Markovac, Zagreb; Ed., Muzika. Mbrships: Musicol. Sect., Assn. of Croatian Comps.; Music Pedagogues Assn. of Croatia. Publs: Pavao Markovac - Selected Articles & Essays (critical ed.), 1957; Pavao Markovac - His Life & Work (monograph), 1965. Contbr. to books & profl. jrnls. Hons: Pedagogic Counsellor, 1962. Address: Marijana Badela 34, 41040 Zagreb, Yugoslavia.

TOMBLINGS, Philip Benjamin, b. 8 June, 1902, London, UK. Organist; Music Educator. Educ: Exeter Cathedral Schl.; Sir Ernest Bullock; RCM, w. Dr Charles Wood & Dr Henry Ley; ADCM; FRCO (CHM); ARCM. m. Margaret Tickner (dec.), 1 d. Career: Organist & Choirmaster, Ide Parish Ch., Devon, 1919-21; St. Matthew's Ch., Exeter, 1921-23; St. Mary's Berkeley Sq., London, 1923-25; Asst. Music Master, Tonbridge Schl., 1925-29; Organist & Music Master, Bloxham Schl., 1929-31; Dir. of Music, St. Lawrence Coll., Ramsgate, Kent, 1931-45; Dir. of Music, Merchant Taylors' Schl., 1946-66; Prof. of Harmony, RAM, 1966-77; Examiner, Assoc. Bd., Royal Schls. of Music, 1948-; Organist, All Sts. Ch., Croxley Green, Herts., 1973-. Comps: var. liturgical & ch. music incl: Missa Sancti Matthaei; Communion Service, Series 3; Intermezzo for Organ; Finale Maestoso; Anthems, carols & settings of the canticles. Contbr. to Composer (jrnl. of CGGB). Mbrships: ISM. Recip: Hon. ARAM, 1968. Address: 76 Frankland Rd., Croxley Green, Rickmansworth, Herts., WD3 3AU, UK.

TOMC, Matija, b. 25 Dec. 1899, Kaplijisca, Metlika, Slovenia, Yugoslavia. Catholic Priest; Professor of Music; Composer. Educ: Acad. of Music, Vienna. Career: Film: Spring in Bela Krajina; Organ concerts on radio; Lectr. on radio & at musical meetings; Comps. on radio & TV. Comps. incl: Ch. Comps. (masses & requiems); Variation on Nat. Song Nizki Rej (suite); Belokranjski plesi (viola-piano); Concert arr. of Slovene Folk Songs (collection Belokranjske). Num. comps. on records. Publs: Modukacija, 1938. Contbr. to Pevec; Cerkveni glasbenik; Music critic, newspaper Slovenec. Mbr. Sci. Coun., Slovene Ethnographic Comm., Slovene Acad. of Sci. & Art. Address: 61230 Domzale, Na Zavrteh 5, Slovenia, Yugoslavia.

TOMEK, Otto, b. 10 Feb. 1928, Vienna, Austria. Radio Editor. Educ: PhD, Univ. of Vienna, Austria, 1953; Vienna Conservatoire of Music. m. Sabine Schumann. Career: Publr., Universal Ed., Vienna, 1953-57; Radio Ed., Music, Westdeutscher Rundfunk, Cologne, Germany, 1957-71; Hd., Music Dept., Suedwestfunk, Baden-Baden, 1971-. Publs: Co-Ed., Neue Zeitschrift fuer Musik, 1967-; Num. scripts for broadcasts featuring contemporary music. Contbr. to sev. music periodicals. Address: Vormberger Strasse 25, D 7573 Sinzheim, Germany.

TOMESCU, Vasile, b. 1 June 1929, Radulesti, Ilfov, Roumania. Musicologist. Educ: Music Conserv., (Theory Sect.), Bucharest; Lycernc en Arts; Doct., musicol., Univ. of Paris. m. Yvonne Mitache, 1 child. Debut: 1953. Career: Music Critic; Ed., the revue, "Muzica"; Writer on hist. of music & Aesthetics of music; Contbr. to radio broadcasts, Congresses & Confs. Publs: Monographs, Dimitrie Cuclin, 1956; Alfonso Castaldi, 1958; Alfred Alessandrescu, 1962; Filip Lazar, 1963; Paul Constantinescu, 1967; Histoire des relations musicales entre la France et la Roumanie, 1973; Contbr. to: Reveues in Roumania; Syntheses, Brussels; Beiträge zur Musikwissenschaft, Berlin; Das Orchester, Mainz; Die Kultur, Vienna. Mbrships: Sec., Union of Roumanian Comps.; French Musicol. Soc.; Assn. Int. des Docteurs ès Lettres de l'Univ. de Paris, (ALDLUPA); Acad. of Social Scis. & Politics of RS

Roumania. Hons: "Ciprian Porumbescu" prize, Roumanian Acad., 1967; Order of Merit, etc. Hobbies: Book-binding; Collecting Art Reproductions. Address: Rue Apusului B1. 49. app. 2, Secteur VII, Bucharest, Roumania.

TOMLINSON, Ernest, b. 1924, Rawtenstall, UK. Composer. Educ: Manchester Cathedral Choir Schl.; MusB, Manchester Univ.; FRCO; FRMCM. m. Jean Garnett Lancaster, 1 s., 3 d. Career: Arr., Arcadia & Mill Music, 1949-55; Organist, 3rd Ch. of Christ Sci., London, 1948-58; specializes in electronic music & recording. Compositions incl: Symphony '65 for jazz & symph. orchs.; Rhapsody & Radio for horn & orch.; Concerto for 5 (5 saxophones & orch.); Head of the Family (opera, after W W Jacobs); Egyptian Princess (ballet); 2 sets of Engl. folk-dances; The Story of Cinderella (radio musical play); background music for films, TV & radio, often under pseudonym of Alan Perry; many songs; chmbr. works; educl. music; electronic music thru' Tomlinson Electrophonics. Mbrships incl: Exec. Committee, Composers' Guild of GB, 1961-66; Chmn., Light Music Soc., 1966-; Dir., PRS, 1966-. Hobbies: Cricket; Football; Radio Constrn. Address: Lancaster Farm, Chipping Rd., Longridge, Preston, Lancs, PR3 2NB, UK.

TOMLINSON, John, b. 22 Sept. 1946, Accrington, UK. Operatic Bass. Educ: BSc, Manchester Univ., 1967; ARMCM (Tchr. & Perf.), Royal Manchester Coll. of Music. m. Moya Tomlinson, 1 s., 2 d. Career incls: Glyndebourne Fest. & Touring Opera, 1970-74; Engl. Nat. Opera, 1974-; apps. w. the New Opera, Kent Opera, BBC Proms, Radio, TV & in concerts w. most major orchs. in Britain. Mbr., Brit. Actors Equity Assn. Hobby: Making Things. Mgmt: Music Int. Address: 53 Southover High St., Lewes, E. Sussex BN7 1JA, UK.

TOMS, Carl, b. 29 May 1927, Kirby-in-Ashfield, Notts., UK. Designer. Educ: Mansfield Coll. of Art; Royal Coll. of Art; Old Vic Schl. Career incls: appointed 1st Hd. of Design for The Young Vic Co., 1970; prods.: Peter Grimes, San Fran. Opera, 1973 & Lyric Opera House, Chgo., 1974, Der Meistersinger, NYC Opera, 1975; Norma: San Diego, 1976; Thais: San Francisco Opera, 1976. Mbrships: Assn. of Cinematograph, TV & Allied Technicians; United Scenic Artist Assn. Hons: Tony (Antoinette Perry) Award for best set design, London & NYC, 1974-75; Drama Desk Award for most outstanding set design, 1975; OBE. Hobbies: Parrots; Gardening; Travel. Mgmt: Trafalgar Perry Ltd., 4 Goodwin's Ct., St. Martin's Lane, London WC2N 4LL, UK. Address: 49 Noel Rd., London N1, UK.

TOMSIC, Dubravka, b. 6 Dec. 1940, Dubrovnik, Yugoslavia. Concert Pianist; Professor of Music. Educ: BSc; Acad. of Music, Ljubljana; Dip. in Piano, Juilliard Schl. of Music, NYC, USA. m. Alojz Srebotnjak, 1 s. Debut: Dubrovnik, aged 5. Career: Concerts throughout Europe inclng. USSR, & in USA, Can., Aust., & E Africa, in recitals & w. major orchs.; TV & radio apps.; Recordings for major European radio stns. & var. Yugolsavian labels; Prof., Acad. of Music, Ljubljana, 1967-; Hd., Piano Dept., ibid, 1972-76. Mbr., Slovenian Soc. of Music Artist. Hons. incl: The Preseren Prize, 1975; AVNOJ Prize, 1976; Orlando Prize, 1978. Hobbies: Driving cars; Swimming; Cooking. Mgmt: Interartists, The Hague, Netherlands. Address: Linhartova 1, 61113, Ljubljana, Yugoslavia.

TONI, Olivier, b. 27 May 1926, Sao Paulo, Brazil. Conductor; Composer; Bassoonist. Educ: Sao Paulo Univ., fac. of Phil.; Studies piano, bassoon, orch. cond. & comp., Sao Paulo; Santa Cecilia Acad., Rome. m. Maria Helena Toni, 2 d., 1 s. Debut: Sao Paulo, 1947. Career: Dir. Sao Paulo Chmbr. Orch.; concerts in all major Brazilian Orchs.; Tours through Europe w. Chmbr. programs dedicated to musicians of the 18th Century, Brazilian Colonial Period. Comps: 3 Variations for orch., 1963; Chmbr. music; Brazilian 18th Century music. Recordings: Bach Cantata 82; Telemann concert in G for 4 violins; Albinoni, oboe concerto. Publs: Articles Monographies about Brazilian Colonial Music; Book of Harmony. Hons: Medal, Smetana, Czech. Repub. & Brazilian Geographical Soc. Hobby: Swimming. Address: Rua Joaquim Tavora, 1060 casa 5, 04015 Sao Paulo, Brazil.

TØNNESEN, Terje, b. 27 Feb. 1955, Oslo, Norway. Violinist. Educ: Veitvedt Music Conserv., Oslo, 1962-72; studies w. Prof. Max Rostal at Bern Conserv. for Music, Switz. Debut: Oslo, 1972. Career: Soloist apps. in Sweden, Germany, GB, Yugloslavia, France, Austria & Switz.; Apps. in Norway with leading orchs.; Radio & TV apps.; App. at Bergen Fest. of Music, 1975; Ldr., Norwegian Chmbr. Orch., 1977-. Mbrships: Norwegian Musicians Soc. Hons: Triple Prize Winner, Jeunesses Musicales Int. Violin Competition, Belgrade, 1976. Mgmt: Impresario A/S, Tollbodgaten 3, Oslo 1, Norway. Hobbies: Reading; Drawing; Painting; Sport. Address: Ole Buues Vei 6A, 2020 Skedsmokorset, Norway.

TOOP, Richard William, b. 1 Aug. 1945, Chichester, UK. Musicologist. Educ: BA in music, Univ. of Hull. Career: Tchng. asst. to Karlheinz Stockhausen & coordinator of Seminar fur Neue Musik, Staatliche Musikhochschule, Cologne; Lectr., Vicenza Summer courses; Lectr., NSW Conserv. of Music, Sydney. Recording: Bussotti, Per tre sul piano (w. others). Contbr. to: Perspectives of New Music; Music Review; Studies in Music; Collage; Musical Quarterly; Contact; Times Lit. Supplement; Musical Times, Miscellanea Musicologica, etc. Hons: Hull Univ. Music Prize, 1967. Address: NSW Conserv. of Music, Macquarie St., Sydney 2000, NSW, Aust.

TOPERCZER, Peter, b. 24 July 1944, Kosice, Czech. Concert Artist - Pianist. Educ: Conserv. Kosice, 1958-62; Acad. of Fine Arts, Prague, 1962-68; Post Grad. Study, ibid, 1969-72. m. Juliana Nevická, 2 s. Career: Concert Perfs., USA, Can., Japan, UK, USSR, Bulgaria, Roumania, Germany, Switz., Spain, Sweden, Turkey, etc. Recordings: Tomásek; Chopin; Schumann; Mozart; Tchaikovsky; Bartok; Prokofiev; Messiaen; Slavický; Debussy; Copland; Burian. Mbr., Slovak Comps. Union. Hons: Semifinal prize, Leeds, 1966; Grand Prize & title of Laureate, Int. Rostrum of Young Interpreters, UNESCO, 1972. Hobby: Painting. Mgmt: Slovkoncert, Bratislava, Czech. Address: Na dolinách 27, 147 00 Prague, Czech.

TOPLANSKY, Herman, b. 12 June 1907, Newark, NJ, USA. Music Teacher; Conductor; Clarinettist; Violist. Educ: MB, Ithaca Coll., NY, 1929; BS, Tchrs. Coll., Columbia Univ., 1935; MA, ibid, 1939; Profl. Dip., 1955. m. Eleanor Silverman, 2 s. Career: Supvsr. of Music, Lititz, Pa., 1929-31; Music Tchr., Public Schls. of Elizabeth, NJ, 1931-; Co-cond., All State Orch., NJ, 1935 & 1939; Fndr.-cond., Elizabeth Civic Orch., 1954; Dir. of Music Educ. for Geo Wash. Schl.-Community Ctr., 1971-; Pvte. Tchr. of Clarinet; Has cond. var. orchs.; Assoc. cond., Union Co. Symph. Orch. Mbrships. incl: Phi Mu Alpha; Am. Schl. Band Dirs. Assn.; Former Libn. for Ctrl. Jersey Music Educators Assn.; Am. Fed. Musicians. Hobbies: Musical Arrangements for Band & Orch., Woodworking; Gardening. Address: 559 Winthrop Rd., Union, NJ, USA.

TORCHINSKY, Abe, b. 30 Mar. 1920, Phila., Pa., USA. University Professor; Tuba Player. Educ: Curtis Inst. of Music, Phila. m. Berta Brenna Torchinsky, 3 d. Career: Solo tuba player w. NBC Symph. under Toscanini, 1946-49; Solo tuba w. Phila. Orch., 1949-72; Prof., Tuba & Euphonium, Univ. of Mich. Recordings: (w. Phila. Brass Ensemble) The Glorious Sound of Brass; A Festival of Carols; Antiphonal Music of Gabrieli; Hindemith Sonatas for Brass Instruments; num. recordings w. NBC & Phila. Orchs. Publs: 20th Century Orchestral Studies for Tuba, 1969; Dance Movements for Tuba, 1974; The Tuba Players Orchestra Repertoire, Vol. 1, 1975. Contbr. to Instrumentalist. Mbr., profl. assns. Hons: Grammy, 1969; Grand Prix du Disque, 1969. Hobbies: Fishing; Model Building. Address: 654 Greenhills Drive, Ann Arbor, MI 48105, USA. 2.

TORÉN, Torvald, b. 29 Sept. 1945, Uppsala, Sweden. Organist. Educ: Dips. in Organ & Piano, Royal HS of Music, Stockholm, 1964-70; Study w. Flor Peeters, Belgium, 1970, 71 & Maurice Duruflé, Paris, 1974, 75. m. Elisabet, 1 s. Career: Organist, Hedvig Eleonora Ch., Stockholm, 1966-; frequent organ recitalist & broadcaster of Swedish Radio & TV; specialist in French music of Romantic & Modern Period. Recording: Kontrapunkt; Lyricon. Address: Artillerigatan 25, 11445 Stockholm, Sweden.

TORGRIMSON, Paul Edward, b. 24 Oct. 1918, Grand Meadow, Minn., USA. Piano Professor. Educ: BS in Music Educ., Univ. of Minn.; MMus, DMus Arts, Eastman Schl. of Music. m. Elva Swenson, 2 s., 1 d. Career: Prof. of Piano, NW State Univ., 1945-; Band Dir., High Schls. in Blooming Prairie, Minn., Pine Island, Minn. & Hot Springs, SD. Contbr. to: LA Musician; SW Musician; LA Schls.; Instrumentalist; Am. Music Tchr. Mbrships: Music Tchrs. Nat. Assn.; Pres., La. MTA; MENC; United Fedn. of Coll. Tchrs.; Phi Mu Alpha Sinfonia; Phi Kappa Phi. Address: Northwestern State Univ., Natchitoches, LA 71457, USA.

TORO, Puli, b. 18 Apr. 1947, San Juan, Puerto Rico. Singer (mezzo-soprano). Educ: New England Conserv. of Music; Mannes Schl. of Music, NYC. m. Luis J Munoz. Debut: NYC Opera, 1974. Career: Singer w. NYC Opera; Kennedy Ctr.; Los Angeles Music Ctr.; Pitts. Opera; NYC Ctr. (operetta); Caracas Municipal Theatre, Venezuela; Channel 13 Nat. Educl. TV; Recitals in USA & Puerto Rico; Broadcasts, Radio WNYC, NY O WIRB, Puerto Rico. Recordings: role of Hansel in Educl. Audio-Visual Prods. Mbrship: PR Chapt., New England Conserv. Alumni Club. Hons. incl: Outstanding Artist of P R Citation, 1976. Mgmt: Joseph Scuro. Address: 1 Sherman Sq., Apt. 4OH, NY, NY 10023, USA.

TORSTENSSON, Thorleif S G, b. 26 June 1949, Nottebäck, Sweden. Composer; Musician (singer, guitar, saxophone, clarinet & flute). Educ: musically self-taught. m. Bittan Edoff, 2 d. Career: apps. on Swedish radio & TV & on Norwegian TV. Comps: num. pop songs. num. recordings. mbr., SKAP. Hobby: Photography. Address: Skeda Norregard, 36017 Nottebäck, Sweden.

TORTELIER, Paul, b. 21 Mar. 1914, France. Cellist; Composer. Educ: Nat. Conserv. of Music, Paris. Career: 1st Cellist, Monte Carlo Orch., 1935-37; 3rd Cellist, Boston Symph. Orch., 1937-40; 1st Cellist, Soc. des Concerts du Conserv. de Paris, 1946-47; Solo cellist w. leading Orchs. in Europe, US, Israel, etc., 1947-56; Prof., Paris Conserv., 1956-. Compositions incl: 2 Cello Concertos; Concerto for 2 Cellos; Symph. Israelienne; Cello Sonata; Suite for unacc. Cello; Trois Petits Tours (cello & piano); duos for 2 cellos; Cadenzas for Concertos by Haydn, Boccherini, Schumann & K P E Bach; 6 studies for cello & piano; Concerto for Violin & Orch.; Edit. of Sammartini Sonata. Mbrships: Soc. of Music Authors, Composers & Eds.; Hon., RAM, London. Address: 14 rue Leon Cogniet, Paris 17e, France.

TORTELIER, Yan Pascal, b. 19 April 1947, Paris, France. Conductor; Violinist. Educ: Conserv. Nat. Superior of Music, Paris; Berkshire Music Center, Tanglewood, USA; Lauréat du Concours Int. Tibor Varga; Direction of Orch. w. Franco Ferrara, Accademia Chigiana, Siena. m. Sylvie Brunet Moret, 1 s. Debut: BBC Proms, Royal Albert Hall, 1962. Career: Apps., most cities & orchs. of UK; Perfs., E & W Europe, USSR, Japan, S Am. & Africa; Marlboro Music Fest., USA; Luzern Fest.; Cond., Royal Phil. Orch., & Toulouse Opera House. Recordings: Saint Saens, Caprice, Prélude de Déluge; Lalo, Symphonie Espagnole; Tschaikovsky, cond. Northern Sinfonia Orch.; Schumann cello concerto (P Tortelier) cond. Royal Phil. Orch.; Ravel & Saint Saens trios (Tortelier Trio). Hobbies: Nature; Skiing. Mgmt: Ibbs & Tillett, London. Address: 39 Avenue de Lavaur, 31500 Toulouse, France.

TORTORELLA, Adalberto, b. 3 Dec. 1927, Buenos Aires, Argentina. Harpsichordist. Educ: Prof. of Music, Nat. Univ. of La Plata, Buenos Aires. Debut: Buenos Aires, 1954. Career: concert apps., radio & TV broadcasts, Argentina, Uruguay, Germany, France, Spain, Belgium, Italy; has perf. for film soundtracks; former Prof., Nat. Conserv. Carlos López Buchardo, & Fac. of Arts, Nat. Univ. of La Plata, both Buenos Aires; Fndr., current Dir., Conserv. Juan José Castro, Min. of Educ. of Buenos Aires. Contbr. to var. jrnls. Mbrships incl: Int. Soc. for Musical Educ. Address: Coronel Diaz 1812, Buenos Aires, Argentina.

TORTORICH, Mary A, b. 8 Dec. New Orleans, La., USA. Vocal Teacher; Singer. Educ: Juilliard Schl. of Music; BMus, Loyola Univ., BMusEd; MFA, Tulane Univ. Debut: Carnegie Hall, NY. Career: Apps. w. New Orleans Symph., radio & TV, New Orleans; Radio, CBS, NY; Radio Music Hall, concerts in Pa. & upstate NY; Concerts & Opera, New Orleans, parts of LA & Miss. Mbrships: Past Bd. Mbr., New Orleans Music Tchrs. Assn.; Past VP, Nat. Assn. of Tchrs. of Singing Inc.; Fac. Advsr., Epsilon Chapt., Phi Beta. Hobbies: Stamp collecting; Photography. Address: 93 E Park Pl., New Orleans, LA 70124, USA.

TÓSZEGHI, András, b. 20 May 1945, Debrecen, Hungary. Violist. Educ: Violin Dip., Lucerne, Switz.; studied w. Prof. B Katona, London, UK; Perf.'s Cert. for Viola, under William Primrose, Ind. Univ., USA. Career: Recitalist, Switz., France, Greece, UK, Austria, Germany, Italy, Netherlands, USA; has made radio recordings. Recordings: 7 LPs of viola music by J S Bach, Schubert, Brahms, Bartók, Juon, Honegger, Haller, Beethoven, Glinka, Bloch, Tamás & Kodály. Mbr., Swiss Musicians' Union. Hons: Edwin Fischer Mem. Prize, 1972; special distinction, Swiss Competition for mod. chmbr. music, 1975. Hobbies: Bridge; Table tennis. Mgmt: Ingpen & Williams, London. Address: Poststr. 53, 8953 Dietikon, Switz.

TOTENBERG, Roman, b. Lodz, Poland. Violinist. Educ: Chopin Conserv., Warsaw; Hochschule Für Music, Berlin; Int. Inst., Paris. m. Melanie Shroder, 3 d. Career incls: Toured S Am. w. Artur Rubinstein; Given jt. recitals w. Karol Szmanowski; Played as Soloist w. most renowned orchs. in Europe, N & S Am.; Hd., String Dept., Boston Univ., USA. Recordings incl: All Bach Solo Sonatas; Schumann Sonatas; Bach Concerti; Beethoven Concerti. Hons: Gold Medal, Chopin Conserv., Warsaw; Mendelssohn Prize, Berlin, 1932; Wieniawski Medal, 1968; Ysaye Medal, 1973. Mgmt: Basil Douglas, London, UK. Address: 15 Day School Lane, Belmont, MA 02178, USA.

TOTH, Margit, b. 20 June 1920, Budapest, Hungary. Ethnomusicologist. Educ: Study of Ethnomusicol., Acad. of Music, Budapest, 1956. Career: Hd., Folk Music Dept., Ethnographical Mus., Budapest. Publs: Co-ed., Hungarian Music Lexicon, 1965; Hungarian Funeral Songs (w. Laszlo Lajtha), 1956; Musical Documentation of the Hungarian Soviet Republic (w. J Njfalussy), 1973; Contbr. to sev. musical periodicals. Mbrships: Int. Musicol. Soc.; Art Fndn. of Hungarian People's Repub.; Assn. of Hungarian Musicians; Employees' Trade Union. Recip: Cert. & Medal of Hungarian Excellent Workers. Hobby: Knitting. Address: Eszek u. 18, 1114 Budapest, Hungary.

TOUCHIN, Colin Michael, b. 3 Apr. 1953, Liverpool, UK. Composer; Performer (recorder & clarinet); Conductor; Teacher. Educ: Keble Coll. Oxford, 1971-74; BA, 1974; cert. of Educ., Manchester Univ., 1974-75; Recorder from age 8, LTCL (perf.), 1969; Clarinet from age 10 w. Graham Turner; Piano from age 11, later w. Hedwig Stein. Debut: Wigmore Hall, London, 1979. Career: Bowden Sinfonietta, 1971-; tutor, Stockport Recorder Coll., 1975-; fndr., BS Wind Band, 1977; fndr. & supporter of Wind Bands & Recorder Orch.; 500 perfs. on clarinet/recorder at univs. as soloist or in orchs. Comps: Rebirth, film score, 1979 (recorded). Contbr. to: Northern Recorder Mag. Mbrships: Musicians' Union; ISM (Manchester branch committee); Soc. of Recorder Players (exec. committee, 1977-79); Clarinet & Saxophone Soc. of GB; N W Arts. Hons: Lennox Berkeley Comp. Trophy & Concerto Medal, Oxford Fest., 1974. Hobbies: Cycling; Hostelling; Reading. Address: 180 Framingham Rd., Brooklands, Sale M33 3RG, UK.

TOUMA, Habib Hassan, b. 12 Dec. 1934, Nazareth, Palestine. Composer; Musicologist. Educ: Grad., Israeli Acad. of Music, 1962; PhD, Free Univ. of Berlin, 1968. m. Monika Kirchberger, 2 d. Compositions: Oriental Rhapsody for 2 flutes & Darabukka, 1958; Samai for Oboe & Piano, 1961; Etude for Flute solo, 1962; Combinations (Flute solo), 1965; Arabian Suite for piano, 1961; Reflexus I for 12 String Instruments, 1966; Taqsim for piano, 1972. Publs: Der Maqam Bayati im arabischen Taqsim, 1968, Engl. ed., 1974; Musik der A-aber, 1975, French ed., 1976. Contbr. to var. music jrnls. Mbrships: Int. Musicol. Soc.; Soc. for Ethnomusicol.; Int. Folk Music Coun.; Int. Inst. for Comp. Music Studies. Hobbies: Photography; Travel. Address: Lohmeyerstr. 16, 1000 Berlin 10, Germany.

TOWER, Ibrook, b. 21 July 1948, Boston, Mass., USA. Clarinettist; Conductor; College Teacher & Director of Instrumental Ensembles. Educ: BMus, BMusEd, Peabody Conserv. of Music, Balt., Md.; MMus, Temple Univ., Phila., Pa. Career incls: Dir. of Instrumental Ensembles & Instructor in Music, Juniata Coll., Huntingdon, Pa.; Perfs. w. Young Audiences Inc., Orchl. Soc. of Phila., Wilmington Chmbr. Orch. etc. Comps: With & Without; Scraps. Contbr. to Music Appreciation & the Child, 1970. Mbrships. incl: Int. Clarinet Soc.; Coll. Band Dirs.' Nat. Assn. Hons. incl: Z T Thomas Prize, 1970; Teaching Fellowship, Temple Univ.-Settlement Music, Schl., 1971. Address: 1401 Washington St., Huntingdon, PA 16652, USA. 28.

TOWER, Joan, b. 6 Sept. 1938, New Rochelle, NY, USA. Composer; Pianist; Teacher. Educ: BA, Bennington Coll.; MA, Columbia Univ.; D Musical Arts, ibid. Career: Pianist, Da Capo Chmbr. Players. Comps: (recorded) Prelude for Five Players; Breakfast Rhythms for Clarinet & 5 Instruments; (published) Movements for Flute & Piano; Percussion Quartet; Hexachords for flute. Mbrships: Bds. of Am. Music Ctr., Am. Comps. Alliance, Meet the Comp., & League of Int. Soc. Contemporary Music. Hons: Nat. Endowment Award, 1974-75; MacDowell Colony Fellowship, 1974; Contemporary Music Soc. Commission, 1976. Mgmt: Judith Liegner Inc. Address: 545 W 111th St. (9D), NY, NY 10025, USA. 5, 16.

TOWN, Christopher, b. 16 Jan. 1945, Bromley, Kent, UK. Teacher; Singer (Tenor); Organist & Choirmaster. Educ: BEd, London Univ.; ACP (Educ.); Organ Schlr., Bishop Otter Coll., Chichester; GSM; LRAM; LGSM; ARCL. Career: Music Master, Burnt Ash Schl., Bromley, 1966-70; Singing Tutor, Southern Music Trng. Ctr., 1968-75; Dpty. Headmaster, Parish Schl., Bromley, 1970-79; Organist, Grove Pk. Hosp., 1971-; Hon. Asst., St. Augustine's Grove Pk., 1972-; Headmaster, St. John's C.E. School, Penge, 1979-; Many solo tenor perfs., oratorios etc, London & elsewhere. Mbrships: Pres., Bromley & Croydon Dist. Organists & Choirmasters Assn., 1976-78; ISM; RSCM; NAHT; Organ Club. Hobbies incl: FA Referee; Recording; Photography; Attending Concerts; Visiting Organs. Address: 96 Ridgeway Dr., Bromley, Kent, BR1 5DD, UK.

TOWN, Robert Lloyd, b. 31 Oct. 1937, Watertown, Wis., USA. Organist; Teacher; Recitalist; Church Musician. Educ: BMus, Eastman Schl. of Music, Rochester, NY, 1960; MMus, Syracuse Univ., NY, 1962; Advanced Grad. Study, Univ. of

Mich., Ann Arbor, 1963-65. Debut: Boston Symph. Hall, Mass., 1964. Career incls: Prof. of Organ, Wichita State Univ., Kan., 1965-; App. as recitalist in Boston Symph. Hall & Methuen Mem. Music Hall, Mass., var. other states & Can. Mbrships: Past Dean, AGO; Phi Mu Alpha; Am. Theatre Organ Soc. Hons: 1st Pl., Boston Symph. Orch.'s Young Artists' Competition, 1963; Nat. Finalist, Ft. Wayne, Ind., 1st Presby. Ch. Nat. Organ Playing Competition, 1965. Address: 1601 Kenmar Dr., Wichita, KS 67208, USA. 8.

TOWNELEY, Simon Peter Edmund Cosmo William, b. 14 Dec. 1921, London, UK. HM's Lord Lieutenant; Autos Rotulonu for Lancashire. Educ: MA, DPhil., Worcester Coll., Oxford. m. Mary Fitzherbert, 1 s., 6 d. Career incls: Lectr. in History of Music, Worcester Coll., Oxford, 1949-55. Publs: Venetian Opera in the Seventeenth Century, 1954, 2nd ed., 1968. Contbr. to: New Oxford History of Music; Grove's Dict., 6th Ed., 5th Ed.; Music & Letters. Hons: KSCJ, 1976; KCSG, 1977; Hon. FRNCM, 1977. Hobby: Playing Chmbr. Music. Address: Dyneley, Nr. Burnley, Lancs., UK. 1.

TOWNHILL Dennis William, b. 29 May 1925, Lincoln, UK. Organist; Music Director; Educator. Educ: BMus, Durham Univ.; FRCO; ADCM; LRAM. m. Mabel Irene Ellingworth, 1 s., 1 d. Career incl: Organist & Master of the Choristers, St. Mary's Episc. Cathedral, Edinburgh; Dir. of Music, St. Mary's Music Schl., Edinburgh; Tchr., (Organ, harpsichord, piano), Royal Scottish Acad. of Music, Glasgow; num. broadcast performances on Radio & TV. Recordings incl. sev. LPs of organ music & w. Cathedral Choir. Mbrships: Inc. Soc. of Musicians; Royal Schl. of Ch. Music; Rotary. Hons. incl: Hon. Dip. RSCM; Read Prize, RCO, 1945. Hobbies: Reading; Swimming; Driving. Address: 3 Grosvenor Cres., Edinburgh EH 12 5EP, UK. 34.

TOWNSEND, David Michael, b. 18 Apr. 1942, Chgo., Ill., USA. Performer & Teacher of Clarinet; Conductor. Educ: BMusEd, Ind. Univ., Bloomington; MMus (perf.), Mich. State Univ., E Lansing. m. Jane Eleanor Schuster Townsend, 1 d. Debut: Bloomington, Ind., 1964. Career: Clarinettist, US Military Acad. Band, West Point, NY, 1965-67; Clarinettist & Soloist, Am. Wind Symph. Orch., Pitts., Pa., 1970; Clarinet Recitalist & Cond., var. Colls., USA, 1970-; currently at Concordia Coll., Moorhead, Minn. Compositions incl: Happy Christmas for Brass, 1975. Mbrships: Int. Clarinet Soc.; NACWPI; Pi Kappa Lambda; Phi Mu Alpha Sinfonia. Hon: Honors Concert Soloist, Mich. State Univ. Orch., 1970. Hobbies: Composing Music for Unaccompanied Clarinet; Reed Making; Swimming; Cycling. Mgmt: PR Office, Concordia Coll., Moorhead, Minn., USA. Address: 906 S 8th St., Moorhead, MN 56560, USA.

TRABICHOFF, Geoffrey Colin, b. 15 Apr. 1946, London, UK. Violinist. Educ: admitted to GSM, 1961; AGSM; LGSM (perfs.), 1967; further study w. Sascha Lasserson. m. Judith Orbach. Debut: Wigmore Hall, 1972. Career: broadcasts for BBC & Israel Radio; Ldr. & Solo Violinist, Gulbenkien Chmbr. Orch., London. Comp. of cadenzas for Mozart Concertos nos. 2, 3, & 4, & Haydn concertos in C & G Major. Mbr., ISM. Hons: Corp. of London Prize, 1961; holder, Martin Musical Scholarship, 1968-74; winner, Royal Amateur Orchl. Soc.'s Soloist Award, 1972-73, & Worshipful Co. of Musician's Prize, 1974. Hobbies incl: Chess. Mgmt: New Era Int. Concerts. Address: 23 Shamrock Way, Southgate, London N14, UK.

TRACEY, Andrew T N, b. 5 May 1936, Durban, S Africa. Ethnomusicologist. Educ: MA, Univ. of Oxford, UK. m. Heather Mary, 2 children. Career: Musical Dir., Wait a Minim, int. stage show, 1962-68; Ethnomusicol. Rsch. in Rhodesia, Mozambique, Malawi, S Africa; Dir., Int. Library of African Music. Recordings: Wait a Minim; Always Something New Out of Africa; Andrew Tracey's Steelband. Contbr. of articles on African music to African Music. Address: ILAM, c/o ISER, Rhodes Univ., Grahamstown 6140, S Africa.

TRACEY, Bradford, b. 7 July 1951, Sydney, NS, Can. Specialist Performer on Historical Keyboard Instruments. Educ: Musicol. & Perf., Toronto Univ.; Harpsichord & Clavichord, Schola Cantorum Basel, Switzerland; Prof. Fritz Neumeyer's Histl. Instrument Collection, Bad Krozingen, German Fed. Repub. Career: Regular soloist, int. concert series, ibid.; Concerts throughout Europe, inclng. German Dem. Repub. by invitation; Radio & TV apps., Can., German Fed. Repub., etc.; Ensemble player w. Krozingen Musik Collegium, Ars Renata Ensemble, & keyboard duo w. Rolf Junghanns. Recordings incl: Harpsichord works of L & F Couperin, Farnaby, Handel; Farnaby, Virginal Music. Mgmt: Hart/Murdock Artists. Address: Schloss, D-7812 Bad Krozingen, German Fed. Repub.

TRACEY, Edmund, b. 14 Nov. 1927, Preston, UK. Production Director English National Opera; Writer. Educ: Lincoln Coll.,

Oxford; GSM; Pvte. study. Career: Music Critic, The Observer, 1958-65; Dir., Sadler's Wells Opera (now Engl. Nat. Opera), 1966-. Comps: Original libretto for Malcolm Williamson's specially commissioned opera Lucky Peter's Journey, 1969; Engl. transl. for new prods., Sadler's Wells Opera incl: Sandrina's Secret (Eng. version of Mozart's La Finta Giardiniera), 1976; New lyrics for A Waltz Dream, 1977; Aida, 1978; Leonore & Fidelio, 1970; The Tales of Hoffmann, 1970; La Traviata, 1973; Manon, 1974; Tosca, 1976. Publs: Engl. libretti: Die Fledermaus; Lucky Peter's Journey; The Seraglio; A Waltz Dream. Hobbies: Reading; Cinema; Walking. Address: c/o Engl. Nat. Opera, London Coliseum, St. Martin's Lane, London, WC2, UK. 3.

TRACK, Ernst, b. 20 Jan. 1911, Vienna, Austria. Composer; Author; Actor; Master of Ceremonies; Singer. Educ: Handelsschule; Autodidact; Pvte. Music Instruction. 1 s. Debut: Singer, Austrian State Radio Network RAVAG, 1937. Career: MC on Austrian Radio & TV; As Singer & Comp. toured Germany, Switzerland, Norway & USA. Comps: Over 250 songs; overtures; marches; violin & piano pieces; waltzes. Recordings as singer & comp. Mbrships: AKM, Austria; Austrian Comp. Soc. Hons. incl: Silver Hon. Medal of Repub. of Austria; Golden Hon. Medal of Austrian Union (OeGB); Golden Hon. Cross of Province of Lower-Austria. Hobbies: Composing; 8 mm Filming. Mgmt: Veranstaltungsdirektion, Roemerfeldgasse 8, Perchtoldsdorf, Austria. Address: Roemerfeldgasse 8, Perchtoldsdorf (NOe), Austria A2380.

TRACK, Gerhard, b. 17 Sept. 1934, Vienna, Austria. Orchestral & Choral Conductor; Composer; Arranger. Educ: BS, Tchr. Trng. Coll., Vienna, 1953; MS, Acad. of Music & Perf. Arts; MA, Paedagogic Inst., Vienna, 1954; MMus. m. Micaela Maihart, 2 s. Debut: Cond., Vienna Boys Choir, 1954. Career incls: Music Dir., Vienna Boys Choir, 1953-58; Assoc. Prof. of Music & Cond., Symph. Orch. & Male Choir, St. John's Univ., Minn., USA; Music Dir., Pueblo Symph. Assn., 1969-; Music Dir., Metropolitan Youth Symph., Minn., 1965-69; Guest Cond. of orchs., choirs, music fests. in USA & Europe. Comps: More than 200 orchestral, choral & chmbr. music works. Num. recordings. Contbr. to profl. mags. & newspapers. Active mbr. num. profl. orgs. Hons. incl: Golden Hon. Cross, Repub. of Austria, 1974; Arts & Humanities Award, 1976. Hobbies: Recording; Radio work. Mgmt: Ernst Track Perchtoldsdorf, Romerfeldgasse 8, Austria; SRO Productions, 2910 Bloomington Ave. S, Minn., MN 55407, USA. Address: 130 Baylor, Pueblo, CO 81005, USA. 3, 8, 21, 23, 28, 29.

TRACK, Micaela Maihart, b. 13 Aug. 1934, Amstetten, Austria. Concert Pianist. Educ: Reifepruefung Degree, Acad. of Music & Performing Arts, Vienna, Austria. m. Gerhard Track, 2 s. Debut: Bad Gastein, Austria, 1955. Career: Concerts in Austria, USA & S Am.; Soloist w. orchs. in Europe, USA & S Am.; TV perfs. in Austria & USA; Pvte. Tchr.; Tchr., Master Class, Univ. Windsor, Can., 1965. Recordings in USA & Austria. Hons: 1st Prize Bad Gastein Musikwettbewerb, Austria, 1955. Hobbies: Swimming; Hiking; Reading. Mgmt: Pueblo Symph Assn., 1117 Lake, Pueblo, Colo., USA; Concert Office Ernst Track, Roemerfeldgasse 8, Perchtoldsdorf/Wien, Austria. Address: 130 Baylor, Pueblo, CO 81005, USA.

TRAERUP, Birthe, b. 9 Oct. 1930, Kolding, Denmark. Ethnomusicologist; Lecturer. Educ: Musicol. & Serbo-Croatian lang. & lit., Univ. Copenhagen. 1 child. Career: Lectr., ethnomusicol., Univ. Copenhagen; Radio Series on folk music, Radio Denmark, Sweden & Norway; Advsr., ethnomusicol. & Yugoslav lit., Royal Lib. Copenhagen. Publs. incl: East Macedonian folk songs, 1970. Contbr. to profl. publs. Mbr. profl. orgs. Hons: Puasesignallegatet, Denmark Radio, & Hon. Mbrship., Soc. Serbian Folklorists, 1972. Address: Bygaden 40 Vetterslev, 4100 Ringsted, Denmark.

TRAFICANTE, Frank Anthony, b. 1 Apr. 1937, Pitts., Pa., USA. University Professor (Musicologist); Player of Viola da Gamba & Lyra Viol. Educ: BA, 1960, MA, 1961, Carnegie-Mellon Univ.; PhD Musicol., Univ. of Pitts., 1965; Rsch., Linacre Coll., Oxford, UK, 1965-66; studied Contrabass & Viola da Gamba w. var. masters. Career: Music Ref. Libn., Music Div., Lib. of Congress, Wash. DC, 1966-68; Asst. Prof.-Assoc. Prof., Schl. of Music, Univ. of Ky., Lexington, 1968-; Vis. Assoc. Prof., Claremont Grad. Schl., Calif., spring 1976; Chmn., Music Dept., ibid, 1976-. Publs: Ed., Tobias Hume, The First Part of Ayres, 1605, & Captaine Humes Poeticall Musicke, 1607, 1969. Contbr. to musical publs. & jrnls. Mbr., profl. assns. Recip., var. rsch. grants. Hobby: Cycle touring. Address: 580 Bucknell Ave. Apt. L, Claremont, CA 91711, USA.

TRAILL, Eric Sinclair, b. 17 Dec. 1904, Cambourne, Dorset, UK. Journalist. m. Nancy Eileen Traill, 1 s. Career: Fndr., Ed.,

Jazz Jrnl. for 30 yrs. Publs: Play That Music, 1954; Concerning Jazz, 1955; Just Jazz, w. Hon. Gerald Lascelles, Volume 1, 1956, Volume 2, 1957, Volumes 3 & 4, 1958; Ain't Misbehavin', w. Ed. Kirkeby, 1966. Contbr. to: Jazz Jrnl.; Melody Maker. Hobbies: Fishing; Woodwork. Address: 3 Wyndham St., Brighton BN2 1AF, Sussex, UK.

TRAJKOVIC, Vlastimir, b. 17 June 1947, Beograd, Yugoslavia. Composer. Educ: Music Acad., Beograd, Bachelor's Degree, 1971, Master's Degree, 1977. Debut: Concert of Belgrade Chmbr. Orch., Beograd, 1968 playing Concerto for Piano & String. Orch. Career: Var. interviews for Radio & TV, Beograd; Asst. to Prof. Radomir Petrovic, Fac. of Music Art, Beograd. Comps. incl: String Quartet; Tempora Retenta; a Study for Symphonic Orch.; Duo for Piano & Orch.; Bells (piano); Epiméthée (organ), 1977. All comps., recorded for Radio Beograd; Bells for Radio Zagreb; The String Quartet for Radio Kiev, USSR. Mbrships: Soc. of Comps. of Serbia. Recip. var. prizes. Address: 11000 Belgrade, Francuska 14 Yugoslavia. 28.

TRAMPLER, Walter, b. 25 Aug. 1915, Munich, Germany. Violist. Educ: State Acad., Munich. m. (1) Margaret Stark, 1 s., 1 d. (2) Karen Phillips. Career: Mbr., Strub Quartet; Violist, German Radio Symph. Orch.; Immigrated to USA, 1939 (naturalized, 1944); entertained troops playing viola & violin, WWII; Fndng. Mbr., New Music Quartet, 1947-56; Guest w. Budapest Str. Quartet, 1955, Juilliard Str. Quartet, 1955; apps. at Casals Fest., 1958, 59, & 60; Soloist, Aspen Music Fest., Colo., 1953, 54, 55 & 56; Assoc. Prof., Rollins Coll. Conserv. of Music, 1939-42; Prof., Juilliard Schl. of Music, NYC, 1962-; extensive tours, USA & abroad. Recordings incl: Hindemith Viola Sonatas; Berlioz's Harold in Italy; Reger Viola Suites; Stravinsky's Élégie for solo viola; Berio chmbr. works (w. Juilliard Quartet); Mozart Str. Quintets (w. Budapest Str. Quartet). Address: 33 Riverside Dr., New York, NY 10023, USA.

TRAN, Quang Hai, b. 13 May 1944, Linh dông xa, Gia Dinh, Vietnam. Musician. Educ: Sorbonne, Paris, France; Nat. Conserv. of Music, Saigon, Vietnam; Dip. of Oriental Music, Inst. of Musicol., Paris, France. m. Bach Yen, 1 d. Debut: 1966. Career incls: Perfs. on radio & TV, France, GB, Belgium, Switzerland, Germany, Italy, Spain, Iran; Participant, many int. music fests. Compositions incl: Nho miên Thuong du, for 16 stringed zither, 1971; Ao thanh, for spoons, 1973. Recordings incl: Cithare Vietnamienne Par Trân Quang Hai, 1971; Tieng Hat Song Huong, 1973; Musiques du Vietnam: tradition du Sud par Trân Quang Hai et Hoàng Mông Thuy, 1976; Music of Vietnam, 1976. Contbr. to profl. publs. Mbr. var. profl. orgs. Hobbies: Listening to other kinds of music; Rsch. in the musical field. Address: 1 Résidence Limeil Village, 94450 Limeil Brevannes, France. 23, 28, 29, 30.

TRANCHELL, Peter Andrew, b. 14 July 1922, Cuddalore, British India. University Lecturer in Music. Educ: Exhnr. in Classics, Schol. in Music, King's Coll., Cambridge Univ.; MA (Cantab.), MusB (Cantab.); Organ & piano study w. D G A Fox, Harold Darke, Boris Ord. Career: Asst. Master, Eastbourne Coll., 1949-50; Asst. Lectr., Cambridge Univ., 1950; Univ. Lectr., ibid, 1953; Fellow, Caius Coll., ibid, 1960-. Compositions incl: Mayor of Casterbridge (opera); Zuleika (musical comedy); Psalms, in New Songs for the Church, 1968; Hymns, in Pilgrim Praise, 1972. Publs: Co-ed., Anthems for Men's Voices, 1965. Contbr. to profl. jrnls. Mbrships: Composers Guild of GB; Perf. Right Soc.; ISM. Hons: John Stewart of Rannoch Prize in Sacred Music, 1947. Hobbies: Antiquity; Travel; Wit; Wine. Address: Caius Coll., Cambridge, Cambs., UK. 3.

TRANTHAM, William Eugene, b. 6 Aug. 1929, Elkland, Mo., USA. Music Educator; Pianist; Organist. Educ: BS, BSE, SW Mo. State Univ., 1951; MM, 1955, PhD, 1966, Northwestern Univ. m. Patsy Ann Starr, 1 s., 1 d. Career: Prof. of Music, SW Bapt. Coll., Bolivar, Mo., 1955-60; Dean, Schl. of Music & Prof. of Music, Ouachita Bapt. Univ., Arkadelphia, Ark., 1960-; Organist-Dir., Westminster Presby. Ch., Hot Springs, Ark., 1975-. Comps: Berceuse (Organ). Contbr. to: Ch. Musician; Jrnl. of Rsch. in Music Educ. Mbrships. incl: Pres., Ark. State Music Tchrs. Assn.; MENC; Am. Musicol. Soc. Hobbies: Gardening; Cooking. Address: 688 Carter Rd., Arkadelphia, AR 71923, USA. 2.

TRAN VAN KHE, b. 24 July 1921, Binh Hoa Dông, Mytho, Vietnam. Professor; Research Director; Player of dan nguyêt (moon-shaped lute), dan tranh (16 stringed zither) & dan nhi (2 stringed fiddle). Educ: Cert. in Phys., Chem. & Biol.; Dip., Inst. of Pol. Studies, Paris; Dr. ès-lettres, musicol., Univ. of Paris; Inst. of Musicol., Paris; Master of traditional music of Vietnam. div., 2 s., 2 d. Career: has made radio & TV apps., France,

Germany, Engl., Belgium, Holland, Switz., Italy, Can., Iran, India & Japan; Dir. of Rsch., French Nat. Ctr. for Sci. Rschs. (Musicol.); Prof. of Vietnamese Traditional Music, Ctr. for Oriental Music Studies; Prof. of Ethnomusicol., Univ. of Paris, Sorbonne. Recordings: Musique du Viet Nam; Viet Nam I & II (2 records); Musique du Viet Nam (on Disque OCORA); Folk Music, Traditional Music, Folk Music Theatre of the Socialist Repub. of Viet Nam - Unesco Collection. Publs: La musique vienamienne, traditionnelle, 1962; Vietnam - Les traditions musicales, 1967. Contbr. to many publs. in field. Mbrships. incl: VP, Int. Folk Music Coun.; Mbr., Scientific Bd., Inst. of Musicol., VietNam; French & Int. Musicol. Socs.; Coun., Soc. of Ethnomusicol.; Pres. of Sci. Bd., Int. Inst. of Comparative Music Studies & Documentation. Hon: Hon. DMus, Univ. of Ottawa, 1975. Hobby: Collecting documents on travels. Address: 44 rue Clement Perrot, 94400 Vitry-sur-Seine, France.

TRAUFFER, Barbara Olive, b. 14 Nov. 1940, Chgo., Ill., USA. Flautist; Piccolo Player. Educ: BMus, Chgo. Musical Coll., Roosevelt Univ.; MusM, Duquesne Univ., Pitts., Pa. Career: Flautist, Calgary Phil., Alta., Can.; Flautist, Youngstown Phil., Ohio; Solo Piccolo, Birmingham Symph. Orch., Ala.; Solo lecture recitals; TV & radio perfs.; Participant, Shenandoah Fest., Moyse seminars; NY & Va. State Symph. Orchs.; Am. Wind Symph.; Birmingham Summer Pops etc.; Flute Instructor, Mount Royal Coll. Algary, Alta., Ala. Schl. of Fine Arts, Mo. Symph. Soc. & Chmbr. Music Symph. Soc. Mbrships: Am. Fedn. of Musicians; Am. Symph. Orch. League; Am. Musical Instrument Soc.; Nat. Flute Soc. Recip., Scholarship, Chgo. Civic Orch. Address: 900 42nd St. S, Birmingham, AL 35222, USA.

TRAUNFELLNER, Peter Carl, b. 1930, Vienna, Austria. Composer. Educ: Univ. Acad. of Music, Vienna. Career: Cond. & Dir. of Stage Music, Opera, Graz, Austria, 1953-57; apps. throughout Europe as Cond. & Pianist; sent by Acad. of Music & Min. of Educ., Vienna, to Kabul, Afghanistan to help found conserv., 1960-63; concerts & lectrs. throughout Middle & Far E; Dir., Viennese Music Schl. III & Tchr., Vienna Conserv., 1963-. Compositions incl: Symph.; Rondo Ostinato; Ballet; Toccata & Sonata for piano; Concert for 4 flutes, piano, vibraphone, bass & orch.; num. chmbr. works & songs; film scores; Music for Flute & Harpsichord. Hobbies: Swimming; Philosophy; Mountaineering; Literature. Address: Schlosselgasse 24, Wien 1080, Austria.

TRAVIS, Roy, b. 24 June 1922, NYC, USA. Composer; Professor of Music. Educ: AB, Columbia Coll., 1947; BS, 1949, MS, 1950, Juilliard Schl. of Music; MA, Columbia Univ., 1951; studied comp. w. var. masters inclng. D. Luening, D. Milhaud, F. Salzer, B. Wagenaar. m. Victoria Khodadad, 2 s., 1 d. Career incl: Instr., Columbia Coll., 1952-53; Instr., Mannes Coll. of Music, 1952-57; Instr.-Full Prof., Univ. of Calif., Los Angeles, 1957-. Comps. incl: (recorded) The Passion of Oedipus; Symphonic Allegro; Switched-on Ashanti Collage; Duo Concertante; African Sonata; Piano Concerto; Songs & Epilogues; Preludes. Contbr. to profl. publs. inclng: The Music Forum (advsry. bd.); Tonal Coherence in 1st movement, Bartok's 4th String Quartet; Yale Jrnl. of Music Theory, 1959, Towards a New Concept of Tonality; Persp. of New Music, 1966. Mbr., ASCAP. Hons. incl: 1st prize, 7th Annual Gershwin Award, 1951; Guggenheim Fellowship, 1972; Nat. Endowment Arts Fellowship - Grants, 1976, 1978. Hobbies: Swimming; Hiking; Sailing. Address: 16680 Charmel Ln., Pacific Palisades, CA 90272, USA.

TREDE, Yngve Jan, b. 17 Dec. 1933, Volksen/Springe, Germany. Composer; Pianist; Harpsichordist. Educ: State Acad. of Music, Hamburg. m. Signe Jahnn. Career: Lectr., Music Theory, Hamburg Acad., 1960-66; Royal Danish Music Conserv., Copenhagen, 1966-73; Prof., Theory & Comp., ibid, 1973-. Compositions: 1st & 2nd Symph.; 1st Str. Quartet; Organ Concerto; 2 Chmbr. Concerti; piano sonatas, other pieces; 2 Fantasias, var. other works, organ; Le chant des oiseaux, wind quintet. Hons: Deutsche Akademie Villa Massimo, Rome, 1961; Forderungespreis der Stadt Stuttgart für junge Komponisten, 1961; Premio Citta di Trieste, 3 premio, 1964. Address: 14 Hartmannsvej, DK 2690 Karlslunde, Denmark.

TREDINNICK, Noël Harwood, b. 9 Mar. 1949, London, UK. Director of Music; Composer; Organist; Conductor; Professor. Educ: Grad., GSM, 1970; Cert. of Educ., Philippa Fawcett Coll., 1971. m. Fiona Jean Couper-Johnston. Organist & Choirmaster, St. Paul's Ch., Beckenham, Kent, 1968-72; Cond., Beckenham Chorale, 1971-72; Asst. Dir. of Music, Langley Pk. Schl., Beckenham, 1971-75; Dir. of Music, All Souls' Ch., Langham Pl., London, 1972-; Prof. of Comp., Keyboard Harmony & Aural Perception, GSM, 1975-; Musical

Dir. & Cond., 4 broadcasts of BBC TV Songs of Praise. Comps: Psalm 150, Brief Encounters (recorded); 8 modern hymn tunes (in the book Psalm Praise). Recordings: as arr./cond., Reflection Records & Word Records. Hons. incl: Sir Augustus Mann Mem. Prize for Organ Playing, 1970. Hobbies: Theatre; Architecture; Country Walks. Address: Flat 1, 139 Cleveland St., London W1P 5PH, UK.

TREE, Michael, b. 19 Feb. 1934, Newark, NJ, USA. Violinist; Violist. Educ: Dip., Curtis Inst. of Music. m. Johanna Kreck, 1 s., 1 d. Debut: Carnegie Hall, 1954. Career: Soloist w. major Am. orchs.; Solo & chmbr. music apps., major fests. inclng. Israel, Athens, Spoleto, Casals, Marlboro; Fndng. Mbr., Guarneri Str. Quartet; on fac., Curtis Inst. of Music, Phila. Recordings: over 50 chmbr. music works (RCA, Columbia & Vanguard) inclng. complete Beethoven quartets & 10 works for piano & strings w. Rubenstein. Hobbies: Tennis; Backpacking. Mgmt: Harry Beall Mgmt. Inc. Address: 45 E 89 St., NY, NY 10028, USA. 2.

TREGASKIS, Herbert Alan, b. 11 June 1918, Geelong, Australia. Organist; Conductor; Educator. Educ: BMus, Durham Univ.; FRCO; FTCL; ARCM; MACE. m. Eileen Mildred White, 3 s. Career: Organist, St. Paul's Cathedral, Melbourne, 1947, S Aust. Symph., 1947-62, Sydney Symph., 1962-70; Cond., Adelaide Univ. Bach Choir, Adelaide Philharmonic, Sydney Univ. Music Soc.; Sr. Lectr., Guild Tchrs. Coll., Sydney; Dir. of Music, Methodist Ladies Coll., Adelaide, Adelaide Boys HS, Barker Coll., Sydney; Lectr., NSW State Conserv. Comps: Suite for Orch.; works for piano, voice, choir, organ. Mbrships: Dir., Nat. Music Camp Assn. of NSW; Coun., Musical Soc. of NSW, Guild Tchrs. Coll.; Aust. Coll. of Educ.; Music Masters Assn. of GB; ISM; ISME. Recip., Harding Prize, RCO, 1970. Hobbies: Gardening; Bowling; Painting. Address: 3 Myoora St., Pymble, NSW, Australia.

TREIBER, Friedrich Georg, b. 2 Jan. 1909, Heidelberg, Germany. Composer; Music Educator. Musical Educ: State exams., Prof. of Music, Hochschule für Musik, Vienna & Karlsruhe; Dr Phil. et Mus., Univs. of Vienna & Heidelberg. m. Else Maria Kreye, 2 children. Debut: 1934. Career: Condcutor, Heilbronn, Liegnitz, Kiel & Stettin, 1934-44; Russian prisoner, 1945-50; Active in civil serv., until 1972; Now free-lance composer; Radio broadcasts. Compositions: Chmbr. music; Klavier-Trio; 5 Streichquartette; Klarinettenquintett; Septett; Orchl. works: Sinfonia Gregoriana; Impulse Inventionen für grosses Orchester; 2 Konzerte für Orchester; Suite für Streichorchester & Schlagwerk; Variationen über ein schwedisches Volkslied; Die Chronik des Dag Hamarskjold (oratorio). Author of Die thüringischsächsische Kirchenkantate zur Zeit des jungen Joh. S Bach, Archiv fř Musikforschung, 1938. Mbr., Deutscher Komponistenverband. Hobbies: Walking; Climbing. Address: Panorama str. 28, 6905 Schriesheim, German Fed. Repub.

TREMAIN, Ronald, b. 9 Oct. 1923, Feilding, NZ. University Professor. Educ: BMus, Univ. of Canterbury; DMus, London Univ., UK; RCM; ARCM; LRAM. m. Anne Severs, 4 children. Career incls: Sr. Lectr., Univ. of Auckland, 1957-67; Vis. Prof., Univ. of Mich., & SUNY at Buffalo, USA, 1967-69; Sr. Lectr., Goldsmith's Coll., London Univ., UK, 1969-70; Chmn., Dept. of Music, Brock Univ., St. Catharines, Ont., Can., 1970-. Comps. incl: Symph. for Strings; 4 Medieval Lyrics; Allegro for Strings; Tenere Juventa; 3 Mystical Songs; 9 Studies for Violin & Viola; 7 Medieval Lyrics (Tenor, chorus & orch.), 1975. Recordings: Music by Ronald Tremain; Choral Works. Mbr., profl. assns. Recip., var. bursaries & scholarships. Hobbies: Swimming; Tennis. Address: Niagara-on-the-Lake, Ont., Canada.

TREMAINE, Ann Kafoury, b. 13 Sept. 1929, Eugene, Ore., USA. Violinist; Professor. Educ: BMus, Univ. of Ore.; MMus, Univ. of Wash. m. Norman V Tremaine, 2 d. Career: Portland Jr. Symph., when 12 yrs. old; Concertmaster, Univ. of Ore. Symph., 3 yrs.; Mbr., Asst. Concertmaster & Soloist on 2 European tours, Little Chmbr. Orch., Portland; Soloist, Portland Chmbr. Orch., Tacoma, Bremerton & Pacific Luth. Univ. Symphs.; Concertmaster, Pacific Luth. Univ. Symph., Tacoma Symph., Tacoma Pops & Tacoma Opera Orchs.; Asst. Prof. of Music, Pacific Luth. Univ. Mbrships: ASTA; Am. Fedn. of Musicians; Mu Phi Epsilon. Hobbies: Walking; Hiking; Reading; Cooking. Address: 7003 Phillips Rd. SW, Tacoma, WA 98498, USA. 5.

TREXLER, Georg Max, b. 9 Feb. 1903, Pirna/Elbe, Germany. Professor; Organist; Conductor; Composer. Educ: Leipzig Univ., 1924-25; Leipzig Conserv., 1926-29, State exam. m. Käte Persike (dec.), 2 d., 1 s.; Elisabeth Meinel. Career: 1930-71, Cath. Ch. Leipzig; 1935, Lectr. Leipzig Conserv.; 1935-70, Music Acad. Leipzig; 1948, Prof.; 1948-55, Choir cond.

Leipzig. Comps. incl: Orch. works; Chmbr. msuic; Gregorian organ works; Ch. music; Vocal music; Folk songs arrs. Recordings: num. own works. Mbrships: var. profl. orgs. Publs. incl: Liturgy and Church Music, Leipzig, 1952; The Motu Proprio Pius X and the New Church Music, Leipzig, 1952. Contbr. to: var. profl. jrnls. Hons: Sylvester Order Pope Paul VI, 1967; Orlando di Lasso Medal, 1969. Hobbies: Painting; Poetry; Model building. Address: Tschaikowski Str. 10, DDR 701, Leipzig, German Dem. Repub.

TRIER, Stephen Luke, b. 13 Mar. 1930, Woolton Hill, UK. Musician (Clarinets & Saxophones). Educ: Fndn. Schrl., RCM, 1947-50. m. Caroline Fraser Scott, 2 d. Career: Bass Clarinet, RPO, 1950-56; LSO, 1956-68; LPO, 1968-; Clarinet, Sadlers Wells, 1953-56; Regular apps. w. BBC Symph., Vesuvius Ensemble, Melos Ensemble, London Wind Soloists etc.; Prof., Saxophone & Bass Clarinet, RCM & GSM. Recordings: num. w. above grps. Publs: Essential Clarinet Repertoire (ed. w. Alan Boustead), 1966; Playing the Saxophone by Jean-Marie Lendeix (Engl. ed.), 1974. Hon: Hon. ARCM. Hobbies: Cooking; Gardening; Tinkering w. woodwind instruments. Address: 31 Brook Green, London W6, 7BL, UK.

TRIFUNOVICH, Vitomir, b. 4 Nov. 1916, Kraljevo, Yugoslavia. Composer. Educ: Grad. Dept. Comp., Music Acad., Belgrade. m. Katherine Kostich, 2 s. Career incls: Comps. performed on TV, Stage & Radio. Comps. incl: Synthesis 4; Antinomia; String Quartets No. 1 & No. 2; Associations; Lamentosso; Heroic Ouverture; Sights (cantata). Recordings of Sights (cantata); Associations. Contbr. to Politics; Borba; Sound. Mbrships: Serbian Assn. of Comps.; Pres., Union of Yugoslav Comps.; Radio Television Belgrade. Hons: Prizes, Serbian Assn. of Comps., 1972; Prizes, Belgrade Radio TV, 1970, 71; Prize of Belgrade Int. Music Fest., 1973; Prize of the Belgrade City Coun., 1976, etc. Mgmt: Sokoj, Misarska 1-3, Belgrade, Yugoslavia. Address: Jove Ilica 89, 11000 Belgrade, Yugoslavia.

TRIMBLE, Valerie, b. 17 Aug. 1917, Enniskillen, Ireland. Pianist. Educ: Royal Acad., Dublin; Cello Schlr., RCM; ARCM. m. John Williams, 2 s., 2 d. Debut: Promenade Concerts, London, 1942. Career: num. broadcasts, 1936-; TV apps.; in duo w. sister Joan Trimble. Mbr., ISM. Recip., Cobbett Prizes for chmbr. music. Hobbies: Cooking; Gardening. Mgmt: Ibbs & Tillett, London. Address: 13 Drayton Gdns., London SW10, UK. 3, 14.

TROMBETTA, Vincent John, b. 24 Dec. 1940, Phila., Pa., USA. Studio Musician & Teacher; Composer; Arranger. Educ: Phila. Conserv. of Music; Juilliard Music Schl.; BMus, Phila. Music Acad.; studied w. Vincent Persichetti, Robert Siederberg, Joseph Castaldo, Boots Mazuli, Phil Woods & Gary McFarland. m. Gayle Marie Tanner, 1 s., 1 d. Debut: Villanova Jazz Fest., 1963. Career: Clarinet & sax. recital, 1962; Perf. on var. record dates; Staff musician, Mike Douglas Show; Tchr., Phila. Music Acad. Over 200 publd. Comps. incl: Four Ives; Wind Trio I; Moods; Saxophone Quartet; Rosee; Bird Lives; Song for my Son, etc. Publs: Studies for Saxophone. Contbr. to: Down Beat; NARAS Awards Guide. Mbrships: ASCAP; Songwriters Guild; Nat. Acad. of Recording Arts & Scis.; Am. Fed. of Musicians. Hons: First Sax., Villanova Jazz Fest., 1963; Charlie Parker Meml. Award, 1963. Hobbies: Sports Cars; Gourds. Address: 278 Park View Dr., Agoura, CA 91301, USA.

TROMBLE, William Warner, b. 15 June 1932, Madrid, Neb., USA. Associate Professor of Music. Educ: AB, Asbury Coll., 1953; MMus, Mich. State Univ., 1960; PhD, Music Educ., Univ. of Mich., 1968. m. Joella Jane Boone, 1 s., 2 d. Career: Hd., Music Dept., Owosso Coll., Mich.; Assoc. Prof., Spring Arbor Coll., Mich.; Dir. of Tchr. Educ. in Music, Olivet Nazarene Coll., Kankakee, Ill. Comps: Freedom Overture (symph. orch.); Song of Easter (SATB cantata); The Creation (brass choir & narrator). Contbr. to jrnls.; Prog. Notes, Kankakee Symph. Orch. Mbrships: MENC; Nat. Assn. of Schls. of Music; Nat. Ch. Music Fellowship; Coll. Music Soc. Hobbies: Writing; Tennis; Photography. Address: Houghton, NY, USA. 12.

TROMBLEE, Maxell Ray, b. 21 Mar. 1935, Woodward, Okla., USA. Conductor; Clarinettist. Educ: BME, Wichita State Univ., 1959; MME, 1967, EdD, 1972, Univ. of Ill. m., 2 s. Career: Prin. Clarinet, Chattanooga (Tenn.) Symph., 1959-65; Clarinet Instr., Sewanee Summer Music Ctr., 1960-62; Band Dir., Lakeview HS, Ga., 1959-65; Grad. Asst., Univ. of Ill. 1966-67; Dept. Chmn., Tchr., Woodwinds, Theory, Band, Stage Band & Orch., Phillips Univ., Enid, Okla., 1967-; Cond., Enid-Phillips Symph., 1970-. Mbrships: Am. Symph. Orch. League; MENC; Enid Music Tchrs. Assn.; Phi Mu Alpha Sinfonia; Phi Beta Mu. Hobbies: Composition; Physical Fitness. Address: 3310 Lookout Dr., Enid, OK 73701, USA.

TROUP, Malcolm, b. 22 Feb. 1930, Toronto, Ont., Canada. Concert Pianist; Director of Music. Educ: DPhilMus, Univ. of York; Assoc., Royal Conserv. of Music, Toronto; FGSM. m. Carmen Lamarca-Bello Subercaseaux, 1 d. Debut: w. CBC Symph. Orch., Toronto, age 17. Career: Recitals & Concertos w. leading orchs. in Europe, N & S Am.; Premieres of important modern works; Frequent broadcaster w. BBC; Hd. Music, The City Univ., London; External Examiner, Univ. of York. Contbr. to: Composer; Music & Musicians; Music Tchr.; 20th Century Music; Ed., GSM Review. Mbrships: Freeman & Liveryman of City of London, Worshipful Co. of Musicians; Gov., Music Therapy Charity Trust UK; Vice Chmn., European Piano Tchrs. Assn.; Int. Jury, Canada Coun. Awards. Hons: Prof., Univ. of Chile; Gold Medal, Canadian Nat. Exhib.; Commonwealth Medal; Int. Music Award, etc. Address: 18 Highgate W Hill, London N6, UK. 3.

TROWBRIDGE, Lynn Mason, b. 29 Apr. 1942, Pt. Washington, NY, USA. Musicologist; French Hornist. Educ: BFA in Music Perf. & in Music Educ., Carnegie-Mellon Univ., 1966; MMus, 1971, PhD Cand., Univ. of Ill. m. Nancy Lee Sietas, 1 s. Career: Instructor in Music, Alma Coll., Mich., 1971-74; positions held w. var. orchs. inclng: Saginaw Symph., Mich., Delta Fest. Orch., Bay City, Mich., & Danville Symph., Ill. Contbr. to profl. publs. Mbrships: incl. Am. & Int. Musicol. Socs.; Music Lib. Assn.; Am. Fedn. of Musicians, NYC. Address: 1539 Hunter St., Urbana, IL 61801, USA.

TRUDIC, Bozidar, b. 24 Mar. 1911, Smederevska, Palanka, Yugoslavia. Composer; Professor of Music. Educ: Dip., Comp. & Cond., Music Acad. of Beograd. m. Dragoslava Trudic, 1 s., 1 d. Career: Dir. & Prof., Music Schl. Stankovic, Beograd, 1948-55; Prof., Music Acad. of Sarajevo, 1955-64; Freelance, 1964-71. Comps. incl: 2 Symphs.; 2 Concertos; 4 Cantatas; 4 orchl. suites; 10 pieces for violin & piano; comps. for wind instruments; choral works; solo songs; folksong arrs.; film stories, etc. Num. recordings. Mbrships: Union of Yugoslav Comps.; Assn. of Serbian Comps. Hons: incl: Gold Medal of Union of Yugoslav Comps., 1970. Hobbies: Maths ; Painting; Esperanto; Inventor of Globe Chess, 1973. Address: 11000 Beograd II, 29 November 118/VI-31, Yugoslavia.

TRUE, Alan Harding, b. 23 Aug. 1939, Collie, WA, Aust. Lecturer. Educ: BA, Univ. of WA, 1972; LMus, 1964; AMusA, 1960; MA. m. Jill Almora Kershaw, 2 d. Career: Tchr., primary schls., 1959-64; Music specialist, secondary schls., 1965-69; Fndn. staff mbr., Mt. Lawley Coll., 1970; Sr. Lectr. in charge of music educ., ibid; 1 yrs. study, Univ. of London, 1979-80. Contbr. to Aust. Jrnl. of Music Educ. Mbrships: V-chmn., WA Chapt., Aust. Soc. of Music Educ.; Organ Soc. of WA (V-chmn., 1976-78); Aust. Coll. of Educ. Hon: Univ. of WA Choral Soc prize, 1965. Hobbies: Following Cricket & Hockey. Address: 119 High St., Sorrento, WA 6020, Aust.

TRUEMAN, Brian William, b. 12 May 1930, Oldham, UK. Professor; Educator; Music Director; Examiner; Piano & Organ Recitalist. Educ: studies w. F E Bailey, F H Wood, Alan Bush; BMus (Dunelm); FRCO; FTCL; LRAM; ARCM; Hon. FLCM. Career: Prof. & Examiner, LCM; Tchr., Herts. County Music Schl.; Tutor, Workers' Music Assn. Summer Schls.; Music Dir., Fest. Ch. of St. John, Waterloo Rd., & at St. Andrew's, Lambeth; Piano & organ recitalist. Hobbies: Special subject - Robert Schumann; Walking. Address: 14A Golders Way, London, NW11, UK.

TRUMBLE, Robert William, b. 15 Apr. 1919, Melbourne, Aust. Composer. Educ: MusB, Melbourne Univ.; DMus, ibid, 1978; postgrad. studies in comp. w. Matyas Seiber in England, 1958. m. Joan Marie Klätte, 1 s., 1 d. Comps: principally for solo instruments & chmbr. groups; Sev. works for orch.; one TV Ballet (La Diabolique); Symph. No. 1, 1976; Antiphonae, for choir & orch., 1976. Recorded works incl: Four Songs without Words for Oboe & Piano; Sonata No. 1 for Violin & Piano; Introduction & Capriccio for String Trio; Sonata No. 1 for Flute & Piano; Music for Woodwind (Intro., Theme & Variations); num. short works for piano solo. Publs. incl: Vincent D'Indy: His Origins, Development, Creative Work & Influences; Aspects of Percy Grainger (some of the material of these books has been used in Radio Broadcasts for the Aust. Broadcasting Commission). Mbrships: Fndr. Mbr., Fellowship of Aust. Comps.; Aust. Perf. Rights Assn. Hobbies: French & English Lit.; Hist. & Lit. of Cricket; Chess, etc. Address: 17 Merton St., Caulfield, Vic. 3161, Aust.

TRÜMPY, Balz (Johann Balthasar), b. 4 Aug. 1946, Basel, Switzerland. Composer. Educ: Konservatorium der Musikakademie Basel; Dips. as Master of Composition, Master of Music Theory. Debut: Basel; Budapest, Hungary. Career: Concerts in Basel, Zürich, St. Moritz, Budapest; BBC Recording. Comps. incl: Stück für Streichorchester, 1969; The Tell-tale

Heart, for violin & piano, 1973; Luzifer (Streichquintett), 1973; Totentanz (grosses orch.), 1974; for violin & piano, 1973; Gesten, Figaren (piano), 1975; Libera (8 voices, elec. organ & synthesizer), 1975; Facetten (violin), 1976; Relief (Kammerorch.), 1976. Mbrships: Schweizerischer Tonkünstherverein; Schweizerischer Musikpadagogischer Verband. Recip. Prize, comp. competition, Humanistisches Gymnasium, Basel, 1964. Hobbies: Reading; Cinema. Address: c/o Prof. Dr. H Trümpy-Meyer, Arabienstrasse 27, CH-4000, Basel, Switz.

TRUSCOTT, Harold, b. 23 Aug. 1914, Ilford, Essex, UK. Musician (Piano). Educ: RCM, 1943-45; ARCM (Tchr. & Perfs.). m. Eleanor Margaret Madge, 1 s., 2 d. Career: Fortnightly piano recitals for Exploratory Concert Soc., 1945-48; Concerto perfs. w. Haydn Orch.; Broadcast recitals, inclng. own works, to 1954; num. broadcast talks, 1951-; Staff Mbr., 1957-, Prin. Lectr., 1970-, Schl. of Music, Huddersfield (Polytechnic, 1970-). Comps. incl: Symph., 1948; 14 piano sonatas; 2 suites for piano; 5 sonatas for violin & piano; Toccata for Organ; many broadcast. Publ: Beethoven's Late String Quartets, 1968. Contbr. to: The Symphony (Pelican); British Music Now, 1975; other books, over 55 articles in musical & other jrnls.; record sleeve notes, etc. Address: St. Clare, 16 Claremont Rd., Deal, Kent, UK.

TRYK, Christian Maureen, b. 20 Jan. 1951, Los Alamos, NM, USA. Horn Player. Educ: Schl. of Music, Univ. of Miami; BMus, Univ. of NM, 1972; Schl. of Music, Yale Univ., 1974. Debut: Yale Univ. Masters Recital, 1974. Career: Prin. Horn, Palm Beach Symphonette, Fla., 1969-70; Albuquerque Symph., NM, 1971-72; Norwegian Radio Orch., 1974-75; Co-Prin. Horn, Iceland Nat. Symph.; Horn Instructor, Iceland Conserv., 1975-77; Horn player, Adelaide Symph. Orch., 1977-. Contbr. to: Horn Call Mag.; New Mexican; NM Mag. Mbrships: Int. Horn Soc.; Phi Kappa Phi; Icelandic Musicians Union. Hons. incl: Alice & Corrin Strong Grant; Am.-Scandinavian Fndn., 1974. Hobbies: Photography; Langs. Address: 57A Norma St., Mile End, SA 5031, Aust.

TRYON, Valerie Ann, b. 5 Sept. 1934, Portsmouth, UK. Concert Pianist. Educ: RAM; ARCM; LRAM.; ARAM; Study w. Jacques Févier, Paris. m. Alan Walker. Debut: Wigmore Hall, London, 1953. Career: Fest. debut, Cheltenham, 1959; Num. recitals, perfs. w. maj. orchs., Europe & N Am. num. recordings. Mbrship: ISM. Hons: Associated Bd. Schlrship. to RAM; Boise Schlrship. for study w. Évrier; Prize, Liszt Competition, Budapest, 1956; Harriet Cohen Award, 1967. Address: 623 Old Dundas Rd., Ancaster, Ont., Canada.

TRYTHALL, Richard Aaker, b. 25 July 1939, Knoxville, Tenn., USA. Composer; Pianist. Educ: BMus, Univ. of Tenn.; MFA, Princeton Univ.; Hochschule für Musik, Berlin. m. Nona Hershey. Solo Pianist, Darmstadt Int., Venice Fests. of Contemporary Music, Breseia-Bergame Fest., Carnegie Hall, NYC, USA, Rome Radio Orch., Recitals throughout Italy. Compositions: Costruzione Per Orch.; Continuums, for large orch.: Suite for harpsichord & tape; Salute to the Fifties, percussion & tape; Bolero, for 3 percussions. Recordings of own works; Coincidences for piano; Variations on a theme by Haydn. Mbrships: ASCAP; Phi Mu Alpha; Fellows of the Am. Acad. in Rome. Hons: Fulbright Fellowship, 1964; Rome Prize, 1965-66-67; Guggenheim Fellowship, 1968. Naumberg Recording Award, 1973; Commissions from Fromm Music Fndn., Dorian Quintet; Kranichstein Musikpreis, Darmstadt Fest., 1969. Hobby: Tennis. Mgmt: Ornella Cogliolo, 79 via Babuino, 00187 Roma. Address: 96 via Quattro Novembre 00187, Rome, Italy.

TRZASKOWSKI, Andrzej, b. 23 Mar. 1933, Krakow, Poland. Composer; Jazz Pianist; Musicologist. Educ: Grad. (musicol.), Jagiellonian Univ., 1957; studied piano w. Olga Axeull, composition & theory of contemp. music w. Boguslaw Schaeffer, & electronic music w. Eugeniusz Rudnik. m. Teresa, 1 s. Debut: 1949. Career: app. at many Jazz Fests. w. own grp., inclng. Wash. DC & Newport, USA, 1962; Lugano, Switz., 1963; Bologna, Italy, 1963 & 64; Bled, Yugoslavia, 1963; Nuremberg, German Fed. Repub., 1966; Pori, Finland, 1968; Dir. & 1st Cond., Polish Radio & TV Orch., Studio S-I., has made radio & TV apps. in most European countries & Hollywood, USA, 1962; has done over 30 scores for full-length films & TV shows & theatre music for 15 plays; has made Tv & radio recordings in many countries w. own grp. & int. known artists. Comps. incl: The Quibble, 1966; Posters; Epitaph for KK, 1969; Double, 1970; Collection, 1970; The Blocks, 1971; Magma, 1972; Requiem for Scotty, 1962; Seant, 1966; Disagreement, 1967; His Better Feelings, 1974. Records incl: Quintet (2 discs); Jazz Workshop (3 discs on 2 labels); Trio. Mbrships: Polish Composers Assn.; Polish Musicians Assn.; European Jazz Fedn. Recip. of Main Prize, competition for TV opera & ballet music, for 'Nihil Est...', 1972. Address: Freta 49/51 m. 7,00-227 Warsaw, Poland.

TSCHACHTLI, Marie-Madeleine b. 8 Sept. 1925, Morat, Switzerland. Violinist. Educ: Virtuoso Dip., Ribaupierre Inst., Lausanne; Dip., Nat. Conserv., Paris, France. m. Henry de Malvesin. Career: Perfs. in recitals & w. orchs., France, Switzerland, Italy, Spain, Germany, England, Russia, Poland, Netherlands; Soloist w. BBC London Philharmonia Orch., Warsaw Phil. Orch., Suisse Romande Orch., Zürich Town Hall Orch.; Tchr., Nat. Conserv., Bobigny. Recip. 1t Prize, for Class, Nat. Conserv., Paris. Hobbies: Reading; Yoga; Walking. Address: 13 Ave. Charles de Gaulle, Le Pecq 78230, France.

TSCHAIKOV, Alan, b. 16 Aug. 1933, London, UK. Musician (clarinet & bass clarinet). Educ: Royal Coll. of Music; BA, Musicol., Hebrew Univ., Jerusalem, Israel. m. Maureen Powell, 4 c. Career: Mbr., Israel Broadcasting Orch.; Tchr., Rubin Conserv. of Music, Jerusalem; Soloist & chmbr. music recitalist throughout Israel & on Israel Radio; num. 1st perfs., Israel. Hobbies: Cooking; Swimming. Address: 4 Rehov, Shmuel Klein, German Colony, Jerusalem 93-103, Israel.

TSCHAIKOV, Basil Nichols, b. 30 May 1925, London, UK. Musician (Clarinet). Educ: ARCM. m. Dorothy Gallon, 2 d. (by previous marriage). Career: LPO, 1943-47; RPO, 1947-55; New Phil. Orch., 1958-; Prof., RCM; Vis. Lectr., Middx. Polytechnic; Dir., Nat. Centre for Orchl. Studies, London Univ., Goldsmith's Coll., 1978-. Comps: First Tunes & Studies; Play the Clarinet. Recordings: Var. Chmbr. Ensembles. Publs: Teachers Handbook for Playing the Clarinet; How To Be A Musician. Mbrships: ISM; Vice-Chmn., EC, MU. Address: Flat 4, 39 Wellbeck St., London W1, UK. 3.

TSUCHIDA, Sadao, b. 14 Apr. 1908, Akita City, Akita Prefecture, Japan. Musicologist. Educ: Grad., Tokyo Univ. m. Wiko Inoue, 1 s. Career: Prof., Nippon Univ., Tokyo Gakugei Univ., Lectr., Keio Univ., Nippon Univ., Dir., Musicol. Soc. of Japan; Judge, NHK Mainichi Music Contest. Publs: incl: Logic of Musical Performance, 1965; Sounds of No Existence - Source of Music & Poem, 1969. Contbr. to: Ongaku Geijutsu; Ongakugaku; Ongakujunpo. Mbrships: Musicol. Soc. of Japan; Int. Musicol. Soc.; Soc. of Oriental Musicol., Recip. Music Critics Prize, Nippon Ongakubunka Kyokai, 1944. Hobbies: Haiku; Mountaineering. Address: 4-3-9 Chofugaoka Chofu-City, Tokyo, Japan.

TSUR, Chaim Asher, b. 2 Sept. 1939, Jerusalem, Israel. Radio Music Editor; Educator. Educ: Hebrew Univ. of Jerusalem; Rubin Acad. of Music, Jerusalem. m. Naomi Sara Tsur, 2 d. Career: Concert Violinist, making sev. recordings for Israeli Radio; Tchr. of violin & guitar; qualified Prod. & Ed. of classical music progs., Israel Radio, currently Hd., Dept. of Non-European Music. Comps. incl: over 300 recorded songs; music for sev. films; childrens' musicals. Publs: Step by Step (guitar tutor in 3 vols.). Mbrships: ACUM; Jeunesse Musicale, Israel. Recip. 1st Prize, Israel Song Fest. for Layl Stav (Autumn Night), 1967. Address: 17 Shohannah St., Jerusalem, Israel.

TSUTSUMI, Tsuyoshi, b. 28 July 1942, Tokyo, Japan. Concert Cellist; Professor. Educ: Toho Gakuen High Schl. of Music, Tokyo; Artist Dip., Ind. Univ., Bloomington, Ind. m. Harue Saji. Debut: Tokyo, 1955. Career: concert apps. in N Am., Europe & Asia; Prof., Univ. of Western Ont., London, Can. 12 recordings. mbr. Violoncello Soc. of NY. recip. 1st prize, Casals Cello Competition, 1963. Hobbies: Trains; Coins; Stamps. Mgmt: Kazuko Hillyer Int., NYC. Address: 1209 Richmond St., Apt. 1502, London, Ont. N6A 3L7, Can. 21.

TSVETANOV, Tsvetan, b. 6 Nov. 1931, Sofia, Bulgaria. Composer. Educ: violin w. Prof. Vladimir Avramov; piano, theory & comp. w. Parashkev Hadjiev; Grad., Sofia Conserv., 1956. m. Gezgana Vladova, 1 d. Career: Asst. Prof., now Assoc. Prof. of Harmony & Comp., Bulgarian State Conserv. Comps: Orpheus and Rhodopa (ballet), 1960; The Great Beginning, symphonic poem for narrator & orch., 1963; The Ladder, ballad for men's choir, alto & orch., 1966; Ballad About Botev's Kiss, poem for mixed choir & orch., 1973; Joyful Overture, 1971; Two Pieces for Flute and Piano, 1952; Sonata for Violin and Piano, 1955; Sonata for cello & piano, 1973; Concertino for piano & chmbr. orch., 1970; Festal Concert, 1975; 4 Symphs.; Four Songs for Mixed Choir, after the words by P R Slaveykov, 1970; Five Songs for Children's Choir, after the words by A Raztsvetnikov; Choral Songs; Arrs. of Folk Songs. Mbr., Union of Bulgarian Comps. Hobby: Football. Address: Uladost - 2, U 206, -C, Sofia, Bulgaria.

TUBIN, Eduard, b. 18 June 1905, Estonia, Tartu. Composer. Educ: Conserv., Tallinn, Estonia. m. Erika Tubin, 2 s. Debut: comp. first perf., 1930. Career: Cond., Wanemuine Theatre,

1931-44; Tchr. of Comp., Tartu, 1940-44. Compositions: 10 symphs.; 2 operas; 1 ballet; 5 suites for orch.; Music for Strings, 2 concertos for violin; 1 concerto for piano; 1 concerto for double-bass; 1 concerto for balalaika; sonatas for piano, cello, violin, viola, sax; songs, etc. Recordings: Symph. No. 6, music for strings, concerto for double-bass, pianomusic (all 'Melodia'). Mbrships: Foreningen Svenska Tonsattare (Swedish Comps. Assn.). Hobbies: Chess; Photography. Address: Nynäsvägen 56, 13640 Handen, Sweden.

TUČAPSKY, Antonin, b. 27 Mar. 1928, Opatovice nr. Brno, Czech. Conductor; Composer; Professor. Educ: Tchrs. Trng. Coll.; PhDr, Brno Univ.; Cond., Choral Music, Janacek Acad. of Music, Brno. m. Beryl Musgrave. Debut: Ostrava, 1962. Career: Cond., var. jr. choirs, 1954-65, Children's Choir, Czech. Radio, Ostrava, 1960-62; Chief Cond., Moravian Tchrs. Choir, 1964-74; apps. on BBC TV & radio, Belgian TV & radio; Adjudicator, choral classes, nat. & int. fests.; currently Assoc. Prof., TCM, UK. Comps. incl: works for choruses; cantatas; piano pieces; instrumental works; etc. Recorded w. Moravian Tchrs. Choir. Publs: Sightreading or Singing at Sight, 1969; Janacek's Male Choruses & their Interpretation, 1971. Contbr. to jrnls. Mbr., PRA; CGGB; ISM; Dvorak Soc. of GB. Recip. var. hons. Hobbies: Skiing; Mountaineering. Address: 10 Stratford Pl., London W1N 9AE, UK.

TUCKWELL, Barry, b. 5 Mar. 1931, Melbourne, Aust. French Horn Player. Educ: Sydney Conserv. m. Hilary Warburton, 2 s., 1 d. Career: Apps. all over the world; Prof., RAM; Mbr. Tuckwell Wind Quintet & Chmbr. Music Soc. of Lincoln Ctr. num. recordings. Publs: Playing the Horn, 1978. Mbr., Athenaeum Club. Hons: OBE; Hon. RAM; Hon. GSM. Address: c/o Athenaeum Club, Pall Mall, London SW1, UK.

TULAN, Frederick Thomas, b. 5 Sept. 1934, Stockton, Calif., USA. Concert Organist; Harpsichordist; Music Editor; Lecturer. Educ: BA, Univ. of the Pacific; Further study, Univs. Md., Ore., Stanford, Calif. at Berkeley, Calif. State at San Fran., Paris (Sorbonne), Mills Coll. & NY Univ.; Pvte. study, USA, France, Germany & UK; PhD. Debut: Paris, 1953. Career: Featured soloist, var. univs., cathedrals etc., USA & Europe; Soloist w. European & Asian Symph. Orchs.; Lectr., Am. Bicentennial & avant-garde keybd. music. var. recordings. Publs. incl: Critical eds. of music by Bach, Bliss, Purcell; Newly Discovered Canons of J S Bach, 1976. Contbr. to profl. jrnls. Mbr. var. orgs. Hons. incl: San Fran. Critics Award, 1971; Pulitzer Prize nominee, 1974, '75. Address: 528 W Walnut St., Stockton, CA 95204, USA. 2, 9, 30.

TUMBLESON, J Raymond, b. 31 Jan. 1922, Sac City, Iowa, USA. Singer (Tenor); Opera Director; Choral Director. Educ: UCLA; BA, Univ. of So. Calif., 1949; Ed.D, Music Educ., ibid, 1965; MA, Columbia Univ., 1951; studied w. Arthur Kraft at Eastman Schl. of Music; Dr. Edouard Lippe & Nathan Stewart, LA; Sidney Dietch, NY; Pietro Pellegrino, Italy (Bari). m. Treva Launer, 2 s., 1 d. Debut: as Tamino in The Magic Flute, USC Opera, 1948 under Ingolph Dahl. Career: Los Angeles, San Fran. Civic Light Opera, 1947 & '52; Savoy Opera, San. Fran., 1948; Talent '50 revue & Seventeen, 1951, Broadway, NY; (films) The Robe, & Pat & Mike; (TV) Show of Shows, Today Show, Perry Como & Ed Sullivan Shows, Musical Comedy Time, NBC; Radio City Music Hall; Music Dir., Rogue Valley Opera Assn., Medford, Ore. Comps: The Green & Blue Cantata, etc. Contbr. to Nat. Opera Jrnl. Mbrships: Nat. Opera Assn.; Nat. Assn. of Tchrs. of Singing; AAUP; Actors Equity, etc. Hons: Fulbright Award, 1951; Carpenter Award, 1964; USO tour of the Orient, 1970-71; Anglo-Int. Fest. of Music, Medal of Distinction, Coventry, 1973. Hobbies: Theatre; Travel. Address: 655 Leonard St., Ashland, OR 97520, USA.

TUNLEY, David Evatt, b. 3 May 1930, Sydney, Aust. University Professor. Educ: BMus (Dunelm), 1958; MMus (Dunelm), 1963; DLitt., (W Aust.), 1970; Dip., NSW State Conserv., Sydney, 1950; Lic. Dip., TCL, 1950. m. Paula Patricia Laurantus, 2 d., 1 s. Career incls: University Professor. Comp: Concerto for Clarinet & Strings, 1966 (recorded). Publs: The Eighteenth Century French Cantata, 1974; Introductory Studies in Tonal Harmony, 1978; Australian Composition in the 20th Century, 1979. Contbr. to: Grove's Dict., 6th Ed.; The New Oxford History of Music; Music & Letters; Musical Quarterly; Musical Times; Recherches; Studies in Music; Miscellenea Musicologica; Aust. Jrnl. of Music Educ. Mbrships: State Pres., Musicol. Soc. of Aust.; State Pres., Aust. Soc. for Music Educ.; Societé française de musicologie; Fellowship of Aust. Comps. Hons: Bourse de Perfectionnement, 1964-65; 1st Prize, Wangaratta Arts Fest. Aust. Comps. Competition, 1962; Fellow of the Aust. Acad. of the Humanities, 1979. Hobbies: Reading; Travel. Address: 100 Dalkeith Rd., Nedlands, W Australia, 6009, Aust. 4, 14.

TUNNELL, John, b. 12 May 1936, Stockton-on-Tees, UK. Violinist. Educ: RAM; Vienna Acad. of Music, Austria. m. Wendy Packard, 2 s., 1 d. Career: Regular concert, radio, TV apps. & foreign tours; Soloist & Ldr. of many chmbr. music grps. inclng. Tunnell Piano Trio, Tunnell Piano Quartet, Vesuvius Ensemble of London, Scottish Chmbr. Orch. Recordings: Num. Chmbr. Music recordings. Hons: FRAM. Hobbies: Golf; Hill Walking; Gardening. Address: Crawhill Manor, By Bathgate, West Lothian, Scotland, UK. 3.

TUNNELL, Susan Mary, b. 26 Aug. 1933, Darlington, UK. Pianist; Harpsichordist. Educ: Royal Manchester Coll. of Music; Paris. m. Maurice J Checker, 1 s., 1 d. Debut: Wigmore Hall, London, 1955. Career: radio & TV broadcasts; concerts, mainly w. Tunnell Trio, throughout UK & in France, Germany & N Am.; currently devoted principally to chmbr. music. Recordings: Brahms Horn Trio; Frank Bridge Piano Trio & Quartet. Mbr., ISM. Fellow, Royal Manchester Coll. of Music, 1970. Hons: Dayas Gold Medal, ibid, 1953; Moulton-Mayer Award, 1955. Hobbies: Reading; Theatre; Cooking; Gardening; Walking. Address: 6 Gt. Stuart St., Edinburgh EH3 6AW, UK.

TUOMINEN, Harri Olavi, b. 1 Apr. 1944, Kuusankoski, Finland. Composer. Educ: Studies w. Prof. Tauno Marttinen & Prof. Amti Sonninen; Study trips to Prague & Budapest. m. Leena S Tuominen, 1 d., 1 s. Career: Choir Dir.; Orchl. Cond. Comps: Approx. 40 choral works; Hyadit; Scholares Voce Pores; Comps. for orch. & soprano; Music for the theatre. Mbrships: Soc. of Finnish Comps. Hons: Kuusankoski Prize, 1971; Kymenlaanin Taid e Palkinto, 1972 (Province of Kymi Art Prize). Hobby: Music. Address: Yhdyskatu 8 as 9, 53100 Lappeenranta 10, Finland.

TURECK, Rosalyn, b. 14 Dec. 1914, Chgo., Ill., USA. Concert Artist (Piano, Harpsichord, Clavichord, Organ); Conductor. Educ: studied w. Sophia Brilliant-Liven, 1925-29, w. Jan Chiapusso, 1929-31; Grad., cum laude, Juilliard Schl. of Music, 1935 (4 yr. fellowship to study w. Olga Samaroff). Debut: Recital & w. Phila. Orch., NY, 1935. Career: Org., Dir. of a Soc. for the perf. of Int. contemp. music, Composers of Today, Inc., 1951-55; Extensive US tours, 1937-; European Tours, 1957-; Formed Tureck Bach Players (London), 1959; Tureck Bach Fests., Glyndebourne, (Dublin),1959-60; Played w. leading orchs. of USA, Canada, Europe, S. Africa, S. Am., Israel; Cond.-Soloist w. London Phil., 1958; NY Phil., 1958 (1st woman to cond. this orch.); Collegium Musicum, Copenhagen; SNO, 1963; Int. Bach Soc. Orch., 1969, etc.; TV series, Granada TV, London, 1961; Num. TV & radio appearances, US, 1961-; Fac. Mbr. of many univs., inclng. Prof. of Music, IV Step, Univ. of Calif., San Diego, 1966-72, Juilliard Schl. of Music, 1972-; Var. world tours. Num. recordings. Publs: An Introduction to the Performance of Bach, 1959-60; Fndr.-Dir., Int. Bach Soc. & Inst. for Bach Studies, 1966 & '68; Fndr.-Dir., Comps. of Today, 1951-55; Hon. Mbr., Advisory Coun., AMS & Soc. Johann Sebastien Bach de Belgique. Recip. num. hons. & awards. Mgmt: Columbia Artists Mgmt. Inc., NY. Address: c/o Columbia Artists Mgmt., 165 West 57th St., NY, NY 10019, USA. 2, 5, 27, 29.

TÜRK, Hans Peter, b. 27 Mar. 1940, Sibiu, Romania. Composer; Pianist; Organist. Acad. of Music, Cluj, 1965; Dr.'s degree in musicol., Cluj, 1979. m. Gerda Herbert, 1 s. Debut: Cluj, 1963. Career: asst., 1965-75, lectr. (harmony & comp.), 1975-, G Dima Acad. of Music, Cluj; perfs. in Romania, German Dem. & Fed. Repubs., Hungary, Austria & Netherlands; apps. on Radio Cluj, Radio & TV Bucharest. Comps: Trio for wind instruments; Meditations on KV 499 for str. quartet; Eco per Collegium Musicum (for flute, oboe, violin, cello & keyboard), 2 mixed choirs a cappella (recorded); 3 choirs, for women's chorus & chmbr. orch.; 8 Saxon popular songs from Transylvania, for mixed choirs & instruments; Resonances, for 24 wind instruments & percussion. Publs: incl. Functional Harmony (3 vols.), 1970, '77, '79; (co-author) Baroque Musical Forms in the Works of J S Bach (vol. 2), 1973. Contbr. to profl. jrnls. Mbrships: Comps. Union of Romania; Int. Stiftung Mozartium, Salzburg. Hobby: Photography. Address: str. Baita 5, ap. 34, 3400 Cluj- Napoca, Romania.

TURNBULL, David Middleton, b. 9 Feb. 1931, Birmingham, UK. Director of Music. Educ: MA, Queens' Coll., Cambridge; Lic., Royal Acad. of Music, Voice culture & class singing; Assoc., Royal Coll. of Music, Piano Tchr. m. Eleanor Diana Wood, 1 s., 2 d. Career: Dir., Music, Solihull Schl., W Midlands. Mbrships: Pres. Elect, Music Masters' Assn.; Incorp. Soc. of Musicians; Royal Soc. of Musicians of GB. Hobbies: Lit.; Drama; Mtn. Walking; Travel; Looking at pictures. Address: 11 Ashleigh Rd., Solihull, W Midlands, B9A, 1AE, UK.

TURNER, Bruce, b. 5 July 1922, Saltburn, Yorks., UK. Jazz Musician (Clarinet, Alto Sax). m. Sandra Lynne, 4 d. Debut:

Cooks Ferry Inn, 1947. Career: Freddy Randall Band, 1946-49; Bandleader, HMS Queen Mary, 1 yr.; Humphrey Lyttelton Band, 1952-56, 1970-79; Own Band, 1956-63; Acker Bilk Band, 1965-69; Num. radio apps.; 1st Jazz Tour, USSR, 1956, Arctic Circle, 1959; Films incl. Tommy Steele Story. Comps. incl: Dadbo; Queen of Spades; Exhibition at the Pictures; Helsinki. Recordings incl: Jazz Masters; The Music of Harry Warren; num. LPs w. Humphrey Lyttelton. Contbr. to: Melody Maker; Crescendo. Hobbies: Symphonic Music; Lit., esp. Shakespeare. Address: 53 Chester Ave., Luton, Beds., UK.

TURNER, (Dame) Eva, b. 1899, UK. Opera Singer (Soprano). Career: Leading operatic roles in UK, USA & Italy; noted for Wagnerian repertoire, also works of Verdi & Puccini, especially in title role of Turandot. Mbrships: Pres., Wagner Soc., 1971-. Recip: DBE, 1962. Address: 26 Palace Ct., London W2, UK.

TURNER, John R., b. Halifax, UK. Cathedral Organist; Lecturer. Educ: FRCO; MA, MusB, Cantab. Career: Num. organ recitals, BBC Radio; Recital & Lecture Tr, Am., 1972-77; Organist Glasgow Cathedral, Scotland; Lectr., RSAMD. Recording: Organ Music in Glasgow Cathedral, 1973; Music from Glasgow Cath., 1975; 6 Famous Brit. Organs, vol. 2, 1977. Hons: Harding Prize, FRCO; Stewart-of-Rannoch Schlr., Cambridge Univ., 1960. Hobbies: Cycling; Gardening. Address: c/o Glasgow Cathedral, Glasgow, G4 0QZ, UK.

TURNER, Lynne Alison, b. 31 July 1941, St. Louis, Mo., USA. Harpist. Educ: studies w. Alberto Salvi & Edward Druzinsky & at Tanglewood Music Fest. (1959); Premier Prix, Primiere Nomme, hors concours., Paris Conserv. (studied under Pierre Jamet), 1960. m. Paul H Singer, 1 s., 1 d. Career: Mbr., Chgo. Symph. Orch., 1962-, & Civic Orch. of Chgo.; Soloist, Chgo., & Balt. Symph., Israel Phil., num. smaller orchs. & many chmbr. grps. inclng. Fine Arts Quartet, NY Woodwind Quintet & Chgo. Symph. Harp Trio; TV apps., USA & Europe; Tchr. of harp; on fac., DePaul Univ. Schl. of Music, Chgo., & Music Ctr. of N Shore, Winnetka, Ill. Mbrships: Am. Harp Soc.; Arts Club of Chgo. Recip. 1st Prize, 2nd Int. Harp Competition, Israel, 1962. Hobbies: Gourmet Cooking; Collecting antiques. Address: 1993 Westgate Terr., Highland Park, IL 60035, USA. 2, 5, 8.

TURNER, Malcolm, b. 9 Oct. 1939, Sheffield, UK. Museum Assistant Keeper. Educ: Univ. Coll., Univ. of Durham, 1958-65; BA (Hons. in Music), 1961; DipEduc, 1962; Registered for PhD, 1962-65 (uncompleted). Career: Joined Brit. Mus., 1965; worked as Asst. Keeper in Dept. of Printed Books, 1965-68 & '71; Asst. Sec. to Bd. of Trustees of Brit. Mus., 1968-71; Asst. Keeper, Music Lib., Brit. Mus. Contbr. of misc. articles for forthcoming 6th edn. of Grove's Dictionary of Music & Musicians. Mbrships: Sec., Royal Musical Assn., 1971-; Sec., Int. Hepertory of Music Lit., UK Br., 1969-; Fellow, Royal Horticultural Soc., 1973-; Bibliographical Soc., 1966-; Museums Assn., 1972-. Hobbies: Gardening; Detective Fiction; Architectural History. Address: 8 Little Green St., London NW5, UK.

TURNER, Marion M, b. 14 Apr. 1929, Arlington, Mass., USA. Flautist - Performer & Teacher. Educ: BS, Univ. of Mass.; MS, Purdue Univ.; Boston Univ. Coll. of Music; Pa. State Univ. m. James R Turner, 2 s., 1 d., 1 step s. Career: Prin. Flautist, Pa. State, Purdue, Pioneer Valley & Univ. of Mass. Symphs.; Am-Art Woodwind Quintet, radio; Purdue Woodwind Quintet, radio; Soloist w. Westmoreland, Carnegie, Wilkinsburg (TV) & Pa. State Symphs.; Num. apps. w. var. chmbr. music ensembles; Prin. Flutist, Westmoreland Symph.; Fine Arts Players, Artists-in-res., Seton Hill Coll.; Flute Tchr., ibid, & pvte. instruction. Mbrships: Pitts. Flute Club; Pitts. Tuesday Musical Club. Hobbies: Gardening; Tennis; Bowling. Address: 1330 Knollwood Dr., Monroeville, PA 15146, USA.

TURNER, Pamela Ann Morgan, b. 10 Nov. 1928, Clapham, London, UK. Lecturer in Music. Educ: Tchrs. Cert., Univ. of London; Acad. Dip. in Educ., Inst. of Educ., ibid; LRAM; Music Tchrs. Cert., Royal Schls. of Music; MA (Mus.Ed.), Univ. of London. m. Leonard R Turner. Career: Mistress i/c of Music, Sydenham Schl. for Girls, 1949-53; Mistress for Music, 1953-59, Hd., Music Dept., 1959-63, Ensham Schl. for Girls; Lectr., 1963-66, Sr. Lectr., 1966-73, Prin. & Hd. of Music Dept., 1973-, Philippa Fawcett Coll. of Educ. Contbr. to: Recorder & Music. Mbrships. incl: ISM; Hon. Sec., Musical Educ. of the Under 13s Assn.; Assn. of Tchrs. in Colls. & Depts. of Educ.; Soc. of Recorder Players. Hobbies: Singing; Gardening; Cooking; Needlework; Riding. Address: Copsley End, Gay House Lane, Outwood, Redhill, Surrey, UK.

TURNER, Robert Comrie, b. 6 June 1920, Montreal, Can. Composer; Professor. Educ: MusB, MusD, McGill Univ.; MMus, George Peabody Coll. for Tchrs.; RCM w. Herbert Howells &

Gordon Jacob; studied w. Roy Harris, USA & Olivier Messiaen, Berkshire Music Ctr. m. Sara Nan Scott, 2 s., 1 d. Career: Sr. Music Producer, CBC, Vancouver, 1952-68; Prof. of comp., Univ. of Man., 1969-. Comps. incl: (orchl.) Nocturne; Children's Overture; Symph. for strgs.; Lyric Interlude; 3 Episodes; (instrumental) 4 Fragments for brass quintet; Sonata for violin & piano; Strg. Quartets Nos. 2 & 3; Little Suite for harp; 6 voluntaries for organ; A Merry-Mournful Mood for piano; (vocal) The Brideship (opera); Choral Piece No. 2; Prophetic Song. num. recordings of own works. Mbrships: Coll. Music Soc. (USA); Can. Assn. of Univ. Tchrs.; Can. Assn. of Univ. Schls. of Music; Can. League of Comps.; CGGB. Hobbies: Reading; Travel; Hiking. Address: 104 Yale Ave., Winnipeg, Man., Can., R3M OL6. 2.

TURNER, Sally Margaret Tudsbery, b. 9 Apr. 1945, Duffield, Derbys., UK. Music Teacher; Pianist; Flautist. Educ: London Univ. Tchrs. Cert., Trent Pk. Coll. of Educ.; LRAM; ARCM. Career: Hd. of Music Dept., Stancliffe Hall Schl., Darley Dale, Matlock, Derbys., 1971-76; Hd. of Music Dept., Derby High Schl., Littleover, Derbys., 1976-. Mbr., ISM. Hobbies: Tennis; Walking; Reading; Antique Clocks; Dressmaking. Address: Jacob's Gdn., 29 Castle Hill, Duffield, Derbys. DE6 4EA, UK.

TURNER, Thomas, b. 30 Sept. 1937, Hamilton, Ohio, USA. Composer; Pianist. Educ: BMus, Univ. of Ariz., 1959; MMus, Univ. of Mont., 1960; Further study, Univ. of Ill.; Participant, Int. Ferienkurse für neue Musik, Darmstadt, 1963, '64; Piano studies w. Webster Aitken, 1962-. m Sara Nix Turner. Debut: Wigmore Hall, London, UK, 1966. Career: Mbr., Music Fac., Univ. of NC, Charlotte; Piano recitals & comps. perf. in USA, UK & Germany; Films for US Educl. TV; 1st perf. of Stockhausen's Klavierstuck IX in UK. Comps. incl: 6 variations for piano, 1966; Phorminx, for 2 harps & string orch., 1977; For If We Believe (choir), 1978; Bottle Music, for 5 singers & 20 bottles, 1978; Modules & Variables, for guitar & piano, 1975. Contbr. to Times Educl. Supplement, 1966. Mbr. Am. Music Ctr. & Coll. Music Soc. Hons: var. grants. Hobbies: Gastronomy; Mycology; Medicinal Herbs. Address: 2001 Eastway Dr., Charlotte, NC 28205, USA.

TURNOVSKY, Martin, b. 29 Sept. 1928, Prague, Czechoslovakia. Conductor. Educ: Prague Acad. of Music. m. Zdenka, 2 children. Debut, w. Prague Symph. Orch., Prague, 1952. Career: Cond., State Phil. Orch., Brno, 1960-63; Music Dir., Pilsen Radio Orch., 1963-67, & Dresden State Opera & State Orch., 1967-68; Guest Cond., num. well-known orchs. inclng. Radio Orch. Berlin, Cleveland Orch., Toronto Symph., Stockholm Phil., Bournemouth Symph., Liverpool Royal Phil. Orch., BBC Northern Orch. (Manchester), etc., 1968-; Music Dir., Norwegian Opera in Oslo, 1975-. Recordings: many on Supraphon label inclng. one of 4th Symphony by Bohuslav Martinu which received Grand Prix du Disque, 1968. Recip. of 1st Prize, Int. Competition for Conds., Besancon, France, 1958. Address: Ulrichgasse 4, 1020 Vienna, Austria.

TUROK, Paul Harris, b. 3 Dec. 1929, NYC, USA. Composer. Educ: BA, Queens Coll., 1950; MA, Univ. of Calif., Berkeley, 1951; Juilliard Schl. of Music, 1951-53. m. Susan Kay Frucht. Career: All-Turok concert at Tully Hall, Lincoln Ctr., May 15, 1970; Comps. perf. by Cinn., Cleveland, Dallas, Indpls., Louisville, Minn., NJ, Phila., St. Louis Symph. Orchs. Comps. incl: Richard III (opera); Scene Domestic (chamber opera); Antoniana (after Vivaldi); Chartres West; Homage to Bach; Great Scott!; Joplin Overture; Symphony in Two Movements; Variations on an American Song (all for orch.); Violin Concerto; Lyric Variations for oboe & strings; 3 string quartets; string trio; wind quintet; brass quintet; Elegy in Memory of Karol Rathaus (brass ensemble); sonatas for horn, trumpet, cello, unacc. viola, unacc. cello, harpsichord, organ, guitar; Passacaglia; Little Suite; Transcendental Etudes (all for piano); songs; choruses. num. recordings. Contbr. to NY Herald Tribune; Music Jrnl. Hons. incl: Comp. in Res., Villa Montalvo, 1955, Ind. State Univ. Contemp. Music Fest., 1971, Wolf Trap Farm for the perf. arts, 1973. Hobby: World Travel. Address: 170 W 74th St., NY, NY 10023, USA.

TURRELL, Frances (Berry), b. 15 Mar. 1903, Portland, Ore., USA. Musicologist. Educ: AB, 1924, MA, 1940, Reed Coll., Univ. of Ariz.; Univ. of Lyon, France, 1925-26; Schola Cantorum, Paris, 1928-29; Sorbonne, 1929-31; studied w. Vincent d'Indy, 1 yr., & A Pirro, 1 yr.; PhD, Univ. of Southern Calif., 1956. M. Charles A Turrell (dec.), 1 s., 1 stepd. Career: Educator, Lewis & Clark Coll., Portland, 1945-52, & Portland State Univ., 1956-69 (Prof. emeritus, 1970). Publs. incl: The Isagoge of Henry Glarean, 1959. Contbr. to profl. jrnls. Mbrships. incl: Chmn., NW Chapt., Am. Musicol. Soc. Recip. Nat. Rsch. Prize, Mu Phi Epsilon, 1962. Hobbies: Music in the Ams. Mgmt: Free Univ. of Ariz., Tucson. Address: 2115 E 8th St., Tucson, AZ 85719, USA. 9, 11, 27.

TURSKI, Zbigniew, b. 16 Oct. 1908, Warsaw, Poland. Composer; Conductor. Educ. in Warsaw. m. Halina Turska, 3 d. Career: Musical Dir., Warsaw Radio, 1936-39; Dir., Baltic Phil. Orch., 1945-46; Lectr., State Superior Theatrical Schl., 1948-49; Cons., Modern Theatre, Warsaw, 1957-. Compositions incl: 3 Symphs.; Sinfonia de Camera; Violin Concerto; 2 String Quartets; Cantatas - The Airs; The Vistula (on poems by Broniewski & Fiszer); Theatre & Film Music. Mbrships: Pres., Polish Union of Composers, 1959-60. Hons: Gold Medal, Olympic Arts Contest, London, 1948; Prize, 2nd Festival of Polish Music, 1955; Union of Composers Award; Min. of Culture Prize, 1957; State Prize, 1968; var. decorations. Address: Union of Polish Composers, Rynek Starego Miastra 27, Warsaw, Poland.

TURTON, Gervaise Mary, b. 16 Oct. 1899, Solihull, Warwicks., UK. Teacher of Piano, Flute, Recorder & Classical Guitar. Educ: Kensington Schl. of Music, 1921-24 (bronze & silver medals); GSM, 1946-50; AGSM; LTCL. Career: in charge of music, var. schls. incl. Solent House, Cowes, & Ascot Priory; asst. music tchr., St. George's Coll., Weybridge, Sir William Perkins Schl., Chertsey, Salesian Girls' Schl. & Boys' Coll., Prin., Chertsey Schl. of Music; retired 1979. mbr. ISM. Hobbies: Collecting Antiques & Copper; Golf; Cricket. Address: Chertsey Schl. of Music, Cloister Garth, Abbey Gn., Chertsey, Surrey, UK.

TUSLER, Robert Leon, b. 1 Apr. 1920, Stoughton, Wis., USA. Professor of Music; Church Music Director; Organist. Educ: BA, BMus, Friends' Univ., Wichita,Kan.; MA, Univ. of Calif., Los Angeles; PhD, Utrecht Univ., Netherlands. m. (1) Adelaide Gest, 1 s., (2) Alida Penters. Career: Fac. Mbr., Univ. of Calif., Los Angeles, 1958-; Dir. of Music, Wilshire Presby. Ch., Los Angeles, 1959-. Publs. incl: The Style of J S Bach's Chorale Preludes, 1956, 1968; The Organ Music of Jan Pieterszoon Sweelinck, 1958; Ed., The California Organist, 51 vols. Contbr. to musical jrnls. Mbr., profl. assns., USA & Netherlands. Hons. incl: Fulbright Rsch. Grant, Netherlands, 1971-72. Hobbies incl: Refinishing old furniture; Swimming; Hiking. Address: 19044 SAnta Rita, Tarzana, CA 91356, USA.

TUTHILL, Burnet C(orwin), b. 16 Nov. 1888. Composer; Conductor; Educator; Writer; Clarinettist. Educ: AB & MA, Columbia Univ.; MMus, Coll. of Music of Cinn. Widower, 2 d. Career: Cond., Columbia Univ. Orch., 1909-13; Peoples' Choral Union, NY, 1913-16; Asst. Cond., NY Oratorio Soc., 1914-16; Plandome Singers, 1919-22; Gen. Mgr., Cinn. Conserv. of Music, 1922-30; Cond., Univ. of Cinn. Glee Clubs, 1922-30; Dir. of Music, Southwestern Coll. at Memphis, 1935-59; Fndr. & Cond., Memphis Symph. Orch., 1938-46; Cond., Southwestern Singers, 1935-59. Compositions incl: works for orch., band, woodwinds, brasses, strings; ensemble music for clarinet; choral works; songs. Recordings: Three Moods for solo flute; Come Seven for Orch.; Sonata for Alto Sax. & Po.; Chip's Pieces for Clarinet & Po. Contbr. to music jrnls. Mbrships: Fndr. & Treas., Soc. for the Publ. of Am. Music, 1919-49; Co-Fndr. & Sec., Nat. Assn. of Schls. of Music, 1924-59. Recip., var. hons. inclng. MusD, Chgo. Musical Coll., 1943 & Southwestern at Memphis, 1972. Hobbies: Bridge; Swimming. Address: 295 Buena Vista Pl., Memphis, TN 38112, USA. 3.

TUTTLE, Thelma Kent, b. 30 Sept. 1902, Waukee, Iowa, USA. Teacher of Piano, Theory; Composer; Educator; Adjudicator. Educ: MMus, Am. Conserv. of Music, Chgo., Ill., 1928; postgrad. work, Juilliard Schl. of Music, NYC, 1952. m. Harold A Tuttle, dec. Career: Tchr. of Piano, Drake Univ., Des Moines, Iowa, 1957-66; Pvte. studio in same city, 1967-; Org. Daytona Beach Jr. Musicale, Fla., 1950, Young Keyboard Players, Daytona Beach, 1953. Audition Ctr. in Daytona Beach, for NGTP, 1951 (Chmn., 1951-57), Helped org. Private Music Tchr. of Volusia Co., Fla., 1955 (VP, 1956-57); Adjudicator, Am. Coll. of Musicians (for NGPT), 1951-. Compositions incl: Piano Tchng. Materials & Shadows in the Lagoon, 1951; Fog Horn Warning, 1952; Sleepy Bugler, 1954; Umbrella in the Wind, solo, 1955; Umbrella in the Wind, duo piano, 1957; Tower Chimes, 1957; Nocturne (solo & duo), 1962; Moods, 1964. Mbr. of many profl. orgs. Hons: Hon. mention awarded for piano solo 'Moods' w. publ. 1964 from the J Fischer & Bro. Centennial Prize Competition. Var. hobbies. Address: 4023 University Ave., Des Moines, IA 50311, USA. 5.

TUUKKANEN, Kalervo, b. 14 Oct. 1909, Mikkeli, Finland. Composer; Conductor. Educ: MA, Helsinki Univ., 1934; Study of comp. w. Leevi Madetoja, theory w. Ilmari Krohn. m. Gunhild Katharina Sigfrids, 1 s. Career: Orch., Choral Cond., 1930-; Cond., num. Finnish nat. fests.; Music Tchr., Instr., Finland, 1935-; Vis. Prof. Chung Chi. Coll., Chinese Univ., Hong Kong, 1967-69; Cond., Concerts of own comps. Viipu , Helsinki, Hong Kong. Num. comps. incl; Symphonic Trilogy of 3 symphs.; 3 other symphs., 2 violin concertos; cello conerto, festive cantatas, Indumati (1-act opera), incidental music to Finnish & for plays, vocal music. Recordings: Bear Hunt (symph. poem for male chorus & orch.); Character Scenes from The Three Musketeers (orch.). Publs: Leevi Madetoja (biog.), 1947; Tuumailuja, 1960; Tuuma tuumalta, 1964. Contbr. to num. profl. jrnls.; Music critic, var. newspapers. Hons: Silver Medal, for Bear Hunt, London Olympic Games, 1948; Sibelius Grant for study in UK, 1951; State Artist Pension, 1972. Hobbies: Engl., Am., Swedish & German lit.; Angling; Photography. Address: Apollonkatu 13 D 31, 00100 Helsinki 10, Finland. 19.

TVEITT, Geirr, b. 19 Oct. 1908, Hardanger, Norway. Composer; Pianist. Educ: Leipzig Univ. & Acad.; State Acad., Vienna; pvte. study w. Honegger, Florent Schmitt & Villa Lobos, Paris. Debut: Leipzig. Career: extensive concert tours as Pianist; num. apps. on radio & TV broadcasts; Cons., Norwegian Broadcasting Co. Comps. incl: many concertos, 5 for piano; many orchl. works; 4 operas, 3 ballets; sonata for piano & for violin; ballads. Author, Tonalithestheorie des Parallen Leittonsystems. Contbr. to jrnls. Mbrships: TONO Soc.; NOPA Soc. Hobby: For. langs. Address: Munthes Gate 39, Oslo 2, Norway. 16.

TVERMOES, Ruth Vibeke, b. 5 Apr. 1907, Ribe, Denmark. Cellist. Educ: Studied w. Ernst Hoeberg, Prof. Heinrich Grunfeld, Guilermina Suggia, Pablo Casals. Debut: Copenhagen, Denmark, 1922. Career: Concerts in Denmark, Germany, Austria, Italy, UK, Portugal, S Am.; Soloist w. var. orchs.; num. radio perfs.; Danish Radio Symphoniorchestra; Sjaellands Symphonieorchestra. Mbr. Musiker og Orkesterferening, Copenhagen. Hobbies: Milieu Conservation; Reading; Walking; Sailing. Address: 30 Odensegade, 2100 Copenhagen , Denmark.

TWARDOWSKI, Romuald, b. 17 June 1930, Wilno, Poland. Composer. Educ: Dips. in Comp. & Piano, Conserv. in Wilno, 1957; Dip. in Comp., Higher Schl. of Music in Warsaw; Postgrad studies w. Nadia Boulanger in Paris, 1963. div. Career incls: Cyrano de Bergerac, opera, first perf. at Silesian Opera House, 1963; Tragedy, opera, Opera House in Lodz, 1969; Magicians Statues, ballet, Opera House in Wroclaw, 1971; Antiphones, for orch., Warsaw Autumn, 1962; Lord Jim, opera, Opera House, Lodz, 1976, Baltic Opera House, Gdansk, 1977; Study in A, for orch., Warsaw Autumn, 1976; Laudate Dominum, for 2 choirs, Warsaw Autumn, 1979. Comps incl: 3 miniatures, for pianos, 2 landscapes, for orch.; Maria Stuart, opera; Capriccio in blue, for violin & piano Many recordings. Mbr., Polish Comps. Union. Hons: Int. Comps. Tribune, UNESCO, Paris, 2nd place for Antiphones, 1963; 1st Prize for Magicians Statues at Int. Competition of Comp., Monaco, 1965; 1st Prize for Sonetti di Petrarca, ibid, Prague, 1965; 1st Prize for Lord Jim, opera, Monaco, 1973. Address: ul. Miaczynska 54 m.61, 02-637 Warsaw, Poland.

TWEREFOO, Gustav Oware, b. 4 April 1934, Nkwatia-Kwahu, Ghana. Research Fellow, Music Education. Educ: Tchrs. Certs. A & B, Tchrs. Training Coll., 1954-59; Univ. of Ghana, Legon, 1964-67; Univ. of Ill.,Urbana, USA, 1973-75; Cert. in Music, Legon, 1964; Dip. Music, 1967; Dip., Orff Schulwerk, 1972; MSc, Music Educ., 1974; MEd, 1975. 8 c. Career incls: Research in Music Educ., Inst. of African Studies, Legon, 1975-; Ldr., Atenteben Ensemble. Recordings: Film, Xylophon Fantasy. Publs: Preparation of Instructional Materials in Music, 1975; The World of Music, 1976; Music as a Life Long Ed., 1976; Overcoming Directional Singing, 1976; Music Ed. With the Handicapped, 1978. Contbr. to: The Conch Review Book. Mbrships: ISME; Research Commission, ISME. Hons: Pi Kappa Lambda, Univ. of Ill. Hobbies: Gardening; Tchng. children piano. Address: Univ. of Ghana, Legon, Africa.

TWOREK, Wandy, b. 25 June 1913. Violinist; Actor; Entertainer. m. Trine Tworek, 1 s. Debut: Copenhagen, aged 6. Career: concert, TV & radio perfs. all over the world. Recordings: Teldec; Decca; Polyphon. Publs: violin method. Mbrships: Hon., Danish Musicians', Artists' & Soloists' Socs.; Rotary Int. Hons: incl: HC Lumbye Prize; Peder Möller Prize. Hobby: Painting. Address: Aakjaer Farm, Moshusevej, Sdr. Stenderup, 6092 Varmark, Denmark.

TYLER, James Henry, b. 3 Aug. 1940, Hartford, Conn., USA. Lutenist; Musicologist; Arranger. Educ: Univ. of Conn.; Hartt Coll. of Music; studied lute w. Joseph Iadone. m. Joyce Geller. Debut: Wash. DC, 1962. Career: has made many apps. in live concerts, & on radio & TV both as soloist & as mbr. of chmbr. ensembles such as Musica Reservata, Early Music Consort of London, Julian Bream Consort; Formed the London Early Music Group, 1976; Arr: score for BBC-TV Merchant of Venice; early music for recordings; Arr. & Dir., prog. of popular Am. music of Edwardian era; Composed music for BBC-TV prodns. of Romeo & Juliet, Measure for Measure & Henry VIII. Recordings incl: Renaissance Duets (w. A Rooley); Lute Music of the Italian Baroque (solo); Songs in Shakespeare's Plays (w. J Bowman); as Dir. of London Early Music Group, What Pleasure Have Great Princes (2 record set); Music for All Seasons (2 record set). Publs: The Early Guitar - A History & Handbook, 1979. Contbr. to var. publs. inclng. Grove's Dictionary, 6th ed. Mbr., Perf. Right Soc. Address: 40 King Edward's Gdns., London, W3, UK. 13.

TYLER, John Malcolm, b. 31 Oct. 1929, Peterborough, UK. County Music Adviser. Educ: Henry Smart Scholar, RAM; FRCO; LRAM; ARAM. Career:Sub-Organist, Peterborough Cathedral, 1950-53, Canterbury Cathedral, 1953-55; Cond.; var. choirs & orchs.; Dir. of Music, King's Coll., Taunton, 1957-62, St. John's Coll., Johannesburg, S Africa, 1962-64; Coun. Music Org., Banffshire, 1964-67, Northants., 1967-; Mbr., ISM. Hobby: Campanology. Address: 34 Church Way, Weston Favell, Northants., UK. 3.

TYNDALL, Jeremy Peter, b. 17 Sept. 1950, London, UK. Festival Organiser. Educ: Charterhouse Schl.; Selwyn Coll., Cambridge; BA in Egyptology (Cantab); Dip., Admin. of the Arts, Polytechnic of Ctrl. London. m. Lindsay Jean Aston. Career: Asst. mgr., Wigmore Hall, London, 1974-79; Festival Organiser, Cheltenham Int. Fest. of Music, 1979-. Address: c/o Town Hall, Imperial Sq., Cheltenham, Glos., UK.

TYRA, Thomas (Norman), b. 17 Apr. 1933, Chgo., Ill., USA. Music Educator; Composer; Arranger; Conductor; College Music Administrator. Educ: BMusEd, Northwestern Univ., 1954; MMus, ibid., 1955; PhD, Univ. Mich., 1971. m. 2 Valerie S Franklin, 3 s., 3 d. Career incls: Dir., Bands, Eastern Mich. Univ., Ypsilanti, 1964-77; Assoc. Prof., Music, ibid., 1964-71; Prof., 1971-77; Chmn., Wind & Percussion Area., 1968-77; Instrumental Student Tchng. Coord., 1971-77; Cond., Ann Arbor Civ. Band, 1969-77; Hd., Dept. of Music, W. Carolina Univ., Cullowhee, 1977-. Comps. incl: Intravention, 1973; Oom Pah Pah (arr. for band), 1974; I'd Do Anything (arr. for band), 1975. Contbr. to profl. jrnls. Mbr. num. orgs. inclng: Grand Nat. Pres., Kappa Kappa Psi, 1973-75. Hobby: Golf. Address: 1421 Pine Valley Blvd., Ann Arbor, MI 48104, USA.

TYREE, Ronald Wayne, b. 17 Oct. 1932, Kan. City, Mo., USA. Music Educator; Bassoonist & Alto Saxophonist. Educ: BA, 1954, MA, 1955, PhD, 1957, Univ. of Iowa, Iowa City. m. Beverly Briggs, 1 d., 1 d. Career: Prin. Bassoonist, 7th Army Symph. Orch., 1958-59; Assoc. Prof., Morningside Coll., Sioux City, Iowa, 1959-65; Dir., Siouxland Youth Symph., 1962-65; Asst. Prof., Schl. of Music, Univ. of Iowa, 1965-70; Assoc. prof., ibid., 1970-; Prin. Bassoonist, Tri City Symph., Davenport, Iowa, 1965-. Mbrships: Galpin Soc.; Nat. Assn. of Coll. Wind & Percussion Instructors; Jr. Fest. Advsr., Nat. Fedn. of Music Clubs. Publs: 4 musical eds. Hobbies incl: Travel; Photography. Address: 3226 Friendship St., Iowa City, IA 52240, USA. 12, 29.

TYSON, Alan, b. 27 Oct. 1926, Glasgow, UK. Musicologist. Career: Fellow, All Souls Coll., Oxford, 1952-; Sr. Rsch. Fellow, ibid., 1971-; Vis. Prof. of Music, Columbia Univ., NYC, USA, 1969-; Lyell Reader in Bibliography, Oxford Univ., 1973-74; Ernest Bloch Prof. of Music, Univ. of Calif. at Berkeley, 1977-78. Publs: The Authentic English Editions of Beethoven, 1963; English Music Publishers' Plate Numbers (w. O W Neighbour), 1965; Selected Letters of Beethoven (ed.), 1965; Thematic Catalogue of the Works of Muzio Clementi, 1967; Beethoven Studies (ed.), Vol. 1, 1973, Vol. 2, 1977. Address: 7 Southcote Rd., London N19, UK.

TYSON, Margaret Lynn, b. 29 Oct. 1948, Independence, Mo., USA. Violinist; Teacher. Educ: B Mus, violin perf., Texas Christian Univ., Ft. Worth, 1970; MMus, Univ. of Mo. at Kansas City, 1972. Career: Prin. 2nd, Ft. Worth Symph., 1967-70; Kansas City Lyric Opera Orch., 1971-74; Kansas City Phil., 1972-74, 1976; San Jose Symph., 1977; San Fran. Ballet Orch., 1977-78; Solo apps. w. var. orchs., 1966-; Solo app., Roehampton Music Fest., 1976, '77, '79. Mbrships: Sigma Alfa Iota; Pi Kappa Lambda. Hons: Dallas Symph. Guild Scholarship, 1970; Recip. Fellowship to Yale Music & Art Acad., 1972. Hobbies: Reading; Painting; Travelling; Photography. Address: 3615 Fruitvale Ave., Oakland, CA 94602, USA.

TYSZKOWSKI, Jerzy Stanislaw, b. 6 May 1930, Warsaw, Poland. Composer. Educ: MA in Comp., Warsaw Conserv., 1957. m. Bogumila Tychowska, 1 s. Career: Chief of Music, Students' Satirical Theatre, Warsaw, 1954-; Music Ed., Warsaw TV, 1960-. Comps. incl: Elegia (symph. orch.), 1964; Alterazioni (str. quartet), 1971; Dispersioni (piano), 1969;

Uwerture (orch.), 1973; (recorded) Tre Impressioni Poetiche, 1961; Preludium quasi una passacaglia e fuga, 1966; Allegro per archi, 1968. Publs: Transl., A Hodeir, Hommes & Problèmes du Jazz, 1961. Mbr., Assn. Polish Comps. ZAIKS. Hons. incl: Winner, Contests for Choral Songs Grunwald, 1961, Poznan, 1967 & Warsaw, 1971; Gold Cross of Merit, 1966; Defence Medal. Hobbies: Skiing; Photography. Address: ul. Zwyciezcow 4c m. 27, Warsaw, Poland.

TYTGAT, Martin Marie Nicholas, b. 18 Dec. 1911, Hasselt, Belgium. Violinist. Educ: Dips., Royal Conserv. of Music, Liège. m. Florette Guilmot, 3 s. Debut: Liège, 1933. Career: 1st Violin, Nat. Orch. of Belgium, 1937-45; Violin Tchr., Conserv. of Louvain, 1938, Royal Conserv. of Music, Antwerp, 1946; Concertmaster, Gt. Symph. Orch. of the Kursaal, Ostend & Knokke, 1947-53; Violin Tchr., 1956, Chmbr. Music Tchr., Dir., 1973-, Jean Absil Music Acad., Etterbeek. Comps: Berceuse for violin & piano; Moto Perpetuo for violin & piano; Moto Perpetuo for violin solo; Study in Octaves for violin solo. Hons: Kt., Orders of Couronne & of Leopold. Address: Ave. Michel-Ange 44, 1040 Brussels, Belgium.

U

UBERTI, Mauro, b. 4 May 1936, Tradate, Italy. Musical Educator. Educ: MA (biol & scis.), Univ. of Siena. m. Giulia Polacco. Debut: Chorus Cond., Milan, Italy, 1967. Career: Fndr. & Cond., Camerata Polifonica di Torino (Renaissance consort of vocal soloists w. ancient instruments); Fndr. & Dir., Municipal Inst. of Music 'Cordero di Pamparato', Pamparato (Cuneo); Prof., interpretation of early music, Conserv. of Parma; Cond., Turin Univ. Chorus, 1974-75; Sci. Collaborator, Dept. of Anthropol., Univ. of Turin. Author on topics related to Italian bel canto & lang. evolution. Contbr. to profl. jrnls. Mbrships: Italian Soc. of Musicol. Hobbies: Mountaineering. Address: via Alpignano 25, 10143 Torino, Italy.

UCHIDA, Ruriko, b. Aug. 1920, Tokyo, Japan. Ethnomusicologist; Singer (Alto); Professor. Educ: Tokyo Univ. Arts; Ethnomusicol., Vienna Univ., Austria; Singing, Vienna Acad. Debut: vocal Recital, Tokyo, 1948. Career: Singer, stage, TV & radio, Japan & Europe, 1945-; Vocal Recital, Vienna, 1962; Prof., Kunitachi Music Coll., Tokyo. Recordings: Ruriko Uchida sings Japanese Contemporary Composers I & II. Publ: Europe ni Uta o motomete, 1963. Mbr. profl. orgs. Hons: Prizes, Japanese Cultural Min., 1949, '66. Hobby: Photography. Mgmt: Shin-ensoka-Kyokai, Tokyo. Address: 3-23-6 Chuo, Nakano-ku, Tokyo, Japan.

UHL, Alfred, b. 5 June 1909, Vienna, Austria. Composer; Professor. Educ: Dip., Music High Schl., Vienna, 1932. m. Friederike Uhl, 1 s. Career: Musical Arr., num. films, Zurich & Vienna; prof., Music High Schl., Vienna. Compositions incl: (publd.) Sinfonischer March, orch.; Divertimento, 4 clarinets; Gitarre-Sonate; Etuden, clarinet, bassoon, viola; 4 Capricen, orch.; Konzertante Symphonie, clarinet & orch.; Introduktion & Variationen, string orch.; oratorio Gilgamesch; cantata Wer Einsam 1st, Der Hat Ws Gut; Chmbr., Choir Music; (recorded) Klarinetten-Divertimento; Str. Quartet; Streichervariationen. Mbrships: Pres., AKM; Austrian Copyright Soc.; Art Senate. Hons: Greater Austrian State Prize, 1959; Greater Music Prize, City of Vienna, 1960. Address: 28 Langackerg, A-1190 Vienna, Austria.

UHL, Fritz, b. 2 Apr 1928, Vienna, Austria. Operatic Singer (dramatic tenor). Educ: State Music Acad., Vienna, 1947-52. m. Erika Stari, 1 s. Debut: Graz, 1952. Career incl: w. Munich State Opera, 1956; Vienna State Opera, 1961-; Festival appearances at appearances throughout Europe & in USA, japan, Korea, Can., Argentina, etc. Recordings incl: Tristan (Decca); Flying Dutchman (Philips); Elektra, Arabella & Antigonae (Deutsche Grammophon); Wozzeck (CBS). Mbrship: Vienna Male Voice Choral Soc., 1947-. Hon: Bayerischer Kammersänger, 1962. Hobbies: Books; Records; Astronomy. Mgmt: R Schultz, Munich & Vladarski, Vienna. Address: Lindauerstr. 9, D-8000 Munich 83, German Fed. Repub.

UJFALUSSY, Jozsef, b. 13 Feb 1920, Debrecen, Hungary. Musicologist; Music Educator. Educ: Grad., Univ. of Debrecen, 1944; Study of composition & orchl. condng., Acad. of Music, Budapest, 1946-49. Career incl: Prof. of aesthetics, Acad. of Music, Budapest, 1955-; Collaborator, Inst. for Musicol., hungarian Acad. of Scis., ibid., 1961-73; Dir., ibid., 1973-. Publs: Bartók Breviärium, 1st ed., 1958, (w. Vera Lampert), 1974; Debussy, 1959; A valósag zenei Képe, 1962; Bartćok Béla, 1965, 3rd ed., 1976, also Engl., Russian & German eds. Mbrships: Pres., Hungarian Acad. of Scis.; pres., Hungarian Musicians Assn. Recip: Kossuth Prize, 1966. Address: Orszägház ut. 9, H-1014 Budapest, Hungary.

UKMAR, Vilko, b. 10 Feb. 1905, Postojna, Yugoslavia. University Professor of Music. Educ: Juridical Degree, Classical Coll.; Acad. of Music, Zagreb; Dip., Musikakademi, Vienna, Austria, 1932. m. Mileva Boltar, 1 s. Career: Prof. of Music, Acad. & Univ., Ljubljana. comps. incl: Lepa Vida (ballet) Godec (ballet); Symphony I (poem), 1957; Symphony II (poem), 1962; Symphony III, 1969; Transformations, 1973; 3 string quartets; sonatas for piano; Expressions (13 comps. for piano); Novels (7 comps. for piano & cello); Alarm (cantata), 1977; comps. for organ; vocal-instrumental comps. Mbrships. incl: Heinrich Schultz Soc. Publs. incl: Through Beauty to Truth, 1972. Contbr. to profl. jrnls. Recip., Preseren's Reward, 1967. Address: Oraznova 3, 61000 Ljubljana, Yugoslavia.

ULLOM, Jack Ralph, b. 31 Oct. 1944, Alameda, Calif., USA. Professor of Music (Orchestra, Strings, Musicianship &

History); Violinist; Conductor. Educ: BA, San Jose State Univ.; MA, Stanford Univ.; studied w. Joachim Chassman; D Mus A, Univ. of Ore., Eugene. m. Jeanne Marie Olsen, 1 d. Career: Dir., Orch. & Choir, Hillsdale High Schl., San Mateo, Calif., 1967-69; Prof. of Music, Santa Barbara City Coll., 1969-; Violinist & Cond., Santa Barbara Youth Symph. Comps: Performing Ed. of Arcangelo Corelli's Sonata No. 3 in C Maj. Opus 5; Michele Mascitti: An Analysis & Performing Ed. of 3 sonatas for Violin & Basso Continuo, Opus 1, Nos. 1 & 3, and Opus 4, No. 8. Mbr. num profl. orgs. inclng: Phi Kappa Phi; Phi Mu Alpha; Phi Kappa Lambda. Hons: Num. awards & fellowships. Hobbies: Woodworking; Tennis. Address: 5082A Calle Real, Santa Barbara, CA 93111, USA.

ULRICH, Boris, b. 10 Aug 1935, Zagreb, Yugoslavia. Composer; Concert Pianist. Educ: Acad. of Music. m. Betty Jurkovic, 1 d. Debut: Zagreb, 1955. Career: As pianist & cond. perf. of own works at concerts, & on TV; Stage music, ballets & TV ballets; Specialist in stage music for dramas, radio plays, & films. Comps. incl: Miniatures, 1954; Intimate Conversations, 1955; Ten Syllogisms for Piano, 1960; Perspectives, concerto for piano & orch., 1970; Multiple Vision (ballet), 1971; Sinfonia Vespro, 1974; Sounds (tapes & chmbr. ensemble), 1975. Mbrships. incl: Croatian Comps. Assn.; Jury of Int. Rostrum of Comps., UNESCO, Paris. Contbr. to The Sound. Recip., sev. hons. Hobbies incl: Film recording & photography. Address: Mesnicka 25, 41000 Zagreb, Yugoslavia.

ULRICH, Homer, b. 27 March 1906, Chicago, Ill., USA. Music Teacher; Administrator; Editor. Educ: MA, Univ. of Chicago, 1939. m. Miriam Elizabeth North, 2 d., 1 s. Career: cello & bassoon, Chicago Symph. Orch., 1929-35. Comps: Rondo Energico, for bassoon & piano, 1934. Publs: Chamber Music, 1948, 1966; The Education of a Concert-Goer, 1949; Famous Women Singers, 1952; Symphonic Music, 1952; Music: A Design for Listening, 1957, 1962, 1970; Designed for Listening (w. Paul A Pisk), 1963; Survey of Choral Music, 1973; Centennial History of Music Teachers National Association, 1976. Contbr. to: Encyclopedia Brittanica; Encyclopedia Americana; World Book Encyclopedia, etc.; Jrnl. of MENC; The Am. Music Tchr. Mbrships: Music Tchrs. Nat. Assn. (Ed. of Am. Music Tchr., 1972-). Hobbies: Photography; Woodworking; Travel. Address: 3587 S Leisure World Blvd., Silver Spring, MD 20906, USA. 1.

ULRICH, Jürgen, b. 21 Nov 1939, Berlin, German Fed. Repub. Lecturer of Theory & Aural Training. Educ: studied comp., theory, ear-trng. (Gehörbildung), piano at Musikhochschule Detmold, 1959-63; Final exams. in musical theory, Gehörbildung, piano, 1962. m. Uta, (née) Krackau, 2 s, 1 d. Career: Piano Tchr., giving elem. music lessons at the Youth Music Schl. in Frankfurt; Educ. of Music Tchrs., Tchrs. Trng. Coll. of The State of Hessen in Jugenheim an der Bergstrasse, 1964-67; Tchr. Theory & Aural Trng., Bergisches Conserv. in Wuppertal, 1967; Prof. Musikhochschule, Detmold. Comps. incl: (orchl. music) Sonata Serena, for bassoon & orch., 1964; Apparitions, for violin & chmbr. orch., 1966; (chmbr. music) 3 Rhapsodic Studies, for guitar, 1965; 2 Denkweisen, for flute, oboe, cello, harpsichord, 1966; Spots, for harpsichord & percussion, 1968; Verwehendes, 2 movements for chamber ensemble, 1968; Im kuehlen August, for piano, flute, string trio, 1970; var. educl. music inclng. High Schl. Symph., 1965. Hons: Stuttgart Prize for Young Comps., 1963, '67; Kuhlau-Competition of Uelzen, 1970; Prize of Musikgesellschaft Braunschweig (chmbr. music), 1977; New Music for Music Schls., Hamm, 1976. Address: Papenrgweg 33, D 4930 Detmold, German Fed. Repub.

ULTAN, Lloyd, b. 12 June 1929, NYC, USA. Professor. Educ: BS, NY Univ.; MA, Columbia Univ.; PhD, State Univ., of Ia. m. Roslye Rita Benson, 4 d. Career: Prof. of Music & Chmn., Dept. of Music, Am. Univ., Wash., DC; Num. TV & Radio apps. as educator, cond., perf. (trombone w. mil. band) & interviewer; Chmn. & Prof., Depts. of Music & Music Educ., Univ. of Minn., Mpls., 1975-. Comps. incl: Rejoice in the Lord; The Man with a Hoe; Symph. No. 1; Symph. No. 2; Sonata for Bassoon & Piano; Sonata for Cello & Piano; Piano Sonata Fuschl Am See; String Quartet; Guitar Quintet; Piano Sextet; Piano/Bass Quintet; Conflicts '74, piano solo; Collaborations for organ & quadraphonic tape; Alleluia (mixed chorus, brass quintet & timpani); Sonata for viola & piano; Carlisle Concerto; Wanaki Win (orchl. overture); Sonata for viola & piano; concerto for organ & chmbr. orch. Author, Composition Problems & practices of the Middle Ages & Renaissance. Contbr. to music jrnls. Mbr., profl. orgs. Hobbies: Gardening; Carpentry; Pets. Address: 5249 Lochloy Dr., Edina, MN 55426, USA. 2, 11, 29, 30.

UMIŃSKA. Eugenia, b. 4 Oct. 1910, Warsaw, Poland. Violinist; Teacher. Educ: Conserv. de Varsovie; Masterclass

Porf. O Sevicik (Czech.); studies w. Georges Enesco (Paris). m. Tomasz Jaworski (2) Nikodem Goldi, 1 d. Debut: Concert w. Warsaw Phil., Warsaw. Career: Concert apps., Europe; Radio & TV apps.; Tchr., Conserv. Nat. Superior, Kraków. Recordings incl: K Szymanowski, 1st Concerto & 2nd Concerto. Contbr. to profl. publs. Mbrships: Assn. des musiciens polonais; Societé Wieniawski - Poznán (Hon. Mbr.); Societé des artistes luthiers polonais (Fndr. Mbr. & Hon. Mbr.); Fndn. E Ysaÿe, Brussels, Paris, Prague, Helsinki, etc. Hons: Prix Nat. Polonais pour Musique, 1957, '64, '74; Prix de Ville de Kraków, 1955, '60; Prix Alfred Jurzykowski Fndn., 1977. Address: Basztowa 15/9, 31 143 Krakow, Poland.

UNDERWOOD, Mark Cecil, b. 5 May 1952, Sydney, Aust. Flautist; Conductor. Educ: DSCM (Hons.), Performing & Tchng. (Flute), Sydney Conserv. of Music, 1970; BMus (Hons), Univ. of Sydney, 1974. Debut: Flute, ABC Instrumental & Vocal Competition, 1971; Conducting, 'Chromattica,' 1973. Career: Played flute w. var. Aust. orchs.; Recitals & chmbr. music concerts, 1970-; Fndr., cond., 'Chromattica,' 15 mbr. ensemble specialising in contemporary music; Cond., ABC 'Gold' concert, 1974; cond. var. orchs. in workshops & concerts; Soloist w. Sydney Symph. Orch., perf. of William Lovelock's Flute Concerto, 1972. Recordings: ABC Studio recordings as flautist & cond. of 'Chromattica'. Publs: An analysis of Anton Webern's op. 24, 1974. Contbr. to Music Now, ABC record annotations. Mbrships: Profl. Musicians Union of Aust. (Sydney); ISCM. Hons: commonwealth runner-up (Orchl. Instruments Section), ABC Instrumental & Vocal Competition, 1971. Hobbies: Reading; Films. Address: 24/38-40 Meadow Crescent, Meadowbank, NSW 2114 Aust.

UNGVARY, Tamas, b. 12 Nov. 1936, Kalocsa, Hungary. Composer; Conductor; Double-Bass Player; Teacher. Educ: Philos., Budapest; Dip., cond., Mozarteum, Salzb urg; Bela Bartok Conserv., Budapest (double-bass). m. Agnes Kadar, 1 d. Career: Hungarian State Phil., 1957; solo double-bass, Camerata Academica, Salzburg, 1967-69; (as comp.); ISCM Fests., 1973, '74, '78; Warsaw Autumn, 1978; all major European radios. Comps. incl: Seul; Basic Barrier; Traum des Einsamen; Incrementum; Akonel No. 2 (flute & tape); Interaction No. 2 (organ & tape); Sinus-Coitus (piano & tape). Contbr. to: Melos; Nytida Musik; Muzsika. Mbrships: Swedish Soc. for Comps.; Fylkingen; Swedish sect., ISCM. Hons: Prize, Swedish Competition for Conds., 1970; Prize, Premio Firenze for young conds., 1971. Address: Hagalundsgatan 31, 17151 Solna, Sweden.

UNVERRICHT, Hubert Johannes, b. 4 July 1927, Liegnita/Schlesien, Germany. Professor for Musicology (Music History & Systematical Musicology). Educ: Humboldt Univ., E Berlin; Freie Univ., W Berlin. m. Renate Richter, 5 children. Career: Joseph Hayden Inst., Cologne, 1956-62; Johannes Gutenberg Univ., Mainz, 1962-; Univ. of Mainz, 1967-, Prof., 1971-. Publs. incl: Die Eigenschriften und die Originalausgaben von Werken Beethovens in ihrer Bedeutung ·für die moderne Textkritik, 1960; Geschichte des Streichtrios, 1969; Die Kammermusik, 1972. Ed. var. works. Contbr. to jrnls. & musical publs. Mbr., Vorsitzender der Arbeitsgemeinschaft für mittelrheinische Musikgeschichte; Herder-Forschungsrat. Recip. var. hons. Address: Hans Böckler-Str. 43a, D 65 Mainz-Bretzenheim, German Fed. Repub.

UPPARD, Peter Garth, b. 17 Jan. 1944, High Wycombe, Bucks., UK. Concert Pianist; Composer; Professor of Piano; Examiner. Educ: Bucks. Schl. Music under Sylvia Ingman & Frederick Bailey; ARAM; RAM under Frederic Jackson & Gordon Green; LRAM (Perfs. & Tchrs.)m. Alison Edith Fowke. Debut: Wigmore Hall, 30 Sept 1970. Career: Sub-prof., RAM, 1965; Prof., ibid., 1972; Staff., Bucks. Schl. Music, 1962-71; Wycombe Abbey Schl., 1970-72; Examiner, Royal Schls. Music, 1972; Piano Recitals, UK. Comps. incl: Scores for films 'The Rainbow Man', 1968, 'Hell Fire Frances', 1971; Musical Plays (words & music) 'One Crowded Hour', 'Scar & Commissar'; Music for Brass, 1976; Vogues, for wind quintet, 1978. Contbr. to RAM Mag. Hons. incl: Lees Prize, RAM; Nora Naismith Schlr. & Munster Schlr., ibid. Hobbies incl: Theatre; Lit. Address: S side, White House Lane, Wooburn Green, High Wycombe, Bucks, UK.

UPPMAN, Theodor, b. 12 Jan. 1920, San Jose, Calif., USa. Bariton (Opera, Recital & Orchestral Soloist). Educ: Coll. of Pacific, Calif.; Curtis Inst. of Music, Phila.; Stanford Univ.; Opera Workshop, Univ. of Southern Calif. m. Jean Seward, 1 s., 1 d. Debut: w. San. Fran. Symph. as Pelléas, Monteux, 1947. Career incls: Creator of Billy in première of Britten, Billy Budd, Covent Garden, UK, 1951; Opera roles incl: Pelléas, Papageno, Sharpless, Guglielmo. Opera Cos. incl: Met Opera; NYC Opera; San. Fran.; Phila. Soloist w. mun. major US orch.; Annual Recital tours, US & Can.; num. fest., radio, TV apps.

Recordings incl: Faure, Requiem. Hons. incl: Gainsborough Award, 1947. Hobbies incl: Gardening; Hiking. Mgmt: Columbia Artists Mgmt., 165 W 57th St., NY, NY 10019, USA. 2.

URAY, Ernst Ludwig, b. 1906, Schladming, Styria. Composer; Teacher; Pianist. Educ: Acad. for Music & Representative Arts, Vienna. m. Herta Fruhwirth, 3 s. Career: w. Acad. of Music, Vienna, 1939-45; Prod., Vienna Radio, 1938-45; Music Dir., Graz Radio, 1946-. compositions incl: num. works for orch.; works for solo instruments w. orch.; chmbr. works; Variations for var. instruments, solo & in ensemble; choral works; Lieder & ballads; film music. Mbrships: Pres., Musical Artists Assn. of Styria, 1961-; Hon. Pres., Austrian Richard Wagner Soc. 1962-; Styrean Musicians Union; Soc. for Contemp. Music. Recip. of many hons. inclng: Schubert Prize, City of Vienna, 1944; Austrian State Prize for Music, 1954. Address: Jandlweg 3, Graz 9, Austria.

URBANNER, Erich, b. 26 March 1936, Innsbruck, Austria. Composer, professor. Educ: state exam, Vienna music acad. m. Edda Gabriel, 2 s. Debut: Innsbruck, 1948. Comps incl: Missa Benedicite gentes, 1958; 5 pieces for violin & piano, 1961; Der Gluckerich (opera), 1963; concerto for oboe & chmbr. orch., 1966; Rondeau for large orch., 1967; Improvisation IV for wind quintet, 1969; 'Solo' for violin, 1971; Double bass concerto, 1973; 'Retrospektiven', 1974; 'Pastorale', 1975. Num. recordings of own works. Hons: Austrian music mag. prize for comp., 1956; Doblinger music competition, 1st prize, 1956; Award for achievement, Vienna, 1963. Address: 1130 Wien, Auhofstr. 237a/1, Austria.

URBANYI-KRASNODEBSKA, Zofia Jadwiga, b. 18 Mar. 1936, Bydgoscz, Poland. Orchestral Conductor. Educ: piano, Second. Schl. of Music, Bydgoszcz, 1954; MA, Dept. of Comp., Theory & Cond., Sect. of Symph. & Opera Cond., HS of Music, Warsaw, 1961. m. Ryszard Kranodebski, 1 s. Debut: w. Scout Symph. Orch., Warsaw Opera House, 1959. Career incl: Choir Asst.-Choir Master-Choir Chief, Gt. Theatre of Warsaw, 1957-72; conducting & lecture posts, HS of Music, Warsaw, 1961-71; Creator & cond., I Musici Cantanti, 1966-72; full-time Orchl. Cond., State Opera House, Wroclaw, 1972-. Mbrships: Polish Classical Musicians Assn.; Fedn. de Jeunesses Musicales. Hobby: Horseback riding. Address: ul. M. Kasprzaka 4-1, 51- 676 Wroclaw, Poland.

URHO, Ellen Alli Marjatta, b. 22 Jan. 1920, Pirkkala, Finland. Music Educator. Educ: MA, Helsinki Univ., 1950; Schl. Music Tchr., Sibelius Acad., Helsinki. m. Valo Urho, 3 c. Career: Lectr., Tchrs. Trng. Coll., Helsinki, 1959-70; Hd., Schl. Music Dept., Sibelius Acad., 1970-75; Vice Dir., Sibelius Acad., 1975-. var. TV, Radio Apps.; Publs: w. Olavi Pesonen, Sanoin ja tanaan I-II, 1973-74; w. Liisa Tenkku, Vihrea Viseryskone, 1972, Sininen Soittorasia, 1974, Punainen Posetiivi, 1976, Keltainen Kellopeli, 1977. Contbr. to var. profl. jrnls. Mbrships: Bd., Northern Scandinavian Music Tchrs., Union; Finnish Music Tchrs. Soc. Address: 16 A 15 Lautta-saarenti, 00200 Helsinki 20, Finland.

URQUHART, Dan Murdock, b. 6 Jan. 1944, Raleigh, NC, USA. Composer; Professor of Music Theory; Director of Electronic Music. Educ: BS, Southern Colo. State Coll., 1965; MA, Eastman Schl. of Music, Rochester, 1967; PhD, ibid, 1969. m. Marilyn K, 1 s., 1 d. Career incl: Asst. Prof. of Music & Dir., Electronic Music Lab., Fla. State Univ. Schl. of Music, Tallahassee. Compositions: Moonscapes for Band; Psalm 149 for Chorus & Tape; Sonatina for Clarinet & Piano. Recording: Music from Caesar; Cinna'a Death; (Nat. Electronic Music Serv., on tape). Contbr. to: Numus; The Fla. Music Dir.; The Coll. Music Symposium. Exchanges, for Bb Clarinet & Tape; Punctus, for flute & Percussion. Mbrships: Coll. Music Soc.; MENC; Chmn., Fla. Coll. Music Educators Committee on Electronic Music. Recip: Woodrow Wilson Nat. Fellowship, 1965-66. Hobbies: Cycling; Woodwork. Address: 2008 Sheridan Rd., Tallahassee, FL 32303, USA.

URUP, Henning, b. 13 May 1931, Hinge, Nr. Randers, Jutland, Denmark. Musicologist. Educ: MS, Tech. Univ. Denmark; MA, Univ. Copenhagen. m. Ida Bocher, 2 children. Career: Rschr., music & dance esp. Danish folk music, 1965-; Music advsr. & tchr., Municipal Music Schl. Copenhagen. Contbr. to: Dansk AArbo gfor Musikforskning VI, 1972; Musik og Forskning I, 1975, & II, 1976; Swedish Jrnl. Musicol., 1975. Mbr., Danish Musicol. Soc. Address: Skolebakken 44, DK-2830 Virum, Denmark.

USHER, Julia, b. 21 July 1945, Oxford, UK. Composer; College Lecturer; Teacher of Handicapped Children. Educ: Newnham Coll., Cam bridge; Tchrs. Cert., York Univ. m.

Rodney Gordon Usher, 2 s. Career: Clarinet Quintet, Encounter, BBC Music in Our Time, 1975; Flute solo, Asolando, BBC Young Comps. Forum, 1977; Ordnance Survey, BBC Young Comps. Forum, 1979. Comps. incl: Season's End (SATB Chorus), 1966; Byzantine Mosaics (Flute), 1968; Encounter, Clarinet Quintet, 1973; Gordale Scar (Orch.), 1974; De Revolutionibus (Orch.), 1975; Asolando (Flute), 1975; Burning Bush (Ensemble), 1976; Exits and Entrances (Double Bass), 1977; Wall (Oratorio), 1978; Ordnance Survey (Tenor & Ensemble), 1978; Rites of Transition, (SATB), 1978; Hey Mr Butterfly (Educational), 1979. Contbr. to: Encyclopaedia Britannica. Mbrships: Comps. Guild; SPNM; Glos. Symph. Orch. (1st flute, 1971-74). Hons: Abingdon Prize (Cambridge), 1967; Stroud Int. Comps. Competition, 1974; Soc. for Modern Music Winter competition, 1968. Hobbies incl: Reading; Archaeology; Mythology; Walking; Travel; Art. Address: 110 Wyatt Park Rd., Streatham, London SW2, UK.

UTAGAWA, Anne, b. 11 Sept. 1948, Tokyo, Japan. Flautist. Educ: Conserv. Nat. Superiur de Musique, Paris, France. m. Dominique Hunziker, 1 s. Debut: Tokyo, 1971. Career: Concerts, Japan, UK, France, Switz. & Germany; TV & radio apps., Japan; Radio apps., Switz. & France. Recordings: Toshiba, Japan; Jecklin, Zurich; Ariola Euro Disc, Germany. Contbr. to: Ongaku no Tomo, Tokyo. Mbr. Assn. Musiciens Suisses, Lausanne. Hons: Bourse d'étude du Govt. Francais, 1967; Werkjahr des Aarrg Kuratoriums, 1974; Auszeichnung durch: Jubiläums-stiftung der Schweiz Bankgesellschaft, 1975. Mgmt: Shin Ensoka Kyokai, Tokyo. Address: Ochsengassli 9, 5000 Aarau, Switz.

UTEN, Eugeen, b. 21 Sept. 1919, Diest, Belgium. Carilloneur. Educ: Studies w. Staf Nees, Jef Van Hoof; Dip. Finaliteit, Dip. Virtuosity, Beiaard Schl., Mechelen. m. Hendrika Moretelmans, 3 c. Debut: Hulp Beiaardier te Mechelen, 1948. Career: TV & Radio apps. Comps: Opus 11; Opus 12. Wev. recordings. Mbrships: Oudleerlingenbond België; Guild of Carilloneurs of USA. Hons. 1st Prize, Nederlands Int. Competition, 1957, for Opus 12; Laureaat in de wedstrijd 1958 te Mechelen. Hobby: Stamps. Mgmt: Stadsbeiaardier te Brugge. Address: Markt 7, 8000 Brugge, Belgium.

UTGAARD, Merton Blaine, b. 2 Nov. 1914, Maddock, ND, USA. Music Educator; Adjudicator; Conductor. Educ: BA, Valley City State Coll., ND; MMEd, Univ. of Minn.; Ed.D., EdD, of Northern Colo. m. Noella Michon, 2 s., 1 d. Career: Dir. of Bands, Univ. of SD, Ball State Univ., Ind., Northern Ill. Univ.; Lectr., Brandon Univ., Man., Can.; Dir., Summer Schl. of the Fine Arts, Int. Music Camp. Contbr. to Instrumentalist Mag. Mbrships: Am. Bandmasters Assn.; Nat. Band Assn.; Chmn., N Ctrl. Div., ibid; MENC; var. Nat. Committees, ibid; Coll. Band Dirs. Assn.; N Am. Band Dirs. Coord. Coun. Hons: Citation of Excellence, Nat. Band Assn., 1971; as Dir., Int. Music Camp Band, 1st Prize, World Music contest, Kerkrade, Holland, 1966, 1970; Bismark Art Assn. Award, 1975; One of the Ten Most Outstanding Music Dirs. in the US, 1976; Governor's Award for the Arts, 1977. Hobbies: Amateur Radio; Sailing. Address: Box 328, Bottineau, ND 58318, USA. 12.

UTHUP, Usha, b. 8 Nov. 1947, Bombay, India. Musician in both Western & Indian Traditions. Educ: Dip., J J Schl. of Art. m. Jani Chacko Uthup, 1 s., 1 d. Debut: Madras, 1969. Career: singer & Guitarist, Western Jazz, Folk & Pop, as well as Indian Music, giving concerts & making night club apps. & radio & TV broadcasts in India; has recorded film soundtracks in sev. dialects. Recordings incl. 3 LPs in Engl: Scotch & Soda; Usha Sings Love Story; Usha Sings Beautiful Sunday. Hobbies: Painting; Sewing; Listening to music. Address: c/o J Thomas & Co. Pvt. Ltd., Nilhat House, Bristow Rd., Cochin 3, Kerala, India.

UUSTALU, Uve-Holger, b. 4 Oct. 1933, Tallinn, Estonia. Hornist; Teacher. Educ: Leningrad Conserv. m. Helene Uustalu, 2 s., 1 d. Debut: w. Brass Band of the Kirov Theatre, Leningrad, 1956. Career: Solo Hornist, Orch. of Estonia Theatre, 1958-69, Estonian State Orch. of Estonia Theatre, 1958-69, Estonian State Symph. Orch., 1969; Hornist, Estonian Phil. Woodwind Quintet (Jaan Tamm), 1959-, Tallinn Chmbr. Orch., 1960-; Tchr. of Horn, Tallinn Conserv. Recordings: Melodiya, Moscow. Mbrships: Estonian Theatre Soc.; Int. Horn Soc. Recip., 1st Prize, Estonian Brass Competition, 1970. Hobbies: Photography; Records; Gardening. Address: Suur-Larka 10-2, Tallinn 200001, Estonia, USSR.

UYTTENHOVE, Yolande, b. 25 July 1925, Leuze, Belgium. Music School Director; Pianist. Educ: 1st prize, & Dip. Supériur in Chmbr. Music, Royal Conserv. of Music, Brussels; LRAM (perf.), London, UK, 1953. m. René De Macq, 2 s. Debut: 1929. Career: Concerts in Belgium, France, Switzerland, UK, Holland, USA & Germany; Radio perfs. for ORTF, Paris, Vara Radio & KRO Radio, Hilversum, & in Belgium; TV app., Lille, France & USA. Dir., Music Schl., Braine-l'Alleud, Belgium. Compositions: Sonatina for Piano, 1962; Sonata for Flute & Piano, 1964; Méthode de Piano; Cancale & Ratour, 1967; Diner á Cajarc (piano), 1967; (educl. works): Rochemaure (piano piece for 6 Hands), 1962; Piéce pour Cor, 1962; Piece triste pour Trompette, 1962; Recueil de Dictées atonales, 1966; Le Sire de Lusigny (piano), 1967. Mbrships: SABAM; Assn. Enseignement Musical Subventionné. Hons: Bronze Medal of Arts, Sci. & Lit., paris, 1950; Dip. of Hon., Int Concours of Pianists, Barcelona, Spain, 1954. Hobby: Music. Address: 128 Rue des Confédérés, B 1040 Brussels, Belgium.

V

VACHALOVA, Libuse, b. 17 Apr. 1932, Prague, Czech. Harpist; Professor. Educ: State Conserv. of Music, 1952. m. Kiri Bousek, 1 s., 1 d. Debut: Prague, 1952. Career: Concerts, Czech. & abroad; Soloist, Film Symphonic Orch.; Prof., State Music Conserv., Prague; Fndr., Artistic Ldr., Lyra Nova musical grp. Num. radio, TV recordings, prize-winning film, Czech Harp. Mbrship: Sect. of Concert Artists. Hons: Artistic Recognition Awards, Musical Fund. Hobbies: Chamber music; Books; Theatre; Knitting; Cooking. Mgmt: Pragoconcert, Prague. Address: Utulna 507, 108 00 Prague 10, Czech.

VACKAR, Dalibor C, b. 19 Sept. 1906, Korcula, Yugoslavia. Composer; Writer. Educ: State Conserv., Prague; Master-Schl., Violin, Comp., Prague. m. Adina Pochman, 2 d., 2 s. Career: Violin Virtuoso, comp., Jrnlst., Writer, 1932-; Mbr. Czech. Broadcasting Co. Symph. Orch., 1934-; freelance Artist, Writer, 1945- Compositions incl: 4 Symphs.; Symphoniette; fantasy Pianoforte Cantata, piano & percussion; 8 concerti for solo instruments w. orch.; Chmbr. Ensemble works; choir, solo vocal music; 24 Filmscores. Publs. incl: 4 books of Poems; book of Short Stories; book of Aphorisms; 12 Plays; 3 opera libretti. Contbr. to: Music Review; Daily News; Lidova Demokracie. Mbrships: Union of Czech. Comps.; Union of Czech. Writers; Author's Safety Union. Named Merited Artist, Czech. State. Hobbies: Sports: Football. Address: 22 Francouzka, 120000 Praha 2, Czechoslovakia.

VACKOVA, Jirlina Marie, b. 25 Jan. 1912, Libstejn, Czechoslovakia. Musicologist; Music Educator. Educ: Grad., Piano Dept., Acad. of Music & Dramatical Arts, Bratislava; PhD, Brno Univ., 1938; CSc, 1969. Career: Tchr. of Piano, Conserv. of Music, Prague, 1940-46; Tchr. of Piano, Hist. of Music & Aesthetics, Chair of Musical Educ.; Pedagogical Fac., Charles' Univ., Prague, 1947-61; Specialized Worker, Antonin Dvorak Mus., Prague, 1961-69; Rsch. Worker, Chair of Musical Educ., Charles Univ., 1969-74. Publs. incl: Julie Reisserová. Life & work, 1948; About the Study of Piano Playing, 1951; Choral preludes of J S Bach, 1952; Problems of the Anthropologie of Music in the Frame of the Complex Science of a Man, 1974. Bozena Nemcová in Music, 1976. Contbr. num. chapts. & articles to publs. in field. Mbr: Musical Soc., Prague. Hobbies: Langs.; Travelling; Nature. Address: Parizská 28, 11000 Praha 1, Czechoslovakia.

VAD, Knud, b. 14 Sept. 1936, Aarhus, Denmark. Organist; Conductor. Educ: Royal Danish Music Conservatoire. 3 children. Debut: Organist, Vor Frelsers Kirke, 1961. Career: Organ Soloist w. apps. in var. countries inclng: USSR, UK, USA, W Germany, Norway; Num. apps. on TV & radio in Denmark & abroad; Organist, Soro Ch.; Music Tchr., Soro Akademi; Artistic Dir. & Fndr., Soro Int. Organ Festival; Organ Tchr., Conserv., Lübeck. Comps: In Principio Erat Verbum (soprano & organ), 1970; Passacaglia and Fugue (organ), 1966. Num. recordings. Contbr. of articles to profl. jrnls. Mbrshjips: Dansk organist og Kantor-Samfund; Koda; Gramex. Hobbies: Music; Concert Tours; Reading; Children. Address: Esbern Snaresvej 17, 4180 Sore, Denmark. 30.

VADAS, Agnes, b., Budapest, Hungary. Violinist. Educ: Artist Dip., Acad. of Music, Budapest. m. Lucal Myers. Career: Child Prodigy; Soloist, State Phil., Hungary; Perfs. w. all maj. Hungarian Orchs.; Tours of Europe & USA Perfs., NYC, & Radio Luxembourg, Stockholm, Munich, Frankfurt radio, others. Recordings: Bartok's Solo Sonata. Hons: Remenyi Prize, Budapest, 1946; Bach Fest., Leipzig, 1950; Flesch Competition, London, 1955. Hobby: Chess. Address: 160 W 106, NY, NY 10025, USA.

VADER, Hans, b. 31 May 1942, Groningen, Netherlands. Cellist. Educ: Dips., Cello Tchng., Solo Perf., Adam Schl. of Music. m. Mellina DeRoo Van Alderwerelt, 2 children. Career: Cellist, Amsterdam Concertgebouw Orch. & Viadana Trio. Sev. radio perfs. recorded. Address: Hugo de Grootlaan 36, Uithourn, Netherlands.

VAIL, James H, b. 15 Mar. 1929, Los Angeles, Calif., USA. Choral Conductor; Organist; Professor. Educ: BMus, Curtis Inst., 1951; MMus, 1956, DMA, Ch. Music, 1960, Univ. of S Calif. m. Barbara Di Iullo, 1 s., 1 d. Career: Organist/Choirmaster, var. Pa. churches, 1947-52; Organist & Choirmaster, ST. John's Episc. Ch., LA, 1954-69, St. Alban's Episc. Ch. Westwood, 19690-; Instr., Organ, Immaculate Heart Coll., LA, 1957-60; Assoc. Prof., Prof. of Music, Univ. of S

Calif., 1961-; Cond., Univ. Concert Choir; Co-dir., Univ. Chorus; Chmn., Schl. of Music Grad. Coun.; Num. organ recitals; cond. all maj. choral works; Adjudicator; Clinician,. Publs: Selective Music Lists (co-compiler), 1968. Contbr. to profl. jrnls. Mbrships: Past Pres. , LA Chapt., Choral Conds. Guild of Calif., Past Dean, LA Chapt., AGO; Am. Choral Dirs. Assn.; Am. Choral Fndn.; MENC; Hymn Soc. of Am.; Eta Chapt., Pi Kappa Lambda. Address: 3005 Motor Ave., Los Angeles, CA 90064, USA.

VAINIO, Matti Olavi, b. 5 July, 1946, Kuopio, Finland. Reader in Musicology; Music Educator. Can. Hum., 1968; MPhil, 1969; Licentiate of Philos., 1972; PhD, 1976; violin studies, Conserv. of Kuopio & abroad, 1953-70; tchr. of music hist., tchrs. Training Coll., 1969. m. Kaisa Hannikainen, 1d. Career: Reader of Musicol., Univ. of Helsinki; tchr., Univ. of Jyväskylä. Publs: Diktonius: A Modernist & a Composer, 1976; The Effectiveness in Teaching Music, 1978; Towards Modernism, 1976; Some Problems of Musicality, 1977, etc. Contbr. to: Musiikki; Kanava. Mbrships: Soc. for Rsch, in Psychol. of Music & Music Educ.; Musicol. Soc. of Finland; Aesthetical Soc. of Finland. Hon: pro Musica, Assn for Finnish Music Tchrs., 1966. Hobbies: Literature. Address: Vänrikki Stoolin katu 8 A 7, 00100 Helsinki 10, Finland.

VAJDA, Igor, b. 16 Mar. 1935, Banská Bystrica, Czechoslovakia. Musicologist; Critic; Publisher. Educ: MPh, Fac. of Philos., Commenius Univ., Bratislava. Debut: Monography about Kantate Eugen Suchon's Zalm zeme podkarpatskej. Career: Prof. of Musical Theory, State Conserv., Kosica; Radio Broadcasts incl: Cycle of Slovac Chmbr. Music; TV broadcasts inc: What Is Opera? & 50 Yrs. of Slovac Nat. Theatre; Currently, Asst., Slovac Acad. of Scis. Publs: Sergej Prokofiev: Popular Mongraphy, Bratislava, 1964; Co-Author, National Artist Eugen Suchon, 1978. Contbr. to profl. jrnls. Mbrships: Union of Slovac Dramatists; Union of Slovac Comps. Hons. incl: Prize of Slovac Lit. Fund, 1972, 74. Hobby: Travel. Address: 811 00 Bratislava 11, Dubnická 4, Czech.

VALACH, Jan, b. 22 Sept. 1925, Hnusta, Czechoslovakia. Conductor; Organ Virtuoso. Educ: Dips. in Organ, Conducting, State Exam. in Pedagogy, Bratislava Conserv., & Acad. of Music, Prague; Study of Musical Sci. & Aesthetics, Bratislava Univ., Charles Univ., Prague. m. Blanka Havlinova. Career: Cond., Choir Dir., Nat. Opera Bratislava; Chief Cond., Artistic Dir., Opera House, Banska Bystrica; Cond., var. choirs; Guest Cond., var. Czech. & for. orchs. & opera houses; Cond., Royal Opera, Antwerp, 1968-. cond., Arti Vocali, Antwerp, 1974-; Tchng. Career: Prof. at conservs. in Zilina, Czech., Cairo, Egypt; Ghent, Belgium. External Prof., High Schl. of Music, Bratislava. Organ Career: Recitals at all maj. European fests.; Soloist, w. Cairo Symph. Orch.; Recitals, most European countries; Radio apps. & recordings, BBC, Berlin, Budapest, Brussels, Antwerp, Cairo, Leipzig, prague, Lugano, Geneva, Zürich, Moscow, Rome, others; TV recordings. Compositions incl. works for mixed, men's children's choirs'. Contbr. to profl. jrnls., books, opera progs. num. recordings. Mbrships: Soc. of Slovak Composers, Bratislava; Alex de Vries Fndn., Antwerp; Georg Schumann Gesell.; Oostervelde Cultureel Centurm, Antwerp. Hons. incl: Awards, var. Competitions, piano, organ, choir; Conducting & Organ Dips. w. Distinction, 1951, '52. Hobbies: Chess; Archaeology; Sports. Mgmat: Denise Tolkowski, Antwerp. Address: Belgiëlei 39, 2000 Antwerp, Belgium.

VALANTE, Harrison R, b. 27 Jan. 1936, Newark, NJ, USA. Conductor. University Departmental Chmn. Educ: BMus, Eastman Schl. of Music; MMus, Manhattan Schl. of Music; MA & Doct., Columbia Univ. m. Sallie Valante, 2 s. Career: Cond.; Bridgeport Civic Orch.; Greater Bridgeport Symph., & Bridgeport Youth Orch. Cond., NJ Chorale, & Conn. Fest. Orch.; Chmn., Dept. of Music, Univ. of Bridgeport. Comps: Marzo Brilliante; (music theatre) The Golden Reign, & You're Not Listening. Contbr. to Univ. of Bridgeport Quarterly, 1970. Mbrships: Phi Mu Alpha; Phi Delta Kappa; Coll. Music Soc. Hons: George Eastman Scholarship; Schumann Music Club Award; Henry B Dupont III Professorship. Hobbies: Boating; Tennis. Address: 36 Burr Farms Rd., Westport, CT 06880, USA.

VALAVANI, Tasso George, b. 7 Jan. 1928, Athens, Greece. Conductor; Pianist; Musicologist. Educ: Dips., Econs. & Pol. Sci., Bus. Admin.; Grad., Nice-Aosta, Cincinnati, Strasbourg, Univ.; Dips. in Piano Lit., Theory of Music, Conducting & Musicol.; PhD., Strasbourg Univ. Career: Cond.; Pianist; Musicologist; Music & Drama film critic; Prof., Athens Grad. Schl. of Jrnlsm. Dir., Athens Grad. Schl. of Musicol.; Chmn., Nat. Hellenic comm., CUNY. Publs: The Futher of the Music Drama; Politics & The Arts. Contbr. of over 2,300 articles to mags., etc. Mbrships: Int. Musicological Soc.; Int. Press Inst.; Nat. Union of Writers; Fijet of Athens; Soc. of Pub. & Int.

Affairs. Awards: Nat. Conserv., in piano, 1961, in Musicol., Athens Apollo Conserv., 1972; Int. Fedn. of Tourist Writers, 1973. Hobbies: Skiing; Golf. Address: 100 Eolos St., PB 39, Athens, Greece.

VALDENGO, Guiseppe, b. 24 May 1920, Torino, Italy. Concert & Opera Baritone. Educ: Dip., G Berdi Conserv., Turin. Debut: Barber Seville, Parma. Career: has appeared at La Scala, Milan, Met. Opera, NYC, San Carlo Opera House, Naples, Opera di Parigi, Teatro Nazionale Praha, etc.; apps. w. NBC Orch., etc.; Artistic Dir., Les Semaines Musicales de St. Vincent. Author: Ho cantato con Toscanini. Address: Via Ponte Romano 93, St. Vincent (Ao), Italy.2.

VALEK, Jiri, b. 4 June 1940, Olomouc, Czechoslovakia. Musician; Flautist. Educ: Studied w. Prof. Robert Slama, Conservatory, Kromeriz, Moravia; Studied w. Prof. Frantisek Cech, Music Acad., Prague. Career: Num. recordings on Czech Nonett, chmbr. ensemble of Czech Phil.; Concert tours in Europe, USA, Canada, Japan, Iran; Tchr., Prague Music Conservatory, 1st Flautist, Czech Phil. Orch., 1975-. Composer of Jazz Music, approx. 20 jazz pieces recorded on Prague radio, some on record. Recordings: Sonatas for flute, Handel; Concertos, Telemann; Suite h moll, Bach; Double Concerto, Martinu; Double Concerto, Schulhof; Sonata, Prokofiev; Triple Concerto, Bach; & others. Hobbies: Jazz music; Films. Mgmt: Pragokoncert, Maltezske Namesti 1, Prague 1. Address: Leninova 661, 16000 Prague 6, Czechoslovakia.

VALEK, Vladimir, b. 2 Sept. 1935, Nový Jicin, Czech. Conductor. Educ: State Conserv. of Kromeriz; Acad. of Musical Arts, Prague. m. Jana Válková, 2 s. Debut: w. Radio Symph. Orch., Prague. Career incls: concerts w. Czech. Philharmony, Prague Symph. Orch., Symph. Orch. of Czech. Radio, FOK; apps., USA, USSR, Italy, Germany, Poland, Yugoslavia, Czech., also at fests. inclng. Prague Spring & Int. Jazz Fest. Prague, noted instrumentalists. Has made over 25 recordings w. noted orchs. Hons. incl: Prize of Czech. Music Fund, Moscow, 1975. Hobbies: Sport; Nature. Mgmt: Pragokoncert, Prague 1. Address Jeremenkova 51, 14 000 Prague 4, Czech.

VALGAEREN, Marcel J F, b. 13 Jan. 1938, Herselt, Antwerp, Belgium. Musician (trumpet). Educ: Dip. trumpet, Music Conserv. of Antwerp, 1962; Tchr's. qualification in Brass instruments, 1970. m. Lea Janssens, 1 d. Career: cornet w. I B Corps Band, Belgian Army, 1957-60; Trumpet soloist w. Nat. Orch. of Belgium, 1961-; 1st trumpet, ibid., 1965-& 1969-; 1st trumpet, Radio chmbr. Orch., Brussels, 1968; 1st trumpet, Art in Brass Quintet; Tchr. of Brass Instruments, Rijksmusick Acad. & Kunsthamaniora & Koninklijk Music Conserv., Antwerp; Adjudicator, var. schls., acads. & music conservs.; Trumpet & piano recitals on radio. Mbr. num. profl. orgs inclng: Koninklijk Music Conserv. Tchrs. Soc., Antwerp. Address: Boniverlei 2A, 2520 Edegem, Belgium.

VAN, Jeffrey Wylie, b. 13 Nov. 1941, St. Paul, Minn., USA. Classical Guitarist; Teacher. Educ: BA, Macalester Coll., St. Paul, Minn., 1963; MFA, Univ. of Minn., 1970; studied w. Albert Bellson & Julian Bream; attended Segovia class. m. Rica Jane Jensen, 2 d. Debut: Macalester Coll., 1962; Wigmore Hall, London, 1972; Carnegie Recital Hall, NY, 1979. Career: num. perfs. in USA & UK; premieres of works by Argento, Fetler, Larsen, De Jong etc.; chmbr. music perfs. Comps. incl: Elegy (solo guitar); Child of Peace (SATB & guitar); sev. transcriptions. Recordings: Jeffrey Van, Guitarist; 20th century Guitar Music; Serenade (w. Vern Sutton, tenor); works by Argento. Mbrships: Pi Kappa Lambda; Guitar Fndn. of Am. Strg. Tchrs. Assn. Hons: 1st prize, Int. Fests. Guitar Competition, 1966; selected to represent Minn. in Bi-Centennial perfs. at Kennedy Ctr., Wash., DC, 1976. Hobbies: Badminton; Ice skating; visiting art galleries. Address: 930 Delaware Ave., W St Paul, MN 55118, USA.

vanACKERE, Jules-Emile, b. 8 Feb. 1914, Heule, Belgium. University Professor. Educ: Univ. of Ghent; Royal Conserv., Ghent. m. Mady Cattebeke, 2 s. Career: num. public confs., perfs.; sev. hundred radio lectures, inclng. complete works of Frederick Delius, P Hindemith, A Schönberg, etc.; Prof., Univ. of Antwerp, Belgium. Publs. incl: Meesterwerken van het Klavier, 1966; Eeuwige Muziek, 1960; De Kamermuziek en het lied, 1967; Claude Debussy; Igor Stravinsky; Aspecten van het melos bij Ravel, 1950; Debussy's Images, 1962; Schubert en de Romantiek, 1963; Bartok's Concertos; Muziek van onze eeuw 1900-1950, 1954; Frederick Delius, Musicien Méconnu, 1968; Arnold Schönberg en Alban Berg, 1978. Contbr. to num. profl. jrnls. Mbrships: Belgian Musicol. Soc.; Advsry. Coun., Algemene Muziekencyclopedie; Correspondent, Music in Geschichte & Gegenwart; Var. Literary Socs. Hons: Grand-Off., Order of Leopold, 1967; Chevalier, Order of the Star of the Republic of Italy, 1972; Laureate of the Royal Flemish Acad. Address: 38 Ave. Jean de Bologne, 1020 Brussels, Belgium. 2, 14.

VAN ALLAN, Richard, b. 28 May 1935, Mansfield, UK. Singer (Bass). Educ: Tchrs. Dip. in Sci., City of Worcester Trng. Coll. div., 1 s. m. (2) Elisabeth Rosemary Pickering. Career: Royal Opera House, Covent Garden; Engl. Nat. Opera Co.; Welsh Nat. Opera Co.; Scottish Opera; Paris Opera; Bordeaux; Nice; San Diego Opera, USA; Phoenix; Boston, Mass; Colon Theatre, Buenos Aires. Recordings: Don Alfonso, Cosi Fan Tutte; Masetto, Don Giovanni; Wurm, Luisa Miller; Uin-Sci, L'Oracolo; Doctor, La Traviata; Tom, Ballo; Brander, Damnation de Faust. Hons: Grammy Award, Nat. Acad. Recording Arts & Scis., 1976. Hobbies: Tennis; Shooting; Golf. Mgmt: John Coast, UK; Claude Stricker, France. Address: 343 Essex Rd., London N1 3PT, UK.

VAN AMERONGEN, Alexander (Alex), b. 15 May 1920, Rotterdam, Holland. Educator; Pianist; Harpsichord Player; Music Critic. Educ: Rotterdam Conserv. Career: Radio recitals, 1945-; sev. radio appearances as soloist w. orch.; World premiere, Piano Concerto, Gagnebin, w. Rotterdam Phil. Orch., 1953; Radio & TV Appearances, Kuala Lumpur, Singapore, Hongkong, 1967; concert tour, Java, 1969. Compositions: Aria for organ; Aria for trumpet & organ, 1949; sonata da chiesa no.1, 1957; Sonata da chiesa no. 2, 1962; Triptiek, for Carillon, 1974. Recordings: Fauré, Piano Music; Baroque Music in the Doelen, Rotterdam; Dussek 4 hand piano music w. V J Sykora; Piano works by Balakirev, 1976. Publs: History of Russian music up to 1917 in 'Muziek Onder Woorden', 1978. Contbr. of articles to music jrnls. and concert reviews for newspapers. Mbrships: Royal Netherlands Soc. Musicians; Netherlands Union Jrnlsts. Hobby: Travel, est. to Far E. Address: Van Slingelandtlaan 26, Rotterdam, 3051HX, Netherlands.

VAN ASPEREN, Bob (Jan Gerard), b. 8 Oct. 1947, Amsterdam, Holland. Harpsichordist; professor of Harpsichord, Royal Conserv., The Hague. Educ: Pvte. studies, piano & harpsichord; Solo Dip., harpsichord, Amsterdam Conserv., 1971; Solo Dip., Organ, ibid, 1972; Pvte. cello studies. m. Mieke van der Sluis. Debut: Concertgebouw, Haarlem, 1966. Career: Num. harpsichord recitals & solo cencerts w. orchs. at almost all major concert halls in the Netherlands, Purcell Room & Queen Elizabeth Hall, London, Bruges (Belgium), Berlin, Frankfurt, Bologna, Padova, Verona, & for Dutch, German, Belgian, French & English Radio Stations. Recordings: Harpsichord solo, Frescobaldi, Couperin, Byrd; C P E Bach Würtemberg Sonatas & Prussion, Sonatas; Haydn clavier trios; J S Bach's Triple Concerto. recip., Edison Prize, 1979. Hobbies: Paintings; Historical Buildings; Piano playing. Address: Zandwerven 54, Spanbraek, The Netherlands.

VAN BAKERGEM, Frits, b. 21 Apr. 1923, Rotterdam, Holland. Musician (flute). Educ: Amsterdam Conserv.; study w. Hubert Barwahser. m. Renee Talens. Debut: Amsterdam, 1947. Career: Frequent recitals on Radio (RONO) & in var. towns w. Orch., piano & organ of classical & modern music; Tchr. & Concert Flautist, Cultural Ctr. 'de Lindenberg', Nijmegen. Contbr. to: Mens en Melodie; Samenklank; Maandblad Huismuziek. Mbrships: Koninklijke Nederlandse Toonkunstenaars Vereniging (Royal Dutch Musicians Assn.); Maatschappj Tot Bevordering der Toonkunst; Nederlandse Vereniging van Huismuziek. Hobby: Nature. Address: Blymarkt 5a, Zwolle, Netherlands.

VAN BARTHOLD, Kenneth, b. 10 Dec. 1927, Sourabaya, Java, Indonesia. Concert Pianist; Teacher; Head of Music. Educ: Musical Scholar, Bryanston Schl.; Paris Nat. Conserv. of Music (Laureat du Conservatoire National de Musique de Paris); LRAM. m. 1) Prudence C Mary, 2) Sarianne May Campbell, 2 s., 1 d. Debut: w. Bournemouth Municipal Orch., 1944 (aged 16); Wigmore Hall, London, 1956. Career: Concerts in UK, Eire, Canada; Var. radio & TV solo perfs.; w. Trinity Coll. of Music, 1959-64; formed Music Dept., City Lit. in 1959; Edinburgh Univ. annual Master Classes during Int. Fest., 1968-; Num. masterclasses, tchng., lecturing, in UK, Eire, Canada; Wrote & presented first BBC TV studio music documentary, 1964; Scriptwriting, presenting, linking, interviewing, perf., etc. in over 25 progs., to date; Adjudicator for first Canadian Nat. jPiano Competition, 1972; Two tours of Canada. Recordings: Decca/Argo. Publs: The Story of the Piano, 1975. Mbrships: ISM; Assn. of Tchrs. in Tech. Insts. Hons: Scriptwriter & narrator fro 1974 Critics Award Best TV Documentary. Hobbies: Reading; Anthropology; History, etc. Mgmt: Trafalgar Perry, 4 Goodwin's Ct., London WC2 N4LL. Address: 54 Blomfield Rd., London W9 2PD, UK. 2.

VAN BLERK, Gerardus J M, b. 14 May 1924, Tilburg, The Netherlands. Concert Pianist. Educ: studied piano w. Prof. W. Andriessen, Amsterdam Conserv.; Piano-soloist (Prix d'excellence); studied w. Yves Nat, Paris, France, 1950-52. m. A van den Brekel. Career: Solo concerts w. Concertgebouw Orch., Residentie Orch., The Hague, Rotterdam Phil. Orch. w. Haitink, Jochum, Fournet, etc.; Recitals, chamber music, accompaniments (instrumental & singers); Prof. of Piano, Royal Conserv., The Hague. Recordings: Hindemith, Kammermusik Nr. 2 Klavierkonzert op. 36 Nr. 1 (Telefunken SLT43110/12); Chopen, Grand duo Concertant, Polonaise brillante op. 3, Son.G mol Op. 65 w. Anner Bijilsma (violoncello) Basf 2521577-6. Hobbies: Chess; Bridge. Mgmt: Interartists, The Hague & Nederlands Impresariaat, Amsterdam. Address: Prinsengracht 1095, Amsterdam, The Netherlands.

van BRANTEGHEM, Luc, b. 8 Jan. 1910, Ostende, Belgium. Professor of History of Music & Secretary-Librarian, Ostende Conservatory of Music; Composer; Musicologist. Educ: Laureat, Royal Conserv. of Music, Brussels; studied composition w. Paul Gilson & Maurice Schoemaker. m. Jeanne de Selliers de Moranville. Career: app. as violinist in chmbr. music trio (violin, piano & cello); has made many radio broadcasts & has spoken to amany works for voice & piano, choir a cappella, as well as instrumental works. Publs: Le concerto pour piano de Bach á Bartok; Variations sans théme (Musique et Musiciens); Le Conservatoire de Musique d'Ostende (Histoire et Organisation); Théorie de la Musique. Contbr. to many periodicals in field; Ed., Revue Musicale Blege, 1930-40. Mbrships: Belgian Soc. of Authors & Composers; Int. & Belgian Musicol. Socs.; Belgian Deleg. to the Eugene Ysaye Fndn. Hons: Kt. Order of Leopold II; Gold Palms of Order of Couronne; Civic Cross; Medal of Honor, Belgian Soc. of Authors & Composers. Hobbies: Collecting 1st ed. musical works of 17th, 18th & 19th centuries; Gardening; Walking; Travel. Address: Dilbeeklaan 11, 8400 Ostende, Belgium.

VANCE, Ann Stockton, b. 4 Dec. 1950, Phoenix, Ariz., USA. Musician (French Horn); Music Therapist. Educ: Assoc. Degree in Music, Mesa Community Coll.; BA in Music, ASU, Tempe, Ariz.; BS, Music Therapy, ibid. Career: Freelance Musician, Chgo. & Phoenix, Ariz.; Music Therapist, Ariz.; Freelance Brass Quintet Mbr. Contbr. to: Research in Music Therapy; Eurhythmics. Mbrships: Musicians Fedn.; Nat. Assn. of Music Therapists; Sigma Alpha Iota. Hons. incl: Outstanding Freshman Music Major, Mesa Community Coll., 1970. Hobbies: Music; Arts & Crafts; Athletics. Address: 1637 E Calle de Caballos, Tempe, AZ 85284, USA.

VAN CLEEMPUT, Werner F P, b. 14 July, 1930, Sint Niklaas, Belgium. composer; Music Teacher Functionary. Educ: Music Acad., Sint Niklaas; IPEM Ghent; pvte. study, N Bulterys. m. Lea Hellemans, 3 children. Comps: music for recorders, piano (incl. Impressions), organ (incl. 4 Inventions); chmbr. music; cantatas w. chmbr. orch.; carillon; (incl. 2 sets of pieces, Dithyramb), (orchl.) both symphonic & wind, (incl. Suite de ballet, Heroic Poem). Hons: De Boeck & Province de Liège Prizes, 1972; Town of Mechlin prize, 1973; Hon. mention Jef Van Hoof Prize & Schnitger Intern. Prize, 1974; Staf Nees Prize, 1975; Hilvarenbeek 2nd prize for comps. for Youth Orch. (band), 1976; SABAM prize (string quartet), 1976; Kempisch Jeugd Orkest Prize (band), 1977; 1st prize, Hilvarenbeek (symphonic windband), 1978. Hobby: Travel. Address: 124 Hertestraat, 2700 Sint Niklaas, Belgium.

VAN DELDEN, Lex, b. 10 Sept. 1919, Amsterdam, Holland. Composer; Pianist; Musicologist. Educ: degree in medicine; piano study. m. Henriette van Dijk, 2 s., 1 d. Career: cond., ballet cos., 1945-47; Radio & TV talks on music. Compositions: 8 symphs.; concertos for piano, flute, harp, trumpet, 2 oboes, 3 trombones, electronic organ, violin; chamber music; songs; incidental music for theatre; ballet scores; film music; oratorios. Music Ed., Het Parool newspaper. Mbrships: Pres., BUMA (Dutch Perf. Rights Soc.); Bd., past Pres., Dutch League Comps.; Bd., Dutch Sect., Int. Soc. Contemporary Music. Hons: Gt. Music Prize of Amsterdam for Rubaiyat, 1948; Prizes, Calif. Harpists Org. for Harp Concerto, 1952 & for Impromptu for Harp, 1956. Hobby: Soccer. Address: Churchill-laan, 184, Amsterdam, Netherlands.

VAN DEN BERG, Sanet, b. 16 Oct. 1953, Pretoria, S Africa. Pianist; Piano Teacher. Educ: RAM w. Hamish Milne; master classes w., Carlo Zecchi, Rome, Jorge Bolet, Edinburgh; BMus, Univ. of Pretoria; LTCL; FTCL; LRAM; UPLM, UTLM, Univ. of S Africa; RAM. Debut: Pretoria. Career: Concert apps.; piano tchng.; recordings for S African TV & radio. Mbr., S African Soc. of Music Tchrs. Hons: sev. scholarships & awards; prizes at Eisteddfods since age 10. Hobbies: Photography; Reading; Tennis; Drawing. Address: 268 Russel St., Rietondale, Pretoria 0084, S Africa.

VAN DEN BOOREN, Jo, b. 14 Mar. 1935, Maastricht, Netherlands, Composer; Trumpeter. Educ: conserv., Maastricht; Trumpet w. Marinus Komst; comp. w. Kees van Baaren & Klaus Hub er. Debuts: (trumpeter): Hat Brabants Orkest, Hertogenbosch, 1953; (comp.): Int. Music Week, Gaudeamus-Bilthoven, 1959. Comps. incl: Strofa per corno solo, 1972; Sinfonia Jubilata per orch., 1975; Birds, a story for 5 flautists, 1975; Hisperica Famina for brass quintet 1975; Potpourri for brass quintet, 1973; Akitob per flauto-violino e viola, 1973; Triptiek, ode to Jeroen Bosch, 1977; Nu Noch, opera buffa, 1978; Logos, divertimento; Eros, for flute, violin, viola & violoncello, 1978. Recording: Spectra per Quintette afiata. Recip., Visset-Heetlandia Prize, 1970. Hobbies incl: Films. Address: Homeruslaan 14, 5216 CV S' Hertogenbosch, Netherlands.

VAN DEN BRIL, Hendrik, b. 12 Nov. 1948, Boom/Antwerp, Belgium. Cellist. Educ: Music Schls.; Royal Conserv. Brussels, Antwerp Mechelen w. Gustaaf Hanssens, Edomond Bert & Hugo Van De Velde; Dip., Chmbr. Music. m. Agnes Van Ballaer, 4 c. Debut: Symph. Orch. Liège, 1970. Career: w. O.S.L., Belgium, 1970; Soloist in Chmbr. Concerts & recitals, 1972; Cello Tchr., 3 Music Schls.; Mbr., Siegerland orch., String Quartet & Piano Trio; Solo Cello, Kreuztaller Chmbr. Orch. Sev. recordings. Mbrships: Int. Soc. of Bassists; Violoncello Soc. Inc., NY. Hons: 1st Prize, Cello, 1970; Chmbr. music prize, 1967, '68. Address: Wittgensteinerstr. 23, 5912 Hilchenbach, German Fed. Repub.

VAN DEN BURG, William, b. 18 Sep. 1901, The Hague, Netherlands. Conductor; Cellist. Educ: Grad., Royal Conserv., The Hague, 1920; Curtis Inst. (cond.), 1935; studies w. Casals & Ravel. m. Jill Olson Van den Burg. Career: solo cellist, Phila. Orch., 1926-35; asst. cond., ibid.; solo cellist & asst. cond., San Francisco Orch.; cond., San Francisco Nat Youth Orch.; solo cellist, Paramount & MGM studios, 1943-; mbr. New Art Strg. Quartet; guest cond. num. orchs; Prof. of Music, Univ. of Calif., Santa Cruz, 1965-. Comps: cadenzas for cello concertos; num. arrs. num. recordings. num. hons. incl: Officer d'Academie (Palms), France, 1937. Hobby: Oil Painting. Address: 820 Club House Dr., Aptos, CA 95003, USA.

VAN DEN HEUVEL, Johannes R, Jr., b. 14 Apr. 1946, Benoni, S Africa. Teacher (piano, organ, recorder, theory & history). Educ: pvte. music study since age 9; Pretoria Conserv. of Music; NAFA Mus Dip;.; NAFA Mus. Perf; ATCL; LTCL. Career: 10 yrs spent establishing Northdean Acad. of Fine Arts (first acad. examining on electronic organ in light music); fndr. mbr., Northdene Acad. of Fine Arts, 1976; chmn., ibid., 1976; Dir. of Examinations, ibid., 1977; Hd. of Music Dept., ibid., 1978. Comps: 5 Little Fugues; Air in C; Medley in F sharp minor; num. studies & peices for use in examinations. Publs: Theory of Music Work Books, Grades Initial - 5, 3 vols., 1977; Aural Trainin for Students, 1977; Famous Pieces for Piano & Organ, 1977; History of Music for Graded Music Examinations, 1979. Mbrships: Nat. Inst. for Contemporary Music (Academic Advsr.); Traansvaal Tchrs. Assn.; Soc. for Music Tchrs.; Int. Soc. for Music Educ. Hobbies: Mountaineering; Philately; Amateur Radio. Address: PO Box 1480, Benoni, T V L 1500, S Africa.

van der BEEK, Andrew Theodorus, b. 25 Feb. 1946, Berkeley, UK. Player of Cornetto, Dulcian, Recorder & other old woodwind instruments. Educ: BSc, Univ. Coll., London. Career: Mbr., Early Music Consort of London, 1972-; The Munrow Recorder Consort, 1972-; The New Excelsior Talking Machine, 1973-; The London Serpent Rio, 1974-; Mgr., The London Cornett & Sackbut Ensemble, 1974. Recordings incl: Instruments of the Middle Ages & Renaissance; Music by Michael Praetorius; The Art of the Recorder; The Art of the Netherlands. Mbrships. incl: Galpin Soc. Hobby: Travel. Address: 30A Scarsdale Villas, London W8 6PR, UK.

VAN DER HALLEN, Arnold Joseph Gustaaf, b. 26 Sept. 1923, St. Laureins, Belgium. Conductor. Educ: Organ, piano, harpsichord, Interdiocesane Kerkmuziekschl. Lemmens Inst., Malines. m. Liliane Leysen, 3 children. Career: Fndr. & cond., Deliciae Musicales, Genootschap voor oude Muziek, 1949; 1st radi app., 1953. Contbr. to: Fontes Artis Musicae. Mbrships: Int. Musicol. Soc.; Int. Assn. Music Libs.; Vereniging voor Muziekgeschiedenis te Antwerpen; Belgische Vereniging voor Muziekwetenschap, Brussels. Hobbies: Drawing; Painting. Address: Groenendaallaan 5, 2060 Merksem, Belgium.

VANDER LINDEN, Albert, b. 8 July 1913, Louvain, Belgium. University Professor. m. Jacqueline Wachsmuth, 2 c. Career incl: Libn. Conserv. of Music & Prof., Univ. of Brussels. Publs: Octave Maus & la Vie Musicale Belge; Atlas Historique de la Musique (w. Paul Collaer). Contbr. to: Revue Belge de

Musicologie. Mbrship: Royal Acad. of Belgium. Address: Ave. de Broqueville 84, 1200 Brussels, Belgium.

VAN DER MEER, Antonious Wiebe (Anton), b. 8 June 1908, Gorredyk, Netherlands. Piano Teacher; Church Organist; Conductor of Choirs. Educ: Dip. Piano. m. (1) Aukje Agter, (2) Geertje van den Bosch, 1 s. Career: TV app. w. bass singer Ritske Numan, 1963; On radio as organist at ch. serv.; Cond. of choirs at Drachten & environs. Comps. incl: Two Songs for Choir: Wintermuggen: & a poem by G Gerelle; A Frisian Song of Douwe Kiestra; 3 Songs. Recordings: Hymns of Fedde Schurer (choir & solo) own organ & choir arrangem ent conducted personally; Songs of Johannes de Heer (bass & choir), cond. P Grin, own organ accomp. Contbr. to The Organ. Mbrships: Soc. of Organists; Soc. of conds. Hobbies: Reading (especially C Dickens); Watching Sports (football & tennis). Address: Kerkstraat 45 c, Velp (G), The Netherlands.

VAN DER MEER, John Henry, b. 9 Feb. 1920, The Hague, Netherlands. Museum Curator. Educ: Law Degree, State Univ. of Utrecht; Dip. Music Theory, Conserv., Utrecht; Dr. Musicol., State Univ., Utrecht. Career: Tchr., Music Hist., Royal Conserv., The Hague, 1949-55; Curator of Music Dept., The Hague Municipal Mus., 1954-62; Curator of Collection of Historic Instruments at Germanisches National-Museum, Nuremberg, 1963-. Publs: Johann Josef Fux als Opernkomponist (Bilthoven), 1961; Contbr. to scientific reviews; Musik in Geschichte und Gegenwart, etc. Mbr. num. profl. orgs. Hons: Corres. of Royal Dutch Acad. of Scis. Address: Günthersbühlerstr. 69 A, D 8500 Nuremberg, German Fed. Repub.

VAN DER MEER, Rudolf Cornelius Adrianus, b. 23 June 1936, Den Haag, Holland. Singer (former Oboist, Choral Conductor). Educ: Oboe, Choir Conducting & Schlmusic, Royal Conserv., The Hague. 2 d. Debut: Singer, Concertgebouw, Amsterdam, 1967. Career: Oboist, The Hague Phil; Schlmusician var. grammar shcl.; cond., variety of choirs; Singer at Concerts, on radio & TV, in W & E Europe, UK, Scandinavia & USA, 1972-; Prof., Conservatorium, Amsterdam, 1975. Recordings: Lieder & oratorio; St. Johns Passion (Grand prix du Disque, 1970. Mbr. KnTV. Hons: Laureate of Int. Vocal Competition, Barcelon, 1970. Hobbies: Ice Hockey. Address: Pomonalaan 22, The Hague Netherlands. 1.

van der MERWE, Derik (Frederik Johannes), b. 11 July 1924, Bethleham, S Africa. University Lecturer; Pianist (Accompanist); Choirmaster. Educ: BMus, Witwatersrand Univ., 1945; Hon. B Mus, Univ. of Orange Free State, 1953; M Mus (w. distinction), Univ. of S Africa, 1977. Career: Sr. Lectr., Dept. of Musicol., Univ. of S Africa, Pretoria; one of leading S African Accomps., perfs. w. major S African & vis. artists; Fndr. & Choirmaster, Musicae Amici, Pretoria, 1970-; Num. TV programes, broadcasts & concerts; Coach, Orange Chmbr. Choir, & Choirmaster &/or Cond., Arts Coun. prods., Orange Free State, 1963-66. Recordings incl: Rosa Nepgen, Hart in die nag, & Cinque Canti. Co-Ed., Ars Nova. Hons: Recip., bursary, Univ. of S Africa for doctoral study, 1978. Hobbies: Theatre; Cinema. Address: 163 Koelman Rd., Ashlea Gdns., pretoria 0181, S Africa.

VAN DER VELDEN, Renier, b. 14 Jan. 1910, Antwerp, Belgium. Composer. Career: 1 st Prod., Belgian Radio & TV. Comps. incl: concertos for violin, flute, trumpet, oboe, etc.; orchl. music; piano music; chmbr. works; ballet music; songs; choral works. Recorded on sev. labels. Mbrships: Royal Acad. of Sci., Lit. & Fine Arts, Belgium; Pink Poëts, Antwerp; SABAM. Hons: Prize for Ballet comp., Antwerp; Prize for serious music, Brussels; prize Visser-Neerlandia, Netherlands; officier in de Kroonorde; Groot-Officier in de Leopoldsorde. Address: Lorte Gasthuisstraat 1-bus, 4, B-2000 Antwerp, Belgium.

van der WYK, Jack A, b. 12 Sept. 1929, Los Angeles, Calif., USA. Timpanist & Percussionist; Teacher; Inventor; Composer. Educ: BA, Univ. of Southern Calif., 1951; studied Musicol., Grad. Schl., ibid. m. 1) (div.), 2 s.; 2) Lucille A Gewinner, 2 d. Debut Timpanist, Pasadena Symph., 1946. Career incls: Percussionist, San Antonio Symph.; Timpanist, San Fran. Ballet Orch., 15 yrs.; Timpanist, 10 yrs., Percussionist, 6 yrs., Oakland Symph. Orch.; Inventor, Baya-Bass glissando attachment to bass drum, US Patent, 1975. Comp: Prelude to the Fulfilment of your Warmest Wishes, 1976. Recordings: Timpanist, Brant, Kingdom Come, & Lazarus, Concerto for Violincello & Orch. Publs. incl: ChoomBoonk Instruction Book, 1974. Address: 6857 Armour Drive, Oakland, CA 94611, USA.

VAN DE VATE, Nancy Hayes, b. 30 Dec. 1930, Plainfield, NJ, USA. Composer; Professor of Music. Educ: AB, Wellesley

Coll., 1952; M Mus, Univ. of Miss., 1958; DMus, Fla. State Univ., 1968; Eastman Schl. Music, 1948-49; Electronic Music Inst., Dartmouth Coll. & Univ. of NH, summer 1972. div., 1 s., 2 d. Career: Assoc. Prof. of Music, Hawaii Loa Coll. Comps: Sonata for Viola & Piano, Woodwind Quartet; Loneliness, 1966; Death is the Chilly Night, Short Suite for Brass Quartet; String Quartet No. 1; 6 Etudes for Solo Viola; Diversion for Brass; Sonata for Oboe & Piano; Cradlesong, Youthful Age; 4 Somber Songs; The Pond; Trio for Strings. contbr. to music jrnls. Mbrships: Pres., Southeastern Comps. League, 1973-75 (sec., 1965-68, 1970-73); ASCAP; Am. Soc. Univ. Comps; Fndr. (1975) & Chairperson, Int. League of Women Comps.; Coll. Music Soc.; Nat. Assn. of Comps. Hons. incl: ASCAM Standard Award, 1973-79; Res. fellowship, Yaddo, 1974; 1st Prize, Instrumental Category, 1975 Delius Comp. Contest. Hobby: Travel. Address: PO Box 23152, Honolulu, HI 96822, USA.

van DRIEM, Adriann Julius August, b. 23 Oct. 1901, Naarden, Netherlands. Violinist; Composer; Teacher. Educ: Dips., Violin master-class & Orchl. Cond., Acad. Chigiana, Siena, Italy. m. Carola Seligmann, 2 d. Debut: soloist, Mozart violin concerto in D major, w. Rotterdam Phil. Orch., Amsterdam; Ldr., Rotterdam, Arnhem. comps: Prelude & Rondo (2 violins); Allegro giocoso (violin & piano); Improvisation (solo violin); Hungaria (viovin & orch.); Serenade Pathetique (violin & piano); Thema & variations (violin & piano). Contbr. to The Strad. Mbr., Nederlandse Toonkunstnaarsraad. Hons: Medal, City of Amsterdam; Hon. Citizen, El Paso, Louisville & Evansville, all USA. Hobbies incl: Para-psychol. Address: Anthony van Dyckstraat 3, Amsterdam, Netherlands. 19.

VAN DYCK, Jeannette, b. 29 Jan. 1925, Utrecht, Netherlands. Lyric Soprano. Educ: Tchrs. Degree, Royal Conserv. of Music, The Hague; Theory & Hist. w. H Brandts Buys; singing w. Joh Zegers de Beyl; Opera acting w. Prof L Wallerstein. m. T Van Duyvandyk, 1 s, 1 d. Debut: Netherlands Opera, Amsterdam, 1957. Career: apps in Concerts & Oratorio w. Amsterdam Concertgebouw, The Hague Phil., Rotterdam Phil., Gurrenich Orch. Cologne; The Radio Phil. Orch. & Capella Coloniensis; Soprano w. Netherlands Opera Co., 30 parts inclng. Marzelline (Fidelio), Micaela (Carmen), Pamina (Magic Flute), Butterfly, Mimi (La Bohéme); Solo song recitals, Netherlands, Belgium, Germany, UK; Regular TV & Radio broadcasts. Recording: Haydn - The Creation. Mbr., Soroptimists, The Hague. Hons: 2nd Prize, Geneva Int. Singing Contest, 1954; Grand Pix du Disque (for The Creation), Paris, 1965. Hobbies: Music; Cooking; Embroidery. Address: Riouwstraat 88c, 2585HE The Hague, Netherlands.

VANECEK, Jaroslav, b. 13 Sept. 1920, Bratislava, Czechoslovakia. Professor of Violin & Viola. Educ: Grad., Prague Conserv. m. Kveta Vanecek, 1 d. Debut: Recital in Prague. Career: Solo Concerts in Czechoslovakia, Poland, Rumania, Netherlands, France, Denmark, Norway, UK, Repub. of Ireland, 1944-65; Concerts w. wife; Sr. Prof., Royal Irish Acad. of Music, Dublin, 1949-55; Coll. of Music, Dublin, 1955-72; Prof. of Violin & Viola, RCM, London. Composer of works for solo violin published in Prague. Hons: Hon. RCM. Address: 28 Wallace Ct., 300 Old Marylebone Rd., London NW1, UK.

VAN ESS, Donald Harrison, b. 11 May 1926, Belvedere, Ill., USA. Musicologist; University Professor. Educ: BM, MacPhail Coll. of Music, Univ. of Minn., 1950; MM, Northwestern Univ., 1952; PhD, Music, Boston Univ., 1963; Study of Counterpoint & Fugue w. Dr Hugo Norden. Career: Tchng. Fellow, boston Univ., 1955-56; Asst. Prof., Music, Carthage Coll., 1956-59; Assoc. Prof., Music, Pa. State Univ., 1959-63; Assoc. Prof., SUNY Brockport, 1963-66; Prof., ibid, 1966-. Educl. musicol. recordings. Publs. incl: The Heritage of Musical Style, 1970; A Listener's Guide to the Heritage of Musical Style, 1970; The Commonwealth of Arts & Man - Readings in the Humanities, 1973. Mbrships: Am. Musicol. Soc.; AAUP; Nat. Assn. for Humanities Educ.; Mbr., NY Regents Schlrship. Exam. Comm. in Music; Pa. State Music Educ. Advsry. Bd., 1960-61; Pi Kappa Lambda. Hons: Tchng. Fellowship, Boston Univ., 1955-56. Hobbies: Golf; Skiing. Address: Dept. of Music, SUNY Brockport, NY 14420, USA.

van FRACHEN, Victor, R R Ph, b. 8 May 1924, St-Ulriks-Kapelle, Belgium. Music-Teacher; Composer; Organist; Singer; Choir & Orchestra-conductor; Commentator; Pedagogue. Educ: laureate of the Royal Music Conserv., Brussels. m. Laurette Bosteels. Debut: aged 6, song & piano. Career: Recitals for Belgian & Luxembourg radio; apps. as singer, choirconductor & composer on special radio progs.; soloist & recitalist at concerts in Belgium, France, Netherlands, Germany, Luxembourg, Spain, Italy, Austria, Yugoslavia, Norway; cond., St. Michiels Choir,

Hekelgem. Comps: vocal music on poems by his mother, Angéle de Bremaeker, his wige Laurette Bosteels & others; folksong arrs.; motets; instrumental music. sev. recordings. Publs. many songs & much keyboard music. Contbr. to: Music & Word; Ars Musica; Echo. Mbrships: Union of Belgian Comps.; SABAM; VEBELMU. num. prizes & awards as comp., cond. & singer. Hobby: Painting. Address: Huize Meizang, Brusselbaan 25, 1790 Hekelgem, Belgium.

VAN GELDER, Hans, b. 25 May 1919, Arnhem, Netherlands. Cellist; Teacher. Educ: Music Lyceum, Amsterdam. m. Else S Krauss, 3 d. Debut: Karlsruhe, Germany, 1946. Career: Mbr., Badische Staatskapelle, Karlsruhe; Tchr., Badische Hochschule fur Musik; Solo Cellist, Radio Phil. Orch., Djakarta, Radio Chamber Orch., Hilversum, Gelders Orch., Arnhem, Holland; Soloist; Chamber Music; Violoncello Tchr. Contbr. to Music & Lit. Mbrships: trade unions ANOUK & KNTV; Mbr., Gelders Chamber Music Soc. Hobby: Thematic philately. Address: Piet Heinlaan 13, VELP/Gld., Netherlands.

VAN GORKOM, Karel, b. 14 Feb. 1946, Breda, Netherlands. Composer; Arranger; Performer on Tenor & Alto Saxophones & Clarinet. Educ: Conserv. m. A A M Struijs, 1 child. Career: Jazz Musician, touring in Netherlands & abroad; apps. w. var. grps. inclng. Anthony Hops, Han Bennink, Willem Breuker, Harry Verbeke, Charles Green, Roy Harris, John Blaine, etc. Comps: Four Movements; Three up, three down; Klimatologie; Poppof; weiebas. Mbrships: European Jazz Fedn.; Beroepsvereniging voor improviserende musici; Genootschap van Nederlandse Componisten; Toonkunstenaarsregister; Delta Sound. Hobbies: Sports; Sailing Fishing. Mgmt: GGM-studio/Delta Sound, Vlietstrat 12 Terheijden, Netherlands.

VAN GUCHT, Georges, b. 23 Apr. 1934, Salies de Béarn, France, Percussionist. Educ: Paris Nat. Conserv. Career: 1st Percussion Soloist, then 1st Kettle Drum Soloist, ORTF, 1957-71; Strasbourg Phil. Orch., 1971-. Recordings: 21st Century Prospective, Strasbourg Percussion, Philips; w. Boulez, FRANTO Records; Marteau without cond., under the direction of P Boulez. Author of book about percussion. Mbr. PAS. Hons: 1st Prize, Percussion, Paris Nat. Conserv.; Solfeggio Medal; Sev. Prizes for Recordings w. Strasbourg Percussion. Hobbies: Tennis; Photography; Mechanics. Address: 24 rue des Fleurs, 67460 Souffelmeyersheim, France.

VAN HARMELEN, Rita, b. 4 Oct. 1933, The Hague, The Netherlands. Soprano; Surgeon. Educ: Univ., specialising in Surg.; pvte. musical studies since 1961. m. Reinier Plomp. Debut: Handel's Messian, Zeist, 1963. Career: All great oratories on the Dutch stage, church concerts, song recitals on stage & on radio. Hons: Prize of the Johan Wagenaar Stichting for a radio perf. of songs by Bernard van den Sigtenhorst Meyer, 1972. Hobbies: work for church & med. orgs. Mgmt: Nederlands Impresariaat, Amsterdam. Address: Jozef Israëlslaan 22, Bosch en Duin, The Netherlands.

van HASSELT, Luc, b. 9 July 1936, Den Helder, Netherlands. Harpsichordist; Pianist; Music Critic. Educ: Amsterdam Univ.; Utrecht Conserv. Career: Radio Perf., 1965-; Newspaper Music Critic, 1968-; Compiler & Presenter, regular Radio Prog., 1971-; Ed., Mens en Melodie, 1976. Publs: Concert Program Notes for var. Dutch Orchs. Mbrships: Int. Musicol. Soc.; Soc. for Music Rsch.; Dutch Musicians Union. Address: 6 Cornelis van der Lindenstraat, Amsterdam 1007, Netherlands.

van HEERDEN, Stephen, b. 23 Dec. 1950, Pretoria, S Africa. Conductor. Educ: BMus, Univ. of Toronto, 1978. Debut: North Bay, Ont. Career: cond., N Bay Symph., Sudbury Symph. & Deep River Symph. Orchs.; Music Dir., Northern Musical Arts Assn., Ont. Mbr: Toronto Musicians Assn.; AFM; Am. Symph. Orch. League. Hons: winner, Ont. Arts coun. Conds. Workshop Scholarship, 1976, '78; Can. Coun. Grant, 1979. Hobbies: Chess; Travel. Address: PO Box 91, Postal Station J, Toronto, Ont. M4J 4X8, Can.

VAN HEMEL, Oscar Louis, b. 3 Aug. 1892, Antwerp, Belgium. Composer. Compositions: 5 Symphonies; Violin concertos; sev. chmbr. orchl. works; 3 act opera 'Viviane'; 1 act opera 'The Prostituée'; choral works, 4 Shakespeare Sonnets & La Ballade des Pendus; num. pieces for viola, piano, violincello, oboe, wind quintets etc. Mbr., Genootschap Nederlands Componisten. Hons. incl: Zesde Strijkkwartet, Visser Neerlandiaprijs, 1964; Cultuurprijs, Gemeente Hilversum, 1964; Cultuurprijs, Provincie N Brabant, 1973. Address: Emma Str. 43, Hilversum, Netherlands.

VAN HOECKE, Daniel Marin, b. 21 Aug. 1926, Ghent, Belgium. Pianist; Carillon. Educ: Conserv., Amsterdam; Dutch Carillon Schl., Amersfoort. m. Trulis Van Dyk, 1 s., 1d. Career: Radio & TV Appearances, playing Carillon; Tchr. of Piano,

Municipal Schl. Music, Arnhem; Carilloneur of cities Arnhem, Nymesen & Doesburg. Compositions: Prelude, Air & Passacaglie; Het Viel Eens Hemels Douwe (Dutch folk song). Mbrships: Duthc Musicians Soc; Dutch Carillon Soc. Hons: 1st Prize, Carillon, Amersfoort, 1963; 2nd Prize, Carillon, Tiel, 1967. Hobbies: Photography; Filming; Travel. Address: Alb. Cuypstraat 2, Arnhem, Netherlands.

van HOEK, Jan-Anton, b. 26 Dec. 1936, Schiebroek, Netherlands. Composer; Musicologist; Performer on Guitar, Lute, Theorbo & Vihuela. Educ: Coll. Dip., 1954; State Dip. in Guitar. m. Antoinett W M't Hoen. Career: concerts & radio broadcasts, Poland & Netherlands; stage & film music; Tchr., Municipal Music Schl., Eindhoven. Comps. incl: 1285 for orch., choir & var. ensembles; num. works for guitar. Publs. incl: Polyphonic Playing on the Guitar; Old House Music; Ancient Polish Music; Polyphonic Guitar Music from Four Centuries. Contbr. to: Poradnik Muzyczny, Poland. Mbrships: Dutch Soc. of Comps.; Royal Dutch Soc. of Musical Artists. Recip., Award for Suite Slave for guitar, 1972. Hobbies: Poetry; Art; Literature; History; Oriental Philosophy; Animals. Address: De Wagenmaker 65, Veldhoven N Br, Netherlands.

VAN IMMERSEEL, Jos, b. 9 Nov. 1945, Antwerp, Belgium. Harpsichordist; Organist; Pianist; Conductor. Educ: Dips., Royal Flemish Conserv., Antwerp. Career incls: Piano Recitalist & Accomp., 1966-; Choirmaster, Alma Musica, Borgerhout, 1967-73; Cond.; Collegium Musicum, Antwerp, 1964-68; Organ & Harpsichord Recitalist, 1966-; Mbr., Belgian Radio & TV Symph. & Chmbr. Orch., 1963-70; Tchr., Antwerp Conserv. Recordings: Musique en Wallonie; Alpha; Erato; CBS; Musica Magna. Recip., 1st Prize, Int. Harpsichord Comp., Paris, 1973. Address: Van Noort St. 15, B-2000 Antwerp, Belgium.

van KAMPEN, Bernhardt Anthony, b. 4 Mar. 1943, Bushey, Herts., UK. Double Bass Player. Educ: Hornsey Coll. of Art; GSM. Career: Art Ed., Aldus Books, 1964-66; Fndr. Mbr., New BBC Orch. (now Acad. of the BBC), 1966; Prin. Bass, ibid, 1967-68; Freelance in London w. LSO, RPO, BBC Symph. Orch. etc.; BBC Symph. Orch., 1972-78; Freelance musician & Artist; Tchr. Recordings w. BBC Symph. Orch. Hobbies: Comp.; Art work esp. graphics & illustrations; Astronomy; Travel; Reading. Address: Borovere, The Chase, Pinner, Middx., HA5 5QP, UK.

VAN KEULEN, Geert Synco, b. 11 Oct. 1943, Amsterdam, Netherlands. Clarinettist; Bass Clarinet & Bassethorn Player; Composer. Educ: Muzieklyceum Conserv., Amsterdam. m. Louisa Stÿlen. Career: Bass Clarinettist, Concertgebouw Orch., Amsterdam, & Bass Clarinet & Bassethorn Player, Netherlands Wind Wnsemble, 1966-. Compositions: Confused Winds (for wind orch.), 1972; Souvenir Nostalgique (flute quartet), 1973; 'Chords,' for 15 winds 1975; 'Music for Her,' for piano, 1975. Recordings: Mozart Wind Music, Richard Strauss Serenade, Sonatina, ete. w. Netherlands Wind Ensemble. Recip. of Vienna Press Prize (Chmbr. Music), 1965. Address: Henri Polaklaan 17, Amsterdam, Netherlands.

van LEEUWEN, Andrianus Cornelis, b. 30 Oct. 1887, Oudewater, Netherlands. Trumpeter; Pianist. Educ: orfe. lessons, trumpet, violin, piano; comp., organ & cond. w. Dr M A Brandts Buys; antique Gregorian music w. A C Cristiaans; musicol. & comp. w. Dr P van Westrhenen. m. Elsebeth de Ridder, 3 s. Career: 1st Cornet, Mil. Band of 8th Reg. Inf., Arnhem, 1903-23; 1st Cornet & Trumpet, 1923-33, Souschef, 1933-36, Royal Gren. Guards, The Hague; Chef, Mil. Band of 6th Regt. Inf., Breda, 1936-45. Comps: 15 Marches for Mil. bands; 4 concert pieces; 10 arrs.; 4 chmbr. music works; 3 orchl. comps. Contbr. to var. mags. Mbrships: Comps. Soc. (Geneco); KNTV (Royal Soc. of Musicians). Recip. Off., d'Acad. Francaise, 1935. Address: Geelgorslaan 5, Arnhem, Netherlands.

van LUIN, Maria Hillegonde, b. 6 Jan. 1911, Amsterdam, Netherlands. Pianist. Educ: 2 dips. for piano; studied w. var. tchrs. m. van Luin, 4c. Career: num. concerts & radio perfs. in Netherlands, Germany, Switz., Belgium, France, UK; fndr., piano duo w. Aus Bonter; co-fndr., Youth Orch. of Jeuneese Musicale, Haarlem; accomp. for flute & singers. Recordings: w. flautist Frans Vester. Mbrships: Dutch Govt. for Jeuneese Musicale; Coun. of Supervision, Music Schl. for the working class, Amsterdam; Royal Dutch Musicians Soc.; Fed. of Profl. Musicians. recip. prize for chmbr. music (w. Frans Vester), Nederlands Impresariaat, Amsterdam. Hobbies: Flowers; Animals. Address: Bronsteeweg 76, Heemstede, Netherlands.

van MEVER, Pieter Adriaan (Piet), b. 27 Jan. 1899, Zaandam, Netherlands. Conductor; Composer; Violinist; Teacher. Educ: Studied Violin w. L Zimmermann, Comp. & Cond. w. Cornelis Dopper & Dodecaphony w. Dr. Paul Pisk, Vienna. m. Barbera

Christina Leguit, 1 s., 1 d. Career incls: Cond. Symph. Orchs. inclng. Rotterdam Phil. Orch.; Cond., Noord-Holland Chmbr. Orch., var. Brass Bands, Choirs, etc. Tchr., Cond. & Instrumentation, Utrecht Conserv. Comps: Num. works inclng. 7 Suites for symph. band, works for symph. orch., brass wind instruments, etc. Publs: Textbook of Instrumentation for Symphonic & Brass Bank (2 parts), 1952; Concise History of the Wind Orchestra, 1974. Mbrships incl: Union of Conds (Gen. Chmn.); Hon. Mbr., Royal Dutch Redn. of Bands. Hons. incl: Kt., Order of Oranje Nassau, 1974; var. prizes for comps. Address: Noorderhoofdstraat 74, Krommenie, (NH), Netherlands

VAN MILAAN-CHRISTIAANSE, Loekie Elsje, b. 20 Sept. 1932, Leiden, The Netherlands. Music Pedagogue; Pianist. Educ: Piano Cl (qualification to teach) & Piano C II (soloist qualification), Royal Dutch Conserv., The Hague; pedagogical Acad., Leiden. Career: Music Tchr. at Schl. for children w. educ. problems. Has comp. var. songs for children. Mbr., Assn. of Tchrs. of Schl. Music. Hobbies: Playing the Irish Harp; Tapestry. Address: Stokroos 25, 2317 EM Leiden, The Netherlands.

van MILL, Rucky, b. 9 Dec. 1922, Amsterdam, Netherlands. Concert Pianist; Harpsichord Player. Educ: Prix d'excellence, Amsterdam Conservatorium, 1938. m. Nicholas Roth. Career: apps. throughout, E Can. (1977), Europe in Salzburg, Bergen (Norway) & Harrogate Fests.; broadcasts on all European radio stns.; tour of Far E, 1976; Prof. of Piano, TCM, UK, 1964-. Recordings incl: Field, 18 Nocturnes; Giordani & Haydn cembalo concertos. Mbr., ISCM. Hon. Fellow, TCM, 1969. Hobbies: Reading in 5 langs; Studying early hist. of mankind. Address: 8 Leven Close, Talbot Woods, Bournemouth, Dorset, UK. 30.

VANN, William Stanley, b. 15 Feb. 1910, Leicester, UK. Master of the Music, Peterborough Cathedral; Conductor, Peterborough Philharmonic Choir & Orchestra. Educ: BMus (Lond); DMus (lambeth); FRCO; ARCM; ATCL. m. Gertrude Frances Wilson, 1 s., 1 d. Career: Asst. Organist, Leicester Cathedral, 1931-33; Chorus Master, Leicester Phil., 1931-35; Organist, Gainsborough PC, Music Master, Grammar & High Schls. & Cond., Gainsborough Musical Soc., 1933-39; Organist, Holy Trinity PC, Lemington Spa, & Fndr.- Cond., Leamington Bach Choir & Warwickshire Symph. Orch.; Master of the Music, Chelmsford Cathedral, cond., Chelmsford Singers & Essex Symph. Orch. & Prof., TCL, 1949-53. compositions incl: carols, motets, evening servs. & a Missa Brevis. Has made recordings as Dir. of Peterborough Cathedral Choir for BBC. Mbrships: Coun. & Examiner, RCO; Examiner, TCL; Adjudicator, Brit., Can. & Hong Kong. Fests. Fedns.; Special Commnr., RSCM; Music Panel, Eastern Arts Assn.; ISM. Hons: D Mus for eminent servs. to ch. music, Archbishop of Canterbury, 1971; Fellow hc TCL, 1953. Hobbies: Photography; Model Railways. Mgmt: The Concert Directory Int. Address: Holly Tree Cottage, Yarwell Rd., Wansford, Peterborough PE 8 6PL, UK. 3.

VAN OOSTVEEN, Klaas, b. 13 Dec. 1911, Den Helder, Netherlands. Senior Lecturer. Educ: PhD; Dips., theory & comp., 1937, conducting, 1944, Amsterdam Conserv. m. Johanna Susanna Suermondt, 1 s. Career: Tchr., music theory, Amsterdam Music Schl., 1942-44, comp., harmony, counterpoint, etc., Amsterdam Music Lyceum, 1946-55; Sr. Lectr., Music Dept., Univ. of Witwtersrand, Johannesburg, S Africa, 1957-74. Publd. Comps: Six Children's Songs. Author: Practische Modulatieleer, 1949. Hons: Prize of Municipality of Amsterdam, for Stabat Mater, 1947; Dip. di Merito for Flute Quintet, Vercelli, 1952. Hobbies: Languages; Chess. Address: 5 Condon Rd., Blairgowrie, Randburg, S Africa.

VAN POOLE, Virginia Cromwell, b. 21 Jan. 1955, Arlington, Va., USA. Bassoonist; Performer on Ranaissance Winds. Educ: BMus Cand., Cath. Univ. of Am. Career: perfs. w. Kansas Univ. Symph. Orch., Kansas Univ. Little Symph., Kansas Univ. Collegium Musicum, Cath. Univ. Symph. & Concert Orchs., Wind Symph. & Cath. Univ. Contemp. Ensemble. Mbrships incl: Mod. Music Masters; Am. Musicol. Soc.; Am. Recorder Soc.; Hon.; USN Band; ALA; Galpin Soc. Hobby: Motoring. Address: 2219 N Roosevelt St., Arlington, VA 22205, USA.

VAN PROOIJEN, Cornelius Anton, b. 22 Nov. 1939, Rotterdam, Netherlands. Music School Director; Composer; Conductor; Pianist; Teacher. Educ: Hd. Masters Cert., Trng. Coll.; Piano & comp., Rotterdam Conserv.; Violin & guitar, Inst. Sonol. m. Sylvia de Ridder, 1 s., 1 d. Career: Cond., Rotterdam String Ensemble, 4 yrs.; Cond.,var. choirs; TV & Radio broadcasts, electronic & expmtl. music for children; Lectr., R Wagner, Indian Music & Electronics; Dir., Stichting Terneuzense Muziekschl., 1965-. Comps. incl: Klinkende

Kleuren; Sea Fantasy. Contbr. to jrnls. Mbr. profl. orgs. Hobbies incl: Geol.; Sailing. Address: Celsius Strat 13, Terneuzen, Netherlands. 4.

van REE-BERNARD, Nelly, b. 24 Nov. 1923, Teteringen N Br., Netherlands. Musician (Psalterium & Clavichord); Harpsichord Teacher; Interior Decorator. Educ: Dip. baccalaureat, Univ. of Toulouse, 1942; Dip. Piano, Acad. Marshall, Barcelona, 1945; Grad., Int. Dec., IVKNO, Amsterdam, 1949; Dept. of Musicol., Banaras Hindu Univ., India, 1969; Dip. Harpsichord, Cons. Muzieklyceum, Amsterdam, 1972; Dip. Clavichord, Belgian Music Coll., Antwerp, 1972. m. Frank van Ree, 2 s. Career: radio perfs., KRO, Holland; Lectures/Courses, Schwartzehuis, Conserv. Muziek-lyceum, Amsterdam, Rotterdams Conserv., Music Schl. Toonkunst, Haarlem, Music Schl. Oss, Utrecht Conserv., Conserv. Sup. Barcelona, & Leiden Univ. Comps: Drie variaties op een 16e eeuwse 'fabordon llano', 1974. Publs. incl: Introduction to the Construction of Hindustani Music, 1974. Contbr. to jrnls. Mbr., Register van Nederlandse Toonkunstenaars, Amsterdam. Address: 7 Kleine Sparrenlaan, Bennebroek Noord/Holland, Netherlands. 3.

VAN REMOORTEL, Edouard-William, b. 30 May 1926, Brussels, Belgium. Conductor. Educ: Attended Geneva Univ., Switzerland; Studied, Brussels, Belgium & Geneva, Switzerland Conservs. & Acad. Chigiana, Siena, Italy. div., 1 s. Debut: Geneva, 1944. Career: Music Dir. & Permanent Cond., St. Louis Symph., USA, 1958-62; Music Advsr., Monte Carlo Nat. Opera Symph., Monaco, 1964-70; Cond., Vienna Symph. Chmbr. Orch., Austria; Prin. Guest Cond., Orquesta Sinfonica Nacional of Mexico, 1974-. Recordings: 32 LPs for Decca, Vox, Columbia (USA), Philips & Genesis. Hons: First prizes in Cello, Chmbr. Music, Conducting & Comp.; Merite Culturel & Ordre des Arts et Lettres, France; Ordre de Leopold, Belgium; Ordre de la Couronne, Belgium. Hobbies: Sailing; Golf. Mgmt: Basil Horsfield, London, UK & H. Beall Mgmt., NYC, USA. Address: 1 Blvd. de Belgique, Monte Carlo, Principality of Monaco.

VAN ROSSUM, Frederik, b. 5 Dec. 1939, Brussels, Belgium. Composer; Musical Director; Teacher. Educ: studied at Royal Conserv. of Music, Brussels: 1st prizes, Solfége, hist. of music, piano, chamber music, practical & written harmony, counterpoint & fugue. m. Marie-Paule Valkenaire, 3 children. Career: Tchr., piano, Royal Conserv., Brussels, 1965-68; Prof., counterpoint, Royal Conserv., Liege, 1968-71; Prof., musical analysis, Royal Conserv., Brussels, 1971-; Dir., Music Acad., Watermael-Boitsfort, Belgium, 1971-; Compositions: Sinfonietta pour orch., op. 7, 1964; Symph. concertante pour cor, piano, percussion et orch. op. 11, 1967; Douze miniatures pour orch. op. 13, 1967; Divertimento pour cordos op. 15, 1967; 'Threni' pour mezzo soprano & orch. op. 22, 1969; 'Der Blauer Reiter' pour orch. op. 23, 1971; 'Requistorie' pour cuivres & percussion op. 28, 1973; var. other pieces inclng., chamber music, theatre music, etc. Recordings: Sinfonietta, Symph. concertante, (Nat. Orch. of Belgium); Epitaphe,; Douze Miniatures,. Hons: Premier Grand Prix for comp., Rome, 1965; Prix Koopal, Brussels, 1972; Grand Prix Paul Gilson, Québec, Can., 1973, etc. Hobby: Chess. Address: Rue de la Montagne 13, 5931 Gerompont, Mont Saint André, Belgium.

VAN SPENGEN, Lilly N H, b. 2 May 1911, Rotterdam, Netherlands. Pianist; Harpsichordist. Educ: Degree of pedagogue, 1932, soloist, 1936, Rotterdam Conserv.; Pvte. study w. Willem Pijper. Career: Recitals in Holland, Belgium & England; Played w. sev. Dutch orchs. inclng. Rotterdam Phil. Orch., Utrecht Symph. Orch.; Many radio recitals of chmbr. music; Accomp.-Harpsichord Played, Bach's Passionen A O, Aldeburgh, UK, 1950; Tchr., Rotterdam Conservatorium, over 40 yrs. Mbrships. incl: KNTV Koninklijke Nederlandse Toonkunstenaars Vereniging. Hobbies: Collecting shells, minerals & antiques; Reading. Address: Hoflaan 94, Rotterdam, Netherlands.

VAN STEENBERGEN, Anna, b. 6 Dec. 1928, Berchem-Antwerpen, Belgium. Manager. Educ: Gen. Music Educ., Piano, Chmbr. Music & Pvte. Studies. Career: Music Libn., CeBeDeM (Belgian Ctr. for Music Documentation), 1954-60; Gen. Sec., ibid., 1960-. Mbr. IAML; VP, Music Information Centers, 1976; Pris., ibid, 1977-. Hons: Chevalier de L'Ordre de la Couronne, 1976. Address: Korte Gasthuisstraat 27 bus 5, B-2000 Antwerp, Belgium.

VÁNTUS, István, b. 27 Oct. 1935, Vaja, Hungary. Composer; Professor. Educ: Comps. Cert., Acad. of Music Ferenc Liszt, Budapest, 1960. m. Judith Gal, 1 s. Debut: 1960. Career: Perfs. on radio & TV; A portrait film; Prof., Acad. of Music, Szeged. Comps: 2 Operas (The Three Wanderers, The Golden Voffin); Orchl. works; Cantatas; Choral works; Comp.

for Chmbr. Orch. Recordings: The Three Wanderers; The Golden Coffin; Hymn to Man (cantata); Elegy, Reflections, Naenia (orchl. works); Inventio Poetica, The Fire (choral works); Suite for Violin. Mbrships: Fedn. of Hungarian Musicians; Art Fndn. of the Hungarian People's Repub. Hons: Art Award of the Town Szedge, 1967; Reward for Creative Art, Town of Szeged, 1975; Erkel Prize, 1976. Hobbies: Re-instrumentation; Rearrangement of old pieces. Address: Petöfi S.sgt. 55-61, 6725 Szeged, Hungary.

VAN VACTOR, David, b. 8 may 1906, Plymouth, Ind., USA. Flautist; Composer; Conductor; Professor of Music. Educ: BM, Northwestern Univ.; MMus, ibid; Vienna Acad.; L'Ecole Normale, & Conservatore, Paris. m. Virginia Landreth, 2 s. Career: Flautist, Chgo. Symph., 1931-43; Instructor Of Music, Northwestern Univ., 1935-47; Asst. Cond., Kan. Phil., 1943-47, Allied Arts Orch., Kan. City; Cond., Knoxville Symph., 1947-72; Hd., Dept. of Fine Arts, Univ. of Tenn., 1947-52; Prof. of Music, ibid, 1947-; 4 tours of S Am. w. N Am. Woodwind Quintet; Guest Cond., Rio & Santiago Orchs., Chgo. Symph., NY Phil., Cleveland Orch., London Philharmonia, Hession Radio Orch. Compositions incl: (publd.) 61 works; (recorded) Symphs. No. 1 & No. 2; Fantasia, Chaconne, Allegro, Scherzo, for orch.; 2 concerti; num. small orchl. & band works. Recordings: Cond., var. orchs., Everest; Composers Recordings Inc. Author, Every Child May Hear. Mbrships: Arts Club, Cliff Dwellers, Chgo.; Fndr. Mbr., Southeastern Comps. League. Hons: comp. Laureate, State of Tenn. Address: 2824 Kingston Pike, Knoxville, TN 37919, USA. 2, 3, 12.

VAN VEELEN, Paul, b. 16 July 1939, Eindhoven, The Netherlands. Organist; Composer. Educ: Trng. Coll. for Tchrs., 1961; Soloist's Dip. for organ & improvisation, 1968; Conserv. of the Soc. Musiclycea, Amsterdam. Career: Recitals in Holland & USA; Organ Tchr. in Music Schl. Compositions incl: works for chamber ensembles, for organ & for radio plays. Recordings: Recital in St. Stephen United Meth. Ch., Mesquite, Tex., USA., 1969. Mbrships: NOV (Soc. of Dutch Organists); GENECO, (Soc. of Dutch Composers). Hobbies: Playing chess; Drinking wine, etc. Address: Kinder Huissingel 48, Haarlem, The Netherlands.

VAN VLIET, Trudy Ann, b. 31 May 1955, Regina, Sask., Can. Trumpet Player. Educ: BMusEd Cand., Univ. of Regina. Career: app. w. Regina Arts Quintet, CBC Radio; CBC-TV broadcast, 1975; Regina Symph.; Regina Arts Quintet. Mbr., Regina Musician's Union, Sask. (Local 446). Hobbies: Skiing; Teaching. Address: 18 McGillivray Cres., Regina, Sask., Canada.

VAN VOORTHUYSEN, Jan, b. 9 Sept. 1911, Zoeterqoude, near Leiden, Netherlands. Musicologist. Educ: Leiden Univ.; Solo Dip., Royal Conserv., The Hague. m. Clasine Marie Blom. Debut: As soloist, 1935. Career: Music Critic, Nieuwe Rotterdamsche Courant & Het Vaderland, 1937-42; worked w. Clandestine Press, 1940-45; Music Ed., Het Parool & Haagsch Dagblad, 1945-47; Haagsche Courant, 1947-72 & Het Vaderland, 1976-; Guest Critic, Louisville Times, Ky. & Dallas Moring News, Tex., USA, 1958-59. Radio Career: Soloist, 1937-42; Histl. Series, 1949; Record Talks Series, 1963-; Mbr., var. panels. Comps: Lost during WWII. Publs: 8500 reviews & 7100 articles. Contbr. to : Algemene Muziekencyclopedie (Belgium); Grote Winkler Prins Encyclopedie (Netherlands); Grote Nederlandse Larousse Encyclopedie (Belgium); num. musical jrnls. Mbrships: Netherlands Soc. of Journalists; past mbr., var. musical orgs. Hons: Kt., Order of Academic Palms, France, 1967; Kt., Order of the Crown of Belgium, 1968. Hobbies: Ancient Books on Dutch History; Curious Gramophone Records; Jazz Musicol.; Reference Books. Address: 18 Resedastraat, 2565 DB The Hague, Netherlands. 19.

van WERKHOVEN, Huber B M, b. 1 Oct. 1944, Rotterdam, Netherlands. Orchestral Manager. Educ: Dr's degree (musicol.), Utrecht Univ., 1970. m. Ineke van Veenendaal, 3d. Career: Music Libn., Dutch Broadcasting Fndn., 1975-79; Mgr., Het Brabants Orkest, 1979-. Contbr. to Fontes. mbr., Vereniging voor Nederlandse Muziekgeschiedenis. Hobby: Fishing. Address: Kamperfoeliestraat 18, 's-Hertogenbosch, Netherlands.

VAN WESSEL, Bernadus Gerhardus, b. 19 June 1931, Etten, Gendringen, The Netherlands. Educ: 3 Dips., Tech. Educ.; Gen. educ. for Brass instruments & saxophones (main instrument trombone); Orchl. Cond., Ha.Fa., 1966. m. AMTh. Abbing, 3 c. cond of 4 orchs. Mbrships: bond van orkestdirigenten in Nederland; Nederlandse toonkunstenaars. Recip. 15 first prizes (3 w. award) in nat. & int. competitions & Prize for conds., Nat. Concours, 1976. Hobby: Sport. Address: Lijsterstraat 57, Ulft, The Netherlands.

VAN WICKEVOORT CROMMELIN, Ankie, b. 4 Apr. 1903, Rotterdam, Netherlands. Soprano; Pianist. Educ: Amsterdam Conserv.; studies w. Cornelie v. Zanten, The Hague. m. E W J Rosenberg. Career: var. Radio concerts in Holland and abroad; concert, oratorio singer w. many famous cond. W Mengelberg, Bruno Walter, Eugen Jochum, Dobrowen, George Czell, A. v. d. Horst, Bach's Matthew Passion. Recordings: 1930, La Patrie des Hirondelles. Mbrships: Royal Dutch Soc. for Musicians; Tchr. Soc. Contbr. to: samenklank, mag. Royal Dutch Soc. for Musicians. Hons: Vienna 1932, Prize and Cert. Hobbies: Walking; Reading about plants and birds. Address: Hollanderstr. 9a, The Hague, Netherlands.

VAN WORMER, Gordon W, b. 20 Mar. 1937, Athens, Pa., USA. Teacher; Percussionist; Composer; Arranger; Choral Director; Recorder Player & Instructor. Educ: BS, Mansfield State Coll., Pa.; MS, Ithaca Coll. Schl. of Music, NY. m. Sandra E Burdick, 2 d. Career: currently HS Tchr. of Vocal Music & Theory. d. Career: currently HS Tchr. of Vocal Music & Theory. Choral comps. publd. incl: Come to the Manger; Make Ye Merry for Him that is Come; That Tiny child; The Captain; I Shall Give Thanks Unto God; A Girl (text of Ezra Pound); An Immorality (Ezra Pound). Publs: Functional Music Theory for the Dilettant, 1979. Mbrships. incl: Am. Recorder Soc.; NEA; Phi Mu Alpha Sinfonia. Hons: NY State Coun. on the Arts Grant, 1975; commn. from BC Pops Orch., Binghampton, NY, 1975. Hobbies: Painting; Drawing; Trout Fishing. Address: 25 Crescent Dr., RD1, Painted Post, NY 14870, USA.

van WYK, Arnold, b. 26 Apr. 1916, Calvinia, S Africa. Composer; Pianist; Lecturer. Educ: Univ. of Stellenbosch; RAM w. Theodore Holland & Harold Craxton; BMus, Durham Univ. Career: staff, BBC, 1939-44; Lectr., Univ. of Cape Town, 1949-60, & Univ. of Stellenbosch, 1961-78; works perf. at ISCM fests. in Brussels, Palermo, Haifa & at Cheltenham Fest.; all van Wyck concert, Wigmore Hall, London, 1968. Comps. incl: 5 Elegies for str. quartet; Str. Quartet No. 1; 3 Improvisations for piano duet (recorded); Song cycle, Van Liefde en Verlatenheid; Pastorale e Capriccio for piano; 4 piano pieces; Vier Weemoedige Liedjies for voice & piano (recorded); Night Music for piano (recorded); unpubls. works incl. 2 symphs.; Missa in Illo Tempore. Hons. incl: FRAM; DMus (hc), Univ. of Cape Town. Hobbies: Gardening; Crossword Puzzles. Address: 4 Thibault St., 7600 Stellenbosch, S Africa. 14.

van WYK, Carl Albert, b. 12 May, 1942, Cape Town S Africa. Senior Lecturer. Educ: BMus, Univ. of Cape Town, 1964; MMus, ibid., 1965; RAM; D Mus., Univ. of Cape Town, 1971. m. Petrusa Trytsman, 2 s., 2 d. Career incl: var. tchng. & leturing posts; Lectr. in music theory, Univ. of Port Elizabeth, 1973-76; Sr. Lectr. in music theory, Schl. of Music, Univ. of the Witwatersrand, 1976-; organist, var. chs.; comps. perf. by orchs. in S Africa. Comps. incl: Derivations; Petrusa Variations; Violin Sonata; Sinfonia 73, Concert Overture; Little Dance for the Piccaninny. publ. var. articles & papers on comp. & tchng. Mbrships: incl. S African Soc. of Comps.; S African Soc. of Music Tchrs. (VP, Transvaal, 1979); committee, Betty Pack Music Fndn. Hons: var. scholarships & bursaries; Manson & West awards, RAM, 1968; Repub. Fest. Competition, SABC, 1966. Hobbies: Electronics; Woodwork; Motor Mechanics. Address: 55 Scott St., Berario, Johannesburg 2195, S Africa.

VAN ZYL, Lorett Elizabeth, b. 27 June 1949, Pietersburg, S Africa. Music Teacher. Educ: Mus. Bach.; Dip., Music Teaching; Tchrs. Lic. in Music for piano; Tchrs. Lic. in Music for French Horn; Tchrs. Lic. in Music for Viola. Career: Profl. Horn player, Symph. Orch. Performing Arts Coun. of Transvaal; Freelance, S African Broadcasting Corp. Orch. as violinist; Freelance in Performing Arts Coun. of Transvaal as percussionist; Hd., Music Dept., Ermelo HS. Recordings: Ermelo HS Symph. Orch. Broadcast for S African Broadcasting Corp. Mbr., Camerata Pretoriana Chmbr. Grp. as Horn Player. Hobbies: Hothouse Gardening; Exotic Flowers. Address: 63 Burger Ave., Lyttelton 0140, S Africa.

VARCOE, Jonathan Philip, b. 23 Apr. 1941, St. Austell, UK. Schoolmaster. Educ: Organ Scholar, Hertford Coll., Oxford, 1960-63; Cert Ed, Bristol Univ., 1964-65; MA; ARCO (Limpus Prize), 1962. m. Margaret Anne Herdman, 2 s., 1 d. Career: Freelance Tchr., Freetown, Sierra Leone, 1963-64; Asst. Dir. of Music, Cheltenham Coll., 1965-68; Dir. of Music, Merchan Taylors' Schl., 1968-75, St. Paul's Schl., 1975-. Compiler, Merchant Taylors' School Hymnbook, 1974. Mbr., ISM. Hobbies: Cornish hist.; Sea & all things maritime; Poetry; Gardening. Address: St. Syllow, 6 Suffold Rd., Barnes, London SW13, UK.

VARELLA, Jane, b. 4 Dec. 1936, Dayton, OH, USA. Percussionist; Educator. Educ: BM, Performer's Cert., Eastman Schl. of Music. div., 1 s., 1 d. Career: apps. on WHAM-TV,

Rochester, NY & WHIO-TV & WLW-TV, Dayton, OH; Tchr. of Percussion, Wright State Univ., Sinclair Community Coll., & Univ. of Dayton; Prin. percussionist & Personnel Mgr., Dayton Phil. Orch.; Pvte. Tchr. of Percussion & Piano. Recordings: w. Eastman Wind Ensemble, Mercury Records, 1956-58. Mbrships: Mu Soc.; Percussive Arts Soc. Address: 331 Nutt Rd., Spring Valley, OH 45370, USA.

VARGA, Tibor, b. 4 July 1921, Gyoer, Hungary. Violinist; conductor. Educ: Univ. of Budapest; Acad. of Music Franz Liszt, Budapest. m. Judith Szava, 1 s, 1 d. Debut: As Solosit w. Orch., Budapest, 1931. Career: Int. Soloist; Tours on all continents; Fndr., Fest. de Sion, Acad. of Music, Sion. Num. recordings. Hons: Hon. Citizen of France & Switz.; Prof. & BVK, German Fed. Repub. Mgmt: Adler, Berlin. Address: CH 1961 Grimisuat, Switz.

VARGYAS, Lajos, b. 1 Feb. 1914, Budapest, Hungary. Ethnomusicologist; Folklorist. Educ: Music Acad., Budapest, 1936-37; Dr. Degree, Univ., 1941. m. Katalin Gálfi, 3 children. Career incls: Libn., Univ. Lib., Budapest, 1942-52; Chief, Music Dept., Ethnography Mus., Budapest, 1952-61; Mbr., Folkmusic Rsch. Grp. of Acad. of Scis., 1961-69; Dir., ibid., 1970-73; Scientific Advsr., Inst. for Musicol., Hungarian Acad. 1974-. Recordings of Mongolian Folk Music. Publs: incl: The Hungarian Folk Ballad and Europe, 1976. Contbr. to profl. jrnls. Mbrships: Ethnographical Soc. of Hungary (Exec. Bd.); Int. Folk Music Coun. Recip. Munkaérdemrend. Golden Degree. Hobbies: Early Hungarian Hist. Address: 1022 Budapest, Bimbó út 4, Hungary. 30.

VARNAI, Péter P, b. 10 July 1922, Budapest, Hungary. Musicologist; Music Critic. Educ: Compositions. cond. of orch., Nat. Conserv., Budapest, Hungary. m. Eva Banyai, 1 c. Career: Prog. Ed., Hungarian Broadcasting Co.; Cond.; Szeged Philharmony; Ldr. of the Musical Sect. of the Hungarian Studio of Documentary Films; Cond., Madach Theatre, Budapest; Ed., Edito Musica, Budapest, 1956-; Music Critic, Magyar Hirlap (newspaper), Budapest, 1968-; Var. activities, Verdi inst.; Parma; Vis. Prof., Univ. of Budapest, 1977-. Compositions: Something to Hum, for mixed choir. Publs incl: Life & Acitivity of G matray, I-II, 1954-55; The role of the unisono in Mozart's Vocal Works, 1957; Verdi in Hungary, I-III, 1962, '69, '73; Leonora & Don Alvaro, 1966; Drama & Music in Nabucco, 1973; Rhythmical Structure as medium of Charracturization in the Vespri Siciliani, 1974. Dictionary of Opera, 1975; The music of Venice, 1974; The book of oratoraios, 1972; Conversations with Luigi Nono, 1978; Conversations with Dallapiccola, 1977; The Operas of Verdi, 1978. Mbr., profl. orgs. Address: Felsoerdosor 12-14, H-1068 Budapest VI, Hungary.

VARNAY, Astrid, b. Stockholm, Sweden. Operatic Soprano. m. Herman O Weigert. Career: concerts, USA, Can., Europe; has appeared in opera in Chgo., Cin., San. Fran. & other W Coast cities, USA, & in Rio de Janeiro; w. Met Opera, NYC, 1941-42; leading roles at Florence May Fest. & Bayreuth Wagner Fest., 1951, 52; has interpreted all Wagnerian soprano roles, also Elektra, Salome, Santuzza, Amelia, Marschallin. Mgmt: Rosset, 570 Seventh Ave., NY, NY, USA. Address: 375 Riverside Dr., NY, NY, USA. 2.

VARON, Neil, b. 24 Feb. 1950, NY, NY, USA. Conductor; Pianist. Educ: BMus, MMus, Juilliard Schl., NY; Mozarteum, Salzburg; Berkshire Music Fest., Tanglewood. m. Katherine Vasil Varon. Debut: Alice Tully Hall, Lincoln Ctr., w. Juilliard Orch., 1972. Career: has cond. Istanbul State Opera, Vienna Chmbr. Opera, city theatres of Krefeld & Monchengladbach, also in Bremen; now 1st cond. (Kapellmeister), Nürnberg Opera House. Hobby: Golf. Mgmt: Paasch Agentur, Düsseldorf. Addres: Am Klosterbach 9, Nürnberg 85, German Fed. Repub.

VASARY, Tamas, b. 11 Aug. 1933, Hungary. Concert Pianist. Educ: Franz Liszt Univ. of Music, Budapest, w. Hernadi, Gat & Kodaly. Solo debut at age 8. Career: Tchr. of Theory, Franz Liszt Acad.; Recitalist in Warsaw, Leningrad & Moscow; Resident in Switzerland, 1958-; London debut, 1961; NY debut, 1962; Subsequent concert tours of num. countries incl. Europe, N & S Am.; S Africa; India; Thailand; Australia, Hong Kong & Japan. Recordings incl: 3 LPs of works of Liszt; 9 records of Chopin (Deutsche Grammophon). Hons: Liszt Prizes - Queen Elizabeth (Belgium) & Marguerite Long (Paris); Chopin Prize in Int. Competitions, Warsaw & Brazil; Bach & Paderewski Medals, London. Address: Villa Vasary, Chardonne sur Vevey, Vaud, Switzerland, & 9 Village Rd., London N3, UK.

VASCONCELLOS CORRÊA, Sergio Oliveira de, b. 16 July, 1934, Sao Paulo, Brazil. Professor of piano, harmony, counterpoint & composition. Educ: Higher course in piano, 1963; Univ., 1973. m. Dina Irene Mazzucato de Vasconcellos

Correa, 3 c. Debut: as comp., 1951. Career: Prof., dept. of music, Inst. of Art, Univ. de Campinas SP & Escola Superior Santa Marcelina, Sao Paula. Comps. incl: Suite piratiningano; Concertino for piano & orch.; Concertino for trumpet & orch; Piano trio; Contrastes, for piano; Desolacao, for flute; Duo, for clarinet & bassoon; Chora Mané, for voice & viola; Concertante for percussion, orch., magnetic tape. num. recordings of own works. Contbr. to jrnls. Mbrships: Cons., Museu da Imagem e do Som, Sao Paulo; Associacao Paulista de Criticos de Arte; Sociedade Pró-Música Brasileira (VP). sev. grants/prizes. Address: Rua Barao de Goiana 76, Aeroporto de Congonhas, Sao Paulo, Brazil.

VAUGHAN, Clifford, b. 23 Sept. 1893, Bridgeton, NJ, USA. Pianist; Accompanist; Organist; Vocal Coach; Conductor; Composer. Educ: Dip., Phila. Conserv. of Music, Pa. m. Frances R. Vaughan, 1 d, 1 s. (dec.) Debut: as Organist, Broad & Arch Sts., Meth. Ch., Phila., Pa. Career: Piano soloist; Accomp. to artists inclng. opera singers (Met.); Cond. & comp. for Ruth St. Denis & Denishawn Dancers throughtout the Orient, USA & Canada; Organist for sev. denominations; Orchestrator w. NBC Broadcasting in NY, 5 yrs.; Over 30 yrs. comp. & orchestrating for motion pictures at Metro Goldwyn Meyer, Universal, Warner Bros., Disney & Columbia. Compositions incl: Four orchl. symphs.; Two tone poems; concerti for violin, cello, piano & organ; Thirty Oriental Translations for small orch.; Two Str. Quartet, & other chamber works, songs. Num. comps. for organ. Recordings: Six Oriental Translations - tapes of 2nd & 3rd symphs. Mbrships incl: AGO; Am. Fed. of Musicians, locals 47 & 802. Recip. approx. a dozen awards from ASCAP. Var. hobbies. Address: 5830 1/2 Lexington Ave., Hollywood, CA 90038, USA.

VAUGHAN, Denis, b. 1926, Melbourne, Aust. Organist; Clavichordist; Harpsichordist; Conductor. Educ: MusB, Univ. of Melbourne; ARCM; FRCO; FAGO; studied w. Andre Marchal & under noted conds. Career: Organist, Melbourne Univ., 1944-46; Recitalist (organ, harpsichord & piano), UK, USA & Europe, 1948-56; Keyboard Soloist & Bass Player, RPO & Philharmonia Orch., 1950-54; did operatic work at Glyndebourne, Munich, Hamburg, Bayreuth, & in Italy; Asst. cond. & Chorus Master to Sir Thomas Beecham, 1954-57; Cond., LPO, Philharmonia Orch. & Turin Radio Orch., & at Bratislava Fest. has recorded w. Naples Orch. & Deller Consort. Publs. incl: Puccini's Orchestration, 1960; Preface on organ playing to The Voluntaries of John Stanley. Mbrships: ISM; Int. Musicol. Soc. Hons: Tagore Gold Medal, RCM; Silver Medal, Worshipful co. of Musicians. Address: Via Angelo Brunetti 33 Int. 8, Rome 00186, Italy.

VAUGHAN, Elizabeth, b. Llanfyllin, Wales, UK. Operatic Soprano. Educ: LRAM; ARAM; FRAM. m. Ray Brown, 1 s., 1 d. Debut: Abigaille, Telsh Nat. Opera Co. Career: prin. soprano,Royal Opera; guest artist, Met. Opera Co. Vienna State Opera, Hamburg Opera, Welsh Nat. Opera, Scottish Opera; roles incl: Amelia, Leonora, Violetta, Aida, Manon Lescaut; Butterfly, Mimi, Tosca, Turandot. recip., Kathleen Ferrier Award. Hobbies: Tennis; Gardining; Driving fast cars. Mgmt: Music Int., London. Address: Oak Hill, Uphampton, Onbersley, Worcs., UK.

VAUGHAN, Margery (Mae), b. 27 Dec. 1927, Vancouver, BC, Can. Associate Professor of Music Education; pianist. Educ: LRSM; MusG (Paed.), Univ. of Western Ont.; MusB, Univ. of Toronto; MLitt, Univ. of Durham, UK; EdD, Univ. of Ga., USA. Career: Prof. of Music Educ., Univ. of Victoria, BC, Can. Contbr. to: Jrnl. of Rsch. in Music Educ.; Music Educators' Jrnl.; Can. Music Educator; Educl. Trends; Music for the Exceptional Child. Mbrships: Can. Music Educators Assn.; Chmn. Rsch. Coun., MENC. Address: 1716 McKenzie Ave., Victoria, BC, Can. V8N 1A7.

VAUGHAN WILLIAMS, Ursula, b. 15 Mar. 1911, Valletta, Malta. Writer. m. 1) Lt-Col. J M J Forrester Wood (dec.); 2) Ralph Vaughan Williams, O.M. (dec.) Career: Author of Libretti for R. Vaughan Williams, Elizabeth Maconchy, Charles Camillieri, David Barlow, Malcolm Williamson & others. Publs: Heirs & Rebels (w. Imogen Holst) 1962; RVW: A Biography, 1964; Ralph Vaughan Williams: A Pictorial Biography, 1972;(novels) Metamorphoses; Set to Partners; 5 vols. of verse. Mbrships incl: Govng. Body, RAM; VP, Morley Coll.; Musicians Benevolent Fund (committee); R. V. W. Trust (committee); Music Info. Ctr. (Chmn., Trustees). Hon. FRAM, 1974; RCM, 1976. Hobbies: Travel; Opera & Theatre-going; Reading; Gardening. Address: 69 Gloucester Cres., London NW1, UK. 3, 30.

VAVRINECZ, Béla, b. 18 Nov. 1925, Budapest, Hungary. Composer; Conductor. Educ: Dip. of Comp., Acad. of Music, Budapest, where studied w. Zoltán Kodály & Dr. ReszóKókai,

1950; Dip. of Cond. as pupil of J. Ferencsik & L. Somogyi, 1952. m. Amália Endrey, 1 s., 6 d. Career: 1st Cond., Phil., Orch., Györ, 1957-58; Chief Cond., Symph. Orch. of Min. of Home Affairs, Budapest, 1961-73; Currently Artist Dir., Hungarian State Dance Ensemble, Budapest, Works frequently broadcas on Radio & TV. Comps. incl: Orchl. Music; Suite No. 1, 1950; Symphony, 1955 revised 1973; Festive Music, 1964; Gypsies from Nagyida (Concert overture), 1972; Hunt, 1976; The Shaman, 1978. Chmbr. Music: Swineherd's Dance, 1973; Funeral song for dulcimer solo, 1975. Chorus & Orch: In Retrospect (chmbr. oratorio), 1965; Kádár Lata. scenic oratorium, 1976. State Works: 1919, 1969; Ballad of Sällösi Erzsi, 1976; Harvest (ballet), 1977. Recordings incl. music by Liszt, & Hungarian Folk Music. Contbr. to Memorial Book of Kodály, 1953. Mbrships. incl: Hungarian Kodály Assn.; Hungarian Musicians Assn.; Liszt Ferenc Soc. Hons: 2 Prizes, World Youth Fest., 1957. Address: H-1141 Budapest, Bonyhádi üt 119, Hungary.

VAZSONYI, Bálint, b. 7 Mar. 1936, Budapest, Hungary. concert Pianist. Educ: Grad., Franz Liszt Music Acad., Budapest, 1956; Vienna Music Acad., 1957-58; MMus., Fla. State Univ., USA, 1960. m. Barbara Whittington, 1 s. Debut: Budapest, 1948. Career: has app. w. all major orchs. in GB; regularly tours Europe, N & Ctrl. Am., & Africa; has made radio broadcasts on BBC & most continental stns. & sev. TV broadcasts inclng. on NBC network in USA; Chronological continuous Beethoven cycles, 1977, NY, Boston, London. Has recorded for Vox, Pye Virtuoso & DGG. Publs: Ernö Dohnányi (biog.), 1971; Schumann's piano Cycles (Schumann - The Man & His Music), 1972. Contbr. to Grove's Dictionary. Recip. of Liberty Bell Award, Mich., 1964. Mgmt: Van Walsum, 20 Priory Rd., Richmond, Surrey, UK. Address: 67 Chambers Lane, London NW 10 2RL, UK. 30.

VEA, Ketil, b. 5 Feb. 1932, Bö, Vesteralen, Norway. Music Teacher; Composer. Educ: as Tchr. & Music Tchr.; Orchl. Cond., Oslo Conserv.; pvte. studies, comp. m. Kari heir. Career: Music Tchr., Tchr. Trng. Schl., Nesna; Comp., works perfd. on radio, TV & in concerts. Comps. incl: Violin Concerto; Piano Concerto; Sev. works for orch., chmbr. groups or solo instruments; Songs; Works for choirs & choir and orch. Publs: Spilleboka, 1962 (rev. 1979); Metodisk Improvisasjon, 1964; Temaboka, 1969; Co-Author, Musikkpedagogisk grunnbok, 1972; Vi gjör musikk, 1977. Contbr. of articles to pedagogical & music mags. Mbr., Norwegian Comps. Soc. Address: 8700 Nesna, Norway.

VEAL, Arthur Edwin, b. Reading, UK Lecturer; Adjudicator; Composer. Educ: Univ. of Durham; Westminster Abbey; York Minster; studied w. Gustav Holst; DMus; FRCO; Dip Ed. Career: Dir. of Music, Bedford Mod. Schl., 1949-51; Co. Music Advsr., Bedford Mod. Schl., 1949-51; Co. Music Advsr., Nottinghamshire, 1951-71; Extramural Lectr., Univ. Nottingham, 1971-76. Publs: Three Greek Pastorals for flute & piano; Modern Flute Pieces; Prelude Interlude & Carillon for organ; Tango for piano duet; Pedlar's Pack; The Sherwood Carols; The Singing Cowboy; many songs, etc. Emeritus Mbr., Music Advsrs. Nat. Assn. Hobbies: Reading unpopular authors; Travel. Address: 11 Glenmore Rd., W Bridgford, Nottingham, UK. 3.

VEAL, Margaret, b. 7 July 1935, Abertillery, Wales, UK. Teacher; Lecturer; Accompanist. Educ: RCM; ARCM (piano & schl. music). div., 1 d. Career: TV & BBC broadcasts; Tchr., Westminster Schl., until 1961; Musical Dir., Intimate Opera Co., until 1973; currently i/c all opera, City Lit. Inst., i/c all choral music, Webber Douglas Acad. of Drama; Repetiteur, Welsh Nat. Opera Co., 8 yrs. Mbr., ISM. Hobbies: Gardening; Reading. Address: 8 Kelvedon Close, Kingston-on-Thames, Surrey, UK. 3.

VEASEY, Josephine, b. 10 July, 1930, London, UK. Opera Singer (mezzo-soprano). m. Andre Anderson, 1951 (div. 1969), 1 s., 1 d. Career: Chorus, Covent Gdn. Opera Co., 1948-50; Soloist ibid, 1955; currently Prin. Mezzo-Soprano, Royal Opera House; num. perfs. abroad, incl. Salzburg Festival; La Scala, Milan; Metropol. Opera, NY; Paris Opera. Recordings of var. works made under conds. incl. Karajan, Solti & Davis. Address: 13 Ballards Farm Rd., S Croydon, Surrey, CR2 7JB, UK.

VÉBER, Gyula, b. 25 Aug. 1929, Kapoly, Hungary. Assistant Professor of Musicology. Educ: Grad., Hungarian Philology, Budapest, 1952; Arabic & Islamic studies, R K Univ. of Nijmegen, The Netherlands, 1963-67; Organ study, Schl. of Music, Györ; Dip., ch. Music, Györ, 1949; Dip. Schl. Music, Budapest, 1952; Degree, musicol., Univ. of Utrecht, 1971; DLitt, 1976. m. Gizella Gasparavˌics. Career: Tchr., Hungarian & Music, 1952-56; Univ. Kib., Nijmegen, 1957-67; Asst.,

Arabic, R K Univ. of Nijmegen, 1967-75; Asst. Prof. of music pedagogy & didactics, Univ. of Utrecht, 1971-; Asst. Prof. of Baroque music, Inst. of Musicol., Univ. of Utrecht, 1975-. Publs. incl: Hungarian-Dutch Dictionary, 1961; Dutch-Hungarian Dictionary, 1966; Hungarian on Journey, 1967, II, 1969, III, 1972, IV, 1975, V, 1977, VI, 1979; Ungarische Elemente in der Opernmusik Ferenc Erkels, 1976. Contbr. to: Tijdschrift van de Vereniging voor Nederlandse Muzukgeschiedenis; Bibliotheca Orientalis; Studia Musicologia. Mbrships: Int. Musicol. Soc., Basle; Vereneging voor Nederlandse Muziekgeschiedenis, Utrecht; Ex Oriente Lux, Leiden. Address: Randwijksingel 10, NL-6581 CE Malden, The Netherlands.

VECCHI, Giuseppe, b. 26 Nov. 1912, Bologna, Italy. University Professor. Educ: Grad. in Letters, Univ. of Bologna, 1939; Grad. in Philos., ibid., 1941; Music studies, Phil. Acad. of Bologna. Appts: Asst., Fac. of Letters. Univ. of Bologna, 1948; Rdr. in Musical Paleography, ibid.; Rdr. in Mediaeval Latin Letters; Prof., Hist. of Music. Mbrships. incl: Phil. Acad. of Bologna; F. Chopin Soc., Warawa; Acad. of Sci., Bologna; Fndr., Antiquae Musicae Italicae Studiosi Assn.; Fndr. & Dir., Quadrivium review, Univ. of Bologna. Author of var. publs. in hist. of music; baroque theatre; rsch. work on musical notation of Nonantola, etc. Address: 32 Via Marsala, Bologna, Italy.

VEENSTRA, Piet, b. 28 Aug. 1929, Rotterdam, Netherlands. Concert Pianist; Teacher. Educ: State Dip., 1951; studied w. Leon Fleisher, Rudolf Serkin, et al. Debut: Diligentia, The Hague, 1955. Career: regular concerts in prin. cities of Netherlands, 1967-; yearly in De Doelen; also concerts in Germany, Austria & France; app. w. Rotterdam Phil. Orch.; Free-lance Music Critic. Recordings: Chopin's Ballades & Nocturnes op. 27; Schubert sonatas. Mbrships: KNTV; Rotterdam Artists Club. Hobbies: Reading; Arts; Theatre; Cinema; Soccer. Address: Kortekade 27b, 3062 GL Rotterdam, Netherlands.

VÉGH, Sándor, b. 17 May 1905, Budapest, Hungary. Violinist; Quartet leader. Educ; Budapest Music Acad. Career: 1935 Fndr. and 2nd violin, Hungarian Quartet, Beethoven, Bartók interpretations; Fndr., Ldr. Végh Quartet; solo recitals in many countries; Master classes a. o. Prussia Grove, Cornwall. Hons: Hubay Prize; Remenyi Prize. Address: c/o Ingpen & Williams, 14 Kensington Court, London, W8 5DN, UK.

VELLA, Joseph Paul, b. 9 Jan. 1942, Victoria, Gozo, Malta. Conductor; Composer; Music Education Officer. Educ: Grad., Malta Coll. Educ.; FLCM; BMus, Dunelm. m. Natalie, 1 s. Career: Tchr.; Educ. Off., music, Educ. Dept.; Cond. & composer, stage, radio & TV. Contbr. to: Sunday Times Malta; Times Malta; Malta News. Mbrships: PRS; Songwriter's Guild GB Hobbies: Woodwork; Fishing. Address: 'It-Tokk' Misrah Kola, Attard, Malta.

VELLEKOOP, Cornelis Kees, b. 10 Nov. 1940, Rotterdam, Netherlands. Musicologist; Musician, Viola Da Gamba, Cello. Educ: Dip., Cello, Schola Cantorum Basiliensis, Basle, Switz. m. Jos Knigge, 2 d. Career: Tchr., Hilversum Conserv.; Cello Tchr., Amsterdam Music Schl.; Doctor Inst. of Musicol., Utrecht, 1968-; Radio Apps. w. Nederlands Muziekcollege; Ed., Stimulus Mag.; prepared var. scores for stage perf. Recordings: Englische Musik für Blockflöten & Gamben-Consort, w. Brüggen-consort. Author, Het Antwerps Liedboek, 1972; Dies ire dies illa, 1978. Contbr. to: Stimulus; Huismuziek; Tijdschrift van de Vereniging voor Nederlandse Muziekgeschiedenis. Mbrships: Vereniging voor Nederlandse Muziekgeschiedenis; Gesellschaft für Musikforschung; Int. Musicol. Soc. Address: 2 Bleyenburgstraat, 3572JN Utrecht, Netherlands.

VELLEKOOP, Gerrit, b. 3 Sept. 1907, Rotterdam, Holland. Teacher (violin, recorders musical direction). Educ: Pvte. studies. m. S Haagberg, 1 s, 2 d. Career: Tchr., violin, recorder, piano, guitar, viola da gamba; Conductor; Ldr., Vereniging voor Huismuziek. Publs: Muziekuitgeverij XYZ De Foorks. Contbr. to: Mens en Melodie; Huismuziek. Mbrships: Vereniging voor Nederlandse Musiekgeschiedenis; Int. Gesellschaft für Musikwissenschaft. Address: Schoutenkampweg 90, Soestzuid, Netherlands.

VENDOME, Richard Andrew John, b. 22 Nov. 1949, Oxford, UK. Musicologist; Keyboard Player; Organist; Teacher. Educ: MA, B Litt., Queen's Coll., Oxford Univ.; Halstead Rsch. Scholar, 1974-75; Royal Schl. of Ch. Music, Croydon; Royal Coll. of Music; FRCO; ARCM. Career: Recitalist, UK & abroad; Organist, Exeter Coll., Oxford, 1974-76; Rsch. on Musicological applications of computer technology. Comps: Motets, organ music & part songs. Recordings: Music from the Dow Part-Book, 1976; The Organ Works of A P F Boëly, 1979.

Publs: Music from the Dow Part-Books: An Anthology. Mbrships: Royal Musical Assn.; Brit. Inst. of Organ Studies; Pres., Eglesfield Musical Soc., 1972-73. Contbr. to: The Organ. Hobbies: Walking; Art; Organ Building. Address: 65A Barns Rd., Oxford, UK.

VENER, Victor, b. 18 June 1945, Pasadena, Calif., USA. Conductor; Horn Player; Music Historian; Music Consultant. Educ: BMus, MMus, DMusA, Univ. of S Calif.; Fromm Fellowship, Berkshire Music Ctr. (Tanglewood); Zeugnis, Mozarteum, Salzburg, Austria. m. Gudrun Vener, 1 s., 1 d. Career incls: Solo Horn, Edmonton Symph., Can., Nürnberg Symph., Germany, Musikkollegium Winterthur, Switz., Freiburg Phil., Germany, Baden State Orch., Germany; Cond., Staff USC Opera Theatre, USA; Music Dir. & Cond., Lamar Phil.; Acting Music Dir., Beaumont Symph.; Guest Cond., Beaumont Chmbr. Orch.; Cond. 3 concerts w. Sommes Akademie des Mozarteums, Salzburg; Artist Dir., Music for Everyone Series & Musica Rara; Cond., Pasadena Fest. of Arts; Music Cons., Calif. Arts Coun., Univ. of S Calif., City of Pasadena, etc.; currently freelance recording artist. Num. recordings. Contbr. to jrnls. Mbrships. incl: Int. Horn Soc.; Coll. Music Soc. Address: 265 S Sierra Bonita Ave., Pasadena, CA 91106, USA.

VENHODA, Miroslav, b. 14 Aug. 1915, Moravské Budejovice, Czechoslovakia. Musicologist; Conductor; Artistic Director, Pargue Madrigal Singers. Educ: Charles Univ., Prague; Pontificio Itit di Musica Sacra, Rome. m., 1 s., 3 d. Career: Fndr., Hd., Schola Cantorum, male voice studio & chorus, 1939-50; Fndr., Prague Madrigal Singers, 1956; Prague Madrigal Singers profl. state chorus at Music Div. of Nat. Mus., Prague, 1956-. Apps. w. Madrigal Singers at all maj. fests., Europe, USA, Canada. Over 50 recordings w. Madrigal Singers, inclng: Les Discophiles Francaises; Lasso's prophetiae Sibyllarum; Gesualdo's Responsoria Sabbati Sancti; Christmas Songs of Old Europe; 2 anthologies of early Bohemian music, 2 of Slovakian music. Publs: Uvod do studia gregorianskeho choralu (Introduction to study of Gregorian chant), 1947; Cantiones medii et renascentis Bohemium aevi, 1966. Hons: Num. awards for recordings inclng. Grand Prix Acad. Charles Cross, L'Orphée d'Or, Acad. du Disque Lyrique, Paris; Feb. Prize, City of Prague, 1970. Address: Dvoreckeho 13, 169 00 Prague, Czechoslovakia. 14.

VEN HORST, (Sister) St. John, b. 12 July 1908, Davenport, Iowa, USA. String Instructor. Educ: BA, St. Ambrose Coll., 1940; MA, Holy Names Coll., 1972; Study of Stringed instruments, DePaul Univ., Eastman Schl. of Music, Oakland Univ.; Mbr., Sisters of Humility. Career: Tchr., Ottumwa Heights Coll.; Apps., KTVO TV. Mbrships: Am. String Tchrs. Assn.; Am. Harp Soc.; Nat. Music Educators Assn.; Nat. Cath. Music Educators Assn.; Ch. Music Assn. of Am. Metrop. Opera Guild. Hons: Nat. Award for String Crusade, 1967-69, '71; Outstanding Educator of Am. Award, 1975. Hobbies: Flowers & flower gardening. Address: Ottumwa Heights Coll., Ottumwa, IA 52501, USA.

VENN, Paul A, b. 20 Sept. 1943, Birmingham, UK. Conductor; Pianist; Vocal Coach; Composer. Educ: Birmingham Schl. of Music, 1960-63; ABSM; RCM, 1963-66; GRSM. Career: Mbr. of Musical Staff, London Festival Ballet, 1966, Sadlers Wells Opera, 1967-68; Cond., Hackney New Symph. Orch., 1968-69, New Music Chamber Orch., Birmingham, 1971-; Mbr. of Acad. Staff, Birmingham Schl. of Music, 1972-; Tutor, Worker's Educl. Assn. Comps. incl: Symph., 1973; Str. Quartet, 1965. Mbr., ISM. Hobbies: Books; Theatre; Tennis; Swimming. Address: 40 Doris Rd., Birmingham, B11 4NE, UK.

VERCHALY, André Paul Joseph, b. 4 Dec. 1903, Angers, France. Pianist; Musicologist. Educ: B Latin-Scis./Maths.; Lic. in Letters; Dip., Inst. of Art & Archaeol.; Dip. of Advanced Histl. Study. m. Simone Viguier. Debut: 1925. Career: Accomp., 1925-39; Tech. Advsr., Music, Min. of Youth, 1945-68; Assoc., Nat. Ctr. for Sci. Rsch., 1955-59; Radio broadcasts, 1945-73. Publs. incl: Songs & Airs of Court, vols. 4 & 5, 1587-1617, 1954; Tunes Court for Voice & Lute (1603-1643), 1961; J Planson, Tunes in 4 Part Settings (w. H Expert), 1966. Contbr. to var. profl. publs. Mbrships. incl: Sec. Gen., French Musicol. Soc., 1949-74. Hons: Kt., Legion of Hon.; Off., Acad. Palms. Hobbies: Lit.; Travel. Address: 17 rue Saint-Saëns, 75015 Paris, France.

VERCOE, Barry Lloyd, b. 24 July 1937, Wellington, NZ. Composer; Computer Musician. Educ: MusB, 1959, BA maths., 1962, Univ. of Auckland; D. Musical Arts, Univ. of Mich., USA, 1968. m. Elizabeth Hendry, 1 s., 1 d. Career: Asst. Prof., Oberlin Conserv., 1965-67; Comp.-in-Res., Seattle-Tacoma Schls., 1967-68; Rsch. in Computer Music, Princeton Univ., 1968-70; Guest Lectr., Yale Univ., 1970-71; Assoc. Prof. Music, & Dir., Studio for Experimental Music, MIT, 1971-

Comps: (recorded) Digressions (also publd.); Synthesism; Synapse for Viola & Computer. Publs: MUSIC 360 Language for Digital Sound Synthesis, 1971. Contbr. to music jrnls. Mbr., profl. assns. Hons: Neil Prize in Comp., NZ, 1959; Ford Fndn. Grant, 1967. Address: Rm 26-311, MIT, Cambridge, MA 02139, USA.

VERDEHR, Walter, b. 31 Aug. 1941, Gottschee, Yugoslavia. Professor of Violin. Educ: BMus, MS, Dr. Musical Arts, Juilliard Schl. of Music, NY, USA; Dip., Vienna Music Acad. m. Elsa Ludewig-Verdehr. Career: Quartet Player, Soloist w. orch. & in recital, under auspices of Jeunesses Musicales, Vienna; Tchr., Chamber Music, Juilliard, 1967-68; Toured NY State as Soloist, under auspices of Lincoln Ctr. Young Artists Prog.; Solo appearances w. orchs. in NY, Calif. & Mich.; Sev. Solo apps. w. Houston Symph.; Num. Mich.; Sev. Solo apps. w. Houston Symph.; Num. perfs., NET-TV; 3 European tours w. Verdehr Trio, 1974, 75, 76; Prof. of Violin, Mich. State Univ., E Lansing. Hons: Fulbright Scholarships; NDEA Fellowship. Mgmt: Barbara Graham, London, UK. Address: 1635 Roseland, E Lansing, MI 48823, USA.

VERDI, Ralph Carl, b. 21 Sept. 1944, NYC, NY, USA. Composer. Educ: BA, Univ. of Dayton, Ohio, 1967; MA, ibid., 1969; MDiv, St. Bernard's Sem., Rochester, NY, 1974; BA Liturgical Music, St. Joseph's Coll., Rensselaer, Ind., 1969; MMus, Eastman Schl. of Music, Univ. of Rochester, NY, 1974. Debut: Nat. Cath. Music Educators Assn., Houston, Tex., 1968. Comps. incl: Mass of the Resurrection, 1968; Fantasy for Organ & Orchestra, 1973; Theatre Music, 1970. Contbr. to var. musical publs. Mbrships. incl: Bd. of Dirs., comps. Forum for Cath. Worship, 1970-74; Coll. Music Soc.; Nat. Cath. Music Educators Assn. Hons. incl: Winner. Young comps. Contest; Nat., Fedn. of Music Clubs, 1964. Hobbies incl: Electronic music. Address: Box 856, ST. Joseph's Coll., Rensselaer, IN 47978, USA.

VEREBES, Robert, b. 15 Nov. 1934, Budapest, Hungary. Violist. Educ: Franz Liszt Acad. of Music, Budapest. m. Eva Lorand, 1 d., 1 s. Career: 1st Violist, Ottawa Phil. Orch., 1957-59; Mbr., 1959-, Second Solo Violist, 1964-, M.S.O. Classical Quartet of MTL; Musica Camerata MTL; Recitals, Chmbr. Music, Soloist; CBC Radio & TV apps. Recordings: Bartok's 3rd & 6th String Quartets; Sev. transcription recordings; Solo & chmbr. music. Publs: Ed., Jean Coulthard's Ode for Viola and Orchestra, 1979. Mbrships: Pres., Musica Camerata, Montreal. Address: 414 Dufferin Rd., Montreal, P.Q. H3X 2Y7, Can.

VERESS, Sandor, b. 1 Feb. 1907, Kolozsvar, Hungary. Composer; Pianist; Music Ethnologist; Professor of Music. Educ: Studied Comp. w. Z Kodaly, Piano w. Bela Bartok, Liszt State Acad. of Music; Dip. for Comp., & Tchrs. Dip. Piano, Budapest. m. Enid Mary Blake. Career incls: Rchs. Asst. to Bartok & Kodaly, Folk Music Dept., Acad. of Scis., 1936; Prof. of Comp., 1950-, Prof. of Music, 1968-, Univ. of Berne, Switz. Vis. Prof., var. Univs., USA. Comps: Num. works for orch., orch. w. chorus, chorus, solo instruments w. orch., chmbr. music, duets, piano pieces, folk songs, etc. Latest works incl: Sonata for Violincello Solo, 1967; Songs of the Seasons, 1967; Trio for Clarinet, Violin & violincello, 1972. Publs: Articles on folk music. Hons. incl: State Prize, Berne, 1975. Address: PO Box 89, 3000 Berne 8, Switz. 14.

VERHAALEN, Marion, b. 9 Dec. 1930, Milwaukee, Wis., USA. Professor. Educ: BMus, Alverno Coll., Milwaukee, 1954; MusM, Cath. Univ., Wash. DC, 1962; EdD, Tchrs. Coll., Columbia Univ., NYC, 1971. Career: Music Tchr., Elem., Secondary Schls. & Coll., 1954-; Clinician, Nat. Piano Fndn., Chgo., Ill., 1964-; Originator of Brazilian implantation, Pace Grp. Piano Prgog., series of workshops, 1973-. Compositions: Phrygian Toccata for Piano, 1962; City Set for Piano, 1968; Duets on Four Brazilian Songs for Piano Duet, 1973; Sev. dozen liturgical compositions, Gregorian Inst. of Am. Publs: Guided Listening Experiences, Volums I & II, 1968; Co-translator & Adaptor, Music for Piano, Skills and Drills (Robert Pace Grp. Piano Prog.) in Portugese, 1973. Contbr. to: Music Educators Jrnl.; Staff Ed., Musart, 1962-69. Mbrships: MENC; Wis. Music Educators Assn.; pres., Wis. Coll. & Univ. Music Education Prof., 1974-75; Zeta Delta Chapt., Delta Omicron. Recip., var. schlrships. Hobbies: Photography; Travel; Sports. Address: 3558 S 92 St., Milwaukee, WI 53228, USA.

VERHAAR, Ary, b. 23 Apr. 1900, The Hague Netherlands. Composer. Music Teacher. Educ: Tchng. Cert., 1918; Caligraphers Schl. Cert., 1922; Royal Acad. of Art, The Hague, 1928. Career: Concert soloist (piano, Clavecymbel), Diligentia, The Hague & Concertgebouw, Hilversum; Music tchr., 1933-78. Comps. incl: 75 works, 1932-75, music for symph. & jazz orchs., recorder grps.; Chmbr. music; Music for solo piano, organ, carillon, str. quartet; Music for oratorios; Songs for soprano, also, tenor, bass; Film music. Recordings: Paysage, Baudelaire (choir & oboe), 1966; Puzzle Book for Piano, 1943; 3 sonatas for Piano, 1958; Music for the film Electronic Microscopy, (Univ. of Leiden), 1968; Sonatine for Piano, 1941. Publs: Het leven van Schubert, 1949; Het leven van Debussy, 1950; Het leven van Bartok, 1951; Het leven van Ravel, 1952. Contbr. to: Haagsch Dagblad, 1960-65. Mbrships: Soc. of Dutch Comps. Soc. of Dutch Musicians; Donemus, Amsterdam. Hons. incl: Num. awards for comps., inclng., Visserneerlandia Prize for Sonatas for Piano, 1959; Kleine Dag-Muziek, Johan Wagenaar Fndn., 1959; 1st prize, Cliqueton Cliquetis, KNTV, 1960; 2nd prize, Muziek voor Clavecymbel, KNTV, 1960; Prize awarded by Dom Ch., The Hague, for Archangeli, (suite for organ), 1960; Viser-Neerlandia Prize, Vivos Voco (str. quartet), 1962; Priamel, Johan Wagenaar Fndn., 1964; Vocalise, Culturele Raad van Zuid-Holland, 1967. Hobbies: Translating; Stereotype Design. Mgmt: Donemus, Amsterdam. Address: Vlierboomstraat 369, The Hague, Netherlands.

VERHEUL, Koos, b. 7 Nov. 1927, Boscoop, Netherlands. Flautist. Educ: Royal Conserv. The Hague, 1950-56. m. Louise Verheul-van der Ploeg, 2 d. Career: since 1959 solo flautist Residential Orch., The Hague; var. concert tours throughout Europe, USA; Int. festivals; Recitals Chambr. music w. pieanist Jan van der Meer, Radio prod.; Tchr. Amsterdam Conserv. Recordings: num. classical and modern comp. Hons: Kranichstein Music Prize, Darmstdt, 1954. Address: Roomburgerweg 14, Leiden, Netherlands.

VERHOEFF, Nicolaas Theodorus (Nico), b. 4 May 1904, Rotterdam, Netherlands. Pianist; Organist; Conductor. Educ: grad., Rotterdam Schl. Music, 1928. m. Wilhelmina Maria Antonia Meeuwisse, 7 c. Debut: Rotterdam, 1926. Career: Cond., Residentiekoor, The Hague, Rotterdam Mixed Choir, Apollo Male Choir, Rotterdam, Oratorium Choir Toonkunst, Gouda, Male Choir Die Delftsche Sanghers, Delft, Delft Ladies Choir; Cond., Residentieorkest, The Hague, Rotterdam Phil. Orch., Udtrecht Municipal Orch., Netherlands Orch. 's-Gravenhage (fndng. mbr.), var. radio orchs. Compositions: vocal comps. & arrangements, inclng. Christmas Songs, Psalms, Pie Jesu, Pater Noster. Contbr. to: Mens en Melodie, etc. Mbrships: Dutch Comps. Soc.; Royal Dutch Assn. Musicians. Hons: Pontifical hons. Pro Ecclesia & Pontifice, 1969; Hon annuity, Netherlands Min. Culture, 1972; Silver Medal, Acad. Francaise, 1974; Knight Order of Orange-Nassau, 1974. Hobbies: Music; Photography. Address: 44 Hofwijckstraat, Voorburg, The Netherlands.

VERNEY, Myra, Educ: BA (Hons.) Oxon; Priv. with Ninon Vallin in France & C Rosser in England, prof: Soprano. ma: Given 1st perfs. of works by Stravinsky, Finzi, Wellesz, etc.; 1st perfs. in France of Walton, Lennox Berkeley, etc., hobbies: mus. comp: philately. Address: 24 Gurney Drive, London, N2 ODG, UK.

VERRETT, Shirley, b. 31 May 1931, New Orleans, La., USA. Mezzo-Soprano. Educ: Juilliard Schl. of Music. m. Louis Lomonaco, 1 d. Career: frequent apps. in leading opera houses, USA, Europe; fest. apps.; concert & recital tours inclng. perfs. in oratorio. Roles incl: Carmen; Amneris, Aida; Eboli, Don Carlos; Lady Macbeth, Macbeth; Dido, Les Troyens. Has recorded. Hobbies: Cooking; Musical biographies; Collecting Engl. & Am. antiques & engravings of famous singers. 16.

VERSCHRAEGEN, Herman Elie Bertha, b. 4 Apr. 1936, Gent, Belgium. organist; Director of Music Academy. Educ: Higher Dip., Organ, Royal Schl. of Music, Gent; Virtuosity-Prize, Organ, ibid, 1965. m. Genevléve Van Hove, 2 c. Debut: Gent, 1957. Career: Organist, St. Josef Ch., Antwerp, 1962-; Master of Music Theory & History, Music Acad. of Wilrijk, 1963-73; Organ Master, Music Acad. of Aalst, 1965-73, Music Acad. of Geel, 1966-73; Dir., Muisc Acad. of Wilrijd, 1974-; Organ Master, Royal Schl. of Music, Brussels, 1976-; Over 450 Organ Concerts & Recitals in Belgium, Denmark, E & W Germany, France, Holland, Austria, Czechoslovakia, Poland, Sweden, Switzerland, USA, Israel, UK, & S Africa. Recordings: Handel, Bach, Couperin, Van den Gheyn; A Verhoeven. Contbr. to: Gamma; var. Flemish music mags. Mbrships: Chmn., Fndr., Orgel Wintercyclus, Antwerp; Mgr., Co. Fndr., Kunst-en Kultuurcentrum Oosterveld Wilrijk; Mgr., Antwerps Bachgenootschap. Recip. num. hons. Hobby: Travel. Address: 5 Schansweg, B-2610 Wilrijk, Antwerp, Belgium.

VESMAS, Tamas, b. 2 June 1944, Simbateni, Rumania. Concert Pianist. Educ: Acad. of Music, Bucharest, 1963-68; studied piano w. Ella Philipp & Florica Musicescu; studies w. Yvonne Lefébure & Monique de la Bruchollerie, French Govt. Scholarship, 1969-71. m. Magdalena Lucia Vesmas. Debut:

Aged 14, Soloist, Timisoara, Rumania. Career: Apps. w. leading Rumanian Symph. Orchs.; tours, num. European countries & S. Africa; Radio & TV broadcasts, Europe; South Bank Piano Recital Series, Queen Elizabeth Hall, 1977; apps. w. Nathan Milstein, Paris; has perfd. w. all BBC Symph. Orchs., Ulster Orch., London Mozart Players, etc. Recordings: Mozart -Sonata K.332, K.570, Rondo K.511, Adagio K.540 & Variations K.265. Hons: 1st Prize, Nat. Competition, Bucharest, 1962; Gold Medal, Int. Competition C Debussy, St. Germain en Laye, France, 1968; Winner, Int. Competition, Orense, Spain, 1971, etc. Mgmt: Ingpen & Williams Ltd. Address: 3 Eastbourne Rd., London SE17 9EG, UK.

VESTER, Frans, b. 22 May 1922, The Hague, Holland. Professor (Flute). Educ: Final Dip., Amsterdam Conserv., 1937-41. Career: Fndr. & Ldr. of Danzi Wind Quintet (Amsterdam); Toured Europe (incl. USSR), USA, Can. & Israel; Prof. of Flute, Royal conserv. of the Hague. Recordings: (on histl. instruments) Mozart-the 5 works for flute & orch.; Wind Quintets by Reicha, Cambini; J S Bach, Trio from the Musical Offering etc.; (on modern instruments) Mozart, Quartets; Telemann, Tafelmusik I, II, III; Telemann, Concerto for flute, recorder & orch.; Schubert, Quartet; Stockhausen, Zielmasse; Schöberg, Wind Quintet; Debussy, Sonata for flute, viola, harp, etc. Publs: Flute repertoire Catalogue, 1967; Studies and Music for flute & chambermusic; The Flute Library - A series of historical flute instruction books. Mgmt: Nederlands Impresariaat, Amsterdam. Address: Royal Conserv., The Hague, The Netherlands.

VESTERGAARD-PEDERSEN, Christian, b. 15 Nov. 1913, Traeden, Horsens, Denmark. Educ: Grad. (as Organist), Royal Danish Conserv. of Music, 1934; Dip. in direction of ch. music, ibid, 1942; Cert. as tchr. of organ playing, music hist. & music theory, 1947; took class in conducting, 1955; Degree in Theol., 1939; MA, Univ of Copenhagen, 1946. m. Randi Andersen. Debut: Copenhagen, 1942. Career: Organist, St. Nicolai Ch., Copenhagen, 1945, & St. Hans Ch., Odense (Fyn), 1946-71; Cond., Odense Motet Choir, 1946-55; Fndr. & Cond., Odense a cappella kor, 1955-67; has given over 400 concerts of ch. music in St. Hans Ch. & num. concerts & radio broadcasts as organist or choir cond., Denmark, Norway, Sweden, Germany, Netherlands & Switz.; Tchr. & Admnstr., Conserv. of Music of Fyn, Odense, 1946-53; Tchr., Royal Danish Conserv., Copenhagen, 1965-70, & Inst. for Musicol., Univ. of Copenhagen, 1967-70, 71-. Comps. incl: Christmas Cantata for choir & organ, 1958-60; Choral Arrangements for Organ, 1964; A volume of service music for use in Danish Churches, 1979; 85 chorale preludes, 1965; many hymn tunes. Publs: incl: Catalogue (2vols.) of works perf. in 181 concerts of ch. music at St. Hans Ch.., 1960 & 71; transl. into Danish, Friedrich Herzfeld's Magie des Taktstocks, 1954. Contbr. to var. jrnls. Hobbies: Ornithol. & Photography. Address: Kgemestervej 10, 3400 Hillerd, DK, Denmark.

VEYRON-LACROIX, Robert, b. 1922, Paris, France. Pianist; Harpsichordist. Educ: Nat. Conserv., Paris. Career: Soloist, ORTF; Mbr. of Int. Jury, Paris Conserv.; Prof., Nice Int. Acac 1959-, & Nat. Higher Conserv. of Music, Paris, 1967-; specializes in rsch. into old music & 1st perfs. of modern works. Publs: Realisations & Adaptations of Older Music. Hons: 1st prize, Harmony & Fugue, Piano & Conducting, Paris; Grand Prix du Disque, 1954, 57, 60 & 65. Hobbies: Tennis; Swimming; Bridge; Motoring. Address: 138 Ave. des Camps Elysées, Paris 8, France.

VIALA, Claude, b. 26 Dec. 1922, Geneva, Switz. Violincellist. Educ: Dip., 1943, Masters degree, 1944, Geneva Conserv. of Music. m. Marguerite Brandt, 1 s., 1 d. Career: Cellist, 1944, 1st Solo Cellist, 1965, Suisse Romande Orch.; Prof., 1953, Dir., 1970-, Geneva Conserv. of Music. Contbr. to: Bulletin, Geneva Conserv. of Music. Mbrships: European Assn. of Conservs. Acads. of Music & Musikhochschulen (Gen. Sec., 1972); Conf. of Dirs. of Swiss Conservs. (Pres., 1972-76) Int. Competition for Musical Execution, Geneva (Pres., 1976); Friends of Suisse Romande Orch. (Pres., 1974). Address: Conservatoire de Musique, Place Neuve, 1204 Geneva, Switz. 16, 19.

VIBERT, Mathieu, b. 15 Dec. 1920, Carouge, Geneva, Switzerland. Composer; Radio-TV Music Manager. Educ: Calvin Coll., Geneva; Geneva Conserv. div., 1 s., 1 d. Debut: Geneva, 1938. Career incls: Music Mgr., Radio-TV of French Switzerland, Geneva Studio, 1944-; Live shows & recordings of works w. Suisse Romande Orch. & for orchs. Comps. incl: (publs.) Symphonic Dance; Concerto for violin & orch.; Symphonie Funébre, dedicated to Jan Masaryk; Humana Missa, for full orch., mixed choirs, children's choirs, 4 soloists; (recordings) Song of Night; Nocturne for soloist & orch.; Epitaphe for full orch.; Symph. No. 2 (rapsodique); Lux et Pax, fragment symphonique. Mbrships. incl: Assn. of Swiss Musicians. Recip. Pro Helvetia Fndn., 1971. Hobby: World lit. Address: 1 rue des Grand'Portes, 1213 Onex/Genéve, Switzerland. 19.

VICCAJEE, Victor Framjee, b. 20 Jan. 1903, Shanghi, China. Chartered Accountant; Violinist. Educ: BA, Univ. of Hong Kong; FCA, England & Wales. Career: Acting Pres., Calcutta Schl. of Music, India; 1st Violin, Calcutta Symph. Orch.; Founder & Cond., Chmbr. Orch. of Calcutta; Organiser, sev. chmbr. music concerts; Apps. in local concerts of baroque music. Hobbies: Pictorial Photography. Address: c/o S R Batliboi & Co., Chartered Accountants, 36 Ganesh Chandra Ave., Calcutta 700 013, India.

VICKERS, Jon, b. 29 Oct. 1926, Prince Albert, Sask., Canada. Concert & Opera Singer (tenor). m. Henrietta Outerbridge, 1953, 3 s., 2 d. Career: Concert & opera singer in Canada; Mbr., Royal Opera House Co., Covent Gdn., London, 1957-; num. perfs. in leading Opera Houses of Europe, etc., incl: Vienna State Opera; La Scala, Milan; Paris Opera; Athens Festival; Bayreuth & Salzburg Festivals, also in USA at San Fran. Opera; Chge. Lyric Opera; Metropol. Opera, NY. Hons. incl: LLD, Univ. of Sask.; CLD, Bishop's Univ. Address: c/o Metropol. Opera Co., NY, NY, USA.

VICTORY, Gerard, b. 24 Dec. 1921, Dublin, Ireland. Director of Music; Composer. Educ: BA; DMus. m. Geraldine Herity; 5 children. Career: Prod., RTE (Irish Radio-TV), 1961-; Dir. of Music, ibid., 1967-. Comps. incl: 2 symphs; 7 operas; Miroirs (recorded); String Quartet (recorded); Heloise & Abelard (opera); An Evening for Three (opera). Contbr. to: Tempo; BBC; RTE. Mbrships: Performing Rights Soc.; Comps. Guild of GB. Recip., Kt., Order of Arts & Leters, Repub. of France; Order of Merit, German Fed. Repub. Hobbies: Philately; Swimming. Address: 29 Lawnswood Pk., Stillorgan. Co. Dublin, Repub. of Ireland.

VIDAL, Augustus Olatunji, b. 20 Feb. 1942, Lagos, Nigeria. Ethno-musicologist. Educ: BA, UCLA, USA; MA (Ethnomusicol), ibid. m. Georgina Ajoke. Career incl: Film on African Music for US Info. Serv., 1971; Video-tape on African Music, Sonoma State Coll., Calif.; TV Prog. of African Music & Dance from Santa Rosa, Calif.; Am. Coun. on Educ. Int. Seminar Series, 1972-73, 1973-74; Sev. stages perfs. in African Music & Dance, Contbr. to African. Arts. Mbrships: AAUP; African Studies Assn., USA, Calif. Music Tchrs. Assn.; Soc. for Ethnomusicol.; Educators to Africa Assn. Hobbies: Soccer; Lawn Tennis; Table tennis; Youth work; Swimming. Address: 1700 26th Ave., Oakland, CA 94601, USA.

VIDOVSZKY, László, b. 25 Feb. 1944, Békéscsaba, Hungary. Composer. Educ: HS of Music, Budapest, 1962-67; GRM, Paris, France, 1970-71. Career: concerts w. Uj Zenei Studio Ensemble, Hungary, 1971-, Musée de l'Art Moderne, Paris, France, 1974, Krakow, Warsaw, Poland, 1973, Warsaw Autumn, 1975. Prin. comps. incl: Kettös (for 2 prepared pianos), 1968-72; Autokoncert, 1972; 405, 1972; Undisturbed (w. Zoltán Jeney & László Sary), 1974; Schroeder halála, 1975; Circus, 1974-75; Hommage á Kurtág (w. others), 1975. Fndn. Mbr., Uj Zenei Studio, 1970-. Address: H-1124 Budapest, Vércse u. 17, Hungary.

VIERTEL, Karl-Heinz Rudolph, b. 29 Nov. 1929, Leipzig, Germany. Musicologist. Educ: Music Acad., Leipzig; Asst., Opera House, Leipzig; Exam. Opera Dir., 1954. m. Elisabeth Breul, 1 d. Debut: Frankfurt/Oder 1954, Altenburg, 1960-63, Gera 1963-68. Career: Karl Marx Univ. Leipzig, 1960-63, 1968-71. Grad. Dip. Phil., 1968; Dr. Phil., 1971. Readings Karl Marx Univ., 1971-; Music Acad., Leipzig, 1975-; Guest Readings, Univ. of Ljubljana, Warsaw, Krakow & Poznan. Publs: Chief Ed., Musica alla corte sassone-polacca. Contbr. to Music & Soc., Berlin. Mbrships: Union of Comps. & Musicologists, German Dem. Repub.; Dist. Bd., Leipzig; Union Theatre Workers. Hons: Hon. Medal, Union of Comps. & Musicologists, 1975. Mgmt: Kunstler-Agentur, German Dem. Repub. Krausenstrasse 9-10, 108 Berlin. Address: Kietzstrasse 9, DDR-7033, Leipzig, German Dem. Repub.

VIERU, Anatol, b. 8 June 1926, Iasi, Romania. Composer; Conductro; Musicologist; Professor. Educ: Bucharest Conserv. (w. Klepper, Silverstri & Rogalski); Moscow Conserv. (w. Khatchaturian). m. Nina Vieru, 2 c. Debut: Enescu Competition, 1946. Career: Cond., Nat. Theatre, Bucharest, 1948; Ed., 'Muzica' (review), 1950; Tchr., Bucharest Conserv., orchestrationclass, 1954-; ibid, Composition, 1956-; comp.-in-Res., W. Berlin, 1973; Cond., Chmbr. Concerts at the Bucharest Phil. Comps. incl: Concerto for Orch., 1954; Concerto for Cello, 1962; Violin Concerto, 1964; 3 Symphs., 1967-78; Jonah, (opera), 1971-6; Electronic Music, The

Stoneland, 1972; The Birth of a Language, piano (4 hands), 1971; 3 String Quartets, 1955-73; Mosaiques, 1972. Recordings: Jeux for piano & orch.; Violin Concerto; Flute Concerto; Cello Concerto; Clepsidra I & II; Stoneland; Museum Music. Mbrships: Union of Romanian Comps. Hons: Nat. Romanian Prize, 1949; Reine Marie Jose Prize, 1962; Enesco Prize of Romanian Nat. Acad., 1967; Union of Romanian Comps. prize, 1977 & '78; Award of the Koussevitsky Fndn., Wash, 1966. Address: Bucharest 70734, str. Stirbei Voda 68, op. 3, Romania.

VIETHEER, Erich Walter, b. 13 Jan. 1930, Toowoomba, Qld., Aust. Singing Teacher. Educ: studied w. (England) Clive Carey, Bruce Boyce, Vera Rozsa, (Germany) Hochschule für Musik, Munich; German student exchange scholarship to study w. Gerhard Hüsch & Loote Lehmann. Debut: Wigmore Hall, London, 1966. Career: Eng. Opera Group & Glydebourne Opera, 1961; recital tours, Aust., Far East, Germany, Sweden, UK; Artist in Residence, NSW Conserv., 1975; lecture tours for Aust. Fed. of Music Tchrs., 1976-78; Artist in Residence, W Aust. Univ., Perth. Mbrship: Pres., Mastersingers Guild, Perth, WA. Hobbies: Breeding Tropical Fish; Restoring Antiques. Address: 176 Iverson Rd., London NW6 2HL, UK.

VIG, Rudolf, b. 25 June 1929, Bogács, Hungary. Ethnomusicologist. Educ: Budapest Musical Gymnasium; Liszt Ferenc High Schl. of Music, Budapest; P I Tchaikovsky Conserv., Moscow; Dip. of Merit in Cond. & Musicol., 1954. m. Anna Kozak, 6 c. Career: Cond., Hungarian State Folk Ensemble, 1954-58; Concerts in Budapest, Paris, Brussels, Amsterdam, Moscow & Leningrad; on Staff at Folk Music Rsch. Grp., Inst. of Musicol., Hungarian Acad. of Sci., 1958-. Recordings: Contemporary Hungarian Choir Comps., Pathe Marconi, Paris, Phillips, Brussels; Gypsy Folk Songs; Hungarian Gypsy Folk Songs. Publs: Ed., Nepek Dalai (Songs of Peoples), 1949; Co-Ed., Ungarische Volksliedtypen, 1964; Gypsy Folk Songs from the Béla Bartók & Zoltán Kodály Collections, 1974. Hons: Grand Prix, Art Fest., 1976; Min. of Ed., Tokyo. Contbr. to Studia Musicologica. Address: H-1029 Budapest, Huba Vezér u 55, Hungary.

VIGAY, Denis, b. 14 May 1926, Brixton, UK. Musician; Violoncellist. Educ: FRAM; ARCM. m. Greta Vigay, 1 s., 2 d. Debut: Wigmore Hall, 1959. Career: Prin. Cello & Soloist, Royal Liverpool Phil. Orch.; Prin. Cello & Soloist, BBC Symph. Orch.; Mbr. of The Acad. of St. Martin-in-The-Fields Chmbr. Ensemble & MKusica da Camera. Recordings w. The Acad. of St. Martin-in-the-Fields; BBC Symph. Orch.; Philharmonia Orch.; Brit. Coun. Mbr. ISM. Hobbies: Sailing; Walking; Reading. Address: 12 Chesterfield Rd., London N3, UK.

VIGNOLES, Roger Hutton, b. 12 July 1945, Cheltenham, UK. Piano Accompanist. Educ: Magdalene Coll., Cambridge, 1962-66; BA, BMus (Cantab); ARCM. m. Tessa Henderson. Debut: Purcell Room, London, 1967. Career: Recitals, esp. London, 1967- inclng. accompanying Rita Streich, Gwyneth Jones, John Shirley-Quirk, Hughes Cuenod, etc.; Repetiteur, Royal Opera House, Covent Gdn., 1969-71; BBC Radio & TV broadcasts. Recordings: Trios by Brahms, Beethoven, Applebaum (Montagnana Trio); Songs by Frank Bridge. Mbr., ISM. Hobbies: Travel; Sailing; Painting. Address: 16a Broadlands Rd., Highgate, London N6 4AN, UK.

VIKÁR, László, b. June 1929, Szombathely, Hungary. Ethnomusicologist. Educ: PhD; Music Tchr. Dip.; ethnomusicol. Dip. m. Katalin Forrai, 2 s., 1 d. Career: Mbr., Folk Music Rsch. Grp., Inst. Musicol., Hungarian Acad. Scis.; Rsch., Hungary, Czech., Romania, China, Korea & esp. among Finno-Ugrian & Turkic peoples, USSR. Prof., Liszt Acad. of Music; Hd. of Folk Music Archives, Inst. of Musicology, Hungarian Acad. Scis. Publs: Cseremisz Nepdalok, 1967; Cheremis Folksongs, 1971; Ed., Finno-Ugrian Music, 1972; Ed., Bela Bartok's Folk Music Research in Turkey, 1976; Chuvash Folksongs, 1978; Ed., Music of the Tatar People, 1978. Contbr. to: Studia Musicologica, Hungarian Acad. Scis.; Jrnl., Int. Folk Music Coun. Mbrships: VP, Int. Kodály Soc.; VP, Hungarian Kodály Soc. Hons: Academic Prize, 1976; Erkel Art Prize, 1977. Address: 1054 Budapest, Bajczy 60, Hungary. 3.

VILEC, Michal, b. 6 Aug. 1902, Bradejovska Nova Ves, Czechoslovakia. Composer; Conductor; Pianist. Educ: Master of Music Arts, Acad. of Music Arts, Budapest, Hungary, 1924. m. Paula Vilec, 1 child. Debut (as Cond.): Wiener Neustadt, Austria. Career: Theatre Cond., Graz, Austria, Bautzen, Germany, & other small towns in Middle Europe; Dir. & chief Cond. of Music Broadcasting, Kosice, Czechoslovakia; Dir. of Bratislava Conserv., Czechoslovakia; now ret'd. compositions incl: Sonata; Two Voice Inventions; Piano Play Schl.; Sonata for 'Cello & Piano; Chmbr. Music; Str. Quartet; Piano Trio; Summer

Recordings for Wind Instruments & Piano; Prelude Eroico for Symph. Orch.; Vocal compositions for Soloists & choirs; 4 Hands Compositions for Piano. Publs: Piano School, 1952. Mbrships: Assn. of Slovak Composers; Slovak Musical Fund. Hons: State Prize for Outstanding Work, 1962; A Meritorious Artists, 1972. Hobbies: Touring; Reading. Address: Skoráncia St. 1/b., Bratislava, Czechoslovakia.

VILLAUME, Jack Waldemar (John Villaume), b. 11 Feb. 1907, Blackall, Qld., Australia. Schools Music Specialist; Conductor; Critic; Pianist; Organist; Accompanist; Composer; Teacher. Educ: LRSM (Pfte.), 1926; LTCL (Pfte. perf.). 1930; Study of violin w. L d'Hage; Singing, Organ & Choral conducting, w. E R Streeten; Composition, w. Dr William Lovelock. m. Doreen May Morgan, 1 s. Career: Solo Piano Recitals, Australian Braodcasting Commission Brisbane Studios, 1938-42; Compere, weekly recording sessions, ibid, 1942-49 & later; Choral Cond., 1930-; Cond., children's choirs, concerts & broadcasts, 1966-76; Guest Cond., Qld. Primary Schls. Music Fest., 1972-73; Adjudicator, music fests. jAustralia, 30 yrs.; Music Specialist, Carmel Coll. for Girls, Wynnum, Qld., 1974-76. Comps. incl: Old John Bax, Aust. ballad for children. Recordings: Tomorrow is A-Dying (w. The Adelaide Singers); Dreamspun, By The Moongate, Carey's Catwalk & The Salutation (w. James Christiansen). Assoc. Music Critic, Courier-Mail, Brisbane. Mbrship: Assoc. Mbr., Australasian Perf. Rights Assn. Ltd. Hons: 1st Prize, Song Competition, Aust. Perf. Rights Assn./Aust. Broadcasting Commission, 1953; 2nd Prize, ibid, 1959. Hobbies: Swimming; Growing roses; Natural history; Research into family history. Address: 27 Herbert St., Toowong, Qld. 4066, Aust.

VINCENT, Lina, b. 25 Jan. 1923, Peshawar, India. Violinist. Educ: studied w. Adila Fachiri & Albert Sammons. m. C T Vincent, 2 s., 1· d. Career: extensive concert tours for CEMA; Ldr., London Music Grp. (founded by Thurston Dart); num. recitals; currently Mbr., Music Dept., St. Mary's & St. Paul's Trng. Colls., Cheltenham. Address: 10 Christ Ch. Rd., Cheltenham, Glos., UK.

VINCENT, Robert William, b. 14 Aug. 1941, Medan, Sumatra, Indonesia. Organist & Harpsichordist. Educ: MA, Magdalen Coll., Oxford; GSM, London; FRCO. m. Sarah Elizabeth Waddle, 1 s., 2 d. Career: Prof., GSM, 1967-77; Organist & Master of Music, St. Martin-in-the-Fields, 1967-77; Organist & Master of the Choristers, Manchester Cathedral, 1977-. Recordings: Organ Music From St. Martin-in-the-Fields. Mbrships: ISM; RSCM; RCO; Rotary. Hobbies: Reading; Gardening; Winemaking; Cooking. Address: The Cathedral, Manchester M3 1SX, UK.

VINCZE, Ottó, b. 9 July 1906, Visegrád, Hungary. Composer; Conductor. Educ: Comp., ch. mus, cond., Franz Liszt Acad. of Music. m. Amalia Tóth, 3 d. Debut: Recital of the 'Falun' in the Village suite for Orch. at 1953 Concert-Orch., Budapest, cond. V Vaszy. Career: Cond., sev. theatres & orchs., film recordings & recordings, 1928-45; Cond., Radio Orch., 1943-45; Musical Dir., Nat. Theatre at Miskolc, 1946-49; Cond., Operett-Theatre & Petofi Theatre, 1957-63. Compositions: (musicals) All About a Specked Calf., Hung. Ed.; Visitor from Paris, H E & Henschel Verlag, Berlin; Adventure at Buda, Disappointments, Barber of Seville, H E; (orchestral) Capriccio, Serenade, Rhapsody, Rhapsody for Flute & Orch.; Let us Remember the Ancients, suite; Fantastic Dances, etc. Var. recordings of Bolero, & sev. light songs. Mbrships: Foundation for Music; Soc. of Hungarian Musicians. Hons: Erkel Prize, 1955 & 57; Prize of the Symphonic Light music contest of the Radio Brussels, 1956; Prize for Quality of the Hungarian Radio, 1959, '64, '66. Hobbies: Car; Bicycle; Travel. Address: Rajk Laszlo 5, 1136 Budapest, Hungary.

VINHOLES, L C, b. 10 Apr. 1933, Pelotas, RS, Brazil. Composer; Lecturer. Educ: Pro-Arte Schl. of Music, São Paulo, 1953-57; Brazilian Inst. of Philos.; Pro Arte Int. Sems. of Music, Teresopolis, Rio de Janeiro; Bahia Univ., Salvador; Tokyo. Univ. of Fine Arts & Music; Music Dept., Imperial Palace, Tokyc. m. Young Soon Vinholes, 1 s, 1 d. Career: Barzilian Deleg. 1961 Tokyo E-W Music Encounter, 1961; Brazilian Observer num. Symposiums inclng: Int. Symposium of Specialists on Art in E & W by UNESCO & AICA, Tokyo, 1966. Comps. incl: Time-Space IX, 1975. Publs: Introduction to Acoustics, 1957 (w. Brito & Novaes). Contbr. to var. publs. Mbr. num. profl. orgs. Hons: Order of Sacred Treasure 5th Class by His Majesty The Emperor of Japan. Hobbies: Concret Poetry; Fishing. Address: Brazilian Embassy, 255 Albert St., Suite 900, Ottawa, Ont., Can. K1P 6A9.

VINQUIST, Mary, b. 17 July 1938, Red Wing, Minn., USA. Musicoligist; Teacher of Recorder. Educ: BMus, St. Olaf Coll.;

MA, Ind. Univ.; PhD, Univ. of NC; Tchrs. Cert. Am.. Recorder Soc. Career: Pvte. Music Tchr., specialising in tchng. of young children; Pt.-time instructor, Applied Music, Univ. of NC. Asst. Prof., Pt.-time, w. Chester State Coll. Publs: Co-ed., Performance Practice, A Bibliography, 1971. Contbr. to: Current Musicol. Mbrships: Student Mbr. of Coun., Sec. of local chapt., Am. Musicol. Soc.; Music Dir., local chapt., Am. Recorder Soc.; Chapel Hill Music Tchrs. Assn.; Phi Beta Kappa, 1960, Recip. of NDEA Title II Grad. Study Grant, 1969. Hobbies: Athletics; Politics. Address: 166 Hamilton Rd., Chapel Hill, NC 27514, USA.

VINSON, Harvey Lee, b. 9 Mar. 1943, San Diego, Calif., USA. Musician (Guitar; Piano). Educ: Univ. Tex.; Queens Coll.; Juilliard Schl. Music. Music. Publs. incl: B B King, 1970; A Folksinger's Guide to the Classical Guitar, 1970; Rock Chord Guide, 1970; The Jefferson Airplane, 1971; Rhythm Guitar, 1971; Chords & Progressions, 1972; Classic Guitar Pieces, 1972; Lead Guitar, 1972; Classic Guitar Duets, 1973; Bass Guitar, 1973; The Complete Guitar Scale Manual, 1973; The Early American Songbook, 1974; Bass Guitar Scale Manual, 1975. Mbrships: incl: Phi Eta Sigma; ASCAP; Am. Fedn. Musicians. Hobbies: Sailing; Skiing; Chess. Address: PO Box 17994, Portland, OR97217, USA.

VINTILA, George, b. 30 Mar. 1924, Husi, Romania. Orchestra & Opera Conductor. Educ: Conserv. of Iasi; studied chem., A I Cuza, Iasi; Conserv. P I Ceaikasvski, Moscow. m. Ersilia Vintila, 1 child. Debut: Liningrad, 1953. Career: apps. in Moscow, Kiev, Liningrad, Minsk, Tashkent, Poland, Czech., German Dem. Repub., German Fed. Repub., Yugoslavia. Contbr. to musical jrnls. Mbr., ATM Bucharest. Hons: Ordinul Muncii Clasa a II-a, 1963; Ordinul Meritul Cultural, 1968. Mgmt: ARIA, Bucharest. Address: Iasi, Strada Stefan Cel Mare, No. 4, Sc. A, et. 3, ap. 9, Romania.

VINTON, John, b. 24 Jan. 1937, Cleveland, Ohio, USA. Freelance Editor; Writer; Administrator in fields of contemporary music, dance & theatre. Educ: Ohio State Univ., 1954-58; NY Univ., 1958-63; Univ. of So. Calif., 1965-66. Career: Editl. & Rsch. Asst. Béla Bartók Archives, NY, 1962-65; Gen. Mgr., Dance Theatre Workshop, Ny, 1971-73; Asst. Music Critic, Wash. Star-News, 1966-67. Publs: Dictionary of Contemporary Music, 1974; Essays After A Dictionary (ca. 1976); Diary of Light (ca. 1976). Contbr. to: Musical Qtly.; Music Review; Music & Letters; Jrnl. of the Am. Musicol. Soc.; Arte Musical; Studia Musicologica; Sohlmans Musiklexikon; Notes, Bucknell Review; Res Facta, Heterofonia. Hobbies: Mycol.; Cooking; Conversation; Creative Writing; Contemporary hist. Address: 167 Hicks St., Brooklyn, NY 11201, USA.

VIOLA, Elizabeth, b. 13 May 1952, Colo. Springs, Colo., USA. Pianist; Recorderist. Educ: BA, Univ. of Northern Colo; currently studying for MMus, ibid. Career: Pt.-time Instr. in Piano, Schl. of Music, Univ. of Northern Colo. Mbrships: Am. Musicol. Soc.; Pi Kappa Lambda; Delta Omicron; Music Tchrs. Nat. Assn.; Colo. State Music Tchrs. Assn. Recip., Hons. Pin, Delta Gamma Chapt., Delta Omicron, 1974. Hobbies: Western horsemanship; Reading; Guitar; Tennis. Address: 1020 9th St., Apt. 1101, Creeley, CO 80631, USA.

VIOLLIER, Renée Marguerite, b. 15 May 1894, Geneva, Switzerland. Musicologist; Music Critic. Educ: studied piano, comp. etc., Geneva Conserv. of Music, 1918; studied singing pvtly.; studied early music w. Wanda Landowska, 1930-35. Career: Music Corres., La Tribune de Genèva, Paris, 1947-; Music Corres., La Revue Musicale Suisse, Zürich. Compositions: Num. adaptations of French music of 17 & 18 centuries, inclng., Ier & 2e concert de Chambre; Les Amours des Dieux, (ballet), La Provencale, (ballet), Jean-Joseph Mouret; L'Horoscope Accomply, (1 Act comedy), Simon Thomas Gueullette; Divertissements, Jean-Joseph Mouret; Les Petes Venitiennes, (opera ballet), André Campra; Arr., operas, by Rameau Platée, Castor et Polliny, Les Fêtes d'Herbe, (2 version), Dardanus, (2 version), Les Paladins, Pygmalion; Jephte, (lyridal tragedy), Michel de Montéclair; Cantique de Noël 'O beate Infantiae', Charles Hubert Gervais; Les Jardins de Sceaux, (cantata), Nicolas Bernier. Num. Recordings inclng., works for chamber orchs., grps. & var. solo instruments. Publs: Jean-Joseph Mouret, 'Le Musicien des Graces', Paris, 1950, 2nd Ed., Geneva, 1974. Contbr. to: La Revue Francaise de Musicol.; Recherches. Mbr., French Soc. of Musicol. Recip., Prix de l'Acad. des Beaux Arts for book publd., Paris, 1951. Address: 7 Villa Emile Bergerat, 92200 Neuilly, France.

VIOZZI, Giulio, b. 5 July 1912, Trieste, Italy. Composer. Educ: Conserv. Tartini, Trieste; Piano Dip., 1931; Comp. Dip., 1937. Debut: Trieste, 1931-; Tchr. of Comp., Conserv. Tartini, Trieste. Comps: (Lyric operas) Allamistakeo, 1954; Un

Intervento Notturno, 1957; Il Sasso Pagano, 1962; La Giacca Dannata, 1967; Elisabetta, 1971; (ballet) Prove di Scena, Scala, 1958; 12 concertos for Solo Instruments; symphonic, chmbr., choral & piano music. Recordings: Transcriptions of popular songs for Cetra. Publs: Musical writings in Italian Newspapers, jrnls., mags., concert progs., etc., & for Italian radio. Dir., Music Sect., Circle of the Arts, Trieste. Hobby: Alpinist. Address: Via San Francesco 6, 34133 Trieste, Italy.

VIRIZLAY, Mihaly, b. 2 Nov. 1931, Budapest, Hungary. Concert Cellist; Professor of Music; Composer. Educ: Artist Dip., Franz Liszt Acad. Music, budapest. m. Paula Skolnick Virizlay, 2 s. Career: Prof. Music, Peabody Conserv., Balt., USA; Solo perfs., Chgo. Symph.; Pitts. Symph.; Balt Symph.; Engl. Chmbr. Orch.; Gstaad Fest.; BBC & CBC apps.; Recitals throughout USA, London & Canada. Comps: Sonata for Unaccompanied Cello; The Emperors New Clothes (for orch.). Recordings incl: Beethoven Duos (w. Ruggiero Ricci); The Art of Mihaly Virizlay; Brahms Trio in A Minor, Op. 114. Hon: Harriet Cohen Int. Award for Violincello, 1962. Hobbies incl: Astron.; Ping-Pong. Mgt: Basil Douglas Ltd., London. Address: 3904 Hadley Sq. W, Baltimore, MD 21218, USA.

VIRIZLAY, Paula Skolnick, b. 21 July 1945, Quantico, Va., USA. Cellist; Teacher. Educ: BA, Stanford Univ.; MMus, Univ. of Southern Calif. m. Mihaly Virizlay, 1 s. Debut: Saint-Saëns Concerto w. Utah Symph. Career: Mbr., Balt. Symph. Orch.; Chmbr. Music Recitalist, USA; participant, Marlboro, Ojai & Carmel Bach Fests. & Shawnigan Int. Fest. of Arts, BC, Can.; Tchr., Peabody Conserv. & Univ. of Md. Mbrships: SAI; Phi Kappa Lambda. Recip. var. hons. Hobby: Art. Address: 3904 Hadley Sq. W, Baltimore, MD 21218, USA.

VIRKAHAUS, Taavo, b. 29 June 1934, Tartu, Estonia. Conductor; Composer; Music Educator. Educ: BMus, Univ. of Miami, Fla., USA, 1955; MMus, Eastman Schl. of Music, Rochester, NY, 1957; DMA, ibid, 1967; student of Pierre Monteux, summers 1960-61; Fulbright Scholar, Cologne, Germany, 1963-64. m. Nancy Herman. Debut: (Cond.) Miami Ballet Guild Orch., 1956. Career: Cond., Opera Theater of Rochester, 1970-; Cond., Rochester Opera Under the Stars, 1972 season; Guest Cond. w. Rochester Phil. Orch., 1969-; Guest Cond., Balt. Symph., 1966, Eastman Chmbr. Orch., 1970-; Dir. of Music, Univ. of Rochester; Assoc. Prof., Eastman Schl. of Music; Cond., All-Univ. Symph. Orch.; Guest Cond., Amarillo Symph., 1975 & Baltimore Symph., 1976; Music Dir., Cond., Duluth-Superior Symph. Orch., Duluth, Minn. Contbr. to var. music jrnls. Mbrships: Am. Symph. Orch. League; Estonian Learned Soc. of Am. Hons: Howard Hanson Prize for composition, 1966; Am. Heritage Award, JPK Lib., 1974. Mgmt: Judith Liegner Artists Mgmt., NYC. Hobbies: Pilot; Tennis; Water skiing; Travel. Address: 321 High St., Duluth, MN 55811, USA. 6, 28.

VIRTUE, Robert Francis (Bobby), b. 8 Dec., Terang, Victoria, Aust. Classical Guitarist & Teacher; Researcher; Composer. Educ: Guitar studies w. Lionel Schneider, Geelong & Don Andrews, Sydney, Aust. Career incls: Played w. Jack Grimsley's Jazz Band & Bobby Bell's Band, Sydney; Rsch. into Classical guitar styles & tchng. methods; Fndr. of the Aust. Spanish Guitar Acad., Roselands Guitar Schl., Lakemba Guitar Schl., Tamworth Guitar Schl.; Tchr., Christian Brothers Coll., Miranda Fair Guitar Schl. Apps. on Geelong, Melbourne & Wollongong Radio accompanying singers. Var. comps. for the classical guitar. Contbr. to mags. & reviews. Mbrships: Musicians Union, Sydney; The Guitar Fndn. of Am.; Mid-Am. Guitar Soc.; Jazz Action Soc., Sydney. Hons: Presented w. the full arr. of Rodrigo's Concierto de Aranjuez by the Spanish Min. of Foreign Affairs, 1973. Hobbies: Music; Comp. of Classical Guitar Music; Oil painting. Address: 6/51 Carthage St., Tamworth, NSW 2340, Aust.

VISCUGLIA, Felix Alfred, b. 13 Jan. 1927, Niagara Falls, NY, USA. Clarinettist; University Teacher. Educ: MusB, New England Conserv. m. Deborah, 2 d. Career: Clarinetist, Boston Symph., 1966-78; Soloist, Boston Symph. & Boston 'Pops'; Chmbr. music perfs. in all major US cities, esp. w. contemporary music ensemble, Collage. Recordings for major record cos. Mbrships: Trustee, New England Conserv. Hobbies: Astronomy; Painting. Address: PO Box 251, Henderson, NV 89015, USA. 2.

VISHNEVSKAYA, Galina Pavlovna, b. 1926, Leningrad, USSR. Singer. Educ: studied w. Vera Garina, 1942-52. Career: Liningrad Musical Theatres, 1944-52; Bolshoi Theatre, 1952-. Roles incl: Leonora, Fidelia; Tatiana, Eugene Onegin (also film); Aida; Kupava, Snow Maidan; Liza, Queen of Spades; Chio-Sio-San, Madame Butterfly; Margaret, Faust; Natasha, War & Peace; Cherubino, Marriage of Figaro. Recordings incl: Shostakovitch, Symphony No. 14. Hons: People's Artist of RSFSR & USSR. 16.

VISSER, Ruth Arienne, b. 16 Sept. 1948, Gorkum, The Netherlands. Musician (Oboe, Oboe d'amore & English Horn). Educ: Dips., tchng. & solo playing, Royal Conserv. of Music, The Hague. Career: English Horn, Rotterdam Phil. Orch.; Chmbr. Music perfs.; TV & Radio apps. Contbr. to: Mens en Melodie. Hons: 2nd Prize, Tromp Concours, 1975; Prix d'excellence, Royal Conserv. of Music, 1976. Hobbies: Reading; Dancing; Horse Riding; Designing & Dressmaking. Address: Palestinastraat 88b, 3061 HP Rotterdam, The Netherlands.

VITALE, Vincent Albert, b. 11 Nov. 1942, Brooklyn, NY, USA. Musician (Trumpet & Guitar). Educ: BA in Music Educ., SUNY at Fredonia; MA Music Educ., ibid; Grad., USN Schl. of Music; Grad., Am. Schl. of Piano Tuning. m. Mary Ann Bielaszka, 1 s., 1 d. Career: Dir. of Bands, Orchard Pk. HS, NY. Comps: Marching Along; March of the Jesters; The Dancing Elephant; Waltz for Two Trumpets; Galloping George; Imperial March; Cha Cha Cantabile; New Empire March; Rock One; Battle at Sandy Hook. Mbrships: NY State Schl. Music Assn.; Orchard Pk. Tchrs. Assn.; NY State Tchrs. Assn.; MENC; Erie Co. Music Educators Assn. Hobbies: Woodworking; Tennis. Address: 35 Burton Lan, Hamburg, NY 14075, USA.

VIVIENNE, Hazel, b. 14 July 1934, Bromborough, Cheshire, UK. Musician (piano); Conductor. Educ: Fellow, Royal Manchester Coll. of Music. Career: Chorus Master, Engl. Nat. Opera, 1964-76; Cond., ibid, 1967-; Hd., Music Staff, 1975-. Recordings: English Wind Music Vol. 1; Recital Record w. John Denman (Clarinet); Clarinet Concerti by Spohr & Stamitz; Cond., Sadlers Wells Orch. w. John Denman as soloist. Hobby: Gardening. Address: 45 Madrid Rd., London SW13 9PQ, UK.

VIVIER, Claude, b. 14 Apr. 1948, Montreal, Can. Composer. Educ: Conserv. de musique de Quebec, Montreal; studied comp. w. G M Koenig, Utrecht, Paul Mefano, Paris & Karlheinz Stockhausen, Cologne & Darmstadt. Career: works perf. in Can., France, Netherlands, Germany & USA. Comps. incl: Ojikawa, for soprano, clarinet & percussion, 1968; Proliferation, for piano, ondes Martenot & percussion (recorded), 1969; Chants, for 7 women's voices)recorded), 1972-73; Lettura di Dante, for soprano & instrumental ensemble (recorded) 1973-74; Pulau Dewata, for percussion or other instruments (recorded), 1977; Shiraz, for piano, 1977; Greetings Music, for cello, flute, oboe & percussion, 1978; Kopernikus (opera), 1978-79. recip. sev. bursaries. Address: 5352 Park Ave., Apt. 35, Montreal, PQ, Can. H2V 4G8.

VIZINO, Sergey, b. 8 June 1946, Wilhelmstahl, Germany. Pianist; Guitarist. div. 1 s., 1 d. Career: recording artist, vocal & guitar, for 3 1/2 yrs.; guest artist, Toronto clubs, Holiday Inn, Fla., USA. nearly 70 comps., 16 recorded. Contbr. to: Music Scene, 1976-79; Cashbox, 1979; Crescendo, 1976-79; Billboard, 1979. Mbrships: Acad. of Country Music Assn.; jPerforming Right Organization of Can.; Teamsters Union; Toronto Musicians Assn. sev. awards. Hobbies: Playing Guitar; Singing; Writing Songs; Outdoor Sports; Inventing. Address: 260 John Garland Blvd., Apt. 231, Rexdale, Toronto, Ont. M9V 1N8, Can.

VIZZA, Nancy J, b. 28 Mar. 1950, Bronx, NY, USA. Freelance Musician. Educ: BMus, Mannes Coll. Music, 1972; MMus, Manhattan Schl. Music, 1974. Debut: Solo recital, Mannes Coll. Music, NY, 8 May 1972. Career incls: Opera perfs. w. Boris Goldovsky, Summer Festival, Southern Mass., 1974; 1st Horn, Bkly. Boro Pk. Symph., 1975-76; num. apps. NYC inclng. St Stephen's Ch., NYC & NY Brass Conf., 1974; Chmbr. music perfs., Schirmer Music Store concert series, NYC, 1976. Mbr., Int. Horn Soc. Recip: Nat. Orch. Award, 1968. Hobbies incl: Drawing; Reading. Address: 234 E 81st St., NY, NY 10028, USA.

VLACH, Joseph, b. 8 June 1923, Ratmerice, Bohemia, CSSR. Violinist; Leader of Chamber Orchestra; Professor of Violin. Educ: Conservatorium of Music & Acad. of Music, Prague. m. Dana Trellova 2 children. Debut: Int. Quartet Competition. Leége. Career: First Violin, Vlach Quartet; Ldr., Czech Chmbr. Orch.; Prof. of Violin, Acad. of Music, Prague; Guest Cond., Czech Phil & Prague Radio Symph. Num. recordings w. Vlach Quartet & Czech Chmbr. Orch. Contbr. to Hudebni Rozhledy, Prague. Hons: 1st Prize, Int. Concours of String Quartets, Liege, Belgium, 1955; Order of Labour, Czechoslovakia, 1963; State Hon. Deserving Artist, 1972. Address: Karpatska 2/1188, 100 00 Praha, 10-Vrsovice, Czechoslovakia.

VLAJIN, Milan, b. 25 Nov. 1912, Timisoara, Romania. Professor of Harmony, Counterpoint, Composition, Violin & Chamber Music. Educ: Acad. of Art & Music, Belgradensis. m. Zorica Vlajin-Radukic. Career: Radio TV Belgrade, Zagreb, Novi Sad, Titograd, Prinstina, Yugoslavia, Timisoara, Bucarest, etc.,

Romania, Mulhouse, France, etc. Comps. incl: Balkan (symphonic suite), 1958; Romanticna Poema (symphonic orch.), 1947; Rondino (oboe & piano), 1956; Sedan Bagatela (horn & piano), 1967; Decje Pesme, 1966; Vizantijska reminisencija (for symph. orch.); Lieder (voice & piano). Mbrships: Servian Soc. of Comps.; Serbiam Soc. of Music Folklorists. Contbr. to: The Music Elements of Krajina; var. profl. jrnls. Recip., Finalist Dip. for comp., Vercelli, Italy. Hobby: Numismatics. Address: 11000 Beograd, Sv. Save 20, Yugoslavia.

VODOVOZ, Anatoly, b. 28 July 1936, Kiev, USSR. Composer; Pianist. Educ: MA, Comp.; MA, Pianist; Moscow State Conserv.; Tashkent Conserv. m. Larisa Vodovoz, 1 s. Debut: w. comp. Upon Earth (vocal & symph. series). Career: Mgr., Or Yehuda Conserv.; Comps. for Tashkent State Theatre of Drama; Radio; Min. of Culture of USSR; Music Fund of USSR. Comps: If I Forget Thee, Jerusalem (voice & piano), 1975; Alleluia (voice & piano), (violin & piano) & (cello & piano), 1976; Piano Variations, 1976. Recordings: Piano Variations, Tel Aviv Radio, 1974; Year Seasons, Radio Jerusalem, 1975. Mbrships: Comps. League; Copyright Protection Org. Recip. ACUM Prize, 1975. Hobbies: Musical Instruments; Recording Equipment. Address: 42/29 Hamachroset str., Bat Yam, Israel.

VODZOGBE, Augustine Kofi, b. 22 Feb. 1924, Tsevie, Repub. of Togo. Teacher (Voice & Piano). Educ: General Music Dip., Univ. of Ghana, Legon, 1967. m. Philomene Evenamede, 10c. Debut: Alto Horn in Anthony Silver Star Band, Lome, Togo, 1938-39. Career: Music Master, Mount Mary Tchr. Trng. Coll., Somanya, Ghana, 1959-64; Music Master, Dzodze Secondary Schl., Ghana, 1967-73; Supvsr., Music Tchng., 1974-76. Comps. incl: Black Art Mass. Publs: Music Workbook for Primary Schools, 1976. Mbrships: Fndr., Ghana MTA; Sec., Catholic Ch. Organists Assn., Keta/Ho Diocese. Hobbies: Painting; Lawn Tennis. Address: PO Box 181, Aflao, Ghana.

VOGEL, Edith, b. Austria. Concert Pianist; Teacher. Educ: Dip., Vienna State Cad.; ARCM. m. Herbert Edward Jeffrey. Debut: Vienna when aged 10. Career: broadcasts & recitals in Vienna; recitals, concerto apps. & BBC broadcasts, London & provinces; Master classes, London & provinces, Dartington Summer Schl.; Prof., GSM; BBC talks on music. Recorded w. Decca & EMI; BBC records & tapes. Mbrships: Fellow, GSM; London Acad. of Music & Dramatic Art; Zool. Soc. of London; ISM. Hobbies: Lit.; Arch.; Biol.; Wildlife. Address: 35A St. Lukes Rd., London W11 1DD, UK. 2, 23, 27.

VOGEL, Ernst, b. 1 Mar. 1926, Stockerau, Austria. Composer. Educ: Pvte. music studies. m. Annemarie Vogel, 1 s., dec., 1 d. Comps: 10 Orch. works; 9 Works of Chmbr. music; 1 Ballet, commissioned by City Theater Heidlberg. Recordings: Octet. Mbrships: Mbr. Of Dir., Vienna Concert Hall Soc.; Pres., Vienna Song Acad.; Mbr. of Dir., Austrian Soc. for Comp. Hons: Cultural Stimulation Prize, Niederösterreich, 1968. Hobbies: Water sport. Address: POX 1, A-2000 Stockerau, Austria.

VOGEL, Howard, b. 21 Feb. 1933, NY, USA. Musician, Bassoon, Guitar, Lute, Recorder; School & Ensemble Director; Assistant Professor of Music. Educ: BMus, Manhattan Schl. of Music, 1955; MMus, ibid, 1960. m. Jodi Vogel. Debut: Carnegie Recital Hall, NYC, 1961. Career: Bassoon, Kan. City Phil., Tchr., Modern Dance, Kan. City Conserv., 1956-58; Guitar Soloist, NC Symph. Tour; Lute Soloist, Robert Shaw Chorale Orch.; Bassoon Soloist, ibid; Recorder Soloist w. Masterwork Chorus; Bassoon, Recorder, Lute, NY Baroque Ensemble, num. Int. Tours; Dir., ibid, 1961-; Dir., Village Music Workshop, 1965-; Asst. Prof. of Music, CUNY; num. Perfs., Bassoon, Contrabassoon, NYC. Recordings: Bassoon Soloist, Bach, B. Minor Mass; var. other orchl. recordings. Contbr. to Sing Out. Mbrships: Galpin Soc.; Am. Lute Soc.; Music Ed.; Am. Lute Soc. Eds., 1966-68; Am. Recorder Soc.; Am. Musical Instrument Soc. Hobbies: Architecture; Carpentry. Address: Box 42, Bonna Creek Hollow, Mt. Tremper, NY 12457, USA.

VOGEL, Karsten, b. 11 Jan. 1943, Copenhagen, Denmark. Alto & Soprano Saxophonist; Composer. Educ: Cand., Univ. of Copenhagen, 1968. m. Jytte Jensen, 2 children. Debut: 1961. Career: Smaller jazz combos, 1961-66; Cadenita Nova Danica, 1966-68; Fndr. & Ldr., Burnin Red Ivanhoe, 1967-74, inclng. concerts in Denmark, Sweden, Norway, Finland, Germany & UK; Fndr., Secret Oyser, 1972-77; Fndr., Ldr., Birds of Beauty, 1976-. Film: Henning Carlsin: Are you scared, 1969. Comps. incl: Inside Thule; Medardus; Gong-Gong; The Elephant Song; Pelican; Delveaux. Recordings incl: Burnin Red Ivanhoe, 7 albums; Secret Oyster, 4 albums; Birds of Beauty, 2 albums. Publs: Rythmic Music, 1978. Mbr., Danish Comps. Guild. Hobbies incl: H C Andersen. Address: Lersa Park Alle 37, 2100 Copenhagen, Denmark. 30.

VOGEL, Martin, b. 23 Mar. 1923, Frankfurt/Oder, Germany. Musicologist. Educ: PhD, Univ. of Bonn, 1954; Habilitation, Philos. Fac., ibid., 1959. m. Hannelove Schlemmer, 3 s., 1 d. Publs. incl: Die Zahl Sieben in der Spekulativen Musiktheorie, 1955; Der Tristanakkord und die Krise der modernen Harmonielehre, 1962; die Zukunft der Musik, 1968; Die Lehre von den Tonbezeihungen, 1975; Chiron, der Kentaur mit der Kithara, 1976. Ed., Orpheus Series of Monographs on Basic Questions in Music. Hobby: Construction of musical instruments. Address: Lotharstrasse 111, 53 Bonn. German Democratic Republic.

VOGEL, Michael P, b. 4 June 1940, San Francisco, Calif., USA. Professional Musician (Oboe, English Horn); Music Resource Teacher. Educ: BMus, MMus, Univ. Southern Calif. Career: Mbr. Pasadena Symph. Orch., 1966-; San Gabriel Valley Symph. Orch., 1968-; Apps: Glendale Symph. Orch.; Los Angeles Bach Festival; Pasadena Opera Co.; Young Musicians Fndn. Debut Orch.; Westside Symph.; Peninsula Symph.; Idyllwild Festival Orch.; Instr., Oboe & Chambr. Music, Univ. Southern Calif's Summer Campus, Idyllwild, Calif.; mbr., Redlands Bowl summer music series; Instr. of double reeds & chmbr. music, Wilwood Music Camp, Idyllwild, Calif. Mbrships. incl: Phi Mu Alpha; Pi Kappa Lambda; Int. Double Reed Soc.; Southern Calif. Band & Orch. Assnl. Schl.; Music Educators Nat. Conference. Recip. num awards. Hobbies: Swimming; Fishing; Photography; Attending Concerts. Address: 1216 37th St., San Pedro, CA 90731, USA.

VOGEL, Richard Friedrich Manfred, b. 21 June 1918, Freiburg, Germany. Chamber Musician; Flautist; Lecturer. m. Christine Mayerlen, 3 c. Career: Flautist, sev. Orchs., inclng., Hofer Sinfoniker, Freiburg Orch., Düsseldorf Symph. Orch.; Lectr., Musikhochschule Rheinland; Düsseldorf Inst. Hobbies: Railways; Photography. Address: D4 Dusseldorf-30, Roferstr, 16, German Fed. Repub.

VOGEL, Vladimir, b. 29 Feb. 1896. Moscow, USSR. Composer. Educ: studied w. Busoni. m. (1) Käthe-Katje Sommer (dec.) (2) Alne Valengin (sep.) m. (3). Career: Prof. of Composition, Klindworth-Scharwenka Conserv.; Lectr., Basle, Zurich, etc. Compositions incl: Composition for 1 & 2 pianos, 1923; Sinfonia Fugata, 1924; Grosse Fugue (str. quartet), 1924; Etude Toccata (piano), 1926; Tyl Klass (oratorio), 1943; Epitaffio per Alban Berg (piano), 1946; Arpiade, 1955; 2 Etudes (orchl.); Wagades Untergand durch die Eitelkeit (oratorio); Ritmica Ostinata (orchl.); Tripartita (orch.); Passacaglia for Orch.; Sept Aspects d'une Série (orchl.); Flucht; Jona ging doch nach Ninére (oratorio); Dramma Oratiorio.

VOGELSANG, Konrad, b. 19 Nov. 1928, Bonn, Germany. Librarian; Pianist; Musicologist; Music Teacher. Educ: Free Univ. Berlin; Univ. Tübingen. m. Hannelore Braemer. Comp.: The World of the Child, 2 vols.; Toccata for piano; Impulse; Studies for expression-dance. Mbrships: Soc. for Musical Rsch.; Int. Soc. for Musicol. Publs.: Alban Berg, biography, 1959, Berlin; Documentation on the Opera Wozzek by Alban Berg. Address: Ts. Sudetenstr. 2, 6243 Falkenstein, German Fed. Repub.

VOGG, Herbert, b. 17 May 1928, Vienna, Austria. Lecturer. Educ: DrPhil, Musikwissenschaft, Germanistik, Univ. of Vienna, 1951; studied piano pvtly. m. Lisbeth Vogg, 2 s, 1 d. Career: Verlag Doblinger, Vienna, 1951-; Lektor, Herstellungsleiter, Prokura 1962; Verlagsdirektor. Publs: 'Diletto Musicale'; Idea & Content of this Series of Old Music (over all: J Haydn & his Contemporaries); Contemporary Music of Austria. Hons: 'Silbernes Ehrenzeichen für Verdienste um die Republik Osterreich', 1971. Hobbies: Family; Literature; Art; Nature. Address: Ahornergasse 9, 1970 Vienna, Austria.

VOICULESCU, Dan, b. 20 July 1940, Saschiz-Sighisoara, Romania. Composer; Professor. Educ: Conserv. G. Dima of Cluj (Acad. of Music), 1958-63 w. Dip. for comp. & piano; classes w. V. Mortari, Venice, 1968 & K. Stockhausen, Cologne, 1971-72. Career: Prof. for Counterpoint, Conserv. G. Dima, Cluj; musicologist; musical critic; radio broadcasts. Comps: Sinfonia ostinato, 1963; Visions cosmiques, 1968; Music for Strings, 1971, Pieces for Orch., 1973; Fables, Dialogs, Sonata, Croquis, Sonantes - for piano solo, Piccola sonata per flauto solo, Sonata for Clarinet solo, Cantata for baritone, choir & orch., 1977; Homage to Blaga; 3 vols. of choral music for children, etc. Mbrships: Union of Romanian Comps. Hons: Prize of the Union of Romanian Comps., 1972, '74 & '76. Address: Aleea Detunata 13, Ap. 15, 3400 Cluj Napoca, Romania.

VOLCKAERT, Edith (Augusta-Marie), b. 27 Aug. 1949, Ghent, Belgium. Violinist. Educ: Pvte. study of violin w. Prof. Carlo Van Neste from age of 4 to 21. Debut: Vevey, Switz., aged 11. Career: Concerts & recitals as soloist in Europe, Am.,

S Am., & Africa; Radio & TV apps.; Prof., Royal Conserv. of Music, Brussels, 1970-78. Recordings: Shostakovitch, Concerto No. 1; Vivaldi, Concerti; De Beriot & De Croes, Violin Concerti; Mozart, Concerti Nos. 216 & 219; Louël, Concerto No. 1. Recip., num. musical prizes & scholarships, 1965-. Mgmt: Alex Saron, PO Box 29, 1260AA Blaricum, Netherlands. Address; Ave. Van Der Meerschen 23/B9, B-1150 Brussels, Belgium.

VOLEK, Jaroslav, b. 15 July 1923, Trencin, Czechoslovakia. University Professor. Educ: PhD, 1952; CSc, 1958; DSc, 1968; Dip. Composition Class, Conserv. of Prague, 1946; Dip., Master Schl., ibid, 1948. m. Miloslava Pirkova, 2 s. Career: Tchr. of Aesthetics & Musicol., 1952-; Docent, 1957; Prof., 1968; Music Dept., Radio Bratislava, 1950-52; Music Critic, Mlada Fronta (daily newspaper). Compositions incl: Quintetto for Strings, 1946; Kalendar (mixed chorus, piano); Phantasy for violin & orch.; Parabola for piano & solo voice. Publs: Ed., Theoretic Foundations of Harmony, 1954; Ed., New Systems of Harmony, 1961; Ed., Foundations of the General Theory of Art, 1968; Ed., Chapts. from the History of Aesthetics, 1969; The Question of the Taxonomy of the Arts, 1971-72. Contbr. to num. music jrnls., etc. Mbrships: Int. Soc. of Musicol.; Union of Czech Composers; Int. Soc. of Empiric Aesthetics. Recip: Prize, Czech Musical Fndn. Hobbies: Table Tennis; Tennis; Skiing; Chess. Address: Prague 2, Americka 22, Czechoslovakia.

VÖLKL, Walter, b. 26 Feb. 1929, Vienna, Austria. Musician (guitar, Clarinet, Saxophone, E bass); Music Teacher; Composer. Educ: conserv. of Music; Cert., music teacher, Acad. of Music. m. Herta Völkl, 2s. Debut: Beethoven Music Schl., Mödling. Career: Band leader; Music tchr.; apps. on Radio Vienna & Radio Hessen. Comps: Folk music, light music, dance music. num. recordings. Publs. incl: My Golden Guitar School; Weltmusik für Gitarre; Alle Jarhe wieder; Heissa Troika; In Dixieland etc. mbr. num. profl. socs. Hons: Der lustige Augustin silver medal for 25 yrs. wind music. Hobbies: Swimming; Fishing. Address: Reisenbauer-Ring 3/2/7, 2351 Wr. Neudorf, Austria.

VOLPÉ, Elizabeth, b. 5 May 1953, Toronto, Can. harpist; formerly Flautist & Pianist. Educ: BMus (Perf.), Univ. of Tronto, 1975 (1st harpist to grad.); studied harp w. Judy Loman, Toronto, Alice Chalifoux, Cleveland, USA, & Edna Phillips, Maine. Debut: Walter Hall, Edward Johnson Building. Career: Flautist, N York Woodwind Quintet; harp soloist, Univ. of Toronto Concert Choir, Bach Youth Ensemble, Oshawa Symph.; perfs. w. Toronto Symph., CBC Fest. Orch., Kingston Symph. N & E York Symphs. & Nat. Youth Orch.; freelance work; 1st harpist, Nat. Ballet of Can.; sev. recitals throughout Can. ; apps. on CBC radio. Mbrships: Am. Harp Soc. Hons: Open Scholarship from Univ. of Toronto, 1975; Music Scholarship from York Mills C I, 1971. Hobbies: Skiing; Tennis; Languages; Stamp Collecting. Address: 3 Daleberry Pl., Don Mills, Ont. M3B 2A5, Can.

VON ALBRECHT, Georg, b. 19 Mar. 1891, Kasan, Russia. Composer; Pianist. Educ: Dip., Stuttgart Conserv.; Leningrad Conserv.; Studied w. Glazounoff & Tanejev, Moscow. m. (1) Wanda Dydziulz (2) Elisabeth Kratz, 1 s, (3) Elisabeth Charlotte Hose. Career: Tchr., Piano & Comp., Stuttgart Conserv., 1925; Prof. of Comp., 1945; Acting Dir., 1946; Tchr. Comp., Heidelberg Conserv., 1956-69. Comps. incl: Piano Sonatas, Violin Concerto, Mass, Requiem. Songs & Dances of the Russian People (violin & piano); Prelude & Fugue (flute & piano); 3 Georgian Songs (violin & piano). Recordings incl: Georg Von Albrecht - Piano Works; 5 Eastern Folk Songs. Mbr. num. profl. orgs. Hons. incl: Joh Wenzel Stamitz Prize, 1966 (Kunstler Gilde Esslingen); Glinka Prize (Belaieff). Hobby: Collector of Eastern Folk & Ch. Music. Address: 6902 Sandhausen, Am Forst 9, German Fed. Repub.

von BARTESCH, Seta K, b. 30 Nov. 1944, Bucharest, Rumania. Pianist. Educ: BMus, MSc, Juilliard Schl. of Music. m. Rudolf von Bartesch, 2 s. Debut: Carnegie Recital Hall, 1973. Career: recitals & TV apps., radio broadcasts, Rumania, USSR, Belgium, German Fed. Repub., Lebanon, USA, Etc. Hons: Juillard Alumni Award; num. scholarships. Hobbies: Writing short stories; Gardening; Homemaking. Address: 56-19 196th St., Flushing, NY 11365, USA.

VON BULOW, Gert Oluf, b. 4 Mar. 1946. Copenhagen, Denmark. Cellist; Composer; Painter. Educ: Dip. (grand prix), Royal Danish Conserv; Studies w. Gregor Piatigorsky & Prof. Pierre Forunier. m. Ingrid Boisen. Debut: Copenhagen & Hamburg. Career: Concerts, Berlin, Hamburg, Hannover, Munchen, Zurich, Brussels, Paris, London, Oslo, Gotenborg, Montreal, Ottawa, Quebec; Danish Rep., official cultural exchanges, Min. Cultural Affairs, on sev. occasions. Comps: Commnd. works for Denmark Radio, Royal Theatre & Cullberg

Ballet. Recordings: Danish Anthol. of Music. Mbr. profl. orgs. Hons. incl: Jacob Gade's Fndn. Prize, 1967; Gladsexe's Music Award, 1968. Hobby: Sailing. Address: PO box 57, 2800 Lyngby, Denmark.

VON BUSCH-WEISE, Dagmar H E, b. 3 Jan. 1926, Kulmbach, Germany. Musicologist. Educ: Dr. W Spilling Music Schl., Nurnberg; Conserv. of Music, ibid. m. Friedrich von Busch, 3 c. Career: Knowledge Asst., Beethoven Archiv, Bonn, 1949-64. Publs incl: Ein Skizzenbuch Beethovens zur Chorfantasie op. 80, vollstandige, mit einer Einleitung und Ammerkungen versehene Ausgabe, 1957; Beethoven, Bilder aus seinem Leben, 9th Ed., 1975; Beethoven, Ein Skizzenbuch zur Pastoralsymphonie (2 vol.), 1961. var. other works on Beethoven. contbr. to: Musikforschung; MGG; Neue Zeitschrift für Musik; Osterr. Musikzeitschrift; var. musicol. books. Mbrships: Int. Musicol. Soc.; German Soc. for Music Rsch.; Study Grp. for Rhenish Music History; Advsr., ibid. Hobbies: Travel; Gardening; House Restoration. Address: Burg Graurheindorf, D53 Bonn 1, German Fed. Repub. 27, 30.

VON EINEM, Gottfried, b. 24 Jan. 1918, Berne, Switz. Composer. Educ: Gymnasium at Ratzeburg; Pvte. studies w. Boris Blacher. m. Lotte Ingrisch, 1 s. Debut: Berlin Phil. Orch. w. Capriccio for Orch., under Leo Borchard, 1943. Career: Coach, Berlin State Opera, Bayreuth Fest., 1938; Dresden State Opera, Comp.; Freelance Comp. Comps: num., publd. By Boosey & Hawkes; Universal Edition; Bote and Bock; Schirmers; AMP. Num. recordings. Publs: Composer & Society. Contbr. to num. profl. jrnls. Mbr. num. profl. orgs. inclng: AKM; Bd., Salzburg Fest. Recip. sev. hons. Hobby: Cooking. Address: A 1030 Vienna, Marokkanergasse 11, Austria.

VON FISCHER, Kurt, b. 25 Apr. 1913, Berne, Switzerland. Professor of Musicology; Pianist. Educ: PhD, Univ. of Berne, 1938; Habilitation, ibid, 1948; Piano Dip., Berne, 1935. m. Esther Aerni, 2 c. Career: Privatdozent, Univ. of Berne, 1948-57; Guest Prof., Univ. Basel, 1956-57 & Univ. if Ill., 1967-71. Full Prof. of Musicol., Univ. of Zürich, 1957-; vis. Prof., Univ. of Ill., USA, 1967 & '71; Gen. Ed. of the 14th Century series of Oiseau Lyre (Monaco); Co-Ed. of the Hindemith Gesamtausgabe; Co-Ed of 'Archiv fur Musikwissenschaft'. Publs incl: Griegs Harmonik und die nordlandische Folklore, Berne, 1938; Die Beziehungen von Form und Motiv in Beethovens Instrumental werken, 1948, '72; Studien zur italienischen Musik des Trecento und fruhen Quattrocento, 1956; Die Variation, 1956, English edn., 1960; Handschriften mit mehrstimmiger Musik des 14, 15 und 16 Jahrhunderts (2 vols. ed. w. Dr. Max Lutolf), 1972. Contbr. to many profl. publs. Mbrships incl: VP, Int. Musicol. Soc., 1964-67; Pres., ibid, 1967-72. Recip. var. hons. inclng: Corresp. fellow of Brit. Acad. Address: Laubholzstr. 46, CH-8703 Erlenbach-Zürich, Switzerland.

von FORSTER, Walter, b. 15 June 1915, Hammer nr. Nürnberg, Germany. Composer; Musicologist. Educ: masterclass in comp. w. Joseph Haas; State exams. in evangelical ch. music & schl. music. m. Gisela Spatz, 1 d. Career: Cantor & Organist; Lectr. then Prof., HS for Music, Munich, 1946-; num. progs. for Bavarian Broadcasting Co., & other networks, 1959-. comps. incl: Allein zu dir, Herr Jesu Christ (choral partita for organ); unpubld. works for orch., choir, piano, harpsichord, etc. has recorded for radio. Publs. incl: Elemente des homophonen Satzes, 1971. Mbrships: Soc. for Music Rsch., Kassel; Int. Musicol. Soc. Address: Graf-Rasso-Str. 19, 8082 Wildenroth, German Fed. Repub.

VON HASE, Hellmuth, b. 30 Jan. 1891, Leipzig, Germany. Music Publisher. Educ: Juristisches Studium, Doctor jur. m. Elisabeth Bierey, 3 d. Career: Head of Breitkopf & Hartel, publishing house. Mbr., German Music Publsrs. Assn. Publs: History of Breitkopf & Hartel, Vol. III. Address: Feuerbach Str. 18, 62 Wiesbaden, German Fed. Repub.

von HEUNE, Friedrich Alexander, b. 20 Feb. 1929, Brelsau, Germany. Instrument Maker, Historical Woodwinds; Musician, Recorder & Baroque Flute. Educ: BA, Bowdoin Coll., USA. m. Ingeborg Reiser, 5 children. Debut: w. Cambridge Consort, Tulley Hall, 1974. Recordings: w. Cambridge Consort, Songs of a Travelling Apprentice, Love & Dalliance in Renaissance France, The World of Adam de la Halle; w. Boston Camerata, The Wandering Musicians, Monteverdi Scherzi Musicali. Contbr. to musical jrnls. Mbrships: Galpin Soc.; Am. Musical Instrument Soc.; Am. Recorder Soc. Recip. w. Cambridge Consort, Walter W Naumburg Award; Recip., Guggenheim Fellowship, 1966-67. Hobbies: Sailing; Travel; Model ships. Address: 7 Oakland Rd., Brookline, MA, USA.

VONK, Hans, b. 18 June 1942, Amsterdam, Netherlands. Conductor. Educ: Dip., solo piano, 1964; studied cond. in

Siena, Salzburg, Hilversum. m. Jessie Follerts. Debut: 1965. Career: Cond. Dutch Nat. Ballet, 1966-69; asst. cond., Concertgebouw Orch., 1969-73; cond., Dutch Radio, 1973-79; Cond., Netherlands Opera, 1976-; Assoc. cond., RPO, London, 1976-; cond., all Dutch orchs. abroad in Rome, Paris, Mexico, San Francisco, Boston, San Diego, Dresden, Berlin, Helsinki, Copenhagen, Brussels & Zürich. num. recordings incl. Schubert's 9th Symph. w. RPO. Hobbies: Chess; Football; Tennis. Mgmt: Harold Holt Ltd., London. Address: Stadionkade 8, Amsterdam, Netherlands.

von KOCH, Erland, b. 26 Apr. 1910, Stockholm, Sweden. Composer; Professor. Educ: Stockholm Conserv. of Music, 1931-35; studied w. Paul Hoeffer, Claudio Arrau, Walther Gmeindl, Clemens Krauss, Tor Mann. m. Ulla Gyllenhammar, 1 d. Debut: 1934. Career: Cond., Stockholm Phil., 1938; Lectr., Royal coll. of Music, Stockholm, 1953-75; Prof., ibid, 1968-75. Comps. incl: (pubId) 5 Symphs.; 12 Solo Concerti; 6 Str. Quartets; 4 Ballets; 2 Orchl. Trilogies; 12 Scandinavian Dances; Orchl. & Instrumental works; songs for vocal solo, choir; TV, Film Scores for Ingmar Bergman & others; (recorded) Oxberg Variations; Saxophone Concerto; 6 Scandinavian Dances; Nordic Capriccio; Piano Concerto No. 3; Dances No. 1-5; Piano Solo Fantasia on Ack, Vaermeland Du Skoena; Sonatina No. 2; Lapland Metamorphosis; Impulsi Trilogy (orch.); String Quartet No. 4, Monologues. Mbrships: Royal Acad. of Music, Stockholm; Soc. of Swedish Comps.; Int. Music Soc. of Swedish Comps. Hons: Christ Johnson Prize, USA, 1958; Kt., Royal Vasa Order, Sweden, 1967; Royal Litteris et Artibus, Sweden, 1979. Hobbies: Ornithology; Nature; Boating. Address: 23 Narvavägen, 11460 Stockholm, Sweden. 14.

VON KOTSCHUBEY, Ruth, b. 9 Feb. 1943, Zug, Switz. Singer (soprano). Educ: Music High Schl., Zürich; Univ. Freiburg i. Br., Germany; studied w. Prof. Confalognieri, Milan, Prof. E Campogalliani, Milan/Mantua: Debut: Mozarteum, Salzburg. Career: Int. Opera Studio, Zürich; Oratorios & Orch. Concerts throughout Europe & USA; Lied concerts and concerts w. organ in chs. & cathedrals; Radio & TV perfs. Sev. recordings. Mbr., Assn. des musiciens suisses. Hobbies: Golf. Mgmt: BUKO S. A. section musique, 6622 Ronco s/A Switz. Address: Obstgartenweg 20, 8708 Maennedorf, Switz.

VON PECHY, Valerie, b. 11 Dec. 1947, Cleveland, Ohio, USA. Harpist; Teacher. Educ: BME, Baldwin-Wallace Coll. Conserv.; MM, Univ. of Miami, Fla. Career: Prin. Harp, Miami Int. Opera, Ft. Lauderdale Symph.; 2nd Harp, Miami Phil. Composer, Sweet Is My Layde Love, harp solo. Recording: The Von Duet, 6 Immortal Melodies For Cello & Harp. Mbr. Am. Harp Soc. Address: 93 Palm Ave., Palm Island, Miami Beach, Fl 33139, USA.

VON PODEWILS, Torsten Hünke, b. 21 Dec. 1909, Kassel, Germany. Dramatic Producer; Composer; Author. Educ: Studied composition, piano & conducting, Klindvorth-Scharwenka-Konservatorium, Berlin. m. Ilsabe Deneke, 1 s., 1 d. Debut: Reichsrundfunk, Berlin. Career: Dir., touring theatre, 1946; Conductor & Composer, Stadtheater, Lüneburg, 1947-52; Radio & Film Composer, Music Critic, 1953-57; Chief Dramatic Prod., 1958-76, Comp. for Stage Music, 1976-, Stadttheater Lüneburg. Compositions: Orch. suite for the comedy Der Diener zweier Herren; Drei Zirkus-Minaturen; Orchl. music; Stage music; Songs. Recordings: Konzert in Lüneburg; Schaumburger Mächensänger. Contbr. to: Landeszeitung, Lüneburg; Bergedorfer Zeitung, & others. Address: Barckhausenstr. 66, 2121Lüneburg, German Fed. Repub.

Von STADE, Frederica, b. 1 June 1945, Somerville, NJ, USA. Singer (mezzo-soprano). Educ: BS, Mannes Coll. of Music, NYC. m. Peter K Elkus. Debut: Metropol. Opera, NYC, 1970. Career: Contract Artist w. Metropol. Opera, 3 seasons, inclng. leading roles in The Magic Flute, Faust, Tales of Hoffman, Rigoletto, Madame Butterfly, Figaro, Romeo & Juliet, etc.; appearances at Covent Gdn. (Barber of Seville), Paris Opera (Cherubino), La Scala Milan (Damnation of Faust); Festival appearances at Salzburg, & Glyndebourne;l Concerts w. leading phil. orchs. inclng. Vienna, Los Angeles & NY; San Fran. Symph.; New Philharmonia, etc. Recordings incl: Duet album w. Judith Blegen (CBS); Solo Album, Mozart & Rossini arias (Philips). Mbr: Am. Guild of Musical Artists. Hobbies: Cooking; Tennis. Mgmt: Columbia Artists Mgmt., NYC. Address: 44 W 62nd St., NY, NY 10023, USA.

VON ULLMANN, Hellmuth, b. 23 June 1913, Kosch, Estland. Composer; Organist; Conductor. Educ: Reval, Berlin; 1936, Dip. musician. m. Benita von Maydell, 1 d.; Elisabeth Hoescheler, 1 s.; Mia Arnhardt, 1 s. Career: Since 1937 Theater cond.; 1942-45 Soldier; After 1945 Theater dir.,

concert cond.; since 1955 comp. for Radio Hamburg, TV prod. Comps. incl: Opera, Goya; Symph. in C, 1951; Concerto for Orch., 1954; Songs; Chmbr. music. Recordings: Symph. in C, 1953; concerto for Orch., 1955; Farewell songs, 1954. Mbrships: Artists' Guild; Soc. for Intellectual Hist. Contbr. to: Melos; var. German newspapers. Hons: comp. commissions: braunschweig, Farewell songs, 1954; Goslar, concerto for Orch., 1955. Hobbies: Gardening; History; Wandering. Address: D-3119 Gruehagen, German Fed. Repub.

von VOLBORTH-DANYS, Diana, b. 18 Jan. 1941, Antwerp, Belgium. Science Librarian; Musicologist. Educ: Sci. Libn., Antwerp Schl. for Libns.; MA, Antwerp Art Histl. Inst.; Doct., Art Hist. & Archaeol.; music studies, Royal Flemish Conserv., Antwerp. m. Carl-Alexander von Volborth. Career: Collaborator, Mus. of Musical Instruments, Brussels, 1960-65; Sci. Libn., Antwerp Zool. Soc., 1962-65; Reoganiser, Royal Flemish Opera Lib., 1963-64; Dept. Hd., Lib. of Tumours, Brussels, 1966-70; Musicol. cons., Belgian Ctr. for Music Documentation, & Promoter, 1970-. Publ: CeBeCeM and its Affiliated Comps., 1978. Contbr. to: radio progs.; num. concert progs., biographical folders on var. Belgian comps.; La Vie Musicale Belge; Fontes Artes Musicae. Address: Jan Van Rijseijcklaan 31,2000 Antwerp, Belgium.

VOORMOLEN, Alexander Nicolaas, b. 3 Mar. 1895, Rotterdam, The Netherlands. Composer; Pianist. Educ: Utrecht Music Schl. of M W Petri, under Ravel & Roussel. 1 d. Career: Apps. world-wide. Comps. incl: 2 Suites Baron Hop; The Three Horsemen (tone poem); Sinfonia; Chaconne & Fuga; Stringquartet; Arethusa; Works performed by Willem Mengleberg, Pedor de Freitas Branco, Carl Schuricht, Paul Van Kempen, etc. Recordings incl: 2 Concertos for oboe; Concerto for 2 pianos & cymbals. Mbr., Royal Lib. at The Hague. Hons. incl: First Music Prize of The Hague, 1931; Wagenaar Prize of The Hague, 1976; Medal of the Town of Rotterdam. Address: Breitnerlaan 47, The Hague, The Netherlands.

VOORN, Josephus Hermanus Maria, B. 16 Oct. 1932, The Hague, Holland. Composer; Music Educator. Educ: Dr. of Dogmatic Theol., Univ. of Nymegen; Dip., Cath. Assn. of Choir Dirs. & organists, 1951; Brabants Conserv., 1966-; Dip. in theory, ibid, 1969; Dip. in piano, 1971. Career: Prof. of Theory, Brabants Conserv., 1969-. Compositions: Cyclus for organ, 1967; Psalm CXIV - In Exitu (soprano, children's choir & orch.), 1968; Three Songs from Lucebert (soprano & piano), 1968-69; Van de twaalfjarige in de tempel (mixed choir), 1969; Ludi & Interludi (piano solo), 1969; Three Songs from Leo Vroman, (baritone & piano), 1970; String Quartet 2, 1970; Nakupenda, trio for flute, viola & violin, 1971; Immobile: Music for Tutankhamun (orch.), 1973; Petit concert du Printempts (flute et cordes), 1975; Quintet for piano, oboe, clarinet, horn & basoon, 1975. Mbrships: Geneco (Assn. of Dutch Composers); Stichting Centrum voor de Kerkzang. Hobbies: Visual Arts; Lit; Transcendental meditation. Address: Sportlaan 4, Berkel Enschot, Netherlands.

VORHOLZ, Dieter, b. 14 Feb. 1932, Ludwigshafen, Germany. Violinist. Educ: Peter Cornelius conserv. m. Eva Zhlbruckner. Career: Ldr. of Frankfurt opera house and mus. orch., from 1961; ldr. of Capella Coloniensis of W German radio, Cologne, from 1969. Recorcings: Collective recordings of piano trios by Mozart, Beethoven & Brahms (w. 'Mannheim Trio'); Mozart-Serenade KV 204 (w. Mainz chmbr. orch.). Publs: Boccherini - Sonate for violin & piano (harpsichord) op. 5 nr, 3 in B, (ed. Peters) 1972; Dvorak - sonatine for violin & piano op. 100, (ed. Peters) 1973; Hons: Kranich steiner Musikpreis 1953 (for interpretation of new music). Address: 638 Bad Homburg 1, Sudetenstr. 21, German Fed. Repub.

VOSS, Aage, b. 18 Sept. 1911, Copenhagen, Denmark. Musician (Saxophone & Clarinet). Educ: studied w. Aage Oxenvad. m. Marga Vigga Marie Nielsen, 1d. Career: Lead Saxophone, num. Danish Dance Bands for 15 yrs.; 1st Clarinet soloist, Saxophone soloist, Danish Radio Light Orch., 20 yrs.; Tchr. of saxophone, Royal Danish conser., 1960-. Recordings: Hans Schreiber, Caprice Romantique; Jimmy Dorsey, Oodles of Noodles; Ronald Binge, Concerto for Saxophone; Bizet, Agnus Dei, for saxophone & organ. Named Kt. of the Danish Flag, 1972. Hobbies: Auto repair; Beach House. Address: 71/3 Peter Bangsvej, 2000 Copenhagen F, Denmark.

VOTAPEK, Ralph, b. 1939, Milwaukee, Wis., USa. Concert Pianist. Educ: Juilliard Schl. of Music; Manhattan Schl. of Music; Northwestern Univ. m. Albertine Baumgartner, 1 s., 1 d. Career: Soloist w. prin. orchs. & Recitalist throughout USA, S Am. & UK. Hons: Naumburg Award, NYC, 1959; 1st Prize, Van Cliburn Int. Piano Competition, 1962. Hobby: Tennis. Address: c/o Sol Hurok Attractions, 730 Fifth Ave., New York, NY 10019, USA.

VOUNDER-DAVIS, Jean, b. 8 July 1917, Sydney, Australia. Pianist; Harpsichordist; Teacher. Educ: MusDoc, Melbourne Univ., Australia; MA, Univ. of Calif., USA; Special studies, Univs. of Edinburgh, UK & Paris, France, TCL; BA, Melbourne Univ.; Musical Therapist's Degree, State of Calif.; Musicol. studies w. Dr. Karl Geiringer of Vienna, Austria; Pupil of Artur Schnabel & Jascha Smvakovsky. m. (dec.), 1 d., 1 s. Debut: Albert Hall, London, UK, at age of 9 yrs. Career: Concerts & solo recitals in Europe, USA & Aust.; Soloist under Sir Malcolm Sergent, Sir Thomas Beecham, Sir Bernard Heinze, Sir Edgar Bainton & others; TV & Radio recitals. Author of History of Music in Aust., 1965. Contbr. to literary & musical jrnls., short stories, TV scripts; Music Critic, sev. leading Am newspapers. Mbrships: Am. Musicol. Soc.; AAUP; Hawaiian Acad. of Sci. Recip. of num. prizes in piano. Hobbies: Fishing; Swimming; Scuba Diving. Address: PO Box 17561, Los Angeles, CA 90017, USA.

VRANEK, Gustav, b. 29 Nov. 1906, Veseli nad Luznic, Bohemia. Violinist. Educ: Prague Conserv., Czechoslovakia. m. Miroslava Englova, 3 c. Career: Violinist, Czech Philharmonic Orch. Compositions edited: Lento, Sonatina; Three Melodies, From Depths of Ages. Mbr., Czech Acad. of Scis. & Arts, 1948. Recordings: February Night. Hons: SCS, 1955 & 1976; PSSU, 1972. Hobbies: Philosophy; Chess; Fishing. Address: 100 00 Prague 10, Solidarita A 116, Czechoslovakia.

VREMŠAK, Samo, b. 29 May 1930, Kamnik, Slovenija, Jugoslavia. Professor of Music; Chorus Director. Educ: Dip. Comp. & Singing, Middle Music Schl., Acad. of Music. m. Rozalija Krajnc, 4 children. Debut: Comp., 1954; Soloist (singing), 1955. Career: Var. comps. executed on stage, radio apps., num. concerts w. male chorus & mixed chorus of Slov. Filharmonija; Chorus Dir., Slovenska Filharmonija, Ljubljana. Comps. incl: 2 Symphs. for grand orch.; Concertino for piano & strings; Sonatina for strings; Dramatical Overture for grand orch.; Sonata Quasi una Fantasia for organ. Recordings of Chorus Comps. Mbr. Assn. of Slovenia Comps. Hons. incl: golden Tablet Jacobus Gallus, 1972; Tomo Brejc Award, 1972; JRTV Award for comp., 1974. Hobby: Walking in the Woods. Address: Kmnik 61240, Maistrova 8/l, Slovenija, Yugoslavia.

VRENIOS, Anastasios Nicholas, b. 24 Aug. 1940, Turlock, Calif., USA. Opera Singer, Tenor. Educ: BVoice, Univ. of Pacific, Calif., 1962; MVoice Perf., Indiana Univ., 1965; Post-Grad. work, ibid, 1965-67. m. Elizabeth Anne Kirkpatrick, 2 s. Debut: Royal Albert Hall, London. Career: Soloist w. num. major Symph. Orchs., USA, Can., UK; Leading Tenor, Spoleto Festival, Italy, Phila. Lyric, Boston, Florentine, San Francisco, Seattle, Santa Fe, Lake George, Chgo. Operas, Am. Nat. Opera Co., & TV Prods. on NET, CBC, BBC; extensive Concert Tours in USA, Can., Europe. Recordings: Les Huguenots, London Records. Mbrships: Am. Guild of Musical Artists; Phi Mu Alpha. Hons: 1st Place, WGN Auditions Of The Air, Chgo., 1967; Nat. Fedn. of Music Clubs Nat. Winner, 1962. Hobbies: Tennis; Hiking; Bicycling. Mgmt: USA, Columbia Artists Mgmt., NYC; Europe, Ingpen Williams Mgmt., London. Address: 6628 32nd St. NW, Washington, DC 20015, USA.2.

VRENIOS, Elizabeth Kirkpatrick, b. 26 Nov. 1940, Healdsburg, Calif., USA. Singer; Professor. Educ: BMus, Univ. of Pacific, 1962; MusM, Northwestern Univ. m. Nicholas Vrenios, 2 s. Career: Soloist w. Nat., Stockton, Saganaw & Alexandria Symphs.; Apprentice Artist, Santa Fe Opera; Artist, Lake George & Colo. Springs Operas; Soloist, Inaugural Ball for Pres. Johnson; Soloist, Wolf Trap, Kennedy Ctr.; Solo recitals inclng. Nat. Gall., Phillips Gall. & Community Concerts; Solo tours of Mid-West & E & W Coasts; Premieres incl. A Cycle of Cities (Siegmeister), The Outcasts of Poker Flat (Beckler), Elephant Steps, (Silverman) & Voice Quintet (Makris). Recording: Songs by Elie Siegmeister. Fndr. & Dir., Am. Univ. Opera Theater; Assoc. Prof. of Music & Chmn., Voice Dept., Am. Univ., Wash. DC. Mbrships: Pi Kappa Lambda; Mu Phi Epsilon; Nat. Fedn. Music Clubs; Alpha Chi Omega. Hobbies: Parapsychology, Gardening. Address: 6628 32nd St. NW. DC 20015, USA.5.

VRHEL, James J, b. 6 Dec. 1920, Chgo., Ill., USA. Double Bass Player. Educ: Northwestern Univ.; Univs. of Ind. & Chgo.; Grad., Alexander Hamilton Inst. of Business; studied music w. Vaclav Jiskra & Franz Holz; profl. trng. w. Chgo. Civic orch. m. Lois P Vrhel. Career: Mbr. of Indpls. Symph. Orch., Cleveland Symph. Orch., etc; Mbr., 32 yrs., Asst. Prin. Bass Player, 20 yrs., Prin. Double Bass Player, 9 yrs., Chgo. Symph. Orch.; WGN TV apps. Recordings for major record Cos. Publs. Ed., Simandl, Bk. II, 1947; Ed., Storch-Hrbe, Etudes for Double Bass, 1948. Mbr., musical & social orgs. Hobbies incl: Yachting; Travel. Mgmt: Orchl. Assn. of Chgo. Address: 3010 S Harlem Ave., Riverside, IL 60546, USA.

VRHOVSKI, Josip B. 20 Feb. 1902, Crecana, Yugoslavia. Composer; Educator. Educ: Music Acad., Zagreb; Hochschule für Musik, Berlin. m. Nada Boskic, 2 children. Career: Dir. & Prof., Music Schl., Varazdin, 1945-51; Cond., Varazdin Theatre, 1945-51; Dir. & Prof. of Music Schl., Cond. of orch., Karlovac, 1953-63; Cond. of Theatre orch. & Prof. of Music Schl., Split, 1951-53. Comps. incl: solo and choral vocal works, church songs, brass quartets, wind quintets, orchl. comps. & opera 'Jana.' Mbrships: Soc. of Croatian Comps., Zagreb; Assn. of Yugoslav Comps., Belgrade. Hons: 6 awards for comp.; Pres. Tito's medal; award for pedagogical work, 1976. Address: Gracani Isce 27, 41070 Zagreb, Yugoslavia.

VRIEND, Jan N M, b. 10 Nov. 1938, Sybekarspel, Netherlands. Composer; Conductor; Theoretician; Pianist; Organist. Educ: Conserv. of Amsterdam; Inst. of Sonol., Utrecht; Schola Cantorum, Paris. 1 d. Career: Cond. of choirs, - 1970; Organist, - 1965; Fndr. & Cond., ASKO-ens. for Contemporary Music, - 1970; Cond. of orchs. & ensembles of contemporary music; Tchr., Conserv., Utrecht, 1968-69; Lectr. for radio & other instns; Theoretical rsch. w. Jos Kunst into logico-mathematical basis of music. Major comps. incl: Ensembles for choir, 1971; Elements of Logic (w. Jos Kunst), for 35 wind instruments, 1972; Kri, for choir & instruments, 1975; Huantan for organ & wind orch. Hons. incl: 1st Prize, Int. Gaudeamus Fest., 1970. Address: Het Laagt 129, Amsterdam, Netherlands.

VRONSKY, Karel, b. 18 July 1918, Vienna, Austria. Violinist. Educ: Prague Conserv., Czechoslovakia; Mistrovska Schl., Prague. m. Karla Tluchorova, 3 children. Debut: Prague. Career: Concertmaster, Czech Philharmony; Concertmaster, Moravian Philharmony; Concertmaster, Pilsen Opera; Prof., Conserv., Pilsen. Concertmaster, recordings of opera, symphs. & chmbr. music. Mbr., Sect. of Perf. Artists, Union of Czechoslovak Composers. Hobbies: Fishing. Mgmt: Pragokoncert. Address: Blatenska 17, 30703 Pilsen, Czechoslovakia.

VUKÁN, George, b. 21 Aug. 1941, Budapest, Hungary. Pianist; Composer; Arranger; Professor. Educ: Music Conserv. Debut: aged 14. Career: (as pianist), classical concerts in Acad. of Budapest; jazz concerts throughout Europe; num. recordings on radio & TV in Hungary & abroad; music for 38 films; Prof. of comp. & arr., Jazz fac., Univ. of Budapest. Comps. incl: 7 Jazz Symphonic Pieces; Concerto for 2 pianos & orch.; music for theatre, film, radio & TV; chmbr. jazz music; num. jazz tunes. num. recordings. Publs: The Vocal Art (I-II); Arrangement (I-V); The Relative Axis - Improvising System. Mbrships: The Hungarian Music Fndn.; ibid., jazz fac. Hons: Comps. prize of Hungarian Radio, 1970; 2nd prize, Montreux, 1969; 1st prize, Hungarian Piano competition, Helikon, 1957; Balasz Bela Prize for film music, 1978. Hobbies. Sport; Tennis. Mgmt: Interconcert, Budapest. Address: Határör ut 19/B II 8, 1122 Budapest, Hungary.

VUKDRAGOVIĆ, Mirjana, b. 1 Sept. 1930, Belgrade, Yugoslavia. Pianist; Professor. Educ: w. Prof. Svetislav Stancić, Acad. of Music, Zagreb. Debut: Zagreb, Belgrade, 1954. Career: Concerts in all major towns in Yugoslavia, Paris, Vienna, Prague, Bratislava, etc., Bucharest, var. towns USSR, Sofia, Finland, Cairo; Prof., Fac. of Music, Belgrade. Recordings for Radio Belgrade, Zagreb. Mbrships: Assn. of Music Artists of Serbia, Belgrade. Address: Dzordza Vasingtona 38-a/V, 11000 Belgrade, Yugoslavia.

VYHNALEK, Ivo, b. 7 Mar. 1930, Milevsko, Bohemia, Czech. Composer; Music Director & Adviser. Educ: Dip. in Comp., Acad of Arts, Prague. m. Dr. Dagmar, 2 s. Debut: w. Czech. Phil. Orch., House of Arts (Rudolfinum), Prague, 1954. Career: Cultural Ed., Czech Radio, 1954-58; Dir. of Music, Czech TV, 1958-64; Hd. of Music Dept., ibid, 1964-68; Cultural Advsr. for Unitel-Film, & Dir., Filmkunst-Musikverlag, Munich, Germany, 1968-. Comps: Mandragora (after Niccolo Machiavelli) - opera, 1958; Gallows-Report, 1963; Expositio in Appocalypsim Beati Joannis Apostoli - oratorio, 1968; SVEJK - musical, 1973; music for over 50 TV & cinema films. Mbrships: Czech TV Rep., Int. Music Ctr., Vienna, 1967-68; Chmn., Film Sect., ibid, 1968-. Hons: State Award for work in Czech TV, 1968; Prize for best TV music of the yr., Union of Film & Theatre Authors, Czech. 1967. Hobby: Study & comparison of religious scis. Address: D-8000 Munich 19, Hofenfelsstr. 1 d, German. Fed. Repub.

VYNER, Michael Geoffrey, b. 3 Jan. 1943, Leeds, Yorks., UK. Artistic Director. Educ: LLB, Univ. of Leeds; Nat., Youth Orch.; Studied violin w. Eta Cohen, 1947-60. Career incls: Artistic Dir., The London Sinfonietta. Hobbies: Playing the violin; Walking. Address: Gypsy Hill Coll., Kingston Polytechnic, Kingston Hill, Kingston-on-Thames, Surrey, UK.

VYVERMAN, (Monsignor) Jules, b. 6 Jan. 1900, Malines, Belgium. Composer; Choirmaster; Inspector of Music Schools. Educ: St Rombaut Coll. Malines; Seminary, ibid; Musical studies at Inst. Lemmens (High Schl. for Sacred Music), ibid. Career: Prof., 1935-52, & Dir., 1952-63, Inst. Lemmens; Cond. St. Rombaut's Choir, & Choirmaster, Malines Cathedral, 1949-67; Ed., jrnl. Musica Sacra, 1952-63; Insp. of Music Schls., 1963-. Compositions incl: Pastor Bonus (oratorio); Kamper Goods (oratorio); Naar U (cantata); La Sainte Fleurdelysée (choir & orch.); Mariacantate (Choirs, orch. & organ); Suite for Orch.; Geen Beeld is't (diptych); 2 Masses; organ music, piano music & num. songs & anthems. Publs: Over Muziek & Componisten, 1935; Muziek op School, 1971. Contbr. to profl. publs. Mbrships. incl: Int. Musicol. Soc.; Rassegna Int. di Cappelle Musicali (Artistic Bd. of Dirs.); Vereniging voor Muziekgeschiedenis (Bd. of Dirs.). Hons. incl: Kt., Order of Leopold, 1954; Secret Chamberlain of His Holiness the Pope (Monsignor), 1959; Officer, Order of the Crown, 1960; Canon Titulary, 1962. Hobbies: Travelling; Books; Records. Address: Lange Sint Annastraat 5, B 2000 Antwerp, Belgium. 3, 19.

W

WAASDORP, Nicolaas Antonius Maria, b. 3 July 1928, Hoofdorp, Netherlands. Organist. Educ: Amsterdam Conserv. m. A H J M Waasdorp-Barel, 4 children. Debut: 1958. Career: apps. & broadcasts, Netherlands; Organist, 1960-, Dir. of choirs, Roman Cath. Ch., Overveen, nr. Haarlem; Organ Tchr., Municipal Conserv. of Zwothe, 1976. Comps: Deus Israel for 2 voices & organ; Trio for organ; Intermezzo for organ. Mbrships: KNTV; KDOV. Address: Berkenlaan 6, Bloemendaal, Netherlands.

WÄCHTER, Eberhard, b. 8 July 1929, Vienna, Austria. opera Singer. Educ: studied w. Elisabeth Rado, Vienna. m. 3 s., 3 d. Debut: Volksoper, Vienna. Career: w. Vienna State Opera, 1955-; apps. in Germany, France, Netherlands, UK, Spain, USA, Italy; participant in fests. inclng. Bayreuth Salzburg & Salzburg. 16.

WADDAMS, Eric William, b. 21 May 1913, Ealing, London, UK. Teacher. Educ: MA, Kings Coll., Cambridge. m. Joan Isobel Colls, 3 d. Career: Commentator, Comp., Cond., Today in the S & W, mag. prog., BBC; Fndr. & Cond., Les Petits Chanteurs de Guernsey. Comps: Carols for St. Nicholas & St. Christopher. Recordings: w. Les Petits Chanteurs de Guernsey & Elizabeth Coll. Choir (Guernsey). Mbrships: VP, Sporting Club. Hons: Les Petits Chanteurs de Guernsey won Class Superierure, French Nat. Choir Fest., 1972; Cup de sec. d'éetatá la Jeunesse, sports et loisir, ibid. Hobbies: Mycology; Ornithology; Heraldry. Address: Monamy, St. Jacques, Guernsey, Channel Islands.

WADE, Frank, b. 25 July 1908, Salford, UK. Pianist; Conductor; Composer. Educ: Manchester Univ.; Hon. FTCL; Hon. GSM. m. Constance Astington. Debut w. BBC Northern Orch. Career: Asst. to Controller, Music, BBC, 1952-55; Hd., Light Music Prog., BBC, 1955-65. Mbrships: Hon. Mbr. Composers Guild of GB; Songwriters Guild; Perf. Right Soc. Hons: Lt. Col., RAC. Hobby: Writing musical criticism. Address: 9 Winchester Court, Worthing, Sussex, UK. 3.

WAGEMANS, Peter-Jan, b. 7 Sept. 1952, The Hague, Netherlands. Organist; Composer; Teacher in music theory. Educ: Organ Dip B, studied w. Wim van Beek, theory & comp. w. Jan van Vlijmen & Klaus Huber. Debut as cond. & comp., Utrecht, 1972. Career: Works have been perf. by Hague Phil., Utrecht Phil., Ned. Sax. Quartet, M Ensemble, in and outside Netherlands; sev. works broadcast. Comps: Symph., Op. 3; Overture, Op. 4; 2 Piano Pieces, Op. 5; Wind Quintet, Op. 6; Muziek I, Op. 7; Saxofoonquartet, Op. 8; Vit de Zangen van Maldoror (ballet), Op. 9; Muziek II, Op. 10; Alla Marcia (tuba concerto), Op. 11; 3 Dances, Nuages Gris (tuba solo), Op. 12. Mbr. Genootschap van Ned. Componisten. Hons: Nicolai Prize for comp., 1975; Fock Medallion for theory of music, 1977. Hobby: Film. Address: 2e Sweelinckstraat 95, The Hague, Netherlands.

WAGENAAR, Nelly, b. 27 Nov. 1898, Utrecht, Netherlands. Concert Pianist; Professor of Piano (Retired). Educ: Dip. cum laude, Utrecht Conserv., 1920; studied w. Artur Schnabel & Bruno Eisner, Berlin, Germany, 1922-23. m. Manuel Steuer. Debut: Utrecht, 1920. Career: Concert pianist; Prof. of Piano, Amsterdam Conserv., 1927-68. Hon. Mbr., Royal Dutch Musicians Assn. Hobbies: Reading; Country Life. Address: van Hoornbeek straat 19, The Hague, Netherlands.

WAGNER, Edyth Elizabeth, b. 15 Oct. 1916, Brooklyn, NY, USA. Pianist; Professor of Piano & Music Education. Educ: Piano Dip., Inst. of Musical Art, NYC, 1941; BS (piano), Juilliard Schl. of Music, 1947; studied w. James Friskin & Josef Raieff, ibid; MMus, (Piano), Univ. of S Calif., 1951; DMA, Music Educ., ibid, 1968. m. Frederick C. Roop. Debut: LaForge Studies, NYC, 1938. Career incl: Taught pvtly. at studio in NYC & at her LI home; Taught at the Juilliard Summer Sessions & the Juilliard Prep. Schl.; Served on facs. of univs. in Tex. & Calif.; Piano Pedagogy Workshops at Univ.; Judge, piano auditions; WQXR Radio, NYC, 1938-39; Piano recitals, NY, Tex., Calif.; Clavichord Recitals, Calif. Recordings: Lesson tapes for the Lib. of Congress, Physically Handicapped Div.; 2 Mozart records & 3 Beethoven piano music on Educo label; w. master lessons; Rec. w. 6 other pianists the entire Int. Lib. of Piano Music, 1973. Publs: Piano Technique for the First Years, 1975; Transl., Brazilian Folk Songs for Beginners; Raymond Burrows & his Contributions to Music Education, 1968. Contbr. to: Clavier, Music Jrnl., etc. Mbrships incl: Am. Musicol. Soc.; Pi Kappa Lambda; Music Tchrs. Nat. Assn.; Life Mbr., MENC. Var. hobbies. Address: 506 Oak Creek Ln., Ojai, CA 93023, USA.

WAGNER, John Waldorf, b. 11 Feb. 1937, Oak Park, Ill., USA. Musicologist; Clarinettist. Educ: BM, DePauw Univ., Greencastle, Ind.; MM, Fla. State Univ., Tallahassee, Fla.; PhD, Ind. Univ., Bloomington. m. Bobbie B Wagner, 2 s. Career: Assoc. Prof. of Music, Newberry Coll., SC; 2nd Clarinettist, Columbia (SC) Philharmonic Orch. Publs: Ed., The Music of James Hewitt (in progress). Contbr. to: Grove's Dictionary of Music & Musicians; Musical Quarterly; Notes; Ga. Histl. Quarterly. Mbrships: Sec.-Treas., SE Chapt., Am. Musicol. Soc.; MENC. Hobbies: Tennis; Playing Jazz. Address: 905 Amelia St., Newberry, SC 29108, USA.

WAGNER, Lavern John, b. 30 Dec. 1925, Bellevue, Iowa, USA. Musicologist; Composer of Sacred Music; Pianist; Trumpet Player; Educator. Educ: BMus, Loras Coll., 1949; BMusEd, Oberlin Coll., 1952; MMus, Univ. Wis., 1953; PhD, ibid., 1957. m. Joan M Ernst, 4 s., 7 d. & 2 s., 1 d. adopted. Career incl: Prof. of Music & Chmn. of Music Dept., Quincy Coll., Ill., 1958-. Comps. incl: Religious hymns; Mass in the Aeolian Mode; Fanfares for a Festival Banquet. Recordings incl: Christmas with the Wagner Family Singers. Publs. incl: Philippe Rogier, 3 Vols., 1974. Contbr. to profl. jrnls. Mbr. num. profl. orgs. Recip. var. fellowships. Hobbies: Accordion playing in German Band; Writing Polkas & Waltzes. Address: 1419 Locust St., Quincy, IL 62301, USA.

WAGNER, Manfred, b. 5 Dec. 1952, Vienna, Austria. Pianist; Professor of Piano. Educ: Dips. as Concert & Chmbr. music Pianist, Acad. of Music, Vienna. Career: Professor of Piano, Acad. of Music, Vienna; Concerts in Austria, Belgium, German Fed. Repub., Turkey, Iran & Egypt & at Vienna Fest. Week, 1975; TV apps. for Austrian Radio Corp., Bavarian Radio & Radio Zagreb, Yugoslavia. Hons: Gold Medal, GB Viotti Int. Music Competition, Vercelli, Italy, 1971. Hobbies: Architecture; Sculpture; Natural Science Books & Photography. Address: Bartensteingasse 8/20, A-1010 Vienna, Austria.

WAGNER, Manfred J, b. 31 Aug. 1944, Amstetten, Austria. High School Professor. Educ: DPh; Studied conducting & comp. m. Doris Neuvians, 2 s. Career: Lehrbeauftragter, Inst. für Aufführungspraxis, Graz, 1970-72; Musikredakteur, Hessischer Rundfunk, 1973; Lehrkanzel für Kultur & Geistesgeschichte, Hochschule f. angew Kunst, Vienna, 1974. Mbr., Internationales Forum Burgenland. Publs: Die Harmonielehre in der Ersten Hälfte des 19 Jarhunderts, 1974; Österreichs Musikkritik in Beispielen, 1976; Opern auf Schallplatten (w. K Blaukopf), 1974. Contbr. to profl. jrnls. Recip., Theodor Körner Prize, 1971. Address: 1010 Vienna, Herrengasse 15/1/10, Austria.

WAGNER, Werner S., b. 3 Dec. 1927, Koeln, Germany. Composer; Concert Agent. Educ: study of composition w. Jacobo Ficher; piano study w. Berta Sujovolsky. m. Maria Julia Pero, 2 children (by prev. marriage). Compositions incl: Sonatina (piano); First String Quartet; Song Cycle (mezzo soprano & woodwind quartet); Ten Miniatures for English Horn & Piano; Lamentaciones (symph. orch.); Concierto de Camara (chmbr. orch.); Suite for Children (string orch.); Concerto (piano & orch.); Rhapsody (cello & orch.); Concerto (piano & orch.); Rhapsody (cello & orch.); Argentine Rhapsody (symph. orch.); Suite No. 1 (string orch.); Suite No. 2 (symph. orch.); Improvisaciones Sinfonicas (symph. orch.); Second String Quartet; Musica Concertante (horn & strings). Contbr. & opera critic to Oper & Konzert, Munich. Mbrships: Past Pres., Assn. of Young Composers of Argentina; Union of Composers of Argentina; Past Sec., Argentine Nat. Music Coun.; Int. Music Committee, UNESCO. Recip. var. awards for compositions. Hobby: Filming. Address: Guido 1612 141B, 1016 Buenos Aires, Argentina.

WAGONER, Ruth Diane, b. 24 May 1954, Greensboro, NC, USS. Cellist. Educ: BMus, Univ. of NC, Chapel Hill; Study w. Alan Smith; Univ. of Texas at Austin w. Phyllis Young. Career: Mbr. Greensbor Symph. Orch., 1975-78; Winston Salem Symph. Orch., 1976-78; NC Schl. of the Arts Orch., 1977-78; Brevard Music Centre Orch.; Eastern & Aspen Music Fests.; Faculty Cannon Music Camp, 1978. Mbr. Violoncello Soc., NY. Recip. acad. hons. Address: 673 Percy Street, Greensboro, NC 27405, USA.

WAITZMAN, Daniel Robert, b. 15 July 1943, Rochester, NY, USA. Flautist; Recorder Player. Educ: BA, Columbia coll., 1965; MA, Columbia Univ., 1968. Debut: Carnegie Recital Hall, NYC, 1971. Career incl: Soloist, Clarion Concerts Orch., Amor Artis Orch., 1974-; Soloist, Queens Symph. Chmbr. Orch., LI Baroque Ensemble; Prin. Recorderist, NBC-TV show, Watch Your Child; Recitalist, major US cities, Alice Tully Hall,

Carnegie Hall, etc. Recordings: Musical Heritage Soc. MHS 1860. Publs: The Art of Playing th Recorder, 1976; sev. eds. of musical works. Contbr. to: Am. Recorder; Recorder & Music; Galpin Soc. Jrnl. Hons: Concert Artists Guild Award, 1971; Int. Bach Soc. Perf. Award, 1973. Mgmt: Podium Mgmt. Assocs., Inc., 75 E 55th St., NY, NY 10022, USA. Address: 28-02 Parsons Blvd., Flushing, NY 11345, USA. 6.

WAKEFIELD, John, b. 21 June 1936, Wakefield, UK. Operatic Tenor; Teacher of Singing. Educ: RAM; LRAM; FRAM. m. Jennifer Phillips, 1 d. Debut: Welsh Nat. & Sadler's Wells Operas, 1961. Career: Glyndebourne debut as Macduff, 1964; Covent Garden debut in Gianni Schicchi, 1965. Recordings: Handel's Messiah; Cavalli's L'Ormindo; Sadler's Wells Opera. Recordings. Hons: Kathleen Ferrier Scholarship, 1956; s'Hertogenbosch Int. Competition, 1960. Hobbies: Golf; Squash; Reading; Eating. Address: 59 Woodstock Rd., London W4 1ED, UK.

WAKELKAMP, Wim Antonie Johannes, b. 17 Oct. 1924, Amersfoort, Netherlands. Composer; Musicologist. Educ: Univ. of Leiden. m. Maria Stuyvenberg, 3 s., 3 d. Career incls: Choirmaster/Organist, Ch. of the Assumption of the Holy Virgin Mary, Master in Cond., Roman Cath. Schl. for Ch. Music, & Cond., var. grps., inclng: Utrecht Chmbr. Choir, Viva la Musica, 1949-61; Choirmaster/Organist, Ch. of the Holy Virgin of Good Counsel; Organist/Choirmaster, RC Ch., Oosterwolds; Cond., Die Haghe Sanghers & Guido van Arezzo; Music Master, Tchrs. Sem., 1961-72; currently Comp. & Musicol. Comps. incl: masses; motets; songs. Mbrships. incl: Cath. Music Dirs. & Organists Assn.; St. Gregorius Soc. Hobbies: Art; Culture. Address: No. 47 Farmhouse Fermate, 8432 PD Haule, Friesland, Netherlands.

WALACIŃSKI, Adam, b. 18 Sept. 1928,Cracow, Poland. Composer; Music Critic. Educ: State Coll. of Music, Cracow, 1947-51; Post grad. Dip. in Comp. m. Anna Walacińska. Career: Violinist, Polish Radio Orch., Cracow, 1949-56; Devoted to comp., 1957-; Tchr., State Coll. of Music, Cracow, 1972-; Lectr., Coll. of Dramatic Art, ibid, 1973-; Comps. perfd. in Europe & USA & at num. int. music fests. inclng. Warsaw & Belgrade, Music Today, Can., 1971, Holland Fest., 1973. Comps. incl: Canzonazca, 1967; Torso, 1971; Divertimento interrotto, 1974; over 120 works for films & TV plays. Mbrships: Chmn., Cracow Sect., Polish Comps. Union. Publs. incl: Szymanowskis Gesamtausgabe, 1974; num. review articles. Recip., Nat. Prize for film music, 1966; Music Prize of Cracow, 1976. Address: ul. Br. Wesolowskiego 4, 30-138 Cracow, Poland.

WALCHA, (Arthur Emil) Helmut, b. 27 Oct. 1907, Leipzig, Germany. Organist; Harpsichordist; Professor. State Music School, Frankfurt-Main; Organist, Three Kings Church, Frankfurt-Main. Educ: Dept. of Sacred Music, Leipzig Conserv. m. Ursula Koch. Compositions: Chorale-Preludes for Organ, Vols. I-III. Recordings: Complete Organ Works of J S Bach, DGG Archiv; Complete Harpsichord Works of J S Bach, Electrola. Publs: Ed., "die Künst der Füge" J S Bach Orgel-Ausgabe; Ed., 12 Orgelkonzerte von G F Händel. Address: 27, Hasselhorstweg, Frankfurt-Main, German Fed. Repub. 3.

WALDEN, William Glenn, b. 21 Apr. 1943, Gadsden, Ala., USA. Bass Trombonist. Educ: BS in Music Educ.; MA, Music Hist. m. Mary Powell Walden. Publs: Igor Stravinsky's Abraham & Isaac, Southern Chapt. of Am. Musicol Soc., 1975. Mbrships: Am. Musicol. Soc.; Int. Webern Soc.; Int. Berg Soc.; Int. Schoenberg Soc.; Pi Kappa Lambda; Am. Recorder Soc.; MENC; Phi Mu Alpha Sinfonia. Hobbies: Electronics; Citizen's Band Radio. Address: 3101 Highland Rd. Apt. 122, Baton Rouge, LA 70802, USA.

WALE, Reginald George, b. 6 Mar. 1925, Nottingham, Uk. Musician (Percussion); Composer; Arranger; Musical Director. Educ: Nottingham Conserv. of Music. Career: Soloist, theatres, 5 yrs.; Musical Dir., RMS Caronia, 2 yrs.; Musical Dir. for Russ Conway, TV incl. Number Please Series, ABC-TV; Russ Conway Show, BBC-TV; Own series, Anglia TV; 15 yrs. as session musician w. bands of Ron Goodwin, Stanley Black, Bill McGuffie, Mancini, etc.; Over 100 broadcasts w. own band. Recordings of own comps. incl: LPs Bouquet; Bach-a-Changing; Merry Vibes of Windsor; Go-Go-Go; Quartet of Modern Jazz Nos. 1 & 2; Quintet of Modern Jazz; Flute 'n Four; Spinning Like A Top; Dimples. Publs: Hymn book - Teach Me How to Look, 1973. Mbrships: Performing Rights Soc.; Musicians Union. Hobby: Golf. Address: 90 Glasgow House, Maida Vale, London W9, UK.

WALKER, Agnes T., b. Thankerton, Biggar, Scotland. Concert Pianist. Educ: LRAM; ARCM. m. William McLellan, 1 d. Debut: Glasgow, Scotland. Career: Concerts in Europe, Am. & Can.;

STV Piano Series; Stirling Festival; Pitlochry Mini-Festival; Tours in Poland, Hungary, Germany & Scandinavia; Orchl. engagements SNO, BBC, Can., Poland, Moscow, etc. Recordings: A Liszt Legend; Chopin; Jane Stirling. Contbr. to Glasgow Herald; Scotsman; Scottish Field; Brit. Inst. of Recorded Sound Mag. Mbrships: Pres., Zonta Club, Glasgow; Sesame Club, London. Recip. Caird Travelling Scholarship in Music. Mgmt: Ibbs & Tillett, London. Address: The Knowe, Thankerton, Biggar, Scotland, UK. 3, 27.

WALKER, Alan, b. 6 Apr. 1930, Scunthorpe, UK. Writer; Teacher; Musicologist. Educ: DMus, Durham Univ.; FGSM; ARCM. m. Valerie Tryon. Career: BBC Music Prod., 1961-71; Prof. & chmn., Music Dept., McMaster Univ., Can. Publs. incl: A Study in Musical Analysis, 1962; An Anatomy of Musical Criticism, 1966; (ed.) Frederic Chopin: Profiles of the Man & his Music, 1970; (ed.) Robert Schumann: The Man & his Music, 1971; Franz Liszt: A Biography, 1971. Contbr. of num. articles to: Ency. Britannica; Times Lit. Supplement; Times Educl. Supplement; Music & Letters; Music Review; The Listener; Musical Times, etc. Hon. FGSM. Hobby: Book Collecting. Address: Dept. of Music, McMaster Univ., Ontario, Can. 14, 28.

WALKER, Arthur Dennis, b. 14 Sept. 1932, Bradford, Yorks., UK. Music Librarian; Musicologist. Educ: Pvte. study of Music. Career: Asst., Bradford Pub. Libs., 1951-57; Sr. Asst., Battersea Pub. Libs., London, 1958-64; Music Libn., Manchester Univ., 1964-. Compositions: Var. works have been performed. Publs: Music Printing: A Bibliography, 1963; Schoenberg, Gurrelieder (transl.), 1966; A Short History of Breitkopf & Härtel, 1969; Handel, dettingen Te Deum, 1970; Bruckner, Overture in G Minor, 1972; G. F. Handel: The Newman Flower Collection in the Henry Watson Music Library, A Catalogue, 1972; Handel, Judas Maccabaeus, 1973; Wagner, Polonaise, 1973; Mozart Symphony K.338/Minuet K.409, 1976. Contbr. to: Music Teacher; Musical Times; Audio Record Review; Music & Letters; Records & Recording; Brio; Lib. Assn. Record; RMA Rsch. Chronicle; Die Musik in Geschichte & Gegenwart. Mbrships: Lib. Assn.; Int. Assn. Music Libs. (UK Br.); Brit. Inst. Recorded Sound; Int. Alban Berg Soc.; Hallé Concerts Soc.; Hallé Club; Brontë Soc.; PRS; Songwriters' Guild. Hobbies incl: Berg; Bruckner; Handel; Mahler; Brontë Family; Trams; Railway History. Address: 15 Maitland Ave., Manchester M21 2ND, UK. 3.

WALKER, Betty Stoller, b. 17 June 1940, Jamesport, Mo., USA. Music Teacher (Accordion, Piano, Voice, Theory). Educ: BMus, 1961, MMus & Perf.'s Cert. in Opera, 1963, Eastman Schl. of Music. m. Jack Walker. Career: Fndr.-Cond., Upstate Accordion Orch., 1967. w. tours of Can., 1972, & Europe, 1973; Dir. Accordion Workshops, Opera roles & perfs. incl Zerlina, Don Giovanni; Concepcion, L'Heure Espagnol. Musical comedy roles incl: Marian in the Music Man; Julie in Show Boat. Contbr. to profl. jrnls., USA & Denmark. Mbrships incl: Nat. MTA (Chmn., Accordion Subject Area, 1976-); Accordion Tchrs. Guild (Pres., 1976-77). Hons: 1st Places w. Orch. in Nat. Accordion Competitions, 1967, 68. Hobbies: Skiing; Sewing; Interior Decorating. Mgmt: Mgr-Walker Music Inc., 18 Sibley Pl., Rochester, NY, 14607, USA. Address: as above.

WALKER, Clyde Phillip, b. 14 June 1944, Farmville, Va., USA. Baritone. Educ: BMus, Univ. of Wash., Seattle. Career: BBC TV; opera, concert & recital apps. throughout the USA in 30 ldng. opera roles, 15 oratorios & a varied song repertoire (Boston Symph., Opera Soc. of Wash. DC, San Fran. Spring Opera, Minnesota Opera, Opera South). Mbrships: Artists Advsry. Bd., Affiliate Artists, Inc.; Am. Guild of Musical Artists. Hons. incl: Winner, Wm. Mattheus Sullivan Fndn., 1972. Hobbies: Piano; Cycling; Cooking; Hiking. Address: The Ansonia, 2109 Broadway, Suite 15-44, NY, NY 10023, USA.

WALKER, Edward, b. 19 Apr. 1909, Stoke-on-Trent, Staffs., UK. Flautist. Educ: FRAM, 1969; FRCM, 1972. m. Mary Reeve, 1 s., 1 d. Career: Scottish Orch., 1929-30; BBC Symph. Orch., 1930-37; LSO, 1937-55; Philharmonia Orch., 1958-75; Prof., RCM, 1950-. Recordings: Mozart & Haydn Flute Quartets; Virtuoso Ensemble. Mbr., Savage Club. Hons: Ross Schlr., RAM. Hobbies: Golf; Sailing. Address: St. John's Cottge, John St., Shoreham-by-Sea, Sussex, UK.

WALKER, Eldon, b. 5 April 1932, Wallasey, Cheshire, UK. Composer. Educ: pvte. studies w. Matyas Seiber & Thomas Wess; BSc, London; MSc, Liverpool. m. Margaret Mary Jefferson. Comps: Elegy; This Bird (Soprano flute, clarinet); Duologne (2 clarinets, bass clarinet); Terzetto (flute, viola, guitar). Mbrships: CGGB; Soc. for the Promotion of New Music; Chmn., Sandon Studios Soc. Music Group, Liverpool, 1967-69; Mercia Music Group, E Anglia. Hobbies:

Photography; Crystallography. Address: Thornleigh, Park Lane, Preesall, Nr. Blackpool, Lancs., UK.

WALKER, Geoffrey Henry, b. 1 Aug. 1948, Stoke-on-Trent, UK. Teacher; Organist; Conductor. Educ: MA, St. Peter's Coll., Univ. Oxford; Dip. Lib. Studies, Univ. Coll., London; Assoc., Royal Coll. Organists. Career: Dir. of Music, Newcastle HS, Staffs., 1974-; Accompanist, 1975-78; Chorus Master, Ceramic City Choir, 1978-; Conductor, St. Cecilia Choral Soc., 1978-; Sev. appts. as organist & choirmaster incl: St. Aloysius Ch., Oxford; HM Prison, Holloway; St. Giles Parish Ch., Newcastle, 1979-. Mbr., Incorp. Soc. of Musicians. Address: 40 The Plaisaunce, Westlands, Newcastle-under-Lyme, Staffs., ST5 3RZ, UK.

WALKER, George Theophilus, b. 27 June 1922, Wash. DC, USA. Composer; Pianist. Educ: MusB, Oberlin Coll.; Artist Dip., Curtis Inst. of Music; DMA, Rochester Univ. Debut: NY Town Hall, 1945. Career: Concert tours of USA & Europe as pianist. Comps. incl: Sonata for cello & piano; 3 Lyrics for chorus; 3 piano sonatas; Perimeters for clarinet & piano (recorded); Spektra for piano (recorded); Lyric for strings; Variations for orch. (recorded); Music for Brass (recorded); Piano concerto; Trombone concerto; Dialogus for Cello & orch.; 2 String Quartets; Mass for Chorus & orch.; Songs, Choral works. Mbr., ASCAP. Hons: Harvey Gaul Prize, 1964; Eastman Alumni Award, 1976; num. Fellowships incl. Rockefeller Fellow, 1971, '74. Hobbies incl: Tennis; Hi-Fi. Address: 323 Grove St., Montclair, NJ 07042, USA.

WALKER, Gerald Alan, b. 8 Jan. 1947, El Centro, Calif., USA. Musician (Oboe; English Horn; Oboe d'amore). Educ: Grad., Calif. State Univ., Los Angeles; w. Julien Shanis, San Fran. Symph.; Royal Conserv., Hague, Netherlands. Career: Mbr., Quartette en Concert; Freelance Musician; Los Angeles Camerata. Mgmt: West Coast Artists Mgmt. Address: PO Box 4100E, LA, CA 90041, USA.

WALKER, James, b. 4 Oct. 1929, Rotherham, UK. Pianist; Composer. Educ: ALCM. m. Dorothy Elizabeth Muffett, 1 s., 1 d. Career: Res. Pianist, Leicester Univ.; Mbr., Archduke Piano Trio; Apps. at fests., recitals, broadcasting. Comps: Shakespeare settings; Miniature Suite; Wind Scherzo; Clarinet Sonatina; Trumpet Sonatina; num. wind comps.; Opera, The Proposal. Recordings: The Hollow Crown; Homage to Kreisler. Mbr. ISM. Hons: MMus, Leicester, 1975. Hobby: Reading. Mgmt: London Artists. Address: Cornerways, 85 S Green Dr., Stratford-upon-Avon, Warwicks., UK.

WALKER, Penelope, b. 12 Oct. 1956, Manchester, UK. Singer. Educ: GSM; AGSM, 1977; cert. of advanced studies, 1978. Debut: Royal Albert Hall, London, 1976. Career: apps. w. most ldng. orchs. in UK; perfs. at South Bank, Wigmore Hall, Three Choirs Fest.; toured w. World of Gilbert & Sullivan; app. on HTV & Austrian radio. Recordings: for Radio Wales, incl. Elgar's Sea Pictures. Mbrships: Equity; ISM. Hons: Countess of Munster Musical Trust Awards, 1977 & 78; Brit. Arts Coun. Award & Bursary from 'The Friends of Covent Garden' to study at Nat. Opera Studio, 1979-80; 1st Prize, Triennial Welsh Young Singers Competition, 1979; Winner, Franz Schubert Inst. Jr. Prize for Interpretation of Lied, 1979. Hobbies: Squash; Cookery; Travel. Mgmt: Concert Directory Int. Address: 33 Shakespeare Tower, Barbican, London EC2, UK.

WALKER, Richard Link, b. 18 Jan. 1940, Lexington, NC, USA. Music Librarian. Educ: BA, High Pt. Coll.; Peabody Conserv., Balt., Md.; MMus, MLS, Univ. NC, Chapel Hill; Clarinet, saxophone & voice, w. var. tutors. m. Judith Rogers Walker, 1 s. Career incls: (Past) Min. Music & Tenor Soloist, United Meth. Ch.; Saxophone soloist & clinician; Saxophone recitals, Univ. NC; Univ. NC New Music Ensemble; Music Libn., Bklyn. Coll.; (Currently) Music Libn., NC Symph. Orch. Publs. incl: A Study of Journals Containing Reviews of Books in the Field of Music, 1971. Mbr. var. profl. orgs. Hobbies incl: Photography; Philately. Address: 228 Monmouth Ave., Durham, NC 27701, USA.

WALKER, Sandra, b. 1 Oct. 1946, Richmond, Va., USA. Opera Singer (Mezzo-Soprano). Educ: Univ. of N Carolina. m. Melvin Brown. Debut: San Fran. Opera, 1972. Career: New York City Opera; Chgo. Lyric Opera; Spoleto Fest., Italy & USA; TV Great Performance Series; Menotti's The Consul (Secretary) & Saint of Bleeker St. (Desideria). Recordings: Ned Rorem's King Midas; Song Cycle for Tenor & Mezzo Soprano (w. John Stewart). Hobbies: Cooking; Entertaining. Address: c/o Kazuko Hillyer Int., 250 W 57th St., NY, NY 10019, USA.

WALKER, Sarah, b. Cheltenham, UK. Mezzo Soprano. Educ: RCM; ARCM; LRAM. m. Graham Allum. Debut: Diana/Giove, Cavalli's La Calisto, Glyndebourne Fest. Opera, 1971. Career:

Glyndebourne, Scottish, Royal Opera House Covent Garden, Chicago, Kent & Engl. Nat. Operas; roles incl: Didon, Les Troyens; Marguerite, La Damnation de Faust; Ottavia, Poppea & Penelope, Monteverdi; Maria Stuarda; Dorabella; Fricka; Herodias; BBC Promenade Concerts; frequent recitals; perfs. of contemp. works w. London Sinfonietta, London & abroad; Recitals w. Graham Johnson, USA & Europe. Recordings: "Voices", w. London Sinfonietta. Mbr., ISM. Recip. var. awards. Hobbies: Reading; Crochet; Gardening; Interior Design. Mgmt: Ibbs & Tillett, 124 Wigmore St., London W1H OAY, UK. Address: 152 Inchmery Rd., London SE6 1DF, UK.

WALKER, William, b. 29 Oct. 1931, Waco, Texas, USA. Baritone. Educ: BMus, Texas Christian Univ., 1956. m. Marci Martin Walker, 1 d., 3 s. Debut: Ft. Worth, Texas, 1956; Metropolitan Opera, 1962. Career: Leading Baritone, Metropolitan Opera, 1962-; Concert apps. w. all major Symph. Orchs. in USA: Recitals, USA, Can., Sweden, Iceland & Poland; Num. TV apps., USA; Operatic apps. w. Metropolitan, Japan, 1975, Theatr Weilki, Warsaw, 1976. Mbrships: Lotos Club (NY); Dutch Treat Club (NY); Canyon Creek Country Club (San Antonio, Tex.). Hons: Disting. Alumnus, Texas Christian Univ., 1970. Hobby: Golf. Mgmt: Columbia Artists Mgmt., NY. Address: 209 Lariat Dr., San Antonio, TX 78232, USA. 2, 30.

WALL, Ashley Grainger, b. 23 Nov. 1945, London, UK. Musician: Tuba. Educ: RCM; ARCM. m. Gillian Flora Westgate. Career: Mbr., RPO, 1969-74; Orch. of Royal Opera House, Covent Garden, 1974-; Prof. of Tuba, TCL, 1976-. Mbrship: Royal Soc. of Musicians of GB. Address: Kingsley Cottage, Little Mill, E Peckham, Tonbridge, Kent, TN12 5JP, UK. 3.

WALLACE, Ian, b. 10 July 1919, London, UK. Singer. Educ: studied singing w. Rodolfo Mele, London; MA (Law), Trinity Coll.,Cambridge. m. Patricia Gordon (née Black), 1 s., 1 d. Debut: w. New London Opera Co., Cambridge Theatre, 1946. Career: operatic apps. in buffo roles, Glyndebourne, Scottish & Welsh Nat. Opera, & in Rome, Venice, Parma, Berlin & Bregenz; num. concert apps. & radio & TV broadcasts; stage career in musicals, revue, pantomime & straight plays. Has many num. recordings. Author, Promise Me You'll Sing Mud, 1975. Mbrships: Pres., ISM, 1979-80; Brit. Actor's Equity; Garrick Club. Hobbies: Golf; Sailing. Mgmt: Raymond Gubbay, Tower Music, 125 Tottenham Ct. Rd., London W1P 9HN, UK. Address: 18 Denewood Rd., Highgate, London N6, 4AJ, UK. 1, 3.

WALLACE, Paul J., b. 24 Mar. 1928, Pontiac, Mich., USA. University Professor; Trombonist; Baritone Horn Player. Educ: BM, Univ. of Mich.; MM, ibid; Grad. study, Univ. of Colo. & Kan. Univ.; Nat. Music Camp, Interlochen, Mich.; Berkshire Music Ctr., Tanglewood, Mass. m. Gwyndolyn M. Wallace, 3 d. Career: Mbr., US Army Band, Wash. DC, 1952-63; Tchr., Brass & Band Instruments, Wis. State Coll., Stevens Pt., 1957-63; Tchr., Brass & Musical Educ., Kan. Univ., 1955-57; Fac. Mbr., Kent State Univ., 1963-; currently Prof. of Music & Assoc. Dir., Schl. of Music, ibid. Compositions: unpubld. arrangements. Mbrships: 1st Ed., catalog of Ms. Music for Winds & Percussion, 1958-63, Ed., NACWPI Bulletin (now NACWPI Jrnl.), 1962-66, Nat. Bd., 1968-72, Nat. Pres., 1968-70, Past Nat. Pres. & Chmn., Coun. of Past Pres., 1970-72, NACWPI; MENC; AAUP; Ohio Music Educ. Assn.; Past Mbr., Phi Mu Alpha, Kappa Kappa Psi, Pi Kappa Lambda & Alpha Kappa Rho; Patron, Delta Omicron; Leblanc Nat. Educator Advsry. Bd. Recip. of Oliver Ditson Schlrship., Univ. of Mich. Hobbies: Reading; Bridge; Swimming. Address: 556 Valley View, Kent, OH 44240, USA.

WALLACE, Robert William, b. 18 Nov. 1945. Pianist & Conductor. Educ: BMus, Manhattan Schl. of Music; MMus, ibid. m. Roxana Tourigny. Debut: Solo w. New Orleans Phil., 1962. Career: Concert accomp.; Vocal & opera coach; Asst. Cond., NYC Opera, 1970-72; also worked w. San Francisco Opera & Met. Opera Studio. Mbrships: Nat. Opera Assn.; Ctrl. Opera Serv. Address: 777 West End Ave., NY, NY, USA.

WALLÉN, Martti, b. Helsinki, Finland. Operatic & Concert Bass Singer. Educ: Sibelius Acad., Helsinki. Debut: Helsinki. Career: Finnish Nat. Opera, 1973-75; Prin. Bass, Royal Opera, Stockholm, 1975-; roles incl. Colline (Boheme), Ferrando, Philip II (Don Carlos), Sparafucile (Rigoletto), Geisterbote (Die Frau ohne Schatten), Dikoj (Katia Kobanova); concert & oratorio perfs. in Scandinavia, UK, Belgium. Mgmt: Artistsekretariat Ulf Törnqvist, Norrtullsgatan 26, tr.4, 11345 Stockholm, Sweden. Address: c/o mgmt.

WALLER, Ronald William, b. 26 Mar. 1916, London, UK. Musician (Bassoon). Educ: TCL; FRAM; ARAM. m. Susanna Evans, 1 s., 2 d. Career: LSO, 1948-55; Philharmonia Orch; London Wind Soloists; New Phil. Orch., 1965-; Virtuoso

Chmbr. Ensemble; Prof. RAM. Recordings: Mozart Divertimenti & Wind Serenades, w. London Wind Soloists; Beethoven Quintet, Sextet, Septet & Octet. Mbrships: RAM Club; Mill Golf Club. Hobbies: Golf; Interior Decoration. Address: 8 St. Mary's Ave., Finchley, London N3, UK. 3.

WALLFISCH, Peter, b. 20 Oct. 1924, Breslau, Germany. Pianist. Educ: Hons. degrees as Tchr. & Perf., Jerusalem Acad. of Music; Cours de Perfectionnement Marguerite Long, Paris. m. Anita Lasker, 2 c. Career: Regular concerts, broadcasts, recitals in practically every country of Europe, also Middle East, S. Am., Far East, USA; Concerts in USA & Can.; Prof., RCM. Recordings: Works by Frank Bridge, Kenneth Leighton, Guillaume Lekeu, Charles de Beriot, Mozart. Mbr., ISM. Hons: Bela Bartok Prize, 1948; Munich, 1952; Vercelli, 1951; Harriet Cohen Bach Medal, 1957; Scheveningen, 1948; Hon. RCM, etc. Hobbies: Travelling; Reading; Pets. Mgmt: Helen Jennings. Address: 27 Chelmsford Sq., London NW10, UK. 3.

WALLS, Geoffrey, b. 26 Mar. 1925, Harrow, UK. Bass Singer; Senior Lecturer in Music (Singing). Educ: BA, MA, Downing Coll., Cambridge; Mackenzie Schl. of Music, Cambridge; studies w. Norman Allin, Charles Webber, Eric Greene. Debut: 1952. Career: num. operatic roles; num. TV apps. & radio broadcasts; Soloist in oratorio; Vis. Singing Tutor, St. Mary's Coll., Strawberry Hill, London, 1967-74; Sr. Lectr. in Music (singing), Mabel Fletcher Tech. Coll., Liverpool, 1974-. Num. recordings inclng. 1st recordings of Strauss' Capriccio & Walton's Troilus & Cressida. Contbr. to jrnls. Mbr. profl. orgs. Hobbies: Cricket; Lit.; Drama. Address: 11 Searle's View, Horsham, Sussex, UK. 3.

WALLS, Robert Boen, b. 24 Dec. 1910, Spirit Lake, Idaho, USA. Choral Director; Voice Teacher; Singer (tenor). Educ: BEd., Minn. State Coll., 1932; MS, Univ. of ND, 1936; voice study w. pvte. tutors. m. Dorothy M Ness, 1 s., 2 d. Career: Supvsr. of Music, Pub. Schls., 1930-36; Hd., Dept. of Music, State Tchrs. Coll., Valley City, ND, 1936-40; Assoc. Prof. of Music, Univ. of Idaho, 1940-47; Dir. of Choral Activities & Voice Tchr., Ore. State Univ., 1947-74; Chmn., Dept. of Music, ibid, 1947-65; Prof. Emeritus, 1974; Radio & TV Broadcasts in Int. Choral Prof., Educl. TV, etc. Comps: Choral - Gloria in Excelsis; Shallow Brown; Hymn of Praise; Kyrie; Bonnie Doon; Comfort Ye; God Bless Our People; The Names of Oregon. Contbr. to var. music jrnls. Mbrships: MENC; ASCAP; Phi Kappa Phi; Phi Mu Alpha; Am. Choral Dirs. Assn.; Nat. Assn. of Tchrs. of Singing. Hons: Ore. State Univ. Alumni Dist. Prof. Award, 1974. Hobbies: Photography; Travel; Writing; Woodwork. Address: 2135 NW Evergree St., Corvallis, OR 97330, USA. 2, 9.

WALN, Ronald Lee, b. 25 June 1931, Cedar Rapids, Iowa, USA. University Professor. Educ: BMusEd., Oberlin Coll., 1957; MA, State Univ. of Iowa, 1959; PhD, ibid, 1971; Flute study w. Maurice Sharp, Robert Willoughby, Ruth Freeman, Nelson Hauenstein, Betty Bang Mather & James Pellerite; Bassoon study w. George Goslee, Louis Cooper, William Polisi & Himie Voxman. m. B. Clara Schlecht, 2 s. Career: Grad. Fellow, Univ. of Iowa, 1957-59; Instr., Fla. State Univ., 1959-65; Asst. & Assoc. Prof., Univ. of Ga., 1965-; Prof. of Woodwinds & Music Educ., ibid, 1978-; Perf. w. Gt. Neck Symph., Brooklyn Orch., Akron Symph., Cedar Rapids Symph., Pensicola Symph., Jacksonville Symph., Tallahassee Symph., etc.; Mbr. of Univ. of Iowa Fac. Woodwind Quintet, Tallahassee Woodwind Quintet, & Univ. of Ga. Woodwind Quintet; Mbr., Univ. of Ga. Baroque Ensemble. Contbr. to var. profl. jrnls. Mbrships: Pres., U. Ga. Chapt., Nat. Pres., NACWPI, 1970-72; Bd. Dirs., Nat. Flute Assoc., 1976-78 (VP, 1978-79, Pres., 1979-80); sev. profl. orgs. Hons: Phi Kappa Lambda, 1965-67; Phi Mu Alpha; Selected to serve on Fulbright Fellowship selection bd. in music, 1972. Address: 499 Brookwood Dr., Athens, GA 30605, USA. 7.

WALTA, Jaring Douwe, b. 12 May 1941, Leeuwarderadeel, Friesland, Netherlands. Violin Player. Educ: Conserv. dip. solo violin player, 1962. Debut: Silver Circle of Friends, 1963. Career: 1st Violin, Concertgebouw Orch., 1962, 65; 1st Concertmaster, Overijssel Phil., 1965, 70; 1st Concertmaster Res. Orch.; Num. solo concerts, radio & TV apps. European String Tchrs. Assn., Pres., 1976-. Address: De Melkpotte 12, Nootdorp, Netherlands.

WALTER, Franz, b. 14 July 1907, Marseilles, France. Cellist; Professor; Music Critic. Educ: Dip., Conserv. of Geneva; studied comp. under Vincent d'Indy, Schola Cantorum, Paris; Sorbonne. m. Odette Mossar, 1 d. Career: Solo Cellist, Orch. de la Suisse Romande, 10 yrs.; Mbr.; Quatuer de Lausanne, 7 yrs.; Prof., Cello & String Quartet, Conserv. of Geneva; Music Critic, Jrnl. de Genève; Artistic Counsellor, European Assn. of Music Fests.; radio & TV broadcasts. Publs: Var. plays (under name

Terval). Mbrships: num. musical & dramatic socs. Hons. incl: Medal, Int. Competition for Cello, Vienna, 1937. Hobbies: Volleyball; Tennis; Crosswords. Address: 9 Blvd. des Philosophes, 1205 Geneva, Switz.

WALTER, Horst, b. 5 Mar. 1931, Hanover, W. Germany. Musicologist. Educ: Univ. Cologne, musicol., German philo., phil.; DPh, 1962. Career: since 1962 sci. co-operator Joseph Haydn Inst., Cologne. Publs. incl: Music History of Lüneburg, from the end of the 16th Century to the beginning of the 18th Century, Tutzing, 1967; Ed. in the Complete Haydn ed.; Symphonies 1764 and 1765 1/4, 1964, 1/17, 1966, XIV/5, 1968, XXV/8, 1976 Haydn's pianos, Haydn Studies 11/4, 1970; The posthorn signal in Haydn and other composers of the 18th Century, Haydn Studies IV/1, 1976. Contbr. to: Music Past and Present (MGG); Grove's Dictionary, 6th ed. Address: Mohnweg 5, 5060 Bergisch Gladbach-Refrath, German Fed. Repub.

WALTER JONES, Elias, b. 24 Jan. 1921, Llanrwst, N Wales, UK. Organist; Harpsichordist; Teacher. Educ: FRCO; LRAM; ARCM; Matthay Schl. of Music, Liverpool; organ study w. Malcolm Boyle, Chester Cathedral. m. Margaret Walter Jones, 1 d. Debut: as Harpsichordist w. Royal Liverpool Phil. Orch., 1963. Career: Organist & Choirmaster, Holy Trinity Ch., Llandudno; Music Master, Rydal Schl., Colwyn Bay; Organ & Harpsichord Continuo w. Royal Liverpool Phil. Orch. & BBC Welsh Symph. Orch. at Royal Phil. Hall, Liverpool & Royal Nat. Eisteddfod, Wales. Mbrships: Life, Old Rydalian Club; Viola Rsch. Inst., W Germany. Hobbies: Viola Playing; Art. Address: Coytmor, 52 St. Hilary's Dr., Deganwy, Gwynedd, N Wales, UK.

WALTERS, Frank, b. 18 Mar. 1915, Malvern, Worcs., UK. Pianist; Organist; Lecturer; Artists Manager; Musical Advisor; Critic (now retired). m. Freda Fussey, 2 d. Career incls: Var. organ appts., Malvern, Worcester, Grimsby & Birmingham, 1930-40; HM Forces, 1940-46; Perf. w. ENSA, Stars in Battledress; Music Off., Southern Cmd.; Critic & Reviewer, num. newspapers & jrnls.; Fndr.-Dir., Wessex Musicians Consortium; Mgr., Kathleen Merritt Orch.; V-Chmn., Southern Orchl. Concert Soc.; Acknowledged authority on Sir Edward Elgar (his Godfather). Publs. incl: Elgar, The Man I Knew. Mbr. Profl. orgs. Hobbies incl: Reading. Address: Scarthoe, 35 Woodbury Ave., Petersfield, Hants, GU32 2ED, UK.

WALTERS, Gareth, b. 27 Dec. 1928, London, UK. BBC Music Producer; Composer. Educ: RAM; Nat. Conserv. of Music, Paris; Accademia Chigiana, Siena; LRAM; ARAM; ARCM. m. Glenys Jones, 4 d. Career: Music Producer, BBC, 1957-; Prof. Jr. Exhibnr. Sect. RAM, 1956-. Compositions incl: Sinfonia Breve; Elegy; Divertimento (strings) Poesies du Soir (soprano & orch.); Salm y Genedl; Primavera. Num. chmbr. works. Recordings: Divertimento; Little Suite; Harpsichord Suites 1 & 2; Elizabethan Suites 1 & 2; Flourish for Brass. Mbrships: Perf. Rights Soc.; MCPS. Hobbies: Swimming; Tennis. Address: 31 Beauchamp Rd., E Molesey, Surrey, UK.

WALTERS, Irwyn Ranald, b. 6 Dec. 1902, Ammanford, S Wales, UK. Organist; Accompanist; Composer; Conductor. Educ: Attended Univ. Coll., Aberystwyth, Wales; BA; BMus; Hon FTCL. m. Margaret Jane, 1 s. Career: Music Tchr., Shebbear Coll., N Devon, Owens Schl., Islington & King Edward Schl., Stafford; First HMI (Music) Appointed in Wales; Overseas Examiner, TCL; Schl. Music Lectr.; Fest. Cond.; Fndr., Nat. Youth Orch. of Wales. Publs: Music & The Physically Handicapped, Enquiry by the Ctrl. Coun. for the Disabled. Mbrships: Music Advsr., Music Panel, Disabled Living Fndn., 1965-67. Hons: OBE. Hobbies: Travel; Languages. Address: 12 Huntington Close, W Cross, Swansea, Glam., UK.

WALTERS, Jess, b. 18 Nov. 1908, Brooklyn, NY, USA. Opera, Concert Singer. Educ: studied w. Mario Pagano, Luigi Giufferida, Frank La Forge; Rossini Opera Workshop. m. Emma C DeFina, 1 s. Debut: Brooklyn Acad. of Music, 1935. Career: New Opera Co., Verdi, Macbeth, NYC, 1941-42; Royal Opera, Covent Gdn., London, UK, 1947-60; Netherlands Opera, Amsterdam, Holland, 1960-65; Prof. of Voice, Univ. of Tex., Austin, 1965-. Recording: Delius, Idyll, Halle Orch., Barbirolli. Mbrships: AGMA; Bd. of Govs., ibid, 1943-46; Pi Kappa Lambda, 1965-; NATS, 1965-. Recip. 1st Place, Baritone Category, Named Best Male Singer, Jrnl. Am. Voice Contest, 1932. Hobbies: Horses; Agriculture. Address: 203 Almarion Way, Austin, TX 78746, USA.

WALTMANS, Marinus Jan Hubert, b. 14 Mar. 1929, Brunssun, Amsterdam, Netherlands. Assistant Professor of Music; Director of Music. Educ: Licentiaat Philos., 1950; Licentiaat Theol., 1955; Grad. Musicol., Univ. Amsterdam; Roman Cath. Priest Roermond, 1955; Studied organ, Conserv.

Royale de Liege. Career incls: Asst. Prof., Inst. of Musicol., Univ. of Amsterdam; Dir. of Music, St. Nicolaas Coll., Amsterdam; Perfs. on Dutch Radio & TV & BRT, WDR, Germany. Comps. incl: Ch. Music; Psalms; Masses. Publs: Kerkorgels te Roermond, Heythuisen, 1956; Johann Gottfried Walther en de Figura-leer Amsterdam, 1969. Mbr. Vereniging voor Nederlandse Muziekgeschiedenis. Hobby: Automobiles. Address: Staalmeesterslaan 252, Amsterdam, The Netherlands.

WALTON, Nigel David, b. 10 June 1944, Bromyard, Herefordshire, UK. Teacher; Organ Recitalist; Composer. Educ: BA Music, Bristol Univ.; Cert. Ed., Queens Coll., Cambridge. Career: Var. posts as Ch. organist from age of 13 yrs.; Currently Dir. of Music, Churchill Schl., Avon. Comps. incl: Chmbr. & choral works; Pop Cantata, David. Mbr. RCO. Hobbies: Eating Out; Driving Fast Cars. Address: Flat 7, 11 Clifton Pk., Bristol, BS8, 3BX, UK.

WALTON, Richard, b. 23 Feb. 1913, Manchester, UK. Trumpet Player; Professor of Trumpet, RCM. Educ: RCM; Hon RCM, 1960; FRCM, 1965. m. Margaret Gunyon, 2 s., 2 d. Career: Prin.-Mbr., LPO, 1932, Prin. Trumpet, 1935-41; LPO; Prin. Trumpet, Royal Phil. Orch., 1948-54, Philharmonia Orch., 1954-59, LPO, 1959-62, BBC Symph. Orch., 1962-. Recordings: w. above orchs. Contbr. to: Felix Weingartner. Mbr., Royal Soc. of Musicians of GB, 1934-. Address: 71A Strand-on-the-Green, Chiswick, London W4 3PF, UK.

WALTON, (Sir) William, b. 29 Mar. 1902, Oldham, England. Composer. Educ: Christ Ch., Oxford. m. Sussana Gil. Compositions incl: Piano Quartet, 1918; Sinfonia Concertante for piano & orch., 1927; Portsmouth Point (chmbr. orch.), 1925; Façade, 1926; Siesta, 1926; Viola Concerto, 1928-29; Belshazzar's Feast (choral), 1931; 1st Symph., 1935; The Quest (str. quartet), 1947; Violin Sonata, 1950; Troilus & Cressida (opera), 1954; Te Deum, 1953; Orb & Sceptre, 1953; Cello Concerto, 1956; Partita, 1958; 2nd Symph., 1960; The Bear (opera), 1967; The Wise Virgins (ballet); Variations on a Theme by Hindemith; Capriccio Burlesco; film music. Recip. of Kthood., 1951. Address: c/o Oxford Univ. Press, 37 Dover St., London W1X 4AH, UK.

WANG, Alfredo, b. 7 June 1918, Vienna, Austria. Violinist; Lecturer. Educ: Master's degree, State Acad. of Music, Vienna. Div., 2 s., 1 d. Debut: Prize-winner, Int. Competition for Violin, 1932, Vienna. Career: Prof., Univ., Sucre, Bolivia, 1940-41; Ldr., Chilean State Str. Quartet, 1941-48; Prof., Music Inst., Univ. of Chile, Santiago, 1944-48; Lectr., Univ. Coll., Cardiff, 1952-; Ldr., Univ. Ensemble, Cardiff, 1952-; Concerts & broadcasts in all Western European countries, N & S Am., Middle & Far East; BBC & ITV. Recordings on: Heritage, USA; Pye & Lyrita, UK. Mbr., ISM. Hobbies: Chamber Music; Reading; Travelling. Address: 17 Queen Anne Sq., Carfidd CF1 3ED, UK. 3.

WANGENHEIM, Volker, b. 1 July 1928, Berlin, Germany. Conductor; Composer. Educ: State Music Acad., Berlin. m. Ewa Olejniczak, 1 d. Career: Fdnr. & chief cond., Berlin Mozart Orch., 1950-59; Cond., Mecklenburg State Opera, Schwerin, 1951-52; Music Dir., City of Bonn, 1957-; Gen. Music Dir., ibid, 1963-76; Cond., Phil. Choir, ibid, 1957-76; Co-fndr. & chief cond., German Nat. Youth Orch., 1969-; Guest cond. in Germany & abroad; Prof. of condng., Cologne Music Acad., 1972-. Comps: Sonatina per orch.; Sinfonietta concertante; Sinfonia Notturna; Sinfonie 1966; Klangspiel I, II; Mass; Psalms 70, 123, 130; Stabat Mater; Hymnus Choralis; Nicodemus cantata. Recordings of Baroque & Classical music. Mbrships: Presidium, German Music Coun. Hons: Arts Prize, City of Berlin, 1954; Fed. Service Cross, 1972; Cross of Merit, Polish Arts, 1978. Address: Hasenweg 7, 5205 St. Augustin 1, German Fed. Repub.

WANTANABE, Akeo, b. 1919, Tokyo, Japan. Conductor. Educ: Tokyo Acad. of Music; studied conducting w. Joseph Rosenstock & w. Jean Morel, Juilliard Schl. of Music, NYC. m. Nobuko Hatoyama, 3 s. Career: Regular Cond., Tokyo City Symph., 1945-46; Permanent Cond., Tokyo Phil. Orch., 1948-54; Fndr. & Music Dir., Japan Phil. Symph. Orch., 1956-66; Prin. Prof., conducting course, Tokyo Univ. of Arts, 1962-67; Music Dir., Kyoto Municipal Symph. Orch., 1970-. Hons: Kt., 1st Class, Order of Finnish Lion, 1958; Kt. of Arms & Letters, France, 1963; Japan Art Acad. Award, 1967. Address: 350-95 Asahigaoka-cho, Ashiya-shi, Hyogo-Ken, Japan.

WARBURTON, Annie Osborne, b. 9 Apr. 1902, Manchester, Lancs., UK. Author. Educ: MusD; FNSM; LRAM; ARCM. m. R H Hawkins. Career: Music Tchr., Manchester HS, etc.; Examiner, Northern Jt. Matriculation Bd.; Trng. Colls.; etc.; Lectr. Publs:

Harmony, Melody, Writing & Analysis: A Graded Music Course for Schools, Books I-IV; Read, Sing & Play, pupils & tchrs. books I & II; Analyses of Music Classics Books I-IV; Basic Music Knowledge; Graded Aural Tests for all Purposes (over a million copies sold). Contbr. to: Music Tchr. Mbrships: Past Warden, Schl. Music Sect., ISM; Past Mbr., Coun. & Exec., ibid. Address: 9 Golf Links Rd., Burnham-on-Sea, Somerset, TA8 2PW, UK.

WARCHAL, Bohdan, b. 27 Jan. 1930, Orlova, Czechoslovakia. Violinist. Educ: Janácek Acad. of Music, Brno. m. Eva Jobová, 1 s. Career: Concertmaster, Slovak Phil. Orch., Bratislava; Fndr., Artistic Ldr. & Cond., Slovak Chmbr. Orch., ibid., 1960-; num. apps. in Europe, USA & Can. as soloist & cond.; TV & radio perfs. Recordings: Corelli, Concerti grossi op. 6; Handel, Concerti grossi op. 6; Soloist, Vivaldi, Four Seasons; works of Purcell, Mozart & num. other baroque & classical comps. Mbr., Union of Slovak Comps. (artistic sect.). Hons: State Title, Artist of Merit, 1969. Hobbies: Do-It-Yourself; Drawing; Repairing Bows & String Instruments. Mgmt: Slovkoncert, 890 36 Bratislava, Leningradska 5. Address: 801 00 Bratislava, Hlavna 50, Czechoslovakia.

WARD, David, b. 3 July 1922, Dumbarton, Scotland. Opera Singer. Educ: RCM, London; RAM; FRCM; LLD, Strathclyde, 1974. m. E V Susan Rutherford. Debut: w. Sadlers Wells Opera. Career: Guest Apps: Royal Opera House, London; La Scala, Milan; Metrop., NY; Colon, Buenos Aires. Recordings: Pélléas & Mélisande; Romeo & Juliet; Messiah; St. John Passion; Walkure, etc. Recip. CBE, 1972. Hobbies: Watching Cricket; Swimming; Golf. Mgmt: Ingpen & Williams. Address: 14 Clarence Terrace, Regents Pk., London NW1, UK. 1.

WARD, David William Bassett, b. 28 Dec. 1942, Sheffield, UK. Pianist (Soloist & Accompanist); Conductor. Educ: Bryanston Schl., Dorset; Caius Coll., Cambridge; RCM; ARCM (tchrs. dip.); LRAM (perfs. dip.); studied w. Nadia Boulanger. m. Elizabeth Gladstone, 1 d., 1 s. Debut: Purcell Room, London, 1970. Career: concerts in UK, Europe, Am.; broadcasts in UK, France, Ireland. Recordings: works by Borodin & Mozart. Hons: var. scholarships & exhibitions incl. French Govt. scholarship for study w. Nadio Boulanger & Leverhulme postgrad. scholarship, RCM. Hobbies: Philosophy; Tai Chi; Walking; Reading; Watching & Listening. Mgmt: Martin Bloomfield, 21 Lower Common S, London SW15. Address: c/o RCM, Prince Consort Rd., London SW7.

WARD, George Jr., b. 27 June 1932, Binghamton, NY, USA. Percussionist; Public School Music Teacher. Educ: BMus, MMus, Syracuse Univ. m. Sandra Gorham, 1 s., 1 d. Career: Marimba Soloist, Tympanist, Gt. Lakes Navy BAnd, 4 yrs.; on Ed Sullivan Show; w. Syracuse Symph., 6 yrs.; w. Utica Symph & other community symphs., 20 yrs., working w. many noted conds.; played for Bolshoi Ballet, & many noted entertainers (Connie Francis, Milton Berle, Trini Lopez, etc.), also for many musicals & operettas; Tchr., Marcellus Publ. Schl., 2 yrs., W Genesee Pub. Schls., 12 yrs., Onondaga Community Coll., 7 yrs., Syracuse Univ., 8 yrs.,in own studio, 22 yrs. Recorded w. La Banda. Ed. Cons., Percussion Curriculum Outline for State of New York. Mbr. profl. orgs. Hobbies incl: Carpentry; Model railroads. Address: 111 Standish Dr., N Syracuse, NY, USA.

WARD, John Owen, b. 20 Sept. 1919, London, UK. Music Publisher & Writer. Educ: MA, Oxford Univ., 1956; London Violoncello Schl. m. Maya Riviere. Career: Ed. Asst. to Percy A Scholes, 1949-56; Mgr., Music Dept., Oxford Univ. Press, NY, 1957-72; Dir. of Serious Music, Boosey & Hawkes, NY, 1972-. Publs: Careers in Music, 1968; Ed., Oxford Companion to Music, 10th ed., 1970; Concise Oxford Dictionary of Music, 2nd ed., 1964; Junior Companion to Music. Contbr. to var. jrnls. Mbrships: Pres., Music Publrs. of USA, Royal Musical Assn.; Int. & Am. Musicol. Assns.; Soc. for Italian Studies. Hobbies: Travel; Chmbr. Music. Address: 325 W 76th St., NYC, NY 10023, USA.

WARD, Joseph, b. 22 May 1942, Preston, Lancs., UK. Singer. Educ: Royal Manchester Coll. of Music; FRMCM; FRNCM. Debut: Royal Opera House Covent Garden, 1962. Career: Prin. Tenor, Am., London, Germany, Portugal, France, Aust.; Asst. Hd. of Vocal Studies, RNCM. Recordings as tenor soloist incl: Norma; Beatrice Di Tenda; Montezuma; Wuthering Heights; Pilgrims Progress; Albert Herring. Hobbies: Swimming; Horse Riding. Address: Royal Northern Coll. of Music, 124 Oxford Rd., Manchester M13 9RD, UK.

WARD, Margaret, b. 21 Sept. 1928, Grand Rapids, Mich., USA. Musician (Viola & Violin). Educ: BMus, Eastman Schl. of Music, Univ. of Rochester, NY. m. Robert Paul Ward, Jr., 1 s., 3 d. Career: Prin. Viola, Eastman Little Symph. & a regular Mbr. of the Rochester Phil., while at Eastman; Has appeared as Soloist w. orchs. in her native Mich. & in recital in such places as Mich., Wash, DC & Beirut, Lebanon; She has appeared in Chamber Music concerts w. the facs. of Mich. State Univ., Univ. of NC., Univ. of Miami, Cath. Univ. of Am. & the Conservatoire Nationale du Liban; Regular mbr. of the Miami Symph. cond. by the late Fabien Sevitzky, 1961-64; Mbr. of the Fac. of the Lebanese Conserv., Prin. Viola of the Conservatoire Chamber Orch. & Guest Violist in concert w. many chamber musicians, Lebanon, 1964-66; Prin. Viola, Filene Center Orch., Wolf Trap Farm Pk. for Perf. Arts during the summers, & w. chamber & orchl. perfs. at the JFK Ctr. for the Perf. Arts, Wash. DC, 1966-; Violist, Balt. Symph. Orch. under Sergiu Commissiona, 1973-; Tchr. of Violin & Viola in pvte. studio. Address: 1101 Playford Ln., Silver Spring, MD 20901, USA.

WARD, Paul Clarendon, b. 29 Aug. 1918, Taunton, UK. Cellist; Conductor. Educ: ARCM (cello perf.). m. Susan Watmough, 1 s., 1 d. Career: Fndr. & Cond., Manchester Mozart Orch.; Cond., Northenden Choral Soc., 1956-59, City of Chester Symph. Orch., 1966-, Stockport Youth Orch., 1955-74; Mbr., Boyd Neel Orch., 1946-48; Sub-Prin. Cellist, Halle Orch., 1948-54; Cellist, Turner Quartet, 1948-53, 1957-63, Wissema Quartet, 1966-76; Continuo Cellist; Tchr., Royal Manchester Coll. of Music, 1948-76, Northern Schl. of Music, 1953-76,. Royal Northern Coll. of Music; var. orchl. courses, Cond. & Cello Tutor; Fest. Adjudicator; Lectr. Contbr. to Music Jrnl. Mbrships: ISM; Musicians Union. Hobbies: Reading; Arch. Address: 5 Belgrave Pl., Camden, Bath, BA1 5JL, UK.

WARD, William Reed, b. 20 May 1918, Norton, Kan., USA. Teacher; Author; Composer. Educ: BMus & BMus Ed, Univ. of Kan., 1941; MMus, Eastman Schl. of Music, Univ. of Rochester, 1942; PhD, ibid., 1954. m. Elizabeth Jane (Adam) Ward, 1 d., 2 s. Career incl: Music Fac., San Fran. State Univ., 1947-; Chmn., Music Dept., ibid., 1954-69; Prof. of Music, ibid., 1959-; Lectr. & Panelist on music for var. insts. & assns.; Choir Dir., United Meth. Ch., Burlingame, Calif., 1967-; Assoc. Dean, Schl. of Creative Arts, San Fran. State Univ., 1977-. Comps. incl: O For a Thousand Tongues to Sing, 1974; O Come, O Come Emmanuel, 1974. Recordings incl: Listen, Lord. Publs. incl: American Bicentennial Song Book, 1975. Mbrships: Am. Soc. of Comps., Authors & Publrs. Address: 120 Occidental Ave., Burlingame, CA 94010, USA. 2.

WARD JONES, Peter Arthur, b. 30 March 1944, Chester, UK. Music Librarian; Conductor; Organist; Harpsichordist. Educ: MA, Balliol Coll., Oxford; FRCO. m. Shirley Bailey. Career: Pt.-time Prof. of Music, RCM, 1967-69; Hd. of Music Dept., Bodleian Lib., Oxford, 1969-; Organist. St. Giles' Ch., Oxford, 1971-; Cond., Oxford Harmonic Soc., 1971-; Harpsichordist, Oxford Pro Musica, 1968-. Contbr. to: Music & Letters; BRIO; Bibliographies to New Oxford History of Music, Vol. 7 & Bibliography of Westrup's Writings in A History of Western Music, Vol. 1; Essays on Opera and English Music, in honour of Sir Jack Westrup. Mbrships: Royal Musical Assn.; RCO; Int. Assn. of Music Libs. Hons: Dr. F J Read Prize, FRCO, 1962. Hobbies: Mountain Walking; Collecting Alpine Books. Address: 25 Harbord Rd., Oxford, UK.

WARD-STEINMAN, David, b. 6 Nov. 1936, Alexandria, La., USA. Composer; Pianist; Professor. Educ: BMus, Fla. State Univ., 1957; MusM, Univ. of Ill., 1958; DMA, ibid, 1961; Vis. Fellow, Princeton Univ., 1970; Summer Schl., Aspen, Colo., Indian Hill Music Workshop, Mass. & Tanglewood, Mass. m. Susan Diana Lucas, 2 children. Career: Prof. of Music, San Diego State Univ.; Orchestral perfs. w. Chgo. Symph., Seattle Symph., Japan Philharmonic Symph., New Orleans Philharmonic Symph. & San Diego Symph. Compositions incl: Piano Sonata, 1956-57; Symph., 1959; Prelude & Toccata for orch., 1962; Fragments from Sappho for soprano, flute, clarinet & piano, 1962-65; Song of Moses, oratorio for narrator, soprano, 2 tenors, baritone, chorus & orch., 1963-64; Western Orpheus, ballet, 1964; Cello Concerto, 1964-66; These Three, ballet for orch.; Jazz Tangents for wind ensemble or band, 1966-67; The Tale of Issoumbochi, for narrator, soprano, flute, clarinet, cello, piano interior celesta & percussion, 1968; Childs Play for bassoon, piano & piano interior, 1968; Tamar, music drama in 3 acts, 1970-74; Sonata for piano; Jazz Tangents & Raga for wind instruments. Contbr. to: Music Educators Jrnl.; Contemporary Music Proj. Num. mbrships. Publs: Comparative Anthology of Musical Forms (2 vols. w. S L Ward-Steinman), 1976. Hon. doctorate, Gracian Inst., Montreal. Address: 9403 Broadmoor Pl., La Mesa, CA 92041, USA. 9.

WARDEN, Anne, Violinist. Educ: RAM; LRAM. Career: solo & sonata recitals; broadcasts & Arts Coun. tours; concerto engagements; Tchr., Sr. Dept., Royal Scottish Acad. of Music, 1952; Free lance orchl. playing, UK & abroad. Mbr., ISM.

Hobbies: Travel; Literature; Motoring. Address: 131 West End Lane, London, W.W.6, UK.

WARD RUSSELL, Gillian, b. 19 Oct. 1953, Maldon, Essex, UK. Organist; Accompanist; Conductor; Private Teacher. Educ: BA, Music Schl., NE Essex Tech. Coll., Colchester; Fellow, Royal Coll. Organists; Assoc., Royal Coll. Music; Lic., Royal Acad. Music; Lic., Trinity Coll. of Music; Pupil of Harrison Oxley & Hilary Macnamara. m. Anthony Russell. Debut: St. Edmundsbury Cathedral, 1976. Career: Musical Dir., Braintree Choral Soc.; Organist, Choirmaster, Coggeshall Parish Ch., Essex; Lectr., Music, Colchester Inst.; Recitals of piano & organ throughout Britain. Recordings: Organ Music at Coggeshall. Publs: Chapt., Essex Organs in book Essex Churches, 1979; Arrangements of car. orchestral works. Mbrships: Incorp. Soc. of Musicians; Braintree Arts Festival Committee. Hons: Canon Jack Award, 1975; Brighton Organ Competition Prize, 1978. Hobbies: Reading; Driving. Mgmt: Anthony Russell. Address: 10 New St., Maldon, Essex, CM9, 6AQ, UK.

WARE, Clifton, b. 15 Mar. 1937, Newton, Miss., USA. Singer (tenor); Associate Professor of Voice. Educ: BA, Millsaps Coll., Jackson, Miss.; MMus, Univ. of S Miss.; DMus, Northwestern Univ., Evanston, Ill. m. Elizabeth Jean Oldham, 3 s. Career: Leading & supporting roles in over 43 opera performances; num. apps. in oratorio & concert recitals; Assoc. Prof. of Voice, Univ. of Minn. Recordings: Clifton Ware sings in Recital; St. Nicolas (B Britten). Publs. incl: Vocal Production in Speech & Song, 2nd ed., 1975; A Guide to Solo Vocal Performance, 1978. Contbr. to: Opera Jrnl. Mbr., num. profl. orgs. Recip: Fisk Award in vocal competition, Northwestern Univ., 1969. Hobbies: Art; Sailing; Camping; Travelling. Address: 3429 Benjamin NE, Mpls., MN 55418, USA.

WARE, John Marley, b. July 1942, Two Rivers, Wis., USA. Musicologist; Composer; Pianist; Organist. Educ: BMus, MMus, Ind. Univ.; PhD Cand., La. State Univ. m. Emily Christine Carlson, 1 s. Comps: Passacaglia for Organ; Deploration on the Death of Rabbi A J Haschel; Sonata for Organ (performed at nat. meeting of Am. Guild of Organists); Num. other works. Contbr. of papers to Regional Meetings of Am. Musicological Soc. at New Orleans, 1971, Chgo., 1975. Mbrships: Am. Musicological Soc.; Southeastern Comps. League; Pi Kappa Lambda. Recip. of Woodrow Wilson Fellowship, 1964. Hobbies: Reading; Hiking; Travel; Swimming. Address: Univ. of the South, Sewanee, TN 37375, USA.

WAREING, Deryck John Highfield, b. 3 Dec. 1944, Farnham, Surrey, UK. Violinist. Educ: RAM, 1963-67; LRAM, 1967. Career: Asst. Music Master, Blundell's Schl., Tiverton, 1967-71; Asst. Music Master, Hurstpierpoint Coll., Sussex, 1971-72; Surrey Co. Music Staff; Cond., Weybridge & Walton Youth Orch., 1972-75; Music Master, Ellesmere Coll. & Moreton Hall, Salop, 1975-77; Res. Violinist, The Dragon Schl. Oxford, 1977-. Mbrships: ISM; RAM Club; European String Tchrs. Assn.; Musicians Union. Recip., Sir Edward Cooper Prize, RAM, 1966. Address: The Dragon Schl., Oxford, OX2 6SS, UK.

WARFIELD, Gerald Alexander, b. 23 Feb. 1940, Ft. Worth, Texas, USA. Composer; Writer; Editor; Administrator. Educ: BA, N Texas State Univ., 1963; MMus, ibid, 1965; MFA, Princeton Univ., 1967. Career: Assoc. Dir. of Index of New Musical Notation, Perf. Arts Rsch. Center, NYPL at Lincoln Center, 1973-75; Ed., Longman Music Series, Longman Inc., NY, 1976-. Comps. incl: The Transformed Prelude, for orch.; A Trophy (song); A Study of Two Pears (song); Romances and Metamorphoses, Fantasy Quintet, ensemble. Recordings: Variations and Metamorphoses, for 2 cellos. Publs: Co-Author, Layer Dictation, 1978; How to Write Music Manuscript, 1977; Writings on Contemporary Music Notation, 1977; Layer Analysis, 1976; etc. Contbr. to num. profl. publs. Mbrships: Chmn., Exec. Committee, Am. Soc. of Univ. Comps., 1972-74; Treas., Am. Comps. Alliance, 1979-; Coun., Coll. Music Soc., 1977-; Conference Committee, Int. Conference on New Musical Notation, Belgium, 1974. Address: 205 W 22nd St., NY, NY 10011, USA. 2.

WARNAS, Huibertus Willem Abraham Christiaan, b. 25 Nov. 1925, Rotterdam, Netherlands. Conductor; Musician (Trombone, Euphonium). Educ: Dips., Trombone & Euphonium, 1956, Cond. Dip., 1959, Royal Conserv. of Music, The Hague. m. Gerry Bosman, 2 d. Career: w. Band of Royal Grenadier Guards, The Hague, 1954-60; 2nd. Cond., Band of the Royal Netherlands Air Force, 1960-76; 1st Cond. (Dir. of Music), 1976-, ibid. Comps: 3 Fanfares & a Marching Fanfare; 3 Marches for Military Trumpets & Drums; Arrs. from Trumpet Blues, Kovanchina, An American in Paris; many choral arrs. Recordings: At the Big Band Ball, No. 1; At the Big Band Ball, No. 2; The Band of the RNAF Play Sousa. Contbr. to: Music

Industry Directory. Mbrships: Assn. of Netherland Conds.; Officers Club, RNAF, Nijmegen; BUMA; STEMRA. Hobby: Home discothèque. Address: Malderburchtstraat 548, 6535 NV Nijmegen, Netherlands.

WARNER, Robert A., b. 5 June 1912, Parkersburg, Iowa, USA. Professor of Musicology; Museum Director. Educ: BA, Univ. of N Iowa; MA, Eastman Schl. of Music, Univ. of Rochester; PhD, Univ. of Mich.; studied piano, violin, viola da gamba. m. Maretta L Martinek, 2 s. Career: Prof. of Music, E III. Univ., 1938-56; Prof. of Music, Univ. of Mich., 1956-; Dir., Stearns Collection of Musical Instruments. Publs: Ed., John Jenkins, Three-Part Fancy-Divisions, 1966. Contbr. to: Ency. Britannica; Music Review; Jrnl. of Am. Musicol. Soc.; Galpin Soc. Jrnl.; Music Educs. Jrnl. Mbrships: Am. Musicol. Soc.; Am. Musical Instrument Soc.; Viola da Gamba Soc. of Am. & UK; Galpin Soc.; Royal Musical Assn.; Mich. Museums Assn. Hobbies: String Quartets; Gamba Ensembles; Swimming; Canoeing; Cross-country Skiing; Bicycling. Address: 1205 Arbor View, Ann Arbor, MI 48103, USA.

WARNER, Sally Slade, b. 6 Sept. 1932, Worcester, Mass., USA. Organist; Choir Director; Carillonneur; Teacher; Record Librarian. Educ: New England Conserv. of Music, 1950-52; ChM, AGO, 1964; AAGO, 1965; Cohasset Carillon Schl., Mass., 1974-; pvte. study of Carillon, Belgium, 1976; Royal Carillon Schl. Jef Denyn, Mechelen, Belgiu, 1978-79. Career: Organist, 1955-; Dir. of Music, 1964-; Ch. of St. John the Evangelist, Beacon Hill, Boston; Asst. to Music Dept., 1973-; Acad. Carillonneur, 1975-; Phillips Acad., Andover, Mass.; Organ recitals, New England; Carillon recitals, New England, Michigan & Bruges, Belgium; Lectr. for AGO. Mbrships. incl: AGO; Guild of Carilloneurs in N Am.; Organ Histl. Soc. Hons. incl: Music Scholarship, Am. Fed. of Women's Clubs, 1951. Hobbies: Candlepin Bowling; Jigsaw Puzzles; Record collecting; Recorder playing. Address: Phillips Academny, Andover, MA 01810, USA. 27.

WARRACK, Guy (Douglas Hamilton), b. 8 Feb. 1900, Edinburgh, Scotland, UK. Composer; Conductor. Educ: Magdalen Coll., Oxford, BA; RCM; Hon. ARCM. m. Valentine Clair Warrack, 3 s., 1 d. Career: Cond.; Handel Soc., 1934 35; BBC Scottish Orch., 1936-45; Music Dir., Sadler's Wells Theatre Ballet, 1948-51. Recordings: Many film scores. Publs: Sherlock Holmes and Music, 1947. Contbr. to: The Times; Musical Times; Music & Letters, etc. Mbrships: ISM; PRS; CGGB. Address: 72 Courtfield Gardens, Flat 9, London SW5 ONL, UK. 1.

WARRACK, John Hamilton, b. 9 Feb. 1928, London, UK. Music Critic. Educ: Winchester Coll., 1941-46; ARCM, RCM. m. Lucy Beckett, 4 s. Career: Asst. Music Critic, Daily Telegraph, 1954-61; Chief Music Critic, Sunday Telegraph, 1961-72; Dir. Leeds Fest., 1976-; Vis. Lectr., Durham Univ., 1975-76; Ed., 19th Century Entries, New Groves Dictionary of Music. Publs: Six Great Composers, 1958; Concise Oxford Dictionary of Opera, 1964, 2nd ed., 1979; Carl Maria von Weber, 1968, 2nd ed., 1976; Tchaikovsky Symphonies & Concertos (BBC Music Guide), 1969; Tchaikovsky, 1973; Tchaikovsky Ballet Music (BBC Music Guide), 1979. Contbr. to: Opera; The Musical Times; Music & Letters; The Gramophone; Times Literary Supplement. Mbrships: Editl. Bd., New Berlioz Edn.; Royal Musical Assn. Hons: Colles Prize (RCM), 1951. Hobbies: Gardening; Cricket; Cooking. Address: Beck House, Rievaulx, Helmsley, York, UK.

WARREN, Edwin Brady, b. 1 Nov. 1910, Fowler, Calif., USA. University Professor; Musicologist. Educ: AB, Fresno State Coll., Calif.; MMus (Theory & Musicology), PhD Musicol., Univ. of Mich.; Post-Grad. work, Harvard Univ. m. Linda Boswell Warren. Career: Professor, Musicologist, S III. Univ., Edwardsville. Recordings: Responses and Amens; Recordings of works of Robert Fayrfax. Publs: Collected Works of Robert Fayrfax (1464-1521), Vols. I-III; Life and Works of Robert Fayrfax, 1969. Contbr. to: Musica Disciplina; Jrnl. of AMS; Music Lib. Assn. Notes. Mbrships: AMS; IMS; PMMS; AAUP; CMS; Pi Kappa Lambda. Hons: Grant from Am. Phil. Soc. for work on Fayrfax; Outstanding Educator of Am., 1975; Edwin B Warren Collegium Music Award established at S III. Univ., Edwardsville, 1975. Address: 6920 Florian Ave., St. Louis, MO 63121, USA. 1, 8, 11, 29.

WARREN, Elinor Remick, b. 23 Feb. Los Angeles, Calif., USA. Composer; Pianist. Educ: Piano study w. var. tchrs.; Study of theory, counterpoint & orchn. w. Dr. Clarence Dickinson & Nadia Boulanger; Hon. DMus, Occidental Coll., Calif. m. Z Wayne Griffin, 2 s., 1 d. Career: Pianist-accompanist for Lawrence Tibbett, Richard Crooks, Lucrezia Bori, etc.; Concert tours & recitals of own compositions throughout USA. Comps. incl: Abram in Egypt (recorded by Roger Wagner Chorale &

LPO); Suite for Orch., recorded by Oslo Symph. Orch., Norway. Mbrships: ASCAP; Nat. League of Am. Pen Women; Assn. of Am. Composers & Cond., etc. Hons: DMus, Occidental Co., LA, 1960; Choral Comp. prize for Abram in Egypt, Gedok, Germany, 1962; Winner, num. nat. comps., Nat. League of Am. Pen Women. Hobbies: Poetry collection; Raising horses. Address: 154 S Hudson Ave., LA, CA 90004, USA. 5, 27.

WARREN, Raymond Henry Charles, b. 7 Nov. 1928, Weston-super-Mare, UK. Composer; Teacher. Educ: MA, MusD, Univ. of Cambridge; studies w. Michael Tippett & Lennox Berkeley. m. Roberta Lydia Alice Smith, 4 children. Career: Lectr. in Music, 1955-66, Prof. of Comp., 1966-72, Queen's Univ., Belfast; Prof. of Music, Univ. of Bristol, 1972-. Comps: The Passion, 1964; String Quartet No. 1, 1967; Violin Concerto, 1967; Songs of Old Age, 1971; Orchestral Suite, Wexford Bells, 1970; String Quartet No. 3, 1977. Mbrships: Chmn., Bristol Ctr., ISM; Comps. Guild of GB. Hobby: Walking. Address: Dept. of Music, Univ. of Bristol, Royal Fort House, Tyndall Ave., Bristol BS8 1UJ, UK.

WARREN, Winifred Merrill, b. Atlanta, Ga., USA. Musician & Professor (violin & viola). Educ: Columbia Univ.; Univ. of Ind.; Cert. in violin, Ia. State Univ.; Dips. Inst. of Musical Art, NYC (now Juilliard Schl.). m. Arthur E Warren. Debut: Series of sonata recitals, Carnegie Chmbr. Music Hall, NYC. Career: Soloist w. Mpls. Symph.; Recitals, Brown Univ., Univ. of Me.; Extensive tours w. Int. Trio; Lectr., music in therapy & concerts for hosps. & serv. units, during WW II; Artist in Residence, violin, Ind. Univ. Schl. of Music; Prof. of violin, viola & chmbr. music. Perfs. of Bach Sonatas for solo violin. Mbrships: Pres., Pi Kappa Lambda, 1954-56; Nat. Arts Club, NYC; Fndr., Musicians' Club of Am.; Patroness, Sigma Alpha Iota; Am. String Assn.; AAUP; VP, Highland Pk. Music Club. Recip. Bessie Collier Award for violin playing, 1925. Hobbies: Short story writing; Gardening. Address: 2766 Summit Ave., Highland Pk., IL 60035, USA. 5, 8.

WARZECHA, Piotr, b. 10 Mar. 1941, Bytom, Poland. Composer; Conductor. Educ: Music Dips. in Comp. & Conducting, Acad. of Music, Katowice. m. Aleksandra Bogustawska, 1 child. Debut: Comp., Internationales Jugendfestspieltreffen, Bayreuth, 1964; Cond., Symph. Orch. of Silesian Phil., 1973. Career incls: Works performed at var. Polish festivals, on radio & TV; Cond., Impressions, 1974; Adjunt, Acad. of Music, Katowice; Cond., Symph. Orch. of Silesian Phil., Katowice. Compositions incl: Arcades for Orch., 1970; Concerto for Orch., 1972. Mbr. Polish Comps. Union. Hons. incl: Award, Malawski Competition, Krakow, 1972. Address: 41-902 Bytom, ul Chorzowska 55 m. 11, Poland.

WASHBURN, Franklin Ely b. 29 Sept. 1911, Houston, Tex., USA. Musician, Violin, Viola; Teacher. Educ: BMus, BMusEd., N Tex. State Univ.; studied w. Paul Berge, Samuel Gardner, Edouard Dethier, James V Lerch. m. Dorothy Gillham, 2 d., 1 s. Career: Houston Symph., 15 yrs.; Mbr. String & Orch. Tchng. Staff, Dallas Independent Schl. Dist., 1957-75; Music Guild String Quartet; Exec. Dir., Musical Acheivement Fndn., Inc., 1956-; Pvte. violin & viola tchr. from age 21; Orch. Cond., Southwestern Univ.; Ed. Good Music Neighbors, music bulletin, Dallas. Mbrships: Am. String Tchrs. Assn.; MTNA; Tex. Music Educs. Assn.; Dallas Music Educs. Assn.; Pres., Dallas MTA. Hobby: Camping. Address: 3208 Drexel Dr., Dallas, TX 75205, USA. 4.

WASHBURN, Jon Spencer, b. 4 July 1942, Rocnelle, III., USA. Conductor, Choral & Orchl.; Viola da Gamba Player; Teacher; Broadcaster. Educ: III. State Univ.; BS in music educ., Univ. of III., 1965; grad. studies, Northwestern Univ. & Univ. of BC. m. (1) Carol Ann Applegate, 1 d., (2) Linda-Lee Thomas. Career: Musical Dir. & Cond., Vancouver Chmbr. Choir & Amity Singers; Viola da Gambist & Co-Dir., Can. early music ensemble Hortulani Musicae; Dir. of Choral Activities, Vancouver Community Coll.; Broadcaster, Can. Broadcasting Corporation; Guest Cond.; Lectr. & Workshops. Comps: Golden Vase Carol. Recordings: 4 w. Vancouver Chmbr. Choir; 1 w. Vancouver Bach Choir; sev. w. var. Can. early music ensembles. Choral records reviewer for CBC Sound Reviews; BC Choral Fedn. Newsletter. Mbrships: Bd., Can. Music Centre; BC Choral Fedn. Hons: Can. Silver Jubilee Medal, 1977; var. cond. prizes from the Netherlands, Poland & UK. Address: 426 W 18th Ave., Vancouver, BC, Can. V5Y 2B1.

WASHBURN, Robert Brooks, b. 11 July 1928, Bouckville, NY, USA. Composer; College Professor. Educ: BS & MS, SUNY; PhD, Eastman Schl. of Music. m. Beverly Darnell Washburn, 1 s., 1 d. Career: Prof. of Music, State Univ. Coll., Potsdam, NY, 1954-. Compositions incl: Two Symphonies; Sinfonietta for Str. Orch.; String Quartet; Concertino for Wind Quintets; Suite for Strings; Suite for Band; Ode to Freedom; Quintet for Woodwinds;

Quintet for Brass; Festive Overture; Synthesis for Orch., Prologue & Dance; St. Lawrence Overture. Recordings: The Music of Robert Washburn. Contbr. to music jrnls. Mbrships: ASCAP; MENC; Am. Music Ctr.; Phi Mu Alpha. Recip. var. grants. Address: RD4, Potsdam, NY 13676, USA. 6.

WASSENAAR, Roelof, b. 27 March 1903, Zaandam, Holland. Conductor; Composer; Musician (guitar & mandolin). Educ: Studies w. Profs. Joh B Kok & Richard Heukenroth. m. Margaretha Antonia Buysman. Career: Cond., Sev. Dutch mandolin & accordion orchs.; currently Cond., Hoorns Mandolinorchestra Entre Nous, Youth Orch. & accordeonorchestra Excelsior, Aartswoud. Comps. for Mandolin Orch. incl: Ans; Elly; Marganto; Prima Vera; Limburgia. Hons: Cond. prizes, Netherlands, France & Luxemburg; Oranje Nassau Orde, 1962; Silver Medal, Hon. Citizen of Hoorn, 1972. Address: Willemsweg 9, Hoorn, Netherlands.

WASSON, Barbara Hickam, b. 12 Feb. 1918, Spencer, Ind., USA. Piano Teacher. Educ: BA, Vassr Coll.; MM, Chgo. Musical Coll.; DePauw Univ.; Ind. Univ.; Pvte. study in piano. m. Audley Jackson Wasson, 1 s., 1 d. Career: Soloist w. Dayton Phil. Orch. & Dayton Jr. Phil. Orch.; Num. recitals apps. in S & Midwest; Piano Tchrs. Workshops in Ohio and S & Midwest; Co-Dir. & Fndr., Wasson Piano Studio; Music Assoc., Wright State Univ. Mbr. num. profl. orgs. inclng: Mu Phi Epsilon; Dayton Music Club; 1st VP, W Dist. Chmn., Ohio MTA; Chmn., Independent Music Tchrs. Hons. incl: Mason Hamlin Tchrs. Recognition Award, E Ctrl. Div., Music Tchrs. Nat. Assn., 1973. Hobby: Playing Piano. Address: 5797 Paddington Rd., Centerville, OH 45459, USA. 5, 8.

WASSON, D. Dewitt, b. 20 Feb. 1921, Orangeburg, NY, USA. Conductor; Organist; Visiting Professor of Music. Educ: Dip. Music, Nyack Coll., 1943; B Sacred Music, Eastern Bapt. Coll., 1944; M Sacred Music, Union Theol. Sem., 1947; D Sacred Music, ibid, 1957; NY State Perm. Tchrs. Cert. in Music; Choirmaster Dip., AGO; summer workshops at Ball State Univ., The Orff Inst. of the Salzburg Mozarteum, New Coll., Oxford Univ. m. Josephine B Diener. Career: Organ concert tours of Europe have included apps. at int. organ fests. at Bonn, Salzburg & Karlsruhe; Frequent apps. as Cond. of the Westchester Baroque Chorus & as Harpsichord Soloist; Vis. Prof. of Music, The King's Coll., NY; Dir., Alumni Bd. of Nyack Coll. Contbr. to music jrnls. Music & Book Reviewer for The Am. Organist. Mbrships: Past Dean, Westchester Chapt. of the AGO; Hymn Soc. of Am.; Gesellschaft der Orgelfreunde. Hobbies: Travelling; Camping, etc. Mgmt: Helma von Bockelmann, Hinseler Feld 9, D-4300 Essen 14, German Fed. Repub. Address: 213 Highland Ave., N Tarrytown, NY 10591, USA.

WATANABE, Mamoru, b. 9 Oct. 1915, Tokyo, Japan. Professor of Musicology & Aesthetics; Director of Japan Cultural Institute, Cologne, Germany. Educ: Grad., Tokyo Univ., 1939; Univ. of Vienna. m. Ilse Watanabe-Wetzel, 1 s., 1 d. Career: Tchr., Japanese Cultural Hist., Univ. of Sofia, Bulgaria; Prof., Tokyo Univ., 1965-76; Advsr. to Polydor Int. Co., Tokyo; Dir., Japan Cultural Inst., Cologne, Germany, 1976-. Publs. incl: The Structure of Music, 1969; Philosophy of Art, 1975; Several transls. German-Japanese & Japanese-German. Mbrships: Comm., Japanese Musicol. Soc.; Commn., Japanese Soc. of Aesthetics; IMG; GMF. Address: Japanisches Kulturinstitut, 5 Cologne 1, Universitätsstrasse 98, German Fed. Repub.

WATANABE, Miwako N., Violinist. Educ: Toho Schl. of Music, Tokyo; Curtis Institute, Phila. m. Dr. Kyozo Watanabe, 2 c. Career: Soloist, Sequoia String Quartet; Chmbr. Music Groups & Chmbr. Orch. incl: LA Chmbr. Orch., Münchener Bach Orch. Hons: Walter W Naumburg Chmbr. Music Award, 1976. Mgmt: Sheldon Soffer Mgmt., NY. Address: LA, CA 90034, USA.

WATANABE, Ruth T., b. 12 May 1916, LA, Calif., USA. Musicologist; Music Librarian; Lecturer; Educator. Educ: BMus (Piano), Univ. of Southern Calif., LA, 1937; AB, ibid, 1939; MA, ibid, 1941; MMus (Piano), ibid, 1942; Schl. of Lib. Sci., Columbia Univ., 1947; PhD (Musicol.), Univ. of Rochester, 1953. Publs: 16 vols. of Prog. Annotations, Rochester Phil. Orch., 1953-74; Introduction to Music Research, 1967; Ed., New Scribner Music Library, vols. V, VI, VIII, 1973; Ed., Five-Part Madrigals of Antonio II Verso (1st Book), in progress. Contbr. to: Notes of Music Lib. Assn.; Music Educators Jrnl.; Columbia Tchrs. Coll. Record; Fontes Artis Musicae; Univ. of Rochester Lib. Bulletin. Mbrships: Int. Assn. Music Libs.; Int. Musicol. Soc.; Music Lib. Assn. (Ed. Bd.); Am. Musicol. Soc.; MENC; Mu Phi Epsilon; AAUW; Int. Fedn. Univ. Women. Hobbies: Travel; Needlework; Photography. Address: Sibley Music Library, Eastman School of Music, Univ. of Rochester, Rochester, NY 14604, USA. 5, 6, 11.

WATERHOUSE, David Boyer, b. 13 July 1936, Harrogate, Yorks., UK. University Teacher. Educ: MA, King's Coll.,

Cambridge Univ.; LRAM (piano), 1956. m. Naoko Matsubara, 1 s. Career: Asst. Keeper, Dept. of Oriental Antiquities, Brit. Mus., 1961-64; Fellow, Ctr. for Asian Arts, Univ. of Wash., Seattle, USA, 1965-66; on staff, 1966-, Prof., 1975-, Dept. of E Asian Studies, Univ. of Toronto. Publs: Harunobu & His Age, 1964; Tawaraya Sotatsu & the Dear Scroll, 1966; Images of Eighteenth Century Japan, 1975; Japanese Woodblock Prints from the J Bruce Varcoe Collection, 1976. Contbr. to profl. jrnls. inclng: Recorded Sound; Groves Dictionary; also to Encyclopedia of Music in Canada & Cross-Cultural Perspectives in Music. Mbr. profl. orgs. Hobbies: Highland pipes; Judo; Antiquarianism. Address: Dept. of E Asian Studies, Univ. of Toronto, Toronto, Ont., Canada.

WATERHOUSE, John Charles Graeme, b. 23 Apr. 1939, Bournemouth, UK. Music Historian; Staff Tutor in Music. Educ: BA, Merton Coll., Oxford Univ., 1960; MA, ibid, 1964; D Phil, 1969. Career: Specialist, 20th Century Italian music; Asst. Lectr. in Music, Extra-Mural Dept., Queen's Univ., Belfast, 1966-67; Lectr. in Music, ibid, 1967-72; Staff Tutor in Music, Extramural Dept., Univ. of Birmingham, 1973-. Contbr. to: Musical Times; Music & Musicians; Tempo; Int. Cyclopedia of Music & Musicians; Ricordiana; Current Musicol.; Rassegna Musicale Curci; Grove's Dict., 6th Ed.; Proceedings of Royal Music Assn.; etc. Mbrships: Life, Royal Musical Assn.; Assn. of Univ. Tchrs. Hobby: Arts esp. visual. Address: Flat B. 1 Ampton Rd., Birmingham, B15 2UP, UK.

WATERHOUSE, William, b. 18 Feb. 1931, London, UK. Bassoonist. Educ: ARCM, RCM, London. m. 3 children. Career: ROH Covent Garden; Italian-Swiss Radio Orch.; LSO; BBC Symph. Orch.; Melos Ensemble; Prof., RNCM, Manchester Juror, Munich Concours, 1965-75. Num. recordings w. Melos Ensemble, etc. Publs: Num. eds. of wind music; Translations, articles for Grove, etc. Mbrships: RAM; ISM; Galpin Soc. Hobbies: Swimming; Skiing; Travel. Address: 86 Cromwell Ave., London, N6 5HQ, UK.

WATERMAN, Fanny, b. 22 Mar. 1920, Leeds, UK. Teacher of Piano; Musical Administrator; Author. Educ: Leeds Univ., 1938-39; RCM, 1940-43; ARCM, 1943. m. Geoffrey de Keyser, 2 children. Fndr. & Chmn., Leeds Int. Pianoforte Competition. Publs. (w. Marion Harewood): First, Second & Third Year Piano Lessons (3 vols.). Ed. (w. Marion Harewood): First, Second & Third Year Piano Repertoire. Hons: Challen Gold Medal, RCM, 1943; MA, Leeds Univ., 1966; FRCM, 1970; OBE, 1970. Address: Woodgarth, Oakwood Grove, Leeds LS8 2PA, UK.

WATERMAN, George Gow, b. 13 Dec. 1935, Poughkeepsie, NY, USA. Musicologist. Educ: BS, MS, Cornell Univ.; PhD Cand., SUNY at Buffalo. m. Greta Albrecht Waterman, 2 children. Career: Tchr. of Music Hist., Orchl. Cond., Bates Coll., Lewiston, Maine, 1974-. Contbr. to Grove's Dict., 6th Ed. Mbr., Am. Musicol. Soc. Hobbies: Sailing; Boatbuilding; Gardening; Backpacking. Address: Cushing Briggs Rd. RFD 2, Box 18 Freeport, ME 04032, USA.

WATERMAN, Ruth, b. 14 Feb. 1947, Harrogate, UK. Violinist. Educ: RMCM; Dip., Juilliard Schl. of Music, NYC, 1969. m. Edmund Arkus. Career: has given concerts in GB & USA; has played for Radio & TV; perf. for Queen, Royal Fest. Hall; played w. Menuhin, Bath Fest., & w. Rosalyn Tureck, NY; Soloist, Henry Wood Promenade Concerts, Aldeburgh Fest. York & Harrogate Fests. (w. major Brit. orchs.). Has recorded for CRI. Adjunct Lectr. Queens Coll., CUNY; 1st violin, Andreas String Quartet; Mus. Dir. & Fndr. of concert series Chamber Music 99; Lectr., NY Univ. Mbrships: Permanent Mbr., Int. Bach Soc.; ISM; Apple Hill Chmbr. Players. Hons: Prizewinner, BBC Violin Competition, 1965; Grants from Youth & Music, Leverhulme Trust fund, US Fedn. of Music Clubs, 1967 & Martha Baird Rockefeller Fund for Music, 1972; NY Recital Debut, Carnegie Hall Corp., 1974. Address: 85-18 123rd St., Kew Gdns., NY 11415, USA. 4.

WATERS, David L, b. 9 Aug. 1940, Houston, Tex., USA. Bass Trombonist; Trombone Instructor. Educ: BMus, Univ. of Houston, 1962; MMus, Univ. of Tex., 1964. Career: Trombone & Tuba, Houston Symph. Orch., 1966-; Instructor, Sam Houston State Univ., Huntsville; Artist Tchr. of Trombone, Rice Univ., Shepherd Schl. of Music. Recordings: Wind Music of Hovaness (w. N Jersey Wind Symph.); Live at Carnegie Hall (Houston Pops Orch.); w. Houston Symph. Orch., works by Samuel Jones, Paul Cooper, Woody Herman, Burt Bacharach. Mbrships: Int. Trombone Assn. Address: 9130 Elizabeth Dr., Houston, TX 77055, USA.

WATERS, J Kevin, b. 24 June 1933, Seattle, Wash., USA. Composer; Professor; Jesuit Priest. Educ: BA, Gonzaga Univ., Spokane, Wash., 1957; MA, ibid, 1958; MA, Santa Clara Univ., 1963; BA (Music), Univ. of Wash., Seattle, 1964; DMus, Univ. of Wash., 1970; Post-doctoral studies in avant-garde techniques w. Bruno Bartolozzi, Florence, Italy. Compositions incl: Mass of the American Martyrs; Psalm of Thanksgiving; Mask of Hiroshima (opera); Ennistymon; Passacaglia for orch.; The Florentine; String Quartet; A Solemn Liturgy; Ballet music for The Eye of the Quetzal; Sinfonia for Independence Day; Opera, Dear Ignatius, Dear Isabel. Contbr. to: America; The Canticle; Catholic World. Num. hons. inclng: Commn. from Hearst Fndn. for the Eye of the Quetzal, 1974. Address: Seattle Univ., Seattle, WA 98122, USA.

WATERS, Marian Elizabeth, b. London, UK. Pianist; Lecturer; Adult Education Tutor. Educ: BA, Dip. in Educ., Univ. of London; LGSM; ARCM. m. Dr. Harold Ellison Roberts, 2 s. Career: BBC recitals, London; Solo Pianist, Royal Opera House Covent Gdn., 1949; Extra-Mural Music Tutor, Univs. of London & Oxford; Specialist Music Tutor, Open Univ., London Reg.; residential courses for the above & for Earnley Concourse, Chichester. Recordings: Solo Recital, Warren Recordings, 1972. Mbr., Solo Perf.'s Sect., ISM. Recip., var. prizes, GSM. Hobbies: Motoring; Cooking; Gardening. Address: Pilgrims' View, St. Alban's Rd., Reigate, Surrey, UK.

WATERS, Vivian, b. 13 Nov. 1936, Bryn Mawr, Pa., USA. Violinist; Violist. Educ: Grad., New Schl. of Music, Phila., Pa., USA; Juilliard Schl. of Music; Mannes Coll. of Music. m. Stanley Ritchie, 2 d. Debut: Violin Soloist, Westminster Choir World Tour, 1956. Career: Mbr. Met. Opera Orch., NYC; Musica Aeterna Chmbr. Orch.; 2nd Prin., Princeton & Trenton, NJ Symphs.; Mbr. NY Contemporary Str. Quartet, NY. Chmbr. Soloists, Apple Hill Chmbr. Players; Fndr., Bloomingdale Trio; Co-Fndr., Colby Quartet; Asst. to Jascha Brodsky, New Schl. of Music, Phila.; Dir., String Dept., Bloomingdale House of Music; developed course of Violin study for Conn. Public Schls. Hobbies: Video-Tape Experiments; Swimming; Horseback Riding. Address: 2912 Eddystone Cres., N Vancouver, BC V7H 1B9, Can.

WATKINS, David Nigel, b. 1 June 1938, Corbridge on Tyne, UK. Harpist; Composer. Educ: RAM. Career: Recitals on radio & TV in most European countries & Hong Kong; Solo recital in Moscow; Prin. Harpist, Royal Opera House, Covent Gdn., London, sev. yrs.; Prin. Harpist, LPO. Comps: Petite Suite for Harp. Recordings: Music for Harp; Spanish Music for Harp; Romantic Music for Harp. Mbrships: ISM; Performing Rights Soc. Publs: An Anthology of English Music for Harp (4 vols.); Complete Method for Harp. Contbr. to profl. jrnls. Hons: Hon. Grad., Moscow Conserv., 1975. Hobbies incl: Looking out of train windows. Address: Vines Farm, Matthews Lane, W Peckham, Kent, UK.

WATKINS, Glenn, b. 30 May 1927, McPherson, Kan., USA. Musicologist; Professor. Educ: BA, MMus, Univ. of Mich.; PhD, Fastman Schl. of Music, Univ. of Rochester; Am. Conserv., Fontainebleau, France. Author, Gesualdo: The Man & His Music, 1973; Co-Ed: Complete Works fo Carlo Gesualdo, 1957-66; complete works of Sigismondo d'India, 1976-. Contbr. to: Jrnl. of Am. Musicol. Soc.; Notes; Groves Dictionary, 6th Ed. Mbr., Am. Musicol. Soc. Recip. var. grants & awards. Address: Schl. of Music, Univ. of Mich., Ann Arbor, MI, USA. 2.

WATKINS, Sara Van Horn, b. 12 Oct. 1945, Chicago, Ill., USA. Principal Oboist; University Lecturer. Educ: BMus, Oberlin Conserv., 1967; Fellowship student, Tanglewood, 1967. Career: Prin. Oboist, Nat. Symph. Orch., Wash. DC, 1973-; Prin. Oboist, Honolulu Symph., 1969-73; Chgo. Chmbr. Orch., 1967-69; Am. Nat. Opera Co., 1967; Grand Teton Music Festival, 1971-73; Soloist w. Fine Arts Quartet, 1968, w. Honolulu Symph., 1970, w. Chgo. Chmbr. Orch., 1968, Nat. Symph.; Lectr. in Oboe, Univ. of Hawaii, 1969-73; Artist in Residence, Claremont Music Festival, Pomona, Calif., 1973. Recordings: Handel Water Music, w. Chgo. Chmbr. Orch., (Vox Turnabout); Tschaikovsky Romeo & Juliet, Fatum, Tempest w. Nat. Symph. Orch. (London); Dalladiccola il Priginiero, Nt. Symph. Orch. (London). Hobby: Tennis. Address: 4763 W Braddock Rd., Apt. 2, Alexandria, VA 22311, USA. 4.

WATLINGTON, Rosalind T G, b. 11 Feb. 1925, Montclair, NJ, USA. Violin & Viola Teacher. Educ: BA, Maryville Coll., Tenn.; Special Cert., Royal Schls. of Music, 1962. m. Francis W Watlington, 1 s., 1 d. Career: Violinist, Bermuda Phil. Soc., 1960-79; Exec. Committee, 1963-65; Orch. Rep., 1965-66, 70-71, 73-75; Violinist, Gilbert & Sullivan Soc. Prods., 1973-78; Violin & viola, My Fair Lady, Bermuda 1978. Mbrships: Amateur Chmbr. Music Players; ASTA; Trustee, Menuhin Fndn., Bermuda; Patron, Bermuda Fest. 1976-; Gilbert & Sullivan Soc. & Bermuda Music & Dramatic Soc., etc. Hobbies: Chmbr. Music; Sports; Art; Travel. Address: 'Coralita', Hidden Lane off Pitts Bay Rd., Pembroke, Bermuda 5-62. 4.

WATSON, Angus James, b. 22 Apr. 1932, Kumming, S China. Master of Music; Violinist; Conductor. Educ: RCM,

London; ARCM (vp); MA, MusB, Magdalene Coll., Cambridge Univ. m. Alison, 3 s., 1 d. Career: Asst. Music Master, Stowe Schl., Bucks., 1955-60; Dir. of Music, ibid, 1960-70; Master of Music, Winchester Coll., 1970-. Contbr. to Making Music. Mbrships: Pres., Cambridge Univ. Music Club, 1953-54; ISM. Recip., Music Scholarship to Magdalene Coll. Hobbies: Gardening; Wine & Beer Making. Address: 9 Kingsgate St., Winchester, UK. 3.

WATSON, Audrey Lee, b. 3 Sept. 1934, Dayton, Ohio, USA. Musician (Piano & Organ); Founder & Director of Audrey Lee Watson Piano Studio. Educ: BMus, MMus, Syracuse Univ. Coll. of Fine Arts; Boston Univ. Coll. of Fine & Applied Arts; Univ. Vienna, Austria. Career incls: Prof. of Music, Wilberforce Univ., Ohio, 1958-60; Fndr. & Dir., Audrey Lee Watson Piano Studio, 1959-; Lectr., Black Hist. & Human Rels., 1965-; Lectr. Pianist in Music Hist. & Lit., 1968-; TV series on Music Hist. & Lit. on TV Stn. WHIO Ohio, 1972; Guest Soloist w. Boston Orch. & Chorale, 1976. Recordings: Dr. Gradus Ad Parnassus by Debussy. Mbrships: incl: Nat. Assn. of Univ. Women; Zeta Phi Beta; Int. Musicol. Soc.; Afro-Am. Music Opportunities Inc.; AAUW. Hobbies: Dancing; Reading; Oil Painting. Address: 1330 Home Ave., Dayton, OH 45407, USA. 4, 5.

WATSON, Jack McLaurin, b. 22 Nov. 1908, Dillon, SC, USA. University Performing Arts Administrator & Teacher; Editor; Author. Educ: Univ. NC, 1926-27; Geneva Coll., 1927-28; BMus, Cinn. Conserv. Music, 1930; MMus, Univ. SC, 1940; MA, Columbia Univ., 1945; PhD, ibid., 1947; Post-doct. study, pt.-time, 1948-50; Juilliard Schl. Music, summers, 1944, '45. m. Corinne Robinson. Career incls: Dean & Thomas James Kelly Prof. Music, Coll.-Conserv. Music, Univ. Cinn., 1963-74; Prof., Creative & Performing Arts, Univ. Cinn., 1974-. Recordings incl: (Arr. & Prod.): Music for Living, 1956. Publs. incl: The Education of School Music Teachers, 1948, reprint, 1972. Contbr. to num. jrnls. Mbr. profl. orgs. Hons. incl: Rosa F & Samuel B Sachs Award, Cinn. Inst. Fine Arts, 1973. Hobby: Travel. Address: 880 Rue de la Paix, CN 45220, USA.

WATSON, Lillian Barbara, b. 4 Dec. 1947, London, UK. Singer (Soprano). Educ: AGSM; Opera Ctr., London. m. Hugh Morgan. Debut: Wexford Fest. Career: Has sung in leading roles for Welsh Nat. Opera, & at Covent Garden, Glyndebourne & Bordeaux; var. operas & concerts, BBC radio 3; Film for Dutch TV of an opera by William Boyce; 2 ITV shows; an opera on Italian radio. Recordings: Monteverdi Madrigals, Raymond Leppard; Le Nozze di Figaro, Colin Davis; Israel in Egypt, Simon Preston. Hobbies: Rugmaking; Reading. Mgmt: Harrison/Parrott. Address: 20 Doughty News, London WC1, UK.

WATSON, Lorne, b. 29 July 1919, Leamington, Ont., Canada. Music Director. Educ: BA (Hons. Music), Toronto Univ.; ATCM (Toronto); LTCM (Toronto); MA, NY Univ. Debut: Toronto, 1949; DMus, Ind. Univ. Career: Concertised throughout Canada; CBC radio appearances; Dir., Schl. of Music, Brandon Univ., Man. Contbr. to Canadian Music Jrnl. Mbrships: Pres., Canadian Assn. of Univ. Schls. of Music; Past Pres., Manitoba Music Educators' Assn.; Past Pres., Man. Registered Music Tchrs. Assn.; Chmn., Eckhardt-Gramatte Competition for perf. of Can. music. Hons: LTCM Gold Medalist, 1941; Canada Coun. Award, 1961; Hon. Fellowship, Royal Hamilton Coll. of Music, 1978. Hobbies: Bridge; Theatre. Address: 2734 Lorne Ave., Brandon, Man., Canada.

WATSON, Mary Baugh, b. 10 Aug. 1890, Pulaski, Tenn., USA. Teacher of Violin, Viola, Piano & Harmony; Church Organist. Educ: 2 yrs., Oberlin, 1 1/2 yrs. Cinn. Conserv. m. Stewart A Watson (dec.). Career: recitalist for over 70 yrs.; apps. on radio in Atlanta & Columbus, Ga.; ch. organist for 40 yrs.; orchs. violinist for 50 yrs. Comps. incl: Sonata for violin & piano; 4 part Fugue; Romance, Dedication; Gulliver & the Liliputians, for unacc. violin. Mbrships: Int. League of Women Comps.; Ga. Music Tchrs. Assn.; Treble Clef Club, Des Moines, Ia.; Tri-Cities Federated Music Clubs. recip. 1st prize (comp.), Tri-Cities, Tri-States, 1929. Hobby: Finding tunes that can be played together. Address: 608 N Jefferson, Albany, GA 31701, USA.

WATSON, Monica, b. Ilford, UK. Pianist. Educ: RAM; LRAM (piano & singing); ARCM (piano). m. Edward Alan Chard, 1 s. Debut: Wigmore Hall, London. Career: in two-piano team w. Elizabeth James, giving recitals, making broadcasts, etc. Mbrships: ISM; Brit. Fedn. of Music Fests.; Treas., York Bowen Soc.; RAM Club. Hobby: Riding. Address: 67 Fitzjohn's Ave., London NW3 6PE, UK. 27, 30.

WATSON, Trevor, b. 31 March 1942, Bexleyheath, Kent, UK. Choir trainer; Schoolmaster. Educ: RAM; GRSM; LRAM (Organ). Career: Organist/Choirmaster, St. Alban, Ilford, 1962; Dir. Music, St. Hugh's, Woodhall Spa, 1964;

Organist, St. Peter, Woodhall Spa & Deanery Rep., RSCM, 1967; Dir. Music, Cargilfield, Edinburgh, 1971; Dir. Music, Bilton Grange, Rugby, 1974. Comps: Negro Spirituals for Treble Voices, 1976. Recordings: Music for Treble Voices, 1978. Mbr., ISM. Hobbies: Hi-Fi; Car Mechanics; Philately; Cooking. Address: Cheam, Headley, Newbury, Berks., UK.

WATSON, Walter Robert, b. 13 Oct. 1933, Canton, Ohio, USA. Composer; Professor of Music; Pianist; Consulting Editor; Organist-Choirmaster. Educ: BFA, 1960, MFA, 1961, Ohio Univ., Athens; PhD, N Tex. State Univ., Denton, 1967. m. Barbara Roush Watson, 2 d. Career: Prof. of Music, Kent State Univ.; Cons. Ed., Ludwig Music Publng. Co.; Organist-Choirmaster, Christ Episcopal Ch., Kent. Comps. incl (orch.): Symphony No. 1; A Folk Fantasia; (symphonic band) American Pastiche; Antiphony & Chorale; (SATB) A Choral Bouquet; The Voice of Jesus. Recordings incl: Five Japanese Love Poems. Mbrsips. incl: ASCAP. Contbr. to The Music Jrnl., 1966. Recip., sev. awards. Address: 1224 Fairview Dr., Kent, OH 44240, USA.

WATT, Alan (James), b. 4 March 1947, Aberdeen, Scotland. Opera & Concert Singer; Recitalist (Baritone). Educ: RSAMD, Glasgow (DRSAM, Tchng. & Perf.). Covent Garden Debut: Morales in Carmen, 1976. Covent Gdn., 1976. Career: Covent Gdn., Morales, Marullo (Rigoletto); Glyndebourne Fest., Morbio (Die Schweigsame Frau), Commerzienrat (Intermezzo), Dog (Cunning Little Vixen); Glyndebourne tour, Marcello, Guglielmo, Figaro (Marriage of Figaro); Kent Opera, Robin Oakapple (Ruddigore), Papageno, Don Alfonso (Cosi Fan Tutte); Guglielmo, Grand Theatre, Tours, France; Apps., num. London Fests.; Debut, Northern Sinfonia, 1976; Regular appls. abroad. Recordings: Israel in Egypt, w. Choir of Christ Ch. Cathedral, Oxford, & English Chmbr. Orch.; Wexford Fest. debut as Ernesto in Haydn's Il Mondo Della Luna, 1978. Hobbies: Squash; Golf; Drawing; Painting. Mgmt: Patricia Greenan, 19B Belsize Pk., London NW3, UK. Address: 3 Bishop's Lane, Ringmer, Nr. Lewes, E Sussex, BN8 5LB, UK.

WATTS, André, b. 20 June, 1946, Nuremberg, Germany. Concert Pianist. Educ: Grad., Peabody Conserv., Baltimore. Debut: w. Phila. Orch., at Children's Concert, age 9. Career: Annual apps. throughout USA w. NY Phil., Los Angeles Phil., Phila. Orch., Chgo. Symph., Boston Symph., Cleveland & other major orchs.; European Debut w. London Symph. Orch., 1966; toured Europe w. Los Angeles Phil., 1967, & USSR w. San Francisco Symph., 1973; frequent tours as soloist & recitalist in Europe, Japan & S America 11 consecutive yrs. on Great Performers series, Lincoln Center; first live recital to be nationally telecast (1976, from Avery Fisher Hall, Lincoln Center). Num. recordings. Hons: Order of the Zaire from Congo, 1970; DMus, Yale Univ., 1973; Lincoln Center Medallion, 1974; Dr. Humanities, Albright Coll., 1975. Address: c/o Judd Concert Artist Bureau, 155 W 68th ST., NY, NY 10023, USA.

WATTS, Helen, b. Haverfordwest, S Wales, UK. Contralto. Career: in Glyndebourne & BBC choruses; toured w. Engl. Opera Grp., USSR, 1964; apps. w. leading orchs. & conds. in Europe; concert tours, USA, 1967-; participant in 4 Promenade concerts, 1974; has appeared in Salzburg, Covent Gdn. & Hong Kong fests. Recordings incl: Handel Arias; Orfeo; B Minor Mass; Beethoven, Mass in C Minor; The Apostles; Götterdämmerung. 16.

WATTS, Lawrence, b. 31 Oct. 1914, London, UK. Teacher of Singing; Tenor Soloist; Lecturer; Adjudicator. Educ: RCM; ARCM; FTCL; studied w. Rodolfa Lhombini, Eric Greene, Lucie Manen & Herbert Caesari. m. Patricia Stanley. Career: Vicar-Choral, St. Paul's Cathedral, 1947-74; tenor soloist in recitals & oratorios; vis. tchr. of singing, King Alfred's Coll., Winchester, 1964-; tchr. of singing, ILEA Ctr. for Young Musicians, Pimlico, 1970-; Prof. of singing, LCM; cond., var. choirs. Mbrships: ISM; Equity; Worshipful Co. of Musicians; Assn. of Tchrs. of Singing; Savage Club. Address: 6 Regent House, 72 Eversholt St., London NW1 1BY, UK.

WATTS, Trevor Charles, b. 26 Feb. 1939, York, UK. Jazz Musician (Alto & Soprano Saxophones). Educ: RAF Schl. of Music & Band, 5 yrs. 1 s. Career: w. New Jazz Orch., 1963; Spontaneous Music Ensemble, 1965; Fndr., Amalgam, 1967, Trevor Watts String Ensemble, 1976, Universal Music Grp., 1978. Comp. & Perf., music for The Connection, 1974; Perfs. at num. major fests., Europe; The Bobby Bradford Quartet; Own Record Co., 'A' Records, 1974. Comps. incl: Ed's Message; Suzie Jay; Prayer for Peace; Tales of Sadness; Ripple; For My Friends; Club 66; Another Time; Jive; Hater; Medication; No Waiting. Recordings incl: Challenge; Oliv; SME for CND; And so What do you Think¿; Love's Dream; Prayer for Peace; Face to Face; Amalgam Play Blackwell & Higgins; Innovation; No Fear;

Deep; Warm Spirits. Mbr., PRS. Hobby: Music. Address: 10 Gt. North Rd., Highgate, London N6, UK. 30.

WAUTERS, Jozef, b. 1 Dec. 1939, St. Niklaas, Belgium. Flautist; Professor of Music; Conductor. Educ: Conserv. Ghent. Career: Solo flute, Belgian Navy Band, Mars, 1960; Prof., Music Acad. St. Niklaas, Belgium & Conserv. Terneuzen, Netherlands; Cond., Military Band of The Belgian Navy, sev. amateur wind & symph. orchs. Comps: Sev. marches for military band. Hons: Sev. 1st prizes, Conserv. Ghent. Address: Ankerstraat 8, 2628 Rupelmonde, Belgium.

WAYENBERG, Daniel Ernest Joseph Carol, b. 11 Oct. 1929, Paris, France. Pianist. Educ: studies w. Margaret Berson (mother), Ary Verhaar & Marguerite Long. Career: num. recitals & concerto perfs. throughout the world; apps. at num. fests. Comps: Solstice (Ballet); Sonata for violin & piano; Concerto for 5 wind instruments & piano; Capella, symph. for orch.; Concerto for 3 pianos & orch. Recordings: Num., incl. works by Brahms, Tchaikovsky, Gershwin, Rachmaninoff. num. hons. Hobbies: Chess; Building miniature railways; Swimming. Mgmt: Concert Direction De Koos, Netherlands. Address: 42 Avenue des Puits, 78170 La Celle St. Cloud, France; 42 Kornoeljestraat, The Hague, Netherlands.

WEAIT, Christopher Robert Irving, b. 27 Mar. 1939, Merton, Surrey, UK. Bassoonist; Instructor of Bassoon. Educ: BS, State Univ. Coll. of Educ., Potsdam, NY, 1961; MA, Tchrs. Coll., Columbia Univ., NYC, 1966. m. Margaret Barstow Weait, 1 s., 1 d. Career: Bassoonist & Contrabassoonist, Chmbr. Symph. of Phila., 1966-68; Co-Prin. Bassoonist, The Toronto Symph., 1968-; Instr. of Bassoon, Fac. of Music, Univ. of Toronto, 1973-78; Prod. & Ed., num. stereo recordings; Soloist, Toronto Symph., 1976, tour of E Can. Comps. incl: Variations for Solo Bassoon, 1975; Lonely Island for Solo Bassoon. Recordings incl: Music for Bassoon by Canadian Composers, w. Monica Gaylord; A Baroque Bouquet (Toronto Baroque Trio w. Melvin Berman & Monica Gaylord); Toronto Winds. Mbrships: Int. Double Reed Soc.; Am. Music Instrument Soc.; Galpin Soc.; Sonneck Soc.; NACWPI. Publs. incl: Bassoon Reed Making: A Basic Technique, 1970. Contbr. to: Applied Radiology. Recip., var. hons. Hobbies incl: Photography. Address: 23 Gaspe Rd., Willowdale, Ont. M2K 2E7, Canada.

WEALE, Malcolm Angus, b. 11 March 1947, London, UK. Principal Trumpet. Educ: GRSM, London, 1969; LRAM; LGSM; ALCM. m. Janet Kerr Corbett, 2 d. Debut: LSO, Fest. Hall, London, 1968. Career: Appeared on Indep. TV, BBC Radio 3, German TV; Recorded as orchl. player w. Bournemouth Symph. Orch., Bournemouth Sinfonietta, & Scottish Nat. Orch.; Prin. Trumpet, Bournemouth Symph. & Bournemouth Sinfonietta Orchs.; Examiner, Assoc. Bd. Exams; Prin. Trumpet, Bolshoi Ballet, 1968-69; Pt.-time Lectr. of Brass, Poole Tech. Coll., Dorset; Brass Coach, Hants. Youth Orch. Recordings: Manfredini Double Trumpet Concerto. Mbrships. incl: ISM. Hobbies incl: Sport; Travelling. Address: 73 Beaufors Ave., Ferndown, Wimborne, Dorset BH22 9RN, UK. 2.

WEARNE, Michael Collin, b. 22 Aug. 1942, Jerusalem, Palestine. Director of Music. Educ: RCM; BMus, Univ. of London; studied piano, organ & comp.; ARCM; LRAM; LMusTCL; FTCL; FLCM. m. Jane Elizabeth Furst, 2 d. Career: Dir. of Music, Lindisfarne Coll., 1965-67; Hd. of Music Dept., Lord Mayor Treloar Coll., 1967-70; Organiser, Kent Music Ctr., 1970-75; Organiser, W Kent Area, 1975-78; Dir., Kent Music Schl., 1978-. Publs: Kent Music, 1975-78. Contbr. of book reviews for Rural Music Schls. Assn. Mbrships: Sec., W Kent Dist., ISM; Exec. Committee, Standing Conf. for Amateur Music; Sec., Kent Co. Music Committee; Music Advisers Nat. Assn. Hobbies: Theatre; Eating Out; Tennis; Sailing; Psychicism. Address: 50 Bower Mt. Rd., Maidstone, Kent ME16 8AU, UK. 29, 30.

WEATHERBURN, Robert James, b. 5 Oct. 1943, Sydney, Aust. Pianist; Composer. Educ: AMus, LMus Aust.; NSW State Conserv. Music w. Alexander Sverjensky; Netherlands Inst. Cultural Rels.; Louis Kentner, London; Conducting w. Dr. Nicolai Malko. Career: Concerts & Recitals, radio & TV, USA, Aust., Singapore, Japan, Iran, Holland, Spain & GB. Comps: Suites for piano; solos; incidental music for stage & ballet inclng. Congreve 'Double Dealer' & Turgenev's 'Month in the Country'. Recordings: Festival Records. Hons. incl: 1st prize, Beethoven competition; Award Netherlands Inst. Cultural Rels.; Best instrumental recording Aust., 'Monuments with Great Composers.' Hobbies incl: Swimming; Chess. Address: Sunyani, 34 W Hill Rd., St. Leonards-on-Sea, Sussex, UK.

WEATHERS-BAKONYI, Felicia, b. 1937, St. Louis, Mo., USA. Opera & Concert Singer. Educ: Wash. Univ., St. Louis; Lincoln Univ., Jefferson City, Mo.; MusB. m. Bela F Bakonyi. Debut:

Zürich, Switz., 1961. Career: made num. apps. in USA & Europe (operatic & concert), 1962; app. at State Opera, Vienna, & in Munich, Germany, 1962, & Hamburg & Cologne, 1963; Mbr., Met. Opera co., 1965-; Guest Artist w. many operas in Europe, USA & S Am.; has made radio & TV broadcasts. Mbrships: Delta Sigma Theta; Roman Catholic Club; Am. Women's Club (Bad Godesberg) Germany; Landshut Flying Club. Hons: DMus; Titcom Award, Met. Opera, 1961. Address: Willroider Str. 6, Suite 104, 8000 Munich 90, German Fed. Repub.

WEATHERSTEN, Nancy Lurline, b. Orange, NSW, Aust. Organist; Pianist; Teacher. Educ: studied w. Oliver Frost of TCL. m. John Weathersten (dec.), 1 s. Career: Choir ldr. & organist for 47 yrs.; apps. in cantatas, amateur theatricals as singer, actress & accomp.; ch. organist; cond., radio choir for 4 yrs. Mbrships: hon. sec., Orange, MEAB; Pres., United Sunday Schl.' Tchrs. Assn.; Hammond Organ Soc. Hons: Western NSW Amateur Artist (soprano), 1940; Piano Duet, 1942; Eisteddfod cond., Junior Choir; Shield Winners for 5 yrs. Hobbies: Music; Gardening; Home; Charity; Ch. Work. Address: 143 Edward St., Orange, NSW 2800, Aust.

WEAVER, Robert Lamar, b. 26 July 1923, Dahlonega, Ga., USA. Professor of Music History and Theory. Educ: BA, Columbia Coll.; MA, Columbia Univ.; PhD, Univ. of NC; Paris Conserv., France; Inst. Phonetiques, Paris; Univ. per gli stranieri, Perugia; Juilliard Schl. of Music; Univ. of Florence, Italy. Prof. of Music Hist., Schl. of Music, Univ. of Louisville, Louisville, KY. m. Norma, 1 s. Recordings: Josquin Des Pres Missa Pange Lingua; Sacred works; Music Lib. Recordings. Publs: Alessandro Melani (Fascicle 8), 1972; Atto Melani (Fascicle 9), 1972; A Chronology of Music in the Florentine Theater, 1590-1750. Contbr. to: Jrnl. of Am. Music Soc.; Notes; Musical Quarterly; Rivista italiana di Musicologia; Jrnl. of Rsch. in Music Educ. Mbrships: Nat. Coun. & Chmn., S. Ctrl. Chapt., Am. Musicol. Soc.; Int. Musicol. Soc.; Italy, 1952-53; Fulbright Rsch. Fellowship to Austria, 1966-67. Hobbies: Tennis; Swimming; Travel. Address: 78 Westwind Rd., Louisville, KY 40205, USA. 11.

WEBB, Brian Patrick, b. 9 Dec. 1948, Auckland, NZ. Assistant Professor of Music. Educ: ATCL Piano, 1966; LTCL Organ, 1970; BMus, Auckland Univ., 1971; MMus, Ind. Univ., USA, 1972; DMus, ibid, 1977. m. Laurene Anne Webb. Career: Asst. Prof. of Music, Norwich univ., Vt., USA, 1974-; Organist-Choirmaster, Christ Ch., Montpelier, Vt., USA, 1974-; Music Dir., Assoc. Opera Artists of Vt., 1975-; Mus. Dir. & Cond., Vt. Phil. Orch., 1977-. Compositions: Drop, Drop Slow Tears (choral), 1972. Mbr. Pi Kappa Lambda. Address: 99 1/2 Coll. St., Montpelier, VT 05602, USA.

WEBB, Julian Barry, b. 6 July 1936, Epsom, Surrey, UK. University Teacher; Conductor; Examiner. Educ: Trinity Coll., Cambridge Univ., 1954-58; MA, MusB; pvte. study w. Leonard Hirsch. m. Heather May Budd, 3 s. Career: Mbr., Nat. & Int. Youth Orchs.; Music Staff, Wellington Coll., 1958-60; Lectr. in Music, Univ. of Manchester, & Mbr., Ad Solem Ensemble (chmbr. music broadcasts & recitals), 1961-66; Lectr.-Sr. Lectr., Univ. of E Anglia, 1966-; Ldr., Str. Quartet, ibid., 1966-73; Dir., Norwich Sinfonia, 1967-; Orchl. Cond., Norwich Phil. Soc., 1971-. Mbr., Assn. Univ. Tchrs. Hobbies: Photography; Travel; Winemaking. Address: Delaware, Church Av. East, Norwich, UK.

WEBB, Marianne, b. 4 Oct. 1936, Topeka, Kan., USA. Organist; Professor of Organ. Educ: BMus, Washburn Univ., 1958; MMus, Univ. of Mich., 1959. m. David N Bateman. Career: Organist, Recitals throughout Europe & Am.; Univ. Organist, Instructor, Organ & Piano, Iowa State Univ., Ames, 1959-61; Asst. Prof. of Organ & Music Lit., James Madison Univ., Harrisonburg, Va., 1963-65; Prof. of Organ & Theory, Univ. Organist, Southern Ill. Univ., Carbondale, 1965-; Cons. in design & bldg. of organs. Recordings: Historical Anthology of Music, P 250, P 251. Contbr. to Music Ministry. Mbrships: AGO; Dean, Southern Ill. Chapt., ibid, 1965-67, 1973-75; Sigma Alpha Iota; VP, Theta Chapt., 1957-58; Phi Kappa Phi; Pi Kappa Lambda. Hons: Sigma Alpha Iota Sword of Hon., Hon. Cert., 1958; Fulbright Grant to Paris, France, 1961-62. Mgmt: Phyllis Stringham Concert Mgmt. Address: Schl. of Music, Southern Ill. Univ., Carbondale,IL 62901, USA. 5, 8.

WEBB, Peter Vincent, b. 27 Apr. 1925, Portsmouth, Hants, UK. Private Practice, Pianoforte, Theory, Composition & Music Therapy. Educ: Litt D, Warsaw Univ.; FLCM; LLCM; LMusLCM; ARCM; DMus, Kansas Univ., USA, 1978. Publs: Music and Its Application as a Therapy in the Treatment of the Physically and Mentally Sub-normal. Contbr. to jrnls. Mbrships: Prof. Music Therapy Nat. Assn. Music Therapy, Kan., USA; Royal Soc. Musicians; Assoc., Royal Phil. Soc.; IGCM; Fellow, Linnaean Soc.

London; Fellow, Royal Geog. Soc.; FRSA; Lic., Royal Soc. Hlth.; Royal Inst. Pub. Hlth. & Hygiene; Hon. Sec., LCM Exams., Portsmouth. Hons: Gold & Silver Medals, Vic. Coll. Music for Comp.; Fellow, Vic. Coll. Music; Fellow, Inst. of Music Therapy, Univ. of Wroclaw, 1978; Award of United Services Chapter for Lit., 1978. Address: 155 Harbour Tower, Trinity Green, Gosport, Hants., PO12 1HF, UK. 1, 28.

WEBB, Richard, b. 16 Jan. 1951, Felixtowe, Suffolk, UK. Baroque Violoncellist; Professor of Music. Educ: GSM; LGSM. m. Susan Brown. Career: Continuo Cello, 17th-18th Century Opera, Lyon Opera, Wexford Fest. Opera, Covent Garden - English Bach Fest., Kent Opera, Sadler's Wells, tours of UK, Athens, Granada, English Bach Fests., Versailles - Opera Royal; Radio recordings, UK, Belgium, France, S Germany (baroque chmbr. recitals); Recitals w. Anthony Pleeth; Mbr., English Concert Acad. of Ancient Music, English Bach Fest. Orch.; Prof. of Music (baroque violoncello), Early Music Dept., GSM. Hobbies: Gardening; Houses; Cooking; Carpentry. Address: 5 Walnut Tree Rd., Greenwich, London SE10, UK.

WEBBER, Nicholas, b. 8 Mar. 1949, Hove, UK. Composer; Critic; Author; Organist. Educ: BMus. Debut: London, 1970. Career: Organist & Master of Music, St. Botolph's, Bishopsgate, 1975-77; Haslemere Parish Ch., 1978-; Dir., Musica Tridentina, 1970-; Specialist writer & critic, Music & Musicians & Records & Recording, 1971-77; Features Ed., Hi-Fi Weekly, 1976-77; Music critic & on staff, Church Times, 1971-74; Classical Ed., Music Week, 1977-78; Prin. Contbr. & reviewing panel, Classical Music Weekly, 1977-; Dir., W G Whittaker Centenary Fest., 1976. Comps. incl: Chmbr. quintet, Ezra Pound, pour l'election de votre sepulchre, Op. 14; Mass of the Angels, Op. 15; Organ Symph. in Albis, Op. 16; Preces & Responses (2nd Set), Op. 17; Summer Idyll, for chorus & orch., Op. 18; Dance-Toccata, Op. 19. Recording of Pontifical High Mass for All Saints' Day. Publs: Contemporary French Organ Music: A Discography, 1976; W G Whittaker, The Centenary, 1977. Contbr. to profl. mags. Mbr., Critics' Panel, Int. Organ Fest., St. Albans, 1979. Hobby: Filling in forms. Address: c/& Rhinegold Publishing, 52A Floral St., London, WC2E 9DA, UK. 29.

WEBBER, Winston, b. 12 Feb. 1949, Detroit, Mich., USA. Conductor; Violinist. Educ: BMus, Univ. of Mich.; studied w. Angel Reyes. Career: mbr., Toronto Symph. Orch. to 1979; now cond. & music dir., Chamber Players of Toronto, Peterborough Symph. Orch. & Oshawa Symph. Orch. Address: 322 Eglinton Ave. E, Apt. 1103, Toronto, Ont. M4P 1L6, Can.

WEBER, Ben, b. 23 July 1916, St. Louis, Mo., USA. Composer. Career: Composer; Private Teacher. Comps: (publd.) 9 orchl. works inclng. 2 Concerti; 8 songs w. instrumental or orchl. accomp.; 20 Chamber Music works; 7 works for piano, 2 for chorus, 1 for organ; (recorded) Symphony On Poems of William Blake, Concerto for Piano & Orch., num. Chamber works. Mbr. Nat. Inst. of Arts & Letters. Hons: Guggenheim Fellowships, 1950, 1953; Fromm Foundation Award, 1953, 1956; Phoebe Ketchum Thorne Fellowship, 1965-68; Award & Citation, Nat. Inst. of Arts & Letters, 1950; elected Life Mbr., ibid, 1970. Hobbies: Reading History, Science; Cooking Address: 418 Ctrl. Pk. W, NY, NY 10025, USA.

WEBER, Sven Fridtjof, b. 28 Sept. 1934, Nykoebing.FL, Denmark. Pianist; Composer; Examiner. Educ: RAM, London; Staatliche Hochschule für Musik, Hamburg; BMus; ARAM; LRAM. m. Marian Lesley Baker, 6 c. Debut: Wigmore Hall, 1964. Career: Var. radio & TV perfs.; Public Concerts; Examiner for Assoc. Bd. of Royal Schls. of Music; Staff Mbr., RAM, RMCM, 1963-75. Comps: Piano Sonata; Clarinet Sonata; Violin Fantasy; many smaller pieces. Contbr. to: Radio Communication. Mbrships: Radio Soc. of GB (Islands Representative); CGGB. Hons: ARAM, 1965. Hobbies: Amateur Radio (GM8ACC); Walking; Photography. Address: Seafield, Stronsay, Orkney, UK.

WEBSTER, Beatrice, b. 12 Apr. 1923, Nelson, NZ. Singer; Voice Teacher. Educ: TCL; RCM; Mozarteum, Salzburg. m. Dr William Kerr Webster, 2 s., 2 d. Career: Lectr., Conserv. of Music, Univ. of Auckland, NZ. Mbrships: Dominion exec., Registered Music Tchrs. of NZ; Int. Soc. for Music Educ.; Engl. Assn. of Tchrs. of Singing. recip., Queen Elizabeth II Arts Coun. award. Address: Midlothian Park, Main Road, RD2, Kumeu, Auckland, NZ.

WEBSTER, Donald Frederick, b. 26 Feb. 1926, Leeds, UK. Lecturer; Conductor; Organist; Adjudicator; Critic. Educ: FRCO (ChM); ADCM; FRCL; LRAM; ARCM; MusB (Dunelm), Leeds Univ. m. Joan Camidge, 1 s. Career incls: Cond., Bradford Old Choral Soc., Huddersfield Glee & Madrigal Soc.; Sub-Organist,

Leeds Parish Ch.; Organist, Palmerston Pl. Ch., Edinburgh; broadcasts of talks; radio & TV broadcasts as organist & cond.; Sr. Lectr., Huddersfield Polytechnic, 1970-76; Sr. Lectr. in Music, Napier Coll. of Commerce & Technol., Edinbrugh, 1976-. Contbr. to: ISM Jrnl.; Sesame; critic & reviewer, Musical Opinion; num. prog. notes for concerts & recitals. Recip., John Brook Mem. Prize for Choir Trng., 1965. Hobbies: Reading; Watching Cricket. Address: Napier Coll. of Commerce & Technol., Sighthill Ct., Edinburgh, UK. 28, 30.

WEBSTER, Ernest Wesley, b. Mt. Vernon, Ill., USA. Concert Accordion Instructor; Teacher; Conductor; Composer. Educ: Royal Schl. Music, Alton, Ill.; Univ. Ariz., Tucson; 1st concert accordionist approved by Fla. State Music Tchrs. Assn. m. Arlene Waite, 2 d. Debut: N Phoenix HS Auditorium, 1947. Career incls: Accordionist, radio stns. KPHO & KOOL, Phoenix, Ariz., 1948-51; Star, educl. filsm, Instructional TV Stn., Channel 22, Ft. Lauderdale. Comps. incl: Suite for Accordion, 1967; Little Poeme, 1968; Little March, 1973; Prelude to Jazz, 1964. Contbr. to jrnls. Mbr. profl. orgs. Hons. incl: Cond.; Webster Accordion Symphonette, winner Fla. State Most Outstanding Performing Accordion Orch., 1963-71. Hobbies incl: Art Galls. Address: Webster Schl. Music, 1232 SW 31 Ave., Ft. Lauderdale, FL 33312, USA.

WEBSTER, Gerald B, b. 6 Jan. 1944, Antioch, Calif., USA. Trumpet Player; Professor. Educ: Univ. of Pacific; BME, MM, Ind. Univ.; Pvte. studies. m. Melinda A Barrett, 1 s. Career incls: Fac., Western Ill. Univ., 1969-70; Washington State Univ.; Freelance perf., soloist, clinician throughout USA; Soloist w. num. bands & orchs. in NW USA; Prin. Trumpet var. orchs. inclng: Spokane Symph.; Solo Trumpet, USMA Band; Fac., Shoreline Music Schl.; Selkirk Coll. Music Schl., Can.; Spokane Jr. Symph. Music Camp; WSU Music Camp; Musical/Artistic Dir., Expo '74. Comps. incl: Num. arrs. for brass ensemble. Recordings: Music Press. Publs: Piccolo trumpet (in progress). Contbr. to: Instrumentalist. Mbr. profl. orgs. inclng: Pi Kappa Lambda; Phi Mu Alpha; Musicians Union. Recip. num. awards & grants. Hobbies: Woodworking; Tennis. Address: NW 340 Larry St., Pullman, WA 99163, USA. 2.

WEDDLE, Robert George, b. 19 Dec. 1941, Amersham, Bucks., UK. Organist & Master of the Choristers, Coventry Cathedral. Educ: MA, Magdalene Coll., Cambridge; ARCO (ChM). m. Catherine Jane Mary Cooke, 2 s. Career: Sub-Organist, Coventry Cathedral, & Asst. Music Master, King Henry VIII Schl., 1964-72; Music Advsr., Univ. of Warwick, 1968-70; Organist, Coventry Cathedral, 1972-; Cond., St. Michael's Singers, 1972-: w. Coventry Cathedral Choir, 1965, 69, 71; The Organ in Coventry Cathedral, 1974; w. City of Coventry Band, 1974. Hobbies: Painting; Good food & conversation. Address: 39 Spencer Ave., Coventry, UK.

WEDGEWOOD, Richard B, b. 21 May, 1942, Cincinnati, OH, USA. University Professor; Pianist; Director of Performances of Contemporary Music. Educ: BM, MacMurray Coll., Jacksonville, Ill.; MMus, Univ. of Ark.; PhD, Univ. of Wis., Madison. m. Mary E Wedgewood. Career: Prof., Music Theory & Comp., Electronic & Computer Music, 20th Cent. Music Hist. & Lit., Piano, currently at Univ. of Sask.; Pianist, as soloist, accomp. & in chmbr. grps., recitals & concert halls & broadcasts on CBC; Dir., Univ. of Sask. Contemp. Chmbr. Ensemble. Comps: Chansons innocentes for soprano & piano; Variations for flute & piano; Solicitude No. 1 for 2 keyboards, contrabass clarinet, bass clarinet, trombone & cello; Nonsense (Fortrees SK 467) for 6 wind instruments; 5 Movements for woodwind quintet. Mbrships. incl: Am. Soc. of Univ. Comps.; Coll. Music Soc.; Am. Musicol. Soc. Hobbies: Sports; Reading; Contemporary Art; Dance & Theatre. Address: 129 Dalhousie Cres., Saskatoon, Sask., Canada S7H 3R4.

WEED, Joseph Laiten, b. 14 Mar. 1917, Athol, Kan., USA. Teacher; Violinist; Administrator. Educ: BM, Bethany Coll., 1938; MusM, Yale Univ., 1942; Postgrad. study, Yale, Harvard Univs., Manhattan Schl. of Music, Aspen Schl. of Music. m. Lucy Palermo. Career: Music Dir., Langdon HS, Kan., 1938-40; Pvte. studio, Hutchinson, Kan., 1940-41; Instr., Sterling Coll., 1940-41; Concertmaster, Hutchinson Symph., 1939-41; Dir. of Conserv., Yankton Coll., SD, 1947-74; Prof. of Music, ibid, 1947-; Mbr., New Haven Symph., 1941-42, 1946-47, Sioux City Symph., 1947-, Sioux Falls Symph., 1960-; Fndr. & Musical Dir., Lewis & Clarke Symphonette, 1961-67; Ed., Co-prod., premiere of The American Volunteer by Felix Vinatieri. Contbr. to profl. jrnls. Mbrships: Pres., SD Music Educators Assn., 1974-76; Mbr., Exec. Coun., W Ctrl. Div., MTNA; Mbr., State Bd. of Control, SD Music Educators Assn.; Pres., local chapt. AAUP; Am. String Tchrs. Assn.; Kiwanis Int. Hons: Full Tuition Schlrship. to Yale Univ. Schl. of Music, 1941; Sioux City Symph. Schlrship. to Aspen, 1963; Gov.'s Rep. to Nat. Coun. of Fine Arts, 1966; Vice-Chmn., SD

Arts Coun., 1967-70; MusD, Morningside Coll., 1968. Hobbies: Chamber music; Swimming. Address: 802 Pine St., Yankton, SD 57078, USA. 3, 8, 12.

WEED, Maurice James, b. 16 Oct. 1912, Kalamazoo, Mich., USA. Composer; Music Educator. Educ: AB, Western Mich. Univ., 1934; BMus, Eastman Schl. of Music, Univ. of Rochester, NY, 1941; MMus, ibid, 1952; PhD, 1954. m. Berneice LaVerne Pope, 2 d. Career incls: Teaching Fellow in Music Theory, Eastman Schl. of Music, Univ. of Rochester, NY, 1951-54; Reg. staff, Summer Session, 1954; Hd., Dept. of Music, Northern Ill. Univ. De Kalb, 1954-61; Prof. of Music, 1961-74; Prof. of Music, Western Carolina Univ., Cullowhee, NC, 1974-. Compositions incl: Introduction & Scherzo, 1959; The Wonder of the Starry Night, 1960; Psalm XIII, 1964; Praise Ye the Lord (Psalm 148), 1968; Over 50 original works altogether. Contbr. to NACWPI Jrnl.; The Ill. Music Educator. Mbrships. incl: Am. Soc. of Univ. Comps.; Am. Music Ctr.; ASCAP; NACWPI; MENC. Recip. of num. hons. Hobbies incl: Gardening; Camping; Mountain Climbing; Jazz. Address: R 1, Box 641, Timberland Rd., Waynesville, NC 28786, USA. 2, 8.

WEEDON, Bert, b. 10 May 1920, East Ham, London, UK. Solo Guitarist; Composer. Career: 5000 radio & TV shows; apps. at London Palladium, Albert Hall, Opera House, Manchester & every theatre in UK. Comps. include num. hit records, rags, guitar solos. num. hit recordings & No. 1 LPs in record charts. Publs: Play in a Day Guitar Tutor, 1956; Play Every Day Guitar Method; num. guitar albums. Contbr. to: Melody Maker; New Musical Express; The Stage. Mbrships: PRS; Variety Club of GB; Stars Org. for Spastics. Hons: voted Britain's Top Solo Guitarist 9 times, 1960-70; gold & platinum awards for sales of LPs. Hobbies: Swimming; Driving. Address: Epperstone House, 45 Penn Rd., Beaconsfield, Bucks., UK.

WEEGENHUISE, Johan Eduard, b. 2 Sept. 1910, Amsterdam, Netherlands. Composer; Pianist; Organist; Choral Conductor; Teacher. Educ. incls: Piano dip., Liège; State Piano Dip., The Hague; Organ Dip.; Schl. of Music, Maastricht. m. Bernadette M G A Nooy, 1 d. Debut: as pianist, aged 12, Maastricht. Career incls: Choirmaster & Organist, var. Roman Cath. Chs., Amsterdam, 1932-67; Music Tchr., pvte., pub. & at Amsterdam Musiclyceum; about 25 broadcasts, Radio Hilversum; Pianist & Organist; Concertgebouw, Amsterdam; perfs. in Paris & London. Comps. incl: 10 masses; 8 piano pieces; 18 comps. for choir a cappella & w. accomp.; 16 organ pieces; 5 orchl. wokrs; Concerto for recorder & strings; 30 pieces for voice; 30 pieces for voice & piano; num. chmbr. & instrumental works. Recordings: principally broadcast. Mbrships: Royal Soc. of Netherlands Musicians; Soc. of Dutch Comps.; Cath. Choirmasters & Organists Soc. Hobbies: Philosophy; History; Politics. Address: Legmeerstraat 12, ND1058 Overtoomseveld, Amsterdam W, Netherlands.

WEEKLEY, Dallas Alfred, b. 15 May 1933, Sparks, Ga., USA. Concert Pianist & Professor of Music. Educ: BMus, MMus, DMus, Ind. Univ., Bloomington. m. Nancy Arganbright, 1 s. Debut: Carnegie Hall. Career: concerts throughout Am. & Europe; Nat. network TV apps. (CBS-TV). Recordings. A Recital of L Hand, One Piano Music. Publs: The One-Piano, Four-Hand Compositions of Franz Schubert. Contbr. to: Clavier; Music Jrnl.; Music & Artists. Mbrships: Pi Kappa Lambda; Phi Mu Alpha; local Chmn., NGPT; MENC; MTNA; Piano Tchrs. Guild. Hons: BBC Award, 1964. Hobbies: Restoring 19th Century Mansion. Mgmt: Edmond Karlsrud, 948 The Parkway, Mamaro Neck, NY. Address: 1532 Madison St., La Crosse, WI 54601, USA. 8, 16.

WEEKLEY, Nancy (Arganbright), b. 29 Mar. 1936, Georgetown, Ind., USA. Concert Pianist; Piano Teacher. Educ: MS, Audiovisual Media, Univ. of Wis.; BMus in Piano Perf., Ind. Univ., Bloomington. m. Dallas A Weekley, 1 s. Debut: Carnegie Hall, 1963. Career: Concerts throughout USA & Europe; Nat. network TV apps. (CBS-TV). Mbrships: Pi Kappa lambda; Mu Phi Epsilon; NGPT. Recip., BBC Award, 1964. Hobbies: Stichery; Gourmet Cooking. Mgmt: Allied Concert Servs., Mnpls. Address: 1532 Madison St., La Crosse, WI 54601, USA. 27.

WEEKS, John Ralph, b. 15 July 1934, Bath, UK. Educator; Composer. Educ: ARCM; BMus, London; LRAM; FRCO. m. June Dorothy Gowen, 2 d. Career: Clarinettist, Irish Guards Band, 1953-56; Freelance work, mainly piano, 1957-60; Clarinettist, Jose Limon European Tour, 1957; Asst. Music Master, Dauntsey's Schl., Wilts., 1960-70; Lectr. in Harmony & Counterpoint, etc., RSAMD, Glasgow, 1970-. Compositions: Jubilate for Brass & Organ; The Rapture; Evening Canticles; Festival Anthem; Oboe Sonatina; When the Fire & the Rose are One. Mbrships: CGGB; RCM Union. Hons: 2nd Prize, Schnitgerprize, Zwolle, 1964; 2nd Prize, Stroud

Festival, 1970. Hobbies: Reading; Walking; Natural Hist. Address: 120 Kylepark Dr., Uddingston, Glasgow G71 7DE, UK. 3.

WEGELIN, Arthur Willem, b. 5 Mar. 1908, Nijmegen, Netherlands. Violin Teacher; Chamber Music Player; Orchestral Violinist; Composer; Theorist; Educator; Director of Conserv. of Music; Professor and Head of Music Department; Researcher. Educ: BMus, MMus, UNISA, Pretoria; FTCL. m. (1) Sophia Betsy Hiebendaal, (2) Wytske Johanna Zoetelief Tromp., 1 s., 1 d. Career incls: Violinist, Utrechtsch Stadelijk Orch., Netherlands; Lectr., RSA, Lectr., Potchefstroom Univ.; Fndr., Conserv. & Dept. Music, Univ. Port Elizabeth; Sr. Rsch. Off., Human Scis. Rsch. Coun., S Africa; Rsch., musical aptitude. Publs. incl: Skoolmusiek vir Suid-Afrika, 1962; Junior & Senior Musical Aptitude Tests, 1977. Contbr. to newspapers & jrnls. Mbr., num. profl. orgs. Recip. several bursaries. Hobby: Woodwork. Address: Zoetelief, Kruinsingel, Montagu 6720, S. Africa.

WEHR, David August, b. 21 Jan. 1934, Mt. Vernon, NY, USA. Educator. Educ: BMus & MMus, Westminster Choir Coll., Princeton, NJ; PHD, Univ. Miami, Coral Gables, Fla., 1971; Studied voice, organ & conducting w. var. tutors. m. Nancy S Wehr, 2 s., 1 d. Career incls: Organist-Choirmaster-Carillonneur, Meth. Cathedral of the Rockies, Boise, Idaho, 1958-68; Currently Prof., & Dir. Choral Activities, Eastern Ky. Univ., Richmond. Comps. incl: (choral) Consider, O My Soul; Now Alien Tongues (carillon) Christmas Carols for Carillon; (handbells) Festival Fanfare; (organ) 4 Festive Pieces for Organ. Contbr. to profl. publs. Mbr. var. orgs. Hons. incl: ASCAP cash award annually 1966-. Hobbies incl: Barbershop Quartet Singing. Address: Rt. 9, Hillcrest Estates, Richmond, KY 40475, USA. 7.

WEHRLE, Heinz, b. 1921, Zürich, Switz. Organist; Harpsichordist; Radio Producer. Educ: studied piano, harpsichord & organ w. Prof. V Schlatter, Zürich Cathedral. m. Anne-Marie Stumpf. Career: 1st Organist, Reformed Ch. of Meilen-Aürich, 1949-; has given many organ & harpsichord concerts in Zürich & Vienna, & over radio; Cond., Meilen Chmbr. Orch., 1950-61; prod., organ & jazz progs., Radio Zürich; presents live jazz concerts on radio; Tchr. of courses on jazz, Wetzikon-Zürich Canton Schl. & Zürich Schl. for Soc. Work. Compositions incl: Fanal for organ; Aria Variata for organ; Chant de paix for organ; Sons d'orgue; Three Choral Fantasies; Requim; music for radio plays. Publs: Schweizerische Radio-und Fernseh-Zeitung. Mbrships. incl: New Jazz Club, Zürich; Assn. of Zürich Organists. Address: Biberlinstr. 39, 8032 Zürich, Switzerland.

WEHRLE, Paul, b. 14 Aug. 1923, Karlsruhe, Germany. Music Teacher; Choral Conductor. Educ: Musikhochschule, Karlsruhe; Univs. Heidelberg & Freiburg; Gymnasial-Professor. m. Üte Wehrle. Career: Cond., Der Karlsruher Kammerchor, Philharmonischer Chor Karlsruhe; Gen. Sec., Fest. Europe Cantat I-VI. Contbr. to: Musik und Bildung. Mbr. & Office holder, num. profl. orgs. Hons: Bundesverdienstkreuz. Address: Sonnenbergstr. 20, 7500 Karlsruhe 41, German Fed. Repub.

WEIGALL, Richard, b. 28 July 1944, London, UK. Orchestral Oboist. Educ: Nat. Youth Orch., 1961-63; studied w. Terence MacDonagh, RCM, 1963-66; pvte. study w. Johann Baptist Schee, Essen, German Fed. Repub., 1966-67. Career: Prin. Oboe, Sadlers Wells (now Engl. Nat.) Opera Orch., 1967-69; Prin. Oboe, City of Birmingham Symph. Orch., 1969-. Hons: Fndn. Scholarship to RCM; Worshipful Co. of Musicians Medal, 1966. Hobby: Painting. Address: 41 The Lindens, off Balden Rd., Harborne, Birmingham 32, UK.

WEIGAND, George Alexander, b. 3 Nov. 1946, Balt., Md., USA. Musician (lute, mandore, orpharion, bandora, cittern & banjo). Educ: BA, E Carolina Univ., NC, USA; MPhil., Warburg Inst., Univ. of London. m. Rosemary Thorndycraft. Debut: as lutenist, USA TV, 1963. Career: TV/radio apps. in UK, German Fed. Repub., Eire & Norway; perf. w. Royal Shakespeare Co.; Dir., Extempore Str. Ensemble; apps. w. Camerata of London, City Waits, Broadside Band, London Early Music Group, Musica Aure (Liège), Jaye Consort, New Excelsior Talking Machine, etc. num. recordings mainly of Renaissance music. Publs: Lute Improvisation, 1977; Playing the Elizabethan Lute, 1978. Contbr. to: Early Music; Galpin Soc. Jrnl. Mbrships: Musicians' Union; ISM. Hobbies: Building Instruments; Painting. Address: 72 Sussex Way, London N7 6RR, UK.

WEINBERG, Anton, b. 25 Nov. 1944, London, UK. Musician (Clarinet, Bass Clarinet, Saxophone). Educ: LRAM; ARCM; BBC Trng. Orch. m. (1) 1 s.; (2) Francesca Crowe. Debut: Wigmore Hall. Career: Solo recitals for BBC Radio; Guest Artist on radio & TV progs.; recitals at Harrogate, Corfu & Coruna Fests. & at

many music clubs; regular perfs. w. RPO, BBC Symph. Orch., London Sinfonietta. Has recorded w. Engl. Chmbr. Orch. (w. Peter Pears), Rick Wakeman, David Essex, also for advertising soundtracks. Contbr. to: Crescendo Mag.; BBC Radio 3. Mbr., ISM. Recip. var. prizes & awards inclng: Arts Coun. award for study of solo repertoire, 1975. Mgmt: Ibbs & Tillett. Address: 22 Cranley Gdns., Muswell Hill N10 3AP, London, UK.

WEINBERGER, Jaromir, b. 8 Jan. 1896, Prague, Czech. Composer. Educ: Prague Conserv.; studied w. Max Reger, Berlin. Career: Prof. of Composition, Ithaca Conserv., NY, 1922-26; Dir. of Opera, Nat. Theatre of Bratislava, 1926; Dir., Eger Schl. of Music, 1926. Compositions incl: Schwanda the Bagpiper (opera - num. recordings), 1926; Christmas Overture, 1929; The Legend of Sleepy Hollow (orchl.), 1939; Under the Spreading Chestnut Tree (orchl.), 1939; Dixie (orchl.).

WEINER, Max, b. 15 Feb. 1920, Austria. Musician; Violinist. Educ: BA, Columbia Univ., NYC; Pvte. studies in music. m. Carolynn Newitt, 1 s., 1 d. Debut: Detroit, Mich., 1938. Career: Performed w. Detroit, Chgo. & Pitts. Symphs. previous to 1946; Mbr., NY Phil., 1946-. Recordings: w. Chmbr. Ensemble (Philharmonia Virtuosi of NY). Hobby: Reading Hist. Address: 2811 215th St., Bayside, NY 11360, USA. 4.

WEINER, Stanley Milton, b. 1925, Balt., Md., USA. Composer; Violinist. Educ: Peabody Conserv., Balt.; David Mannes Music Schl.; Manhattan Schl. of Music, NYC. 1 d. m. (2) Jacquelin Devreux. Career: Concert Master, NYC Symph. under Leonard Bernstein, 1947-48, & Indpls. Symph. Orch., 1950-53; Concert tours as soloist in Europe & Am.; Tchr., Grenzland Inst., Aachen, 1975-77; Prof. of Violin, State Acad. of Music, Hamburg, Germany, 1976-. Comps. incl: Noah's Ark, for Narrator & Orch.; Symphs. No. 2 & 3; 7 Caprices for violin solo; Concerto No. 4 for violin & orch.; Sonata for flute solo; Phantasy for trombone & piano; Concerto for trumpet & orch.; 2 String Quartets; chmbr. music. Hobbies: Photography; Philately. Address: 12 Ave. des Narcisses, B-1180 Brussels, Belgium. 3.

WEINTRAUB, Eugene, b. 10 March 1904, Stalnoye, USSR. Publisher. Educ: Violin studies w. Victor Küzdö; Cond., Juilliard Schl., NY. Career: Dir., Am-Rus Music Corp., 1940; Hd., Dept. of Soviet Music, Leeds Music Corp., 1944-50; Fndr., Weintraub Music Co., 1950, specializing in works of modern Am. comps. Contbr. of articles on Arturo Toscanini, NY Times, LA Times, The Music Jrnl.

WEIR, Gillian Constance, b. 17 Jan. 1941. Concert Organist & Harpsichordist. Educ: RAM, 1962-65; LRAM; ARCM; LCTL; Hon. FRCO. m. Lawrence Phelps. Debut: Royal Festival Hall, 1965. Career incls: concert apps. w. leading orchs. & ensembles in UK & abroad; yearly concert tours in USA; Solo apps. at major fests., UK & Europe; regular broadcasts on BBC-3, also TV broadcasts; master classes, UK & Am.; Adjudicator, Int. competitors, France, USA, Can. & UK; 1st perfs. of var. contemp. works; Vis. Lectr., Royal Northern Coll. of Music; Artist-in-Res., Wash. Univ., 1976, Univ. of Western Aust., 1977, '78, '79, Univ. of Melbourne, 1978, '79, Univ. of Cape Town, 1978. Recordings incl: complete organ works, Clerambault, Couperin, Roberday; Messiaen (1979), etc. Contbr. to musical publs. Mbrships: Fac. of Music, Cambridge Univ.; ISM; Coun., RCO. Recip. many hons. Hobby: Theatre. Mgmt: Clarion Concert Agency, 64 Whitehall Pk., London N19, 3TN, UK. Address: Univ. Women's Club, 2 Audley Sq., S Audley St., London W1, UK. 27, 30.

WEIS, Carl Flemming, b. 15 Apr. 1898, Copenhagen, Denmark. Organist; Composer; Music Critic. Educ: Royal Conserv. of Copenhagen. m. Ingeborg Trier, dec., 1 s., 1 d. Career: Organist, Anna Ch., Copenhagen, 1929-68; Music Critic, 'Politiken', 1963-. Compositions incl: Serenade for wind quintet (rec.); Diverting music for flute & strings (rec.); 12 monologues for piano (rec.); Sine Nomine for orch., 1973; Chaconne for orch., 1975; Three Sisters for solo cello, 1974 (rec.); Tree Aspects, for solo guitar, 1975 (rec.); String Quartet, 1977. Contbr. to var. periodicals. Mbrships: Bd. Mbr., Danish Sect., ISCM, 30 yrs.; Chmn., ibid, 1942-56; Hon. Mbr., 1956-; Bd. Mbr., Danish Composers Soc., 1956-; Chmn., ibid, 1967-71; Hon. Mbr., 1978, ibid; Chmn., Soc. for Publishing Danish Music. Hons: Kt. of the Order of Danebrog, 1952; Kt. of First Degree, 1962. Hobbies: Gardening; Collecting butterflies & moths. Address: Gotfred Rodesveg 20, 2920 Charlottenlund, Denmark. 19, 23, 30.

WEISBROD, Annette Jeanne, b. 9 Dec. 1937, Blackburn, UK. Pianist. Educ: Tchr. Dip. & Chmbr. Music Dip., Zürich Conserv., Switz.; Concert Dip., Basle Conserv. m. Charles Kirmess. Debut: London, 1960. Career: Concerts all over Europe as soloist & in chmbr. music ensembles; Mbr., Swiss Fest. Trio;

Num. radio & TV apps.; Master Class, Berne Conserv.; Num. recordings, inclng. complete recording of all Haydn Trios. Mbrships: Schweizerischer Tonkünstler-Verein; Schweizerischer Musikpädagogishcer Verband; Lyceum-Club. Hobbies: Art; Cookery; Nature. Mgmt: K Kirmess, Heuelst. 33, 8032 Zürich, Switzerland.

WEISGALL, Hugo, b. 1912, Ivancice, Czechoslovakia. Composer; Conductor; Teacher. Educ: PhD, Johns Hopkins Univ.; Dips., Curtis Inst.; studied composition w. Roger Sessions. m. Nathalie Shulman, 1 s., 1 d. Career: Dir., Balt. String Symph., 1937-39, Balt. Inst. of Musical Arts, 1949-50, Hilltop Opera Co., 1951-54, & Balt. Chmbr. Music Soc., 1951-60; Disting. Vis. Prof., Pa. State Univ., 1959-60; Chmn. of Fac., Cantors Inst., NYC, 1951-; Instructor, Juilliard Schl. 1956-; Prof., Queens Coll., 1960-. Compositions incl: 7 operas (Six Characters in Search of an Author, The Tenor, Nine Rivers from Jordan, etc.); A Garden Eastward (cantata for high voice & orch.); Soldier Songs (cantata for medium voice & orch.); Outpost (ballet); Quest (ballet); many songs & choral pieces; radio & TV music. Contbr. to jrnls. Address: 81 Maple Drive, Gt. Neck, NY, USA.

WEISGARBER, Elliot, b. 5 Dec. 1919, Pittsfield, Mass., USA. Composer; Conductor; Research & Performer of Japanese music. Educ: BMus, MMus, Perfs Cert. in clarinet, Eastman Schl. of Music, Univ. of Rochester; studies in clarinet, chmbr. music, comp. & Japanese music. m. Bethiah Setter, 1 d. Career incls: Instr.-Asst. Prof.-Assoc. Prof., Woman's Coll., Univ. of NC, USA, 1944-60; Asst. Prof.-Assoc. Prof.-Prof., Univ. of BC, Can., 1960-. Comps. incl: Concerto for violin & orch., 1974; A Pacific Trilogy (full orch.); Fantasia a Tre (horn, violin, piano); Illusions of Mortality; Song cycle for soprano & piano (poems by Clive Simpson); Crown of Fire, film music; Music for the Morning of the World, for wind & percussion ensembles; Quintet, for flute, oboe, clarinet, horn & bassoon. Num. recordings. Contbr. to jrnls., books & poetry in MS. Mbr. profl. orgs. Recip. var. awards & many commissions. Address: 4042 W 33rd Ave., Vancouver, BC V6N 2J1, Canada.

WEISMANN, Wilhelm, b. 20 Sept. 1900, Wurttemberg, BRD. Composer; Music Writer. Educ: Conserv., Stuttgart; Music Acad., Leipzig; State Exam. m. (1) Dorothea Braungart (d. 1943), (2) Ernestine Vogel, 4 s., 3 d. Debut: Italian Madrigals, 1925. Career: Ed., Music Mag., 1924-28; Lectr. & Ed., Peters Publrs., Leipzig, 1929-65; Tchr. & Professorship, Music Acad., Leipzig, 1946-55, 1961-72. Comps. incl: Songs from Goethe's W-E Collection, 1967; Suite in H, 1960. Recordings: 23rd Psalm, 1954; Songs & choral works; Madrigals; song cycles. Contbr. to Music Mag.; German Annual for Musicol. Mbrships: Community of Comps. & Musicologists of DDR; Cultural Soc. DDR. Hons. incl: State Prize for Popular Arts; Hon. Mbr., Art Acad. of DDR. Address: Kdt. Prendel-Allee 116, 7027 Leipzig, German Democratic Repub.

WEISS, Edward, b. 6 Sept. 1892, New York, NY, USA. Concert Pianist. Educ: Master Pupil: Xaver Scharwenka, Berlin; Ferruccio Busoni, NY, Zurich & Berlin. m. Gustava Weiss. Career incls: Apps. w. Berlin Phil.; NY Phil.; Recitals at Town Hall; Artistic Dir., Liederkranz Musicales; Apps. in USA & all European countries; Honoured by Jean Sibelius while on tour of Finland. Recordings incl: Busoni Sonata & Busoni's Indian Diary accepted by Signor Gronchi, Pres. of Italy, for his pvte. record collection. Contbr. to Music Jrnl., NY; Music Jrnl., Mexico. Mbrships: Liederkranz Club, NY; Bohemians, NY; Nat. Arts Club, NY. Hons: Finnish Cross of the Lion. Address: 853 Seventh Ave., New York, NY 10019, USA.

WEISS, Elizabeth B, b. 7 Feb. 1940, Atlanta, Ga., USA. Symphonic Musician; Violist. Educ: BMus, La. State Univ., 1961. m. Howard A Weiss. Career: Prin. Violist, Baton Rouge Symph. & Mobile Symph.; Mbr., Atlanta Pops Orch. & Chgo. Chmbr. Orch.; Mbr., Rochester Phil. Orch., 1967-; Hartwell String Quartet, 1975-78; Fac. Mbr., Eastern Music Fest., Greensboro, NC, 1976-. Hobbies: Cooking; Reading; Needlework; Skiing. Address: 228 Castlebar Rd., Rochester, NY 14610, USA.

WEISS, Ferdinand, b. 6 June 1933, Vienna, Austria. Composer; Conductor; Teacher. Educ: Univ. of Vienna; Dip. for Comp., 1958, Dip. as Cond., 1960, Dip. for Flute, 1961, Acad. of Music, Vienna. m. Ingeborg Scheibeweiss, 1 s. Debuts: (composer) Eisenstadt, 1957; (cond.) Vienna, 1960. Career: Cond. in theatres inclng. Theater an der Wien, Vienna; Flautist in var. orchs. in Austria & Germany; Fndr., Chmbr. Ensemble for concerts in Lower Austria; About 200 perfs. of comps. in concerts & on radio. Comp. of 140 works. Recordings: Concertpiece for Oboe & String Orchestra. Mbr., var. music assns. Recip., sev. prizes. Hobbies incl: Hist. Address: A-2500 Baden, Christalnigg-Gasse 11/2, Austria.

WEISS, Howard A, b. 6 Feb. 1939, Chgo., Ill., USA. Concertmaster; Music Director; Conductor; Violinist. Educ: BMus, Chgo. Musical Coll. of Roosevelt Univ., 1960; MMus, ibid, 1966. m. Elizabeth B Weiss. Debut: Chgo., aged 14. Career: Soloist w. Youth Orch. of Greater Chgo.; Mbr., Cleveland Orch.; Concertmaster, San Fran. Ballet Orch., Va. Symph. & Chgo. Chmbr. Orch.; Concertmaster, Rochester Phil. Orch., 1967-; Music Dir., Cond., Rochester Phil. Youth Orch., 1970-; Ldr., Hartwell String Quartet, 1975-78; perf. 30 violin concertos w. num. Am. Orchs.; Concertmaster, Eastern Music Fest., Greensboro, NC, 1976-; num. fest. apps., master classes; Chmbr. music coach. Recordings: Elegy for Violin & Orch. (w. Rochester Phil.); 5 LP records & TV apps. w. Rochester Phil. Youth Orch. Hobbies: Chamber Music; Sports. Address: 228 Castlebar Rd., Rochester, NY 14610, USA.

WEISS, Manfred, b. 12 Feb. 1935, Niesky o/L, German Dem. Repub. Composer; Lecturer. Educ: Music Studies Halle, Berlin; State exam, 1957; German Art Acad. Berlin, 1957-59. m. Angelika Weiss, 4 c. Career: Since 1959 Lectr. Music Acad. Dresden; Radio prod. of own works. Comps. incl: To My Compatriots, Brecht Cantata; Str. Quartet, 1965; Studies; 4 Works for Str. Quartet; Piano Trio II; Octet; Sonata for piano; Piano Trio op. 8; Organ concerto; Piano concerto. Mbrships: Assn. for Comp. & Musicologists German Dem. Repub., mbr. bd. of dir. Address: Hartmannstr. 37, 8021 Dresden, German Dem. Repub.

WEISS, Piero Ernesto, b. 26 Jan. 1928, Trieste, Italy. Musicologist; Pianist; Teacher. Educ: AB, Columbia Coll., 1950; PhD, Columbia Univ., 1970; studied piano w. Isabelle Vengerova; comp. w. Karl Weigl; chamber music w. Adolf Busch & Rudolf Serkin. m. Carole Anne Severson, 1 s., 1 d. Debut: Town Hall, NY, 1953. Career: Piano recitals, sonata recitals w. violin, concertos w. orchs., mainly from 1949-61 in USA, England (Wigmore Hall, 1955), Norway, Holland, Germany, Austria, Switz., Italy; On Music Fac. of Columbia Univ., 1965- & at Brooklyn Coll., NY, 1973-. Recordings: Schumann's 'Carnaval'; music of Debussy & Ravel. Publs: Letters of Composers Through Six Centuries (compiled & edited), 1967; Carlo Goldoni, Librettist: The Early Years, 1970; num. articles, transls., reviews in profl. publs. Mbrships: Int. Musicol. Soc.; Am. Musicol. Soc. Address: 180 Riverside Dr., NY, NY 10024, USA.

WEISSENBERG, Alexis, b. 1929, Sofia, Bulgaria. Pianist. Educ: studied piano & comp. under Pancho Viadiguerov at age 3 yrs.; studied under Olga Samarov at the Juilliard Schl. of Music, NY, USA, 1946. Debut: in concert at Carnegie Hall w. the NY Phil. under George Szell. Career: First orchl. concert in Israel, 1944, & concert tour of S Africa in the same yr.; Coast-to-coast tour of USA w. Phila. Orch. & Eugene Ormandy; Concerts in Paris, Vienna, Madrid, Milan, 1951; Appeared w. Herbert von Karajan, playing Tchaikovsky First Piano Concerto w. the Berlin Phil. Orch., 1966; Invited to play w. many great conductors & orchs. all over the world, inclng. Abbado, Bernstein, Celibidache, Giulini, Karajan, Ormandy, etc., 1967; Var. recent world-wide tours; w. Maazel & New Phil. Orch., Royal Fest. Hall, London, UK, 1974. Has-recorded w. RCA & EMI. Mgmt: S A Gorlinsky Ltd., 35 Dover St., London, UK & Michel Glotz, 141 Blvd. St. Michel, Paris, France.

WEISSENSTEINER, Raimund, b. 14 Aug. 1905, Hoheneich nr. Gmund, Austria. Professor of Music; Chaplain. Educ: Dip, Vienna Coll. of Music, 1934. Career: Chaplain, Votivkirche, Vienna; Comp.; Dir., yearly concerts of own works for Friends of Music Soc., Vienna & Vienna Concert House Soc.; Prof. of Comp., Hochschule für Musik, Vienna. Comps: 95 works inclng 3 str. quartets; num. orchl. works inclng: 11 symphs.; many works for violin & piano, solo piano, & var. other chmbr. combinations; vocal & choral works inclng. masses & oratorios. Mbrships: Austrian Comps. Union; Soc. of Authors, Comps. & Music Publrs., Vienna. Recip. var. hons. Mgmt: Edition Oberon, Vienna. Address: Amtsstr. 21-25, 1210 Vienna, Austria. 3.

WEKRE, Frøydis Ree, b. 31 July 1941, Oslo, Norway. Musician; Horn. Educ: studied w. Wilhelm Lanzky-Otto, Vitalij Boujanovsky. Debut: Oslo, 1961. Career: 3rd Horn, Oslo Opera Orch., 1960-61, Oslo Phil. Orch., 1961-65; Co-Prin. Horn, Oslo Phil., 1965-; Soloist, var. amateur & profl. orchs. & bands, Norway & Denmark; num. TV apps.; mbr. Oslo Wind Soloists, The Norwegian Brass Quintet; Jury Mbr., Competition for Musical Interpretation, Geneva, 1971; Tchr., Perf., 5th & 6th Annual Horn Workshops, USA. Recordings: w. Oslo Wind Quintet, Philips. Mbr. Int. Horn Soc. Recip. 3rd Prize, Woodwind & Horn Competition, Trondheim, Norway, 1965. Hobby: Nature; Other People. Address: 7 Dalsbergstien, Oslo 1, Norway.

WELFFENS, Peter, b. 7 May 1924, Antwerp, Belgium. Composer; Pianist; Conductor. Educ: Royal Flemish Acad. of

Music, Antwerp; Mozarteum, Salzburg, Austria; studied comp. w. Fortner & orchl. dir. w. Igor Markevitch. m. Louisa Delen, 1 s., 1 d. Career: Musical Dir., Royal Youth Theatre, Antwerp; work in radio, TV & film. Comps. inlc; 2 symphs.; sev. ballets; Concerto for harpsichord & orch.; Stroppelacorde (opera); stage & film music; works for chmbr. orch.; songs; chmbr. music; etc. Comps. recorded: 2nd Symphony; Table music for guitar & cello. Contbr. to mags. Mbr., Belgian Comps. Union. Hons. incl: Lodewijk Mortelmans prize for song cycle Orpheus & Eurydice, 1975. Address: Menegemlei 60, B-2100 Deurne/Antwerpen, Belgium. 3.

WELITSCH, Ljuba, b. Bozissovo, Bulgaria. Opera Singer (soprano). Career: Mbr.,Sofia Cathedral Choir, age 13; Mbr., Vienna State Opera, 1946-; opera performances at Covent Gdn.; Metropol. Opera, NYC; Brussels Opera; Salzburg Festival, etc.; leading roles incl: Salome; Donna Anna; Tosca; Aida; Tatiana; Senta; Leonora. Address: c/o Vienna State Opera, 1010 Vienna, Austria.

WELIVER, E. Delmer, b. 18 July 1939, Crawfordsville, Ind., USA. Music Librarian; Horn Player. Educ: BMusEd, Arkansas State Univ.; MA (music perf.), Univ. of Iowa. m. Evelyn R Van Bockern, 1 d., 1 s. Career: Formerly played horn w. The United States Army Band, Wash. DC & L'Orchestre Symphonique de Quebec, Can.; currently Prin. Horn, Northwestern Mich. Symph. Orch.; Music Librarian, Interlochen Center for the Arts. Mbrships: Int. Horn Soc.; Am. Fedn. of Musicians; Bd. of Dirs., Northwestern Mich. Symph. Orch. Hobbies: Sailing; Cross-country Skiing; Photography. Address: 8846 Park Lane, Interlochen, MI 49643, USA.

WELLEJUS, Henning, b. 23 Aug. 1919, Roskilde, Denmark. Composer. Educ: studied w. Svemd Erik Tarp, Giovanni Di Bella. m. Inge Osterby, 2 c. Debut: Copenhagen. Comps. incl: 3 Symphs.; 3 Concerti, for violin & orch., oboe & orch., cello & orch.; Symphonic Fantasies - The History of the Year, Nina; Our Childhood's Friends, and from Hans Christian Andersons picturebook, 2 suites from ballet, 'The Swan'; Wind Quintet; Flute Serenade just for Fun; 2 Str. Quartets, sev. songs, trio for clarinet, viola & piano; The Dream, ballet; Passacaglia, for orch.; A Freedom Overture; Copenhagen Rhapsody; A Danish Summer Pastorale; Grates Nunc Omnes Reddamus Domini, for soprano, chorus & orch.; A Trio for Piano, Violin & Oboe; A Symphonic Fantasy, 'Dionysia'; Operas - The Changed Bridegroom, Barbara; num. others. Contbr. to: Frederiksborg Amts Avis; Venstre Pressens Bureau. Mbr. Dansk Komponistforening. Hons: Lange-Muller Stipendiet, 1956; Aksel Agerbys Mindelegat, 1957; Det Anckerske Legat, 1958; Cross, Order of Kt. Hood, Denmark. Hobby: Summer Cottage. Address: 99 Godthaabsvej, Copenhagen 2000F, Denmark.

WELLER, Walter, b. 30 Nov. 1939, Vienna, Austria. Violinist; Conductor. Educ: Violin study, HS for Music & Dramatic Art, Vienna. m. Elisabeth Samohyl. Career: Mbr., Vienna Phil. Orch., 1946-; soloist, ibid, 1951-; Fndr. & ldr., Weller Quartet, 1958-; toured Europe, Asia & N Am. w. Weller Quartet; Cond., Vienna State Opera, 1969-, inclng. tours of Germany, Switzerland, UK & Japan; Prin. cond., Royal Liverpool Phil. Orch., 1979-. Recordings: var. works on Decca label. Hons: Beethoven Gold Medal; Mozart Invitation Prize. Hobbies: Magic; Stamps; Railways. Address: c/o Royal Liverpool Phil. Orch., Phil. Hall, Hope St., Liverpool L1 9BP, UK.

WELLINGTON, Christopher Ramsay, b. 5 Feb. 1930, London, UK. Violist; Viola d'Amore Player. Educ: BA, Queen's Coll., Oxford Univ.; ARCM. m. Joanna Donat, 1 s., 1 d. Career: Sadler's Wells Opera & Philharmonia Orchs.; currently Prin. Viola, London Bach Orch.; played w. Zorian Str. Quartet, Amici Str. Quartet, Nemet Str. Trio; currently Mbr., Music Grp. of London; Fndr. & Mbr., Musica Intima (contralto, viola, piano), Tre Corde (str. trio); Soloist, Berlioz's Harold in Italy, Mozart's Sinfonia Concertante, Vaughan Williams' Flos Campi, etc. Has recorded w. Music Grp. of London. Mbr., ISM. Hobby: Sailing. Address: 17 Grove Terr., London NW5 1PH, UK.

WELLITSCH, Ljuba, b. 10 July 1913, Borissowo, Bulgaria. Opera Singer. Educ: High Schl. for Music & Art. div. Debut: Nedda in Bajazzo, Graz. Career: State Opera in Hamburg, Dresden, Munich, Vienna, London (Covent Garden), Edinburgh Fests., Glyndebourne, Metre NY, St. Louis, Baltimore, Phila., Chgo.; Num. films in Germany & Austria; approx. 35 TV plays during last 15 yrs. Num. recordings. Hons: Gold Prize of Merit, Republic of Austria; Gold Medal, City of Vienna. Hobbies: Reading. Address: Ditscheinergasse 3/9, 1030 Vienna, Austria.

WELLS, James Roy, b. 22 Feb. 1932, St. Peters, Pa., USA. Professor of Music. Educ: BS (Music Educ.), W Chester State Coll., Pa., 1954; MEd, Temple Univ., 1961; DEd, Columbia

Univ., 1974. m. Joanne M Noble, 2 s., 1 d. Career: Music Co-ord., Oley Valley Area Schls., 1954-63; Asst. Prof.,Kutztown State Coll., 1963-67; Prof. of Music, W Chester State Coll., 1968-; Dir., W Chester State Coll. Marching Band, Nat. Music Festival, Atlantic City, 1976. Publs: The Marching Band in Contemporary Music Education, 1976; 6 Instrnl. Manuals & 19 films on instrumental music, 1973-76; Instruments of the Band; The Marching Band Instructional Series. Mbrships: incl: MENC; Pa. Music Educators; Coll. Band Dirs. Nat. Assn.; NEA; Pa. Educ. Assn.; Phi Mu Alpha. Hobbies: Yoga; Weightlifting. Address: 907 Nicholson Ave., Douglassville, PA 19518, USA. 6.

WELSH, Moray Meston, b. 1 March 1947, Haddington, Scotland, UK. Cellist. Educ: BA, York Univ.; ARCM; LRAM. Moscow Conserv., USSR; studied w. Joan Dickson, Martin Lovett, Mstislav Rostropovitch. Debut: Wigmore Hall, London, 1972. Career: apps., Royal Fest. Hall, South Bank, Albert Hall Proms, Radio & TV; Perfs. w. LSO, Halle, Liverpool Phil., SNO & BBC Orchs.; Mbr., Staff, Royal Northern Coll. of Music; Perfs., Netherlands, Italy, Carnegie Hall, NY, etc. Recordings: (Solo) Hugh Wood Cello Concert; (Chmbr. Music) Brahms Sextets; Schubert Quintet; Bach Sonatas. Mbrships: ISM; European String Tchrs. Assn.; Musicians Union. Hons: Brit. Coun. Anglo-Soviet Scholarship, 1969-71; Gulbenkian Fndn. Fellowship, 1971-74. Hobbies: Theatre; Instrument Making. Mgmt: Raymond Gubbay. Address: 37 Lansdowne Rd., London W11, UK.

WELTON, Frederic Percy, b. 4 Jan. 1926, Alderley Edge, UK. Music Lecturer; Examiner; Adjudicator (piano, violin). Educ: Northern Schl. of Music, GNSM, LRAM (pianoforte, aural training, voice culture, schl. music); ARCM (pianoforte); MusB (Dublin); FRNCM. m. Winifred Anne, 2 s., 1 d. Career: Schl. music posts, 1951-65; Sr. Lectr., Didsbury Coll. of Educ., 1965-71; Prin. Lectr., Asst. Hd. of Schl. of Academic Studies, RNCM, 1971-; Hd., ibid, 1980. Publs: Careers with Music, 1978; Ed., Music Matters. Mbrships: Coun., ISM; British Fedn. of Music Fests. Hobby: Photography. Address: 1 Nursery Lane, Wilmslow, Cheshire, SK9 5JG, UK.

WENDT-WALTHER,Ursula, b. 13 Mar. 1939, Berlin, Germany. Opera Singer. Educ: Music High School, Berlin; Dip., ibid. m. Wolfgang Walther. Debut: Staatstheater, Hannover. Career: apps. at num. fests & regularly at Nürnberg Opera House; guest artist at opera houses at Bremen, Lübeck, Hannover, Cologne, Darmstadt, Mannheim, Karlsruhe, Wiesbaden, Zürich, Vienna, Venice & Florence. Hobbies: Antique Furniture; Gardening. Address: Nibelungenstr. 49, 8501 Lindelburg, German Fed. Repub.

WENINGER, Richárd, b. 21 Dec. 1934, Versec, Hungary. Professor of Harp-playing. Educ: Liszt Ferenc Music Acad. m. Clara Weninger. Debut: Budapest, 1960. Career: Gov., Liszt Ferenc Musical Acad., Tchrs. Coll. for conservatoires, Szeged Sect. Mbrships: Sec., S Hungarian Sect., Assn. of Hungarian Musicians. Hons: Minister's Prize, 1971. Hobby: Fine Arts. Address: Dózsa u.5, 6720 Szeged, Hungary.

WENKOFF, Spas, b. 23 Sept. 1928, V. Tarnovo, Bulgaria. Opera Singer. Educ: Pvte. studies. m. Hannelore Wenkoff, 1 s. Debut: 1955. Career: Staatsoper Berlin; Staatsoper Dresden; Theatro alla La Scala Milan; Wiener Staatsoper; Hamburgische Staatsoper; Bayerisches Nationaltheater Munich; Baden-Württhembergisches Staatstheater Stuttgart; Bayreuth Fest.; Metropolitan Opera, NY; San Francisco Opera, etc.; Film, Tännhauser, 1978; Sev. radio perfs. sev. recordings. Mgmt: Columbia Artists Mgmt. Inc. Address: Rudolf Seiffert Str. 6, 1156 Berlin, German Dem. Repub.

WENNER, Gene C, b. 21 Dec. 1931, Catasauqua, Pa., USA. Trumpet Player Educ: BS, Music Educ., W Chester State Coll., Pa., 1953; MEd, Music Educ., Pa. State Univ., 1954; Course completed DEd, ibid. m. Carole Brunner, 2 children. Career: Mbr., Phila. Orch. Chorus, 1958-59; Advsr. to NY Phil., Denver Symph. & Pitts. Symph., 1975-76. Comps: Robert's Theme & The World of Sound, scripts & music for Adventures in the Arts, WITF-TV, Hershey Pa., 1968; Chorale of Dedication, 1974; Turn Thou to Me, 1975. Recordings w. Phila. Orch. Chorus. Publs. incl: Dance in the Schools, 1973. Contbr. to profl. jrnls. Mbrships: MENC; Nat. Art Educ. Assn. Hons. incl: Best Musical Dir., Little Theatre of Alexandria, Va., 1971. Hobbies: Ice-skating; Tennis. Address: JDR 3rd Fund, 50 Rockefeller Plaza, NY, NY 10020, USA. 3.

WENSTRÖM-LEKARE, Lennart Helge, b. 14 Apr. 1924, Huddinge, Sweden. Music Educator. Educ: Militar musik direktors examen, Royal HS of Music, Stockholm, 1949; Musiklararexamen, 1953; Studied comp. w. Prof. Lars-Erik Larsson, 1953-56. m. Inger Wenstrom, 1 s., 1 d. Career: Horn

& Viola Player in mil. bands & orchs., 1942-49; Tchr. of Music, Music Hist., var. educl. insts. inclng. Univ. of Stockholm & Musik Institutet vid Stockholms Borgarskola, 1949-69; Headmaster, Music Schl. in Sundbyberg, 1969-; currently Music Tchr., Samskolan Djursholm; var. comps. (songs & chamber music) perf. on Swedish Radio & TV. Compositions: Unga Toner, collection for amateur & schl. orchs.; Liten Danssvit, small dancing suite; religious & secular songs. Publs: Musik och Musikhistoria, 1963, '67, '74. Recip. 1st & 2nd prize in competition for comps., 1973. Hobbies: Nature; Cooking. Address: Ynglingävägen 6, 18262 Djursholm, Sweden.

WENZEL, Eberhard, b. 22 Apr. 1896, Pollnow, Pomerania. Church Music School Director. Educ: Sternsches Konservatorium & Univ., Berlin, 1914; Cert. Acad. Inst. for Ch. Music, Berlin; Further pvte. study w. Fritz Heitmann, Julius Dahlke, Arnold Ebel; Dr. Theol., hc, Univ. of Heidelberg, 1962. m. Marga Wenzel (von Wedel) (decd.), 2 d. Career: Schl. musician & organist, Berlin, 1921-25; Organist & Choirmaster, Neubrandenburg, 1925-30; Choirmaster & Organist, Peterskirche & Dir., Singakademie & Bachchor, 1930-50; Dir., newly founded ch. music schl., Halle (Salle), 1951-65; Choirmaster, St. Ulrich, 1951-65. Composer of works for choir & orch., choral works w. instruments (also solo voice), works for full choir a cappella, organ works, works for wind instruments w. organ or choir, orchl. works, works for solo voice, chmbr. music, piano. Recordings, as conductor, incl: David, Deutsche Messe; Distler, Es ist das Heil uns kommen her; Wenzel, Nicaenum; Handel, Dixit Dominus. Publs: Bach - Schemelli; Händel, Dixit Dominus. Mbrships. incl: Deutscher Komponisten Verband; Verband Ev. Kirchenmusiker in Württemberg. Recip. of hons. Address: Schlossstr. 3, 7103 Schwaigern b. Heilbronn, German Fed. Repub.

WENZINGER, August, b. 14 Nov. 1905, Basle, Switz. Cellist; Conductor; Educator. Educ: Dip., tchr. & soloist, Univ. of Basle, 1926; Univ. of Cologne, Germany, 1927-29. m. Ilse Hartmann. Career: 1st Cello, Bremen Symph. Orch., 1929-34; Co-Ldr., Kammermusikkreis Scheck-Wenzinger, 1936-43; Co-Fndr., 1934, Tchr. viola da gamba & ornamentation, 1934-170, Schola Cantorum Basiliensis; Solo Cellist, Allg. Musikgesellschaft Basel; Prof. of Music, Acad. Basle, 1936-70; Cond., Capella Coloniensis, 1954-66, Baroque Opera, Hannover-Herrenhausen, 1958-66, & var. chmbr. orchs.; Musical Dir., Baroque Perf. Inst., Oberlin, Ohio, USA; Guest Prof. for Viola da Gamba, Hochschule für Musik, Vienna, 1976-; concert tours, USA, Europe, Asia. Num. recordings. Publs: Gambenubung I & II, 1935; J. S. Bach Solosuiten fur Cello, 1950; Monteverdi, Orfeo, 1955; J. Chr. Fr. Bach Sonata in A, 1950. Hons: Hon. Dr., Univ. Basle, 1960; Fellow, Könige Schwedischen Acad. for Music, 1965. Address: 3 Zehntenfreistr., CH-4103 Bottmingen, Switz. 2.

WERDIN, Eberhard, b. 19 Oct. 1911, Spenge, Westfalen, Germany. Composer. Educ: Schl. Music & Comp. m. Anny Werdin, 2 c. Career incls: Dir., Musikschule Leverkusen. Comps. incl: Kindermesse, for choir & instrument (recorded); Concertino, for flute, guitar & string orch. (recorded); Ungarische Suite; Childrens Choral Songs; youth operas; choral works; cantatas; orchl. works; Educl. music, etc. Address: Dellbrucker Hauptstrasse 164, 5 Köln-Dellbruck, German Fed. Repub.

WERION, Rudi, b. 12 June 1935, Berlin, Germany. Composer; Pianist; Clarinettist. Educ: Acad. of Music, Berlin; Humboldt Univ., Berlin. Comps. incl: dance music; 18 film scores; 2 musicals; 6 musical comedies; theatrical music; TV music; approx. 60 recorded works; Clarinettque (for clarinet & orch.). Mbrships: Union of Comps. & Musicols. of the German Dem. Repub. Hons: Bronze Medal, Union of Comps. & Musicols. of the German Dem. Repub; FDGB-Kunstpeis, German Dem. Repub., 1971. Address: Oderberger Strasse 54, GDR 1058 Berlin, German Dem. Repub.

WERNER, Jean-Jacques, b. 20 Jan. 1935, Strasbourg, France. Composer. Educ: Strasbourg Conserv.; Schola Cantorum, Paris. Comps. incl: (publs.) Elevation, for soprano & orch.; 1st Symph., 1962; Capriccio, for orch., 1964; Horn Concerto, 1962; Sonata, for violin & piano, 1963; 5 Ballads of Olden Days, for guitar, 1971; Notes Taken in New York, for soprano & tenor & piano, 1964; 3 Circular Movements, for piano, 1970; Da Pacem Domine, for organ, 1960; Psalm VIII, choral music w. instrumental ensemble, 1970; Folk for Kate, for 2 flutes (children), 1975; (recordings) 4 Canadian Songs; Toccata. Address: 31 Rue de Verdun, 94260 Fresnes, France.

WERNER, Leszek, b. 27 April 1937, Nowe Miasto, Lubawskie, Poland. Professor; Reader in Music. Educ: Dip., Acad. of Music, Cracow, 1962; Summer Course, Accademia

Musicale Chigiana, Siena, Italy, 1962; Conserv. S Cecilia, Rome, 1962-63; Akademie am Mozarteum, Salzburg, 1963. m. Janina Romańska. Debut: 1964. Career: Organ recitals, Poland, Austria, Belgium, Denmark, Can., USSR, Sweden, Italy, German Fed. Repub., German Dem. Repub., Mexico, Greece, USA; Prof., Reader of Music, Acad. of Music, Cracow; Guest Artist, Polish Radio & TV. Contbr. to: Koszalin Musical Assn. & PWSM Gdansk. Mbrships: SPAM; Assn. Polish Artists & Musicians. Hons: 2nd Prize, First Polish Old Music Competition, Lódź, 1961. Hobbies: Travel; Swimming. Mgmt: PAGART, Pl. Zwyciestwa nr 9, Warsaw. Address: ul. Komandosów nr 23 m 26, 30-334 Craków, Poland.

WERNER, Sven Erik, b. 21 Feb. 1937, Copenhagen, Denmark. Composer; Director. Educ: BA, Univ. of Copenhagen, 1964. Career: Sec., Danish Radio, 1964-70; Tchr., Acad. of Music, Odense, 1970; Prin. Ed., Dansk Musiktidsskrift, 1972-74; Dir., Acad. of Music, Odense, 1974. Comps. incl: Conditiones (2 choirs a cappella), 1968; The Holy Communion (opera), 1973; Epluchure III (16 voices w. organ), 1974; So Much has been Created (mass for TV), 1974. Publs: incl: The Diaries of Charles Burney (Danish transl.), 1967. Mbrships: DUT, Copenhagen; Comps.' Union, ibid. Recip. State Scholarship, 1969-72, State Award, 1973. Address: Hojby Skovvej 40, 5793 Hojby Fyn, Denmark.

WERNICKE, Helmuth, b. 21 Mar. 1909, Berlin, Germany. Composer; Arranger; Pianist; Organist; Bandleader. Educ: Stern'sches Konservatorium, Berlin; Klindworth-Scharwenka Conserv., Berlin. m. Ramhilde Wernicke, dec. Debut: Age 14. Career: num. Concerts; TV, Film Perfs., Germany; Radio Perfs., Berlin, Hamburg, Cologne, & Switzerland; Perf. in num. theatres, night clubs, Germany; presently at Hotel Bristol, Kempinski. Compositions incl: Pop Evergreen; Das Fräulein Gerda; Golfstrom; var. Jazz comps. Recordings: w. Helmuth Wernicke Trio; Instrumental Septet Helmuth Wernicke; w. Rex Stewart, Frank Goudie, Chet Baker, Lionel Hampton. Contbr. to Horst H. Lange, Die Geschichte der Jazz in Deutschland. Mbrships: German Comps. Grp.; Union of German Musical Conductors; German Musicians Union. Recip. 3rd Place, Jazz Pianist, Gondel Jazz Poll, Germany, 1953-54. Hobbies: Collecting Jazz Records; Swimming. Address: 1 Buelowstr., 1000 Berlin 37, German Fed. Repub.

WESOLOWSKA, Anna Krystyna, b. 9 Jan. 1949, Lodz, Poland. Pianist. Educ: Grad. w. Hons., Hochschule für Musik, Lodz, 1972; Dip., ibid, 1977; Dip., Music Acad., Vienna. m. Stanislaw Firlej. Debut: playing Ravel's G-major concerto w. Phil. Orch. in Lodz, 1967. Career: radio & TV broadcasts; fests. in Poland & abroad; European concerts; Soloist, Chmbr. Musician; frequent perfs. for Jeunesses Musicales; Nohant Fest., France, Polish Piano Fest., Stupsk & Czech. Jeunesses Musicales Fest., 1976. Mbrships: Music Soc., Lodz; Jeunesses Musicales de Pologne. Hons: Music Competitions in Bucharest, 1970, Prague, 1973 & Vercelli, 1975; Rotterdam, 1976; 5th Prize, Dip. w. hons for best accomp., s'Hertogenbosch, Netherlands, 1974; 1st Prize, Chmbr. Music, Poland, 1971. Hobbies: Books; Music. Mgmt: Pagart. Address: Rodakowskiego 9m. 10, 93-277 Lodz, Poland. 4, 30.

WESSELY, Helene, b. 29 July 1924, Vienna, Austria. Musicologist. Educ: Tchrs. Trng. Coll., Vienna; PhD, Univ. of Vienna, 1950. m. Othmar Wessely. Career: Asst., Commn. for Musicol., Austrian Acad. of Scis., 1954-56; Musicol. studies, Italy, 1956-58, 1960. Publs: Henry Purcell als Instrumentalkomponist, 1955; Romanus Wichlein, 1958; Lelio Colista, 1961; Romanus Weichlein: Encaenia musices, 1974; New Eds., 7 Trio sonatas of Lelio Colista, 1952, 1960, 1978. Contbr. to var. jrnls. & encys. Mbrships: Austrian Musicol. Soc. Hobbies: Painting; Photography. Address: Währinger Str. 55, A-1090 Vienna, Austria.

WESSELY, Othmar, b. 31 Oct. 1922, Linz, Austria. Professor of Musicology. Educ: PhD, Univ. of Vienna, 1947; Bruckner Conserv., Linz; Acad. of Music & Dramatic Art, Vienna. m. Dr. Helene Wessely. Career: Archivist, State Opera, Vienna, 1948-49; Sec., Publng. Soc. of Monuments of Music in Austria, 1949; Asst., Univ. of Vienna, 1950-63; Instr., Musicol., ibid, 1959-63; Prof. of Musicol., Univ. of Graz, 1963-71 & Univ. of Vienna, 1971-. Publs. incl: Fruhmeister des stile nuovo in Osterriech, 1973; Johann Joseph Fux, la donna forte nella madre de'sette Maccabei, 1976; Philippus de Monte, Il Primo libro de Madrigali a 5 voci, 1977. Mbrships. incl: Corresp., Austrian Acad. of Scis., 1967-; Pres., Publng. Soc. of Monuments in Music in Austria, 1974-; VP Austrian Soc. of Musicol., 1974-; VP, J J Fux Soc., 1978-. Address: Wahringer Str. 55, A-1090 Vienna IX, Austria.

WESSENIUS, (Sten) Henry, b. 26 July 1926, Örebro, Närke, Sweden. Pianist; Music Director; Piano Teacher. Educ: Dips. in piano tchng., solo piano, music direction at Royal Acad. of Music, Stockholm; studied piano w. Olof Wibergh, Sven Brandel, Stockholm, Robert Riefling, Oslo & Martha Mayer-Reinach, Örebro. m. Runa Wessenius, 1 s. Career: Piano tchr., Stokholms Kommunala Musikskola, 1953-; piano broadcasts on Swedish & N W German radio; concerts in Sweden, W Germany. Publs: Kompendiums in Piano Pedagogy. Mbr. Svenska Piano pedagogforbundet. Hobby: Book Collecting. Address: Hornsgatan 33A, 11649 Stockholm, Sweden.

WEST, Edward (Ted) Randall Kenneth, b. 4 Feb. 1944, Victoria, BC, Can. High School Director of Music; Organist & Choir Director; Performer on Trombone & Euphonium. Educ: BA, McGill Univ., 1967; Class I Tchng. Dip., Macdonald Coll., 1968; Highest Grade in Piano, McGill Conserv. of Music. m. Donna Dell Bouck. Career: Dir. of Music (Band & choir), Hudson-Macdonald HS, Montreal; Organist & Choir Dir., var. chs. in Montreal; Classical & commercial perfs.; Dir., prize-winning HS concert & jazz bands, var. competitions inclng. CNE Band Contest, Toronto, & Berklee Jazz Fest., Boston, Can. Stage Band Fest (Nat. Winner). Recordings: Hits A Go-Go, 1967. Mbrships: Can. Band Dirs. Assn.; Can. Stage Band Fest. Assn. Recip. var. hons. Hobbies incl: Computers; Rebuilding pipe organ in own home; Physical training; Weight lifting. Address: 314 Acadia Dr., Beaconsfield, Quebec, H9W 2K2, Canada.

WEST, John Calvin, b. 25 Oct. 1938, Cleveland, Ohio, USA. Concert & Opera Singer (Bass). Educ: French Horn & Piano, Eastman Schl. of Music; Dip., Curtis Inst., 1962. Debut: Missa Solemnis, Carnegie Hall, 1963. Career incls: apps. w. num. Am. Opera Cos.; Mexico City Opera; Musik Theater im Revier, Gelsenkirchen, German Fed. Repub.; Caracas Opera; Niedersachsiches Staatstheater, Hannover, Germany; Num. Fest. apps.; Orchl. & Oratorio perfs., major cities & orchs. of Am.; Recitals, USA, Can., Italy, Hessischer Rundfunk; fac., Juilliard Schl. of Music. Hons: Tchaikovsky Int. Competition; Munich Int. Competition; Martha Baird Rockefeller Fund for Music; W M Sullivan Fndn.; Phila. Orch. Young Artists Award; Metropolitan Opera Auditions. Hobbies: Cooking; Reading. Addres: 114 W 70th St., NY, NY 10023, USA.

WESTBROOK, James Earl, b. 19 Nov. 1938, Winfield, Ala., USA. University Professor; Teacher-Performer (Flute, Piccolo). Educ: BME, Univ. Southern Miss., 1962; MMus, Univ. Miss., 1968; AMusD, Univ. Wis., 1974. div. Career incls: Solo Flute num. orchs. inclng: Jackson Symph.; Mobile Symph.; Memphis Symph.; Meridian Symph.; Stevens Point Symph.; Flute & Piccolo, Green Bay Symph.; Madison Symph.; Flute, Heritage Trio; Solo Flute, touring orch. of Rudolf Nureyev, 1974; Flute, quartet & quintet, Ohio State Fac. Baroque, 1974-75; Solo Flute, Orch. Panov Ballet Co., 1975-. Publs: A Beginning Flute Book for Adults. Mbrships. incl: Kappa Kappa Psi. Num. awards. Hobbies: Reading; Sailing; Tennis; Camping. Address: 231 E Patterson, Columbus, OH 43202, USA.

WESTBY, Øivind, b. 2 Jan. 1947, Oslo, Norway. Player of Trombone, Bass Trombone, Tuba & Euphonium; Arranger; Composer. m. Solveig Hjerkinn Westby. Career: Trombonist, Oslo Phil. Orch., 1968-69; Bass Trombonist, Norwegian Opera Orch., 1969-71; Norwegian Radio Symph., 1971-. Mbrships: Norwegian Comps. & Musicians Socs.; Int. Trombone Assn.; Norwegian Comps. of Light Music. Recip., Comp. of the Yr. shared w. 6 others, 1974, w. 1 other, 1975. Address: Drammensveien 201B, Oslo 2, Norway.

WESTEN, Theo, J H, b. 21 Jan. 1909, Groningen, The Netherlands. Conductor; Composer. Educ: sev. private docents & Conservatorium, Groningen. m. Joh. C W Ferrari, 5 c. Career: Violoncellist, Noordelijk Filharmonisch Orkest, 1929-74; Cond., Choir of the Paterskerk, 1935-56; Cond., Male Choir of Students for the Univ. Groningen, 1963-; Cond., Bach's Passionen NicolaiKerk - Appingedam, 1963-; Cond., Gronings-Politie-Muziekcorps, 1942-71; Cond. of symph., concerts throughout the Netherlands. Comps: Missae (3X) for male choir & organ; Missa Pro Pace for 5 string, choir & brass; 2 symphs. for orch.; Victimae, variations for orch. (on a Gregorian melody); songs for voice & piano; Operetta in Gronings dialect 'Laifde in de Meulenhorn' & 'Lubbe van Leerms'. Publs: Grunneger Zangbouk (2 parts). Hons: Music Prize, Culturele Prijs Provincie Groningen, 1968; Ridder in de Orde van Oranje-Nassau, 1971. Address: de Savornin Lohmanplein 1A, Groningen, The Netherlands.

WESTENHOLZ, Elisabeth, b. 6 Aug. 1942, Copenhagen, Denmark. Pianist; Organist. Educ: Organ Dip., Royal Acad. of Music, Copenhagen. m. Preben Steen Petersen, 2 s. Debut: Piano, 1968; Organ, 1969. Career: Concerts in Denmark, Sweden, Germany, Austria, France & Russia; Apps. on radio & TV. Mbrships: Solistforeningen af 1921; DOKS. Hons: Bequest

in memory of Victor Schioler; Carl Nielsen-Prisen; Music Prize, Gladsaxe; Artist Prize, Circle of Music Critics. Mgmt: Wilhelm Hansen, Copenhagen. Address: Wiedeweltsgade 52, 2100 Copenhagen O, Denmark.

WESTERLINCK, Wilfried, b. 3 Oct. 1945, Leuven, Belgium. Producer, Chamber Music Department, Belgian Radio/TV. Educ: Study of Piano, Leuven; Study of Oboe & Harmony, Conserv. of Brussels; Musical Forms, Analysis & Composition, Cond. Conserv. of Antwerp. m. Beatrys Schilders, 2 c. Career: Accompanist; Dir., 'De Filharmonie' of Antwerp, & Belgian Radio Orch.; Music Prod., Lightmusic, radio dance orch.; Prod., Chmbr. Music Dept., Belgian Radio; Prof., Music Analysis, Royal Conserv. of Antwerp, 1972-. Compositions: 2 Yugoslavian Portraits, for recorder quartet; Cheerful Studies for a Summerwork, wind quartet; Suite for Harpsichord Solo; Landscapes for woodwind quintet, 1977; String quartet, 1978. Var. songs, recorded on tape for radio; Metamorfose for Full Orch., for Dept. of Educ. Contbr. to profl. jrnls. Hons: Prize Winner for Metamorfose, Tenuto Competition, 1972; 2nd Prize in Province of Antwerp, for Landscapes, 1977. Hobbies: Reading; Walking. Address: Huib Hostelei 2, B-2540 Hove, Belgium.

WESTON, Pamela Theodora, b. 17 Oct. 1921, London, UK. Clarinettist; Teacher; Writer. Educ: LRAM; GRSM; ARCM. Debut: London, 1948. Career: Concert Artist, inclng. BBC recitals, 1948-65; Prof., Clarinet, GSM, 1951-69; Writer & Pvte. Tchr., 1965-; Eds., arrs., clarinet music. Publs: Clarinet Virtuosi of the Past, 1971; The Clarinet Teacher's Companion, 1976; More Clarinet Virtuosi of the Past, 1977. Contbr. to jrnls. & Grove's Dictionary. Mbrships: ISM; Fedn. of Fests.; Int. Clarinet Soc.; Galpin Soc. Hons: Fndn. Schlrship., GSM; Orchestral Prize; Wind Prize. Hobbies: Painting; Driving; Gardening. Address: 1 Rockland Rd., London SW15 2LN, UK.

WESTOVER, Wynn Earl, b. Lincoln, Neb., USA. Violinist; Conductor; Teacher of Mental Hearing. Educ: BA, Wesleyan Univ., 1950; Coll. of Physns. & Surgs., Columbia Univ., 1950-54; Trinity Coll., London; ATCL, 1961; LTCL (perf.), 1963; LTCL (tchng.), 1963; PhD, Anthony Univ., 1976; Study of chmbr. music w. Adolph Baller, Dominican Coll., Calif., 1964-65; Conds. Seminars w. Paul Douglas Freeman. m. Virginia Lucier. Debut: Cond., San Fran., 1968; Operatic Baritone, in Amahl & the Night Visitors, 1969-70. Career: Violin Soloist; Music Dir. & Cond., John F Kennedy & Martin Luther King, Jr., Mem. Concerts, San Fran., 1968-69, Laetrile Concert, Port Costa, Calif., 1971; Chmbr. Music Series, San Fran., 1968-71; Gen. Mgr., Music from Bear Valley, Calif., 1970-72. Composition: Laetrile, pt. 1 (symphonic poem). Recording: Laetrile at Port Costa. Publs: Violin Bowing, 1961; Music Theory through Sight Singing (Mental Hearing), 1962; Ed., Violin Technik by Blado Kolitsch, 1965; Num. sci., med. & environmental publs., 1972-; Ear Training & Mental Hearing for Musicians, 1974. Contbr. to sci. publs. Mbrships: Am. Symph. Orch. League; Amateur Chmbr. Music Soc. hon. mention, Festival of Rome, 1976. Hobbies: Keyboard improvisations; Scientific research. Address: POB 853, Sausalito, CA 94965, USA.

WESTPHAL, Frederick William, b. 25 Apr. 1916, Walnut Ridge, Ark., USA. Consulting Editor; Professor of Music; Professional Clarinettist & Saxophonist. Educ: BS, 1937, BMus, 1938, Univ. of Ill.; MMus, 1939, PhD, 1948, Perf.'s Cert. in Clarinet, 1947, Eastman Schl. of Music. m. Hinda Wood Cunningham, 2 s. Career: Asst. Prof., Tex. Women's Univ., Denton, 1939-46; Prof., Calif. State Univ., Sacramento, 1948-; Ed. over 75 coll. level texts, William C Brown Co. Publs: Guide to Teaching Woodwinds, 2nd ed., 1974; Woodwind Ensemble Method; Beginning Class Instruction, 3rd ed., 1976. Mbrships. incl: MENC; NACWPI; Int. Clarinet Soc. Hobby: Photography. Address: 201 Sandburg Dr., Sacremento, CA 95819, USA.

WETHERELL, Eric David, b. 30 Dec. 1925, Tynemouth, UK. Conductor. Educ: Queen's Coll., Oxford; RCM; BA; BMus; FRCO. m. (1) Jean Mary (2) Elizabeth Mary Major, 1 s., 2 d. Career: Instrumentalist; Conductor; Composer; Chief Cond., BBC Northern Ireland Orch., 1976; Horn Player, Repetiteur, Covent Garden. Comps. incl: TV, Film Music; Airs & Graces (Orchl.); Welsh Dresser (Orchl.). Mbrships: ISM; Savage Club. Hobbies: Films; Theatre. Mgmt: Arthur Baker. Address: 1 Limerick Rd., Bristol BS6 7DX, UK.

WETTSTEIN, Peter, b. 15 Sept. 1939, Zürich, Switz. Composer; Conductor; Violinist. Educ: Violin tchr. Dip., Music Acad., Zürich, 1961; Composer's Dip., Music Acadd., Detmold, 1964; Conductor's exam., ibid., 1965. m. Elisabeth Wille, 2 s. Career: Theory tchr., Music Acad., Zürich, 1965; Lehrauftrag Universitt Zürich (Akustik/Gehöbildung), 1973;

Vice-Dir., Conserv. & Music High Schl., Zürich, 1976. Comps: Works for choir & orch.; Chamber music. Publs: Akustik und Instrumentenkunde, 1976. Mbrships: Scweizerischer Tonkünstler verein; Schweizerischer Musikpädagogischer Verband. Address: Seestrasse 146, 8700 Küsnacht, Switz.

WEYDAHL, Hanna-Marie, b. 30 June 1922, Tjome, Norway. Pianist; Lecturer. Educ: Ecole Normale de Musique, Paris, 1937; Premier Prix avec distinction, Conserv. Royal de Musique, Brussels, 1948; studies w. Elisabeth Onarheim & Reimar Riefling; courses, Norsk Korrespondanseskole & Linguaphone Inst. widow, 1 s., 2 d. Debut: Oslo, 1940. Career: recitals, all Scandinavian countries, Belgium, France, GB; radio broadcasts, Scandinavia, Austria, Poland; TV broadcasts in Norway; Soloist w. major Norwegian orchs. Recordings: Piano Music by Fartein Valen; Finn Arnestad's Toccata. Contbr. to jrnls. Mbr. Profl. orgs. Recip. Harriet Cohen Int. Prize for perf. of contemp. music, 1966. Hobbies: Langs.; Skiing; Swimming. Address: Asdalsveien 9, Oslo 11, Norway. 19, 27, 30.

WEYERS, Raymund Wolfgang, b. 3 May 1949, Cologne, German Fed. Repub. Educ: Studied Philos. & Musicol., gained PhD degree. Pvte. musical studies. Mbrship: Gesellschaft für Musikforschung. Publs. incl: Arthur Schopenhauers Philosophie der Musik, 1976. Hobby: Theory of Music. Address: 5000 Cologne Herwarthstr. 23, German Fed. Repub.

WHALLON, Evan, b. 24 July 1923, Akron, Ind., USA. Conductor. Educ: BMus, MMus, Eastman Schl. of Music. m. Jean Borgman (dec.), 2 s. Debut: Phila. Orch. Career: Cond. & Music Dir., Columbus, Ohio, Symph. Orch. & Chautauqua Opera Assn.; Guest Cond., Phila. Orch., Cleveland Orch., NYC Opera, Prague Symph., Budapest Symph., Rumanian Symph. & Timisora Opera. Hons: Docts., Denison Univ.; Otterbein Univ. & Ohio Dominican Univ. Address: 101 E Town St., Columbus, OH 43215, USA. 2, 8, 21.

WHAPLES, Miriam K, b. 16 Dec. 1929, Bridgeport, Conn., USA. Musicologist; Pianist; Harpsichordist. Educ: BA, Music, 1950, MM, Piano, 1954, PhD, Musicol., 1958, Ind. Univ. m. George Whaples, 1 s., 2 d. Career: W. Md. Coll., 1960-66; Asst. Prof., 1966-72, Assoc. Prof., 1972-, Univ. of Mass. Publs: Bach Aria Index, 1971, Carmina Burana, 1975. Contbr. to num. profl. jrnls. Mbrships: Am. Int. Musicol. Socs. Address: Dept. of Music, Univ. of Mass., Amherst, MA 01003, USA. 5.

WHEAR, Paul William, b. 13 Nov. 1925, Auburn, Ind., USA. Composer; Conductor; Teacher. Educ: BNS, Marquette Univ.; AB, DePauw Univ.; MMus, ibid; PhD, Western Reserve Univ. m. Nancy Voiers, 2 s., 1 d. Career: Instructor, Baker Univ.; Asst. Prof., Mount Union Coll.; Assoc. Prof., Chmn. Music Dept., Doane Coll.; Prof. of Music, Res. Comp., Marshall Univ.; Cond., Huntington Chamber Orch; Comp. Fac., Nat. Music Camp, Interlochen; Cond., Ohio Univ. Symph. Orch.; TV apps., commercial TV. Comps. incl: (publd.) over 80 works; Symph. No. 2 (recorded) Antietam; Catharsis Suite; Psalms of Celebration; Joyful-Jubilate; The Chief Justice (oratorio); Kedushah (cantata); Symph. No. 3, The Galleries; The Devil's Disciple (opera); String Quartet No. 3, The Phoenix. Recordings: The Music of Paul W Whear. Contbr. to: Instrumentalist Mag.; Music Jrnl.; Music Educators Jrnl.; The World of Music. Mbrships: ASCAP; Am. Soc. of Univ. Comps.; Pi Kappa Lambda; Phi Mu Alpha Sinfonia. Recip. num. hons. Hobbies: Sailing; Ship Models; Printing. Address: 524 9th Ave., Huntington, WV 25701, USA. 21.

WHEELER, Douglas B, b. 30 July 1946, West Chester Pa., USA. Percussionist; Teacher. Educ: BS; MEd, W Chester State Coll., Pa. m. Lynn H Wheeler, 1 s., 2 d. Career: Percussionist, USAF Acad. Band; Prin. Percussionist, Colo. Springs Symph. Orch.; Instructor in Music, Delta State Univ., Cleveland, Miss. Mbr., Percussive Arts Soc. Recip., Bandsman of the Quarter Award, USAF Acad. Band, July-Oct. 1975. Hobbies: Hiking. Address: 1224 Deering St., Cleveland, MS 38732, USA. 2.

WHEELER, Gerald, b. 26 Mar. 1929, Richmond, Surrey, UK. Organist; Harpsichordist; Pianist; Choral Director. Educ: RCM, London, 1949-52; ARCM, piano perf.; LRAM, piano teaching; FRCO. m. Jennifer Taylor, 1 s., 3 d. Career: Sub Organist, St. Paul's Cathedral, 1953-56; Organist, St. Matthew's, Ottawa, Can., 1956-65; Organist, Christ Ch. Cathedral, Montreal, 1965-. Recording: Organ Plus, 1976. Chmn., Montreal Ctr., Royal Can. Coll. of Organists, 1971-72. Hobby: Cross country skiing. Address: 129 Dobie Ave., Montreal, H3P 1S3, Can.

WHEEN, Natalie Kathleen, b. 29 July 1947, Shanghai, China. Musical Journalist & Broadcaster. Educ: London Univ.; RCM; BMus, ARCM. Career: Staff Mbr., BBC, working in TV & Radio prod., 1968-73; Prod./Interviewer, weekly music mag. prog. 'Music Now', 1972- (freelance, 1973-). Contbr. to: Tablet (one-time critic); Music & Musicians; BBC Radio 3 & 4.

Hobbies: Exotic Travel; Musical Affairs; Politics. Address: 19 Drayton Gdns., London SW10 9RY, UK.

WHELEN, Christopher, b. 17 Apr. 1927, London, UK. Composer; Conductor. Educ: New Coll., Oxford Univ.; Worksop Coll.; Birmingham Coll. of Music. Debut: as Cond., Bournemouth, 1948; as Comp., London (Old Vic), 1952. Career: Asst. Cond., Bournemouth Orch., 1948-52; Music Dir., Old Vic, 1952-55; Asst. Cond., Birmingham Orch., 1955-57. Compositions: 5 operas for BBC TV & radio (commissioned plus two entries for Italia Prize in 1969 & '72); many scores for film, radio, TV, theatre, ballet, inclng. music for practically all Shakespeare's plays; 5 musicals; Bridges, own play w. music; The Restorer, own play w. music. Recip., Sprague Coolidge Medal, 1956. Hobbies: Collecting paintings; Swimming, etc. Address: 15a Courtfield Rd., London SW7, UK.

WHETTAM, Graham Dudley, b. 7 Sept. 1927, Swindon, UK. Composer. m. Janet Rosemary Lawrence, 4 s., 1 d. Compositions incl: (orchl. works) Sinfonia Concertante; Sinfonietta Stravagante; Cello Concerto; Sinfonia Contra Timore; The Masque of the Red Death; Variations for Oboe, Bassoon & Strings; (instrumental & chamber music) Prelude, Scherzo & Elegy, for piano; Night Music for Piano; Prelude & Scherzo Impetuoso, for piano; Str. Quartet No. 1; Sonatina for Clarinet & Piano; Prelude, Allegro & Postlude, for flute, oboe & piano; Fantasy for Ten Wind Instruments; Music for Brass; 2 Oboe Quartets; Woodwind Sextet; Trio for Violin, horn & piano; Trio for oboe, clarinet & bassoon; (choral) Do not go gentle into that good night; (educl.) 6 into 37 (Part I); 3 times 6 (Part II); The Chef who wanted to Rule the World; The Kitchen (Percussion Ensemble); Suite for Youth (orchl.). Mbrships: V-Chmn., Brit. Copyright Coun., 1972-; Chmn., CGGB, 1971-; Dir., Mech. Rights Soc.; Musicians Union; ISM. Hobbies: Being among hills; Good food cigars & wine; Reading, etc. Address: Flat 1, Felden Hall, Coll. of Educ., Kirby Corner Rd., Coventry, CV4 8EE, UK. 3, 14.

WHISTON, David, b. 8 Oct. 1941, S Elmsall nr. Pontefract, Yorks., UK. Violinist. Educ: Major Scholar, RCM, 1958-61; studied w. Antonio Brosa, Erich Gruenberg, Dr. Herbert Howells, Michael Mulliner, Bernard Walton. m. Maureen Tomlin. Debut: Leighton House Art Gall., London, 1960. Career: Ldr., Nat. Youth Orch.; Prin. 1st Violin, LPO & RPO; Mbr., LSO; Ldr., New London Ballet Orch.; Solo Prin. Violin, Tonhalle Orch., Zürich, Switz.; Concertmaster, Netherlands Radio Orch., Hilversum. Num. recordings w. London symph. orchs. Hons. incl: Ricketts Prize, RCM, 1958. Hobbies: Gardening; Bernese mtn. dog. Address: 21 White Hart Ln., Hockley, Essex, UK.

WHITAKER, Margaret Joy, b. 30 Oct. 1926, Sunderland, UK. Piano Teacher. Educ: RAM, London; LRAM; ARCM; LRAM. Debut: Harrogate Lunch Time Concert, 27 Apr. 1944. Career: Num. piano recitals, violin & piano recitals; Music therapy; Pt.-time tutor, adv. piano study dip. work & tchng. techniques, Bretton Hall, Wakefield, 1949-51; Vis. piano tchr., St. Peter's Schl., York & Allerton HS, Leeds, 1952-63; Asst., piano & jr. class music, M M Walthamstow Schl., Sevenoaks, 1963; Dir. Music, Harrogate Coll., 1964-65; Vis. piano tchr., Queen Margaret's Schl., York, 1965-66; Pvte. tchr., 1966-. Mbr. profl. orgs. incl: European Pianoforte Tchrs. Assn.,Yorks. Br. Hons: Bronze medal, piano & aural trng., 1943; Silver, 1944; Cert. Merit, 1945. Hobbies incl: Cardiac rsch.; Geology; Architecture. Address: 133 Wetherby Rd., Harrogate, HG2 7SH, N Yorks, UK. 3, 27, 30.

WHITCOMB, Mervin W, b. 18 Feb. 1913, Minneapolis, Minn., USA. Prof. of Music; Musician (Violin, viola, organ & piano). Educ: BMus, EdM, Boston Univ.; EdD, Columbia Univ.; Dip., New England Conserv. of Music; study of violin w. Richard Burgin & Felix Winternitz. m. Ella E, 1 s., 1 d. Career incl: Music Dir., Radio Str. WHDH; Asst. Concert Master, Bridgeport Symph. Orch., Conn.; Asst. Concert Master, Honolulu Symph. Orch., Hawaii; Prof. of Music, Western Conn. State Coll. Comps: Dawn; When I Was in Love; When I Was One & Twenty; Go Marry; Happy as can Be; No One's Awake, Not Even You; Face of God; The Wide World; Hand of God; Caribbean Charisma; String Music for Concert & Study. Contbr. to Music Educators Jrnl. Mbrships: Nat. Music Educators Assn.; Am. String Tchrs. Assn. Hons: Winner, RI comp. for Strings; Prize winner for Marching Song, USAF. Hobbies: Golf; Tennis; Travel. Address: 198 Southern Blvd., Danbury, CT 06810, USA.

WHITE, Andrew Nathaniel, III, b. 6 Sept. 1942, Washington, DC, USA. Saxophonist; Oboist; English Horn Player; Recording Engineer; Composer; Arranger; Conductor; Musicologist; Publisher; Impresario. Educ: BMus, Music Theory, Howard Univ., Wash., DC, 1960-64. m. Jocelyne H J Uhl. Debut: Solo app., Carnegie Hall, NYC, 1974. Career: (Jazz saxophonist)

JFK Quintet, 1960-64; New Jazz Trio, 1965-66; Soloist & Leader, 1966-; (Oboist & English Horn Player) Ctr. of Creative & Performing Arts, 1965-67; Prin. Oboe & Eng. Horn, Am. Ballet Theatre, 1968-70; (Electric Bassist - Jazz & Rock) Stevie Wonder, 1968-70; The 5th Dimension, 1970-76; The Jupiter Hair Co., 1971-; Motown Record Corp., 1968-70; Weather Report (recording), 1972-73. Comps: Concerto (1963); Concertina (1963) Shepherd Song (1963); sev. jazz comps. Num. recordings. Publs. incl: The Works of John Coltrane, Vols. I-V; 209 trans., Vols. VI-X, 212 trans.; Treatise on Improvisation, on Transcription, on Practice Methods, on Professionalism in the Music Business. Mbrships: Pi Kappa Lambda. Hons: num. grants for music studies in US & Europe. Mgmt: Andrew's Musical Enterprises Inc. Address: 4830 S Dakota Ave., NE Wash, DC, USA.

WHITE, Chappell, b. 16 Sept. 1920, Atlanta, Ga., USA. Educator; Musicologist. Educ: BA, Emory Univ., 1940; Westminster Choir Coll., BMus, 1947; MFA, 1950, PhD, 1957, Princeton Univ.; Am. Conserv. Fontainebleau, 1938. m. Barbara Tyler, 2 d., 1 s. Career: Assoc. Prof. of Music, Emory Univ., 1952-74; Prof. of Music, Dir. of Grad. Studies, Kansas State Univ., 1974-. Vis. Prof. of Music, Ind. Univ., 1973, Univ. of Ga., 1971; Music Critic, Atlanta Jrnl., 1960-72. Publs: Introduction to the Life and Works of Richard Wagner, 1967; Ed., Four Violin Concertos by G B Viotti, 1976; Ed., Coll. Music Symposium, vols. 13-15, 1973-75. Contbr. to: Musical Quarterly; Jrnl. of Am. Musicol. Soc.; Fontes Artis Musicae; Symposium; Musical America; Opera News; Choral Jrnl. Am. Choral Review; Grove's Dict., 6th ed. Mbrships: Coll. Music Soc. (Pres., 1979-81, Coun., 1976-78); Am. Musicol. Soc. (Chmn., S Central Chapt., 1967). Hobbies: Golf; History. Address: 500 Wickham Rd., Manhattan, KS 66502, USA.

WHITE, Duane Craig, b. 29 June 1947, Seattle, Wash., USA. Violinist. Educ: BA, Music Educ., Univ. of Wash., Seattle, 1969; studied w. Emanuel Zetlin, Stanley Chapple. Debut: Mendelssohn Violin Concerto, Thalia Symph., Seattle, 1965. Career: Concertmaster, Univ. of Wash. Concert Orch., 1965; Prin., Univ. of Wash. Symph., 1967-69; Asst. Prin., Spokane Symph., 1969-70 & Second Honululu Symph., 1970-74; Siegerland Orch., Cologne Opera, 1976-77; Honolulu Symph., 1970-75, 1977-. Mbrships: AFM; Int. Congress of Symph. & Opera Musicians. Recip., William O. Just Award Seattle, 1965. Address: 1249-G Matlock Ave., Honolulu HI 96814, USA.

WHITE, Elwood L, b. 5 May 1941, Rome, Ga., USA. Musician, French Horn. Educ: BA, 1970; MA, 1974; M.Ln., 1975; EST, 1978; studied w. Dr. Joseph A. White, Verne Reynolds, A. Robert Johnson m. Dorothy Craig Stamps. Career: Prin. Horn, Am. Ballet Theatre, 1967-69; Asst. Prin. Horn, Atlanta Symph., 1969-71; Horn Instructor, Univ. of Ga., 1971-72; Atlanta Chamber Orch., 1977-78. Mbr. Am. Fedn. of Musicians, Local 148-462; Local 802, ibid. Hons: Fla. State Univ. Musicianship Awards, 1957, 1958; Phi Mu Alpha Sinfonia Musicianship Award, 1958; Ritter Medal, 1959; Atlantic Steel Fellowship, 1972. Hobbies: Hiking; Boating; Riflery. Address: 409 Oakdale Rd., Atlanta, GA 30307, USA.

WHITE, Hilda Naomi, b. 2 Feb. 1892, London, UK. Pianist; Violinist; Music Teacher (Singing). Educ: Grad., Brit. Tchr. Trng. Coll., Fulham (Now Furzedown Trng. Coll.), UK; Ont. Pub. Schl. Tchrs. Cert. m. John R. White, dec. Career: Tchr., many schls. in London & in Can.; did much volunteer work w. Girl Guides. Mbrships: Life Mbr., Royal Soc. of Tchrs., UK; local 198 (Niagara Falls) Am. Fedn. of Musicians; Craft Guild; Histl. Soc., Niagara Falls; Horticultural Soc., Niagara Falls, Niagara District Art Assn.; Ont. Registered Music Assn.; Bd. of Dirs., Niagara Strings. Hobbies: Travel; Art; Historical Events. Address: 4468 Philip St., Niagara Falls, Ont. L2E 1A6, Canada.

WHITE, John, b. 28 May 1938, Leeds,UK. Lecturer; Professor; Viola Player. Educ: RAM (Charles Oldham Scholar); ARAM; ARCM. m. Carol Susan Shaw, 1 s., 1 d. Career: Sr. Lectr., Hockerill Coll. of Educ., Bishops Stortford, Herts.; Prof. of Viola, RAM, 1976-; Profl. Viola Player, recitals at schls., colls., music clubs, etc.; Mbr. of Stadler Trio, 1967-; Mbr., Alberni Str. Quartet, 1961-67; Adjudicator at Music Fests.; Cond. & Coach at music courses, etc.; Appeared on radio & TV at home & abroad w. Alberni Str. Quartet; Viola, in schls. music workshop progs. Recordings: Haydn str. quartets (Saga) & Rawsthorne Str. Quartets (Argo) w. Alberni Str. Quartet. Edited 3 Miniature Str. Quartets by Richard Stoker, 1967-68, w. St. George's Canzonia To Blow the Cold Winter Away, on CRD. Contbr. to Strad Mag. Mbrships: ESTA; ISM; MU; BFMF; Brit. Rep., Viola Rsch. Soc. Recip. var. music prizes whilst at RAM. Hobbies: Football; Pitch into viola; Concerts. Address: 36 Seeleys, Harlow, Essex, CM17 OAD, UK. 3.

WHITE, John David, b. 28 Nov. 1931, Rochester, Minn.,USA. Composer; Cellist; Author. Educ: BA, Univ. of

Minn., 1953; MA, Eastman Schl. of Music, 1954; PhD, Univ. of Rochester, 1960; Perfs. Cert., Cello, Eastman Schl. of Music, 1960. m. Marjorie White, 2 s., 1 d. Career: Fac. Schls. of Music, Univ. of Mich., & Kent State Univ.; Prin. Cellist, 7th Army Symph., 1955-56, Eastman Philharmonia, 1959; presently Dean, Schl. of Music, Ithaca Coll., NY; Ed., Music & Man; Vis. Prof. of Music, Univ. of Wis., 1976. Comps. incl: (publd.) 3 madrigals for Chorus & Orch.; The Monkey's sonnet, SATB, piano; The Passing Of Winter, SATB, piano; The Turmoil, SATB, piano; Why Not?, piano (recorded) Variations for Clarinet & Piano. Publs: w. A Cohen Anthology of Music for Analysis, 1965; Understanding & Enjoying Music, 1968; Music in Western Culture, A Short History, 1972; The Analysis of Music, 1976. Contbr. to: Jrnl. of Music Theory; Music Jrnl.; Int. Musician. Recip. num. hons. for comps. Hobbies: Tennis; Skiing. Address: 634 Highlands Rd., Ithaca, NY 14850, USA.

WHITE, John Maurice, b. 10 Feb. 1940, London, UK. Oboist; Performer on Cor Anglais & Oboe d'Amore. Educ: Nat. Youth Orch. of GB; Fndn. Scholarship, RCM, 1959-61; ARCM. Career: Freelance Musician; Mbr. 1961-, currently 1st Oboe, Sadler's Wells, not Engl. Nat. Opera. Hobbies: Photography; Model Engrng.; Golf; Tennis. Address: 49 Langley Dr., Wanstead, London E11 2LN, UK.

WHITE, John S., b. 4 March 1910, Vienna, Austria. Managing Director, NYC Opera. Educ: PhD, linguistics & philos., Vienna Univ.; Sorbonne Paris; Perugia, Italy; Besancon, France; pvte. piano studies. Career: Instructor for German & French Lit., Vienna; New Schl. for Social Rsch., Lycée Francais, NY; Managing Dir., NYC Opera, New York. Publs: Renaissance Cavalier, 1959; Psyche & Tuberculosis, 1967. Contbr. to: Social Rsch.; Psychiatry; American Imago. Hobbies: Dressage Riding; Swimming. Address: 57 W 58th St., NY, NY 10019, USA. 2.

WHITE, Marie Elizabeth Fox Warren, b. 14 June 1908, Chattanooga, Tenn., USA. Professor of Piano & Organ; Teacher. Educ: Profl. Tchrs. Cert., Am. Colls. of Music Certification; Approved Music Profl. Tchrs. Cert. m. Charles W White (dec.). Career: Apps. on TV & radio; Band Dir. in High Schls.; Choir Dir., High Schls. & Chs.; Tchr., organ, accordion, guitar; Theatre Mgr.; Dir. of Plays; Mgr. of Music Depts. in retail business. Compositions incl: Arrangements recorded for tchng. in studios & coll. Contbr. to: Staff Notes. Mbrships. incl: Nat. Fedn. of Music Clubs; State Tchrs. Assn.; Nat. Guild of Piano Fac. & Adjudicator. Num. awards. Hobbies: Writing; Reading; Travel; Dining Out; Walking. Address: PO Box 643, Maple Shade Rd., Alma, AR 72921, USA. 2, 27.

WHITE, Martin John, b. 26 Dec. 1941, Southall, Middx., UK. Organist; Recitalist; Conductor. Educ: RAM; London Univ. Inst. of Educ; FRCO (CHM); GRSM; LRAM; ARCM. Career: Organist & Choirmaster, Harrow Parish Ch., 1963-68; Organist & Master of the Choristers, Armagh Cathedral, 1968-; many organ recitals broadcast on BBC Radio 3 & Radio Eireann; Recital tour, Belgium & Germany, 1975; Specialist in organ improvisation.; Hons: Stewart Macpherson Prize for Improvisation, 1965; John Brook Prize for Choir trng., 1967. Hobbies: Camping; Electronics. Address: 8 Vicars' Hill, Armagh, BT61 7ED, Northern Ireland, UK.

WHITE, Peter Gilbert, b. 21 Jan. 1937, Plymouth, Devon, UK. Organist; Educator. Educ: MusB, MA, Cambridge Univ.; RAM; LTCL (organ perf.); FRCO (CHM). m. Doreen Elizabeth Storey, 2 s. Career: Asst. Cathedral Organist, Chester, 1960-62; HQ Choirmaster, RSCM, 1962-67; Dir. of Music, Merchant Taylor's Schl., 1967-70; Master of the Music, Leicester Cathedral, 1970-; Hd. of Music, City of Leicester Schl., 1979-. Comps: Urbs Beata (organ toccata for a Dedication Fest.); Carillon (organ piece); Christ is Risen. Recordings: Hear My Prayer & Tallis & Weelkes w. choir of St. John's Coll., Cambridge; Organ Music for a Golden Jubilee (on Leicester Cathedral Organ); Carols of Praise (Cond. Leicester Bach Choir). Mbr. Cathedral Organists Assn. Recip. var. hons. inclng. ARSCM, 1967. Hobbies: Reading; Walking. Address: The Cathedral, St. Martins, Leicester, LE1, 5FX, UK.

WHITE, Raymond Eric, b. 22 July 1944, Wyndham, Southland, NZ. Cathedral Organist; Principal of Music School. Educ: MusB, Univ. of Otago, Dunedin, NZ; PhD, Univ. of St. Andrews, Scotland, UK; FTCL; LRSM; ARCO; post-grad. study, RSCM. Career: Organist & Master of the Choristers, Christ Ch. Cathedral, Nelson, & Prin. of Nelson Schl. of Music, 1971-; regular organ broadcasts, Radio NZ; recitals throughout NZ & Aust. Recordings: Organ Music from Christ Church Cathedral, Nelson; Christmas Cards from the Choir of Christ Church Cathedral, Nelson. Mbr., RCO. Hons: Jeannie MacAndrew Prize, Univ. of Otago, 1964; scholarships. Hobbies: Travel; Rsch. on 16th & 17th Century Scottish ch. music. Address: 359 Trafalgar St., Nelson, NZ.

WHITE, Samuel Driver, b. 19 Sept. 1938, St. Marys Platt, Kent, UK. Solicitor; Festival Administrator. Educ: Summer Fields, Rugby Schl.; qualified solicitor of Supreme Court. m. Elizabeth Christine White, 2 d. Career: Dir., Elgar Fndn.; Dir., Three Choirs Fest. Assn.; Admnstr., Worcester Three Choirs Fest. since 1974; chmn., Worcester Concert Club; Exec. mbr., Worcester Arts Coun. Hobbies: Music; Horses; Squash. Address: 5 Deansway, Worcester, UK.

WHITEAR, Sheelagh Lesley, b. 1 Sept. 1959, Bishops Stortford, UK. Mezzo Contralto; Piano Teacher. Educ: NE Essex Tech. Coll. & Schl. of Art Colchester; LRAM; LGSM; ARCM; Cert. in Educ. London Univ., 1973. Career: Freelance Singer in oratorio & Recitalist in UK & abroad. Mbr., ISM; Eastern Arts Assn. Hons. incl: Artistic Singing Cup, NEETC, 1969. Hobbies: Dressmaking; Gardening; Theatre. Address: Ivy Farm House, Surrex, Coggeshall, Essex, UK.

WHITEHEAD, Gillian, b. 23 April 1941, Hamilton, NZ. Composer. Educ: BMus, Wellington, NZ, 1964; MMus, Sydney, Aust., 1966; Pvte. studies w. Peter Maxwell Davies, 1966-67. Career: Freelance work for publishing houses, Europe; Lectr., Tchr., NZ, 1975; Tchr. of Comp., Auckland Univ., 1975; currently Comp. in Res., Northern Arts, UK. Comps. incl: Missa Brevis, SATB, 1963; Fantasia on Three Notes, piano solo, 1966; Te Ahua Atarangi, quartet, 1970; Tristan & Iseult, chmbr. opera for 4 singers, mimes, puppets, chmbr. ensemble, 1975; Tinea, 1978; Hoata, for chmbr. orch., 1979. Recordings: Fantasia on Three Notes; Qui natus est; La Cadenza sia corta. Address: Newonstead, Great Bavington, Capheaton, Newcastle-upon-Tyne, UK.

WHITEHOUSE, Richard St. Clair, b. 7 March, 1952, Wolverhampton, UK. Pianist; Composer; Arranger. Educ: Toronto Conserv. of Music; Berklee Coll. of Music, Boston, Mass.; Univ. of Vic. Music Dept. Career: TV apps. as accomp. Mbrships: Musicians Assn. of Toronto; Am. Fedn. of Musicians. Address: Apt. 101, 27 Hamilton St., Toronto, Ont. M4M 2C6, Can.

WHITEMAN, Sibyl, b. 30 Dec. 1937, Cape Town, S Africa. Pianist; Clarinettist; Teacher of Piano & Clarinet. Educ: RAM, London, UK; LRAM (piano tchrs. & perf.); Muzieklyceum, Amsterdam; ARCM; LRSM (piano perf.); UTLM, UPLM (piano lics., Univ. of S Africa); UPLM (clarinet); Orchl. Dip., Muzieklyceum, Amsterdam, Netherlands. m. Alan Morris, 2 s. Debut: Cape Town, 1955. Career: Num. concerto perfs., S Africa; Broadcasts, S Africa & Netherlands; Recitals, S Africa, Netherlands, UK, German Fed. Repub.; Freelance orchl. player; Sr. Lectr. in Piano, Univ. of Port Elizabeth, 1966-68. Contbr. to: S African Music Tchr. Mbr.; S African Soc. Music Tchrs. Hons: Donemus Prize, Netherlands, 1962; Prix d'Excellence, Amsterdam, 1964. Hobbies incl: Reading; Photography. Address: 5 Vine Rd., Bergvliet, Cape 7800, S Africa.

WHITENER, David, b. 22 Dec. 1944, Seattle, USA. Orchestra Musician (French Horn). Educ: Grad., Ind. Univ.; studies w. Philip Farkas & Michael Höltzel. Career: Stuttgart Phil.; former solo horn, Dutch Nat. Ballet Orch.; currently solo horn, Nat. Theater-Orch., Mannheim, German Fed. Repub. Recordings: W A Mozart, Harmoniemusik from Entführung aus dem Serail & Figaro's Hochzeit, w. Mannheimer Bläsersolisten. Hobbies: Swimming; Jogging; Watching gold prices. Addres: Keplerstr. 29, 6800 Mannheim, German Fed. Repub.

WHITFIELD, Charles, b. 24 June 1939, Huddersfield, UK. Baritone Singer; Musicologist; Lecturer. Educ: Licencié es Lettres (music), Univ. of Paris IV (Sorbonne), Capes d'éducation musicale; dip., Conserv. Européen de Paris; Wiener Meisterkurse; studies w. Paul Schilawsky, Salzburg, & Ré Koster, Paris. Career: TV apps. in France & Switz.; radio perfs. in France, Italy & Spain; fest. apps. incl. Avignon, Aix-en-Provence, Ascona, Avila, Prague & Wallonie. Recordings: works by Cl. Le Jeune & Jannequin. Contbr. of transls. of texts for Arion recordings. Mbrships: Pres., Ensemble Polyphonique de France; Société française de Musicologie; Guilde des Artistes solistes. Hons: Grand Prix du Disque français for record of Le Jeune's Le Printemps. Hobbies: Walking; Swimming; Old Houses; Musical Instruments. Address: 43 rue de Saintonge, 75003, Paris, France.

WHITMORE, Keith Baden, b. 28 Jan. 1929, Biggleswade, Beds., UK. Musical Administrator; Educator; Musician (horn). Educ: Guildhall Schl. of Music. m. Muriel Jean West, 1 s. Career: Prin. Horn London Phil. Orch., 1953-56 & Royal Phil. Orch., 1956-59; Returned to LPO, 1959-; Bd. Dirs., ibid., 1959-; Chmn., 1962-75; Asst. Prin. Horn, 1969; Gen. Admnstr., Western Orchl. Soc. Ltd. (Bournemouth Symph. Orch. & Bournemouth Sinfonietta), 1975-; Prof. of Horn, Royal Acad. of Music, 1968-75. Mbrships: Rotary; Fellow, Royal

Soc. of Arts; Royal Soc. of Musicians. Hon: ARAM, 1972. Hobbies: Photography; Golf. Address: 9 Marlborough Pl., Wimborne, Dorset, BH21 1HW, UK. 28, 29, 30.

WHITNEY, Maurice Cary, b. 25 Mar. 1909, Glens Falls, NY, USA. Educator; Composer; Organist; Choir Director. Educ: BS, Ithaca Coll., NY; MA, NY Univ.; Columbia Univ.; Westminster Choir Coll.; New England Conserv.; Williams Coll. m. Betty Sanders, 1 s., 1 d. Career: Dir., Music Dept., Hudson Falls, NY, Public Schls., 1932-45, Glens Falls, NY, City Schl. Dist., 1945-69; Visiting Prof. of Music, Adirondack Community Coll., Glens Falls, 1969-71; Organist & Choir Dir., Ch.'s in Ithaca, Hudson Falls, Glens Falls, 1930-71. Compositions incl: 25 anthems; 15 choral works; 12 orchl. pieces; 35 band pieces; 10 organ works; 30 instrumental solos & ensembles; piano paraphrases, songs, study materials. Publs: Backgrounds in Music Theory, 1954; Backgrounds in Harmony, 1961; Freeman-Whitney Band Reader, 1954; Essentials of Musicianship for Band, 1970; Contbr. to num. profl. jrnls. Mbr. & Off., num. profl. orgs. Recip. var hons. & prizes incl: Hon. Doct. (LHD), Elmira Coll., 1966. Hobbies: Early music & early instruments; chamber music; duo piano playing. Address: 1508 Danbury Dr., Sun City Ctr., FL 33570, USA. 6.

WHITTENBERG, Charles, b. 6 July 1927, St. Louis, Mo., USA. Composer; Professor of Music. Educ: BMus, Eastman Schl. of Music, Rochester Univ., 1945; FAAR, Am. Acad. in Rome, 1965. M. Mary C. Walsh. Career: Assoc. Prof., Music, Univ. of Conn., Storrs; Maj. Advsr., Grad Schl. Prog. in Music Composition; Prof. Emeritus; ret'd. 1978. Compositions perf. in Europe, Asia, USA. Recordings: String Quartet in One Movement; Games of Five for Wind Quintet; Triptych for Brass Quintet; Variations for 9 Players. Contbr. to profl. jrnls. Mbrships: Am. Soc. of Univ. Composers; Am. Composers Alliance; Am. Soc. of Aesthetics; Broadcast Music Inc. Hons: 2 Guggenheim Fellowships, Composition, 1963-64; Tchng. Grant, Am. Coun. of Learned Socs.; Var. other grants & endowments. Hobby: Hunting. Address: 15 N Maple St., Enfield, Connecticut, USA. 11, 14.

WHITTERIDGE, Janet Mary, b. 2 Mar. 1942, Oxford, UK. Flautist. Educ: Corp. of London Woodwind Schlr., GSM, 1961-65; AGSM, 1964; LTCL, 1977; FTCL, 1978. Career: Royal Ballet Touring Co., 1967-68; BBC Scottish Symph. Orch., 1968-77; Dir. of Music, Craigflower Schl., 1967-. Hons: GSM Chamber Music Prize, 1965; TCL Phillips Prize, 1977. Hobbies: Singing; Skiing. Address: The Cottage, Crombie Point, By Dunfermline, Fife, UK.

WHITTLE, William James Bartlett, b. 12 Apr. 1928, Castle Cary, Somerset, UK. Director of Music; Organist; Singer. Educ: Surrey Coll. of Music; FRCO; LRAM. m. Anne Rosemary Eveleigh, 1 s., 1 d. Career: Director of Music, Wells Cathedral Schl.; num. radio & TV apps. in connection w. trng. of gifted children, & work at Wells Cathedral Schl. Mbrships: ISM; RCO. Hobbies: Gardening; Wine Making. Address: Ripple Farm House, Henton, Wells, Somerset, BA5 1PD, UK.

WHITTOW, Marion Frances, b. 13 Apr. 1947, Lyndhurst, Hampshire, UK. Solo Recitalist, Orchestral & Chamber Music Player on Oboe, Oboe d'Amore & cor Anglais. Educ: GSM, 1965-69; AGSM Perf.'s Dip. Debut: Wigmore Hall, 1972. Career: w. Royal Ballet, 1969-70; w. D'Oyly Carte Opera, 1971-73; Max Jaffa Seasons (also broadcast), 1973-75; has played w. Ulster Orch., Engl. Symph. Orch., Engl. Nat. Orch., Les Musiciens du Roi, Bournemouth Sinfonietta, London Mozart Players, English Sinfonia, etc.; 1977-78 w. Icelandic Symph. Orch. in Reykjavik inclng. broadcasting & solo recording. Mbr: Musicians Union. Hons: GSM Chmbr. Music & Orchestral Prizes, 1968 & 69. Hobbies: Skiing; Swimming; Painting; Cooking; Writing; Wine-Making; Singing. Address: 47, S Hill Park, London NW3 2SS, UK.

WHITWELL, George Frederick, b. 26 Feb. 1907, Handsworth, Birmingham. Pianoforte & Clarinet Teacher. Educ: TCL; LRAM, clarinet tchr.; ARCM, clarinet perf.; LTCL, pianoforte tchr.; LGSM, pianoforte tchr.; MRST. m. Ellen McHugh, 2 s. Career: Prin. Clarinet Int. Ballet Orch., 1945-46; Sub Prin. Clarinet, City of Birmingham Symph. Orch., 1946-54; Music Master, Hately Heath Schl., W Bromwich, 1955-56; Lodge Farm Co. Secondary Schl., Redditch, 1956-64; Hd., Music Dept., Kingshurst Comprehensive Schl., Birmingham, 1964-72. Mbr. ISM. Scholarship, TCL; Hons. & Silver Medal, GSM, 1939. Hobbies: Swimming; Radio amateur. Address: 29 St. Ledger's Rd., Queen's Park, Bournemouth, BH8 9BA, UK.

WHITWORTH, John Anthony, b. 27 Dec. 1921, Ely, Cambs., UK. Music Adviser; Singer (counter-tenor). Educ: MA (Cantab.); Choral Scholar, King's Coll., Cambridge; ARCM. m. Patricia Fitzgerald, 3 d. Career: Alto Lay Vicar, Westminster Abbey,

1949-71; Counter-tenor soloist (over 100 broadcasts); Mbr., Golden Age Singers & Well-tempered Singers; Music Dir., Renaissance Soc., 1965-71; Organist, Christchurch, Chelsea, 1964-65; Organist, St. Paul's, Covent Garden, 1965-70; Asst. Music Adviser, Leics., 1971-. Comps: Arrs. of folk songs (The Mermaid, O Waly Waly, Begone, dull care); Eds. of early music; music to Zodiac. Recordings: Purcell, The Fairy Queen, The Indian Queen; Elizabethan Restoration Music; Songs of William Shakespeare; Purcell, Come Ye Sons of Art; Music of King Henry VIII; Mediaeval Lyrics, etc. Contbr. to: English Ch. Music. Mbrships: ISM. Hobbies: Vintage Cars; Aircraft. Address: 16 Stoop Lane, Quorn, Leics. LE12 8BU, UK. 3.

WHONE, Herbert, b. 14 June 1925, Bingley, Yorks., UK. Violinist. Educ: MusB, Manchester Univ.; ARMCM. 5 children. Career: BBC Symph. Orch.; Covent Gdn.; Dpt. Ldr., Nat. Orch.; Solo recitals, BBC Radio 3; Hd. of Strings, Huddersfield Polytechnic Schl. of Music. Publs: The Simplicity of Playing the Violin, 1972; The Hidden Face of Music, 1974; The Integrated Violinist, 1976. Hobby: Art. Address: 46 Duchy Rd., Harrogate, Yorks., UK.

WIBAUT, Frank (Stephen), b. 10 Nov. 1945, London, UK. Concert Pianist. Educ: Royal Coll. of Music; ARCM. m. Kay Alexander, 1 d. Debut: Wigmore Hall, 1969. Career: Concert performances in Holland, Belgium, Denmark, Germany, Ireland, Spain & Malta; Frequent broadcaster on Radio & TV; Mbr., The Camarilla Ensemble. Recordings: The Romantic Chopin; Favourite Piano Classics; Elgar's From the Bavarian Highlands (in original form); Piano Quintets by Elgar, Suk, etc. Mbrships: Musicians Union; Inc. Soc. of Musicians. Hons. incl: Jr. Exhib., RCM, 1956; Sr. Fndn. Schlrship., Leverhulme Schlrship. & Countess of Munster Award, ibid; 1st prize, Chopin Competition, London; Chappell Gold Medal; BBC Piano Competition, 1968. Hobbies: Driving; Do-it-Yourself; Washing up. Mgmt: Helen Jennings. Address: Highfield Lodge, 68 Harborne Rd., Edgbaston, Birmingham B15 3HE, UK.

WIBERG, Tore, b. 9 Aug. 1911, Stockholm, Sweden. Pianist. Educ: Royal Acad. of Music, Stockholm, 1927-33; Pvte. studies w. Gottfried Boon, Vivian Langrish (London) & Algot Haquinius. m. Marianne Torndahl, 2 c. Debut: Konserthuset, Stockholm, 1935. Career: Soloist, Ensemble player & Accomp., N Europe; Soloist, Stockholm Phil. Orch., 1937-; Accomp. to artists incl. Enrico Mainardi, Gaspar Cassadó, Cecilia Hansen, Andre Navarra & Ruggiero Ricci. Mbrships: Sällskapet Idun. Address: Hornsgatan 38, 117-20 Stockholm, Sweden.

WICEBLOOM, Sidney Leonard, b. 5 Oct. 1930, Colombo, Ceylon. Violinist. Educ: RCM; ARCM (violin perf.). m. Patricia Ann Lissack, 1 s., 1 d. Career: Violinist, Liverpool Phil. Orch., 1953-54, HPO, 1955-. Mbr., ISM. Hons: Dove Prize, 1951, & Natchez Prize, 1952, both RCM. Hobby: Philately. Address: 24 Hillside Grove, London NW7 2LR, UK. 3.

WICK, Denis Gerald, b. 25 June 1931, Braintree, UK. Trombonist. Educ: RAM; LRAM; LTCL; FGSM. m. Audrey Smith, 1 s., 2 d. Career: Prin. Trombone, London Symph. Orch. Address: c/o Boosey & Hawkes (Musical Instruments) Ltd., Deansbrook Rd., Edgware, Middx., UK.

WICKENS, Dennis John, b. 6 Apr. 1926, Croydon, UK. Music Adviser. Educ: BMus, (London); TCL; AMusTCL. m. Muriel E Vaughan, 2 s., 1 d. Career: Gentleman, Choir of the Queen's Chapel of the Savoy, 1954-59; Lay Clerk, Choir of Worcester Cath., 1959-66; Dir. of Music, Worcester Royal Grammar Schl., 1961-66; Co. Music Adviser, Isle of Wight Educ. Committee, 1967-. Compositions: Five songs for tenor & orch. (broadcast by BBC); Song Cycle; The Everlasting Voices (broadcast by BBC); Double Concerto for Harmonica & Violin, & Sinfonia, (both commissioned by Orchestra da Camera); Concertante Music for Brass & Percussion; Miniature Str. Quartet (Novello); Jubilate (OUP); Motet: O vos omnes omnes, Worcester Cath. Choir. Mbrships: ISM; Composers Guild of GB; Music Advisers' Nat. Assn. Hobbies: Tennis; Reading. Address: 19 Marina Ave., Appley, Ryde, Isle of Wight, UK. 3.

WICKENS, Nigel, b. 27 July 1937, Hales-Owen, UK. Concert Singer; Professof of Singing. Educ: MA, Pembroke Coll., Oxford; RAM; LRAM; Hochschule für Musik, Berlin. Career: Solo baritone specialising in French Song, Lieder, Oratorio. Mbr., ISM. Hobbies: Architecture; Country Pursuits. Address: 8 The High St., Orwell, Nr. Royston, Herts., UK. 3.

WICKES, Jean Kim, b. 5 May 1947, Korea. Concert Signer. Educ: BMus, MMus, DMus (Voice), Ind. Univ.; Vienna Inst. of Music & Dramatic Arts. Career: (is totally blind) Billy Graham Evangelistic Assn., Vocal Soloist, 1974-; Chmn., Kim's Ministries, Inc., 1976-; TV app., Robert Schuller's Hour of Power. Recordings: The Love of God; The Lord Is My Light. Mbrships: Chorister, Mu Phi Epsilon, 1969-70; Pi Kappa Lambda, 1968-; G M A, 1978. Hons: Nat. Assn. of Tchrs. of Singing, Upper Div., 1st place, 1969; Fulbright Scholar, Vienna, Austria, 1973-74. Hobbies: Swimming; Knitting; Bible Study; Cooking; Hula hooping. Mgmt: Kim's Ministries, Inc. Address: Kim's Ministries, Inc., P.O. Box 1370, W Memphis, AR 72301, USA.

WICKETT, William Herbert, b. 4 May 1919, Port Hope, Ont. Canada. Organist; Teacher. Educ: Conserv. of Music, Toronto, Assocs. in Piano, 1937; Organ, 1942 (Gold Medal); Can. Coll. of Organists, (ACCO & FCCO, 1955). Career: Organist & Choir Dir., sev. Ont. Chs.; Accomp., Choirs, Instrumentalists & Soloists; Tchr., Music for 2 yrs., Coll. Inst.; Organ Recitals; European Tour as Organist for The Choir of Gentlemen & Boys from St. Thomas, Ont., 1969; Toured England as Organist w. Luke's Cathedral Choir of Sault Ste. Marie, Ont., 1976; Organist & Choir Dir., St. Peter's Cathedral Basilica, London, Can., 1978-. Mbr., Bd. of Examiners, Western Ont. Conserv. of Music, London, Ont. Contbr. to: Jubilate Deo (ch. music mag.). Mbrships: Exec. Coun. & Chmn. Local Branches, RCCO & Ont. Reg. Music Tchrs. Assn.; Hymn Soc. of Am. Hons: Silver Medal, Art, Sciences, Lettres, Paris, 1972. Hobbies: Photography; Swimming; Chess. Address: 509 Clarence St., Apt. 2, London, N6A 3N1 Ont., Canada.

WIDDER, Roger Henry, b. 9 Sept. 1923, Milwaukee, Wis., USA. Professor of Music; Department Chairman; Musician, Woodwinds. Educ: BMusEd, Northwestern Univ.; MMus, ibid; Univ. of Wis.; Univ. of Idaho. m. Kathryn Horner Widder, 4 s. Career: Oboist, Bassoonist, var. orchs.; Recitalist, Soloist, Oboe, Baroque Oboe, Bassoon, Baroque Bassoon, Flute, Recorder, Renaissance Woodwinds; Prof. of Music, Chmn., Music Dept., Univ. of Ark. Contbr. to The Dir. Mbrships: Pi Kappa Lambda; Phi Mu Alpha Sinfonia; Hon. Kappa Kappa Psi; NACWPI; Int. Double Reed Soc.; Am. Recorder Soc.; MENC; Music Tchrs. Nat. Assn. Hobbies: Boy Scouts of Am.; Photography; Hiking; Fishing. Address: 1660 Markham Rd., Fayetteville, AR 72701, USA.

WIDDICOMBE, Gillian, b. 11 June 1943, Aldham, Suffolk, UK. Critic; Journalist. Educ: RAM; Gloucester Cathedral. Career: BBC Music Div., 1966; Glyndebourne Fest. Opera, 1969; Critic & Jrnlst., var. publs. inclng. Financial Times, 1970-76; The Observer, 1977-. Mbr., Chmn., Critics' Circle Music Sect., 1976-. Address: 23 Grevill Rd., London NW6, UK.

WIDEMAN, Nena Plant, b. 21 Dec. 1905, Doyline, La., USA. Piano Teacher. Educ: BA, NW State Univ., La.; BM, Centenary Coll.; MM, Chgo. Musical Coll. m. Yandell Wideman (dec.), 2 s. Career: Tchr., Judson Coll., Ala.; Chmn., Fine Arts, S State Univ., Ark.; Hd., Wideman Schl. of Music, 12 yrs; Vis. Prof., La. Tech. Univ., 1 yr.; Centenary Coll. Schl. of Music, 1966-; Concerts, var. southern states; Adjudicator, music fests.; Fac. Mbr., NGPT. Num. mbrships. incl: Co-fndr., Mbr., 1st Bd., 1st Soloist, now Hon. Bd. Mbr., Shreveport Symph.; Org., annual benefit concerts, ibid, 1959-; Past State Chmn. for Piano, La. Music Educators Assn. & La. Music Tchrs.; Past Pres., Music Forum; Past Educl. Chmn., Symph. Women's Guild; Past Mbr., Cultural Comm., Chbr. of Comm.; Chmn., Shreveport Symph. Annual Contest, 12 yrs.; Past Artist Mbr., La. Fedn. of Music Clubs. Hons: Ganz Piano Schlrships, 2 yrs., Chgo. Musical Coll.; Hall of Fame, NGPT & Gtr. Music Tchrs. Assn.; Hon. Mbr., Chgo. Musical Coll. Alumni Assn. Hons: Alumni Award, Northwestern State Univ. Address: 524 Gladstone, Shreveport, LA, USA. 5.

WIENAND, Karl D, b. 15 Dec. 1941, Ft. Smith, Ark., USA. Assistant Professor, Organ, Music Theory, Harpsichord, Collegium Musicum. Educ: BMusEd, Ctrl. Meth. Coll., Fayette, Mo., 1963; MMus, Wash. Univ., St. Louis, Mo., 1966; DMusArts, Univ. of Colo., Boulder, 1973; studied w. Luterh Spayde, Helmut Walcha, Karel Paukert, Anton Heiller, Susi Jeans, Isolde Ahlgrimm, Hans Kneihs; Studio for Early Music, Munich, Germany, 1964. m. Marilyn Marie Mogensen, 2 s., 1 d. Career: Fndr. Mbr., Collegium Musicum, Univ. of Colo.; Interim Instructor, Fndr. Collegium Musicum, Hastings Coll.; Asst. Prof., Fndr. Collegium Musicum, Musical Dir., Fac. Ancient Instruments Ensemble, Adams State Coll., Alamose, Colo.; Dir. of Cultural Enrichment, ibid.; num. tours w. Ancient Instruments Ensemble. Contbr. to The Diapason. Publs: 2 Anthems. Recordings: Ancient Instruments Ensemble in Concert. Mbrships: Am. Musicol. Soc.; AGO; Am. Recorder Soc. Recip. Fulbright Scholarship, 1963. Hobbies: Building Musical Instruments; Camping. Address: 205 W Ave., Alamosa, CO 81101, USA. 9, 28, 29.

WIENAND, Marilyn M, b. 6 June 1942, Ontario, Ore., USA. College Instructor; Singer; Pianist; Early Music Specialist. Educ:

Acad. for Music, Vienna; BMus, Wash. Univ., St. Louis, 1966; MMus, Univ. of Colo., 1971; Study w. Anton Heiller, Howard Kelsey, Leslie Chaby, Axel Schiotz, John Paton. m. Karl D Wienand, 2 s., 1 d. Career: vocal recitals; Denver, Colo., TV show Colo. Camerata; Soloist, oratorios; Accomp. & Coach; tours w. Ancient Instruments Ensemble, Mexico & western USA; Ch. Organist, Children's Choir Dir.; Fndng. Mbr. Collegium Musicum, Univ. of Colo.; Fndng. Mbr., Collegium Musicum, Hastings Coll..& fac. Ancient Instruments Ensemble, Adams State Coll., Alamosa, Colo.; Soloist, in concerts, Austria; Profl. choir, Vienna. Recordings: The Ancient Instruments Ensemble of Adams State Coll. in Concert. Mbr., Nat. Assn. of Tchrs. of Singing. Hobbies: Nutrition; Travel. Address: 205 West Ave., Alamosa, CO 81101, USA.

WIENANDT, Elwyn Arthur, b. 23 Dec. 1917, Aniwa, Wis., USA. Musicologist; University Administrator. Educ: BMus, Lawrence Coll., 1939; MMus, Univ. of Denver, 1948; PhD, Univ. of Iowa, 1951. m. Lois Patricia Trachsel, 2 s., 1 d. Career: Assoc. Prof. of Music, NM Highlands Univ., 1951-56; Vis. Lectr. in Musicol., Univ. of Iowa, 1954; Assoc. Prof. of Musicol., 1956, Prof., 1957, Chmn. of Grad Studies, 1957, Assoc. Dean, 1973, Schl. of Music, Baylor Univ. Compositions: more than 115 works, eds., arrangements & transcriptions for vocal & instrumental ensembles w. leading publrs. Publs: Choral Music of the Church, 1965; The Anthem in England & America (w. Robt. H Young), 1970; Opinions on Church Music, 1974; The Bicentennial Collection of American Music (in 3 vols.), vol. 1, 1974. Contbr. to: Jrnl. of the Am. Musicol. Soc.; Western Folklore; Music Review; Music Lib. Assn. Notes; Diapason; Christian Century; Grove's Dicitonary of Music & Musicians, 6th ed. Mbrships: Pres., SW Chapt., Am. Musicol. Soc., 1961-63; Music Lib. Assn.; AAUP. Recip., num. hons. Hobbies: Gardening; Golf. Address: 1216 Cliffview Rd., Waco, TX 76710, USA. 2, 7, 11, 29.

WIENCKOWSKI, Jean Ellen, b. 6 Dec. 1947, Washington, Ga., USA. Violist. Educ: BMus Perf., Univ. of Mich.; BM in Music. Career: Profl. Violist w. Baritone, Tulsa Opera Chorus. num. perfs. 1956-; 1st Oboe, Northeast Okla. Symph. Orch., 1961-63; 3rd Oboe, Tulsa Phil. Orch., 1966-71; Choir Dir., Memorial Christian Ch., 1967-68, Will Rogers Christian Ch., 1969, & 2nd Presby. Ch. 1970-, all Tulsa. Mbr., Am. Fedn. Musicians. Hobbies: Photography; Canoeing; Camping. Address: PO Box 688, Gordon, GA 31301, USA.

WIENER, Julia, b. 17 June 1932, Sofia, Bulgaria. Opera Singer. Educ: Sofia Conserv. of Music. m. Dimiter Chenisher. Debut: Leonora, Trovatore, Nat. Opera, Sofia, 1954. Career: Bulgarian Nat. Opera, Sofia; Staatsoper DDR, Berlin; Theater de la Monnaye. Recordings: Prince Igor; Aida; Verdi Requiem; 3 Recitals of Opera, Rachmaninov Songs, etc. Mbr., Bulgarian Union of Musicians. Hons: Kammersängerin, DDR; Nat. Artist, Bulgarian Repub.; Bearer of Dimitrov's Prize, Bulgaria. Mgmt: Bulgarian Nat. Opera. Address: 11th Auguststr. A13, Sofia, Bulgaria.

WIERSZYLOWSKI, Jan, b. 11 Aug. 1927, Jablonna, Warsaw, Poland. Conductor; Pianist; Scientist. Educ: Piano, Schl. of Music, Warsaw, 1952; Dip., Dept. of Theory, Comp. & Cond., Higher Schl. of Music, Warsaw, 1958; MA, Univ. of Warsaw, 1958; PhD (Psychol. of Music), ibid, 1967. m. Zofia Janowska, 1 s., 1 d. Debut: w. Musicae Antiquae Collegium Varsoviense, Warsaw Nat. Philharmonic Orch., Int. Chopin Congress, Warsaw, 1960. Career: w. Inst. of Musicol., Univ. of Warsaw, & Higher Schl. of Music, Warsaw; has given regular concerts w. Warsaw Philharmonic Orch. old music ensemble, choir & chmbr. orch.; apps. in cities throughout Poland & on radio & TV. Recordings: From the Musical Treasury of the Polish Millenium, Polskie Nagrania, annually 1960-74. Publs: Zarys Psychologii Muzyki (Introduction to the Psychology of Music), 1966; Psychologia Muzyki (Psychology of Music), 1970. Contbr. to: Muzyka; Ruch Muzyczny. Mbr., Polish Union of Composers. Hobbies: Gardening; Flowers; Playing guitar w. the children. Address: ul. Wigury 1, Wesola k/Warszawy^05-440, Poland.

WIESEHAHN, Willem, b. 31 May 1914, Amsterdam, The Netherlands. Conductor; Composer. Educ: pupil of Fred. Roeske, Spaanderman, Stroomenbergh, etc.; Dip. of The Royal Oratory Soc. m. Helena Wiesehahn-Schipperijn, 2 s. Debut: 1932. Career: Cond. choirs at approx. 500 concerts in Holland, Belgium, Switzerland, Germany & England w. Het Amsterdams Phil. Orch., The Radio Phil. Orch., LSO, Het Residentie Orch. (The Hague), Het Utrechts Symph. Orch., Luzerner Festwochen Orch., etc.; Many radio appearances; Cond., The Amsterdam Mixed Choir; The Oratory Soc., etc. Compositions incl: Orch. - Te Deum for mixed choir, Soprano; Te Deum for male choir & organ; A Christmas Cantata; comps. for male voice choir & female voices, etc. Recordings: Mijne Moedertaal. Contbr. to

Euphonia. Mbrships: Royal Musicians Soc.; The Dutch Conductor Soc., etc. Hobbies: Fishing. Address: Sonneveld 43, Amsterdam (Buitenveldert), The Netherlands.

WIESER, Gerhard, b. 7 Feb. 1930, Zürich, Switzerland. Musician; Viola Player; Manager. Educ: Studies in Paris, Zürich, Geneva. m. Ruth Pletscher, 2 s. Career: Viola, Winterthur Symph. Orch., 4 yrs.; Viola Solo, Radio-Orch. Beromünster, Zürich, 8 yrs.; Viola Solo, Tonhalle-Orch. Zürich (Opera House), Mbr., Collegium Musicum Zürich & Piraccini-Stucki-Quartet, Cond., Rüti-Orch., 5 yrs. Recordings: Viola Concerto (Paul Müller-Zürich); Arpiade (Wladimir Vogel). Mbrships: Schweizerischer Tonkünstler-Verein; Schweizerischer Musikerverband. Hobbies: Photography; Books; Engl. pipes; House; Ships; Model railways. Address: Auf der Bürglen 7, 8627 Grüningen, Switzerland.

WIGGINS, John, b. 29 May 1924, Sutton, Surrey, UK. Flautist; Teacher of Flute. Educ: Recip. of Open Schlrship. to RCM, 1940; St. Marys Hosp. Med. Schl., 1947-49; GSM, 1949-50; studied pvtely. w. Robert Murchie & w. Geoffrey Gilbert, GSM. m. Margaret Helen Burlton, 1 s., 2 d. Career: Mbr., BBC Scottish Symph. Orch., 1950-; Prin. Flute, ibid, 1954-; Tchr. of Flute, RSAM, 1958-. Hobbies: Keyboard Instruments; Motoring; Electronics. Address: 59 Rowan Drive, Bearsden, Glasgow, G61 3HH, UK. 3, 4.

WIGGINS, William Bramwell, b. 28 Sept. 1921, London, UK. Trumpet Player. Educ: TCL & RAM; ARAM; LRAM; ARCM; LTCL. m. Betty Doreen Rouse, 2 d. Career: LSO, 1946-57; Dir. of Music, Moose Jaw Jr. Band Assoc., Sask., & CBC (Winnipeg) Orch., Can., 1957-60; Philharmonia, RPO & Engl. Chmbr. Orch., 1960-66; Music Master, Stowe Schl., 1966-. Comps: Works for Band (brass & concert); Music for brass grps.; First Tunes & Studies for Trumpet; First Tunes & Studies for Trombone; Arrangements for School Wind Band. Contbr. to: Sounding Brass; Brit. Bandsman; Making Music. Mbrships: Royal Soc. of Musicians; ISM; RAM Club; C'wlth. Club. Hobbies: Painting; Golf; Canadiana; Candle & wine making. Mgmt: Ibbs & Tillet Ltd. Address: 'Anlow', Dadford nr. Buckingham, Bucks. MK 18 5LB, UK. 3.

WIGGLESWORTH, Frank, b. 3 Mar. 1918, Boston, Mass., USA. Composer; Teacher. Educ: BS, Columbia Univ.; MMus, Converse Coll.; studied comp. w. Otto Luening, Henry Cowell & Edgar Varese. m. Anne Parker, 2 c. Comps: Lake Music; Duo for Oboe & viola; Woodwind quintet; Brass quintet; Telesis; Three portraits; many songs & choral pieces. Recordings: Lake Music for solo flute; Duo for oboe & viola; Symphony No. 1 (Vienna Phil.); two masses, etc. Contbr. to: Notes; Ipswich Chronicle. Mbrships: Editl. Bd., CRI; 1st VP, Am. Comps. Alliance; Pres., Composers Forum. Hons: Alice M Ditson Award in Comp., 1943; Inst. of Arts & Letters Award in comp., 1951; Fellow, Am. Acad. in Rome, 1951-54; Fellow, McDowell Colony, 1962 & '70. Hobbies: Chamber Music. Address: 19 Downing St., NY, NY 10014, USA.

WIGGS, Sheila N, b. 7 Dec. 1946, Irvine, Ayrshire, Scotland. UK. Musician; Music Teacher; Musicologist; Accompanist. Educ: RCM, 1965-69; ARCM (piano); ARAM (oboe); GSRM MMus, 1971. Career incls: Tchr., Sutton High Schl., 1968-70, Westminster Schl., 1970-, Westminster Abbey Choir Schl., 1970-, RCM, 1970-, Mander Portman Woodward Tutors, 1973-; Asst. Curator, Museum of Instruments, RCM, 1970-74; Pvte. music tchr.; Freelance oboist & piano accomp. Publs: Musica da Camera series of 18th Century Music; Eds. of Wind Music, Oxford Univ. Press, 1975. Contbr. to Grove's Dictionary of Music, 1976. Mbrships: ISM; Royal Musical Assn. Hobbies: Reading; Langs.; Tennis; Cooking; Musical rsch.; Crosswords. Address: Glenesk, 19 Tadorne Rd., Tadworth, Surrey, UK.

WIGHTMAN, Brian Robin, b. 8 Oct. 1942, Ilford, Essex, UK. Bassoonist. Educ: TCL, LTCL. m. Joanna Graham, 1 s., 1 d. Career: Prin. Bassoon, Sadlers Wells-Engl. Nat. Opera, 1966-; Bassoonist w. Nash Ensemble & others. Recordings: chmbr. music w. Nash Ensemble. Hobbies: Travel; Boating; Real Ale; Chess. Address: 20 Park Ave., Finchley, London N3, UK.

WIGSTON, Frederic Roland, b. 31 May 1914, London, UK. Orchestral Musician; Double Bassist. m. Joan Mavin Hobson, 2 s. Career: Mantovani, 1937-39; BBC Theatre Orch., 1946; Liverpool Phil., 1946; Royal Opera, Covent Garden, 1947-57; 2nd Prin., RCH, 1957-65; Prin., ibid, 1965-; Prof., double bass, Trinity Coll. of Music, London. Mbr., London Orchl. Assn. Hobbies: Classical Guitar; Art; Photography. Address: 67 Salesbury Dr., Billericay, Essex CM11 2JH, UK. 3.

WIHLBORG, Hans Ferdinand, b. 10 Mar. 1916, Malmo, Sweden. Singing Teacher. Singing pedagogy exam., RAM &

Royal Music HS, Stockholm, 1953; Piano pedagogy, ibid, 1954; Singing studies w. var. tutors. m. Wira Eleonora Wihlborg, 1 d. Career incls: Singer, choir master, Royal Opera, Stockholm, 1939-55; Drottningholm Theatre, Stockholm, 1949; Currently Tchr., solo singing, singing pedagogy & ensemble singing, Music HS, Stockholm & Music Schl., Ingesund, Arvika. Recordings incl: The Medieval Ballad; num. w. Singing Quartet 'Synkopen'. Contbr. to profl. jrnls. Mbr. num. orgs. Hons: Grant, Royal Opera, Stockholm, 1955. Address: Gambrinusgatan 5, I, S 112 31 Stockholm, Sweden.

WIKMAN, (Arne) Bertil, b. 18 May 1944, Stockholm, Sweden. Pianist; Lecturer. Educ: BA, 1969; piano studies, Richard Andersson's Music Schl., Stockholm & w. Ellen Anberg, Molin, Stockholm. m. Solveig Wikman, 2 s. Debut: Stockholm, 1967. Career: concerts in Sweden as Soloist & in Piano Duo w. wife; broadcasts on Swedish TV & radio; int. debut of piano duo, Berlin, 1975; lectr. in musicol. Recordings: Swedish Piano Music for Four Hands (2 discs); Music for Two Pianos; Piano Solo & Duet (2 discs). Contbr. to Swedish music reviews. Recip. state art scholarship, 1973, 75. Address: Mardvägen 18, 14600 Tullinge, Sweden.

WIKMAN, Solveig Inga-Lill, b. 20 Sept. 1942, Viskafors, Sweden. Pianist; Piano Teacher. Educ: studied piano w. var. tchrs. inclng. Gottfrid Boon, Stockholm, Bruno Seidlhofer, Salzburg, & Wilhelm Kempff, Italy; studied romance interpretation w. Erik Werba; Piano Tchrs.'s Exam., 1965; studied musicol., Stockholm Univ. m. Bertil Wikman, 2 s. Debut: 1975. Career: has given concerts in Sweden as Soloist & in Piano Duo w. husband Bertil; Piano Duo apps. on Swedish TV & radio. Recordings: Swedish Piano Music for Four Hands (2 discs); Music for Two Pianos; Piano Solo & Duet (2 discs). Hons: Art Schlrship. of the State, 1973, 1975. Address: Mardvägen 18, 14600 Tullinge, Sweden.

WIKNER, Stephen Charles Nevill, b. 7 Nov. 1948, Moascar, Egypt. Violinist; Composer. Educ: ARCM., 1969; Eastman Schl. of Music, Univ. of Rochester, NY. m. Madeleine Kranenburg, 1 s. Career: Violinist/Libr., Cape Town Symph. Orch., S Africa, 1971-74; Int. (perf.) Promotion, Oxford Univ. Press Music, 1975-. Comps: Oboe Quartet; Five Pieces for String Orch.; Cyclophony I. Mbr. Comp's. Guild of GB. Hobbies: Food; Wine; Astronomy. Address: 22 Dunster Dr., London, NW9 8EJ, UK.

WIKSTROM, Inger Elvi Margareta, b. 11 Dec. 1939, Gothenburg, Sweden. Pianist. Educ: Stockholm Borgarskola; Piano Pedagogical exam., 1958; Pvte. study w. Gottfried Boon, Stockholm, & Ilona Kabos, London. m. Caspar Lundquist, 1 d.; (2) David Bartov, 1 s. Debut: Stockholm, Lond, Berlin, 1959; NYC, 1963. Career: Worldwide tours, inclng. 4 in USA, 4 in USSR, S. Am., Israel; Num. apps., radio & TV; Guest, Vienna, Spoleto, Dubrovnik, Stockholm Fests. Recordings: 10 albums for RCA, Decca & Swedish Soc. Hons: Göteburgs-Tidningens Debut Prize, 1960; Swedish Soloist of Year, 1961; San Michele Schrlship., 1961; Cavaleiro da Ordem de Rio Branco, Brazil, 1969. Hobbies: Reading; Painting; Skiing. Mgmt: van Wyck, London. Address: Lokattsvägen 48, 16137 Bromma, Sweden. 3.

WILBRAHAM, John, b. 15 April 1944, Bournemouth, UK. Trumpet Player. Educ: RAM; LRAM; ARCM. m. Susan Drake. Career: New Philharmonia Orch., 1966-68; Royal Phil. Orch., 1968-72; BBC Symph. Orch., 1972-. Recordings incl: trumpet concertos by Haydn, Hummel, Mozart, Telemann, Torelli. Mbrships: Savage Club; ISM. Recip., Silver Medal, Worshipful Co. of Musicians, 1965. Hobby: Cooking. Address: 14B Elizabeth Mews, London NW3 4TL, UK.

WILD, Earl, b. 26 Nov. 1915, Pitts., Pa., USA. Pianist; Composer. Educ: Carnegie Tech. Coll., Pitts.; studied w. Selmar Jansen, Egon Petri, Helene Barrere, Volya Cossack & Paul Doguereau. Career: apps. w. symph. orchs. inclng. NBC Orch. under Toscanini, 1942; recitals in many countries; has performed for 7 US presidents, inclng. inauguration of J F Kennedy; Music Dir. Palm Springs Mus. num. recordings. Comps. incl: The Turquoise Horse (choral); ballet; oratorio; piano music; songs. Hobby: Writing poetry. 16.

WILD, Jean Marion, b. 30 June 1950, Nottingham, UK. Music Teacher. Educ: London Coll. of Music, 1968-71; Grad., ibid.; Lic., ibid. for violin & piano teaching; Assoc., ibid.; Dip., Educ., Homerton Coll., Cambridge, 1971-72. m. Stuart Gregory Wild. Career: Music Mistress, Loughborough HS for Girls, 1972-73; Berkhamsted Schl. for Girls, 1973-; Examiner, London Coll. of Music, 1975-. Mbr., Incorp. Soc. of Musicians. Hobbies: Ch. Choir Mbrship.; Scottish Country Dancing; Cooking; Walking. Address: Aljustrel, 1 Egerton Rd., Berkhamsted, Herts., HP4 1DT, UK.

WILDE, David, b. 12 Nov. 1944, Hereford, UK. French Horn Player; Chamber Musician; Conductor; Director. Educ: Kneller Hall; pvte. study (comp.) w. Carmello Pace, Malta; Cardiff Coll. of Music; Open Univ.; Lancaster Univ. Debut: Malta TV, 1967. Career: apps. in Hong Kong, Germany, USA, UK. Malta; mbr., Etesian Wind Ensemble until recently; mbr.; resident wind ensemble, Loughborough Univ.; premieres of works of C Pace, Peter Crump & A Wilson-Dickson; Dir., Nat. French Horn Convention, Loughborough Univ., 1979. var. recordings. mbr., ISM. Hobbies: Reading; Travel; Organising French Horn Conventions. Address: 43 Goscote House, Sparkenhoe St., Leicester LE2 0TD, UK.

WILDE, David Clark, b. 25 Feb. 1935, Stretford, Lancs., UK. Pianist; Conductor; Teacher. Educ: Studied w. Franz Reizenstein, 1945-47; w. Iso Elinson, Royal Manchester Coll. of Music, 1948-53; ARMCM Perf.'s Dip. 1951, Tchrs. Dip., 1953; studied w. Nadia Boulanger, France, 1963 & other masters. m. Jeanne Lukey, 1 s., 1 d. Career: BBC Staff Accomp., Glasgow, 1959-62; Prof., RAM, 1965-67, Royal Manchester Coll. of Music, 1967-69; Concert perfs. from age 6; Concerts w. all major UK orchs., & in Europe & USA; num. solo recitals, lecture recitals & broadcasts; Masterclasses, UK & USA; TV progs. incl. Liszt & London, Bartok's Breakthrough; Chmbr. music w. Tatrai Quartet, Elisabeth Soderstrom, Yfrah Neaman, etc. Recordings incl: Bush, Variations Nocturne, Finale on an English Sea Song; Liszt Recital. Contbr. to Liszt, the Man & his Music, ed. A. Walker, 1970. Mbrships: Brit.-Hungarian Friendship Soc. (VP); ISM; Assoc., Royal Phil. Soc. Hons. incl: 1st Prize, Int. Liszt-Bartok Competition, Budapest, 1961; 1st Queens Prize, London, 1962; FRMCM, 1966; Arts Coun. Award, 1967; ARAM, 1968. Hobbies: Swimming; Reading; Good Company. Mgmt: Liesl Stary Artists Mgmt., 2/2 Mandeville Pl., London W1. Address: 30 Conifer Gdns., London SW16, UK. 3.

WILDER, Michael David, b. 8 June 1955, Ames, Iowa, USA. Clarinettist; College Instructor. Educ: BMus, Iowa State Univ., 1977; MMus, Univ. of Mich., 1978. Career: Des Moines Symph. (Bass Clarinet), 1975-77; Wichita Symph. Orch. (2nd Clarinet), 1978-; Southwestern Coll., Instructor of Woodwinds, 1978-; Prin. Clarinet, Wichita Metropolitan Ballet Orch., 1978. Mbrships: MENC; Pi Kappa Lambda; Kansas Music Educs. Assn. Hons: Ames Int. Orch. Fest. Assn. Scholarship, 1973-77. Hobbies: Ceramics; Woodworking; Plants; Graphic Design. Address: 323 1/2 Coll. Ave., Winfield, KS 67156, USA.

WILDER, Stephen Gilbert, b. 21 July 1952, Hammersmith, London, UK. Accompanist & Repetiteur. Educ: ARCM (piano perf.); GRSM. m. Kathleen Mary Parker. Debut: Wigmore Hall, 1974. Career: var. concert apps., London & provinces; Official Accomp., Ferrier Competition, Richard Tauber Competition & Boise Scholarships; Repetiteur, Glyndebourne Fest. Opera; Kent Opera; Welsh Nat. Opera; Pvte. Singing Coach. BBC recording w. Julie Kennard. Hons. incl: Percy Buck Award, 1975; Clytie Mundie & Van Someren Godfrey Accomp. Prizes. Hobbies: Swimming; Photography; Gardening. Address: 17 Tintern Rd., Wood Gn., London N22 5LU, UK.

WILDING-WHITE, Raymond, b. 22 Oct. 1922, Caterham, Surrey, UK. Composer; Teacher; Author. Educ: Juilliard Schl., NYC, USA, 1947-49; New England Conserv. of Music, Boston, Mass.; MMus, ibid.; DMA, Boston Univ., 1962. m. Glennie Brown, 2 s., 1 d. Career: Kulas Chair of Music, Case Inst. of Technol.; Fndr., Case Electronic Music Studio, Case Experimental Music Presentations, & Cleveland Portfolio Concert Series; Assoc. Prof. of Music, DePaul Univ.; Fndr., DePaul Electronic Music Studio & The Loop Group (multi-media ensemble); frequent broadcaster, Stns. WCLV-FM, Chgo. & WFMT-FM. Compositions: over 70 works incl: For Mallets (percussion ensemble), 1962; Space Madrigals (mixed chorus & soprano solo), 1950; Paraphernalia - A Regalia of Madrigalia from Ezra Pound (voice, trumpet, oboe, clarinet, violin & harpsichord), 1959; My Nannie O (Scotch Ballad), 1965. Hons incl: F. S. Coolidge Award (twice); Cleveland Fine Arts Award. Address: 715 Ridgeland Ave., Oak Pk., IL 60304, USA.

WILDMAN, John Edward Jr, b. 25 May 1922, Chgo., Ill., USA. Instrumental Music Teacher; Oboist; Adjudicator; Clinician. Educ: BSc, music educ., Univ. Cinn. & Cinn. Conserv. Music; DMA Cand., ibid. m. Pansy Buyer, 3 children. Debut: Prin. Oboe, Dayton Phil. Orch., 1946. Career: Mbr., Dr. Frank Simon Radio Band Am; Pt.-time oboist w. Chattanooga, Cinn. Symph., Columbus, Hamilton, Huntington, Lima & Springfield Orchs.; Prin. Oboist, Dayton Phil. Orch. Assn.; Ohio; Instrumental music tchr., Troy Pub. Schls., Ohio. Mbr. profl. orgs. Hons. incl: Rocekfeller Grant, Tchrs. Perf. Inst., Oberlin Conserv. Music, Ohio, 1968. Hobbies incl: Electronics. Address: 242 Robin Hood Lane, Troy, OH 45373, USA.

WILES, Margaret Jones, b. 25 Dec. 1911, Hamilton, Ohio, USA. Violinist; Violin & Viola Instructor; Conductor. Educ: Mus B, De Pauw Univ., Ind.; RAM, London, 1933-34; studied w. Raphael Bronstein, NYC. m. Gordon Pitts Wiles, 2 s. Career incls: Violin soloist w. broadcasting & symph. orchs. in S Africa, 1937-51, incl. Virginia Radio Quartet, 1942-45, Durban Symph. Orch., 1941-45; Asst. Concertmaster, E Conn. Symph., 1957-71; Violin & Viola Instr., Conn. Coll., 1957-75; Cond., Conn. Coll. Symph. Orch., 1957-75. Comps: 50 str. quartets performed over S African Broadcasting Ed., Viola Instruction Book. Contbr. to Outspan, S Africa. Mbrships: AAUP; Mu Phi Epsilon; Alpha Phi. Hons: Gold Dip., Viola, Eisteddfod, S Africa, 1937; Elected Cond. Emeritus, Conn. Coll., 1975. Hobbies: Camping; Gardening; Viola Da Gamba. Address: 30 Colony Rd., E Lyme, CT 06333, USA. 5, 6, 27.

WILHELM, Rolf Alexander, b. 23 June 1927, Munich, Germany. Composer; Conductor; Pianist. Educ: Hochschule fur Musik, Vienna, 1942-45, w. Prof. J Marx; Hochschule fur Musik, Munich, 1946-48, w. Hans Rosbaud, masterclass. m. Helga Neuner, 1 s., 1 d. Debut: Cond., own comps. for radio-plays, 1946. Career: 300 radio-plays, 1946; approx. 150 TV plays, 1954; first movie, 1954; now over 50 film scores. Compositions: chamber music; songs for soprano & string orch.; piano concerto; 3 Fantasias for orch.; violin concerto, etc. Recordings: sev. sound tracks of film scores; 3 Fantasien uber Dtsch. Volkslieder; Plays for Children. Publs: Richard Strauss Jahrbuch 'Die Donau', 1954. Mbrships: Deutscher Komponisten Verband; GEMA; Music Union; Munich Golf Club. Hobbies: Antiques; History of Art; Golf; Painting. Address: Hubertus-str. 64, D 8022 Gruenwald, Munich, German Fed. Repub.

WILIMEK, Eduard, b. 8 Dec. 1904, Vienna, Austria. Composer. Educ: High Schl. for Music, Vienna, 20 yrs. Comps. incl: Violin-Concerto; Bürgenland-Rhapsodie; Bürleske for Piano & Orch.; Concertante Symphonia; 2 Sinfoniettas; Concertino for Clarinet & String Orch.; 2 Suites for Orch.; Musick in C (orch.); 3 Klavier Quintets; 5 String Quartets; 2 Divertimenti for Chmbr. Orch.; Choral & Chmbr. Music; 2 Cantatas; Lieder. Recordings: Divertimento for String Orch.; Concertino for Clarinet & String Orch.; Musik in C (orch.). Mbrships. incl: Komponistenbund; Österreichische Gesellschaft für Zeitgenössische Musik. Hons. incl: Verdienstzeichen, Vienna & Theodor Körner Prize; Professoren-Titel. Hobbies: Reading; Gardening; Car travel. Address: Stromstrasse 20/8/9, A1200 Vienna, Austria. 4.

WILK, Peter Rudolph, b. 12 Sept. 1940, Montreal, Quebec, Can. Accordion Player. Educ: BSc in Electronics Engineering; Accordion study w. Eric Mundinger; Studied Theory w. Dr. H R Goodwin. m. Bogdanna (Donna) Ann Danilewicz, 3 c. Career: Past Mbr., Mundinger Accordion Orch.; currently perf. solo & in small groups, Toronto. Recordings: Mendelssohn Concerto in E minor, 3rd Move. Mbr., Toronto Musicians Assn. Hons: Winner, 1st Annual Hohner Cup, 1960; Solo First Awards, Kiwanis Music Fest., Under 19 yrs. 1953& '54, Open Competition, 1961. Hobbies: Swimming; Travel; Photography. Address: 72 Glentworth Rd., Willowdale, Ont. M2J 2E8, Can.

WILKES, Sandra Ann, b. Breaston, Derbyshire, UK. Soprano. Educ: ARCM, 1965; RCM. m. Neil Jenkins, 1 s. Debut: Royal Albert Hall, 1968. Career: Oratorio Soloist, many Brit. choral socs.; Recitalist, London recitals (ISM, Worshipful Co. of Musicians, Kirckman Concert Socs.), also Duet Recitals w. Neil Jenkins; toured Germany, 1970, Iceland, 1972, '73, Can. & USA (inclng. perfs. at Kennedy Ctr., Wash. DC, & Carnegie Hall, NYC), 1973, France, 1977, '79; Singing Tutor, Froebel Inst. & Digby Stuart Coll., 1978-. Recordings: BBC Time & Tune Record. Mbr., ISM. Hons. incl: Agnes Nicholls Trophy, 1967; Clara Butt, Vaughan Williams Trust & Countess of Munster Musical Trust Awards, 1968. Mgmt: Ibbs & Tillett. Address: 17 Birchwood Gr., Hampton, Middx. TW12 3DU, UK.

WILKINS, Margaret Lucy, b. 13 Nov. 1939, Kingston-upon-Thames, Surrey, UK. Composer; Senior Lecturer. Educ: TCM; BMus, Univ. of Nottingham; LRAM; Post-grad. Music Tchrs.' Cert., Uaniv. of London. m. Dr. Nigel Edward Wilkins, 2 d. Career: Comps. performed at Wigmore Hall, London, Queen Elizabeth Hall, London, Purcell Room, London, Edinburgh Fest., City Hall, Glasgow; BBC broadcasts on Radios 3 & 4; Perfs. abroad, Switz., & Can. Comps. incl: Concerto Grosso; The Silver Casket; Witch Music; Instrumental Interludes. Mbrships. incl: Exec. Comm. & Chmn., Scottish Br., Composers' Guild of GB; Recip., var. hons. Hobbies: Motoring; Sewing. Mgmt: Scottish Music Archive, 7 Lilyband Gdns., Glasgow G12 8RZ, UK. Address: 39 Butternob Rd., Beaumont Park, Huddersfield HOH 7AR, Yorks., UK.

WILKINS-OPPLER, Nancy Dorothy, b. 25 Nov. 1923, Fulham, London, UK. Musician: Violin, Viola. Educ: LRAM, RAM. m. Richard Wilkins-Oppler, 1 s. Career: Freelance orchestral player; Violin, viola tchr.; Schl. recitalist. Mbrships: Solo Performers Sect., ISM. Hobbies: Gardening; Tennis; Swimming. Address: Apple Acre, Garlinge Green, Petham, Nr. Canterbury, Kent, UK.

WILKINSON, Alan, b. 29 Nov. 1929, London, UK. Violinist. Educ: RAM, London; Accademia Musicale Chigiana, Siena, Italy; Int. Acad. Chmbr. Music, Rome; studies w. Paul Beard, Yehudi Menuhin, Alberto Lysy & other masters. m. Lucy Mary Lucas, 2 s., 1 d. Career: Specialist in Violin & Piano duo; partnerships w. Malcolm Troup, David Gwilt, & 1967- w. Janet Gare; European tours; Perfs. of complete Bartok works for violin & piano, & complete Beethoven sonatas, Newcastle Fests., 1973 & 1975; Gen. Admnstr., Christ's Hosp. Arts Ctr., 1974-. Mbr. ISM (Solo Perfs. sect.). Hons: ARAM. Hobbies: Golf; Fishing; Reading; Arts in General. Address: Newlands, Christ's Hospital, Horsham, Sussex, UK.

WILKINSON, Jennie Gaudio (also known as GAUDIO, Jennie), b. Gary, Ind., USA. Violinist; Teacher. Educ: Sherwood Music Schl.; Chgo. Conserv.; studied pvtely. w. Adolph Pick & Paul Stassevitch of Chgo.; De Paul Univ. m. William R Wilkinson, 1 s. Career: Toured w. Monte Carlo Opera Ensemble as violin soloist, appearing in 15 states; Appeared as Soloist in Orchestral Hall w. The Sherwood Symph. Orch. playing the Tschaikovsky Concerto; Commencement concert of Chgo. Conserv. w. mbrs. of Chgo. Symph. Orch.; Former Mbr. of Fac. of Sherwood Music Schl. & of Pro Musica Quintette, Chgo.; Former Concertmaster of Sherwood Symph. Orch.; w. Rockford Symph. Orch., Ill. & Am. Opera co. Orch., Chgo.; Var. tours as soloist; Mbr., Chgo. Artists Trio for 8 yrs.; First Concertmaster of Gary Symph. Orch., serving for 10 yrs. (also appearing as soloist sev. times); Approved Tchr., Ind. Univ., Gary Ctr.; Mbr. of Gaudio Trio, Gary & Dangremend Trio, Chgo., etc. Now tchng. privately. Mbrships incl: Lakeview Musical Soc.; Past Pres., Gary Music & Arts Soc.; Chgo. Musicians Club of Women. Winner of Fest. Concerts. Address: 5767 Taft Pl., Merrillville, IN 46410, USA. 3, 8.

WILKINSON, Kenneth Roy, b. 20 June 1933, Liversedge, Yorks., UK. Schoolmaster; Director of Music; Adjudicator; Examiner. Educ: Organ Scholar, Sidney Sussex Coll., Cambridge; MA; ARCM; GRSM. m. Elizabeth Scott, 1 s., 1 d. Career: Dir. of Music, City of London Schl.; Dir. of Music, Marlborough Coll.; Examiner for Assoc. Bd. of Royal Schls. of Music. Mbrships: ISM; Music Masters Assn. Hobbies: Gardening; Antiques; Reading Address: Hamelin, Marlborough, Wilts., UK.

WILKINSON, Marc, b. 27 July 1929, Paris, France. Composer; Conductor; Lecturer. Educ: Studied comp. w. Edgard Varese & Oliver Messiaen; MA, Columbia Univ., NYC; MFA, Princeton, Univ., NJ. m. Fanny Yen, 1 d. Career: Dir. of Music, Nat. Theatre of GB, 1965-; Created & developed Music Dept., ibid.; Comp. & Dir. of Music for Royal Shakespeare Theatre, Royal Ct. Theatre, London, & sev. theatres in London & abroad; Music has featured in sev. plays on Broadway, NYC; Cond. of music for many plays, film scores & concert works. Comps. incl: (Film & theatre music) If...; The Hireling; (Concert music) Voices. Contbr. to var. publs. Hobbies incl: African & other ethnic art objects. Mgmt: London Mgmt., 235-41 Regent St., London W1, UK. Address: 119 Lansdowne Rd., London W11 2LF, UK. 1, 3.

WILKINSON, Philip George, b. 28 Aug. 1929, London, UK. Professor of Harmony & Composition. Educ: RAM, London Univ.; DMus, London; MMus, RCM; FRCM; ARCM (piano perf.); LRAM (piano perf.). m. Margaret Matterson, 1 s., 1 d. Career: Mbr., Music Staff, Cranleigh Schl., 1953-59; Prof., RCM & Examiner to Assoc. Bd. of Royal Schls. of Music, 1959-. Comps: Shakespearean Suite; Symph.; Miniature Symph. (all orch.); Miniature Str. Quartet; Num. songs, part-songs & children's songs; Ensemble music; Piano & piano duet music; 100 score-reading exercises. Contbr. to RCM Mag. Mbrships: PRS; ISM. Hons: Madrigal Soc.'s Prize, 1960; Royal Phil. Socs. Prize, 1961. Hobbies: Cosmogony; English Grammar; Woodwork; Mountain Walking. Address: Lyndhurst, Avenue Rd., Cranleigh, Surrey GU6 7LE, UK.

WILKOMIRSKA, Wanda, b. 1931, Warsaw, Poland. Violinist. Educ: Lodz Conserv., & in Budapest & France. m. Mieczyslaw F Rakowski, 1952, 2 s. Debut: age 7. Career: 1st orchl. appearance in Cracow, 1946; regular appearances w. leading orchs. throughout the world. Hons: State Awards, 1952, 1964; Var. for. prizes; num. decorations. Hobbies: Lit.; Theatre. Address: Dabrowki 13, Warsaw Saska Kepa, Poland.

WILKOMIRSKI, Józef, b. 15 May 1926, Kalisz, Poland. Conductor; Composer; Broadcasting Musical Popularizer &

Lecturer; Freelance Journalist. Educ: studied Hist. & Anthropol., Univ. of Lodz; Dip., Warsaw Acad. of Music, 1950; MA. m. 3 children. Debut: Warsaw Philharmonic, 1950. Career: Over 1000 concerts & perfs. in 16 countries of Europe, Am. & Asia; Also in Radio & TV. Compositions: (Ballet) The Fairy-tale of Prince Fair; Harp Concerto; Two symphoniettas; Symphonic suite 'The Royal Castle in Warsaw'; Symphonic poems; Sonatas for violin, cello, double bass; trio; Songs & other works; concerto for 4 harps; string quartet; sonata for viola; concertina for cello; double concerto for violin, cello & orch., 1977. Recordings for the broadcasting cos. of Poland, Ireland & Luxembourg. Mbr., Assn. of Polish Comps. Hons: The 'Pomeranian Gryphon' Medal, 1960; The Musical Prize, 1961; Cross of the Order 'Polonia Restituta', 1963; Medal for Merit in Culture, 1967; Prize for Public Cultivation of Music, 1970. Hobbies: Literature; History; Psychology. Address: Moniuski St. 41, 38-500 Walbrzych, Poland.

WILKOMIRSKI, Kazimierz, b. 1 Sept. 1900, Moscow, Russia. Cellist; Conductor; Composer. Educ: Imperial Conserv., Moscow; Dip. w. hon. mention, Nat. Conserv., Warsaw, 1923. m. (1) Maria Fryde; (2) Teresa Lisica-Sulkowska, 1 d. Debut: Wilkomirski Trio, Moscow, 1915. Career: Cellist, mbr. of chmbr. grps., 60 yrs.; Cond., symph. & opera, Poland, USSR, Czech., Hungary, Romania, France, Bulgaria, Iran, Israel, Cuba, E & W Germanies, 50 yrs.; radio & TV apps.; Prof., Conservs. in Lodz, Wroclaw, Gdansk & Warsaw; Dir., operas & symphs., Dansk & Wroclaw. Comps: str. quartet; 6 pieces & 12 études for cello. Recordings incl: P E Bach & Vivaldi cello concertos, 1967; Tchaikovsky trio; unaccompanied Bach suites, 1974. Publs: Cello technique & interpretation problems; Reminiscences (autobiog.). Contbr. to Ruch Muzyczny. Mbr. musical orgs. Recip. state & fest. prizes. Address: Hoza 54 m. 63, 00-682 Warszawa, Poland.

WILKSTRÖM, Inger E M, b. 1939, Göteborg, Sweden. Concert Pianist. Educ: Music Pedagogical Examn., Borgaskola, Stockholm, 1958; studied piano w. Prof. Gottfrid Boon, Prof. Bruno Seydlhofer & Illona Kabaos. Career: Guest Artist, Stockholm, Vienna, Spoleto & Dubrovnik Fests.; has made 4 tours of USA & 3 in USSR; makes frequent apps. thru'out Europe. Recordings: 10 albums w. Decca & RCA-Victor labels. Hobbies: Lit.; Skiing; Painting. Address: Champ Soleil, 1295 Tannay, Switzerland.

WILLANDER, Alfred, b. 24 Feb. 1947, Baden, Austria. Administrator; Director. Educ: Dr., musicol., Univ. of Vienna; pvte. study of piano & singing. m. Christa Fitzinger, 2 d. Career: Musikreferent der NÖ Landesregierung; Dir., Haydn Museum, Rohrau. Publ: Beiträge zur Musikgeschichte der Stadt Baden und das Archiv der Stadtpfarrkirche St. Stefan zu Baden. Contbr. of sev. bibliographical articles. Mbrships: NÖ Tonkünstlerorchester (chmn. of Bd. of Dirs.); Wiener Musikseminar (exec. Bd.); Baden Kammerchor (Pres.); hon. mbr., treas., nieder-österreichischer musikalische Vereine. Hobbies: Music; Travel; Playing piano w. others. Address: Mozartstr. 20, 2500 Baden, Austria.

WILLCOCKS, (Sir) David, b. 30 Dec. 1919. Director of the Royal College of Music. Educ: RCM, 1938-39; King's Coll., Cambridge Univ. (Organ Scholar), 1939-40 & 45-47; MA, 1948; MusB, 1946; FRCO, 1938; CHM, 1939, ARCM, 1939; ADCM, 1946. m. Rachel G Blyth, 2 s., 2 d. Career: Fellow, King's Coll., Cambridge, 1947-51; Cond., Cambridge Phil. Soc., 1947; Organist, Salisbury Cath., 1947-50; Organist, Worcester Cath., 1950-57; Cond., City of Birmingham Choir, 1950-57; Cond., Bradford Fest. Choral Soc., 1955-74; Fellow & Dir. of Music, King's Coll., Cambridge Univ., 1957-73; Cond., Cambridge Univ. Music Soc., 1958-73; Univ. Organist, Cambridge, 1958-74; Lectr., Cambridge, 1957-74; Music Dir., The Bach Choir, 1960-; in present position since 1974. Comp. of misc. ch. music & organ music. Over 70 recordings w. King's Coll. Choir, The Bach Choir, Acad. of St. Martin-in-the-Fields, LSO, etc. Gen. Ed., Oxford Ch. Music, 1960-; Jt. Ed., Carols for Choirs, vols. I, II, & III & Anthems for Men's Voices, vols. I & II. Mbrships: VP (Pres. 1966-68) RCO; Coun. Mbr., RSCM; VP, Rural Music Schls.; VP, Cambridge Phil. Soc. Hons: MC, 1944; CBE, 1971; Hon. MA, Bradford Univ., 1973; Hon. DMus, Exeter Univ., 1976; FTCL, 1976; FRNCM; FRCM; FTCL; DMus, Leicester Univ., 1977. Address: Royal Coll. of Music, Prince Consort Rd., London SW7, UK. 1, 3, 14, 28.

WILLETT, Susan Mary, b. 19 May 1954, Bunbury, UK. Soprano; Teacher of Piano & Singing. Educ: Lic., Royal Acad. of Music; Britten-Pears Schl. for Advanced Musical Studies. Debut: Westminster Abbey. Career: Perf. of Messiah, 1976. Mbr., Incorp. Soc. of Musicians. Hons: Gertrude Norman Prize, Royal Acad. of Music, 1975. Hobbies: Embroidery; Engl. Hist. Address: 6 Churchyardside, Nantwich, Cheshire, CW5 5S1, UK.

WILLETTS, Pamela Joan, b. 9 April 1929, Kingston-on-Thames, UK. Deputy Keeper. Educ: BA (Cantab.); LTCL, piano. m. Edgar Gordon, 1 s. Career: Deputy Keeper, Dept. of MSS, British Library. Publs: The Henry Lawes Manuscript, 1969; Beethoven and England, 1970; Handlist of Music Manuscripts acquired 1908-67, 1970. Contbr. to: Music and Letters; Musical Times; British Museum Quarterly; British Library Jrnl.; Chelys, etc. Hobbies: Practical Music (violin, viol, baroque cornett); Languages. Address: Glenburn, Cardigan Rd., Barnes, London SW13, UK. 14.

WILLIAMS, Adrian, b. 30 Apr. 1956, Watford, UK. Composer; Pianist. Educ: Watford Schl. of Music; TCL; RAM; RCM; LRAM & ARCM (piano perf.). Career: Comp.-in-Residence, Charterhouse Schl., 1980-83; piano & chmbr. music recitals; accomp., choirs & instrumentalists; fest. adjudicator; arranger; copyist; tchr. Comps: Explorations & Metamorphoses, op. 13 for orch. (perf. on Radio London). Contbr. to RCM Mag. Mbrships: ISM; Composers' Guild; Performing Right Soc.; RCM Union; Ecology Party. Hons: Leverhulme Scholarship, 1977; Howells Prize & Hopkinson Silver Medal (piano), 1977; Horowitz Prize, 1978; Menuhin Prize, 1978; Charterhouse Award, 1979. Hobbies: Railways; Canals; Walking; Cycling; Poetry; Lit.; Cartography; Photography. Address: Charterhouse Schl., Godalming, Surrey GU7 2DX, UK.

WILLIAMS, Carol Janice, b. 23 Oct. 1950, Adelaide, Aust. Musicologist. Educ: BMus, Adelaide Univ.; PhD studies, ibid.; AMEB, Grade 7 (piano), Grade 5 (theory). m. Richard G D Roberts, 1 d. Career: Pt. time tchng., Adelaide Univ. & Sturt Co. of Advanced Educ.; present lectr. in musicol., Monash Univ., specialising in 14th century music. Contbr. to Miscellanea Musicologica. Mbrships: Musicol. Soc. of Aust. (sec., 1979-80); Musicol. Soc. of S. Aust.; Musicol. Soc. of Vic. Hobbies: Cooking; Reading. Address: 10A Black St., Middle Brighton, Vic. 3186, Aust.

WILLIAMS, David Russell, b. 21 Oct. 1932, Indpls., Ind., USA. Assistant Professor of Music Theory. Educ: AB, Columbia coll., NYC; MA, Columbia Univ., NYC; PhD, Univ. of Rochester, NY. m. Elsa Buehlmann. Career: Asst. Prof. of Music Theory, Administrator, MMus. in Perf. & Lit., Sect. of the Fac., Eastman Schl. of Music, Rochester, NY. Compositions: Five States of Mind, for orch.; Suite for Oboe; Fanfare, brass quintet; Recitation for Trombone Choir. Recordings: Rsch. Asst., Meantone Temperament in Theory & Practice, & The Theory & Practice of Just Intonation. Publs: Bibliography of the History of Music Theory, 2nd Ed., 1971; Ed., Opera Volume, New Scribner Music Library, 1972. Mbrships: Sec., Coll. Music Soc., 1973-; Coun., ibid, 1972-74; NY State Chmn. of Theory & Comp., Music Tchrs. Nat. Assn.; State Exec. Bd., ibid, 1970-74; Pres., Bd. of Dirs., Opera Theatre of Rochester, 1974; Corporate Bd., Hochstein Schl. of Music, Rochester; Am. Music Ctr., Am. Musicol. Soc.; Nat. Assn. of Schls. of Music; Phi Beta Kappa; Phi Mu Alpha; Pi Kappa Lambda; Rochester Club. Hons: Eastman Schl. of Music Publ. Award, 1970; 3rd Prize, Edward Benjamin Contest for Tranquil Music, 1963. Hobby: Puzzles; Cryptograms. Mgmt: ASCAP. Address: 520 East Ave., Rochester, NY 14607, USA. 6, 23, 28, 29.

WILLIAMS, Edgar, b. 11 Mar. 1926, Porth-Rhondda, Wales, UK. Principal Lecturer; Bassoonist. Educ: TCL. m. Patricia Ann Jones, 2 d. Career: Prin. Bassoon, Bournemouth Symph. Orch., 1951-63; Freelance w. prin. London Orchs., 1963-70; Hd., Wind instrument Dept., RSAM, 1970-; Perf. in Fests. in Aldeburgh, Edinburgh, Berlin, Moscow, Prague, Warsaw, USA. Recordings: Num. recordings w. LSO, RPO, English Chmbr. Orch., Melos Ensemble & other grps. Hobbies: Theatre; Reading. Address: Westbourne Gardens, Glasgow, G12, UK.

WILLIAMS, Edwin Lynn, b. 9 July 1947, Crawfordsville, Ind., USA. Professor of Brass, Theory; Assistant Director of Bands. Educ: BMus, DePauw Univ., 1969; MMus, Ind. Univ., 1971; Vienna Acad. of Music, 1973; Doctl. Cand., Coll.-Conserv. of Music, Univ. of Cincinnati, 1975-. m. Rosemary Zika Williams. Career: Soloist, US State Dept. sponsored Orchs. in Europe; 1st Trumpet, Cinn. Ballet Orch.; Cinn. Opera Orch.; Cinn. Symph. May Fest.; Prin. Trumpet, Lima Symph. Orch., 1973-; Dir., Lima Area Youth Orch., 1975-. Mbrships: Phi Mu Alpha Sinfonia; Nat. Band Assn.; Nat. Jazz Educators Assn.; Coll. Band Dirs. Nat. Assn.; MENC; Ohio Music Educators Assn.; Int. Trumpet Guild; Kappa Kappa Psi. Recip. Fulbright-Hayes Scholarship, 1972-73. Hobby: Hiking. Address: 216 E College Ave., Ada, OH 45810, USA. 29.

WILLIAMS, (Horace) Robert, b. 14 Nov. 1932, Norristown, Pa., USA. Hornist; Music Educator. Educ: BS in Music Educ., Pa. State Coll., West Chester; MM in Music Educ., & postgrad. study, Eastman Schl. of Music. m. Geraldine Hubbard, 1 s., 2 d.

Career: Hornist, US Army, Columbia, SC, & with Symph. Orchs. of Lancaster, Pa., Greece, NY, & Livermore, Calif.; Music Educator in Lancaster, Pa., Webster, NY, Alburquerque, NM & Oakland, Calif.; Classical music announcer & commentator, Radio WBFB, Rochester, NY, 1965-70; Cond., Pleasanton Community Band, 1978-. Recordings: w. Franklin & Marshall Coll. Ensembles, Lancaster, Pa., 1959-62; Lancaster Opera Theatre, 1962-64; as Cond., Webster, NY Band Fest., 1970. Life Mbr., MENC. Hobbies: Skiing; Sailing; Gardening. Address: 7119 Valley Trails Dr., Pleasanton, CA 94566, USA.

WILLIAMS, Huw Tregelles, b. 13 Mar. 1949, Gowerton, Swansea, S Wales, UK. BBC Music Producer-Wales. Educ: BMus, MA, Univ. Coll., Cardiff, 1967-72; FRCO. Career: Radio 3 Organ Recitalist. Mbr., RCO. Hons: 1st Class Hons., BMus, 1970; John Morgan Lloyd Mem. Scholarship, Univ. Coll. of Wales, & Turpin Prize, RCO, both 1971. Hobbies: Reading; Good food; Listening to all kinds of music. Address: c/o Music Dept., Broadcasting House, Llandaff, Cardiff, UK.

WILLIAMS, John Ratcliffe, b. 24 Sept. 1920, Swansea, Wales, UK. Organist; Professor. Educ: Chorister, All Saints Ch., Margaret St., London; Choral Scholar, St. John's Coll., Cambridge; MusB., MA; FRCO; hon. RCM. m. Valerie Trimble, 4 c. Career: Organist & Master of the Music, The Chapel Royal of St. Peter-ad-Vincula, Her Majesty's Tower of London; Prof., RCM; former organist & choirmaster, All Saints Ch., Margaret St., London; radio apps. as cond. & speaker. Recording: Music for Kings & Queens of England; Music at the Tower. Contbr. to The Times (music reviews). Hobbies: Sailing; Cooking; Walking. Address: 13 Drayton Gdns., London SW10, UK.

WILLIAMS, Maria Elizabeth, b. 7 Sept. 1952, Barry, S Glamorgan, Wales, UK. Concert & Opera Singer (Soprano). Educ: Welsh Coll. of Music & Drama; London Opera Ctr.; FTCL; LTCL; LWCMD; LRAM (double dip.). Career: num. freelance apps. incl. Royal Fest. Hall, Fairfield Hall, Sadler's Wells & Collegiate Theatres; apps. w. Handel Opera Soc., Unicorn Opera, Oxford Univ. Fac. of Music; guest soloist w. major Welsh choirs; concert & recital apps. throughout UK; fest. apps. incl. Lower Machen, Rhymney Valley Arts, Llantilio Crossenny. Mbrships: ISM; Equity. Hons: Creative Arts Award, 1974; Worshipful Co. of Musicians Silver Medal, 1974; Peter Moores Fndn. Award, 1977; Welsh Arts Coun. Scholarship, 1976; R V Williams Trust Fund Award, 1978. Hobbies: History; Historical Buildings; Exhibitions; Cooking; Antiques. Address: Harton House, 67 Tynewydd Rd., Barry, S Glamorgan CF6 6BA, Wales, UK.

WILLIAMS, Mary Ruth, b. London, UK. Opera Singer (soprano). Educ: LRAM (Singing Tchr.). Debut: Kaiserlautern, Germany. Career: Operatic soprano, Kaiserlautern, 2 yrs.; Osnabruck, 1 yr., Kiel, 2 yrs. & other guest appearances in W Germany; currently w. Engl. Nat. Opera. Hobbies: Fast Cars; Painting; Pottery. Address: 21 Almorah Rd., Islington, London N1, UK.

WILLIAMS, Meirion, b. 19 July 1901, Dyffryn, Merioneth, UK. Composer; Pianist; Organist; Adjudicator. Educ: 2 Dips. in Music, Univ. of Wales; ARAM, LRAM. m. Gwendolyn Roberts, 1 d. Debut: Piano recital, Grotrian Hall, London. Career: Pianist, Accompanist, BBC Radio, TV & HTV; Organist, St. Benet Welsh Ch., London; Adjudicator, Nat. Eisteddfod of Wales, other maj. Welsh Fests.; Piano recitals, Welsh Arts Coun. Compositions: Songs & Partsongs (publd. & recorded). Contbr. to Welsh Music Mag. Mbrship: Guild for Promotion of Welsh Music. Hobbies: Gardening; Fishing. Address: 18 Grasmere Ave., Wembley, Middx., UK. 3.

WILLIAMS, Patrick Joseph, b. 18 Sept. 1951, Liverpool, UK. Performer on Flute & Piccolo. Educ: Perf.'s Course, Royal Manchester Coll. of Music, 1968-72. Debut: Belfast, 1972. Career: freelance engagements w. most leading Brit. Orchs. beginning w. BBC Northern Symph. Orch.; permanent engagements w. Ulster Orch., 1972-73 & Welsh Philharmonia, 1973-75; currently Prin. Flute, Royal Ballet Orch., Covent Gdn. Mbr., ISM. Recip. Award for most promising young musician, Pernod of Paris, 1971. Hobbies: Tennis; Football; Cricket; Reading. Address: 13 Belmont Dr., Newsham Pk., Liverpool, L6 7UW, UK.

WILLIAMS, Peter Fredric, b. 14 May 1937, Wolverhampton, UK. Director of Russell Collection of Harpsichords & Clavichords, Edinburgh. Educ: MA, MusB, PhD, Univ. Cambridge; Studied harpsichord w. Thurston Dart & Gustav Leonhardt. Career: Perf. specialized concerts & recordings, mostly J S Bach. Recordings: Extensive series, BBC Sound Archives discs of Couperin, Bull, Bach, etc. Publs: The European Organ, 1966; Figured Bass Accompaniment, 1970; Organ Music of J S Bach, 1972; Ed., Organ Yearbook, 1969-; Transl. The Organ in the Netherlands, Peeters/Vente. Contbr. to

profl. mags. Address: Dept. of Music, University of Edinburgh, Edinburgh, UK.

WILLIAMS, Richard, b. 8 Sept. 1939, Long Beach, Calif., USA. Conductor. Educ: BA Music Theory, Calif. State Univ., Long Beach; MA, Cond., Brigham Young Univ. m. Linda, 4 s., 1 d. Career: Musical Dir., Cedar Rapids Symph. Orch., 1970-; Amici Della Musica, 1964-69; Cabrillo Summer Fest., 1969; Guest Cond., Czech. Phil., BBC Scottish Symph. Orch., BBC Welsh Symph. Orch., Calgary Phil., Orchestre Regionale de Mulhouse (France), Dutch Radio Phil.; Gen. Music Dir., Nat. Theatre of Kenya Opera Prods. Publs: Translation - Shostakovich: Symph. No. 13 (English). Mbrships: Am. Symph. Orch. League; Iowa Arts Coun. Hobby: Tennis. Address: 201 Liberty Dr. SE, Cedar Rapids, IA 52403, USA.

WILLIAMS, Roger Bevan, b. 30 Aug. 1943, Swansea, Wales, UK. Music Lecturer; Conductor; Harpsichordist. Educ: BMus, Hons., Univ. Coll., Cardiff; PhD, Kings Coll., Cambridge; PGTC, Univ. of London, Goldsmith's Coll.; FTCL; ARCM; ARCO. Career: Lectr., Univ. of Aberdeen. Comps: Quartet for guitars, 1976; Cinq Chansons, 1978. Mbrships: Royal Musical Assn.; ISM. Hobbies: Cooking; Dominoes; Chess; Go. Address: Music Dept., Univ. of Aberdeen, Powis Gate, College Bounds, Old Aberdeen, UK.

WILLIAMS, Rosemary Zika, b. 13 Sept. 1949, Chicago, Ill., USA. Lecturer in Piano. Educ: BMus, Ind. Univ., 1971; Hochschule für Musik und Darstellende Kunst, Vienna, Austria, 1972; Cinn. Coll. Conserv. of Music, 1975-. Piano study w. Alfonso Montecino, Walter Panhofer & Jeanne Kirstein. m. Edwin Lynn Williams. Career: Perfs. in Austria, NY, Ill., Ind. & Ohio; piano arrs. Mbrships: Tau Beta Sigma; Mu Phi Epsilon; NGPT; Am. Music Scholarship Assn.; S Ohio Music Educs. Assn. Hobbies: Reading; Crafts; Bicycling. Address: 216 E Coll. Ave., Ada, OH 45810, USA. 5, 29.

WILLIAMS, Sioned, b. 1 July 1953, Mancot, Clwyd, N Wales, UK. Harpist. Educ: Welsh Coll. of Music & Drama, 1971-74; LWCMD; LRAM; Advanced Course, RAM, 1974-76; Dip. RAM. m. Kim A L Sargeant. Debut: Purcell Room - Park Lane Group Young Artists/20th Century Music, 1977; Carnegie Hall, NY, 1980. Career: Apps. world-wide incl. apps. w. LSO, Philharmonia, LPO, BBCSO, CBSO, Royal Ballet, London Sinfonietta, Royal Opera House, SNO; Solo, chmbr. & concerto perfs.; Theatre, Radio, TV & Fest. apps.; Prof. of Harp, RCM Junion Dept. Comps: Cyfres I'r Delyn, 1973 (Special prize, 17th Int. Harp Week). Solo debut recording. Contbr. to: UKHA Mag. Mbrships: Telynores Garmon in Bardic Circle; ISM; UK Harpists Assn. Recip., num. prizes, scholarships, etc. Hobbies: Embroidery; Reading. Address: 37A Curzon Rd., London N10 2RB, UK. 27.

WILLIAMS, William Sidney Gwynn, b. 1896, Plas Hafod, Llangollen, N Wales. Composer; Editor; Publisher; Adjudicator; Administrator. m. Elizabeth Eleanor Davies. Career: Organiser of Music, Gorsedd of Bards, Wales, 1923-; Gen. Ed., The Gwynn Publishing Co., Llangollen, 1937-77; Music Dir., Llangollen Int. Music Eisteddfod, 1946-77; Chmn., Music Committee, Nat. Eisteddfod, 1953-; Vice Chmn., Union of Welsh Publrs. & Booksellers, 1954-, Chmn., 1963; Vice Chmn., Brit. Fedn. of Music Fests., 1969-77; Chmn., Welsh Amateur Music Fedn., 1969-. Comps. incl: songs, part-songs, piano & violin solos & orch. miniatures of Welsh character. Publs. incl: Welsh National Music & Dance, 1932, 5th Ed., 1975; Ed. of many collections of Welsh folksongs & dances inclng. Old Welsh Folk Songs, 1927 & '50, Caneuon y Cymry, 1933, Caneuon y Gymanfa, 1936, Traditional Songs of the Welsh, Vols. I & II, 1961 & '63; Harp Tunes of Wales, 1962. Mbrships: Sec., Welsh Folk Song Soc., 1942-58, Ed., 1946-, Chmn., 1958-; Treas., Int. Folk Music Council, 1947-; Chmn., Welsh Folk Dance Soc., 1949-; Corres. Mbr., Acad. Petrarca, Italy. Hons: OBE; MA; FRSA; Hon. RAM; Hon. RCM; Hon. FTSC; Cavaliere al Merito della Repubblica Italiana. Address: Plas Hafod, Llangollen, N Wales, LL20 8SN, UK. 3.

WILLIAMS-JONES, Pearl, b. 28 June 1931, Washington, DC, USA. Afro-American Gospel Singer; Pianist; Music Educator; Lecturer, Research, Writer, Consultant on Afro-American Gospel Music. Educ: BMus, Howard Univ. Schl. of Music, 1953; MMus, ibid., 1957; HHD, Lycoming coll., Pa. m. William V Jones, 1 s., 1 d. Career: Gospel Music Concert Artist w. concerts in chs., schls. & univs.; Apps. at Town Hall, NYC; Wigmore Hall, London, Sophiensalle, Munich; Am. Cultural Ctr., Paris, 1966; Currently Asst. Prof. of Music, Fed. City Coll., Wash. DC. Num. recordings. Contbr. to profl. jrnls. Mbrships. incl: Pi Kappa Lambda. Hons. incl: Grant from Nat. Endowment for Arts, 1974. Hobby: Travel. Address: 4720 16th St. NW, Washington, DC 20011, USA.

WILLIAMSON, John Ramsden, b. 31 Oct. 1929, Manchester, UK. Teacher; Composer; Pianist. Educ: Royal Manchester Coll. of Music, 1949-52; Assoc., ibid., 1952; Lic., Royal Acad. of Music, 1961; BMus, Dunelm, 1973; Fellow, London Coll. of Music, 1977. m. Valmai Roberts, 2 s. Career: Schl. Music Tchr., 5 schls. in Engl. & Wales, 1952-76; Piano Tutor, Notre Dame Coll. of Educ., Liverpool; Pvte. tchr. of piano & harmony. Compositions incl: Piano concerto; 3 Piano Sonatas; Sonatina; Cantata; String Quartet; Song Cycle; 13 piano preludes. Mbrships: Incorp. Soc. of Musicians; Composers' Guild of GB. Hons. incl: Barlow Cup for Composition, Chester Musical Festival, 1972, 1978, 1979; 1st Prize, Rhys James Eisteddfod, Lampeter, 1971. Hobbies: Cyling; Gardening. Address: 11a Calthorpe Dr., Prestatyn, Clwyd, Wales, LL19, 9RF, UK.

WILLIAMSON, Malcolm Benjamin Graham Christopher, b. 21 Nov. 1931, Sydney, NSW, Aust. Composer; Pianist; Organist. Educ: Sydney Conserv.; pvte. study of comp. w. Sir E Goossens, Elizabeth Lutyens & Erwin Stein. m. Dolores Irene Daniel, 1 s., 2 d. Debut: (Organ) London, UK, 1956. Career: Soloist w. num. orchs. inclng. LPO, LSO, BBC Symph., Engl. Chambr. Orchs., Halle, Danish Radio Orch., Ulster, Vienna, Lusaka, Haifa, Sydney & Melbourne Symphs. Comps. incl: Operas: Our Man in Havana, 1963; The Violins of St. Jacques, 1966; The Red Sea, 1972. Ballets: Sinfonietta, 1965; Spectrum, 1967. Orchl. Works: Concerti; Ensemble Works; Miniature Operas; Organ Works; Vocal, Choral & Piano Music; TV & Film Music. (recorded) The Happy Prince, Julius Caesar Jones (operas); Sonata No. 2; Violin Concerto. Contbr. to var. papers & jrnls., UK, USA & Sweden. Mbrships incl: CGGB. Hons: Sir A Bax Memorial Prize, 1963; DMus, Westminster Choir Coll., Princeton, NJ, USA, 1971; Creative Arts Fellowship, Aust. Nat. Univ., Canberra, 1973, Master of the Queen's Musick, 1975. Hobbies: Literature; Swimming. Mgmt: John Coast, Park Close, London SW1. Address: 32 Hertford Ave., London SW14, UK. 1, 3, 15, 16, 21.

WILLIAMSON, Paul, b. 16 Jan. 1947, Frome, Somerset, UK. Performer; Instrument Maker. Educ: Dip. Music Educ., Dartington Coll. of Arts. m. Hilary Jean Williamson, 1 s., 1 d. Career incls: Music Tchr. & Cond., Bucks., UK, 1968-72; Musical Instrument Maker & Profl. Perf. w. The Oriana Early Music Consort; Mbr., Quintain; Apps. w. Peasants All on BBC radio & TV, also ITV, in music clubs & theatres throughout Engl.; Early Percussion instruments made and sold to countries inclng. Japan, Argentine, Aust., Can., Europe & UK; Perf. on viol, crumhorn, psaltery, rebec, recorder, medieval bagpipes, pipe & tabor. Recordings: A Handful of Pleasant Delites; Countrie Faire. Mbrships: ISM; FOMRHI. Mgmt: Plant Life Records & Agency. Address: The Red Last, Shepeau Stow, Whaplode Drove, Spalding, Lincs., UK.

WILLIS, Stephen Charles, b. 17 Dec. 1946, Collingwood, Ont., Can. Musicologist; Archivist. Educ: Assoc. of Music, Western Ont. Conserv. of Music, 1965; BA, Univ. Western Ont., 1969; MA, Columbia Univ., 1971; PhD, ibid., 1975. m. Louise-Marie Pauline Courtemanche-Willis, 1 child. Career: Hd. Manuscript Collection, Music Div., Nat. Lib. of Can., 1977-. Contbr. to Current Musicol.; Can. Assn. of Music Libns. Newsletter. Mbr. num. profl. orgs. Hons. incl: Columbia Univ. Fellowship, 1969-72; Can. Coun. Doct. Fellowship, 1972-74. Hobbies: Philately; Numismatics; Choral Singing; Swimming; Cross-country Running; Gardening. Address: 89 Cockburn St., Richmond, Ont. KOA 2ZO, Canada.

WILLIS, Suzanne Eileen, b. 25 May 1951, New Brunswick, NJ, USA. Graduate Student in Physics. Educ: BA, Mt. Holyoke Coll., 1972; MPhil, Yale Univ., 1974. m. Arthur Lane Dana. Career: perf. in Aleksandr Nevsky cantata w. Mt. Holyoke Coll. Glee Club & Detroit Symph. Orch., Detroit, Carnegie Hall, NYC & Kennedy Ctr., Wash. DC, 1971. Recordings: w. Mt. Holyoke Glee Club & Chmbr. Singers, 1st United Meth. Ch. of Los Alamos Choir. Mbrships: Los Alamos Chapt., Am. Recorder Soc.; Choir of 1st United Meth. Ch., Los Alamos, NM; Los Alamos Choral Soc.; Los Alamos Arts Council. Hobbies: Physics of Musical Instruments; Backpacking; Needlepoint. Address: 2329B 33rd St., Los Alamos, NM 87544, USA.

WILLISEGGER, Hansruedi, b. 22 Apr. 1935, Etiswil/Lucerne, Switz. Professor of Piano, Organ, Theory, Music Instruction, Improvisation & Dancing Instruction. Educ: Tchrs. & Concert Dip. in Piano; Tchrs. Seminar, Hitzkirch, Lucerne; Dip., Organ, cond., theory, comp. & schoolmusic. m. Nella Bussmann, 3 d. Career: Fndr. & Dir., Lucerne Singers, 1966 & the Lucerne Singers Ensemble, 1970; Dir., Emmenbrücke Mixed Choirs; Tchr., Hitzkirch Tchrs. Seminar; Piano Tchr., Lucerne Conserv.; Tchr. of dancing instrn. & improvisation, Acad. for Schl. & Ch. Music. Comps. publd: religious music; folksongs; large organ works; 6 choral & orchl. pieces. Recordings: discs w. Lucerne Singers. Publs: Kleine Chorschule, 1973. Contbr. of music criticism to var. jrnls. Mbrships. incl: Exec., European Fedn. of Youth Choirs; Co-Fndr., Swiss Fedn. of Youth Choirs; VP, Lucerne Dist., Swiss Music Educ. Assn. Recip., hons. as choral dir. & comp. of organ works. Address: Alpstr. 34, CH-6020 Emmenbrücke/Lucerne, Switz.

WILLMAN, Allan Arthur, b. 11 May 1909, Hinckley, Ill., USA. Pianist; Composer; Music Educator. Educ: BMus, Knox Coll., Galesburg, Ill., 1928; MMus, Chgo. Musical Coll. Ill., 1930; pvte. study w. Natia Boulanger & Thomas de Hartmann, Paris, France, 1935-36. m. Regina Hansen Willman (dec.). Career: Num. apps. as soloist & w. var. artists in USA; Duo recitals w. Rudolf Kolisch (violin) in Germany, Austria, Switzerland, France, UK (for BBC) & Ireland; European tour for US Dept. of State; Broadcasts of Am. piano music, France & Switzerland; Judge, Int. Competiton, Contemporary Music Fest., Darmstadt, Germany; Vis. Lectr., Univ. of Calif. at Berkeley; currently Emeritus Prof. Dept. of Music, Univ. of Wyo. Compositions: Works performed by Boston Symph. Orch., NBC Radio Orch. & other major orchs., chmbr. grps. & artists; (publd.) Songs & minor piano pieces. Publ: Tran., A Honneger, I Am A Composer (w. W O). Mbrships. incl: Nat. Assn. Music Execs. in State Univs.; Am. Music Ctr.; MTNA; Wyo. Music Tchrs. Assn. (Fndr. & Pres.); Pi Kappa Lambda. Hons. incl: 1000 Dollar Paderewski Award for orchl. work, 1935. Hobby: Collecting Old Books on Music. Address: Dept. of Music, Univ. of Wyoming, Laramie, WY 82071, USA.

WILLOUGHBY, Louis Philippe Charles, b. 23 April 1903, London, UK. Violinist; Composer. Educ: Studied violin w. Sascha Lassarson, Russian Conserv. & Carl Flesch; Comp. w. Matyas Seiber. m. Beatrice Emma, 2 s., 2 d. Career: Soloist; Ldr. of Boyd Neel String Orch.; Willoughby String Quartet; Albion Trio; Fndr. & one of Dirs. of Pro Ar Orch.; Tchr. Mbr. Royal Soc. of Musicians. Mbr., Theosophical Soc. Hobby: Horticulture. Address: 8A The Drive, Sevenoaks, Kent TN13 1HB, UK.

WILLS, Arthur, b. 19 Sept. 1926, Coventry, UK. Organist; Composer. Educ: BMus, Dunelm; FRCO. (CHM); ADCM; ARSCM. m. Mary Elizabeth Wills, 1 s., 1 d. Career: Organist, Ely Cathedral, 1958-; Prof., RAM, 1964-; Dir. of Music, King's Schl., Ely, 1953-65; Supvsr., Univ. of Cambridge, 1966-; Examiner, RSM, 1966-; 6 recital tours of N Am., tours of Holland, France & Scandinavia. Comps. incl: Concerto for Organ; Strings & Timpani; Sonata for Organ; Trio-Sonata for Organ; Sonata for Guitar; 5 Pieces for Organ; Christmas Meditations; Variations on a Carol; Variations on 'Amazing Grace'; 2 Preludes & Fugues; num. short works for organ & choral works. Author, The Art of Organ Improvisation, 1975. Contbr. to: Musical Times; Comp. Mag.; Organist Review. Mbrships: Cathedral Organists Assn.; RAM Club; Savage Club; CGGB. Hons: Hon. RAM, 1974; Hon. FLCM, 1966. Hobbies: Antiques; Travel; Indian Philos.; Lit. Mgmt: Music Int. Address: The Old Sacristy, The Coll., Ely, Cambs., UK. 1, 3, 28.

WILLSHIRE, James Havilland, b. 25 July 1953, Lapford, Devonshire, UK. Piano Teacher; Pianist. Educ: Postgrad. Cert. in Educ., Univ. Manchester; Grad., Royal Northern Coll. of Music (merit in perf.); Assoc., ibid. (Piano tchr.); Assoc., ibid. (Perf. Dip. in Accompaniment); Assoc., ibid. (Solo Perf. Dip.). Career: Recordings & Broadcasts as soloist & accompanist for BBC Radio; Piano Recitals; Pvte. Piano Tchr.; Piano Tchr., Wigan Educ. Auth. Mbr., Incorp. Soc. of Musicians. Hobbies: Hist.; Lit.; Motoring. Address: 22 Okehampton Crescent, Sale, Cheshire, M33 5HR, UK.

WILLSON, Meredith, b. 18 May 1902, Mason City, Iowa, USA. Flautist; Composer; Conductor; Author. Educ: Pvte. study w. Henry Hadley, Julius Gold, Bernard Wagenaar, Georges Barrere, Damrosch Inst. of Music. m. (1) Elizabeth Wilson (div.), (2) Ralina Zarova (dec.), (3) Rosemary Sullivan. Debut: Mason City, Iowa. Career: 1st-Chair flautist w. J P Sousa; Asst. 1st chair flautist, NY Phil. Compositions incl: May the Good Lord Bless & Keep You; You & I; 76 Trombones; Goodnight My Someone; Till There Was You; Libretto & score for The Music Man; Score for The Unsinkable Molly Brown & Here's Love. Publs. incl: The Music Man; And There I Stood with My Piccolo; Eggs I Have Laid. Contbr. to jrnls. Mbrships. incl: ASCAP; The Family, San Fran.; Am. Guild of Authors & Comps.; Comps. & Lyricists Guild of Am.; Nat. Acad. of Recording Arts & Scis. Hons. incl: Edwin Franko Goldman Citation, 1964; 3 hon. docts. Hobbies incl: Barbershop quartet singing; Croquet; Swimming. Address: 1750 Westridge Rd., LA, CA, USA. 2, 3, 9.

WILMA-BAGNIUK, Sofia Anna, b. 8 June 1929, Warsaw, Poland. Vocalist. Educ: BA, Warsaw Acad. of Music. m. Kazimierz Bagniuk, 1 d. Debut: as Blonde in The Abduction from the Seraglio, Warsaw Phil. Hall & in Rostock, German Dem. Repub. Career: Wolksteater, Rostock; Grand Opera House, Warsaw; Warsaw Chmbr. Music Opera broadcast of Telemann's Pimpinone; radio broadcasts, Polish Radio & Radio Hilversum. Recordings: Polskie Nagranie; Veriton. Mbrships: Soc. of Polish Musicians; Warsaw Soc. of Musicians. Hons. incl: Hungarian Radio & TV Prize, Ferenc Erkel Int. Competition, Budapest, 1960; 1st Prize, Int. Music Competition, s'Hertogenbosch, Holland, 1962. Hobbies: Knitting; Crochet; Literature. Mgmt: Pagart. Address: ul. Wiślicka 1 m 18, 02-114 Warsaw, Poland.

WILMERS, Catherine Claire, b. 30 May 1952, London, UK. Cellist. Educ: RAM; LRAM; ARCM; Hochschule für Musik, Vienna. Debut: Wigmore Hall, London, 1979. Career: sub-prin. cellist, Engl. Nat. Opera Orch., 1976-79; sub-prin. cellist, LPO, 1979-; mbr., Parnassus Piano Trio. Mbrships: ISM; Musicians' Union. Hon: ISM Young Artists Wigmore Hall Recital, 1979. Hobbies: Skiing; Theatre; Travel. Address: 3 Kara Lodge, 14 Newton Grove, Bedford Pk., London W4, UK.

WILSON, Alfred, b. 12 June 1901, Perth, Scotland, UK. Organist. Educ: Perth; Glasgow; Toronto; pvte. musical educ. m. Dawn MacLeod. Debut: Perth Cathedral, aged 17. Career: Organist & choirmaster, Perth Baptist Ch., aged 14; Paisley Abbey, 1937; St. Andrew's, 1931, Toronto; num. recitals; Examiner, TCL since 1944; 25 overseas tours as examiner; Dir. of Music, St. Felix Schl. for Girls, 1966. Comps: works for choir, solo voice, organ & piano, perf. in 4 countries. Publs: East & West, 1968. Contbr. to profl. jrnls. Mbrships: Coun., RCCO, 1934; Pres., Glasgow Soc. of Organists, 1942. Hons: represented Can. as recitalist, NY, Int. Convention of Organists, 1935. Hobbies: Black & White Photography; Art Subjects. Address: 6 West End, Cove, Berwickshire, Scotland, UK. 29.

WILSON, Allan Harold, b. 5 Sept. 1949, London UK. Freelance Trumpet Player (also Natural Trumpet & Cornetto); Brass Teacher & Conductor. Educ: LRAM; LGSM; MMus, SUNY at Fredonia, USA. Debut: w. E Ham Symph. Orch., 1965. Career: Res. Cond., The Hanwell Band; TV app., Can.; perfs. on BBC radio w. Hendon Band, Hanwell Band, & Acad. of BBC Orch., Bristol; Solo perfs., UK, Can. & USA. Hons: John Solomon Prize (wind), & Sidney Langston Prize (brass), RAM, 1973. Hobbies: Music Writing & Arranging; Travel. Address: 109 Waters Drive, Mormede Pk., Staines, Middx. TW18 4RP, UK.

WILSON, Carolyn Patricia, b. 1 Nov. 1954, Wanstead, London, UK. Oboe & Violin Performer & Teacher. Educ: Lic., Royal Acad. of Music (Oboe Tchr.); Profl. Cert., ibid. Career: Participant, var. orchestral works; Working on book of arpeggios for oboe. Mbrships: Incorp. Soc. of Musicians; Royal Acad. of Music Club. Hobbies: Instructing on RAC/ACU Motorcycling scheme; Photography; Ice skating. Address: 19 Tree Tops, Brentwood, Essex, CM15 9DE, UK.

WILSON, Catherine, b. Glasgow, UK. Opera Singer. Educ: RAM. m. Leonard Hancock. Debut: w. Sadler's Wells Opera Co. Career: Glyndebourne; Sadler's Wells; Scottish Opera; Welsh Nat. Opera; Edinburgh Fest.; Cologne Opera; Engl. Opera Grp.; Geneva Opera; Santa Fe Fest.; Houston Grand Opera. Recordings: Albert Herring; Dido & Aeneas. Recip. Hon. Fellow, Royal Manchester Coll. of Music. Hobbies: Gardening; Cooking. Address: 18 St. Mary's Grove, London N1, UK.

WILSON, Cecelia Kaye, b. 3 July 1952, Nashville, Tenn., USA. Violinist; Pianist. Educ: BME, Geo Peabody Coll. for Tchrs., Nashville, Tenn. Career: Prin. 2nd Violinist, Tenn. All State Orch., 1968; Prin. 2nd Violinist, Quad State Orch., 1968; Asst. concertmistress, Nashville Youth Symph., 1972; 2nd Violinist, Nashville Symph. Orch. Mbrships: Iota Phi Chapt., Sigma Alpha Iota; Kappa Delta Epsilon. Hons: Myra Jackson Blair Schlrship., 1967-68, 1968-69; Schrlship., Univ. of Kan. Summer Music Camp, 1967, '68, '69; Nat. Order of Elks 'Most Outstanding Student' Schlrship., 1970-71; Elizabeth Buford Shepherd Schlrship., 1970-71, 1971-72, 1972-73, 1973-74; Music Schlrship., Music City Chapt., Am. Bus. Women's Assn., 1974-75. Hobbies: Cooking; Sewing; Reading; Travel. Address: 1208 McAlpine Avenue, Nashville, Tenn. 37216, USA.

WILSON, Charles Mills, b. 8 May 1931, Toronto, Can. Composer; Conductor; Teacher. Educ: BMus, DMus, Toronto Univ. m. Jennifer Wilson, 1 d., 2 s. Career: Music Supervisor, Public Schl., Guelph; Music Dir., Guelph Collegiate; Music Dir., Georgetown HS; Fac., Univ. of Sask., 1 yr.; Theory Tchr., McMaster Univ.; Tchr. of Hist. & Theory, Brock Univ.; Music Dir., Chalmers United Ch. Guelph; Fndr., Dir., Guelph Opera & Concert Singers (Cond. & Stage Dir.); Cond., Bach-Elgar Choir of Hamilton & Bach-Elgar Singers; Fndng. Pres., Ont. Choral

Fedn.; currently Tchr. of Comp., Univ. of Guelph & Chorusmaster, Can. Opera Co. Comps. incl: Three Song Cycles; (choral) Three Madrigals on Latin Lyrics; Dona Nobis Pacem, choir & brass; Cristo Paremus Canticam, choir & orch.; Missa Brevis, choir & brass/organ; (Orchl.) Symph. in A; Music for a Ballet; Conductus for piano & chmbr. orch.; var. chmbr. music & stage music. Recordings: Dona Nobis Pacem; Brass Trio. Contbr. to: Opera Can. Mbrships: Can. League of Comps.; Fndng. Pres., Ont. Choral Fedn. Hobby: Model Railways. Address: 395 Lakeshore Rd. E, Oakville, Ont., Can.

WILSON, Christopher Robert, b. 1 Oct. 1952, Hull, Yorks., UK. Oboist; Organist; Music Historian. Educ: BA, MA, Univ. of Oxford. Debut: Hull, 1960. Career incl: Mbr., Nat. Youth Orch., 1969-71; Solo oboe w. Schola Cantorum Oxon., BBC, 1973; Organist, Parish Ch. of St. Mary the Virgin, Iffley, Oxon.; Mbr., CESR, tours, 1977; Temporary Lectr., Univ. of St. Andrew's, 1978; Researcher for English Ayres prog., BBC, 1978-79. Publs: Musical Appendix to Jonson's Epicoene, 1979; Carol, Three Magi (w. F. W. Sternfeld), 1978. Contbr. to: Music & Letters; The Library. Mbrships: Royal Musical Assn.; RCO. Hons: J. I. Halstead Scholarship, 1976,'77; Louise Dyer Award, 1977; Grad. Scholarship., St. Cross Coll., Oxford, 1977, '78. Hobbies incl: Reading; Cinema; Gardening. Address: 4 St. Lawrence Rd., South Hinksey, Oxford, UK. 30.

WILSON, Clive, b. 23 Mar. 1932, Leeds, UK. Festival Director. Educ: Pvte. & Public Schls. Career: Fndr. & Dir., Harrogate Int. Fest., 1966-; co-fndr., Harrogate Concert Soc., 1961; chmn., ibid, 1967-; Mbrships: Chmn., Music Panel, Yorkshire Arts Assn., 1970-76; Committee, Leeds Int. Piano Competition, 1966-; Coun., Engl. Nat. Opera N, 1978-. Hobbies: European, Am. & Eng. Lit.; Record Collecting; Maintaining small country house. Address: Riseley House, Wormald Gn., Harrogate, N Yorks., UK.

WILSON, Donald M, b. 30 June 1937, Chgo., Ill., USA. Composer. Educ: BA, Univ. of Chgo., 1959; MA, Cornell Univ., 1962; DMA, ibid, 1965. m. Claire P. Wilson, 2 d. Career: Mgr. Cornell Univ. Orchs., 1960-64; Asst. to Music Dir., WRVR-FM, NYC, 1964-65; Music Dir., WUHY-FM, Phila., 1965-66; Prog. Dir., ibid, 1966-67; Instr. in Composition & Theory, Bowling Green State Univ., 1967-69; Asst. Prof., ibid, 1969-72; Assoc. Prof., 1972-; Dept. Chmn., 1973-77. Publs. Compositions for str. orch., 1960; Quintet for clarinet & str. quartet, 1960-61, rev. 1962; Doubles, a game-piece for 2 woodwinds, vs. 2 strings, 1964; Visions, 4 songs for mixed chorus & symph. band, 1969-70; Dedication for string orch. (recorded). Contbr. to Am. Music Tchr.; Contemp. Music Newsletter. Mbrships: Am. Composers Alliance, 1967-; Am. Music Ctr., 1964-; Phila. Composers Forum, 1966-67; Ohio Theory Composition Tchrs., 1968-; Ohio Music Tchrs. Assn., 1968-. Hons: 2nd Place, Joseph H Bearns Prize, Columbia Univ., 1963; Composition Award, Sr. Category, Ohio Music Tchrs. Assn., 1968-76; Instrumental Best-in-Category Award, Delius Competition, 1974. Hobbies: Chess; Cinema. Address: 550 W Wooster St., Bowling Green, OH 43402, USA. 6.

WILSON, James, b. Marion, Ohio, USA. Concert & Opera Singer (tenor). Educ: BMus, DePauw Univ.; MMus, New England Conserv. m. Sandra Darling, 1, 1 d. Debut: Concert, Carnegie Recital Hall, 1975. Career: w. off-Broadway Am. Savoyards; NYC Ctr. Gilbert & Sullivan Co.; opera appearances w. Toledo Symph., Goldowsky Opera, Little Orch. Soc., Ctrl. City Opera, Bronx Opera; Concert performances w. Symph. Orchs. of Dallas, Buffalo, Balt., Portland (Me.) & Detroit; Charter Mbr., the First Gilbert & Sullivan Quartette. Hobby: Reading. Address: 12 45 Longfellow Ave., Teaneck, NJ 07666, USA.

WILSON, James Robert, b. 3 Oct. 1928, Spokane, Wash., USA. Trumpeter. Educ: BA (Educ.), Eastern Wash. Coll., Cheney; MA (Music), Univ. of Wash., Seattle. m. Diane K, 2 s. Career: Trumpeter, USAF 560th Band, Spokane Symph., Tucson "Pops" Orch.; 1st Trumpet, Tucson Symph. & Ariz. Brass Quartet; Band Dir., College Place Public Schl., Wash., 1950-51, Heppner HS, Ore., 1953-56, Hood River HS, Ore. Sunnyside HS, (Chmn. of The Fine Arts, Band Dir., Stage Band Dir.), Tucson, Ariz., 1958-75. Contbr. to: Ariz. Music News. Mbrships: Am. Schl. Band Dir.'s Assn.; Ariz. Unit Pres., Nat. Assn. of Jazz Educators; 2nd VP, Ariz. Music Educators Assn.; Chmn., Southern Dist., Ariz. Band & Orch.; Dir.'s Assn.; Deleg., NEA. Hons: Copper Letter of Outstanding Citizen, City of Tucson, 1975. Hobbies: Golf; Travel. Address: 1518E Nevada Dr., Tucson, AZ 85706, USA. 28.

WILSON, Peter Gardner Wotherspoon, b. 19 Apr. 1936, Airdrie, Scotland, UK. Editor; Adjudicator; Conductor. Educ: Pt.-time studies, Royal Conserv. fo Music, Toronto, Can. m. Jean Campbell MacReavie Edmondson, 1 s., 1 d. Career: Prin.

Euphonium, Scottish CWS Band, 1958-61; Musical Dir., Kirkintilloch Silver Band, 1950-65; Musical Dir., Broxburn Band, 1965-70; Organising Sec., Nat. Brass Band Championships, 1971-77; Ed., British Bandsman, 1977-. Contbr. to Brit. Bandsman. Hobbies: Reading; Church Music; Art. Address: 151 Tudor Way, Rickmansworth, Herts., UK.

WILSON, Phillips Elder Jr. (Phil), b. 19 Jan. 1937, Belmont, Mass., USA. Trombonist; Composer; Arranger. Educ: New Engl. Conserv., 1955-58. m. Patricia Ann Ferry, 1 s., 1 d. Career incls: Instr., Admnstr., Berkelee Coll., 1965-74; on fac., Nat. Stage Band Camps, 1965-; Chmn., Afro-Am. Dept., New Engl. Conserv., 1974-; Music Dir., Big Money (TV show); Fndr., Outrageous Records, 1977; Instr., Beriller Coll., 1977. Comps. incl: Basically Blues; The Sound of the Wasp; Buttercrunch. Num. recordings w. noted jazz artists, titles incl: Live & Cookin'; Phil Wilson, Outrageous No. 3. Co-Author, Chord Studies for Trombone, 1967. Contbr. to jrnls. Mbr., Bd. of Dirs., Int. Trombone Assn. Hobbies: Jogging; Swimming; Music. Address: 8 Hammond Rd., Belmont, MA 02178, USA. 2.

WILSON, Sydney Virginia Payne, b. 28 Dec. 1942, Great Bend, Kan., USA. Professional Harpist; Music Educator. Educ: BA, N Tex. State Univ., Denton, Tex.; MMus, The New England Conserv. of Music, Boston, Mass.; Cert. as Sr. Tchr., Yamaha Music Schl., Downey, Calif., 1973. m. Allen F Laudenslager Jr., div., 2 s., 1 d. Career: Freelance work inclng. Brockton Symph., Mass., 1968; Prin. Harp, Ft. Worth Symph., 1968-; Tchr., Piano & Harp, Tarrant Co. Jr. Coll., Ft. Worth, Tex., 1972-; Tchr., Harp, Tex. Christian Univ., 1972-; Tchr., Yamaha Music Schl., Ft. Worth, Tex., 1973-. Recordings: Brahms' Vier Gesange w. Tex. Girls Choir, 1968; The Ceremony of Carols by Britten w. Tex. Boys Choir, 1974. Mbrships: Mu Phi Epsilon Music Sorority; Pi Kappa Lambda; Ft. Worth Symph. League. Hons: Music Schlrships. to Tex. Christian Univ., 1960-62, N Tex. State Univ., 1962-64, New England Conserv., 1964-65, Tanglewood Berkshire Music Fest., 1964; Fellowship, New England Conserv., 1965-66. Hobbies: Sewing; Cooking; Reading; Dancing. Address: 2820 W Fuller, Ft. Worth, TX 76133, USA.

WILSON, Thomas Brendan, b. 10 Oct. 1927, Trinidad, Colo., USA. Professor, Glasgow Univ. Educ: MA, Glasgow Univ., Scotland, UK, 1951; BMus, ibid, 1953; ARCM, 1954. m. Margaret Rayner, 3 s. Career: Lectr., Glasgow Univ., 1957-72; Reader, ibid, 1972-. Compositions incl: Variations for Orch.; Toccata for Orch.; Pas De Quoi; The Charcoal Burner (opera); Sequentiae Passionis; Carmina Sacra; Missa Pro Mundo Conturbato; Te Deum; Nigh Songs; Str. Quartet No. 3; Canti Notturni; Complementi; Ritornelli per Archi; Cello Sonata; Fantasia for Cello; Clarinet Sonatina; Concerto de Camera; Coplas Del Ruisenor; Soliloquy; 3 Pieces for Guitar; Piano Sonata; Piano Sonatina; Sinfonia A 7; Piano Trio; Confessions of a Justified Sinner (opera), 1976; Ubi Caritas et Amor; Songs of Hope & Expectations; String Quartet No. 4. Mbrships. incl: Vice Chmn., Scottish Br., CGGB; Advsy. Committee, Scottish Music Archive; Scottish Arts Coun., 1968-74; Bd., Govs., RSAMD; PRS. Hons: Goudie Prize, 1948; McEwen Comp. Prize, 1959. Hobby: Golf. Address: 120 Dowanhill St., Glasgow G12 9DN, UK. 3.

WILSON, Timothy, b. 10 Oct. 1942, Bklyn., NY, USA. Flautist. Educ: Wesleyan Univ., Cann., 2 yrs.; Columbia Univ.; Paris Conserv., France, 2 yrs.; BMus, Manhattan Schl. of Music, 1973. Career: Prin. Flute, Hong Kong Phil. Orch.; Prin. Flute, 4th & 8th US Army Bands, 1967-69. Address: 19 Broadwood Rd., Hong Kong.

WIMBERGER, Gerhard, b. 30 Aug. 1923, Vienna, Austria. Composer; Conductor. Educ: studied comp. & cond. w. Clemens Krauss, Johann Nep. David, Bernhard Paumgartner, Mozarteum. m. Eva Wimberger, 2 s. Career: Coach, Volksoper, Vienna, 1947; Cond., Salzburger landestheater, 1948-51; Tchr., Mozarteum, 1953-; Hd. of Cond. & Comp. Class, ibid, 1968-; Prof. 1971-; Mbr., Bd. of Dirs. of the Salzburger Fest. Compositions: (operas) Schaubudengeschichte; La Battaglia; Dame Kobold; Lebensregeln; (ballets) Der Handschuh; Hero und Leander; (orch. works) Figuren und Phantasien; Stories; Risonanze; Chronique; Plays; Motus; Concerto a dodici; Multiplay; (cantatas) Heiratspostkantate; Ars amatoria; (vocal works) Prevert-Chansons; Kästner-Liederbuch; Memento Vivere; Mein Leben mein Tod. Songs; Singsang; chamber music for Radio & TV. Recordings: Stories; Heiratspostkantate; Signum for Organ; Chronique for orch. Mbr., Rotary Int. Hons: Recip., Austria State Prize for Comp., 1967. Address: Wallmannweg 13, Salzburg, A 5020, Austria. 19, 30.

WIMBERLY, Anne Elizabeth Streaty, b. 10 June 1936, Anderson, Ind., USA. Professor of Music. Educ: BS Educ., Ohio

State Univ., Columbus, Ohio, 1957; MMus, Boston Univ., 1965; Doctoral Cand., ibid. m. Edward Powell Wimberly. Career incls: Elementary Music Specialist, Detroit Pub. Schls., Mich., 1958-64; Dir., Dist. Chorus, ibid, 1960-63; Doct. Tchng. Fellow, Boston Univ. Schl. of Fine Arts, 1964-66; Elementary Vocal Music Cons., Newton Pub. Schls., Mass., 1966-67; Elementary Vocal Music Cons., Worcester Pub. Schls., Mass., 1968-73; Asst. Prof. of Music Educ., Worcester State Coll., 1973-75; Asst. Prof. of Music, Atlanta Jr. Coll., Ga., 1975-; Vocal concert, Winchendon, Mass., 1967; Num. solo apps.; Organist & choir Dir., E Grand Blvd. Methodist Ch., Detroit, Mich., 1962-64; Mbr., Advsry. Committee, Music Dept., Worcester Pub. Schls., 1973-75; Clinician, Workshop on Older Adults as Non-Traditional Students, 1978. Publs: Music Curriculum Guide, The official guide of the Worcester Pub. Schls., 1973. Contbr. to num. profl. publs. Mbrships: MENC; Int. Soc. for Music Educ.; Ga. Music Educs. Assn. (Chairperson, 1977-78, 5th Dist. Coll. Div.); Nat. Educ. Assn.; Ga. Assn. of Educs.; UNICEF. Address: 2738 Aquamist Dr., Decatur, GA 30034, USA.

WINBERGH, Gösta, b. Stockholm. Operatic Tenor. Educ: study w. Martin Öhman & Erik Saedén; Stockholm Opera Schl. Debut: as Rodolfo in La Boheme, Gothenburg. Career: Prin. tenor, Royal Opera, Stockholm, 1973-; apps. in San Francisco, Hamburg, Madrid, Copenhagen, Stuttgart, Amsterdam, Paris, Geneva, etc.; apps. on German radio & TV; roles incl. Alfredo (La Traviata), Duke (Rigoletto), Ottavio (Don Giovanni), Fenton (Falstaff), David (Die Meistersinger), Almaviva (Barber), Tamino (Magic Flute). Mgmt: Artistsekretariat Ulf Törnqvist, Norrtullsgatan 26, tr. 4, 11345 Stockholm, Sweden. Address: c/o mgmt.

WINCENC, Joseph, b. 16 Oct. 1915, Buffalo, NY, USA. Professor of Music; Symphony Conductor. Educ: Oberlin Coll. Conserv. of Music; Juilliard Schl. of Music; MM, State Conserv. of Music, Prague, Czechoslovakia; MA, Tchrs. Coll., Columbia Univ.; DHL, Canisius Coll., NY. m. Margaret Dorothy Miller, 3 d. Debut: Violin Recital, 20th Century Club, Buffalo, NY, 1937. Career incls: Violinist, Cond. of num. Symph. Orchs.; Conducted over 1,500 concerts; Apps. incl: Radio, TV, Musicals, Opera, Oratorio, Chmbr. Music; Music Instr., 10 public schls. in USA. Recordings w. num. Festival Orchs. Mbr., profl. orgs. inclng: Pi Kappa Lambda. Recip., var. citations & awards. Hobbies: Golf; Travel; Gardening; Cards; Coin Collecting. Address: 45 Irving Pl., Buffalo, NY 14201, USA. 12.

WINCH, Ruth Hazel, b. Southsea, Hampshire, UK. Accompanist; Soloist; Piano Teacher. Educ: Assoc., Royal Coll. of Music for piano teaching; Assoc., ibid. for schl. music; Lic., Royal Acad. of Music for accompanying; Assoc., Trinity Coll. of Music, London for piano perf. m. D J Nicholson, 2 d., 1 s. Mbr., Incorp. Soc. of Musicians & EPTA. Recip. Gold Medal, Trinity Coll. of Music, 1937. Hobbies: Composing Children's pieces; Needlework; Gardening; Playing duets. Address: The Coach House, Stitchill Rd., Torquay, Devon, TQ1 1PZ, UK.

WINCKEL, Fritz, b. 20 June 1907, Bregenz, Austria. Professor; Institute Director. Educ: Dipl.-Ing. (telecommunications & musical acoustics), Tech. Univ., Berlin, 1932; rsch. on electronic music & audiovision, Heinrich-Hertz Inst. & Acad. of Music, Berlin; Dr.-Ing., 1952; studied piano & solo singing for purposes of rsch., 1948-53. Career: worked w. phys. Walter Nernst, Univ. of Berlin, to dev. Neo-Bechstein-Flügel (1st electrified grand piano), 1932-34; Fndr. w. composer Boris Blacher of Tonmeister Schl., Acad. of Music, Berlin, & Studio for Expmntl. Music, Tech. Univ. of Berlin, 1953; Prof., Tech. Univ., Berlin-W; Dir. of Inst. of Communication Scis. of Music & Speech, & of Studio of Expmntl. Music; w. Boris Blacher & Studio of Electronic Music, Berlin, has composed 'Zwischenfälle bei einer Notlandung' (opera) & num. electronic works, & 5 audiovisual films; Student & Lectr. in med. (larynx & ear) & arch.; Cons. in acoustics & constrn. of concert halls; Lectr., info. theory & cybernetics; studies of neurocontrol of singers' voices for electronic measuring device. Recordings: Boris Blacher. Publs. incl: Klangwelt unter de Lupe, 1952; Klangstruktur der Musik (ed. & jt. author), 1955; Experimentelle Musik (ed. & jt. author), 1970. Contbr. to var. jrnls. Mbr., profl. socs. Address: Höhmannstrasse 9, D-1 Berlin 33, Germany. 19.

WINFIELD, John Michael Tyson, b. 20 Oct. 1937, Preston, Lancs., UK. Tenor. Educ: Royal Manchester Coll. of Music. m. Jennifer Anne Newman, 2 s. Debut: Cenerentola, Sadler's Wells Opera, 1966; Khovanschina, Covent Gdn., 1972. Career: Apps. w. Sadler's Wells Opera (Engl. Nat. Opera); Royal Opera House, Covent Gdn.; Scottish Opera; Welsh Nat. Opera; Radio & TV apps. for BBC & BBC TV. Recordings: Moses und Aaron; Sir John in Love; Saul. Hons: Ricordi Opera Prize, 1961;

Imperial League of Opera Prize, 1961. Mgmt: Neil Dalrymple, Music Int. Address: 60 Yaverland Dr., Bagshot, Surrey, UK.

WING, Winifred Gladys, b. 19 Mar. 1934, Redruth, Cornwall, UK. Music Teacher; Piano, Singing, Theory & Organ. Educ: Assoc., Royal Coll. of Music; Assoc., Trinity Coll. of Music, London. m. Ronald Wing, 2 s. Career: Pvte. tchr., 1952-70; Off. Accompanist, Camborne Music Festival, 1973-76; Organist, 1948-70; Conductor, Circuit Wives Choir, 1969-79; Accompanist, Redruth Amateur Operatic Soc.; Staff Mbr., Cornwall Rural Music Schl., 1970-; Hd. of Music, Treliske Preparatory Schl., Truro, 1977-. Recordings w. Camborne Circuit Wives Choir. Contbr. to: ISM Journal. Mbrships: Incorp. Soc. of Musicians; Cornwall Meth. Music Comm. since 1975; Cornwall Organists' Assn. Hobbies: Trng. & Presenting Youth Choirs; Sewing; Knitting; Gardening; Decorating. Address: 10 Jethan Drive, Camborne, Cornwall, UK.

WINICK, Steven D, b. 7 July 1944, Brooklyn, NY, USA. Music Educator; Trumpet & Cornel Player. Educ: BMus, 1966, MMus, 1968, D Musical Arts, 1973, Eastman Schl. of Music. m. Sharon Smolensky Winick, 1 d., 1 s. Career: Solo Cornet, Eastman Wind Ensemble, 1967-68; Trumpet, Rochester Phil. Orch., 1966-69, & Atlanta Symph. Orch., 1972-; Chmn., Dept. of Music, & Cond., Wind & Jazz Ensembles, Ga. State Univ., Atlanta. Comps: Confrontation (brass trio); Equinoctial Points (solo trumpet). Recordings incl: American Music for Symphonic Winds; Fiesta (both w. Eastman Wind Ensemble). Publ: Rhythm, An Annotated Bibliography, 1974. Contbr. to Instrumentalist; Int. Trumpet Guild Jrnl. Mbr., profl. assns. Hons: NDEA Fellowship, 1966-69. Hobbies: Skiing; Swimming; Tennis. Address: 2877 St. Andrews Way, Marietta, GA 30062, USA.

WINKLER, David, b. 11 Oct. 1948, Chgo., Ill., USA. Composer; Pianist. Educ: BA in Music, Univ. of Calif. at Los Angeles, 1970; MA in Music, Columbia Univ. Career: One-hour radio interview, inclng. 40 mins. of own music, radio WQXR, 1974. Comps. incl: Frische Schatten, meine Freude (vocal), 1975; Intermezzo for Piano, 1976; 3 Pieces for Violoncello Solo, 1976; 3 Sonnets for Soprano & Piano, 1976; Chamber Concerto 2 Pianos & Percussion, 1976; Chmbr. Concerto (flute, piano & percussion), 1974; Concerto for Piano & 12 Instruments, 1974; Double Concerto for Flute, Bass Clarinet, Strs. & Percussion, 1973. Mbrships. incl: Guilf of Comps. Inc. (treas.); BMI; Am. Comps. Alliance. Hons: Bernstein Comps. Fellowship, Tanglewood, 1972; BMI Student Comp. Award, 1972; Commission, From Music Fndn., 1974; Rapaport Prize, 1976. Address: 362 Broadway 3rd Floor, NY, NY 10013, USA.

WINKLHOFER, Sharon, b. 24 Jan. 1947, Santa Fe, NM, USA. Musicologist; Music Critic. Educ: BA, Stanford Univ., 1969; MA, 1974, PhD, UCLA, 1978. Career: Specialist in Liszt schlrship. Mbrships: Am. Musicol. Soc.; AAUP; Liszt Soc. of England. Contbr. of more than 200 music reviews to The Los Angeles Times, 1973-. Recip. Atwater Kent Prize in Musicol., 1976. Address: c/o Music Dept., UCLA, Los Angeles, CA 90024, USA. 29.

WINOLD, Helga Ulsamer, b. 16 April 1937, Munich, Germany. Cellist. Educ: Hochschule für Musik, Cologne; DMus, Ind. Univ. m. Allen Winold, 2 d. Debut: Radio Cologne, 1956. Career: Soloist; Chmbr. Music Player; Apps. w. Munich Phil. & other orchs.; Tchr., Ind. Univ. Schl. of Music; Clinics in US, Can. & Europe. Publs: Musical Aspects of Motion Analysis. Hons: Pi Kappa Lambda. Address: 2233 Moore's Pike, Bloomington, IN 47401, USA.

WINSOR, Philip Gordon, b. 10 May 1938, Morris, Ill., USA. Composer. Educ: BMus, Ill. Wesleyan Univ.; MA, San Fran. State Univ. m. (1) Julia Sentman Winsor, 2 s., 2 d., (2) Michele-Louise. Career: Currently Chmn., Theory-Comp. Dept., DePaul Univ. Schl. of Music. Comps: Over 20 works, inclng. Gorge (5 str. basses), Asleep in the Deep (5 tubas), Melted Ears (2 pianos, recorded), Coronation (5 trumpets), Honeycomb (full orch. & tape), multimedia works. Contbra. to Numus West mag. Mbrhips: Broadcast Music Inc.; Am. Comps. Alliance. Recip., num. awards & fellowship, inclng. Prix de Rome, 1966-67; Ford Fndn. Fellowship, 1973; Nat. Endowment for the Arts Comp. Fellowship, 1977. Mgmt: Beryl Zitch, 2528 Jerome St., Chgo. Address: 3836 N Marshfield Ave., Chgo., IL 60613, USA.

WINSTEAD, William, b. 11 Dec. 1942. Composer; Musician (bassoon, piano & harp). Educ: BMus, Curtis Inst. of Music; MMus, W Va. Univ. Career incl: Performer, Marlboro Music Festival, 7 yrs.; Festival of Two Worlds; Chmbr. music recitals in Eastern USA & Can.; Mbr., Opera Orchs. inclng. Lake George Opera & Goldovsky Inst.; Soloist w. Pitts. Symph. & Phila.

Orch. Compositions: The Moon Singer; piano Transcriptions of 10 Vivaldi Bassoon Concerti. Recordings: as Prin. Bassoon under Pablo Casals, Beethoven's 7th Symph.; Mozart's Prague Symph.; Brahms Haydn Variations, etc. Hons. incl: Nat. Endowment for the Arts grant, 1976. Address: D-12 La Mesa Ct., Morgantown, WV 26505, USA.

WINTER, James Hamilton, b. 18 Oct. 1919, Minneapolis, Minn., USA. University Professor of Music; Artist - Teacher of French Horn; Hornist. Educ: BA magna cum laude Carleton Coll.; MMus Northwestern Univ.; PhD, Univ. of Iowa. m. Pearl Bowman Winter, 2 s. Career: Prin. Honr, Fresno Phil., 25 yrs.; Prin. Horn/Soloist, Music from Bear Valley Fest.; Prof., Calif. State Univ., Fresno, 1947-; Asst. Dean, Arts & Scis., ibid, 1967-69; Chmn., Music Dept., ibid, 1972-76. Comps: Bourree for Horn Trio; Three Canons for Two Horns; Suite for a Quartet of Young Horns; Chorale-Prelude, Komm Süsser Tod. Recordings: IHS Workshops IV, V, VI, in solo & ensemble. Publ: The Brass Instruments, 1964. Contbr. to profl. jrnls. & mags. incl. Ed., The Horn Call. Mbr., num. profl. orgs. incl: Phi Mu Alpha Sinfonia (Fac. Advsr. & Province Gov.); Pi Kappa Lambda; Phi Kappa Phi. Hobbies: Tennis; Woodworking. Address: 1386 E Barstow, Fresno, CA 93710, USA. 9.

WINTERBOTTOM, Herbert Wager, b. 26 Dec. 1921, Oldham, Lancs., UK. Chairman, Dept. of Music, Univ. of Salford; Concert Organist; Harpsichord Player; Conductor. Educ: Manchester Coll. of Sci. & Technol.; Northern Schl. of Music; FRSA; MSc; FNSM; FTCL; LRAM; ARCM. m. J M Wilcock, 2 c. Career: Lectr., Manchester Coll. of Sci. & Technol. & at Rochdale Tech. Coll.; Prof. of Organ, Northern Schl. of Music & RNCM. Contbr. to profl. mags. & jrnls. Mbrships: AFRAES; ISM. Hobbies: Walking; Climbing; Swimming. Address: Chandos, 16 Alstone Rd., Heaton Chapel, Stockport, Cheshire SK4 5NH, UK.

WINTERS, Geoffrey, b. 17 Oct. 1928, Chingford, Essex, UK. Composer; Lecturer. Educ: RAM, 1945-47, 1949-52; LRAM; GRSM. m. Ch on BBC w. these ensembles). Publs: Pleasure & practice with the Recorder (6 books); Read & Play (2 books); 2 Minuets from Brahms Op. 11 arr. for recorder quartet; School Recorder Book of Carols; Pleasure & Practice Music Cards (3 books); Ways with Music; recorder tutors; A Handbook for Recorder Players. Contbr. to num. profl. jrnls. Mbrships: ISM; Brit. Fed. of Music Fests.; Royal Musical Assn.; Affiliate of Inst. of Linguists; Lancia Motor Club. Hobbies: Theatre; French; Wine; Motoring. Address: 23 Mount View Rd., N Chingford, London E4 7EF, UK. 28, 29.

WINTERS, George Archer, b. 3 Dec. 1950, St. Paul, Minn., USA. Double Bassist; Music Director. Educ: BMus, Univ. of Colo., Boulder; MMus, Eastman Schl. of Music, Rochester, NY. Career: w. San Antonio Symph.; Music Dir., Winters Chmbr. Orch. Comps: 2 String Quartets; Dance Suite for Strings; 2 Brass Quintets; Fanfare for Strings & Brass; Nocturne for Chmbr. Orch.; Serenade for 2 Horns & Strings. Recordings: Brahms & Verdi Requiems. Mbrships: Bruno Walter Soc.; Am. Fedn. of Musicians; Am. Symph. Orch. League; Int. Soc. of Bassists; Cum Laude Soc. Hons: Scholarship, Aspen Music Fest., 1976; Participating Cond., Brockport Conds. Fest., 1978. Hobbies: Basketball; Golf; Collecting symphonic recordings; Astronomy; Archaeol. Address: 6515 Spring Well No. 3, San Antonio, TX 78249, USA. 3, 28.

WINTERS, Leslie John, b. 22 June 1923, London, UK. Educator; Musician; Author. Educ: Goldsmiths' Coll., Univ. of London; LRAM; AMusTCL; London Univ. Cert. of Educ. m. Nancy Cowling, 3 s. Career: Former Hd. of Music Dept., var. schls.; freelance lectr., adjudicator, tchr. of piano, recorder & theory; fndr., cond., Leslie Winters Jr. Singers & Dir., Leslie Winters Consort (apps. on BBC w. these ensembles). Publs: Pleasure & practice with the Recorder (6 books); Read & Play (2 books); 2 Minuets from Brahms Op. 11 arr. for recorder quartet; School Recorder Book of Carols; Pleasure & Practice Music Cards (3 books); Ways with Music; recorder tutors; A Handbook for Recorder Players. Contbr. to num. prof. jrnls. Mbrships: ISM; Brit. Fed. of Music Fests.; Royal Musical Assn.; Affiliate of Inst. of Linguists; Lancia Motor Club. Hobbies: Theatre; French; Wine; Motoring. Address: 23 Mount View Rd., N Chingford, London E4 7EF, UK. 28, 29.

WINTERS, Ross, b. 19 Apr. 1951, Walthamstow, UK. Recorder Playeer; Professor of Recorder. Educ: Queen's Coll., Oxford; BA (Oxon.); LTCL (recorder perf.); ARCM (piano perf.); Muzieklyceum, Amsterdam w. Walter van Hauwe. m. Cilla Attfield. Debut: Macnaghten Concert, 1961. Career: perfs. w. London Pro Musica, Ars Nova, Engl. Concert, Hanart Ensemble & Vivaldi Players; apps. as soloist in major London halls; recitals w. Alan Wilson (harpsichord); recorder tchr. for ILEA, 1974-; Balls Pk. Coll., 1974-78, RCM Jr. Dept., 1975-, Sr. Dept.,

1978-; Recorder in Educ. Summer Schl., 1974-78; Adjudicator. Recordings for BBC. Contbr. to Recorder & Music mag. Mbrships: ISM; Musicians' Union; Soc. of Recorder Players. Hobbies: Being w. People; Squash; Swimming; Piano Playing; Reading. Address: c/o RCM, Prince Consort Rd., London SW7, UK.

WIREN, Dag Ivar, b. 15 Oct. 1905, Striberg, Sweden. Composer. Educ: Royal Conserv. Music, Stockholm, 1926-31. m. Noel McKenzie Franks, 1 d. Compositions: 5 Symphs.; Sinfonietta; Serenade for String; concertos for cello, violin, piano, & orch.; minor orchl. works; 5 str. quartets; 2 piano trios; Sonatine for Piano, violin & cello; piano pieces. Mbrships: Swedish Comps. Soc.; Royal Musical Acad. Address: Asevägen 5, 18235 Danderyd, Sweden.

WIRSTA, Aristide, b. 22 Mar. 1922, Bukovina, Ukraine. Musicologist; Violinist; Violin Teacher. Educ: Dip. (violin), Conserv. Supérieur de Musique, Paris, France, 1949; Dip., Acad. Musicale Chigiana, Siena, Italy (Class of G. Enesco), 1953; Doct. in Musicol., Univ. of Paris, 1955; Doct. d'Etat ès Lettres & Sciences Humaines, 1974. m. Hélène Hunder, 2 d. Debut: Concertmaster, Symph. Orch., Belo Horizonte, Brazil, 1950-51. Career: Num. broadcasts in Paris, Munich, Stuttgart, Zürich, Berne & Geneva on musicol. & Ukrainian music, & as a violinist. Recordings: Les Anciens présentent leurs Instruments. Publs: Ecoles de Violon au 18 ième siecle, 1955; l'Abbèle Fils, Principes du Violon, 1961; L'Enseignement du Violon au XIXième siecle, 1971. Contbr. to musical jrnls., encys. & dictionaries. Mbrships: Int. Musicol. Soc.; Soc. Française de Musicol.; Assn. Int. des Docteurs de l'Université de Paris (VP); European String Tchrs. Assn.; Assn. Académique Ukrainienne à Paris, (Pres., 1960-). Hon: Medaille d'honneur (Gold), 1975. Hobby: Collector of String Instruments. Address: 1 Rue Albert Camus, 92340 Bourg la Reine, France. 19.

WISE, Patricia, b. 31 July 1944, Whichita, Kansas, USA. Opera Singer. Educ: BMusEd., Univ. of Kansas. Debut: Susanna, Marriage of Figaro, Kansas City Lyric Opera. Career: Apps. w. num. operas cos., USA, UK, Austria, Germany, Switz. & Italy, incl. NYC Opera, Royal Opera, London, Vienna State Opera, Munich State Opera, Rome Opera; Num. roles; Apps. w. num. orchs. Recordings: Mozart-Coronation Mass, Vesperoe di Domenica, Domenicus Mass. Recip., num. hons. incl: M B Rockefeller Fund Grant, 1969-70; Sullivan Fndn. Grant, 1970; Morton Baum Memorial Award, 1971. Hobbies: Playing Piano; Painting; Cooking. Mgmt: Columbia Artists, NY; John Coast, UK; Raab Agentur, Vienna. Address: Albertplatz 8120, A-1080 Vienna, Austria. 1.

WISHARD, France Anne, b. 18 May 1900, Greenwood, Ind., USA. Pianist; Harpsichordist; Organist; Recorder Player; Teacher. Educ: Franklin Coll., Ind., 2 yrs.; BMus, Jordan Schl. of Music, Butler Univ., Indlps.; studied recorder & music crafts, Dushkin Schl. of Music, Winnetka, Ill.; pvte. study of organ w. Carrie Hyatt Kennedy, Indpls., Ind.; MMus., Univ. of Southern Calif., LA; studied harpsichord w. Alice Ehlers. Career: Perf. in sev. ensemble progs., WFBM radio, Indpls., & in chmbr. music radio; Pianist w. Orloff Quintet, Columbia Club, Indpls.; Tchr., Piano & Theory, Jordan Schl. of Music, Piano & Recorders, Univ. of Southern Calif. Schl. of Music, Recorder Workshops, Idyllwild Schl. of Music & the Arts, Univ. of Southern Calif., Piano, Organ, Theory & Early Childhood Educ. Tchr. Trng., Univ. of Calif., Santa Barbara; Hd., Music Dept., Orchard Schl., Indpls.; Organist, chs. in Ind. & Calif.; Curator, Human Rels. Area Files, Univ. of Southern Calif., LA, for 16 yrs. Contbr. to Educ. Sect., Christian Sci. Monitor. Mbr., Off. Holder, num. profl. orgs. Recip., scholarships. Address: 2927 S Hoover St., Los Angeles, CA 90007, USA. 4.

WISHART, Betty Rose, b. 22 Sept. 1947, Lumberton, NC, USA. Composer. Educ: BMus, Queens Coll., Charlotte, NC; MMus, Univ. of NC at Chapel Hill; studied piano & comp. w. var. masters. m. Eugene H Howard. Career: Perfs. at Int. Conf. of Delta Omicron, Kentucky, Evening of New Music, Charlotte, NC; Eisteddfod, Llangollen, UK; Delta Omicron Concert, Columbia, SC; 14 City tour, An Evening w. Wishart; Comps. concert Series, Chapel Hill NC, Seoul Nat. Univ., Korea; var. fests. Comps: Experience; Ch'ien; Memories of Things Unseen; Sounds; The Kohinoor Sonata; Illusions (piano suite); Etherea; Strings Quartet no. 2; The Eights Key (instrumentalists & dancer); Hymn for the Children. Mbrships: Delta Omicron (area chmn).; League of Women Comps.; ASCAP. Hons. incl: Star of Delta Omicron, 1969; Outstanding Yooung Women of Am., 1973, '75. Hobbies: Swimming; Genealogy. Address: 200 Locust St. 31-D, Phila., PA 19106, USA.

WISHART, Peter, b. 25 June 1921, Crowborough, Sussex, UK. Composer; Conductor. Educ: BMus, Birmingham Univ.; studied in Paris pvtly. w. Nadia Boulanger; FGSM. m. Maureen Lehane, 1 s., 1 d. Career: Lectr., Birmingham Univ.,

1950-59, GSM, 1961-, Kings Coll., London Univ., 1971-77; Prof., Reading Univ. 1977-; Comps. incl: 4 operas, The Captive, Two in the Bush, The Clandestine Marriage, Clytemnaestra; 2 symphs.; Concertos; Choral Works; Num. songs, chmbr. works. Recordings: Carols; Music for Movement 1 & 2. Publs: Harmony, 1956; Key to Music, 1971; Messiah Ornamented (Ed.), 1975; Co-ed., Purcell Songs, 3 vols., 1976. Mbr., ISM. Hons: FGSM, 1970. Hobbies: Cooking; Gardening; Walking. Address: Bridge House, Great Elm, Frome, Somerset, UK. 3, 14.

WISHART-HODGSON, James Bentham, b. 30 Jan. 1930, Lancaster, Lancs., UK. Director of Music; Organist. Educ: RMCM; Reading Univ.; GRSM; ARMCM; ARCO; LRAM. Career: Yorkshire Bank, 1946-61; Asst. Organist, Liverpool Cathedral, 1961-65; Dir. of Music, Lancaster Royal Grammar Schl., 1965-; organist, Lancaster Priory, 1972-; Superintendant, Lancaster City Organ, 1977-. Mbrships: ISM; Assn. of Asst. Masters. Hobby: Gardening. Address: 27 Newlands Rd., Lancaster, UK.

WISSMER, Pierre Alexandre, b. 30 Oct. 1915, Geneva, Switzerland. Composer. Educ: Law, Univ. of Geneva; Geneva Conserv.; Schola Cantorum, Paris; Paris Conserv. m. Laure-Anne Etienne. Career: Hd., Chmbr. Music Sect., Geneva Radio; Dir. of Progs., Télé-Luxembourg; Dir., Schola Cantorum, Paris; Dir., Nat. Schl. of Music, Dance & Dramatic Art, le Mans; Prof. of Comp., Conserv., Geneva. Comps. incl; (for theatre) Marion, 1951-52; Capt. Bruno 1955 (ballsts) Beautiful Sunday, 1944; Christina & her Idle Dreams, 1972. Mbrships: incl: Prog. Committee, ORTF; Hon. Pres., Int. Dance Ctr., Paris. Hons. incl: Grand Music Prize, City of Paris, 1967. Hobbies: Skiing; Water Skiing; Travel. Address: Residence Rivoli, 9 Square de Mondovi, Parly II, 78150 Le Chesnay, France.

WISZNIEWSKI, Zbigniew, b. 30 July 1922, Lwow, Poland. Composer. Educ: Univ. Lodz; MA, Acad. of Music, Lodz. Debut: Polish Radio, 1949. Career: Apps. in films, w. Ballet Orch. & on Polish Radio; W. Edition Schott, Mainz, W Gemany, 1966-68; Redactor, Polish Radio, Warsaw, 1968-. Comps: Electronic Music incls: Three Postludes, 1962; Burlesque, 1963; Chmbr. Music: Kammermusik No. 4, 1975; Duo per flauto & viola, 1967; Radio Operas: Neffru, 1958; Paternoster, 1972; Var. Var: Concerto for clarinet & strings, 1972; Ad Hominem (ballet), 1974. Contbr. to Das Musikinstrument, Germany; Ruch Muzyczny, Poland. Mbrships: Union of Polish Comps.; Assn. of Authors; Assn. of Polish Bibliopolists. Hons. incl; 2nd Prize (Italian Radio), Int. Competition; Prix Italia, 1959; 1st Prize, Int. Competition, Monaco for TV oratory Genesis, 1969; Gold Cross of Merit, 1973. Address: Swarzewska str. 58, 01 821 Warsaw, Poland.

WIT, Antoni, b. 7 Feb. 1944, Crakow, Poland. Conductor. Educ: Jagiellonien Univ., 1969; Conserv. of Music, Crakow, conducting w. Henryk Cryz, comp. w. K Penderecki, 1967. m. Zofia Cwikilewicz. Debut: Crackow, 1964. Career: Asst. Cond., Warsaw Phil., 1967-69; Cond., Poznan Phil., 1970-72; Music Dir., Bydgoszoz Phil., 1974-77; Music Dir., Polish Rado & TV Orch., Crakow, 1977-. Hons: 2nd Prize, H von Krajan, Berlin, 1971. Mgmt: Pagart. Address: 31041 Crakow, Sienna 14/4, Poland.

WITKOWSKI, Leon, b. 13 Dec. 1908, Slawkowo, Poland. Docent of University. Educ: Magister of Musigology & Classical Philology; Dr. Class Philology. Publs: Transl. in Polish lang. & musical adaptation of opera Turandot by G Puccini; Transl. in Polish lang. & musical adaptation of opera Szekely Fono by Z Kodaly. Mbrships: Int. Fellowship of Hymnology; Polksie Towarzystwo Filologiczne; Towarzystwo Naukowe w. Toruniu; Bydgoskie Towarzystwo Naukowe, Winckelmann-Gesellschaft Stendal. Num. articles in profl. jrnls. & mags. Recip. Golden Cross of Merit. Hobbies: Gardening; Sports. Address: Mickiewicza 52m 6, 87-100 Torun, Poland. 4.

WITOSZYNSKYJ, Leo, b. 23 June 1941, Vienna, Austria. Guitarist; Professor. Educ: DJ, Univs. Vienna & Graz, 1966; Grad., Vienna Acad. Music, 1964. m. Eleonore Kujal, 2 s. Debut: Nuremberg, Dec. 1964. Career: Prof., Musikhochschule, Graz; Apps., ORF, BBC, & Yorks. TV; ORTF, RAI, Swiss, Czech., Venezuelan & Turkish Radio; Recitals, num. countries Europe, Nr. E, Venezuela & USA. Recordings: Classics for Pleasure; Colosseum; Supraphon; Musical Heritage Soc.; Tudor; Christophorus, etc. Contbr. to jrnls. Hon: Winner, 1st Int. Competition for Guitar, Alessandria, 1968. Hobbies incl: Art. Address: Sclusselgasse 5/13, A-1040 Vienna, Austria.

WITTLICH, Kate, b. 3 Dec. 1935, Tallinn, USSR. Pianist. Educ: Musikhochschule Berlin, Germany; Musikhochschule Vienna, Austria. div., 1 c. Debut: Vienna. Career: Concerts, Europe, Can., USA; Fest. apps., Royan (France), Salzburg

(Austria), Berlin (Germany), Vienna (Austria); TV Film of 3rd Sonata, Pierre Boulez, w. Ircam, Paris, 1978. Recordings: Pierre Boulez, Structures I & II. Mbrships: Int. Soc. of Contemporary Music; IGNM Austria. Address: Liechtensteinstrasse 60/15, A-1090 Vienna, Austria.

WITZENMANN, Wolfgang, b. 26 Nov. 1937, Munich, German Fed. Repub. Composer; Musicologist. Educ: Music HS, Stuttgart, 1957-60; DPh, Univ. of Tübingen, 1965. m. Charlotte Veit (div.) Career: Apps. in Int. Fest. Gaudeamus, Netherlands, 1967, 68, 70, 71, Int. Ferienkurse für Musik, Darmstadt, 1969, Autunno Musicale, Como, 1975; Prods. for radio & TV in sev. countries. Comps. incl: Oden I-V (voice & piano), 1962; Perspektiven (piano), 1971;...pars (cycle of 5 expmtl. pieces for sev. instruments, live electronic & tape), 1969-74. Mbrships. incl: Dept. Hist. of Music, German Hist. Inst., Rome. Publs: incl; Ed., Mazzocchi, Sacrae concertationes, 1976. Contbr. to profl. jrnls. Hobbies incl: Lit. Address: Via Lucilio 36, I-00136 Rome, Italy.

WOESS, Kurt, b. 2 May 1914, Linz, Austria. Conductor; Musical Director. Educ: Acad. of Music, Vienna; MA; MusB. m. Margareta Gnad, 2 s., 1 d. Career: Permanent Cond., Tonkuenstler Orch., Vienna, 1949-51; Chief Cond., NHK Symph. Orch., Tokyo, 1951-54; Victoria Symph. Orch., Melbourne, Aust., 1956-60; Musical Dir., Opera House, Linz, Austria, 1961-; Chief Cond., Bruckner Orch., Linz, 1968-74; now freelance. Publs: Advice for the Interpretation of Anton Bruckner's Symphonies. Mbrships: Kiwanis Club; Savage Club. Hobbies: Reading; Tennis. Mgmt: S A Gorlinsky, London. Address: Kantgasse 3, Vienna 1, Austria.

WOHLAFKA, Louise Ann (George), b. 14 Oct. 1946, Manchester, NH, USA. Soprano; Trombonist. Educ: BS, educ., State Univ. Coll., Fredonia, NY; Ithaca Coll.; Elmira Coll.; SUNY, Binghamton & Potsdam; Univ. Southern Ill. m. Gary B Wohlafka. Debut: Violetta, 'La Traviata', Tri-Cities Opera, Binghamton, 1970. Career: Var. roles inclng. Juliette, 'Romeo & Juliette', Tri-Cities Opera, Binghamton; Pamina, 'Magic Flute' Syracuse Opera; Concert apps. w. Buffalo Phil., Binghamton, Syracuse & Niagara Falls Symphs; Metropolitan Opera, NY, 1978; Lectr. on competitions & voice. Hons. incl: Top Hon., Montreal Int. Competition, 1977; Female Achievement of the Yr. Award, 1977; Young Artist Grant, 1977. Hobbies incl: Sewing. Address: 37 Mason Ave., Binghamton, NY 13904, USA.

WÖHNHAAS, Theodor, b. 4 July 1922, Kirchheimbolanden, Germany. Academic Director of Music. Educ: Music, Erlangen Univ., 1946-49, 1955; Dr. Phil., 1958. Publs: 'Süddeutsche Orgeln aus der Zeit vor 1900' in 'Beiträge zum Orgelbau in Süddeutschland' (Essays on south German organ building) vol. 1, 1973; Georg Friedrich Steinmeyer, 1978. Contbr. to Jahrbuch für fränkische Landesforschung; Kirchenmusikalisches Jahrbuch; Jahrbuch für Augsburger Bistumsgeschichte. Mbrships. incl: Soc. for music rsch.; Soc. for Frankish History; Swabian rsch. soc. of Bavarian Acad. of Learning. Hons: Prize from town of Nuremberg for distinguished efforts in learning. Address: Erlangen, Hartmannstr. 89, German Fed. Repub.

WOICZYŃSKA, Maria, b. 16 Nov. 1945, Cracow, Poland. Musicologist. Educ: Master's degree, State Higher Schl. of Music, Cracow, 1969; doct. cand. Career: Polish Music Publications, 1969-73; Rsch. worker into 20th century music, State Higher Schl. of Music, Cracow, 1973-. Publs: (articles) Instrumental Theatre, 1970; In Search of 'Lost' Form, 1973; K Misiek's Phantom Sonata, 1978, etc. Contbr. to: Forum Musicum; Muzyka. Hobbies: Literature; Philosophy; Art; Water Sports; Hiking. Address: Dietla 80/34, 31073 Cracow, Poland.

WOJTKO, Donnamarie Zwolinsky, b. 27 June 1951, Portsmouth, Va., USA. Music Teacher in Public School System, Vocal & Instrumental (Woodwinds & Brass). Educ: BA Music Educ., Glassboro State Coll., NJ. m. Edward J Wojtko. Debut: Sr. Recital, Glassboro State Coll., NJ, 1973. Career: Music Tchr., Mt. Holly, NJ. Public Schl. System; Dir., Mt. Holly Fife & Drum Corps.; Co-Dir., Ch. Folk Grp.; Oboist, Engl. Horn, Haddonfield Symph. Orch.; 1st Oboe, Burlington Co. Pops Symph. Orch. Mbrships: Delta Omicron; Local 336, AF of M. Hobbies: Crafts; Tennis; Treasure Hunting. Address: 114 Dawn Dr., Holly, NJ 08060, USA.

WOLDIKE, Mogens, b. 5 July 1897, Copenhagen, Denmark. Conductor. Educ: Studied w. Carl Nielsen & Thomas Laub. m. Edith Moritz, 1 d. Career: Organist, Copenhagen Cathedral; Cond., Symph. Orch. of Radio Denmark, 1937-; Fndr., 1924, Ldr., Copenhagen Boys Choir. Compiler (w. Jens Peter Larsen): Official Hymn Book of the Danish Church, 1954. Comp. chorale preludes for organ. Mbr., Swedish Royal Acsd.

Hons: Sonning Music Prize, 1976; Dr. phil. hc., Univ. of Copenhagen. Address: 2 Trondhjemsgade, 2100 Copenhagen, Denmark. 2.

WOLF, Doris, b. 27 Sept. 1927, Graz, Austria. Concert Pianist. Educ: Landeskonservatorium, Graz; Dip., Akademie für Musik und darstellende Kunst, Vienna. m. Manfred Blumauer. Debut: Vienna, in Beethoven's 3rd concerto. Career: Concerts & recitals in nearly all countries of Europe & in the Near East; Prof. of piano. Hobby: Gardening. Address: Oberberg 72, 8052 Graz, Austria.

WOLF, Ilse, b. 7 June 1921, Düren, Germany. Singer. Educ: studied w. Emmy Hein & Helene Isepp. Career: lieder & oratorio singer; num. concert, recital, TV & radio apps. since 1947. Recordings: Bach, Monteverdi, lieder. recip., hon. FTCL. Address: 55A Hartswood Rd., London W12 9NE, UK.

WOLF, James Gary, b. 28 June 1933, Benton, Kan., USA. Pianist; College Music Teacher. Educ: BME, Wichita State Univ., 1955; MMus, Eastman Schl. Music, 1960; DMA, ibid., 1964; Fulbright Schlr., Mozarteum, Salzburg, Austria, 1960-61; Cert. Profl. Advancement, Fla. State Music Tchrs. Assn., 1973. m. Carolyn Ann Lygrisse, 1 s., 1 d. Debut: Recital, Town Hall, NY, 1973. Career incls: Soloist, Mozarteum Orch., 1961; Piano soloist, chmbr. music performer & concerto soloist; App. many Am. Matthay Piano Fests.; Coll. Music Tchr.; Chmn.; Music Dept.; Fla. Technol. Univ., Orlando. Recording: Music for English Horn & Piano (Golden Crest Records). Mbr. profl. orgs. Recip: Naftzger Young Artist Award, Wichita, Kan., 1951. Address: 2142 Chinook Trail, Maitland, FL 32751, USA.

WOLF, Jürgen, b. 31 July 1938, Braunschweig, Germany. Cellist. Educ: studied w. Walter Lutz, Berlin & Rudolf von Tobel, Berne. Career: num. solo recitals & concerto perfs.; 1st solo cellist, Düsseldorfer Sinfoniker; mbr., Streichtrio Pro Musica; Mbr., Detmolder Klaviertrio; apps. on radio & TV; Tchr., Robert Schumann Konservatorium; Düsseldorf. Recordings: Haydn/Boccherini, cello concerto; Offenbach, cello duets; Richard Strauss, cello sonata. Hobby: Mozart Research. Address: Theodor-Fontanestr. 65, 4047 Dormagen 5 - Zons, German Fed. Repub.

WOLF, R Peter, b. 5 Dec. 1942, Wash., DC, USA. University Professor; Musicologist; Harpsichordist. Educ: AB, Harvard Univ., 1965; Amsterdam Conserv., Netherlands, 1965-66; Harpsichord w. Gustav Leonhardt, 1965-66, & Ralph Kirkpatrick, 1966-70; MPhil, Music Hist., Yale Univ., 1969; PhD in Music Hist., ibid. 1977. Career: Num. concerts as Harpsichord Soloist & Continuo Player; Musician-in-Res., NC State Univ. at Raleigh, 1971-72; 2 TV shows, NC educl. network, 1972; Instructor in Music, SUNY at Stony Brook; Prof. (Musicol.), Univ. of Utah; Mbr., Bowers-Wolf duo; Salt Lake Chmbr. Ensemble. Recordings: Pvte. recording of works by Rameau, J S Bach, C P E Bach. Contbr. to: The Musical Quarterly; Recherches; Jrnl. of Am. Musical Instrument Soc. Mbrships: Am. Musicol. Soc.; Int. Musicol. Soc.; Am. Musical Instrument Soc.; New Bach Sec. (Am. Chapt.); Am. Fedn. of Musicians. Hons: Fulbright-Hays Fellowship, 1965-66. Address: Music Dept., The Univ. of Utah, Salt Lake City, UT 84112, USA.

WOLFENSBERGER, Rita, b. 28 May 1928, Schaffhausen, Switz. Pianist; Musical Journalist. Educ: Dip., École Normale de musique, Paris; Grad., Accademia Musicale Chigiana, Siena. Career: Concerto perfs., solo recitals, chmbr. music perfs. in Switz., Italy, France, Germany, Netherlands, UK, Austria; perfs. on radio in Rome, Zurich, Lugano, Lausanne, Munich & Madrid. Recordings: Folklore in der Trioliteratur; Virtuoso cellomusik (w. Rama Juciker). Publs: Erste Biographie über Clara Haskil, 1961. Contbr. to num. Swiss jrnls. Mbrships: Zentral Vorstand des Schweiz. Musikpädagogischen Verbandes; Redaktorin des Mitteilungsblattes desselben Verbandes; Schweiz. Tonkünstlerverein; former pres., Zontaclub. recip., medal from Int. Musikwettbewerb Genf, 1956. Address: Riethaldenweg 34, 8200 Schaffhausen, Switz.

WOLFF, Arthur Sheldon, b. 19 Feb. 1931, Cleveland, Ohio, USA. Professor of Music Theory; Musicologist; Composer. Educ: BM, DePauw Univ., 1955; MM, Composition, Univ. of Redlands, 1958; PhD, Musicol., N. Tex. State Univ., 1970. m. Kathlyn Veazey, 2 s., 1969-70; Prof. & Chmn. Theory Dept., Okla. Bapt. Univ., 1964-69; Theory Prof., Eastman Schl. of Music, Univ. of Rochester, 1971-74; Prof., Wichita State Univ. Coll. of Fine Arts, Div. of Music, 1974-. Compositions incl: Fantasy Variations for Piano, 1956; Overture to a Tragedy (orch.); Woodwind Quintet. Publs. inclk: Speculum, A Handlist of Musically Related Articles & Book Reviews, 1963 & 65; Casanatense 2856, Its History, Purpose & Music, 2 vols., 1970; Speculum, 1971. Mbrships: Am. Musicol. Soc.; Phi Mu Alpha Sinfonia; Coll. Music Theory Assn. Hons: Charles

Wakefield Cadman Grad. Schlrship. in Composition, Univ. of Redlands, 1956-57; Doctoral Fellowship, N Tex. State Univ., 1960-63, 1969. Hobbies: Painting; Hiking; Crafting; Cycling. Address; 3260 Oneida, Wichita, KS 67208, USA.

WOLFF, Christoph, b. 24 May 1940, Solingen, Germany. Historical Musicologist. Educ: Schls. of Music, Berlin & Freiburg; Staatsexamen, 1963; studied Musicol., Philos., Art Hist., Free Univ. of Berlin, Univ. of Erlangen; Dr. Phil. in Musicol., 1966. m. Barbara Mahrenholz Wolff, 3 d. Career: Lectr. in Musicol., Univ. of Erlangen-Nuremberg, 1966-69; Assoc. Prof. of Musicol., Univ. of Toronto, Can., 1968-70; Prof. of Musicol., Columbia Univ., NY, 1970-76; Vis. Prof., Princeton Univ., 1973 & '75; Prof. of Musicol.; Dir. of Grad. Studies, Harvard Univ., Cambridge, Mass. Publs. incl: Der stile antico in der Musik J S Bachs, 1968; Ed., Bach Jahrbuch, 1975-; Ed., W A Mozart, Klavierkonzerte K. 246, 271, 365, 413-15, Neue Mozart-Ausgabe V/15, 2-3, 1976; Musikalisches Opfer, Neue Bach-pAusgabe VIII/1, 1974; J S Bach, Klavierubung IV, 14 Kanons Neue Bach-Ausgabe V/2, 1976; P Hindemith, Cardillac, Hindemith-Gesamtausgabe 1/2, 1976. Contbr. to var. profl. publs. Mbr., profl. orgs. Hons: Dent Medal, Royal Musical Assn., London, 1978. Address: 182 Washington St., Belmont, MA 02178, USA.

WOLFF, Hellmuth Christian, b. 23 May 1906, Zürich, Switzerland. Musicologist. Educ: PhD, Berlin, 1932; Dr. habil. (2nd degree), Kiel, 1942. m. Liselotte Zeman, 2 c. Career: Mgr., Niedersächsiche Music Soc., Braunschweig, 1942; Prof. of Musicol., Univ. of Leipzig, 1947-71. Comps: Esther (opera-oratorio), 1946; Der Tod des Orpheus, 1948; Ich lass mich scheiden, 1950; Sonata for Flute & Piano, op. 38, 1969. Publs. incl: Die Händel-Oper auf der Modernen Bühne, 1957; Die Barockoper in Hamburg, 2 vols., 1957; Jugend-Sinfonien von Felix Mendelssohn-Bartholdy (Nr. I-XII), 3 vols., 1965-72; Oper-Szene und Darstellung von 1600 bis 1900 (mg. in Bilden), 1968; Ordnung und Gestalt-die Musik von 1900-1950, 1978. contbr. to profl. jrnls. & New Accademia Filarmonica, Bologna, 1975: Italian & Int. Socs. of Musicol. Hobby: Painting (exhibs. Leipzig 1961, 63 & 66, Düsseldorf 1965). Address: Springerstr, 23, 7022 Leipzig, German Dem. Repub.

WOLFF, Konrad, b. 11 Mar. 1907, Berlin, Germany. Pianist; Piano Teacher; Musicologist. Educ: studied piano w. Joseph Lomba, 1921-22, Willy Bardas, 1922-23, Bruno Eisner, 1923-25, Frank Muehlbauer, 1932-33 & Artur Schnabel, 1936-47 (intermidttently); Dr. jur., Berlin, 1930; 2 Diplômes d'Etudes supérieures, Sorbonne, 1935; MA musicol., Columbia Univ., NY, 1957. m. Ilse Bing. Career: Recitals in NY. Wash., Balt. Boston, etc.; West European recitals in 1954; Many lecture-concerts in USA & England; Frequent Chamber music appearances. Publs: Co-author, Erich Itor Kahn, 1958; The Teaching of Artur Schnabel, London & NY, 1972, in Japanese, 1975, German, 1979; Ed., Robert Schumann. 'On Music & Musicians', NY, 1946 & frequent reprints (also paperback), Contbr. to: Musical Qtly.; Piano Qtly.; Clavier; Music Survey; Am. Record Guide. Mbr. Music Tchrs. Nat. Assn.; Am. Int. Musicol. Soc. Hons: Cert. of Merit, Peabody Conserv., 1974. Address: 210 Riverside Dr., NY, NY 10025, USA. 6, 11, 21.

WOLFF, Marguerite, b. London, UK. Concert Pianist. Educ: FTCL; RAM. m. Derrick Moss (dec.), 2 d. Career: Soloist, LSP, RPO, Philharmonia, Bournemouth & Birmingham Orchs.; radio & TV broadcasts w. major orchs.; Toured USA, Europe & Far East. Recorded Bliss Piano Sonata. Mbrships: Coun., Liszt Soc.; ISM. Winner, Int. Bambridge Competition. Hobbies: Reading; Walking. Address: 9 Deanery St., Park Lane, London W1, UK. 30.

WOLFF, Moss Leonardus Herman, b. 30 Jan. 1907, The Hague, Netherlands. Musician (Violin, Viola, Recorders); Director; Composer. Educ: Royal Conserv., The Hague (Violin, Alto Comp.); studied Choir Direction w. Bond v. Kourdirigenten in Nederland. m. Jenny Hirsch, 1 d. Career: Tchr., Violin, Viola, Recorders. Gen. Musical Educ. & Theory; Perfs. in Haag, Piano Quartet, and as cond. in Gouda, Liedertufell; Director own Comp., Valerius Triptych, w. Choir & Radio Phil. Orch. Compositions: The Lords Prayer, 1951; Complainte & De Goede Garen (2 songs for tenor & piano), 1952; Ik Sla De Trom (male choir); De 18 Doden (Jan Campert) declamation, viola & piano), 1953; Vocalise (bass & piano), 1969; Paasleis (mixed choir); Kinderliedjes. Mbrships: Royal Dutch Soc. of Musicians; Dutch Performing Rights Soc. (Geneco); Federatie van Kunstenaarsverenigingen. Hobbies: Educational Psychology; Parapsychology. Address: van Diepenburchstraat 106, The Hague, Netherlands.

WOLFORD, Darwin K, b. 19 Oct. 1936, Logan, Utah, USA. Professor; Organist; Composer; Editor. Educ: BS, Utah State Univ.; MMus, Univ. of Utah; PhD. m. Julie Lofgren Wolford, 3 s., (1 dec.), 1 d. Comps. (publs.) incl: Nine Psalms for Organ, 1967; Suite à la Mode (piano), 1976; Pastels (piano solo); Seascape (organ solo); var. piano, organ, & vocal solos. Publs. incl: The Beginning Organist, Vols. i & II; Just for Manuals, Vols. I & II; Organ Studies for the Beginner; Songs of Praise by Contemporary Composers. Hons: 1st Symph. performed by Utah Symph., 1968; Other works performed by Salt Lake Mormon Tabernacle Choir on CBS Radio. Hobby: Travel. Address: 4 N Mill Hollow Dr., Rexburgh, ID 83440, USA.

WOLFRAM, Victor, b. 3 May 1920, NY, NY, USA. Concert Pianist & Harpsichordist; Professor of Music. Educ: Dip., Juilliard Schl. of Music, 1937; BSc, ibid., 1940; MSc, ibid., 1941; Post-Grad. Dip., ibid., 1946. m. Esta Bablan Wolfram. Debut as Pianist, Chgo., Ill., 1944; as Harpsichordist, San Antonio, Tex., 1970. Career: Soloist, Omaha Symph. Orch., Okla. City Symph; TV appearances on ETV; Prof. of Music & Chmn., Keyboard Fac., Okla. State Univ. Recordings: Haydn, Debussy, Werner Josten, Mozart, Beethoven, Educo Records. Author, The Sostenuto Pedal, 1965. Contbr. to: Diapason; High Fidelity; The Harpsichord; Cimarron Review; The Am. Music Tchr. Mbrships: Music Tchrs. Nat. Assn.; Am. Assn. of Univ. Profs. Recip. Fellowship, Juilliard Grad. Schl., 1941-46. Hobbies: Ornithology; Swimming; Reading. Address: Dept. of Music, Okla. State Univ., Stillwater, OK, USA.

WOLLENBERG, Susan Lesley Freda, b. 28 Apr. 1949, Manchester, UK. University Lecturer in Music. Educ: Junior Dept., RNCM; BA, D Phil., Oxford Univ. m. Dr. L S Wollenberg, 1 s. Contbr. to: Grove's Dict., 6th Ed.; Music and Letters; Musical Times; Proceedings of the Royal Musical Assn.; Encyclopaedias, etc. Mbrships: Fellow of Lady Margaret Hall, Oxford; Royal Musical Assn.; Int. Soc. for 18th Century Studies. Recip., sev. acad. hons. Hobbies: Literature (English, French, German). Address: Fac. of Music, 32 Holywell, Oxford, UK.

WOLMER, Jan, b. 18 Oct. 1909, Oslo, Norway. Pianist; Composer & Orchestrator. Educ: Studied Piano w. var. Norwegian masters, in Riga, 1932-35, & Berlin, 1934, 36, 39, & w. A Rubinstein & H Wasserman, Calif., USA, 1948-50; studied orchestration w. var. masters, USA & Norway. Career: Concerts in Scandinavia, Netherlands, Spain, Canary Islands, USA; ret'd. through illness, 1960. Compositions: 5 Orchl. Suites; Piano Sonata; about 50 piano pieces, songs, etc. Recordings: Berceuse op. 2 number 2, & Poem op. 11 number 1, Kjell Bakkelund; Gavott & Menuet op. 5, Valse C sharp minor op. 8 number 1, Capriccio op. 12 number 5, Nostalgic Suite, Kringkastings Orch., oslo; Si Mon Amour, Pascal. Mbr., NOPA. Address: Setravej 26, Holmenkollen, Oslo 3, Norway.

WOLPERT, Franz Alfons, b. 11 Oct. 1917, Wiesentheid, Germany. Composer; Pianist. Educ: Regensburg; Mozarteum, Salzburg. m. Elfie Bauer, 1 s. Debut: Mozarteum, Salzburg, 1940. Career: Tchr. of Music & Theory, Mozarteum, Salzburg, 1941-44; Tchr., Schls. of Salem, 1950-74. Comps: 2 Sonatas, for piano; Ritornell, for viola or cello & piano; Banchetto Musicale Nos. I & II; Concerto for Piano, Cello & Orch.; Concerto for Violin & orch.; Urworte, for Choir, soloist & orchs.; opera Der Eingebildete Kranke. Publs: Neue Harmonik, Kurzfassung, 1951; Neue Harmonik, Neufassung, 1972; Schubert-Variationen for Orch., 1975; Der goldene Schuh, opera. Mbrships: Deutscher Komponistenverband; GEMA. Hons: Chmbr. Music Prize, Salzburg, 1944; Robert-Schumann-Preis fur Komposition, Dusseldorf, 1959; Joseph-Haydn-Preis, 1966. Address: D 8714 Wiesentheid bei Würzburg, German Fed. Repub.

WOLSING, Waldemar, b. 3 May 1910, Hellerup, Denmark. Solo Oboist. Educ: studied oboe w. Svend Chr. Felumb, 1927-32, Henry Munck, 1933-35, Louis Bleuzet, Paris, 1932-37, Marcel Tabuteau, 1950, 53, 64. m. Ingrid Wichmann. Career: Mbr., Tivoli Concert Hall, Orch., 1935-40, Radio Symph. orch., 1941; Solo Oboist, 1946. Mbrships: Chmn. of Bd., Danish Radio Symph. Orch., 1942-50, 56-; Bd., Dansk Tonekunstnerforening, 1966. Recip. Kt. of Dannebrog, 1st degree. Address: Islands Brygge 13, 2300 Copenhagen S, Denmark.

WOLTER, Detlef Franz Emil, b. 11 Mar. 1933, Berlin, Germany. Composer; Pianiat. Educ: Studied music w. Herbert Wolter (father), Anneliese Koch & Ernest G Naumanni; State Music Acad., Munich, 1955-57. Debut: Rias, Berlin, 1953. Career: Radio, TV, Concert & Theatre perfs., Germany & abroad. Comps: Orchl., Dramatic, Chmbr. & Vocal works. Mbrships: German Comps. Union; GEMA. Hons: German Youth Music Prize, 1953. Address: Guardinistr. 131, D8000 Munich 70, German Fed. Repub.

WOLTERS, Klaus, b. 23 Apr. 1926, Winterthur, Switzerland. Pianist. Educ: Conservs. of Zürich, Vienna &

Rome/Siena; Tchr.'s Dip. & Soloist's Dip., 1947/50. m. Esther Winter, 2 -s. Debut: 1953. Career: Recitals, symphonic concerts, radio recordings; Prof., Winterthur Conserv., 1947-, Bern Conserv., 1957-66, Profl. Class; Zürich Conserv., 1974-; Dir., Diploma Examinations (Swiss Soc. for Music Educ.). Comps; Erstes Speil zu vier Händen. Volkslieder (Barenreiter). Recordings: Dances by Schubert (op. 171) & Weber (op. 65, Amadeo). Publs: Handbuch der Klavierliteratur, 1967; Das Klavier, 3rd ed., 1975; Orientierungsmodelle für den Instrumentalunterricht: Klavier, 1975. Contbr. to Schweizerische Musikzeitung. Mbr. profl. orgs. Recip. Gt. Prize, Zürich Conserv., 1952. Address: Lärchenstr. 13, 8442 Hettlingen, Switz.

WONNACOTT, Olwen Elizabeth, b. 10 Aug. 1930, Aberystwyth, UK. Piano Teacher; Accompanist; Performer. Educ: Study at Univ. Coll. of N Wales, Bangor, UK w. Miles Coverdale; RAM, LRAM (Performer Pianoforte), 1950; GRSM, 1951; Studied w. Harold Craxton, 1948-52. Postgrad. studies w. Frederick Jackson, 1952. m. Cyril Howard Wonnacott, 1 d. Debut: Soloist, w. Nat. Youth Orch. of Wales, Nat. Eisteddfod, 1952. Career: 1st piano recital, Cardiff, 1948; Num. recitals, 1948-52; Recital broadcast w. BBC Welsh Orch., 1956; App. as soloist, ITV, Cardiff, 1959; Tchr., Music Staff, St. Gabriel's Trng. Coll., London; Dpty. Organist, Westminster Chapel, London, 1954-56; Tchr., Royal Naval Schl., Haselmere, Surrey, 1957; Piano tchr., Penrhos Coll., Colwyn Bay, 1963-64; Piano tchr., Clarendon Schl., 1964-70; Piani tchr., Tockington Manor Schl., Nr. Bristol, 1976-. Recordings: Accomp. for Lyndon Baglin (Euphonium), 'Showcase for the Euphonium,' (Saydisc), 1975. Mbrships: ISM, RAM Club. Hons: Assoc. Bd. Scholarship, 1948; 1st prize, Llangollen Int. Eisteddfod, 1947. Hobbies: Helping farmer husband; Piano teaching. Address: Lower Hazel Farm, Rudgeway, Bristol BS12 2QP, Avon, UK.

WON-SIK, Lim (pen name - Unpa), b. 24 June, 1919, Korea. Conductor; Educator. Educ: Tokyo Schl. of Music, Japan; Juilliard Schl. of Music, NYC. Career: Regular Cond., Koryo Symph. Orch., 1946, Seoul Symph. Orch., 1949; Prof., Ewha Women's Univ., 1949; Prof., Coll. of Music, Seoul Nat. Univ., 1953; Fndr. & Cond., Seoul Ctrl. Broadcasting Stn. Orch., 1956; Prin., Seoul Art HS, 1961-; Guest Cond., Japanese & Korean orchs., 1963-. Mbrships: Korean Deleg., UNESCO Int. Music Conf., 1953, 56. Hons: May Lit.-Art Award, Educ. Min., Korea, 1964; Seoul City Cultural Award, 1965; decorated w. order, German Fed. Repub., 1966; Contribution Award, Nat. Acad. of Arts, Korea, 1970. Address: 236-39 Shindang-dong, Songdong-gu, Seoul, Korea.

WOOD, Anne, b. 2 Aug. 1907, Crawley, UK. Singer (retired); Teacher; Arts Administrator. Educ: Higher Cert. in Engl., French & Hist. Debut: Bach's B Minor Mass, St. Martin-in-the-Field. Career: Concerts, recitals, oratorio perfs., some opera; radio apps. in UK, Germany, etc.; Gen. Mgr., Phoenix Opera Ltd. mbr., ISM. Hobbies: Travel; Gardening; Reading. Address: 59 Marlborough Pl., London NW8, UK.

WOOD, Graham Edwin, b. 13 Sept. 1930, Melbourne, Vic., Aust. Violinist. Educ: MusB (Melbourne); BMus (WA); MMus (WA); ALCM; A Mus A. m. Patricia Mary, 1 s., 1 d. Career: Melbourne Symph. Orch.; Royal Opera House, Covent Garden; LPO; WA Symph. Orch. (Asst. Concert Master till 1972); currently Sr. Lectr., Dept. of Music, Univ. of WA. Var. recordings as Ldr. of Oriel String Quartet, of Contemporary Aust. Comps. Contbr. to: Aust. Jrnl. of Music Educ. Mbrships: Dir. of Nat. Camps, Fed. Coun. of Nat. Music Camp Assn., 1979, '80; State Rep., Aust. String Tchrs. Assn.; Committee, Musica Viva. Hobbies: Golf; Philately. Address: 86 Adelma Rd., Dalkeith, WA 6009, Aust.

WOOD, Hugh Bradshaw, b. 27 June 1932, Parbold, Lancs., UK. Composer. Educ: BA, New Coll., Oxford Univ.; ARCM (pvte. study w. Dr. Lloyd Webber), 1954-56; study of Harmony & Counterpoint w. Anthony Milner, 1957-60; study of Comp. w. Iain Hamilton, 1956-58, Matyas Seiber, 1958-60. m. Susan McGaw, 3 children. Career: Extra-mural Dept., London Univ., 1956-60; Evening Teaching, Morley Coll., London, 1958-67; Prof. of Harmony, RAM, 1962-65; Cramb Rsch. Fellow in Comp., Univ. of Glasgow, 1966-70; Lectr., in Music, Univ. of Liverpool, 1971-73; Pt.-time Lectr., ibid, 1973-; Frequent Broadcasts inclng. Beethoven (1970) & series on The Symphony. Compositions incl: (publd.) Variations for Viola & Piano, op. 1, 1958; Trio for Flute, Viola & Piano, op. 3, 1961; Capriccio for Organ, op. 8, 1968; (to be publd.) Chmbr. Concerto op. 15, 1971; Violin Concerto, op. 17, 1972; Song Cycle to Poems of Neruda, op. 19, 1974; (recorded) Str. Quartet No. 1, 3 Piano Pieces. Contbr. to European Music in the 20th Century, ed. Hartog; profl. jrnls. Mbrships: PRS; CGGB; Soc. for Promotion of New Music (Chmn. 1964-66). Hobby:

Broadcasting & Writing on Music. Address: Lowood, Lyndhurst Rd., Liverpool L18 8AU, UK.

WOOD, Joseph, b. 12 May 1915, Pitts., Pa., USA. Composer; Teacher. Educ: BS, Julliard Schl. Music, NY; MA, Columbia Univ., ibid; Dip. in Piano, Inst. Musical Art; Dip. in Comp., Juilliard Grad. Schl. m. Wendy Bradley, 1 d. Career: Staff Comp., Michael Checkhov Theatre Studio, 1939-40; Freelance Comp. O Arranger for theatre, radio O publrs., NY, 1940-50; US Army, 1943-46; Fac., Oberlin Conserv. Music, Ohio, 1950-. Compositions: Symphs. I, II O III; Poem for Orch.; Str. Quartets, I, II O III; Overture to Twelfth Night; Sonata for Viola O Piano; Sonata for Violin O Piano; Piano Sonata; Concerto for Violin O Orch.; Concerto for Viola, Piano O Orch.; Divertimento for Piano O small Orch.; The Progression, for speakers, chorus O wind ensemble; Quintet for tenor saxophone O string quartet; songs; choral pieces; paino pieces; vocal O instrumental arrangements. Recordings: Poem for Orch. Contbr. to Choice mag. Mbrships. incl: Am. Comps. Alliance; Nat. Assn. Am. Comps. O Conds. Hons. incl: Huntington Hartford Fellowship, 1960; Villa Montalvo Fellowship, 1957. Address: 261 W Lorain St., Oberlin, OH 44074, USA. 8.

WOOD, Judith Ellis, b. 10 Jan. 1945, Ashtabula, Ohio, USA. Singer (Mezzo-soprano). Educ: BMus, Coll. of Wooster, 1966; Juilliard Schl. of Music, 1966-67; MMus, Ind. Univ., 1972. div., 2 d. Debut: Annapolis Opera, Md., 1974. Career: Lady Billows in Albert Herring, 0 Act II finale, Cenerentola, Wolf Trap Co., Vienna, Va., 1973; Mother, Amahl O the Night Visitors, Univ. of Ill., 1974; major recitals incl. Tanglewood, 1966, Westmar Coll., Iowa, 1968, Ind. Univ., 1967, 1972, Shenandoah Conserv., Va., 1973, 0 Univ. of Ill., 1975 O Phillips Gallery, Wash., DC, 1977; instr. of Voice, Univ. of Ill., Urbana, Ill., 1974-. Mbr., Nat. Assn. Tchrs. of Singing. Hons. incl: State Winner, Iowa Advanced Div., Nat. Assn. Tchrs. of Singing, 1969; Rosanna M Enlow Award, Evansville, Ind., 1972. Hobbies: Sewing; Cooking. Address: 1909 Alton Drive, Champaign, Il 61820, USA.

WOOD, Richard, b. 15 Sept. 1910, Crawley, Sussex, UK. Singer. Educ: New Coll., Oxford; pvte. music studies. 2 children. Debut: Wigmore Hall. Career: Singer, lieder, oratorio 0 on radio; Dir. of Singers in Consort; Tchr. of singing O voice prod.; Dir. of courses; Adjudicator; Lectr. (adult educ.) in music 0 drama. Mbrships: ISM; Brit. Fedn. of Music Fests. Hobbies: Walking; Countryside; Art. Address: 67 Hamilton Terr., London NW8 9QX, UK 3.

WOOD, Ruzena Alenka Milena, b. Macclesfield, Cheshire, UK. Musicologist; Composer; Writer; Viennese Zither player; Translator; Poet. Educ.: MA, Edinburgh Univ.; studied comp. w. John Brydson O Ronald Stevenson. Career: Music Dept., Nat. Lib. of Scotland, Edinburgh, 1959-; specialising in music exhibition design, music documentaries etc. Comps: Choral works, songs 0 chmbr. music. Publs: The Palace of the Moon, 1980. Contbr. to: Brio (Ed., 1964-74); Int. Assn. of Music Libs. Jrnl. Mbr., Royal Musical Assn. Hobbies: Czech lit.; Christian 0 Jewish theology; Theatre; Central European cooking; Tapestry. Address: 50 Spottiswoode St., Edinburgh EH9 1DG, UK.

WOOD, Vivian Poates, b. 19 Aug. 1928, Wash. DC, USA. Mezzo-Soprano; Educator. Educ. incls: BMus, Hartt Coll. of Music, 1968; MMus, 1971, PhD, 1973, Wash. Univ., St. Louis; studies w. noted tchrs. Debut: 1953. Career: num. concerts in Ams.; Soloist 0 Recitalist; Chosen to app. in Wanda Landowska Mem. Concert, Landowska Ctr., Lakeville, Conn.; Assoc. Prof., Voice, Asst. Dean, Coll. of Fine Arts, Univ. of Southern Miss. Publs: The Songs of Francis Poulenc for Voice 0 Piano (w. transls. of poems), 1973. Mbrships. incl: Nat. Assn. Tchrs. of Singing; Am. Musicol. Soc. Recip. many awards 0 hons. Hobby: Sailing. Address: Coll. of Fine Arts, Box 264, Southern Stn., Univ. of Southern Miss., Hattiesburg, MS 39401, USA.

WOOD, William, b. 3 Aug. 1935, San Francisco, Calif., USA. Associate Professor of Music; Composer. Educ: AA, Sacramento Jr. Coll., 1955; BA, Sacramento State Coll., 1957; MA, Univ. Ore., 1958; DMus Arts, Estman Schl. of Music, 1965, m. Erin S Armstrong, 2 s. Career: Comps. performed in USA 0 Europe; Comp. in res., Univ. NM. Comps. incl: Trios for flute, oboe, clarinet, amplified piano O percussion (recorded); Sonata for violin O piano (recorded); Vortrag for Oboe O Piano (recorded). Mbrships: Am. Soc. Univ. Comps.; Int. Webern Soc. Recip. Prize, Prague Spring Festival Int. Comps. Competition, 1966. Hobbies: Baseball; Basketball; Hiking; Reading. Address: 12508 Prospect Ave., NE, Albuquerque, NM 87112, USA.

WOODAGE, Wesley, b. 23 Apr. 1917, Exeter, UK. Orchestral Player (Trumpet, Cornet, etc.); Teacher 0 Conductor of Brass. Educ: ARCM. m. Decima Kathleen Ellen, 1 s., 1 d. Debut: w. LPO, 1938. Career: LPO, 1938-39; Royal Marines Staff Band, 1939-47; LPO, 1947-50; BBC Symph. Orch., 1950-71; currently on staff i/c Brass, Haberdasher's Aske's Schl., Elstree, O King's Hs. Prep. Schl., Richmond, Surrey, UK; Freelance Player, Cond.; Coach O Tchr.; Coach to Herts. County Youth Band. Mbrships: ISM; Asst. Masters Assn.; MCC; Musician's Union. Recip. Kent Scholarship, RCM, 1935-39. Hobbies: Sports, esp. cricket; Gardening. Address: 'Timbers', St. Nicholas Close, Elstree, Herts WD6 3EW, UK.

WOODBURY, Ward, b. 23 July 1922, Durango, Colo., USA. Music Educator; Pianist; Conductor. Educ: BA, Western State Coll. of Colo., 1943; MA, 1945, Perf.'s Cert., 1949, PhD, 1954, Eastman Schl. of Music. m. Anna Jean McInturf, 3 children. Career incls: Music Dir. O Cond., Winter Pk. Bach Fest., 1966-; Dir. of Music, 1966-, Prof. of Music Rollins Coll., Winter Pk., Fla.; Cond., Fla. Symph.-Rollins Chmbr. Orch., 1967-; Brevard Music Ctr. (chorus, orch., opera), 1967-. Mbrships. incl: Dir., Coun. of Arts O Scis. of Ctrl. Fla O Civic Music Assn.; Am. Chapt. New Bach Soc.; Nat. Assn. Schls. of Music; MENC; Music Tchrs. Nat. Assn. Contbr. to profl. publs. Hobby: Private Aviation. Address: Box 2371, Rollins Coll, Winter Park, FL 32789, USA. 7.

WOODHOUSE, Francis Michael, b. 24 May 1944, N Fitzroy, Melbourne, Aust. Singer (Bass Baritone). Educ: Grad., Aust. Nat. Theatre Opera Schl., Melbourne. m. Yvonne Elizabeth. Debut: 'South Pacific', Palais Theatre, St Kilda, Melbourne . Career: 1st TV perf., 'Quem Queritis', Melbourne Town Hall, 1973; Stage roles incl: Mephistopheles, 'Faust'; Collatinus, 'Rape of Lucretia'; Sarastro, 'Magic Flute'; Sparafucile, 'Rigoletto'; Prince Gremin, 'Eugene Onegin'; Don Basilio, 'Barber of Seville'; Brit. premieres, Hecules, 'Giasone', 1975, O Viliotto, 'La Vera Constanza', 1976. Recip: Schlrship. to Aust. Nat. Theatre Opera Schl. Address: 32 Punchcroft, New Ash Green, Kent, UK.

WOODLAND, Rae, b. Nottingham, UK. Concert, Oratorio O Operatic Soprano. Educ: Pvte. vocal study W. Roy Henderson O at Opera Schl. w. Joan Cross; Dip., ibid. m. Denis Stanley. Debut: Queen of the Night in The Magic Flute, Engl. Nat. Opera, Sadlers Wells. Career incl: opera performances w. Glyndebourne, Covent Gdn., Engl. Nat. Welsh Nat. Scottish Nat., Stadtschouburg Amsterdam, Flemish, Antwerp, Aixen-Provence, Rome Radio O num. Aldeburgh Festivals; Visits to USSR, Brussels O Scandinavia; Oratorio performances w. leading choral soc. O symph. orchs. of UK O W. Europe; Regular broadcaster on BBC radio O TV; Tours w. Royal Ballet O Festival Ballet. Recordings: incl: Midsummer Night's Dream; Montezuma; Sir Arthur Bliss Birthday Record; Glamourous Night. Mbrships: Equity; Inc. Soc. of Musicians; Royal Phil. Soc. Hobbies incl: Gardening, Cooking, Collecting Antiques O China. Address: 33 Moss Ln., Pinner, Middx., UK.

WOODS, Elaine, b. 5 May 1946, Radcliffe, Lancs., UK. Soprano Singer. Educ: St. Anne's Coll., Oxford; BA (Oxon.); studied w. Elsie Thurston, 1964-75, & Marjorie Thomas, 1975-; RMCM, 1970-73. m. Daniel Powell. Debut: as Violetta w. Kent Opera, Edinburgh Fest., 1979. Career: Recitals, apps. w. choral socs. & orchs. throughout UK; apps. w. Engl. Nat. Opera & Kent Opera; perf. at Wexford Fest.; perfs. for BBC. Mbr., ISM. Recip., 2nd prize, Int. Vocalisten Concours, 's-Hertogenbosch, 1978. Hobbies incl: Walking; Reading; Antiques; Birdwatching. Address: 6 Netherfield Rd., London N12 8DP, UK.

WOODS, Richard Stanley, b. 9 Dec. 1952, London, UK. School Music Director. Educ: Haberdashers' Aske's Schl., Elstree, Herts.; Royal Acad. of Music, London; Grad., Royal Schl. of Music; Lic., Royal Acad. of Music; Assoc., Royal Coll. of Music; Lic., Guildhall Schl. of Music; Lic., Trinity Coll. of Music, London; Postgrad. Cert. in Educ. Bishop Otter Coll. Chichester, W. Sussex. Career: Mbr., Piano Master Class, Nat. Youth Orch. of GB. Mbrships: Incorp. Soc. of Musicians; Brit. Fedn. of Music Festivals, Music Tchrs. Assn.; Royal Acad. of Music Club. Recip. York Bowen Prize, Royal Acad. of Music, 1974. Address: Waltham, The Bramblings, Rustington, W Sussex, BN16 2DA, UK.

WOODWARD, Enid McClure, b. 10 Sept. 1908, Wash. CH, Ohio, USA. Professor of Conducting, Organ, & Piano. Educ: BA, Western Coll. (now Miami Univ., Ohio), 1936; BMus, 1930, MMus, 1936, Coll. of Music of Cinn. (now Univ. of Cinn.). m. Henry Lynde Woodward, 1 s., 1 d. Career: Coll. of Music, Cinn., Ohio; Western Coll., Oxford, Ohio; Carleton Coll., Northfield, Minn.; Prof. Emeritus, ibid. Mbrships. incl: Assoc., Am. Guild of Organists; Coll. Music Soc. Publs. incl: An Organ Primer, 1959; Library of Organ Music (ed. w. husband) (4 vols.), 1966.

Recip., Minn. State Arts Coun. Award, 1974. Hobby: Cooking. Address: 209 W Univ. Dr., Chapel Hill, NC 27514, USA.

WOODWARD, Henry Lynde, b. 18 Sept. 1908, Cinn., Ohio, USA. Professor of Music Theory & History, & Organ. Educ: AB, Miami Univ., Ohio, 1936; BMus, 1929, MMus, 1932, Coll. of Music of Cinn.; AM 1942, PhD 1952, Harvard Univ. m. Enid McClure, 1 s., 1 d. Career: Vassar Coll., Poughkeepsie, NY, 1938-39; Carleton Coll., Northfield, Minn., 1942-73; Prof. Emeritus, ibid. Comps. incl: O Clap Your Hands (anthem); var. short organ pieces. Mbrships: incl: Past VP & Treas., Coll. Music Soc.; Past Coun., Am. Musicol. Soc. Publs. incl: Notes for the Study of Harmony, 1959, 3rd ed. 1970. Contbr. to profl. publs. Mbr. (archivist) Coll. Music Soc. Recip., Minn. State Arts Coun. Award, 1974. Hobbies incl: Woodworking. Address: 209 W Univ. Dr., Chapel Hill, NC 27514, USA. 2.

WOODWARD, Kerry Russell, b. 31 July 1939, Barry, Wales, UK. Conductor; Pianist; Editor. Educ: BMus, Cardiff Univ.; MTC, London Univ.; Conducting Scholar, GSM, London. m. Julie Anne Woodward, 1 d. Career: Cond., Netherlands Opera, London Sinfonietta, BBC Welsh Orch., BBC Scottish Orch., London Studio Strings, London Studio Players, Orch. of Royal Ballet, Covent Gdn.; Assoc. Cond., BBC Singers; Cond., Netherlands Chmbr. Choir. Comps: Ed., Der Kaiser Von Atlantis, one-act opera by Viktor Ullmann; Arr. of 4 Xmas Carols; Incidental music for radio plays. Num. recordings w. var. orchs. Contbr. to Musical Opinion. Hobbies incl: Family; Tennis. Mgmt: Horowitz Mgmt. Address: 42 Belsize Ave., London NW3, UK.

WOODWARD, Roger Robert, , b. 20 Dec. 1944, Sydney, NSW, Aust. Pianist. Educ: State Conserv. of Music, Sydney, Aust.: MusM O advanced studies in Piano, Comp. O Cond., State Acad. of Music, Warsaw, Poland. Career: Org. O Dir. of Annual Series of New Music Concerts in London O Sydney; Has worked w. num. Comps. inclng. Boulez, Barragué, Cage, Xenakis, Feldman, Penderecki, Bussotti, Stockhausen O Meale; Has appeared w. all leading Orchs. O at major Music Fests. throughout world, inclng. Proms., Albert Hall, London (BBC), La Scala Opera House, Festival Hall O var. tours of USA, Japan, Aust. O Europe; Has worked w. num. Conds., inclng. Boulez, Maazel, Mehta, Rowicki, Ozawa, Leinsdorf, Masur O Susskind. Recordings: Barraqué; Bussotti; Brouwer; 2 Chopin Recitals; Rachmaninoff Préludes; Skryabin; Prokofiev; Shostakovich; Meale; Sculthorpe; Edwards; Complete Takemitsu, 1974; Beethoven Sonata, Op. 57, 1974; Brahms Piano Concerto No. 1, 1977. Hons: Comps. Award for Services to New Music in Aust.; Winner, Int. Gaudeamus Competition for Contemporary Music, Holland, 1970. Hobbies: Films; Beach: Collecting O Investigating of Original Musical Scores. Mgmt: Ibbs O Tillett, 124 Wigmore St., London, UK. Address: 94 Effra Parade, London, SW2, UK.

WOOLDRIDGE, David, b. 24 Aug. 1931, Seal, Kent, UK. Conductor; Composer. Educ: RAM; FCTL; BMus, PhD, London Univ; MM, Ind. Univ. m. 1) Anita Visconti (div); 2) Angela Smythe-Browne (dec); 1s. Career: Staff cond., Bavarian State Opera, 1954-56; Musical Dir., Lebanese Nat. Orch., 1961-65; Musical Dir., Cape Town Symph. Orch., 1965-66; Guest cond., Royal Ballet, 1967; Vis. Prof., Ind. Univ. Schl. of Music, 1968-70, Grinnel Coll., 1970-71, Univ. of Calif., 1972 O 1976-77; Guest cond., RPO, Cleveland, Boston, BBC, num. radio orchs. Comps: Viola concerto (recorded); 4 Ballets; Partita for orch. (recorded); Movements for 10 soloists (recorded); 5 Italian songs (recorded); 4 string quartets; 6 settings of Ezra Pound (recorded); film O theatre music. Publs: Conductor's World, 1970; From the Steeples O Mountains: A Study of Charles Ives, 1974. Contbr. to: Tempo; Musical Am.; JAMS. Mbr. profl. socs. Hons: Royal Phil. Soc. Prize, 1950; Harkness Fellowship, 1955-57; Chapelbrook Fellowship, 1969-70. Hobbies: Driving; Riding; Chess. Address: Bridgewater, CT 06752, USA.

WOOLFENDEN, Guy Anthony, b. 12 July, 1937, Ipswich, UK. Composer; Conductor. Educ: Westminster Abbey Choir Schl.; Christ's Coll., Cambridge; MA (Cantab.); GSM; LGSM. m. Jane Aldrick, 3s. Career: Music Dir., Royal Shakespeare Co., Stratford-on-Avon; comp. 70 scores for this co.; also comp. scores for Burgtheater, Vienna, O Comedie Francaise, Paris, O for films, radio O TV; cond., most Brit. Symph. Orchs; cond., concerts in Can., Germany O Paris; cond., opera for BBC radio O TV O for Scottish Opera, 1979; arr. Tchaikovsky score for Australian Ballet of Anna Karenina. Recordings: Music for Royal Shakespeare Co.; Music for The Winter's Tale; Songs of Ariel. Mbrships: Musicians' Union; Performing Right Soc., Mechanical Copyright Protection Soc.; Comps. Guild; ISM. Hons: PRS Ivor Novello Award for best Brit. musical, 1976-77, O Soc. of W End Theatre Award for best Brit. Musical, 1977 (both for The Comedy of Errors). Mgmt: Trafalgar Perry Ltd., London.

Address: Malvern House, Sibford Ferris, Banbury, Oxon. OX15 5RG, UK. 13.

WOOLFORD, Delia, b. 2 Aug. 1931, Petworth, UK. Contralto Singer. Educ: pvte. 0 at RCM; ARCM (singing perf. 0 piano tchng). m. Eric Waddington. Career: recitals for BBC of oratorio, lieder, English 0 French Songs; apps. in UK, Netherlands, Germany 0 France in Bach's St. Matthew Passion; oratorio 0 recital perfs. throughout UK 0 Europe. Recordings: Bach's St. Matthew Passion; Blow's Venus 0 Adonis. Mbrships: ISM; RCM Union. recip., London Musical Soc. prize, circa 1951-52. Hobbies: Reading; Swimming; Home; Family 0 Friends; France: Food 0 Wine. Address: Langley, Pathfields Close, Haslemere, Surey GU27 2BL, UK. 27, 29, 30.

WOOLLAM, Kenneth Geoffrey, b. 16 Jan. 1937, Chester, UK. Opera Singer. Educ: Chester Cathedral Choir Schl.; RCM. m. Phoebe Elizabeth Scrivenor, 3 children. Debut: Sadler's Wells, London, 1972. Career: Apps. w. Engl. Nat. Opera., Scottish Opera, Royal Opera, Ghent; roles incl. Walther (Die Meistersinger), Adolar (Euryanthe), Siegfried (The Ring), Bacchus (Ariadne auf Naxos), Boris (Katya Kabanova) Laca (Jenufa) 0 Husband in world premiere of John Tavener's Gentle Spriit at Bath; 3 films - Canio (I Pagliacci), Alfredo (La Traviata) 0 Hoffmann (Tales of Hoffmann); concerts 0 oratorios w. leadning socs. Mbrships: ISM; Savage Club; The Glass Circle. Hobby: Antique Glass. Mgmt: Music Int. Address: 20 Burnaby Gdns., Chiswick, London W4 3DT, UK.

WOOLLEN, Russell, b. 7 Jan. 1923, Hartford, Conn., USA. Composer; Pianist; Organist; Harpsichordist; Professor of Music. Educ: BA, St. Mary's Univ., Balt., Md., 1944; MA, Theol. & Romance langs., Cath. Univ. Am., Wash. DC, 1948; MA, Music, Harvard Univ., 1954; Grad. study, ibid., 1954-57; var. pvte. tutors & summer schls. m. Carolyn Fox, 1 d. Career incls: Music Fac., Cath. Univ. Am., 1948-62; Howard Univ., 1968-74; Staff keybd. artist, Nat. Symph. Orch., Wash. DC, 1956-. Comps. incl: Missa Antiphonalis, Latin 1961, Engl. 1962; Symphony No 1, 1961; Resurrection for Mixed Chorus (text John Donne), 1972. Mbr. profl. orgs. Hons. incl: Geo. Arthur Knight Prize, chmbr. music, Harvard, 1954; Ernst Bloch Choral Award, 1962. Hobbies incl: French lit. Address: 4747 Berkeley Terr. NW, Washington, DC 20007, USA.

WOOLLEY, Clara Virginia, b. 11 Aug., 1938, Warren, Ind., USA. Musician (violin, piano, organ); Music Educator. Educ: BS, Manchester Coll., 1960; MS, Ind. State Univ.; Life License for tchng. music in Ind. m. Daniel Joseph Woolley, 1 d. Career: Public schl. music tchr., 1960-70; Pvte. studio for piano & organ tchng.; Organist, 1st United Ch. of Christ; Violinist, South Bend Symph.; Pt.-time Instr. in Music, Ancilla Coll., Ind. Mbrships: Locals 58 & 278, Am. Fedn. of Musicians; Nat. Guild of Piano Tchrs.; Music Educators Nat. Conference; Ind. Music Educators Assn. Hobbies: Sewing; Travel. Address: 708 S Michigan St., Plymouth, IN 46563, USA. 5, 23, 27, 29, 30.

WORDSWORTH, William Brocklesby, b. 17 Dec. 1908, London, UK. Composer. m. Frieda Nellie Robson, 2 s., 2 d. Compositions incl: Symposium (for solo violin, strings, percussion, etc.), 1972; The Solitary Reaper (song for soprano, piano & clarinet), 1973; Adonais, for 5 solo voices, 1974; 5 Symphs.; 3 Concertos; 3 Overtures; other orchl. works; 6 String Quartets; 2 Quintets; 3 trios; Confluence. op 100, for full orch., commissioned for opening of Eden Court Theatre, 1976. Other chamber works: Symphony No. 6, op. 102, Full Orch., with Voices, 1976; Reflections (Harp & Piano), op. 101; Four Shakespeare Songs, op. 103, 1977. Contbr. to Composer. Mbrships: CGGB (chmn., 1959); Scottish br. chmn., 1966-70); Chmn., Badenoch Arts Soc., 1968-77. Hons: 1st Prize, Clements Mem. Prize, 1941; 1st Prize, Edinburgh Int. Festival, 1950. Hobbies: Golf; Carpentry; Gardening. Mgmt: Scotus Music Publications of Edinburgh. Address: Ard Insh, Kincraig, Kingussie, Inverness-shire PH21 1NA, UK. 3.

WORKMAN, William, b. 4 Feb. 1940, Valdosta, Ga., USA. Singer (Lyric Baritone). Educ: BA, Davidson Coll.; Artist Dip., Curtis Inst. of Music, Phila. m. Elizabeth Parker, 1 d. Debut: Hamburg State Opera. Career: Res. Leading Baritone, Hamburg State Opera, German Fed. Repub., 1965-72, & Frankfurt Opera, 1973-; Guest perfs., Paris Opera, Geneva, Amsterdam, Rome, Stuttgart, Aix-en-Provence, Bordeaux, Strasbourg, Santa Fe, Marlboro, Teatro Colon, Buenos Aires; Aust. Broadcasting Commission Tour, Aust.; Film roles: Papageno, Zauberflöte, & Tony, Globolinks (created at world premiere). Hons: Oberdorfer Prize, 1970. Hobbies: Sport; Reading. Mgmt: Thea Dispeker; Lies Askonas; Claude Stricker. Address: 638 Bad Homburg, Kaiser Friedrich Promenade 167, German Fed. Repub.

WORM, Dieter Gerhardt, b. 31 Aug. 1930, Zittau, Germany. Conductor. Educ: Cond. w. Prof. Abendroth, Dresden &

Weimar; Theory of Music w. Profs. W Vetter & E H Meyer, Berlin. m. Gudrun Götz, 4 c. Debut: w. Dresden Phil. Orch., 1962. Career: Chief Prod., VEB Deutsche Schallplatten, 1956-72; Dir. Berlin State Orch., 1973-78; Chief Cond., Städtische Theater, Karl-Marx-Stadt, 1975-; Prof. of Cond., Int. Summer Acad. Mozarteum, Salzburg. Hobbies incl: Family. Address: Waidinannsweg 49, 1405 Glijuicke, German Dem. Repub.

WORMHOUDT, Pearl Shinn, b. 27 Oct. 1915, Knoxville, Iowa, USA. Singing Teacher. Educ: BA, Ctrl. Coll., Iowa; MA, Columbia Univ.; Pvte. voice study w. Douglas Stanley, Paola Novikova; Song & Opera coaching w. Stevenson Barrett & others; Opera workshop w. Herbert Graf. m. Arthur L Wormhoudt, 1 s. Career: Voice Tchr., 22 yrs.; design, 9 yrs., Vocal pedagogy, master classes, vocal adjudicator; Curator, William Penn Coll., Jones Mid-East Collection; Lectr., Mid-East Music & Art. Publs: The Voice as an Instrument, a Handbook for Singing Teachers & Students, 1979. Mbrships: Int. Assn. for Experimental Rsch. in Singing; Past Pres., Iowa Chapt., Nat. Comm. Mbr., Singing in Contemp. Soc., Nat. Assn. of Tchrs. of Singing. Hobbies: Sculpture & ceramics; Research in music history & in performance psychology; Dance; Economics. Address: 1818 Kemble Dr., Oskaloosa, IA 52577, USA.

WORRALL, Peter Clement, b. 11 Feb. 1946, Leeds, UK. Cellist. Educ: RAM, London, 1963-67; Recital Dip., 1966; ARAM, 1977; Dip. di Merito, Accademia Chigiana, Siena, 1966-67; French Govt. Scholar, Paris, 1967-68; studied w. André Navarra. m. Ruth Lifshitz, 1 s., 1 d. Career: Freelance Cellist, London (apps. w. ECO, LPO, etc.), 1968-70; Prin. Cellist, Edmonton Symph. Orch., Atla., Can., 1970-72; Can. Premier, Britten Cello Symph., 1972; Co-Prin. Cello, Israel Chmbr. Ensemble, Tel Aviv, 1972-73; Mbr., Israel Phil. Orch., 1974-75; Prin. Cello, Hallé Orch., Manchester, 1975-. Mbr., Musicians Union. Hons: ARAM, 1977. Hobbies: Driving; Swimming; Camping; Reading. Mgmt: Hallé Concerts Soc. Address: 5 Motcombe Farm Rd., Heald Green, Cheadle, Cheshire SK8 3RW, UK.

WORRALL, William Charles (Bill), b. 23 Mar. 1936, London, Ont., Can. Publisher. Educ: Univ. of Calif., Irvine Ext.; NY Univ., Notre Dame Coll. Ext.; Long Beach City Coll. Appts: Publisher, Keyboard Wld. Mag.; The Organist Mag.; Fndr., Int. Young Organists Assn.; Dir., Home Organist Fests. Organist; organist, pianist, concerts in USA, Can., Mexico, Aust. Recordings: 4 LPs. Mbrships: Pres., 1971-72, Long Beach Profl. Organists Assn.; Dir., 1973-74, Vol. Servs., Exceptional Childrens Fndn.; Bd., Elect. Arts Fndn.; Hollywood Comedy Club; Los Angeles Wld. Affair Coun.; Pres., 1977 Orange Co. Profl. Organists. Hons: Finalist Judge, Yamaha Electone Can. Fest., 1976. Address: 8525 S Passons Blvd., Pico Rivera, CA 90660, USA.

WORTHINGTON, Roger Paul, b. 24 May 1951, London, UK. Composer; Freelance Viola Player 0 Teacher. Educ: ARCM (piano 0 viola); Univ. of Exeter. m. Elizabeth Mary Suwala. Career: Among other orchs. 0 ensembles has played with LSO, Royal Ballet, 0 London Fest. Ballet; Gave chairty recital w. wife, London, 1974. Comps: var. chmbr works inclng. music for contemporary dance. Mbrships: Comps. Guild of GB; ISM. Address: White Lodge, 21 Hazelmere Rd., Petts Wood, Kent, UK.

WORTON-STEWARD, Andrew, b. 20 Feb. 1948, Kent, UK. Composer; Teacher; Recitalist (organ). Educ: BA, Univ. of Newcastle-upon-Tyne; Coll. Conserv. of Music, Univ. of Cinn., USA; DMus; Dip. Ed; ARCO. Career: Recitals of Comps. in USA 0 England. Num. comps. Recordings: Chamber Music. Contbr. to: Comp. Mbrships: Hon. Music Soc. of Am. Hons: Winner, BBC Young Comps. Forum, 1978; Organ Scholarship, 1969; Grad. Assistantship to Univ. of Cinn., 1973. Hobbies: Reading; TV; Walking. Address: c/o 28 St. Leonards Rd., Hove, Sussex, UK.

WOUDENBERG, Pierre Willem Hubert, b. 19 Dec. 1949, The Hague, Netherlands. Clarinettist. Educ: Solosit Dip., Royal Dutch Conserv., The Hague, 1975. Career: Free-lance Clarinettist, maj. Dutch orchs.; Mbr., Aulos-Amsterdam Wind Quintet, sev. yrs.; Mbr., Schoenberg Ensemble, The Hague; Clarinettist 0 Es-Clarinettist, Rotterdam Phil. Orch., 1975-; Mbr., Rotterdam Wind Ensemble, 1975-; Hons: 1st Prize w. Aulos-Amsterdam Wind Quintet, Nat. Chamber Music Competition, 1973; Rock-Medaille, for best instrumental examination, Royal Dutch Conserv., 1975. Address: Breitnerlaan 65, The Hague, Netherlands.

WOYTOWICZ, Boleslaw, b. 5 Dec. 1899, Dunajowce, USSR. Composer; Pianist; Editor. Educ: Univ. of Keiv, USSR; Univ. of Warsaw; Warsaw Conserv., Dip. in Piano, 1924; Comp. studies w. Nadia Boulanger, Paris, 1930-32 (Polish State

Scholarship). Career: Concerts, recitals, TV O radio apps., W Europe; USA; Prof. of Piano, Warsaw Conserv., 1935-39; Prof. of Comp. O Piano, Ktowice Conserv., Warsaw Conserv., Krakow Conserv., 1946-70. Comps. 2 sets of Piano Etudes; 3 Symphs.; 4 Cantatas; 2 String Quartets. Recordings: Chopin Etudes, complete (2 discs). Publs: Ed., Debussy, Complete Works for Piano, 1970; Ed., Beethoven, 11 Sonatas for Piano Solo, Piano-Violin, Piano-Cello, 1975; Var. works of Tchaikovsky, Grieg, etc., 1975. Mbrships: Life Mbr., Union of Polish Comps. Hons: Dip w. Distinction, Int. Chopin Piano Competition, Warsaw, 1927; French Gold Medal for Comp. (Ballet Score - Le Retour), 1932. Hobbies: Literature; Philosophy. Mgmt: Polish Artists Agency (PAGART). Address: Kilinskiego 50, Katowice, Poland.

WOYTOWICZ, Stefania, b. 1922, Orynin, Poland. Concert Singer. Educ: State HS of Music, Cracow. m. Stanislaw Rudnicki. Career: has app. thr'out world as Recitalist & Soloist w. major orchs. under noted conds.; has premiered many works by contemp. Polish composers; sings oratorio. Hons. incl: Golden Cross of Merit; Polonia Restituta; State Prize of Merit; Orpheus Prize of Polish Musicians' Assn.; 1st Prize, J S Bach Competition, Poland, 1950; 1st Prize, Prague Spring Fest., 1957. Address: A1. Przuaciol 3-13, Warsaw, Poland.

WRAGG, Gerald, b. 10 Mar. 1931, Chesterfield, UK. Conductor; Accompanist. Educ: Royal Manchester Coll. of Music. m. Alison Jane Anthony, 1 s., 1 d. by previous marriage. Debut: as child for ENSA. Career: Free-lance Cond. & Accomp.; Pianist for Arts Council Opera for All, 1954; Asst., Rome Opera, 1956-58; Accomp., Soc. Musicales di Gioventu D'Italia, 1956-58; TV apps. for BBC; Accomp. BBC recitals; Visiting Lectr., Capetown Univ., 1966; Dir. of Opera, City of Leeds Coll. of Music, 1968-. Recordings: w. the Wondertones. Contbr. to: Modern Dance by Jane Winearls, 1968; Musical Opinion. Hons: Max Mayor Prize, RNCM, 1952. Hobbies: Fishing; Crime Fiction; Photography. Address: 14 Oakfield Terrace, Leeds 6, UK.

WRANCHER, Elizabeth Ann, b. 19 Oct. 1930, Indpls., Ind., USA. Opera Singer; Concert Artist; Teacher. Educ: BMus, Ind. Univ., 1955; Hochschule für Musik, Munich, Germany. Debut: Landes-Theater, Detmold, Germany. Career incls: Contracts & Guest Perfs., maj. opera houses, Germany; App. extensively in Belgium, Switz. & Austria; Guest Soloist, radio, Munich, Cologne; Tchr., Univ. of S Fla., USA, 6 yrs.; Hd., Vocal Prog., Fla. Technol. Univ., Orlando. Recordings: Music of Thomas Beversdorf. Mbrships. incl: Nat. Soc. of Arts & Letters; Mu Phi Epsilon. Recip. Fulbright Scholarship, 1955. Hobby: Study of philosophies & religs. Address: 200 St. Andrews Blvd. Apt. 3607, Winter Park, FL 32789, USA. 3, 27.

WRIGHT, Alfred George James, b. 23 June 1916, London, UK. Professor; College Administrator; Band & Symphony Conductor; French Horn Player; Writer. Educ: BA, Univ. of Miami, Fla., 1937; MEd, ibid., 1947. m. Gladys Stone Wright, 2 d. Career: Played French Horn in Opera & Symph. Orchs.; Dir. of Music, Cond. of the Bands, Purdue Univ., Lafayette, Ind., 1954-; Contributing Ed., Instrumentalist Mag., 1955-; Bd. of Advsrs., Music Jrnl., 1965-. Bd. Advsrs., Int. Music Fests., 1971-; Pres., Int. Tours Inc., Elected to Acad. of Wind & Percussion Arts, 1968-. 680 Perfs. in Radio City Music Hall, NYC. Recordings: Rhythm & Colour; Great Marches for Band; Purdue Band; Big Ten Salute; Glory of the Gridiron. Publs: Marching Band Fundamentals, 1963; The Show Band, 1957. Contbr. to: NIMAC Manual, 1963; Music Education in Action, 1960; The Band Directors Guide, 1964; The Instrumentalist, 1948-; num. other profl. jrnls. Mbrships: var. offices in num. profl. orgs. Hons: Kappa Kappa Psi, 1956; Phi Beta Mu, 1956. Hobbies: Ecology; Wild Animal Protection. Address: 344 Overlook Dr., W Lafayette, IN, USA. 8.

WRIGHT, Anthony Paul, b. 28 Aug. 1951, Taplow, Bucks., UK. Organist; Conductor; Recitalist, Teacher. Educ: BA (Cantab.); MA, ibid; FRCO; FTCL; ARCM. m. Sheila Brenda Emms. Debut: Royal Albert Hall, aged 15 (organ). Career: Many London apps. at Wigmore Hall, South Bank, Royal Albert Hall etc.; 4 organ recital tours of USA. 3 yrs. work as Musical Dir. in profl. theatre; sub-organist, Coventry Cathedral. Comps: Missa Brevis for men's voices. Hobbies: Sport; Reading; Cinema. Address: Coventry Cathedral, 7 Priory Row, Coventry, UK.

WRIGHT, Brian James, b. 4 Aug. 1946, Tonbridge, Kent, UK. Conductor. Educ: Gulbenkian Scholar, Guildhall Schl. of Music; AGSM (Condng. O Singing); Munich Music Acad., Germany. M. Susan Jane. Debut: Royal Festival Hall, London, 1972 (Messiah). Career: Profl. singer (tenor) w. Engl. Opera Grp.; Recitals, Wigmore Hall, 1971 O Purcell Room, 1972; Assoc. Cond., Goldsmiths Choral Union, 1972; Musical Dir., ibid,

1973; Cond., Highgate Choral Soc., 1972; Asst. Cond., London Symph. Orch., 1974-75; Guest Cond., Philharmonia, BBC Symph. Orch., RPO, etc. O in Portugal, Switz., Belgium O Germany, 1975-78; Cond., BBC Symph. Chorus, 1976-. Hons. incl: 2nd Prize, Rupert Fndn. Competition, London, 1974; Silver Medal, Guido Cantelli Competition, Milan, 1975. Hobbies incl: Singing; Reading; D-I-Y. Mgmt: Norman McCann Ltd. Address: 34 Priory Rd., London N8 7EX, UK.

WRIGHT, David Arthur, b. 16 Apr. 1934, Leamington Spa, UK. Organist; Conductor; Director of Music; Lecturer; Examiner. Educ: Lichfield Cathedral Choir Schl.; Exeter Coll., Oxford (organ scholar); BMus, MA (oxon.); FRCO. m. Joan Mavis Gelsthorp, 1 s. Career: Asst. organist, New Coll., Oxford, 1956-57; organist O choirmaster, Boston Parish Ch.; Dir. of Music, Boston Grammar Schl.; cond., Boston Choral Soc. O Orch., 1957-; tutor, Etra-Mural Dept., Nottingham Univ., 1958-69; Examiner, Assoc. Bd., 1969-; TV O radio broadcasts; recitals. Comps: Ch. O Educ. music. s/sev. recordings. fndr., pre., S O S Lincs. Organists' Assn. recip., FRCO Limpus Prize, 1955. Hobbies: Photography; Motor Car Mechanisms. Address: 118 Fishtoft Rd., Boston, Lincs. PE21 ODG, UK.

WRIGHT, Desmond Elliston, b. 23 Nov. 1940, Durban, S Africa. Pianist. Educ: ARCM; Studies w. Myra Hess, 2 yrs. m. Annagret Ginsig, 1s. Career: Concerts as Soloist O in Chmbr. Music in Austria, Germany, Switzerland, Italy O S Africa; Mbr., Teaching Staff, Hochschule Mozarteum, 1972-. Recordings incl: As Mbr. of Das Mozart Trio, Sämtliche Kaviertrios (Mozart); Sämtliche Sonaten für Klavier und Violine (Mozart). Address: Wartgutstr. 1, 8413 Neftenbach, Switz.

WRIGHT, Edred John, b. 14 Feb. 1911, London, UK. Director of Music. Educ: MusB, Cantuar; ARSCM. m. Jane Gannaway, 1s., 1 d. Career: St. Michael's Coll., Tenbury, Worcs.; Choirmaster, RSCM, Canterbury, O Addington Palace, Croydon; Dir. of Music, The King's Schl., Canterbury, Kent; Special Commissioner, RSCM. Publs: Basic Choirtraining; Musical Ed., King's School Hymn Book; King's School Psalter. Mbrships: Music Master's Assn., ISM; Music Panel, S eastern Arts Assn; Canterbury Arts Coun.; Marlowe Theatre Trust, Canterbury; Trustee, Kent Opera, Canterbury. Hobbies: Theatre; Gardening. Address: 2 Summer Hill, Harbledown, Canterbury, Kent, UK.

WRIGHT, Maurice Willis, b. 17 Oct. 1949, Front Royal, Va., USA. Composer; Educator; Lecturer. Educ: BA, Duke Univ., NC, 1972; MA, Columbia Univ., NYC, 1974; studied w. noted tchrs. Career: Comp., instrumental, vocal O electronic music for concert O cinema; Music Lectr., Columbia Univ. O Columbia-Princeton Electronic Music Ctr.; Music Co-ord. Cons., Creative Artists Prog. Serv. Proj., NY State Coun. for Arts; Dir. of Electronic Music, Boston Univ. Comps. publd. incl: A Noise Did Rise Like Thunder in My Hearing (concerto for bass trombone O 5 instruments); Cantata for Tenor, Percussion O Electronic Sound; Five Pieces for Viola; Stellae, new music for orch. O quadraphonic electronic sound; Night Watch, song cycle; Country Music (computer processed animal sounds). Recordings: Electronic Composition. Mbrships. incl: Am. Comps. Alliance; Pres., Guild of Comps.; Sec./Treas., Center for Computer Music O Studies in the Computer Arts. Recip. sev. awards. Address: 415 Riverside Dr. No. 3B, NY, NY /&& °; USA.

WRIGHT, Rosemarie, b. Chorley, UK. Concert Pianist. Educ: Dip., Vienna State Acad.; RAM w. Harold Craxton; LRAM; ARAM; studied piano w. Edwin Fischer, chamber music w. Pablo Casals. m. Michel Brandt, 2s. Debut: Vienna, 1960. Career: Concerts w. orch., recitals O broadcasts in France, Germany, Austria, Italy, Switz., Portugal, Greece, Turkey, Holland, Belgium, Norway, Denmark, USA, UK; Perfs. at num. fests.; Pianist in Residence, Southampton Univ., 1972-; Prof. of piano, RNCM, 1973-78; Prof of Piano, RAM, 1978-. Hons: Albanesi Prize; Chappell Silver Medal; Kate Steel Prize; Matthay Fellowship; Haydn Prize, Vienna, 1959; Bösendorfer Prize 1960. Hobbies: Art; Educ. Address: 84 Filsham Rd., Hastings, E Sussex, UK. 27, 30.

WRIGHT, Thomas Gordon, b. 21 March 1929, Indianapolis, Ind., USA. Concert Pianist; Professor of Music. Educ: BM, Butler Univ.; MS, Ind. Univ.; Grad. study equal to Music Doc., Columbia Univ., Dip, Arthur Jordan Conserv. of Music. Single, 1 d. Career: Concert Pianist, Gershwin specialist, num. apps. w. major US orchs., concerts throughout USA; TV, radio perfs.; Prof., Music, Fla. State Music Tchrs. Assn.; Past Pres., Fla., State Univ. Chapt., Phi Kappa Phi; Pi Kappa Lambda; Phi Mu Alpha; Gold Key; Sigma Delta Pi; Alpha Epsilon Rho; Omicron Delta Kappa. Hons. incl: Fac. of Yr. Award, Gold Key, Fla. State Univ.; Baldwin Artist List; Outstanding Educator of Am., 1975; Oglesby Award, 1975; An Evening w. Gershwin (concert) Hon.

by special resolution of Fla. legislature. Hobbies: Antique aircraft; Hist. of air war, WWI. Mgmt: Artist Bur., Fla. State Univ.; Alkahest Agency, PO Box 12403, Northside Station, Atlanta, GA 30355, USA. Address: Schl. of Music, Fla. State Univ., Tallahassee, FL 32301, USA.

WRIGHT, Wayne Paul, b. 4 Oct. 1936, Dowagiac, Mich., USA. Violinist; Teacher. Educ: BMus, W Mich. Univ.; MMus, Mich. State, Northwestern O Boston Univs. Career: Perf. in orchs., SE USA; Violinist, Str. Quartet, Charlotte, NC; 1st Violin, Louisville Symph. Orch. Mbrships: Chgo. Fedn. of Musicians; NEA. Hons: Undergrad. scholarships; Grad. assistantships; Concertmaster of univ. orchs. Hobbies: Attending lectures; Growing fruit, vegatables O flowers; Participating in theol. activities. Address: 407 Oak St., Dowagiac, MI 49047, USA.

WRONSKI, Tadeusz, b. 1 Apr. 1915, Warsaw, Poland. Musician; Professor; Violinist. Educ: MA (w. distinction), Warsaw State Conserv. of Music, 1939; Conserv. Royale de Musique, Brussels (1st prize w. distinction). m. Halina Radlinska, 1 d. Career incl: concert tours in USSR, UK, Germany, Italy, Turkey, India, Japan, Czech., Bulgaria, Hungary, etc. as soloist O chmbr. music player; Prof., Ind. Univ. Recordings: Muza Poland; Brahms O Berg concertos; Brahms sonatas; Debussy sonata; Turski concerto. Publs: Intonation, 1957; Fingering, 1961; Technology of Violin Playing, 1965; Physiological Approach to Violin Playing, 1970; Bach Sonatas O Partitas, 1970; Talented O Untalented Students, 1979. Mbrships: former Pres., Polish Musicians Assn.; Hon. mbr., Polish Violin Makers Assn.; Hon. mbr., Japanese Strg. Tchrs. Assn. Hons: State Prize for musical achievement, Poland, 1950. Hobbies: Chess; Philosophy. Address: (office) Schl. of Music, Ind. Univ., Music Bldg., Bloomington, In 47405, USA; (home) UL Promyka 41, 01604 Warsaw, Poland. 28, 30.

WU, Enloc Ruth, b. 31 Oct. 1946, Shanghai, China. Concert Pianist. Educ: RCM; ARCM; LRSM. m. Ting Hoi To, 1 d. Debut: London, 1967. Career: Far Eastern tour; BBC Radio & TV broadcasts; concerts, var. music fests.; solo apps. w. major orchs. inclng. London Mozart Players; regular concert tours of UK. Hons: Royal Overseas League C'wlth. Prize, 1966; Chappell Gold Medal, 1967; Nat. Fedn. of Music Socs. Prize, 1968. Hobbies: Bridge; Painting. Mgmt: Helen Jennings Concert Agcy. Address: 76 Halegrove Gdns., Mill Hill, London NW7, UK. 3.

WUENSCH, Gerhard, b. 23 Dec. 1925, Vienna, Austria. University Professor; Composer; Musicologist. Educ: PhD (musicol.), Univ. of Vienna, 1950; Artist's dip. in piano & comp., State Acad. of Music, Vienna, 1952. div., 1 s. Career: Comp. for Austrian radio network RAVAG, 1950-54; theatre & film comp. for var. Austrian cos. Comps. incl: 2 pieces for organ, op. 23; Music for 7 brass, op. 27; Vexilla Regis (cantata), op. 36; Suite for trumpet & organ, Op. 40 (recorded); A Merry Suite, for harpsichord, Op. 26; 4 Mini Suites, for accordion, op. 42 (recorded); Glimpses for piano (excerpts recorded), op. 37; Spectrum, for piano, op. 41; Cameos, for flute & piano, op. 46 (excerpts recorded). Contbr. of articles on Max Reger to Mitteilung des Max Reger-Instituts, 1971 & Festschrift Erich Schenk, 1975. Mbrships: Can. League of Comps.; Can. Assn. of Univ. Schls. of Music; Phi Kappa Lambda; CAPAC. Hons: Benjamin Award (NC Symph.), 1955. Fulbright Grant to Tex., 1954-56; Can. Coun Rsch. grants, 1972, '78. Hobby: Stamp Collecting. Address: 141 Sherwood Ave., London, Ont. N6A 2E4, Can.

WÜHRER, Friedrich Anton Franz, b. 25 June 1900, Vienna, Austria. Pianist. Educ: State Acad. of Music, Vienna; Univ. of Vienna. m. Margaret Jungbluth. Career: Recitalist & solo pianist w. leading orchs. in Europe, Asia, N Africa & USA; appearances w. var. chmbr. ensembles; accompanist; Tchr., pvte. classes & in master classes at Vienna & Salzburg. Recordings: 35 LPs inclng complete piano sonatas of Schubert (Vox label). Mbrships: Comm., Austrian Sect., Int. Soc. for Contemporary Music, 1923-; Assoc., Richard Wagner Acad. Recip: Liszt Prize. Address: Richard-Wagner-Str. 33, D-68 Mannheim, German Fed. Repub.

WULSTAN, David, b. 18 Jan. 1937, Birmingham, UK. University Teacher; Conductor. Educ: Royal Masonic Schl.; Magdalen Coll., Oxford, 1967. m. Susan Nelson Graham, 1 s. Career: num. Apps., BBC Radio 3, BBC TV, Thames TV; Cheltenham Fest.; Cond., The Clerkes of Oxenford. Comps. incl: (publd.) Christmas carols; var. others; (recorded) Let My Prayer Come Up. Recordings: var., inclng. Christmas Music By The Clerkes Of Oxenford; Music of Tallis; Music of John Sheppard. Publs: Orlando Gibbons, Verse Anthems, 1966; An Anthology of Carols, 1968; An Anthology of English Church Music, 1970. Recordings of Music by Robert White, Sheppard,

O. Gibbons & Tallis. Contbr. to: Music & Letters; Jrnl. of Theol. Studies; Iraq; Musical Times; Brit. Jrnl. of Radiology; Medium Aevum. Mbr., Publs. Sec., Plainsong & Medieval Music Soc. Hons: Academical Clerk, 1960, Sr. Scholar, 1963, Fellow by Examination, 1964, Magdalen Coll., Oxford. Hobbies: Farming; Gardening; Badminton; Tennis. Address: Whitehill House, Tackley, Oxford, UK.

WUORINEN, Charles, b. 9 June 1938, NYC, USA. Composer. Educ: BA, 1961, MA, 1963, Columbia Univ.; Hon. DMus, Jersey City State Coll., 1971; Studied comp. w. Otto Luening, Jack Beeson, Vladimir Ussachevsky. Career incls: apps. as Pianist, Cond. or Overseer of amplification w. noted orchs. & on radio & TV broadcasts; on staff, Manhattan Schl. of Music, 1971-; Fndr. & Co-Dir., Group for Contemp. Music, 1962-; Bd. of Govs., 1962-, VP, 1969-71, Am. Comps. Alliance; Cons., Manhattanville Music Curric. Proj. (US Off. of Educ.), 1967-; Bd., Am. Music Ctr., 1971-, & Comps. Recordings Inc.; Advisory Bd., Am. Music Soc. (England); 'Meet The Comp.' Comps. incl: about 140 works inclng. stage works; electronic music; percussion music; vocal & choral music; works for standard & non-standard instrumental ensembles. Num. recordings. Publs: Simple Composition, 1979. Recip. num. commissions. Pulitzer Prize & many awards & hons. Hobbies incl: Chinese lang. & culture; Travelling. Mgmt: Ruth Uebel, 205 E 63rd St., NY, NY 10021, USA. Address: 870 W End Ave., NY, NY 10025., USA.

WÜRZ, Anton, b. 14 July, 1903, Munich, Germany. Writer. Composer; Teacher. Educ: Munich Univ. m. Edda Antonia Winter. Career: Free-lance Writer on Music contbng. to var. newspapers & jrnls.; Free-lance Music Tutor, 1928-45; Music Critic, Münchner Telegramzeitung; Music Cons., Bayerischen Staatszeitung, 1950-. Comps. incl: Die Weise von Liebe und Tod des Cornets Chr. Rilke, 1942 (publd. 1964); 6 string quartets, 3 string trios, 4 quintets, piano trio, 5 duo sonatas w. piano (all recorded on tape); approx. 200 songs w. piano. Publs. incl: Franz Lachner als dramatischer Komponist, 1928; Reclams Operettenführer, 1962-75. Contbr. to num. publs. in field, inclng: Grove's Dict., 6th ed.; Musik in Geschichte & Gegenwart. Mbrships. incl: Assn. of Munich Musicians; Int. Gustav Mahler Soc.; Hans Pfitzner Soc.; Hon. Mbr., Bavarian Nat. Educ. Soc., 1973. Num hons. Address: Angerlohstr. 62, D 8000 Munich 50, German Fed. Repub.

WÜRZL, Eberhard, b. 1 Nov. 1915. Vienna, Austria. Professor of Music Education in Secondary Schools O Organ. Educ: Trng. Coll. for Tchrs.; Dips. in Music Educ. O Sacred Music, Acad. of Music, Vienna. Career: Holds Chair for Music Educ.; Ed., Musikerziehung (periodical), 1961-. Publs: Austrian Song-Books for children O youths, 1965 O 71. Contbr. to int. music educ. jrnls. Mbrships: Arbeitsgemeinschaft der Musikerzieher Osterreichs; Pres., Osterreichisches Volksliedwerk. Hobbies: Mountaineering; German O Russian Lit. Address: Radetzkystrasse 27/20, A-1030 Vienna, Austria.

WYCKOFF, Lou Ann, b. Berkeley, Calif., USA. Opera Singer. Educ: Pvte. music study. Debut: as Donna Elvira in Don Giovanni, Spoleto Festival, 1967. Career: Opera O concert singer, radio O TV in Germany, Italy, Switzerland, France, Belgium, Spain, Holland, UK O USA; Mbr., Deutsche Oper, Berlin, 1969-, inclng. appearances in world premieres of Nabokov's Love's Labours Lost O Wahren's Fettklosschen. recordings: Rameau-Zoroastre Excerpts (Turnabout label); Rienzi Highlights from Wagner (Euro-disc). Hons: Martha Baird Rockefeller Grants, 1965-68; Matthew Sullivan Fndn. Award, 1968; 1st Prize, Artists Advsry. Coun., 1968. Mgmt: Thea Dispeker, NYC. Address: Kurfürstendamm 59/60, 1 Berlin 15, Germany.

WYLIE, Ruth Shaw, b. 24 June 1916, Cincinnati, Ohio, USA. Composer; Teacher. Educ: AB, 1937, MA, 1939, Wayne State Univ.; PhD, Eastman Schl. of Music, Rochester, NY, 1943. Career: Hd., Theory O Comp., Univ. of Mo., 1943-49; Prof O Hd. of Comp., 1949-69, Prof. Emeritus, 1969-, Wayne State Univ. Comps. publd: 6 Little Preludes; 5 Easy Pieces; 5 Piano Preludes; 3rd String quartet; Incubus for flute, clarinet, percussion O large cello ensemble. Comps. recorded: Psychogram 1968, CRI. Contbr. to: Am. Jrnl. of Aesthetics; Criticism; Dance Mag.; etc. Mbrships. incl: Am. Soc. of Univ. Comps.; League of Women Comps.; Am. Music Ctr.; ASCAP; Am. Women Comps.; US Chess Fedn. Recip., acad. O musical awards; NEA Grant, 1978. Hobbies: Chess; Hiking; Skiing; Bowling; Golf; Painting. Address: 1251 Country Club Dr., Long's Peak Rt., Estes Park, CO 80517, USA. 3, 5.

WYMAN, Dann Coriat, b. 13 Nov. 1923, Boston, Mass., USA. Composer; Performer (Viola, Violin, Double Bass). Educ: BA, Northeastern Univ.; Harvard Univ. Fine Arts; studied piano w. Faelton Schl.; Extensive musical studies w. Arthur Fiedler O classes given by Hindemith. m. Irene Wyman, 1 d. Debut: (as

Comp.) 1939. Career incls: Mbr., Szathmey Str. Quartet, O Zevitsky Musical Ensemble; player w. orchs., USA O Europe; Fndr. O Dir., Newton Symph. Orch., O Charles Playhouse for Contemporary Theatre, Boston. Comps. incl: Str. Quartet No. 1 (also recorded); Overture for Orch.; Aloness (viola); Ode to Viola (str. orch. O viola); Impressions (full orch.); Sonatas. Mbrships incl: Nat. Assn. Comps. O Conds. Hon. Mention for Comp., NBC Awards, 1939. Hobbies: Tournament Tennis; Yacht racing. Address: 220 Hobart Rd., Chestnut Hill, MA 02167, USA.

WYNER, Yehudi, b. 1 June 1929, Calgary, Canada. Composer; Pianist; Conductor. Educ: Dip., Juilliard Schl. of Music, 1946; BA, Yale Coll., 1959; BMus., 1951, MMus., 1953, Yale Schl. of Music; MA, Harvard Univ., 1952, m. Nancy Braverman, 2 s., 1 d.; (2) Susan Davenny. Career: Tchr., Lectr., Hofstra Coll., Queens Coll., Hebrew Union Coll., 1959-60; Music Dir., Westchester Reform Temple, NY, 1959-68; Music Dir., Turnau Opera Assn., 1961-64; Asst. Prof., Theory, Yale Schl. of Music, 1963-69; Assoc. Prof., Yale Schl. of Music, 1969-; O Chmn., Composition Dept., ibid, 1969-73; Music Dir., New Haven Opera Soc., 1968-; Mbr., Bach Aria Grp., 1968-; Composer-Cond., Tanglewood, 1961; Active Career as Pianist, Cond. Num. compositions incl. music for piano, organ, wind, string instruments, voice incidental music for plays. Recordings of own works: Serenade for 7 instruments; Concerto Duo for Violin O Piano; 3 Short Fantasies for Piano. Mbrships: Past Bd. of Dirs., Am. Composers Alliance; Broadcast Music Inc.; Am. Assn. of Univ. Composers; Past Bd. of Dirs., Int. Soc. for Contemp. Music Num. hons. incl: Rome Prize in Composition, 1953-56; A E Hertz Fellow in Composition Univ. of Calif., 1953-54; Guggenheim Fellow, 1959; Am. Inst. of Arts O Letters Grant, 1961; Brandeis Creative Arts Award, 1963; Commissions from Yale Univ., Mich. Univ., Fromm Fndn., Ford Fndn., Koussevistzsky Fndn., Park Ave. Synagogue. Hobbies: Chinese cooking; carpentry, cabinetry. Address: 78 Lyon St., New Haven, CT 06511, USA. 2.

WYNNE, David, b. 2 June 1900, Hirwaun, Mid-Glam., Wales, UK. Teacher; Lecturer; Composer. Educ: Univ. Coll., Cardiff; Bristol Univ.; pvte. studies; BMus; DMus; Dip. Ed. m. Eirwen Evans. Comps: 3 Symphs.; many orchl. works, concertos, chmbr. music, vocal O choral works, 3 works for theatre. Recording of own comps: Piano Sonata No. 2; String Quartet No. 3; Song Cycle, Evening Shadows. Contbr. to: Anglo-Welsh Review; Artists in Wales No. 1; Welsh Music. Mbrships: PRS; Mechanical Rights Soc.; CGGB; Guild for the Promotion of Welsh Music. Hons: Alfred J Clements Prize for Chmbr. Music, 1944. Hobbies: Walking; Gardening; Reading. Address: Highfield, Tabor Rd., Maesycwmmer, Hengoed, Mid-Glam., CF8 7PU, UK.

WYSOCKI, Zdzislaw, b. 18 July 1944, Poznan, Poland. Composer; Pianist. Educ: Hochschule für Musik, Poznan O Wien; Mag. Art, 1968, bzw Dip., 1973, for Comp. m. Eva Barisits, 1 c. Debut: as comp. O Pianist, 1963. Career: Comps. perfd. on radio O TV; Mbr., Chmbr. music group, Die Kontraste (piano). Comps: Orchl., Chmbr. music: Organ music; Choral O Cantatas. Recordings: Tonbandaufnahmen. Mbrships: IBNM;Österr. Komponistenbund; Polnischer Komponistenbund. Hons: Preis für Klavierkomposition bei Wettbewerb, Poland, 1968; T Szeligowski Preis, Poland, 1966; Theodor Korner Preis, Förderungspreis Stadt Wien, 1977, Austria. Hobbies: Chess, Bridge, Mountains. Address: Wien 12, Laskegasse 41/5, A-1120 Wien, Austria.

WYTON, Alec, b. 3 Aug. 1921, London, UK. Organist; Choirmaster; Composer. Educ: BA, MA, Oxford Univ.; MusD, Susquehanna Univ.; RAM, London; FRCO (CHM); FRAM; FRSCM; FAGO; FRCCO. Career: Organist, Choirmaster, St. Matthew's Ch., Northampton, UK, 1946-50, Christ Ch. Cathedral, St. Louis, Mo., USA, 1950-54; Cathedral of St. John the Divine, NY, 1954-74; Adj. Prof. of Music, Union Thol. Sem., NY, 1956-73; Vis. Prof. of Ch. Music, Westminster Choir Coll., Princeton, NY, 1974-; Co-ord. of Music, Episcopal Ch., USA, 1974-. Comps: Opera, The Journey with Jonah; Song Cycle, The Psalm of Christ; num. works for choir, organ, orch. Contbr. to var. music jrnls. Mbrships: Pres. AGO, 1964-69; ISM; ASCAP; The Bohemians; RCO; RCCO. Hons: Annual Award, ASCAP, 1967-. Hobbies: Reading; Walking. Address: 865 Madison Ave., NY, NY 10021, USA. 2,3,12.

WYTTENBACH, Jurg, b. 2Dec. 1935, Berne, Switzerland. Composer; Pianist; Conductor. Educ: Studied w. Prof. Dr. Kurt V Fischer O Sandor Varass, Konservatorium, Berne; w. Yvonne Lefebure O Joseph Calvert, Conservatoira Nat. Sup., Paris. m. Janka Brun, 2 children. Comps. incl: Sonate (oboe solo), 1962; Drei Satze (oboe), 1963; Konzert (orch), 1964; Divisions, 1964; Drei Klavierstucke, 1969; Ad Libitum, 1969; Sutil und Laar (chorus), 1964; Vier Kanzonen (soprano), 1964; Two Nonsense Verses, an Epigram O a madrigal (soprano), 1964; De Metalli (baritone O orch.), 1964; Execution ajournee 1, 1960; ajournee, II, 1970; Kunstucke, die Zeit Totzuschlagen, 1972. Address: St. Alban, Vorstadt 18, CH 4000 Basel, Switzerland.

X

XENAKIS, Iannis, b. Romania. Composer; Architect; Civil Engineer. Educ: Polytech. Schl., Athens; comp. studies w. Hermann Scherchen, Oliver Messiaen, Darius Milhaud; Dlitt., Univ. of Paris, 1976. Career: Greek resistance fighter; collaborated w. Le Corbusier in architecture for 12 yrs; introduced probability calculus & set theory into instrumental, electroacoustic & computerized comp.; fndr. & dir., Centre d'Etudes de Mathématique et Automatique Musicales; Assoc. prof., Ind. Univ., 1967-72. Comps: 67 to date for all media, internationally perf. & recorded. Publs: Musiques Formelles, 1963; Formalized Music, 1971; Musique Architecture, 1976, '76. Contbr. to profl. publs. Hons: Maurice Ravel Gold Medal, 1974; hon. mbr. Am. Acad. of Arts & Letters & Nat. Inst. of Arts & Letters; Beethovan Prize, Bonn, 1977. Address: 17 rue Victor Massé, 75009 Paris, France.

Y

YADYKH, Pavel, b. 30 Nov. 1922, Vinnitsa, the Ukraine, USSR. Conductor. Educ: Cond. of opera & symph. orch. & Violinist, Kiev Conserv. m. 1 d. Debut: w. State Symph. Orch. of USSR, Kiev. Career: Cond-in-Chief. N-Ossetia. Symph. orchs; Voronezh, Yaroslavl. Recordings: Sev. w. orchs. of Moscow & Leningrad; num. w. State Orch. of N-Ossetia. Regularly conds. symph. orchs. in major cities of USSR. Contbr. to periodicals. Mbrships: Russian Theatrical Soc.; Comm. of Trade Union of Culture Wkrs. Hons: People's Artist of N-Ossetia, 1960; Order of Symbol of Hon., 1961; Acknowledged Magister of Arts of Russia, 1972; prize Winner, Kosta Khetafurore's Nat. Prize, 1974. Hobbies Philately; Chess. Address: Borodinskaya St. 19, Flat 9, Ordzhonikidze, N-ossetia, USSR.

YAMAGUCHI, Hideo, b. 27 Sept. 1933, Kyoto, Japan. Violinist. Educ: Bachelor of Law, Doshisha Univ., Japan; Ind. Univ.; Univ. of Utah, Meadowmount; Violin Schl. Aspen Music Schl., USA. m. Junko Yamaguchi. Career: Perfs. in N & Central Am., Europe, Middle & Far East as mbr., Cinn., New Orleans & Utah Symphs.; fac. mbr., Utah State Univ.; Mbr., Osaka Phil.; currently mbr., Honolulu Symph. Recordings: num., as mbr. of Cinn., New Orleans & Utah Symphs. Publs: Translation of A Violinist's Notebook (Joseph Szigeti), 1967. Hobbies: Reading; Photography, etc. Address: 112-2 Puwa Pl., Kailua, HI 96734, USA.

YAMASH'TA, Stomu, b. 1947, Kyoto, Japan. Percussionist. Educ: Kyoto Music Acad.; Interlochan Summer Music Schl., Mich.; Art Acad. Coll. of Music; Boston Berkely Acad. of jazz. m. Career: Solo Percussionist, Kyoto Philharmonic Orch., 1960; film studio recordings; Fac., Art Acad. Coll. of Music; has played w. Jackie Byard, Int. Mod. Jazz Quintet, Toshiko Akiyoshi & Metropolitan Opera Orch.; UK apps. at Aldeburgh Fest., 1970 & Inst. of Contemp. Arts, London; app. in 'The Man from the East' w. Sun Treader under Morris Pert; Mbr., Red Buddha Theatre. Compositions: film score for Ken Russell's 'The Devils.'(w. Peter Maxwell Davies); theme music for 'Images'; other film work. Recordings incl: Floating Magic & The Man from the East.

YANAGITA, Masako, b. 30 Mar. 1944, Tokyo, Japan. Violinist. Educ: Dip., Mannes Coll. of Music, NYC; studied w. Eijin Tanaka, Louis Graeler, William Kroll. m. Abba Bogin. Debut: Tokyo, 1966. Career: Concert Apps. throughout USA, Europe, Near East & Far East; Soloist w. orchs. in Japan, England, Germany, Philippines, USA; 1st Violin, toured w. Vieuxtemps String Quartet; Fac. Mbr., Mannes Coll. of Music & Queensborough Coll., NYC. Hons: Silverstein prize, Berkshire Music Ctr., Tanglewood, Mass., 1966; Carl Flesch Competition, London, UK, 1968; Paganini Competition, Genoa, Italy, 1968; Munich Int. Competition, 1969. Mgmt: Raymond Weiss Artists Mgmt. NY, NY, USA. Address: 838 West End Ave., NY, NY 10025, USA.

YANCHUS, Judith, b. 18 Dec. 1939, Wilkes Barre, Pa., USA. Violinist. Educ: BMus, Boston Conserv., Mass.; Pupil of Joseph Fuchs, Raphael Bronstein & Ivor Karman in NY; Studied chmbr. music w. William Kroll. Career: Mbr: Buffalo Phil.; Rotterdam Phil.; Minneapolis Symph.; Met. Opera; Concertmaster, Boston Women's Symph.; Violinist w. String Trio of NY; Performed chmbr. music & as soloist in many Am. cities; Appeared w. String Trio of NY at Carnegie Recital Hall, 1975. Hobby: Golf. Mgmt: New Era Int. Concerts Ltd., London, UK. Address: 9 W 64th St., New York, NY 10023, USA.

YANCICH, Milan Michael, b. 11 Dec. 1921, Whiting, Ind., USA. French Horn Player. Educ: BMus Ed., Univ. of Mich., 1946; MM, Northwestern Univ., 1951. m. Paulina White, 3 s., 1 d. Career: 1st horn, Columbus Phil., 1946-48; Asst. & Assoc. 1st horn, Chgo. Symph., 1948-51; 1st horn, Cleveland Symph., summer 1951; 3rd horn, ibid., 1951-52; Solo horn, ABC Radio, Chgo., 1952; horn, all positions, Rochester Phil. 1958-; Solo horn, Lake Placid Sinfonietta, 1952-; Fac. mbr., Eastman Schl. of Music, Univ. of Rochester, 1958; Publ. & Ed., Wind Music, Inc. Publs: A Practical Guide to French Horn Playing; Method for French Horn (2 vols.); 15 Solos for French Horn & Piano, arr. Yancich. Contbr. to profl. jrnls. Mbr. ASCAP. Hobby: Chess. Address: 153 Highland Parkway, Rochester, NY 14620, USA.

YANKEY, James Adumli, b. 1 Sept. 1942, Axim, Ghana. Music Teacher; Performer (Atenteben Bamboo Pipe; Drums).

Educ: Tchrs. Cert. A, Ghana; Music Educ. Dip., Legon. m. Grace Amoah, 2 s., 2 d. Comps. incl: (songs) Ghanaman ma mo nsore; Mede ne ale ene; Yeybe mo; Obiara nsomu bi; Arr., Go Down Moses; Akposa, 1 & 2 (piano trio); Nyame Katakyi (piano & cello); Play Time (orch.); The Past & the Present (piano & atenteben); Wandering (strings); about 50 others. Mbr., Ghana Music Tchrs. Assn. hons: 2nd Prize, Ghana Nat. Patriotic Songs Competition, 1975. Hobbies: Swimming; Draughts Playing; Gardening. Address: National Academy of Music, P.O. Box 25, Winneba, Ghana.

YANNICOSTA, Melita Elisabeth, b. 19 Nov. 1928, Athens, Greece. Concert Pianist. Educ: Baccalauréat és Lettres; musical studies in Switz.; Dip. of Soloist, w. highest hons. (Gold Medal), Athens Conserv.; studied w. Louis Kentner, London, UK. Career: Recitals & apps. w. orchs., Greece, The Balkans, Switz., Netherlands, Engl., Asia; broadcasts from Athens, Salonica, Hilversum, Beromünster & Sottens (German & French Switz.), BBC London. Soloist Mbr., ISM, London Recip. 1st Prize, Concerto competition, under auspices of LPO, Hastings, 1961. Hobbies incl: Interest in preservation of natural environment. Address: 66 Hurlingham Rd., London SW6 3RQ, UK.

YARON, (Papper) Izhar, b. 8 July 1910, Tel Aviv, Israel. Composer; Musicologist; Music Critic. Educ: BA., Tel Aviv Univ.; Studied comp. w. A U Boscovitch, Oden Partos. m. Sima Kremenchugsti, 1 s., 1 d. Career: Var. song recitals; Radio appearances. Compositions: Music for documentary of Youth Dept. of Jewish Agcy., The flame has not lessened; Rinot, songs & dances, songs for voice & piano, songs for choir, 1965; Agadat Yarchei Hashana (legend of the months of the year), children's opera, 1966. Author of The Human Voice, 1964. Ed., music dept., Al Hamishmar, daily newspaper. Mbrships: League of Israeli Comps.; Acum; League of Israeli Musicologists. Address: Kibbutz Ein Hashofet, Israel.

YASSER, Joseph, b. 16 Apr. 1893, Lodz, Poland. Organist & Musicologist. Educ: Dip. Hon. Citizen, Imperial Schl. of Commerce, Moscow, Russia, 1912; MA, State Conserv. of Moscow, 1917. m. Marie Luirié. Debut: Moscow, 1918. Career: Prof. of Moscow Conserv.; Organist, Moscow Grand Opera (Bolshoi), 1918-20; Cond., 'Shangha Songsters', Choral Soc., China, 1921-22; Organist & Choirmaster, Temple Rodeph Sholom, NY, 1929-59; VP, Am. Lib of Musicol., 1932-41; Mbr. of Fac., Cantor Inst., Jewish Theol. Sem., NY, 1952-59. Publs: A Theory of Evolving Tonality, 1932; Medieval Quartal Harmony, 1938. Contbr. to num. jrnls. Mbrships: Chmn., NY Chapt., Am. Musicol. Soc., 1935-37; Pres., Jewish Music Forum, 1945-48. Hons: DMus, Musical Arts Conserv. of W Tex., Amarillo, 1950. Hobbies: Painting; Philos. lit. Address: 905 West End Ave., Apt. 53, NY, NY 10025. USA. 4, 14.

YBARRA, Ramon, b. 8 Aug. 1930, Habana, Cuba. Professor; Master Concert Guitarist. Educ: Master in Theory & Master in Guitar, Conservatorio Municipal de la Habana; Master's Degree in Civil Engrng., Univ. of Utah, USA. m. Maria Concepcion Rubio Camin, 2 s., 1 d. Debut: pro Arte Musical Soc., Habana, 1937. Career incls: Radio & TV, Habana; Concerts throughout Cuba; 300 concerts, Radio & TV, fests., Spain; Radio & TF, concerts, France; 200 concerts inclng. 3 at Carnegie Hall, USA. Recordings incl: Sortileges de la Guitare. Mbrships. incl: Nat. String Conf.; Guitar Fedn. of Am. Hobbies: Painting; Theatre. Address: Arcade Gdns., Bldg. 15, Apt. 5, Old Bridge, NJ 08857, USA.

YELVERTON, Vera, b. 12 Nov. 1917, Negri Sembilan, Malaysia. Piano Teacher. Educ: studied w. Madeline Evans, Frederick Haggis at Goldsmiths Coll., Norman Anderson at GSM (5 yrs.), & Alfred Kitchin (4 yrs.); ARCM. m. Fritz Gottlieb (dec.), 1 s. Career: concert apps. & concertos w. orchs., UK; Dir., Vera Yelverton Schl. of Music. Publs: Music for GCE 'O' level (w. Jane Corbett), 1962, now in 5th ed.; Contbr. to var. jrnls. Hobbies: Hist.; Gardening; Bridge; Travel. Address: 39 Wood Vale, London N 10 3DJ, UK.

YEPES, Narciso, b. 14 Nov. 1927, Lorca (Murcia), Spain. Concert Guitarist. Educ: Dip., Conservatorio Superior, Valencia; Studied w. Enesco & Gieseking. m. Marysia Szumlakowska, 3 children. Debut: Madrid 1947. Career: Perfs. exclusively on 10-string Guitar of own creation since 1961; Apps. at concerts & recitals in all maj. world music ctres. inclng: E & W Europe, USA, S Am., & Orient. Recordings incl: Five Centuries of Spanish Music; Complete works of J S Bach for lute. Hons. incl: Kt. Cmdr., Order of Isabel la Catolica. Hobbies: Chess; Sailing; Astronomy. Mgmt: Mariedi Anders, 535 El Camino del Mar, San Francisco, CA 94121, USA. Address: San Julio 7, Madrid 2, Spain.

YEPES de ACEVEDO, Fabio, b. 12 Feb. 1937, Medellin, Colombia. Opera Singer. Educ: PhD, Univ. of Naples, 1963; conserv. San Pietro a Majella, Naples; Acad. Santa Cecilia, Rome. m. Susanne, 2 s., 1 d. Debut: as Ernesto, Haydn's Il mondo della Luna, Teatro Massimo, Palermo, 1964. Career: perfs. at Teatro Massimo, San Carlo, Naples, Opera of Rome, etc.; tours in N & S Am., USSR, Western Europe; radio & TV broadcasts, Italy, Denmark, Colombia, etc.; apps. in sev. Italian films; Asst. Tchr. in Opera, Conserv. S Pietro a Majella, Naples, & Acad. Alfani Tellini, Rome; Instr. of Performing Arts, Gladsaxe Ungdomsscene, Denmark, 1971-. Contbr. to var. jrnls. Mbr., Artisti Lirici e Cinema, Italy. Recip. var. hons. Hobby: Horses. Mgmt: Koncertdirection: Wilhelm Hansen, Copenhagen. Address: Collinsgade 7, 2100 Copenhagen &, Denmark.

YFFER, Louis Alexander, b. 25 Nov. 1925, Vienna, Austria. Violinist. Educ: studied under Max rostal, Dr. D C Dounis & Maxim Jacobsen. m. Muriel Frances Arts, 1 s., 3 d. Career incls: Staff, Royal Opera House, Covent Gdn.; 1st Violin, Phil. Orch.; Ldr., London Fest. Ballet, 1966-74; New Opera Co. (Sadler's Wells); Ballet Rambert, Pro Arte Chmbr. Orch.; Ldr., Christchurch Symph. Orch. (NZ), 1966-74; Supvsr., Christchurch Schl. of Instrumental Music; Lectr., Tchrs. Coll.; Regd. Mus. Tchr. (NZ), 1974-; Acting Concertmaster, Tasmanian Symph. Orch.; Concertmaster, Elizabethan Trust Melbourne Orch., 1974-75. Mbr., NZ Music Tchrs. Assn. Address: Villa 4, 38 Grange Rd., Toorak, Vic. 3142, Aust.

YODER, Dorinné Lou, b. 22 Jan. 1936, Long Beach, Calif., USA. Harpist. Educ: Seattle Pacific Coll. m. Lee E Yoder, 1 s., 2 d. Career: num. stage & TV Appearances, Seattle, LA, San Diego, Phoenix; Fndr. & Mgr.-Dir., Hidden Valley Harp Quintet (composed of the 5 mbrs. of Lee Yoder family); harpist, Fanfare Recording Studios, Calif.; Ptnr. w. Lee Yoder in bldg. & selling folk harps known as Hidden Valley Harps; Tchr. of concert & folk harp. Recording: Sacred Harp Selections. Contbr. to Folk Harp Jrnl. Mbr., Am. Harp Soc. Hobbies: Arranging sacred harp music; Travel; Reading. Address: 1444 Calle Pl., Escondido, CA 92027, USA.

YOFFE, Shlomo (Solomon), b. 19 May 1909, Warsaw, Poland. Composer. Educ: Tchr.'s Sem., Poland; Agricl. Schl., Czech.; Acads. of Music, Jerusalem & Tel-Aviv, Israel. m. Shulamit, 2 s. Debut: w. 'Ruth' (suite), perf. by JSO, Israel, 1953, Compositions incl: 3 symphs.; 4 suites; 3 symph - poems; concertos for violin, for oboe & for cello; 6 cantatas on biblical themes; 2 str. quartets; film scores; music for chmbr. ensembles & for choirs. Mbrships: League of Composers in Israel; ACUM Ltd. Hons. incl: Min. of Educ.'s Prize for Alilot Gilboa Cantata, 1955; Engel Prize for Violin Concerto, Tel Aviv, 1957; ACUM Prize for Str. Quartet, 1962; Hebrew Union Coll. Prize for Religious Cantata for tenor, choir & chmbr. orch., 1970. ACUM prize for 'Lamentation' for mixed choir, 1975; Prize of the Int. Competition for a comp based on the theme 'Holocaust & Rebirth', 1978. Address: Kibutz Bet-Alfa, DN Gilboa, Israel.

YORK, John, b. 20 March 1949, Eastbourne, UK. Pianist; Teacher. Educ: GSM; Paris Conserv.; Vienna Hachschule. Debut: Wigmore Hall, 1974. Career: Radio apps., England, Can., USA, France, Ireland, Germany; Concerts, UK, USA, Can., Brazil, Norway, Austria, France, Germany, Ireland, etc. Recordings: 4 Records w. James Campbell. Mbr., ISM. Hons: concours Debussy 1st prize, Paris, 1973. Mgmt: Helen Ranger and Assocs., London W5 1ND, UK. Address: 84B Vanbrugh Park, Blackheath, London SE3 7AJ, UK.

YOST, Oliver, b. 3 Feb. 1924, Tuscarora, Pa., USA. Music Educator. Educ: MRE, Schl. of Relig. Educ., The So. Bapt. Theol. Sem., Louisville, Ky.; BMus. & MMus, Eastman Schl. of Music, Univ. of Rochester, NY; MSM, Schl. of Ch. Music, So. Bapt. Theol. Sem. m. Julia Lincoln Yost, 3 s., 1 d. Career: Has served as Organist-Dir. of ch. choirs; Min. of Music & Educ: Adjudicator for the NGPT in NC, SC, Ga. & Ky.; Judge, choir fests. in NC; Adjudicator for Nat. Fedn. of Music clubs in NC & SC; Adjudicator for SC Music Tchrs. Assn. (piano); Chmn. Music Dept., Bapt. Coll. at Charleston, SC Music Critic, Charleston Evening Post. Mbrships: 2nd VP, SC Music Tchrs. Assn.; Fac. Mbr., Am. Coll. of Musicians of the NGPT; Pres., Summerville Music Club, affil. w. the Nat. Fedn. of Music Clubs. Hons: Geo. Eastman Hon. Scholarship, Eastman Schl. of Music, 1949-50. Var. hobbies. Address: 507 Dogwood Circle, Summerville, SC 29483, USA.

YOUNG, Alexander, b. London, UK. Concert & Opera Singer (Tenor); Educator. Educ: RCM; studied w. Prof. Stefan Pollmann, London. m. Jean Anne Prewett, 1 s., 1 d. Debut: as Scaramuccio, Ariadne Auf Naxos, Glyndebourne Co.,

Edinburgh, 1950. Career incls: num. apps. in opera & oratorio, UK & abroad; created title role in Brit. of Stravinsky's The Rake's Progress, 1953; many recitals w. accomps. Rex Stephens, Harold Lester & Keith Swallow; regularly broadcasts for BBC, but has also broadcast for Dutch & German radios & European Broadcasting Union; Hd., Schl. of Vocal Studies, Royal Northern Coll. of Music, Manchester, 1973-. Has made over 50 recordings of opera, oratorio, song recitals, etc. Hons: Fellow, RNCM, 1977. Mbrships: Brit. Actors Equity. Hobby: Photography. Address: Spring Bank, Start Ln., Whaley Bridge, Stockport, Cheshire, UK. 3.

YOUNG, Anne Lloyd, b. 9 Sept. 1936, Chgo., Ill., USA. Clarinettist; Pianist; Recorder Player. Educ: BMusEduc., Oberlin Conserv. of Music, 1958; BMus, ibid., 1959; MA, Calif. State Univ., Los Angeles, 1964; Doctoral studies, Univ. of Southern Calif. m. Larry A Young, 1 d., 1 s. Debut: Soloist w. Evansville Phil. Orch., 1954. Career: Soloist w. Rio Hondo Symph. Orch., Pasadena Community Orch.; Prin. Clarinettist w. Nat. Virtuosi Sinfonietta; Prin. Clarinettist w. Rio Hondo Symph.; Recitals in Europe, USA (Midwest, S Calif.) as chmbr. musician; Artist in Res., Whittier Coll.; Fac. Mbr., Santa Monica Coll. Mbrships: Pi Kappa Lambda; Artist Patron, Phi Beta; Los Angeles Oberlin Alumni Assn., past Pres.; Music Assn. of Calif. Community Coll.; S Calif. Piano Assn.; Am. Recorder Soc.; Rio Hondo Symph. Assn. Bd. Hons: Coleman Chmbr. Music Award, 1960; Rotarian Award, 1954; Lions Club Award, 1954; DAR, 1954. Hobbies: Skiing; Swimming; Gardening. Address: 6018 S Friends Ave., Whittier, CA 90601, USA.

YOUNG, Frederick John, b. 19 May 1931, Buffalo, NY, USA. Contrabass Tubist. Educ: BS, 1953, MA, 1954, PhD, 1956, Carnegie Inst. of Technol.; musical studies w. noted tchrs. m. Beverly Hall, 3 s. Debut: Carnegie Hall, Pitts., Pa., 1949. Career: Contrabass Tubist, Pitts. Symph., 1950-; Prof., Carnegie-Mellon Univ., 1956-70, Pa. State Univ., 1974-; Inventor, 'Dr. Young' tuba mouthpiece; made 1st prediction of frequencies of open tones of brass instruments based on their taper functions. Var. arrs. for tuba ensembles. Recordings: Rite of Spring, Capitol, 1954. Contbr. to musical publs. Mbrships: Phi Mu Alpha Sinfonia; Sigma Xi; Phi Kappa Phi; Tubist Universal Brotherhood Assn. Recip. var. hons. Hobbies incl: Magnetohydrodynamics; Electrodynamics; Magnetism. Address: 762 Devonshire Dr., State College, PA 16801, USA.2.

YOUNG, John, b. 22 June 1946, Margaret, Ala., USA. Concert Pianist; Assistant Professor of Music. Educ: BMus, MMus, Manhattan Schl. of Music, NYC. Debut: NY, 1979. Career: Perfs. throughout USA, Switzerland, Austria; TV, Radio & Symph. Orchs. in USA; Num. Fests. & Seminars; Piano Workshop & Lecture Recitals; Instructor of Piano, Harlem Schl. of the Arts, NY, 1969-73; Asst. Prof. of Music, W Chester State Coll., Pa., 1976; Asst. Prof. of Music, Artist in Res., Lincoln Univ., Pa., 1972-. Mbrships: Am. Liszt Soc.; Nat. Assn. of Negro Musicians. Hobbies: Swimming; Jogging; Cooking. Mgmt: Adeline Leslie, 233 W 77th St., NY, NY 10024, USA. Address: PO Box 72, Lincoln Univ. Pa., USA.

YOUNG, Percy Marshall, b. 17 May 1912, Northwich, Cheshire, UK. Musician; Writer. Educ: Selwyn Coll., Cambridge; MusB, MA; Mus D, Trinity Coll., Dublin. m. Renee Morris. Career: Dir. of Music, Stranmillis Tchrs. Trng. Coll., Belfast, 1934-37; Advsr. on Music, City of Stoke-on-Trent Educ. Auth., 1937-44; Dir. of Music, Wolverhampton Coll. of Technoloigy, 1944-65. Comps: More than 30 published reconstructions, orchestrations, accomps., arrs., etc; More that 20 published comps. inclng: Fugal Concerto in g minor, 1954; Festival Te Deum, 1961. Publs: More than 50 books. Contbr. to profl. jrnls., etc. Mbr. num. profl. orgs. Hons: incl: Var. Scholarships & Awards. Hobbies: Sports; Gardening. Mgmt: A P Watt & Son. Address: 72 Clark Rd., Wolverhampton, WV3 9PA, UK.

YOUNG, Phyllis, b. 20 Oct. 1925, Milan, Kan., USA. String Educator; Cellist; University Professor. Educ: BMus, Univ. of Tex., 1949; MMus, ibid, 1950; studied w. Horace Britt, NYC & Mexico City, & Andre Navarra, Chigiana Acad., Siena, Italy. m. James M young. Career: apps. incl. num. solo & chmbr. music recitals, USA & Italy; Prin. Cellist, Austin Symph., sev. seasons; perfs. w. Britt Cello Ensemble; Str. Clinician for var. pedagog. bodies; w. Music Fac., Univ. of Tex., Austin, 1953-; currently Prof. of Music & Dir. of Univ. of Tex. Str. Proj.; ibid. Publs: Playing the String Game: Strategies for Teaching Cello & Strings, 1978. Contbr. to: Am. Str. Tchrs. Assn., 1972-74; Sword of Hon., Sigma Alpha Iota; Pi Kappa Lambda; MENC; Tex. Orch. Dirs. Assn. Pres., Am. String Tchrs. Assn., 1978. Recip. Special Citation in recognition of disting. ldrship. & serv. in trng. str. tchrs. & developing young talent, Am. Str. Tchrs.

Assn., 1974. Hobbies: Painting; Gardening. Address: 7304 W. Rim Dr., Austin, TX 78731, USA. 5.

YOUNG, Robert Floyd, b. 3 Mar. 1924, Allentown, Pa., USA. Chairman, Music Department; Associate Professor of Music. Educ: BMus, Syracuse Univ., 1949; MMus, ibid., 1950. m. Vivian G Young, 2 s. Career: Voice concerts in Minn., Iowa, Wis., ND, Norfolk, Va.; Lead Opera Roles in Barber of Seville, Tosca, La Traviata, Camelot, Music Man, Mikado; Dir. of Hansel & Gretel & La Boheme; Asst. Prof., Voice, St Olaf Coll., Northfield, Minn., 1950-56; Chmn., Music Dept. & Assoc. Prof. of Music, Old Dominion Univ., Norfolk, Va. Mbrships: incl: Phi Mu Alpha Sinfonia; Pres., Va. Chapt., Nat. Assn. Tchrs. of Singing. Recip. Tuition Scholarships, Syracuse Univ. Hobby: Photography. Address: 5900 Powhatan Ave., Norfolk, VA 23508, USA.

YOUNG, Sareen Anne, b. 17 Oct. 1953, Cape Town, S Africa. Teacher of Piano & Theory. Educ: BMus, (Wits.); MEd (Wits.); LTCL (Tchrs.); LRSM (Tchrs.). m. Richard Michael Young, 1s, 1d. Mbrships: SASMT. Hons: 4 Bursaries awarded by UNISA, 1963-66. Hobbies: Pottery; Needlework. Address: 6, Taling Street, Sunward Park, Boksburg, 1460 Transvaal, S Africa.

YOUNGBLOOD, Jessie Orian, b. 7 Feb. 1941, Wichita Falls, Tex., USA. Professionsl Clarinettist; College Teacher of Clarinet & Woodwinds. Educ: BMus, Clarinet Perf., N Tex. State Univ., 1963; MMus, (w. distinction), Ind. Univ., 1965; currently preparing D Musical Arts. N Tex. State Univ. Career: 1st Chair Clarinet, 761st & 752nd USAF Bands, 1965-69; 1st Chair clarinet, Anchorage, Alaska, Symph., 1968; 1st Chair Clarinet w. Fest. Orch., & Clarinet Tchr., Alaska Fest. of Music, 1968; currently 1st chair Clarinet, Wichita Falls, Tex., Symph. Orch. Mbrships: Int. Clarinet Soc.; NACWPI; Tex. Flute Club. Hobbies: Tennis; Swimming; Hunting. Address: 2111 Wenonah, Wichita Falls, TX 76309, USA.

YTTESEN, Peter Holling, b. 1 May 1946, Odense, Denmark. Trumpeter. Educ: Dip., Acad. of Music; Educl. Dip., ibid; Scholarship from The French State to study w. Roger Delmotte. Career: 2 yrs. w. Aalborg Symph. Orch., 1970-72; Chmn., Trumpet Sect., Symph. Orch., Odense (1st solo trumpet). Address: Langelinic 97, 5000 Odense, Denmark.

YTTREHUS, Rolv, b. 12 Mar. 1926, Duluth, Minn., USA. Composer; Teacher. Educ: BS, Univ. of Minn, 1950; MMus, Univ. of Mich., 1953; Dip. Acad. di St. Cecelia, 1962; study w. var. leading tutors & at Princeton Seminar in Advanced Musical Studies, 1959. Career incl: composer of var. works performed by St Cecilia Orch., Rome; Festival of Contemporary Am.

Music, New England Conserv.; Am. Acad., Rome; Festival of Contemporary Music, tanglewood, Mass.; Carnegie Recital Hall & other NYC concert halls. Compositions: Music for Winds; percussion & Viola, 1961; Expressioni per Orch., 1962; Music for winds, percussion, cello & voices, 1969; Perf. on ISCM World Music Days, 1976. Sextet, 1964-70; Perf. on ISCM World Music Days, 1976. Sextet, 1964-70; for soprano & percussion, 1971; Wuintet, 1973 League ISCM concert NY, 1975. Var. works recorded on Capra & CRI labels. Mbrships: Am. Composers Alliance; Am. Soc. of Univ. Composers; Am. Music Ctr. Hons. incl: Fulbright Schlrship., 1953-54; Martha Baird Rockefeller Fndn. Recording Subsidy, 1974. Address: 847 Oak St., Oshkosh, WI 54901, USA.

YU, Chun Yee, b. 12 July 1936, Shanghai, China. Concert Pianist. Educ: LRSM; ARCM. m. Isabella Miao, 2 s. Debut: recital, London, 1962; Royal Fest. Hall, 1963. Career: represented Singapore at 1st Asian Music Fest., Hong Kong, 1962; concerts in Far E, Brit. Isles & some European countries; prof. of Piano, RCM. London. Hons: Ricordi Prize.; Prize Winner, Int. Piano Competition, Paris, 1961. Hobbies: Motoring; Sports; Reading. Mgmt: Ibbs & Tillett, London. Address: The Red Cottage, 34 Creswick Rd., London W3 9HF, UK.

YUIZE, Shinichi, b. 30 Oct. 1923, Fukagawa City, Hokkaido, Japan. Private Teacher of traditional Japanese instruments, koto (harp) & sangen (3-stringed banjo); Composer; Concert Artist; Musicologist. Educ: BA Otaru Coll. of Commerce; BA, Dept. Music, Tokyo Univ. of Arts; Pvte. studies; Columbia Univ., USA. m. Yasuko Nakashima Yuize, 2 children. Debut: participant in Nat. Competition in Japanese Traditional Music. 1st Place Hons. Contbr. to Music Educ.; The traditional Japanese Music Wuarterly; Music Companions. Mbrships: Int. House of Japan. Inc.; Int. Music Congress; Contemporary Japanese Comps. League; Asian Comps. League; Seiha Schl. of Traditional Japanese Music. Hobby: Pottery-ware Collecting. Address: 4-22-5 Honcho, Kokubunji-shi, Tokyo, Japan T 185.

YUN, Isang, b. 17 Sept. 1917, Tongyong, Korea. Composer. Educ: univs. in Korea & Japan 1939-43; Paris conserv. & Berlin, 1956-9. m. Sooja Lee, 1 s., 1 d. Career: Tchr/lectr., schls. & univs., Korea, 1946-56; Lectr. coll. of music, Hannover, 1969-70; lectr. of comp. State Coll. of music, Berlin, from 1970; prof., Berlin acad. of arts. Comps. incl: Butterfly Widow, 1968; Sim Tjong, 1972; Reak, 1964; Namo (3 soprano & orch.) 1971; Konzertante Figuren für kleines Orchester, 1972; Loyang, 1962; Garak für flöte und Klavier, 1963; An der Schwelle, 1975; Konzert fur Violoncello & Orchester, 1976; Shao Yang Yin (harpsichord) 1966; Tuyaux sonores (Organ), 1967. Hons: 2 Korean art awards; Kulturpreis, Kiel, 1970. Mgmt: Bote & Bock, 1 Berlin 12, Hardenbergstr. 9a, German Fed. Repub.

Z

ZABALETA, Nicanor, b. 7 Jan. 1907, San Sebastian, Spain. Concert Harpist. Educ: Harp Grad., Madrid Royal Conserv., 1920; Mbr. of Jury at Paris Conserv. (Harp grad.); Mbr. of Jury, Israel Int. harp Contests, 1961 & '70. m. Graciela Torres, 1 s, 1 d. Debut: Salle Erard, Paris, 1925. Career: Soloist w. orchs. & concerts all over the world, inclng. most the Music Fests. Compositions: (for harp) Beethoven, Six easy variations on a Swiss theme; Spanish Comps. 16th & 17th Century; Dussek, Sonata in C minor. Many comps. have dedicated works to Zabaleta. Recordings for D G & EMI - solo recitals & soloist w. following orchs.: Berlin Phil., Berlin Radio Orch., Paris Nat. Orch.; Madrid Orquesta Nacional de Espana; Paris Kuentz Chamber Orch. Contbr. to Am. Harp Jrnl. Hons: Grand Prix National du Disque, France, 1960; Grand Prix Edison, Holland, 1971. Hobbies: Lecturing. Mgmt: Tower Music, London, UK; Anders Artists Mgmt., San Fran., Calif., USA. Address: Villa Izar, Aldapeta, San Sebastian, Spain.

ZABLUDOW, Michael, b. Wallasey, Cheshire, UK. Teacher of Violin. Educ: Pvte. study w. Max Rostal. m. Margaret Harris. Career: Mbr., LPO, BBC Symph. Orch., others. Contbr. monthly series of articles, Fundamentals of Violin Technique to The Strad. Hobbies: Walking; Photography; Tennis. Address: 82 Stapleton Hall Rd., London N4 4QA UK.

ZACHARIAS, Helmut, b. 27 Jan. 1920, Berlin, Germany. Musician (Violin); Arranger; Composer. Educ: Studied w. Prof. Havemann, Hochschule für Musik, Berlin. m. Hella Konradat, 2 s., 1 d. Debut: 1926. Career: Musical Prod. for Radio; TV & records Concert tours. Compositions: Tokyo Melody; Bells & Little Bells; Fantasie über 3 Eigene Themen; Frag den Wind; Wie ein Roman; Rhapsodie in Jazz. Recordings: About 550 titles. publ: Die Jazz-Violine, 1950. Mbrships: GEMA, Berlin; Künstler-Club, Ascona, Switzerland. Hons: Fritz Kreisler & Bernard Molique Prizes, Hochschule für Musik, Berlin; Grand Prix du Disque, Olympia, Paris, France, 1955; Maschera d'Argento, Italy, 1961; Coque d'or, Rio de Janeiro, Brazil, 1966; Popularity Prize, Caracas, Venezuela, 1972. Hobbies: Golf; 8 mm. Movies. Mgmt: EMI Electrola, Cologne, Germany. Address: Casa La Campanella, CH 6612 Ascona, Switz.

ZACHARIASSEN, Uffe Eilif, b. 27 Feb. 1935, Kliplev, Denmark. Musician (harpsichord, clavichord, organ). Educ: Degrees in Song, Harpsichord & Organ, Royal Danish Conserv., Copenhagen. m. Lydia Catherine Zachariassen, 1 d, 1 s. Debut: Harpsichord, 1963. Career: Num. apps., Danish radio & TV; Concerts in Scandinavia; Organist, Thomas Kingo's Ch., Odense. Recordings: 4 Suites (for harpsichord) by Froberger, L couperin, F Couperin, Bach. Contbr. to: Fyens Stiftstidende, Odense (Music Reviewer). Mbrships: Danish Soloists' Assn. of 1921; Danish Soc. of Organists & Choirmasters. Hons: Musikanmelderringens Kunstnerpris, 1964 (Prize of the Copenhagen Guild of Music Critics). Hobby: Photography. Address: Poppelvej 14, DK-5230 Odense M, Denmark.

ZACK, George, b. 8 July 1936, Pine bluff, Ark., USA. Conductor; Instrumentalist. Educ: BMus, Wichita State Univ., 1958; MusM, Univ. of Mich., 1960; PhD, Fla. State Univ. 1972. m. Kerry Sheehan, 1 d. Career: 'Form in Music', 5 pt. NBC TV Series; Cond. & Dir., Warren Chmbr. Orch., Ohio; Lexington Philharmonic Orch.; Lexington Musical Theater Soc. Mbrships: Am. Symph. Orch. League; AAUP. Hobbies: Sailing; Photography; Fishing. Address: 237 Woodspoint Rd., Lexington, KY 40502, USA.

ZAGAJEWSKA-SZLEZER, Zofia Barbara, b. 4 Apr. 1926, Stanislav, Ukraine. Pianist. Educ: Conserv. of Music, Stanislav, 1939; Coll. of Joteyko, Cracow, Poland, 1948; Dip., High Schl. of Music, ibid., 1952; Dip. MMus (Aspirantura), ibid., 1957. m. Zbigniew Szlezer, 1 s. Debut: Stanislav, 1936. Career incls: Solo & chmbr. music perf., USSR radio, 1943-46; Concerts, 1947-63; perfs. w. Cracow Str. Quartet, Polish TV & Radio, 1950-63; Sonata concerts w. husband (violin), 1960-75; Prof., Coll. of Music, 1958-; Asst. Prof., High Schl. of Music, 1973. Recordings: Tapes w. Cracow of Merit, 1975. Hobbies: Literature; Art Exhibitions; Walking Tours. Address: 31-141 Cracow, ul. Krowoderska 19Ç6, Poland.

ZAGORZANKA, Barbara, b. 31 Aug. 1938, Kazimierzow, Poland. Singer (Soprano). Educ: Dip. (Vocal), Govt. Schl. of Music, Szczecin, 1960. m. Mieczyslaw Pozarski, 1 s., 1d. Debut: State Opera, Bydogoszcz. Career: Apps. in State Opera Houses, all Polish cities; Soloist, symph. concerts; TV perfs.,

Lucia of Lammermoor, & Fra Diavolo, & concerts; Apps. in Belgium, France, German Fed. & Dem. Repubs., Italy, Romania, Czechoslovakia, Bulgaria; radio perfs. Roles incl. about 30 leading soprano parts from world opera. Mbr., Assn. Polish Artists-Musicians. Hons: Winner, Int. Singers Competition, Czechoslovakia, 1967. Hobbies: Books; Travel; Knitting. Mgmt: St. Moniuszko State Opera, ul. Fredry 9 Poznań. Address: Os. Przyjaźni 10HÇ105, 61-685 Poznań, Poland.

ZAHORSKY, Philip C., b. 20 May 1951, ChampagneÇUrbana, Ill., USA. Professor of Music; Bass Trombonist. Educ: BA, San Jose State Univ.; MA, ibid. m. Margo Welch. Career: Prof. of Music, Ohlone Coll., Fremont & San Jose State Univ.; Bass Trombonist, San Jose Symph., Vintage Brass Ensemble; Extra trombonist, San Fran. Symph. & Opera, Am. & Joffrey Ballet Cos. Recordings: Mike Vax, Art Pepper Big Band. Mbr., MENC. Hobbies: Travelling; Backpacking; Skiing. Address: 3555 MacGregor Lane, Santa Clara, CA 95050, USA.

ZAIMONT, Judith Lang, b. 8 Nov. 1945, Memphis, Tenn., USA. Composer; Pianist; Teacher. Educ: Artist's Dip., Master in Piano, Long Island Inst. of Music, 1966; BA, Queen's Coll., CUNY, 1966; MA, Columbia Univ., 1968; pvte. study with André Jolivet, Paris, France, 1971-72. m. Gary Edward Zaimont. Career: Concert career as duo-pianist w. Doris L Kosloff, 1960-67; Carnegie Hall debut, 1963; Apps. throughout continental USA; TV apps. Comps. incl: A Calendar Set (12 Preludes for piano); Greyed Sonnets, for soprano & piano; Sacred Service for the Sabbath Evening, for baritone, chorus & Orch.; Sunny Airs & Sober (madrigals for 8 part chorus); Piano Concerto. Recordings: Concerto for 2 pianos; Vocal Music of Judith Lang Zaimont. Mbrships: ASCAP; Am. Women Comps., Inc. (VP); Am. Music Center. Hons. incl: ASCAP Standard Awards; MacDowell Colony Fellowships; Gottschalk Centernary Comp. Competition, 1st prize. Hobbies incl: Comparative Linguistics. Address: 264-20 82nd Avenue, Floral Park, NY 11004, USA.

ZAKOTNIK, Breda, b. 10 Nov. 1945, Maribor, Yugoslavia. Pianist. Educ: Musicol., Univ., Ljubljana; Piano, Maribor, Ljubljana & Vienna; Concert Dip., 1969; Master Courses, Budapest, Paris; Chmbr. Music, Vienna, Portugal & UK. Debut: aged 12. Career: Concerts, mainly chmbr. music, Yugoslavia, Austria, Germany, Italy, Spain, Portugal, France, Belgium, UK; Radio recordings, Austria, Spain, Yugoslavia; TV, ibid.; Soloist specializing in Mozart & Hammer Klavier. Hon: Debussy Prize, 1968. Hobby: Nature. Address: Neufanggasse 5, A-5020 Salzburg, Austria.

ZANDER, Benjamin David, b. 9 Mar, 1939, Gerrards Cross, Bucks., UK. Cellist; Conductor; Chamber Music Teacher. Educ: BA, London Univ.; Dip., Hochschule, Cologne, Germany; Study w. Gaspar Cassado, Italy, Germany & Spain, 5 yrs. m. Patricia, 1 d. Career: cond., Civic Symph. Orch. of Boston & New England Conserv. youth Chmbr. Orch., USA; Co-Chmn., Chmbr. Music Dept. & Tchr. of Cello, New England Conserv. Hobbies: Music; Opera; Drama; Students; Family. Address: 12 Ellsworth Ave., Cambridge, MA 02139, USA.

ZANINELLI, Luigi, b. 30 Mar. 1932, Raritan, NJ, USA. Composer; Conductor; Pianist; University Professor. Educ: Dip., Curtis Inst. Music, Phila., Pa. m. Joanne Zasucha, 4 d. Debut: Juilliard Schl. Music, NYC, 1951. Career: Composer-cond., RCA Italiana, Rome, Italy; Music Dir., Met. opera Star, Anna Moffo, ibid., Prod.-Dir., CBC-TV series, 20th Century Music, Canada; Music critic, CBC Radio. Comps. incl: music for 5 films, US, Canada & Italy; 'The Tale of Peter Rabbit', New Orleans Symph.; over 250 works for symph. orch., symphonic band, etc. Recordings: Golden Crest; RCA Victoria; Shawnee Press Ref. Recordings. Publ: Hearing & Singing, 1956. Mbr. profl. orgs. Hons. incl: ASCAP Standard Award Winner, 1964-; Outstanding achievement in Music, Prov. Alberta, 1972. Hobbies: For. sports cars. Address: 501 Court St., Hattiesburg, MS 39401, USA.

ZARET, Peter H, b. 21 Feb. 1939, NYC, USA. Violinist. Educ: BS, MS, Juilliard Schl.; DMA cand., Univ. of Mich.; pvte. study w. Joseph Fuchs, Ivan Galamian, Louis Persinger, Raphael Bronstein, Paul Makanovitsky, Juilliard Str. Quartet, & Berl Senofsky. Career: Concertmaster, Richmond (Va.) Symph., Springfield (Ohio) Symph., & (currently) Norfolk (Va.) Symph. & Va. Opera Assn.; Artist-in-Res., Norfolk State Coll.; former 1st Violin, Va. C'wlth. Univ. Str. Quartet; has made num. broadcasts on local TV & radio stns. Recordings: num. pop records & commercials. Hobbies: Photography. Address: 601 Pembroke Ave., Norfolk, VA 23507, USA.

ZARZO, Vicente, b. 6 May 1938, Benaguacil Valencia, Spain. Musician; French Horn Player. m. Maria del Carmen Sabater, 4

s., 1 d. Career: Nat. Orch. of Reykjavik, Iceland; Am. Wind Symph., Pitts., USA; Nat. Orch. of Mexico; Played solo in Mexico, Holland, Germany, Ireland, USA & Can.; Perf., Dutch radio & TV. Recordings incl: Sinfonia No. 3 for Wind Orch. w. 'Corno Obligatto' (Eduardo Mata). Mbr., Bureau des Informations Musicales, Moudon, Switz. Recip. Dip. as best instrumentalist of the yr., Unión Mexicana de Críticos de Teatro y Música, 1963. Hobbies: Pvte. Lib. of horn music; Horn collection. Mgmt: Alex Saron, Box 29, Blaricum, Netherlands. Address: Florence Nightingalelaan 1, Pijnacker, Netherlands.

ZASLAW, Neal Alexander, b. 28 June 1939, NYC, USA. Flautist & Musicologist. Educ: BA, Harvard Coll., 1961; MS, The Juilliard Schl. of Music, 1963; MA, Columbia Univ., 1965; PhD., ibid, 1970; Flute studies w. James Pappoutsakis & Julius Baker. m. Ellen Faust. Career: Solo & chamber music apps. in Boston, New Haven, NY, Wash. DC., etc, 1958, 3 seasons (1962-65) w. Am. Symph. Orch. under Leopold Stokowski; Instr. in Muisc, City Coll. of CUNY, 1968-70; Asst. Prof. of music, Cornell Univ., 1970-74; Assoc. Prof. of Music, ibid, 1974-; Assoc. Ed., Current Musicology, 1966-67; Ed.-in-Chief, ibid, 1967-70; Book Review Ed., Notes, the Qtly, Jrnl. of the Music Lib. Assn., 1970-. Publs: Performance Practice: A Bibliography, 1971; Edward A MacDowell, 1964. Contbr. to var. profl. publs. Mbrships. incl: Am. Musicol. Soc.; Royal Musical Assn, UK; Soc. Francaise de Musical Hons: Senior Fellowship (Nat. Endowment for the Humanities) for rsch. in London, 1976-77. Address: 132 South Hill Terr., Ithaca, NY 14850, USA.

ZASTROW, Joyce Ruth, b. 27 Feb. 1929, Milwaukee, Wis., USA. Professor of Music; Lyric Soprano. Educ: BA, Valparaiso Univ., Ind.; MMus, Ind. Univ.; D Musical Arts, Univ. of Ill.; Berkshire Music Ctr.; Aspen Schl. of Music; Fontainebleau Schl. of Music, France; Mozarteum, Salzburg, Austria. Career: Perfs. in opera, oratorio & recital, esp. in field of contemporary music, throughout Mid-west; Contemporary Music Fests., Oberlin Coll., Ball State Univ. & Ind. State Univ.; Assoc. Prof. Music, Western Mich. Univ., Kalamazoo. Publs: A Study of Musical Settings of the 3 Soliloquies of Gretchen from Goethe's Faust, 1973. Contbr. to Am. Music Tchr. (reviews). Mbr. & Officeholder, profl. assns. Hobbies: Sewing; Golf; Swimming. Address: 1933 Stevens Ave., Kalamazoo, MI 49008, USA.

ZATHEY, Janusz Romuald, b. 7 Feb. 1927, Warsaw, Poland. Pianist; Assistant Professor. Educ: Dip. in piano, 1953, in comp., 1956, State High Schl. of Music, Cracow. m. Janina Drzewinska Zathey. Debut: Philharmony, Cracow, 1948. Career: num. apps., radio, TV & concert halls as Soloist, Accomp. & Chmbr. Musician, 1949-; at State High Schl. of Music, Cracow, 1953-; Lectr., ibid, 1966; Asst. Prof. ibid, 1975-; Prodekanus, ibid, 1978-; Comps. incl: Suita Zartobliwa for clarinet & piano, 1954; Sonata for violin & piano (recorded by Polish Radio). Recordings: w. violinists K Danczowska, T Globówna & W Kwasny, for radio. Publs: Ed., var. piano scores for string concertos. Contbr. to: Ruch Muzyczny. Mbrships: Soc. of Polish Musicians; Assn. of Polish Tchrs. Recip., state & civic hons. Hobby: Tinkering. Address: Karmelicka 5 m 4, 31-133 Cracow, Poland.

ZAYAS, Juana, b. 25 Dec. 1940, Havana, Cuba. Pianist. Educ: Peyrellade Conserv., Havana, 1951; Nat. Conser. of Music, Paris, France, 1958-61; pvte. study w. Adèle Marcus & David Bar-Illan. m. Henri P M Fromageot, 3 s. Debut when aged 5. Career: Mbr., Albany Symph. Orch., 1969-73; num. solo recitals incl. Alice Tully Hall, NY, 1977; has appd. as soloist w. Albany, Berkshire, Schenectady & Dallas Civic, Venezuela Symph. Orchs. Hons: 1st prizes, Piano & Chmbr. Music, Medals in Sight-reading & Solfege, Nat. Conserv. of Music, Paris; Medal w. Distinction, Int. Piano Competition, Geneva, Switz., 1962; 3rd prize, Teresa Carreño Latin Am. piano competition, Venezuela, 1976. Hobby: Folkdancing, Mgmt: ConeÇSusman, NY. Address: 1171 Van Antwerp Rd., Schenectady, NY 12309, USA.

ZBINDEN, Julien-Francois, b. 11 Nov. 1917, Rolle, Vaud, Switzerland. Deputy Head of Music Broadcasting. Educ: Tchr.'s Dip., Vaud Coll. of Educ., 1938; Lausanne Conserv. m. Marie-Madeleine Martignier. Debut: Profl. Jazz Pianist, 1938. Career: Pianist, Franch Switzerland Radio, 1947; Hd., Musical Serv., Lausanne Studio, 1956; Dpty. Hd., Music Broadcasting, 1965-. Comps. incl: (publs). 2 Symphs.; Opera; Oratorio; 10 concertos; Num. Chmbr. music works, vocal & choral works, film music, radiophonic music; (recordings) Concerto da camera, for piano & strings; Erato; concertino for Trumpet. Contbr. to Musical Review, French Switzerland. Mbrships. incl: Pres., Assn. of Swiss Musicians, 1973. Recip. num. prizes. Hobbies: Astrol.; Flying. Address: rte. de Berne 59, 1010 Lausanne, Switzerland.

ZDRAVKOVITCH, Gika (Zdravković Zivojin), b. 24 Nov. 1914, Belgrade, Yugoslavia. conductor. Educ: Philos. Fac., Carl's Univ., Prague; Music Acad., Belgrade; Conserv., Prague; High Master Degree for Conducting & Comp., w. Vaclav Talich, Prague. m. Jevrosima, 1 d. Debut: w. prague Chmbr. Orch., 1948. Career: Music Dir., Belgrade Phil. Orch.; had conducted in major ctr. through world excepting Aust.; over 200 TV & radio broadcasts; Prof., Belgrade Music Acad. Recordings for Decca, Electrola, Philips, Jugoton, RTB. Publs., articles & books in Yugoslavia. Mbr., Int. Juries (Music Competitions). Hons: Hon. Prize, Yugoslavian Govt., 1950; decorations from govts. of Libya, 1961, UAR, 1962, & Yugoslavia, 1971. Hobby: Tennis. Address: pariska 14, 11000 Belgrade, Yugoslavia.4.

ZDZITOWIECKA, Krystyna Maria, b.12 May 1943, Tomaszow Maz, Poland. Soprano. Educ: Music Coll., Warsaw, 1965. m. Pankracy Zdzitowiecki, 1 s. Debut: Polskie Radio, Warsaw. Career: Recitals, radio & TV, Poland; Play registrations, Radio Berlin; Soloist concerts, Paris. Recordings: Opera, chmbr. & light music. Mbr., Assn. Polish Musician Artists, Warsaw. Hon: Prize, best recording 1973 for 'Vocalisse' by S Rachmaninoff. Hobbies: Motor cars; Touring. Address: ul. Konopacka 16 m.5, 03-428 Warsaw, Poland.

ZECHLIN, Dieter, b. 30 Oct. 1926, Goslar, Germany. Pianist. Educ: Studied in Leipzig, Weimar. m. Sascha Zechlin, 1 d. Career: concerts in Europe, Japan, S Am.; App. on TV series on Beethoven & Popular Educ. Recordings incl: Beethoven (32 Sonatas); Schubert; Bartok; Mozart. Mbrships: VP, Akademie der Kunste, Berlin (DDR); Pres., Musikrat der DDR; IMC. Hons. incl: Nationalpreis der DDR; Vaterlandischer Verdienstorden Kunstoreis der DDR, Schuman preis Zwickan. Address: Waldstr. 30 1197 Berlin, German Demorcratic Repub.

ZECHLIN, Ruth, b. 22 June 1926, Grosshartmannsdorf bei Freiberg, Germany. Composer: Professor of Composition. Educ: Study of piano, organ & composition w. Rohden, Ramin, Straube & David. div., 1 d. Career incl: Prof. of Composition, Berlin Acad. of Music. Compositions incl: Sonatinas; Trio; 6 String Quarters, 2 Chmbr. Symphs.; 3 Symphs; Concertos for violin, oboe; flute; harpsichord; piano; organ. Amor. & Psyche (chmbr. music); opera - Reineke Fuchs; Canzoni olla notte, for baritone & orch.; Letters, for orch.; An Aphrodite (chamber music); var. pieces for organ, harpsichord, choral works, Lieder, etc. Var. works recorded. Mbrships: Acad. of Arts of German Fed. Repub. Hons. incl: Goethe Prize, 1962; Art Prize of German Dem. Repub., 1965; Nat. Prize, ibid., 1975; Hanns-Eisler Prize, 1968. Hobby: Harpsichord. Address: Bielckenweg 8, 1115 Berlin-Buch, German Dem. Repub. 21.

ZEHM, Friedrich, b. 22 Jan. 1923, Neusalz, Schlesien, Germany. Composer and Music Publisher's Reader. Educ: Mozarteum, Salzburg, Austria; PMP, Music High Schl., Freiburt/Breisgau. m. Roswitha Zehm, 3 s. Career: Pianist, Concert, Radio Perfs. of own works; Educator; Music Cons., America House, Freiburg, 1956-63; Reader, B Schott's Sons, Music Publrs., Mainz, 1963-. Compositions incl: Konzert, flute & orch.; Concerto in Pop, for Pop group & orch.; Concerto da camera, oboe & string orch.; Capriccio, for perc. & orch.; Divisions on Let it Be, for guitar & strings; 5 variations for cembalo; Introduction & Ragtime for 12 cellos; Alla Danza, 3 Latin American dances for instrumental groups; var. orchl. works; 14 Chmbr. works; 5 Keyboard works; 6 Lieder, var. vocal solos; Mass, cantata Nonstop-Songs, var. works for choir & orch. or ensemble; 4 Heitere Chorlieder, 5 Polnische Volkslieder, unaccomp. choir. 8 Duets for 2 clarients, 1975; Fünf Gedichte für mittlere Stimme und Klavier, 1976. Mbrships: German Comps. Grp.; GEMA. Recip. num. Hons. Address: 6 Schlichterstr., 62 Wiesbaden, German Fed. Repub.

ZEIGLER, Lynn Jay, b. 1 Aug. 1946, Rochester, Minn., USA. Organist; University Teacher. Educ: BMus, Oberlin Conserv. of Music; MMus Northwestern Univ., Evanston; Conserv. de Musique, Geneva. Switz.; Cert., Haarlem Summer Organ Acad., Netherlands. Debut: Switz., 1972. Career: num. concerts, Switz., Germany, France, Belgium, Netherlands, USA, inclng. Mangadino Organ Fest., Switz.; EUROVISION broadcast, Brusio, Switz.; num. recordings for Swiss & Netherlands radios; Organ Tchr., Duke Univ., USA, 1974-75, Iowa State Univ., 1975-. Mbrships: Am. Musicol. Soc.; AGO. Hons. incl: 1 Prix de Virtuosité, Genevas Conserv., 1973; 1 Prix, Concours de la TV & Radio Suisse, 1973, & Concours d'Orgue de la Jeunesses Musicales de Suisse, 1972; 4th Prize, Nurnberg Int. Organ Competion, 1975. Address: Iowa State Univ., Music Dept., Ames, Iowa 50011, USA.

ZEITLIN, Zvi, b. 21 Feb. 1923, Dubrovna, USSR. Concert Violinist; Professor of Violin. Educ: Juilliard Schl. of Music, Hebrew Univ., Jerusalem. m. Marianne Langner, 1 s., 1 d.

Debut: NY, 1951. Career: Prof., Eastman Schl. of Music, Univ. of Rochester; Hd., Violin Dept., Music Acad. of the West, Santa Barbara, Calif.; Concert tours all over the world; Appearances w. leading world symphs.; Broadcasts on TV & radio. Ed., newly unearthed Nardini concerto, 1958; Currently working on 6 other Nardini Concerto. Author of articles on Biblical Cantillation. Recordings: Schoenberg Violin Concerto; Rochberg Variations; Schumann Sonateas; Schuleit w. Eastman Trio. Mbrships: The Behemians, NY; Univ. of Rochester Fac. Club; NY State Tchrs. Assn.; Am. Fedn. of Musicians. Hons: Am. Israel Soc. Award, for furthering cultural rels. between USA & Israel, 1957; Commission of Paul Ben-Haim Violin Concerto for Zeitlin, Am. Israel Cultural Fndn; Prof. at Univ. of Rochester, 1975. Mgmt: Thea Dispeker, NY. Address: 204 Warren Ave., Rochester, NY 14618, USA. 6, 14, 28.

ZELENKA, Istvań, b. 30 July 1936, Budapest, Hungary. Composer. Educ: BMus, comp., Hochschule für Musik und darstellende Kunst, Vienna, 1962. Comps. incl: Requiem pro viventibus; Gué; Dove, dove, Signore, Signori?; The birds, the end & the remembrance (ª plays for musical theatre); Trio; Voulez-vous voler librement.....?; you do remember all the circumstance?; Union Libre 1977; Glock Glück 1st? Recordings made by European TV & radio stns. Mbr. var. profl. orgs. Hons: 1st prize, comp. contest, Innsbruck, 1966; Special Broadcast Portraits, ORF, Vienna, 1972 & SSR, Geneva, 1974, 78. Mgmt: Franz Konig, Tonos-Verlag, Ahastrasse, Darmstadt, Germany. Address: 134 Chemin de la Montagne, 1224 Chene-Bougeries, Switzerland.

ZELLAN-SMITH, Georgina, b. 26 Sept. 1931, Milburn, Otago, NZ. Concert Pianist; Professor. Educ: BMus, Otago Univ., NZ; LRAM; ARCM; BMus, London Univ. Debut: Wigmore Hall, 1961. Career: Solo recitals, UK, Europe, Hong Kong, Singapore, Aust., NX, S Am., W Indies, also broadcasts; TV broadcasts in UK, Hong Kong, NZ & Trinidad; Soloist, NZ Proms; Concerto Soloist w. major Engl. orchs.; Prof. of Music, RAM. Recordings: Liszt Recital (Peerless Records). Mbrships: Royal Soc. of Musicians; ISM; RAM Club. Recip. FRAM, 1975. Hobbies incl: Home crafts & cooking. Address: 83 Dora Rd., London SW19 7JT, UK.

ZEMAN, Anton, b. 17 Oct. 1937, Resita, Romania. Composer; Conductor. Educ: Conserv. Ciprian Porumbescu, Bucharest, Romania. m. Mariana, 2 c. Debut: 1964. Career: Comp.; Prof., Conserv. George Enescu, Iasi, Romania. Comps: Small Poem; Suite for mixed choir; Sonata for piano; Elaboration for Orch. No. 1; childhood of a Flight (Suite for Children's Choir); The Wonderful Forest, for Children's Choir; From Ancient Timnes, for mixed choir, Recordings: I Symph.; II Symph.; Elaboration for Orch. Nos. I & II; Arches Over Time for Choir & Orch.; Suite for mixed choir; Sonata for Piano; Cuttings for Instrumental Camera Group; Images for 2 Violins. Mbrships: Union of Comps. of Romania; Comps. Bureau Office, Iasi. Hons: Prizes, Union of Comps., 1969, '71, '73; Prize of Acad. of George Enescu, Romania. Hobby: Travelling. Address: Str. Eternitate, No. 84, Iasi, Romania.

ZEMAN, Jiří, b. 20 Nov. 1934, Prague, Czech. Teacher; Singer; Musicologist. Educ: Tchrs. Dip., Tchrs. Trng. Inst., prague, 1954; musicol., Fac. of Philos., Charles Univ., Prague. m. Milada Nussbauer, 1 s. Career: Violist, St. James & St. Francis Ch. Orch.; Mbr., Tchrs. Vocal Ensemble, Artisitic Ensemble, Czech Phil. Choir; Sec. & Ed., State Publing. House of Music; Vice-Mgr., Czech Music Fund; currently Ext. Collaborator, Swiss Radio, Stn. Basle & Sec., Ctrl. Rsch., Ciba-Geigy Ltd., Basle. Has recorded w. Czech Phil. Choir. Publs: The Jubilant Czech Philharmonic Choir, 1964. Contbr. articles to var. periodicals & lectures to Swiss Radio. Hons: 1st Prize, 1954 Radio Prague Musical Instrument-Detection Competition; Extraordinary Mbr., Czech Phil.'s Inst., 1962. Hobbies: Gardening; Hiking; Swimming; Skiing. Address: Allschwilerstr. 2, Postfach 404, 4104 Oberwil/BL, Switz.

ZEMANEK, Heinz, b. 1 Jan. 1920, Vienna, Austria. Director & Researcher of Computer Arts. Educ: Dip., Ing., 1944; Dr. Tech., 1954; Lectr., 1959; Prof., 1964. m. Maria Assumpta Lindebner, 1 d., 1 s. Career: Univ. of Tech., Vienna, 1947-61; IBM. Laboratory Dir., 1961-76; IBM Fellow, 1976-81; 10 TV films for Austrian TV & ZDF. Publs: (co-author), Computer - Werzeug der Information. Contbr. to tech. jrnls. Mbrships: incl: Acad. of Arts, Berlin; past pres., Int. Fed. of Information Processing. Hons: Grosses Ehrenzeichen für Verdienste um die Republik Osterreich; Golden Stefan Exner Medal; Prechtl-Medal. Hobby: Hist. of Computers & Automata. Address: Blutgasse 3, 1010 Vienna I, Austria.

ZEMTSOVSTY, Jzalij Josifović, b. 22 Feb. 1936, Leningrad, USSR. Ethnomusicologist; Folklorist. Educ: Univ. of Liningrad;

Leningrad Conserv. dv., 1 d. Career incls: Concertmaster (pianist), Leningrad Schl. of Music, 1958-60; Sr. Sci., Folklore Sect., State, Inst. for Theatre, Music & Cinematography, Leningrad., 1960-. Author of many books in field, incl. Folklore & composer, 1978. Contbr. to newspapers & profl. jrnls. Mbrships: Union of Comps. of USSR; Soc. for Ethnomusicol. Inc., USA; Int. Folk Music coun. Recip. Medal, All-Union Competition of sci. students' work, 1959. Hobby: Philately. Address: Leningrad 190000, Jsaakievskaja ploshchad', Dom 5, USSR.

ZENATTI, Ariette, b. 23 Feb. 1931, paris, France. Hd. of Research in Musical Psychology; Pianist. Educ: Lic. ès Lettres; PhD, Psychol., Univ. of Paris; 1st Prizes, Piano, Hist. of Music, Musicol., Nat. Sup. Conserv., Paris. Career: Piano Concerts throughout France, 1953-; Prof., Piano, Nat. Sub. Music Conserv., Mans, 1964-70; Hd. of Rsch., (Music Conserv., Mans, 1964-70; Hd. of Rsch., (Music Psychol), Nat. Ctr. for Scientific Rsch., 1970-; Chief Ed., Sciences de l'Art-Scientific Aesthetics. Publs: Le prélude dans la musique profane de clavier en France, de Louis Couperin au déclin du Romantism, Paris, 1962; Preceptionet intelligence musicale chez l'enfant, Paris, 1967; Le développement génétique de la perception musicale, Paris, 1969. Mbrships: French Psychol. Soc.; Int. Soc. of Empirical Aesthetics; Int. Soc. for Music Educ.; French Musicol. Soc. Recip., Bronze Medal, Nat. Ctr. for Scientific Rsch., 1968. Hobby: Gardening. Address: 3 ter, r. rue de Brévannes, 94370 Sucy-en-Brie, France.

ZENDER, Johannes Wolfgang Hans, b. 22 Nov. 1936, Wiesbaden, Germany. Conductor; Composer. Educ: Dips., Cond., Piano, Comp., Music Conserv., Freiburg. m. Gertrude Achenbach. Career: Cond., Freiburg, 1959; Prin. Cond., Bonn., 1964; Gen. Music Dir. of the City of Kiel, 1969; Prin. Cond., Saar Broadcasting, 1971-; Guest cond., Berlin Phil., LSO, BBC, Residentie-Orkest, Tonhalle Zurich, Opera Houses of Munich, Stuttgart, Cologne; Hamburg, Festival of Bayreuth (Parsifal). Compositions: Vexilla Regis; Quartett, Flute, Cello, piano & percussion; Trifolium, flute, cello, piano; Les Sirenes chatent, soprano & instruments; Bremen wodu, electronic work; Schachspiel, orch.; Zeitstrome, orch.; Canto's I-V, voices & instruments; Muji no kyo, trio & instruments tutti ad lib.; Modelle I-XII, Orchl. Grps. Recordings: Wergo; DGG. Mbrships: GEMA; Int. Soc. for Contemporary Music; German comps. Grp. Recip. num. Hons. for Comp. Hobbies: Arts; Literature. Mgmt: Allied Artists Agency, London; Adler, Berlin; Concertdirectie Dr. G de Koos, Netherlands. Address: 3 Am Gegenortschacht, 6602 Dudweiler/Saar, German Fed. Repub.

ZENGERINK, Herman(us) Joannes, b. 3 Aug. 1918, Hoofddorp/Haarlemmermeer, Netherlands. Library Official; Music publisher. Educ: Choral Cond. Dip., Cath. Choirmasters & Organists Soc., 1950; Musicol. Dip. Drs. (doctl. cand.), Utrecht Univ., 1972. Career: Music Office Mgr., Wed. J R van Rossum, music publr. & dealer, Utrecht, also ed., arr., etc., 1944-70; Owner, Publr., van Rossums & Herman Zengerink, Amsterdam-Utrecht, 1970-; Official, Lib., Inst. of Musicol., Utrecht Univ. 1974-; Mbr., VNM Publications, 1978-. Comps. incl: songs & choral works; about 200 choral arrs. Recordings of choral works & arrs. Mbr. profl. orgs. Hobbies incl: Organ; Violin; Drawing; Painting; Photography; Poetry. Address: Urlusstraat 24, 3533 SN Utrecht, Netherlands.

ZERASCHI, Helmut, b. 25 Oct. 1911, Sarichen nr. Gorlita, Germany. Musicologist. Educ: Musikhochschule Halle/Saale; Staatsdip., PhD, Karl-Marx-Universität, Leipzig. m. Ingeborg Kagelmann. Career: Rsch. worker, Musikinstrumenten-Museum, Leipzig, 1958-61; Dir. ibid., 1974-76; Pres., Breitkopf und Härtel, Friedrich Hofmeister & Deutscher Verlag für Musik, Leipzig, 1961-74. Comp: Kleine Musik für Streichtrio. Publs: Das Buch von der Drehorgel, 1971; Die Drehorgel in der Kirche, 1973; Drehorgelstücklein aus dem 18. Jahrh., 1973; Drehorgeln, 1976; Geschichte des Musikinstrmenten-Museums Leipzig, 1977; Die Musikinstrumente unserer Zeit, 1978; books for children. Mbr., Verband der Komponisten und Musikwissenschaftler der DDR. Address: Katherinenstr. 2, 701 Leipzig, German Dem. Repub.

ZETHELIUS, Gudrun, b. 14 Apr. 1918, Stockholm, Sweden. Organist. Educ: Teol.kand. (BD), Fil.kand. (BA), Uppsala; 3 higher exams. for organists, Royal Coll. of Music, Stockholm. Career: Organist & choir ldr., Burträsk Ch.; Cond., Assn. of Ch. Choirs, diocese of Lulea. Contbr. to: Svensk Kyrkomusik; Svenskt Gudstjänstliv. Mbrships: Hon. Sec., Riksfürbundet Svensk Kyrkomusik (Assn. of Swedish Ch. Choirs); Hon. Sec., Laurentius Petri Soc. Address: Ringvägen 16, 930 20 Burträsk, Sweden.

ZETTERHOLM, Finn Tore, b. 4 Aug. 1945, Taby, Sweden. Folksinger; Guitarist; Author. Educ: Fil.kand., 1969. m. Kristina

Niklasson, 2 d. Debut: 1966. Career: apps. in most Swedish concert halls; about 100 radio & TV broadcasts. Comps: about 75 ballads & songs. Recordings: visor i trotzaldern, 1966; Visor ur wrangstrupen, 1968; Hemfjorda visor, 1970; OBS. Taxten, 1971; Joe Hill pa svenska, 1969; Lillfar och Lillmor, 1970; Forsta Jaj, 1973; Alskog, 1974; Varldens minsta LP, 1974; Folklar, 1977; Längfansglaa elepant, 1977. Publs: Barnvisan i Sverige, 1969; Svensk Foklpiesi, 1972; Svenska Folkvisor, 1975. Mbrships: YTF; Sveriges Forfattarforening; SKAP. Address: Lovängsvagen 6, 13012 Alta, Sweden.

ZETTY, Claude Elias, b. 2 May 1924, Quakertown, USA. Choral conductor & University Professor. Educ: BS, Cornell Univ.; Westminster Choir Coll.; BMus & MMus, Ind. Univ. 3 c. Career: Choirmaster & Instr., Dept. of Music, Culver Mil. Acad., 1951-61; Dir. of Choral Activities & Prof., Dept. of Music, Trinity Univ., 1961-. Recordings: Music for 'The Protestant Hour', Trinity Univ. Choir; Ceremony of Psalms, William Thornton. Contbr. to var. music jrnls. Edited a series of 13 articles in the area of ch. music for The Choral Jrnl., 1968-72. Mbrships: Am. Choral Dirs. Assn; Tex. Choral Dirs. Assn.; Assn. of Am. Choral Conds.; Presbyn. Assn. of Musicians; Pi Kappa Lambda. Hons: Sigma Kappa Epsilon Award of Merit for outstanding contbn. to Trinity Univ. 1969; Chi Beta Epsilon & Bengal Lancer Outstanding Prof. Award, Trinity Univ., 1972-73. Hobbies: Gardening. Address: 1923 Howard no. D, San Antonio, TX 78212, USA.

ZETZER, Alfred, b. 3 July 1916, Cleveland, Ohio, USA. Clarinettist & Bass Clarinettist. Educ: BMus; Grad. w. virtuoso hons., Cleveland Inst. of Music, 1940; sutdied w. Daniel Bonade. m. Gertrude, 2 s. Debut: Solo Clarinettist, Kansas City Phil. Career: Solo Clarienttist w. Ballet Russe de Monte Carlo, Kansas City Phil., Pitts. Symph. & San Antonio Symph.; Bass Clarinettist of Cleveland Symph. under George Szell & Lorin Maazel, 1949-. Recordings w. Cleveland Symph. Orch. Hobbies: Collecting Antique Clarients & Spode China. Address: 3284 Enderby Rd., Shaker Heights OH 44120, USA.

ZEUTHEN, Morten B. 19 June 1951, Copenhagen, Denmark. Cellist. Educ: Studies w. var. tchrs. incl. Asger Lund Christiansen & Paul Tortelier. Debut: Copenhagen, 1976. Career: Asst. solo cellist, The Royal Danish Orch., 3 yrs.; Solo cellist, Danish Radio Symfoniorkestra; Tours as soloist & chmbr. musician, Europe; Mbr., The Kontra String Quartet. Recordings: Mostly of Danish modern chmbr. music. Hons. incl: Gade Prize, 1973. Hobby: Mbr. of Scandinavian Folk Music Group De Nordiske Spillemand. Mgmt: Wilhelm Hansen, Gothersgade 9-11, Copenhagen. Address: Ronnebaervej 28, 2840 Holte, Denmark.

ZHURAYTIS, Algis, b. 1928, USSR. Conductor. Educ: Vilnius & Moscow Conservs. Career: Cond., Lithuanian Opera & Ballet State Theatre, 1951-54; Cond., Bolshoi Theatre, 1960-; cond. of radio broadcasts, 1955-. Address: State Academic Bolshoi Theatre of USSR, 1 Ploschchad Sverdlova, Moscow, USSR.

ZIAK, Siegbert Karl Gustav, b. 5 Dec. 1909. University Professor; Pianist. Educ: Dr. Jur., Vienna Univ., Austria, 1936; Studied under Walter Kerschbaumer, Carlo Zecchi & Friedrich Wührer; State Exam., Acad. of Music & Performing Arts, Vienna, 1933. Career: Tchr., Public Conserv., Vienna, 1937-38; Tchr., City Schl. of Music, ibid, 1938-41; Tchr., Klagenfurt Conserv., 1941-55; Tchr., Graz Conserv., 1955-63; Prof., Acad. of Music & the Performing Arts, Graz, 1963-; Full Prof., ibid, 1972-. concerts as soloist w. orch. & Chmbr. music, Vienna, Graz, Klagenfurt/Franfurt/Main, Dresden, Leipzig & Prague. Mbrships. incl: commn. for Univ. planning, Conf. of Austrian Rectors, 1970-. Hobbies: Photography; Filming & Travel. Address: A 8010 Graz, Rudolfstr. 123 d, Austria.

ZICHOVA, Zorka, b. 4 June 1920, Bratislava, Czechoslovakia. Pianist. Educ: Conserv. of Music, Prague; Dip., Acad. of Music, prague. m. Jaroslav Zich. Career: apps. as chmbr. pianist, Czech., Poland, German Dem. Repub., German Fed. Repub., Bulgaria; piano Accomp., int. instrumental competitions, France, Switz., German Fed. Repub., Czech.; about 600 radio broadcasts, Prague, Stuttgart, Munich, Paris, Warsaw; about 12 TV broadcasts, prague; Instr., Acad. of Music, Prague, 1968-. Recordings: Supraphon; Panton; Chante du Monde. Mbr., Guild of Czech. Comps. & Concert Artists, Prague. Hobbies: Travel; Mountain Walks. Mgmt: Pragokoncert. Address: Bubenec, Raisova 5, 1600 Prague 6, Czechoslovakia.

ZIERITZ, Grete von, b. 10 Mar. 1899, Vienna, Austria. Composer. Educ: Conserv. of Styrian Music Soc., Graz., 1912-17; studied comp. w. Franz Schreker, Musikhochschule,

Berlin, 1926-31. div., 1 d. Debut: Graz, 1913. Career: Concert Tours in Austria & abroad; Piano & Comp. Evenings; Int. Radio recordings of own & contemporary works. Comps. incl: 129 Lieder & songs w. piano & other instruments; 24 songs w. orch.; 49 Chmbr. music works, 13 for Orch., 31 for Choir; 1 Flute Concerto; Concerto for 2 solo trumpets & orch. Mbrships: Deutscherr Komponistenverband; VDMK; Hon. mbr., Steir. Tonkb., Graz. Hons: Mendelssohn State Prize for Comp., Berlin, 1928; Schubert Scholarship, Columbia Phonographic Co., NY, 1928; named Professor By Austrian Federal Pres., 1958; Plakette für Kunst und Wissenschaft of the Berlin Salon. Hobbies: Occult Studies; Study of Precious Stones & Crystal; Travelling; Solitude. Address: Marburgerstrasse 16, D-1000 Berlin 30, German Fed. Repub.

ZIGON, Marko, b. 11 Feb. 1929, Ljubljana, Yugoslavia. Conductor; Composer. Educ: Dip., Musical Acad. m. Jarija Zigon, 1 s. Career: Cond., Maribor Opera, 1956-78; opera recordings on TV; tchr. of music. Comps: Overture; Prelude for piano; comp. for violin & piano; Sonatina for violin & piano; Quartet for flute, oboe, clarinet, bassoon; Strg. Quartet; Trio for flute, oboe, clarinet; 3 Sonatinas for piano; songs, etc. Hobbies: Nature; Books. Address: 63320 Velenje, Sercerjeva 17, Slovenia, Yugoslavia.

ZIJDERLAAN, Johan (Hans), b. 13 Nov. 1923, Hilversum, Netherlands. Music Publisher. Educ: studied piano, conducting & theory, Amsterdam Conserv.; pvte. study w. Hans Brandts Buys. m. Klaske de Visser, 5 children. Career: Music Publr., 1946-; Dir., Harmonia-Utgave, Hilversum. Mbrships: Pres., Dutch Music Publrs.; Dutch Performance Right Soc. (BUMA); Fndr., Dutch courses for music dealers & publrs., & Harmonia Fndn. Recip. Dutch Music Publrs. Prize, 1965. Hobbies: Botany; Sport; Baroque music. Address: Koloniepad 2, Blaricum NH, Netherlands. 19.

ZIKMUNDOVA, Eva, b. 4 May 1932, Kromeriz, Czech. Opera Singer (Soprano). Educ: State Conserv., Brno; Music Acad., prague. div., 1 s. Debut: Opera House, Ostrava. Career: Mbr., Opera Co. of Nat. Theatre, Prague, 1958-; Guest apps., State Opera Berlin, Hannover, Venice, Naples, Lausanne, Vienna, Edinburgh; recitals for Czech. radio & TV; Prof. of Singing, State Conserv., Parague, 1971-. Recordings: Dvorak, St. Ludmila & Moravian duets; Janacek, The Cunning Little Vixen; also recordings of arias & duets. Recip. Suprahon Annual Award for Cunning Little Vixen, 1974. Mgmt: Pragokoncert, Prague 1, Maltézské námestí 1. Address: Mánesova 23, Prague 2, Czecholsovakia.

ZIMBALIST, Efrem, b. 9 Apr. 1889, Russia (US Citizen). Violinist; Composer. Educ: St. Petersburg Conserv., w. Leopold Auer. m. (1) Alma Gluck (dec. 1938); (2) Mary Louise Curtis (dec. 1970). Debut: Berlin, 1907. Career: Noted concert performer in major cities of Europe & USA; gave 1st US perf. of Glazunov's Concerto in A Minor; Dir., Curtis Inst. of Music, Phila., Pa., 1941-. Compositions incl. works; string quartet; violin sonata; vocal & piano works. Address: 866 Skyline Blvd., Reno, NV 89502, USA.

ZIMMER, Ján, b. 16 May 1926, Ruzomberok, Czechoslovakia. Composer; Pianist. Educ: State Conserv., Bratislava (Dips. in organ, piano & composition); HS of Music, Budapest; Salzburg Seminar in Am. Studies. Div., 1s. Career: Musical mgr., Broadcasting Corp., Bratislava, 1945-48; Prof. State conserv., ibid, 1948-52; Freelance composer & pianist, 1952-. Compositions incl: 9 symphs.; 6 piano concerts; 5 sonatas for piano; 4 sonatas for 2 pianos; Concerto da Camera, oboe & strings; Concerto Grosso, 2 pianos, 2 string orchs. & percussion; Concerto for organ, strings & percussion; Oedipus Rex - opera in 2 acts; The Broken Time, opera; Tatras, 2 suites for orch; Phantasie for piano, orch. & choir; var. chmbr. music & music for films. Var. works recorded. Contbr. to var. Czech musical jrnls. Mbrships: British coun. & Am. Infor. Serv., 1946-52. Hobbies: Sports; Swimming; Photography; Motoring; Travel. Address: St rachotova 13, Bratislava 830 00, Czech.

ZIMMERMANN, Heinz Werner, b. 11 Aug. 1930, Freiburg, Germany. Composer. Educ: Staatliche Musklehreprüfung für Komposition und Musiktheorie, 1953; Study of comsosition w. Julius Weismann, Wolfgang Fortner; Theory, at Evangelisches Kirchenmusik Inst., Heidelberg; Music Hist., Heidelberg Univ. m. Renate Marx, 1 d. Debut: Baden-Baden, 1955. Career: Instr., Composition & Music Theory, Evangelisches Kirchenmusik Inst., Heidelberg, 1954; Prof., Composition & Music Theory, Dir., Berlin Schl. of Sacred Music, 1963-74; Prof. for comp. & music theory, Staatliche Musichochule, Frankfurt am Main. Compositions incl. choral music, motets; Psalmkonzert, for 3 trumpets, vibrahone, string bass, baritone solo & 5-part chorus; Vespers, for vibrahone, harpsichord, string bass & 5-part chorus; 3 Spirtuals, for 8-12 part mised chorus a capella. Contbr. to jrnls. Mbrships: German Performance Rights Soc.; VP, Direktorenkonferenz der Deutschen Kirchenmusik-Schulen. Hons: Prize, Junge Komponisten Ernster Musik, Stuttgare, 1962, '65; Prize, Junge Generation, W Berlin, 1966; DM, Wittenberg Univ., Ohio, USA, 1967. Address: Berliner Kirchenmusikschule Evang. Johannesstit, Schönwalder Allee, 1 Berlin 20, German Fed. Repub.

ZIMMERSCHIED, Dieter, b. 1 July 1934, Danzig (now Gdansk), Poland. Professor of Music Education. Educ: Abitur, 1954; Studium (school music, research etc.) 1954-58, Staatsexamen; Musikzieher am Schlossgymnasium Mainz, 1960-76; Promotion, 1967. m. Christa Brauch, 1 d. Career: Ldr. of Music Cultural Commission, 1970-73; Music advisor to Ministry of Culture, Rhineland-Pfalz, 1969-76; Prof. of Music Pedagogy, Music High Schl. Mainz, 1976-; Ldr., Schl. music sect., Musikhochschule, Stuttgart, 1977-; mbr. of team, Funk-Kolleg Musik, 1976-78. Publs. Incl: Die Kammermusik Johann Nepomuk Hummels, 1967; Perspektiven never Musik, 1974; Tendenzen der Musikdidaktik, 1978. Contbr. to Musik und Bildung (monthly), Mainz. Mbrships: Verband Deutscher Schulmusikerzieher e.V. Address: Weidmanstr. 43, 6500 Mainz, German Fed. Repub.

ZINSSTAG, Gérard, b. 9 may 1941, Zürich, Switz. Composer; Flautist. Educ: Univ. of Geneva; Dip. (flute), Conserv. Geneva; Conserv. Nat. Superiur, Paris; studied chamber music at Acad. Chigiana, Siena, comp. w. H U Lehmann (Zürich) & H Lachenmann. div., / d. Debut: Tonhalle Orch., Zurich, 1967. Career: Prof. of Flute, Zurich Conserv. 1974-; tours of Europe as free lance musician & broadcasts, 1962-66. Comps. incl: Pentaphonie (woodwind quintet); Tastatenfelder (music theatre); Suono Reale (for choked piano); Alternances (for 2 orch. groups); Hülsen..oder die Irrfahrt des Kerns (for 20 speakers, string sextet, 4 vocalists & ° tapes); Innanzi (for Double Bass & Orch.); first autodidac. comp. Publs: Ed., Edition Modern Munich. Mbrships: Tonkünstlerverein, Swits. Hons. incl: scholarship for chamber music, Acad. Chigiana, Siena; Medal, concours Int. Geneva, 1968; Sev. Commissions from cities of Zürich, Basle, Baden-Baden, TV etc. Address: Froschaugasse 20, 8001 Zürich, Switz. 2.

ZIPP, Friedrich, b. 20 June 1914, Frankfurt am Main, Germany. Composer. Musical Educ: Hockschule für Musikerziehung; Hochschule für Kirchenmusik. m. Elfriede Duthweiler, 1 d. Compositions (publd. & recorded) incl: Piano, harpsichord & organ works; Chmbr., music; Orchl. works; Youth music; Works for solo voice & choir a cappela & w. instruments (cantatas); Works for brass instruments. Author of Vom Wesen der Musik - Grundlagen musikalischen Schaffens & Erlebens, 1974. Contbr. to books & jrnls. inclng: Musica; Lied & Chor; Der Kirchenmusiker; German Studies (Sec.I), 1972. Mbrships: Verband Evangelischer Kirchenmusiker Deutschlands; Deutsches Hochstift. Hons. incl. 1st Prize, Hausmusik competition, Hochschule für Musikerziehung, Berlin, 1937. Hobbies: Hist of lit. & art; Walking. Address: Neuhausstr. ' 2, 6 Frankfurt am Main, German Fed. Repub. 19.

ZIVKOVIC, Mirjana, b. 3 May 1935, Split, Yugoslavia. Composer. Educ: MA, Acad. of Music Belgrade. Debut: 1958. Career: Comps on Radio, TV & Yugoslav Stages; Tchr. of Music, Conserv. Josip Slavenski, Belgrade. Compositions: Works for Symph. Orchs: Sinfonia Polifonica; Torso Symphonic; Chmbr. Music: Variations for violin & piano; Incantation for voice & four tympales; Wind instruments quintet; Soloistic Music: Comps, for piano, violin, violincello, songs for voice and piano. Publs: Analytical study of Josip Slavanski's Musical Language, Contbr. to Pro Musica; Mbr. Comps. Assn. of Yugoslavia. Hons. incl: 1st Prize, Conserv. of Fontainebleau. Hobbies: Flower; Gardening. Address: 11000 Beograd, Stanislava Sremcevica 4, Yugoslavia.

ZIVONI, Yossi, b. Dec. 1939, Tel-Aviv, Israel. Violinist. Educ: Grad., Israeli Music Acad., Tel-Aviv & Brussels Conserv. m. Jeanne, 1 d. Career: Tours in Europe, Aust., S Africa, Can., Israel. Hons: Prizewinner, Paganini Int. Competition, 1960, Munich Int. Competition, 1961, Queen Elisabeth Int. Competition (Brussels) 1963. Address: 18 Midholm, London NW11,UK.

ZOEBELEY, Hans Rudolf, b. 27 May 1931, Mannheim, Germany. Conductor; Organist; Music Instructor; Musicologist. Educ: Piano; organ & comp., Heidelberg Univ.; Musicol., Munich Univ.; PhD. m. Margarete Busch, 2 s., 2 d. Recordings: Orlando di Lasso 'Heiter-Komoediantisch' (Christophorus-Verlag); Heinrich Schutz, Mehrchorige geistliche Konzerte (ibid.). Publ: Die Musik des Buxheimer Orgelbuchs. Mbr.,

Muenchner Tokuenster-Verband. Hons: 2nd prize, Int. Choir Competition, Arezzo, Italy, 1966; 1st prize, Int. Choir Competition, Spittal, Austria, 1967. Address: 19 Birkerstrasse 8 Munich 19, German Fed. Repub.

ZOEPHEL, Klaus Joachim, b. 16 July 1929, Plauen/Vogtland, DDR. Conductor; Composer; Music Teacher. Educ: Music Acad., Leipzig; State Examination Comp. & Cond. m. Anneliese Zansler, 1 s. Debut: Leipzig, 1952. Career: Dir., State Cultural Orch., Senftenberg, 1953-56; Cond., Kresitheater, Dobelin, 1956-57; Choirmaster & Cond., Nat. Theatre, Weimar, 1957-61; Cond., Municipal Theatre, Zwickau, Muhlhausen, 1962-63; Mus. Dir., State Orch. Pirna, 1963-; Univ. tchr., Music Acad., Dresden. Comps. incl: Symph. in D; Sinfonietta; Chmbr. music; Songs & choral works. Recordings: All works broadcast on Radio DDR. Mbr. of Soc. Conds. & Musicologists in DDR. Hons. incl: 1st Prize Competition Commission for Cultural Affairs, DDR, 1952; Carl-Maria-von-Weber Prize, 1959. Address: Tiergartenstr. 83, 8020 Dresden, German Dem. Repub.

ZOLL, Klaus, b. 27 Dec. 1944, Alsfeld, W Germany. Concert Pianist. Educ: Abitur Exam, Goethe Gynnasium, Frankfurt, W Germany, 1965; Hochschule für Musik, Frankfurt; RAM, London, UK. m. J Zoll. Debut: W New Phil. Orch., Royal Festival Hall, London, UK. Career: Concerts throughout Europe & USA w. maj. orchs. inclng: New Phil., London; Engl. Nat. Orch.; Rheinische Phil.; Munich Phil., etc. Radio & ÇTV apps. over most maj. European Stns. & USA. Hons: German Chmbr. Music Prize, 1966; 1st Prize, London Int. Competition, 1967. Hobbies: Sports: Football; Chess. Mgmt: Konzertdirektion Delseit, 5 Köln 41, W Germany, Emmastr. 3. Address: 16 Ely Close, Stevenage, Herts., UK.

ZOLLMAN, Ronald, b. 8 Apr. 1950, Antwerp, Belgium. Conductor. Educ: Final Dip. in cond. (w. greatest Distinction), Brussels Conserv; Dip. di merito, Acad. Chigiana, Siena. m. Dominique Mols. Career: Has cond. all Belgian orchs. & given concerts in Switz., Germany, Netherlands, Sweden, France, S America, S Africa & USSR, all with major orchs. Hd, Cond. Fac., Brussels Conserv. Recordings of Belgian music for Min. of Culture, Brussels. Hons: 1st prize for cond., Brussels Conserv.; Laureate, Premio Firenze for conds., 1972. Mgmt: De Koos, Laren, Netherlands. Address: 30 Parvis St. Henri, 1200 Brussels, Belgium.

ZOLTAI, Dénes, b. Mar. 1928, Gyula, Hungary. Educator. Educ: Doctorate & Cand. of Philos., Univ. of Budapest, Fac. of Arts, Hungary. m. Judit Karkovány, 2 c. Career: Prof. of Aesthetics, Fac. of Arts, Univ. of Budapest, Hungary. Publs: Ethos und Affekt - Geschichte der philosophischen Musikasthetik von den Anfangen bus zu Hegel, Berlin/Budapest, 1970; The Concept of Man in Modern Music, Budapest, 1969, German ed., 1978. Contbr. to: Muzika & Magyar zene, Hungary. Mbrships: VP, Nat. Comm. of Hungarian Aestheticians; Assn. of Hungarian Musicians. Address: Torokvesz ut 12/b, 1022 Budapest, Hungary.

ZOMER, Hans, b. 18 June 1933, Wageningen, Netherlands. Concert Singer (Bass-baritone). Dubut: 1966. Career: Apps.: Concertgebouw, Amsterdam; Tonhalle, Zürich, Switzerland; Warchau, Cracow & Stettin, Poland; Essn, W Germany; & on Dutch Musical Soc. Hobby: Architecture. Mgmt: Wil Viser, Koninginnéweg 164, Amsterdam. Address: de Kappel, Darthuizerweg 3, Leersum, Netherlands.

ZONN. Wilma Zapora, b. 7 June 1936, Alden, Pa., USA. Oboist; Teacher. Educ: BMus., Univ. of Miami, Fla., 1958; MMusA, Univ. of Iowa, 1966; studied w. Harold Gomberg & Ray Still. m. Paul Zonn, 1 d. 1 s. Career: has made nat. TV apps. at Tanglewood & as soloist at Berkshire Fest.; Solo Apps., Carnegie Recital Hall, Donnell Lib. & Grace Rainey Auditorium, all NYC, & at Univ. of Chgo.; Soloist w. Portland Symph., Ore., & Iowa & NW Woodwind Quintets; Artist-in-Res., Univ. of Hawaii; Lectr. & Recitalist, 2nd. Annual Convention, Int. Double Reed Soc. Recorded Chroma (by Paul Zonn) on CRI. Dialogue, (by F Furner); Gifts, (by S Smith); Liberation I, (by P Zonn). Contbr. to: Contemporary Instrumental Techniques (chapt. on oboe); jrnls. in field. Mbrships: Int. Double Reed soc.; Am. Fedn. of Musicians. Local 802, NYC. Hons: Best Musician of Yr., Sigma Alpha Iota, 1958; compositions specially written by well-known composers. Hobbies: Gardening: Cooking; Animals; Sports. Address: 308 Pond Ridge Lane, Urbana, IL 61801, USA.

ZOOK, Mary Ann, b. 10 Aug. 1939, Mifflintown, Pa., USA. Educator. Educ: BS, Pa. State Univ., 1961; MMus., Ind. Univ., Bloomington, 1963. Career: Asst. Prof. of Music, Hartwick Coll., Oneonta, NY, 1963-; Apps. in var. recitals as soloist & accomp. Recordings: records and tapes made at Pa. State

Univ., Ind. Univ. & Hartwick Coll. Contbr. to Mini course in Music, Ed. Frederic F. Swift, 1973. Mbrships: Mu Phi Epsilon; Pi Lambda Theta; Int. Soc. Music Educ.; MENC (advsr. of coll. chapt., Hartwick Coll.); NY State MTA (past chmn., dist 8); Nat. MTA; AAUP. Hobby: Travel. Address: 4 East St., Oneonta, NY 13820, USA.

ZOON, Gerrit, b. 1 Jan. 1918, Sommelsdyk, Netherlands. Pianist; Conductor; Church Organist; Music Master. Educ: State Examination Piano, 1951. Comps: For male choir: Gloria, 1955; De Rivier, Jubilate Deo (Psalm 65); Van de Zee, 1976; For choir, soprano, string band: Kyrie eh Sanctus; For choir, piano, tenor, cornet, kettledrums: Te Deum; For choir, organ, soprano, trumpets, kettledrums: Delta Symphoie, 1973 (to commemorate flood of 1953 in S W Netherlands); Num. works for male, female & mixed choirs. Mbrships: Vereniging BUMA; Nederlands organisten Vereniging; Nederlandse Dirigenten Organisatie. Recip. num. awards & hons. inclng: Gold Medal, Order Of Oranje Nassau. Hobbies: Antiques; Painting. Address: Voorstraat 6, Sommelsdyk, Netherlands.

ZOTTOVICEANU, Elena, b. 8 Apr. 1933, Chisinau, Romania. Musicologist. Educ: Degree in Music, Conserv., Ciprian Porumbescu, Bucharest (piano dept.) 1956. Career: Main rsch. worker, Inst. of History of Art, Bucharest. Publs: 2 chapts. in monograph, George Enescu, 1971; The War of Independence & 19th century Romanian Music, etc. Contbr. of over 50 aarticles on hist. of Romanian music to var. scholarly jrnls. Mbrships: Union of Comps. & Musicologists of Romania (musicol. Bd.); Assn. of theatres & musical insts. of Romania; Fellow of Salzburg Seminar in Am. Studies. Hons: Romanian Acad. Prize, 1971; Union of Comps. Prize, 1971-72; Bernier Prize of the Acad. des Beaux Arts, Inst. of France, 1971-72. Hobbies: Lit.; Cinema; Mountaineering. Address: Intr. Buciumeni nr. 1, Of. 22, 71154 Bucharest, Romania.

ZUBROD, Paul Frederick, b. 28 Sept. 1949, Gahanna, Ohio, USA. Percussionist. BMusEd, Ohio State Univ. m. Rebecca Zubrod. Career incls: Percussion Instructor, var. schls., colls. etc.; Percussion Clinician & Adjudicator; Toured w. Americana Braqss, 14 months; Backer var. perfs.; Tour w. Panov's Ballet Duo, NY Repertoire Co. Publs: Cadences in Colour (Permus Publs.). Mbr., Columbus Symph. Orch. & Columbus Symph. Orch. Percussion Trio. Recordings: columbia Records: RCA. Mbrships: incl Phi Mu Alpha; Ohio State Univ. Jazz Ensemble. Recip. Ohio State Marching Band Scholarship. Hobbies: Antique collecting, esp. musical things. Address: 3171 Iremont Rd., Upper Arlington, OH 43221, USA.

ZUBRZYCKI, Boguslaw, b. 25 July 1929, Cracow, Poland. Pianist. Educ: Dip. Piano, State Coll. of Music, Krakow, 1956. m. Anna Przybyta, div. Debut: Soloist, Cracow Phil. Orch., 1955. Career incls: Soloist w. num. symphs.; Performed in Cracow w. Nat. Phil. Orch.; Solo recitals of music by Debussy, Ravel, etc. on stage & Polish radio; Recitals at Conservatoir, Corbeil, near Paris, France, 1969-71. Comps. incl: Sketches, miniature studies in series Per-Painoforte. Num. recordings w. Polish Radio orch., Cracow; Solos in collection of tape recordings of Polish Radio. Mbr. Assn. of Polish Musicians. Hobby: Motorcycle Riding. Address: 7 ul Pokoju 46, 31-548 Cracow, Poland.

ZUCKERMAN, Pinchas, b. 16 July 1948, Israel. violinist. Educ: Israel Conserv.; Acad. of Music, Tel-Aviv; Juilliard Schl. of Music; studied w. Ivan Galamian. Debut: w. Ny Phil., 1969. Career: world-wide concerts & recitals, Dir., tours & plays w., Engl. Chmbr. Orch.; apps. at Spoleto, Pablo Casals, Edinburgh & Brighton Fests. num. recordings. Recip. Leventritt Award, 1967. 16.

ZUCKEROVA, Olga, b. 11 July 1933, Plzen, Czechoslovakia. Editor. Educ: Pedagogical Fac., Charles Univ., prague, 1954; Philos. Fac., ibid, 1956. m. Jiri Zucker, 1 d. Career: Ed.; Classicai authors dept., Supraphon Publng. House, Prague. Publs: Edits. of J V H Vorisek: Composizioni per Piano, Editio Musica Antique bohemica Vol. 52, 1962-; Staré lovecké fanfáry (Old Hunting Fanfares), 1-4 horns (instrumental revn. Jiri Stefan), 1970; J V H Vorisek: Grande ouverture in C minor for 2 pianos op. 16, Edit. the 19th Century, 1971; Ze stoleteho kapsáre ceského hudebniho sisku (Anthol. of Curiosities of 19th Century Czech musical press), 1973. Contbr. to var. music mags. & to Radio Prague, 1960-. Hobby: Music humour. Address: 140 00 Prague 4, Svatoslavova 15, Czechoslovakia.

ZUKOFSKY, Paul, b. 1943, B'klyn., NY, USA. Violinist; Composer; Conductor. Educ: BMus., MS; Juilliard Schl. of Music. Career: Fromm Fellow & Asst., Contemp. Music Activities, Berkshire Music Ctr., Tanglewood, 1963-; Artist in Res., NY Univ., Stony Brook; Creative Assoc., Ctr. of Creative & Perf. Arts. SUNY, Buffalo, 1964; Violinist & Lectr., Contemp.

Chmbr. Ensemble, Rutgers Univ., 1965-67; vis. Assoc. in Perf., Swarthmore Coll., pa., 1966-. Compositions incl: No. 19 for orch. & pre-recorded reciter; Catullus Fragmenta for 2 voices & string trio; No. 13 for 3 mallet-men & percussion player; var. other chmbr, works. Recordings: Paganini's 24 Caprices for Solo Violin; works by Ives, Sessions, Penderecki, Busoni, etc. Publs: Ed., Charles Ives Largo for Violin & Piano. Recip. of many awards. Address: 77 7th Ave. (19M), NYC, NY 10011, USA.

ZUMBACH, André, b. 4 mar. 1931, Geneva, Switzerland. Composer; organist. Educ: Coll. & Univ. of Geneva; Acad. of Music, Geneva; Studio di Fonologia de la Ral, Milan. m. 1 s. 1 d. Career: Sound Engr. for musical recordings (Tonmeister) at Radio Geneva, 1955-62; Hd. of Ancient, Contemporary & Experimental Music Serv. & Artistic Dir. of Centre de Recherches Sonores of Radio Suisse Romande, Geneva, 1962-. Comps: Popular musical & folk dances inclng: Les Fauteurs de Miracles; La Route, 1972; Les Accordailles, 1976. Num. recordings. Contbr. to Le Robot; La Bete et l'Homme; Ed., La Baconniere Micromegas Musique; Ed., Stauffenegger & Cie. Mbr. num profl. orgs. Hobby: Wine Making. Address: Saconex d'Arve, CH-1228 Plan-le-Ouates, Geneva, Switzerland.

ZUPANOVIC, Lovro, b. 21 July 1925, Sibenik, Croatia, Yugoslavia. Composer; Musicologist. Educ: finished Slavistic & Romanistic studies, Fac. of Philos., Zagreb, 1950; Hist. of Music, Acad. of Zagreb, 1953; Dr Musicol., Fac. of Philos., Ljubljana, 1965; Composition, Music Acad. of Ljubljana, 1971. m. Vera Pinter-Zupanović. 1 child. Debut (as composer): 1947. Career: engages in musicol. rsch. in hist. of Croatian music thru' 16-19th centuries. Comps. incl: sev. works for orch.; 2 str. quartets; many works for solo instruments; Pisava, Master of One's Own Body (opera in 2 acts); An Unusual Romance (music for radio play by T Williams); cantatas, song cycles, shoral works & popular & childrens songs. Contbr. num. works to field of musicol.; Fndr., Ed., Annual Spomenici hrvatske glazbene proslosti, Soc. of Croatian Comps., 1970-74; Croatia Concert 1975-. Mbrships: Soc. of Croatian Composers; Union of Yugoslav Composers; Int. Musicol. Soc. Recip. of about 30 prizes inclng: Zagreb City Award, 1970; V Lisinski prize of Soc. of Creatian Composers, 1970, 73. Hobbies: Visiting Archaeol. Sites; Car Outings. Address: Vrbanićeva 37 (Fiserova 3), 41000 Zagreb, Yugoslavia. 14.

ZUR, Menachem, b. 6 Mar. 1942, Tel-Aviv, Israel. Composer; Teacher of Theory & Composition. Educ: Tchrs. Dip., Coll. for Tchrs. of Music, Tel-Aviv, 1964; Dip., Rubin Acad. of Music, Jerusalem, 1967; BMus, Mannes Coll. of MLusic, NYC, USA, 1971; MFA, Sarah Lawrence Coll., ibid., 1972; D Musical Arts, Columbia Univ., 1975. m. Lila Zur, 1 d. comps. incl: Affairs; Pictures; Fantasy for Piano; concertino for Woodwind Quintet; Sonata for Cello & Piano; 3 + 2 (5 instruments); Cantata for Choir, Magnetic Tape, Percussion, Brass quartet; sev. works for tape. Mbr., profl. assns., Israel & USA. Hons: Winner, Int. Electronics Music Competition, 1975; 1st Prize, ORR Contest. Israel, 1973. Address: Rubin Acad. of Music, 7 Pevetz Smolenskin St., Jerusalem, Israel.

ZURAWLEW, George, b. 22 Jan. 1887, Rostov-on-the-Don, USSR. Pianist; Professor of Piano. Educ: Hon. Distinction Dip., Warsaw Acad. of Music; Prof., ibid. m. Ann Sophie Gerstin. Debut: w. Warsaw, Phil., 1911. Career: Concerts w. orch. & recitals in Poland & abroad; Num. Radio & TV apps.; Creator of Int. Frederic Chopin Competitions; Initiator & organizer of 1st Frederic Chopin competition, Warsaw, 1927; Jury Mbr., Chopin Competitions; Fndr. of several higher schls. of music. Num. long-playing records. mbrships: Frederic Chopin Soc., Poland & Czech.; Assn. of Polish Musicians. Hons: Highest Polish State hons., prizes & distinctions; French Legion d'Honneur, 1937. Hobbies: Painting; Sculpture. Address: Swietokryska 16 ap. 14, 00-050 Warszawa, Poland.

ZURBRUEGG, Eva, b. 29 Aug. 1941, Bern, Switz. Violinist. Educ: Bern Conserv.; Music Acad. Basel, TD, concert dip. Career: Var. concerts w. Paul Klecki, Carl Schuricht, Sir M Sargent, Paul Kempe, Paul Sacher; Tchr. Bern Conserv. Mbrships: Bern Str. Quartet. Hons: 1st prize, Paris Conserv., 1961; Carl Flesch Prize, London, 1964. Hobbies: Philosophy; Psychology. Address: Thunstr, 163, 3074, Bern, Switz.

ZWART, Jaap, b. 23 May 1924, Zaandam, Netherlands. Organist; Choral Conductor. Educ: Amsterdam Conservatorium; Nederlandse Beiaard-school te Amersfoort, 1973-75. m. Klaziena Sara van der Sijde, 8 children. Debut: (organist) 1948; (choral cond.) 1952. Career: (as organist): many recitals in the Netherlands; sev. recordings for Dutch radio & TV; Invitation to tour Can., 1967; Organist, Amersfoort & Reformed Westerkerk; (choral cond.): Cond. of sev. oratorio-choirs; perfs. of oratorios of Bach, handel, mendelssohn, etc.

Mbrships. incl: Vereniging voor Nedarlandse Muziekgeschiedenis. Contbr. to profl. jrnls. Hobby: Theol. Address: Maasstraat 21, Amersfoort, The Netherlands.

ZWICKY, Conrad Fridolin, b. 14 May 1946, Basel, Switzerland. Orchestral Musician (Viola); Organist; Teacher of Viola & Organ. Educ: Dips. for Viola & Organ Teaching, Basel Conserv. m. Elisabeth Kaeppeli, 2 children. Career: Concerts as Soloist, Switzerland, France, Germany, Austria, UK & Norway; Radio apps., Norway & Switzerland. Recordings: Brahms & Schubert, Sonatas for Viola & Piano; Mozart, Duo No. 2 for Violin & Viola; Piano Quintets of Boccherini, Dvorak, martin & Martinu. Hobby: Railway Modelling. Mgmt: Int. concerts, Zürich. Address: Hasenbuehlstrasse 42, 8910 Affoltern/Albis, Switzerland.

ZYKAN, Otto Mathäus, b. 29 Apr. 1935, Vienna, Austria. Comp. Educ: Music Acad., piano, comp. m. Sigrid Schuster, 1 d. Debut: Vienna. Career: Concerts w. own comp. in Vienna, Salzburg, Frankfurt, Hamburg, Berlin, Warschau, Graz; Prod. for Austrian TV, Radio cologne (WDR(. Comp. incl: Singer's Sewing machine is the Best; Study; State Music. Recordings: Schönberg's Piano works; Ossiach Live; For Example Theatre Music. Publs: Art as Living Ritual. Hons: Winner Darmstadt Piano Competition, 1958; All Austrian Comp. Prizes. Hobbies: Tennis. Address: postfach 11, 1192 Vienna, Austria.

ZYLIS-GARA, Teresa, b. 23 Jan. 1935, Wilno, Poland. Soprano. Educ: Lodz Music Acad.; pvte. study w. Prof. Olga Olgina, Lodz. Debut: Cracow, 1957. Career: has sung w. major opera cos. in Belgium, Czech., France, Germany, Austria, Netherlands, Hungary, Italy, Mexico, Monte Carlo, Spain, Switz., UK, USA; also sings lieder, oratorio & w. orchs. Has recorded for Angel, EMI, Seraphim & DGG labels. Hons. incl: Winner, Int. Singing Competition, Munich, 1960; Mozart Gold Medal, Mexico City; Polish Nat. Award, great distinction for artistic achievement. Mgmt: Columbia Artists Mgmt. Inc., 165 W 57th St., NY, NY 10019, USA.

ZYTOWSKI, Carl Byrd, b. 17 July 1921, St. Louis, MO., USA. Professor of Music; Professional Singer. Educ: BMus, St. Louis Inst. of Music, 1949; MA, Univ. of Wash., 1951; Nat. Schl. of Opera, London, 1951. Debut: St. Louis Grand Opera Guild, 1947. Career: Concert & Opera Singer in USA, Austria, Germany, France, Holland, England & Canada; Prof. of Music, Univ. of Calif., Santa Barbara; Opera & Song Translator; Composer & Arranger; Conductor. Publs: Classic Song (w. Van A Christy), 1970; He That Hath Ears; Two Morale Chorales. Contbr. to: Nat. Opera Assn. Jrnl.; Ed., Quodibet, Jrnl. of the Intercollegiate Musical Coun., Guest Ed., Opera Jrnl. Mbrships: Pres., Intercollegiate Musical Coun., Bd. Dirs., Nat. Opera Assn.; Am. Chroal Dirs. Assn.; Ctrl. Opera Serv. Hons: Plous Award for Creative Activity, Univ. of Calif., 1959. Hobbies: Photography; Writing. Address: 4013 Pala Lane, Santa Barbara, CA 93110, USA. 11.

APPENDIX A

ORCHESTRAS

So far as it has been possible to ascertain, all orchestras in this Appendix are fully professional.

ARGENTINA

Buenos Aires
Banda Sinfonica de Ciegos, Hipolito Yrigoyen 2850.
Banda Sinfonica Municipal, Avda. Corrientes 1530. Conductor: Armando Nalli. Manager: Marta Parenti.
Ensamble Musical de Buenos Aires, Corrientes 1665, 3°, p., Dto. A. Contact: Alejandro Szterenfeld.
Grupo de Camara de Buenos Aires, Viamonte 372, 4°, p., Dto. 27.
Melos Ensamble de Buenos Aires, Santa Fe 38886.
Orquesta Estable del Teatro Argentino de La Plata, Calle 53 No. 725.
Orquesta Estable del Teatro Colon, Cerrito 618/36.
Orquesta Filarmonica de Buenos Aires, Cerrito 618/36. Musical Director: Pedro I. Calderon.
Orquesta Sinfonica de Bahia Blanca, Dorrego 120, Bahia Blanca. Musical Director and Manager: Alberto Guala.
Orquesta Sinfonica Municipal de Mar del Plata, Rioja 1650.
Orquesta del Instituto de Musica, Sarmiento 109, Avellaneda. Conductor: Claudio Guidi Drei.
Orquesta Sinfonica de la Municipalidad de Olavarria, Dirección Municipal de Cultura. Musical Director: Alfredo José Rossi. Manager: Octavio Sabattini.
Orquesta Sinfonica Nacional, Cordoba 1155-p11. Musical Director: Jacques Bodmer.

Cordoba
Banda Sinfonica de la Dirección Gral. de Cultura, Artistica de Cordoba, Abda. Velez Sarsfield 365.
Orquesta Sinfonica de Cordoba, Teatro Rivera Indarte, Avda. Velez Sarsfield 317.

Mendoza
Orquesta Filarmonica de Mendoza, Catamarca 31, Galeria Tonsa, Local A24.

Parana-Entre Rios
Orquesta Sinfonica de Parana, 25 de Junio 26.

Rosario
Orquesta Sinfonica Provincial de Rosario, Cordoba 1331, 2000 Rosario. Conductor: Juan Carlos Zorzi. Manager: Carlos Bortolotto.

AUSTRALIA

A.C.T.
Canberra Symphony Orchestra, PO Box 92, Canberra 2600. Conductor: Ernest Llewellyn. Manager: Maeva Galloway.

NEW SOUTH WALES
Sydney
Australian Chamber Orchestra, Suite 3, 8th Floor, 36-38 Clarence St., Sydney 2000. Conductor: John Harding. Manager: Donald B McDonald.
Elizabethan Symphony Orchestra, PO Box 137, Kings Cross 2011.
Lionel Huntington Orchestra, PO Box 372, Artamon 2064. Musical Director: Lionel H Huntington.
Sydney Symphony Orchestra, Australian Broadcasting Commission, GPO Box 47, Sydney 2001.

QUEENSLAND
Brisbane
Queensland Symphony Orchestra, Australian Broadcasting Commission, GPO Box 293E, Brisbane 4001. Chief Conductor: Patrick Thomas. Manager: Robert Shepherd.

SOUTH AUSTRALIA
Adelaide
Adelaide Symphony Orchestra, Australian Broadcasting Commission, GPO Box 1419H, Adelaide 5001. Musical Director: Elyanum Shapirra. Manager: Laurence Casey.
Sinfonia of Adelaide, 52 McLaren St., Adelaide 5000. Conductor: Joannes Roose.

TASMANIA
Hobart
Tasmania Symphony Orchestra, Australian Broadcasting Commission, PO Box 205B, Hobart, 7001. Publicity Officer: Mrs C Forward.

VICTORIA
Melbourne
Elizabethan Melbourne Orchestra, St. Peter's Hall, Gisborne St., E Melbourne 3002. Orchestral Manager: Judith Kolecany.
Melbourne Philharmonic Orchestra, PO Box 197,, Eltham 3095. Musical Director/-Administrator: Paul Coppens.
Melbourne Symphony Orchestra, Australian Broadcasting Commission, Waverley Studios, Waverley Road, East Malvern, Melbourne 3145. Orchestral Manager: G. Wraith.
Victorian Concert Orchestra, c/o Ministry of Tourism, 276 Collins St., Melbourne 3000. Musical Director: Harold Badger. Secretary: L. Fernando.

WESTERN AUSTRALIA
Perth
Western Australia Arts Orchestral Foundation, PO Box 131, West Perth 6005.
Western Australian Symphony Orchestra, Australian Broadcasting Commission, 187-193 Adelaide Terr., Perth 6000. Chief Conductor: David Measham. Manager: Ray Irving.

AUSTRIA

Baden
Orchester des Stadttheaters Baden, Theaterplatz 1, 2500 Baden. Musical Director: Gerhard Lagrange. Manager: Dr. Günter Alvin.

Dornbirn
Städtisches Orchester Dornbirn, Musikschule, 6850 Dornbirn. Conductor: Guntram Simma. Management: Musikschule Dornbirn.

Graz
Philharmonisches Orchester Graz, Opernhaus, 8010 Graz. Conductor: Berislav Klobucar. Manager: Gustav Cerny.

Innsbruck
Städtisches Sinfonieorchester Innsbruck, Museumstrasse 17a, 6020 Innsbruck. Musical Director: Karl Randolf.

Klagenfurt
Orchester des Stadttheaters Klagenfurt, Theaterplatz 4, 9020 Klagenfurt.

Linz
Brucknerorchester Linz, Promenade 39, 4020 Linz. Chief Conductor: Theodor Guschlbauer. Manager: Adolf Holschan.
Linzer Konzertverein, Hörzingerstrasse 40,4020 Linz. Artistic Director: Leopold Mayer. Manager: Wolfram Ziegler.

St. Pölten
Orchester des Stadttheaters St. Pölten, Rathausplatz 11, 3100 St. Pölten. Musical Director: Walter Breitner.

Salzburg
Mozarteum Orchester, Schwarzstrasse 4/iv, 5020 Salzburg. Musical Director: Leopold Hager. Administrator: Josef Linden.
Orchester des Stadttheaters Salzburg, 5020 Salzburg.

Vienna
Niederösterreichisches Tonkunstlerorchester, Kolingasse 19,1090 Vienna. Musical Director: Walter Weller. Administrative Director: Hans Plescher.
Orchester des Raimund-Theaters, Wallgasse 18-20, 1060 Vienna.
Orchester des Theaters an der Wien, Lehargasse 5, 1060 Vienna.
Orchester der Wiener Volksoper, Währingerstrasse 78, 1090 Vienna. Musical Director: Bill Bauer-Theussl.
ORF Symphonie Orchester, Argentinierstrasse 30a, 1041 Vienna. Musical Director: Leif Segerstam. Manager: Dr. Otto Sertl.
Wiener Johann Strauss-Orchester, Gusshausstrasse 16, 1040 Vienna. Artistic Director: Theo Cieplik.
Wiener Philharmoniker, Bösendorferstr. 12, 1010 Vienna. Pres: Prof A Altenburger.
Wiener Symphoniker, Bayerngasse 1/15, 1030 Vienna. Conductor: Carlo Maria Giulini. Director: Karl Peter Pietsch.

BELGIUM

Antwerp
Antwerps Kamermuziekgezelschap, Korte Gasthuisstraat 6.
Antwerp Philharmonic Orchestra, J. van Gentstraat 4, 2000 Antwerp.
Orkest van de Koninklijke Vlaamse Opera, Van Ertbornstraat 8, 2000 Antwerp.

Berchem
Het Percussieorkest, Kardinaal Mercierlei 37, 2600 Berchem.

Bonlez
Ensemble Musique Nouvelles, Chemin du Fort des voiles 12, 5963 Bonlez.

Brugge
Het West-Vlaams Orkest, Carmerstraat 16, 8000 Brugge.

Brussels
Belgian National Orchestra, 155 rue de la Loi, 1040 Brussels. Conductor: Georges Octors. Manager: Jan Symoens.
Belgian Radio Symphony Orchestra, 18 place Eugene Flagey, 1050 Brussels. Conductor: Daniel Sternfeld.
Ensemble Jean-Sebastian Bach de Belgique, Rus Jacques Jordaens 19, 1050 Brussels.
Musique des Guides, Avenue Fonsny 6, 1060 Brussels.
Orchestre de Chambre de Bruxelles, Rue du Prevot 121, 1050 Brussels.
Orchestre de Chambre des Concerts de Midi, Rue Vilain XIIII 38, 1050 Brussels.
Orchestre de Chambre du TRM, Place de la Monnaie, 1000 Brussels.
Orchestre du Theatre Royal, Place de la Monnaie, 1000 Brussels.

Gent
Orkest van de Koninklijke Opera, Schouwburgstraat 3, 9000 Gent.
Vlaams Mobiel Kamerensemble, Jan Verspeyenstraat 18, 9000 Gent.

Gentbrugge
Les Solistes de Belgique, Voetbalstraat 6, 9219 Gentbrugge.

Heusy
Orchestre de Chambre de Verviers, Ave. Prince Baudouin 37, 4802 Heusy.

Kraainem
Ensemble Cappella Concertante, Clos de Mimosas 8, 1950 Kraainem.

Liège
Orchestre de Chambre des Concerts de Midi, Place du 20 Août 14, 4000 Liège.
Orchestre du Centre Lyrique de Wallonie, Theatre Royal de Liège, Rue des Dominicains 1, 4000 Liège.
Orchestre Symphonique de Liège, Rue Forgeur 14, 4000 Liège.

Mons
L'Ensemble d'Archets Eugene Ysaye, Hotel de Ville, 7000 Mons.
Orchestre Symphonique de Mons, Conservatoire Royal de Musique, Rue de Nimy 7, 7000 Mons.

Rixensart
Orchestre Mozart de Belgique, Ave. Léopold 58A, 1330 Rixensart.

Sterrebeek
Het Vlaams Kamerorkest van Brussel, Sparrenhof, 10, 1960 Sterrebeek.

Wenzembeekoppem
Les Solistes de Liège, Rue du Fer à Cheval 49,1970 Wezembeekoppem.

BOLIVIA
La Paz
National Symphony Orchestra, Ministerio de Educacion y Cultura. Conductor: Leonard Atherton.

BRAZIL

Rio de Janeiro
Brazilian Symphony Orchestra, Avenido Rio Branco 135, Room 918/920. Musical Director: Isaac Karabtchevsky. Manager: João Carlos R. M. Alvim Corrêa.
National Symphony Orchestra, Praca de Republica 141-A. Conductor: Marlos Nobre. Manager: Undine Ferreira de Mello.
Symphony Orchestra of Teatro Municipal do Rio de Janeiro, Praca Floriano, S/N Centro.

Rio Grande do Sul
Symphonic Orchestra of Porto Alegre, Rua Desembargador Andre da Rocha 50. Musical Director: David Machado.

San Paulo
San Paulo Philharmonic Orchestra, Praca Roosevelt 200, 10 andar. President: Aldo Travaglia. Artistic Director: Simon Blech. Executive Secretary: Arthur E. Kauffman.

BULGARIA

Sofia
Sofia State Philharmonic Orchestra U1. Benkovski 1. Conductor: Dimitar Manolov. Deputy Director: Ilya Lippavtzov.
Symphony Orchestra of the Committee for Television and Radio, 4 Dragan Tzankow Blvd. Musical Directors: Vassil Stephanov and Stephan Vladkov. Secretary: Petko Dramsasov.

CANADA

ALBERTA
Calgary
Calgary Philharmonic Orchestra, 300-330 9th Ave. S.W. T2P1K6. Musical Director: Franz-Paul Decker. Manager: Kurt Trachsel.

Edmonton
Edmonton Symphony Orchestra, 11712-87 Avenue, T6E 4T2. Musical Director: Pierre Hetu. Manager: W. R. Palmer.

Lethbridge
Lethbridge Symphony Orchestra, PO Box 1101. Musical Director: Lucien Needham. Manager: Mike Thomas.

BRITISH COLUMBIA
Vancouver
Baroque Strings of Vancouver, 17, 1460 Esquimalt Ave., W. Vancouver. Manager: Judith Fraser.

Canadian Broadcasting Corporation Vancouver Chamber Orchestra, 6409 Larch Street, Vancouver 13. Conductor: John Avison.
Metropolitan Orchestra, 1595 W. 10th Ave. Vancouver 9. Conductor: Capt. Leonard Camplin. Manager: A. A. Cone.
Vancouver Symphony Orchestra, 566 Hornby St., Vancouver 1. Conductor: Simon Streatfield. Manager: Victor White.

Vernon
Festival Players. Conductor: Jan Warnars.

Victoria
Victoria Symphony Society, 631 Superior St., V8V 1V1. Musical Director: Paul Freeman. Manager: Robert J. McGifford.

MANITOBA
Winnipeg
Winnipeg Symphony Orchestra, Centennial Concert Hall, 117-555 Main St., Main and Market, Winnipeg R3B 1C3. Conductor: Piero Gamba. Manager: A. R. D'Amato.

NOVA SCOTIA
Halifax
Atlantic Symphony Orchestra, 2011 Elm St., B3L 2Y2. Musical Director: Victor Yampolsky. Exec. Director: Lionel D. Smith.

ONTARIO
Barrie
Huronia Symphony Orchestra, 21 Marwendy Drive. Conductor: Barry Devereux. Manager: Mrs. Muriel Leeper.

Hamilton
Hamilton Philharmonic Orchestra, PO Box 2080, Station A, L8N 3Y7. Musical Director: Boris Brott. Manager: Mark Warren.

Kingston
Kingston Symphony Orchestra, PO Box 1616, K7L 5C8. Musical Director: Alexander Brott. Manager: Mrs. Patricia Beharriell.

Kitchener
Canadian Chamber Ensemble, Box 2, Waterloo N2J 3Z6. Conductor: Raffi Armenian. Manager: Daniel S. Donaldson.
Kitchener/Waterloo Symphony Orchestra, Box 2, Waterloo N2J 3Z6. Conductor: Raffi Armenian. Manager: Daniel S. Donaldson.

London
Aeolian Hall Orchestra, Box 2121, M6A 4E3. Musical Director: Gordon D. Jeffery.
London Symphony Orchestra, 520 Wellington St., N6A 3R2. Acting Conductor: Victor Feldbrill. General Manager: Erling Alfee.

Oakville
Oakville Symphony Orchestra, 196 Sabel St. Conductor: Kenneth R. R. Hollier.

Oshawa
Oshawa Symphony Orchestra, 146 Simcoe St. N. Conductor: Jacob Groob.

Ottawa
National Arts Centre Orchestra, Box 1534, Station B, K1P 5W1. Musical Director: Mario Bernardi. Manager: Andreas C. Hackh.

Thunder Bay
Lakehead Symphony Orchestra, PO Box 4, Postal Station P. Conductor: Boris Brott. Manager: David Lewis.

Toronto
Chamber Players of Toronto, 66 Hillholme Road, Toronto 7. Conductor: Victor Martin. Manager: Mrs. Mabel H. Laine.
East York Symphony Orchestra, 20 Rolph Road, Toronto 17. Conductor: Orval Ries. Manager: Mrs. Dorothea Wiley.

Toronto Symphony Orchestra, 215 Victoria St., M5B 1V1. Musical Director: Andrew Davis. Manager: Walter Homburger.

Windsor
Windsor Symphony Orchestra, 682 Ouellette Avenue. Musical Director: Laszlo Gati. Manager: Mrs. Barbara Kersey.

PRINCE EDWARD ISLAND
Charlottetown
Charlottetown Festival Orchestra, c/o Confederation Arts Centre, PO Box 848. Artistic Director: Alan Lund.
Prince Edward Island Symphony Orchestra, Music Dept., University of Prince Edward Island. Conductor: Alan Reesor. Manager: Hubert Tersteeg.

QUEBEC
Montreal
McGill Chamber Orchestra, 1745 Cedar Avenue, H3G 1A7. Musical Director: Alexander Brott. Manager: Mrs. Alexander Brott.
Montreal Philharmonic Orchestra, 3601 Sainte-Famille, Box 703, Montreal 130.
Montreal Symphony Orchestra, 200 Ouest Blvd. de Maisonneuve Blvd. W, H2X 1Y9. Musical Director: Charles Dutoit. Manager: Madeleine Panaccio.

SASKATCHEWAN
Saskatoon
Regina Symphony Orchestra, 200 Lakeshore Drive. Musical Director: F. Vernon. Manager: Beverly Moose.

CHILE

Santiago
Chile Symphony Orchestra, Casilla 2100. Manager: José Vasquez.
Orquesta Sinfonica de la Universidad de Chile, Compañia 1264. Musical Director: Victor Tevah T. Management: Direccion General de Expectaculos.
Santiago City Philharmonic Orchestra, Casilla San Antonio 149. Conductor: Juan Carlos Zorzi.

COLOMBIA

Bogota
Colombia Symphony Orchestra, Centro Administrativo Nacional, Edifico Mineducacion, p. 3. Musical Director: Olav Roots.
Municipal Philharmonic Orchestra, Town Hall. Musical Director: Jose Carlos Antos.

COSTA RICA

San José
Orquesta Sinfonica Nacional, Apdo. 1035. Musical Director: Gerald Brown. Manager: Miguel Serrano.

CUBA

Havana
National Symphonic Orchestra, Amadeo Roldan Theatre. Conductors: Enrique Gonsalez Mantici and Manuel Duchesne Cuzan.
National Theatre Orchestra, Garcia Lorca Theatre. Conductor: Felex Guerrero.

CZECHOSLOVAKIA

Banska Bystrica
Regional Symphony Orchestra, Pedagogickafakulta. Conductor: Vladimir Gajdos.

Bratislava
Bratislava Radio Symphony Orchestra, Zochova 1, 897 11 Bratislava. Musical Director: Ondrej Lenárd. Manager: Vlastimil Horák.

Slovak Philharmonic Orchestra, Palackeho 2. Musical Director and Manager: Ladislav Slovák.

Brno
Brno State Philharmonic Orchestra, Komenského nám 8. Conductor: Jiři Waldhans.

Františkovy Lázně
Regional Symphony Orchestra, Ruská 14. Conductor: Stanislav Hondlik.

Gottwaldov
State Symphony Orchestra, Dum uměni. Conductor: Zdeněk Bilek.

Karlovy Vary
Karlovy Vary Symphony Orchestra, trída Jednotných odburu 21, 36001 Karlovy Vary. Conductor: Radomil Eliska. Manager: Oldřich Kurzawa.

Kosice
Kosice State Philharmonic Orchestra, Dum uměnia. Conductor: Bystrik Režucha.

Mariánské Lazně
Westbohemian Symphony Orchestra, 353-21 Mariánské Lazně, PO Box 50/B. Musical Director: Miloslav Bervid.

Olomouc
Moravian Philharmonic Orchestra, Nám Miru 23, 77200 Olomouc. Musical Directors: Jaromir Nohejl and Přemsyl Chudoba. Manager: Vratislav Nevrlý.

Ostrava
Ostrava Janáček Philharmonic Orchestra, Ostrava 5, Michálkovická 181. Conductor: Otakar Trhlik.
Ostrava Radio Orchestra, Dr. Smerala 2, Ostrava 1. Conductor: Pavel Staněk.

Plzen
Plzen Radio Symphony Orchestra, Nám Miru 4. Conductor: Bohumir Liška.

Podebrady
Central Bohemian Symphony Orchestra, Jiřiho nám 41. Musical Directors: O. Nedoma and M. Zelenka, L. Hlaváček.

Prague
Czechoslovakian Philharmonic Orchestra, Dum umělcu, Alšovo Nábř 12. Conductor: Václav Newmann.
Prague Chamber Orchestra, Hudebni Studio, Valdštejnská 10, 118 01 Prague 1. Manager: Jan Líbal.
Prague Radio Symphony Orchestra, Vinohradská 12, Prague 2. Conductor: Jaroslav Krombholc.
Prague Symphony Orchestra, Obecnidum, 110 00 Prague 1. Musical Director: Jindřich Rohan. Manager: Ladislav Šíp.

Teplice
Northern Bohemia Symphony Orchestra, Mao Ce-ıTungova 1. Conductor: Jaroslav Soukup.

DENMARK

Aalborg
Aalborg Symphony Orchestra, Aalborghallen, 9000 Aalborg. Musical Director: Janos Fürst. Manager: Kaj Birkeholm.

Aarhus
Aarhus Symphony, Guldsmedgade 3, 8000 Aarhus. Musical Director: Ole Schmidt.

Copenhagen
Danish Radio Symphony Orchestra, Rosenørnsalle 22, 1999 Copenhagen V. Musical Director: Herbert Blomstedt. Manager: Kield Neiiendam.
Royal Life-Guards' Music Band, Adjutanten v/Livgarden, 2B Oster Voldgade, Copenhagen O.

Royal Orchestra, Theatre Royal, Holmens Kanal 3, Copenhagen. Musical Directors: John Frandsen and Poul Jørgensen. Chairman: Eyvind Rafn.
Sjaelland Symphony Orchestra, Bernstorffsgade 9, 1577 Copenhagen V. Manager: H. H. Jensen.
Tivoli Symphony Orchestra, Tiroli Vesterbrog 3, Copenhagen V. Musical Director: Eifred Eckhard Hausen.

Esbjerg
West Jutland Chamber Ensemble, Islandsgade 50. Manager: Lisbeth Hass.
West Jutland Symphony Orchestra, Islandsgade 50, Esbjerg 6700. Conductor: Peder Holm. Manager: Lisbeth Hass.

Odense
Odense Symphony Orchestra, Kongensgade 68, 5000 Odense. Musical Director: Karol Stryja. Manager: Ejner Gylling.

Randers
Randers Municipal Orchestra, c/o Gronborg, Brodregade.

Silkeborg
Silkeborg Municipal Orchestra, 22 Vertergade.

Sonderborg
Southern Jutland Symphony Orchestra, Skovvej, Sonderborg 6400. Musical Director: Carl von Garaguly. Manager: Jørgen Billesbølle.

DOMINICAN REPUBLIC

Santo Domingo
National Symphony Orchestra, Palacio de Bellas Artes. Conductor: Manuel Simó. Manager: Isais Paez Soler.

EDUADOR

Quito
Orquesta Sinfónica Nacional, Venzuela 666. Musical Director: George Monseur. Manager: Marcia de Arrata.

EGYPT

Cairo
Cairo Symphony Orchestra, 27 Abdel Khalek Tharwat. Director: Yousef El-Sisi.

EIRE

Dublin
New Irish Chamber Orchestra, 4 Templemore Avenue, Rathgar. Manager: Lindsay Armstrong.
Radio Telefis Eireann Concert Orchestra, Donnybrook, Dublin 4. Musical Director: Proinnsías Ó Duinn.
Radio Telefis Eireann Symphony Orchestra, Radio Centre, Donnybrook, Dublin 4. Manager: Val Keogh. Co-Principal Conductors: Albert Rosen and Colman Pearce.
Ulysses Ensemble, c/o P. J. Carroll & Co., Grand Parade, Dublin 6. Musical Director: Colman Pearce. Manager: Peter Healy.

EL SALVADOR

San Salvador
El Salvador Symphony Orchestra, 8a ave. Norte 228. Musical Director: Gilberto Orellana. Manager: Omar Mejía.

FINLAND

Helsinki
Helsinki Philharmonic Orchestra, Finlandia Hall, Karamzininkatu 4, SF-00100 Helsinki 10. Musical Director: Paavo Berglund, Manager: Reijo Jyrkiäinen.

Radion Sinfoniarkesteri, Unioninkatu 16, 00130 Helsinki 13. Musical Director: Okko Kamu. Manager: Kalevi Kuosa.
Töölönranta Chamber Orchestra, Finlandia Hall, 00100 Helsinki 10. Secretary: Helena Kuoppamäki.

Joensuu
Orchestra of Joensuu, Koskikatu 15, 80100 Joensuu 10. Conductor: Pekka Haapasalo. Manager: Helena Grahn.

Jyväskylä
Jyväskylä City Orchestra, Killerjärvi 40630 Jyväskylä 63. Musical Director: Onni Kelo. Manager: Lasse Allonen.

Kotka
Kotka City Orchestra, Satamakatu 4, 48100 Kotka 10. Musical Director: Jukka Hapuoja. Manager: Esko Bly.

Kouvola
Kouvola City Orchestra, Torikatu 10, 45100 Kouvola 10. Musical Director: Eero Bister. Manager: Reijo Peuravaara.

Kuopio
Kuopio City Orchestra, Niiralankatu 28, 70600 Kuopio 20. Musical Director: Lauri Siimes. Manager: Kalevi Lehtinen.

Lahti
Lahti City Orchestra, Sibeliuksenkatu 8, 15110 Lahti 11. Musical Director: Urpo Pesonen. Manager: Ritva Frisk.

Oulo
Oulo City Orchestra, Asemakatu 15A 13, 90100 Oulo 10. Musical Director: Rauno Rännäli. Secretary: Mrs. Outi Sipila.

Pori
Pori City Orchestra, Länsipuisto 15, 28100 Pori 10. Conductor: Juhani Numminen. Manager: Rae-Marja Vataja.

Savonlinna
Savonlinna Orchestra, Olavinkatu 35, 57130 Savonlinna 13. Conductor: Kyösti Haatanen. Manager: Helena Kettu,

Tampere
Tampere Philharmonic Orchestra, Aleksis kiven katu 14, SF 33210 Tampere 21. Musical Director: Paavo Rautio.

Turku
Turku Philharmonic Orchestra, Sibeliuksenkatu 2, 20110 Turku 11. Musical Director: Pertti Pekkanen. Manager: Karl-Erik Tiittanen.

Vaasa
Vaasa City Orchestra, Ylätori 2A9, 65100 Vaasa 10. Conductor: Ralf Sjöblom. Manager: Jan-Erik Backman.

FRANCE

Angers
Loire Regional Orchestra, AMCA rue Toussaint, 4900 Angers. Musical Director: Michel Découst.

Array
Atelier Musique de Ville d'Array, 10 rue de Marnes, 92410 Ville d'Array. Conductor: Jean-Louis Petit. Manager: George Lafon.

Caen
Orchestre de Chambre de Caen, Hôtel de Ville, Esplanade Jean-Marie Louvel, 14034 Caen. Musical Director: Jean-Pierre Dautel. Manager: Jean-Pierre Daragon.

Grenoble
Municipal Orchestra of Grenoble,, 6 Chemin des Gordes, 38000 Grenoble.

Lyons
Orchestre Symphonique de Lyon, Auditorium M. Ravel, 149 rue Garibaldi, 69003 Lyon. Musical Director: Serge Baudo. Manager: Claude Jacquemin.

Marseille
Ensemble Instrumental de Provence, 47 rue Camille Jullian, 13004 Marseille. Musical Director: Clement Zaffini.

Metz
Municipal Orchestra of Metz, Hôtel de Ville, 57000 Metz.

Mulhouse
Municipal Orchestra, 2 Pierre Curie, 68000 Mulhouse.

Nancy
Orchestre Symphonique de Nancy, Conservatoire National de Region, 4 rue Chanzy, 54000 Nancy. Musical Director: L. Noel.

Nice
Orchestre Philharmonique de Nice, Théâtre de l'Opéra. Musical Director: Antonio de Almeida.

Nogent-sur-Marne
Orchestre de Chambre Français, 4 place Maréchal Leclerc, 94 Nogent-sur-Marne. President/Founder: Jacques Michon.

Paris
André Colson Chamber Orchestra, Domaine de Vernou, BP22 Langeais. Director: Andrée Colson.
Ars Nova Ensemble, 16 rue des Fioses-St-Jacques, 75005 Paris. Musical Director: Marius Constant. Manager: L. O. Houdia.
Ensemble Instrumental, 252 Fbg. St. Honoré, 75008 Paris. Artistic Director: Suzy Haim.
Jean-François Paillard Orchestra, 194 rue du Lauriston, 75016 Paris. Director: Jean-François Paillard.
Musique Vivante Ensemble, 286 Blvd. St.-Germain, 75007 Paris. Conductor: Diego Masson.
Orchestre de Chambre de l'O.R.T.F., Maison de l'O.R.T.F., 116 ave. du President Kennedy, 75016 Paris.
Orchestre de Chambre Jean-Louis Petit, 39 Blvd. des Capucines, 75002 Paris. Musical Director: J.-L. Petit. Manager: Bianca Colonna.
Orchestre Natonal de la Radiodiffusion Française, 28 rue Felician-David, Paris 16e.
Orchestre Fernand Oubradous, Salle Gaveau, 45 rue La Boetie, 75008 Paris.
Orchestre de Paris, 2 Place de la Porte Maillot, Paris 8e. Musical Director: Daniel Barenboim. Manager: J. P. Guillard.
Orchestre de Chambre Paul Kuentz, 144 Faubourg St. Antoine, 75012 Paris. Musical Director: Paul Kuentz. Manager: Gabrielle Josso.

Rouen
Rouen Chamber Orchestra, Hôtel de Ville, 76000 Rouen. Director: J. S. Bereau.

Strasbourg
Strasbourg Philharmonic Orchestra, Avc. de la Marseillaise 7, 6700 Strasbourg. Musical Director: Alain Lombard.

Toulouse
Toulouse Chamber Orchestra, 18 rue Agathoise, 3100 Toulouse. Director: Louis Auriacombe.

Tours
Municipal Orchestra of Tours, 34 rue de la Sellerie, 3700 Tours.

GERMAN DEMOCRATIC REPUBLIC

Berlin
Berliner Sinfonieorchester, 108 Berlin, Oberwallstr. 6-7. Musical Director: Kurt Sanderling.
Deutsche Staatskapelle Berlin, 108 Berlin, Unter den Linden 7. Musical Director: Ottmar Suitner.
Orchester der Komischen Oper, 108 Berlin, Behrenstr. 55-58. Musical Director: Gaza Oberfrank.
Rundfunksinfonieorchester Berlin, 116 Berlin, Nalepastr. 18-50. Musical Director: Heinz Rögner.

Dresden
Dresdner Philharmonie, 801 Dresden, Kulturpalast am Altmarkt. Musical Director: Günter Herbig. Manager: Dr. Dieter Hartwig.
Staatskapelle Dresden, 801 Dresden, Julian-Grimau-Allee 27. Musical Director: Herbert Bloomstedt.

Erfurt
Städtisches Orchester, 50 Erfurt, Gorkistr. 1. Musical Director: Ude Nissen.

Frankfurt/Oder
Philharmonisches Orchester, 12 Frankfort/Oder, Gerhart-Hauptmannstr. 3. Musical Director: Wolfgang Botha.

Gera
Staatliches Sinfonieorchester, 65 Gera, Dimitroffallee. Musical Director: Günter Schubert.

Gotha
Staatliches Sinfonieorchester Thüringen, 58 Gotha, Reinhardsbrunnerstr. 23. Musical Director: Gerhard-Rolf Bauer.

Halle
Hallesche Philharmonie, 402 Halle/Saale, Brüderstr. 2. Musical Director: Olaf Koch.
Handel-Festspielorchester, 402 Halle, Universitätsring 24. Musical Director: Volker Rhode.

Jena
Jenaer Philharmonie, 69 Jena, Prof.-Ibrahim-Str. 12. Musical Director: Gunter Blumhagen.

Karl-Marx-Stadt
Städtisches Orchester, 90 Karl-Marx-Stadt, Theaterplatz 2. Musical Director: Christian Kluttig.

Leipzig
Gewandhaus zu Leipzig, 701 Leipzig, Katharinenstr. 23. Musical Director: Kurt Masur. Manager: Karl Zumpe.
Rundfunksinfonieorchester Leipzig, 7022 Leipzig, Springerstr. 24. Musical Director: Herbert Kegel.

Magdeburg
Städtisches Orchester, 301 Magdeburg, Boleslav-Bierut-Platz 13. General Musical Director: Roland Wambeck.

Neubrandenburg
Staatliches Sinfonieorchester Neubrandenburg, 20 Neubrandenburg, Treptowerstr. Musical Director: Hermann Josef Nellessen.

Potsdam
DEFA-Sinfonieorchester, 15 Potsdam-Babelsberg. Musical Director: Manfred Rosenberg.
Sinfonieorchester des Hans-Otto-Theaters, 15 Potsdam, Zimmerstr. 10. Musical Director: Hans-Dieter-Baum.

Rostock
Philharmonisches Orchester, 25 Rostock, Patriotischer Weg 33. Musical Director: Gerhard Puls.

Schwerin
Staatskapelle Schwerin, 27 Schwerin, Alter Garten. Musical Director: Hartmut Haenchen.
Staatliches Sinfonieorchester Schwerin, 27 Schwerin, Schlachterstr. 2. Musical Director:
Walter König.

Sonderhausen
Staatliches Loh-Orchester, 54 Sonderhausen, Loh 2. Musical Director: Horst Förster.

Suhl
Staatliches Sinfonieorchester, 60 Suhl, Strasse des 7. Oktober 7. Musical Director:
Siegfried Geissler.

Weimar
Weimarische Staatskapelle, 53 Weimar. Musical Director: Lothar Seyfarth.

GERMAN FEDERAL REPUBLIC

Bad Reichenhall
Bad Reichenhall Philharmonic Orchestra, Postfach 123, 8230 Bad Reichenhall. Musical
Director: Wilhelm Barth. Manager: Lothar Thiel.

Baden-Baden
Baden-Baden Radio Symphony Orchestra, Postfach 820, 7570 Baden-Baden. Conductor: K.
Kord. Manager: Olaf Seesemann.

Bamberg
Bamberg Symphony Orchestra, Altes Rathaus, Postfach 3180, 8600 Bamberg. Musical
Director: Eugen Jochum.

Berlin
Berlin Philharmonic Orchestra, Matthäikirchstr. 1, 1000 Berlin 30. Musical Director: Herbert
von Karajan. Intendant: Wolfgang Stresemann.
Berlin Radio Symphony Orchestra, Kaiserdamm, 26, 1000 Berlin 19. Conductor: Lorin
Maazel.
Berlin Symphony Orchestra, Paulsbornerstr. 88, 1000 Berlin 31. Musical Director: Theodore
Bloomfield. Manager: Franz Offermanns.

Bochum
Bochum Symphony Orchestra, Geschäftsstelle, Königsallee 178, 4630 Bochum. Musical
Director: Othmar M. F. Maga. Manager: Gerhard Sohl.

Bonn
Beethoven Halle Orchestra, Flensburgerstr 39, D-53 Bonn. Contact: Mr. Heckmann.
Chur Cologne Orchestra, Marienstr. 17, 5300 Bonn. Musical Director: Herbert Beissel.

Bremen
State Philharmonic Orchestra, Domshof 26, 2800 Bremen. Conductor: Hermann Michael.

Cologne
Cologne Chamber Orchestra, An der Joch 33, 5000 Cologne. Musical Director: Hans Müller-
Brühl.
Cologne Radio Symphony Orchestra, Funkhaus, 5000 Cologne. Musical Director: Hiroshi
Wakasugi. Manager: Bär von Randow.
Rhine Chamber Orchestra, 11 Steinfeldergasse, 5000 Cologne. Musical Director: Jan
Corazolla. Manager: Ingenborg Schäfer.

Detmold
Tibor Varga Chamber Orchestra, Bruchstr. 25, Postfach 528, 4930 Detmold. Musical
Director: Tibor Varga. Manager: Mrs. B. Watts.

Dortmund
Dortmund Philharmonic Orchestra, Kuhstr. 12, 4600 Dortmund. Conductor: Wilhelm
Schüchter.

Duisburg
Duisburg Symphony Orchestra, Stadtverwaltung-Kulturamt, 4100 Duisburg.

Düsseldorf
Düsseldorf Symphony Orchestra, Direktion Tonhalle, Ehrenhof 1, 4 Düsseldorf, 1. Musical Director: Bernhard Klee. Manager: Julius Dellert.

Frankfurt/Main
Frankfurt Radio Symphony Orchestra, Bertramstr. 8, 6000 Frankfurt/Main. Conductor: Eliahu Inbal. Manager: Heinz Enke.
Hesse Chamber Orchestra, Kluberstr. 15,6000 Frankfurt/Main.
Museum Society Orchestra, Untermainanlage 11, 6000 Frankfurt/Main. Musical Director: Christoph von Dohnányi.

Göttingen
Göttingen Symphony Orchestra, Postfach 609, Hainholzweg 3-5, 3400 Göttingen. Musical Director: Andreas von Lukacsy.

Hamburg
Hamburg Chamber Orchestra, Dammtorwall 46, 2000 Hamburg 36. Musical Directors: Heribert Beissel & August Wenzinger. Manager: Peter Hinrichs.
Hamburg Radio Symphony Orchestra, Rothenbaum Chausee, 2 Hamburg 13. Conductor: Moshe Atzmon. Manager: Christoph Vollmer.
Hamburg State Philharmonic Orchestra, Staatsoper, Hamburg 36. Musical Director: Aldo Ceccato. Manager: Ernst Schönfelder.
Hamburg Symphony Orchestra, Dammtorwall 46, 2 Hamburg 36. Manager: Herbert Beissel.

Heidelberg
City Orchestra of Heidelberg, City Theatre, Friedrichstr. 5, 6900 Heidelberg. Musical Director: Christian Süss.

Herford
North West German Philharmonic Orchestra, Stiftbergstr. 2, 4900 Herford.

Hilchenbach
Siegerland Orchestra, 5912 Hilchenbach, Postfash 1320. Musical Director: Jorge Rotter. Intendant: Gerhard Hartmann.

Hof
Hof Symphony Orchestra, Karollnenstr. 19, 8670 Hof.

Koblenz
Rhenish Philharmonic Orchestra, Clemensstr. 4, 5400 Koblenz. Musical Director: Pierre Stoll. Intendant: Erhard May.

Konstanz
Bodensee Symphonie-Orchester, Spanierstr. 3, 7750 Konstanz. General Musical Director: Tamás Sulyok. Managers: Werner Pöpplein & Renate Roth.

Ludwigshafen
Pfälz Philharmonic Orchestra, Mundheimenstr. 220, 67 Ludwigshafen. Musical Director: Christoph Stepp. Intendant: Erhard May.

Marl
Philharmonica Hungarica, Theater der Stadt Marl, PO Box 1422, 4370 Marl. Musical Director: Antal Dorati.

Mönchengladbach
City Orchestra of Krefeld and Mönchengladbach, Combined City Theatre, Hindenburgstr. 73, 4050 Mönchengladbach.

Munich
Bavarian Radio Symphony Orchestra, Rundfunkplatz 1, 8000 Munich 2. Musical Director: Rafael Kubelik. Manager Erich Mauermann.
Graunke Symphony Orchestra, Wilhelm-Mayr-Str. 15, 8000 Munich. 21. Conductor: Kurt Graunke.
Munich Philharmonic Orchestra, Rindermaktt 3-4, 8000 Munich. Musical Director: Sergiu Celibidache. Manager: F. X. Ohnesong.

Oberhausen
Orchester des Theater Oberhausen, Ebertstr., 4200 Oberhausen. Musical Directors: Fritzdieter Gerhards & Edwin Scholz.

Pforzheim
South West German Chamber Orchestra, Jahnstr. 31, 7530 Pforzheim. Musical Director: Paul Angerer. Manager: Uta Nagel.

Recklinghausen
Westphalian Symphony Orchestra, Städtische Saalbau Dorstenerstr. 16, 4350 Recklinghausen. Musical Director: Karl Anton Rickenbacher. Manager: Harald Birk.

Remschied
City Orchestra, Schützenstr. 5, 5630 Remschied. Musical Director: Alexander Rumpf. Manager: E. Senftleben.

Reutlingen
Swabian Symphony Orchestra, am Markt, Wilhelmstr. 71, 7410 Reutlingen. Musical Director: Dmitri Agrafiotis. Manager: Manfred Hermann.

Saarbrücken
Saarbrücken Radio Symphony Orchestra, Funkhaus Halberg, 6600 Saarbrücken. Conductor: Hans Zender. Manager: Ulf Thomson.

Stuttgart
Stuttgart Chamber Orchestra, Charlottenplatz 17, 7000 Stuttgart. Musical Director: Karl Münchinger. Manager: Nora Nill.
Stuttgart Philharmonic Orchestra, Schickhardstr. 5, 7000 Stuttgart. 1. Conductor: Hans Zanotelli. Manager: Nora Nill.
Stuttgart Radio Symphony Orchestra, Postfach 837, 7000 Stuttgart. Conductor: Hans-Müller Kray. Manager: Otto Tomek.

Ulm
City Orchestra, Bayerstr. 54, 7900 Ulm.

GREECE

Athens
Athens Radio Symphony Orchestra, Aghia Paraskevi, Attiki.
Athens State Orchestra, Kapodistriu Str. 2, Athens 147. Musical Director: Manos Hadjidakis.
Symphony Orchestra of the City of Athens, Dimarcheion Athinon.

Salonica
Thessaloniki State Orchestra, Iktinoy Street 3. Director George Thymis.

Thessaloniki
State Orchestra of N. Greece, 6 Aristotelous St.

GUATEMALA

Guatemala City
National Symphony Orchestra, Teatro de Bellas Artes, 3a Avda. 7-40, Zona 1. Musical Director: Ricardo de Carmen.

HONG KONG

Hong Kong
Hong Kong Philharmonic Orchestra, PO Box 13858. Conductor: Ling Tun. Manager: John Duffus.

Kowloon
Wang Kwong Chinese Orchestra, 407 Lily House, So UK Estate. Chairman of Executive Committee: Ho Yuk Kwong.

HUNGARY

Budapest
Budapest Chamber Orchestra, Verhalom 9b, Budapest 2. Musical Director: András Mihály.
Budapest MAV Symphony Orchestra, 1800 Budapest, Magyar Radio. Musical Director: György Lehel. Manager: András Sebastyén.
Budapest Philharmonic Orchestra, Nepkoz tarsasag u 22, Budapest 6. Conductor: András Koródy.
Franz Liszt Chamber Orchestra, Korhaz u. 19, 1035 Budapest. Manager: Pal Kelemen.
Hungarian State Symphony Orchestra, Budapest V, Semmelweiss. u.

Debrecen
MAV Philharmonic Orchestra, Simonffy u/c.

Györ
Municipal Philharmonic Orchestra, Czuczor u. 28. Musical Director: János Sándor.

Miskolc
Municipal Symphony Orchestra, 3525 Miskolc, Déryné u.5. Musical Director: Peter Mura. Manager: Laszlo Kerekgyarto.

Pecs
Municipal Philharmonic Orchestra, Szinhazter 2. Musical Director: Tamas Breitner.

Szeged
Municipal Symphony Orchestra, Festo u.6, 6721 Szeged. Musical Director: Tamás Pál. Manager: Imre Nagy.

ICELAND

Reykjavik
Sinfoniuhljomsveet Islands, PO Box 120, Lindargata 9a. Manager: Gunnar Gudmundsson.

INDIA

Calcutta
Calcutta Symphony Orchestra, 43 Rafi Ahmed Kidwai St. Calcutta 16. Conductor: Hussain Mohammed.

IRAN

Teheran
Teheran Symphonic Orchestra, Kh. Kamal-ol-Molk. Contact: Heshmat Sanjan.

ISRAEL

Haifa
Haifa Symphony Orchestra, 50 Pevsner St. Director: Michael Mendelson.
Pro Musica Orchestra, PO Box 7191. Musical Director: Dalia Atlas. Manager: Esther Anderman.

Jerusalem
Jerusalem Symphony Orchestra, Israel Broadcasting Authority, Y.M.C.A. Building, King David St. Chief Guest Conductor: Sidney Harth. Managing Director: Yehuda Fickler.

Tel Aviv
Israel Chamber Orchestra, Asia House Ltd., 2 Dafna St. Musical Director: Rudolf Barshai. Director: Roni Abramson.
Israel Philharmonic Orchestra, 1 Huberman St., PO Box 11292. Musical Director: Zubin Mehta. Administrator: Abe Cohen.

ITALY

Florence
Orchestra del Maggio Musicale Fiorentino, Teatro Communale, Via Solferino 15, 50100 Florence. Musical Director: Riccardo Muti. Superintendent: Masimo Bogiakino.

Milan
Orchestra Sinfonica della Radiotelevisione Italiana, Corso Sempione 22. 20154 Milan.
Orchestra of La Scala, Teatro alla Scala, via Filodrammatici 2.

Palermo
Sicilian Symphony Orchestra, via la Farina 29, 90121 Palermo. Musical Director: Roberto
Pagano. Permanent Conductor: Gabriele Ferro. Manager: Dr. Vincenzo Rossitto.

Rome
Italian Radio and TV Symphony Orchestra, Foro Italico, 00100 Rome. Conductor: Armando
la Rosa Parodi.
Orchestra dell'Academia Nazionale di S. Cecilia, Via Vittoria 6. Conductor: Fernando
Previtali.
Rome Opera Orchestra, Teatro dell'Opera, via Firenze 63.

Trieste
Trieste Opera Orchestra, Teatro Communale 'Giuseppe Verdi', piazza Verdi.

Turin
Italian Radio and TV Symphony Orchestra, via Montebello 12, 10124 Turin. Conductor:
Pierre Bellugi.

Venice
Opera Orchestra, Teatro 'La Fenice.'

JAPAN

Gumma
Gumma Symphony Orchestra, c/o Municipal Library, 1 Takamaksu-cho, Takasaki-shi,
Gumma-ken. Permanent Conductor: Kôtaro Sato. Manager: Shinji Tôyama.

Kyoto
Kyoto Municipal Symphony Orchestra, 103 Izumoji Tatemoto-cho, Kita-ku, Kyoto 603.
Principal Conductor: Stewart Kershaw. Principal Guest Conductor: Hiroshi Wakasugi.
General Director: Jiro Sunada.

Osaka
Osaka Philharmonic Orchestra, 4-55 Kitahama, Higashi-ku, Osaka 530. Musical Director:
Takashi Asahina. Manager: Kosuke Noguchi.

Sapporo
Sapporo Symphony Orchestra, Nishi 13, Odori Chuo-ku, Sapporo 060. Musical Director:
Hiroyuki Iwaki. Manager: Seiji Taniguchi.

Takasaki
Gumma Symphony Orchestra, 1 Takamatsu-cho, Takasaki 370.

Tokyo
I Commidianti in Musico, 8-8-21 Nishi Gotanda, Shinagawa-ku, Tokyo 141. Artistic
Director: Victor C. Searle.
Japanese Broadcasting Corporation Symphony Orchestra, 2-16-49 Takanawa, Minato-ku.
Musical Director: Iwaki Hiroyuki. General Manager: Daigoro Arima.
New Japan Philharmonic Orchestra, 22 Mori Bldg, 4-3-20 Toranomon Minatoku, Tokyo
105. Conductors: Seiji Ozawa & Kazohiro Koizumi. General Manager: Hirofumi Aoyama.
Tokyo Metropolitan Symphony Orchestra, 5-45 Ueno Park, Taito-ku. Musical Director: Akeo
Watanabe. Manager: Shinzo Kusakari.
Tokyo Philharmonic Orchestra, 2-3-12 Nishi-Shimbashi, Tokyo 105.
Nippon/Yomiuri Symphony Orchestra, c/o Yomiun Shimbun, 1-7-1 Ohtemachi, Chiyoda-ku,
Tokyo 100. Conductor: Seiichi Mitsuishi. Manager: Toshiharu Kubo.

KOREA

Seoul
Korean National Symphony Orchestra, Korean Broadcasting System, 8 Yejang-Dong,
Chong-ku, Seoul 100. Conductor: Yun Taik Hong.

Seoul Philharmonic Orchestra, 81-3 Sejong-ro, Chongro-ku, Se-Jong Cultural Centre. Conductor: Chai Dong Chung. Manager: Du Hoon Moon.

LUXEMBOURG

Luxembourg
Luxembourg Radio Symphony Orchestra, Villa Louvigny. Conductor: Louis de Fromont.

MEXICO

Jalisco
Guadalajara Symphony Orchestra, Teatro Degollado, Guadalajara. Musical Director: Kenneth Klein.
Orquesta Sinfonica del Noroeste, Rio de Janeiro 2594, Colonia Providencia, Guadalajara.

Mexico DF
National Symphony Orchestra, Dolores 2. Conductor: Luis Herrera de la Fuente.
Orquesta Filarmonica de la UNAM, 10 Piso Torre de la Rectoria, Ciudad Universitaria, Mexico 20. Musical Director: Héctor Quintanar. Manager: Gloria Carmona.

Puebla
Puebla Symphony Orchestra, Departamento de Diffusion Cultural, Universidad de Puebla. Conductor: Idelfonso Cedillo.

Sin
North Eastern Symphony Orchestra, Universidad de Smaloa, Culican. Conductor: Luis Zimenez Caballero.

MONACO

Monte Carlo
National Orchestra, The Opera House. Musical Director: Lovro von Matacic. General Manager: Tibor Katona.

THE NETHERLANDS

Amsterdam
Amsterdam Philharmonisch Orkest, Valeriusstraat 96. Conductor: Anton Kersjes. Manager: Jan Willem Loot.
Concertgebouworkest, Jacob Obrechtstraat 51. Musical Director: Bernard Haitink. Business Manager: A. M. van Dantzig. Artistic Manager: Hein van Royen.
Nederlands Ballet Orkest, Singel 259. Manager: Julia van Delden.
Nederlands Kammerorkest, Jan Willem Brouwersplein 4, Amsterdam 1007. Conductor: Antoni Ros-Marba. Manager: G. L. van Mourik.

Arnhem
Het Gelders Orkest, Velperbuitensingel 12. Musical Director: Yoav Talmi. Manager: A. Henrichs.

Delft
Gewestelijk Orkest Nieuwe Plantage 63. Musical Director: Frits Kox. Manager: Detlev Weers.

Enschede
Overijssels Philharmonisch Orkest, Postbus 1321. 7500 BH Enschede. Musical Director: Hein Jordans. Managing Director: H. P. van der Braak.

Groningen
Noordelijk Filharmonisch Orkest, Palmslag 10. Musical Director: Charles de Wolff. Manager: R. Ottes.

Haarlem
Noordhollands Philharmonisch Orkest, Lange Begijnestraat 13 rd. Musical Director: Jerzy Katlewicz. Manager: R. Mulder.

The Hague
Hague Philharmonisch Orkest, Statenlaan 28. Residentie Orkest, Statenlaan 28. Musical Director: Hans Vonk. Manager: H. B. van der Meer.

's-Hertobenbosch
Brabants Orkest, 'Sweelinckhuis', Postbox 442. Conductor: André Vandornoot. Manager: H. B. M. van Werkhoven.

Hilversum
Metropole Orkest, Heuvellaan 32. Conductor: Dolf van der Linden.
Omroeporkest, Heuvellaan 32. Musical Director: Kenneth Montgomery.
Promenade Orkest, Heuvellaan 32. Conductor: Jan Stulen.
Radio Filharmonisch Orkest, Heuvellaan 32. Musical Director: Jean Fournet. Manager: Jan Eerenberg.
Radio Kammerorkest, Heuvellaan 32. Musical Director: Ernest Bour. Manager: Wim Baarens.

Leewarden
Frysk Orkest, Johan Willem Frisostraat 3. Musical Director: Zsolt Deaky. Manager: H. J. Smink.

Maastricht
Limburgs Symphonie Orkest, Henric van Veldekeplein 23, 5001 Maastricht. Musical Director: Andreé Rieu. Manager: G. J. G. Bronckers.

Rotterdam
Rotterdams Philharmonic Orkest, De Doelen, Kruisstraat 2, Rotterdam 3002. Musical Director: David Zinman. Manager: Dr. J. Oosterlee.

Utrecht
Utrecht Symphonie Orkest, Vredenburg 8 III. Conductor: Cornelius Dumbraveanu.

NEW ZEALAND

Auckland
Symphonia of Auckland, Box 6663, Auckland 1. Musical Director: Juan Mateucci.

Christchurch
Christchurch Symphony Orchestra, PO Box 13-164. Musical Director: Peter Zwartz. Chairman: Dr. D. Shelley.

Wellington
Lindsay String Orchestra, PO Box 10328. Musical Director: Alex Lindsay.
New Zealand Symphony Orchestra, PO Box 2092. Manager: Peter Averi.

NORWAY

Bergen
Musikselskabet 'Harmonien', Engen 15 5000 Bergen. Musical Director: Karsten Andersen. Manager: Laila Kismul.

Kristiansand
Town Orchestra of Kristiansand, Postboks 777, 4600 Kristiansand. Chairman of Board: Byrge Birkeland.

Oslo
Kringkastingorkestret, NRK Marienlyst, Oslo 3. Conductor: Olivind Bergh.
Oslo Philharmonic Orchestra, Tollbugt 24, Oslo 1. Musical Director: Okko Kamu. Manager: Alv Rasmussen.

Stavanger
Symfoniorkestret i Stavanger, Asylgaten 15, 4000 Stavanger. Musical Director: Björn Woll. Manager: Olaf Backlund.

Trondheim
Trondheim Symphony Orchestra, Kongensgt 3, 7000 Trondheim. Musical Director: Finn Avden Oftedal. Manager: Else Marie Dalaker.

PARAGUAY

Asuncion
Orquesta Sinfonica de Asuncioñ. Associate Director: Luis Szarañ. Manager: Nicolas Escurra.

PERU

Lima
Orquesta Sinfonica Nacional, Teatro Municipal. Conductor: Leopoldo la Rosa.

THE PHILIPPINES

Manila
Filipino Philharmonic Orchestra, 1665 Taft Ave. Conductor: Luis Valencia.
Manila Symphony Orchestra, Room 225, Manila Hilton, United Nations Ave. Musical Director: Regolada Jase. Manager: Suzie Moya Benitez.
National Philharmonic Orchestra, PO Box 865. Musical Director: Redentor Remero.

POLAND

Bialystok
State Symphony Orchestra, ul. Podeśna 2, 15-227 Bialystok. Musical Director: Tadeusz Chachaj.

Bydgoszcz
Ignacy Paderewski Pomeranian State Philharmonic Orchestra, Libelta 16. Musical Director: Antoni Wit. Manager: Andrzej Szwalbe.

Cracow
Orchestra of the Musical Theatre, ul. Senacka 6, 31-002 Cracow. Musical Director: Krzyszk of Missona. Manager: Lucyna Kolodziejczyk.
Polish Radio and Television Symphony Orchestra, Wislna 8. Musical Director: Antoni Wit. Manager: Jan Bogocz.

Czestochowa
State Symphony Orchestra, Braci Kakielow 16. Musical Director: Zygmunt Hassa.

Gdansk-Wrzeszcz
State Philharmonic Orchestra, Al Zwyciestwa 15. Musical Director: Zbigniew Chwedczuk.

Katowice
Katowice Philharmonic Orchestra, Katowice ul. Gen. Zawadzkrego 2.
Polish Radio and Television Symphony Orchestra, Plebiscytowa 3. Musical Director: Stanislaw Wislocki. Manager: Marian Wallek-Walewski.
Silesian State Philharmonic Orchestra, Zawadzkiego 2. Musical Director: Karol Stryja. Manager: Marian Bukowski.

Kielce
Oskar Kolberg State Philharmonic Orchestra, Sienkiewicza 18. Musical Director: Karol Anbild.

Koszalin
Stanislaw Moniuszko State Philharmonic Orchestra, Harcerska 1. Musical Director: Zygmunt Rychert. Manager: Tadeusz Maszkowski.

Lodz
State Philharmonic Orchestra, Narutowicza 20. Musical Director: Henryk Czyz. Manager: Kazimierz Mikolajczak.

Lublin
Henryk Wieniawski State Philharmonic Orchestra, ul. J. Osterwy 7. Musical Director and Manager: Adam Natanek.

Olsztyn
Feliks Nowawiejski State Philharmonic Orchestra, Jagiellonska 57. Musical Director: Janusz Prsybylski.

Opole
State Philharmonic Orchestra 'Josef Elsner', Krakowska Nr. 24, 45-075 Opole. Musical Director: Marek Tracz. Manager: Marta Wagilewicz.

Poznan
State Philharmonic Orchestra, Armii Czerwonej 81. Musical Director: Renard Czajkowski.

Rzeszow
Artur Malawski State Philharmonic Orchestra, Okrzei 7, Rzeszow 1. Musical Director: Stanislaw Michalek.

Szczecin
Mieczyslaw Karlowicz State Philharmonic Orchestra, Dzierzynskiego 1. Musical Director: Stefan Marczyk. Manager: Jadwiga Igiel.

Warsaw
National Philharmonic Orchestra, Jasna 5, Warsaw 00-950. Musical Director: Witold Rowicki. Manager: Eugeniusz Libera.

Wroclaw
State Philharmonic Orchestra, Swirczewskiego 17. Musical Director: Tadeusz Strugala. Manager: Wanda Stanislawska.

Zielona Gora
State Symphony Orchestra, Powstancow Wielkopolskich 1. Musical Director: Kazimierz Morski.

PORTUGAL

Lisbon
Lisbon Philharmonic Orchestra, Rua des Caetanos 29. Musical Director: Ivo Cruz.
National Radio Symphony Orchestra, Rua do Quelhas 2, Lisbon 2. Assistant Musical Director: Frederico de Freitas.

ROMANIA

Arad
Philharmonic Orchestra, Piata George Enescu 1. Musical Director: Eliodor Rau.

Bacau
Philharmonic Orchestra, 6 rue Cuza Voda. Musical Director: Ovidio Balan.

Botosani
Philharmonic Orchestra, 72 Blvd. Lenin, 12775 Botosani. Musical Director: Cichirdan Modest. Manager: Turcanu Ion.

Brasov
Filarmonica de Stat 'Gh. Dima', Str. Ciucas 8. Musical Director: Ilarion Ionescu-Galati. Secretary: Stela Mitu.

Bucharest
Philharmonic Orchestra 'Georges Enescu', 2 rue Exarcu. Musical Director: Dumitru Capoianu.
Romanian Radio Symphony Orchestra, Strada Nuferilor 60. Conductor: Iosif Conta.

Cluj
Philharmonic Orchestra, Strada Kogalniceanu 3. Musical Director: Sigismund Toduta.

Craiova
Philharmonic Orchestra, 52 Calea Unirii. Musical Director: Theodor Costin.

Galati
Philharmonic Orchestra, 50 rue Mihai Bravu.

Iasi
'Moldova' State Philharmonic Orchestra, Strada Cuza Voda 29. Musical Director: Ion Baciu.

Oradea
Philharmonic Orchestra, 4 Piata Republicii. Musical Director: Alexandru Firez.

Ploiesti
Philharmonic Orchestra, Strada Anton Pann 5. Conductors: Horia Andreescu & Cristian Brâncuşi.

Satu Mare
Philharmonic Orchestra, 8 Piata Libertatii. Musical Director: Stefan Gregorovicio.

Sibiu
Philharmonic Orchestra, Strada Filarmonica 2. Musical Director: Petre Sbârcea. Manager: Toma Tohati.

Timisoara
Philharmonic Orchestra 'Banatul', Blvd. Victoriei 2. Musical Director: Adriana Iacob. Conductors: Nicolae Boboc & Remus Georgescu.

Tirgu-Mures
Philharmonic Orchestra, Strada George Enescu 2. Musical Director: Lorand Szalman.

SOUTH AFRICA

Cape Town
CAPAB Orchestra, PO Box 11399. Musical Director and Manager: David Tidboald.
Cape Town Symphony Orchestra, City Hall. General Manager: Benito Moni. Manager: Stephen Lindner.
South African Broadcasting Corporation Orchestra Band, South African Broadcasting Corporation.
South African Navy Band, Simonstown.

Durban
Durban Symphony Orchestra, City Hall. Conductor: Alfred Walter.
South African Broadcasting Corporation Orchestra Band, South African Broadcasting Corporation.

Johannesburg
Johannesburg Promenade Orchestra, PO Box 6233, Johannesburg 2000. Musical Director: Solly Aronowsky.
National Symphony Orchestra of South African Broadcasting Corporation, PO Box 4559, Johannesburg, 2000. Manager: Head of Music, SABC.
Springs Concert Band, PO Box 62379. Contact: Bill Holding.

Pretoria
S.A.A.F. Band, S.A. Air Force HQ, Pvte. Bag X119. Musical Director: Commandant B. C. Griffiths.

Simonstown
South African Navy Band, Naval Training Command, Simonstown 7995. Musical Director: Cdr. R. R. Marlow. Manager: WOI D. Elliott.

Transvaal
Hugenote Seune Hoerskool Band, Springs.
South African Permanent Force Band, Voortrekkerhoogte.

SINGAPORE

Singapore Symphony Orchestra, 8th Floor, Pub. Building, Somerset Rd., Singapore 0923. Musical Director: Choo Hoey. Manager: Henry Lau Li Hien.

SPAIN

Barcelona
Barcelona City Orchestra, Carrer del Bruc 110-112, Barcelona 9. Conductor: Salvador Mas. Manager: August Valera.

Bilbao
Bilbao Symphony Orchestra, c/o Excmo Ayuntamiento. Conductor: Pedro Pirfano.

Madrid
Madrid Philharmonic Orchestra, Donoso Cortes 35. Conductor: Odón Alonso.
National Orchestra, Alcala 34, Madrid 14. Conductor: Rafael Frühbeck de Burgos.
Spanish Radio Symphony Orchestra, c/o Ministerio de Informacion y Turism. Conductor: Igor Markevitch.

Malaga
Malaga Symphony Orchestra, c/o Conservatorio de Musica. Conductor: José G. La Puente.

Seville
Seville Philharmonic Orchestra, Excmo Ayuntamiento. Conductor: Luis Izquierdo.

Valencia
Valencia City Orchestra, c/o Excmo Ayuntamiento. Conductor: Luis Antonio.

SWEDEN

Göteborg
Göteborg Symphony Orchestra, Stenhammarsgatan 1, 41256 Gotebörg. Musical Director: Charles Dutoit. Manager: Sven Kruckenberg.

Malmö
Malmö Symphony Orchestra, Box 17009, 20010 Malmö. Musical Director: Janos Fürst. Manager: Olof Hult.

Stockholm
Stockholm Philharmonic Orchestra, Konserthuset, Box 40083, 10342 Stockholm. Musical Director: Gennadi Rozjdestvensky. President: Bengt Olof Engström.
Swedish Radio Symphony Orchestra, Radiohuset, Oxenstrernsgatan 20, 10510 Stockholm. Musical Director: Stig Westerberg. Manager: Magnus Enhörning.

SWITZERLAND

Basle
Basle Chamber Orchestra, Leonhardstr. 4, 4051 Basle. Musical Director: Paul Sacher. Manager: Kathrin Klingler.
Basle Symphony Orchestra. Musical Director: Hans Ziegler.
Radio Symphony Orchestra, Münsterplatz 18,4000 Basle.

Bid/Bienne
City Orchestra, Stadheater Bid.

Berne
Berner Sinfonieorchester, Münzgraben 2, 3011 Berne. Musical Director: Gustav Kuhn.

Geneva
Suisse Romande Orchestra, Promenade du Pin 3, 1200 Geneva. Musical Director: Wolfgang Sawallisch. Manager: Ron Golan.

Lausanne
Lausanne Chamber Orchestra, Chemin du Devin 72, 1012 Lausanne. Artistic Director: Armin Jordan. Secretary-General: Jean W. Bezmann.

Lucerne
Allgemeine Musikgesellschaft Luzern, Huenenbergstr. 24, 6006 Lucerne. Musical Director: Ulrich Meyer. Manager: Werner Schaerli.

Lugano
Italian-Swiss Radio Orchestra, Radiotelevisione della Svizzera Italiana, 6903 Lugano. Musical Director: Marc Andreae. Manager: Dr. Ermanno Briner.

Winterthur
Stadtorchester, Winterthur

Zürich
Tonhalle Orchester.
Collegium Musicum Zürich, Konzertgesellschaft, Steinwiesstr. 2, 8032 Zürich. Conductor: Paul Sacher. Manager: Samuel Hirschi.
Kammerorchester Zürich, Sekretariat Kreuzstr. 55, 8032 Zürich. Conductor: Edmond de Stoutz. Manager: Alexander Chasen.
Swiss Festival Orchestra, Brunnenhofstr. 9. Manager: Andrée Raoult.

TAIWAN

Taipei
Taiwan Symphony Orchestra, PO Box 8-7, Taichung, Taiwan. Musical Directors: Deng Han-Ching & Lee Tai-Shiang.

UNITED KINGDOM

Barnet
Geraint Jones Orchestra, The Long House Arkley Lane, EN5 3JR. Musical Director: Geraint Jones.

Beckenham
Les Musiciens du Roi, 6 Aldersmead Rd, BR3 1JN. Artistic Director: Lionel Sawkins.

Belfast
BBC Northern Ireland Orchestra, Broadcasting House, 25-27 Ormeau Ave. BT2 8HQ. Musical Director: Kenneth Alwyn.
Ulster Orchestra, 181a Stranmillis Rd., BT9 5DU. Artistic Director & Principal Conductor: Bryden Thomson. General Manager: Anthony Finigan.

Biggin Hill
English National Orchestra, 'Alwyn', Lilly Rd., Biggin Hill, Kent. Principal Conductor & Artistic Director: William Rutledge. Orchestra Manager: Stephen Hope.

Birmingham
City of Birmingham Symphony Orchestra, 60 Newhall St. B3 3RP. Musical Director: Simon Rattle. Manager: Edward Smith.
Orchestra da Camera, 75 Edmund St., B3 3HA. Musical Director: Kenneth Page. Chairman: John Engleheart.

Bournemouth
Bournemouth Sinfonietta, 2 Seldon Lane, Poole, Dorset BH15 1UF. General Administrator: Keith Whitmore.
Bournemouth Symphony Orchestra, Western Orchestral Society, 2 Seldon Lane, Poole, Dorset BH15 1UF. General Administrator: Keith Whitmore.

Brentwood
Eastern Sinfonia Orchestra, 18 Meadsway, Gt. Warley, Brentwood, CM13 3DQ. Musical Director: Eric Stanley. Manager: Roy Haines.

Brighton
Brighton Philharmonic Orchestra, 50 Grand Parade, BN2 2QA. Musical Director: John Carewe. Secretary: Jill Mason. .

Bristol
Bristol Sinfonia, 16 Foye House, Bridge Rd., Leigh Woods, BS8 3PE. Musical Director: Sidney Sager. Manager: W. T. Lane.

Cambridge
Cambridge Symphony Orchestra, 6 King's Parade, CB2 1SN. Musical Director: Lawrence Leonard. Manager: Susan Smith.
Cambridge Players, 6 Luard Close, CB2 2PL. Musical Director: Christopher Brown. Secretary: Elizabeth Gaster.

Cardiff
BBC Welsh Symphony Orchestra, Broadcasting House, Llandaff CF5 2YQ.

Orchestra of the Welsh National Opera, John St., CF1 4SP. Musical Director: Richard Armstrong. Manager: James Michell.

Cheltenham
Cheltenham Chamber Orchestra, Hillcrest, Birchley Rd., GL52 6NX. Musical Director: Laurence Hudson. Secretary: Mrs. E. Godfrey-Jones.

Didcot
Apollo Chamber Orchestra, 39 Park Rd., OX11 8QL. Musical Director: Andrew Massey. Manager: Miss F. Royals.

Edinburgh
Pro Arte Players. c/o Pro Arte Musica, 5 Lonsdale Terrace. EH3 9HN. Musical Director: Eric Roberts. Manager: John Nicoll.
Scottish Baroque Ensemble, 14 Albany Street, EH1 3QB. Musical Director: Leonard Friedman. Administrator: Ursula Richardson.
Scottish Chamber Orchestra, 14 Albany Street, EH1 3QB. Musical Director: Roderick Brydon. Administrator: Ursula Richardson.
Scottish Philharmonia, 14 Albany Street, EH1 EQB. Administrator: Ursula Richardson.

Glasgow
BBC Scottish Radio Orchestra, BBC, Queen Margaret Drive, G12 8DG. Musical Director: Brian Fahey. Orchestral Assistant: Mrs. Jenny Wales.
BBC Scottish Symphony Orchestra, BBC, Queen Margaret Drive, G12 8DG. Musical Director: Christopher Seaman. Manager: Pauline I. Dodd.
Scottish National Orchestra, 150 Hope St., G2 2TH. Musical Director: Alexander Gibson. General Administrator: David Richardson.

Guildford
Guildford Philharmonic Orchestra, 1st Floor, 72 North St., GV1 4AW. Musical Director: Vernon Handley. Manager: Kathleen M. Atkins.

Kingswood
Commonwealth Philharmonic Orchestra, Poynings. Waterhouse Lane, Kingswood, Surrey KT20 6HU. Musical Director: Michael Bialoguski.

Leeds
Yorkshire Sinfonia, 2 Oxford Place, LS1 3AX. Musical Director: Manoug Parikian. Manager: Harry Tolson.

Liverpool
Liverpool Sinfonietta, 40 Caulfield Drive, Greasby, Wirral L49 1SW. Musical Director: Anthony Ridley.
Royal Liverpool Philharmonic Orchestra, Philharmonic Hall, Hope St., L1 9BP. General Manager: Stephen Gray. Principal Conductor: David Atherton.

London
Academy of St. Martin-in-the-Fields, 21 Aberdare Gardens, N.W. 6. Musical Director: Neville Marriner. Manager: Sylvia Holford.
BBC Concert Orchestra, BBC, 16 Langhan St., W1. Musical Director: Ashley Lawrence. Manager: H. C. Trotman.
BBC Symphony Orchestra, BBC, Yalding House, 156 Gt. Portland St., W1N 6AJ. Chief Conductor: Gennadli Rozhdestvensky.
Ben Uri Chamber Orchestra, 21 Dean St., W1V 5AH. Musical Director: Sydney Fixman. Secretary: Barry Fealdman.
Capriol Orchestra of London, 33 Holly Park Gardens, N3 3NG. Musical Director: Roy Budden. Manager: Charles Pemell.
City of London Sinfonia, c/o Ibbs & Tillett, 450-452 Edgeware Rd., W2. Musical Director: Richard Hickox. Manager: Ian Ritchie.
English Bach Festival Orchestra, 15 S Eaton Pl., SW1. Artistic Director: Lina Lalandi. Manager: Louise Honeyman.
English Chamber Orchestra, 1A Bloemfontein Way, W12 7BU. Musical Director: Raymond Leppard. Manager: Michael Storrs.
English Ensemble, 10 Burrard Rd., NW6 1DB. Musical Director: Jack Rothstein. Manager: Louise Honeyman.

English National Opera Orchestra, Coliseum Theatre, St. Martin's Lane, WC2N 4ES. Musical Director: Charles Mackerras. Manager: Neil Feiling.

English Symphony Orchestra, 10 Burrard Rd., NW6 1DB. Manager: Louise Honeyman.

Fine Arts Chamber Orchestra, 10 Burrard Rd., NW6 1DB. Musical Director: Jack Rothstein. Manager: Louise Honeyman.

Haydn Orchestra, 10 Burrard Rd., NW6 1DB. Musical Director: Harry Newstone. Manager: Louise Honeyman.

Jacques Orchestra, c/o Helen Jennings Concert Agency, 60 Paddington St., W1M 3RR.

Little Symphony of London, 23 The Bridle Road, Purley, CR2 3JB. Musical Director: Arthur Davison.

London Bach Orchestra, 10 Burrard Rd., NW6 1DB. Musical Director: Martindale Sidwell. Manager: Louise Honeyman.

London Chamber Orchestra, 17 Red Lion Square, WC1. Musical Director: Emanuel Hurwitz. Manager: John Honeyman.

London Chanticleer Orchestra, Allfarthings, Hermitage Rd., Kenly, CR2 5EB. Musical Director: Ruth Gipps. Secretary: Robert Baker.

London Concert Orchestra, 125 Tottenham Court Rd., W1P 9HN. Administrator: Raymond Gubbay.

London Jazz Composers' Orchestra, 6 Hassendean Rd., Blackheath, SE3 8TS. Musical Director & Manager: Barry Guy.

London Mozart Players, 105 11a Queen's Rd., SW19 8NG. Musical Director: Harry Blech. Manager: Michael de Grey.

London Philharmonic Orchestra, 53 Welbeck St., W1M 7HE. Musical Director: Sir George Solti. Manager: Eric Bravington.

London Sinfonietta, Kingston Hill Place, Kingston Hill, Kingston-upon-Thames, KT2 7LX. Artistic Director: Michael Vyner. Manager: Anthony Whitworth-Jones.

London Symphony Orchestra, 1 Montagu Street, WC1B 5BT. Principal Conductor: Claudio Abbado.

Melos Sinfonia, 10 Burrard Rd., NW6 1DB. Musical Director: Gervase de Peyer. Manager: Louise Honeyman.

Menuhin Festival Orchestra, c/o Harold Holt Ltd., 122 Wigmore St., W1H 0DJ. Musical Director: Yehudi Menuhin.

New Cantata Orchestra, 82 Shaftesburg Ave., W1V 7DG. Artistic Director: James Stobart. Secretary: Geoffrey Grey.

New London Ensemble, 8 The Limes, Linden Gardens, W2 4ET. Musical Director: Richard Bradshaw. Manager: Undine Concannon.

Orchestra of St. John's, Smith Square, 174 Uxbridge Rd., W12 7JP. Musical Director: John Lubbock.

Oxford Wind Ensemble, 5 Southwood Lawn Rd., N6 5SD. Musical Director: Anthony Sargent. Secretary: Jennie Fisher.

Park Lane Music Players, 10 Stratford Place, W1H 9AE. Administrator: John Woolf.

Philharmonia Orchestra, 12 De Warden Court, 85 New Cavendish St., W1M 7RA. Principal Conductor: Riccardi Muti. Manager: Christopher Bishop.

Philomusica of London, Suite 33, 20-21 Took's Court, EC4A 1LB. Artistic Director: David Littaur. Administrator: Anne Collis.

Polyphonia, 45 Redbourne Ave., N3 2BP. Musical Director: Bryan Fairfax. Secretary: Michael Oliver.

Priory Concertante, Flat 11, 19 Hanson St., W1P 7LN. Musical Director: Frank Stiles. Secretary: E. Lewis.

Pro Arte Orchestra, 48 Clarewood Ct. Seymour Place, W1H 5DE. Musical Director: Eugene Cruft.

Richard Hickox Orchestra, 62 Briarwood Road, SW4. Musical Director: Richard Hickox. Administrator: Richard Apley.

Royal Ballet Orchestra, Royal Opera House, Covent Garden, WC2E 7QA. Conductor: Barry Wordsworth. Manager: Clarissa Melville.

Royal Opera House Orchestra, Royal Opera House, Covent Garden, WC2E 7QA. Musical Director: Colin Davis.

Royal Philharmonic Orchestra, 97 New Bond St., W1Y 9LF. Principal Conductor: Walter Weller. General Manager: David Harvey.

Serenata of London, 66 Cromwell Ave., N6 5HQ. Musical Director: Emanuel Hurwitz. Manager: Helen Anderson.

St. John's Smith Square, Orchestra, 12 Elsworthy Rd., NW3 3DJ. Conductor: John Lubbock.

Symphonica of London, 11 Heron Place, 3 George St., W1H 5PA. Musical Director: Wyn Morris. Manager: Isabella Wallich.

Tilford Bach Festival Orchestra, 60 Stanley Road, SW14 7DZ. Musical Director: Denys Darlow.
The Twenty-four, 4 Hanover Terrace Mews, NW1 4RH. Principal Conductor: Andrew Parrott.

Manchester
BBC Northern Symphony Orchestra, New Broadcasting House, Oxford Rd. Musical Director: Raymond Leppard.
Hallé Orchestra, 30 Cross St., M2 7BA. Principal Conductor: James Loughran. Manager: Clive Smart.
Manchester Camerata, 19 Moorland Rd., M20 0BB. Musical Director: Szymon Goldberg. Manager: John Whibley.
Northern Philharmonic Orchestra, 19 Moorland Rd., M20 0BB. Manager: John Whibley.

Newcastle-upon-Tyne
Northern Sinfonia Orchestra, Sinfonia Centre, 41 Jesmond Vale, NE2 1TG. Musical Director: Christopher Seaman. Manager: Christopher Yates.

Nottingham
English Sinfonia, 72 St. James's St., NG1 6FJ. Musical Director: Neville Dilkes. Manager: James Allaway.

Oxford
Oxford Pro Musica, 40 George St., OX1 2AQ. Musical Director: Yannis Daras. General Manager: John King.

Penrith
Cumbria Concertante, 37 Frenchfield Gardens, CA11 8TX. Conductor: Denis McCaldin. Manager: John Upson.

Preston
Northern Concert Orchestra, Lancaster Farm, Chipping Rd., Longridge, PR3 2NB. Musical Director: Ernest Tomlinson.

Purley
Virtuosi of England, 23 The Bridle Road, CR2 3JB. Musical Director: Arthur Davison.

Reading
Reading Concert Orchestra, 65 Henwick Lane, Thatcham, Berks. Musical Director: Michael Evans. Manager: Les Lawrence.

York
Lemare Orchestra, 10 St. Nicholas Croft, Askham Bryan, York. Musical Director: Iris M. E. Lemare.

Wakefield
Yorkshire Philharmonic Orchestras, Torridon House, 104 Bedford Rd., Wrenthorpe, Wakefield. General Manager: Brian Greensmith.

U.S.S.R.

Alma-Ata
Kazakh SSR Symphony Orchestra. Conductor: S. H. Kazhgaliev.

Baku
Gadzhibekov Symphony Orchestra, U1 Kommunischcheskaya 2.

Dnepropetrovsk
Dnepropetrovsk Symphony Orchestra. Conductor: G. A. Karapetyan.

Donetzk
Donetzk Symphony Orchestra. Conductor: I. Gamkalo.

Dushanbe
Dushanbe Symphony Orchestra, U1 Aini 31. Conductor: Y. Yevseyev.

Gorky
Gorky Symphony Orchestra, U1 Sverdlova 29. Conductor: I. B. Gusman.

Irkutsk
Irkutsk Symphony Orchestra. Conductor: V. N. Barsov.

Kazan
Kazan Philharmonic Orchestra. Conductor: N. G. Rakhlin.

Khabarovsk
Far East Symphony Orchestra. Conductor: V. Z. Titz.

Kiev
Kiev Chamber Orchestra. Conductor: I. I. Blazhkov.
Ukranian Radio & Television Symphony Orchestra. Conductor: V. B. Gnedash.
Ukranian SSR State Symphony Orchestra, Vladimirsky spusk 2. Conductor: V. M. Kozhukhar.

Kishinev
Kishinev Symphony Orchestra, U1 25 Oktyabra 78. Conductor: T. I. Gurtovoy.

Kislovodsk
Kislovodsk Symphony Orchestra, Zeliony Park.

Kuibyshev
Kuibyshev Philharmonic Orchestra. Conductor: S. D. Dudkin.

Leningrad
Leningrad Philharmonic Orchestra, U1 Brokskogo 2. Conductor: Yevgeni Mravinsky.

Lugansk
Lugansk Symphony Orchestra. Conductor: Y. V. Olesov.

Lvov
Lvov Symphony Orchestra, U1 Tchaikovskogo 7. Conductor: D. K. Pelekhaty.

Makhachkala
Dagestan Radio & Television Symphony Orchestra. Conductor: A. V. Romankov.

Minsk
Byelorussian State Symphony Orchestra. Conductor: V. V. Katayev.

Moscow
Moscow Chamber Orchestra, U1 Gertzena 13, Moscow K9.
Moscow Radio & Television Symphony Orchestra, U1 Pyatnitskaya 25. Conductor: Gennadi Rozhdestvensky.
Moscow State Philharmonic, Ulitsa Gorkogo 31. Conductor: Kiril Kondrashin.
U.S.S.R. State Symphony Orchestra, U1 Gertzena 13, Moscow K9. Conductors: Yevgeni Svetlanov, Maxim Shostakovich.

Nalchik
Kabardino-Balkar Philharmonic Orchestra. Conductor: I. Shcherbakov.

Novosibirsk
Novosibirsk Philharmonic Symphony Orchestra, U1 Michurian 12. Conductor: A. M. Katz.

Odessa
Odessa Philharmonic Orchestra. Conductor: V. I. Aliev.

Omsk
Omsk Philharmonic Orchestra. Conductor: S. Cohen.

Ordzhonikidze
North Osetian Philharmonic Orchestra. Conductor: P. A. Yadykh.

Riga
Latvian Radio & Television Symphony Orchestra. Conductor: Leonid Vigner.

Rostov-on-Don
Rostov-on-Don Symphony Orchestra. Conductor: L. S. Katz.

Sverdlovsk
Sverdlovsk Symphony Orchestra, U1 K Libnekhta 38A. Conductor: M. I. Paverman.

Tallin
Estonian Radio & Television Symphony Orchestra, U1 Kreitsvaldi 14. Conductor: N. Järvi.

Tashkent
Uzbeck State Symphony Orchestra. Conductor: Zakhid Haknazarov.

Tbilisi
Georgian State Symphony Orchestra, Pr Plekhanova 123. Conductor: Z. Z. Khurodze.
Tbilisi Radio & Television Symphony Orchestra. U1 Lenina 68. Conductor: L. G. Kiladze.

Tomsk
Tomsk Philharmonic Orchestra. Conductor: I. F. Kovalev.

Ulyanovsk
Ulyanovsk State Symphony Orchestra, 5 Lenin Square. Conductor: Eduard Serov.

Vilnius
Lithianian State Symphony Orchestra. Conductor: I. Domarakas.

Vladivostok
Primorsky Radio and Television Symphony Orchestra. Conductor: V. A. Krasnoshchyok.

Voronezh
Voronezh Philharmonic Symphony Orchestra, Pl. Lenina 12. Conductor: Y. I. Nikolayevsky.

Yalta
Crimean State Philharmonic Orchestra, Litkens str. 13. Musical Director: A. F. Gulyamitsky.
Manager: V. P. Pankov.

Yaroslavl
Yaroslavl Philharmonic Orchestra. Conductor: Y. A. Pertzev.

Yerevan
Armenian State Symphony Orchestra, Pl. Lenina 46. Conductor: R. Z. Vartanyan.

U.S.A.

ALABAMA
Birmingham
Birmingham Summer Symphony Orchestra, 807 City Hall Building, 35203.
Birmingham Symphony Orchestra, 807 City Hall Building 35203. Musical Director: Amerigo
Marino. General Manager: Gordon G. Andrews.

Huntsville
Huntsville Chamber Orchestra, 1304 Cleermont, 35801.
Huntsville Symphony Orchestra, c/o The Arts Council, 311 Clinton Ave. W. 35801.

Juneau
Juneau Symphony Orchestra, 326 4th St., No. 905, 36801. Contact: Jane Harlow.

Mobile
Mobile Symphony Orchestra, PO Box 1988, 36601.

ALASKA
Anchorage
Anchorage Symphony Orchestra, Box 213, 99501. Musical Director: Maurice Bonney.
Manager: Mike Benson.

ARIZONA
Phoenix
Phoenix Symphony Orchestra, 6328 N. 7th St., 85014. Musical Director: Theo Alcantara. Managing Director: Ralph Rizzolo.

Sun City
Sun City Symphony Orchestra, 10606 Deanne Drive, 85351.

Tucson
Tucson Symphony Orchestra, 443 S. Stone Avenue, 85701. Musical Director: Gregory Millar. Manager: Dan Pavillard.

ARKANSAS
El Dorado
South Arkansas Symphony Orchestra, 510 1st National Bank Building 71730.

Fort Smith
Fort Smith Symphony Orchestra, PO Box 723, 72901. Musical Director: Walter Minniear. President: James Ellis.

Little Rock
Arkansas Symphony Orchestra, 604 E 6th St., 77202. Musical Director: Kurt Klippstatter. Exec. Director: Tom McGuire.

CALIFORNIA
Berkeley
San Francisco Chamber Orchestra, 907 Keeler Ave., 94708. Musical Director: Edgar J. Braun. Manager: David Meblin.

Fresno
Fresno Philharmonic Orchestra, 1362 N. Fresno St., 93703. Musical Director: Guy Taylor. General Manager: Stewart Comer.

Granada Hills
San Fernando Valley Symphony Orchestra, 17715 Chatsworth St., Suite 107, 91344. Conductor: Elmer Bernstein.

Long Beach
Long Beach Symphony Orchestra, 121 Linden Ave., 90802. Musical Director: Alberto Bolee. Manager: John L. Hyer.

Los Angeles
California Chamber Symphony Orchestra, 6380 Wilshire Blvd., 1715, 90048. Musical Director: Henri Temianka. Administrator: Rosalee Sass.
Los Angeles Chamber Orchestra, 1777 N. Vine St., 400, 90028. Musical Director: Neville Marriner.
Los Angeles Philharmonic Orchestra, 135 N. Grand Avenue, 90012. Musical Director: Zubin Mehta. Executive Director: Ernest Fleischmann.

Ontario
West End Symphony Orchestra, 217 S. Lemon Ave., 91761. Musical Director: Keith Moon. Manager: Marci Ruggles.

Pasadena
Pasadena Symphony Orchestra, 300 E. Green St., 91101. Musical Director: Daniel Lewis. Manager: Mrs Dori Barnes.

Redding
Shasta Symphony Orchestra, 1065 N. Old Oregon Trail Road, 96001. Musical Director: Olando Tognozzi.

Redondo Beach
Beach Cities Symphony Orchestra, PO Box 248, 90277. Musical Director: Louis Palange. Manager: Jeanne Jefferson.

Riverside
Riverside Symphony Orchestra, PO Box 1601, 95202. Musical Director: James Guthrie. Manager: Dr. Edward Clinkscale.

San Diego
San Diego Symphony Orchestra, PO Box 3175, 92103. Musical Director: Peter Eros. Manager: Robert Christian.

San Francisco
San Francisco Chamber Orchestra, 907 Keeler Ave., Berkeley 94708. Music Director: Edgar J. Braun. Manager: David Meblin.
San Francisco Symphony Orchestra, Room 107, War Memorial Veterans' Building, 94102. Principal Conductor: Edo de Waart. Exec. Director: Peter Pastreich.

San Jose
San Jose Symphony Orchestra, 170 Park Center Plaza, Suite 100, 95113. Musical Director: George Cleve. General Manager: Richard H Wright.

San Rafael
Marin Symphony Orchestra, Box 127, 94902. Musical Director: Hugo Rinaldi. Manager: Chris Jennings.

COLORADO
Denver
Denver Symphony Orchestra, Suite 611, 1615 California St., 80202. Musical Director: Brian Priestman. Executive Director: Oleg Lobanov.

Golden
Jefferson Symphony Orchestra, 1938 Mt. Zion, 80401. Conductor: T. Gordon Parks. Manager: John J. Galland.

Greeley
Greeley Philharmonic Orchestra, PO Box 1535, 80632. Conductor: Howard Skinner. Manager: William Jamieson.

CONNECTICUT
Bridgeport
Greater Bridgeport Symphony Orchestra, Bernhard Center, University of Bridgeport, 06602. Musical Director: Gustav Meier. Manager: Dr. Harrison R. Valante.

Greenwich
Greenwich Philharmonic Orchestra, PO Box 35, 06830. Conductor: John Nelson.

Hartford
Hartford Symphony Orchestra, 15 Lewis St., 06103.
New Britain Symphony Orchestra, PO Box 34, 06050. Conductor: Jerome Lasziofly. President: Charles Boos.
New Haven Symphony Orchestra, 33 Whitney Avenue, 06510. Musical Director: Murry Sidlin. Manager: Harold Kendricks.

New London
Eastern Connecticut Symphony Orchestra, PO Box 627, 06320. Musical Director: Victor Norman. Manager: Pauline Chapman.

Waterbury
Waterbury Symphony Orchestra, PO Box 1728, 06920. Manager: Mrs. E. E. Stauff.

West Hartford
Connecticut String Orchestra, 25 Bainbridge Rd., 06119. Musical Director: Renato Bonacini.

DELAWARE
Wilmington
Delaware Symphony Orchestra, PO Box 1870, 19899. Musical Director: Stephen Gunzenhauser. Manager: Jeffrey M. Ruben.

DISTRICT OF COLUMBIA
Washington
Baroque Arts Chamber Orchestra of Washington, PO Box 39083, D.C., 20016.

National Gallery Orchestra, Sixth and Constitution Ave., N.W., D.C. 20565.
National Symphony Orchestra, 2480 16th St., N.W., D.C. 20009. Musical Director: Antal
Dorati. Manager: William L. Denton.

FLORIDA
Jacksonville
Jacksonville Symphony Orchestra, The Galleria. Musical Director: Willis Page. Manager:
Florence Young.

Miami Beach
Miami Beach Symphony Orchestra, 420 Lincoln Rd., 33139. Musical Director and Manager:
Barnett Breeskin.
Florida Symphony Orchestra, 150 S.E. 2nd Ave., 33131. Musical Director: Brian Priestman.
Manager: Azim Mayadas.

Sarasota
Florida West Coast Symphony Orchestra, PO Box 1107, 33578. Musical Director: Paul
Wolfe. Manager: Colleen Pope.

Tampa
Florida Gulf Coast Symphony Orchestra, PO Box 449, 44601. Musical Director: Irwin
Hoffman. Office Manager: Deborah Sampson.

GEORGIA
Atlanta
Atlanta Symphony Orchestra, 1280 Peachtree St., N.E., 30309. Musical Director: Robert
Shaw. Manager: Stephen Sell.

Savannah
Savannah Symphony Orchestra, PO Box 9505, 31402. Musical Director: Christian Badea.
Manager: John A. Berg.

HAWAII
Honolulu
Honolulu Symphony Orchestra, Suite 303, 1000 Bishop St., 96813. Musical Director:
Robert La Marchina. General Manager: Gordon T. Coats.

IDAHO
Boise
Boise Philharmonic Orchestra, PO Box 2205, 83701. Musical Director: Daniel Stern.
Manager: Vivian Garets.

Twin Falls
Magic Valley Symphony Orchestra, PO Box S, 83301. Conductor: Del Slaughter. Manager:
Mrs. R. A. Sutcliff.

ILLINOIS
Chicago
Chicago Artists' Orchestra, 410 S. Michigan, No. 524, 60605.
Chicago Chamber Orchestra, 332 S. Michigan Avenue, 60604. Musical Director: Dieter
Kober. Manager: Ralph B. Block.
Chicago Symphony Orchestra, 220 S. Michigan Avenue, 60604. Musical Director: Sir
George Solti. Exec. Vice-President: John S. Edwards.

Elmhurst
Elmhurst Symphony Orchestra, PO Box 345, 60126. Musical Director: Gordon Peter.
Manager: Brenda Born.

Rockford
Rockford Symphony Orchestra, 1111 E. State St., 61108. Musical Director: Crawford
Gates. Secretary: Virginia Millard.

INDIANA
Bloomington
Bloomington Symphony Orchestra, 2920 E. 10th St., 47401. Musical Director: E. Kent
Hart. Manager: H. Walter Johnson.

Fort Wayne
Fort Wayne Philharmonic Orchestra, 927 Harrison, 46802. Musical Director: Thomas Briccette. Manager: Richard P. Eistenstein.

Indianapolis
Indianapolis Symphony Orchestra, PO Box 88207, 46208. Musical Director: John Nelson. Manager: Fred H. Kumb, Jr.
Philharmonic Orchestra of Indianapolis, 3200 Cold Spring Rd., 46222. Musical Director: Wolfgang Vacano.

Marion
Marion Philharmonic Orchestra, PO Box 272, 46952. Musical Director: Benjamin Delvecchio. Manager: Edward Hermanson.

South Bend
South Bend Symphony Orchestra, 215 W. North Shore Drive, 46617. Musical Director: Herbert Butler. Manager: Elizabeth M. Cullity.

IOWA
Cedar Rapids
Cedar Rapids Symphony Orchestra, Dows Building. Musical Director: Richard Williams. Manager: Karla Mason.

Des Moines
Des Moines Symphony Orchestra, 318 Securities Building, 50309. Musical Director: Yuri Krasnapolsky. Manager: Franklin Brewster.

Dubuque
Dubuque Symphony Orchestra, PO Box 881, Five Flags Center, 52001. Musical Director: Parvis Mahmoud. Business Administrator: Mary C. FitzPatrick.

KANSAS
Hutchinson
Hutchinson Symphony Orchestra, PO Box 1241, 67501.

Ottawa
Ottawa Little Symphony Orchestra, PO Box 555, 66067.

Wichita
Wichita Symphony Orchestra, 225 W. Douglas Avenue, No. 207, 67202. Musical Director: François Huybrechts. Manager: Paul Stapel.

KENTUCKY
Lexington
Lexington Philharmonic Orchestra, PO Box 838, 40501. Conductor: George Zack. Manager: Linda G. Moore.

Louisville
Louisville Orchestra, 333 W. Broadway, 40202. Musical Director: Jorge Mester. Manager: Jack M. Firestone.

Owensboro
Owensboro Symphony Orchestra, 122 E. /th St., 42301. Musical Director: Leon Gregorian. General Manager: George Alexsovich.

LOUISIANA
New Orleans
New Orleans Philharmonic Orchestra, Suite 207, 333 St. Charles Avenue, 70130. Musical Director: Werner Torkanowsky Manager: Thomas Greene.

Shreveport
Shreveport Symphony Orchestra, PO Box 4057, 71104. Musical Director: John Shenaut. Manager: General Manager: Russell P. Allen.

MAINE
Portland
Portland Symphony Orchestra, 30 Myrtle St., 04111. Musical Director: Paul Vermel. Manager: Russell I. Burleigh.

MARYLAND
Baltimore
Baltimore Symphony Orchestra, 5204 Roland Ave., 21210. Musical Director: Sergiu Comissiona. Manager: Joseph Leavitt.
Gettysburg Symphony Orchestra, c/o 1800 Cromwell Bridge Road, 21234. Musical Director & Manager: William Sebastian Hart.

MASSACHUSETTS
Boston
Boston Pops Orchestra, Symphony Hall, 02115. Manager: Thomas W. Morris.
Boston Symphony Orchestra, Symphony Hall, 02115. Musical Director: Seiji Ozawa. Manager: Thomas W. Morris.

Brockton
Brockton Symphony Orchestra, 1076 Main St., 02401.

Reading
Reading Symphony Orchestra, 43 Oak Ridge Road, 01867.

Springfield
Springfield Symphony Orchestra, 49 Chestnut St., 01103. Musical Director: Robert Gutter. Manager: John Gidwitz.

Wellesley
Wellesley Symphony Orchestra, 324 Washington St., 02181.

MICHIGAN
Battle Creek
Battle Creek Symphony Orchestra, PO Box 1319, 49016. Musical Director: William Stein. Manager: Kathleen Samra.

Dearborn
Dearborn Orchestra, PO Box 1015, 48121. Conductor: Nathan Gordon. Manager: James R. Irwin.

Detroit
Detroit Symphony Orchestra, Fort Auditorium, 48226. Musical Director: Antal Dorati. Managing Director: Ralph O. Guthrie.

Grosse Pointe
Grosse Pointe Symphony Orchestra, 689 Reward Blvd., 48230. Musical Director: Felix Resnick.

Kalamazoo
Kalamazoo Symphony Orchestra, 426 South Park St., 49007. Musical Director: Yoshimi Takeda. Business Manager: Horace T. Maddux.

Lansing
Lansing Symphony Orchestra, 113 1/2 W. Michigan Ave., 48933.

St. Clair Shores
St. Clair Shores Symphony Orchestra, 22427 Statler Blvd., 48081.

MINNESOTA
Minneapolis
Minnesota Orchestra, Orchestra Hall, 1111 Nicollet Mall, 55403. Musical Director: Neville Marriner. Managing Director: Richard Bass.
Minneapolis Symphony Orchestra, 110 Northrop Memorial Auditorium.

Rochester
Rochester Symphony Orchestra, City Hall, 55901. Musical Director: Wolfgang Balzer. Manager: Marianne Segura.

St. Paul
St. Paul Chamber Orchestra, St. Paul Building, 5th & Wabash St., 55102. Musical Director: Dennis Russell Davies. General Manager: James Howland.

MISSISSIPPI
Greenville
Greenville Symphony Orchestra, PO Box 750, 38701. Manager: R. K. Haxton Jr.

Jackson
Jackson Symphony Orchestra, PO Box 4584, 39216. Musical Director: Lewis Dalvit. Manager: Ramona Boughan.

Meridian
Meridian Symphony Orchestra, PO Box 3173, 39301. Musical Director: Vernon Raines. Manager: Tom Lawrence.

Starkville
Starkville Symphony Orchestra, PO Box 1587, 39762. Musical Director: Charles E. Lewis. Manager: Glenn D. Bryant.

Tupelo
Tupelo Symphony Orchestra, PO Box 466, 38801. Musical Director: Kenneth Peeler. Manager: Wade H. Lagrone.

MISSOURI
Kansas City
Kansas City Philharmonic Orchestra, 210 W 10th St., 64105. Musical Director: Maurice Peress. Manager: Nancy Sies.

St. Joseph
St. Joseph Symphony Orchestra, 510 Francis, 64501. Conductor: Russell Waite. Executive Secretary: Golden Patten.

St. Louis
Gateway Festival Orchestra of St. Louis, 8016 Cornell, 63130. Musical Director: William Schatzkamer. Executive Director: Lily L. Kaufman.
St. Louis Symphony Orchestra, Powell Symphony Hall, 718 N Grand Blvd., 63103. Musical Director: Leonard Slatkin. Exec. Director: David J. Hyslop.

Springfield
Springfield Symphony Orchestra, 1675 E Sunshine, Suite G-100, 65804. Musical Director: Charles E. Bontrager. Manager: Rita Ann Preston.

MONTANA
Billings
Billings Symphony Orchestra, PO Box 602, 59103. Musical Director: George Perkins. Manager: Marjorie L. Homza.

Butte
Butte Symphony Orchestra, 1009 Placer St., 59701. Musical Director: Rick Hartwig. Manager: Robert T. Taylor.

NEBRASKA
Lincoln
Lincoln Symphony Orchestra, Route 8, 68505. Musical Director: Leo Kopp. Manager: Louis Babst.

Omaha
Omaha Symphony Orchestra, 478 Aquila Court, 68102. Musical Director: Thomas Bricceti. Manager: Roger R. Jones.

NEW JERSEY
Bloomfield
Bloomfield Symphony Orchestra, 84 Broad St., 07083. Musical Director: Edward Napiwoki. Manager: Victor M. Krygowski.

Dumont
Ridgewood Symphony Orchestra, 59 Andover Avenue, 07628. Manager: Robert V. Keihner.

Haddonfield
Haddonfield Symphony Orchestra, PO Box 212, 08033. Musical Director: Arthur Cohn. President: Frank M. Travaline Jr.

Long Branch
Monmouth Symphony Orchestra, 448 Ocean Avenue, 07740. Musical Director: Louis Miraglia. Manager: M. H. Goldwasser.

Newark
New Jersey Symphony Orchestra, 213 Washington St., 07101. Musical Director: Max Rudolf. General Manager: Kenneth R. Meine.

Summit
Summit Symphony Orchestra, 81 Beekman Rd., 07901. Musical Director: Harry Hannaford.

Trenton
Greater Trenton Symphony Orchestra, 28 W Slate St., Room 821, 08608. Musical Director: William Smith. Manager: Joseph Cellini.

Union City
Union Symphony Orchestra, 1035 Bertram Terrace, 07083. Musical Director: Leo Rindler. Secretary: Lillian Paul.

Verona
South Orange Symphony Orchestra, 33 Westview Rd., 07044. Musical Director: Robert Helmacy.

West Caldwell
North Jersey Wind Symphony Orchestra, 108 Park Avenue, 07006. Musical Director: Keith Brion. Manager: Edmond Modgrack.

NEW MEXICO
Albuquerque
New Mexico Symphony Orchestra, PO Box 769, 87103. Musical Director: Yoshimi Takeda. Executive Administrator: William L. Weinrod.

Roswell
Roswell Symphony Orchestra, PO Box 1321, 88201. Director: John Farrer.

NEW YORK
Albany
Albany Symphony Orchestra, 19 Clinton Avenue, 12207. Musical Director: Julius Hegy. Manager: Fred Leise.

Binghampton
Binghampton Symphony Orchestra, 19 Chenango St., 13905. Musical Director: David Loebel. Manager: Ernest Rose.

Brooklyn
Brooklyn Philharmonia, 30 Lafayette Avenue, 11217. Musical Director: Lukas Foss. Manager: Maurice Edwards.
Rockaway Five Towns Symphony Orchestra, 59 Auerbach Lane, Cedarhurst. Musical Director: Myron Levite. Manager: Armand Grunberg.

Buffalo
Buffalo Philharmonic Orchestra, 26 Richmond Avenue, 14222. Musical Director: Michael Tilson Thomas. Manager: Harold Lawrence.
Buffalo Symphonette, 14 Cheltenham Drive, 14216. Musical Director: Fred Ressel. Manager: R. M. Sherrard.

Chautauqua
Chautauqua Symphony Orchestra, Chautauqua, NY 14722. Musical Director: Sergiu Comissiona. President: Robert R. Hesse.

Forest Hills
Queens Symphony Orchestra, 99-11 Queens Blvd., Rego Park, 11374. Musical Director: Davit Katz. Executive Director: Judith Linden.

Huntingdon
Huntingdon Symphony Orchestra, 12 New St., 11743. Musical Director: Seymour Lipkin. Manager: William Kupferberg.

Newburgh
New York State Symphony Orchestra, Powder Mill Rd., 12550.

New York City
American Symphony Orchestra, 200 W 57th St., 10019. Musical Director: Leopold Stokowski.
Guggenheim Concerts Band, 300 Madison Ave., 10017. Musical Director: Ainslee Cox.
Mozart Festival Orchestra, 33 Greenwich Ave., 10014. Musical Director: Baird Hastings. Manager: Mrs. Lily Hastings.
New Little Orchestral Society Orchestra, 1860 Broadway, 10023. Musical Director: Thomas Scherman. Manager: John J. Jones.
New York Philharmonic Orchestra, Avery Fisher Hall, 65th St. at Broadway, 10023. Musical Director: Pierre Boulez. Managing Director: Albert K. Webster.
Symphony of the New World, Carnegie Hall, 881 7th Ave., Suite 303, 10019. Musical Director: Everett Lee. Executive Director: Robert B. Patterson.
Symphony for United Nations (SUN), 2112 Broadway, Suite 504, 10023. Musical Director: Joseph Eger. Manager: Mildred White Solomon.
Westchester County Symphony Association, PO Box 333 Scarsdale, 10583. Musical Director: Stephen Simon. Manager: Robert Gewald.
West End Symphony Orchestra, 685 West End Ave., 10025. Musical Director: Eugene R. Gamiel. Secretary: Roslyn Gamiel.

Orchard Park
Orchard Park Symphony Orchestra, 6721 Jewett Holmwood Rd., 14127. Musical Director: J. Wincenc.

Poughkeepsie
Hudson Valley Philharmonic Orchestra, PO Box 191, 12602. Musical Director: Imre Pallo. Manager: Carla Smith.

Rochester
Rochester Philharmonic Orchestra, 20 Grove Place, 14605. Musical Director: David Zinman. Manager: Tony H. Dechario.

Scarsdale
Westchester Symphony Orchestra, PO Box 445, 10588. Musical Director: Anton Copolla. Manager: Mrs. Alfred Bright.

Shrub Oak
Northern Westchester Symphony Orchestra, PO Box 445, 10588. Musical Director: Earl Groner. Manager: Martin Harner.

Syracuse
Syracuse Symphony Orchestra, Suite 40, Civic Center, 411 Montgomery St., 13202. Musical Director: Christopher Keene. Manager: Sandor Kallai.

NORTH CAROLINA

Asheville
Asheville Symphony Orchestra, 419 City Bldg., 28801.

Charlotte
Charlotte Symphony Orchestra, Spirit Sq., 110 E 7th St., 28202. Musical Director: Leo B. Driehuys. General Manager: Karen R. Dobbs.

Fayetteville
Fayetteville Symphony Orchestra, PO Box 3513, 28305. Manager: Robert Downing.

Greensboro
Greensboro Symphony Orchestra, 200 N Davie St., 27401. Musical Director: Peter P. Fuchs. Manager: Mrs. Margaret B. Faison.

Raleigh
North Carolina Symphony Orchestra, PO Box 28026, 27611. Musical Director: John Gosling. Manager: Hiram Black.

Winston-Salem
Winston-Salem Symphony Orchestra, 610 Coliseum Drive, 27106. Musical Director: John Luele. Manager: William C. Jackson III.

NORTH DAKOTA
Fargo
Fargo-Moorhead Symphony Orchestra, PO Box 1753, 58102. Musical Director: J. Robert Hanson. Manager: Evelyn Hanson.

Grand Forks
Greater Grand Forks Symphony Orchestra, PO Box 1294, 58201.

OHIO
Akron
Akron Symphony Orchestra, Thomas Hall, Center and Hill St., 44304. Musical Director: Louis Lane. Manager: Robert L. Henke.

Canton
Canton Symphony Orchestra, 1001 Market Avenue N, 44702. Musical Director: Thomas Michalak. Manager: Nancy McPeek.

Cincinnati
Cincinnati Symphony Orchestra, 1241 Elm St., 45210. Musical Director: Michael Gielen. Manager: Steven Monder.

Cleveland
Cleveland Orchestra, Severance Hall, 44106. Musical Director: Lorin Maazel. Manager: Kenneth Haas.

Dayton
Dayton Philharmonic Orchestra, 210 N Main St., 45402. Musical Director: Charles Wendelkin-Wilson. Manager: Richard C. McCauley.

Lakeside
Lakeside Symphony Orchestra, 236 Walnut St., 43440. Musical Director: R. L. Conquist. Manager: Barbara J. Sauvey.

New Philadelphia
Tuscarawas County Philharmonic Orchestra, PO Box 406, 44663. Musical Director: Margery Henke. Manager: Charolette H. Bohse.

Springfield
Springfield Symphony Orchestra, PO Box 1374. Musical Director: John E. Ferritto. Manager: Richard S. Wommack.

Toledo
Toledo Symphony Orchestra, Suite 134, 1 Stranahan Square, 43604. Musical Director: Serge Fournier. Manager: Robert Bell.

Warren
Warren Chamber Orchestra, 1000 Springrun NE, 44484. Musical Director: George Zack. Manager: H. A. Pendleton.

Youngstown
Youngstown Symphony Orchestra, 260 W Federal St., 44503. Musical Director: Franz Bibo. Manager: Jack W. Hynes.

OKLAHOMA
Oklahoma City
Oklahoma Symphony Orchestra, 512 Civic Center Musical Hall, 73102. Musical Director: Ainslee Cox. Manager: John H. Deford.

Tulsa
Tulsa Philharmonic Orchestra, 2210 S Main St., 74114. Musical Director: Murry Sidlin. Resident Conductor: Joel Lazar. Manager: Karen Kimes.

OREGON
Eugene
Eugene Symphony Orchestra, 1245 Charnelton, 97401. Musical Director: Lawrence Maves. Administration: Reginald S. Tonry.

Portland
Oregon Symphony Orchestra, 1119 SW Park, 97205. Manager: John E. Graham.

Seaside
North Coast Chamber Orchestra, PO Box 1016, 97138. Musical Director: James R. Smith. Manager: Gainon Meriott.

PENNSYLVANIA
Allentown
Allentown Symphony Orchestra, 23 N 6th St., 18104. Musical Director: Donald Voorhees. Executive Director: Virginia E. Wartman.

Erie
Erie Philharmonic Orchestra, 409 G. Daniel Baldwin Building, 16501. Musical Director: Walter Hendl. Manager: Earle C. Batchelder.

Philadelphia
Philadelphia Orchestra, 230 S 15th St., 19102. Manager: Boris Sokoloff.
Philadelphia Accordion Concert Orchestra, 105 S 18th St., 19103. Musical Director: Jacob Neupauen. Manager: Karen Farst.

Pittsburgh
Pittsburgh Symphony Orchestra, Heinz Hall for the Performing Arts, 600 Penn Avenue, 15222. Musical Director: André Previn. Managing Director: Seymour L. Rosen.

Reading
Reading Symphony Orchestra, 219 N 5th St., 19601. Musical Director: Louis Vyners. Executive Secretary: Louise M. Harris.

RHODE ISLAND
Providence
Rhode Island Civic Orchestra, 27 The Arcade, 02903. Musical Director: Ron Morris. Executive Director: John A. D'Errico.
Rhode Island Philharmonic Orchestra, 334 Westminster Mall, 02903. Musical Director: Francis Madeira. Manager: Muriel Port Stevens.

SOUTH CAROLINA
Columbia
Columbia Philharmonic Orchestra, 1527 Senate St., 29201. Musical Director: Arpad Daraza. Manager: Leon Harrelson.

SOUTH DAKOTA
Rapid City
Rapid City Symphony Orchestra, Rapid City Recreation Department, 617 6th St., 57701. Musical Director: John C. Knowles.

Sioux Falls
Sioux Falls Symphony Orchestra, 101 W 37th St., 57105. Musical Director: Ardeen Foss. Manager: Lois Lundin.

TENNESSEE
Chattanooga
Chattanooga Symphony Orchestra, 730 Cherry St., 37402. Musical Director: Richard Cormier. Manager: John G. Wend.

Jackson
Jackson Symphony Orchestra, PO Box 3098, 38301. Musical Director: James Petty. Manager: Vivian Towwater.

Johnson City
Johnson City Symphony Orchestra, PO Box 533, 37601. Musical Director: W. G. Oxendine. Chairman: Dr. Paul Clark.

Kingsport
Symphony Orchestra of Kingsport, Fine Arts Center, Church Circle, 37660. Musical Director: Willem Bertsch. Treasurer: Mrs. Vernon M. Howe.

Memphis
Memphis Symphony Orchestra, 1503 Monroe Avenue, 38104. Musical Director: Vincent de Frank. Manager: Walter Hehmeyer.

Nashville
Nashville Symphony Orchestra, 1805 W. End Avenue, 37203. Musical Director: Thor Johnson. Manager: George Carpenter.

TEXAS
Abilene
Abilene Philharmonic Orchestra, 310 N. Willis, Suite 228, 79603. Musical Director: George Yaeger. Manager: Ed Allcorn.

Amarillo
Amarillo Symphony Orchestra, Box 2552, 78105. Musical Director: Thomas Conlin. Manager: Lt. Col. James M. Alfonte.

Corpus Christi
Corpus Christi Symphony Orchestra, PO Box 495, 78403. Musical Director: Maurice Peress. Manager: Mrs. John Kline.

Dallas
Dallas Symphony Orchestra, PO Box 26207, 75226. Musical Director: Eduardo Mata. Manager: Leonard D. Stone.

Fort Worth
Fort Worth Symphony Orchestra, 3505 W. Lancaster, 76107. Musical Director: John Giordano. Manager: Beverly Cardona.

Houston
Houston Symphony Orchestra, Jesse J. Jones Hall, 615 Louisiana, 77002. Musical Director: Sergiu Comissiona. Principal Guest Conductor: (1981-) Sir Alexander Gibson. Exec. Director: Michael Woolcock.

Longview
Longview Symphony Orchestra, 29 Country Place, 75601. Musical Director: James Snowden.

Midland
Midland-Odessa Symphony Orchestra, Box 6266, 79701. Musical Director: Thomas Hohstadt. Manager: Samuel Woodward.

San Antonio
San Antonio Symphony Orchestra, 109 Lexington, Suite 207, 78205. Manager: Nat Greenberg.

Sherman
Sherman Symphony Orchestra, Box 1592, Austin College, 75090. Musical Director and Manager: Cecil Isaac.

Wichita Falls
Wichita Falls Symphony Orchestra, 702 Hamilton Bldg. 76301. Musical Director: William H. Boyer. Manager: Virginia Pierce.

UTAH
Provo
Utah Valley Symphony Orchestra, 461 E. 2875 N., 84601. Musical Director: Glenn Williams. Manager: Beverly D. Dunford.

Salt Lake City
Utah Symphony Orchestra, 123 W. South Temple, 84103. Musical Director: Robert E. Henderson. Manager: Herold L. Gregory.

VERMONT
Middlebury
Vermont State Symphony Orchestra, PO Box 548, 05735. Musical Director: Alan Carter. Manager: Phyliss Franze.

Montpelier
Vermont Philharmonic Orchestra, PO Box 826, 05602. Musical Director: Jon Borowicz. Manager: Bernard Folta.

VIRGINIA
Newport News
Peninsula Symphony Orchestra, PO Box 1392, Newport News, 23601.

Norfolk
Norfolk Symphony Orchestra, PO Box 26, 23501. Musical Director: Russell Stanger. Manager: Matthew F. M. Werth Jr.
Virginia Orchestra Group, PO Box 26, 23501. Musical Directors: Russell Stanger, Walter Noona, Cary McMurray. Exec. Director: Francis Crociata.

Richmond
Richmond Symphony Orchestra, 15 South Fifth St., 23219. Musical Director: Jacques Houtmann. Manager: Joan T. Briccetti.

Roanoke
Roanoke Symphony Orchestra, St. John's Parish House, Elm House, S.W., 24009. Musical Director: Gilbert Morrissey. Administrator: G. Councill.

WASHINGTON
Burien
Highline Symphony Orchestra, PO Box 666235, 98166.

Port Angeles
Port Angeles Symphony Orchestra, PO Box 991, 98362. Manager: David Andre.

Spokane
Spokane Symphony Orchestra, The Flour Mill, Suite 203, W. 621 Mallon, 99201. Musical Director: Donald Thulean. Manager: Maxey Adams.

WEST VIRGINIA
Charleston
Charleston Symphony Orchestra, PO Box 2292, 25328. Musical Director: Charles Schiff. Manager: Edward Beulike

WISCONSIN
La Crosse
La Crosse Symphony Orchestra, PO Box 623, 54601.

Milwaukee
Milwaukee Symphony Orchestra, 929 N. Water St., 53202. Musical Director: Kenneth Schermerhorn. Manager: Richard C. Thomas.

WYOMING
Cheyenne
Cheyenne Symphony Orchestra, Box 851, 82001.

URUGUAY

Montevideo
City Orchestra, Teatro Solis, Buenos Aires 678. Conductor: Hugo Lopes. Orquesta Sinfonica del Sodre Andes, 1465 Montevideo. Artistic Director: Pedro Ipuche-Riva.

VENEZUELA

Caracas
Orquesta Sinfonica Venezuela, Ed/Corporacion Felman, Cipreses a Miracielos Ave/Lecuna. Musical Director: Gonzalo Castellanos. Manager: Luis Morales Dance.

YUGOSLAVIA

Belgrade
Belgrade Philharmonic Orchestra, Studentski/trg. 11, 11000 Belgrade. Musical Director and Manager: Gika Zdravkovitch.

Dubrovnik
Dubrovnik Symphony Orchestra, Kovacka 3/11,, 50000 Dubrovnik. Musical Director: Nikola Debelič. Secretary: Ivo Breskovič.

Ljubljana
Slovenian Philharmonic Orchestra, TRG Osvoboditve 9. Musical Director: Marijan Gabrijelčič. Manager: Dragisa Ognjanovič.

Sarajevo
Sarajevo Philharmonic Orchestra, Obala 9, 71000 Sarajevo. Musical Director and Manager: Romanić Teodor.

Skopje
Macedonian Philharmonic Orchestra. Conductor: Todo Skalovski.

Zagreb
Zagreb Philharmonic Orchestra. Conductor: Milan Horvat.

APPENDIX B

MUSIC ORGANIZATIONS

ARGENTINA

Asociación Argentina de Compositores (Association of Argentina Composers), Bonpland 2042, Buenos Aires. Secretary: Alicia Terzian.

Asociación Argentina de Profesores de Musica y Artes Afines (Association of Argentine Professors of Music and Fine Arts), Colodrero 2675, Buenos Aires. President: Prof. Gregorio Surif.

Asociación Filarmónica de Mendoza (Philharmonic Association of Mendoza), Catamarca 31, Galeria Tonsa, Local 24, Mendoza.

Asociación Filarmónica de Olavarria (Philharmonic Association of Olavarria), Alsina 3183, Olavarria, Buenos Aires. Secretary: Miguel M. Llorensi.

Asociación Guitarristica Argentina (Argentine Guitar Association, Avda. de Mayo 702, Buenos Aires.

Asociación Guitarristica de Salta (Salta Guitar Association), Necochea 562, 4400 Salta. Secretary: Prof. Rafael B. Ramos.

Asociación del Profesorado Orquesta (Association of Orchestral Teachers), Sarmiento 1682, Buenos Aires. Secretary: Mr. Bassi.

Asociación de Profesores Nacionales de Musica de Rosario (Association of Professors of Music), 9 de Julio 80, Buenos Aires.

Asociación Tárrega de Cultura Guitarristica (Association of Guitar Culture of Tárrega), Presidente Roca 1952, Santa Fe.

Consejo Argentino de la Música (National Committee of the International Music Council), Avenida Madero 235, 6 671 Buenos Aires. Secretary: Ana Lucia Frega.

Internaciónal Encuentro de Contemporánea Música (International Centre for Contemporary Music), Bonpland 2042, Buenos Aires. Director: Mrs. Alicia Terzian.

Juventudes Músicales de la Argentina (Jeunesses Musicales of Argentine), Corregidores 1551, Buenos Aires. Secretary: Mme. Arnolda Hirsch.

Sindicato Argentino de Músicos (Musicians' Union of Argentine), Paraguay 1162, Buenos Aires.

Sociedad Argentina de Autores y Compositores de Música (Argentine Society of Authors and Composers of Music-a performing right society), Lavalle 1547, Buenos Aires. President: Ariel Ramirez.

Sociedad Argentina de Música Contemporánea (National Section of the International Society for Contemporary Music), Medrano 747.1 G, Buenos Aires. Secretary: Regina Benavente.

Los Solistas de Buenos Aires (Soloists of Buenos Aires), Berutti 3866. p., Buenos Aires.

Union de Compositores de la Argentina (Argentine Union of Composers), Corrientes 127, 4 407, Buenos Aires. Secretary: Horacia Lopez de la Rosa.

AUSTRALIA

Accordeon Society of Australia, 579 Princes Highway, Rockdale, NSW 2216. Federal President: Mrs. E. N. Brandman.

Arts Council of Australia, ADC Building, 77 Pacific Highway, North Sydney 2060. Federal Administrator: Jennifer Knox.

Association for Education of Youth through Music, 10 Mayfair St., Mt. Claremont, WA 6010. Secretary: Jean Parker.

Australasian Performing Right Association Ltd., 25-27 Albany St., Crows Nest, NSW 2065. Secretary: Miss Glenda Maria Callaghan.

Australia Council, PO Box 302, North Sydney, NSW 2060. Director, Music Board: Antony Jeffrey. General Manager: John Cameron.

Australia Music Centre, PO Box N9, Grosvenor, Sydney 2000. National Director: James Murdoch.

Australian Broadcasting Commission, SPO Box 487, Sydney 2000. Director of Music: Harold Hort.

Australian Cello Society, 24 Lynwood Crescent, Lower Plenty, Vic. 3093. President: Daniel Kahans.

Australian College of Organists (NSW), 11 Macleay Place, Earlwood, NSW 2206.

Australian Copyright Council, 24 Alfred St., Milsons Point 2016. Secretary: David Catterns.

Australian Elizabethan Theatre Trust, PO Box 137, Potts Point, NSW 2011. Administrator of Trust Orchestras: K. Mackenzie-Forbes.

Australian Folklore Unit, PO Box 162, Paddington, NSW 2021. Secretary: Warren Fahey.

Australian Institute of Aboriginal Studies, PO Box 553, Canberra, ACT 2601. Research Officer (Ethnomusicol.): Dr. Alice Moyle.

Australian Music Examinations Board, c/o Univ. of WA, Redlands, WA 6009. Director: Wallace Tate.

Australian Music Publishers Association, 8th floor, 215-217 Clarence St., Sydney, NSW 2000. Secretary: A. J. Turner.

Australian Music Therapy Association, PO Box 161, Wahroonga, NSW 2076. President: Ruth Bright.

Australian National Council of Orff-Schulwerk Associations, c/o N Brisbane College of Advanced Education, PO Box 117, Kedron, Qld. 4031. President: K. Smith. Secretary: Bernie Hoesman.

Australian National Folk Trust, c/o Australia Council. Secretary: Jon Fogarty.

Australian Society for Keyboard Music, 9 Glenroy Ave., Middlecove, NSW 2068. Secretary: Julienne Horn.

Australian Society for Music Education, PO Box £°, Grosvenor St., Sydney, NSW 2000. Exec. Officer: Barbara Hamer.

Australian Society of Saxophonists, c/o Music Dept., Melbourne State College, 757 Swanston St., Carlton, Vic. 3053. President: Peter Clinch.

Australian String Teachers Association. F21/26 Raglan St., Mosman, NSW 2088. Treasurer: Raymond Jenkins.

Australian Tape Recording Society, PO Box 9, Crows Nest 2065. Secretary: D. N. James.

Australian Trumpet Guild, 170 Elizabeth St., Sydney, NSW 2000. President: Norman Harris.

Australian Youth Orchestra, Carclew Arts Centre, 11 Jeffcott Street, North Adelaide. South Australia 5006.

Bach Society of Queensland, Unit 5, 235 Cavendish Rd., Coorparoo, Brisbane, Qld. 4151. Secretary: Leonie Scotney.

Bartok Society of Australia, 5 Milner St., Mosman, NSW 2066. Secretary: W. Scarlett.

Centre for Aboriginal Studies in Music, 28 Twin St., Adelaide, SA 5000. Director of Music: L. Rankine.

Classical Guitar Society, 12 Benning Ave, Turramurra, NSW 2074.

Composers & Songwriters Guild of Australia, 19 Bickleighvale Rd., Mooroolbark, Vic. 3138. Secretary: Bruce Rowland.

Composers Guild of Australia, 3/4 Studley Avenue, Kew, Vic. 3201. Secretary: Claire Thonemann.

Dalcroze Society of Australia, 9 Grantham St., Burwood, NSW 2134. Secretary: Greta Deem.

Federated Music Clubs of Australia, Box 790 G.P.O., Sydney 2001. Secretary: Doris Shirley.

Federation of Australian Music Teachers' Associations, c/o NSW Conservatorium of Music, Macquarie St., Sydney, NSW 2000. Secretary: Noel Cislowski.

Fellowship of Australian Composers, Box 522 P.O. Strathfield NSW 2135. Secretary: Anne Carr Boyd.

Friends of the Australian Opera, Box J194, P.O., Brickfield Hill, NSW 2001. President: Carol Walton.

International Society for the Music Education, c/o Univ. of WA, Redlands, WA 6009. Treasurer: Prof. Frank Callaway.

International Trombone Association, 49 Coronga Crescent, Killara, NSW 2071. Secretary: Alan Mewett.

Jazz Action Society, PO Box N9, Grosvenor St., Sydney, NSW 2000.

Kodaly Institute, PO Box 110, Baulkham Hills, NSW 2153. Secretary: Gwen Rosen.

Music Arrangers' Guild of Australia, 10 Grange Avenue, Canterbury 3126. Secretary: Neil Whitford.

Musica da Camera, 73 Doyle Terrace, Chapman, ACT 2611. Manager: Don McFeat.

Musica Viva Australia, Musica Viva House, 68-70 Clarence St., Sydney, NSW 2000. Manager: Suzanne Gleeson.

Musicians' Union of Australia, 65 Wellington St., Windsor, Vic., 3181. General Secretary: D. A. Cushion.

Musicological Society of Australia, Union Box 300, Univ. of NSW, Music Dept., PO Box 1, Kensington, NSW 2033. Secretary: Dr. Michael Kassler.

National Band Council of Australia, Kincumber, 11 Mooramie Ave., Kensington, NSW 2033. Secretary: C. D. Goodchild.
National Lieder Society of Australia, 53 View St., Woollahra, NSW 2025. Secretary: Heather Snedden.
National Music Camp Association, Carclew Arts Centre, 11 Jeffcott St., North Adelaide, South Australia 5006. Administrator: Michael G. Elwood.
Organ Historical Trust of Australia, PO Box 200, Camberwell, Vic. 3124. Chairman: John Maidment.
Professional Musicians Association Cooperative Ltd., PO Box 48, Woollahra, NSW 2025. Secretary: Frank Norman.
Viola da Gamba Society of Australia, 12 Union St., Richmond, Vic. 3121. Organiser: Peter G. Kahane.

AUSTRIA

A.K.M., staatl.genehmigte Gesellschaft der Autoren, Komponisten und Musikverleger (Performing Right Society), Baumannstrasse 8-10, 1030 Vienna. Managing Director: Ernst Huemer.
Arbeitsgemeinschaft der Musikerzieher Österreichs, Landstr. 31, 4020 Linz. Secretary: Dr. Josef Mayr-kern.
Europäisches Lisztzentrum, Schloss Esterhazy, Eisenstadt.
Gesellschaft der Musikfreunder in Wien, Bösendorferstrasse 12, 1010 Vienna. Secretary: Prof. Rudolf Gamsjager.
Gewerkschaft Kunst Medien und Freie Berufe-Sektion Musiker, Maria Theresien-str. 11, 1090 Vienna. Secretary: Prof. Friedrich Gartner.
International Confederation of Music Publishers, Postfach 3, 1015 Vienna. General Secretary: Guy Kaufmann.
Internationale Bruckner Gesellschaft, Backerstr 18, 1010 Vienna.
Internationale Gesellschaft für Neue Musik, Hanuschgasse 3, 1010 Vienna. Secretary: Dr. Peter Burwik.
Internationale Gustav Mahler Gesellschaft, Wiedner Gurtel 6/2, 1040 Vienna. Secretary: Mrs. Emmy Hauswirth.
Internationale Richard Strauss Gesellschaft, Staatsoper, 1010 Vienna. Secretary: Dr. Gunter Brosche.
Internationale Hugo Wolf Gesellschaft, Backerstr. 18, 1010 Vienna.
Internationales Institut für Musik, Tanz und Theater, Metternichgasse 12, 1030 Vienna. Director: Kurt Blaukopf.
Internationales Musikzentrum Wien, Lothringerstr. 20, 1030 Vienna. Secretary-General: Dr. Wilfried Scheib. Executive Secretary: Dr. G. Rindauer.
Internationales Opernarchiv, Billrothstr. 74, 1190 Vienna. Secretary: C. M. Gruber.
Internationale Schönberg Gesellschaft, Ferdinand-Buchbergergasse 11, 2340 Mödling. General Secretary: Walter Szmolyan.
Musikalische Jugend Österreichs, Bösendorferstr. 12, 1010 Vienna. General Secretary: Dr. Thomas Angyar.
Österreichische Gesellschaft für Musik, Hanuschgasse 3, 1010 Vienna. Secretary: Dr. Harald Goertz.
Österreichischer Komponistenbund, Baumannstr. 8-10, 1031 Vienna. Secretary: Mrs. Vera Huemer.
Österreichischer Musikrat, Lothringerstr. 18, 1030 Vienna. Secretary: Dr. Sigrid Wiesmann.
Österreichischer Richard Wagner Verband, Kärtner Ring 10, Vienna. Franz Schmidt Gesellschaft, Postfach 9, 1014 Vienna. Secretary: Dr. Friedrich Jolly.
Johann Strauss Gesellschaft, Neues Rathaus, Vienna. Director: Prof. F. Salmhofer.
Wiener Beethoven Gesellschaft, Pfarrplatz 3, 1190 Vienna. President: Klemens Kramert.
Wiener Konzerthaus Gesellschaft, Lothringerstr. 20, 1030 Vienna. General Secretary: Dr. Hans Landesmann.

BELGIUM

Académie Royale des Sciences, des Lettres et des Beaux-Arts de Belgique, Palais des Académies, Rue Ducale 1, 1000 Brussels.
Association Franz Liszt de Belgique, 29 rue du College, 1050 Brussels. Secretary: Paul Raspe.
Peter Benoit-Fonds, c/o Maatschappij voor Dierkunde van Antwerpen, Koningin Astridplein 26, 2000 Antwerp.

Centre Belge de Documentation Musicale, rue de l'Hôpital 31, bte 2, 1000 Brussels. Secretary General: Miss Anna van Steenbergen.
Centre de Rechenche Musicale de Wallonie, Rue Forgeur 3, 4000 Liège.
Centre de Sociologie de la Musique, Ave. Jeanne 44, 1050 Brussels.
Centrum voor Muziekopvoeding Halewijnstichting, Van Putlei 33, 2000 Antwerp.
Cercle et Centre de Documentation Antonio Vivaldi, Rue Bosquet 12, 1060 Brussels.
Chambre Syndicale des Editeurs de Musique de Belgique, Rue Madeleine 13, 1000 Brussels.
Confederation Musicale de Belgique, Square P. Hauwaerts 10, 1140 Brussels.
Conseil National de Musique (National Committee of International Music Council), 11 rue Baron Horta, 1000 Brussels. Secretary: Hadelin Donnet.
Fédération Belge du Spectacle, Place Fontainas 9, Brussels. Secretary: F. van Stichel.
Fédération Internationale Jeunesses Musicales, Palais des Beaux-Arts, Rue Royale 10, 1000 Brussels. Secretary-General: Harald Kurth.
Fédération National Jeunesses Musicales, Palais des Beaux-Arts, Rue Royale 10, 1000 Brussels.
Internationale Heinrich Schütz Gesellschaft, Heistraat 86, 2700 Sint-Niklaas.
Musique Vivante, BP4, 6000 Charleroi IV. President: Claude R. Roland.
Radiodiffusion Television Belge, Place Eugéne Flagey 18, 1050 Brussels.
Ruckers Genootschap, Museum Vleeshuis, Vlieshouwersstraat 38-40, 2000 Antwerp.
Société Belge des Auteurs, Compositeurs et Editeurs, Rue d'Arlon 75-77, 1040 Brussels.
Société Belge de Musicologie, 30 rue de la Régence, 1000 Brussels. Secretary: Henri Vanhulst.
Société Internationale de Musique Contemporaine (Belgian Section of ISCM), Muinkkaai 45, 9000 Gent.
Société Liègeoise de Musicologie, Place du Vingt Août, 4000 Liège.
Studio de Musique Electronique, c/o APELAC, Place J. Jacobs 11, 1000 Brussels.
Union de la Presse Musicale Belge, Maison de la Presse, Blvd. Charlesmagne 1, 1040 Brussels.
Union des Compositeurs Belges, Avenue du Cor de Chasse, 1, 1170 Brussels. President: Willem Pelemans.
Union Wallonne des Organistes, Rue Romainville 26, 5228 Bas-Oha.
Vereniging voor Muziekgeschiedenis, Desguinlei 25, 2000 Antwerp.

BRAZIL

Associacäo de Canto Coral (Chorus Singing Association), Rua des Marrecas 40, 9 andar, Rio de Janeiro. President: Moacyr Villas-Boas.
Associacäo Nacional de Música (National Music Association), Av. Princesa Isabel 38, Apartment 603, Copacabana, Rio de Janeiro.
Consejo Internaciónal de Música (National Committee of the International Music Council), Palacio Itamarati, rua Marechal Floriano 196 (ZC-78), Rio de Janeiro. President: Renato Almeida.
Institute de Música da Bahia (Bahia Music Institute), Rua Carlos Gomes 101, Salvador, Bahia.
Institute Músical de São Paulo (Sao Paulo Music Institute), Ruados Est Volantes 32, Säo Paulo. Principal: Hercilia Castilho Gardosa.
Madrigal Renascentista Fundacão de Arte, Rua Gonçalves Dias 142-Sala 904, 30000 Bela Horizonte.
Movimento Candango de Musica Contemporanea, SQN 107/Bloco B/Apto. 104, 70000 Brasilia.
Ordem dos Músicos do Brasil (Order of Brazilian Musicians), Av. Almirante Barroso 72, 7 andar, Rio de Janeiro.
Sindicato dos Compositores, Artisticos, Musicais e Plásticos do Estado de São Paulo (Society of Composers, Musicians and Artists of São Paulo (Society of Composers, Musicians and Artists of Sao Paulo), São Paulo.
Sociedade Brasileira de Autores, Compositores e Editores de Musica (Brazilian Society of Authors, Composers and Editors of Music-a performing right society), Rua Buenos Aires 58, Rio de Janeiro. President: Mario Rossi.
Sociedade Brasileira de Realizaçoes Artistico Culturais (Brazilian Society for Artistic and Cultural Promotions), Av. F. Roosevelt 23, S/310, Rio de Janeiro. Secretary: Liana Nunes.
Uniao Brasileira de Compositores (Union of Brazilian Composers), Rua Visconde de Inhaurma 134, Rio de Janeiro.
Uniao dos Músicos do Brazil (Union of Brazilian Musicians), Av. Rio Branco 185, Rio de Janeiro.

BULGARIA

Institute of Musicology, Dimiter Paljanoff-str. 21, 1504 Sofia. Secretary: Prof. Agapia Balorieva.
International Music Council, Office of the Secretary General, 13-a Pencho Slaveykov Bld., 1606 Sofia. Secretary: Dr. Dimiter Christoff.
Jeunesses Musicales de Bulgarie, c/o Union of Musicians in Bulgaria.
Union of Bulgarian Composers, 2 Ivan Vazov Str. 1000 Sofia. Secretary: Jules Levi.
Union of Musicians in Bulgaria, 52 Alabin str., Sofia. Secretary: Prof. Alexander Nejnski.

CANADA

American Federation of Musicians, Suite 510, 207 W. Hastings St., Vancouver, B.C. V6B 1J6. President: Robert A. Reid.
American Federation of Musicians of the U.S. and Canada, 630 8th Avenue, Suite 703, Calgary 2, Alberta.
Alberta Registered Music Teachers' Association, 2807 Conrad Drive, N.W. Calgary, Alta., T2L 1B3. Secretary: Dawn Lhenen.
Association of Canadian Television and Radio Artists (ACTRA), 105 Carlton St., Toronto, Ontario M5B 1M2. General Secretary: Paul Siren.
Brantford Music Club, 64 Lorne Crescent, Brantford, Ont. N3T 4L7. Secretary: Mary Jane Mintern.
Association of Musicians in Quebec, 1406 St.-Cyrille O, Winnipeg.
Atlantic Federation of Musicians, 6307 Chebucto Road, Halifax, Nova Scotia.
BMI Canada Ltd., 41 Valleybrook Drive, Don Mills 405, Ontario. General Manager: Harold Moon.
British Columbia Registered Music Teachers' Association, 202-1488 Dallas Rd., Victoria, B.C. V8S 1A2. Secretary: S. G. Smillie.
Calgary Musicians' Association, Local 547, American Federation of Musicians, 703, 630-8th Avenue S.W. Calgary, Alberta T2P 1G6. Secretary-Treasurer: Ray Petch.
Canada Council, PO Box 1047, Ottawa, K1P 5V8. Director: Charles Lussier.
Canadian Amateur Musicians, PO Box 353, Westmount, Que. H3Z 2T5. Secretary: Rachel LaForest.
Canadian Association of Music Libraries, c/o Music Libraries, 559 Avenue Rd., Toronto, Ont.
Canadian Association of University Schools of Music, École de Musique, Université Laval, Que. President: Prof. Armand Ferland.
Canadian Band Directors' Association, 875 Kelley Avenue, London, Ontario. President: Martin Boundy.
Canadian Broadcasting Corporation, 354 Jarvis St., Toronto 116, Ontario.
Canadian Bureau for the Advancement of Music, Exhibition Place, Toronto, Ontario M6K 3C3. Managing Director: Lt. Col. C. O. Hunt.
Canadian Conference of the Arts, Suite 707, 141 Laurier St. W, Ottawa, Ont. K1P 5J3. Secretary: Gordon Johnston.
Canadian Federation of Music Teachers' Associations, 812 Haig Road, Ancaster, Ontario L9G 3G9. Secretary/Treasurer: Mrs. Doris Phillips.
Canadian Independent Record Production Association, 39 Hazelton Avenue, Toronto, Ontario M5R 2E3. Secretary: Arlene Ezrin.
Canadian League of Composers, 1263 Bay St., Toronto, Ontario. Secretary: Josette Fitch.
Canadian Music Centre, 1263 Bay St., Toronto, Ont. M5R 2C1. General Manager: John P. L. Roberts.
Canadian Music Council, 36 Elgin, Ottawa, Ont. R1P 5K5. Secretary: Guy Huot.
Canadian Music Educators' Association, C.M.E.A. Resource Centre, RR 2, Lakeshore Road, St. Catherines, Ontario, L2R 6P8. Executive Secretary: Wallace Laughton.
Canadian Music Publishers Association, 111 Avenue Rd., Toronto, Ont. M5R 3J8.
Canadian Recording Industry Association, 89 Bloor St. E, Toronto, Ont. M4W 1A9. Administrative Assistant: Daisy C. Falle.
Canadian Recording Manufacturers' Association, Room 618, 57 Bloor St., Toronto 189, Ontario. Secretary: A. L. Betts.
Centaur Foundation for Performing Arts, 454 St. Francois-Xavier, Montreal 125, Quebec.
Community Arts Council of Vancouver, 315 West Cordova St., Vancouver, B.C. V6B 1E5. Secretary: Miss Karen Pilkington.
Composers', Authors' and Publishers' Association of Canada, 1263 Bay St., Toronto 185, Ontario. General Manager: John V. Mills.
Edmonton Musical Club, 4903-114 St., Edmonton, Alberta. Secretary: Mrs. G. Schuler.

Federation of Canadian Music Festivals, 304-310 Donald St., Winnipeg, Manitoba R3B 2H4. Secretary: G. Murray Campbell.

Halifax Ladies' Musical Club, 1792 Oxford St., Halifax, Nova Scotia. Secretary: Mrs. H. A. MacDonald.

International Institute of Music of Canada, 106 Dulwich, St. Laurent, Quebec. Director: Monique Marcil.

International Society for Contemporary Music (Canadian Branch), 287 MacLaren, Suite 500, Ottawa, Ontario K2P OL9. Secretary: Guy Huot.

Jeunesses Musicales of Canada, 5253 Park Avenue, Suite 600, Montreal, Quebec H2V 4G9. Director: Jean-Claude Picard.

JMC Orford Arts Centre, PO Box 280, Magoq, Quebec. Director: Collette Maurice.

Jewish Women's Musical Club, 538 Atlantic Avenue, Winnipeg, Manitoba. Secretary: Mrs. D. Ferdman.

Ladies' Morning Musical Club, 1410 Guy St., Room 32, Montreal H3H 2L7. Secretary: Mme. Suzanne Gamache.

Musicians' Guild of Montreal, 1500 de Maisonneuve Blvd. East, Suite 201, Montreal, Quebec H2L 2B1. Secretary/Treasurer, Claude Landry.

Musiciens Educateurs du Quebec, 25 Chouinard, Suite 214, Hull, Quebec. Secretary: Constance Mainville.

National Arts Centre Corporation, Box 1534, Station 'B'. Ottawa, Ontario K1P 5W1. Secretary: Donald Stephenson.

New Brunswick Registered Music Teachers' Association, 72 Bridge St., Sackville, New Brunswick E0A 3C0. Secretary: Mrs. Vivien Hay.

Nova Scotia Registered Music Teachers' Association, R.R.2, Wolfville, Nova Scotia, Box 563, B0P 1X0. Secretary: Dr. Peter Riddle.

Ontario Registered Music Teachers Association, 27 Shirley Ave., Barrie, Ont. L4N 1M8. Secretary: June M. Melenbacher.

Quebec Registered Music Teachers' Association, 117 Taywood Drive, Beaconsfield, Quebec H9W 1A7. Secretary: Mrs. Margaret Ronald.

Regina Music Club, 4164 Princess St., Regina, Saskatchewan. Secretary: Mrs. J. Tureski.

Royal Canadian College of Organists, 300A-212 King St., W., Toronto, Ontario, M5H 1K5. Secretary: Mrs. Rita Carlson.

Saskatchewan Registered Music Teachers' Association, 819-11th St. E., Saskatoon, Saskatchewan S7N 0G7. Secretary: Miss Mary Friesen.

Saskatoon Women's Musical Club, 1340 Elliott St., Saskatoon, Saskatchewan. Secretary: Mrs. R. F. Schnell.

Société de musique contemporaine du Quebec, 4858 Côte-des-Neiges, app. 1403, Montreal, Quebec H3V 1G8. Secretary: Miss Louise Ostiguy.

Toronto Musicians' Association, 101 Thorncliffe Park Drive, Toronto, Ontario M1E 2K7. Secretary/Treasurer: Victor E. Bridgewater.

Vancouver Cello Club, 1407 Haywood Avenue, W. Vancouver, B.C. V7T 1V5. Secretary: Ernest S. Collins.

Vancouver Women's Musical Club, 717 Williams Road, Richmond, B.C. Secretary: Mrs. Patrick Killeen.

Wednesday Morning Musicale, 441 Cambridge St., Winnipeg 9, Manitoba. Secretary: Mrs. V. Fox.

Winnipeg Musicians' Association, 205 Confederation Building, Winnipeg, Manitoba.

Women's Association for Symphony Orchestras, 345 Redfern Avenue, Montreal, Quebec H3Z2G4. President: Mrs. Michael Bell.

Women's Musical Club of Toronto, 44 Glen Watford Drive, Agincourt, Ontario M1S 2C3. Secretary: Mrs. Sylvia G. MacMillarr.

Women's Musical Club of Winnipeg, 14 Birkenhead Avenue, Winnipeg, Manitoba R3P OP1. Secretary: Mrs. W. Reid Waters.

CHILE

Asociacion Interamericana de Directores de Coro, Casilla No. 3133, Santiago. Secretary-General: Waldo Aranguiz Thompson.

Centre of Professors of Musical Education, Casilla 2804, Santiago.

Choral Association of Chile, Casilla 1037 Correo 35, Santiago.

Federacion Nacional de Coros de Chile, Casilla 10473, Santiago. National President: Waldo Aranguiz Thompson.

Interamerican Institute of Musical Education, Agustinas 1572-B, Santiago. Director: Eliana Breitler.

International Music Council (National Committee), Casilla 10473, Santiago. Secretary General: Federico Heinlein.
Performing Right Society, San Antonio 427, 2 piso, Santiago. Director: Homero Zamorano Cubillos.
Sindicato Profesional Orquestal, Teatrinos 740, 3 = P, Casilla 14420, Santiago. Secretary: Benicio Sanchez Abarca.

COLOMBIA

Asociación Colombiana de Músicos Profesionales, Carrera 8 No. 11-15, Of. 202, Bogota.
Consejo Nacional de Música, Centro Administrativo Nacional, Edificio Mineducacion, p. 3, Bogota.
Sindicato Nacional de Trabajadores de la Música, Carrera 38, No. 44-7, Barranquilla. President: Dagoberto Almanza.

CUBA

Centro Nacional de Derecho de Autor, Calle Línea 365, esq.a G, El Vedado, Havana. Director: Miguel Cossio Woodward.
International Music Council, (National Committee), Avenida Kohly y 32, Nuevo Vedado, Havana 6. Executive Secretary: Odilio Urfe.
Juventudes Musicales de Cuba, Calle 32, No. 858, entrée 26J41, Nuevo Vedado, Havana 6. Director: M. Silvio Rodriguez.
Musical Institute of Cuba, On 56, Vedado, Havana.
National Music Direction, F y 9 Vedado, Havana 4. Director: Julio Bidopia.
National Music Seminar, Inglesia Iglesia de Paula, Avenida del Puerto, Havana 1. Director: Odilio Urfe.
National Union of Writers and Artists of Cuba (Music Section), 17 y H, Vedado, Havana 4. President: Jose Ardevol.

CZECHOSLOVAKIA

Authors' Association for Protection of Rights in Musical Works, Cš armády 20, 160 56 Prague 6. General Manager: Ivo Jirasek.
Association for the Protection of Performing Artists' Rights, Na Pořiči 27, Prague 1. Chairman: L. Slovák.
Czechoslovak Federal Committee of Cultural Unions, Gorkého nám. 23, Prague 1. Chairman: Václav Pubal.
Czech Music Foundation, Besedni 3, 118 00 Prague 1. Director: Vladimir Sevcik.
Czech Society for Chamber Music, Barrandov 327, 150 00 Prague. Chairman: Dr. Vladimír Čelakovský.
Guild of Czech Composers and Concert Artists, Valdštejnské nám. 1, 118 01 Prague. General Secretary: Dr. Václav Kučera.
International Music Council (National Committee), c/o Association of Czechoslovakian Composers, Valdštejnske nám. 1, Prague 1. Secretary: Ladislav Morkrý.
International Society for Contemporary Music (Czechoslovakian section), c/o Association of Czechoslovakian Composers, Valdštejnské nám. 1, Prague 1. Secretary: Dr. Václav Kučera.
Music Information Centre, Fučíkova 29, 801 00 Bratislava. Director: Jindra Felixová.
Music Information Centre of the Czech Music Foundation, Besední 3, 118 00 Prague 1. Director: Dr. Jan Ledeč.
Slovak Authors' Rights Union (Performing Right Society), Živnostenská ul.č.l, 883 27 Bratislava. Director: Andrej Gaduš.
Slovak Music Foundation, Fucikova 29, 801 00 Bratislava.
Union of Slovak Composers, Sládkovičova 11, 301 88 Bratislava. President: Eugen Suchoň.

DENMARK

ARTE (Concert organisation), Hvidkildevej 64, Copenhagen NV. Managing Director: Kjeld Hansen.
Association of Danish Music Librarians, Statsbibliotheket, 8000 Arhus.
Association of Music Publishers in Denmark, 9-11 Gothersgade, 1123 Copenhagen K. Chairman: Lone Wilhelm Hansen.

Association of Music Teachers in Secondary Schools, 'Solbakken', Lundum, 8700 Horsens, Denmark. Secretary: Knud Lindum Poulsen.
Association of Young Professional Musicians, Hammerensgade 3, Copenhagen K.
Choir Conductors' Association, Margrethevej 12, Rungsted Kyst. President: Cai Wendelboe-Jensen.
Church Music Circle, Bagsvaerdveg 147A, 2800 Lyngby. Secretary: Ulrich Teuber.
Danish Artists Federation, Vesterbrogade 31, Copenhagen 1620.
Danish Association of Authors and Composers of Revues, Strandvejen 67A, 2100 Copenhagen Ø. Secretary: Henrik Blichmann.
Danish Carl Nielsen Society, Royal Library, 8 Christians Brygqe, 1219 Copenhagen K. Secretary: Torben Schousboe.
Danish Choral Association, Grundtvigsvej 14a, Copenhagen V.
Danish Composers' Society, Valkendorfsgade 3, 1151 Copenhagen K. Secretary: Mrs. Käthie Kirk.
Danish Music Dealers' Association, Frederiksberg Alle 29, Copenhagen V.
Danish Music Educationalists' Association, Abildbardsparken 6, 3460 Birkerod. Contact: Birgitte Mandel.
Danish Musical Society, Radhusstraede 1, Copenhagen K. Secretary: S. Heering.
Danish Organists' and Precentors' Society, 147A Bagsvaerdveg, Kongens, Lyngby.
Danish Society of Composers, Authors and Editors of Music, Rosenvaengets Hovedvej 14, 2100 Copenhagen. Contact: E. Larsen.
Danish Society for Musicology, Åbenrå 34, 1124, Copenhagen K.
Danish Soloists' Association, Sundholmsvej 49, 2300 S Copenhagen. Secretary: Mrs. Helene Hartvig.
Dansk Kapelmesterfoérening, Rosenvangsvej 47, 2670 Greve Strand. Director: Robert Svanescøe.
Dansk Musikbiblioteksforening (Danish Branch of AIBM), c/o Royal Library, Christians Burgqe 8, 2119 Copenhagen K. Librarian: Birthe Heien.
Dansk Musiker Forbund, Vendersgade 25, 1363 Copenhagen K. Secretary: Mrs. N. Hansen.
Danske Populaerautorer (Danish Songwriters Guild), Strandvgen. 67A, 2100 Copenhagen Ø. Secretary: Henrik Blichmann.
Det Danske Selskab, Biblioteksgården 2, Kulturvet, 1175 Copenhagen K. Head of Administration: R. Ostenfeld.
International Music Council (National Committee), Nybrogade 2, 1203 Copenhagen K. Secretary: Steffen Heering.
International Society for Contemporary Music (Danish Section), Montergade 6a, 116 Copenhagen K. President: Peter Ernst Larsen.
International Society for Music Education, 133 Carinaparken, 3460 Birkerod. Secretary: Henning Bro Rasmussen.
International Antonio Vivaldi Society, Hyldegaards Tvaervej 45, 2920 Charlottenlund.
Kobenhavns Musiker og Orkesterforening, Vendersgade 23, 1363 Copenhagen. General Manager: Arne Spliid.
KODA (Performing Right Society), Rosenvaengets Hovedvej 14, 2100 Copenhagen Ø. President: Prof. H. Lund Christiansen.
Music Board, Ministeriet for kulturelle anliggender, Nybrogade 2, Copenhagen K.
Music and Youth, Hvidkildevej 64, 2400 Copenhagen NV. Secretary General: Kjeld Hansen.
Musical Artists Foundation, 7-9 V. Voldgade, Copenhagen V.
Musicological Institute, Copenhagen University, Klerkegade 2, Copenhagen K.
Samfundet tli Udgivelse of Dansk Musik (Music Information Centre), Grabrødretory 7, 1154 Copenhagen.
Société Internationale Antonio Vivaldi, c/o Instituto Italiano di Cultura, Gjoerlingsvej 11, 2900 Hellerup.
Society of Danish Church Singing, Lindevangsvej 4, 8240 Risskov.
Society for the Management of International Rights of Composers in Denmark, Rosenvaengets Hovedvej 14, 2100 Copenhagen Ø. Chairman: Flemming Weis.
Society for Publishing Danish Music, Valkendorfsgade 3, 1151 Copenhagen K. Secretary: Mrs. Käthie Kirk.
Soloists' Association, Frederiksberg alle 25, 1820 Copenhagen V. Chairman: Prof. A. Lund Christiansen.
Statens Musikråd (State Music Council), Nybrogade 2, 1203 Copenhagen K. Secretary: Lasse Lindhard.
Union of Danish Singers, Ørumsgade 30, 8000 Arhus.
Union of Danish Singing Teachers, Stalhojen 14, 8240 Risskov. Secretary: Ejnar Ege Moller.
Union of Music Teachers in Training, Jyllandsgade 48, 9520 Skørping. Secretary: Jorgen Ebbesen.
Young Musicians' Association, 6a Møntergade, Copenhagen K.

EGYPT

Egyptian Music Association, 9 Adly Pasha St., Cairo.
Higher Council for Arts, Literature and Social Science, 9 Hassan Sabri St., Zamalek, Cairo. Secretary: Mahmoud Kamel.
International Music Council (National Committee, 9 Hassan Sabri St., Zamalek, Cairo. General Secretary: Saraf Eddine Soliman.

EIRE

Arts Council, 70 Merrion Square, Dublin 2. Music Officer: Marion Creely.
Association of Irish Traditional Musicians, 32/33 Belgrave Square, Monkstown, Co. Dublin. General Secretary: John Keenan.
Association of Irish Musical Societies, Peira-Cava, Newtownpark Avenue, Blackrock, Co. Dublin. Secretary: Joyce Tunstead.
Association for the Promotion of Music in Education, 6 Derrynane Court, Donnybrook, Dublin 4. Secretary: Margaret Prandy.
Association of Young Irish Composers, 25 Flower Grove, Dun Laoghaire, Co. Dublin. Secretary: Brian Beckett.
Comhaltas Ceoltóirí Éireann (Traditional Irish singing and dancing society), 6 Harcourt St., Dublin 2. Secretary: Séan Ó Cianain.
Folk Music Society of Ireland, 157 Claremont Ct., Glasnevin, Dublin 11. Secretary: Nicholas Carolan.
International Heinrich Schütz Society, 4 Chelmsford Road, Dublin 6. Secretary: June Croker.
Irish Association of Brass & Military Bands, 50 Davitt Rd. S., Wexford. Secretary: M. Curran.
Irish Church Music Association, Milltown Park, Dublin 6. Secretary: Eoin Garrett S. J.
Irish Federation of Musicians and Associated Professions, Cecilia House, 63 Lower Gardiner St., Dublin 1. General Secretary: Jack Flahive.
Mechanical Copyright Protection Society, 15 Herbert St., Dublin 2. Manager: David Buskell.
Music Association of Ireland Ltd., 3 Suffolk St., Dublin 2. Secretary: Joan Cowle.
Performing Right Society Ltd., 4 Clare St., Dublin 2. Manager: Pat Condon.
Radio Telefís Éireann, Donnybrook, Dublin 4.
Society of Recorder Players, 110 Kincora Ave., Clontarf, Dublin 3. Secretary: Patricia Flanagan.

ETHIOPIA

International Music Council (National Committee, PO Box 704, Addis Ababa. President: Ashenafi Kebede.

FINLAND

Association of Finnish Music Institutes, Kampinaktu 8 C 30,00100 Helsinki 10. Secretary: Mrs. Outi Sipilä.
Association of Finnish Musical Artists, Tarkk'ampujankatu 14,00150 Helsinki 15. Secretary: Lassi Rajamaa.
Association of Finnish Soloists, Sepäankatu 19 A 26,00150 Helsinki 15. President: Kauko Kuosma.
Association of Finnish Symphony Orchestras, Kauppakatu 17 A 7,40100 Jyväsklyä 10. Executive Manager: Mrs. Anna-Maija Poussa.
Association of Military Conductors, Box 13,00251 Helsinki 25. Secretary: Bandmaster Jukka Vrolio.
Association of Swedish Speaking Church Musicians, Aningaisgatan 1 c 25, Abo. Secretary: Gunvor Helander.
Composers of Film and Popular Music, Runeberginkatu 15 A 11,00100 Helsinki 10. Secretary: Mrs. Taimi Kyyro.
Concert Centre, Kampinkatu 8 C 30,00100 Helsinki 10. Secretary: Miss Mirja Aro.
Finnish Composers' International Copyright Bureau, Lauttasaarentie A, 00200 Helsinki 20. Managing Director: Pekka Kallio.
Finnish Music Council, Finlandia-hall, 00100 Helsinki 10. Secretary: Mrs. Helena Kuoppamäki.
Finnish Music Information Centre, Runeberginkatu 15 A 1,00100 Helsinki 10. Secretary: Kauko Karjalainen.

Finnish Musicians' Union, Undenmaankatu 36 D 21,00120 Helsinki 12. General Secretary: Raimo Vikström.

Foundation for the Promotion of Music in Finland, Piluittärenpolku 7, 02100 Esjoo 10. Secretary: Veikko Katajainen.

International Musical Council (National Committee), Kampinkatu 8 C 30,00100 Helsinki 10. Secretary: Miss Mirja Aro.

Internatonal Society for Contemporary Music (Finnish Section), c/o Finnish Broadcasting Company, Fabianinkatu 15,00130 Helsinki 13. Secretary: Mrs. Sisko Ramsay.

Music Educators' Union of Finland, Frederikinkatu 61A, 3rd Floor, 00100 Helsinki 10. Bureau Chief: Anitta Rissanen.

Musicological Society of Finland, Lyhdekuja 1 D, 02200 Nittykumpu. Secretary: Teuvo Väätainen.

Jean Sibelius Society, Pohjoinen Rautatiekatu 9,00100 Helsinki 10. Chairman: M. Raatikainen.

Society of Finnish Composers, Kampinkatu 8 C 30,00100 Helsinki 10. Secretary: Miss Mirja Aro.

Turko Music Society, Sibelius Museum, Piispankatu 17, Turku. Secretary: Heikki Lang.

Union of Finnish Music Associations, Runeberginkatu 15 A 11, 00100 Helsinki 10. Secretary: Mrs. T. Kyyrö.

FRANCE

Les Amis de l'Orgue, 52 rue Boileau, 75016 Paris. Secretary General: Pierre Denis.

Association des Choeurs et Organistes Liturgiques de France, 30 rue de Toulouse, 35400 Saint-Malo.

Association Européene des Directeurs de Bureaux de Concerts et Spectacles, 11 ave. Delcassé, 75008 Paris. Secretary: Michael Rainer.

Association Française pour la Propagande de la Musique, 107 rue du Cherche-Midi, 75006 Paris. President: Pierre d'Arquennes.

Association Française pour la Recherche et la Creation Musicales, 9 rue Chaptal, Paris 9e. Secretary: André Jauve.

Association Générale des Musiciens Aveugles, 5 rue Duroc, 75007 Paris. Secretary: M. Bonamy.

Association Nationale des Directeurs d'Écoles de Musique, Conservatoire Régional de Reims, 14 rue Carnot, 51000 Reims. President: Jacques Murgier.

Association Nationale de Formation des Organistes Liturgiques, Square Albert 1er, 62000 Arras. Secretary: Abbé Podevin.

Association des Professeurs d'Education Musicale de l'Enseignement Catholique, École Sainte-Marie, Beauchamps-Ligny, 59134 Fournes-en-Weppes.

Association des Professeurs d'Education Musicale de l'université, 135 rue Blomet, 75015 Paris. President: Mlle. Levallous.

Centre Européen d'échange Musical, 3 rue Pauline, 94 Fontenay-sous-Bois. President: Pierre Hoste.

Centre 'France Lyrique', 6 ave. Pierre 1er de Serbie, 75116 Paris. Director: Robert Geay.

Centre d'Information et d'Action Musicales, 6 ave. Pierre 1er de Serbie, 75116 Paris. Contact: Anne Chiffert.

Centre National de Pastorale Liturgique, 4 ave. Vavin, 75006 Paris. Secretary: Rev. Daniel Milon.

Chambre Syndicale des Éditeurs de Musique, 175 rue St. Honoré, 75001 Paris. President: Claude A. Leduc.

Chambre Syndicale des Administrateurs de Concerts de France, 252 rue du Faubourg Saint-Honoré, 75008 Paris. Secretary: R. de Saint-Ours.

Comité National de la Musique, 252 rue du Faubourg Saint-Honoré, 75008 Paris. Secretary General: Jacques Masson-Forestier.

Confédération Internationale des Sociétés d'Auteurs et Compositeurs, 11 rue Keppler, 75116 Paris. Secretary General: Jean-Alexis Ziegler.

Confédération Musicale de France, 121 rue Lafayette, 75010 Paris. Secretary: Claude Quemy.

Conseil International de la Musique (National Committee), 252 rue du Faubourg Saint-Honoré, 75008 Paris. General Secretary: Raymond Lyon.

Conseil International de la Musique Populaire, Palais de Chaillot, 75016 Paris. President: Mme. Claudil Dubois.

Fédération Française des 'Pueri Cantores', 1 rue Garaucière, 75006 Paris. Secretary: Père Jean Valentin.

Fédération Musicale Populaire, 13 rue de Montyon, 75009 Paris. Secretary: Emmanuel Jacquin.

Fédération Nationale d'Associations Culturelles d'Expansion Musicale, 23 rue Asseline, 75014 Paris. President: Jacques Serres.

Fédération Nationale des Industries et Commerce de la Musique, 1 rue de Courcelles, 75008 Paris.

Fédération Nationale de la Musique, 1 rue de Courcelles, 75008 Paris. Secretary General: Pierre Chesnais.

Groupe des Instruments Anciens de Paris, 8 rue de Kabylie, 75019 Paris.

Guilde Française des Artistes Soloistes, 37 rue du Général Foy, 75008 Paris. General Secretary: Mme. Janine Weill.

Institut de Musicologie, 3 rue Michelet, 75006 Paris. President: Jacques Chailley.

Institut de Musique Liturgique, 21 rue d'Assas, 75270 Paris. Director: Jean Bihan.

International Music Council (with UNESCO), Unesco House, 1 rue Miollis, 75732 Paris. Secretary-General: Prof. Tibor Sarai. Exec. Secretary: Jack Bornoff.

Jeunesse et Musique, 107 ave. de Villiers, 75017 Paris. President: Armand Ferté.

Jeunesses Musicales de France, 14 rue François Miron. 65008 Paris. Director-General: Jean-Pierre de Lavigne Les Musicoliers, 6 ave. Pierre 1er de Serbie, 75116 Paris. Director: Philippe Gondamin.

Music Information Centre, Bibliothèque Musicale, 116 ave. due Président Kennedy, 65016 Paris. Director: Henri Courbon.

Ordre des Musiciens, 121 rue Lafayette, Paris 10e. Secretary General: Mme. Viguié.

Société pour l'Administration du Droit de Reproduction Mécanique des Auteurs, Compositeurs et Editeurs, 225 ave. Charles-de-Gaulle, 92521 Neuilly sur Seine. Director General: Jean Ferraton.

Société des Amis de la Musique, 24 rue de la Mésange, 67000 Strasbourg. Secretary: Albert Weber.

Société des Auteurs, Compositeurs et Éditeurs de Musique (SACEM), 225 ave. Charles-de-Gaulle, 92251 Neuilly sur Seine. President: Georges Auric.

Société Française de Musicologie, 2 rue Louvois, 75002 Paris. Secretary: Dr. Marc Honegger.

Société Internationale de la Musique Contemporaine (French Section) Bureau de Concerts Marcel de Valmalete, 7-11 ave. Delcassé, 75008 Paris. President: Henri Martelli.

Société Nationale de Musique, Bureau de Concerts Marcel de Valmalete, 11 ave. Delcassé, 75008 Paris. Secretary General: Henri Martelli.

Syndicat National des Artistes Musiciens, 21 bis rue Victor-Masse, 75009 Paris. Secretary General: Jean Berson.

Syndicat National des Auteurs et Compositeurs, 80 rue Taitbout, 75442 Paris. General Secretary: Roger Fernay.

Le Triptyque (Association de Musique Contemporaine), 107 rue du Cherche-Midi, 75006 Paris. President: Pierre d'Arquennes.

Union Européene des Écoles de Musique, c/o Musique et Instruments, 39 rue du Général Foy, 75008 Paris.

Union Fédérale Française de Musique Sacrée, 6 ave. Vavin, 75006 Paris. Secretary: Abbé Sebastien Deyrieux.

Union Internationale des Éditeurs (Section de Musique), 4 Place de la Madeleine, 75008 Paris. General Secretary: G. Kaufmann.

Union des Sociétés Musicales de Paris, 45 rue Clisson, 75013 Paris.

GERMAN DEMOCRATIC REPUBLIC

Akademie der Künste der DDR (Sektion Musik), Robert-Koch-Platz 7, 104 Berlin. Secretary of Music Section: Siegfried Matthus.

Anstalt zur Wahrung der Aufführungsrechte auf dem Gebiete der Musik, Storkower Strasse 134,1055 Berlin. Director General: Klaus Eisenbarth.

Arbeitsgemeinschaft der Musikverleger der DDR, Deutscher Verlag für Musik, Karlstr. 10,701 Leipzig. President: Dr. Helmut Zeraschi.

Internationaler Musikrat (National Committee), Leipzigerstr. 26, 108 Berlin. Secretary: Vera Reiner.

Nationales Zentrum Musikerziehung der DDR, Leipzigerstr. 26,108 Berlin. President: Paul Michel.

Verband Deutscher Komponisten und Musikwissenschaftler, Leipzigerstr. 26, 108 Berlin. Secretary: Wolfgang Lesser.

Zentrale Arbeitsgemeinschaft für Instrumentalmusik beim Zentralhaus für Kulturarbeit, Dittichring 4,701 Leipzig. Secretary: Helmut Grimmer.

Zentralhaus für Kulturarbeit der DDR, Dittrichring 4,701 Leipzig. Secretary: Helmut Grimmer.

Zentralinstitut für Musikforschung, Leipzigerstr. 26,108 Berlin. Director: Konrad Neimann.

GERMAN FEDERAL REPUBLIC

Allgemeiner Cäcilien-Verband, Kölnstr. 415, 53 Bonn. Secretary: Dr. Peter Lambertz.

Arbeitsgemeinschaft deutscher Blasmusik, Albstr. 10,7209 Gosheim u Spaichingen. President: Eugen Weber.

Arbeitsgemeinschaft der Direktoren der stadtischen Musikhochschulen, Escherhaimerlandstr. 33,6000 Frankfurt/Main. Chairman: Philipp Möhler.

Arbeitsgemeinschaft Musik in der evangelischen Jugend, Am Tiasbusch 5, 3542 Willingen (Upland)-Stryck. Director: Jochen Schwarz.

Arbeitsbemeinschaft der Musikdozenten an Pädagogischen Hochschulen, Sültenweg 57,3140 Lüneberg. Chairman: Gottfried Küntzel.

Arbeitsgemeinschaft der Musikpädagogischen Seminare, Karlstr. 2,7217 Trossingen. Chairman: Guido Waldmann.

Arbeitskreis für Musik in der Jugend, Hoffman-von-Fallerslebenstr. 8,3340 Wolfenbüttel. General Secretary: Mrs. Elke Jacobs.

Arbeitskreis für Schulmusik und allgemeine Musikpädagogik, Gründgensstr. 16,200 Hamburg 80. Federal Chairman: Dr. Werner Krützfeldt.

Bund Deutscher Liebhaberorchester, Stadtländerstr. 21,2800 Bremen 33. Secretary: Dr. Wolfgang Schäfer.

Bundersverband der Deutschen Musikinstrumenten-Herstelle, Bockenheimer Anlage 1a,6000 Frankfurt/Main. Secretary: Notker Anton.

Bundersverband Schallplatte, Katherinenstr. 11,2000 Hamburg 11. Chairman: Ladislaus Veder.

Deutsche allgemeiner Sängerbund, Marienstr. 16,3000 Hanover. Chairman: Willi Voss.

Deutsche Gesellschaft fur Musik des Orients, Drümmerstr. 48,1 Berlin 33. Chairman: Dr. Artur Simon.

Deutsche Harmonika-Verband, Haldeleweg 10,7204 Wurmlingen/Krs. Tuttlingen. President: Joseph Zepf.

Deutsche Mozart-Gesellschaft, Karlstr. 6,8900 Augsburg. Secretary: Mathilde Steiner.

Deutsche Orchestervereinigung, Charlotte-Niese-Strasse 8,2000 Hamburg 52. Secretary: Dr. Peter Girth.

Deutsche Sängerbund, Bernhardstr. 166,5000 Cologne. President: Walter Weidmann.

Deutscher Komponisten-verband, Bergengruenstr. 28,1000 Berlin 38. Director: Mrs. Marianne Augustin.

Deutscher Musikrat (National Committee of the International Music Council), Michaelstr. 4a,5300 Bonn-Bad Godesberg. Contact: Dr. Gojouy.

Deutscher Musikverleger-verband, Friedrich Wilhelmstr. 31,5300 Bonn. Secretary: Dr. Hans-Henning Wittgen.

Deutscher Musikverband in der Gewerkschaft Kunst, Besenbinderhof 67, 2000 Hamburg 1. Chairman: Willi Suhr.

Europäische Föderation Junger Chöre, Sonnhalde 48, 7803 Gundelfinger, Stupferich. General Secretary: Christoph Kühlewein.

Fachgruppe 'Freie musikwissenschaftliche Forschungsinstitute', Blumenthalstr. 23,5000 Cologne 1. Secretary: Dr. Georg Feder.

GEMA - Gesellschaft für Musikalische Aufführungs-und mechanische Vervielfaltigungsrechte (Performing Right Society), Bayreutherstr. 37-38, 1000 Berlin. General Manager: Dr. Erich Schulze.

Gemeinschaft deutscher Musikverbände, Friedrich-Wilhelmstr. 31,5300 Bonn. Secretary: Dr. Hans-Henning Wittgen.

Gesamtverband Deutscher Musikfachgeschäfte, Friedrich-Wilhelmstr. 31,5300 Bonn. Secretary: Dr. Hans-Henning Wittgen.

Gesellschaft für Musikforschung, Heinrich-Schütz-Allee 35,3500 Kassell-Wilhelmshöhe. Secretary: Mrs. Elisabeth Wenzke.

Gesellschaft für Neue Musik Mannheim, Staatl. Musikhochschule L15,16,6800 Mannheim. Secretary: Prof. Hermann Fischer.

Institut für Neue Musik und Musikerziehung, Grafenstr. 26,6100 Darmstadt. Secretary: Mrs. Werner.

International Institute for Comparative Music Studies & Documentation, Winklerstr. 20,1000 Berlin 33. Secretary: Dr. Rudolf Heinemann.

Internationale Gesellschaft für neue Musik (National Section of the International Society for Contemporary Music), Nieder-Ramstädterstr. 190,6100 Darmstadt. Secretary: Ernst Thomas.

International Vereinigung der Musikbibliotheken, Deutsches Rundfunkarchiv, Bertramstr. 8,6000 Frankfurt/Main 1. Secretary General: Harald Heckmann.
Internationales Musikinstitut Darmstadt, (Music Information Centre), Nieder-Ramstädterstr. 190,6100 Darmstadt. Director: Ernst Thomas.
Konferenz der Leiter Katholischer kirchen-musikalischer Ausbildungs-statten Deutschlands, St. Ingberterstr. 84,6600 Saarbrücken 3. Chairman: Hans Lonnendonker.
Musikalische Jugend Deutschland, Marktplatz 12, 6992 Weikersheim. Secretary-General: Jörg Steidl.
Verband der Deutscher Konzertdirektion, Geisbergstr. 40, 1 Berlin 30.
Verband Deutscher Musikerzieher und Konzertierender Künstler, Hirschgartenallee 19,8000 Munich 19. President: Dr. Eckart Rohlfs.
Verband Deutscher Oratorien und Kammerchöre, Kempenerstr. 5, 4060 Viersen 12. Secretary: Heribert Allen.
Verband Deutscher Schulmusikzieher, Weihergarten 5,6500 Mainz. Secretary: Bertold Marohl.
Verband Evangelischer Kirchenchöre Deutschlands, Königstr. 28,3205 Bockenem 1. Chairman: Dr. Hans-Christian Dromann.
Verband Evangelischer Kirchenmusiker Deutschlands, Domplatz 5,6720 Speyer. President: Erich Hübner.
Wergemeinschaft Lied und Musik, Am Carl-Mosterts-Platz 1, 4000 Düsseldorf. Chairman: Gunter Bernert.

GHANA

Brass Bands' Union, c/o Arts Council of Ghana, 28th February Road, PO Box 2738, Accra.
Church Choirs' Union, c/o Arts Council of Ghana, 28th February Road, PO Box 2738, Accra.
Copyright Owners' Protection Society, PO Box 5206, Accra. Secretary: James D. Mason.
Dance Bands' Union, c/o Arts Council of Ghana, 28th February Road, PO Box 2738, Accra.
Ghana Music Teachers' Association, c/o National Academy of Music, PO Box 25, Winneba. National Secretary: George K. Ogbe.
Guitar Bands' Union, c/o Arts Council of Ghana, 28th February Road, PO Box 2738, Accra.
International Music Council (African Regional Secretariat), Institute of African Studies, Univ. of Ghana, PO Box 73, Legon. Secretary: Ms. Nyamafo Chapman Nyaho.
National Music Association, Arts Council of Ghana, 28th February Road, PO Box 2738, Accra. Secretary: S. Geoffrey Boateng.
Singing Bands' Union, c/o Arts Council of Ghana, 28th February Road, PO Box 2738, Accra.
Traditional Musicians' Association, c/o Arts Council of Ghana, 28th February Road, PO Box 2738, Accra.

GREECE

Hellenic Association for Contemporary Music.
International Society for Contemporary Music (Greek Section).
Documentation Centre for Contemporary Greek Music.
Electronic Music Studio, 8 Patroou St., and 25 Mitropoleos St., Athens 118. General Secretary: John G. Papaioannou.
Federation of Music Associations of Greece, 3 Averoff St., Athens.
Hellenic Society for the Protection of Authors' Rights, 14 rue Deligianni, Athens 148. Contact: C. Kyprianos.
International Music Council (National Committee), 38 Mitropoleos St., Athens. General Secretary: Theodoros Karyotakis.
Jeunesses Musicales de Greece, 11-13 Rue Aristoyitonos, Athens 112. Secretary-General: Maria Gazis.
League of Greek Composers, 38 Metropoleos St., Athens. Secretary: Dr. Costa-Notis Santorineo.
Pan-Hellenic Musical Association, Odos Halkokondyli 24, Athens. General Secretary: Costas Clavvas.
Society of Skalkottas' Friends, 7 Mourouzi St., Athens 138. General Secretary: John G. Papaioannou.
Society of Teachers of Recognised Schools of Music, Ipirou 41, Athens 109. Secretary: Prof. Panayotis Tsakarisianos.
Studio of Contemporary Music, Goethe Institute, 14 Phidiou St., Athens 142. Adviser and Co-founder: John G. Papaioannou.
Union of Greek Musicians, 38 Mitropoleos St., Athens.

GUATEMALA

Asociación Alejandro von Humboldt, 10 calle 152, Zona 1.
Consejo Nacional de Musica de Guatemala, 3a Av 4-61, Zona 1.

HONG KONG

Composers & Authors Society of Hong Kong, Room 1217, Hong Kong Arts Centre, Harbour Rd., Hong Kong. Secretary: Chong Kou-Li.
Hong Kong Music Society, 10th floor, 124 Temple St. Director: Yuen Siu Fai.
Hong Kong Musicians' Union, Marador Mansions, 7th floor, A1, 54 Nathan Road, Kowloon.
Hong Kong Schools Music and Speech Association, 4/F Kam Chung Building, 54 Jaffe Rd., Wanchai. Secretary: Mrs. Valerie J. Fry.
Performing Right Society Ltd., Room 304, Lansing House, 41–47 Queen's Road Central. Agent: David K. W. Wong.
Yuet Sing Musician Association, 2nd floor, 124 Temple St., Yaumati, Kowloon. Secretary: Fung Wah.

HUNGARY

ARTISJUS, Hungarian Office for Copyright Protection, P.B.67, Vörösmarty tér 1,1364 Budapest. General Manager: Dr. István Timár.
Association of Hungarian Musicians, PO Box 47, Vörösmarty tér 1, 1364 Budapest. Secretary General: Prof. István Lang.
Council of Hungarian Choirs, Vörösmarty tér 1, 1364 Budapest. General Secretary: Gyula Maróti.
Institute of Musicology of the Hungarian Academy of Sciences, Országházu. 9,1014, Budapest. Director: Dr. Zoltán Falvy.
International Concert Management, 'Interconcert', Vörösmarty tér 1, 1364 Budapest. Director General: József Horváth.
International Music Council (National Committee), Vörösmarty tér 1, 1364 Budapest. General Secretary: Tibor Sárai.
International Society for Contemporary Music (Hungarian Section), Vörösmarty tér 1,1364 Budapest. General Secretary: Tibor Sarái.
Ferenc Liszt Society, Liszt Ferenc tér 8,1061 Budapest. General Secretary: M. Forral.
Music Information Centre, c/o Association of Hungarian Musicians.
Union of Hungarian Musicians, Gorkijfasor 38,1068 Budapest. Secretary: Mrs. Ibolya Balázs.
Youth and Music of Hungary, c/o Interconcert, Postafiok 239,1368 Budapest. Secretary-General: Tamas Kleniansky.

ICELAND

Félag tonlistar-kennara, Bragagötu 16, Reykjavik. Secretary: Arndis Steingrimsdottir.
Iceland Composers' Society, c/o Bandalag Islenskra Listamanna, PO Box 629 Reykjavík.
Iceland Music Information Centre, Freyjugata 1, PO Box 978 121 Reykjavik. Secretary: Thorkell Sigurbjörnsson.
Icelandic Musicians' Union, Laufásvegur 40, Reykjavík. General Secretary: Sverrir Gardarsson.
International Music Council (National Committee), PO Box 495, Reykjavík. Secretary: Thorkell Sigurbjörnsson.
International Society for Contemporary Music (Icelandic Section), Tonskaldafelag Islands, Laufasvegur 40, Reykjavík. Secretary: Thorkell Sigurbjörnsson.
Reykjavík Music Society, Gardastraeti 17, Reykjavík.
Society of Icelandic Musicians, Dalsel 8, Reykjavík. Chairman: Halldor Haraldsson.
Union of Authors and Copyright Owners, Laufásvegur 40, Reykjavík. General Manager: S R Petursson.

INDIA

Indian Music Association, Lucknow.
Indian Performing Right Society, Ltd., A-12, Meherinia, Nepean Road, Bombay 400036. Secretary: B Kaicker.

International Cultural Centre, 16 Hailey Road, New Delhi. Secretary: Mrs. Madhun Dayal.
National Centre for the Performing Arts, Nariman Point, Bombay 400 021. Executive Director: Dr. Narayana Menon.
Performing Right Society, 26 Chowringhee Road, Calcutta 13.
Sangit Mahabharati (Organisation for Research & Training in Performing Arts of India), A/6 10th Road, Juhu Scheme, Vile Parle (West), Bombay 400 049. Founder-Director: Shri Nikhil Ghosh.

INDONESIA

Federation for Cultural Co-operation, Djalan Gudjah Mada 13, Bandung.
International Music Council (National Committee), 60 dj H. A. Salim, Djakarta. Secretary: Bernard Suryabrata.

IRAN

International Music Council (National Committee), c/o 182 av. Hoghoughi, Tehran.
Jeunesse Musicales d'Iran, 43 Ave. Iranshahr, Tehran 15.
Ministry of Culture and Arts, Kamalolmolk St., Tehran.
National Iranian Radio and Television, Pahlavi Road, Jame Jam Avenue, PO Box 33-200, Tehran.
Music Council of Radio Iran, Maidan Ark, Tehran.

IRAQ

Institute of Fine Arts (Dept. of Music), PO Box 402, Baghdad. Director: Sekman Shukur Daood.
Iraqi Musicians Association, Nidhal Str. No. 204, PO Box 2444, Baghdad. Secretary: Riad Arthur Gilder.
Iraqi National Council of Music (National Committee of the International Music Council), PO Box 402, Baghdad. Secretary: Adjulwahab Bilal.

ISRAEL

Authors', Composers' and Music Publishers' Society (ACUM), Ltd., Rothschild Blvd 118-120, Tel-Aviv. Secretary: Jochanan Ben-David.
International Music Council (National Section), POB 176, Jerusalem. Secretary: Dr. J. Hirshberg.
International Society for Contemporary Music (National Section). c/o Israel Composers' League, Tel-Aviv.
Israel Composers' League, PO Box 11180, Tel Aviv. Chairman: Prof. Tzvi Avni.
Israel Music Institute, PO Box 11253, Tel-Aviv. Director: William Elias.
Jeunesses Musicales d'Israel, F. R. Mamm Auditorium, PO Box 11292, Tel-Aviv. Secretary: Moshe Hoch.
National Union of Musicians in Israel, General Federation of Labour in Eretz-Israel, 93 Arlossoroff St. National Secretary: Isaac Litvak.

ITALY

Gioventù Musicale d'Italia, 13 Corso Vittorio Emmanuele II, 20122 Milan. Executive Secretary: Giuseppe Colombo.
International Centre of Sacred Music, Piazza S. Agostino 20/A Rome. President: Jacques Chailley.
International Centre of Studies for the Diffusion of Italian Music, Via dei Greci 18, Rome.
International Music Council (National Committee), c/o Comitato Nazionale dell'UNESCO, Piazza Firenze 27, 00186 Rome. Secretary: Firmino Sifonia.
International Society for Contemporary Music (Italian Section), Via Vipiteno 15, 00135 Rome. President: Mario Peragallo.
Instituto Musicale 'Luisa d'Annunzio (Music Information Centre), Via Leopoldo Muzii 7, 65100 Pescara.
Italian Association of Music Publishers, Piazza del Liberty 2, 20121 Milan. Secretary: Emanuele Daniele.

Italian Institute for the History of Music, Via Vittoria 6, 00187 Rome. President: Prof. Luigi Ronga.
Italian Musical Syndicate, Via de Villa Albani 8,00198 Rome. Secretary: Prof Carlo Marinelli.
Italian Society of Authors and Editors, Viale della Letteratura 30, Rome. General Manager: Luigi Conte.
Italian Society for Musicology, Via del Conservatorio 2, Parma. Secretary: Maripiera Mantovani.
Italian Union for Performing Artists, Via Tacito 10,00193 Rome. Secretary General: Arturo Abba.
Jeunesse Musicales of Italy, Via dei Greci 18,00187 Rome. President: Giovanni Elkan.
National Music Syndicate, Via Palestro 36, Rome.

JAMAICA

Jamaican Federation of Musicians, PO Box 24, Kingston 3. Secretary: Tony Wilson.
Jamaican Federation of Musician's Unions, 38 Smith Lane, Kingston.
Jamaican Festival Commission, 5 Belmont Road, Kingston 5. Secretary: Mrs. Thelma Campbell.
Performing Right Society Ltd., 36 Duke St., Kingston. Agent: Donald S. Scott.

JAPAN

Agency for Cultural Affairs, 3-2-2 Kasumigaseki, Chiyoda-ku, Tokyo.
Classical Music Society, 145 Umegaoka, Setegaya-ku, Tokyo 154. Contact: Juro Milame.
Council of Music Education, c/o Musashino University of Music, 1013 Hazawa, Nerima-ku, Tokyo 176.
Japan Academy of Arts, Ueno Park, Tokyo 110.
Japanese Musicological Society, c/o Tokyo University of Arts, Ueno Park, Taito-ku, Tokyo. Secretary: Prof. Keiichiro Watanabe.
Japanese National Committee of the International Music Council (UNESCO), 33 Shinanomachi, Shinjuku-ku, Tokyo PC160. Secretary-General: Kunio Toda.
Japanese Recital Musicians' League, Dai Schichi Building, 1-3 Ginza, Tokyo 104.
Japanese Section of International Society for Contemporary Music ISCM), 31-9, 3 chome, Kasugacho, Nerima-ku, Tokyo 176. Secretary: Dr. Yori-Aki Matsudaira.
Japanese Society of Rights of Authors and Composers (Performing Right Society), JASRAC House, 7-13, 1-chome Nishishimbashi, Minato-ku, Tokyo 105. Manager, International Department: Hiroaki Miyazawa.
Minon Concert Association, 1-32-13 Kitashinjuku, Shinjuku-ku, Tokyo 160. Senior Managing Director: Kimitsune Anekoji.
Seishonen Ongaku Nihon Rengo (Youth & Music), c/o Kyodo Building, 41-1 Udagawa-cho, Shibuya-ku, Tokyo. Secretary-General: Akira Masuyama.
Society for Research in Asiatic Music, c/o Ishikawa, 4-17-8 Jungu-mai, Shibuya-ku, Tokyo 150. Secretary: Dr. Goro Kakinoki.

JORDAN

Culture and Arts Department, PO Box 6140, Amman.

KOREA

Korean Musicians' Union c/o General Federation of Literature and Arts of Korea, Pyongyang, North Korea.
National Classical Music Institute, San 14-67 Changchung-dong 2-ka Chung-ku, Seoul, South Korea. Director: Dr. Bang-song Song.
Music Association of Korea (National Committee of the International Music Council, FACO Building, Room 303, 81-6 Sechongro, Chongro-ku, Seoul 110, South Korea. President: Sang Hyun Cho.
Youth & Music, PO Box 4143, Seoul. Secretary-General: Lee Sang-Mun.

LEBANON

Institute of Musicology, University of Saint-Esprit of Kaslik, Jounieh.
International Music Council (National Committee), Academie Libanaise, 221 rue Mousseibeth, Beirut. Contact: Alexis Boutros.
Jeunesses Musicales du Liban, c/o Hotel Carlton, Beyrouth. President: Antoine Medawar.

LUXEMBOURG

International Confederation of Popular Societies of Music, 23A rue des Ardennes. General Secretary: Yvron Christnach.

International Music Council (National Committee), rue des Romains, Bertrange. Secretary: Edmond Cigrand.

Jeunesses Musicales de Luxembourg, 18 place d'Armes, Luxembourg-ville. Secretary-General: Jean-Pierre Oestreicher.

MADAGASCAR

International Music Council (National Committee), Dept. des Arts, Ministere des Affaires Culturelles, 55 rue Romain Desfosses, Tananarive. Secretary General: Sylvestre Randafison.

MALTA

Guild of Maltese Composers and Authors, 111/5 Lucia St., Valetta. General Secretary: F. X. Pisani.

Malta Cultural Institute (Dept. of Music).

MEXICO

Association of Friends of Music, Culiacan, Sin.

International Music Council (National Committee), c/o Dept. de Musica, Instituta de Belles Artes, Dolores 2, Mexico 1 DF. Secretary: Hector Quintanar.

Juventudes Musicales de Mexico, Santisimo 25, Mexico 20 DF. President: Dolores Carrillo.

National Institute of Fine Arts and Literature, Dept. of Music, Palacio de Belles Artes, Mexico 1 DF. Promotions Chief: Carola Rodriquez Zozaya.

Sociedad de Autores y Compositores de Musica, San Felipe 143, Co. General Anaya, Mexico 13, DF. Director General: Carlos Gomez Barrera.

MONACO

Comité National de la Musique, (Monaco Section of International Music Council) Ministère d'Etat - Monaco - Ville. Secretary General: Antoine Battaini.

Jeunesses Musicales de Monaco, c/o Direction de L'Instruction Publique, Ministère d'Etat, Monte-Carlo. Secretary-General: Antoine Battaini.

MOROCCO

Association of Friends of Music, Andolouse, Casablanca. Director: Driss Benjelloun.

Jeunesses Musicales du Maroc, 3 Av. Moulay Youssef, Rabat. President: Abdeslan Bennis.

NETHERLANDS

Amateur Music Making Council, Mozartstr. 4, Kaatsheuvel. Administrator: Wim de Ruiter.

Arts Council of the Netherlands, R. J. Schimmelpennincklaan 3, The Hague. General Secretary: Rob. S. Sakko.

Association of Music Dealers and Publishers in the Netherlands, Amstel 52, Amsterdam. Secretary: C. Smit Jr.

Eduard van Beinum Foundation (International Musicians' Centre), Queekhoven House, Zandpad 39, 2580 Breukelen. Director: André G. Jurres.

BUMA (Bureau voor Muziekaiteursrecht - Performing Right Society), Marius Bauerstr. 30, Amsterdam 17. General Manager: G. Willemsen.

Contact Organisation for Electronic Music, PO Box 30, Bilthoven. Secretary: Chr. Walraven.

Contact Organisation for Orchestras in the Netherlands, Van Baerlestraat 138, Amsterdam. Secretary: P. van den Bos.

Council of Organisations of Musicians in the Netherlands, Valeruisplein 20, Amsterdam. Contact: R. C. Broek.

Donemus Foundation (Music Information Centre), Jacob Obrechtstraat 51, Amsterdam O.Z. Managing Director: Chr. Walraven.

Gaudeamus Foundation (National Section of the International Society for Contemporary Music), PO Box 30, 3720 AA Bilthoven. General Director: W. A. F. Maas.

Groningen Bach Association, Paulus Potterweg 26, 9761 HP Felde. Secretary: Dr. R. J. Snuif.

International Music Council (Netherlands Committee), Fred. van Eedenlaan 32, Hilversum. Secretary: André Jurres.

International Society of Organ Builders, Drift 21, Utrecht. Secretary: Dr. M. A. Vente.

Instituut voor Muzikale Vorming (Lennards Institute) Steegstraat 16, Roermond. Director: Lukas Lindeman.

Kunstenaarsorganisatie NVV, Passeerdersgracht 32, 1016 XH Amsterdam. Secretary: Mrs. J. van Laar.

Musicians' Union of the Netherlands, Herengracht 163, Amsterdam. General Secretary: Jan Sevenstern.

Netherlands Bach Association, Juliana van Stolberglaan 98, Naarden.

Netherlands Broadcasting Foundation, Postbox 10, Hilversum. Director, Orchestra and Choir Dept: P. C. Heuwekemeijer.

Netherlands Choral Association, Van Baerlestraat 138, 1071 BE Amsterdam. Manager: Dr. G. H. M. Post.

Performers' Union of the Netherlands, Plein 4&-45 No. 1, Amsterdam W.

Royal Netherlands Association of Musicians, van Miereveldstraat 13, Amsterdam. Secretary: Th. van Eijk.

Society for the Advancement of Music, Jacob van Campenstraat 59, Amsterdam. Secretary: Wouter Paap.

Society of Dutch Composers, Mariusbauerstraat 30, Amsterdam 1017. Secretary: Lucas Vis.

Society for Netherlands Musical History, Drift 21, 3512 BR Utrecht. Secretary: Dr. A. Annegarn.

Standing Conference of Music Schools, Huis Randebroek, Amersfoort. Director: H. J. Waage.

Wagner Society: Gabriél Metsustr. 32, Amsterdam. Secretary: Evert Cornelius.

Youth and Music, Roemer Visscherstraat 42, Amsterdam 1013. Secretary: J. C. Eekman.

NEW ZEALAND

Australasian Performing Right Association Ltd., BNSW Building, 318-24 Lambton Quay, PO Box 11-168, Wellington. Branch Manager: Miss P. A. Bell.

International Society of Music Education, c/o Prof. John Ritchie, School of Music, University of Canterbury, Christchurch 1.

Music Federation of New Zealand Inc., PO Box 3391, Wellington. Administrator: Miss Elizabeth Airey.

New Zealand Federation of Chamber Music Societies, Hannah's Building, Eva St., Wellington.

New Zealand Musicians' Union, PO Box 5694, Wellesley St., Wellington. Secretary: Neil V. McGough.

New Zealand Society for Contemporary Music (National Section, International Society for Contemporary Music), c/o Music Dept., University of Canterbury, Christchurch. Contact: David Sell.

Queen Elizabeth II Arts Council of New Zealand, PO Box 6040. Te Aro, Wellington. Director: M. A. Rickard.

NORWAY

Association of Friends of Music, Riddervoldsgate 10, Oslo 2. Secretary: Einar O. Solstad.

International Music Council (National Committee), Rektorhaugen 5, Oslo 8. President: Kristian Lange.

International Society for Contemporary Music (Norwegian Section), Klingenberggate 5, Oslo 1. President: Kare Kolberg.

Music Society 'Harmonien,' Engen 15,5000 Bergen. Contact: Laila Kismul.

National Association of Norwegian Composers of Light Music, Klingenberggate 5, Oslo 1. Secretary: Christian Hartmann.

Norwegian Association of Musical Artists, Edkersbergsgate 57a, Oslo 2. Secretary: Egil Nordsjø.

Norwegian Composers' Association, Klingenberggate 5, Oslo 1. Secretary: Miss Benthe P. Larsen.

Norwegian Cultural Council, Rosenkrantzgaten 11, Oslo 2. Director: Asmund Oftedal.

Norwegian Music Information Centre, c/o Norwegian Composers Association. Director: Diane Hanisch.

Norwegian Musicians' Union, Stortingsgt. 28, Oslo 1. President: Sigurd Lønseth.
Organisation of Amateur Town Orchestras, Dronningensgt. 50, 8501 Narvik. President: Skjoldulf Malm.
State Travelling Concerts Organisation, Munkedamsvn 59B, Oslo 2.
Youth & Music (Landslaget Musikk i Skolen, Eckersbergsgt. 57A, Oslo 2. President: Egil Nordsjø.

PAKISTAN

Arts Council of Pakistan (Dept. of Music), M. R. Kayani Rd., Karachi. Executive Director: Irfan Husain.
International Music Council (National Committee), National Commission for UNESCO, Ministry of Education, Islamabad.
Music Foundation of Pakistan, c/o Dr. Home Kharas, 5 Buch Terracce, Preedy St., Karachi 3. Director: Ferose Buchome.
Performing Right Society, PO Box 137, Chowk, Karachi.

PANAMA

National Institute of Music, Apdo 1414, Panama 1.

PARAGUAY

Association of Authors of Paraguay (Performing Right Society), Asuncion. President: Don Angel Peralta Arellano.

PERU

Association of Authors and Composers of Peru (Performing Right Society), 1206 Ave. Washington, Lima. President: Mario Cavagnaro Llerena.
International Music Council (National Committee), c/o Banco Hipotecario del Peru, Carebaya 421, Lima. President: Ernesto Araujo Alvarez.
Philharmonic Society, Jirón Ica 426, Lima.

PEOPLE'S REPUBLIC OF CHINA

Circle of Musical Culture, Macao.
Union of Chinese Musicians, c/o All China Federation of Literature and Art Circles, Peking. Chairman: Lu Chi.

PHILIPPINES

Artists Guild of the Philippines, 163 E. Meridiola St., Manila. President: Jovita Fuentes.
Filipino Society of Composers, Authors and Publishers, Room 243, Republic Supermart Building, Rozal Ave., Manila. Secretary: Simplicio U. Suarez.
International Music Council (National Committee), UNESCO Office, 1580 Taft Ave., Manila. Executive Secretary: Lucrecia R. Kasilag.
League of Filipino Composers, 1665 Taft Ave., Manila. Chairman: Lucrecia R. Kasilag.
Music Promotion Foundation of the Philippines, Ysmael Building, 1845 Taft Ave., Manila. Chairman: Jovita Fuentes.
Philippine Society for Music Education, Office of Philippines Women's University, Taft Ave., Manila. Vice-President: Prof. Crispina C. Garcia.
Youth & Music, c/o UNESCO Office, 1580 Taft Ave., Manila.

POLAND

Association of Authors and Composers ZAKR (Performing Right Society), ul. Hipoteczna 2, 00-092 Warsaw. Managing Director: Wladyslaw Jakubowski.
Association of Polish Musicians, ul. Krucza 24/26,00-526 Warsaw. General Secretary: Teodor Liese.
Association of Polish Violin Makers, Krakowskie przedmiescie 16-18, Warsaw. Secretary: Michal Wieckowski.
Frederic Chopin Society, ul. Okolnik 1,00-368 Warsaw. Director General: Wiktor Weinbaum.

International Music Council (National Committee), Rynek Starego Miasta 27, 00-272 Warsaw. General Secretary: Józef Patkowski.
International Society for Contemporary Music (Polish Section), c/o Union of Polish Composers, Rynek Starego Miasta 27,00-272 Warsaw. General Secretary: Henryk Schiller.
Jeunesses Musicales of Poland, Okolnik 1, 00-368 Warsaw. Secretary General: Marek Bykowski.
Polish Music Centre, Rynek Starego Miasta 27, OO-272 Warsaw. Director: Barbara Zwolska.
Polish Musicological Society, Plac Kultury i Nauki, 8 pietro, Warsaw.
Society of Authors 'ZAIKS,' ul. Hipoteczna 2,00-092 Warsaw. President: Karol Malcuzyński.
Union of Lyric Writers and Composers of Light Music, ul. Hipoteczna 2, 00-092 Warsaw.
Union of Polish Composers, Rynek Starego Miasta 27,00-272 Warsaw. General Secretary: Wladyslaw Slowiński.
Union of Polish Composers, Musicological Section, Rynek Starego Miasta 27,00-272 Warsaw. Secretary: Dr. E. Witkowska-Zaremba.

PORTUGAL

Circle of Musical Culture, Rossio 45, Lisbon 4. President: Luis G. Gomes.
Fundacao Calouste Gulbenkian (Music Information Centre), Av. de Berna 45, Lisbon 1.
International Music Council (National Committee), Instituto de Alta cultura, Praca do Principe Real 14, Lisbon. Secretary: Edgard dos Santos.
Jeunesses Musicales of Portugal, Rua Rosa Araujo ; 3°, Lisbon 2. Secretary-General: Dr. Luis Filipe Pires.
National Society of Music, Rua de Arroios 5, Lisbon 1. Director: Cap Valente.
Society of Portuguese Authors and Composers, Avenida Duque de Loulé 31, 1098 Lisbon. General Manager: Dr. Luiz Francisco Rebello.

ROMANIA

Association of Theatre Artists and Musicians, Str. Episcopiel 9, Bucharest. Secretary: Mrs Dina Cocea.
Central House of Popular Creative Art (Music Dept.), Strada Popa Soare 39, Bucharest 3. Director: Nicolas Nistor.
International Music Council (National Committee), Calea Victoriei 141, Bucharest. Secretary: Mircea Bude.
State Committee for Culture and Education (Music Dept.), Piata Scinteii 1, Bucharest. Director: Nicolae Călinoiu.
Theatre Artists & Musicians Association, Strada Filimon Sirbu 16, Bucharest 1. President: Dina Cocea.
Union of Composers and Musicologists in Socialist Republic of Romania, Calea Victoriei 141, 7000 Bucharest 22. President: Ion Dumitrescu.

SENEGAL

International Music Council (National Committee), Ecole des Arts, BP 3111, Dakar. Secretary: Abdourahmane Diop.

SINGAPORE

Performing Right Society, 1st floor, Meyer Chambers, Raffles Place.
Singapore Music Teachers' Association, 5, Jalan Kechil. Secretary: Miss Maria Chen.
Young Musicians' Society, c/o Extra-curricular Activities Centre, Ministry of Education, Northumberland Road, Singapore 8. Secretary: David Lim Kim San.

SOUTH AFRICA

International Library of African Music, ISER, Rhodes University, Grahamstown 6140. Director: Dr. Andrew Tracey.
Cape Musicians' Association, 10 Waterbury Road, Plumstead, Cape Town. Secretary: A. E. Frazer.
Natal Musicians' Association, PO Box 2698, Durban. Chairman: Ken Varner.
Society of South African Music Teachers, 73 Milner St., Waterkloof, Pretoria. Chairman: Mrs Joyce Joubert.

South African Co-ordinating Performing Arts Council, PO Box 4107, Silverton, Pretoria, 0001. Secretary: Peter Koster.
South African Military and Brass Band Association, PO Box 23117, Joubert Park, Johannesburg. Secretary: D. L. Sergeant.
South African Music Rights Organisation (Performing Right Society), SAMRO House, De Beer and Juta Sts., Braamfontein, Johannesburg. Secretary: P. J. Roos.
South African Navy Band, S. A. Navy Headquarters, Simonstonw 7995. Secretary: W. O. Il T. Dunlop.
Transvaal Musicians' Union, Cor. Main & Von Wielliah Sts., Johannesburg. Secretary: Mrs. Mildred Herbert.

SPAIN

Comisaria General de la Música, Ministerio de Educación y Ciencia, Alcala 34, Madrid.
Comite Español del Consejo Internacional de la Música, Martin de los Heros 56, Madrid 8. General Secretary: Antonio Iglesias.
Juventudes Musicales Espanolas, Diagonal 430, Barcelona. Secretary-General: German Beascoechea.
Sociedad General de Autores de España, Fernando VI, Madrid 4. Secretary: Carlos Galiano.
Sociedad Internaciónal de Música (Spanish Section of International Society for Contemporary Music), Ave. Reina Victoria 58, Madrid 3. Secretary General: Antonio Iglesias.

SRI LANKA

Cultural Council of Sri Lanka, 135 Dharmapata Mawatha, Colombo 7. Administrative Trustee: R. L. Wimaladharma.
Ministry of Education and Cultural Affairs (Dept. of Music), Colombo 3. Performing Right Society, 243 Hulftsdorp St., Colombo 12.

SWEDEN

Association of Male Voice Choirs, Mariatorget 1, Stockholm.
Association of Swedish Choirs, Box 14052, 10440 Stockholm. Chairman: Torgil Ringmar.
Association of Swedish Musical Artists, Tavastgatan 30, Stockholm. Secretary: L. Sellergren.
Association of Swedish Musicians, Upplandsgatan 4, 11123 Stockholm. Secretary: Yngve Akerberg.
Association of Swedish Symphony Orchestras, Båtsmanvägen 25, 19148 Sollentuna. Secretary: Einar Persson.
International Association of Music Libraries (IAML), Svenskt musikhistoriskt arkiv, Sibyllegatan 2,11451 Stockholm. Secretary: Anders Lönn.
International Music Council (National Committee), c/o Musikaliska akademien, Blasieholmstorg 8,11148 Stockholm. Secretary: Hans Åstrand.
International Society for Contemporary Music (Swedish Section), Prästgatan 28, Stockholm. Secretary: Gunnar Ahlen.
Musical Art Association, Blasieholmstorg 8,11148 Stockholm. Secretary Gösta Percy.
Royal Academy of Music, Blasieholmstorg 8,11148 Stockholm. Permanent Secretary: Hans Åstrand.
Society of Music Teachers in Sweden, Fasanvagaen 13, Ektorp. Secretary: B. Agnestig.
Society of Swedish Church Musicians, Kvarngatan 2, Frödinge, 59800 Vimmerby.
Society of Swedish Composers, Box 5091, Birger Jarlsgatan 6b,10242 Stockholm. Secretary: Miklós Maros.
Society of Swedish Light Music Composers, Box 5091, 10242 Stockholm. Secretary: Mrs. Britt-Marie Malmros.
Society of Swedish Music Publishers, Drottninggatangla, Stockholm C.
Society of Swedish Piano Teachers, Kata Dálströmsgata 10iii, 12666 Hägersten-Stockholm. Secretary: Mrs. Carla Lundqvist.
Swedish Broadcasting Association, Dept. of Music, 10510 Stockholm. Head of Serious Music Section: Bengt Emil Johnson.
Swedish Music History Archives, Strandvägen 82,11527 Stockholm. Director: Dr. Axel Helmer.
Swedish Musicians' Union, Box 43 10120, Stockholm. Secretary: Kjell Ivri.
Swedish Music Information Centre, Birger Jarlsgatan 6b, PO Box 5091, 10242 Stockholm.

Swedish Society of Composers, Authors and Editors, STIM, (Performing Right Society), Box 1539,11185 Stockholm. Secretary: Mrs. Monica Agerkrans.
Swedish Society for Musicology, Strandvagen 82,11527 Stockholm. Secretary: Per-Erik Brolinson.
Swedish Society for Musical Research, Uppsala University, 75221 Uppsala.
Swedish Society of Music Teachers, Multragatan 114, Vallingby. Secretary: T. Lewander.
Youth & Music, Box 1225, 111 82 Stockholm.

SWITZERLAND

Association of Concert Giving Societies of Switzerland, Münsterplatz 18, 4000 Basle. Secretary: Hans Ziegler.
Association of Swiss Conductors, Avenue du Général-Guisan 33, 1009 Pully.
Association of Swiss Musicians, Av. du Grammont 11 bis, Case postale 153,1000 Lausanne 13. General Secretary: Dr. Dominque Creux.
European Association of Concert Managers, Rennweg 15,8022 Zürich. President: Klaus Menzel.
European Association of Music Festivals, 122 rue de Lausanne, 1202 Geneva. Secretary: Mrs. Marianne Dentan.
Federation of International Music Competitions, 12 rue de l'Hôtel de Ville, 1204 Geneva. General Secretary: Franco Fisch.
Goethe Foundation for Arts and Sciences, Birchstrasse 155,8050 Zürich-Oerlikon.
International Federation of Musicians, Hofackerstr. 7,8032 Zürich. General Secretary: Rudi Leuzinger.
International Music Council (National Committee), Case 203,4001 Basle. Executive Secretary: Mrs. Huguette Zimmermann.
International Musicological Society, POB 588, 4001 Basle. Secretary General: Dr. Rudolf Häusler.
International Society for Contemporary Music c/o Association of Swiss Musicians, Av. du Grammont 11 bis, case postale 153,1000 Lausanne. Secretary General: Bernard Geller.
Jeunesses Musicales de Suisse, Case Postale 233,1211 Geneva 8. Secretary-General: François Page.
National Association of Orchestras, Gartenstrasse 4,6210 Sursee. President: Dr. Alois Bernet.
National Association of Singers, Burgstr. 1, 4143 Dornach. President: Max Diethelm.
National Music Association, Postfach 139,4901 Langenthal. President: Ernst Müller.
Performing Right Society of Switzerland, Bellariastr. 82,8038 Zürich. Contact: Dr. H. J. Stern.
'Romand' Centre of Sacred Music, POB 204, Champel, 1211 Geneva. 12. Secretary: Miss Georgette Albrecht.
Schola Cantorum Basiliensis, Leonhardstr. 4,4051 Basle.
Society of Friends of Old Musical Instruments, Muhlebachstrasse 174,8008 Zürich. Secretary: Siegfried Brenn.
Swiss Association of Accordion Teachers, Wildenstr. 15,8049 Zürich. President: Willy Vogt.
Swiss Association for Church Singing, Bernstr. 85,3018 Berne. President: Hans Leuenberger.
Swiss Association of Mixed Choirs, Rainallee 68,4125 Riehen. Vice-President: Louis Loeliger-Schneider.
Swiss Association of Professional Conductors, Fronwaldstr. 132,8046 Zürich. Secretary: Ferdinand Lackner.
Swiss Association of Professional Musicians, Elisabethenstr. 2,4051 Basle. Secretary: Dr. Peter Kuster.
Swiss Music Archives, (Music Information Centre), Bellariastr. 82,8038 Zürich. Director: Hans Steinbeck.
Swiss Music Education Association, Forchstr. 375,8008 Zürich. Secretary: Mrs. Hanna Brandenberger.
Swiss Music Interpreters Society, Talaker 35,8001 Zürich. Managing Director: Dr. V. Hauser.
Swiss Music Teachers Association, Forchstr. 376,8008 Zürich. Secretary: Hanna Brandenberger.
Swiss Romand Sacred Music Association, Abbaye Saint-Maurice, 1890 Saint Maurice/Valais. Secretary: Georgette Albrecht.
Swiss Society of Music Teachers, Rue da la Porcelain 4, 1260 Nyon. Secretary: Edouard Garo.

Swiss Society of Music Teachers at Secondary Schools, Haffnerstr. 18,4500 Solothurn. Secretary: Dr. Alfred Rubeli.
Swiss Society for Musical Research, 25 Passwangstr., Basle. Secretary: Dr. Jurg Stenzl.
Swiss Society for National Music, Am Chapholz, 8126 Zumikon. Secretary: L. Walter Ramspeck.
Swiss Study Group for Youth Music and Music Education, Sonnengartenstr. 4,8125 Zollokerberg.
Swiss Workers' Music Association, Schermenweg 133,3072 Ostermundigen. President: R. Schüpbach.
Union Suisse des Chorales, Obere Zäune 22, 8001 Zürich. Chairman: Max Diethelm.

TRINIDAD

Trinidad Music Association, Bishop Anstey High School, Abercromby St., Port of Spain.
Trinidad and Tobago Music Festival Association, c/o Ministry of Education & Culture, PO Box 388, Port of Spain.

TUNISIA

International Music Council (National Committee), National Conservatory of Music, Dance and Dramatic Art, 5 rue Zarkoun, Tunis. Secretary General: Mme. Hedia Chedi.
Jeunesses Musicales de Tunisie, 20 Ave. de Paris, Tunis. President: Féthi Zghonda.
Society of Tunisian Authors and Composers (Performing Right Society), 11 rue Al-Djazira, Tunis.

U.S.S.R.

Azerbaijan Composers' Union, Ulitsa Khagani 27, Baku. First Secretary: Kuliev Tofick Aleckperogly.
Composers' Union of Georgia, Tiflis.
Estonian Composers' Union, Blvd. Estonia 4, Tallin.
International Music Council (National Committee), c/o Union of Soviet Composers, ul. Nyezhdavovoi 8-10, Moscow K9.
Kirghiz SSR Union of Composers, Frunz.
Ukrainian Composers' Union (Lviv Branch), Chaikovsky Street 7,290000 Lviv-centre, Ukraine. Secretary: Anatol Ossypovych Kos-Anatolskyi.
Union of Composers of the U.S.S.R., Gertzena 45, Leningrad. Chairman: A. P. Petrov.
Union of Soviet Composers, ul. Nyezhdavovoi 8-10, Moscow K9.

UNITED KINGDOM

Accordion Teachers' Guild, Somerset House, Cranleigh, Surrey. Secretary: J. J. Black.
Arts Council of Great Britain, 105 Piccadilly, London W1V 0AU. Music Director: John Cruft.
Asian Music Circle, 63 Arlington Avenue, London, N1 7BA. Contact: Shankar Angadi.
Associated Board of the Royal Schools of Music, 14 Bedford Square, London, WC1. Secretary: Philip Cranmer.
Association of Band Traders, 60 Whalley House, Wood Road, Manchester M16 9RL. Secretary: Edward C. Buttress.
Association of British Orchestras, 11 Little Britain, London, EC1A 7BX. Secretary: John May.
Association of Musical Instrument Industries, 62 Park View, Hatch End, Pinner, Middlesex HA5 4LN. Secretary: D. A. Michell.
Association of Touring and Producing Managers, Suite 41/43, 18 Charing Cross Road, London, WC2. Secretary: Nat Day.
Australian Musical Association, c/o Australia House, The Strand, London WC2B 4LA. Secretary: G. Chard.
Barbirolli Society, 8 Tunnel Road, Retford, Notts., DN22 7TA. Chairman: Pauline Pickering.
Sir Thomas Beecham Society, 46 Wellington Avenue, Westcliff-on-Sea, Essex, SS0 9XB. Chairman: Denham Ford.
British Arts Festivals Association, 33 Rufford Road, Sherwood, Notts., NG5 2NQ.
British Association of Concert Agents, 44 Castlenau Gardens, Arundel Terrace, London SW13 9DU. Secretary: Miss P. M. Nunn.
British Broadcasting Corporation, Music Dept., Yalding House, 156 Great Portland Street, London, W1N 6AJ.

British Copyright Council, 29-33 Berners Street, London, W1. Secretary: Geoffrey Adams.
British Copyright Protection Association, 29-33 Berners St., London, W1. Secretary: Reynell Wreford.
British Council, Music Dept., 97/99 Park St., London, W1Y 4HQ. Head of Music Section: Barrie Iliffe.
British Federation of Brass Bands, 32 Cedar Dr., Ibstock, Leicester LE6 1HX. Secretary: David Johnson.
British Federation of Music Festivals, 106 Gloucester Place, London W1. Secretary: Eileen Craine.
British Institute of Recorded Sound, 29 Exhibition Road, London SW7 2AS. Director: Patrick Saul.
British Music Information Centre, 10 Stratford Place, London W1N 9AE. Librarian: Roger Wright.
British Music Society, 40 Laburnum Rd., Maidenhead, Berks. SL6 4DE. Secretary: John Dodd.
British Society for Electronic Music, 277 Putney Bridge Road, London SW15 2PT. Secretary: Dr. Peter Zinovieff.
Gerald Burley Research Foundation, 32 Arlington Way, London EC1R 1YH. Secretary: Anthony Burley.
Cathedral Organists' Association, c/o Royal School of Church Music, Addington Palace, Croydon CR9 5AD. Secretary: Lionel Dakers.
Choir Schools' Association, Cathedral Choir School, Ripon, North Yorkshire. Secretary: Rev. Duncan Thomson.
Chopin Society, 20 Princes Gate, London SW7. Founder and Secretary: Mrs. L. Swiatek.
Cobbett Chamber Music Club, 47 Sterling Avenue, Edgware, Middlesex. Secretary: Donald Sehlackman.
Composers' Guild of Great Britain, 10 Stratford Place, London, W1N 9AE. General Secretary: Elizabeth Yeoman.
Concert Artists' Association, 20 Bedford Square, London, WC2E 9HP. Secretary: Carmel Maguire.
Contemporary Concerts Co-ordination, c/o SPNM, 1 Montague St., London WC1B 5BP. Chairman: John Woolf.
Council of Brass Bands Associations, 60 Whalley House, Wood Road, Manchester M16 9RL. Secretary: E. C. Buttress.
Delius Society, 16 Slade Close, Walderslade, Chatham, Kent. Secretary: J. K. White.
Dolmetsch Foundation, 136 High St., Marlborough, Wiltshire. Secretary: Mrs. Angela Evans.
Eastern Arts Association, 8-9 Bridge St., Cambridge CB2 1UA. Music Officer: Gillian Longfield.
Eastern Authorities' Orchestral Association, 10 Stratford Pl., London W1N 9AE. General Manager: Anthony Burley.
Elgar Society, 7 Batchworth Lane, Northwood, HA6 3AU. Secretary: E. W. A. Jackson.
Entertainment Agents' Association, 3 Golden Square, London W1R 3AD. Secretary: Gordon Blackie.
English Music Theatre Company, 45 Floral St., London WC2. Artistic Directors: Colin Graham/Stuart Bedford.
European Community Youth Orchestra, 24 Cadogan Sq., London SW1X 0JP. Secretary-General: Joy Bryher.
Executives and Managers' Association, 337 Grays Inn Road, London WC1X 8PX. Secretary: Ivor Gayus.
Glasgow Society of Musicians, 73 Berkeley St., Glasgow C3.
Guild for the Promotion of Welsh Music, Angel Chambers, 94 Walter Road, Swansea SA1 5QA. Secretary: Huw Rogers.
Hallé Concerts Society, 30 Cross Street, Manchester, M2 7BA. Secretary and General Manager: Clive F. Smart.
Harmonica Guild, Somserset House, Cranleigh, Surrey. Secretary: J. J. Black
Haydn-Mozart Society, 70 Leopold Road, Wimbledon, London SW19 7JQ. Secretary: Mrs. Marion Blech.
Huddersfield Choral Society, High Warren, Stocks Bank Road, Mirfield, Yorks, WF14 0EY. General Secretary: Richard Barraclough.
Hymn Society of Great Britain & Ireland, 17 Little Cloister, Westminster Abbey, London SW1P 3PL. Secretary: Rev. Alan Luff.
Incorporated Association of Organists, St. Catherine's College, Cambridge CB2 1RL. Secretary: Glyn Jenkins.
Incorporated Guild of Church Musicians, Forde House, 51 Clothfair, London EC1A 7JL. Registrar: A. T. Pinder.

Incorporated Society of Authors, Playwrights and Composers, 84 Drayton Gardens, London SW10.

Incorporated Society of Musicians, 10 Stratford Place, London W1N 9AE. General Secretary: Susan M. Alcock.

Institute of Contemporary Arts, Nash House, The Mall, London SW1.

International Association of Music Libraries (U.K. Branch), Library, Birmingham School of Music, Paradise Circus, Birmingham B3 3HG. Secretary: Susan M. Clegg.

International Concertina Association, 42 St. Barnabas St., London SW1W 8QE. Contact: J. Harvey.

International Federation of Musicians, 29 Catherine Place, Buckingham Gate, London SW1E 6EH. President: John Morton.

International Federation of Producers of Phonograms and Videograms, 123 Pall Mall, London SW1Y 5EA. Director-General: John Hall, Q.C.

International Federation of Youth Orchestras and the Performing Arts, 24 Cadogan Square, London, SW1X 0JP. Secretary General: Mrs. Joy Bryher.

International Liszt Centre for 19th Century Music, 53 Priory Rd., London NW6 3NE. Secretary: Mariann Meier.

International Louis Spohr Society, 69 Bloomfield Road, Bromley, Kent. Contact: M. F. Powell

International Society for Contemporary Music, British Section, 105 Piccadilly, London W1V 0AU. Secretary: Annette Morreau.

Jewish Music Council, 21 Dean Street, London W1. Contact: Barry Feldman.

Lincolnshire & Humberside Arts, St. Hugh's, 23 Newport, Lincoln, LN1 3ON. Music Officer: Miss E. Parker.

Liszt Society Ltd., 32 "Chivelston," 78 Wimbledon Park Side, Wimbledon, London SW19 5LH. Secretary: Eunice Mistarz.

London Association of Organists, St. Jude-on-the-Hill, Central Square, London NW11. Secretary: Peter Lea-Cox.

London Federation of Music Societies, 29 Exhibition Road, London SW7 2AD.

London Musical Club, 21 Holland Park, London W11 3TE. Secretary: Mrs. Eve Spooner.

London Orchestral Association, 13 Archer St., London W1V 7HG. Secretary: A. Fawcett.

London Orchestral Concert Board Ltd., Royal Festival Hall, London SE1 8XX. Secretary: George Mann.

London Philharmonic Society, 53 Welbeck St., London W1M 7HE. Membership Secretary: Shirley Whitfield.

London Symphony Orchestra Club, Regent Arcade House, 19/25 Argyll St., London W1V 2LN. Secretary: Miss L. Sykes.

Lute Society, 71 Priory Road, Kew Gardens, Richmond, Surrey TW9 3DM. Administrator: Francesca McManus.

Mechanical Copyright Protection Society, 380 Streatham High Road, London SW16 6HR. General Manager: John M. Edwards

Merseyside Arts Association, 6 Bluecoat Chambers, School Lane, Liverpool L1 3BX. Secretary: Peter Bevan.

Midland Sinfonia Concert Society, 72 St. James's St., Nottingham NG1 6FJ.

Musical Advisers' National Association, Education Office, 22 Northgate St., Warwick. Secretary: David M. Jones.

Music Directors' Association, 88 Rochester Row, London, SW1P 1JP. Secretary: B. W. Owen.

Music Masters' Association, Orchard House, Benefield Road, Oundle, Peterborough PE8 4EU. Secretary: R. B. Miller

Music Publishers' Association Ltd., 73/75 Mortimer St., London W1N 7TB. Secretary: David Toff.

Music Trades Association, 5 Denmark St., London, WC2H 8LP. Secretary-General: A. F. Spencer-Bolland.

Musicians' Union, 60/62 Clapham Rd., London SW9. General Secretary: John Morton.

National Accordion Organization of Great Britain, Somerset House, Cranleigh, Surrey. Secretary: J. J. Black.

National Association of Brass Band Conductors, No. 1 Centre, 10A Kathleen Road, London, SW11 2JS. Secretary: Herbert J. Mepham.

National Association of Teachers in Further and Higher Education (Music Section), Derby Lonsdale College, Mickleover, Derby. Secretary: B. M. Sims.

National Federation of Gramophone Societies, Bollin Cross School, Styal Wilmslow, Cheshire SK9 4HX. Secretary: G. H. Sidery.

National Federation of Music Societies, 1 Montague St., London WC1B 5BS. General Secretary: John Crisp.

National Music Council of Great Britain, 35 Morpeth Mansions, Morpeth Terrace, London SW1P IEU. Chairman: James Archibald.

National Operatic and Dramatic Association, 1 Crestfield St., London WC1H 8AU. Secretary: A. W. Denyer.

National School Brass Band Association, 2 Gray's Close, Barton-le-Clay, Bedford MK45 4PH. Secretary: E. Charles Sweby.

North Wales Arts Association, 10 Wellfield House, Bangor, North Wales. Secretary: D. Llion Williams.

Northern Arts, 31 New Bridge St., Newcastle upon Tyne, NE1 8JY. Director: David Dougan.

Northern Concert Artists, 3 Manor Square, Otley, Yorks.

Northern Ireland Musicians' Association, Crown Chambers, 64 Royal Avenue, Belfast BT1 1EJ. General Secretary: William D. McAlpine.

The Organ Club, 5 Frognal Mansions, London NW3 6XT. General Secretary: Frederic Symonds.

Park Lane Group, 1 Montague St., London WC1B 5BP. Executive Chairman: John Woolf.

Performing Right Society Ltd., 29/33 Berners St., London W1P 4AA. Secretary: George M. Neighbour.

Personal Managers' Association, 91 Regent St., London W1R 8RU. Chairman: Peter Dunlop.

Philharmonia Concert Society, 61 Carey St., London WC2.

Pipers' Guild, 11 Lambourn Way, Tunbridge Wells, Kent TN2 5HJ. Secretary: Mrs. Phyllis R. Morris.

Plainsong and Medieval Music Society, The Church Lodge, Wimborne St. Giles, Wimborne, Dorset. Secretary/Treasurer: S. G. A. Kiddell.

Pro Corda (National Association for Young Chamber Music Players), Silver Birches, Crossfield Place, Weybridge, Surrey KT13 0RG. Director: Elizabeth G. Hewlins.

Ernest Read Music Association, 143 King Henry's Road, London NW3 3RD. Secretary: Peter Avis.

Royal Air Force Headquarters Music Services, R.A.F. Uxbridge, Middlesex. Director: Sqn. Leader Eric Banks.

Royal Choral Society, Royal Albert Hall, Kensington Gore, London SW7. General Manager: Michael Heyland.

Royal College of Organists, Kensington Gore, London SW7 2QS. Hon. Secretary: Sir John Dykes Bower.

Royal Liverpool Philharmonic Society, Philharmonic Hall, Hope St., Liverpool L1 9BP. Secretary: Stephen Gray.

Royal Musical Association, Music Library, British Library, Gt. Russel St., London WC1B 3DG. Secretary: Hugh Cobbe.

Royal Philharmonic Orchestra Club, 97 New Bond St., London, W1. Secretary: Joanne R. Hallgren.

Royal Philharmonic Society, 124 Wigmore St., London W1H 0AX. Hon. Secretary: Dr. William Cole.

Royal Society of Musicians of Great Britain, 10 Stratford Place, London W1N 9AE. Secretary: Mrs. Marjorie Gleed.

Rural Music Schools' Association, Ibberson Way, Benslow Lane, Hitchin, Herts. SG4 9RB. Director: Norman Hearn.

Schools' Music Association, 4 Newman Road, Bromley, Kent. Secretary: Stephen S. Moore.

Schubert Society of Great Britain, Garden Flat, 125 Grosvenor Avenue, London N5. Secretary: Alan Tabelin.

Scottish Amateur Music Association, 7 Randolph Crescent, Edinburgh EH3 7TE. Secretary: Alex. A. Soutar.

Scottish Arts Council, 19 Charlotte Square, Edinburgh EH2 4DF. Music Director: Christie Duncan.

Society for the Promotion of New Music, 1 Montague St., London WC1B 5BP. Administrator: John Woolf.

Society of Recorder Players, 26 Delamere Road, London W5 3JR. Secretary: Joan Davis.

Society for Research in Psychology of Music and Music Education, Dept. of Education, Manchester University, Manchester M13 9Pl. Secretary: Dr. Aubrey Hickman.

Society of Women Musicians, 18 Albert Bridge Road, London SW11. Secretary: Miss D. Orpen.

Songwriters' Guild of Great Britain, Ascot House, 52/53 Dean St., London W1V 5HJ. General Secretary: Bill Cochran.

South East Arts' Association, Marlowe Theatre, St. Margaret's St., Canterbury, Kent.

South Place Sunday Concert Society, Conway Hall, Red Lion Square, London WC1R 4RL. Secretary: George Hutchinson.

South West Arts, 23 Southernhay East, Exeter, EX1 1QL. Music Officer: John de la Cour.

Southern Arts Association, 19 Southgate St., Winchester, Hants. Music Officer: Patricia Reynolds.

Standing Conference for Amateur Music, 26 Bedford Square, London WC1B 3HU. Secretary: David Ogborn.

Traditional Music and Song Association of Scotland, 29 Sunnyside, Straithkinnes, Fife.

Ulster Orchestra Association, 181A Stranmillis Road, Belfast BT9 5DU. Secretary: Harold Wilkin.

United Kingdom Harpists' Association, 50 West Hill, Wembley Park, Middlesex. Contact: Michael Jeffries.

Viola da Gamba Society, 2 Northfield, Braughing, Ware SG11 2QQ. Secretary: G. D. Davidson.

Visiting Orchestras Consultative Association, 32 Arlington Way, London EC1R 1YH. Secretary: Anthony Burley.

Wagner Institute, Marcol House, 293 Regent St., London W1R 8AA. Secretary: Philip Saul.

Welsh Arts Council, 9 Museum Place, Cardiff CF1 3NX. Music Director: Roy Bohana.

West Midlands Arts, Lloyds Bank Chambers, Market St., Stafford ST16 2AP. Music Officer: Dorothy Wilson.

West Wales Association for the Arts, Dark Gate, Red St., Carmarthen. Secretary: T. D. Scourfield.

Western Orchestral Society Ltd., 2 Seldown Lane, Poole, Dorset BH 15 1UF. General Administrator: Keith B. Whitmore.

Workers' Music Association, 236 Westbourne Park Road, London W11 1EC. Secretary: Mrs. Anne Gilman.

Worshipful Company of Musicians, 4 St. Paul's Churchyard, London EC4M 8AY. Clerk: W. R. I. Crewdson.

Yorkshire Arts Association, Glyde House, Glydegate, Bradford BD5 0BQ. Music Officer: Richard Phillips.

Youth and Music, 22 Blomfield Street, London EC2M 7AP. Administrator: Alan Fluck.

U.S.A.

Accordion Teachers' Guild, 12626 W. Creek Road, Minnetonka, MN 55343. Executive Secretary: Carl E. Hane.

Affiliate Artists Inc., 155 W. 68 St., NY 10023. President: Richard Clark.

All American Association of Contest Judges, 518 Hicks Avenue, Plainwell, MI 49080. Commissioner: Granville B. Cutler.

Amateur Chamber Music Players, Inc., 15 West 67th St., New York, NY 10023. Secretary: Helen Rice.

America First Society, Univ. of Florida, Gainesville, FL 32611. Chairman: Dr. David Z. Kushner.

American Academy & Institute of Arts & Letters, 633 W. 155 St., NY, NY 10003. Exec. Director: Margaret Mills.

American Academy of Teachers of Singing, 75 Bank St., NY, NY 10014. Secretary: William Gephart.

American Accordionists' Association, 224 W. 4th St., NY 10014. President: Charles Magnante.

American Bandmasters' Association, 2019 Bradford Drive, Arlington, TX 76010. Secretary/Treasurer: Jack H. Mahan.

American Choral Directors' Association, P.O. Box 17736, Tampa, FL 33612. Secretary: R. Wayne Hugaboom.

American Choral Foundation, Inc., 130 West 56th St., New York, NY 10019. Administrative Director: Sheldon Soffer.

American College of Musicians, National Guild of Piano Teachers, P.O. Box 1807, Austin, TX 78767. Exec. Secretary/Vice President: Walter Merchant.

American Composers' Alliance, 170 W. 74th St., New York, NY 10023. Executive Director: Francis Thorne.

American Federation of Musicians, 1500 Broadway, New York, NY 10036. Secretary/Treasurer: J. Martin Emerson.

American Guild of Authors and Composers, 40 West 57th St., New York, NY 10019. Executive Director: Lewis M. Bachman.

American Guild of Music, P.O. Box 3, Downers Grove, IL 60515. Secretary: Elmer Herrick.

American Guild of Musical Artists, 1841 Broadway, New York, NY 10023. National Executive Secretary: DeLloyd Tibbs.

American Guild of Organists, 630 5th Avenue, Suite 2010, New York, NY 10020. Secretary: Barbara F. Mount.

American Harp Society, 6331 Quebec Drive, Hollywood, CA 90068. Office Manager: Dorothy Remsen.

American International Managers' Society, 250 W. 57th St., New York, NY 10019. President: Sara Tornay.

American International Music Fund, Inc., 30 West 60th St., New York, NY 10023. Executive Secretary: Karen Van Outryve.

American Liszt Society, Dept. of Music, University of Florida, Gainesville, FL 32611. Chairman: Dr. David Z. Kushner.

American Lute Seminars, 5821 Rolling Road, Woodland Hills, CA 91364. Secretary: Dr. Cheryl Lew.

American Matthay Association, School of Music, University of Oklahoma, Norman, OK 73069. President: Lytle Powell.

American Music Center, 250 West 57th St., Room 626-7, New York, NY 10019. Exec. Director: Margaret Jory.

American Music Conference, 150 East Huron St., Chicago, IL 60611. President: Theodore M. McCarty.

American Musicological Society, 201 South 34th St., Philadelphia, PA 19174. Exec. Director: Prof. Alvin H. Johnson.

American Recorder Society, 141 West 20th St., New York, NY 10011. Secretary: Clara M. Whittaker.

American School Band Directors' Association, 3200 East Shawnee, Muskogee, OK 74401. Secretary: Jerry Huffer.

American Society of Composers, Authors and Publishers, 1 Lincoln Plaza, New York, NY 10023. President: Stanley Adams.

American Society of Music Arrangers, 224 West 49th St., New York, NY 10019. President: M. Russel Goudey.

American Society of University Composers, 250 West 57th St., Room 626-7, New York, NY 10019. Chairman: Richard Brooks.

American String Teachers' Association, 2596 Princeton Pike, Lawrenceville, NJ 08648. Executive Director: Robert Marince.

American Symphony Orchestra League, P.O. Box 66, Vienna, VA 22180. Secretary: Mrs. Robert H. Barnes.

American Theatre Organ Society, P.O. Box 1002, Middleburg, VA 22117. Secretary: Erwin A. Young.

Artists in Action, Inc., 131 Cambridge St., Boston, MA 02114.

Artists' Representative Association, 1270 Avenue of the Americas, New York, NY 10020. President: David C. Baumgarten.

Associated Councils of the Arts, 1564 Broadway, New York, NY 10036. President: John M. MacFadyen.

Associated Male Choruses of America, Inc., 1338 Oakcrest Drive, Appleton, WI 54911. Executive Secretary: Elmer C. Rehbein.

Association of Choral Conductors, 130 West 56th St., New York, NY 10019. Administrator: Sheldon Soffer.

Association of College, University and Community Arts Administrators, Inc., P.O. Box 2137, Madison, WI 53701. Executive Director: Dr. William M. Dawson.

Birmingham Chamber Music Society, 22 Clarendon Road, Birmingham, AL 35213. Contact: Ruth Shugerman.

Boston Recorder Society, 5 Commonwealth Avenue, Boston, MA 02116.

Broadcast Music Inc., 320 West 57th St., New York, NY 10019. Secretary: Edward W. Chapin.

Broadcasting Foundation of America, 52 Vanderbilt Avenue, New York, NY 10017. Vice-President and Executive Director: Howard L. Kany.

Bruckner Society of America, P.O. Box 1171, Iowa City, IA 52240. President: Charles L. Eble.

Casals Archives, 169-05 Northern Blvd., Flushing, NY 11358. Secretary: Jose D. Alfaro.

Center for the Study of Comparative Folklore and Mythology, 1037 GSM Lib. Wing, University of California, Los Angeles, CA.

Chinese Musical and Theatrical Association, 181 Canal St., NY 10013. Director of Music: Stanley Chiu.

Choral Conductors' Guild, Box 714, Mount Vernon, NY 10551. Contact: Roy Anderson.

Church Music Association of America, Boys Town, NE 68010. Secretary: Rev. Ralph S. March.

Civic Musical Society of Utica, Inc., 255 Ynesee St., Utica, NY 13501. General Manager: Mrs. Terry W. Evans.

College Band Directors' National Association, Ohio University, Athens, OH 45701. Secretary: Guy N. Duker.

College Music Society, Regent Box 44, Univ. of Colorado, Boulder, CO 80309. Secretary: Dr. D. R. Williams.

Colorado Music Educators' Association, 840 Tucson St., Aurora, CO 80011. Contact: Byron L. Gillett.

Columbia Broadcasting System, Inc., 51 West 52nd St., New York, NY 10019.

Community Music Center of Boston, 48 Warren Avenue, Boston, MA 02116. Executive Director: Michael Garroway.

Composers in Performance, Inc., Carnegie Hall, Suite 1203, New York, NY 10019. Executive Director: Benjamin Patterson.

Composers and Lyricists Educational Foundation, Inc., 40 West 57th Street, Suite 410, New York, NY 10019. Executive Director: Lewis M. Bachman.

Composers' and Lyricists' Guild of America, 6565 Sunset Blvd., Suite 419, Hollywood, CA 90028.

Composers Theatre, 225 Lafayette St., NY, NY 10012. Director: John Watts.

Concentus Musicus, 905 4th Avenue S., Minneapolis, MN 55404. Administrative Director: Ann-Chinn Maud.

Concert Artists' Guild, Carnegie Hall, Studio 136, New York, NY 10019. Administrative Assistant: Simeon Westbrook.

Connecticut Music Educators' Association, McNeil Road, Bethel, CT 06801. Secretary: Lenore Pogonowski.

Danbury Music Center, 240 Main St., Danbury, CT 06810. Secretary: June K. Goodman.

Flute and Fiddle Club, 1623 Sylvester Place, Highland Park, IL 60035. Director: Everett L. Millard.

French Society of Authors, Composers and Publishers, 435 Spring Valley Road, Paramus, NJ 07652.

Friday Morning Music Club Foundation, 1649 K St., N.W., Washington, DC 20006. Director: Mrs. Sidney Shear.

Friends of Music, Inc., Box 369, Westport, CT 06880. President: Herbert L. Cohen. Secretary: Mrs. Josephine Barnett.

Georgia Music Educators' Association, Inc., Box 784, Conley, GA 30027. Secretary: Ms. Margaret M. Swain.

Hymn Society of America, Wittenberg University, Springfield, OH 45501. Executive Director: W. Thomas Smith.

Idaho Music Educators' Association, 3432 N. 33rd, Boise, ID 83703. Secretary: Roger Fordyce.

Institute of High Fidelity, 516 5th Avenue, New York, NY 10036. President: Walter Goodman.

Instituto de Cultura Puertorriqueña, Box 4184, San Juan, PR 00905. Director of Music Program: Hector Campos Parsi.

Inter-American Music Council, 1889 "F" St. N.W., 5th Floor, Washington, DC 20006. Secretary-General: Efrain Paesky.

Intercollegiate Music Council, Dept. of Music, Emory University, Atlanta, GA 30322. President: William Lemonds.

International Association of Music Libraries - U.S. Branch, Northwestern University Music Library, Evanston, IL 60201. Secretary: Don L. Roberts.

International Association of Organ Teachers, USA, 7938 Bartram Ave., Hammond, IN 46324. Secretary/Treasurer: Jack C. Greig.

International Bach Society, Inc., 165 West 57th St., New York, NY 10019. Secretary/Treasurer: Miss Alice H. Bonnell.

International Alban Berg Society, Music Dept., Paul Arts Centre, University of New Hampshire, Durham, NH 03824. Secretary: Mark DeVoto.

International Chopin Foundation, Inc., 11341 Jos. Campau Avenue, Detroit, 12, MI. Secretary: Mrs. Sophie Myslowski.

International Horn Society, 337 Ridge Avenue, Elmhurst, IL 60126. Secretary/Treasurer: Nancy Fako.

International Jazz Federation, 1697 Broadway, Suite 1203, NY, NY 10019. Exec. Director: Jan A. Byrczek.

International Pianists' Guild, 885 Westwood Drive, Abilene, TX 79603. Chairman: E. Edwin Young.

International Society of Performing Arts Administrators, 615 Louisiana St., Houston, TX 77002. Secretary: James Bernhard.

International Society of Violin and Bow Makers, 2039 Locust St., Philadelphia, PA 19103. President: William Moenig Jr.

International Trombone Association, 1812 Truman Drive, Normal, IL 61761. Secretary: Dr. G. B. Lane.

Jeunesses Musicales, Carnegie Hall, 154 W. 57th St., NY, NY 10019. National Secretary: Carolyn Criddle.

League of Composers-International Society for Contemporary Music (National Section), c/o American Music Center. Secretary: Dr. P. A. Levi.

League of Women Composers, P.O. Box 23152, Honolulu, HI 96822. Chairperson, Exec. Bd.: Dr. Nancy Van de Vate.

Leschetizky Association, 105 West 72nd St., New York, NY 10023. President: Mrs. Genia Robinor.
Louisville Bach Society, 2549 Woodcreek Road, Louisville, KY 40205. Director: Melvin Dickinson.
Louisville Society for the Classical Guitar, 1137 Everett, Louisville, KY 40204.
Lute Society of America, P.O. Box 194, Topanga, CA 94022. Secretary: Donna Curry.
Madison Civic Music Association, 211 N. Carroll, Madison, WI 53703. Manager: Robert R. Palmer.
Major Symphony Managers' Association, San Antonio Symphony, S. Texas Bldg., San Antonio, TX 78205. Chairman: Chris Hutchinson.
Massachusetts Music Educators' Association, 132 June St., Worcester, MA 01602. Exec. Secretary: David Kaplan.
Masterwork Music and Art Foundation, 300 Mendham Road, Morristown, NJ 07960. Public Relations Director: Mrs. Lois F. Bell.
Metropolitan Symphony Managers' Association, c/o American Symphony Orchestra League, P.O. Box 66, Vienna, VA 22180.
Mobile Chamber Music Society, 401 Auditorium Drive, Mobile, AL 36602.
Modern Music Masters' Society, P.O. Box 347, Park Ridge, IL 60068. Executive Secretary: Mrs. Frances M. Harley.
Moravian Music Foundation, Drawer Z, Salem Station, Winston-Salem, NC 27108. Director: Dr. Karl Kroeger.
Music Club of Westfield, 819 E. Broad St., Westfield, NJ 07090.
Music Council of Puerto Rico, c/o Instituto de Cultura Puertorriquera, San Juan, PR. Director: Ricardo E. Alegria.
Music Critics Association, Inc., and M.C.A. Educational Activities, Inc., 6201 Tuckerman Lane, Rockville, MD 20852. Executive Secretary: Richard D. Freed.
Music Editors' Association, Box 714, Mount Vernon, NY 10551. Contact: Roy Anderson.
Music Educators' National Conference, 1902 Association Drive, Reston, VA 22091. Executive Director: Donald W. Dillon.
Music in the Garden, Franklin St., Vineyard Haven, MA 02568. Contact: Sydna White.
Music Library Association, Inc., 2017 Walnut St., Philadelphia, PA 19103. President: Dr. Ruth Watanabe.
Music Publishers' Association of the U.S., 810 7th Avenue, NY 10019. Philip B. Wattenberg.
Music Teachers' National Association, 2113 Carew Tower, Cincinnati, OH 45202. Exec. Director: Mrs. M. H. Clinton.
Musical Theatre Guild, 5 Hartford Conservatory, 834 Asylum Avenue, Hartford, CT 06105.
Musicians' Club of America, 322 Navarre Avenue, Coral Gables, FL 33134. Chairman of the Board: Dr. Ralph Harris.
National Academy of Recording Arts and Sciences, 4444 Riverside Drive, Burbank, CA 91505. Executive Director: Mrs. Christine M. Farnon.
National Association of Composers, U.S.A., New York Chapter, 133 West 69th St., New York, NY 10023. President: Dr. Larry Paul Lockwood.
National Association of Music Executives in State Universities, Dept. of Music, University of Tennessee, Knoxville, TN 37616.
National Association of Music Merchants, Inc., 35 E. Wacker Drive, Chicago, IL 60601. Executive Vice-president: William R. Gard.
National Association for Music Therapy, Inc., 610 Kentucky, Suite 206, P.O. Box 610, Lawrence, KS 66044. Exec. Director: Margaret Sears.
National Association of Negro Musicians, 4512 S. Vincennes Avenue, Chicago, IL 60653. President: Theodore Charles Stone.
National Association of Organ Teachers, Inc., 7938 Bertram Avenue, Hammond, IN 46324. Administrative Director: Jack C. Greig.
National Association of Pastoral Musicians, 1029 Vermont Ave. N.W., Washington, DC 20005. Founder & President: Rev. Virgil C. Funk.
National Association of Schools of Music, 11250 Roger Bacon Drive 5, Reston, VA 22090. Executive Director: Samuel Hope.
National Association of Teachers of Singing, Inc., 250 West 57th St., New York, NY 10019. Secretary: James Francis Browning.
National Band Association, Band Office, Northwestern University, Evanston, IL 60201. Secretary: Maxine Lefever.
National Convention of Gospel Choirs and Choruses, 4154 S. Ellis Avenue, Chicago, IL 60653. President: Thomas A. Dorsey.
National Council of State Supervisors of Music, c/o Music Educators' National Conference, 1902 Association Drive, Reston, VA 22091. Chairman: Malone Coakley.
National Educational Television, 10 Columbus Circle, New York, NY.

National Federation of Music Clubs, 220 East 80th St., New York, NY 10021. President: Dr. Merle Montgomery.

National Guild of Community Music Schools, Third St. Music School Settlement, 55 East 3rd St., New York, NY 10003. President: Harris Danziger.

National Institute of Arts and Letters, 633 West 155 St., New York, NY 10032. Secretary: William Meredith.

National Music Council, 250 West 57th St., Suite 626, New York, NY 10019. Secretary: Mrs. Doris O'Connell.

National Music Publishers' Association, Inc., 110 East 59th St., New York, NY 10022. President: Dr. Leonard Feist.

National Orchestra Association, 111 West 57th St., Room 1500, New York, NY 10019. Director for Community Relations: Constance O'Sullivan.

National Piano Foundation, 435 N. Michigan Avenue, Chicago, IL 60601. Executive Director: George M. Otto.

National Piano Manufacturers' Association of America, 435 N. Michigan Avenue, Chicago, IL 60611.

National School Orchestra Association, 1126 South Oak, Freeport, IL 61032. Secretary: Myron McLain.

New Bedford Chamber Music Society, 144 Campbell, New Bedford, MA 02740. Manager: David Sachs.

Organ and Piano Teachers' Association, 436 Via Media, Palos Verdes Estates, CA 90274. Secretary: Phyllis MacFadden.

People-to-People Music Committee, Inc., c/o John F. Kennedy Center for the Performing Arts, Washington, DC 20566. Executive Director: Mrs. Ruth Sickafus.

Percussive Arts Society, Inc., 130 Carol Drive, Terre Haute, IN 47805. Executive Secretary/Treasurer: Neal Fluegel.

Performing Arts Foundation, Inc., 500 Riverside Drive, New York, NY 10027. Secretary: Mrs. Herman Rottenberg.

Phi Mu Alpha Sinfonia, 10600 Old State Rd., Evansville, IN 47711. Exec. Director: Dr. D. E. Beeman.

Pro Arte Musical of Puerto Rico, San Juan, PR.

Public Broadcasting Service, 485 L'Enfant Plaza West, S.W., Washington, DC 20024.

Recording Industry Association of America, Inc., 1 East 57th St., New York, NY 10022. Executive Director: Henry Brief.

Rochester Civic Music Association, 60 Gibbs St., Rochester, NY 14604. Executive Manager: Howard Scott.

San Mateo County Chamber Music Society, 829 Vega Circle, Foster City, CA 94404. Executive/Musical Director: Helen Beyer.

Screen Composers' Association, 9250 Wilshire Blvd., Beverly Hills, CA 90212. President: Nathan Scott.

Seesaw Music Corporation, 177 East 87th St., New York, NY 10028. President: Raoul R. Ronson.

SESAC Inc., (Performing Right Society), 10 Columbus Circle, New York, NY 10019. President: Mrs. Alice H. Prager.

Sinfonia Foundation, 10600 Old State Road, Evansville, IN 47711. Secretary: Alan E. Adams.

Society of Black Composers, 148 Columbus Avenue, New York, NY 10023. Secretary: Carmen Moore.

Society of the Classic Guitar, 409 East 50th St., New York, NY 10022. Music Director: Miss Martha Nelson.

Society for Ethnomusicology, Inc., Room 513, 201 South Main St., Ann Arbor, MI 48108. Secretary: Dr. Charlotte Frisbie.

Southeastern Composers' League, University of Maryland, College Park, MD 20742. Exec. Secretary: Dr. Ralph Turek.

Texas Music Educators' Association, 1011 W. 31st, P.O. Box 14707, Austin, TX 78761. Exec. Secretary: Bill Cormack.

United Choral Conductors of America, c/o Mozart Hall, 328 East 86th St., New York, NY 10028. President: Leonard A. Temme.

U.S. Army, Navy and Air Force Bandsmen's Association, P.O. Box 1826, New Haven, CT 06508. Secretary: Major A. R. Teta.

U.S. Information Agency, Music Section, 1717 H. St., N.W., Room 414, Washington, DC 20547. Music Advisor: Daryl D. Dayton.

Washington Music Educators' Association, Federal Way School District, Federal Way, WA 98002. Vice-president: Vern Niclaus.

Wolftrap Foundation for the Performing Arts, 1624 Trap Road, Vienna, VA 22180. Assistant to Director of Programming: Mary Therese Mennino.

Women Band Directors' National Association, 130 Christopher Circle, Ithaca, NY 14850. President: Mrs. Nora Arquit.
Women's Association for Symphony Orchestras, 5100 Park Lane, Dallas, TX 75220. President: Mrs. Theodore Strauss.
Worcester County Music Association, Memorial Auditorium, Worcester, MA 01608. Executive Director: Mrs. Stasia B. Hovenesian.
Young Concert Artists, 75 East 55 St., New York, NY 10022. Secretary: Judith Kurz.

URUGUAY

Asociación General de Autores del Uruguay (Performing Right Society), Canelones 1130, Montevideo. Secretary: Luis Eduardo Etchegonchelhay.
Asociación Uruguaya de Músicos, Maldonado 1130, Montevideo.
Centro Cultural de la Música, 18 de Julio 1006, piso 6, Cepto 5, Montevideo. Director: Jorge Calvetti.
Consejo Internaciónal de Música (National Committee), Andes 1424, Montevideo. President: Carlos Estrada.
Juventudes Músicales del Uruguay, Rio Negro 1228, Montevideo. Secretary-General: Maria Tania Siver.
Sociedad Uruguay de Música Contemporanea (National Section), Casilla de Comeo 1328, Montevideo. Secretary: Coriún Aharonián.

VENEZUELA

Asociación Venzolana de Autores y Compositores (Performing Right Society), Edificio Camuri, calle Real Sabana Grande, Caracas. Director: Maria Luisa Escobar.
Consejo Internaciónal de Música (National Committee), Edificio Macanao, av. Paris, Las Mercedes, Caracas. Secretary General: Mrs. Nellie Mele Lara.
Insituto Interamericano de Etnomusicologia y Folklore, Apartado 6238, Caracas. Director: Isabel Aretz.
Juventudes Músicales Venezolanas, 10 Transversal de la Castellana, Edificio Habitat apto. 13B, Caracas Secretary-General: Renata Tomaselli.
Sociedad de Autores y Compositores de Venezuela, Avenida Andres Bello, Edificio VAM, Torre Oeste, 9 piso, Caracas. Secretary-General: Luisa Helena Gonzáles.

YUGOSLAVIA

Cultural Centre of FIJM, 52393 Grožnjan.
Institute of Musicology, Knez Mihailova 35, Belgrade. Director: Dr. Dimitrije Stefanović.
International Federation of Festival Organizers (FIDOF), P.O. Box 370, 58000 Split. Secretary General: Prof. Armando Moreno.
International Music Council (National Committee), Mişarka 12, Belgrade. Secretary: Vojislav Kostic.
International Society for Contemporary Music (Yugoslav section), Remetinacka 75, Zegreb. Secretary General: Natko Devcic.
Union of Composers' Organisations of Yugoslavia, Mišarska 12-14, 11000 Belgrade. President of the Executive: Dane Škerl.
Union of Yugoslav Performing Artists, Terazije 26, Belgrade. Secretary: Stanislow Kovacevic.
Youth & Music, Terazije 26/II, 11000 Belgrade. Contact: Vera Stojanović.

ZIMBABWE

National Arts Foundation of Zimbabwe, P.O. Box UA463, Union Avenue, Salisbury. Chief Executive: D. A. Huggins.

APPENDIX C

MAJOR COMPETITIONS AND AWARDS

In most cases competitions and awards have been listed under the names of the organizing bodies. Others, particularly major international competitions have been listed under the title of the competition or award.

It should be remembered that in many cases, values of awards and restrictions on entry may vary from year to year and interested readers are advised to contact organizations directly for fuller information.

Except where an award is marked International or it is otherwise stated, it should be assumed that only those born or residing in the country concerned may apply. Government and general awards have been excluded. Many of the institutions listed in Appendix E also run scholarship schemes.

ARGENTINA

ASOCIATION FILARMONICA DE MENDOZA
Catamarca 31, local A-24 Mendoza. *El Concurs Internacional para Jovenes Pianistas* (International Competition for Young Pianists). Annual competition for those born or resident in the Mendoza region only. Age limit: 30. 1st prize: 2,000 pesos + concert performances; 2nd prize: 1,500 pesos + concert performances; 3rd prize (Prize of the Secretary of Culture of Mendoza): 1,000 pesos + concert performance.

ASOCIACION FILARMONICA DE OLAVARRIA
Alsina 3183, Olavarria, Provincia de Buenos Aires. A number of annual scholarships and awards made to young musicians.

LATIN AMERICAN CENTER FOR ADVANCED MUSICAL STUDIES
Torcuato di Tella Institute, Supero 1502, Belgrano R. Buenos Aires. Approx. 10 annual scholarships in composition and music teaching available for residents of Canada, U.S.A., or Latin America. Tenable: for 2 years at the Latin American Center. Value: $U.S.200 per month.

ORQUESTA SINFONICA PROVINCIAL DE ROSARIO
calle Cordoba 1331, Rosario (SF). Biennial competitions for chamber and symphonic compositions. Biennial competitions for young solo instrumentalists.

AUSTRALIA

AUSTRALIAN BROADCASTING COMMISSION
PO Box 487, Sydney, N.S.W. 2000. *A.B.C. Vocal and Instrumental Competition.* Annual competitions for pianists, orchestral instrumentalists & singers. Age limits: Singers between 16 & 29 inclusive; others below 29. Prizes worth $A2,000 in each category.

AUSTRALIAN COUNCIL FOR THE ARTS
PO Box 302, N. Sydney, N.S.W. 2060. A number of annual scholarships to enable young musicians to continue their musical education.

AUSTRALIAN MUSIC EXAMINATIONS BOARD
University of Melbourne, Parkville, Victoria 3052. 1 scholarship awarded biennially. Tenable: for 2 years study outside Australia. Age limits: 16-21 (instrumentalists); 16-24 (vocalists). Value: $1,600 per year.

AUSTRALIAN OPERA AUDITIONS
'Fairwater,' 560 New S. Head Road, Double Bay, N.S.W. 2028. A number of scholarships awarded annually at competitive auditions.

MUSIC TEACHERS' ASSOCIATION OF SOUTH AUSTRALIA
4 Toronto Ave., Clapham, S. Australia 5062. *Gwen Robinson Award.* Biennial award for

- piano students. Tenable: for 2 years. Age limits: 13-15. Value: $100 per annum. *Norman Sellick Memorial Scholarship.* Annual award to instrumental students. Age limit: 12. Value: $100.

SUN NEWSPAPER
235 Jones St., Broadway, N.S.W. 2007. *Sun Aria Competition.* Annual opera contest for those born or residing in Australia, New Zealand, United Kingdom or the Commonwealth. Tenable: for overseas study. 1st prize: $1,500 + scholarship worth $3,000; 2nd prize: $250; 3rd prize: $250; 4th prize: $125; 6th prize: $125.

AUSTRIA

DEPARTMENT OF CULTURE OF THE CITY OF INNSBRUCK
Fallmerayerstrasse 6,6010 Innsbruck. *Paul Hofhaimer-Wettbewerb der Landeshaupstadt Innsbruck.* (Paul-Hofhaimer Competition of the County Town of Innsbruck). Annual award for the interpretation of organ music.

FERNSEH-OPERNPREIS DER STADT SALZBURG
(Television Opera Prize of the City of Salzburg). Argentinierstrasse 22, 1041 Vienna. Triennial composition competition. for operas written for television, of up to 120 minutes duration. Open to all broadcasting organizations belonging to the European Broadcasting Union. 1st prize: AS: 125.000.

HOCHSCHULE FÜR MUSIK UND DARSTELLENDE KUNST IN GRAZ
Nikolaigasse 2 8023 Graz. *Wettbewerb der Hochschule für Musik und darstellende Kunst in Graz, (Competition of the College of Music and Dramatic Art in Graz).* Biennial competition for organ improvisation.

INTERNATIONAL CHORWETTBEWERB
(International Choral Competition). Kulturamt der Stadt Spittal an der Drau, Burgplatz 1, 9800 Spittal/Drau. Annual competition for choirs. Category A (mixed choirs): 1st prize, 15,000 Austrian Schillings; 2nd prize, 10,000 Schillings; 3rd prize, 5,000 Schillings. Category B (folk song, mixed choirs): 1st prize, 8,000 Schillings; 2nd prize, 6,000 Schillings; 3rd prize, 4,000 Schillings.

INTERNATIONAL ORGAN IMPROVISATION COMPETITION
PO Box 959, 1011 Vienna. Annual competition for organists. Age limit: 30. Prizes vary.

MUSIKALISCHE JUGEND ÖSTERREICHS
Max Tendlerstr. 16, Postfach 14, 8700 Leoben. *'Jugend Musiziert' Instrumentalwettbewerb für die Jugend Österreichs.* ('Youth Makes Music' Instrumental Competition for Young People of Austria). Biennial competition (1981: 1983) featuring a different instrument each year. Age limits: 10-25.

UNIVERSITY OF VIENNA
Dr. Karl-Lueger-Ring 1,1010 Vienna 1. A number of scholarships in the history of music open to applicants who must have spent at least 1 year at a European University or 2 years at a European College. Tenable: at the University of Vienna Summer School. International.

BELGIUM

LES AMIS DE MOZART
39 rue Fritz-Toussaint, 1050 Brussels. *Belgian International Song Competition.* Annual competition for vocalists. Age limit: 35.

CONCOURS DE COMPOSITION 'PRIX DE ROME'
c/o Ministère de la Culture Française, Direction générale des Arts et des Lettres, Avenue de Cortenbergh 158, 1040 Brussels.

CONCOURS INTERNATIONALE DE COMPOSITION MUSICALE POUR CARILLON (MALINES)
c/o Beiaardschool, Frederik De Mérodestraat, 2800 Mechelen.

CONCOURS MUSICAL INTERNATIONAL REINE ELISABETH
(Queen Elisabeth International Music Competition). 11 rue Baron Horta, 1000 Brussels.

1980 Violin; 1982 Composition. Prizes approx. 1,335,000 Belgian francs. Age limits for violinists: 17-30.

FESTIVAL VAN VLAANDEREN
(Festival of Flanders) Collaert Mansionstraat 30,8000 Bruges. Annual international festival featuring a competition for different instruments each year. 1981 Early Music Competition (ensembles). 1982 J. S. Bach organ competition. Prizes worth at least £4,000. Age limit for soloists, 33; for ensembles, average of 30.

INTERNATIONAL SINGING COMPETITION
6 rue de Gymnase, 48000 Verviers. Annual competition for vocalists. Age limit: 35.

INTERNATIONAL SINGING CONTEST
rue de Chene 10,1000 Brussels. Annual competition for vocalists. Age limit: 33.

INTERNATIONAL STRING QUARTET COMPETITION
66 rue de Joie, 4000 Liège. An annual competition with the following sections: Composition for string quartet. 1st prize: 60,000 francs. Interpretation of a string quartet composition. 1st prize: 80,,000 francs. String quartet performance. 1st prize: 175,000 francs.

PRIX QUADRIENNAL DE COMPOSITION MUSICALE 'CAMILLE HUYSMANS'
c/o CeBeDem, Rue de L'Hôpital 31, Gte. 2, 1000 Brussels. Quadrennial (next 1982) competition for Belgian composers.

BRAZIL

SOCIEDADE BRASILEIRA DE REALIZACOES ARTISTICO-CULTURAIS.
Ave. Franklin Roosevelt 23, Sala 310, Rio de Janeiro. 1981: Rio de Janeiro International Singing Competition. Prizes: US $6,500 and medals. Age limit: 32 or under.

CANADA

ASSOCIATION OF CANADIAN TELEVISION AND RADIO ARTISTS
105 Carlton St., Toronto, Ontario MB IM2. Over 20 annual awards to composers, lyricists and musical performers. Limited to Canadian citizens or landed immigrants.

CANADA COUNCIL
PO Box 1047, Ottawa, Ontario K1P 5V8. A large number of grants and awards including: *Arts Awards.* Several annually. Tenable: for 4-12 months in Canada or elsewhere. Value: Approx. $8,000 + travel allowance. *Art Bursaries.* Approx. 195 awarded annually. Tenable: for 6-12 months in Canada or elsewhere. Value varies. *Canadian Broadcasting Corporation/Canada Council for Young Composers.* Annual composition competition. Age limit: 29. Prizes vary.

COMPOSERS, AUTHORS AND PUBLISHERS ASSOCIATION OF CANADA
1240 Bay St., Toronto M5R 2C2. Various awards for composition.

HUMANITIES RESEARCH COUNCIL OF CANADA
151 Slater St., Suite 415, Ottawa, Ontario K1P 5H3. *Aids to Publication Programme.* Financial aid is offered to musicologists to help them publish manuscripts.

INSTITUT INTERNATIONAL DE MUSIQUE DU CANADA
106 ave. Dulwich, St-Lambert, Province of Quebec. *Montreal International Competition.* Annual for three years then a break of one year. Competition for musical performance. One of the following is featured each year: piano, violin, voice. 1980, piano; 1981, voice; 1983, violin. Age limits: 16-30 (violinists and pianists); 20-35 (vocalists). Prizes total $22,000 and include: 1st 'Grand Prize' of $10,000.

EDWARD JOHNSON MUSIC FOUNDATION
PO Box 1091, Guelph, Ontario N1H 6N3. *Scholarship Competition.* Annual, open to those born or living in Guelph region. Age limits: 16-30 (instrumentalists); 19-30 (vocalists). 1st prize: 'Robert Markon Prize'; $500; other awards of $100-300.

KIWANIS MUSIC FESTIVAL
Room 127-119 W. Pender, Vancouver 3, British Columbia. Annual competitive festival for amateur musicians. Prizes vary.

LETHBRIDGE SYMPHONY ASSOCIATION
PO Box 1101, Lethbridge, Alberta. 3-5 annual scholarships. Value: $75.

MANITOBA MUSIC COMPETITION FESTIVAL
304-310 Donald St., Winnipeg 1, Manitoba. Annual competitive festival with a number of sections and various awards. For amateurs.

MONTREAL SYMPHONY ORCHESTRA
Place des Arts, Montreal, Quebec H2X 1Y9. *Montreal Symphony Orchestra Competition.* Annual musical performance competition featuring piano and voice one year, strings, woodwind and brass the following year. 1980, wind & strings; 1981, piano & voice; 1982, wind & strings. Prizes (1980) $7,5000 + concert with Montreal Symphony Orchestra for 1st prizewinner. Age limits: strings & piano, category A, 18-25; category B, 17 & under; winds, 16-25; voice, 18-30.

ORGAN COMPOSITION COMPETITION
First-St. Andrew's United Church, 350 Queens Ave., London 14, Ontario. Annual competition for organ music.

CHILE

INTERNATIONAL COMPETITION 'ENRICO CARUSO'
Santiago. Annual competition for vocalists.

CZECHOSLOVAKIA

ACADEMY OF ARTS
Smetanova Nabr. 2, Prague 1. A number of scholarships awarded annually to music graduates. Tenable: for 4-5 years at the Academy of Arts. Value: Covers cost of music tuition + expenses.

BEETHOVEN'S 'HRADEC PRIZE' NATIONAL COMPETITION
747 Hradec nad Moravici. Competition of violin performance. Age limits in the following sections: under 18; 18-21; 21-30.

FREDERIC CHOPIN CZECHOSLOVAK PIANO COMPETITION
353 01 Mariánské Lázné. Age ranges in two sections: under 20; 2&-30.

CZECHOSLOVAK RADIO
Concertino Praga International Radio Competition for Young Musicians. Annual musical performance competition open to all members of the International Radio and Television Organization and the European Broadcasting Union, who may nominate one entrant for each section. Sections: clarinet; flute; French horn; oboe; trumpet. Age limit: 16. Two prizes in each class. Further information from: Czechoslovak Radio, Vinohradska 12, 120 99, Prague 2. *Musical Prize of Radio Brno.* Annual competition for radio musical programmes open to all radio organizations throughout the world. Sections: editorial treatment; interpretation; quality of sound. Prizes in each class. This competition is held at the annual International Music Festival in Brno. Further information from: Czechoslovak Radio, Beethovenova 4, Brno.

DUSEK'S COMPETITION OF MUSICAL YOUTH
Nusle, Pod. Vilami 28, Prague 4. Annual competition for chamber ensembles (though for instrumentalists & singers in some years). Age limits: instrumentalists, 21 & under, singers, 18-25. Honorary prizes.

THE GOLDEN MACE
Vinohradska 12, 120 00 Prague 2. Annual composition award for a military song.

GOLDEN WREATH OF BRATISLAVA
Suché Mýto c 17,801 00 Bratislava. Annual award for vocalists.

HERAN VIOLONCELLO COMPETITION
Usti nad Orlici. Annual musical performance competition. Age limit: 16. Prizes vary.

INTERNATIONAL ROSTRUM OF YOUNG INTERPRETERS
Polackého 2,898 20 Bratislava. Annual competition for musical interpretation.

INTERPRETATION COMPETITION OF THE CZECHOSLOVAKIAN SOCIALIST REPUBLIC
Valdstejnska 10, 11000 Prague 1. Annual musical performance competition open to students and graduates of musical schools in Czechoslovakia. Sections: brass; chamber ensembles; wind. Age limits: average age to be under 35 (chamber ensembles); 18-30 (brass and wind). Prizes in each class.

KOCIAN'S VIOLIN COMPETITION
Usti nad Orlici. Annual. Age limit: 16. Prizes vary. International.

LYRE OF BRATISLAVA
Leningradská 5,890 36 Bratislava. Annual award for a composition open to composers from Czechoslovakia and other socialist countries. Prizes: National 10,000 crowns. International 12,000 crowns.

PIESTANY INTERNATIONAL MUSIC FESTIVAL
Postova St. 1,921 34 Piestany. An annual competitive festival. *Original Composition Competition.* Vocal, chamber or orchestral composition. 1st prize: 7,000 Czech crowns + a performance of the winning work at the Festival. Restricted to those of Czech nationality.

PRAGUE SPRING INTERNATIONAL MUSIC COMPETITION
Alesova Nabrezi 12, Dom umelcu, Prague 1. Annual competition of musical performance. Age limit: 30. 1st prize: 20,000 Czech crowns; 2nd prize: 15,000 Czech. crowns; 3rd prize: 10,000 Czech. crowns. 1978: Singing, horn, trumpet, trombone. 1979: organ, string quartet.

SMETANA PIANO CONTEST
Park of Rest and Culture, Armady 300, Hradec Kralore. Biennial (1980: 1982). Two categories: 25 & under; 19 & under. Prizes: 7,000 Czech crowns & upright piano.

DENMARK

RADIO DENMARK
Radiohuset Rosenorns Alle 22, 1999 Copenhagen V. *Nicolai Malko International Competition for Young Conductors, 1977.* Periodical. Age limit: 30. 1st prize: Approx. 12,000 Danish kroner + conducting engagements with Danish symphony orchestras. 2nd prize: 6,000 Danish kroner; 3rd prize: 5,000 Danish kroner.

EIRE

CASTLEBAR SONG CONTEST
c/o David J. Flood, Main St., Castlebar, Co. Mayo. Annual song composition contest. Prizes total £10,000.

CORK INTERNATIONAL CHORAL AND FOLK DANCE FESTIVAL
15 Bridge St., Cork. Annual competitive festival for amateurs with numerous choral and dance competitions including: *Mixed Choirs Contest. Female Choirs Contest. Male Choirs Contest. School Choirs Contest.* Trophies & monetary prizes.

IRISH ARTS COUNCIL
70 Merrion Square, Dublin 2. Student performers awards varying between £1,200 & £3,600 to a total of £14,000. Composition awards totalling £5,000. *Macauley Fellowship.* Composition award of £2,500.

OIREACHTAS FESTIVAL
6 Harcourt St., Dublin 2. Annual festival for the performance of music in the Irish style with competitions for solo singers and choirs.

FINLAND

ASSOCIATION OF FINNISH SOLOISTS
Sepänkatu 19 A 26,00150 Helsinki 15. A number of annual scholarships for vocalists.

FINNISH NATIONAL OPERA FOUNDATION
Bulevardi 23-27, Helsinki 8. A number of annual grants to opera singers.

FOUNDATION FOR THE PROMOTION OF MUSIC IN FINLAND
Pilvettätenpolku 1,02100 Tapiola. Numerous prizes and awards to music teachers, students of music, performers and composers. Value varies.

INTERNATIONAL JEAN SIBELIUS VIOLIN COMPETITION
Pohj Rautatiekatu 9, Helsinki 10. 4th International violin competition 1980. Prizes total US $17,600. Age limits 16-33.

FRANCE

LES AMIS DE L'ORGUE
(Friends of the Organ) 52 Rue Boileau, 75016 Paris. From time to time they organize musical composition and performance competitions. 1977 Composition; limited to French composers under 35.

CONCOURS INTERNATIONAL DE CHANT DE PARIS
14 bis, ave. du President Wilson, 75116 Paris. Biennial (next 1982). Prizes total 85,000 French francs. Age limits: women 32; men 34.

CONCOURS INTERNATIONAL DE CHANT
Théâtre du Capitole, 31000 Toulouse. Annual competition for vocalists. Age limits: 18-33. Prizes total 60,000 francs.

CONCOURS INTERNATIONAL DE JEUNES CHEFS D'ORCHESTRE
(International Competition for Young Conductors) Parc des Expositions, Planoise, 25000 Besancon. Annual. Age limit: 30. A number of prizes including 1st prize: Prix Emile Vuillermoz + Lyre d'Or + conducting engagements with major orchestras.

CONCOURS INTERNATIONAL D'ORGUE 'GRAND PRIX DE CHARTRES'
(International Organ Competition 'Grand Prize of Chartres) 75, rue de Grenelle, 75007 Paris. Annual competition with two sections: improvisation; interpretation. Competitors may enter for one section only. Age limit: 35. Prize in each section: Medal + 10,000 francs.

CONCOURS INTERNATIONAL DE PIANO ET DE VIOLON 'MARGUERITE LONG-JACQUES THIBAUD'
(International Piano and Violin Competition 'Marguerite Long-Jacques Thibaud') 11 ave. Delcassé, 75008 Paris 8e. Competition with two sections: piano, violin. Age limit: 15-32. Prizes total approx. 135,000 francs. 1st prize in each section: 30,000 francs. 1977 and 1979.

FESTIVAL ESTIVAL
5, place des Ternes, 75017 Paris. 1981. 5th Concours International de Clavecin. 1st prize, 20,000 francs; 2nd prize, 10,000 francs; 3rd prize, 5,000 francs. Age limit: 32.

FONDATION DES ETATS-UNIS
15, Blvd. Jourdan, 75690 Paris 14. *Harriet Hale Wolley Scholarships*. 4 scholarships for music and art offered annually to U.S. citizens only. Tenable: for 1 year to continue studies in Paris. Age limits: 21-34. Value: U.S.$1,700.

FONDATION DE FRANCE
67 rue de Lille, Paris. *Arthur Honegger Prize*. Annual award for musical interpretation.

FONDATION MAEGHT
06, St. Paul, Paris 8e. A number of grants and scholarships awarded annually.

INTERNATIONAL IMPROVISATION PRIZE
Hôtel de Ville, 69 Lyon. Annual musical performance competition with the following sections: classical piano; jazz piano; organ. Age limit: 45. Prizes in each section.

INTERNATIONAL PIANO COMPETITION
85 rue d'Hauteville, Paris 10e. Annual competition for musical performance. Age limit: 32.

INTERNATIONAL STRING QUARTET COMPETITION
Festival d'Evian, Casino Royal Hotel, Chateau de Blonay, 74500 Evian. Competition for String Quartets whose members are under 30.

RENCONTRES INTERNATIONALES D'ART CONTEMPORAIN DE LA ROCHELLE
11 rue Chef de Ville, 17000 La Rochelle. *1981 Concours Rostropovitch.* International cello competition for contemporary music. 1st prize: 15,000 francs + concert engagements. Other prizes worth 26,000 francs. Age limit: 33. *1982 Concours Olivier Messiaen.* International piano competition for contemporary music. Details from above address.

RENCONTRES INTERNATIONALES DE CHANT CHORAL
Boite Postale 1452,37000 Tours. *Concours de Chant Choral.* Annual choral competition for the following classes: mixed choirs; women's & children's voices; men's voices; vocal ensembles. Open only to amateur choirs. Composer's competition for choral composition.

SOCIÉTÉ DES AUTEURS, COMPOSITEURS ET EDITEURS DE MUSIQUE
(Society of Authors, Composers and Editors of Music) 10, rue Chaptal, 75441 Paris 9. A number of awards including: *Georges Enesco Prize.* Annual award to a young violinist who must be an ex-pupil of the Paris Conservatory. *Grand Prize for Chamber Music.* Annual award for a chamber music composition. Age limit: 40. *Grand Prize for Light Symphonic Music.* Annual award for a light symphonic composition. Age limit: 40. *Grand Prize for the Promotion of Symphonic Music.* Annual award for a symphonic composition. Age limit: 40. *Grand Prize for Singing.* Annual vocalists award.

GERMAN DEMOCRATIC REPUBLIC

INTERNATIONAL 'JOHANN SEBASTIAN BACH' COMPETITION
Grassistr 8,701 Leipzig. Annual competition for musical performance with the following sections: organ; piano; violin; voice. Age limit: 33. Prizes total 104,000 Marks.

INTERNATIONAL 'ROBERT SCHUMANN' COMPETITION FOR PIANISTS AND SINGERS
Münzstrasse 12,9500 Zwickau. Annual competition. Prizes (1981): for pianists, 8 prizes with a total value of approximately 20,000 marks; for singers, 6 prizes with a total value of approximately 18,000 marks. Age limits: Pianists, 18 & over; Singers, 20 & over.

GERMAN FEDERAL REPUBLIC

BAYERISCHER RUNDFUNK
Rundfunkplatz 1, 8000 Munich. *Internationaler Musikwettbewerb* (International Musical Competition). Annual competitions. 1980: Voice, Viola, Piano Duo, Trumpet, Wind Quintet. 1981: Piano, Violin, Oboe, Trombone, Trio for Piano & Strings. 1982: Voice, Cello, Clarinet, Guitar, String Quartet. Prizes total (1980) DM. 122,500. Age limits: 17-30.

BERLIN PHILHARMONIC ORCHESTRA
Matthäikirehstrasse 1,1 Berlin 30. *Conductors' Competition.* Annual. Age limits: 20-30. 1st prize: 10,000 Marks; 2nd prize: 7,500 Marks; 3rd prize: 5,000 Marks. *Youth Orchestra Competition.* Annual. 1st Prize: Gold Medal; 2nd prize: Silver Medal.

FOLKWANG-HOCHSCHULE, ESSEN
43 Essen-Warden, Abtei. 10-15 scholarships awarded annually. Tenable: for 1 term at the Hochschule. Age limits: 16-30. International.

INTERNATIONALES MUSIKINSTITUT DARMSTADT
(Darmstadt International Music Institute) Nieder-Ramstaedter Strasse 190,6100 Darmstadt. A number of annual scholarships and also: *Kranichsteiner Musikpreis.* Award for composition and interpretation during vacation courses. Age limit: 30. Prize: 10,000 Marks.

MUSICAL YOUTH OF GERMANY
Hirschgartenallee 19,8 Munich 19. A number of scholarships awarded annually to cover the cost of International Summer music courses. Age limits: 16-30.

STIFTUNG ETTERZHAUSEN DER REGENSBURGER DOMSPATZEN
(Etterzhausen Foundation of the Regensburg Domspatzen) 8411 Etterzhausen. A number of annual scholarships.

HERBERT VON KARAJAN FOUNDATION
Bundesallee 1-12, 1 Berlin 15. *Competition for Youth Orchestras.* Biennial. *Conductors'
Competition.* Biennial. Prize: Herbert von Karajan Gold Medal.

GIBRALTAR

GIBRALTAR SONG FESTIVAL
c/o Gibraltar Tourist Office, Cathedral Square. Annual competitive festival with awards for
singers, composers and lyricists. 1st prize (1980), £2,000 + trophy.

GREECE

'ATHENAEUM' INTERNATIONAL SONG CONTEST
International Cultural Centre 'Athenaeum', 2 Pausaniou St., Athens TT501. Annual
competition for vocalists with sections for men and women. Age limits: 20-32 (men); 20-30
(women). Prizes total U.S. $3,400.

GREEK SONG FESTIVAL OF THESSALONIKI
Thessaloniki International Trade Fair, Thessaloniki 36. Annual Competition for Greek song
composers & lyricists. 3 prizes.

HUNGARY

BELA BARTOK INTERNATIONAL CHOIR CONTEST
Hunyadi U. 1-3, 4026 Debrecen. Biennial competition (1980: 1982) for amateur choirs in
the following classes: men's choirs; women's choirs; mixed choirs; children's choirs. 3
prizes in each section.

BUDAPEST MUSIC WEEKS
Vörösmarty tér 1, Budapest 5. Age limit: 32. Awards total 100,000 forints. 1978.
International Bartok Seminar. Competition for string quartets; organ. 1979. Competition for
violin; violoncello.

HUNGARIAN RADIO AND TELEVISION
Commerce and Public Relations Office, Felszabadulas tér 1, 1053 Budapest. *International
Conductor Competition of Hungarian Television.* Annual competition for young conductors.
Age limit: 35. 1st prize: 40,000 Ft. + a televised engagement to conduct the symphony
orchestra of the Hungarian Radio and Television; 2nd prize: 30,000 Ft.; 3rd prize: 20,000
Ft.

INTERNATIONAL MUSIC COMPETITION
Vörösmarty tér 1, 1366 PO Box 80, Budapest 5. Competition for various instruments,
varying each time. Age limit: 32. Large monetary prizes.

WEINER STRING-QUARTET COMPETITION
c/o Budapest Office of Music Competitions, PO Box 80, 1366 Budapest 5. Annual musical
performance competition. 1st prize: 60,000 Ft.; 2nd prize: 40,000 Ft.; 3rd prize: 20,000
Ft. (All amounts are approx.).

INDIA

NATIONAL CENTRE FOR THE PERFORMING ARTS
89 Bhulabhai Desai Roadd, Bombay 400 036. *Kesarbai Kerkar Scholarship.* Annual award of
approx. £250 to young professional trained in Indian classical music.

ISRAEL

INTERNATIONAL HARP FESTIVAL
52, Nachlat Benjamin St., PO Box 29874, Tel-Aviv. *International Harp Contest.* Triennial
competition for harpists (next: 1982). Age limit: 35. 1st prize: Lyon and Healy Concert
Harp; other cash prizes.

INTERNATIONAL ARTUR RUBINSTEIN PIANO MASTER COMPETITION
PO Box 29404, 5th Floor, Shalom Tower, Tel-Aviv. Annual competition for pianists. Prizes

vary. Age limits: 18-32. Candidates must have won prizes at other competitions or be recommended by artists of International stature.

LEAGUE OF COMPOSERS IN ISRAEL
PO Box 11180, 73, Nordau Blvd., Tel-Aviv. *Lieberson Prize Contest.* Annual competition for an instrumental composition. Prizes vary.

ITALY

GASPAR CASSADO INTERNATIONAL VIOLONCELLO CONTEST
c/o Teatro Comunale, Via Solferino 15,50123 Firenze. Biennial cello competition. Age limit: 31. 1st prize, 2,300,000 lire + concert engagements throughout Italy.

ALESSANDRO CASAGRANDE INTERNATIONAL PIANO COMPETITION
via S. Lucio 25,00165 Rome. Annual competition for pianists. Age limit: 35.

ALFREDO CASELLA INTERNATIONAL COMPETITION
c/o Accademia Musicale Napoletana, Via S. Pasquale a Chiara 62,80121 Napoli. Annual awards for pianists and composers. Age limits: 18-32 (pianists - no age limits for composers). 1st prize (pianists): 1,500,000 lire and Silver cup; 1st prize (composers): Gold Medal.

CHIGIANA MUSIC ACADEMY FOUNDATION
Via di Citta 89,53100 Siena. A number of annual scholarships to enable music students to attend summer courses.

ALBERTO CURCI FOUNDATION
via Nardones 8,80132 Naples. *International Violin Competition.* Biennial competition for violinists. Age limit: 32. Prizes total 3,500,000 lire.

GUIDO D'AREZZO INTERNATIONAL CHORAL COMPETITION
Piazza Grande 6,52100 Arezzo. Annual competition for vocalists.

INTERNATIONAL GUIDO CANTELLI CONDUCTING COMPETITION
Ente provinciale per il Turismo, Corso Cavour 2,28100 Novara. Annual competition for young conductors. Age limit: 32.

INTERNATIONAL CENTRE FOR STUDIES FOR THE DIFFUSION OF ITALIAN MUSIC
Via dei Greci 18, Rome. A number of annual scholarships available to those with a degree or diploma from a musical academy or conservatory. Tenable: for study in Rome or Venice. Age limit: 35. Value: 90,000 lire per month.

INTERNATIONAL COMPETITION FOR CHAMBER ORCHESTRA COMPOSITION
piazza S. Angelo, 20121 Milan. Annual award for an orchestral composition of 15-25 minutes duration. 1st prize (Premio Angelicum): 800,000 lire.

INTERNATIONAL COMPETITION OF THE CITY OF TRIESTE
Palazzo Municipale, Piazza dell'Unita d'Italia 4,3412 Trieste. Annual award for an orchestral composition. 1st prize 3,000,000 lire + performance of winning composition.

INTERNATIONAL COMPETITION 'CONQUEST OF THE CLASSICAL GUITAR'
Viale Marche 31,20125 Milan. Annual competition of musical performance. Minimun age limit: 13. 1st prize: 150,000 lire + Classical Guitar.

INTERNATIONAL ORCHESTRAL CONDUCTING COMPETITION
c/o Accademia Nazionale de S. Cecilia, via Vittorio 6,00187 Rome. Triennial competition for young conductors. Age limit: 35. 1st prize: 2,000,000 lire + conducting engagements; 2nd prize: 1,000,000 Lire.

INTERNATIONAL 'NICOLO PAGANINI' VIOLIN PRIZE
Palazzo Tursi, Via Garibaldi 9, Genova. Annual competition for musical performance. Age limit: 35. 1st prize (Paganini Prize): 5,000,000 lire + public performances.

INTERNATIONAL PIANO COMPETITION 'F. BUSONI'
c/o Conservatorio C. Monteverdi, Piazza Domenicani 19,391000 Bolzano. Annual

competition for pianists. Age limits: 15-32. 1st prize: 1,000,000 lire + concert engagements: 2nd prize: 500,000 lire.

INTERNATIONAL PIANO COMPETITION 'ETTORE POZZOLI'
Commune di Seregno, 20038 Seregno. Biennial competition for pianists. 1st prize includes: 1,000,000 lire + 5 public concert performances; 2nd prize: 500,000 lire; 3rd prize: 300,000 lire; Extra prize awarded to youngest finalist: Gold Medal 'Giulio Confalonieri.'

INTERNATIONAL 'RICCARDO ZANDONAI' COMPOSITION COMPETITION
c/o Tourist Office, Rovereto. Annual competition for a composition for two pianos of 5-10 minutes duration. Age limit: 35.

DANIELE NAPOLITANO COMPOSITION PRIZE
c/o Accademia Musicale Napoletana, Via S. Pasquale a Chiara 62, 80121 Naples. Biennial award for a composition for trio, quartet or quintet with optional piano.

SOCIETA ITALIANA DEGLI AUTORIED EDITORI
(Italian Society of Authors and Editors) Foro Bonaparte 18, Milan. *Premio musicale guida valcarenghi.* Annual award for musical, operatic or theatrical composition.

SOCIETA DEL QUARTETTO
Casella Postale 127, 13100 Vercelli. *Viotti International Music Competition.* Annual competition for different performers. 1080: Voice, Piano, Percussion, Composition. 1981: Voice, Piano, Trombone, Composition. 1982: Voice, Piano, 2 piano duo, Composition. Prizes total 8,000,000 lire.

ERCOLE VARZI FOUNDATION
Ave. Enrico Cabella, Via del Lauro 3,20120 Milan. A number of annual prizes and scholarships.

JAPAN

MIN-ON MUSIC COMPETITION
Min-On Concert Association, 32-13 Kita-Shinjuko, 1-chome, Shinjuko-ku, Tokyo 160. Annual competition for different performers each time. Prizes total 1,700,000 yen + concert engagements. Age limit: 36.

TOKYO BROADCASTING SYSTEM
5-3-6 Akasaka, Minato-ku, Tokyo. *International Contest.* This song competition is held annually at the Tokyo Music Festival, sponsored by the above organization. Awards are for vocal compositions of up to 3 minutes duration. Grand Prize: Trophy + 3,000,000 yen; Golden Award: Trophy + 1,000,000 yen; Silver Awards: Trophies + 600,000 yen; Bronze awards: Trophies + 300,000 yen.

WORLDWIDE 'MADAME BUTTERFLY' COMPETITION
4-4, 1-chome, Akasaka, Minato-ku, Tokyo. Competition for sopranos and tenors under 35. Prizes total over 5,000,000 yen.

KOREA

MUSIC ASSOCIATION OF KOREA
Room no. 303, FACO Building, 81-6 Sechon-Ro, Chongro-Ku, Seoul. A number of annual awards including: *Prize of Musical Culture.* Awarded annually to a musician of any kind.

MALTA

GOLDEN CROSS FESTIVAL
An annual competitive festival with twelve competitions for vocal compositions of up to 3 1/2 minutes duration. 1st prize: Golden Cross; 2nd prize: Trophy. International.

MONACO

PRIX DE COMPOSITION MUSICALE PRINCE PIERRE DE MONACO
(Prince Pierre of Monaco Composition Prize) Palais princier, Monaco. Annual competition for

composers. 1981: Chamber Music for a maximum of 12 performers. 1982: Symphonic and Ballet Music. Prize: 30,000 French francs. No age limits.

THE NETHERLANDS

DONEMUS FOUNDATION
Jacob Obrechtstraat 51, Amsterdam. Provides a number of annual grants and scholarships to musicians.

FEDERATION OF DUTCH SINGERS' ASSOCIATION
PO Box 496, The Hague. *International Choral Festival.* Biennial contest for vocalists (next: 1977). Value of awards varies.

GAUDEAMUS FOUNDATION
Contemporary Music Centre, PO Box 30, Bilthoven. *International Gaudeamus Competition for the Interpretation of Contemporary Music.* Annual contest for vocalists and musicians of all kinds. Age limit: 35. A number of prizes including: 1st prize: 4,000 Dutch florins. Each prize-winner has the chance of concert performances. *International Gaudeamus Composers' Competition.* Annual contest for compositions for any of the following: chamber music ensemble; chamber orchestra; choir; symphony orchestra or electronic music. Age limit: 35.

INTERNATIONAL JUBILEE COMPETITION FOR DUTCH CHAMBER MUSIC
c/o B.U.M.A., Marius Bauerstraat 30, Amsterdam 1017. Annual musical performance competition for chamber music ensembles of 3-6 players. Prizes total 60,000 Dutch florins.

INTERNATIONAL KOORFESTIVAL
(International Choir Festival). Postbus 496, The Hague. Biennial competitive festival with the following sections: childrens choirs; female choirs; male choirs; mixed choirs; youth choirs. Age limits: 16 (childrens choirs); 16-25 (youth choirs). Competitions in 1981, 1983.

INTERNATIONAL ORGAN COMPOSITION COMPETITION
Emmawijk 2, Zwolle. Annual contest for organ composition. Prizes vary.

INTERNATIONAL SINGING COMPETITION 'S-HERTOGENBOSCH
POB 1225, 's-Hertogenbosch. Annual competition for singers. Prizes total 22,500 guilders. Age limit: 32.

WERELDMUZIEK CONCOURS KERKKADE
(World Music Contest) Quadrennial competition with the following sections: bands; conducting; instrumentalists; orchestras; vocalists. Age limit: 30. Prizes vary. International.

NEW ZEALAND

QUEEN ELIZABETH II ARTS COUNCIL OF NEW ZEALAND
Box 6040, Wellington. Numerous annual awards made on a competitive basis. Tenable: for study in New Zealand or abroad. Values vary.

UNIVERSITY OF OTAGO
Dunedin, New Zealand. *Mozart Fellowship.* Annual award to a young musician under 27. Must be born or resident in New Zealand. Value $6,000 New Zealand.

NORWAY

ASSOCIATION OF FRIENDS OF MUSIC
Riddervolds gate 10, Oslo 2. *Debutant Prize.* Biennial award for musical performance.

EDMUND RUDD AND KATE AND ALICE WALLENBERG'S SCHOLARSHIPS
Tollbodgaten 27, Oslo. Annual scholarships awarded to female vocalists, citizens of Norway or Sweden.

PERU

FUNDACION CODESA
PO Box 5715, Lima. *C. Harshmanini Keyboard and Harp Award.* Annual award for pianists and harpists. No age limit. Value varies.

THE PHILIPPINES

MANILA SYMPHONY SOCIETY
PO Box 664, Manila. *Manila Symphony Orchestra Scholarships.* Annual scholarships awarded to instrumental music students. *Manila Symphony Orchestra Young Artists Competition.* Annual competition for young musical performers.

POLAND

ASSOCIATION OF POLISH MUSICIANS
Krucza 24-26, 00-526 Warsaw. *Orpheo Award.* For the best interpretation of Polish Music at the International Warsaw Autumn Festival. *Maria Andrzejewska Prize.* Annual award for contributions to the development of Polish music. *Gold Award.* 5 annual awards made to the most meritorious members of the Association. *Prize of the Association of Polish Musicians.* Annual award for contributions to music generally. Also 3 annual prizes are made to music critics for the best articles in periodicals, radio and television.

COMPETITION FOR YOUNG POLISH COMPOSERS
Rynek Starego Miasta 27,00-272 Warsaw. Annual competition for musical composition of any kind.

GRZEGORZ FITELBERG COMPETITION FOR COMPOSERS
Plebiscytowa 3,40-035 Katowice. Biennial composition contest for members of Polish Composers Union.

INTERNATIONAL PIANO COMPETITION 'FREDERIC CHOPIN'
ul. Okolnik 1,00-953 Warsaw 37. Annual competition for pianists. Age limits: 15-28. A number of awards including: 1st prize: 60,000 zlotys + gold medal.

ARTUR MALAWSKI COMPETITION FOR COMPOSERS
Bohaterów Stalingradu 3,31-038 Craców. Annual contest for musical composition.

HENRYK WIENIAWSKI SOCIETY
Wodna Street 27,61-781 Poznań. *Henryk Wieniawski International Violin Competition.* Competition held approx. every 5 years. Age limit: 30. 1981: for violinists & violin makers. Numerous prizes.

PORTUGAL

CONCORSO INTERNACIONAL VIANNA DA MOTTA
(Vianna da Motta International Competition) Ave. Conselheiro Fernando Sousa SRF-r/c, Lisbon. Biennial competition for musical performance featuring the piano one time, violin the next. Next: (1981) will be for the violin. Age limits: 17-30. Many prizes including: 1st prize (Grand Prix Vianna da Motta): $U.S.4,000 + concert engagements in Portugal and other European countries + medal + recording contract; 2nd prize (Gulbenkian Prize): $U.S.3,000; 3rd prize (City of Lisbon Prize): $U.S.1,500; 4th prize (Luis Barbosa Prize): $U.S.1,000; 5th prize: $U.S.300; 6th prize: $U.S.200.

ROMANIA

GEORGE ENESCU INTERNATIONAL COMPETITION
I strada Stirbei Voda, Bucharest. Competition for violinists, pianists, singers. Triennial.

SOUTH AFRICA

ELLIE MARX MEMORIAL SCHOLARSHIP
Ladywood, Hillwood Ave., Claremont 7700, Cape. Annual award for performance on a stringed musical instrument. Tenable: for 3 years at an appropriate institution outside S. Africa. Value: Approx. R400.

SOUTH AFRICAN BROADCASTING CORPORATION
PO Box 4559, Johannesburg 2000. *South African Broadcasting Corporation Music Prize.* Annual award usually made for piano playing but other instruments have been included. Age

limits: 18-30, 1st prize: R 2,000; 2nd prize (South African Music Rights Organization Prize): R 1,000; 3rd prize: R 800. Open to South Africans and residents of 4 years standing.

SOUTH AFRICAN MUSIC RIGHTS ORGANIZATION
SAMRO House, De Beer and Juta Sts., Braamfontein, Johannesburg. *Scholarship for South African Composers.* Biennial award (next: 1982) open to residents of S. Africa, S.W. Africa, Botswana, Lesotho, Swaziland. Tenable: for 2 years. Value: R 1,000 per annum. *Scholarship for South African Performing Artists.* Biennial award (next: 1981). Conditions and value of award as for Composers' Scholarship.

SPAIN

CONCURSO DE ARTISTAS NOVELES
(Competition for New Artists) La Voz de Espana, San Sebastian. Annual competition for musical performance with the following sections: instrumental, vocal, vocal duet, vocal group. International.

CONSERVATORIO DE MUSICA DE ORENSE
plaza Mayor 2, Orense. *Conservatory of Music International Competition.* Annual competition for pianists.

GUIPUZCOA CHORAL FESTIVAL
Bajos del Teatro Victoria Eugenia, San Sebastian. Annual competitive festival for vocalists. No age limits.

INTERNATIONAL MUSIC COMPETITION 'MARIA CANALS'
Gran Via 654, Barcelona 10. Annual competition for various performers. Prizes total approximately 800,000 pesetas. Age limits: 18-32.

INTERNATIONAL SINGING CONTEST 'FRANCISCO VINAS'
Bruch 125, Barcelona 9. Annual contest for vocalists. Age limits: 18-32 (women); 20-35 (men). For both men and women there are the following awards: 1st prize: 60,000 pesetas + commemorative medal; 2nd prize: 40,000 + commemorative medal; 3rd prize: 30,000 + commemorative medal. There are also many other special prizes and awards connected with this contest.

PREMIO CIUDAD DE SAN SEBASTIAN DE ACORDEON
(Accordion Prize of the City of San Sebastian) Theatre, San Sebastian. Annual competition for accordionists.

PREMIO INTERNACIONAL DE MUSICA 'OSCAR ESPLA'
(International Oscar Espla Prize) Town Hall, Alicante. Annual competition for a symphonic composition of 15-25 minutes duration. Award: 250,000 pesetas.

SWITZERLAND

CONCOURS INTERNATIONAL DE COMPOSITION MUSICALE OPERA BALLET
(International Competition for the Composition of Opera and Ballet) Maison de la Radio, 66 blvd. Carl-Vogt, 1211 Geneva. 1981: Ballet Music.

CONCOURS INTERNATIONAL D'EXECUTION MUSICALE
(International Competition for Musical Performers) 12 rue de L'Hôtel de Ville, 1204 Geneva. Annual contest with the following sections in 1977: voice; viola; piano; oboe; piano; trio. Age limits: 15-30. Prizes total 80,000 francs.

FESTIVAL DE MUSIQUE MONTREUX-VEVEY
c/o Festival de Musique, Case Postale 124, 1820 Montreux. Annual competitive festival with a number of competitions including: *Concours Clara Haskil, 1981 & 1983.* (Clara Haskil Competition). Competition for pianists. Age limit: 32. Prize: 10,000 Swiss francs + concert appearances + recording opportunity. International.

GOLDEN ROSE TELEVISION FESTIVAL
c/o Tourist Office, 42 Grand-Rue, 1820 Montreux. Annual competitive festival with awards for winning musical television programmes. Prizes: 10,000 Swiss francs + Gold, Silver or Bronze Rose.

PRIX DE COMPOSITION MUSICALE 'REINE MARIE-JOSÉ'
(Queen Marie-José Prize for Composition) Merlinge-Gy, 1249 Geneva. Biennial contest for a
chamber music composition of 10-30 minutes duration. No age limit. 1st prize: 10,000
francs. International.

U.S.S.R.

INTERNATIONAL TCHAIKOVSKY COMPETITION
ul Neglinnaya 15, Moscow. Competitions in the following sections: cello; piano; violin;
voice. Age limits: singers 18-32; instrumentalists 16-30. Prizes total over 10,000 rubles,
medals, badges, etc. + concert tour.

UNITED KINGDOM

ANGLO-AUSTRIAN SOCIETY
46 Queen Anne's Gate, London SW1H 9AU. *Richard Tauber Memorial Scholarship, 1980.*
For British or Austrian singers. Award includes travel bursary, study grant and recital in
London.

ARTS COUNCIL OF GREAT BRITAIN
105 Piccadilly, London W1V 0AU. *Henry and Lily Davis Fund.* Biannual awards for British or
Commonwealth post graduate musical performers to continue their studies. Tenable: for up
to 6 months. Age limits: 21-30. *Dio Fund.* 1 annual award for a British or Commonwealth
student as a commission fee for an instrumental and/or vocal work. Value: £50. *Miriam
Licette Scholarship.* 1 annual award for a female singer. Tenable: for 1 year to study in Paris.
Age limit: 30. Value: Approx. £1,000. *Guilerminia Suggia gift for the Cello.* 1 annual award
for a cellist. Age limit: 21. International. *H. A. Thew Fund.* A number of annual awards for
musicians and musical organizations in the Liverpool and Merseyside area only.

ANTHONY ASQUITH MEMORIAL FUND
2 Soho Square, London W.1. Annual award to a composer for the 'most apt and imaginative
use of music in a film or television feature.' Prize: Wedgwood Plaque.

ASSOCIATED BOARD OF THE ROYAL SCHOOLS OF MUSIC
14, Bedford Square, London WC1B 3JG. 6 annual scholarships. Tenable: at one of the Royal
Schools of Music for 3-4 years. Age limits: 16-20 (instrumentalists); 18-25 (vocalists).
Value: £100 per annum. 7 annual scholarships for overseas scholars. Tenable: at one of the
Royal Schools of Music for 2-4 years. Age limits as above. Value: Cost of fees + cost of
travel to and from U.K. + help towards living expenses. Further particulars from the
Secretary.

ASSOCIATION OF MUSICAL INSTRUMENT INDUSTRIES
8 Hollywood Way, Woodford Green, Essex. 1 annual award for the best violin made by a
student of music trades at the London College of Furniture. Value: Approx. £4.

AUDIO RECORD REVIEW
Heathcock Press Ltd., Heathcock Court, London W.C.°. Awards: 5-10 annual awards for
best long playing recordings of the year. Prizes are given to individuals on behalf of their
companies. Prizes: Statuettes.

BARBER INSTITUTE OF FINE ARTS
University of Birmingham, Birmingham B15 2TS. *Cunningham Scholarship in Music.* 1
annual award.

BIO-STRATH INTERNATIONAL VIOLIN SCHOLARSHIP
24 Cadogan Square, London SW1. Irregular awards of scholarships to violinists.

BOISE FOUNDATION
14 Bedford Square, London WC1B 3JG. Two scholarships for musical performers. Tenable:
for further study in U.K. or abroad. Age limit: 30. Value: £650 each. Candidates must be
nominated for audition by a nominator authorised by the Foundation.

BRITISH ACADEMY
Burlington House, Piccadilly, London W1V 0NS. Annual grants for research into the history
or theory of music, mainly of post-doctoral standard.

BRITISH BROADCASTING CORPORATION
Kensington House, Richmond Way, London W14 0AX. A number of awards including: *BBC Piano Competition.* An irregular competition for British or Commonwealth pianists. Age limit: 30. 1 prize only. For further information about this competition write to: Room 104, PO Box 27, Manchester M60 1SJ. *BBC-TV Young Musician of the Year Competition.* Annual competition for UK residents who have passed Grade 8 with distinction. Prizes total (1980) £5,000.

GEORGE BUTTERWORTH MEMORIAL TRUST
Clarendon Laboratory, Oxford. A number of grants for composers.

SIR JAMES CAIRD TRUST
136 Nethergate, Dundee DD1 4PA. *Sir James Caird's Travelling Scholarships in Music.* 1 annual scholarship for Scottish singers, instrumentalists, or composers. Tenable: for one year. Value: £500 or above at discretion of Trustees. *Wiseman Prize.* 1 annual award for the best musical performance of the year by a Scot at the Trust's auditions.

CHOWN MUSIC SCHOLARSHIP FUND
Toynbee Hall, 28 Commercial St., London E1 6LS. Annual awards for musicians living in the East End of London to continue their musical education. Minimum age limits: 17. Value: Approx. £30.

CITY OF NOTTINGHAM EDUCATION COMMITTEE
Exchange Buildings, Nottingham NG1 2DF. *Helena Monica Hayton Scholarship.* 1 awarded annually for singers wishing to become professionals, who are living in the Nottingham area. Tenable: for three years at an approved college or institute. Minimum age limit: 17. Value: Approx. £40 per annum. *Amy Stockwin Music Scholarship.* 1 awarded annually for instrumentalists wishing to become professionals, who are living in the Nottingham area. Tenable: at the Royal Academy of Music or a similar institution for one year. Minimum age limit: 17. Value: Approx. £40.

CLEMENTS MEMORIAL PRIZE
St. Margaret's, Broomfield Ave., London N/3 4JJ. 1 awarded biennially for a chamber music composition for 3-6 instruments of 15-30 minutes duration. No age limits. Prize: £250.

CRAMB UNIVERSITY TRUSTS
190 St. Vincent St., Glasgow G2 5SP. *Cramb Bursaries Fund.* 2-3 bursaries awarded annually to students of music at Glasgow University. Value: Total of £100. *Lectureship Fund.* 1 annual award to a visiting lecturer at Glasgow University. Value: £400. *Poorer Students Fund.* Annual awards to help students of music at Glasgow University. Value: Total of 4100. There are no restrictions on age, nationality or instruments played for any of these awards.

HAROLD CRAXTON MEMORIAL TRUST
39a Portsmouth Road, Cobham, Surrey. A number of annual awards to musicians.

CROYDON SYMPHONY ORCHESTRA
18 Temple Road, Croydon CR0 1HT. *Croydon Symphony Orchestra Soloist Award.* Annual competition for singers and solo instrumentalists resident in Surrey, Sussex, Kent or a Greater London Borough South of the Thames. Age limits: 28. 1st prize: £20 + solo performance with Croydon Symphony Orchestra in a concert at Fairfield Hall.

DENNE GILKES MEMORIAL FUND
Grants to young people studying music or drama, generally as a supplement to other grants and for special purposes.

DISC AND MUSIC ECHO
Dorset House, Stamford St., London SE1. Numerous awards in the field of light music.

DRAPERS' COMPANY
Drapers' Hall, Throgmorton St., London EC2. Annual awards to students of music, Value varies.

FRIENDS OF COVENT GARDEN
Royal Opera House, Covent Garden, London WC°. A number of annual scholarships to the London Opera Centre and the Royal Ballet School, including one £1,000 prize for singing.

GLYNDEBOURNE TOURING OPERA AWARD.
c/o Glyndebourne Opera, Lewes, Suffolk. Annual grant for further study for young singers appearing with Glyndebourne Touring Opera.

GUILDHALL SCHOOL OF MUSIC AND DRAMA
John Carpenter St., London EC4Y OAR. A number of scholarships for students of the school. *Carl Flesch International Competition.* Biennial competition for violinists. Age limit: 32. 1st prize: £1,000 Carl Flesch Medal + a number of solo engagements; 2nd prize: £750; 3rd prize: £500.

HAYDN-MOZART SOCIETY
105 Hartfield Road, London SW19 3TJ. *Mozart Memorial Prize.* For U.K. residents under 30. Prize: £100 + concerts.

HOME OFFICE
Prison Dept., 89 Eccleston Square, London S.W.1. *Arthur Koestler Awards.* Annual awards to prisoners showing promise in the field of music.

INCORPORATED SOCIETY OF MUSICIANS
48 Gloucester Place, London W1A 4LN. *ISM/NatWest Festival Days.* Annual awards for young professional musicians who are members of the Society. Prizes: Wigmore Hall recitals. Age Limits: 28-40.

INTERNATIONAL COMPETITION FOR JUNIOR VIOLINISTS
Glasgow Arts Centre, Washington Building for the Arts, 12 Washington St., Glasgow G3 9AZ. Annual. Age limits: 12-18. 1st prize: £500. Three other cash prizes.

INTERNATIONAL FESTIVAL OF YOUTH ORCHESTRAS
24 Cadogan Square, London SW1X OJP. *Israel Fieff Violin Scholarship.* Annual award to most promising young violinist attending the festival. Tenable: for 1 year to study in Berne, Switzerland. Value: Varies. *Young Composers' Competition.* Annual award for an orchestral work of up to 10 minutes duration, for those born in or resident in Scotland only. Age limit: 25. Value £500.

INTERNATIONAL ORGAN FESTIVAL SOCIETY
PO Box 80, St. Albans AL1 1BY. *Interpretation Competition.* Biennial award for organ music to be held 1981 & 1983. Age limit: 31. 1st prize: £800 + at the Royal Festival Hall and other places. *Tournemire Prize.* Biennial award for improvisation on the organ. Age limit: 31. A monetary award + a recital in Paris. The above competitions are held at the biennial International Organ Festival.

JULIUS ISSERLIS SCHOLARSHIP
c/o Royal Philharmonic Orchestra, 97 New Bond St., London W1Y 9LF. Award for 2 years study abroad to young pianist normally resident in UK. Age limits: 15-20.

ITALIAN INSTITUTE
39 Belgrave Square, London SW1X8NX. A number of annual scholarships for musicians and vocalists. Tenable: in Italian music academies and conservatories. Available to British music graduates or undergraduates.

CATHERINE AND LADY GRACE JAMES FOUNDATION
Pantyfedwen, Market St., Aberystwyth, Dyfed. A number of annual grants to enable students to continue their music education. Welsh male students only.

MABEL LANDER MEMORIAL SCHOLARHSIPS
46 Clarendon Road, London W.11. A number of annual awards.

THE LECHE TRUST
7 Relton Mews, London SW7 1ET. *Sir Thomas Beecham Scholarship.* 1 annual award to a young opera singer. Tenable: for 4 1/2-9 months to continue opera training abroad. Age limits: 25-35. Value: Approx. £100 per month. Further information from the above address. Applications to: Secretaries to the Trust, Gartmore Investment Ltd., Cayzer House, 2 St. Mary Axe, London EC3A 8BP.

LEEDS INTERNATIONAL PIANOFORTE COMPETITION
University of Leeds, Leeds LS2 9JT. Triennial competition for piano playing. Age limit: 30. Prizes: total approximately £6,000 + concert engagements.

LEEDS NATIONAL MUSIC PLATFORM
c/o Bursar's Department, University of Leeds, Leeds LS2 9JT. Triennial competition for performing musicians other than solo pianists. Competitors must be British or British residents and must have been bona fide students in U.K. Prizes total £1,500 + many concert engagements in U.K. Age limit: 30.

LIGHT MUSIC SOCIETY
10 Heddon St., Regent St., London W1R 8QB. *Light Music Society Competition for New Orchestral Works.* Annual award for light orchestral compositions of up to 9 minutes duration.

LLANGOLLEN INTERNATIONAL MUSICAL EISTEDDFOD
International Eisteddfod Office, Llangollen LL20 8NG, Clwyd, N. Wales. An annual eisteddfod with numerous choral and dance competitions including: *Mixed Choirs Contest.* For mixed choirs with up to 80 voices. Minimum age limit: 16. Various prizes. *Female Choirs Contest.* For female choirs with up to 60 voices. Minimum age limit: 16. Various prizes. *Male Choirs Contest.* For male choirs with up to 60 voices. Minimum age limit: 16. Various prizes. Also competitions for children's choirs, solo singers, folk song & chamber groups.

GREATER LONDON ARTS ASSOCIATION
25 Tavistock Place, London WC1H 9SF. Annual Young Musicians & Young Jazz Musicians scheme of assistance with concert fees. For professional performers under 26 (singers under 28). Average age if Jazz groups must be 28 or under.

LONDON MOZART PLAYERS
11A Queen's Rd., London SW19. *Mozart Memorial Prize.* Biennial competition for the interpretation of the work of Mozart. Sections: piano or violin; flute, oboe, bassoon or horn; voice. Age limit: 30. 1st prize: £100 + performance in concert at the Royal Festival Hall + one other concert performance. Limited to residents of, or students in UK.

LONDON MUSICAL COMPETITION
102 Wendover Court, Chiltern St., London W1M 1PN. Annual competition for musical performance.

MECHANICAL-COPYRIGHT PROTECTION SOCIETY LTD.
Elgar House, 380 Streatham High Road, London SW16 6HR. An annual award for composition, open only to students of music of the University of Surrey. Value: £50.

MELODY MAKER
161 Fleet St., London E.C.4. Numerous annual awards in the field of light music.

MENDELSSOHN SCHOLARSHIP
14 Bedford Square, London WC1B 3JG. 1 biennial scholarship for composition. Tenable: for studies in the U.K. or abroad. Age limit: 30. Value: £2,000.

MERCHANT TAYLORS' COMPANY
Bursary, Merchant Taylors' Hall, 30 Threadneedle St., London EC2R 8AY. 1 annual award for a vocalist or instrumentalist attending the Merchant Taylors' School. Award: Scholarship to Guildhall School of Music and Drama. Value: £100.

COUNTESS OF MUNSTER MUSICAL TRUST
Wormley Hill, Godalming GU8 5SG. Approx. 50 annual awards to British or Commonwealth vocalists, instrumentalists, conductors or composers. Tenable: for 1 year to study music in U.K. or abroad. Age limits: 11-30. Value: varies according to financial position of applicants.

NATIONAL FEDERATION OF MUSIC SOCIEITES
1 Montague St., London WC1B 5BS. *National Federation of Music Societies' Award.* Annual awards for young concert artists. Competition changes each year, in 1980 it is for women singers, 1981 wind players, 1982 men singers. Prizes total at least £500. Age limit: 25 (27 for singers). Limited to British citizens.

NATIONAL ORGAN COMPETITION
Holy Trinity Church, Southport. Biennial competition for organ music. Prizes: 1st, 2nd and Rushworth Trust Memorial Prize.

NEW MUSICAL EXPRESS
15-17 Long Acre, London WC2. Numerous annual awards in the field of light music.

JAMES CHALMERS PARK MEMORIAL TRUST
1a St. Chad's View, Leeds LS6 3AQ. Annual award to a young musician.

J. W. PEARCE MUSIC TRUST
Pearce Fund Trustees, The Polytechnic, Queensgate, Huddersfield HD1 3DH. *Mrs. Sunderland Musical Competition.* Annual award for those born or living in the Huddersfield area, for a performance of up to 15 minutes duration. Monetary prizes + trophy + concert engagements. Age limits: 16-25.

FRANCIS PEARMAN MUSIC TRUST
Chief Executive's Office, Council House, Birmingham B1 1BB. Annual awards to local organizations to improve the standard of music in Birmingham. Total of awards: Approx. £1,200.

POLISH CULTURAL INSTITUTE
16 Devonshire St., London W1N 2BS. 1 annual scholarship for composition awarded to a graduate of a British music college. Tenable: for 1 year at one of the Polish Academies of Music at Cracow, Warsaw or Katowice.

RADCLIFFE MUSIC AWARD
11 Coulson St., London SW3. 2 biennial award to a U.K. or Commonwealth citizen or resident for a chamber music composition. Age limit: 40. 1st prize: £300. 2nd prize £200.

ROYAL ACADEMY OF MUSIC
Marylebone Road, London NW1 5HT. 162 annual awards open to all students of musical instruments and voice including: competitive prizes; entrance scholarships; bursaries; awards as a result of annual examinations. Age limits are usually: 18-21. Values: range from £10-£1,000.

ROYAL AMATEUR ORCHESTRAL SOCIETY
19 Nireh Court, Haywards Heath, Sussex. *Royal Amateur Orchestral Society Silver Medal Award.* 2 annual award for a young solo instrumentalist or singer under 28. Bronze medal for runner-up.

ROYAL COLLEGE OF MUSIC
Prince Consort Road, London SW7. Numerous awards including: Limited number of annual scholarships for singers, instrumentalists and composers. Age limits: 16-25. Tenable: for 3 years at the Royal College of Music. Value: £160 per annum. 6 annual exhibitions to a first year student. Tenable: for up to 3 years at the Royal College of Music. Value: £80 per annum. (Scholarships confined to British subjects. Exhibitions open to all students.

ROYAL COLLEGE OF ORGANISTS
Kensington Gore, London SW7 2QS. *Bonwick Bequest.* A number of annual awards for young organists. Tenable: for 1 year to continue musical education. Age limit: 20. Value: £30.

ROYAL NATIONAL EISTEDDFOD OF WALES
Pen-y-Garreg, Porthaethwy, Ynys Mon, Gwynedd. An annual eisteddfod with numerous compositions in the following sections: instrumental; choral; brass band; composition. Awards: Many prizes ranging from £2-£500.

ROYAL NORTHERN COLLEGE OF MUSIC
124 Oxford Road, Manchester M13 9RD. *Walter Carroll Memorial Scholarship.* Annual award to a school leaver.

ROYAL OVER-SEAS LEAGUE
Over-Seas House, London SW1A 1LR. *Stella Murray Memorial Prize.* 1 annual award for New Zealanders only in any branch of music. Age limit: 30. Value: £50. *Eric Rice Memorial Prize for Accompanists.* 1 annual award open to UK and Commonwealth accompanists at the Royal Over-Seas League Music Festival. Value: £50. *Royal Over-Seas League Music Festival.* Annual competitive festival with awards in the following sections: vocal; instrumental, open to UK and Commonwealth students only. Age limits: 25 (instrumentalists); 30 (vocalists). In each section there is a first prize of: £250.

ROYAL PHILHARMONIC SOCIETY
124 Wigmore St., London W1H 0AX. *Emily Anderson Prize for Violin Playing.* Held every

4-5 years. Age limits: 18-30. 1st prize: £750. International. *Kathleen Ferrier Memorial Scholarship*. Annual award for a British singer aged 21-26. Tenable: for further study in U.K. or abroad. Value: £750. *Royal Philharmonic Society Composition Prize*. Annual award for composition open only to past or present students of the following establishments: Guildhall School of Music and Drama; Royal Academy of Music; Royal College of Music; Royal Northern College of Music; Royal Scottish Academy of Music and Drama; Trintiy College of Music. Age limit: 26.

RUPERT FOUNDATION
Rupert Foundation Conductor's Scholarship. Annual scholarship for a conductor with some professional experience. Age limits: 22-30. Award: £5,000 + conducting engagements.

WILLIAM RUSHWORTH MEMORIAL TRUST
Liverpool Council of Social Service, 14 Castle St., Liverpool L2 0NJ. A number of annual grants to societies and individuals operating in the Liverpool area towards the encouragement of musical activity, education and appreciation.

SCOTTISH ARTS COUNCIL
11 Rothesay Terrace, Edinburg 3. Numerous awards in all fields of music.

SCOTTISH NATIONAL ORCHESTRA
150 Hope St., Glasgow G2 2TH. *Ian Whyte Award*. Triennial award for an unpublished and unperformed orchestral composition. Age limit: 35.

SONG WRITERS' GUILD OF GREAT BRITAIN
Performing Right Society Ivor Novello Awards. Numerous annual awards to lyricists, composers, music publishers and record manufacturers. Sections for all kinds of music with the following awards in each: 1st prize: Bronze statuette; 2nd prize: Certificate of Honour. The Performing Right Society has taken over financial responsibility for these important awards but judging is organized by the Song Writers' Guild of Great Britain.

STROUD FESTIVAL
c/o Miss A. M. C. Shaw, Lenton, Houndscroft, Stroud, Glos. GL5 5DG. *Antiphon Competition*. Annual award to a composer for the setting of a prescribed text for four parts & organ. *International Composers' Competition*. Annual competition contest. Conditions vary each year. Prizes total £600. Age limit: 40.

MAGGIE TEYTE PRIZE
75 Woodland Rise, London N10 3UN. Biennial award for a female vocalist. Age limit: 30. Value: 100 guineas.

TRINITY COLLEGE OF MUSIC
Mandeville Place, London W1M 6AQ. A number of annual scholarships. Tenable: at Trinity College of Music. Age limits: 16-23. International.

ULSTER ORCHESTRA
26-34 Antrim Road, Belfast BT15 2AA. *Ulster Orchestra Composers' Competition*. Irregular competition for a composition for strings or orchestra of 5-15 minutes duration. For N. Ireland residents only. Age limit: 25.

UNIVERSITY OF OXFORD
University Registry, Clarendon Building, Broad St., Oxford OX/ 3BD. *Donald Tovey Memorial Prize*. Triennial grant awarded to assist in the furtherance or publication of research in understanding or history of music. Value: £400. International.

WESTERN ORCHESTRAL SOCIETY
2 Seldown Lane, Poole, Dorset BH15 1UF. *Imperial Tobacco Conductors' Competition*. Annual. Monetary prize + concert engagements. Age limit: 30. *Imperial Tobacco Cello Awards*. Annual. Monetary prizes + gold, silver & bronze awards. No age limits.

CITY OF WESTMINSTER ARTS COUNCIL
Marylebone Library, Marylebone Road, London NW1 5PS. *Menuhin Competition for Young Composers*. Triennial. Age limit: 30. 1st prize: £1,000 + public performance of the winning work in London + possibility of publication, broadcasting and recording of composition. Restricted to residents of U.K. Further details from: Menuhin Prize Management Committee at the above address.

IAN WHYTE AWARD FOR BRITISH COMPOSERS
c/o General Administrator, Scottish National Orchestra Society Ltd., 150 Hope St., Glasgow G2 2TH. Triennial competition (next 1981) for a work for symphony orchestra. Monetary prize + performance.

SIR THOMAS WHITE'S EDUCATION FOUNDATION
c/o General Charities Office, Old Bablake, Hill St., Coventry CV1 4AN. *Music Scholarship.* Annual award for instrumental or vocal music to music students born or resident in Coventry. Tenable: at any institution for higher education in music. Value: £500 (can be divided between several applicants).

WORSHIPFUL COMPANY OF MUSICIANS
4 St. Paul's Churchyard, London EC4M 8AY. A number of awards including: *W. T. Best Memorial Scholarship.* Annual award to an organist. Tenable: for 3 years to further musical education. *John Clementi Collard Fellowship.* Triennial award to a professional musician in one of the following fields: composition; research; performance; conducting. *Maisie Lewis Young Artists' Fund.* Annual awards to young musicians to enable them to take part in concerts. Age limit: 28.

U.S.A.

ACCORDION TEACHERS' GUILD
12626 W. Creek Road, Minnetonka, MN 55343. 3 annual cash prizes for accordian playing.

AKRON YOUTH SYMPHONY
E. J. Thomas Hall, Center and Hill Sts., Akron, OH 44304. A number of annual scholarships awarded through competitive instrumental auditions. Value: $100.

AMERICAN ACADEMY AND INSTITUTE OF ARTS AND LETTERS
633 W 155th St., NY, NY 10003. *Richard Rodgers Production Award for Musical Theater.* Candidates must be nominated by a member of the Academy and Institute, but members themselves are not eligible.

AMERICAN ACADEMY OF ARTS AND SCIENCES
280 Newton St., Brooklin Station, Boston, MA 02146. A number of annual awards in all fields of music.

AMERICAN ACADEMY IN ROME
101 Park Ave., New York, NY 10017. 15 fellowships awarded annually in a number of subjects including musical composition. Tenable: for 1 year at the American Academy in Rome. Value: $4,600 + residence and other allowances.

AMERICAN BACH FOUNDATION
1211 Potomac St., NW Washington, DC 20007. *Johann Sebastian Bach International Competition.* Annual competition for pianists. Age limits: 17-35. A number of awards including: 1st prize: $1,000 + solo appearance with the Cologne Chamber Orchestra + a grant to stay in the Federal Republic of Germany to attend musical events.

AMERICAN BANDMASTERS' ASSOCIATION
7414 Admiral Drive, Alexandria, VA 22307. *Ostwald Band Composition Contest.* Annual competition for a band composition. Prize: $1,000 + $250 travel expenses.

AMERICAN COMPOSERS' ALLIANCE
170 W. 74th St., New York, NY 10023. *Laurel Leaf Award.* Annual award for distinguished achievement in American music. Award: Parchment scroll.

AMERICAN CONSERVATORY OF MUSIC
116 S. Michigan Ave., Chicago, IL 60603. *Collins Memorial Scholarships.* Available for full time senior or graduate students. $3,000 to be divided in 3 awards.

AMERICAN MUSIC CONFERENCE
c/o The Philip Lesly Co., 33 N. Dearborn St., Chicago, IL 60602. Annual awards for the use of music in advertising non-musical products or services. Awards: Certificates.

AMERICAN MUSICOLOGICAL SOCIETY
201 S. 34th St., Philadelphia, PA 19174. *Alfred Einstein Award*. Annual award for a musicological article in the American or Canadian press. Age limit: 40. Award: $400. *Otto Kinkeldey Award*. Annual award to a musicologist. *Noah Greenberg Award*. Annual award of $1,000. All restricted to members of the Society.

AMERICAN OPERA AUDITIONS
4509 Carew Tower, Cincinnati, OH 45202. Annual competitive auditions for opera singers. Age limits: 28 (sopranos); 32 (tenors and baritones); 34 (mezzo sopranos, contraltos and bass). Awards: 3-6 singers selected to perform opera in Europe, all expenses paid.

AMERICAN SOCIETY FOR COMPOSERS, AUTHORS AND PUBLISHERS
1 Lincoln Plaza, New York, NY 10023. *ASCAP-Deems Taylor Awards*. Annual awards for book, newspaper or magazine articles on music. Prizes (in each section): 1st prize: $1,000; 2nd prize: $500; 3rd prize: $300. Numerous other annual awards for standard or popular music composition. Value: $100-2,000.

MARIAN ANDERSON SCHOLARSHIPS
762 S. Martin St., Philadelphia, PA 19146. 2 annual scholarships for vocalists. Tenable: to further musical training in the U.S.A. Age limits: 16-30. Value: $1,000 and $600.

AUGUSTA SYMPHONY ORCHESTRA
PO Box 3684, Hill Station, Augusta, GA 30904. *William S. Boyd Competition for Young Pianists*. Annual award for pianists. Age limits: 16-25. 1st prize: $1,000 + appearance with the Augusta Symphony Orchestra. Other prizes.

BERKSHIRE MUSIC CENTER AT TANGLEWOOD
Winter: Symphony Hall, Boston, MA 02115. Summer: Tanglewood, Lenox, MA 01240. Fellowships for residency at Tanglewood for young professional musicians. Selection by audition.

MARY LOUISE CURTIS BOK FOUNDATION
1726 Locust St., Philadelphia, PA 19130. A number of annual scholarships to young musicians. Value varies.

BOSTON SYMPHONY ORCHESTRA
Symphony Hall, Boston, MA. *Berkshire Music Centre Fellowships*. Annual awards to young musicians for advanced study, covering tuition, accommodation and board, travel if necessary.

BOYS' TOWN MUSIC DEPARTMENT
Boys' Town, NB 68010. *Boys' Town Medal of St. Cecilia*. 1 annual bronze medal awarded for achievement in the field of liturgical music.

BRAEMAR CONTEST
Hebraic Arts Chamber Series-Adath Jeshurun, Old York Road at Ashbourne, Elkins Park, PA 19117. Annual contest for a musical composition and performance by an Hebraic string quartet. Prize varies.

BROADCAST MUSIC INC.
589 Fifth Ave., New York, NY 10017. *Broadcast Music Inc. Awards to Student Composers*. Annual awards for vocal or instrumental compositions to residents of N. or S. America. Age limit: 26. Prizes total $15,000. 1st prize: $2,000.

CHAUTAUQUA INSTITUTION
Chautauqua, New York, NY 14722. Annual scholarships awarded to instrumentalists and vocalists. Tenable: for 7 weeks at courses held by the Institution.

CLEVELAND INSTITUTE OF MUSIC
11021 E. Blvd., Cleveland, OH 44106. A number of annual scholarships and teaching fellowships. Value varies. Robert Casadesus International piano competition 1981. 1st prize: $4,000 + performance with Cleveland Orchestra. 2nd prize: $2,000. Age limits: 17-32.

VAN CLIBURN INTERNATIONAL QUADRENNIAL PIANO COMPETITION
3505 W. Lancaster, Fort Worth, TX 76107. Quadrennial competition for pianists (next 1981). Prizes total $34,000. Age limit: 30.

COLUMBIA UNIVERSITY
New York, NY 10027. *Joseph H. Bearns Prizes in Music.* Annual awards for musical composition. Age limits: 18-25. 1st prize: $1,200; 2nd prize: $900. *Alice M. Ditson Conductors' Award.* Annual award for a young conductor. Value: Citation + $1,000.

COMPOSERS' LYRICISTS' EDUCATIONAL FOUNDATION
50 W. 57th St., New York, NY 10019. A number of annual scholarships including: *Duke Ellington Scholarship. Dorothy Fields Scholarship.* Values vary.

COMPOSITION CONTEST FOR 'GEBRAUCHSMUSIK' FOR RECORDER CONSORT
7777 S.W. 74th St., Miami, FL 33143. Annual composition competition for recorder music.

CONCERT ARTISTS' GUILD
Carnegie Hall, Studio 136, 154 W. 57th St., New York, NY 10019. *Carnegie Hall Recital Award.* 10 annual awards to vocalists or instrumentalists. Age limit: 32 (Singers 35). Value: Debut recital at Carnegie Hall to which NY critics are invited.

CURTIS INSTITUTE OF MUSIC
1726 Locust St., Philadelphia, PA 19103. A number of annual scholarships. Tenable: at Curtis Institute. Age limit: 21. International.

DARTMOUTH ARTS COUNCIL
Electronic Music Studio, Dartmouth College, Hanover NH 03755. Annual award for composition of electronic music.

DAYTON PHILHARMONIC ORCHESTRA ASSOCIATION
15 E. 1st St., Dayton, OH 45402. *Young Peoples' Auditions.* Annual competitive auditions in the following areas of music: brass; piano; strings; voice; woodwinds. Awards: Scholarships to: Cincinnati Conservatory of Music; University of Dayton: Wright State University.

DIABLO SYMPHONY ASSOCIATION
PO Box 2222, Dollar Ranch Station, Walnut Creek, CA 94595. *Young Musicians' Contest.* Annual competition featuring a different instrument each year. 1st prize: Cash + performance with Diablo Symphony of Walnut Creek. Age limits: 16-25 1980, violists.

EASTMAN SCHOOL OF MUSIC
University of Rochester, 20 Gibbs St., Rochester, New York, NY 14604. Approx. 6 annual awards to music graduates. Tenable: for 1 year at the Eastman School of Music. Value: up to $1,750. International.

FONTAINEBLEAU FINE ARTS AND MUSIC SCHOOLS ASSOCIATION
1083 5th Ave., New York, NY 10028. A number of annual scholarships. Tenable: at Summer Schools for Music in the U.S.A. Age limit: 30.

FRIDAY MORNING MUSIC CLUB FOUNDATION
1649 K. St. N.W., Washington, DC 20006. *Washington International Competition.* Annual musical performance competition featuring a different instrument each year. Age limits: 18-28. Number of awards. 1980, Voice; 1981, Piano; 1982, Strings.

FRIENDS OF MUSIC AT TANGLEWOOD
Friends Office, Tanglewood, Lenox, MA. A number of awards for composition, conducting and performance. The awards are made at the Berkshire Festival.

FROMM MUSIC FOUNDATION
1028 W. Van Buren St., Chicago, IL 60607. Numerous annual awards to musicians of all kinds. Values vary.

GOTTSCHALK COMPETITION FOR PIANISTS AND COMPOSERS
1028 Connecticut Ave., Washington, DC 20036. Annual contest for composers and instrumentalists, with a number of prizes.

JOHN SIMON GUGGENHEIM MEMORIAL FOUNDATION
90 Park Ave., New York, NY 10016. *Guggenheim Fellowships.* Annual fellowships in music

for composers or scholars who are residents of U.S.A., Canada or other American states. Tenable: for 6-12 months. No restrictions on place of tenure. Age limits: 30-45.

INSTITUTE OF INTERNATIONAL EDUCATION
809 United Nations Plaza, New York, NY 10017. Contact: Robert F. Morris, Secretary of Music Committee. *Cintas Fellowship Program.* Annual fellowships to Cuban composers of serious music. Value: $4,000. *International Music Competitions Project.* A number of annual awards made to allow young musicians to travel abroad to compete in International music competitions.

INTERNATIONAL COMPETITION FOR SINGERS
3530 N. Dickerson St., Arlington, VA 22207. Triennial competition for vocalists. Age limit: 29.

INTERNATIONAL COMPETITION FOR STRING PLAYERS
3530 N. Dickerson St., Arlington, VA 22207. Triennial competition for instrumentalists.

INTERNATIONAL PIANO FESTIVAL AND COMPETITION
c/o University of Maryland, College Park, MD 20742. Annual competition for pianists with three main prizes. Age limits: 16-30. 1st prize: $2,500 + concert engagements.

ISLAND ORCHESTRA SOCIETY
12 New St., Huntington, NY 11743. *Composers' Competition.* Annual. Prizes vary. *Youth Solo Competition.* Annual competition for solo instrumentalists. Prizes vary.

JUILLIARD SCHOOL OF MUSIC
Lincoln Center Plaza, New York, NY 10023. A number of annual scholarships. Tenable: at Juilliard School of Music. Age limits: 18-30. Values vary.

KOSCIUSZKO FOUNDATION
15 E. 65th St., New York, NY 10021. *Chopin Scholarship for Pianists.* Annual award. Age limits: 15-21. 1st prize: $1,000; 2nd prize: $500; 3rd prize: $250.

KOUSSEVITZKY MUSIC FOUNDATION
Room 1000, 250 Park Ave., New York, NY 10017. A number of annual awards and scholarships of varying amounts. The organization also grants commissions for the composition of new music with no restrictions on age or nationality. Awards include: *Koussevitzky Memorial Conducting Prize.* Annual award made at the Berkshire Festival. Prize: $300. *Koussevitsky Tanglewood Composition Prize.* Annual award made at the Berkshire Festival. Prize: $250.

LANSING SYMPHONY ASSOCIATION
Suite, F, 230 N Washington Square, Lansing, MI 48933. *Young Artist Competition.* Annual competition for young musicians; different instruments or singing each year. Monetary prize + performance with Lansing Symphony Orchestra.

LEVENTRITT FOUNDATION
1175 Park Ave., New York, NY 10028. *International Leventritt Competition.* Annual musical performance competition for violinists. Value of awards varies.

LIMA SYMPHONY WOMEN'S GUILD
Memorial Hall, Lima, OH 45801. A number of annual scholarships and competitions including: *Young Musicians' Competition.* Annual musical performance competition with sections for piano and orchestral winds one year, voice and strings the next. 1st prize: Cash + appearance with the Lima Symphony Orchestra.

LONGBY SCHOOL OF MUSIC
1 Follen St., Cambridge, MA 02138. A number of annual scholarships. Tenable: for 1 year at the Longby School of Music. Values vary.

LONGVIEW SYMPHONY ORCHESTRA
29 Country Place, Longview, TX 75601. *Piano Concerto Competition.* Annual competition for pianists open only to those residing in N.E. Texas. 1st prize: $50 + performance with the Longview Symphony Orchestra; 2nd prize: $25 + possibility of performance with the Longview Symphony Orchestra.

MANHATTAN SCHOOL OF MUSIC
238 E. 105th St., New York, NY 10029. A number of annual scholarships. Tenable: for 1 year at the Manhattan School of Music. International.

MASTERWORK MUSIC AND ART FOUNDATION
300 Mendham Road, Morristown, NJ 07960. A number of annual scholarships for vocalists. Value varies.

METROPOLITAN OPERA NATIONAL COUNCIL
Lincoln Center, New York, NY 10023. A number of annual awards and scholarships to opera singers. Value of awards totals $106,000.

DMITRI MITROPOULOS INTERNATIONAL COMPETITION FOR CONDUCTORS
130 E. 59th St., New York, NY 10022. Annual contest for young conductors. Age limits: 20-33.

MUSIC ACADEMY OF THE WEST
1070 Fairway Road, Santa Barbara, CA 93108. *Music Academy of the West Summer Festival.* Annual competitive festival with various awards. *Scholarships.* A number of annual scholarships made to instrumentalists and vocalists. Tenable: for 8 weeks at the Academy. Value: $600-700. International.

MUSIC AND ARTS INSTITUTE OF SAN FRANCISCO
2622 Jackson St., San Francisco, CA 94115. 10 annual scholarships awarded to full-time students at the Institute. International. These include: *W. Waldo Freeman Scholarship. Harp Scholarship.*

NATIONAL ACADEMY OF RECORDING ARTS AND SCIENCES
21 W. 58th St., New York, NY 10019. *Grammy Awards.* Annual awards in recognition of achievement in the field of musical recording. The 46 categories include: Best Chamber Music Performance; Best Choral Performance (awards to both conductor and choral director); Best Classical Performance (award to conductor); Best Classical Performance of Instrumental Soloist or Soloists; Best Classical Vocal Soloist Performance; Best Opera Recording (awards to both conductor and producer); Classical Album of the Year (awards to both artist and producer) etc.

NATIONAL ASSOCIATION FOR AMERICAN COMPOSERS AND CONDUCTORS
15 W. 67th St., New York, NY 10023. A number of annual awards for service to music, including: *Henry Hadley Medal.* Annual award, to composers or conductors for contributions to American music.

NATIONAL ASSOCIATION OF TEACHERS OF SINGING
250 W. 57th St., New York, NY 10019. *Artists' Awards.* Annual awards to vocalists. Values vary.

NATIONAL CATHOLIC MUSIC EDUCATORS' ASSOCIATION
Riggs Building, Suite 228, 7411 Riggs Road, Hyattsville, MD 20783. *Piano Competition.* Annual competition for musical performance. 1st prize: Certificate of Recognition + at least one performance with a major symphony orchestra.

NATIONAL ENDOWMENT FOR THE ARTS
Washington, DC 20506. A number of annual fellowships and grants including: Fellowships of up to $2,500 for the promotion of outstanding composers' careers; Fellowships of up to $5,000 to lirettists or translators; Fellowships of up to $10,000 to composers for the creation of new works; Much larger grants are available to orchestral and operatic companies for the creation of special projects.

NATIONAL INSTITUTE FOR ARTS AND LETTERS
633 W. 155th St., New York, NY 10032. A number of annual grants and medals awarded for distinguished achievement in all fields of music including: *March Blitzstein Award for the Music Theatre.* Annual award for a composer, librettist or lyricist. Value: $2,500.

NATIONAL SCHOOL ORCHESTRA ASSOCIATION
330 Bellevue Drive, Bowling Green, KY 42101. *National School Orchestra Association Composition Contest.* Annual competition for an orchestral composition of up to 7 minutes duration. 1st prize: $1,000.

WALTER W. NAUMBURG FOUNDATION INC.
144 W. 66th St., New York, NY 10023. *Music Competition.* Open to any nationally. Age limits: 17-30. 1980, Voice; 1981, Violin. Prize (1980): $5,000 + Alice Tully Hall recital.

NEW HAVEN SYMPHONY ORCHESTRA
33 Whitney Ave., New Haven, CT 06510. *State Wide Competition for Young Artists.* Annual contest open to all student instrumentalists resident in Connecticut. 1st prize: $600; 2nd prize $300; 3rd prize: $100. *Young Musicians' Contest.* Annual Contest open to student instrumentalists of brass, piano, string or woodwind, resident in Connecticut. 1st prize (Harry Berman Memorial Award): $100 + appearance with the New Haven Symphony Orchestra.

NEW ORLEANS BAPTIST THEOLOGICAL SEMINARY
3939 Gentilly Blvd., New Orleans, LA 70126. *Performance Awards.* A number of annual awards made in recognition of performance in all areas of music. Tenable: at the New Orleans Baptist Theological Seminary. Value: $100.

NEW SCHOOL FOR MUSIC STUDY INC.
353 Nassau St., Princeton, NJ 08540. 4 annual scholarships for musical performance. Tenable: for 1 year at the New School for Music Study. Value: $240-480. International.

PEABODY CONSERVATORY OF MUSIC
1 E. Mount Vernon Place, Baltimore, MD 21202. A number of annual scholarships in all fields of music. Tenable: for 1-2 years at the Conservatory. Value: $300-1,500.

PRESSER FOUNDATION
Presser Place, Bryn Mawr, PA 19010. A number of annual grants to students of music - usually to those intending to become teachers. Awards total: $400.

PUEBLO SYMPHONY ASSOCIATION
1117 Lake Avenue, Pueblo, CO 81004. *Young Artists Competitions.* 1981, piano; 1982, strings. Competition on two levels. Level 1: Age limit 25. 1st prize $1,000 + performance with Pueblo Symphony Orchestra. Level 2: Age limit 17. 1st prize $400 + performance with Pueblo Youth Symphony Orchestra.

PULITZER PRIZE IN MUSIC
702 Journalism, Columbia University, New York, NY 10027. Annual award for ballet, opera, chamber, choral or orchestral music composition performed during previous year.

RECORD INDUSTRY ASSOCIATION OF AMERICA
1 E. 57th St., New York, NY 10022. Numerous annual awards made to record companies for singles selling more than a million copies and for albums selling more than a million dollars worth of copies.

REDLANDS COMMUNITY MUSIC ASSOCIATION
PO Box 466, Redlands, CA 92373. Numerous annual awards made in all fields of music at the Redlands Bowl Festival. Available to school students in the locality between the ages of 15 & 26. Prizes to the value of $300.

MARTHA BAIRD ROCKEFELLER FUND FOR MUSIC
1 Rockefeller Plaza, New York, NY 10020. Numerous annual grants awarded to the following: composers; musicologists; professional soloists just beginning their careers. Age limits: 35 (performers); 45 (composers). Value: $1,000-$6,000 per year. Limited to U.S. citizens or permanent residents in U.S.A.

ROSARY COLLEGE
7900 W. Division St., River Forest, IL 60305. A number of annual scholarships to graduate musicians. Tenable: for 1 year at the Villa Schifanoia Graduate School of Fine Arts, Florence, Italy. Age limit: 39. Value: $1,000.

SAN FRANCISCO CONSERVATORY OF MUSIC
1201 Ortega St., San Francisco, CA 94122. *Performance Scholarships in Music.* Annual awards to musicians of all kinds. Tenable: for 1 year at the Conservatory. Age limit: 24. Value: $650-1,150. International.

SINFONIA FOUNDATION
10600 Old State Road, Evansville, IN 47711. *Research Assistance Grants.* A number of annual awards available for research into American music or music education. Value varies.

SPRINGFIELD SYMPHONY ORCHESTRA
PO Box 1374, Springfield, OH 45501. *Annual Competition for High School Students.* Contest for solo instrumentalists. *Statewide Instrumental Concerto Competition.* Annual contest for student instrumentalists. 1st prize: Cash + performance with Springfield Symphony Orchestra.

WILLIAM MATHEWS SULLIVAN MUSICAL FOUNDATION
410 E. 57th St., New York, NY 10022. Annual awards to professional singers beginning their careers.

SYMPHONY ORCHESTRA ASSOCIATION OF KINGSPORT
Fine Arts Center, Church Circle, Kingsport, TN 37660. A number of annual scholarships tenable at summer music camps and also: *Concerto Competition.* Annual contest open to instrumentalists and vocalists. 1st prize: Appearance with the Symphony Orchestra of Kingsport.

UNIVERSITY OF ILLINOIS
College of Fine and Applied Arts, 110 Architecture Building, University of Illinois at Urbana-Champaign, IL 61801. *Kate Neal Kinley Memorial Fellowship.* 1 annual award open to graduates of the college. Tenable: in U.S.A. or abroad. Age limit: 25. Value: $2,500.

UNIVERSITY OF MISSOURI
Conservatory of Music, 4420 Warwick Blvd., Kansas City, MO 64111. A number of annual scholarships in all fields of music for varied amounts, also an annual jazz contest.

BRUCE YARNELL MEMORIAL AWARD
War Memorial Opera House, San Francisco, CA 94102. Annual award to baritones. Age limits: 20-32. Award: $1,000.

YOUNG CONCERT ARTISTS' INC.
75 E. 55th St., New York, NY 10027. Biennial award to an instrumentalist. Winners eligible for Michaels award (solo recital, Alice Tully Hall and engagements with major U.S. orchestras) or for Philip M. Faucett String Prize (Alice Tully Hall recital).

URUGUAY

CITY OF MONTEVIDEO INTERNATIONAL PIANO COMPETITION
Enrique Munoz 815, Montevideo. Irregular competition. Age limits: 15-32. Value of awards totals $5,000 + concerts. Next: 1978.

YUGOSLAVIA

BELGRADE SPRING FESTIVAL OF LIGHT MUSIC
c/o Cara Dusana ul. 96,11000 Belgrade. Annual competitive festival. Honorary Prizes.

FESTIVAL SOLIDARNOSTI
c/o RTV Skopje, Redakcija zabavne muzike, 91000 Skopje. Annual competitive festival.

SARAJEVO SONG FESTIVAL
Danijela Ozme-7, 71000 Sarajevo. Annual competitive festival for vocalist, lyricists and composers.

SLOVENIAN SONG FESTIVAL
c/o Tavcarjeva - 17,61000 Ljubljana. Annual competitive festival for vocalists, lyricists and composers.

SONG FESTIVAL ZAGREB
Udruzenje Kompositora SRH, 41000 Zagreb. Annual competitive festival for vocalists, lyricists and composers.

SPLIT SUMMER
c/o Dalmacijakoncert, Trg. Republike 1, 58000 Split. Annual competitive festival with sections for music and song.

YOUTH FESTIVAL
Dom Kulture, Gradska Kuca, 2400 Subotica. Annual competitive festival with sections in all branches of music.

YUGOSLAV TV SONG FESTIVAL
c/o Dezmanov Prolaz 10, 41000 Zagreb. Annual competitive festival for vocalists, lyricists and composers.

ZIMBABWE

AFRICAN ARTS FESTIVAL
PO Box 1976, Salisbury. Annual competitive festival with numerous awards.

BULAWAYO EISTEDDFOD SOCIETY
PO Box 2379, Bulawayo. Many annual awards and scholarships all for instrumental performers including: *Chassay Cup and Prize.* Minimum age limit: 15. *Eugene Gordon Trophy.* No age limits. *William Walton Cope Cup.* Age limit: 20.

INSTITUTE OF ALLIED ARTS
PO Box 1273, Salisbury. Numerous annual awards and occasional bursaries to musicians of all kinds.

APPENDIX D

MUSIC LIBRARIES

AUSTRALIA

Australian Capital Territory
CANBERRA SCHOOL OF MUSIC, William Herbert Place, Canberra City 2601. Librarian: Ann Wellman. Collection: Music, scores, records and books for teaching and performance.

NATIONAL LIBRARY, Canberra 2600. Music Librarian: Prue Neidorf.

New South Wales
CITY OF SYDNEY PUBLIC LIBRARY, Queen Victoria Building, 473 George St., Sydney 2000. Music Librarian: Elizabeth Maher. Collection: c. 3,000 items, mostly scores; emphasis on opera & operetta scores.

MUSIC LIBRARY, Australian Broadcasting Commission, GPO Box 487, Sydney 2001. Librarian: J. Hyde.

PUBLIC LIBRARY OF N.S.W., Macquarie St., Sydney 2000.

N.S.W. STATE CONSERVATORY OF MUSIC, Macquarie St., Sydney 2000. Librarian: Margaret Horton. Collection: Music, scores, records and books for teaching and performance.

Queensland
QUEENSLAND CONSERVATORY OF MUSIC, Gardens Point, George St., Brisbane 4000. Librarian: D. S. Barkla. Collection: Scores, records, films, books and serials for teaching and performance.

STATE LIBRARY OF QUEENSLAND, William St., Brisbane 4000.

Victoria
PUBLIC LIBRARY OF VICTORIA, Melbourne 3000. Chief Librarian: K. A. R. Honn.

STATE LIBRARY OF VICTORIA, 328 Swanston St., Melbourne 3000. Music Librarian: Joyce Veronica McGrath. Collection: Music, scores, records, manuscript and oral history tapes. Special items: Louise Dyer Collection of British choral music, Library of the Musical Society of Victoria, MSS of Dorian La Galliene, Fritz Hart, Clive Douglas and Louis Lavater; unpublished music of Peggy Glanville Hicks; papers of Sir Bernard Heinze, recorded music of European ethnic communities in Australia.

Western Australia
CENTRAL MUSIC LIBRARY, 102 Beaufort St., Perth 6000. Librarian: Haydn Sugden. Collection: Reference collection of music materials and recordings; loan collection of scores.

STATE LIBRARY OF WESTERN AUSTRALIA, Perth 6000.

AUSTRIA

Klagenfurt
BIBLIOTHEK DES KARTNER LANDESKONSERVATORIUM, Miesstalerstr. 8, Karten, 9020 Klagenfurt. Librarian: Oar Josef Inzko. Collection: Music, scores and books used for the work of the Conservatoire.

St. Florian
STIFTSBIBLIOTHEK, 4490 St. Florian. Librarian: Dr. Karl Rehberger. Collection: Archives relating to Anton Bruckner, his pupil Franz X. Muller and many other composers.

Salzburg
HOCHSCHULBIBLIOTHEK "MOZARTEUM", Mirabellplatz 1, A-5020 Salzburg. Chief-Librarian: Dr. Werner Rainer. Collection: 50,000 volumes of music, 30,000 books, 140 periodicals, 5000 records and tapes, 12000 slides.

Vienna
BIBLIOTHEK DER HOCHSCHULE FÜR MUSIK UND DARSTELLENDE KUNST, Lothringerstr. 18, 1037 Vienna. Librarian: Dr. Wolfgang Pernauer. Collection: c. 77,000 volumes of which 50,000 are for practical musical use. Special items: Church music, Dance music, items for teaching; Bruno Walter memorial room.

MUSIKSAMMLUNG DER ÖSTERREICHISCHEN NATIONALBIBLIOTHEK, Augustinerstr. 1, 1010 Vienna. Music Librarian: Dr. Franz Grasberger. Collection: Many printed books, music, MSS. Special items: Fugger collection, Emperor Leopold I collection, Emperor Charles V collection, Vienna "Hofmusikkapelle" collection, Vienna opera archives, MSS of masterworks. Recent acquisitions: First and early editions of works by Anthony van Hoboken.

ÖSTERREICHISCHES VOLKSLIEDWERK, Fuhrmannsgasse 18, 1080 Vienna. Librarian: Dr. Gerlinde Haid. Collection: folk music, song and dance; marches; folk drama. Special items: MSS, pictures and sound recordings; Raimund Zodex folk dance archives.

BELGIUM

Antwerp
ROYAL CONSERVATORY OF MUSIC, Desguinlei 25, 2000 Antwerp. Librarian: Marie-Therese Buyssens. Collection: c. 240,000 volumes including music, scores and books for teaching and performance. Special items: c. 6,500 MSS. of works by Belgian composers, particularly those of 19th and 20th centuries.

Brussels
ARCHIVES DE LA VILLE DE BRUXELLES, Hôtel de Ville, Grand Place, 1000 Brussels. Archivist: Melle Mertens. Collection: 19th Century orchestral & operatic material.

BIBLIOTHÈQUE MUSICALE DE LA RTB, 18 Place Flagey, 1050 Brussels. Keeper: Edouard Niffle.

BIBLIOTHÈQUE ROYALE ALBERT 1ER, Boulevard de L'Empereur. Chief Music Librarian: Bernard Huys. Collection: Scores, books, microfilms and records. Special items: fétis & Van Hulthem collections. Recent acquisitions: Private collections of Eugène Ysaye, Arthur de Greef and Edgar Tinel.

CeBeDem, rue de L'Hopital 31, 1000 Brussels. General Secretary: Melle Anna Van Steenbergen. Collection: MSS of contemporary composers.

CONSERVATOIRE ROYAL DE MUSIQUE, 30 rue de la Régence, Brussels. Keeper: Dr. Albert Van der Linden.

Leuven
LEMMENSINSTITUUT, Herestraat 53, 3000 Leuven. Chief Music Librarian: Van Reeth Michel. Collection: 19th century music. Special items: Vocal scores, works by De Monte.

Liège
BIBLIOTHÈQUE DU CONSERVATOIRE ROYAL DE MUSIQUE DE LIÈGE, 14 rue Forgeur, 4000 Liège. Chief Music Librarian: Dr. M. Barthélémy. Collection: Library of music and books. Special items: Old (16th-17th centuries) and modern (19th-20th centuries) MSS: rare editions. Recent acquisitions: Léopold Charlier collection; part of the Ysaye collection.

Mons
BIBLIOTHÈQUE DE LA VILLE. Collection: Includes works by Orlando di Lassus.

Verviers
LIBRARY OF THE CONSERVATOIRE, 6 rue Chapuis, Verviers. Chief Librarian: Jean-Marie Troupin. Collection: Instrumental and vocal music.

CANADA

Ottawa
NATIONAL LIBRARY OF CANADA, 395 Wellington St., Ottawa, Ontario K1A 0N4. Chief of Music Division: Helmut Kallmann. Collection: Basic world musical literature (printed material), Comprehensive Canadian collection of scores, books, periodicals, sound recordings, manuscripts, programmes, pictures etc. Special items: Canadian copyright deposits, Percy Scholes library and information files, early Berliner discs; Papers of Canadian composers Healey Willan, Alexis Contant, Claude Champagne and others. Recent acquisitions: Papers of Robert Fleming, R. Murray Schafer and Arnold Walter.

Toronto
EDWARD JOHNSON MUSIC LIBRARY, Faculty of Music, University of Toronto, Ontario M5S 1A1. Librarian: K. McMorrow. Collection: Reference and research collection of scores, periodicals, monographs, recordings; printed collection of 90,000 volumes; 60,000 records. Special items: Small rare books collection for teaching purposes, local music history materials. Recent acquisition: Sidney Fisher collection of scores, books and flutes.

CHILE

Santiago
BIBLIOTECA CENTRAL, Dpto, de Música, Faculdad de Ciencias y Arts Músicales, Compania 1264, Santiago de Chile, Casilla 2100. Librarian: Mary Elizabeth Smith Rodriguez. Collection: Good collection of books, scores, microfilms relating to teaching, research and performance; anthologies of medieval, renaissance and baroque music; complete works of Bach, Beethoven, Brahms, Chopin, Orlando di Lasso, Mozart, Scarlatti and Schütz. Special items: Scores by Chilean composers; many works by Schubert and Schönberg.

COLOMBIA

Bogota
BIBLIOTECA DEL DEPARTAMENTO DE MÚSICA, Faculdad de Artes, Departmento de Música, Universidad Nacional. Librarian: Ines Londono Gutierrez. Collection: Large collection of books, scores, music for teaching, research and performance. Special items: Small collection of popular Colombian music and music by Colombian composers.

DENMARK

Copenhagen
MUNICIPAL LIBRARY, Kultorvet 2, 1175 Copenhagen K. Music Librarian: Bente Honoré Kjeldsen. Collection: c. 14,000 volumes of music, musical literature, scores, c. 70 periodicals, c. 15,000 records. Special items: Small collection of pre-1800 music; card index of songs.

EIRE

Dublin
MUSIC LIBRARY, City of Dublin Public Libraries, Lr. Kevin St., Dublin 8. Music Librarian: Miss B. Boland. Collection: Extensive collection of scores, books, reference material, periodicals; records and cassettes in classical and light classical fields as well as jazz and spoken word. Special items: Irish music.

NATIONAL LIBRARY OF IRELAND, Dublin. Collection: most important works are contained in the Joly collection of 23,500 volumes, mostly 18th century works.

TRINITY COLLEGE LIBRARY, Dublin. Collection: Copyright Deposit Library. Special items: Ebenezer Prout library; some 16th-18th century music including lute books of W. Ballet and T. Dallis.

FINLAND

Helsinki
HELSINKI UNIVERSITY LIBRARY, Unionink. 36, P.O. Box 312, 00171 Helsinki 17. Collection: finnish music.

LIBRARY OF THE SIBELIUS ACADEMY, Pohjois Rautatiekatu 9, 00100 Helsinki 10. Librarian: Pentti Soini. Collection: Music, musical literature and records. Special item: E. Katila's musical library.

SIBELIUSMUSEUM (MUSICOLOGICAL INSTITUTION AT ÅBO ACADEMY), Biskopsgatan 17. Head: Prof. Fabian Dahlström. Collection: Musical literature, music, scores, documents, instruments, records, tapes etc. Special item: Sibelius collection. Recent acquisitions: Sibelius manuscripts; library of Prof. Otto Andersson; musical instruments.

FRANCE

Aix-en-Provence
BIBLIOTHÈQUE MEJANES, Hôtel de Ville, 13616, Aix-en-Provence. Librarian: Mme. Suzanne Esteve. Collection: Musical manuscripts of 14th and 16th centuries; manuscript scores of 17th and 18th centuries. Special items: Archives of the Metropolitan Choir School of Aix-en-Provence. Recent acquisitions: Three autograph manuscripts by Darius Milhaud; 1739 score of André Campra's ballet, L'Europe Galante.

Avignon
BIBLIOTHÈQUE CALVET, 65 rue Joseph Vernet, 84000 Avignon. Librarian: Helene Lieutiez. Collection: Many musical scores in folio, quarto and octavo, 539 manuscripts, mostly opera. Special items: Library of the old Avignon theatre, consisting of opera scores of the 17th, 18th and 19th centuries.

Besançon
BIBLIOTHÈQUE MUNICIPALE, 1 rue de la Bibliothèque, 25000 Besançon. Chief curator: J. Mironneau. Collection: Liturgical manuscripts of the middle ages; motets by Campra and others; sonatas, cantatas and religious music of 17th and 18th centuries, operas, ballets and divertissements by Lully and other 17th and 18th century composers; lute and theorbo music by Jacquesson, Visée and others.

Caen
BIBLIOTHÈQUE MUNICIPALE DE CAEN, Place Louis Guillouard, 14034 Caen. Music Librarian: Mlle. M. J. Carbonelle. Collection: Books, records and periodicals.

Carpentras
BIBLIOTHÈQUE INGUIMBERTINE, 234 Boulevard Albin-Durand 84200 Carpentras. Librarian: Henri Dubled. Collection: mostly music of 17th, 18th and 19 centuries. Special items: Jean-Bonaventure Laurens collection of MSS and musical autographs.

Paris
BIBLIOTHÈQUE NATIONALE, Departement de la Musique, 2 rue Louvois, 75002 Paris. Music Librarian: François Lesure. Collection: c. 1,000,000 MSS, printed music, books and periodicals from 16th to 20th centuries. Special items: Folklore collection, engravings. Recent acquisitions: Unedited manuscript of 12 canons by J. S. Bach; Kochno collection of Russian ballet; MSS of French composers.

COLLECTION ANDRÉ MAYER, 148 Boulevard Malesherbes, 75017 Paris. Collection: Manuscripts, drawings, instruments, pictures. Special items: Manuscript of Stravinsky's "Sacré du Printemps"; Manuscript of Debussy's "Pelleas et Mélisande." Recent acquisition: contemporary portrait of Monteverdi.

Strasbourg
BIBLIOTHÈQUE NATIONALE ET UNIVERSITAIRE DE STRASBOURG/SECTION SCIENCES HUMAINES, 6 place de la République, BP 1029, 67070 Strasbourg. Librarian: Mlle. L. Greiner. Collection: Small collection of theoretical works and scores written before 1919. Special item: Georges Migot collection.

Valenciennes
BIBLIOTHÈQUE MUNICIPALE, 2-6, rue Ferrand 59300 Valenciennes. Collection: Five MSS (9th-19th centuries), some printed music of 16th-18th centuries.

GERMAN DEMOCRATIC REPUBLIC

Berlin
DEUTSCHE STAATBIBLIOTHEK, Postfach 1312, 1806 Berlin. Music Librarian: Dr. Karl-Heinz Köhler. Collection: A large collection which is now believed to include priceless MSS of major works by Bach, Haydn, Mozart, Beethoven, Schubert and others, removed to Poland during World War II and recently (1977) rediscovered there.

Dresden
SÄCHSISCHE LANDESBIBLIOTHEK, Marienallee 12,806 Dresden. Music Librarian: Dr. Wolfgang Reich. Collection: 95,000 volumes, including 14,000 MSS; 40,000 LPs, including source collection, lending library; bibliographic centre, sound recordings library. Recent acquisitions: Annaberger Chorbücher (c. 1535); Exner collection (18th century); Jacobi collection (17th/18th centuries); Waver collection.

Leipzig
DEUTSCHE BÜCHEREI, Deutscher Platz, 7010 Leipzig. Collection: since 1943 the library has been collecting printed music from all over Germany.

MUSIKBIOLIOTHEK DER STADT LEIPZIG, Ferdinand-Lassallestr. 21,701 Leipzig. Librarian: Ellen Roeser. Collection: c. 100,000 volumes of printed and manuscript music, 12,000 records and some musical portraits. Special items: C. F. Becker collection, Peters Music library including autograph by J. S. Bach, Mendelsohn, Schumann, Brahms, Grieg and Reger, R. Hagedorn's Wagner library, J. S. Bach archives, Heinrich Besseler library. Recent acquisition: Library of the Leipzig Singakademie.

Schwerin
WISSENSCHAFTLICHE ALLGEMEINBIBLIOTHEK DES BEZIRKES SCHWERIN, Am Dom 2, 27 Schwerin. Music Librarian: Raimund Jedeck. Collection: music from the Schwerin Court, mostly from 18th and 19th centuries, including c. 4000 MSS. Special items: works by Mecklenburg composers. Recent acquisitions: collection of works by the composers E. F. Rohloff (1884-1947), E. A. Hawacker (1889-1972), Adolf Emge (1874-1951) and Konrad Blumenthal (1895-1960).

Weimar
BIBLIOTHEK DER HOCHSCHULE FÜR MUSIK "FRANZ LISZT," Platz der Demokratie 2, 53 Weimar. Librarian: Dr. Beate Grimm. Collection: large collection of teaching material. Special items: music by Franz Liszt; music by Thuringian composers.

GERMAN FEDERAL REPUBLIC

Berlin
STAATLICHES INSTITUT FÜR MUSIKFORSCHUNG PREUSSISCHER KULTURBESITZ, Stauffenbergstr. 14, 1000 Berlin 30. Librarian: Dr. Imogen Fellinger. Collection: musicology in general, history and theory of music, music therapy, history of musical instruments, psychology, ethnology, musical acoustics and technology, musical education and bibliography. Special items: complete collection of international literature on the history of musical instruments, rarities of the 17th and 18th centuries, important technical periodicals, archives (autographs, letters, MSS.). Recent acquisition: autograph letters of Giacomo Meyerbeer.

STAATSBIBLIOTHEK PREUSSISCHER KULTURBESITZ MUSIKABTEILUNG, Archivstr. 12-14, 1000 Berlin 33. Librarian: Dr. Rudolf Elvers. Collection: largest in Germany; more than 18,000 MSS. and autographs from the 10th to 20th centuries; c. 250,000 volumes of printed music; libretti collection; books on music. Special items: collections of works by Busoni, Erk, von Pretlack (1716-81), Mendelssohn.

Cologne
HISTORISCHES ARCHIV DER STADT KÖLN, Severinstr. 222-228, 5 Cologne 1. Senior Archive Consultant: Dr. Gertrud Wegener. Collection: bequests and collections of archives and books relating to famous Cologne musicians. Special items: Offenbach collection; Ferdinand Hiller bequest.

Darmstadt
HESSISCHE LANDES-UND HOCHSCHULBIBLIOTHEK, Schloss, 6100 Darmstadt. Music Librarian: Dr. Oswald Bill. Collection: c. 4000 Manuscripts, mainly instrumental music of the first half of the 18th century. Special item: part of the Breitkopf and Härtel Archives. Recent acquisition: Hermann Heiss collection.

Düsseldorf
HEINRICH-HEINE-INSTITUT, Bilkerstr. 14, 4 Düsseldorf 1. Director: Dr. Joseph A. Kruse. Collection: autographs of Robert and Clara Schumann, Mendelssohn, Burgmüller, Hiller, Wasiliewski, Joachim and Max Bruch, etc. Special items: Schumann collection.

Frankfurt am Main
STADT-UND-UNIVERSITÄTSBIBLIOTHEK, Bockenheimer Landstrasse 134-138, 6 Frankfurt am Main. Music Librarian: Dr. Hartmut Schaefer. Collection: chiefly 17th-20th centuries, including c. 850 works by Telemann in manuscript; autograph letters, libretti, portraits, programmes, archives of music and collected printed editions. Special items: opera house, Frankfurt, collection; bequests of papers of Humperdinck, Ferdinand Hiller and Julius Stockhausen.

Fulda
HESSISCHE LANDESBIBLIOTHEK, Heinrich-von-Bibra-Platz 12, 64 Fulda. Music Librarian: Dr. Artur Brall. Collection: mainly concerned with the musical history of Fulda and includes many musical MSS of medieval sacred music as well as much material relating to Fulda composers and publishers. 333 MSS, 7,527 volumes of printed music, c. 600 gramophone records. Special items: Henkel collection, Hockner archives, C. 770 libretti.

Hamburg
STAATS-UND-UNIVERSITÄTSBIBLIOTHEK, Moorweidenstr. 40, 2 Hamburg 13. Music Librarian: Dr. Bernhard Stockmann. Collection: MSS. printed music, books and records. Special items: Handel and Brahms collections.

Hannover
STAATLICHE HOCHSCHULE FÜR MUSIK UND THEATER BIBLIOTHEK, Emmichplatz 1, 3000 Hamburg. Librarian: Hans Janssen. Collection: 95,000 volumes of books and music, 3,000 records.

Lübeck
BIBLIOTHEK DER HANSESTADT LÜBECK, Hundestr. 5-17, 2400 Lübeck. Music Librarian: Renate Schleth. Collection: old printed music, church music, old vocal music, piano music. Special item: old textbooks.

Munich
BAYERISCHE STAATBIBLIOTHEK MÜNCHEN MUSIKSAMMLUNG, Postfach 150, 8 Munich 34. Music Librarian: Dr. Robert Münster. Collection: in extent and continuity the richest learned musical library in the Federal Republic. Large collection of records. Special items: Choir books (15th and 16th centuries) of the Munich Hofkapelle; 16th century printed music; collections of works by 100 composers. Recent acquisitions: music autographs of Richard Strauss, Pfitzner, Reger and K. A. Hartmann.

STÄDTISCHE MUSIKBIBLIOTHEK MÜNCHEN, Salvatorplatz 1, 8000 Munich 2. Librarian: Brigitte Kohl. Collection: 137,000 volumes; large reference library with complete editions, other printed music, scores, c. 8,500 records etc. Special items: Richard Strauss autographs of songs and "Till Eulenspiegel."

Nuremberg
BIBLIOTHEK DES GERMANISCHEN NATIONALMUSEUM, Kartäusergasse 1, 8500 Nuremberg. Director of the Library: Dr. Elisabeth Rücker. Collection: literature concerning historic instruments.

STADTBIBLIOTHEK NÜRNBERG, Abteilung Musikbibliothek, Burg 2, 8500 Nuremberg. Music Librarian: Angelika Bieberbach. Collection: music, musicological books, records and cassettes, studio for recording, practice room for pianists.

Regensburg
BISCHÖFLICHE ZENTRALBIBLIOTHEK - Proske-Musiksammlung, St. Petersweg 11-13, 8400 Regensburg. Director: Dr. Paul Mai. Collection: musical Antiquities of Ratisbon, Proske

library of portfolios, Choral music, theoretical works, Mettenleiter and Haberl libraries. Special items: manuscripts and printed music of the 16th and early 17th centuries.

Wiesbaden
HESSISCHE LANDESBIBLIOTHEK WIESBADEN, Rheinstr. 55157, 62 Wiesbaden. Music Librarian: Dr. Schwitzgobel. Collection: complete editions, music and scores from all eras, specimens of Breitkopf and Härtel publications in Wiesbaden. Special items: old printed music; Miroslav Weber (1854-1906) collection.

Wolfenbüttel
HERZOG AUGUST BIBLIOTHEK, Postbox 227, Lessingplatz 1, 3340 Wolfenbüttel. Music Librarian: Dr. Hans Haase. Collection: printed music and treatises, particularly of the 16th and 17th centuries; MSS of the Notre-Dame school; songbook, Bavarian Mass choirbook from around 1500; MS. of Heinrich Schütz. Special items: keyboard and plucked instrument tablatures; libretti (cf. catalogue by E. Thiel 1970).

Würzburg
UNIVERSITÄTSBIBLIOTHEK, Domerschulstr. 16, 87 Würzburg. Music Librarian: Dr. Martin Seelkopf. Collection: a few MSS and c. 100 printed volumes from 16th to 20th centuries; selection of important books on music (biographies, handbooks etc.).

GREECE

Patmos
LIBRARY OF THE MONASTERY OF ST. JOHN THE THEOLOGIAN, Monastery of St. John the Theologian, Patmos. Librarian: Father Chrysostomos Florentis. Collection: Ecclesiastical music. Special items: MSS of Byzantine ecclesiastical music 12-th-20th centuries.

HUNGARY

Budapest
GORKY STATE LIBRARY, Music Department, Pf. 17, VII Gorkij fasor 45, 1406 Budapest. Music Librarian: Ferenc Gyimes. Collection: c. 50,000 library units with music, books, records, tapes. Special items: Eastern European music, contemporary composers, Hungarian choral music.

INSTITUTE OF MUSICOLOGY OF THE HUNGARIAN ACADEMY OF SCIENCES, P.f. 28, 1250 Budapest. Librarian: Gábor Albert. Collection: Musicological books, scores, manuscripts, specialising in Hungarian music. Special items: Bartok archives; folk music collection, c. 100,000 items.

Esztergom
LIBRARY OF THE CATHEDRAL, Bajcsy Zsilinsky u. 28,2500 Esztergom. Director: Dr. Zoltán Kovách. Collection: medieval and other liturgical manuscripts, antiphons, graduals etc; printed liturgical and other music.

INDIA

New Delhi
NATIONAL ACADEMY OF MUSIC, DANCE AND DRAMA, Rabindra Bhavan, Ferozeshah Road, New Delhi 110001. Music Librarian: Oommen Varkey. Collection: Indian music, with books, music with Indian notation, theoretical works, Indian folk music and Indian instruments. Special items: large collection of Indian music on disc and tape. Recent acquisitions: rare books on Hindu, Isai and oriental music.

ISRAEL

Jerusalem
AMLI LIBRARY AT THE RUBIN ACADEMY OF MUSIC, 7 Peretz Smolenskin St. Director: Claude Abravanel. Collection: books, scores, records, periodicals, manuscripts. Special items: Jewish and Israeli music.

Tel-Aviv
AMLI-CENTRAL LIBRARY FOR MUSIC AND DANCE, 26 Bialik St. Director: Yaakov Snir.
Collection: books, music, records, periodicals, films, slides. Special items: Huberman and
Menashe Ravina archives. Joachim Stuchevsky collection.

ITALY

Bassano-del-Grappa
MUSEO, BIBLIOTECA E ARCHIVIO DI BASSANO-DEL-GRAPPA, via Museo 4, 36061
Bassano-del-Grappa. Deputy Director: Dr. Fernando Rigon. Collection: a few MSS donated
by Oscar Chilesotti.

Bologna
BIBLIOTECA DEL CONSERVATORIO DI MUSICA "G. B. MARTINI," piazza Rossini 2,40126
Bologna. Librarian: Dr. Oscar Mischiati. Collection: chiefly modern music and musicological
material. Special items: Bertocchi archives (19th century MSS. printed music, practical and
theoretical books); Dono Ivaldi collection of piano music. Recent acquisition: Verdi'
correspondence with Maria Massari Waldmann.

Cesena (Forli)
BIBLIOTECA COMUNALE MALATESTIANA, piazza Bufalini 1,47023 Cesena (Forli).
Director: Dr. Antonio Brasini. Collection: c. 100 musical works printed from 16th to 18th
centuries (see catalogue by S. Paganelli in "Collectanea historiae musicae, Vol II, Florence
1956). Special items: 14 choral MSS of 15th century, including many autographs by
composers of the Ferrara school.

Ferrara
BIBLIOTECA COMMUNALE ARIOSTEA. 44100 Ferrara. Collection: Small collection of
Italian printed music of the 15th-18th centuries.

Florence
BIBLIOTECA MEDICEA LAURENZIANA, piazza San Lorenzo 9,50121 Florence. Librarian:
Dr. Antonietta Morandini. Collection: no special music collection; codices are stored and
arranged in different sections of the library. Recent acquisition: codice Varzi, Acquisition and
bequest 666 (cf. facsimile and edition by E. E. Lowinsky "The Medici Codex of 1518,"
Chicago 1968).

BIBLIOTECA NAZIONALE CENTRALE, piazza Cavalleggeri 1,50100 Florence. Director: Dr.
Anna Lenzuni. Collection: MSS. collection, printed music of 16th-19th centuries; modern
editions; large collection of libretti; books and periodicals on musical history. Special items:
18th-19th century MSS; old music in editions of 16th-18th centuries; music of 19th-20th
centuries.

CONSERVATORIO STATALE DI MUSICA "LUIGI CHERUBINI," piazzetta delle Belle Arti.
Librarian: Prof. Vinicio Gai. Collection: Pitti endowment; Basevi Endowment.

Milan
BIBLIOTECA DEL CONSERVATORIO DI MUSICA "G. VERDI," via Conservatorio 12.
Librarian: Prof. Agostina Zecca Laterza. Collection: nearly all music printed in Milan province
from 1800 till now; 60 collections of complete works and another 50 memorial and
collected editions. Principal compositions of Italian and foreign composers; MSS opera
scores of works given in Milan 1816-56. Special items: S. Barbara Gonzaga,
(1530-c.1630). Noseda endowment (MSS and printed material of 18th century).

Modena
BIBLIOTECA ESTENSE, piazza S. Agostino 337,41100 Modena. Director: Dr. Silvana
Verdini. Collection: Many important collections from the first half of the 15th century until
now.

Noto
BIBLIOTECA COMUNALE, viz Matteo Raeli 8,96017 Noto. Director: Dr. G. Santocomo
Russo. Collection: General music collection.

Padua
BIBLIOTECA UNIVERSITARIA, via S. Biagio 7. Director: Dr. Eugenia Govi. Collection: 32

codici and 27 fragments of MSS, described in "Indice speciale dei codici musicali," 1559 edition (Sec. XVI-XX), described in the alphabetical catalogue of composers.

Perugia
BIBLIOTECA COMUNALE, 06081 Perugia. Director: P. Gino Zanotti. Collection: includes Catalogue of the musical collection at the Biblioteca Comunale of Assisi, Milan 1962.

Pesaro
BIBLIOTECA DEL CONSERVATORIO "G. ROSSINI," piazza Olivieri 5,61100 Pesaro. Librarian: Marta Mancini. Collection: MSS and printed works from 16th to 20th centuries. Special item: collection of string quartets printed in late 18th and early 19th centuries.

BIBLIOTECA OLIVERIANA, via Mazza 96,61100 Pesaro. Music Librarian: Prof. Antonio Brancati. Collection: numerous medieval and later codici and modern works of particular value. MSS include an 18th century treatise on musical theory and polyphonic composition; Domenican liturgical music, the earliest tablature for French lute (16th century). Printed music includes c. 300 opera libretti from 1600, many of them unique; also F. Gafurius "Practica musicale" published in Brescia 1497.

Reggio Emilia
BIBLIOTECA MUNICIPALE A. PANIZZI, via Farini 3,42100 Reggio Emilia. Director: Dr. Maurizio Festanti. Collection: a variety of secular and sacred music.

Rimini
BIBLIOTECA CIVICA "GAMBALUNGA," via Gambalunga 27. Music Librarian: Prof. Piero Meldini. Collection: small but precious collection of about 50 MSS. Special items: Mattei-Gentile bequest, including MSS and printed music - 2,000 MSS of scores of 16th-19th centuries, 1,500 printed scores 17th-19th century.

Rome
ACCADEMIA NAZIONALE DEI LINCEI BIBLIOTECA, Via della Lungara 10. Director: Dr. Amelia Cosatti. Collection: Important collections of old and modern music. Special items: Chiti and Corsini collections of old MSS.

BIBLIOTECA CASANATENSE, via S. Ignazio 52. Music Librarian: Marta Corsanego. Collection: 994 MSS covering the period 11th-19th centuries; 681 printed works of the period 15th-20th centuries. Special items: Baini collection of MS and printed works; 90 autographs and manuscripts of works by Paganini; Compagnoni-Marefoschi bequest of 604 MSS.

BIBLIOTECA VALLICELLIANA, piazza della Chiesa Nuova 18. Collection: MSS and printed music, mainly 17th century; early laudi, sacred music and other works.

PONTIFICIO ISTITUTO DI MUSICA SACRA, piazza S. Agostino 20a,00186 Rome. Music Librarian: Mgr. Dr. Ferdinand Haberl. Collection: Renaissance polyphonic music, Gregorian chant, organ and instrumental music, liturgical music. Special items: Beethoven and Mozart; Denkmäler der Tonkunst in Österreich, Patrologia greca, Patrologia latina etc.

Siena
ARCHIVIO DELL'OPERA DELLA METROPOLITANA DI SIENA, piazza del Duomo 8. Rector: Prof. E. Carli. Collection: MSS and printed sacred music from 17th to 19th centuries from the Cathedral.

Turin
ARCHIVIO ARCIVESCOVILE, via Arcivescovado 12. Archivist: Canon Gallo Giuseppe. Collection: Houses the library of Turin Cathedral.

CIVICA BIBLIOTECA MUSICALE "ANDREA DELLA CORTE," via Roma 53,10125 Turin. Collection: 35,170 books and pamphlets, 54,285 scores, 2,904 opera libretti, 376 MSS, 210 periodicals, 7,455 records. Special items: opera libretti of the former Scuola di canto corale municipale, Societa di Concerto di Teatro Regio and Banda Civica. Recent acquisitions: Andrea della Corte bequest (1968) of 14,783 books, periodicals and scores.

Venice
BIBLIOTECA NAZIONALE MARCIANA, S. Marco, n. 7,30124 Venice. Director: G. A. Ravalli Modoni. Collection: one of the finest in Italy, containing many early MSS and printed works;

MSS include works by Marcello, the Scarlattis (e.g. 13 volumes of Harpsichord sonatas), Cavalli (27 operas), Galuppi, Graun, Monteverdi, Haydn etc; printed music is rich in madrigal part books, chiefly Venetian editions; also many cantatas, arias, songs etc. in both MSS and early printed editions. Special items: Pietro Canal collection; Contarini collection (operas, some autograph, of the Venetian school). Recent acquisitions: Gino Tagliapietra collection of over 50 MSS; Dini collection of 42 MSS and 110 printed works.

KOREA

Seoul
SEOUL NATIONAL UNIVERSITY LIBRARY, San 56-1 Sinlim-Dong Gwanac, Gu, Seoul 151. Music Librarian: Woon-Tai Kim. Collection: 6,000 books, 5,000 scores, 4,500 records, 1,300 tapes etc. Special item: Yuk Young-Su memorial record collection.

LEBANON

LIBRARY OF MUSIC AND MUSICOLOGY, Institute of Musicology, University of the Holy Spirit.

NETHERLANDS

Amsterdam
PUBLIC MUSIC LIBRARY, Prinsengracht 587. Librarian: Huib Deetman. Collection: 46,000 volumes of scores and music, 15,000 volumes of books on music, 40,000 records.

TOONKUNST-BIBLIOTHEEK, Prinsengracht 587. Librarian: Paul W. van Reijen. Collection: Research collection, containing first and early editions, MSS, modern scholarly music editions and books on music. Special items: Former library of Dutch Music History.

Bilthoven
LIBRARY OF THE GAUDEAMUS FOUNDATION, P.O. Box 30, 3720 AA Bilthoven. Librarian: G. van Inger. Collection: Contemporary music only; 10,000 scores, 1,500 records, 2,000 tape recordings.

The Hague
MUSIC LIBRARY OF THE HAAGS GEMEENTEMUSEUM, Stadhouderslaan 41. Music Librarian: D'. van den Hul. Collection: research library; early printings of music, opera, theory, libretti; archives of Dutch composers and musicians (1800-1950). Recent acquisitions: Abraham Burggraf von Dhona collection (17th century); Mengelberg archives.

Utrecht
LIBRARY OF THE INSTITUTE OF MUSICOLOGY OF THE UNIVERSITY, Drift 21. Librarian: Dr. A. Annegarn. Collection: part of the University's main library, used for study and musicological research.

LIBRARY OF THE UTRECHT CONSERVATORY, Librarian: Miss Bernadette Harperink. Collection: Miss Bernadette Harperink. Collection: for professional musical training; 10,000 volumes of music, books, periodicals, choral and orchestral music; 1,500 records, 200 tapes, 1,000 slides.

NEW ZEALAND

Auckland
CITY OF AUCKLAND CENTRAL LIBRARY, P.O. Box 4138. Collection: c. 22,000 scores, c. 8,000 books on music, c. 10,000 records. Special items: New Zealand composers' published works, manuscripts and records; chamber music.

UNIVERSITY OF AUCKLAND, Dept. of Anthropology, Private Bag. Director: Mervyn McLean. Collection: archive of Maori and Pacific music.

UNIVERSITY OF AUCKLAND MUSIC LIBRARY, Conservatorium of Music, 31 Princes St. Collection: c. 30,000 scores, 5,630 records; comprehensive collection of complete works in scholarly edition. Special items: Medieval and early Renaissance music; Slavonic music; 20th century music; published works of New Zealand composers.

Christchurch
UNIVERSITY OF CANTERBURY LIBRARY, Private Bag, Christchurch. Collection: c. 5,000 scores, 500 records.

Dunedin
UNIVERSITY OF OTAGO LIBRARY, P.O. Box 56, Dunedin. Collection: c. 10,000 scores, 1,000 records. Special items: Renaissance and avant-garde music.

Wellington
ALEXANDER TURNBULL LIBRARY, National Library of New Zealand, P.O. Box 12-349, Wellington. Collection: c. 500 scores (including those of New Zealand composers), 800 records. Special items: historical discs of Maori music; archive of New Zealand music, including MSS, published scores etc.

NATIONAL LIBRARY OF NEW ZEALAND, Headquarters, Private Bag, Wellington. Collection: c. 2,600 scores including complete works of major composers in scholarly editions and a growing collection of 20th century music.

RADIO NEW ZEALAND MUSIC LIBRARY, P.O. Box 98, Wellington. Collection: c. 100,000 scores; keyboard, instrumental, orchestral and choral music. Special items: choral music, light music and some MSS of New Zealand composers.

VICTORIA UNIVERSITY OF WELLINGTON LIBRARY, P.O. Box 196, Wellington. Reference Librarian: Mrs. Dorothy Freed. Collection: c. 10,000 scores and 1,000 records; scores reflect needs of teaching staff and students; 20th century composers well represented; complete works in scholarly editions. Special items: copies of Douglas Lilburn MSS and printed scores and records.

NORWAY

Bergen
BERGEN PUBLIC LIBRARY, Music Department, Stromgt. 6, 5000 Bergen. Music Librarian: Karen Falch Johannessen. Collection: 31,000 volumes of sheet music, scores and books; 4,000 records. Special items: Edvard Grieg's testamentary collection which consists of 110 items of Grieg's own MSS, c. 340 letters from Grieg and c. 5,000 letters to Grieg; also 34,000 items of first and pirated editions of Grieg's work; some MSS by Grieg's friend Richard Nordraak.

Oslo
NATIONAL MUSIC COLLECTION, Observatoriegaten 1, Oslo 2. Librarian: Oystein Gaukstad. Collection: Norway's largest musical collection: 14,000 MSS (including about 15,000 Norwegian folk tunes), 130,000 items of printed music (including 25,000 Norwegian composers) and a selection of theoretical, biographical and historical literature. Special items: Norwegian Sound Archives, with about 20,000 78 r.p.m. records, 4,000 LPs, 1,000 phonogram recordings and 1,000 tapes; also special collection of Beethoven's and Schubert's music. Recent acquisitions: MSS bequests by several Norwegian composers.

NORWEGIAN ACADEMY OF MUSIC LIBRARY, Nordahl Brunsgt. 8, Oslo 1. Librarian: Tone Elogsson. Collection: 30,000 items of sheet music, 4,000 books, 3,000 records, 400 tapes.

Stavanger
STAVANGER LIBRARY, Music Section, Haakon VII'sgt. II, 4,000 Stavanger. Music Librarian: Ragnhild Vetrhus. Collection: 14,000 scores, c. 1,000 books, 20 periodicals, c. 3,500 gramophone records covering the classical field, jazz, folk, pop and religious music.

POLAND

Cracow
JAGELLONIAN UNIVERSITY LIBRARY, Music Department Library, A1. Nickiewecza 22,

30-059 Cracow. Music Librarian: Agnieszka Mietelska-Ciepierska. Collection: old printed editions pre-1800, especially Polish. Deposit library for modern music and books. Special items: Library of Cracow Music Society; libretti; periodical 19th and 29th centuries. Recent acquisition: autograph of Chopin's "Variations in D major" for piano duet.

Gdańsk
GDAŃSK LIBRARY OF THE POLISH ACADEMY OF SCIENCES, Watowa 15, 80-858 Gdańsk. Deputy Director: Dr. Edmund Kotarski. Collection: 724 MSS from 17th-19th centuries, mainly religious music by Polish, Italian, French and German composers; c. 586 items of printed music from 16th-18th centuries, mainly religious works, but also secular occasional music. Special items: George Knophius collection of 162 volumes of Italian madrigals and motets.

Katowice
LIBRARY OF THE ACADEMY OF MUSIC, Katowice, ul. 27 stycznia 33, 40-025 Katowice. Librarian: Dr. Karol Musiol. Collection: c. 75,000 items including MSS, printed music both old and new, books, records and tapes. Special items: archives of musical culture in Silesia. Recent acquisitions: MSS collections of Silesian composers, old Polish musical posters, the first printed composition by Chopin with the composer's autograph.

Kórnik
KÓRNIK LIBRARY OF THE POLISH ACADEMY OF SCIENCES, Music Section, Kórnik-Zamek.

Lódź
UNIVERSITY LIBRARY, Music Section, Matejki str. 34/38, 90-950 Lódź. Music Librarian: Krystyna Bielska. Collection: 22,000 volumes of sheet music, orchestral and vocal scores; complete Polish music editions since 1945; Polish music of the 19th and 20th centuries; works of foreign composers including complete editions; world contemporary music. Special items: collection of 580 opera titles, scores and piano reductions, including 175 first editions of French operas of 18th and 19th centuries. Recent acquisitions: first editions of works by Chopin and Moniuszko; new audio equipment including tape recorders.

Lublin
CATHOLIC UNIVERSITY LIBRARY, Music Section, ul. Chopina 27, 20-023 Lublin.

Toruń
UNIVERSITY LIBRARY, Music Section, ul. Gagarina 13, 87-100 Toruń.

Warsaw
NATIONAL LIBRARY, Music Section, Plac. Krasińskich 5, 00-207 Warsaw.

LIBRARY OF THE ACADEMY OF MUSIC, Okólnik 2, 00-368 Warsaw.

LIBRARY OF THE WARSAW MUSIC SOCIETY, ul. Zakroczymska 2, 00-225 Warsaw.

LIBRARY-ARCHIVE OF THE FREDERIC CHOPIN SOCIETY, Okolnik 1, 00-368 Warsaw.

UNIVERSITY LIBRARY, Music Section, ul. Zwirki i Wigury 93, 02-093 Warsaw.

WARSAW PUBLIC LIBRARY, ul. Koszykowa 26. Music Librarian: Mrs. Danuta Heckermann. Collection: 12, 124 musical items, many scores published in Poland since 1945 and received as deposit copies; 1,515 records.

Wroclaw
UNIVERSITY LIBRARY, Music Section, ŚW. Jadwigi 3/4, 50-266 Wroclaw.

PORTUGAL

Coimbra
UNIVERSITY OF COIMBRA LIBRARY, Coimbra. Collection: MSS of secular and sacred music of the 15th-18th centuries; printed music, theoretical works, early secular and sacred polyphonic music.

Lisbon
ARQUIVA DE MÚSICA, Fábrica da Sé Patriarcal, Largo da Sé. Music Librarian: M. S. Kastner.

Collection: Mainly 18th and 19th century church music by Portuguese and Italian composers; a few books of 16th and 17th century polyphony.

BIBLIOTECA DA AJUDA, Palacio Nacional da Ajuda, Lisbon 3. Collection: MSS of 18-19th centuries; printed music 19th-20th centuries.

ROMANIA

Bucharest
BIBLIOTHÈQUE MUSICALE - documentaire de l'Union des Compositeurs Roumains, str. Constantin Esarcu 2, 70149 Bucharest. Librarians: Mihaela Marinescu and Sanda Nenoiu. Collection: Scores, books on musical history and aesthetics, manuscripts, periodicals, orchestral parts. Special items: MSS. by Enescu, Dinu Lipatti, Bartok, a letter of Beethoven's, etc; rare copies of Byzantine and oriental music; Glareanus's "Dodekahordon" (1547), Reicha's "Traité de Mélodie" (1814), etc.

LIBRARY OF "CIPRIAN PORUMBESCU" ACADEMY OF MUSIC, 33 Stirbey Voda St., Bucharest 7. Music Librarian: Verona Ienciu. Collection: 198,491 volumes (scores, books on musicology, manuscripts, records, museum exhibits). Special items: "Carmen" choral record office, MSS of the forerunners of Roumanian music. Recent acquisitions: G. Pantîru "La Notation de la musique byzantine"; I. D. Petresco "Etudes de paléographie musicale byzantine."

Iasi
BIBLIOTECA CONSERVATORULUI DE MUZICĂ "GEORGE ENESCU," str. Cuza Veda 29. Librarian: Ana Dumitrescu. Collection: 75,000 volumes on all musical subjects including, scores, printed sheet music, books on history and aesthetics, folklore, ethnography etc.

SOUTH AFRICA

Cape Town
UNIVERSITY OF CAPE TOWN MUSIC LIBRARY, S. A. College of Music, Main Road, Rosebank, 7700. Librarian: Mrs. J. Skutil. Collection: 9,000 books, 37,000 items of printed music, 9,000 records, periodicals. Special item: Collection of South African music. Recent acquisitions: MSS of Dr. Erik Chisholm, Denkmäler der Tönkust in Österreich, Denkmäler der Deutschen Tönkunst.

Grahamstown
INTERNATIONAL LIBRARY OF AFRICAN MUSIC, I.S.E.R., Rhodes University, Grahamstown 6140. Director: Andrew Tracey.

SPAIN

Madrid
BIBLIOTECA NACIONAL, Seción de Música y Archive de la Palabra Hablada, Avda. de Calve Sotelo 20. Music Librarian: Nieves Iglesias Martinez. Collection: Musical literature, theoretical works, scores, records and cassettes, particularly relating to the musical culture of Spain. This is a copyright deposit library. Special items: F. A. Barbieri (1823-94) library; MSS of 17th, 18th and 19th centuries; original MSS of works by Spanish composers. Recent acquisition: library of the composer Gerado Gombau (1906-1972).

BIBLIOTECA DE PALACIO, Palacio Real, plaza de Oriente, Madrid 13. Music Librarian: Justa Moreno Garbayo. Collection: Chiefly music of the 18th and 19th centuries, with an extensive collection of operas. Special items: "Cancionero Musical de Palaccio" - MSS of 15th and 16th centuries.

SWEDEN

Stockholm
ROYAL THEATRE MUSIC LIBRARY, The Royal Theatre, AB Box 16094, 103 22 Stockholm.

Music Librarian: Mats Farell. Collection: Opera and ballet scores, orchestral and vocal parts from 18th century onwards.

Uppsala
UPPSALA UNIVERSITETSBIBLIOTEK, Box 510, 751 20 Uppsala. Music Librarian: Dr. Carl-Otto von Sydow. Collection: Printed music and MSS from the 16th century onwards. Special items: Düben collection of 17th and 18th century MSS, including Buxtehude autographs; Gimo collection of Italian MSS of 18th century; German, French and Italian printed music of 16th and 17th centuries.

SWITZERLAND

Basle
BIBLIOTHEK DER MUSIKAKADEMIE, Leonhardsstrasse 4-6, 4051 Basle. Librarian: Dr. Ruedy Ebner. Collection: scores and parts of all kinds. Special items: Pre-1800 works on performing practice.

ÖFFENTLICHE BIBLIOTHEK DER UNIVERSITÄT BASEL, Schönbeinstr. 18-20, 4056 Basle. Music Librarian: Dr. Hans Peter Schanzlin. Collection: Practical and theoretical works, both MSS and printed, from late middle ages until today. Special items: Collection of Lucas Sarasin and Collegium musicum Basel (18th century MSS); Swiss composers' MSS; Refardt collection concerning history of Basle music; Library and archive of Swiss Musicological Society.

Berne
SWISS NATIONAL LIBRARY, Music Division, Hallwylstr. 15, 3003 Berne. Music Librarian: Robert Wyler. Collection: Helvetica (Music by Swiss composers, music printed in Switzerland, MSS, sound recordings, microfilms or other copies of non-printed Swiss music). Special items: J. Liebeskind collection: Operas and symphonic music of late 18th and early 19th centuries, especially Gluck and Dittersdorf.

Einsiedeln
STIFTSBIBLIOTHEK MUSIC DEPT., Kloster, 8840 Einsiedeln. Music Librarian: P. Lukas Helg. Collection: Music and books since 1550. Music of the music is in portfolios of which there are c. 1050; several thousand books. Special items: Copies and autographs from the Italian region of the country by J. C. Bach, Sammartini; music from Salzburg and important German monasteries. Robert Pearsall library acquired in 1862.

Zürich
BIBLIOTHEK DER ALLGEMEINE MUSIKGESELLSCHAFT, c/o Zentralbibliothek, Zürich. Librarian: Dr. Gunther Birnker. Collection: Manuscript and printed music of 17th-19th centuries. Recent acquisition: MS of Brahms's 4th symphony.

KONSERVATORIUM UND MUSIKHOCHSCHULE ZÜRICH, Florhofgasse 6, 8001 Zürich. Librarian: Lisbet Thew. Collection: Material relating to the teaching and performance of music. Special items: part of the estate of Xaver Schnyder von Wartensee.

U.S.S.R.

Moscow
LENIN STATE LIBRARY, pr. Kalinina 3, 101000 Moscow. Music Librarian: G. B. Koltypina. Collection: over 300,000 volumes of printed music, Russian (from 18th century), Soviet and foreign; books on music and musicology, records, periodicals. Special items: B. V. Asafiev music collection; rare printed music of 17th and 18th centuries; manuscripts. Recent acquisitions: B. B. Borissovsky collection of viola music.

UNITED KINGDOM

Aberdeen
UNIVERSITY OF ABERDEEN MUSIC LIBRARY, King's College Library, Old Aberdeen. Librarian: Catherine Drummond. Collection: extensive collection of miniature scores, full scores, vocal scores; expanding collection of chamber music: standard historical editions.

Special items: copyright collection (early 19th century); Taylor collection of Psalmody; Gavin Greig collection of folksongs. Recent acquisition: Murdoch Henderson collection of Scottish music.

Aberystwyth
NATIONAL LIBRARY OF WALES, Aberystwyth, Dyfed, SY23 3BU. Keeper of Printed Books: P. A. L. Jones. Collection: divided between Welsh and Celtic music, and other music. All forms of music acquired under the Copyright Act of 1911. Special items: Welsh music collection.

Belfast
QUEEN'S UNIVERSITY OF BELFAST, Belfast BT7 1NN. Collection: designed for research and study, not performance; many editions of composers' complete works. Special items: Sir Hamilton Harty collection of orchestral scores (including MSS of Harty's own works); Edward Bunting collection of transcripts of 18th century versions of Irish folk melodies.

Birmingham
UNIVERSITY OF BIRMINGHAM MUSIC LIBRARY, Barber Institute of Fine Arts, P.O. Box 363, Birmingham B15 2TS. Librarian: P. S. Wilson. Collection: general library of books, records, scores, collected editions, anthologies and periodicals for teaching and postgraduate work. Special items: pre-1801 printed music; Granville Bantock MSS and printed works. Recent acquisitions: 1976 - Gloria Rose collection of 17th and 18th century MSS.

Cambridge
CAMBRIDGE UNIVERSITY LIBRARY, West Road, Cambridge, CB3 9DR. Music Librarian: D. W. Williams. Collection: copyright deposit library; research library with no especial emphasis on performing material; foreign publications. Special items: 16th and 17th century lute music MSS; Hook autographs; Warlock autographs; Arnold bequest; Marion Scott bequest; Picken Collection (Ethnomusicology); Ely Cathedral MSS on deposit.

FITZWILLIAM MUSEUM, Trumpington St. Librarian: P. Woudhuysen. Collection: 1,200 volumes (10,000 items); large number of autograph MSS by Blow, Purcell, Bach, Scarlatti, Haydn, Mozart, Beethoven and others. Special items: Handel collection.

KING'S COLLEGE, ROWE MUSIC LIBRARY. Music Librarian: Mrs. M. Cranmer. Collection: rich in collected editions, scores and printed music; large collection of pre-1800 printed music and c. 500 MSS. Special items: L. T. Rowe library, part of the A. H. Mann collection, library of Boris Ord and papers of E. J. Dent.

MAGDALENE COLLEGE, PEPYS LIBRARY. Librarian: The Pepys Librarian. Collection: MSS and printed collection of Samuel Pepys.

PEMBROKE COLLEGE LIBRARY, Trumpington St. Assistant Librarian: W. S. Hutton. Collection: c. 80 volumes of printed music (17th-19th centuries); c. 200 volumes of general use to music students and performers. Special items: 6 bound volumes of MSS anthems and Services (Tallis, Gibbons, Child et al.) 17th and 18th centuries.

PENDLEBURY LIBRARY OF MUSIC, University Music School, West Rd. Librarian: Richard M. Andrewes. Collection: Musical scores and literature for loan to members of the University; sound recordings and microfilms for teaching purposes only. Special items: Bequests and gifts from E. J. Dent, B. Ord, J. B. Trend and Picken.

Cardiff
CARDIFF PUBLIC LIBRARIES, Central Library, The Hayes (Music section). Collection: large general collection of books, music, scores etc. Special items: Aylward Collection of English sacred music and organ music; Bonner Morgan collection of 17th and 18th century music, including 10 MS volumes of early Italian opera.

Croydon
ROYAL SCHOOL OF CHURCH MUSIC, Addington Palace. Librarian: M. P. M. Fleming. Collection: Church music, liturgy and related subjects.

Edinburgh
EDINBURGH CITY LIBRARIES, Central Library, George IV Bridge, Edinburgh EH1 1EG. Music Librarian: Lorna Mill. Collection: reference and lending collection of books and music,

including much early Scottish printed music. Special items: Edinburgh Musical Society archives 1728-95; Marr bequest, Cowan bequest, Niecks bequest.

NATIONAL LIBRARY OF SCOTLAND, George IV Bridge, Edinburgh EH1 1EW. Music Librarian: Roger Duce, M.A. Collection: copyright deposit library; over 100,000 scores, mostly post-1850. MSS of Scottish music (including bagpipe music), 17th century lute and bass viol music from France, Percy Grainger works. Special items: Glen, Inglis collections of Scottish music; Balfour Handel collection. Recent acquisitions: Murdoch Henderson collection of Scottish music; Hopkinson Berlioz and Verdi collections.

REID MUSIC LIBRARY, Alison House, Nicolson Square, Edinburgh EH8 9DF. Librarian: Michael S. Anderson. Collection: Library of the Faculty of Music, Edinburgh University, containing more than 60,000 items (scores, books, records etc); much 20th century music; rare and early prints and MSS. Special items: Weiss collection of Beethoven literature; Niecks collection, Tovey collection.

Glasgow
MITCHELL LIBRARY, North St., Glasgow, G3 7DN. Music Librarian: George R. Barr. Collection: reference library of 44,000 volumes representative of all types of music. Special items: Kidson collection of old English music; Moody Manners collection of opera scores. Recent acquisition: F. G. Scott manuscripts.

ROYAL SCOTTISH ACADEMY OF MUSIC AND DRAMA, 58 St. George's Place, Glasgow G2 1BS. Librarian: Kenneth F. Wilkins. Collection: general collection of music, books, records, choral and orchestral parts relating to the teaching of the Academy.

Hereford
HEREFORD CATHEDRAL LIBRARY, The Cathedral, Hereford, HR1 2NG. Hon. Librarian: Penelope E. Morgan. Collection: chiefly sacred music, including 18th and 19th century MSS; also glees and madrigals; piano music formerly owned and autographed by Fanny Kemble. Special items: Hereford Breviary c. 1720; Roger North's autographed MSS of his 'Musicall Grammarian' and 'Memoires of Musick'; MSS of Elgar, S. S. Wesley etc.

London
BRITISH LIBRARY REFERENCE DIVISION, Great Russell St., London WC1B 3DG. Music Librarian: O. W. Neighbour. Keeper of Manuscripts: Dr. D. P. Waley. Collections: Copyright deposit library; comprehensive collection of printed music; c. 10,000 volumes of manuscript music.

CENTRAL MUSIC LIBRARY, Westminster City Libraries, 160 Buckingham Palace Road, London SW1W 9UD. Music Librarian: Alan Sopher. Collection: large collection (c. 100,000 items) of printed music, books, sets of orchestral parts and periodicals, combining functions of a loan and a reference library; plays an important part in the interlending of music in the ·U.K.

GUILDHALL SCHOOL OF MUSIC AND DRAMA, Barbican, London EC2. Librarian: Paul Holden. Collection: comprehensive and expanding collection of 40,000 scores, books, plays and sound recordings; sets of orchestral parts and vocal scores; teaching material. Special items: Appleby collection of guitar music (over 6,000 items, many unique); Rosenczweig collection of Jewish music; Alkan Society Collection of scores and recordings of the music of Charles Alkan.

HORNIMAN MUSEUM AND LIBRARY, London Road, Forest Hill, London SE23 3PQ. Collection: organology and ethnic musical instruments and music; no printed music. Special item: Adam Carse collection and MSS.

ROYAL ACADEMY OF MUSIC, Marylebone Road, London NW1 5HT. Librarian: M. J. Harington. Collection: scores, books on music, records; early printed music; some MSS. Special items: Henry Wood Library of orchestral music.

ROYAL COLLEGE OF MUSIC - PARRY ROOM LIBRARY, Prince Consort Road, London SW7 2BS. Librarian: The Keeper. Collection: Antiquarian music. Special items: Sacred Harmonic Society Library.

VAUGHAN WILLIAMS MEMORIAL LIBRARY OF THE ENGLISH FOLK DANCE AND SONG SOCIETY, Cecil Sharp House, 2 Regent's Park Road, London, NW1 7AY. Collection: 8,000 volumes of folk music, folk song, folk dance, principally British but also some foreign material; material on customs, folklore; 3,500 records, 250 tapes. Special items: MSS collections of early folk song and dance from Anne Gilchrist, Lucy Broadwood, H. E. D. Hammond, George Gardiner, George Butterworth, Cecil Sharp (copy), Vaughan Williams (copy of folk song MSS); collection of original broadsides.

Manchester
HENRY WATSON MUSIC LIBRARY, Central Library, Manchester M2 5PD. Librarian: Leonard W. Duck. Collection: lending (380,000 items) and reference (15,000 items) of music and books on music. Special items: 2,000 items of early published music and MSS.

Oxford
BODLEIAN LIBRARY, Oxford OX1 3BG. Music Librarian: P. A. Ward Jones. Collection: copyright deposit library; c. 350,000 items of printed music, 13,000 books, c. 1,000 MSS. Special items: former Oxford Music School collection; Osborne Wight bequest; W. N. H. Harding collection. Recent acquisitions: Deneke Mendelssohn collection of autograph MSS, diaries, letters, personal library; W. N. H. Harding collection of English and French songs and opera, American sheet music.

OXFORDSHIRE COUNTY LIBRARIES, Central Library, Westgate, Oxford, OX1 1DJ. Music Librarian: 7,000 scores, parts, miniature scores and books on music; 6,000 records; 250 reference books; computerised catalogue by subject and alphabetically, 400 pp. Special items: English madrigal school sets 55 volumes presented by the Friends of Music in Oxfordshire.

Welwyn Garden City
HERTFORDSHIRE COUNTY MUSIC LIBRARY, Central Library, Campus West, Welwyn Garden City, Herts. Music Librarian: Philip Robinson. Collection: scores, books on music, libretti, orchestral parts, sets of vocal scores, records and cassettes.

U.S.A.

CALIFORNIA

Los Angeles
LOS ANGELES PUBLIC LIBRARY, 630 West 5th St., CA 90071. Music Librarian: Katherine E. Grant. Collection: 25,000 books; 44,000 scores; 1,750 orchestral scores and parts; Musicians Index; song index; symphonic programme notes; 256 periodicals. Special items: complete editions; solo, instrumental and chamber music; operatic and musical comedy scores; sheet music.

San Francisco
SAN FRANCISCO CONSERVATORY OF MUSIC LIBRARY, 1201 Ortega St., CA 94122. Librarian: Mrs. Viola L. Hagopian. Collection: designed to support the teaching work of the Conservatory; includes scores, books, chamber music, choral and orchestral parts, over 5,000 records and tapes; periodicals and serials. Special items: large collection of Ethnomusicological records; piano/vocal scores of operas; classical guitar music and records. Recent acquisitions: MSS autographs of contemporary American composers.

San Marino
HUNTINGTON LIBRARY, San Marino, CA 91108. Librarian: Daniel H. Woodward. Collection: Mainly English and American music from 1500-1875. cf. Catalogue of music in the Huntington Library printed before 1801, San Marino 1949. Recent acquisitions: several American music books before 1800; a number of 19th century American songbooks.

CONNECTICUT

New Haven
YALE UNIVERSITY MUSIC LIBRARY, Yale University, 98 Wall St., New Haven, CT 06520. Music Librarian: Harold E. Samuel. Collection: research library consisting of 100,000 books and scores, 15,000 LP records, 75,000 early recordings, 1,000 MSS and several archival collections. Special items: Lowell Mason collection (12,000 items acquired before 1860, including the private library of J. C. H. Rinck); complete papers and musical MSS of Charles E. Ives, Carl Ruggles, Leo Ornstein, Horatio Parker, Quincy Porter, Richard Donovan and

others; private library of Dragan Plamenac. Recent acquisitions: complete papers and MSS of Virgil Thompson and Thomas de Hartmann.

DISTRICT OF COLUMBIA

Washington
LIBRARY OF CONGRESS, Music Section, 20540. Collection: c. 3,500,000 items of music and music literature; c. 500,000 sound recordings on disc and tape; probably the largest and most extensive music library in existence, extremely rich in early MSS and printed works; as it is impossible to describe it here, reference can be made to the Annual Reports of the Librarian of Congress (1903-42) and subsequently the Library of Congress Quarterly Journal of Current Acquisitions.

ILLINOIS

Chicago
NEWBERRY LIBRARY, 60 West Walton St., 60610. Curator of modern manuscripts: Diana C. Haskell. Collection: Primary and secondary material for the study of Western music from the middle ages, and of American music from its beginning. Strongest holdings are for early theory; Renaissance and Baroque scores and literature; opera scores and libretti; early American psalmody and religious music; sheet music, periodicals, complete editions; manuscripts. Special items: "Euridice" 1600; Cortot collection; Hubert Platt Main library; J. Francis Driscoll collection of 80,000 pieces of American sheet music, (mainly 1761-1865); Frederic G. Gleason bequest etc.

Evanston
NORTHWESTERN UNIVERSITY MUSIC LIBRARY, 60201. Music Librarian: Don L. Roberts. Collection: 25,000 books, 39,000 scores, 21,000 recordings and 5,000 manuscripts - a general collection but emphasising the 20th century. Recent acquisitions: "Ricordi" collection; part of the Moldenhauer Archives.

Urbana
MUSIC LIBRARY, Music Building, University of Illinois at Urbana-Champaign, 61801. Librarian: William M. McClellan. Collection: Teaching, research and reference materials including books, scores, manuscripts, periodicals, microfilms, etc. Special items: pre-1801 MSS and editions on microfilm; American popular sheet music 1830-1970.

INDIANA

Bloomington
MUSIC LIBRARY, Indiana University, 47401. Librarian: Dr. David E. Fenske. Collection: 86,000 items of books, solo and chamber scores, periodicals, 53,000 records and tapes; 181,000 orchestral scores and parts and multiple copies of choral music. Special items: Apel collection; Paul Nettl papers; Black Music and Latin American Music collections.

Indianapolis
MARION COUNTY PUBLIC LIBRARY, 40 E. St. Clair St., 46204. Head, Arts Division: Helen Barron. Collection: basic collection of music, scores, books and sound recordings. Special items: Collection of old American popular songs.

KENTUCKY

Lexington
UNIVERSITY OF KENTUCKY MUSIC LIBRARY, Fine Arts Building, University of Kentucky, 40506. Librarian: Adelle G. Dailey. Collection: Research library of 35,000 books and scores, 8,000 recordings. Special items: Alfred Cortot collection of early theory books.

Louisville
LOUISVILLE FREE PUBLIC LIBRARY, Fourth and York Sts., 40203. Head of Fine Arts Division-Main Library: Timothy J. Hellner. Collection: A circulating collection of c. 13,000 LP records distributed throughout the Library System (including 24 branches and 4

Bookmobiles) and comprising classical music, bluegrass, country, folk, jazz and pop. Special items: Listening access (not for circulation) to an archive collection of over 100,000 discs of classical performances.

MARYLAND

Baltimore
PEABODY CONSERVATORY LIBRARY, 21 East Mount Vernon Place, 21202. Librarian: Edwin A. Quist Jr. Collection: c. 60,000 items including books, music and sound recordings. Special items: Caruso memorabilia; 19th century opera (piano/vocal scores); MSS of Peabody Composers.

ENOCH PRATT FREE LIBRARY, 400 Cathedral St., 21201. Music Librarian: James D. Dickson, Head of Department. Collection: general collection of c. 25,000 volumes and 18,000 records. Special items: c. 15,000 pieces of popular song from mid-19th century onward.

MASSACHUSETTS

Boston
BOSTON PUBLIC LIBRARY MUSIC DEPARTMENT, Copley Square, 02117. Music Librarian: Ruth Bleecker. Collection: 90,000 volumes of scores, parts, reference material in many languages, history, theory, musicology etc.; popular music, folk collections, periodicals; sound recordings. Special items: Allen A. Brown collection. Recent acquisitions: Koussevitsky archives, Handel and Haydn Society archives, Beerbohn Tree Theatre Music collection.

Cambridge
HARVARD UNIVERSITY LIBRARY, 02138. Collection: large general collection of music and books etc. Special items: (in the Eda Kuhn Loeb and Houghton Libraries) 90,000 sheet music songs; folk lore collection; over 200 volumes of manuscript including words of c. 1,500 Italian operas. MSS includes five volumes of Boccherini chamber music and autographs of Bellini, Haydn, Fauré and many American composers; Isham Memorial Library of microfilms of early music prints and MSS; Coke Theatre Papers, MSS mainly concerning the introduction of Italian opera at the Haymarket Theatre, London, 1705-15.

Northampton
FORBES LIBRARY, 20 West St., 01060. Music Librarian: Daniel J. Lombardo. Collection: 17,000 scores, 3,000 music history and related books, 5,000 records; superb collection of 19th century sheet music. Special items: Alfred Moffat library of late 18th and early 19th century editions; several earlier rare items on dance and dance music; complete editions.

WERNER JOSTEN LIBRARY FOR THE PERFORMING ARTS, Smith College, 01060. Music Librarian: Mrs. Mary M. Ankudowich. Collection: library to support the music curriculum of the College, including collected sets, performing editions, books, periodicals and sound recordings. Special items: instrumental and vocal music of 16th-18th centuries, copies by Dr. Alfred Einstein.

Worcester
AMERICAN ANTIQUARY SOCIETY, 185 Salisbury St., 01609. Director and Librarian: Marcus A. McCorison. Collection: includes sacred and secular music printed in America up to 1876; both books and sheet music.

MICHIGAN

Ann Arbor
UNIVERSITY OF MICHIGAN MUSIC LIBRARY, 48109. Music Librarian: Wallace Bjorke. Collection: 60,000 volumes for undergraduate and postgraduate scholars, including books, music, sound, recordings and microfilms. Special items: rare book material, particularly strong in 18th century material; much of the rare book material is part of the Stellfeld purchase.

Detroit
DETROIT PUBLIC LIBRARY, Music and Performing Arts Dept., 5201 Woodward Ave., 48202. Chief Music Librarian: Agatha Pfeiffer Kalkanis. Collection: c. 43,000 scores, 12,500 books, 25,000 recordings and 4,500 periodicals for practical and scholarly needs. Special items: Michigan collection; Azalia Hackley collection (Afro-American music).

MINNESOTA

Minneapolis
MINNEAPOLIS PUBLIC LIBRARY, 300 Nicollet Mall, 55401. Music Librarian: Mrs. Marlea Warren. Collection: comprehensive collection of books, records, tapes, scores and sheet music; popular sheet music of late 19th-20th centuries. Special items: collected editions of major composers.

MONTANA

St. Louis
PIUS XII LIBRARY OF ST. LOUIS UNIVERSITY, 221 N. Grand St. Music Librarian: Miss Constance Smith. Collection: microfilms of many Vatican Renaissance and Baroque MSS; fairly large collection of Americana; several collected editions.

NEW JERSEY

Newark
NEWARK PUBLIC LIBRARY, Art and Music Department, 5 Washington St., 07101. Music Librarian: William J. Dane. Collection: extensive library of literature of music, scores, recordings, periodicals; largest circulating collection in New Jersey. Special items: Choice collection of music autographs and MS material from the John Tasker Howard Donation gathered for his book "Our American Music."

Princeton
PRINCETON UNIVERSITY LIBRARY, P.O. Box 190, 08540. Music Librarian: Miss Paula Morgan. Collection: c. 13,500 books, 12,600 scores, 20,000 records, 1,700 microfilms, 70 periodicals; strong on Eastern and Western chant, medieval and renaissance music, Bach, Beethoven, Handel and Wagner. Special items: Scheider Photographic archives of J. S. Bach contains photocopies of the primary sources, especially vocal music. Recent acquisitions: 1973 - Handel collection assembled by Dr. James S. Hall of Walmer, Kent, containing 18th century printed editions as well as MS copies, libretti and other materials.

NEW YORK

Buffalo
BUFFALO AND ERIE COUNTY PUBLIC LIBRARY, Lafayette Square, 14203. Music Librarian: Norma Jean Lamb. Collection: 68,000 volumes include collected works, historical and national anthologies, performance scores and parts, instructional material, books, periodicals; 64,000 records and tapes. Special items: extensive collection of American sheet music from late 18th century onwards; the former NBC Symphony collection of orchestral scores and parts.

Ithaca
CORNELL UNIVERSITY MUSIC LIBRARY, 225 Lincoln Hall, Cornell University, 14853. Music Librarian: Michael A. Keller. Collection: strong in complete works, Denkmäler, music dictionaries and encyclopedias; also in opera and opera history; includes 62,000 books and scores, 12,000 pieces of sheet music; musical periodicals; 27,000 records. Special items: Donald J. Grout collection; Locked Press (rare books - c. 2,000 pre-1800 or delicate books and scores). Recent acquisitions: full score MS of A. Scarlatti's "La Caduta de Decimviri"; Bks I-IV of Marin Marais Pieces de Violes; first and second editions of Orpheus Brittanicus.

New York
GENERAL LIBRARY AND MUSEUM OF THE PERFORMING ARTS, New York Public Library at

Lincoln Centre, 111 Amsterdam Avenue, 10023. Music Librarian: George Louis Mayer. Collection: strong performing arts collection for circulation including c. 96,000 scores, 85,000 books, 37,000 recordings, dance, drama and children's collection; broad coverage of classical, popular and folk music.

NEW YORK PUBLIC LIBRARY, Music Division, 111 Amsterdam Avenue, 10023. Music Librarian: Frank C. Campbell. Collection: large general collection of books, scores, MSS, sheet music and sound recordings. Special items: Americana; early theoretical works; MSS of 17th century English instrumental music; Drexel collection of rare books; Toscanini memorial archives; Rodgers and Hammerstein archives of recorded sound. Recent acquisitions: Petrucci "Odhecaton" A(1504); Chirk Castle MSS; Harry G. Schumer collection of opera scores.

NEW YORK UNIVERSITY, MUSIC LIBRARY, Bobst Library, 70 Washington Square, S. 10012. Music Librarian: Mrs. Ruth B. Hilton. Collection: University research collection including recordings and microfilms. Special items: archives of the American Institute for Verdi Studies.

OHIO

Berea
RIEMENSCHNEIDER BACH INSTITUTE LIBRARY OF BALDWIN-WALLACE COLLEGE, Merner-Pfeiffer Hall, 49 Seminary St., 44017. Director and Chief Librarian: Dr. Elinore Barber. Collection: c. 9,000 volumes including first editions, collected works, periodicals; 1,200 records; special strength in the works of J. S. Bach and his contemporaries; many first editions of other composers. Special items: Riemenschneider collections (c. 300 Bach items, 50 others); Martin collection (Bach and others). Recent acquisitions: Hans T. David collection; Tom Villella recording collection begun 1974.

Cincinnati
GORNO MEMORIAL MUSIC LIBRARY, 101 Emery Hall, University of Cincinnati, 45221. Music Librarian: Robert O. Johnson. Collection: scores, books, periodical, music, records, microfilms in support of undergraduate curriculum, broadcasting, musical theatre and dance; and graduate programmes in applied music, theory, education. Special items: Everett Helm collection, of 18th century opera full scores, first and early editions of Handel, Beethoven, Mendelssohn, Schumann etc; Leigh Harline collection, Anatole Chujoy Memorial Dance collection. Recent acquisitions: Personal library of Thomas Schippers.

HEBREW UNION COLLEGE, Jewish Institute of Religion, Clifton Avenue, 45220. Librarian: Herbert C. Zofre. Collection: Jewish music.

Oberlin
MARY M. VIAL MUSIC LIBRARY, Oberlin Conservatory of Music, Oberlin College, 44074. Librarian: John E. Druesedow, Jr. Collection: 65,000 books and scores, 25,000 records, 5,200 microfilms. Special items: Karl Gherkens collection of music education materials; Best collection of musicians' autographs. Recent acquisitions: M. Felix Raugel's collection, acquired 1972-3.

OREGON

Portland
LIBRARY ASSOCIATION OF PORTLAND, 801 S.W. 10th Avenue, 97205. Music Librarian: K. Padden. Collections: c. 18,000 scores and sheet music, 8,000 books, c. 21,000 records. Special items: John McCormack record collection.

PENNSYLVANIA

Philadelphia
CURTIS INSTITUTE OF MUSIC LIBRARY, 1720 Locust St., 19103. Librarian: Elza Ann Viles. Collection: c. 50,000 volumes of music, mostly performing editions. Special items: Leopold Stokowski collection.

EDWIN A. FLEISHER COLLECTION OF ORCHESTRAL MUSIC IN THE FREE LIBRARY OF PHILADELPHIA, Logan Square, 19103. Curator: Sam Dennison. Collection: World's largest lending library of orchestral performance materials; over 13,000 orchestrations complete with scores and parts; works under copyright available with permission of copyright holder; public domain works available without restriction. Special items: Collection of reference scores; collection of tapes and phonodiscs; permanent composer files; microfilms. Recent acquisitions: Complete orchestral works of Isadore Freed; Harrison Kerr; Nicolai Lopatnikoff; Karl Weigl; Louis Gruenberg; Robert Cassadesus; Eduard Steuermann; Franz Bornschein; and many others. Special emphasis upon acquisition of American composers.

MUSIC DEPARTMENT, THE FREE LIBRARY OF PHILADELPHIA, Logan Square, 19103. Music Librarian: Frederick James Kent. Collection: The state's largest collection of materials on music and dance, c. 100,000 vols., including books, scores, periodicals (current subscriptions, 212) and recordings (46,000 discs) with many special and rare items available for reference. Special items: Drinker Library of Choral Music (347,500 choral scores, orchestral parts); uncataloged vocal and piano sheet music (135,000); chamber music in parts (over 17,000 works) and the Library of the Musical Fund Society (Keffer Collection of Early American Imprints, the Choral and Orchestral Library) on loan to the Free Library. Recent acquisitions: Duplicates of the American Antiquarian Society (2,000 vols.); Harry Dichter Collection of Sheet Music (c. 70,000 items); Arnold Dolmetsch Collection.

Pittsburgh
CARNEGIE LIBRARY OF PITTSBURGH, 4400 Forbes Avenue, 15213. Music Librarian: Ida Reed. Collection: c. 100,000 volumes; especially strong in early American and German music periodicals; over 100 pre-1800 publications; 28,000 records. Special items: Karl Merz Musical Library (1,400 volumes); Charles N. Boyd Memorial collection (3,000 volumes). Recent acquisitions: Donald S. Steinfirst Memorial Record Collection.

THEODORE M. FINNEY MUSIC LIBRARY, University of Pittsburgh, Music Building, 15260. Librarian: Dr. Norris L. Stephens. Collection: research library containing over 30,000 volumes of music and music literature; 1,000 films; 9,000 recordings; manuscripts; over 1,000 pre-1800 imprints. Special items: libraries of Adolph Foerster, Ethelbert Nevin and Fidelis Zitterbart. Recent acquisitions: Libraries of T. M. Finney and William Steinberg.

VATICAN CITY

BIBLIOTECA APOSTOLICA VATICANA, 00120 Cittá del Vaticano. Collection: chiefly liturgical and theoretical works, particularly rich in early MSS from 10th century onwards; French troubadour songs of 13th-14th centuries; MSS with music by Dunstable, Binchois and others. Special items: Sistine Chapel Collection; Barberini collection; Chigiana collection.

APPENDIX E

CONSERVATORIES OF MUSIC

AFGHANISTAN

Kabul
Kabul Art School, Dept. of Music, Bibi Mahro.

ALGERIA

Algiers
Conservatoire de Musique et de Declamation, 2 blvd. Ché Guévara.

Oran
Conservatoire Municipal de Musique et de Déclamation, 5 rue d'Igli.

ARGENTINA

Buenos Aires
Conservatorio de Música "Manuel de Falla," Sarmiento 1551.
Conservatorio Nacional de Música "Carlos Lopez Buchardo," Callao 1521.
Escuela Superior de Música, General Urqueza Plaza 2687.
Faculdad de Artes y Ciencias Músicales, Humberto I 656.
Latin American Center for Advanced Musical Studies, Supero 1502.

AUSTRALIA

AUSTRALIAN CAPITAL TERRITORY
Canberra
Canberra School of Music, P.O. Box 804, Canberra 2603.

NEW SOUTH WALES
Newcastle
Newcastle Conservatorium of Music, Laman St., Newcastle 2300.

Sydney
New South Wales State Conservatorium of Music, Macquarie St., Sydney 2000.

QUEENSLAND
Brisbane
Queensland Conservatorium of Music, 259 Vulture St., S. Brisbane 4101.

Innisfail
North Queensland Conservatorium of Music, P.O. Box 882, Innisfail 4860.

SOUTH AUSTRALIA
Adelaide
Elder Conservatorium of Music, Univ. of Adelaide, Adelaide 5001.

TASMANIA
Hobart
Tasmanian Conservatory of Music, GPO Box 1415P.

VICTORIA
Melbourne
Victorian College of the Arts, School of Music, 234 St. Kilda Road, Melbourne 3004.

AUSTRIA

Graz
Hochschule für Musik und darstellende Kunst, Leonhardstr. 15, 8010 Graz.

Innsbruck
Konservatorium der Stadt Innsbruck, Museum strasse 17a, 6020 Innsbruck.

Klagenfurt
Kärntner Landeskonservatorium, Miesstaler Strasse 8, 9020 Klagenfurt.

Linz
Bruckner-Konservatorium des Landes Oberösterreich, Postfach 95, 4041 Linz.

Salzburg
Hochschule für Musik und darstellende Kunst "Mozarteum," Frohnburgweg 55, 5020 Salzburg.
Orff-Institut, Frohnburgweg 55, 5020 Salzburg.

Vienna
Hochschule für Musik und darstellende Kunst, Lothringerstrasse 18, 1037 Vienna.
Horak-Konservatorium für Musik und darstellende Kunst, Hegelgasse 3, 1010 Vienna.
Konservatorium für Musik und dramtische Kunst. Mühlgasse 28-30, 1040 Vienna.
Konservatorium der Stadt Wien, Johannesgasse 4a, 1010 Vienna.
Österreichische Akademie der Wissenschaften, Fleischmarkt 22, 1010 Vienna.
Privatkonservatorium für Musik und darstellende Kunst, Vienna 4.

BELGIUM

Antwerp
Centrum voor Muziekopvoeding, Halewijn Stichting v.z.w., Van Putlei 33, 2000 Antwerp.

Koninklijk Vlaams Muziekconservatorium, Desquinlei 25, 2000 Antwerp.

Argentevil-Waterloo
Chapelle Musical Reine Elisabeth, Chaussée de Tervuren 445, 1410 Argentevil-Waterloo.

Brugge
Stedelijk Muziekconservatorium, Sint-Jacobsstraat 23, 8000 Brugge.

Brussels
Conservatoire Royal de Musique de Bruxelles, 30 rue de la Régence.

Charleroi
Conservatoire de Musique, Rue A. Biarent 1, 6000 Charleroi.

Ghent
Koninklijk Muziekconservatorium, Hoogport 54, 9000 Ghent.

Leuven
Hoger Instituut voor Kerkmuziek, Herestraat 51, 3000 Leuven.
Stedelijk Muziekconservatorium, Koning Albertsquare 1, 3000 Leuven.

Liège
Conservatoire Royal de Musique de Liège, rue Forgeur 14, 4000 Liège.

Hasselt
Stedelijk Muziekconservatorium, Maastrichtstraat 61, 3500 Hasselt.

Huy
Conservatoire de Musique, Rue Saint-Pierre 48, 5200 Huy.

Kortrijk
Stedelijk Muziekconservatorium, Begijnhofstraat 7, 8500 Kortrijk.

Mechelin
Beiaardschool, Frederik de Merodestraat, 2800 Mechelin.
Stedelijk Muziekconservatorium, Melaan 3-5, 2800 Mechelin.

Mons
Conservatoire Royal de Musique de Mons, 7 rue de Nimy, 7000 Mons.

Namur
Conservatoire de Musique, Chaussée de Louvain 121, 5000 Namur.
Institut de Musique Sacrée, Rue Juppin 28, 5000 Namur.

Ostend
Stedelijk Muziekconservatorium, Romestraat 36, 8400 Ostend.

Tournai
Conservatoire de Musique, Rue Saint-Martin 64, 7500 Tournai.

Verviers
Conservatoire de Musique, Rue Chapuis 4, 4800 Verviers.

BRAZIL

Bahia
Instituto de Musica de Bahia, Rua Carlos Gomes 101.

Parana
Escola de Musica e Belas Artes do Parana, Rua Emiliano Pernata 179.

Rio de Janeiro
Conservatorio Brasileiro de Musica, Av Graca Aranha, 57-12°.

Saõ Paulo
Conservatorio Dramatico e Musical de Saõ Paulo, av. Saõ Joaõ 269.
Instituto Musica de Saõ Paulo, Ruados Estudantes 32.
Instituto Musica "Santa Marcelina," Rua Cardoso de Almeida 541.

BULGARIA

Sofia
Bulgarian State Conservatoire of Music, U1, K1. Gottwald 11.

BURMA

Mandalay
State School of Music and Drama.

Rangoon
State School of Music and Drama.

CANADA

ALBERTA
Banff
Banff School of Fine Arts.

Calgary
Calgary Conservatory of Music, 329A 8th Ave., South West, Calgary 2.
Mount Royal Conservatory of Music and Speech Arts, 4825 Richard Rd. SW, T3E 6K6.

BRITISH COLUMBIA
Victoria
Victoria Conservatory of Music, 1050 Joan Crescent.

NOVA SCOTIA
Halifax
Maritime Conservatory of Music, 5835 College St.

ONTARIO
Cornwall
Ecole Musica, 822 est, rue Première.

Guelph
Guelph Academy of String Arts, 35 Galt St.

Hamilton
Royal Hamilton Conservatory of Music, 126 James St. South.

London
Western Ontario Conservatory of Music, Talbot College, University of Western Ontario, N6A 3K7.

Toronto
Royal Conservatory of Music, 273 Bloor St. West, Toronto 5.
St. Michael's Choir School, 66 Bond St., Toronto M5B 1X2.

QUEBEC
Montréal
Collége de Musique Sainte-Croix, 637 boulevard Ste-Croix, St.-Laurent, Montréal 379.
École de Musique, Université Laval.
Conservatoire de Musique de Montréal, 1700 rue Berri.
École de Musique Vincent-D'Indy, 200 Avenue Vincent-d'Indy, Outremont, Montréal H2V 2T3.
École Normale de Musique, 4873 ave Westmount, Montréal 217.

Saint-Hyacinthe
École de Musique Présentation-de-Marie, 605, rue Girouard, J26 2Y5.

CHILE

Santiago
Conservatorio Nacional de Musica, Compania 1264.

Valparaiso
Universidad Catolica de Valparaiso, Escuela & Educacion Musical, Blanco Veal 596, Cerra Barón.

CHINA

Peking
Central Conservatory of Music.

COLOMBIA

Antioguia
Conservatorio de Musica, Ciudad Universitaria Bloque 25.

Barranquilla
Conservatorio de Musica, Calle 68, no. 53-45.

Bogota
Conservatorio Nacional de Musica, Ciudad Universitaria.

Popayan
Conservatory of Music, Apartado Nacional 113.

Tolima
Conservatorio de Musica del Tolima, Calle 9, No. 1-18.

CUBA

Havana
Conservatorio de Musica "C. A. Peyrellade."

CZECHOSLOVAKIA

Bratislava
Academy of Arts, Sturova 7.
College of Music and Dramatic Arts, Sturova 7.
State Conservatory of Music, Rybnenam 7.

Brno
Conservatory of Music in Brno, Trida kpt Jarose 45.
Janacek Academy of Music and Dramatic Art, Komenského námesti 6. Brno 600 00.

Kosice
Conservatory of Music, Leninova 93.

Prague
Academy of Arts, Alšovo nábřezi 12, Prague 1.
Conservatory of Music in Prague, Na Rejisti 1, Prague 1.

DENMARK

Äarhus
Folkemusikskole, Guldsmedgade 3, 8000 Åarhus.
Jutland Conservatory of Music, 26 Fuglsangsallé.

Alborg
North Jutland Academy of Music, Sohngardsholmsvej, 9000 Alborg.

Copenhagen
Copenhagen Boys' Choir, Sct. Anae Gymnasium, 135 Sjaelor Blvd., Copenhagen 2500.
Copenhagen Music High-School, 57 Kobmagergade, Copenhagen K.
Italian Bel Canto School, 7-9 V. Voldgade, Copenhagen V.
Musical-Dramatic School, 18 Uraniavej, Copenhagen K.
Copenhagen University, Musicological Institute, 2 Klerkegade, 1308 Copenhagen K.
Royal Danish Academy of Music, Niels Brocksgade 1, 1274 Copenhagen.

Esberg
West Jutland Conservatory of Music, Kunstpavillonen, Havnegade.
Academy of Music, Islandgade 50, 6700 Esbjerg.

Odense
Det Fynske Musikkonservatorium, Islandsgade 2, 5000 Odense C.

DOMINICAN REPUBLIC

San Cristobal
Liceo Musicale.

Santa Domingo
Academia de Musica.
Conservatorio Nacional de Musica, Ave. George Washington.
Escuela Elemental de Musica.

Santiago
Liceo Musicale 'José Ovidio Garćia, Duvergé No. 14.

Villa Consuelho
Academia de Musica.

Villa Francisca
Academia de Musica.

La Vega
Liceo Musicale.

ECUADOR

Cuenca
Conservatorio de Musica "José Maria Rodgriquez."

Quito
Conservatorio Nacional de Musica, Apdo 274.

EGYPT

Cairo
Higher Institute of National Music, Cité des Arts, Ave. des Pyramides, Gizeh.

EIRE

Dublin
Royal Irish Academy of Music, Westland Road.

ETHIOPIA

Addis Ababa
National School of Music, c/o Ministry of Education & Fine Arts.
Yared High School of Music, Box 30097.

FINLAND

Åbo-Turku
Sibelius Museum, Biskopsgatan/Piispankatu 17, 20500 Åbo-Turku.
Turan Musikkiopisto, Linnankatu 43A, 20100 Åbo-Turku.

Espoo
Espoo Musiikkiopisto, Jousenkaari 10, 02120 Espoo.

Hämeenlinna
Hämeenlinnan musiikkiopisto, Hattelmalantie 25, 13130 Hämeenlinna 13.

Helsinki
Helsingin Konservatorio, Fredrikinkatu 34B, 00100 Helsinki 10.
Sibelius Academy, P. Rautatiekatu 9, 00100 Helsinki 10.

Hyvinkää
Gyvinkään musiikkiopisto, Hyvinkääkatu 1, 05800 Hyvinkää.

Joensuu
Joensuun musikkiopisto, Koskikatu 10, 80100 Joensuu 10.

Jyväskylä
Jyväskylän Konservatorio, Gummeruksenkatu 6, 40100 Jyväskylä 10.

Kajaani
Kainuun musiikkiopisto, Kasarminkatu 18, 87100 Kajaani 10.

Kemi
Länski-Pohjan Musiikkiopisto, Meripuistokatu 19, 94100 Kemi.

Kokkola
Keski-Pohjanmaan musiikkiopisto, Jungsborg, 67200 Kokkola 20.

Kotka
Kotkan seudun musiikkiopisto, Koulukatu 21, 48100 Kotka 10.

Kouvola
Pohjois-Kymen musiikkiopisto, Salpausselänkatu 38, 45100 Kouvola 10.

Kuopio
Kuopion musiikkiopisto, Haapaniemenkatu 10, 70100 Kuopio 10.

Mikkeli
Mikkelin musiikkiopisto, Mikonkatu 1, 50100 Mikkeli 10.

Oulu
Oulun kaupungin musiikkiopisto, Ojakatu 2, 90100 Oulu 10.

Pori
Porin musiikkiopisto, Vähäuusikatu 17, 28100 Pori 10.

Savonlinna
Savonlinnan musikkiopisto, Kirkkokatu 17, 57100 Savonlinna 10.

Seinäjöki
Etelä-Pohjanmaan musikkiopisto, Koulukatu 41 D, 60100 Seinäjöki 10.

Tampere
Tampereen musiikkiopisto, Lundelininpolku 2, 33230 Tampere 23.

Tapiola
Espoon musiikkiopisto, Jousenkaari 10, 02120 Tapiola.

Tikkurila
Vtaan musiikkiopisto, Orvokkitie 13, 01300 Tikkurila.

FRANCE

Aix en Provence
École Nationale de Musique et de Danse, Conservatoire Darius Milhaud, 3 rue Joseph Cabassol, 13100 Aix en Provence.

Amiens
École Nationale de Musique, 3 Rue Desprez, 80 Amiens.

Angers
École National de Musique, 73 Rue Plantaganet, 49000 Angers.

Avignon
École Nationale de Musique, Place du Palais, 84 Avignon.

Bordeaux
Conservatoire National de Region, 124 Rue du Dr. Albert Barraud, 33 Bordeaux.

Boulogne sur Mer
École Nationale de Musique, Blvd. du Prince Albert, 62 Boulogne sur Mer.

Boulogne-Billancourt
École Nationale de Musique, 22 Rue de la Belle Feuille, 92100 Boulogne-Billancourt.

Bourges
École Nationale de Musique, Esplanade Marceau, 18 Bourges.

Brest
École Nationale de Musique, 16 Rue du Chateau, 29200 Brest.

Caen
Conservatoire Nationale de Region, Esplanade Jean Marie Louvel, 14000 Caen.

Calais
École National de Musique, 43 rue du 11 novembre, 62100 Calais.

Cannes
Conservatoire de Musique, 5 Rue d'Oran, 06 Cannes.

Chalons-sur-Marne
École de Musique Sacrée, 21 rue Titon.

Clermont Ferrand
Conservatoire Nationale de Region, 3 Rue du Maréchàl Joffre, 63000 Clermont Ferrand.

Dijon
École Nationale de Musique et d'art dramatique, Rue de l'École de Droit 5.

Douai
Conservatoire Nationale de Region, Rue de la Fonderie, 59500 Douai.

Grenoble
Conservatoire regional de Musique d'art dramatique et de danse classique. Ch. de Gordes 6.

Lille
Conservatoire National de Musique de Region, Place du Concert, 59000 Lille.

Lorient
École Nationale de Musique, Cité des Oeuvres Sociales, 12 Rue Colbert, 56 Lorient.

Lyon
Conservatoire Régional de Musique, 4 Moutée de Pourviere 69005 Lyons.

Marseille
Conservatoire de Musique et de Declamation, Rue de la Bibliotheque 1, 13001 Marseille.

Montpelier
Conservatoire National de Musique de Region, 14 Rue Eugene Lisbonne 3400 Montpelier.

Montreuil sous Bois
École Nationale de Musique, Rue Estienne d'Orves, 93 Montreuil sous Bois.

Nantes
Conservatoire Nationale de Region, Rue Gaëtan Rondeau-Ile Beaulieu, 44000 Nantes.

Nice
Conservatoire Regional de Musique, 24 Blvd. de Cimiez, 06000 Nice.

Paris
Conservatoire National Superieur de Musique, 14 rue de Madrid, Paris 7.
Fondation des Etats-Unis, 15 blvd. Jourdan, 75 Paris 14.
Schola Cantorum, École Supérieure de Musique, de Danse et d'Art Dramatique, 269 rue St. Jacques, Paris 5.

Reims
Conservatoire National de région de Musique et danse, rue Carnot 14 51093 Reims.

Rennes
Conservatoire National de Musique, 30 Rue Hoche, 35000 Rennes.

Roubaix
École Nationale de Musique, 65 Rue de Soubise, 59 Roubaix.

Rouen
Conservatoire National de Region, Ave. de la Porte des Champ, 76000 Rouen.

Saint Brieuc
École Nationale de Musique, 6 Rue Henri Servain, 22 Saint Brieuc.

Saint Maur les Fosses
École Nationale de Musique, 73 Avenue Diderot, 94 Saint Maur les Fosses.

Saint Omer
École Nationale de Musique, Place Saint Jean, 62 Saint Omer.

Strasbourg
Conservatoire Régional de Musique, 7 Place de la Republique, 67 Strasbourg.

Toulouse
Conservatoire Régional de Musique, 12 Rue du Conservatoire, 31 Toulouse.

Tourcoing
École Nationale de Musique, 6 Rue Paul Doumer, 59 Tourcoing.

Tours
Conservatoire Régional de Musique, 8 Rue J Simon, 37 Tours.

Troyes
École Nationale de Musique, 2 Rue Diderot, 10 Troyes.

Valenciennes
École National de Musique, 8 Rue Ferrand, 59300 Valenciennes.

Versailles
Conservatoire Régional de Musique, 24 Rue de la Chancellerie, 78 Versailles.

GERMAN DEMOCRATIC REPUBLIC

Berlin
Deutsche Hochschule für Musik, Wilhelmstr 63, Berlin W.8.
Deutsche Hochschule für Musik "Hans Eisler," Otto-Grotewohlstr. 19, 108 Berlin.

Dresden
Hochschule für Musik "Carl Maria Von Weber," Blochmannstrasse 2/4, 801 Dresden.

Leipzig
Hochschule für Musik Leipzig, Grassistr. 8, Leipzig C.I.
Franz Lizst Hochschule, Platz der Demokratie.

GERMAN FEDERAL REPUBLIC

Aachen
Grenzland-Konservatorium, Aureliusstr. 9, Aachen 9.

Augsburg
Leopold Mozart Konservatorium, Maximilianstrasse 59, 8900 Augsburg.

Berlin
Berlin State Conservatory, Bundesallee 1-2, Berlin W 5.
Hochschule der Künste, Ernst-Renter Platz 10, 1000 Berlin 10.
Hochschule für Musik, Fasanenstr 1, Berlin-Charlottenburg.
Julius-Stern-Institut der Staatlichen Hochschule für Musik and darstellende Kunst Berlin, Bundesallee 1-12, Berlin 15.

Bonn
Musik Wissenschaftliches Seminar der Universität Bonn, Am Hof 34, 5300 Bonn.

Braunschweig
Niedersächsische Musikschule, Theaterwall 12.

Cologne
Staatliche Hochschule für Musik, Degobertstrasse 38.

Darmstadt
Internationales Musikinstitut, Nieoter-Ramstädterstr. 190, 6100 Darmstadt.

Detmold
Music Academy of North West Germany, Neustadt 12.
Staaliche Hochschule für Musik, Allee 22 (Palais).

Düsseldorf
Staatliche Hochschule für Musik Rheinland, Robert Schumann Institut, Fischerstr. 110, 4000 Düsseldorf.

Essen
Staatliche Hochschule für Musik Ruhr, Abtei, 43 Essen.

Frankfurt-am-Main
Staatliche Hochschule für Musik, Escherheimer Landstrasse 33, Postfach 2326.

Freiburg
Staatliche Hochschule für Musik, Munsterplatz 30, 78 Freiburg im Brisgau.

Hamburg
Hochschule für Musik und darstellende Kunst, Harvestehuderweg 12, 2000 Hamburg 13.

Hannover
Hochschule für Musik und Theater, Emmichpl. 1, 3000 Hannover.

Heidelberg
Staatliche Hochschule für Musik Heidelberg-Mannheim, Friedrich-Ebert-Anlage 92, 6900 Heidelberg.

Lübeck
Schleswig-Holsteinische Musikakademie, Jerusalemberg 4.

Mainz
Staatliche Hochschule für Musik, Binger Str. 26, 6500 Mainz.

Munich
Richard-Strauss Konservatorium, Ismaninger Str. 29, 8080 Munich.
Staatliche Hochschule für Musik, Arcisstrasse 12, Munich 2.

Saarbrücken
Musikhochschule des Saarlandes, Bismarckstrasse 1, 66 Saarbrücken.

Stuttgart
Staatliche Hochschule für Musik und darstellende Kunst, Urbansplatz 2.

Trossingen
Staatliche Hochschule für Musik, Schultheiss-Koch-Platz 5, 7218 Trossingen.

Wuppertal
Staatliche Hochschule für Musik Rheinland, Brillerstr. 2, 5600 Wuppertal.

Würzburg
Bavarian State Conservatory of Music, Megentheimerstrasse 76.
Hochschule für Musik, Hofstallstr. 6-8, 8700 Würzburg.

GHANA

Winneba
National Academy of Music, P.O. Box 25.

GREECE

Athens
Odeion Athenon, Odos Piraeus 35.

Odeion Ethnikon, Odos Maizonos 8.
Odeion Hellenikon, Odos Phidiou 3.

Thessaloniki
Odeion Thessaloniki, Ploutarchou St. 4.

GUATEMALA

Guatemala
Conservatorio Nacional de Musica, 3a Avenida 4-61, zona 1.

HAITI

Port-au-Prince
Conservatoire National de Musique.

HONDURAS

Tegucigalpa
Escuela Nacional de Musica, 2a Ave. 307.

HUNGARY

Budapest
Béla Bartók Conservatory of Music, Nagymezo u.1, Budapest VI.
Budapest Academy of Music, Nagymezo u.1, Budapest VI.
Franz Liszt Academy of Music, Liszt Ferenc-tér 8, 1391 Budapest.

Debrecen
Zoltan Kodaly Music Academy, Var u.

Pécs
Pécs Conservatory of Music.

Szeged
Szeged Conservatory of Music, Lenin Krt. 77.

ICELAND

Reykjavik
College of Music, Skipholti 33.

INDIA

Bombay
Sangit Mahabharati (Conservatoire of Music), A/6 10th Rd., Juhu Scheme, Vile Parle (West), Bombay 400 049.
Sharatiga Vidya Bhavan, Chaupatty Road, Bombay 7.

Madras
Music Academy, 306 Mowbray's Road, Royapettah, Madras 600 014.

Mysore
Sri Varalakshmi Academies of Fine Arts, 668 Ramavilas, Kashipathy Agrahar, Chamaraja Double Rd., Mysore 4.

New Delhi
National Academy of Music, Dance and Drama, Rabindra Bhavan, New Delhi 1.

IRAN

Teheran
High School for National Music.

ISRAEL

Holon
Conservatory of Music, 7 Bilo St., Holon 58-334.

Jerusalem
Rubin Academy of Music, 7 Smolenskin St.

ITALY

Bari
Conservatorio di Musica Niccolo Piccinni, Via Brigata Bari 26, Bari 70124.

Bologna
Conservatorio Statale di Musica G. B. Martini, Piazza Rossini 2.

Bolzano
Conservatorio Statale di Musica "C. Monteverdi," Piazza Domenicani 19, 39100 Bolzano.

Cagliari
Conservatorio di Musica, Via Baccareda, 09100 Cagliari.
Conservatorio Statale di Musica "G. Pier Luigi de Palestrina," Piazza Palazzo 1.

Florence
Conservatorio di Musica "L. Cherubini," Piazzetta delle Belle arti.

Milan
Conservatorio de Musica G. Verdi, Via del Conservatorio 12.

Naples
Conservatorio di Musica "S. Pietro a Maiella 35.

Palermo
Conservatorio di Musica "V. Bellini," Via Squarcialupo 45.

Parma
Conservatorio di Musica "A. Boito," Via Conservatorio 27, 43000 Parma.

Pesaro
Conservatorio di Musica, "Gioacchino Rossini," Piazza Oliviera 5, 61100 Pesaro.

Pescara
Conservatorio di Musica, L. D'Annunzio, Via Leopoldo Muzii 7, 65100 Pescara.

Rome
Conservatorio di Musica "Santa Cecilia," Via Dei Greci 18.
Pontificio Istituto di Musica Sacra, Piazza S. Agostino 20a, 00186 Rome.

Siena
Accademia Musicale Chigiana, Via Città n 89, 53100 Siena.

Trieste
Conservatorio di Musica Giuseppe Tartini, Via Carlo Ghega 12.

Turin
Conservatorio Statale di Musica "Giuseppe Verdi," Via Mazzini 11.

Venice
Conservatorio di Musica, Palazzo Pisani, 30124 Venice.
Conservatorio di Musica Benedetto Marcello, San Marco 2810.

JAPAN

Hiroshima
Elizabeth University of Music, 4-15 Noboricho.

Osaka
Osaka College of Music, 1-70 Shonai Saiwai-cho, Toyomaka-shi.

Tokyo
Kunitachi College of Music, 5-5-1 Kashiwa-cho, Tachikawa City, 190 Tokyo.
Musashino College of Music, 1-13 Hanezawa, Nerima-Ku.
Music University, 2-12-19 Nishi, Kunitachi City.
Toho Gakuen School of Music, 1-41-1 Wakabacho, Chofu-shi.
Tokyo National University of Fine Arts and Music, Ueno Park, Taito-Ku.
Tokyo College of Music, 3-530 Zoshigaya-cho, Toshima-Ku.
Ueno Gakuen College of Music, 24-12, 4-chome, Higashi-Ueno, Taito-Ku.

JORDAN

Amman
Jordan Conservatory of Music.

KENYA

Nairobi
Kenya Conservatoire of Music, P.O. Box 41343.

KOREA

Seoul
Surabul College of Art and Music, San 3-1, Donam-Dong, Sungbuk-ku.

LUXEMBOURG

Esch-sur-Alzette
Conservatoire de Musique, rue de l'Eglise 10.

Luxembourg
Conservatoire de Musique, de la Ville de Luxembourg, Rue du St. Esprit 14-16.

MEXICO

Mexico City
Conservatorio Nacional de Musica, Avenida Presidente Masaryk 582, Mexico 5.
Escuela Superior de Musica, Fernandez Leal 31, Coyoacan, Mexico 21 DF.

Michoacan
Conservatorio de las Rosas, Jardin Las Rosas 347, Morelia.

MONACO

Monaco
Academie de Musique Prince Ranier III, 10 Rue princesse Florestine.

MOROCCO

Casablanca
Conservatoire de Musique.
School of Andulasian Music.

Fez
Conservatoire Dar Adyel.

Marrakesh
Conservatoire National de Musique.

Rabat
Conservatoire National de Musique, de Danse et D'Art.

Tangier
Conservatoire de Tangier.

Tetouan
École National de Musique et de Dance de Tetouan.

NETHERLANDS

Amersfoort
Nederlandse Beiaardschool-Stadhuis, c/o Fahrenheitstraat 12.
Netherlands Carillon School, Grote Spui 11, 3811 GA Amersfoort.

Amsterdam
Conservatorium van de Vereniging het Muzieklyceum, Keizersgracht 62-64.
Sweelinck Conservatorium Amsterdam, P.O. Box 7168, 1007 JD Amsterdam.

Arnhem
Stedelijk Conservatorium, Weversstraat 16.

Groningen
Stedelijk Conservatorium, St. Jansstraat 7-9.

Haarlem
Stichting Muziekschool van de Maatschappij tot Bevordering van de Toonkunst, Nieuwe Gracht 41.

The Hague
Koninklijk Conservatorium voor Muziek en Dans, 7 Korte Beestenmarkt.

Hilversum
Stichting Vereningde Muzieklyceaa, Koninginneweg 25.

Leeuwarden
Gemeentelijk Institut, Schans 44.
Stedelijke Muziekpedagogische Akademie, Schrans 44.

Maastricht
Conservatorium Maastricht, Lenculenstraat 31.
Conservatorium voor Muziek en Dramatische Kunst, Bonnefantenstraat 15.

Rotterdam
Rotterdams Conservatorium, Pieter de Hoogweg 122, 3024 BJ Rotterdam.

Tilburg
Brabants Conservatorium, Kempenbaan 27, 5022 KC Tilburg.

Utrecht
Institute of Musicology, Drift 21, 3152 BR Utrecht.
Nederlands Instituut voor Katholieke Kerkmuziek, Plompetorengracht 3, 3512 CA Utrecht.
Utrechts Conservatorium, Mariaplaats 28, 3511 LL Utrecht.

Zwolle
Stedelijk Conservatorium, Bloemendaalstraat 14.

NORWAY

Bergen
Musik-Konservatoriet, Olav Kyrresgt. 59.

Oslo
Norwegian Academy of Music, Nordal Brunsgt 8, Oslo 1.

Stavanger
Stavanger Musikkonservatorium, Sandeidgt. 12.
Rogaland Musikkonservatorium, Bjergsted, 4000 Stavanger.

PANAMA

Panama City
Escuela Nacional de Musica, Ave. A No. 106, Apdo. 1414, Panama 1.

PARAGUAY

Asuncion
Conservatorio Municipal de Musica, Fulgencio R. Moreno 1635.

PEOPLE'S REPUBLIC OF CHINA

Ch'eng-tu
Southwestern Music Institute, Szechwan.

Hsi-an
Northwestern Music Institute, Shensi.

Rei-ching
Central Conservatoire.

Shenyang
Northeastern Music Institute, Liaoning.

T'ien-ching
Central Conservatoire, Hopei.

Wuhan
Central-Southern Music Institute, Hupei.

PERU

Arequipa
Escuela Regional de Musica de Arequipa.

Ayacucho
Escuela Regional de Musica de Ayacucho.

Cuzco
Escuela Regional de Musica del Cuzco.

Huanuco
Escuela Regional de Musica de Huanuco.

Lima
Conservatorio Nacional de Musica, Mineria 180, Apdo. 2957.

Piura
Escuela Regional de Musica de Piura.

Trujillo
Escuela Regional de Musica de Trujillo.

PHILIPPINES

Manila
St. Scholastica's College, 2560 Leon Guinto St.

POLAND

Cracow
Academy of Music, U1. Bohaterow Stalingradu 3, 31-038 Cracow.

Gdansk
School of Music, U1. Lagiewniki 3, 80-847 Gdansk.

Katowice
State Higher School of Music, 27 Stycznia 33.

Lodz
State Higher School of Music, ul. Gdanska 32, 90-716 Lodz.

Poznan
State Higher School of Music, U1. Armii Czerwonej 87.

Warsaw
Frederik Chopin Academy of Music, U1. Okolnik 2, 00-368 Warsaw.

Wroclaw
Academy of Music, U1. Powstancow Slaskich 204, 53-140 Wroclaw.

PORTUGAL

Lisbon
National Academy of Music, Rua dos Caetanos 29.

Porto
Conservatory of Music of Porto, Rua da Maternidade 13, 4000 Porto.

ROMANIA

Bucharest
Conservatoire 'Ciprian Porumbescu,' 33 rue Stirbey Voda.

Cluj
Conservatoire 'George Dima,' 25 rue 23 August, 3400 Cluj-Napoca.

Iasi
Conservatoire 'George Enescu,' 29 rue Cuza Voda.

SENEGAL

Dakar
École des Arts, BP 3111.

SIERRA LEONE

Freetown
National College of Music.

SOUTH AFRICA

CAPE PROVINCE
Stellenbosch
Conservatory of Music, University of Stellenbosch, Van Riebeek St.

TRANSVAAL
Pretoria
Department of Performing Arts & Technikon Pretoria Opera School, 420 Church St. East.

SPAIN

Barcelona
Academia de Música 'Ars Nova,' Avenida Jose, Antonio 654, Barcelona 10.
Centre d'Estudis Musicals de Barcelona, Avda. Vallvidrena 73, Barcelona 17.
Conservatorio Superior Municipal de Música de Barcelona, Calle Bruch 112, Barcelona 9.

Cadiz
Conservatorio de Música 'Manuel de Falla,' Calle del Tinte 1.

Cordoba
Conservatorio Superior de Música y Escuela de Arte Dramatico, Calle Angel de Saavedra 1.

Madrid
Escuela Superior de Música Sagrada y de Pedagogia Musical Escolar, Victor Pradera 65 bis, Madrid 8.
Real Conservatorio Superior de Música de Madrid, Plaza de Isabel II.
Royal Academy of Music, San Bernardo 44.

Murcia
Conservatorio Superior de Música y Escuela de Arte Dramatico, Plaza Romea.

San Sebastian
Conservatorio Superior Municipal de Música, Victor Pradeva 39.

Seville
Conservatorio Superior de Música, Calle Jesus del Gran Poder 49. Seville 2.

Valencia
Conservatorio Superior de Música y Escuela de Arte Dramatico y Danza, Plaza San Esteban 3.

SRI LANKA

Colombo
State College of Fine Arts.

SWEDEN

Göteborg
Musikhögskolan i Göteborg, Dicksonsgatan 10, 41256 Göteborg.

Malmö
Musikhögskolan i Malmö, Fridhemsvagen 2, 21774 Malmö.

Stenhammarsgatan
Göteborgs Musikkonservatorium, Konserthuset, Stenhammarsgatan 1.

Stockholm
Musikhögskolan i Stockholm, Valhallavägen 103-109, 11531.
Royal Swedish Academy of Music, Blasieholmstorg 8, 11148 Stockholm.

SWITZERLAND

Baden
Music School of the Baden Region, Burghaldestr, 5400 Baden.

Basle
State Music Academy of Basle, Leonhardsstrasse 4-8.

Bern
Conservatory of Music, Kramgasse 36, 3011 Bern.

Chur
Music School of Chur, Rhätisches Volkhaus, 7000 Chur.

Delémont
École Jurassienne de Musique, rue de la Promenade 6.

Fribourg
Conservatory and Academy of Music, rue Pierre Aeby 228A, 1700 Fribourg.

Geneva
Academy of Music.
Conservatory of Music, Place Neuve, 1024 Geneva.

La-Chaux-de-Fonds
Conservatoire de La-Chaux-de-Fonds et du Locle, 34 Ave. Léopold Robert, 2300 La-Chaux-de-Fonds.

Lausanne
Conservatory of Music, 6 rue du Midi.

Lucerne
Conservatory of Lucerne, Dreilindenstr. 82, 6000 Lucerne.

Neuchâtel
Conservatory of Music, Faubourg de l'Hôpital 106, 2000 Neuchâtel.

Schaffhausen
Music School of Schaffhausen, 8200 Schaffhausen.

Sion
Conservatoire Cantonal de Musique, 1950 Sion.

Winterthur
Music School and Conservatory of Winterthur, Aychenbergstr. 94, 8400 Winterthur.

Zürich
Music Academy of Zürich, Florastrasse 52, 8008 Zürich.

SYRIA

Aleppo
Aleppo Institute of Music.

Damascus
Arab Conservatory of Music, Ata Ayubi St.

TUNISIA

Tunis
Conservatoire National de Musique, de Danse et d'Arts Populaires, 20 ave. de Paris.

TURKEY

Ankara
State Conservatoire.

Istanbul
Conservatoire Municipal, Cemberlitas.

Izmir
Izmir State Conservatoire.

U.S.S.R.

Alma Ata
Kazakh SSR Kurmangazy State Institute of Arts, prospekt 90, Kommunistichesky.

Astrakhan
Astrakhan State Conservatoire, Sovietskaya U1. 28.

Baku
Azerbaijan SSR U Gajibekov State Conservatory, U1. Dimitrova 98.

Donetsk
Donetsk Musical-Pedagogical Institute, U1. Artena 44.

Erevan
Erevan Komitas State Conservatoire, U1. Sayatnovy la.

Frunze
Kirghiz State Institute of Fine Art, U1. Pavlodarskaya 115.

Gorky
Gorky M.I. Glinka State Conservatoire, U1. Piskunova 40.

Kazan
Kazan State Conservatoire, U1. Boshaya Krashaya 38.

Kharkov
Kharkov State Institute of Arts, Ploshchad Teveleva 1113.

Kiev
Kiev P. I. Tchaikovsky Conservatoire, U1. K. Marxa 1-3/11.

Kishinev
Kishinev G. Musichesku State Conservatoire, U1. Sadovaya 87.

Leningrad
Leningrad N. A. Rimsky Korsakov State Conservatoire, Teatralnaya pl. 3.

Lvov
Lvov M. V. Lysenka State Conservatoire, U1. Boyko 5.

Minsk
Byelorussian State Conservatoire, Internatsionalnaya U1. 30.

Moscow
Gnesiny State Musical and Pedagogical Institute, U1. Vorovskogo 30/36, Moscow G-69.
Moscow P. I. Tchaikovsky State Conservatory, U1. Gerzena 13, Moscow K-9.

Novosibirsk
Novosibirsk M. I. Glinka State Conservatory, Sovetskaya U1. 31, Novosibirsk 99.

Odessa
Odessa A. V. Nezhdanova State Conservatory, U1. Ostrovideva 63.

Riga
Latvian S.S.R. Yazep Vitol State Conservatoire, U1. Krishyana, Barma 1.

Rostov-on-Don
Rostov State Institute of Pedagogics and Music, Budennovsky pr. 23.

Saratov
Saratov L. V. Sobinov State Conservatoire, Prospekt Kirova 1.

Sverdlovsk
Urals M. P. Mussorgsky State Conservatoire, Pr. Lenina 26.

Tallin
Estonian SSR State Institute of Theatrical and Musical Art, Vabaduse pst. 130.
Tallin State Conservatoire, Bulvar Sivorova 3.

Tashkent
Tashkent State Conservatoire, Pushkinskaya 31, Uzbek.

Tbilisu
Tbilisu V Sarjishvil State Conservatory, U1. Griboedova 8.

Ufa
Ufa State Institute of Fine Arts, 14 Bashkir.

Vilnius
Lithuanian State Conservatoire, Pr Lenin 42.

Vladivostock
Far-Eastern Pedagogical Institute of Arts, U1. 1 Maya 3.

UNITED KINGDOM

Belfast
City of Belfast School of Music, 99 Donegal Pass, Belfast BT7 1DR.

Birmingham
Birmingham School of Music, Paradise Circus, Birmingham B3 3HG.

Cardiff
Welsh College of Music and Drama, Castle Grounds, Cathays Park, Cardiff CF1 3ER.

Croydon
Royal School of Church Music, Addington Palace, Croydon CR9 SAD.

Edinburgh
St. Mary's Music School, Manor Place.

Glasgow
Royal Scottish Academy of Music and Drama, St. George's Place, Glasgow G2 1BS.

Harrow-on-the-Hill
Purcell School, Oakhurst, Mount Park Road, HA1 3JS.

Leeds
City of Leeds College of Music, Cookridge St., Leeds LS2 8BH.

London
Central Tutorial Schl. for Young Musicians, Heath House, London NW3.
Curwen Institute, 108 Battersea High St., London SW11 3HP.
Guildhall Schl. of Music and Drama, The Barbican, London EC2Y 8DT.
London College of Music, 47 Great Marlborough Street, London W1V 2AS.
National Centre for Orchestral Studies, 21 St. James, New Cross, London SE14 6AD.
Royal Academy of Music, Marylebone Road, London NW1 5HT.
Royal College of Music, Prince Consort Road, London SW7.
Tanya Polunin School of Pianoforte Playing, Casita, Lansdowne Road, London W11 3LS.
Tonic Sol-fa College, 108 Battersea High St., London SW11 3HP.
Trinity College of Music, 11 Mandeville Place, London W1M 6AQ.

Manchester
Chetham's School of Music, Long Millgate, Manchester M3 1SB.
Royal Northern College of Music, 124 Oxford Road, Manchester M13 9RD.

Stoke D'Abernon
Yehudi Menuhin School, Stoke D'Abernon, Cobham, Surrey KT11 3QQ.

Twickenham
Royal Military School of Music, Kneller Hall, Twickenham, Middlesex.

U.S.A.

ALABAMA
Birmingham
Birmingham Conservatory of Music, 1100 8th Ave., 35204.

CALIFORNIA
San Francisco
San Francisco Conservatory of Music, 1201 Otrega St., 94122.

Santa Barbara
Music Academy of the West, 1070 Fairway Road, 93108.

Valencia
California Institute of the Arts, School of Music, 24700 McBean Parkway, 91355.

DISTRICT OF COLUMBIA
Washington
Washington Musical Institute, 1730 16th St., 20013.

GEORGIA
Macon
Wesleyan College Conservatory and School of Fine Arts, 31201.

ILLINOIS
Chicago
American Conservatory of Music, 116 S. Michigan Ave., 60603.
Chicago Conservatory College, 64 E. Van Buren St., 60605.
Sherwood Music School, 1014 S. Michigan Ave., 60605.
Vandercook College of Music, 3219 S. Michigan Ave., 60616.

MARYLAND
Baltimore
Peabody Conservatory of the City of Baltimore, 1 E. Mt. Vernon Place, 21202.

MASSACHUSETTS
Boston
Berkeley School of Music, 1140 Boylston St., 02215.
Boston Conservatory of Music, 8 The Fenway, 02215.
New England Conservatory of Music, 290 Huntingdon Avenue, 02115.

Cambridge
Longy School of Music, 1 Follen St., 02138.

MICHIGAN
Detroit
Detroit Institute of Musical Art, 48202.

MINNESOTA
Minneapolis
MacPhail College of Music, 55403.

MISSOURI
St. Louis
St. Louis Institute of Music, 7801 Bonhomme Ave., 63105.

NEW JERSEY
Princeton
Boychoir School of Princeton, Lambert Dr., 08540.

New School for Music Study, Inc., 353 Nassau St., 08540.
Westminster Choir College, 08540.

NEW MEXICO
Taos
Taos School of Music, P.O. Box 12, 87571.

NEW YORK
Brooklyn
Brooklyn Academy of Music, 30 Lafayette Ave., 11217.
Brooklyn Conservatory of Music, 58 7th Ave., 11217.

Flushing
Long Island Institute of Music, 78-39 Parsons Boulevard, 11357.

New York City
Juilliard School of Music, Lincoln Center Plaza, 10023.
Manhattan School of Music, 120 Claremont Ave., 10027.
Mannes College of Music, 157 East 74th Street, 10021.

Rochester
Eastman School of Music, 26 Gibbs St., 14604.

Westchester
Febbraio School of Music.

OHIO
Cleveland
Cleveland Institute of Music, 11021 E. Blvd., 44106.

OREGON
Portland
Portland School of Music, 1017 S.W. Morrison, 97205.

PENNSYLVANIA
Philadelphia
Combs College of Music, 100 Pelham Road, 19119.
Curtis Institute of Music, 1726 Locust St., Rittenhouse Square, 19103.
Grandoff School of Music, 2118 Spruce St., 19103.
Neupauer Conservatory of Music, 105 S. 18th St.
Philadelphia Academy of Performing Arts, 1617 Spruce St., 19103.

VIRGINIA
Winchester
Shenandoah Conservatory of Music, 22601.

URUGUAY
Mayo
Conservatorio Nacional de Musica, 25 de Mayo 692.

Montevideo
Conservatorio Universitario de Musica, Paysandu 843.

VATICAN CITY STATE
Rome
Pontificio Istituto Musica Sacra, 20A Piazza S Agostino.

VENEZUELA
Caracas
Academia de Musica Fischer, Edif. Leon de San Marco.

Academia de Musica 'Padre Sojo,' Avenida Los Granados, P.O. Box 60479, Este.
Conservatorio Italiano de Musical, Edif. Centro Venezolano-Italiano de Cultura.
Escuela Nacional de l'Opera, Direcion de Cultura y Bellas Artes del Ministerio de l'Educacion,
Este 2 consur 25.
Escuela Superior de Musica 'Jose Angel Lamas,' Verves a Santa Capilla.

DEMOCRATIC REPUBLIC OF VIET-NAM

Hanoi
Music School.

YUGOSLAVIA

Belgrade
Musical Academy, Marsala Tita 50, 11000 Belgrade.

Ljubljana
Musical Academy, Gosposka 8.

Sarajevo
Musical Academy, Markovica i/11.

Zagreb
Musical Academy, Gundulićeva 6, 41000.

ZAIRE

Kinshasa
Institut National des Arts, B.P. 8332.

ZIMBABWE

Bulawayo
Kwanongoma College of Music, P. Bag T 5392.
Zimbabwe Academy of Music, P.O. Box 1678.

Gwelo
Midlands Academy of Music, P.O. Box 142.

Salisbury
Zimbabwe College of Music, Civic Centre, Rotten Row, Salisbury C3.

APPENDIX F

MASTERS OF THE KING'S/QUEEN'S MUSICK

It has long been the tradition for the Kings of England to retain a band of musicians as part of their household.

In 1660, Charles II established a band of performers of stringed instruments popularly known as the 'four and twenty fiddlers.' After the death of Charles the band was kept up but no longer consisted exclusively of stringed instruments. Its duties were mainly those of entertaining the King, playing in the royal chapel and the performance of music composed annually for the King's birthday and New Year's day.

The office of Master of the Musick is now honorary and it is usual, though not obligatory, for the holder of the post to compose on important state occasions.

The following is the succession of the Masters of the King's/Queen's Musick from the Restoration onwards. Unfortunately, complete records have not always been kept so there is doubt concerning some of the dates:

Nicholas Lanier: 1660.
Louis Grabu: 1666.
Dr. Nicholas Staggins: 1674.
John Eccles: 1700.
Dr. Maurice Greene: 1735(?).
Dr. William Boyce: 1755.
John Stanley: 1779.
Sir William Parsons: 1786.
William Shield: 1817.
Christian Kramer: 1829.
Francois Cramer: 1834.
George Frederick Anderson: 1848.
Sir William George Cusins: 1870.
Sir Walter Parratt: 1893-1924.
Sir Edward Elgar: 1924-34.
Sir Walford Davies: 1934-41.
Sir Arnold Bax: 1941-53.
Sir Arthur Bliss: 1953-75.
Malcolm Williamson: 1975-.